Immigration Law and Practice in the United Kingdom

PLEASE DONATE YOUR OLD EDITION OF THIS BOOK TO THE
INTERNATIONAL LAW BOOK FACILITY

If you still have the old edition of this book, why not donate it to the
International Law Book Facility (ILBF)? This title is particularly needed by
law schools, law societies, pro bono groups and other institutions and
individuals in Africa, Asia and the Caribbean.

The ILBF is establishing itself as a charity which aims to provide key legal
texts to worthy recipients in developing jurisdictions. It is headed by a Board
and Operating Committee consisting of solicitors, barristers and legal librar-
ians, as well as by officers of Book Aid International, The Law Society, The
Bar Council, The International Bar Association, Sweet & Maxwell and
LexisNexis Butterworths. The Chairman of the Board is Lord Justice Thomas
of the Court of Appeal.

Your help is needed both in donating old editions and donating funds to cover
the costs of shipment. To make a donation, please send cheques payable to
'ILBF' to the ILBF at the following address. To donate your old edition of this
book, simply send it DX or post, to DX 149121 Canary Wharf 3 (10 Upper
Bank St, London E14 5JJ).

ISBN 0-406-96972-8

9 780406 969729

Immigration Law and Practice in the United Kingdom

Sixth edition

General Editors

Ian A Macdonald QC
Garden Court chambers

Frances Webber
Garden Court chambers

Contributors

Kathryn Cronin
Garden Court chambers

Nadine Finch
Garden Court chambers

Laurie Fransman QC
Garden Court chambers

Stephanie Harrison
Garden Court chambers

Louise Hooper
Garden Court chambers

David Jones
Garden Court chambers

Peter Jorro
Garden Court chambers

Patrick Lewis
Garden Court chambers

Sonali Naik
Garden Court chambers

Julia Onslow-Cole
partner at CMS Cameron McKenna LLP

Melanie Plimmer
Garden Court North

Nicola Rogers
Garden Court chambers

Sadat Sayeed
Garden Court chambers

Rick Scannell
Garden Court chambers

Ronan Toal
Garden Court chambers

Philip Trott
partner at Bates, Wells & Braithwaite

Amanda Weston
Tooks chambers

LexisNexis® Butterworths

Members of the LexisNexis Group worldwide

United Kingdom	LexisNexis Butterworths, a Division of Reed Elsevier (UK) Ltd, RSH, 1–3 Baxter's Place, Leith Walk EDINBURGH EH1 3AF and Halsbury House, 35 Chancery Lane, LONDON WC2A 1EL
Argentina	LexisNexis Argentina, BUENOS AIRES
Australia	LexisNexis Butterworths, CHATSWOOD, New South Wales
Austria	LexisNexis Verlag ARD Orac GmbH & Co KG, VIENNA
Canada	LexisNexis Butterworths, MARKHAM, Ontario
Chile	LexisNexis Chile Ltda, SANTIAGO DE CHILE
Czech Republic	Nakladatelství Orac sro, PRAGUE
France	Editions du Juris-Classeur SA, PARIS
Germany	LexisNexis Deutschland GmbH, FRANKFURT and MUNSTER
Hong Kong	LexisNexis Butterworths, HONG KONG
Hungary	HVG-Orac, BUDAPEST
India	LexisNexis Butterworths, NEW DELHI
Italy	Giuffrè Editore, MILAN
Malaysia	Malayan Law Journal Sdn Bhd, KUALA LUMPUR
New Zealand	LexisNexis Butterworths, WELLINGTON
Poland	Wydawnictwo Prawnicze LexisNexis, WARSAW
Singapore	LexisNexis Butterworths, SINGAPORE
South Africa	LexisNexis Butterworths, Durban
Switzerland	Stämpfli Verlag AG, BERNE
USA	LexisNexis, DAYTON, Ohio

First edition 1983
Second edition 1987
Third edition 1991
Fourth edition 1995
Fifth edition 2001
Reprinted 2002
Sixth edition 2005

© Reed Elsevier (UK) Ltd 2005

Published by LexisNexis Butterworths

A CIP Catalogue record for this book is available from the British Library.

ISBN 0 406 969728

Typeset by Letterpart Ltd, Reigate, Surrey

Printed and bound in Great Britain by William Clowes Limited, Beccles, Suffolk

Visit LexisNexis Butterworths at www.lexisnexis.co.uk

Preface

In the preface to the last edition, we referred to the 'most momentous changes' in immigration and asylum law which had taken place since the previous edition. Of these, the most momentous were the setting up of the Special Immigration Appeals Commission (SIAC), the coming into force of the Human Rights Act 1998 and the manifold changes to immigration and asylum procedures and appeals brought about by the Immigration and Asylum Act 1999. The four years since the last edition have witnessed changes to all aspects of the law, from work permits to asylum support, nationality and appeals – at an unfeasibly fast pace.

There have been two major Acts dealing with immigration and asylum since 2001. The Nationality, Immigration and Asylum Act 2002 rivalled the 1999 Act in size, with its 164 sections and nine schedules and the Asylum and Immigration (Treatment of Claimants etc) Act 2004. We summarise the provisions of these Acts in Chapter 1 and give all the details in the appropriate chapters. But behind these two Acts and the numerous Regulations and Orders which come out of them, there lies another story.

Since the last edition there has been one major development, which reaches far beyond the confines of immigration or asylum law, and into the heart of the constitutional arrangements within the state between government and the judiciary.[1]

The Immigration and Asylum Act 1999 made legal aid available on a much wider scale than ever before to give refugee claimants legal representation before adjudicators and the Tribunal. There was available a sizeable cadre of well trained immigration lawyers to meet the need and to provide a large measure of guidance and training for those coming to the subject for the first time.

The 1999 Act initiative ranks alongside the government's campaign to 'bring human rights home', heralded by the Human Rights Act 1998, which came into force in October 2000. Again there was a corps of practitioners, judges and academics available to carry out a massive training programme of the profession and judiciary.

While this was going on, the number of applications for refugee status almost doubled, from 46,000 in 1998 to 80,000 in 2000 and 84,000 in 2002, before dropping back to 49,000 in 2003, coinciding with a general fall across

---

[1] We are grateful to Dr Richard Rawlings for letting us have an advance copy of his article *Review Revenge and Retreat* (2005) 68 (3) MLR 378–410, which we have made use of in this Preface.

Europe.[2] Decisions on applications leapt from 31,500 in 1998 and 33,000 in 1999 to 98,500 in 2000 and 125,500 in 2001 before falling off to 68,000 in 2003.[3]

No-one doubts the pressure these figures put on an already creaky administration. The administrative burden alone was bound to affect the nature and quality of what has been called 'frontline decision-making'. But the figures also helped to fuel the domestic political controversy over asylum and the arguments that Britain was a soft touch for asylum seekers. Inevitably the whole decision-making process has been affected. Add to this a long list of criticisms raised by practitioners in the field, such as hostile and aggressive questioning by officials of refugees' accounts, defective assessment of conditions in country of flight, inadequate treatment of medical evidence, and a widespread culture of disbelief among those with the power to make potential life or death decisions.

The whole mix gave adequate, inevitable and necessary scope for successful legal intervention on behalf of applicants whose refugee claims had been rejected by the Home Office. And so it happened right through the appellate and other judicial processes. In this edition we look at the detail of what has taken place. What we see is a widening, broadening and internationalising of the process of appeal and of judicial review, in which this book, we hope, has played a part. In the course of things some important decisions have gone in favour of appellants, others have confirmed and upheld the Secretary of State's position. It has never been a one way trend.

But the government's reaction has been unprecedented and initially, at least, quite disproportionate. Governments in the past have used new laws to overturn courts' decisions they did not like;[4] they have previously tried to oust jurisdiction of the courts,[5] including discretionary decisions under nationality laws. But in the case of asylum, the government went further than any previous administration. Statute now seeks to curtail judges' decisions on factual issues, such as claimants' credibility and the safety of particular countries. Statute now limits the judicial function in interpreting the meaning or ambit of the Refugee Convention. And statute has now drastically reduced legal aid to refugee claiming appellants, so that it has become like gold dust. The immigration appellate authority has been telescoped from a two-tier system to one tier. The right of effective appeal before removal has been progressively curtailed by the system of 'non-suspensive' appeal rights; and everything now has to be done on the hurry-up, with the inevitable risk that bad decision-making will go unchecked in large numbers of cases. We describe these developments in Chapters 12 and 18.

This unprecedented statutory attack on the judicial and appellate process has been called a 'revenge package' by one academic.[6] We agree. It has come all wrapped up in a government campaign of the most unrestrained attack on the judiciary and on lawyers who represent refugee applicants. According to

[2] HO Asylum Statistics 2003. National Audit Office *Asylum and Migration: a review of HO statistics* HC 625 session 2003–04. We have rounded the figures to the nearest 500.
[3] Ibid.
[4] *Burmah Oil Co (Burma Trading) Ltd v Lord Advocate* [1965] AC 75, HL: reversed by subsequent legislation.
[5] *Anisminic Ltd v Foreign Compensation Commission* [1969] 2 AC 147, [1969] 1 All ER 208, [1969] 2 WLR 163, 113 Sol Jo 55, HL. See BNA s 44, ch 2.
[6] Rawlings, p 378.

Mr Blunkett, the former Home Secretary, who became the main spokesperson of the elective dictatorship, it was 'time for judges to learn their place'.[7] It was his successor who refused to accept gracefully the decision of the House of Lords in *A v Secretary of State for the Home Department*[8] that indefinite detention without trial of foreign terror suspects was in breach of European Convention of Human Rights.

The denouement of the whole process was the attempt in the 2004 Asylum and Immigration Treatment of Claimants Bill to introduce the mother of all ouster clauses, a magnificently drafted chef d'oevre of the parliamentary draughtsman, which would have left the courts with little option, but to lie down like pussycats, or alternatively to take constitutional law to new places, by putting new limits on the ambit of the sovereignty of Parliament. The constitutional stand-off never in fact took place, because the government backed down. However, the debate on the constitutional position and the rule of law continues.

The year 2000 saw the extension of the prohibition on race discrimination to public authorities by the Race Relations Amendment Act 2000, with exemptions given to ministers and their delegates performing immigration functions. Since then, the Administrative Court has emphasised the narrowness of the statutory exemptions and the need to construe them strictly, in the *Tamil Information Centre* case.[9] In *Roma Rights*,[10] the House of Lords, reversing the Court of Appeal's judgment,[11] held that the pre-entry screening operation conducted at Prague airport to prevent Roma would-be asylum claimants from boarding UK-bound aircraft (which did not have the sanction of a ministerial authorisation) constituted direct and systematic discrimination against Roma which could not be justified. And Lady Hale's important speech in *Hoxha and B*[12] should usher in a more enlightened attitude to the issue of gender persecution, which had stalled since the seminal case of *Shah and Islam*[13] in 1999.

Other important judgments of the House of Lords resolved the issue of 'extra-territoriality' in human rights by confirming that expulsion may in principle engage all Articles of the Human Rights Convention, although only the prospect of flagrant breaches of qualified rights in the destination country engage the UK's responsibility.[14] Too late for inclusion in the text comes the

---

[7] Rawlings, pp 378 and 397.

[8] [2004] UKHL 56, [2005] 2 WLR 87.

[9] *R (on the application of the Tamil Information Centre) v Secretary of State for the Home Department* [2002] EWHC 2155 (Admin).

[10] *European Roma Rights Centre v Immigration Officer at Prague Airport (United Nations High Commissioner for Refugees intervening)* [2004] UKHL 55, [2005] 2 AC 1.

[11] *European Roma Rights Centre v Immigration Officer at Prague Airport (United Nations High Comr for Refugees intervening)* [2003] EWCA Civ 666, [2004] QB 811; *revsd sub nom European Roma Rights Centre v Immigration Officer at Prague Airport (United Nations High Commissioner for Refugees intervening)* [2004] UKHL 55, [2005] 2 AC 1.

[12] *R (on the application of Hoxha) v Secretary of State for the Home Department; R (on the application of B) v Same* [2005] UKHL 19, [2005] 1 WLR 1063.

[13] *Islam v Secretary of State for the Home Department (United Nations High Comr for Refugees intervening); R v Immigration Appeal Tribunal, ex p Shah (United Nations High Comr for Refugees intervening)* [1999] 2 AC 629, [1999] 2 All ER 545, [1999] 2 WLR 1015, [1999] Imm AR 283, [1999] INLR 144, HL

[14] *R (on the application of Ullah) v Special Adjudicator; Do v Secretary of State for the Home*

House's decision in *Bagdanavicius*[15] (upholding the Court of Appeal) that the *Horvath* test of state protection applies equally to human rights claimants as to those seeking refugee status.

The House's decision in *N*[16] reflects political preoccupations with the danger of the health service being swamped by health tourism rather than humanitarian ones. Having accepted the illogicality of distinguishing (for the purpose of expulsion) between terminally ill people and those saved from death by anti-retroviral treatment who will assuredly revert to a state of terminal illness shortly after expulsion, for want of suitable treatment in the country of return, their Lordships followed this doleful distinction, in delimiting the UK's obligation to refrain from expulsion, in a decision which faithfully follows a line of less than satisfactory Strasbourg cases and thereby risks condemning many hundreds of AIDS patients currently receiving treatment in the UK to despair and death in their countries of origin. Since then, in *J*,[17] the Court of Appeal has held that suicide on return to the country of origin requires a higher threshold to engage the UK's responsibilities under the Convention than suicide here. We deal with human rights in Chapter 8.

Asylum law is an area which is becoming subject to increasing regulation under a European floor of rights. Already, three Council Directives – the qualification directive,[18] the reception conditions directive[19] and the temporary protection directive[20] apply to different areas of asylum law, the first having persuasive effect since its adoption (it must be transposed by October 2006), the other two having direct effect, since the period for transposition is expired and indeed, both have been transposed into domestic law by statutory instruments and by changes to the Immigration Rules.

These are in addition to the Dublin II Regulation, the successor to the 1990 Dublin Convention. An asylum procedures directive[21] is due for adoption in the near future. All impose minimum standards of protection. All (with the possible exception of the Dublin II Regulation) bestow or will bestow rights which individuals may vindicate by court action in the UK (and if necessary, in the ECJ). These, and the many developments in asylum case law and statutory law, are dealt with in Chapter 12. Meanwhile, free movement for EEA nationals and their family members is becoming freer, with the *Baumbast*

Department [2004] UKHL 26, [2004] 3 WLR 23, *reversing* [2002] EWCA Civ 1856 [2003] INLR 74; *R (on the application of Razgar) v Secretary of State for the Home Department* [2004] UKHL 27, [2004] 2 AC 368.

[15] *R (on the application of Bagdanavicius) v Secretary of State for the Home Department* [2005] UKHL 38, [2005] 2 WLR 1359, on appeal from [2003] EWCA Civ 1605.

[16] *N v Secretary of State for the Home Department (Terrence Higgins Trust intervening)* [2005] UKHL 31, [2005] 2 AC 296.

[17] *J v Secretary of State for the Home Department* [2005] EWCA Civ 629.

[18] Council Directive 2004/83/EC on minimum standards for the qualification and status of third country nationals and stateless persons as refugees or persons who otherwise need international protection, OJ 2004 L 304/12.

[19] Council Directive 2003/9/EC on minimum standards for the reception of asylum seekers, OJ 2003 L 31/18.

[20] Council Directive 2001/55/EC on minimum standards for giving temporary protection in the event of a mass influx of displaced persons and on measures promoting a balance of efforts between member states in receiving such persons and bearing the consequences thereof, OJ 2001 L 212/12.

[21] Amended proposal for a Council Directive on minimum standards on procedures in Member States for granting and withdrawing refugee status (COM (2000) 578, 20 Sep 2000; OJ 2001 C 62 E/231); amended proposal (COM (2002) 326, 18 June 2002; OJ 2002 C 291 E/143.

principle extended to carers of EEA infants in *Man Lavette Chen*[22] and subsequently incorporated into the UK's EEA regulations and the immigration rules. The Citizens' Directive, due to replace a myriad directives on family reunion rights in 2006, will for the first time recognise unmarried partners as equivalent to spouses, provided a civil partnership has been registered. Practitioners must look to EC law for answers in ever broader fields of law. EC law is dealt with in Chapter 7.

Another area where the pace of change is hard to keep up with has been work and business. There was a significant liberalisation in the criteria for entry and stay in work and business categories, which for the first time included unskilled categories other than the long-established seasonal agricultural workers' scheme. Changes were made to the immigration rules creating new categories of the talented, the bright and the plain rich, and allowing switching among and between various categories including degree-level students, working holiday makers, science and engineering graduate scheme participants, postgraduate medical and dental students, trainees and observers, work permit holders, business persons, highly skilled migrants, innovators and investors. These categories, and the switching rules between them, are set out in Chapters 9 and 10. However, at the time of writing, the pendulum appears to be about to swing towards a more restrictive policy, at least for the less qualified breeds. Already, restrictions have been imposed on working holiday makers, who must come from countries with which the UK has bilateral arrangements, and may not work for more than 12 months during their working holiday.

This brief and selective review indicates the speed of change in all areas of immigration law. There have been changes in nationality law too, brought about by two Acts which confer rights to British citizenship on residuary categories of British national, and by the Nationality, Immigration and Asylum Act 2002, which makes citizenship more difficult to obtain for those who must naturalise, and easier to lose. These are touched on in Chapter 2. Huge changes in adoption law are dealt with in Chapter 11, which is expanded in this edition to describe in detail the relationship between immigration and family law.

This sixth edition describes the law as at 5 April 2005.

Our thanks are due to a number of colleagues and others who provided invaluable assistance at various stages, including Mark Symes, Stephen Knafler, Duran Seddon, Lois Kawa Walker, Tania Poscotis, ILPA and John Dean of EIN. Mistakes are, of course, our sole responsibility.

Ian Macdonald QC and Frances Webber
Garden Court chambers
London
June 2005

---

[22] *Chen v Secretary of State for the Home Department: C-200/02* [2005] QB 325, [2005] All ER (EC) 129, [2004] 3 WLR 1453, ECJ.

Contents

Chapter 1
INTRODUCING IMMIGRATION LAW

Chapter 2
RIGHT OF ABODE AND CITIZENSHIP

Chapter 3
CONTROL OF ENTRY

Contents

Chapter 8
HUMAN RIGHTS LAW

Chapter 9
VISITS, STUDY AND TEMPORARY PURPOSES

Chapter 10
WORKING, BUSINESS, INVESTMENT AND RETIREMENT IN THE UK

Contents

Chapter 11
FAMILIES, PARTNERS AND CHILDREN

Chapter 12
REFUGEES, ASYLUM AND EXCEPTIONAL LEAVE

Chapter 13
ASYLUM SUPPORT, COMMUNITY CARE AND WELFARE BENEFITS

Chapter 14
PENAL AND CARRIER SANCTIONS

Chapter 15
DEPORTATION AND REPATRIATION

Chapter 16
REMOVAL AND OTHER EXPULSION

Chapter 17
DETENTION AND BAIL

Contents

Chapter 18
IMMIGRATION APPEALS

Appendix 1
LEGISLATION AND MATERIALS

Contents

Contents

Table of Statutes

Table of Statutory Instruments

Table of Statutory Instruments

Table of Statutory Instruments

Table of Immigration Rules

Table of Immigration Rules

Table of Conventions and Agreements

Table of European Legislation

Table of Cases

Table of Cases

Table of Cases

PARA

Table of Cases

Table of Cases

Table of Cases

Table of Cases

PARA

C

Table of Cases

Table of Cases

Table of Cases

Table of Cases

Table of Cases

PARA

Table of Cases

I

Table of Cases

Table of Cases

Table of Cases

PARA

Table of Cases

Table of Cases

Table of Cases

Table of Cases

PARA

PARA

PARA

Table of Cases

V

Table of Cases

Table of Cases

Table of Cases

PARA

Table of Cases

Table of Cases

Chapter 1
INTRODUCING IMMIGRATION LAW

INTRODUCTION

1.1 The cornerstone of UK immigration law is still the Immigration Act 1971, which came into force on 1 January 1973, and the Immigration Rules made under it. However, the 1971 Act has been significantly amended and added to by a vast accretion of statute law: the British Nationality Act 1981, the Immigration (Carriers' Liability) Act 1987, the Immigration Act 1988, the Asylum and Immigration Appeals Act 1993, the Asylum and Immigration Act 1996, the Special Immigration Appeals Commission Act 1997, the Immigration and Asylum Act 1999, the Nationality, Immigration and Asylum Act 2002 and the Asylum and Immigration (Treatment of Claimants, etc) Act 2004. Only the Immigration (Carriers' Liability) Act 1987 has been repealed in full by later Acts, but its provisions have been re-enacted and enlarged by the 1999 Act. Some consolidation has been done, but nine separate statutes still have to be consulted. In addition, the 1971 Act provisions have been modified as regards entry through the Channel Tunnel by the Channel Tunnel (International Arrangements) Order 1993.[1] As well as the Immigration Rules made under the 1971 Act, which have been made and amended, recast and consolidated on many occasions, there is a large body of statutory instruments, most made under provisions of the 1999 Act which, despite its size, often does no more than sketch fields, ranging from asylum support to the provision of immigration services, within which the regulations operate. There are further statutory instruments made under the 2002 and 2004 Acts, Codes of Practice under the 1996 and 1999 Acts, setting out how employers can avoid racial discrimination and how lorry drivers, coach operators and others can avoid carriers' liability, and procedure rules and practice directions for the new Asylum and Immigration Tribunal, which in April 2005 replaced the adjudicators and Immigration Appeal Tribunal which had been in existence since 1969. The Special Immigration Appeals Commission hears immigration appeals in national security cases, which are subject to their own procedure rules and practice directions. The Asylum and Immigration Tribunal is designed as a one-tier appeal system, which will sit in various combinations from a single immigration judge to a three-person legally qualified Tribunal headed by a a High Court judge as President. The Special Immigration Appeals Commission also boasts a presiding High Court judge. A vast body of case law has come into being, both from the Tribunal and the courts, and is reported in two different sets of specialist reports as well as in various on-line sites.

[1] SI 1993/1813, amended by SI 1996/2283, 2000/913, 2000/1775, 2001/178, 2001/418, 2001/1544, 2001/3707, 2003/2799.

1.2 At the same time, British immigration law is becoming more integrated with European law. The free movement provisions of EC law are reflected in domestic law, in the Immigration Act 1988 and the Immigration (European Economic Area) Regulations 2000[1] (replacing the European Economic Area Order 1994),[2] and practitioners are becoming ever more familiar with the small print of Association Agreements, and applying EC criteria in deportation and expulsion cases. A number of Directives and Regulations impose common minimum standards and criteria in asylum claims and in reception conditions for asylum claimants, make provision for temporary protection in humanitarian crises, govern the responsibility of the UK government vis-à-vis its European counterparts in dealing with asylum claims, and provide for common action on border control, including carrier sanctions, provision of passenger information and joint expulsions.[3]

[1] SI 2000/2326.
[2] SI 1994/1895.
[3] See 7.30ff below.

1.3 Refugee law is part of international humanitarian law, rather than of immigration law, and it is only the exclusionary policies of the UK and other western governments which have linked it inexorably with immigration law. The appellate authorities and the courts have become very familiar with the refugee definition in the UN Convention Relating to the Status of Refugees (Geneva, 1951) and its Protocol of 1967 (referred to collectively as the 'Refugee Convention'). Nor did practitioners in the field wait until the coming into force of the Human Rights Act 1998 in October 2000 to urge compliance with the 1950 European Convention on Human Rights (ECHR) – although now at least these demands must be heard. Cases in the field have contributed to the development of administrative accountability and to the broadening and deepening of fundamental human rights. Immigration law has developed from small beginnings into an important and valuable branch of law.

A BRIEF HISTORY OF IMMIGRATION LAW

Aliens, British subjects and the prerogative[1]

1.4 Aliens have traditionally been divided into alien friends and alien enemies. Alien enemies have no civil rights or privileges unless they are here under the protection and by the permission of the Crown. Alien friends, on the other hand, have long since been treated in reference to civil rights as if they were British subjects.[2] Friendly aliens were never controlled by the prerogative power, at least since the 1770s. In a directive issued to all British missions in 1852, the Foreign Secretary, Earl Granville, made it clear that –

> 'By the existing laws of Great Britain, all foreigners have the unrestricted right of entrance and residence in this country ... No foreigner, as such, can be sent out of the country by the Executive Government, except persons removed by treaties with other States, confirmed by Act of Parliament, for the mutual surrender of criminal offenders.'[3]

According to Dr Vincenzi, every removal or exclusion of aliens during the last 200 years or more has been taken to Parliament for authorisation, whether temporary in effect[4] or permanent.[5] Likewise the Foreign Deserters Act 1852 and the Extradition Act 1870 'enabled' the Crown to hand over deserters and fugitive offenders to foreign powers. In none of these statutes, passed while the country was at peace, is there any mention of a Crown prerogative relating to aliens, or any reservation of one.[6] The first appearance of a reservation is in the Aliens Restriction Act 1914, passed on the outbreak of World War I,[7] intended to preserve the Crown's prerogative power in relation to enemy aliens.[8] The Immigration Act 1971 contains a similar power, never used but no doubt intending to preserve the same powers. Dicta in the Privy Council cases of *Musgrove v Toy, Attorney General for Canada v Cain* and in the Scottish case of *Johnstone v Pedlar* which support the existence of a prerogative power in relation to all aliens,[9] and further dicta in the mid-twentieth century cases of *R v Brixton Prison Governor, ex p Soblen* and *Schmidt v Secretary of State for the Home Department*, which contain very firm assertions of the existence of such a power,[10] are not matched by the practice or views of successive British governments.

1   Following a critical review of the history section of this book's previous edition, Dr Prakash Shah very kindly drew our attention to a number of academic Articles and books, including Dr Christopher Vincenzi's important Article *Aliens and the judicial review of Immigration Law* (1985) Pub L 93, which we have used heavily in this section, as well as his own book *Refugees, Race and The Legal Concept of Asylum in Britain* (Cavendish Publishing 2000), which we have also used.
2   *Porter v Freudenberg* [1915] 1 KB 857, per Lord Reading CJ, dictum approved in *Ertel Bieber & Co v Rio Tinto Co* [1918] AC 260, at 268. Contrast *Silvester's Case* (1701) 7 Mod 150 (alien enemy), cited by Vincenzi, p 107.
3   State Papers, vol 42 (1852–1853), quoted by Vincenzi at p 107, Shah, below, at p 24, and B Porter *The Refugee Question in Mid Victorian Politics* (Cambridge CUP 1979) p 149.
4   Aliens Act 1793 33 George III c 4; Aliens Act 56 George III c 86; Aliens Act 1848 11 & 12 Victoria c 20.
5   For example, the Aliens Act 1905, the Aliens Restriction Act 1914. For a full history see Prakash Shah, ch 3.
6   Vincenzi at p 107.
7   Aliens Restriction Act 1914 s 1(6).
8   See *R v Commandant of Knockaloe Camp, ex p Forman* (1917) 82 JP 41.
9   *Musgrove v Toy* [1891] AC 272, 282; *A-G for Canada v Cain* [1906] AC 542, 546, and *Johnstone v Pedlar* [1921] 2 AC 262, 283, where Lord Atkinson said: 'Aliens, whether friendly or enemy, can be lawfully prevented from entering this country and can be expelled from it ...'
10 *R v Brixton Prison Governor, ex p Soblen* [1963] 2 QB 243, 300, CA and *Schmidt v Secretary of State for Home Affairs* [1969] 2 Ch 149, 168.

1.5 These decisions have been given detailed scrutiny by Dr Vincenzi in his Article and are found wanting. We need not repeat his telling deconstruction here. Undoubtedly the *Musgrove* judgment has been identified as a turning point in legal thinking[1]. At about the same time the US Supreme Court, drawing inspiration from *Vattel*, in the case of a Japanese national, declared that according to international law a State had the discretion to admit whomsoever it saw fit.[2] This view has proved persistent to the present day, influencing a judicial perception that excluded aliens are not deserving of a detailed scrutiny of their claims. Dr Shah goes further.[3] He says:

'What is significant is that such case law developed as a result of the exclusion of particular racial groups (blacks, Japanese, Chinese and South Asian) that were not deserving of an equal right of free movement, and that judges in legal systems across the Anglo-Saxon world tended to accommodate legislative demands to exclude such people.'

1 At the time it gave rise to a lively academic debate: see Craies 'The Right of Aliens to Enter British territory' (1890) 6 Law Quarterly Revue 27–41 and Haycraft 'Alien Legislation and The Prerogative of the Crown' (1897) 13 Law Quarterly Review 165–168; Shah p 28. Referred to by Shah p 28.
2 *Nishimura Ekiu v US* 142 US 651 at 659. Cited by Shah at p 29. See also Richard Plender *International Migration Law* (2nd edn, 1988) p 64ff. In these judicial pronouncements, the views of international jurists who took a less tenacious perspective were totally ignored; Plender pp 72–75.
3 Shah p 29.

1.6 The position of British subjects is not at all clear. The traditional view is that their situation stood in direct contrast to that of aliens.[1] It is said that at common law all British subjects had a right of abode in the UK. Prior to 1962 they enjoyed this right whether they lived in the UK or elsewhere, and whether or not they were citizens of the United Kingdom and Colonies (CUKCs). Under the British Nationality Act 1948 British subjects were also known as 'Commonwealth citizens' and the two terms were interchangeable until 1983.[2] British Protected Persons were not British subjects and, therefore, had no right of abode, but they were under British protection.[3] In *DPP v Bhagwan*[4] Lord Diplock referred to this right of abode:

'Prior to the passing of the Commonwealth Immigrants Act 1962, the Respondent as a British Subject had the right at common law to enter the United Kingdom without let or hindrance when and where he pleased and to remain here as long as he liked. That right he still retained in 1967 save insofar as it was restricted or qualified by the provisions of the Act.'[5]

This was first time such a right had been mentioned in any case, and it was made without any reference to authority. So far as we know there is none. However, bearing in mind Sir Robert Megarry's famous quote about the difference between directly enforceable nominate rights and liberties:

'England ... is a country where everything is permitted except what is expressly forbidden.'[6]

and applying it to Lord Diplock's speech, it is possible to read his 'right' as no more than one aspect or consequence of the British subject's right not to be restrained without lawful authority. But here is the rub. As we have seen, friendly aliens were in exactly the same position.[7] They could not be restrained except by lawful authority. It was already well established by 1772 that an alien in territorial waters could secure his or her release by *habeas corpus*, as in *Somersett v Stewart*,[8] where Lord Mansfield ordered the release of an African-born slave being detained on board a ship bound for the American colonies. So, as Dr Vincenzi argues, 'the more accurate way of describing the position of both subjects and aliens would be to say that neither has rights of entry into the United Kingdom as such, at common law, only a freedom from restraint, in the absence of statutory authority, at the port of entry'.[9] With that qualification we can accept Lord Diplock's dictum, but, if we are right, it also means that aliens still retained that right 'save insofar as it was restricted or qualified' by statute.

1 This was the view taken in previous editions of this book, We quoted *Calvin's Case* (1608) 2 State Tr 559; *Musgrove v Chun Teuong Toy* [1891] AC 272; and *A-G for Canada v Cain*; *A-G for Canada v Gilhula* [1906] AC 542. It was an easy assumption to make, given that at the time of the passing of the British Nationality Act 1948 aliens were controlled by the Aliens Order 1953, but no restrictions were placed on British subjects or Common-wealth citizens, as they were also called: British Nationality Act 1948, s 1(2).
2 British Nationality Act 1948, s 1(2); British Nationality Act 1981, s 51.
3 British Nationality Act 1948, s 1(3); *R v Secretary of State for the Home Department, ex p Thakrar* [1974] QB 684, [1974] 2 All ER 261, CA; *R v Chief Immigration Officer, Gatwick Airport, ex p Singh* [1987] Imm AR 346, QBD.
4 [1972] AC 60, [1970] 3 All ER 97, HL.
5 [1970] 3 All ER 97 at 99.
6 Sir Robert Megarry VC in *Malone v Commisioner of Police of the Metropolis (No 2)* [1979] Ch 344, at 366, cited at Vincenzi, p 97.
7 1.4–1.5 above.
8 (1772) 20 St Tr 1; *R v Lesley* (1860) Bell CC 20; *Ex p Lo Pak* (1888) IX NSWR 221 (application for habeas corpus, in which the Prerogative was raised by the Crown, but rejected by the High Court of New South Wales as a bad return); *Ex p Leong Kum* (1888) IX NSWR 250. These cases are all cited by Vincenzi at p 98.
9 Vincenzi, pp 98–99.

1.7 Do these matters have any bearing on what is happening to-day? In nearly all the case law under the ECHR, involving the removal of immigrants or asylum seekers, references are made to the right which sovereign States possess under international law to regulate the entry of aliens into their territory. This right, it is said, applies subject to any treaty obligation of a State or rule of the State's domestic law which may apply to the exercise of that control.[1] In Strasbourg cases the court makes frequent reference to this right, always making it clear that it is subject to any treaty obligations the State has entered into.[2] The British courts do the same, but usually embellish the description of the international law right by a reference to the fact that in English law, control derived from the prerogative, which gave the Crown an unfettered discretion over aliens.[3] The reference to the international law right in the Strasbourg case law is twofold. First the need to uphold and protect the individual's Convention rights is a qualification or limitation upon the exercise of immigration control. Secondly, in the case of qualified rights, the exigencies of immigration control may call into play one or more of the public interests, economic wellbeing, prevention of crime and so on, named in Article 8(2) and the other qualified rights. However, if immigration law is seen as some kind of extension to an unfettered prerogative power, it is all too easy to argue, in the human rights context, that the ECHR was not intended by its signatories to constrain 'their rights under international law to refuse entry to or to remove aliens from their territory'.[4] It then becomes much easier for court to treat the right to control immigration as one which 'outweighs or trumps' the Convention right.[5] The embellishment of immigration control with an unfettered prerogative background gives it more weight, when it comes to be used as one side of a fair balance. But suppose that this aspect of immigration control is, as has been suggested, built upon the weakest and sandiest of foundations, it must lose some of its aura and weight. Maybe the elaboration of immigration policy is not a paradigm of the responsibility of elected government, as Laws LJ once put it.[6] Maybe it does not trump, as the Master of the Rolls put it in *Ullah*, unless the individual can come up with some exceptional countervailing human rights story. The working out of the balance between the public interest as defined by government, and the rights and liberties of the individual, is one of the major themes of this edition of the book.

[1] See per Lord Slynn in *R (on the application of Saadi) v Secretary of State for the Home Department* [2002] UKHL 41, [2002] 1 WLR 3131, para 31.
[2] *Vilvarajah v United Kingdom* (1991) 14 EHRR 248, para 102; *Chahal v United Kingdom* (1996) 23 EHRR 413, para 73; *D v United Kingdom* (1997) 24 EHRR 423, para 46; *Bensaid v United Kingdom* (2001) 33 EHRR 205, para 32; *Boultif v Switzerland* (2001) 33 EHRR 1179, para 46.
[3] *R (on the application of Saadi) v Secretary of State for the Home Department* [2002] UKHL 41, [2002] 1 WLR 3131, at para 31: *R (on the application of Ullah) v Special Adjudicator* [2004] UKHL 26, [2004] 2 AC 323 at para 6. In *European Roma Rights Centre v Immigration Officer at Prague Airport* [2004] UKHL 55, [2005] 2 WLR 1, at para 9 Lord Bingham quoted with approval a reference by Sir William Holdsworth (*A History of English Law*, Vol X, pp 395–396) to a judgment by Jeffreys CJ in *East India Company v Sandys* (1685) 10 State 371, at 530–531, when he said: 'I conceive the King had an absolute power to forbid foreigners, whether merchants or others, from coming within his dominions, both in times of war and in times of peace, according to his royal will and pleasure; and therefore gave safe-conducts to merchants strangers, to come in, at all ages, and at his pleasure commanded them out again.'
[4] *R (on the application of Ullah) v Special Adjudicator* [2002] EWCA Civ 1856, [2003] 1 WLR 770 at para 21, per Lord Phillips MR.
[5] [2002] EWCA Civ 1856, [2003] 1 WLR 770 at para 24.
[6] *N v Secretary of State for the Home Department* [2003] EWCA Civ 1369, [2004] INLR 10, at para 38.

1.8 Commonwealth citizens were first made subject to statutory immigration control in the UK by the Commonwealth Immigrants Act 1962. This Act was brought into force mainly as a result of a campaign against black Commonwealth citizens already here. The Act made a distinction between CUKCs and citizens of independent Commonwealth countries, and based control upon the kind of passport held by the would-be immigrant. All Commonwealth citizens became subject to immigration control except the following:

(a)   persons born in the UK;
(b)   holders of UK passports issued by the UK government as opposed to those issued on behalf of the government of a Crown colony or of some other part of the Commonwealth;[1]
(c)   other persons included in the passport of one of the persons excluded from immigration control under (a) or (b) above.

[1] Commonwealth Immigrants Act 1962, s 1(2) and (3); *R v Secretary of State for the Home Department, ex p Bhurosah* [1968] 1 QB 266, [1967] 3 All ER 831, CA. Other exemptions from control were given to diplomats (s 17(1)); certain members of Commonwealth armed forces (s 17(2)); persons exempted by the Secretary of State for the Home Department

(Commonwealth Immigrants (Control of Immigration) Exemption Order 1965, SI 1965/153); and persons who landed in the UK and spent 28 days without submitting to examination by immigration officers (Commonwealth Immigrants Act 1962, Sch 1, para 1(2), as amended by Commonwealth Immigrants Act 1968, s 4; and see *R v Governor of Brixton Prison, ex p Ahsan* [1969] 2 QB 222, [1969] 2 All ER 347).

1.9 In short, CUKCs were exempted from control, except those who were born in Crown Colonies and obtained their passports there. CUKCs who were born in independent Commonwealth countries and who retained that status after independence were exempted from control provided they had a UK passport. A passport issued by the High Commissioner would normally qualify. This category of CUKC comprised, among others, large sections of the Asian community in Kenya, who had expressly been given the option of UK citizenship by the Kenya Independence Act 1963 on exactly the same basis as the European settlers. Similar provisions had been made when Uganda became independent. Under the Commonwealth Immigrants Act 1962 all of these persons were entitled to come to Britain as of right, and many did so, because of the policy of Kenyanisation adopted by the Kenyan government and a similar policy of preference to their own citizens adopted by other East African countries.[1]

1 On 'The Legal Basis for the Asian Exodus from Kenya' see Alan H Smith in *Law Guardian* (November 1970). It should also be noted that Asians who opted for Kenyan citizenship rather than UK citizenship after independence were unaffected. Those who opted for UK citizenship, however, clearly did so because they assumed (rightly at the time) that it offered greater security. See further Plender *International Migration Law* (2nd edn, 1988) pp 88–93 and 156.

1.10 The Commonwealth Immigrants Act 1968 sought to change all this. Its aim was to bring the East African Asians under immigration control;[1] its method was to divide holders of UK passports into two separate categories, those who could enter Britain without restriction and those who could not. A CUKC, who was the holder of a UK passport issued by the UK government, was now subject to immigration control unless he or she, or at least one parent or grandparent, was born, adopted, naturalised or registered as a CUKC in the UK. Ancestral connection to the UK became the key factor in determining which CUKCs were subject to immigration control. The intention was to keep out East African Asians and it was not difficult to see that the mechanism for doing this was the section defining the necessary ancestral connection. The immediate precedent was to be found in the British Nationality Act 1964, the main aim of which had been to preserve the right to resume UK citizenship to white settlers in Africa who were then under pressure to assume the citizenship of newly-independent African countries. It is a formula which enables politicians and officials to proclaim that there is nothing racist about such laws. In 1971 the requirement of an ancestral connection was further refined by the enactment of the 'patrial' section in the Immigration Act 1971. When British nationality was reformed by the British Nationality Act 1981, 'patriality' was replaced by an extended definition of 'British citizenship', which we look at in chapter 2 below.

1 See in particular *East African Asians v United Kingdom* (1973) 3 EHRR 76, paras 76, 83–84, 96.

1.11 By the time of the Commonwealth Immigrants Act 1968, the UK had already granted individuals the right to petition the European Commission on Human Rights in Strasbourg over alleged breaches of their human rights, a right whose first exercise was by Commonwealth immigrants, with mixed success.[1] But it was the Asian CUKCs excluded from their country of nationality by the 1968 Act who really began the trend of using the ECHR to seek redress for immigration grievances. Their common law right to enter the UK freely was replaced by a discretionary scheme of special vouchers. Many also lost the right to remain and work in the countries where they were living. Some became destitute. But when they tried to enter Britain they found themselves being shuttlecocked in and out, or being kept in prison.[2] The International Commission of Jurists criticised the 1968 Act at the time of its passing as a violation of international law.[3] In *East African Asians v United Kingdom*[4] complaints by a large number of applicants, that their human rights had been infringed by the operation of the 1968 Act, were upheld, and in particular the Commission found as a fact that, notwithstanding the neutrality of the language of the statute, it had racial motives and targeted a racial group, and that the racial discrimination in its operation constituted degrading treatment.[5] The special voucher system continued until March 2002, when it was abolished. Under provisions of the Nationality and Immigration Act 2002 any remaining British nationals who have no other citizenship can register as British citizens.[6] The huge opposition to the 1962 and 1968 Acts, and the real sense of grievance within the immigrant communities, may have been among the factors leading to the setting up of the Committee on Immigration Appeals,[7] whose report led to the Immigration Appeals Act 1969. The 1969 Act gave appeal rights only to Commonwealth citizens (these were extended to aliens by the Immigration Act 1971), and instituted the two-tier system of appeal which survived until 4 April 2005, when the two tiers were amalgamated into one, depriving immigrants and asylum claimants of one level of judicial protection.

1   *Mohammed Alam v United Kingdom* (2991/66); *Harbajan Singh v United Kingdom* (2992/66) (1967) Times, 12 October.
2   'Return to Sender, Report on Shuttlecocks' (September 1970) JCWI p 1.
3   Bulletin No 34, pp 36–37.
4   (1973) 3 EHRR 76.
5   (1973) 3 EHRR 76, at paras 197, 202 and 207.
6   Nationality, Immigration and Asylum Act 2002, s 12; British Overseas Territories Act 2002, ss 3, 4. See 2.19 below.
7   Chaired by Rir Roy Wilson QC, Cmd 3387.

1.12 The Immigration Act 1971 repealed all previous legislation, with minor exceptions, and spelled the end of large-scale primary immigration for settlement from the 'new Commonwealth'. The benefits of the right of abode had shrunk to a small, exclusive, largely white group of 'patrials', defined by their connection to the UK through their ancestry. On the same day that the 1971 Act came into force, 1 January 1973, the Treaty of Rome provisions came into force in the UK, giving rights of free movement for work and establishment in business or self-employment to all citizens of the EEC's Member States.[1] The 1971 Act virtually assimilated Commonwealth citizens with aliens, although the former had some residual benefits: some were eligible for the right of abode (which aliens could never have, except on naturalisation), or for exemption from deportation on fulfilling certain residence requirements; and there was a standstill clause preventing the rules on settlement from becoming more restrictive than those enjoyed before 1973 (which operated mainly to exclude Commonwealth citizens seeking family reunion from having to comply with maintenance and accommodation requirements). The standstill clause was repealed in 1988. Commonwealth citizens, in addition, have never had to register with the police.

[1]   At that time France, Germany, Belgium, Netherlands, Luxembourg, Ireland and Italy.

1.13 The concept of patriality was introduced to entrench the division between persons with the right of abode and those who needed leave to enter. All aliens were non-patrial, as were some Commonwealth citizens and some UK citizens. Thus the harmony between nationality and free movement was destroyed between 1962 and 1971. The British Nationality Act of 1981 attempted to re-align nationality with immigration rights, and in doing so created further confusion and anger. The 1981 Act created out of the former UK and Colonies citizenship several different types of British nationality, only the first of which, British citizenship, carried the right of abode. The other 'citizens', British Dependent Territories citizens, British Overseas citizens, British subjects without citizenship, and British Nationals Overseas, remained subject to immigration control. The return of Hong Kong to Chinese control in 1997, and the resulting dramatic reduction in the numbers of British Dependent Territories citizens and British Nationals (Overseas) with no other citizenship, enabled the government to offer the few remaining British Dependent (now Overseas) Territories citizens and British Nationals (Overseas) British citizenship.[1] The other main category of former CUKCs given lesser citizenship status by the 1981 Act, the British Overseas citizens, a category with no right of entry anywhere, may now register as British citizens if they have no other nationality.[2]

[1]   British Nationality (Hong Kong) Act 1997; White Paper *Partnership for Progress and Prosperity* (1999); British Overseas Territories Act 2002, ss 3, 4.
[2]   Nationality, Immigration and Asylum Act 2002, s 12.

1.14 The politics of immigration and race continued to play a decisive role in developing the law in the 1970s and 1980s. Rules on family settlement became tighter and ever more strictly applied, with virginity tests for brides from the Indian sub-continent causing a furore in the late 1970s[1] and the primary purpose rule[2] keeping husbands out throughout the 1980s and 1990s. The 'standstill' clause preventing the application of harsher rules to Commonwealth settlement after 1973 was repealed in 1988,[3] and appeal rights on deportation were curtailed for those who had been in the UK for less than seven years.[4] By the mid-1980s the first visa controls had been imposed on Commonwealth citizens,[5] and these were swiftly followed by the first carriers' liability measure, the Immigration (Carriers' Liability) Act 1987, pushed through in response to the arrival of visa-less Tamils fleeing Sri Lanka.

[1]   See Yellowlees report on medical examination of immigrants, 15 December 1980.
[2]   HC 394, para 50 (1980); the burden of proof shifted to the couple to prove that the primary purpose was not settlement in HC 66, para 54 (1982).
[3]   Immigration Act 1988, s 1.

4   Immigration Act 1988, s 5.
5   India, Sri Lanka, Bangladesh, Ghana, Nigeria.

1.15 The introduction of visa controls on Commonwealth citizens, and of carrier sanctions, were the first domestic manifestation of a pan-European policy to deal with the increasing numbers of asylum seekers arriving in Europe, and it is asylum which has become the big issue in the past two decades. Britain and most European countries had signed up to the 1951 Refugee Convention and its 1967 Protocol. But when Britain and Europe sought unskilled migrant labour during the fifties and sixties to rebuild their ravaged infrastructure and economy, their governments neither knew nor cared what the migrants' motives were. Many who came from Africa and Asia may have been eligible for refugee status under the Convention, but so long as migration for work was possible, asylum was not an issue. The closing of all avenues of migration (save for the highly educated or talented, through the work permit scheme, and the wealthy, through the business and independent means categories) took away a possible escape route when upheavals, sudden regime change, breakdowns and murderous civil wars left devastation in the home country. Asylum became the big issue. Developments in immigration law in the 1980s and 1990s reflected the battle between the exclusionary imperatives of European immigration policy to the poor countries of the world, on the one hand, and the humanitarian imperatives of international humanitarian law on the other. Visa controls and carrier sanctions were thus calculated to stop refugees and others arriving in Europe. Non-British and non-EU travellers from 'refugee-producing' countries required visas and could not get them.[1] Airlines would not sell tickets to those without visas. Thus the trade in false passports and documents began, and the trafficking trade, with which many of the laws of the 1990s and the early years of the new century deal.

1   A person is not a 'refugee' under the 1951 Refugee Convention unless he or she is outside his or her own country, and so it is impossible to obtain a 'refugee visa'. For the territorial limitations of the Refugee Convention see *European Roma Rights Centre v Immigration Officer at Prague Airport* [2004] UKHL 55, [2005] 2 WLR 1 (12.9 and 12.37 below).

1.16 The Immigration Act 1971 did not deal with asylum, and rules made under it merely recorded that full account was to be taken of the UK's obligations under the 1951 Refugee Convention when a person seeking to enter or being removed claimed asylum or indicated a fear of persecution. This changed with the Asylum and Immigration Appeals Act 1993, which, with new Immigration Rules introduced in 1994 and asylum procedure rules, made up a statutory scheme for asylum determination and appeals. The scheme gave effect to the developing inter-governmental initiatives in the EEC, in particular the Dublin Convention 1990[1] and the London Resolutions 1992[2] which indicated a common approach to asylum seekers who had travelled through 'safe third countries', or whose claims were otherwise believed to be manifestly ill-founded. On the one hand, the 1993 Act gave in-country appeal rights to all asylum seekers, including those who had travelled through a 'safe' third country, although appeals in such cases were subject to an accelerated procedure. On the other hand, the 1993 Act began the process of placing asylum seekers in a class apart, subjecting them to mass fingerprinting and to separate and inferior provision in the fields of housing and social security. The 1993 Act also removed appeal rights from visitors and other groups defined by the purpose or length of their proposed stay, or by their lack of appropriate documents or other qualifying conditions. It also replaced the right to seek judicial review of Immigration Appeal Tribunal final determinations by a direct appeal to the Court of Appeal on a point of law.

1   Convention determining the State responsible for examining applications for asylum lodged in one of the Member States of the European Communities, Dublin, 15 June 1990.
2   Resolution on a harmonised approach to questions concerning host third countries (SN 4823/92 WGI 1283 AS 147); Resolution on manifestly unfounded applications for asylum (SN 4822/92 WGI 1282 ASIM 146), adopted 30 November 1992 and 1 December 1992 by immigration ministers of the EU States; in *Key texts on Justice and Home Affairs in the EU* Vol 1 (1976–1993) (1997) Statewatch Publications.

1.17   The Asylum and Immigration Act 1996 reduced the rights of immigrants and asylum seekers, without any compensatory improvements. Accelerated appeal procedures were extended from third-country cases to whole new categories of asylum seekers.[1] The 1996 Act responded to widespread concern among adjudicators about the admissibility procedures of several European countries, particularly Italy, France and Belgium, by abolishing the suspensive appeal in the case of removal of asylum seekers to an EU destination, leading to a series of judicial review challenges.[2] The 1996 Act also introduced employer sanctions to ensure that those subject to prohibitions on taking employment did not work, provisions which are still in force although subject to very light touch enforcement where employers are concerned.[3] But the other, more shocking, change was the wholesale removal from entitlement to basic subsistence benefits of virtually everyone subject to immigration control except for port asylum claimants. Regulations to this effect were introduced in February 1996,[4] but were declared *ultra vires* in their application to asylum seekers in July 1996, because they 'necessarily contemplate for some a life so destitute that ... no civilised nation can tolerate it ... Something so uncompromisingly draconian can only be achieved by primary legislation'.[5] The government duly obliged, enacting the condemned regulation as section 11 of the 1996 Act.

1   The 'white list' of so-called safe countries under the Asylum (Designated Countries of Destination and Designated Safe Third Countries) Order 1996, SI 1996/2671, included Pakistan, from which women, Ahmadis, Christians and political activists had been found to be refugees. See *Ahmed (Iftikhar) v Secretary of State for the Home Department* [2000] INLR 1 (Ahmadis); *Islam v Secretary of State for the Home Department; R v Immigration Appeal Tribunal and Secretary of State for the Home Department, ex p Shah* [1999] 2 AC 629, [1999] INLR 144, HL (women). The designation of Pakistan was held unlawful in *R (on the application of Javed) v Secretary of State for the Home Department* upheld [2001] EWCA Civ 789, [2002] QB 129.
2   See eg *R v Secretary of State for the Home Department, ex p Canbolat* [1997] Imm AR 442; *Kerrouche v Secretary of State for the Home Department* [1997] Imm AR 610; *Iyadurai v Secretary of State for the Home Department* [1998] Imm AR 470; *R v Secretary of State for the Home Department, ex p Adan* [1999] Imm AR 521, CA; [2001] INLR 44, HL: see chapter 12 below.
3   See 14.84 fn 5 below.
4   Social Security (Persons from Abroad) Miscellaneous Amendments Regulations 1996, SI 1996/30.
5   *R v Secretary of State for Social Security, ex p Joint Council for the Welfare of Immigrants* [1997] 1 WLR 275, per Simon Brown LJ.

1.18 In the same year, the lack of due process afforded to those liable to removal on national security grounds came in for condemnation by the ECHR in *Chahal v United Kingdom*.[1] The extra-statutory advisory panel, whose recommendation did not bind the Secretary of State, and before which there was a right to appear but not to know the basis for removal, was not a 'court', and did not provide an effective remedy for possible breaches of Article 3 of the ECHR involved in the removal of such persons. The judgment led to the setting up of the Special Immigration Appeals Commission and a system of special advocates by the Special Immigration Appeals Commission Act 1997, which provides a parallel appeal system for 'national security' cases aiming both to safeguard the rights of the subject and to pay due regard to security concerns. In 2001 after 11 September, SIAC was given jurisdiction to hear appeals from foreign nationals who had been certified as suspected international terrorists linked to Al Qaeda under the Anti-terrorism Crime and Security Act 2001. This lasted until December 2004, when the House of Lords held that the whole system of indefinite detention of foreign nationals was unlawful under ECHR law as being discriminatory and disproportionate, and quashed the derogation order which had allowed it to happen.[2] The legislation has now lapsed and has been replaced by new laws which no longer come within the ambit of immigration law.[3] SIAC will now continue with its proper immigration appellate jurisdiction, hearing appeals which involve issues of national security.

[1]   (1996) 23 EHRR 413.
[2]   *A and X v Secretary of State for the Home Department* [2004] UKHL 56, [2005] 2 WLR 87.
[3]   Prevention of Terrorism Act 2005, which enacts a system of control orders for suspected terrorists, British or foreign, on the basis of reasonable suspicion.

1.19 Then came three Acts, which form the bulk of modern immigration and asylum law and are the source material for much of this edition – the Immigration and Asylum Act 1999, the Nationality Immigration and Asylum Act 2002 and the Asylum and Immigration (Treatment of Claimants, etc) Act 2004. Together they constitute a vast reorganisation of the law and practice in the field of immigration, asylum and to a lesser extent nationality. The changes have not been introduced in any coherent fashion, but bit by bit, changing something one year and then re-amending it later, or worse still, giving the Secretary of State power to amend by statutory instrument. The 1999 Act, like its 2002 successor, is a vast and rambling piece of legislation, spreading over several fields. Perhaps its main innovation was the introduction of a new system of asylum support and a new Home Office organisation to run it, called the National Asylum Support Service or NASS,[1] which has been embellished by the other two Acts. Apart from its section 2, which makes it a criminal offence for an asylum seeker to attend an interview without a passport or other identity document without a reasonable excuse,[2] and its ss 19–25, which restricts the right to marry (which probably compete for the vote as the nastiest new clauses of 2004) the main claim to fame of the 2004 Act is its recasting of the immigration appellate authority into a one tier Asylum and Immigration Tribunal and consigning adjudicators to the dustbin of history. We refer in detail to all these new laws in the chapters which follow. Below we give an Act-by-Act summary.

1   Immigration and Asylum Act 1999, Part V and Schs 5–7.
2   See *R v Wang (Bei Bei)* [2005] EWCA Civ 293, a guideline case under s 2, where a
     ten-month sentence was reduced to two months and a recommendation for deportation
     quashed against an 18-year-old Chinese girl who had pleaded guilty to the offence, having
     complied with the agent's instruction to return the travel document to him.

OUTLINE OF CURRENT IMMIGRATION AND ASYLUM LAW

The Immigration Act 1971

1.20 The Immigration Act 1971 contains the structure of immigration law, making provision for the right of abode,[1] for leave to enter and remain for those who do not have the right of abode,[2] defining a common travel area between the United Kingdom, the Islands and the Republic of Ireland where normal controls are modified,[3] for exemption from control for diplomats, crew members, armed forces and others,[4] and for the removal of those whose conduct is seen to merit removal[5] or (with the 1999 Act) who have no right to remain.[6] It delineates responsibility for immigration control: immigration officers at the port, dealing with leave to enter and with illegal entrants; the Secretary of State for the Home Department dealing with leave to remain and enforcement against overstayers.[7] It creates myriad offences to do with avoiding or obstructing or helping others to avoid or obstruct immigration controls,[8] as well as the unique offence of helping people to obtain the fundamental human right of claiming asylum,[9] although it is no longer the only immigration measure which creates criminal offences.[10] The corresponding powers of arrest, entry, search and seizure are spelt out in detail.[11] The 1971 Act contains the basic rule-making power enabling the Secretary of State to make detailed rules as to eligibility for entry and stay for persons coming for employment, for visits or for family reunion.[12] Schedule 2 to the Act sets out immigration officers' administrative powers of examination, detention and removal and ancillary powers of entry, search and seizure, and provisions for release on temporary admission or bail, while Schedule 3 sets out parallel detention, release and removal powers of the Secretary of State in relation to deportation. The 1971 Act used to contain provisions for appealing against immigration decisions, but these are now contained in the 2002 and 2004 Acts, below.

1   Immigration Act 1971, s 2.
2   Immigration Act 1971, s 3.
3   Immigration Act 1971, ss 1(3), 9, Sch 4.
4   Immigration Act 1971, ss 8 (exemption), 8A (inserted by Immigration and Asylum Act 1999 s 7) (persons ceasing to be exempt).
5   Immigration Act 1971, ss 3(5), 3(6), 5, 6 (deportation). Section 8B (inserted by Immigration and Asylum Act 1999, s 8) provides for certain individuals named or specified in UN or EU resolutions as war criminals etc to be refused entry.
6   Immigration Act 1971, Sch 2, para 9 (removal of illegal entrants); Immigration and Asylum Act 1999, s 10 (removal of overstayers). The provisions for deportation and removal also provide for members of the family of the principal to be deported or removed, subject to safeguards.
7   Immigration Act 1971, s 4. This neat division of responsibility is maintained by the Immigration (Leave to Enter and Remain) Order 2000, SI 2000/1161, which provides for cancellation abroad of leave to enter by immigration officers and of leave to remain by the Secretary of State, but has been blurred by the Immigration (Leave to Enter) Order 2001,

SI 2001/2590, which empowers the Secretary of State to grant or refuse leave to enter to a person who has made an asylum or human rights claim.

8   Immigration Act 1971, ss 24–27.

9   Immigration Act 1971, s 25A. Gain is an essential ingredient of the offence: see chapter 14 below.

10 Although many new offences created by subsequent legislation have been inserted into the 1971 Act (by ss 24A, 25A, 25B, 26A and 26B), the 1999 Act retains various offences concerning asylum support, as well as regulatory offences concerning unauthorised provision of immigration advice or services, detention centres, provision of information etc. The 2002 Act contains further offences relating to failure to provide information, and the AI(TC)A 2004 deals with the offences of failure to produce a passport on arrival, failure to cooperate with removal, and trafficking for exploitation. The offence of trafficking for prostitution, originally contained in the 2002 Act, has now been broadened to trafficking for sexual exploitation and is contained in the Sexual Offences Act 2003 ss 57–59 (see 14.46 below).

11 Immigration Act 1971, ss 28A–28K (inserted by the 1999 and 2002 Acts). The AI(TC)A 2004 adds new powers of arrest for immigration officers, on reasonable suspicion of an array of offences including fraud, bigamy, theft, perjury as well as trafficking, and applies the Immigration Act 1971 powers of entry, search and seizure to them (s 14).

12 Immigration Act 1971, s 1(4).

1.21 Sections 3A and 3B of the Immigration Act 1971, inserted by the Immigration and Asylum Act 1999, enabled the Secretary of State to change the structure of control. The Immigration (Leave to Enter and Remain) Order 2000[1] made under these sections, provides that leave to enter may be granted and refused, curtailed and varied abroad, and that in various circumstances defined in the Order, it does not lapse, as before, when the holder leaves the UK. The changes make control more flexible, allowing frequent travellers to continue travelling while applying to extend their stay, and removing for the most part the dual control of entry clearance followed by lengthy port procedures. A more profound effect of the changes is the possibility it creates for asylum seekers to be granted – or refused – leave to enter abroad, something canvassed by the British government in Europe at the instigation of a former Home Secretary both as a means of legalising refugees' travel to the UK (which would of course be welcome) and, more controversially, to reduce numbers by applying a quota, which could have an adverse impact on the right of asylum.[2] This was seen in operation in the *European Roma Rights Centre* case, where a pre-clearance scheme was operated at Prague airport to screen out potential asylum claimants before they embarked on their journey. The House of Lords confirmed that the Refugee Convention had no extra-territorial reach, so that there was nothing to prevent the Secretary of State from preventing the arrival of asylum claimants. It was the flagrant discrimination against Roma passengers which rendered the refusal of leave unlawful in that case.[3] Section 3C, also inserted by the 1999 Act, replaced 'VOLO' leave (deemed leave following the expiry of leave, pending the determination of an in-time extension application) by a new statutory leave which continues pending appeal against refusal.[4] Section 31A, inserted by the 1999 Act, requires applications for leave to remain under the Act to be made in a prescribed form.

1   SI 2000/1161.

2   Jack Straw 'An effective protection regime for the twenty-first century', speech to IPPR, 6 February 2001.

3   *European Roma Rights Centre v Immigration Officer at Prague Airport* [2003] EWCA Civ 666, [2003] INLR 374, revsd [2004] UKHL 55, [2005] 2 WLR 1.

⁴ Provided that the appeal too is lodged in time. VOLO leave was leave granted under the Variation of Leave Order 1976.

The Immigration Act 1988

1.22 The relevant parts of the 1988 Act which are still in force restrict the exercise of the right of abode of more than one wife in a polygamous marriage,[1] and most importantly, provide that persons exercising Community rights do not require leave to enter or remain in the UK under the 1971 Act.[2]

¹ Immigration Act 1988, s 2.
² Immigration Act 1988, s 7.

The Asylum and Immigration Appeals Act 1993

1.23 The only section of the 1993 Act which is still in force is section 2, which provides that nothing in the immigration rules under the 1971 Act shall lay down any practice which is contrary to the Refugee Convention. Judicial opinion has been divided as to the extent to which that section operates to incorporate the Refugee Convention into domestic law,[1] but the House of Lords affirmed in the *European Roma Rights* case that the Convention has been fully incorporated.[2]

¹ The House of Lords held in *R v Secretary of State for the Home Department, ex p Siva-kumaran* [1988] AC 958 at 990 that the Convention had been for all practical purposes incorporated by references in the immigration rules; in *R v Uxbridge Magistrates' Court, ex p Adimi* [2001] QB 667, [2000] 3 WLR 434, [1999] 4 All ER 520 the Divisional Court believed that the Convention may have been incorporated by legitimate expectation, a view subsequently resiled from by Simon Brown LJ and rejected by Laws LJ in *European Roma Rights* in the Court of Appeal: *European Roma Rights Centre v Immigration Officer at Prague Airport* [2003] EWCA Civ 666, [2003] INLR 374.
² *European Roma Rights Centre v Immigration Officer at Prague Airport* [2004] UKHL 55, [2005] 2 WLR 1, paras 7 (Lord Bingham) 41–42 (Lord Steyn), 50 (Lord Hope).

The Asylum and Immigration Act 1996

1.24 Apart from amendments to the 1971 Act, the sections of the 1996 Act which are still in force and relevant concern employer sanctions. Section 8 provides that employing someone who is not entitled to work in the UK is a criminal offence, and sets out a statutory defence. Section 8A provides for a Code of Practice for employers to avoid the racial discrimination in employment which was widely perceived as bound to follow. The provisions have not been rigorously enforced so far as employers are concerned, and made no dent in the exploitation to which irregular migrants are exposed.[1] Section 13 defines persons subject to immigration control, a definition still in use for housing provision.

¹ See 14.84 below.

The Special Immigration Appeals Commission Act 1997

1.25 The 1997 Act establishes an alternative forum for immigration appeals in cases in which national security, political or diplomatic considerations are engaged, either underlying refusal, deportation or removal, or as a reason for non-disclosure of evidence supporting such a decision.[1] The Commission provides exactly the same appeal rights as those provided by the 2002 Act, below,[2] but provides a procedure which allows some of the material on which the Secretary of State relies to be withheld from the appellant and his or her legal representatives, but disclosed to a 'special advocate' who is briefed to test the 'closed' evidence on behalf of the appellant.[3] The role of the Special Immigration Appeals Commission was extended to review the derogation from the ECHR and the detention of suspected international terrorists under the Anti-terrorism, Crime and Security Act 2001[4] between 2001 and 2005, but the relevant provisions lapsed in March 2005 and the Commission's role reverts to deciding appeals and applications under the 1997 Act. SIAC appeals are dealt with at 18.160 below.

[1]   Ie, appeals certified under Nationality, Immigration and Asylum Act 2002, s 97.
[2]   Special Immigration Appeals Commission Act 1997, s 2.
[3]   By rules made under s 5 Special Immigration Appeals Commission Act 1997; see SI 2003/1034.
[4]   Anti-terrorism, Crime and Security Act 2001, ss 21–27.

The Immigration and Asylum Act 1999

1.26 As indicated above, much of the Immigration and Asylum Act 1999 consists of amendments to the 1971 Act, which we do not need to traverse again. But in addition, the 1999 Act contains the schemes for carriers' liability, the regulation of immigration service providers, asylum support and the regulation of detention centres (now renamed removal centres), as well as dealing with removal of overstayers and others in breach of control, finger-printing and the use of force in performing immigration functions, and imposing new procedures on marriage registrars. Much of the meat of the 1999 Act, like its successors, is not in the text of the Act itself but is to be found in the plethora of Orders and Regulations to which it has given birth.

Part I of the Immigration and Asylum Act 1999 contains a random grouping of disparate measures:

(i)   *Leave and fees.* These include the provisions about leave to enter or remain described above,[1] and a power to charge fees on applications for leave[2] and for travel documents.[3]

(ii) *Financial bonds.* Sections 16 and 17, not yet in force, provide for financial bonds or security to be taken by the government as a condition of the grant of entry clearance and extensions of leave. The government has not implemented the scheme, but has indicated an interest in doing so in the context of admitting unskilled workers, in its five-year strategy.[4]

(iii) *Information and control facilities.* There are various administrative measures for obtaining passenger and criminal intelligence information,[5] for monitoring refusals of entry clearance,[6] and for the provision of immigration control facilities at ports of entry.[7]

(iv) *Accommodation.* Section 4 deals with the provision of accommodation for those temporarily admitted or released from detention and was clearly intended to reduce the need to detain people who have no address to go to. As amended, it also provides for accommodation for failed asylum seekers,[8] the group of persons who have made the most use of the provision.[9]

(v) *Overstayers.* One of the most significant and controversial changes made by the 1999 Act was the placing of overstayers and others who breach conditions on the same footing as illegal entrants subject to summary removal, with a consequent loss of appeal rights against deportation.[10]

(vii) *Criminal offences.* Apart from the additional criminal offences inserted into the Immigration Act 1971 by sections 28 to 30, section 31 is a response to the Divisional Court decision in *Ex p Adimi*[11] which held that the prosecution of asylum seekers for travelling with false documents is a breach of Article 31 of the 1951 Refugee Convention, providing a statutory defence based on Article 31, but in more limited circumstances than those set out in the judgments in *Adimi*.[12]

(viii) Registrars are required to report suspected 'sham' marriages to the Home Office,[13] a power which goes hand-in-hand with a new regime governing the celebration of all marriages, not just those with an immigration slant, contained in Part IX.[14] These provisions have been built on by the AI(TC)A 2004: see below.

1   Immigration and Asylum Act 1999, ss 1–3; see 1.21 above.
2   Immigration and Asylum Act 1999, s 5. The Nationality, Immigration and Asylum Act 2002, s 122 adds the power to charge for the issue of immigration employment documents, while the Asylum and Immigration (Treatment of Claimants, etc) Act 2004, s 42 permits the Secretary of State to charge more than the administrative costs of processing the applications, to reflect the benefits likely to accrue by the grant.
3   Immigration and Asylum Act 1999, s 27. This refers to Geneva Convention travel documents and to certificates of identity for those granted humanitarian protection or discretionary leave: see 12.178 below.
4   Controlling our borders, making migration work for Britain: Five-year strategy for immigration and asylum, Cm 6472, February 2005.
5   Immigration and Asylum Act 1999, s 18–20, amending the Immigration Act 1971.
6   Immigration and Asylum Act 1999, s 23.
7   Immigration and Asylum Act 1999, s 25–26. In committee the Government stated that that the supply of information to the Home Office would be subject to the requirements of the data protection laws and the Human Rights Act 1998 (protection of privacy).
8   Subsections (2)–(4) were inserted by Nationality, Immigration and Asylum Act 2002, s 49, which also changed the heading of the section from 'bail hostels'. Subsections (5)–(9), added by the Asylum and Immigration (Treatment of Claimants, etc) Act 2004 s 10 from 31 December 2004 (SI 2004/2999), enable regulations to be made setting out the criteria for support under the amended section. See now the Immigration and Asylum (Provision of Accommodation to Failed Asylum Seekers) Regulations 2005, SI 2005/930, in force 31 March 2005.
9   See *R (on the application of Salih) v Secretary of State for the Home Department* [2003] EWHC 2273 (Admin), [2003] All ER (D) 129 (Oct).
10 Immigration and Asylum Act 1999, s 10 and Sch 14, para 44. Section 9 provided a regularisation period from 1 February to 1 October 2000; see Immigration (Regularisation Period for Overstayers) Regulations 2000, SI 2000/265. Those whose deportation is

conducive to the public good and family members of deportees can still be deported and will have a merits appeal against deportation as before. Overstayers may appeal on human rights grounds before removal, unless their claim is certified clearly unfounded. See chapter 18 below.

11 *R v Uxbridge Magistrates' Court, ex p Adimi* [1999] 4 All ER 520, [1999] INLR 490, DC. See further chapter 14 below; Jill Francis 'Section 31 of the Immigration and Asylum Act – Defences based on Art 31(1) of the Refugee Convention' (2000) INLP 81.
12 The High Court has held that is the statutory defence which reflects the UK's incorporation of Article 31 and which should be relied on by defendants, and not the *Adimi* judgment: *R (on the application of Pepushi) v Crown Prosecution Service* [2004] EWHC 798 (Admin), (2004) Times, 21 May.
13 Immigration and Asylum Act 1999, s 24.
14 Immigration and Asylum Act 1999, ss 160–163 and Sch 14, paras 1–32.

1.27 Provisions for automatic bail hearings enacted in Part III of the Act were never brought into force, and all that survives is a power to make regulations in relation to bail applications, and the extension of bail to deportation cases under the 1971 Act.[1] The extension of the powers of immigration officers in Part VII of the 1999 Act include greatly increased fingerprinting powers[2] and the power to use force,[3] which enable immigration officers to act as fully fledged immigration police. Part VIII regulates detention centres (now known as 'removal centres') and their staff.[4] Part II, dealing with carriers' liability, re-enacted and extended the 1987 carriers' liability legislation, imposing civil penalties for failure to fulfil the extensive duties to check and control passengers and to ensure that no clandestine entrants are carried.[5] Part II was extensively amended by the 2002 Act after its provisions for penalties and forfeiture of vehicles carrying clandestine entrants were declared incompatible with the ECHR by the Court of Appeal.[6] These are dealt with in chapter 14 below.

1 Immigration and Asylum Act 1999, ss 53, as amended by Nationality, Immigration and Asylum Act 2002, ss 62, 114, Sch 7, para 28; s 54 (brought into force 10 February 2003, SI 2003/2).
2 Immigration and Asylum Act 1999, s 141ff.
3 Immigration and Asylum Act 1999, s 146.
4 The name was changed by Nationality, Immigration and Asylum Act 2002 s 66. See also Immigration and Asylum Act 1999, Schs 11 and 12, and the Detention Centre Rules 2001, SI 2001/238.
5 Immigration and Asylum Act 1999, ss 32–43 and Sch 1, as amended by Nationality, Immigration and Asylum Act 2002 s 125, Sch 8. See also the Carriers' Liability (Clandestine Entrants) (Code of Practice) Order 2000, SI 2000/684; Carriers' Liability (Clandestine Entrants and Sale of Transporters) Regulations 2000, SI 2000/685 as amended by SI 2001/311; Carriers' Liability (Application to Rail Freight) Regulations 2001, SI 2001/280; Carriers' Liability (Clandestine Entrants) (Code of Practice for Rail Freight) Order 2001, SI 2001/312; Carriers' Liability Regulations 2002, SI 2002/2817. See 14.88 below.
6 *International Transport Roth GmbH v Secretary of State for the Home Department* [2002] EWCA Civ 158, [2002] 3 WLR 344.

1.28 Part V of the Immigration and Asylum Act 1999 contains the scheme for the registration and supervision of those advising on immigration and asylum matters who have no professional qualification as solicitors or barristers. An Immigration Services Commissioner and an Immigration Services Tribunal oversee registration and disciplinary measures. The provisions, together with amendments under the Asylum and Immigration (Treatment of Claimants, etc) Act 2004, make it a criminal offence for unregistered advisers to provide or to advertise advice or services, or to obstruct the Commissioner, who has powers of entry, search and seizure in the investigation of offences. Although members of the legal profession are exempt, there are powers to bring them into the scheme at a later date, and the Commissioner has powers in relation to discipline by professional bodies.[1]

[1] Immigration and Asylum Act 1999, ss 82–93; Schs 5–7, as amended by Asylum and Immigration (Treatment of Claimants, etc) Act 2004 ss 37–41 from 1 October 2004 (SI 2004/2523).

1.29 Part VI of the Immigration and Asylum Act 1999 contains the main scheme of support for asylum seekers, given meat by the Asylum Support Regulations.[1] Persons subject to immigration control, as defined in this Part, are removed from social security benefits and related provisions. Instead, asylum seekers receive their support through a Home Office-run system,[2] which largely replaces benefits and support under the National Assistance Act 1948 and the Children Act 1989. Access to this compulsion-based system of support is controlled by a test of destitution. Part VI also provides the framework for the involuntary dispersal of asylum seekers throughout the UK. To make this stringent scheme more palatable, there are appeals to Asylum Support Adjudicators against refusal of support.[3] The new provisions are described fully in chapter 13 below. This basic scheme has been amended by the 2002 and 2004 Acts; see below. The 2002 Act excludes from NASS support late asylum claimants who have no dependent children,[4] and additionally excludes from social services support other classes of person including EEA nationals and family members, persons unlawfully in the UK and failed asylum claimants.[5] These provisions and the changes summarised at 1.34, below are dealt with in chapter 13.

[1] SI 2000/704, as amended by SI 2002/472, SI 2002/2619, SI 2002/3110, SI 2003/241, SI 2004/1313, SI 2005/11, SI 2005/738; see also Asylum Support (Interim Provision) Regulations 1999, SI 1999/3056, as amended by SI 2002/471, SI 2004/566, SI 2005/595. The provisions of Part V and Sch 8 impact on the whole welfare field, including homeless persons, social security, allocation of housing, council tax, income related benefits, jobseekers' allowance and NHS charges. See chapter 13 below, and see Willman, Knafler and Pierce *Support for asylum seekers* (2nd edn, 2004), Legal Action Group.
[2] The National Asylum Support Service (NASS), effective from April 2000; see Immigration and Asylum Act 1999, Schs 8–10. Schedule 9, which came into force in December 1999, provided an interim support scheme which is similar in outline but which is run by local authorities. It still runs in parallel with the Home Office scheme.
[3] Immigration and Asylum Act 1999, s 103.
[4] Nationality, Immigration and Asylum Act 2002, s 55. Support must be provided when required to prevent a breach of human rights obligations.
[5] Nationality, Immigration and Asylum Act 2002 s 54, Sch 3. Support must be provided when required to prevent a breach of human rights obligations.

The Race Relations (Amendment) Act 2000

1.30 The Race Relations (Amendment) Act 2000 extends the scope of the Race Relations Act 1976 in relation to public authorities, outlawing race discrimination in functions not previously covered. The new section 19B makes it unlawful for a public authority to do any act which constitutes discrimination. This covers all public authorities carrying out immigration and nationality functions, such as the Home Office, Foreign Office, and local authorities involved in providing for asylum seekers. However, the ambit of the new power is severely curtailed. A minister of the Crown and immigration officials[1] are never allowed to discriminate on grounds of *race* or *colour*[2] in immigration and asylum matters, but a minister acting personally, and an immigration officer acting in accordance with a ministerial authorisation, may do so on grounds of *nationality* or *ethnic or national origins*.[3] Under such an authorisation, Kurds or Afghans may be given a harder time by immigration officers simply because of who they are.[4] Authorisations based on nationality cover examination of passengers seeking entry, prioritisation of asylum claims, permission to work outside the immigration rules, and language and document analysis.[5] This licence to discriminate has been rightly criticised by some commentators,[6] and the courts have attempted to ensure that it is applied strictly. In the *Tamil Information Centre* case, Forbes J held *ultra vires* a ministerial authorisation which allowed immigration officers to discriminate when examining passengers on the basis of intelligence or statistics, because it unlawfully delegated the analysis of the intelligence and statistics, and the decision to discriminate, to officers, when this should have been exercised personally by the Secretary of State.[7] Since July 2003, ministerial authorisations allowing discrimination in the examination of passengers seeking entry have been issued monthly on a transparent statistical basis.[8] Discrimination which is not expressly authorised by a ministerial authorisation remains unlawful. The House of Lords so held in a resounding decision in the *European Roma Rights* case;[9] the justification for the discrimination against the Roma which denied them access to aircraft coming to the UK, that they were more likely to claim asylum on arrival than non-Roma, was rejected on the simple basis that direct discrimination, unlike indirect discrimination, can never be justified.[10] The House of Lords issued another resounding decision a week later, holding the derogation from Article 5 and the indefinite detention of foreign nationals under the Anti-terrorism, Crime and Security Act 2001 discriminatory and unlawful, but by reference to Article 14 ECHR rather than domestic race relations law.[11] No similar amendment has been made to the Sex Discrimination Act 1975, and it therefore continues to be of no relevance to immigration decisions.[12] Where the immigration service is involved in the investigation and prosecution of offences in Part III of the Immigration Act 1971, they are in the same position under the Race Relations Act 1976 as the police.[13]

---

[1] Race Relations Act 1976, s 19D(2), as amended by Race Relations (Amendment) Act 2000.

[2] Race Relations Act 1976, s 19D(1).

[3] Race Relations Act 1976, s 19D(3). The 2000 Act amendment allowed for discrimination in nationality functions, but the Nationality, Immigration and Asylum Act 2002, s 6 removed that limb of the exception. Section 19D(4) and (5) (as amended by the 2002 and 2004 Acts) define these as functions exercisable by virtue of the Immigration Acts (save for the powers of entry, search and seizure under s 28A–K of the 1971 Act and s 14 of the Asylum and Immigration (Treatment of Claimants, etc) Act 2004), the Special Immigration Appeals Commission Act, provisions under s 2 of the European Communities Act 1972 and Community law provisions relating to immigration and asylum. The Secretary of State no longer issues authorisations to discriminate on grounds of ethnic or national origins, only on nationality grounds: see 2nd report of the immigration race monitor, on IND website.

4   See the Race Relations (Immigration and Asylum) Authorisations, in IDI Feb 03, Ch 1, s 11, Annex EE, EE1, EE2. Astonishingly, the authorisation of March 2001, which came into force on 2 April 2001, was still posted on the IND website at the time of writing, despite the fact that it is no longer used, after being held *ultra vires* in *R (on the application of Tamil Information Centre) v Secretary of State for the Home Department* [2002] EWHC 2155, (2002) Times, 30 October.

5   These authorisations are not to be found anywhere on the Home Office website (see fn 4 above), but are described in independent race monitor Mary Coussey's second annual report (2003/4), presented to Parliament in March 2004. They are generally circulated by ILPA.

6   Ann Dummett 'The immigration exceptions in the Race Relation (Amendent) Act 2000', ILPA, 2001. In her second annual report (fn 5 above), the independent race monitor expressed concern about apparent case hardening and cynicism in dealing with asylum claims from certain nationalities, which could become self-perpetuating, and recommended more stringent quality control, training and an independent element in initial decision-making (paras 14–21).

7   *R (on the application of Tamil Information Centre) v Secretary of State for the Home Department* [2002] EWHC 2155, (2002) Times, 30 October.

8   See fn 5, and 3.3 below.

9   *European Roma Rights Centre v Immigration Officer at Prague Airport* [2004] UKHL 55, [2005] 2 WLR 1. The operation conducted by UK immigration officials at Prague Airport in an attempt to stop Roma people coming to the UK to claim asylum was unlawful under both domestic and international law: see further at 8.98 and 8.114 below.

10 As opposed to indirect discrimination (imposing a qualification which can be met by fewer persons in the applicant's group than the comparator group, which may be justified. Article 14 ECHR makes no distinction, and allows States to discriminate if such discrimination is objectively justified and proportionate: see fn 12 below and see 8.98.

11 *A and X v Secretary of State for the Home Department* [2004] UKHL 56, [2005] 2 WLR 87. The decisive factor for the House of Lords was the security services' acceptance that British nationals (who could not be interned) were just as likely to be engaged in terrorist activity as foreign nationals.

12 *Re Amin* [1983] 2 AC 818, HL.

13 Race Relations Act 1976, s 19D(5)(a) (as amended).

1.31 Section 71 of the Race Relations Act 1976 is replaced by a new section[1] imposing a duty on public authorities to have due regard to the need to eliminate unlawful discrimination and to promote equality of opportunity and good relations between persons of different racial groups. Public authorities such as the Home Office, which carry out immigration and nationality functions, are subject to these duties insofar as they require the promotion of good race relations between persons of different racial groups.[2]

1   Race Relations Act 1976, s 71, as amended by Race Relations (Amendment) Act 2000, s 2. A whole raft of statutory instruments flesh out the general statutory duty.

2   Race Relations Act 1976, s 71A, as amended by Nationality, Immigration and Asylum Act 2002, s 6, modifying the general statutory duty in relation to immigration and nationality functions as inserted.

1.32 Where complaints of race discrimination are made relating to immigration decisions,[1] they should be brought before the Asylum and Immigration Tribunal in the same way as an appeal on human rights grounds, rather than in the county court,[2] but the Act does not permanently exclude the jurisdiction of the country court, to which a discrimination claim may be brought if the Tribunal does not deal with the issue on appeal.[3] An immigration appeal may be allowed solely on the ground that there has been unlawful discrimination,[4] and the Tribunal or Special Immigration Appeals Commission can then refer the case to the county court for assessment of a claim for damages.[5] A county court cannot question an immigration decision.[6]

1 Race Relations Act 1976, s 57A(2), inserted by Race Relations (Amendment) Act 2000, s 6.
2 Race Relations Act 1976, s 57A(1).
3 *Bibi v Immigration Appeal Tribunal* [2005] EWHC (Admin) 386, Hughes J.
4 Nationality, Immigration and Asylum Act 2002, s 84(1)(b).
5 Race Relations Act 1976, s 57A(3).
6 Race Relations Act 1976, s 57A(4).

The Nationality, Immigration and Asylum Act 2002

1.33 The Nationality, Immigration and Asylum Act 2002, like the 1999 Act, covers a number of distinct areas in its 164 sections and nine schedules. Part 1 amends the British Nationality Act 1981 in a number of distinct ways, including a new allegiance ceremony for those who acquire British citizenship by registration or naturalisation,[1] a new power to deprive British citizens of their citizenship for doing anything seriously prejudicial to the vital interests of Britain or an overseas territory, and new appeal rights against deprivation;[2] it also gives British overseas citizens, who lost their special voucher rights in 2002, a right to register as British citizens if they have no other citizenship or nationality; the same right applies to British subjects under the British Nationality Act 1981 and to British Protected Persons.[3] Section 11 defines the phrase 'in breach of the immigration laws' for the purpose of nationality.[4] We deal with these and the other nationality changes in chapter 2.

1 Nationality, Immigration and Asylum Act 2002, ss 1, 3, Sch 1, amending British Nationality Act 1981 by replacing s 42, inserting s 42A, amending Sch 1 and replacing Sch 5.
2 NIAA 2002, s 4, replacing British Nationality Act 1981, s 40 and inserting a new s 40A (amended by Asylum and Immigration (Treatment of Claimants, etc) Act 2004, Sch 2, para 4). British citizens by birth may be deprived of citizenship under the new provisions, unless they would otherwise be stateless.
3 NIAA 2002, s 12, inserting new British Nationality Act 1981, s 4B.
4 An important effect of the section is to ensure that persons on temporary admission following a port asylum or human rights claim may naturalise (according to the provisions of the 1981 Act), following the grant of indefinite leave to remain, without being penalised for the time spent on temporary admission. The section does not apply to illegal entrants or overstayers granted temporary admission while their claims are decided, however. The definition is applied to exclusion from various forms of support under Sch 3, para 7 ('Fourth class of ineligible person: person unlawfully in UK'): see chapter 13 below.

1.34 Parts 2 and 3 of the 2002 Act deal with asylum support, and Part 3 additionally deals with other support and assistance. Part 2 provides for the housing of asylum claimants in accommodation centres.[1] The original plan was to hold 750 claimants, including family members, in each remote centre, with on-site medical and educational facilities.[2] The plans have been scaled down since. At the time of writing, no accommodation centre is open. Section 18 redefines 'asylum seeker' for the purpose of asylum support to include a requirement that an application is made at a specified place, rather than anywhere, as before.[3] Part 3 amends the 1999 Act asylum support provisions,[4] to give the Secretary of State further powers to decide how, when and whether to provide support.[5] It provides for the exclusion from support of certain persons[6] and for late claimants.[7] Part 3 also provides for assistance for voluntary leavers, previously catered for in the 1971 Act,[8] and enables the Secretary of State to participate in international projects to reduce migration, assist or ensure the return of migrants or their settlement (in the UK or elsewhere) and allied purposes.[9] We deal with asylum support at chapter 13 below.

1   Nationality, Immigration and Asylum Act 2002, ss 16–42.
2   The public justification was 'swamping' of schools and doctors' surgeries by asylum seekers, but this blatant populism was disavowed by the Secretary of State in parliament, where he revealed that the true purpose of the centres was to prevent integration, which made removal of failed claimants difficult: see Hansard HC 24 April 2002, col 353.
3   See 13.39 and 13.41 below.
4   NIAA 2002, ss 44–47 (not wholly in force), 48 (amending Immigration and Asylum Act 1999, s 4 to add failed asylum seekers to those who may be provided with accommodation under that section), 50 (adding provisions as to conditions of support), 53 (revising the appeals provisions of the 1999 Act).
5   For example the Home Office can stop providing 'support only' to destitute asylum claimants with their own accommodation (not yet in force): Nationality, Immigration and Asylum Act 2002, s 43; see also s 51, enabling the Secretary of State to decide which form of support under the 1999 and 2002 Acts to offer.
6   Those with refugee status abroad, citizens of EEA States or their dependants, former asylum seekers who have failed to cooperate with removal directions and persons unlawfully in the UK are ineligible for support (whether NASS or the various forms of welfare support provided by local authorities) unless they are children, British citizens or support is necessary to prevent a breach of human rights obligations: s 54, Sch 3. See 13.178 below.
7   See 13.55ff.
8   NIAA 2002, s 58. The Immigration Act 1971, s 29 provisions were designed to assist voluntary repatriation of those with leave to remain. The new provisions contain no such limitation, and may be used for 'explore and return' programmes for failed asylum claimants.
9   NIAA 2002, s 59. The provisions are wide enough to include funding UNHCR in setting up quota schemes for refugees (whereby refugees are screened abroad for settlement), and the International Organisation for Migration in its return programmes. Human Rights Watch has expressed concern that IOM does not consider itself bound by *non-refoulement* obligations; see Joint Statement by Amnesty International and Human Rights Watch to IOM Governing Council, 2–3 December 2002, on Human Rights Watch website.

1.35 Part 4 of the 2002 Act, headed 'Detention and removal', enables the Secretary of State to exercise detention and bail powers similar to those of immigration officers,[1] ensures that any use of force by officials is confined to what is reasonable,[2] deals with the powers and duties of detainee custody officers,[3] changes the name of detention centres to removal centres,[4] and provides that persons who cannot be removed may still be treated as liable to detention.[5] More details are at chapter 17. It also enables asylum seekers to be sent to induction centres for a fortnight to be 'educated about the nature of the asylum process',[6] and allows restrictions to be imposed on visitors and students who claim asylum.[7] It defines 'particularly serious crimes' for the purpose of exclusion from the *non-refoulement* protection of the Refugee Convention,[8] and allows refugees' indefinite leave to remain to be revoked for actions inconsistent with the status.[9] It amends provisions relating to removal of family members of overstayers and other immigration offenders under the 1999 Act,[10] and re-states the protection against removal provided for asylum claimants and for all manner of appellants.[11] In other words it covers a whole farrago of bits and pieces.

1   Nationality, Immigration and Asylum Act 2002, ss 62 (detention), 68 (bail).
2   NIAA 2002, s 63.
3   NIAA 2002, ss 64, 65.
4   NIAA 2002, s 66.
5   NIAA 2002, s 67, enacted in response to the decision of the High Court in *R (on the application of Khadir) v Secretary of State for the Home Department* (CO/5118/2001, 29 July 2002) that Iraqis who could not be removed were not 'liable to be detained' and so could not be subjected to the immigration limbo of temporary admission indefinitely. As a result of the enactment of s 67, the decision was reversed at [2003] EWCA Civ 475, [2003] INLR 426, and at time of writing, was on appeal in the House of Lords.
6   NIAA 2002, s 70, allowing for the imposition of a residence condition to stay in such a centre. See chapter 12.
7   NIAA 2002, s 71. The power to impose restrictions under this section appears to be additional to any conditions which may be attached to the leave under s Immigration Act 1971, s 3C, for which see 4.17 below.
8   NIAA 2002, s 72; Nationality, Immigration and Asylum Act 2002 (Specification of Particularly Serious Crimes) Order 2004, SI 2004/1910.
9   NIAA 2002, s 76, putting into statutory form Article 1C(1)–(4) of the Refugee Convention.
10 NIAA 2002, s 73. It also amends the removal powers under Immigration and Asylum Act 1999, s 10 (s 74) and updates Immigration Act 1971, s 7 (exemption from deportation) (s 75).
11 NIAA 2002, ss 77–79. Provisions relating to removal of asylum claimants to safe third countries have been repealed and replaced by the Asylum and Immigration (Treatment of Claimants, etc) Act 2004 (below).

1.36 Part 5 of the 2002 Act, with its AI(TC)A 2004 amendments, sets out the new system of immigration appeals. Immigration decisions, defined by section 82, may be appealed to the recently formed Asylum and Immigration Tribunal[1] on grounds which are comprehensively set out in the statute.[2] Exceptions to appeal rights[3] and special 'upgrade' asylum appeals[4] are provided. The Act also outlines the matters to be considered in determining an appeal,[5] the powers of the Tribunal,[6] and whether the appeal is to be in-country or abroad,[7] suspensive of removal or not. Appeals against removal on asylum and human rights grounds do not suspend removal if the Secretary of State certifies them clearly unfounded, and claims in relation to specified countries are subject to a quasi-presumption to that effect.[8] A one-stop appeal system requires applicants and appellants to state all grounds on which they seek to remain, and precludes appeals where there has been an earlier opportunity to raise the ground now relied on.[9] Decisions involving national security, diplomatic or political considerations are hived off to SIAC (see 1.25 above). From the Tribunal, an appeal may either go to the High Court or its Scottish or Irish equivalents for reconsideration, or to the Court of Appeal or Court of Session, depending on the composition of the Tribunal which decided the appeal and whether the decision was itself a reconsideration.[10] The Act defines when an appeal is pending[11] and enables regulation of notices of immigration decisions and procedure on appeals, and for practice directions, funding of reconsideration and subsequent appeals, and other ancillary matters.[12] Fuller details are at chapter 18, below.

1   Nationality, Immigration and Asylum Act 2002, s 81, substituted by Asylum and Immigration (Treatment of Claimants, etc) Act 2004 s 26(1) from 4 April 2005. As originally enacted, s 81 provided for adjudicators who heard first-instance appeals, with s 101 (repealed by the AI(TC)A 2004, s 26(5)) providing an appeal to the IAT on a point of law.
2   NIAA 2002, s 84. Section 109 enables regulations to make provision for EEA appeals: see the Immigration (European Economic Area) Regulations 2000, SI 2000/2326, as amended by SI 2003/3188, 2004/1236 and 2005/47.

3   NIAA 2002, ss 88–91 (s 88A inserted by Asylum and Immigration (Treatment of Claimants, etc) Act 2004, s 29(1) 1 October 2004 (SI 2004/2523).
4   NIAA 2002, s 83 as amended by Asylum and Immigration (Treatment of Claimants, etc) Act 2004, s 26(3) as from 4 April 2005.
5   NIAA 2002, s 85.
6   NIAA 2002, ss 86, 87 (s 87 amended by Asylum and Immigration (Treatment of Claimants, etc) Act 2004, Sch 2, para 19 from 4 April 2005).
7   NIAA 2002, s 92, amended by Asylum and Immigration (Treatment of Claimants, etc) Act 2004, s 28 from 1 October 2004 (SI 2004/2523).
8   NIAA 2002, s 94, amended by Asylum and Immigration (Treatment of Claimants, etc) Act 2004, s 27 from 1 October 2004. There is provision for a monitor of clearly unfounded claims in s 111.
9   NIAA 2002, ss 120, 96 (s 96 amended by Asylum and Immigration (Treatment of Claimants, etc) Act 2004, s 30 from 1 October 2004).
10 NIAA 2002, ss 103A–E, inserted by Asylum and Immigration (Treatment of Claimants, etc) Act 2004, s 26(6) from 4 April 2005.
11 NIAA 2002, s 104, amended by Asylum and Immigration (Treatment of Claimants, etc) Act 2004, Sch 2 para 20, from 4 April 2005.
12 NIAA 2002, ss 105–107, amended by Asylum and Immigration (Treatment of Claimants, etc) Act 2004, Sch 2, paras 21ff, from 4 April 2005. Public funding of reconsideration appeals is dealt with in s 103D and by procedure rules; funding of SIAC appeals by s 116 and of Northern Ireland appeals by s 117. Section 110 enables grants to be made to voluntary organisations providing advice and assistance to appellants.

1.37 Part 6 of the 2002 Act contains miscellaneous provisions on immigration procedure. It amends the provisions of the 1971 Act governing applications and statutory leave,[1] and enables fees to be charged for work permits.[2] It amends carriers' liability provisions, and enables the Secretary of State to set up an authority to carry scheme[3] and to implement juxtaposed controls (whereby UK and French immigration controls are exercised at each other's borders);[4] requires applicants to provide biometric data on demand[5] and gives the Secretary of State increased powers to demand information from a range of public bodies and private persons.[6] It makes minor amendments to the regulation of immigration service providers,[7] and establishes the Advisory Panel on Country Information.[8] Part 7 of the Act amends the criminal provisions of the 1971 and 1996 Acts, amending and adding offences and creating more powers of arrest and ancillary powers. Part 8 provides consequential, interpretative and final provisions.

1   Nationality, Immigration and Asylum Act 2002, s 118, amending statutory leave under s 3C of the Immigration Act 1971 (inserted by Immigration and Asylum Act 1999, s 3); s 119, making a minor amendment to the provisions for examination of passengers under Sch 2, para 6 of the 1971 Act; s 120 (requirement to state additional grounds of application) (replacing the complicated one-stop provisions of ss 73–76 of the Immigration and Asylum Act 1999); s 121 (formalities for valid applications, amending s 31A of the 1971 Act).
2   NIAA 2002, s 122.
3   NIAA 2002, s 125 and Sch 8 replace the draconian and unlawful provisions relating to carriers of clandestine entrants under ss 32ff of the 1999 Act; s 124 sets out the framework for an authority to carry scheme, whereby carriers will be required to provide advance passenger information to the Home Office and may not allow passengers to embark without authorisation (see 14.100 below).
4   NIAA 2002 s 141 enables provisions for juxtaposed controls to be made in accordance with the Le Touquet agreement and any similar agreement; see Nationality, Immigration and Asylum (Juxtaposed Controls) Order 2003, SI 2003/2818 (at 3.28 below).
5   NIAA 2002, ss 126, 128 (compulsory provision): see Immigration (Provision of Physical Data) Regulations 2003, SI 2003/1875 as amended by SI 2004/474 and SI 2004/1834, 3.16 below; s 127 (voluntary provision), see 2nd annual report of the independent race monitor, March 2004, referring to 'frequent flyer' schemes at Miami and Madrid.

6   NIAA 2002, ss 129 (local authorities, on whereabouts of suspected immigration offenders), 134–135 (employers and financial institutions, on suspected immigration or asylum support offenders). The Inland Revenue may provide information but may not be compelled (s 130). Failure to comply with a requirement is an offence: s 137. Character information may be provided by police and other law enforcement agencies under s 20 Immigration and Asylum Act 1999 in connection with naturalisation applications: s 131, and documents or Articles provided under s 20 may be retained for immigration purposes: s 132. Medical inspectors may make disclosure of health information about an individual to a health service body: s 133.
7   NIAA 2002, ss 123, 140.
8   NIAA 2002, s 142. See 12.126 below.

The Asylum and Immigration (Treatment of Claimants, etc) Act 2004

1.38 The centrepiece of the AI(TC)A 2004 is the radical revision of the appeals regime, which we have dealt with at 1.36 above. The Act creates a number of new criminal offences. For example it is now a criminal offence to flee from persecution, if you arrive, but cannot produce a passport or other satisfactory identity document at your interview with immigration officer and cannot prove you have a reasonable excuse for your delinquency. After this, there is a serious new offence of trafficking people for exploitation, existing offences are amended and immigration officers are given a range of new police powers.[1] There is now a statutory presumption that certain kinds of behaviour, listed in the Act, such as destroying a passport, will be treated as damaging an asylum claimant's credibility.[2] Then there are provisions dealing with support and accommodation for failed asylum seekers[3] and the backdating of benefits and the grant of 'integration loans' to refugees.[4] The Act makes it easier to remove asylum claimants to safe third countries, by extending presumptions of safety under both the Refugee and Human Rights Conventions, or under the Refugee Convention only, to a wider range of countries, and preventing any appeal inconsistent with the presumption.[5] There are minor amendments to passenger information and control provisions.[6] Charges may exceed the administrative cost of processing applications, and may be levied for transferring leave stamps to a new passport.[7] Major changes wrought by the AI(TC)A 2004 require those subject to immigration control to get written permission to marry from the Secretary of State unless they came with entry clearance for marriage,[8] or can find a friendly vicar to marry them in church. Finally, the Act provides for release on bail or temporary admission to be subject to a condition of electronic monitoring.[9]

1   See Asylum and Immigration (Treatment of Claimants, etc) Act 2004, s 1 (amending s 25 Immigration Act 1971), s 3 (amending s 5 Forgery and Counterfeiting Act), s 6 (amending s 8 Asylum and Immigration Act 1996, s 7 (enabling the Director of Public Prosecution to give advice to immigration officers), (all in force 1 October 2004, SI 2004/2523); s 14 (immigration officers' powers of arrest) (in force 1 December 2004, SI 2004/2999).
2   AI(TC)A 2004, s 8, in force 1 October 2004 for the purpose of making regulations: SI 2004/2523. See the Immigration (Claimant's Credibility) Regulations 2004, SI 2004/3263.
3   AI(TC)A 2004, ss 9, 10 (in force 1 December 2004, SI 2004/2999, amending Nationality, Immigration and Asylum Act 2002 Sch 3 and Immigration and Asylum Act 1999, s 4); Immigration and Asylum (Provision of Accommodation to Failed Asylum Seekers) Regulations 2005, SI 2005/930. Section 11 (in force 4 January 2005: SI 2004/2999) prevents recognised refugees from asserting a local connection with the area from which they were dispersed, reversing the effect of *Al-Ameri v Royal Borough of Kensington and Chelsea; Osman v London Borough Council of Harrow* [2004] UKHL 4, [2004] 2 AC 159.

4   AI(TC)A 2004, ss 12–13 (not yet in force). Back-dating of benefits for refugees was provided in exchange for removal of statutory benefits for asylum seekers under the 1999 Act.

5   AI(TC)A 2004, s 33, Sch 3, in force 1 October 2004 (SI 2004/2523).

6   AI(TC)A 2004, s 15 (amendment of s 141 Immigration and Asylum Act 1999 to enable fingerprints to be taken on service of immigration decision, in force 1 October 2004, SI 2004/2523); s 16 (amendment of Sch 2 para 27B Immigration Act 1971, provision of copies of passengers' documents (tickets etc) on demand, not yet in force); s 17 (retention of documents, in force 1 December 2004, SI 2004/2999); s 18 (insertion of para 2A(2A) into Sch 2 to 1971 Act, enabling cancellation of advance leave granted for different purpose, in force 1 October 2004, SI 2004/2523).

7   AI(TC)A 2004, ss 42, 43 (in force 1 October 2004: SI 2004/2523).

8   AI(TC)A 2004, ss 19–25, in force 1 February 2005 (SI 2004/3398); see the Immigration (Procedure for Marriage) Regulations 2005, SI 2005/15.

9   AI(TC)A 2004, s 36, in force 1 October 2004 (SI 2004/2523) for the purpose of making regulations, although none had been issued at the time of writing.

UK and EU law

1.39   The free movement provisions of the EC Treaty are reflected in section 7 of the Immigration Act 1988 and in the Immigration (European Economic Area) Regulations 2000.[1] The integration of domestic law with EU law on free movement, immigration and asylum proceeds in fits and starts. It was hoped that Articles 17 (ex Article 8) and 18 EC (ex Article 8a) would confer real citizenship rights on citizens of the EU, and particularly that the right of free movement would be an attribute of citizenship rather than ancillary to economic activity within the Community. That hope has been realised to a great extent through the *Baumbast*,[2] *Avello*[3] and *Chen*[4] cases, and free movement has detached itself from the status of worker, student or self-employed person exercising rights of establishment, although it is still contingent on financial independence in these situations, and is still not available as against the national authorities of citizens' own States.[5] The ECJ has also rejected the fiction of temporary admission in *Yiadom*,[6] in holding that the safeguards against expulsion of those enjoying Treaty rights apply equally to those physically in the country for a period of time pending a decision on admission. The ECJ confirmed in *Akrich* that the motive for the exercise of free movement rights was not something which should concern Member States' authorities.[7] Attempts to strengthen the human rights foundation of EC law have met with scant success outside the field of family life, where Article 8 ECHR has been applied to good effect in *Carpenter*[8] and *MRAX*.[9] In *Manjit Kaur*[10] the ECJ refused to get embroiled in the argument about the extent to which fundamental human rights contained in Protocols of the ECHR not signed by all Member States form part of the *corpus* of human rights on which the Community is founded. The terms of the treaties whereby ten new States joined the EU allow Member States to derogate from the free movement rights of nationals of eight of them,[11] and the UK has done so to a limited extent, by requiring registration of employment as a prerequisite for stay in the country as a worker, and precluding reliance on welfare benefits for a period.[12]

1   SI 2000/2326, as amended by SI 2001/865, SI 2003/549, SI 2003/3188, SI 2004/1236, SI 2005/47 and SI 2005/671.

2   *Baumbast v Secretary of State for the Home Department* C-413/99 [2003] INLR 1.

3   *Avello v Belgium* C-148/02 [2004] All ER (EC) 740.

4   *Chen v Secretary of State for the Home Department*: C-200/02 [2005] QB 325, ECJ.

5   Except on return from the exercise of EC Treaty rights elsewhere in the EEA, as in Case
    C-370/90: *R v Immigration Appeal Tribunal and Surinder Singh, ex p Secretary of State for
    the Home Department* [1992] 3 All ER 798, [1992] Imm AR 565, ECJ; Immigration
    (European Economic Area) Regulations 2000 reg 11.
6   *R (on the application of Yiadom) v Secretary of State for the Home Department* C-357/98
    [2001] All ER (EC) 267, ECJ.
7   *Secretary of State for the Home Department v Akrich* C-109/01 [2004] QB 756, [2004]
    INLR 36.
8   *Carpenter v Secretary of State for the Home Department* C-60/00 [2003] QB 416, ECJ.
9   *Movement contre le racisme, l'antisemitisme et la xénophobie ASBL v Belgium* C-459/99
    [2002] ECR I-6591, ECJ. The principles of Art 8 also underlie the *Baumbast and R*
    decision (fn 2 above).
10 *R v Secretary of State for the Home Department, ex p Kaur (Manjit)* (7 March 2001,
    unreported), ECJ.
11 See 7.7 below.
12 Accession (Immigration and Worker Registration) Regulations 2004, SI 2004/ 1219.

1.40 The institutional framework of the EU has been modified by the Treaty
of Amsterdam, which incorporates into the framework of the EU the two
Schengen agreements made in 1985 and 1990 and various measures taken to
implement them (collectively known as the Schengen *acquis*). These, together
with Articles 14 and 61 to 63 of the consolidated EC Treaty, lay the
foundations for a common European immigration and asylum policy, including control of external frontiers, common visa policy, expulsion measures,
harmonised family reunion measures and common asylum criteria and procedures. Because the UK was not prepared to lift immigration controls at
internal frontiers, the UK and Ireland have been allowed to opt out of the
Schengen *acquis* and Articles 61 to 63, with a choice to opt in to any measure,
subject to the procedures agreed. There are Commission and Council directives and regulations in a number of areas covered by these Articles, which the
UK has opted in to, notably regulations allocating responsibility for dealing
with asylum claims and for fingerprinting asylum claimants, directives laying
down minimum conditions for the reception of asylum seekers and on the
criteria for refugee and subsidiary status and the content of international
protection, directives on temporary protection, expulsion and carrier sanctions. For the full list see 7.34–7.37 below. These pieces of Community
legislation have direct effect, and are likely to assume increasing importance as
they are litigated in UK courts. Chapter 7 below, deals with EU law.

UK refugee law

1.41 Substantive refugee law is governed by the 1951 Convention relating to
the Status of Refugees and its 1967 Protocol, known collectively as the
Refugee Convention. Section 2 of the Asylum and Immigration Appeals
Act 1993, still in force, gives primacy to the Convention over any UK
Immigration Rules, and the Convention is effectively incorporated into
domestic law.[1] The most litigated matters in UK refugee law, apart from
procedural and credibility issues, concern the definition of 'refugee' in
Article 1A(2) of the Convention. Recent case law establishes that the Convention does not operate extra-territorially so as to oblige States to enable asylum
claimants to travel to the UK;[2] that a person in fear of persecution from
non-State agents may be a refugee if his or her State is unable to provide a

sufficiency of protection;[3] that the protection may be provided by a body to which the powers of the State have been transferred,[4] but it must be available on the ground, not merely as a matter of theory;[5] that the fear may be based on unreasonable activities[6] or even ones performed in bad faith;[7] but that the ordinary risks inherent in civil war do not found a refugee claim,[8] and nor does punishment for conscientious objection,[9] unless it is based on refusal to participate in acts contrary to international law;[10] that the fundamental purpose of the Convention is counteracting discrimination and persecution based on gender or other immutable characteristic founds refugee status;[11] that where persecution is localised, a person may be a refugee if internal relocation would be unduly harsh;[12] and that in assessing a claim, all the available evidence must be weighed for what it is worth[13] and the focus of the inquiry is on the future risk of persecution.[14] Chapter 12 below gives a comprehensive exposition of current UK asylum law.

[1] *R v Secretary of State for the Home Department, ex p Sivakumaran* [1988] AC 958; *R v Uxbridge Magistrates' Court, ex p Adimi* [1999] INLR 490; *European Roma Rights Centre v Immigration Officer at Prague Airport* [2004] UKHL 55, [2005] 2 WLR 1. The EC Directive 2004/83 (the 'Qualification Directive) (OJ 2004 L 304/12) provides minimum standards for the interpretation and application of the Convention, and has direct effect.

[2] *European Roma Rights Centre v Immigration Officer at Prague Airport* [2004] UKHL 55, [2005] 2 WLR 1 (upholding, on this issue, [2003] EWCA Civ 666 [2003] INLR 374).

[3] *Horvath v Secretary of State for the Home Department* [2000] Imm AR 552, HL. Where the agents of persecution are 'rogue' State agents, the standard of protection required of the home State is higher: *Svazas v Secretary of State for the Home Department* [2002] EWCA Civ 74, [2002] INLR 197.

[4] *R (on the application of Vallaj) v Immigration Appeal Tribunal* [2001] INLR 455, QBD, upheld as *Canaj v Secretary of State for the Home Department* [2001] EWCA Civ 782, [2001] INLR 342.

[5] *Kinuthia v Secretary of State for the Home Department* [2001] EWCA Civ 2100, [2002] INLR 133; *McPherson v Secretary of State for the Home Department* [2001] EWCA Civ 1955, [2002] INLR 139 (a human rights case, but the courts have held that the test for protection is the same in *Dhima v Immigration Appeal Tribunal* [2002] EWHC 80 (Admin), [2002] Imm AR 394, [2002] INLR 243 and *R (on the application of Bagdanavicius) v Secretary of State for the Home Department* [2003] EWCA Civ 1605, [2004] INLR 163 (currently on appeal to the HL).

[6] *Ahmed (Iftikhar) v Secretary of State for the Home Department* [2000] INLR 1. The difficult issue now is whether fear of persecution which forces someone to conceal the offending attribute (eg sexuality or religion) can itself amount to persecution. The Australian and New Zealand authorities have said "yes", in *Appellant S395/2002 v Minister for Immigration and Multicultural Affairs* [2003] HCA 71, and *Refugee Appeal No 74665/03* (NZRSAA), 7 July 2004; the UK courts have so far sidestepped the issue (see *Z v Secretary of State for the Home Department* [2004] EWCA Civ 1578, [2004] All ER (D) 32, a human rights case, where similar principles apply).

[7] *Danian v Secretary of State for the Home Department* [2000] Imm AR 96, CA.

[8] *Adan v Secretary of State for the Home Department* [1999] 1 AC 293, HL.

[9] *Sepet v Secretary of State for the Home Department* [2003] UKHL 15, [2003] 3 All ER 304.

[10] *Krotov v Secretary of State for the Home Department* [2004] EWCA Civ 69, [2004] INLR 304.

[11] *R v Immigration Appeal Tribunal and Secretary of State for the Home Department, ex p Shah, Islam v Immigration Appeal Tribunal* [1999] 2 AC 629, HL. The issue in the recent case law is whether the failure of protection must emanate from institutional discrimination enshrined in law, as in *Shah and Islam*: see *R (on the application of Ivanauskiene) v Special Adjudicator* [2001] EWCA Civ 1271, [2002] INLR 1; *WS (Social Group – woman – forced marriage) (Afghanistan) CG* [2004] UKIAT 00328 'Reported'.

[12] *R v Secretary of State for the Home Department, ex p Robinson* [1998] QB 929, CA. In *AE and E v Secretary of State for the Home Department* [2003] EWCA Civ 1032, [2003] Imm AR 609, [2003] INLR 475, the Court of Appeal said that conditions must be compared with the site of persecution, not the UK, in a refugee case. It was on appeal to the HL at the time of writing.

[13] *Karanakaran v Secretary of State for the Home Department* [2000] 3 All ER 449, [2000] Imm AR 271, [2000] INLR 122, CA.

[14] *Karanakaran* above; *Ravichandran v Secretary of State for the Home Department* [1996] Imm AR 97, CA.

UK immigration-related human rights law

1.42 It is well established that immigration decisions such as exclusion and expulsion engage obligations under international human rights law.[1] When, for the first time, the human rights guaranteed by the ECHR became enforceable in all UK courts and tribunals as a result of the coming into force of the Human Rights Act 1998,[2] and it was no longer necessary to go to Strasbourg to get redress,[3] immigration lawyers expected great things. The expected honeymoon was more like a big freeze, however, as the higher courts responded with severity to attempts to use human rights where asylum claims had failed and rules and policies gave no relief. The human rights ceiling has at times felt very close to the floor in the immigration field. The years since incorporation have seen a thaw in some areas. They have been marked by battles over issues such as:

- the extra-territorial reach of the Convention, concluded with the House of Lords' acceptance in *Ullah* that removal may engage qualified ECHR rights as well as absolute ones where the risk is of flagrant violation in the receiving country;[4]
- the proper role of the courts in deciding whether an immigration decision is proportionate, where the House of Lords held in *Razgar* that the appellate authority exercises an independent judgment on the materials before it;[5]
- the scope of the discretionary area of judgment or deference in a statutory appeal, where the Court of Appeal held in *Huang* that the immigration rules and policies expressed parliament's view of where the public interest lay in striking the balance inherent in qualified obligations such as Article 8;[6]
- the scope of positive and negative obligations under the Convention, discussed in *Lord Saville of Newgate*[7] and *Pretty v Secretary of State for the Home Department*,[8] and fought over in *Limbuela*[9] and *Bagdanavicius*[10] (on appeal to the House of Lords);
- the lawfulness of a derogation from the right to liberty which affected foreign nationals only, which the House of Lords held in *A* discriminatory and disproportionate;[11]
- the proper threshold for Article 3 in cases of removal of sick and vulnerable people to countries where they are likely to die for want of treatment, held to be engaged only in most exceptional cases by the Court of Appeal, and now upheld by the House of Lords in *N*.[12]

Since 2 October 2000 it has been possible to appeal against an immigration decision on the ground that the decision is incompatible with fundamental human rights.[13] Amendments to the rules dealing with the admission of unmarried partners,[14] improved rules on admission for contact with UK-based children,[15] and leave to remain on the basis of long residence,[16] and policies on residence and family ties in the context of removal are designed to give effect to family and private life rights in Article 8 of the Convention. Article 8 has also affected the maintenance and accommodation rules for family reunion[17] and their interpretation.[18] Chapter 8 below looks in detail at the UK's human rights obligations and their implementation.

1 *Abdulaziz, Cabales and Balkandali v United Kingdom* (1985) 7 EHRR 471; *Soering v United Kingdom* (1989) 11 EHRR 439.
2 In England and Wales as from 2 October 2000; in Scotland as from the same date, except where it affected devolution, when the date was 1999.
3 Strasbourg is, of course, still available if earlier attempts in the domestic courts are unsuccessful.
4 *R (on the application of Ullah) v Special Adjudicator* [2004] UKHL 26, [2004] 3 WLR 23, reversing [2002] EWCA Civ 1856, [2003] INLR 74.
5 *R (on the application of Razgar) v Secretary of State for the Home Department* [2004] UKHL 27, [2004] 3 WLR 58.
6 *Huang v Secretary of State for the Home Department* [2005] EWCA Civ 105, 149 Sol Jo LB 297.
7 *R (on the application of A) v Lord Saville of Newgate (No 2)* [2001] EWCA Civ 2048, [2002] 1 WLR 1249.
8 *R (on the application of Pretty) v DPP (Secretary of State for the Home Department Intervening)* [2001] UKHL 61, [2002] 1 AC 800.
9 *R (on the application of Adam) v Secretary of State for the Home Department, R (on the application of Limbuela) v Secretary of State for the Home Department, R (on the application of Tesema) v Secretary of State for the Home Department* [2004] EWCA Civ 540, [2004] QB 1440 (support for asylum claimants).
10 *R (on the applicatin of Bagdanavicius) v Secretary of State for the Home Department* [2003] EWCA Civ 1605, [2004] INLR 163 (expulsion to lack of protection against ill-treatment).
11 *A v Secretary of State for the Home Department* [2004] UKHL 56, [2005] 2 WLR 87.
12 *N v Secretary of State for the Home Department* [2003] EWCA Civ 1369, [2004] 1 WLR 1182, [2004] INLR 10; [2005] UKHL 31.
13 Section 65 of the Immigration and Asylum Act 1999 provided a free-standing appeal on human rights grounds against any decision relating to entitlement to enter or remain in the UK. It was repealed and replaced by the human rights grounds of appeal against an immigration decision (Nationality, Immigration and Asylum Act 2002, ss 82, 84).
14 HC 395, paras 295A–O, inserted by Cm 4851 (2 October 2000), and amended by HC 538, Cm 5597, Cm 5949, Cm 6339.
15 HC 395, paras 246–248F, substituted and inserted by Cm 4851 (2 October 2000).
16 HC 395, para 276A–D, inserted by HC 538 (31 March 2003).
17 HC 395, para 6A, inserted by Cm 4851 (2 October 2000).
18 *R v Secretary of State for the Home Department, ex p Ali (Arman)* [2000] INLR 89, QBD; *Abdulla (Intekab)* [2002] UKIAT 07516.

SOURCES OF IMMIGRATION LAW AND PRACTICE

Immigration statutes and the orders and regulations made under them

1.43 The main sources of immigration and asylum law are the Immigration Act 1971 and the amending and other statutes described in the previous sections.[1] The 1971 Act contains the rule-making power, and it and the other legislation provide for implementing Orders and Regulations, usually to be made by statutory instrument, sometimes by Order in Council. The Immigration and Asylum Act 1999 is the worst offender. On a rough count there are

12 instances of powers to make Orders by statutory instrument; 26 for regulations; seven for rules; seven codes of practice will apply; two sets of directions; one Order in Council; and one set of arrangements.[2] Not all these powers have been or will be used, but the list of Orders and Regulations, covering a very wide span, is formidable. All are subject to change. Increasingly, it is going to be necessary for readers to consult an immigration encyclopaedia or the internet to check the up-to-date position.[3] The key rules are still *The Statement of Immigration Rules*, made under the 1971 Act and usually published as a House of Commons paper (currently HC 395), setting out the criteria for entry and stay in the various immigration categories. A consolidated version of the current Immigration Rules is available on the Home Office website, and the most recent Statements of Changes are also available separately. In the year prior to publication, there were at least eight such changes, and it is very important to keep abreast of them. Then come the rules of procedure for immigration and asylum appeals[4] and the regulations for the service of notices in connection with appeals.[5] The validity of these subordinate rules and regulations may be challenged.[6]

1   There is very little left of the Immigration Act 1988, the Asylum and Immigration Appeals Act 1993 and the Asylum and Immigration Act 1996: see 1.22–1.24 above.
2   The Nationality, Immigration and Asylum Act 2002 has 15 instances of powers to make Orders and two dozen for regulations, with two Lord Chancellor's rules, a code of practice and two sets of guidance.
3   Useful websites are set out in Appendix 2.
4   Asylum and Immigration Tribunal (Procedure) Rules 2005, SI 2005/230. There are separate rules for fast track appeals: Asylum and Immigration Tribunal (Fast Track Procedure) Rules 2005, SI 2005/560.
5   Immigration (Notices) Regulations 2003, SI 2003/658.
6   In *R v Immigration Appeal Tribunal, ex p Begum (Manshoora)* [1986] Imm AR 385, QBD, a provision of an Immigration Rule was held so unreasonable as to be invalid. A procedure rule met the same fate in *R v Secretary of State for the Home Department, ex p Asifa Saleem* [2000] INLR 413, and designation of a safe country in a statutory instrument in *R (on the application of Javed) v Secretary of State for the Home Department* (2001) Times, 9 February, upheld [2001] EWCA Civ 789, [2002] QB 129. See also *R v Secretary of State for Social Security, ex p Joint Council for the Welfare of Immigrants* [1997] 1 WLR 275. The Human Rights Act 1998 s 6(1), (2) offers further scope for challenge on the basis that the rule or regulation in question infringes ECHR rights and is not required to do so by the primary legislation. If the primary legislation requires the infringement, the High Court can make a declaration of incompatibility under s 4(4): cf *International Transport Roth GmbH v Secretary of State for the Home Department* [2002] EWCA Civ 158, [2002] 3 WLR 344; *A v Secretary of State for the Home Department* [2004] UKHL 56, [2005] 2 WLR 87. See chapter 8 below.

The prerogative

1.44 The prerogative powers of the Secretary of State for the Home Department are another source of immigration law. Section 33(5) of the Immigration Act 1971 states that the Act 'shall not be taken to supersede or impair any power exercisable by Her Majesty in relation to aliens by virtue of her prerogative'. A similar reservation was made in the Aliens Restriction Act 1914, which was passed at the beginning of World War I. The view then was that it referred to a prerogative power to deal with enemy aliens, and it is thought that this is also the full and correct ambit of the reservation in the

Immigration Act 1971. See 1.4–1.5 above. The issue of passports to British citizens involves a quite separate preogative power, which we describe at 2.66–2.68 below.

1.45 Where the Secretary of State overrules an immigration officer, grants someone discretionary leave to remain when the Immigration Rules say he or she should go, or adopts a policy that people of a particular class or nationality should get leave outside the immigration rules, or grants a general amnesty, the source of the discretion – prerogative or statute – has caused some difficulty. Our view is that it derives from the Secretary of State's and the immigration officers' statutory powers, and, in particular, from the discretion under section 4(1) of the Immigration Act 1971, which is a very broad discretion, not made subject to the Immigration Rules. The Secretary of State can, therefore, waive a requirement of the Rules in an individual case as a matter of statutory discretion. But there are dicta in two cases which suggest that the power to treat an immigrant more favourably than the Rules dictate derives from prerogative rather than statute.[1] This cannot, in our view be a reference to the prerogative power referred to in section 33(5), because that applies only to enemy aliens, as we have previously argued (at 1.4–1.5 above) It is difficult to identify any other prerogative power to which the judges could be referring, unless it is the Crown's prerogative as 'fountain of justice.'[2] In *Ahmed and Patel*[3] the parties were agreed that the Secretary of State was using prerogative powers in the formulation and application of extra-statutory policies such as those on long residence or marriage and children in relation to removal. But the court held that a Treaty entered into by the executive, such as the ECHR or the UN Convention on the Rights of the Child, could have no greater effect in relation to the exercise of a discretion under the prerogative than in the case of a statutory discretion.[4]

[1] *R v Secretary of State for the Home Department, ex p Kaur* [1987] Imm AR 278, DC; *R v Secretary of State for the Home Department, ex p Ounejma* [1989] Imm AR 75. In *R v Secretary of State for the Home Department, ex p Northumbria Police Authority* [1989] QB 26 Purchas LJ approved of this kind of residual use of the prerogative power, stating that:

> 'where the executive action is directed towards the benefit or protection of the individual, it is unlikely that its use will attract the intervention of the courts ... Before the courts will hold that such executive action is contrary to legislation, express and unequivocal terms must be found in the statute which deprive the individual from receiving the benefit or protection intended by the exercise of the Prerogative power'.

[2] See Chitty *Treatise on the Law of the Prerogative of the Crown* (1820) ch 7; *R v Secretary of State for the Home Department, ex p Northumbria Police Authority* [1989] QB 26, [1988] 1 All ER 556 at 563, CA.

[3] *R v Secretary of State for the Home Department, ex p Ahmed and Patel* [1998] INLR 570.

[4] See also *R (on the application of Acan) v Immigration Appeal Tribunal* [2004] EWHC 297 (Admin), [2004] All ER (D) 193 (Feb), where Gibbs J held that it was unnecessary to decide whether exceptional leave was granted outside the terms of the Act, under the prerogative, or within the Act but outside the rules.

1.46 The prerogative powers in relation to national security affected immigration law adversely until very recently, overriding normally applicable Immigration Rules[1] or the obligations under the 1951 Refugee Convention.[2]

The courts retained no more than a nominal power to quash the decision on normal judicial review grounds.[3] But this changed following (i) the *Chahal* case,[4] where the European Court held that the applicant's rights not to be subjected to torture, inhuman and degrading treatment (under Article 3 of the ECHR) overrode any interests of national security; and (ii) the enactment of the Special Immigration Appeals Commission Act 1997, passed as a direct response to the European Court in *Chahal*, which set up the Special Immigration Appeals Commission to hear appeals involving national security. We deal with these in later chapters. The higher courts have made it clear that, in deciding whether a decision or action is lawful, it is the subject matter, not the source of the power, which is determinative,[5] and have recently shown a willingness to entertain challenges to decisions in prerogative areas traditionally held not justiciable, such as foreign relations,[6] defence[7] and declaring war.[8] The issue of whether a power derives from prerogative or statute is now largely of historical interest only.[9]

1   *R v Secretary of State for the Home Department, ex p Hosenball* [1977] 3 All ER 452, [1977] 1 WLR 766, CA; *NSH v Secretary of State for the Home Department* [1988] Imm AR 389, CA; *R v Secretary of State for the Home Department, ex p Chahal* [1994] Imm AR 107, CA.
2   Although the Secretary of State was under an obligation to asylum seekers lawfully in the UK to balance their interests under the 1951 Refugee Convention against the interests of national security: see *NSH v Secretary of State for the Home Department* above; *Ex p Chahal* above.
3   See *The Zamora* [1916] 2 AC 77, PC; the speech of Lord Atkin in *Liversidge v Anderson* [1942] AC 206, [1941] 3 All ER 338, HL; *Council of Civil Service Unions v Minister for the Civil Service* [1985] AC 374 at 420–423, HL, per Lord Roskill; *Hussain v Secretary of State for the Home Department* [1993] Imm AR 353, CA; *Ex p Hosenball* above; *NSH v Secretary of State for the Home Department* above; *Chahal* above.
4   *Chahal v United Kingdom* (1996) 23 EHRR 413, ECtHR.
5   *Council of Civil Service Unions v Minister for the Civil Service* [1985] AC 374, *R (on the application of Abbasi) v Secretary of State for Foreign and Commonwealth Affairs* [2002] EWCA Civ 1598.
6   *R (on the application of Abbasi) v Secretary of State for Foreign and Commonwealth Affairs* [2002] EWCA Civ 1598, (2002) Times, 8 November (failure to intervene in the detention of British nationals in Guantánamo).
7   *R (on the application of Bancoult) v Secretary of State for Foreign and Commonwealth Affairs* [2001] QB 1067 (expulsion of Ilois from their homes for defence purposes, where the Divisional Court concluded that the British Indian Ocean Territory Order 1965 was made under prerogative rather than statutory power, but that the prerogative power did not permit the Queen to exile her subjects from the territory where they belong).
8   *R (on the application of Campaign for Nuclear Disarmament) v Prime Minister* [2002] EWHC 2777 (Admin), (2002) Times, 27 December.
9   See *Council of Civil Service Unions* case, fn 5 above; *R (on the application of Acan) v Immigration Appeal Tribunal* [2004] EWHC 297 (Admin), [2004] All ER (D) 193 (Feb) at 1.45 fn 4 above.

Decisions of the Tribunal and courts

1.47 The most voluminous source of immigration and asylum law is the case law of the higher courts and the former Immigration Appeal Tribunal, now the Asylum and Immigration Tribunal, on the meaning, effect, and application of the primary and subordinate legislation, the Immigration Rules and Home Office policies outside the Rules. Decisions of the House of Lords and Court of Appeal are binding on those courts and on the lower courts and on the

Tribunal. Decisions of the High Court also bind the Tribunal. Tribunal decisions are not strictly binding, but in 2001 the then President, Mr Justice Collins, instituted a system of key decisions, known as starred cases, decided by legal panels, which are meant to be binding on the Tribunal in subsequent cases, in order to end the previously common situation where there were conflicting decisions by different Tribunals.[1] The starred cases system was later followed by the system of 'Country Guideline' cases (factual precedent cases, referred to at 18.142 below)[2] and finally, the system of 'Reported' cases introduced in 2003. The current Practice Direction[3] brings the three systems together, and has exhaustive directions on their citation. It stipulates that no unreported decision of the Tribunal (and no adjudicator determination) may be cited unless either a member of the family of the current appellant was a party or the appellate authority has given permission, and the conditions for obtaining permission are very stringent indeed.[4] Reported decisions of the Tribunal, anonymised and referred to by their neutral citation, are available in the Supreme Court and Law Society Libraries and, in electronic form, through the Tribunal website, BAILII and the Electronic Immigration Network.[5] Administrative Court, Court of Appeal and House of Lords decisions, if not reported in the paper reports, are similarly available in the Libraries, on BAILII and the Electronic Immigration Network, and as full transcripts in electronic form.[6] With two competing sets of specialist immigration law reports, the official websites and the EIN, more decisions of importance are now reported or otherwise available to practitioners. In this situation we have included more recent unreported cases than in previous editions, although we have tried to purge the text of references to old and inaccessible unreported Tribunal decisions. In addition to the reports of decisions of domestic courts, there is a growing body of European decisions from both Luxembourg[7] and Strasbourg.[8] We refer to these in the text, and to Commonwealth case law, which is also widely available in electronic form.[9]

---

1   The Tribunal should follow an earlier starred decision unless it is satisfied that the decision is clearly wrong: *Sepet v Secretary of State for the Home Department* [2001] EWCA Civ 681, [2001] INLR 33, per Laws LJ, para 99. Starred IAT and Tribunal decisions are binding unless inconsistent with other binding authority: Asylum and Immigration Tribunal Practice Directions 2005, 18.1.

2   A reported determination of the Tribunal or of the IAT with the letters 'CG' is to be treated as an authoritative finding by the Tribunal on the country guidance issue identified in the determination on the evidence before that Tribunal, and unless expressly superseded or replaced by a later 'CG' determination, is to be followed by the Tribunal in any subsequent appeal on that issue, so far as it depends on the same or similar evidence: Practice Directions, 18.2; *BD (application of SK and DK) Croatia* [2004] UKIAT 00032. A list of current CG cases is maintained on the Tribunal website, with which the parties will be expected to be conversant: 18.3.

3   Asylum and Immigration Tribunal Practice Directions, 2005. The directions on citation of determinations (s 17) are in very similar terms to the Practice Direction No 10/2003, [2003] INLR 358.

4   Practice Directions, 17.6ff. Permission will be given only in exceptional cases, and even more rarely in the case of single-member determinations. An application for permission to cite an unreported case must include a full transcript, identify the proposition for which it is to be cited, certify that the proposition is not found in any reported determination of the Tribunal or the IAT and has not been superseded by a decision of higher authority, and be accompanied by a summary analysis of all other decisions of the Tribunal and all available decisions of higher authority relating to the same issue, promulgated in the period beginning six months before the date of the relevant decision and ending two weeks before the date of the instant hearing: 17.8. A party citing an unreported pre-2003 IAT

determination must be able to certify that the proposition for which it is cited has not been the subject of more recent, reported determinations of the IAT or the Tribunal: 17.11.

5　The Tribunal website, www.ait.gov.uk, contains all reported and country guidance IAT and Tribunal cases. BAILII (British and Irish Legal Information Institute), www.bailii.org, is a free website with a vast database of cases from the Tribunal, the higher courts, and Irish and Commonwealth law. The Electronic Immigration Network website is at www.ein.org and its public resources homepage is an excellent gateway into most websites which immigration practitioners would need. The Tribunal decisions, and those of the higher courts, the ECJ and the ECtHR, are available by subscription on ein.

6　Through the website of the Court Service, www.courtservice.gov.uk, and that of shorthand writers Smith Bernal, at www.casetrack.com (by subscription). House of Lords decisions are available on the House of Lords website, at www.parliament.the-stationery-office.co.uk.

7　ECJ judgments and Opinions are available on the Internet at www.curia.eu.int.

8　ECtHR judgments are available at www.echr.coe.int.

9　The New Zealand refugee cases are at www.refugee.org.nz. Australian cases are on AUSTLII (sister to BAILII). Canadian and South African cases can be found through a Google search of the relevant court. There are some specialist websites on refugee law, such as www.refugeecaselaw.org.

The Immigration Rules

1.48 These are made by the Secretary of State for the Home Department in accordance with sections 1(4) and 3(2) of the Immigration Act 1971. Statements of the Rules must be laid before Parliament and they then take effect, unless either House votes against them. The same procedure applies to changes in the Rules. There are few statutory or other restrictions on the rule-making power.[1] Section 1(4) of the 1971 Act provides that the Rules must include provisions for the admission of persons coming for employment and study, and as visitors or dependants. There is no similar requirement for 'after entry' rules. The general rule-making power is contained in section 3(2) of the 1971 Act and it expressly provides that in framing the Rules there is no need to have uniform provisions as regards admission of persons for employment, study or as visitors of dependants and account may be taken of citizenship or nationality. It is not subject to the provisions of the Human Rights Act 1998 which make it unlawful for public authorities to act in a way which is incompatible with a right protected by the ECHR,[2] or the provisions of the Race Relations Act 1976 prohibiting racial discrimination by public authorities,[3] thus preserving parliamentary sovereignty. But a rule which infringes basic rights such as the right of access to a tribunal, which is not expressly or by necessary implication authorised by an Act of Parliament, is *ultra vires*.[4]

1　The Asylum and Immigration Appeals Act 1993, s 2 provides that nothing in the Immigration Rules shall lay down any practice which would be contrary to the 1951 Refugee Convention. Before its repeal by Immigration Act 1988, s 1, s 1(5) of the 1971 Act imposed mandatory and negative obligations on the rule-making power of the Secretary of State for the Home Department, by providing that the Rules should be so framed that Commonwealth citizens settled in the UK on 1 January 1973, and their wives and children, were no less free to come into and go from the UK than if the 1971 Act had not been passed. In *R v Immigration Appeal Tribunal, ex p Haque, Ruhul* [1987] Imm AR 587 the Court of Appeal held that an Immigration Rule infringing the mandatory and negative obligations contained in s 1(5) was *ultra vires* and void, but that could not lead to a resurrection of any of the pre-1973 rules. For standstill clauses in EC law, see *R (on the application of Tum) v Secretary of State for the Home Department, R (on the application*

of Dari) v Secretary of State for the Home Department [2003] EWHC 2745 (Admin),
[2004] 1 CMLR 1091, upheld [2004] EWCA Civ 788, [2004] INLR 442; referred to the
ECJ at [2004] UKHL, 7.162 below.
2   Human Rights Act 1998, s 6.
3   Race Relations Act 1976, s 19, as amended by Race Relations (Amendment) Act 2000.
4   *R v Secretary of State for the Home Department, ex p Saleem (Asifa)* [2000] INLR 413.

1.49 The rule-making power is a statutory one and the Immigration Rules
must conform to the statutory parameters; they cannot require officials to do
what the statute does not allow. The Rules might be challenged as *ultra vires* if
they impose an unlawful fetter on the discretion of the immigration official or
unlawfully delegate a discretionary power. Such challenges have been made
unsuccessfully in relation to rules which provide for mandatory refusal of
leave for those arriving in the UK without a proper visa or entry clearance.[1]
The *vires* of an Immigration Rule may also be challenged on the basis that it is
unreasonable, in the sense of being impartial or unequal in its operation as
between classes; manifestly unjust; made in bad faith; or involving such
oppressive or gratuitous interference with the rights of those affected by them
as could find no justification in the minds of reasonable persons.[2] In *R v
Immigration Appeal Tribunal, ex p Manshoora Begum* a provision in one of
the family rules was struck down on this ground.[3]

1   *R v Secretary of State for the Home Department, ex p Kaur (Rajinder)* [1987] Imm AR
278, DC; *R v Secretary of State for the Home Department, ex p Hassan* [1989] Imm AR
75, DC.
2   Per Lord Russell CJ in *Kruse v Johnson* [1898] 2 QB 91. Applied in *R v Immigration
Appeal Tribunal, ex p Begum (Manshoora)* [1986] Imm AR 385, QBD. In *R v Immigration
Appeal Tribunal, ex p Begum (Hasna)* [1995] Imm AR 249, QBD the court held that HC
251, para 3, dealing with polygamous marriages (now HC 395, para 278), was not *ultra
vires*.
3   *R v Immigration Appeal Tribunal, ex p Begum (Manshoora)* [1986] Imm AR 385, QBD.

1.50 Where changes are made to the Immigration Rules, it is sometimes
difficult to establish whether the old or new Rules apply. The transitional
provisions in the current rules, HC 395, provide that applications extant prior
to their coming into force will be decided under the previous rules.[1] We
suggest that the same logic should apply with regard to the amendments, so
that applications made before the amendments take effect should be dealt with
under the unamended rules. Any other rule penalises the applicant for Home
Office delays. New editions of the Rules often contain transitional provisions
which may give rise to problems of interpretation.[2]

1   See HC 395, para 4; *R v Immigration Appeal Tribunal, ex p Nathwani* [1979–80] Imm AR
9, QBD.
2   For reported decisions on transitional provisions see *Shamseddin v Secretary of State for
the Home Department* [1981] Imm AR 66; *Kamry v Secretary of State for the Home
Department* [1981] Imm AR 118; *Pope* [1987] Imm AR 10; *Minah Begum v Secretary of
State for the Home Department* [1990] Imm AR 38; *Pardeepan v Secretary of State for the
Home Department* [2000] INLR 447. See also 18.44 below.

1.51 There has been considerable debate about the legal status of the
Immigration Rules – whether they are rules of law or not. In *Pearson v
Immigration Appeal Tribunal*[1] the Court of Appeal stated that although the
Rules are not delegated legislation or rules of law, but rules of practice laid

down for the guidance of those entrusted with the administration of the Act, they had the force of law for those hearing immigration appeals.[2] This is made clear by section 86(3) of the Nationality, Immigration and Asylum Act 2002, which provides that the Tribunal 'must allow the appeal if it thinks that a decision against which the appeal is brought or is treated as being brought was not in accordance with the law (including immigration rules)'. It is, therefore, clear that the rules are far more a source of law than, for example, the Code of Practice under section 8A of the Asylum and Immigration Act 1996, which is a relevant consideration in deciding whether an employer has discriminated unlawfully in hiring or refusing to hire someone. The Rules have more immediate and binding effect, as any cursory reading of the reported decisions of the Tribunal and the IAT makes clear. The appellate authorities are always concerned to see whether immigration officials have followed the Immigration Rules applicable to the case. If they have failed to do so, the appeal must be allowed.[3] If the Rule gives the immigration official a discretion, the Tribunal can review the exercise of that discretion and decide that it ought to have been exercised differently.[4] If, however, the wording of the Rule is in mandatory terms and the immigration officer has followed it, the prevailing view is that there is no exercise of discretion by the immigration officer to review on the merits and so there is no room for any decision under section 86(3)(b).[5] As immigration law becomes more sophisticated, the Immigration Rules tend to be drafted in a more comprehensive form.[6] The current Rules make it mandatory to refuse entry clearance, leave to enter, or a variation for a purpose not covered by the Rules,[7] putting at risk all those whose immigration status is and remains regulated outside the Rules, such as carers of UK-based relatives, and asylum seekers granted exceptional leave. However, more and more concessionary policies have been incorporated into the rules since October 2000, in accordance with the requirements of consistency and transparency mandated by the ECHR.[8]

1   [1978] Imm AR 212.
2   See further *R v Secretary of State for the Home Department, ex p Hosenball* [1977] 3 All ER 452, [1977] 1 WLR 766, CA.
3   Nationality, Immigration and Asylum Act 2002, s 86(3)(a), amended by Asylum and Immigration (Treatment of Claimants, etc) Act 2004, Sch 2, para 18.
4   NIAA 2002, s 86(3)(b) as amended.
5   NIAA 2002, s 86(3) as amended. See eg *Kausar* [1998] INLR 141 (decided under the 1971 Act). Such a decision may be not in accordance with the law because of incompatibility with the Refugee or Human Rights Convention, or race discrimination, or because it contravenes general principles of administrative law: see 18.49 below.
6   For a discussion of the appellate jurisdiction under the old rules, see the fourth edition at 2.51.
7   HC 395, paras 320(1) and 322(1). See also *Somasundaram v Entry Clearance Officer* [1990] Imm AR 16.
8   Former policies incorporated into the immigration rules include those on domestic workers in private households (now HC 395, paras 159A–H, inserted by Cm 5597 on 27 August 2002); ministers of religion not admitted in that capacity (now HC 395, paras 173, 174A–B, inserted by Cm 6297 on 3 August 2004); exercising access rights to a UK-based child (now HC 395, paras 246–248F, substituted and inserted by Cm 4851 on 2 October 2000); long residence (now HC 276A–D, inserted by HC 538 on 31 March 2003); Gurkhas and foreign or Commonwealth citizens discharged from HM forces (now HC 395, paras 276F–276Q, inserted by HC 1112 on 18 October 2004; domestic violence (now HC 395, para 289A–D, inserted by HC 104, 26 November 2002); unmarried partners (now HC 395, paras 295A–O, inserted by Cm 4851 on 2 October 2000); children brought to the UK for adoption (now HC 395, para 316A–D, inserted by Cm 5829 on 30 May 2003).

1.52 The Immigration Rules also play a very important role in judicial review where the decisions of immigration officers and the appellate authorities are challenged in the Administrative Court. In this context, the Rules are not rules of law, because they are not made by statutory instrument but are described in the Immigration Act 1971 as rules of practice to be followed in the administration of the Act for regulating entry to and stay in the UK. This characterisation of the rules has a number of consequences:

(i) the language of the Rules is that of the administrator rather than that of the parliamentary draftsman. Often, they are no more than descriptive. They are, therefore, to be given a purposive rather than a strict construction unless, the words used are wholly unambiguous;[1]

(ii) the power to make any decision on entry, stay or deportation comes from the 1971 Act, not the Rules, and is unfettered.[2] In particular, it is not made subject to the Immigration Rules;[3]

(iii) the existence of a residuary discretion outside the Rules means that the Secretary of State can make some Rules mandatory without risk of unlawfully fettering his or her discretion, because in each case, he or she can decide whether to depart from the Rules.[4] It is probably also why an immigration officer who gives leave mistakenly is not acting outside his or her authority;[5]

(iv) the Rules are not binding on the Administrative Court in the way that statutes are. Indeed, as we have seen, in exceptional cases, the court may strike out a Rule as being wholly or in part invalid for unreasonableness or unnecessary infringement of human rights.[6] In most cases however, the court is concerned with the interpretation, rather than the *vires* of the Rules.

---

1 *Alexander v Immigration Appeal Tribunal* [1982] 2 All ER 766, [1982] 1 WLR 1076, HL; *Singh v Immigration Appeal Tribunal* [1986] 2 All ER 721, [1986] Imm AR 352, HL; *R v Immigration Appeal Tribunal, ex p Rahman* [1987] Imm AR 313, CA; *Gurdev Singh v Immigration Appeal Tribunal* [1988] Imm AR 510, CA; *R v Immigration Appeal Tribunal, ex p Manshoora Begum* [1986] Imm AR 385, QBD; *R v Immigration Appeal Tribunal, ex p Zanib Bibi* [1987] Imm AR 392, QBD; *Bombay Entry Clearance Officer v De Noronha* [1995] Imm AR 341, CA; *R v Secretary of State for the Home Department, ex p Arman Ali* [2000] INLR 89.

2 Immigration Act 1971, s 4(1).

3 See 1.44ff above for a discussion on the source of the residuary discretion.

4 See *Pearson v Immigration Appeal Tribunal* [1978] Imm AR 212, CA; per Banks LJ in *R v Port of London Authority, ex p Kynoch Ltd* [1919] 1 KB 176 at 184, CA; *British Oxygen Co Ltd v Minister of Technology* [1971] AC 610, [1970] 3 All ER 165, HL. A good example of a fettering of discretion is *R v LCC, ex p Corrie* [1918] 1 KB 68 – a decision of the London County Council to refuse all further permits, without exception, to distribute literature in London public parks. In considering the exercise of the discretion outside the Immigration Rules, the Secretary of State is entitled to act so as to ensure that generally speaking the Rules are followed, to ensure fairness between applicants: *R v Secretary of State for the Home Department, ex p Ahmed* [1995] Imm AR 210, CS.

5 See *R v Secretary of State for the Home Department, ex p Ram* [1979] 1 All ER 687, [1979] 1 WLR 148.

6 *R v Immigration Appeal Tribunal, ex p Manshoora Begum* [1986] Imm AR 385; *R v Secretary of State for the Home Department, ex p Dhahan* [1988] Imm AR 257, QBD; *R v Secretary of State for the Home Department, ex p Saleem (Asifa)* [2000] INLR 413, CA. See 1.48 above. However, the Court of Appeal has held in *Huang v Secretary of State for the Home Department* [2005] EWCA Civ 105, 149 Sol Jo LB 297 that the immigration rules, in prescribing which classes of aliens (sic) will in the ordinary way be allowed to

enter the UK and which will not, have themselves struck the balance between public interest and private right for the general run of cases, so that the courts will accord very considerable respect for the balance so struck (paras 57–58, per Laws LJ).

Administrative practice and discretion outside the Immigration Rules

1.53 Unfortunately, the Immigration Rules are not a comprehensive code of all the practices regulating entry into the UK. There are still gaps, some of which are covered by well-known practices, which in some cases have an almost equivalent status to the Rules but for reasons best known to the Home Office are not incorporated into them. For example, the policy to grant refugees indefinite leave to remain immediately is not mentioned in the Rules,[1] although family reunion for refugees has now been incorporated.[2] Secondly, the Secretary of State or immigration official is frequently asked to sanction a waiver of part of a Rule, or a departure from the Rule, based on the particular personal circumstances of the applicant, usually of a compassionate nature. Alternatively, the departure may be of such general application that it has become something of a practice or general concession, at least for the time being. For example, under current Home Office policy, those given humanitarian protection may be granted settlement if at the end of three years, following review of their circumstances, it is decided that further protection is needed, while those granted discretionary leave are normally eligible to apply for settlement only after six years.[3] Most of these policies are now collected and put into the Immigration Directorate Instructions (IDI), Asylum Policy Instructions (API), Nationality Instructions (NI) and the Operational Enforcement Manual (OEM), published (or partly published – large parts of these documents are withheld) by the Home Office since 1998 as part of its commitment to greater transparency or openness. These instructions are an invaluable guide, not just to policies outside the Rules but also to latest Home Office practice in the interpretation of the Rules. They are available on the Home Office website.[4] The equivalent policies and practices in dealing with entry clearance applications are the Diplomatic Service Procedures (DSP), available on the UK Visas website. We refer to relevant IDI, API, DSP etc throughout this work. The Home Office has also recently published its European Directorate Instructions (EDI). These fall into a different category, since they merely represent Home Office interpretation – sometimes contentious – of binding EC law. As such, they should not be relied on as authoritative.

1   The policy is set out in 'New measures for dealing with asylum claims', Asylum and Appeals Policy Directorate letter, April 1999, in *Butterworths Immigration Law Service*, 2B, 27 [14]. The policy is arguably incorporated by reference into primary legislation, ie Nationality, Immigration and Asylum Act 2002 s 76, which refers to revocation of ILR if the refugee acts inconsistently with his or her status.
2   HC 395, paras 352A–F, inserted by Cm 4851 and amended by Cm 5597.
3   API, Humanitarian protection, para 8; Discretionary leave, para 5.4.
4   IDI and API (formerly Asylum Directorate Instructions, ADI) were made available to the public under the government's *Code of Practice on Access to Government Information*. They are available, with the other instructions and guidance, at www.ind.homeoffice.gov.uk/ind/en/home/laws_policy/policy_instructions/. The Home Office also publishes guidance on work permits at www.workingintheuk.gov.uk.

1.54 Although some of these general practices or concessions are of a temporary nature, designed to deal with political upheaval in a particular country, we refer to all of them as established practices or concessions because they are sufficiently detailed, well known and consistently applied. A failure to take such a practice or policy into account, or a misinterpretation or misapplication, might well open the decision to a successful challenge, either on appeal on the basis that the decision is not in accordance with the law,[1] or on judicial review on the basis that it is unreasonable or unfair.[2] The existence of the policy may give rise to a legitimate expectation that it will be invoked in the applicant's favour.[3] It used to be thought that if a policy was unpublished, no legitimate expectation would arise, although it was held that it would be unreasonable for the Secretary of State to apply such a policy inconsistently or unfairly as between one person and another.[4] But in *Rashid*,[5] Davis J held that the issue of publication was irrelevant: applicants had a legitimate expectation that the Home Office would apply any relevant policy to them. The application of an unpublished policy not to release a person in immigration detention in circumstances where the published policy indicated that there would be a release was held unfair in *Nadarajah and Amirthanathan*.[6] Problems arise when a beneficial policy is discontinued, or superseded by a more restrictive one. Which policy applies? In *Nadarajah*,[7] an asylum seeker who married in the UK sought the benefit of a Home Office policy against removing asylum seekers with family ties in the UK to a safe third country. He brought judicial review against the Secretary of State's refusal to apply the policy to him, and after the grant of permission, the Home Office changed the policy to stipulate that asylum seekers could not rely on family relationships entered into post-arrival. Stanley Burnton J held that the claimant had no right to have his claim reconsidered under the previous policy.[8] In *Joseph*,[9] a policy to grant exceptional leave to remain to failed asylum seekers from Sierra Leone was erroneously not applied to the claimant. His claim for judicial review, brought after the policy had ended, was rejected: it was held that the policy did not constitute an unqualified practice or promise and did not give rise to any legitimate expectation. But in *Rashid*, the failure to give the claimant the benefit of an unpublished but universally applied policy was held so unfair as to demand rectification by the grant of refugee status even though the circumstances giving rise to the policy no longer existed.[10]

1   *Abdi v Secretary of State for the Home Department* [1996] Imm AR 148, CA; *Hersi v Secretary of State for the Home Department* [1996] Imm AR 569 at 580, CA, per Otton LJ.
2   *A-G of Hong Kong v Ng Yuen Shiu* [1983] 2 AC 629, [1983] 2 All ER 346, PC; *R v Secretary of State for the Home Department, ex p Khan* [1985] 1 All ER 40, [1984] 1 WLR 1337, CA; *R v Immigration Appeal Tribunal, ex p Bastiampillai* [1983] 2 All ER 844, [1983] Imm AR 1; *Khan (Asif Mahmood) v Immigration Appeal Tribunal* [1984] Imm AR 68, CA.
3   *Gyeabour* [1989] Imm AR 94; *Ahmed v Secretary of State for the Home Department, Patel v Secretary of State for the Home Department* [1999] Imm AR 22, CA (marriage and deportation); *R v Secretary of State for the Home Department, ex p Najem* [1999] Imm AR 107, QBD (travel documents; grounds for grant of exceptional leave to remain); *Warsame v Entry Clearance Officer, Nairobi* [2000] Imm AR 155, CA (Somali family reunion); *R v Secretary of State for the Home Department, ex p Singh (Tarlok)* [2000] Imm AR 508, QBD (children and deportation).
4   *R v Secretary of State for the Home Department, ex p Amankwah* [1994] Imm AR 240, QBD (policy on marriage and deportation DP2/93); see also *R v Secretary of State for the Home Department, ex p Ozminnos* [1994] Imm AR 287, QBD.

⁵   *R (on the application of Rashid) v Secretary of State for the Home Department* [2004] EWHC 2465 (Admin), [2004] All ER (D) 316 (Oct), para 51, citing Hobhouse LJ in *Ahmed v Secretary of State for the Home Department, Patel v Secretary of State for the Home Department* [1998] INLR 570 at 591 to the effect that legitimate expectation is a principle of fairness, which is objective and not based on the state of knowledge of those affected.
⁶   *Nadarajah v Secretary of State for the Home Department* [2003] EWCA Civ 1768, [2004] INLR 139.
⁷   *R (on the application of Amirthanathan) v Secretary of State for the Home Department* [2002] EWHC 2595, [2003] All ER (D) 29 (May).
⁸   Part of the judge's reasoning was that the Secretary of State might have lawfully excluded the claimant under the previous policy.
⁹   *R (on the application of Joseph) v Secretary of State for the Home Department* [2002] EWHC 758 (Admin), [2002] All ER (D) 149 (Apr).
¹⁰ *R (on the application of Rashid) v Secretary of State for the Home Department* [2004] EWHC 2465 (Admin), [2004] All ER (D) 316 (Oct), per Davis J. He reached this conclusion on the basis that the policy was in universal and unqualified terms, admitting of no exception, and that the Secretary of State had no good reason for failing to apply it to the claimant at the relevant time. In those circumstances it would be substantively unfair to allow the Secretary of State to rely on the change of circumstances to deny the claimant the benefit of it. At the time of writing, the Secretary of State's appeal to the Court of Appeal was pending.

European Community law

1.55 On the same day that the Immigration Act 1971 came into effect, the UK's membership of the EC also took effect. Joining the Common Market, as it was then known, has meant that the development of domestic immigration law has gone hand in hand with that of EC law on free movement rights.[1] Now, as a result of the Treaty of Amsterdam, EC law has expanded to take in third-country immigration, expulsion and asylum issues. The Immigration Acts are not the last word; their provisions must yield to EC law, when it is applicable.[2] Where national courts have to interpret domestic law in a field governed by EC law, the courts must interpret that law in the light of the wording and purpose of EC law, so far as it is possible for them to do so.[3] The 'so far as possible' principle of interpretation contained in *Marleasing* has now been incorporated into the Human Rights Act 1998[4] in order to minimise conflict between domestic law and the ECHR.[5] It is now a requirement of European law that the rights guaranteed by the ECHR are respected as general principles of EC law.[6] This means that in imposing limitations on the right of free movement of EU nationals (such as deportation), Member States must respect any relevant provision of the ECHR.[7] By this process, parts of the ECHR which are not included in the list of substantive rights set out in the Human Rights Act 1998 because they are unratified, such as the fourth Protocol, may also find their way into UK domestic law, as part of the *corpus* of law to be taken into account in construing EC law.[8] Reports of decisions of the ECJ are published on the internet[9] and in the European Court Reports (ECR),[10] and in the commercially published Common Market Law Reports and European All ERs. A useful summary of ECJ judgments and opinions of the Advocate General is published and distributed from Luxembourg each month.

¹   See 1.39–1.40 above; chapter 7 below.

2   See European Communities Act 1972, s 2; Treaty Establishing the European Community (consolidated version of Treaty of Rome), Art 10 (ex Art 5); *R v Secretary of State for Employment, ex p Equal Opportunities Commission* [1995] 1 AC 1, HL.
3   *Marleasing SA v La Comercial Internacional de Alimentacion SA* [1990] ECR I-4135, ECJ; applied by the HL in *Litster v Forth Dry Dock and Engineering Co Ltd* [1990] 1 AC 546.
4   Human Rights Act 1998, s 3(1).
5   See 1.56 below.
6   Treaty on European Union, Art 6 (ex Art F); *Elliniki Radiophonia Tileorass AE v Pliroforissos and Kouvelas* [1991] ECR I-2925, ECJ.
7   *B v Secretary of State for the Home Department* [2000] Imm AR 478, [2000] INLR 361, CA.
8   This argument was not, however, addressed by the ECJ in *R v Secretary of State for the Home Department, ex p Manjit Kaur* C-192/99 (20 February 2001, unreported).
9   At www.curia.eu.int.
10 The official reports published by the ECJ registry.

The European Convention of Human Rights

1.56 The ECHR and its case law, consisting mainly of judgments of the European Court of Human Rights in Strasbourg and (previously) opinions of the European Commission on Human Rights,[1] has long been a necessary part of the immigration lawyer's briefcase and we have dealt with its very considerable impact on immigration law in all of the previous editions of this work. Unlike EC law, ECHR law does not have primacy over UK domestic legislation, unless it is applied as part of the *corpus* of EC law.[2] However, all domestic courts and tribunals must 'so far as it is possible' read and give effect to primary and subordinate legislation in a way which is compatible with Convention rights.[3] If this is not possible, Convention rights will have to yield to the UK provisions in the time-honoured way, and only a higher court (not the Tribunal) can then declare the law to be incompatible with the Convention rights. By section 2 of the Human Rights Act 1998 a court or tribunal determining a question which has arisen in connection with a Convention right must take into account the case law of the ECtHR, the opinions and decisions of the EComHR, and decisions of the Committee of Ministers. This whole body of law must, therefore, become an essential part of the immigration lawyer's repertoire. The case law is to be found on the court's website, which also gives access to press releases of forthcoming cases and summaries of recent decisions;[4] in the printed decisions of the ECtHR or the EComHR (the Series A reports); the case law summaries published by the court; and the commercially published Human Rights Law Digest (for decisions of the Committee of Ministers up to 1998), the European Human Rights Reports and the European Human Rights Law Review.

1   Abolished by Protocol 11 of the ECHR as from 1 November 1998.
2   See 1.55 above.
3   Human Rights Act 1998, s 3(1).
4   At www.echr.coe.int.

The Convention Relating to the Status of Refugees

1.57 The Convention Relating to the Status of Refugees (Geneva, 1951) and its 1967 Protocol (collectively the Refugee Convention) and the very considerable body of UK and foreign case law are key sources of asylum law, to be read with the provisions of the UK statutes and rules which give effect to the Convention in this country.[1] The Convention is a primary source of asylum law and its provisions are now construed routinely by the courts. In doing so, the courts use a number of UNHCR materials as aids to interpretation, in particular the UNHCR *Handbook*[2] and Executive Committee (ExCom) recommendations and conclusions. These may also be relevant to the exercise of a broad discretion, even though they are not themselves the source of obligations and duties.[3] Although the Convention is an international instrument, there is no supra-national court which can provide an international interpretation of its provisions. Inevitably, therefore, any examination of a particular provision by the courts will involve looking at a wide range of case law from different countries. Some familiarity with the leading case law of countries such as Canada, the US, New Zealand and Australia has been, and no doubt will continue to be, essential for those practicing in this field. Much of this case law is available on the internet, through the Electronic Immigration Network or law libraries' websites.[4]

[1] Asylum and Immigration Appeals Act 1993, s 2; see 1.23 above.
[2] UNHCR *Handbook on Procedures and Criteria for Determining Refugee Status* (1979), 'the *Handbook*'.
[3] See 12.14 below.
[4] The Electronic Immigration Network website is at www.ein.org. For other websites see 1.47 above, and Appendix 3.

International treaties and obligations

1.58 Until the last decade, international instruments other than the Refugee Convention and the ECHR have played a rather background role in immigration and asylum, because they were not part of domestic law and their role as sources of immigration law was either very obscure or barely counted. For example, there are a number of Conventions which have led to the adoption of particular provisions in the Immigration Rules, such as the rule providing for settlement after four years in employment, which derives from the International Labour Organisation Convention regarding Migration for Employment, or the long residence concession, which derives from the European Convention on Establishment. With the incorporation of the ECHR into British law, UK courts and tribunals are expected to develop their own human rights jurisprudence. A number of other human rights instruments and the case law built round them is both relevant and helpful. These have already played a role in the development of Strasbourg jurisprudence. They are recognised as important aids to construction in the Convention itself. Article 53 provides that nothing in the Convention shall be construed as limiting or derogating from any of the human rights and fundamental freedoms under any other agreement to which any High Contracting Party is a party. These include the International Covenant on Civil and Political Rights and decisions of the UN Human Rights Committee set up to receive complaints under this Covenant; the International Covenant on Economic, Social and Cultural Rights; the Convention on the Rights of the Child; the Convention for the Elimination of all Forms of Racial Discrimination; the Convention on the Elimination of all Forms of Discrimination Against Women; the UN Convention Against Torture and Other Cruel, Inhuman and Degrading Treatment; the

European Convention for the Prevention of Torture and Inhuman and Degrading Treatment or Punishment; and the UN Body of Principles on All Forms of Detention (1988). Texts of these and a whole host of other important international documents can be found in Plender's *Basic Documents on International Migration Law*[1] and on websites such as that of the UN. The *Commonwealth Human Rights Digest* is another source of information.

[1]   2nd edn (1999) Nijhoff.

THE PERSONNEL OF IMMIGRATION CONTROL

1.59 Control of immigration and asylum, as we have just seen, is administered within the framework of the Immigration Act 1971 and subsequent primary and subordinate legislation, EC law, the 1951 Refugee Convention, the ECHR and, of course, the Immigration Rules. All this has created a lot of officials and has placed onerous responsibilities and duties on airlines and other carriers, road hauliers, employers, local authorities, marriage registrars and others. It has generated a whole industry of advisers, some more caring, scrupulous and competent than others. The purpose of the remainder of this chapter is to describe the key elements of the administration of immigration control, by looking at the principal personnel and the main sources and limits of their power. At one level it is all about the Home Office, immigration officers, airlines and immigration advisers. But at another level it is about power, legality, and the particular tools of trade of a very large and powerful administrative organisation and the attempt to involve and regulate those involved in asylum or immigration for commercial reasons.

The Home Office and Secretary of State for the Home Department

1.60 The Home Office is responsible for immigration control. The Secretary of State for the Home Department is the minister in charge. But the statutes make no express reference to either. The Immigration Act 1971 refers only to the Secretary of State. Under Schedule 1 to the Interpretation Act 1978 it is provided that in every Act the expression 'Secretary of State' shall mean 'one of Her Majesty's principal Secretaries of State for time being'. In practice, it is the Secretary of State for the Home Department (the Home Secretary) who is in overall control and has the last word.[1] In Scotland it might be thought that the powers would be exercisable by the Secretary of State for Scotland, but it has been held that this is not so, and the Home Secretary in London can validly order someone who is within the Scottish jurisdiction to be deported,[2] or in some cases, admitted.[3] The administration of immigration control is not, however, entirely run by the Home Secretary: entry clearance officers in overseas posts are usually attached to the Foreign and Commonwealth Office,[4] and the Lord Chancellor is responsible for appointing members of the Asylum and Immigration Tribunal[5] and making rules of procedure for appeals.[6] The Immigration and Nationality Directorate at the Home Office now[7] comprises an asylum section, an appeals directorate, the National

Asylum Support Service and managed migration, which includes all non-asylum casework, work permits and British nationality. There is now a bewildering array of departments and units within these Home Office departments, all referred to by acronym, such as RESCU, DEPMU, WICU, OASIS and NEAT.[8]

1　*Pearson v Immigration Appeal Tribunal* [1978] Imm AR 212, CA.
2　*Agee v Murray* (23 February 1977, unreported), CS, per Lord Kincraig. However, the appointment of immigration officers and medical inspectors in Scotland is transferred to Scottish ministers: Scotland Act 1998 (Transfer of Functions to the Scottish Ministers) Order 1999, SI 1999/1750.
3　In 2000 the Home Secretary ordered the admission of boxer Mike Tyson, who had a conviction for rape, to enable him to box in Scotland, a decision upheld in *R v Secretary of State for the Home Department, ex p Bindel* [2001] Imm AR 1, QBD.
4　The Home office and Foreign Office have formed a Joint Entry Clearance Unit (JECU) which is responsible for coordination of entry clearance policy and practice.
5　Nationality, Immigration and Asylum Act 2002, Sch 4 (substituted by Asylum and Immigration (Treatment of Claimants, etc) Act 2004, s 26(4), Sch 1, from 4 April 2005: SI 2005/565.
6　Nationality, Immigration and Asylum Act 2002, s 106 as amended by Asylum and Immigration (Treatment of Claimants, etc) Act 2004, Sch 2, para 21.
7　Since internal reorganisation in 2003.
8　Respectively (so far as we can ascertain) Resettlement and Coordination Unit; Detainee Escorting and Population Management Unit; Warnings Index Computerised Unit (reporting on overstayers); Operational Advisory Services for Immigration Service; and NASS Eligibility and Assessment Team). We have attempted to list as many of these acronyms as possible in a glossary: see Appendix 4.

1.61 Within the Home Office there was previously a clear division of responsibility between the Secretary of State and immigration officers – under section 4(1) of the Immigration Act 1971, immigration officers are responsible for giving leave to enter and the Secretary of State for giving leave to remain or varying leave – but this clear division has been blurred by section 62 of the 2002 Act, which allows the Secretary of State to give leave to enter. The Secretary of State also has responsibility for making the Immigration Rules and laying them before Parliament,[1] and for making various Orders, rules and regulations under the 1971 Act and the other Immigration statutes. The various tasks of the Secretary of State are normally carried out by responsible departmental officials operating within normal *Carltona* principles,[2] but certain decisions such as the exclusion of persons on grounds of national security must be taken by the Secretary of State in person.[3] The signing of deportation orders is normally done by the Secretary of State in person, reflecting the significance of his or her decision.[4] In *R v Secretary of State for the Home Department, ex p Oladehinde*[5] the House of Lords held that although immigration officers had independent statutory powers, they were members of the Home Office and accordingly the Secretary of State could devolve decisions to deport to them.

1　Immigration Act 1971, s 3(2).
2　*Carltona Ltd v Works Comrs* [1943] 2 All ER 560, CA.
3　Immigration and Asylum Act 1999, ss 60(9), 62(4), 64(2).
4　Earlier rules reflected this: HC 251, para 175, but not the current Immigration Rules. See per Woolf LJ in *R v Secretary of State for the Home Department, ex p Alexander and Oladehinde* [1990] 2 WLR 1195 at 1202, DC; further *Re Khan (Amanullah)* [1986] Imm AR 485, QBD.
5　[1991] 1 AC 254, [1990] 3 All ER 393, HL. See also *Jazayeri* [2001] UKIAT 00014, [2001] INLR 489.

1.62 The Secretary of State for the Home Department is expected to carry out his or her functions in accordance with the established principles of administrative law and not to do anything which breaches any person's human rights.[1] As a public authority he or she must not discriminate unlawfully on racial grounds, although discrimination on grounds of nationality or ethnic or national origin in certain areas is permissible.[2] He or she must keep within the limits of the statutory powers, under which decisions are taken, and must exercise prerogative powers fairly (see 1.46 above). In situations covered by the Immigration Rules, the Secretary of State must act in accordance with them, unless it be to make a decision more favourable to an immigrant (see 1.44 above). The Secretary of State is now fully susceptible to control by the courts and may be restrained by interim or final injunctions and is guilty of contempt of court if he or she breaches an injunction or undertaking given to the court.[3]

[1] Human Rights Act 1998, s 6.
[2] Race Relations Act 1976, ss 19B, 19D, as amended by Race Relations (Amendment) Act 2000.
[3] *Re M* [1994] 1 AC 377, sub nom *M v Home Office* [1993] 3 All ER 537, HL.

Immigration officers

1.63 Immigration officers are part of the immigration service, which consists of immigration officers, chief immigration officers and immigration inspectors, all of whom are appointed by the Secretary of State under the Immigration Act 1971.[1] They have their own statutory functions as immigration officers, but they are also civil servants[2] and can, therefore, be asked to make decisions to deport on behalf of the Secretary of State.[3] Their main functions are to examine those who arrive in this country[4] and to grant, refuse, suspend or cancel leave to enter.[5] They also have important policing functions under sections 28A-K and Schedules 2 and 3 to the 1971 Act, Part VII of the Immigration and Asylum Act 1999 and section 14 of the Asylum and Immigration (Treatment of Claimants, etc) Act 2004. It is a criminal offence to obstruct immigration officers in carrying out their functions under the 1971 Act.[6]

[1] Immigration Act 1971, Sch 2, para 1(2). The paragraph enables customs officers to be employed as immigration officers by arrangement with the Commissioner of Customs and Excise. In Scotland, immigration officers are appointed by the Scottish ministers: Scotland Act 1998 (Transfer of Functions to the Scottish Ministers) Order 1999, SI 1999/1750.
[2] See per Woolf LJ in *R v Secretary of State for the Home Department, ex p Oladehinde and Alexander* [1990] 2 WLR 1195 at 1203.
[3] *R v Secretary of State for the Home Department, ex p Oladehinde* [1991] 1 AC 254, [1990] 3 All ER 393, HL. See also *Jazayeri* [2001] UKIAT 00014, [2001] INLR 489.
[4] And at Eurostar stations, on Eurostar and in ports at Dover, Calais, Boulogne and Dunkirk, to be extended to Belgian ports: see modifications made to Immigration Act 1971, Sch 2 by the Channel Tunnel (International Arrangements) Order 1993, SI 1993/1813 as amended; Nationality, Immigration and Asylum (Juxtaposed Controls) Order 2003, SI 2003/2818. See further 3.27–3.28 below.
[5] Immigration Act 1971, Sch 2, paras 2–6, as amended by Immigration (Leave to Enter and Remain) Order 2000, SI 2000/1161. In doing so they are entitled to mark passports: *R v Secretary of State for the Home Department, ex p Raju* [1986] Imm AR 348, QBD.
[6] Immigration Act 1971, s 26(1)(g). For this and other criminal offences see chapter 14 below.

1.64 In exercising their statutory functions immigration officers must act in accordance with the law, the Immigration Rules, and any instructions given to them by the Secretary of State for the Home Department, provided these are not inconsistent with the Immigration Rules,[1] and they must not do anything which breaches a person's human rights[2] or constitutes unlawful racial discrimination.[3] The need to act in accordance with the law and the Immigration Rules is consistent with the general principles of administrative law and includes the duty to act fairly, which we look at in more detail below. But it also derives quite specifically from section 86(3) of the Nationality, Immigration and Asylum Act 2002,[4] which requires the Asylum and Immigration Tribunal to allow an appeal if the decision is not in accordance with the law, including the Immigration Rules. Uncertainty still hangs over the extent of the Tribunal's jurisdiction in respect of a decision which is *Wednesbury* unreasonable, taken in bad faith or unfairly (see chapter 18 below), but this does not affect the clear restraints placed upon the immigration officer's powers and the manner in which they must be exercised. It appears that immigration officers share the Secretary of State's discretion to depart from the Rules in a manner favourable to the immigrant,[5] an issue the court left open in *Ex p Ounejma*.[6]

1   Immigration Act 1971, Sch 2, para 1(3).
2   Human Rights Act 1998, s 6.
3   Race Relations Act 1976, s 19B, as amended by Race Relations (Amendment) Act 2000. Immigration officers may discriminate on grounds of nationality or ethnic or national origins pursuant to specific ministerial authorisation, but not otherwise: s 19D; *R (on the application of the Tamil Information Centre) v Secretary of State for the Home Department* [2002] EWHC 2155 (Admin), (2002) Times, 30 October; *European Roma Rights Centre v Immigration Officer at Prague Airport* [2004] UKHL 55, [2005] 2 WLR 1. See 1.30 above.
4   Previously Immigration and Asylum Act 1999, Sch 4, para 21, and before that, Immigration Act 1971, s 19(1)(a)(i).
5   See 1.45 and 1.52 above.
6   [1989] Imm AR 75.

1.65 In *Ex p Safira Begum*[1] the Divisional Court said there was no obligation on immigration officers to make any inquiries on their own initiative in an attempt to assist would-be entrants; they could merely stand at their bench and wait for intending entrants to say what they had to say. This may be an overstatement of the immigration officer's position. In their dealings with immigrants they must act honestly and fairly.[2] This means that in all cases the would-be entrant should be given a real opportunity of satisfying the immigration officer that he or she should be admitted,[3] and where immigration officers' suspicions are aroused they must make them known to the immigrant and give him or her a chance to explain.[4] An immigration officer who makes insufficient inquiries may be failing to act reasonably. Thus in one case, a simple inquiry of the Home Office would have revealed a Home Office report that a woman passenger's marriage was genuine.[5] In *Ex p Mughal* the Court of Appeal emphasised that immigration officers were administrative officers engaged in administrative inquiries and that the rules of natural justice must not be stretched too far.[6] So when immigration officers obtained further information which confirmed their suspicions there was no need to tell immigrants of this or give them a further opportunity to explain. In *Ex p Ajekukor,* where a passenger was found to have a forged stamp in her passport and could give no explanation, the immigration officer was held to be under no duty to make further inquiries and a failure to do so was not a breach of the rules of natural justice.[7] But in *Ex p Moon* the Divisional Court held that it was unfair not to give a visa applicant an opportunity to deal with objections to his admission.[8] This later decision brings the position of immigration officers vis-à-vis the duty of fairness closer to that of departmental officers making decisions on asylum[9] or naturalisation applications.[10] In carrying out investigations, arrests, searches and other policing functions immigration officers are subject to modified Police and Criminal Evidence Act 1984 (PACE) Codes of Practice.[11]

[1] *R v Secretary of State for the Home Department, ex p Begum (Safira)* (1976) Times, 27 May, QBD.
[2] *Re HK (infant)* [1967] 2 QB 617 at 630, per Lord Parker CJ; *Re Arif (an infant)* [1968] Ch 643, sub nom Hanif v *Secretary of State for Home Affairs* [1968] 2 All ER 145, CA; *R v Chief Immigration Officer, Lympne Airport, ex p Singh (Amrik)* [1969] 1 QB 333, [1968] 3 All ER 163; *R v Secretary of State for the Home Department, ex p Mughal* [1974] QB 313, CA.
[3] *Ex p Mughal* above, at 331, per Scarman LJ.
[4] *Ex p Mughal* above at 325, per Lord Denning MR.
[5] *R v Secretary of State for the Home Department, ex p Ramnial* [1983] LS Gaz R 30, DC.
[6] *Ex p Mughal* above. See further *Kumar v Entry Clearance Officer, New Delhi* [1985] Imm AR 242 (entry clearance officers exercising administrative, not judicial function, when carrying out interviews).
[7] *R v Immigration Officer, ex p Ajekukor* [1982] Imm AR 3, DC.
[8] *R v Secretary of State for the Home Department, ex p Moon* (1995) Times, 8 December.
[9] *Secretary of State for the Home Department v Thirakumar* [1989] Imm AR 402, CA; *Mapah v Secretary of State for the Home Department* [2003] EWHC 306 (Admin), [2003] Imm AR 395; *R (on the application of the Refugee Legal Centre) v Secretary of State for the Home Department* [2004] EWHC 684 (Admin), [2004] All ER (D) 580 (May).
[10] *R v Secretary of State for the Home Department, ex p Fayed* [1997] 1 All ER 228, CA.
[11] See chapter 14 below.

Police

1.66 Although immigration officers have taken over much of the policing of immigration control with the powers given to them under Part VII of the Immigration and Asylum Act 1999 and section 14 of the Asylum and Immigration (Treatment of Claimants, etc) Act 2004, the police retain a considerable role. They are responsible for the registration of foreign nationals[1] and remain jointly responsible for the enforcement of those parts of the criminal law, including immigration offences, which involve immigration. Like immigration officers, they have powers under the Immigration Act 1971 to arrest suspected overstayers, illegal entrants and absconders for the purposes of administrative detention,[2] as well as immigration offenders.[3] They can arrest illegal entrants and others, and can obtain warrants for the search and arrest of such persons.[4] In addition to these powers, the police may be used for the service of documents such as decisions to deport, and have been used in the collection of information about the home circumstances of sponsors wishing to bring relatives and family into this country and on applicants for naturalisation. Immigration law makes a distinction between police acting in the execution of the Immigration Acts (ie performing an administrative function given to them under the Acts) and police exercising common law powers to investigate crime.[5]

1   Immigration Act 1971, s 4(3); Immigration (Registration with Police) Regulations 1972, SI 1972/1758 (amended on many occasions only in respect of the fee for issue of a certificate of registration).
2   Immigration Act 1971, Sch 2, para 17.
3   Immigration Act 1971, s 28A(1), as amended by Immigration and Asylum Act 1999 (arrest without warrant for certain immigration offences).
4   Immigration Act 1971, s 28B.
5   *R v Clarke* [1985] AC 1037, [1985] 2 All ER 777, HL.

Entry clearance officers

1.67   The citizens of approximately one hundred countries now need visas even for a visit to the UK, and visas or entry clearance are also required for citizens of every non-EEA country who wish to come to the UK for work, business or family reunion. Soon, visas will be required for everyone who seeks entry for more than six months.[1] Visas and entry clearances are granted by entry clearance officers and visa officers, who work under the aegis of the Foreign Office, rather than the Home Office.[2] A Joint Entry Clearance Unit was set up in 1999 to ensure proper co-ordination between entry clearance officers and the Home Office. Its objective is 'to regulate entry to and settlement in the United Kingdom effectively in the interests of sustainable growth and social inclusion'.[3] It is a joint Home Office and Foreign and Commonwealth Office initiative to manage and staff entry clearance posts abroad and monitor their performance.[4] 'Entry clearance' is defined in the Immigration Acts[5] and in many cases there is an appeal against refusal.[6] Yet entry clearance officers are not mentioned, as such, in the Acts, which is surprising in view of the vitally important role they play in granting entry clearances which operate as leave to enter,[7] and in determining in the country of origin whether someone is eligible for admission to the UK.[8] However, the immigration rules HC 395, as amended, place entry clearance officers in the same position as immigration officers vis-à-vis the application of the rules, which includes of course the obligation to act in accordance with the UK's obligations under the ECHR. They are also 'public authorities' for the purpose of the Human Rights Act.[9] They are also subject to the prohibition on discrimination on racial grounds, and on grounds of nationality, ethnic or national origin unless this is authorised by specific ministerial authorisation.[10] All the requirements of legality and fairness set out above in relation to immigration officers apply with equal force to entry clearance officers.[11]

1   Ministerial written statement: changes to immigration practice, June 2003; see 3.8 below.
2   See *R v Secretary of State for the Home Department, ex p Phansopkar* [1976] QB 606, [1975] 3 All ER 497, CA. In many cases entry clearance officers refer applications back to London for decision. In some cases this is mandatory; in others optional.
3   UK Visas Annual Report 2004. In 2003, entry clearance officers processed over 2 million applications for visas at 162 posts. The reports of the entry clearance monitor (1.68 below) give a useful insight into the operation of entry clearance.
4   The Foreign and Commonwealth Office website, www.fco.gov.uk, provides access to entry clearance posts, up-to-date information on fees and e-mail addresses of posts. The JECU website, UKVisas, contains the Diplomatic Service Procedures (instructions to entry clearance officers on the operation of the rules and on concessions and policies outside the rules) which are the equivalent of the IDI used by immigration officers.
5   Immigration Act 1971, s 33(1); Immigration and Asylum Act 1999, s 167(2).
6   Nationality, Immigration and Asylum Act 2002, s 82(2)(b).

7 Immigration Act 1971, s 3A, inserted by Immigration and Asylum Act 1999, s 1; Immigration (Leave to Enter and Remain) Order 2000, SI 2000/1161, Arts 2–4.
8 See *R v Secretary of State for the Home Department, ex p Ounejma* [1989] Imm AR 75, DC for the suggestion that they may be creatures of the prerogative.
9 Human Rights Act 1998, s 6.
10 Race Relations Act ss 19B, 19D, 67 as inserted and amended by Race Relations (Amendment) Act 2000. See *European Roma Rights Centre v Immigration Officer at Prague Airport* [2004] UKHL 55, [2005] 2 WLR 1, where the House of Lords held that the operation conducted by UK immigration officials at Prague Airport in an attempt to stop Roma people coming to the UK to claim asylum was unlawful under both domestic and international law: see 8.98 below.
11 *Kumar v Entry Clearance Officer* [1985] Imm AR 242; *R v Secretary of State for the Home Department, ex p Moon* (1995) Times, 8 December, QBD.

Monitors

1.68 The Secretary of State has appointed a number of monitors to oversee functions which require an element of accountability which is not provided through the appellate system, including the following:

- The Immigration Race Monitor, appointed by virtue of section 19E of the Race Relations Act,[1] monitors the effect of ministerial authorisations to discriminate issued under section 19D of the Act on the operation of immigration functions. She reports annually to Parliament, and may produce interim reports to the minister. Her reports are published on the IND website.

- The Independent Monitor of Certification of Claims as Unfounded[2] reviews the operation and use of the power to certify an asylum claim or human rights claim (or both) as unfounded, and the quality and effectiveness of decisions made under this procedure. She reports annually to the Secretary of State, who will then lay a copy of the report before the House.[3] The consideration of whether countries are suitable for addition to the list of countries designated under section 94 is not within the terms of appointment of the unfounded claims monitor.[4]

- The Accommodation Centres Monitor, appointed under section 34 of the Nationality, Immigration and Asylum Act 2002, is required to observe the operation of accommodation centres, and in particular, to consider the quality and effectiveness of accommodation and other facilities provided at the centres, including the nature and enforcement of conditions of residence, the treatment of residents, and whether, in the case of any accommodation centre, its location prevents a need of its residents from being met. He or she will provide an annual report to the Home Secretary, which will be laid before Parliament.[5]

- The Independent Monitor for entry clearance refusals which do not attract the right of appeal is appointed by the Secretary of State for Foreign and Commonwealth Affairs.[6] The type of refusals that the entry clearance monitor reviews are those which have no right of appeal in accordance with sections 90 and 91 of the 2002 Act, such as those for entry clearance as a visitor. The monitor looks at the overall quality of refusal decisions, paying particular attention to fairness, consistency and the procedures used to reach those decisions. Entry Clearance Posts do not know in advance which cases have been chosen for review. The findings of the Independent Monitor are given in a report to the Foreign Secretary, who submits it to Parliament.[7]

In addition, HM Chief Inspector of Prisons inspects Home Office removal centres,[8] and reports on the treatment of detainees and the conditions of detention. His or her inspection reports go to the Secretary of State, and annual reports are presented to Parliament.[9] An escort monitor, who is a Crown servant, is said to keep escort arrangements under review, inspect the conditions under which detained persons are transported, investigate allegations against detainee custody officers, and report to the Secretary of State, who is, however, under no statutory duty to publish the monitor's reports or present them to Parliament.[10]

1   Inserted by Race Relations (Amendment) Act 2000.
2   Ie, under s 94 of the Nationality, Immigration and Asylum Act 2002.
3   Nationality, Immigration and Asylum Act 2002, s 111. No reports are yet available.
4   Government response to the Constitutional Affairs Select Committee on Immigration and Asylum Appeals, June 2004.
5   Home Office website, July 2004. No accommodation centres are yet built. The contract has been awarded to GSL (UK), whose running of the immigration detention estate has a controversial history involving three separate Prison Service enquiries (see below). In addition to the monitor, the Secretary of State has power to appoint an advisory group in relation to each centre, to visit the centres and hear complaints by residents, under s 33 of the 2002 Act.
6   Under Immigration and Asylum Act 1999, s 23, as amended by Nationality, Immigration and Asylum Act 2002, Sch 7, para 27.
7   The reports of the independent monitor for the past three years are on the UKVisas website. The monitor's 2003 report (published in June 2004) concluded that up to 10,000 visitors and students were being wrongly denied appeals annually, and that refusals of visit visas were frequently taken on subjective and judgmental grounds unrelated to the criteria of the rules.
8   Under the Prisons Act 1952, s 5A(5a), inserted by Immigration and Asylum Act 1999, s 152(5), amended by Nationality, Immigration and Asylum Act 2002, s 66.
9   All the inspection reports on removal centres are available on the Home Office website.
10 Immigration and Asylum Act 1999, Sch 13, para 1.

Private security firms

1.69 A source of increasing concern is the involvement of the private sector in the detention and removal of immigrants. Private security companies such as Securicor and Group 4 have been involved for decades in the running of immigration detention centres. Concerns about the treatment of detainees, and of those being removed from the UK, have emerged from time to time, but are more difficult to investigate than if the establishments and officers concerned were under the direct control of the Secretary of State.[1] In *Quaquah v Group 4 and the Home Office*,[2] the High Court struck out a claim in tort against the Home Office for events at Campsfield House detention centre in 1997 which resulted in the prosecution of the plaintiff, holding that the Home Office was not liable for the tortious actions of an independent contractor to whom it had delegated the running of a detention centre, provided it exercised reasonable care over the selection of that contractor. The 1999 and 2002 Acts have established a regulatory regime at removal centres, but have also given staff employed by the private companies extensive disciplinary powers, including the use of reasonable force, and powers of entry into premises, search and seizure when accompanying an immigration officer.[3] The companies concerned are however 'public authorities' when exercising these functions.[4] The Secretary of State may intervene in the running of a contracted out removal centre if the manager has lost control of the centre or any part of it, or appears likely to, or in the interests of safety or prevention of damage to property.[5]

[1] One of the companies which runs a number of removal centres, GSL (a former subsidiary of Group 4) has been the subject of at least three official inquiries, including one into the events at Yarl's Wood on 14 February 2002 which led to the centre burning down; an inquiry into allegations of racism and abuse at Yarl's Wood, where the Prisons Ombudsman found the incidence of force 'disproportionate', and an ongoing inquiry into racism and abuse at Oakington Immigration Reception Centre and at Heathrow during escort of deportees, depicted by a BBC programme, 'Asylum Undercover' in March 2005 (see ministerial statement by Des Browne, Hansard 3.3.05, Col 95WS). Despite this record, the company has been awarded the contract to design, build and run the accommodation centres established under Part 2 of the Nationality, Immigration and Asylum Act 2002 (see IND website).

[2] *Quaquah v Group 4 (Total Security) and the Home Office* (01/TLQ/0340) (23 May 2001, unreported).

[3] See Immigration and Asylum Act 1999, ss 147–157; Schs 11–13; Nationality, Immigration and Asylum Act 2002, s 64.

[4] Human Rights Act 1998, s 6; this was conceded in *Quaquah v Group 4* fn 2 above.

[5] Immigration and Asylum Act 1999, s 151.

Airlines and other carriers

1.70 Airlines and other carriers which bring passengers to the UK have responsibilities for checking passengers' passports and visas and now perform public law duties and have public law powers in respect of immigration control beyond any rights and liabilities arising from the contract of carriage.[1] The Immigration Act 1971 and the Immigration and Asylum Act 1999 make special provision for them. First, they are generally expected to call or, in the case of trains, stop only at specified ports of entry or terminal control points.[2] There they are under a duty to co-operate with the immigration authorities in ensuring that passengers embark and disembark in designated controlled areas and observe the conditions and restrictions which apply.[3] During the journey they must supply passengers with landing or embarkation cards as required.[4] The captain of a ship or aircraft and the manager of a train arriving in the UK is required to stop passengers disembarking, except in accordance with the arrangements made for their examination by immigration officers,[5] and is required to furnish immigration officers with lists of passengers and crew members and other passenger information,[6] arrival times of ships, trains or aircraft expected to carry non-EEA nationals,[7] and copies of passengers' documents,[8] as required.

[1] See generally 5 *Halsbury's Laws* (4th edn) para 301ff; Carriage by Air Act 1961.

[2] Immigration Act 1971, Sch 2, para 26(1), modified in relation to Channel Tunnel trains by the Channel Tunnel (International Arrangements) Order 1993, SI 1993/1813, Sch 4 para 1(11)(r).

[3] Immigration Act 1971, Sch 2, para 26(2), as modified for the Channel Tunnel by SI 1993/1813.

[4] Immigration Act 1971, Sch 2, para 5, modified in relation to Channel Tunnel trains by SI 1993/1813, para 1(11)(g); Immigration (Landing and Embarkation Cards) Order 1972, SI 1972/1666, as amended by SI 1975/65.

5   Immigration Act 1971, Sch 2, para 27(1), modified in relation to Channel Tunnel trains by SI 1993/1813, para 1(11)(r).
6   Immigration Act 1971, Sch 2, paras 27(2) and 27B, inserted by Immigration and Asylum Act 1999, s 18, modified in relation to Channel Tunnel trains by SI 2000/913; Immigration (Particulars of Passengers and Crew) Order 1972, SI 1972/1667, as amended; Immigration (Passenger Information) Order 2000, SI 2000/912.
7   Immigration Act 1971, Sch 2, para 27C, inserted by Immigration and Asylum Act 1999, s 19, modified in relation to Channel Tunnel trains by SI 2000/913.
8   Immigration Act 1971, Sch 2, para 27B(4A), inserted by Asylum and Immigration (Treatment of Claimants, etc) Act 2004, s 16, not yet in force at time of writing.

1.71 Carriers or their agents may be required to remove or make arrangements for the removal from the UK of any passengers who are refused leave to enter or are illegal entrants.[1] Normally the cost of removal will fall on the carrier, but in the case of passengers refused admission there is a two-month time limit for the giving of directions for their removal, after which the cost of removal falls on the Secretary of State for the Home Department.[2] Carriers are also liable to pay up to 14 days' detention costs for those refused leave to enter, illegal entrants and certain crew members who overstay their shore leave.[3] The costs of detaining illegal entrants by deception is not payable, however, unless their leave was cancelled within 24 hours of the conclusion of their examination.[4] In the case of deportees, the owners or agents of any ship, train or aircraft or the captain are required to comply with the directions given by the Secretary of State for the removal of the person from the UK.[5] The captain of a ship or aircraft, or a train manager, may also be required to prevent the escape of a person placed on board pending removal from the UK and has power to detain such person in custody for this purpose.[6] Breaches of their respective duties under the Immigration Act 1971 by either the owners, their agents or the captain or manager may make them liable to criminal penalties under section 27 of the 1971 Act.[7] If passengers arrive in the UK without proper documentation, the carrier may, in addition to the cost of removal and detention, be liable to pay a penalty of up to £2000.[8] Carriers' liability is treated in detail in chapter 14 below.

1   Immigration Act 1971, Sch 2, paras 8–9, modified in relation to Channel Tunnel trains by SI 1993/1813, Sch 4, para 1(11)(h)–(l); see also *R v Immigration Officer, ex p Shah* [1982] 2 All ER 264, [1982] 1 WLR 544; *Parshotam Singh v Secretary of State for the Home Department* [1989] Imm AR 469, CA.
2   IA 1971, Sch 2, paras 8(2) and 10(3).
3   IA 1971, Sch 2, paras 19(1) and 20(1), as amended by Asylum and Immigration Act 1996, Sch 2, paras 8, 9, modified in relation to Channel Tunnel trains by SI 1993/1813, Sch 4, para 1(11)(q).
4   IA 1971, Sch 2, para 20(1A), inserted by Asylum and Immigration Act 1996, Sch 2, para 9(2).
5   IA 1971, Sch 3, para 1(1) and (2), modified in relation to Channel Tunnel trains by SI 1993/1813, Sch 4, para 1(12).
6   IA 1971, Sch 2, para 16(4) and Sch 3, para 1(3), modified in relation to Channel Tunnel trains by SI 1993/1813, Sch 4, para 1(11)(p), 1(12).
7   Modified in relation to Channel Tunnel trains by SI 1993/1813, Sch 4, para 1(9).
8   Immigration and Asylum Act 1999, s 40(2), substituted by Nationality, Immigration and Asylum Act 2002 s 125, Sch 8.

Marriage and civil partnership registrars

1.72 Section 24 of the Immigration and Asylum Act 1999 imposes a duty on registrars to whom notice of marriage has been given, and those who have attested a declaration accompanying the notice, to report to the Secretary of State for the Home Department any suspicion on reasonable grounds that the marriage is, or will be, a sham marriage.[1] A 'sham marriage' is defined as one involving a non-EEA national, entered into for the purpose of avoiding the effect of a provision of UK immigration law or the Immigration Rules.[2] This definition is considered at 11.62 below. The registrars must report their suspicions without delay. They are given powers to require specified evidence from persons giving notice of marriage to them.[3] When the Civil Partnership Act is in force, exactly the same provisions apply to civil partnership registrars in respect of sham civil partnerships, defined in the same way.[4] In addition, sections 19–25 of the Asylum and Immigration (Treatment of Claimants, etc) Act 2004 preclude a superintendent registrar (in England and Wales), a district registrar (in Scotland) or a prescribed registrar (in Northern Ireland), from entering notice of a marriage in the marriage notice book unless satisfied that a party who is subject to immigration control either has entry clearance for the purpose of marriage, or has the Secretary of State's written permission to marry in the UK, or falls within a specified class.[5]

1   Immigration and Asylum Act 1999, s 24; see also the Reporting of Suspicious Marriaages and Registration of Marriages (Miscellaneous Amendments) Regulations 2000, SI 2000/3164 (in Northern Ireland, SI 2000/3233).
2   IAA 1999, s 24(5).
3   Marriage Act 1949, ss 28A and equivalent in Ireland, inserted by Immigration and Asylum Act 1999, s 162.
4   IAA 1999, s 24A, not yet in force, prospectively inserted by the Civil Partnerships Act 2004, s 26(1), Sch 27, para 162 (not yet in force).
5   Asylum and Immigration (Treatment of Claimants, etc) Act 2004, ss 19–24, in force 1 February 2005 (SI 2004/3398). The Immigration (Procedure for Marriage) Regulations 2005, SI 2005/15, specify persons settled in the UK as those who may marry without permission.

Immigration advisers

Unqualified practitioners

1.73 The Immigration and Asylum Act 1999 made provision for the regulation of immigration advisers and service providers, following widespread public concern at the incompetent and sometimes unscrupulous advisers who were active in this field, taking advantage of the vulnerability and lack of proficiency in the English language of their clients. The scheme of Part V of the 1999 Act focuses on non-legally qualified advisers, but there is scope for control of professionally qualified practitioners, should the professional bodies fail. It is now unlawful for any person to provide immigration advice or services[1] unless he or she is (i) registered by the Immigration Services Commissioner or by an equivalent body in the EEA; (ii) authorised to practice by a designated professional body in the UK or the EEA; (iii) a Crown officer or employee of a government department acting in that capacity; (iv) exempt under the terms of the 1999 Act; or (v) works for or under the supervision of any of the above.[2] Voluntary bodies such as immigration aid units, and publicly funded bodies like CABx or the Refugee Legal Centre must apply for exemption, and have to comply with the requirements of the scheme. The

Commissioner has developed a Code of Standards and Guidance on Competences detailing the regulatory requirements for organisations seeking exemption.[3] Advisers charging for their services must register with the Commissioner, and will need to show that they are capable of complying with the Commissioner's Rules and Codes of Standards.[4] Registration may be at level 1 (generalist advice), level 2 (detailed advice) or level 3 (specialist advice), according to a competence assessment by the Commissioner. The fees for registration depend on the level of competence and the number of advisers.[5] Those authorised to practice by a designated professional body whose members are regulated by that body (eg the Bar Council or the Law Society)[6] do not need to apply for exemption or registration, and nor does anyone working under the supervision of such a person. Contravention of the prohibition on unqualified advice or services is an offence,[7] as is advertising services which the adviser is not registered to provide. We deal with offences and the OISC's investigatory powers in chapter 14 below.

[1]   As defined in Immigration and Asylum Act 1999, s 82.
[2]   IAA 1999, s 84. The provisions of s 84 do not apply to educational institutions, students' unions acting on behalf of their members and health sector bodies: Immigration and Asylum Act 1999 (Part V Exemption: Educational Institutions and Health Sector Bodies) Order 2001, SI 2001/1403.
[3]   Under the Immigration and Asylum Act 1999, Sch 5, para 3.
[4]   IAA 1999, Sch 5, paras 1–3.
[5]   The current fees are £555 for first or continuing registration of a level one adviser, and otherwise range from £1700 for first registration of an organisation with 1–4 advisers (£1,250 for continuing registration) to £2,300 and £2,050 respectively for an organisation with ten or more advisers: Immigration Services Commissioner (Registration Fee) Order 2004, SI 2004/802, Arts 4, 5.
[6]   IAA 1999, s 86.
[7]   IAA 1999, s 91.

1.74 The scheme covers the whole spectrum of immigration, nationality and asylum work in connection with the UK and the EEA, including appeals and judicial review. Criminal proceedings are not covered by the regulation,[1] but advice on unlawful entry is, and also bail applications in the context of immigration detention.[2] Advice and applications for immigration employment documents are covered,[3] unless made on behalf of the applicant's own employee or prospective employee.[4] The Act provides for limited forms of registration, by reference to specified fields, or specified categories (eg work permits, or asylum claimants), and registration may be varied to or from such limited effect.[5] The regulation and registration of immigration advisers is the responsibility of the Immigration Services Commissioner.[6] An Immigration Services Tribunal, an independent body, with its own rules of procedure,[7] will hear disciplinary charges laid by the Commissioner and deal with appeals from the Commissioner's decisions, such as a refusal to register or to continue the registration of an adviser.[8] The Commissioner has a wide range of powers and responsibilities. First, he or she has a general duty to promote good practice, and will be concerned with the competence and scruples of advisers.[9] Secondly, he or she is in charge of the registration and exemption schemes and must keep and maintain registers of qualified advisers.[10] Thirdly, he or she may make rules to regulate the professional practice, conduct and discipline of immigration advisers,[11] and may prepare a Code of Standards for all immigration advisers, except members of the professional bodies.[12] The Commissioner must also establish a complaints system for the public.[13]

1   Immigration and Asylum Act 1999, s 82(1) under the definition of 'immigration advice'.
2   IAA 1999, s 82(1) under the definition of 'relevant matters'.
3   IAA 1999, s 82(1)(ba), inserted by Nationality, Immigration and Asylum Act 2002 s 123 (in force 1 April 2004).
4   IAA 1999 Part V Exemption: Relevant Employers) Order 2003, SI 2003/3214. Advice or help to an accession State national in applying for workers' registration is not regulated, but any advice or services relating to UK residence is: see OISC website.
5   IAA 1999, Sch 6, para 2, 3A (para 3A inserted by Nationality, Immigration and Asylum Act 2002 s 140).
6   IAA 1999, s 83(1) and (2) and Sch 5, Pt II. The first Commissioner, John Scampion, was appointed in May 2000, and the prohibition on unregulated advice came into force in April 2001.
7   IAA 1999, s 87(1) and Sch 7; Immigration Services Tribunal Rules 2000, SI 2000/2739, as amended by SI 2002/1716.
8   IAA 1999, s 87(3) and (4).
9   IAA 1999, s 83(3) and (5).
10 IAA 1999, s 85 and Sch 6.
11 IAA 1999, Sch 5, paras 1 and 2.
12 IAA 1999, Sch 5, paras 3 and 4. The Commissioner has prepared two such Codes, one for those who are to register and the other for exempt organisations.
13 IAA 1999, Sch 5, paras 5–10. See the Commissioner's annual reports, on the OISC website, for details of complaints, prosecutions, etc.

Professionally qualified practitioners

1.75 Concern has also been voiced about members of the legal profession, both by the Lord Chancellor and the Legal Aid Board, the predecessor to the Legal Services Commission. In 1998 the Lord Chancellor's Advisory Committee on Legal Education and Conduct reported that immigration law was an area where solicitors and barristers lack both knowledge and expertise, involving as it did many non-traditional sources such as the quantity of administrative guidance, with some of which many practitioners were unfamiliar.[1] The Legal Aid Board went further, complaining of a significant increase in poor quality, ill-supervised and sometimes unnecessary work.[2] To meet the criticisms, there have been several reforms, including franchising and immigration contracts, which involve solicitors demonstrating compliance with key quality criteria; and the Law Society's setting up of a specialist panel of immigration practitioners who meet fairly rigorous criteria of competence and proper case management. The most recent initiative has been the Law Society's Accreditation Scheme. From August 2005, no publicly funded work may be undertaken by a practitioner who is not accredited.[3] So far as the Bar is concerned, the Bar Council has a voluntary accreditation scheme for barristers in the immigration, nationality and asylum fields.

1   Advisory Committee on Legal Education and Conduct, *Improving the quality of immigration advice and representation: A report* (July 1998).
2   Legal Aid Board (now Legal Services Commission) *Access to quality services in the immigration category* (May 1999). We deal in chapter 18 below with funding of immigration and asylum appeals.
3   Accreditation, like registration of unqualified advisers, is at three levels. For details of accreditation scheme, see the Law Society's website.

Chapter 2

RIGHT OF ABODE AND CITIZENSHIP

INTRODUCTION

2.1 British citizenship now largely determines who obtains the right of abode in UK domestic law and who obtains the right of free movement and residence as a European citizen. However, the meaning of British citizen for the purpose of the right of abode and freedom from immigration control in the UK domestic context is different from the meaning of British nationals under international human rights law or UK nationals for the purpose of free movement and residence under EC law. In this chapter we explain the link between British nationality, British citizenship and the right of abode and refer to the new and easier means of acquiring British citizenship following the enactment of the British Overseas Territories Act 2002 and the Nationality Immigration and Asylum Act 2002. The meaning of UK nationals in the EU is explained in chapter 7. The following abbreviations are used in this chapter:

AI(TC)A 2004	Asylum and Immigration (Treatment of Claimants, etc) Act 2004
BC	British citizen
BDTC	British Dependent Territories citizen (now called BOTC)
BNA 1981	British Nationality Act 1981 (into force on 1 January 2083)

BN (O)	British National (Overseas)
BOC	British Overseas citizen
BOTA 2002	British Overseas Territories Act 2002 (main parts in force 26 February 2003)
BOTC	British Overseas Territories citizen (rename of BDTCs)
BPP	British Protected Person
CUKC	Citizen of the United Kingdom and Colonies
NIAA 2002	Nationality Immigration and Asylum Act 2002

THE RIGHT OF ABODE

2.2 When British nationality was reorganised in 1948, possession of British citizenship gave an automatic right of abode to all British nationals, not just Citizens of the UK and Colonies (CUKCs). It was a common law concept. After Commonwealth immigration control was introduced in 1962, the right of abode became a status of enormous importance. Between 1962 and 1973, when the Immigration Act 1971 came into force, it remained a common law concept, subject to such derogations as were required by clear provisions of the Commonwealth Immigrants Act 1962.[1] After 1973 it took on a statutory form, and became quite separate from the broad concept of British nationality and the status of Commonwealth citizen or British subject which went with it. But the definition of persons who had a right of abode was still linked to one or more of the categories of British subject. It is therefore necessary to look at the outlines of British nationality law.

[1] *DPP v Bhagwan* [1972] AC 60, [1970] 3 All ER 97, HL.

2.3 Under the Immigration Act 1971, section 1(1) it is provided that all those who are expressed to have the right of abode in the UK shall be free to live in, and to come and go into and from, the UK without let or hindrance except such as may be required by the Act to enable their right to be established or as may be otherwise lawfully imposed on any person. For example, they may be asked to produce their passports on entry,[1] and they may be refused entry if they do not have the requisite passport or certificate to prove their entitlement. Under section 3(9) of the 1971 Act they must have either:

(a) a UK passport describing them as a British citizen or as a CUKC having the right of abode; or
(b) a certificate of entitlement certifying that they have such a right.[2]

There are two groups of people who have a right of abode:

(1) British citizens;[3] and
(2) Commonwealth citizens who for the purpose of the Immigration Act 1971 are treated as British citizens.

By virtue of the right of abode, all these people are free from immigration control and cannot be deported or (except by extradition) removed,[4] unless they are unable to prove their status. The possession of British citizenship confers a status on the holder, and normally it can only be acquired by a strict application of nationality law or the exercise of a discretion under it by a minister or governor. This means that there is normally no room for the grant of citizenship by a representation from an immigration official or member of the staff at a High Commission or consulate that a person is entitled to it, unless possibly that person is acting on behalf of a minister or governor who has authority to grant citizenship.[5]

1   Immigration Act 1971, s 1(1) and Sch 2, paras 2 and 3. For the equivalent EC law requirement see *Re Wijsenbeek* [2000] INLR 336, ECJ.
2   Immigration Act 1971, ss 3(9)(b) as amended by NIAA 2002, s 10(5) from 1 April 2003 (SI 2003/754), and 33(1) as amended by NIA 2002, s 10(5)(b) from a date to be appointed. A 'Confirmation of Right of Abode' document was issued between 1 January 1983 and 1 August 1988 to those entitled to the right of abode under s 2(1)(a) and (b) of the Immigration Act 1971 as originally in force. Although it is no longer issued it remains valid with the validity of the passport to which it is attached. If someone with a Confirmation of Right of Abode obtains a new passport he or she will be issued with a certificate of entitlement: IDI Ch 1, s 1, Annex A.
3   These include dual nationals, who may be travelling on the passport of another country.
4   Immigration Act 1971, ss 2, 3(1), (5) and (6); Immigration and Asylum Act 1999, s 10. See *M v Islington London Borough Council* [2004] EWCA Civ 235, [2004] 4 All ER 709, 2.8 below.
5   *Christodoulidou v Secretary of State for the Home Department* [1985] Imm AR 179; *Gowa v A-G* (1984) 129 Sol Jo 131, CA, upheld in HL on different grounds: [1985] 1 WLR 1003.

2.4 The right of abode must be distinguished from: (1) rights of free movement within the common travel area comprising the UK, Channel Islands, Isle of Man and the Republic of Ireland; (2) exemptions from immigration control conferred on diplomats and others; (3) EC rights of free movement and residence; and (4) settlement or indefinite leave to remain granted to persons who are subject to immigration control and do not have the right of abode. The distinctions are to some extent technical and artificial, but behind them lies the difference between different degrees of immigration control and coming or going without let or hindrance.

2.5 What has to be understood is that essentially the right of abode stems from citizenship and is an automatic benefit of it, whereas the other rights (common travel, free movement, exemption, settlement) flow from separate quite specific provisions of the Immigration Act 1971. Only EC law is comparable. Since 1993 the right of free movement and residence within Europe is for the first time tied to citizenship, and a fledgling European right of abode is discernible. Who benefits from the right of abode under UK law cannot be understood until we have dealt with the main provisions of citizenship and nationality law.

Right of abode and international human rights law

2.6 Protocol 4 of the European Convention on Human Rights (ECHR) contains provisions which give the nationals of signatory States rights which are akin to the right of abode in UK domestic law. First, it provides that no-one shall be deprived of the right to enter the territory of the State of which he or she is a national.[1] Secondly, no-one shall be expelled, by means of a collective or individual measure, from the territory of the State of which he or she is a national.[2] Thirdly, once lawfully in the country, everyone (not just nationals) has a right to move freely throughout the territory, to choose a residence and to leave the country,[3] subject to such restrictions as are in accordance with the law and are necessary in a democratic society in the interests of national security or public safety, for the maintenance of public order, the prevention of crime, the protection of health and morals or for the protection of the rights and freedoms of others.[4] However, the right of abode in UK domestic law is not conferred on all British nationals and so there are important groups of British nationals, who do not enjoy its benefits. Protocol 4 would give them a broadly equivalent right, which is the principal reason why it has not been ratified so far by the British government.[5] Notwithstanding this, the principles of the Protocol are still important for UK immigration law. First, the wording of Article 3(2) 'no-one shall *be deprived of* the right to enter …' (our emphasis) is posited on the existence of a right of entry of nationals.[6] This reflects the position in international human rights law, under which there is a duty on a State to admit its own nationals.[7] Secondly, notwithstanding the non-ratification of Protocol 4 by the UK, the ECHR and all the human rights contained in it (including the Protocols) are part of the *corpus* and general principles of EC law,[8] and may therefore be used in the construction of EC law.[9] Thirdly, the Government is gradually moving into line with the international human rights position by a series of law changes which have extended the territorial reach of British citizenship to all British overseas territories and have conferred a much more extensive entitlement to registration as a BC on certain BOCs, British subjects and BPPs.[10]

1   ECHR, Protocol 4, Art 3(2).
2   ECHR, Protocol 4, Art 3(1).
3   ECHR, Protocol 4, Art 2(1) and (2).
4   ECHR, Protocol 4, Art 2(3).
5   See Laurie Fransman 'Human Rights and British Nationality' in Butterworth's *A Guide to the Human Rights Act 1998* (1999) pp 134ff.
6   See *East African Asians v United Kingdom* (1973) 3 EHRR 76, para 242, per Professor JES Fawcett.
7   See eg the UN International Covenant on Civil and Political Rights, 1966 Art 12(4) which provides that no one shall be arbitrarily deprived of the right to enter his own country. For texts see Brownlie and Goodwin-Gill *Basic Documents on Human Rights* (4th edn, 2002) OUP. See further Universal Declaration of Human Rights, Art 13(2), Brownlie and Goodwin-Gill *op cit*; Fransman fn 5 above, para 3.1. This right has in fact been relied on by the British Government in arguing (unsuccessfully) against the application of EC law to the return to the UK of a British national who has gone to another Member State of the EU in the exercise of her free movement rights: *ex p Surinder Singh* [1992] Imm AR 565, ECJ, at 22, quoted in *Fransman* above.
8   EU Treaty, Art 6 (ex Art F.1); *Elliniki Radiophonia Tiléorassi AE v Pliroforissis and Kouvelas* [1994] ECR I-2951 ECJ; *B v Secretary of State for the Home Department* [2000] Imm AR 478, paras 13–14.
9   In the referred application of *Manjit Kaur* it was argued that Art 3(2) of Protocol 4 could and should be used as an aid to the construction of Art 8 of EC Treaty (now after amendment Art 17 EC), so as to entitle a British Overseas citizen to enter and remain in the UK. This question was not dealt with in the judgment of the court: see Case C-192/99: *R (on the application of Kaur) v Secretary of State for the Home Department* [2001] ECR I-237, [2001] All ER (EC) 250, ECJ.
10 See BOTA 2002, ss 3 and 4 and NIAA 2002, s 12.

Restrictions on the right of abode

2.7 The statutory definition of the right of abode refers to 'let or hindrance' which may be lawfully imposed on any person. The extent of this exception is uncertain and untested, but is thought to include the following six restrictions:

(i)   lawful imprisonment and other restrictions (eg bail conditions restricting residence) imposed by criminal courts in the exercise of their normal jurisdiction;[1]

(ii) lawful detention and other restrictions imposed under other statutory powers, for example, under the Mental Health Act 1983;

(iii) restrictions lawfully imposed on the movement of children by an order of a court in matrimonial, wardship and Children Act 1989 proceedings;[2]

(iv) restraints imposed by the issue of a writ *'ne exeat regno'*, restraining the subject from leaving the kingdom, now largely superseded by injunction;[3]

(v)   restrictions, other than normal bail conditions, requiring surrender of a passport and a ban on foreign travel. This concerns measures taken, for example to deal with football hooliganism and foreign travel by paedophiles;

(vi) restrictions on entry of polygamous wives.[4]

[1]   See *R v Saunders*: Case 175/78 [1980] QB 72, [1979] 2 All ER 267 at 275, ECJ where a similar exemption with regard to EC free movement provisions is discussed. Any loss of liberty must also be justifiable under ECHR, Art 5: see 8.58 below.

[2]   See *Re Arif (Mohamed) (an infant)* [1968] Ch 643, sub nom *Re A (an infant), Harif v Secretary of State for Home Affairs* [1968] 2 All ER 145, CA.

[3]   For discussion of the writ *'Ne exeat regno'* see the fourth edition of this work at 6.6.

[4]   Immigration Act 1988, s 2.

2.8 An example of lawful restrictions which may be imposed on the right of abode is contained in the much amended Football Spectators Act 1989.[1] Under this Act banning orders may be imposed on those convicted of a football related offence or who have at any time caused or contributed to violence or disorder in the UK or abroad, where the Court is satisfied that there are reasonable grounds to believe that the banning order will help prevent violence and disorder at football matches.[2] So far as matches abroad are concerned, the subjects of banning orders are prevented from travelling by having to surrender their passports and to report to their local police stations over the period of the match or tournament.[3] A second example of restraints on foreign travel is contained in the Sexual Offences Act 2003. Under section 114 the police may apply for a foreign travel order to prevent convicted paedophiles from travelling outside the UK, if this is needed to protect children abroad from serious sexual assault. But an infant child's right of abode in the UK means more than merely a right to choose to live in the UK on her majority, and precludes a local authority from discharging its support responsibilities in a way that encourages or in practice enforces the expulsion of the child before the effect of her citizenship has been decided by the proper authority for that purpose.[4]

[1]   The Football (Offences and Disorder) Act 1999 (now superseded), the Football (Disorder) Act 2000 and the Football (Disorder) (Amendment) Act 2002 consist almost entirely of amendments to the Football Spectators Act 1989. Relevant parts of these are printed and

commented upon in Archbold *Criminal Pleading Evidence and Practice* (2005) Sweet & Maxwell, paras 5–821ff, including amendments made by the Anti-Social Behaviour Act 2003 as from 20 January 2004 and the Courts Act 2003.

2   Football Spectators Act 1989 as amended, ss 14A and 14B. An order under the Act preventing British citizens from leaving the UK to attend international football matches is not a 'penalty' within Article 7 ECHR and is not in breach of it: *Gough v Chief Constable of Derbyshire; R (on the application of Miller) v Leeds Magistrates' Court; Lilley v DPP* [2001] EWHC Admin 554, [2002] QB 45.

3   FSA 1989, ss 14(4)(b) and 14E(3).

4   *Obiter* per Buxton LJ, paras 15–21 of *M v Islington London Borough Council* [2004] EWCA Civ 235, [2004] 4 All ER 709, where the local authority's attempt to discharge its responsibility under the Children Act 1989 to the British child of a woman unlawfully in the UK by offering the child's mother tickets for both of them to go to Guyana, the mother's country of nationality, was quashed on different grounds.

2.9 Section 2 of the Immigration Act 1988 applies to women who acquired the right of abode through their polygamous marriage to a former CUKC, British subject or Commonwealth citizen who became a BC on commencement of the BNA 1981.[1] It provides that such a woman may not enter the UK in exercise of the right of abode, or be granted a certificate of entitlement, if another of the man's wives (or widows) has entered the UK or been granted a certificate of entitlement on the basis of the marriage.[2]

1   It does not apply to women who married and came to the UK before the coming into force of the Act: Immigration Act 1988, s 2(1)(b), (the burden of proving these facts is on them: s 2(5)); or to women who first came to the UK after the Act, when they were the only spouse: IA 1988, s 2(4).

2   Entry as a visitor or as an illegal entrant is to be disregarded: Immigration Act 1988, s 2(7). The ban also applies if an application for a certificate of entitlement is pending from another wife or widow: IA 1988, s 2(9).

The right of abode 1973 to 1983

2.10 Immediately prior to 1 January 1983 the statutory right of abode depended on whether or not a person was 'patrial' as defined in the Immigration Act 1971, section 2. Since that date (when the British Nationality Act 1981 came into force) it depends on the definition of 'British citizen' set out in the new section 2. Under pre-1983 law, patriality was conferred on certain citizens of the UK and Colonies (CUKCs) and certain other Commonwealth citizens. The British Nationality Act 1981 redefined citizenship and divided up former CUKCs into three new categories of citizenship and, as a result, changed the definition of those who have the right of abode. Under the Immigration Act 1971, before amendment, the following (broadly speaking) were patrials:

(i)   CUKCs by birth, adoption, naturalisation or registration in the UK;[1]

(ii)   CUKCs with similar connections to the UK through a parent or grandparent;[2]

(iii) CUKCs who had been ordinarily resident in the UK for five years;[3]

(iv)   Commonwealth citizens with a parent born in the UK;[4]

(v)   Commonwealth women who become patrial through marriage.[5]

1   Immigration Act 1971, old s 2(1)(a).

2   Immigration Act 1971, old s 2(1)(b).

3   Immigration Act 1971, old s 2(1)(c).

4   Immigration Act 1971, old s 2(1)(d).
5   Immigration Act 1971, old s 2(2).

RIGHT OF ABODE AFTER BRITISH NATIONALITY ACT 1981

2.11 Under the new provisions of the British Nationality Act 1981 the old category of 'patrials' was swept away. The old section 2 of the Immigration Act 1971 was entirely replaced by a new section 2.[1] Those who have the right of abode are defined in terms of British citizenship. But this has been given a special extended meaning for the purpose of the Immigration Act 1971. 'British citizens' has one meaning for nationality purposes (getting a passport and EU citizenship) and a somewhat different meaning in the amended section 2 of the 1971 Act, which preserves the right of abode for those Commonwealth citizens who were not CUKCs but had the status of 'patrial'. They are classed as 'British citizens' for immigration control purposes under the amended section 2. They consist mainly of those who were previously patrial under the old section 2(1)(d) of the Immigration Act 1971 because one of their parents was born in the UK.

1   BNA 1981, s 39.

2.12 Those who have the right of abode under the post-1983 definition of British citizenship under the amended section 2 of the Immigration Act 1971 are:

(i)   Those who automatically became British citizens on the coming into force of the British Nationality Act 1981.[1] These will include all the former CUKCs who prior to commencement had a right of abode because they were 'patrials', ie CUKCs born, adopted, registered or naturalised in the UK, those with the necessary ancestral connections with the UK, and those who were ordinarily resident here for five years free of immigration restrictions;[2]

(ii)   Commonwealth citizens[3] who immediately before commencement had the right of abode by virtue of having a parent who was born in the UK under the old section 2(1)(d) of the Immigration Act 1971; and

(iii)   Women Commonwealth citizens who immediately before commencement had a right of abode under the old section 2(2) of the 1971 Act by virtue of their marriage to a patrial.

Since only CUKCs who became British citizens obtained an automatic right of abode under the British Nationality Act 1981, this meant that resident CUKCs who were free from immigration conditions and who would previously have expected to become patrial after five years' ordinary residence in the UK,[4] lost out. If they merely became British Dependent Territories citizens or British Overseas citizens, they lost the automatic right to acquire patrial status after five years' ordinary residence. In its place, they obtained a right to register as BCs if they meet the requirements of section 4 of the IA 1981. This applies to all BDTCs (now known as BOTCs), BN (O)s, BOCs, British subjects under the Act, and BPPs who have spent the last five years in the UK (without absence for more than 450 days during the whole period and 90 days in the final 12 months), have had indefinite leave for at least the last 12 months and have not been in breach of the immigration laws during the five-year period.[5] This way of acquiring the right of abode will be of diminished importance in view of the new rights to become BCs under the two Acts of 2002 (see below 2.14).

1   BNA 1981, s 11.
2   IA 1971, s 2(1)(c), before amendment.
3   Commonwealth citizens are all those who are citizens of the countries set out in BNA 1981, Sch 3.
4   IA 1971, s 2(1)(c), before amendment.
5   See BNA 1981, s 4.

2.13 The second main change made by the British Nationality Act 1981 was that women Commonwealth citizens no longer automatically obtained a right of abode by marriage to British men. Since 1 January 1983 they must naturalise as British citizens under section 6 of the 1981 Act, if they are to acquire a right of abode. The third main change is that Commonwealth citizens born after commencement of the 1981 Act will not obtain a right of abode by virtue of having a parent born in the UK, as used to happen under the old section 2(1)(d) of the Immigration Act 1971, as originally in force. Commonwealth citizens born after commencement of the 1981 Act will only obtain a right of abode if they acquire British citizenship by descent, naturalisation or because they have dual BOTC status.[1] Fourthly, it should be noted that Commonwealth citizens born before 1 January 1983 (the commencement date of the 1981 Act) who were patrial do not lose this status, provided they have not ceased to be Commonwealth citizens in the meanwhile.[2] Commonwealth citizens who were not patrial had a five year window to register as BCs after completing five years' ordinary residence, but this entitlement ended in 1988.[3]

1   Under BNA 1981, s 2(1), BC status can now be inherited from either the mother or the father, and the old rules which prevented an illegitimate child inheriting the father's status have now been swept away by the NIAA 2002: BNA 1948, s 50(9), as amended by NIAA 2002, s 9(1) from a date to be appointed.
2   IA 1971, s 2(1)(b), as amended.
3   BNA 1981, s 7(1).

RIGHT OF ABODE AFTER THE TWO ACTS OF 2002

2.14 In 1983 BDTCs from Gibraltar and the Falkland Islands were granted privileged access to British citizenship, not available to other BDTCs, especially those from Hong Kong.[1] By 1997 Hong Kong had reverted to China and limited safeguards had been put in place to protect the British connections of the people of Hong Kong (see 2.20 below). This cleared the way for fuller integration into full British citizenship of the people from the remaining dependent territories. In 1999 the Government published a White Paper, proposing to extend full access to all remaining BDTCs.[2] This has now been done in the BOTA 2002 as from 21 May 2002.[3] Meanwhile moves to ease the position of other residual groups of British nationals and BPPs were taking place and resulted in significant nationality provisions in Part I of the NIAA 2002, much of which came into force on 30 April 2003: see 2.19 below.

1   BNA 1981, s 5 (Gibraltar); British Nationality (Falkland Islands) Act 1983 (Falkland Islands).
2   *Partnership for Progress and Prosperity – Britain and the Overseas Territories*, Cm 4264, March 1999.
3   British Overseas Territories Act 2002 (Commencement) Order 2002, SI 2002/1252.

2.15 Sections 1 and 2 of BOTA 2002 deal solely with name changes. All references in statutes and subordinate legislation to a Dependent Territory are changed to British Overseas Territory and BDTCs become BOTCs. These changes took effect as soon as the Act came into force on 26 February 2002. The substantive changes put all BOTCs on a similar footing as the Falkland Islanders as from commencement on 21 May 2002.[1] Section 3 confers British citizenship, and a right of abode in the UK, on anyone who was a BOTC immediately before commencement, automatically, without their having to make any kind of application.[2] The one exception to this rule concerns persons who are BOTCs by virtue only of a connection with the Sovereign Base Areas in Cyprus, which remains outside the 'qualifying territories' for all purposes connected with the Act.[3] An important amendment during the passage of the Bill deals with the special position of the British Indian Ocean Territory islanders, the Ilois, who come from the Chagos Islands. During the late 1960s and early 1970s, 2000 of these islanders were forced by the British Government to leave their homes to make way for a US military base on the largest island, Diego Garcia. They went to Mauritius or other Indian Ocean Islands. This meant that many of those born while the Ilois were in exile from their islands would not qualify for British citizenship under the main provisions of the new Act. In 2001 the High Court held that the forced exile and exclusion from their homelands was unlawful.[4] There was, therefore a grave injustice to rectify, and special provision was made in section 6 of the Act to close this important loophole. Exceptionally it extends the grant of citizenship to those islanders, who were born outside the British Indian Ocean Territory on or after 26 April 1969 and before 1 January 1983, whose fathers were not British and who were unable to inherit their mother's British nationality under the discriminatory provisions of nationality law at the time. Depending on their particular circumstances, the section makes them BCs[5] or BOTCs[6] and thus puts them in the same position as the other beneficiaries of the new law, so that they either qualify automatically for BC status or can become the beneficiaries of a discretionary registration under new section 4A of the BNA 1981.[7]

1   British Overseas Territories Act 2002 (Commencement) Order 2002, SI 2002/1252.
2   British Overseas Territories Act 2002, s 3(1). The person becomes a BC by descent if he or she was a BOTC by descent: BOTA 2002, s 3(3).
3   BOTA 2002, s 3(2). See further Cyprus Act 1960 s 2(1) and Sovereign Base Areas of Akrotiri and Dhekelia (Boundaries) Order in Council 1962, SI 1962/396, as amended by SI 1966/1415; and Sovereign Base Areas of Akrotiri and Dhekelia Order in Council 1960, SI 1960/1369, as amended by SI 1966/1415.
4   *R (on the application of Bancoult) v Secretary of State for the Foreign and Commonwealth Office* [2001] 2 WLR 1219.
5   BOTA 2002, s 6(1). They become BCs by descent: BOTA 2002, s 6(2).
6   BOTA 2002, s 6(3), (4).
7   Inserted into the BNA 1981 by BOTA 2002, s 4.

2.16 So far we have dealt with the position of those who were BOTCs immediately before commencement. Section 5 and Schedule 1 deal with the position after commencement. In essence the schedule extends the territorial application of British nationality law to all overseas territories other than the sovereign bases in Cyprus from the time of the 'appointed day', which is 21 May 2002.[1] The territories to which the new provisions apply are referred to as 'qualifying territories'.[2] Thus British citizenship is acquired by birth, abandonment or adoption in a qualifying territory after the appointed day on exactly the same basis as in the UK under section 1 of the BNA 1981.[3] It extends to the qualifying territories the same principles of acquisition of citizenship by descent contained in section 2 of the BNA 1981[4] and allows for registration of minors born outside the UK and a qualifying territory on the basis of ancestral connection to the UK and prior parental presence in the UK or a qualifying territory, and, in the case of stateless minors, if they merely have the ancestral connection.[5]

[1] British Overseas Territories Act 2002 (Commencement) Order 2002, SI 2002/1252 (made under BOTA 2002 s 8(2)).

[2] There are 13 qualifying overseas territories: Anguilla, Bermuda, British Antarctic Territory, British Indian Ocean Territory, British Virgin Islands, Cayman Islands, Falkland Islands, Gibraltar, Montserrat, Pitcairn Islands, St. Helena and Dependencies, Turks and Caicos Islands, and South Georgia and the South Sandwich Islands. The Sovereign Bases in Cyprus of Akrotiri and Dhekelia are an overseas territory, but not a qualifying territory: see BOTA 2002, Sch 1, para 5(2), inserting the definition of 'qualifying territory' into s 50(1) of BNA 1981. The full list of overseas territories is set out in BNA 1981, Sch 6.

[3] BNA 1981, s 1, as amended by BOTA 2002, Sch 1, para 1.

[4] BNA 1981, s 2, as amended by BOTA 2002, Sch 1, para 2.

[5] BNA 1981, s 3(2) and (3), as amended by BOTA 2002, Sch 1, para 3.

2.17 Despite the far-reaching effect of the changes brought about by the BOTA 2002, a small number of persons will continue to keep or to acquire BOTC status. For example, there are all those connected to the Sovereign Base Areas in Cyprus. They are and will continue to be BOTCs.[1] Then there are those who were born stateless in either the UK or a British overseas territory (including the Sovereign bases in Cyprus). They are entitled to register as BCs or BOTCs if they have spent a specified amount of time in either the UK or an overseas territory (no matter which) during the five years prior to the date of their application to register.[2] If the majority of that time was spent in the UK, they become a BC; if not they become a BOTC. The application can be made anytime up to the age of 22. A previous requirement that applicants have reached the age of 10 has been repealed.[3] Except for those connected to the Sovereign Base areas in Cyprus and those who have renounced their British citizenship, any remaining BOTCs will be able to apply for discretionary registration as BCs under the new section 4A of BNA 1981.[4] People who only have BOTC status because of their connection to the Cyprus bases and people who have renounced their BC status will only be able to acquire or reacquire BC status, if they come to the UK and live here for five years[5] or they can persuade the Home Secretary to register them as a BC under the discretionary power to register minors under section 3(1) of the BNA 1981. Only then will they have the right of abode in the UK.

[1] The Sovereign Bases were contained in the list of dependent territories in BNA 1981, Sch 6, and those connected with the Bases will have acquired BDTC status by virtue of one of the provisions set out in BNA 1981, ss 15–23. That status now becomes BOTC under BOTA 2002, s 1(1).

2.17 Right of Abode and Citizenship

2 Under BNA 1981, Sch2, para 3, as amended by NIAA 2002, s 8, which came into force on 1 April 2003: see NIAA 2002, s 162(4) and SI 2003/754, Art 2(2).
3 By BOTA 2002, s 8.
4 Inserted by BOTA 2002, s 4.
5 BNA 1981, s 4. Registration under BNA 1981, s 4A, inserted by BOTA 2002, s 4 is available to all BOTCs except those who are BOTCs *only* by virtue of a connection with the Cyprus Bases. If they have the status by virtue of a connection with another overseas territory, eg, because one their parents was born there, they can apply straight away for discretionary registration under s 4A, which came into force on 21 May 2002: British Overseas Territories Act 2002 (Commencement) Order 2002, SI 2002/1252 (made under BOTA 2002, s 8(2)).

2.18 Although BOTA 2002 widens the number of territories a connection with which qualifies a person for acquiring British citizenship, the right of abode does not have an equivalent territorial scope. It still remains a right confined to the territory of the UK.[1] The position of people who wish to move from one overseas territory to another or from the UK to one of the overseas territories is not dealt with in UK legislation. One possibility is that the position will be regulated by reviving and adapting the common law right of abode;[2] another is that it will remain a matter for local law. BOTA 2002 applies to the UK, the Channel Islands, the Isle of Man, and all the overseas territories.[3] It should not be difficult for Parliament to clarify the position. If you have a universal British citizenship covering a wide stretch of territories, it is no great matter to enact that there is a right of abode with the same territorial reach.

1 Immigration Act 1971, s 1(1).
2 *DPP v Bhagwan* [1972] AC 60, [1970] 3 All ER 97, HL.
3 BOTA 2002, s 8(4).

2.19 A number of provisions in the NIAA 2002 widen the scope for acquiring BC status and, therefore, the right of abode in the UK. The amendments to the provisions relating to the registration of stateless children are referred to in 2.16 above. The other changes are as follows:

(i) *Legitimacy.* Section 50(9) of BNA1981 defined the relationship between father and child in a way which meant that a child born illegitimate did not have a father for nationality purposes, unless the child was legitimated by the subsequent marriage of the parents. Section 9 of NIAA 2002 amends section 50(9) as from a date to be appointed, and changes all this.[1] The effect of the section, when in force, will be to allow those proved to be fathers, by DNA testing or otherwise, to be recognised as the fathers of their illegitimate children for nationality purposes. Other differences in the treatment of legitimate and illegitimate children will be removed.[2] People previously not recognised as BCs will now be so and will acquire the right of abode;

(ii) *Registration of BOCs, BPPs and British Subjects.* After the ending of the special voucher scheme[3] without warning on 5 March 2002, many BOCs were left without the possibility of acquiring a right of abode in the UK and were unable to do so in any other country, because they had no other nationality. The same was true of BPPs and British subjects. Section 4B of the BNA 1981, inserted by section 12 of the NIAA 2002,[4] now gives each of these groups an entitlement to register as BCs provided they have no other citizenship or nationality and have not after 4 July 2002 (the date when the new provision was made public) renounced, voluntarily relinquished or lost through action or inaction any other citizenship or nationality which would keep them out of the ambit of the new provisions, if it was effective.

(iii) *Discrimination.* Prior to 1983, a British woman who had married a foreign national and was living abroad could not pass on her CUKC status to her foreign born children. To be British they would need to have been born in the UK. In an identical situation children of a CUKC father, who lived abroad with his foreign wife, became British by descent.[5] On 6 February 1979 a policy was introduced to register the children born outside the UK to British mothers so long as the children were under 18. But not everyone knew of the practice and many missed the opportunity. Then the BNA 1981 provided for the first time that citizenship could descend through either the mother or the father.[6] But this still left many people born overseas to British mothers prior to 1983 without British citizenship. Such people, if born between 1961 and 1983, are entitled to register as BCs, under the new section 4C of the BNA 1981.[7] Notwithstanding these changes, some discrimination remains. Those born abroad to British mothers before 7 February 1961 still do not have the right to register, unless it can be said that the new section 4C gives the Home Secretary a discretion to waive the conditions of registration in the section.[8]

1   NIAA 2002, s 9 comes into force on a date to be appointed: see NIAA 2002, s 162(1); for effect see s 162(5). According to the Home Office, the section will not have retrospective effect, and children born before its coming into force will have to rely on the policy of discretionary registration of such children: see Lord Filkin to Fiona Mactaggart MP, 5 February 2003.
2   BNA 1981, ss 3(6)(c) and 17(6)(c) (registration of the children of BCs and BOTCs by descent).
3   A quota scheme introduced when CUKCs were stripped of their entitlement to enter the UK by the Commonwealth Immigrants Act 1968: see previous edition of this work at 8.85ff.
4   NIAA 2002, s 12 came into force on 30 April 2003: see SI 2003/754, Art 2(1), Sch 1.
5   See British Nationality Act 1948, s 5.
6   BNA 1981, s 2.
7   As inserted by NIAA 2002, s 13, which came into force on 30 April 2003: see SI 2003/754, Art 2(1), Sch 1. The change was preceded by a concessionary policy allowing discretionary registration of children born abroad to British mothers between 1961 and 1979: see Home Office to ILPA 3 October 2003.
8   The editors of *Butterworths Immigration Law Service* (at [2612]) say that the section does not prohibit the Secretary of State from exercising his discretion to address the sex discrimination in the cases of those born before 7 February 1961.

HONG KONG AND THE RIGHT OF ABODE

2.20 At the time of the handover of Hong Kong to the People's Republic of China in 1997, there were some 3.2 million BDTCs, most having acquired that status by virtue of their birth in Hong Kong, but others by registration or naturalisation. In the run-up to the handover three significant changes were made.[1] First, the British Nationality (Hong Kong) Act 1990 made provision for some 50,000 selected key people to be awarded British citizenship and, therefore the right of abode in the UK, even though many of them had little intention of taking up their option. This affected an elite of selected people. Secondly, it was made clear that British Dependent Territories citizenship which was based on a Hong Kong connection would come to an end on handover. The Hong Kong (British Nationality) Order 1986 enacted that BDTCs who had that citizenship only by virtue of a Hong Kong connection, would cease to be such citizens on 1 July 1997,[2] and that Hong Kong would then be removed from the list of Dependent Territories.[3] Thirdly, the same Order created a new category of citizenship to be known as British National (Overseas).[4] It was open to all BDTCs who were to lose their BDTC status on handover, but would apply only to those who registered. The advantages were fourfold. First, the status would continue after handover. Secondly, all BN(O)s are Commonwealth citizens.[5] Thirdly, BN(O)s are able to use a British travel document after that date and were in fact able to keep and use their passports showing BDTC citizenship. Fourthly, if the holder of the new citizenship comes to the UK to live, he or she has a right to register as a BC after five years under section 4(1) of the BNA 1981. The great disadvantage is that by losing BDTC status, none of the Hong Kong BDTCs can take advantage of the new rights of BOTCs to register as BCs under the BOTA 2002. Section 14 of the NIAA 2002 makes it clear that there is no way back into BOTC status by registration under the BNA 1981 for those who would have to rely on a Hong Kong connection. Indeed it seems very likely that the removal of some 3.2 million potential BCs of Chinese origin paved the way for the new liberalism of the 2002 Acts.

[1] For fuller details see the 4th edition of this work at 6.82–6.88.
[2] Hong Kong (British Nationality) Order 1986, SI 1986/948, Art 3.
[3] SI 1986/948, Art 5.
[4] SI 1986/948, Art 4.
[5] BNA 1981, s 37(1)(a). BN(O)s now number about 3.5 million. They continue to receive consular and passport services from HMG. The UK Residence Permit (UKRP) Scheme has been running successfully in Hong Kong since 2003 free of charge to BN(O)s and as at December 2004 they have visa-free access to 101 countries: *Six-monthly Report on Hong Kong* Jul-Dec 2004, paras 77–79, (2005) Cmd 6484.

PROVING ENTITLEMENT TO RIGHT OF ABODE

2.21 Proving entitlement to British citizenship and, therefore, to a right of abode has been a matter of particular statutory concern. Under section 3(8) of the Immigration Act 1971 it is provided that when any question arises under the Immigration Acts whether or not a person is a British citizen, it lies on the person asserting the claim to prove it. This will arise when people apply for a passport or a certificate of entitlement or pass through immigration control in the course of their travel to the UK. Section 3(9) makes provision for the means of proof for someone seeking to enter the UK and claiming a right of abode. Proof is provided by the production of a UK passport[1] describing the person as a British citizen or as a CUKC having the right of abode, or of a certificate of entitlement.[2] The passport must be a current one.[3] Until now the procedure for applying for a certificate of entitlement has been unregulated, except as regards fees and a right of appeal against refusal,[4] and there is no case law or immigration rules to give guidance,[5] as there is, for example, in the case of entry certificates (see 3.16). Section 10 of NIAA 2002 now enables the Secretary of State to make regulations, specifying such matters as the person to whom an application should be made, where it is to be sent, the form of the application, the documents which are to accompany it, and the fee to be paid.[6] The regulations may also provide for the certificate to be revoked where it has been obtained by fraud, or to cease to have effect after a specified time.[7] The validity of existing certificates may also be protected. Section 10 is in force but no regulations had been made at the time of writing.[8]

[1] The reference to a UK passport means a full passport, not a British visitor's passport, which is insufficient: *Minta v Secretary of State for the Home Department* [1992] Imm AR 380, CA. The British Visitor's Passport was discontinued in 1995. For the legal consequences of producing the requisite passport see 2.63 below.

[2] From a date to be appointed, granted under the NIAA 2002, s 10, certifying that a person has the right of abode in the UK: Immigration Act 1971, ss 3(9)(b) and 33(1) as amended by NIAA 2002, s 10(5) from a date to be appointed; see *Akewushola v Immigration Officer* [1999] INLR 433, CA.

[3] *Akewushola* above.

[4] NIAA 2002, s 82(2)(c).

[5] But there is guidance on the websites of the Home Office and of a number of High Commissions. See eg IDI, Ch 1, s 1 and Annexes, on the right of abode and applying for a certificate of entitlement.

[6] NIAA 2002, s 10(2). The Asylum and Immigration (Treatment of Claimants, etc) Act 2004, s 42 provides for regulations or Orders in Council to be made enabling the Secretary of State or consular officers to charge fees for the issue of a certificate of entitlement at a level which exceeds administrative costs, so as to reflect the benefit likely to accrue if the application is successful. That part of the fee would be refundable if the application is rejected. The British Nationality (Fees) (Amendment) Regulations 2005, SI 2005/651, increased fees for naturalisation and registration but not for a certificate of entitlement to the right of abode, which remains at £20.

[7] Nationality, Immigration and Asylum Act 2002, s 10(2)(g) and (h).

[8] NIAA 2002, s 10(1)–(4) and (6) came into force at Royal Assent: NIAA 2002, s 162(2)(c).

2.22 In most cases proving a right of abode is not a problem and involves collecting the necessary birth, marriage or death certificates and applying for a passport or a certificate of entitlement.[1] The problem areas arise where:

(i) persons cannot prove an essential ingredient of the claim to British citizenship, such as their place of birth, their parent's nationality at the relevant time, or that a birth certificate relates to them;

(ii) the Home Office or immigration officer disputes the validity of an existing full UK passport or certificate of entitlement.

In the first situation the burden remains throughout on the applicant.[2] In the second case the burden of proving any alleged fraud or deception will be on the Home Office or immigration officer, and since the allegation involves fraud or deception, proof will need to be by a preponderance of probability.[3]

[1] Certified copies of documents are acceptable as an alternative to original documentation submitted in support of nationality applications: IND to ILPA 7 February 2002. The Passport Office holds cassettes containing the name, date of birth and passport number of all passport holders from 1898 onwards, and is prepared to disclose its records in the public interest provided the subject of the records is dead and sufficient information is provided to enable a search. This would normally be full name and date of birth, and sometimes passport number and/or date of issue: Home Office (Record Management Services) to James & Co Solicitors, 15 August 2003.

2   *Re Bamgbose* [1990] Imm AR 135, CA; *Mokuolo v Secretary of State for the Home Department* [1989] Imm AR 51, CA. On an application for a declaration of British citizenship, the High Court will assess the facts for itself: *R (on the application of Harrison) v Secretary of State for the Home Department* [2003] EWCA Civ 432, [2003] INLR 284.

3   *R v Secretary of State for the Home Department, ex p Obi* [1997] 1 WLR 1498, [1997] Imm AR 420; *Khawaja v Secretary of State for the Home Department* [1984] AC 74, [1983] 1 All ER 765, HL. See 2.63 below.

OUTLINES OF BRITISH NATIONALITY LAW

2.23 The right of abode started out as a right unambiguously linked to a broad concept of British nationality which included citizens of independent Commonwealth countries as well as those of the UK and Colonies. It then became something much narrower, as British nationality was split up into more distinct species of citizenship. Now citizens of independent Commonwealth countries are out of the nationality equation, except for a small exceptional group, who still have a right of abode, as we have seen. Otherwise the tendency is towards an eventual consolidation of all the different sub-categories of British citizenship back into a single British citizenship, where the right of abode will once more be a concomitant right of British national status. To understand this trend and the processes by which British citizens achieve their status, it is necessary to look at the outlines of British nationality law and the changes that have taken place since 1948.[1]

1   We do so only to identify the right of abode. Anyone wishing to deal with the wider issues of nationality should consult Fransman's *British Nationality Law* (2nd edn, 1998) Butterworths.

2.24 Before the 1948 Act, the status of British subject belonged to all those who owed allegiance to the Crown in whichever Crown territory they were born. A subsidiary category was the status of British Protected Person, that is to say people who had placed themselves under the protection of the British Crown without becoming the subject of the Sovereign. Unlike British subjects, their position was regulated by prerogative rather than common law. They are not Commonwealth citizens nor aliens, as we shall see at 2.41 below. With the break-up of the British empire and the creation of separate citizenships in the self-governing dominions, it was thought necessary to devise citizenship laws which were appropriate to a number of self-governing units within a unified Commonwealth. The principle of separate citizenships for each of the self-governing units was expressly recognised, but at the same time the universal status of 'British subject' or 'Commonwealth citizen' was retained. For our purposes, the point about having the status of British subject or Commonwealth citizen (the two terms then had the same meaning) [1] was that it gave an unqualified common law right of abode to such persons in the UK. [2] Aliens alone were subject to immigration control.

1   British Nationality Act 1948, s 1(2). Now, all British subjects are Commonwealth citizens, but not vice versa: see British Nationality Act 1981, s 37.

2   *DPP v Bhagwan* [1972] AC 60, [1970] 3 All ER 97, HL.

2.25 Although entry to the UK for British subjects was unrestricted, this did not mean that the same thing applied to independent Commonwealth countries or to colonial territories. The opposite was the case, and had been so for many years. In fact the mechanisms of immigration control introduced for the UK in 1962 had been tried and tested many years earlier in the dominion territories in attempts to keep out Chinese, Japanese and Indian migrants.[1] But in 1948 the status of British subject or Commonwealth citizen gave an unrestricted right of entry to the UK. When immigration controls were later imposed by the Commonwealth Immigrants Act 1962 and its amending Act of 1968,[2] the method used was to make subdivisions within the three main categories of Commonwealth citizen:

- CUKCs
- citizens of independent Commonwealth countries
- British subjects without citizenship.

Initially, under the 1962 Act the dividing line between a continuing right of abode and being subject to immigration control depended on the place of issue of the person's British passport. Under the 1968 Act, the need for an ancestral connection to the UK was introduced, cutting across and undermining ties to Britain of British nationality. By the time of the Immigration Act 1971, birth in and ancestral connection to the UK were the principal distinctions between 'patrials' and 'non-patrials'.[3] Patrials had a right of abode; non-patrials were subject to control. Possession of British nationality no longer qualified British nationals for the right of abode in their country of nationality. The British Nationality Act 1981 formally reconnected the right of abode to British citizenship, but only by creating the hierarchy of British nationalities set out in 2.1 above.

[1]   See the third edition of this work, pp 12–15.
[2]   Commonwealth Immigrants Act 1968.
[3]   There were other ways of acquiring patriality, e g by residence in the UK or marriage to a patrial: see Immigration Act 1971, s 2 (before amendment).

2.26 Throughout the period from 1948 to 1971 all classes of British subject were to be distinguished from: (i) Irish citizens; (ii) aliens, ie all foreigners other than Irish citizens, and (iii) British Protected Persons. So far as aliens and British Protected Persons are concerned, they never became 'patrial' under the Immigration Act 1971 unless they had dual nationality[1] or acquired the status of CUKC through marriage or naturalisation. Some Irish citizens were Commonwealth citizens and could therefore be patrial, though this was really an unimportant category because Ireland was part of the common travel area and later a Member State of the EEC. The right of abode of an Irish citizen, therefore, usually only arose when there was an issue of deportation.

[1]   The status of British Protected Person was not inconsistent with that of CUKC and so a person could be both CUKC and British Protected Person – a sort of domestic dual nationality: *Motala v A-G* [1992] 1 AC 281, [1992] Imm AR 112, HL, overruling CA [1991] 2 All ER 312 at 315.

Dual nationality

2.27 Some countries forbid their citizens to have dual nationality, but this is not the case in the UK. So the fact that a person has another nationality, and travels under another country's passport, does not mean that he or she is not a CUKC or, under the British Nationality Act 1981, a British citizen. For example, there are large numbers of persons living in Malaysia and Singapore who are citizens of those countries and British Overseas citizens at the same time. Indeed, the 1981 Act quite clearly confers dual nationality on possibly quite large numbers of persons. For example, as we shall see, CUKCs who were patrial through five years' residence in the UK became British citizens on commencement, but may have become, by virtue of their connection to a dependent territory, British Dependent Territories citizens as well or, in other cases, British Overseas citizens.[1] Under the pre-1983 patriality provisions of the Immigration Act 1971, one category of patrial citizens was Commonwealth citizens with a parent born in the UK.[2] This provision was intended for holders of Australian, New Zealand, and other 'old' Commonwealth passports, but in fact if their fathers were born in the UK they had dual nationality – Australian or New Zealand by birth and CUKC by descent through their father. Under the 1981 Act, British citizenship can descend through the mother as well as the father and this has created large numbers of Commonwealth citizens who have dual nationality. However, there are limits. British citizenship is a unitary concept, which does not give rise to classes of such citizenship, such as full citizenship and citizenship by descent. So BCs by descent cannot use the process of naturalisation under BNA 1981 to become full BCs, who can transmit their citizenship to their children.[3]

[1] This sort of domestic double nationality was expressly approved of by the House of Lords in *Motala v A-G* [1992] 1 AC 281, [1992] Imm AR 112, HL; see further *Patel v Secretary of State for the Home Department* [1993] Imm AR 509, CA. In both these cases it was held that a British Protected person could simultaneously be a CUKC.

[2] Immigration Act 1971, s 2(1)(d).

[3] *R (on the application of Ullah) Secretary of State for the Home Department* [2002] QB 525, [2001] Imm AR 439, CA.

CITIZENSHIP UNDER BRITISH NATIONALITY ACT 1948

2.28 In order to understand the concept and status of 'British citizen', it is necessary to go back to the three main classifications of British national used in the British Nationality Act 1948. But beware! In this part of this chapter we set out what is at best a very brief summary. For fuller treatment it is essential to refer to a specialist textbook on British nationality law.[1]

[1] Fransman *British Nationality Law* (Butterworths, 2nd edn, 1998) which contains a full account and texts of the relevant provisions of every Commonwealth country as well as the UK.

Citizens of Commonwealth countries

2.29 Each independent Commonwealth country has its own citizenship laws which determine who are citizens of that country. The list of countries is set out in Schedule 3 to the BNA 1981, as amended. Once a country achieves political independence with its own constitution and laws, the determination of its citizenship is no longer a matter for UK law[1] or the UK Parliament. All UK law determines is that for the purposes of UK law citizens of independent

Commonwealth countries are Commonwealth citizens. Nothing more. To find out whether someone is or becomes a citizen of an independent Commonwealth country it is always necessary to look at that country's own citizenship laws. Depending upon the answer to that question, UK nationality law may have something to say about that person's status, for example, whether they remain British citizens or not.

---

[1] See *Oppenheimer v Cattermole* [1976] AC 249, [1975] 1 All ER 538, HL. Although the question of whether a person is a citizen of a Commonwealth country is under English private international law a matter for the law of that country, one English court has determined that question as one of purely domestic English law when it affects a claim to British citizenship, even though it reached a conclusion different from that of the governing authorities of the country concerned: *Bibi v Secretary of State for the Home Department* [1987] Imm AR 340, CA.

2.30 The difficulties do not arise so much with regard to persons born in a Commonwealth country after independence,[1] but with those born before independence and living there or in the UK at the time of independence. CUKCs who acquired their citizenship through connection with a colony may have lost that citizenship when the colony became independent. This often happened through the operation of statute, without the person realising it. A person from Grenada or St Lucia might have been a UK citizen with the right of abode as a result of five years' ordinary residence one day and have ceased to be so on the next day following independence. In all cases where there is a history of this kind it is necessary to examine the particular statute that granted independence and the new citizenship laws of the newly independent country, in order to find out who lost and who retained their status as a CUKC.[2] On decolonisation the usual provision was that any persons who acquired citizenship of the new Commonwealth country lost their former citizenship of the UK and colonies, unless they had a parent or grandparent who was born in the UK or in a country which remained a colony at that time. But the formulations differed from country to country. In order to discover whether a person acquired citizenship of the new country, it is always necessary to examine the constitution or citizenship laws of the new country. In East Africa, some CUKCs were specifically permitted to retain their UK citizenship.[3] At the time of decolonisation, these CUKCs were free from immigration control, although they continued to live in East Africa. In 1968, however, they became subject to immigration control under the Commonwealth Immigrants Act 1968. So when living in East Africa was made difficult or they were expelled, they had nowhere to go. This is the source of what was referred to as the 'problem' of the East African Asians.[4]

---

[1] Although there is always a question of whether such persons are British citizens or some other citizen by descent.
[2] See Fransman *British Nationality Law* (2nd edn, 1998) Butterworths, where all the independence statutes and Commonwealth citizenship laws are gathered.
[3] For the position in Kenya see *Mohammed (AA) v Secretary of State for the Home Department* [1979–80] Imm AR 103.
[4] See *East African Asians v United Kingdom* (1973) 3 EHRR 76.

Citizens of the UK and Colonies (CUKCs)

Birth

2.31 Under the British Nationality Act 1948 a person born in the UK and Colonies before or after commencement (1 January 1949) became a CUKC by birth, unless the person's father was a foreign diplomat or an enemy alien and the birth occurred in enemy-occupied territory.[1] Thus those born in the Channel Islands of a German father during the 1939–45 war would not have become British subjects at birth and would not become CUKCs on 1 January 1949.

[1]   British Nationality Act 1948, ss 4 and 12(1)(a).

Adoption

2.32 Adopted children could also acquire citizenship. In England and Wales the Adoption Acts of 1949 and 1976 and in Scotland the Adoption (Scotland) Act 1978 provided that a child adopted in the UK by a CUKC became a CUKC, if not already one, from the date of the adoption order. In the case of a joint adoption, where the adopting parents had different nationalities, the child only became a CUKC if that was the male adopter's nationality. An adoption outside the UK did not confer the British nationality of the adoptive parent.[1]

[1]   *R v Secretary of State for the Home Department, ex p Brassey and Brassey* [1989] FCR 423, [1989] Imm AR 258, DC.

Descent

2.33 Citizenship by birth in the UK or colonies was the most common method of acquiring the status of CUKC. This was citizenship by *jus soli* (country of birth). But English law also recognises the *jus sanguinis* (citizenship by descent).[1] Persons born outside British territory could therefore be CUKCs by descent if their father was such a citizen[2] at the time of the person's birth.[3] This applied in general to persons born before and after 1948.[4] However, for persons born after 1948 the right to become a CUKC by descent was limited where the person's father himself acquired this citizenship by descent.[5]

[1]   See British Nationality Bill 1948 (Cm 7326) p 9.
[2]   British Nationality Act 1948, s 5(1).
[3]   *R v Immigration Appeal Tribunal, ex p Uddin* [1989] Imm AR 391, QBD.
[4]   British Nationality Act 1948, s 12(2).
[5]   For exceptions, such as registration at a British consulate, see British Nationality Act 1948, s 5(1)(a)–(d) and (2).

2.34 Citizenship by descent could only be acquired through the father under the British Nationality Act 1948, never through the mother, and not if the child was illegitimate. An illegitimate child was not considered to be the child of its father for nationality purposes unless legitimated by the subsequent marriage of its parents.[1] A legitimate child born after the death of his or her father would acquire the status of the father at the time of the father's death.[2]

1 British Nationality Act 1948, ss 32(2) and 23.
2 British Nationality Act 1948, s 24.

Registration

2.35 An important method of acquiring the status of CUKC after 1948 was by registration. In some cases it was a right; in others it was within the Secretary of State's discretion. Registration was only open to Commonwealth citizens, citizens of the Republic of Ireland, their children, and to women, alien or Commonwealth, who married CUKCs. Registration could be completed in the UK or outside. In the UK it was done by the Secretary of State, in the Colonies usually by the Governor and in Commonwealth countries by the British High Commissioner.[1] With the coming into force of successive Immigration Acts between 1962 and 1973 the right of Commonwealth citizens to register was much changed from the originally enacted position in 1948.[2] For women married to CUKCs the right was almost an absolute one, unless they had gained the right to registration by fraudulent or other criminal means.[3]

1 British Nationality Act 1948, s 8.
2 See fourth edition 6.21–6.23.
3 British Nationality Act 1948, s 6 and see *R v Secretary of State for the Home Department, ex p Puttick* [1981] QB 767, [1981] 1 All ER 776.

Naturalisation

2.36 Naturalisation was the mechanism under the British Nationality Act 1948 by which aliens and British Protected Persons could become CUKCs, although the residence requirements differed.[1] The grant was a matter of discretion. Decisions were unappealable and section 26 of the 1948 Act provided that no reasons need be given and the decision was not reviewable in any court. The same ouster clause was inserted in the British Nationality Act 1981,[2] which we examine at 2.56 below.

1 British Nationality Act 1948, s 10 and Sch 2 as amended by Commonwealth Immigrants Act 1962, s 20(2).
2 British Nationality Act 1981, s 44(2).

Loss of citizenship of the UK and Colonies

2.37 The status of CUKC, as we have seen, could be acquired in a number of ways. It could also be lost. This happened in three ways. The first was the most common:

(i) CUKCs connected with a Crown colony could lose their citizenship when the colony became independent;[1]

(ii) Persons having dual nationality or acquiring a new nationality could lose their UK citizenship by making a declaration of renunciation;[2]

(iii)   CUKCs could be deprived of their UK citizenship by the Secretary of State for the Home Department if they had acquired it by registration or naturalisation.[3]

¹   See *Motala v A-G* [1992] 1 AC 281, [1992] Imm AR 112, HL; *Patel v Secretary of State for the Home Department* [1993] Imm AR 508, CA; *R v Secretary of State for Foreign and Commonwealth Affairs, ex p Shah* [1993] Imm AR 261, QBD; *Patel v Secretary of State for the Home Department* [1988] Imm AR 521, IAT; *Liew v Secretary of State for the Home Department* [1989] Imm AR 62, IAT.
²   British Nationality Act 1948, s 19.
³   British Nationality Act 1948, s 20, which conferred a right to a hearing before an independent tribunal. A naturalisation or registration could be of no effect and s 20 would not come into play if the applicant could not prove that he was the person named in the certificate: *R v Secretary of State for the Home Department, ex p Akhtar (Parvaz)* [1981] QB 46, [1980] 2 All ER 735.

Resumption of citizenship

2.38 Resumption of citizenship following renunciation was governed by section 1(1) of the British Nationality Act 1964. A person who was obliged to renounce their CUKC status in order to avoid being deprived of another citizenship (a circumstance which arose when a number of Commonwealth countries became independent) and had a qualifying connection with the UK and colonies or a protectorate or protected State or, if a woman, had been married to such a person, was able to apply for registration.

British subject without citizenship

2.39 The British Nationality Acts 1948 and 1965 created a number of residual categories of British subject. These were people who were neither citizens of independent Commonwealth countries nor CUKCs.[1] They were:

(a)   British subjects without citizenship, who consisted of:
    (i)   persons who were regarded by the British Nationality Act 1948 as potential citizens of an independent Commonwealth country, but who did not become citizens of that country when they passed citizenship laws;[2] and
    (ii)   persons who are declared to be British subjects without citizenship. They are persons who before 1 January 1949 ceased, on the loss of British nationality by a parent, to be a British subject and, but for this, would have become British subjects without citizenship;[3]
(b)   married women who registered as British subjects under the 1965 Act.[4] These are alien women who married a man who was within one or other of the residual categories of British subject;
(c)   Irish citizens born before 1949 who were also British subjects and remained such if they wrote to the Home Secretary and claimed to remain such.[5]

The British Nationality Act 1981 continues these categories of citizenship and refers to them as British subjects under the Act.[6] Under both the 1948 and

1981 Acts, they are Commonwealth citizens.[7] Clearly they are a diminishing group, who now lose their British subject status if they acquire any other citizenship or nationality in whatever circumstances.[8]

1 See Ann Dummett *Citizenship and Nationality* (1976) Runnymede Trust, p 23.
2 British Nationality Act 1948, s 13. Such persons did not become CUKCs under s 13(2) of the 1948 Act as might have been supposed because of the definition of citizenship law in s 32(8) of that Act.
3 BNA 1948, s 16.
4 British Nationality Act 1965, s 1.
5 BNA 1948, s 2.
6 British Nationality Act 1981, ss 30 and 31.
7 BNA 1948, s 1(2) and BNA 1981, s 37(1)(a).
8 BNA 1981, s 35.

BECOMING A BRITISH CITIZEN

2.40 The British Nationality Act 1981 recast British citizenship and replaced the existing definition of patriality by an entirely new section 2 of the Immigration Act 1971. This defined the right of abode in terms of the new categories of citizenship. The right of abode and British citizenship are now more or less equated. To understand who has the right of abode it is therefore necessary to know what became of CUKCs and who become British citizens. The 1981 Act divided CUKCs into three new categories of citizenship:[1]

● British citizens
● British Dependent Territories citizens
● British Overseas citizens.

The Hong Kong (British Nationality) Order 1986[2] added another citizenship: that of British National (Overseas). Other categories of Commonwealth citizens are virtually unaltered. Irish citizens who are British subjects and British subjects without citizenship are referred to as British subjects under the Act. The overall category of 'Commonwealth citizen' is retained. So under the 1981 Act Commonwealth citizens comprise:[3]

● British citizens
● British Dependent Territories (now British Overseas Territories) citizens
● British Overseas citizens
● British subjects under the Act
● Citizens of independent Commonwealth countries.

1 British Nationality Act 1981, s 51(3).
2 SI 1986/948, in force 1 July 1987.
3 BNA, ss 37, 51 (as amended by British Overseas Territories Act 2002, s 2).

2.41 British Protected Persons are not Commonwealth citizens,[1] but they are also excluded from the definition of aliens.[2] Traditionally they were excluded from being classed as British nationals in domestic law[3] or being treated as UK nationals under ECHR law,[4] but they have been equated with British Dependent (now Overseas) Territories citizens, British Overseas citizens, and British subjects under the 1981 Act as having a right to register as BCs after five years' residence in the UK,[5] and now have a right to register as BCs alongside BOCs and British subjects, provided they have no other nationality (see 2.19 above). They are increasingly being included in modern legislation in the list of UK nationals.[6]

1   British Nationality Act 1981, s 38.
2   BNA 1981, s 50(1).
3   *R v Secretary of State for the Home Department, ex p Thakrar* [1974] QB 684, [1974] 2 All ER 261, CA.
4   *East African Asians v United Kingdom* (1973) 3 EHRR 76.
5   BNA 1981, s 4.
6   See L Fransman 'A Right to British Nationality' in Butterworth's *A Guide to the Human Rights Act 1998* (1999) p 131 where he cites definitions of UK nationals in Antarctic Act 1994, s 31(1), Chemical Weapons Act 1996, s 3(4), and Outer Space Act 1996, s 2(2). A BPP is included in the definition of a UK national in the International Criminal Court Act 2001, s 67(1).

Becoming a British citizen on commencement of the 1981 Act

CUKCs

2.42   With two exceptions, a person who immediately before commencement of the British Nationality Act 1981 was a CUKC and had the right of abode under the Immigration Act 1971 became a British citizen upon commencement.[1] The two exceptions are:

(i)   an illegitimate and formerly stateless person who became a CUKC by registration under the British Nationality (No 2) Act 1964;[2]

(ii)   a British subject who became a CUKC by registration outside the UK by reason of an ancestral connection with the UK.[3]

1   British Nationality Act 1981, s 11(1).
2   BNA 1981, s 11(2). Such a person is likely to have become a British Dependent Territories citizen (BNA 1981, s 23(1)) or a British Overseas citizen (s 26). If the person was already resident in the UK but had not completed five years' residence, he or she had a right to register as a British citizen on completion of the five years under BNA 1981, s 4.
3   BNA 1981, s 11(3). Such a person may in fact have qualified for a right of abode by another route, eg by completing five years' ordinary residence in the UK prior to 1983, and thus qualifying as patrials under the former s 2(1)(c) of the Immigration Act 1971. If they did not qualify under the pre-1983 regime and are resident in the UK, they qualify to register as British citizens on completion of five years' residence under BNA 1981, s 4.

Falkland Islanders

2.43   Persons from the Falkland Islands who would normally have become British Dependent Territories citizens on commencement in fact became British citizens, if immediately before commencement:

(i)   they were CUKCs born, naturalised or registered in the Falkland Islands; or

(ii)   one of their parents was such a CUKC or would have been but for their death; or

(iii)   in the case of a woman she was at any time married to a man who benefits from provisions (i) or (ii) above.[1]

1   British Nationality (Falkland Islands) Act 1983, s 1(1).

Becoming a British citizen after commencement

Birth in the UK or an Overseas Territory

2.44 The British Nationality Act 1981 abolished citizenship by birth in the UK, pure and simple. Children born in the UK after commencement of the BNA 1981 will only become British citizens if one of their parents is a British citizen or is settled in the UK.[1] Children born in the Falkland Islands after that date also became British citizens, if one of their parents was a British citizen or was settled in the Falkland Islands at the time of the birth, but, rather surprisingly, the legislation did not extend the acquisition of this status, where the only British link was that one or both parents were settled in the UK.[2] This has now been remedied. The provisions of the BNA 1981 are now extended to all persons born in a qualifying territory (meaning an overseas territory other than the Sovereign Base Areas in Cyprus), if one of their parents is a BC or is settled in the UK or that territory at the time of the birth.[3] One gap in the new law concerns the baby born in a qualifying territory, whose qualifying parent or parents is or are settled in a different qualifying territory at the time of the birth. This person does not become a BC, because neither parent is settled in 'that territory'.[4] As originally enacted the BNA 1981 allowed a child to trace entitlement through either parent, provided that the child was legitimate or had been legitimised by the subsequent marriage of its parents. An illegitimate child could only trace entitlement through its mother.[5] This is to change with the prospective coming into force of section 9 of the NIAA 2002. Illegitimacy is no longer to be a bar to tracing nationality through the father.

[1] British Nationality Act 1981, s 1.
[2] British Nationality (Falkland Islands) Act 1983, s 1(2), which is repealed and incorporated into the amendments made to BNA 1981 by BOTA 2002 as from 21 May 2002: SI 2002/1252, Art 2(c). See above 2.14.
[3] British Nationality Act 1981, s 1, as amended by BOTA 2002, s 5 and Sch 1. Commencement of the Sch 2 amendments took place on 21 May 2002, the appointed day under SI 2002/1252, Art 2(a).
[4] BNA 1981, s 1(1)(b), as amended above.
[5] BNA 1981, s 50(9), before amendment by NIAA 2002, s 9. *The illegitimacy rules were held not to be in breach of Art 8 or of Art 8 read with Art 14 of ECHR: R (on the application of Montana) v Secretary of State for the Home Department* [2001] 1 WLR 552, CA. In fact the Secretary of State for the Home Department could always use his or her discretion under BNA 1981, s 3(1) to register as a British citizen the illegitimate child of a British father. Since March 2000, IND policy has been to register the illegitimate child of a British citizen father where: (a) they are satisfied about paternity; (b) they are satisfied that the father is a British citizen; (c) they have the consent of all those with parental responsibility; (d) they are satisfied that the conditions for registration would have been met if the child had been legitimate and (e) there is no reason to refuse on character grounds: Nationality Instructions (NI) Ch 9, s 9. The NI give guidance on the evidence needed to prove paternity.

2.45 A child may trace entitlement to British citizenship through a parent who died before his or her birth. Under the British Nationality Act 1981 the definition of 'parent' includes the parent of a child born posthumously. The status of the mother or father shall be the status of the parent in question at the time of that parent's death.[1]

[1] British Nationality Act 1981, s 48.

2.46 Where a child wishes to trace entitlement through its parent, it is the status of the parent at the time of the birth, or in the case of posthumous children, at the time of the death, which counts. If the parent becomes a British citizen, for example by registration, naturalisation or operation of law, after the birth of the child, the child does not automatically become a British citizen by birth but is entitled to be registered as such on making an application under section 1(3) of the British Nationality Act 1981.

2.47 The alternative to having a parent who is a British citizen is to have a parent who at the time of the child's birth is settled in the UK or in a qualifying territory (meaning a British overseas territory other than the Sovereign Bases in Cyprus: 2.15 above). Under section 50(2) of the British Nationality Act 1981 a person is settled for the purposes of the Act if he or she is 'ordinarily resident in the United Kingdom or a British overseas territory ... without being subject under the immigration laws to any restriction on the period for which he may remain'.[1] Section 50(3) of the 1981 Act excludes from this definition people who are in the UK as diplomats, international functionaries or as members of Commonwealth or visiting armed forces and are exempt from immigration control.[2] In some cases persons who have been entitled to a diplomatic exemption may be able to bestow British citizenship on their children born in the UK if they were settled in the UK before they took up their diplomatic posts.[3]

[1] Freedom from immigration restrictions and conditions is the first requirement of settlement. Ordinary residence is the second requirement. This is discussed in detail at 5.5–5.6 below. Section 50(5) of the British Nationality Act 1981 provides that a person is not to be treated as ordinarily resident in the UK when he or she is in the UK or a British overseas territory in breach of the immigration laws. The 'immigration laws' are defined by BNA 1981, s 50(1) in relation to the UK as meaning the Immigration Act 1971 and 'any law for purposes similar to that Act which is for the time being or has at any time been in force in any part of the UK'.

[2] See Immigration Act 1971, s 8(3) and (4)(b) and (c). But Gurkhas serve in the UK as members of the home forces, and can be regarded as settled in the UK, so as to confer British citizenship on their UK-born children: see NI, Ch 3, Annex A; see also IND to JCWI 23 August 2001.

[3] BNA1981, s 50(4).

2.48 From this short account it can be seen that disputes about whether a child's parents were 'settled' in the UK or a British overseas territory at the time of the birth may be a contentious issue when determining the nationality of the child.[1] In relation to the UK, the government recognised that doubts about parents' immigration status might arise many years after the birth of the child, and so modified the effect of the rule by providing for citizenship by registration for children born in the UK whose parents could not meet the settlement requirement. So section 1(4) of the British Nationality Act 1981 provides that a person born in the UK who has not been out of the country for more than 90 days in each of the first ten years of his or her life may register as a British citizen at any time. The immigration status of the person is irrelevant, and his or her residence may have been lawful or unlawful.[2] Registration as a British citizen under s 1(4) can occur in adulthood. It is also provided that where a child's parents become settled after the birth of the child, that child gets an automatic right to be registered as a UK citizen under section 1(3) of the 1981 Act. The application for registration under s 1(3) must be made while the child is still a minor. Limited provision is also made for people born in the UK who would otherwise be stateless. In some cases they automatically become British citizens and in other cases they may register.[3] These registration provisions only apply to persons born in the UK. However, as a result of BOTA 2002, the Secretary of State has a general discretion to register any BOTC as a BC, other than those who are BOTCs only by virtue of a connection with the Sovereign Bases in Cyprus or who have previously renounced their British citizenship.[4]

[1]   This is particularly so where EEA nationals are involved: see Fransman, *British Nationality Law* (2nd edn, 1998) Butterworths, para 11.2.
[2]   NI, Ch 8, s 1 (Entitlement: UK-born person).
[3]   British Nationality Act 1981, s 36 and Sch 2, paras 1 and 3.
[4]   BNA 1981, s 4A, as inserted by BOTA 2002, s 4.

Abandoned infants

2.49 Where a newborn infant has been found abandoned in the UK, after commencement of the BNA 1981, section 1(2) provides that the qualifying conditions for citizenship in section 1(1) are deemed to apply to that child unless the contrary is shown. The same applies to babies abandoned in the Falkland Islands at any time after commencement of the 1981 Act and to other overseas territories (other than the Sovereign Bases in Cyprus) at any time after the appointed day for the commencement of that part of BOTA 2002.[1] There is no definition of 'newborn' in the Act and this must be construed as a matter of fact by the Secretary of State and possibly the courts.[2] Children who have been found abandoned but are patently not newborn may be registered under section 3(1) at the minister's discretion.

[1]   British Nationality (Falkland Islands) Act 1983, s 1(3) as from commencement of the BNA 1981; repealed and incorporated into the British Nationality Act 1981, s 1 (2), as amended by BOTA 2002, Sch 1 as from 21 May 2002 (SI 2002/1252).
[2]   Of course, the precise age of the child is unlikely to be known by the very circumstances of abandonment. In the committee stages of the British Nationality Bill the minister suggested that a child of about 12 months might be considered to be newborn in certain circumstances; it would be the minister's intention to give the phrase a generous interpretation: HC Official Report (5th series) col 212, 26 February 1981, 6th sitting.

Adoption

2.50 Under the BNA 1981 as enacted, an adoption order made in a UK court automatically confers British nationality on a child who is not a British citizen, where at least one of the adopters is a British citizen, but an adoption order abroad has no such effect.[1] The Adoption (Intercountry Aspects) Act 1999 amends the law in order to give effect to the 1993 Hague Convention on Protection of Children and Co-operation in respect of Intercountry Adoption.[2] In relation to nationality, it implements Article 26(2) of the Convention which requires a Contracting State, where an adoption has the effect of terminating a pre-existing legal parent-child relationship, to ensure that:

'the child shall enjoy in the receiving State, and any other Contracting State where the adoption is recognised, rights equivalent to those resulting from adoptions having this effect in each such State'.

The amendment, which came into force on 1 June 2003,[3] ensures that the adopted child enjoys the same status from the making of a Convention adoption order as he or she would if the adoption was made in the UK. Amended section 1(5) of the British Nationality Act 1981 now provides that a child without British nationality, who is adopted either in any UK court or outside the British Islands under a Convention adoption,[4] automatically acquires British citizenship. This is subject to two requirements:[5] first, that at least one of the adoptive parents is a British citizen at the time the adoption order is made or the Convention adoption is effected; and secondly, in the case of a Convention adoption, the adopter or, in the case of an adoption by a married couple, both of the adopters are habitually resident in the UK. The 1999 Act does not extend to Northern Ireland, but covers the whole of the British Islands, including the Channel Islands and the Isle of Man. However, an adoption order made in Northern Ireland would qualify to confer citizenship, as an adoption order made by a court 'in the United Kingdom'.[6]

1 British Nationality Act 1981, s 1(5) and (6). See Adoption Act 1976; Adoption (Scotland) Act 1978; Adoption (Northern Ireland) Order 1987. The courts are aware of the immigration consequences of adoption and regard them as a relevant factor, and have held that benefits from the acquisition of British nationality which occur during childhood are benefits to which first consideration should be given under s 6 of the Adoption Act 1976: *Re B (Adoption Order: Nationality)* [1999] INLR 125, HL. Home Office policy was to register children adopted by British citizens overseas in the circumstances set out in the NI, Ch 9, s 8, or where adoption was demonstrably in the child's best interests. For the provisions of the Immigration Rules dealing with the admission of adopted children to join their parents in this country see chapter 11 below.
2 The Convention is printed as the Adoption (Intercountry Aspects) Act 1999, Sch 1.
3 BNA 1981, s 1(5) as substituted by Adoption (Intercountry Aspects) Act 1999, s 7: SI 2003/362, Art 2(a).
4 'Convention adoption' is an adoption effected under the law of a Convention country outside the British Islands and certified under Art 23(1) of the Convention: see Adoption Act 1976, s 72(1); Adoption (Scotland) Act 1978, s 65(1), as amended by Adoption (Intercountry Aspects) Act 1999, s 8. This definition applies for nationality purposes; BNA 1981, s 1(8), as amended by Adoption (Intercountry Aspects) Act 1999, s 7(3). This provision, but not the definition, is likely to be superseded by Adoption and Children Act 2002, s 66(1)(c), when it comes into force.
5 BNA 1981, s 5(5A), as inserted by Adoption (Intercountry Aspects) Act 1999, s 7.
6 Adoption (Intercountry Aspects) Act 1999, s 18(4) and (5).

Adoption in the British Overseas Territories

2.51 Adoption in the Falkland Islands and other qualifying overseas territories is being brought into line with the provisions operating in the UK, so as to confer British citizenship on minors who are adopted by British citizens in those territories.[1] The complication is that there is a gap between the start of the BOTA changes and the coming into force of the Adoption (Intercountry Aspects) Act 1999. BOTA started operating on 21 May 2002 and the 1999 Act on 1 June 2003. It has, therefore, been necessary for the legislators to make provision for BOTA 2002 coming into force first. The two amendments to BNA 1981, section 1(5) come to the same thing,[2] by ensuring that a minor who is not a British citizen, will automatically become one where an adoption order is made on or after the appointed day (ie 21 May 2002) by any court in a qualifying territory. However, Convention adoptions only confer British nationality on minors adopted abroad by parents living in an overseas territory after 1 June 2003, and in such cases the adoptive parents will have to have been habitually resident in the UK; habitual residence of the adopters in an overseas territory will not suffice.[3]

1   British Nationality (Falkland Islands) Act 1983, s 1(4) conferred BC status, where an adoption order was made in any court in the Falklands. On the appointed day (21 May 2002) it was repealed and replaced by the general provision for qualifying territories (meaning all British overseas territories other than the Sovereign Bases in Cyprus): BOTA 2002, ss 5, 7 and Sch 1, paras 1(4) and (5).
2   BNA 1981, s 1(5) as substituted by the Adoption (Intercountry Aspects) Act 1999, s 7 and amended successively by BOTA, Sch 1, paras 1(4) and (5).
3   BNA 1981, s 1(5A)(b), as inserted by Adoption (Intercountry Aspects) Act 1999, s 7.

Descent

2.52 Where a child is born outside the UK, the British Nationality Act 1981 as enacted provides for automatic transmission of citizenship from parent to child for just one generation.[1] The Act provides that persons born overseas after commencement automatically become British citizens from birth if their mother or father was a British citizen otherwise than by descent at the time of their birth, or was in Crown or similar designated service outside the UK or was working for a Community institution somewhere outside the UK.[2] But children born after 21 May 2002, the appointed day under BOTA 2002, in one of the qualifying overseas territories to a parent, who is a British citizen by descent, will no longer be subject to the 'one generation' rule; in fact these children will be BCs by birth, although their children born overseas (ie outside the UK or a qualifying territory) will be subject to the descent rules. Similarly, under the BOTA amendments, Crown and other designated services is given a broader definition and the 'one generation' rule will not apply to BCs in such Crown or other designated service, where recruitment has taken place in the UK or a qualifying territory.[3] The 'one generation' rule may nevertheless produce some harsh results and so citizenship by descent is complemented by a scheme of registration to alleviate its deficiencies.[4]

1   British Nationality Act 1981, s 2. Citizenship by descent is defined in the BNA 1981, s 14. See further British Nationality (Hong Kong) Act 1997, s 2. It should also be noted that BOTCs, who become BCs under s 3 of BOTA 2002 and were BOTCs by descent immediately before commencement of that section, are BCs by descent, unless they have become BCs otherwise than by descent: see BOTA 2002, s 3(3).
2   BNA 1981, s 2(1)(b) and (4).
3   BNA 1981, s 2, as amended by BOTA 2002, Sch 1, para 2.
4   BNA 1981, s 3(2)–(6). See also the amendments to these provisions in BOTA 2002, Sch 1 para 3. In *R (on the application of Ullah) v Secretary of State for the Home Department* [2001] EWCA Civ 659, [2001] Imm AR 439, the Court of Appeal held that a British citizen by descent cannot naturalise so as to confer citizenship on future children born abroad.

Registration

2.53 Under the British Nationality Act 1981 previous entitlements to register as CUKCs were swept away either immediately the Act came into force or after a transitional period and were generally replaced by naturalisation, except for minors, where registration is still available in a variety of circumstances,[1] and for residual classes of British nationals and British Protected persons resident in the UK who wish to upgrade to British citizens.[2] Registration for these citizens is an entitlement, provided all the conditions are fulfilled, but the Secretary of State has a discretion to waive unfulfilled conditions in the 'special circumstances of any particular case'.[3] To qualify the person must have been in the UK for a period of five years prior to the application without being in breach of the immigration laws and must have had no restrictions attached to their leave in the twelve months prior to the application.[4] This provision continues to operate, but has been largely overtaken by the automatic grant of British citizenship to BOTCs by BOTA 2002 and by the new right to register as a BC given by section 12 of NIAA 2002 to BOCs, British subjects under the Act and BPPs, unless they have another nationality: see 2.14–2.19. It will obviously still be of use to those who cannot qualify under BOTA 2002, or because of dual nationality.

[1] For registration of those born in the UK see 2.48 above. Additionally, children born abroad to British citizens by descent are entitled to register as British citizens subject to various conditions: British Nationality Act 1981, 3(2), 3(5). There is provision for discretionary registration in s 3(1). Home Office policy is to register the illegitimate children of British citizen fathers (NI, Ch 9, s 9), the second- or subsequent generation children born abroad to British citizens on long-term business or service overseas (Ch 9, s 10); mentally disabled minors (Ch 9, s 11) and minors needing British citizenship to follow a particular career (eg police, armed forces or civil service) (Ch 9, s 13). The main general criteria for discretionary registration are that the child's future should clearly be seen to lie in the UK, that there are close connections (either through a parent or otherwise) and that a child of 13 or over has lived in the UK for two years. See further NI Ch 9. The consent of the court is needed if the child is a ward, and the consent of all those with parental responsibility where Children Act orders have been made: NI, Ch 9, ss 17, 20–22.

[2] BNA 1981, s 4.

[3] BNA 1981, s 4. For the circumstances when residence conditions will be waived see NI Ch 12 Annex A.

[4] Having no restrictions attached to leave will usually mean having indefinite leave to remain, but it can also include having an exemption from control or even being in breach: see NI Ch 12 Annex A. The circumstances in which a person is in the UK in breach of the immigration laws are exhaustively set out in NIAA 2002, s 11(2); see 2.54 fn 4 below.

Naturalisation

2.54 An application for naturalisation can be made under section 6(1) of the British Nationality Act 1981 or, in the case of persons (men or women) married to British citizens, under section 6(2). There is a residence qualification, which is different in each case. In the non-marriage cases the applicant must have been in the UK for five years without any absences in excess of 450 days.[1] In the case of spouses the period of required residence is three years with no absence in excess of 270 days.[2] Absences in excess of those number of days may be ignored at the Secretary of State's discretion.[3] Similarly, although the rule is that the applicant must not have been in breach of the immigration laws during either residence period,[4] breaches may be overlooked.[5] A condition which cannot be waived is that the applicant must have been physically present in the UK on a date five (or three) years before the making of the application.[6] In addition to the requirement of a fixed period of residence in the UK, the applicant must also be free from any restrictions on his or her length of stay in the UK.[7] A spouse can apply immediately after receiving indefinite leave, but others must normally wait 12 months, although the Home Secretary may ignore this requirement in a suitable case.[8] There is no requirement that a person be 'settled' in the UK to be naturalised.[9] Applicants other than spouses must also intend, if naturalised, to live principally in the UK or work in Crown or similar service, or for a UK-established company.[10] It used to be the normal practice of the government to treat any person resident in the UK in exercise of a right conferred by the EC Treaty, as extended by the European Economic Area Agreement 1992, as being a person with unrestricted stay in the UK, for these purposes.[11] This should probably be treated as an exercise of the Home Secretary's waiver discretion, because Regulation 8 of the EEA Regulations[12] now contains a very limited definition of EEA nationals who are to be regarded as free from a time restriction on their stay. Anyone within the groups set out in regulation 8 will, therefore, qualify as free from any immigration restriction on their length of stay for naturalisation purposes. Other EEA nationals, such as workers and the self-employed, will have to wait four years, until they qualify for and are granted permission to remain indefinitely under paragraph 255 of HC 395, as amended, and will (subject to discretionary waiver) be required to have held such permission for the twelve months preceding the application.[13]

---

1   British Nationality Act 1981, Sch 1, para 1(2)(a).
2   BNA 1981, Sch 1, para 3.
3   BNA 1981, Sch 1 paras 1(2)(a), 2(a), 3(a) and 4(b). Criteria for the exercise of discretion to waive excess absence are set out in NI Ch 18 Annex B, paras 4 and 5.
4   BNA 1981, Sch 1, paras 1(2)(d) and 3(d). What is meant by 'in breach of the immigration laws' is now exhaustively set out in NIAA 2002, s 11(2). Although the provision is not intended to change the law (see Lord Filkin, Parliamentary Under-Secretary of State for the Home Office in *Hansard* HL Report, 8 July 2002, vol 637, no 165, col 550), it may in fact do so in respect of EEA nationals, who will be treated as being in the UK in breach of the immigration laws, if they have neither an entitlement to be here under European community law nor permission to be here: see view set out in *Butterworths Immigration Law Service*, A[2610] (Issue 41). The NI (Vol 2: General Information: EEA and Swiss Nationals, paras 10–11) state that EEA nationals remaining in the UK without rights of residence under Community law or leave under the 1971 Act are to be regarded as subject to restrictions on the period for which they can remain, but are not to be regarded as in breach of the immigration laws. One effect of NIAA 2002, s 11(3), which applies Immigration Act 1971, s 11(1) for the purposes of this section, is to ensure that a person is not to be treated as being in breach of the immigration laws at any time when he or she was still in the immigration control area or had been detained or temporarily admitted pending a decision on his or her eligibility to enter. This had been Home Office policy where a person on temporary admission pending admission was granted leave to enter, but not where he or she was removed. Overstaying by an asylum seeker after a claim is not treated as residence in breach: NI Ch 18 Annex B, para 9.9. The application of s 11(1) of the 1971 Act affects the legality of a person's residence in the UK, but not the calculation of the duration of their stay: see Beverley Hughes MP, Minister of State in the Home Office to Fiona Mactaggart MP, 18 July 2002. For a summary of the position see 5.10 below.
5   BNA 1981, Sch 1, paras 2(d) and 4(b). See *Fransman* 2.48 fn 7, para 11.2. For policy on disregarding breaches see NI Ch 18, Annex B, para 8.
6   BNA 1981, Sch 1, para 1(2)(a), 3(a). Where an applicant misses the requirement by three months or less, the application may be returned to be re-signed and re-dated to arrive on a date when it can be met: NI Ch 18, Annex B para 3.
7   BNA 1981, Sch 1, paras 1(2)(c) and 3(c).
8   BNA 1981, Sch 1, para 2(c).
9   Freedom from restrictions will normally mean that the person is also settled, but it does not have to; it could mean residence pursuant to an exemption from control, or residence in breach of control (which can be waived): NI Ch 18 Annex B. Irish nationals are

considered to be free from time limits on their stay and therefore do not require ILR: Home office to Law Centre (Northern Ireland) 20 March 2003.

10   BNA 1981, Sch 1, para 1(1)(d). For the meaning of UK-established company see *R v Secretary of State for the Home Department, ex p Mehta* [1992] Imm AR 512. Normally the IND expects evidence that employment will continue for five years as a reasonable minimum alternative to an intention to make a permanent home in the UK: NI Ch 18 Annex F, para 7. An employee of a multinational company seconded to an associate non-UK registered company (parent or subsidiary) would be expected to have a contract of employment with the UK-established company or will be regarded as one of its own career staff: NI Ch 18 Annex F, para 5.

11   The UK Passport Agency continued to accept EC nationals exercising EC Treaty rights as 'settled': see Fransman, para 11.2.1.8, and Immigration and Nationality Directorate letter to Walthamstow CAB, 6 December 1999. Prospective applicants were advised to apply for indefinite leave to remain under the Immigration Rules as a precautionary measure.

12   Immigration (European Economic Area) Regulations 2000, SI 2000/2326, reg 8 provides that, essentially, retired workers and self-employed people and those with permission to stay indefinitely, and their family members, are to be regarded as not subject to a restriction on their length of stay.

13   IND to Kingsley Napley, 9 September 2002. There are indications that there will be a degree of waiver and that there will be no need for them to wait 12 months once they have obtained indefinite permission to remain or if they are to be treated as subject to no time restriction under reg 8, and fulfil all the other conditions of the 1981 Act: Letter from Immigration and Nationality Directorate to Cameron McKenna, 5 October 1998.

2.55 New requirements for naturalisation have now been introduced by the NIAA 2002[1] and previous differences between the naturalisation of spouses and non-spouses, other than the residence requirements referred to in the previous paragraph, have gone. First, all applicants have to show that they are of full age and capacity,[2] and of good character.[3] These are old provisions. A criminal record is taken into account, but is not fatal. Someone with a life sentence can qualify, if he or she was released at least 20 years ago, has been above suspicion ever since, has no further convictions, and has made sustained attempts to contribute to society since release.[4] Illegal employment of an overseas domestic worker is unlikely to count against the employer, if the worker's position was later regularised under the domestic workers' concession, but a current or recent attempt to assist someone in the evasion of immigration control is likely to result in refusal.[5] Secondly, it is now necessary for spouses as well as non-spouse applicants to have sufficient knowledge of the English, Welsh or Scottish Gaelic language[6] and sufficient knowledge about life in the UK (the 'jingle bells' test), unless it would be unreasonable to expect the applicant to fulfil either requirement because of age or physical or mental condition.[7] Regulations to deal with knowledge of English are in force, but none to deal with knowledge of life in Britain.[8] Successful applicants, provided they are of full age, will now have to take an oath and pledge loyalty to the UK and democracy at a citizenship ceremony.[9] Details of this are set out in a new section 42 and Schedule 5 to the BNA 1981.[10] The citizenship ceremony applies to adults being registered as BCs as well as those who are naturalised.[11] Registration or naturalisation are contingent on payment of a fee,[12] and new fees have recently been set for registration and naturalisation, including a fee for the citizenship ceremony.[13]

1   NIAA 2002, ss 1–3 and Sch 1; British Nationality Act 1981, Sch 1, para 1(2)(c).

2   Mental illness or disability does not disqualify, but the person 'should be able to grasp, however dimly, the purpose of the application': NI, Ch 18 Annex A.

3   The Secretary of State is entitled to adopt a high standard in assessing 'good character' for naturalisation, and need not limit it to criminal convictions: *R v Secretary of State for the Home Department, ex p Fayed* [2001] Imm AR 134. The Home Office would not consider applicants to be of good character if there was information on file to suggest that they did not respect and were not prepared to abide by the law (ie were, or were suspected of being, involved in crime), or their financial affairs were not in order (eg failure to pay taxes for which they were liable), or their activities were notorious and cast serious doubt on their standing in the local community, or they had practised deceit, eg in their dealings with the Home Office, DSS, Inland Revenue or Customs and Excise: NI Ch 18 Annex D.

4   NI Ch 18 Annex D, para 3.4.3.

5   NI Ch 18 Annex D, para 7.

6   BNA 1981, Sch 1, paras 1(1)(c), 3(e), as amended by NIAA 2002, s 2(1)(a).

7   BNA 1981, Sch 1, paras 1(1)(ca) and 2(e), 3(e) and 4 as amended.

8   The British Nationality (General) Regulations 2003, SI 2003/548, reg 5A as inserted by the British Nationality (General) (Amendment) Regulations 2004, SI 2004/1726; and the British Nationality (General) (Amendment No 2) Regulations 2004, SI 2004/2109, made under BNA 1981, s 41(1)(ba), (bb), inserted by NIAA 2002, s 1(3) and (4). See also the British Nationality (British Overseas Territories) (Amendment) (No 2) Regulations 2003.

9   NIAA 2002, s 3 and Sch 1, substituting BNA 1981, s 42 and Sch 5 and adding new ss 42A and 42B. See also British Nationality (General) Regulations 2003, SI 2003/548, as amended by SI 2003/3158, SI 2004/1726, SI 2004/2109.

10   Inserted by NIAA 2002, Sch 1.

11   BNA 1981, s 42(1) as substituted.

12   Asylum and Immigration (Treatment of Claimants, etc) Act 2004, s 42 allows the Secretary of State to prescribe fees for applications under the BNA 1981 which exceed the administrative costs of determining the application, and reflect benefits believed likely to accrue if the application is successful.

13   The British Nationality (Fees) Regulations 2003, SI 2003/ 3157, as amended by the British Nationality (Fees) (Amendment) Regulations 2005, SI 2005/651. Fees for registration have increased on 1 April 2005 from £85 for an adult and £144 for a minor to £120 and £200; for naturalisation from £150 (£146 for a spouse) to £200, including spouse, with an unchanged fee of £68 for the citizenship ceremony.

Challenging registration and naturalisation decisions

2.56 In some registrations and in all naturalisations, the award of British citizenship is discretionary.[1] The Nationality Instructions now provide guidelines on the way in which that discretion should be exercised, but there is no appeal to the Asylum and Immigration Tribunal and, until recently, the Secretary of State was not obliged to give reasons for any refusal and his decision on such applications was not subject to 'appeal to or review in' any court.[2] That has all changed. Now, although there is still no right of appeal against refusal to register or naturalise as a British citizen, reasons for any refusal must be given and the ouster clause has gone.[3] So the decision can be challenged on all judicial review grounds, not just lack of jurisdiction or unfairness.

1   The Secretary of State is not authorised to discriminate on grounds of nationality, ethnic or national origin: see Race Relations Act 1976, s 19D(1) as amended by NIAA 2002, s 6(2).

2   British Nationality Act 1981, s 44 (2) and (3). Ouster clauses, however, have never usually been able to oust challenges on the basis of (i) lack of jurisdiction; see *Anisminic Ltd v Foreign Compensation Commission* [1969] 2 AC 147 at 171B–D, HL; *A-G v Ryan* [1980] AC 718, PC; *South East Asia Fire Bricks Sdn Bhd v Non-Metallic Mineral Products Manufacturing Employees Union* [1981] AC 363, [1980] 2 All ER 689, PC; *Re Racal Communications Ltd* [1981] AC 374, [1980] 2 All ER 634, HL; *Gowa v A-G* [1985] 1 WLR 1003, HL; *R v Secretary of State for the Home Department, ex p Mehta* [1992] Imm AR 512, QBD (very restricted view of the meaning of a company 'established in the

United Kingdom' wrong and s 44(2) did not oust court's jurisdiction to say so); or (ii) lack of fairness; see *A-G v Ryan* above; *R v Secretary of State for the Home Department, ex p Fayed* [1997] 1 All ER 228, CA.

3   NIAA 2002, s 7. Judicial review is the only proper route of challenging an erroneous refusal of registration: *Harrison v Secretary of State for the Home Department* [2005] EWHC 706, Ch.

Loss of British citizenship

2.57 Under the scheme of the British Nationality Act 1981 those connected with a dependent territory (now British overseas territory) lost their CUKC status and became British Dependent Territories citizens (now BOTCs), not British citizens.[1] But this process has run its course, and loss of citizenship in this way would only occur if some overseas territory became an independent country. New legislation would be required. Under current law, loss of British citizenship can occur in two ways:

(i)   by renunciation, where BCs with dual nationality or about to acquire another nationality renounce their British citizenship by a declaration of renunciation;[2]

(ii)   by deprivation, where the Secretary of State for the Home Department makes an order depriving someone of British citizenship. Previously this only applied to those who have acquired it by registration or naturalisation,[3] but now there is a new power to deprive persons who acquired British citizenship at birth, provided this does not make that person stateless.[4]

1   British Nationality Act 1981, s 23.
2   BNA 1981, s 12 (BCs), s 24 (BDTCs/BOTCs), s 29 (BOCs), and s 34 (British subjects).
3   BNA 1981, s 40.
4   BNA 1981, s 40(2), as substituted by NIAA 2002, s 4(1) which came into force on 1 April 2003: SI 2003/754.

Renunciation and resumption of citizenship

2.58 Renunciation of citizenship can only take place if the person renouncing already has or will acquire within the next six months another citizenship or nationality.[1] Then it is a fairly straightforward matter, provided the prescribed procedure is followed.[2] Merely making an informal declaration of renunciation, for example, where someone becomes a citizen of the USA, is not enough. There is also a fee to be paid.[3] Once renounced, can British citizenship be resumed? And in what circumstances? This is a more difficult question.

1   BNA 1981, s 12(3) (which also applies to ss 24, 29 and 34).
2   See British Nationality (General) Regulations 2003, SI 2003/548, paras 8, 9 and Sch 5.
3   British Nationality (Fees) Regulations 2003, SI 2003/3157, as amended by SI 2005/651. The fee is £120.

2.59 Where a person had acquired the right to resume citizenship as a CUKC (under the British Nationality Act 1964), the British Nationality Act 1981 gave a right to register either as a British citizen or as a BDTC, provided that the person had what was known as 'an appropriate qualifying connection' either with the UK (for BCs) or with a British Dependent Territory (now British Overseas Territory) (for BDTCs, now BOTCs).[1] These were people, as we have seen at 2.38 above, with a qualifying connection to the UK or a colony, who had been obliged to renounce their CUKC status in order to avoid being refused or deprived of citizenship of a newly independent Commonwealth country. For them, registration is a right. For other people who renounced their CUKC status, registration as a BC or BOTC is still a possibility, if they have the appropriate qualifying connection, but at the discretion of the Home Secretary.[2] Although these are transitional provisions for people who had renounced their CUKC status prior to commencement of the BNA 1981, they continue to operate today, and the number of potential beneficiaries has been widened by section 5 of the NIAA 2002, which allows resumption of citizenship by all spouses of those with an appropriate qualifying connection, and not just wives, as before.[3] However, the Act of 2002 does nothing about the fact that qualifying connections can be gained only by the person or through his or her father or the father's father. They cannot be acquired through the maternal line.

1 British Nationality Act 1981, s 10(1) (BCs) and s 22(1) (BDTCs). The meaning of 'an appropriate qualifying connection' in s 10(4), 22(4) was considered in *R v Secretary of State for the Home Department, ex p Patel and Wahid* [1991] Imm AR 25, QBD.
2 BNA 1981, s 10(2) (BCs) and s 22(2) (BDTCs). Registration may be appropriate where the purpose of renunciation was to acquire a spouse's citizenship, and the marriage has now ended, or to acquire another citizenship to assist in a career, and the person now wishes to return or come to the UK for settlement: NI Ch 16.
3 BNA 1981, s 10(1) and (2) (BCs) and s 22(1) and (2) (BDTCs), as amended. The amendments to the BNA 1981 apply to all applications made after 7 November 2002 as well as to applications made, but not determined by this date: NIAA 2002 s 162(3).

2.60 A person who makes a declaration of renunciation after the BNA 1981 came into force is entitled to resume citizenship only if the renunciation of British citizenship was necessary in order to retain or acquire some other citizenship or nationality.[1] This resumption is achieved by an application to the Secretary of State for the Home Department for registration by a person of full capacity. In addition to the right to resume under section 13(1) of the BNA 1981, there is also a general discretion to allow resumption under section 13(3).[2]

1 BNA 1981, s 13(1).
2 The discretion is intended primarily to benefit those who renounced citizenship in order to acquire the nationality of a spouse or to assist in a career, and the marriage or career has now ended and the person wishes to remain in or return to the UK for settlement: NI Ch 17.

Deprivation of citizenship

2.61 The grounds upon which a British citizen may be deprived of citizenship under the 1981 Act, as amended by the NIAA 2002 as from 1 April 2003 are as follows:

(a)   where the Secretary of State is satisfied that the person has done anything 'seriously prejudicial to the vital interests' of the UK or a British overseas territory;[1]

(b)   where registration or naturalisation has been obtained by fraud, false representation or concealment of material facts.[2]

For the first time, those acquiring British citizenship by birth or descent may be deprived of citizenship, provided that they would not thereby become stateless.[3] The new deprivation provisions, including the new right of appeal, apply to cases where the person has acquired citizenship by registration or naturalisation under the law in operation before 1 April 2003, if the Secretary of State is satisfied that the registration or naturalisation was obtained by fraud, false representation or concealment of a material fact.[4] In exercising the powers under new section 40, the Secretary of State is not confined to evidence coming into existence after commencement, but can have regard to anything which occurred before commencement on which he or she could have relied (alone or with other matters) in making an order under section 40 before commencement.[5] The language of these provisions suggest that the new powers do not have retrospective effect in relation to deprivation of citizenship acquired by birth or descent.[6]

[1]   British Nationality Act 1981, s 40(2), as substituted by Nationality, Immigration and Asylum Act 2002, s 4. The phrase 'seriously prejudicial to the interests' is taken from the European Convention on Nationality (Strasbourg 6 Sept 1997) which the government intends to ratify: see *Butterworths Immigration Law Service*, A[2604].
[2]   BNA 1981, s 40(3) as substituted.
[3]   BNA 1981, s 40(2), (4) as substituted; cf s 40(3) (as enacted) (deprivation of citizenship for disloyalty, trading with the enemy etc), which applied only to certain registered or naturalised citizens.
[4]   BNA 1981, s 40(6), as substituted by NIAA 2002, s 4(1).
[5]   NIAA 2002, s 4(4).
[6]   This view accords with that set out in *Butterworths Immigration Law Service*, A[2604].

2.62 Decisions of the courts under the former section 40 and its predecessor, section 20 of the British Nationality Act 1948, drew a distinction between deprivation, which requires a positive act by the Secretary of State for the Home Department, and cases where the Secretary of State can treat the registration or naturalisation as of no effect.[1] In *Mahmood*,[2] the applicant had obtained entry into the UK and subsequently registration as a CUKC by assuming the identity of a dead man. The Court of Appeal held that he had never become a CUKC. In *Akhtar*[3] the applicant had obtained his registration as a CUKC on the basis that he was the son of WA, but WA later denounced him and said he was not his son. The Court of Appeal held that, since the applicant could not prove that he was the son of WA as claimed in the certificate of registration or that he was the person named in the certificate, he could not rely on it. The court preferred to rest their decision on an absence of proof, rather than on a distinction between void and voidable registrations. In *Ejaz*,[4] the applicant was naturalised as a British citizen on the basis of her marriage, but it later turned out that her husband had never become a British citizen. The Secretary of State claimed that her naturalisation was a nullity on the ground that the Secretary of State has no power to grant naturalisation where the husband is not in fact a British citizen. The Court of Appeal rejected that argument and held that she became a British citizen as from the date on which her certificate of naturalisation was granted under British Nationality Act 1981, section 42(5) and remained such unless and until the Secretary of

State invoked the deprivation machinery under section 40. In cases of registration the same rule applies; so the date of registration and not the date of application determines when citizenship is granted.[5]

1   The NI, Ch 55, draw a distinction between deprivation and nullity, the latter being impersonation cases, the former where some other fraud was practised to obtain citizenship.
2   *R v Secretary of State for the Home Department, ex p Mahmood* [1981] QB 58n, [1980] 3 WLR 312n, CA.
3   *R v Secretary of State for the Home Department, ex p Akhtar (Parvaz)* [1981] QB 46, [1980] 2 All ER 735, CA.
4   *R v Secretary of State for the Home Department, ex p Ejaz* [1994] QB 496, [1994] 2 All ER 436, CA.
5   *R v Secretary of State for the Home Department, ex p Bibi (Amina)* [1995] Imm AR 185, QBD.

Disputed claims to citizenship

2.63   As noted at 2.21 above, section 3(8) of the Immigration Act 1971 places the burden of proving a claim to British citizenship on the claimant, and section 3(9) provides the means of doing so – by production of a passport or certificate of entitlement. In cases of disputed citizenship, where the applicant has neither the requisite British passport nor a certificate of entitlement, section 3(8) of the 1971 Act has been crucial.[1] In such cases the court has expressly rejected the argument that other evidence (such as the applicant's British visitor's passport or birth certificate) is prima facie proof of citizenship so as to shift the burden to the immigration authorities to disprove citizenship.[2] On the other hand where the claimant is able to produce the required means of proof, the position is different. In *Ex p Obi*[3] Sedley J held that the production of a genuine UK passport, issued to the applicant and describing him as a British citizen, discharges the burden of proof and there was no need for further proof, even though the Secretary of State for the Home Department called into question the applicant's identity. This, however, does not stop the Home Office trying to rebut the presumption of citizenship created by the passport by trying to prove that it or the certificate of registration or naturalisation, on which the passport has been issued, was obtained by fraud, false representation or concealment of a material fact. At that point *Khawaja* will have a bearing. The burden of proving that citizenship or a certificate of entitlement was obtained by fraud will be on the Home Office and must be proved to a high degree of probability.[4] In *Obi* there was no question but that the passport was issued to the applicant. In such cases, it will clearly be for the Secretary of State to put the machinery of deprivation into motion and to prove that the conditions for a deprivation under section 40(3) are satisfied. But where there is an allegation of impersonation, it remains to be seen whether the Secretary of State will seek to assert that registration or naturalisation did not take effect since it was issued to a person other than the applicant, as in *Akhtar*,[5] or will invoke the deprivation procedure on the basis that citizenship was obtained by fraud. Although a disputed claim for citizenship may be resolved by an application to the Administrative Court for a declaration, and in such proceedings the Court will resolve the dispute on the merits by deciding the precedent facts for itself,[6] the appeal procedure is likely to be more convenient.

1 *Minta v Secretary of State for the Home Department* [1992] Imm AR 380; *Re Bamgbose* [1990] Imm AR 135, CA; *Mokuolo v Secretary of State for the Home Department* [1989] Imm AR 51, CA.
2 In both *Minta* and *Bamgbose* (fn 1 above), the Court of Appeal held that *Khawaja v Secretary of State for the Home Department* [1984] AC 74, [1983] 1 All ER 765, HL has no bearing on the question of British citizenship, which is expressly dealt with by section 3(8).
3 *R v Secretary of State for the Home Department, ex p Obi* [1997] Imm AR 420, QBD.
4 *Khawaja v Secretary of State for the Home Department* [1984] AC 74. See *Minta*, above; *R v Secretary of State for the Home Department, ex p Rouse and Shrimpton* (13 November 1985, unreported), QBD.
5 *R v Secretary of State for the Home Department, ex p Akhtar (Parvaz)* [1981] QB 46, [1980] 2 All ER 735, CA.
6 *R (on the application of Harrison) v Secretary of State for the Home Department* [2003] EWCA Civ 432, [2003] INLR 284, where a New Zealander claimed that his father was born on a British-registered vessel, making him a British citizen. His claim for a declaration that he was a British citizen or had a right to register as such was struck out at [2005] EWHC 706 (Ch).

APPEALS

2.64 No appeal lies against the refusal of the Secretary of State for the Home Department to register or naturalise a person as a British citizen. The only remedy is, therefore, by way of judicial review. But in disputed claims to citizenship and right of abode an appeal to the Asylum and Immigration Tribunal is possible. A right of appeal is available to those who are refused a certificate of entitlement.[1] The appellant is entitled to appeal while he or she is in the UK, where the application was made in the UK.[2] Under the old appeal regime, the appellate authority treated passport refusals and disputed claims to a right of abode as constituting certificate of entitlement appeals even though no formal request for a certificate has been made.[3] It is doubtful if such a view would hold good today and it is, therefore, advisable to apply for a certificate of entitlement in all cases of doubt or dispute over citizenship or entitlement to a right of abode. This view is reinforced by the new provisions of the NIAA 2002, which have provided for greater formality in applications for certificates of entitlement.[4] Secondly, there is a variety of other possible appeals, where the issue of disputed citizenship or right of abode may also arise from one of the other appealable immigration decisions.[5] Occasionally, the ambit of the appeal will be limited to dealing with whether the passport is a forgery or the person seeking to enter is the same as the person described in the passport, and will not permit the appellant to prove his or her citizenship or right of abode by any admissible means.[6]

1 Nationality, Immigration and Asylum Act 2002, s 82(2)(c); its precursors were Immigration Act 1971, s 13(2) and Immigration and Asylum Act 1999, s 59.
2 NIAA 2002, s 92(2).
3 Under Immigration Act 1971, s 13(2); see *Secretary of State for the Home Department v Antoniades* [1993] Imm AR 57; *Menon v Entry Clearance Officer, Kuala Lumpur* [1993] Imm AR 577.
4 NIAA 2002 s 10, which gives power to make regulations governing the application for and granting of certificates of entitlement. Although the section is in force, no regulations had been made at the time of writing.
5 Ie, one of the decisions set out in NIAA 2002, s 82(2), e g refusal of leave to enter or refusal of entry clearance.
6 *Akewushola v Immigration Officer, Heathrow* [1999] INLR 433, CA.

2.65 Previously, the only remedy in a case of deprivation was a right of inquiry before a specially-appointed committee of inquiry.[1] Now there is a right of appeal to the Asylum and Immigration Tribunal, with the possibility of an appeal to the Court of Appeal or the Court of Session.[2] No order of deprivation may be made until any appeal has been finally determined or the time for appealing has expired.[3] In national security case there is provision for cases to be heard by the Special Immigration Appeals Commission.[4]

[1] British Nationality Act 1981, s 40(6)–(9) as enacted. See British Citizenship (Deprivation) Rules 1982, SI 1982/988. There were similar provisions for the deprivation of British Dependent Territories citizenship in s 40 and British Dependent Territories Citizenship (Deprivation) Rules 1982, SI 1982/989.
[2] BNA 1981, s 40A, as inserted by NIAA 2002, s 4 (1) and as amended by Asylum and Immigration (Treatment of Claimants, etc) Act 2004, Sch 2, para 4(a) from 4 April 2005: SI 2005/565.
[3] BNA 1981, s 40A(6), as inserted by NIAA above.
[4] Special Immigration Appeals Commission Act 1997, s 2B, inserted by NIAA 2002, s 4(2).

THE RIGHT TO A BRITISH PASSPORT

A prerogative power

2.66 Travellers may be refused a British passport because their citizenship is not recognised. We have dealt with the remedies for this situation in the last section. But passports may also be withheld from British citizens for a variety of reasons, and this will obviously affect their ability to travel and, therefore, to enjoy the benefits of their statutory right of abode. The power to issue passports is not statutory but is derived from the prerogative.[1] Passports are issued by the UK Passport Agency, which is an executive agency of the Home Office, referred to as the Passport Office. Overseas they are issued by British consulates, British High Commissions and British dependent territory authorities. A passport is not an entry clearance document for the purposes of an appeal under section 82(2) of NIAA 2002 or its statutory precursors. Thus where a person succeeds in proving a disputed relationship and by reason of that relationship is a British citizen by descent, the appellate authority cannot require the entry clearance officer to issue a passport, only a certificate of entitlement.[2] On the other hand, for the purposes of entry a passport is proof that the holder has a right of abode.[3] It is, therefore, a very valuable and essential document. Yet, so far no court or tribunal has been willing to sanction the existence of any implied duty to order the issue of a passport.

[1] Wade and Forsyth do not regard this as a true prerogative power for the highly questionable reason that the grant or cancellation of a passport involves no direct legal consequences; see *Administrative Law* (7th edn, 1994) Clarendon pp 249 and 383. This may be based on an early judicial view of a passport as a document merely to be used for purposes of consular protection: see *R v Brailsford* [1905] 2 KB 730 at 745. In *R v Secretary of State for Foreign and Commonwealth Affairs, ex p Everett* [1989] QB 811, [1989] 1 All ER 655, CA O'Connor LJ said it was a prerogative power.
[2] *Kassun (Khatoori)* (4272).
[3] Immigration Act 1971, s 3(9). See *R v Secretary of State for the Home Department, ex p Obi* [1997] Imm AR 420, QBD.

2.67 It was stated in the House of Lords in 1958: 'No British subject has a legal right to a passport. The grant of a UK passport is a royal prerogative exercised through Her Majesty's ministers and in particular the Foreign Secretary.'[1] Details of how the prerogative was usually exercised were given to the House. These reasons were amplified in 1974 and 1981.[2] There are five reasons for refusal or withdrawal of a passport. These are:

(a)   minors being taken out of the jurisdiction illegally, or contrary to the wishes of a parent or other person awarded parental rights;

(b)   applicants wishing to leave the country where there is good evidence to believe that they wish to avoid prosecution;

(c)   applicants whose conduct is so demonstrably undesirable that continued enjoyment of passport facilities is contrary to the public interest;[3]

(d)   persons repatriated at the public expense who have not refunded the cost of their repatriation;[4]

(e)   persons for whose arrest a warrant has been issued in the UK[5] or who are wanted for serious crime in the UK.[6]

[1]   209 HL Official Report (5th series) col 860 (PQ). See David W Williams 'Without Let or Hindrance' [1973] NLJ 605; JUSTICE *Going abroad.*

[2]   See 881 HC Official Report (5th series) written answers col 265, 15 November 1974; 416 HL Official Report (5th series) written answers col 558, 22 January 1981.

[3]   Only about 20 people were denied passports on political grounds between 1945 and 1968. Then there were the exceptional cases during the Rhodesian rebellion; see 764 HC Official Report (5th series) col 1107, 14 May 1968. British citizens who had been held at Guantánamo as suspected international terrorists had passports withdrawn or refused on their release and repatriation to the UK, although it is not clear why. See *Guardian* 17 February 2005.

[4]   This was said to occur only once or twice a year and the practice was confirmed in 792 HC Official Report (5th series) col 232. In 1968 it was stated in a parliamentary question that 2,400 passports had been impounded since 1951 (764 HC Official Report (5th series) col 183); a later debate in the House of Commons revealed that the overwhelming majority of these 2,400 refusals or withdrawals were people who had run out of money on holiday and handed in their passports to get their fares home paid: 764 HC Official Report (5th series) col 1107, 14 May 1968; see further David W Williams 'Without Let or Hindrance' [1973] NLJ 605.

[5]   *R v Secretary of State for Foreign and Commonwealth Affairs, ex p Everett* [1989] QB 811, [1989] 1 All ER 655, CA.

[6]   It is not clear how far (b) and (e) overlap.

Challenging refusals

2.68 Since it is now possible to challenge decisions taken under the prerogative on judicial review,[1] it is also possible to challenge a refusal to issue a passport. In *Ex p Everett*,[2] the Court of Appeal held that the Secretary of State for Foreign and Commonwealth Affairs was entitled to refuse a passport, but had to give reasons for doing so. Where the refusal was because of an outstanding arrest warrant, the applicant should be told when and where the warrant was issued and what for. When notifying the applicant he or she should be told to tell the Secretary of State of any exceptional grounds for issuing a passport, for example, when the applicant was ill in a foreign country. *Everett* focuses on the need to give reasons after the decision is made, but there may now also be cases where it will be necessary as a matter of fairness for the passport office to indicate areas of concern to applicants *before* the decision in sufficient detail to enable them to make representations.[3]

¹   *Council of Civil Service Unions v Minister for the Civil Service* [1985] AC 374, [1974] 3 All ER 935 at 948, 951 and 956, HL. See further *R v Secretary of State for the Home Department, ex p Bentley* [1994] QB 349, [1993] 4 All ER 442 (challenge to the prerogative of mercy).
²   *R v Secretary of State for Foreign and Commonwealth Affairs, ex p Everett* [1989] QB 811, [1989] 1 All ER 655, CA.
³   *R v Secretary of State for the Home Department, ex p Fayed* [1997] 1 All ER 228, CA.

A new approach

2.69 Today an unfettered prerogative power to refuse a passport is probably a thing of the past. First, a passport is not just a document to be used for the individual's protection as a British subject.¹ It may also be needed to give effect to the statutory right under section 1 of the Immigration Act 1971 to leave or enter the UK. Under EC law there is an obligation to allow British nationals to leave the country in pursuit of their free movement rights (see chapter 7 below). In our view neither this right nor the right to reside in another EC country in pursuit of free movement rights can be impeded by the refusal of the passport or other suitable identity document, except on public policy grounds within the terms of EC Council Directive 64/221.

¹   Per Lord Alverstone in *R v Brailsford* [1905] 2 KB 730 at 745.

2.70 The question is whether a passport can be withheld for travel outside the EC. We have already referred to Articles 2(2) and 3(2) of the Fourth Protocol of the ECHR at 2.6 above.¹ However, there is a much older common law right of a British subject to come and go without let or hindrance referred to in *DPP v Bhagwan*.² This echoes Blackstone's view that an Englishman had a right at common law to leave the realm, subject only to the restraints of the writ *ne exeat regno*.³ The right is now a statutory right, set out in section 1(1) of the Immigration Act 1971. However, without a passport it is largely useless. Does this mean that there is now a concomitant right to a passport, which can only be withheld in the limited circumstances to which section 1(1) relates?⁴ Or are the restraints set out in the parliamentary answers referred to in 2.67 above ones which can be lawfully imposed? *Everett* was argued on the basis that such restraints were not to be questioned and the only issue dealt with in that case was unfairness. The question must be open to argument in a future case.

¹   Identical provisions on the right to leave are contained in Art 12(2) and (3) of the UN International Covenant on Civil and Political Rights 1966. Britain is a party to this but not to the optional protocol which gives individuals a right to complain to the Human Rights Committee. The Covenant may give a right of complaint but it has not been incorporated into UK municipal law and it is, therefore, thought unlikely that it could found a judicial review challenge on any refusal or withdrawal of a passport. For text see Brownlie and Goodwin-Gill, *Basic Documents on Human Rights* (4th edn, 2002) OUP.
²   [1972] AC 60, [1970] 3 All ER 97.
³   See 2.7 above.
⁴   See 2.8 above.

Chapter 3

CONTROL OF ENTRY

INTRODUCTION

3.1 Since the last edition of this work, the Government, working with its EU partners, has worked on physical and legislative measures to make immigration control as extra-territorial as far as possible, so as to prevent the arrival in the UK of undocumented passengers or passengers likely to make an asylum claim. Quite apart from the increased use of high-tech devices, such as heartbeat detectors, thermal imaging and gamma scanners,[1] to detect clandestine entrants it has pushed immigration control back from Dover to Calais, Boulogne, Dunkirk, Lille, Paris, and Brussels, using powers under the IA 1971 (modified by the Channel Tunnel (International Arrangements) Orders)[2] and juxtaposed controls under the NIAA 2002,[3] and from Heathrow to Prague and points east, using 'pre-entry clearance' powers under section 3A of the IA 1971.[4] It is piloting the use of biometrics in entry clearance applications,[5] and is advancing plans to use powers under the NIAA 2002,[6] together with increased powers to demand passenger information from carriers before boarding,[7] to create a 'virtual control', whereby immigration officers will refuse carriers authority to board passengers whose faces don't fit (literally).[8] Meanwhile, we are in Phase I of the UK residence permit scheme,[9] whereby all passengers arriving for more than six months will require entry clearance (in Phase 1, the requirement applies only to specified nationals).[10] In this brave new world, where arrival without documents can be a criminal offence,[11] borders are more and more secure, but the 'safe haven' is increasingly hard to find.[12] Many of these developments – increased immigration officers' powers, criminal offences and carrier sanctions – are dealt with below in chapter 14. Here we examine the law and practice on visas, entry clearance and leave to enter the UK. A helpful development has been the construction of the UKvisas website, including extensive Diplomatic Service Procedures or 'DSPs' which set out FCO/IND policy guidance to entry clearance officers in a clear and easily accessible manner.

1   See Home Office press release 273/2003, 6 October 2003, claiming that 4,000 people were prevented from reaching the UK in the previous six months because of the introduction of these devices in Zeebrugge and Ostend.
2   Channel Tunnel (International Arrangements) Order 1993, SI 1993/1813, as amended by SI 1994/570, SI 1994/1405, SI 1996/2283, SI 2000/913, SI 2000/1775, SI 2001/1544, SI 2001/3707; see 3.27 below.
3   Nationality, Immigration and Asylum Act 2002, s 141; Nationality, Immigration and Asylum (Juxtaposed Controls) Order 2003, SI 2003/2818. See 3.28 below.
4   Section 3A was inserted by the Immigration and Asylum Act 1999, s 1 and the Immigration (Leave to Enter and Remain) Order 2000, SI 2000/1161, Art 7 was made under it. See *European Roma Rights Centre v Immigration Officer at Prague Airport* [2004] UKHL 55, [2005] 2 WLR 1; 3.25 below.
5   Immigration (Provision of Physical Data) Regulations 2003, SI 2003/1875 as amended by SI 2004/474 and SI 2004/1834, made under Nationality, Immigration and Asylum Act 2002, s 126. See 3.16 below.
6   Immigration Act 1971, Sch 2, para 27B, as inserted by Immigration and Asylum Act 1999, s 18 and amended from a date to be appointed by Asylum and Immigration (Treatment of Claimants, etc) Act 2004, s 16.
7   Nationality, Immigration and Asylum Act 2002, s 124, not yet in force, enabling an authority-to-carry scheme to be set up in which carriers would require advance authorisation to carry passengers.
8   Nationality, Immigration and Asylum Act 2002, s 126, enabling regulations to be made compelling passengers to provide external physical characteristics including irises. Regulations under the section so far only require provision of fingerprints; see fn 5 above.
9   UK Residence Permit scheme (formerly EU residence permit), with effect from 13 November 2003 (phase I). See 3.9 below.
10   For the specified nationals under Phase I: see 3.8 below.
11   Asylum and Immigration (Treatment of Claimants, etc) Act 2004, s 2, in force 22 September 2004. See 14.33 below.
12   *Secure Borders, Save Haven* (Cm 5387), February 2002.

3.2 Until the changes brought about by the Immigration and Asylum Act 1999, control on entry was exercised geographically and by particular personnel. Pre-entry control meant visas and entry clearance, always obtained abroad from entry clearance officers or visa officers. On-entry control meant the grant or refusal of leave to enter, always exercised at the port by immigration officers. Post-entry control, meaning the grant or variation of leave to remain (disregarding enforcement), was always exercised in the UK by the Secretary of State for the Home Department. The 1999 Act changes removed the geographical and to some extent the personnel nexus and eroded the boundaries between the forms of control. These boundaries have been further eroded by the 2002 and 2004 Acts. Now, entry clearance may operate as leave to enter. Leave to enter may be granted (or refused) before the traveller embarks for the UK or during the journey, and it may be granted or refused in the UK by the Secretary of State rather than an immigration officer. Leave does not normally lapse when the holder leaves the UK, but may be cancelled while the holder is abroad. An immigration officer at the port may grant, refuse, suspend or cancel leave to enter and may vary leave to remain on behalf of the Secretary of State. Leave may be varied by the Secretary of

State while the holder is abroad. The concept of extra-territorial immigration control has been taken considerably further by the extended use of 'juxtaposed controls' whose statutory derivation and impact are described more fully at 3.28 below. The implications for travellers are plain: it is more difficult to monitor examinations and control procedures conducted abroad to ensure their fairness and their compatibility with fundamental rights. Those attempting to access the UK in order to seek protection or re-unite with family members are effectively prevented from accessing UK protection procedures,[1] legal advice, or remedies for unlawful decisions. We comment elsewhere on the destructive effect that the carrier sanctions and airline liaison officer schemes have on those fleeing persecution or other ill-treatment, and on the protection duties of the UK.[2] Legislative changes have enabled the use of new technologies in controlling immigration: passengers from designated countries must now provide a biometric with their application for entry clearance, while leave to enter may now be granted by e-mail or telephone as well as by a stamp or sticker in the passport. These procedures need careful monitoring to ensure that injustice does not result from haste or lack of care in considering applications. However, the procedure at the port is likely to be speeded up considerably for those deemed 'low risk passengers',[3] and one effect of the increased use of new technologies is to put an end to the legal questions arising from illegible stamps. There is a comprehensive account of the law in this area in the 4th edition of this work at 3.47–3.60.

[1]   See eg *European Roma Rights Centre v Immigration Officer at Prague Airport* [2004] UKHL 55, [2005] 2 WLR 1; [2003] EWCA Civ 666, [2003] INLR 374
[2]   See 12.9 below.
[3]   For 'high risk' passengers see 3.3 and 3.21 below.

Discrimination

3.3 Immigration officers, entry clearance officers and all staff of the Home Office Immigration and Nationality Directorate (referred to throughout as IND) will, according to rule 2 of the Immigration Rules,[1] carry out their duties without regard to the race, colour or religion of persons seeking to enter or remain in the UK, and in compliance with the Human Rights Act 1998. However, section 19D of the Race Relations Act 1976 (as amended by the Race Relations (Amendment) Act 2000) allows officers acting in accordance with ministerial authorisation to discriminate on grounds of nationality or ethnic or national origins in carrying out immigration functions.[2] There has been concern for decades about assumptions, stereotypes and attitudes in the immigration service and among consular staff based on race and nationality or national origins,[3] and that concern continues.[4] The Independent Race Monitor warned in her second report against the 'self-perpetuating' nature of discrimination on grounds of nationality,[5] and Forbes J ruled in the *Tamil Information Centre* case[6] that the 'licence to discriminate' provided by the Act must be subject to strict control. Current ministerial authorisations, issued monthly since January 2003,[7] allow entry clearance and immigration officers to exercise coercive information-gathering powers on grounds of a passenger's nationality alone; immigration officers may conduct a more rigorous examination of entrants, detain them or impose conditions or restrictions on temporary admission on such grounds, and give priority to removing those passengers.[8]

1   HC 395, as amended by Cm 4851.
2   But no longer in relation to nationality functions: see Nationality, Immigration and Asylum Act 2002, s 6 deleting nationality from the permitted fields of discrimination and making further amendments to s 19 of the 1976 Act. The Concluding Observations of the UN Committee on the Elimination of Racial Discrimination (63rd session, Aug 2003, CERD/C/63/CO/11) recommended the abolition of s 19D 'to ensure full compliance with the Convention'.
3   See eg two Runnymede Trust sponsored studies in 1974 and 1978: *Where Do You Keep Your String Beds?* (1974) and *Appeal Dismissed* (1978). Commission for Racial Equality (CRE) *Report on Immigration Control Procedures* (1985); Joint Council for the Welfare of Immigrants *Target Caribbean* (1990); National Association of Citizens' Advice Bureaux *A right to family life* (1996).
4   See the House of Lords' finding of anti-Roma discrimination in relation to the pre-clearance scheme at Prague airport in *European Roma Rights Centre v Immigration Officer at Prague Airport* [2004] UKHL 55, [2005] 2 WLR 1; see 3.6 below.
5   Annual report of the independent race monitor, Mary Coussey, 2003/04, paras 11, 19.
6   *R (on the application of Tamil Information Centre) v Secretary of State for the Home Department* [2002] EWHC 2155 Admin, (2002) Times, 30 October.
7   See Race Relations Act 1976, section 19D Ministerial Authorisation, 25 July 2003, for the current criteria. The latest authorisation to be posted on the Home Office website at the time of writing, however, dates from 21 November 2002: IDI Feb 03, Ch 1, Annex EE1.
8   See 3.31 below.

LEAVE TO ENTER

3.4 Leave to enter is the cornerstone of UK immigration law. No one may enter the UK without leave except:

(i)   British citizens and Commonwealth citizens who have the right of abode;[1]

(ii)   persons arriving from Ireland or another part of the common travel area, in circumstances where leave is not required;[2]

(iii) persons exempt from control, such as diplomats, crew members and others;[3]

(iv)   persons exempt from the requirement of leave under section 7 of the Immigration Act 1988 (as set out in the Immigration (European Economic Area) Regulations 2000);[4]

(v)   prisoners being brought to the UK to give evidence in drug trafficking cases.[5]

Unfortunately, the description in the Immigration Rules of those requiring leave to enter continues to be inadequate, misleading and wrong,[6] although the IDI and the DSP fortunately give more accurate guidance.

1   Immigration Act 1971, ss 3(1), 2(1)(b), 2(2). See chapter 2 above.
2   Immigration Act 1971, s 9; Immigration (Control of Entry through Republic of Ireland) Order 1972, SI 1972/1610 as amended. See chapter 6 below.
3   Immigration Act 1971, s 8. For the full list see the Diplomatic Service Procedures, Entry Clearance, Volume 1, General Instructions (DSP), available on the UK Visas website, Ch.5 and annexe 5.1. See also chapter 6 below.
4   Ie, 'qualified persons' (EEA nationals entering the UK as workers, self-employed, to provide or receive services, students or self-sufficient persons, and their family members; SI 2000/2326, as amended by SI 2003/549, SI 2003/3188 (extending the definition of 'family members') and modified by 2002 SI 2002/1241 (extending EEA free movement rights to Swiss nationals), regs 12 and 14.
5   Criminal Justice (International Co-operation) Act 1990, s 6.

6   HC 395, para 7, as substituted by Cm 4851. It omits a number of categories of persons who do not require leave to enter the UK.

3.5 Leave to enter used only to be granted or refused on arrival in the UK. Arrival and entry are two distinct concepts in immigration law. Section 11 of the Immigration Act 1971 defines the point at which someone who arrives in this country is treated as having entered. First, it provides that persons arriving by ship or aircraft are not deemed to 'enter' unless and until they disembark.[1] Secondly, on disembarkation they are still deemed not to have entered so long as they remain in any part of the port which has been approved for use for immigration control. They only enter once they pass through immigration control. Thirdly, they will still not be treated as having entered if they are detained pending examination or removal or are temporarily admitted or released while liable to such detention.[2] This is of practical importance given the increasing use and length of temporary admission, and means that a person on temporary admission may be physically in the UK for years, and may have married and had children, but has not 'entered' for the purposes of section 11 and will still require leave to enter.[3]

1   Immigration Act 1971, s 11(1). For those coming by train through the Channel Tunnel, they 'enter' the UK when they leave a designated control area or stay on a through train after it has ceased to be in a control area: Immigration Act 1971, s 11(1), as modified by Channel Tunnel (International Arrangements) Order 1993, SI 1993/1813, Sch 4, para 1(5). See also, in relation to frontier controls between the UK, France and Belgium, the Channel Tunnel (Miscellaneous Provisions) Order 1994, SI 1994/1405, Art 7.
2   Immigration Act 1971, s 11(1) as amended by the Nationality, Immigration and Asylum Act 2002 to include detention by the Secretary of State under s 62 and temporary admission under s 68 of that Act.
3   In *R v Secretary of State for the Home Department, ex p Yiadom* (C-357/98) [2001] All ER (EC) 267, [2001] INLR 300, the ECJ condemned the 'fiction' of temporary admission, holding that an EU national so admitted was entitled to the safeguards attending expulsion on refusal of leave to enter: see 7.147 below. A period of temporary admission can count as lawful residence for the purpose of naturalisation under the British Nationality Act 1981: see the Nationality, Immigration and Asylum Act 2002, s 11(3); and see 3.3 above.

3.6 Now, however, leave to enter will be granted and refused in the country of departure in many cases. The Immigration (Leave to Enter and Remain) Order 2000,[1] made under section 3A of the Immigration Act 1971,[2] provides that leave to enter may be given or refused before the person leaves for or arrives in the UK. In most cases, entry clearance obtained at a British post abroad will operate as advance leave to enter.[3] However, there are other cases of advance leave or refusal of leave to enter, such as the pre-entry clearance scheme operated at airports of countries whose nationals did not require visas.[4] The 'juxtaposed controls' whereby UK immigration officers examine passengers seeking entry at French and Belgian ports do not operate by means of advance leave to enter, however, but by modifying the meaning of 'arrival' and 'entry' to include embarkation ports, called 'control zones'.[5] We deal with this at 3.27 below. The power to give or refuse leave to enter was previously to be exercised only by immigration officers but there is now provision for the power to be exercised by the Secretary of State (and his or her officers).[6] Immigration officers and the Secretary of State are authorised to examine applicants more rigorously, demand documents, or decline to grant or refuse advance leave to enter by reason of a person's nationality, if justified by statistical evidence showing adverse decisions against or breach of immigration laws by persons of that nationality.[7]

1 SI 2000/1161.
2 Inserted by Immigration and Asylum Act 1999, s 1.
3 Immigration (Leave to Enter and Remain) Order 2000, SI 2000/1161, Art 2.
4 See the notorious *European Roma Rights Centre* case [2003] EWCA Civ 666, [2003] INLR 374, in which the Court of Appeal endorsed this scheme and its objective of preventing Czech Roma asylum seekers from coming to the UK and, with Laws LJ dissenting, held that their intensive questioning and higher refusal rate (conducted without reference to a relevant ministerial authorisation under s 19D) were not racially discriminatory, but justified since (as Roma were more likely than others to be asylum seekers) they were more likely to lie about their intentions to get to the UK. But the House of Lords reversed the decision at [2004] UKHL 55, [2005] 2 WLR 1, holding that 'the operation was inherently and systemically discriminatory and unlawful' (per Lady Hale at para 97).
5 Through the Channel Tunnel (International Arrangements) Order 1993, SI 1993/1813, as amended, the Channel Tunnel (Miscellaneous Provisions) Order 1994, SI 1994/1405 and the Nationality, Immigration and Asylum Act 2002, s 141.
6 See the Immigration (Leave to Enter) Order 2001, SI 2001/2590, made under the Immigration Act 1971, s 3A (as inserted), enabling the Secretary of State to give or refuse leave to enter where an immigration officer has begun but not completed an examination. The most obvious application of the order is in relation to asylum claimants, whose claims are not dealt with by immigration officers at the port but referred to the Home Office. The provision enables Home Office civil servants to take the immigration decision (grant or refusal of leave to enter) at the same time as granting or refusing asylum, instead of (as before) having to return the papers to the port for the immigration officer to issue the relevant decision. The order includes consequential provisions designed to deal with the '24-hour rule', for which see 3.40 below.
7 See 3.3 above and 3.31 below.

3.7 Leave to enter may be granted for a limited or indefinite period.[1] If limited leave is given, it may be subject to conditions[2] restricting employment or occupation in the UK; requiring the holder to maintain and accommodate himself or herself and any dependants without recourse to public funds; or requiring him or her to register with the police.[3] Conditions will not be imposed by reason of the foreigner's nationality.[4] Indefinite leave to enter (or remain) may not be made subject to any conditions.

1 Immigration Act 1971, s 3(1)(b): leave may be limited in time (eg six months) or to a period of employment: see *R v Immigration Appeal Tribunal, ex p Coomasaru* [1983] 1 All ER 208, [1983] 1 WLR 14, CA.
2 The immigration officer may require a person arriving in the UK and granted leave to enter to submit to a medical examination after entry, under the Immigration Act 1971, Sch 2, para 7, but this is not a condition of leave under the 1971 Act. See IDI Mar 04, Ch 1, s 8, para 2.11.
3 Immigration Act 1971, s 3(1)(c); see Immigration Rules HC 395 (as amended by HC 194 from 4 February 2005), paras 325–326 and Appendix 2 (listing 'relevant foreign nationals' subject to registration requirements).
4 Letter from Beverley Hughes MP, then minister of state at the Home Office, to Immigration Law Practitioners' Association, 20 May 2003, announcing the deletion of that part of para 3(2)(e) of the ministerial authorisation which allowed an immigration officer to impose a condition or restriction on leave to enter by virtue of the passenger's nationality. The power to impose such a condition on temporary admission by virtue of nationality remains: see Race Relations Act 1976, section 19D Ministerial Authorisation, 25 July 2003, para 3(2)(e).

ENTRY CLEARANCE

3.8 As we indicated above, everyone seeking leave to enter for other than temporary purposes, and all visa nationals, will have had to obtain an entry clearance, which will, in most cases, operate as advance leave to enter.[1] By the end of 2005, entry clearance is planned to be mandatory for everyone seeking leave to enter the UK for more than six months.[2] Entry clearances under the Immigration Act 1971 consist of visas for visa nationals, stateless persons and refugees[3] and entry certificates for non-visa nationals and British nationals other than British citizens.[4] An entry clearance may be for a single journey or for multiple visits. A multiple entry visa is available for frequent visitors and is usually valid for a period of two years, although it may have a five or ten-year validity. It may be for simple visits or for business trips. Since October 2000, entry clearance has taken the form of a sticker or 'vignette' affixed to the passport or travel document.[5] There are two forms of vignette: uniform format visas (UFV)[6] (issued for visits, and for airside transit and transit visas, for which see 3.11 below), and Category D entry clearance (for long-stay visas, all categories of non-visa nationals and EEA family permits).[7] The entry clearance will be endorsed with the period of its validity (unless it is for indefinite leave to enter).[8] Before October 2000, an entry clearance which was not a multiple entry visa was only valid for one visit and was not re-usable for further visits within the same period.[9] The Immigration (Leave to Enter and Remain) Order 2000 provides that a visit visa which has effect as leave to enter is good for multiple entries within the period of its validity.[10] When the holder of an entry clearance arrives in the UK, admission is not automatic and entry to the UK may still be refused.[11]

1   HC 395, para 25A; Immigration (Leave to Enter and Remain) Order 2000, SI 2000/1161, Arts 2–4 as amended by SI 2004/475.
2   The first phase of the scheme, affecting the nationals of ten countries (Australia, Canada, Hong Kong (other than BNOs), Japan, Malaysia, New Zealand, Singapore, South Africa, South Korea and USA, came into force on 13 November 2003: HC 395 as amended by HC 1224, para 6, Appendix 3. These are referred to in the rules as 'specified nationals'.
3   See 3.10 below.
4   HC 395, para 25. The statutory definition in Immigration Act 1971, s 33(1) includes other documents but excludes a work permit.
5   IDI Jun 02, Ch 1 s 4, para 1.
6   IDI Ch 1, s 4, para 3. The UFV, issued in accordance with Council Regulation (EC) 1683/95 of 29 May 1995 laying down a uniform common format for visas, has visual and machine-readable fields, details of which are set out in the IDI.
7   Category D entry clearances are endorsed with the purpose and length of the permitted stay. They too have machine-readable fields (see IDI para 5).
8   Normally the visa or entry clearance is valid from the date of issue, but the ECO can delay the 'valid from' date for up to three months to correspond with the date of travel: IDI, Ch 1, s 4, para 4.4 (visit visas), 5.5 (Cat D ec).
9   *Andronicou* [1974] Imm AR 87, IAT.
10 SI 2000/1161, Art 4.
11 See below, 3.49 for grounds on which leave to enter may be refused to holders of entry clearance

3.9 Article 62 (formerly Article 73) of the Consolidated EC Treaty provides for (i) common lists of third countries whose nationals must possess a visa and for those who need not, (ii) common rules on the issue of short-stay visas, and (iii) a uniform format for visas. This Article is optional so far as the UK and Ireland are concerned,[1] but earlier EC Regulations on a uniform common format for visas[2] and on the third countries whose nationals must be in possession of a visa when crossing the external borders of the Member States,[3] are binding.

¹   See Protocol No 4 (1997) on the position of the UK and Ireland, providing that the UK and Ireland are not bound by any provision of Title IV (measures on immigration and asylum) but may opt in by giving notice. See chapter 7. Council Regulation (EC) 539/2001 of 15 March 2001, listing the third countries whose nationals must be in possession of visas when crossing the external orders and those whose nationals are exempt, does not apply in the UK and Ireland: see Preamble, para 4.
²   Council Regulation (EC) 1683/95, made under Art 100c of the EC Treaty.
³   Council Regulation (EC) 574/99, made under Art 100c of the EC Treaty.

Who needs entry clearance

3.10 Visa nationals require an entry clearance whatever the purpose of their travel to the UK and will normally be refused entry if they do not have one.[1] The list of visa countries is set out in Appendix 1 to the current Immigration Rules. It includes stateless persons and persons who hold non-national documents. This list is frequently amended and care should be taken to ensure that a particular country has not been added to the list or removed from it. Those who do not need a visa are:

(i)   returning residents (those with indefinite leave who return within two years of departure from the UK);[2]

(ii) those seeking to re-enter during the period of their original leave and for the same purpose, unless it was for a period of six months or less, or was granted by statute;[3]

(iii) those who obtained a visa and are re-entering the UK within the period of validity of their original visa and for the same purpose, unless it was for a period of six months or less, or was granted by statute;[4]

(iv) visitors returning to the UK within the period of validity of their visit visa;[5]

(v)   nationals of the People's Republic of China holding passports issued by the Hong Kong or Macao Special Administrative Region;[6]

(vi) schoolchildren who are visa nationals living in other EU States travelling in school groups, if the group is accompanied by a teacher and their names are included on the official form to be obtained by the school;[7]

(vii) foreign seamen settled in the UK who signed on in the UK who are discharging from a vessel or arriving as passengers having signed off abroad, foreign seamen arriving in the UK as crew members for discharge or for temporary shore leave, or those with a seafarer's identity document who come to join a ship in the UK, and aircrew who are to leave within seven days.[8]

Refugees resident in countries signatories to the Council of Europe Agreement on the Abolition of Visas for Refugees 1959 used not to require a visa for visits of three months or less, but the UK suspended its obligations under the Agreement in February 2003, since when such refugees have required visas to enter the UK.[9] If visa nationals arrive in the UK from Ireland and have no visa for the UK, they must obtain leave to enter.[10] Note that visa nationals will require a visa if they intend to enter the UK *en route* to another destination.[11]

¹   HC 395, para 24. The imposition of visa requirements on Commonwealth citizens under the Immigration Rule is not *ultra vires: R v Secretary of State for the Home Department, ex p Suresh Kumar* [1986] Imm AR 420, QBD. The discrimination inherent in the concept

of visa nationals, and in the differential treatment of applicants according to nationality, is made lawful in domestic law by s 19D of the Race Relations Act 1976 (inserted by the Race Relations (Amendment) Act 2000): see 3.3 above.

2   HC 395, as amended, Appendix 1, para 2(a).
3   HC 395, as amended, Appendix 1, para 2(b). See also SI 2000/1161, Art 13(2)–(4): for such persons, their original leave now does not lapse when they leave the UK, unless their leave was extended by the Secretary of State and after the extension, only six months or less was left, or it was extended by s 3C Immigration Act 1971 (as now substituted by Nationality, Immigration and Asylum Act 2002), s 118, ie statutory leave pending a decision on an application to vary, or pending appeal.
4   HC 395 as amended, Appendix 1, para 2(f) (which seems to add little if anything to para 2(b), fn 3 above); SI 2000/1161, Art 13(2)–(4).
5   SI 2000/1161, Art 4.
6   HC 395 as amended, Appendix 1, para 2(d) and (e), inserted by HC 735 on 16 April 2002.
7   IDI, Ch 1, s 4, para 8, Annex V para 4, referring to an EU Council Agreement to waive visa requirements. This concession is not incorporated into the rules.
8   See DSP (7 March 2003) Ch 22, and chapter 6 below.
9   See 12.103 below.
10   Immigration (Control of Entry through Republic of Ireland) Order 1972, SI 1972/1610, Art 3. See also *Mohan v Secretary of State for the Home Department* [1989] Imm AR 436. If they have gone from Ireland to one of the Islands without the appropriate visa, they require leave. If they fail to get it and proceed to the UK, they will be illegal entrants. See chapter 6 below.
11   Visitors in transit are dealt with at paras 47–49 of HC 395. The 'Transit Without a Visa' (TWOV) scheme (outside the rules) gives immigration officers discretion to allow visa nationals to transit the UK without requiring them to hold a visa for that purpose where the sole intention is to pass in transit between eg two airports in the UK if they have a confirmed booking on a flight departing within 24 hours to their country of destination, and the documents required to gain entry at that destination, including if appropriate any transit visa which may be required for any other country en route; or they are arriving on a cruise ship and intend to leave within 24 hours: DSP Ch 11.

TRANSIT VISAS

3.11 Nationals of particular countries[1] and holders of travel documents issued by certain authorities[2] designated under the Immigration (Passenger Transit Visa) Order 2003[3] must obtain a direct airside transit visa (DATV) when passing through the UK to another country, even though they do not enter.[4] There are a number of exemptions: those with the right of abode in the UK, EEA nationals, citizens of the People's Republic of China with passports issued by the Special Administrative Region of Hong Kong or Macao,[5] those with valid visas for Australia, New Zealand, the US or Canada and tickets to travel there via the UK,[6] those with residence rights in Australia, New Zealand, the US, Canada or an EEA Member State, and others.[7]

1   The list of countries, set out in Sch 1 to the Immigration (Passenger Transit Visa) Order 2003, SI 2003/1185 as amended by SI 2003/2628, SI 2004/1304 and SI 2005/492 is: Afghanistan, Albania, Algeria, Angola, Bangladesh, Belarus, Burma, Burundi, Cameroon, Colombia, Congo, Democratic Republic of Congo, Ecuador, Eritrea, Ethiopia, Former Yugoslav Republic of Macedonia, Gambia, Ghana, Guinea, Guinea-Bissau, India, Iran, Iraq, Ivory Coast, Kenya, Lebanon, Liberia, Moldova, Mongolia, Nepal, Nigeria, Pakistan, Palestine Territories, People's Republic of China, Rwanda, Senegal, Serbia and Montenegro, Sierra Leone, Somalia, Sri Lanka, Sudan, Tanzania, Turkey, Uganda, Vietnam and Zimbabwe.
2   The authorities are the 'purported Turkish Republic of Northern Cyprus, the former Socialist Republic of Yugoslavia, the former Federal Republic of Yugoslavia and the former Zaire: Immigration (Passenger Transit Visa) Order 2003, SI 2003/1185 as amended, Art 2(3).

³ SI 2003/1185 as amended.
⁴ SI 2003/1185 as amended, made under Immigration and Asylum Act 1999, s 41.
⁵ SI 2003/1185 as amended, Art 2(4).
⁶ The requirements for the exemptions are fairly detailed, and are set out in full in SI 2003/1185 as amended, Art 3A.
⁷ Other categories include those travelling from Australia, New Zealand, the US or Canada within six months of their last admission there, who have a valid visa for their destination country, and persons with diplomatic or service passports issued by the PRC, India or Vietnam: SI 2003/1185 as amended, Art 3A(b), (g)–(i).

3.12 Most non-visa nationals have no need for an entry clearance if they come for a visit, to study or for certain other temporary purposes, or are returning residents or are born in the UK. Entry clearance is necessary for all other purposes.[1] Non-visa nationals from ten countries (referred in the immigration rules as 'specified nationals') seeking leave to enter for over six months for any purpose require entry clearance,[2] and by the end of 2005, this requirement is planned to be universal for those seeking to enter for more than six months.[3] Non-visa nationals and non-specified nationals who do not need entry clearance may obtain one if they wish to ascertain in advance that they satisfy the requirements for leave.[4] The fact that entry clearance is made mandatory for almost all purposes in the Immigration Rules is not unlawful. The courts have held that it is not *ultra vires* the Secretary of State's rule-making power, either as being an unlawful delegation of power to entry clearance officers or as a fetter on the discretionary powers of immigration officers to give or refuse leave to enter under section 4(1) of the Immigration Act 1971.[5] First, the Home secretary, as the rule maker, still has a residual discretion whether or not to make an exception in the circumstances of the particular case.[6] Secondly, the immigration officers' discretion is retained in the new dispensation, where entry clearance operates as leave to enter,[7] through their power to cancel leave.[8]

¹ Entry clearance requirements are set out for entry in all immigration categories as they are dealt with: see chapters 9–11 below.
² HC 395, para 24, as amended by HC 1224, Appendix 3 (as inserted). The nationals specified in the Appendix are those of Australia, Canada, Hong Kong (other than BN(O)s), Japan, Malaysia, New Zealand, Singapore, South Africa, South Korea, USA.
³ This accompanies the introduction of UK Residence Permits, as from 13 November 2003, following a new common EU-wide format to allow easy identification across the EU. See ministerial written statement: changes to immigration practice, June 2003, Annex B.
⁴ See HC 395, para 23A (inserted by HC 1224).
⁵ See *R v Secretary of State for the Home Department, ex p Rofathullah* [1989] QB 219, [1988] Imm AR 514, CA; *R v Secretary of State for the Home Department, ex p Ounejma* [1989] Imm AR 75, DC. See further *R v Secretary of State for the Home Department, ex p Kaur* [1987] Imm AR 278, DC, a challenge to the *vires* of rules made under the Commonwealth Immigrants Act 1962.
⁶ See *Pearson v Immigration Appeal Tribunal* [1978] Imm AR 212, at 225, per Stephenson LJ, CA; *R v Port of London Authority, ex p Kynoch Ltd* [1919] 1 KB 176, at 184, per Bankes LJ; *British Oxygen Co Ltd v Board of Trade* [1971] AC 610.
⁷ Immigration (Leave to Enter and Remain) Order 2000, SI 2000/1161, Art 6; HC 395, para 25A (inserted by HC 704); see 3.22 below.
⁸ Under Immigration Act 1971, Sch 2, para 2A, inserted by Immigration and Asylum Act 1999, Sch 14, para 57.

Making an application for entry clearance

3.13 Applications for entry clearance are to be considered in accordance with the provisions of the Immigration Rule relating to the grant or refusal of leave to enter, subject to the Human Rights Act 1998, and the term 'entry clearance officer' may be substituted for the term 'immigration officer' where this is appropriate.[1] To qualify for the grant of an entry clearance as a visitor, family member, business person or whatever, the person must fulfil the requirements of the particular Immigration Rule which deals with that particular type of entrant. But qualifying in this way may not be enough. Entry clearance may still be refused on a number of general grounds which apply across the board. These are described at 3.49ff below.

[1]   HC 395, para 26.

Where to apply

3.14 First, all applicants must be outside the UK and Islands at the time of application.[1] Secondly, the application has to be made to the British Embassy or High Commission, a British Consular post or special authorised person outside the UK and Islands.[2] A list of designated posts is published by the Foreign and Commonwealth Office.[3] A distinction is made between visit entry clearances and others. Visitors, transit passengers and applicants for EEA family permits can apply to any post designated by the Secretary of State to accept applications from that category of applicants. They do not need to be in the country where they live. All other visa applications have to be made in the country where the applicant 'is living', unless there is no designated post in that country able to receive applications for that purpose from that category of applicants. Then the visa can be applied for and obtained elsewhere.[4] DSPs state that 'where they live' means 'the place where a person is present in any capacity other than as a short term visitor and has permission from the relevant authorities to be so present'.[5] Closure of some embassies following attacks, and heightened security in others, has led to lengthy delays and severe difficulties for applicants in a number of countries.[6] In particular cases, it may be necessary for advisers to contact the Embassy or Consulate concerned to ascertain the prevailing practice but it should normally be sufficient to refer to the DSP and contact UKVisas (the joint initiative of the FCO and Home Office) in the event of difficulty.[7]

[1]   HC 395, para 28.
[2]   HC 395, para 29.
[3]   It is available on the UKVisas website, whose address is www.ukvisas.gov.uk.
[4]   For example, since 1991 Somalis have applied for entry clearance to posts at Addis Ababa and Nairobi. Under the Somali Family Reunion policy which operated until 1994, UK sponsors obtained indications from the Home Office on the likely outcome of visa applications which were then formally made at the post: see *Secretary of State for the Home Department v Dahir and Abdi* [1995] Imm AR 570, CA. Until 1 November 1999 a concession allowed Vietnamese refugees in the UK to apply direct to the Home Office by letter for their relatives in Vietnam to join them, but all such concessions have now been withdrawn: API *Family Reunion*.
[5]   DSP, Ch 8, para 8.1. An unreasonable refusal to entertain an application where an applicant is not living (because of insuperable difficulties in compliance) might be challengeable if fundamental human rights were at issue. See chapter 8 below.
[6]   After attacks on embassy premises, visa offices in Pakistan were closed in May 2002 and applications were made through a private contractor, Gerry's Fedex. As at May 2005 the British High Commission Islamabad was accepting visa applications in all categories save working holiday makers and first time visitors under 25. In *R (on the application of Mire) v Entry Clearance Officer, Kampala* [2002] EWHC 3157 (Admin) (permission hearing),

the policy of preventing would-be applicants without a valid national passport or refugee card or laissez-passer from UNHCR from entering the British High Commissions in Kampala and Nairobi because of the security threat was upheld as reasonable. Following the attack on the British Consulate in Istanbul in November 2003, the Consulate in Ankara was accepting only limited applications, by post or courier service only, excluding applications from spouses; in December 2003 the Home Office indicated that although it would not waive the requirement for entry clearance, it would consider granting discretionary leave to spouses already in the UK who satisfied the other requirements of the rule, until consular services were resumed: Beverley Hughes (then Minister of State at the Home Office) to Fiona Mactaggart MP, 10 December 2003.

7   See the UK Visas website, fn 3 above.

3.15 Fees are charged for the issue of visas and entry clearances.[1] Previously this requirement applied only to aliens, but from 1 January 1985 Commonwealth citizens have also been charged. Posts have a discretion to waive fees where appropriate. All fees and gratis visas are now listed on the UK Visas website. Visa fees are not payable where the sponsor in the UK has been recognised as a refugee and the applicants are coming as his or her dependants.[2] There is a reduced fee for dependants of those on exceptional leave.[3] There is power to waive the fee in other circumstances.[4] An application for entry clearance is not made until any fees have been paid.[5] The level of fees charged for family settlement may be prohibitive in some cases, for example, where a spouse and a number of dependent children seek entry, and could constitute a disproportionate obstacle to the right to respect for family life. Refusal by an entry clearance officer to process an application in such circumstances could, we suggest, be susceptible to challenge by way of judicial review.[6]

1   The Consular Fees Order 2002, SI 2002/1627 sets out the current fees, which range from £36 for a single entry visit or student visa to £260 for a settlement visa for a spouse, fiancé(e) or child.
2   *Abdi* (11000); *Ibrahim* (9347). The rules on refugee family reunion are silent on this, but see DSP Ch 7.4(g), which states that refugees and their pre-flight dependants qualify for waiver.
3   DSP Ch 7.2 and Ch 16. The fee for immediate family members of people with exceptional leave to remain is £75.00.
4   The list of persons to be granted gratis visas, set out in the DSP at Ch 7, is a motley one, including reputable journalists, members of Anglophile societies, nationals of Kyrgistan and destitute persons. Joint Entry Clearance Unit (JECU) guidance on destitution is that it is for the applicant to pay the fee or demonstrate destitution, and the ECO is entitled to consider what support the applicant may reasonably expect to receive from the sponsor. For this purpose ECOs should seek details of any savings held by the sponsor. If the sponsor is paying for the applicant's travel, the ability to pay the entry clearance fee 'should be inferred'. Receipt of income support by the sponsor point to but are not conclusive of financial incapacity: JECU Operations Section draft guidance to posts, Jan 2002.
5   HC 395, para 30, reversing *Entry Clearance Officer, Port Louis v Ross* [1992] Imm AR 493, IAT. However, an immigration rule does not change the law; it merely changes the practice, and a reading of the DSP, especially para 8.2, suggests that r 30 of HC 359 does not accurately describe the practice. For example, you cannot consider whether fees should be waived for reasons of destitution, without having an application before you to consider. A better description of the practice would be that the ECO will not normally consider an application before the fees are paid. That interpretation of the practice would not stop the application being 'made' or 'received' before that date.
6   A consent order was made in *R v British Embassy Addis Ababa, ex p Jama*, CO 3338/1999, on the FCO accepting that the applicant was destitute.

The application

3.16 The date when an application for entry clearance is made is important because, although the key date for judging whether someone is eligible for a visa or entry certificate is usually the date of the decision rather than the date of the application,[1] the date of the application may count in certain cases.[2] For example, in the case of a child wishing to join parents who are settled in the UK, eligibility will depend upon the age of the applicant at the time when the application for entry clearance is made, and an application may not be refused solely on account of an applicant becoming over-age between the date of the application and the date of the decision on it.[3] The rules for entry clearance applications, unlike those for variations of leave from persons already in the UK, do not prescribe the use of particular forms, so that although the overseas posts all have stocks of standard forms (and the forms are available for downloading from the UK Visas website) their use is not mandatory. Before HC 395 the case law had established that an application for entry clearance did not require any particular formality, merely a request 'in quite unambiguous terms for an entry certificate to be issued to a particular person'.[4] The Court of Appeal has held, however, that an inquiry by relatives in the UK as to the likely outcome of an application for entry clearance and a reply from the Home Office did not amount to an application.[5] The Rules attempt to overcome the uncertainties of the case law by saying that an application is not made until the fees are paid.[6] Where there are local difficulties which make it impossible to enclose the fee with the postal application an exception may be made. Also where a delay between the receipt of the application and the fee places the applicant outside the rules (eg regarding an age requirement) the date of receipt of the *application* form should be treated as the material date of application provided that the applicant attends and pays the fee on the appointed day.[7] Applications made to posts in specified countries must be accompanied by a record of the applicant's fingerprints.[8] Failure to provide fingerprints entitles the entry clearance officer to treat the application as invalid.[9]

1   HC 395, para 27.
2   In *R v Immigration Appeal Tribunal, ex p Bibi and Purvez* [1986] Imm AR 61, DC the date of application was used to determine whether the Pakistani wife and children of a Commonwealth citizen settled in the UK on 1 January 1973 should be treated as Commonwealth citizens or aliens. The date of application is often the important date in transitional provisions for new rules and policies.
3   HC 395, para 27. For some unexplained reason, children of students, work permit holders, businessmen, etc do not benefit from the concession in para 27, although refusal of admission in these categories on the ground that the child has become over-age by the date of decision may be irrational and unfair, and may also engage Art 8 of the ECHR.
4   *Brown v Entry Clearance Officer, Kingston* [1976] Imm AR 119; *Prajapati v Immigration Appeal Tribunal* [1982] Imm AR 56, CA; *Malik v Secretary of State for the Home Department* [1982] Imm AR 183. See further *R v Immigration Appeal Tribunal, ex p Kobir* [1986] Imm AR 311, QBD.
5   *Secretary of State for the Home Department v Dahir and Abdi* [1995] Imm AR 570. See 3.13 fn 4 above.
6   HC 395, para 30.
7   DSP Ch 8 at para 8.2.
8   See the Immigration (Provision of Physical Data) Regulations 2003, SI 2003/1875 as amended by SI 2004/474 and SI 2004/1834, made under Nationality, Immigration and Asylum Act 2002, s 126 specifying applications made in Djibouti, Eritrea, Ethiopia, Kenya, Rwanda, Sri Lanka, Tanzania and Uganda. Children under 16 may only be fingerprinted in

the presence of a parent, guardian or other responsible adult: SI 2003/1875, reg 4. The government proposes to extend this requirement to all visa applicants by 2008: see *Controlling our borders: Making migration work for Britain: Five year strategy for asylum and immigration*, Cm 6472, Feb 2005.
9   SI 2003/1875 as amended, reg 5.

3.17 Once an application for entry clearance is made, it must be considered by the visa or entry clearance officer.[1] Sponsorship and other documentation must be in place.[2] Often there will be an interview. In spouse and family cases it is a central feature of the application. Like immigration officers, entry clearance officers have a duty to be fair. Like immigration officers, they are under a duty not to act in a way which breaches a person's fundamental human rights,[3] nor in a way which discriminates on grounds of race or colour.[4] In the interview the entry clearance officer should check that the person being interviewed is well and understands the questions. Unfair questions should not be put. Leading questions do not particularly advance the case against an applicant or assist the interview, but entry clearance officers are carrying out administrative, not judicial, functions and there is, therefore, nothing improper in asking such questions.[5] An entry clearance officer should afford an applicant an opportunity to address any adverse evidence or conclusions which will affect his or her decision.[6] The conduct of interviews will now also be subject to the scrutiny of the Independent Race Monitor,[7] and (in cases where there is no right of appeal) of the Entry Clearance Monitor.[8] Complaints are to be directed to UK Visas.[9]

1   DSPs, Ch 8, paras 8.2 and 8.5 provide that applications for entry clearance should routinely be screened before acceptance in order to avoid the costs and other adverse implications of a formal refusal. Only a formal refusal will give rise to rights of appeal, but appeal rights will accrue (subject to the statutory exceptions) despite an application not having been made in accordance with the geographical, financial or other procedural requirements of the rules.
2   The UK Visas website contains all the relevant leaflets which give guidance as to documentation required: www.ukvisas.gov.uk.
3   Human Rights Act 1998, s 6(1).
4   Race Relations Act 1976, s 19B, inserted by Race Relations (Amendment) Act 2000. However, s 19D allows discrimination on grounds of nationality, ethnic or national origin in the performance of immigration functions, making the amendment of little value. See Dummett, *The immigration exemptions in the Race Relations (Amendment) Act 2000*, ILPA, April 2001.
5   *Kumar v Entry Clearance Officer, New Delhi* [1985] Imm AR 242.
6   *R v Secretary of State for the Home Department, ex p Moon* [1997] INLR 165; see also *Secretary of State for the Home Department v Thirukumar* [1989] Imm AR 270, QBD, 402, CA (on entry); *R v Secretary of State for the Home Department, ex p Fayed* [1997] 1 All ER 228, CA.
7   Race Relations Act 1976, s 19E, inserted by Race Relations Amendment Act 2000, s 1. Annual reports are published on the Home Office website.
8   The annual reports of the Independent Monitor (currently Fiona Lindsley) are published on the UK Visas website. The reports usefully analyse refusal of entry clearance by nationality as well as pointing to problems such as the wrongful denial of appeal rights.
9   UK Visas, Foreign & Commonwealth Office, King Charles Street, London SWA 2AH and see the email links on the website.

3.18 Although entry clearance officers are applying the Immigration Rules, this is not a mechanical exercise of applying rules to the facts of applications as presented to them. They are entitled to and do carry out their own investigations,[1] sometimes arranging DNA tests (with the applicant's consent)[2] or making surprise village visits.[3] Sometimes these will prove the existence of a relationship previously in doubt, but their inquiries may also prove that an applicant is disqualified in some other way, for example, because a child seeking entry to join a parent has married. Usually entry clearance officers are not precluded from acting on the results of their investigations.[4] Applications may also be referred back to the Home Office for inquiries to be made in the UK, for guidance to be given in a complicated case or because of a special policy.[5]

[1]   *R v Immigration Appeal Tribunal, ex p Hoque and Singh* [1988] Imm AR 216, CA.
[2]   *For DNA testing in the context of family reunion applications see IDI Ch 8 Annex N.*
[3]   See eg IDI Dec 04, Ch 8, Annex X which deals with village visits in dependent relatives' applications.
[4]   *R v Immigration Appeal Tribunal, ex p Kobir* [1986] Imm AR 311, QBD. But they should not act on anonymous denunciations or statements made by persons who are not prepared for the applicant to be aware of their evidence: IDI Sep 04, Ch 9, s 1, 'Adverse decisions', para 2.2. The DSP Ch 8 para 8.14 suggest a slightly different approach to denunciations, ie, not to mention them in refusals even where they may have been taken into account.
[5]   For the circumstances in which referral is likely, see DSP Ch 25.

3.19 In the past, applications by persons seeking to enter the UK for marriage caused problems if applicants were unsure how long they intended to remain in the UK after marriage. At one time the Tribunal said that the onus was on applicants to define their position and bring themselves within either the visit or the fiancé rule,[1] but this approach has since been held to be a misapplication of the Rules.[2] Applicants do have to make clear the factual foundation of what they want, but applications are not formal documents and there is certainly no need for an applicant to specify any applicable Immigration Rule. That, it is thought, is the task of the entry clearance officer, who, like an immigration officer, must consider all relevant rules without having to conduct a roving expedition through all conceivably relevant rules.[3]

[1]   *Hussain v Entry Clearance Officer, Islamabad* [1989] Imm AR 46.
[2]   *R v Immigration Appeal Tribunal, ex p Rafique* [1990] Imm AR 235, QBD. There is now specific provision in the Immigration Rules for visits for marriage, see HC 395, paras 56D–F, inserted by HC 346 from 15 March 2005.
[3]   *Ali v Secretary of State for the Home Department* [1988] Imm AR 274, CA. An application should not be refused where someone unfamiliar with the rules asks for more than the rules permit, eg when a spouse seeks settlement rather than entry for the probationary period: IDI Sep 04, Ch 9, s 1, para 6.

3.20 Where there has already been a successful application but the entry clearance was for some reason not used, and the applicant has had to re-apply, the previous application is strong evidence in favour of the applicant.[1] Where an applicant has successfully appealed against the refusal of entry clearance, it is wholly improper for an attempt to be made to circumvent the adjudicator's decision by pursuing fresh inquiries with a view to denying entry on a different basis, but in such cases entry clearance officers are entitled to ask questions in order to see if there has been a change of circumstances or there has been fraud or deception.[2] All this means that there may be considerable delay before applications are decided. The queues in India, Pakistan and Bangladesh are notorious and result in inordinate delay in some cases.[3] The existence of delay, however, does not invalidate the need for entry clearance,[4] although in a particular case it might give rise to a challenge on the ground of unfairness, and failure to take a decision after a reasonable period of time may be challenged by an application for a mandatory order.

1   *Visa Officer, Islamabad v Channo Bi* [1978] Imm AR 182; *Begum (Sarwar)* [1986] Imm AR 192.
2   *R v Secretary of State for the Home Department, ex p Yousuf* [1989] Imm AR 554, QBD.
3   The longest waiting time for interviews as at 30 June 2004 was at Dhaka (45 weeks for settlement): UK Visas website. See also 3.14 above.
4   *R v Secretary of State for the Home Department, ex p Rofathullah* [1989] QB 219, [1988] Imm AR 514, CA.

Revocation of entry clearance

3.21   After an entry clearance has been issued, an entry clearance officer may revoke it[1] if satisfied that:

(i)   whether or not to the holder's knowledge false representations were employed or material facts were not disclosed, either in writing or orally, for the purpose of obtaining the entry clearance; or

(ii)   a change of circumstances since the issue of the entry clearance has removed the basis for admission to the UK, except where the change of circumstances amounts solely to a child coming for settlement becoming over-age since the issue of the entry clearance; or

(iii)   the holder's exclusion from the UK would be conducive to the public good.

There is no right of appeal against a decision to revoke or cancel entry clearance.[2] In order to prevent unfair circumvention of appeal rights, policy guidance is that where revocation is necessary (and the power to do so should be exercised sparingly), the application should be reconsidered immediately and, where appropriate, a formal refusal issued, triggering appeal rights.[3] Failure to follow the policy could render revocation vulnerable to challenge by way of judicial review. The rule enabling entry clearance to be revoked or cancelled before departure for the UK is similar to (although not as extensive as) immigration officers' powers to refuse leave to enter to an entry clearance holder.[4]

1   HC 395, para 30A, added by HC 329 from 3 June 1996.
2   It is not an immigration decision for the purposes of Nationality, Immigration and Asylum Act 2002, s 82. See also IDI, Ch 1, s 4, para 10.1.
3   See IDI above, para 10.1.
4   See 3.49 below.

ENTRY CLEARANCE AS LEAVE TO ENTER

3.22   Section 3A of the Immigration Act 1971 (inserted by section 1 of the Immigration and Asylum Act 1999) created 'greater flexibility in the way permission to enter the UK may be granted'[1] by empowering the Secretary of State to make Orders which (inter alia) allow entry clearance to have effect as leave to enter the UK, thereby reducing the role of immigration officers at the port of entry. The substance of the provision is contained in the subordinate legislation, the Immigration (Leave to Enter and Remain) Order 2000.[2] Under this Order, entry clearance will have effect as leave to enter provided it specifies the purpose for which the holder wishes to enter the UK[3] and is endorsed with the conditions to which it is subject,[4] or a statement that it is to have effect as indefinite leave to enter the UK.[5] Entry clearances which do not operate as leave to enter are those endorsed on refugees' Convention travel documents on or after 27 February 2004,[6] certificates of entitlement, EEA family permits, exempt visas[7] and direct airside transit visas.[8] Visit visas are to have effect as leave to enter on an unlimited number of occasions during their period of validity[9] unless issued pursuant to the 'ADS agreement with China.[10] Leave to enter as a visitor will be for a period of six months where six months or more remain of the visa's period of validity and, where less than six months remain, for the remaining period.[11] Entry clearances for purposes other than visit(s) are, according to the Order, to have effect as leave to enter the UK on one occasion only during the period of their validity,[12] whether that leave to enter is for an indefinite period[13] or endorsed with conditions.[14] In practice, such entry clearances operate as leave to enter on every entry during the period of leave which they grant, since such leave does not lapse on the holder's departure.[15]

1   Explanatory notes to the Immigration and Asylum Act 1999, para 7.
2   SI 2000/1161, as amended by SI 2004/475.
3   SI 2000/1161, Art 3(2).
4   SI 2000/1161, Art 3(2)(a).
5   SI 2000/1161, Art 3(2)(b). For power to refuse on the basis of nationality, see 3.3 above.
6   SI 2000/1161, Art 3(4), inserted by SI 2004/475. This does not apply to holders of travel documents issued by the UK, who do not require entry clearance.
7   Because such passengers do not require leave to enter. See IDI Jun 02, Ch 1, s 4, para 2.
8   Because such passengers do not enter the UK (within the meaning of Immigration Act 1971, s 11(1)). See IDI above, para 2.
9   SI 2000/1161, Art 4(1). 'Period of validity' is defined in Art 4 as 'the period beginning on the day which the entry clearance becomes effective and ending on the day on which it expires'. Most visit visas only run for six months, but can run for up to five years for frequent travellers. Normally the 'valid from' date is the date of issue, but the ECO may delay this date for up to three months to correspond with the date of travel: IDI, Ch 1, s 4, para 4.4. If this has not been done and a visitor had less than six months left on entry to the UK, he or she may be granted a short extension to make up the full six months: IDI, Ch 1, s 9, para 2.7.
10 SI 2005/1159, Immigration (Leave to Enter & Remain) (Amendment) Order 2005 in force 1 April 2005, limiting visit visas, granted under the Approved Destination Status (ADS) 'tourist groups' agreement with China, to leave to enter on one or two occasions only, as endorsed.
11 SI 2000/1161, Art 4(2). See fn 9 above. Visitors under the ADS agreement above will be granted 30-day visas: HC 395, para 56G, inserted by HC 486 from 5 April 2005.
12 SI 2000/1161 Art 4(3).
13 SI 2000/1161, Art 4(3)(a).
14 SI 2000/1161, Art 4(3)(b). The conditions which can be imposed will be those which can be imposed on leave to enter under Immigration Act 1971, s 3(1)(c), ie restricting employment, precluding recourse to public funds and requiring registration with police.
15 SI 2000/1161, Art 13. See 4.5 below.

3.23   Where entry clearance operates as leave to enter, the immigration officer may examine the holder at the port to decide whether the leave to enter should be cancelled.[1] An immigration officer may cancel an entry clearance, if the holder arrives in the UK before the day on which it becomes effective,[2] or seeks leave to enter for a different purpose.[3] In the former case, if satisfied that the passenger is seeking entry on the same basis and qualifies for leave to enter, the immigration officer may, while cancelling the entry clearance, grant leave to enter.[4] If leave is sought for a different purpose, the immigration officer would normally cancel the entry clearance, unless it is appropriate to grant leave to enter exceptionally without entry clearance.[5] Other criteria for cancellation of entry clearance operating as leave to enter are stricter. For detailed consideration of these grounds see 3.44–3.47 below. Where entry clearance operates as leave to enter, cancellation by an immigration officer on entry attracts a right of appeal, which was exercisable from the UK,[6] but no longer is, since section 28 of the Asylum and Immigration (Treatment of Claimants, etc) Act 2004 came into force, in cases where there has been deception or a change of circumstances or entry is sought for a different purpose than that for which the entry clearance was granted.[7] We deal with cancellation of leave and port examinations below. Where entry clearance does not operate as leave to enter (for example, where it is endorsed on a Convention travel document),[8] when the holder seeks leave to enter it may be refused on the same grounds as those on which the entry clearance officer may revoke entry clearance, set out at 3.18 above. These are that false representations were made or material facts not disclosed for the purpose of obtaining entry clearance, or that there has been a relevant change in circumstances, or that exclusion is conducive to the public good. These grounds are considered in detail below, together with the additional grounds on which leave to enter may be refused, or cancelled, where entry clearance operated as leave to enter.

[1]   Immigration Act 1971 Sch 2, para 2A (inserted by Immigration and Asylum Act 1999, amended by Nationality, Immigration and Asylum Act 2002).
[2]   Immigration (Leave to Enter and Remain) Order 2000, Art 6(2)(a); HC 395 para 30C, inserted by HC 704.
[3]   SI 2000/1161 Art 6(2)(b).
[4]   See IDI, Ch 1, s 4, para 10.3.
[5]   See IDI, Ch 1, s 4, para 10.3.
[6]   Nationality, Immigration and Asylum Act 2002 s 82(2)(a) read with s 92(3) and Immigration Act 1971, Sch 2, para 2A(8), (9) (inserted by Immigration and Asylum Act 1999, amended by Nationality, Immigration and Asylum Act 2002), prior to amendment by 2004 Act.
[7]   Nationality, Immigration and Asylum Act 2002, s 92(3), (3A), (3B) as inserted by s 28 Asylum and Immigration (Treatment of Claimants, etc) Act 2004 from 1 October 2004: SI 2004/2523).
[8]   SI 2000/1161, Art 3(4).

Other advance grant (or refusal) of leave

3.24 We saw at 3.6 above that, quite apart from the entry clearance system and co-existing with it, section 3A of the Immigration Act 1971, inserted by the Immigration and Asylum Act 1999, gave the Secretary of State the power to introduce a scheme enabling immigration officers to grant or refuse leave to enter extra-territorially.[1] The immigration rules provide that 'where a person is outside the UK but wishes to travel to the UK an immigration officer may give or refuse him leave to enter ...'.[2] The provisions were implemented at Prague airport, by agreement with the Czech government, and were used to refuse numbers of Czech Roma would-be passengers leave to enter the UK before they boarded (and to stop them from doing so). The House of Lords held that the system of 'pre-entry clearance' checks as operated at Prague Airport was unlawful and discriminatory, overturning the majority decision in the Court of Appeal.[3]

1   See Immigration (Leave to Enter and Remain) Order 2000, SI 2000/1161, Art 7 (made under Immigration Act 1971, s 3A as inserted).
2   HC 395, para 17A, inserted by HC 704.
3   *European Roma Rights Centre v Immigration Officer at Prague Airport* [2004] UKHL 55, [2005] 2 WLR 1.

Pre-arrival immigration checks and juxtaposed controls

3.25 The other way in which immigration controls have been made extra-territorial is through provisions which deem parts of Europe as ports of entry for immigration control purposes. These provisions initially related to the Channel Tunnel but have been expanded to include other ports of embarkation for the UK. What these provisions do is to make parts of French and Belgian territory, trains travelling through it and potentially part of every EEA port of embarkation for the UK, effectively part of the UK for immigration purposes.

The Channel Tunnel

3.26 The Channel Tunnel Act 1987, passed to implement the Canterbury Treaty of 12 February 1986, included provision for the construction and operation of the Channel Tunnel; for the incorporation of the British part of the tunnel system into England and the district of Kent and for English law to apply accordingly;[1] for the application and enforcement of law in relation to it and otherwise for the regulation of the tunnel system and matters connected with it. The principal order made under the Act is the Channel Tunnel (International Arrangements) Order 1993,[2] which came into force on 2 August 1993, initially covering arrangements with France, but amended by the Channel Tunnel (Miscellaneous Provisions) Order 1994[3] so as to cover both France and Belgium.

1   Channel Tunnel Act 1987, s 10.
2   SI 1993/1813, as amended by the Channel Tunnel (Security) Order 1994, SI 1994/570, and the Channel Tunnel (International Arrangements) (Amendment) Orders, SI 1996/2283, SI 2000/913, SI 2000/1775, SI 2001/178, SI 2001/418, SI 2001/1544, SI 2001/3707 and SI 2004/2589.
3   SI 1994/1405.

3.27 The Channel Tunnel (International Arrangements) Order 1993[1] incorporates into UK law[2] the terms of the agreements between France and the UK for the running of the tunnel system and associated policing and immigration control, referred to as the 'International Articles' being the incorporated parts of the Sangatte Protocol[3] and Additional Protocol.[4] The Order and its 1994 counterpart[5] enable UK immigration officers to operate on French and Belgian territory and vice versa and allow immigration controls to be carried out on the trains running between London, Calais, Paris and Lille,[6] and Brussels. The Orders extend the powers of immigration officers under the Immigration

Act 1971 to carry out immigration control within 'control zones' (and supplementary control zones) within French and Belgian territory.[7] A 'control zone' means that part of French or Belgian territory within which immigration officers (and now also the Secretary of State for the Home Department)[8] are empowered to effect immigration and other controls.[9] The provisions of the Immigration Act 1971 are modified in relation to those entering and leaving through the tunnel system, so as to include leaving a control zone in the definition of entry,[10] and to allow examination, and the grant, refusal or cancellation of leave, to take place in control zones as if they were at the port of entry in the UK.[11] The Additional Protocol to the Sangatte Protocol, which came into force in May 2001, provides for the establishment of control bureaux at Waterloo, St Pancras and Ashford, in UK territory, and in Paris Gare du Nord, Calais and Lille in French territory.[12]

[1] SI 1993/1813, as amended by the Channel Tunnel (Security) Order 1994, SI 1994/570, and the Channel Tunnel (International Arrangements) (Amendment) Orders, SI 1996/2283, SI 2000/913, SI 2000/1775, SI 2001/178, SI 2001/418, SI 2001/1544 SI 2001/3707 and SI 2004/2589.
[2] SI 1993/1813, Art 3(1).
[3] Signed at Sangatte on 25 November 1991.
[4] Signed at Brussels on 29 May 2000.
[5] Channel Tunnel (Miscellaneous Provisions) Order 1994, SI 1994/1405 in force 1 December 1997 implementing the provisions of the Tripartite Agreement and Protocol made at Brussels 15 December 1993.
[6] International Articles Art 7 (set out in SI 1993/1813 Sch 2); SI 1993/1813, Art 5A (inserted by SI 2001/1544).
[7] International Articles 5, 8, 9 and 10, contained in Sch 2 to SI 1993/1813; Sch 3, para 2(2)(a) as amended by SI 2001/1544; Art 4(1) of the Channel Tunnel (Miscellaneous Provisions) Order 1994, SI 1994/1405.
[8] Immigration Act 1971, s 3A(7) and (8), as inserted by Immigration and Asylum Act 1999, s 1.
[9] See Art 1(2)(g) of the International Articles in Sch 2 to SI 1993/1813.
[10] Immigration Act 1971, s 11, as modified by SI 1993/1813, Art 7 and Sch 4.
[11] SI 1993/1813, Sch 4, para 1(11)(d), as substituted by SI 2001/1544, Art 6(3).
[12] Supplementary Articles Art 2 (set out in Sch 2A to SI 1993/1813 as amended by SI 2001/1544).

3.28 The project to re-position UK borders on the other side of the Channel continued with section 141 of the Nationality, Immigration and Asylum Act 2002, which gave the Secretary of State wide powers to make orders giving effect to international agreements allowing for UK laws to have effect in EEA ports. The first Treaty to which effect has been given by an order under the section is the Le Touquet Treaty, which came into force on 1 February 2004.[1] The Order giving effect to it is the Nationality, Immigration and Asylum (Juxtaposed Controls) Order 2003,[2] which provides for additional control zones in ports at Dover, Calais, Boulogne and Dunkirk.[3] Article 11 of the 2003 Order sets out those provisions of domestic law which are to have effect in a control zone in France.[4] The Channel Tunnel agreements and orders resulted in UK immigration controls at Coquelles and at Eurostar stations; since 1 February 2004, all UK-bound passengers travelling from Calais and Dunkirk have been subject to UK immigration control before boarding. Immigration officers grant or refuse leave to enter as if they were in a UK port.[5]

1 Treaty between the Government of the UK and the Government of France concerning the implementation of frontier controls at the sea ports of both countries on the Channel and North Sea.
2 SI 2003/2818.
3 SI 2003/2818, Sch 1.
4 These are the Immigration Act 1971; Schs 7 and 8 to the Terrorism Act 2000; the Code of Practice for examining officers under the Terrorism Act 2000; the Immigration (Leave to Enter and Remain) Order 2000; and the Immigration (European Economic Area) Regulations 2000.
5 Further control zones have been agreed for the Eurostar terminal at Brussels-Midi, and negotiations have begun with the Dutch authorities for similar control zones at ports in the Netherlands: see Home Office press release 15 April 2004.

3.29 How do juxtaposed controls work in practice? Clearly there is no problem if a passenger is granted leave to enter. But if he or she is refused, how are appeal rights effective? Although the government has stated that passengers refused entry who have a right of appeal from abroad will be served with a notice of refusal which will include information about the Refugee Legal Centre and the Immigration Advisory Service,[1] it is not clear how the would-be appellant would in practice be able to access any advice from those organisations. Will those whose leave is cancelled, but who have in-country appeal rights, be allowed to board the ferry in order to access those rights? The 2002 Act is not one of the enactments which has effect in control zones; what effect does this omission have on appeal rights? All these matters await clarification, and possibly litigation. If the immigration officer requires the passenger to submit to further examination, the powers of detention under the Immigration Act 1971 apply. But what about temporary admission? The Home Office has stated that immigration officers operating at juxtaposed controls may consider alternatives to detention, which means either releasing passengers and 'asking them to come back the next day' or 'handing them back to the French authorities'.[2] Article 4 of the Additional Protocol to the Sangatte Protocol provides that an application for asylum made in a control zone to the officers of the 'state of arrival' is to be examined by the authorities of the 'state of departure'.[3] This means that no asylum seekers will reach the UK through Calais or Dunkirk (or the other control zones, including Eurostar stations and trains), unless they enter illegally, since an admission that asylum is sought will result in being handed over to the French authorities, regardless of the reasons for wishing to claim in the UK.[4] One suspects that reducing the number of asylum claimants reaching the UK was the main reason for the whole exercise.[5]

1 See Consultation Process Report government response to comments on legal representation, available on the IND website.
2 Note of meeting between the Home Office and NGOs, 13 January 2004.
3 Set out in Sch 2A, SI 1993/1803 (as amended by SI 2001/1544).
4 Presumably, however, the Dublin regulation will operate to enable the French authorities to transfer claimants to the UK if they satisfy the criteria (such as having family members in the UK as refugees).
5 See responses by Refugee Council Jan 2003 (available at www.refugeecouncil.org.uk) and ILPA.

Examination abroad for the grant of leave

3.30 As we have seen above, an immigration officer, whether or not in the UK, may give or refuse a person leave to enter the UK at any time before that person's departure for the UK, or in the course of their journey.[1] To determine whether or not to give leave to enter, and if so for what period and subject to what conditions, the immigration officer may seek the information and documents that he or she would be entitled to obtain in an examination at the port.[2] Since the immigration officer examining someone abroad cannot refer the applicant to the port medical inspector, an up-to-date medical report can be requested instead.[3] Failure to provide the information, documents or medical report is a ground for refusal of leave.[4] The immigration officer or Secretary of State is authorised to use the power of examination in a discriminatory way against persons of a particular nationality if justified by statistical information indicating that persons of that nationality have an above average refusal rate or have breached immigration laws.[5]

[1]   Immigration (Leave to Enter and Remain) Order, SI 2000/1161, Art 7(1).
[2]   SI 2000/1161, Art 7(2).
[3]   SI 2000/1161, Art 7(3).
[4]   SI 2000/1161, Art 7(4). Presumably it is a discretionary ground. See 3.53 below.
[5]   See Race Relations Act 1976, section 19D Ministerial Authorisation, 25 July 2003, replacing the Race Relations (Immigration and Asylum) Authorisation 2001, para 4(2)(b), 6. See 3.6 above.

EXAMINATION AT THE PORT OF ENTRY

Who is examined

3.31 All passengers arriving at a port of entry in the UK (or in a control zone)[1] are required to submit to examination by immigration officers. This applies to British citizens,[2] other citizens of the EU,[3] and other people who do not require leave to enter. In order to retain these frontier controls, which run counter to the establishment in the EC of a single market without internal frontiers,[4] the UK has negotiated a special protocol to the Consolidated Treaty of the EC.[5] In order to find out who is eligible and if so on what conditions they should be given leave to enter, immigration officers are given power under the Immigration Act 1971 to examine all those who have arrived in the UK by ship, aircraft or train, even if they are merely in transit and do not wish to enter the UK.[6] The purpose of doing so is to establish:

(i)   whether any of them are British citizens (or Commonwealth citizens with a right of abode); and

(ii)   if subject to control, whether they can or cannot enter without leave; and

(iii)   if they may not, whether they have been given leave which is still in force;

(iv)   if not, whether they should be given leave and for what period and on what conditions (if any); or

(v)   should be refused it.

In respect of passengers arriving with leave to enter which is in force but was given before their arrival, the immigration officer's examination is to establish:

(i)   whether there has been such a change in the circumstances of the case that it should be cancelled;

(ii) whether the leave was obtained as a result of false information given by the passenger or his or her failure to disclose material facts;

(iii) whether there are medical grounds on which leave should be cancelled;[7]

(iv) whether it would be conducive to the public good for the leave to be cancelled;[8]

(v) whether the purpose for which entry is sought is different to the purpose specified in the entry clearance.[9]

It is a criminal offence to refuse to submit to this examination.[10] Normally, examination of holders of UK passports describing the holder as a British citizen or as a citizen of the UK and Colonies having the right of abode in the UK, will be cursory. Similarly those with EEA passports (who do not require leave to enter) will normally be waved through.[11] Passengers who have certificates of entitlement, and those who have continuing leave to enter or remain will normally have a fairly cursory examination. Ministerial authorisation under the Race Relations Act[12] enables the immigration officer to subject passengers to a more rigorous examination, require them to submit to further examination, examine and detain their documents, search them, detain them and impose conditions on temporary admission by reason of their nationality,[13] if there is statistical evidence showing a trend of adverse decisions on or breach of the immigration laws by persons of that nationality.[14] The current ministerial authorisation allows immigration officers to target nationals in respect of which nationalities adverse decisions and immigration breaches reach more than 50 in total (it is not specified over which period) and five of every one thousand persons.[15] The 'licence to discriminate' provided by the Act must not be 'at large' but specific, justified and subject to close personal scrutiny and supervision by the Minister.[16]

1   The term includes areas, ports and trains in France and Belgium defined as control zones under the Channel Tunnel (International Arrangements) Order 1993, SI 1993/1813, as amended. See 3.27–3.29 above.
2   Immigration Act 1971, ss 1(1), 3(9).
3   Immigration (European Economic Area) Regulations 2000, SI 2000/2326, reg 24.
4   See Art 14 EC (formerly Art 7a).
5   See Protocol on the application of certain aspects of Art 14 of the Treaty establishing the European Community to the UK and to Ireland.
6   Immigration Act 1971, Sch 2, para 2(1); *R v Secretary of State for the Home Department, ex p Connhye* [1987] Imm AR 478, QBD.
7   Immigration Act 1971, Sch 2, para 2A(2), inserted by the Immigration and Asylum Act 1999, Sch 14, para 57.
8   Immigration Act 1971, Sch 2, para 2A(3) as inserted.
9   Immigration Act 1971, Sch 2, para 2A(2A), inserted by Asylum and Immigration (Treatment of Claimants etc) Act 2004, s 18.
10   Immigration Act 1971, s 26(1)(a).
11   The 'Bangemann wave' (holding the passport aloft and waving it at the immigration officer on passing the control desk) was the historic compromise between the UK government's demand to retain immigration controls at internal frontiers and the other EU governments' demand that they be removed. In practice EEA nationals' passports are examined as cursorily as those of British citizens.
12   Race Relations Act 1976, s 19D, inserted by Race Relations (Amendment) Act 2000.
13   Race Relations (Immigration and Asylum) Authorisation 2001, in IDI, Ch 1, s 11, Annex EE replaced by Ministerial Authorisation dated 23 May 2003 (not yet published on Home Office website, where the latest ministerial authorisation to be published is that of 21 November 2002 (IDI, Ch 1, Annex EE1).
14   Tamils, Kurds, Pontic Greeks, Roma, Somalis, Albanians, Afghans and ethnic Chinese presenting Malaysian or Japanese travel documents have been targeted: see Written Answer 1 May 2001, col 636W, HC. The criteria for discrimination were tightened after

the *Tamil Information Centre* case (see below). Intelligence showing a likelihood of future breaches has been replaced by statistical evidence showing actual breaches in the past, although the criteria also include above-average adverse decisions, which introduces an element of self-fulfilling prophecy to the exercise.

15 Written ministerial statement 23 February 2004: Hansard HC Column 5WS. The statement indicated that immigration officers may target passengers of Somali ethnic origin for linguistic analysis, and may demand fingerprints from passengers from Iraq, Turkey, Sudan, Somalia and Iran for inter-country fingerprint comparisons. The authorisation was renewed by the Minister on 24 May 2004: Hansard HC Col. 74WS. The most recent authorisation to be published on the Home Office website is that of November 2002 (see fn 13 above), containing significantly looser criteria for discrimination which are insufficiently specific to comply with the judgment in the *Tamil Information Centre* case (see below).

16 *R (on the application of the Tamil Information Centre) v Secretary of State for the Home Department* [2002] EWHC 2155 (Admin).

3.32 Apart from refugees and passengers relying on provisions of the ECHR, all other travellers to the UK must be in possession of some kind of documentation to obtain entry under the Immigration Act 1971 and the Immigration Rules.[1] The main kinds of document needed on arrival at a port of entry are:

- passport or recognised travel document;
- identity card;
- medical certificate;
- certificate of entitlement;
- visa;
- entry certificate;
- work permit; and
- landing card.

A valid national passport or other document 'satisfactorily' establishing identity and nationality must be produced by every passenger arriving at a port of entry if demanded by an immigration officer.[2] However, inability to produce such a document may render the passenger liable to prosecution under section 2 of the Asylum and Immigration (Treatment of Claimants etc) Act 2004,[3] but does not, thereby make the passenger an illegal entrant.[4] EC nationals can travel with valid national identity cards instead of passports.[5] If a person has a passport or travel document from a country which either is not recognised as a State by the UK, or is not dealt with as a government by the UK, or does not accept valid UK passports for its own immigration control, or does not comply with international passport practice, the person should normally be refused leave to enter on that ground alone.[6]

1 Those with the right of abode are entitled to come and go without let or hindrance except such as may be required under the Act to enable their right to be established: Immigration Act 1971, s 1(1). If their right of abode is disputed, they must prove it by means of a passport or a certificate of entitlement: s 3(9); HC 395, paras 12, 13.
2 Immigration Act 1971, Sch 2, para 4(2)(a); HC 395, para 11.
3 See 14.33 below.
4 Before the offence was created under the 2004 Act, mere inability to produce a document under Sch 2, para 4 did not render the passenger an illegal entrant: *R v Naillie* [1993] AC 674; [1993] 2 All ER 782, HL. The new offence does not change this, because the decision on entry does not depend on the absence or not of a passport without reasonable excuse, but on whether the person is or is not a refugee or has some other good claim to entry. See further chapter 16 below.

5   Immigration (European Economic Area) Regulations 2000, SI 2000/2326, reg 12.
6   HC 395, para 320(10). See 3.54 below; note the concessions and the fact that leave may not be cancelled on this ground.

3.33 Passengers in transit to another country outside the common travel area will not normally be given any detailed examination once it is established that they are in transit, have the means and intention of proceeding at once to another country, are assured of entry there and intend to leave the UK within 48 hours.[1] Leave to enter may be given for 48 hours, no more.[2] Transit passengers, however, can be stopped and detained and removed to a different destination.[3] Leave to enter will be refused if an immigration officer is not satisfied about the passenger's intentions, means, or that he or she will be admitted to the country of destination.[4]

1   HC 395, para 47.
2   HC 395, paras 48 and 50.
3   HC 395, para 49; Immigration Act 1971, Sch 2, paras 8 and 16. See the case of *Williams, ex p* [1970] Crim LR 102, a black civil rights leader, who was detained in transit while on his way back from China to the US.
4   HC 395, para 49; see *R v Secretary of State for the Home Department, ex p Connhye* [1987] Imm AR 478; affd (1988) Independent, 20 April, CA, where it was held proper for an immigration officer to examine the financial means of a transit passenger.

3.34 In order to assist immigration officers in their task, a duty is cast on all persons who are examined by immigration officers (either on arrival or departure) to answer any questions put to them, say what documents they may be carrying and to produce their passport or other identity document.[1] These may be retained by the immigration officer until either leave to enter is granted or, if it is refused, until the passenger is about to be removed following refusal of leave.[2] Landing cards are also required for all passengers over 16 who are not British citizens, except on journeys within the common travel area.[3] It is a criminal offence to give false information or documents to an immigration officer,[4] or not to give information which is required or to refuse to hand over documents, unless there is a reasonable excuse.[5] There is no duty to volunteer unsolicited information, and a person will not be an illegal entrant if they accidentally and without intention to mislead offer incorrect information, but silence accompanied by conduct can in some circumstances amount to a false representation.[6]

1   Immigration Act 1971, Sch 2, para 4.
2   Immigration Act 1971, Sch 2, para 4(2A). The IDI state that once a passenger has been refused leave to enter, the passport should not be returned before removal unless there is a valid reason (eg to obtain a foreign visa or have it revalidated). The chief immigration officer must be satisfied that there is no risk of the passenger absconding or defacing the passport to frustrate removal: IDI Sep 04, Ch 9, s 6, para 6.
3   Immigration Act 1971, Sch 2, para 5; Immigration (Landing and Embarkation Cards) Order 1975, SI 1975/65, Art 4. They are supplied by the carriers: Art 4(2).
4   Immigration Act 1971, s 26(1)(c).
5   Immigration Act 1971, s 26(1)(b). See 14.58 below.
6   See *Khawaja v Secretary of State for the Home Department* [1984] AC 74, [1983] 1 All ER 765, HL. There is no commensurate duty to attend for interview with an entry clearance officer or to provide documents, but failure to do so may result in an adverse inference being drawn (*R v Immigration Appeal Tribunal, ex p Hubbard* [1985] Imm AR 110, QBD) or even in the entry clearance officer deeming the application to have been withdrawn. See also *R v Secretary of State for the Home Department, ex p Awan* [1996] Imm AR 354,

QBD. The Asylum and Immigration (Treatment of Claimants, etc) Act 2004, s 8 obliges adverse inferences to be drawn from such failure in the asylum context: see 12.164 below.

3.35 In carrying out their examination, immigration officers can search the person, baggage or vehicle of an entrant, and any ship, aircraft or vehicle on which he or she arrived, for any documents that they wish to see.[1] Normal practice is to return any documents produced or found in a search, after examination, unless they are needed for an appeal or for a criminal prosecution, in which case they may be kept for as long as necessary.[2] There are limits on the documents they may take. Like police powers of search and seizure, where, broadly speaking, only documents which are relevant to some crime may be seized, only documents relevant to the discharge of immigration control may be taken by immigration officers.[3] According to the Home Office, immigration officers may, in appropriate cases, make photocopies of documents belonging to those seeking entry to the UK.[4] The main use of these powers is to discover whether an entrant possesses documents which might show that the real purpose of coming to the UK is something other than that stated. A number of refusals have resulted from such searches.[5] Section 141 of the Immigration and Asylum Act 1999 contains power to fingerprint passengers who fail on request to produce a valid passport or other identification, unless they have a reasonable excuse. Fingerprints may also be taken from asylum seekers, illegal entrants, overstayers and other defined groups, and their dependants.[6] Those seeking leave to enter who present a UN Convention travel document endorsed with entry clearance are required to provide a record of fingerprints.[7] The very extensive powers of examination and search described here are inappropriate for citizens of the EU and others exercising their rights under EC law. Even if they are making a journey from outside the EU, they do not require leave to enter and extensive examination is unnecessary.[8]

[1]   Immigration Act 1971, Sch 2, para 4(3).
[2]   IDI Sep 04, Ch 9, s 6, para 6. Passengers wanting a receipt for their documents must ask for one.
[3]   See (in relation to police powers) *Chic Fashions (West Wales) Ltd v Jones* [1968] 2 QB 299, [1968] 1 All ER 229, CA; *Ghani v Jones* [1970] 1 QB 693, [1969] 3 All ER 1700, CA. For detailed powers of search and seizure see 14.12–14.13 below.
[4]   See IDI, Ch 9, s 6. The photocopying of documents relating to an international conference organised by the South West Africa Peoples Organisation in 1971 was surely not an appropriate case (Guardian, 26 December 1971).
[5]   See *Baldacchino v Secretary of State for the Home Department* [1972] Imm AR 14 at 15, where the search of the immigrant's baggage was crucial. In *R v Secretary of State for the Home Department, ex p Hindjou* [1989] Imm AR 24, QBD, the immigration officer drew unreasonable inferences from letters found in the passenger's luggage, and the refusal of leave to enter was quashed.
[6]   Immigration and Asylum Act 1999, s 141(7), (10). The power is exercisable by immigration officers, police and prison officers: s 141(5). See 14.19 below for fingerprinting powers.
[7]   Immigration (Provision of Physical Data) Regulations 2003, SI 2003/1875 as amended by SI 2004/474, made under the Nationality Immigration and Asylum Act 2002, s 126. For fingerprint records in the context of entry clearance see 3.16 above.
[8]   See Council Directive (EEC) 68/360, Arts 2(1) and 3(1); and Council Directive (EEC) 73/148, Art 3(1)(2); chapter 7 below.

Passenger information

3.36 The immigration officer may come to this examination holding information about the passengers. Carriers bringing passengers to the UK (whether owners or agents of ships or aircraft or the operators of the Channel Tunnel through trains) must on request supply information about the passengers to the immigration officer.[1] The information to be supplied by shipping companies and airlines includes not just name and nationality, as previously, but also gender, date of birth, type of travel document held and expiry date, ticket number, date and place of issue, how it was paid for, the passenger's itinerary, the names of all other passengers appearing together on one reservation, and (if the passenger is in a vehicle) its registration number.[2] See further 14.26 below.

[1] Immigration Act 1971, Sch 2, para 27, modified in relation to the Channel Tunnel by SI 1993/1813, Sch 4, para 1(11)(r), allows the Secretary of State for the Home Department to make Orders requiring the provision of passenger lists giving names and nationality of passengers and crew. Paragraph 27B requires carriers to provide passenger information. Paragraph 27C requires them to notify the Secretary of State of the arrival of any ship or aircraft expected to carry non-EEA nationals.

[2] Immigration (Passenger Information) Order 2000, SI 2000/912.

3.37 An immigration officer may want to ask further questions or obtain further information before deciding whether or not to admit a passenger. In that case, he or she may require the passenger to submit to further examination.[1] The passenger may be arriving with or without advance leave. This power may also be exercised by the Secretary of State where a passenger makes an asylum or human rights claim, or seeks leave to enter outside the rules, since in such a situation the Secretary of State is empowered to grant or refuse leave to enter.[2] The requirement to submit to further examination must be in writing.[3] In the case of a passenger with advance leave, the leave to enter may be suspended during the examination or pending further examination.[4] The request to submit to further examination does not prevent a transit passenger or a member of a crew from leaving on his or her intended ship, aircraft or train.[5] Passengers arriving without leave, or those whose leave has been suspended, may be detained under the authority of the immigration officer or the Secretary of State pending the examination or further examination and pending a decision to give, refuse or cancel leave to enter.[6] In deciding whether to detain a passenger pending examination or further examination, the immigration officer or Secretary of State is entitled to discriminate on nationality grounds if justified by statistical information.[7] The power of detention is usually enforced without any need to arrest, but a backup power of arrest is available.[8] The passenger may be released on temporary admission instead of being detained.[9] Detainees awaiting further examination may be eligible for bail.[10] During interviews a passenger may be represented by a friend or lawyer, but there is no right to have a representative present at the interview. This is a matter for the interviewing officer, who must, however, exercise the discretion properly.[11] Where a person who has been released on temporary admission pending a decision fails to report for further examination as required, the immigration officer or Secretary of State may direct that the person's examination is concluded and refuse or cancel leave to enter forthwith.[12]

1   Immigration Act 1971, Sch 2, paras 2(3), 2A(5).
2   Immigration (Leave to Enter) Order 2001, SI 2001/2590 (made under s 3A(7) Immigration and Asylum Act 1999), Arts 2, 3.
3   Immigration Act 1971, Sch 2, paras 2(3), 2A(5) and 2A(10).
4   Immigration Act 1971, Sch 2, para 2A(7). The suspension of leave must also be in writing: para 2A(10). The Secretary of State does not have the power to suspend leave under SI 2001/2590, probably because it is assumed that asylum and human rights claimants and those seeking leave to enter outside the rules have not obtained advance leave.
5   Immigration Act 1971, Sch 2, para 2(3), 2A(6), SI 1993/1813, Sch 4, para 1(11)(e), (ea), inserted by SI 2000/1775.
6   Immigration Act 1971, Sch 2, para 16(1), (1A) (immigration officers); Nationality, Immigration and Asylum Act 2002, s 62 (Secretary of State).
7   Ministerial authorisations made under Race Relations Act 1976, s 19D (inserted by Race Relations (Amendment) Act 2000; see 3.3 above.
8   Immigration Act 1971, Sch 2, para 17. See 14.10 and chapter 17 below.
9   Immigration Act 1971, Sch 2, para 21, applied to the Secretary of State by Immigration (Leave to Enter) Order 2001, SI 2001/2590, Art 3.
10 Immigration Act 1971, Sch 2, para 22. See further chapter 17 below.
11 *R v Secretary of State for the Home Department, ex p Lawson* [1994] Imm AR 58, QBD. For asylum interviews see 12.123 below.
12 Immigration Act 1971, Sch 2, para 21(3), (4), applied to the Secretary of State by Immigration (Leave to Enter) Order 2001, SI 2001/2590, Art 3.

Medical examination

3.38 Anyone seeking to enter the UK may be examined by a medical inspector.[1] The power to require further examination applies to medical examinations as well as others.[2] This is dealt with at 3.37 above. If the immigration officer decides to grant leave to enter (or, in the case of advance leave, not to cancel it), but that (on the advice of a medical inspector or other qualified practitioner) a further medical test or examination may be required in the interests of public health, the passenger may be given notice in writing requiring him or her to report to a medical officer for any further tests or examination that person deems necessary.[3] This requirement is not, however, a condition of leave under section 3(1)(c) of the Immigration Act 1971, so failure to comply cannot found a decision to remove, or to curtail or refuse to extend leave, as a breach of conditions (although it might found a decision to deport, or a refusal to extend leave on public good grounds, in extreme cases). Failure to comply with a direction to report to a medical officer of health, or to attend or submit to a medical examination, is, however, a criminal offence.[4] Information regarding the health of the person examined may be disclosed to a health service body, together with the inspector's opinion as to any action which the health service body should take.[5]

1   Immigration Act 1971, Sch 2, paras 2(2), 2A(4).
2   Immigration Act 1971, Sch 2, paras 2(3), 2A(5).
3   Immigration Act 1971, Sch 2, para 7. The power to direct a person to submit to medical examination may also be exercised by the Secretary of State, in a case where the Secretary of State is taking a decision on an asylum or human rights application or an application outside the rules: Immigration (Leave to Enter) Order 2001, SI 2001/2590, Arts 2, 3.
4   Immigration Act 1971, s 24(1)(d): see 14.56 below.
5   Nationality Immigration and Asylum Act 2002, s 133.

3.39 As indicated above, the examination powers extend to control zones in France and Belgium under the modifications to the Immigration Act 1971 made by the Channel Tunnel international arrangements and the Juxtaposed Controls Order.[1] Immigration officers also have power to board any ship, aircraft or Channel Tunnel train to carry out their examination on board.[2] These powers have been used, sometimes with unfortunate consequences, where large numbers of asylum seekers are expected to arrive from a particular refugee hot spot.[3] Treating passengers in haste has led to asylum claims being overlooked. Secondly, because of the pressure on airlines and the threat of penalties under the carriers' liability provisions in Part II of the Immigration and Asylum Act 1999,[4] there may be a temptation for airlines and ferry captains to prevent a passenger landing and to call in immigration officials to conduct an on-the-spot examination. In both such cases there is a grave risk of the examination being carried out in an unfair manner, and because abuses can be carried out unseen, and the victim may be quietly removed, the power is a dangerous one.[5] It seems to us that the cases where an 'on board' examination is justified must be very few and far between.

1   See 3.28–3.30 above.
2   Immigration Act 1971, Sch 2, para 1(4), as modified in relation to the Channel Tunnel by SI 1993/1813, Sch 4, para 1(11)(a).
3   See Alison Stanley 'The Legal Status of International Zones, the British experience' [1992] 6 Immigration & Nationality Law & Practice at 126.
4   As amended by Nationality Immigration and Asylum Act 2002, s 125 and Sch 8 following the declaration of incompatibility in *International Transport Roth GmbH v Secretary of State for the Home Department* [2002] EWCA Civ 158, [2002] 3 WLR 344, CA; see 14.89 below.
5   These concerns are accentuated by the provisions authorising discrimination on grounds of nationality, ethnic or national origin in s 19D of the Race Relations Act 1976 (inserted by Race Relations (Amendment) Act 2000) and the specific authorisation of nationality-based discrimination in pre- and on-entry controls discussed at 3.31 above.

Examination, decision and the 24-hour rule

3.40 Passengers with advance leave to enter (by means of entry clearance or otherwise) whose leave is not to be suspended or cancelled will emerge from the examination by the immigration officer with no further passport stamp or notice, just as British citizens do. Other passengers need notice of a decision. Previously, where leave was granted, written notice had to be given to the person affected and this was usually done by a stamp in the passport.[1] The Immigration and Asylum Act 1999 gave the Secretary of State the power to add to the ways in which leave may be given, refused or varied. Leave to enter need no longer be granted or refused in writing, but may be given by fax and e-mail,[2] and in the case of visitors, may be given orally, including by telecommunication.[3] Leave to enter may also be given or refused by a notice to a responsible third party,[4] who might include the person appearing to be in charge of a group of people arriving together, a tour operator, a carrier, a control port manager or a British Embassy or consulate official.[5] The notice does not need to name the individuals covered by it, but can describe them by reference to a group.[6] However, if leave is refused orally or to a responsible third party, a notice in writing must be given as soon as practicable, confirming the refusal and giving the reasons.[7] If the refusal attracts a right of appeal under section 82 of the 2002 Act, written notice must be given under the Immigration (Notices) Regulations 2003,[8] and notice under the Notices

Regulations is good notice under the Immigration (Leave to Enter and Remain) Order 2000.[9] A notice which is irregular in that it fails to tell of rights of appeal or gives incorrect information is still a good notice under the 1999 Act and its defects can be corrected.[10] Notice need not be signed.[11] If leave to enter is to be granted, this can be done by the immigration officer who carries out the initial examination. But if leave is to be refused, or advance leave cancelled, immigration officers cannot take the decision on their own but must obtain the authority of a chief immigration officer or an immigration inspector in all cases.[12]

[1] Immigration Act 1971, s 4(1). In granting or refusing leave immigration officers are entitled to mark the passport: *R v Secretary of State for the Home Department, ex p Raju* [1986] Imm AR 348, QBD.

[2] Immigration (Leave to Enter and Remain) Order 2000, SI 2000/1161, Art 8(1), (2). The power to grant or refuse leave to enter otherwise than by notice in writing to the person affected applies to the Secretary of State in appropriate cases: see Immigration (Leave to Enter) Order 2001, SI 2001/2590, Art 2(5).

[3] SI 2000/1161, Art 8(3). The immigration officer may decline to use these methods on the basis of the passenger's nationality: Race Relations (Immigration and Asylum) Authorisations made under Race Relations Act, s 19D as inserted.

[4] SI 2000/1161, Art 9(1).

[5] SI 2000/1161, Art 1(3).

[6] SI 2000/1161, Art 9(2).

[7] SI 2000/1161, Art 10(1). In the case of someone who is illiterate or unable to understand the notice, it may be sent to a representative if there is one: *R v Chief Immigration Officer of Manchester Airport, ex p Begum (Insah)* [1972] 1 All ER 6; affd [1973] 1 All ER 594, [1973] 1 WLR 141, CA.

[8] SI 2003/658. This does not apply where an appeal may only be brought on Refugee or Human Rights Convention grounds see reg 5(6). A decision to grant limited leave which is appealable under s 83 of the 2002 Act must also be in writing, inform the person of a right of appeal and be accompanied by a statement of the reasons for the rejection of the claim for asylum: regs 4(2) and 5(2). On the power to change the reasons for refusal, see *Dagdalen v Secretary of State for the Home Department* [1988] Imm AR 425, CA. This will usually be regarded as a refinement of the notice and will not require a new notice: *Hettierarachchi v Secretary of State for the Home Department* [1991] Imm AR 499, CA; see further *Rajendran v Secretary of State for the Home Department* [1989] Imm AR 512, IAT: see 18.83 and 18.111 below.

[9] SI 2000/1161, Art 10(2).

[10] *Labiche v Secretary of State for the Home Department* [1991] Imm AR 263, CA; *R v Secretary of State for the Home Department, ex p Lateef* [1991] Imm AR 334, QBD. See further *R v Secretary of State for the Home Department, ex p Abeywickrema* [1991] Imm AR 535, QBD; *(Defective Notice of Decision) Iraq* [2004] UKIAT 00194.

[11] *R v Secretary of State for the Home Department, ex p Kondo* [1992] Imm AR 326, QBD.

[12] HC 395, para 10.

3.41 After completing the examination of a person arriving in the UK without advance leave and wishing to enter in a capacity attracting limited leave, the immigration authorities normally have 24 hours in which to give their decision, failing which the passenger is deemed to have been given six months' leave to enter with a condition prohibiting employment.[1] This provision, known as the '24-hour rule', used to be of considerable importance before 1988, when failure to give proper notice resulted in the deemed grant of indefinite leave. The courts held that an illegible passport stamp was not good notice, since it did not notify the entrant of the terms of the leave, and so passengers whose passports had been stamped illegibly on entry obtained indefinite leave. In 1988 the paragraph was amended to grant a deemed leave of only six months, meaning that only those who should not have been granted leave at all, or transit passengers who would not have expected as much as six months' leave, gained from it. The effect of the 24-hour rule has been further eroded by Article 12 of the Immigration (Leave to Enter and Remain) Order 2000,[2] which deals with the situation where an examination has begun but has been adjourned for further inquiries, or the applicant has been required to submit to further examination, after which the immigration officer considers that the applicant does not need to be re-interviewed. In such a situation, any notice which is subsequently given in conformity with the requirements of the Order is deemed to comply with the requirement to give notice within 24 hours. This provision does away with much of the old case law dealing with when an examination comes to an end and the 24-hour time limit begins to run.[3] In addition, the Immigration Act 1971 provides that if a passenger who is on temporary admission pending further examination fails to report to an immigration officer as required, his or her examination may be treated as concluded and there is no need for notice to comply with the 24-hour rule.[4]

1   Immigration Act 1971, Sch 2, para 6(1), as amended.
2   SI 2000/1161, Art 12. This provision is applied to the situation where the Secretary of State takes over an examination begun by an immigration officer (e g where the passenger has made an asylum or human rights claim or has sought leave to enter outside the immigration rules), by the Immigration (Leave to Enter) Order 2001, Art 4.
3   See the 4th edition of this work, at 3.37–3.40.
4   Immigration Act 1971, Sch 2, para 21(3), (4).

What is an examination?

3.42 The problem remains, however, as to whether any 'examination' at all has taken place. Not everyone passing through immigration control comes face to face with an immigration officer. Not everyone is interrogated. For example, babes in arms, persons on excursions or named in a collective passport may never be spoken to by an immigration officer on their way through immigration control. These situations are now dealt with by the provision that leave, and notice of it, may be given collectively, to the responsible third party in charge of the group.[1] Examination of all passengers is not mandatory, but permissive;[2] the important thing is that leave is granted to all those who need it. The responsible third party includes anyone who appears to be in charge of a group travelling together,[3] and a family is of course a group *par excellence*. This provision would avoid the result in *Ex p Ghazalgoo*,[4] where a 16-year-old Iranian boy was included on his father's passport. They arrived together at immigration control, but only the father was asked questions. The passport was stamped for the father only and the boy was completely ignored. The court held that there had been no examination of the boy, no leave given to him, and he was an illegal entrant – an absurdly harsh decision.

1   Immigration Act 1971, Sch 2, para 6(4); SI 2000/1161, Art 9; see 3.40 fn 4 above.
2   *R v Secretary of State for the Home Department, ex p Kumar* [1990] Imm AR 265, QBD.
3   SI 2000/1161, Art 1(3).
4   [1987] Imm AR 448.

Leave given by mistake

3.43 Immigration officers are fallible and do make mistakes. Sometimes they stamp a passport with indefinite leave to enter. This is what happened in *Ex p Ram*.[1] A mistake had been made, and the applicant was given indefinite leave. The Divisional Court held that the immigration officer had been acting within his powers under section 4 of the Immigration Act 1971; it could not be said in the absence of any fraud or dishonesty on the part of the applicant that he had no authority to act as he did. And so an immigrant, given a leave by mistake, is allowed to keep it. We suggest that the same doctrine applies to a leave granted abroad, since the mistaken grant of leave is not one of the grounds for cancellation of leave when a passenger arrives at the port.[2]

[1] *R v Secretary of State for the Home Department, ex p Ram* [1979] 1 All ER 687, [1979] 1 WLR 148.
[2] For grounds for cancellation of leave: see 3.74 below.

Illegible stamps

3.44 The doctrine of grant of deemed leave by an illegible stamp in a passport is now, we suggest, for all practical purposes a dead letter. When the grant of leave to enter had to be by notice in writing to the person affected, an illegible stamp was held not to be an effective notice and so, under the provisions of Schedule 2, paragraph 6 to the Immigration Act 1971, indefinite leave, later amended to a six months' leave, with a prohibition on employment, was deemed to have been granted.[1] But now that leave to enter may be granted in other ways, a passenger may have other evidence of the grant of leave, and it will only be in those cases where there is no other evidence of leave having been granted that the defective stamp will need to be relied on. It is only transit passengers who might benefit from the deemed leave to obtain something more than they would otherwise have been entitled to; in *Low*[2] the Tribunal held that if transit leave is all that is intended, the leave stamp must make that clear; otherwise a visitor leave will be granted (with a right to apply for an extension and to appeal). The replacement of ink stamps with stickers is another reason for the redundancy of the 'illegible stamp' issue.

[1] Immigration Act 1971, Sch 2, para 6 provides that leave must be granted or refused 24 hours after the end of the immigration officer's examination; if not, leave of six months is deemed given. An ineffective notice did not operate to grant leave, thus engaging para 6. See *R v Secretary of State for the Home Department, ex p Tolba* [1988] Imm AR 78, QBD; *Katoorah v Secretary of State for the Home Department* [1996] Imm AR 595, CA; *Minton v Secretary of State for the Home Department* [1990] Imm AR 199, CA.
[2] *Low v Secretary of State for the Home Department* [1995] Imm AR 435.

No stamp given

3.45 A doctrine which deserves to fall by the wayside is that of illegal entry by the immigration officer's failure to stamp a passport. The demise of this pernicious and unfair doctrine is long overdue. It arose because a person who requires leave to enter and enters the UK without obtaining such leave is in breach of section 3(1) of the Immigration Act 1971 and is an illegal entrant.[1]

When the only way that leave could be granted was by a stamp in the entrant's passport, the lack of such a stamp was held to mean that no leave had been granted. The lack of stamp could have been the fault of the immigration officer, who mistakenly believed that the person had a right of abode or was exempt from immigration control. The doctrine originated in *Rehal*,[2] where the applicant was a British Overseas citizen but the immigration officer who examined him, thinking he was a British citizen, waved him through without stamping his passport. It had been thought that where a mistake of this kind was made, the immigrant always obtained the benefit of a deemed leave to enter,[3] but the Court of Appeal rejected this view, holding that this was limited to cases where the immigration officer intended either to grant or refuse leave and had no application to any other case.[4] In this way innocent travellers became stigmatised as illegal entrants and liable to removal through immigration officers' mistakes. The only remedy was to seek leave to remain from the Secretary of State for the Home Department,[5] and to challenge refusal, or the exercise of discretion to remove as an illegal entrant, as irrational, as failing to take into account a legitimate expectation of admission to the UK, created by the error of the immigration officer without any inaccurate representation on behalf of the immigrant.

1   Immigration Act 1971, ss 3(1), 33(1).
2   *Rehal v Secretary of State for the Home Department* [1989] Imm AR 576, CA.
3   By virtue of Immigration Act 1971, Sch 2, para 6; see 3.41 above.
4   The argument that the immigrant in this situation benefited from deemed leave had been accepted in *Amoako* (4679) and consensually in *R v Secretary of State for the Home Department, ex p Malik* (2 October 1987, unreported), QBD, with the sensible result that innocent persons did not become illegal entrants.
5   See chapter 4 below.

3.46 Now that leave to enter does not have to be in writing in all cases, but can be by fax, e-mail, telephone or oral, the lack of a passport stamp no longer leads to the inference that the passenger entered without leave. He or she may have been granted leave orally or benefited from a collective grant of leave to a responsible person.[1] However, the person in the situation of Mr Rehal would be no better off, if unable to prove that leave had been granted or intended in one of these ways.[2]

1   See 3.40 text and fn 4 above.
2   The burden of proof that leave has been granted in one of these ways is on the entrant: Immigration (Leave to Enter and Remain) Order 2000, SI 2000/1161, Art 11.

Date stamp only

3.47 Where the passport is stamped with a rectangular date stamp and nothing more, the effect of the stamp seems to depend on the factual situation; if there are indications in the factual matrix suggestive of indefinite leave to enter, following *Ex p Badaike*,[1] the rectangular stamp in the passport would amount to a written notice of indefinite leave to enter, and would be an effective leave unless the Secretary of State could prove otherwise (for example, if the immigration officer was misled by the applicant). In *Bagga*[2] the Court of Appeal held that such a stamp did not confer indefinite leave to enter if it was placed in the passport by an immigration officer in the belief that the holder was exempt from immigration control, so that, following *Rehal*,[3] there was no room for the operation of paragraph 6(1) of Schedule 2 to the Immigration Act 1971. This would have the same effect as no stamp at all, that is, it would mean that the person had been granted no leave and was therefore an illegal entrant.[4] The problem starts with *Rehal*, and the court's interpretation of the examination powers of immigration officers, in particular paragraphs 2(1) and 6(1) of Schedule 2 to the 1971 Act. The Court interpreted the words 'where a person examined by an immigration officer ... *is to be given* a limited leave etc' as referring to the immigration officer's *intentions* after conducting the examination. This subjective approach means that paragraph 6(1) deals with delays only, but not mistakes. In *Rehal* the court rejected an objective interpretation of the words 'is to be given'. In other words, if, on a proper examination, a person does not have a right of abode, then he or she is a person who 'is to be given' leave. At a stroke, all the present injustices would go. Instead of mistakes turning innocent people into illegal entrants, they would get an automatic six months' leave and an opportunity of resolving the position with the Home Office.

[1]   *R v Secretary of State for Home Affairs, ex p Badaike* (1977) Times, 4 May, DC.
[2]   *R v Secretary of State for the Home Department, ex p Bagga* [1991] 1 QB 485, [1990] Imm AR 413, CA.
[3]   *Rehal v Secretary of State for the Home Department* [1989] Imm AR 576, CA.
[4]   See 3.45 above.

3.48 A person who has been granted leave to enter on arrival may have his or her leave cancelled up to 24 hours after the conclusion of the immigration officer's examination.[1] This happens most frequently when someone is given leave to enter by immigration control and then passes through to customs, who discover large quantities of drugs in his or her baggage.[2] In the same way, a person refused leave to enter at the port may have that refusal cancelled; in this case the 24-hour time limit does not apply, but if indefinite or limited leave is not granted at the same time that the original refusal of leave is cancelled, then six months' leave is deemed granted.[3]

[1]   Immigration Act 1971, Sch 2, para 6(2), as amended.
[2]   See eg *Villone v Secretary of State for the Home Department* [1979–80] Imm AR 23.
[3]   Immigration Act 1971, Sch 2, para 6(3), as amended.

GENERAL GROUNDS FOR REFUSING ENTRY CLEARANCE OR LEAVE TO ENTER

3.49 An application for leave to enter, or for entry clearance, will be determined according to the detailed Immigration Rules dealing with the particular purpose for which the applicant wishes to come to the UK – visit, study, business, family reunion and so forth. Qualifying under these rules does not, however, guarantee that leave to enter will be granted, because the person may fail on general grounds, relating, broadly, to past conduct, lack of proper documents, non-cooperation with the immigration authorities, restricted returnability, public policy or public health. The immigration rules set out these general grounds for refusal in two additional lists – one where leave to enter or entry clearance 'is to be refused' and one where it 'should normally be refused'. They do not apply in cases where the person seeking entry already has entry clearance because in that situation the grounds for refusing leave to enter are much more restricted. These are set out at 3.71–3.73 below. Entry clearance or leave to enter is to be refused[1] under HC 395, paragraph 320 in the following cases:[2]

(1) entry is being sought for a purpose not covered by the Rules;
(2) the person seeking entry is currently the subject of a deportation order;
(3) failure to produce a valid national passport or other document satisfactorily establishing identity and nationality;
(4) failure to show that he or she is acceptable to the immigration authorities in another part of the common travel area to which the applicant wishes to travel;
(5) failure to produce entry clearance, if one was required;
(6) the Secretary of State has personally directed that exclusion is conducive to the public good;
(7) refusal on medical grounds (unless the person is settled in the UK or there are strong compassionate circumstances).

Grounds on which entry clearance or leave to enter should normally be refused are as follows:

(8) failure by a person arriving in the UK to provide information to the immigration officer;
(8A) failure, by a person outside the UK, to provide information, documents or medical reports required to the immigration officer;
(9) failure by a returning resident to meet the requirements of paragraph 18 of the Rules;
(10) production of a passport which is from an unrecognised territory or which is otherwise unacceptable;
(11) failure to observe the time limit or conditions attached to a past leave;
(12) obtaining a previous leave by deception;
(13) restricted returnability of a person other than those eligible for admission for settlement or a spouse eligible for admission under paragraph 282;
(14) refusal by a sponsor to give an undertaking in writing to be responsible for the applicant's maintenance and accommodation for the period of any leave granted;
(15) the making of false representations or the failure to disclose any material fact for the purpose of obtaining a work permit;
(16) failure, in the case of an unaccompanied child under the age of 18 years other than an asylum seeker, to provide written consent to the application from his parent(s) or legal guardian;
(17) save in relation to a person settled in the United Kingdom, refusal to undergo a medical examination;
(18) save where admission would be justified for strong compassionate reasons, conviction in any country of a serious criminal offence;
(19) exclusion is conducive to the public good in the light of the person's character, conduct or associations.
(20) failure to comply with a requirement relating to the provision of physical data (eg, fingerprints) required by regulations made under section 126 of the Nationality Immigration and Asylum Act 2002.[3]

1   The IDI make clear that even the 'mandatory' grounds are not wholly mandatory, and that 'in practice, there are occasions where refusal is not appropriate': IDI Jun 04, Ch 9 s 2.
2   We use the numbering of the immigration rule. This Rule must be read with HC 395, para 26, which allows the word 'entry clearance officer' to be used for 'immigration officer' where appropriate, and para 39 which gives entry clearance officers the same discretion in relation to medical examinations as immigration officers.
3   Inserted by HC 370 from 27 February 2004.

The mandatory and discretionary grounds

3.50 A distinction is sometimes made between mandatory and discretionary decisions of immigration officials. The distinction is not as clear cut as it sounds, because even where words like 'is to be refused' are used, a reading of the IDIs, for example, will often show that there is an element of residual discretion remaining, and under public law the doctrine of 'fettering discretion' means that the circumstances of every case have to be considered, and, even if they do not meet the 'mandatory' requirements of a particular rule, a decision must still be taken whether or not to make an exception. Nevertheless the distinction remains an important and useful way of classifying things in this area, not least because the ambit of the right of appeal, as we shall see, may depend on whether a discretion is exercised under the Rules or outside them. The first part of HC 395 paragraph 320,which states that leave or entry clearance 'is to be refused', is generally regarded as containing mandatory guidance to be followed by immigration officials. The second list, which contains the instruction that leave or entry clearance 'should normally be' refused, is generally regarded as presuming refusal, but leaving a large measure of discretion to the immigration official.

Entry not covered by the rules

3.51 Leave to enter or entry clearance is to be refused if admission is sought for a purpose not covered by the Immigration Rules.[1] The Rules are drafted so narrowly that large numbers of people and purposes are omitted. Although provision is now made for unmarried partners, there is still no provision in the Rules for the admission of certain relatives, such as step-children or step-parents where the natural parent is still alive. Nor is there provision for the admission of the family members of those in the UK with exceptional leave to remain. Earlier rules were silent on these categories, but since 1994 the Rules have provided for mandatory refusal. This does not prevent immigration officers exercising discretion to admit them outside the Rules,[2] but it deprives applicants of an appeal against an adverse decision,[3] unless human rights are engaged.[4]

1   HC 395, para 320(1).
2   *Kuku v Secretary of State for the Home Department* [1990] Imm AR 27, CA; *Adac-Bosompra* [1992] Imm AR 579, IAT. See IDI Jun 04, Ch 9, s 2; immigration officers should consider eligibility under any concession as well as under the Rules.
3   See 18.21 below.
4   See chapter 8 below.

3.52 Other mandatory guidance requires little explanation. A person who is the subject of a current deportation order is to be refused leave to enter or entry clearance[1] since the deportation order prohibits entry to the UK.[2] A deportation order is not invalidated by leave to enter granted in error. However, if the deportation followed a conviction which is spent, refusal is not automatic.[3] A person who is subject to an Irish deportation order is not to be refused for that reason alone.[4] Passengers who do not satisfy the entry clearance officer or immigration officer of their identity or nationality are to be refused,[5] unless there are strong compassionate or other reasons for granting leave.[6] When they seek leave to enter, whether they are in the UK or abroad, they must submit to examination and produce valid documents establishing identity and nationality.[7] Those who are travelling to another part of the common travel area but are not acceptable to the authorities there must be refused entry to the UK.[8] Those seeking leave to enter (whether in the UK or abroad) who are required to hold entry clearance but do not have one, are to be refused.[9] The Secretary of State for the Home Department may give a personal direction not to grant leave to enter or entry clearance on the ground that exclusion is conducive to the public good.[10] That ground is considered further below, as are medical grounds for exclusion, which are in discretionary terms although categorised with the mandatory grounds (3.57–3.60).

[1]   HC 395, para 320(2).
[2]   Immigration Act 1971, s 5(1).
[3]   IDI Jun 04, Ch 9, s 2, para 3.3.
[4]   IDI Ch 9, s 2, para 3.3.
[5]   HC 395, para 320(3).
[6]   IDI Ch 9, s 2, para 4, revealing a discretion even in 'mandatory refusal' cases.
[7]   Immigration Act 1971, Sch 2, para 4 (persons arriving in the UK); Immigration (Leave to Enter and Remain) Order 2000, SI 2000/1161, Art 7(2), (4) (persons seeking leave to enter abroad).
[8]   HC 395, para 320(4).
[9]   HC 395, para 320(5).
[10] HC 395, para 320(6).

The discretionary grounds

3.53 The second list, contained in HC 395 paragraph 320, gives the immigration official a large measure of discretion[1]. Normally the existence of one of these grounds will lead to a refusal of, leave to enter or entry clearance but not always. That is where the discretion comes in. The grounds are wide-ranging, and many are self-explanatory. We examine some of them in detail below.

[1]   The Tribunal has underlined the importance of the reviewable discretion in non-mandatory refusals in *R (on the application of Mauritius) v Entry Clearance Officer, Port Louis* [2003] UKIAT 00030.

Unacceptable passports

3.54 The immigration officer may refuse entry to persons using passports issued by governments of entities not recognised by the UK government.[1] Currently these are the Turkish Republic of Northern Cyprus (TRNC), Republic of China (Taiwan) and Palestine. However, the IDI state that Turkish

Republic of Northern Cyprus passport holders should not be refused entry under this paragraph, although their passports should not be endorsed. Taiwanese passports may be stamped notwithstanding non-recognition. Palestinian Authority travel documents are acceptable for travel to the UK and may be endorsed, although the IDI hasten to add that 'this does not imply recognition of a separate State of Palestine'.[2]

1   HC 395, para 320(10).
2   IDI Ch 9, s 2, para 12.4. See also DSP Ch 4 and Vol 2 Ch 1, which sets out in full those travel documents acceptable for the purposes of entry clearance.

Restricted returnability

3.55 Passengers who do not satisfy the immigration officer that they would be admitted to another country after a stay in the UK may be refused leave to enter.[1] This Rule expressly exempts persons who are eligible for admission for settlement or to a spouse who is admitted for an initial two-year probationary period with a view to settlement, but it applies to everyone else, including unmarried partners entering with a view to settlement,[2] and is not disapplied just because the passenger holds an entry clearance.[3] Where a person's returnability to another country is restricted, leave to enter may nevertheless be given, subject to severe limits on the length of stay.[4]

1   HC 395, para 320(13).
2   However, the IDI, Ch 9, s 2, state that this paragraph should not be used when a person seeks entry with a view to settlement (para 15).
3   See *R v Secretary of State for the Home Department, ex p Sadiq* [1990] Imm AR 364, QBD.
4   See HC 395, paras 21–23.

Previous breaches of immigration law

3.56 Previous breaches of immigration control form separate grounds for refusal. Overstaying or breach of conditions on a previous stay, such as working or recourse to public funds, can give grounds for refusing leave to enter or entry clearance,[1] but should not do so unless the breach was reasonably serious.[2] Obtaining a previous leave to enter or remain by deception also grounds refusal of leave to enter or of entry clearance.[3] A person who has a work permit may be refused leave to enter if, whether or not to his or her knowledge, false representations were employed or material facts not disclosed, for the purpose of obtaining it.[4]

1   HC 395, para 320(11). See *Marquez v Immigration Officer, Gatwick North* [1992] Imm AR 354, which mirrors *R v Secretary of State for the Home Department, ex p Sadiq* [1990] Imm AR 364, QBD (student working in breach of conditions on earlier stay). Emergency recourse to public funds should not ground refusal; see next fn.
2   See 4.27 and 4.28 below. If the breach is not serious enough to warrant refusal of variation of leave, it should not ground refusal of leave to enter or entry clearance. The IDI, Ch 9, s 2 state that this ground should be relied on only against persons shown by their previous conduct to have contrived in a significant way to frustrate the purpose of the rules. It should not be used in a punitive manner, such as relying on a minor period of overstaying (para 13).

3   HC 395, para 320(12). The IDI, Ch 9, s 2 state that the materiality of the deception is relevant, and the decision-maker should ask whether disclosure of the true facts would have led to refusal (para 14). The deception does not need to be that of the applicant, under this Rule, so a person brought in illegally as a child could be penalised years later when seeking to enter as an adult. In these circumstances, however, refusal on this basis could be held unfair or irrational.

4   HC 395, para 320(15). This Rule parallels the Rule allowing immigration officers to refuse leave to enter to those with entry clearance: see 3.71ff below.

Medical grounds

3.57 Entry clearance officers abroad have a discretion to refer intending travellers for medical examination and a power to require a medical report, and leave to enter may be refused if examination is declined or such a report is not produced.[1] Immigration officers at the port may refer anyone seeking leave to enter on arrival in the UK, and anyone arriving with advance leave, to a medical officer for medical examination.[2] The Immigration Rules state that a passenger who intends to stay in the UK for more than six months should normally be referred to the medical inspector for examination.[3] Passengers mentioning health or medical treatment as a reason for their visit, or who appear not to be in good mental or physical health, should also be referred to the medical inspector.[4] Immigration officers have a discretion, which should be exercised sparingly, to refer for examination in any other case.[5] Doctors should be used only to determine whether there are medical reasons for refusing admission or making admission subject to a requirement that the person has further examination or treatment. It is quite wrong to use doctors for other purposes in the administration of immigration control.[6] Refusal to undergo a medical examination is a ground for refusal of leave to enter except where the person is a returning resident.[7] If a person refused entry or detained further examination threatens or attempts suicide, the opinion of the medical inspector on the person's state of mind will be sought immediately, and removal will not be effected in such a case without reference to the casework section.[8] Immigration officers may require any person on board or disembarking from an aircraft to produce a valid international vaccination certificate, and may detain anyone who embarked in a local infected area and who is unable to produce such a certificate to await the arrival of a medical inspector, for up to three hours.[9] Passengers requiring urgent medical treatment should be required to submit to further examination; those taken to hospital before any examination by an immigration officer remain liable to examination and to the requirement to obtain leave to enter.[10]

1   Immigration (Leave to Enter and Remain) Order 2000, SI 2000/1161, Art 7(3) and (4); HC 395 paras 39 and 320(17). The DSP Ch 24 at para 24.2 state that each post should adopt an appropriate policy on medical referrals.

2   Immigration Act 1971, Sch 2, para 2; 2A(4). See 3.38 above

3   HC 395, para 36. An immigration officer will normally waive the requirement for medical examination for passengers intending to remain longer than six months if they are returning from short visits abroad, or are passengers of international repute or good standing, or are teachers coming for authorised employment, or are students sponsored by the British Council (who will have had a medical before being granted a scholarship), or dependants of US Forces (who will have had a medical before leaving the US), or where the medical inspector is not immediately available, or in any other case where the immigration officer feels it unnecessary: IDI Mar 04, Ch 1, s 8, para 2.10. Examination may also be

waived for passengers coming for private medical treatment sponsored by their government, those with entry clearance for medical treatment, or where the nature of the
proposed treatment makes it clear that the medical inspector would not advise against
entry: IDI Mar 04, Ch 1, s 8, para 2.10.

4   HC 395, para 36.
5   The IDI, Ch 1, s 8 suggest that a person who is 'obviously unwell or [who] appears bodily
    dirty' could be referred (para 2.2).
6   In 1979, after the 'virginity testing' scandal, the Secretary of State gave instructions that
    medical inspectors should not be asked to examine passengers to establish whether they
    have borne children or have had sexual relations. In 1982 the Secretary of State gave
    further instructions that medical inspectors should not be asked to X-ray persons for the
    purpose of assessing their age. The IDI stress that it is essential that these instructions be
    strictly observed (para 2). A woman should not be referred for confirmation of a suspected
    pregnancy unless there is strong evidence that the purpose of her visit is to take advantage
    of NHS facilities: IDI, Ch 1, s 8, para 2.6. But seeking to take such advantage is not a
    ground for refusal of entry. So what is the point of referral?
7   HC 395, paras 38 and 320(17).
8   IDI, Ch 1, s 8, para 2.8.
9   Under the Public Health (Aircraft) Regulations 1970: see IDI, Ch 1, s 8, Annex Z.
10 IDI, Ch 1, s 8, Annex Z, para 2.1.

3.58 Where the medical inspector at the port advises that for medical reasons
it is undesirable to admit someone, the immigration officer must refuse leave
to enter unless the person is settled here or there are 'strong compassionate
reasons justifying admission.'[1] According to the IDI, the medical inspector
would normally certify that it is undesirable to admit a passenger who is
found or suspected to be suffering from pulmonary tuberculosis, venereal
disease, leprosy or trachoma, or if the passenger is heavily infested with lice, is
bodily dirty or is suffering from scabies.[2] The IDI indicate that medical
inspectors may also issue a certificate if the nature of the person's condition
would interfere with his or her ability to comply with the no recourse to
public funds requirements.[3] However, medical inspectors should only certify
that it is undesirable to admit a passenger to the UK when satisfied that his or
her condition represents a significant risk to public health.[4] This suggests that
a medical certificate of undesirability based on economic rather than public
health criteria might be unlawful, although para 37 of the Rules clearly
empowers immigration officers to have regard to economic considerations in
deciding whether to refuse leave to enter. A passenger who is diagnosed as
suffering from AIDS or HIV infection, or any other serious illness, should not
be refused on public health grounds alone.[5] The IDI state that immigration
officers are entitled to take into account the cost of any treatment which may
be required. Since NHS treatment does not count as 'public funds', leave could
not be refused to a passenger who otherwise qualifies on the ground that he or
she is likely to seek such treatment, and the immigration officer would
therefore have to justify refusal of leave or entry clearance to an AIDS or HIV
sufferer on other grounds.[6]

1   HC 395, para 320(7).
2   IDI Mar 04, Ch 1, s 8, para 2.1.
3   IDI Ch 1, s 8, para 2.1; see also HC 395 para 37.
4   IDI Ch 1, s 8, para 2.2.
5   IDI Ch 1, s 8, para 2.5.
6   For eligibility for NHS treatment see 13.201 below.

3.59 The Rule appears to give medical inspectors enormous powers, as
refusal is based (a) on the medical inspector's diagnosis and (b) on his or her

views on the desirability of admission, and the wording of the Rule is that immigration officers can only overrule the medical inspector if 'strong compassionate grounds' warrant admission. The Tribunal in *Al-Tuwaidji v Chief Immigration Officer, Heathrow* took the view that refusal was mandatory even if independent medical evidence puts into question the diagnosis or advice of the medical inspector. It held that a medical inspector's diagnosis of schizophrenia could not be challenged on appeal, and that in the absence of compassionate circumstances leave should be refused.[1] We suggest that this decision cannot stand today, since it embodies fundamental unfairness,[2] as well as involving unlawful delegation of power from immigration officers to medical inspectors which is not warranted by the terms of the Immigration Act 1971. A better view of HC 395, paragraph 320(7), and one which accords better with the other relevant rule, para 37, would be to treat the medical advice as a factor to be taken into account by immigration officers in the exercise of their own discretion, enabling them to take into account alternative medical diagnosis and opinions as well as the advice of the medical inspector.[3]

1   [1974] Imm AR 34. Followed in *Mohazeb v Immigration Officer, Harwich* [1990] Imm AR 555.
2   See chapter 8 below.
3   See *Pearson v Immigration Appeal Tribunal* [1978] Imm AR 212, CA; *R v Secretary of State for the Home Department, ex p Ounejma* [1989] Imm AR 75, QBD where a similar argument as regards mandatory entry clearance was rejected. See further *R v Secretary of State for the Home Department, ex p Rofathullah* [1989] QB 219, [1988] Imm AR 514, CA. This is also the view of the Home Office: see IDI Mar 04, Ch 1, s 8, para 2.2; IDI Jun 04, Ch 9, s 2, para 8.1.

3.60 The Tribunal has in the past mitigated the effect of the mandatory refusal by a liberal interpretation of strong compassionate circumstances warranting admission.[1] The fact that a patient has undergone a cure would itself be a compassionate circumstance.[2]

1   See *Entry Clearance Officer, Bombay v Sacha* [1973] Imm AR 5.
2   See *Parvez v Immigration Officer, London (Heathrow) Airport* [1979–80] Imm AR 84, and *Immigration Officer, London (Heathrow) Airport v Bhatti* [1979–80] Imm AR 86n.

Criminal record

3.61 Certain persons who have committed a criminal offence are to be refused leave to enter or entry clearance unless the entry clearance officer or immigration officer considers admission to be justified on strong compassionate grounds.[1] The Rule applies to spouses or children under 18 coming for settlement, but in those cases there are more likely to be strong compassionate reasons.[2] Offences which count are those which, if committed in the UK, are punishable with imprisonment for a term of 12 months or more or, if committed outside the UK, would be so punishable if the conduct constituting the offence had occurred in the UK. Where the fact of conviction is disputed the burden is on the immigration officer.[3] It is unclear whether a 'conviction' can be disregarded if it was obtained without due process or *in absentia*, but the entry clearance officer or immigration officer may in such circumstances exercise discretion to grant leave or entry clearance.[4] Spent convictions must be disregarded.[5] If the passenger is exempt from deportation (by virtue of being a Commonwealth citizen with long residence in the UK),[6] it would be perverse to refuse him or her leave to enter in reliance on a criminal conviction or on conducive grounds.[7]

1   HC 395, para 320(18).
2   But see *Vasiljevic v Secretary of State for the Home Department* [1975] Imm AR 100.
3   *Hashim* (6421) IAT, unreported.
4   *Hashim* (6421) IAT, unreported.
5   See IDI Mar 04, Ch 9, s 2, para 20.
6   Ie, under Immigration Act 1971, s 7.
7   *R (on the application of Harris) v Secretary of State for the Home Department* [2001] EWHC 225 (Admin), [2001] INLR 584. For conducive grounds see 3.65 below.

3.62   In decisions under the old rules, the Tribunal held that admission would only be allowed if there are 'strong compassionate circumstances'.[1] 'Strong compassionate circumstances' are not further defined or qualified in the Immigration Rules and ought to be given their ordinary meaning. Thus in *Liberto*[2] it was held that strong compassionate circumstances did not include the need personally to be present in order to prosecute civil proceedings in the English courts. In another case it was held that there were strong compassionate grounds where the appellant had been convicted for possession of a small amount of cannabis, but had a wife and children born in the UK who, for family reasons, did not want to leave and who had had previous visits without incident or complaint.[3] What constitutes compassionate circumstances is largely a question of fact in each case. The seriousness of the offence and the immigrant's propensity to re-offend will be relevant.[4] In *Palacio*[5] the applicant, who had a conviction for fraud, wished to visit this country for one week in order to see his fiancée and two of his children by a former marriage. He was refused entry and this was upheld by the Tribunal, ruling that the circumstances were not 'of a totally exceptional and compelling nature' so as to justify admission.[6] The Divisional Court said the Tribunal was wrong to redefine 'strong compassionate circumstances', but did not reverse the decision, suggesting instead that the appellant make a fresh application.

1   *Vasiljevic v Secretary of State for the Home Department* [1975] Imm AR 100; *Sanchez* (4731) following *R v Secretary of State for the Home Department, ex p Guediche* (18 December 1985, unreported), DC.
2   [1975] Imm AR 61. However, the equality of aims requirements of Art 6 ECHR might dictate a different conclusion today; see *R v Immigration officer, ex p John Quaquah* [2000] INLR 196, QBD.
3   *Bailey* (3670).
4   *Langridge v Secretary of State for the Home Department* [1972] Imm AR 38.
5   *R v Immigration Appeal Tribunal, ex p Palacio* [1979–80] Imm AR 178.
6   A test formulated by the Tribunal in *Visa Officer, Jerusalem v Awadallah* [1978] Imm AR 5.

3.63   However, the Rule is not mandatory in terms but discretionary, and it is not necessary for there to be strong compassionate circumstances in order for discretion to be exercised in the applicant's favour. The fact that there is a residual discretion under which a person to whom the paragraph applies may be given leave to enter the UK was emphasised by Sullivan J in the Mike Tyson case,[1] in which Justice for Women challenged the Secretary of State for the Home Department's instruction to admit the heavyweight boxer, who had been sentenced to six years' imprisonment in the US for rape. He pointed out that it may be considered that it is in the public interest that that person be permitted to come to the UK, given some learning, entertainment or economic value that he can bring to this country. Whether those advantages are such as to justify an exception being made to the normal rule is a matter, in normal cases, for the immigration officer to decide. But he expressly upheld the general discretion to admit in the absence of strong compassionate circumstances – a discretion belonging both to the immigration officer and to the Secretary of State.

[1] *R v Secretary of State for the Home Department, ex p Bindel* [2001] Imm AR 1, QBD.

3.64 The criteria for exclusion under HC 395, paragraph 320(18) for having a criminal record remain distressingly vague. Those entitled to rely on EC law are much better off, since exclusion must be much more rigorously justified.[1] Care must also be taken to ensure that the right to family life is not interfered with in a manner contrary to Article 8 of the ECHR by taking disproportionate measures which are not necessary in a democratic society (see chapter 8 below). No one claiming asylum can be refused leave to enter on the basis of this or any other general Immigration Rule; the Convention criteria for exclusion must be applied.[2] Similarly, no one claiming a fear of treatment contrary to Article 3 of the ECHR may be refused leave to enter by virtue of this Rule, or any other.[3]

[1] See C-348/96 *Calfa (Donatella)* [1999] INLR 333, ECJ. See chapter 7 below.
[2] See chapter 12 below.
[3] See chapter 8 below.

Exclusion for the public good

3.65 The Immigration Rules provide for refusal of leave to enter or of entry clearance, or cancellation of advance leave on arrival, on 'conducive to the public good' grounds in two distinct situations. Refusal is mandatory, where the Secretary of State for the Home Department personally has so directed.[1] But even where there is no such direction, leave should normally be refused,[2] or is to be cancelled,[3] where the immigration officer has information which makes it seem right to refuse leave to enter, for example, in the light of the passenger's character, conduct or associations. Refusal on 'conducive grounds' may thus result from a prior ban imposed by the Secretary of State or from an on-the-spot decision by an immigration officer. An example of a prior blanket ban was that imposed on Scientologists in 1968 on the grounds that Scientology was 'socially harmful' and a 'serious danger to ... health'.[4] This ban was only lifted in 1980.[5] The Secretary of State has imposed bans on notorious racists such as Ku Klux Klan imperial wizard Bill Wilkinson,[6] and on US Nation of Islam leader Louis Farrakhan.[7] An example of an on-the-spot refusal is the case where a man is given leave to enter by the immigration officer and passes through to Customs, where drugs are discovered in his baggage and he is refused leave on 'conducive' grounds.[8]

[1] HC 395, paras 320(6) and 321A(4).
[2] HC 395, para 320(19).
[3] HC 395, para 321A(5).
[4] 769 HC Official Report (5th series) written answers col 189.

5   988 HC Official Report (5th series) written answers col 578. See further Case No 41/74: *Van Duyn v Home Office* [1975] Ch 358, [1974] ECR 1337, ECJ.

6   (1978) Guardian, 17 February.

7   This ban was upheld by the Court of Appeal in *R (on the application of Farrakhan) v Secretary of State for the Home Department* [2002] EWCA Civ 606, [2002] QB 1391, [2002] 3 WLR 481, [2002] 4 All ER 289, [2002] Imm AR 447, [2002] INLR 257 reversing the judgment of Turner J in the Administrative Court ([2001] EWHC Admin 781).

8   *Villone v Secretary of State for the Home Department* [1979–80] Imm AR 23. Whether refusal would be justified in this situation depends on whether the quantity and questioning indicate commercial or personal use: IDI Jun 04, Ch 9, s 2, para 21.2–4. Other examples might be where someone has no criminal record but is suspected to be involved in organised crime (for someone refused entry on these grounds and because of their criminal record see *R v Immigration Appeal Tribunal, ex p Palacio* [1979–80] Imm AR 178).

3.66 In determining whether a person should be refused admission on 'public good' grounds, the discretion is wide, but the reasons are not to be trivial or light.[1] This, however, has not prevented refusals for possession of trivial amounts of cannabis,[2] or preventing the entry of someone who has been tried and acquitted of a charge of illegal importation of drugs, just because the immigration officer took a different view from the jury.[3] Nor has it prevented the Tribunal suggesting that there is a general rule that it is conducive to the public good to refuse admission to anyone attempting to import opium.[4] The upshot is that in drug smuggling cases, the offender or suspect is unlikely to obtain admission and the Immigration Rules will be administered without regard to any of the principles governing deportation recommendations by a criminal court or decisions to deport by the Home Office. In deception cases, however, there is likely to be a greater cross-reference to the deportation decisions, particularly since the House of Lords held in *R v Immigration Appeal Tribunal, ex p Patel*[5] that past dishonest deception was covered by the power to deem deportation conducive to the public good.[6] Refusal of entry on conducive grounds based on serious deception, past or present, is unlikely to be struck down as unreasonable on a judicial review challenge.[7]

1   *Scheele* [1976] Imm AR 1.

2   *Villone* as above. Now, however, the IDI Jun 04, Ch 9, s 2, para 21.2 indicate a different attitude. Dealing with those caught at the airport in possession of drugs, they say that if the quantity is small and the passenger has enough money to pay the fine and cover his or her proposed stay in the UK, he or she should be admitted. Refusal of leave should only follow if there is good reason to believe that the drugs are intended for sale, or if the passenger is an addict or regular user: IDI Jun 04, Ch 9, s 2, para 21.2.

3   *Nkiti v Immigration Officer, Gatwick* [1989] Imm AR 585, CA. Now, however, the immigration officer must be satisfied 'beyond reasonable doubt' before refusing on the basis that a passenger is a trafficker in pornography, although seizure of material by Customs would constitute prima facie grounds for refusal.

4   *Khazrai v Immigration Officer, London (Heathrow) Airport* [1981] Imm AR 9.

5   [1988] AC 910, [1988] 2 All ER 378.

6   Immigration Act 1971, s 3(5)(a). Knowing use of a forged document may ground refusal under this head as well as under para 320(3): IDI, Ch 9, s 2, para 21.5.

7   See *R v Secretary of State for the Home Department, ex p Kwapong* [1993] Imm AR 569 (Nigerian with indefinite residence facilitates an illegal entry by bringing with him a child travelling on a false passport); *R v Secretary of State for the Home Department, ex p Sanyaolu* [1993] Imm AR 505 (applicant had obtained his previous leave by saying he was supported by an uncle, when in fact he was working in breach of conditions).

3.67 Before the Tribunal the test is not so stringent. It is dealing with an appeal on the merits and can assess the exercise of discretion by the immigration officer. This means that Tribunal decisions can often throw greater light on the proper exercise by immigration officers of their discretion. In *Olufosoye*[1] the Tribunal gave guidance on public good refusals, where the holder of a multiple entry visit visa had worked in breach of her leave conditions on a first visit, and was refused entry when she returned to the UK. First, the Tribunal held that where the immigration authorities contended that exclusion was conducive to the public good, whether on a decision to deport or a refusal of leave to enter, it was for them to satisfy the appellate authority that the decision was justified. In so far as the justification consists of deception or other criminal conduct, the standard of proof will be at the higher end of the spectrum of balance of probability. Secondly, in the light of the provisions of HC 395, paragraph 320(11) and (12), it was necessary to prove grounds other than those set out in those paragraphs to justify exclusion as conducive to the public good. The general reasons for refusing the grant of an entry clearance, such as breach of the time limit or conditions of a previous leave, are a different set of criteria from exclusion on conducive grounds, and paragraph 320(19) should not be used as a back door so as to import into paragraph 321 extra grounds for refusing leave to the holder of an entry clearance. Thirdly, the fact that particular conduct would not provide the basis for a decision to deport on conducive grounds was relevant in considering whether the same conduct should lead to a refusal of leave to enter on 'conducive grounds'.[2] Where a decision on conducive grounds is based on conduct which has been the subject of previous investigation or adjudication, the immigration officer should not normally depart from the results of that inquiry.[3]

[1]   [1992] Imm AR 141.
[2]   In *ECO Amsterdam v Bishop* [2002] UKIAT 05532 the IAT did not consider that a history of threats and aggressive behaviour coupled with deception, rendered exclusion conducive to the public good.
[3]   See *Ali v Secretary of State for the Home Department* [1984] 1 All ER 1009, [1984] 1 WLR 663, CA; see also (in another context) *R v Secretary of State for the Home Department, ex p Danaie* [1998] Imm AR 84.

3.68 Refusal on conducive grounds will normally be made in the light of the passenger's character, conduct or associations, but it need not be confined to reasons of this kind. This was made clear by the Divisional Court in *Ajaib Singh*.[1] There a man had obtained an entry certificate to come to the UK for marriage. At the time, however, his bride-to-be was only 14½ years old. This had been overlooked by the entry clearance officer, although fully disclosed, but was spotted by the immigration officer on his arrival and leave to enter was refused. If the reason had been merely to correct an executive or administrative error by the entry clearance officer, the Divisional Court suggested that refusal would be wrong. But more was involved. The discretion to refuse on public good grounds was deliberately left in wide terms so that an immigration officer could exercise a wide discretion. The public good rule has thus been invoked to exclude a man who obtained his prior residence status by a marriage of convenience.[2]

[1]   *R v Immigration Appeal Tribunal, ex p Ajaib Singh* [1978] Imm AR 59. This situation is now covered by HC 395, para 277.
[2]   *Osama v Immigration Officer, London (Gatwick) Airport* [1978] Imm AR 8. See also *R v Immigration Appeal Tribunal, ex p Cheema* [1982] Imm AR 124, CA.

EC joint list of persons to be refused entry

3.69 The Schengen Information System, set up under the Schengen Agreements of 1985 and 1990, is a system for the exchange of information concerning persons who for one reason or another – commission of criminal offences, immigration irregularities, football hooliganism, suspected involvement with banned organisations – are considered undesirable for entry into Member States. The UK has opted out of the Schengen *acquis* which now forms part of the 'framework' of the EU,[1] but has indicated its intention to be part of the Schengen Information System. It is probable that persons whose names come up on the computer from other Member States are in fact refused on conducive grounds by an operational practice of co-operation which is not fully transparent.

[1]   Protocol 2 to the Consolidated EC Treaty incorporates the Schengen *acquis* into the framework of the EU, but acknowledges that the UK and Ireland are not parties to the Agreements, although they should be allowed to opt in to some parts. See 7.28ff below.

Excluded persons under international obligations

3.70 Section 8B of the Immigration Act 1971 (inserted by section 8 of the Immigration and Asylum Act 1999) provides for mandatory refusal or cancellation of leave to enter of 'excluded persons', defined as persons named or described by UN Resolution or EU Council instrument in designated Orders under the 1971 Act.[1] Such persons are also to be stripped of diplomatic exemption.[2] The Immigration (Designation of Travel Bans) Order 2000[3] provides that persons named by, or under, or described by a designated instrument (as set out in the Schedule) need not be excluded from the UK if admitting them would not be contrary to the obligations in the designated instruments listed in Article 2 of the Order; or if their exclusion breached the UK's obligations under the ECHR or the Geneva Convention. The designated list is contained in Schedule 1 to the Order.[4] Clearly, these provisions are designed to exclude war criminals and persons of that ilk, rather than football hooligans. However, they may well be used to exclude members and supporters of organisations perceived as terrorist under the very wide new definitions on the domestic and European plane, and the designation orders should therefore be monitored with care.

[1]   Immigration Act 1971, as amended, s 8B(4).
[2]   Immigration Act 1971, s 8B(3).
[3]   SI 2000/2724, in force 10 October 2000 as amended by SI 2001/2377 and SI 2003/3285.
[4]   The most recent version of the Schedule, amended by SI 2003/3285 (in force 9 December 2003), refers to UN Security Council resolutions in respect of Al Qua'ida, the Taleban, Liberia and Sierra Leone and also EU Council instruments relating to Bosnia-Herzegovina, Burma, FRY, Liberia, Moldovan Republic, Sierra Leone and Zimbabwe.

False representation to obtain entry clearance

3.71 Entry clearance may be revoked,[1] or leave to enter refused,[2] if the entry clearance officer or immigration officer is satisfied that false representations were used to obtain entry clearance, whether or not to the holder's know-ledge.[3] Here we are not talking about an entry clearance which operates as a leave to enter, where different considerations apply. The representations may be written or oral. It is incumbent on the officer to prove the case to the requisite standard, ie prove a representation, its falsity and the fact that it was made for the purpose of gaining entry clearance.[4] The Court of Appeal has ruled that a false representation is simply a representation that is inaccurate, and does not necessarily connote fraud.[5] Where fraud is alleged the standard of proof will have to be higher. A representation will not be false if it is only a statement of the existence of facts on a certain day, and not a continuing representation of future matters. Does the false representation have to be material in the sense of decisive of the application? In *Sukhjinder Kaur*,[6] a woman coming to join her husband for settlement in the UK failed to mention to the entry clearance officer that he was in prison on remand for homicide. The Court of Appeal upheld the immigration officer's refusal of leave to enter, following its earlier decision in *Akhtar*,[7] and holding that the false represen-tation does not need to have been determinative in the sense that the entry clearance officer would have been bound to refuse entry clearance if he or she had known the true facts.[8] All that is required is that the immigration officer should be satisfied that false representations were employed for the purposes of obtaining the clearance. The court also held that the false representations did not need to be false in a material respect .[9] If the entry clearance operated as leave to enter, however, different considerations apply. First, the matter is dealt with by statute and not just the immigration rules.[10] Secondly, that leave may only be cancelled where false information has been given, if the false information has been given by the by the applicant and not some third party.[11] Thirdly, in contrast to the position described above, the false information must be 'material', because in the words of the statute, the leave must have been obtained 'as a result of' the false information.[12]

---

[1]   HC 395, para 30A(i).

[2]   HC 395, para 321(i).

[3]   Examples of third-party false representations given in the IDI are a father applying for entry clearance for a child to be accompanied by the child's mother, knowing that the mother does not intend to stay (so-called 'courier wives'), and an employer intending to fire a worker posted to the UK: IDI Feb 02, Ch 9, s 3, Refusal of leave to enter for holders of entry clearance, para 3.3.

[4]   The standard required will be particularly high where the entry clearance has been issued following a successful appeal, where the starting point is a binding decision in favour of the appellant: *R v Secretary of State for the Home Department, ex p Miah* [1983] Imm AR 91, DC; *Ali v Secretary of State for the Home Department* [1984] 1 All ER 1009, [1984] 1 WLR 663, CA. See also *R v Secretary of State for the Home Department, ex p Danaie* [1998] Imm AR 84, CA.

[5]   *Akhtar v Immigration Appeal Tribunal* [1991] Imm AR 326, CA.

[6]   *Kaur (Sukhjinder) v Secretary of State for the Home Department* [1998] Imm AR 1, CA.

[7]   *Akhtar v Immigration Appeal Tribunal* above.

[8]   This was the old test in the illegal entry cases on false representation to secure entry: see *R v Secretary of State for the Home Department, ex p Jayakody* [1982] 1 All ER 461, Imm AR 205, CA; *R v Secretary of State for the Home Department, ex p Ming* [1994] Imm AR 216, QBD.

[9]   *Kaur (Sukhjinder)* above. In *Akhtar* the CA left this question open; in *Eusebio* (4739) the Tribunal had held that false representations had to be material. In *Kaur* the Court said that the position was quite different from case of non-disclosure, where there needs to be materiality in order to place limits on the wide scope of the duty of candour: [1998] Imm AR 1 at 9–10. For refusal on the ground of a *previous* deception, the IDI (Jun 04, Ch 9, s 2, para 14) state that the materiality of the deception is highly relevant: see 3.56 above.

10 Immigration Act 1971, Sch 2, para 2A(2) and (8) and HC 395, para 321A(2).
11 Immigration Act 1971, Sch 2, para 2A(2) and (8) and HC 395, para 321A(2).
12 These changes are reflected in HC 395, para 321A, inserted by HC 704 on 28 July 2000.

Non-disclosure of material facts

3.72 The second main ground for revoking an entry clearance or refusing leave to enter on an entry clearance which is ineffective as leave to enter is where the immigration officer is satisfied that material facts were not disclosed for the purpose of obtaining entry clearance. Here, the critical question is the meaning of 'material'. In *Sukhjinder Kaur*[1] the Court of Appeal again adopted a different approach from that taken in the illegal entry cases, holding that 'material' did not mean 'decisive', as the court had previously held in *Jayakody*,[2] but it was only necessary that the facts not disclosed would be likely to have influenced the decision. All that immigration officers need show is that passengers have failed to disclose facts which they knew or ought to have known would be relevant in considering whether to grant the visa. However, in practice the scope of relevant questions is usually determined by those posed in the application form and any oral questions. In determining whether facts are 'material', the critical question is the effect they would have had on the application actually made. Where the entry clearance operated as leave to enter, it can only be cancelled on this ground if the failure was that of the applicant, not if a third party was responsible.[3] An immigrant who has obtained an entry clearance on an inaccurate basis cannot replace the actual application with a wholly different application on arrival and argue that since he or she might have been admitted on this new application the previous non-disclosures are immaterial.[4] As we have seen, an immigration officer may cancel an entry clearance if the holder seeks leave to enter for a different purpose.[5] If the entry clearance operated as leave to enter, however, different considerations apply. First, the matter is dealt with by statute and not just the immigration rules. [6] Secondly, that leave may only be cancelled where it is the applicant's failure to disclose material facts and not some third party. [7] Thirdly, the failure to disclose must be 'material' and the leave must have been obtained 'as a result of' the failure to disclose material facts. [8]

1 [1998] Imm AR 1, CA. See also *Marquez* [1992] Imm AR 354.
2 *R v Secretary of State for the Home Department, ex p Jayakody* [1982] 1 All ER 461, [1981] Imm AR 205, CA; see also *R v Secretary of State for the Home Department, ex p Ming* [1994] Imm AR 216, QBD.
3 HC 395, para 321A(2).
4 *Bugdaycay v Secretary of State for the Home Department* [1987] AC 514 at 525, HL.
5 Immigration (Leave to Enter and Remain) Order, SI 2000/1161, Art 6(2); HC 395, para 30C.
6 Immigration Act 1971, Sch 2, para 2A (2), (2A) and (8), and HC 395, para 321A(2).
7 Immigration Act 1971, Sch 2, para 2A (2), (2A) and (8), and HC 395, para 321A(2).
8 Immigration Act 1971, Sch 2, para 2A (2), (2A) and (8), and HC 395, para 321A(2).

Change of circumstances since issue

3.73 The entry clearance officer or immigration officer may revoke entry clearance[1] or refuse leave to enter, or cancel it if the entry clearance operated as leave to enter, if a change of circumstances since the issue of entry clearance has removed the basis of the holder's claim to admission.[2] This does not include children, including children adopted under recognised adoption procedures, coming to join parents settled in the UK who become over-age between the issue of entry clearance and travelling to the UK.[3] The change of circumstances must be sufficient to remove the basis of the holder's claim to admission, so only decisive changes will suffice, such as marriage by a child seeking entry as a dependant of his or her parents.[4] Other changes may often be a matter of degree and will depend on the facts.[5] Marriage by a dependent child is perhaps the most frequent decisive change, but there has to be a valid marriage and the burden of proving that is on the immigration officer. Where a decision on entry has been delayed and the entrant has been on temporary admission, the change of circumstances may arise after arrival in the UK. Thus, where an Iranian was a genuine visitor on arrival but decided to remain as a businessman prior to the decision to grant or refuse entry, this was a change of circumstances.[6] Decisions on this provision are sometimes very harsh, as in cases where the sponsor or the accompanying parent dies between the date of issue of the entry clearance and arrival in the UK.[7]

[1]   HC 395, para 30A(ii).
[2]   Immigration Act 1971, Sch 2, para 2A(2)(a) and HC 395, paras 321(ii) and 321A(1).
[3]   HC 395, paras 321(ii) and 310. Paragraph 321 does not apply to children joining parents who are not settled or in a category leading to settlement.
[4]   The burden of proof is on the immigration officer. See *R v Immigration Appeal Tribunal, ex p Begum (Suily)* [1990] Imm AR 226, QBD.
[5]   *Immigration Officer, Heathrow v Salmak* [1991] Imm AR 191, IAT; *Olufosoye* [1992] Imm AR 141, IAT. Cancellation of leave to a student who had ceased to attend classes and was working 39 hours a week was upheld by the Tribunal in *B (Nigeria) v CIO Heathrow* [2004] UKIAT 55. The IDI refer to withdrawal of a job offer or of student sponsorship, or the permanent departure of the sponsor of children, as changes of circumstance justifying refusal of leave to enter: IDI Feb 02, Ch 9 s 3, Refusal of leave to enter to holders of entry clearance, para 4.
[6]   *Teflisi* (3522) unreported.
[7]   See *Arshad* [1977] Imm AR 19; *R v Secretary of State for the Home Department, ex p Begum (Angur)* [1989] Imm AR 302, QBD.

Additional grounds for refusal or cancellation of leave to enter

3.74 Apart from the three general grounds on which entry clearance may be revoked or leave to enter refused or cancelled (false information or representations, non-disclosure of material facts and change of circumstances), there are additional grounds which do not entitle the entry clearance officer to revoke entry clearance but which entitle him or her, or an immigration officer on arrival, to refuse or cancel leave to enter.[1] Leave to enter may be refused to an entry clearance holder (but not cancelled if it operates as leave to enter) on grounds of restricted returnability, if the passenger cannot satisfy the immigration officer that he or she would be admitted to another country after staying in the UK.[2] Leave may be refused or cancelled on medical grounds;[3] at the personal direction of the Secretary of State for the Home Department on grounds of public good; or that it would be conducive to the public good to cancel leave. Leave to enter may be cancelled where the passenger's purpose in arriving in the UK is different from that stated in the entry clearance.[4]

¹   Immigration (Leave to Enter and Remain) Order 2000, SI 2000/1161, Art 13(7); Immigration Act 1971, Sch 2, para 2A(2)–(8); HC 395, paras 321, 321A.
²   HC 395, para 321(iii); see *R v Secretary of State for the Home Department, ex p Sadiq* [1990] Imm AR 364. See 3.55 above.
³   See 3.57–3.60 above.
⁴   Immigration Act 1971, Sch 2, para 2A(2A), inserted by Asylum and Immigration (Treatment of Claimants, etc) Act 2004, s 18 from 1 October 2004: SI 2004/2325.

Re-determining admissibility

3.75 Where the validity of a visa or an entry certificate has been effectively undermined by false representations, a failure to disclose material facts or by a change of circumstance, the reality is that in most cases a refusal or cancellation of leave will be the inevitable consequence. But there will always be a residue of cases where this is not necessarily so. The Court of Appeal decision in *Akhtar*¹ leaves undecided the consequences of a finding by the immigration officer that false representations were employed in obtaining entry clearance. Can immigration officers re-determine admissibility in any case, or must they refuse or cancel leave to enter and treat the entry clearance as ineffective in all cases? The wording of the rule relating to cancellation of advance leave (whether or not granted by entry clearance) is mandatory: leave to enter or remain which is in force 'is to be cancelled' on these grounds.² The consequence of cancellation of advance leave to enter is that the entry clearance ceases to have effect.³ This contrasts with the language of the earlier rule relating to refusal of leave to enter of those holding entry clearance, which is on its face discretionary, but which was held to be mandatory in effect. The arcane debate on the extent to which entry clearance remains 'current' for the purposes of appeals⁴ is, we suggest, made redundant by the provision in the Immigration Act 1971 that cancellation of leave to enter is deemed a refusal of leave to enter while holding entry clearance.⁵ This gives rise to a right of appeal, which we deal with in the next paragraph.

¹   [1991] Imm AR 326, CA.
²   HC 395, para 321A.
³   Immigration (Leave to Enter and Remain) Order 2000, SI 2000/1161, Art 6(1).
⁴   See 4th edition, 3.21–3.23.
⁵   Immigration Act 1971, Sch 2, para 2A(8).

RIGHTS OF APPEAL

3.76 A refusal of an entry clearance or a refusal of leave to enter on arrival gives rise to a right of appeal only where detailed conditions relating to age, possession of relevant documents and category of entrant are met, unless the appeal is brought on race discrimination or Refugee/Human Rights Convention grounds.¹ Visitors (except for family visitors), short-term students, prospective students who have not yet been accepted on a course and their dependants, have no right of appeal against refusal of entry clearance, except on race discrimination or human rights grounds.² Section 92(3) of the 2002 Act as originally enacted provides that refusal or deemed refusal of leave to enter³ to a person holding entry clearance or a work permit attracted an in-country right of appeal. This is now amended by the Asylum and Immigration (Treatment of Claimants, etc) Act 2004,[4] so that the in-country right of appeal only applies to those with entry clearance (possession of a work permit is no longer enough unless the passenger is a British national),[5] and does not apply where advance leave is cancelled on the grounds of a change of circumstances, the giving of materially false information, medical grounds or that the passenger seeks entry for a different purpose than that for which the entry clearance was issued.[6] Someone seeking leave in one capacity and refused may have rights of appeal on grounds raised subsequently to the refusal (ie asylum or human rights grounds) under the appeals provisions of the Nationality Immigration and Asylum Act 2002. All of these rights of appeal are dealt with in detail in chapter 18 below.

1   Nationality, Immigration and Asylum Act 2002, ss 82, 88 and 89.
2   NIAA 2002, ss 90, 91. There is no right of appeal on Refugee Convention grounds. The Immigration and Asylum Act 1999, s 23 provides for the monitoring of refusals of entry clearance where there is no right of appeal. The reports of the independent monitor are available on the Foreign and Commonwealth Office website at www.fco.gov.uk. They recommend general procedural improvements, but do not deal with the merits of any individual case.
3   Ie, passengers whose advance leave to enter (entry clearance operating as leave to enter) is cancelled on arrival: Immigration Act 1971, Sch 2, para 2A(9).
4   Asylum and Immigration (Treatment of Claimants, etc) Act 2004, s 28, in force from 1 October 2004: SI 2004/2523.
5   NIAA 2002, s 92(3)(b), (3D), as substituted and inserted by AI(TC)A 2004, s 28, as from a date to be appointed. The categories of British national whose possession of a work permit gives rise to an in-country appeal are British Overseas Territories citizens, British Overseas citizens, British Nationals (Overseas), British Protected persons and British subjects: s 92(3D)(c) as inserted.
6   NIAA 2002, s 92(3A)–(3C) as inserted by the AI(TC)A 2004, s 28, as from 1 October 2004: SI 2004/2523.

Chapter 4
CONTROL AFTER ENTRY

4.1	Extending and varying leave
4.24	Exercising the discretion to vary leave
4.36	Registration with the police
4.40	Hotel registers
4.41	Control of departure

EXTENDING AND VARYING LEAVE

4.1 In the last chapter we looked at leave to enter. In this chapter we look at leave to remain. Section 4(1) of the Immigration Act 1971, as originally enacted made a clear distinction between the two and made it clear that in general immigration officers were responsible for leave to enter and the Secretary of State's officials for leave to remain. However, these distinctions have become blurred, as immigration officers have taken on functions of varying leave at ports and the Secretary of State has taken responsibility for specified applications for leave to enter.[1] The permissive system of immigration control which was represented by these two kinds of permission – leave to enter and leave to remain – stands in contrast to the rights-based system of European free movement law.[2] Under the domestic system of immigration control envisaged by the IA 1971 as originally enacted, rights belonged to those outside immigration control, through the right of abode or the common travel area, while the entry of those requiring leave was a matter of discretion. All these distinctions are further blurred with the UK's opt-in to the European residence permit scheme.[3] In this chapter we discuss these developments in the context of the general framework of post-entry control; the powers of the Secretary of State for the Home Department and civil servants to extend, refuse to extend, or curtail leave to enter or remain in the UK; requirements to register with the police, and for hotels to keep registers of guests. We do not deal with formal qualifications needed by students, businessmen and so forth, who are seeking extensions of leave, because these topics have their own chapters; we deal here with the general policies. A person may qualify for an extension of leave under the formal rules relating to students or business persons, but may still not succeed in obtaining an extension, because of a bad immigration record or a serious criminal offence coming to light.

4.2 The European Community institutions not only make laws governing the free movement rights of EU citizens and their families; increasingly Community law sets common norms and standards governing the entry and stay of third country nationals and refugee claimants, through Directives, Regulations and Joint Actions. The UK Government opted in to the Residence Permit Scheme[1] in 2002, and is now implementing the provisions in stages, from 13 November 2003. A Residence Permit is an authorisation issued by a Member State of the European Union allowing a non-EEA national to stay legally in its territory. The EC Council Regulation provides that all such authorisations should be in a uniform format.[2] From February 2004, all leave to remain in the UK for more than six months is in the form of a residence permit.[3] Immigration officers cannot grant leave to enter for more than six months at the port.[4] The Home Office plans to require everyone who wishes to stay in the UK for longer than six months to obtain prior entry clearance, which will be in the same form as the residence permit, for the full period of the proposed stay.[5] From 13 November 2003, under Phase 1 of the Home Office scheme, 'specified nationals'[6] must have an entry clearance for the purpose for which they seek entry.[7] From the same date, all work permit holders (except those coming to the UK for six months or less, nationals of the accession States[8] and British nationals),[9] require entry clearance.[10] With an Entry Clearance, they will not need to apply for a UK Residence Permit. The Entry Clearance is in the form of a vignette or sticker placed in a passport at a visa-issuing post overseas. Nationals of other countries wishing to stay for more than six months will be given six months' leave to enter and advised to apply to the Home Office for leave to remain, which will be in the form of the residence permit.[11]

1   Council Regulation (EC) No 1030/2002 of 13 June 2002 laying down a uniform format for residence permits for third country nationals, OJ L157, 15.6.02. For its direct effect see 7.42 below.
2   The residence permit is a sticker containing security features, which goes into the holder's passport.
3   The Home Office stated that they expected all grants of leave to remain, including successful asylum applicants granted more than six months' leave to enter or remain, to be issued by way of UK residence permits by the end of February 2004: IND Change and Reform Directorate to ILPA (13 January 2004; IND Appeals Directorate to ILPA 16 January 2004).
4   HC 395, para 23A, inserted by HC 1224.
5   Home Office: UK Residence Permits: Questions and Answers (June 2003).
6   Ie, nationals of Australia, Canada, Hong Kong, Japan, Malaysia, New Zealand, Singapore, South Africa, South Korea and USA seeking to enter the UK as students or work permit holders for six months or more.
7   HC 395, para 6, as amended by HC 1224; Appendix 3, as inserted.
8   Ie, the States which became members of the EU on 1 May 2004.
9   BN(O)s, BOTCs, BOCs, BPPs and BSs (see chapter 2).
10 HC 395 para 128 as amended by HC 1224, HC 95, HC 176 and HC 523.
11 Home Office Questions and Answers (fn 5 above).

4.3 As indicated above, the distinction between the functions of immigration officers and those of the Secretary of State, performed by officials of the Home

Office, has become somewhat blurred since the early days of the Immigration Act 1971. In *Oladahinde*[1] the House of Lords held that, although immigration officers held a distinct statutory office, they were still employees of the Home Office and the Secretary of State could, accordingly, devolve making decisions to deport to them. In the same way immigration officers may be asked to exercise the Secretary of State's power to vary someone's leave at the port on return to the UK, if that leave has not lapsed by the person's departure from the common travel area.[2] Recent legislation has further blurred the distinction. First, the Secretary of State now has the power to prescribe circumstances in which he or she may grant leave to enter.[3] Secondly, the Immigration (Leave to Enter) Order 2001[4] provides that the Secretary of State may give or refuse leave to enter to (and exercise other examination, detention and removal powers in respect of) a person who has made a claim for asylum, a person who has made a claim that it would be contrary to the UK's obligations under the ECHR for him to be removed, and a person who seeks leave to enter for a purpose not covered by the immigration rules.[5] Nevertheless, despite these changes, the basic rule remains that, once someone has entered the UK, the power to give leave to remain or to vary any leave is to be exercised by the Secretary of State.[6]

[1]   *Oladahinde v Secretary of State for the Home Department* [1991] 1 AC 254, [1990] 3 All ER 393, HL.
[2]   HC 395, para 31A, inserted by HC 704. The Immigration (Leave to Enter and Remain) Order 2000, SI 2000/1161, Art 13(6) allows the Secretary of State to vary leave while the person is abroad.
[3]   Immigration Act 1971, s 3A(7), inserted by Immigration and Asylum Act 1999, s 1. SI 2000/1161, SI 2001/2590 (below) and SI 2004/475 were made under the powers conferred by the section.
[4]   SI 2001/2590.
[5]   SI 2001/2590, Arts 2 and 3.
[6]   Immigration Act 1971, s 4(1). We discussed in the previous chapter the point at which someone who arrives in this country is treated as having entered: see 3.5 above. This very clear distinction was thrown into confusion by the Divisional Court in *Singh v Hammond* [1987] 1 All ER 829, [1987] 1 WLR 283—a case which has not been followed and was confined to its particular facts. The distinction was crucial in *R v Naillie* [1993] AC 674, HL.

Leave to remain

4.4 People who entered the UK illegally and people who have overstayed the duration of their leave, may have their position regularised; they will be given leave to remain, which may be a limited or indefinite leave. Then there are those who entered the UK without any leave to enter, either because they were exempt, or had a right of abode or came in under EC free movement rights. A change in their circumstances may mean that they require leave. So the main categories who may need to seek leave to remain[1] include:

(i)   former Commonwealth citizens (mainly CUKCs and British citizens) and Irish citizens who had a right of abode[2] or the benefit of uncontrolled travel under the common travel area,[3] but have lost it by renouncing or losing their nationality;

(ii)   citizens of the EEA[4] and members of their families who cease to be entitled to remain under EC free movement law and have not been given leave to enter or remain in the UK;

4.4 *Control after Entry*

(iii)   members of the crew of a ship or aircraft who have entered lawfully without leave,[5] but wish to remain in the UK;

(iv)   diplomats and others exempted under section 8(2) and (3) of the Immigration Act 1971, who are treated as having been given 90 days' leave to remain when they cease to be exempt, and wish to remain longer in the UK;[6]

(v)   illegal entrants[7] who seek to be allowed to stay.

As with leave to enter, leave to remain may be of limited or indefinite duration, and, if limited, may be subject to conditions[8] (see 3.7). The only difference is that since leave to remain is granted under different powers from the immigration officers' examination powers under Schedule 2, no condition of submitting to a medical test or examination[9] may be imposed. Since 1996 the Secretary of State has had power to impose a condition requiring the person to maintain him or herself without recourse to public funds,[10] in addition to conditions restricting or prohibiting employment or occupation and (for foreign nationals) a condition of reporting to police. These are the only conditions which may lawfully be attached to leave.[11] Failure to comply renders a person liable to removal,[12] as well as to potential prosecution.[13] From February 2004 leave to remain which extends a stay to more than six months will take the form of a UK Residence Permit stuck into the passport.[14]

---

1   Immigration Act 1971, s 3(1)(b).
2   Immigration Act 1971, s 1(1).
3   Immigration Act 1971, s 1(3); Immigration (Control of Entry through the Republic of Ireland) Order 1972, SI 1972/1610, as amended.
4   Immigration Act 1988, s 7(1) and Immigration (European Economic Area) Regulations 2000, SI 2000/2326, as amended.
5   Immigration Act 1971, s 8(1).
6   Immigration Act 1971, s 8A(2), inserted by Immigration and Asylum Act 1999, s 6.
7   Immigration Act 1971, s 33(1).
8   Immigration Act 1971, s 3(1)(c) and 3B(2)(b), inserted by Immigration and Asylum Act 1999, s 2. No further conditions, other than those set out in s 3(1)(c), have been imposed by regulations.
9   See Immigration Act 1971, Sch 2, para 7.
10   Immigration Act 1971, s 3(1)(c)(ii), inserted by Asylum and Immigration Act 1996, Sch 2, para 1. For the definition of 'public funds' see HC 395, para 6.
11   The requirements of the rules under which leave to remain is sought are not conditions of leave, so that failure to comply eg with attendance requirements as a student cannot found removal or prosecution for breach of conditions.
12   Immigration and Asylum Act 1999, s 10.
13   Immigration Act 1971, s 24(1)(b)(ii).
14   See 4.2 above.

4.5 Until the amendments brought about by the Immigration and Asylum Act 1999, a person's leave to enter or remain in the UK lapsed on his or her leaving the common travel area. This meant that many persons with limited leave (as students, for example) who left the UK for a short holiday were refused leave to enter on their return, even if it was the middle of term or they had exams to sit. To add insult to injury, they were told that they could not stay in the UK to appeal against the refusal of leave to enter (unless they had obtained a visa to return to the UK, which, after a short holiday in mid-course, was unheard of). Nor would the High Court listen to judicial review applications, citing the right to appeal from abroad as the 'alternative remedy', even although this was likely to be quite ineffective, since appellants could never be present at the appeal.[1] The provisions of the Immigration (Leave to Enter and Remain) Order 2000[2] have put an end to this absurdity. Leave to enter or remain does not lapse when the holder goes abroad, if it was conferred by an entry clearance (other than a visit visa) or by an immigration officer or the Secretary of State for more than six months.[3] There appear to be two exceptions. First, section 3C of the Immigration Act 1971,[4] which extends leave where an application for further leave is made during the currency of the original leave but not decided before that leave expires, provides that leave extended as a result of that section will lapse if the person leaves the UK.[5] Secondly, where leave has already been varied by the Secretary of State and, following the variation, there is less than six months left, it will lapse on leaving the UK.[6] Students, and everyone who had entry clearance which operated as leave to enter, except for visitors, can leave the country during the period of their leave without worrying that they will be excluded on return. So can those granted leave by the Secretary of State after arrival. Their leave only lapses if they remain outside the UK for more than two years, if it has not expired by then.[7] But leave granted by an immigration officer on arrival after 13 November 2003 will lapse, since such leave cannot exceed six months.[8] The position has now been formalised by the introduction of the UK Residence Permit; holders of the permit will not have to obtain fresh leave on re-entry.[9]

[1]   See *R v Secretary of State for the Home Department ex p Swati* [1986] 1 All ER 717, [1986] Imm AR 88, CA; but see per Lord Denning in *R v Chief Immigration Officer, Gatwick Airport ex p Kharrazi* [1980] 3 All ER 373, [1981] 1 WLR 1396, CA.
[2]   SI 2000/1161, made under Immigration Act 1971, ss 3A and 3B (inserted by Immigration and Asylum Act 1999, ss 1 and 2).
[3]   Immigration (Leave to Enter and Remain) Order 2000, SI 2000/1161, Art 13(2). A fiancé(e) visa (HC 395, para 291) should confer non-lapsing leave, since, although it does not exceed six months, it is leave conferred by means of an entry clearance under Arts 3 and Art 13(2)(a).
[4]   Immigration Act 1971, s 3C, as substituted by the Nationality, Immigration and Asylum Act 2002, s 118.
[5]   Immigration Act 1971, s 3C(3) as substituted.
[6]   SI 2000/1161, Art 13(3). This might apply where a fiancé(e) extends his or her visa because the projected marriage has been delayed.
[7]   SI 2000/1161, Art 13(4).
[8]   HC 395, para 23A, inserted by HC 1224. See 4.2 above.
[9]   It will be those applicants who qualify for non-lapsing leave (by entry clearance other than visit visas, and leave to remain for over six months, who will be given UK residence permits.

Variation of leave to enter or remain

4.6 As we have seen, leave to enter or remain may be either for a limited or an indefinite period.[1] Indefinite leave cannot be varied, but it may lapse,[2] or be revoked.[3] A person in the UK with limited leave may have that leave varied, whether by restricting, enlarging or removing the limit on its duration, or by adding, varying or revoking conditions.[4] But if the limit on its duration is removed, any conditions attached to the leave shall cease to apply. In other words, when someone is given settlement, with indefinite leave, any conditions restricting or prohibiting employment or recourse to public funds, and any requirements to register with the police, cease to have effect.

1   Immigration Act 1971, s 3(1)(b).
2   If the holder remains out of the UK for two years: Immigration (Leave to Enter and Remain) Order 2000, SI 2000/1161, Art 13(4)(a).
3   Nationality Immigration and Asylum Act 2002, s 76.
4   Immigration Act 1971, s 3(3).

Applying for variation of leave

4.7 Applications for variation of leave or for all time limits to be removed should always be made before the expiry of the existing leave. A late application is inadvisable for three reasons:

(i)   the application may be refused on the grounds that the applicant has failed to comply with the conditions of his or her leave;[1]
(ii) the right of appeal is lost;[2] and
(iii) there is a risk of being removed for overstaying.[3]

Except for applications to remain for asylum, or by persons seeking to remain for business or self-employment pursuant to rights under EC Association Agreements, all applications for leave to remain or for a variation of leave by non-EEA nationals must be made on compulsory prescribed application forms.[4] The Immigration (Leave to Remain) (Prescribed Forms and Procedures) Regulations 2005 prescribe the relevant forms necessary for each application for limited or indefinite leave to remain.[5] Since 1 April 2004 a prescribed form has been required for an application for limited leave to remain for work permit employment, as a highly skilled migrant, or a seasonal agricultural worker, for the purpose of employment under the Sectors-Based Scheme, or for Home Office approved training or work experience.[6] Applications for leave to remain for dependants may be included on the application form of the principal applicant.[7]

1   If overstaying one's leave is a breach of conditions; Immigration and Asylum Act 1999, s 10; HC 395, para 322(3). In practice, this ground of refusal is rarely used, certainly not on its own.
2   Section 82(2)(e) and (f) of the Nationality, Immigration and Asylum Act 2002, like the Immigration Act 1971, s 14, requires extant leave in order to appeal against refusal to extend it. See 4.15 below.
3   Immigration and Asylum Act 1999, s 10.
4   Immigration Act 1971, s 31A, inserted by Immigration and Asylum Act 1999, s 165 from 1 August 2003 (SI 2003/1862), and amended by NIAA 2002, s 121 from 1 February 2003 (SI 2003/1); Immigration (Leave to Remain) (Prescribed Forms and Procedures) Regulations 2005, SI 2005/771. Regulations 8(3) and 11(3) exempt asylum claimants and their dependants, and EC Association Agreement applicants from using the forms. Persons seeking leave on the grounds that to remove them would breach Art 3 ECHR are equated with asylum claimants for this purpose. Those seeking leave to remain on the basis of Article 8 should apply on the appropriate form: FLR(M) for spouses and unmarried partners, FLR(O) for parents or children.
5   The forms are attached in the Schedules to SI 2005/771. Examples are FLR(M) (limited leave to remain for spouses or unmarried partners), FLR(S) (students, including those seeking to re-sit exams or write up a thesis, and student nurses), FLR(O) (other temporary purposes, permit-free work and other categories within the rules), SET(M) (settlement for spouse or unmarried partner), SET(F) (settlement for family members), SET(O) (settlement for work and other categories within the rules), BUS (sole representatives, business persons, retired persons of independent means, investors and innovators), FLR(IED) (leave to remain for holders of immigration employment documents), FLR(SEGS) (leave to remain under the Science and Engineering Graduate Scheme). Form FLR(O) is prescribed

for an application for limited leave to remain for any other reason or purpose for which provision is made in the immigration rules but which is not covered in the other forms (reg 8(2), Sch 6). Multiple forms for students and others are available, owing to the introduction of new fees on 1 April 2005: see information about single payment for multiple applications on the IND website. Non-compulsory forms are also provided for EEA nationals and family members (EEC1–3), persons seeking to remain under the EC Association Agreements (ECAA), persons granted exceptional or humanitarian leave who now seek indefinite leave (ELR), for a certificate of approval for marriage (COA) and for transfer of a limited orindefinite leave to remain stamp to a new passport (TOC and NTL): see 'Application Forms' on IND website. Since these forms are not compulsory, they cannot be declared invalid if they are not filled in correctly or if the necessary supporting documentation is not enclosed.

6   See the Immigration (Leave to Remain) Prescribed Forms and Procedures) (Amendment) Regulations 2004, SI 2004/581, now repealed and replaced by SI 2005/771.

7   SI 2005/771, reg 12.

4.8 The application must be completed as required, and signed by the applicant, or, in the case of a minor, by the parent or legal guardian, and must be accompanied by the documents and photographs specified in the form.[1] However, a failure to do either of these things 'to any extent' will only invalidate an application if the applicant does not provide an explanation of the failure, which the Secretary of State 'considers to be satisfactory', and does not remedy the failure within, at the latest, 28 days of being notified.[2] An application which is treated as invalid is not refused; it is treated as not having been made. Thus, rejection of an application as invalid can have very serious consequences. The decision on whether an application is acceptable is made by the Initial Consideration Unit, Work Permits (UK) or, for those attending in person, a Public Enquiry Office, as appropriate. The forms and accompanying documents are checked for compliance, and the merits of the application are disregarded at that stage. Applications which contain deficiencies in the signing and dating of forms, or in the supply of the specified documents and photographs will be returned to applicants or their advisers within 21 days, endorsed with the defects which need remedying, and the applicant then has 28 days at most, in which to comply with the requirements. An initial reading of the 2005 Regulations suggests that no other defects in the form-filling can lead to the invalidation of the application.

1   Immigration (Leave to Remain) (Prescribed Forms and Procedures) Regulations 2005, SI 2005/771, reg 13(1)–(3).

2   Immigration (Leave to Remain) (Prescribed Forms and Procedures) Regulations 2005, SI 2005/771, reg 14.

4.9 It is clearly vitally important that the application is completed to the satisfaction of the Initial Consideration Unit, Work Permits (UK) or Public Enquiry Office. A checklist of good practice to ensure this might include the following:

(i)   the correct form for the application must be used. In *Sithole*,[1] a Tribunal decision, which may need to be reconsidered, an application made on the wrong form was held to be invalid, and since no valid application was made in time, there was no right of appeal against refusal of leave;

(ii) if the application is phrased in the alternative, more than one of the forms may be appropriate. Applicants should not be afraid to use more than one form;

(iii) the form should be completed and an answer given to every applicable question;

(iv) alteration of the form will not invalidate the application, but where this happens, it is always safer to write a covering letter, setting out any qualifications and explanations;

(v) covering letters may also be used to complement answers, but the form should still be properly completed and should not merely state 'see covering letter';

(vi) the original of every document requested should be provided or, if it is not available or only a photocopy is available, a clear explanation should be given as to why the original cannot accompany the form;

(vii) the correct fee for the application should be included;[2]

(viii) the application should be made well before the current leave expires in order to avoid becoming out of time if the first attempt at the application is rejected as invalid;

(ix) lastly, if an application is returned as potentially invalid, time is of the essence and the form should be made compliant with the Regulations as quickly as possible.

If the application is returned as invalid but finally completed to the satisfaction of the Home Office, its initial rejection will have caused no prejudice. Even if the application is rejected, it will be considered a valid application at the date of its original submission provided any defects have been promptly remedied.[3] But if the revised application is rejected and the Secretary of State claims it is invalid, significant and difficult questions of law may arise. If refusal of a valid application attracts a right of appeal, to safeguard the applicant's position, a notice of appeal to the appellate authorities should be lodged, stating clearly that a preliminary issue arises as to whether the rejection of the application as invalid is correct and whether it should be considered as a valid application.[4] The issue for the Tribunal would be whether the application was valid or should have been treated as valid. In *Derouiche*,[5] the Tribunal found that the wording of the form FLR(S) was misleading and imprecise and that, since it had to be used by applicants who may not speak or understand English, rejection of an application for a minor non-compliance was unfair and unjust. The 2005 Regulations would appear to endorse that position,[6] but the language of the Regulation is quite cautious and does not represent the final word. In *Ravichandran and Jeyeanthan*[7] the Court of Appeal indicated that whether an application or notice was invalid because of a failure to comply with statutory requirements about its content was a much more nuanced question than much of the case law suggested, and that in each case the court or tribunal should concentrate on what the rules intended should be the just consequence of non-compliance. The first question is whether there has been substantial compliance with the procedural requirements, even if there has not been strict compliance. The second is whether the non-compliance is capable of being waived, and if so, whether it has been. That will not arise in this situation, which is predicated on the Secretary of State's refusal to waive the non-compliance. The third is what are the consequences of non-compliance.[8] The draconian consequences of non-compliance[9] are such that the Tribunal should, we suggest, lean in favour of a generous approach and find substantial compliance whenever reasonably possible.

1   *Sithole (Hettie)* (00TH 1969) (7 August 2000, unreported), IAT (Collins J).
2   See 4.10 below.
3   This is the effect of SI 2005/771, reg 14 (4.8 text and fn 2 above).
4   The Asylum and Immigration Tribunal (Procedure) Rules 2005, SI 2005/230, r 45(4)(d)(i) gives the Tribunal power to direct a matter to be dealt with as a preliminary issue. Clearly, the issue of validity, and therefore whether a right of appeal exists, is apt for this procedure.
5   *Derouiche* [1998] INLR 286.
6   SI 2005/771, reg 14 (fn 3 above).
7   *R v Immigration Appeal Tribunal, ex p Jeyeanthan; Ravichandran v Secretary of State for the Home Department* [2000] Imm AR 10.
8   *Ravichandran* above, per Woolf MR at 17.
9   *Ravichandran* above, at 13.
10   This sentence, which appeared in the last edition of this work, was disapproved by Maurice Kay J in *R (on the application of Campbell) v Secretary of State for the Home Department* [2003] EWHC 2681 (Admin), where however significant parts of the form were not completed, making it impossible for the Secretary of State to decide the application. This is not 'substantial' compliance. Applicants now have the benefit of the procedures introduced by the 2003 regulations, SI 2003/1712 (reproduced in SI 2005/771) which allow time to make good deficiencies before a form is rejected as invalid.

Fees

4.10 The appropriate fee must also be enclosed with the application. Section 5 of the Immigration and Asylum Act 1999 gave the Secretary of State the power to charge fees for applications for leave to remain, and section 52 of the Asylum and Immigration (Treatment of Claimants, etc) Act 2004 allows these fees to be set exceeding the administrative costs, and reflecting the benefits deemed likely to accrue to successful applicants.[1] Regulations made under the section[2] introduce massive fee increases. All applications made in person must be accompanied by a £500 fee. Applications made by post cost £335, except student applications, which cost £250, and applications to transfer a leave stamp, which cost £160.[3] In all cases a single fee is payable where the application includes one or more of the applicant's dependants.[4] No fee is payable where an application for indefinite leave to remain is made on the grounds of domestic violence, where the applicant appears destitute,[5] or where the applicant is an asylum seeker or applies on Article 3 ECHR grounds, or is the dependant of such a person,[6] or where leave is varied at the port on arrival,[7] or where the applicant is a child being assisted, accommodated or maintained by a local authority, or a person who applies for further leave to remain who was granted leave outside the rules when under 18,[8] or a person who was granted leave to remain outside the rules on the rejection of an asylum claim and is seeking further leave to remain outside the rules.[9] In employment cases, an additional fee will have been paid by employers when they applied for a work permit or other employment document, which varies according to the type of employment.[10] No fees are payable in respect of citizens or nationals of excepted countries (comprising mainly EEA and ECAA countries).[11] Applications submitted without the appropriate fee will be rejected and deemed invalid.

4.10 *Control after Entry*

1   The Immigration (Application Fees) Order 2005, SI 2005/582 specifies functions and matters which may be taken into account in fixing fees. These include the costs of appeals and recovery of past deficits.
2   SI 2004/3105, SI 2005/654, amending SI 2003/1711.
3   SI 2003/1711, reg 3, as amended by SI 2005/564. No fee is payable by nationals of States which have ratified the Council of Europe Social Charter of 1961 or the Revised Social Charter of 1996: SI 2003/1711, reg 5(c) as substituted. Apart from EEA nationals (to whom these provisions do not apply), the States concerned are Armenia, Bulgaria, Moldova, Romania, Croatia and Turkey.
4   SI 2003/1711, reg 4. But where dependants are over-age, or apply separately, a separate fee will be charged: Guidance Notes attached to application forms.
5   SI 2003/1711, reg 5(e). It is unlikely that the Secretary of State would make an exception to the fees requirement in other cases, save in the most exceptional and compelling compassionate circumstances: IND (Managed Migration) to Wandsworth & Merton Law Centre, 30 September 2003.
6   Immigration and Asylum Act 1999, s 5(3)(a). But those seeking leave to remain on the basis of long residence or under the seven-year concession would be liable to pay the prescribed fee: IND (Managed Migration) to Wandsworth & Merton Law Centre, 30 September 2003, as would applicants seeking leave on Art 8 (family life) grounds. But it is not IND policy to charge for an Art 8 application where this is linked to an asylum or Art 3 ECHR claim: IND to Hackney Community Law Centre, 27 January 2005.
7   SI 2003/1711, reg 5(b), substituted by SI 2004/580. The leave thus granted will not exceed six months: HC 395, para 23A.
8   SI 2003/1711, reg 5(d), inserted by SI 2004/3105.
9   SI 2003/1711, reg 5(f), inserted by SI 2005/654.
10   The Immigration Employment Document (Fees) Regulations 2003, SI 2003/541, as amended by SI 2003/1277, SI 2003/2447, SI 2003/2626, SI 2004/1004, SI 2004/1485 and SI 2005/627, made under the Nationality, Immigration and Asylum Act 2002, s 122 set a fee of £153, except for persons seeking to enter or remain as Highly Skilled Migrants or as seasonal agricultural workers, where the fees are £315 and £12 respectively. There are special arrangements for teachers and for groups of employees.
11   Immigration Employment Document (Fees) Regulations 2003, SI 2003/541, as amended, reg 5.

4.11 Non-employment or business-related applications should be sent by prepaid post to the IND or can be submitted in person at a Public Enquiry Office (PEO) of the IND. Applications for leave to remain for work permit employment, as a seasonal agricultural worker, for the purpose of employment under the Sectors-Based Scheme, or for Home Office training or work experience must be sent by prepaid post or by courier to Work Permits (UK) at the IND or submitted in person to Croydon PEO.[1] Applications under the Highly Skilled Migrants Programme, and business applications (including sole representatives, retired persons of independent means, investors and innovators, may not be submitted in person but must be sent by post or courier, to Work Permits (UK) for highly skilled migrants, and to IND for the rest.[2] Where an application is sent by post, the Regulations provide that the date on which the application is made is the date of posting.[3] This accords with Home Office practice to treat an application as having been made on the date of the sending by post rather than of its receipt, and the Tribunal case of *Lubetkin*,[4] the authority for this proposition, is still good law. Recorded delivery is better than the ordinary post because this will provide clear proof of the date of posting. For applications handed in personally at the PEO or delivered by courier, the date of application is the date of delivery.[4]

1   Immigration (Leave to Remain) (Prescribed Forms and Procedures) Regulations 2005, SI 2005/771, reg 13(2)(c). For details of the quite separate applications by employers for work permits and other employment documents, visit the Work Permits (UK) website (www.workpermits.gov.uk). See chapter 10.

²   SI 2005/771, reg 13(1)(c), 13(2)(c).
³   Immigration (Leave to Remain) (Prescribed Forms and Procedures) Regulations 2005, SI 2005/771, reg 14(2)(a).
⁴   *Lubetkin v Secretary of State for the Home Department* [1979–80] Imm AR 162.
⁵   SI 2005/771, reg 14(2)(b), (c).

4.12 The date of the application is important for three reasons. First, as indicated above, it is essential to apply before the current leave expires if the person is to have a right of appeal under section 82 of the Nationality, Immigration and Asylum Act 2002.[1] Secondly, the date of the application is a decisive date, where the applicant is a child who becomes over-age before the date of the decision.[2] Thirdly, the date of the application is important if there have been rule changes, since in a number of the transitional provisions in the immigration rules, this date determines which set of rules applies. [3]

¹   See 4.17 below.
²   See eg HC 395, para 27.
³   See eg HC 395 para 4.

Withdrawal and lapsing of applications

4.13 Normally, applications duly made must be considered by the Home Office, although there is no particular order in which applications must be considered. They can be put in a queue or given priority.[1] There is no power to cancel an application unilaterally.[2] Only a clear, unambiguous request in writing by the applicant for consideration of the application to be discontinued will the application be considered withdrawn.[3] And during a period where an expired leave is continued under section 3C of the Immigration Act 1971 pending a variation decision, the applicant is not entitled to make any more applications for variation of leave to enter or remain.[4] So even someone who marries after making an application to remain as a student cannot, while they have leave under section 3C, make a fresh application on the basis of the marriage.[5] On the other hand, it is possible to vary the grounds of an application already made, even by introducing something completely new.[6] After all, amended section 3C of the Immigration Act 1971 expressly provides that an application may be varied without in any way imposing a limitation on the time when it is to be made. So, according to Home Office instructions, a student application can be varied so as to include marriage grounds.[7] As a result, there may be little difference in practice between a fresh application and a request to vary an existing application. The IDI go further. A second or third application made while section 3C leave is running cannot be regarded as a request to withdraw the first application, unless this is specifically stated.[8] It should be treated as a variation of that original application. The IDI make two important points. First, if the applicant makes it absolutely clear that the new grounds are to be considered instead of the grounds put forward initially, then the original grounds need not be considered.[9] Secondly, it should not be assumed that an applicant wishes to withdraw the original grounds simply because they appear incompatible with later grounds.[10] For example, if a person asks for leave to remain as a foreign spouse after an initial application to remain as a student, it may well be that the marriage application casts the gravest doubt on the applicant's intention to leave the UK at the end of the period of study. Nevertheless, it will be necessary to make a decision on the student point as well as the marriage grounds.

1   *R v Secretary of State for the Home Department, ex p Khasawneh* [1995] Imm AR 315, QBD, where the division of applications into queues and the prioritisation of newer applications under the Asylum and Immigration Appeals Act 1993 were held lawful.

2   *Dungarwalla v Secretary of State for the Home Department* [1989] Imm AR 476.

3   See IDI, Ch 1, s 5, 'Section 3C of the Immigration Act 1971 as amended', para 4.2.

4   Immigration Act 1971, s 3C(4) and (5), as amended by NIAA 2002, s 118. The substituted s 3C applies to all applications made after 1 April 2003, and to applications made before that date but not decided by then: Nationality, Immigration and Asylum Act 2002 (Commencement No 4) Order 2003, SI 2003/754, Sch 2, para 2(2), as amended by SI 2003/1040.

5   IDI Ch 1, s 5, para 3.2.

6   IDI Ch 1, s 5, para 3.2.

7   IDI Ch 1, s 5, para 3.2.

8   IDI Ch 1, s 5, para 4.3.

9   IDI Ch 1, s 5, para 4.3.

10 IDI Ch 1, s 5, para 4.3. But see *R v Immigration Appeal Tribunal, ex p Majid* [1988] Imm AR 315, QBD, where the Secretary of State was held entitled to treat an application as lapsed by being superseded by a later one.

Leaving the UK

4.14 Where a person makes an application and then goes abroad before the application is determined, does it lapse or does it remain a valid application, which requires a decision by the Home Office? If the applicant has sent in his or her passport with the application, as is required in every single prescribed application,[1] and has to make a request for its return before being able to travel, is the application treated differently from that of the person who has a second passport and can travel without any need to ask for the return of the passport lodged with the Home Office? And will the Home Office ever be prepared to return a person's passport without treating the application as lapsed? If a passport is requested to open a bank account or get a driving licence, the Home Office will make appropriate arrangements and will not treat the application as lapsed.[2] The problems arise when the passport is withdrawn for travel abroad. Prior to the Immigration and Asylum Act 1999, when someone left the common travel area, his or her leave lapsed[3] and there was nothing left to vary; so technically the application would also lapse, but there remained a discretion to continue dealing with it. In the previous edition we argued that this position was changed by the Immigration (Leave to Enter and Remain) Order 2000,[4] notwithstanding the apparently inconsistent immigration rule regarding the effect of a request for a return of a passport in order to travel outside the common travel area.[5] This Order provides that an original leave of over six months and a varied leave with six months or more to run will not lapse when a person goes outside the common travel area;[6] and it expressly provides for a power to vary leave, even when the applicant is outside the UK.[7] So what is the position? First, there is no immigration rule which deals with the person who has two passports, but in practice the variation application of such a person is not withdrawn by travel outside the CTA on the second passport. Secondly, rule 34 of the Immigration rules provides that where an applicant requests the return of a passport for travel outside the common travel area, the application for variation of leave shall (provided it has not been determined) be treated as withdrawn as soon as the passport has been returned in response to the request.[8] However, rule 34 is merely referring to the practice which the Secretary of State's officials will normally follow. It is not a rule of law, and therefore allows of exceptions and variations at the discretion of the Secretary of State, and the government has indicated that good sense would prevail in the exercise of the Home Office's discretion to treat an application for a variation of leave as withdrawn, if for instance the person left for a good reason.[9] This clarifies the position in a way, but the sheer complication of the rules is likely to lead to inconvenience, hardship and injustice. There are many people who need to travel frequently on business, or for family reasons, but still need to have their application for a variation of leave dealt with without all the inconvenience and complication of it being treated as withdrawn.

1   Ie, under Immigration (Leave to Remain) (Prescribed Forms and Procedures) Regulations 2003, SI 2005/771, and see Guidance Notes accompanying application forms (available on Home Office website, www.ind.homeoffice.gov.uk. A certified copy is acceptable provided there is a reasonable explanation for not sending in the original, and the original is sent in later.
2   See 'Making an application' and 'Return passports' on the Home Office website.
3   Immigration Act 1971, s 3(4).
4   SI 2000/1161, Art 13(1)–(4). See the previous edition of this work, 4.12.
5   HC 395, para 34, as amended by Cm 4851.
6   SI 2000/1161, Art 13(2).
7   SI 2000/1161, Art 13(6).
8   HC 395, para 34, as amended by Cm 4851. See also IDI, Ch 1, s 5, para 4.1. The Home Office will consider expediting consideration of an application so that the applicant can travel if there is an emergency medical reason such as a family illness abroad, evidence of which must be faxed in English from a doctor or hospital abroad: 'Return passports' on Home Office website.
9   See *Hansard* (HL) 31 October 2002, col 408 (Lord Bassam of Brighton).

4.15 There are three possible scenarios. First, if the applicant has a section 3C leave it will end in any event when the person leaves the UK.[1] In most cases it will end earlier, because the Home Office will normally grant one calendar month's leave on the same conditions as before, before returning the passport.[2] When the applicant goes to a country outside the common travel area this new leave will lapse, because it will not meet the conditions of the Immigration (Leave to Enter and Remain) Order 2000.[3] The applicant will be forced, at great inconvenience and cost, to apply for entry clearance to get back in. Secondly, there are those whose original leave has not yet expired, when their passport is returned to them, but that leave does not meet the conditions of the Immigration (Leave to Enter and Remain) Order 2000; so, on going outside the common travel area, their leave will lapse and their application for a variation will be treated as withdrawn. They too will have to obtain an entry clearance to get back in. On the other hand, there is a third group with a leave to enter or remain, which has not expired, when they get their passport back, and which does not lapse, because it meets the conditions of the Immigration (Leave to Enter and Remain) Order 2000. But because they have asked for their passport back, their application to vary is treated as withdrawn.[4] They can apply to vary from abroad,[5] or on return, at the port,[6] but may (depending on the time left on their non-lapsed leave) prefer to make a fresh variation application once they are back in the UK, after being readmitted on their original leave, unless that leave has by then expired. Of course, they might not know about this complicated nonsense and do nothing either abroad or when they get back. Will the immigration service be kind to them? Will they get back in? Or will calamity beckon? Cases are awaited. Where a person, having left the common travel area with a leave which remains in force under Article 13 of the 2000 Order, applies from abroad for a variation of that leave, it is not entirely clear whether that leave can be extended under section 3C of the Immigration Act 1971, as amended, if it has expired before the application is decided.

1   Immigration Act 1971, s 3C(3), as inserted by NIAA 2002, s 118. See 4.17 fn 8 below.
2   See IDI, Ch 1, s 5, para 4.1. The leave stamp will indicate to immigration officers and entry clearance officers that the person concerned was not an overstayer. There is no right of appeal against this decision (because an in-time applicant has no right of appeal against a variation decision, unless the effect of the decision is that the applicant has no leave at all: Nationality, Immigration and Asylum Act 2002, ss 82(2)(d) and (e)).
3   See Immigration (Leave to Enter and Remain) Order 2000, Art 13(2).
4   HC 395, para 34.
5   Immigration (Leave to Enter and Remain) Order 2000, Art 13(6) and (8).
6   HC 395, para 31A, inserted by HC 704.

Variation of leave

4.16 The Secretary of State may vary leave, including any conditions to which it is subject, in such form and manner as permitted by the Immigration Act 1971.[1] Leave may, as we have seen, be varied by restricting it as well as enlarging it. The Immigration (Leave to Enter and Remain) Order 2000 enables the Secretary of State to vary the leave of someone who, having left the common travel area, has a leave to enter or remain, which remains in force.[2] The Order and the Immigration rules[3] clearly envisage applications for variation being made while the person is outside the UK. However, the Secretary of State is not obliged to consider such applications.[4] Similarly, an immigration officer may grant a variation of leave at the port (or a control zone) on a person's return, but is not obliged to entertain the application.[5] Neither applications for variation made abroad nor those made at the port need be made on the forms prescribed for all other variation applications.[6] Leave (including any conditions to which it is subject) may be varied in such form and manner as permitted for the giving of leave to enter.[7] This means that, in order to consider whether to vary leave, the Secretary of State (by his or her officers, including immigration officers) has power to seek the information and documents that an immigration officer would be entitled to seek in an examination on arrival.[8]

1   Immigration Act 1971, s 3(3).
2   SI 2000/1161, Art 13(6) and (8).
3   HC 395, para 33A, inserted by HC 704.
4   HC 395, para 33A.
5   HC 395, para 31A, inserted by HC 704. If the immigration officer declines, a variation application is made to the Home Office in the normal way: HC 395, para 31A.
6   HC 395, para 32.
7   SI 2000/1161, Art 13(6) and HC 395, para 33A.
8   SI 2000/1161 Art 13(8). For immigration officers' powers of examination see 3.31 above.

Variation of leave by statute

4.17 The time taken to consider applications for leave varies. Some may take a long time, involving lengthy investigations and, possibly, an interview with the applicant and his or her spouse. Others are quite routine and can be dealt with in a straightforward manner without fuss or difficulty. Yet these variations in time can have a serious adverse impact on the subsequent appeal rights of unsuccessful applicants. Under section 82 of the Nationality, Immigration and Asylum Act 2002 there is, in general, a right of appeal where an immigration decision is made in respect of a person, including a refusal to vary a person's leave to enter or remain in the UK if the result of the refusal is that the person has no leave to enter or remain. In the past, delay by the Home Office in reaching a decision until after the person's leave had expired could affect whether there was a subsequent right of appeal.[1] This obvious injustice was remedied by making provision for leave to be extended by law if an application to extend it was submitted before it expired. This is now achieved by section 3C of the 1971 Act.[2] Technically, the leave is 'extended'. To benefit, a person must have existing leave to enter or remain at the time when the application to vary is made.[3] If that leave expires before a decision is taken section 3C extends it during any period when:[4]

(i) the application for variation is neither decided nor withdrawn;
(i) an in-time appeal under section 82 of the 2002 Act may be brought;
(i) a section 82 appeal is pending.[5]

However, the original leave is only extended in this way if the application to vary is made to the Secretary of State before the expiry of the original leave.[6] The purpose of extending leave in this way is to preserve the right of appeal under section 82 of the 2002 Act and to ensure that people who make valid in-time applications are not prejudiced by routine Home Office delays. So if leave has been extended under this provision, and during this extension a further application for a variation of leave is made by the applicant, there will be no further extensions, and consequently no further right of appeal.[7] Statutory leave lapses on departure from the UK.[8]

---

[1]   See Immigration Act 1971, s 14 (now repealed) and *Suthendran v Immigration Appeal Tribunal* [1977] AC 359, [1977] Imm AR 44.
[2]   Inserted by the Immigration and Asylum Act 1999, s 3, and substituted by Nationality, Immigration and Asylum Act 2003, s 118 in respect of applications made after 1 April 2003 and applications made earlier but outstanding on that date: see Nationality, Immigration and Asylum Act 2002 (Commencement No 4) Order 2003, SI 2003/754, Sch 2, para 2(2), as amended by SI 2003/1040. Formerly, leave was extended by the Immigration (Variation of Leave) Order 1976, or VOLO, and the phrase 'VOLO leave', meaning statutory extension of leave, is still encountered in the case law.
[3]   Immigration Act 1971, s 3C(1) as substituted.
[4]   Immigration Act 1971, s 3C(2) as substituted.
[5]   An appeal is pending until it is finally determined, withdrawn or abandoned, and is not finally determined while a further in-time application for reconsideration or appeal may be brought or is pending, or an appeal has been remitted for reconsideration, but an appeal to the Tribunal is treated as abandoned if the appellant leaves the UK, if he or she is granted leave to enter or remain in the UK or a deportation order is made against him or her: Nationality, Immigration and Asylum Act 2002, s 104(1)–(5) as amended by Asylum and Immigration (Treatment of Claimants, etc) Act 2004, Sch 2, para 20. See 18.106 below.
[6]   Immigration Act 1971, s 3C(1)(b) as substituted.

7   Immigration Act 1971, s 3C(4) as substituted. See further *Moussavi v Secretary of State for the Home Department* [1986] Imm AR 39. Applications made during a period of statutory leave under the provisions of the 1976 Order or the 1999 Act (see fn 2 above) may attract further appeal rights: Magrath & Co to ILPA 22 May 2003.
8   Immigration Act 1971, s 3C(3), as substituted.

4.18 Extensions of leave under section 3C of the Immigration Act 1971 are examples of an automatic grant or extension of leave by statute. Another concerns diplomats and other beneficiaries of an exemption from immigration control under sections 8(2) and 8(3) of the Immigration Act 1971 Act.[1] When their exemption ended (because they left their post, for example), the position under the pre-1999 Act law was that they were in the UK without leave. Now, by virtue of section 8A of the 1971 Act,[2] they are treated as if they have 90 days' leave to remain from the date when their exemption ends, unless they already had a shorter leave, in which case that leave operates.[3] In addition, the Secretary of State has powers under sections 3B and 4(1) to make orders by statutory instrument for general variations of leave and the conditions attached to it, in respect of any class of persons. The only Order made so far was one made during the Gulf War in 1991, which required all Iraqi nationals with limited leave to register with the police.[4]

1   See chapter 6 below.
2   Inserted by Immigration and Asylum Act 1999, s 7.
3   Immigration Act 1971, ss 8(2) and (3), and 8A, as amended by the 1999 Act, ss 6 and 7; s 8A(2)(b).
4   Immigration (Variation of Leave) Order 1991, SI 1991/77.

4.19 Apart from these statutory extensions of leave, all other extensions are granted or refused by the Home Office dealing with each case on an individual basis. Section 4(1) of the Immigration Act 1971, which requires the Secretary of State to exercise the power to give leave to remain or to vary any leave by notice in writing given to the person affected, is modified by section 3B, inserted by the Immigration and Asylum Act 1999, allowing the Secretary of State by Order to make provision for changes in the form or manner in which leave may be given, refused or varied.[1] No such changes have yet been made, although the Immigration (Leave to Enter and Remain) Order 2000[2] now permits the grant or refusal of leave to *enter* otherwise than by notice in writing.[3] It is likely that leave will soon be varied or refused by e-mail. But for now, where leave is varied, this is usually effected by an entry in the passport, travel document or registration certificate, which serves as the section 4(1) notice. Sometimes there is only a letter, and sometimes a combination of letter and stamp in the passport. Stamps have, since February 2004, been replaced by UK residence permit stickers.[4] In *Hashmi*[5] the Court of Appeal decided that a letter written to an applicant's MP, in which it was decided exceptionally to grant indefinite leave to remain, amounted in itself to a decision, which the Home Office could not reverse, in the absence of fraud. This was notwithstanding the absence of a stamp in the passport, the Court of Appeal noting that the stamping of passports in itself does not amount to a decision. It may evidence a decision which has previously been made but the stamping is an administrative act following a decision. However, in *Robina Rafiq*[6] the Court of Appeal held that in the light of the requirement of notice, communication was essential to a decision.[7] Hence where, in response to an application for indefinite leave to remain, an indefinite leave stamp had been endorsed in a passport which had not been returned to the holder, the Secretary of State could cancel the stamp and refuse the application.[8] In *Hashmi* it was accepted that the letter written to the applicant's MP when she was acting as a representative of the applicant was capable of constituting notice in writing to the applicant as required by section 4(1). If a notice letter indicates that leave is varied for a limited period, but omits to say what that period is, it does not constitute proper notice and, in consequence, the Secretary of State has not exercised his or her power to vary leave. What then is the position? In *Ah-Time*[9] the Tribunal pointed out that for variation of leave there is no equivalent to paragraph 6(1) of Schedule 2 to the Immigration Act 1971 (which deems a six-month grant of leave to enter in the absence of proper notice of the decision), and so no deemed leave takes effect. Instead, by virtue of what is now section 3C of the 1971 Act, the applicant's original leave would be extended until the Secretary of State corrected the mistake or reached a fresh decision. Where the notice granting leave is ambiguous over the date from which the leave is to run, this ambiguity should be construed in favour of the immigrant.[10]

[1] Immigration Act 1971, s 3B(1), (2)(a), inserted by Immigration and Asylum Act 1999, s 2.
[2] SI 2000/1161.
[3] SI 2000/1161, Art 8, made under Immigration Act 1971, s 3A, inserted by Immigration and Asylum Act 1999, s 1. See chapter 2 above.
[4] See 4.2 above.
[5] *R (on the application of Hashmi) v Secretary of State* [2002] EWCA Civ 728, [2002] INLR 377, CA.
[6] *Rafiq v Secretary of State* [1998] INLR 349, CA.
[7] See also the important decision of the House of Lords in *R (on the application of Anufrijeva v Secretary of State for the Home Department* [2003] UKHL 36, [2003] Imm AR 570 (on uncommunicated asylum decisions and their effects on asylum support), where Lord Steyn said: 'A constitutional State must accord to individuals the right to know of a decision before their rights can be adversely affected ...[the idea] that an uncommunicated decision can bind an individual is an astonishingly unjust proposition'.
[8] The requirement for communication cuts both ways. In *R v Secretary of State for the Home Department, ex p Popatia; R v Secretary of State for the Home Department, ex p Chew* [2001] Imm AR 46, Sullivan J held that a deportation order which never actually came to the notice of its subject did not 'stop the clock' for the purpose of the long residence concession. See now HC 395 para 276B.
[9] *Ah-Time v Secretary of State for the Home Department* [1989] Imm AR 340, IAT. If the purported grant of leave is sent out in response to an out-of-time application, it might amount to an 'authorisation' by the Secretary of State to remain in the UK: see *Idrish* [1985] Imm AR 155 at 168, IAT.
[10] *Secretary of State for the Home Department v Behrooz* [1991] Imm AR 82, IAT.

4.20 At present, as indicated above, section 4(1) of the Immigration Act 1971 requires a written notice to be given to the unsuccessful applicant. He or she must also be given written notice under the Immigration (Notices) Regulations 2003, if he or she has a right of appeal.[1] The notice must set out the reasons for refusal, and give details of any right of appeal and how to exercise it.[2] Thus there is a double requirement to give notice: (i) in all cases under section 4(1) and (ii) in cases where there is a right of appeal, under the Notices Regulations. The two requirements are married by regulation 6 of the Notices Regulations, which provides that the notice can be the same one for both purposes, provided that it contains all the necessary information. A notice is deemed to have been received on the second day after posting by first-class post.[3] In addition, where leave is refused and the decision attracts a right of appeal, section 120 of the 2002 Act empowers the Secretary of State to serve a notice on the applicant requiring him or her to state any additional grounds he or she may have for wishing to stay in the UK.[4]

1   The Immigration (Notices) Regulations 2003, SI 2003/658 are made pursuant to ss 105 and 112 of the Nationality, Immigration and Asylum Act 2002.
2   SI 2003/658, reg 5. The requirement to notify of the right of appeal does not apply if the only right of appeal is on asylum or human rights grounds: reg 5(6); see chapter 18 below.
3   SI 2003/658, reg 7(4)(a). Notices sent abroad are deemed received 28 days after posting: SI 2003/658, reg 7(4)(b).
4   Nationality, Immigration and Asylum Act 2002, s 120(2). The one-stop warning may be issued at any time, not just on refusal, although this is the most likely time. See 18.87 below.

What constitutes an extension of leave?

4.21 In complicated cases considerable correspondence may pass between the applicant and the Home Office. Sometimes Home Office letters appear to indicate that an existing leave has been extended, when in fact, this was not the intention of the Home Office. Thus in *R v Immigration Appeal Tribunal, ex p Ahluwalia*[1] the applicant had received a letter from the Home Office in reply to her application for variation of her leave to remain, which stated: 'Meanwhile this acknowledgement may be regarded as authority for the holder to remain in the UK pending a decision on any application made for an extension of stay'. This was held to be leave. In contrast, a letter, which drew the applicant's attention to the statutory protection provided by section 14 of the Immigration Act 1971, 'the appellant will not be required to leave the UK while the appeal is pending', was held not to constitute leave in *R v Immigration Appeal Tribunal, ex p Subramaniam*.[2] Misunderstandings of this kind are less likely to occur, now that leave is extended automatically pending a decision and any subsequent appeal.[3] The Home Office now grants 28-day leave in a number of situations, for example, to enable a fresh application to be made or to enable someone who has withdrawn his or her passport for travel to do so without being treated as an overstayer on embarkation.[4] There is now a clearer distinction between a grant of leave and a decision to refrain from removal without granting leave, which leaves people in limbo.[5]

1   [1979–80] Imm AR 1. See further *Secretary of State for the Home Department v Enorzah* [1975] Imm AR 10.
2   [1977] QB 190, [1976] Imm AR 155, CA.
3   Nationality, Immigration and Asylum Act 2002, s 3C; see 4.15 above.
4   See eg IDI, Ch 1, s 5, para 4.1; see also 'Post-Refusal decisions: Variation (Curtailment of Leave to Remain)', on Home Office website. Discharged NATO soldiers are given 28 days' leave to enable them to make an application or to leave the UK.
5   Many failed asylum seekers are in the latter situation, either because of country-specific policies, practical difficulties of return or simple failure by the Home Office to enforce removal. See *R (on the application of Hwez) v Secretary of State for the Home Department* [2002] EWHC 1597 (Admin), [2002] All ER (D) 439 (Jul); revsd because of a change in the law sub nom *R (on the application of Khadir) v Secretary of State for the Home Department* [2003] EWCA Civ 475, [2003] LS Gaz R 37, [2003] All ER (D) 47 (Apr) and on appeal to the HL), and see *R (on the application of Guveya) v Secretary of State for the Home Department* [2004] EWCA Civ 1280 (perm).

'Packing-up time'

4.22 Where an application has been refused and the applicant has been allowed a short period to organise his or her affairs, pack up and leave, the view of Lord Russell in *Suthendran v Immigration Appeal Tribunal*[1] was that such 'packing up time' constituted a fresh grant of leave.[2] However this view is, we believe, no longer tenable, at least where the Secretary of State makes it clear that the intention is not to grant further leave but merely to assure an applicant that no action will be taken to enforce departure pending the taking of an exam, the selling of a house or the birth of a child.[3] See the previous paragraph.

[1]   [1977] AC 359 at 372, HL.
[2]   He repeated his view in *Halil v Davidson* [1979–80] Imm AR 164, HL.
[3]   See *R v Immigration Appeal Tribunal, ex p Bhanji* [1977] Imm AR 89, CA; *Theori v Secretary of State for the Home Department* [1979–80] Imm AR 126, IAT; *R v Secretary of State for the Home Department, ex p Smith* [1996] Imm AR 331.

Cancellation of leave to remain

4.23 Under section 3B of the Immigration Act 1971[1] the Secretary of State may make provision with respect to the giving, refusing or varying leave to remain, including any appropriate supplemental provision, which may include a power to cancel leave to remain in appropriate cases. Cancellation on arrival of advance leave to enter is not unfamiliar, since it is similar to the power to refuse entry to someone holding an entry clearance.[2] But cancellation of leave to remain is unfamiliar. There is an automatic cancellation of leave to enter or remain, when someone becomes an 'excluded person' under section 8B(2) of the Immigration Act 1971,[3] but there is no general power to cancel leave to remain. Article 13(7) of the Immigration (Leave to Enter and Remain) Order 2000 provides that non-lapsing leave may be cancelled while its holder is outside the UK, in the case of a leave to enter by an immigration officer, and by the Secretary of State in the case of a leave to remain.[4] The power to seek information and documents is the same as that of an immigration officer conducting an examination at the port, with the additional power of calling for a medical report (since there is no power to refer the person abroad to a medical inspector). A failure to provide the requested information, documentation or report is itself a ground for cancellation of leave.[5] The Immigration rules state that an immigration officer at the port may cancel leave to remain,[6] although in fact this may not be correct, since Schedule 2 to the 1971 Act gives immigration officers at the port powers to cancel leave to enter, but there is no mention of cancellation of leave to remain.[7] Cancellation of leave to enter is dealt with at 3.23 above.

[1]   Inserted by Immigration and Asylum Act 1999, s 2.
[2]   See chapter 3. Under the Immigration Act 1971, Sch 2, para 2A(9) such cancellation is treated as a refusal of leave to enter at a time when the person refused had a current entry clearance, except where entry is sought for a different purpose from that in the entry clearance. This ensures an in-country right of appeal: NIAA 2002, s 82(2)(a) read with s 92(3)(a), subject to the exception: see AI(TC)A 2004 s 18, 28.
[3]   Immigration Act 1971, s 8B, inserted by Immigration and Asylum Act 1999, s 8 (war criminals).
[4]   SI 2000/1161, Art 13(7)(a) and (b).

5   SI 2000/1161, Art 13(8), (9).
6   HC 395, para 10B, inserted by HC 704.
7   Immigration Act 1971, as amended by Immigration and Asylum Act 1999, Sch 14, para 57, Sch 2, para 2A(1).

EXERCISING THE DISCRETION TO VARY LEAVE

Formal requirements of rules

4.24 In determining whether to vary leave, refuse to vary it or curtail it, the Secretary of State has to consider not only the formal requirements of the immigration rules regarding visitors, students, and so forth, but also certain general rules. Where someone is granted discretionary leave outside the rules, the Secretary of State is entitled to apply the rules when a variation of leave is sought, provided that the wording of the rule fits the applicant's case.[1] Similarly, in dealing with the formal requirements of the rules, the Secretary of State has a general discretion to vary leave outside the rules, and can for example extend leave for someone whose case falls partly within one category and partly in another ('cross-fertilisation'), but if he or she declines to do so the appellate authority cannot 'bend' the rules itself.[2] In *R v Immigration Appeal Tribunal, ex p Martin*,[3] decided under earlier rules, an Australian woman only had sufficient means to maintain herself if she combined her earnings as a self-employed seamstress with a private income received from her father, but neither source was sufficient by itself. The adjudicator held that she could qualify as a person who 'set up in business' and that her private income could be taken into account, albeit that it was not large enough for her to qualify as a person of independent means. The Tribunal's reversal of this decision was upheld by the Divisional Court, which held that an applicant for an extension of leave must clearly bring herself within one or other of the categories in the immigration rules.[4]

1   *Mamon v Immigration Appeal Tribunal* [1988] Imm AR 364, CA in respect of exceptional leave to remain.
2   'Bending' the rules is not the same as giving them a construction which accords with their general humanitarian purpose: *R v Immigration Appeal Tribunal, ex p Singh (Swaran)* [1987] Imm AR 563, CA; or with the ECHR: *R v Secretary of State for the Home Department, ex p Ali (Arman)* [2000] INLR 89.
3   [1972] Imm AR 275.
4   See further *R v Immigration Appeal Tribunal, ex p Ali (Aisha Khatoon)* [1979–80] Imm AR 195, qualified by *R v Immigration Appeal Tribunal, ex p Coomasaru* [1983] 1 All ER 208, [1983] 1 WLR 14, CA.

4.25 Just as cross-fertilisation of the different categories is allowed to the Secretary of State but not to the Tribunal on appeal, so too it has been held that the appellate authorities cannot construe the immigration rules so as to extend the categories of dependent relatives eligible for entry under the rules on family reunion.[1] However, as a public authority, the Tribunal must act compatibly with the ECHR[2] and must construe the rules purposively to give effect to the rights protected by the Convention, which might involve reading words in where necessary.[3]

1   *Nisa v Secretary of State for the Home Department* [1979–80] Imm AR 20. But see *R v Secretary of State for the Home Department, ex p Ali (Arman)* [2000] INLR 89.

2   Human Rights Act 1998, s 6; see chapter 8 below.
3   Human Rights Act 1998, s 3.

The 'no switching' rule

4.26 Prior to 1980, persons in the UK as visitors, students and other temporary entrants could obtain extensions of leave to set up in business[1] or become persons of independent means. Since then, the policy has swung against such changes being allowed, and is now swinging back again. The current immigration rules generally prevent switching categories, but contain some important exceptions. For example, visa nationals in the UK as visitors cannot become students,[2] and neither visitors nor students may remain as au pairs or working holidaymakers.[3] Visitors may not remain (under the Rules) for employment,[4] investment[5] or to set up in business,[6] but students may be granted extensions of stay for Department of Employment-approved training,[7] or for post-graduate medical or dental training,[8] and graduates, student nurses, trainee doctors and dentists, working holiday-makers, highly skilled migrants and innovators may switch to work permit employment,[9] as may doctors admitted for a PLAB test or on clinical attachment and dental observers;[10] anyone from an Association Agreement country may apply to remain for business or self-employment under the Agreement,[11] and graduates, medical trainees, working holidaymakers, work permit holders and innovators can apply to remain as highly skilled migrants,[12] who in turn, together with the other groups, may remain as innovators.[13] Work permit holders, highly skilled migrants, innovators and business persons may remain as investors.[14] Men or women admitted in a temporary capacity can stay on if they qualify under the unmarried partners' rule[15] or (if granted leave for more than six months or as a fiancé(e)) the marriage rules,[16] and those admitted for marriage or unmarried relationship whose relationship has broken down may stay for contact with the children of the relationship.[17] Finally, people visiting family members settled in the UK may apply to remain with them permanently as dependent relatives.[18]

1   Visitors could set up in business, but the wording of HCs 80 and 82 may have excluded students. The old rules are relevant because of the 'standstill' provisions of the EC-Turkey Association Agreement: see fn 6 below.
2   HC 395, para 60(i).
3   HC 395, paras 92(i) (au pair), 98(i) (working holidaymaker).
4   HC 395, para 128. A concession operates to allow switching into shortage occupations in exceptional circumstances: see 10.57 below.
5   HC 395, para 227.
6   HC 395, para 206. However, Turkish nationals admitted as visitors may be entitled to remain to set up in business under the 'standstill' provisions of the EC-Turkey Association Agreement and its additional protocol: *R v Secretary of State for the Home Department, ex p Savas* [2000] INLR 398, ECJ.
7   HC 395, para 119(i).
8   HC 395 para 73.
9   HC 395, para 132, inserted by HC 346, with reference to paras 131A–F, inserted by Cmnd 5597, Cm 5949, Cm 6339..
10 HC 395, para 132 as inserted, with reference to para 131G, as inserted.
11 HC 395, para 217.
12 HC 395, para 135E, inserted by HC 346, with reference to paras 135DA–135DD, inserted by Cm 6339, 135DE–135DF, inserted by HC 1112, and 135DG, inserted by HC 346.
13 HC 395, para 210D–210DF, 210E, inserted by Cm 6339, HC 538, amended by HC 1112.

14 HC 395, para 227A–D, inserted by HC 346.
15 HC 395, para 295D.
16 HC 395, para 284, as amended by Cm 5959.
17 HC 395, para 248A, inserted by Cm 4851.
18 HC 395, paras 298(ii)(a) and 299; 317 and 318.

General grounds for refusing variations and curtailing leave

4.27 Prior to 1994, an application for leave to remain for a purpose not covered by the immigration rules, if refused, attracted a right of appeal on its merits.[1] The loophole was closed by the 1994 rules,[2] which provided that (1) a variation of leave 'is to be refused' if leave is being sought for a purpose not covered by the rules. The Secretary of State may of course still allow such an application outside the rules, but a refusal is not appealable on the merits.[3] In addition to this general ground on which an extension of leave must be refused under the rules, there are further grounds on which such an application 'should normally' be refused.[4] These are:

(2)   the making of false representations or the failure to disclose any material fact for the purpose of obtaining leave to enter or a previous variation of leave;

(3)   failure to comply with any conditions of leave;

(4)   failure by the person concerned to maintain or accommodate himself and any dependants without recourse to public funds;

(5)   the undesirability of permitting the person concerned to remain in the light of his or her character, conduct or associations or because of a threat to national security;

(6)   refusal by a sponsor to give an undertaking in writing to be responsible for maintenance and accommodation or failure to honour such an undertaking;

(7)   failure by the applicant to honour any declaration or undertaking given orally or in writing as to the intended duration and/or purpose of his or her stay;

(8)   failure, except by those who qualify for settlement or who are married to someone settled in the UK, to satisfy the Secretary of State that he or she will be returnable to another country if allowed to remain in the UK for a further period;

(9)   failure to produce within a reasonable time documents or other evidence required by the Secretary of State to establish a claim to remain under the Rules;[5]

(10) failure, without providing a reasonable explanation, to attend for interview;

(11) failure in the case of a child (other than an asylum seeker) making an application to remain other than in conjunction with his or her parents, to produce written consent to the application from a parent or legal guardian to the Secretary of State, if required to do so.

Rule 323 provides that a person's leave to enter or remain may be curtailed on any of the grounds set out in paragraphs (2)–(5) above or if the person ceases to meet the requirements of the Rules under which leave to enter or remain was granted.

1   Since there was no applicable rule, there was no application to depart from the immigration rules, and so the appellate authority was not precluded from exercising its own discretion: see eg *Rahman (Jinnah) v Secretary of State for the Home Department* [1989] Imm AR 325.
2   HC 395, para 322(1).
3   The refusal will be appealable on asylum or human rights grounds if as a result of the refusal, the person has no leave to enter or remain: Nationality, Immigration and Asylum Act 2002, ss 82(2)(d), 88(4) and 84(1)(b), (c), (g). See chapter 18 below.
4   HC 395, para 322(2)–(11). We retain the numbering of the sub-paragraphs here.
5   See *R v Secretary of State for the Home Department, ex p Animashaun* [1990] Imm AR 70, QBD. The asylum equivalent of this rule, HC 395, para 340, combined with absurdly short compliance times, led to over a third of asylum claims being rejected on non-compliance grounds at one time, and to widespread anger at the cynical abuse of the procedure by the Secretary of State to inflate refusal figures for political purposes.

4.28 The general considerations at (2)–(5) above expressly apply to a variation of leave which curtails it, as well as refusal to vary.[1] Curtailment of leave is rather more drastic than a refusal to vary it, and it will normally only be used in exceptional circumstances.[2] It will not be used if less than six months' leave remains.[3] There is only one situation where curtailment is routinely considered, and that is where a person who is in the UK in a temporary capacity, such as student or au pair, applies for asylum which is refused.[4] If the person does not qualify for humanitarian protection or discretionary leave, was warned of his or her liability to curtailment, and does not qualify for leave under any other provision of the immigration rules, leave may be curtailed on the basis that the applicant ceases to meet the requirements of the immigration rules (usually the requirement that they intend to leave the UK at the end of their stay).[5] Exceptions are persons married to British citizens or to EEA nationals exercising Treaty rights; holders of leave in a category leading to settlement (work or business); or passengers who are terminally ill.[6] Curtailment of humanitarian protection or discretionary leave might follow if the person ceases to meet the requirements of the concession under which it was granted, or travels to the country fear of return to which formed the basis of the leave.[7]

1   HC 395, para 323.
2   Curtailment should not follow automatically when the basis of stay no longer exists: IDI, Ch 9, s 5, para 2.6. The IDI on maintenance and accommodation for spouses suggest that curtailment would only be appropriate where someone has persistent recourse to public funds shortly after marriage and the situation is unlikely to change: IDI Ch 8, Annex F, para 8; see also IDI, Ch 9, s 5, para 2.3.
3   IDI, Ch 9, s 5.
4   API, 'Curtailment of limited leave in cases where an asylum or human rights application is refused', para 3.
5   API, 'Curtailment of limited leave ...' above, para 3.1.
6   API, 'Curtailment of limited leave ...' above, para 3.2.
7   IDI, Ch 9, s 5, para 3.

4.29 So far as refusal to vary leave is concerned, the long list of specific reasons suggests that a person who satisfies the formal qualifications of the particular rule, as a student or employee for example, and does not fall foul of one of the listed general considerations, would be entitled to a variation. Many of the features of the general grounds for refusing extensions are to be found in the general grounds for refusing leave to enter set out in chapter 3[1] and little further explanation is needed. Other general grounds are self-evident and no further explanation is given. Our further comments are set out in the paragraphs which follow.

1   At 3.49 above.

False representations and non-disclosure

4.30 False representations must have been made or material facts not disclosed in order to obtain leave to enter or a previous variation of leave.[1] An innocent failure will not be enough. Although the Court of Appeal has held that a false representation is simply a representation which is inaccurate, and does not necessarily connote fraud,[2] it is still incumbent on the Home Office to prove the case to the requisite standard; ie prove a representation, its falsity and the fact that it was made for the purpose of obtaining leave or an earlier variation. Where fraud is alleged, the standard of proof will have to be higher.[3] Where non-disclosure is relied on, the applicant should not be punished for a failure to realise that facts not disclosed were material.[4] Otherwise, one effect of the rule will be to rectify mistakes by immigration officials in granting earlier leave, at the expense of the innocent applicant. See further 3.71–3.72 above.

1   HC 395, para 322(2). Note that, by virtue of s 24A(1)(a) of the Immigration Act 1971 (inserted by Immigration and Asylum Act 1999, s 28) it is a criminal offence to obtain leave to remain by means which include deception. The IDI (Ch 9, s 5, para 2.1) indicate that it would be more usual to proceed to administrative removal under s 10 Immigration and Asylum Act 1999, or to treat the applicant as an illegal entrant.
2   *Akhtar v Immigration Appeal Tribunal* [1991] Imm AR 326, CA. See 3.71 above.
3   *Khawaja v Secretary of State for the Home Department* [1984] AC 74, [1983] Imm AR 139, HL.
4   On what is meant by 'material' see 3.72 above, 16.21 below.

Failure to comply with conditions attached to stay

4.31 A failure to comply with conditions attached to stay[1] will lead to refusal of further leave only where a person has shown by his or her conduct that he or she has deliberately and consistently breached conditions of stay. It is not intended that the paragraph should be used indiscriminately where, for example, a person has overstayed leave unintentionally or an application was submitted a few days late.[2] The fact that a past breach has been overlooked, in the sense that further leave has been granted despite it, does not mean that it has been condoned in the sense of full forgiveness. Thus, where a student had overstayed once but had been given an extension, and had then overstayed a second time, the first overstay could be used to ground a refusal.[3] However, in all cases, the decision must be personal to the applicant and it would still be wrong to refuse a variation solely to deter others from overstaying or breaching their conditions.[4] Conditions attached to stay do not equate with requirements of the rules,[5] and failure to attend classes is not a breach of conditions of leave to remain as a student, although further leave may be refused, or leave curtailed, on the ground that the person no longer satisfies the requirements of the student rules.[6]

1   HC 395, para 322(3).
2   IDI, Ch 9, s 4.
3   *Secretary of State for the Home Department v Sidique* [1976] Imm AR 69.
4   *Lee v Secretary of State for the Home Department* [1975] Imm AR 75.
5   For conditions attached to leave see Immigration Act 1971, s 3(3), 3.7 above; for requirements of the rules see the relevant immigration rule.
6   *R (on the application of Zhou) v Secretary of State for the Home Department* [2003] EWCA Civ 51, [2003] INLR 211.

Recourse to public funds

4.32 If leave was subject to a condition of no recourse to public funds (which would be stamped in the passport), the previous paragraph could be used to refuse further leave. If no such formal condition was imposed, this paragraph could be relied on to refuse applicants who have failed to maintain and accommodate themselves and any dependants without recourse to public funds.[1] 'Public funds' covers housing under Part VI or VII of the Housing Act 1996 and Part II of the Housing Act 1985 and the equivalent enactments in Scotland and Northern Ireland, attendance allowance, severe disablement allowance, carers' allowance and disability living allowance under Part III, income support, council tax benefit and housing benefit under Part VII, social fund payments under Part VIII and child benefit under Part IX of the Social Security Contribution and Benefits Act 1992, income-based jobseeker's allowance under the Jobseekers Act 1995, state pension credit under the State Pension Credits Act 2002, child tax credit and working tax credit under Part I of the Tax Credits Act 2002, and the equivalent benefits in Northern Ireland.[2] The definition is often amended and should be checked in the current version of the immigration rules. An applicant is not treated as having recourse to public funds by relying on funds provided to the sponsor in his or her own right, provided that the applicant's presence in the UK has not resulted in increased entitlement for the sponsor,[3] or if he or she is not excluded from specified benefits under section 115 of the Immigration and Asylum Act 1999 by regulations under that section or under section 42 of the Tax Credits Act 2002.[4] Refusal (or curtailment) on this ground might be appropriate if the person is clearly going to be a continuing and significant burden on the State, but not where he or she has claimed for a short time in an emergency,[5] and a spouse should not be refused settlement in reliance on this paragraph if, without fault, there has been strictly temporary assistance from public funds.[6]

1   HC 395, para 322(4).
2   HC 395, para 6 as most recently amended by HC 346 with effect from 15 March 2005.
3   HC 395, para 6A, inserted by Cm 4851.
4   HC 395, para 6B, inserted by HC 346 above.
5   IDI, Ch 9, s 5, para 2.3.
6   IDI, Ch 8, Annex F, para 8.

Character, conduct or associations

4.33 Refusal or curtailment may occur if it is deemed undesirable to permit the applicant to remain in the UK in the light of his or her character, conduct or associations.[1] These are wide-ranging words which give the Secretary of

State a discretion in the light of an applicant's criminal record, or other bad behaviour or associations. Curtailment is unlikely since the Secretary of State can use deportation powers, which carry a prohibition on re-entry.[2]

1   HC 395, para 322(5).
2   Immigration Act 1971, ss 3(5)(a), 5. There would be a right of appeal against either decision under Nationality, Immigration and Asylum Act 2002, s 82.

Breach of undertakings

4.34 An application for variation of leave may be refused if the person has failed to honour any declaration or undertaking given orally or in writing as to the intended duration and/or purpose of that person's stay.[1] The situation arises most often when a family visitor decides to apply for leave to remain in the UK with the sponsoring family member, having said on arrival or at entry clearance interview that he or she would return home at the end of the visit. A 'declaration' must, we suggest, be something more definite than a mere statement of intention, but exactly what will amount to a 'declaration' or how cogent the evidence must be to prove a 'declaration' is still unclear. So far as 'undertakings' are concerned, Tribunal authorities under earlier rules held that the only undertakings which count are those which amount to false representations. In other words, a genuine change of circumstances since the 'undertaking' will not prevent an extension of leave.[2] This appears to be the way the rule is interpreted by the Home Office in the IDI, which state that where there is good reason for the applicant's change of mind, such as unforeseen circumstances, leave may be granted; only where there does not appear to be a good reason, and particularly where there is reason to doubt the applicant's future intentions, should leave be refused.[3]

1   HC 395, para 322(7).
2   *Ridha* (3060), unreported; *Perera* (3063), unreported.
3   IDI, Ch 9, s 4, para 8.

4.35 The current immigration rules provide that they do not generally apply to EEA nationals.[1] Curtailment or refusal to renew residence permits or other leave granted to EEA nationals who benefit from the free movement provisions must all be justifiable by reference to EC law and, in particular, to the public policy provisions (see chapter 7 below).

1   HC 395, para 5.

REGISTRATION WITH THE POLICE

4.36 Under the Immigration Act 1971 the government has power to make any group of immigrants register with the police. The present policy is to limit this to aliens,[1] but this can be changed at any time, subject to annulment in Parliament.[2] The current regulations are the Immigration (Registration with Police) Regulations 1972.[3] They apply only to aliens who have a limited leave to enter or remain in the UK which is for the time being subject to a condition requiring registration with the police.[4] In practice not all aliens are required to register, only 'relevant foreign nationals', namely, those from countries listed in Appendix 2 of the immigration rules, stateless persons, and those holding non-national travel documents.[5]

¹ An alien means a person who is neither a Commonwealth citizen nor a BPP nor a citizen of the Republic of Ireland: British Nationality Act 1981, s 50(1), as applied by SI 1972/1758, reg 2.
² Immigration Act 1971, s 4(3). The Police Federation opposed the registration with police of Commonwealth citizens under the 1971 Act. It cannot have been because of the administrative burden, because only 15 new personnel would have been required: see 813 HC Official Report (5th series) col 51.
³ SI 1972/1758, amended on many occasions in respect of the fee for issue of a certificate of registration. The fee for registration now stands at £34: see the Immigration (Registration with Police) (Amendment) Regulations 1995, SI 1995/2928.
⁴ SI 1972/1758, reg 3.
⁵ HC 395, para 325, substituted by HC 194 from 4 February 2005.

4.37 The current immigration rules[1] provide that a condition requiring registration will normally be imposed on any relevant foreign national[2] aged 16 or over who is given limited leave to enter for more than six months, or is given limited leave to remain which has the effect of allowing him or her to remain in the UK for longer than six months, whether or not a condition of registration was imposed on entry.[3] Exceptionally, a requirement to register with the police may be imposed in any other case in order to ensure that a foreign national complies with the terms of his or her leave.[4] This condition cannot be imposed on children under 16, and should not normally be imposed on those given leave to enter or remain as seasonal agricultural workers, ministers of religion, missionaries and members of religious orders, diplomats' private servants, spouses and unmarried partners of persons settled in the UK or those granted asylum.[5] EEA nationals and their non-EEA family members are not required to register, since such a condition is contrary to free movement rights under EC law.

¹ HC 395, paras 325 and 326, as substituted by HC 194 from 4 February 2005.
² Foreign nationals are synonymous with aliens; see 4.36 above fn 1.
³ HC 395, para 326(1).
⁴ HC 395, para 326(3) as substituted.
⁵ HC 395, para 326(2) as substituted. The IDI add other groups of relevant foreign nationals who are exempt from registration: members of non-NATO forces admitted for courses at British military establishments or with private companies; Community Service Volunteers; civilian components of NATO forces; non-visa nationals who are employees of contractors to US Armed Forces in the UK or of the American Battle Monuments Commission; and the dependants of those not required to register: IDI, Ch 10, s 1, para 3.

4.38 Registration involves going to the local police station within seven days of the requirement to register[1] and giving detailed particulars, including name, address, marital status, details of employment or occupation, including employer's name and address, a photograph, and paying the registration fee.2 While the person is required to register, changes of address must be notified to the police within seven days, and changes in marital status, nationality and employment or occupation within eight days of the change.[3] In return the foreign national receives from the police a certificate of registration. The requirement to register continues in the case of relevant foreign nationals until they are granted indefinite leave to remain.

¹ SI 1972/1758, reg 5.
² See 4.36 fn 3 above. A further fee is not payable on re-registration by a relevant foreign national who keeps his police registration certificate on leaving the UK and returns within a year: IDI Jan 04, Ch 10, s 1, para 4.3.
³ SI 1972/1758, reg 7 (changes of residence or address) and 8 (other changes).

4.39 Someone who, without reasonable excuse, fails to comply with any of the registration requirements, ie fails to register or fails to notify a change of particulars, commits a criminal offence under section 26(1)(f) of the Immigration Act 1971. This is a summary offence with a six-month time limit. It is continuous up to the time when limited leave expires, but once the period of leave has expired, the registration regulations cease to apply, although offences against the regulation committed prior to the date of expiry of leave might still be prosecuted within the six-month time limit.¹ Additionally, such a person may not be granted further leave to remain, having breached the conditions of leave,² and may be summarily removed under s 10 of the Immigration and Asylum Act 1999.³

¹ *R v Naik* (1978) Times, 26 July, CA.
² *Under HC 395, para 322(3); see* 4.27 and 4.31 *above.*
³ *See* 16.32 *below.*

HOTEL REGISTERS

4.40 The Immigration Act 1971 contains power to make regulations requiring hotels and guest houses to keep records of persons staying there,¹ and under the Immigration (Hotel Records) Order 1972, hotels and other premises where lodging or sleeping accommodation is provided for reward must normally keep registers.² All visitors over the age of 16 who stay there must on arrival inform the keeper of the premises of their full name and nationality. That applies to everyone. Aliens (non-Commonwealth citizens) must also give passport details and inform the hotel of their next address.³ The keeper of the premises must record this information and keep it available for inspection for at least 12 months.⁴ It is not clear how effective or how necessary is the maintenance of hotel registers.

¹ Immigration Act 1971, s 4(4).
² SI 1972/1689.
³ SI 1972/1689, Art 3.
⁴ SI 1972/1689, Art 5.

CONTROL OF DEPARTURE

4.41 UK immigration law does not expressly recognise a right of departure from the UK, though one might be tempted to think that it does, because of the grandiloquent opening to the Immigration Act 1971: ¹

'all those who are in this Act expressed to have the right of abode in the United Kingdom shall be free to live in, and to come and go into and from the United Kingdom without let or hindrance ...'

This, however, is subject to two limitations affecting the right to depart. First, the right to go without let or hindrance is subject to such limits as may be 'lawfully imposed' on any person.[2] Secondly, the right to depart depends upon the person being able to acquire a passport.[3] Although the position in UK law is somewhat obscure, under EC law there is a clearly defined right to depart.[4] British citizens wishing to exercise their right to depart for a Community purpose can invoke these provisions of EC law if they are refused a passport or other travel document valid in the territories of other EC countries. For a full discussion, see 2.66–2.68 above.

[1]   Immigration Act 1971, s 1(1).
[2]   Immigration Act 1971, s 1(1). See 2.7–2.8 above.
[3]   The refusal of a passport is now subject to judicial review: *R v Secretary of State for Foreign and Commonwealth Affairs, ex p Everett* [1989] QB 811, [1989] Imm AR 155, CA. See 2.66 above.
[4]   See chapter 7 below.

Right to depart – immigration officers' powers

4.42 An immigration officer may examine someone seeking to leave the UK for the purpose of determining whether he or she has the right of abode and, if not, in order to establish his or her identity.[1] For the purpose of this examination, the immigration officer can require the person wishing to leave the UK to produce either a valid passport with photograph or some other document which satisfactorily establishes the person's identity and nationality or citizenship.[2] Immigration officers may also require the provision of other documents and may carry out searches, as on entry.[3] But there is no express power to detain or require a person to submit to further examination, and there is certainly, except in the limited situation referred to below, no power to prevent the person's departure for any immigration reason. Clearly there is power to arrest and detain under other powers, for example if there is a warrant for the arrest of the person in connection with a criminal offence.[4] But immigration powers of detention do not apply to persons leaving the UK.

[1]   Immigration Act 1971, Sch 2, para 3(1).
[2]   IA 1971, Sch 2, para 4.
[3]   IA 1971, Sch 2, para 4. On 14 April 1998, ports ceased to endorse passports or issue/collect embarkation cards on passengers' departure from the United Kingdom.
[4]   For immigration officers' powers of arrest see chapter 14.

Emergency and safety powers

4.43 Under section 3(7) of the Immigration Act 1971 power is given to make provision for prohibiting nationals or citizens of a particular country from leaving the UK, or from doing so other than at a port of exit or for imposing conditions or restrictions on them when they wish to leave. Such an order can only be made where it appears to Her Majesty proper to do so by reason of restrictions or conditions imposed on British citizens when they want to leave a particular country or territory. Provision may also be made by Order in Council to prohibit all those who do not have the right of abode in the UK from leaving on a ship or aircraft specified or indicated in the prohibition in the interests of safety.[1] Where such an order is in force, an immigration officer has additional powers of examining persons who are leaving or seeking to leave the UK to determine:

(a)   whether any of the provisions of the order apply to them; and
(b)   whether, if so, any power conferred by the order should be exercised in relation to them and in what way.[2]

No such order has been made or is in force since the Immigration Act 1971 came into force.

[1]   Immigration Act 1971, s 3(7).
[2]   IA 1971, Sch 2, para 3(2).

Chapter 5

SETTLEMENT AND RETURN

5.1   Settlement
5.20   Return to the UK

SETTLEMENT

Definition

5.1 A person with the right of abode does not need to qualify for admission to the UK under the Immigration Act 1971 or the Immigration Rules. The concept of a 'right of abode' is to be distinguished from the concept of 'settlement' or the right to permanent residence. The right to permanent residence, or settled status, does not confer freedom from immigration control. Being 'settled' means being ordinarily resident without being subject under the immigration laws to any restriction on the period of stay.[1] Ordinary residence and being free from restrictions on the length of permitted stay under the Immigration Rules are the two key elements. The word 'settled', therefore, covers persons with a right of abode and those with indefinite leave to enter or remain, provided each is ordinarily resident in the UK. The phrase 'settled in the United Kingdom' is defined by the Immigration Rules to mean that the person concerned is (a) free from any restriction on the period of stay (excluding those exempt from control under section 8), and (b) ordinarily resident in the UK without (c) having entered or remained in breach of immigration laws or, having entered or remained unlawfully, has subsequently entered lawfully or has been granted leave to remain and is so resident.[2]

[1]   Immigration Act 1971, s 33(2A), as amended by British Nationality Act 1981, s 39(6) and Sch 4, para 7. See also British Nationality Act 1981, s 50(2)–(4), where a more comprehensive definition (necessary for the purpose of nationality law) is given: see below. For EEA nationals reg 8 of the Immigration (European Economic Area) Regulations 2000, SI 2000/2326 defines those who are to be treated as not subject to any restriction on their period of stay.
[2]   HC 395, para 6.

5.2 A similar definition of settlement applies for the purposes of the British Nationality Act 1981, except that for nationality purposes residents in the

Channel Islands or Isle of Man, as well as in the UK, are included.[1] Persons who are subject to exemptions from immigration control, such as diplomats, consuls, members of visiting forces and so forth, are not normally regarded as 'settled' during any period when they are entitled to exemption.[2] Limited exceptions apply to enable the children of an 'exempted' parent to obtain British citizenship by birth in the UK under section 1 of the British Nationality Act 1981.[3]

[1]   British Nationality Act 1981, s 50(1), (2).
[2]   In those cases where the Act says that 'the provisions of this Act ... shall not apply', this would mean that the definition of 'settled' in s 33(2A) would also not apply. Whether this is the reason for the accepted view that settled status cannot be achieved during a period of exemption, unless special provision is made, is not entirely clear. See Immigration Act 1971, s 8(5). See also British Nationality Act 1981, s 50(3).
[3]   Immigration Act 1971, s 8(5A), as amended; British Nationality Act 1981, s 50(4).

No restriction on the period of stay

5.3 Whether a person is free from immigration restrictions on their length of stay is not normally difficult to determine, in those cases where the person is subject to the permissive system of control used in UK domestic law. Thus, a person with a six-month or 12-month leave has a restriction on their period of stay and cannot be regarded as 'settled'. The Immigration Act 1971 distinguishes between a limited leave and indefinite leave,[1] and normally the person must have been granted one or other of them, there being no half-way house between the grant of leave and entry without leave.[2] Limited leave is subject to a time restriction; indefinite leave is not, as section 33(2A) of the Immigration Act 1971 makes clear. The position is different for those with exemptions from immigration control, whom we deal with at 5.4 below, and EEA nationals and their families, who come to Britain under EEA free movement rights. EEA nationals enter as of right and are not, on entry, subject to the normal permissive system of getting a leave to enter. So it was thought they were not subject to any restrictions on their period of stay. But that has changed. The rights of workers and the self employed, it is said, are conditional, presumably, on the continuance of their economic activity. It is a debatable point.[3] The upshot is that their position is now regulated by regulation 8 of the Immigration (European Economic Area) Regulations 2000, under which the general rule is that freedom from restrictions on length of stay only occurs if indefinite permission is granted or in other specified circumstances.[4]

[1]   Immigration Act 1971, s 3(1).
[2]   *Mokuolo v Secretary of State for the Home Department* [1989] Imm AR 51, CA.
[3]   For a fuller discussion, see 7.121 below.
[4]   Immigration (European Economic Area) Regulations 2000, SI 2000/2326, reg 8, which (apart from EEA nationals and their family members who have indefinite permission to remain in the UK), cover retired self-employed persons, their family members, and family members of deceased workers and of other qualified persons who fulfil various conditions. Giving a domestic law status in line with indefinite leave is probably necessary in the light of EC Directives and regulations, which only refer to permanent stay in relatively few cases: eg Directive 73/148, Art 4(1) (self employed); Directive 75/34, Art 2.1 (retired persons); Directive 75/34, Art 3(2) (family members of deceased self employed person); Regulation 1250/70, Art 3(2) (family members of deceased worker). The right of residence for those providing services is for the period during which services are provided: Directive

73/148, Art 4(2). In the case of workers the period of stay is restricted for seasonal workers and may be for other workers following voluntary unemployment: Directive 68/360, Arts 6 and 7. The residual right of residence to all EU citizens is time restricted residence; Directive 90/364, Art 2(1); so too for the retired and those with invalidity pensions; Directive 90/365, Art 2(1). The right of residence to which students are entitled is restricted to the duration of their studies: Directive 93/96, Art 2(1).

5.4 Indefinite leave may be notified by letter, which is a valuable document to keep. It is also usually indicated in one of two ways: either by a stamp in the passport endorsed by the immigration officer on entry or by the Immigration and Nationality Directorate after entry; or by an indication on an entry certificate, which is now treated as a leave to enter.[1] A stamp in a passport indicating leave to enter or remain for an indefinite period is clearly an express grant of indefinite leave.[2] Difficulties have arisen, however, where all that has been used is a rectangular stamp with a date but no clear words indicating any sort of leave, limited or unlimited. In the case of returning residents, such a stamp would be enough to constitute indefinite leave to enter, but in other cases, this is unlikely. The Court of Appeal has held that in the circumstances of the particular case such a stamp was not the grant of a leave to enter at all, but merely a record of the person's passage through immigration control.[3] Illegible stamps in passports (which once gave rise to indefinite leave to enter) are deemed to grant six months' leave with a condition prohibiting employment.[4] Settlement can only occur where there is no time limit on stay.

[1] Under Arts 2–4 of the Immigration (Leave to Enter and Remain) Order 2000, SI 2000/1161 a visa or other entry clearance may have effect as indefinite leave to enter if (a) it specifies the purpose of entry, and (b) states it is to have effect as indefinite leave to enter (arts 3(3)(b) and 4(3)(a)). See generally chapter 3 above.

[2] *R v Secretary of State for the Home Department, ex p Bagga* [1991] 1 QB 485, [1990] Imm AR 413, CA: see 3.47 above.

[3] An 'indefinite leave stamp' includes a sticker or other attachment: Immigration and Asylum Act 1999 s 5(5) (as amended by Asylum and Immigration (Treatment of Claimants, etc) Act 2004, s 43).

[4] Since an illegible stamp is not an effective 'notice giving or refusing leave' as required by Immigration Act 1971, s 4(1); Sch 2, para 6(1), as amended, applies.

Ordinarily resident

5.5 The term 'ordinarily resident' is used in a number of different statutes, including the Immigration Act 1971 and the British Nationality Acts 1948 and 1981. The term is also used as a criterion of eligibility for educational and other social services provided by central and local government.[1] A trend towards defining ordinary residence in terms of immigration status in the context of education was rejected in *Shah v Barnet London Borough Council*,[2] where the House of Lords held that an overseas student habitually and normally resident in the UK for study, apart from temporary or occasional absences of long or short duration, was 'ordinarily resident' in the natural and ordinary meaning of those words used in the Education Acts and implementing regulations. Lord Scarman, who gave the leading speech, unhesitatingly subscribed to the view that 'ordinarily resident' referred to persons' abode in a particular place or country which they had adopted voluntarily and for settled purposes as part of the regular order of their life for the time being, whether of short or long duration. The purpose might be one or several, specific or general, and did not require that the person intended to stay indefinitely; indeed, the person's purpose might be for a limited period. Education, business or profession, employment, health, family, or merely love of the place sprang to mind as common reasons for a choice of regular abode. All that was necessary was that the purpose of living where one did had a sufficient degree of continuity to be properly described as settled. It was wrong to attach any decisive importance to the immigration status of the persons claiming to be ordinarily resident, except in the case of a person whose presence was unlawful.[3] Further, the notion that ordinary residence required a permanent or indefinitely enduring purpose derived from a confusion of ordinary residence with domicile. The 'real home' test did not apply to determining ordinary residence.[4]

1   But increasingly immigration status rather than 'ordinary residence' defines eligibility for housing, social services and social security (as well as employment): see chapter 13 below.
2   [1983] 2 AC 309, [1983] 1 All ER 226.
3   See *R v Secretary of State for the Home Department, ex p Margueritte* [1983] QB 180, [1982] 3 All ER 909, CA; *Immigration Appeal Tribunal v Chelliah* [1985] Imm AR 192, CA.
4   See *Stransky v Stransky* [1954] P 428, [1954] 2 All ER 536.

5.6 Thus ordinary residence is to be distinguished from the more traditional concept of domicile, which is used in private international law. Ordinary residence may be acquired without any intention permanently to reside in the country, whereas an intention permanently to remain is essential to the acquisition of a new domicile.[1] Thus persons who come to the UK for a visit and remain for reasons beyond their control may be ordinarily resident though they cannot acquire a domicile of choice because of absence of any necessary intention.[2] At common law, persons may be ordinarily resident although they are liable to removal or deportation under the immigration laws,[3] but it is not clear whether they may be ordinarily resident if their residence in the UK is not voluntary because, for example, they are in prison or a psychiatric institution.[4] A person may be ordinarily resident in two places at one time.[5] It is also clear that ordinary residence is not lost through temporary absences abroad,[6] though clearly this is always a matter of degree. In *R v Hussain*[7] an absence abroad for a period of 20 months was held to break the period of ordinary residence for the purposes of exemption from deportation under the Commonwealth Immigrants Act 1962. On the other hand, in *R v Edgehill*[8] a sentence of less than six months' imprisonment imposed by a foreign court did not prevent a defendant from having been 'ordinarily' and 'continuously' resident here for five years so as to exempt him from deportation under the 1962 Act. In *R v Immigration Appeal Tribunal, ex p Siggins*,[9] a nine-month absence in the US was insufficient to break the period of ordinary residence. In each case the test to apply is whether the applicant intends to return to the UK so that the break in residence is a merely temporary one. Where the applicant intends to reside in a new country for the foreseeable future, ordinary residence in the UK will end.[10]

1   See *Hopkins v Hopkins* [1951] P 116 at 121–122 and *Stransky v Stransky* [1954] P 428 at 437. For a fuller discussion of domicile see chapter 11.

2   *Re Mackenzie* [1941] Ch 69, [1940] 4 All ER 310; and cf *Re Bright, ex p Bright* (1903) 51 WR 342, CA; *R v Denman, ex p Staal* (1917) 86 LJKB 1328; *Pittar v Richardson* (1917) 87 LJKB 59.

3   *Boldrini v Boldrini and Martini* [1932] P 9, CA; *May v May and Lehmann* [1943] 2 All ER 146; *Cruh v Cruh* [1945] 2 All ER 545.

4   See *IRC v Lysaght* [1928] AC 234, per Viscount Sumner at 243; contrast *Re Mackenzie* [1941] Ch 69, per Morton J at 77. Lord Scarman in *Shah v Barnet London Borough Council* [1983] 2 AC 309 at 344, doubted whether imprisonment had the necessary voluntary character to found ordinary residence.

5   *Re Norris, ex p Reynolds* (1888) 4 TLR 452, CA (bankrupt ordinarily resident in Brussels and London); see further *Fox v Stirk and Bristol Electoral Registration Officer* [1970] 2 QB 463, [1970] 3 All ER 7, CA, per Lord Denning MR at 475 (a person may have two residences); *Shah v Barnet* above at 342F.

6   See *Hopkins v Hopkins* [1951] P 116, [1950] 2 All ER 1035; *Stransky v Stransky* [1954] P 428, [1954] 2 All ER 536; *Lewis v Lewis* [1956] 1 All ER 375, [1956] 1 WLR 200; *R v Immigration Appeal Tribunal, ex p Siggins* [1985] Imm AR 14, QBD; *Secretary of State for the Home Department v Haria* [1986] Imm AR 165. The Court of Appeal in *Ikimi v Ikimi* [2001] EWCA Civ 873, [2001] 3 FLR 672 equated 'ordinary residence' with 'habitual residence', and held that it required a degree of continuity.

7   *R v Hussain* (1971) 56 Cr App Rep 165, CA.

8   [1963] 1 QB 593, [1963] 1 All ER 181, CCA.

9   [1985] Imm AR 14, above.

10 *R v Immigration Appeal Tribunal, ex p NG* [1986] Imm AR 23, QBD; *Ex p Siggins* above.

5.7 The ordinary residence of children may cause problems. In *Re P (GE) (an infant)*[1] it was held that the ordinary residence of children too young to decide for themselves where to live was the home of their parents, even while they were away at boarding school. They did not lose that status by temporary absence abroad or by being abducted by one of the parents without the consent of the other. In an Australian case[2] it was held that though a child spent more time at boarding school than at her parents' home, she was nevertheless ordinarily resident with her father because this had been her permanent home at all times and the time spent at school was for the special purpose of education. This is in contrast to the position of adult students, for whom study may be a 'settled purpose' which establishes ordinary residence: see *Shah v Barnet* above.

1   [1965] Ch 568, [1964] 3 All ER 977, CA.

2   *Clark v Insurance Office of Australia Ltd* [1965] 1 Lloyd's Rep 308, SC of Victoria.

Residence in breach of the immigration laws

5.8 For the purposes of immigration and nationality law, ordinary residence contains statutory requirements over and above those in the common law. The Immigration Act 1971 and British Nationality Act 1981 both deal with the question whether a person can be ordinarily resident while in breach of the immigration laws. For purposes of exemption from deportation, once ordinarily resident, a person does not cease to be so while in breach of the immigration laws.[1] But for other Immigration Act purposes, it is expressly provided that a person cannot be ordinarily resident at a time when he or she is in breach of the immigration laws.[2] A similar qualification is made under the British Nationality Act 1981: a person is not to be treated as ordinarily resident for the purposes of that Act when he or she is in the UK in breach of the immigration laws.[3]

1   Immigration Act 1971, s 7(2).
2   IA 1971, s 33(2).
3   British Nationality Act 1981, s 50(5). Under the British Nationality Act 1948 no such qualification was made, but in *R v Secretary of State for the Home Department, ex p Margueritte* [1983] QB 180, [1982] 3 All ER 909, the Court of Appeal held that lawful presence was imported into the meaning of ordinary residence under that Act, distinguishing *Azam v Secretary of State for the Home Department* [1974] AC 18, [1973] 2 All ER 765, HL where in a number of their Lordships' speeches it was assumed that a person could be ordinarily resident although an illegal entrant.

5.9 In *Shah v Barnet London Borough Council*,[1] the House of Lords, going further than the statutes required, held that unlawful residence could never be relied on by the resident as establishing ordinary residence,[2] a holding not adopted in its entirety in other contexts.[3] We suggest that, for the purposes of immigration law, there are four situations where someone will be held not to be ordinarily resident on account of breaches of the immigration laws: (1) where the person is in breach of a deportation order;[4] (2) where a person who requires leave to enter enters without leave,[5] even if the person has acted quite innocently;[6] (3) where leave to enter or remain has been obtained by a material deception;[7] and (4) where the person has overstayed the time limited by a leave to enter, even if this is done innocently through ignorance or oversight. For the purpose of qualifying for indefinite leave by reason of long residence in the UK under HC 395, paragraph 276A, lawful residence means continuous residence pursuant to (i) existing leave to enter or remain; (ii) temporary admission within section 11 of the 1971 Act,[8] where leave is subsequently granted; or (iii) an exemption from immigration control, including where an exemption ceases to apply if it is immediately followed by a grant of leave to enter or remain.

1   [1983] 2 AC 309 at 343.
2   Although such residence could be relied on by the Crown for tax purposes: [1983] 2 AC 309 at 343.
3.   In the context of matrimonial proceedings, the Court of Appeal held in *Mark v Mark* [2004] EWCA Civ 168 that habitual residence (equated with ordinary residence in *Ikimi v Ikimi* [2001] EWCA Civ 873, [2001] 3 FLR 672) was a question of fact, to which illegal status might be relevant, and that the rule of public policy relied on by the HL in *Shah v Barnet London Borough Council* was not absolute.
4   Immigration Act 1971, s 33(1).
5   See *Azam v Secretary of State for the Home Department* above.
6   *R v Governor of Ashford Remand Centre, ex p Bouzagou* [1983] Imm AR 69, CA; *Rehal v Secretary of State for the Home Department* [1989] Imm AR 576, CA.
7   See chapter 16 below.
8   *Immigration Appeal Tribunal v Chelliah* [1985] Imm AR 192, CA; *Sui-Ling Lui v Secretary of State for the Home Department* [1986] Imm AR 287.
9   For temporary admission see 17.11 below.

5.10 For the purposes of nationality law,[1] section 11 of the Nationality Immigration and Asylum Act 2002 sets out exhaustively the circumstances in which a person would be in the UK in breach of the immigration laws. A person is in the United Kingdom in breach of the immigration laws if (and only if) he or she :

(a)   is in the United Kingdom,
(b)   does not have the right of abode in the UK,[2]

(c)   does not have leave to enter or remain in the UK (whether or not he or she previously had leave),

(d)   is not a qualified person,[3] who is entitled to reside in United Kingdom without leave (whether or not he was previously a qualified person),

(e)   is not a family member of a qualified person (whether or not he or she was previously a family member of a qualified person),

(f)   is not entitled to enter and remain in the UK as a crew member,[4] (whether or not he or she was previously entitled), and

(g)   does not have the benefit of an exemption under section 8(2) to (4) of the Act of 1971 (diplomats, soldiers and other special cases) (whether or not he or she previously had the benefit of an exemption).

A person is not to be treated as having been here in breach of the immigration laws during any time when he or she is in the immigration control area or is detained or temporarily admitted pending a decision on his or her eligibility to enter.[5] But although detention or temporary admission of this kind does not affect the legality of someone's presence in the UK, the time spent in this way can be calculated as part of the duration of the time spent in the UK for nationality purposes. Except as regards qualified persons and their families, the 2002 Act statement of circumstances in which a person is in breach of the immigration laws has retrospective effect.[6]

---

[1]   The British Nationality Act 1981, s 4 and Sch 1 require applicants for registration and naturalisation to have been ordinarily resident in the UK for a specified period, and s 50(5) states that ordinary residence does not include residence in breach of the immigration laws.

[2]   Within the meaning of the Immigration Act 1971, s 2.

[3]   Within the meaning of the Immigration (European Economic Area) Regulations 2000, SI 2000/2326, reg 5.

[4]   By virtue of the Immigration Act 1971, s 8(1).

[5]   Nationality Immigration and Asylum Act 2002, s 11(3), applying Immigration Act 1971, s 11 to this provision.

[6]   Nationality, Immigration and Asylum Act 2002, s 11(4).

Consequences of being settled

5.11 Settlement brings many advantages. Persons subject to immigration control who are 'settled' have in general a right to permanent residence in the UK, provided they continue living here, although they are potentially liable to deportation, unless they have an exemption,[1] and may be deported if they commit serious crimes or their presence is no longer conducive to the public good for this or some other reason.[2] Revocation of indefinite leave is now possible for a number of reasons under the Nationality, Immigration and Asylum Act 2002.[3]

---

[1]   Immigration Act 1971, s 7.

[2]   Immigration Act, s 3(5)(a) and (6).

[3]   Nationality Immigration and Asylum Act 2002, s 76, covering those liable to deportation but who cannot be deported for legal reasons, such as refugees excluded from protection by Art 33(2) of the Refugee Convention (commission of a particularly serious crime and representing danger to community), who are likely to face ill-treatment engaging Art 3 ECHR if deported (s 76(1); see 12.97 below); those who obtained indefinite leave to remain by deception but who cannot be removed for similar reasons or for practical reasons (s 76(2)); and refugees whose voluntary act (eg returning home or taking another

nationality) attracts the cessation clauses Art 1C(1)–(4) of the Refugee Convention (s 76(3), see 12.84 below). Revocation of indefinite leave attracts a right of appeal under NIAA 2002, s 82(2)(f).

5.12 Other important consequences of being 'settled' are that persons who were previously tied to doing a particular job can change employment without permission[1] or go into business if they choose; and all can take the full benefits of the welfare state, unless they were given leave to enter or remain as a result of a maintenance undertaking.[2] Another important practical consequence is that the 'settled' person is in a position to call for members of their family and other dependants to join them in the UK, provided the necessary accommodation is available and there will be no additional recourse to public funds as a result.[3] There is a wider range of options for family reunion for those settled in the UK than for those with only a limited leave.[4] Foreign nationals who previously were required to register with the police no longer need to do so on being granted settlement.[5] Having the right to settle leads to eligibility for naturalisation or registration as a British citizen.[6] Settlement enables a parent to qualify his or her child for British citizenship, if the child is born in the UK,[7] although this is not a precondition of registration or naturalisation.[8]

[1]   Under Immigration Act 1971, s 3(1) restrictions on employment can only be imposed on a person with limited leave.
[2]   Immigration and Asylum Act 1999, ss 115(9)(c), 116(1A), and 117(4A); the exception is modified by Social Security (Immigration and Asylum) Consequential Amendments Regulations 2000, SI 2000/636, Sch, paras 2–4. See 13.6 below.
[3]   HC 395, paras 6, 6A (inserted by Cm 4851), 281 (spouse), 290 (fiancé), 295A (unmarried partner), 297 (child), 301 (adopted child) and 317 (other dependent relative). The maintenance and accommodation requirements do not apply to the family members of discharged Gurkhas and foreign and Commonwealth soldiers from HM Forces who obtain settlement under HC 395, para 276G–P (inserted by HC 1112 from 18 October 2004): see paras 276R–276AB (inserted by HC 164 from 1 January 2005).
[4]   Compare eg HC 395, paras 194–199 with para 298.
[5]   HC 395, paras 325–326.
[6]   British Nationality Act 1981, ss 4 and 6.
[7]   British Nationality Act 1981, ss 1(1) and 50(4).
[8]   British Nationality Act 1981, ss 4, 6 and Sch 1.

Settlement under the Immigration Rules

5.13 Under the Immigration Rules certain categories of immigration status never lead to settlement, for example, visitor,[1] student,[2] working holiday,[3] au pair,[4] work training,[5] seasonal agricultural worker[6] and teachers and language assistants on approved exchange schemes.[7] In all these cases the person is expected to leave at the end of the allotted period and they cannot generally switch into a category which qualifies for settlement.[8] But in other categories settlement is given straightaway or the persons are admitted for a limited period with a view to eventual settlement. Thus spouses are given a two-year initial period before qualifying for settlement, unless they have already been married for four years, when indefinite leave should be granted.[9] Unmarried partners, whether of the same or opposite sex, are also given a two-year leave with a view to settlement.[10] So too are any children who come with the spouse or unmarried partner.[11] Otherwise, children and other dependent relatives obtain immediate settlement on arrival.[12] Children born in the UK who are not British citizens may also qualify for immediate settlement if one of their parents qualifies for it, or acquires a right of abode, or the child goes into local authority care.[13] Bereaved spouses and unmarried partners of settled persons who died during the initial two-year probationary period qualify for settlement,[14] as do non-custodial parents exercising access rights to children resident in the UK (for whom the qualifying period is 12 months).[15]

1   HC 395, para 44.
2   HC 395, paras 60 and 67.
3   HC 395, para 98.
4   HC 395, para 92.
5   HC 395, para 119.
6   HC 395, para 107 (amended by HC 1224).
7   HC 395, para 113.
8   There are exceptions for certain students, trainees and for working holiday-makers, who may now switch into work permit employment: see Ch 10.
9   HC 395, para 282. Not all of this time need be spent in the UK: *Qureshi* (18312) [1999] 5 ILD 4 at 23; IDI, Ch 8, s 1. NB this used to be a period of 12 months, but was extended to two years from 1 April 2003 by Cmd 5949 and is now in line with the position for unmarried and same-sex partners under para 295B. Spouses of former Gurkhas and foreign or Commonwealth members of HM Forces applying under paras 276R–W (inserted by HC 164 from 1 January 2005) need to have been married for only two years to obtain immediate settlement.
10 HC 395, para 295B, G, inserted by Cm 4851, para 32.
11 HC 395, para 302.
12 HC 395, paras 299, 308 and 317.
13 HC 395, paras 305–308. Indefinite leave is generally granted where children are likely to remain in care for the foreseeable future. See IDI, Ch 8, s 3, Annex P, and Ch 11 below.
14 HC 395, para 287(b), inserted by Cm 4851, para 30 (spouses), HC 395, paras 295M-O as inserted (unmarried partners).
15 HC 395, para 248D, inserted by Cm 4851, para 22.

5.14 Apart from family reunion the other categories of applicant who may qualify for eventual settlement are work permit holders,[1] highly skilled migrants,[2] those in permit-free employment,[3] business and self-employed persons,[4] innovators,[5] writers, composers and artists,[6] investors and retired persons of independent means[7] and Commonwealth citizens with grandparents born in the UK who wish to take or seek employment in the UK.[8] Under the Immigration Rules, these last groups of people qualify for settlement if they have 'spent a continuous period of four years in the UK in this capacity'.[9] The Rules require continuity of residence in the UK for four years while in a particular capacity. A person whose continuity of residence in the UK has been broken would only qualify for an extension of stay in the same capacity and not for settlement. The general practice is to disregard absences of three months in any one year, and, exceptionally, longer periods.[10] While the legal effect of settlement is to allow people to change jobs or business, its grant is dependent in many cases on the prospect of being able to continue in the existing capacity. In employment cases, continuation with the present employer is an express requirement and the employer must give a certificate to this effect.[11] In business cases, evidence of the continuing viability of the business and the applicant's involvement with it is required.[12]

1   HC 395, para 134. The government plans to remove settlement rights from unskilled categories of work permit holders, to increase the minimum qualifying period from four years to five and to impose language and culture tests similar to those imposed by the

NIAA 2002 to applicants for naturalisation: see *Controlling our borders: Making migration work for Britain: Five year strategy for asylum and immigration*, Cm 6472, Feb 2005.
2   HC 395, para 135G, as inserted by HC 538.
3   HC 395, paras 142, 150, 158, 167, 176 and 184.
4   HC 395, paras 209 and 222 (self employed or business under EC Association agreement). The government plans to increase the qualifying period of settlement to five years: see fn 1 above.
5   HC 395, para 210G.
6   HC 395, para 238.
7   HC 395, paras 230 and 269.
8   HC 395, para 192.
9   This phrase recurs in almost all of the settlement rules just referred to, viz paras 134, 142, 150, 158, 167, 176, 184, 192, 209, 210G, 222, 230, 238 and 269. Paragraph 135G (dealing with highly skilled migrants) provides more flexibility, envisaging movement between this and other work or business categories during the four-year period. See further 10.107 below.
10   In *Shahbakhti* (16978) [1999] 5 ILD 1 at 30, 20 months' absence in four years was too long for a work permit holder.
11   HC 395, para 134.
12   HC 395, para 209.

5.15 Although the grant of settlement after four years in a particular capacity depends upon the exercise of discretion by the Home Office, settlement is normally given as a matter of course where the requirements of the Immigration Rules are satisfied, and before refusing settlement the Secretary of State must remain unsatisfied about one or more of these requirements unless a general ground for refusing indefinite leave is relied on, such as breach of a condition or undertaking or bad character.[1] But while under earlier rules a failure to fulfil one of the requirements of the rules during the four-year period could be overlooked,[2] it leads to mandatory refusal under the current Rules. In such a situation, settlement may only be given as a concession outside the Rules, an exercise of discretion which cannot be reviewed as to its merits on appeal.

1   The general grounds for refusing variation of leave are set out at HC 395, para 322: see 4.27 above. The Secretary of State is entitled to delay a decision on an application for indefinite leave to remain, despite the existence of compassionate circumstances, to await the outcome of a police investigation: *R v Secretary of State for the Home Department, ex p Hina Memon* [1999] Imm AR 85. See 5.14 fn 1 above for government proposals to impose additional requirements.
2   *Fanous v Secretary of State for the Home Department* [1993] Imm AR 200, IAT.

5.16 In addition to these Rules, special provision is made for the removal of the time limit on the stay of EEA nationals and their families.[1] The basis of these provisions is dealt with in chapter 7 below.

1   HC 395, paras 255–257.

Other methods of acquiring settlement

5.17 Settlement within the Immigration Rules may also be given to a variety of people. Many of the categories below were previously dealt with as discretionary policies outside the rules, but most have now been brought within the rules. First, there are refugees. The current practice, introduced in

1998, is to give refugees settlement immediately.[1] Those refused asylum may be given Humanitarian Protection or Discretionary Leave outside the immigration rules. This takes the form of a limited leave to enter or remain. Under the new policy, which is set out in the latest API, there is no presumption towards settlement or further leave to remain at the end of that period.[2] Secondly, settlement may also now be given under the Rules to persons who have lived in the UK for a continuous period of ten years, if here lawfully, and 14 years if any part of that time has been unlawful.[3] Thirdly, a policy which remains outside the rules provides that British Overseas citizens who have been in the UK with limited leave for seven years may be granted settlement.[4] Another circumstance which may result in the grant of settled status under the Rules is domestic violence occurring during the two-year initial period following admission.[5] There are also rules allowing for the grant of settlement to bereaved spouses, unmarried partners and bereaved unmarried partners, all cases which were brought within the framework of the Immigration Rules in October 2000.[6] In addition, persons benefiting from the Secretary of State's policies precluding enforcement action against overstayers and illegal entrants on family life grounds may be eligible for a discretionary grant of settlement.[7] The same may also result from the application of ECHR, Article 8, although current Home Office policy is to grant an initial period of limited leave before granting indefinite leave.[8] A concession whereby Gurkhas and other foreign and Commonwealth soldiers serving in HM Forces were granted settlement on discharge has now been brought within the immigration rules.[9]

[1]   See 12.175 below. Previously those recognised as refugees were granted settlement after four years. The White Paper of July 1998, *Fairer, Faster and Firmer – A Modern Approach to Immigration and Asylum,* announced the removal of the qualifying period for settlement.
[2]   APU Notice 01/2003. Until 1 April 2003, exceptional leave to remain was granted to asylum seekers not recognised as refugees but with humanitarian or compassionate reasons for being allowed to stay. They qualified for settlement after four years (reduced from seven years by the White Paper of 1998: see fn 1 above); see 12.176 below. A one-off exercise was announced in October 2003 to grant settlement to asylum seeking families with dependent children in the UK since 2 October 2000: see 12.178 below.
[3]   HC 395, paras 276A–D, commonly referred to as the 'ten year rule' and '14 year rule'. Previously this operated as a long-standing policy outside the rules. See 16.47 below.
[4]   See letter from the Home Office to JCWI referred to in *R v Secretary of State for the Home Department, ex p Patel* [1993] Imm AR 257, QBD and 392, CA. This form of settlement is likely to become redundant, because BOCs with no other citizenship or nationality can now register British citizens and obtain a right of abode. See 2.18 above.
[5]   See HC 395, paras 289A–C.
[6]   See HC 395, paras 287(b) (bereaved spouses), 295G (unmarried partners) and 295M (bereaved unmarried partners).
[7]   See DP3/96 (previously DP2/93, replaced on 16 March 1996), DP4/96 dealing with divorced or separated parents, and DP5/96 dealing with families with children resident in the UK for seven years (reduced from ten years by a ministerial statement of 24 February 1999) (for these policies see *Butterworths Immigration Law Service,* D[61B], D[67], D[83], D[87], D[188]). See 11.74 and 11.122 below.
[8]   *R (on the application of Isiko) v Secretary of State for the Home Department* [2001] 1 FLR 633, CA. See IDI and API on discretionary leave, following a claim for asylum.
[9]   HC 395, paras 276E–Q, inserted by HC 1112 from 18 October 2004. Former soldiers who have completed at least four years' service and were discharged on completion of their engagement are eligible if they were not discharged more than two years before the date of application, and either have entry clearance or leave to enter or remain. If discharged in the UK, they can be granted 28 days' leave on discharge to enable them to apply: IDI Ch 15 s 2 (Apr 05), para 4.2. There are transitional provisions enabling Gurkhas without leave to remain, and those who retired from the British army over two years ago and after 1 July

1997 to benefit, and the family reunion provisions do not require maintenance and accommodation without recourse to public funds, and allow for the discretionary admission of dependants over 18, and of orphaned children of former soldiers: see IDI May 05, Ch 15 s 2A; HC 395, paras 276R–276AC (inserted by HC 164 from 1 January 2005).

Settlement on the coming into force of the Immigration Act 1971

5.18 So far we have dealt with those who are granted indefinite leave to enter or remain in the exercise of the discretion of an immigration officer or the Home Office. There is a further category of persons who were granted indefinite leave by statute. These are all persons who were either settled in the UK before the coming into force of the Immigration Act 1971 on 1 January 1973 or were given unconditional admission or leave to land under the earlier immigration laws. Section 1(2) of the 1971 Act provides that indefinite leave to enter or remain shall be treated as having been given under the 1971 Act to those in the UK at its coming into force, if they were then settled there and not exempt from immigration control. The benefit of section 1(2) only applies to those physically present in the UK on 1 January 1973. Where the protection of that section is claimed, the burden is on the immigrant to show that he or she was settled.[1]

[1]   *R v Secretary of State for the Home Department, ex p Mughal* [1974] QB 313, [1973] 3 All ER 796, CA.

5.19 If such persons had not yet become ordinarily resident by 1 January 1973, or they were absent from the UK on that date, they may still rely upon the provisions of section 34(2) and (3) of the Immigration Act 1971. Section 34(2) provides that leave to land by virtue of earlier legislation is to be treated as leave to enter under the Immigration Act 1971. Section 34(3) provides that a person treated as having leave to enter is to be treated as having indefinite leave if that person was not, on 1 January 1973, subject to a condition limiting his or her stay in the UK. These provisions cannot, however, benefit persons who were illegal entrants.[1]

[1]   *Azam v Secretary of State for the Home Department* [1974] AC 18, [1973] 2 All ER 765, HL; *R v Secretary of State for the Home Department, ex p Razak* [1986] Imm AR 44, DC; affd (25 March 1986, unreported), CA; *R v Secretary of State for the Home Department, ex p Miah* [1990] 2 All ER 523, [1989] Imm AR 559, CA; *R v Secretary of State for the Home Department, ex p Khan* [1990] 2 All ER 531, [1990] Imm AR 327, CA.

RETURN TO THE UK

5.20 Under section 3(4) of the Immigration Act 1971, all leave, including indefinite leave,[1] lapses on leaving the common travel area,[2] unless the holder returns in circumstances in which leave to enter is not required, in which case the previous leave, and the conditions attached to it, continue to apply. The section applies equally to visa nationals and those not requiring visas by virtue of their nationality.[3] Prior to the passage of the Immigration and Asylum Act 1999[4] and the making of the Immigration (Leave to Enter and Remain) Order 2000[5] under it, the exemption from obtaining leave on return applied only to very limited classes of people, such as certain government officials and Commonwealth citizens on day trips to the continent.[6] The automatic lapsing of leave for everyone else gave rise to absurdity and injustice, as students midway through degree courses found themselves barred from re-entering the UK after a mid-term break in Paris, and long-settled immigrants on contracts abroad lost their right of permanent residence when they returned for short visits, because they did not utter the magic words 'returning to resume settlement'. Section 3(4) still remains the general rule, but now has effect subject to the Immigration (Leave to Enter and Remain) Order,[7] whose provisions have enormously eroded its scope. Leave to enter does not lapse on leaving the common travel area, if it was conferred by means of an entry clearance (other than a visit visa).[8] Nor does leave to enter or remain granted in the ordinary way, if it was for more than six months.[9] We examine below how these new provisions work.

[1]   *Ghassemian and Mirza v Home Office* [1989] Imm AR 42, CA.
[2]   See chapter 6 below.
[3]   *Re Wijesundera* [1989] Imm AR 291, CA; *Kuku v Secretary of State for the Home Department* [1990] Imm AR 27, CA.
[4]   Immigration and Asylum Act 1999, ss 1 and 2, inserting new ss 3A and 3B into the Immigration Act 1971.
[5]   Immigration (Leave to Enter and Remain) Order 2000, SI 2000/1161.
[6]   Immigration Act 1971, s 8(2); Immigration (Exemption from Control) Order 1972, SI 1972/1613, as amended: see 6.42–6.43 below.
[7]   SI 2000/1161, Art 13(10).
[8]   SI 2000/1161, Art 13(2)(a).
[9]   SI 2000/1161, Art 13(2)(b) and (3).

Travellers on temporary leave

5.21   The effect of the Immigration (Leave to Enter and Remain) Order 2000[1] provisions is that leave to enter and remain given for a period of more than six months and any leave given by an entry clearance (other than a visit visa), however long or short, will remain in force so as to enable students, au pairs, working holidaymakers and others on temporary leave to go abroad and return on the same leave and subject to the same conditions (non-lapsing leave). Only visitors,[2] and those given less than six months stay by immigration officials in the UK,[3] will find that their leave lapses on departure. But even those with visit visas gain protection from the Order. Article 4 provides that during the period of validity of a visit visa, it has the effect of leave to enter on an unlimited number of occasions.[4] On each occasion that the visitor arrives in the UK, he or she is to be treated as having been granted before arrival leave to enter for six months, beginning on the date of arrival, if six months or more remain of the visa's period of validity, and for the visa's remaining period of validity if it has less than six months to run.[5] In cases where leave is granted by entry clearance, leave will continue in force until the date of expiry of the entry clearance, unless, of course, it has been varied.[6] Thus visa nationals who leave the UK during the period of leave do not need to obtain a further visa to re-enter.

[1]   SI 2000/1161.
[2]   SI 2000/1161, Art 13(2)(a). The visit visa might be a five-year multiple entry one, but visit leave always lapses on departure. See below.

³ SI 2000/1161, Art 13(3).
⁴ SI 2000/1161, Art 4(1).
⁵ SI 2000/1161, Art 4(2). Although a visit leave may not exceed six months under the Immigration Rules (HC 395, paras 42 and 52), a visit visa may well have a much longer validity, eg multiple visit visas are usually valid for a period of two years.
⁶ SI 2000/1161, Art 4(3)(b).

5.22 The purpose and likely effect of the provisions is to obviate the need for repeated scrutiny on each return to the UK of those whose application for entry to or stay in the UK has previously been approved by an immigration officer or a Home Office civil servant. Such persons may still be examined at the port on re-entry, but they do not have to establish a case for re-entry, as was the case under the old law.[1] The object of the immigration officer's examination on re-entry is to establish whether leave previously granted is still in force,[2] and if so, whether there has been a change of circumstances such that it should be cancelled;[3] whether it was obtained by false information given by the passenger or by his or her failure to disclose material facts;[4] whether there are medical grounds for the cancellation of leave;[5] whether entry is sought for a purpose other than that for which entry clearance was obtained;[6] or whether cancellation is conducive to the public good.[7] The passenger may be required to submit to further examination,[8] or to be examined by a medical inspector,[9] and the leave may be suspended pending further inquiries.[10] In this event the ordinary powers of detention and temporary admission apply.[11] If leave is cancelled,[12] the passenger has an in-country right of appeal against cancellation,[13] unless cancellation is on the ground that the passenger seeks entry for a different purpose from that on the entry clearance.[14] It is noteworthy that for the purposes of cancellation of leave any false information or failure to disclose material facts must be attributable to the passenger and not to any third party, in contrast to the provisions of the previous law.[15]

¹ See *Secretary of State for the Home Department v Patel* [1992] Imm AR 486, CA.
² Ie because it has not lapsed by virtue of Art 13 of the Immigration (Leave to Enter and Remain) Order 2000, SI 2000/1161 or because, as a visit leave, it is deemed to have been granted afresh abroad under Art 4. Immigration Act 1971 Sch 2, para 2(1)(c)(i), substituted by Immigration and Asylum Act 1999, Sch 14, para 56.
³ Immigration Act 1971, Sch 2, para 2A(2)(a).
⁴ Immigration Act 1971, Sch 2, para 2A(2)(b).
⁵ Immigration Act 1971, Sch 2, para 2A(2)(c).
⁶ Immigration Act 1971, Sch 2, para 2A(2A), inserted by Asylum and Immigration (Treatment of Claimants, etc) Act 2004, s 18 (from 1 October 2004: SI 2004/2325).
⁷ Immigration Act 1971, Sch 2, para 2A(3).
⁸ Immigration Act 1971, Sch 2, para 2A(5).
⁹ Immigration Act 1971, Sch 2, para 2A(4)
¹⁰ Immigration Act 1971, Sch 2, para 2A(7).
¹¹ Immigration Act 1971, Sch 2, para 16(1A), 21.
¹² Immigration Act 1971, Sch 2, para 2A(8).
¹³ Immigration Act 1971, Sch 2, para 2A(9) read with Nationality Immigration and Asylum Act 2002, ss 82(2)(a) and 92(3)(a).
¹⁴ Nationality, Immigration and Asylum Act 2002, s 92(3B), inserted by Asylum and Immigration (Treatment of Claimants, etc) Act 2000, s 28 (from 1 October 2004: SI 2004/2325).
¹⁵ Immigration Act 1971, Sch 2, para 2A(2)(b).

5.23 The Immigration (Leave to Enter and Remain) Order 2000[1] also provides that leave to enter or remain may be varied (or cancelled) while the holder is abroad.[2] For that purpose, immigration officers (or Home Office officials) may seek information and documents which they would be entitled to obtain in an ordinary immigration examination under Schedule 2 to the Immigration Act 1971,[3] and may require the holder of the leave to supply an up to date medical report.[4] Failure to provide the information, documents or report requested is a ground for cancellation of leave.[5] These provisions enable a person whose continuing leave expires while he or she is abroad, or who wishes to change the basis of leave (say, from student to trainee or spouse) to apply for an extension or variation while abroad. They also enable leave to be cancelled while the holder is abroad if, for example, it was discovered that the passenger had used deception to obtain the leave or if terrorist activities became known such that cancellation of leave would be conducive to the public good. Previously, there was no provision for appeal against a refusal to vary leave, or curtailment of existing leave, if this took place abroad. The NIAA 2002 now makes provision for a right of appeal where a refusal to vary leave or a curtailment of leave abroad means that the person has no leave to enter or remain.[6] Furthermore, if leave carries on while the holder is abroad, and an extension can be applied for while abroad, it seems logical that an application to vary leave should also continue until it is determined, and not lapse, as at present, if the applicant goes abroad before it is determined.[7]

1 SI 2000/1161.
2 SI 2000/1161, Art 13(6), (7).
3 SI 2000/1161, Art 13(8).
4 SI 2000/1161, Art 13(8).
5 SI 2000/1161, Art 13(9).
6 Nationality, Immigration and Asylum Act 2002, s 82(2)(d). The wording of the appeals provisions of the 1999 Act (Immigration and Asylum Act 1999, s 61), couched in terms of being 'required to leave the UK within 28 days', manifestly precluded appeals against variation or refusal to vary leave while the holder was abroad. This wording was not repeated in the 2002 Act.
7 See 4.14 above.

5.24 The provisions of the Immigration (Leave to Enter and Remain) Order 2000[1] abolish the need for visas on return to the UK within the period of leave (or to resume residence pursuant to indefinite leave, as to which see below). At a stroke the body of law which was developed over the years to mitigate the harshness of the unmodified section 3(4), on the effect of the section 3(3)(b) stamp and the grant of earlier leave and whether these were capable of giving rise to a legitimate expectation of re-entry, became redundant.[2] The only categories of passenger who do not benefit from the Order are non-visa nationals granted leave to enter as visitors or in some other capacity at the port for six months or less and those granted leave to remain by the Secretary of State which is due to expire in less than six months. These persons' leave lapses on their departure from the common travel area and does not take effect as a new pre-arrival leave to enter under Article 4. Additionally leave lapses if, during the period of leave, the holder remains outside the UK for longer than two years.[3] Although section 3(3)(b) of the Immigration Act 1971 is not repealed, its scope is now limited to these residual categories. Unlike the old section 3(3)(b) stamp, the cancellation of continuing leave on re-entry gives rise to a right of appeal before removal, except where leave is sought on re-entry for a different purpose.[4] This applies equally to family visitors with visas who re-enter during the validity of the visa.

1 SI 2000/1161.
2 See the 4th edition of this work 5.22–5.26.
3 SI 2000/1161, Art 13(4)(a).
4 Immigration Act 1971, Sch 2, para 2A(9) read with Nationality, Immigration and Asylum Act 2002, ss 82(2)(a) and 92(3)(a). There is no in-country appeal, however, if leave was cancelled on the ground that the passenger sought entry for a different purpose than that specified in the entry clearance (which would have operated as a grant of leave): Nationality, Immigration and Asylum Act 2002, s 92(3B), inserted by Asylum and Immigration (Treatment of Claimants, etc) Act 2004, s 28 with reference to Immigration Act 1971, Sch 2, para 2A(2A) as inserted by Asylum and Immigration (Treatment of Claimants, etc) Act 2004, s 18.

Returning residents

5.25 A variety of returning resident rights are catered for by the Immigration Rules. The two main categories are those who can return freely however long they have been away and those who should return within two years. Once British nationals without the right of abode, such as British Overseas citizens, have been given indefinite leave to enter or remain, they may be in a better position to return to the UK than other returning residents. The Rules reflect the piecemeal history of the imposition of immigration control on British nationals and the quirks of policy and practice in the past.

Holders of UK passports issued in the UK or Ireland

5.26 Paragraph 16 of HC 395 provides that British Dependent Territories citizens, British Nationals (Overseas), British Overseas citizens, British Protected persons, or British Subjects under the British Nationality Act 1981, who can produce a passport issued in the UK and Islands or the Republic of Ireland before 1 January 1973, should be admitted freely unless the passport has been endorsed to show that they were subject to immigration control.[1] This Rule reflects the rights of residual categories of former nationals of the UK and protected persons who were not subject to control prior to the coming into force of the Immigration Act 1971 but who did not become patrial under that Act or British citizens under the 1981 Act. The Rule seems to require the actual production of the historic passport that gives rise to the right, but if a replacement passport has been endorsed with the right of re-admission, the passport holder should be entitled to rely on that, even if the historic document has been lost; the endorsement in a current passport would give rise to legitimate expectations of admission unless a person's nationality has changed.[2] It may, however, be necessary to produce the historic passport or its replacement to obtain the endorsement in any subsequent passport. A further question arises where the historic passport was issued to a parent but is endorsed with details of a dependent child during its currency; can the child obtain admission years later in reliance on such a document? This remains unclear.

1   See IDI, Ch 1, s 3, Annex M. The reference in the rules and the IDI is to British Dependent
     Territories Citizens, although they have been renamed British Overseas Territories Citizens:
     see chapter 2 above.
2   See *Liew v Secretary of State for the Home Department* [1989] Imm AR 62. See further
     Lee (21753) [2000] 6 ILD 1 at 36, IAT.

5.27 British Overseas citizens who hold a UK passport, wherever issued, and
can satisfy the immigration officer that they have been given indefinite leave to
enter the UK since 1 March 1968, should be given indefinite leave to enter.[1]
There is thus no obligation to comply with the two-year rule, and the presence
of any intervening limited leave will not prevent such re-admission. Previous
versions of this Rule referred to British Overseas citizens 'who have previously
been admitted for settlement'. This was held only to cover those who had been
admitted at a time when they were subject to immigration control.[2] It would
appear that British Protected Person voucher holders who are admitted for
settlement will have to comply with the two-year rule in respect of absences
abroad.

1   HC 395, para 17. See IDI, Ch 1, s 3, Annex M.
2   *R v Secretary of State for the Home Department, ex p Himalyaishwar* (1984) Times,
     21 February, QBD.

Refugees

5.28 Persons recognised as refugees and issued with a Convention travel
document must be re-admitted at any time during the validity of the
document.[1] They need not comply with the two-year rule.

1   1951 Convention relating to the status of refugees (Geneva, 1951) Sch, para 13(1).

Return within two years

5.29 The system of non-lapsing leave described in paras 5.21–5.24 above
applies equally to those with indefinite leave to remain, provided that they
have not stayed outside the UK for a continuous period of more than two
years.[1] The change is of great benefit to settled residents who return to the UK
within two years. In the past, because leave lapsed every time they went
abroad, every time they returned to the UK they had to apply for leave to
enter anew. Workers on a contract abroad coming to the UK for a short visit
found themselves losing their returning resident status by having their passport stamped with visit leave. Now, leave continues and will be suspended or
cancelled only for good reason.[2]

1   Immigration (Leave to Enter and Remain) Order 2000, SI 2000/1161, Art 13(4)(a).
2   See 5.22 above.

5.30 Under the Immigration Rules,[1] returning residents must satisfy the
immigration officer that they had indefinite leave to enter or remain in the UK
when they *last* left, they have not been away longer than two years, they did
not receive public assistance towards the cost of leaving, and they *now seek
admission for the purpose of settlement*.[2] Under the Immigration (Leave to

Enter and Remain) Order 2000[3] a passenger with continuing leave who does not intend to resume ordinary residence may have leave cancelled,[4] but the Home Office has accepted that where there is some continuity of connections or residence, a short return visit should not lead to the cancellation of indefinite leave. The IDI state that:

> 'a person returning temporarily to the United Kingdom is not necessarily a visitor. Many people who have their home in the United Kingdom may spend substantial periods overseas on short term business contracts or for studies and return to the United Kingdom for only a short period during holidays. This will not disqualify a person from readmission as a returning resident provided he is normally resident in the United Kingdom, at the time of admission he considers himself to be domiciled in the United Kingdom, and he has not been away from the United Kingdom for more than two years and he intends to return to the United Kingdom for settlement in the future on completion of his employment, business or studies etc.'[5]

Cancellation attracts an in-country appeal as a refusal of leave to enter,[6] but cancellation and the imposition of limited leave instead does not,[7] since leave to enter has been granted, albeit in a different capacity. If there is no right of appeal in this situation, judicial review would be available to challenge the decision.[8] But the big difference from the previous law is that in the past, the onus was on the returning resident to obtain a fresh leave by satisfying the immigration officer that he or she fulfilled the criteria; the immigration officer had no obligation to offer admission for settlement if the passenger did not ask for it.[9] When a passenger was granted limited leave instead of indefinite leave on return, Home Office policy was to grant returning resident status on an after-entry application if the applicant always wanted to be and could have been treated as a returning resident when he or she last entered the UK, but was misunderstood or was refused indefinite leave on entry.[10] It did not apply to those who were unaware that they could have sought entry as a returning resident, or to those who changed their mind since seeking entry as a visitor.[11] Now, the onus is on the immigration officer to justify cancelling leave by reference to a change in circumstances. In the vast majority of cases little examination should be necessary. Returning residents may have their leave cancelled if on inquiry it is discovered that the original leave to enter was secured by their deception.[12] The requirement that returning residents had indefinite leave to remain in the UK when they last left used to pose a problem for passengers whose passport had been stamped with visit leave on their last return to the UK and, in haste or inadvertence, they had failed to remedy the situation before leaving the UK. A person who has lost indefinite leave in this way might still benefit from the discretion in paragraph 19 of HC 395 to grant fresh leave as a returning resident.[13] With the change in the law, however, this scenario is now very unlikely; only those whose indefinite leave has been cancelled and replaced by visit leave will be affected, a process which will have involved full inquiry into the passenger's intentions.

---

[1]   HC 395, para 18. By para 19A, added by Cm 4851, spouses accompanying members of HM Forces, of British diplomats and of comparable UK-based staff members of the British Council who are serving overseas are exempt from the two-year rule and from the rule preventing travel at public expense (sub-paras (ii) and (iii)).

[2]   In *Cawte* (HX 00639) the Tribunal held, following *R v Immigration Appeal Tribunal, ex p Coomasaru* [1983] 1 All ER 208, that an appellant could qualify as a returning resident if she intended to return as such, even if she did not tell the immigration officer on arrival. See fn 5 below. See also *Ali Yazidi* (16387) (16 April 1998, unreported), IAT.

3 SI 2000/1161.

4 The IDI, Ch 1, s 3, para 2.2, state that a person who is returning only for a limited period (eg as a visitor) simply so as to show a period of residence here within two years of departure, should not be re-admitted. But see below.

5 IDI, Ch 1, s 3, para 2.2. See also *R v Secretary of State for the Home Department, ex p Chugtai* [1995] Imm AR 559 where Collins J accepted that a person may retain ordinary residence although working outside the UK for a substantial or indefinite period.

6 Immigration Act 1971, Sch 2, para 2A(9) read with Nationality Immigration and Asylum Act 2002, ss 82(2)(a) and 92(3)(a).

7 *Ishaq v Secretary of State for the Home Department* [1996] Imm AR 80, decided under the previous law but still good.

8 Permission was granted in *R v Secretary of State for the Home Department, ex p Pearson* (CO 1397/1998) and a grant of leave to enter as a visitor quashed by consent and indefinite leave reinstated.

9 *R v Secretary of State for the Home Department, ex p Tolba* [1988] Imm AR 78, QBD. See also *R v Immigration Appeal Tribunal, ex p Coomasaru* [1983] 1 All ER 208, [1982] Imm AR 77, CA where the court held that if this had been the intention of the passenger he was entitled to returning resident status. Sharp practice in obtaining a visa may deprive an applicant of this advantage: *Nazari* 2000 6 ILD 1 at 36.

10 IDI, Ch 1, s 3, Annex L. The policy has survived the change in law which makes the occasion for its operation very unlikely. Perhaps the likeliest field of application is where a returning resident has been away for more than two years, so that ILR has lapsed, and the passenger must persuade the immigration officer to exercise discretion under HC 395, para 19 to reinstate it (see below).

11 IDI, Ch 1, s 3, Annex L. Discretion will be exercised to grant indefinite leave to remain outside the rules in 'wholly exceptional cases', such as where the applicant has lived in the UK for most of his or her life.

12 Immigration Act 1971, Sch 2, para 2A(2)(b); see *Sattar v Secretary of State for the Home Department* [1988] Imm AR 190, CA; *Ali v Secretary of State for the Home Department* [1988] Imm AR 274, CA; *R v Secretary of State for the Home Department, ex p Musk* (CO 3956/1996) (26 March 1996, unreported), QBD. However, the dicta on the standard of proof may not apply to this situation, since leave is not being merely refused, but cancelled.

13 *Entry Clearance Officer, Bombay v de Noronha* [1995] Imm AR 341, CA, which held otherwise, only applied to the old immigration rules and not to HC 395. See further *Macdalla* (L00010) [2000] 4 ILD No 4, p 33; IDI, Ch 1, s 3, Annex L, para 2.

Return after two years

5.31 The leave of persons who have been away from the UK longer than two years lapses.[1] Such former residents may nevertheless be admitted for further settlement at the discretion of the immigration authorities under the provisions of HC 395, paragraph 19.[2] One example given is persons who have lived here for most of their lives.[3] But it is only an example, and a combination of a shorter period of residence and family or other ties may be sufficient.[4] Ties in the UK constituting family life or private life for the purposes of Article 8 of the ECHR would clearly be highly relevant to the exercise of discretion under the paragraph.[5] In *Buckle*[6] the Tribunal said the question was whether the facts point to an intentional break of residence or not; children are in a special position, as it is less easy for them to make an intentional break.

1 Immigration (Leave to Enter and Remain) Order 2000, SI 2000/1161, Art 13(4).

2 Spouses accompanying British soldiers, diplomats or other comparable staff members of the British Council on tours overseas are not obliged to return to the UK within two years: HC 395, para 19A, inserted by Cm 4851.

3 HC 395, para 19. The phrase 'most of his life' does not mean 'most of his adult life': *Peart* [1979–80] Imm AR 41.

4   *Costa v Secretary of State for the Home Department* [1974] Imm AR 69.
5   See eg *Forou* (00TH01101) (28 April 2000, unreported), IAT.
6   (15012) IAT, 8 May 1997, 1999 5 ILD No 1, p 29. See also *Gomez (Joffrey)* (00TH02294)
     (5 October 2000, unreported), where parental obstruction of a young adult's attempts to
     return to the UK from Ecuador constituted grounds for the exercise of discretion to admit
     him.

5.32 The purpose of this discretionary Rule is to avoid injustice or undue hardship which might arise from an inflexible application of the two-year rule and 'the discretion must be exercised in a manner to give effect to this purpose.' In *Armat Ali*[1] it was suggested that the guidelines, set out in *Costa's* case,[2] that the person 'must show strong connections with this country by a combination of length of residence and family or other ties' were applicable when the applicant for re-entry had voluntarily stayed away for more than two years, but not where the absence was involuntary. In *Ex p Ademuyiwa*[3] Farquharson J did not dissent from the *Armat Ali* interpretation where the applicant had originally left because of family illness but had remained to engage in business. In considering whether to admit such a person as a returning resident, he said, the immigration officer or the minister has to review a number of matters, such as: (i) the length of the original residence of the applicant; (ii) the time the applicant has been outside the UK; (iii) the reason for the delay which has extended the applicant's absence beyond two years – was it at the applicant's own wish or through no fault of the applicant?; (iv) what is the purpose and intent of the applicant in returning at the particular time?; (v) what is the nature of the family ties? – how close are they and to what extent has the applicant maintained them while absent from the UK?; (vi) whether the applicant has a home in this country and if admitted to the UK, is it his or her intention to remain and live in that home? The IDI adopt the criteria in *Armat Ali* in giving guidance on when those remaining abroad over two years may be re-admitted. In addition, the instructions set out other more specific circumstances which might apply in favour of an individual as: travel and service abroad with a particular employer prior to returning with him or her; service abroad for the UK government, as an employee of a quasi/government body, a British company or a UN organisation; employment abroad in the public service of a friendly country by a person who could not reasonably be expected to settle in that country permanently; a prolonged period of study abroad by a person who wished to rejoin their family here at the end of their studies; prolonged medical treatment abroad of a kind not available here; and whether the person contacted a post abroad within two years to express their future intention to return to the UK.[4]

1   *Ali* [1981] Imm AR 51.
2   [1974] Imm AR 69 at 74.
3   *R v Secretary of State for the Home Department, ex p Ademuyiwa* [1986] Imm AR 1,
     followed by the Tribunal in *Secretary of State for the Home Department v Agyen-
     Frempong* [1986] Imm AR 108 (upheld by CA at [1988] Imm AR 262).
4   IDI, Ch 1, Annex K, para 2.1. This is not a realistic option for most people, as there is no
     formal mechanism to record such an expression of intention and it would be a long,
     expensive and wasteful journey to the relevant British post.

5.33 In cases where the absence has been prolonged beyond the two years through no fault of the applicant, Tribunal decisions have tended to be favourable to the applicant. Examples are where a passport had to be surrendered because of legal proceedings abroad, and delay caused by illness,[1] accident or civil disturbance.[2] On the other hand, the longer the period which an applicant has remained out of the UK the more difficult it will be to qualify for admission under Immigration Rule, para 19.[3]

[1] *Khokhar v Visa Officer, Islamabad* [1981] Imm AR 56n.
[2] *Gokulsing* (1632) (1978, unreported). See also *Gomez (Joffrey)* (00TH02294) (parental obstruction).
[3] *R v Secretary of State for the Home Department, ex p Ademuyiwa* [1986] Imm AR 1, DC; *Agyen-Frempong* [1986] Imm AR 108; *R v Immigration Appeal Tribunal, ex p Saffiullah* [1986] Imm AR 424, DC. An appellant who had been out of the country for six years and acquired citizenship of another country on marriage succeeded in *Cawte* (HX00639) (8 February 2000, unreported); another away for nearly seven years succeeded because of his four children in the UK (*Forou* (00TH01101)).

5.34 Refusal of leave to enter to a returning resident away for over two years will not attract an in-country right of appeal in the absence of entry clearance (unless human rights issues are raised),[1] but would be challengeable by judicial review.[2] However, an appeal, albeit outside the country, is often preferable because of the power of the appellate authority to reverse decisions to refuse entry on the merits in what are often finely balanced cases.[3] Refusal of entry clearance as a returning resident whose leave has lapsed would attract a right of appeal.[4]

[1] Nationality, Immigration and Asylum Act 2002, ss 82(2)(a), 88(2)(b), (3), 92(2) (subject to s 94(1A), inserted by Asylum and Immigration (Treatment of Claimants, etc) Act 2004, s 27) from 1 October 2004 (SI 2004/2325), which precludes an in-country appeal if the Secretary of State certifies the human rights claim clearly unfounded.
[2] The principle that judicial review may not be sought where there is a statutory right of appeal, even when this is less convenient (*R v Secretary of State for the Home Department, ex p Swati* [1986] Imm AR 88) has never been held to apply to returning residents, even those who have remained out of the country for over two years.
[3] See comments of Carnwath J in *R v Secretary of State for the Home Department, ex p Musk* (CO 3956/1996) (26 March 1996, unreported).
[4] Nationality Immigration and Asylum Act 2002, s 82(2)(b).

Chapter 6

COMMON TRAVEL AREA, CREW MEMBERS AND EXEMPTED GROUPS

INTRODUCTION

6.1 This chapter deals with a number of special cases under UK immigration law. First, there are Irish citizens who, because of the common travel area, can come and go more or less as they like, but who are still subject to exclusion, deportation and removal. Then there are the inhabitants of the Channel Islands and the Isle of Man, who nominally have their own immigration control, but whose laws are, in fact, closely integrated with those of the mainland. Like Irish citizens, they too are part of the common travel area. Then there are such anomalous groups as seamen, airline and train crews, diplomats and military personnel. This chapter is about these groups.

COMMON TRAVEL AREA

6.2 The common travel area predates the development in Europe of free movement rights in the original Common Market and now in the EU. The Single European Act of 1987 envisaged within the EU an internal market 'without internal frontiers'. Although this is not yet fully effective, the adoption into Community law of the Schengen *acquis* by the Treaty of Amsterdam in 1997[1] has brought an EU without internal frontiers even closer, at least for those countries within the EU who have fully signed up. This does not include Ireland and the UK, whose governments have, so far, opted out of this part of the Schengen *acquis*. That is one reason for the continued importance of the common travel area. But it does not just embrace Ireland

and the UK. The Channel Islands, Guernsey and Jersey, and the Isle of Man, referred to hereafter as the Islands, are involved as well. Since they are not fully integrated into the EC, the common travel area provides an important ongoing link with the UK, which preserves their special constitutional position, but at the same time operates on the basis of very close harmony between the immigration laws of mainland and Islands.

¹ See chapter 7 below.

6.3 Until the Immigration Act 1971, the common travel area was a purely administrative arrangement allowing free travel between Northern Ireland and the Republic of Ireland, between Britain and Ireland, and between these places and the Isle of Man and the Channel Islands. Since 1971 the common travel area has been given full statutory recognition, but this has also meant it has become hedged around by quite complicated rules, as we shall see.

6.4 The first principle of the common travel area is that local journeys within it are exempt from control, but journeys which start from or extend outside it are not. Thus section 1(3) of the Immigration Act 1971 provides that, subject to exceptions, arrivals in and departures from the UK on local journeys 'shall not be subject to control under this Act,¹ nor shall a person require leave to enter the UK on so arriving'. A local journey is one which begins and ends in the common travel area and is not made by a ship or aircraft which:

(i) arrives in the UK, but began its voyage from a place outside the common travel area or has called at such a place during its voyage; or

(ii) leaves the UK, but is due to end its voyage at a place outside the common travel area or to call at such a place in the course of its voyage.²

The common travel area consists of the UK, the Republic of Ireland, the Channel Islands and the Isle of Man.³ The Immigration Rules state that a person who has been examined for the purpose of immigration control at the point at which he or she entered the area does not normally require leave to enter any other part of it.⁴ However, there are exceptions, most, but not all of which deal with Ireland.⁵ The rules also provide that passengers arriving in the UK or seeking to enter through the Channel Tunnel are to be refused leave, if there is reason to believe they are headed for another part of the common travel area where they would not be acceptable to the immigration authorities.⁶ Statutory provision is made to change the boundaries of the common travel area if the immigration laws of the Islands get out of line with those of the UK, or for specified purposes in Ireland.⁷

¹ 'Control under this Act' refers to the control on entry envisaged by ss 3 and 4 of the Immigration Act 1971, by the Immigration (Leave to Enter and Remain) Order 2000, SI 2000/1161, by the Immigration (Leave to Enter) Order 2001, SI 2001/2590, and to the examination provisions in Immigration Act 1971, Sch 2, paras 2–7. We refer to it loosely in the text as passport or frontier control, which is to be contrasted with immigration control, to which all non-British citizens are subject irrespective of their right to cross a border without submitting to any passport control or obtaining leave to enter.
² Immigration Act 1971, s 11(4).
³ Immigration Act 1971, ss 1(3), 11(4) and 33(1).
⁴ HC 395, para 15.

5   Immigration Act 1971, s 9(4), Sch 4, para 4 and Immigration (Control of Entry Through the Republic of Ireland) Order 1972, SI 1972/1610, as amended, Art 3(2).
6   HC 395, para 320(4).
7   Immigration Act 1971, s 9(5) and (6).

6.5 The Immigration Act 1971 clearly intended to retain the notion of a travel area which is free from frontier immigration control. On the other hand, the government did not want the common travel area (especially entry through Ireland) to become a loophole in an otherwise strict immigration control.[1] A compromise is therefore struck between a frontier-free area and the exceptions. The existence of the common travel area means that:

(i)   all British and Irish citizens and EEA nationals are free to travel between Ireland, the UK and the Islands without any passport control. This does not mean that there is no immigration control. That still exists, in that Irish citizens and EEA nationals may still be subject to exclusion or to deportation on public policy grounds, and can then be refused entry. We deal with this at 6.6 below;

(ii) immigration controls imposed in the Islands by their immigration officials have effect in the UK and vice versa. Thus third country nationals who have settled status in any of the Islands are free to travel to the UK to take up employment or occupation and residence; there is no such reciprocal arrangement between the UK and the Republic of Ireland, and it is not clear whether third country nationals with settled status in the Republic are free from immigration control within the common travel area;

(iii) people with limited leave to enter or remain in any of the Islands are free to travel to the UK and to remain there for the remainder of their leave, subject to the same conditions as were imposed by the immigration authorities there;

(iv) the absence of frontier control is subject to a series of exceptions, which make it necessary to obtain leave, on local travel from both the Islands and Ireland, and there are further exceptions as between the UK and Ireland, including the automatic imposition of limited leave to enter and conditions prohibiting employment;

(v)   the exceptional requirement to obtain leave and the automatic imposition of leave and conditions are complicated and difficult for lay person and specialist to follow, but can have serious consequences. Those who fail to obtain leave become illegal entrants and can be removed.[2] Those who overstay the limited leave, of which they have had no notice,[3] become overstayers and liable to summary removal.[4] No doubt these restrictions stop loopholes, but they also lay serious traps for the unwary and innocent, who can find themselves arrested, held in custody, and removed from the UK.[5]

1   See *Qureshi v Harrington* [1970] 1 All ER 262, [1970] 1 WLR 138 (a decision under the Commonwealth Immigrants Act 1962).
2   See *R v Governor of Ashford Remand Centre, ex p Bouzagou* [1983] Imm AR 69, CA.
3   In the past notice of leave has normally been given by a stamp in the passport: see Immigration Act 1971, s 4(1) and Sch 2, para 6, but this is no longer necessarily the case: see 3.40 above.

4 Immigration and Asylum Act 1999, s 10. Prior to 2 October 2000, overstayers were subject to deportation under the Immigration Act 1971, s 3(5)(a) (before amendment) which applied to automatic restrictions imposed on travel from Ireland by virtue of s 9(3): see *Kaya* [1991] Imm AR 572.
5 *Bouzagou* above.

The general exceptions

6.6 Section 9(4) of the Immigration Act 1971 sets out the general exceptions, which apply to persons arriving in the UK from any other part of the common travel area. They affect deportees, persons banned from the UK for reasons of national security, and those who have been previously refused leave to enter. We deal with each in turn:

(i) *Deportees.* Section 1(3) of the Immigration Act 1971 does not affect the operation of a deportation order.[1] This means that anyone who is subject to a deportation order in Ireland or the Islands is not free to enter the UK. Further provision is made in Schedule 4 for deportation orders made in the Islands to be enforceable by the UK authorities if the deportee comes to Britain.[2] The provision in section 9(4) also means that where an Irish citizen has been deported from the UK, he or she can be refused leave to enter. The exercise of this power must, however, be in accordance with the EC Public Policy Directive (see chapter 7 below). Deportees may be covered by these general exceptions, but illegal entrants, overstayers and breachers of conditions attached to their stay are not. All of these categories are covered as regards the Islands by Schedule 4 to the IA 1971, but as regards Ireland, only illegal entrants are dealt with, as we shall see.[3] Overstayers coming from Ireland and those in breach of their conditions there are still covered by the section 1(3) arrangements, but are likely to be subject to the automatic imposition of a limited leave and conditions.[4]

(ii) *Exclusion orders notified on arrival.* The existence of the common travel area does not prevent the Secretary of State from banning non-British citizens from the UK for reasons of national security.[5] But under section 9(4) notice of the exclusion order must be given on arrival in the UK and exclusion is limited to cases involving national security. Where a person is not examined and given the exclusion notice at the time of his or her arrival, that person remains exempt from control under section 1(3) and cannot be removed if encountered in the UK after arrival,[6] unless he or she arrived from the Republic of Ireland when there were directions for the person's exclusion from the UK on public good grounds; in which case the person will be an illegal entrant.[7] Although this power is mainly targeted on Irish citizens, it prevents anyone else who is subject to such a ban from entering the UK through Ireland or the Islands.

(iii) *Previous refusal of leave to enter the UK.* Where a person has been refused leave to enter the UK at any time in the past and has not subsequently been granted leave, leave to enter is required and may be refused.[8] A grant of subsequent leave need not necessarily be one given by UK immigration officials. For example, if someone has been given leave in one of the Islands, that counts as a leave in the UK, if it is still current.[9] Secondly, if someone has been given an advance leave under the Immigration (Leave to Enter and Remain) Order 2000,[10] that will also count as a subsequent leave and will override this exception to section 1(3) of the IA 1971. Thirdly, EEA nationals exercising their free movement rights do not require leave to enter, and these rights override the provisions in s 9(4)(b) requiring leave to enter, where the person has an outstanding past refusal.[11]

1   Immigration Act 1971, s 9(4).
2   See 6.12 below.
3   See 6.7 below.
4   See 6.8 below.
5   Immigration Act 1971, s 9(4).
6   See IDI Ch 1, s 2, paras 2(4) and 2(6) (Apr 04).
7   Under Art 3(1)(b)(iv) of the Immigration (Entry through the Republic of Ireland) Order 1972, SI 1972/1385, a person subject to such a direction, who has entered from the Republic of Ireland, requires leave to enter and will be an illegal entrant, if he or she fails to obtain such leave.
8   Immigration Act 1971, s 9(4)(b).
9   Immigration Act 1971, Sch 4, para 4. See 6.12 below.
10   SI 2000/1161, in force since 30 July 2000.
11   See 6.10 text and fn 1 below.

The Irish exceptions

Leave required

6.7 Section 1(3) of the Immigration Act 1971 exempts from control people travelling within the common travel area. However, in addition to the circumstances set out in the previous paragraph, Article 3 of the Immigration (Control of Entry Through the Republic of Ireland) Order 1972 makes further exceptions for certain people who enter the UK through the Republic of Ireland.[1] Persons in the following categories may not enter the UK, from the Republic of Ireland, without leave from an immigration officer:

(i)   *transit passengers.* Passengers (by ship or aircraft) from outside the common travel area who have merely stopped in transit in the Republic of Ireland *en route* to the UK, without being given leave to land there, if they catch a local flight or boat to the UK;[2]

(ii)   *no visa.* Visa nationals on a local journey from Ireland who have no valid visa for entry into the UK;[3]

(iii)   *illegal entrants to Ireland.* Those who arrive in the UK on a local journey, having entered the Republic unlawfully from a place outside the common travel area;[4]

(iv)   *illegal entrants to the UK* Persons who entered the UK unlawfully who go to Ireland and then try to return to the UK on a local journey;[5]

(v)   *expired UK leave.* Under the original Order, persons whose limited leave expired whilst in the United Kingdom or Islands, did not require leave to enter on returning to the United Kingdom from the Republic. Now they do.[6] However, a person who re-entered the United Kingdom in these circumstances before 1 August 1979, and who has not left the United Kingdom or Islands since, or been given leave to enter or remain, should be given indefinite leave to remain.[7] An overstayer who re-entered after 1 August 1979 without leave is an illegal entrant. Amended Article 3(1)(b)(iii) of the Order does not apply to someone who was exempt from UK immigration control and travelled to Ireland after the exemption came to an end,[8] or to cases in which persons whose leave expired whilst in the United Kingdom entered the Irish Republic after first going to a place outside the common travel area;[9]

(vi) *public good exclusions.* As we have seen, any non-British citizen, including Irish citizens, can be barred from entry to the UK, if the Secretary of State directs that there are national security reasons for their exclusion, and this applies whether the person is travelling from Ireland or one of the Islands.[10] In the case of travel from Ireland the power is more extensive. The Secretary of State can bar entry by giving a direction that exclusion is conducive to the public good without any mention of the interests of national security.[11] Anyone who enters in defiance of such a direction is an illegal entrant and can be removed. However, the power can only be exercised against Irish and other EEA nationals in a manner consistent with the scope and procedural requirements of the public policy derogation under EC law (see chapter 7).

Where a person who requires leave by virtue of s 9(4) of the Immigration Act 1971, or by Article 3 of the 1972 Order, or a person in respect of whom a deportation order is in force, enters or seeks to enter the UK from the Republic of Ireland, the removal powers of the 1971 Act apply with modifications to take into account the land border between the United Kingdom and Ireland.[12]

1 SI 1972/1610, as amended. The IDI on the common travel area has a flow chart which attempts to set out the position: see IDI Feb 04, Ch 1, s 2, Annex I.
2 Immigration (Control of Entry Through the Republic of Ireland) Order 1972, SI 1972/1610, as amended, Art 3(1)(a). Under the Aliens (Visas) Order 2001, SI 36/2001, as amended in December 2003, aliens arriving in Ireland from outside the common travel area will not be given leave to land, unless they have a valid transit visa, if they are nationals of Afghanistan, Albania, Bulgaria, Cuba, Democratic Republic of Congo, Ethiopia, Eritrea, Federal Republic of Yugoslavia (Serbia and Montenegro), Ghana, Iran, Iraq, Lebanon, Moldova, Nigeria, Romania, Somalia, Sri Lanka. See also IDI Apr 04, Ch 1, Annex G, para 1.1.
3 SI 1972/1610, Art 3(1)(b)(i).
4 SI 1972/1610, Art 3(1)(b)(ii).
5 SI 1972/1610, Art 3(1)(b)(iii).
6 The Immigration (Control of Entry through the Republic of Ireland) (Amendment) Order 1979, in effect 1 August 1979, amending Art 3(1)(b)(iii).
7 IDI Apr 04, Ch 1, Annex G, para 1.5.
8 SI 1972/1610, Art 3(1)(b)(iii). *R v Secretary of State for the Home Department, ex p Wuan* [1989] Imm AR 501, QBD.
9 IDI Apr 04, Ch 1, Annex G, para 1.5.
10 Immigration Act 1971, s 9(4)(a).
11 Immigration (Control of Entry through Republic of Ireland) Order 1972, SI 1972/1610, as amended, Art 3(1)(b)(iv).
12 See the Immigration (Entry Otherwise than by Sea or Air) Order 2002, SI 2002/1832, Art 2 and Schedule.

Automatic time limit and conditions prohibiting employment

6.8 Then there are those who do not require leave to enter, but are liable, under Article 4 of the 1972 Order, to the imposition of automatic time limits on their stay in the UK and conditions prohibiting their taking employment.[1] Section 9(3) of the Immigration Act 1971 provides for the restrictions to have the same effect as if the leave had been given under the Act. So, firstly, they must apply for their leave to be extended before their time limit runs out, if they wish to stay on. Secondly, a refusal to vary or extend the time limit attracts a right of appeal under section 82 of the NIAA 2002 if the result of the refusal means that the person has no leave to enter or remain, or there is a variation which has the same result.[2] The imposition of automatic leave and conditions by Article 4 of the Order does not apply to persons who:

(i)   have the right of abode;[3]
(ii) are British or Irish citizens or EEA nationals;[4]
(iii) have obtained an advance leave to enter the UK under the Immigration (Leave to Enter and Remain) Order 2000 or have a non-lapsing leave under that Order;[5] or
(iv) have been excluded from the benefits of the common travel area for any of the reasons set out in 6.6 and 6.7 above.[6]

Automatic restrictions on length of stay and conditions apply to persons:

(a)   who come to the UK on a local journey from Ireland, 'after having ... entered the Republic ... on coming from a place outside the common travel area'.[7] They are subject to an automatic time limit on their stay (three months normally, but one month if they have a 'short-visit' visa), and a condition prohibiting them from engaging in any occupation for reward or any employment.[8] If they have a 'short-stay' visa and are over 16, they must also register with the police;[9]
(b)   who come to the UK on a local journey, 'after having entered the Republic ... after leaving the UK' while having a limited leave to be in the UK and this leave has since expired.[10] On their return to the UK from Ireland they become subject to an automatic limit on their stay of seven days[11] and, unless they are EC nationals, to a condition prohibiting them from engaging in any occupation for reward or any employment.[12] If they have a 'short-visit' visa and are over 16, they must also register with the police.[13]

---

[1]   Under Immigration Act 1971, s 9(2) and Immigration (Control of Entry through the Republic of Ireland) Order 1972, SI 1972/1610, Art 4(1). See IDI, Ch 1, s 2, Annex I for a flow chart illustrating the position.
[2]   See chapter 18. There is no longer an appeal against the imposition of conditions, or against the grant of a shorter leave than that requested: see NIAA 2002, s 82(2)(d) and (e).
[3]   Immigration (Control of Entry through the Republic of Ireland) Order 1972, SI 1972/1610, Art 4(1).
[4]   According to the IDI Apr 04, Ch 1, s 2, para 3.1, Art 4 of the Order does not apply to EEA nationals. This must be correct, but it is not consistent with the very strange wording of Art 4(4)(b) and (c). See fn 7 below.
[5]   SI 2000/1161; Immigration (Control of Entry through the Republic of Ireland) Order 1972, SI 1972/1610, Art 4(2), as amended by SI 2000/1776, which together mean that anyone with extant leave granted by the UK authorities is subject to the time limit granted by and conditions imposed by that leave.
[6]   SI 1972/1610, Art 4(2).
[7]   Immigration Act 1971, s 9(2)(a); SI 1972/1610, Art 4(4).
[8]   SI 1972/1610, Art 4(4), 4(5), as amended by SI 1980/1859, SI 1985/1854 and SI 1987/2092. Art 4(4) contains a very outdated exemption from the employment prohibition for EC nationals other than those of Portugal or Spain, who at that time

enjoyed the right of establishment, but not yet the rights of worker movement. There is also an exemption from the condition prohibiting engagement in an occupation, but it is confined to EC nationals and does not extend to all EEA nationals: SI 1972/1610, Art 4(4)(b) and (c). These deficiencies do not particularly matter, because the provisions of EC law cover the situation quite adequately: see chapter 7 below.

9   SI 1972/1610, Art 4(6).
10   Immigration Act 1971, s 9(2)(b); SI 1972/1610, Art 4(1)(b).
11   SI 1972/1610, Art 4(7).
12   SI 1972/1610, Art 4(4)(b) and (c), as amended: see fn 3 above.
13   SI 1972/1610, Art 4(6).

6.9 There are a number of difficulties and objections to these provisions. First, the words used in section 9(2)(a) of the 1971 Act and Article 4 of the 1972 Order are ambiguous. Do the words: 'after having entered the Republic ... on coming from outside the common travel area' mean 'shortly after'; immediately after'; 'any time after'; or 'a reasonable time after'? On the face of it there would appear to be no limit on the length of time between arrival in Ireland and departure for the UK. So someone who has been settled in Ireland for many years and comes to the UK and stays here for over three months could find herself in serious trouble. Arguably, there is a world of difference between a person who arrives in Dublin, works there for five years and then travels to the UK and someone who only stays there for three days, having come there as part of a package tour. The purpose of the restrictions is to close loopholes, not to set traps for long-time residents of the Republic. The real problem is that in imposing these restrictions, the UK legislators have had no regard for conditions of stay granted by the Irish authorities. There is no reciprocation of leave, as in the case of the UK and the Islands.[1] A person with a limited leave to land in the Republic will, therefore, be subject to the automatic imposition of three months' leave and conditions on arrival in the UK,[2] irrespective of the length of his or her leave in Ireland. But what of the traveller who has been given settlement in the Republic, and who has an immigration status which does not depend on which route he or she came to Ireland, but on the possession or acquisition of a status or on the fulfilment of certain conditions while in the Republic? On the face of the 1971 Act and the 1972 Order, it appears that they are in the same position vis-à-vis UK immigration control as the traveller coming from Ireland with limited leave. However, it is certainly arguable that both section 9(2) of the 1971 Act and Article 4(1) of the 1972 Order are referring to local journeys which cannot be regarded as free from immigration control, because they have characteristics which give them a different quality, either because they started outside the common travel and are not, therefore, strictly speaking, local journeys or trips, or because the person's immigration status within the common travel area has become unregularised. The words 'after having ... entered Ireland' in section 9(2)(a) may thus be read in the context of a longer journey, which started outside the Republic, but which is reasonably close in time to the arrival in the UK. Similarly, the words 'after having ... left the United Kingdom ...' in section 9(2)(b) are to be read as referring to a period of time during which the traveller has an unregularised immigration status in any part of the common travel area. This is why in previous editions of this work, we have argued that:

'third country nationals who have settled status in any part of the common travel area (including the Republic) are free to travel to any other part and to take up employment or occupation and residence there'.

The question, however, is not free from doubt.

1   Under Immigration Act 1971, Sch 4. See 6.13 below.
2   Under the Immigration (Leave to Enter and Remain) Order 2000, SI 2000/1161, Art 4(4).

Effect of EC law on travel from Ireland

6.10 The control on entry provisions of the common travel area outlined above have to be read in conjunction with free movement and residence rights under EC law. It is not just Irish citizens who are affected, but all EEA nationals and members of their families. Where EC law is engaged there is a right to enter without any need for leave under UK domestic law.[1] This right prevails over the common travel area provisions covering travel from Ireland to the UK where there is a conflict. Similarly, where there are conditions imposed prohibiting employment or occupation for gain, they must yield to the requirements of EC law, not in the terms set out in the Control of Entry Order,[2] but on the terms of current EC law.

1   *R v Pieck* [1981] QB 571, ECJ. The Immigration Act 1988, s 7(1) and Immigration (European Economic Area) Regulations 2000, SI 2000/2326 give effect in domestic UK law to EC law. Though reg 12 of SI 2000/2326 is premised on the EEA national entering through a recognised control point, reg 14 makes it clear that the right to remain in the UK derives directly from EC law without any need for a leave under domestic law. The right to enter under EC law is, of course, subject to public policy considerations: see *Shingara v Secretary of State for the Home Department* [1999] Imm AR 257 and 7.131ff below.
2   See 6.8 text and fns 4 and 7 above.

Immigration laws in the Islands

6.11 The Channel Islands and the Isle of Man have nominally separate immigration laws from the UK. In practice the Immigration Acts of 1971 and 1988 extend to the Islands, with modifications, and although the Islands have their own immigration rules (called Directions in Jersey), they closely follow the UK ones.[1] Following the enactment of the Immigration and Asylum Act 1999, further changes were not made to update the Islands' laws and keep them in step until 2003.[2] This is done in the following way:

(i)   Orders in Council extend the provisions of the UK Acts with any necessary changes to each of the Islands. In the case of Guernsey, the Order is the only effective immigration law, but in the case of Jersey the 1937 Loi sur les Etrangers still operates in addition to the extended Immigration Act, and in the Isle of Man employment is controlled by the Control of Employment Act 1975, as amended;

(ii)   machinery is laid down in the Orders and in Schedule 4 to the Immigration Act 1971 for decisions taken in the Islands to apply in the UK and vice versa.

1   IDI Jul 04, Ch 1, s 2, Annex H.

2   Immigration and Asylum Act 1999 (Jersey) Order 2003, SI 2003/1252, which came into force on 5 June 2003; Immigration and Asylum Act 1999 (Guernsey) Order 2003 SI 2003/2900, which came into force on 11 December 2003. No Order has been made in relation to the Isle of Man and no Orders have been made applying any of the provisions of the NIAA 2002.

6.12 Schedule 4 to the 1971 Act, as amended by the Immigration and Asylum Act 1999, provides inter alia:

(a)   any leave to enter or remain and time limit or conditions attached to it by the immigration authorities in the Isle of Man, Jersey or Guernsey will still apply to a person who subsequently arrives in the UK from one of the islands before the expiry of any time limit;[1]

(b)   in the case of limited leave, application can then be made to the Home Office for further extensions or the revocation of conditions as if the leave and conditions had originated under UK immigration law. If an extension of leave is refused, the normal rights of appeal under UK law apply;[2]

(c)   a deportation order or its equivalent made in one of the Islands operates in the UK, where it has the same effect as a deportation order made in the UK, except where the person is a British citizen, EEA national, member of the family of an EEA national, or the member of the family of a British citizen who is neither a British citizen or EEA national.[3] Except in the case of British citizens (who cannot be deported from the UK),[4] the Secretary of State can decide to enforce an Island deportation against one of these people,[5] but must bear in mind the public order provisions of EC law. These categories of Island deportees can appeal against an adverse decision.[6] From October 2000 the Secretary of State can no longer revoke an Island deportation order which is operating in the UK.[7] It is not unlawful for a deportee to enter the UK in transit to a place outside the UK;[8]

(d)   there are integrated removal powers after a refusal of leave. Anyone refused leave to enter one of the Islands is treated as if they had been refused leave to enter the UK.[9] The Island authorities can arrange for the UK authorities to remove that person;

(e)   there are also integrated removal powers for illegal entrants. Paragraph 4 provides that notwithstanding the principle of travel without leave 'it shall not be lawful for a person who is not a British citizen to enter the UK from any of the Islands where his presence was unlawful under the immigration laws of the Island, unless he is given leave to enter'. So, if someone with leave to enter the UK goes to one of the Islands, and his or her leave then expires, that person's return to the UK, without getting further leave, makes that person an illegal entrant. The same applies to persons who overstay leave given to them in one of the Islands and then travel to the UK.[10]

Immigration officers in the Islands act in liaison with the Immigration Service in the UK.[11]

1   Immigration Act 1971, Sch 4, para 1(1) and (2); *Teixeira* [1989] Imm AR 432.
2   IA 1971, Sch 4, para 1(3).
3   IA 1971, Sch 4, para 3(1) and (2), as amended.

⁴ IA 1971, s 3(5), (6).
⁵ IA 1971, Sch 4, para 3(4), as amended
⁶ IA 1971, Sch 4, para 3(7), as amended. The paragraph extends appeal rights under
   Immigration and Asylum Act 1999, s 80, which was however repealed by Nationality,
   Immigration and Asylum Act 2002, ss 114, 161, Sch 9, as from 1 April 2003
   (SI 2003/754); the equivalent right of appeal is now NIAA 2002, s 82.
⁷ IA 1971, Sch 4, para 3(3), as amended.
⁸ IA 1971, Sch 4, para 3(5), as amended.
⁹ IA 1971, Sch 4, para 1(1).
¹⁰ IA 1971, Sch 4, para 4; IDI, Ch 1, s 2, Annex G, para 2.
¹¹ IDI, Ch 1, s 2, Annex H.

6.13 In the Islands the same integration of their laws with those of the UK and other Islands is achieved by the provisions in the various Orders in Council which extend and adapt Schedule 4 to the particular Island. So leave given in the UK continues to operate when someone travels to one of the Islands; UK deportation orders have effect there; and the island authorities can deal with UK or other Island overstayers and illegal entrants.

6.14 This integration nevertheless leaves some areas of autonomy to each of the Islands. Though the content of each Island's immigration law is almost identical to the mainland Immigration Acts of 1971 and 1988, each administers its own controls and therefore retains a large measure of discretion over whom to admit or refuse. This is particularly important in the area of employment, where each Island retains full control over the granting of work permits and is therefore able to fit immigration control into any existing employment restrictions. Apart from the retention of administrative control over immigration, perhaps the most important difference between the laws operating in the Islands and in mainland UK is the continuing absence of any appeal machinery in the Channel Islands. Only the Order in Council for the Isle of Man extends the rights of appeal set out in Part II of the IA 1971. We look at this in the next paragraph.

Isle of Man

6.15 The provisions of the UK Immigration Acts are extended here by the Immigration (Isle of Man) Orders 1991 and 1997.¹ The appointment of immigration officers and the administration of control is under the Lieutenant-Governor. Changes in the Immigration Rules must be laid by Tynwald. Under the 1997 Order, the rights of appeal operating under Part II of the Immigration Act 1971 are applied with suitable modifications to the Isle of Man, the High Bailiff and Deputy High Bailiff acting as adjudicators.² Part II of the IA 1971 was repealed by the Immigration and Asylum Act 1999, whose appeal provisions have in turn been replaced by those of the Nationality, Immigration and Asylum Act 2002 (chapter 18 below). The conundrum is whether the repealed 1971 provisions or the unincorporated 2002 ones – or neither – apply to those seeking to challenge Manx decisions.

¹ SI 1991/2630 and SI 1997/275.
² SI 1997/275, Sch, para 1. There was never a further right of appeal to the IAT:
   SI 1997/275, Sch, para 9.

6.16 Apart from immigration controls applying to non-British citizens under the extended Immigration Act 1971, there is also strict control over the employment in the Isle of Man of anyone who is not an 'Isle of Man worker' as defined by the Control of Employment Act 1975, as amended in 1983. This status is acquired by birth or long residence in the Isle, or descent from or marriage to an Islander. Subject to exceptions, anyone who is not an 'Isle of Man worker' needs a work permit from the Isle of Man Board of Social Security. EC law rights of free movement are excluded.[1]

[1] See *Department of Health and Social Security v Barr* [1991] 3 CMLR 325, ECJ, for an examination of these provisions applying to a British citizen seeking employment in the Isle of Man.

6.17 In the Isle of Man, entry from the Republic of Ireland is subject to similar restraints to those operating under UK law. The same categories of person who require leave to enter the UK from Ireland require leave to enter the Isle of Man from there.[1] Secondly, an automatic time limit and condition prohibiting employment is imposed on non-British or Irish citizens arriving in the Isle of Man from Ireland, who entered the Republic from a place outside the common travel area; or who left the Isle of Man while having a limited leave to be there and this leave has since expired.

[1] SI 1991/2630, Art 3 and Sch 1, para 9; see 6.7 above.

Guernsey

6.18 The UK Immigration Acts are extended here by the Immigration (Guernsey) Order 1993,[1] the Asylum and Immigration Act 1996 (Guernsey) Order 1998, [2] and the Immigration and Asylum Act 1999 (Guernsey) Order 2003, which came into force on 11 December 2003.[3] Control under these Orders is exercised by immigration officers, who have power to give or refuse leave to enter, the Lieutenant-Governor, who has power to vary the length of any leave, and the Board of Administration, which deals with restrictions and prohibitions on employment and registration with the police as well as making the Immigration Rules. These have to be laid before the States of Guernsey. The power to make subordinate Orders under the extended Act is divided between the States and the Lieutenant-Governor. The 1998 Order gave the 1951 Refugee Convention statutory force in Guernsey for the first time.

[1] SI 1993/1796.
[2] SI 1998/1264.
[3] SI 2003/2900. This extends to Guernsey provisions of the IAA 1999 such as the s 3A and 3B insertions into the Immigration Act 1971, relating to new forms in which leave can be granted, provisions for administrative removal of overstayers, extended criminal offences, changes to carrier sanctions, greater powers to officials to enter and search premises, to take fingerprints and to detain.

6.19 Special provision is made for entry into Guernsey from the Republic of Ireland. The restraints are almost identical to those operating under UK law. Leave to enter Guernsey from Ireland is required for the same category of persons as require leave to enter the UK from there,[1] and similar restrictions are placed on persons arriving in Guernsey from Ireland (1) who entered Ireland from a place outside the common travel area or (2) who left Guernsey having a limited leave to be there and this leave has since expired.

¹   SI 1993/1796, Art 3, Sch 1; see 6.7 above.

Jersey

6.20   The UK Immigration Acts are extended to the Bailiwick of Jersey by the Immigration (Jersey) Order 1993,¹ the Asylum and Immigration 1996 (Jersey) Order 1998,² and the Immigration and the Immigration and Asylum Act 1999 (Jersey) Order 2003.³ Asylum control is exercised by immigration officers, who have power to give and refuse leave to enter, and by the Lieutenant Governor, who is responsible for after entry control and for making the immigration rules, which are called 'Directions' in Jersey. The Orders are not the Island's only legislation governing the admission and control of non-British citizens. In addition there is the 1937 Loi sur les Etrangers. The administration of control is divided between the States of Jersey Defence Committee, which deals with the regulation of employment and registration with the police, and the Lieutenant-Governor who has overall direction and authority.

¹   SI 1993/1797.
²   SI 1998/1070. This gives statutory force to the 1951 Refugee Convention in Jersey for the first time.
³   SI 2003/1252. This extends to Jersey provisions of the IAA 1999 such as the s 3A and 3B insertions into the Immigration Act 1971, relating to new forms in which leave can be granted, provisions for administrative removal of overstayers, extended criminal offences, changes to carrier sanctions, greater powers to officials to enter and search premises, to take fingerprints and to detain.

6.21   The extended UK Acts apply to all non-British citizens, alien and Commonwealth, but the 1937 Loi only applies to aliens. Under it no aliens can take jobs in the Island without a work permit, whatever their status on the mainland.¹ They may need a guarantor as a condition of getting a permit² and if, within a year of arrival, they become chargeable to the public of the Island they may be removed,³ with the guarantor, no doubt, having to foot the bill for removal. A register of aliens is kept and it is the duty of aliens over the age of 15 who reside in the Island for over three months to register.⁴ In addition to the deportation powers given under the extended Immigration Act, the 1937 Loi expressly retains the powers of 'banishment and of repatriation possessed by the Royal Court of Jersey'.⁵ The same provision is made for entry into Jersey from the Republic of Ireland, as applies in the case of Guernsey and the Isle of Man: see 6.17 and 6.19 above.⁶

¹   1937 Loi sur les Etrangers, Art 4.
²   1937 Loi sur les Etrangers, Art 5.
³   1937 Loi sur les Etrangers, Art 8.
⁴   1937 Loi sur les Etrangers, Arts 12(1) and 15.
⁵   1937 Loi sur les Etrangers, Art 24.
⁶   SI 1993/1797, Art 3, Sch 1.

The Islands and the EC

6.22 The Channel Islands and the Isle of Man enjoy a special relationship with the EC, as opposed to full membership.[1] But the extent of it is unclear. The Islands are within the definition of the UK for the purpose of British nationality law,[2] and so connection to the Islands as opposed to mainland UK makes not the slightest bit of difference to the acquisition or possession of full British citizenship. Furthermore, Islanders are included in the declaration by the UK government on the meaning of a British national for the purposes of the European Treaties. On the other hand, when Britain joined the Common Market, Channel Islanders and Manxmen were expressly excluded from the free movement provisions of the EEC Treaty by Protocol 3 of the Treaty of Accession of the UK to the Common Market (as it was then known).[3] Under Article 6 of the Protocol, the following definition is given of a Channel Islander and a Manxman:

> 'In this Protocol, Channel Islander or Manxman shall mean any citizen of the United Kingdom and Colonies[4] who holds that citizenship by virtue of the fact that he, a parent or grandparent was born, adopted, naturalised or registered in the island in question; but such a person shall not for this purpose be regarded as a Channel Islander or Manxman if he, a parent or a grandparent was born, adopted, naturalised or registered in the United Kingdom. Nor shall he be so regarded if he has at any time been ordinarily resident in the UK for five years.'

On the basis of this definition, Islanders, although EU citizens, enjoy no free movement rights, unless they have been ordinarily resident in the UK at any time for a period of five years. In practice this provision is either a dead letter or virtually unenforceable. A passport shows place of birth, but does not show places of residence during a person's lifetime, and says nothing about the place of birth of parents or grandparents. The real effect of the Protocol is that it prevents free movement rights into the Islands and thus protects the residence and employment restrictions operating there. This is, we think, the clear effect of Article 3 to the Protocol read with Article 4, as interpreted by the European Court of Justice. Article 4 requires the Islands to apply 'the same treatment to all natural and legal persons of the Community'. This means that they must treat the nationals of other Member States in the same way as they treat British nationals, who have visiting rights by virtue of the common travel area but are subject to restrictions on residence and employment. These restrictions will thus also apply to those from the EEA. The principle of non-discrimination could not, therefore, give employment rights to EEA nationals in the Isle of Man.[5]

[1] Article 227(5) of EC Treaty (now, after amendment, Art 299(6)(c)) and Protocol No 3 to Treaty of Accession.
[2] British Nationality Act 1981, s 50(1). They were also part of the UK for the purpose of the 1948 Act: British Nationality Act 1948, s 3(1).
[3] Article 2 of Protocol No 3 to Treaty of Accession. See further chapter 7 below.
[4] For the meaning of 'citizen of the UK and Colonies' see now British Nationality Act 1981, s 51(3)(a), which provides that after 1 January 1983 it means a British citizen, a British Dependent (now Overseas) Territories citizen or a British Overseas citizen.
[5] *Department of Health and Social Security v Barr* [1991] 3 CMLR 325, ECJ, where the court warned that the exclusion could not be permitted to operate in a discriminatory manner as between those excluded from the right.

Immigration law in the Republic of Ireland

6.23 In order to complete the picture of immigration control within the common travel area, it is necessary to consider briefly the immigration laws operating in the Republic of Ireland. The enabling statute is the Aliens Act 1935. The Aliens Order 1946[1] is the principal order made under it, and this has been amended at various times.[2] Two more recent amendments have been the Refugee Act 1996, which deals with asylum claims in the Republic, and the Immigration Act 1999, which gives statutory effect to most of the previous delegated legislation under the Aliens Act 1935 and refines the law in relation to deportation, exclusion, crime and asylum appeals, which now go to the newly constituted Refugee Appeal Tribunal. Under the Act and Orders the system of control to some extent parallels that of the UK, but is not nearly so complicated. 'Aliens' are all those who are not citizens of Saorstat Eireann[3] or British citizens.[4] Secondly, it is made clear that the system of control set out in these Orders does not affect the operation of the free movement provisions of the EC, of which the Republic is a member.[5]

[1] SR & O 1946/395.
[2] See Aliens (Amendment) Order 1975, SI 1975/128; Aliens (Amendment) (No 3) Order 1997, SI 1997/277; Aliens (Amendment) Order 1999, SI 1999/17; Aliens (Exemption) Order 1999, SI 1999/97. There are frequent minor amending Orders, mainly adjusting visa requirements.
[3] Aliens Act 1935, s 2; SI 1999/17; 1999/97. On the acquisition of Irish citizenship see Irish Nationality and Citizenship Act 1956, as amended in 2001; see *Zhu and Chen v Secretary of State for The Home Department* Case C-200/02 [2005] INLR 1, ECJ.
[4] Aliens (Amendment) (No 2) Order 1999, SI 1999/24.
[5] SI 1975/128, Art 8.

6.24 As in UK law, the controls distinguish between those who arrive from another part of the common travel area and those who come from outside. Those who come from outside must present themselves to an immigration officer for leave to land.[1] Immigration officers have wide discretion to refuse leave.[2] One ground for refusal is that the alien 'intends to travel (whether immediately or not) to Great Britain or Northern Ireland and the officer is satisfied that the alien would not qualify for admission to Great Britain or Northern Ireland if he arrived there from a place other than the State ... '.[3] In other words in deciding whether to admit an alien into the Republic, Irish immigration officers can take into account the UK immigration rules, and refuse admission to someone who they consider would not qualify under them.

[1] Aliens Order 1946, SR & O 1946/395, Art 5(1), as amended by Aliens (Amendment) Order 1975, SI 1975/128, Art 3 and Aliens (Amendment) (No 2) Order 1999, SI 1999/24.
[2] SR & O 1946/395, Art 5(2), as amended.
[3] SR & O 1946/395, Art 5(2)(j), as amended by SI 1999/24. This matches the reciprocal rule in the UK Immigration Rules: HC 395, para 320(4).

6.25 Aliens entering the Republic of Ireland through the common travel area, that is from Great Britain, the Channel Islands or Northern Ireland, were until 1997 not required to submit to examination by immigration officers on arrival. Now, they may be examined by immigration officers in the same way as those arriving from elsewhere, and may be refused leave to land on the same grounds.[1] If they are not so examined, they are automatically subject to time limits on their stay. In the case of workers and those wishing to establish themselves in business, the time limit is one month and in the case of everyone else, three months. They must obtain extensions from the Minister of Justice.[2] Anyone in contravention commits an offence[3] and can be arrested without warrant[4] and eventually deported.[5]

[1] Aliens Order 1946, SR & O 1946/395, Art 5(7)(a), as amended by Aliens (Amendment) (No 3) Order 1997, SI 1997/277.
[2] Aliens Order 1946, SR & O 1946/395, Art 5(7)(d) and (e), as amended by Aliens Order 1975, SI 1975/128, Art 3. Those coming for work are required to register with police within seven days: Art 5(7)(d) and (e).
[3] Aliens Act 1935, s 6.
[4] SR & O 1946/395, Art 17.
[5] SR & O 1946/395, Art 13; Immigration Act 1999, s 3(2)(g).

Entering UK en route to another part of common travel area

6.26 Where passengers arrive in the UK intending to travel on to the Republic of Ireland or one of the Islands, special rules apply. Guidance is contained in the current practice, given in the IDI.

(i)   The Republic of Ireland

Visas. Where a person needs a visa to enter the Republic, and is not in possession of one, the immigration officer should contact the Department of Justice, Dublin, to establish whether or not the person will be acceptable to the immigration authorities there.[1] If not, leave to enter should be refused under paragraph 320(4) of HC 395.[2]

Visitors, intending to travel to the Republic, who appear acceptable there and who would normally qualify for leave as a visitor if they were intending to remain in the United Kingdom for the whole of their stay, may be given leave to enter as a visitor for six months.[3] Those who do not qualify for a full six months' leave, but a refusal is not appropriate, should be granted leave to enter for one month.[4]

Persons who qualify for indefinite leave to enter the United Kingdom, who intend to travel to the Republic, should be given such leave.[5]

Persons intending employment in the Republic of Ireland, who are seeking entry to the United Kingdom en route to the Republic should be refused leave to enter unless they are in possession of an Irish labour permit or official confirmation that the permit has been or will be granted. Holders of Irish labour permits or other official documentation should be given leave to enter for one month.[6]

Other persons, who are intending to travel to the Republic of Ireland, for example, as a student or a seaman joining a ship in the Republic, and including those resident in the Republic, should be given leave to enter for no more than one month.[7]

(ii)   The Channel Islands and the Isle of Man

Visas. Unless otherwise exempted from the requirement to produce a visa, visa nationals seeking entry in transit to any of the Islands, who are not in possession of the appropriate visa will normally be refused leave to enter.[8]

Work permit holders, in possession of a permit to take employment in Jersey or Guernsey or the Isle of Man, should be given leave to enter for the validity of the permit if they are non-visa nationals. A copy of the landing card will be forwarded to the Island authorities.[9]

Persons with indefinite leave to enter or remain in any of the Islands should be dealt with under the returning resident provisions of the UK Immigration Rules (HC 395, paras 18 and 19). They should be given indefinite leave to enter if they qualify for admission.[10]

Other returning residents. Persons who have extant leave to enter or remain in the Islands may be given leave to enter for the remaining period, provided that they still qualify for entry.[11]

Other categories. A person travelling to any of the Islands in any other category may be given leave to enter as if he or she were seeking entry to the United Kingdom only. Doubtful cases should be referred to the appropriate Island Immigration Department.[12]

1   IDI Jul 04, Ch 1, Annex H, para 2.1.
2   Paragraph 320(4) of the Rules should only be used as a reason for refusal of leave to enter in cases where a passenger seeks entry in transit to another part of the common travel area and there is reason to believe that he is not acceptable there. Before such a passenger is refused entry for that reason the appropriate authority in the Islands or the Republic of Ireland should be contacted: IDI, as above, para 4.
3   IDI, Ch 1, Annex H, para 2.2.
4   IDI, Ch 1, Annex H, para 2.2.
5   IDI, Ch 1, Annex H, para 2.2.
6   IDI, Ch 1, Annex H, para 2.3. Irish work permits are issued by the Minister of Labour, Dublin.
7   IDI, Ch 1, Annex H, para 2.4.
8   IDI, Ch 1, Annex H, paras 3.1 and 4.1.
9   IDI, Ch 1, Annex H, para 3.2. The Isle of Man Department of Trade and Industry issues two types of work permit: (i) those issued under the Immigration Act 1971, as extended to the Isle of Man, which are similar in appearance to the work permits issued by Work Permits (UK); and (ii) permits under the Isle of Man Control of Employment Act 1975, which are issued to persons who are not members of the Isle of Man labour force but who are permitted to work in the Isle of Man. Persons holding such documents are likely to be British citizens or persons with indefinite leave in the United Kingdom. These permits are not relevant to the Immigration Act and are not 'work permits' as defined in s 33(1) of the IA 1971. A person seeking leave to enter or remain in the UK, presenting one of these permits, does not qualify under para 128 of HC 395: see IDI, Ch 5, Annex A, para 11.2.
10   IDI Jul 04, Ch 1, Annex H, para 3.3.
11   IDI, Ch 1, Annex H, para 3.4.
12   IDI, Ch 1, Annex H, para 3.5.

6.27 Leave to enter the UK should not be refused on general grounds, according to the IDI, unless the immigration officer has reason to believe that any passenger arriving in the UK en route to another part of the common travel area would not be acceptable there.[1] Before any refusal, the immigration officer is expected to contact the appropriate immigration authority in the Republic of Ireland or the Islands. Leave may also be refused if the immigration officer believes that the passenger's real intentions are to use his or her documentation to remain in the UK.[2]

1   IDI Jul 04, Ch 1, s 2, Annex H, para 4.
2   IDI Ch 1, s 2, Annex H, para 4.

Irish citizens and terrorism laws

6.28 The existence of the common travel area does not mean that Irish citizens are totally exempt from UK immigration control. Citizens of the Republic, unless they also have British citizenship, are subject to immigration control. Though they can normally come to the UK without needing leave to enter, they may, as we have seen, be refused entry as security risks; they may be deported, and cannot then return without leave or until the deportation order is revoked; they may also be refused admission to the UK on EC public policy grounds.[1] Before the peace process in Northern Ireland these were important powers, but could only be used against Irish citizens and did not deal with movement and travel between Northern Ireland and mainland UK. This was dealt with through extensive powers of exclusion or banishment, in order to prevent acts of terrorism, contained in the Prevention of Terrorism (Temporary Provisions) Act 1989. Under this Act the Secretary of State for the Home Department could make an exclusion order against anyone he or she was satisfied was involved in terrorism, including British citizens, who could be restricted to living either in Northern Ireland or in Great Britain (England, Scotland or Wales).[2] The Act also contained draconian powers of arrest and detention, which gave rise to considerable case law.[3]

1   Council Directive (EEC) 64/221. See chapter 7 below.
2   Prevention of Terrorism (Temporary Provisions) Act 1989, ss 5(1), 6(1), 7(1).
3   Prevention of Terrorism (Temporary Provisions) Act 1989, s 14. See the Northern Ireland High Court in *Hanna v Chief Constable of the Royal Ulster Constabulary* [1986] 13 NIJB 71 (Carswell J); *Brogan v United Kingdom* (1988) 11 EHRR 117, where the ECtHR held that four people who had been arrested and detained for periods of at least four days and six hours under the Prevention of Terrorism Act 1984 had been detained in violation of Art 5(3) and (5) of the ECHR; *Brannigan and McBride v United Kingdom* (1993) 17 EHRR 539, ECtHR, where the ECtHR upheld the UK government's later derogation from its Convention obligations. As regards the validity of exclusion orders under EC law, see the references in *R v Secretary of State for the Home Department, ex p Gallagher* [1996] 1 CMLR 557, ECJ; and *R v Secretary of State for the Home Department, ex p Adams* [1995] All ER (EC) 177, DC, a reference subsequently withdrawn by CA after revocation of the exclusion order.

6.29 The peace process in Northern Ireland has made the exclusion powers in the 1989 Act redundant and the whole Act has in fact been repealed by the Terrorism Act 2000.[1] Although various special powers are still retained for Northern Ireland, the Secretary of State can no longer make exclusion orders banning suspected terrorists from travel between Northern Ireland, Great Britain and the Republic. The Terrorism Act 2000[2] re-enacts provisions similar to those in the 1989 Act dealing with port and border controls on travel to and from Northern Ireland, using police, immigration and customs officers,[3] who have extensive powers of examination and search of vehicles, aircraft and ships in order to identify people concerned in the commission, preparation or instigation of acts of terrorism.[4] The Anti-Terrorism Crime and Security Act 2001 and the Prevention of Terrorism 2005 amend existing powers and provide a whole batch of new ones in relation to terrorism, but continue to use the definition of terrorism contained in the TA 2000.

1   Terrorism Act 2000, Sch 16.
2   In force February 2001.
3   Terrorism Act 2000, s 53 and Sch 7.
4   Terrorism Act 2000, s 40(1)(b). Terrorism is given a very wide definition in s 1 of the Act, which may conflict with international law definitions, particularly as regards 'action' outside the UK: see s 4(4)(a).

CONTROL OF SHIP, AIRCRAFT AND TRAIN CREWS

6.30 Members of the crews of ships, aircraft and Channel Tunnel trains are in fact subject to more rigorous control than other groups of travellers. Their admission, unless they are resident in the UK or qualify in some other capacity, is always temporary – usually dependent on the turn-around time of their ship, aircraft or train – and they are liable to instant removal without time limit or any effective right of appeal if they overstay. But, because they are usually given temporary admission until the next departure of their ship, aircraft or train and do not normally need to obtain the express leave of an immigration officer on arrival, they are an exempt category,[1] and so are dealt with in this chapter.

1   The exemptions arise from the application under UK immigration law of international standards and practices which have been adopted in order to expedite international travel and to prevent unnecessary delays owing to immigration procedures. Under the 1958 Seafarers' National Identity Documents Convention parties to the Convention are obliged to admit the holder of a seaman's card for temporary shore leave to enable him to join a ship or to transfer to another. Under the International Labour Organisation (ILO) Convention No 108 seamen with a Convention document do not require a visa when they are travelling as a crew member to or through countries which have ratified the Convention. A list of countries which have ratified is contained in IDI Dec 00, Ch 16, Annex A. For a fuller account, see Goodwin-Gill *International Law and the Movement of Persons between States* (1978), pp 156–159; Turack *The Passport in International Law*, chs 14 and 15.

Meaning of crew member

6.31 Normally there is no difficulty in telling who is a member of the crew of a ship, aircraft or train[1] and who is not. Under section 33(1) of the Immigration Act 1971 the crew means all persons 'actually employed in the working or service' of the ship, aircraft or through train or shuttle train, including the captain or train manager.[2] But in one case the tribunal had to decide whether the wives of two ship's officers were members of the crew. In the ship's Articles they were listed as stewardesses, but they were not actually engaged in any duties on board ship and only received pay at a nominal rate. They were East Germans and would normally require a visa. They had none. The immigration officer refused to treat them as crew members or let them enter, and the Immigration Appeal Tribunal agreed with him. In the definition of 'crew' the words 'actually employed' were intended to differentiate between persons who are necessary to the working and service of the ship and others, like these wives, who are supernumerary and carry out no duties.[3]

1 'Aircraft' is defined to include hovercraft: Immigration Act 1971, s 33(1).
2 Immigration Act 1971, s 33(1), modified in relation to trains by the Channel Tunnel (International Arrangements) Order 1993, SI 1993/1813, Sch 4, para 1(10). Crew members on ships can include croupiers, waiters, hairdressers, painters and repairmen, but not supernumeraries, stowaways or passengers, whose names may have been entered in the ship's Articles as crew: see IDI, Ch 16, s 1, para 3. For detailed guidance on special classes of seamen see IDI, Ch 16, Annex B. Air crew do not include airline security guards: IDI Ch 16 s 2.
3 *Diestel* [1979] Imm AR 51. See the Court of Appeal's definition of 'operational staff' of airlines in *Attivor v Secretary of State for the Home Department* [1988] Imm AR 109, CA. The IDI state that dependants of air crews are not exempt and require leave to enter: IDI, Ch 16, s 2, para 7.

Automatic shore leave or break between flights or trains

6.32 Under section 8(1) of the Immigration Act 1971 no leave to enter is normally needed for crew members of a ship who are contracted to leave the UK on the same ship, or air or train crew between flights or trains. Ships' crews are given until their ship departs; air and train crews do not necessarily go out on the same plane or train that they came in on, and are, therefore, in effect given seven days. But if there is a delay in the departure of a particular aircraft, they are entitled to remain until their plane leaves.[1] Visa requirements are waived for visa nationals who arrive and leave as aircrew within seven days.[2] This leave-free entry does not operate in the case of crew members who are subject to deportation orders, who were refused leave on their last visit or who are required to submit to examination by an immigration officer.[3] Air crews whose breaks between flights exceed seven days may also be exempt from the need to obtain leave to enter if they had a limited leave before their last flight and they returned to the UK within the period of that leave.[4] If that happens, the limited leave does not lapse but continues to have effect as before.[5]

1 Immigration Act 1971, s 8(1), modified in relation to train crews by Channel Tunnel (International Arrangements) Order 1993, SI 1993/1813, Sch 4, para 1(4). For the government's explanation of this provision see 817 HC Official Report, cols 1006–1007.
2 IDI, Ch 16, s 2, para 2.2. For the position of seamen, see 6.39 below.
3 Immigration Act 1971, s 8(1)(a), (b), and (c), repeated in IDI, Ch 16, s 1, para 2.
4 Immigration (Exemption from Control) Order 1972, SI 1972/1613, Art 5(1)(e).
5 Immigration Act 1971, s 3(4).

Leave to enter for shore leave or longer breaks

6.33 Crew members of ships or aircraft who wish to enter the UK for longer periods will normally be required to obtain leave, as will deportees, those refused entry on a previous visit[1] and anyone required to submit to examination by an immigration officer, who may decide to examine any or all crew members.[2] Notice granting leave will usually require them to leave on a ship or aircraft specified or indicated in the notice,[3] or within a specified period in accordance with the arrangements to be made for their return home.[4] But where leave is given to enable crew-members to get hospital treatment, they are allowed to stay until completion of the treatment and will then be required to leave the UK in accordance with the arrangements made for their return home.[5] These provisions do not apply to train crews.

[1] Immigration Act 1971, s 8(1).
[2] Immigration Act 1971, Sch 2, para 2(1). This will usually happen because the vessel or certain crew members have been identified as problems: IDI, Ch 16, s 1. The requirements for leave to enter for temporary shore leave are set out in IDI, Ch 16, s 1, paras 4 and 5.
[3] Immigration Act 1971, Sch 2, paras 12(1), 13(1)(a) (transferring to another ship).
[4] Immigration Act 1971, Sch 2, para 13(1)(c) (repatriation). There is a concession outside the Immigration Rules allowing for air crew of certain airlines to be based in the UK; they may be granted leave for up to 12 months at a time for this purpose and may be joined by family members. See IDI, Ch 16, Annex E.
[5] Immigration Act 1971, Sch 2, para 13(1)(b) (hospital treatment).

Coming to join a ship or aircraft

6.34 Crew members coming to the UK to join a ship or aircraft, hovercraft, hydrofoil or international train service require leave. Notice granting leave will usually require them to leave on a ship or aircraft specified or indicated in the notice.[1] Extensions of stay will only be given if it is necessary to fulfil the purpose for which leave to enter was given or the crew member meets the requirements for an extension of stay as a spouse under HC 395, paragraph 284.[2] Under the immigration rules relating to those seeking leave to enter for work permit employment, seafarers joining ships in British waters are required to possess a work permit *unless* they are under contract to join a ship due to leave British waters.[3] This means that, generally speaking, permits will be needed where the ship in question does not leave British waters for a foreign port, or is operating wholly or largely within British waters. Under Guidelines operating from 1 August 1996, work permits were needed for those working on dredgers and boats doing domestic ferry voyages between two United Kingdom ports.[4] With effect from 1 June 2000, the existing work permit requirement was extended to include scheduled domestic freight services between UK ports.[5]

[1] Immigration Act 1971, Sch 2, para 12(1).
[2] HC 395, para 324 (there is no equivalent on-entry rule); *Immigration Officer, Heathrow v Ekinci* [1989] Imm AR 346. Since the spouse rule was amended, it can benefit only those whose leave has permitted them to stay for over six months: para 284(i).
[3] HC 395, para 128. If a ship is bound for an overseas port, the requirements of para 128 of HC 395 are met and work permits are not required. This should be taken to include scheduled *passenger and freight* vessels leaving British waters, since the period of 'employment' in the UK will be short: IDI, Ch 16, Annex B. The fact that a vessel leaves British waters for a short period will not enable a seafarer to circumvent this requirement.
[4] This does not include voyages to the Isle of Man or the Channel Islands: IDI, Ch 16, Annex B. The fact that a vessel leaves British waters for a short period will not enable a seafarer to circumvent the work permit requirement: ibid.
[5] There was a grace period of six months from 1 June 2000, so that from 1 January 2001 all non-EEA seafarers working on ships engaged in scheduled domestic freight services must have a valid work permit. The work permit requirements are to be extended to other types of ship which operate solely or mainly in British waters: IDI, Ch 16, Annex B, para 4.1.

Discharged seamen

6.35 Where seamen are discharged from their ship on its arrival in the UK, they do not qualify for automatic shore leave and will require leave to enter. If the immigration officer is satisfied that they have the proper documents, do not intend to take employment (unless transferring to another ship due to leave British waters), intend to leave the UK, have made satisfactory arrangements for their onward travel and there are no general grounds for refusal, leave to enter will normally be given for a limited period pending departure.[1] If they require hospital treatment, the owners or agents must be willing to meet all the costs involved and to arrange for repatriation at the end of the treatment.[2] Discharged seamen may also be given leave to enter as visitors in a suitable case.[3] Visa requirements are waived.[4] Certain seamen who are discharged from their ship on their arrival in the UK are exempt from the need to obtain leave. These are Commonwealth citizens who hold a British seaman's card and Irish citizens if (in either case) they were engaged as crew members of a ship in a place within the common travel area.[5] The assumption behind this exemption is that seamen within this group are based in the UK or Ireland, and will be seeking their next engagement within the common travel area.

[1] IDI, Ch 16, s 1, para 5.4.
[2] IDI, Ch 16, s 1, paras 5.4 and 5.6.
[3] IDI, Ch 16, s 1, para 5.12.
[4] IDI, Ch 16, s 1, para 5.5.
[5] Immigration (Exemption from Control) Order 1972, SI 1972/1613, Art 5(1)(d).

Arrest, detention and removal of crew members

6.36 In each of these cases the temporary nature of the crew members' stay is emphasised and reinforced by the powers given to the immigration service to deal with those who do not comply. Under Schedule 2 to the Immigration Act 1971, crew members who remain beyond the time allowed by section 8(1) or by any express leave can be arrested, detained and summarily removed from the UK.[1] Jumping ship is put on a par with illegal immigration or overstaying. In fact the powers may be more severe. Crew members can be arrested, detained and removed not only if they have actually failed to comply, but also if they are 'reasonably suspected' by an immigration officer of intending to do so. The right of appeal which existed under previous legislation was removed by the 2002 Act, but has now been reinstated.[2] There is no time limit on the exercise of the powers of removal. Someone who jumped ship ten years ago is as liable to removal, it seems, as someone who did so last week. Train crews are liable to removal if they fail to return to their train or remain beyond the time allowed by their exemption under section 8(1).[3]

[1] Immigration Act 1971, Sch 2, paras 12(2) and 13(2).
[2] Removal of crew members under Immigration Act 1971, Sch 2, paras 12(2) and 13(2) was not an 'immigration decision' conferring a right of appeal under Nationality, Immigration and Asylum Act 2002, s 82 as enacted, but carries a right of appeal under s 82(2)(ia) of that Act, inserted by Asylum and Immigration (Treatment of Claimants, etc) Act 2004, s 31 as from 1 October 2004: SI 2004/2523.
[3] Immigration Act 1971, Sch 2, para 13(2), modified by the Channel Tunnel (International Arrangements) Order 1993, SI 1993/1813, Sch 4, para 1(11)(n).

Shipwrecked seamen

6.37 Where a ship is wrecked, shipwrecked seamen should normally be given leave to enter.[1] They will usually be cared for by a local shipping agent, the Shipwrecked Mariners Society or the Mission of Seamen. Seamen for this purpose include non-professional seamen.[2]

[1] IDI, Ch 16, s 1, Annex B, para 8.
[2] IDI, Ch 16, s 1, Annex B, para 8.

Seamen's documents

6.38 Seamen's documents may be issued by governments, not only to their own citizens but also to seamen of other countries. Although the holder of a seamen's document is not a national of the issuing country, the document may be accepted as evidence of identity and status and may exempt the holder from visa requirements, if the issuing country is a signatory to the International Labour Organisation Convention No 108.[1] The main effect of the Convention, to which the United Kingdom is a party, is that a seaman holding a document to which it applies:

- shall be readmitted to the country which issued the document both during its validity and during a period of at least one year after any date of expiry; and
- does not require a visa when travelling in the course of his duties to or through countries which have ratified the Convention.

The provisions of the Convention cover joining or transferring to a ship, passing in transit to join a ship in another country or for repatriation and temporary shore leave while the ship is in port.[2] Seamen travelling on national passports or holders of documents issued by countries which have not ratified the ILO Convention are subject to the normal visa requirements.[3]

[1] See IDI, Ch16, Annex A, para 6.1.
[2] A list of the countries which have ratified the Convention as of 31 December 1995 is contained in IDI, Ch 16, Annex A, para 6.1. Seamen travelling on documents issued by former Soviet Union States, other than the Baltic States, arriving without entry clearance should be refused leave to enter: IDI, Ch 16, Annex A, para 6.1.
[3] IDI, Ch 16, Annex A, paras 6.1 and 6.5.

The British Seamen's Card

6.39 The British Seamen's Card, which is red in colour, is issued by the Department of Transport and contains a notice that it is a seafarer's document for the purposes of the ILO Convention. It is issued to persons who qualify under the terms of the Merchant Shipping (Seamen's Documents) Regulations 1987.[1] According to the current IDI these are:

- British Citizens with right of abode;
- British passport holders without right of abode but who have indefinite leave to enter;
- Commonwealth citizens with indefinite leave to enter; and

- Irish citizens.

Non-Commonwealth nationals are not entitled to apply for a British Seaman's Card. Persons travelling on British Seamen's Cards are exempt from immigration control when arriving as a member of a crew of a ship, having signed on in the Common Travel Area.[2]

[1] SI 1987/408, regs 2 to 14. 'British seamen' are defined in Merchant Shipping Act 1995, s 79(3) as 'persons who are not aliens within the meaning of the British Nationality Act 1981 [s 50(1)] and are employed, or ordinarily employed, as masters or seamen'. Under the regulations the cards must be given to persons with a right of abode; to other non-aliens the grant is discretionary: see SI 1987/408, regs 5 and 11. See further IDI Ch 16, Annex A, para 6.2. British seaman's cards should not be confused with British Discharge Books, which are blue in colour and also issued by the Department of Transport to British and foreign seamen employed on United Kingdom registered vessels: see Merchant Shipping (Seamen's Documents) Regulations 1987, SI 1987/408, regs 15 to 24, as amended by SI 1999/3281, made under the Merchant Shipping Act 1995 s 80. They should not be endorsed by the immigration officer: IDI, Ch 16, Annex A, para 6.2. Nor should Indian Seamen's Discharge Books: Ch 16, Annex A, para 6.3. UK seamen who are refugees or stateless, are entitled to have their Home Office documents endorsed 'The Convention relating to Seafarers' National Identity Documents dated 13 May 1958 applies to this document': Ch 16, Annex A, para 6.4.

[2] IDI, Ch 16, Annex A, para 6.2.

GROUPS COVERED BY EXEMPTION ORDER

6.40 Section 8(2) of the Immigration Act 1971 enables the Secretary of State to exempt any person or class of persons from all or any of the provisions of the Act relating to those who are not British citizens. The exemption may be conditional or unconditional.[1] Exemptions of classes of persons must be done through statutory instrument, and the relevant exemptions are set out in the Immigration (Exemption from Control) Order 1972, which has been amended several times to add new classes.[2]

[1] Immigration Act 1971, s 8(2). Exemptions under this section and the Order are in addition to diplomatic exemption (covered by s 8(3): 6.44 below), and exemption for armed forces (6.51 below).

[2] Immigration (Exemption from Control) Order 1972, SI 1972/1613, as amended by SI 1975/617; SI 1977/693; SI 1982/1649, SI 1985/1809, SI 1997/1402, SI 1997/2207.

Consular officers and employees

6.41 Consular officers are appointed by their governments to live in a foreign port or city, chiefly as a representative of their country's commercial interests. They differ from diplomats, who are dealt with at 6.44ff below. There is also a distinction between full and partial exemption. Full exemption means not only freedom to enter and leave the country freely but also freedom from deportation. Partial exemption means officials are exempt from all control except deportation. Where consular Conventions have been concluded between the UK and another State,[1] full exemption from immigration control is given to any consular officer or employee[2] in the service of that State, and to any member of the family of such a person who forms part of his or her household.[3] Consular employees only get the exemption if they are in the full-time service of the State concerned and are not engaged in the UK in any private occupation for gain.[4]

1   The list of States with which the UK has concluded such Conventions is set out in SI 1972/1613, but it has not been updated since 1997. For an up-to-date list see IDI Ch 14, s 1.
2   For definitions see Consular Relations Act 1968, Sch 1, para 1(d), (e).
3   Immigration (Exemption from Control) Order 1972, SI 1972/1613, as amended, Art 3(1).
4   SI 1972/1613, Art 3(2).

6.42 Exemption from all immigration control except deportation[1] is given under the Immigration (Exemption from Control) Order 1972[2] to the following:

(i)   members of foreign governments on official business and consular officers and employees of States who have not signed a consular convention with the UK;[3]

(ii) senior officials from international organisations like the International Monetary Fund, International Bank for Reconstruction and Development, International Finance Corporation, International Development Association, the Hong Kong Economic and Trade Office, the Independent International Commission on Decommissioning and the North Atlantic Salmon Conservation Organisation;[4]

(iii) persons connected with international organisations or international tribunals who attend certain conferences in the UK;[5]

(iv) representatives of Commonwealth countries attending conferences[6] or performing consular functions;[7]

(v)   officials of the Commonwealth Secretariat who are entitled to limited immunities under Schedule 6 to the Commonwealth Secretariat Act 1966, but not to full diplomatic immunity.[8]

In each of these cases the exemption also applies to any member of the family forming a part of the exempted person's household.[9]

1   Under Immigration Act 1971, s 3(5)(a) and (b).
2   SI 1972/1613, made under Immigration Act 1971, s 8(2).
3   SI 1972/1613 as amended, Art 4(a), (h), (i).
4   SI 1972/1613 as amended, Art 4(b), (c), (d), (k), (l), (m).
5   SI 1972/1613 as amended, Art 4(g). The IDI have a full list of organisations whose delegates would be exempt: IDI, Ch 14, Annex B.
6   SI 1972/1613 as amended, Art 4(e).
7   SI 1972/1613 as amended, Art 4(f).
8   SI 1972/1613 as amended, Art 4(j).
9   SI 1972/1613 as amended, Art 4(n). Family members for these purposes include dependent offspring over 18 who are still in full-time education, dependent relatives forming part of the household abroad and other close relatives with no one else to look after them: IDI, Ch 14, s 1, para 6. For the position of unmarried and same-sex partners of consular officials see IDI, Ch 14, s 1, para 6. There is an issue as to whether family members benefit if the relevant person is a British citizen. The Home Office argues that Art 4 of the Immigration (Exemption from Control) Order 1972, SI 1972/1613 provides exemption from any provisions of the Immigration Act 1971 relating to those who are not British citizens and that British citizens (and therefore their families) are not exempt. The alternative view is that a British citizen can be both exempt and have a right of abode; and where Parliament wants to limit exemption to non-British citizens it uses the formula in Art 5 of the 1972 Order: 'the following persons who are not British citizens are exempt ...'

Other exempted groups

6.43 Under the Immigration (Exemption from Control) Order 1972,[1] made under section 8(2) of the Immigration Act 1971, the following classes of persons, not already referred to, who are not British citizens, have a limited exemption from the requirement under section 3(1)(a) of the 1971 Act to obtain leave to enter:[2]

(i) any Commonwealth citizen included in a collective passport issued in the UK or Islands;[3]

(ii) any Irish or Commonwealth citizens returning from an excursion to France, Belgium or the Netherlands who hold a valid identity document issued for such excursions;[4]

(iii) certain holders of a British seamen's card and certain members of the crew of an aircraft.[5]

These exemptions do not apply to any person against whom there is a deportation order in force, or who has previously entered the UK unlawfully and has not subsequently been given leave to enter or remain.[6] For these purposes Commonwealth citizens include British Protected persons.[7]

---

[1] SI 1972/1613.
[2] SI 1972/1613, Art 5. Former citizens of the UK and Colonies (CUKCs) (British Dependent Territories and British Overseas citizens) holding a British visitor's passport are expressed to be exempt under Article 5(1)(a) of SI 1972/1613, but British visitor's passports have now been abolished, so this exemption has been omitted from the main text.
[3] SI 1972/1613, Art 5(1)(b).
[4] SI 1972/1613, Art 5(1)(c).
[5] SI 1972/1613, Art 5(1)(d) and (e). See 6.33 and 6.39 above.
[6] SI 1972/1613, Art 5(2).
[7] SI 1972/1613, Art 5(3).

DIPLOMATIC EXEMPTION

6.44 Representatives of foreign governments and of international organisations, such as the UN, and their families are exempt from control under either the Immigration (Exemption from Control) Order 1972[1] made under section 8(2) of the Immigration Act 1971 or under section 8(3). In some cases full exemption is given, and in others officials are exempt from all control except deportation. Consular exemption, described at 6.41–6.42 above, is sometimes full exemption, meaning freedom to enter and leave the UK and freedom from deportation during the period of exemption, and sometimes partial, meaning that deportation is still possible. Diplomatic exemption, which we now consider, is always full exemption.

---

[1] SI 1972/1613 as amended.

Diplomats and their staff

6.45 Diplomatic staff carry on the diplomatic relations of the State they represent in the country to which they have been appointed. Members of diplomatic missions and members of their families who form part of their household are fully exempt under section 8(3) of the Immigration Act 1971. The Diplomatic Privileges Act 1964 divides those members of diplomatic missions entitled to diplomatic immunity into three categories:

(i)   diplomatic agents, who are heads of the mission and members of their diplomatic staff;

(ii)   members of the administrative and technical staff, consisting of clerical staff, translators, coding clerks, press representatives, etc; and

(iii)   members of the service staff, who are chauffeurs, cooks, cleaners, etc.[1]

Each of these categories is entitled to differing degrees of immunity from civil and criminal proceedings, but all are exempt from immigration control under section 8(3) of the 1971 Act, except staff recruited in this country. Section 8(3A), as amended by the Immigration and Asylum Act 1999, provides that members of a mission, other than diplomatic agents, are only exempt if (a) they were resident outside the UK, and were not in the UK, when they were offered their post, and (b) they have not ceased to be a member of the mission after having taken up the post.[2]

1   See Diplomatic Privileges Act 1964, Sch 1, para 1.
2   The original s 8(3A) of the Immigration Act 1971 was inserted by Immigration Act 1988, s 4. It ensured that foreign nationals in the UK, who took up posts in diplomatic missions, other than as diplomatic agents, were not exempt from immigration control. But there was a lacuna in the law. If these locally recruited people left the UK and then returned while still in post, the original s 8(3A) operated to free them from immigration control on their return. By the Immigration and Asylum Act 1999 amendment, the new s 8(3A) closes this loophole, but at the same time ensures that they do not remain subject to immigration control for ever. A person who has held such a post in the past, but has subsequently left it, and has then been appointed from abroad, will enjoy full diplomatic exemption.

6.46   The distinction between service staff who are exempt from control and other employees of a mission is sometimes difficult to make. In practice the distinguishing feature appears to be whether or not they are liable to pay UK tax. Under Article 37(3) of the Vienna Convention, members of the service staff of the mission are exempt from local taxes. Thus in *Kandiah*[1] the Tribunal held that a messenger working for a mission was not exempt from immigration control where it was a condition of his employment that he paid local taxes.[2] Equally, it is doubtful if a housekeeper in the household of the deputy head of mission would be exempt from control, even if he or she has his or her contract with the government concerned.[3] The service staff of the mission is not the same as the service staff of one of its members. The Tribunal, however, seemed to take a different view in the case of *Florentine*.[4] The private servants of heads of State have total exemption unless the Secretary of State otherwise directs.[5]

1   (2699) unreported.
2   See *Pintucan* (16451) [1999] 1 ILD 27.
3   The test of exemption is not the mere fact of being employed at a diplomatic mission. The IDI Ch 14, Annex A, para 2.1, distinguishes between a servant of the head of the mission paid by the country, and one paid by the head of mission, the latter being a private servant in a diplomatic household requiring leave to enter under HC 395, paras 152 to 159. Arts 1 and 37(4) of the Vienna Convention contained in Sch 1 to the Diplomatic Privileges Act 1964 (and given force of law by s 1 thereof) is not particularly helpful in shedding light on this distinction.
4   (4811) unreported.

⁵ State Immunity Act 1978, s 20(3). See IDI, Ch 14, s 1, para 2.3. However, the IDI, Ch 14 Annex A, para 2.2 indicates that servants of Heads of State are subject to control and should be treated as domestic servants in private households. We prefer the former guidance, which fits the statutory position.

UN officials

6.47 Persons entitled to like immunity from jurisdiction as is conferred by the Diplomatic Privileges Act 1964 on 'diplomatic agents' are fully exempt from immigration control.[1] Like immunities are conferred on high officers of a number of international organisations, such as the UN, by Orders in Council made under the International Organisations (Immunities and Privileges) Act 1950, as continued by the International Organisations Act 1968, section 12(5), and on senior officers of the Commonwealth Secretariat under the Commonwealth Secretariat Act 1966. The range of employees covered and whether the exemption extends to any member of the person's family forming part of his or her household depends upon the terms of the agreement reached with each organisation.[2]

[1] Immigration Act 1971, s 8(3).
[2] IDI, Ch 14, s 1, Annex B, para 2. The family has exemption because they obtain like immunity under the relevant agreement, not because of any express mention of a family in Immigration Act 1971, s 8(3).

Members of the diplomat's family

6.48 Subject to the above, in all the immunities granted to diplomats and international functionaries, the exemption extends to members of their family who form part of their household.[1] This can be a difficult issue. In *Gupta*[2] the question in issue was whether the widowed sister of an Indian diplomat qualified. She claimed she was entitled to remain here as a member of her brother's family who formed part of his household within the meaning of section 8(3) of the Immigration Act 1971. The High Court held that she was exempt from control. The IDI now give some guidance, giving the term a more generous interpretation than that used for persons subject to immigration control and having more in common with the EC definition.[3] It extends to children over 18 who are still in full-time education; dependent relatives forming part of the household abroad; and other close relatives with no one else to look after them.[4] The IDI give a mixed message about unmarried partners (including same sex partners). On the one hand unmarried partners are said not to be exempt from control, but may seek leave to enter under the Immigration Rules.[5] On the other hand unmarried partners (common law or same sex relationships) are to be considered as members of households, where the relationship is recognised as durable by the sending State and is one that is akin to marriage and where the parties intend to live together in the United Kingdom for the duration of the posting.[6]

[1] See eg Immigration Act 1971, s 8(3); Immigration (Exemption from Control) Order 1972, SI 1972/1613, Art 3(1)(c) and 4(l).
[2] [1979–80] Imm AR 52. See *Florentine* [1987] Imm AR 1.
[3] In Council Regulation (EEC) 1612/68, Art 10.
[4] IDI, Ch 14, s 1 para 6.

5   IDI, Ch 14, s 1, para 9.
6   IDI, Ch 14, s 1 para 6.

Locally engaged staff (non-diplomats) of diplomatic missions working in the UK

6.49 *Locally engaged staff recruited prior to 1 August 1988.* Under section 8(3) of the Immigration Act 1971 (as originally in force) the locally engaged members of missions in the non-diplomatic categories of administrative and technical staff and service staff, and their families, were entitled to exemption from control. The position of persons recruited in the above categories prior to 1 August 1988 is not affected by subsequent amendments of the Immigration Act 1971 and their exemption will continue.

Locally engaged staff recruited between 1 August 1988 and 1 March 2000. Under section 8(3) of the Immigration Act 1971,[1] missions were able to engage locally only persons in the above categories, whose status allowed them to take employment, or persons whose appointments were notified to the Protocol Department of the Foreign and Commonwealth Office under Article 10 of the Vienna Convention on Diplomatic Relations.[2] If the Foreign and Commonwealth Office were satisfied that the persons were in bona fide employment and entitled to privileges and immunities, employment was permitted.[3] They were, however, subject to control. Staff recruited between 1 August 1988 and 1 March 2000 who had travelled abroad before 1 March 2000 became exempt upon their return by virtue of returning as a member of a diplomatic mission.[4] Locally engaged staff of missions currently in the UK who have not acquired exempt status by travelling abroad before 1 March 2000 are subject to immigration control, and if they travel abroad on or after 1 March 2000, they will remain subject to immigration control upon their return to the UK.[5]

Locally engaged staff recruited after 1 March 2000. Under the new section 8(3A) of the 1971 Act,[6] members of missions other than diplomatic agents will only benefit from exemption if they were resident outside the UK and were not present in the UK when offered a post as a member of a mission; and if they have not ceased to be a member of the mission after taking up the post. However, they do not remain subject to immigration control for ever. A person who has held such a post in the past, but has subsequently left it and has been appointed abroad to the current post, is to be treated like any other member of that mission appointed outside the UK.[7]

1   As amended by the Immigration Act 1988.
2   IDI, Ch 14, s 1, Annex A, para 3.
3   IDI, Ch 14, s 1, Annex A, para 3.
4   Immigration Act 1971, s 8(3A), as inserted by Immigration Act 1988.
5   IA 1971, s 8(3A), as substituted by IA 1999, s 6.
6   Originally inserted by the Immigration Act 1988, s 4; then substituted by the Immigration and Asylum Act 1999, s 6.
7   IA 1971, s 8(3A)(b), as amended by IAA 1999. See commentary in *Butterworths Immigration Law Service*, para **A [622]**.

CEASING TO HAVE DIPLOMATIC AND OTHER EXEMPTION

6.50 When diplomats and others exempted under section 8(2) and (3) of the Immigration Act 1971 cease to be exempt on or after 1 March 2000, and, as a result, require leave to remain, they are treated as if they had been given leave for a period of 90 days, beginning on the day exemption ceases.[1] If, however, the person already has a leave which expires before the end of the 90-day period, his or her leave is treated as expiring at the end of the shorter period.[2] If the ex-diplomat wishes to remain in the UK, an application to do so will be considered in the normal way under the immigration rules.[3] The provisions of section 8A of the IA 1971, together with the new section 8(3A), which came into force on 1 March 2000,[4] disposes of many of the practical problems of diplomatic exemption referred to in the previous editions of this work.[5] The position now is:

(i)   if clearly indicated indefinite leave was given on arrival in the UK, prior to 1 March 2000, and before taking up the diplomatic post, this will remain unaffected by the exemption. Since under section 8(3) 'the provisions of this Act ... shall not apply ... so long as' the person remains exempt, such leave will not lapse due to trips overseas,[6] and the former diplomat will be free to remain;[7]

(ii)   a mere rectangular stamp in a passport with a date but no words indicating any sort of leave does not operate as the grant of indefinite leave.[8] Further, a grant of indefinite leave on arrival in the UK is unlikely, since it is now the law that those who come from overseas to take up a diplomatic post become members of the mission on arrival in the UK, and not when they actually take up the appointment or when the appointment is officially notified to the UK government;[9]

(iii) persons with prior limited leave are dealt with by sections 8(5) and 8A(3)(b) of the 1971 Act. If they wish to remain longer they need to apply before the end of the period of their leave in the normal way;

(iv)   there is uncertainty as to the effect of an express grant of leave (indefinite or limited) given to somebody who is exempt from control as a diplomat.[10]

A period of exemption from immigration control counts towards 'lawful residence' for the purposes of the long residence rule.[11]

---

[1]   Immigration Act 1971, s 8A(2), inserted by the Immigration and Asylum Act 1999, s 6 and in force on 1 March 2000.

[2]   Immigration Act 1971, s 8A(3).

[3]   IDI, Ch 14, s 1, Annex C, para 2.

[4]   SI 2000/168.

[5]   4th edn 7.46ff.

[6]   As would have been the case under IA 1971, s 3(4); the provisions of the Immigration (Leave to Enter and Remain) Order 2000, SI 2000/1161 would now in any event prevent the lapsing of indefinite leave.

[7]   IDI, Ch 14, s 1, para 8.4. For further details of the pre-March 2000 position, see IDI, Ch 14, s 1, Annex D.

[8]   *R v Secretary of State for the Home Department, ex p Bagga* [1990] Imm AR 413, CA.

[9]   *Bagga* above, overruling *R v Governor of Pentonville Prison, ex p Teja* [1971] 2 QB 274, [1971] 2 All ER 11; *R v Lambeth Justices, ex p Yusufu* [1985] Crim LR 510; *Re Osman (No 2)* (21 December 1988, unreported), DC; and *Rahi v Secretary of State for the Home Department* [1987] Imm AR 293 on the issue that immunity depends on notification and acceptance.

10   One argument is that such leave is ineffective as contrary to s 8(3) of the Immigration
     Act 1971. The opposing argument is that exemption from the requirement to obtain leave
     does not preclude reliance being placed subsequently on such a leave when the person
     ceases to be exempt. In practice the Home Office recognises that there has been a pledge of
     public faith by immigration officials and the grant of leave is usually honoured: IDI, Ch 14,
     s 1, para 8.5. This does not apply if the leave was limited and expires within three months
     of the exemption ending: IDI, Ch 14, s 1.
11   HC 395 para 276A(b)(iii) (inserted by HC 538).

MILITARY PERSONNEL

6.51 Section 8(4) of the Immigration Act 1971 also gives a limited exemption
to members of the home forces subject to service law,[1] to members of
Commonwealth forces training with the home forces and to members of a
visiting force, such as US servicemen, posted in the UK.[2] The exemption is
limited since it exempts from control on and after entry, but not from
deportation. On ceasing to be exempt (eg by discharge from the armed
forces), military personnel do not benefit from any period of statutory leave,
and those who remain in the UK will become overstayers unless they had leave
before their exemption, in which case that leave will resume, or apply for fresh
leave.[3] However, under new arrangements, the Home Office grants 28 days'
leave to Gurkhas and foreign and Commonwealth forces of whose discharge it
has been sent advance notice, to take effect on discharge, so as to enable them
to regularise their position.[4] The dependants of those with a military exemption are not themselves exempt, but should normally be granted leave to enter
or remain for the duration of the principal's training or posting.[5]

1   This includes Gurkhas, and foreign and Commonwealth soldiers in HM Forces: IDI Jun
    04, Ch 15, s 1.
2   Immigration Act 1971, s 8(4) and (6). See *R v Secretary of State for the Home Department,
    ex p Wuan* [1989] Imm AR 501, QBD. For further details see IDI, Ch 15, s 1 and Annexes
    A and C.
3   Immigration Act 1971, s 8A does not apply to those who were exempt under IA 1971,
    s 8(4). See IDI, Ch 14, s 1 Annex D; IDI, Ch 15, s 2. For NATO civilian employees see IDI,
    Ch 15, s 3.
4   IDI Apr 05, Ch 15, s 2, para 4.2. Gurkhas and foreign and Commonwealth forces who
    have served for over four years are eligible for indefinite leave to remain under HC 395,
    paras 276E–276Q, inserted by HC 1112, from 25 October 2004. For details see chapter 5.
5   IDI Jun 04, Ch 15, s 1, para 4.

CHILDREN BORN IN THE UK

6.52 Generally speaking, those exempt from control are not to be regarded as
settled in the UK,[1] but the British Nationality Act 1981 made provision[2] for
the Secretary of State for the Home Department to treat as settled in the UK
(for the purposes of section 1 of the 1981 Act) any person or class of person
who is exempted by Order from immigration control. This will apply to
parents of children born in the UK after 1983, but who do not acquire British
citizenship by birth. The 1972 Order as amended provides that where an
exempt person (other than a diplomat)[3] becomes a parent of a UK-born child,
the parent will be treated as settled (enabling the child to be a British citizen

by birth) if he or she had indefinite leave to remain before becoming exempt from control and was ordinarily resident in the UK from that time until the time of the child's birth.[4]

[1] Immigration Act 1971, s 8(5).
[2] British Nationality Act 1981, s 39(4) inserted a new s 8(5A) into the Immigration Act 1971.
[3] The Article does not apply if a parent has diplomatic immunity under the Diplomatic Privileges Act 1964.
[4] Immigration (Exemption from Control) Order 1972, Art 6 (inserted by SI 1982/1649).

Chapter 7

EUROPEAN COMMUNITY LAW AND RELATED OBLIGATIONS

INTRODUCTION

7.1 This chapter is concerned with the impact on immigration law of rights of freedom of movement and associated provisions afforded under the Treaty of Rome 1959 (the EEC Treaty), as amended by the Single European Act 1987, the Treaty on European Union 1993 (the Maastricht Treaty), and the Treaty of Amsterdam 1997. The UK became a member of the European Communities with effect from 1 January 1973.[1] Since this date the Treaty, and directives and regulations made under it, are binding in the UK by virtue of the European Communities Act 1972.[2] So also are decisions and interpretations on these provisions by the European Court of Justice (ECJ).[3] Contrary to the general policy of the Immigration Act 1971, whose clear purpose is to restrict the right of individuals to enter or remain in the UK, the main characteristic of these freedom of movement provisions is that they grant rights directly to individuals and restrict the powers of the national authority. Interpretation of the Community texts by the ECJ tends, therefore, to favour the individual rather than the Member State. This is in sharp contrast to the interpretation of domestic immigration law, which tends to give fuller recognition to the extensive discretionary power of the immigration authorities at the expense of the individual. From its inception, the freedom of movement of persons was characterised as one of the European Economic Community's (EEC's) principal foundations, along with freedom of movement for goods, services and capital.[4]

[1] European Communities Act 1972 (ch 68), as amended. The Act has been amended on many occasions, as new treaties have been signed and there have been accessions of new States to the Community and Union, the latest of which is the European Union (Accessions) Act 2003, which received the Royal assent in November 2003 and marked the accession of the 10 latest Member States to join.

[2] European Communities Act 1972, s 2.

[3] European Communities Act 1972, s 3; see *EC Commission v Luxembourg* [1997] ECR I-3207, [1996] 3 CMLR 981; *Orfinger v Belgium* [2000] 1 CMLR 612, ECJ.

[4] See Case 167/73 *EC Commission v France* [1974] ECR 359, [1974] 2 CMLR 216, ECJ; Preamble to Council Regulation (EEC) 1612/68.

7.2 Since 1 November 1993 and the amendments made at Maastricht by the Treaty on European Union (TEU) the EEC is now known as the European Community (EC). This suggests that the Community is concerned with political and social rights as well as purely economic ones. From this date the Member States of the EC have formed the European Union (EU) which includes, but is a different body from, the EC.[1] A national of a Member State is now, by virtue of that nationality, also a citizen of the EU.[2] The free movement rights of EU citizens and members of their families remain the core of Community law as it affects immigration, but the Treaty on European Union also provided a structure for inter-governmental co-operation on asylum and immigration of third-country nationals in what became known as the third pillar of the EU. On 2 October 1997 Member States signed the Treaty of Amsterdam with a view to improving the efficiency, democracy and transparency of the EU, and to prepare it for the next enlargement of membership.[3] The central change has been the integration into the framework of the EU of the Schengen *acquis*[4] and a new Title IV of the EC Treaty, containing the power to make new Community law on immigration and asylum, matters which had previously been dealt with on an inter-governmental basis under the Justice and Home affairs provisions of the Treaty on European Union (the 'third pillar'). As a result of Amsterdam, the EC Treaty has been extensively amended and renumbered (see 7.24 below).[5]

[1] Selected Articles of the EC and EU Treaties are set out in the Appendix. For the full texts see *Butterworths Immigration Law Service*, F[31] (EC Treaty), F[201] (Treaty on European Union). The TEU was adopted in the UK by the European Communities (Amendment) Act 1993, which received the Royal Assent in July 1993. Implementation was delayed until the House of Commons voted on the UK's opt-out of the Protocol on Social Policy. A challenge was also made to the power of the Secretary of State for Foreign Affairs to conclude the Treaty (*R v Secretary of State for Foreign and Commonwealth Affairs, ex p Rees-Mogg* [1994] QB 552, [1993] 3 CMLR 101). The Treaty on European Union had also to receive approval from the German and French Constitutional courts (see *Brunner v European Union Treaty* [1994] 1 CMLR 57).

[2] Article 17 EC (ex Art 8).

[3] See Kay Hailbronner 'The Treaty of Amsterdam and Migration Law' 1999 EJM & L 9.

[4] The Schengen *acquis* is a body of compensatory measures on border controls etc, derived from agreement on the gradual abolition of checks at common borders signed by other EC Member States on 14 June 1985 and 19 June 1990. See 7.25ff below.

5 For the renumbered texts, see *Butterworths Immigration Law Service*, F[31]; British Management Data Foundation *Treaty of Amsterdam in Perspective* (2nd edn, 1998).

7.3 The EC Treaty gives powers to the EC and the Member States to enter into Association Agreements with other States.[1] These are binding in Community law. Some were made with Eastern European countries, such as Poland and Hungary, which have now become full members. Of the others, perhaps the most significant for immigration lawyers are the Ankara Agreement 1963 with Turkey, and the Agreements with North African States, which we deal with at 7.151 below, and the 1999 Agreement with Switzerland below.

1 Article 310 EC (ex Art 238 of the EEC Treaty, as amended by the Single European Act 1987).

7.4 Not all these agreements are with individual States. Some are with other international entities. For example, a completely new entity, the European Economic Area (EEA) was created by an agreement made with the former European Free Trade Association countries under the EC Treaty, giving the same free movement rights within the area to both EU nationals and to nationals of Norway, Iceland and Liechtenstein.[1] It has an advanced institutional structure, including a distinct Court and Surveillance Authority.[2] In June 1999 the EC and Switzerland entered into an agreement intended to extend full free movement rights between the community and Switzerland. It came into force in the UK on 1 June 2002.[3] The Agreement on the European Economic Area 1992 has the force of law in the UK by virtue of the European Economic Area Act 1993, which amends the European Communities Act 1972. The freedom of movement rights under the 1992 Agreement were implemented in UK law as from 20 July 1994 by the European Economic Area Order in Council 1994.[4] This has now been replaced since 2 October 2000 by the Immigration (European Economic Area) Regulations 2000.[5] In the 2000 Regulations a national of a State that is party to the EEA Agreement is called a 'qualified person' irrespective of whether or not he or she is a national of an EU Member State. In this chapter, in considering free movement rights we will refer to EEA nationals rather than EC or EU nationals, and this will include Swiss nationals, unless separate consideration is required for any particular group.[6] The rights accruing under association agreements will be considered separately in 7.151ff.

1 See European Economic Area Act 1993, applying the Agreement on the European Economic Area signed at Oporto on 2 May 1992, as adjusted by the Protocol signed at Brussels on 17 March 1993 OJ L86 20.4.1995. The implementation of the Agreement was delayed until the ECJ was satisfied that the joint committee established to monitor the Agreement did not impinge on the court's jurisdiction; see ECJ Opinion 1/92 given on 10 April 1992. For the rules of the joint committee and the EEA Court see [1994] 1 CMLR 84. On 1 May 2004 the ten new Member States of the EU became parties to this agreement, ie the Czech Republic, Estonia, Cyprus, Latvia, Lithuania, Hungary, Malta, Poland, Slovenia, and Slovakia: see Accession Treaty, Art 2; Act of Accession Art 6.
2 See S Peers 'The EC-Switzerland Agreement on Free Movement of Persons: Overview and Analysis,' 2000 EJM & L 127.
3 Agreement between the European Community and the Swiss Confederation on The Free Movement of Persons (30 Apr/02 OJ L114/6). The Immigration (Swiss Free Movement of Persons) Regulations 2002 (SI 2002/1012) were made to give effect to the Agreement. Those Regulations, however, contained the wrong commencement date. They were, therefore, revoked by the Immigration (Swiss Free Movement of Persons) (No 2)

Regulations 2002 (SI 2002/1013) and replaced by the current Immigration (Swiss Free Movement of Persons) (No 3) Regulations 2002, which apply the Immigration (European Economic Area) Regulations 2000 in relation to a Swiss national, and to any person related to that national, as if the Swiss national were an EEA national and Switzerland an EEA State (reg 2 (1)). They also confer rights of entry and residence on employees of Swiss nationals or Swiss companies that provide or seek to provide services in the United Kingdom and send their employees to the United Kingdom for that purpose ('posted workers') (reg 2(2)). This accords with Arts 1 and 17 of Annex 1 of the Agreement. See 7.75 below.

4 SI 1994/1895.
5 SI 2000/2326, as amended.
6 The Agreement confers on Swiss nationals and their family members broadly similar rights of entry into and residence in the United Kingdom as are enjoyed by EEA nationals, but these are subject to the modifications set out in the Schedule to the Swiss Free Movement Regulations. The modifications are required to take account of the difference between the situation of EEA nationals and those covered by the Agreement between the EC and Switzerland.

ACCESSION OF NEW MEMBER STATES

7.5 Prior to 1 May 2004, the Member States of the EU were Austria, Belgium, Denmark, Finland, France, Germany, Greece, Holland, Ireland, Italy, Luxembourg, Portugal, Spain, Sweden and the UK. On 1 May 2004 they were joined by ten new members: the Czech Republic, Estonia, Cyprus, Latvia, Lithuania, Hungary, Malta, Poland, Slovenia, and Slovakia, under an Accession Treaty signed in Athens on 16 April 2003 ('the Accession Treaty').

7.6 The Accession Treaty consists of three Articles which tell us who are the new Member States, the date on which they join, and incorporate the Act of Accession (see Article 1(2)), which contains detailed rules about accession. Then there are the 17 Annexes to the Act of Accession, which are concerned with specific adaptations to be made by each new Member State. More importantly, for our purposes, they contain the detailed rules on a transitional period which could last up to seven years before the eight Eastern European new Member States attain the right to full free movement of workers and services.

Free movement of persons under the Accession Treaty

7.7 What then is the position under the Accession Treaty as regards free movement? First, it grants nationals of Cyprus and Malta the same rights to work in another Member State as are currently enjoyed by nationals of the existing Member States. Secondly, however, nationals of the other eight relevant States are subject to transitional provisions, set out in Annexes V, VI, VIII, IX, X, XII, XIII and XIV of the Act of Accession.[1] Their effect can be demonstrated by examining the agreement with Slovakia in Annex XIV.[2] Thirdly, nationals of the eight new relevant Member States enjoy free movement rights as regards each other, although these may be suspended at the Commission's discretion during the first seven years of membership (until 1 May 2011).[3] Fourthly, where the free movement of nationals of one of the relevant new Member States is restricted during any part of the transitional period by any of the existing States, the new Member State can take equivalent measures against the nationals of the Member State or States in question.[4] Fifthly, existing Member States applying national law during the derogation period, cannot make their national rules more restrictive than they were on 1 May 2004,[5] but they may introduce, under national law, more liberal rules if they wish, 'including full labour market access'.[6] This is what has happened in the UK (see below). From 1 May 2006 such a State can at any time decide to stop relying on national law and apply the full EC rules.[7] It is important to keep in mind that if a Member State only applies national rules which are more liberal, rather than the EC rules, the interpretation of those rules is presumably outside the jurisdiction of the EU courts, unless they allegedly infringe the accession treaty.[8] Even those Member States which apply full free movement of workers have a special safeguard for seven years (until 1 May 2011), if there are serious threats to the standard of living or the level of employment due to disturbances in its labour market.[9]

1   Chapter 2 of each Annex contains the relevant material on each Member State.
2   We follow the example of Professor Steve Peers of the University of Essex, who prepared the Statewatch comments on the EU Accession Treaty, by which we have been guided in part in the preparation of the text. These are accessible on the Statewatch website (see Appendix 3 below). There are standard rules which apply to each of the eight relevant new Member States, although in fact all the Annex XIV references below are taken from the rules for Slovakia.
3   Annex XIV, para 11.
4   Annex XIV, para 10.
5   Annex XIV, para 14. This paragraph also obliges existing Member States to give preference to workers from the accession States over third country nationals as regards access to their labour market, and they may not treat non-EU nationals more favourably than workers and their families from the accession States. Equally new Member States cannot treat nationals from existing Member States and their families, who are in the new Member State, less favourably than third country nationals.
6   Annex XIV, para 12.
7   Annex XIV, para 12.
8   Statewatch Comments, above.
9   Annex XIV, para 7. However, any decision to suspend free movement rights will be at the discretion of the Commission, whose decision can be overturned by the Council. It is also possible for Member States to apply the safeguard unilaterally 'in urgent and exceptional cases'.

7.8 The scope of the derogation needs to be understood. It only applies to free movement of workers and services. It does *not* apply to freedom of establishment (of the self-employed) or movement for any other purpose (as students, pensioners or self-sufficient persons) or the limited temporary movement of workers to provide services, as defined in Article 1 of Directive 96/71/EC.[1] Those freedoms apply immediately upon the entry into force of the Accession Treaty. Secondly, the derogation from the full free movement of workers and services applies in three distinct stages. There is an initial period of two years after accession, during which period national immigration law or measures resulting from bilateral agreements will apply.[2] (paragraph 2). Prior to the end of this period, ie prior to 1 May 2006, any Member State that has not imposed restrictions on free movement of workers from the eight relevant States, or has relaxed them in the interim, is free to impose them or re-impose them.[3] From 1 May 2006, Member States must either grant nationals from the eight relevant States the right to move freely for the purpose of work in accordance with Community law, or continue to apply national measures or bilateral agreements for a further three-year period, up to 30 April 2009.[4] If the option to extend the period of derogation until that date is not taken up, full free movement rights apply.[5] After five years, Member States may extend the derogation until the end of a seven-year period (1 May 2011), if they have notified the Commission before then that there are 'serious disturbances of its labour market or threats thereof.' [6] In the absence of any notification the derogation automatically comes to an end. Thirdly, even if full free movement rights have come into play before the end of the seven-year period, an individual Member State, which 'undergoes or foresees disturbances of its labour market which could seriously threaten the standard of living or level of employment in a given region or occupation', can apply to the Commission to suspend worker rights wholly or in part. The Commission then has two weeks in which to determine the application and decide on the terms of a derogation.[7]

[1] The derogation only applies to the free movement rights contained in Arts 39 and 49 of the EC Treaty (other than those involving the temporary movement of workers), and those rights contained in Arts 1–6 of Regulation 1612/68, such as the right to take up an activity as an employed person in another Member State (para 2). Since the provisions of Directive 68/360/EEC cover much the same ground as Arts 1–6 of Regulation 1612/68 and cannot be disassociated from them, derogation from those provisions is also allowed by para 9.

[2] Annexe XIV, para 2.

[3] This is the view set out in the Government Guide to the European Union (Accessions) Bill. Paras 2 and 3, however, speak of the 'present Member States ...', suggesting a collective rather than individual choice to continue derogation; contrast paras 5 and 7 which speak of '... a Member State ...'.

[4] Annex XIV, para 3.

[5] Annex XIV, para 3.

[6] Annex XIV, para 5.

[7] Annex XIV, para 7. There is also provision in Art 37 of the Act of Accession for a safeguard to be applied until 1 May 2007, which allows new members to apply for authorisation to take protective measures, including derogations from the rules of the EC Treaty, if they have serious economic difficulties. These could be relevant to freedom of establishment or freedom to provide services as well as the free movement of workers. Article 38 provides for a similar safeguard regarding the 'internal market'.

7.9 What about the free movement of workers who were admitted under the domestic law (for example, on a work permit) of one of the Member States either before or after 1 May 2004? The Annexes provide that Accession State workers legally employed on that date and admitted for over 12 months for employment will enjoy continued access to the labour market of that Member State.[1] The same will apply to those admitted to the labour market for a 12-month period after enlargement.[2] So, even though the work permit regime of the particular country restricts employment to a specified job with a specified employer, the Accession State worker will be able to change jobs without having to seek further permission from the authorities. Furthermore, it will be impossible for an existing Member State to remove people on economic grounds if they have already been admitted or are later admitted for longer-term employment during the transitional period.

[1] Annex XIV, para 2.

[2] Annex XIV, para 2.

7.10 The position of the worker may be clear, but there is or may be a problem with the position of family members. Since only Articles 1–6 of Regulation 1612/68 (workers' right to take up an activity as an employed person in another Member State and ancillary rights) are expressly made part of the derogation, implicitly, then, the *other* provisions of that Regulation (concerning equal treatment while in employment, (Articles 7–9) family reunion and the right of family members to employment and education) (Articles 10–12) will apply, *if* a Member State authorises an Accession State national to enter its territory as a worker.[1] The EC rules on social security, expulsions and mutual recognition of qualifications will also apply. However, Annex XIV, paragraph 8 modifies the application of Article 11 of Regulation 1612/68 regarding access to employment. Those family members legally residing in an existing Member State with a worker on the date of accession (1 May 2004) have immediate access to employment if the worker has been authorised to stay there for 12 or more months.[2] Otherwise they will only have access to employment if they have lived there for over 18 months, or from the third year following the date of accession (1 May 2007), whichever comes earlier.[3] It is not expressly stated that the family members have equal access to the labour market, though this must be inferred from the non-discrimination clause in the Annex[4] and from the general provisions of the EC Treaty.[5] Nevertheless, there is a clear problem with this provision. All eight of the relevant new accession States had previously entered into Association Agreements with the European Communities.[6] In each of these agreements, there was a general clause saying that the legally resident spouse and children of a worker employed in the territory of a Member State should, subject to exceptions, have access to the labour market of that Member State during the period of the worker's authorised employment.[7] No waiting period for access was provided for (although conversely there is no right of family reunion under the Agreements). It follows that for family members joining workers during the first three years following enlargement, their right of access to employment will be more limited than it was before accession, and more limited than it remains for nationals of Romania and Bulgaria, who have not yet joined the EU.[8]

---

1   See Statewatch Comments, above.
2   Annex XIV, para 8.
3   Annex XIV, para 8.
4   Annex XIV, para 14.
5   EC Treaty Art 12 (ex Art 6).
6   See below 7.165.
7   See Agreement with Poland, Art 37 (1) 2nd indent, printed in *Butterworths Immigration Law Service* F[6001].
8   See below 7.165 and Statewatch Comments, above.

Implementation in UK law of the Accession Treaty

7.11 In order to give effect in UK law to the Accession Treaty, the European Union (Accessions) Act 2003 amends the definitions of 'the treaties' and 'the Community treaties' in the European Communities Act 1972 to include the 2003 Treaty. In broad terms, it does two things. First, it enables the Accession Treaty to be implemented in UK law, by granting automatic effect to directly applicable Treaty provisions. Secondly, it provides the power to make regulations amending existing UK legislation, to the extent necessary to give nationals of the Czech Republic, Estonia, Latvia, Lithuania, Hungary, Poland, Slovenia and Slovakia ('the eight relevant States') the same rights to work in the UK from 1 May 2004 as are enjoyed by nationals of the States in the European Economic Area (EEA).[1] In fact the Regulations do no such thing, but instead create a complicated registration system, as we shall see, for Eastern European workers, which puts them in the weakest possible bargaining position as against their employers and entirely at the mercy of cockle picking gang masters and the like.

1 The European Economic Area comprised the 15 Member States of the EU, together with Norway, Iceland and Liechtenstein prior to the new accessions.

Registration scheme for workers in accession period

7.12 In order to give force in UK national law to the provisions which regulate the position of nationals from the relevant new Member States of the EU during the transitional period before full free movement rights for workers and their families comes into force, the government has made Regulations which amend the Immigration (European Economic Area) Regulations 2000 ('the 2000 Regulations') and establish a worker registration scheme for workers from the eight relevant States.[1] They came into force on 1 May 2004. If it is right that in setting up the registration scheme and its ancillary provisions, the UK is applying national law, not EC law, the new scheme will be outside the jurisdiction of the European Court.

1 Accession (Immigration and Worker Registration) Regulations 2004, SI 2004/1219.

7.13 *Regulation 3* amends the definition of 'EEA State' in regulation 2(1) of the 2000 Regulations so that it now includes the existing EU countries, the Accession States, Switzerland,[1] Iceland, Liechtenstein and Norway.[2] This will extend the European Community free movement rights, transposed by the 2000 Regulations, to Accession State nationals and their family members, subject to the qualifications made in relation to Accession State workers.

1 The Immigration (Swiss Free Movement of Persons) Regulations 2002, SI 2002/1012, reg 2(1).
2 Accession (Immigration and Worker Registration) Regulations 2004, SI 2004/1219, regs 1(2)(f) and 3, amending the Immigration (European Economic Area) Regulations 2000, SI 2000/2326, reg 2(1).

7.14 *Regulation 4* gives effect to the derogation provided for in the Accession Treaty to regulate access to the United Kingdom labour market by accession State nationals. Under regulation 4(2), nationals from the relevant accession States who come to the United Kingdom to seek work during the transitional period, will not have a right to reside in the United Kingdom by virtue of their work seeker status, but will only be able to do so if they are self-sufficient.[1] The idea of this provision is to deter so called 'benefit scroungers'.[2]

7.14 *European community law and related obligations*

1   Accession (Immigration and Worker Registration) Regulations 2004, SI 2004/1219, reg 4(3). 'Self-sufficient person' is defined in the Immigration (European Economic Area) Regulations 2000, SI 2000/2326, reg 3(1)(e).
2   For EEA workers and benefits see chapter 13 below. However, the detailed implications of the accession regime for social security law are beyond the scope of this work, and for a fuller discussion on access to welfare benefits for nationals of accession States see Nicola Rogers and Rick Scannell *Free Movement of Persons in the Enlarged European Union* (Sweet & Maxwell, 2004), ch 28.

7.15 Some workers from the relevant new Accession Member States may have already acquired settled or similar status under UK domestic immigration law or they may have transitional rights under the Accession Treaty as described above. They will not come within the new transitional registration scheme, which comes into force after 1 May 2004 and can last until 30 April 2009. This is dealt with by regulations 5, 7 and 8. Then there are those who arrived before accession day and were admitted under the ordinary immigration regime with conditions restricting employment, but who now come under the 2000 Regulations, including the registration scheme. Regulation 6 deals with their position.

7.16 Regulation 5 modifies the application of the 2000 Regulations to workers from the relevant accession States who are 'Accession State workers requiring registration', as defined in regulation 2. Broadly speaking, the following rules define those who are required to register under the new transitional regime:

- An 'Accession State worker requiring registration' means a national of a relevant accession State working in the UK during the accession period.[1]
- Someone who, on 30 April 2004, had leave to enter or remain in the UK under the 1971 Act and that leave was not subject to any condition restricting his employment is not an accession State worker requiring registration.[2]
- Someone who was legally working in the UK on 30 April 2004 and had been legally working here without interruption throughout the previous 12 months is not an accession State worker requiring registration.[3]
- Someone who legally works in the United Kingdom without interruption for a period of 12 months falling partly or wholly after 30 April 2004 ceases to be an accession State worker requiring registration at the end of that period of 12 months.[4]
- Someone who is a dual national and is also a national of (a) the United Kingdom; (b) another EEA State, other than a relevant accession State; or (c) Switzerland is not an accession State worker requiring registration.[5]
- A person is not an Accession State worker requiring registration during any period in which he or she is (a) a posted worker; [6] or (b) a family member[7] of a Swiss or EEA national who is in the UK as (i) a worker, other than as an accession State worker requiring registration; (ii) a self-sufficient person; (iii) a retired person; (v) a self-employed person or (v) a student.[8]

1   Accession (Immigration and Worker Registration) Regulations 2004, SI 2004/1219, reg 2(1).

2   SI 2004/1219, reg 2(2).
3   SI 2004/1219, reg 2(3). Someone, who is 'legally working' is defined in reg 2(7). The meaning of 'without interruption' is contained in reg 2(8).
4   SI 2004/1219, reg 2(4). See above fn for the meaning of the key words used.
5   SI 2004/1219, reg 2(5).
6   SI 2004/1219, reg 2(6). 'Posted worker' is defined in reg 2(9)(b).
7   'Family member' is defined in SI 2004/1219, reg 2(9)(c).
8   SI 2004/1219, reg 2(6), as amended by the Immigration (European Economic Area) and Accession (Amendment) Regulations 2004 SI 2004/1236, reg 3(2). 'Self sufficient person' is defined in SI 2004/1219, reg 1(2)(j) and SI 2000/2326, reg 3; 'retired person' and 'student' in reg 3 of SI 2000/2326.

7.17 Under regulations 5(2) to (4) those who are 'Accession State workers requiring registration' will generally only have a right of residence in the UK as workers under the 2000 Regulations during a period in which they are working for an employer for whom they are authorised to work under the workers' registration scheme in Part 3 of these Regulations. Whilst they require registration, neither they nor their family members[1] will be entitled to have a residence permit or document.[2] However, the Immigration Appeal Tribunal has held that Accession nationals who were in the UK at the date of accession should not be removed unless they pose a threat to public health, public policy or public security.[3]

1   'Family member' is defined in Accession (Immigration and Worker Registration) Regulations 2004, SI 2004/1219, reg 2(9)(c), as amended by the Immigration (European Economic Area) and Accession (Amendment) Regulations 2004, SI 2004/1236, reg 3(2).
2   SI 2004/1219, reg 5(5) and (6).
3. Ie, on the same grounds as other EEA nationals (see 7.127ff): *MH (Slovakia)* [2004] UKIAT 00315 'IAT Reported'.

7.18 Part 3 of the Accession Regulations sets out the Accession State worker registration scheme, which will apply to Accession State workers requiring registration.[1] Under regulation 7, workers requiring registration, who are already in legal employment on 30 April 2004, can continue to work for the employer concerned without further registration.[2] Workers requiring registration who begin work on or after 1 May 2004 have to apply, within one month of beginning working, for a registration certificate authorising them to work for the employer concerned if they are to be authorised to work for that employer for more than a month.[3] Regulation 8 sets out the registration procedure. Workers requiring registration will be issued with a registration card and a registration certificate authorising them to work for the employer concerned. A fee of £50 will be changed for the first registration to cover the administrative costs of registration. Regulation 9 makes it an offence for an employer to employ a worker who is not authorised under the registration scheme to work for that employer.

1   Accession (Immigration and Worker Registration) Regulations 2004, SI 2004/1219, regs 7 to 9.
2   SI 2004/1219, reg 7(2)(a).
3   SI 2004/1219, reg 7(2)(b) and (3). Special provision is made in reg 7(4) in relation to seasonal agricultural workers until 31 December 2004.

THE SOURCES AND INSTITUTIONS OF EC LAW

7.19 The EEC Treaty (Treaty of Rome), by which the Common Market was first established In 1959, remains the fundamental source of the constitution of the EC, and distributes functions between the Council, the European Commission, the ECJ and the European Parliament.[1] The Council and the Commission are given the task of making regulations, issuing directives, taking decisions, making recommendations or delivering opinions in accordance with the provisions of the Treaty.[2] The ECJ has the task of interpretation of the Treaty and the acts of Community institutions.[3] Community law consists of the totality of legally enforceable obligations; a wider concept is the *acquis communitaire* which includes the actions and opinions of Community institutions. The *acquis communitaire* is to be respected and built upon by the EU.[4]

[1] See Pt V, Title 1, Arts 189–267 EC (ex Arts 137–198). A full description of the workings of Community law and its institutions is beyond the scope of this work. The reader is referred to Vaughan *Law of the European Communities* (Butterworths); Wyatt and Dashwood *European Union Law* (4th edn, 2000), Sweet & Maxwell; Craig and De Burca (eds) *The Evolution of EU Law* (1999), OUP; Craig and De Burca, *EU Law* (2nd edn, 1998), OUP; Lasok *Law and Institution of the European Union* (7th edn, 2001), Butterworths.

[2] Article 249 EC (ex Art 189). As well as initiating Community legislation the Commission has the task of ensuring that Member States comply with their obligations under Community law and can bring proceedings before the ECJ if they have failed to do so, despite the issue of a Commission opinion: see Art 226 EC (ex Art 169).

[3] Article 234 EC (ex Art 177).

[4] Article 3 EU (ex Art C).

7.20 In its original form the EEC Treaty provided in general terms for the progressive reduction of all the barriers preventing the free movement of nationals of member countries from one EEC country to another.[1] Free movement rights were specifically provided for in connection with economic activities. The key Articles are Articles 39 and 40 EC (ex Articles 48 and 49) which deal with the free movement of workers, [2] Articles 43 EC (ex Article 52) *et seq*, which deal with the right of establishment, including the right to engage in and carry on self-employed occupations, and Articles 48 EC (ex Article 58) *et seq*, which deal with the provision of services in another Member State.[3] Effect is given to these Articles by Community legislation in the form of directives and regulations. Following the Amsterdam Treaty, new Community law may now be adopted under Title IV EC on the position of third-country nationals lawfully resident in the EU.

[1] Article 3(c) EEC.

[2] Article 39 EC (ex Art 48) refers to workers or workers of Member States, Council Regulation (EEC) 1612/68 refers to workers who are nationals of Member States. This has led to a debate as to whether Community competence in respect of 'workers of Member States' extends to a broader class than merely workers who are nationals of such States: See Elspeth Guild 'Discretion, Competence and Migration in the European Union' (1999) EJ M& L 61 at 72–77; R Plender 'Competence, European Community Law and Nationals of Non-Member States' [1990] 39 ICLQ 599; T Hoogenboom 'The Position of those who are not Nationals of the Community Member States' in Cassese, Clapham, Weiler (eds) *Human Rights in the European Community. Methods of Protection* (1991); P Stangos 'Les Ressortissants d'etats Tiers au sein de L'ordre Juridique Communautaire, Cahiers des Communautés Européenes vis-à-vis des Ressortissants de Pays Tiers' in Den Boer (ed) *The Implementation of Schengen: First Widening, now Deepening* (1997).

[3] The text of these Articles is set out in Appendix 1 below.

7.21 The **Single European Act 1987**, which came into force on 1 July 1987, carried the process further and required the Community to adopt measures with the aim of progressively establishing the internal market, which comprises an area 'without internal frontiers in which the free movement of goods, persons, services and capital is ensured in accordance with the provisions of this Treaty'.[1] Shortly before this happened, Germany, France and the three Benelux countries entered into the first Schengen Agreement in 1985, aimed at reducing frontier control between their countries. The Agreement was supplemented by the Schengen Convention of 1990, which came into force in 1995. Schengen marks an important stage in the recent development of EC and EU law and we shall come back to it in more detail at 7.25 below.

[1]   Article 14 EC (ex Art 7a).

7.22 The next stage was the **Maastricht Treaty** or the **Treaty on European Union (TEU)**, which came into force on 1 November 1993. It contained important amendments to the EEC Treaty (the old Treaty of Rome), which now became the EC Treaty. These amendments included the creation of a European citizenship[1] with concomitant rights, of which the most controversial is the right to move and reside freely in the territory of the Member States.[2] It also created the European Union (the EU), which has been described as a temple supported by three pillars. These are: the European Community (based on the old EEC Treaty, as amended), co-operation on a common foreign and security policy (Title V) and co-operation in the fields of justice and home affairs (Title VI). Linking the three aspects of the EU is the European Council—the lintel over the columns, to pursue the architectural metaphor.[3] Under Title VI (the third pillar) a new dimension was added to European immigration law; asylum, border control and immigration policy became matters 'of common interest' to Member States, although dealt with on an inter-governmental basis outside the competence of the EC. The next stage was to bring them within that competence. This was done by the **Treaty of Amsterdam** which entered into force on 1 May 1999. Under it the EC acquired jurisdiction to deal with wider questions of immigration and asylum, bringing the possibility of much greater impact than ever before on the substance of UK immigration law. The Treaty created the framework for future action and legislation. The main changes were to (i) integrate the Schengen *acquis* into the framework of the EU and (ii) move immigration, asylum and civil cooperation from the third pillar of the union into the first pillar (EC) under the new Title IV EC, whilst leaving police, criminal and customs co-operation in the third pillar (Title VI EU). One consequence of all this is that these topics have now become part of EC law within the competence of the EC institutions (the Council, Commission and ECJ).

[1]   Article 17 EC (ex Art 8).
[2]   Article 18 EC (ex Art 8a).
[3]   Treaty on European Union (TEU), Title 1, Arts C, D, E and F (now, after amendments, Arts 3, 4, 5 and 6 EU).

The EC and the EU

7.23 Following the Maastricht and Amsterdam treaties we can now distinguish EC law, the law of the Community, including free movement law, and

243

7.23 *European community law and related obligations*

EU law, the law of the Union, which comprises EC law (the law of the first pillar) and all the inter-governmental co-operation, falling within EU Justice and Home Affairs or the third pillar of the Union.[1] So far as the EC Treaty is concerned, there have been considerable amendments and the whole Treaty has been renumbered. There has also been considerable rewriting of the Treaty on European Union and Articles have been given numbers where previously they had letters, but there have also been some substantial changes. Article 1 EU now also provides that decisions are to be taken 'as openly as possible' to the citizen. Article 2 EU now includes a far more detailed objective than merely 'to develop close co-operation on justice and home affairs'. Now the objective is 'to maintain and develop the Union as an area of freedom, security and justice, in which the free movement of persons is assured in conjunction with appropriate measures with respect to external border controls, asylum, immigration and the prevention and combating of crime'. Article 6(1) EU now provides that 'the Union is founded on principles of liberty, democracy, respect for human rights and fundamental freedoms, and the rule of law'. A new Article 7 EU sets out a procedure by which a Member State judged to be in 'serious and persistent breach' of these principles might have certain of its EU and EC Treaty rights suspended.[2]

[1]   The processes and results of this co-operation have been charted in detail in Peers' *EU Justice and Home Affairs Law* (2000), Pearson Education.
[2]   Peers, above, p 12.

Referring to renumbered Articles of the Treaties

7.24 The renumbering of the Treaties is part of a process to simplify and update. Some Articles and paragraphs which have lapsed and are no longer relevant have been removed. Owing to the potential confusion over renumbering, the ECJ has decided that in identifying the Articles in the various Treaties, the following designations will be used:

(1)   Treaty on European Union – EU;
(2)   Treaty establishing the European Community – EC;
(3)   Euratom Treaty – EA;
(4)   European Coal and Steel Community – CS.

These designations will appear after the Article number, eg Article 23 EC. In addition the court will refer to Articles as they stood before the Amsterdam changes as follows:

(1)   where the Article number but not the text has changed: 'Article 23 EC (ex Article 9)';
(2)   where the text and Article number have changed: 'Article 9 of the EC Treaty (now, after amendment, Article 23 EC)'.

The Schengen Agreements

7.25 The original Schengen Agreement of 14 June 1985[1] had two objectives:

(1)   to reduce common frontier controls by instituting 'a simple visual check on private vehicles crossing the common frontier at a reduced speed without requiring the vehicle to stop';[2]

(2)   to abolish internal controls on all persons, whatever their origins.

The Schengen Convention of 19 June 1990, which came into force on 26 March 1995, aimed to create a zone with only one external border and free movement within it. In order to achieve this, the 1990 Convention established common conditions of entry,[3] including a common visa[4] for non-EU nationals wishing to cross the external borders of the Schengen States.[5]

[1]   See *Butterworths Immigration Law Service*, F[6551].
[2]   Schengen Agreement 1985, Art 2.
[3]   Schengen Convention 1990, Art 9.
[4]   Schengen Convention 1990, Art 10.
[5]   Airports are now considered to be external borders for flights to or from third countries and internal borders for flights between Schengen States. The same applies to seaports. See *Butterworths Immigration Law Service*, F[6508].

Abolition of internal borders

7.26 The Schengen Agreements were a forerunner to the adoption by the Community of measures to get rid of all internal borders between participating States.[1] The first community measure was the insertion of Article 8a (later Article 7a and now Article 14 EC) into the EEC Treaty by the Single European Act 1987, agreed in late 1985 and coming into force in 1987. It requires the EC 'To adopt measures with the aim of progressively establishing the internal market over a period expiring on 31 December 1992...'[2] At the time it came into force, it promised more than it could deliver, since the EC lacked competence under the existing Treaty provisions to adopt the necessary measures.[3]

[1]   Elspeth Guild 'Discretion, Competence and Migration in the European Union' (1999) EJML 61 at 82; D O'Keefe 'Free Movement of Persons and the Single Market' (1992) Eur Law Review 17 at 3–13.
[2]   The internal market means 'an area without internal frontiers in which the free movement of goods, persons, services and capital is ensured in accordance with the provisions of this Treaty'.
[3]   The Commission tried but failed in its attempt to use Art 100 EC for a directive on illegal immigration and employment law: see *Peers* above, p 65.

7.27 This lack of competence is now remedied by the Amsterdam Treaty, with its integration of the Schengen *acquis* into the framework of the EU and the new Title IV, which enables the Community to introduce measures in respect of the movement and residence of third country nationals. The underlying principle remains the completion of the internal market and the abolition of intra-Community borders,[1] even although Title IV gives a 'flanking' Community competence to regulate immigration and asylum, but without any clearly defined goals or objectives, other than the establishment of an area of freedom, security and justice.[2] We deal first with the Schengen *acquis* and then with Title IV.

1   Elspeth Guild 'Discretion, Competence and Migration in the European Union' [1999] EJM & L 61 at 84.
2   Article 61(a) EC.

Schengen acquis

7.28 The Schengen *acquis* consist of the Schengen Agreement of 14 June 1985, the Schengen Convention 1990, the accession protocols and agreements creating new members of Schengen, and the decisions and declarations adopted by the Schengen Executive Committee, as well as the acts adopted for its implementation.[1] Protocol 2 which is annexed to the Treaty on European Union and EC Treaty, applies the Schengen *acquis* to the 13 participating Member States,[2] and brings the provisions of the Schengen *acquis* into the framework of the EU, the idea being that these provisions will be split up and allocated to the relevant part of the EU and EC Treaties, while at the same time preserving a special 'pick and choose' position for the UK and Ireland,[3] and an associate participation for two non-EU States, Norway and Iceland.[4]

1   Annexe to Protocol 2 to TEU and TEC; see *Butterworths Immigration Law Service* F[62]–[76].
2   The participating Member States are Austria, Belgium, Denmark, France, Finland, Germany, Greece, Italy, Luxembourg, Netherlands, Portugal, Spain and Sweden.
3   Now an 'opt out' with the right to opt in; see Peers *EU Justice and Home Affairs Law* (2000), Pearson Education, p 56; 7.33 below.
4   Protocol 2, Art 6. The Council concluded an agreement with Norway and Iceland in 1999 (OJ 1999 L 176/35) setting out procedures for their 'association' with existing Schengen *acquis* and measures building on it, and together with Ireland and the UK made a separate agreement with Norway and Iceland on the one hand and the UK and Ireland on the other to the extent that the UK and Ireland opted in to the Schengen *acquis*: see *Peers* above, p 57.

7.29 In May 1999 the Council agreed on the allocation of all the Schengen *acquis* with the exception of the Schengen Information Services (SIS), which is used by police and customs to prevent crime and by the immigration authorities to control entry and is, therefore, difficult to place in either the Treaty on European Union or the EC Treaty.[1] In dealing with the allocation it was decided that not all the *acquis* would be allocated.[2] For example, the asylum provisions of Schengen had been overtaken by the ratification of the Dublin Convention and did not, therefore, need to be allocated.[3] After allocation, measures building upon the *acquis* became regular parts of EC or EU law with no special rules applying, or as Peers puts it: 'Conceptually, this is the legal equivalent of breaking a large lump of sugar into two separate lumps, and then dissolving these lumps into two separate cups of tea.'[4] In the immigration field, the Schengen *acquis* thus form a further basis for community legislation on border controls and the position of third-country nationals within the EC.

1   Decision of May 1999 (OJ 1999 L 176/17). Peers *EU Justice and Home Affairs Law*, 2000, Pearson Education, p 59. As a result of the failure to allocate the Schengen Information Services provisions the 'default' position operates and they are to be regarded as third pillar Acts based on Title VI of the Treaty on European Union: see Protocol 2, Art 2.1.
2   *Peers* above, p 57.

³   *Peers* above, p 57.
⁴   *Peers* above, p 57.

EC TITLE IV PROGRAMME AND DEVELOPMENT

Programme

7.30 Title IV of the EC Treaty, contained in Articles 61 to 69 sets a programme of legislation to be carried out by the Council in a number of fields, including immigration and asylum.[1] In the field of immigration and asylum, Article 61 provides that the Council shall adopt:

(a)   measures within five years to complete the establishment of the internal market under Article 14 EC and to put in place directly related 'flanking' measures on external border controls, asylum and immigration, and measures to prevent and combat crime;[2]

(b)   other measures in the fields of asylum, immigration and safeguarding the rights of third-country nationals;[3]

Article 62 EC provides that the Council shall adopt within five years:

(1)   measures with a view to ensuring, in compliance with Article 14, the absence of any controls on persons, whether citizens of the Union or nationals of third countries, when crossing internal borders;

(2)   measures on the crossing of the external borders of the Member States including standards and procedures to be followed by Member States in carrying out checks on persons at such borders, and rules on visas.

(3)   measures setting out the conditions under which nationals of third countries shall have the freedom to travel within the territory of the Member States during a period of no more than three months.

Article 62 complements Article 14 EC (ex Article 7a) and provides the legal base for the measures which the Community will need to take in order to achieve the goal of abolishing internal borders. But its provisions also match closely the bulk of Articles 2 to 27 of the Schengen Convention 1990, and it is no surprise that the bulk of these provisions have in fact been allocated by the Council, when it allocated the Schengen *acquis,* to parts of Article 62.[4] If Article 14 still has any independent legal effect separate from Title IV, it will be open to all national courts and tribunals in all Member States to refer questions to the ECJ for interpretation. In respect of Article 62 the jurisdiction of the ECJ is much more limited, as we shall see.[5]

¹   Article 61(a) EC. The Council must normally act unanimously: see Article 67 EC. However, in framing new measures under Article 62, the Council may act on a qualified majority on a proposal from the Commission and after consultation with the European Parliament: Article 67(3) EC. This contrasts with the position on the rest of Title IV.
²   Article 61(a) EC.
³   Article 61(b) EC.
⁴   Final decision on allocation of Schengen *acquis* OJ 1999 L 176/17. A few of the provisions on legal and illegal migration were allocated to Article 63(3) EC.
⁵   See 7.47 below. There may be a further problem with Article 62(2)(b)(i) and (ii) EC, which deal with common visas. These sub-paragraphs re-enact ex-Article 100C, which was repealed by the Amsterdam Treaty. This was one of the areas which was under Community

competence after the Treaty on European Union and was subject to two regulations: (i) on a uniform visa format (Council Regulation (EC) 1683/95) and (ii) on the list of third-country nationals who need visas to enter the EC (Council Regulation (EC) 539/01 of 15 March 2001, which replaced Council Regulation (EC) 574/99). Both Regulations are binding on all EU Member States, including the UK and Ireland. Ex-Article 100C was limited, as is Article 62(2)(b)(i), to visas 'when crossing the external borders'. In 1998 the ECJ held that the Article was not drafted widely enough to enable joint measures on the airside transit visa (ATV): Case C-170/96 *EU Commission v EU Council* [1998] 2 CMLR 1092. According to a Commission working paper, Article 62 may not be wide enough to accommodate a proposed regulation on the same subject, because the relevant sub-sections are taken from ex-Article 100C (Commission Staff Working Paper on Visa Policy, 16 July 1999, SEC (1999) 1213, para 6. Initiative of Finland with a view to adoption of Council Regulation on airport transit arrangements 10867/99 DGH1).

7.31 As regards asylum, Article 63 EC requires the Council to adopt within five years:[1]

(1)   Measures of asylum in accordance with the Refugee Convention of 1951 and the Protocol of 1967 and other relevant treaties, within the following areas:

    (a)   criteria and mechanisms for determining which Member State is responsible for considering an asylum application submitted by a third country national in one of the Member States;

    (b)   minimum standards on the reception of asylum seekers in Member States;

    (c)   minimum standards with respect to the qualification of nationals of third countries as refugees;

    (d)   minimum standards on procedures in Member States for granting or withdrawing refugee status.

(2)   Measures on refugees and displaced persons within the following areas:

    (a)   minimum standards for giving temporary protection to displaced persons from third countries who cannot return to their country of origin and for persons who otherwise need international protection;

    (b)   promoting a balance of effort between Member States in receiving and bearing the consequences of receiving refugees and displaced persons.

Title IV does not provide for Community powers over every aspect of immigration policy, and the precise scope is still a matter for debate.[2] Legal and illegal migration is now addressed in Articles 63(3) and (4) of the EC Treaty, which enable the Council to adopt measures on immigration, including conditions of entry and residence, family reunion, and removal of illegal immigrants.

[1]   These provisions were drafted with many of the pre-existing EU asylum measures in mind. Article 63(1)(a) EC refers to the old Dublin Convention; Art 63(1)(b) EC to the aborted Joint Position; 63(1)(c) EC to the 1996 Joint Position and so forth (See Peers' *EU Justice and Home Affairs Law* (2000), Pearson Education at p 127). The only part of Art 63 EC which is not matched by previous efforts under the EU is Art 63(2)(a) EC, which clearly refers to subsidiary protection. Then there is Protocol 6, which deals with asylum for EC nationals: see 12.107 below.

[2]   See Hailbronner 'European Immigration and Asylum Law after the Amsterdam Treaty' (1998) 35 CMLR 1047; 'Treaty of Amsterdam and Migration Law' (1999) EHML 12; Monat 'Justice and Home Affairs in the Treaty of Amsterdam' (1998) 23 ELR EV 320; *Peers* fn 1 above, pp 100–101.

7.32 In dealing with the new powers, it should also be noted that all the pre-Amsterdam EC law competences on migration still apply, including the working conditions of third-country nationals after the integration of the Agreement on Social Policy into the main EC Treaty under Article 137(3) EC. In *El-Yassini* the ECJ ruled that, in some circumstances, immigration status falls within the concept of 'working conditions'.[1] Lastly it should be noted that Article 64 EC substantially re-enacts the 'national safeguard' clauses contained in ex Article 100C(2) and (5). These are no longer confined to safeguards on visas, but cover the whole Title IV package, providing for Council measures to meet a 'sudden inflow' to any particular Member State of third country nationals[2] and to make clear that Title IV does not affect each Member State's responsibility for the maintenance of law and order and safeguarding its own internal security.[3]

[1] Case C-416/96 *El-Yassini v Secretary of State for the Home Department* [1999] ECR I-1209.
[2] Article 62(2) EC.
[3] Article 64(1) EC.

UK and Ireland

7.33 However, notwithstanding the integration of the Schengen *acquis* into the framework of the EU and all the new EC provisions in Title IV enabling the Community to issue regulations and directives on immigration, asylum and the common visa, the UK and Ireland have decided not to surrender sovereignty over immigration and asylum policy, but to keep their own systems of immigration control for the time being. This is done in a number of ways. First, Protocol 2, which integrates the Schengen *acquis* into the framework of the EU, gives the UK and Ireland an extraordinary 'opt out, opt in' position.[1] Secondly, Protocol 3, which is annexed to both Treaties, specifically exempts the UK and Ireland[2] from any EC laws or measures requiring the abolition of border controls and allows them to exercise frontier control over persons seeking to enter.[3] The third exempting measure is Protocol 4, which provides that the UK and Ireland are to take no part in the adoption of the new Community legislation under Title IV on immigration, asylum or visas,[4] unless either or both have notified the President of the Council that they wish to do so.[5] Similarly, neither country is bound by any of the provisions of Title IV of the Treaty establishing the EC, any measure adopted pursuant to that Title, or provision of any international agreement concluded by the Community pursuant to it, or any decision of the ECJ interpreting any such provision or measure.[6] They only become bound by new asylum or immigration measures adopted by the Council under this Title, if they notify the Council and Commission that they wish to accept them.[7] They can do so at any time.[8] A separate Protocol exempts Denmark in much the same way as the UK and Ireland, except that it is not exempted from measures relating to a common entry visa.[9]

[1] Protocol 2, Art 4 and 5. So far the UK has indicated that it wishes to take part in the criminal and policing rules of the Schengen *acquis*, except for cross-border pursuits, with related Schengen Information Services access, plus Arts 26 (carriers' liability) and 27 (illegal immigration). This was agreed by the EC Council on 2 December 1999, except for the territorial scope and partial access to Schengen Information Systems. The UK has also

opted in to the asylum provisions set out in Article 63: see below. For a clear exposition of opt-outs in this area see *Statewatch* Briefing: 'Vetoes, opt-outs and EU immigration and asylum law', October 2004, *Statewatch* website.

2   Protocol 3, Arts 1 and 2. The exemption of Ireland is conditional on the continuance of the common travel area.

3   Protocol 3, Art 1. Art 2 further entitles the UK and Ireland to maintain the common travel area and to check individuals coming from other Member States, no matter what the Treaties say or what measures other Member States may take. Art 3 allows other Member States to have reciprocal control on persons seeking to enter their territory from Ireland or the UK.

4   Protocol 4, Art 1.

5   Protocol 4, Art 3.

6   Protocol 4, Art 2.

7   Protocol 4, Art 4. In March 1999 the UK government indicated that in principle it would opt into all civil co-operation and asylum measures, along with many immigration and external border control ones: Peers *EU Justice and Home Affairs Law*, 2000, Pearson Education, p 55. Ireland's position is set out in Unilateral Declaration 4 to Amsterdam Treaty; see *Butterworths Immigration Law Service*, at F[281].

8   Article 11(3) EC, as adapted by Protocol 3, Art 4.

9   Protocol 5, Art 4.

Title IV Developments

Asylum

7.34   In the field of asylum, measures have been adopted across a wide range. They are: (1) Decision 2000/596 on the European Refugee Fund;[1] (2) Regulation 2725/2000 establishing the Eurodac system of fingerprinting for the effective application of Dublin II;[2] (3) Directive 2001/55 on minimum standards for giving temporary protection in the event of a mass influx of displaced persons;[3] (4) Regulation 407/2002 implementing Eurodac;[4] (5) Directive 2003/9 on reception conditions, setting out the minimum standards for the conditions of reception for asylum seekers;[5] (6) Dublin II Regulation 343/2003;[6] (7) Regulation 1560/2003 implementing Dublin II;[7] (8) Directive 2004/83 on the refugee definition and the content of international protection, setting out the minimum standards required to qualify as a refugee or person otherwise needing international protection and the content of the protection to be granted.[8] The terms of the Directive on Asylum Procedures[9] have been agreed, but it has not yet been adopted. The UK has opted into all of these measures; Ireland into all except Directive 2003/9 on reception conditions. Various other measures are on the table, such as a draft Regulation on safe third countries proposed by Austria (OJ 2003 C 17); a proposed Decision on an extension of the European Refugee Fund; and a proposal for a Directive on long-term resident status for refugees and persons with subsidiary protection (March 2004). However, the Member States have become deadlocked on trying to agree a list of safe countries of origin, some of them even agreeing that a country should be included, when their comments make it clear that they do not regard the country as safe.[10]

1   OJ 2000 L 252/12.

2   OJ 2000 L 316/1, in operation on 15 January 2003.

3   OJ 2001 L 212/12, to be implemented by 31 December 2002.

4   OJ 2002 L 62/1.

5   OJ 2003 L 31/18.

6   OJ 2003 L 50/1, in force 1.9.03. The direct effect of this measure in asylum law is of particular importance: see 12.150 below.
7   OJ 2003 L 222/3, in force 6 September 2003.
8   OJ 2004 L304/12, in force 20 October 2004; measures in compliance to be brought in by Member States by 10 October 2006 (Art 38). This means that any provisions of the Directive which are of direct effect can be relied on in the national courts of any Member State as from 20 October 2004. The second date is the date on which Member States must have enacted measures to give effect to the provisions of the Directive. For direct effect see 7.41ff below.
9   COM (2000) 578); amended COM (2002) 326, 18 Jun 2002 (OJ 2002 C 291 E/143).
10   *Statewatch* Press Statement 27 September 2004; see *Statewatch* website.

Borders and visas

7.35 Council Directive 2004/82/EC on the obligation of carriers to communicate passenger data to immigration authorities came into force on 5 September 2004,[1] amidst controversy over the additional power to transmit this data to law enforcement agencies, which may exceed the Council's mandate under Articles 62(2)(a) and 63(3)(b). The UK and Ireland have opted in these measures. When it comes to other new measures which have been adopted on border control and visas, the UK has opted out of all them, except those dealing with visa stickers and a common visa format. Ireland has said 'no' to all of them. The following is the list of adopted measures, all of them Regulations: (1) Regulation 539/2001 establishing visa list;[2] (2) Regulation 789/2001 on the procedure for amending Common Consular Instructions;[3] (3) Regulation 790/2001 on the procedure for amending borders manual;[4] (4) Regulation 1091/2001 on freedom to travel for holders of long-term visas;[5] (5) Regulation 2414/2001 moving Romania to the 'white list' of nationals not requiring visas;[6] (6) Regulation 333/2002 on visa stickers for persons coming from unrecognised entities;[7] (7) Regulation 334/2002 amending Regulation 1683/95 on common visa format;[8] (8) Regulation 415/2003 on visas at the border and visas for seamen;[9] (9) Regulation 453/2003 on the visa list;[10] (10) Regulation 693/2003 on 'Facilitated Travel Documents';[11] (11) Regulation 694/2003 on format for facilitated travel documents;[12] (12) Regulation 1295/2003 on special rules for the Olympic games;[13] (13) Regulation 871/2004 on new functions for the Schengen Information System, including in the fight against terrorism;[14] (14) Regulation 2007/2004 establishing a European Agency for the Management of Operational Cooperation at the EU External Borders;[15] (15) Regulation 2133/2004 on the requirement to stamp the travel documents of third country nationals when they cross EU external borders.[16] In addition to the Regulations there have been a number of implementing decisions of a very technical nature, most of which are of no concern to the UK, the government having opted out of them. Then there are a whole lot more measures in the pipeline, the only one in which the government shows any interest being a manual containing a standard form of refusal and standard rules for checks on minors; necessary but not very exciting stuff.

1   OJ 2004 L 261/24.
2   OJ 2001 L 81/1. The UK 'appears to have' opted in to this, according to the Statewatch legislative observatory, citing Council document 14241/01 of 23 November 2001.

³ OJ 2001 L 116/2. The UK 'appears to have' opted in to this: see fn 2 above. The validity of this and the next Regulation (ie Regs 789 and 790) is under challenge in the European Court in Case C-257/01, *Commission v Council* [2005] All ER (D) 115 (Jan).
⁴ OJ 2001 L 116/5.
⁵ OJ 2001 L 150/4.
⁶ OJ 2001 L 327/1. The issue of whether Romanians need visas is before the European Court in Case C-51/03 *Georgescu*.
⁷ OJ 2002 L 53/4.
⁸ OJ 2002 L 53/7.
⁹ OJ 2003 L 64/1.
¹⁰ OJ 2003 L 69/10.
¹¹ OJ 2003 L 99/8.
¹² OJ 2003 L 99/15.
¹³ OJ 2003 L 183/1.
¹⁴ OJ 2004 L 162/2.
¹⁵ OJ 2004 L 349/1. The Agency took up its responsibilities on 1 May 2005.
¹⁶ OJ 2004 L 369/5.

Irregular migration

7.36 As regards irregular migration, the UK and Ireland have opted in to all the new measures. The following have been adopted: (1) Directive 2001/40 on the mutual recognition of expulsion decisions;[1] (2) Directive 2001/51 on carrier sanctions;[2] (3) Regulation 2424/2001 on funding SIS II;[3] (4) Decision 2001/886/JHA on funding SIS II;[4] (5) Framework Decision on trafficking in persons;[5] (6) Directive 2002/90 defining the facilitation of unauthorised entry, transit and residence;[6] (7) Directive 2003/110 on assistance with transit for expulsion by air,[7] (8) Directive 2004/82 on the transmission of passenger data, referred to above,[8] (9) Conclusions on transit for expulsion by land or sea;[9] (10) Decision on joint flights for expulsion.[10] The UK has opted out of Directive 2004/81 on residence permits for victims of human trafficking or facilitation,[11] the only measure designed for a humanitarian purpose.

¹ OJ 2001 L 150/47; to be implemented by 2 December 2002.
² OJ 2001 L 187/45; to be implemented by 11 February 2003.
³ OJ 2001 L 328/4.
⁴ OJ 2001 L 328/1.
⁵ OJ 2002 L 203/1.
⁶ OJ 2002 L 328/17.
⁷ OJ 2003 L 321/26.
⁸ OJ 2004 L 261/24, 7.35 above.
⁹ Replacing a proposed Directive, at OJ 2003 C 223. The Conclusions as adopted are not yet published.
¹⁰ OJ 2004 L 261/28.
¹¹ OJ 2004 L 261/19. Other measures include Regulation 871/2004 on future functionalities for SIS (OJ 2004 L 162/29). Proposed measures include a Decision on costs of expulsion, implementing Art 24 Schengen and Dir 2001/40 (COM (2003) 49) which the UK has opted into; a Decision on an early warning system proposed by the Commission (COM (2003) 727, 25.11.2003). Other developments include an Action Plan on illegal immigration (OJ 2002 C 142) and a Commission proposal for a Directive on minimum standards on return.

Legal migration

7.37 The following measures have been adopted: (1) Regulation 1091/2001 of 28 May 2001 on freedom of movement with a long-stay visa, which enables long term visa holders to travel more than once to other Member States, which the UK has opted out of;[1] (2) Regulation 1030/2002 on a uniform residence permit;[2] (3) Regulation 859/2003 on third-country nationals' social security;[3] (4) Directive 2003/86 on family reunion;[4] (5) Directive 2003/109 on long-term residents,[5] and (6) Directive 2004/114 on the conditions of admission of third-country nationals for the purposes of studies, pupil exchange, unremunerated training or voluntary service.[6] The UK and Ireland have opted into numbers (2) and (3) only. Proposed measures include a Directive on economic migration,[7] which only the Irish have opted into. Then there is a proposal for amending residence permits to allow the insertion of biometric details.[8]

1   OJ 2001 L 150/4.
2   OJ 2002 L 157/1.
3   OJ 2003 L 124/1.
4   OJ 2003 L 251/12.
5   OJ 2004 L 16/44.
6   OJ L375/12, entered into force 12 January 2005.
7   COM (2001) 386, OJ 2001 C 332 E/248.
8   COM (2003) 558, 24.9.03 (proposed regulation amending Regulation 1683/95 on visa format).

THE APPLICATION OF EC FREE MOVEMENT LAW

7.38 There are three principal ways in which effect is given to EC law in the domestic legal systems of Member States: (i) the enactment of national measures to give effect to Community obligations; (ii) the duty of national courts to interpret general legislation to conform with Community obligations; and (iii) finally, the doctrine of direct effect, where aggrieved individuals can rely on the Community duty as directly applicable, although not specifically so enacted. There is an inter-relationship between the three. In the area of free movement, for example, we find effect being given to EC law by section 7 of the Immigration Act 1988, by the Immigration Rules, and by the Immigration (European Economic Area) Regulations 2000.[1] At the same time, measures of EC law are directly applicable, in ways we explore below. Thirdly, UK courts are bound by Community jurisprudence to interpret all measures within the field of Community competence in accordance with the principles and policy of the Community obligation giving rise to these measures. This has been described as the 'teleological' principle of construction, frequently at odds with the common law concept of strict statutory construction.[2] Courts must interpret all statutes and inferior measures, whether passed before or after the obligation arose, so that they accord with the requirements of Community law, if it is possible to do so without distortion.[3] This principle of construction has now been adopted for UK courts dealing with human rights by section 3 of the Human Rights Act 1998.[4]

1   SI 2000/2326.
2   See Lord Denning in *James Buchanan & Co Ltd v Babco Forwarding and Shipping (UK) Ltd* [1977] 1 All ER 518 at 522, CA; *Freight Transport Association Ltd v London Boroughs Transport Committee* [1991] 3 All ER 915, [1991] 1 WLR 828, HL; *R v Secretary of State for the Home Department, ex p Adams* [1995] All ER (EC) 177, DC.
3   *Duke v GEC Reliance Ltd* [1988] AC 618, [1988] 1 All ER 626, HL; Case C-106/89 *Marleasing SA v La Comercial Internacional de Alimentacion SA* [1990] ECR I-4135, [1992] 1 CMLR 305, ECJ.

⁴   It has been described as a 'new canon of interpretation' and 'a strong adjuration' by Lord Cooke in *R v DPP, ex p Kebeline* [1999] 4 All ER 801, at 837.

National measures

7.39   In the UK, the duty of giving effect to EC Treaty rights is achieved by the European Communities Act 1972. The Act has been extensively amended as the Community has developed from Common Market to European Union. The latest amendments are by the European Union (Accessions) Act 2003, which makes provision for the consequences of the accession of ten new Member States to the EU on 1 May 2004 (see 7.6 and 7.11 above). The key sections of the 1972 Act, as amended, are set out in the Appendix. We do not print those parts of the amending Acts of 1993 or 1998 which stand alone, because they do not relate to free movement of persons.¹ The European Economic Area Act 1993 was passed to make provision in respect of the EEA following the Agreement on the European Economic Area of 2 May 1992 and Protocol of 17 March 1993. The 1992 Agreement is a Community Treaty and has direct effect by virtue of the 1972 Act.³ Section 2 of the European Economic Area Act 1993 makes provision for a consistent application of EC law to the whole of the EEA, and section 3 ensures that implementing Orders in Council, passed under the powers set out in the 1972 Act, apply to the EEA.

¹   See 17 *Halsbury's Statutes* (4th edn) for the full text of all relevant statutes.
²   See European Communities Act 1972, ss 1 and 2.

7.40   By section 2 of the European Communities Act 1972, provision is made for regulations and directives of the EEC to have effect in the UK. This means that Community legislation is directly applicable in accordance with the principles discussed at 7.41–7.43 below. It creates rights which British courts must protect. The UK government initially sought to implement the free movement directives by provisions in the Immigration Rules relating to EC nationals. But this was woefully inadequate; it left in place the statutory regime of requiring EC nationals to obtain leave to enter, which was a breach of Community law.¹ The right to enter for a Community purpose flows directly from EC law rather than from permission given by an official. Thus a residence permit issued under Community law is only evidence of this right and not the source of it.² Visas and other formalities not envisaged by Community law cannot be required; under EC law the only formal requirement at the frontier is production of a passport or national identity document.³ This fundamental principle of EC law was eventually given effect in UK statute law by section 7 of the Immigration Act 1988, which expressly absolved EC nationals from the need to obtain leave when exercising enforceable Community law rights,⁴ and enabled the Secretary of State for the Home Department to make provision for a limited period of automatic leave to be given to EC nationals who do not benefit from an EC free movement right. Section 7 was not brought into force until the Immigration (European Economic Area) Order 1994 took effect on 20 July 1994.⁵ Now the main implementing measure is the Immigration (European Economic Area) Regulations 2000,⁶ which came into effect on 2 October 2000.

1 See especially Case C-157/79 *R v Pieck* [1981] QB 571, [1981] 3 All ER 46, ECJ; Case 321/87 *EC Commission v Belgium* [1989] ECR 997, [1990] 2 CMLR 492, ECJ.

2 *R v Pieck* above; *Commission v Belgium* above; Case C-59/85 *Netherlands v Reed* [1986] ECR 1283, [1987] 2 CMLR 448; Case C-357/89 *Raulin v Minister van Onderwijs en Wetenschappen* [1992] ECR I-1027, [1994] 1 CMLR 227, ECJ.

3 See Council Directive (EEC) 68/360, Art 3; Immigration (European Economic Area) Order 1994, SI 1994/1895, Art 12.

4 See Immigration Act 1988, s 12(3) and (4) and the Immigration Act 1988 (Commencement No 1) Order 1988, SI 1988/1133.

5 SI 1994/1923.

6 SI 2000/2326, as amended by the Amendment Regulations SI 2001/865, 2003/549, 2003/3188, 2004/1219, 2004/1236, 2005/47 and 2005/671, and modified in relation to Swiss nationals, family members and posted workers by SI 2002/1241.

Direct effect

7.41 The doctrine of direct effect began as a way of bringing into effect provisions of the common market Treaties, even though Member States were dragging their feet over completion of timetables set out in the Treaties. Once the timetable for implementation has expired, the doctrine allows aggrieved individuals or institutions to seek direct implementation of a Community measure against the State or its emanations if the obligation is sufficiently precise to be capable of direct enforcement.[1] This is the so-called vertical effect, as opposed to the horizontal effect, which applies when one private citizen or corporation sues another.[2] Plainly, individuals who have free movement rights or other rights under Community law which the UK has failed to implement may invoke the direct applicability of the measure, and thus come within its 'vertical effect'. Decisions in the national courts suggest that direct effect may be relied on by organisations such as the Equal Opportunities Commission, as well as individuals aggrieved by particular decisions.[3]

1 Case 26/62 *Algemene Transport-en Expeditie Onderneming van Gend & Loos NV v Nederlandse administratie der belastingen* [1963] ECR 1, [1963] CMLR 105, ECJ; Case 104/81 *Hauptzollamt Mainz v C A Kupferberg & Cie KG* [1982] ECR 3641, [1983] 1 CMLR 1, ECJ; Case 152/84 *Marshall v Southampton and South West Hampshire Area Health Authority* [1986] ECR 723, [1986] 1 CMLR 688, ECJ; Case C-188/89 *Foster v British Gas* [1991] 2 AC 306, [1991] 2 All ER 705, HL; *Webb v Emo Air Cargo (UK) Ltd* [1992] 4 All ER 929, [1993] 1 WLR 49, HL; Case C-127/92 *Enderby v Frenchay Health Authority* [1994] 1 All ER 495, [1994] 1 CMLR 8, ECJ. Article 39 (ex Art 48) EC may also have horizontal effect: see Case 36/74 *Walrave* [1974] ECR 1405.

2 See *Angonese Cassa di Risparmio di Bolzano SpA* Case C-281/98 [2000] All ER (EC) 577, where the ECJ stated at para 36 that the prohibition of discrimination in Art 39 EC (ex Art 48) applies to private persons as well as public bodies; see also Case 36/74 *Walrave and Koch v Association Union Cycliste Int* [1974] ECR 1405, para 16 (rules made by private persons or bodies aimed at regulating gainful employment in a collective manner); *Union Royale Belge des Societos de Football Association ASBL v Bosman* [1995] ECR I-4921, at paras 84 and 87 (agreements or acts concluded by private persons or bodies which determine the terms on which professional sportsmen can engage in professional sport); Joined Cases C-51/96 and C-191/97 *Deliège* and *Lehtonen* 11 April 2000 (judo and basketball rules); *Wilander v Tobin* [1997] 2 CMLR 346, CA (rules of Tennis Federation regarding drugs).

3 *R v Secretary of State for Employment, ex p Equal Opportunities Commission* [1995] 1 AC 1, [1994] 1 All ER 910, HL. The decisions on *locus standi* in judicial review have also established that representative organisations with a proven interest in the subject-matter of the decision may be able to challenge decisions on grounds of Community law: *R v Inspectorate of Pollution, ex p Greenpeace* [1994] 4 All ER 321, [1994] 1 WLR

570, CA; *R v Secretary of State for the Environment, ex p Friends of the Earth Ltd* [1994] 2 CMLR 760. Thus, organisations such as the Joint Council for the Welfare of Immigrants (JCWI) or the Immigration Law Practitioners' Association (ILPA) could seek judicial review of Immigration Rules that are not in accordance with Community law.

Direct effect of Treaty obligations

7.42 Articles 39, 43 and 50 EC (ex Articles 48, 52 and 60) are now directly applicable.[1] The free movement provisions contained within them are subject to important qualifications which give Member States an element of discretion in enforcement, on grounds of public policy, public security or public health. However, the ECJ has ruled that this is no bar to the direct effectiveness of these provisions.[2] There is a distinction between obligations which are sufficiently precise to be binding and those which have the character of a general programme or aspiration. The existence of direct effect turns on the context of the Article in question, so similar words in different measures may result in different interpretations as to direct effect. Thus the provisions for free movement in the EC/Turkish Association Agreement were held not to be capable of direct effect notwithstanding the expiry of the transitional period, whereas the specific decisions of the Association Council established under that Agreement could be if they produced clear and precise obligations not subject to the adoption of any subsequent measure.[3] In *Savas*[4] the court held that a standstill provision in Article 41(1) of the Additional Protocol to the Turkish Agreement was of direct effect, which means that the UK has to apply the 1973 business rules to Turkish business people seeking to establish themselves in the UK. In *El-Yassini*[5] an anti-discrimination clause, Art 40 of the EEC Moroccan Cooperation Agreement, was held to be of direct effect. The ECJ has held that a provision in an agreement with non-Member States is directly effective when, regard being had to its wording and the purpose and nature of the agreement, the provision contains a precise and clear obligation which is not subject in its implementation or effects to the adoption of any subsequent measure.[6]

---

[1] Case 2/74 *Reyners v Belgium* [1974] ECR 631, [1974] 2 CMLR 305, ECJ; Case 33/74 *Van Binsbergen v Bestuur van de Bedrijfsvereniging voor de Metaalnijverheid* [1974] ECR 1299, [1975] 1 CMLR 298, ECJ. If a provision of national law is incompatible with a directly applicable provision of the EEC Treaty and is retained unchanged, this in itself constitutes an infringement of the Treaty: Case 168/85 *Commission v Italy* [1986] ECR 2945, [1988] 1 CMLR 580, ECJ; Case 147/86 *Commission v Greece* [1988] ECR 1637, [1989] 2 CMLR 845, ECJ. For the superior position of EC law in the UK see Case C-213/89 *R v Secretary of State for Transport, ex p Factortame (No 2)* [1991] 1 AC 603, [1990] ECR I-2433, ECJ and *(No 3)* [1992] QB 680, [1991] ECR I-3905, ECJ.

[2] Case 41/74 *Van Duyn v Home Office (No 2)* [1974] ECR 1337, [1975] 1 CMLR 1, ECJ. See further on direct applicability of Arts 59 and 60 EC Case 33/74 *Van Binsbergen v Bestuur van de Bedrijfsvereniging voor de Metaalnijverheid* [1974] ECR 1299, [1975] 1 CMLR 298, ECJ.

[3] Case 12/86 *Demirel v Stadt Schwäbisch Gmünd* [1987] ECR 3719, [1989] 1 CMLR 421, ECJ; Case C-192/89 *Sevince v Staatsecretaris van Justitie* [1990] ECR I-3461, [1992] 2 CMLR 57, ECJ; *R v Secretary of State for the Home Department, ex p Narin* [1990] 2 CMLR 233, CA; Case C-237/91 *Kus v Landeshauptstadt Wiesbaden* [1992] ECR I-6781, [1993] 2 CMLR 887, ECJ. See also Case C-312/91 *Metalsa Srl v Public Prosecutor (Italy)* [1994] 2 CMLR 121, ECJ where the court gave a different interpretation to a provision of the EEC-Austria free trade Agreement identical to the EEC Treaty.

[4] *R v Secretary of State for the Home Department, ex p Savas* Case C-37/98 [2000] 1 WLR 1828; see 7.162 below.

5   *El-Yassini v Secretary of State for the Home Department* Case C-416/96 [1999] ECR
     I-1209, ECJ.
6   Case C-432/92 *R v Ministry of Agriculture, Fisheries and Food, ex p Anastasiou
     (Pissouri) Ltd* [1995] 1 CMLR 569, ECJ (Original Protocol to EEC Cyprus Association
     Agreement held to be of direct effect).

Direct effect of regulations and directives

7.43 The position with regulations and directives is simpler. Under Article 249 EC (ex Article 189), regulations are 'binding in their entirety and take direct effect in each Member State', and directives are 'binding as to the result to be achieved'. As regards regulations, this means that they are to be treated as law, and national courts must take judicial notice of them in their entirety. Depending on their proper interpretation, specific provisions may bestow on individuals rights as against other individuals or a Member State.[1] Although there is no mention of directives having direct effect, a series of court decisions has in effect put them on exactly the same footing as regulations. In Case 41/74 *Van Duyn v Home Office (No 2)*[2] the ECJ stated that a directive which itself imposed substantive obligations could be directly effective. Otherwise the 'useful effect' of the directive would be weakened. What this means in practice is that Community rules are to be enforced by national courts and take precedence over the provisions of national law. This was stated quite clearly by the ECJ in *Rutili v Minister for the Interior*,[3] where the court referred to some of the free movement provisions contained in directives and said:

> 'The effect of all these provisions, without exception, is to impose duties on Member States, and it is, accordingly, for the courts to give the rules of the Community Law which may be pleaded before them precedence over the provisions of national law.' (paragraph 16)

The doctrine of direct effect is likely to have a considerable impact on asylum law, through the Dublin regulation and the Directives governing qualification and procedures for obtaining refugee status.[4]

1   Case 43/71 *Politi v Italian Ministry of Finance* [1971] ECR 1039, para 9; Case 93/71
     Leonesio v Italian Ministry of Agriculture and Forestry [1972] ECR 287 at 300. See Wyatt
     and Dashwood 7.19 fn 1, pp 84–88.
2   [1974] ECR 1337, [1975] 1 CMLR 1, ECJ.
3   Case 36/75 [1975] ECR 1219, [1976] 1 CMLR 140, ECJ. The superiority of Community
     law to municipal law, both common law and statutory, was exemplified most clearly in *R v
     Secretary of State for Transport, ex p Factortame (No 2)* [1991] 1 AC 603, [1991] 1 All ER
     70, HL. See further Case C-473/93 *EC Commission v Luxembourg* [1997] ECR I-3207,
     [1996] 3 CMLR 981, para 37; *Orfinger v Belgium* [2000] 1 CMLR 612, paras 8–10,
     Belgian Conseil d'Etat.
4   For these directives see 12.106 and 12.150 below.

7.44 In *Re Watson and Belmann*[1] the court spelt out what was meant by the binding effect of both the Treaty provisions on free movement and the implementing regulations and directives:

> 'Article 48 of the Treaty and the measures adopted by the Community in application thereof implement a fundamental principle of the Treaty, confer on

persons whom they concern individual rights which the national courts must protect and take precedence over any national rule which might conflict with them.'

1   Case 118/75 [1976] ECR 1185, [1976] 2 CMLR 552, ECJ.

The European Court of Justice

7.45 Where a Member State fails to fulfil an obligation under the EC Treaty, it may be taken to task by the Commission[1] or another Member State[2] before the ECJ. Without going into detail on the available sanctions, one remedy which the ECJ has endorsed is that damages can be awarded to aggrieved individuals, where a Member State fails to implement a directive.[3] Public law bodies may also be liable for damages, instead of or in addition to central government.[4]

1   Article 222 EC (ex Art 169).
2   Article 227 EC (ex Art 170).
3   Case C-6, 9/90 *Francovich and Bonifaci v Italy* [1991] ECR I-5357, [1993] 2 CMLR 66, superseding the dicta to the contrary in *Bourgoin SA v Ministry of Agriculture, Fisheries and Food* [1986] QB 716, [1985] 3 All ER 585. See also Case C-334/92 *Wagner Miret v Fondo de Garantía Salarial* [1993] ECR I-6911; *R v HM Treasury v British Telecommunications* Case C-392/93 [1996] All ER (EC) 411, [1996] 2 CMLR 217, ECJ; C-46 and 48/93 *Brasserie du Pêcheur v Germany, Factortame v UK* [1996] QB 404, [1996] 1 CMLR 889, ECJ; Case C-594 *R v Ministry of Agriculture, Fisheries and Food, ex p Hedley Lomas* [1997] QB 139, [1996] ECR I-2553, ECJ; Case C-178–190/94 *Dillenkofer v Germancy* [1997] QB 259, [1996] All ER (EC) 917, ECJ; cf *R v Secretary of State for the Home Department, ex p Gallagher (No 2)* [1996] 2 CMLR 951, CA (damages refused, because no causal link between the violation and exclusion of the EU national).
4   Case C-424/97 *Haim v Kassenzahnarztliche Vereinigung Nordrhein*, 4 July 2000, ECJ.

7.46 The clear effect of the EC Treaty and the ECJ decisions is that national courts must apply Community law. Where doubtful points about the effect of Community law arise, they can be settled by a reference of the point to the ECJ under Article 234 EC (ex Article 177).[1] A reference can be made by any court or independent tribunal, if it considers that a decision on the question is necessary to enable it to give judgment. In the UK, magistrates' courts, adjudicators and the Immigration Appeal Tribunal have made references,[2] and clearly immigration judges have a discretion to do so.[3] The decision whether to make a reference to the ECJ where a Community law point requires determination is discretionary, save in courts against whose decisions there is no judicial remedy under national law.[4] Where a reference is inevitable it should be made as soon as possible to avoid extra delay.[5] The criteria for a reference by a national court, other than a final Appeal Court, have been set out by the Master of the Rolls in *R v International Stock Exchange of the United Kingdom and the Republic of Ireland Ltd, ex p Else*:[6]

'If the facts have been found and the Community law issue is critical to the court's final decision, the appropriate course is ordinarily to refer the issue to the Court of Justice itself unless the national court can with complete confidence resolve the issue itself. In considering whether it can with complete confidence resolve the issue itself, the national court must be fully mindful of the differences between national and Community legislation, of the pitfalls which face a national court venturing into what may be an unfamiliar field, of the need for uniform interpretation throughout the Community and of the great advantages enjoyed by the Court of Justice in construing Community instruments. If the national court has any real doubt it should refer.'

1   See CPR Sch 1, RSC Ord 114 for the procedure for a reference in the High Court. A reference need not be made if the question is *acte claire* or the issues can be disposed of without determining the point of Community law: *R v Plymouth Justices, ex p Rogers* [1982] QB 863, [1982] 2 All ER 175, QBD; *Polydor Ltd and RSO Records Inc v Harlequin Record Shops and Simons Records* [1980] 2 CMLR 413, CA; *R v Henn and Darby* [1980] AC 850, [1980] 2 All ER 166, HL; *HP Bulmer Ltd v J Bollinger SA* [1974] Ch 401, [1974] 2 All ER 1226, CA; Case 166/73 *Rheinmühlen Düsseldorf v Einfuhrñund Vorratsstelle für Getreide und Futtermittel* [1974] ECR 33, [1974] 1 CMLR 523, ECJ. Even if the meaning of an instrument seems clear to the national court, it may still make a reference, if it considers it appropriate to do so by reason of the importance of the issue raised or otherwise: *CILFIT Srl v Ministry of Health* [1982] ECR 3415. The House of Lords referred the case of *R (on the application of Tum) v Secretary of State for the Home Department* [2004] UKHL (on appeal by the Secretary of State) citing its concern for the numbers of Turkish asylum seekers who benefit from the Court of Appeal's interpretation (at [2004] EWCA Civ 788, [2004] INLR 442) of the standstill provision in the Ankara Agreement.
2   Case 30/77 *R v Bouchereau* [1978] QB 732, [1977] ECR 1999, ECJ (magistrates court); Case C-356/98 *Kaba v Secretary of State for the Home Department* [2000] All ER (EC) 537, ECJ (adjudicator); Case C-416/96 *El-Yassini v Secretary of State for the Home Department* [1999] ECR I-1209 (adjudicator); *Baumbast* (21263) IAT; Case C-60/00 *Carpender*, IAT.
3   *R v Immigration Appeal Tribunal, ex p Antonissen* [1992] Imm AR 196; *El-Yassini* above; Case C-195/98 *Osterreichischer Gewerkschaftsbund v Republik Osterreich*, 30 November 2000, ECJ. See further Dine, Douglas-Good and Derscard, *Procedure in the European Court* (1991) p 55.
4   Article 234 EC (ex Art 177). Usually in the UK this is the House of Lords, the Privy Council in devolution cases, and the High Court of Justiciary in Scottish criminal cases, from which there is no right of appeal to the HL: *McIntosh v Lord Advocate* (1876) 2 App Cas 41.
5   *R v Pharmaceutical Society of Great Britain and Secretary of State for Social Services, ex p Association of Pharmaceutical Importers* [1987] 3 CMLR 951, CA.
6   [1993] QB 534 at 545. For the principles on which interim relief may be granted restraining the implementation of a national law pending a reference see *R v HM Treasury, ex p British Telecom plc* [1994] 1 CMLR 621.

7.47 Modifications have been made to the powers of the ECJ as a result of the Treaty of Amsterdam. Article 234 EC (ex Article 177) remains so far as the free movement provisions in Part III of the EC Treaty are concerned and all courts may make references. But when it comes to visas, immigration and asylum under Title IV of the EC Treaty, the powers of national courts to make references are more limited. Under Article 68(1) EC only a court from which 'there is no judicial remedy under national law' can make a reference, and it must do so if a decision of the ECJ on the question is necessary to enable that court to give judgment. Requests can also be made by the Council, Commission or a Member State for a ruling on the interpretation of Title IV or of acts of the institutions of the Community based on it.[1] But where the EC has adopted measures requiring the abolition of internal border controls under Article 62(1) EC, the ECJ has no jurisdiction to rule.[2] As regards the remaining third pillar in the EU Treaty (Title VI), the ECJ has a mandatory jurisdiction over dispute settlement, but its role still falls short of its role under the first pillar.[3] But the Treaty of Amsterdam has now formally granted the ECJ power to interpret the human rights clause contained in Article 6(2) EU (formerly Art F(2)), a power which it did not previously possess. Article 45 EU now allows the ECJ jurisdiction over Article 6(2) EU with regard to actions of the institutions, insofar as the court has jurisdiction under the Treaties establishing the European Communities and under the Treaty on European Union. No doubt this is a purely formal amendment (see below), but it still has symbolic importance. As regards the Schengen *acquis*, the ECJ has the powers it otherwise has under the relevant applicable provisions of the Treaties once the Council has determined the legal basis for each of the provisions or decisions which constitute the Schengen *acquis*, except that it has no jurisdiction on measures or decisions relating to the maintenance of law and order or the safeguarding of internal security.[4]

1   Article 68(3) EC.
2   Article 68(2) EC.
3   See Peers *EU Justice and Home Affairs Law* (2000), Pearson Education, pp 46–48.
4   Protocol 2, Art 2.1.

European Court of Justice and human rights

7.48 The European Community is under an obligation, contained in Article 6(2) EU, to respect fundamental rights as guaranteed by the ECHR as general principles of Community law. The Treaty of Amsterdam has now brought Article 6(2) directly within the jurisdiction of the ECJ. This is a formal rather than a substantive change.[1] Though it means that the court can interpret and apply the different rights and freedoms contained in the ECHR, the court is not bound to follow Strasbourg case law or to have regard to it, and has not always done so.[2] ECJ decisions cannot be challenged before the Strasbourg court, since Article 34 of the ECHR only allows complaints against one of the High Contracting Parties and not against the EU or Community.[3] Individual recourse to the ECJ is very limited,[4] and offers no realistic possibility of challenge to the provisions of EC law or the implementation of any measure, which is in breach of the ECHR. The European Court of Human Rights has made it clear that anyone wishing to go to Strasbourg on an EC law issue will face formidable hurdles. First, in *Matthews v UK*[5] the court has stated that acts of the EC as such cannot be challenged before the court, because the Community is not a contracting party. However, the court went on to rule that in certain circumstances an individual could bring complaints against a Member State for a failure to secure Convention rights for that individual as regards the implementation of EC law. *Matthews* dealt with the responsibility of contracting States as regards the provisions of the EC Treaties. The court reasoned that if the provision of a Treaty could not be challenged before the ECJ, then the only available recourse would be before the court in Strasbourg. Normally, no such obstacle would apply in the case of directives or regulations. Can a Member State be taken to task for failing to apply these? In *Cantoni v France*[6] the court suggests that there is a similar responsibility on Member States to secure human rights as regards EC Council Directives, as in the case of Treaties. If the rationale for interference is not based on the fact that the ECJ has no jurisdiction, then there is no reason why Strasbourg competence should not extend to regulations and Council Directives as well. At least one commentator has remarked that while the ECJ has been criticised for overlooking relevant Strasbourg case law, the court in Strasbourg is capable of being equally at sea with EC law. Unlike UK courts fulfilling their new jurisdiction under the Human Rights Act 1998, there is no obligation on either of the European courts to have regard to the relevant case law of the other.[7]

1   The ECJ was already applying ECHR law: see the ERT case: *Elliniki Radiophonia Tileorassi AE v Pliroforissis and Kouvelas* Case C-260/89 [1994] 4 CMLR 540, ECJ.
2   Case 374/87 *Orkem v Commission* [1989] ECR 3283, ECJ. See Lord Hope 'Human Rights – where are we now?' [2000] EHRLR 439, where he discusses other cases of divergence.
3   See further *Matthews v UK* (1999) 28 EHRR 361.
4   Article 230 EC (ex Art 173).
5   *Matthews* above (case concerned voting rights in Gibraltar under Art 3 of Protocol 1 of the ECHR).
6   *Cantoni v France* (17862/91, 15 November 1996).
7   ILPA European Update (October 1999) p 8.

SCOPE OF FREE MOVEMENT RIGHTS

Territorial, personal and material scope

7.49 Entitlement to free movement rights depends on the personal and territorial scope of the EC and EEA Treaties. Thus Art 47 of Council Regulation (EEC) 1612/68, the main regulation dealing with the free movement of workers and their families, applies the regulation to the territories of Member States and to their nationals. If someone is within the territorial and personal scope of the Community provisions, questions then arise regarding rights of entry and residence of workers and their families or persons seeking to establish themselves, or whether and to what extent Member States can discriminate on grounds of nationality or have conditions or requirements which hinder free movement. Rules regarding these questions fall within the material scope of Community law. We shall be mainly concerned with the personal and material scope of the Treaties, but the territorial scope assumes importance with regard to Overseas Countries and Territories, such as the Cayman Islands and places such as the Channel Islands, Isle of Man and Gibraltar.

Territorial scope

7.50 Article 299(1) EC (ex Article 227(1) applies the EC Treaty to the territories of each of the Member States.[1] Article 299(2) EC provides that it applies to the French Overseas Departments, the Azores, Madeira and the Canary Islands,[2] but the Council may adopt specific measures aimed at laying down the conditions of application of the Treaty to these regions, including common policies. When Spain joined the Community, Article 25 of the Treaty of Accession applied free movement rights to the Canary Islands, Ceuta and Melilla without derogation, but Andorra is outside Community territory.

1   The territorial scope of Community law is established by Art 299 EC, but it should be noted that the territory which applies for free movement rights is not the same as the territory for customs' purposes: See Martin and Guild *Free Movement of Persons in the European Union* (1996), p 48.

2   The Treaty of Amsterdam amends Art 299(2) EC and simplifies the position. In Case 148/77 *Hansen* [1979] 1 CMLR 604, the ECJ held that the provisions of the Treaty and derived rights apply automatically to the French overseas territories from 1 January 1960, inasmuch as they are an integral part of the French Republic, but that it always remains possible subsequently for specific measures to be adopted in order to meet the needs of those territories. This view was upheld in Case C-163/90 *Administration des Douanes et Droit Indirects v Legros* [1992] ECR I-4625, ECJ. In 1964, Council Decision 64/350 applied the Treaty provisions regarding the right of establishment to these territories. In 1968, Decision 68/359 did the same for workers. In the light of *Hansen* and *Legros* and the latest amendment to former Article 227, these decisions seem unnecessary: see further Martin and Guild above, pp 182–183 on the position prior to the Treaty of Amsterdam.

7.51 Special arrangements for association with a number of countries and territories, which have special relations with Denmark, France, the Netherlands and the UK, are contained in Articles 182 to 187 EC (ex Articles 131 to 136a). They are, therefore, within the territorial scope of the EC Treaty for some purposes, although not generally for freedom of movement.[1] The countries and territories are Greenland, British Indian Ocean Territory, British Antarctic Territory, French Southern and Antarctic Territories, Pitcairn, British Virgin Islands, Bermuda, Cayman Islands and the Falkland Islands.[2] Apart from this list, no other countries or territories having a special relationship with the UK are included.[3] However, the Treaty applies to those European territories for whose external relations a Member State is responsible.[4] This provision covers Gibraltar, and British Dependent (now Overseas) Territories citizens with a Gibraltarian connection are included in the definition of a UK national for the purposes of the Treaty. But it does not cover the Sovereign Base Areas of the UK in Cyprus, nor the Faroe Islands.[5] It applies to the Channel Islands and the Isle of Man 'only to the extent necessary to ensure the implementation of the arrangements for those Islands' as set out in Protocol 3 to the Treaty of Accession of the UK to the EC. We have already dealt with the special position of the Islands at 6.11 above. In Italy, the Republic of San Marino is part of the customs territory of the EU, but is a State independent of Italy and for whose external relations Italy is not responsible, and is, therefore, outside the territorial scope of the EU. The same applies to the Vatican for the same reasons.[6] Lastly, the EC Treaty applies to the Åland Islands (Finland) in accordance with the arrangements set out in Protocol 2 to the Treaty of Accession for Austria, Finland and Sweden.[7]

1   Article 299(3) EC (ex Art 227(3)).
2   Annex II to EC Treaty. Greenland was defined as an Overseas Country from 1 February 1985 by a Treaty amendment of 13 March 1984 (OJ L89 1.2.85 p 1); see Martin and Guild *Free Movement of Persons in the European Union* (1996), p 48, and is the subject of specific provisions detailed in Protocol 15 to the EC Treaty.
3   Article 299(3) EC (ex Art 227(3)).
4   Article 299(4) EC (ex Art 227(4)).
5   Article 299(6) EC (ex Art 227(5)).
6   Martin and Guild *Free Movement of Persons in the European Union* (1996), p 48.
7   Article 299(5) EC; OJ L75 4.4.95 p 18.

7.52 The geographical application of the EC Treaty is defined in Article 299 EC (ex Article 227), as we have seen, but that Article does not preclude Community rules from having effects outside the territories of the Community.[1] The European case law has consistently held that EC law may apply to professional activities pursued outside Community territory, so long as the employment relationship retains a sufficiently close link with the Community. The starting premise is that in an employment relationship between a Community undertaking and a national of another Member State, the rules on freedom of movement for workers (particularly those prohibiting discrimination on grounds of nationality) are in principle applicable. The case law makes it clear that their application in principle is not affected by the fact that the work is carried out abroad (ie, outside the territories of the Community), whether temporarily and occasionally,[2] or permanently and exclusively.[3] The criterion for applying these rules to an employment relationship existing abroad is the existence of a 'sufficiently close link with the Community'. In *Boukhalfa*[4] the Advocate General's opinion was that it was a matter for the national court to determine whether such a link actually exists. This, however, was not endorsed by the ECJ, which concluded that a Belgian woman working in the German embassy in Algeria, who was paid less than her German colleagues, was sufficiently linked to German law as to come within the Community provisions on discrimination. In determining the existence of the link, the ECJ or national court will look at a number of factors, such as whether the employment relationship was entered into by a EU national and an undertaking of another Member State, whether recruitment took place in a Member State, whether the Community worker was established in a Member State at the time of the recruitment, where the employer is established, whether the contract of employment is governed by the law of a Member State and so forth.

1   Case C-214/94 *Boukhalfa v Germany* [1996] 3 CMLR 22, para 14.
2   Case 36/74 *Walrave & Koc v Association Union Cycliste Internationale* [1974] ECR 1405, ECJ; Case 237/83 *Prodest* [1984] ECR 3153, para 6.
3   Case 9/88 *Da Veiga v Staatssecretaris van Jushtie* [1989] ECR 2989, [1991] 1 CMLR 217, para 15; Case C-60/93 *Aldewereld v Staatssecretaris van Financien* [1994] ECR I-2991, para 14.
4   *Boukhalfa* fn 1 above.

7.53   The Immigration (European Economic Area) Regulations 2000[1] do not address the question of the territorial scope of the EC Treaty, but deal with 'qualified persons' purely in terms of the personal scope of the Treaties. Regulations 12 and 14 give effect in UK domestic law to the right of admission and right of residence of 'qualified persons' as regards the UK. The Channel Islands and Isle of Man are within Community territory for customs purposes,[2] but not for free movement and the provision of services. The 2000 Regulations do not address the position of EEA nationals arriving in the UK under free movement rights and moving on to one or other of the Islands. That is dealt with under a different regime, as we have seen in chapter 6 above. Under the various Orders in Council dealing with the Islands it is provided that EEA nationals, who are entitled to enter and remain in the UK by virtue of an enforceable Community right, do not need leave to enter or remain in that particular Island.[3]

1   SI 2000/2326.
2   EC Treaty, Protocol 3, Art 1.
3   Immigration Act 1988, s 7, as applied to the Islands by Immigration (Isle of Man) Order 1991, SI 1991/2630, Sch 1, Pt IV, para 2; Immigration (Guernsey) Order 1993, SI 1993/1796, Sch 1, Pt III, para 2; Immigration (Jersey) Order 1993, SI 1993/1797, Sch 1, Pt III, para 2.

PERSONAL SCOPE (1) NATIONALS

EU and EEA nationals

7.54 Although Article 39 EC (ex Article 48) refers only to 'workers' and does not contain any words limiting its application to nationals of a Member State, the ECJ and the subsidiary regulations and directives have all made it clear that this provision may only be relied on by nationals of Member States.[1] Articles 43 EC (ex Article 52) (right of establishment) and 49 EC (ex Article 59) (provision of services) are expressly limited to nationals of Member States. To come within the personal scope of EC free movement rights someone must, therefore, be a national of an EU Member State, which now qualifies him or her as an EU citizen under Article 17 EC (ex Article 8). Because the EEA Treaty extends EC free movement rights to all EEA nationals, being a national of an EEA State can properly be described as the main requirement to come within the personal scope of free movement rights. In this context, EEA nationals include UK nationals. However, as regards admission to the UK, a narrower definition of 'EEA nationals' is used in UK domestic law. Under the Immigration (European Economic Area) Regulations 2000, as recently amended, EEA nationals means nationals of all EEA States, including the 10 new EU Member States since 1 May 2004, but not the UK.[2]

[1] Council Regulation (EEC) 1612/68, Arts 1 and 2; Council Directive (EEC) 68/360, Art 1; Case 238/83 *Meade* [1984] ECR 2631; see Martin and Guild *Free Movement of Persons in the European Union* (1996), p 95.

[2] Immigration (European Economic Area) Regulations 2000, SI 2000/2326, reg 2(1), as amended by The Accession (Immigration and Worker Registration) Regulations 2004, SI 2004/1219, reg 3. The list of EU Member States is set out at 7.5 above. Note that UK Nationals are EEA nationals for the purpose of the EEA Agreement and their free movement rights, whenever they enter another EEA Member State.

7.55 This group broadly corresponds with those who are within the definition of a 'qualified person' in the UK's Immigration (European Economic Area) Regulations 2000,[1] which give effect to obligations under the EC Treaty and the Agreement on the European Economic Area 1992. A 'qualified person' is any national of an EEA Member State other than the UK, who is in the UK as a worker, self-employed person, provider of services, recipient of services, self-sufficient person, retired person, student, or a person who has ceased activity. During the 'accession period' (1 May 2004 to 30 April 2009) nationals of the eight new Eastern European Member States, who are required to register as workers, will be qualified persons only during a period in which they are working in the UK for an authorised employer[2] and will not be treated as qualified persons as regards the issue of residence pemits and residence documents.[3] Dependants and members of an EEA member's household are not qualified persons, but family members may be, in a very limited group of cases, where the qualified person has died.[4] We shall look at each of these categories in turn. In reading the 2000 Regulations, it is important to note their limitations. First, they are a national measure intended to give effect to Community law as regards entry into and stay in the UK. This is made clear by regulations 12 to 14. They do not, therefore, deal with the free movement rights of UK nationals, who wish to exercise their rights on the territories of other Member States. 'Qualified persons' do not, therefore, include any UK nationals, unless they are dual nationals having the nationality of one of the other Member States. Similarly, apart from the *Surinder Singh* situation, which is expressly dealt with by Regulation 11 (see 7.60) they do not acknowledge that UK nationals who have exercised one or more of their Community rights in another Member State may be covered by Community law on their return to the UK,[5] and may, for example, be 'workers' [6] entitled to the benefit of EC rules on non-discrimination and access to social security and welfare benefits. Thirdly, where they conflict with EC law, Community law prevails.

[1] SI 2000/2326, reg 5.
[2] The Accession (Immigration and Worker Registration) Regulations 2004, SI 2004/1219, reg 5(2).
[3] SI 2004/1219, reg 5(6).
[4] SI 2000/2326, reg 5(1)(h) and (4).
[5] Case C-19/92 *Kraus* [1993] ECR I-1663 (obtaining qualifications recognised by EC law); Case C-370/90 *R v Immigration Appeal Tribunal and Surinder Singh, ex p Secretary of State for the Home Department* [1992] ECR I-4265, [1992] 3 All ER 798 (working on the territory of another Member State); Case C-60/00 *Carpenter* [2002] ECR I-6279, [2002] INLR 439 (providing or receiving services on the territory of another Member State)
[6] All Community nationals, whatever their place of residence or nationality, who have exercised a free movement right and have worked in another Member State come within Art 39 (formerly 48) EC and are to be classed as 'workers': see Case C-419/92 *Scholz v Opera Universitaria di Caligari and Anzia Porcedda* [1994] ECR I-505, [1994] 1 CMLR 873, ECJ; Case C-443/93 *Vougioukas v Idrima Koinon Asphalisseon (IKA)* [1995] ECR I-4033.

7.56 Only nationals of a State party to the EEA Agreement can take direct advantage of free movement rights. But there are circumstances, such as membership of the family or household of an EEA national, that bring collateral rights of free movement to non-nationals.[1] Nationality is the principal connecting factor so far as natural persons are concerned, but it is inappropriate for companies. Article 48 EC (ex Article 58) therefore provides that a company or firm which has its registered office, central administration or principal place of business within the Community will be treated in the same way as a natural person who is a Community national. Companies so defined have the right of establishment in the territory of another Member State.[2] In some cases residence in Community territory is required, in addition to nationality. Thus a period of residence in the UK is necessary before British citizens from the Channel Islands and Isle of Man can benefit from the free movement provisions.[3] Similarly, nationals of Denmark who are resident in the Faroe Islands are outside the personal scope of the EC Treaty.[4]

[1] See 7.60 and 7.86ff below.
[2] Article 48 EC (ex Art 58).
[3] See 6.22 above.
[4] Article 4 of Protocol 2 to Danish Act of Accession; see also Art 299(6)(a) EC (ex Art 227).

7.57 Whether someone is or is not a national of a Member State depends on each State's municipal law.[1] The criteria for obtaining nationality vary from State to State. In theory each State can unilaterally expand or reduce the scope of the free movement provisions by changing its nationality law. Thus those born in the UK after 1 January 1983 will not automatically acquire the free movement rights they would have done following birth in the UK in the ten years prior to that date.[2] Equally, it has been possible for Member States on joining the EC to create for EC purposes special definitions of nationality which derive from, but are different to, the normal definition of nationality in that State's municipal law. The issue has not yet presented real problems, except for Germany[3] and the UK. In the UK the problem arises because British nationality is subdivided into a number of different citizenships which carry different immigration rights.

1   See *Oppenheimer v Cattermole* [1976] AC 249, [1975] 1 All ER 538, HL; *Stoeck v Public Trustee* [1921] 2 Ch 67; *Bibi (Mahaboob) v Secretary of State for the Home Department* [1987] Imm AR 340, CA. This also accords with the rule of public international law that in general each State may determine who are its nationals: see Plender *International Migration Law* (2nd edn, 1998) p 39ff.
2   British Nationality Act 1981, s 1.
3   The German definition of citizenship according to its Constitution prevailed for EC purposes, and this extended German nationality not only to East German nationals but also a wider range of persons of German extraction, thus bringing them within the personal scope of free movement rights. German reunification has caused the problem to vanish.

UK nationals for EC purposes

7.58 At the time of signing the Treaty of Accession to the EEC, the British government made a declaration on the meaning of a UK national for the purposes of the Treaties.[1] Since then the government has made a further declaration, which took effect on 1 January 1983, when the British Nationality Act 1981 came into force.[2] So far as the UK is concerned, the term 'national' or 'nationals' in any Community document now means:

(a)   British citizens;
(b)   British subjects under the British Nationality Act 1981[3] who have the right of abode in the UK;
(c)   British Dependent (now Overseas) Territories citizens who acquire that citizenship from a connection with Gibraltar.

Two features of the declaration should be noted. First, it excludes those citizens of a Commonwealth country who have obtained the right of abode in the UK, but not British citizenship.[4] Secondly, it includes Gibraltarians, who can move to any other country of the EU but might otherwise be denied entry to the UK under UK immigration law. This can be overcome if they register as British citizens under the British Nationality Act 1981.[5] Just as Gibraltarians can move to other Member States, nationals of those States can move to Gibraltar, to whose territory freedom of movement is extended in accordance with Article 299(4) EC (ex Article 227(4)). The validity of the UK Declaration was upheld by the ECJ in *R (on the application of Kaur) v Secretary of State for the Home Department*.[6]

1   (1972) (Cm 4862) p 118. Under this declaration a UK national was a citizen of the UK and Colonies (CUKC) or a British subject without citizenship, having in either case the right of abode, or a CUKC by connection with Gibraltar.
2   28 January 1983, (1983) OJ C 23, p 1, (1983) (Cmd 9062). There may be some doubt as to the legal authority for this declaration. It is a unilateral declaration not a treaty document. It is made without any statutory authority or parliamentary approval. It is not the judgment of a competent court.

3   British Nationality Act 1981, ss 30–32.
4   Immigration Act 1971, s 2(1)(b).
5   British Nationality Act 1981, s 5.
6   Case C-192/99 [2001] All ER (EC) 250.

7.59 Some people may have the nationality of more than one State. Dual nationality does not hinder the enjoyment of fundamental freedoms under Community law where this applies. This will be the case where the person is both a national of a Member State and of a third State or is a national of two Member States at the same time. In *Micheletti* the ECJ held that a Member State may not restrict the effects of the grant of nationality of another Member State by imposing conditions (such as a habitual residence requirement on the territory of the Member State in question) for recognition of that nationality with a view to the exercise of one of the Treaty's fundamental freedoms. Effectively the Member State is precluded from treating a person who is both an EU national and a national of a non-Member State as if he or she were not such an EU national.[1] In the UK this issue has arisen most frequently with respect to Irish nationals. Thus in *Ex p Aradi*[2] a dual Irish and British citizen had never been out of the UK in her whole life. Her possession of dual nationality was held, therefore, not to bring into play the more beneficial provisions of EEC law on family reunion in what would otherwise be a purely internal British situation. This authority is not compatible with more recent decisions of the ECJ. In *Avello*,[3] two dual Belgian and Spanish national children who had lived all their lives in Belgium were found by the ECJ to enjoy the status of citizen of the Union conferred by Article 17 EC. The court recalled that the scope of the Treaty is not extended to purely internal situations which have no link with Community law. However it considered that as they were nationals of one Member State lawfully resident in the territory of another Member State a link with Community law had been established. The fact that people may not need to rely on their EC nationality to gain admission does not mean that rights incidental to such a claim are ineffective.[4] Where an applicant claims that he or she is a citizen of a particular Member State, the burden of proof is on the applicant and no different principle is imported because of the implications of Community law.[5]

1   Case C-369/90 *Micheletti v Delegacion del Gobierno en Cantabria* [1992] ECR I-4239; see also Jauler Carrescosa in (1994) 8 INLP 1. This principle was applied in *Chen and Zhu v Secretary of State for the Home Department* C-200/02 (19 October 2004, unreported) to the situation of an infant whose mother went to Ireland to give birth to her child to enable the child to obtain Irish nationality; the child's Irish nationality conferred free movement rights under Art 18 EC and Directive 90/364 and it would be contrary to EU law to impose further conditions over and above possession of that nationality.
2   *R v Immigration Appeal Tribunal, ex p Aradi* [1987] Imm AR 359, QBD.
3   Case C-148/02 *Avello (Carlos Garcia) v Etat Belge* [2003] ECR I-11613.
4   Cases C-389 and 390/87 *Echternach v Minister van Onderwijs en Wetenschappen* [1989] ECR 723, [1990] 2 CMLR 305, ECJ; Case C-370/90 *R v Immigration Appeal Tribunal and Surinder Singh, ex p Secretary of State for the Home Department* [1992] 3 All ER 798, [1992] Imm AR 565, ECJ.
5   *Surinder Singh* above.

7.60 In *Surinder Singh*[1] the European Court held that where a British citizen had exercised Community rights in another part of the EU or the EEA and returned to the UK with non-national family members, he or she was exercising Community as well as national rights of entry, and the family members could not be treated less favourably than required by Community law. The Immigration (European Economic Area) Regulations 2000[2] now expressly deal with this situation in regulation 11, which seeks to implement the ECJ judgment, by extending Community rights (in certain circumstances) to family members of a UK national. The circumstances included a need to prove (by whom is not clear) that the UK national did not leave the UK 'in order to enable his family member to acquire rights under these regulations and thereby evade the application of UK immigration law'. This provision was withdrawn in the light of the decision of the ECJ in *Akrich*.[3] In that case the ECJ affirmed its previous jurisprudence in the case of *Levin*[4] that Member States are not entitled to take account of motives which may have prompted a worker to seek employment in another Member State or indeed in seeking to return to his or her home country. However in what appears to be a qualification of the *Surinder Singh* principle, the ECJ alluded to the fact that spouses of EU citizens, who are living unlawfully in the citizen's home State, have no right under Article 10 of Council Regulation 1612/68 to install themselves in another Member State. This would appear to be confined to cases concerning citizens who seek to return their own Member State relying on Community law and whose spouses were not lawfully residing in the Member State of origin of the EU citizen. This aspect of the ECJ's judgment does not sit easily with other decisions, in cases such as *Carpenter*[5] and *MRAX*,[6] and is questionable as authority, given that this aspect was not put to the parties at any stage during the proceedings.[7] In his opinion in *Commission v Spain*,[8] the Advocate-General, referring to *MRAX*, has re-affirmed that Member States are not entitled to require prior long-term visas for the entry of third-country national family members. However, the Immigration (European Economic Area) Regulations have been amended following *Akrich* to incorporate the requirement that where a UK national seeks to rely on the *Surinder Singh* principle to bring a non-EEA national family member with him or her on return from another Member State, that family member must be lawfully resident in an EEA State.[9]

1   Case C-370/90 *R v Immigration Appeal Tribunal and Surinder Singh, ex p Secretary of State for the Home Department* [1992] 3 All ER 798, [1992] Imm AR 565, ECJ.

2   SI 2000/2326. See the amendments brought about by the Immigration (European Economic Area) (Amendment) Regulations 2005, SI 2005/47, fn 9 below.

3   Case C-109/01 *Secretary of State for the Home Department v Akrich (Hacene)* 23 September 2003.

4   Case 53/81 *Levin v Secretary of State for Justice* [1982] ECR 1035.

5   Case C-60/00 *Carpenter (Mary) v Secretary of State for the Home Department* [2002] ECR I-6279, [2002] INLR 439 .

6   *Mouvement contre le Racisme, l'antisemitisme et la Xenophobie ASBL v Belgium* C-459/99, [2002] ECR I-6591, ECJ.

7   For further comments, see 'Family reunion in Community law', by Steve Peers, Professor of Law, University of Essex, in Walker (ed) *Europe's Area of Freedom, Security and Justice* (2004) OUP.

8   C-157/03 *Commission v Spain* (9 November 2004, unreported), ECJ, per A-G Stix-Hackl.

9   SI 2005/47, reg 2, amending SI 2000/2326, reg 11(2)(b). It also amends reg 13 to provide that a non-EEA national family member applying for a family permit in an EEA Member State will not be eligible if he or she is not lawfully resident in any Member State. There are transitional provisions protecting applications made before the amendments are in force (7 February 2005). Clarification of the ECJ's judgment in *Akrich* (fn 3 above) is being sought in Case C-1/05 *Jia*, referred by a Swedish court on 30 December 2004.

Non-nationals

7.61 Non-nationals are normally outside the personal scope of the Treaty provisions relating to citizens and free movement. They do fall within the scope of measures taken under Title IV but these do not generally create free movement rights. But, as always, there are exceptions These are:

(1)   family members of qualified persons;[1]

(2)   directors and staff of a company constituted in one Member State and carrying out services in another. A company providing services in another Member State may travel with the whole of its staff for the duration of the work undertaken.[2] See 7.73–7.76 below;

(3)   stateless persons and refugees recognised in one Member State, who have been admitted to the territory of another, are entitled to carry with them accrued social security rights in the same way as EC nationals.[3] As regards free movement rights, the Council declared in 1964 that refugees moving from one Member State to another to seek employment should receive 'the most favourable treatment possible', and their entry 'must be given especially favourable consideration'. This declaration has no direct effect and does not bring refugees within the personal scope of the EC, but it is the strongest possible invitation to Member States to take the declaration into account when considering the grant of leave to enter.[4]

Once the Council puts into effect the measures on immigration and asylum under Title IV of the EC Treaty, there will inevitably be a widening of the personal scope of the EC Treaty, but it will apply to Title IV immigration and asylum provisions and not to free movement rights.

[1] Case 131/85 *Gül v Regierungspräsident Düsseldorf* [1986] ECR 1573, [1987] 1 CMLR 501, ECJ. But the Community national member of the family must have exercised free movement rights. Community law has no application to a wholly internal situation: see 7.62 below.

[2] Case C-113/89 *Rush Portuguesa Lda v ONI* [1990] ECR I-1417, [1991] 2 CMLR 818; see also the important decision of the ECJ in Case C-43/93 *Van Der Elst v OMI* [1994] ECR I-3803 where a Moroccan worker lawfully resident in Belgium was held entitled to work for a Belgian company undertaking a project in France.

[3] Council Regulation (EEC) 1408/71, which deals with social security benefits for migrant workers.

[4] See further Martin and Guild 7.50 fn 1 above, chapter 21. It is arguable that the Home Office must have regard to the words quoted in deciding whether to admit Convention refugees recognised in another Member State: *R v Secretary of State, ex p Obomalayat* (16 August 1978, unreported), QBD cited in *Vaughan* 7.19 fn 1 above, para 15.363. See further 12.104 below.

Internal situations

7.62 Article 39 EC (ex Article 48) only applies to situations within the scope of Community law, namely the free movement of workers, and envisages someone moving from one Member State to another to seek or take up employment. Those who have never exercised a free movement right within the Community do not come within Article 39 and cannot be classified as 'workers'. In *R v Saunders*[1] it was held that the free movement provisions of the EC Treaty cannot apply to situations which are wholly internal to a Member State. In *Morson and Jhanjan*[2] this was interpreted to mean that where workers have never exercised a right to free movement within the Community there is no EC link, and the Member State in question cannot be prevented by EC law from refusing entry or stay to the non-EC parents or spouse of a local national. The purely internal situation does not just apply to Article 39 and workers. The provisions on freedom of establishment do not apply to obstacles which affect nationals of Member States on their own territory without any connecting factor to a situation covered by EC law. In the same way Article 49 EC (ex Article 59) cannot be applied to activities which are confined in all respects within a single Member State. Thus a company operating in one Member State with its head office there does not come within Community law by simply extending its activities in that country.[3]

1   Case 175/78 [1980] QB 72, [1979] ECR 1129, ECJ; Case C-206/91 *Poirrez* [1992] ECR I-6685, ECJ.
2   Case 35, 36/82 *Morson and Jhanjan v Netherlands* [1982] ECR 3723, [1983] 2 CMLR 221, ECJ; Cases C-297/88 and 197/89 *Dzodzi v Belgium* [1990] ECR I-3763. A hypothetical possibility of professional activity in another Member State is not enough: Case 180/83 *Moser v Land Baden-Württemberg* [1984] ECR 2539, ECJ, nor is a mere intention to become an EC worker without any practical steps being taken: *Bouanimba v Secretary of State for the Home Department* [1986] Imm AR 343, IAT. In Case 44/84 *Hurd v Jones* [1986] QB 892, [1986] 2 CMLR 1, ECJ the same principles were applied to a UK national employed at the European Community School. He was the only teacher not granted a tax exemption by the UK government, but the court held that he could not invoke the non-discrimination provisions of what was then Art 7 of the Treaty against the UK government because he had never exercised his free movement right and was not, therefore, within the protection of Art 48. See further *R v Immigration Appeal Tribunal, ex p Aradi* [1987] Imm AR 359, QBD (but see 7.59 above); *R v Secretary of State for the Home Department, ex p Tombofa* [1988] Imm AR 400, CA. Case 147/87 *Zaoui v CRAM de l'Ile de France* [1987] ECR 5511, [1989] 2 CMLR 646, ECJ. Other examples where the ECJ has held a situation to be wholly internal are Case C-60/91 *Re Morais* [1992] ECR I-2085, [1992] 2 CMLR 533, ECJ (prosecution of a driving instructor); Case C-147/91 *Ministerio Fiscal v Ferrer Laderer* [1992] 3 CMLR 273, ECJ (prosecution of an estate agent); Case C-332/90 *Steen v Deutsche Bundespost* [1992] ECR I-341, [1992] 2 CMLR 406 (recruitment of a German national to the post office); Case C-153/91 *Petit v Office National des Pensions* [1992] ECR I-4973, [1993] 1 CMLR 476 (adopted child not exercising community rights).
3   Case C-134/94 *Esso Española SA v Comunidad Autonoma de Canaries* [1995] ECR I-4223.

7.63 On the other hand, where there is a sufficient link to a situation envisaged by EC law, the matter is no longer purely internal and EC law can be invoked. Some examples might be a travel agent with offices in London and Brussels, or a restaurant owner with restaurants in Dublin and Paris. So where a broadcasting body establishes itself in another Member State in order to avoid the legislation applicable in the receiving State to domestic broadcasters, its broadcasts were regarded as services within the meaning of Article 49, irrespective of its motive for relocating.[1] Where a national of a Member State has entered into a contract of employment with an employee in another Member State with a view to exercising gainful employment, the situation cannot be called a purely internal one, even if the offer of employment is never taken up. This is what happened in the case of *Bosman*,[2] a Belgian footballer who was prevented by the Belgian FA's transfer rules from moving to a French club. The ECJ held that this was not an internal situation. Where a worker has exercised the right of free movement within the Community by taking employment in another Member State, he or she is entitled to rely upon Community law on returning to his or her own State. The decision of the ECJ in *Surinder Singh*[3] upheld the conclusion of the Immigration Appeal Tribunal, that where there has been a genuine exercise of Community rights, the returning national and the non-national spouse or relative are entitled to any more favourable treatment provided by Community law, despite the fact that there is also a right of entry under national law. This case was followed in *Kraus v Land Baden-Württemberg*,[4] where a German national wished to use a university title received following study in the UK on return to his native Germany. See 7.60 above. In *Carpenter* the ECJ considered that a national residing in his own Member State could benefit from free movement rights in his own Member State, in that case the right to family reunion, if he was providing services in another Member State, even where that provision of services was on a very temporary and infrequent basis.[5]

1   Case C-23/93 *SA v Commissariaat voor de Media* [1994] ECR I-4795, [1995] 3 CMLR 284, ECJ.
2   Case C-415/93 *Union Royal Belge des Societies de Football Assciation ASBL v Bosman* [1995] ECR I-4921, [1996] 1 CMLR 645, paras 88–91, ECJ.
3   Case C–370/90 *R v Immigration Appeal Tribunal and Surinder Singh, ex p Secretary of State for the Home Department* [1992] ECR I-4265, ECJ, [1992] Imm AR 565.
4   Case C-19/92 [1993] ECR I-1663.
5   Case C-60/00 *Carpenter (Mary) v Secretary of State for the Home Department* [2002] ECR I-6279, [2002] INLR 439, ECJ.

7.64   Prior to 1993, the sole fact of moving residence from one Member State to another did not constitute a sufficient connecting factor, as the ECJ held in *Werner v Finanzant Aachen-Innenstadt*.[1] This case pre-dates the introduction of Article 18 EC (ex Article 8a) which for the first time confers directly on every citizen of the EU the right to move and reside freely within the territory of the Member States. The case of *Avello* makes clear that the sole fact of residence in another Member State is sufficient to engage Community law.[2] In *Avello* the children wishing to benefit from Community law were not exercising any particular community right and, in fact, were born in the Member State in question and had lived there all their lives.

1   Case C-112/91 [1993] ECR I-429.
2   C-148/02 *Garcia Avello v Etat Belge* [2004] All ER (EC) 740; see also C-200/02 *Chen v Secretary of State for the Home Department* (19 October 2004, unreported), ECJ, para 19, where the court cited *Avello* in holding that 'the situation of a national of a Member State born in the host Member State, who has not made use of the right to freedom of movement, cannot for that reason alone be assimilated to a purely internal situation'.

PERSONAL SCOPE (2) WORKERS

7.65   A national of an EEA Member State only comes within the personal scope of Article 39 EC if he or she is a worker. Regulation 3(1) of the Immigration (European Economic Area) Regulations 2000 defines a 'worker' as a worker within the meaning of Article 39 of the EC Treaty.[1] It thus relies entirely on the interpretation given to this term by Community law. Although Article 39 refers to 'freedom of movement for workers', 'workers of the

Member States' and 'workers of other Member States' and Article 50 EC envisages a programme to encourage the exchange of 'young workers', the Treaty does not define the term 'worker'. However, at an early stage of the EEC it was established by the ECJ[2] that the term must have a Community meaning rather than definitions given by laws of individual Member States.[3] Under the EC Treaty, rights of 'workers' are distinguished from those relating to 'establishment' and 'services', and this suggests that a worker is a person employed, actually or potentially, under a contract of employment and is not a self-employed person, who would be eligible to benefit from freedom of establishment (Article 43, formerly 52) and freedom to provide services (Article 49, formerly 59).[4]

1   Immigration (European Economic Area) Regulations 2000, reg 3(1)(a).
2   Case 75/63 *Hoekstra (née Unger) v Bestuur der Bedrijfsvereniging voor Detailhandel en Ambachten* [1964] ECR 177 at 184, ECJ.
3   Case 17/76 *Brack v Insurance Officer* [1976] ECR 1429 at 1448, ECJ; Case 53/81 *Levin v Secretary of State for Justice* [1982] ECR 1035 at 1049, ECJ.
4   See C Maestripieri *La Libre Circulation Des Personnes et des Services dans la CEE* (1972) p 46. Sometimes it is difficult to distinguish a worker from the self-employed or a service provider. See Case C-106/91 *Ramrath v Ministre de la Justice* [1992] 3 CMLR 173; Case C-202/90 *Ayuntamiento de Sevilla v Recaudadores de Tributas de la Zonas primera y segunda* [1994] 1 CMLR 424, ECJ; Case C-3/87 *R v Ministry of Agriculture, Fisheries and Food, ex p Agegate* [1990] 2 QB 151, [1990] 1 CMLR 366, ECJ.

7.66 Early decisions of national courts and tribunals gave a narrow and restrictive definition to 'workers' and suggested that the term excluded casual, intermittent and part-time employment.[1] The ECJ, however, has made it clear that, since the terms 'worker' and 'activity as an employed person' define the spheres of application of one of the fundamental freedoms guaranteed by the Treaty, they may not be interpreted restrictively.[2] In *Levin*[3] a woman with a part-time job as a hotel chambermaid was a worker. The court held that an income less than the minimum required for subsistence is enough, provided only that the person pursues an activity as an employed person which is effective and genuine, and it does not matter what the motive was for taking it. Thus, contrary to what regulation 11(2)(b) of the Immigration (European Economic Area) Regulations 2000[4] says, an EEA national wife may take part-time employment for the purpose of giving her non-EEA national husband rights under Community law. In *Lawrie-Blum v Land Baden-Württemberg*[5] the ECJ stated that the essential characteristic of the employment relationship is the fact that during a given time one person provides services for and under the direction of another in return for remuneration. This applies to trainees and apprentices if they do work for an employer for pay, however low, even though they are under supervision and the work is preparation for a qualifying exam or to qualify the employee for work elsewhere.[6] Remuneration appears to be the key. However, payment need not be enough to live on or it may be in kind, rather than a formal wage. In *Kempf v Staatssecretaris van Justitie*[7] the court went further. A person may still be a worker even if the pay is so low that he or she needs to supplement it with unemployment benefit or has to apply for sickness benefit during a period of illness, provided that the effectiveness and genuineness of the activities as an employed person are established. In *Steymann v Staatssecretaris van Justitie*[8] a German plumber went to Holland and joined a religious community, which secured its economic independence by commercial activities, such as the operation of a bar, discotheque and launderette. The claimant worked for them and in return was provided with his material needs, including pocket money. The court held that where commercial activity was an inherent part of membership of the community, the upkeep of the member of the community could be regarded as an indirect countervailing charge for their work, even though it was not a formal wage. Provided the work is genuine and effective (which is a question for the national courts) and not purely marginal and incidental, it can be considered an economic activity. The purpose of the work is irrelevant, whether it be of a non-commercial nature, such as State education, or part of the public service.[9] Playing sport is not usually regarded as an economic activity, but it is in the case of professional or semi-professional sports players, who thereby become workers.[10] The employer need not be an undertaking; all that is required is the existence of or the intention to create an employment relationship.[11]

[1] *Re Expulsion of an Italian National* [1965] CMLR 285; *R v Secchi* [1975] 1 CMLR 383 at 393; *City of Wiesbaden v Barulli* [1968] CMLR 239; *Nijssen v Immigration Officer, London (Heathrow) Airport and Immigration Officer, Sheerness* [1978] Imm AR 226.

[2] Case 53/81 *Levin v Secretary of State for Justice* [1982] ECR 1035 at 1052, ECJ; but see Case C-171/91 *Tsiotras v Landeshauptstadt Stuttgart* [1993] ECR I-2925, ECJ.

[3] See *Levin* above.

[4] SI 2000/2326.

[5] Case 66/85 [1986] ECR 2121, [1987] 3 CMLR 389. Followed in respect of Turkish 'workers' in Case C-36/96 *Günaydin v Freistaat Bayern* [1997] ECR I-5143. Employment from 10 up to 18 hours a week has been acceptable in *Kempf* fn 7 below; Case C-171/88, *Rinner-Kühn v FWW Spezial-Gebäudereinigung* [1993] 2 CMLR 932; Case C-102/88; *Ruzius-Wilbrink v Bestuur van de Bedrijfsverieiniging voor Overheidsdienten* [1991] 2 CMLR 202, ECJ; Case C-444/93 *Megner and Scheffel v Innungskrankenkasse Vorderpfalz* [1996] All ER (EC) 212, [1996] IRLR 236, ECJ. Low productivity does not prevent a person from being a worker: Case 344/87 *Bettray v Staatsecretaris van Justitie* [1989] ECR 1621, [1991] 1 CMLR 459, ECJ.

[6] *Gunaydin* above; Case C-27/91 *Union de Recouvrement des Cotisations de Securite Sociale et d'Allocations familiales de la Savoie (URSSAF) v Hostellerie le Manoir Sarl* [1991] ECR I-5531, ECJ (trainee employed over the summer months in a hotel school).

[7] Case 139/85 [1986] ECR 1741, [1987] 1 CMLR 764, ECJ.

[8] Case 196/87 [1988] ECR 6159, [1989] 1 CMLR 449, ECJ.

[9] Work which merely constitutes a means of rehabilitation or re-integration of a person into the workforce may not be regarded as effective and genuine: *Bettray* above. The issue of rehabilitative employment will be considered shortly by the ECJ again in *Trojani v Centre public d'aide sociale de Bruxelles (CPAS)* Case C-456/02 in which a French national carried out chores for some 30 hours a week in a Salvation Army hostel in Brussels where he lived as part of a rehabilitation project.

[10] Case C-415/93 *Union Royale Belge des Societas de Football Association ASBL v Bosman* [1996] 1 CMLR 645, ECJ; Case 36/74 *Walrave and Koch v Association Union Cycliste Internationale* [1974] ECR 1405, [1974] 1 CMLR 320, ECJ; Case 13/76 *Donà v Mantero* [1976] ECR 1333 at 1340, ECJ; see also C-438/00 *Deutsch Handballbund ev Kolpak* 8 May 2003.

[11] *Bosman* above, para 74.

7.67 The term 'worker' does not cover only actual workers, but also job seekers,[1] those between jobs,[2] workers undergoing vocational training in their own field or in some cases retraining in a different field,[3] the involuntarily unemployed, and sick,[4] injured and retired workers. The fact that a contract of employment was for a fixed term does not necessarily lead to the conclusion that, once that contract expired, the employee concerned is automatically to be regarded as voluntarily unemployed.[5] In the case of *Bernini*[6] an Italian national who had undergone occupational training in the Netherlands retained the status of worker when undergoing full-time study in Italy where there was a link between the previous occupational activity and the studies in question. The amount of time given to job seekers to find work is not fixed. The effectiveness of Article 39 EC is secured if they have a reasonable time in which to do so. Member States may allow them to remain for a reasonable period, but cannot require them to leave at the end of that period, if the person concerned produces evidence that he or she is continuing to seek employment and has genuine chances of being engaged.[7] Workers who have not yet found employment may not be entitled to the fuller rights available to those who have found employment. In particular the right to enjoy the same social and tax advantages may not accrue until employment is found.[8] The conduct of the person concerned before and after the period of employment was not relevant in establishing the status of worker.[9] The Immigration (European Economic Area) Regulations 2000 do not expressly deal with the time allowed to find work, but they do deal with those who cease to be qualified. They state that a worker does not cease to be a qualified person solely because (a) he or she is temporarily incapable of work as a result of illness or accident or (b) is involuntarily unemployed, if that fact is duly recorded by the relevant employment office.[10]

1   Case C-292/89 *R v Immigration Appeal Tribunal, ex p Antonissen* [1991] ECR I-745, [1991] 2 CMLR 373, para 10.
2   Case 75/63 *Hoekstra (née Unger) v Bestuur der Bedrijfsvereniging voor Detailhandel en Ambachten* [1964] ECR 177 at 184, ECJ.
3   Case 39/86 *Lair v Hanover University* [1988] ECR 3161, [1989] 3 CMLR 545, ECJ, as qualified by Case 197/86 *Brown v Secretary of State for Scotland* [1988] ECR 3205, [1988] 3 CMLR 403, ECJ.
4   *Lair* above. See also *Giangregorio v Secretary of State for the Home Department* [1983] 3 CMLR 472, [1983] Imm AR 104, IAT; *Monteil v Secretary of State for the Home Department* [1983] Imm AR 149, [1984] 1 CMLR 264, IAT. Case C-302/90 *Caisse Auxiliaire díAssurance Maladie-Invaliditié v Faux* [1991] ECR I-4875.
5   Case C-413/01 *Ninni-Orsache (Franca) v Bundesminister Fur Wissenschaft, Verkehr Und Kunst* (2003) ECJ (Sixth Chamber) 6/11/2003.
6   Case C-3/90 *Bernini v Minister van Onderwijs en Wetenschappen* [1992] ECR I-1071. For another case on the interrelation of studies and work see Case C-357/89 *Raulin v Minister van Onderwijs en Wetenschappen* [1992] ECR I-1027, [1994] 1 CMLR 227, ECJ.
7   See *EC Commission v Belgium* Case C-344/95 [1997] 2 CMLR 187, ECJ; Case C-292/89 *R v Immigration Appeal Tribunal, ex p Antonissen* [1991] ECR I-745, [1991] 2 CMLR 373.
8   See Council Regulation (EEC) 1612/68, Art 7. The directive makes a distinction between work seekers and those who have found employment, although they may be workers for the purpose of Art 39.
9   Case C-413/01 *Ninni-Orsache* fn 5 above.
10   Immigration (European Economic Area) Regulations 2000, SI 2000/2326, reg 5(2).

Employment in the public service

7.68 Article 39(4) EC (ex Article 48(4)) takes account of the legitimate interest of each Member State in the protection of its national interest by restricting employment in the public service to its own nationals.[1] But, since the exercise of this power is a derogation from the fundamental principle that workers in the Community should enjoy freedom of movement without discrimination on nationality grounds, it must be construed in such a way as to limit its scope to what is strictly necessary for safeguarding the interests which that provision allows Member States to protect.[2] According to the established case law, the derogation must be restricted to activities which in themselves are directly and specifically connected with the exercise of official authority.[3] The test is not the status of the civil servant, but whether the employee is responsible for exercising powers conferred by public law or for safeguarding the general interests of the State. There has to be direct and specific participation in the exercise of official authority. The exemption presupposes the existence of a special relationship to the State and the posts excluded are limited to those which, on account of the tasks and responsibilities attaching to them, are likely to have the characteristics of special administrative activities in these areas.[4] Rather surprisingly, the post of head, technical office supervisor, principal supervisor, work supervisor, stock controller, municipal night watchman and municipal architect in Belgium have been held to fall within the meaning of public service.[5] On the other hand trainee locomotive drivers, loaders, plate-layers, shunters and signallers with the Belgian National Railway, and unskilled workers with a local Belgian railway company, as well as hospital nurses, children's nurses, plumbers, carpenters, electricians and garden hands with the City of Brussels and the Commune of Auderghem have been held to be outside the category.[6] A nurse and trainee teacher, though having the status of civil servant, have also been held outside the exemption.[7] Court officials may be outside the exemption, but not judges.[8] Masters of ships and chief mates of merchant ships with flag flying duties have been held to fall within the exception.[9] In the case of research scientists, only those with duties of management or advising the State on scientific and technical questions would qualify.[10]

[1] Case C-443/93 *Vougioukas v Idrima Koinonikon Asphalisseon (IKA)* [1995] ECR I-4033, ECJ.

[2] Case C-147/86 *Commission v Greece* [1989] 2 CMLR 845, para 7, ECJ; Case C-114/97 *Commission v Spain* [1999] 2 CMLR 701, para 34, ECJ.

[3] *Commission v Spain* above, para 35; Case 2/74 *Reyners v Belgium* [1974] 2 CMLR 305, para 45, ECJ; Case C-42/92 *Thijssen v Controldienst voor de Vorzekeringen* [1993] ECR I-4047, para 8, ECJ.

[4] Case C-42/92 *Thijssen v Controldienst voor de Verzekeringen* [1993] ECR I-4047, ECJ (insurance commissioners in Belgium not covered by exemption); Case C-4/91 *Bleis v Ministère de l'Education Nationale* [1991] ECR I-5627, [1994] 1 CMLR 793, ECJ (school teachers not exempt); Case C-213/90 *ASTI (Association de Soutien aux Travailleurs Immigrés) v Chambre des Employés Privés* [1991] ECR I-3507, [1993] 3 CMLR 621, ECJ (guilds with policy advisory function not exempt).

[5] Case 149/79 *Commission v Belgium (No 2)* [1982] ECR 1845 at 1851, ECJ.

[6] *Commission v Belgium* above, at 1852; see also [1980] ECR 3881 at 3898, ECJ.

[7] Case 66/85 *Lawrie-Blum v Land Baden-Württemberg* [1986] ECR 2121, [1987] 3 CMLR 389, at para 28, ECJ (trainee teachers); Case 307/84 *Commission v France* [1986] ECR 1725, [1987] 3 CMLR 555, ECJ (nurses in public hospital); Case C-4/91 *Bleis v Ministere de l'Education Nationale* [1991] ECR I-5627, [1994] 1 CMLR 793, para 7, ECJ (secondary school teachers); Case C-259/91 *Allue v Universita degli Shidi di Venezia and University deglie Stidi di Parma* [1993] ECR I-4309, ECJ (university teachers); *Commission v Luxembourg* Case C-473/93 [1997] ECR I-3207, at para 33–34 (primary school teachers).

[8] Case 2/74 *Reyners v Belgium* [1974] ECR 631 at 655, ECJ. But for insurance commissioners see Case C-42/92 *Thijssen v Controldienst voor de Vorzekeringen* [1993] ECR I-4047, ECJ.

[9] Case C-405/01 *Colegio de Oficiales de la Marina Mercante Espanola v the State Administration* (2003) ECJ 30/9/2003.

¹⁰   *Lawrie-Blum*, above; Case 225/85 *Commission v Italy* [1987] ECR 2625, [1988] 3 CMLR 635, ECJ.

7.69   The interests which the public service exception allows Member States to protect are satisfied by the power to restrict the admission of foreign nationals to certain activities in the public service. But Article 39(4) EC goes no further than this, and cannot be used to justify discrimination as regards pay or other terms and conditions of employment against non-national workers once they have been admitted to the public service.¹ However, Article 39(4) may allow the exclusion of nationals of other Member States from the benefit of certain promotions or transfers within the public service, if these involve performing functions required to safeguard the general interests of the State.²

¹   Case 152/73 *Sotgiu v Deutsche Bundespost* [1974] ECR 153, ECJ; Case 225/85 *Commission v Italy* [1988] 3 CMLR 635, ECJ; Case 390/87 *Echternach v Minister van Onderwijs en Welenschappen* [1990] 2 CMLR 305, ECJ; Case 33/88 *Allué and Coonan v Universita degli Stidi di Venezia* [1991] 1 CMLR 283, ECJ.
²   See further Martin and Guild 7.50 fn 1 above, pp 44–47.

PERSONAL SCOPE (3) ESTABLISHMENT

7.70   Free movement rights apply to nationals of Member States and thereby to all EEA nationals who wish to establish themselves in another Member State or EEA country in business or as a self-employed person.¹ They apply to natural persons and to companies. The main provision is contained in Article 52 EC (now after amendment Article 43 EC). Article 43(1) now 'prohibits' restrictions on the freedom of establishment by nationals of a Member State in the territory of another Member State, including the setting up of agencies, branches or subsidiaries. Article 43(2) states that the freedom of establishment includes the right to take up and pursue activities as a self-employed person as well as the right to set up and manage undertakings. These measures are implemented by Council Directive (EEC) 73/148, Article 1 of which provides that freedom of movement rights extend to those who wish to establish themselves in a Member State. So, just as job seekers can benefit from free movement rights under Article 39, so also can those seeking opportunities for self-employment. This is mirrored in the Immigration (European Economic Area) Regulations 2000.² Regulation 5(1)(b) includes among 'a qualified person' an EEA national who is in the UK as 'a self-employed person'. 'Self-employed person' is then defined in regulation 3(1)(b) as someone who 'establishes himself in order to pursue activity as a self-employed person in accordance with Article 43 of the EC Treaty or who seeks to do so'. Although the right of establishment extends to companies, we are only dealing with the effect on people.

¹   The expression 'self-employed' is defined in Case 300/84 *Van Roosmalen v Beshiur van der Bedrijfscoreiniging voor de Gezonheid, Geestelijke en Maatschappelijke Belangen* [1986] ECR 3097, [1988] 3 CMLR 471, ECJ and in Case C-268/99 *Jany* [2001] ECR I-8615. Self-employment in Community law is defined as genuine and effective economic activity carried out outside of a relationship of subordination. For the position of families see 7.86ff below.
²   SI 2000/2326.

7.71 Although Article 43 EC (ex Article 52) confers a direct right of establishment free of restrictions based on nationality and non-discriminatory obstacles, it will only be a complete right when each Member State recognises training and educational and professional qualifications, obtained or recognised in other Member States, as equivalent to its own. There is a whole body of EC law dealing with the harmonisation of professional qualifications, their standardisation and mutual recognition which is outside the scope of the present work.[1]

[1] See, for example, Council Directives (EEC) 75/362 and 75/363 relating to the free movement of doctors. Free movement is limited to those doctors who are EEA nationals and who hold basic medical qualifications gained within the EEA. This excludes doctors of Asian origin who qualified outside the EEA. See Council Directive (EEC) 92/51 of 18 June 1992 (OJ L209 24.7.92 p 25) on a general system for recognition of professional education and training; Council resolution concerning nationals of Member States who hold a diploma awarded in a third country (OJ C187 24.7.92 p 1); Case C-309/90 *Commission v Greece* [1991] ECR I-5311, ECJ (architects' qualifications); Case C-313/89 *Commission v Spain* [1991] ECR I-5231, ECJ (midwives); Case C-351/90 *Commission v Luxembourg* [1992] 3 CMLR 124, ECJ (medical, dental and veterinary practitioners); Case C-377/90 *Commission v Belgium* [1992] ECR I-1229, ECJ (waterway transporters); Case C-166/91 *Bauer v Conseil National de l'Ordre des Architectes* [1993] 1 CMLR 141, ECJ; Case C-106/91 *Ramrath v Ministre de la Justice* [1992] 3 CMLR 173, ECJ (restrictions on practice as auditors); Case C-61/89 *Re Bouchoucha* [1990] ECR I-3551, [1992] 1 CMLR 1033, ECJ (non-recognition of osteopathy qualification gained in the UK); Case C-294/89 *Commission v France* [1991] ECR I-3591, [1993] 3 CMLR 569, ECJ (restriction of rule that local lawyer must be retained when non-national lawyers exercising Treaty rights).

7.72 Under Article 45 EC (ex Article 55) Member States are allowed to exclude from the equal treatment rule certain official activities, if they are activities which in the Member State are connected, even occasionally, with the exercise of official authority.[1] It is for each Member State to decide what constitutes official authority, but since the exception derogates from the fundamental rule of freedom of establishment, its scope is limited to what is strictly necessary in order to safeguard the interests which it allows the Member State to protect.[2] Setting up a supplementary school, a language school, a music school or a vocational training centre, or giving private tuition from home do not fall within the Article 45 exception.[3] The profession of 'notary' belongs within the exception,[4] but not that of lawyer.[5]

[1] Article 45 EC (ex Art 55). See 7.68 above, regarding employment in the public service.
[2] Case 147/86 *Commission v Greece* [1988] ECR 1637, [1989] 2 CMLR 845, ECJ. See also 7.68 above with respect to excluded categories of workers.
[3] *Commission v Greece* above.
[4] Martin and Guild 7.50 fn 1 above, p 67.
[5] Case 2/74 *Reyners v Belgium* [1974] ECR 631, [1974] 2 CMLR 305, ECJ. Other activities which have been excluded from the exception are: a lottery concessionaire and activities relating to the design, programming and operation of data systems for the public service (Case C-272/91 *Commission v Italy 'Public supply contract 3 – loto'* [1994] ECR I-1409, [1995] 2 CMLR 673, ECJ); activities of traffic accident experts (Case C-306/89 *Commission v Greece* [1991] ECR I-5863, [1994] 1 CMLR 803, ECJ); and the post of approved insurance commissioner (Case C-42/92 *Thijssen v Controldienst voor de Vorzekeringen* [1993] ECR I-4047, ECJ).

PERSONAL SCOPE (4) PROVISION AND RECEIPT OF SERVICES

Providing services

7.73 Akin to the right of establishment is the right given by the EC Treaty to provide services in another member country. The idea is that persons established in one country, for example, doctors, plumbers, tailors, etc, should be able to provide their services in other member countries. Article 49 EC (ex Article 59) prohibits restrictions on this right. Article 50 EC (ex Article 60) provides that the person providing a service may, in order to do so, temporarily pursue his activity in the State where the service is provided. The right to provide services includes the right to travel to the other country and to remain there long enough to perform them.[1] The right applies to companies as well as persons[2] but there are four conditions. First, the service provider, who is a natural person, must be a national of a Member State (an EEA national in our wider context). Secondly, he or she must be 'established' in a Member State.[3] Thirdly, the provision of services must normally involve the engagement by the provider in some sort of economic activity.[4] Fourthly, the right only arises if the provider of the services is established in country A and wishes to travel to country B. Visits to country B are clearly envisaged as temporary. If anything more permanent is intended, the provisions relating to establishment or workers will apply.[5] A Member State may not make the provision of services in its territory subject to compliance with all the conditions required for establishment.[6]

[1] Council Directive (EEC) 73/148, Art 1(1)(a); Case 186/87 *Cowan v Trésor Public* [1989] ECR 195 and Case C-68/89 *Commission v Netherlands* [1991] ECR I-2637, para 10). This right is reflected in reg 3(1)(c) and 5(1)(c) of the Immigration (European Economic Area) Regulations 2000, SI 2000/2326.
[2] Articles 48 EC (ex Art 58) and 55 EC (ex Art 66).
[3] An employed person, whether in his or her own State or in another, may benefit from Art 49 EC as someone 'established': see Case C-106/91 *Ramrath v Ministre de la Justice* [1992] ECR I-3351, [1992] 3 CMLR 173, ECJ; Case 143/87 *Stanton and SA Belge D'Assurances L'Etoile 1905 v INASTI (Institute National D'Essurance Sociales pour Travailleurs Indépendants)* [1988] ECR 3877, [1989] 3 CMLR 761, ECJ.
[4] Taking part in sporting events may involve engaging in economic activity, and therefore be the provision of services by the organisers of the event, even though those taking part are amateur athletes or players: Cases C-51 and 191/97 *Deliège v Ligne Francophone de Judo* (11 April 2000, unreported), ECJ.
[5] Case 196/87 *Steymann v Staatssecretaris Van Justitie* [1988] ECR 6159, [1989] 1 CMLR 449, ECJ. See further Case 220/83 *Commission v France* [1986] ECR 3663, [1987] 2 CMLR 113, ECJ (co-insurance services); Case C-113/89 *Rush Portuguesa Lda v ONI* [1990] ECR I-1417, [1991] 2 CMLR 818, ECJ.
[6] See the judgments in Case C-154/89 *Commission v France* [1991] ECR I-659, para 12, and in Case C-76/90 *Saeger v Dennemeyer* [1991] ECR I-4221, para 13.

7.74 The right to provide services is a kind of mini-right of establishment. It allows such persons to leave their own country,[1] to enter the territory of another Member State[2] and gives a right of residence 'of equal duration with the period during which the services are provided'.[3] For visits of less than three months, no formalities other than having an identity card or passport are needed, but if the visit exceeds three months the person becomes entitled to be issued with what is referred to in the directive as a 'right of abode as proof of the right of residence'.[4] Family members are included in the free movement rights on the same basis as those of workers.[5] The restriction of rights in the case of the exercise of official authority are the same as for business people.[6]

1   Council Directive (EEC) 73/148, Art 2.
2   Council Directive (EEC) 73/148, Art 3.
3   Council Directive (EEC) 73/148, Art 4(2).
4   Council Directive (EEC) 73/148, Art 4.
5   See 7.86 below.
6   See 7.72 above.

Posted workers

7.75 Where companies carry out contracts in another Member State, they will usually bring with them a mixture of employees. Some will be nationals of Member States (or EEA nationals). They will often qualify as 'workers' and be covered by Article 39 EC. But in other cases posted personnel may properly be considered as falling within the scope of Article 49 EC rather than Article 39, although it may be difficult to determine which.[1] In either case, the concern (especially in the building trade) is whether the posted workers are being subjected to an exploitative regime. Although normally national legislation in the receiving State is unable to restrict the provision of services, the public interest relating to the social protection of workers may constitute an overriding requirement, justifying such a restriction, if there is insufficient protection in the State where the service provider is established.[2] However, other posted personnel may be third country nationals, whom the service-providing company wishes to bring with it. Here we have one of the most significant developments with regard to the provision of services by companies. In the *Rush Portuguesa* case[3] it was held that a company established in the EC has the right to transfer its non-EC national labour force to another Member State for the duration of the project. It is unnecessary to obtain work permits for the posted non-EC national employees and a failure to do so cannot make the employer liable to penal sanctions, as happened in the *Vander Elst* case,[4] where the posted worker was a Moroccan who was settled in Belgium and posted to France. However, there is nothing in Article 49 or the case law to prevent the employer recruiting his or her labour force from nationals of a third country, who habitually work in that third country, for example in a subsidiary of the main undertaking. Although posted workers do not need work permits, it is unclear whether they enter and reside as of right, although this would seem to be a necessary consequence of the case-law.[5] Given the uncertainty, it seems that at present they will need to comply with the host State's laws regarding entry.[6] Posted workers working for Swiss employers are in a different position; they are given an express right of entry under the EC-Switzerland Free Movement Agreement.[7]

1   Case C-106/91 *Ramrath v Luxembourg* [1992] ECR I-3351, paras 15–16, ECJ.
2   Case C-272/94 *Guiot* [1996] ECR I-1905, ECJ.
3   Case C-113/89 *Rush Portuguesa Lda v ONI* [1990] ECR I-1417, [1991] 2 CMLR 818, ECJ.
4   Case C-43/93 *Vander Elst v Office des Migrations Internationales* [1994] ECR I-3803, ECJ.

5   See *Vander Elst*, above, at paras 19–22, where the issue is alluded to but not dealt with. The EEA Regulations SI 2000/2326 as amended by SI 2002/1241, regs 3(1)(ba) and 12(3) only deal with posted workers employed by Swiss nationals or Swiss undertakings and neatly avoid the issue of posted workers from other Member States.

6   However those rules on entry cannot be unnecessarily restrictive, see *Commission v Luxembourg* Case C-445/03 (14 October 2004, unreported). The problem is that under UK domestic law posted workers, other than those coming from from Switzerland, have no existence either in the EEA Regulations SI 2000/2326 as amended or in the Immigration rules; see 7.117ff, below. The practice of UK Embassies has been to require posted workers to have been employed for at least one year by the company abroad. In the light of *Commission v Luxembourg* this requirement cannot be strictly applied.

7   Agreement between the European Community and the Swiss Confederation on The Free Movement of Persons (30 April 2002 OJ L114/6). Article 1 of Annex I of the Agreement provides that 'the Contracting Parties shall allow ... posted persons within the meaning of Article 17 of this Annex to enter their territory simply upon production of a valid identity card or passport.' Article 17 defines posted persons as '... employees, irrespective of their nationality, of persons providing services, who are integrated into one Contracting Party's regular labour market and posted for the provision of a service in the territory of another Contracting Party ...'

7.76 The Posted Workers Directive intends to ensure the trans-national provision of services under conditions of fair competition and of guaranteed workers' rights.[1] The directive obliges EEA States to ensure that, whatever the law applicable to the employment relationship may be, the undertakings guarantee workers posted to their territory the terms and conditions of their employment. Thus it regulates the legal framework of working conditions and applicable employment legislation, so as to alleviate concerns that posted workers would not access the same protection as other employees. It applies to both nationals of Member States and third country nationals. In addition to the Directive the EC principles of non-discrimination and not placing obstacles in the way of free movement also apply.[2] Where the requirements of the host State create obstacles to free movement rights, a breach of Article 39 EC may occur without any need to consider whether there has been indirect discrimination on nationality grounds under Article 39(2) EC.[3]

1   Directive 96/71/EC of the European Parliament and of the Council of 16 December 1996 concerning the posting of workers in the framework of the provision of services, (OJ L 018, 21/01/1997 p 0001–0006).

2   See Case C-369/96 *Criminal Proceedings against Arblade* [1999] ECR I-8453.

3   Case C-18/95 *Terhoeve (FC) v Inspecteur van de Belashingdiens Parhailiere Ondernemingen Buitenland* [1999] ECR I-345.

Receiving services

7.77 Where the provisions dealing with services broke new ground was in the implementing provisions. Article 1(1)(b) of Council Directive (EEC) 73/148 provides that *recipients* of services, not just providers, are entitled to enter the territory of another Member State to receive services. The far-reaching nature of these provisions was established in the landmark decision in *Luisi and Carbone*.[1] There the ECJ held that the freedom to provide services includes the freedom, for the recipients of the services, to go to another Member State in order to receive a service there, and that tourists, persons receiving medical treatment and persons travelling for the purpose of education and business are to be regarded as recipients of services. This decision was followed by *Cowan* *v Trésor Public*[2] where it was held that a British tourist to Paris was exercising rights to seek services, and therefore could not be excluded from compensation for criminal injuries on the grounds of nationality.

[1]   Joined Cases 286/82 and 26/83 *Luisi and Carbone v Ministero del Tesoro* [1984] ECR 377, [1985] 3 CMLR 52, ECJ. To qualify as a person who can be said to be in receipt of services under the free movement rights, there needs to be something more substantial than listening to Radio Luxembourg (see *R v Secretary of State for the Home Department, ex p Tombofa* [1988] 2 CMLR 609, [1988] Imm AR 400, CA), or pursuing a court case in the Family Division of the High Court in the UK (see *Liem* (5983), IAT, unreported). Normally there will have to be a crossing of the frontiers of one EC State to another to bring Art 49 into play. See further *Tisseyre* (6052), IAT, unreported, where the visit was to a friend and the only services used would be those needed to travel there; held not sufficient to bring into play Art 49 EC.

[2]   Case 186/87 *Cowan v Trésor Public* [1989] ECR 195, [1990] 2 CMLR 613, ECJ.

7.78 In *Belgium v Humbel*[1] the court restricted the principle, so far as students are concerned, to services 'normally provided for remuneration'. These will include services of an industrial and commercial character as well as the activities of craftsmen and professionals, but not courses of study provided within the framework of the national education system, even where pupils of parents have to pay fees or make other financial contributions. Students at State institutions may not benefit, but it is thought that genuine students at private educational establishments and tourists both benefit, as well as their spouses.[2] Vocational students in State education now qualify for residence during their studies under Council Directive (EEC) 93/96, which we consider at 7.81 below. The court recently held in the case of *Chen* that recipients of services should be receiving those services on a temporary basis, not long-term or permanently.[3]

[1]   Case 263/86 [1988] ECR 5365, [1989] 1 CMLR 393, ECJ. For confirmation that fee-paying students are receiving services, see Case C-109/92 *Wirth v Landeshauptstadt Hannover* [1993] ECR I-6447, ECJ.

[2]   See Case C-357/89 *Raulin v Minister van Onderwys en Welenschappen* [1992] ECR I-1027.

[3]   Case C-200/02 (1) *Chen (Man Lavette)* (2) *Zhu (Kunqian Catherine) v Secretary Of State For The Home Department, judgment* (19 October 2004, unreported), para 22. Recipients of services are covered in the EEA Regulations SI 2000/2326, regs 3(1)(d) and 5(1)(d).

7.79 The nationality of the provider of services is crucial for the application of Articles 49 and 50 EC rights, but in *Svensson* the ECJ held that nationality was irrelevant so far as concerned the recipient of services.[1] Does this mean that a recipient of services, who happens to be a third country national, may move within the Community in order to enable the provider of a service effectively to provide that service? Does the application of Article 49 to third country nationals, as recipients of services, allow them to travel freely to another Member State, if that is an essential element of the provision of the services? It is much more likely that the proposition only holds good when considering the free movement rights of the provider of services, but not vice versa.

[1]   Case C-484/93 [1995] ECR I-3955.

PERSONAL SCOPE (5) STUDENTS, THE SELF-SUFFICIENT AND
THE RETIRED

Students

7.80 We have already seen that fee-paying students will qualify for admission
to another Member State as recipients of services.[1] Dependants of EC workers
or the self-employed will also have rights of access to general and vocational
education and consequential rights to remain under the directive dealing with
family members.[2] Vocational training referred to in Article 150 EC (ex
Article 127) has long been an indispensable element in the Community, to be
available to nationals of Member States without discrimination.[3] But it was
not thought to give a right of entry or general residence.[4] In order to give
effect to free movement in the single market, it was considered necessary to
make some provision for those who do not enjoy rights under other parts of
Community law.

[1] See 7.78 above. For a general summary of the position of EEA students see 9.30 fn 1
   below.
[2] Council Regulation (EEC) 1612/68, Art 12. For discussion on the breadth of these rights
   see 7.84 below.
[3] Case 293/83 *Gravier v City of Liège* [1985] ECR 593, ECJ; *Belgium v Humbel* [1988]
   ECR 5365; *Blaizot v University of Liège* [1988] ECR 379; Case 42/87 *Commission v
   Belgium: Higher Education Funding* [1988] ECR 5445; Case C-47/93 *Commission v
   Belgium* [1994] ECR I-1593.
[4] The right of residence implied by the non-discrimination requirement is limited to the
   purpose and duration of the studies: Case C-357/89 *Raulin v Minister von Ordernijs*
   [1992] ECR I-1027. However more recently the decision in the case of *D'hoop (Marie-
   Nathalie) v Office National de l' Emploi* (Case C-224/98 – (2002) ECJ 11/7/2002) suggests
   that an EU citizen who moved to another Member State in order to study exercises a
   Community law freedom.

7.81 Council Directive (EEC) 93/96 provides for a right of residence during
the duration of a course of studies at a recognised educational establishment,
if the principal purpose of the enrolment is to follow a vocational training
course.[1] The ambit of the Directive is quite limited, and students are likely to
be better off relying on other provisions of Community law if they can. First,
there is no right to any maintenance grant.[2] Secondly, students must be
covered by sickness insurance in respect of all risks in the Member State.[3]
Thirdly, they must show that they have 'sufficient resources to avoid becoming
a burden on the social assistance system of the host Member State during their
period of residence'.[4] The ECJ has qualified this last requirement by hold that
students are to avoid becoming an 'unreasonable' burden on Member States.
A temporary need for social assistance would not cause a student to fall foul
of this requirement, particularly if the student had been lawfully resident and
studying in the Member State for a substantial length of time.[5] Vocational
training is given a broad definition and is likely to include any courses beyond
primary education which are linked to preparation for a career or professional
qualifications.[6]

[1] Council Directive (EEC) 93/96, Art 1(1). But see Case C-209/03 *R (on the application of
   Bidar) v London Borough of Ealing v Secretary of State for Education and Skills* (2005)
   ECJ 15 March 2005, where the Court held that, while it is permissible for Member States
   to ensure that assistance to students from other Member States does not become an

unreasonable burden, the non-discrimination provisions of the Treaty cover assistance given to students, and were breached by domestic law provisions limiting student grants and loans to those settled in the UK, since this restriction excluded EU citizens who were integrated into the host Member State.

2   Council Directive (EEC) 93/96, Art 3.

3   Council Directive (EEC) 93/96, Art 1.

4   Council Directive (EEC) 93/936, Art 1. See the EEA Regulations, SI 2000/2326, reg 3(1)(g), 5(1)(g).

5   Case C-184/99 *Grzelczyk (Rudy) v Centre public d'aide sociale d'Ottignies-Louvain-la-Neuve* (20 September 2001, unreported).

6   Case C-295/90 *Parliament v Council* [1992] ECR I-4193, [1992] 3 CMLR 281, ECJ; *Gravier* above; *Humbel* above.

7.82 Students qualifying under the Council Directive (EEC) 93/936 can be joined by a spouse and dependent children but do not enjoy the rather more generous family provisions for the self-sufficient and retired. Family members joining a student can take employment irrespective of their nationality.[1]

1   Council Directive (EEC) 93/936, Arts 1(1) and 2(2). See the EEA Regulations, SI 2000/2326, reg 6(2). See also the support requirements in reg 3(4) (as amended by SI 2004/1236).

The self-sufficient

7.83 Nationals of Member States who do not work but have sufficient resources to avoid becoming a burden on the social assistance system of the host Member State are entitled to a right of residence if they do not qualify under some other provision of Community law, provided that they and their families are covered in respect of all risks by sickness insurance during the period of residence.[1] The conditions placed on those wishing to exercise this right of residence must be applied in a manner which is proportionate, so that a temporary need for social assistance or failure to provide evidence of sickness insurance may not result in the automatic refusal of the host Member State to recognise the right of residence.[2]

1   Council Directive (EEC) 90/364, Art 1(1). These provisions are reflected in the EEA Regulations, SI 2000/2326 (as amended by SI 2004/1236), reg 3(1)(e) and (2). They were applied to an infant child in *Chen and Zhu v Secretary of State for the Home Department* C-200/02 (19 October 2004, unreported), ECJ.

2   Case C-413/99 *Baumbast v Secretary of State for the Home Department* [2003] INLR 1.

7.84 The family members who can join the self-sufficient are a spouse and any dependent descendants of that person, or the spouse and any of their dependent relatives in the ascending line (ie parents and grandparents).[1] The spouse and dependent children are entitled to take employment or self-employment irrespective of whether they are nationals of a Member State.[2] Where the self-sufficient person is an infant child, her parent who is her primary carer is allowed to accompany her in order to give meaning to the child's free movement and residence rights.[3]

1   Council Directive (EEC) 90/364, Art 1(2), reflected in the EEA Regulations, SI 2000/2326 (as amended by SI 2001/865), reg 6(4).

2   Council Directive (EEC) 90/364, Art 2(2).

3   *Chen and Zhu v Secretary of State for the Home Department* C-200/02 (19 October 2004, unreported), ECJ. Following the judgment, new immigration rules regulate the entry of the primary carer and relatives of such EEA national self-sufficient children: see HC 395, paras 275C–275E, inserted by HC 164 (in force 1 January 2005).

The retired

7.85 Workers and the self-employed who reach pensionable age or are invalided out of work or incapacitated in the host country are entitled to remain in permanent residence under the provisions of Council Directive 90/365 (EEC) which also applies to those who wish to move to another Member State after retirement without having previously exercised economic activity there. To qualify for this right a retired person must be in receipt of an invalidity or early retirement pension, or old age benefits or a pension in respect of an industrial accident or disease. The funds so received must be sufficient to avoid the person and any family members becoming a burden on the social security system of the host Member State during the period of residence.[1] The person and accompanying family members must be covered by sickness insurance in respect of all risks. The family reunion rights are the same as for self-sufficient persons.[2]

1   Council Directive (EEC) 90/365, Art 1(1), reflected in the EEA Regulations, SI 2000/2326 (as amended by SI 2004/1236), reg 3(1)(f), (3), reg 5(1)(f).
2   Council Directive (EEC) 90/365, Art 1(2); SI 2000/2326, reg 6(4).

MEMBERS OF THE FAMILY

7.86 In addition to workers, the self-employed, students and those providing or receiving services, the right of free movement is also given to the spouse and other family members of such persons. This is principally done through Part I, Title III of Council Regulation (EEC) 1612/68, and Council Directives (EEC) 68/360 and 73/148, all of which are printed in the Appendix.[1] Although the exercise of family rights depends on the exercise of Community rights by the principal, in content they are virtually the same as the principal's right to enter, reside in and remain in another EEA country.[2] They are given irrespective of the sex or nationality of the family members. Thus the Pakistani or American husband of a woman who is an EU national is entitled to accompany his wife when she exercises her right to set up in business, to seek work or to receive or provide services. The provisions in Community law relating to family members are designed to give effect to the free movement rights of the EU national, and are based upon the notion that obstacles to workers being joined by their families and integrated into the host State are obstacles to free movement within the EU.[3] The ECJ has stressed that the integration of EEA nationals and their family members into the host State is a fundamental objective required to ensure that workers and their families resident in a host State enjoy no disadvantage with respect to those who are nationals of the host State.[4] In Case C-308/89 *Di Leo v Land Berlin*[5] (a case involving the right to education for children of EU workers) the court stated:

'... the aim of Regulation 1612/68, namely freedom of movement for workers, requires for such freedom to be guaranteed in compliance with the principles of liberty and dignity, the best possible conditions for the integration of the Community worker's family in the society of the host country.'

The ECJ has emphasised the need to give effect to fundamental rights and in particular the right to respect for family life protected by Article 8 of the European Convention on Human Rights:[6]

'Moreover, in accordance with the case-law of the Court, Regulation No 1612/68 must be interpreted in the light of the requirement of respect for family life laid down in Article 8 of the European Convention. That requirement is one of the fundamental rights which, according to settled case-law, are recognised by Community law.'

It is notable that the ECJ fully endorses the approach to Article 8 ECHR taken by the European Court of Human Rights in the case of *Boultif*,[7] and the application of Article 8 by the ECJ has been favourable to applicants.[8]

[1] Article 10 of Council Regulation (EEC) 1612/68 is incorporated into Council Regulation (EEC) 1251/70 and Directive 72/194; Art 1 of Council Directive (EEC) 73/148 is incorporated by Council Directive (EEC) 75/34. Council Directives (EEC) 90/364, 90/365 and 90/366 have their own definitions of family members. For a full discussion of EC rights of family reunion see Prof Steve Peers 'Family reunion in Community law', in Walker (ed) *Europe's Area of Freedom, Security and Justice* (2004) OUP. Note that these provisions will all be amended or replaced by Council Directive 2004/38 on 30.04.06 (European Citizens' Directive).

[2] Case 131/85 *Gül v Regierungspräsident Düsseldorf* [1986] ECR 1573, [1987] 1 CMLR 501, ECJ.

[3] The recital of the third Preamble to Council Regulation (EEC) 1612/68 recognises that 'freedom of movement constitutes a fundamental right of workers and their families' and the fifth recital affirms that in order for the right to be exercised with freedom and dignity 'equality of treatment shall be secured in fact and in law'.

[4] Case 249/86 *EC Commission v Germany* [1989] ECR 1263, paras 11–12; [1990] 3 CMLR 540; see also Case 267/83 *Diatta v Land Berlin* [1985] ECR 567, [1986] 2 CMLR 164, paras 14–18 and 20, ECJ. In the context of Association Agreements see Case C-351/95 *Kadiman v Freistaat Bayern* [1997] ECR I-2133, para 30.

[5] [1990] ECR I-4185, para 13. See more recently Case C-459/99 *Mouvement Contre Le Racisme, L'Antisemitisme et la Xenophobie ASBL) v Belgium* [2002] ECR I-6591, 25/7/2002.

[6] Case C-413/99 *Baumbast and R v Secretary of State for the Home Department* [2003] INLR 1, para 77.

[7] *Boultif v Switzerland* [2001] 2 FLR 1228.

[8] Case C-60/00 *Carpenter (Mary) v Secretary of State for the Home Department* [2002] ECR I-6279, [2002] INLR 439.

7.87 The Immigration (European Economic Area) Regulations 2000[1] replace, refine and extend the 1994 definition of 'family member', which was limited to a spouse, descendants of EEA nationals or their spouse who are under 21 years of age or dependent, and dependent relatives in the ascending line.[2] This definition met the requirements of Article 10(1) of Council Regulation (EEC) 1612/68 but did not give effect to the broader obligation in Article 10(2) to facilitate the admission of family members, not coming within the above list, if they are dependent on the person with the primary right or were living under their roof in the country from which they have come.[3] The 2000 Regulations are more comprehensive and attempt to give effect to the broad scope of family rights provided under Community law. Under regulation 6 of the 2000

Regulations, the range of family members who are entitled to join the EEA national depends on the primary right exercised by the EEA national, so that:

(1)   *students* – can be joined by spouse and dependent children;[4]
(2)   *other cases (including workers, the self-sufficient and retired)* – can be joined by spouse, descendants of either spouse under 21 or dependent; dependent relatives in the ascending line of either spouse.[5]

So the categories of persons who may benefit are:

- spouse;
- children under 21 or dependent on their parents;
- dependent grandchildren;
- non-dependent grandchildren under 21 (in the case of workers only);
- dependent relatives in the ascending line (eg parents, grandparents).

The regulations provide that students, self-sufficient and retired persons (but not workers or self-employed persons), who bring their families to the UK, must ensure that they have sufficient resources to avoid becoming a burden on the social assistance system of the UK, and that all members of the family are covered by sickness insurance.[6]

1   SI 2000/2326 as amended by SI 2001/865, SI 2003/549, SI 2003/3188, SI 2004/1236 and SI 2005/47.
2   Immigration (European Economic Area) Order 1994, SI 1994/1895, Art 2.
3   Council Regulation (EEC) 1612/68, Art 10(2).
4   SI 2000/2326, reg 6(2).
5   SI 2000/2326, reg 6(4). Regulation 6(3) has been deleted by SI 2001/865.
6   SI 2000/2326 (as amended by SI 2004/1236), reg 3(2)–(5). This provision does not preclude assistance by way of a student grant or loan to integrated EU citizens: see *R (on the application of Bidar) v London Borough of Ealing v Secretary of State for Education and Skills* Case C-209/03 (15 March 2005, unreported) ECJ.

Spouse

7.88   Currently, a spouse means a person who is formally contracted in a legal marriage.[1] The Immigration (European Economic Area) Regulations 2000 do not give any definition, except to exclude 'a party to a marriage of convenience'.[2] This is a controversial limitation the effect of which has never been authoritatively decided.[3] The EC Regulation and Directives refer simply to 'spouse'. Community law does not permit an examination into how the couple met or why they married. The right of residence must be acknowledged by the host State on production of the documents identified by Community legislation.[4] Thus there has never been any equivalent notion of a 'primary purpose' test in Community law.[5] The Home Office view is that such a marriage is outside the protection of Community law and does not give rise to rights; hence the definition of 'spouse' in the Immigration (European Economic Area) Order 1994 and now the Immigration (European Economic Area) Regulations 2000.[6] The Tribunal has also taken the same line,[7] concluding that a marriage of convenience which does not involve cohabitation or family life at all is unlikely to be relevant to the purposes of the legislation. The furthest the ECJ has gone in this regard is to note that fraudulent conduct or use of Community law to evade national provisions is not permitted.[8] The reference to fraudulent conduct suggests that, to derogate from the directives and regulation on family reunion, it will be necessary to rely on grounds of public policy, public security or public health, as interpreted in Community law.[9]

1 Case 59/85 *Netherlands v Reed* [1986] ECR 1283; Compare Case T-65/92 *Arauxo-Dumay v EC Commission* [1993] ECR II-597. See *R v Secretary of State for the Home Department, ex p Morono Lopez* [1997] Imm AR 11, QBD.
2 SI 2000/2326, reg 2(1). See 11.61 below.
3 A Council Resolution on marriages of convenience makes a broad statement of policy against such arrangements and a commitment by Member States to combat their use to obtain admission and residence, but is expressly stated to be 'without prejudice to Community law'.
4 The Member State may only require from the spouse the document on which he or she entered the territory and a document issued by a competent authority proving the relationship. See eg Council Directive (EEC) 68/360, Art 4(3).
5 See below; however, EU policy on third-country nationals suggests that governments are attracted to some such test as propounded by the UK: see London Resolution of European Council, December 1992.
6 SI 2000/2326, reg 2(1), Immigration (European Economic Area) Order 1994, SI 1994/1895, Art 2(2). The minister introducing the 1994 Order in Parliament recognised that 'EC law does not enable us to apply all the provisions of the immigration rules, such as the primary purpose test, in EEA marriage cases, but we do not accept that a party to a marriage of convenience has any right to benefit from EC law relating to the admission and residence of family members. We intend to maintain a strong line against bogus marriages and we will ensure that non-EEA nationals are not able to use marriages of convenience as a way of obtaining residence in the United Kingdom'. (HC Official Report (6th series) col 68, 9 May 1994).
7 *Yee-Kee Kwong* (10661); *Kam Yu Lau* (10859), applied in *Desmond* (15063), *Yuen* (18283) (16 June 1998, unreported), IAT.
8 Case C-370/90 *R v Immigration Appeal Tribunal and Surinder Singh, ex p Secretary of State for the Home Department* [1992] Imm AR 565 at 569–570; [1992] ECR I-4265, ECJ. This was more recently confirmed in *Secretary of State for the Home Department v Akrich*, Case C-109/01 [2004] INLR 36, where the ECJ stated that there would be an abuse if Community law were invoked in the context of marriages of convenience entered into in order to circumvent national immigration laws (see para 57).
9 Council Directives (EEC) 64/221 and 73/148, Art 8. In the case of *R v Immigration Appeal Tribunal, ex p Cheema and Ullah* [1982] Imm AR 124 the CA held that it was in the public interest to deport those who had gained admission by marriages of convenience, and thereby undermined a fundamental institution of society. At first instance Woolf J had interpreted the power to deport under s 3(5)(b) (now s 3(5)(a)) of the Immigration Act 1971 by reference to the EC concept of public policy under Council Directive (EEC) 64/221 and held that deportation on such grounds was permissible. See 7.127 below.

7.89 These issues were to be litigated in the case of *Ex p Clinton*,[1] where permission was granted to challenge the expulsion of a spouse of a Community national whose marriage was alleged to be one of convenience. One of the grounds of challenge was that the Immigration (European Economic Area) Order 1994[2] violated Community law in excluding such spouses from the definition of family member, and that expulsion was only possible if the Secretary of State for the Home Department could establish a public policy derogation.[3] However, the case was conceded and the claimant was granted indefinite leave to enter in the light of the affidavit evidence suggesting that the marriage was not one of convenience.[4] In *Chang*,[5] a starred Tribunal held that Article 4(3) of Council Directive (EEC) 68/360 did not preclude fuller investigation of a relationship which came into existence after the applicant last entered the UK, and that Community law did not prevent the UK from regulating marriage. On the facts, the appellant's marriage was one of convenience, and he was not a family member of an EU national.

1   (CO 3111/94) 27 October 1994, Turner J.
2   SI 1994/1895.
3   Likewise, leave to appeal to the Court of Appeal was granted in *Kwong* (10661) on the central issue of whether the nature of the marriage or a public policy derogation determined the status of the spouse, but the appeal was withdrawn.
4   This contrasts with the refusal of permission in *R v Immigration Appeal Tribunal, ex p Cheung* [1995] Imm AR 104 where Popplewell J assumed without deciding that the Tribunal in *Kam Yu Lau* (10859) was correct, and determined the application on a *Wednesbury* basis, concluding that there was material upon which a reasonable Secretary of State for the Home Department could conclude that the marriage was one of convenience.
5   *Chang* (01TH00100) (starred) (24 April 2001, unreported), IAT.

7.90 In our opinion, it is inappropriate for national legislation to qualify Community rights by giving a restrictive definition of spouse when there is no definition of 'marriage of convenience' in the directives or regulations, when opinions differ as to the meaning of this phrase and when the proper approach must be through the public policy derogation. In correspondence arising from the parliamentary debate in respect of the Immigration (European Economic Area) Order 1994,[1] the minister offered the following definition:

> 'A marriage of convenience is regarded as a sham marriage which is entered into solely for immigration purposes where the partners have no intention of living with the other as man and wife in a settled and genuine relationship.'[2]

The implication that cohabitation is necessary to avoid a finding of a marriage of convenience is at odds with Community law, which does not require a couple to live under the same roof, so that a genuine relationship as man and wife can exist irrespective of cohabitation.[3] The ECJ's judgment in *Akrich* suggests that a marriage of convenience is one which is entered into solely for the purpose of circumventing immigration control.[4] Furthermore, evidence of some disqualifying aspect to the marriage may be hard to find. There is no power of compulsory interview for any alien (EEA citizen or not) *after* entry to the UK. Detailed and intrusive questioning as to the couple's motives is inconsistent with the swift and summary procedure for obtaining confirmation of the rights of admission under EC law. It may be that if a Member State's authorities can demonstrate that a marriage to an EEA national possesses all the disqualifying characteristics, then a residence permit can be refused or expulsion initiated in the absence of other grounds to remain. The burden of proof is firmly on the State, and since under the Immigration (European Economic Area) Regulations 2000[5] admission under EC law depends on the definition of 'spouse', and is, therefore, a matter of jurisdiction, proof that a marriage is one of convenience should be treated as a 'precedent fact'. The issue has not been resolved in the Administrative Court.[6] If public policy permits Member States to take measures to deny residence to those prima facie entitled to it, the derogation must be strictly construed, and the exercise of such power should not be used to apply some version of the discredited primary purpose rule, with its concomitant paraphernalia of delay, humiliating investigation, separation and suffering.

1   SI 1994/1895.

2   Lord Annaly to Lord McIntosh, 24 May 1994. This test is stricter than the definition under the previous Immigration Rules (see *R v Immigration Appeal Tribunal, ex p Mahmud Khan* [1983] QB 790, [1982] Imm AR 134).
3   See Case 267/83 *Diatta v Land Berlin* [1986] 2 CMLR 164, ECJ.
4   Case C-109/01 *Secretary of State for the Home Department v Akrich* [2004] INLR 36 ECJ.
5   SI 2000/2326.
6   See 7.89 above.

7.91 In *Reed v Netherlands*[1] the ECJ ruled that cohabiting but unmarried heterosexual couples could not be included in the definition of spouse. The court acknowledged the need to give a purposive approach to Community legislation, but decided that it could not yet give such a broad interpretation, in the absence of evidence of a clear consensus within the Member States of the Community, to treat common law relationships on the same basis as marriage.[2] In *Reed* it was not argued that an unmarried partner may qualify under the broader provisions of Article 10(2) of Council Regulation (EEC) 1612/68, which refers to 'any other family member'. Instead, the court ruled that since the Netherlands allowed cohabiting partners of Dutch nationals to obtain residence in the country on the basis of the relationship, it violated the principles of non-discrimination to refuse to extend the same benefit to the unmarried partners of EU nationals. The presence of such a partner was recognised as a 'social advantage' for the purposes of the non-discrimination provision of Article 7 of regulation 1612/68.[3] The non-discrimination principle can found a right of residence.[4] Although the Commission hinted in a Communication that the ECJ had not had to rule on the question of cohabiting couples recently, in a 1999 staff case, the Court of First Instance found that cohabiting couples could not be treated as spouses.[5]

1   Case 59/85 *Netherlands v Reed* [1986] ECR 1283, [1987] 2 CMLR 448, ECJ.
2   Two decades later this conclusion should, we suggest, be revisited, given the social developments and increased recognition afforded to cohabiting relationships within the Union.
3   Article 7 of Council Regulation (EEC) 1612/68 prohibits discrimination on the grounds of nationality in respect of the conditions of employment and work (Arts 7(1) and (4)), and provides for equality of treatment in respect of social and tax advantages (Art 7(2)), and in the conditions for access to training in vocational schools and retraining centres (Art 7(3)).
4   See Case C-237/91 *Kus v Landeshauptstadt Wiesbaden* [1992] ECR I-6781, para 28, where the ECJ recognised, in the context of the Turkish Association Agreement, that the right of residence must necessarily be implied to give effect to the non-discrimination provisions.
5   Case T-264/97 *D-Council* ECR Staff Cases [1999].

7.92 Disappointingly, the recently adopted Citizen's Directive does not extend Community law to give cohabiting couples family reunion rights, although it does codify existing practice, achieved through the non-discrimination provisions recognised in the *Reed* decision.[1] There is still scope for much improvement in this field to bring Community law in line with societal and demographic changes.[2] Home Office policy is to apply the unmarried partners rule to unmarried partners of EEA nationals.[3]

1   A 'family member' includes a partner with whom the Union citizen has contracted a registered partnership under the legislation of the host Member State, if such legislation treats registered partnerships as equivalent to marriage: Directive 2004/38/EC, Art 2(2)(b). Other partners in durable relationships, duly attested, are admissible in accordance with national legislation: Art 3(2)(b). The Directive comes into force in April 2006.

2   It remains open to the court to extend the legal definition of spouse to reflect changes in social norms since 1968 and since the judgment in *Reed* in 1986; compare Case T-43/90 *Diaz Garcia v European Parliament* [1992] ECR II-2619 ('legal responsibility to maintain' in staff regulations does not apply to a cohabitee).

3   Unmarried partners (including same sex partners) would be given two years' leave to remain in the first instance, and then a further three years. After four years they could apply for settlement: letter from HO International Policy Directorate to Clifford Chance, 16 July 2002. For the unmarried partners' rule see 11.70 below. Fiancé(e)s are not treated as family members of EEA nationals until after their marriage: HO International Policy Directorate to Northern Ireland Law Centre, 18 November 2002.

7.93 The spouse's right of residence is generally dependent on that of the principal. Thus where the worker leaves the territory permanently, adjectival rights will generally cease. In the case of *Sandhu*[1] the couple separated and the applicant's EEC spouse had gone back to Germany. The Court of Appeal in England held that the applicant was no longer within EEC protection and his residence in the UK could, therefore, be curtailed. The House of Lords dismissed an appeal, concluding that the decision in *Diatta* rendered the question *acte claire*.[2] In *Botta*[3] a deportation order was made against the EEC wife of a non-EEC alien, and the English court held that he lost his EEC right of residence as from that moment. The position for childless couples, or couples with no dependent children or grandchildren living with them, can now be summarised as follows: A non-EEA spouse in the UK loses the benefit of EC law if (a) the parties divorce, but not if they separate and remain in the UK;[4] (b) they separate and the EEA spouse leaves the UK to live permanently in another country; or (c) the EEA national is deported. Even those positions are not absolutes. In the unusual circumstances where a couple divorce but remain living together in a relationship akin to marriage and later re-marry, they can include the intervening period as constituting family life protected by Community law.[5] The situation for couples looking after dependent children or grandchildren has been transformed since the case of *Baumbast and R*,[6] where the ECJ considered the rights of a third country national divorcée and of a third country national whose spouse was working outside the EU. In both cases, their dependent children were resident in the UK. The ECJ decided that the children, who were the children of an EU national formerly working in the UK, had acquired the right to enter general education and thereby the right to remain for the duration of their studies in the UK through Article 12 of Regulation 1612/68. Their mother, who was their primary carer with no other right to remain in the UK, was said to facilitate the exercise of their Community law rights. If unable to remain with her children, this would constitute a breach of Community law having regard to Article 8 ECHR. The case had a significant impact, leading to changes in the Immigration (European Economic Area) Regulations[7] so that, where there are dependent descendants under 19 in full-time education, the definition of 'family member' includes the divorced spouse, and the spouse or divorced spouse of an EEA national who has left the UK, provided that he or she is the primary carer of the children.[8]

1   *R v Secretary of State for the Home Department, ex p Sandhu* [1983] 3 CMLR 131, CA.
2   (1985) Times, 10 May.
3   *R v Secretary of State for the Home Department, ex p Botta* [1987] 2 CMLR 189, QBD.
4   *The domestic violence concession does not apply to family members of EEA nationals, but the Home Office accepts that a separated spouse continues to qualify as a family member and will issue residence documents accordingly: Home Office European Directorate to*

Waltham Forest CAB Legal Service, 6 June 2001. *Spouses and partners who are victims of domestic violence will not lose rights of residence on divorce, annulment of marriage or termination of registered partnership under Art 13(2)(c) of the Citizens' Directive, 2004/38/EC, which will come into force in April 2006.*

5   Case C-65/98 *Safet Eyüp v Landesgeschaftstille des Arbeitsmarktservice Vorarlberg* [2000] ERC I-4747. This case concerned the application of Decision 1/80 of the Council of Association of the EC-Turkey Association Agreement where the period of time spent together as a family member is important if that family member is to acquire certain rights of residence under the Decision.

6   Case C-413/99 *Baumbast and R v Secretary of State for the Home Department* [2003] INLR 1.

7   See Immigration (European Economic Area) (Amendment) Regulations 2003, SI 2003/549, and Immigration (European Economic Area) (Amendment) (No 2) Regulations 2003, SI 2003/3188.

8   Immigration (European Economic Area) Regulations 2000 as amended, reg 6(2A), (2B). A divorced spouse of an EEA national admitted to the UK as a family member who is not the primary carer of the children but wishes to remain for contact with them may apply under HC 395 para 248A, and will be treated as a person who had leave to remain as a spouse: HO Policy Directorate to Philip Barth, 17 July 2003.

7.94 Special provision is made in the case of the death of the person with the primary right. If the principal dies during his or her working life and before acquiring the right to remain under national or Community law, the members of the family can remain permanently if any one of the following conditions is fulfilled:

(i)   the deceased resided continuously in the host country for the two years before death; or

(ii)   he or she died from an accident at work or an occupational disease; or

(iii)   the surviving spouse was a national of the host State, but lost that nationality on marriage to the deceased.[1]

In *Givane* the ECJ made clear that the deceased must have resided in the host country for two years immediately preceding his death.[2]

1   Council Regulation (EEC) 1251/70 and Directive (EEC) 75/34, Art 3(2), given effect in the EEA Regulations, SI 2000/2326, reg 5(4).

2   Case C-257/00 *Givane v Secretary of State for the Home Department* [2003] ECR I 345, [2003] INLR 259.

Descendants: children

7.95 There is no definition of descendants in the Immigration (European Economic Area) Regulations 2000,[1] nor is there any authoritative case law. The notion of descendant is wider than children. It plainly covers all blood children, legitimate or not, and whose parents are divorced or not, as well as grandchildren, great-grandchildren and so forth. The purposive approach to interpretation of Treaty rights would strongly suggest that it would include step-children[2] and adopted children, including children in *de facto* adoptions where there was clear evidence of the assumption of parental responsibility and dependency.[3] In any event the scope should not be less favourable than that provided in domestic law[4] and practice, in order to keep within the non-discrimination provisions. Further children, who are not descendants but who are part of the EEA worker's household, may qualify under Article 10(2) of regulation 1612/68 as any other member of the family (see below).

1   SI 2000/2326.
2   The ECJ ruled in Case C-275/02 *Ayaz v Land Baden-Wurttemberg* [2004] All ER (D) 188, ECJ that a step-son of a Turkish worker who is under 21 or dependent on the worker is a family member for the purposes of the EC-Turkey Association Agreement.
3   See Hartley *EEC Immigration law* (1978), North Holland, p 132; Vaughan *Law of European Communities* (1986), Butterworths, paras 15.16, 15.11. In interpreting Community law the ECJ will have regard to the obligations of the contracting States under the ECHR: Case C-260/89 *Elliniki Radiophonia Tileorassi AE v Pliroforissis (ERT)* [1991] ECR I-2925; and the opinion of Advocate General Jacobs in Case C-168/91 *Konstantinidis v Stadt Altensteig Standesamt* [1993] ECR I-1191.
4   See Immigration Rules, HC 395, rule 6 where the definition of 'parent' would mean the inclusion of certain step-children, children born outside marriage and certain adoptive children.

7.96 Children of migrant workers, therefore, have rights of residence derived from their EEA national parent under Article 10(1) of Council Regulation (EEC) 1612/68. They also have a right under Article 12 to be admitted to the host State's general educational and other training and vocational courses under the same conditions as nationals of the host State.[1] The Member States also have an obligation 'to encourage all efforts to enable such children to attend these courses under the best possible conditions'.[2] Interpretation of Article 12 by the ECJ means that children of migrant workers retain rights of their own under Community law, notwithstanding the departure of their EEA national parent, where they have entered the educational system of the host State at a time when the parent was exercising Treaty rights. In the case of *Echternach and Moritz*[3] a student had entered the general educational system of a host State while his father was working there. The employment of the father in that State ceased and the family left the territory. The student discovered that there were difficulties in proceeding to further education in the country of origin in the light of the qualifications received in the host State. He therefore returned there and entered further education. The court held that he was entitled to a grant under Article 12 of Regulation 1612/68 notwithstanding the departure of the father. The Article 12 right is not, however, freestanding, and the position is different if the child was not installed with his or her parents when they exercised their free movement rights.[4] However the right to remain in education continues even if the EU worker leaves the host Member State and the children remain behind.[5]

1   Council Regulation (EEC) 1612/68, Art 12 covers general measures intended to facilitate educational attendance and not just rules of admission: Case 9/74 *Casagrande v Landeshauptstadt München* [1974] ECR 773, [1974] 2 CMLR 423, ECJ; Case 68/74 *Alamio v Préfet du Rhône* Case [1975] ECR 109, [1975] 1 CMLR 262, ECJ Case C-389, 390/87 *Echternach* fn 3 below; Case C-308/89 *Di Leo Land Berlin* [1990] ECR I-4185. This, coupled with Art 7(2) non-discrimination, has resulted in broad application of this measure to ensure State assistance for educational purposes, especially the funding of grants: *EC Commission v Belgium* [1988] ECR 5445, including for non-dependent children over the age of 21 as in Case C-7/92 *Landsamt für Ausbildurgsförderung Nordrhein-Westfalen v Gaal* [1995] ECR I-1031, ECJ.
2   Council Regulation (EEC) 1612/68, Art 12. Case 42/87 *EC Commission v Belgium: Re Higher Education Funding, Re* [1989] 1 CMLR 457, ECJ. These rights continue after the child is 21 and/or no longer dependent.
3   Case C-389, 390/87 *Echternach and Moritz v Minister van Onderwijs* [1989] ECR 723, [1990] 2 CMLR 305, ECJ.

4   Thus, a child of a migrant worker was not entitled to an educational grant, although residing in a host Member State where his parents had exercised Community rights before the child's birth: *Brown* [1988] 3205; Case C-7/92 *Gaal* [1995] ECR I-1031. If the child is an EEA national, however, different considerations may apply, in the light of *Chen and Zhu v Secretary of State for the Home Department* C-200/02 (19 October 2004, unreported) and *R (on the application of Bidar) v London Borough of Ealing v Secretary of State for Education and Skills* Case C-209/03 (15 March 2005, unreported), ECJ.

5   Case C-413/99 *Baumbast and R v Secretary of State for the Home Department* [2002] ECR I-7091; Immigration (European Economic Area) Regulations 2000, SI 2000/2326 (as amended by SI 2003/549 and SI 2003/3188), reg 6(2B)(b), extends this principle to descendants of EEA nationals and their spouses, who are under 21 or are their dependants, and who have been attending an educational course in the UK when the qualified person was residing in the UK and are continuing to attend such a course. 'Educational course' is defined with reference to Art 12 of Regulation (EEC) No 1612/68: reg 6(2C). Home Office practice is to extend the benefit of the provision to children at nursery school (communication from Philip Barth).

7.97 In the case of *Gal*[1] the Immigration Appeal Tribunal followed *Echternach and Moritz*[2] in holding that children who had entered primary school before the departure of their father had a right to continue their education, notwithstanding the permanent departure of the EEA worker. The right to admission to the educational system implies a right to remain in the UK for this purpose.[3] The case of *Baumbast* confirms the right of children exercising their right to be admitted to the general education system to have installed with them their non-EU national parent who is their primary carer:[4]

'where the children enjoy, under Article 12 of Regulation 1612/68, the right to continue their education in the host Member State although the parents who are their carers are at risk of losing their rights of residence as result, in one case, of a divorce from the migrant worker and, in the other case, of the fact that the parent who pursued the activity of an employed person in the host Member State as a migrant worker has ceased to work there, it is clear that if those parents were refused the right to remain in the host Member State during the period of their children's education that might deprive those children of a right which is granted to them by the Community legislature'.

The decision is consistent with the European Court's well-established position that Council Regulation (EEC) 1612/68 should be interpreted consistently with the rights under Article 8 of the ECHR,[5] and that measures incompatible with the observance of human rights would not be acceptable under Community law.[6]

1   *Gal* (10620) INLP vol 8(2) 1994 p 69.
2   Case C-389, 390/87 *Echternach and Moritz v Minister van Onderwijs* [1990] 2 CMLR 305, ECJ.
3   For another instance of such an implication see Case C-237/91 *Kus v Landshasplstadt Wiesbaden* [1993] 2 CMLR 887, ECJ where a right to a renewal of a work permit for a Turkish national imported a right to renewal of a residence permit.
4   *Baumbast v Secretary of State for the Home Department*, Case C-413/99 [2003] INLR 1, para 71. These rights are now reflected in the EEA Regulations, which enable primary carers of dependent children under 19 in full-time education to remain as 'family members' despite divorce or the departure of the EEA spouse: see 7.93 above.
5   Case 4/73 *Nold v Commission* [1974] ECR 491, para 13.
6   Case C-260/89 *Elliniki Radiophonia Tileorassi AE v Pliroforissis* (ERT) [1991] ECR I-2925. See for further examples Case 44/79 *Hauer v Rheinland Pflaz* [1979] ECR 3727, para 17; Case 63/83 *R v Kirk* [1984] ECR 2689, para 22; Case C-404/92P *X v EC Commission* [1994] ECR I-4737, para 17; Case C-415/93 93 *Union Royale Belge des*

Societies de Football Association ASBL v Bosman [1995] ECR I-4921, para 79; Case C-199/92P *Hüls v Commission* [1999] ECR I-1000, paras 149–150; Case C-235/92P *Montecatini v European Commission* [1999] ECR I-4539, para 37.

7.98 A child is entitled to the rights set out in Council Regulation (EEC) 1612/68 if he or she is under 21 years of age or is dependent on the worker. Accordingly, a handicapped child who is prevented from acquiring the status of a worker because of the handicap and qualifies during minority for benefits for the handicapped, remains entitled to equality of treatment even after attaining the age of 21.[1]

[1]   Case 7/75 *F v Belgium* [1975] ECR 679, [1975] 2 CMLR 442, ECJ. See also Case C-7/92 *Gaal* [1995] ECR I-1031, [1995] 3 CMLR 17.

7.99 When a child of a worker or self-employed person who is also an EEA national takes up employment, he or she can rely on the provisions of the Treaty and Council Regulation (EEC) 1612/68 even if he or she was born in the host Member State and/or has never exercised free movement rights.[1]

[1]   Case 235/87 *Matteucci v Communaute Française Belgique* [1988] ECR 5589; see also by way of illustration Case C-243/91 *Belgium v Taghavi* [1992] ECR I-4401.

Relatives in the ascending line

7.100 The notion of relatives in the ascending line covers not only the father and mother of the worker and his or her spouse, but also grandparents and great-grandparents and, on the basis of the above analysis, step-parents and adoptive parents. In an interesting twist to the right to install relatives in the ascending line, the ECJ has held that children who exercise a general right of residence under Article 18 EC and Directive 90/364 have the right to install their parents who are their primary carers, in order to give content to their own rights of residence, following the *Baumbast* principle, despite the fact that the Directive does not expressly provide for relatives in the ascending line and even though the children who are in fact infants, can only be said to be exercising such rights by virtue of their parents being self-sufficient and thereby making the family collectively self-sufficient.[1]

[1]   Case C-200/02 *Chen and Zhu v Secretary of State for the Home Department* [2005] QB 325. Primary carers of EEA national self-sufficient children are not included in the EEA Regulations as 'family members' (although the primary carers of children in education under Art 12 of Regulation 1612/68 EEC have been included: see 7.93 above), but instead have been made the subject of new immigration rules regulating their entry: see HC 395, para 257C–257E, inserted by HC 164 from 1 January 2005.

Other family members

7.101 Regulation 10 of the Immigration (European Economic Area) Regulations 2000[1] attempts to give effect to the provisions of regulation 10(2) of Council Regulation (EEC) 1612/68.[2] It applies to dependants and members of the household of EEA nationals who are workers or self-employed.[3] Family permits, residence permits or residence documents (as the case may be)[4] can be issued to relatives of EEA nationals or their spouses[5] if they:

(a)   are dependent on the EEA national or his or her spouse;
(b)   are living as part of the EEA national's household outside the UK; or
(c)   were living as part of the EEA national's household before the EEA national came to the UK.[6]

[1]   SI 2000/2326.
[2]   Article 10(2) of Council Regulation (EEC) 1612/68 creates an obligation to 'facilitate the admission of any member of the family not coming within paragraph 1 if dependent upon the worker ... or living under the same roof in the country whence he comes'.
[3]   SI 2000/2326, reg 10(5).
[4]   SI 2000/2326, reg 10(1).
[5]   The 'relative' requirement was added by the Immigration (European Economic Area) (Amendment) Regulations 2001, SI 2001/865, in force 2 April 2001.
[6]   SI 2000/2326, reg 10(4). The Tribunal has held that the regulation requires the relative to have been living with the principal in another EEA Member State before arrival in the UK, in *PB (Goa: EEA discretionary permit: interpretation) India* [2005] UKIAT 00082 'IAT Reported'.

7.102 The concept of 'relative' is not defined in the Immigration (European Economic Area) Regulations 2000[1] and is not found in Community law. It will need to be interpreted consistently and purposively in line with the broad scope of 'member of the family' in Article 10(2) of Council Regulation (EEC) 1612/68. Whilst persons such as aunts, uncles, brothers, sisters or cousins will fall within regulation 10 of the 2000 Regulations, Community law requires a purposive approach to the definition of 'member of the family' which gives practical effect to the central principles of free movement and integration in the host State. The definition goes beyond formal legal relationships and is not restricted to marriage or blood/biological relationships.[2] Where de facto relationships such as cohabitation or adoption are concerned, it ought properly to be a question of evidence as to the duration, nature and stability of the relationship which determines whether it has the characteristics of family, and not some biological hurdle that can never be crossed. Unmarried partners are clearly an important category, and there is no decided authority on the issue of heterosexual relationships, although the Turkish Association Agreement case of *Safet Eyüp*[3] is the closest the court has yet come to considering this point. An argument was advanced on behalf of Mrs Eyüp that 'the family of a migrant worker includes a cohabitee'. Advocate General La Pergola gave his opinion in favour of this construction, placing considerable reliance on Article 8 of the ECHR[4] and concluding that 'members of the family' includes 'the extra-marital cohabitee provided there is a serious and stable family bond between the two people ...'.[5] Mr and Mrs Eyüp had lived together for a continuous period of 13 years during which time they had divorced and later remarried, and had had several children together, some born while they were divorced. The ECJ ruled in the Eyüps' favour, but on different grounds, and was silent as to the approach of the Advocate General on the construction of family. The Citizens' Directive, which comes into force in April 2006, recognises unmarried partners in registered civil partnerships as members of the family.[6]

[1]   SI 2000/2326.

2   It is perfectly conceivable and consistent with the broad and purposive approach to envisage a person, such as a nanny who has been in long service in the household, as being a member of the family without distorting the concept and in order to give effect to the primary right of free movement.
3   Case C-65/98 *Eyüp (Safet) v Landesgeschaftsstelle des Arbeitsmarktservice Vorarlberg* [2000] ECR I-4747. See further 7.157 fn 2.
4   Opinion delivered 18 November 1999, paras 24–25.
5   Opinion above, Conclusion, para 39(1).
6   Directive 2004/38/EC, Article 2(2)(b): see 7.92 fn 1 above.

7.103 As far as same-sex couples are concerned, the Administrative Court in *R v Secretary of State for the Home Department, ex p McCollum*[1] refused to construe membership of the family so as to include a long-standing and stable same-sex relationship. The court declined to follow the approach and the definition of family member as including a same-sex partnership, which the House of Lords applied to the Rent Acts in *Fitzpatrick v Sterling Housing Trust*.[2] Nor did the court place reliance on the fact that it is the practice of the Home Office to treat cohabiting relationships, including those between same-sex partners, as akin to marriage.[3] As regards transsexuals, the European Court of Justice in *KB* found that there was an inequality of treatment which related to the inability of a transsexual to marry on basis of her acquired gender.[4] The ECJ relied on the ECHR decision in *Goodwin v United Kingdom*[5] to conclude that the legislation making it impossible for transsexuals to marry on the basis of their acquired gender was incompatible with the Treaty. In *Goodwin* the European Court of Human Rights had held that since it was impossible for a transsexual to marry a person of the sex to which he or she belonged prior to gender reassignment surgery, the UK was in breach of Article 12 ECHR (the right to marry and found a family). While *KB* concerned pensions legislation, no legislation or decision which flows from the impossibility of a transsexual to marry on the basis of his or her acquired gender could be considered compatible with Community law. From April 2006, registered civil partnerships between same-sex and transsexual couples will ensure their recognition as family members, under the Citizens' Directive which will come into force then.[6]

1   CO 589/99, 24 January 2001, CA.
2   [2001] 1 AC 27. The House of Lords adopted the following as the hallmarks of what were described as '*de facto* relationships capable of creating membership of the ... family', namely: 'there should be a degree of mutual interdependence, of the sharing of lives, of caring and love, of commitment and support.'
3   An appeal to the Court of Appeal was withdrawn on the Home Office indicating its willingness to issue a residence permit, so the question of principle was not decided. For Home Office policy on unmarried partners see 7.92 above.
4   Case C-117/01 *KB v NHS Pensions Agency and Secretary of State for Health* [2004] All ER (EC) 1089, ECJ.
5   (2002) 35 EHRR 18.
6   See 7.102 fn 6 above.

7.104 Regulation 10(1) of the Immigration (European Economic Area) Regulations 2000[1] gives a broad discretion to the decision maker to issue a residence permit to persons falling within regulation 10(4) 'if in all the circumstances it appears ... appropriate to do so'. There is no equivalent provision in the Immigration Rules and it is likely that if such indeterminate grounds were used to refuse a residence permit to a member of the family who satisfied the substantive conditions of the 2000 Regulations, the refusal would be impermissible in Community law, either as a failure to facilitate admission or as a discriminatory measure.

1   SI 2000/2326.

Dependency

7.105 If regulation 10(4) of the Immigration (European Economic Area) Regulations 2000[1] is to be read consistently with the Community law provision in regulation 10(2) of Council Regulation (EEC) 1612/68, then regulation 10(4)(a) of the 2000 Regulations must be disjunctive, ie in the alternative to 10(4)(b) and 10(4)(c) of the 2000 Regulations. Otherwise it is incompatible with regulation 10(2) of 1612/68, which speaks of the family member being 'dependent ... or living under his roof ...' (our emphasis). Dependency in Community law is a factual question only. There is no need to establish the reason for the dependency nor that it be a dependency of necessity (in contrast to the domestic Immigration rules). A person may be dependent even if able to take up employment in his or her own right.[2] The fact that the family member applies for or receives social assistance does not mean that he or she is no longer dependent. To hold otherwise would deny equality of treatment between nationals.[3] Furthermore, dependency need not have arisen before admission to the UK.[4] The contrary was held in a refusal of permission for judicial review in the case of *R v Secretary of State for the Home Department, ex p Yenin*[5] but *Lebon* was not cited, nor a Tribunal case of *Mustafa*[6] which had considered the point in detail and concluded that dependency need not arise prior to admission.

1   SI 2000/2326.
2   Case 316/85 *Centre Public d'Aide Sociale v Lebon* [1987] ECR 2811.
3   In *Lebon* above the assistance was the Belgian 'minimex' and in Case 256/86 *Frascogna v Caisse des dépôts et Consignations* [1987] ECR 3431 at para 7 an old-age allowance.
4   *Lebon* above.
5   [1995] Imm AR 93.
6   (11495), IAT.

7.106 It would therefore seem that an opportunity has been missed in the 2000 Regulations and their amendments to provide a comprehensive and clear domestic code giving effect to the full ambit of Article 10 of Council Regulation (EEC) 1612/68. This means that litigation on the scope of Community law rights for family members of workers will continue, and direct reliance on the Community regulations and questions of compatibility of domestic law will continue to arise.

MATERIAL SCOPE (1) FREE MOVEMENT RIGHTS

Abolishing discrimination and other obstacles to free movement

7.107 Our principal concern is with the rules relating to entry into and stay in the UK arising from EC rules on free movement. But a large part of free movement law is concerned with the removal of restrictions and obstacles, which put the incomer at a disadvantage as against nationals of the receiving Member State, or simply act as an unjustifiable obstacle to free movement. No account of free movement rights would be complete without some mention of two of the key elements in the material scope of free movement rights, but this is a vast subject with an extensive case law and within the scope of this work we can only highlight the main outlines:

(i)   the abolition of any discrimination based on nationality; and
(ii) the abolition of non-discriminatory obstacles.

Non-discrimination

7.108 The principle of non-discrimination is one of the fundamental principles of Community law. Article 12 EC (ex Article 6) provides:

> 'Within the scope of application of this treaty and without prejudice to special provisions therein any discrimination on the grounds of nationality shall be prohibited.'

The Article, although renumbered, is in that part of the EC Treaty entitled 'Principles' and constitutes the foundation stone upon which the Treaty rests, its fundamental base.[1] It is the express statement of the general principle of equality and is the source of specific provisions elsewhere in the Treaty prohibiting discrimination in different Treaty fields. It applies independently only to situations governed by Community law, where the Treaty contains no specific prohibition of discrimination. In practice, most of the direct beneficiaries of Article 12 in the past have been students.[2] In a landmark decision in *Avello*, however the court held that EU national children resident in another Member State could rely on Article 12 EC not to suffer discrimination on grounds of nationality vis-a-vis the rules governing the change of surnames, a matter that would not normally fall within the competence of Community law at all.[3] All the other areas of free movement contain their own express prohibitions. Article 39(2) EC (ex Article 48(2)) outlaws discrimination based on nationality between workers of Member States as regards employment, remuneration, and other conditions of work and employment. Article 7(1) of Council Regulation (EEC) 1612/68 provides for non-discrimination on the grounds of nationality in the field of employment and vocational training,[4] and Article 9 relates to the field of housing.[5] Article 7(2) provides that an EU worker in the territory of a host Member State must enjoy the same 'social and tax advantages' as nationals of the host State. Thus even where there are no Community law rights to a social security benefit, it may be unlawful to provide it to own nationals but not to other EEA nationals.[6] In *Collins,*[7] the applicant was an Irish citizen who had lived outside the EU for 17 years. His initial claim for Jobseekers' Allowance was rejected on the basis that he did not satisfy the habitual residence test. The court held that although the applicant, as a newly arrived jobseeker, was not a worker within Part II of Regulation 1612/68,[8] access to a benefit such as the jobseekers' allowance, which was intended to assist the applicant seeking work, had to be provided in a non-discriminatory manner. Thus whilst it considered that it might be justifiable to require a link to the employment market of the Host State, and that this might be established by a period of residence, there could be no discrimination on the application of any rules on the basis of nationality. Similarly, the court has interpreted social advantage very broadly. Thus a national provision allowing those who are nationals or permanently settled to be joined by their common law partners has to be extended to EEA workers in the host State.[9] Anti-discrimination provisions are also contained in Articles 43 EC (ex Article 52) (right of establishment) and 54 (ex Article 65) (services). These provisions are extensive in their application and the ECJ's case law is extensive.[10] It covers direct discrimination, where less favourable treatment is given to one set of nationals,[11] and indirect discrimination, where one set of nationals can fulfil more easily conditions applicable to everyone.[12] For the purposes of immigration law the aggregate effect of these various non-discrimination provisions is much wider than the protection of wages and other conditions of employment referred to in Article 39(2) (ex Art 48(2)) or the housing, education and trade union rights dealt with by regulation 1612/68. They are fundamental to the enjoyment of free movement rights. Advocate General Jacobs expressed it thus in his opinion in the case of *Phil Collins*:[13]

'The nationals of each Member State are entitled to live, work, and do business in other Member States on the same terms as the local population. They must not simply be tolerated as aliens, but welcomed by the authorities of the host State as Community nationals who are entitled, within the scope of application of the Treaty "to all the privileges and advantages enjoyed by the nationals of the host State". No other aspect of Community law touches the individual more directly or does more to foster the sense of common identity and shared destiny without which "the ever-closer union among the peoples of Europe" proclaimed by the preamble to the Treaty would be an empty slogan.'

[1]   Martin and Guild 7.50 fn 1 above, p 14.
[2]   See 7.80 above. As regards the Turkish Association Agreement, see *Sürül v Bundesanstalt für Arbeit* Case C-262/96 [1999] ECR I-2685; 7.160 below. See most recently *D'Hoop v Office National de l' Emploi*, Case C-224/98 [2002] ECR I-6191; *R (on the application of Bidar) v London Borough of Ealing v Secretary of State for Education and Skills*, Case C-209/03 (2005) 15 March 2005 ECJ (non-discrimination provisions of the Treaty breached by domestic law provisions limiting assistance to students to those settled in the UK, excluding integrated EU citizens).
[3]   *Avello (Carlos Garcia) v Etat Belge* Case C-148/02, [2003] ECR I-11613.
[4]   Case 293/83 *Gravier v City of Liège* [1985] ECR 593, [1985] 3 CMLR 1, ECJ; Case 235/87 *Matteucci v Communaute Française de Belgique* [1989] 1 CMLR 357, ECJ; Case 24/86 *Blaizot v University of Liège* [1988] ECR 379, [1989] 1 CMLR 57, ECJ; Case 263/86 *Belgium v Humbel* [1989] 1 CMLR 393, ECJ; Case 42/87 *Re Higher Education Funding: EC Commission v Belgium* [1989] 1 CMLR 457, ECJ; Case 197/86 *Brown v Secretary of State for Scotland* [1988] 3 CMLR 403, ECJ; Case 261/83 *Castelli v ONPTS* [1987] 1 CMLR 465, ECJ; Case 39/86 *Lair v University of Hanover* [1989] 3 CMLR 545, ECJ.
[5]   Case 63/86 *Re Housing Aid: EC Commission v Italy* [1989] 2 CMLR 601, ECJ.
[6]   Under Art 42 EC (ex Art 51) the Council was required to set up a system to enable workers to overcome obstacles with which they might be confronted in national social security rules. It did so by the enactment of Council Regulations (EEC) 1408/71 and 574/72. A notable application of the principle of non-discrimination in social security is Case C-18/90 *Office National de l'Emploi v Kziber* [1991] ECR I-199, ECJ a decision on the Morocco Association agreement. *Kziber* has been followed by the ECJ in Case C-58/93 *Yoursfi v Belgium* [1994] ECR I-1353, ECJ despite attempts by Member States to persuade the court to overturn it.
[7]   Case C-138/02 *Collins v Secretary of State for Work and Pensions* [2005] QB 145.

8   The concept of 'worker' is not used in Regulation No 1612/68 in a uniform manner. While in Title II of Part I the term covers only persons who have already entered the employment market, in other parts of the same regulation the concept of 'worker' must be understood in a broader sense. The court's case law draws a distinction between Member State nationals who have not yet entered into an employment relationship in the host Member State where they are looking for work and those who are already working in that State or who, having worked there but no longer being in an employment relationship, are nevertheless considered to be workers (see Case 39/86 *Lair v University of Hanover* [1988] ECR 3161, paras 32 and 33). Only those who have already entered the employment market may, on the basis of Art 7(2) of Regulation No 1612/68, claim the same social and tax advantages as national workers (see in particular, *Lebon*, cited above, paragraph 26, and Case C-278/94 *EC Commission v Belgium* [1996] ECR I-4307, paragraphs 39 and 40): *Collins*, above at paras 30–32.

9   Case 59/85 *Netherlands v Reed* [1987] 2 CMLR 448, ECJ.

10   See in particular Case 2/74 *Reyners v Belgium* [1974] ECR 631, [1974] 2 CMLR 305, ECJ; Case 33/74 *Van Binsbergen v Bestuur* [1974] ECR 1299, [1975] 1 CMLR 298, ECJ; Case 36/74 *Walrave and Koch v Association Union Cycliste Internationale* [1974] ECR 1405, [1975] 1 CMLR 320, ECJ; Case 11/77 *Patrick v Ministre des Affaires Culturelles* [1977] ECR 1199, [1977] 2 CMLR 523, ECJ; Case 136/78 *Ministère Public v Auer* [1979] ECR 437, [1979] 2 CMLR 373, ECJ; Case 107/83 *Ordre des Avocats v Klopp* [1985] QB 711, [1985] 1 CMLR 99, ECJ; Case 222/86 *Union Nationale des Entraineurs v Heylens* [1989] 1 CMLR 901, ECJ. Case C-179/90 *Merci Convenzionali Porto di Genova Spa v Siderurgica Gabriella SpA* [1991] ECR I-5889, ECJ; Case C-360/89 *EC Commission v Italy* [1992] ECR I-3401, ECJ; Case C-419/92 *Scholz v Opera Universitaria di Cagliari* [1994] ECR I-505.

11   See *R v Trinity House Pilotage Committee, ex p Jensen and Leu* [1985] 2 CMLR 413, QBD; *R v Inner London Education Authority, ex p Hinde* [1985] 1 CMLR 716, QBD; Case C-293/83 *Gravier v City of Liege* [1985] 3 CMLR 1, ECJ.

12   Case 152/73 *Sotgiu v Deutsche Bundesport* [1974] ECR 153, ECJ; Case 1/78 *Kenny v National Insurance Comr* [1978] ECR 1489, [1978] 3 CMLR 651, ECJ; Case 182/83 *Robert Fearon & Co v Irish Land Commission* [1985] 2 CMLR 228, ECJ; Case 41/84 *Pietro Pinna v Caisse D'Allocations Familiales de la Savoie 1* [1988] 1 CMLR 350; Case 33/88 *Allue v Università degli Studi Venezia* [1989] ECR 1591, [1991] 1 CMLR 283; ECJ; Case C-175/88 *Biehl v Luxembourg* [1990] ECR I-1779, [1990] 3 CMLR 143; Case C-204/90 *Bachmann v Belgium* [1992] ECR I-249, [1993] 1 CMLR 785, ECJ.

13   Case C-92/92 *Collins (Phil) v IMTRAT Handelsgesellschaft mbH* [1993] 3 CMLR 773 at 785.

7.109 The material scope of any free movement right is usually to be determined by the yardstick of what the local nationals can do. All EEA nationals must be put on the same footing as nationals of the host State. Thus in *Watson and Belman*[1] it was held that although penalties could be imposed for illegally entering or remaining in a country, they must be comparable to penalties attaching to local nationals for breaches of provisions of equal importance and should not be so disproportionate that they become an obstacle to free movement.[2] Clearly the comparison between the position of own nationals and those of another Member State is not an exact one in this kind of situation, and this is always likely to be the case as regards rights of entry or stay. Normally the court does not draw such a distinction when dealing with the grant of a social advantage. Thus in *Sala*[3] the principle of equal treatment precluded the Member State from requiring a national of another Member State to be in possession of a residence permit in order to be granted a social advantage when no such requirement was imposed on its own nationals.[4] However, exceptions to the principle of discrimination have been acknowledged by the court many times on the basis of 'objective discrimination', which arises from the simple fact that certain requirements are necessary for non-nationals or non-residents which would not apply to own nationals, such as the requirement to hold their national driving licence;[5] to notify the appropriate authorities of the person's presence on the territory;[6] or to have a passport or identity document.[7] In *Kaba*[8] the distinction was made and it was said that the UK could rely on 'any objective difference' between the position of its own nationals and those of another Member State so far as the obtaining of settlement was concerned. The distinction between *Kaba* and a case like *Sala* is that in *Kaba* the claimed 'social advantage' was indefinite leave. This was something which no own national either needed to or could acquire. If on the other hand the claimed 'social advantage' was some social security benefit or a family allowance, it could be acquired by own nationals, and like could be compared with like. It should also be noted that the public policy exceptions, allowing exclusion or expulsion on public policy grounds, can by definition only apply to other nationals and not to own nationals, but this does not constitute discrimination.[9]

[1] Case 118/75 *Re Watson and Belmann* [1976] ECR 1185, [1976] 2 CMLR 552, ECJ. See Case 8/77 *Sagulo, Brenca and Bakhouche, Re* [1977] ECR 1495, [1977] 2 CMLR 585, ECJ and Case 157/79 *R v Pieck* [1981] QB 571, [1981] 3 All ER 46, ECJ at paras 12 and 13, where the need to bring the position of workers of other Member States into line with that of local nationals is referred to.
[2] See further Case 321/87 *EC Commission v Belgium* [1990] 2 CMLR 492, ECJ.
[3] Case C-85/96 *Sala v Freistaat Bayern* [1998] ECR I-2691, ECJ.
[4] See further Case C-262/96 *Sürül v Bundesanstalt für Arbeit* [1999] ECR I-2685, ECJ.
[5] Case 16/78 *Choquet v Germany* [1978] ECR 2293.
[6] Case 118/75 *Watson and Belmann, Re* [1976] ECR 1185, [1976] 2 CMLR 552, ECJ.
[7] Case 8/77 *Re Sagulo, Brenca and Bakhouche, Re* [1977] ECR 1495, [1977] 2 CMLR 585, ECJ.
[8] Case C-356/98 [2000] All ER (EC) 537, ECJ.
[9] Case 41/74 *Van Duyn v Home Office* [1975] Ch 358, [1975] 3 All ER 190, ECJ; Joined Cases C-65/95 and 111/95 *Shingara and Radiom v Secretary of State for the Home Department* [1997] 3 CMLR 703, ECJ.

7.110 Although the wording of Articles 39(2), 43 and 54 EC suggests that the principle of equal treatment applies without exception, the ECJ now accepts that in cases of indirect discrimination, where a measure applies to everyone irrespective of nationality, the discrimination may be justified if based on objective considerations independent of the nationality of the workers concerned, and they are proper to the legitimate aim pursued by the national law and not disproportionate.[1]

[1] Case C-237/94 *O'Flynn v Adjudication Officer* [1996] ECR I-2617. In another line of cases, the test for justification of indirect discrimination is imperative reasons relating to the public interest: Case 33/88 *Allué v Università degli Studi Venezia* [1989] ECR 1591, ECJ; Case C-175/88 *Biehl v Luxemburg* [1990] ECR I-1779, ECJ; Case C-204/90 *Bachmann v Belgium* [1992] ECR I-249; Case C-398/92 *Mund and Fester v Hatrex Internahmaal Transport* [1994] ECR I-467, ECJ; Case C-80/94 *Wielockx v Inspecteur der Directe Belasligen* [1995] ECR I-2493, ECJ.

Non-discriminatory obstacles to free movement

7.111 This development in the case law is closely connected to a further development – that of non-discriminatory obstacles to free movement, which gained particular prominence in the *Bosman* case, concerning the effect of football transfer fees on free movement. The concept was borrowed from earlier case law on the freedom of movement of goods, which held that Article 28 EC (ex Article 30) prohibited not only discriminatory measures in relation to the movement of goods, but also unjustifiable non-discriminatory obstacles.[1] In *Kraus*[2] the ECJ held that Articles 48 and 52 (now Articles 39 and 43 EC) did not permit any national measure relating to the conditions for use of a postgraduate university degree acquired in another Member State, which, even though applied without discrimination on the basis of nationality, was capable of hindering or making less attractive the exercise of fundamental freedoms contained in the Treaty by Community nationals, including nationals of the Member State which had taken the measure. This rather startling innovation was later confirmed and clarified by the court in *Bosman* and *Gebhard*. In *Bosman*[3] the court held that provisions which preclude or deter nationals of a Member State from leaving their country of origin in order to exercise their right of free movement constitute an obstacle to that freedom, even if they apply without regard to the nationality of workers. In *Gebhard*[4] the court held that where national measures are liable to hinder or make less attractive the exercise of fundamental freedoms guaranteed by the Treaty, they must fulfil four conditions: (i) they must be applied in a non-discriminatory manner; (ii) they must be justified by imperative requirements of the general interest; (iii) they must be suitable for securing the attainment of the objective which they pursue; and (iv) they must not go beyond what is necessary in order to attain it. Here the court was repeating the reasoning already handed down in an earlier decision on the application of Article 59 EC (now Article 49).[5] More recently, the ECJ has confirmed that where obstacles to free movement rights have been identified there is no need to consider whether there is indirect discrimination on grounds of nationality.[6] In an extension of its previous case law the Court has held that the inability to enjoy family life can constitute an obstacle the exercise of free movement rights. In *Carpenter*, the court held that the expulsion by the UK authorities of the non-EU national wife (who was an overstayer) of a British national exercising free movement rights as a service provider in other Member States, would constitute a breach of Community law since she facilitated the exercise of the British national's Treaty rights by looking after his family:[7]

'the Community legislature has recognised the importance of ensuring the protection of the family life of nationals of the Member States in order to eliminate obstacles to the exercise of the fundamental freedoms guaranteed by the Treaty ... It is clear that the separation of Mr and Mrs Carpenter would be detrimental to their family life and, therefore, to the conditions under which Mr Carpenter exercises a fundamental freedom. That freedom could not be fully effective if Mr Carpenter were to be deterred from exercising it by obstacles raised in his country of origin to the entry and residence of his spouse'.

[1]   Case 8/74 *Procureur du Roi v Dassonville* [1974] ECR 837, ECJ; later limited in Case C-267/91 *Keck* [1993] ECR I-6097.
[2]   Case C-19/92 *Kraus v Land Baden-Würtemberg* [1993] ECR I-1663, ECJ.
[3]   Case C-415/93 *Union Royale Belge des Societies de Football Association ASBL v Bosman* [1996] All ER (EC) 97, [1995] ECR I-4921, ECJ.
[4]   Case C-55/94 *Gebhard v Consiglio dell'Ordine degli Avvocati e Procuration di Milano* [1995] ECR I-4165, ECJ.
[5]   Case C-288/89 *Stichting Collective Antennevoorziening v Gouda v Commissariat voor de Media* [1991] ECR I-4007, ECJ.

⁶ Case C-18/95 *Terhoeve v Inspecteur van de Belastingdienst Particulieren Ondernemingen Butenland* [1999] ECR I-345, ECJ; Case C-337/97 *Meeusen v Hoofddirecte van de Informake Beheer Groep* [1999] ECR I-3289, ECJ.
⁷ Case C-60/00 *Carpenter (Mary) v Secretary of State for the Home Department* [2002] ECR I-6279, [2002] INLR 439, ECJ.

Reverse discrimination

7.112 Non-discrimination is important for the protection of other EEA nationals coming to the UK and of UK nationals going to other EEA countries. But can it assist UK nationals who suffer discrimination at the hands of the UK government? This practice is referred to as 'reverse discrimination'.¹ There is clear reverse discrimination by the UK government in the field of family rights. Other EEA nationals in the UK have few problems in being joined by members of their families. British citizens, on the other hand, have a host of obstacles to overcome: intention to live together, maintenance and accommodation, sole responsibility, exceptional compassionate circumstances are a few of them. There is no doubt that the non-discrimination provisions can apply to Member States in respect of their own nationals in certain circumstances. This was first recognised in *Knoors*² where a Dutch plumber who had practised his trade in Belgium for seven years was refused a permit to practise by the Dutch government on his return to Holland. He claimed that this was contrary to EC law. The ECJ stated that the wording of Article 43 EC (ex Article 52), which refers to 'nationals of one Member State in the territory of another', did not exclude 'own' nationals from the benefit of EC law or from the application of non-discrimination provisions. An 'own' national could qualify where, by lawful residence on the territory of another Member State, his or her situation has become assimilated to that of any other persons enjoying the rights and liberties guaranteed by the Treaty. A State cannot discriminate against its own nationals who are within the protection of one or other provision of EC law. The principle is now widely accepted³ and extends to non-discriminatory measures adopted by the home State, which are obstacles to a home national's free movement.⁴ The problem in these cases is not 'reverse discrimination' but establishing a link to a provision of Community law, which removes the case from a wholly internal situation.⁵

¹ See D Pickup 'Reverse Discrimination and Freedom of Movement for Workers' (1986) 23 CML Rev 135.
² Case 115/78 *Knoors v Secretary of State for Economic Affairs* [1979] ECR 399, [1979] 2 CMLR 357, ECJ, at para 24. In Case 1/78 *Kenny v National Insurance Comr* [1978] ECR 1489, [1978] 3 CMLR 651, ECJ the court held that discrimination by a Member State against its own nationals, as much as discrimination by a Member State against nationals of another Member State, was forbidden. In Case 136/78 *Ministère Public v Auer* [1979] ECR 437, [1979] 2 CMLR 373, ECJ the court indicated at para 28 that EEC nationals were protected against their own State, provided that the other conditions for the application of the rule on which they rely are fulfilled. See further Case 292/86 *Gullung v Conseil de l'Ordre des Avocats* [1990] 1 QB 234, [1988] 2 CMLR 57, ECJ.
³ *Union Royale Belge des Societes de Football Association ASBL v Bosman* [1996] All ER (EC) 97 above; Case C-379/92 *Peralta, criminal proceedings against* [1994] ECR I-3453, ECJ.
⁴ See 7.111 fn 6, above.
⁵ See *Phull v Secretary of State for the Home Department* [1996] Imm AR 72, CA.

7.113 Where there is a link to some provision of EC law and where reverse discrimination applies, the advantage which own nationals can take of it is nevertheless restricted in the circumstances of the criminal law. The ECJ in *Saunders* noted:[1]

> 'Although the rights conferred upon workers by Article 48 may lead the Member State to amend their legislation, where necessary, even with respect to their own nationals, this provision does not however aim to restrict the power of the Member States to lay down restrictions, within their own territory, on the freedom of movement of all persons subject to their jurisdiction in implementation of domestic criminal law.'

Putting someone in prison after conviction and sentence in the criminal courts is undoubtedly a restriction on that person's freedom of movement, but is not in any way intended to be restricted by any of the free movement provisions. The English High Court extended this rule to extradition procedures and the handover procedure under the Visiting Forces Act 1952.[2] The rationale was explained by Robert Goff LJ in *Ex p Healy*.[3] Using the purposive construction of Article 48 EEC (now Article 39) by the ECJ in *Saunders* he stated that Article 48 (now Article 39 EC) did not aim to restrict the power of Member States to lay down restrictions within their own territories on the freedom of movement of all persons subject to their jurisdiction in the implementation of extradition procedure or the handover procedure under the Visiting Forces Acts.

1   Case 175/78 *R v Saunders* [1979] ECR 1129, [1980] QB 72, ECJ (application of restrictions of domestic criminal law to own national); Case 180/83 *Moser v Land Baden-Würtemberg* [1984] 3 CMLR 720, ECJ (denial to own national of access to further education); Case 298/84 *Iorio v Azienda Autonoma delle Ferrovie dello Stato* [1986] 2 CMLR 665, ECJ (dispute by own national with state railway over limited access to trains); Joined Cases 35 and 36/82 *Morson and Jhanjan v Netherlands* [1982] ECR 3723, [1983] 2 CMLR 221, ECJ (own nationals who have never worked outside home country); Case 44/84 *Hurd v Jones, Inspector of Taxes* [1986] QB 892, [1986] 2 CMLR 1, ECJ; Case C-104/91 *Colegio Oficial de Agentes de la Propriedad Inmobiliaria v Aguirre Borrell Newman* [1992] ECR I-3003 and Joined Cases C-330/90 and 331/90 *Ministerio Fiscal v A Lopez Brea and C H Palacios* [1992] 2 CMLR 397, ECJ (proceedings against Spanish estate agents).
2   *R v Governor of Pentonville Prison, ex p Budlong* [1980] 1 All ER 701; *Re Budlong and Kember* [1980] 2 CMLR 125, DC; *Re Virdee* [1980] 1 CMLR 709, QBD.
3   *R v Governor of Pentonville Prison, ex p Healy* [1984] 3 CMLR 575, DC.

MATERIAL SCOPE (2) RIGHT TO LEAVE, ENTER AND RESIDE

Right to leave own country

7.114 In EC law the right to depart is expressly given to workers and the self-employed and those providing or receiving services. Article 2(1) of Council Directives (EEC) 68/360 (workers) and 73/148 (self-employed) requires Member States to grant workers the right to leave their territory. What this means is that Member States must be prepared to let any EC workers leave their territory on production of a valid identity card or passport, and in the case of their own nationals to issue to them and renew their identity cards and passports, which should state the holder's nationality.[1] A passport must be valid at least for all Member States and for countries through which the holder must pass when travelling between Member States (for example Switzerland and Austria in the case of travel from Italy to Germany or vice versa).[2] Where a passport is the only document on which the holder can lawfully leave the country, its period of validity should be not less than five years.[3] Member States cannot demand any exit visas or equivalent document.[4] Where a country has issued an identity card or passport it must allow the holder to re-enter its territory without any formality, even if the document is no longer valid or the nationality of the holder is in dispute.[5] Thus the right to leave your country is matched by a right under EC law to re-enter it.

[1]   Council Directives (EEC) 68/360 and 73/148, Art 2(1).
[2]   Council Directives (EEC) 68/360 and 73/148, Art 2(2).
[3]   Council Directives (EEC) 68/360 and 73/148, Art 2(3).
[4]   Council Directives (EEC) 68/360 and 73/148, Art 2(4).
[5]   Council Directive (EEC) 64/221, Art 3(4).

Right to enter

7.115 Various provisions of EC law give rights of entry to another Member State and these rights are extended to all EEA States by the Agreement on the European Economic Area,[1] and to Switzerland by the EC- Swiss Confederation Agreement on the Free Movement of Persons.[2] Article 39 (ex Article 48) of the EC Treaty clearly gives a right to enter to those seeking work as well as to workers who have definite jobs to go to and this is spelt out in more detail in the subsidiary legislation.[3] A similar right to enter is given to business people, the self-employed, and providers and recipients of services, and those covered by the June 1990 directives: students, the self-sufficient and the retired. All these are referred to by the Immigration (European Economic Area) Regulations 2000 as 'qualified persons'.[4] In addition rights of entry are given to family members,[5] and, under the Swiss Agreement, to posted workers employed by a Swiss national or Swiss undertaking.[6] Under EC law the right involves both entry and internal free movement,[7] and is exercisable by EEA nationals 'simply on production of a valid identity card or passport'.[8] No prior leave to enter or permission is required, because the right to enter flows directly from EC law.[9]

[1]   The Agreement on the European Economic Area signed at Oporto on 2 May 1992, as adjusted by the Protocol signed at Brussels on 17 March 1993 OJ L86 20.4.1995.
[2]   Agreement between the European Community and the Swiss Confederation on The Free Movement of Persons (30 Apr/02 OJ L114/6).
[3]   Article 1 of Council Regulation (EEC) 1612/68 refers to the right to take up activity as an employed person and the right to take up available employment in the territory of another Member State on the same priority as the nationals of that State. The case law has made it clear that the right includes the right to enter to find available employment and to respond to offers of employment. See 7.65 above.
[4]   SI 2000/2326, reg 5.
[5]   See 7.86, above.
[6]   Agreement between the European Community and the Swiss Confederation on The Free Movement of Persons (above), Arts 1 and 17 of Annex 1.
[7]   Case 36/75 *Rutili v Minister for the Interior* [1975] ECR 1219, [1976] 1 CMLR 140.
[8]   Council Directive (EEC) 68/360, Art 3(1) and 73/148, Art 3(1). Recently the ECJ has held that it is contrary to Art 49 EC for an EU national to be required in another Member State to present a valid identity card or passport in order to prove their nationality, when that State does not impose a general obligation on its own nationals to provide evidence of

identity, and permits them to prove their identity by any means allowed by national law. This is despite the provision in Art 3(1) of Directives 73/148 and 68/360. Case C-215/03 *Oulane*, 17 February 2005.
9 Case 157/79 *R v Pieck* [1981] QB 571, [1981] 3 All ER 46, ECJ; Case 321/87 *EC Commission v Belgium* [1990] 2 CMLR 492.

7.116 The entitlement to enter is given effect in UK domestic law by section 7 of the Immigration Act 1988 and by the 2000 Regulations, which provide that admission must be granted to EEA nationals if they produce on arrival a valid passport or national identity card issued by another EEA State.[1] This also applies to posted workers, working for a Swiss employer, but in addition they may apply for a posted worker authorisation prior to departure, which avoids any problems on arrival.[2] In addition to a passport or identity document, family members who are not EEA nationals need 'an EEA family permit' or residence document if they are either visa nationals or coming to install themselves with the qualified person.[3] In all other cases, a document proving that the holder is a family member of the qualified person will be enough.[4] Family permits are issued by entry clearance officers free of charge to family members of EEA nationals who are already qualified persons or will be so on arrival in the UK.[5] The EEA Regulations provide that an EEA permit can be refused if the entry clearance officer is not satisfied that the applicant is a family member of a qualified person and not a person subject to exclusion on grounds of public policy, public security or public health.[6] The Regulations incorporate the power of examination under Schedule 2 to the Immigration Act 1971 for family members of EEA nationals and those who might fall to be excluded from the UK on public policy grounds.[7] In *MRAX*,[8] a test case brought before the European Court by a Belgian pressure group, the court considered the right of non-EU national family members of EU nationals exercising Treaty rights to enter a Member State where they were not in possession of the correct visas. The court held that in order that full effect is given to Article 3(2) of Directive 68/360 and Article 3(2) of Directive 73/148 (which state that Member States are to accord family members of EU nationals exercising Treaty rights every facility for obtaining any necessary visa) a visa must be issued without delay and as far as possible at the place of entry into the territory of the Member State. The right to respect for family life underlay its decision that a Member State may not send back at the border a third country national married to a national of a Member State who attempts to enter the Member State without being in possession of a valid identity card, passport or visa:

> 'In view of the importance which the Community legislature has attached to the protection of family life, it is in any event disproportionate and, therefore, prohibited to send back a third country national married to a national of Member State where he is able to prove his identity and the conjugal ties and there is not evidence to establish that he represents a risk to the requirements of public policy, public security or public health'.[9]

The A-G has reaffirmed in his opinion in *Commission v Spain* that Member States may not require prior long-term visas for the entry of third-country national family members.[10]

1 Immigration (European Economic Area) Regulations 2000, SI 2000/2326, reg 12(1).
2 SI 2000/2326, regs 12(3) and 13A.

3   SI 2000/2326, reg 12(2).
4   SI 2000/2326, reg 13.
5   SI 2000/2326, reg 13.
6   SI 2000/2326, reg 21.
7   SI 2000/2326, reg 24. A person who has been deported on public policy grounds can be
    refused re-admission under Community law rather than treated as an illegal entrant under
    national law: *R v Secretary of State for the Home Department, ex p Shingara and Radiom*
    (3 February 1995, unreported), QBD, citing Case 115/89 *Adoui* [1982] ECR 1665 at
    1709.
8   Case C-459/99 *Mouvement contre le racisme, l'antisémitisme et la xénophobie ASBL v
    Belgium* [2002] ECR I-6591.
9   *Mouvement contre le racisme, l'antisémitisme et la xénophobie ASBL v Belgium* above,
    para 61.
10 C-157/03, 9 November 2004.

Right of residence

7.117 After admission to the territory of a Member State, Community law
enables qualified persons to obtain a residence permit as confirmation of their
right of residence.[1] It is important to note that the residence permit is not the
source of rights or a permission to remain, and a qualified person does not
lose rights through the absence of a residence permit.[2] Non-national family
members are given a residence document which must be of equivalent
validity.[3] In the UK the Immigration (European Economic Area) Regulations 2000[4] bring together the rights to a residence permit under the various
EC Directives. It is granted to EEA nationals upon production of the
document on which the person entered the territory and proof that they are a
qualified person.[5] In the case of workers such proof need not be more than
confirmation of employment from an employer.[6] There is no requirement to
give a residence permit to workers who are temporary workers engaged for
under three months,[7] frontier workers who return to their residence in another
Member State at least once a week,[8] or seasonal workers whose contracts
have been approved by the Department for Education and Employment.[9]
Persons providing or receiving services for no more than three months have a
right of residence, but need not be given a residence permit.[10] Posted workers
working for a Swiss employer have a right of residence under the EC-Swiss
Agreement,[11] but need not be given a residence document under the 2000
Regulations, if their authorised period of residence is 90 days or less.[12] Posted
workers working for employers from an EEA country are not at present
regarded as having any entitlement to enter and reside under EC law (a
dubious proposition) [13] and are not dealt with under the 2000 Regulations or
under the immigration rules. Family members of a qualified person receive a
'residence permit' if they too are EEA nationals, and a 'residence document'
(which will usually be in the form of a stamp in the passport),[14] if they are
not.[15] They need to have their identity document or passport and a 'family
permit' if that was required for admission, or other proof that they are a
family member of the qualified person.[16] In *MRAX* the court held that a
Member State may neither refuse to issue a residence permit to a third country
national who is married to a national of a Member State and entered the
territory of that Member State lawfully, nor issue an order expelling him from
the territory, on the sole ground that his visa expired before he applied for a
residence permit.[17] Further, the court held that a Member State is not

permitted to refuse to issue a residence permit to someone who is able to furnish proof of his or her identify and of his or her marriage to a national of a Member State on the sole ground that he or she entered the territory of the Member State concerned unlawfully.[18] This decision confirms the declaratory nature of residence permits and the fact that the right to install family members flows directly from EU legislation. Member States may derogate from the duty to issue a residence permit on grounds of public policy, public security or public health.[19] Under Article 5 of Council Directive (EEC) 64/221, a decision to grant or refuse a first residence permit is to be taken as soon as possible and not later than six months from the date of application.[20] During this period the applicant is allowed to remain temporarily in the country concerned.

1   Member States are required to grant workers the right of residence under Council Directive (EEC) 68/360, Art 4(4), and the right of permanent residence to those who are established or wish to be established or provide or receive services under Council Directive (EEC) 73/148, Art 4. Little turns on the distinction, which is not reflected in the Immigration (European Economic Area) Regulations 2000, SI 2000/2326. In the case of workers, the residence permit must include the wording set out in the Annex to Directive 68/360, which is as follows: 'this permit is issued pursuant to regulation (EEC) number 1612/68 of the Council of the European Communities of 15 October 1968 and to the measures taken in implementation of the Council Directive of 15 October 1968'.

2   Case 48/75 *Royer, Re* [1976] ECR 497, [1976] 2 CMLR 619; Case 8/77 *Sagulo, Brenca and Bakhouche, Re* [1977] ECR 1495, [1977] 2 CMLR 585; *R v Pieck* [1981] QB 571; Case 59/85 *Netherlands v Reed* [1986] ECR 1283, [1987] 2 CMLR 448; Case C-363/89 *Roux v Belgium* [1991] ECR I-273, at para 9; Case C-459/99 *Mouvement contre le racisme, l'antisémitisme et la xénophobie ASBL v Belgium* [2002] ECR I-6591, at para 74; Case C-138/02 *Collins v Secretary of State for Work and Pensions* [2005] QB 145, para 40.

3   Council Directives (EEC) 68/360, Art 4(4) and 73/148, Art 4(3). The IAT held in *Layne* [1987] Imm AR 243 that the rights attached to the non-national document must be the same. Under para 255 of HC 395 holders of both residence permits and documents can apply for indefinite permission to remain under the Immigration Rules.

4   SI 2000/2326.

5   SI 2000/2326, reg 15(1).

6   SI 2000/2326, reg 15(3).

7   SI 2000/2326, reg 16(1)(a), Council Directive (EEC) 68/360, Art 8(1)(a).

8   SI 2000/2326, reg 16(1)(b), Council Directive (EEC) 68/360, Art 8(1)(b). Special rules are also made for EC nationals who are non-nationals of country A who wish to work in country B while retaining their residence in country A. If they have been workers or self-employed in country A for three years, they can go on living there, and work in country B provided they return home (country A) 'as a rule, each day or at least once a week'. They become entitled to permanent residence in country A under Council Directive (EEC) 75/34 (self-employed) or Council Regulation (EEC) 1251/70 (workers).

9   SI 2000/2326, reg 16(1)(c) (which has not been amended to reflect the split in functions and change in nomenclature between the Department for Education and Skills and the Department for Work and Pensions), Council Directive (EEC) 68/360, Art 8(1)(c).

10   SI 2000/2326, reg 16(1)(d).

11   Agreement between the European Community and the Swiss Confederation on The Free Movement of Persons (30 Apr/02 OJ L114/6), Art 17 of Annex 1.

12   SI 2000/2326, modified in relation to Swiss nationals and posted workers by SI 2002/1241 by the insertion of reg 16A.

13   See 7.75 above.

14   SI 2000/2326, reg 17(2).

15   SI 2000/2326, reg 15(2).

16   SI 2000/2326, reg 15(2).

17   Case C-459/99 *Mouvement contre le racisme, l'antisémitisme et la xénophobie ASBL v Belgium* [2002] ECR I-6591, para 91.

18   *Mouvement contre le racisme, l'antisémitisme et la xénophobie ASBL v Belgium* above, para 80.

[19] Council Directive (EEC) 68/360, Art 10 and 73/148, Art 8, and there are equivalent provisions in the June 1990 Directives. See SI 2000/2326, reg 22(1).

[20] The Commission has successfully brought infringement proceedings against Spain for the failure by the Spanish authorities to make decisions on residence permit applications expeditiously and in any event with six months (see Case C-157/03 *Commission v Spain* (14 April 2005)). It is alarming that the present European Directorate Instructions to IND caseworkers (EDI) warn caseworkers to deal with applications within six months only where representatives insist on expedition, although compliance with Art 5 of Directive 64/221 means that all applications, however complex and whatever issues of public policy or public security they raise, must be dealt with within that time.

Duration of first residence permit

7.118 The first residence permit must normally be valid for at least five years and be renewable,[1] but a lesser period is permitted:[2]

(i)   if the employment is for between three and 12 months, for the duration of the employment;

(ii) if seasonal employment is for more than three months, for the duration of the employment;

(iii) in the case of provision or receipt of services, for the period of such provision;

(iv) in the case of students, for the duration of the studies, or for 12 months in the first instance in the case of studies exceeding 12 months;

(v)   in the case of a retired or self-sufficient person, two years in the first instance, followed by revalidation.

The validity of a residence permit is not affected by absence from the UK for periods of up to six months or absence on military service.[3]

[1] Immigration (European Economic Area) Regulations 2000, SI 2000/2326, regs 18–20, applying the requirements of the Council Directives (EEC) 68/360, 73/148, 90/364, 90/365 and 93/96; Directives 90/364 and 365 for the self-sufficient and retired. Article 2 states that the residence permit may be limited to five years on a renewable basis but Member States may where they deem it necessary require revalidation of the permit at the end of the first two years of residence.

[2] SI 2000/2326, reg 18 (modified by SI 2002/1241 in relation to Swiss nationals, their family members and posted workers).

[3] SI 2000/2326, reg 18(7).

Renewal of residence permit

7.119 Residence permits are renewable on the basis that the person remains a qualified person or the family member of such a person.[1] Family membership continues as long as the parties are not finally divorced and the qualified person has not permanently abandoned residence in the UK, or, if the parties are divorced or the qualified person has left the UK, so long as the person is a descendant in full-time education or the primary carer of such a person.[2] Cohabitation under the same roof is not necessary.[3] A worker remains qualified despite periods of sickness or unemployment. Council Directive (EEC) 68/360, Article 7(2) provides that when a worker's residence permit is first renewed, the period of residence may be restricted (but to no less than 12 months) where the worker has been involuntarily unemployed in the Member

State for more than 12 consecutive months.[4] The implication of such a provision is that no such restriction on a worker's residence can be imposed where the residence permit is renewed for a second or subsequent time; and it also suggests that no grounds other than 'voluntary' unemployment, or public policy, public security or public health (see Article 10 of Council Directive (EEC) 68/360) can justify restricting the period of residence even on a first renewal. This is certainly the view of the Immigration Appeal Tribunal, which has allowed a number of appeals against government attempts to curtail the residence of EEA citizens because they have become a charge on public funds.[5] Persons who have been involuntarily unemployed for more than 12 consecutive months will not have completed four years' employment by the end of their first full-length residence permit, and will not qualify for permanent residence in national law after four years' residence with a permit.[6] For those covered by Council Directive (EEC) 73/148 who remain established for business purposes in the UK, renewal of a residence permit is automatic and residence is described in Article 4(1) as 'permanent'. Regulation 19 of the Immigration (European Economic Area) Regulations 2000[7] provides for renewal of a residence permit on application, subject to the Secretary of State's powers under regulation 22 of the 2000 Regulations to revoke or refuse to renew a residence permit or document:

(i)   where the revocation or refusal is justified on grounds of public policy, public security or public health; or

(ii) the person to whom the residence permit or residence document was issued has ceased to be a qualified person, or is not, or has ceased to be, the family member of a qualified person.

Students with a 12-month first residence permit may have the renewed permit limited to periods of one year, as may workers who have been involuntarily unemployed in the UK for more than one year.[8]

1   Immigration (European Economic Area) Regulations 2000, SI 2000/2326, regs 19, 20, 22(2).
2   See above, 7.93 (spouses) and 7.95 (descendants).
3   See *Diatta v Land Berlin* and the discussion of family membership at 7.93 above. Home Office policy is to grant ILR to separated third country national spouses of EEA nationals who have obtained permanent residence by exercise of Treaty rights, even where decree nisi has been pronounced and decree absolute is being delayed just to benefit from *Diatta*: Home Office to Philip Barth, 17 November 2003.
4   For 'voluntary' unemployment, see below. The 2000 Regulations reflect this provision in SI 2000/2326, reg 19(2).
5   See *Giangregorio v Secretary of State for the Home Department* [1983] Imm AR 104, [1983] 3 CMLR 472, IAT; *Monteil v Secretary of State for the Home Department* [1983] Imm AR 149, [1984] 1 CMLR 264, IAT; *Lubbersen v Secretary of State for the Home Department* [1984] Imm AR 56, [1984] 3 CMLR 77, IAT.
6   Unless they were able to qualify as self-sufficient: HC 375, para 255; see 7.121 below.
7   SI 2000/2326.
8   SI 2000/2326, reg 19(2) and (3).

Public funds and voluntary unemployment

7.120 A detailed analysis of when an EEA national is entitled to claim public funds under the social security system of the UK is beyond the scope of the present work,[1] although many of the ECJ cases on free movement turn on this issue. Here we are concerned solely with the question of what effect recourse to public funds has on an EEA national's right to remain. The EC Directives distinguish between recourse to such funds prior to the issue of a first residence permit and thereafter. The ECJ decision in *Antonissen* has provided some guidance as to when a person retains Community law rights as a worker after admission to the territory of the host State but before a residence permit is issued, and may be summarised as follows:

(i) a reasonable period (which may be six months) is prima facie sufficient for a person seeking employment to have obtained it. During that period a person will remain a worker, and cannot be discriminated against on social security grounds compared with UK nationals;

(ii) thereafter a person who claims to be considered as a worker will have to produce evidence of attempts to seek employment in order to meet the Community definition of worker and thus remain a qualified person;

(iii) if employment is obtained a residence permit cannot be refused solely on the ground of recourse to public funds.[2]

Regulation 5(2) of the Immigration (European Economic Area) Regulations 2000[3] provides that a worker does not cease to be a qualified person on the ground of unemployment if he or she is temporarily incapable of work as a result of illness or accident or is involuntarily unemployed and that fact is duly recorded by the relevant employment office. Thus whilst a worker is registered as seeking employment, he or she will not be considered as voluntarily unemployed. Community law envisages that evidence other than registration for work with the employment office will demonstrate that the person is still actively seeking work and remains a qualified person.[4] Where the worker is employed and relies on public funds to supplement his or her income, there is no incompatibility with the free movement provisions relating to workers, as has been held by the ECJ in *Kempf*.[5] The same must apply to those relying on the right of establishment. A former worker may also qualify under some other provision of Community law, but, apart from those permanently disabled by industrial accident, permanent reliance on the social security system of a host State is likely to become incompatible with the provisions of free movement. If someone leaves a job in order to obtain a better one or to enter further education or training, this is not voluntary unemployment which might lead to a curtailment of residence. In *Hoekstra-Unger*[6] the ECJ held that someone who had left one job and was capable of taking another one was still a 'worker entitled to the protection of the free movement provisions'. The case concerned a woman who became pregnant and left her employment. This certainly suggests that a person who is claiming unemployment or social security benefit and is actively seeking another job is still covered by the provisions of Article 39 EC, since it provides that a worker is someone who is seeking employment in the territory of another Member State. Someone who gives up their current job to return to study or training in order to obtain better qualifications does not necessarily lose their status of 'worker', as the ECJ has held in *Lair*.[7] In such circumstances claiming unemployment or social security benefits or seeking an education grant can be done without risk of penalty.[8] In *Grzelczyk* the ECJ held that a student does not automatically cease to be lawfully resident by accessing social security benefits since Directive 93/96 only precludes students from becoming an 'unreasonable burden' on the host Member State. A temporary or marginal need for social assistance would not constitute an unreasonable burden if the student has otherwise remained self-sufficient for the duration of his studies.[9]

1   Chapter 13 below contains an outline, including the concept of 'habitual residence'.
2   Case C-292/89 [1991] ECR I-745, (1991) 2 CMLR 373, ECJ. See also Case 53/81 *Levin v Secretary of State for Justice* [1982] ECR 1035, [1982] 2 CMLR 454, ECJ and Case 139/85 *Kempf v Staatssecretaris van Justitie* [1987] 1 CMLR 764, ECJ.
3   SI 2000/2326. This applies to self-employed persons, but only if they are temporarily incapable of work through illness or accident: see reg 5(3).
4   *Antonissen* above.
5   Case 139/85 [1987] 1 CMLR 764, ECJ.
6   Case 75/63 *Hoekstra (née Unger) v Bestuur der Bedrifsvereinigung voor Detailhandel en Ambachten* [1964] ECR 177.
7   Case 39/86 *Lair v University of Hanover* [1989] 3 CMLR 545; Case C-357/89 *Raulin v Minister van Onderwijs en Wontschappen* [1994] 1 CMLR 227, ECJ.
8   See *R (on the application of Bidar) v London Borough of Ealing v Secretary of State for Education and Skills* Case C-209/03 (15 March 2005) (student grants).
9   Case C-184/99 *Grzelczyk v Centre public d'aide sociale d'Ottignies-Louvain-la-Neuve* [2001] ECR I-36199.

Permanent residence in the UK

7.121 The entitlement to a residence permit discussed above presupposes that the person concerned fulfils the criteria of a qualified person or family member at the time of issue or renewal. Thus, a person who is established in business and has a right to a permanent residence may lose that right if he or she ceases to carry on business, unless he or she qualifies as a retired or self-sufficient person. There is a difference between the right of permanent residence under Community law and the grant of indefinite or permanent leave to remain under UK domestic immigration law. It is not clear whether and in what circumstances permanent residence can be revoked or curtailed under EC law other than for public policy reasons, nor exactly at which point a temporary or conditional right of residence turns into a permanent one.[1] The position under UK domestic law, on the other hand, is clear, and domestic law has also made provision for Community rights of residence to take effect as permanent permission under domestic law.[2] This, it seems, is the only permissible meeting point for the two systems; for the English Court of Appeal has made it very clear that the two systems of law are distinct and no reliance can be placed on an amalgam of the two.[3] So indefinite leave has to be pursued down the domestic route without tacking on helpful bits of EC law. Furthermore, the ECJ has held in *Kaba*[4] that even though the spouse of a UK national can achieve indefinite leave to remain in 12 months, the fact that it takes four years to achieve the same thing for the spouse of another EEA national is not a breach of the EC's rules against discrimination on nationality grounds. In this situation of uncertainty, the only sure path is to rely on the grant of permanent permission or indefinite leave given to EEA nationals under the Immigration Rules. The right to remain permanently under domestic law for those who have entered and remained under Community law is conveniently summarised in paragraphs 255 to 257 of the UK Immigration Rules (HC 395).

1   For nationality purposes, the Immigration (European Economic Area) Regulations 2000, SI 2000/2326 treat a very small group of EEA qualified persons, comprising retired self-employed persons and their families, and family members of deceased workers, as not being subject to restrictions on the period for which they may remain: reg 8(1) and (2). Significantly, workers and the self-employed are outside the group. In Case C-356/98 *Kaba v Secretary of State for the Home Department* [2000] All ER (EC) 537 the ECJ stated that EC migrant workers' rights of residence are not unconditional, but did not say why (para 30).

2   HC 395, paras 255–257.

3   *Secretary of State for the Home Department v Sahota; Zeghraba v Secretary of State for the Home Department* [1997] Imm AR 429, CA; *Boukssid v Secretary of State for the Home Department* [1998] INLR 275, CA.

4   Case C-356/98 [2000] All ER (EC) 537, ECJ.

7.122 Paragraph 256 of the Immigration Rules permits self-employed EEA nationals who have ceased economic activity in the UK, and their family members, to remain in the UK indefinitely. The term 'ceased economic activity' is itself defined by regulation 4(2) of the Immigration (European Economic Area) Regulations 2000[1] and means:

(i)   a person who has reached the State retirement age when he or she terminates activity, after having been self-employed in the UK for 12 months, and who has resided in the UK for more than three years;[2]

(ii)   a person who has resided in the UK for more than two years and has terminated that activity as a result of permanent incapacity to work;[3]

(iii) a person who has resided in the UK and pursued self-employment but has terminated the activity as a result of permanent incapacity to work owing to an accident at work or occupational illness entitling the person to a State pension;[4]

(iv)   a person who has been continuously resident and active in a self-employed capacity in the UK for three years, and is also active in a self-employed capacity in the territory of another Member State but returns to his or her residence in the UK at least once a week.[5]

Spouses of UK nationals do not have to satisfy length of residence conditions in the first two categories, nor the self-employment condition in the first (retirement).[6] Family members of self-employed persons who die can also obtain permission to remain indefinitely if the qualified person resided in the UK during their working life continuously for more than two years or their death resulted from an accident at work or occupational disease.[7]

1   SI 2000/2326.
2   SI 2000/2326, reg 4(1)(a).
3   SI 2000/2326, reg 4(1)(b).
4   SI 2000/2326, reg 4(1)(c).
5   SI 2000/2326, reg 4(1)(d).
6   SI 2000/2326, reg 4(2).
7   HC 395, para 257(v) applying Council Directive (EEC) 75/34 EEC, Art 3(2).

7.123 Workers and their families qualify for permanent residence if:

(i)   they are permanently incapacitated for work, due to an accident at work, an occupational disease entitling the person to a State disability pension, or (after two years continuous residence in the UK) from any other cause;[1] or

(ii) they have been continuously resident in the UK for three years, have been in employment in the UK or any other EEA State for the preceding 12 months, and have reached the State retirement age.[2]

Family members of workers who die can also obtain permission to remain indefinitely if the qualified person had resided in the UK during their working life continuously for more than two years or their death resulted from an accident at work or occupational disease.[3]

[1] HC 395, para 257(ii)–(iii), applying Council Regulation (EEC) 1251/70, Art 2.
[2] HC 395, para 257(i), applying Council Regulation (EEC) 1251/70, Art 2.
[3] HC 395, para 257(v), applying Council Regulation (EEC) 1251/70, Art 3. The two-year residence period must immediately precede the worker's death in order to give rise to the family's right of permanent residence: Case C-257/00 *Givane v Secretary of State for the Home Department* [2003] INLR 259, ECJ.

7.124 These provisions of the UK Immigration Rules reflect the EC Directives, and the regulations also refer to the fact that workers and self-employed persons can choose to retire irrespective of the period of qualifying residence in the host country if they are married to a spouse who is or was a national of that country.[1] Such persons would almost certainly qualify for settlement under UK immigration law in any event. Continuity of residence, where it is required, is not affected by temporary absences of up to three months per year, nor by longer absences due to compliance with the obligations of military service.[2] Periods of involuntary unemployment or absences due to illness or accident count as periods of employment for these purposes.[3] No formalities are needed in order to exercise the right to remain.[4] Those exercising the right to remain after retirement are entitled to a residence permit, which, like all EC residence permits, must be valid throughout the territory of the Member State issuing it, last for at least five years and be renewable automatically.[5]

[1] Immigration (European Economic Area) Regulations 2000, SI 2000/2326, reg 4(2)(a), reflecting Council Directive (EEC) 75/34, Art 3(2) and regulation (EEC) 1251/70, Art 3(2).
[2] SI 2000/2326, reg 4(4)(a) (for self-employed persons), reflecting Council Directive (EEC) 75/34 and regulation (EEC) 1251/70, Art 4(1). Home Office policy is not to allow absences from the UK to penalise an application. Periods spent in the exercise of a Treaty right may be amalgamated, and only in the case of very long absences would consideration be given to refusing the application: HO European Directorate to Clifford Chance, 4 December 2001.
[3] SI 2000/2326, reg 4(4)(b) (for self-employed persons), reflecting Council Directive (EEC) 75/34 and regulation (EEC) 1251/70, Art 4(2).
[4] Council Directive (EEC) 75/34 and regulation (EEC) 1251/70, Art 5(2).
[5] Council Directive (EEC) 75/34 and regulation (EEC) 1251/70, Art 6.

7.125 In addition to reflecting Community rights, the Immigration Rules also provide that indefinite permission to remain may be granted to the holder of a residence permit or document valid for five years, who has remained for four years in accordance with the Immigration (European Economic Area) Order 1994[1] or the Immigration (European Economic Area) Regulations 2000[2] and continues so to do.[3] Permanent residence of this kind given under national law entitles the recipient to remain irrespective of their subsequent economic activity or later recourse to public funds. Although the Rules avoid the use of the word 'indefinite leave to remain', given that these nationals do not require leave to enter, the holder of this endorsement will be in a similar position in practice to someone who has an indefinite leave stamp.[4] The endorsement will also certainly remove any doubt about the eligibility of the EEA national to naturalise as a British citizen.[5] All attempts to cut short the waiting period using EC law have so far failed.[6]

1   SI 1994/1895.
2   SI 2000/2326.
3   HC 395, para 255.
4   This status does not lapse after a visit abroad: see Immigration Act 1971, s 3(4).
5   See 7.121 fn 1 above for discussion of whether there is any restriction on the period for which such nationals may stay.
6   *Sahota; Boukssid; Kaba* at 7.121 above, fnn 1, 3 and 4.

Appeals against adverse decisions of UK immigration authorities

7.126 EEA nationals or family members who are excluded from the UK, refused a residence permit or residence document, or whose permit or document is withdrawn, may appeal against the refusal under appeal rights contained in Part VII of the Immigration (European Economic Area) Regulations 2000.[1] We deal with all the appeals affecting EEA nationals in chapter 18 below.

1   SI 2000/2326, regs 27–36, as substituted by SI 2003/549 and amended by SI 2005/671.

TERMINATION OF THE RIGHT TO RESIDE: CESSATION OF ENTITLEMENT AND EXCLUSION

Cessation and public policy

7.127 We have seen in the previous section that Community rights granted to the economically active continue whilst that activity is being exercised, with exceptions for retirement and permanent disability. What happens if it stops? An able-bodied EEA national below the age of retirement might cease to be economically active. The question then arises of whether a right to remain ceases to exist or can be terminated by non-renewal of a residence permit, and whether there is a power of expulsion which can then be exercised. In practice, the issue is unlikely to arise except in the case of an EEA national who is looking to long-term reliance on social security and public funds without any prospect of exercising any economic activity provided for by Community law. An EEA national who is self-supporting has a good chance of qualifying under one or other of the directives discussed above.[1]

1   See 7.80ff above. It is only recourse to income support that leads to cesser of qualification.

7.128 In *Antonissen*[1] an EC national who had not worked in the UK had committed drugs offences during the course of his stay, and the question was whether he could rely on Community rights in the deportation appeal. He was held not to be a worker, and therefore had no rights in EC law. There are several early Immigration Appeal Tribunal decisions upholding refusals of admission to EC nationals on the grounds that they had not been working on previous visits to the UK and were not seeking to enter under one of the directives 68/360 or 73/148. Some of these cases must be regarded as unsound in the light of the later ECJ case law defining a 'worker' as including someone genuinely seeking work.

1   Case C-292/89 [1991] ECR I-745, (1991) 2 CMLR 373, ECJ. It may be that the ruling in *Antonissen* is restricted to the case where an EU national has never obtained employment at all, and different considerations apply as to cesser of qualification after a number of years employment in the host State. See also *Monteil v Secretary of State for the Home Department* [1983] Imm AR 149, [1984] 1 CMLR 264, IAT; *Lubbersen v Secretary of State for the Home Department* [1984] Imm AR 56, [1984] 3 CMLR 77, IAT.

7.129 The UK stance on the possibility of removal of EEA nationals who cease to qualify is set out in the Immigration (European Economic Area) Regulations 2000. Under Regulations 21(3), and 22(2), ceasing to qualify is a ground for revoking or refusing to renew a residence permit or document,[1] and for removal from the UK.[2] However, it is still uncertain whether an attempt to exclude an EEA national purely on the grounds of ceasing to qualify would be successful without any other aspect of conduct that brings public policy into play. Ceasing to qualify is not like overstaying leave – a clear breach of the conditions of leave which is met with the sanction of removal. They are conceptually quite different. A major difficulty facing the Home Office, which has the burden of proof,[3] would be to identify the moment when a person ceased to qualify. A person may remain a worker even when not actually in work or seeking work, for example, if employment is interrupted by pregnancy, illness or vocational training.[4] The EEA Regulations provide[5] that a person who is to be removed for ceasing to be a qualified person or the family member of a qualified person is to be treated in the same way as an overstayer under section 10 of the Immigration and Asylum Act 1999.[6]

1   SI 2000/2316, reg 22(2)(b).
2   SI 2000/2316 reg 21(3)(a).
3   See observations of IAT in *Giangregorio v Secretary of State for the Home Department* [1983] Imm AR 104, [1983] 2 CMLR 472, IAT; decision of ECJ in *Antonissen* [1991] 2 CMLR 373.
4   See 7.120 above.
5   SI 2000/2326, reg 26(1), (2).
6   The explicit application of s 10 to such persons gets over the problem that EEA nationals and others relying on EC rights do not require leave to enter, they do not become overstayers or in breach of conditions and could not be removed as such under the section.

7.130 The implications of Article 18 EC (ex Article 8a) of the EEC Treaty, as amended by the Treaty on European Union, also fall to be considered. The UK avoids these questions in the Immigration (European Economic Area) Regulations 2000[1] by elision of the rights of EU nationals and the rights of other EEA nationals under the EEA agreement. But EU nationals have the right to move and reside freely within the territory of Member States, 'subject to the limitations and conditions laid down in this Treaty and the measures adopted to give it effect'.[2] Expulsion of an EU national on the ground that he or she is no longer a qualified person within the meaning of the 2000 Regulations would materially affect the right of residence. In *Baumbast*[3] the ECJ considered the scope of Article 18 EC and nature of the limitations and conditions referred to in Article 18. The court pointed out that the Treaty does not require that citizens of the Union pursue an economic activity in order to enjoy the right of citizenship of the Union and certainly access to citizenship rights does not cease when economic activity comes to an end. Whilst Article 18 EC refers to the right of citizens to reside within the territory of another Member State being subject to the limitation and conditions laid down in the Treaty and measure adopted to give it effective, those limitations and conditions '*do not prevent the provisions of Article 18(1) EC from conferring on individuals rights which are enforceable by them and which the national courts must protect*'.[4] Thus the ECJ held that even if conditions of the general right of residence directive, Directive 90/364, are not strictly met for instance, the right of residence should not be denied for the reason that:

> 'the limitations and conditions laid down in secondary legislation must be applied in compliance with the limits imposed by Community law and in accordance with the general principles of that law, particular the principle of proportionality'.[5]

On the facts, the ECJ considered that as Mr Baumbast has previously worked in the UK he should not be deprived of a right of residence if he failed to provide evidence of sickness insurance as required by Directive 90/364 on general rights of residence.

1 SI 2000/2326.
2 See *R v Secretary of State for the Home Department, ex p Vitale* [1995] NLJR 631.
3 Case C-413/99 *Baumbast v Secretary of State for the Home Department* [2002] ECR I-7091.
4 *Baumbast* above, para 86.
5 *Baumbast* above para 91. See also the discussion of proportionality in the application of restrictions on the right of residence of EU nationals in *Chen and Zhu v Secretary of State for the Home Department* C-200/02, [2005] QB 325.

Public policy

7.131 The free movement provisions of the EC Treaty are all subject to what EC law calls 'the public policy proviso', although public policy is but one limb. For workers, Article 39(3) EC (ex Article 48(3)) says that the free movement provisions, but not the provisions for the abolition of discrimination based on nationality, shall be 'subject to limitations justified on grounds of public policy, public security or public health'. So far as concerns the right of establishment, Article 46(1) EC (ex Article 56(1)) says:

> 'the provisions of this Chapter and measures taken in pursuance thereof shall not prejudice the applicability of provisions laid down by law, regulation or administrative action providing for special treatment for foreign nationals on grounds of public policy, public security or public health.'

So far as services are concerned, Article 55 EC (ex Article 66) of the Consolidated Treaty of Rome provides that the provisions of Articles 45–48 EC (ex Article 55–58) apply also to the matters covered in the chapter concerning services. This means that the provisions of Article 46(1) EC apply to the provision of services as well as to the right of establishment. Although the wording of the public policy proviso is slightly different as between workers and those relying on the right of establishment, the ECJ has made it clear that in practice there should be no difference.[1] The rights of free movement of the self-sufficient, the retired and vocational students are also subject to the public policy proviso.[2]

[1] Case 48/75 *Royer, Re* [1976] ECR 497, [1976] 2 CMLR 619.
[2] See Council Directives (EEC) 90/364, 90/365 and 93/96 relating to residence rights of self-sufficient and retired persons and students respectively.

Implementation of the public policy proviso

7.132 The public policy proviso is implemented by Council Directive (EEC) 64/221 of 25 February 1964. This applies to nationals of a Member State who are workers, self-employed persons or providers or recipients of services, and their families. Its provisions are also expressly made to cover those who have ceased to be economically active as a result of retirement or incapacity, to the economically self-sufficient, and to students.[1] The Directive applies to all measures on grounds of public policy, public security or public health concerning entry into, the issue or renewal of residence permits in and expulsion from an EU country.[2] In the UK the provisions of the Directive are reflected in the Immigration (European Economic Area) Regulations 2000,[3] regulation 21(1), dealing with exclusion from the UK; regulation 21(3)(b), dealing with removal; regulation 22(1), dealing with refusal to issue a residence permit or document; regulation 22(2)(a), dealing with revocation of or refusal to renew a residence permit or document; and regulation 22(4)(a), dealing with an immigration officer's power to revoke an EEA family permit on arrival in the UK. They apply to all EEA nationals and their families, and to persons exercising rights under Association Agreements.[4] A Member State cannot invoke the public policy proviso to serve economic ends, such as protecting the employment prospects of its own nationals as against other EEA nationals.[5] The Directive also makes it clear that the expiry of the travel documents or passports, which EEA nationals had on arrival, is not a good reason for their expulsion from the country, and that despite their expiry such nationals are free to travel back to their own country.[6] It also imposes important substantive[7] and procedural limits on the operation of the public policy proviso.[8]

[1] See Council Directive (EEC) 72/194, Art 1, applying Council Directive (EEC) 64/221 to retired workers; Council Directives (EEC) 90/364 and 90/365, Art 2, applying it to self-sufficient and retired persons; and Council Directive (EEC) 93/96, Art 2, applying it to students. A useful account of Directive 64/221 is given in the Commission Communication to the Council and the European Parliament, August 1999. Note that Council Directive (EEC) 64/221 will be replaced by Council Directive 2004/38 on 30.04.06 (European Citizens Directive).
[2] Council Directive (EEC) 64/221, Art 2(1).
[3] SI 2000/2326, as amended by the Immigration (European Economic Area) (Amendment) Regulations 2001, SI 2001/865.
[4] By Article 14 of Commission Decision (ECSC) 1/80 under the Ankara Agreement: see C-340/97 *Nazli v Stadt Nürnberg* [2000] ECR I-957, para 63.
[5] Council Directive (EEC) 64/221, Art 2; SI 2000/2326, reg 23(a).
[6] Council Directive (EEC) 64/221, Art 3(3) and (4).
[7] Council Directive (EEC) 64/221, Art 3(1): see below.
[8] Council Directive (EEC) 64/221, Arts 8 and 9.

7.133 In a series of important early decisions, the ECJ made it clear that (in contrast to the position in UK immigration law) the principle of free movement within the EEA is far more important than any exceptions to it. First, it stipulated that in any case in which a Member State is relying on the public policy proviso, it has to show that the measure in question is justified on the basis of some objective which forms part of public policy, public security or public health.[1] Secondly, the ECJ has repeatedly held that free movement is a fundamental general principle and that the public policy proviso is an exception which, like all derogations from a fundamental principle of the EC Treaty, should be construed restrictively.[2] Thirdly, the court has repeatedly emphasised that exclusion or expulsion on the ground of public policy should not occur unless the person's 'presence or conduct constitutes a genuine and sufficiently serious threat to public policy'.[3] So the person's presence must not only be a genuine threat to the public policy objective, but also a sufficiently serious one.

[1] Case 48/75 *Royer, Re* [1976] ECR 497, [1976] 2 CMLR 619, ECJ.
[2] Case 41/74 *Van Duyn v Home Office* [1974] ECR 1337; Case 67/74 *Bonsignore v Stadt Köln* [1975] ECR 297; Case 36/75 *Rutili v Minister for the Interior* [1975] ECR 1219, [1976] 1 CMLR 140, ECJ; Case 139/85 *Kempf v Staatssecretaris van Justitie* [1986] ECR 1741; Case C-348/96 *Calfa (criminal proceedings against)* [1999] ECR I-11; Case C-340/97 *Nazli v Stadt Nürnberg* [2000] ECR I-957.
[3] Case 30/77 *R v Bouchereau* [1977] ECR 1999; *Bonsignore, Calfa, Nazli* above.

7.134 Article 3(1) of Council Directive (EEC) 64/221 provides that measures taken on the grounds of public policy or public security should be based exclusively on the personal conduct of the individual concerned.[1] What is meant by this was explained in two early cases before the ECJ. In *Van Duyn v Home Office (No 2)*[2] a member of the Church of Scientology challenged her refusal of entry to Britain under the general ban on scientologists, and her case was referred to the ECJ. The court explored the term 'personal conduct' and concluded that, while a person's past association does not in general suffice, present association 'which reflects participation in the activities of the body or organisation and identification with its aims and designs' may be considered a voluntary act of the person concerned and thus part of his or her personal conduct. Being a member of the Church of Scientology was personal conduct by which the UK government could justify her exclusion from the UK on the ground that her presence was not conducive to the public good. But if the ban or expulsion is for reasons that go much wider than the personal conduct of the person concerned, this may not be allowed. In *Bonsignore*[3] an Italian worker resident in Cologne purchased a Beretta gun from an unidentified source, and while manipulating the gun he accidentally killed his younger brother. He was found guilty by a German court of illegal possession of firearms and causing death by negligence. The German authorities wanted to deport him, but clearly the only reason for doing this was as a general deterrent and not because Bonsignore was likely to commit similar offences again. The ECJ held that Article 3(1) of the Directive made it clear that EEC nationals could not be subjected to decisions made on grounds extraneous to their personal and individual cases. Read together with Article 3(2) it barred Member States from expelling EEC nationals in order to deter other aliens from committing identical or similar offences, that is to say for 'general preventive' or 'deterrent' reasons. This reasoning has been upheld in subsequent cases so as to prevent the automatic expulsion of persons committing drugs offences in particular.[4]

1   Reflected in the EEA Regulations, SI 2000/2326, reg 23(b).
2   Case 41/74 [1974] ECR 1337, [1975] Ch 358.
3   Case 67/74 [1975] ECR 297, [1975] 1 CMLR 472.
4   Case C-348/96 *Calfa (criminal proceedings against)* [1999] ECR I-11; Case C-340/97 *Nazli v Stadt Nürnberg* [2000] ECR I-957, ECJ.

7.135 Article 3(2) of Council Directive (EEC) 64/221, on which the court relied in *Bonsignore*, provides that previous criminal convictions shall not in themselves constitute grounds for the taking of measures on the grounds of public policy or public security.[1] The *Bonsignore* case makes it clear that exclusion or deportation of an EEA national cannot be justified on the grounds of general deterrence. The Article also means that a country's authorities cannot apply a blanket rule excluding from their territory anyone with a criminal record,[2] and certainly renders inapplicable to EEA nationals immigration rules preventing the entry of persons convicted of an extraditable offence unless there are 'strong compassionate reasons'.[3]

1   Reflected in the EEA Regulations, SI 2000/2326, reg 23(c).
2   C-441/02 *Commission v Germany* is pending on the question of Germany's mandatory exclusion of persons who have committed certain criminal offences.
3   See HC 395, r 320(18).

7.136 In *Bonsignore* the court further held that public policy measures should only be applied if there is a likelihood that the offender will commit further offences or in some other way infringe public security or policy. In *R v Bouchereau*,[1] a case concerning a French national who pleaded guilty to drug offences before an English court which wished to recommend him for deportation, the ECJ described the public policy limitation as follows:

'In so far as it may justify certain restrictions on the free movement of persons subject to Community law, recourse by a national authority to the concept of public policy presupposes, in any event, the existence, in addition to the perturbation of the social order which any infringement of the law involves, of a genuine and sufficiently serious threat to the requirements of public policy affecting one of the fundamental interests of society.'

The court held that a criminal conviction can be taken into account only in so far as the circumstances which gave rise to the conviction are evidence of personal conduct:

'constituting a present threat to the requirements of public policy ... Although, in general, a finding that such threat exists implies the existence in the individual concerned of a propensity to act in the same way in the future, it is possible that past conduct alone may constitute such a threat to the requirements of public policy.'

1   Case 30/77 *R v Bouchereau* [1978] QB 732, [1977] ECR 1999, ECJ.

7.137 There was uncertainty in the UK case law applying these principles as to whether a propensity to re-offend was required and in what circumstances it might not be required. In considering a recommendation for deportation of a convicted rapist, the Court of Appeal in *R v Secretary of State for the Home Department, ex p Santillo*[1] considered that future risk posed by the possibility of re-offending was required as a matter of Community law and common sense. In *R v Secretary of State for the Home Department, ex p Al-Sabah*[2] the Court of Appeal doubted these remarks, regarding them as inconsistent with *Bouchereau*. In *Marchon*[3] a Portuguese doctor who had been convicted of importing 4.5 kilos of heroin and sentenced to 14 years' imprisonment was held not to need any propensity to re-offend in order to merit deportation on public good grounds. The court regarded this conduct by a doctor as particularly disgraceful, and indicative of a disregard for the basic or fundamental moral tenets of society.

[1]   [1981] QB 778, CA.
[2]   [1992] Imm AR 223, CA.
[3]   *R v Secretary of State for the Home Department, ex p Marchon* [1993] Imm AR 384, CA.

7.138   The confusion has, we believe, been cleared up by more recent ECJ cases such as *Nazli v Stadt Nürnberg*,[1] involving a Turkish worker exercising rights under the Ankara Agreement and Commission Decision (ECSC) 1/80 under it in Germany. Mr Nazli had been convicted of a drugs-related offence in circumstances indicating no propensity to re-offend, but German aliens' law provided for mandatory expulsion after conviction of drugs offences.[2] The court held that a person enjoying Treaty rights and rights analogous to them under the Association Agreement could not be expelled 'as a deterrent to other aliens without the personal conduct of the person concerned giving reason to consider that he will commit other serious offences prejudicial to the requirements of public policy in the host Member State'.[3] Earlier in its judgment the court referred to the requirement that the expulsion measure 'is justified because ... personal conduct indicates a risk of new and serious prejudice to the requirements of public policy'. This means that in every case the personal conduct of the person involved, and in particular the indications of future risk of threats to public policy, must be assessed. Criminal convictions even for the most heinous crimes will, we suggest, never be enough by themselves.

[1]   Case C-340/97 [2000] ECR I-957, ECJ.
[2]   See also Case C-348/96 *Calfa (criminal proceedings against)* [1999] 2 CMLR 1138, ECJ, a case involving a tourist expelled for life under Greek law for possession of drugs.
[3]   *Nazli* fn 1 above, para 64.

Proportionality

7.139   Measures taken by Member States in respect of nationals of other Member States must be reasonable and not disproportionate to the gravity of their conduct. As the Court of Appeal observed in *International Traders' Ferry*,[2] proportionality 'requires the court to judge the necessity of the action taken as well as whether it was within the range of courses of action that could reasonably be followed', and it may be a more exacting test than a *Wednesbury* formulation.[3] In *B v Secretary of State for the Home Department*[4] Simon Brown LJ pointed out that even if the deportation of an EC national could be justified by the existence of 'a genuine and sufficiently serious threat to the requirements of public policy affecting one of the fundamental interests of society',[5] the requirement of proportionality was held to mean that deportation 'must be both appropriate and necessary for the attainment of the public policy objective sought—the containment of the threat—and also must not impose an excessive burden on the individual, the deportee'. In that case, which pre-dated the coming into force of the Human Rights Act 1998, the Court of Appeal considered the proportionality of a proposed deportation on public good grounds of an EU national convicted of persistent sexual abuse of his daughter, both through the free movement provisions of the EC Treaty and also through the constitutional requirement to respect fundamental rights as guaranteed by the ECHR, enshrined in Article 6 of the consolidated Treaty on European Union (formerly Article F), which gave statutory force to the case law of the ECHR as applied by the ECJ.[6] It held that although the Tribunal was entitled to find the existence of a relevant threat to the requirements of public policy arising both from the intrinsic seriousness of the appellant's offending and from a propensity to re-offend, the remaining and determinative issue was that of proportionality, which was a matter of law.[7] In the circumstances of the case, given the appellant's extremely long residence in the UK, the court held deportation a disproportionate response. The ECJ has held that the expulsion of EU nationals or their family members for failure to comply with immigration laws or complete formalities would be manifestly disproportionate to the interference with Community law rights.[8]

1   *R v Bouchereau* [1978] QB 732 at 743, per Advocate General Warner.
2   *R v Chief Constable of Sussex, ex p International Trader's Ferry Ltd* [1997] 2 CMLR 164, CA. The House of Lords upheld the CA's decision that the Chief Constable's refusal to police the port more than twice a week, meaning that export of live animals was restricted on other days because of demonstrators, was a proportionate measure to maintain public order, although it had a restrictive effect on exports, and was therefore justified under Article 36 EC (now Art 30): [1999] 1 All ER 130.
3   In *Wilander v Tobin* [1997] 2 CMLR 346 the Court of Appeal, holding that mandatory drug testing of sporting competitors was justified by compelling reasons of public interest, observed that proportionality was close to concepts of reasonableness and natural justice, and that the combination of safeguards such as the review body, the appeal committee and the courts made the measure proportionate (assuming without deciding that it restricted Art 39 EC free movement rights).
4   [2000] Imm AR 478.
5   *R v Bouchereau* [1978] QB 732 at 760.
6   Case 260/89 *Elliniki Radiophonia Tileorassi AE v Pliroforissis and Kouvelas* [1991] ECR I-2925.
7   *B v Secretary of State for the Home Department*, fn 4 above. This aspect of the judgment has given rise to endless controversy; see 8.31 below.
8   Case C-459/99 *Mouvement contre le racisme, l'antisemitisme et la xenophobie ASBL (MRAX) v Belgium* [2002] ECR I-6591, para 90.

7.140 Although the application of the proviso depends on the personal conduct of the person involved, the ECJ has held that the activities in question need not be illegal for public policy to be invoked; the activities of scientologists which led to the blanket ban on their immigration to the UK in *Van Duyn* are sufficient. The decision in *Van Duyn*[1] indicates that a ban on the immigration of foreign nationals for public policy reasons is not invalidated merely because no such ban has been imposed on its own nationals. Under international law it is not normally possible for a country to ban its own nationals. The decision makes it clear that the application of the public policy proviso to EC immigration law inevitably involves some discrimination against foreign nationals. However, it is doubtful to what extent a host State can take measures on public policy grounds that it cannot take against own nationals. *Rutili v Minister for the Interior*[2] concerned an Italian national who had spent most of his life in Alsace-Lorraine. He was a political activist who had been involved in the 'events' of May 1968 in France, but had never been convicted of any offence. The French Ministry of the Interior made an order banning him from Alsace-Lorraine. The ECJ ruled, amongst other things, that the public policy proviso does not apply to the right to move freely within the territory of a particular Member State, and so a partial residence prohibition, restraining a migrant from working in one part of the territory of a Member State, could only be applied in those circumstances when such a limitation would be justified under national law in the case of a national.

1   [1975] Ch 358, [1974] ECR 1337.
2   [1975] ECR 1219, [1976] 1 CMLR 140, ECJ.

7.141 Further in *Adoui and Cornuaille*[1] the court considered the applicability of expulsion on grounds relating to prostitution, which was not specifically prohibited by Belgian law. The court noted:

'Although Community law does not impose upon the Member States a uniform scale of values as regards the assessment of conduct which may be considered as contrary to public policy, it should nevertheless be stated that conduct may not be considered as being of a sufficiently serious nature to justify restrictions on the admission of nationals of another Member State in a case where the former Member State does not adopt, with respect to the same conduct on the part of its own nationals, repressive measures or other genuine and effective measures intended to combat such conduct.'

Applying this dictum to the Church of Scientology case, it would appear that unless the UK is prepared to take repressive measures on the grounds of adherence to Scientology against all, including own nationals, it is not entitled to refuse admission to EEA nationals on this ground alone.

1   Case 115/81 [1982] ECR 1665, [1982] 3 CMLR 631.

Public health

7.142 Article 4 of Council Directive (EEC) 64/221 provides that the only diseases or disabilities justifying refusal of entry into a territory or refusal to issue a first residence permit are those listed in the Annexe. These are infectious or contagious diseases requiring quarantine, active tuberculosis, syphilis, and other infectious or contagious diseases if they are the subject of provisions for the protection of nationals of the host country. Drug addiction and profound mental disturbance are listed as diseases and disabilities which might threaten public policy or public security. Article 4(2) makes it clear that a disease or disability occurring after a residence permit has been issued for the first time does not justify a refusal to renew the permit or to order the expulsion of the person from the country. Article 4(3) states that EC countries may not introduce new provisions or practices which are more restrictive than those in force at the date of the Directive. In the UK these provisions are reflected in regulation 23(d) and (e) and Schedule 1 to the Immigration (European Economic Area) Regulations 2000.[1]

1   SI 2000/2326.

Procedural safeguards

7.143 In addition to the substantive limitations on the power of Member States to apply the public policy proviso, Council Directive (EEC) 64/221 also includes important procedural safeguards, namely the right to be given reasons when a decision is made on public policy grounds, and the right to some form of judicial review.

Reasons

7.144 Article 7 of Council Directive (EEC) 64/221 gives the persons concerned the right to be notified of any decision to refuse the issue or renewal of a residence permit or to expel them from the territory. The notice should also state the period allowed for leaving the territory and, except in cases of urgency, this period should be not less than 15 days if the person has not yet been granted a residence permit and not less than one month in all other cases. Article 6 of the Directive provides that where any decision is taken on grounds of public policy, public security or public health, that person shall be informed of the ground, unless this is contrary to the interests of the security of the State involved.[1] In the *Rutili* case[2] the ECJ stated that this provision meant giving the immigrant 'a precise and comprehensive statement of the grounds for the decision' to enable him or her to take effective steps to prepare a defence.

1   See Immigration (European Economic Area) Regulations 2000, SI 2000/2326, reg 23(f).
2   Case 36/75 *Rutili v Minister for the Interior* [1975] ECR 1219, [1976] 1 CMLR 140, ECJ.

Review and appeal

7.145 Article 8 of Council Directive (EEC) 64/221 requires Member States to provide for persons relying on EC rights the same legal remedies in respect of decisions concerning entry, or refusing the issue or renewal of a residence permit, or ordering expulsion from the territory, as are available to nationals of the State concerned in respect of acts of the administration. In *Shingara and Radiom* the ECJ held that this does not mean that EEA nationals refused entry should be given the same rights of appeal as British citizens whose claim is disputed,[1] since nationals of the Member State have a right of entry which is not comparable with the situation of a national of another Member State whose exclusion might be justified on public policy or national security grounds.[2] Article 9 of the Directive grants further rights to those refused a renewal of their residence permit or ordered to be expelled. Where there is no appeal, or where the appeal goes only to the legal validity of the decision and not to the merits, or is not suspensive, they are entitled to the opinion of a competent authority which is different from the one which makes the decision[3] so as to enable an exhaustive examination of all the facts and circumstances, including the expediency of the proposed measure, to be carried out before the decision is finally taken.[4] In *R v Secretary of State for the Home Department, ex p Santillo*[5] the court held that a recommendation for deportation by a criminal court could constitute such an opinion. Although Article 9 imposed obligations on Member States which may be relied on by individuals, it left a margin of discretion to the State to define the 'competent authority'. It needed to be independent of the administrative body which made the decision, and the person affected by the decision must enjoy the right of representation and defence before it.[6]

1 Under Nationality, Immigration and Asylum Act 2002, s 82.
2 Joined Cases C-111/95 and C-65/95 *Shingara v Secretary of State for the Home Department* [1997] ECR I-3343; [1997] 3 CMLR 703, ECJ.
3 A decision to refuse the first issue of a residence permit, or to expel someone before issue of the permit, may on request be referred to an independent competent authority under Council Directive 64/221, Art 9(2), in cases where there is no effective or suspensive appeal: *Shingara and Radiom* above.
4 *Santillo* fn 5 below; Case 115/81 *Adoui and Cornuaille v Belgian State* [1982] ECR 1665; Case C-175/94 *R v Secretary of State for the Home Department, ex p Gallagher* [1995] ECR I-4253; [1996] 1 CMLR 557, ECJ.
5 [1980] ECR 1585, [1980] 2 CMLR 308, ECJ.
6 See also *Adoui and Cornuaille* above.

7.146 In *Gallagher*[1] the ECJ held that Article 9 of Council Directive (EEC) 64/221 did not preclude the authority which made the order from appointing the competent authority, provided the latter performed its duties independently and without being subject to the body making the decision. The court also confirmed that in cases under Article 9(1) where there is no effective appeal, the opinion of the competent authority as to deportation must be obtained before the decision to expel.[2] This is the case in recommendations for deportation under section 3(6) of the Immigration Act 1971, where the criminal court recommending deportation has been held to be a competent authority.[3] In cases where there is an appeal before the Asylum and Immigration Tribunal or the Special Immigration Appeals Commission, the decision precedes the appeal, but no order is made unless the decision is upheld on appeal. Regulation 29 of the Immigration (European Economic Area) Regulations[4] provides appeal rights for EEA nationals reflecting those of non-EEA nationals.

1 [1996] 1 CMLR 557.
2 Case C-175/94 *R v Secretary of State for the Home Department, ex p Gallagher* [1995] ECR I-4253; [1996] 1 CMLR 557, ECJ.
3 *R v Secretary of State for the Home Department, ex p Dannenberg* [1984] QB 766.
4 SI 2000/2326.

7.147 In *Yiadom*[1] the ECJ held that the safeguards of Article 9 of Council Directive (EEC) 64/221 did not apply to persons excluded from the territory, ie refused leave to enter. In that case, the applicant had been on temporary admission under paragraph 21 of Schedule 2 to the Immigration Act 1971 for seven months awaiting a decision on leave to enter. The court condemned the fiction of temporary admission and said that for EC purposes, a decision to remove an EU national pursuant to a refusal of leave to enter after such a protracted period on temporary admission was in fact an expulsion decision, and attracted the appropriate safeguards of Article 9. The lack of in-country appeal rights in cases of refusal of leave to enter has been the subject of domestic legal challenge[2] on the ground of disproportionate interference with freedom of movement and with the right to a fair trial and equality of arms.[3] In *Shingara* the court held that, since the prohibition of entry derogated from a fundamental principle and could not therefore be of indefinite duration, Community nationals were entitled to have their situation re-examined if they thought the circumstances justifying their refusal of entry no longer existed.[4] The new decision may be the subject of an appeal on the basis of Article 8 and, where appropriate, Article 9 of the Directive.[5]

[1] Case C-357/98 R *(on the application of Yiadom) v Secretary of State for the Home Department* [2001] All ER (EC) 267, ECJ.

[2] In *Darwiche* (CO 413/1998) April 2000 an application for judicial review which challenged the lack of suspensive appeal against on-entry refusal of an EEA national with permanent residence was settled by consent after the grant of permission.

[3] In *Loutchansky*, however, the applicant, who was subject to an exclusion order on the personal direction of the Secretary of State for the Home Department, and had a pending Special Immigration Appeals Commission appeal, wished to enter the UK to pursue legal proceedings. On refusal of leave to enter he took proceedings alleging breach of Article 6 equality of arms, and the matter was settled by the Home Office issuing him with a multiple-entry 'laissez-passer' enabling him to come and go to and from the UK, and granting him temporary admission on arrival, although the exclusion order remained in place.

[4] *Shingara* 7.145 fn 2 above, para 40.

[5] *Shingara* above, para 42.

Recommendation for deportation

7.148 In *Santillo*[1] an EC national had been sentenced to a long prison sentence for rape and the Secretary of State for the Home Department signed an order at the beginning of the sentence pursuant to a recommendation for deportation made by the sentencing court. The ECJ accepted that, since the criminal courts in the UK were independent of the administration and the person concerned had a right to be represented and to exercise his or her rights of defence before such courts, a recommendation for deportation by a criminal court at the time of conviction could constitute an 'opinion' under Article 9 of Council Directive (EEC) 64/221. But, it added, the criminal court must take account in particular of the provisions of Article 3 of the Directive inasmuch as the mere existence of criminal convictions cannot automatically constitute grounds for deportation. The ECJ was concerned at the time lapse between the making of a recommendation and its implementation by the Secretary of State. A long prison sentence may have intervened. The court stated that the opinion of the competent authority must be sufficiently proximate in time to the decision ordering expulsion to ensure that there are no new factors to be taken into consideration, and that both the administration and the person concerned are in a position in the normal case to take cognisance of the reasons which led the competent authority to make its recommendation. A lapse of time amounting to several years between the recommendation and the decision to deport is liable to deprive the recommendation of its function as an opinion within the meaning of Article 9. It is essential that the social danger resulting from a foreign national's presence be assessed at the very time when the deportation decision is made against him or her, as the facts to be taken into account, particularly those concerning his or her conduct, are likely to change in the course of time. When the case returned to the Court of Appeal[2] it held that a lapse of four-and-a-half years was not, in the particular circumstances, sufficient to deprive the recommendation of its function as an 'opinion'. In *R v Secretary of State for the Home Department, ex p Dannenberg*[3] the Court of Appeal held that, where a criminal court's recommendation to deport constitutes the opinion of the competent authority for the purposes of Article 9, it must be reasoned to such a degree as to enable the deporting agency to monitor its lawfulness and the alien to decide whether to challenge it. This meant that magistrates had to give reasons for a decision to recommend deportation of an EC national, even though they do not normally give reasons when imposing a sentence.[4]

1   [1980] ECR 1585.
2   [1981] QB 778, [1981] 2 All ER 897.
3   [1984] QB 766.
4   The European Commission has taken action against Germany, Case C-441/02 for mandatory expulsions from Germany of Association Agreement nationals (who have the same rights as EU nationals in this field, see 7.150 below) following certain criminal convictions. The Commission clearly takes the view that mandatory expulsion of any EU national without access to the courts fall foul of Community law.

Appeal to the Asylum and Immigration Tribunal

7.149 The Nationality, Immigration and Asylum Act 2002 provides for a right of appeal against a decision to deport, whether following a recommendation or not.[1] Expulsion on grounds of public policy, public security or public health equates with deportation on public good grounds in domestic law. All EEA deportations will thus come before the Tribunal, except for those involving national security (see below). In *Marchon* the Court of Appeal held that the failure of the criminal court to make a recommendation was irrelevant to the appellate authority's consideration of public policy.[2] But if a criminal court has considered a recommendation and decides that the criminality involved does not merit one, it is difficult to see how such comments are irrelevant, especially as this is the expression of an opinion as required by the Council Directive (EEC) 64/221. Even if the opinion is not binding on the competent authority, regard must be had to it.[3] The Tribunal must consider the question of public good, in the light of the Community rules discussed above: thus the mere existence of the conviction is insufficient, and sufficient reasons must be given to justify the deportation of a qualified person on grounds of public policy.

1   Nationality, Immigration and Asylum Act 2002, s 82(1) (as amended by the Asylum and Immigration (Treatment of Claimants, etc) Act 2004 Sch 1), (2)(j).
2   *R v Secretary of State for the Home Department, ex p Marchon* [1993] Imm AR 384, CA.
3   See *R v Secretary of State for the Home Department, ex p Dannenberg* [1984] QB 766 at 775F–H.

National security cases

7.150 Where a decision to exclude, or to refuse a residence permit or expel an EEA national is the personal decision of the Secretary of State for the Home

Department for political or diplomatic reasons, or is based on national security grounds, regulations 29 and 31 of the Immigration (European Economic Area) Regulations 2000[1] apply and the appeal is to the Special Immigration Appeals Commission instead of theTribunal. In national security cases there is a derogation from the duty of giving reasons.[2] The Special Immigration Appeals Commission procedure would undoubtedly be deemed compliant with the reduced duty, given the procedural safeguard of the special advocate who sees all the national security evidence not available to the appellant and represents the appellant's interests in relation to that evidence.

[1] SI 2000/2326 (appeal provisions of Part VII substituted by SI 2003/549, from 1 April 2003, as amended by SI 2005/671 from 4 April 2005).
[2] Council Directive (EEC) 64/221, Art 6; SI 2000/2326, reg 23(f).

RIGHTS UNDER ASSOCIATION AGREEMENTS

7.151 The EC Treaty provides, under Article 310 EC (ex Article 238), that the Community may conclude with a third State, a union of States or an international organisation, an agreement establishing an association, involving reciprocal rights and obligations, common actions and special procedures. Article 300 EC (ex Article 228) provides that such agreements shall be negotiated by the Commission, and concluded by the Council, after consulting the European Parliament where required. Agreements concluded under these conditions shall be binding on the institutions of the Community and on Member States.[1] Agreements entered into by both the EC and Member States with a third country are mixed agreements, but do not for that reason cease to be enforceable in Community law.[2] A number of these agreements have implications for immigration rights of nationals of the countries with which such agreements have been concluded.[3] In practice the two most important have been the Turkish Association Agreement and those concluded with East and Central European countries, both of which have given rise to a considerable body of case law. Three main points emerge from this. First, the trend of the decisions is to hold that key provisions of the Association Agreements have direct effect in Member States, because they contain clear and precise obligations, which are not subject, in their implementation or effects, to the adoption of any subsequent measure, and nationals from the associated States may, therefore, rely directly on the rights conferred on them by the agreements.[4] Secondly, the principles of free movement enshrined in the EC Treaty should be extended, so far as possible, to the interpretation of directly effective provisions of the agreements,[5] but only where it can be said that the aim pursued by each provision in its own particular context is the same.[6] Thirdly, the application of a national system of prior or post entry control is permissible if the domestic controls are exercised compatibly with the directly effective rights established under the Agreements.[7] Eight of the ten new accession States in May 2004 were Central and East European countries formerly with association agreements. Of these only Bulgaria and Romania remain outside the EU. Finally, Association Agreements have been signed between the EC and Algeria in April 2002 and between the EC and Lebanon on 17 June 2002, but they have not yet come into force.

[1] Article 300(2) EC (ex Art 228(2)).

² Case 12/86 *Demirel v Stadt Schwäbisch Gmünd* [1987] ECR 3719, [1989] 1 CMLR 421, ECJ.

³ There is a vast array of agreements between the European Union and third countries. Many of these include non-discrimination provisions for workers, which do not provide any right of entry to the territory of the Member States but do provide some protection to workers from those third countries already lawfully resident in Member States. For discussion of these agreements see Rogers and Scannell *Free Movement of Persons in the Enlarged European Union* (Sweet & Maxwell, 2004), ch 15.

⁴ So, although neither Art 12 (*Demirel*, above) nor 13 (Case C-37/98 *R v Secretary of State for the Home Department, ex p Savas* [2000] ECR I-2927, [2000] 3 CMLR 729, ECJ) of the Association Agreement are directly applicable in the internal legal order of a Member State, Art 41(1) of the Additional Protocol is: *Savas*, above, para 54; so too Art 13 of Decision No 1/80: Case C 192/89 *Sevince* [1990] ECR I-3461, para 26, and Cases C-317/01 and C-369/01 *Abatay and Sahin* [2003], para 58. On Art 6(1) of Decision No 1/80, see, for example: Case C-192/89 *Sevince v Staatsecretaris van Justitie* [1992] 2 CMLR 57; Case C-237/91 *Kus v Landeshaupstadt Wiesbaden* [1993] 2 CMLR 88, and Case C-373/02 *Oztürk v Pensionversicherungsanstalt der Arbeiter* [2004], para 60; on Art 7(1) of Decision No 1/80: *Kadiman* [1997] ECR I-2133, at paras 27 and 28; Case C-329/97 *Ergat v Stadt Ulm* [2000] ECR I-1487, para 34; Case C-69/98 *Eyüp* [2000] ECR I-4747, para 25; on Art 3(1) of Decision No 3/80 Case C-262/96 *Sürül v Bundesanstalt für Arbeit* [1999], para 74; Case C-102/98 *Kocak (Ibrahim) v Landesversicherunsanstalt Oberfranken und Mittelfranken; Ramazan Örs v Bundesknappschaft* [2000] ECR I-1287, para 36. In Case C-235/99 *R v Secretary of State for the Home Department, ex p Kondova* [2001] ECR I-6427, Art 45(1) of the Bulgarian Association Agreement was held to be directly applicable, notwithstanding Art 59(1) which allows Member States to lay down rules under domestic law regulating entry, stay and establishment: paras 33–39; see also Case C-257/99 *R (on the application of Barkoci) v Secretary of State for the Home Department* [2001] ECR I-6357, ECJ and Case C-63/99 *R v Secretary of State for the Home Department, ex p Gloszczuk* [2001] ECR I-6369, on identical provisions under the Czech and Polish agreements, and Case C-162/00 *Land Nordrhein-Westfalen v Pokrzeptowicz-Meyer* [2002] ECR I-0049, ECJ on the non-discrimination clause in relation to workers in Art 37(1) of the Polish Agreement.

⁵ See 7.153, below in respect of the Turkey Agreement; C-162/00 *Pokrzeptowicz-Meyer* 2002] ECR I-0049.

⁶ See Case C-235/99 *R v Secretary of State for the Home Department, ex p Kondova* [2001] ECR I-6427, at paras 51–53; Case C-257/99 *R (on the application of Barkoci) v Secretary of State for the Home Department* [2001] ECR I-6357 at paras 51–53, and Case C-63/99 *R v Secretary of State for the Home Department, ex p Gloszczuk* [2001] ECR I-6369, paras 48–50.

⁷ *R v Secretary of State for the Home Department, ex p Savas* Case C-37/98 [2000] INLR 398, at para 65; Case C-317/01 *Abatay v Bundesanstalt für Arbeit* [2003] (21 October 2003), at paras 63–67; Case C-329/97 *Ergat v Stadt Ulm* [2000] ECR I-1487, at paras 37–38; *Kondova, above*, at para 57; *Barkoci*, above at para 57, and *Gloszczuk*, above, paras 58 and 68.

Turkish Association Agreement

7.152 On 12 September 1963 at Ankara the EC signed the Turkey EEC Association Agreement, which was supplemented on 23 November 1970 by the Brussels Protocol.¹ These Agreements aimed to establish free movement provisions between Turkey and the EC within 22 years, and this itself was intended as a step towards full Turkish membership of the EC. These aspirations have never been achieved by implementing measures, and full Turkish membership has not yet happened. However, the Agreement provided for a Council of Association on which the various parties are represented.² By Article 36 of the 1970 Protocol, the Council of Association is given the power to decide on the rules necessary to implement the progressive stages for the free movement of workers within the 20-year period.[3] The Association Council adopted three decisions: Decisions 2/76 of 20 December 1976, 1/80 of 19 September 1980 and 3/80 of the same date,[4] which for long were unpublished but have become important for Turkish nationals already resident in the EU by reason of a series of decisions of the ECJ starting with the decisions in *Sevince*[5] and *Kus*.[6]

[1] Association Agreement approved and confirmed on behalf of the Community by Council Decision 64/732/EEC (OJ 1973 C 133, p 1); Additional Protocol approved and confirmed by Council Regulation (EEC) No 2760/72 (OJ 1972 L 293, p 1). A full description of the Association Agreement and its Protocol is not possible within the confines of this volume, but the reader is referred to Rogers and Scannell *Free Movement of Persons in the Enlarged European Union* (2004); Martin and Guild *Free movement of persons in the European Union* (1996).
[2] Ankara Agreement 1963, Art 6, OJ C113/2 24.12.1963.
[3] Additional Protocol signed at Brussels, 23 November 1970, Art 36, OJ C/113/2 24.12.1973. There is also a power to make recommendations in Art 38, but it is the rules which are binding.
[4] The decisions are not published in the OJ, but are set out in full in Rogers *A Practitioner's Guide to the Turkey-EC Association Agreement*, ILPA (2000, Kluwer).
[5] Case C-192/89 *Sevince v Staatsecretaris van Justitie* [1992] 2 CMLR 57.
[6] Case C-237/91 *Kus v Landeshaupstadt Wiesbaden* [1993] 2 CMLR 887, ECJ. Followed in *Eroglu v Land Baden-Württemberg*: Case C-355/93 [1994] ECR I-5113, ECJ.

7.153 The decisions of the ECJ in *Demirel*[1] and *Sevince*[2] held that the programme for free movement of persons between Turkey and the EC by the end of 1985 was not itself of direct effect and therefore gave no rights to Turkish nationals to enter the territory of the EC, even though the Turkey-EC Association Agreement was potentially capable of giving rise to individual rights, if the rules on direct effect were met.[3] However, in *Sevince* the court held that some decisions of the Association Council were sufficiently clear and precise as to be capable of direct effect, although the decision in question was of no assistance to the particular applicant in that case because he was not legally employed. It was only in *Kus*[4] that a Turkish worker succeeded in using an Association Council decision to obtain a fresh work and residence permit in reliance on Community law. The crucial provision relied on in *Kus* is Article 6 of Decision 1/80. This provides:

> '1. Subject to Article 7 on free access to employment for members of his family, a Turkish worker duly registered as belonging to the labour force of a Member State:
> – shall be entitled in that Member State, after one year's legal employment, to the renewal of his permit to work for the same employer, if a job is available;
> – shall be entitled in that Member State, after three years of legal employment and subject to the priority to be given to workers of Member States of the Community, to respond to another offer of employment, with an employer of his choice, made under normal conditions and registered with the employment services of that State for the same occupation;
> – shall enjoy free access in that Member State to any paid employment of his choice, after four years of legal employment.'[5]

[1] [1987] ECR 3719, [1989] 1 CMLR 421, ECJ.
[2] Case C-192/89 *Sevince v Staatsecretaris van Justitie* [1992] 2 CMLR 57.

3 Following *Demirel* the Court of Appeal in the UK held that Art 12 of the Ankara Agreement of 12 September 1963 gave no free movement rights to Turkish nationals: *R v Secretary of State for the Home Department, ex p Narin* [1990] 2 CMLR 233, CA.
4 [1993] 2 CMLR 887.
5 Decision 1/80, Art 6.

7.154 This right only applies after Turkish nationals have entered a Member State and taken up lawful employment there. It does not grant a right to enter or obtain a work permit, and it does not allow a Turkish worker to move from one Member State to another, so it is different from the rights of EEA nationals to seek and obtain work. It is not a free movement right, but gives Turkish workers a progressive series of rights over a four-year period, leading to their eventual integration into the host State's workforce. In setting out the considerable ambit and scope of these rights, the ECJ considers that Article 6 of Decision 1/80 forms part of and thus constitutes a further stage in securing freedom of movement of workers on the basis of Articles 39 to 41 EC, and so says it is essential to extend so far as possible the principles in the EC Articles to Turkish workers.[1] This is consistent with Article 12 of the Ankara Agreement, which states:

'The contracting parties agree to be guided by Articles 48, 49 and 50 [now Articles 39–41] of the Treaty establishing the Community for the purposes of progressively securing freedom of movement for workers between them.'

Thus 'worker' is given the same meaning as under Article 39 EC.[2] Administrative documents are declaratory and evidential, rather than conditions of entitlement, in the case of Turkish workers, as is the case with residence permits under Article 39.[3] The public policy derogation is interpreted in the same way as under Council Directive (EEC) 64/221.[4] The position of the children of Turkish workers compares with those of workers under the main EC Treaty.[5]

1 Case C-98/96 *Ertanir v Land Hessen* [1997] ECR I-5179, para 21; Case C-434/93 *Bozkurt v Staatssecretaris van Justitie* [1995] ECR I-1475, paras 14, 19 and 20; Case C-171/95 *Tetik v Land Berlin* [1997] ECR I-329, para 20; Case C-340/97 *Nazli v Stadt Nürnberg* [2000] ECR I-957, ECJ, paras 50–55; Case C-188/00 *Kurtz v Land Baden-Württemburg* [2002] ECR I-1069, ECJ, para 30.
2 Case C-36/96 *Günaydin v Freistaat Bayern* [1997] ECR I-5143, para 31, ECJ; Case C-98/96 *Ertanir v Land Hessen* [1997] ECR I-5179, ECJ, para 43; Case C-1/97 *Birden v Stadtgemeinde Bremen* [1998] ECR I-7747, ECJ, paras 25 and 28; Case C-188/00 *Kurtz v Land Baden-Württemberg* [2002] ECR I-10691, ECJ, paras 31–32.
3 *Bozkurt* above; Case C-329/97 *Ergat v Stadt Ulm* [2000] ECR I-1487, ECJ. Cf Case 48/75 *Royer, Re* [1976] ECR 497.
4 Case C-340/97 *Nazli v Stadt Nürnberg* [2000] ECR I-957, ECJ; *Ergat* above, ECJ.
5 Case C-210/97 *Akman v Oberkreisdirektor des Rheinische-Bergischen-Kreises* [1998] ECR I-7519, ECJ.

7.155 In a series of cases on the application of Article 6 of Decision 1/80, the ECJ has established the following guidelines for Turkish nationals:

(1) he or she has to be a worker and not self-employed, that is, someone bound by an employment relationship covering a genuine and effective economic activity pursued for the benefit of and under the direction of another for remuneration.[1] It makes no difference to the definition that employment is for the sole purpose of preparing the employee to work

elsewhere;[2] is specific work for a specific employer for a limited period;[3] or is a paid apprenticeship.[4] A person may qualify as a worker even although the job is a temporary one to enable recipients of social assistance to integrate into working life and takes place at a cultural centre funded by public money and not in competition with undertakings in the general labour market;[5]

(2)   he or she has to be duly registered as belonging to the labour force ('appartenant au marché regulier' in the French version) of a Member State.[6] This means being in employment which is either located within the territory of a Member State or which retains a sufficiently close link with it, as in the case of an international lorry-driver who has sufficient links with one Member State.[7] To establish a close link with a particular Member State, it will be necessary to take into account the place where the worker was hired, the territory on which or from which employment is pursued, and the applicable national legislation in the field of employment and social security.[8] A worker will be treated as duly registered if he or she is employed on the same conditions of work and pay as those claimed by workers who pursue identical or similar activities,[9] and complies with the requirements laid down by the rules and regulations in the Member State concerned;[10]

(3)   he or she has to be in legal employment. This means having a stable and secure position in the labour force and an undisputed right of residence.[11] Legal employment is a concept of Community law, which must be defined objectively and uniformly in the light of the spirit and purpose of Article 6 of Decision 1/80.[12] Accordingly, it does not matter that the worker may have been aware of the restrictions imposed by the host State.[13] Employment of less than 12 months may not have sufficient stability to qualify,[14] but the fact that employment contracts are temporary is of no relevance.[15] The immigration status of the Turkish worker is of relevance to the issue of a stable and secure position. Where a worker has obtained his or her residence permit in fraudulent circumstances, he or she will not qualify,[16] nor does one who is resident on a provisional basis awaiting the grant of a residence permit,[17] or someone who is authorised to work while he or she appeals against a decision refusing a right of residence.[18]

(4)   it is settled case law that once Turkish workers have lawfully entered the territory of the host Member State and have entered into lawful employment, as described above, they can enjoy the rights conferred on them by Article 6 (1), irrespective of whether or not the authorities of the host Member State issue a specific administrative document, such as a work permit or residence permit.[19] This is of particular importance once workers have completed four years in employment and are fully integrated into the host Member State (7.155). It also applies to family members after five years' legal residence (7.158).

(5)   it is also settled case-law that Article 6(1) does not make the recognition of any rights, which it confers on Turkish workers, subject to any condition connected with the reason for which the right to enter, work, or reside was initially granted.[20] So if someone is given leave to do an apprenticeship,[21] or was allowed to work while their spouse was in full

time education, these circumstances would not prevent them enjoying the rights conferred by Article 6(1).

1   Case C-36/96 *Günaydin v Freistaat Bayern* [1997] ECR I-5143, ECJ; Case C-1/97 *Birden v Stadtgemeinde Bremen* [1998] ECR I-7747, ECJ. For the situation of the self-employed, see 7.162 below.
2   *Günaydin* above.
3   Case C-98/96 *Ertanir v Land Hessen* [1997] ECR I-5179, ECJ.
4   Case C-188/00 *Kurtz v Land Baden-Württemberg* [2002] ECR I-10691, ECJ.
5   *Birden* above.
6   *Kurtz, above,* at paras 37–44.
7   Case C-434/95 *Bozkurt v Staatssecretaris van Justitie* [1995] ECR I-1475, ECJ, at paras 22–23.
8   *Bozkurt* above.
9   *Günaydin* above, at para 29.
10 *Birden* above, at para 33.
11 Case C-192/89 *Sevince v Staatssecretaris van Justitie* [1990] ECR I-3461, para 30; Case C-237/91 *Kus v Landeshauptstadt* [1992] ECR I-6781, para 12; *Bozkurt* above, para 26; *Birden* paras 47–55, above. Case C-285/95 *Kol v Land Berlin* [1997] ECR I-3069, para 21.
12 *Ertanir* above, at para 39.
13 *Ertanir* above.
14 Case C-306/95 *Eker* [1997] ECR I-2697.
15 *Günaydin,* above at paras 36–40; *Birden,* above at paras 37–39 and 64; *Kurtz, above,* at para 55.
16 *Kol* above.
17 *Kus* above, para 21.
18 *Sevince* above, para 31.
19 *Bozkurt,* paras 29–30; *Günaydin* paras 36–40; *Ertanir,* para 55; *Birden* para 65; and *Kurtz* para 54.
20 *Kus* above, paras 21–22; *Günaydin* para 52; *Birden* para 57; and *Kurtz* para 56.
21 For example, *Kurtz, above*

7.156 Under the first indent of Article 6 of Decision 1/80, workers have to work continuously for the same employer. If they change employers during the first year, they cannot benefit.[1] Similarly, to qualify under the second indent of Article 6, a worker must continue working for the same employer.[2] It is only at the end of three years' continuous employment that a Turkish worker is entitled to accept offers of work from a different employer, but even then he or she must remain in the same occupation as before, and the new employer must respect the right of priority of Community nationals. At the end of four years' employment, the worker can then choose any job in any occupation with any employer. Workers in this position may then voluntarily terminate their existing employment to look for new work on the same conditions as Community work seekers. They must remain duly registered as belonging to the labour force, and this may mean registering with the local employment office as a person seeking employment.[3]

1   Case C-306/95 *Eker* [1997] ECR I-2697.
2   Case C-355/93 *Eroglu v Land Baden-Württemberg* [1994] ECR I-5113.
3   Case C-171/95 *Tetik v Land Berlin* [1997] ECR I-329.

7.157 Article 6(2) of Decision 1/80 deals with continuity of employment. Annual holidays and absences for reasons of maternity or accident at work, or short periods of sickness, are treated as periods of legal employment. Periods of involuntary unemployment, duly certified by the relevant authorities, and long absences on account of sickness, are not treated as periods of legal employment, but do not break continuity. Article 6(2) of the Decision states that they shall not affect rights acquired as the result of the preceding period of employment. The ECJ has held that short interruptions between the expiry of a residence permit and the obtaining of a new one do not affect the Turkish worker's rights.[1] In *Nazli*[2] a lengthy period in prison on remand did not destroy the worker's right of access to employment, and the ECJ held that he continued to have his rights provided he found a job again within a reasonable period after his release. In that case and in *Tetik*,[3] the court has recognised that once Turkish workers are free to change their jobs under Article 6, they should have a reasonable period to seek new employment in the same way as Community nationals.[4]

1 Case C-98/96 *Ertanir v Land Hessen* [1997] ECR I-5179, ECJ.
2 Case C-340/97 [2000] ECR I-957, ECJ, at paras 40–41. A 16 year prison sentence following a drugs conviction meant that the applicant ceased to be duly registered as belonging to the labour force of the UK when he was detained following conviction: *R (on the application of Samaroo) v Secretary of State for the Home Department* [2001] EWCA Civ 1139, [2002] INLR 55, and *R (on the application of Sezek) v Secretary of State for the Home Department* [2001] EWCA Civ 795, [2001] 1 WLR 348, [2001] Imm AR 657.
3 Case C-171/95 [1997] ECR I-329, ECJ, at para 46. See also Case C-188/00 *Kurtz v Land Baden-Württemberg* [2002] ECR I-10691, ECJ, at para 59.
4 See Case C-292/89 *R v Immigration Appeal Tribunal, ex p Antonissen* [1991] ECR I-745, [1991] 2 CMLR 373.

Family members from Turkey

7.158 Article 7 of Decision 1/80 deals with the employment rights of family members of Turkish workers, and has been held to be directly effective.[1] Under Article 7, two distinct rights are given to family members of Turkish workers. First, members of the family of a Turkish worker who is duly registered as belonging to the labour force of a Member State are entitled after a time to take up job offers, if they 'have been authorised to join' him or her.[2] Secondly, children of Turkish workers who have completed a course of vocational training in the host country have a right to take any job once one of their parents has been in legal employment for a certain period. We look at each of these entitlements in more detail.

1 Case C-351/95 *Kadiman* [1997] ECR I-2133.
2 For the definition of 'family' see 7.88, 7.95, 7.101 above. In *Eyup* Case C-69/98 [2000] ECR I-4747, the ECJ declined to hold that a cohabitee could be a member of the family, but held that a Turkish couple who had married, then divorced and later re-married, but who had always lived together, had 'constantly maintained a common legal residence' within the meaning of Art 7(1) of Decision 1/80. In *Ayaz* Case C-275/02, 30 September 2004, the ECJ held that family members would include step-children for the purposes of Article 7 of Decision 1/80.

7.159 First, the right of family members only arises if they have been authorised by the host State to join the primary worker or were born there.[1] If they have entered for some other purpose it does not arise. Secondly, there needs to be a period of cohabitation. In *Kadiman*[2] the ECJ held that the words in the first paragraph of Article 7(1) of Decision 1/80, 'authorised to join him', cannot be interpreted as merely requiring the host Member State to have authorised a family member to enter its territory to join a Turkish worker, without at the same time requiring the person concerned to reside there continually with the migrant worker until he or she is entitled to enter the labour market. In other words, there has to be a specified period of cohabitation in a household with the primary worker before any employment rights accrue. This rather strict condition is at odds with the more lax rules for family members under Council Regulation (EEC) 1612/68, and was prompted by fears of the rules being manipulated by sham marriages. Conscious of the harshness of its interpretation, the court stated that allowances can be made if the person's job or training takes him or her away from home. It is for the national court to determine whether the circumstances justify living apart. It remains to be seen whether domestic violence would constitute such a circumstance.[3] Apart from the hurdle of an initial period of cohabitation, family members are entitled to respond to any offers of employment, subject to the priority to be given to workers of Member States, once they have been legally resident for at least three years. After five years they are free to take any job, without any need to give priority to Community workers. At that point they have independent rights of residence, even if they no longer live with the family member they had been authorised to join.[4] During the periods of legal residence absences for reasonable periods and for legitimate reasons, such as holidays, do not break continuity.[5]

1   *Cetinkaya v Land Baden-Wurttemberg* Case C-467/02 (10 Jun 2004, unreported).
2   Case C-351/95 *Kadiman* [1997] ECR I-2133, paras 37–42.
3   For domestic violence in relation to EEA family members, see 7.93 fn 4 above.
4   Case C-329/97 *Ergat v Stadt Ulm* [2000] ECR I-1487, ECJ.
5   *Kadiman* above, paras 37–42.

7.160 Under the second paragraph of Article 7 of Decision 1/80, children of Turkish workers who have completed a course of vocational training in the host State are free to take any job, irrespective of the time they have spent there, provided that one of their parents has been legally employed in the Member State concerned for at least three years. In *Eroglu*[1] the court held that the second paragraph of Article 7 gives a Turkish national who satisfies the conditions a right to respond to any offer of employment and to rely on the right in order to obtain a new work permit; secondly that the right necessarily implies a recognition of a right of residence, giving the person an opportunity to look for job opportunities; and thirdly, that the right is not subject to any conditions concerning the ground on which the right to enter and stay was granted. So it was immaterial that the person was given leave to enter the host State as a student and not as a family member. Once a child has completed his or her education and acquired the right, conferred directly by Article 7 (2) of Decision No 1/80, of access to the employment market of the host country, and, as a result, the right to obtain a residence permit for that purpose, it is not necessary that the parent of the child still has the status of worker or continues to reside in that Member State.[2]

1   Case C-355/93 *Eroglu v Land Baden-Württemberg* [1994] ECR I-5113, ECJ.
2   Case C-210/97 *Akman v Oberlsreisdirektor des Rheinische-Bergischen-Kreises* [1998] ECR I-7519, ECJ; Case C-329/97 *Ergat v Stadt Ulm* [2000] ECR I-1487, ECJ, at para 44.

7.161 Decisions made under the Turkey Association Agreement also deal with discrimination on grounds of nationality, in relation to education of the children of Turkish workers and as regards social security. Under Article 9 of Decision 1/80, such children are entitled to education on the same footing as own nationals. This accords with the rights such children would have under Article 2 of Protocol 1 of the ECHR, read with Article 14. In *Sürül*[1] the ECJ held that Article 9 of the Decision was of direct effect. The case dealt with Article 3 of Decision 3/80, under which the applicant claimed family allowance in Germany. She was refused on the basis that, although she was lawfully resident, she had only a limited stay. The court held that this was discriminatory, since a Member State cannot impose on Turkish nationals more or stricter controls than those imposed on own nationals, for whom the only requirement was domicile or habitual residence.

---

1   Case C-262/96 *Sürül v Bundesanstalt für Arbeit* [1999] ECR I-2685, ECJ. See further joined cases C-102 and 211/98, *Kocak (Ibrahim) v Landesversicherunsanstalt Oberfranken und Mittelfranken; Ramazan Örs v Bundesknappschaft* [2000] ECR I-1287, ECJ.

7.162 The provisions of Decision 1/80 are subject to limitations based on public policy, public security or public health.[1] Turkish nationals who benefit from the provisions will therefore face deportation on the same basis as EEA nationals.[2] In *Nazli*[3] the ECJ held that the same principles applied as in public policy cases under Article 39(3) EC.[4] So a Turkish worker could not be expelled as a deterrent to others without his or her personal conduct giving reason to believe that he or she would commit other serious offences prejudicial to the requirements of public policy in the host Member State. The same applies to family members.[5]

---

1   Decision 1/80, Art 14(1).
2   See discussion at 7.133ff above.
3   Case C-340/97 *Nazli v Stadt Nürnberg* [2000] ECR I-957, ECJ. See also *Cetinkaya v Land Baden-Wurttemberg* Case C-467/02 (10 June 2004, unreported).
4   See *R v Bouchereau* [1978] QB 732.
5   See Case C-329/97 *Ergat v Stadt Ulm*, [2000] ECR I-1487, ECJ.

Establishment under Turkey Agreement

7.163 As regards establishment, Article 13 of the Ankara Agreement states that the parties agree to be guided by Articles 52 to 56 EC (now 42 to 46) for the purpose of abolishing restrictions on the freedom of establishment between them. Article 14 made similar provision for services. Article 41 EC is a standstill provision, which requires the Parties to refrain from introducing between themselves any new restrictions on the freedom of establishment and the freedom to provide services.[1] In *Savas*[2] a Turkish couple who had overstayed their leave in the UK set up a very successful business and wished to regularise their position. The UK authorities wished to deport them. The case was referred to the ECJ, which ruled that Articles 13 and 41(2) did not have direct effect, but that the standstill clause in Article 41(1) prohibited the introduction of new national restrictions. It was for the national court to determine if the rules applied were less favourable than before the time that the Additional Protocol came into force. However, the clause is not in itself capable of conferring upon a Turkish national the benefit of the right of establishment or of residence which goes with it. The upshot of this is that so far as the UK is concerned no rules more onerous than the 1973 business rules

(HC 510) will apply to Turkish nationals. These rules do not make entry clearance a pre-condition of entry[3] and they are very much less onerous than the current rules, containing no minimum capital requirement or a need to create new jobs.

[1] For the UK this means no new restrictions after 1 January 1973, the date of the UK's adherence to the EEC.

[2] Case C-37/98 *R v Secretary of State for the Home Department, ex p Savas* [2000] INLR 398, ECJ; extended to services in Cases C-317/01 and C-369/01 *Abatay and Sahin v Bundesanstalt für Arbeit* [2003] 1 All ER (D) 342 (Oct), ECJ, paras 61–67. In *R (on the application of A) v Secretary of State for the Home Department* [2002] EWCA Civ 1008 [2003] CMLR 14, 353, the Court of Appeal said *Savas* settled the position in community law and there was no need to make a further reference to the ECJ on this subject.

[3] Thus persons admitted as visitors or for education or other purpose may apply for leave to establish themselves. In *R (on the application of Tum) v Secretary of State for the Home Department* [2004] EWCA Civ 788, the CA held that the Secretary of State was wrong to apply the current business rules to two failed Turkish asylum seekers, who were on temporary admission to the UK, and to refuse them leave to enter. On appeal by the Secretary of State, the House of Lords referred the issue to the ECJ.

The Maghreb Cooperation Agreements

7.164 The EC has entered into Cooperation Agreements with Morocco, Tunisia and Algeria[1] (the Maghreb Agreements) (they are all in similar terms, so references hereafter are to the Morocco Agreement). In the case of Tunisia and Morocco these have been supplemented by Euro-Mediterranean Agreements.[2] Despite this, there have been no specific free movement rights granted to Maghreb workers. But there are provisions prohibiting discrimination in the field of employment and social security. In the case of *Office National de l'Emploi v Kziber*[3] the ECJ held that an Article of the Morocco Agreement prohibiting discrimination in the field of social security had direct effect. Following *Kziber* the ECJ held in *El-Yassini*[4] that Article 40 of the Morocco Cooperation Agreement was of direct effect. The case concerned a Moroccan who married a British citizen and was given 12 months leave to enter the UK. He obtained a job. Before he qualified for indefinite leave to remain the marriage broke down. He argued that refusing to extend his leave to remain amounted to discrimination as regards his working conditions contrary to Article 40 EC. This provides that as regards working conditions and remuneration there should be no discrimination as against nationals of the Member State where the Moroccan workers are employed. The court rejected this argument. 'Working conditions' did not cover the conditions of residence and Article 40 EC did not give any further right of residence.

[1] See OJ 1978 L 264, 27 September, and Council Regulation (EEC) 2211/78 26 September 1978 annexing the Morocco Agreement which provides that the regulation shall be binding in its entirety and directly applicable. The Tunisian and Algerian Agreements are set out in the ensuing pages of the Official Journal.

[2] See OJ 1998 L 97/2 (Tunisia); OJ 2000 L 70/2 (Morocco); see also Euro-Mediterranean Agreement with Israel OJ 2000 L 147/3. The Tunisian Agreement is also set out in *Butterworths Immigration Law Service*, F[5761].

[3] Case C-18/90 *Office National de l'Emploi v Kziber* [1991] ECR I-199, ECJ; the decision was followed in Case C-58/93 *Yousfi v Belgium* [1994] ECR I-1353, ECJ and *Zailika Krid* [1995] ECR I-719, ECJ.

[4] Case C-416/96 *El-Yassini v Secretary of State for the Home Department* [1999] ECR I-1209, [1999] All ER (EC) 193, ECJ.

Lomé Convention with African, Caribbean and Pacific countries

7.165 The EC has also entered the Lomé Agreements with African, Caribbean and Pacific (ACP) countries, but ACP nationals who are workers in the EU have obtained little benefit by way of free movement provisions from these Conventions.[1] In the case of *Poirrez*[2] neither the non-discrimination provisions of the EC Treaty nor the ACP-EEC Convention assisted a claim to benefit by an Ivory Coast national who was the adopted child of a French worker who had never exercised Community rights. In the earlier decision of *Ratzanatsimba*[3] the non-discrimination provision of the 1975 Lomé Convention did not prohibit different treatment between EC and ACP nationals, or even between different ACP nationals with respect to training as a pupil barrister.[4]

[1] The new Lomé Convention, agreed in February 2000, contains draconian rules on the repatriation of people illegally in the EU: see (2000) 10 Statewatch 2.
[2] Case C-206/91 *Poirrez v CAF de la Seine Saint Denis* [1992] ECR I-6685, ECJ.
[3] Case 65/77 *Ratzanatsimba* [1978] 1 CMLR 246. Article 62 of the 1975 Lomé Convention provided:

> 'As regards arrangements that may be applied in matters of establishment and provisions of services, the ... Member States shall treat nationals and companies or firms of the ... ACP States respectively on a non-discriminatory basis. However if, for a given activity, a ... State is unable to provide such treatment, the (other) State shall not be bound to accord such treatment for this activity.'

[4] This tentative non-discrimination clause may have resulted in the conclusion that discrimination was not prohibited.

Central and Eastern European Agreements

7.166 The EC and the Member States also entered into association agreements between 1991 and 1999 with Hungary, Poland,[1] Romania, Bulgaria, Slovenia, the Czech and Slovak Republics, Estonia, Latvia and Lithuania.[2] All of these are history, except those with Romania and Bulgaria, because the other countries, as we have seen, all become Member States of the EU and EC on 1 May 2004. Essentially the agreements for these two countries give a right of establishment and to set up in self employment, and, to provide services. For workers there are provisions for non-discrimination in working conditions similar to the Maghreb Co-operation Agreements discussed above.[3] Generally speaking the legally resident spouse and children of a worker who is legally employed have a right to work during the period when the worker is authorised to be in employment. This operates for Bulgarians and Romanians coming into the EU and vice versa.[4] The Agreements also provide for an Association Council to co-ordinate social security measures for nationals of association agreement States in the EU and vice versa.[5]

[1] The text of the Agreements with Romania and Bulgaria are available at www.europa.eu.int/ under references OJ 1994 L 358 (Bulgaria) and L 357 (Romania).
[2] The agreements with Lithuania, Latvia and Estonia came into force on 1 February 1997, but only *companies* could take advantage until 1 January 2000, when they applied to the *self-employed*: IND letter 23.6.99. Agreements with the Czech and Slovak Republics, Bulgaria and Romania came into force on 1 February 1995: OJ L/357 L/358, L360/4 (31 December 1994).
[3] Eg Article 38(1) of the Bulgarian Agreement.

4   Bulgarian Agreement, Art 38(2). Spouses of Accession State Nationals, which were
    previously associated States, like Poland, may no longer have this right to work under the
    transitional provisions of the Accession Treaty; see 7.10, above.
5   Bulgarian Agreement, Art 39.

7.167 It is the measures to promote freedom of establishment and the supply of services that give rise to immigration law issues. Article 45(1) of the Bulgarian Agreement[1] provides that:

> 'Each Member State shall grant from entry into force of this Agreement, for the establishment of Bulgarian companies and nationals and for the operation of Bulgarian companies and nationals established in its territory atreatment no less favourable than that accorded to its own companies and nationals ...'

Establishment includes the right to take up and pursue economic activities as self-employed persons and to set up and manage undertakings, in particular companies, which they effectively control; but self-employment shall not extend to seeking or taking employment in the labour market, nor does it confer a right of access to the labour market of another party.[2] A relevant company is essentially defined by its place of registration, but if the enterprise has only its registered office in the territory of the Community or Bulgaria or Romania, its operations must possess a real and continuous link with the economy of one of the Member States or the relevant Associated State respectively.[3]

1   Article 45(1) of the Bulgarian Agreement of March 1993, entered into force on Feb/95
    (OJ 1994 L 358).
2   Article 45(5) of the Bulgarian Agreement; Art 44(5) of the Romanian Agreement.
3   Article 49(1) of the Bulgarian Agreement and 49(1) of the Romanian one.

7.168 The European Court has held that the very similarly worded Articles 45(3) of the Czech, 44(1) of the Polish, and 45(1) of the Bulgarian Agreements (and by implication the equivalent Article in the Romanian Agreement) are directly effective in each of the Member States of the EU.[1] This means that rights of entry and residence are conferred, as corollaries of the right of establishment, on Association Agreement nationals wishing to pursue activities of an industrial or commercial character, activities of craftsmen, or activities of the professions in a Member State.[2] But this right has to be read with the Articles equivalent to Article 59(1) of the Czech Agreement, which allows the parties to apply domestic laws and regulations regarding entry and stay, work, labour conditions and establishment of natural persons and supply of services, providing these do not nullify or impair the rights accruing under the Agreement.[3] In the light of this provision, the European Court has held that the rights of entry and residence, conferred on Association Agreement nationals as corollaries of the right of establishment, are not 'absolute privileges', and their exercise may, where appropriate, be limited by the domestic rules of the host Member State.[4] This has two main consequences. First a Member State's immigration authorities can reject an application on the sole ground that when the applicant made the application for leave to remain he or she was residing unlawfully in the Member State.[5] However, the domestic power of regulation does not preclude a new application being made for entry, so that the person may have his or her situation reviewed [6] Secondly, the member State can make leave to enter subject to a requirement of prior entry clearance – a matter which we consider in the next two paragraphs in the light of the UK immigration rules.

1   See Case C-235/99 *R v Secretary of State for the Home Department* , *ex p Kondova* [2001] ECR I-6427, at paras 51–53; Case C-257/99 *R (on the application of Barkoci) v Secretary of State for the Home Department* [2001] ECR I-6357, at paras 51–53, and Case C-63/99 *R v Secretary of State for the Home Department* , *ex p Gloszczuk* [2001] ECR I-6369, paras 48–50.
2   See above cases and Case 48/75 *Royer, Re* [1976] ECR 497, paras 31 and 32, and Case C-37/98 *R v Secretary of State for the Home Department* , *ex p Savas* [2000] ECR I-2927, paras 60 and 63.
3   Article 45(5) of the Bulgarian Agreement.
4   *See*, for example, *Barkoci and Malik*, above at para 54 and *Gloszczuk*, above, at para 51. Thus the host Member State cannot refuse admission and residence, for example, on grounds of the nationality of applicants or their country of residence, or because the national legal system provides for a general limitation on immigration, or makes the right to take up an activity as a self-employed person in that State subject to confirmation of a proven need in the light of economic or labour-market considerations: *Gloszczuk*, above, at para 59.
5   *Kondova;* above at para 90; *Gloszczuk*, above para 85.
6   Ibid.

7.169 The UK has recognised that these provisions are of direct effect and has sought to give effect to them in paragraphs 211 to 223 of HC 395, which make special rules for those Bulgarian and Romanian nationals who seek to come to the UK to establish themselves in a business. 'Business' means an enterprise as a sole trader, a partnership or a company registered in the UK.[1] The substantive requirements for admission are that the person is investing sufficient money under his or her control in the business to establish him or herself in the UK.[2] The share of the profits of the business must provide a sufficient income to maintain and accommodate the person and any dependants without recourse to employment outside the business or to public funds, and there must be sufficient funds for this purpose until the business becomes profitable.[3] Those establishing themselves in a company must have a controlling interest in it and be actively involved in the promotion and management of the company. The company must be registered in the UK and be trading or providing services here.[4] Self-employed Association Agreement nationals must be actively trading and own the assets of the business solely or jointly with any partners, and in the case of partnership their role must not amount to disguised employment.[5] Those taking over an existing business must provide audited accounts.[6] An entry clearance is necessary for admission.[7] Entry is given for 12 months,[8] which is renewable,[9] and settlement may be given after four years.[10]

1   HC 395, para 211.
2   HC 395, para 212(ii).
3   HC 395, para 212(ii) and (iv).
4   HC 395, para 213.
5   HC 395, para 214.
6   HC 395, para 213(vi), r 214(v).
7   HC 395, paras 215 and 216. As to whether this requirement conforms with Community law, see below.
8   HC 395, para 215.
9   HC 395, para 220.
10   HC 395, para 222.

7.170 These provisions reflect the old 1973 business rules and certainly do not require a minimum investment, profit margins or the creation of new employment.[1] In so far as they set minimum standards for establishing a genuine enterprise within the terms of the Association Agreement, they are consistent with the European case-law, and have, indeed, received approval by the European Court of Justice in the batch of cases decided on reference from the English Courts in September 2000.[2] This is how the court put it in *Barkoci*,[3] a case concerning Czech nationals, using almost identical words to those in the Bulgarian case of *Kondova*:

> 'Articles 45(3) and 59(1) of that Association Agreement, read together, do not in principle preclude a system of prior control which makes the issue by the competent immigration authorities of leave to enter subject to the condition that the applicant must show that he genuinely intends to take up an activity in a self-employed capacity without at the same time entering into employment or having recourse to public funds, and that he possesses, from the outset, sufficient financial resources and has reasonable chances of success. Substantive requirements such as those set out in paragraph 212 of the United Kingdom Immigration Rules (House of Commons Paper 395) have as their very purpose to enable the competent authorities to carry out such checks and are appropriate for achieving such a purpose.'

This issue has received further attention from the court in *Panayotova v Minister voor Vreemdelingenzaken en Integratie*,[4] which deals with the requirement of mandatory prior entry clearance. In HC 395 paragraph 216 the refusal of leave to enter in the absence of prior entry clearance is phrased in mandatory terms. The same applies to the recently amended HC 395 para 217,[5] whereby Associated State nationals are only allowed to switch into this kind of economic activity, when they apply for leave to remain, if they had entry clearance on arrival in the UK. The ECJ approved the entry clearance requirement in *Panayotova*, holding that the terms of the Association Agreements did not preclude national legislation which allowed host Member States to reject an application to remain under one of the Association Agreements without considering the merits, if the applicant has not obtained prior entry clearance from the diplomatic or consular authorities of that Member State in the applicant's country of origin or permanent residence.[6] However, the scheme applicable to such residence permits issued in advance must be based on a procedural system which is easily accessible and capable of ensuring that the persons concerned will have their applications dealt with objectively and within a reasonable time. Secondly, refusals to grant a permit must be capable of being challenged in judicial or quasi-judicial proceedings.[7] According to the IDI, the position in the UK is that switching will only be allowed if it would be disproportionate to require the person to go home for an entry clearance, and this will usually only happen where the viability of the application is 'clear and manifest'.[8]

---

[1] See HC 80, para 21 and note comment on Turkish Agreement at 7.159 above.

[2] Case C-235/99 *R v Secretary of State for the Home Department, ex p Kondova* [2001] ECR I-6427 at paras 51–53; Case C-257/99 *R (on the application of Barkoci) v Secretary of State for the Home Department* [2001] ECR I-6357, at paras 51–53, and Case C-63/99 *Gloszczuk* [2001] ECR I-6369 paras 48–50.

[3] *Barkoci and Malik* at para 65.

[4] Case C-327/02, 16 November 2004.

[5] HC 395, para 217, as amended by Cmd 6297 in August 2004.

6   *Panayotova* Case C-327/02, fn 4 above, para 39.
7   Case C-327/02, para 39.
8   IDI Aug 04, Ch 6, s 2.

7.171 The Agreements require the parties to permit the temporary admission of natural persons who provide services[1] or are employed by a service provider as key personnel. They can enter to negotiate the provision of services, but not to make direct sales to the public or to supply services themselves.[2] Such provisions are well accommodated within the business visitor rules, but in any judicial review proceedings to challenge a refusal of admission to any Association Agreement national business person, reference should be made to the Community law obligations and not just the UK Immigration Rules. A belief by an immigration officer that a person may stay longer than the period asked for should not prevent temporary admission to carry out activities covered by the Agreement.

1   In Case C 268/99 *Jany v Staatssecretaris van Justitie* [2001] ECR I-8615, the ECJ held that self-employed prostitutes engage in economic activity which is covered by the Agreements, although Member States were free to impose restrictions on prostitution, provided they were non-discriminatory, and for the protection of public order.
2   Bulgarian and Romanian Agreements, Art 56(2).

Chapter 8

HUMAN RIGHTS LAW

INTRODUCTION

8.1 Of the numerous international human rights instruments to which the UK is a party,[1] the European Convention of Human Rights (ECHR)[2] had already become the most significant and most frequently cited source of rights outside the common law well before 2 October 2000, when the Human Rights Act 1998 brought its provisions within the reach of the domestic courts. Since the coming into force of the 1998 Act, the ECHR has taken its place at the heart of UK human rights law. This chapter will look at the Convention, at how the 1998 Act incorporates it, and at some of the incorporated rights as they affect immigration law. It will also briefly look at the UK's international obligations outside the incorporated rights, both under the ECHR and outside it.

[1] Of which the most important are the UN Universal Declaration of Human Rights 1948 (UDHR), the UN International Covenant on Civil and Political Rights 1966 (ICCPR), the UN Convention Against Torture 1984 (UNCAT), the UN Convention on the Rights of the Child 1989 (COROC), the Convention on the Elimination of all forms of Discrimination against Women (CEDAW) and the UN Convention against Torture and Inhuman and Degrading Treatment 1984.
[2] To give it its full title, the European Convention for the Protection of Human Rights and Fundamental Freedoms, Rome, 4 November 1950.

HISTORY OF THE ECHR

8.2 The ECHR was produced by the Council of Europe, an inter-governmental body formed in 1949 by ten Member States[1] to foster European unity and reduce the risk of future wars. The Charter of the Council of Europe required Member States to subscribe to the rule of law and to afford human rights and fundamental freedoms to all within their jurisdiction.[2] The Convention was one of the Council's earliest projects. Its two principal objectives were to maintain and further realise human rights and fundamental freedoms, and to foster effective political democracy.[3] It was designed to 'secure the universal and effective recognition and observance' of the rights set out in the Universal Declaration of Human Rights 1948, by making contracting States responsible under public international law for ensuring that their laws and practices gave effect to such rights and creating mechanisms of enforcement if they did not. Article 19 of the Convention set up the Commission and the Court. Article 25 provided that contracting States could recognise individuals' right to petition the Commission and Article 46 provided that they could accept the compulsory jurisdiction of the court. Article 13 required States to provide an effective remedy in their domestic courts for violation of the rights in the Convention. The Commission has now gone and Articles 25, 44 and 46 of the original Convention have since been repealed and no longer form part of the Convention. The jurisdiction of the court is now compulsory (Art 32) and individuals have a right to apply to the court (Art 34). But the focus of the Convention is still on securing observance by Member States of minimum standards in the protection of the human rights set out in the Convention. Member States are bound by Article 46(1) to abide by the final judgment (or decision) of the court in any case to which they are parties. Article 26 of the Vienna Convention on the Law of Treaties, expressing customary international law, requires States parties to a treaty to perform it in good faith. The expectation therefore is, and has always been, that a Member State found to have violated the Convention will act promptly to prevent a repetition of the violation, and in this way the primary object of the Convention is served. The Convention has always, however, made provision for affording just satisfaction to the injured party.

---

[1] Belgium, Denmark, France, Ireland, Italy, Luxembourg, Netherlands, Norway, Sweden and the UK. As of March 2005 there were 46 Member States: Albania, Andorra, Armenia, Austria, Azerbaijan, Belgium, Bosnia and Herzegovina, Bulgaria, Croatia, Cyprus, Czech Republic, Denmark, Estonia, Finland, France, Georgia, Germany, Greece, Hungary, Iceland, Ireland, Italy, Latvia, Liechtenstein, Lithuania, Luxembourg, Malta, Moldova, Monaco, Netherlands, Norway, Poland, Portugal, Romania, Russian Federation, San Marino, Serbia and Montenegro, Slovakia, Slovenia, Spain, Sweden, Switzerland, former Yugoslav Republic of Macedonia, Turkey, Ukraine and the UK.

[2] Statute of the Council of Europe 1949 (Cmd 7778).

[3] See judgment of Lord Steyn in *Brown v Stott (Procurator Fiscal, Dunfermline)* [2003] 1 AC 681, [2001] 2 All ER 97, PC.

8.3 The right of individual petition and the compulsory jurisdiction of the court are the mechanisms behind the success of the ECHR as a living and well-used instrument. The UK did not recognise the right, or submit to the compulsory jurisdiction of the court, until 1966,[1] citing the superiority of British law, concern that a 'flood of fatuous or insincere applications would roll in', causing extra work and adverse publicity,[2] and arguing that 'the State, not the individual, is the proper subject of international law'.[3] The real reason for the delay was Britain's colonial situation—in the course of fighting against the liberation warriors of the colonies, the UK had issued ten derogations from Article 5 (the right to liberty and security of person) from 1953 to May 1960.[4] Once the right of individual petition was recognised in the UK, it was frequently used to challenge immigration control measures. The very first British case where the individual right of petition was exercised was an immigration case.[5] The UK renewed the right of petition and its submission to the compulsory jurisdiction every five years. Since November 1998, contracting States have been obliged to recognise the right of individual petition and to submit to the compulsory jurisdiction of the court.[6] Further changes in the procedures of the court are envisaged in new Protocol 14, agreed on 13 May 2004, which is designed to amend and streamline Convention machinery for admission of new cases. More details are at 8.113.

[1] For the full text of the letters from the UK government see (1966) 15 ICLQ 539.
[2] HC Official Report (5th Series) 23 May 1960, col 174.
[3] HC Official Report (5th Series) 23 May 1960, col 180.
[4] HC Official Report (5th Series) 23 May 1960, col 174 and 182: 'Among emerging communities political agitators thrive, and one may well imagine the use which political agitators would make of the right of individual petition.' See further Ian Macdonald, foreword to *A Guide to the Human Rights Act 1998* 1999 *Butterworths Immigration Law Service* Special Bulletin.
[5] Application 2991/66, *Alam v United Kingdom* (1967) Times, 12 October, relating to the refusal to allow a 12-year-old boy to join his father in the UK. It led to a friendly settlement. This was followed by *Harbahjan Singh v United Kingdom* (Application 2992/96), reported at (1967) Times, 12 October. The fact that individual immigrants were invoking the right of individual petition as soon as it became available contributed to the introduction in 1969 of the immigration appellate system. See chapter 18 below.
[6] With the coming into force of ECHR, Protocol 11 on 1 November 1998.

THE UK AND THE ECHR

8.4 As noted above,[1] the UK government's approach to the ECHR was always ambivalent; on the one hand, it took part in the drafting, and in 1953 accepted that the Convention applied to 42 overseas territories,[2] while on the other, it feared a stream of cases from those same territories if it recognised the right of individual petition. In fact, the first time the UK stood in the dock was an inter-state case, *Ireland v United Kingdom*,[3] which exposed the practices of hooding, wall-standing, exposure to white noise, deprivation of sleep, food and drink inflicted on Republican internees in Northern Ireland, which the ECHR condemned as inhuman and degrading treatment. After the right of individual petition had been recognised, all the early cases were immigration ones,[4] culminating in the *East African Asians* case,[5] where the Commission made a finding of rank racial discrimination, amounting to degrading treatment under Article 3 of ECHR, in the application of the Commonwealth Immigrants' Act 1968, which excluded UK and Colonies citizens from the UK on grounds of race.[6]

[1] See 8.3 above. For a fuller description, see the first edition of this work.
[2] Declaration of Her Majesty's Government of 23 October 1953, Cmd 9045. See HC Official Report (5th Series) 23 May 1960, cols 174–181; HC Official Report (5th Series) 19 May 1960 written answers cols 133–134. An irony of the colonial situation was the

willingness of the UK government to see guarantees of fundamental rights inserted into the constitutions of the newly independent ex-colonies: see De Smith *Constitutions of the Commonwealth* chapter 5, above.

3   (1978) 2 EHRR 25.
4   See 8.3 fn 5 above.
5   (1973) 3 EHRR 76.
6   'Publicly to single out a group of persons for differential treatment on the basis of race might in certain circumstances constitute a special form of affront to human dignity, and ... might be capable of constituting degrading treatment when differential treatment on some other ground would raise no such question': (1973) 3 EHRR 76, para 207.

8.5 Before incorporation of the ECHR, judicial opinion in the UK was divided on the relevance of the Convention to the interpretation of statute and the proper exercise of administrative powers. The arguments are still relevant today in the debate on the permissible application in domestic law of rights under other unincorporated international Conventions. The clash between two rules – the rule that international treaties do not confer rights enforceable in the domestic courts without incorporation,[1] and the presumption that Parliament did not intend to enact laws that were contrary to the UK's international obligations[2] led to a difference between the school of judicial thought which believed that, wherever possible, a statute should be construed in conformity with those obligations (the *Garland*[3] view), and the restrictive school, which held that regard should be had to the Convention only in the construction of ambiguous statutes (the *Brind*[4] view).[5] The *Brind* view prevailed, meaning that the Secretary of State was not obliged to have regard to the Convention when framing rules or directives under primary legislation. Where a statutory administrative power was enacted in general terms, a government official did not need to consult or have regard to the Convention in reaching decisions, since the power was 'unambiguous'.[6] To hold otherwise, the House of Lords ruled, would be to incorporate the Convention through the back door, usurping Parliament's function.[7] Nevertheless, prior to incorporation, the ECHR played a large part in developing the common law and, through it, developing a much more comprehensive review of administrative discretion, where a breach of human right has been involved.[8] There is now an open recognition that a decision which breaches an individual's or group's human rights requires 'justification' and that the degree of justification required must be proportionate to the scale and level and importance of the breach of human rights. But the formulation of the new and developing process shows a reluctance by many of the judges, as yet, to break with the traditional language and categories of public law review. Thus the courts speak of a varying intensity of review depending on the nature of the rights affected—building on the dictum of Lord Bridge in *Bugdaycay*[9] a decade earlier. A similar approach was taken in *Saleem*[10] where the Court of Appeal quashed a procedure rule deeming service of an adjudicator's determination to have been effected regardless of whether it had in fact been received, and held that the right of access to a tribunal is a fundamental right.

1   *Malone v Metropolitan Police Comr* [1979] Ch 344 at 379; *J H Rayner (Mincing Lane) v Department of Trade and Industry* [1990] 2 AC 418, 476–7. Article 46 ECHR (the UK's obligation to abide by a judgment of the ECHR), was held to be an international obligation not directly enforceable in the domestic courts in *R v Lyons* [2002] UKHL 44, [2003] 1 AC 976, [2002] 4 All ER 1028 (para 104, per Lord Millett). For the debate on incorporation see the 4th edition of this work, 13.102 fn 2. For a full description of the

attitude of the courts see Murray Hunt *Using human rights law in the English courts* (Hart Publishing, 1997). See also Feldman *Civil liberties and human rights in England and Wales* (OUP, 2002); McCrudden *A common law of human rights? Transnational judicial conversations on constitutional rights* 2000 20(4) OJLS 499.

2   See Bennion *Statutory Interpretation* (3rd edn); *Salomon v Customs and Excise Comrs* [1967] 2 QB 116, per Diplock LJ; *Waddington v Miah* [1974] 2 All ER 377 where the House of Lords decided, having regard to Art 7 ECHR (no retrospective criminality), that the penal provisions of the Immigration Act 1971 were not retrospective.

3   *Garland v British Rail Engineering Ltd* [1983] 2 AC 751 at 771, per Lord Diplock (this was, however, a case involving EC law). See also *R v Secretary of State for the Home Department, ex p Simms* [2000] 2 AC 115, where Lord Hoffmann thundered: 'Fundamental rights cannot be overridden by general or ambiguous words ... In the absence of express language or necessary implication, the courts ... presume that even the most general words were intended to be subject to the basic rights of the individual.'

4   *R v Secretary of State for the Home Department, ex p Brind* [1991] 1 AC 696 at 748.

5   In *Pan American World Airways Inc v Department of Trade* [1976] 1 Lloyd's Rep 257 Scarman LJ said that an international Convention should be consulted in three situations: where Parliament expressly or implicitly requires it; when two courses are reasonably open, only one of which would lead to a result consistent with obligations under the Convention; and where statutory words have to be construed or a legal principle formulated in an area of law where the government has accepted international obligations, as part of the full context or background.

6   The Court of Appeal had previously held in *Chundawadra v Immigration Appeal Tribunal* [1988] Imm AR 161 that immigration officers did not have to have regard to the ECHR in deciding whether to grant leave to enter, following Lord Denning's recantation in *Salamat Bibi* [1976] 3 All ER 843, [1976] 1 WLR 979, CA of remarks in *R v Secretary of State for the Home Department, ex p Bhajan Singh* [1976] QB 198 to the effect that immigration officers ought to bear in mind the principles stated in the Convention. For a recent application of this principle to the Refugee Convention see *European Roma Rights Centre v Immigration Officer at Prague Airport* [2003] EWCA Civ 666, [2004] QB 811, para 51 (Simon Brown LJ), 98–101 (Laws LJ). The Lords, however, held that the Refugee Convention was incorporated into domestic law.

7   But in *R v Secretary of State for the Home Department, ex p Thompson and Venables* [1998] AC 407, the House of Lords held, in relation to the UN Convention on the Rights of the Child, that 'it is legitimate ... to assume that Parliament has not maintained on the statute book a power capable of being exercised in a manner inconsistent with the treaty obligations of this country' (per Lord Browne-Wilkinson at 499).

8   For details see the 5th edition of this work at 8.14–8.20; also *R v Secretary of State for the Home Department, ex p Brind* [1991] 1 AC 696 at 748 and 751; *R v Secretary of State for the Home Department, ex p McQuillan* [1995] 4 All ER 400, per Sedley J, who drew on the Article by Sir John Laws 'Is the High Court the Guardian of Fundamental Human Rights?' in (1993) PL 59; Simon Brown LJ's judgment in *R v Secretary of State for Social Security, ex p Joint Council for the Welfare of Immigrants* [1997] 1 WLR 275 at 292: 'So basic are the human rights here at issue that it cannot be necessary to resort to the ECHR to take note of their violation'; *R v Ministry of Defence, ex p Smith* [1996] QB 517 at 554 per Lord Bingham MR (the 'gays in the military' case); *R (on the application of A) v Lord Saville of Newdigate (No 2)* [2001] EWCA Civ 2048, [2002] 1 WLR 129 at para 37 (on anonymity for soldiers testifying to the Saville Inquiry on Bloody Sunday).

9   The most fundamental right is the individual's right to life, and when an administrative decision under challenge is said to be one which may put the applicant's life at risk, the basis of the decision must surely call for the most anxious scrutiny: *Bugdaycay v Secretary of State for the Home Department* [1987] AC 514, HL.

10   *R v Secretary of State for the Home Department, ex p Saleem* [2000] 4 All ER 814, [2000] Imm AR 529, [2000] INLR 413, upholding Hooper J at [1999] INLR 621. See also *R v Secretary of State for the Home Department, ex p Simms* [2000] 2 AC 115, 8.5 fn 3 above. But the limits of judicial freedom were drawn in *R v Lyons* [2002] UKHL 44, [2003] 1 AC 976, [2002] 4 All ER 1028, where Lord Hoffmann pointed out that 'If Parliament has plainly laid down the law, it is the duty of the courts to apply it, whether that would involve the Crown in breach of an international treaty or not.'

8.6 The various ways in which the courts may have regard to international obligations are of course still highly relevant. The UK has, after all, international obligations respecting human rights, even fundamental human rights, which are not expressed in the ECHR, of which perhaps the most important are rights of children,[1] the right to work, to shelter and subsistence[2], and to health care[3]. So, while it may be possible to enlarge the scope of some of the rights protected by the ECHR in the domestic courts, by approaching them through the medium of the common law,[4] through the construction rule contained in Article 53 of the ECHR,[5] and by use of Commonwealth jurisprudence,[6] on the other hand it will always be necessary to persuade the courts to have regard to other international obligations which past and present governments have seen fit to sign up to without incorporating them into domestic law.[7] A summary of the relevant principles relating to rights protected by unincorporated Conventions is as follows:

(i)   the courts assume that Parliament does not intend to legislate in a manner incompatible with the UK's international legal obligations, and will interpret legislation in a manner consistent with those obligations wherever possible, even where there is no obvious ambiguity:[8]

(ii)   when a statute is enacted to fulfil an international obligation, the courts will assume it is intended to be effective for that purpose and will interpret the legislation accordingly;[9]

(iii)   where the common law is uncertain or there are gaps in the law, the courts will seek to make a decision which is compatible with international obligations;[10]

(iv)   where possible, the courts will exercise their discretion compatibly with international obligations;[11]

(v)   in reviewing the exercise of discretion by public authorities, the courts will subject decisions or actions interfering with fundamental human rights to particularly anxious scrutiny, and such decisions or actions require particularly strong justification if they are not to be regarded as irrational or disproportionate and therefore unlawful;[12]

(vi)   it is part of legal public policy that courts give effect to established rules of international law;[13]

Whether persons having dealings with government bodies have a legitimate expectation that they will be dealt with compatibly with international human rights standards, in the absence of incorporation, is a matter of dispute.[14]

---

1   The Government has appointed a Children's Commissioner to protect children's rights (see Children Act 2004) but has failed to lift the reservation to the UN Convention on the Rights of the Child in respect of immigration and asylum, despite the urging of the Joint Committee on Human Rights: see Joint Committee on Human Rights: Tenth report 2002/3: UN Convention on the Rights of the Child, 24 June 2003 (HL 117/HC 81); Joint Committee on Human Rights: 19th report 2003/4: Children Bill, 21 September 2004 (HL 161/HC 537).

2   While the courts have accepted that a complete lack of shelter and subsistence engages Art 3 in extreme circumstances (see 8.55 below), there is no free-standing right.

3   Similarly, access to health care may engage Art 3 or 8 if denial (or withdrawal in the context of expulsion) causes extreme suffering or severe damage to physical or psychological integrity as an aspect of private life (see 8.52 and 8.87 below) but not otherwise. All these rights are contained in the UN's companion to the ICCPR, the International Covenant on Economic, Social and Cultural Rights 1966 (ICESCR), but the ICESCR has no enforcement mechanism at the suit of individuals, although States are monitored and

have reporting obligations. The Joint Human Rights Committee identifies gaps in the protection of these rights in its 21st report 2004/5: International Covenant for Economic, Social and Cultural Rights, 2 November 2004 (HL 183/HC 1188). Another right as yet unrecognised by the ECtHR is the right to conscientious objection to military service, accepted by the (non-binding) EU Charter of Rights: see *Sepet and Bulbul* [2001] EWCA Civ 681, upheld by [2003] UKHL 15, [2003] 3 All ER 304.

4   In accordance with the injunctions of Lord Lester of Herne Hill QC. See per Lord Steyn in *R v Secretary of State for the Home Department, ex p Thompson and Venables* [1998] AC 407; see also Lord Bingham in *R (on the application of Amin) v Secretary of State for the Home Department* [2003] UKHL 51, [2004] 1 AC 653, para 30. But Sedley LJ's attempt to create a right of privacy by judicial development of the common law, distinct from Art 8 ECHR, in *Douglas v Hello! Ltd* [2001] QB 967, was firmly rebuffed in *Wainwright v Home Office* [2001] EWCA Civ 2081, [2002] QB 1334 (paras 97ff).

5   In *T and V v United Kingdom* (1999) 30 EHRR 121 the ECtHR had regard to the UN Convention on the Rights of the Child and the Beijing Rules (a non-binding declaration) to determine the international consensus on the age of criminal responsibility. See also *Jersild v Denmark* (1994) 19 EHRR 1, where the ECtHR took account of Art 4 of the International Convention on the Elimination of All Forms of Racial Discrimination and interpreted Art 10 ECHR in the light of the International Covenant on Civil and Political rights (ICCPR).

6   See e g the discussion in *R (on the application of Pretty) v DPP* [2001] UKHL 61 [2002] 1 AC 800 of Canadian jurisprudence on the principle of personal autonomy, and the citation of Indian case law in support of the right to life in *Amin* (fn 4 above). But caution was expressed by Brooke LJ in *A v Secretary of State for the Home Department* [2002] EWCA Civ 1502, [2004] QB 335 (para 94) about referring to an interpretation of a different human rights charter as a guide to the provisions of the ECHR.

7   The House of Lords reiterated in *R v Lyons* [2002] UKHL 44, [2003] 1 AC 976, [2002] 4 All ER 1028 that any customary international law duty (or one arising from an unincorporated international instrument) was overridden by express and unqualified statutory provision; but where no such express prohibition exists, the courts have shown themselves willing to push forward the boundaries to uphold fundamental rights; see e g *R v Secretary of State for the Home Department, ex p Simms* [2000] 2 AC 115. In *R (on the application of Abbasi) v Secretary of State for Foreign and Commonwealth Affairs* [2002] EWCA Civ 1598, the Court of Appeal held it was not prevented from reviewing the legitimacy of the actions of a foreign sovereign State where fundamental rights were in play, but that there was no *ius cogens* (peremptory international law norm) requiring the UK's intervention.

8   *Garland v British Rail Engineering* [1983] 2 AC 751; *Litster v Forth Dry Dock and Engineering Co* [1990] 1 AC 546.

9   *R (on the application of Mullen) v Secretary of State for the Home Department* [2002] EWCA Civ 1882, [2003] QB 993.

10   *DPP v Jones* [1999] 2 AC 240, HL.

11   *Rantzen v Mirror Group Newspapers (1986) Ltd* [1994] QB 670, CA.

12   *Bugdaycay v Secretary of State for the Home Department* [1987] AC 514, HL; *R v Secretary of State for the Home Department, ex p Simms* [2000] 2 AC 115, HL; *R v Ministry of Defence, ex p Smith* [1996] QB 517, CA; *R v Secretary of State for the Home Department, ex p Thompson and Venables* [1998] AC 407, HL.

13   *Oppenheimer v Cattermole* [1976] AC 249; *Blathwayt v Baron Cawley* [1976] AC 397; *European Roma Rights Centre v Immigration Officer at Prague Airport* [2004] UKHL 55, [2005] 2 WLR 1 per Lady Hale at paras 98ff.

14   See discussion at 8.31 below.

THE EC AND ECHR

8.7   Prior to the incorporation of the ECHR into British domestic law, it was possible to have full regard to its provisions in the domestic courts in cases involving EC law.[1] Article 6(2) of the revised Treaty on European Union (formerly Article F(2)) requires the Union to 'respect fundamental rights as guaranteed by the ECHR and as they result from the constitutional conditions common to the Member States, as general principles of Community law'. This means that, although the EU cannot be a party to the ECHR, because it is a supra-national institution,[2] its standards have become part of EC law.[3] So all EC law on immigration and asylum under Articles 61–64 of the revised Treaty of the European Communities, and any national law based on it, will need to be compatible with the Convention.[4] The EU's judicial institutions must have regard to the Convention in interpreting and formulating the requirements of EC law.[5] Thus, even rights contained in Protocols to which the UK is not a party, such as the right of nationals to enter their own country, are, in our view, part of the *corpus* of law to be taken into account in construing the Treaty.[6] The possibility of the EU acceding to the ECHR is currently under discussion,[7] and will be legally possible when Protocol 14 of the ECHR comes into force.[8]

[1] See *Elliniki Radiophonia Tileorassi AE v Pliroforissis and Kouvelas* [1991] ECR I-2925, [1994] 4 CMLR 540, ECJ, the rationale of which is now contained in Art 6(2) EU (formerly Art F(2)); see further *B v Secretary of State for the Home Department* [2000] Imm AR 478, CA.

[2] *Re the Accession of the Community to the ECHR* (Opinion 2/94) [1996] 2 CMLR 265, ECJ.

[3] Case 29/69 *Stauder v City of Ulm* [1969] ECR 419; Case 11/70 *Internationale Handelsgesellschaft mbH v Einfuhr und Vorratstelle für Getreide und Futtermittel* [1970] ECR 1125; Case 4/73 *Nold v EC Commission* [1974] ECR 491.

[4] In *Elliniki Radiophonia* above (the ERT case), the Court of Justice held that, when considering national legislation falling within the field of application of EC law, it 'must provide the national court with all the elements of interpretation which are necessary in order to enable it to assess the compatibility of that legislation with the fundamental rights as laid down in particular in the European Convention on Human Rights, the observance of which the Court ensures'.

[5] The ERT case, fn 1 above.

[6] *R v Immigration Appeal Tribunal and Surinder Singh, ex p Secretary of State for the Home Department* [1992] Imm AR 565, ECJ, para 22. In *Jersild v Denmark* (1994) 19 EHRR 1, the ECtHR in effect incorporated Art 20(2) of the ICCPR ('Any advocacy of national, racial or religious hatred that constitutes incitement to discrimination, hostility or violence shall be prohibited by law.') into the interpretation of Art 9 and 10 ECHR, an interpretation which would be valid in UK courts, even though the ICCPR is not incorporated into UK law.

[7] See *Memorandum of the European Court of Human Rights for the Third Summit of the Council of Europe, 2005; see also House of Lords EU Select Committee Sixth Report on The Future Status of the EU Charter of Fundamental Rights, 3 February 2003.*

[8] See the discussion on Protocol 14 below.

8.8 In *Rutili v Ministry of Interior*[1] the Court of Justice held that the ECHR provisions applied to measures taken by Member States in derogation of free movement rights. Thus an order banning free movement in a part of France could infringe the ECHR, Article 11 right of freedom of association, holding out the possibility that a removal or refusal of entry involving EC free movement rights could be challenged on the basis that it infringes a Convention right such as family life.[2] This possibility was realised in *Carpenter*,[3] where the ECJ held that to require a Philippines wife of a British citizen living in the UK but exercising Treaty rights by conducting frequent business trips to Europe to return to the Philippines to apply for entry clearance to re-join him because her immigration position was irregular was a disproportionate interference with family life.[4] In the domestic context, the Court of Appeal in *B*[5] used the EU route to apply proportionality principles to a decision to deport which was said to infringe the applicant's combined rights of free movement and family life.[6] So far as third country nationals are concerned, the EC Qualification Directive,[7] which sets out minimum standards for States for the provision of international protection for refugees and for other persons in need of international protection, signally fails to refer anywhere to the ECHR, although it does incorporate a reference to the EU Charter of Fundamental Rights.[8]

[1] 36/75 [1975] ECR 1219. See also *Pecastaing v Belgium*: 98/79 [1980] ECR 691; *Johnston v Chief Constable of the Royal Ulster Constabulary*: 222/84 [1986] ECR 1651; *Dzodzi v Belgium* C-297/88, C-197/89, [1990] ECR I-3763; *Society for the Protection of Unborn Children v Grogan* C-159/90, [1991] ECR I-4685.

[2] See also the opinion of Advocate General Jacobs in *Konstantinidis v Stadt Altensteig-Standesamt*: C-168/91 [1993] 3 CMLR 401.

[3] *Carpenter (Mary) v Secretary of State for the Home Department* C-60/00, [2002] INLR 439.

[4] See also *Mouvement contre le Racisme, l'antisemitisme et la Xenophobie ASBL v Belgium* C-459/99, [2002] ECR I-6591, ECJ.

[5] *B v Secretary of State for the Home Department* [2000] Imm AR 478, CA.

[6] See also *R v Secretary of State for Employment, ex p Equal Opportunities Commission* [1995] 1 AC 1, HL.

[7] Council Directive 2004/83/EC on minimum standards for the qualification and status of third country nationals and stateless persons as refugees or persons who otherwise need international protection (OJ 2004 L304/12).

[8] Charter of Fundamental Rights of the European Union, OJ 2000 C 364/1, December 2000.

THE HUMAN RIGHTS ACT 1998

8.9 The Human Rights Act 1998 is designed to 'make more directly accessible the rights which British people already enjoy under the Convention'[1] by providing access to those rights through the domestic courts.[2] The two principal mechanisms for giving effect to Convention rights are the interpretative obligation[3]—to interpret all legislation compatibly with the Convention whenever possible—and the obligation imposed on all public authorities, including courts, to act compatibly with Convention rights.[4] Lord Hope expressed the view that the Act would 'subject the entire legal system to a fundamental process of review and, where necessary, reform by the judiciary',[5] but without offending against the sovereignty of Parliament, which is not a public authority[6] and so is exempt from the obligation to act compatibly with the Convention (although there is a clear expectation that it will do so). The interpretative obligation does not affect the validity of primary legislation which is incompatible with the Convention,[7] nor does a declaration of incompatibility affect its validity or oblige Parliament to remedy the incompatibility.[8] The remedy is available but not compulsory. New legislation may be incompatible with the Convention, so long as it declares itself so;[9] and public authorities are not required to act compatibly with the Convention if primary legislation prevents them from doing so. These features of the 1998 Act, designed to reassure those sceptics who feared a shift in the constitutional balance in favour of the judiciary, sets it apart from most Bills of Rights and constitutions, which allow courts to strike down incompatible legislation, and from EC law, which takes precedence over incompatible national law.[10] Much of the debate in the courts since October 2000 has concerned this constitutional balance.

1   *Thoburn v Sunderland CC* [2002] EWHC Admin 195, [2002] 4 All ER 156 (the 'metric martyrs' case).
2   *Rights Brought Home* (Cm 3782, 1997) para 1.19. Sedley LJ's phrase is 'patriating' the ECHR rights: see The Hamlyn Lectures *Freedom, Law and Justice* (1999).
3   Human Rights Act 1998, s 3.
4   HRA 1998, s 6.
5   *R v DPP, ex p Kebeline* [1999] 4 All ER 801, 838.
6   HRA 1998, s 6(3).
7   See *R v Lyons* [2002] UKHL 44, [2003] 1 AC 976, [2002] 4 All ER 1028, para 27.
8   HRA 1998, s 4. See in particular the defiant stance of the government, from December 2004, when the House of Lords ruled that indefinite detention under the Anti-terrorism Crime and Security Act 2001 was unlawful under ECHR, until March 2005, when it was able to introduce a regime of control orders under the Prevention of Terrorism Act 2005.
9   HRA 1998, s 19.
10 *R v Secretary of State for Transport, ex p Factortame (No 2)* [1991] 1 AC 603, HL.

8.10 The rights protected under the Human Rights Act 1998 are the substantive ECHR rights set out in Articles 2–12 and 14, Articles 1–3 of Protocol 1, and Articles1 of Protocol 13, all as read with Articles 16–18.[1] Article 1 of the Convention, the obligation to secure the Convention rights and freedoms to everyone within the jurisdiction, is effected by the 1998 Act itself. The same reason is given for the omission of Article 13 (the right to an effective remedy for violations of the Convention),[2] and clearly courts' and tribunals' powers should be construed with Article 13 in mind.[3] The rights protected have effect subject to designated derogations and reservations.[4] At the time of the entry into force of the Act, the UK derogated from Article 5(3) (the right of a detained person to be brought before a court),[5] and had a reservation in respect of Article 2 of Protocol 1 (education in conformity with parental convictions).[6] The derogation was revoked in April 2001,[7] only to be replaced by a derogation from Article 5(1) in December 2001 to enable the indefinite detention without trial of suspected international terrorists under the Anti-Terrorism Crime and Security Act 2001, which was in turn withdrawn in 2005.[8] The 1998 Act contains provisions for monitoring derogations and reservations to ensure they are not retained after the need for them has gone.[9] Derogations are to have a life of five years,[10] unless extended by Order.[11] Reservations are to be reviewed after five years and the minister must report to Parliament on the review.[12] There is scope for amendment of the Act by Order[13] to bring within the Act further rights in Protocols to be ratified, or signed with a view to ratification, in the future.[14]

1   Human Rights Act 1998, s 1(1). Article 1 of Protocol 13 (prohibition of death penalty in all circumstances) replaced Arts 1 and 2 of Protocol 6 (prohibition of death penalty in peacetime) in the Schedule on 22 June 2004: SI 2004/1574.
2   Lord Irvine, 583 HL Official Report (5th series) col 475, 18 November 1997.
3   583 HL Official Report (5th series) col 479, 18 November 1997. Article 13 'reflects the long-standing principle of our law that where there is a right there should be a remedy. Parliament's intention was, of course, that the Human Rights Act itself should constitute the UK's compliance with Article 13, but this makes it if anything more important that the courts ... should satisfy themselves so far as possible that the common law affords adequate control ... of the legality of official measures which interfere with personal autonomy': *R (on the application of K) v Camden and Islington Health Authority* [2001] EWCA Civ 240, [2002] QB 198. See 8.100 below.
4   HRA 1998, s 1(2).
5   See HRA 1998, s 14 and Sch 3, Pt I (as originally enacted).
6   The reservation was made on 20 March 1952, and shows no signs of being removed. See Human Rights Act 1998, s 15 and Sch 3, Pt II.

⁷ Repealed by SI 2001/1216, Art 4.

⁸ In *A and X v Secretary of State for the Home Department* [2004] UKHL 56, [2005] 2 WLR 87, the House of Lords ruled that the derogation from Article 5 of ECHR was discriminatory and disproportionate, and quashed the derogation order. Part I of Sch 3 to the 1998 Act, containing the derogation, was repealed by the Human Rights Act 1998 (Amendment) Order 2005, SI 2005/1071.

⁹ HRA 1998, ss 16 and 17.

¹⁰ The quashed derogation in *A and X* above had no time limit, so the default provisions of s 16 would have come into play if it had still been in force in December 2006. The indefinite detention provisions of the Anti-terrorism, Crime and Security Act 2001 (ss 21–23) were set to expire 15 months after enactment (14 December 2001) unless extended by order; they were so extended for one year (to 14 March 2004) by the Anti-terrorism, Crime and Security Act 2001(Continuance in Force of Sections 21–23) Order 2003, SI 2003/691, and for a further year by SI 2004/751.

¹¹ HRA 1998, s 16(2); the power to make orders under this section is exercisable by statutory instrument subject to affirmative resolution: s 20(4). See SI 2005/1071.

¹² HRA 1998, s 17.

¹³ HRA 1998, s 1(4). Orders under this section are also subject to the affirmative resolution procedure under s 20(4).

¹⁴ ECHR, Protocol 4 (rights of nationals and aliens in respect of entry, movement within the territory and expulsion) was signed by the UK in 1963, but never ratified because of concerns about the scope of the obligation giving the right of entry to own nationals. The government did not intend to ratify it, according to Lord Williams of Mostyn, Parliamentary Under-Secretary at the Home Office, during the Committee stage in the House of Lords (583 HL Official Report (5th series) col 504, 18 November 1997). Protocol 7 gives aliens procedural rights on expulsion and deals with double jeopardy, appeal rights and compensation in criminal cases, and with spousal equality in marriage. The government indicated its intention to sign and ratify it in due course during the passage of the Act, but has not done so. Protocol 12 (free-standing right not to be discriminated against) has not been signed or ratified by the UK, but Protocol 13 (prohibition of death penalty in any circumstances) has been, and came into force, so far as the UK is concerned, on 1 February 2004. See fn 1 above.

The importance of Strasbourg case law

8.11 The interpretative obligations are set out in sections 2 and 3 of the Human Rights Act 1998. Section 2 requires a court or tribunal determining questions in connection with ECHR rights to take into account the jurisprudence of the ECtHR[1] (and of the Commission before its demise,[2] and of the Committee of Ministers)[3] whenever it was made or given.[4] There is provision under section 2(2) for rules which will indicate how evidence of the relevant jurisprudence is to be given.[5] In practice, Court judgments, Commission opinions and admissibility decisions (of the Commission and now of the court) are the most useful and used jurisprudence. The jurisprudence which must be taken into account is not limited to that on the incorporated Articles; the Lord Chancellor confirmed during the passage of the Act that courts could have regard to jurisprudence on Article 13 of the ECHR, which ought to be of considerable significance for issues such as the intensity of review required by the court.[6]

¹ Including not only judgments (Arts 29, 42, 44), but also decisions (on admissibility under Arts 29 and 35, striking out under Art 37, friendly settlement under Art 39, and on just satisfaction under Art 41), declarations (of admissibility, Arts 28 and 45), and advisory opinions under Art 47: s 2(1)(a). See further per Lord Bingham in *R (on the application of Ullah) v Special Adjudicator* [2004] UKHL 26, [2004] INLR 381 at para 20; *A-G's Reference No 4 of 2002; Sheldrake v DPP* [2004] UKHL 43, [2005] 1 AC 264 at para 33 (UK courts must take the lead from Strasbourg).

2   Human Rights Act 1998, s 2(1)(b), (c) and 21(2). Before the coming into force of Protocol 11, the Commission made the decision on admissibility under Arts 26 and 27 of the (unamended) ECHR, and if the application was declared admissible, would (unless a friendly settlement was reached) prepare a Report stating its opinion on whether the facts found disclosed a breach of the Convention, under Art 31. Decisions and opinions of the Commission under the transitional provisions of Protocol 11 are included: s 21(4).

3   HRA 1998, s 2(1)(d). The Committee of Ministers, comprising political representatives of the Council of Europe's Member States, took unreasoned decisions on the merits in secret under Art 32 of the unamended ECHR, and supervised the implementation of judgments under Art 54. The former function has been removed with Protocol 11 and the only reports which will emanate from it under Art 46 will be on implementation of judgments. As Grosz *et al* remark (Grosz, Beatson and Duffy *Human Rights: the 1998 Act and the European Convention* (2000, Sweet & Maxwell) at para 2.17), the nature of their past proceedings means little juridical significance can attach to their pronouncements.

4   Ie before or after the coming into force either of Protocol 11 or of the Human Rights Act 1998.

5   Rules have been made in relation to Scotland only: see Act of Adjournal (Criminal Procedure Rules Amendment No 2) (Human Rights Act 1998) SSI 2000/315 and Act of Sederunt (Rules of the Court of Session Amendment No 6) (Human Rights Act 1998) SSI 2000/316. ECtHR jurisprudence is in practice cited in the same way as other authority.

6   See in particular, the observations of the court in *Chahal v United Kingdom* (1996) 23 EHRR 413, paras 153–154; *Smith and Grady v United Kingdom* (1999) 29 EHRR 493, para 136; *Lustig-Prean and Beckett v United Kingdom* (1999) 29 EHRR 548.

8.12   The obligation under section 2 of the Human Rights Act 1998 holds the balance between bringing ECHR rights into UK law and retaining the internal constitutional arrangements of the UK, and its common-law case-by-case jurisprudence, by requiring that the courts take Strasbourg jurisprudence into account rather than making that case law binding.[1] UK courts are thus free to develop their own human rights jurisprudence, mindful always that an aggrieved person still has the right to go to the European Court in Strasbourg, once local remedies have been exhausted.[2] Although the Strasbourg case law is not binding, it is likely to be highly persuasive. The House of Lords has held that in the absence of special circumstances, the courts should follow any 'clear and constant' jurisprudence of the European Court.[3] At the same time it has to be remembered that, since the Convention is a living instrument, to be interpreted purposively[4] and dynamically in the light of current conditions,[5] the ECtHR is not itself bound by its own previous case law.[6] In deciding on the scope and content of the rights protected by the Convention, it will often be fruitful to refer to Privy Council cases and to the jurisprudence of Commonwealth countries, with which the UK shares a legal tradition.[7]

1   A judgment of the ECtHR is binding on the UK, not directly binding as a matter of domestic law on the courts: *R v Lyons* [2002] UKHL 44, [2003] 1 AC 976, [2002] 4 All ER 1028 at para 105, per Lord Millett. In *R (on the application of Ullah) v Special Adjudicator* [2004] UKHL 26, [2004] INLR 381, Lord Bingham pointed out (para 20) that the Convention was an international instrument whose authoritative interpretation came from the Strasbourg court, and the national court should not without strong reason dilute or weaken the effect of Strasbourg case law.

2   *Rights brought home,* para 2.5, Home Secretary Jack Straw at 306 HC Official Report (6th series) col 769, 16 February 1998. 'Our courts must be free to develop human rights jurisprudence ... and to move out in new directions': Lord Chancellor, 583 HL Official Report (5th series) col 783, 24 November 1997. The Lord Chancellor also said that 'it is possible that [our courts] might give a successful lead to Strasbourg': 583 HL Official Report (5th series) col 514, 18 November 1997. The 'dialogue' between the higher courts and the European Court has ranged from the House of Lords correcting ECtHR misconceptions about English law (see e g *Lyons* (fn 1 above) para 46; *Z v United Kingdom*

(2001) 34 EHRR 97, correcting its reasoning in *Osman v United Kingdom* (1998) 29 EHRR 245) to the most careful analysis and adoption of the Strasbourg case-law (see *R (on the application of Ullah) v Special Adjudicator* [2004] UKHL 26, [2004] INLR 381 and *R (on the application of Razgar) v Secretary of State for the Home Department* [2004] UKHL 27, [2004] 2 AC 368).

3   In *R (on the application of Alconbury Developments Ltd) v Secretary of State for the Environment, Transport and the Regions* [2001] UKHL 23, [2003] 2 AC 295 (per Lord Slynn); *R (on the application of Ullah) v Special Adjudicator* [2004] UKHL 26, [2004] INLR 381 at para 20. See also *R (on the application of Anderson) v Secretary of State for the Home Department* [2002] UKHL 46, [2003] 1 AC 837, [2003] UKHRR 112, and *R (Amin) v Secretary of State for the Home Department* [2003] UKHL 51, [2004] 1 AC 653. The Court of Appeal could find no such 'clear and constant' jurisprudence on the issue of damages for a breach of Art 8 ECHR, in *Anufrijeva v Southwark London Borough Council; R (on the application of N) v Secretary of State for the Home Department; R (on the application of M) v Secretary of State for the Home Department* [2003] EWCA Civ 1406, [2004] 1 All ER 833. In *N v Secretary of State for the Home Department* [2003] EWCA Civ 1369, [2004] 1 WLR 1182 Laws LJ reluctantly followed ECtHR jurisprudence on Art 3, but gave it a highly restrictive application: see below 8.52.

4   The objectives of the ECHR should be taken into account, particularly its aim to give full and practical effect to human rights: *Golder v United Kingdom* (1975) 1 EHRR 524; *Artico v Italy* (1980) 3 EHRR 1. However, the Privy Council's observation in *Boyce (Lennox) and Joseph (Jeffrey) v R* (PC appeal 99/2002, 7 July 2004), on the Barbados Constitution is apposite: 'the living instrument principle has its reasons, logic and limitations. It is not a magic ingredient which can be stirred into the judicial pot, together with 'international obligations', 'generous construction' and other such phrases, sprinkled with a cherished aphorism or two and brewed up into a potion which will make the Constitution mean something it obviously does not.'

5   See 8.33 below. For similar 'dynamic interpretation' in the UK courts see e g *Fitzpatrick v Sterling Housing Association Ltd* [1999] 4 All ER 705, [2000] 1 FLR 271, HL; *Ghaidan v Mendoza* [2004] UKHL 30, [2004] 3 All ER 411, HL.

6   Although for legal certainty and the orderly development of the case law it usually follows its own precedents (*Sheffield and Horsham v United Kingdom* (1998) 27 EHRR 163), in *Goodwin v United Kingdom* [2002] 2 FCR 577 the court departed from the decision in *Sheffield and Horsham* to rule that, in the light of rapidly changing ideas about relationships and marriage, the UK's failure to give recognition to post-operative trans-sexuals was now in breach of Arts 8 and 12.

7   The citation of Commonwealth authority has already become common in human rights cases; see e g *Ahmed v Secretary of State for the Home Department, and Patel v Secretary of State for the Home Department* [1998] INLR 570, approving the Australian case of *Minister for Immigration and Ethnic Affairs v Teoh* (1995) 183 CLR 273. The House of Lords considered New Zealand and Australian law in the post-Goodwin case of *Bellinger v Bellinger* [2003] UKHL 21, [2003] 2 AC 467 (incompatibility of law, not recognising the change of sex of post-operative transsexual, with Arts 8 and 12 ECHR), and Canadian law in *R (on the application of Ullah) v Special Adjudicator* [2004] UKHL 26, [2004] INLR 381 (para 23) and *R (on the application of Pretty) v DPP* [2001] UKHL 61, [2002] 1 AC 800 (assisted suicide).

Interpretative obligation to achieve compatibility with Human Rights

8.13 The second interpretative obligation requires all legislation—primary and subordinate, past and future—to be read and given effect so far as possible in a way which is compatible with ECHR rights.[1] This interpretative formula is borrowed from EC law,[2] but is a fundamental break with normal principles of statutory interpretation (the 'true meaning',[3] the 'plain meaning of the words',[4] the 'intention of the legislature',[5] so as to ensure that domestic law in time conforms to the basic human rights norms expressed in the Convention.[6] In cases engaging fundamental rights, the courts must 'strive to find an interpretation of legislation which is consistent with Convention rights so far as the language of the legislation allows, and only in the last resort to conclude that the legislation is simply incompatible with them'.[7] This does not depend on statutory ambiguity, as the House of Lords said it did in *Brind*.[8] In seeking a meaning which will prevent incompatibility, the courts are not bound by previous interpretations,[9] and are becoming accustomed to 'reading in' safeguards by way of provisos to apparently absolute restrictions.[10] They are also learning to 'read down' provisions which are on their face incompatible with Convention rights,[11] by limiting the scope and effect of the words to enable compatibility.[12]

---

[1]   Human Rights Act 1998, s 3(1)(a). It does not affect the validity and continuing operation or enforcement of incompatible legislation, however—another balancing mechanism with parliamentary sovereignty: s 3(1)(b) and (c). Although the rule of construction in s 3 applies to all legislation, whenever enacted, it cannot be used to introduce retrospective rights or to change the substantive law retrospectively, so as to apply the Act to events pre-dating it, except in the limited circumstances covered by s 22(4): *Wainwright v Home Office* [2001] EWCA Civ 2081, [2002] 3 WLR 405; see also *R v Lambert* [2001] UKHL 37, [2001] 3 WLR 206, HL; *R v Kansal (No 2)* [2001] UKHL 62, [2002] 2 AC 69; *Pearce v Governing Body of Mayfield Secondary School* [2001] EWCA Civ 1347.

[2]   *Marleasing SA v La Comercial Internacional de Alimentacion SA* C-106/89 [1992] 1 CMLR 305, ECJ.

[3]   In practice this will mean 'a rebuttable presumption in favour of an interpretation consistent with Convention rights': Lord Steyn 'Incorporation and Devolution—A few reflections on the changing scene' [1998] EHRLR 153. A ministerial statement of compatibility under s 19 of the Human Rights Act 1998 (see 8.24 below) will support such a presumption.

[4]   Bennion *Statutory Interpretation* (4rd edn, 2002) Butterworths, pp 467ff.

[5]   Bennion above, pp 819ff.

[6]   *R v DPP, ex p Kebilene* [1999] 4 All ER 801 at 838.

[7]   583 HL Official Report (5th series) col 535, 18 November 1997.

[8]   *R v Secretary of State for the Home Department, ex p Brind* [1991] 1 AC 696; see 8.5 above.

[9]   Starmer *European Human Rights Law* (1999) LAG, p 16.

[10]   As *in R v A* [2001] UKHL 25, [2001] 1 AC 45, where the House of Lords read in a discretion into what on its face was a mandatory requirement to limit cross-examination of a rape victim, to ensure compatibility with fair trial rights. In *R (on the application of Zenovics) v Secretary of State for the Home Department* [2002] EWCA Civ 273, [2002] INLR 219, the Court of Appeal read words into Sch 4, para 9(2) to the Immigration and Asylum Act 1999 (certification limiting appeal rights) to avoid the unintended effect of depriving an appellant of a human rights appeal when the Secretary of State certified his or her asylum claim manifestly unfounded. However, the boundary between interpretation and judicial trespass on the legislative function was reached in *Re S (Care Order: Implementation of Care Plan)* [2002] UKHL 10, [2002] 2 AC 291, where the House of Lords reversed the Court of Appeal's attempt to write in a mechanism for further review of care orders which Parliament had omitted; this was an 'impermissible amendment of a statutory scheme which (if necessary for compatibility with the Convention) only Parliament could effect'. And in *Bellinger v Bellinger* [2003] UKHL 21, [2003] 2 AC 467 the House of Lords emphasised that judges' function is to interpret, not to legislate (paras 67, per Lord Hope, 98, per Lord Hobhouse). See also *R (on the application of Anderson) v Secretary of State for the Home Department* [2002] UKHL 46, [2003] 1 AC 467.

[11]   See *R v Secretary of State for the Home Department, ex p Pierson* [1998] AC 539 at 573–575, per Lord Browne-Wilkinson, 587–590, per Lord Steyn.

[12]   See eg *R v DPP, ex p Kebilene* [1999] 4 All ER 801, HL; *R v A* [2001] UKHL 25, [2001] 1 AC 45, at para 44, per Lord Steyn. See further *R v Lambert* [2001] UKHL 37, [2002] 2 AC 545; *R v Johnstone* [2003] UKHL 28, [2003] 1 WLR 1736; and *A-G's Reference No 4 of 2002; Sheldrake v DPP* [2004] UKHL 43 on when (on the same wording) a reverse burden of proof on a defendant in a criminal trial should be read as 'evidential' and when 'persuasive' to ensure compatibility with Art 6 fair trial rights.

8.14 The interpretative obligation also applies to subordinate legislation such as immigration rules.[1] Thus in *Boadi*[2] the Court of Appeal held that the requirement that an adopted child has 'lost or broken her ties with her family of origin' must be read as referring to ties of responsibility, not of affection, to be compatible with Article 8 ECHR.[3] If it is impossible to interpret a provision in subordinate legislation in a way which is compatible with ECHR rights, and there is nothing in the parent Act requiring this incompatibility,[4] the offending provision may be disapplied or struck down as *ultra vires* the parent Act, as the Court of Appeal did with the rule preventing access to the Tribunal in *Saleem*.[5] However, it should be noted that the Tribunal has no power to strike down incompatible rules,[6] although it can set aside an immigration decision which is unlawful as being incompatible with the appellant's Convention rights, regardless of whether it is in accordance with the rules.[7]

[1] In *R v Secretary of State for the Home Department, ex p Arman Ali* [2000] INLR 89, Collins J interpreted the rules relating to recourse to public funds so as to give effect to Art 8 ECHR obligations.
[2] *Boadi v Entry Clearance Officer, Ghana* [2002] UKIAT 01323, [2003] INLR 54.
[3] See also *Abdulla (Intekab)* [2002] UKIAT 07516, where the Tribunal read para 281(v) of the immigration rules (for admission of spouse, the couple must have no recourse to public funds) as allowing the spouse to depend on the sponsor's savings from disability allowance 'to ensure compliance with ECHR obligations. To prevent someone qualifying for family reunion solely on the basis of inevitable financial hardship could in certain circumstances, particularly where disability prevents a sponsor working, amount to disrespect for private and family life or discrimination contrary to Art 14 with Art 8.'
[4] For example, if the rules are made in exercise of a general rule-making power such as that under Immigration Act 1971, s 3(2).
[5] *R v Secretary of State for the Home Department, ex p Saleem* [2000] 4 All ER 814, [2000] Imm AR 529, [2000] INLR 413.
[6] See *Pardeepan v Secretary of State for the Home Department* [2000] INLR 447; *Koprinov* (01TH00095) and 18.107 below.
[7] Nationality, Immigration and Asylum Act 2002, s 84(1)(c), (g); but see now the restrictions placed upon this power by the Court of Appeal in *Huang v Secretary of State for the Home Department* [2005] EWCA Civ 105, (2005) Sol Jo LB 297.

8.15 If incompatibility of primary legislation cannot be remedied by the new method of construction, or subordinate legislation cannot be read compatibly because the parent Act prevents this, the only remedy is a declaration of incompatibility.[1] A declaration of incompatibility may be made only by the higher courts, ie the High Court, the Court of Appeal, the Privy Council and the House of Lords, and in Scotland the High Court of Judiciary (except when it sits as a trial court) and the Court of Session.[2] The Special Immigration Appeals Commission may make a declaration of incompatibility in a derogation matter.[3] It is a discretionary remedy; the court may decide to leave the incompatibility (although it is hard to reconcile this with its own duty as a public authority to act compatibly with the ECHR, under section 6).[4] If a court is considering making a declaration, the Crown is entitled to notice[5] and to be joined as a party.[6] In another example of the balancing of judicial guardianship of fundamental rights with parliamentary sovereignty, a declaration of incompatibility does not affect the continuing validity, operation and enforcement of the incompatible legislation, nor does it bind the parties.[7] If a minister insisted on action (such as removal) under legislation which has been held incompatible with the Convention, however, it is likely that the court would grant a stay pending parliamentary consideration of a remedial amendment. The declaration empowers, but does not oblige Parliament to remedy the incompatibility,[8] and if Parliament does not do so the victim can apply to the ECtHR as before.

1   Human Rights Act 1998, s 4(1)–(4). In the first two years of the Act's operation, nine declarations of incompatibility were made: see 'Two years of the Human Rights Act', in (2003) EHRLR 14–23. Recent cases involve the right of transsexuals to marry (*Bellinger v Bellinger* [2003] UKHL 21, [2003] 2 AC 467) and the rights of mental patients: *R (on the application of M) v Secretary of State for Health* (2003) UKHRR 746. In *International Transport Roth GmbH v Secretary of State for the Home Department* [2002] EWCA Civ 158, [2003] QB 728, the Court of Appeal held the statutory scheme penalising carriers of clandestine entrants (Immigration and Asylum Act 1999, ss 32–37) incompatible with Art 6 and Protocol 1, Art 1 because of the mandatory and inflexible nature of the penalties, the lack of fair proceedings to challenge penalties and the draconian powers of detention of transporters: see 14.69 below. Measures denying all support to late asylum claimants (Nationality, Immigration and Asylum Act 2002, s 55) avoided a similar fate by saving provisions enabling support to be given 'to the extent necessary to prevent a breach of an applicant's Convention rights': see *R (on the application of Q) v Secretary of State for the Home Department* [2003] EWCA Civ 364, [2003] UKHRR 607, [2003] 2 All ER 905.
2   Human Rights Act 1998, s 4(5).
3   Anti-terrorism, Crime and Security Act 2001, s 30(2). On an appeal originating from a decision by SIAC under this section in *A and X v Secretary of State for the Home Department* [2004] UKHL 56, [2005] 2 WLR 87 the House of Lords ruled that the derogation from Art 5 ECHR was discriminatory and disproportionate, quashed the Derogation Order and and declared s 23 of the Anti-terrorism, Crime and Security Act 2001, which allowed indefinite detention without trial of foreign nationals, incompatible with Arts 5 and 14 of ECHR, since it addressed only the threat of terrorism posed by non-nationals, while that threat was as likely to emanate from nationals.
4   Human Rights Act 1998, s 6(3)(a); see below. But in *Bellinger v Bellinger* [2003] UKHL 21, [2003] 2 AC 467, the House of Lords rejected the Crown's submissions to the effect that a declaration was unnecessary since the government was committed to changing the law after the adverse decision of the ECtHR in *Goodwin v United Kingdom* (28957/95) [2002] IRLR 664, holding it desirable 'in a sensitive case that this House, as the court of final appeal in this country, should formally record that the present state of statute law is incompatible with the Convention.'
5   HRA 1998, s 5(1).
6   HRA 1998, s 5(2). The court will also be sympathetic to public interest organisations applying to be joined as interveners: see 8.26 below.
7   HRA 1998, s 4(6). The purpose of the declaration is to put Parliament under pressure to remedy the incompatibility: Lord Chancellor, 583 HL Official Report (5th series) col 546, 18 November 1997. Since the offending legislation continues in force, there can be no award of damages when a declaration is made: *Re K (a child)* [2001] 2 All ER 719, CA, paras 128–130, although costs should be awarded.
8   Parliament is not a 'public authority' for the purposes of the Human Rights Act 1998: s 6(3) (except for the judicial committee of the House of Lords: s 6(4)), and has no obligation to act compatibly with the ECHR, save under international law. Detailed description of the mechanism for remedying statutory incompatibility is beyond the scope of this work. In essence, the offending legislation may simply be amended when there is parliamentary time, or in cases where the minister considers there are compelling reasons not to wait, he or she may amend the legislation by an order under s 10, known as a remedial order. HRA 1998, Sch 2 contains the fairly complex procedural requirements for a valid remedial order.

The duty on public authorities

8.16   The interpretative obligation is one of the two mechanisms to ensure the compliance of UK law with the ECHR. The other is the obligation on public authorities to act compatibly with the Convention. Section 6 of the Human Rights Act 1998 makes it unlawful for a public authority to act in a way incompatible with a Convention right,[1] unless the authority could not have acted differently because of a provision of primary legislation,[2] or because it was acting to enforce or give effect to such an (incompatible) provision.[3] An act includes a failure to act.[4] A public authority includes a court or tribunal[5] but not Parliament (except the House of Lords in its judicial capacity),[6] and also includes a person[7] some of whose functions are of a public nature.[8] The jurisprudence relating to judicial review will be relevant in determining who is a 'public authority',[9] as will be the Strasbourg jurisprudence on bodies which engage the responsibility of the State for the purposes of the Convention.[10] Purely public authorities such as immigration officers must always act compatibly; private bodies which have private and public functions must do so only in relation to their public functions.[11] Thus, while a security company is delivering bullion (a commercial operation) it has no obligation to act compatibly with the Convention;[12] but while it is running a removal centre, it clearly does; it is a public authority in performing this function.[13] The Court of Appeal applied a restrictive test in *R (on the application of Heather) v Leonard Cheshire Foundation*,[14] but the House of Lords moved to a more realistic (and generous) approach to the exercise of public functions by private bodies in *Aston Cantlow*.[15] They ruled that a function is a public one when the government has taken responsibility for it in the public interest, and the attribution of public authority responsibilities to private sector bodies is justified on the basis that a private body operating to discharge a government programme is likely to exercise a degree of power and control over the realisation of the individual's Convention rights which in the absence of delegation would be State power and control.[16] Despite this guidance, the lower courts have continued to apply an institutional rather than a functional approach to 'public functions' which, as the Joint Committee on Human Rights[17] has commented, leaves real gaps and inadequacies in human rights protection through inconsistent and restrictive interpretation.[18] However, an airline or other carrier refusing boarding to an inadequately documented passenger performs a commercial, as opposed to a public function on the current interpretation of the law.[19]

---

[1]   Human Rights Act 1998, s 6(1).
[2]   HRA 1998, s 6(2)(a). The provision of primary legislation must of course be read compatibly if possible, and if this is possible, or if the legislation does not compel the authority to act in the way it has, the authority cannot rely on this exception. See *Hampson v Department of Education and Science* [1991] 1 AC 171, [1990] 2 All ER 513, and see discussion in Grosz, Beatson and Duffy, 8.11 fn 3 above, paras 4.21ff.
[3]   HRA 1998, s 6(2)(b).
[4]   HRA 1998, s 6(6). This accords with Strasbourg jurisprudence on positive obligations: see 8.34 below. A decision whether or not to prosecute is an 'act' for these purposes: *Brown v Stott* [2001] 2 All ER 97, [2001] 2 WLR 817, PC; *R (on the application of Pretty) v DPP* [2001] UKHL 61, [2002] 1 AC 800 (para 75, per Lord Hope) (refusal to give undertaking not to prosecute is justiciable in exceptional circumstances where the matter cannot be tested at a criminal trial or on appeal). But a failure to make a decision is not a 'decision' for the purpose of an immigration appeal: *Bouras* [2002] UKIAT 00772 (decided under the Immigration and Asylum Act 1999, s 65 which gave a right of appeal against a 'decision relating to ... entitlement to enter or remain'). Failure to take a decision is challengeable by way of judicial review: see *R v Secretary of State for the Home Department, ex p Phansopkar* [1976] QB 606 (common law).
[5]   HRA 1998, s 6(3)(a). A 'public authority' does not have to be in the UK, so would include consular officials such as entry clearance officers acting in relation to UK immigration control.

⁶ HRA 1998, s 6(3), (4). Thus, failure to bring legislation into force (such as the repealed automatic bail provisions of Part 4 of the 1999 Act, which were never brought into force) is not an 'act' capable of being unlawful: HRA 1998, s 6(6).

⁷ This includes legal persons, ie companies such as Group 4, but probably not unincorporated associations.

⁸ HRA 1998, s 6(3)(b).

⁹ A body is 'public' if (for example) the source of its power is statutory or prerogative or it' is institutionally or structurally controlled by government, whether the power it exercises is 'governmental in nature' and would be exercised by government if not by the body concerned: *R v Panel on Take-overs and Mergers, ex p Datafin plc* [1987] QB 815.

¹⁰ For a useful discussion on the scope of 'public authorities' and 'public functions' see Grosz, Beatson and Duffy (at 8.11 fn 3 above), paras 4.02–4.15.

¹¹ HRA 1998, s 6(5). The Lord Chancellor accepted that a private security company would be exercising public functions in its management of a contracted-out prison: 583 HL Official Report (5th series) col 811, 24 November 1997.

¹² *Griffiths v Smith* [1941] AC 170 at 205.

¹³ Under Immigration and Asylum Act 1999, ss 148–157 and Schs 11–13. The element of compulsion was held important in *R (on the application of A) v Partnerships in Care Ltd* [2002] EWHC 529 (Admin), [2002] 1 WLR 2611, where the Court of Appeal held that private sector care providers who were authorised to detain patients under the Mental Health Act 1983 were performing a public function.

¹⁴ [2002] EWCA Civ 366, [2002] 2 All ER 936, holding that a private charitable organisation which houses vulnerable people who have been placed there and funded by a local authority or housing authority is not exercising a public function; the fact that a body performs an activity which otherwise a public authority would be under a duty to perform does not mean such performance is inevitably public, and the role performed by the charity was 'manifestly' not public; it was not standing in the shoes of the public authority, unlike the housing association in *Poplar Housing and Regeneration Community Association Ltd v Donoghue* [2001] EWCA Civ 595, [2002] QB 48, [2001] 4 All ER 604 (a registered social landlord which took transfers of properties from a London borough, which was held to stand in the Council's shoes as a 'public authority'). According to this formulation, landlords contracting with NASS or local authorities to provide accommodation for asylum seekers would not be public authorities for the purposes of the Act.

¹⁵ *Aston Cantlow and Wilmcote with Billesley Parochial Church Council v Wallbank* [2003] UKHL 37 [2003] UKHRR 919, HL.

¹⁶ *Aston Cantlow and Wilmcote with Billesley Parochial Church Council v Wallbank.*

¹⁷ For the Joint Committee on Human Rights see 8.24 below.

¹⁸ Joint Committee on Human Rights, 7th report 2003–4 session, 'The meaning of "public authority" under the Human Rights Act', 3 March 2004, HL 39/HC 382.

¹⁹ See *R v Secretary of State for the Home Department, ex p Hoverspeed* [1999] INLR 591. Even if this was held to be a public function, the carrier might still argue that it is giving effect to provisions of primary legislation, ie the carriers' liability provisions of the Immigration and Asylum Act 1999, s 40 and is therefore not obliged to act compatibly with the ECHR: HRA 1998, s 6(2)(b).

8.17 The requirement that courts and tribunals act compatibly with the ECHR embraces both judicial and procedural or administrative functions of the court. Despite the jurisprudence of the ECtHR indicating that immigration and asylum matters do not relate to 'civil rights and obligations' and so are not within the province of Article 6 ECHR,[1] the legislation on immigration and asylum appeals, and the procedure rules, are clearly intended to reflect Article 6 requirements of due process, openness and fairness.[2] In cases involving human rights, the appellate authorities and the courts thus have a dual function: to review the decision of an immigration officer or the Secretary of State, or of a lower court or tribunal, for compatibility with the Convention, and to act compatibly with the Convention themselves.[3] In the performance of this dual function, the courts are bound to determine for themselves whether the act the appellant complains of is unlawful. This involves determining:

(a)   whether there is a Convention right in play;

(b)   whether any exceptions are permitted in respect of that right under the Convention or whether any reservation or derogation applies;

(c)   if so, whether the exception is provided for by the domestic law (ie the Immigration Acts or the Rules, or any relevant published policy);

(d)   in the case of a qualified right, whether the government has a legitimate aim in applying the exception;

(e)   in such a case, whether the application of the exception is necessary to achieve the legitimate aim, ie is proportionate to it.

1   *Maaouia v France* (2001) 33 EHRR 42. See 8.72 below.
2   The language of the Asylum and Immigration Tribunal (Procedure) Rules 2005, SI 2005/230, r 54, setting out exceptions to the norm of public hearings, mirrors the language of ECHR, Art 6(1), for example. See 18.150 below.
3   However, the argument that the courts, as an organ of State, are obliged to give effect to the State's international obligations, is a fallacy which would completely undermine the principle that the courts apply domestic law, not international treaties: *R v Lyons* [2002] UKHL 44, [2003] 1 AC 976, [2002] 4 All ER 1028 at para 40, per Lord Hoffmann. The Tribunal has referred to its own function as a public authority in ensuring human rights-compliant decisions in *MNM* (00TH02423) and in *SK* [2002] UKIAT 05613 (starred). But the requirement that the court, as a public authority, act compatibly with the Convention does not give it a roving commission to detect breaches of human rights not raised by the applicant, or to ignore procedural requirements such as time limits: *Xhezo* (01TH00625) (12 July 2001, unreported), IAT.

Proportionality and deference

8.18   The proportionality test is clearly more rigorous, objective and intrusive (in demanding a greater degree of justification) than the *Wednesbury* test whose borders, even in a human rights case, are set by mere rationality. The ECtHR has repeatedly made clear that, in determining whether a breach of the ECHR can be justified under Articles 8(2) or 10(2), the court's supervision goes beyond ascertaining whether discretion has been exercised reasonably, carefully or in good faith, and requires it to determine whether it was 'proportionate to the legitimate aim pursued' and whether the reasons adduced by the national authorities to justify it are 'relevant and sufficient'.[1] In the 'gays in the military' cases of *Smith and Grady v United Kingdom* and *Lustig-Prean and Beckett*[2] the court held that 'the threshold at which the High Court and Court of Appeal[3] could find the Ministry of Defence policy, of dismissing gays from the army, irrational was placed so high, that it effectively excluded any consideration by the domestic courts of the question of whether the interference with the applicants' rights answered a pressing social need or was proportionate to the national security and public order aims pursued, principles which lie at the heart of the court's analysis of complaints under Article 8 of the Convention'.[4] In *Daly*,[5] Lord Steyn pointed out that 'There is a material difference between the *Wednesbury* and *ex p Smith* grounds of review and the approach of proportionality applicable in respect of review where Convention rights are at stake.' He adopted the threefold test applied in *de Freitas*:[6] whether (i) the legislative objective is sufficiently important to justify limiting a fundamental right; (ii) the measures designed to meet the legislative objective are rationally connected to it; (iii) the means used to impair the right or freedom are no more than is necessary to accomplish the objective, emphasising the importance of the third criterion, that of necessity. The proportionality test, he added, would require attention to be given to the weight of the factors involved and not merely whether they had been taken into consideration: 'It may require the reviewing court to assess the balance which the decision-maker has struck, not merely whether it is within the range of rational or reasonable decisions. It may require attention to be paid to the relative weight accorded to interests and considerations ... even the heightened scrutiny test developed in ex p *Smith* is not necessarily appropriate to the protection of human rights.'[7] Lord Cooke, concurring, said it was time to bury *Wednesbury* in human rights cases.[8] *Samaroo*[9] was the first post-Human Rights Act attempt of the Court of Appeal to apply the proportionality test as set out in *Daly* in an immigration context. The test was held to be whether the decision-maker has struck 'a fair balance' between the interests of the individual and those of the community, a test which has been followed in countless subsequent cases.[10] In *Huang* the Court of Appeal emphasised once more that the proportionality test, not a *Wednesbury* review, was to be applied in human rights cases.[11]

[1]   *Sunday Times Ltd v United Kingdom (No 2)* (1991) 14 EHRR 229; *Hertel v Switzerland* (1998) 28 EHRR 534.
[2]   (1999) 29 EHRR 493; *Lustig-Prean and Beckett v United Kingdom* (1999) 29 EHRR 548.
[3]   *R v Ministry of Defence, ex p Smith* [1996] QB 517.
[4]   *Smith and Grady v United Kingdom* at para 138.
[5]   *R (on the application of Daly) v Secretary of State for the Home Department* [2001] UKHL 26, [2001] 2 AC 532.
[6]   *de Freitas v Ministry of Agriculture, Fisheries, Lands and Housing* [1999] 1 AC 69, [1998] 3 WLR 675.
[7]   *R (on the application of Daly) v Secretary of State for the Home Department* [2001] UKHL 26, [2001] 2 AC 532 at para 27.
[8]   *Daly* at para 32.
[9]   *R (on the application of Samaroo) v Secretary of State for the Home Department* [2001] EWCA Civ 1139, [2001] UKHRR 1150, [2002] INLR 55 and *R (on the application of Sezek) v Secretary of State for the Home Department* [2001] EWCA Civ 795, [2002] 1 WLR 348.
[10] The test derives from *Sporrong and Lonnroth v Sweden* (1982) 5 EHRR 35, a decision relating to a successful claim under Art 1 of Protocol 1 that the complainants' right to peaceful enjoyment of properties they owned in central Stockholm had been blighted by planning laws.
[11] *Huang v Secretary of State for the Home Department* [2005] EWCA Civ 105, (2005) Sol Jo LB 297, but see 8.20–8.21 below.

8.19   There has been intense debate as to the existence and scope of the 'margin of discretion' or 'discretionary area of judgment' to be afforded to ministers and lower courts by the court reviewing the decision for compatibility with the ECHR,[1] and whether the same margin applies in judicial review and statutory appeal. In *ex p Kebilene*[2] Lord Hope said of the 'discretionary area of judgment':

'In this area difficult choices may have to be made by the executive or the legislature between the rights of the individual and the needs of society. In some circumstances it will be appropriate for the court to recognise that there is an area of judgment within which the judiciary will defer, on democratic grounds, to the considered opinion of the elected body or person whose act or decision is said to be incompatible with the Convention ... It will be easier for such an area of judgment to be recognised where the Convention itself requires a balance to be struck, much less so where the right is stated in terms which are unqualified.

It will be easier for it to be recognised where the issues involve questions of social or economic policy, much less so where the rights are of high constitutional importance or are of a kind where the courts are especially well placed to assess the need for protection ...'

Lord Hope saw this as a constitutional question, marking out the boundaries between the considered opinions of the elected body and those of the judiciary.[3] The constitutional basis of deference, and its flexibility in different contexts, has been emphasised by the Court of Appeal in a string of cases since. In *Roth*[4] Laws LJ said that the reach of deference which judges would pay to the democratic decision-maker, their giving and withholding of it, was the 'second means by which the courts resolve the tension between parliamentary sovereignty and fundamental rights in our intermediate constitution' (the first was the rule of construction under section 3). More deference would be due, he said, to an Act of Parliament than to a decision of the executive; more when the right itself was balanced, more where the subject-matter is peculiarly within executive or legislative constitutional responsibility (such as defence and security of borders, including immigration control), and more or less according to whether the subject matter lies more readily within the potential experience of what he called the democratic powers or the courts.[5] In *Farrakhan*[6] the Court of Appeal emphasised the Secretary of State's relatively wide margin of discretion in immigration cases. This was a judgment which involved the personal decision of the Secretary of State and could, therefore, be classed as the opinion of an elected representative and set apart from more routine immigration decisions. The trend in the domestic case law, however, extends this deference well beyond personal ministerial decisions. Routine decisions to deport and so forth, which used to be the bread and butter of adjudicators, were treated as matters of policy, requiring a large margin of executive discretion to be accorded to the Secretary of State, the high watermark of this trend being the careful deconstruction of proportionality by Dyson LJ in *R (on the application of Samaroo) v Secretary of State for the Home Department*,[7] and its application beyond judicial review to statutory appeal, which we deal with in the next paragraph. The Court of Appeal decision in *Huang* rightly rejected the *Wednesbury* approach and re-armed immigration judges with full power to carry out a merits review on proportionality grounds, not some neo-*Wednesbury* test. However, the focus of this review is so reduced in cases involving acknowledged departure from the immigration rules or relevant policy that the only issue for the immigration judge is whether the case is truly exceptional.[8]

[1] See Lester and Pannick *Human Rights Law and Practice* (2nd edn, 2004, Butterworths), p 74, para 3.21.

[2] *R v DPP, ex p Kebilene* [1999] 3 WLR 972, per Lord Hope at 993–994, and see *Brown v Stott* [2001] 2 All ER 97, PC.

[3] See also Lord Steyn in *Daly* above para 28.

[4] *International Transport Roth GmbH v Secretary of State for the Home Department* [2002] EWCA Civ 158, [2003] QB 728, paras 83–87.

[5] Thus, deference may be due because of the particular knowledge and expertise of the decision maker; see *R v Chief Constable of Sussex, ex p International Trader's Ferry Ltd* [1999] 2 AC 418 (involving the deployment of scarce police resources, where the court deferred to the considered opinion of the chief constable), or of a tribunal with specialist knowledge of the subject matter: see *B v Secretary of State for the Home Department* [2000] Imm AR 478, paras 24–27, per Sedley LJ. See also Singh, Hunt and Demetriou, 'Is there a role for the "Margin of Appreciation" in national law after the Human Rights

Act?' [1999] 1 EHRLR 15–22, which suggests other relevant factors, including whether the aim of the measure under review is to promote other human rights, whether the applicants are particularly vulnerable or eg members of unpopular minorities, and whether the context is one of fairly constant standards throughout democratic societies or one where no discernible standards have yet emerged. And see Clayton and Tomlinson *The Law of Human Rights* (2000, OUP), p 253.

6   *R (on the application of Farrakhan) v Secretary of State for the Home Department* [2002] EWCA Civ 606, [2002] QB 1391, [2002] 3 WLR 481, [2002] Imm AR 447, [2002] INLR 257,where the court ascribed the wide margin of discretion (i) to the weight attached by the Strasbourg court to the right under international law to control the entry of aliens and (ii) to the democratic accountability of the Secretary of State.

7   *R (on the application of Samaroo) v Secretary of State for the Home Department* [2001] EWCA Civ 1139, [2001] UKHRR 1150, [2002] INLR 55 and *R (on the application of Sezek) v Secretary of State for the Home Department* [2001] EWCA Civ 795, [2002] 1 WLR 348.

8   *Huang v Secretary of State for the Home Department* [2005] EWCA Civ 105, (2005) Sol Jo LB 297, paras 46, 49 and 60.

8.20 How, in practice, do the proportionality test and due deference work together? The relationship between the courts and the executive in the court's exercise of the proportionality review required by the statute has given rise to some difficulty. In *Mahmood*,[1] the Master of the Rolls stated that the primary decision on proportionality was for the executive, subject to a *Wednesbury*-style review:

'The court does not substitute its own decision for that of the executive. It reviews the decision of the executive ... there will often be an area of discretion permitted to the executive of a country before a response can be demonstrated to infringe the Convention ...

When anxiously scrutinising an executive decision that interferes with human rights, the court will ask the question, applying an objective test, whether the decision-maker could reasonably have concluded that the interference was necessary to achieve one or more of the legitimate aims recognised by the Convention.'

As we have seen, the House of Lords disapproved of this formulation of scrutiny and review in *Daly*.[2] But subsequently the courts returned to what we have called the neo-*Wednesbury* approach of *Mahmood*, paying the merest lip service to the criticisms in *Daly* and usually citing the passage in Lord Steyn's speech to the effect that the more intense review under the proportionality approach does not mean a shift to a merits review. In *Samaroo*,[3] the Court of Appeal carefully explained the neo-*Wednesbury* position. First, *Daly* did not assist in determining the proper test to apply. Secondly, it is not the task of the court to make up its own mind on the question of proportionality. The function of the court is to decide whether the Secretary of State has struck the balance fairly between the conflicting interests between the individual and the State. Thirdly, in doing this the court must recognise and allow to the Secretary of State a discretionary area of judgement. Fourthly, in an Article 8 case involving the deportation of a foreign national convicted of serious drug offences, the margin of discretion should be a significant one. Fifthly, the right to respect for family life is not regarded as a right which requires a high degree of constitutional protection. In *Edore* [4] Simon Brown LJ said it was 'unhelpful' to characterise proportionality as a question of law, and went on to approve the formulation of Moses J in *Ala*:[5]

'... a breach will only occur where the decision is outwith the range of reasonable responses as to where a fair balance lies between the conflicting interests ... the decision of the Secretary of State in relation to Article 8 cannot be said to have infringed the claimant's rights *merely because a different view as to where the balance should fairly be struck might have been reached.*' (our emphasis)

Samaroo was a judicial review of the Secretary of State's refusal to revoke a deportation decision and did not involve the powers of the appellate authority on a statutory appeal. But in *M (Croatia)*, a starred tribunal took the dicta in *Ala* and *Edore* to their logical conclusion, ie back to the *Wednesbury* formulation disapproved of in *Daly*: and applied it to adjudicators, who 'should normally hold that a decision to remove is unlawful *only when the disproportionality is so great that no reasonable Secretary of State could remove*'.[6] (our emphasis)

1 *R v Secretary of State for the Home Department, ex p Mahmood* [2001] 1 WLR 840, [2001] Imm AR 229, para 40.
2 *R (on the application of Daly) v Secretary of State for the Home Department* [2001] UKHL 26, [2001] 2 AC 532, para 27.
3 *R (on the application of Samaroo) v Secretary of State for the Home Department* [2001] EWCA Civ 1139, [2001] UKHRR 1150, [2002] INLR 55 and *R (on the application of Sezek) v Secretary of State for the Home Department* [2001] EWCA Civ 795, [2002] 1 WLR 348. The test is very little different from the pre-2000 approach in the line of cases starting with *Brind* (*R v Secretary of State for the Home Department, ex p Brind* [1991] 1 AC 696 at 748 and 751; *R v Ministry of Defence, ex p Smith* [1996] QB 517 at 554 per Lord Bingham MR (the 'gays in the military' case); *R (on the application of A) v Lord Saville of Newdigate (No 2)* [2001] EWCA Civ 2048, [2002] 1 WLR 129 at para 37(on anonymity for soldiers testifying to the Saville Inquiry on Bloody Sunday) with the added bit about large margins of discretion to decision makers in the Home office. In fact the individual is probably worse off than in the pre-Human Rights era.
4 *Edore v Secretary of State for the Home Department* [2003] EWCA Civ 716, [2003] Imm AR 516, [2003] INLR 361, at para 20.
5 *R (on the application of Ala) v Secretary of State for the Home Department* [2003] EWCA 521 (Admin), [2003] All ER (D) 283 (Mar), paras 44–45. At para 44 the judge said: 'A decision maker may fairly reach one of two opposite conclusions, one in favour of a claimant, the other in favour of his removal. Of neither could it be said that the balance had been struck unfairly ... Once it is accepted that the balance could be struck fairly either way, the Secretary of State cannot be regarded as having infringed the claimant's Article 8 rights by concluding that he should be removed.'
6 *M (Croatia) v Secretary of State for the Home Department* [2004] UKIAT 24, [2004] INLR 327, at para 28.

8.21 This neo-*Wednesbury* approach, however, was rejected by the House of Lords in *Razgar*, where their Lordships made it clear that in statutory appeals the adjudicator was to exercise an independent judgment on the issue of proportionality, based on all the materials adduced on the appeal.[1] As had happened with the decision in *Daly*,[2] the judgments in *Razgar* were ignored on this point. However, the Court of Appeal in *Huang* came to the same conclusion.[3] The court stated that if the matter were free from authority, 'we would regard it as plain that the *Wednesbury* test is inapt to the adjudicator's task.' [para 30]. After examining *Edore* and *Ala* and *Razgar* both in the Court of Appeal and in the House of Lords, they concluded that the earlier decisions could not stand [para 39] and held that the adjudicator is obliged to do more than conduct a *Wednesbury* review [para 43]. The court held that the principle by which a margin of appreciation is to be accorded to the primary decision maker out of respect for the democratic claims of elected government has no application. In these appeals, adjudicators were not called upon to decide whether any policy was proportionate to its legitimate purpose or to pass judgment on government policy at all [para 55]. Then came the sting in the tail: the policy, the court held, was set out in the statute and, in particular, the immigration rules [para 56]. 'The Rules themselves', said the court, 'have struck the balance between the public interest and the private right' [paras 57 and 58]. Accordingly, 'the true position ... is that the HRA and section 65(1)⁴ require the adjudicator to allow an appeal against removal *if, but only if*, he concludes that the case is *so exceptional* on its particular facts that *the imperative of proportionality demands* an outcome in the appellant's favour, notwithstanding that he cannot succeed under the Rules (para 59)'. It is a signal feature of the adjudicator's task that he is bound to respect the balance struck between public interest and private right by the Rules, with Parliament's approval. That is why the appellant will only win, if his or her case is *'truly exceptional'* [para 60].⁵

1   *R (on the application of Razgar) v Secretary of State for the Home Department* [2004] UKHL 27, [2004] 2 AC 368 at paras 20 (Lord Bingham) and 60 (Lady Hale). The other members of the Committee agreed (paras 26, 27, 77).
2   *R (on the application of Daly) v Secretary of State for the Home Department* [2001] UKHL 26, [2001] 2 AC 532; see above.
3   *Huang v Secretary of State for the Home Department* [2005] EWCA Civ 105, (2005) Sol Jo LB 297.
4   See now Nationality, Immigration and Asylum Act 2002, s 84(1)(c), (g).
5   Lord Bingham had stated in *Razgar* (fn 1 above) that 'decisions taken pursuant to the lawful operation of immigration control will be proportionate in all save a small minority of exceptional cases' (para 19), but there was no suggestion in his speech that the immigration rules embodied the control in and of themselves: see below.

8.22   This ruling is of some concern. First, immigration law is a conglomeration of many different policies, by no means all of which relate to the list of interests set out in Article 8(2) of ECHR. One important policy is family reunion, the very thing that Article 8 rights are about. There is no antithesis of public against private interests here. Another of its driving forces, which has never been mentioned in a single case, is the appeasement of the racist lobby and the xenophobic outpourings against asylum seekers in much of the populist press. Ministers often explain that they are tightening up on 'illegal immigrants' and asylum seekers in order that the government does not lose out to the hate parties of the far right. Further, many of the immigration rules, such as those on family reunion for elderly dependent relatives, are very old, remain cast in the same deeply restrictive terms, and have not been amended since the Human Rights Act came into force. With this background, it seems to us that to suggest that the immigration rules are embodiments of policies which balance immigrants' human rights against the economic well-being of the country or the prevention of crime and disorder is highly disputable and totally unproven. Yet this one of the underlying premises of much of the domestic case-law under Article 8(2). The equation of immigration control with economic wellbeing or the prevention of crime and disorder is taken as a given and has become part of a deeply ingrained trend which it will be hard to displace. Our second concern with the premise of *Huang's* guidance is this. We have always understood that the policy of immigration law and practice has never been to treat the rules as the final arbiter of who should come in and who should not; of who should be deported and who should not; they are rules of practice.[1] They are complemented by employment policies, which do deal with the economic wellbeing of the country, but are largely separate and not part of the Rules. First, the Rules themselves have a built-in flexibility. Those who have been in the country a long time will only be removed once a whole set of factors have been considered and a balance has been struck.[2] Secondly, the Home Secretary always has a residual discretion to admit, when the rules do not permit it.[3] The immigration rules do not, and never have, represented a rigid policy yardstick of where the balance lies between the claims of democratic power and the claims of individual rights.[4] There is no reason why they should now. It is also true that cases which are capable of overcoming the absence of any qualifying immigration rule very often have exceptional features, but sometimes the applicant may miss coming within the rules by a very narrow margin. So describing the Tribunal's task in such rigid and imperious tones would seem to exclude the flexibility which has always been a feature of immigration practice. The sting in the tail also sits uneasily with the recent liberalising trend in the Strasbourg case-law on Article 8, which we discuss at 8.82–8.84 below.

1   Immigration Act 1971, ss 1(4) and 3(2).
2   See HC 395, paras 364 and 395C.
3   Immigration Act 1971, s 4(1).
4   See *Shala v Secretary of State for the Home Department* [2003] EWCA Civ 233, [2003] INLR 349, CA. In *Boultif v Switzerland* [2001] 2 FLR 1228, (2002) 33 EHRR 50, ECtHR, and *Sen v Netherlands* (2003) 36 EHRR 76, the European Court set out some guiding principles on the relevant criteria to assess each individual case, which have none of the rigidity of the English approach. See also *Jakupovic v Austria* (Application 36757/97) [2003] 2 FCR 361, ECtHR; *and Yildiz v Austria* (2003) 36 EHRR 32, ECtHR.

8.23 There remain situations where little or no deference is due to the executive or to immigration rules. In cases involving Article 3 claims, no deference is paid to the executive's view of what constitutes treatment contrary to Article 3, because the right is absolute and cannot depend on differing interpretations of inhuman treatment or torture.[1] Little or no deference is paid to the Secretary of State's view of the reality of a risk, since 'whether a sufficient risk exists is a question of evaluation and prediction based on evidence; in answering such a question the executive enjoys no constitutional prerogative.[2] In *Turgut*,[3] a case involving an evaluation of likely mistreatment of the appellant on his return to Turkey, the court concluded that 'what has been called the "discretionary area of judgment"… is a decidedly narrow one'. The court also affords little deference to the executive in questions of detention.[4]

1   See eg *R (on the application of T) v Secretary of State for the Home Department* [2003] EWCA Civ 1285, [2004] HLR 254. This corresponds with the lack of any margin of appreciation to contracting States on Art 3: see Callewaerts, Johann 'Is there a margin of appreciation in the application of Arts 2, 3 and 4 of the Convention?' [1998] 19 HRLJ 6–9.
2   *Rehman v Secretary of State for the Home Department* [2001] UKHL 47, [2001] 3 WLR 877, [2002] INLR 92, para 54, per Lord Hoffmann, who (at para 57) contrasted the lack of deference to the executive in answering this question with the assessment of a national security risk, where the appellate body allows a wide margin to the decision maker. See also *R (on the application of A) v Lord Saville of Newdigate (No 2)* [2001] EWCA Civ 2048, [2002] 1 WLR 1249, para 34.

³   *R v Secretary of State for the Home Department, ex p Turgut* [2000] Imm AR 306. This
    passage was cited in the ECtHR in *Hilal v United Kingdom* (Application 45276/99) (2001)
    11 BHRC 354, in support of the court's conclusion that judicial review was an effective
    remedy for the purposes of Art 13 in cases raising asylum or Art 3 issues.
⁴   'Liberty ... is a right which English law has guarded with jealous care since at least the time
    of Edward I; [it is] one of the rights of high constitutional importance in which relatively
    slight deference to the executive is appropriate': *R (on the application of Amirthanathan) v
    Secretary of State for the Home Department* [2003] EWHC 2595 (Admin) (although the
    decision in this case was upheld by the Court of Appeal on the narrowest of grounds: see
    Nadarajah v Secretary of State for the Home Department [2003] EWCA Civ 1768). See
    also *A and X v Secretary of State for the Home Department* [2004] UKHL 56, [2005]
    2 WLR 87 per Lord Bingham at para 36.

Statement of compatibility

8.24 In accordance with the constitutional balance of the Human Rights
Act 1998, Parliament is excluded from the definition of a public authority for
the purposes of compliance with the ECHR, as noted above, as is any person
exercising functions in connection with proceedings in Parliament.¹ A failure
to introduce or propose legislation or to make any primary legislation or
remedial order is not 'an act' which can be challenged in the courts.² The one
obligation imposed on ministers is that of stating, before second reading of
any Bill, whether in his or her view the Bill's provisions are compatible with
the Convention rights (a 'statement of compatibility') or not. The purpose of
this is twofold: to ensure that ministers and Parliament address compatibility
with the Convention when legislation is debated (which itself makes the
legislation more likely to be compatible), and to create a presumption that it is
so compatible, in the face of apparently incompatible provisions. The Joint
Committee on Human Rights, a Select Committee formed by both Houses of
Parliament in July 2001 to consider human rights issues in the UK and
proposals for remedial orders under the Act,³ scrutinises bills and prepares
reports on their compatibility with the Convention, enabling ministers to
reconsider provisions about which the Committee expresses concern.⁴

¹   Human Rights Act 1998, s 6(3); see 8.16 above.
²   HRA 1998, s 6(6).
³   Under HRA 1998, s 10(2).
⁴   See the Committee's regular reports on scrutiny of Bills; see also its 5th and 14th reports of
    2003/4, on the Asylum and Immigration (Treatment of Claimants) Bill, 10 February 2004
    (HL 35/HC 304) and 5 July 2004 (HL 130/HC 828, its 6th report, on the Anti-terrorism,
    Crime and Security Act 2001, 24 February 2004 (HL 38/HC 381), and its 5th report of
    2004/5 on the Identity Cards Bill, 2.2.05 (HL 35/HC 283). JCAR also scrutinises
    subordinate legislation which raises human rights concerns; see its 22nd report of 2003/4,
    on the Nationality, Immigration and Asylum Act 2002 (Specification of Particularly
    Serious Crimes) Order 2004, 3 November 2004 (HL 190/HC 1212).

Who may bring proceedings

8.25 Sections 7–9 of the Human Rights Act were intended to lay down a
remedial structure for giving effect to the Convention rights.¹ A victim of an
unlawful act may bring proceedings for a breach or proposed breach of an
ECHR right under section 7(1) of the Human Rights Act in an appropriate
court or tribunal,² or may rely on the Convention right in any legal

proceedings.[3] The intention behind the subsection appears to be to ensure that Convention rights may be relied on in any legal proceedings, whether brought by the public authority or not, and whether the public authority is a party or not.[4] Section 7(11) gives the minister power to enlarge the jurisdiction of a tribunal hearing a human rights case, both as regards the grounds on which it may allow an appeal and as to the remedies it may afford, but no such enlargement has been ordered in the immigration sphere.

1   *Brown v Stott* [2001] 2 WLR 817, per Lord Hope at 847B.
2   Human Rights Act 1998, s 7(1)(a).
3   HRA 1998, s 7(1)(b). 'Legal proceedings' for the purposes of this sub-section includes proceedings brought by the authority or at its instigation (the most obvious example being a criminal case) and an appeal against the decision of a court or tribunal: s 7(6); *R v Kansal (No 2)* [2001] UKHL 62, [2002] 2 AC 69, [2001] 3 WLR 1562; *Pearce v Governing Body of Mayfield School; Macdonald v Advocate-General for Scotland* [2003] UKHL 34, [2004] 1 All ER 339, [2003] IRLR 512. It must also include an appeal against the decision of the public authority, eg an immigration appeal.
4   Where the proceedings were brought by or at the instigation of a public authority, ECHR rights may be relied on even if the unlawful act complained of happened before the Human Rights Act 1998 came into force: s 22(4). But an administrative decision to exclude or expel cannot be categorised as a 'proceeding', much less a 'legal proceeding', and so a decision to refuse entry before the Act came into force on 2 October 2000 could not be impugned after that date on Convention grounds under the Act: see *Pardeepan* [2000] INLR 447, IAT, decided under the provisions of the Commencement Order. The Secretary of State gave an undertaking in that case that human rights claims made after a pre-October 2000 refusal of asylum would attract a separate right of appeal on human rights grounds. In *R v Secretary of State for the Home Department, ex p Mahmood* [2001] 1 WLR 840 the Court of Appeal considered and rejected an argument that the Human Rights Act 1998 applied to a pre-October 2000 decision to remove because in substance the challenge was to its future implementation, cf *Chahal v United Kingdom* (1996) 23 EHRR 413; *Nasri v France* (1995) 21 EHRR 458.

8.26   Only a 'victim' of an unlawful act or proposed act may bring proceedings or rely on ECHR rights under section 7 of the Human Rights Act 1998,[1] and 'victim' is to have the same meaning as in the Strasbourg jurisprudence on Article 34 of the ECHR.[2] Article 34 allows applications from 'any person, non-governmental organisation or group of individuals claiming to be the victim of a violation', and includes all those directly affected or potentially affected by an act or omission.[3] But the definition of victim is considerably narrower than the 'sufficient interest' test for standing to bring judicial review proceedings, and precludes public interest organisations such as the Joint Council for the Welfare of Immigrants from challenging rules or policy as contrary to the Convention.[4] The action or decision complained of does not need to have caused prejudice to the person claiming victim status,[5] which means that an organisation of asylum seekers (rather than one assisting them) could bring a challenge to rules which might affect them.[6] The concern that the narrowness of the 'victim' test would inhibit the use of judicial review to raise issues of general importance involving Convention rights[7] has however been allayed to some extent by the courts' readiness to accept intervention by third parties, in particular by public interest organisations.[8] The need to wait or search for a 'victim' in order to remedy an incompatibility affecting thousands is clearly unsatisfactory, however, and there seems no good reason for the restrictive approach to survive in UK jurisprudence. The 'victim' provision has caused some difficulty in statutory appeals, because the wording of the immigration appeal statutes unjustifiably narrows the scope of the appeal to the sole issue of whether the appellant's Convention rights have been breached, while in Article 8 cases it is often those of UK-based family members which are affected.[9] Family members of those to be removed do have standing for judicial review as 'victims' under section 7, however.[10]

1 Human Rights Act 1998, s 7(1).
2 HRA 1998, s 7(7).
3 Under Article 43, those potentially at risk qualify as victims: *Norris v Ireland* (1988) 13 EHRR 186 (victim of legislation penalising homosexual activities even if risk of prosecution under legislation minimal). In *Open Door Counselling and Dublin Well Woman v Ireland* (1992) 15 EHRR 244, the class of victims was all women of childbearing age, since all could be adversely affected by a ban on the dissemination of information about abortion. In *Klass v Germany* (1978) 2 EHRR 214, the class was all users or potential users of post and telecommunications, who could be adversely affected by secret surveillance. See also *Marckx v Belgium* (1979) 2 EHRR 330.
4 As in *R v Secretary of State for Social Security, ex p Joint Council for the Welfare of Immigrants* [1997] 1 WLR 275.
5 *Lüdi v Switzerland* (1992) 15 EHRR 173, para 34. See also *Open Door Counselling* fn 3 above.
6 *In Segi and Gestoras Pro-Amnistia v Fifteen States of the EU* (6422/02, 9916/02, 23.5.02) the court held that the EU Common Positions 2001/930/CFSP and 2001/931/CFSP which listed the applicant organisations as 'groups involved in terrorist acts' were not directly applicable and gave rise to no binding obligations on the part of Member States, so the situation did not confer on the associations the status of victims of a violation. Clearly, had the lists been adopted in domestic laws, the applicant organisations would have had victim status.
7 See Lord Lester, 583 HL Official Report (5th series) cols 823–837, 24 November 1997; Lord Slynn and Lord Lester, vol 585, cols 805–812, 5 February 1998.
8 For example, Liberty intervened in *A and X v Secretary of State for the Home Department* [2004] UKHL 56, [2005] 2 WLR 87 (on whether derogation from Art 5 ECHR and internment of foreign terrorist suspects breached Arts 5 and 14), Liberty and the Joint Council for the Welfare of Immigrants intervened in *R (on the application of Q) v Secretary of State for the Home Department* [2003] EWCA Civ 364 [2003] 2 All ER 905 (on whether refusal of support under NIAA 2002, s 55 breached Art 3 ECHR); the Terrence Higgins Trust in *N v Secretary of State for the Home Department* [2003] EWCA Civ 1369, [2005] UKHL 31 (on whether Art 3 was engaged by expulsion of an AIDS sufferer to a country where lack of resources meant no or inadequate treatment). Previously, Amnesty International, the Medical Foundation, Redress, Human Rights Watch and organisations of relatives of the 'disappeared' were allowed to intervene, either orally or by written submissions, in *R v Bow Street Metropolitan Stipendiary Magistrate, ex p Pinochet Ugarte* [1998] 4 All ER 897; *(No 2)* [1999] 1 All ER 577. See also Lord Woolf's endorsement of the Justice/Public Law Project report on public interest interventions in *R v Chief Constable of North Wales Police, ex p AB* [1998] 3 WLR 57 at 66. Public interest organisations may be permitted to intervene in Strasbourg: see *HLR v France* (1997) 26 EHRR 29.
9 Nationality, Immigration and Asylum Act 2002, s 84(1)(c) and its predecessor, Immigration and Asylum Act 1999, s 65(1). In *Kehinde* (01TH2668) (starred), a starred Tribunal held that the appellate authority is concerned only with the human rights of the appellant, not of family members. The relationships in that case were found to be without real substance. In *R (AC) v Immigration Appeal Tribunal* [2003] EWHC Admin 389 [2003] INLR 507, a judicial review of a Tribunal's preliminary ruling that the Art 8 rights of the (non-appellant) infant child of a deportee were irrelevant to her appeal, Jack J held (para 33) that the effect of the proposed interference on all those sharing the family life in question must be considered and taken into account, an approach consistent with ECHR jurisprudence (see *McCann v United Kingdom* (1995) 21 EHRR 97; see also Harris, O'Boyle and Warbrick *Law of the European Convention on Human Rights* (Butterworths, 1995), p 637. In Art 8 cases on family life, in the Strasbourg jurisprudence, all members of a family are victims). He distinguished between the human rights of other family members, which were not the subject of an appeal, and the impact of deportation on others, which were relevant (para 37).

[10] In *R (on the application of Holub) v Secretary of State for the Home Department* [2001] 1 WLR 1359, the parents of a child whose rights to education were alleged to be breached by proposed removal had standing under the Act.

8.27 Victim status is lost once the breach has been effectively remedied. But partial reparation does not necessarily prevent an applicant from retaining victim status to bring proceedings,[1] and the grant of a temporary or provisional status to someone who claims that removal would violate an ECHR right does not necessarily bring victim status to an end so as to preclude recourse to a court.[2]

[1] *Chevrol v France* (49646/99), 13 February 2002.
[2] *Ahmed v Austria* (1996) 24 EHRR 278: a stay on expulsion for a renewable period of a year, with a right of recourse to a court if renewal were refused did not prevent the applicant from arguing that his deportation, if it ever happened, would breach Art 3. But cf *Vijayanathan v France* (1992) 15 EHRR 62, where rejection of asylum claims did not give the applicant the status of victim because no expulsion measure had been taken; see also *BB v France* (Application 30930/96) (7 September 1998), where the court struck out an Art 3 claim over the expulsion of an AIDS sufferer after a compulsory residence order was made.

Just satisfaction

8.28 Article 41 of the Convention, repeating the substance of Article 50 of the original version, now provides:

'Just satisfaction

> If the court finds that there has been a violation of the Convention or the protocols thereto, and if the internal law of the High Contracting Party concerned allows only partial reparation to be made, the court shall, if necessary, afford just satisfaction to the injured party.'

Article 41 is not one of the Articles scheduled to the Human Rights Act 1998, but it is reflected in section 8 of the Human Rights Act 1998.[1] Under that section a court or tribunal, which finds a breach of the ECHR, is empowered to grant any relief or remedy or make any order within its powers which it considers just and appropriate.[2] However, no award of damages is to be made unless the court is satisfied, taking account of all the circumstances of the particular case, that an award of damages is necessary to afford just satisfaction to the person in whose favour it is made.[3] Often a finding of violation will, in itself, be just satisfaction for the violation.[4] This reflects the point that the focus of the Convention is on the protection of human rights and not the award of compensation.[5] Under section 8(4) of the 1998 Act the domestic court must take into account the principles applied by the European Court of Human Rights in relation to the award of compensation under Article 41 of the Convention. It is, therefore, to Strasbourg that British courts must look for guidance on the award of damages.[6] For the position regarding compensation for detention, see 8.69 below.

[1] *R v Secretary of State for the Home Department, ex p Greenfield* [2005] UKHL 14.
[2] Human Rights Act 1998, s 8.

3   For the issue of damages under the HRA 1998 see Law Commision Paper No 266 of October 2000. Even the enforceable right to compensation under Art 5(5) of the Convention does not mean that compensation must always be awarded; what the Article requires is a mechanism for the judicial determination of a compensation claim for unlawful detention: *Nikolova v Bulgaria* (2001) 31 EHRR 3. See *R (on the application of KB) v Mental Health Review Tribunal and Secretary of State for Health* [2003] EWHC 193 (Admin), [2004] QB 936; *R (on the application of H) v Secretary of State for the Home Department* [2003] UKHL 59, [2004] 2 AC 253.

4   See the exhaustive survey of ECtHR jurisprudence in *Anufrijeva v Southwark LBC, R (N) v Secretary of State for the Home Department, R (on the application of M) v Secretary of State for the Home Department* [2003] EWCA Civ 1406, [2004] 1 All ER 833, in which no 'clear and constant' jurisprudence on the recovery of damages for human rights breaches other than detention was found. For the principles of just satisfaction in the ECHR see Grosz, Beatson and Duffy *Human Rights: The 1998 Act and the European Convention* (2000, Sweet & Maxwell), paras 6.19–21.

5   *Greenfield*, above, para 9; *Anufrijeva v Southwark London Borough Council* above, paras 52–53, where the Court of Appeal held that the remedy of damages generally plays a less prominent role in actions based on breaches of the Articles of the Convention, where the concern will usually be to bring the infringement to an end and any question of compensation will be of secondary, if any, importance. It is noteworthy that, in exercising its former jurisdiction under the original Art 32, the Committee of Ministers did not, before 1987, award compensation at all, even where a violation was found: D J Harris, M O'Boyle and C Warbrick *Law of the European Convention on Human Rights* (1995, Butterworths), p 699.

6   *Greenfield*, above, para 6.

8.29 The ECtHR has upheld the rule of domestic law that in general no civil action will lie against a public authority for failure to comply with statutory duties.[1] In *Wainwright v Home Office*[2] the Court of Appeal sought to grapple with a claim for damages for a strip-search conducted in breach of Article 8, but Buxton LJ said it was wholly unclear what the rules of remoteness were in a claim under the Human Rights Act, whether breaches were actionable *per se* and what heads of damage and amounts were recoverable. The court sought to answer some of these questions in *Anufrijeva*[3], in which it gave guidance on claims for damages for breach of Article 8 rights arising out of maladministration, which it held would only infringe Article 8 where the consequences were serious, that damages would be awarded on an equitable basis only where necessary to provide just satisfaction, that awards would be modest and that claimants should seek other routes, such as ADR or the Ombudsman, before launching expensive proceedings in the Administrative Court. Awards under the Act are intended to compensate, not punish, so exemplary damages would rarely be appropriate.[4]

1   See eg *W v Home Office* [1997] Imm AR 302 (no damages for wrongful administrative acts causing loss in the absence of negligence, misfeasance or false imprisonment). In *Osman v United Kingdom* (1998) 29 EHRR 245 the court criticised the 'immunity from suit' of police and other public authorities, but withdrew the criticism in *Z v United Kingdom* (2002) 34 EHRR 3, (2001) 10 BHRC 384 and *Clunis v United Kingdom* (45049/98) (11 September 2001, unreported) after it was pointed out by the House of Lords that the rule was not a procedural immunity but a substantive rule of law. See now *ID v Home Office* [2005] EWCA Civ 38, [2005] All ER (D) 253 (Jan): 17.54 below.

2   [2001] EWCA Civ 2081, [2002] QB 1334.

3   *Anufrijeva v Southwark LBC, R (on the application of N) v Secretary of State for the Home Department, R (on the application of M) v Secretary of State for the Home Department* fn 5 above. See also *R (on the application of Bernard) v Enfield London Borough Council* [2002] EWHC 2282 (Admin) (award of £10,000 appropriate for 20 months' unsuitable accommodation provided in breach of Art 8 ECHR); *R (on the application of Gezer) v Secretary of State for the Home Department* [2003] EWHC 860

(Admin), [2003] HLR 972 (dispersal to dangerous area where family subjected to racial attacks did not attract liability on the facts but if it had, £5,000 would have been appropriate for exacerbation of psychiatric injuries) (the issue of damages was not dealt with by the Court of Appeal at [2004] EWCA Civ 1730).

4   *Russell v Home Office* [2001] All ER (D) 38 (Mar), QBD.

8.30 As noted above, the Tribunal does not have the power to strike down immigration rules or subordinate legislation,[1] but clearly it has power to disapply a rule to give effect to fundamental rights in a particular case, deriving from its duty to allow an appeal against an unlawful decision,[2] and may issue directions for the grant of entry clearance or leave to remain even if the refusal appealed against is in accordance with the rules. The section does not allow the appellate authority to grant a remedy it has no statutory power to grant, such as damages, although in appropriate cases it may recommend the award of an *ex gratia* payment of compensation for violation of Convention rights (the Secretary of State has a scheme for 'consolatory payments' for maladministration, including delays, causing injustice, set up at the recommendation of the Parliamentary Ombudsman)[3] but an award of damages is within the powers of the Administrative Court on judicial review.

1   *Pardeepan*, see 8.14 fn 6 above.
2   Nationality, Immigration and Asylum Act 2002, s 86(3).
3   Disclosed in a statement produced to the court in *R (on the application of M) v Secretary of State for the Home Department* [2003] EWHC 319.

8.31 Section 11 of the Human Rights Act 1998, broader in its terms than Article 53 of the ECHR, ensures that a person's reliance on a Convention right does not restrict any other right or freedom conferred on that person by or under any law having effect in any part of the UK. It has been suggested that one possible interpretation of this section is that it allows reliance on rights conferred by other incorporated or partly incorporated Conventions, such as the Refugee Convention and the UN Convention against Torture, and on unincorporated rights from other Conventions, which have been ratified by the UK, on the basis that the Crown's ratification of, or entry into, a treaty might be capable of giving rise to a legitimate expectation upon which the public in general would be entitled to rely.[1] However, the proposition runs counter to older authority[2] and has been given short and scathing shrift in more recent judicial dicta. In *European Roma Rights Centre*,[3] Laws LJ rejected the idea of incorporation through legitimate expectation as a 'constitutional solecism'. 'We must not,' he warned, 'be seduced by humanitarian claims to a spurious acceptance of a false source of law'.[4] This categoric and persuasive rejection of incorporation by 'legitimate expectation does not undermine the reliance on rights recognised by unincorporated Conventions which the decision maker has purported to recognise and apply to the applicant's case,[5] on rights identified and recognised by the common law,[6] and unincorporated treaties and conventions used as an aid to the interpretation of ECHR rights and freedoms in accordance with Article 53 of the ECHR.[7]

1   See *R v Secretary of State for the Home Department, ex p Ahmed and Patel* [1998] INLR 570, CA where Lord Woolf MR accepted that the entering into a Treaty could give rise to a legitimate expectation that the Secretary of State would act in accordance with the Treaty obligations, and an applicant would be entitled to relief if the Secretary of State, without reason, acted inconsistently with those obligations (at 583G). The Treaty in question was,

however, not the ECHR but the UN Convention on the Rights of the Child 1989, which contains express reservations relating to immigration control in respect of the principle that the welfare of the child should be the paramount consideration in court proceedings. He endorsed the judgment of the High Court of Australia in *Minister for Immigration and Ethnic Affairs v Teoh* (1995) 183 CLR 273 to that effect. This approach was followed by the Divisional Court in *R v Uxbridge Magistrates Court, ex p Adimi* [1999] INLR 490 in respect of obligations under the Refugee Convention 1951 not expressly incorporated into UK law by the Asylum and Immigration Appeals Act 1993.

2   In *Chundawadra* [1988] IAR 161 the Court of Appeal held that ratification of the European Convention on Human Rights created no justiciable legitimate expectation that the Convention's provisions would be complied with. In *Behluli* [1998] IAR 407, CA the court came to a like conclusion in relation to the Dublin Convention.

3   *European Roma Rights Centre v Immigration Officer at Prague Airport* [2003] EWCA Civ 666, [2003] INLR 374, at paras 98. The House of Lords confirmed that the Refugee Convention was incorporated into domestic law without resorting to legitimate expectation, at [2004] UKHL 55, [2005] 2 WLR 1.

4   *European Roma Rights Centre* (CA) above paras 99–101. Simon Brown LJ expressed his conclusion in *Adimi* (fn 1 above) as 'superficial and suspect' (para 51).

5   *R v Secretary of State for the Home Department, ex p Launder* [1997] 3 All ER 961.

6   Such as the 'law of common humanity' which prevents foreigners from starving, *R v Eastbourne Inhabitants* (1803) 4 East 103 cited by Simon Brown LJ in *R v Secretary of State for Social Security, ex p Joint Council for the Welfare of Immigrants* [1997] 1 WLR 275.

7   See 8.6 above.

Home Office policy

8.32 To to extent that the immigration rules themselves do not afford adequate protection to the human rights of those affected by them,[1] the Home Office gives effect to human rights considerations by a grant of humanitarian protection (HP) or discretionary leave (DL).[2] Humanitarian Protection will be granted to anyone who is unable to demonstrate a claim for asylum but who would face a serious risk to life or person arising from:

- the death penalty;
- unlawful killing;
- torture, inhuman or degrading treatment or punishment.

Serious criminals, including war criminals; terrorists or others who raise a threat to national security and anyone who is considered to be of bad character, conduct or associations will be excluded.[3] Discretionary leave may be granted to persons who would qualify for asylum or humanitarian protection but have been excluded,[4] and additionally to those with a good Article 3 claim on medical or severe humanitarian grounds, or a good Article 8 claim.[5] Humanitarian protection should be granted for up to three years, and then if protection is still needed, claimants will usually received indefinite leave to remain; otherwise those with no other basis of stay in the UK will be expected to leave.[6] Discretionary leave is not granted for more than three years, and is frequently granted for much shorter periods,[7] although it is renewable, and may lead to indefinite leave to remain after six years (save for those excluded from asylum or HP, who are excluded from ILR, although they have a possibility of applying under the long residence rule).[8] It is not intended to be granted to those who cannot be removed for practical reasons, such as lack of a travel document.[9] Until 2007, transitional provisions apply to individuals who were granted exceptional leave to enter or remain before the change to HP and DL on 1 April 2003; they will be considered for the grant of ILR after four years, in line with the policy then in force.[10]

¹ See the analysis in *Huang v Secretary of State for the Home Department* [2005] EWCA Civ 105, (2005) Sol Jo LB 297 at paras 56–7.

² The criteria for humanitarian protection and discretionary leave are set out in the Asylum Policy Instructions (API), APU notice 1/2003, April 2003. To the extent that the policy provides lesser protection than that required by the EC Qualification Directive (Council Directive 2004/83/EC on minimum standards for the qualification and status of third country nationals and stateless persons as refugees or persons who otherwise need international protection (OJ 2004 L 304/12), the Directive, which has direct effect, prevails.

³ The 'exclusion clauses' are broader and more subjective than exclusion from refugee status under Article 1F of the Refugee Convention (see 12.88ff below). It would however be possible to challenge an exclusion from HP by judicial review.

⁴ APU notice 1/2003 (fn 2 above).

⁵ Ibid. For Art 3 claims on medical or humanitarian grounds see also APU notice 3/2003, and 8.53 below, and see the separate Home Office policy regarding medical (and particularly HIV/AIDS) cases at 8.53 text and fn 3. For claims based on Art 8, see 8.79ff. In addition, DL will be granted to unaccompanied asylum seeking children (UASCs) for whom adequate reception arrangements are not available in their own country (generally for three years or until their 18th birthday, whichever is earlier, but if they come from a State listed in NIAA 2002, s 94 other than Bolivia, Brazil, Ecuador, South Africa or Ukraine, DL is granted for 12 months: APU notice 2/2003). Additionally, DL is granted to others who can demonstrate 'particularly compelling reasons why removal would not be appropriate': APU 1/2003.

⁶ HP may be revoked, on grounds analogous to Refugee Convention cessation grounds, if for example the holder has taken to spending periods of time in the country, fear of return to which led to the grant, but not simply because he or she has re-acquired or used that country's nationality, unless this is incompatible with the basis of the grant: see API: Post-refusal decisions: Humanitarian Protection, para 7.1. Time spent on other forms of leave, including DL, does not count towards the three years' HP threshold for ILR.

⁷ In Art 8 cases, DL should be granted for two years if the claim is based on marriage, otherwise three years; three years is the appropriate grant in Art 3 cases; three years or until 18th birthday for UASCs (see fn 5 above); 6 months for those excluded from asylum or humanitarian protection and for those whose need is likely to be short-lived: see API: Post-refusal decisions: Discretionary Leave, para 5. It would not normally be appropriate to withdraw DL simply because holders have travelled to their own country: ibid para 6.1.

⁸ Formerly the long residence concession, now HC 395, paras 276A–D. The API: Post-refusal decisions: Discretionary Leave, para 8 say that those granted DL because excluded from asylum or HP are eligible for ILR after 10 years (towards which time in prison does not count), unless a personal decision to refuse on conducive grounds is taken by a minister.

⁹ See API: Post-refusal decisions: Discretionary Leave, para 1.

¹⁰ Ibid: Humanitarian Protection, para 11.

ECHR PRINCIPLES

8.33 The ECHR is based on the obligation of contracting States to give effect to the core values of a democratic society: pluralism, openness and broad-mindedness,[1] the rule of law,[2] freedom of expression,[3] and is designed to maintain and promote those values.[4] It is a living instrument which must be interpreted in the light of present-day conditions.[5] This approach, in contrast with that of the common law, decreases the role of precedent as the court re-determines issues in the light of changing conditions.[6] In *Selmouni v France*[7] the court observed that:

'certain acts which were classified in the past as "inhuman and degrading treatment" as opposed to "torture" could be classified differently in future ... the increasingly high standard being required in the area of the protection of human rights and fundamental liberties correspondingly and inevitably requires greater firmness in assessing breaches of the fundamental values of democratic societies.'

The 'living instrument' or dynamic approach to Convention rights applies with force to areas affected by rapidly changing views of private morality,[8] and in particular to the rights of sexual minorities in the context of protection of private life.[9] It also applies to rights to fair trial, as the requirements of fairness have evolved considerably in the court's case law.[10] We shall consider later the relevance of Article 6 'fair trial' requirements to immigration and asylum cases.[11]

[1]   *Handyside v United Kingdom* (1976) 1 EHRR 737, para 49.
[2]   See Preamble; *Golder v United Kingdom* (1975) 1 EHRR 524, para 34; *Klass v Germany* (1978) 2 EHRR 214, para 55.
[3]   *Handyside v United Kingdom* above.
[4]   Preamble; *Kjeldsen v Denmark* (1976) 1 EHRR 711, para 53.
[5]   *Tyrer v United Kingdom* (1978) 2 EHRR 1, para 31; *Marckx v Belgium* (1979) 2 EHRR 330; *Loizidou v Turkey* (1995) 20 EHRR 99, at para 71. This means that the content and scope of rights might be deepened and broadened over time, see eg *Sutherland v United Kingdom* [1998] EHRLR 117, but not that entirely new rights are created: *Johnston v Ireland* (1986) 9 EHRR 203; *Feldbrugge v Netherlands* (1986) 8 EHRR 425.
[6]   See eg *Goodwin v United Kingdom* (28957/95) [2002] IRLR 664 where the court departed from its previous jurisprudence relating to the private lives of transsexuals and found that in the light of present-day conditions there were no longer any significant factors of public interest to weigh against the interest of a transsexual obtaining legal recognition of her gender re-assignment.
[7]   (1999) 29 EHRR 403.
[8]   *Marckx v Belgium* (1979) 2 EHRR 330.
[9]   *Dudgeon v United Kingdom* (1981) 4 EHRR 149; *Smith and Grady v United Kingdom* (1999) 29 EHRR 493, para 97 (homosexuals); *Goodwin v United Kingdom* (fn 6 above).
[10] See *Borgers v Belgium* (1991) 15 EHRR 92, para 24.
[11] See 8.72 below.

8.34 The concept of State responsibility for the protection of fundamental rights is at the heart of the ECHR. States have negative and positive obligations under the Convention: not to interfere with core human rights, and to protect those within their jurisdiction from violations.[1] A positive obligation may also require action to give effect to rights, such as the provision of legal aid to enable access to a court to be effective,[2] or the promotion of family life through the admission of a family member to the country.[3]The positive obligation to protect against killing and torture extends to an effective investigation when individuals have been killed (whether by State agents or private individuals) or when they allege torture.[4] In accordance with the ideas expressed in the Preamble and Article 1, the Convention is intended to guarantee rights that are practical and effective, not theoretical and illusory.[5] Thus, rights must not be subject to conditions for their exercise which render them useless.[6]

[1]   By, for example, not sending someone to a country where their human rights will be violated: *Soering v United Kingdom* (1989) 11 EHRR 439, or by preventing a death which was eminently foreseeable: *Osman v United Kingdom* (1998) 29 EHRR 245, para 115. See also *A v United Kingdom* (1998) 27 EHRR 611 (prevention of assaults on children by

appropriate criminal penalties); *Platform Ärzte fur das Leben v Austria* (1988) 13 EHRR 204, para 32 (dealing with threats of violence by opponents on demonstrations to ensure freedom of assembly).

2   *Airey v Ireland* (1979) 2 EHRR 305, para 24. See also *Marckx v Belgium* (1979) 2 EHRR 330: 'Fulfilment of a duty under the Convention on occasion necessitates some positive action on the part of the State; in such circumstances the State cannot simply remain passive.'

3   *Sen v Netherlands* (2003) 36 EHRR 7. The distinction between positive and negative obligations, in the context of family reunion and separation, was held to be of lesser significance by Judge Martens in *Gul v Switzerland* (1996) 22 EHRR 93, see 8.81 below. For discussion on the relative precision, intensity and scope of negative and positive obligations see *R (on the application of Pretty) v DPP* [2001] UKHL 61, [2002] 1 AC 800; *R (on the application of A) v Lord Saville of Newdigate (No 2)* [2001] EWCA Civ 2048, [2002] 1 WLR 129; *R (on the application of Ullah) v Special Adjudicator* [2004] UKHL 26, [2004] INLR 381 (para 34); see also *R (on the application of Q) v Secretary of State for the Home Department* [2003] EWCA Civ 364, [2004] QB 36. See also *R (on the application of Limbuela) v Secretary of State for the Home Department* [2004] EWCA Civ 540, [2004] QB 440), *R (on the application of Gezer) v Secretary of State for the Home Department* [2004] EWCA Civ 1730, see 8.55 below.

4   *Kaya v Turkey* (1998) 28 EHRR 1; *Gülec v Turkey* (1998) 28 EHRR 121, para 78; *Kaya (Mahmut) v Turkey* (28 March 2000, unreported), ECtHR, para 106–107.

5   *Airey* above; *Golder v United Kingdom* (1975) 1 EHRR 524, paras 28–36.

6   *Winterwerp v Netherlands* (1979) 2 EHRR 387, para 60; *Artico v Italy* (1980) 3 EHRR 1, para 33; *Ashingdane v United Kingdom* (1985) 7 EHRR 528, para 57.

8.35 The ECHR allows the State a margin of appreciation in deciding how best to give effect to the rights enshrined in it pursuant to its obligations under Article 1 and Article 13 (provision of effective remedies for violation of the rights).[1] The margin of appreciation has been defined as the degree of latitude accorded to the national authorities and courts in recognition of the fact that 'by reason of their direct and continuous contact with the vital forces of their countries, the national authorities are in principle better placed than an international court to evaluate local needs and conditions'.[2] By conceding a margin of appreciation to each national system, the ECtHR has recognised that the Convention does not need to be applied uniformly by all States, but may vary in its application according to local needs and conditions.[3] The margin applies in relation to justification for derogation[4] from or interference with a Convention right,[5] the scope of positive obligations[6] and in assessing what constitutes objective and reasonable justification for discrimination under Article 14.[7] It reflects the principle of subsidiarity.[8] But the Court must give the final ruling on whether a restriction is reconcilable with protected rights, and its supervision is not limited merely to ascertaining whether a State exercised its discretion reasonably, carefully and in good faith.[9] The limits of the 'margin of appreciation' vary according to the importance of the rights at stake, the purpose pursued by the State and the degree to which opinions within a democratic society may reasonably vary. The limits are wider in cases involving national security,[10] planning policy,[11] tax,[12] social and economic policy,[13] and narrower in the fields of criminal law, free speech and private morality.[14] The technique is not available to the national courts, when they are considering Convention issues arising in their own countries.[15] However, as Lord Hope pointed out in *Kebilene*, something akin to the margin of appreciation may operate in some circumstances in the domestic jurisdiction, because the alleged breach of the Convention may involve an area of judgment within which the judiciary will defer to the considered opinion of the minister or departmental official.[16]

1   'The State has a choice of various means, but a law that fails to satisfy the requirement [protection of family life] violates Article 8': *Marckx v Belgium* above, para 31.
2   *Handyside v United Kingdom* (1976) 1 EHRR 737, paras 48–49; *Buckley v United Kingdom* (1996) 23 EHRR 101, paras 74–75.
3   *R v DPP, ex p Kebilene* [1999] 4 All ER 801 at 844B, per Lord Hope.
4   Ie, in deciding whether a 'public emergency threatens the life of the nation' under Art 15: *Ireland v United Kingdom* (1978) 2 EHRR 25, para 207. See 8.42 below.
5   *Handyside* above fn 2.
6   *Abdulaziz, Cabales and Balkandali v United Kingdom* (1985) 7 EHRR 471, para 67; *Osman v United Kingdom* [1999] 1 FLR 193.
7   *Rasmussen v Denmark* (1984) 7 EHRR 371, para 40.
8   Clayton and Tomlinson *The Law of Human Rights* (2000, OUP); R Ryssdall 'The coming of age of the European Convention on Human Rights' [1996] EHRLR 18–27. See further Lord Mackenzie-Stuart 'Subsidiarity – a busted flush?' in Curtin and O'Keefe *Constitutional adjudication in European Community law and national law* (1992, Butterworths).
9   *Sunday Times v United Kingdom* (1979) 2 EHRR 245, para 59.
10   The concept was developed initially to ensure freedom of action for national governments in derogating from the ECHR under Art 15: *Lawless v Ireland* 332/57 (1960) 1 EHRR 1, A61.501, 48–49, Commission. See also *Brannigan and McBride v United Kingdom* (1993) 17 EHRR 539.
11   *Buckley v United Kingdom* (1996) 23 EHRR 101, para 129.
12   *Gasus-Dosier-und Fördertechnik GmbH v Netherlands* (1995) 20 EHRR 403.
13   *Hatton v United Kingdom* (Grand Chamber) (2003) 37 EHRR 28.
14   *Smith and Grady v United Kingdom* (1999) 29 EHRR 493.
15   *R v Stratford Justices, ex p Imbert* [1999] 2 Cr App Rep 276 at 286, per Buxton LJ; *R (on the application of Mahmood) v Secretary of State for the Home Department* [2001] 1 WLR 840 at para 31, per Laws LJ.
16   See the majority of the HL in *A and X v Secretary of State for the Home Department* [2004] UKHL 56, [2005] 2 WLR 87 (on the need for derogation) (8.42 below; *Mahmood* above at para 33; *R (on the application of Daly) v Secretary of State for the Home Department* [2001] UKHL 26, [2001] 2 AC 532. See also Lester and Pannick *Human Rights Law and Practice* (2nd edn, 2004, Butterworths) para 3.21; Tomlinson, fn 8 above, paras 6.32, 6.37, 6.82ff; Singh, Hunt and Demetriou 'Is there a role for the "Margin of Appreciation" in National Law After the Human Rights Act?' [1999] 1 EHRLR 15–22.

8.36 The margin of appreciation involves a recognition by the ECtHR that the ECHR need not be applied uniformly by all States, but may vary according to local needs and conditions. But this is limited in practice by another strand of the Strasbourg jurisprudence, namely the principle that terms such as 'civil rights and obligations',[1] 'criminal charges',[2] 'penalty',[3] 'property', 'law' and 'association'[4] have an autonomous meaning under the Convention[5] and cannot be redefined by States so as to avoid their obligations.[6]

1   *König v Germany* (1978) 2 EHRR 170, para 95. See 8.72 below.
2   *Engel v Netherlands* (1976) 1 EHRR 647, para 82; *Deweer v Belgium* (1980) 2 EHRR 439, para 46. But the fact that, for example, a breach of the peace is categorised as a criminal offence for the purposes of Art 5 (*Steel v United Kingdom*) (1998) 28 EHRR 603) does not mean that the UK courts must so characterise it for the purposes of the Police and Criminal Evidence Act: *Williamson v Chief Constable of West Midlands* [2003] EWCA Civ 337, [2004] 1 WLR 14, para 26.
3   *Welch v United Kingdom* (1995) 20 EHRR 247, para 27; *Lauko v Slovakia* (1999) EHRLR 105.
4   *Chassagnou v France* (1999) 7 BHRC 151, 29 EHRR 615, para 100.
5   *Adolf v Austria* (1982) 4 EHRR 313, para 30.
6   This rationalisation of the concept was given in *Chassagnou* fn 4 above.

8.37 There are three kinds of rights protected under the ECHR:

(i) Absolute rights, which apply without qualification and from which States may not derogate even in time of war or public emergency threatening the life of the nation.[1] These are the right to life,[2] the right not to be condemned to death or executed,[3] the right not to be subjected to torture or to inhuman or degrading treatment or punishment,[4] the right not to be held in slavery or servitude,[5] freedom of conscience[6] and the right not to be punished by retrospective laws.[7]

(ii) Rights which are written in unqualified terms but which in practice are qualified and limited. They include rights to liberty and security[8] and to fair[9] and open trial,[10] of appeal in criminal matters,[11] to compensation for wrongful conviction,[12] not to be tried or punished twice[13] and the right to education.[14]

(iii) qualified rights, which may be limited in strictly defined circumstances, and must thus be balanced against, and if necessary may give way to, other public interests. They include rights to family life,[15] to freedom to manifest religion or beliefs,[16] expression,[17] assembly and association,[18] to protection of property,[19] to freedom of movement,[20] the right of aliens to procedural safeguards relating to expulsion,[21] to equality between spouses[22] and the right to enjoy Convention rights and freedoms without discrimination.[23]

[1] By Art 15(1).

[2] Article 2. But death may be inflicted in self-defence, to effect a lawful arrest or to prevent the escape of a lawfully detained person, or in quelling a riot, if it results from the use of force which is no more than absolutely necessary: see *McCann v United Kingdom* (1995) 21 EHRR 97; *Ogur v Turkey* (Application No 21594/93), 20 May 1999, para 78.

[3] Protocol 6 (which prohibits the death penalty except in time of war) and Protocol 13 (in force 1 July 2003, 1 February 2004 in UK) (which prohibits the death penalty in all circumstances).

[4] Article 3. See *Chahal v United Kingdom* (1996) 23 EHRR 413, para 79. So far as Art 3 refers to violence, this does not include the lawful use of violence in self defence, making a lawful arrest, or used reasonably for the prevention of crime; per Laws LJ in *R (on the application of Tesema) v Secretary of State for the Home Department; R (on the application of Adam) v Secretary of State for the Home Department; R (on the application of Limbuela) v Secretary of State for the Home Department* [2004] EWCA Civ 540, [2004] QB 1440.

[5] Article 4(1). See *Ould Barar v Sweden* (1999) 28 EHRR CD 213.

[6] Article 9. Contrast freedom to *manifest* belief, which is qualified.

[7] Article 7.

[8] Article 5, which spells out situations where detention is lawful, and is derogable under Art 15, but only a narrow interpretation of the exceptions is consistent with the aim and purpose of the provision, which is to ensure that no-one is arbitrarily deprived of his or her liberty: *Quinn v France* (1995) 21 EHRR 529; see 8.57 below. Article 1 of Protocol 4 (not ratified by the UK) prohibits imprisonment for debt.

[9] The right to a fair trial is absolute, but the subsidiary rights contained in it (eg the presumption of innocence) are not: *Brown v Stott (Procurator Fiscal, Dunfermline)* [2001] 2 All ER 97, PC.

[10] Article 6, which provides for less than open justice when circumstances require and is derogable under Art 15.

[11] Protocol 7, Art 2.

[12] Protocol 7, Art 3.

[13] Protocol 7, Art 4.

[14] Protocol 1, Art 2.

[15] Article 8.

[16] Article 9.

[17] Article 10.

[18] Article 11.

[19] Protocol 1, Art 1(2).

²⁰ Protocol 4, Art 2(3). This has not yet been ratified by the UK government.
²¹ Protocol 7, Art 1(2). This has not yet been ratified by the UK government.
²² Protocol 7, Art 5. This has not yet been ratified by the UK government.
²³ Article 14.

8.38 The right to respect for private and family life, home and correspondence, which is protected by ECHR, Article 8, permits interference which is in accordance with the law, and is necessary in a democratic society in the interests of national security, public safety, the economic well-being of the country, for the prevention of disorder or crime, for the protection of health or morals, or for the protection of the rights and freedoms of others.[1] Other qualified rights permit interference in similar, though not identical, terms. These interests are the legitimate aims which might justify interference with the protected rights. They are exhaustive, not illustrative,[2] and are to be construed strictly.[3] In *Miailhe v France*[4] the ECtHR stated that the exceptions in Article 8(2) are to be interpreted narrowly and the need for them in a given case must be convincingly established. The permitted restrictions must not be applied for any collateral purpose.[5]

[1] Article 8(2).
[2] *De Wilde, Ooms and Versyp v Belgium* (1971) 1 EHRR 373; *Golder v United Kingdom* (1975) 1 EHRR 524, para 44. In cases such as *Abdulaziz, Cabales and Balkandali v United Kingdom* (1985) 7 EHRR 471 and *D v United Kingdom* (1997) 24 EHRR 423, the ECtHR has referred to the right of States to control immigration. This undoubted international law right is however not one of the legitimate aims justifying interference with the qualified rights, but in the UK jurisprudence on Article 8 it is sometimes treated as if it were a free-standing 'legitimate aim' rather than a means of promoting one of the listed aims such as economic well-being or the prevention of disorder or crime. See the comment by Lord Phillips MR at para 44 of *R (on the application of Ullah) v Special Adjudicator* [2004] UKHL 26, [2004] INLR 381, not dealt with by the House of Lords when it reversed the Court of Appeal's decision.
[3] *Sunday Times v United Kingdom* (1979) 2 EHRR 245; *Smith and Grady v United Kingdom* (1999) 29 EHRR 493 ('pandering to the prejudices of members of the population is not a legitimate aim').
[4] (1993) 16 EHRR 332, para 38; see also *Funke v France* (1993) 16 EHRR 297, para 55; *Klass v Germany* (1978) 2 EHRR 214; *Lustig-Prean and Beckett v United Kingdom* (1999) 29 EHRR 548 (need for particularly serious reasons where restrictions concern a most intimate part of individuals' private life).
[5] Article 18.

8.39 Once it is established that the interference has a legitimate aim as defined within the relevant Article of the ECHR, assessing permissible interference with or restriction of qualified rights requires consideration of legality and proportionality. An interference which is not in accordance with domestic law will breach the Convention regardless of whether it is justified.[1] But legality, or the requirement that interference with rights is 'in accordance with the law' or 'prescribed by law', does not merely refer back to whether interference is allowed by domestic law[2] but it also relates to 'the quality of the law, requiring it to be compatible with the rule of law, a concept inherent in all Articles of the Convention'.[3] To comply with the rule of law the law itself must be sufficiently accessible[4] and precise[5] to enable the citizen to regulate his or her conduct[6] and avoid all risk of arbitrariness.[7] To conform with the requirements of accessibility and precision, a law conferring discretion must indicate its scope and set out the way discretion is to be exercised.[8]

1 See eg *Poltoratskiy v Ukraine* (38812/97) 29 April 2003; *GK v Poland* (Application 38816/97) (20 January 2004).
2 Including subordinate legislation: *Barthold v Germany* (1985) 7 EHRR 383.
3 *Dougoz v Greece* (2002) 34 EHRR 61, para 55.
4 *Malone v United Kingdom* (1984) 7 EHRR 14; *Halford v United Kingdom* (1997) 24 EHRR 523. See also *Zamir v United Kingdom* (1983) 40 DR 42, paras 90–91; *Steel v United Kingdom* (1998) 28 EHRR 603. For a discussion of the effect of late promulgation of an Act of Parliament on the legality of action taken under it see *R (on the application of ZL and VL) v Secretary of State for the Home Department* [2003] EWCA Civ 25, [2003] Imm AR 330, [2003] INLR 224, sub nom *R (on the application of L) v Secretary of State for the Home Department* [2003] All ER 1062, where the Secretary of State certified claims as clearly unfounded, depriving asylum seekers of an in-country right of appeal, before the 2002 Act containing the certification provisions was published. Home Office internal policy guidelines are not 'accessible' unless they are published: *Malone v United Kingdom*. Since 2 October 2000 (the date the Human Rights Act 1998 came into force), many Home Office discretionary policies have been incorporated into the immigration rules (eg on unmarried partners, victims of domestic violence and domestic workers, while some remaining discretionary policies are posted on the Home Office website. But not all: in *R (on the applicatin of Salih) v Secretary of State for the Home Department* [2003] EWHC 2273 (Admin) the Secretary of State's failure to make known to those eligible his policy of providing 'hard cases' support to failed asylum seekers was held unlawful having regard to the 'fundamental requisite of the rule of law' that the law should be made known. See also *R (on the application of Amirthanathan) v Secretary of State for the Home Department* [2003] EWCA Civ 1768, [2004] INLR 139, sub nom *Nadarajah v Secretary of State for the Home Department* (detention under unpublished policy unlawful).
5 *Amuur v France* (1996) 22 EHRR 533, para 50; *Camenzind v Switzerland* (1997) 28 EHRR 458, para 45; *Hashman and Harrup v United Kingdom* [2000] Crim LR 185 (bind over to 'be of good behaviour' not sufficiently precise).
6 *Sunday Times v United Kingdom* (1979) 2 EHRR 245, para 49. Unwritten law may fulfil these criteria: para 47.
7 *Dougoz v Greece* (2002) 34 EHRR 61.
8 *Silver v United Kingdom* (1983) 5 EHRR 347. See also *Huvig v France* (1990) 12 EHRR 528 (what is required is detailed rules setting out when intrusive measures may be carried out); *Leander v Sweden* (1987) 9 EHRR 433.

8.40 The balance between the protection of individual rights and the interests of the wider community is at the heart of the ECHR,[1] and a fair balance is achieved when interference with the individual's rights is strictly proportionate to the legitimate aim pursued in restricting it.[2] As Sedley LJ put it succinctly in *B*:[3]

'A measure which interferes with a human right must not only be authorised by law but must correspond to a pressing social need and go no further than is strictly necessary in a pluralistic society to achieve its permitted purpose; or, more shortly, must be appropriate and necessary to its legitimate aim.'[4]

The requirement that a restriction on a fundamental right be 'necessary' is strict; 'necessary' is not so flexible a term as 'useful' or 'desirable',[5] and the phrase 'necessary in a democratic society' refers to a pluralistic, tolerant and broadminded society.[6] In *Sunday Times Ltd v United Kingdom (No 2)*[7] the ECtHR stated:

'The court's task, in exercising its supervisory jurisdiction, is not to take the place of the competent national authorities but rather to review under Article 10 the decision they delivered pursuant to their powers of appreciation. This does not mean that the supervision is limited to ascertaining whether the respondent exercised its jurisdiction reasonably and carefully and in good faith; what the court has to do is to look at the interference complained of in the light of the case as a whole and determine whether it was "proportionate to the legitimate aim pursued" and whether the reasons adduced by the national authorities to justify it are "relevant and sufficient".'

1   *Sporrong and Lönnroth v Sweden* (1982) 5 EHRR 35, para 52.
2   *Handyside v United Kingdom* (1976) 1 EHRR 737, para 49. For the principle of proportionality see Clayton and Tomlinson (at 8.19 fn 5 above), para 6.40ff; Lester and Pannick *Human Rights Law and Practice* (1999, Butterworths), para 3.10; Grosz, Beatson and Duffy *Human Rights* (2000, Sweet & Maxwell), pp 112–114; Starmer *European Human Rights Law*, pp 169–180; Wadham and Mountfield (1999, Blackstone) *The Human Rights Act* 1998, pp 13–16; De Smith, Woolf and Jowell *Judicial Review of Administrative Action* (5th edn, 1995, Sweet & Maxwell), pp 593–606.
3   *B v Secretary of State for the Home Department* [2000] Imm AR 478.
4   Para 17. It was accepted by both parties that the test of proportionality under the ECHR was the same as that in EU law: para 7. See chapter 7 above.
5   *Chassagnou v France* (1999) 7 BHRC 151.
6   *Handyside* fn 2 above; *Dudgeon v United Kingdom* (1981) 4 EHRR 149 (criminalisation of homosexual acts disproportionate to aim of protection of morals).
7   (1991) 14 EHRR 229, para 50. See further *Hertel v Switzerland* (1998) 28 EHRR 534, para 46; *Grigoriades v Greece* (1997) 27 EHRR 464, para 44.

8.41 Factors relevant to assessing the proportionality of a restriction have been held to include the extent of the interference[1] and whether there was a less restrictive alternative;[2] and whether there are fair procedures[3] and safeguards against abuse.[4] The absence of relevant and sufficient reasons for the restriction[5] is likely to result in a finding that the restriction was not necessary or was disproportionate. The principle of proportionality is not limited to the rights in respect of which interference is expressly defined, but also applies, for example, to detention under Article 5,[6] to Article 6 rights,[7] to the prohibition of discrimination in the enjoyment of ECHR rights under Article 14[8] and to the scope of positive obligations under the Convention.[9]

1   Restrictions which impair the 'very essence' of the right in question will be disproportionate: *F v Switzerland* (1987) 10 EHRR 411, para 40; *Rees v United Kingdom* (1986) 9 EHRR 56, para 50.
2   *Informationsverein Lentia v Austria* (1993) 17 EHRR 93, para 40; *Campbell v United Kingdom* (1992) 15 EHRR 137. The question of a 'less restrictive alternative' (proportionality as to means) was held irrelevant to cases involving expulsion in *R (on the application of Samaroo) v Secretary of State for the Home Department* [2001] EWCA Civ 1139, [2001] UKHRR 1150, [2002] INLR 55 and *R (on the application of Sezek) v Secretary of State for the Home Department* [2001] EWCA Civ 795, [2002] 1 WLR 34855, where the issue is to expel or not.
3   *W v United Kingdom* (1987) 10 EHRR 29, para 62; *Buckley v United Kingdom* (1996) 23 EHRR 101, para 76.
4   *Klass v Germany* (1978) 2 EHRR 214, paras 55, 59; *Camenzind v Switzerland* (1997) 28 EHRR 458, para 45.
5   *Observer and Guardian v United Kingdom* (1991) 14 EHRR 153, para 59; *Vogt v Germany* (1996) 21 EHRR 205, para 52.
6   See 8.37 above.
7   Thus the right of access to a court may be limited, but limitation will not be compatible with Art 6(1) ECHR unless it pursues a legitimate aim and there is a reasonable relationship of proportionality between the means employed and the aim sought to be achieved: *Ashingdane v United Kingdom* (1985) 7 EHRR 528, para 57.
8   'Very weighty reasons would have to be advanced before a difference in treatment on grounds of sex could be considered compatible with the Convention': *Abdulaziz, Cabales and Balkandali v United Kingdom* (1985) 7 EHRR 471, para 78. See 8.98 below.
9   See *Powell and Rayner v United Kingdom* (1990) 12 EHRR 355.

extension' of the territoriality principle to postulate that the Convention requires a State to take positive action to prevent or mitigate the effects of violations of human rights that take place outside the jurisdiction and for which the State has no responsibility. In *R (on the application of Suresh) v Secretary of State for the Home Department* [2001] EWHC Admin 1028, [2002] Imm AR 345, an attempt to seek entry of a leading LTTE member to the UK to prevent his expulsion from Canada to Sri Lanka, where he feared torture, was dismissed on the basis there was no duty on the Secretary of State to prevent a breach of Art 3 by another country, either on the basis of the applicant's entry clearance application or because he had family members in the UK.

⁴ *Bankovic v Belgium* above, para 71. See *Loizidou v Turkey* (1995) 20 EHRR 90 (Turkish occupation of northern Cyprus).

⁵ *Bankovic v Belgium* above, para 73. See *Xhavara v Italy and Albania* (39473/98, 11 January 2001 (interception by Italian naval vessel of ship carrying refugees); *Öcalan v Turkey* (46221/99) (2003) 15 BHRC 297 (seizure of suspect abroad). Lord Bingham expressed the greatest doubt whether this included the actions of British immigration officers in Prague in *European Roma Rights Centre v Immigration Officer at Prague (United Nations High Comr for Refugees Intervening)* [2004] UKHL 55, [2005] 1 All ER 527 at para 21. But see *R(B) v Secretary of State for the Foreign and Commonwealth Affairs* [2004] EWCA Civ 1344, [2005] 2 WLR 618, para 66. And consider the Haitians, intercepted at sea when trying to reach the coast of the US, whose plight was considered in *Sale, Acting Comr, Immigration and Naturalisation Service v Haitian Centers Council Inc* 509 US 155 (1993), p 183, fn 40. The United States authorities' treatment of them was understandably held by the Inter-American Commission of Human Rights (Report No 51/96, 13 March 1997, para 171) to breach their right to life, liberty and security of their persons as well as the right to asylum protected by Article XXVII of the American Declaration of the Rights and Duties of Man (para 163. The Commission also found the United States to be in breach of Art 33(1) of the Refugee Convention: paras 156–158, a view shared by Blackmun J in his dissent in *Sale*).

⁶ *Soering v United Kingdom* (1989) 11 EHRR 439.

⁷ *Cruz Varas v Sweden* (1991) 14 EHRR 1; *Vilvarajah v United Kingdom* (1991) 14 EHRR 248; *Chahal v United Kingdom* (1996) 23 EHRR 413; *D v United Kingdom* (1997) 24 EHRR 423; *HLR v France* (1997) 26 EHRR 29; *Gonzalez v Spain* (Application No 43544/98, 29 June 1999, unreported); *Dehwari v Netherlands* (2000) 29 EHRR CD 74; and *Hilal v United Kingdom* (2001) 33 EHRR 31.

⁸ *R (on the application of Ullah) v Special Adjudicator* [2004] UKHL 26, [2004] INLR 381.

⁹ *R (on the application of Razgar) v Secretary of State for the Home Department* [2004] UKHL 27, [2004] 2 AC 368.

¹⁰ *Ullah* at paras 7 and 9.

THE ECHR RIGHTS

8.44 The main ECHR rights of potential relevance in immigration law are: the right to life (Article 2) and the prohibition of the death penalty (Protocol 6, Article 1 and Protocol 13); the prohibition of torture and inhuman or degrading treatment or punishment (Article 3); the prohibition of slavery and forced labour (Article 4); the right to liberty and security (Article 5); the right of access to courts and due process (Article 6); rights to the protection of private and family life (Article 8) and the prohibition of discrimination in the enjoyment of these rights (Article 14). Other rights of some relevance, particularly in asylum appeals, are freedom of conscience, expression and assembly (Articles 9–11).¹ The right to marry and found a family (Article 12) has recently assumed some significance, although it is generally of less relevance than might be supposed. For reasons of space we refer here only to the main Articles of relevance to immigration and asylum law.²

¹ See 12.46 below for an exposition of the common human rights foundation of the Refugee and Human Rights Conventions.

Right to life

8.45   Article 2 of the ECHR states that:

'1   Everyone's right to life shall be protected by law. No one shall be deprived of his life intentionally save in the execution of a sentence of a court following his conviction of a crime for which this penalty is provided by law.

2   Deprivation of life shall not be regarded as inflicted in contravention of this Article when it results from the use of force which is no more than absolutely necessary:

   (a)   in defence of any person from unlawful violence;
   (b)   in order to effect a lawful arrest or to prevent the escape of a person lawfully detained;
   (c)   in action lawfully taken for the purpose of quelling a riot or insurrection.'

Article 1 of Protocol 13 states that:

'The death penalty shall be abolished. No one shall be condemned to such penalty or executed.'

The Protocol, ratified by the UK and in force as regards the UK on 1 February 2004, replaced Protocol 6, which provided that the death penalty could be used in time of war, in the Schedule of Convention Rights in the Human Rights Act in June 2004. The obligation under Article 2 comprises a negative obligation not to take life except in clearly defined circumstances, and a positive obligation to protect life.[1] The obligation:

'extends beyond its primary duty to secure the right to life by putting in place effective criminal law provisions to deter the commission of offences against the person backed up by law-enforcement machinery for the prevention, suppression and sanctioning of breaches of such provisions ... Article 2 may well also imply in certain well-defined circumstances a positive obligation on the authorities to take preventive operational measures to protect an individual whose life is at risk from the criminal acts of another individual.'[2]

The duty applies to persons in custody where the risk derives from self-harm,[3] and acts and omissions in the field of health care may engage State responsibility under Article 2, in particular putting life at risk by denial of health care available to the general population.[4] The *Osman* duty was considered in the *Widgery Soldiers* case, where it was held that the threshold of State responsibility was lower when the risk was occasioned by the act of the public authority.[5] As regards the negative obligation not to take life, the use of lethal force by agents of the State must be 'absolutely necessary', which is a 'stricter and more compelling test of necessity than that normally applicable when determining whether State action is 'necessary in a democratic society' under paragraph 2 of Articles 8 to 12.[6] The obligation under Article 2 extends to carrying out an effective investigation where individuals have been killed as a result of the use of force, in particular to 'secure the accountability of agents of the State for their use of lethal force'.[7] It also extends to cases where a death occurs in custody, or may be attributed to negligence by State agents.[8]

[1] *Pretty v United Kingdom (2002) 35 EHRR 1: 'The consistent emphasis in all the cases before the court has been the obligation of the State to protect life' (para 39). As Lord Bingham said in R (on the application of Amin) v Secretary of State for the Home Department* [2003] UKHL 51, [2004] 1 AC 653, 'A profound respect for the sanctity of human life underpins ... the jurisprudence under Articles 1 and 2 of the Convention.'

[2] *Osman v United Kingdom* (1998) 29 EHRR 245, para 115. But 'bearing in mind the difficulties involved in policing modern societies, the unpredictability of human conduct and the operational choices which must be made in terms of priorities and resources, such an obligation must be interpreted in a way which does not impose an impossible or disproportionate burden on the authorities'. Article 2 would be breached only if 'the authorities do not do all that could be reasonably expected of them to avoid a real and immediate risk to life of which they have or ought to have knowledge' (para 116).

[3] *Keenan v United Kingdom (2001) 33 EHRR 38.*

[4] *Nitecki v Poland* (65653/01) 21 March 2002. Thus, legislation denying life-saving treatment to certain groups such as asylum seekers would be incompatible with Art 2. However, in the removal cases, there is usually also an Art 3 claim, which the court prefers to deal with first, as it covers much the same ground; see *D v United Kingdom* (1997) 24 EHRR 423. In the domestic court, Art 2 was held engaged where an HIV positive mother on asylum support was provided with insufficient money to buy formula milk, giving rise to a real risk that she would breast-feed her child and transmit the virus to her: *R (on the application of T) v Secretary of State for Health, Secretary of State for the Home Department* [2002] EWHC 1887 (Admin), para 87.

[5] The court was referring there to the current responsibility engaged by the summoning of soldier witnesses to Derry, where, the court held, they were at risk of revenge attacks, rather than the historic one of the Bloody Sunday killings themselves: *R (on the application of A) v Lord Saville of Newdigate (No 2)* [2001] EWCA Civ 2048, [2002] 1 WLR 129, para 28. The court was not referred to *R v Secretary of State for the Home Department, ex p Fadli* (C/00/2682) [2001] 02 LS Gaz R 40, an asylum case which held that Art 2 does not extend to an obligation to protect the life of a serving soldier, whose life is by definition a hazardous one.

[6] *Ogur v Turkey* App no 21594/93, 20 May 1999. See also *McCann v United Kingdom* (1995) 21 EHRR 97.

[7] *Kaya v Turkey* (1998) 28 EHRR 1; *Güleç v Turkey* (1998) 28 EHRR 121.

[8] *Aktas v Turkey* (24351/99) 24 April 2003; *Edwards v United Kingdom* (2002) 12 BHRC 190; *Salman v Turkey* (2002) 34 EHRR 425. In *R (on the application of Amin) v Secretary of State for the Home Department* [2003] UKHL 51, [2004] 1 AC 653 (on the investigative duty where a young offender in detention was killed by a racist cellmate) the House of Lords said that the ECtHR jurisprudence drew no clear dividing line (in terms of the investigate duty) between cases where an agent of the State kills, and those where the system is such that a killing occurs; the guarantees of a public investigation and next-of-kin involvement were minimum requirements (para 42). For the investigative duty in the context of NHS negligence see *R (on the application of Khan) v Secretary of State for Health* [2003] EWCA Civ 1129, [2003] 4 All ER 1129.

8.46 The prohibition on the death penalty in all circumstances under Protocol 13 of the ECHR, superseding its partial prohibition (in time of peace) under Protocol 6, was ratified by the UK in 2004.[1] In Öcalan[2] the ECtHR considered that the *de jure* abolition of the death penalty in 43 of the 44 Contracting States, and a moratorium in the remaining death penalty state (Russia), the signing by all Contracting States of Protocol 6 and its ratification by 41 States,[3] and the Council of Europe's policy requiring new Member States to undertake to abolish capital punishment as a condition of admission, meant that the territories encompassed by Member States of the Council of Europe comprised a 'zone free of capital punishment': 'Against such a consistent background, it can be said that capital punishment in peacetime has come to be regarded as an unacceptable, if not inhuman, form of punishment which is no longer permissible under Article 2'.[4] In the immigration context, this means that no one may be returned to a State where he or she will be subject to the death penalty.[5] But the ECtHR's application of Article 2 to expulsion cases has been problematic. In *Bahaddar*[6] the Commission held that expulsion to a real risk of death did not engage the first sentence of Article 2, and would not constitute 'intentional deprivation of life' unless the expelling State 'knowingly puts the person concerned at such high risk of losing his life as for the outcome to be a near-certainty', although if there was a real risk of death, expulsion would amount to inhuman treatment.[7] Thus, unless expulsion means that death is 'a near certainty', the European Court will find a violation of Article 3, but not of Article 2. Home Office policy (and the EC Qualification Directive)[8] dictates the grant of humanitarian protection to a person at risk of the death penalty or of unlawful killing.[9]

[1] See 8.45 above. *Article 1 of Protocol 13 replaced Arts 1 and 2 of Protocol 6 in the Schedule to the Human Rights Act 1998 in June 2004: see the Human Rights Act 1998 (Amendment) Order 2004, SI 2004/1574.*

[2] *Öcalan v Turkey* (46221/99) (2003) BHRC 297.

[3] *Apart from Turkey, Armenia and Russia.*

[4] *Öcalan v Turkey* (fn 2 above) paras 195–6.

[5] In the light of the *Öcalan* judgment, extradition *to a real risk of the death penalty would now breach Art 2 (an argument rejected by the court in Soering v United Kingdom (1989) 11 EHRR 439). See also Cruz Varas v Sweden (1991) 14 EHRR 1; R (on the application of St John) v Governor of Brixton Prison [2001] EWHC Admin 543, [2002] 2 WLR 221 (extradition to USA).*

[6] *Bahaddar v Netherlands* (25894/94) (1998) 26 EHRR 278, ECtHR (report of Commission adopted 13 September 1976).

[7] *Bahaddar* (fn 6) para 76. This reasoning was adopted in *Dehwari v Netherlands* (2000) 29 EHRR CD 74 (where there was a real risk that the death penalty would be imposed in Iran).

[8] Council Directive 2004/83/EC on minimum standards for the qualification and status of third country nationals and stateless persons as refugees or persons who otherwise need international protection (OJ 2004 L304/12), Arts 2, 15, stipulating that Member States must grant subsidiary protection in these situations (inter alia), subject to exclusion clauses akin to those under the Refugee Convention.

[9] See 8.32 above.

Exposure to torture or inhuman or degrading treatment or punishment

8.47 Article 3 of the ECHR states that:

'No one shall be subjected to torture or to inhuman or degrading treatment or punishment.'

Torture is not defined in the ECHR. It implies deliberately inflicted suffering of particular intensity and cruelty.[1] In the UN Convention Against Torture[2] it comprises three elements: severe pain or suffering, physical or mental; intentionally inflicted for purposes such as obtaining information or a confession or for punishment, for intimidation or coercion or from discrimination; inflicted by or at the instigation of, or with the consent or acquiescence of, a public authority or person acting in an official capacity.[3] But the

ECtHR does not require official involvement to find a breach of Article 3.[4] The Convention being a living instrument, acts which were previously classified as inhuman treatment could now be classified as torture, as standards in the protection of human rights and fundamental liberties rise.[5] It may be inflicted gratuitously without any intention to obtain information.[6] Rape has been recognised as torture,[7] and rape of a detainee by a State official is a specially grave and abhorrent form of ill-treatment because of the vulnerability and weakened resistance of the victim.[8] But a finding of torture is not required to found a violation of Article 3:

> 'Ill-treatment [must] attain a minimum level of severity and involve actual bodily injury or intense physical or mental suffering. Where treatment humiliates or debases an individual, showing a lack of respect for, or diminishing his or her human dignity, or arouses feelings of fear, anguish or inferiority capable of breaking an individual's moral and physical resistance, it may be classified as degrading and also fall within the prohibition.'[9]

Inhuman treatment requires less serious suffering than torture, although the threshold is still high, and it need not be deliberately inflicted.[10] What constitutes inhuman treatment will depend on the characteristics of the individual such as their age, sex and state of health.[11] A threat of torture, if sufficiently real and immediate, may give rise to such mental suffering as to constitute inhuman treatment,[12] as may a callous disregard for the anguish of relatives of the 'disappeared'.[13] Conditions of detention such as severe overcrowding, constant lighting, inadequate sanitation and lack of opportunities for outdoor exercise or human contact, may constitute inhuman treatment,[14] as may subjection to a death sentence,[15] or the agony of waiting on death row.[16] An excessively long sentence may also give rise to a finding of inhuman treatment or punishment.[17] The authorities are under a particular obligation to protect the health of detainees, and the lack of appropriate medical treatment in custody may amount to treatment contrary to Article 3.[18] The suffering which flows from naturally occurring illness, physical or mental, may be covered by Article 3 where it is, or risks being, exacerbated by treatment, whether flowing from conditions of detention, expulsion or other measures, for which the authorities can be held responsible.[19] Article 3 contains within it a duty to investigate any ill-treatment for which the State may be held responsible.[20]

---

[1] *Ireland v United Kingdom* (1978) 2 EHRR 25 where the 'five techniques' of hooding, wall standing, subjection to noise, sleep deprivation and deprivation of food and drink were held not to occasion suffering of the particular intensity and cruelty implied by the word 'torture', although they constituted inhuman or degrading treatment.

[2] Article 1, UN Convention against Torture and other Cruel, Inhuman or Degrading Treatment or Punishment 1984. The prohibition against torture is a *ius cogens*, a binding obligation in international customary law: *R v Bow Street Metropolitan Stipendiary Magistrate, ex p Pinochet Ugarte (No 3)* [1999] 2 WLR 827, per Lord Browne-Wilkinson.

[3] In the absence of central government, armed factions (eg in Somalia) could be 'public officials': *Elmi v Australia* [1999] INLR 341 (UN Committee Against Torture).

[4] *HLR v France* (1997) 26 EHRR 29; see further below 8.50.

[5] *Selmouni v France* (1999) 29 EHRR 403, para 97.

[6] No intention to obtain information is necessary for a finding of torture: *Selmouni* above; *R v Secretary of State for the Home Department, ex p Singh* [1999] INLR 632 at 637, although such an intention may turn lesser violence into torture; cf *Denizi v Cyprus* (23 May 2002, unreported) (beating not torture as purpose not to extract information).

7   *Aydin v Turkey* (1997) 3 BHRC 300, 25 EHRR 251. A risk of sexual abuse and gang attacks in Jamaica were held to engage Art 3 in *A v Secretary of State for the Home Department* [2003] EWCA Civ 175, [2003] All ER (D) 151 (Jan); see also *Kaba* [2002] UKIAT 02289; *Kaur (Joginder)* [2002] UKIAT 07599; *Nkangala* [2002] UKIAT 05518, all Tribunal cases where the threat of rape or sexual violence precluded removal.

8   *Aydin v Turkey* para 83. See also the International War Crimes Tribunal for the former Yugoslavia judgment in *Furundzija* (IT-95–17/1-T) (10 December 1998, unreported).

9   *Pretty v United Kingdom* (2002) 35 EHRR 1.

10 The techniques in *Ireland v United Kingdom*, fn 1 above, were held to constitute inhuman treatment since, without causing bodily injury, they caused intense physical and mental suffering and led to psychiatric disturbances during interrogation. In *Tomasi v France* (1992) 15 EHRR 1 a 40-hour interrogation including slapping, kicking, punching, being threatened with a firearm and made to stand for long periods handcuffed or naked was held to constitute inhuman and degrading treatment. See also *Ribitsch v Austria* (1995) 21 EHRR 573, para 38: any recourse to physical force against a person deprived of his liberty, not made strictly necessary by his own conduct, diminishes human dignity and is in principle an infringement of Art 3 rights.

11 *Tyrer v United Kingdom* (1978) 2 EHRR 1; *Campbell and Cosans v United Kingdom* (1982) 4 EHRR 293, paras 28–30; *Soering v United Kingdom* (1989) 11 EHRR 439, para 100. In *Selçuk and Asker v Turkey* (1998) 26 EHRR 477 the destruction of the homes and property of two elderly residents of a Turkish village by security forces, 'carried out contemptuously and without respect for the feelings' of the applicants, was held to constitute inhuman treatment.

12 *Campbell and Cosans v United Kingdom* (1982) 4 EHRR 293.

13 *Kurt v Turkey* (1998) 27 EHRR 373; *Timurtas v Turkey* (23531/94), 13 June 2000.

14 The *Greek case* (1969) 12 YB 186; *Cyprus v Turkey* (1984) 4 EHRR 482; *Loukanov v Bulgaria* (1995) 19 EHRR CD 65; *Dougoz v Greece* (40907/98) (2001) 10 BHRC 306; *Kalashnikov v Russia* (47095/99), *Van der Ven v Netherlands* (50901/99) (4 February 2002, unreported) (conditions in maximum security prison, and weekly strip search); *Poltoratskiy v Ukraine* (38812/97, 29 April 2003); *Khokhlich v Ukraine* (41707/98) (29 April 2003, unreported). Solitary confinement is not *per se* inhuman treatment but is capable of being so depending on the particular conditions, the duration and stringency of the measure, its objective and its effects. Complete sensory and social isolation may be so by virtue of its effect of breaking down the personality: *Ensslin, Baader and Raspe v Germany* (1978) 14 DR 64.

15 In *Öcalan v Turkey* (46221/99) (2003) 15 BHRC 287, the court held that the imposition of a death sentence did not violate Art 2 (8.46 above) but was inhuman and degrading, and violated Art 3.

16 *Soering v United Kingdom* (1989) 11 EHRR 439.

17 *Weeks v United Kingdom* (1988) 10 EHRR 293, para 47; *Hussain v United Kingdom* (1996) 22 EHRR 1, para 53. But it is not enough that the sentence is more severe than might apply in other European States: *C v Germany* 46 DR 179. The continued detention of a prisoner with cancer violated dignity and caused suffering in excess of that inevitably associated with a custodial sentence and treatment for cancer, giving rise to a breach of Art 3: *Mouisel v France* (67263/01) (14 November 2002, unreported).

18 *Keenan v United Kingdom* (2001) 33 EHRR 38, para 115; see also *Kudla v Poland* (30210/96) (2000) 10 BHRC 269; *Price v United Kingdom* (33394/96) (2001) Times, 13 August.

19 *Pretty v United Kingdom* (2002) 35 EHRR 1, para 52. (But no positive obligation to sanction actions intended to terminate life can be derived from Art 3.)

20 See cases cited at 8.45 fn 7 and 8 above. Where an individual is taken into custody in good health but is found to be injured on release, it is incumbent on the State to provide a plausible explanation of how the injuries were caused, failing which an issue arises under Art 3: *Tomasi v France* (1992) 15 EHRR 1.

8.48 *Degrading treatment.* In the case law on Article 3, the same treatment (particularly in detention) may be both 'inhuman' and degrading', but they are separate concepts. Degrading treatment is treatment which is grossly humiliating, arousing feelings of 'anguish and inferiority capable of humiliating and debasing' the victim.[1] In considering whether treatment or punishment is degrading, the court will have regard to whether the object is to humiliate and debase,[2] but the absence of an intention to degrade does not preclude a finding of degrading treatment.[3] Corporal punishment has been held to constitute degrading punishment.[4] Race discrimination is capable of constituting degrading treatment, as 'publicly to single out a group of persons for differential treatment on the basis of race might ... constitute a special form of affront to human dignity'.[5]

[1] *Ireland v United Kingdom* (1978) 2 EHRR 25. See *Hurtado v Switzerland* (1994) Series A, 280A where the Commission found degrading treatment where a detainee was not permitted to change his clothes after he had soiled his trousers, and *Gurdogan v Turkey* (1986) 76 DR 9 (smearing excrement on the mouths of Kurdish villagers).

[2] *Raminen v Finland* (1998) 26 EHRR 563, para 55; *Keenan v United Kingdom* (2001) 33 EHRR 38, para 109.

[3] *Peers v Greece* (2001) 33 EHRR 1192; *Price v UK* (33394/96) (2001) Times, 31 August, unreported. See also *Kalashnikov v Russia, Poltoratskiy v Ukraine* (47095/99). A strip search in front of a prison officer of the opposite sex was held degrading in *Valašinas v Lithuania* (44558/98) (24 July 2001, unreported). See 8.65 below.

[4] In *Tyrer v United Kingdom* (1978) 2 EHRR 1 (judicial birching of a 15-year-old which was 'institutionalised violence' on someone 'in the power of the authorities'). But cf *Costello-Roberts v United Kingdom* (1993) 19 EHRR 112 where smacking the bottom of a 7-year-old boy in a private school was held not to reach the minimum necessary level of severity. In *A v United Kingdom* (1998) 27 EHRR 611, however, a parent's beating of his 9-year-old stepson, leaving bruising, was held sufficiently serious.

[5] *East African Asians v United Kingdom* (1973) 3 EHRR 76, Commission. The Commission in this case said treatment is degrading if 'it lowers [a person] in rank, position, reputation or character, whether in his own eyes or in the eyes of other people', and reaches a certain level of severity. The applicants in that case were being deprived of their livelihood and being left destitute in Africa, and were reduced to the status of second-class citizens by the UK government, which denied them admission to their country of nationality. The 'shuttle-cocking' of refugees was held capable of engaging Art 3 in *Giana v Belgium* 21 DR 73 and *Harabi v Netherlands* 46 DR 112. In *X and Y v United Kingdom* App 5302/71, 44 CD 29, Kenyan Asians had gone to India where they were established and had strong family links. Their application was declared inadmissible, since 'unlike their fellow citizens in East Africa they had work and a place to live'. See also *Lalljee v United Kingdom* (1985) 8 EHRR 84 where a quota system for immigration was held not to be degrading. The Administrative Court held that Art 3 might arguably be engaged by a claim that Roma children were at risk of being sent to special schools in the Czech Republic in *R (on the application of Kurecaj) v Secretary of State for the Home Department* [2001] EWHC Admin 1199.

8.49 The right not to be tortured or subjected to inhuman or degrading treatment contrary to Article 3 of the ECHR is an unqualified right and can never be balanced or give way to competing considerations. It:

'enshrines one of the fundamental values of democratic societies, prohibits in absolute terms torture or inhuman or degrading treatment or punishment, irrespective of the victim's conduct. Unlike most of the substantive clauses of the Convention ... it makes no provision for exceptions and no derogation from it is permissible even in the event of a public emergency threatening the life of the nation ... the activities of the individual in question, however undesirable or dangerous, cannot be a material consideration.'[1]

However, some domestic confusion has been caused by the court's observations in *Soering*:[2]

'What constitutes inhuman or degrading treatment or punishment depends on all the circumstances of the case. Furthermore, inherent in the whole of the

Convention is a search for a fair balance between the demands of the general interests of the community and the requirements of the protection of the individual's fundamental rights. As movement becomes easier and crime takes on a larger international dimension, it is increasingly in the interests of all nations that suspected offenders who flee abroad should be brought to justice. Conversely, the establishment of safe havens for fugitives would not only result in danger for the State obliged to harbour the protected person but also tend to undermine the foundations of extradition. These considerations must also be included among the factors to be taken into account in the interpretation and application of notions of inhuman or degrading treatment or punishment in extradition cases.'[3]

The court confirmed in *Chahal* that there is no 'balancing' of interests in Article 3 cases:

'It should not be inferred from the court's remarks about the risks of undermining the foundations of extradition, as set out in para 89 of [*Soering*], that there is any room for balancing the risk of ill-treatment against the reasons for expulsion in determining whether a State's responsibility under Article 3 is engaged.'[4]

And in *Tyrer*, the court took the view that 'no local requirements relevant to the maintenance of law and order would entitle any of [the Contracting States] ... to make use of a punishment contrary to Article 3'.[5]

[1]   *Chahal v United Kingdom* (1996) 23 EHRR 413. See also *Ahmed v Austria* (1996) 24 EHRR 278, para 41.
[2]   *Soering v United Kingdom* (1989) 11 EHRR 439.
[3]   (1989) 11 EHRR 439 at para 89. In *Ullah v Special Adjudicator* [2002] EWCA Civ 1856, [2003] INLR 74 (para 38) and in *N v Secretary of State for the Home Department* [2003] EWCA Civ 1369, [2004] 1 WLR 1182 (para 30) the Court of Appeal used this passage to hold that the public interest in extradition or immigration control could be a relevant factor in deciding on the severity of ill-treatment in a receiving State which would preclude removal. The main legal holding in *Ullah* was reversed *in the House of Lords ([2004] UKHL 26 [2004] INLR 381), but* the speeches in the HL judgment in *N* [2005] UKHL 31 clearly had such considerations in mind: see 8.53 below. For criticism of the 'questionable recourse to the principle of proportionality' for the purpose of setting the minimum level of severity for triggering Art 3 see F Sudre, 'Article 3' in Decaux, Imbert and Pettiti, eds, *Commentaires par Articles de la Convention* (Paris, Economica, 1995) p 160.
[4]   *Chahal* (fn 1 above).
[5]   *Tyrer v United Kingdom* (1970) 2 EHRR 1. 'A relativisation of the scope of one of the Convention's most fundamental rights would not only be both absurd and disturbing; it would also occur in the very midst of the western community of nations that is fond of stressing the universality of human rights on the international scene ... If ever there was an area symbolising such universality, it is ... the one covered by Article 3.' Callewaert 'Is there a margin of appreciation in the application of Articles 2, 3 and 4 of the Convention?' (1998) 19 HRLJ 1, pp 6–9.

8.50 The landmark case of *Soering*[1] established that extradition to a country where there is a real risk of treatment contrary to Article 3 of the ECHR engages the UK's responsibility under Article 3.[2] The principle has since been extended to expulsion of rejected asylum seekers,[3] deportation on national security grounds[4] and other removals. In *Vilvarajah*[5] the court held that the expelling State's responsibility was engaged:

'where substantial grounds have been shown for believing that the person concerned faces a real risk of being subjected to torture or inhuman or degrading treatment or punishment in the country to which he is returned.'[6]

The assessment of this risk must be thorough, in view of the importance of Article 3, and is carried out by reference both to the applicant's personal history and to the human rights conditions in the destination country, in much the same way as a Refugee Convention assessment.[7] The ECtHR has shown its willingness to review and reverse domestic courts' adverse credibility findings in carrying out the assessment.[8] The automatic and mechanical application of rigid procedural requirements for asylum claimants is at variance with the protection of the fundamental values embodied in Article 3.[9] In *Pretty v United Kingdom*, the ECtHR held that the act of expulsion is 'treatment' within the scope of the negative obligation;[10] thus, expulsion which exposes a person to a real risk of ill-treatment abroad is a breach of a negative obligation.[11]

[1] *Soering v United Kingdom* (1989) 11 EHRR 439, where the applicant was awaiting extradition to the US, where he faced the prospect of waiting on death row for many years. The court upheld the principle that the sending State was responsible under Art 3 for 'all and any foreseeable consequences of extradition suffered outside their jurisdiction'.

[2] See Alleweldt, Ralf *'Protection against expulsion under Article 3 ECHR'* in (1993) 4 EJIL 360–376, www.ejil.org/journal.

[3] In *Cruz Varas v Sweden* (1991) 14 EHRR 1 the court held that the test in *Soering* applied *a fortiori* to expulsions of aliens. See also *Hilal v United Kingdom* (2001) 33 EHRR 2, [2001] INLR 595: rejection of claim of Tanzanian and decision to remove him breached Art 3.

[4] *Chahal v United Kingdom* (1996) 23 EHRR 413. See also, in the domestic court, *R v Secretary of State for the Home Department, ex p McQuillan* [1995] 4 All ER 400 (exclusion under the Prevention of Terrorism (Temporary Provisions) Act 1989).

[5] *Vilvarajah v United Kingdom* (1991) 14 EHRR 248.

[6] See also *Matumbo v Switzerland* (1994) 15 HRLJ 164, a case on the UN Convention Against Torture. This standard of proof—substantial grounds for believing that a real risk of the prohibited harm exists—has been held to be the same to all intents and purposes as that under the Refugee Convention: *Kacaj* [2001] INLR 354, [2002] Imm AR 213 (starred) (reversed by the Court of Appeal on other grounds).

[7] See eg *Chahal v United Kingdom* (1996) 23 EHRR 413; *Jabari v Turkey* (40035/98) [2001] INLR 136. The historical position is of interest insofar as it may shed light on the current situation and its likely evolution, but it is the present conditions which are decisive: *Ahmed v Austria* (1997) 24 EHRR 278. The Court of Appeal held in *Hariri v Secretary of State for the Home Department* [2003] EWCA Civ 807, (2003) 147 Sol Jo LB 659 (following *Iqbal (Muzafar)* [2002] UKIAT 02239) that where there is nothing to distinguish the applicant from others, he or she would need to show a 'consistent pattern of gross and systematic violations of fundamental rights' in the destination country to succeed on an Art 3 claim. However, in *Batayav v Secretary of State for the Home Department* [2004] EWCA 1489, [2004] INLR 126, the Court of Appeal emphasised the danger of assimilating 'real risk' to 'probability' by the use of the test in *Hariri* (para 39); see also *R (on the application of Kpangui) v Secretary of State for the Home Department* (21 April 2005), per Munby J.

[8] See *Hatami v Sweden* (Commission) (32448/96) paras 95–106; see also *Hilal v United Kingdom* (fn 2 above). The court also obtains evidence for itself, eg by taking oral evidence, in appropriate cases.

[9] *Jabari v Turkey* (fn 7 above): the imposition of a rigid five-day registration requirement as a condition of having an asylum claim examined prevented scrutiny of a claim based on a fear of inhuman and degrading punishment in Iran for adultery.

[10] *Pretty v United Kingdom* (2002) 35 EHRR 1, [2002] 2 FCR 97, para 52.

[11] For positive and negative obligations, see 8.34 above.

8.51 Article 3 read with Article 1 contains a positive obligation to protect against inhuman or degrading treatment emanating from persons or groups who are not public officials, and State responsibility for a breach of Article 3 may be engaged where the framework of law fails to provide adequate protection[1] or where the authorities fail to take reasonable steps to avoid a real risk of ill-treatment about which they knew or ought to have known.[2] In the expulsion context, Article 3 may apply where the risk from non-State actors is real and the authorities of the receiving State are unable to obviate it by providing appropriate protection.[3] The ECtHR jurisprudence suggests that the standard of protection required by the receiving State to exclude responsibility by the UK must be such as to remove the real risk of ill-treatment. In the expulsion cases the sole issue is the existence of a real risk of prohibited harm to the applicant; the court is not concerned with the issue of protection in the receiving State except in its impact on the risk.[4] First, it is the responsibility of the expelling State and not that of the receiving State which is relevant.[5] Secondly, in a removal case, we are not talking about the protective responsibilities of the expelling State, except and to the extent that the treatment of removing (a negative obligation not to breach Article 3) may also involve a positive duty to protect by not removing. That is the full extent of any protective obligations which the removing signatory State may have. Thirdly, in removal cases, we are not dealing with the quite different question of the ambit and extent of a signatory State's positive obligations to protect against prohibited harm by non-State agents within that State's own territory.[6] This brings us to the attempt by the higher English courts (in what is binding authority) to conflate sufficiency of protection in refugee law with the requirements of Article 3 (and Article 2) of ECHR. In our view there is a conceptual difference between protection under the Refugee Convention 1951, whose rationale and prerequisite is the failure of protection by the individual's own State,[7] and the common responsibility for the observance of human rights underlying the ECHR (see the Preamble), which makes the *Horvath* test inappropriate in the ECHR context. But the domestic courts have emphasised the equivalence of the tests and, it seems to us, have got into a quagmire of difficulty and complication.[8] Finally, it should be noted that measures taken by the receiving State are required to be effective in practice as well as in theory, and an applicant who can show that remedies in the receiving State are unlikely to be an effective deterrent against non-State harm will have shown that her removal would violate Article 3.[9] More cases in this difficult area are expected soon.

[1]   *A v United Kingdom* [1998] 3 FCR 597 (para 22); *Z v United Kingdom* [2001] 2 FCR 246 (protection against child abuse and neglect). The test under Art 3 does not require it to be shown that but for the failure of the authorities, the ill-treatment would not have occurred; a failure to take reasonably available measures which could have had a real prospect of altering the outcome or mitigating the harm is sufficient to engage State responsibility: *E v United Kingdom* (33218/96) [2002] 3 FCR 700.

[2]   *Osman v United Kingdom* (1998) 29 EHRR 245; *Kaya (Mahmut) v Turkey* (22535/93) (28 March 2000, unreported).

[3]   *HLR v France* (1997) 26 EHRR 29 (fear of death at the hands of the Colombian drug mafia). See also *Ahmed v Austria* above and *Barar (Ould) v Sweden* (1999) 28 EHRR CD 213 (fear of punishment by slave master).

[4]   See *HLR v France* (1997) 26 EHRR 29, at para 40: '... it must be shown that the risk is real and that the authorities of the receiving State are not able to obviate the risk by providing appropriate protection'. This cannot be taken to mean that the receiving State must be a guarantor of safety or non-violation: see Sedley LJ in *McPherson v Secretary of State for the Home Department* [2001] EWCA Civ 1955, [2002] INLR 139, at para 22.

[5]   *TI v United Kingdom* [2000] INLR 211, ECtHR.

[6]   In cases such as *R (on the application of Limbuela, Tesema, Adam) v Secretary of State for the Home Departmen* [2004] EWCA Civ 540, [2004] QB 1440 and *R (on the application of Gezer) v Secretary of State for the Home Department* [2004] EWCA Civ 1730, (2004)

Times, 23 December, Laws LJ has argued that the distinction between positive and negative obligations is less important than that between cases involving State violence and those involving hardship resulting from the State's lawful administrative acts (which might expose the person to equal violence, but from a different source), where, he argues, the Art 3 threshold is much higher. *Limbuela* is on appeal to the House of Lords.

7   See *Horvath v Secretary of State for the Home Department* [2000] INLR 239, HL, 12.52 below).

8   Although in *R (on the application of Dhima) v Immigration Appeal Tribunal* [2002] EWHC 80 (Admin), [2002] Imm AR 394, [2002] INLR 243, the court said that what was critical (in the receiving State) was a combination of willingness and ability to provide protection *to the level that can reasonably be expected to meet and overcome the real risk of harm* (para 33, our emphasis), the court in *R (on the application of Bagdanavicius) v Secretary of State for the Home Department* [2003] EWCA Civ 1605 [2004] INLR 163 equated the sufficiency of protection falling short of a guarantee of safety (*Horvath*) with that reducing a 'real risk' to a 'possibility' of harm (*Dhima*) in Art 3 cases. *Bagnadavicius* is on appeal to the House of Lords.

9   *McPherson v Secretary of State for the Home Department* [2001] EWCA Civ 1955, [2002] INLR 139. See also *Skenderaj v Secretary of State for the Home Department* [2002] EWCA Civ 567 [2002] INLR 323; *Koci (Dashemir) v Secretary of State for the Home Department* [2003] EWCA Civ 150 (although the standard is one of relative sufficiency, not an absolute guarantee of protection, where police are unable to provide protection, the failure to seek it is irrelevant).

Application of Article 3 to illness

8.52 The European Court has made it clear that, in the light of the fundamental importance of Article 3, it may be engaged by expulsion when the source of the harm in the destination country is not human agency at all, but the exacerbation of a naturally occurring severe illness, whether physical or mental, because of inadequate medical provision or the lack of carers in the receiving State.[1] In the 1987 case of *Fadele*[2] the Commission held admissible under Article 3 of the ECHR (as well as Art 8) the refusal of admission to the UK of a Nigerian father with a bad immigration history after the mother of the UK-based children was killed, leading to the children having to move to Nigeria, where they suffered from illness, isolation, lack of education and loss of the facilities they had enjoyed in the UK. A friendly settlement meant that the issues were not adjudicated on their merits, but a decade later, the case of D established that expulsion to sufficiently severe harm may engage the expelling State's responsibility under the Article where 'the source of the risk of proscribed treatment in the receiving country stems from factors which could not engage, either directly or indirectly, the responsibility of that country, or which, taken alone, do not in themselves infringe the standards of the Article'.[3] In that case, it was held to be in breach of Article 3 to implement a decision to remove a terminal AIDS sufferer from a situation where he enjoyed treatment and support to a country where there was a serious danger that the conditions of adversity awaiting him would further reduce his already limited life expectancy and subject him to acute mental and physical suffering.[4] The court emphasised the need to subject all the circumstances to rigorous scrutiny, especially the applicant's personal situation in the expelling State.[5] The principle was set out in *SCC v Sweden*:[6]

'Aliens who are subject to expulsion cannot in principle claim any entitlement to remain in the territory of a Contracting State in order to continue to benefit from medical, social or other forms of assistance provided by the expelling

State. However, in exceptional circumstances, implementation of a decision to remove an alien may, owing to compelling humanitarian considerations, result in a violation of Article 3.'

The principle has been reaffirmed in a number of cases, including *BB*,[7] and *Pretty*.[8] In *Bensaid* the court accepted that the same principles applied to psychiatric illness which, if untreated, would cause acute suffering and damage to psychological and perhaps physical integrity.[9] In all cases, whether physical or mental health is at risk, factors which have assumed significance in the court's view have included the severity of the applicant's condition, its prognosis, the assumption of responsibility by the expelling State (by the provision of treatment), the availability (including accessibility and affordability) of appropriate treatment for the condition in the receiving State, whether family support is available, and the likely impact on the individual of withdrawal of treatment.[10]

[1]   *Pretty v United Kingdom* (2002) 35 EHRR 1, para 52.
[2]   *Fadele v United Kingdom* (13078/87) (1990) 1 CD 15.
[3]   *D v United Kingdom* (1997) 24 EHRR 423, para 49.
[4]   (1997) 24 EHRR 423, para 52–53.
[5]   (1997) 24 EHRR 423, para 49.
[6]   *SCC v Sweden* (Application 46553/99) (15 February 2000).
[7]   *BB v France*, 30930/96, 9 March 1998 (Commission), 7 September 1998 (Court), where the Commission held that the expulsion of a severely ill AIDS sufferer to Zaire would breach Article 3 because of the length of time he had lived in France, the assumption of responsibility for his health care by the French authorities and the lack of a treatment programme in Zaire. In *Tatete v Switzerland* (Application 41874/98) (18 November 1999) an Art 3 claim involving the removal of another AIDS sufferer to Zaire was held admissible; but a number of health-based claims have been held inadmissible, either because the applicant had no significant symptoms, or because he or she had not shown that treatment or family support would not be available to him or her in the receiving State, so that the risk of the severity of suffering required to engage Art 3 was not reached: see *Karara v Finland* (Application 40900/98) (29 May 1998, unreported) (Commission), *MM v Switzerland* (1999) 27 EHRR 356CD; *Karagoz v France* (Application 47531/99) (15 November 2001, , unreported); *Henao v Netherlands* (Application 13669/03) (24 June 2003, unreported); *Ndangoya v Sweden* (Application 17868/03) (22 June 2004, unreported), *Amegnigan v Netherlands* (Application 25629/04) (25 November 2004, unreported).
[8]   *Pretty v United Kingdom (fn 1 above)*.
[9]   *Bensaid v United Kingdom* (2001) 33 EHRR 205, [2001] INLR 325 (Algerian schizophrenic fearing relapse on return, failed on its facts because of the availability of treatment and speculative nature of the risk of harm).
[10]   *Bensaid v United Kingdom* (2001) 33 EHRR 205.

Domestic application of D

8.53 Following *D*,[1] the Home Office developed a policy on expulsion of those with serious health problems. The July 1998 policy[2] required 'credible medical evidence that return, due to the medical facilities in the country concerned, would reduce the applicant's life expectancy and subject him to acute physical and mental suffering, in circumstances where the UK can be regarded as having assumed responsibility for his care', for the applicant to be granted exceptional leave to remain (ELR). In April 2001 the policy was amended to require in addition 'a complete absence of medical treatment' in the receiving country,[3] and the policy was amended again in March 2004 to require 'exceptional and extreme' circumstances.[4] The extent of Article 3 obligations in this field has been defined restrictively by the House of Lords in the case of *N*,[5] a Ugandan AIDS sufferer who had been very ill but whose health had improved considerably with highly active anti-retroviral treatment (HAART) in the UK, an innovation which had been developed since the time of *D*'s case. The evidence indicated that without such treatment, which would not be reliably available or accessible to the appellant in Uganda, her mental and physical health and her life expectancy would collapse, subjecting her to acute suffering and early death. The Court of Appeal, by a majority, refused to hold that her removal would breach Article 3. The majority advocated a test requiring that the 'humanitarian appeal of the case [be] so powerful that it could not in reason be resisted by the authorities of a civilised State'.[6] On appeal, the House of Lords upheld the Court of Appeal, on different grounds.[7] The judges plumped for the same test, following a close analysis of the relevant Strasbourg caselaw, perhaps most vividly set out in Lady Hale's speech:

> '... the test, in this sort of case, is whether the applicant's illness has reached such a critical stage (ie he is dying) that it would be inhuman treatment to deprive him of the care which he is currently receiving and send him home to an early death unless there is care available there to enable him to meet that fate with dignity'.

They rejected as unhelpful a test based on humanitarian appeal, acknowledging that it was hard to distinguish on humanitarian grounds between cases of expulsion of the terminally ill, and expulsion of those whose good health depended wholly on treatment which would effectively be ended by the act of expulsion.[8] Their Lordships accepted the humanitarian appeal of all such cases. They rested their dismissal of N's appeal on other considerations. Analysis of post-*D* Strasbourg jurisprudence (which they criticised for its fudging of the criteria applied by the court and of issues of availability of treatment and family support)[9] by Lords Hope and Brown yielded the oft-repeated principle that aliens could not claim any entitlement to remain to benefit from medical or other assistance.[10] Emphasis on this principle, and on the exceptional circumstances disclosed by the *D* case, indicated the extremely limited circumstances in which Article 3 could be deployed to resist expulsion of AIDS sufferers. The breach of Article 3 in *D*'s case did not lie in the denial of treatment which would ensure his long-term survival (there wasn't any at that time), but on the denial of the opportunity to die in dignity, in a caring environment.[11] This was what was exceptional in *D*'s case, and in general, their Lordships held, terminal illness would be required in order to rely on Article 3 to resist expulsion.[12] Article 3 did not require Contracting States to allow aliens to remain for indefinite medical treatment and associated welfare benefits, and to interpret it as imposing such an obligation would be to extend the reach of the Convention further than Contracting States would be prepared to accept.[13] Thus, the fact that expulsion is itself a death sentence becomes irrelevant. Further Strasbourg elucidation of the relevant principles is urgently needed.

In principle psychological illness is capable of engaging Article 3 just as physical illness is,[14] particularly where there is a significantly increased risk of suicide because of removal. In such a case, it is not the lack of treatment which will lead to the prohibited harm, but the act of expulsion itself, and cases such as *Keenan v United Kingdom*[15] are more apposite than *D*. The Court of Appeal has held that a real risk of a significantly increased risk of suicide is capable of engaging Article 3.[16]

1   *D v United Kingdom* (1997) 24 EHRR 423. The principle in *D* had been applied in the domestic courts before the coming into force of the Human Rights Act, in *R v Secretary of State for the Home Department, ex p M* [1999] Imm AR 548, QBD; *R v Secretary of State for the Home Department, ex p Kebbeh* (30 April 1998, unreported), QBD; and in relation to a likely psychiatric relapse because of unavailability of treatment save at exorbitant cost see *R (on the application of Njai) v Secretary of State for the Home Department* (CO 3391/1999) (1 December 2000), QBD.

2   *Asylum Directorate Instructions* July 1998, Ch 5, s 2.1 (eligibility criteria). In *R v Secretary of State for the Home Department, ex p Kasasa* (7 January 1999, upheld by the Court of Appeal as *K v Secretary of State for the Home Department* [2001] Imm AR 11, both applications for permission) the court accepted a submission 'from the bottom of the barrel' that this policy applied only to failed asylum seekers, not to others seeking to remain on the basis of severe illness.

3   IND to Terrence Higgins Trust, 24 April 2001. The policy was set out in the IDI Jun 01, Ch 1, s 8, but was superseded in June 2004 (see below). 'Complete absence of treatment' in the home country was held to be capable of making a case exceptional by Lord Hope in *N v Secretary of State for the Home Department* [2005] UKHL 31, para 50. Otherwise, unavailability of treatment to the applicant (including unaffordability: *JB (Ghana)* [2005] UKAIT 00077) and of family support in the home country are relevant only where other circumstances render the situation exceptional, such as terminal illness: *N* para 68, per Lady Hale.

4   IDI Mar 04, Ch 1, s 8, para 3.4. This states that factors required for a successful Art 3 claim include the following: being in the terminal stages of illness, with a short life expectancy even with treatment, or removal which would both significantly shorten his or her life expectancy and result in acute mental or physical suffering (this factor may not, on its own, always be enough to mean the Art 3 threshold is met), or receipt of the relevant treatment in the UK for over four years and dependency on it to sustain life even for a short period (eg kidney dialysis patients). Following the House of Lords' decision in *N* (above) in May 2005, these instructions may well become more restrictive.

5   *N v Secretary of State for the Home Department* [2003] EWCA Civ 1369, [2005] UKHL 31.

6   *N v Secretary of State for the Home Department* [2003] EWCA Civ 1369, per Laws LJ at para 38. Carnwath J dissented, holding that a combination of adverse factors in the receiving State could engage Art 3.

7   [2005] UKHL 31 per Lords Hope (para 50) and Brown (para 94) and Lady Hale (para 69)

8   [2005] UKHL 31 per Lord Nicholls at para 13, Lord Hope at para 49, Lord Brown at para 91. Lord Walker agreed. Their Lordships accepted that the humanitarian appeal of N's case was very high: per Lord Nicholls at para 14, Lord Hope at para 20, Lady Hale at para 67, Lord Brown at paras 97–99.

9   [2005] UKHL 31 per Lord Nicholls at para 14, Lord Hope at para 35, Lord Brown at para 91.

10   See *SCC v Sweden*, 8.52 text and fn 6 above.

11   [2005] UKHL 31, per Lord Hope at para 36, Lady Hale at para 68, Lord Brown at para 93.

12   [2005] UKHL 31, per Lord Hope at para 48, Lady Hale at para 69, Lord Brown at para 94. Lords Nicholls and Hope and Lady Hale acknowledged that other circumstances might be sufficiently exceptional to engage Art 3, at paras 9, 50 and 70 respectively. In *CA v Secretary of State for the Home Department* [2004] EWCA Civ 1165, the exposure of an infant child to death through the lack of potable water in Ghana, which would require a mother with HIV/AIDS to breastfeed the child, was held extreme enough (under Laws LJ's humanitarian principles) to engage Art 3.

13   [2005] UKHL 31, per Lord Nicholls at paras 15 and 17, Lord Brown at para 92. Lord Brown treated the case as one imposing a positive obligation of affording treatment, rather than merely a negative obligation of refraining from expulsion (para 88).

[14] *Bensaid v United Kingdom* (2001) 33 EHRR 10, [2001] INLR 325; *R (on the application of Finna) v Secretary of State for the Home Department* [2002] EWHC 777 (Admin), [2002] All ER (D) 16 (Mar). The Home Office acknowledged, in a response to the Medical Foundation in early 2002, that 'circumstances may arise where it may be possible to demonstrate that the UK would be in breach of its obligations under Art 3 to return a person suffering from post-traumatic stress disorder to their home country'. Cited in Henderson *Best Practice Guide to Asylum and Human Rights Appeals*, ILPA/RLC, 2003, para 1.78.

[15] *Keenan v United Kingdom* (2001) 33 EHRR 38.

[16] *R (on the application of Razgar) v Secretary of State for the Home Department* [2003] EWCA Civ 840 [2003] Imm AR 529, [2003] INLR 543; *R (on the application of Kurtolli) v Secretary of State for the Home Department* [2003] EWHC Admin 2744, [2003] All ER (D) 217 (Nov).

8.54 Article 3 is also capable of being engaged by general conditions in the receiving country, such as absence of water, food or basic shelter, where their effect on particularly vulnerable individuals (such as infants or old and infirm people) reaches the threshold of inhuman treatment,[1] although such cases must now be viewed through the restrictive lens of *N*, described above. Article 3 of the ECHR is thus considerably broader in its application than the Refugee Convention. There are no exclusions from Article 3 protection on national security or criminality grounds;[2] there is no need to show that the harm feared is for reasons of the applicant's race, religion, nationality, membership of a particular social group or political opinion;[3] the harm feared need not have the character of 'persecution'[4] or even be attributable to aggressive action.[5] In *Chahal* the ECtHR said that given the irreversible nature of the harm that might occur if the risk of ill-treatment materialised and the importance the court attaches to Article 3, the notion of an effective remedy under Article 13 required independent scrutiny of the claim that there exist substantial grounds for fearing a real risk of treatment contrary to Article 3.[6]

[1] *The Home Office acknowledges this in its API on Post-refusal decisions: Humanitarian Protection, para 2.4; see Fadele v United Kingdom (Application 13078/87) (1990) ICD 15, and see CA v Secretary of State for the Home Department, 8.53 fn 12 above.*

[2] *Chahal v United Kingdom* (1996) 23 EHRR, 413; *Ahmed v Austria* (1997) 24 EHRR 278; cf *T v Immigration Officer* [1996] AC 742, HL (a Refugee Convention case). However, the EC Qualification Directive (Council Directive 2004/83/EC on minimum standards for the qualification and status of third country nationals and stateless persons as refugees or persons who otherwise need international protection (OJ 2004 L304/12)) Art 17 provides for the exclusion from subsidiary protection on grounds akin to those under the Refugee Convention (for which see 12.88ff below), and the grant of short periods of leave. These provisions are not binding, since the Directive sets out minimum standards of protection, leaving Member States free to be more generous.

[3] For 'Convention grounds' under the Refugee Convention see 12.64ff.

[4] For 'persecution' under the Refugee Convention see 12.46 below.

[5] *D v United Kingdom* (1997) 24 EHRR 423.

[6] *Chahal v United Kingdom* (1996) 23 EHRR 413, para 151.

8.55 Although Article 3 of the ECHR will mainly be engaged in relation to proposed removal, it also has application in relation to conditions in which asylum seekers are detained,[1] and the manner of their support or the deprivation of all support in the UK.[2] Although the humiliating and degrading voucher system of asylum support was abolished,[3] the denial of all support to asylum seekers not making their claim as soon as practicable[4] has led to a spate of cases dealing with when Article 3 is engaged by destitution.[5] In the leading case of *Q*,[6] the Court of Appeal accepted that the regime imposed on asylum seekers who are denied support by reason of section 55(1) constitutes 'treatment' within the meaning of Article 3, but held that the degree of degradation that must be demonstrated in order to engage Article 3 falls significantly below the statutory definition of 'destitition'.[7] The 'real risk' test was, the court held, inappropriate where the feared harm was controllable by the court. Thus, it was not unlawful for the Secretary of State to decline to provide support unless or until it was clear that charitable support is not forthcoming and that the individual is incapable of fending for him- or herself. But where the condition of an applicant verges on that described in *Pretty*[8] (see 8.47 above), section 55(5) permits and Human Rights Act 1998 section 6 obliges the Secretary of State to provide support.[9] These principles would also apply to failed asylum claimants who are not removed because of practical difficulties or concerns about their countries of destination which do not merit the grant of discretionary leave. In *R (on the application of T) v Secretary of State for the Home Department*,[10] the court said that there was no simple way of deciding when Article 3 would be engaged; each case had to be examined on its facts. 'It is not enough for a claimant to feel that he has suffered a loss of dignity. How he sees himself and how he is seen by others are relevant but not determinative.' Psychiatric illness through sleeping rough and begging, resulting in loss of weight and malnutrition, crossed the line, but living at the airport, amid constant noise and light preventing rest and sleep, and being constantly moved on, did not, since there was shelter, sanitary facilities and the applicant had some money for food. In *Limbuela*[11] the Court of Appeal (Laws LJ dissenting) upheld the Administrative Court's approach in each of the three joined cases that once it was established that refusal of support would force the claimant on to the streets, very little more was required to establish a breach of Article 3. The majority preferred this approach to that of Newman J in *Zardasht*,[12] who had held that, the burden being on the applicant to show he or she had suffered to the extent required, detailed evidence was needed to establish the condition to which destitution had brought him or her, and to show that no charitable or self-support was available. Laws LJ, dissenting, and developing his analysis in *N* (8.53 above), described Article 3 cases as a spectrum, at one end of which stood the 'paradigm case of violation of Article 3' of State-sanctioned violence, which is always prohibited, and at the other end were administrative acts in the implementation of lawful government policy, which might expose persons to equally intense suffering but which would not engage Article 3 unless the suffering was sufficiently extreme. Where the point of engagement of the Convention lay depended on the severity of the threatened suffering, its cause and the purpose of the administrative acts. But:

> 'where Article 3 is deployed to challenge the consequences of lawful government policy whose application consigns the individual to circumstances of serious hardship, Article 3 is ... the law's last word. It operates as a safety net, confining the State's freedom of action only in exceptional or extreme cases.'[13]

This approach appears at first sight to beg a number of questions, first, the lawfulness of a policy which deprives destitute people of the means of survival, and secondly, the basis for seeking to reduce Article 3 from an absolute to a qualified right, when there is no valid basis for making a distinction between violence and other types of inhuman and degrading treatment or punishment.[14]

1   *Cyprus v Turkey* (1984) 4 EHRR 482, 541; *CG v Austria* (1994) 18 EHRR CD 51; *Dougoz v Greece* (2002) 34 EHRR 61 (conditions of detention of alien held pending expulsion). However the threshold is high: see *Zhu v United Kingdom* (Application 36790/97) (12 September 2000) (18-month detention with racist abuse and intimidation from other prisoners held not severe enough to give rise to arguable breach of Art 3 ECHR: manifestly unfounded).

2   The common law had paved the way in 'the law of common humanity' which prevents foreigners being allowed to starve; see *R v Inhabitants of Eastbourne* (1803) 4 East 103, cited by Simon Brown LJ in *R v Secretary of State for Social Security, ex p Joint Council for the Welfare of Immigrants* [1997] 1 WLR 275.

3   For the voucher scheme and its effects see the previous edition of this work, 13.26 and 13.27 text and fn 6.

4   Under Nationality, Immigration and Asylum Act 2002, s 55(1); see 13.56 below.

5   In *O'Rourke v United Kingdom* (Application 39022/97) (26 June 2001, unreported) and *Larioshna v Russia* (Application 56869/00) (23 April 2002, unreported), the ECtHR accepted that in principle eviction leading to homelessness (O'Rourke), or payment of a wholly insufficient pension (Larioshna) could raise an issue under Art 3 if it caused damage to physical and mental health of sufficient severity, but ruled the applications manifestly unfounded on their facts. In the Commission report on *BB v France* (30930/96), Cabral Barreto, in a concurring opinion, said: 'I consider that a seriously ill foreigner living in a country as a kind of illegal alien, unable to benefit fully and as of right from the social security regime, is in a situation which fails to meet the requirements of Article 3.'

6   *R (on the application of Q) v Secretary of State for the Home Department* [2003] EWCA Civ 364, [2003] 2 All ER 905.

7   *R (on the application of Q)* paras 56, 59.

8   *Pretty v United Kingdom* (2002) 35 EHRR 1.

9   *R (on the application of Q)* fn 6 above para 119.

10   *R (on the application of T) v Secretary of State for the Home Department* [2003] EWCA Civ 1285, [2004] HLR 254.

11   *Secretary of State for the Home Department v Limbuela, Tesema, Adam* [2004] EWCA Civ 540, [2004] QB 1440.

12   *R (on the application of Zardasht) v Secretary of State for the Home Department* [2004] EWHC 91 (Admin), [2004] All ER (D) 196 (Jan).

13   *Limbuela* above at paras 70, 77.

14   The case is on appeal to the House of Lords. Meanwhile, these arguments were further developed in *R (on the application of Gezer) v Secretary of State for the Home Department* [2004] EWCA Civ 1730, [2005] HLR 219 (upholding Moses J at [2003] EWHC Admin 860, [2003] HLR 977), a case about the dispersal of a very vulnerable family to a Glasgow estate notorious for racist activity. See Lord Brown's endorsement of Laws LJ's analysis in *N v Secretary of State for the Home Department* [2005] UKHL 31 para 88.

Slavery and forced labour

8.56 Article 4 of the ECHR states that:

'1   No one shall be held in slavery or servitude.

2   No one shall be required to perform forced or compulsory labour.

For the purposes of this Article the term "forced or compulsory labour" shall not include:

    (a)   any work required to be done in the ordinary course of detention imposed according to the provisions of Article 5 of this Convention or during conditional release from such detention;

(b)   any service of a military character or, in the case of conscientious objectors in countries where they are recognised, service exacted instead of compulsory military service;

(c)   any service exacted in case of an emergency or calamity threatening the life or well-being of the community;

(d)   any work or service which forms part of normal civic obligations.'

Article 4(1) absolutely prohibits slavery and servitude. The prohibition, like that in Article 3, is unqualified. There has been only one reported Strasbourg case on Article 4 in relation to expulsion to slavery, which was lost on its facts.[1] Escape from, or a fear of return to forced labour or forced prostitution underlie a fair number of claims for protection in the UK,[2] but Article 4 has very rarely been relied on.[3] There is much more potential for its use where expulsion could give rise to enslavement by gangs trafficking in women or children for prostitution purposes, although this scenario would engage Article 3 in any event.[4] Article 4(2) expressly permits military service or forced labour in lieu in those countries which recognise a right to conscientious objection. Article 4(2) is a sanction for forced labour in limited terms, but it is not a denial of a right of conscientious objection. Indeed it has been held that punishment for refusal to perform military service which is motivated by religious beliefs may breach Article 9 (freedom of conscience and religion).[5] The provision in section 10 of the Asylum and Immigration (Treatment of Claimants, etc) Act enabling the Secretary of State to make hard cases support contingent on the performance of community work was said by the Joint Committee on Human Rights to give rise to a significant risk of a breach of Article 4, and of Article 14 together with Article 4: see Joint Committee on Human Rights 14th report Session 2003–2004: Asylum and Immigration (Treatment of Claimants) Bill, additional clauses, 5 July 2004 (HL 130/HC 828).[6]

[1]   *Barar (Ould) v Sweden* (1999) 28 EHRR CD 213 (fear of punishment by slave master).
[2]   See eg *Dzhygun* (00TH00728), a Refugee Convention case in which the Immigration Appeal Tribunal held Ukrainian women trafficked for prostitution to be a 'particular social group' within the Convention; *K (Albania)* [2003] UKAT 23 (trafficked woman from Albania faced a real risk of inhuman and degrading treatment on return); *Kacaj* [2001] INLR 354, [2002] Imm AR 213 (starred) (trafficked Albanian woman; Tribunal found no real risk on return on remittal from Court of Appeal at [2002] UKIAT 07146); *Sultan* [2002] UKIAT 02683 (fear of abduction and sale of children by Afghani Pathan moneylenders: lost on facts); *Kamara* [2002] UKIAT 05842 (fear of subjection to forced labour by Sierra Leonean rebels: lost on facts).
[3]   The only domestic case we have been able to find which relied on Art 4 (unsuccessfully on the facts) was *R (on the application of Ali) v Immigration Appeal Tribunal* [2004] EWHC 98 (Admin), [2004] All ER (D) 194 (Jan), a member of a minority clan in Somalia who feared subjection to forced labour as a condition of protection by a more powerful clan.
[4]   See eg *K (Albania)* (fn 2 above), where Art 3 was successfully argued.
[5]   *Thlimmenos v Greece* (2001) 31 EHRR 411. *For Art 9 and conscientious objection to military service see 8.94 below.*
[6]   See the Immigration and Asylum (Provision of Accommodation to Failed Asylum Seekers) Regulations 2005, SI 2005/930, reg 4.

Detention

8.57   Article 5 of the ECHR states that:

'1 Everyone has the right to liberty and security of person. No one shall be deprived of his liberty save in the following cases and in accordance with a procedure prescribed by law:

(a) the lawful detention of a person after conviction by a competent court;

(b) the lawful arrest or detention of a person for non-compliance with the lawful order of a court or in order to secure the fulfilment of any obligation prescribed by law;

(c) the lawful arrest or detention of a person effected for the purpose of bringing him before the competent legal authority on reasonable suspicion of having committed an offence or when it is reasonably considered necessary to prevent his committing an offence or fleeing after having done so;

(d) the detention of a minor by lawful order for the purpose of educational supervision or his lawful detention for the purpose of bringing him before the competent legal authority;

(e) the lawful detention of persons for the prevention of the spreading of infectious diseases, of persons of unsound mind, alcoholics or drug addicts or vagrants;

(f) the lawful arrest or detention of a person to prevent his effecting an unauthorised entry into the country or of a person against whom action is being taken with a view to deportation or extradition.

2 Everyone who is arrested shall be informed promptly, in a language which he understands, of the reasons for his arrest and of any charge against him.

3 Everyone arrested or detained in accordance with the provisions of paragraph 1(c) of this Article shall be brought promptly before a judge or other officer authorised by law to exercise judicial power and shall be entitled to trial within a reasonable time or to release pending trial. Release may be conditioned by guarantees to appear for trial.

4 Everyone who is deprived of his liberty by arrest or detention shall be entitled to take proceedings by which the lawfulness of his detention shall be decided speedily by a court and his release ordered if the detention is not lawful.

5 Everyone who has been the victim of arrest or detention in contravention of the provisions of this Article shall have an enforceable right to compensation.

The ECtHR has consistently emphasised the importance of the Article 5 protection as a cornerstone of the rule of law and the need to construe it strictly so as to confine the power of the State to interfere with the liberty of the person in a democracy.[1] The central purpose of the Article, the right to liberty and security of person, is designed to protect against arbitrary detention.[2] This is both a substantive and procedural right. Deprivation of liberty must be in accordance with a procedure prescribed by law and, in the immigration context, is lawful only if its purpose is to prevent the person effecting an unauthorised entry into the country, or with a view to removal.[3]

---

[1] *Aksoy v Turkey* (1996) 23 EHRR 553; *Brogan v United Kingdom* (1988) 11 EHRR 117.

[2] *Winterwerp v Netherlands* (1979) 2 EHRR 387, paras 37–39, *Aksoy v Turkey* above, para 76. The list of exceptions to the right to liberty secured in ECHR, Art 5(1) is an exhaustive one and only a narrow interpretation of those exceptions is consistent with the aim and purpose of that provision, namely to ensure that no one is arbitrarily deprived of his or her liberty: *Quinn v France* (1995) 21 EHRR 529, para 42.

[3] Article 5(1)(f).

8.58 Article 5(1) is concerned with the deprivation of liberty rather than its mere restriction, but the distinction is a matter of degree rather than substance, depending on factors such as the nature of the interference with liberty, its duration and the effect on the individual.[1] Thus, the interference with liberty involved in a short examination at the port to establish identity and qualifications for entry would probably not constitute detention so as to engage Article 5. But an equally short detention for fingerprinting or a compulsory medical examination might attract the protection of the Article, because of the element of compulsion and intrusion on privacy.[2] Restrictions on freedom of movement such as residence conditions imposed on temporary admission[3] probably do not involve sufficient deprivation of liberty to amount to detention,[4] although other Convention rights might be engaged.[5] But restrictions amounting to house arrest or severe restrictions falling short of this with conditions prohibiting access to phones or email, as in the government's recently enacted control orders for suspected terrorists,[6] would be sufficient deprivations of liberty to come within the ambit of Article 5.[7] In *Amuur*[8] the French government argued that asylum seekers held at the 'international zone' of the airport were not detained because they could 'at any time have removed themselves from the sphere of application of the measure'. The argument was rejected by the ECtHR, both on the ground that the 'international zone' was a fiction and was French territory, and that an asylum seeker's decision to remain on the territory to make a claim could not be construed as voluntary detention.[9] Detention must also be fair.[10]

[1]   *Guzzardi v Italy* (1980) 3 EHRR 333, para 92; *Amuur v France* (1996) 22 EHRR 533, para 42, *Engel v Netherlands* (1976) 1 EHRR 647 at paras 58–59.
[2]   See eg App 8278/78 18 DR 154.
[3]   Under Immigration Act 1971, Sch 2, para 21(2)–(2B), under which regulations may prohibit unauthorised absence from designated accommodation.
[4]   In *Guzzardi v Italy* (1980) 3 EHRR 333 (fn 1 above) compulsory residence of a suspect on a small island under strict police supervision was a deprivation of liberty engaging Art 5, while restriction on a larger island subject to a less strict regime was not.
[5]   Notably Art 8, because of restrictions on private life and home resulting from the restrictions.
[6]   Prevention of Terrorism Act 2005.
[7]   Interference with liberty short of actual confinement has been held to be a deprivation of liberty, see *Guzzardi v Italy* (fn 4 above. House arrest such as that imposed on a detainee G released on bail by SIAC with conditions as to residence, curfew, tagging surveillance and restrictions on who and how he may contact others (described in *A and X v Secretary of State for the Home Department* [2004] UKHL 56, [2005] 2 WLR 87 para 35) would also constitute a deprivation of liberty; see also *NC v Italy* (24952/94) at para 33.
[8]   *Amuur v France* (1996) 22 EHRR 533.
[9]   *Amuur v France* (1996) 22 EHRR 533, paras 43, 46, 52.
[10]   *Conka v Belgium* (51564/99) (2002) 11 BHRC 555, where a stratagem securing the arrest and detention for deportation of a large number of Slovak Roma, involving conscious deception to make deprivation of liberty easier (requiring them to report to police on the pretext that files needed to be completed) was held unlawful.

Purpose

8.59 The permissible grounds for detention in Article 5 must be construed strictly and narrowly.[1] The two categories of authorised detention directly relating to those subject to immigration control are contained in Article 5(1)(f) and cover (i) prevention of unauthorised entry and (ii) pending deportation.

Preventing unauthorised entry: on its face this is a limited power restricted to a State's legitimate concern to stop people illegally entering countries and attempting to circumvent immigration control. The words indicate it is to prevent such activity and is not a broad ranging power of prolonged detention pending full determination of a claim to entry, and in particular its exercise must not impair or interfere with the right to seek asylum and the protection of the Refugee and Human Rights Conventions.[2] The use of the power to detain asylum seekers on arrival, and those who, having entered illegally, present themselves at the first opportunity, has proved controversial.[3] On any view these persons are seeking authorised entry to the UK and exercising their right to seek international protection.[4] It is not immediately apparent that the purpose of detention, in these circumstances, is to prevent unauthorised entry, unless there is evidence justifying a belief that the person would abscond or not comply with conditions of release. In *Saadi*[5] the House of Lords, however, ruled that detention on arrival of asylum seekers who present no risk of absconding, for the purpose of speedy determination of a claim for asylum, was within the first limb of Article 5(1)(f).[6] The Lords ruled that:

(i)   detention in order to determine the claim for asylum was to prevent unauthorised entry because, (turning the phrase on its head) until the claim was determined and granted, entry was not authorised, and the State has power to detain without violating Article 5, until the application has been considered and entry 'authorised'. The power was wider than to prevent evasion of immigration control, and would include the assessment of the merits of the asylum claim;[7]

(ii)   to be permissible under Article 5(1)(f), detention need not be 'necessary' to prevent unauthorised entry, even if there is an alternative means of processing the claim for asylum that does not require confinement [para 37]. Here the court relied on the judgment of the ECtHR in *Chahal*[8] that detention under the second limb of Article 5(1)(f) need not be necessary to ensure deportation; all that was required is action being taken with a view to deportation for the power to detain to be invoked;[9]

(iii) the detention was a proportionate response to the reasonable requirements of immigration control, given the established need for speedy decision making to process large numbers of claimants, taking into account its limited duration of around seven days in reasonable conditions [para 45].

This judgment has in principle given the Article (5)(1)(f) ground for detention the widest possible basis. Once the focus is shifted from unauthorised to authorised entry, anyone presenting themselves at the border is liable to detention under the paragraph, since all are seeking authorised entry whatever their immigration status, whether they are British nationals, are exercising Community law rights, have indefinite leave to remain or some other limited leave, or are foreigners and have no leave at all. It is our view that this could not possibly have been the intention of the framers of Article 5, and resort to the 19th century notion of unrestrained rights 'to regulate the entry of aliens'[10] is not a sufficient basis for a power as broad and wide as this to deprive a person of their liberty. It remains to be seen whether administrative convenience as a ground for detention is allowed to prevail beyond asylum seekers to other categories of lawful entrant.

1   *McVeigh, O'Neill and Evans v United Kingdom* (1981) 25 DR 15.
2   *Amuur v France* (1996) 22 EHRR 533, para 43.
3   See chapter 12 above, and 17.32ff below.
4   See Art 14 of the Universal Declaration of Human Rights.
5   *R (on the application of Saadi) v Secretary of State for the Home Department [2002] UKHL 41, [2002] 1 WLR 3131, [2002] INLR 523, at para 35.*
6   The House of Lords upheld the Court of Appeal's judgment at [2001] EWCA Civ 1512, which reversed that of Collins J, who had found the detention contrary to Art 5 at [2001] 1 WLR 356.
7   On the basis that if the claim was 'a pack of lies' the claimant would be seeking unauthorised entry: *Saadi* above, para 36 and 43.
8   *Chahal v United Kingdom* (1996) 23 EHRR 413, para 112.
9   'Necessary' in this context can only go to the vires or power to detain and not to the issue of proportionality, as is illustrated in the judgment in *R (on the application of Saadi) v Secretary of State for the Home Department, above.*
10 *R (on the application of Saadi) v Secretary of State for the Home Department, above* para 31, but see 1.4–1.5 above.

Action with a view to deportation

8.60   To justify detention with a view to deportation, all that is required under Article 5 is that 'action is being taken with a view to deportation'.[1] This means that detention need not be necessary to effect removal or to ensure compliance with the enforcement process. In *Chahal v United Kingdom* the ECtHR expressly rejected the idea that Article 5(1)(f) required a connection between detention and the conduct of the person; detention need not be 'reasonably considered necessary, for example, to prevent his committing an offence or fleeing'.[2] However, the power to detain under this provision is limited to circumstances where deportation proceedings are actually in progress and removal can be effected; where the proceedings are being pursued with due diligence; where the overall period of detention is not excessive; and where proper explanation is given for any delay.[3] These Convention restrictions match the limitations on the power to detain in domestic common law. Thus, the detention of a Somali national was held to be outwith Article 5(1)(f) because expulsion to Somalia was practically impossible since the individual did not have the relevant travel documents.[4] In *Chahal* a lengthy detention pending deportation was held not to violate Article 5(1) of the Convention, given the complexity of the issues in the proceedings, which were pursued diligently, and the seriousness of the case, given that it involved national security.[5] The conduct of the detainee is a factor and if he or she has contributed to the length of the detention by delaying proceedings this will be a relevant consideration.[6]

1   *Chahal v United Kingdom* (1996) 23 EHRR 413, para 413.
2   *Chahal* above, at para 112; see also *Bozano v France* (1986) 9 EHRR 297 para 60.
3   *Chahal* above, at para 113.
4   *Ali v Switzerland* (1998) 28 EHRR 304.
5   *Chahal* above, at paras 109 and 117.
6   *Kolompar v Belgium* (1992) 16 EHRR 197.

Legality

8.61   Article 5 of the ECHR requires that any detention conform to the substantive and procedural rules of national law. A detention which is unlawful in domestic law will necessarily be unlawful under the ECHR.[1] In addition, the provisions for detention must conform to the norms of Convention legality and be sufficiently accessible and precise to prevent arbitrary detention.[2] This means that they must be formulated with sufficient clarity to enable those affected to understand them and to regulate their conduct accordingly.[3] The principle, which underlies Convention legality, is, therefore, legal certainty.[4] In *Amuur v France* the ECtHR explained that the words in Article 5 'prescribed by law' refer to the quality of the domestic law and other legal rules.[5] It is in this context that the existence and application of a policy governing detention is of paramount importance. A detailed policy such as that provided in the Operational Enforcement Manual is not an optional extra for the immigration service; it is essential to ensure that the wide power to detain those subject to immigration control is not exercised in an arbitrary fashion. It is also an essential requirement of the common law necessary to meet the demands of fairness and consistency.[6] The Secretary of State's frequent refrain that his policy is more generous than the Convention is in this respect disingenuous: the policy is a fundamental requirement of compliance with Article 5 and the common law. For this reason a failure to apply stated policy is incompatible with Article 5, as is having unpublished criteria for detention, such as the 1991 and 1994 instructions (now published),[7] or an undisclosed practice which is inconsistent with stated policy,[8] or policies whose meaning is not sufficiently clear and foreseeable. Detention may also be arbitrary if insufficient information is provided to the detainees or their representatives to determine the basis of the decision to detain and in order to mount an effective challenge to the decision.[9]

[1] *Raninen v Finland* (1997) 26 EHRR 563 para 46 and *R v Governor of Brockhill Prison, ex p Evans (No 2)* [2000] 3 WLR 843 per Lord Hope.

[2] The three requirements of Convention legality have been formulated by the ECtHR as follows: (i) the interference in question must have some basis in domestic law; and (ii) the law must be accessible; and (iii) the law must be formulated so that it is sufficiently foreseeable: *Sunday Times v United Kingdom* (1979) 2 EHRR 245; *Silver v United Kingdom* (1983) 5 EHRR 347; *Malone v United Kingdom* (1984) 7 EHRR 14; *Halford v United Kingdom* (1997) 24 EHRR 523. See also *Zamir v United Kingdom* (1983) 40 DR 42, paras 90–91; *Steel v United Kingdom* (1998) 28 EHRR 603. In *R (on the application of Nadarajah) v Secretary of State for the Home Department, R (on the application of Amirthanathan) v Secretary of State for the Home Department* [2003] EWCA Civ 1768 the Court of Appeal held that the Secretary of State's policy on detention for removal was not sufficiently accessible, in that his policy of disregarding an intimation of judicial review proceedings when considering whether removal was 'imminent' was not known.

[3] *G v Germany* (1989) 60 DR 256 approved in *De Freitas v Permanent Secretary of Ministry of Agriculture, Fisheries, Lands and Housing* [1998] 3 WLR 675.

[4] *De Freitas v Permanent Secretary of Ministry of Agriculture, Fisheries, Lands and Housing* [1998] 3 WLR 675 per Lord Clyde at 681.

[5] *Amuur v France* (1996) 22 EHRR 533, para 50; see also *Dougoz v Greece* (2002) 34 EHRR 61, (2001) 10 BHRC 306, paras 56–58.

[6] See *R (on the application of Alconbury Developments Ltd) v Secretary of State for the Environment, Transport and the Regions* [2001] UKHL 23, [2003] 2 AC 295 at para 143 per Lord Clyde: 'policies are an essential element in securing the coherent and consistent performance of administrative functions'. For the Operational Enforcement Manual, and the Secretary of State's detention policy, see 17.27ff below.

[7] *Butterworths Immigration Law Service*, D[971]; see 17.7 below.

[8] *R (on the application of Nadarajah) v Secretary of State for the Home Department, R (Amirthanathan) v Secretary of State for the Home Department* [2003] EWCA Civ 1768.

[9] *Garcia Alva v Germany* 13 February 2001 para 39.

Proportionate

8.62 For detention not to be considered arbitrary, in accordance with international law principles, it must be necessary and proportionate to its legitimate aim. Detention may be arbitrary if it is disproportionate in its effect on the individual measured against the aim pursued in detaining the person.[1] The concept of proportionality is also at the heart of the common law in relation to detention.[2] In *Amuur*[3] the court accepted some confinement of asylum seekers to enable States to prevent unlawful immigration, but held that States must ensure the presence of suitable safeguards and that the length of confinement was proportionate to the process of examination. Confinement should not 'above all ... deprive the asylum seeker of the right to gain effective access to the procedure for determining refugee status'.[4] Detention may also be disproportionate if it is used in circumstances where alternatives to incarceration are available[5] and it is not a recourse of last resort.[6] This approach has been applied by the UN Human Rights Committee, applying the equivalent provisions of the International Covenant on Civil and Political Rights, in several cases against Australia.[7] These cases do not appear to have been cited to the Court of Appeal in *Sezek*,[8] when the court stated that 'there is nothing in the Convention nor any authority to support [the] assertion that Mr Sezek's detention is incompatible with Article 5(1)(f) if other ways of preventing him absconding are available'. In *Saadi* the House of Lords considered proportionality as an important aspect of whether the detention under the Oakington regime was compliant with Article 5.[9] The House determined that although alternatives to incarceration were available, they were not as effective as a short period of detention in securing the speedy processing of asylum claims and determining whether or not to authorise entry. Furthermore the limited period of detention in reasonable physical conditions was important in demonstrating that the detention was a proportionate measure balanced against this policy consideration.[10]

---

1   *Winterwerp v Netherlands* (1979) 2 EHRR 387 and *Caprino v United Kingdom* (1980) 4 EHRR 97, EComHR, para 67. *The proportionality test was accepted by the House of Lords in R (on the application of Saadi) v Secretary of State for the Home Department [2002] UKHL 41, [2002] 1 WLR 3131, [2002] INLR 523, and in R v Governor of Brockhill Prison, ex p Evans (No 2) [2000] 3 WLR 843, and by the Court of Appeal in A, X and Y v Secretary of State for the Home Department [2003] 2 WLR 564 and (implicitly) in R (on the application of I) v Secretary of State for the Home Department [2002] EWCA Civ 888, [2003] INLR 196, [2002] All ER (D) 243 (Jun).*

2   See eg *R v Governor of Durham Prison, ex p Singh* [1984] 1 WLR 704, [1983] Imm AR 198, and 17.39ff below.

3   *Amuur v France* (1996) 22 EHRR 533.

4   *Amuur* at para 43.

5   *Tomasi v France* (1992) 15 EHRR 1.

6   *Litwa v Poland (26629/95)* (2000) 63 BMLR 199, ECtHR, a case involving the detention of a drunk, the court emphasised that 'detention of an individual is such a serious measure that it is only justified where other, less severe, measures have been considered and found to be insufficient to safeguard the individual or the public interest'.

7   For example in *A v Australia* [1997] Communication No 560/1993, [1997] 4 BHRC 210, UN HRC, it was held that detention of an asylum seeker can be considered arbitrary if it is 'not necessary in all the circumstances of the case, for example to prevent flight or interference with evidence: the element of proportionality becomes relevant in this context'. See also *B v Australia* (Communication No 1014/2001, 18 September 2003) at para 7.2, where the Committee held that the State had failed to demonstrate that 'there

were not less invasive means of achieving the same ends, that is to say compliance with the State's immigration policies by, for example, imposition of reporting obligations, sureties or other conditions'.

8   *R (on the application of Sezek) v Secretary of State for the Home Department* [2002] 1 WLR 348, at para 13.
9   *R (on the application of Saadi) v Secretary of State for the Home Department* [2002] *UKHL 41, [2002] 1 WLR 3131, [2002] INLR 523* at para 44.
10   *Saadi* above, at paras 45–47.

8.63 Difficulty has arisen in the domestic courts over the ECtHR's ruling in *Chahal* that detention with a view to deportation did not have to be necessary to prevent the commission of offences or absconding.[1] This was applied to entry by the House of Lords in *Saadi*.[2] However, the question of whether detention is a proportionate measure is a different issue from whether or not Article 5(1)(f) should be construed so as to restrict the use of the power to circumstances where it is demonstrably necessary to achieve those ends. The *Chahal* ruling goes to the *vires* or power to detain, but not to the issue of proportionality. Thus the rejection in *Saadi* of the test of necessity was made in the context of the power to detain; having dealt with that the House of Lords then went on to deal with the question of proportionality.[3] But this does not mean that in any individual case, evidence of effective alternatives to detention will be irrelevant to the overall question of whether, assuming the power to detain exists, its exercise is disproportionate. In *Nadarajah and Amirthanathan*[4] the Court of Appeal appears to have conflated the two issues; whilst it was correct to state that Article 5(1)(f) does not 'itself import the test of proportionality', proportionality is an element of the broader requirement that the detention is prescribed by law and not arbitrary.[5] Outside of the Oakington regime, the detention of someone not facing imminent removal, with no history of absconding or other adverse factors, would in our view be disproportionate.[6]

1   *Chahal v United Kingdom (1996) 23 EHRR 413, para 112.*
2   *R (on the application of Saadi) v Secretary of State for the Home Department* [2002] *UKHL 41, [2002] 1 WLR 3131, [2002] INLR 523.* The House upheld administrative detention for seven days at Oakington Barracks to enable the Secretary of State to process claims, accepting that it was compatible with Art 5(1)(f) provided that detention was not continued longer than necessary for this purpose (ie, proportionate to the legitimate aim), but held that detention did not have to be 'necessary' either in the sense that the claimants would otherwise abscond and make an unauthorised entry, or in the sense that the claims could not be investigated without detention.
3   See above.
4   *Nadarajah v Secretary of State for the Home Department* [2003] EWCA Civ 1768, [2004] INLR 139.
5   In *R v Governor of Brockhill Prison, ex p Evans (No 2)* [2000] 4 All ER 15, [2000] 3 WLR 8443, the House of Lords considered that a detention that is lawful in domestic law may 'nevertheless be open to criticism on the ground that it is arbitrary because, for example, it was resorted to in bad faith or was not proportionate', referring to *Engel v Netherlands* [1976] 1 EHRR 647 para 58 and *Tsirlis and Kouloumpas v Greece* (1997) 25 EHRR 198, para 56.
6   In such circumstance the policy would dictate release.

8.64 The conditions and circumstances of detention are also relevant to the question of whether or not the detention is proportionate. There must be 'some relationship between the ground of permitted deprivation of liberty relied upon and the place and conditions of detention',[1] such that it would not be lawful to detain an asylum seeker or immigrant with serious mental health problems in an immigration detention centre. In *Saadi* the physical conditions and relaxed regime at Oakington were important factors in the Lords conclusion that the short period of detention was not disproportionate.[2] Factors such as the age, mental and physical health of the detainee, as well as the actual conditions in the detention centre are all relevant to the question of whether or not the detention is a proportionate measure. In *Dougoz v Greece*[3] the ECtHR found that the detention of an asylum seeker who had been convicted of a series of serious offences and whose expulsion from the territory was ordered violated Article 5 (and 3) in a number of ways: Mr Dougoz was held for a substantial period of time in overcrowded holding cells without adequate health, recreational or social facilities, and in conditions condemned by the Committee for the Prevention of Torture;[4] on his release from the sentence for drug smuggling he was detained by the decision of the deputy prosecutor in a remand centre pending his expulsion, without any independent court decision being taken as to whether he was likely to re-offend;[5] his requests for discretionary release were unanswered and the court that reviewed the decision to expel him did not expressly consider the need to continue to detain him.[6] His detention in these circumstances was held to be arbitrary.

[1]   *Aerts v Belgium* (2000) 29 EHRR 50, para 46 and *Bouamar v Belgium* (1988) 11 EHRR 1.
[2]   *R (on the application of Saadi) v Secretary of State for the Home Department [2002] UKHL 41, [2002] 1 WLR 3131, [2002] INLR 523.*
[3]   *Dougoz v Greece* (2002) 34 EHRR 61, [2001] 10 BHRC 306.
[4]   *Dougoz v Greece above,* at para 46, 48.
[5]   *Dougoz v Greece* at para 56–58.
[6]   *Dougoz v Greece* at para 62, 63.

8.65   Detention, and more often its continuation, may have serious repercussions for the health especially mental health of a detainee and may give rise to a breach of Article 8 or, if more severe, Article 3 of the ECHR.[1] The obligation on the detaining authority is to ensure that 'a person is detained in conditions compatible with respect for human dignity and that the manner and method of the execution of the measure does not subject [the detainee] to distress and hardship of an intensity exceeding the unavoidable level of suffering inherent in detention and that, given the practical demands of imprisonment, [the detainee's] health and wellbeing are adequately secured'.[2] When assessing the conditions of detention account must be taken of the cumulative effect of the conditions.[3]

[1]   *Dougoz v Greece* (above) and *Kalashnikov v Russia* (2003) 36 EHRR 34 paras 101–103 in respect of prison conditions; and more generally *Bensaid v United Kingdom* (2001) 33 EHRR 10. For Art 8 see 8.87 below.
[2]   *Kalashnikov* para 95, approved by the Court of Appeal in *Batayav v Secretary of State for the Home Department* [2003] EWCA Civ 1489, [2004] INLR 126.
[3]   *Dougoz* para 45 and *Kalashnikov* at para 95. The cases of *Peers v Greece* (2001) 33 EHRR 1192, para 74 and *Price v United Kingdom* (2002) 34 EHRR 53 both concerned conditions of detention which were held to give rise to Art 3 violations. Both applicants were disabled prisoners and in neither case was there any intention to inflict suffering or debase the individual, a factor which is not a necessary condition for an Art 3 violation. They were both detained in intolerable conditions, held to constitute degrading treatment.

8.66 In determining whether the detention of immigrants and asylum seekers is arbitrary, the UN Working Group on Arbitrary Detention considers whether the person concerned is able to enjoy all or some of the following guarantees:

(1)   to be informed, at least orally, in a language he or she understands, of the grounds for proposed refusal at the border;

(2)   to have the detention decision taken by an authorised official with a sufficient level of responsibility;

(3)   determination of the lawfulness of the detention by automatic and prompt recourse to a judge or body of equivalent competence, independence and impartiality, or the possibility of appealing to a judge or such a body;

(4)   entitlement to review of detention by higher court or equivalent body;

(5)   written and reasoned notification of detention measure in a language understood by the applicant;

(6)   the possibility of communicating effectively by phone, fax or email with, in particular, a lawyer, consular representative and relatives;

(7)   assistance by counsel (of the detainee's choice or officially appointed) through visits in the place of custody and at any hearing;

(8)   detention in dedicated detention centres or separation from criminal prisoners;

(9)   up-to-date register of those detained with reasons;

(10)   not to be held for an excessive or unlimited period, with a maximum statutory period;

(11)   information of guarantees provided in disciplinary rules;

(12)   procedure for incommunicado detention;

(13)   alternatives to administrative detention;

(14)   access to places of custody by UNHCR, International Committee of the Red Cross and specialised NGOs.[1]

UNHCR's view of required safeguards in respect of detention of asylum seekers[2] includes (i) prompt and full communication of any order of detention, together with the reasons for the order, and the rights in connection with the order, in a language and in terms they understand; (ii) to be informed of the right to legal counsel. Where possible, they should receive free legal assistance; (iii) to have the decision subjected to an automatic review before a judicial or administrative body independent of the detaining authorities, followed by regular periodic reviews of the necessity to continue detention; (iv) either personally or through a representative, the right to challenge the necessity of the deprivation of liberty at the review hearing.

[1]   *Civil and political rights, including questions of torture and detention* UN Commission on Human Rights, 55th Session, 18 December 1998, E/CN.4/1999/63, para 69. See also Report on visit to UK and Isle of Man by the Committee for the Prevention of Torture and Inhuman or Degrading Treatment or Punishment, March 2005 (CPT Inf/2005 1).

[2]   UNHCR *Guidelines on applicable criteria and standards relating to the detention of asylum seekers* (February 1999), Guideline 5 *Butterworths Immigration Law Service*, 2C[261]. See also UNHCR EXCOM Conclusion 44 ('Detention of Refugees and Asylum seekers') UN Doc A/AC.96/688.

Articles 5(2) and (4)

8.67 Detention must be adequately reasoned[1] and subject to prompt and regular review by a court to comply with the procedural requirements of

ECHR, Article 5(2) and 5(4). Article 5(2) states that anyone arrested or detained must be 'informed promptly, in a language which he understands, of the reasons for the arrest and of any charge against him'. This applies to all cases and not just criminal charges.[2] It requires that the detainee must be told at least the essential legal and factual basis for his detention and something that goes beyond simple reference to the source of the power.[3] The giving of reasons is an essential safeguard against arbitrary detention.

1   *X v United Kingdom* (1981) 4 EHRR 188, para 66; *Fox, Campbell and Hartley v United Kingdom* (1990) 13 EHRR 157, para 40.
2   *Van der Leer v Netherlands* (1990) 12 EHRR 567, paras 27–29.
3   *Fox, et al v United Kingdom* (1990) 13 EHRR 157, paras 40–41.

8.68 Article 5(4) of the ECHR requires speedy access to a court to determine the lawfulness of detention, and release if the detention is not lawful.[1] Its purpose is to ensure judicial supervision of the lawfulness of the measure to which they are subjected.[2] The scope of the supervision and the degree of scrutiny under Article 5(4) depends upon the context and the procedure must give to the individual concerned 'guarantees, appropriate to the kind of deprivation of liberty in question, of [a] judicial procedure the forms of which may vary from one domain to another'.[3] The procedure must be adversarial and ensure equality of arms.[4] In *Chahal v United Kingdom*[5] the ECtHR found a violation of ECHR, Art 5(4) because there was no court which could properly review the detention and the national security grounds for it. To meet the requirements of Article 5(4) the review must be wide enough to bear on those conditions which are essential for the lawful detention of a person according to Article 5(1).[6] In *Dougoz v Greece*[7] an Article 5(4) violation was found where release from detention pending deportation was entirely at the discretion of the Minister of Justice with no right of independent review. The court in *Amuur* held that deprivation of liberty is not compatible with the Convention if the courts are unable to review the conditions under which individuals are being held,[8] or to impose a limit on the length of detention or to provide legal, humanitarian or social assistance.[9] The court stressed that 'account should be taken of the fact that detention is applied 'not to those who have committed criminal offences but to aliens who, often fearing for their lives, have fled from their own country'.[10] Failure to keep to a timetable of periodic review may lead to violations of Article 5(4).[11] This has been a problem in domestic jurisdiction, especially with Mental Health Review Tribunals,[12] but the absence of speedy access to a court for immigration bail could also lead to incompatibility with Article 5(4).[13] Volume of applications and workload is not a sufficient justification for delay on the part of judicial bodies in providing access to review.[14] Because the grounds for detention may change over time, periodic review is required.[15] The court must be able to determine the legality of the detention, not merely according to the provisions of domestic law but also those of Convention law.[16] *Habeas corpus* was not an adequate remedy for asylum seekers detained under the Immigration Act 1971, Schedule 2, paragraph 16 prior to the coming into force of the Human Rights Act 1998, because it was concerned merely with the lawfulness of detention under domestic law.[17] A court on a *habeas corpus* application is now required to apply ECHR requirements of legality—including proportionality—to ensure that the decision to detain is compatible with ECHR, Article 5 rights.

[1] *Amuur v France* (1996) 22 EHRR 533, para 43. The court must be able to examine not only whether conditions precedent for detention under domestic law are met (which the High Court does in *habeas corpus*) but also whether detention is necessary or proportionate: *Amuur*, para 53. See also *X v United Kingdom* (1981) 4 EHRR 188; *Brogan v United Kingdom* (1988) 11 EHRR 117, para 65.

[2] *De Wilde, Ooms and Versyp v Belgium* (1976) 1 EHRR 373, para 76. In *Hutchinson Reid v United Kingdom* (50272/99) 20 Febuary 2003 the imposition on the applicant of the burden of proof that he no longer required to be detained violated Art 5(4), as did refusal of access to the detention file which contained documents essential for determining the lawfulness of the detention: see also *Shishkov v Bulgaria* (38822/97).

[3] *De Wilde* above, paras 76–78.

[4] *Sanchez-Reisse v Switzerland* (1986) 9 EHRR 71; *Toth v Austria* (1991) 14 EHRR 551; *Kampanis v Greece* (1995) 21 EHRR 43; *Nikolova v Bulgaria* (31195/96) (25 March 1999, unreported); *Garcia v Germany* (23541/94) (13 February 2001, unreported) para 39.

[5] *Chahal v United Kingdom* (1996) 23 EHRR 413. The decision led to the creation of the Special Immigration Appeals Commission; see chapter 18 below.

[6] *Chahal v United Kingdom above*, at para 127.

[7] *Dougoz v Greece* (2002) 34 EHRR 61, (2001) 10 BHRC 306.

[8] *Amuur v France* above. See also *R (on the application of H) v Secretary of State for the Home Department* [2003] UKHL 59, [2004] 2 AC 253, where the House of Lords held that there was a violation of Art 5(4), where a Mental Health Review Tribunal ordered a conditional discharge of a patient but the applicant could not be released because the conditions could not be met and the legislation did not allow the Tribunal to reconsider its decision in light of the changed circumstances.

[9] *Amuur* above, para 53.

[10] *Amuur* above, para 43.

[11] In *Sanchez-Reisse v Switzerland* (1986) 9 EHRR 71, 31 days was held not to meet the requirements of speedy review in an extradition case but much shorter periods were held unlawful in *De Jong v Netherlands* (22 May 1984, unreported) Series A No 77 and *GB and MB v Switzerland* (30 November 2000, unreported).

[12] In *R (on the application of C) v Mental Health Review Tribunal* [2001] EWCA Civ 1110, [2002] 1 WLR 176, the Tribunal's practice of listing all hearings of patients detained under the Mental Health Act for a uniform specified period after the date of the request was held in breach of Art 5(4) requirements of speedy determination of the lawfulness of the detention. The court held that the Convention requires a hearing within the period reasonably necessary to adjudicate on the application, which will be dependent on the facts of each case.

[13] A system of automatic bail hearings for immigration detainees in Part 3 of the Immigration and Asylum Act 1999, designed to ensure compliance with the procedural requirements of Art 5, was never brought into force and was repealed by the Nationality, Immigration and Asylum Act 2002. In this connection, the seven-day bar on bail applications for new arrivals contained in the Immigration Act 1971, and the repeal of the eight- and 36-day automatic bail references means that there is no time requirement on access to the courts. This compares unfavourably with the review afforded to detained criminal suspects (see fn 11, above) and may not be compatible with Art 5(4). See UN Working Group on Arbitrary Detention *Report on a visit to the UK on the issue of immigrants and asylum seekers*, E/CN.4/1999/63/Add.3 (1998).

[14] *Bezicheri v Italy* (1989) 12 EHRR 210 para 25.

[15] *Bezicheri*, above.

[16] *Amuur v France* above, paras 50 and 53.

[17] *X v United Kingdom* (1981) 4 EHRR 188, paras 58–61; *Weeks v United Kingdom* (1987) 10 EHRR 293. However, in *Zamir v United Kingdom* (1983) 40 DR 42, para 100, judicial review was found to be sufficient to establish the lawfulness of detention under Art 5(1)(f).

Just satisfaction

8.69 Everyone who has been the victim of arrest or detention in contravention of the provisions of Article 5 of the ECHR must have an enforceable right to compensation.[1] Damages for breaches of section 6 of the Human Rights Act 1998 may not be awarded against a court or Tribunal for judicial acts done in good faith, but there is an exception in section 9(3) of the HRA where the award is for compensation for breaches of Article 5.[2] In *KB v the Mental Health Review Tribunal* [3] the court considered, in the context of significant delay in access to the Mental Health Review Tribunal in breach of Article 5(4), whether an enforceable right to compensation means that damages must always be awarded for any breach of Article 5 and concluded that it does not: damages are not mandatory, even where damage flows from the deprivation of liberty, but discretionary, and a declaration of illegality may be sufficient. The court was unable to identify any clear and constant jurisprudence on the issue but two principles could be discerned namely (i) damages are not recoverable in the absence of a deprivation of liberty [4] and (ii) damages are available for distress.[5] Establishing a deprivation of liberty will be inevitable if the detention is unlawful under Article 5(1) but the more difficult question arises in the context of the absence of appropriate procedural rights as required by Article 5(4). There it will need to be established that the applicant would not have been detained or would have been released sooner had he or she had the benefit of the procedural guarantees.[6] *Chahal v United Kingdom* is an example of this approach where the the ECHR declined to award monetary compensation for the applicant despite finding Article 5(4) breached by the lack of judicial supervision of the detention,[7] and a challenge by judicial review of the Secretary of State's refusal to provide compensation was rejected by the Court of Appeal on the basis that the lack of judicial supervision did not affect the lawfulness of the actual detention.[8]

1 ECHR, Art 5(5). See *W v Home Office* [1997] Imm AR 302.
2 *R v Governor of Brockhill Prison, ex p Evans (No 2)* [1999] QB 1043 [2000] 3 WLR 843. In *ID v Home Office* [2005] EWCA Civ 38 the Court of Appeal rejected a claim by the government that immigration officers as well as judges were exempt from civil actions for damages. See 17.54 below.
3 *KB v the Mental Health Review Tribunal and the Secretary of State for Health* [2003] EWHC 193 (Admin).
4 Although even where there is such deprivation damages may not be recovered: see *Fox, Campbell and Hartley v United Kingdom* (1990) 13 EHRR 157 (merits) and (1991) 14 EHRR 108 (just satisfaction).
5 *R (on the application of KB) v Mental Health Review Tribunal*, above at paras 41 and 42.
6 *KB* at paras 41 and 64, applying ECtHR cases including *Nikolova v Bulgaria* (Application 43125/98) (2001) EHRR 3 and *Migon v Poland* (24244/94) and not following other Strasbourg court decisions, where compensation was awarded for frustration and distress without unlawful detention in the context of Art 5(4): see *Delbec v France* (43125/98) (18 June 2002, unreported); *LR v France* (33396/96) (27 June 2002, unreported); *DM v France* (041376/98) (27 June 2002, unreported), and *Laidin v France* (43191/98) (5 November 2002, unreported).
7 *Chahal v United Kingdom* (1996) 23 EHRR 413, para 158.
8 *R v Secretary of State for the Home Department, ex p Chahal* (1999) Times, 10 November, CA.

8.70 In *R (on the application of KB) v Mental Health Review Tribunal*,[1] the court rejected the Secretary of State's submission on the measure of damages to the effect that a European standard should be applied (which was generally extremely modest)[2] and held that the court is free to depart from the European scale in order to award adequate, but not excessive damages judged by the conditions in the UK.[3] In general those awards should reflect awards made in comparable torts.[4] Thus the level of damages for a breach of Article 5(1) should be no different from those for false imprisonment, and the court should make a global assessment of the loss, drawing a distinction between cases where the person has been detained lawfully for a period and those where the entire period of detention was unlawful.[5] In *Anufrijeva v London Borough of Southwark*[6] the Court of Appeal endorsed the approach of Stanley Burnton in *KB* and ruled that the level of damages awarded in respect of torts did provide some rough guidance, as did the guidance from the Judicial Studies Board, awards made by the Criminal Injuries Compensation Board and the Parliamentary and Local Government Ombudsmen where the consequences of the infringement of human rights are similar. In the past damages have been awarded against the Home Office for unlawful detention on a scale similar to that obtaining in actions against the police.[7] This should continue under the Human Rights Act 1998. It is also strongly arguable that those detained under Immigration Act powers are in a similar category to *Lunt*[8]— they are administrative detainees, who have not been convicted of criminal offences and are otherwise of good character. Incarceration for asylum seekers can be particular distressing because of a previous experience of torture or other abuse and they invariably find it difficult to understand why, when they are seeking sanctuary, they find themselves incarcerated. Exemplary damages were held not to be available for a breach of Article 5 on the basis that section 8(3) of the Human Rights Act 1998 prohibits damages otherwise than by way of compensation and exemplary damages by their very nature are punitive.[9] On this reasoning, however, aggravated damages can be available.

1   *R (on the application of KB) v Mental Health Review Tribunal* [2003] EWHC 193 (Admin), [2004] QB 936.
2   See *Curely v United Kingdom* (2000) 31 EHRR 14, referred to at para 44 of *KB*, above.
3   *R (on the application of KB) v Mental Health Review Tribunal* para 48. See, however, the admonitions of the House of Lords on the need to have regard to the Strasbourg case-law in *R (on the application of Greenfield) v Secretary of State for the Home Department* [2005] UKHL 14, which was a case dealing with an Art 6 breach. See 8.28 above.
4   The court adopted the approach of Sullivan J in *Bernard* and of the Law Commission and rejected Lord Woolf's extra-judicial observation that damages under the HRA should be lower than tort damages, an observation he resiled from in *Anufrijeva v Southwark London Borough Council* [2003] EWCA Civ 1406, [2004] QB 1124 at para 73.
5   *R (on the application of KB) v Mental Health Review Tribunal*, above at para 53, referring to the cases of *Thompson v Metropolitan Police Comr* [1998] QB 498 at 516 and the approach of the Court of Appeal in *R v Governor of Brockhill Prison, ex p Evans (No 2)* [1999] QB 1043, especially Lord Woolf at 1059–60, which the court found particularly helpful. Damages for 59 additional days imprisonment were increased from £2,000 to £5,000, to reflect the fact that Ms Evans was properly convicted of a serious criminal offence, had adjusted to serving a prison sentence during that period, had no reason to think that she was not properly incarcerated, and had committed a disciplinary offence which was the cause of the additional days. Her position was contrasted with the case of *Lunt v Liverpool City Justices* (5 March 1991, unreported), CA, where a man of previous good character and reputation was imprisoned for default on payment of his rates. In his case an award of £13,500 was increased on appeal to £25,000 for 42 days of false imprisonment, the entire period having been unlawful.
6   *Anufrijeva v Southwark London Borough Council* [2003] EWCA Civ 1406, [2004] QB 1124, at para 74.
7   £17,000 was awarded for detention of a British citizen and her infant child for approximately five days following a successful judicial review of her detention in *R v Secretary of State for the Home Department, ex p Ejaz* [1994] Imm AR 300, CA. The same amount was awarded for a four-day detention over Christmas following a judgment that the refusal of leave to enter on which the detention depended was irrational: *R v Secretary of State for the Home Department, ex p Honegan*, 13 March 1995, QBD. £2,000 was

awarded against police for a four-hour detention for immigration status check in *Okot v Metropolitan Police Comr*, 1 September 1995, CLCC (1996) Legal Action February, p 12.

8   *Lunt v Liverpool City Justices* (5 March 1991, unreported), CA, fn 5 above.

9   *R (on the application of KB) v Mental Health Review Tribunal* [2003] EWHC 193 (Admin), [2004] QB 936 at para 60.

8.71 Article 5 is one of the rights from which derogation can be made in time of war or other public emergency threatening the life of the nation.[1] Such a derogation, affecting Article 5(1), was made on 11 November 2001[2] by reference to the events of 11 September 2001, to enable the indefinite detention of suspected international terrorists, alleged to be linked to Al Qaeda.[3] It was quashed by the House of Lords in December 2004 in *A and X*,[4] on the grounds that it was discriminatory and disproportionate.[5] The House made a declaration that the certification provisions of the 2001 Act which allowed indefinite detention were incompatible with Articles 5 and 14 of ECHR. Indefinite detention has now been replaced by 'control orders' which may also infringe Article 5 and require derogation, but these are no longer within the ambit of immigration law.[6]

1   Article 15(1) ECHR. See 8.42 above.
2   See the Human Rights Act 1998 (Designated Derogation) Order 2001, SI 2001/3644; Human Rights Act 1998, Sch 3 (as amended). This refers to UN Security Council Resolution 1373 (2001), which requires Member States to take measures (not including detention) to prevent the commission of terrorist attacks, and to the provisions of the Anti-terrorism, Crime and Security Act 2001.
3   Anti-terrorism, Crime and Security Act 2001, ss 21– 23, now expired.
4   *A and X v Secretary of State for the Home Department* [2004] UKHL 56, [2005] 3 All ER 169.
5   Schedule 3 to the Human Rights Act 1998 was amended to delete the derogation by the Human Rights Act 1998 (Amendment) Order 2005, SI 2005/1071.
6   Prevention of Terrorism Act 2005.

Fair trial

8.72 Article 6 of the ECHR states (so far as relevant) that:

'1   In the determination of his civil rights and obligations or of any criminal charge against him, everyone is entitled to a fair and public hearing within a reasonable time by an independent and impartial tribunal established by law. Judgment shall be pronounced publicly but the press and public may be excluded from all or part of the trial in the interests of morals, public order or national security in a democratic society, where the interests of juveniles or the protection of the private life of the parties so require, or to the extent strictly necessary in the opinion of the court in special circumstances where publicity would prejudice the interests of justice.'

2   Everyone charged with a criminal offence shall be presumed innocent until proved guilty according to law.

3   Everyone charged with a criminal offence has the following minimum rights:

a)   to be informed promptly, in a language which he understands and in detail, of the nature and cause of the accusation against him;

b)   to have adequate time and facilities for the preparation of his defence;

c)   to defend himself in person or through legal assistance of his own choosing or, if he has not sufficient means to pay for legal assistance, to be given it free when the interests of justice so require;

d)   to examine or have examined witnesses against him and to obtain the attendance and examination of witnesses on his behalf under the same conditions as witnesses against him;

e)   to have the free assistance of an interpreter if he cannot understand or speak the language used in court.'

The right to fair administration of justice holds a central place in a democratic society[1] and Article 6 of the ECHR is the most frequently invoked provision of the Convention. Article 6 guarantees rights to a fair and public hearing within a reasonable time by an independent and impartial tribunal established by law in the determination of civil rights and obligations or of criminal charges.[2] In the ECtHR and domestic jurisprudence, the right to a fair trial guaranteed by Article 6 has been held not to apply to decisions about the entry and residence of aliens,[3] nor about the determination of British citizenship,[4] since 'civil rights' is an autonomous concept equated by and large with private law rights as opposed to administrative discretions.[5] Substantive Convention rights such as the right to liberty[6] and family life rights[7] are 'civil rights', even if they involve the exercise of discretion, so that bail hearings and hearings relating to contact with children attract Article 6 guarantees of equality of arms.[8] The common law also recognises the rights guaranteed by Article 6 as applicable to cases before the immigration appellate authorities,[9] and clearly this is an area where the common law can influence the development of domestic Article 6 jurisprudence, or can continue to develop and complement it.

[1]   *Delcourt v Belgium* (1970) 1 EHRR 355, para 26.
[2]   Article 6(1). Criminal proceedings are proceedings instituted to determine the veracity of an accusation, where the potential outcome is a sanction whose degree and severity belongs to the criminal sphere: *Engel v Netherlands* (1976) 1 EHRR 647; *Ezeh and Connors v United Kingdom* (39665/98, 40086/98) [2004] Crim LR 472. Article 6 has been held to apply to extradition proceedings: *R v Secretary of State for the Home Department, ex p Johnson* [1999] QB 1174, QBD.
[3]   *Agee v United Kingdom* (1976) 7 DR 164; *P v United Kingdom* (13162/87) (1987) 54 D & R 211; *Alam and Khan v United Kingdom* (1967) 10 Yb 478; *Uppal v United Kingdom* (1980) 3 EHRR 391; *Maaouia v France* (2001) 33 EHRR 42; *Ilic v Croatia* (42389/98) (19 September 2000, unreported). The IAT has held in the starred case of *MNM* [2000] INLR 576, that Art 6 does not apply to asylum appeals.
[4]   *S v Switzerland* (1988) 59 DR 256; *Karassev v Switzerland* (314144/96) (14 April 1998, unreported); *see R (on the application of Harrison) v Secretary of State for the Home Department* [2003] EWCA Civ 432, [2003] INLR 284.
[5]   *König v Germany* (1978) 2 EHRR 170. Proceedings classified under national law as being part of 'public law' could come under ... civil rights if their outcome is decisive for private rights and obligations': *Ferrazzini v Italy* (2002) 34 EHRR 1068. Rights to social security and social assistance have been recognised as 'civil rights' attracting Art 6 protection: *Feldbrugge v Netherlands* (1986) 8 EHRR 425; *Salesi v Italy* (1993) 26 EHRR 187; *Schüler-Zgraggen v Switzerland* (1993) 16 EHRR 405. Although the drafting of asylum support provisions (in the Immigration and Asylum Act 1999) is in discretionary terms, the provisions are not genuinely discretionary, and the support received by destitute asylum seekers is a civil right within the meaning of Art 6: *R (on the application of Husain) v Asylum Support Adjudicator* [2001] EWHC Admin 832, (2001) Times, 15 November.
[6]   *Aerts v Belgium* (1998) 5 BHRC 382, 29 EHRR 50. In *A, X and Y* [2002] EWCA Civ 1502, [2005] 3 All ER 169 the Court of Appeal rejected the submission of the appellants that a certificate under s 21 of the Anti-Terrorist Crime and Security Act 2001 amounted to

a criminal charge within the meaning of Art 6 but confirmed that detention under s 23 of the Act (now lapsed) engaged Art 6 civil rights.

7   *W v United Kingdom* (1987) 10 EHRR 29.
8   *Toth v Austria* (1991) 14 EHRR 551, para 84; *Lamy v Belgium* (1989) 11 EHRR 529, para 29.
9   See *R v Secretary of State for the Home Department, ex p Saleem* [2000] 4 All ER 814, [2000] Imm AR 529, [2000] INLR 413.

8.73 The ECHR, Article 6(1) requires independence from the executive and from the parties.[1] The Tribunal's independence does not have to be established by statute; the argument that, because the Home Office appoints asylum support adjudicators and is a party to appeals before them, they do not satisfy the requirement of independence was rejected in *Husain,* where the most important factor ensuring independence was held to be security of tenure.[2] 'Impartiality' requires a lack of either actual bias or the appearance of bias to a fair-minded and informed observer.[3] It has been held that the requirement of impartiality has not been automatically breached when a tribunal has previously been involved in the case at a pre-trial stage,[4] but the presence on the Tribunal of a chair whose refusal of permission to appeal was successfully challenged on judicial review might give rise to concerns under Article 6(1).[5] The ethnicity or nationality of an immigration judge is not on its own a sound basis for a complaint of partiality.[6] A two-tier process in which the first tier is administrative rather than judicial, and not independent and impartial, may satisfy Article 6 requirements where there is the added safeguard of judicial review.[7] The openness of hearings is dealt with in procedure rules whose exceptions mirror those set out in Article 6(1).[8]

1   The involvement of the Home Secretary in fixing sentences for mandatory lifers was held incompatible with Art 6 independence requirements in *R (on the application of Anderson) v Secretary of State for the Home Department* [2002] UKHL 46, [2002] 4 All ER 1089.
2   *R (on the application of Husain) v Asylum Support Adjudicator* [2001] EWHC Admin 832, (2001) Times, 15 November. Stanley Burnton J indicated the desirability of publishing the adjudicators' terms of employment. See also *Bryan v United Kingdom* (1995) 21 EHRR 342, para 38 (planning inspector in quasi-judicial role appointed by Secretary of State not independent). Cf EU case law: *Adouai and Cornuaille v Belgium* [1982] ECR 1665; *R v Secretary of State for the Home Department, ex p Gallagher* [1994] 3 CMLR 295 (on EC Directive 64/221, Art 9).
3   *Porter v Magill* [2001] UKHL 67, [2002] 1 All ER 465, para 85; *Director-General of Fair Trading v Propietary Association of Great Britain* [2001] EWCA Civ 1217, [2002] 1 All ER 853.
4   *Bulut v Austria* (1996) 24 EHRR 84, para 33.
5   The Court of Appeal held in *Mwakulna v Secretary of State for the Home Department* (98/7306/4) 4 March 1999 that this gave rise to no problem, although the Tribunal held in *Huang* (14058) that it would be inappropriate for a member who had made adverse credibility findings to hear the appeal.
6   *R (on the application of Krishnarajah) v Secretary of State for the Home Department* [2001] EWHC Admin 351 (Tamil asylum seeker's complaint that adjudicator's Sinhalese ethnicity gave rise to danger of bias rejected).
7   See below.
8   See eg Asylum and Immigration Tribunal (Procedure) Rules 2005, SI 2005/230, r 54, at 18.150 below. The ECtHR accepts that 'in some cases it may be necessary to withhold certain evidence from the defence [in criminal cases] so as to preserve the fundamental rights of another individual or to safeguard an important public interest' (to the extent strictly necessary): *Edwards and Lewis v United Kingdom* (39647/98, 40461/98) (22 July 2003, unreported).

8.74 The rule of law implies effective judicial control of executive action, such control offering the best guarantees of independence, impartiality and proper procedure.[1] Since the rule of law, central to the Convention and set out in its Preamble, is scarcely conceivable without access to the court, the right to a fair hearing presupposes access to a court.[2] Lack of access to a court to challenge the imposition of carrier sanctions or to seek mitigation was one of the factors rendering the sanction scheme under sections 32–37 Immigration and Asylum Act 1999 incompatible with Article 6 in *International Transport Roth GmbH v Secretary of State for the Home Department.*[3] The right of access is fundamental and cannot be blocked by unnecessary procedural obstacles or restrictions.[4] There must be access to a court of 'full jurisdiction' for compliance with Article 6(1),[5] but an appellate body does not have to be able to remake findings of fact for it to be a court of 'full jurisdiction', so long as it can review the decision-maker's factual findings.[6] In deciding whether the individual's civil rights have been determined by an independent and impartial tribunal established by law, the whole of the adjudication system, including rights of appeal and rights to judicial review, must be considered.[7] Thus, in *R (Q) v Secretary of State for the Home Department*[8] the Court of Appeal held that, although the blocking of the appeal mechanism for asylum support under section 55(10) Nationality, Immigration and Asylum Act 2002 was lawful, since 'judicial review today is capable of affording to an asylum seeker who is denied support ... recourse to an independent, impartial tribunal which has, in the Strasbourg sense, full jurisdiction' (para 115), the inadequacies of the NASS procedure made it impossible for officials to make an informed decision, and left the court on judicial review equally unable to do so. Thus, the process as a whole, which had to be capable of fairly determining the civil rights in play, did not do so, and was incompatible with Article 6. Article 6 does not necessarily require a statutory right of appeal against all executive decisions, provided that judicial review is available.[9] Where there is no statutory right of appeal, the decision-maker is obliged to give the individual notice of adverse considerations and an opportunity to address them.[10] Access to a court does not necessarily require an oral hearing, and the procedure for statutory review of Tribunal decisions 'on the papers' is compatible with Article 6 requirements.[11] However, ouster of higher courts' jurisdiction over manifest errors of law and breaches of natural justice would represent a fundamental breach of these requirements, and seriously damage the rule of law.[12]

[1]   *Klass v Germany* (1978) 2 EHRR 214, para 55.
[2]   *Golder v United Kingdom* (1975) 1 EHRR 524, paras 34–36.
[3]   [2002] EWCA Civ 158 [2002] 3 WLR 344: see 14.88 below.
[4]   *Aït-Mohoub v France* (1998) 30 EHRR 382 (security for costs); *R v Lord Chancellor, ex p Witham* [1998] QB 575 (court fees); *Tinnelly & Sons Ltd v United Kingdom, McElduff v United Kingdom* (1998) 27 EHRR 248 (public interest immunity certificates). Procedural restrictions such as time limits and rules allowing appeals to be determined without a hearing, e g SI 2005/230, r 19 (made under Nationality, Immigration and Asylum Act 2002, s 106) are allowable provided they do not impair the essence of the right, and provided there is effective supervision by judicial review. The previous rules, which permitted determination without consideration of the merits for procedural non-compliance (SI 2003/652, r 45), have not been repeated in the current rules; in our view they certainly impaired the essence of the right.
[5]   *Le Compte, Van Leuven and De Meyer v Belgium* (1981) 4 EHRR 1, para 51.
[6]   See *Kaplan v United Kingdom* (1980) 4 EHRR 64, para 158; *Bryan v United Kingdom* (1995) 21 EHRR 342, para 44, and see discussion in Grosz, Beatson and Duffy, 8.11 fn 3, paras 5.32ff.
[7]   *Tehrani v United Kingdom Central Council for Nursing, Midwifery and Health Visiting* [2001] IRLR 208

8   *R (on the application of Q) v Secretary of State for the Home Department* [2003] EWCA Civ 364, [2003] 2 All ER 905, at para 115.

9   But in *R (on the application of Husain) v Asylum Support Adjudicator* [2001] EWHC Admin 832, (2001) Times, 15 November, para 78. Stanley Burnton J said that where a decision is likely to depend to a substantial extent on disputed questions of primary fact, judicial review would probably not suffice to produce compliance with the Article, since the scope for review of the primary facts is too narrow to be considered 'full jurisdiction' (para 78). 'The courts should lean against accepting judicial review as a substitute for the independence of the tribunal; [otherwise] the incentive for the executive and the legislature to ensure the independence of tribunals is considerably weakened' (para 79). His appears to be a minority view; see the CA's decision in Q (fn 8 above).

10 *R v Secretary of State for the Home Department, ex p Thirukumar* [1989] Imm AR 270; *R v Secretary of State for the Home Department, ex p Fayed* [1997] 1 All ER 228; see also Q (fn 8 above).

11 See the provisions of Nationality, Immigration and Asylum Act 2002, s 103A (inserted by Asylum and Immigration (Treatment of Claimants, etc) Act 2004, s 26), formerly s 101(2), (3).

12 As was proposed by the Asylum and Immigration (Treatment of Claimants) Bill; see Joint Committee on Human Rights, 5th Report 2003–04, 10 February 2004, HL 35/HC 304; Constitutional Affairs Committee, 2nd report of 2003–2004 on Asylum and Immigration Appeals, 2 March 2004, HC 211.

8.75 The right of access to a court implies the right to legal assistance when this is compulsory or if it is made necessary by reason of the complexity of the procedure or of the case,[1] or if the applicant is a detainee challenging the legality of his or her detention.[2] It is central to the concept of a fair trial, in civil as in criminal proceedings, that a litigant is not denied the opportunity to present his or her case effectively before the court.[3] In such circumstances, if the applicant cannot pay for legal aid, denial of it can amount to a breach of the right of access to a court.[4] However, as the court has recently ruled in *Steel and Morris v United Kingdom*, whether the provision of legal aid is necessary for a fair hearing must be determined on the basis of the particular facts and circumstances of each case and will depend inter alia upon the importance of what is at stake for the applicant in the proceedings, the complexity of the relevant law and procedure and the applicant's capacity to represent him or herself effectively.[5] The right of access to a court is not, however, absolute and may be subject to restrictions, provided that these pursue a legitimate aim and are proportionate.[6] It may therefore be acceptable to impose conditions on the grant of legal aid based, inter alia, on the financial situation of the litigant or his or her prospects of success in the proceedings.[7] Moreover, it is not incumbent on the State to seek through the use of public funds to ensure total equality of arms between the assisted person and the opposing party, as long as each side is afforded a reasonable opportunity to present his or her case under conditions that do not place him or her at a substantial disadvantage vis-à-vis the adversary.[8] Delays in determination procedures and appeal hearings may violate the right to have a hearing within a reasonable time, particularly where the delay causes prejudice, such as loss of benefits;[9] once again, the ECHR accords with the common law, which has long held that 'justice delayed is justice denied', and mandatory orders are available against foot-dragging.[10] Asylum support appeals have strict time limits in recognition of the need for speed because of the potentially irremediable hardship and injustice to which appellants are subjected by denial of all support.[11]

1   *Airey v Ireland* (1979) 2 EHRR 305 para 26. In deciding whether the interests of justice require free legal assistance, the seriousness of the possible consequences of the case and its complexity are relevant: *Benham v United Kingdom* (1996) 22 EHRR 293.

² *Golder v United Kingdom* (1975) 1 EHRR 524; *Airey v Ireland* (1979) 2 EHRR 305; *Megyeri v Germany* (1992) 15 EHRR 584, para 27. See also *A v Australia* (1997) 4 BHRC 210. Legal aid was always available for *habeas corpus* and judicial review applications (subject to means) and since January 2000 has been available for bail applications under the Immigration Act 1971.

³ *Steel and Morris v United Kingdom* (68416/01) (15 February 2005, unreported); *Airey v Ireland* (1979) 2 EHRR 305.

⁴ *Aerts v Belgium* (1998) 29 EHRR 50, para 60, where the ECtHR held that, where the law required legal representation the refusal of legal aid by the Legal Aid Board on the ground that the applicant's challenge to his detention did not appear well-founded impaired the applicant's right of access to a court. Legal aid was made available for all UK immigration appeals in the immigration appellate authority (subject to means and merits tests) from 1 January 2000, although in the Special Immigration Appeals Commission only as from 1 April 2003 (Access to Justice Act 1999, Sch 2, para 2(1)(ha), added by Nationality, Immigration and Asylum Act 2002, s 116). However, there are now concerns that severe legal aid cutbacks are seriously impairing the rights of asylum seekers to effective access; see the Fourth Report 2002–03 of the Constitutional Affairs Committee on Immigration and Asylum: the Government's proposed changes to publicly funded immigration and asylum work, 31 October 2003, HC 1171, and the government's response, printed as an Appendix to the CAC 2nd Special Report 2003–04, 29 January 2004, HC 299.

⁵ *Steel and Morris*, above, at para 61.

⁶ *Steel and Morris*, para 62; see *Ashingdane v United Kingdom*, judgment of 28 May 1985, Series A no 93, pp 24–25, para 57.

⁷ *Steel and Morris*, above, at para 62; *Munro v United Kingdom* (Application 10594/83) (1987) 10 EHRR 516.

⁸ *Steel and Morris*, above, at para 62; see *De Haes and Gijsels* (24 February 1997, unreported), *Reports* 1997–1, para 53, and also *McVicar v United Kingdom* (46311/99), paras 51 and 62.

⁹ *Zimmerman v Switzerland* (1983) 6 EHRR 17; *Guincho v Portugal* (1984) 7 EHRR 223.

¹⁰ *R v Secretary of State for the Home Department, ex p Phansopkar* [1976] QB 606. The Privy Council has held that where there is no constitutional right to judgment within a reasonable time, a delay in producing a judgment is capable of depriving the individual of the protection of the law (rendering it unlawful) where it meant the judge could no longer produce a proper judgment, or the parties could not obtain from the decision the benefit they should: *Boodhoo and Jagram A-G of Trinidad and Tobago* [2004] UKPC 17.

¹¹ See Asylum Support Appeals (Procedure) Rules 2000, SI 2000/541 as amended by SI 2003/1735.

8.76 The right to a fair hearing under Article 6 of the ECHR and under the common law embraces the principle of equality of arms, which affords parties a reasonable opportunity of presenting their case to the court under conditions which do not place them at a substantial disadvantage vis-à-vis their opponents.¹ So far as it is relevant in the immigration context, the principle requires adequate reasons for an administrative decision which may be the subject of an appeal,² and disclosure of all relevant evidence in the possession of the authorities.³ In *Quaquah* deportation which would severely hamper a claimant in the preparation of his civil action against the Home Office for malicious prosecution was held to violate the principle of equality of arms.⁴

¹ *Kaufman v Belgium* (1986) 50 DR 98; *Delcourt v Belgium* (1970) 1 EHRR 355; *Neumeister v Austria* (1968) 1 EHRR 91; *De Haes and Gijsels v Belgium* (1987) 25 EHRR 1. The application of retrospective legislation affecting current proceedings was held to be an unacceptable interference by the legislature in the administration of justice designed to influence judicial determination in *Stran Green Refineries and Stratis Andreadis v Greece* (1995) 19 EHRR 293; see also *Pressos Compania Naviera SA v Belgium* (1995) 21 EHRR 301 (Comm).

² *X v United Kingdom* (1981) 4 EHRR 188, para 66.

³ *Lamy v Belgium* (1989) 11 EHRR 529, para 29; *McMichael v United Kingdom* (1995) 20 EHRR 205, para 82; *Shishkov v Bulgaria* (38822/97).

4   *R v Immigration Officer, ex p Quaquah* [2000] INLR 196,. The Home Office now
     generally agrees not to remove litigants whose claims are pending before the UK courts.

8.77 In Special Immigration Appeals Commission cases, and particularly
'derogation' cases involving allegations of suspected international terrorism,
the Article 6 guarantees applicable to civil proceedings clearly apply, and it is
arguable that the criminal standards might also apply.[1] However, this jurisdiction has now lapsed and the new system of 'control orders' under the
Prevention of Terrorism Act 2005, which replaces the indefinite detention
regime, is no longer dealt with as an immigration matter but comes under the
jurisdiction of the High Court or the Court of Sessions. Our very considerable
concerns about the low standard of proof, the presumption of innocence,
inequality of arms and the receipt of evidence extracted under torture[2] now
belong to a different textbook.

1   The latter argument was rejected by the Court of Appeal in *A v Secretary of State for the
     Home Department, X v Secretary of State for the Home Department* [2002] EWCA Civ
     1502, [2004] QB 335; see 8.72 fn 6 above.
2   *A, B, C, D v Secretary of State for the Home Department* (SC/1, 6, 7, 9, 10/2002)
     2 October 2003, paras 83–84, upheld by the Court of Appeal as *A and 9 others v Secretary
     of State for the Home Department* [2004] EWCA Civ 1123, and now on appeal to the
     House of Lords. See Amnesty International 'Justice perverted under the Anti-terrorism,
     Crime and Security Act 2001', EUR45/029/2003, 11 December 2003.

8.78 In *Soering*[1] the European Court acknowledged that an expulsion could
engage Article 6 ECHR in circumstances where the fugitive has suffered or
risks suffering a flagrant denial of a fair trial in the receiving country[2]. This
view has now been confirmed by the House of Lords in *Ullah*.[3]

1   *Soering v United Kingdom* (1989) 11 EHRR 439.
2   *Soering v United Kingdom* (1989) 11 EHRR 439, para 113. In *Einhorn v France*
     (71555/01), 16 October 2001, the court, following *Soering*, held that in a case where an
     applicant had been unfairly convicted *in absentia*, extradition would be likely to raise an
     issue under Art 6 if substantial grounds existed for believing he could not get a retrial and
     would be imprisoned to serve his sentence. The IAT found no flagrant violation of fair trial
     rights such as to render the return of a conscientious objector to Israel in breach of Art 6 in
     Nikulin [2002] UKIAT 06719; see also *Din (Jamal)* [2002] UKIAT 06585 (Pakistan). See
     also *Lodhi v Governor of Brixton Prison* [2001] EWHC Admin 178, [2001] All ER (D)
     136 (Mar), DC (extradition case).
3   *R (on the application of Ullah) v Special Adjudicator* [2004] UKHL 26, [2004] INLR 381.

Family and private life

8.79 Article 8 of the ECHR states that:

'1   Everyone has the right to respect for his private and family life, his home
      and his correspondence.
2   There shall be no interference by a public authority with the exercise of
      this right except such as is in accordance with the law and is necessary in
      a democratic society in the interests of national security, public safety or
      the economic well-being of the country, for the prevention of disorder or
      crime, for the protection of health or morals, or for the protection of the
      rights and freedoms of others.'

Article 8(1) protects the right to respect for four separate rights: to family life, private life, home and correspondence. Only the first two are important for most immigration purposes, although the other two may be relevant on occasion.[1] Article 8 rights will most often be engaged by decisions to refuse entry or to remove or deport someone with relevant ties to the UK, although they may be engaged in other contexts such as detention and asylum support. Article 8(2) qualifies those rights as set out above.

[1]   In particular the rights to respect for home and correspondence would be engaged by the search and seizure provisions of Immigration Act 1971, as amended by Pt VII of the Immigration and Asylum Act 1999 and Pt VII of the Nationality, Immigration and Asylum Act 2002: see 8.93 below.

8.80 A lawful and genuine marriage will be enough to constitute family life between two people,[1] even if the couple are not cohabiting,[2] but a sham marriage will not give rise to family life.[3] A formally invalid marriage believed valid by the parties gives rise to family life.[4] Although the most important 'family' relationships are those between husband and wife and parent and child, relationships between siblings, between grandparents and grandchildren,[5] and uncle and nephew[6] are all potentially within the scope of 'family life',[7] depending on the strength of the emotional ties. A child born of an existing marital union will usually become part of the family from birth and will only cease to be so in exceptional circumstances,[8] even where there has been a voluntary separation between the parents and child.[9] The presumption in favour of family life between parent and child operates between a child and its natural father, provided he continues to have a level of contact with the child.[10] Family ties may be established through adoption[11] and fostering[12] as well as through biological connections. But the Commission has held that Article 8 of the ECHR was not engaged by the deportation of a woman with her children from a country where her parents and sisters lived, on the ground that she and her children formed an independent family unit, so that the relationship with the extended family did not constitute family life.[13] Whether relationships between adult siblings or adult children and their parents fall within the scope of Article 8 is a question of fact as to whether there exist ties strong enough to constitute family life within the meaning of the Article.[14] In the landmark decision of the Court of Appeal in *Singh v Entry Clearance Officer, Delhi*[15] the court recognised that with the enormous social and cultural changes whicgh have taken place in the last decades, much greater flexibility may be applied to what constitutes family life. The appellant was a seven year old boy who had been adopted in India by his uncle and aunt who lived in the UK. The adoption had been carried out within the family in accordance with a social, religious and cultural tradition which served a humane purpose. Although the child was still living with his natural parents, there had been a genuine transfer of parental responsibility, and the court held that he had become a member of his adoptive parents' family for the purposes of Article 8 of ECHR. Clearly these cases are fact sensitive. Whether a relationship amounts to 'family life' depends on substance as much as form;[16] so informal heterosexual relationships of sufficient substance and stability have been classified as 'family life,'[17] although stable homosexual relationships have not.[18]

[1]   *Abdulaziz, Cabales and Balkandali v United Kingdom* (1985) 7 EHRR 471, para 62.

2   *Abdulaziz* above; *Wakefield v United Kingdom* (1990) 66 DR 251. Cohabitation is not a
    sine qua non of family life: *Kroon v Netherlands* (1994) 19 EHRR 263; *Berrehab v
    Netherlands* (1988) 11 EHRR 322, para 21; *Boughanemi v France* (1996) 22 EHRR 228;
    but will be relevant in deciding whether interference is proportionate: *Söderbäck v Sweden*
    (1998) 29 EHRR 95.
3   However the definition of a 'sham' marriage in Immigration and Asylum Act 1999, s 24(5)
    is almost certainly too wide, since many of the marriages caught within it are based on
    genuine relationships which would in any event attract ECHR, Art 8 protection. See
    11.61ff below.
4   *A and A v Netherlands* (1992) 72 DR 118. In *R v Secretary of State for the Home
    Department, ex p Glowacka* (26 June 1997, unreported), QBD, the Home Office agreed to
    treat the parties to an invalid Roma marriage as if they were validly married for the
    purposes of refugee family reunion following the grant of permission for judicial review. In
    relation to polygamous marriages, the ECtHR has held it legitimate on public policy
    grounds to prevent two wives living together with their husband: *Bibi v United Kingdom*
    (19628/92).
5   *Marckx v Belgium* (1979) 2 EHRR 330, para 45.
6   *Boyle v United Kingdom* (1995) 19 EHRR 179, Commission. The boy's father had died
    and the uncle stayed frequently. See *R (on the application of Lekstaka) v Immigration
    Appeal Tribunal* [2005] EWHC (Admin), 18 April 2005 (*de facto* family life with uncle
    and aunt).
7   *Moustaquim v Belgium* (1991) 13 EHRR 802; *X v Germany* (1978) 9 YB 449.
    Immigration Rules providing for the admission of only certain categories of 'distressed
    relatives' will need to be read so as to include other categories, not mentioned, to avoid
    offending against Art 8.
8   *Berrehab v Netherlands* fn 2 above, para 21; *Ciliz v Netherlands*, [2000] 2 FLR 469,
    paras 33, 44.
9   *Sen v Netherlands* (2003) 36 EHRR 7.
10 Even if at the time of the birth the relationship between the parents had ended: *Keegan v
    Ireland* (1994) 18 EHRR 342. See also *Boughanemi v France* (1996) 22 EHRR 228. The
    presumption may be defeated in the face of a total lack of interest or contact by the father.
11 *X v France* (1992) 31 DR 241; *Lebbink v Netherlands* (45582/99) (1 June 2004,
    unreported; *Pini v Romania* (78028/01) (22 June 2004). The European Court is to
    consider the compatibility of para 310 of the Immigration Rules HC 395 and the Adoption
    (Designation of Overseas Adoptions) Act 1973 with the ECHR in *Singh (Pavittar) v United
    Kingdom* (60148/00), declared admissible on 3 September 2002, on the refusal to grant
    entry clearance to a child adopted in India (not a designated country under the 1973 Act:
    see 11.109 above). But see now *Singh v Entry Clearance Officer, Delhi* [2004] EWCA Civ
    1075, [2004] INLR 515.
12 (Application 8257/78) 13 DR 248.
13 *A and family v Sweden* (1994) 18 EHRR CD 209. See also *Papayianni v United Kingdom*
    (5269/71) [1974] Imm AR 7, 39 CD 104; cf *Uppal v United Kingdom* (8244/78) (1979)
    3 EHRR 391, a case where family life between children, parents, grandparents and married
    sisters forming a large and close family unit was argued, held admissible and subject of a
    friendly settlement.
14 See *Nasri v France* (1995) 21 EHRR 458; *Beldjoudi v France* (1992) 14 EHRR 801 and
    Moustaquim v Belgium (1991) 13 EHRR 802. In *Advic v United Kingdom* 20 EHRR CD
    125, the ECommHR said that Art 8 did not cover links between adult brothers living apart
    for a long period and not dependent on each other, and that there must be more than the
    normal emotional ties between adult siblings or parents and adult children, for family life
    to exist within the meaning of Art 8. For UK courts and Tribunal application of this
    restrictive approach see eg *Kugathas v Immigration Appeal Tribunal* [2003] EWCA Civ
    31, [2003] INLR 170 (where however there had been too little contact for family life to be
    real and effective); *R (Serbia and Montenegro)* [2004] UKIAT 78. But in *Senthuran v
    Secretary of State for the Home Department* [2004] EWCA Civ 950, [2004] 4 All ER 365
    the Court of Appeal warned that each case is fact sensitive, and held both the length of
    time a young adult had been with his family in the UK, and the Secretary of State's
    unreasonable delay in determining his application, relevant to the existence of family life
    and the proportionality of any interference with it. See also *R (Johnson) (Renford) v
    Secretary of State for the Home Department* [2004] EWHC 1550 (para 16).
15 *Singh v Entry Clearance Officer, Delhi* [2004] EWCA Civ 1075, [2004] INLR 515. The
    failure to grant the child entry clearance to come to the UK was a violation of Art 8.

¹⁶ *Marckx* above, para 31; *Kroon v Netherlands* (1994) 19 EHRR 263; *Attafuah* [2002] UKIAT 05922.

¹⁷ *Johnston v Ireland* (1986) 9 EHRR 203; *Marckx v Belgium* above.

¹⁸ *X v United Kingdom* (1983) 32 DR 220; *S v United Kingdom* (1986) 47 D & R 274, para 2; *Kerkhoven v Netherlands* (19 May 1992, unreported) (relationship between a woman and the child of her long-term, same-sex partner not 'family life'). Homosexual relationships have been considered instead in the context of private life: *Roosli v Germany* (Application 28318/95) (15 May 1996), DR 85, p 149. Most recently in *Karner v Austria* (2003) 2 FLR 623 the ECtHR found it 'unnecessary' to consider whether homosexual relationships fell within the scope of 'family life'. The European Court of Justice in *Grant v South West Trains Ltd* [1998] ECR I-621 has similarly failed to recognise homosexual relationships as constituting family life. With the advent of homosexual marriages in European countries such as the Netherlands and the wider legal recognition of homosexual relationships it is difficult to see that the European courts will be able to maintain this distinction between homosexual and heterosexual couples. In *X, Y and Z v United Kingdom* (1997) 24 EHRR 143, the relationship between a transsexual, her female partner and their child was '*de facto*' family life. And in the UK a stable same-sex partner has been held to be 'part of the family' for the purposes of succession to a tenancy: *Fitzpatrick v Sterling Housing Association Ltd* [1999] 4 All ER 705, [2000] 1 FLR 271, HL (reversing [1998] Ch 304, CA); in *Ghaidan v Mendoza* [2004] UKHL 30, [2004] 3 All ER 411, HL a same-sex partner was equated with a spouse. This is another area where the common law can fertilise ECtHR jurisprudence in the UK courts.

8.81 Not every exclusion or removal from the country of residence of the applicant's family constitutes an 'interference' with the right to respect for family life. Article 8 of the ECHR does not expressly deal with immigration. Indeed, the right of a foreigner to enter or remain in a country is not as such guaranteed by the ECHR, but as the court observed in its landmark decision of *Abdulaziz, Cabales and Balkandali*, immigration controls have to be exercised consistently with the obligations under the Convention, although the right to family life is to be seen in the context of the right of States to control the entry of non-nationals onto their territory and consequently Article 8 does not oblige States to respect the choice by married couples of their matrimonial residence or to accept the non-national spouse for settlement in the country.[1] In the years that followed *Abdulaziz* there emerged two types of cases: those involving the expulsion of long-term residents, normally following criminal conviction, and those involving the expulsion or failure to admit third country nationals with family members in the Contracting State. The position of long-term residents would be more easily secured if they had family members in the Contracting State.[2] In considering whether an expulsion amounted to a breach of Article 8, the court would weigh the nature of any offence committed by the applicant and the extent to which links with his country of origin had been severed, although the outcomes generally favoured State control.[3] In cases concerning the expulsion or refusal to admit other third country nationals with close family members in the Contracting State, the family would need to demonstrate that there were 'obstacles' to family life being established elsewhere. In the 1990s the Commission's jurisprudence was extremely tough on this issue; thus even the deportation of the mother of a British citizen child was declared compatible with the ECHR, as the child was of an adaptable age'.[4] In similar vein, the court upheld a refusal to admit a child into a Contracting State where his parents had been granted humanitarian leave to remain, holding that there were no real obstacles to the parents returning to their country of origin.[5] Divorced or separated parents had an apparent advantage, since the non-national parents were likely to encounter obstacles to enjoying their family life with children staying in the State of residence of the other parent, who could not be expected to accompany the non-national abroad.[6] The case law of the court also made a distinction between decisions on admission of a non-national to the territory of a State and expulsion, reflecting a difference in approach to positive and negative obligations under Article 8 ECHR.[7]

1   *Abdulaziz* above, para 68. In *Begum (Husna) v Entry Clearance Officer, Dhaka* [2001] INLR 115, an entry clearance case, the Court of Appeal held that the ability of the family to live together in the country of origin was not always crucial and that family reunion could operate to enable a family member 'left behind' to join family in the UK.
2   In *Boughanemi v France* (1996) 22 EHRR 228 the court found the expulsion of a Tunisian national who had lived in France for 20 years since the age of eight, but had been sentenced to less than four years' imprisonment, did not violate Art 8 ECHR, cf *Moustaquim v Belgium* (1991) 13 EHRR 802.
3   See for instance *Boujlifa v France* (1997) 30 EHRR 419, where the applicant had lived in France since the age of five and had extensive family there, but had been convicted of armed robbery justifying expulsion; in *Bouchelkia v France* (1997) 25 EHRR 886 the applicant had lived in France since the age of two but a conviction for rape justified his expulsion.
4   *Sorabjee v United Kingdom* (Application 23938/93), 23 October 1995, unpublished. *PP v United Kingdom* (1996) 21 EHRR CD 81; *Jaramillo v United Kingdom* (24865/94).
5   *Gul v Switzerland* (1996) 22 EHRR 93.
6   *Berrehab v Netherlands* (1989) 11 EHRR 322. See also *Ciliz v Netherlands* [2000] 2 FLR 469.
7   'As far as those positive obligations are concerned, the notion of "respect" is not clear-cut; having regard to the diversity of practices followed and the situations obtaining in the Contracting States, the notion's requirements will vary considerably from case to case': *Abdulaziz, Cabales and Balkandali v United Kingdom*, para 67.

8.82 The emphasis of the case law of the European Court has changed significantly in the last five years – a change that, in our view, has not been fully appreciated by the domestic courts or immigration practitioners who argue before them. In the court's jurisprudence there has been a considerable softening of the *Abdulaziz* principle on a State's right to control immigration, such that whilst Contracting States are not prohibited by Article 8 from exercising immigration control, the need for fair processes that 'afford due respect to the interests safeguarded by Article 8' is now urged upon States.[1] There are now clear principles that emerge from the court's jurisprudence that can be applied to all types of immigration cases, whether long-term residents facing expulsion or those without any other legal entitlement seeking to remain with close family members. The court's judgment in *Boultif* lays down guiding principles in assessing the likelihood that a decision will interfere with family life and if so, its proportionality to its legitimate aim:

'the court will consider the nature and seriousness of the offence committed by the applicant; the length of the applicant's stay in the country from which he is going to be expelled; the time elapsed since the offence was committed as well as the applicant's conduct in that period; the nationalities of the various persons concerned; the applicant's family situation, such as the length of the marriage; and other factors expressing the effectiveness of a couple's family life; whether the spouse knew about the offence at the time when he or she entered into a family relationship; and whether there are children in the marriage, and if so, their age. Not least, the court will also consider the seriousness of the difficulties which the spouse is likely to encounter in the country of origin, though the mere fact that a person might face certain difficulties in accompanying her or his spouse cannot in itself exclude an expulsion.'[2]

In a later case following *Boultif*, the court made clear that, in considering the proportionality of deportation as a response to criminal convictions, it will place considerable emphasis on the future threat that a person might pose to public order, rather than confining itself to consideration of the past.[3]

[1] *Ciliz v Netherlands* [2000] 2 FLR 469, para 66.
[2] *Boultif v Switzerland* (2001) 33 EHRR 50; followed in *Amrollahi v Denmark* (56811/00), 11 July 2002, where the applicant was convicted of drugs trafficking offences but had left Iran 15 years earlier and was married to a Danish woman with a child; *Yildiz v Austria* (2003) 36 EHRR 32, where the applicant had been subject of a five-year residence ban following serious traffic offences but had a wife (from whom he was divorced by the time of hearing) and a child in Austria making the residence ban disproportionate; *Mokrani v France* (52206/99), 15 July 2003, where the applicant had been convicted of drugs trafficking offences but his family ties in France meant that removal would breach Art 8 ECHR. *Boultif* has also been cited with approval by the European Court of Justice in *Carpenter v Secretary of State for the Home Department* Case C-60/00 [2003] QB 416.
[3] *Yildiz v Austria* (2003) 36 EHRR 32. In *Jakupovic v Austria* [2003] INLR 499, where the applicant joined his mother in Austria four years before the convictions for burglary relied on for expulsion, the court found a violation of Art 8, holding that 'very weighty reasons' would be needed to justify the expulsion of a 16-year-old, alone, to a country which had recently experienced armed conflict and where he had no close relatives.

8.83 It is clear that the court, which had in the past rarely found in favour of applicants even where they had close family members in the Contracting State, has lowered the threshold for finding a violation of Article 8 based on obstacles to the family relocating elsewhere in the world – and this shift appears to be a quite deliberate shift of emphasis, from the right of States to control their borders to their duty to respect their international obligations in doing so.[1] In *Boultif* it recognised that the existence of real difficulties (such as lack of ties or language difficulties) for some family members in the deportee's country of origin, is likely to lead to the conclusion that the family cannot be expected to follow the deportee and that expulsion is a breach of Article 8 unless there are serious public order reasons for it. In *Sen*[2] the court took this one stage further in acknowledging that long-term residents in Contracting States can themselves face obstacles in returning to their countries of origin, such that refusal by a Contracting State to admit a family member who had remained behind in the country of origin, could breach its obligations under Article 8.[3] The duty to admit family members in these circumstances flows from the positive obligation placed on a Contracting State by Article 8 ECHR to foster family life and to consider where family life might best develop, reflecting decisions made in family care cases and echoing what the court had stated in *Ciliz v Netherlands*.[4] Ciliz concerned a divorcé who was attempting to re-establish contact with his child through the courts when the State proposed to remove him for immigration reasons. Confirming its approach to positive obligations under Article 8, the court:

'reiterates that the essential object of Article 8 is to protect the individual against arbitrary action by the public authorities. There may in addition be positive obligations inherent in effective "respect" for family life. However the boundaries between the State's positive and negative obligations under this provision do not lend themselves to precise definition. The applicable principles are, nonetheless, similar.'[5]

1   See *Boultif v Switzerland*, para 48; see also the Concurring Opinion of Judges Baka, Wildhaber and Lorenzen, which lists all the previous case law of the court relating to expulsion where no breach of Art 8 ECHR had been found.
2   *Sen v Netherlands* (2003) 36 EHRR 7.
3   In the domestic context see *Begum (Husna) v Entry Clearance Officer, Dhaka* [2001] INLR 115, where the Court of Appeal held that while it may be relevant to a family reunion application that members of the family had chosen to live in the UK, leaving a relative in the country of origin, it was not universally the case that family reunion could not apply.
4   *Ciliz v Netherlands* (2000) 2 FLR 469, para 66.
5   See the strong dissenting judgment of Judge Martens in *Gul v Switzerland* (1996) 22 EHRR 93, suggesting that the differences were now indistinguishable.

8.84 The court's recent case-law reflects a general acceptance that removal will normally constitute an interference with family life. Rather than requiring the applicant to establish that there would be insurmountable obstacles to family life being established elsewhere, the court has placed the burden of proof on the Contracting State to establish that an expulsion decision or refusal to admit would not constitute an interference with family life. In *Yildiz*[1] the court stated

> 'Nevertheless, the court considers that, as regards the possible effects of the residence ban on his family life, the authorities *failed to establish* whether the second applicant could be expected to follow him to Turkey, in particular whether she spoke Turkish and maintained any links, other than her nationality, with that country.'(our emphasis)

It is settled law that it is for the State to demonstrate that any interference is in accordance with the law (in both its meanings), corresponds to a pressing social need and is proportionate to the legitimate aim pursued.[2] In *Jakupovic v Austria*[3] the court required 'very weighty reasons' to justify the expulsion of a 16-year-old to a country which had recently experienced armed conflict, where he had no close relatives, separating him from his mother, despite his criminal convictions.

1   *Yildiz v Austria*, 8.32 fn 3 above, para 43.
2   *Moustaquim v Belgium* (1996) 13 EHRR 802; *Beldjoudi v France* (1992) 14 EHRR 801; *Sporring and Lönroth v Sweden* (1982) 5 EHRR 35 (para 69); *Cossey v United Kingdom* (1990) 13 EHRR 622.
3   [2003] INLR 499.

8.85 Whilst the focus of *Boultif* and cases that have followed it has been on 'family life', the court had previously begun to take cognisance of the fact that second generation migrants and long-term residents in Contracting States develop whole networks of social ties constituting 'private life'. In *Lamguindaz*,[1] a case involving the proposed deportation on conducive grounds of a Moroccan youth who had lived in the UK since the age of seven, Judge Schermers, in his concurring opinion, said:

> 'Even independent of human rights considerations I doubt whether modern international law permits a State which has educated children of admitted aliens to expel these children when they become a burden. Shifting this burden to the State of origin of the parents is no longer so clearly acceptable under modern international law.'[2]

In *Beldjoudi*[3] Judge Martens, in his concurring opinion, said that 'mere nationality' should not constitute an:

'objective and reasonable justification for the existence of a difference as regards the admissibility of expelling someone from what may be called "his own country"... An increasing number of member States of the Council of Europe accept the principle that such "integrated aliens" should be no more liable to expulsion than nationals, an exception being justified if at all, only in very exceptional circumstances.'

[1] *Lamguindaz v United Kingdom* (1993) 17 EHRR 213.
[2] The government has accepted, in the amended policy DP5/96 (published in *Butterworths Immigration Law Service*, D[651]) relating to the removal of families with children, that children who have lived in the UK for seven years cannot be expected to adapt to life abroad. See 11.122 below.
[3] *Beldjoudi v France* (1992) 14 EHRR 801.

8.86 There is clearly an emerging view in the jurisprudence of the European Court that it is wrong to review deportations or removals, especially of 'integrated aliens', in the context of protection of family life, without also considering the obligation of States to give protection to private life. As Judge Martens stated,

'Expulsion severs irrevocably all social ties between the deportee and the community he is living in and ... the totality of those ties may be said to be part of the concept of private life'[1]

The principle seemed to have been accepted by the court by the late 1990s. In *C v Belgium*,[2] relying on its approach in *Niemietz v Germany*,[3] having looked at the family life of a long-term resident and proposed deportee, it examined his 'private life' in some detail:

'Mr C established real social ties in Belgium. He lived there from the age of 11, went to school there, underwent vocational training there and worked there for a number of years. He accordingly also established a private life there within the meaning of Article 8 (art. 8), which encompasses the right for an individual to form and develop relationships with other human beings, including relationships of a professional or business nature (see, mutatis mutandis, the Niemietz v Germany judgment ... para 29).'[4]

[1] *Beldjoudi v France* (1992) 14 EHRR 801. This position was defended by other judges such as Judge Wildhaber in *Nasri v France* (1995) 21 EHRR 458. Judge Morenilla in *Nasri v France* and Judge De Meyer in *Beldjoudi v France* had gone further and expressed the view that the deportation of an integrated migrant per se would breach Art 3 ECHR. Judge Morenilla stated:

'The deportation of such dangerous "non-nationals" may be expedient for a State which in this way rids itself of persons regarded as "undesirable", but it is cruel and inhuman and clearly discriminatory in relation to "nationals" who find themselves in such circumstances. A State which for reasons of convenience, accepts immigrant workers and authorises their residence, becomes responsible for the education and social integration of the children of such immigrants as it is of the children of its "citizens". Where such social integration fails, and the result is anti-social or criminal behaviour, the State is also under a duty to make provision for their social rehabilitation instead of sending them back to their country of origin, which has no responsibility for the behaviour in question and where the possibilities of rehabilitation in a foreign social environment are virtually non-existent. The treatment of offenders whether on the administrative or criminal level should not therefore differ according to the national origin of the parents in a way which – through deportation – makes the sanction more severe in a clearly discriminatory manner.'

2   *C v Belgium* (7 August 1996, unreported), para 25. The application failed on the facts.
3   (1992) 16 EHRR 97.
4   This was acknowledged in the domestic context in the case of *R v Immigration Officer, ex p James* (CO 2187/1999) where the Home Office accepted 16 years' residence, a close circle of friends, home and employment in the UK as engaging private life considerations.

8.87 The right to respect for private life is linked with personal autonomy, physical and psychological integrity, and the guarantee afforded by Article 8 of the ECHR is primarily intended to ensure the development, without outside interference, of the personality of each individual in his or her relations with other human beings.[1] Thus, enforcement action against carers who enable disabled or ill friends or relatives to live an independent and dignified life at home may constitute a disproportionate interference with the private life rights of the person cared for.[2] Same-sex relationships are an aspect of private life protected by Article 8.[3] Although as yet there has been no ECtHR case in which interference with a homosexual relationship by removal or exclusion of a partner has been held to violate the right of respect to private life, now that such relationships are recognised under the UK Immigration Rules as conferring rights of residence in domestic law on a par with cohabiting heterosexual couples,[4] there can no longer be any justification for a differential approach to interference with these relationships in the domestic courts. In a different context, destitution, isolation and social marginalisation to which late and failed asylum seekers may be subjected, raise issues relating to the right of respect for private life under Article 8.[5]

1   *Botta v Italy* (1998) 26 EHRR 241, para 32; *Niemietz v Germany* (1992) 16 EHRR 97, para 29.
2   The invaluable role of carers is recognised in the government White Paper *Caring for People* (Cmd 849) and policy guidance *Community Care in the next decade and beyond*. The Home Office policy on carers (set out in the IDI Jun 01, Ch 17, s 2, is heavily restricted in time and, insofar as it insists on institutional care as a viable long-term alternative to allowing family members to remain as carers, may well breach Art 8 ECHR. The importance of care provided by friends or relatives was held to outweigh immigration control considerations in *R v Secretary of State for the Home Department, ex p Zakrocki* [1996] COD 304; cf *R v Secretary of State for the Home Department, ex p Green*, 29 October 1996, QBD, 31 January 1997, CA.
3   *Dudgeon v United Kingdom* (1980) 3 EHRR 40, paras 96–97; *Modinos v Cyprus* (1993) 16 EHRR 485; *Sutherland v United Kingdom* [1998] EHRLR 117; *Smith and Grady v United Kingdom* (1999) 29 EHRR 493.
4   HC 395, as amended by Cm 4851, paras 295A and D.
5   See *Smirnova v Russia* (46133/99, 48183/99) (24 July 2003, unreported), where the court held that the failure of the authorities to return identity papers following the applicant's release from prison, which led to difficulties in obtaining work, medical services etc, was a continuing violation of private life rights. See also *Ahmed v Austria* (1996) 24 EHRR 278, [1998] INLR 65. But cf *Mehemi v France* (53470/99), where no violation was found to arise from the legal limbo of an unenforceable exclusion order.

Article 8 in the domestic courts

8.88 The case law of the UK courts reflects a much more conservative approach to Article 8 ECHR than that of Strasbourg. The Court of Appeal's judgment in *Mahmood*[1] set the benchmark from which courts have been very reluctant to depart. How long this will continue remains to be seen, given the rejection by the Court of Appeal in *Huang*[2] of the jurisprudential underpinning of *Mahmood* and many subsequent decisions, which have relied on what we have called a *neo-Wednesbury* approach to proportionality in Article 8(2).[3] The fact that *Huang* has erected another shibboleth in its attempt to give a principled description of the proper approach to proportionality[4] should not detract from the blow it has struck against the ongoing authority of *Mahmood*. In *Mahmood* the Master of the Rolls considered that an applicant who had married or had children at a time when his or her immigration status was 'precarious' would be unlikely to succeed in an argument that removal would breach Article 8. The court set out guidelines which have, in subsequent case-law, been virtually reduced to the catch-phrase 'insurmountable obstacles':[5]

'(1) A State has a right under international law to control the entry of non-nationals into its territory, subject always to its treaty obligations.

(2) Article 8 does not impose on a State any general obligation to respect the choice of residence of a married couple.

(3) Removal or exclusion of one family member from a State where other members of the family are lawfully resident will not necessarily infringe Article 8 provided that there are no insurmountable obstacles to the family living together in the country of origin of the family member excluded, even where this involves a degree of hardship for some or all members of the family.

(4) Article 8 is likely to be violated by the expulsion of a member of a family that has been long established in a State if the circumstances are such that it is not reasonable to expect the other members of the family to follow that member expelled.

(5) Knowledge on the part of one spouse at the time of marriage that rights of residence of the other were precarious militates against a finding that an order excluding the latter spouse violates Article 8.

(6) Whether interference with family rights is justified in the interests of controlling immigration will depend on:
  (i)   the facts of the particular case and
  (ii) the circumstances prevailing in the State whose action is impugned.'[6]

Despite the European Court of Human Rights' decision in *Boultif*[7] and subsequent cases which place less emphasis on 'precarious' immigration status and put this factor in the balance against a range of other factors that might act in the applicant's favour, the *Mahmood* dictum has prevailed.

---

[1] *R (on the application of Mahmood) v Secretary of State for the Home Department* [2001] 1 WLR 840.

[2] *Huang v Secretary of State for the Home Department* [2005] EWCA Civ 105, (2005) Sol Jo LB 297, paras 46, 49 and 60. See 8.19ff.

[3] See 8.20–8.21 above.

[4] See 8.22 above.

[5] This is particularly the case in the Tribunal, where the phrase is too often parroted to avoid a careful analysis of the difficulties which family members would face in the destination country.

[6] *Mahmood* at para 55.

[7] (2001) 33 EHRR 50; see 8.83 above.

8.89 The most common situation where *Mahmood* is cited is in the context of the removal of failed asylum seekers who have married British citizens or non-EEA nationals in the UK while waiting for their asylum claim to be determined, in support of the Home Office argument that they should join the queue for entry clearance.[1] An exception to this was identified in *Shala*,[2] where the Court of Appeal accepted that the same considerations should not apply in a case where the applicant would have been granted asylum (whether refugee status or some other leave under a policy) but for significant delay in processing his or her claim for international protection, during which time the applicant's family life ties had been formed. In such a case, immigration controls did not require an application for entry clearance to be made from outside the UK, since if leave had been granted near the time of arrival the applicant could have subsequently applied for further leave to remain on the basis of marriage. Removal in such circumstances was said to breach Article 8 ECHR. However, the Court of Appeal in *Janjanin*[3] and the Immigration Appeal Tribunal in *R (Serbia & Montenegro)*[4] have ensured that the *Shala* principles are confined to cases where the Secretary of State had a firm policy of granting leave to enter to persons of the applicant's nationality or ethnicity at the time when he or she arrived in the UK, and there has been significant delay in the processing of his or her claim during which time the relevant family ties were forged.[5] Arguments that the application of the Immigration Rules would tend towards refusal and therefore permanent separation of the family if entry clearance were sought have generally met with little success, since according to *Huang* it is only the exceptional case that does not fall within the Immigration Rules that will succeed under Article 8.[6]

---

1   Laws LJ ruled that it was unfair for such applicants to 'jump the queue': *Mahmood* above at para 26. Whether in fact entry clearance was likely to be granted was held to be irrelevant in *R (on the application of Ekinci) v Secretary of State for the Home Department* [2003] EWCA Civ 765, [2003] All ER (D) 215 (Jun), where the Court of Appeal held that that was a matter for the ECO and if necessary, for the intervention of the court at that stage. Two other questions arise. (i) what is the queue and in which countries does it exist? And (ii) is the need to join the queue necessary in the interests of national security, public safety, economic well-being, or for the prevention of disorder or crime?

2   *Shala v Secretary of State for the Home Department* [2003] EWCA Civ 233, [2003] All ER (D) 407 (Feb), followed in *R (on the application of Ala) v Secretary of State for the Home Department* [2003] EWHC 521 (Admin).

3   *Janjanin and Musanovic v Secretary of State for the Home Department* [2004] EWCA Civ 448, [2004] 2 FCR 200. See *also R (on the application of Bekteshi) v Immigration Appeal Tribunal* [2004] EWHC 803 (Admin).

4   [2004] UKIAT 78 *R (Serbia and Montenegro)* 'Reported', following *J* [2004] UKIAT 16, where the *Shala* principles were summarised. The Tribunal in *R* was willing to apply the *Shala* principle to someone who would have qualified under the immigration rules, but dismissed the appeal on the facts.

5   Delay *per se* is not determinative, but the consequences of delay may be significant: see *Alihajdaraj v Secretary of State for the Home Department* [2004] EWCA Civ 104. In *Mthokozisi v Secretary of State for the Home Department* [2004] EWHC 2964 (Admin), the court held that the Secretary of State had wrongly ignored a four-year delay in deciding a minor's application (he was 13 on arrival), which caused him not to be granted ELR or ILR, in assessing whether removal would be a disproportionate interference with his private life.

6   *Huang v Secretary of State for the Home Department* [2005] EWCA Civ 105, (2005) Sol Jo LB 297, see 8.21–8.22 above. But see *R (on the application of Lekstaka) v Immigration Appeal Tribunal* [2005] EWHC 745 (Admin), where Collins J held that a decision maker should contemplate whether the case fell within the spirit of the Immigration Rules and Home Office policies if not the letter of them in determining whether the case is exceptional.

8.90 The domestic courts have also departed from the European Court of Human Rights' guidance in *Boultif* and *Sen* in their reluctance, by and large, to take into account a wide range of factors affecting the ability of families to enjoy family life in another country.[1] In *Vujnovic*[2] the Court of Appeal considered that the fact that an individual might be separated from his family on return due to compulsory military service was irrelevant. In the same case the court found irrelevant the ties between an applicant and his brother and mother, with whom he had fled his home country having shared dreadful experiences.[3] Only in the context of local authority support for children and their parents has the Court of Appeal upheld the right of a British citizen child to live in the UK and not to be forced out by the effective expulsion of a parent.[4] As part of this trend it is significant that in *Huang*[5] the Court of Appeal questioned the importance of *Boultif* and *Sen* because they were 'insufficient' and contained no 'patent reasoning' to support the Strasbourg approach. The speech of Baroness Hale in *Razgar* conveyed the respect which authorities of an expelling State should afford to the right to family life, and the relevance of conditions in the receiving State for the purpose of assessing the proportionality of any interference;[6] the inferior courts should take heed, and act accordingly.

[1] See eg *Secretary of State for the Home Department v G (Somalia)* [2003] UKIAT 175; *G (Azerbaijan)* [2003] UKIAT 155; *G (Algeria)* [2003] UKIAT 78 'reported'; *N (Kenya)* [2004] UKIAT 9, upheld [2004] EWCA Civ 1094, [2004] INLR 612.

[2] *Secretary of State for the Home Department v Vujnovic* [2003] EWCA Civ 1843.

[3] See also *Kugathas (Navaratnam) v Immigration Appeal Tribunal* [2003] EWCA Civ 31, [2003] All ER (D) 144 (Jan) where the Court of Appeal considered that only in an exceptional case would the courts accept that family life exists between an adult and his or her parent or siblings. But cf *Senthuran v Secretary of State for the Home Department* [2004] EWCA Civ 950; *R (on the application of Johnson) v Secretary of State for the Home Department* [2004] EWHC 1550 (Admin); 8.80 fn 14 above.

[4] In *R (on the application of M) v Islington* [2004] EWCA Civ 235, [2004] 4 All ER 709, per Buxton LJ at paras 26ff.

[5] *Huang v Secretary of State for the Home Department* [2005] EWCA Civ 105, (2005) Sol Jo LB 297, at para 48. For a fuller discussion of the case, see 8.21, above.

[6] *R (on the application of Razgar) v Secretary of State for the Home Department* [2004] UKHL 27, [2004] 2 AC 368, para 50, in which she also indicates that the effect upon the spouse or child left behind must be considered and might well be determinative, and comments that 'the court is unsympathetic to actions which will have the effect of breaking up marriages or separating children from their parents'. See also para 52. Although her speech dissented on the facts, her analysis and conclusions on the ECtHR jurisprudence on Art 8 ECHR family life are authoritative and compelling.

8.91 In entry clearance cases, there has been a gravitation towards the view of the Tribunal expressed in *H (Somalia)*[1] that only in exceptional cases would refusal to grant entry clearance breach Article 8 in circumstances falling outside the immigration rules and any relevant policy:

> 'It would normally be the position that the combination of the provisions of the Immigration Rules and extra-statutory policy and discretion would provide a proportionate basis for any interference with or lack of respect for family life in the light of the well-established right of a State to control entry, whether or not that is to be regarded as a free-standing restriction on the scope of Article 8 or as falling within the qualification in Article 8(2).'[2]

Such an approach neither requires the Secretary of State to demonstrate the legitimate aim of the rules or policy in question, nor engages with the balancing act that must be carried out in every case on its own facts, and appears contrary to the approach of cases such as *Sen v Netherlands*.[3]

1   *H (Somalia)* [2004] UKIAT 27. See now *Huang v Secretary of State for the Home Department* [2005] EWCA Civ 105, (2005) Sol Jo LB 297; *MB (Croatia)* [2005] UKAIT00092.
2   *H (Somalia)* above, para 46.
3   (2003) 36 EHRR 7; see 8.83 text and fn 2 above. The Administrative Court's decision in *R v Secretary of State for the Home Department, ex p Ali (Arman)* [2000] INLR 89 however suggests that where third party support is offered in place of support from the sponsor, a failure to meet the immigration rules on maintenance and accommodation should not be fatal given that the purpose of the restrictions is to meet one of the aims of Art 8(2) ECHR. If the applicant is to be supported without recourse to public funds then any aim of protecting the economic interests of the State has been met.

8.92 The domestic courts have been even slower to find in applicants' favour where removal is said to interfere with physical or moral integrity as an aspect of private life. However, in *Razgar*[1] the House of Lords accepted that in an Article 8 claim reliance may in principle be placed on the consequences for a person's mental health of removal to the receiving country. 'Private life' in Article 8 extended to those features which are integral to a person's identity or ability to function socially as a person. This must be taken as a more definitive statement of the ambit of and meaning of 'private life' than that of the Court of Appeal which considered that 'there must be a sufficiently adverse effect on physical and mental integrity and not merely on health' for Article 8 to be engaged. The House of Lords judgment must also call into question the decision in *Djali*,[2] where the Court of Appeal found that the removal of a woman with severe post-traumatic stress disorder suffered as a result of her ill-treatment in Kosovo would not engage Article 8, since at worst it would merely imperil her prospects of a better recovery,[3] and added that even if Article 8(1) had been engaged, the decision-maker would inevitably regard the interests of immigration control, as the imperative and overriding factor, given the grave problems of asylum overload.[4] In *Jegatheeswaran*,[5] the High Court held that removal of a child with severe hearing loss and learning difficulties to Germany could breach Article 8, since he would be unable to communicate in any spoken language. The Tribunal dismissed the risk to physical integrity from depleted uranium in Kosovo as 'remote' in *FZ*.[6]

1   *R (on the application of Razgar) v Secretary of State for the Home Department* [2004] UKHL 27, [2004] 2 AC 368, at para 9, quoting with approval an Article by Professor Feldman 'The Developing Scope of Article 8 of the European Convention on Human Rights' (1997) EHRLR 265, at 270.
2   *Djali v Immigration Appeal Tribunal* [2003] EWCA Civ 1371, [2004] 1 FCR 42.
3   *Djali* above, para 17.
4   *Djali* above, para 26, per Simon Brown LJ. One has to ask whether the 'interests of immigration control', which is not one of the factors listed in Art 8(2), is factored into the 'fair balance' not by virtue of its connection to any of these factors, but because of the international law rule that States have a right to control the entry and expulsion of aliens. It is certainly the darling concept of some sections of the judiciary, but like any unruly pet, it needs to kept in its proper place: see in particular Lord Bingham in *European Roma Rights Centre v Immigration Officer at Prague Airport* [2004] UKHL 55, [2005] 1 All ER 527, para 11ff. See also *R (on the application of Ay) v Secretary of State for the Home Department* [2003] EWCA Civ 1, where the Court of Appeal considered that the harm suffered by children on removal to Germany had to be weighed against the interests of the public and the consequences flowing from the fact that the children might benefit from the unlawful actions of their parents who had remained in the UK in breach of immigration controls and evaded return to Germany.

⁵ *R (on the application of Jegatheeswaran) v Secretary of State for the Home Department* [2005] EWHC, CO/4101/2004, 14 April 2005.

⁶ [2003] UKIAT 315, [2003] Imm AR 633.

8.93 The rights to respect for private life, home and correspondence are engaged by searches of premises,[1] which must be a proportionate measure in all the circumstances,[2] justified by relevant and sufficient reasons and accompanied by adequate and effective safeguards.[3] The ECtHR has given a broad interpretation to 'home', requiring no legal right of occupation but constituting a haven against intervention by public authorities.[4] The right to respect for home may be engaged by a refusal of readmission after a long absence, where the applicant has no other home.[5]

¹ *Funke v France* (1993) 16 EHRR 297; *Miailhe v France* (1993) 16 EHRR 332; *Niemietz v Germany* (1993) 16 EHRR 97; *Chappell v United Kingdom* (1989) 12 EHRR 1.

² *McLeod v United Kingdom* (1998) 27 EHRR 493.

³ *Camenzind v Switzerland* (1997) 28 EHRR 458, para 45.

⁴ *Wiggins v United Kingdom* (1978) 13 DR 40; *Buckley v United Kingdom* (1996) 23 EHRR 101.

⁵ *Gillow v United Kingdom* (1986) 11 EHRR 335 where refusal of a resident's licence to live in a house in Guernsey built by the applicant after 18 years' absence was held to breach Art 8 ECHR.

Freedom of thought, conscience and religion

8.94 Article 9 of the ECHR provides that:

'1   Everyone has the right to freedom of thought, conscience and religion; this right includes freedom to change his religion or belief and freedom, either alone or in community with others and in public or private, to manifest his religion or belief, in worship, teaching, practice and observance.

2   Freedom to manifest one's religion or beliefs shall be subject only to such limitations as are prescribed by law and are necessary in a democratic society in the interests of public safety, for the protection of public order, health or morals, or for the protection of the rights and freedoms of others.'

The right in paragraph 1 includes the absolute and non-derogable right to freedom of thought, conscience and religion, reflecting the ECtHR's general understanding that it is 'one of the foundations of a "democratic society" '.[1] Although the manifestation of beliefs (paragraph 2) is a qualified right, the importance of religious freedom means that States' margin of appreciation is limited.[2] The obligation to ensure the peaceful enjoyment of religious rights[3] may in certain circumstances require an exception to laws of general application.[4] The communal aspect of religious worship has also been recognised.[5] The House of Lords held in *Ullah* that interference with religious freedoms in a receiving State will ground a challenge to expulsion, if there is a real risk of a flagrant denial or gross violation, where the very essence of the right will be completely denied or nullified in the receiving country.[6] Article 9 may in principle be engaged by the removal of a member of a UK congregation,[7] or by dispersal within the UK.[8]

¹ *Kokkinakis v Greece* (1993) 17 EHRR 397, para 31.

2   *Sidiropolous v Greece* (1999) 27 EHRR 633.
3   *Otto Preminger Institut v Austria* (1994) 19 EHRR 34.
4   *Thlimmenos v Greece* (2000) 9 BHRC 12, para 44.
5   Restrictions placed on freedom of movement which impair a population's ability to observe their religious beliefs, and in particular, their access to places of worship outside their own area and their participation in other aspects of religious life were held to violate Article 9 rights in *Cyprus v Turkey* (25781/94) (2001) 11 BHRC 45. See also *Wang v MIMA* [2000] FCA 1599) Fed Ct Aust).
6   *R (on the application of Ullah) v Special Adjudicator* [2004] UKHL 26, [2004] INLR 381.
7   *R (on the application of Lithuania)* [2003] UKIAT 24 (lost on the facts).
8   *R (on the application of Kazema) v Secretary of State for the Home Department* [2002] EWHC Admin 2157, [2003] Imm AR 100 (on the facts, dispersal to Bolton, where no religious services were conducted in the appellant's mother tongue, did not breach Art 9 ECHR as her English was improving.)

8.95 One of the significant areas of application of Article 9 in the ECtHR jurisprudence has been in relation to conscientious objection to military service, in conjunction with ECHR, Article 4, which leaves open the possibility that failure to take account of the individual's beliefs may violate his or her human rights.[1] There is growing support in international human rights law for the proposition that there is a human right of conscientious objection to military service, although no international human rights instrument as yet expressly recognises such a right.[2] In 1973, the Commission found that Article 9, as qualified by Article 4(3)(b), 'does not impose on a State the obligation to recognise conscientious objectors and ... does not prevent a State ... from punishing those who refuse to do military service'.[3] But this case law is now thought to be out of date. All countries in the Council of Europe, except three, now recognise such a right in their domestic law. Such recognition is now required before new members are admitted to the Council, and in *Thlimmenos v Greece*[4] the Commission members accepted (without deciding) that punishment for refusal to perform military service which is motivated by religious beliefs may breach Article 9 (freedom of conscience and religion).[5] By 1979, the UNHCR's position was that 'it would be open to contracting States to grant refugee status to persons who object to performing military service for genuine reasons of conscience'.[6] In *Sepet and Bulbul*[7] the Court of Appeal, by a majority, held that the right to conscientious objection was not so established that denial of it constituted persecution for the purposes of the Refugee Convention, while acknowledging that Article 9 might in future lay the foundations for a general right of conscientious objection. The majority's conclusion was upheld by the House of Lords.

1   See Goodwin-Gill, Guy, report in *Sepet and Bulbul*, para 48.
2   See Asbjørn Eide and Chama Mubanga-Chipoya 'Conscientious Objection to Military Service,' UN document E/CN/4/Sub/2/1983/30/Rev.1; Commission on Human Rights Resolution 1998/77, 22 April 1998: 'Conscientious Objection to Military Service', recalled in Resolution 2000/34, 20 April 2000. See also judgment of Waller LJ in *Sepet v Secretary of State for the Home Department* [2001] EWCA Civ 681, [2001] Imm AR 452.
3   *X v Austria* (1973) 43 CD 161.
4   (Application 34369/97) (2000) 31 EHRR 411, ECtHR.
5   *Thlimmenos v Greece*, Commission opinion above at para 44–45. The court based its judgment on ECHR, Art 14, and did not deal with this aspect of the case.
6   *Handbook*, para 173.
7   *Sepet v Secretary of State for the Home Department* [2001] EWCA Civ 681; [2003] UKHL 15, [2003] 3 All ER 304; see 12.75 below.

Freedom of expression

8.96 Article 10 of the ECHR provides that:

1. Everyone has the right to freedom of expression. This right shall include freedom to hold opinions and to receive and impart information and ideas without interference by public authority and regardless of frontiers ...

2. The exercise of these freedoms, since it carries with it duties and responsibilities, may be subject to such formalities, conditions, restrictions or penalties as are prescribed by law and and are necessary in a democratic society, in the interests of national security, territorial integrity or public safety, for the prevention of disorder or crime, for the protection of health or morals, for the protection of the reputation or rights of others, for preventing the disclosure of information received in confidence, or for maintaining the authority and impartiality of the judiciary.

Article 10 is rarely engaged in the immigration context, but was litigated in *Farrakhan*,[1] in which the Court of Appeal, reversing the High Court, held exclusion proportionate to the legitimate aim of prevention of disorder. The court held that Article 10 was engaged by an exclusion imposed largely to prevent the exercise of freedom of expression in the UK, but not by the exercise of control not directed at those rights, which prevents their exercise. In *A*, it was held that there was no breach of Article 10 arising from arrangements for monitoring journalists' interviews with asylum seekers detained as suspected terrorists.[2]

[1] *R (on the application of Farrakhan) v Secretary of State for the Home Department* [2002] EWCA Civ 606, [2002] 3 WLR 481.
[2] *R (on the application of A) v Secretary of State for the Home Department* [2003] EWHC Admin 2846, [2003] All ER (D) 402 (Nov).

The right to marry and found a family

8.97 Article 12 of the ECHR provides that:

'Men and women of marriageable age have the right to marry and found a family according to the national laws governing the exercise of his right.'

The right to marry and found a family is one right, not two, and it is at least questionable whether it applies only to persons of opposite biological sex.[1] Separation of fiancés by immigration measures could breach Article 12, but has usually been litigated under Article 8. The refusal of a marriage registrar to marry a couple could engage Article 12,[2] although since the Commission has held that the same qualifications should be read into Article 12 as appear in Article 8(2),[3] there would only be an interference with the right if the couple were unable to marry elsewhere or that it would be disproportionate to expect them to do so. There are likely to be claims under Article 12 (either alone or read with Article 14) in relation to the restrictions on marriage under sections 19–25 of the Asylum and Immigration (Treatment of Claimants, etc) Act 2004, which require those subject to immigration control to obtain the permission of the Home Office before engaging in a civil marriage.[4] It is open to Anglicans in England and to Presbyterians in Scotland to marry in church without Home Office permission, but not to Muslims and persons of other faiths.[5] The ECtHR has held that the arrest of an illegal entrant immediately before his or her marriage could found an Article 12 claim if it had the effect of preventing or substantially delaying it.[6]

1   The right of 'a man and a woman' to marry does not assume that these terms must refer to a determination of gender by purely biological criteria: *Goodwin v United Kingdom* (28957/95), 11 July 2002, departing from its earlier decisions in *Rees v United Kingdom* (1986) 9 EHRR 56, para 49 and *Cossey v United Kingdom* (1990) 13 EHRR 622 para 43. The House of Lords refused to follow *Goodwin* in *Bellinger v Bellinger* [2003] UKHL 21, [2003] 2 AC 467, holding it was for Parliament to remedy the incompatibility of the Matrimonial Causes Act.
2   But registrars are merely giving effect to primary legislation, Immigration and Asylum Act 1999, s 24(5) and so would not be liable under the Human Rights Act 1998. For discrimination in pre-marriage checks see *Tejani v Superintendent Registrar for the District of Peterborough* [1986] IRLR 502, CA. Article 12 ECHR should be read with Art 14.
3   App 8166/78, 13 DR 241; App 7175, 6 DR 136.
4   The Joint Committee on Human Rights warned the government before passage of the Act that its provisions carried a significant risk of violating Art 12, either alone or read with Art 14, since the restrictions were not rationally connected to their purpose, were too broad, may impair the essence of the right and discriminated on religious grounds with no objective or reasonable justification: Joint Committee on Human Rights 14th report Session 2003–2004: Asylum and Immigration (Treatment of Claimants) Bill, additional clauses, 5 July 2004 (HL 130/HC 828).
5   For the restrictions see further 11.67 below.
6   *Shahara and Rinea v Netherlands* (Application 10915/85), held inadmissible because the marriage was only deferred for nine days.

Non-discrimination

8.98   Article 14 of the ECHR prevents discrimination in the enjoyment of the Convention rights on grounds of sex, race, colour, language, religion, political or other opinion, national or social origin, association with a national minority, property, birth or other status. The Article does not create a free-standing right not to be discriminated against,[1] but one linked to enjoyment of Convention rights.[2] It is not necessary to show a breach of a substantive right, however, to establish a breach of Article 14.[3] The questions which arise in relation to a claim engaging Article 14 are similar to those arising in respect of a qualified right: has there been a difference in treatment in an area within the ambit of the Convention;[4] if so, was it on a 'status' ground such as race, sex etc, [5] did the differential treatment have a legitimate aim, and an objective and reasonable justification, ie was there a reasonable relationship of proportionality between the means employed and the aim sought to be realised?[6] Certain forms of discrimination, such as those based on race,[7] sex[8] or legitimacy,[9] are identified as particularly serious. They are marked by a consensus in the Member States to eliminate such forms of discrimination, backed by international instruments,[10] and in such cases a heavier burden is placed upon the State to justify the difference in treatment.[11] An unjustifiable difference in treatment in the operation of the Immigration Rules regarding admission of spouses on grounds of gender was held to constitute a breach of the anti-discrimination provision of ECHR, Article 14 in conjunction with Article 8 in *Abdulaziz*.[12] However, in the same case the

ECtHR rejected the argument that the Rules also discriminated on grounds of race, an argument which relied on the disproportionate impact the Rules had on immigrants from the Indian sub-continent as constituting indirect discrimination. The broad margin of appreciation which the court gave there to the domestic authorities meant it could not establish any ulterior discriminatory purpose behind government policy. This approach can of course be avoided by looking at the discriminatory *effect* of policy rather than seeking a discriminatory *purpose*, the approach of the European Court of Justice and of the UK courts under the Equal Treatment Directive[13] and the Sex Discrimination and Race Relations Acts.[14] Since *Abdulaziz* the Strasbourg Court has inched closer to acceptance of indirect discrimination as founding an Article 14 claim, but the question is still open.[15]

[1] Such a free-standing right is created by ECHR, Protocol 12, adopted by the Committee of Ministers in June 2000 and opened for signature in November 2000. The UK has not signed or ratified it, and by March 2004 there were only six ratifications. It requires ten Council of Europe States to ratify it to come into force.

[2] The Secretary of State's refusal to register as a British citizen an illegitimate child of a British father was held not to violate Art 14 ECHR together with Art 8 in *R (on the application of Montana) v Secretary of State for the Home Department* [2001] 1 WLR 552, CA, as the right to nationality is not within the ambit of the Convention, and the discrimination did not in fact impact on family life.

[3] The court has also recognised that the right not to be discriminated against is also violated when States without objective and reasonable justification fail to treat differently persons whose situations are significantly different: *Thlimmenos v Greece* (2001) 31 EHRR 411 (ban on civil service employment for those with criminal convictions caught an applicant with a conviction for conscientious objection, and thus discriminated in the enjoyment of rights of conscience).

[4] *Inze v Austria* (1987) 10 EHRR 394.

[5] The prohibited grounds set out in Art 14 are illustrative, not exhaustive. In *R (on the application of T) v Secretary of State for Health* [2002] EWHC 1887, (2002) Times, 5 September, the status of 'asylum seeker' was held to be a status within Art 14 such that discriminatory denial of fundamental rights of asylum seekers could breach the ECHR.

[6] *Belgian Linguistics Case (No 2)* (1968) 1 EHRR 252; *Marckx v Belgium* (1979) 2 EHRR 330; *Rasmussen v Denmark* (1984) 7 EHRR 371; *Abdulaziz, Cabales and Balkandali v United Kingdom* (1985) 7 EHRR 471. The Court of Appeal has set out the 'structured task' it faces in assessing an Art 14 claim: has there been (i) a difference in treatment (ii) in an area within the ambit of the Convention; (iii) is the chosen comparator analogous; (iv) is there an objective or reasonable justification for the differential treatment: *Wandsworth London Borough Council v Michalak* [2002] EWCA Civ 271, [2003] 1 WLR 617, para 20.

[7] *East African Asians v United Kingdom* (1973) 3 EHRR 76. The court held differential entitlement to emergency social security assistance as between nationals and non-nationals to violate Article 14 with Protocol 1 Article 1, as not based on any objective and reasonable jusitfication, in *Gaygusuz v Austria* (1997) 23 EHRR 364.

[8] *Abdulaziz,* fn 6, above. It is no longer appropriate for the State to discriminate against transsexuals in the enjoyment of family and private life: *Goodwin v United Kingdom* (2000) 34 EHRR 18. The same applies to sexual orientation. Differences in treatment based on sexual orientation require particularly serious reasons by way of justification: *Smith and Grady v United Kingdom* (1999) 29 EHRR 493; *SL v Austria* (45330/99) (9 January 2003, unreported) para 37; *L v Austria* (39392/98, 39829/98) (2003) 13 BHRC 594, para 37; *Karner v Austria* (40016/98) [2004] 2 FCR 563.

[9] *Marckx* fn 6 above.

[10] Convention for the Elimination of All forms of Discrimination Against Women 1978 (CEDAW); Convention for the Elimination of all forms of Racial Discrimination (CERD).

[11] *Abdulaziz* above.

[12] *Abdulaziz* above, where the court rejected the government's attempt to justify on economic grounds and grounds of 'public tranquillity' the rules which made it more difficult for foreign husbands to join wives in the UK than vice versa.

[13] ETD 76/207.

14 Sex Discrimination Act 1975; Race Relations Act 1976. See the House of Lords' application of the proportionality test to a situation of indirect discrimination in *R v Secretary of State for Employment, ex p Equal Opportunities Commission* [1995] 1 AC 1.
15 See *Singh (Pavittar) v United Kingdom* (60148/00) (3 September 2002, unreported), where a claim that the immigration rules on adoption discriminated against Indian intra-family arrangements was held admissible. This problem may now be solved because of developments in domestic law: see *Singh v Entry Clearance Officer, New Delhi* [2004] EWCA Civ 1075, [2004] INLR 515.

8.99 The common law has long held that in the field of administrative decisions unjustified discrimination on grounds of race, colour, gender, religion or any other irrational ground is unlawful,[1] and the constitutional principle of equality developed domestically by the English courts is wider than that protected by the ECHR, since it does not depend on showing an impact on another fundamental right.[2] In *Ali (Arman)*[3] Collins J held that the immigration rules requiring spouses to support and accommodate themselves and their dependants without recourse to public funds as a prerequisite of admission must be read so as to include the possibility that they could be maintained indefinitely by third parties or by their nominal dependants, so as to ensure compatibility with ECHR, Article 8 rights. Otherwise the Rule could discriminate on grounds of disability or age against couples too old or ill to work but with family support. The decision led to a change in the rules regarding recourse to public funds,[4] and has been applied by the Tribunal in analogous situations.[5] In the *Roma Rights* case[6] the House of Lords held that the fact that Roma passengers were questioned more intensively, sceptically and for longer, and refused boarding more often than non-Roma passengers at Prague airport, amounted to unlawful discrimination under domestic[7] and international law.[8] Although there was an authorisation, which might have exempted the immigration service, the Prague operation was not in fact operating under it. The government's case was that there was no discrimination at all. The House came to the inevitable conclusion that the operation was inherently and systemically discriminatory and unlawful. In *A and X v Secretary of State for the Home Department*[9] the detention of foreign terrorist suspects was held incompatible with Article 14 read with Article 5 in the derogation case, on the grounds that it applied only to foreign nationals and not to British citizens who were also part of the threat. Discrimination against homosexuals in an immigration context, which was formerly accepted as legitimate by the ECtHR,[10] would no longer be upheld.[11]

1 *Kruse v Johnson [1898] 2 QB 91; Matadeen v Pointu* [1999] 1 AC 98 (PC). Discrimination on grounds of race, gender or disability is prohibited by statute (Race Relations Act 1976 (as amended by the Race Relations Amendment Act 2000), Sex Discrimination Acts 1975 and 1986, Disability Discrimination Act 1995). But discrimination on grounds of nationality, national or ethnic origin is not unlawful if carried out by a 'relevant person' in carrying out immigration and nationality functions (Race Relations Act as amended, s 19D), although it remains unlawful to discriminate on grounds of race or colour. The distinction between 'race' and 'ethnic origin' is problematic. In *R (on the application of the Tamil Information Centre) v Secretary of State for the Home Department* [2002] EWHC 2156, the court interpreted the exceptions very narrowly. See 1.30 above.
2 See lecture of 18 September 2002 in honour of Lord Cooke of Thoronden, quoted in *Gurung v Ministry of Defence* [2002] EWHC Admin 2463, [2003] 06 LS Gaz R 25, in which Lord Steyn emphasised the importance of the principle of equality: 'Individuals are ... comprehensively protected from discrimination by the principle of equality. This

constitutional right has a continuing role to play. The organic development of constitutional rights is therefore a complementary and parallel process to the application of human rights legislation.'

3   *R v Secretary of State for the Home Department, ex p Ali (Arman)* [2000] INLR 89.
4   HC 395 para 6A was inserted on 2 October 2000, providing that the 'no recourse to public funds' rule for spouses did not prevent a British spouse enjoying public funds in his or her own right, provided that the arrival of the partner did not result in additional recourse. See 11.52 below.
5   See eg *Abdulla (Intekab)* [2002] UKIAT 07516, where the Tribunal accepted that savings made by a sponsor from public funds could satisfy the 'no recourse' requirements and that a generous interpretation of the rules was required to attain compatibility with Art 8 read with Art 14, particularly where disability prevented a spouse from working.
6   *European Roma Rights Centre v Immigration Officer at Prague Airport* [2004] UKHL 55, [2005] 1 All ER 527.
7   Section 19B of the Race Relations Act 1976 as amended by the Race Relations (Amendment) Act 2000, which came into force on 2 April 2001.
8   *Roma Rights* case, above, per Lady Hale at para 98: 'In this respect it was not only unlawful in domestic law but also contrary to our obligations under customary international law and under international treaties to which the United Kingdom is a party.' At para 103 she also noted that the General Assembly of the UN has 'urged all States to review and where necessary revise their immigration laws, policies and practices so that they are free of racial discrimination and compatible with their obligations under international human rights instruments' (UNGA Resolution 57/195, para I.6, adopted 18 December 2002; see also UNGA Resolution 58/160 adopted on 22 December 2003). The UN Committee on the Elimination of Racial Discrimination has expressed its concern at the application of section 19D, which it considers 'incompatible with the very principle of non-discrimination' (UN doc CERD/C/63/CO/11, para 16, 10 December 2003).
9   *A and X v Secretary of State for the Home Department* [2004] UKHL 56, [2005] 2 WLR 87.
10   *S v United Kingdom* (1986) 47 DR 274, para 7; *B v United Kingdom* (1990) 64 DR 278, para 2.
11   There has been no recent ECHR jurisprudence on homosexual partners' family or private life rights in the immigration context, but see ECtHR's observations in *Smith and Grady v United Kingdom* (1999) 29 EHRR 493; *Goodwin v United Kingdom* (2002) 34 EHRR 18. The UK immigration rules were amended to admit same-sex partners on 2 October 2000 (HC 395 para 295A, see 11.71 below). In another context, a same-sex partner was held equivalent to a spouse, reading the interpretation of the phrase 'wife or husband' in the Rent Acts (for succession to a tenancy) compatibly with Art 14 with Art 8, in *Ghaidan v Mendoza* [2004] UKHL 30, [2004] 3 All ER 411, HL.

Effective remedy

8.100 Article 13 of the ECHR provides that:

> 'Everyone whose rights and freedoms as set forth in this Convention are violated shall have an effective remedy before the national authority notwithstanding that the violation has been committed by persons acting in an official capacity.'

Article 13 requires a remedy at national level to enforce the substance of Convention rights and freedoms in whatever form they have to be secured in the domestic legal order.[1] It does not stand alone, but has to be considered in conjunction with other Convention rights. The 'remedy' must consider the substance of an arguable complaint under the Convention, and grant appropriate relief. It must be effective in practice and in law,[2] and its exercise must not be unjustifiably hindered by the acts or omissions of the respondent State authorities.[3] Article 13 is not among the Convention rights listed in the

Human Rights Act 1998, because the Lord Chancellor believes that section 8 of the Act meets the UK's obligations under Article 13.[4] Judicial review has been held to constitute an effective remedy in expulsion cases raising Article 3 issues in *Soering v United Kingdom*,[5] and subsequent cases, on the basis that the courts could effectively control the legality of executive discretion on substantive and procedural grounds and quash decisions.[6] In *Chahal v United Kingdom*[7] the court found the scope of review, and so the effectiveness of the remedy, restricted because of the national security element. That has now been remedied by the Special Immigration Appeals Commission mechanism.[8] However, in *Smith and Grady v United Kingdom*[9] it was held that judicial review was ineffective to comply with the requirements of Article 8(2) in a case in which homosexuals were banned from the armed forces. The ECtHR held that the domestic court placed the threshold of irrationality 'so high that it effectively excluded any consideration by the domestic courts of the question whether the interference with the applicants' rights answered a pressing social need or was proportionate to the national security and public order aims pursued'.[10] In *Daly*[11] the House of Lords affirmed that the courts' intensity of review in human rights cases had to be more rigorous than before. The government's proposal in late 2003 to oust the jurisdiction of the higher courts over decisions of the appellate authority which may be flawed by errors of law or procedural unfairness, contained in the Asylum and Immigration (Treatment of Claimants) Bill, [12] which was withdrawn after being greeted with outrage by (among others) senior judges, would have meant the loss of an effective remedy for significant numbers alleging that their removal would breach fundamental human rights.

---

[1] *Boyle and Rice v United Kingdom* (1988) 10 EHRR 425, para 52.

[2] There must be a rigorous and independent scrutiny of the claim and (in the context of removal to potential Art 3 ill-treatment) the possibility of suspending the implementation of the measure impugned: *Jabari v Turkey* [2001] INLR 136. A discretionary stay on expulsion is not sufficiently effective, since the implementation of the remedy is too uncertain to enable the requirements of Art 13 to be satisfied: *Conka v Belgium* (51564/99) 5 February 2002. The lack of an expeditious avenue of complaint for a prisoner, capable of quashing a punishment before its execution, and the lack of an effective remedy for bereaved persons to establish responsibility for a death in prison and obtain compensation, were held to breach Art 13 in *Keenan v United Kingdom* (2001) 33 EHRR 38.

[3] *Aksoy v Turkey* (1996) 23 EHRR 553; *Aydin v Turkey* (1997) 25 EHRR 251; *Hilal v UK* (2001) 33 EHRR 2 (para 75); *Kaya v Turkey* (1999) 28 EHRR 1 (para 106). An extradition despite an interim measure under rule 39 (request for a stay) was held to preclude the effective examination of complaints and to render nugatory the right to individual application in *Mamatkulov v Turkey* (46827/99, 46951/99) (2003) Times, 13 March.

[4] HL Official Report (5th series) cols 476–477, 18 November 1997. Article 13 'reflects the long-standing principle of our law that where there is a right there should be a remedy. Parliament's intention was, of course, that the Human Rights Act itself should constitute the UK's compliance with Article 13, but this makes it if anything more important that the courts ... should satisfy themselves so far as possible that the common law affords adequate control ... of the legality of official measures which interfere with personal autonomy': *R (on the application of K) v Camden and Islington Health Authority* [2001] EWCA Civ 240, [2002] QB 198.

[5] (1989) 11 EHRR 439; *Vilvarajah v United Kingdom* (1991) 14 EHRR 248; *Hilal v United Kingdom* (fn 3 above). The increasing breadth and depth of judicial review was noted in *R (on the application of Q) v Secretary of State for the Home Department* [2003] EWCA Civ 364, [2003] 2 All ER 905.

[6] *Hilal v United Kingdom* above, paras 77–78.

[7] (1996) 23 EHRR 413.

[8] Special Immigration Appeals Commission Act 1997; see 18.160. Whether proceedings before SIAC are capable of constituting an effective remedy for breaches of Arts 3 and 8 arising from indefinite detention and/or conditions of detention is currently being litigated in *G v Secretary of State for the Home Department* [2004] EWCA Civ 65.

[9] (1999) 29 EHRR 493.

[10] (1999) 29 EHRR 493, paras 136–139.

[11] *R (on the application of Daly) v Secretary of State for the Home Department* [2001] UKHL 26, [2001] 2 AC 532. See 8.18ff above.

[12] Clause 11 of the Bill.

HUMAN RIGHTS APPEALS

8.101 Sections 6 and 7 of the Human Rights Act 1998 are given effect so far as statutory immigration appeals are concerned by section 84(1)(c) and (g) of the Nationality, Immigration and Asylum Act 2002, which enable an appeal to be brought against an immigration decision[1] on the ground that it is unlawful under section 6 of the Human Rights Act as being incompatible with the appellant's Convention rights,[2] or that removal from the UK in consequence of the immigration decision would be so unlawful.[3] Section 84(1)(c) is appropriate for those seeking to enter the UK, as well as those facing expulsion, and could refer to the positive obligations entailed by admission.[4] The human rights ground of appeal may stand alone, where no other ground of appeal exists under the Act or the rules, or may be one of several grounds, but it is only triggered by an 'immigration decision', which is much more narrowly defined than 'a decision relating to the applicant's entitlement to enter or remain in the UK' under the predecessor section, section 65 of the Immigration and Asylum Act 1999.[5] A decision which is incompatible with Convention rights is 'not in accordance with the law', enabling the Asylum and Immigration Tribunal to allow the appeal even though the decision conforms with the immigration rules.[6]

[1] As defined by Nationality, Immigration and Asylum Act 2002, s 82(2).

[2] NIAA 2002, s 84(1)(c).

[3] NIAA 2002, s 84(1)(g). Where national security issues are involved, an appeal lies to SIAC instead: see Special Immigration Appeals Commission Act 1997, s 2 (as substituted by NIAA 2002, s 114(3), Sch 7, para 20). See *Singh (Mukhtiar and Paramjit) v Secretary of State for the Home Department* (31 July 2000, unreported) (substantial grounds for believing appellants at real risk of torture if deported); appeal allowed despite appellants' exclusion from Refugee Convention under Art 1F, and the danger to national security they represented).

[4] See eg *Sen v Netherlands* (2003) 36 EHRR 7.

[5] Immigration and Asylum Act 1999, s 65, as amended by Race Relations (Amendment) Act 2000, s 6(4) and Sch 2, para 32. Section 65 covered a decision to refuse an application made by an overstayer or illegal entrant, not accompanied by a decision to remove, which is not an 'immigration decision' as defined by s 82(2). It also covered the issue of removal directions pursuant to an earlier decision: *R (on the application of Kariharan and Koneswaran) v Secretary of State for the Home Department* [2002] EWCA Civ 1102, [2002] INLR 383, [2003] Imm AR 163. However, even s 65 did not allow the appellate authority to consider the consequences of non-removal (eg withdrawal of NASS support): *Secretary of State for the Home Department v Chawish* [2002] UKIAT 01376. If there is no 'immigration decision' under s 82, the only means of challenging the decision will be by way of judicial review (as to which see 18.183 below).

[6] See NIAA 2002, s 86(3)(a).

8.102 The 2002 Act was the first measure to remove in-country appeal rights from appellants who fear human rights violations in the country to which they are to be removed.[1] Human rights appeals are generally suspensive of removal,[2] but if the Secretary of State certifies a claim as 'clearly unfounded', the effect is to deprive the appeal of suspensive effect,[3] although judicial review is available to challenge the certificate.[4] Section 94 of the Nationality, Immigration and Asylum Act 2002 allows the Secretary of State to certify any human rights claim as clearly unfounded,[5] and requires him or her to do so, unless satisfied that the claim is *not* clearly unfounded, if the claimant is entitled to live in one of the States specified in the section.[6] Those States are listed in section 94(4),[7] and initially comprised the ten aspiring (now new) EU Member States. Now, those listed are other States or parts of States where the Secretary of State is satisfied that there is in general no serious risk of persecution of persons entitled to live in that State or part, or no serious risk to persons of the description of the claimant, and that removal there would not in general contravene the UK's obligations under the Human Rights Convention.[8] The other situation where the Secretary of State can certify a claim as clearly unfounded, depriving a human rights claimant of an in-country appeal, is where a person claims asylum in the UK and the Secretary of State proposes his or her removal is to a third 'safe' country, that is, a country of which the claimant is not a national. The provisions are described in detail at 12.132ff below.

1   The Immigration and Asylum Act 1999 removed only one layer of appeal—to the Immigration Appeal Tribunal—in cases certified manifestly unfounded (by Sch 4, para 9), where the adjudicator upheld the certificate, and third-country claimants (ie, asylum claimants whom the Secretary of State proposed to remove to a third, 'safe' country under ss11 or 12) were the only group who had no right to appeal in-country if their human rights claim was certified manifestly unfounded.
2   Nationality, Immigration and Asylum Act 2002, s 92(4)(a).
3   NIAA 2002, s 94(7). An appeal may be brought outside the UK, and the appellant is treated as still in the UK (s 94(9); otherwise the appeal would be treated as abandoned on removal from the UK, under s 104(4)(b); see 18.106 below).
4   The right to challenge a certificate by way of judicial review is necessary to ensure an 'effective remedy' under Art 13 ECHR: see 8.100 above. The Secretary of State indicated in *R (on the application of L) v Secretary of State for the Home Department* [2003] EWCA Civ 25, [2003] Imm AR 330, [2003] INLR 224 that further representations and evidence would be considered after certification and after judicial review proceedings have been lodged.
5   NIAA 2002, s 94(2).
6   NIAA 2002, s 94(3). This does not apply to persons facing extradition: s 94(6A), inserted by Asylum and Immigration (Treatment of Claimants, etc) Act 2004, s 27.
7   For the list of countries set out in the section see 12.160 above.
8   NIAA 2002, s 94(5)–(5C) (sub-ss (5A)–(5C), as inserted). The Secretary of State may add further States (or parts of States): s 94(5), or remove States from the list: s 94(6). A country specified in a certificate from the Secretary of State enjoys a statutory presumption that life and liberty are not threatened by reason of race, religion, nationality, membership of a particular social group or political opinion, and that it would not *refoule* in breach of the Refugee Convention: s 94(8).

8.103 The criteria for certifying a human rights claim as 'clearly unfounded' were laid down by the House of Lords in *Yogathas*,[1] which was decided under the provisions for dealing with 'manifestly unfounded' claims under the 1999 Act,[2] and is seen as the leading case on the subject. Lord Bingham said that 'the Home Secretary is entitled to certify if … he is reasonably and conscientiously satisfied that the allegation must clearly fail'.[3] Lord Hope added: 'By adopting the language of the international instruments, Parliament has made it clear that the issue as to whether the allegation is manifestly unfounded[4] must be approached in a way that gives full weight to the UK's obligations under the ECHR. The question to which the Secretary of State has to address his mind ... is whether the claim is so clearly without substance that the appeal would be bound to fail'.[5] And Lord Hutton, concurring, formulated the test as: 'An allegation is manifestly unfounded if it is plain that there is nothing of substance in the allegation.'[6] The Court of Appeal, applying the *Yogathas* principles to the provisions of the 2002 Act, noted that the provisions were objective, depending 'not on the Secretary of State's view but upon a criterion which a court can readily reapply once it has the materials which the Home Secretary had. A claim is either clearly unfounded or it is not.'[7] The court set out the process to be gone through:

> 'The decision maker will
>
> (i)   consider the factual substance and detail of the claim,
> (ii)   consider how it stands with the known background data;
> (iii) consider whether in the round it is capable of belief;
> (iv)   if not, consider whether some part of it is capable of belief;
> (v)   consider whether, in the event it is believed in whole or part, it is capable of coming within the Convention.
>
> If the answers are such that the claim cannot on any legitimate view succeed, then the claim is clearly unfounded. If not, not. If on at least one legitimate view of the facts or the law the claim may succeed, it will not be clearly unfounded. If that point is reached, the decision maker cannot conclude otherwise.'[8]

Where there is conflicting evidence from reputable sources, the decision on whether a claim is clearly unfounded can only proceed on the basis of the evidence most favourable to the claimant.[9]

---

1   *R (on the application of Thangarasa) v Secretary of State for the Home Department* [2001] EWHC Admin 420, [2001] All ER (D) 08 (Jan); affd sub nom *R (on the application of Yogathas and Thangarasa) v Secretary of State for the Home Department* [2002] UKHL 36, [2002] 3 WLR 1276, [2002] INLR 620.
2   Immigration and Asylum Act 1999, s 72(2)(a) (which applied only to third-country cases).
3   *Yogathas* fn 1 above, para 14.
4   The IAA 1999 referred to 'manifestly unfounded' claims, the 2002 Act to 'clearly unfounded' ones. They mean the same thing: *R (on the application of L) v Secretary of State for the Home Department* [2003] EWCA Civ 25, [2003] Imm AR 330, [2003] INLR 224.
5   *Yogathas* fn 1 above, para 34.
6   *Yogathas* fn 1 above, para 72.
7   *ZL and VL* fn 4 above, para 56.
8   *ZL and VL* fn 4 above, paras 57, 58. The court indicated that certification would not be appropriate in cases involving allegations of severe ill-treatment requiring medical evidence, or where the authenticity of evidence was disputed, and adverse credibility would not render a claim clearly unfounded unless it was wholly unbelievable. However, a claim may be certified clearly unfounded even though it is clear that rights under Art 8(1) ECHR are engaged, where the Secretary of State reasonably concludes there is no arguable case that interference with those rights is not justified under Art 8(2): *R (on the application of Razgar) v Secretary of State for the Home Department* [2003] EWCA Civ 840, [2003] Imm AR 529, [2003] INLR 543, para 31. This is analogous with the Strasbourg jurisprudence. In *Razgar*, all three certificates were quashed, in claims based on the psychiatric effect of removing vulnerable and disturbed asylum seekers to a third country for their asylum claims to be determined there. The decision was upheld by a majority in the House of Lords at [2004] UKHL 27, [2004] INLR 349.

⁹ *R (on the application of Ahmadi) v Secretary of State for the Home Department* [2002] EWHC 1897 (Admin), para 48. This was another claim where the Secretary of State's certificate was quashed, although the Secretary of State argued successfully against bringing the appellants back to the UK for their appeal, which was subsequently held by video link with Germany and lost. In *R (on the application of Changuizi) v Secretary of State for the Home Department* [2002] EWHC 2569 (Admin), [2003] Imm AR 355 the Secretary of State was ordered to return the claimants wrongly removed to Germany, after the certificate was quashed.

8.104 Most human rights appeals are against refusal of leave to enter or a removal decision relating to an illegal entrant or overstayer, on quasi-asylum, health, or private or family life grounds. Claims based on family life involve consideration of the impact of decisions on other family members. But since the jurisdiction under section 84(1)(c) or (g) requires consideration of whether the decision is compatible with the *appellant's* Convention rights, the rights of a UK sponsor or child, for example to respect for family life with the appellant, may not be the subject of an appeal in their own right. A starred Tribunal held in *Kehinde*[1] that the human rights of individuals other than the appellant are irrelevant save insofar as they relate to the human rights of the appellant him- or herself. This injunction appeared to be contraverted in the later (but unstarred) decision of *Sula*,[2] involving one of the same panel, which concluded that

> 'Within the context of a [human rights] appeal, it is essential that the relevant decision taker (the immigration authority or the appellate authority) take account of the human rights not only of the appellant but also of any other persons who stand to be directly affected by a decision made against the appellant ... the decision on the appellant's appeal must not amount to an act which is incompatible with the human rights of any relevant members of his family', although 'it has to be demonstrated that the threatened wellbeing of a family member is in fact integrally related to the threatened wellbeing of the appellant'.

The Administrative Court ruled in *AC*[3] that the impact of the exclusion or removal of an appellant on a UK sponsor must be considered in the appellant's appeal, and in *Razgar*, Baroness Hale held that it might be determinative.[4]

1 *Kehinde* (01TH02668) (starred) (unreported).
2 *Sula (Met)* [2002] UKIAT 00295, paras 71–72.
3 *R (on the application of AC) v Immigration Appeal Tribunal* [2003] EWHC 389.
4 *R (on the application of Razgar) v Secretary of State for the Home Department* [2004] UKHL 27, [2004] 2 AC 368.

8.105 In a human rights appeal (whether free-standing or as one of a number of grounds of appeal) the process which appellate authorities need to go through to ensure that a decision is 'in accordance with the law' is of a different order from that in the customary appeal. When a decision is in accordance with the Immigration Rules (as to which see below), it will no longer be sufficient to 'ascertain that the decision-maker has adverted to a policy, correctly appreciated relevant facts, and considered whether to exercise discretion in the appellant's favour'.[1] The Tribunal must scrutinise the exercise of discretion outside, as well as inside, the Rules, to determine, if appropriate, whether the decision violates an absolute right,[2] or constitutes a disproportionate restriction on a qualified right.[3] The latter assessment requires the

Tribunal to exercise its own judgment on the evidence before it.[4] We have dealt with how this exercise is performed at 8.21–8.22 above. The Tribunal must deal with all the human rights grounds before them.[5]

[1] The Tribunal's view of its task in deciding whether a decision is in accordance with the law in *Kausar v Entry Clearance Officer* [1998] INLR 141.
[2] See cases cited at 8.37 above. A starred Tribunal in *Kacaj* [2001] INLR 354, [2002] Imm AR 213 held that the standard of proof in Art 3 cases is the same as in asylum appeals.
[3] See 8.39 above.
[4] *R (on the application of Razgar) v Secretary of State for the Home Department* [2004] UKHL 27, [2004] 2 AC 368; *Huang v Secretary of State for the Home Department* [2005] EWCA Civ 105, (2005) Sol Jo LB 297.
[5] *McPherson v Secretary of State for the Home Department* [2001] EWCA Civ 1955, [2002] INLR 139: where an adjudicator allowed an appeal on Art 3 ECHR grounds but failed to deal with the ground under Art 8, the Tribunal should have dealt with it, particularly since the appellant had expressly sought to keep it alive.

8.106 Secondly, the Tribunal must have regard to relevant ECtHR jurisprudence,[1] and must interpret both primary and subordinate legislation so as to give effect to ECHR rights wherever possible.[2] This means reading rules and statutes in a way which ensures compliance with Convention rights. This was done (even before the entry into force of the Human Rights Act) in *Ali (Arman)*, in which the requirement in the immigration rules that parties to a marriage 'maintain and accommodate themselves' without recourse to public funds was read to embrace third-party support, so as to ensure compatibility.[3] A 'human rights-compliant' reading must also be given to procedure rules;[4] the appellate authority should, for example, strive to avoid disposal of a human rights appeal for procedural non-compliance without consideration of the merits;[5] and adjournments might be more necessary in this context in order to obtain relevant and cogent evidence.[6] For procedural requirements see also Article 6, at 8.72ff above. In this connection, there are complaints that the restrictions on publication and citation of Tribunal cases, in Practice Directions of 2003 and 2005, might be incompatible with requirements of equality of arms.[7]

[1] The Tribunal's Practice Direction No 4 [2001] INLR 216, [2001] Imm AR 172 provides that copies of any Strasbourg cases relied on must be submitted 14 days in advance of the hearing, a requirement frequently honoured in the breach, and not repeated in current Practice Directions.
[2] See 8.13 above.
[3] *R v Secretary of State for the Home Department, ex p Ali (Arman)* [2000] Imm AR 134, [2000] INLR 89. See also *Boadi v Entry Clearance Officer, Ghana* [2002] UKIAT 01323 [2003] INLR 54 (construction of immigration rules on admission of adopted children).
[4] See *MNM* [2000] INLR 576, (starred) para 17, *SK* [2002] UKIAT 05613 (starred).
[5] *Muhammad (Ishaq Saqi)* (01TH1233); see also *Haddad (Ali)* [2000] INLR 117, under the Refugee Convention. In *R v Immigration Appeal Tribunal, ex p Jeyeanthan* [1999] 3 All ER 231, [1999] INLR 241 the Court of Appeal held that where fundamental rights were engaged, minor procedural non-compliance should generally be overlooked.
[6] See *R (on the application of Fanna) v Secretary of State for the Home Department* [2002] EWHC Admin 777, [2002] All ER (D) 16 (Mar). See also *R (on the application of Tataw) v Immigration Appeal Tribunal* [2003] EWCA Civ 925, [2003] All ER (D) 223 (Jun), where judicial review was granted to ensure that the claimant obtained an oral hearing of her appeal, despite the lack of fault on the Tribunal's part. For the rules on adjournments to produce evidence see SI 2005/230, r 47, 18.125 below.
[7] The Secretary of State, as a party to all appeals, will receive a copy of all determinations, while appellants will be unable to access unreported determinations. Determinations will not be reported if, in the Tribunal's view, they contain no new principle of law or matter of

real and generally applicable guidance to parties: Practice Direction No 10 of 2003 (Immigration Appeal Tribunal); Practice Direction CA3 of 2003 (Chief Adjudicator) [2003] INLR 358. See now Practice Direction 2005, para 17. The criteria seem reasonable, but given the long-standing concern at the criteria for reporting cases in the Immigration Appeal Reports (when they were the only reports available), the restrictions, together with the reforms to the appellate structure which remove a tier of appeal rights, provoke disquiet.

8.107 If it is impossible to read Immigration Rules or other subordinate legislation so as to give effect to Convention rights, the Tribunal's duty as a public authority and its appellate jurisdiction require it to disapply rules whose application in a particular case would result in a breach of human rights.[1] The Tribunal has no power to strike down such rules; its powers under the Human Rights Act 1998 are confined to granting 'such relief or remedy … within its powers as it considers just and appropriate'.[2] The appellate authority may not disapply primary legislation which cannot be read compatibly with Convention rights, nor subordinate legislation made as an inevitable result of primary legislation.[3] Nor may it declare such legislation incompatible with Convention rights. It must leave such a declaration of incompatibility to the higher courts, which must in turn leave the decision to remove the offending legislation to Parliament.[4]

[1]   For example, the restrictions on the relatives who may join family members in the UK (HC 395, para 317) might amount to a disproportionate obstacle to the enjoyment of family life contrary to Art 8 ECHR, particularly where comparison is made with family reunion rights of EEA nationals, which might engage Art 14, ECHR, in conjunction with Art 8. See the considerably more generous family reunion provisions of Council Regulation (EEC) 1612/68, Art 10 and the Immigration (European Economic Area) Regulations 2000, SI 2000/2326, and those for beneficiaries of temporary protection, vis-à-vis other immigrants and refugees, at HC 395 part 11A (paras 354–356B), inserted by HC 164, in effect 1 January 2005, see 12.173 above. See *Huang v Secretary of State for the Home Department* [2005] EWCA Civ 105, (2005) Sol Jo LB 297, and discussion at 8.21–8.22 above.
[2]   Human Rights Act 1998, s 8(1). In *Koprinov* (01 TH 00091) the Tribunal held it had no jurisdiction to strike down rules.
[3]   HRA 1998, s 6(2).
[4]   HRA 1998, s 4.

8.108 Despite the introduction in October 2000 of a 'one-stop' appeal structure, it is not uncommon for an appellant to have a second appeal, on human rights grounds, which might be based on similar facts to an earlier asylum appeal. Initially, this occurred because, immediately after the entry into force of the Human Rights Act 1998, the Tribunal decided in *Pardeepan*[1] that it had no jurisdiction to decide whether transitional provisions in a commencement order, denying asylum appellants the opportunity to argue on human rights grounds if their claims had been rejected before the coming into force of the Act, violated the Human Rights Convention, so the Home Office undertook that asylum claimants whose claims were decided before 2 October 2000 would have the opportunity to raise human rights objections to removal which, if rejected, could be the subject of a later appeal.[2] An appellant might also have more than one human rights appeal, because of a change in circumstances since the dismissal of the first appeal. The proper approach to a human rights appeal based on the same facts as a previously rejected asylum or human rights appeal was discussed in *Devaseelan*,[3] where the Tribunal held that:

(1)   the first adjudicator's determination should always be the starting point, as an authoritative assessment of the appellant's status at the time it was made;

(2)   facts happening since then can *always* be taken into account by the second adjudicator;

(3)   facts happening before the first adjudicator's determination but not relevant to the issues before him or her then can *always* be taken into account by the second adjudicator;

(4)   facts personal to the appellant which were not before the first adjudicator but were relevant to the issues before him or her should be treated with the greatest circumspection by the second adjudicator, unless they are not in dispute, or unless there is a very good reason why the failure to adduce the evidence should not be held against the appellant; adjudicators should be very slow to conclude that an appeal before another adjudicator has been materially affected by a representative's error or incompetence, and should always report such a finding to the Immigration Services Commissioner.[4]

However, the Secretary of State frequently attempts to block a second human rights appeal by use of paragraph 353 of the Immigration Rules, on the basis that the content of the new claim is not significantly different from the previous claim so as to give a real prospect of success,[5] or by certifying under section 96 of the Nationality, Immigration and Asylum Act 2002 that the new issue or new material could and should have been raised or adduced on an earlier claim or appeal, and that there is no satisfactory reason why this was not done.[6] Such a certificate can be challenged in judicial review proceedings.

---

[1]   *Pardeepan* [2000] INLR 447, decided under the Immigration and Asylum Act 1999 (Commencement No 6, Transitional and Consequential Provisions) Order 2000, SI 2000/2444, Arts 3(1), 4(2).

[2]   An undertaking which it then tried to renege on, but was prevented by the Administrative Court.

[3]   *Devaseelan* [2003] Imm AR 1 (starred).

[4]   *Devaseelan* [2003] Imm AR 1, paras 39–42. In *SK* [2002] UKIAT 05613, (starred) para 22, the Tribunal held that it was not precluded by the terms of IAA 1999, s 77(4) from considering any question relating to the appellant's rights under any Article of the Convention as at the date of the hearing. See now NIAA 2002, s 85.

[5]   Note the change from the old 'fresh claim' provisions of HC 395 para 346; see 12.170 below.

[6]   Nationality, Immigration and Asylum Act 2002, s 96(1), (2), substituted by Asylum and Immigration (Treatment of Claimants, etc) Act 2004, s 30 from 1 October 2004. The provision applies whether or not the person has left the country and returned since the previous claim or appeal. A certificate under s 96 before amendment used to require 'no other legitimate purpose' for making the fresh claim other than to delay removal. This condition generated considerable litigation. In *R (on the application of Vemenac) v Secretary of State for the Home Department* [2002] EWHC 1636 Admin, [2002] Imm AR 613, [2003] INLR 101 'no other legitimate purpose' in the precursor of s 96(1), IAA 1999, s 73(8), was held to mean that the case put forward was so hopeless as not to be properly arguable. In *R (on the application of Ngamguem) v Secretary of State for the Home Department* [2002] EWHC 1550 (QB), [2003] Imm AR 69, the phrase was held to mean that no new material of substance had been placed before the Secretary of State which went beyond that presented to the adjudicator. The Court of Appeal reviewed the

conflicting decisions in *Balamurali v Secretary of State for the Home Department* [2003] EWCA Civ 1806, [2003] EWCA Civ 1806 and held that both the merits and the timing of a second or subsequent human rights/asylum application were relevant. Under s 120, a failure to raise human rights grounds when given an opportunity to do so by service of a one-stop notice is likely to result in a s 96 certificate in response to a later human rights claim. For the one-stop provisions of the 2002 Act see 18.43 below.

8.109 A successful human rights appeal should lead to the grant of humanitarian protection or discretionary leave, in accordance with the Secretary of State's policy set out at 8.31 above. The right to such leave would be defeated only by very clear evidence of fraud or other similarly weighty supervening event.[1] The Tribunal may direct the grant of such leave,[2] but any direction should not be unreasonable; given that the normal maximum grant of HP or DL is three years, a direction for the grant of indefinite leave is likely to be successfully challenged unless it is rigorously justified by reference to the appellant's extreme vulnerability and need for security and stability.[3] There is no necessary contradiction between dismissing a human rights appeal and making an extra-statutory recommendation.[4]

1   *R (on the application of Saribal) v Secretary of State for the Home Department* [2002] EWHC 1542 (Admin), [2002] INLR 596, [2002] All ER (D) 379 (Jul).
2   Nationality, Immigration and Asylum Act 2002, s 87 as amended by Asylum and Immigration (Treatment of Claimants, etc) Act 2004, Sch 2, para 19. For directions generally see 18.69 below.
3   See *Sharif* [2002] UKIAT 00953. We consider the Tribunal's ruling in that case, that the only permissible direction was not to remove the appellant, to understate the proper ambit of the appellate authority's discretion.
4   *R (on the application of Shillova) v Secretary of State for the Home Department* [2002] EWHC Admin 1468, [2002] INLR 611; for extra-statutory recommendations see 18.74 below.

GOING TO EUROPE

8.110 For those cases where the applicant cannot obtain an effective remedy from the Tribunal or the courts in the UK, there remains the possibility of applying to the ECtHR. A detailed exposition of the procedures of the court is beyond the scope of this work, but a brief summary follows.[1] The court became full-time and took over the functions of the Commission in November 1998, with the coming into force of Protocol 11 of the ECHR in an attempt to streamline the procedure and reduce the huge delay in getting a case heard in Strasbourg.[2] With the abolition of the Commission, the court decides on admissibility of applications itself.[3] It is organised into Committees of three judges and Chambers of seven judges, and a Grand Chamber of 17 judges.[4] Committees may declare applications inadmissible by unanimous decision,[5] and if not, a Chamber decides on admissibility and merits.[6] Cases concerning serious questions affecting the interpretation of the Convention or Protocols may go to the Grand Chamber, unless one of the parties objects.[7] The role of the Committee of Ministers has been reduced to supervising the execution of judgments.[8] Much of this may change once Protocol 14 comes into force: see 8.113 below.

1   The reader is referred to Starmer *European Human Rights Law* (1999) LAG for a clear and concise summary of procedures.

² Unfortunately the backlog has in fact increased enormously since then with the addition of new Member States to the Council of Europe bringing the total number of Member States to 45. In 2003 38,435 applications were lodged with the Registry of the European Court of Human Rights. See further 8.113 fn 13.

³ Fewer than 1% of applications considered in 2003 were declared admissible.

⁴ ECHR, Art 27.

⁵ ECHR, Art 28.

⁶ ECHR, Art 29.

⁷ ECHR, Art 30.

⁸ ECHR, Art 46(2).

Procedure

8.111 An application should be made on the application form provided by the Registry.[1] The application must contain (in addition to the applicant's personal details and a clear and concise statement of the facts and relevant domestic law) the ECHR provisions relied on, the object of the application, details of domestic remedies pursued and any judgments or decisions obtained. If it does not, it may not be registered.[2] Individuals may submit applications themselves but legal representation is recommended and is required for hearings or once an application has been declared admissible.[3] There is a legal aid scheme for applicants but legal aid is not available until after a case has been communicated to the respondent government.[4] Following receipt of the application, a judge rapporteur is appointed to examine the application, request further information, decide whether to refer the case to a committee or to a chamber and prepare a report to that body.[5] A chamber has the power to request or take evidence.[6] In cases which are not obviously inadmissible, the respondent government is usually asked to submit observations on an application.[7] There may be an oral hearing on admissibility.[8] A Committee may decide, by unanimous vote, to declare inadmissible or strike out an application where it can do so without further examination. If an application is declared admissible its merits will be considered by a chamber. The chamber may attempt a friendly settlement[9] while pursuing the merits of the case. A hearing on the merits may be requested if there was no hearing at admissibility stage, otherwise it is at the chamber's discretion.[10] The President of the Chamber may grant leave for third-party interventions, either in writing or, in exceptional cases, orally.[11]

¹ Rules of the European Court of Human Rights, r 47(1). There is provision for urgent applications to be made otherwise: rr 47(i) and 47(5).

² Rules of the European Court of Human Rights, r 47(4).

³ Rules of the European Court of Human Rights, r 36.

⁴ Rules of the European Court of Human Rights, r 91. Legal aid rates are not comparable with those in the UK and do not reflect the amount of work that an application usually entails. Legal aid is not available to bring proceedings in the Strasbourg court from the UK Legal Services Commission

⁵ Rules of the European Court of Human Rights, r 49.

⁶ Rules of the European Court of Human Rights, r 42. The power has been frequently used in recent years in respect of applications under ECHR, Arts 2 and 3 from Turkey, where the government disputes the facts. See eg *Akdivar v Turkey* (1996) 23 EHRR 143.

⁷ Rules of the European Court of Human Rights, r 54(3).

⁸ Rules of the European Court of Human Rights, r 54(4).

⁹ Rules of the European Court of Human Rights, r 62.

¹⁰ Rules of the European Court of Human Rights, r 59.

¹¹ Rules of the European Court of Human Rights, r 61.

Interim measures

8.112 The court has no power to grant an injunction against the respondent State, but if the applicant is about to be expelled or deported, the application may contain a request for an interim measure under Rule 39 of the court's procedure rules, which provides that the Chamber or, where appropriate, its President may 'indicate to the parties any interim measure which it considers should be adopted in the interests of the parties or of the proper conduct of the proceedings before it'. This would include a request not to proceed with a removal.[1] The power to adopt a Rule 39 indication is used very sparingly. Until recently the Rule 39 was not considered binding on States.[2] However the court has toughened its stance and has considered that the failure to comply with a Rule 39 indication may constitute an interference with the right of individual petition protected by Article 34 ECHR.[3] An application under Rule 39, like any other application to the court, can be made only once all possible domestic remedies have been exhausted.[4] In addition, even if domestic remedies are exhausted, the risk must be imminent for the court to indicate interim measures. In removal cases, this means that there should be a deportation, expulsion or extradition order pending against the applicant. A Rule 39 indication will only be adopted in cases where there is substantial evidence that there will be 'irreversible harm' to the applicant if expelled and there is good reason to believe that removal will breach Article 3 ECHR.[5]

1   See eg *Hilal v United Kingdom* (2001) 33 EHRR 2, para 5
2   See eg *Cruz Varas v Sweden* (1991) 14 EHRR 1.
3   *Mamatkulov and Abdurasulovic v Turkey* (46827/99 and 46951/99) (2003) Times, 13 March, in which two nationals of Uzbekistan were extradited from Turkey despite a Rule 39 indication having been made by the President of the Court.
4   Article 35(1) ECHR
5   *Cruz Varas*, para 103.

Admissibility

8.113 Most cases fail at admissibility stage, and therefore if an application is to have a chance of proceeding to consideration on its merits, careful attention must be paid to the admissibility criteria.[1] An application will be declared inadmissible if it fails to comply with the requirements of Article 35 of the ECHR. The Rules set out there are:

(i)   the six-month rule: the application must be communicated within six months of the last domestic decision.[2] This is strict and cannot be waived. The time limit may not be relevant in the case of complaints of continuing breaches, although these are strictly interpreted;[3]

(ii)   exhaustion of domestic remedies: the application will be inadmissible if available remedies were not pursued,[4] whether this was because of an adviser's failure or for other reason, unless the failure was due to the respondent State's obstruction.[5] But this rule only requires potentially effective remedies to be exhausted; where a binding authority meant certain failure, a domestic remedy need not be pursued. In such a case the opinion of a senior lawyer should be provided to the court. But a remedy may be effective even if success is not guaranteed;[6]

(iii) manifestly ill-founded applications, ie those disclosing no prima facie breach of a Convention right, or where the complaint is unsubstantiated or the applicant has ceased to be a victim,[7] and applications considered an abuse of the right of application,[8] will be rejected as inadmissible. The 'manifestly ill-founded' provision is very broadly interpreted by the court, which may declare an application to be manifestly ill-founded after examining it in considerable detail;[9]

(iv) Anonymous complaints are inadmissible.[10] An applicant must disclose his or her identity when applying, although there is provision for non-disclosure of identity to the public;

(v) Repetitive applications are inadmissible, although if the complaint is based on new factual information it will not be disqualified;[11]

(vi) Applications which are incompatible with the Convention are inadmissible. A claim is incompatible if it falls outside the terms of the Convention, either in terms of time (eg a claim based on a Protocol not ratified by the respondent State at the time of the alleged violation), or place (ie there is no territorial link with the respondent State), or because it covers matters not within the terms of the Convention at all, such as a right to work in a particular occupation,[12] or matters covered by a derogation.[13]

Further changes in the procedures of the court are envisaged in new Protocol 14, agreed on 13 May 2004, which is designed to amend Convention machinery by (i) the process of filtering out unmeritorious cases; (ii) a new admissibility criterion requiring an applicant to have suffered a 'significant disadvantage', a term not defined in the Protocol; (iii) measures for dealing with repetitive cases; and (iv) improving the process for execution of court judgments.[14]

---

1 In 2004 only 20 applications against the UK government were declared admissible. This represents less than 2 percent of applications made against the UK government (approximately 1,400 applications are lodged per year against the UK based on statistics for 2002 to 2004). See Council of Europe's Survey of Activities for 2004 of the European Court of Human Rights.

2 ECHR, Art 35(1).

3 Application 9852 *United Kingdom and Ireland, Re* (1985) 8 EHRR 49. See also *Yavuz (Bulut and Hatice) v Turkey* (73965/01) (28 May 2002, unreported), where the court considered that even in the case of an alleged continuing violation of the Convention, applicants should make their applications under Art 34 ECHR once they become aware that domestic remedies will be ineffective.

4 ECHR, Art 35(1).

5 See eg *Hilton v United Kingdom* (1978) 3 EHRR 104.

6 See *Soering v United Kingdom* (1989) 11 EHRR 439. On non-exhaustion of effective remedies see Starmer, *European Human Rights Law* (1999) LAG, p 706ff.

7 Eg by accepting damages in settlement of a civil claim: see *Hay v United Kingdom* (41894/98) (17 October 2000, unreported).

8 Eg with no legal foundation, to make a political or other point.

9 *TI v United Kingdom* [2000] INLR 101.

10 ECHR, Art 35(2)(a).

11 ECHR, Art 35(2)(b).

12 *X v Germany* (Application 6742/74) (1975) 3 DR 98.

13 *Brannigan and McBride v United Kingdom* (1993) 17 EHRR 539.

14 The Protocol was prompted by the enormous increase in the court's caseload; for example, it had given 61,633 judgments in the five years since 1998, compared with 38,389 in the previous 44 years; see Joint Committee on Human Rights *Report on Protocol no 14 to the European Convention of Human Rights,* 1st Report of Session 2004–2005, HC 106,

para 3.i. The UK has signed (13 July 2004) but not yet ratified Protocol 14. Ten ratifications are required to bring the Protocol in force. The Council of Europe is anxious to bring the Protocol into effect as soon as possible to relieve the burden on the court.

OTHER INTERNATIONAL OBLIGATIONS

8.114 Many of the obligations under the ECHR are also provided for in the International Covenant on Civil and Political Rights (ICCPR), ratified by the UK in 1976.[1] But the Covenant contains rights not in the ECHR, or contained in Protocols which the UK has not signed, such as the right to enter a person's own country.[2] The UN Human Rights Committee expressed concern in 2001 at the UK's failure to incorporate the Covenant, and its failure to accede to the first Optional Protocol (providing a right of individual petition to the Committee).[3] It also expressed concern at the use of detention against asylum seekers in circumstances not covered by the Covenant, such as for administrative reasons.[4] Following the decisions in *Ahmed and Patel*[5] and *Adimi*[6] it might have been possible to argue that the UK's ratification of the Covenant gave rise to a legitimate expectation that the rights contained in it would be respected. But the UK has made a general reservation from the Covenant rights concerning immigration and nationality, and has consistently refused to withdraw it. The UK has made similar reservations from the UN Convention on the Rights of the Child, a reservation which the Committee monitoring compliance has recommended should be withdrawn.[7] These remarks fall short of express condemnation, and so the rights contained in these international instruments cannot be directly invoked to call into question UK immigration and nationality laws and practices. The ICCPR, however, remains an important source of principles of international human rights law. Concern has been expressed about the compatibility of UK legislation with other international instruments.[8] The UN Committee on the Elimination of Racial Discrimination has expressed concern on both the ability of immigration officers to discriminate on grounds of ethnicity under section 19D of the Race Relations Amendment Act[9] and the detention powers contained in the Anti-terrorism, Crime and Security Act (now lapsed).[10]

[1] The text of this, as of other UN Conventions, is available on the UN website at www.unhchr.ch/intlinst.htm. See also Harris and Joseph *The International Covenant on Civil and Political Rights and United Kingdom Law* (1995).

[2] International Covenant on Civil and Political Rights, Art 12(4), reflecting Protocol 4, Art 3(2) of ECHR, not signed by the UK.

[3] See the UN Human Rights Committee report, CCPR/CO/73, 6/12/2001, para 7.

[4] See the UN Human Rights Committee report, CCPR/CO/73. 6/12/2001, para16.

[5] *R v Secretary of State for the Home Department, ex p Ahmed and Patel* [1998] INLR 570, CA.

[6] *R v Uxbridge Magistrates' Court, ex p Adimi* [1999] INLR 490, QBD. But see the reservations expressed in *European Roma Rights Centre v Immigration Officer at Prague Airport* in the Court of Appeal, at 8.31 above.

[7] Committee on the Rights of the Child, CRC/C/15/Add.188, 9 October 2002. The Joint Committee on Human Rights has also urged the government to drop its reservation: see its Tenth report 2002/3: UN Convention on the Rights of the Child, 24 June 2003 (HL 117/HC 81), and its 19th report 2003/4: Children Bill, 21 September 2004 (HL 161/HC 537).

[8] See Tom Obakota, 'Human Trafficking, Human Rights and the Nationality, Immigration and Asylum 2002' (2003) 4 EHRLR 410 for a discussion of the extent to which anti-trafficking provisions contained in the NIAA 2002 comply with international human rights standards.

9   See further *European Roma Rights Centre v Immigration Officer at Prague Airport [2004] UKHL 55, at paras 98ff per Lady Hale, who gave the lead speech on discrimination.*
10 Concluding observations of the Committee on the Elimination of Racial Discrimination, 10/12/2003 CERD/C/63/CO/11. These provisions were the subject of concerns raised by the UN Human Rights Committee at the end of 2001, see note 3 above, para 6.

THE RIGHT TO ENTER THE COUNTRY OF NATIONALITY

8.115 As we stated above,[1] the UK has refused to ratify Protocol 4 of the ECHR, which recognises the right of nationals to enter and reside in the country of his or her nationality, and during the passage of the Human Rights Act 1998 the minister indicated that there were no plans to do so. The traditional view in international law, that the State's obligation to admit its own nationals applies only as between States and is not an obligation to the nationals, was invoked during the passage of the Commonwealth Immigrants Act 1968.[2] That Act, passed to prevent UK citizens of Asian descent who were threatened with expulsion from Kenya from coming to Britain, removed the previous common law right of certain UK citizens without ancestral connections with the UK to enter the country. A less restrictive interpretation of international law acknowledges that the State's duty to admit its own nationals is the corollary of the individual's right to enter the territory of his or her own State, deriving from the Universal Declaration on Human Rights, international instruments such as the International Covenant on Civil and Political Rights, and the general principles of customary international law.[3] The judgment of Orr LJ in *R v Secretary of State for the Home Department, ex p Thakrar*[4] indicates the extent to which municipal law recognises this duty, to the effect that it is limited to cases of expulsion from the country of residence where the applicant has nowhere else to go. Successive UK governments, despite failing to give full acknowledgement or effect to the duty towards individuals, made arrangements whereby most categories of British nationals—at least those with no other nationality—could be admitted to the UK somehow or another. The longest-lived scheme was the 'Special Voucher scheme' whereby heads of households of British Overseas citizens were granted the right of residence in the UK on fulfilment of a number of less than onerous conditions.[5] The scheme was abolished without warning on 5 March 2002, but from July 2003, the Nationality, Immigration and Asylum Act 2002 makes provision for BOCs, British subjects and British Protected Persons who have no other nationality (and who did not renounce another nationality after 4 July 2002) to British citizenship on application.[6] The same solution—the grant of full British citizenship—was previously used for British Overseas Territories citizens (formerly British Dependent Territories citizens)[7] and for British Nationals (Overseas).[8]

1   See 2.6 and 8.10 fn 14 above.
2   See Plender *International Migration Law* (2nd edn, 1988), pp 133ff for the debate.
3   Universal Declaration on Human Rights, Art 13(2); International Covenant on Civil and Political Rights, Art 12(4); International Covenant on the Elimination of all forms of Racial Discrimination, Art 5(d)(ii); ECHR, Protocol 4, Art 3(2); see also UN Human Rights Committee General Comments No 27 on Free Movement, 1999.
4   [1974] QB 684, CA.
5   For the detailed provisions of the Special Voucher scheme, see the previous edition of this work, 8.85–8.89.

6   Under the Nationality, Immigration and Asylum Act 2002, s 12, in force 30 April 2003
      (SI 2003/754). The date of 4 July 2002 as the cut-off point after which renunciation of
      another citizenship does not confer eligibility, was the date the proposal (an amendment to
      the Bill then going through parliament) was announced.
7   Under the British Overseas Territories Act 2002, ss 3, 4.
8   Under the British Nationality (Hong Kong) Act 1997.

STATELESSNESS

8.116 Persons born in the UK who would otherwise be stateless are eligible
for British citizenship in accordance with provisions to reduce statelessness
under the British Nationality Act 1981, pursuant to the UK's obligations
under the 1961 Convention on the Reduction of Statelessness. The Convention was ratified by the UK in 1966 and came into force in 1967. Stateless
persons are not refugees under the 1951 Refugee Convention simply by virtue
of being stateless,[1] but they may be refugees if they are fleeing persecution in
their country of habitual residence.[2] Deprivation of the benefits of citizenship
may itself constitute persecution.[3]

1   *Revenko v Secretary of State for the Home Department* [2000] INLR 646, CA; *Azam
      (Ghulam)* [2002] UKIAT 05810.
2   See below 12.35.
3   *Lazarevic v Secretary of State for the Home Department* [1997] Imm AR 251, CA.

8.117 The 1954 Convention on the Status of Stateless Persons was ratified by
the UK in 1959.[1] It contains provisions very similar to those in the 1951
Convention on the Status of Refugees, and affords similar rights to stateless
persons with regard to employment, education and welfare. Articles 27 and
28, common to both Conventions, provide for the issue of identity and travel
documents. Article 31 of the 1954 Convention provides that contracting
States shall not expel stateless persons lawfully in their territory except on
national security or public order grounds, and in such cases requires procedural safeguards. Overstaying was held to justify expulsion on public order
grounds in *Kelzani*.[2] However, where no other country will receive a stateless
person, there is no defiance of immigration control and no strong public order
grounds for removal (quite apart from the actual impossibility of removal).

1   Cmnd 1098, 1960. The text is to be found on the UN website, at www.unhchr.ch/
      intlinst.htm, or in Plender *Documents on International Migration Law* (2nd revised
      edition, 1999) Nijhoff.
2   *Kelzani v Secretary of State for the Home Department* [1978] Imm AR 193, IAT.

Chapter 9

VISITS, STUDY AND TEMPORARY PURPOSES

INTRODUCTION

9.1 In this chapter we deal with the formal requirements of the Immigration Rules relating to visits, study, and admission for other temporary purposes. It should be noted, however, that compliance with these Rules may not be sufficient to gain entry and the general requirements for refusal of entry may apply. Passengers who qualify formally for admission may be refused entry because of their restricted returnability, their past immigration or criminal record, for medical reasons or for the other general reasons already referred to.[1] Similarly, extensions of leave may be refused on any of the general grounds contained in the Immigration Rules, even though the formal requirements for an extension are satisfied.[2] In addition, section 8B of the Immigration Act 1971[3] provides for the mandatory exclusion of 'excluded persons' named or described in a designated UN Security Council Resolution or an instrument of the EU Council as war criminals.[4]

---

[1]   HC 395, para 320. Grounds (1) to (7) specify circumstances in which entry clearance or leave to enter *is* to be refused and (8) to (19) where it *should normally* be refused. It was with reference to sub-para (18) that a group representing women victims of violence sought judicial review of the admission of boxer Mike Tyson in 2000, on what the Secretary of State for the Home Department submitted were the 'exceptional circumstances' of not wishing to disappoint third parties, ie businessmen and ticket holders: *R v Secretary of State for the Home Department, ex p Bindel* [2001] Imm AR 1, Sullivan J. The wide scope of such circumstances employed by the Secretary of State in this case may be of benefit to other less famous applicants. See 3.49ff above.

[2]   HC 395, para 322(1) where leave *is to* be refused, and (2)–(11) where leave *should normally* be refused. See 4.27ff above.

[3]   Inserted by Immigration and Asylum Act 1999, s 8.

[4]   The Schedule to the Immigration (Designation of Travel Bans) Order 2000, SI 2000/2724 (as amended by SI 2003/3285 and SI 2004/3316), made under Immigration and Asylum Act 1999, s 8B, designates five UN Security Council resolutions, relating to Al Qa'ida, The

Taliban, Liberia and Sierra Leone, and seventeen EU Council instruments, relating to Bosnia-Herzegovina, Burma, the Federal Republic of Yugoslavia, Liberia, Moldovan Republic and Zimbabwe. See 3.70 above.

9.2 All visa nationals require a visa. Entry clearance is not essential for non-visa nationals coming for purposes considered in this chapter, unless they are coming as working holidaymakers,[1] or are specified nationals seeking leave to enter for more than six months (ie as au pairs or students).[2] However, prior entry clearance, although not compulsory, may be desirable in the case of au pairs[3] and students from non-visa countries, to ensure that they do not waste the cost of travel, and in the case of students, that they do not waste an academic year by a refusal at the port of entry. Entry clearance operates as a grant of leave to enter.[4] Refusal of entry clearance attracts no right of appeal in the case of short-term and prospective students and non-family visitors. The Asylum and Immigration Appeals Act 1993 abolished rights of appeal against refusal of entry clearance for all visitors, short-term and prospective students. The Immigration and Asylum Act 1999 re-introduced appeal rights for family visitors and its 2002 successor continues these and provides rights of appeal on discrimination and human rights grounds where appropriate.[5] The effect of the 1993 removal of appeal rights has been a dearth of recent tribunal authority in relation to visitors, and almost the only challenges in recent years in visitor cases have been by way of judicial review.

[1] HC 395, para 95(ix). For visa nationals see 3.10 above.
[2] HC 395, para 24 and App 3, as amended and inserted by HC 1224. For more detail on specified nationals see 3.10 above.
[3] HC 395, para 90 (which offers this express advice to proposed au pairs).
[4] Immigration (Leave to Enter and Remain) Order 2000, SI 2000/1161, Art 2, HC 395 para 25A (inserted by HC 704). See 3.22 above.
[5] See now Nationality, Immigration and Asylum Act 2002, ss 82, 84, 90, 91.

VISITORS

9.3 People may visit this country for a variety of reasons – as tourists, to see relatives or friends, to transact business, to take part in a conference or in some sporting competition or to seek medical treatment. A visit is any temporary stay in the UK for a purpose which does not place the person in a different category of the Immigration Rules.[1] It is perfectly proper for a person to seek entry as a visitor in order to give evidence at his or her own appeal,[2] to take over domestic responsibilities temporarily or to care for a sick relative,[3] to look after a child temporarily,[4] to visit a spouse who is a student[5] or a working holidaymaker,[6] or for the purpose of marriage (although there are now special rules for 'marriage visitors').[7]

[1] *Secretary of State for the Home Department v Xi* [1993] Imm AR 519; *Kelada v Secretary of State for the Home Department* [1991] Imm AR 400.
[2] *Patel v Visa Officer, Bombay* [1991] Imm AR 97; *Patel v Entry Clearance Officer, Bombay* [1991] Imm AR 273. In *Gaud* (16386) 1999 2 IAS No 6, the Tribunal held that visitor was the correct category for someone in the UK awaiting trial for a criminal offence. The IDI Jun 03, Ch 2, s 1, Annex B, para 2 point out that since 1 October 1996 an appeal is deemed abandoned if the appellant leaves the UK, so that appellants will be seeking leave to enter as visitors to attend entry-clearance appeals or other appeals from outside the UK.
[3] See IDI Jun 03, Ch 2, s 1, Annex B, para 5; IDI Jun 01, Ch 17, s 2 (carers).

4 *Entry Clearance Officer, Manilla v Magalso* [1993] Imm AR 293; IDI Jun/03, Ch 2, s 1, Annex B, para 6; see below.

5 *Secretary of State for the Home Department v Xi* [1993] Imm AR 519.

6 *Deen* (9563) unreported; referred to in [1993] INLP 73.

7 In addition to the requirements imposed on all visitors, marriage visitors must demonstrate that they are free to marry and that they intend to marry or give notice of marriage whilst in the UK, and can produce satisfactory evidence of arrangements for doing so: HC 395, para 56D–F, inserted by HC 346 from 15 March 2005.

9.4 The IDI refer to a number of 'special classes of visitor',[1] such as academic visitors,[2] persons coming to the UK for job interviews[3] and to apply for visas for settlement in third countries,[4] volunteers on archaeological excavations,[5] temporary childminders for close relatives (as long as they do not enter into an employment relationship),[6] carers of sick relatives (who may be admitted for a period of up to three months initially),[7] amateur entertainers and sportspersons.[8] Professional sportspersons and entertainers may be admitted as visitors, though this is described as entry under a permit-free concession outside the Immigration Rules which would otherwise fall foul of the no employment provision of the visit rules.[9] There are a number of similar categories where admission may be given, such as British Universities North America Club (BUNAC) students,[10] unpaid volunteers for certain charitable organisations and registered charities.[11] Parents accompanying children under 12 at school in the UK have now been brought within the rules.[12] Previously this was a concession outside the rules for mothers only. Other 'special classes of visitor' are now set out in the immigration rules, including. marriage visitors,[13] and doctors coming for Professional and Linguistic Assessment Board (PLAB) tests.[14]

1 IDI Ch 2, s 1, Annex B (Jun 03).

2 IDI Ch 2, s 1, Annex B, para 1. They may be post-graduate researchers sponsored by the Royal Society, the British council, a charity, a national research council or university or on an EU programme, or privately funded academics on sabbatical or formal exchange programmes, or eminent doctors or dentists coming for research, teaching or clinical practice. They may perform up to two paid lectures without requiring a work permit, but may not otherwise receive payment other than scholarships, grants, bursaries, expenses or honoraria. Academic visitors may be given leave for up to 12 months, but may not switch to work permit employment.

3 IDI Ch 2, s 1, Annex B, para 12. They must be prepared to leave if they get the job, and seek entry clearance abroad.

4 IDI Ch 2, s 1, Annex B, para 13. The timescale must be short and clearly defined, and the passenger must be returnable elsewhere.

5 IDI Ch 2, s 1, Annex B, para 3.

6 IDI Ch 2, s 1, Annex B, para 6. See 9.15 below.

7 IDI Jun 03, Ch 2, s 1, Annex B, para 5; see also IDI Jun 01, Ch 17, s 2.

8 IDI Jun 03, Ch 2, s 1, Annex B, para 9.1.

9 IDI, Ch 2, s 1, Annex B, para 9.2. See also IDI Oct 01, Ch 17, s 5. They may conduct personal appearances, promotions, sign contracts and sponsorship deals but may not perform: see chapter 10 below.

10 IDI Jun 02, Ch 17, s 1, Annex C. See also Race Relations (Immigration and Asylum) Authorisation 2002, IDI Feb 03, Ch 1, s 11, Annex EE1, and 9.56 below.

11 IDI Jul 03, Ch 17, s 9, Annex C.

12 HC 395, para 56A-C, inserted by Cm 4851 on 2 October 2000.

13 See 9.4 fn 7 above.

14 HC 395 para 75A–F, inserted by HC 346 from 15 March 2005. We deal with doctors coming for PLAB tests at 9.45 below.

9.5 Save for visitors in transit and medical visitors, and subject to the additional requirements for marriage visitors, the same considerations apply whatever the purpose of the visit, although the purpose may influence the decision whether or not to admit. Independent tourists are likely to receive less attention from immigration officers than persons coming to visit relatives and friends who have themselves come from overseas and settled in the country. Another factor influencing the immigration officer's assessment of whether a person is a genuine visitor or not is the country from which a visitor comes and the general standard of living there. The IDI advise that the proposed purpose of the visit must bear some reasonable relationship to the financial means of the passenger and his or her family, social and economic background.[1] From the immigration statistics it used to be possible to calculate the ratio of admissions to refusals for nationals of different countries.[2] They invariably showed a much higher refusal rate from countries such as Ghana, Nigeria, Pakistan, Bangladesh and Jamaica (whose nationals all require visas)[3] compared with the US, Canada, Australia or New Zealand (whose nationals do not).[4] Nowadays, the Home Office publishes 'selected' statistics, which makes this information less easy to find.

1   IDI Aug 04, Ch 2, s 1, Annex A, 'General guidance', para 1. See para 9.10 below.
2   See eg *Control of Immigration Statistics* – UK, published annually by HMSO.
3   The refusal rate for Jamaican nationals drastically increased from 1 in 650 in 1984 to 1 in 67 in 1991 to 1 in 23 in 1999, which compared with a 1 in 2,014 refusal rate for US nationals in 1991, falling to 1 in 4,390 in 1999: *Control of Immigration Statistics*: UK (Cm 4876, October 2000) Table 3.2. The most recent statistics (Cm 6053 Nov 2003) reveal a 500% increase in refusal of entry clearance for Jamaican nationals, from 425 Jamaicans refused entry in 2001 compared with 2635 refused the following year. Similar increases have occurred for nationals from Zimbabwe, Kenya and the DRC. See further *Report of the Independent Monitor* June 2004 (the annual report of the independent monitor of entry clearance refusals); Target Caribbean: *The rise in visitor refusals from the Caribbean* (JCWI, 1990); S Leigh *An Analysis of Racial Discrimination in Law and Practice of Immigration Control*; also CRE 'Immigration Control Procedures; Report of a Formal Investigation' (1985) p 78. Discrimination on the basis of nationality and ethnic origin is expressly authorised by the Race Relations Act 1976, s 19D inserted by the Race Relations (Amendment) Act 2000, and by the ministerial authorisation set out in IDI Feb 03, Ch 1, s 11, Annex EE1. See 3.31 above. With effect from 11 April the British High Commission in Nigeria is not accepting visa applications from first-time visitors aged 18–30, except those with urgent compassionate reasons for travelling such as the death or serious illness of a close relative: see UKVisas website.
4   The position may in fact be worse than is suggested by the statistics, because of the practice of telling applicants for entry clearance that they should withdraw their application, because the entry clearance officer is minded to refuse. This has been done twice to the author's Pakistani aunt on proposed visits sponsored by the author.

9.6   The high refusal rates from West Africa and the Indian subcontinent were institutionalised by the late 1980s by making citizens of Bangladesh, Ghana, India, Nigeria, Pakistan, Sri Lanka, Uganda and Zaire visa nationals,[1] meaning that since then, these citizens have had to obtain a prior entry clearance even if they only wish to come for a visit, although they are Commonwealth countries with allegiance to the Crown, whose nationals are not aliens, nor 'foreign nationals' for the purpose of registration with the police.[2] The list of countries whose nationals require a visa now includes Jamaica, and all the refugee producing countries including Afghanistan, Iran, Iraq, Sudan and Zimbabwe. There is a common list of countries, whose nationals must have a visa to enter the European Union (known as the European common visa list), but it does not apply to the UK or Ireland.[3]

Special arrangements are in force for tourist groups from the People's Republic of China, pursuant to the Approved Destination Status agreement signed in January 2005.[4]

1   HC 395, Appendix 1. The imposition of a visa requirement on Commonwealth citizens is
     not *ultra vires*: *R v Secretary of State for the Home Department, ex p Suresh Kumar* [1986]
     Imm AR 420.
2   HC 395, paras 325–326 (substituted by HC 194 from 1 February 2005).
3   Council Regulation (EC) 539/01 (OJ 2001 L 81/1), as amended by Regulation 453/03
     (OJ 2003 L 69/10). See chapter 7 above.
4   See HC 486, amending HC 395 with effect from 5 April 2005.

General rules on admission

9.7 The rules relating to the admission of visitors are contained in HC 395, paragraphs 40–46. The IDI give further guidance.[1] Under paragraph 41 passengers seeking entry as visitors must satisfy the immigration authority that:

(i)   they are genuinely seeking entry for a limited period as stated by them, not exceeding six months; and
(ii)   they intend to leave the UK at the end of the period of the visit; and
(iii) they do not intend to take employment in the UK; and
(iv)   they do not intend to produce goods or provide services within the UK, including the selling of goods or services direct to members of the public; and
(v)   they do not intend to study at a maintained school; and
(vi)   they will maintain and accommodate themselves and any dependants adequately out of resources available to them without recourse to public funds or taking employment, or will, with any dependants, be maintained and accommodated adequately by relatives or friends; and
(vii) they can meet the cost of the return or onward journey.

Leave to enter is discretionary and will not, as a general rule, be given for a period exceeding six months[2] and will be subject to a condition prohibiting employment. The immigration officer must be satisfied that each of the requirements of paragraph 41 is met;[3] otherwise, leave will be refused.[4] Persons entering the UK under the Approved Destination Status (ADS) Agreement with the People's Republic of China will be granted leave for a maximum of 30 days.[5]

1   IDI Aug 04, Ch 2, s 1.
2   HC 395, para 42, but academic visitors, volunteers on archaeological digs and other
     'special' categories may be granted 12 months: IDI Jun 03, Ch 2, Annex B.
3   HC 395, para 42.
4   HC 395, para 43.
5   HC 395, para 56H, inserted by HC 486 from 5 April 2005. Paragraph 41(i) is modified in
     line in its application to such visitors: para 56G as inserted.

Specifying the length of stay

9.8 The first thing someone wishing to visit Britain must do is to specify the length of the proposed visit. Under the current Immigration Rules it must not exceed six months. Though six months is understood to be the norm, the Rules give no guidance and the exact time given is a matter within the immigration officer's discretion.[1] The courts have said that it is the job of immigration officers to consider what period would be suitable given the visitor's financial and other circumstances.[2] Persons who are extremely vague about their length of stay may fail to satisfy the immigration authorities that they could support themselves without working for the period of visit as stated by them,[3] or the length of the proposed visit may be too vague.[4] On the other hand, where, in the nature of the visit, it is not possible to give an exact date for leaving, leave should still be given if the visit is for an ascertainable period of less than six months and the visitors can show that they would leave when the purpose of the visit had been achieved.[5] The Rules make no reference to a visitor who leaves the UK before the expiry of six months but then returns for another substantial period shortly thereafter. In *Powell*[6] it was held that as long as the appellant was a genuine visitor who intended to leave the country within the period stated by her, the immigration officer should not have been concerned with the number of visits that had been made. The IDI point out that there is no restriction on the number of visits a person may make to the UK nor any requirement that a specified time must elapse between successive visits, and the fact that a person has made a series of visits with only brief intervals between them would not, in the absence of any other relevant factors, constitute a sufficient ground for refusal.[7] But a visitor should not normally spend more than six out of any 12 months in this country.[8] A multiple visit visa (for example, of two or five years' duration) can be used on an unlimited number of occasions and operates as leave to enter on each occasion the holder enters the UK, usually for a period of six months.[9] A change of circumstances after a visitor's visa was issued is not necessarily a ground for cancellation, if the passenger was seeking a limited period of stay.[10]

1   HC 395, paras 42 and 44. Three months is the norm for the common European visa, but so far the government has shown no intention to harmonise downwards on this. For visitors entering the UK under the Approved Destination Status (ADS) Agreement with the People's Republic of China the maximum period is 30 days: HC 395, para 56G–H, inserted by HC 486 from 5 April 2005.

2   *R v Secretary of State for Home Affairs, ex p Harniak Singh* [1969] 1 WLR 835; *Khan* (18 April 1969, unreported), CA, referred to in *Immigration Officer, London (Heathrow Airport) v Schönenburger* [1975] Imm AR 7 at 9.

3   *Immigration Officer, London (Heathrow Airport) v Schönenburger* [1975] Imm AR 7.

4   *Hashim v Secretary of State for the Home Department* [1982] Imm AR 113 – a vague period of medical treatment.

5   *R v Secretary of State for the Home Department, ex p Arjumand* [1983] Imm AR 123, QBD (a period depended on father's health and winding up of his business); *Patel v Entry Clearance Officer, Bombay* [1991] Imm AR 273 (entry clearance sought for visit to give evidence at entry clearance appeal, no date for the appeal having been fixed). The IDI state that the likely timescale for the appeal should be considered before leave is granted: IDI, Ch 2, s 1 Annex B, para 2.

6   (3129) unreported.

7   IDI Aug 04, Ch 2, Annex A, para 4.

8   IDI Ch 2, Annex A, para 4.

9   Immigration (Leave to Enter and Remain) Order 2000, SI 2000/1161, Art 4. See further 9.20 below. The background notes to the July 2000 Changes in Immigration Rules refer to long-term visit visas with a validity of up to five years. An ordinary visit visa of six months' validity also operates as leave to enter on unlimited occasions if the holder leaves the UK and returns within the period of its validity.

10 *Corte* (12708) (1996) 10 INLP.

Genuine visit

9.9 Before granting admission the immigration authority has to be satisfied that the applicant is genuinely seeking entry for the period of the visit as stated by him or her and does not intend to overstay or take employment. An application should not be refused on the basis of one ambiguous answer in interview, particularly by someone who has previously complied with visit requirements.[1] If the immigration authority is satisfied that the applicant will leave, but not within the period stated, this does not necessarily mean it is not a genuine visit.[2] For reasons we have discussed, the exact length of stay may be difficult to ascertain, and it is quite wrong for the immigration officer to refuse leave, merely because he or she thinks the passenger may seek an extension of stay.[3] Most disputed cases, however, are concerned with visitors who, according to the immigration authorities, intend to stay on at the end of their leave. In considering these cases the person's incentives to stay or leave are clearly of great importance. In one case the evidence was that a widower, whose two sons lived in England, had money of his own and property in India and could not live in a cold climate because of his rheumatoid arthritis. This showed a clear incentive to leave at the end of the stated period of visit and persuaded a tribunal to reverse earlier decisions to refuse entry.[4] Employment to return to in another country may well be a material consideration, and evidence confirmatory of such employment and a period of leave is frequently helpful.[5] But loss of such employment between issue of entry clearance and arrival here might amount to a change of circumstances that enables the immigration officer to go behind the entry clearance and cancel the deemed leave to enter.[6]

1   *R v Entry Clearance Officer, Chennai, ex p Sundamoorthy* (CO 4896/99) (20 June 2000, unreported).
2   *Visa Officer, Cairo v Malek* [1979–80] Imm AR 111.
3   *R v Secretary of State for the Home Department, ex p Arjumand* [1983] Imm AR 123, QBD.
4   *Singh (Bhagat) v Entry Clearance Officer, New Delhi* [1978] Imm AR 134. See also *Afzal v Entry Clearance Officer, Islamabad* [2002] UKIAT02732, where a Pakistani farmer's proposed visit to his Birmingham-based cousin to explore UK farming methods was upheld as genuine. Conversely, a lack of apparent incentive to return from a family visit might be fatal to an application: see eg *R v Entry Clearance Officer, ex p Abu-Gidary* (CO 965/1999) (8 March 2000, unreported).
5   *Huda v Entry Clearance Officer, Dacca* [1976] Imm AR 109; see also *Visa Officer, Cairo v Ashraf* [1979–80] Imm AR 45. The onus is on the applicant to prove her case, not on the ECO to undertake investigations about claimed employment: *E (Cameroon)* [2004] UKIAT00077 'Reported'.
6   See IDI Feb 02, Ch 9, s 3. Refusal of leave to enter for holders of entry clearance, para 4; see further 3.23 above.

9.10 Other factors which may be taken into account in deciding whether a person genuinely seeks entry as a visitor include the family's immigration history,[1] the length and purpose of the visit and their means and position in their own country.[2] Previous immigration history and evidence of a pattern of family migration, both here and abroad, may be taken into account. The IDI state that a visitor's proposed purpose in coming to the UK must bear some reasonable relationship to his or her financial means and his or her family, social and economic background.[3] Sometimes the Tribunal is not clear about what is or is not a relevant factor. For example, whether possession of a UK passport is relevant or not is the subject of contradictory decisions. In *Mohamed Din*[4] the fact that the applicant was a non-patrial UK passport holder, and therefore unlikely to be removed from the UK if he overstayed, was held not of itself to be a relevant consideration when determining whether the applicant intended more than a visit, unless there were indications of bad faith. His appeal was allowed. But in *Patel*[5] a differently constituted Tribunal held that the possession of a UK passport was a matter which the immigration authority must take into account, and this together with other factors, meant that the applicant had been properly refused a visit. The position probably no longer needs resolving, because of the new nationality provisions, giving automatic British citizenship to some of these visitors and a right to register as British citizens to others.[6]

[1]   *R v Secretary of State for the Home Department, ex p Kurumoorthy* [1998] Imm AR 401; *R v Entry Clearance Officer, ex p Abu-Gidary* (CO 965/1999) (8 March 2000, unreported), distinguishing *R v Entry Clearance Officer, ex p Edebali* (CO 3237/97) (21 October 1997, unreported), where Sedley J disapproved the adverse inferences drawn from previous family migration. See also *Dalvi* [2002] UKIAT 07201, where the Tribunal relied on a family pattern of migration, as well as evasion and embellishment by the applicant and her sponsor, to uphold a refusal of entry clearance for a family visit.
[2]   Persons of means and position in their own country might well be accepted as genuine visitors even if their declared intention was 'only to visit the maze at Hampton Court', but where it was proposed that a considerable sum of money should be expended by a family with limited resources, the immigration authorities were entitled to consider carefully the reasons for the expenditure: *Manmohan Singh v Entry Clearance Officer, New Delhi* [1975] Imm AR 118, IAT.
[3]   IDI Aug 04, Ch 2, s 1, Annex A, para 1. However, the mere fact that parents on whom a young person finishing education was financially dependent lived in the UK could not justify refusal of entry clearance for a visit to them: *R v Entry Clearance Officer, Chennai, ex p Sundamoorthy* (CO 4896/99) (20 June 2000, unreported).
[4]   *Mohamed Din v Entry Clearance Officer, Karachi* [1978] Imm AR 56.
[5]   *Patel v Entry Clearance Officer, Bombay* [1978] Imm AR 154.
[6]   See 2.14–2.20, above.

9.11 In considering an applicant's intentions, a distinction has to be drawn between a wish and an intention. The distinction was drawn in another context in *Masood v Immigration Appeal Tribunal*,[1] where Glidewell LJ said that a wish is not an intention, unless there is some reasonable prospect of its being fulfilled. The previous expression of a wish to settle or study in the UK is not necessarily prejudicial to a subsequent application for a visit.[2] Otherwise, someone who discloses an earlier wish to settle could never subsequently qualify as a *bona fide* visitor.[3] On the other hand, the distinction between a wish and an intention will disappear if, taking that and the other circumstances of the case into consideration, there is a strong inference of an intention not just to visit but to stay for study or work.[4] By way of an exception, the Immigration Rules allow overseas doctors who come to the UK for the Professional and Linguistic Assessment Board (PLAB) test to remain, if they are successful, for training as a postgraduate doctor or trainee general practitioner; to undertake a clinical attachment; or as a work permit holder or as a doctor under the highly skilled migrant programme,[5] so that an intention to remain for any of those purposes would not disqualify the entrant. A person coming to look after children and learn English may qualify as a visitor, although the application may look like an 'au pair' application, so long as the intention is to leave at the end of the visit and what is sought is not employment,[6] but if the purpose is quite different from a visit, for example, to claim asylum, seeking entry as a visitor will make the person an illegal entrant.[7]

[1]   [1992] Imm AR 69, CA at 78. See also *R v Immigration Appeal Tribunal, ex p Shaikh* [1981] 3 All ER 29, [1981] 1 WLR 1107, QBD.

[2]   *Patel v Immigration Appeal Tribunal* [1983] Imm AR 76, CA, per Dillon LJ at 80, CA; *Ex p Arjumand*, above.

[3]   *Entry Clearance Officer, Hong Kong v Lai* [1974] Imm AR 98; *El Atrash* (3209) and *Ghailane* (3648) where the appellant had made an application in the alternative either for settlement to join his wife and children or to visit them; see also *Karachiwalla* (4726) where the appellant was held to be a genuine visitor despite a wish to settle in the UK with her family.

[4]   *R v Secretary of State for the Home Department, ex p Brakwah* [1989] Imm AR 366, DC; see further *Adesina v Secretary of State for the Home Department* [1988] Imm AR 442, CA (both illegal entry cases): see 9.38–9.39, below. But a genuine visitor may study during the visit: *R v Secretary of State for the Home Department, ex p Montezano* (CO 1000/2000) (9 November 2000, unreported), QBD.

[5]   HC 395 para 75A(iv)(a)–(c), inserted by HC 346 with effect from 15 March 2005. Transitional provisions allow doctors who entered the UK as visitors before that date specifically to take the test to benefit from the new switching provisions: IDI Mar 05, Ch 3, s 7, para 1.2.

[6]   *Gusakov* (11672). *Entry Clearance Officer, Bombay v Shaikh (Salmaben)* [2002] UKIAT 02732.

[7]   *Bugdaycay v Secretary of State for the Home Department* [1987] AC 514; *Rasmish Al-Zahrany v Secretary of State for the Home Department* [1995] Imm AR 510, CA. See also *R (on the application of Montezano) v Secretary of State for the Home Department* [2001] EWHC Admin 285, where the Administrative Court held that, where an entrant's answers to the immigration officer admit two possible bases for entry (visit or study) the IO does not act reasonably or lawfully if he or she considers only one of the activities.

9.12 It is always the applicant's intentions which count rather than those of the sponsoring relative or friend in this country.[1] It is the intention on the present visit that is critical rather than any previous deception.[2] The fact that the sponsor is likely to ensure the applicant's departure is a relevant factor to be taken into account, since it tends to show an intention to depart.[3] But immigration officers are warned that it is not possible to enforce guarantees by sponsors that a passenger will abide by conditions of stay or leave the UK at the end of a specific period, and no such written guarantee or undertaking should be either sought or accepted.[4]

[1]   *Ragavan* (3418) and cases cited therein.

[2]   *Chaudhury* (3157).

[3]   *Entry Clearance Officer, New Delhi v Kumar* [1978] Imm AR 185; *Chaudhury* (3157).

[4]   IDI Aug 04, Ch 2, s 1, Annex A, para 6.2.

Maintenance and accommodation

9.13 The ability of visitors to maintain and accommodate themselves using resources available to them without taking employment or becoming a charge on public funds is always an important factor.[1] Obviously, ordinary tourists will need to have their own funds. In the case of persons staying with relatives or friends, it does not matter whether they maintain themselves or are maintained by their relatives. The Immigration Rules now allow indirect reliance on public funds provided to the sponsor, so long as the passenger's presence does not result in entitlement to an increased amount.[2] But notwithstanding this relaxation, the provisions regarding visitors make it much more difficult for poor people to be allowed to visit this country than the well-off. As well as being less likely to be accepted as genuine visitors, they have a much greater chance of being rejected on maintenance and accommodation grounds, even though, as 'persons from abroad' for the purposes of social security and homelessness legislation, they are ineligible to claim any assistance.[3] Since 1994 the Immigration Rules have provided that a sponsor may be asked to give an undertaking in writing to be responsible for the visitor's maintenance and accommodation for the period of any leave granted, including any further variation.[4] The Department of Social Security may seek to recover from the person giving such an undertaking any income support paid under the social security legislation to meet the needs of the person in respect of whom the undertaking has been given.[5]

[1] HC 395, para 41(vi). The IDI Aug 04, Ch 2, s 1, Annex A, General Guidance, advises immigration officers to check the source of funds which passengers claim to hold, and if the funds are held abroad, to check their transferability (para 5).

[2] HC 395, para 6A, inserted by Cm 4851.

[3] See eg Income Support (General) Regulations 1987, SI 1987/1967, reg 21(3)(a), Sch 7; Housing Benefit (General) Regulations 1987, SI 1987/1971, reg 7A; Asylum and Immigration Act 1996, s 11; Immigration and Asylum Act 1999, s 115; Social Security (Immigration and Asylum) (Consequential Amendments) Regulations 2000, SI 2000/636; see chapter 13 below.

[4] HC 395, para 35. The undertaking does not need to be on any prescribed form and need only be a document expressing in reasonably clear language a future promise or agreement to maintain a sponsored immigrant: *R (on the application of Begum) v Social Services Commissioner* (2003) Times, 4 December; *Ahmed v Secretary of State for Work and Pensions* [2005] EWCA Civ 535.

[5] Social Security Administration Act 1992, s 78(6)(c) (England and Wales), Social Security Administration (Northern Ireland) Act 1992 (for Northern Ireland, where the collecting agency is the Department of Health and Social Services).

Visits for family reasons and for marriage

9.14 Under early Immigration Rules, visits for family purposes for quite long periods at a time were allowed.[1] In *Hamilton v Entry Clearance Officer, Kingston, Jamaica*[2] a three-year visit by a mother, while her daughter did a teachers' training course, was allowed. Family visits to be with older children have long been impossible, because of the six-month time limit,[3] but there is now specific provision in the Rules for the parents of young children (under 12) at independent fee-paying schools, who have their main home outside the UK, to be given leave to remain for 12 months at a time.[4] Thus the parent who wishes to remain continuously in the UK with a child during his or her primary education may do so, provided they are not seeking to make the UK their main home. Visitors seeking to enter for the purpose of marriage must show that they intend to give notice of marriage or to have a wedding ceremony in the UK and provide satisfactory evidence of arrangements for doing so.[5] A couple seeking to marry in the UK need not have any connection with the country, and neither spouse needs to be British or settled here. But even if one prospective spouse is British or settled, entry as a visitor for the purpose of marriage does not entitle a person to remain in the UK as a spouse after the marriage; for that, a fiancé(e) visa would be required.[6]

1   See Cmnd 4298 (pre-1973 Rules), para 12; *Afoakwah v Secretary of State for the Home Department* [1972] Imm AR 17.
2   [1974] Imm AR 43. See *Nourai v Secretary of State for the Home Department* [1978] Imm AR 200; *Obeyesekere v Secretary of State for the Home Department* [1976] Imm AR 16.
3   *Kelada v Secretary of State for the Home Department* [1991] Imm AR 400.
4   HC 395, para 56A–C, inserted by Cm 4851 in Sep 2000. The Rule requires satisfactory evidence of adequate and reliable funds for maintaining a second home in the UK and compliance with all the visitor requirements save the six-month time limit.
5   HC 395, para 56D–F, inserted by HC 346 from 15 March 2005, which require the marriage visitor to satisfy all the requirements of the visit rules, including an intention to leave at the end of the visit. Visitors who have not entered with a marriage visit visa will not be allowed to marry without Home Office permission: see 11.67 below.
6   See 11.68 below.

9.15 The Immigration Rules offer no other route for the admission and stay of carers, either of children or of sick relatives or friends, but visitors may obviously perform these functions,[1] so long as they are not paid for them.[2] The IDI state that visitors may act as temporary child-minders for close relatives where neither parent is able to supervise the daytime care of the child, provided it is not simply an arrangement to enable both parents to take paid employment or to study,[3] and the visitor will not receive a salary (as opposed to board, accommodation and pocket money) and intends to remain in the UK for no longer than six months. Neither parent must be in a category leading to settlement.[4]

1   For the position of visitors seeking leave to remain to care for a sick relative or a friend suffering from a terminal illness, see IDI, Ch 17, s 2; see 'Extensions of stay as a visitor' 9.19 below.
2   See *Goodluck* (4244) (undertaking child-minding duties for a young mother and her baby for payment was employment, not just a visit); *Tan (Swee Hong)* (5212) (looking after a sister's baby for payment was employment). The IDI (Jun 03, Ch 2, s 1, Annex B, para 6) make it clear that a childminder may be provided with board, accommodation and pocket money.
3   The point of this requirement is that the childminding must be temporary, i e not meeting a permanent need but filling a gap caused by e g illness or while the sponsor is arranging longer-term arrangements.
4   IDI Ch 2, s 1, Annex B, para 6. It is not clear what this last requirement means, and refusal of leave to enter as a visitor for temporary child-minding purposes merely on the basis that the sponsor is in a category leading to settlement could be unlawful.

Business visits

9.16 Passengers do not qualify as visitors if they intend to take employment or to produce goods or provide services in the UK, including selling goods and services direct to the public.[1] They are normally prohibited from taking employment by a condition stamped in their passport,[2] and sometimes the stamp also prohibits them from entering any business or profession, although there is no provision for this condition in the Acts or the immigration rules. However, neither prohibition prevents business visitors from transacting business during their visit. Under the Immigration Rules a visitor includes a person living and working outside the UK who comes to transact business, including attending meetings and briefings, fact finding, negotiating or making contracts with UK businesses to buy or sell goods or services.[3] The 'list of typical business visitors' in the current IDI[4] also includes those coming to purchase trade goods and those coming for training in techniques and work practices used in the UK, provided that the training is confined to observation, familiarisation and classroom instruction. Others accepted as business visitors under the instructions as a matter of administrative policy, although strictly falling outside the visitor provisions, include:

- those delivering goods and passengers from abroad, such as lorry drivers and coach drivers, provided they are genuinely working an international route;[5]
- tour group couriers who are contracted to a firm outside the UK, who seek entry to accompany a tour group and intend to leave with that group;
- those coming as speakers at a 'one-off', non-commercial conference;
- advisers, consultants, trainers, trouble-shooters, etc who are employed abroad (directly or under contract) by the same company or group of companies to which the client firm in the UK belongs. Their involvement must not extend to actual project management or to providing advice or consultancy services direct to clients of the UK company. Training should be for a specific 'one-off' purpose (eg in the use of products manufactured overseas, or specific to the operation of the group of companies of which the UK firm is a member), should not go beyond classroom instruction and should not otherwise be readily available here;
- representatives of computer software companies coming to install, debug or enhance their products. They may also be admitted as visitors to be briefed as to the requirements of a UK customer but may not use their expertise to make a detailed assessment of a potential customer's requirements, which is regarded as consultancy work for which a work permit is required;
- representatives of foreign manufacturers coming to service or repair their company's products within the guarantee period;
- representatives of foreign machine manufacturers coming to erect and install machinery too heavy to be delivered in one piece, as part of the contract of purchase and supply;
- monteurs—workers coming for up to six months to erect, dismantle, install, service, repair or advise on the development of foreign-made machinery.

In addition, permission may be given to allow a visitor entry for purposes which arguably involve provision of a service such as giving professional advice or taking instructions, where the visit is short (for a day or so), is 'one-off' and without significant implications for the resident workforce.[6]

1   HC 395, para 41(iii), (iv). For special dispensation to enter as a visitor for recognised festivals and charity concerts, which would normally require a work permit, see 10.101; and see IDI Jul 03, Ch 17, s 3 for a list of such events.
2   HC 395, para 42.
3   HC 395, para 40.
4   IDI Jun 03, Ch 2, s 1, Annex B.

5   The majority of long-distance lorry-drivers come from the EEA in any event, or are employed by an EEA-established company; in either case they are covered by the EC free movement provision: *Rush Portuguesa Lda v Office National d'Immigration* [1990] ECR I-1417; see chapter 7 below.

6   IDI Ch 2, s 1, Annex B, para 4. Ministers of religion and preachers may come as visitors for preaching tours lasting no longer than six months, provided this is not disguised employment: DSP Mar 03, Ch 10 'Visit requirements' para 10.4.

9.17 Most of the above guidance deals with the distinction between employment and a visit and leaves untouched the distinction between transacting business and establishing a business, which determines whether a passenger should be admitted as a business visitor or should be required to return home and obtain a visa for the purpose of setting up a business.[1] In one tribunal case it was held that forming a company, setting up an office and training a partner went too far.[2] The DSP state that self-employed consultants, employees of overseas firms whose involvement with a UK subsidiary amounts to employment here, and those undertaking productive work which could be undertaken by local or EEA labour, and trainers (unless exempted) are not business visitors.[3] Essentially it will be a question of fact in each case.

1   HC 395, paras 200–205; see chapter 10 below. Visitors from Europe Agreement countries may set up in business after entry as visitors, however: see 9.25 below.

2   *Hossain (Sardar) v Immigration Officer, Heathrow* [1990] Imm AR 520. In *Ayoola v Secretary of State for the Home Department* [1992] Imm AR 170, CA it was held that becoming a director of a UK-incorporated company went beyond transacting business.

3   DSP (Mar 03) Ch 10 'Visit requirements' para 10.5.

Time limits and other conditions on stay

9.18 The immigration authority will always impose a time limit on the period of the visitor's stay and of any dependants. A period of six months will normally be appropriate[1] unless there are particular circumstances, such as restricted returnability, or if the passenger is booked out on a particular charter flight, or the visitor's case ought to be subject to early review by the Home Office.[2] Visitors are normally prohibited from taking employment.[3] Visitors from the Commonwealth never have to register with the police, and foreign nationals[4] may only be required to do so in exceptional cases.[5]

1   HC 395, para 42. Visitors seeking leave to enter under the Approved Destination Status (ADS) Agreement with China will be granted leave to enter for a maximum period of 30 days: HC 395 para 56H, inserted by HC 486 from 5 April 2005. The IDI tell immigration officers to give holders of Council of Europe travel documents travelling without visas three months, but otherwise to grant six months unless the passport is endorsed with a visa for a specified period: IDI, Ch 2, s 1, para 2.6, 'Visitors: general guidance' (Aug 04). The DSP tell entry clearance officers that they should normally endorse for six months: DSP (07/03/03) 10.13.

2   *Visa Officer, Aden v Thabet* [1977] Imm AR 75.

3   HC 395, para 42. They are also normally subject to a condition prohibiting recourse to public funds, but this is not reflected in the rules. These conditions are imposed under the Immigration Act 1971, s 3(1)(c).

4   See Appendix 2 to the Immigration Rules HC 395, added by Cm 3953, May 1998.

5   HC 395, para 326(3), substituted by HC 194 from 4 February 2005.

Extension of stay as a visitor

9.19 Six months is, as a general rule, the maximum permitted leave which may be granted to a visitor.[1] A visitor who has been given less than six months on entry may, however, extend his or her visit up to the six-month period.[2] To obtain such an extension a visitor must continue to meet the requirements for a visit, in particular the maintenance and accommodation provisions and the ability to meet the cost of the return or onward journey. If these requirements continue to be met an extension may be granted,[3] but otherwise refusal is mandatory.[4] Where a visitor had leave for less than six months and seeks an extension which, if granted, would take him or her over the maximum, the Secretary of State should not refuse an extension outright but should consider granting leave up to the six month limit, and if this is refused there is a right of appeal.[5] Those caring for sick or disabled relatives may obtain extensions of stay under the carers' concession, which provides for the grant of three months' leave to remain in the first instance, and further leave of 12 months at a time if medical and social services' evidence warrants it.[6]

1   HC 395, para 44. However, 12 months' leave may have been given to special categories such as academic visitors, including postgraduate researchers sponsored by particular bodies, privately funded researchers, visiting lecturers, etc (IDI Ch 2, s 1, Annex B, para 1), and volunteers on archaeological excavations (IDI Ch 2, s 1, Annex B, para 3). For visitors under the ADS Agreement with China see 9.18 fn 1 above.
2   HC 395, para 44(ii). Visitors under the ADS Agreement with China may not extend their leave: HC 395, para 44(iii), inserted by HC 486 from 5 April 2005.
3   HC 395, para 45.
4   HC 395, para 46. But see fn 1 above. Persons in these categories may obtain extensions taking them over the six months' limit, and sometimes over the 12 months, outside the Rules.
5   *Wong* [1995] Imm AR 451. Refusal on the ground that the passenger seeks leave for a period greater than that permitted by the rules is not appealable: see Nationality, Immigration and Asylum Act 2002, s 88(2)(c).
6   The concession is applied to those caring for a patient suffering from terminal illness or from mental or physical disability. Leave to remain to care for a friend will be granted only in an emergency, where there is no-one else to provide care, and only for three months unless there are wholly exceptional circumstances warranting a further extension. Leave to remain to care for a relative should normally be granted for three months on the strict understanding that arrangements will be made for the patient's future care by a person not needing leave to enter outside the rules: see IDI Jun 01, Ch 17, s 2 ('Employment outside the rules'), which sets out the evidential requirements. See also *R v Secretary of State for the Home Department, ex p Zakrocki* [1996] COD 304.

Departure and return

9.20 A visit visa operates as leave to enter on each occasion on which the holder enters the UK during the period of its validity. The holder will be treated as having been granted six months' leave to enter beginning on the date of arrival where six months or more remain of the period of validity, and the period left if less than six months.[1] To operate as leave to enter, the entry clearance must be endorsed with any conditions to which it is subject.[2]

1   Immigration (Leave to Enter and Remain) Order 2000, SI 2000/1161, Art 4(1), (2).
2   SI 2000/1161, Art 3(3)(a).

Visitors in transit

9.21 Visitors who arrive in the UK in transit to another country are dealt with separately under the Immigration Rules and the IDI.[1] First, they must be in transit to a country outside the common travel area; secondly, they must have both the means and the intention of proceeding there at once; thirdly, they must be assured of entry there; and fourthly, they must intend and be able to leave the UK within 48 hours.[2] Passengers meeting these conditions will be given a leave not exceeding 48 hours with a prohibition on employment.[3] Otherwise leave is to be refused.[4] Forty-eight hours is the maximum permitted leave and any application for an extension beyond this period is to be refused.[5] Where a woman on a tour party was given 48 hours by an immigration officer who wished to treat her as a transit passenger, but did not make this clear in the leave stamp, the Tribunal held that she was to be treated as an ordinary visitor with a right to apply for an extension and, if necessary, to appeal against a refusal.[6] The IDI provide that visa requirements may be waived for air travellers with a confirmed flight within 24 hours of arrival, and for cruise passengers and others arriving by ship and leaving on the same ship within 24 hours.[7] The visa waiver concession does not apply to nationals of the countries specified in the Immigration (Passenger Transit Visa) Order 2003.[8] These nationals require a UK visa even when transiting airside without passing through the immigration control.[9]

1   HC 395, paras 47–50; IDI Jul 01, Ch 2, s 2, Annex D.
2   HC 395, para 47.
3   HC 395, para 48.
4   HC 395, para 49.
5   HC 395, para 50.
6   *Low v Secretary of State for the Home Department* [1995] Imm AR 435.
7   IDI Ch 2 s 2 Annex D; see also DSP (Mar 03) Ch 10. Visa nationals using the ship as a hotel and going ashore on successive days require a visa.
8   SI 2003/1185, as amended by SI 2003/2628, SI 2004/1304 and SI 2005/492. For countries specified in the Order and for the exemptions from transit visa requirements see 3.11 above. The IDI have not yet been amended to reflect the revocation of the 1993 Transit Visa Order in May 2003.
9   IDI, Ch 2, s 2, para 1.1.

Medical treatment

9.22 Under the Immigration Rules visitors may be admitted for private medical treatment at their own expense, provided that they meet the ordinary requirements of the visitor rule (no work or provision of services, no study at a maintained school, maintenance and accommodation and ability to meet the costs of the return or onward journey).[1] In the case of a passenger suffering from a communicable disease, the medical inspector must be satisfied that there is no danger to public health.[2] If required to do so, the passenger must be able to show that any proposed course of treatment is of finite duration and that he or she intends to leave the UK at the end of it,[3] but the passenger is not required to be precise about the length of it.[4] Before being admitted for medical treatment a passenger may be required to produce evidence of his or her medical condition, of the arrangements for consultation and treatment, the estimated costs, the likely duration and the availability of sufficient funds in the UK to meet the cost, and may be required to give an undertaking to this effect.[5] The IDI state that the treatment may be from a GP or alternative medical practitioner, but that leave granted for such treatment will not be extended beyond six months.[6] The reference in the Rules to consultation or treatment 'at his own expense' does not mean that the visitor must necessarily pay personally.[7] Nor is the availability of treatment in the passenger's own country a ground for refusing admission.[8] Where leave is granted it will normally be for a period not exceeding six months, subject to a condition prohibiting employment.[9] If the passenger cannot meet all the requirements of the Rules, leave is to be refused.[10]

[1]   HC 395, para 51(i), referring to para 41(iii)–(vii).
[2]   HC 395, para 51(ii).
[3]   HC 395, para 51(iii) and (iv).
[4]   See *Foon v Secretary of State for the Home Department* [1983] Imm AR 29 and *Onofriou* (2704).
[5]   HC 395, para 51(v).
[6]   IDI Dec 01, Ch 2, s 3, Annex F, para 6.
[7]   See *Foon v Secretary of State for the Home Department* [1983] Imm AR 29.
[8]   *Mohan v Entry Clearance Officer, Lahore* [1973] Imm AR 9.
[9]   HC 395, para 52.
[10] HC 395, para 53.

9.23 An extension of stay for a medical visit can only be granted if the requirements for entry continue to be met.[1] In addition, evidence must be produced from a registered medical practitioner, who holds an NHS consultant post, of satisfactory arrangements for private medical consultation or treatment and its likely duration; and, where treatment has already begun, its progress.[2] Patients must also be able to show that they have met any costs and expenses incurred in relation to their treatment in the UK out of the resources available to them,[3] and that they have sufficient funds available in the UK to meet further likely costs and intend to do so.[4] If sufficient evidence of these matters is produced, an extension of stay will normally be given.[5] If there is reason to believe the treatment will be at public expense or that the applicant does not intend to leave the UK at the end of the treatment,[6] or if insufficient evidence of the other matters is available, leave will be refused[7]. There is no provision in the Immigration Rules for the dependant of a person admitted for private medical treatment to be granted an extension of stay beyond the six-month period given for a visitor, but one may be given where, for example, someone is having fertility treatment.[8]

[1]   HC 395, para 54(i). A passenger admitted under the ADS Agreement with China (see 9.6 fn 4 above) may not be granted an extension of leave for medical treatment: para 54(v), inserted by HC 486 from 5 April 2005.
[2]   HC 395, para 54(ii). The IDI indicate that it is reasonable for Home Office caseworkers to scrutinise carefully the likely duration and success of, for example, fertility treatment which could have been going on for some years without success. It would be acceptable (with the applicant's consent) to approach the consultant direct to ask about the likelihood of eventual success of the treatment (IDI Dec 01, Ch 2, s 3, Annex F, para 2).
[3]   HC 395, para 54(iii).
[4]   HC 395, para 54(iv).
[5]   HC 395, para 55(vi).
[6]   See *Foon v Secretary of State for the Home Department* [1983] Imm AR 29 and *Onofriou* (2704).
[7]   HC 395, para 56.
[8]   IDI, Ch 2, s 3, Annex F, para 2.

NHS treatment

9.24 The Immigration Rules do not provide for persons to be granted leave for the sole purpose of receiving free treatment under the NHS, and normally entry clearance or leave to enter for this purpose will be refused.[1] There are exceptional arrangements for the admission of a handful of people each year from countries with which the UK has reciprocal arrangements.[2] Additionally, applications for leave to remain to complete a course of NHS treatment which has already begun will not be refused if it would clearly be unreasonable to require the applicant to leave the UK (eg because he or she was in hospital following an accident).[3]

1   IDI, Ch 2, s 3, Annex F.
2   See the National Health Service (Charges to Overseas Visitors) Regulations 1989, SI 1989/306, as amended by SI 2004/614; the IDI, Ch 2, s 3, Annex F, paras 3.4 and 3.7 contains lists of countries where a very small selection of residents or nationals may come to the UK for free NHS treatment; see also 13.203 below.
3   IDI, Ch 2, s 3, Annex F.

Visitors—switching categories

9.25 Visitors who wish to remain in the UK in order to do something else have quite limited options. They can switch from an ordinary visit to a medical or parent visit,[1] or they can apply for indefinite leave, if they are Gurkhas, foreign or Commonwealth citizens, who have seen service in the British armed forces.[2] But they cannot switch to other temporary categories such as trainee,[3] au pair[4] or working holidaymaker;[5] switching to student status is also difficult. Visitors may only become students if they do not come from one of the visa countries listed in Appendix 1 to the Immigration Rules, and even then their choice is limited to becoming a student nurse or being accepted for a degree-level or higher course or postgraduate medical or dental training.[6] People who wish to visit with a view to enrolling on a course or going to college need to obtain a prospective student visa before leaving home. A non-visa national who obtains entry as a visitor while harbouring an intention to study risks summary removal as an illegal entrant.[7] Specified nationals, ie those from the countries listed in Appendix 3 to the Immigration Rules, may not remain in the UK for more than six months without entry clearance, so may not switch to study which takes them over this limit.[8] Under the current Rules it is not possible for visitors to remain for employment,[9] as investors,[10] retired persons of independent means,[11] writers, composers, artists[12] or in business,[13] unless they are able to establish themselves in business under the relevant EC Association Agreements, which currently apply to Bulgarian and Romanian nationals.[14] It was thought that these nationals could establish themselves in business or self-employment without having to obtain entry clearance in that capacity, if, at least, they 'manifestly and clearly' satisfied the substantive requirements of the immigration rules,[15] but the recently amended rules say otherwise.[16] The position of Turkish visitors is much clearer, as they may take advantage of the 'standstill' clause of the Ankara Agreement to set up in business and that harks back to a time, before March 1980, when switching into business was permitted.[17]

1   HC 395, paras 54 and 56A.

2   HC 395, paras 276I (Gurkhas) and 276O (foreign and Commonwealth citizens), as inserted by HC 1112, 18 Oct 04.
3   HC 395, para 119(ii).
4   HC 395, para 92(i).
5   HC 395, para 98(i).
6   HC 395, paras 60(i) (as amended by Cm 6339 from September 2004) (students), 67(ii) (student nurses), 73, ID1 Dec 04, Ch 3, s 3, para 3.10. Transitional provisions enable non-visa national visitors to switch to studies below degree level if they entered the UK before 22 July 2004, or applied for student leave before 30 September 2004: IDI Ch 3, s 3, para 3.10.2. A visa national who comes in as a visitor cannot switch to student status and refusal of an extension is mandatory (*Okello v Secretary of State for the Home Department* [1995] Imm AR 269, CA).
7   See *Adesina v Secretary of State for the Home Department* [1988] Imm AR 442, CA; *Re Olusanya* [1988] Imm AR 117, DC; *R v Secretary of State for the Home Department, ex p Brakwah* [1989] Imm AR 366, QBD.
8   HC 395, Appendix 3, inserted by HC 1224 from 12 November 2003; see 3.8 above.
9   HC 395, paras 131(i) (work permit holders), 139(i), 147(i), 155(i), 164(i), 173(i), 181(i) (categories of permit-free employment).
10 HC 395, para 227(i).
11 HC 395, para 266(i).
12 HC 395, para 235(i).
13 HC 395, para 206(i).
14 HC 395, paras 211–223.
15 *R (on the application of Barkoci) v Secretary of State for the Home Department* Case C–257/99 [2001] INLR 152, at para 74, ECJ.
16 HC 395, paras 211–223 as amended by HC 523 on 1 May 2004. See 7.170 above.
17 See *R v Secretary of State for the Home Department, ex p Savas* [2000] INLR 398, ECJ; *R (on the application of Tum) v Secretary of State for the Home Department* [2004] EWCA Civ 788, [2004] 2 CMLR 1131 (this case has now gone to the ECJ on a reference from the HL on the Secretary of State's appeal; HC 82 (Control After Entry – EEC and non-Commonwealth Nationals, laid before Parliament on 25 January 1973) allowed switching to business and the no switching rule only came into effect under HC 394, laid before Parliament on 20 February 1980). See further 7.163 above.

9.26 There are further exceptions to the no-switching rule. Commonwealth citizens with a UK-born grandparent may stay to seek and take employment;[1] close relatives of persons settled in the UK may apply to remain with them;[2] and a visitor may apply for leave to remain as the unmarried partner of someone in the UK,[3] but not as a married partner.[4] Visitors who came to visit their close relatives in the UK may apply for indefinite leave, but clearly they must satisfy all the requirements regarding the admission of relatives for settlement. Because of the possibility of switching and the relative ease that a parent or parents over 65 have in meeting the requirements of the Immigration Rules, there is a danger of their being refused visit visas on suspicion that they may apply to switch. Those who do not wish to settle in the UK, or cannot be persuaded to by their family members in the UK, may thus suffer from pre-emptive action against application of this rule. Normally those seeking leave to remain in another capacity should have genuinely changed their mind since entry; otherwise there is a risk of the application being refused under the general considerations[5] or, worse still, of treatment as an illegal entrant.[6] Persons with visit leave may apply at any time for asylum[7] or for Humanitarian Protection or Discretionary Leave on human rights grounds.[8]

1   HC 395, para 189.
2   HC 395, paras 298(ii) (children generally), 306 (children born in UK), 314(xi) (adopted children), and 317, 318 (parents, grandparents and dependent relatives).

³ HC 395, para 295D(i), inserted by Cm 4851. The couple must already have been living together in a relationship akin to marriage for two years.
⁴ HC 395 para 284(i), as amended on 25 August 2003 by Cm 5949.
⁵ Eg under HC 395, para 322.
⁶ *Bugdaycay v Secretary of State for the Home Department* [1987] AC 514.
⁷ See chapter 12 below.
⁸ See chapter 8 above.

Appeals by visitors

9.27 Visitors refused leave to enter have no right of appeal (except on race discrimination, human rights or asylum grounds) unless they held a current entry clearance at the time of refusal,[1] and may not appeal against refusal of entry clearance (except on discrimination or human rights grounds) unless they are family visitors.[2] In addition, they have no right of appeal (except on discrimination, human rights or asylum grounds) if they are seeking entry for a period in excess of the Immigration Rules.[3] Visa holders may exercise their right of appeal without leaving the country.[4] Visitors refused an extension may appeal to an adjudicator, unless the variation asked for would result in the duration of their leave exceeding six months (in the case of a non-medical visit).[5] There is no right of appeal against refusal of an extension (except on discrimination, human rights or asylum grounds) if the visitor's leave has already exceeded the period permitted by the Immigration Rules,[6] even if the Secretary of State has a policy providing for extension beyond the usual maximum under the rules.[7] Refusal or cancellation of leave on conducive grounds by the Secretary of State in person or on his or her direction attracts rights of appeal as above, but to the Special Immigration Appeals Commission rather than to the Tribunal.[8]

¹ Nationality, Immigration and Asylum Act 2002, s 89(1)(a), (2), (3).
² Nationality, Immigration and Asylum Act 2002, s 90; see below.
³ Nationality, Immigration and Asylum Act 2002, s 88(1), (2)(c), (3).
⁴ Nationality, Immigration and Asylum Act 2002, s 92(3). However, as from 1 October 2004, there is no in-country appeal if the holder sought entry for a different purpose than that specified: s 92(3) as amended by Asylum and Immigration (Treatment of Claimants, etc) Act 2004, s 28.
⁵ Nationality, Immigration and Asylum Act 2002, s 88; HC 395, para 44.
⁶ *R v Immigration Appeal Tribunal, ex p Sam* [1996] Imm AR 272.
⁷ This is because there is a distinction between policy and rules, and leave exceeding the maximum permitted under the rules deprives the Tribunal of jurisdiction to hear an appeal. Considerations of whether the decision is 'in accordance with the law' under Nationality, Immigration and Asylum Act 2002, s 84(1)(e) do not therefore arise.
⁸ Nationality, Immigration and Asylum Act 2002, ss 97–98; Special Immigration Appeals Commission Act 1997, s 2(1).

9.28 An applicant who applied to enter the United Kingdom to visit a family member has the right to appeal against the refusal of an entry clearance.[1] A 'family visitor' is a person who applies for entry clearance to visit a spouse, father, mother son, daughter, grandfather, grandmother grandson, granddaughter, brother, sister, uncle, aunt, nephew, niece or first cousin, the father, mother, brother or sister of his or her spouse, the spouse of his or her son or daughter, his or her stepfather, stepmother, stepson, stepbrother or stepsister, or unmarried partner with whom he or she has lived for two of the last three years before the day on which his application for entry clearance was made.[2] It is not clear whether this covers adoptive relationships. Anyone not covered by the list would have a right of appeal on discrimination or human rights grounds only.[3] The right of appeal attaches only to refusal of entry clearance, not to the refusal of leave to enter in this capacity. Thus application for entry clearance is essential to obtain appeal rights. A fee used to be payable in order to exercise this right of appeal, but has now been abolished.

1   Nationality, Immigration and Asylum Act 2002, s 90.
2   Immigration Appeals (Family Visitor) Regulations 2003, SI 2003/518, reg 2(2). The government plans to restrict this appeal to papers only: *Controlling our borders: Making migration work for Britain: Five year strategy for asylum and immigration*, Cm 6472, Feb 2005, para 34. Such a move would deprive the Tribunal of the opportunity to hear the sponsor, who is often able to provide reassurance about the motives and duration of the proposed visit.
3   For appeals and judicial review see chapter 18.

9.29 Visitors who have no right of appeal against refusal of entry clearance or refusal of leave to enter or remain may apply for judicial review if they can show unfairness or an error of law by the immigration officer,[1] but those with a right of appeal should exercise it rather than seek judicial review.[2] Judicial review of refusal of leave to enter as a visitor may be pursued after an applicant has left the UK,[3] if it is not purely academic (ie because refusal might affect future plans to visit).

1   *R v Secretary of State for the Home Department, ex p Arjumand* [1983] Imm AR 123, QBD.
2   *R v Secretary of State for the Home Department, ex p Swati* [1986] 1 All ER 717, [1986] Imm AR 88, CA. This is so even if the appeal can only be exercised after departure.
3   In *R v Secretary of State for the Home Department, ex p Kekana* [1998] Imm AR 136 Potts J held that it was academic to pursue such an action where the applicant had already left the UK; in *R v Secretary of State for the Home Department, ex p Honegan* (10 April 1995, unreported), Tucker J held that it was not, and an application to set aside leave in *R v Secretary of State for the Home Department, ex p Dombaj* (CO 3150/1997) was dismissed by Owen J on 25 March 1998 (reported in *Legal Action* November 1998; the immigration officer's decision was quashed on 1 December 1998).

STUDENTS

9.30 The admission of students is dealt with in HC 395, paragraphs 57–87. These rules are separate from the educational rights given to EEA nationals and their families under EC law, which are touched on briefly in chapter 7.[1] The main point about overseas students is that they must be full-time and able to pay for their course and living expenses, and they must be seeking entry on a course with a registered education provider. Student nurses, graduates from British institutions, doctors, and dentists are allowed to switch into work permit employment[2] (or if they are science or engineering graduates on courses approved by the DfES, to remain to seek and take employment)[3] and although the rules still require them to intend to leave the UK at the end of their studies, in practice the requirement is waived.[4] All other students must intend to return home when their studies are complete.[5] The student rules cover ordinary students, student nurses,[6] postgraduate doctors and dentists and trainee GPs, prospective students and their spouses and children. Entry as a student requires acceptance for a course of study. Those whose plans are not so advanced or definite may, however, come as prospective students provided their intentions of studying are genuine and realistic.[7] The student rules, as we shall see, are fairly complicated, and, although non-visa nationals who are not specified nationals[8] do not require entry clearance, it is usually advisable, in order to avoid unnecessary difficulties at the airport and the possible waste of an academic year. Visa nationals require entry clearance whether they are coming as actual or prospective students. If they arrive without a visa, refusal of entry is mandatory[9]. Irrespective of the length of the course, a student visa should be issued where an applicant qualifies under the student provisions: a visit visa should not be issued simply because a course is only, for example, one week long.[10] There is, however, nothing to prevent a person who is given leave to enter as a visitor undertaking a short course of studies.

1 Once he or she has been in employment, an EEA migrant has a right to vocational training on the same conditions as UK nationals: Art 7(2) and (3) of Regulation 1612/68. Vocational training is given a wide definition: see *Gravier v City of Liège* 293/83 [1985] ECR 593, ECJ and *Blaizot v Université de Liège* 24/86 [1988] ECR 379, ECJ. EEA workers retain the right of residence as a worker, if they give up their job and undertake a course of study which is linked to their employment: *Lair v Universität Hanover* 39/86 [1988] ECR 3161, para 39. Spouses (of whatever nationality) have the same educational opportunities as the migrant workers, but their children have access to general education and can remain in the Member State, even if their parents have returned home: *Echternach v Minister van Onderwijs en Wetenschappen* [1989] ECR 723, ECJ. The principle of equality of access means students from EEA countries cannot be charged higher fees: *Forcheri v Belgium* 152/82 [1983] ECR 2323, ECJ.
2 HC 395 para 131A and B, inserted by Cmnd 5597, amended by HC 104: see 10.57 below.
3 HC 395 para 135R, inserted by Cm 6339.
4 DSP Mar 03, Ch 12, ss 5, 18.
5 HC 395, para 57.
6 HC 395, para 65ff confirms the position reflected in early Tribunal determinations that student nurses are classed as students and not as trainees: *Secretary of State for the Home Department v Oh* [1972] Imm AR 236; *Kulatilake v Secretary of State for the Home Department* [1992] Imm AR 257.
7 HC 395, para 82(i).
8 Ie, nationals of countries set out in Appendix 3 of HC 395: see para 6 as amended by HC 1224; see 3.8 above.
9 HC 395, para 320(5).
10 DSP Ch 12.

Ordinary students

9.31 The requirements to be met by an ordinary student are contained in paragraph 57 of HC 395. There are six main requirements, which we explain more fully below. First, students must have been accepted on a course of study to be provided by an organisation which is included on the DfES' register of Education and Training Providers, and is at a university or similar institution, a private college or a fee-paying school outside the maintained sector.[1] Secondly, the studies must be full-time and not consist of a collection of part-time courses at a number of educational establishments. Thirdly, children under 16 must be in full-time schooling meeting Education Acts requirements. Fourthly, students must, as a general rule, intend to leave at the end of their course of study. Fifthly, they must not intend to engage in business or to take work other than approved part-time or vacation jobs. Sixthly, they must be able to meet all their costs without having to work or have recourse to public funds. A student who meets all these requirements will be given leave to enter for an appropriate period, depending on the length of the student's course of study and means, and with a condition restricting, but not prohibiting, his or her freedom to take employment.[2] Unless each of the requirements of the rules is met, leave to enter as a student is to be refused.[3] Behind this detailed checklist of requirements, there is plenty of scope for immigration officials to make subjective assessments of students' abilities and intentions, and it is, therefore, important to look at a number of the issues thrown up by the requirements in more detail.

1   Courses at state schools do not qualify students for admission under the student rules. There are limited exceptions for exchange students: see 9.59 below.
2   HC 395, para 58. See below 9.51 for the duration of student leave.
3   HC 395, para 59.

Educational institution

9.32 From 1 January 2005, the institution at which the student proposes to study must be one which is on the Department for Education and Skills' Register of Education and Training Providers, and applications will be refused if the institution is not on the DfES Register.[1] There no transitional provisions to protect students who had enrolled before that date at schools or colleges which do not seek or obtain registration.[2] The Immigration Rules envisage acceptance on a course of study at three types of educational institution, which are referred to in somewhat obscure terms, and appear to incorporate meanings borrowed from education law. They are set out in the following paragraphs.

1   HC 395, para 57(i), substituted by HC 164 from 1 January 2005. The list of registered education and training providers is on the DfES website at www.dfes.gov.uk/providersregister.
2   See IDI Dec 04, Ch 3, s 3.4.

9.33 *Publicly funded institutions of further and higher education.*[1] Further and higher education are both defined by the Education Act 1996,[2] and are quite distinct types of education.[3] Learning and Skills Councils (in Wales, the Council for Education and Training, CETW) are responsible for arranging the provision of further education, including adult and community learning, which they or local education authorities may provide.[4] Institutions of further education for which the Learning and Skills Councils or CETW are responsible will count as publicly funded, although this is not spelt out anywhere in the Immigration Rules. The position of institutions of higher education is perhaps clearer. The former distinction between universities and polytechnics was abolished and a single funding structure, known as the Higher Education Funding Council for England and Wales, channels government money into universities.[5]

1   HC 395, para 57(i)(a).
2   'Higher education' means education provided by means of the following: (i) a course for further training of teachers or youth and community workers; (ii) a postgraduate course (including a higher degree course); (iii) a first degree course; (iv) a course for the diploma of higher education; (v) a course for Higher National Diploma or Higher National

Certificate of the Business and Technician Education Council, or the Diploma in Management Studies; (vi) a course for the Certificate in Education; (vii) a course in preparation for a professional examination at a higher level; (viii) a course providing education at a higher level 'whether or not in preparation for an examination': Education Reform Act 1988, s 120(1), Sch 6, paras 1, 2 and 3. 'Further education' means: (a) full-time and part-time education for persons over compulsory school age; and (b) organised leisure-time occupation provided in connection with the provision of such education: Education Act 1996, s 2(3)–(5) (as amended by the Education Act 2002, s 215(2), Sch 22, Pt 3).

³   Education Act 1996, s 2(3) (as amended).
⁴   Learning and Skills Act 2000, Pts I–III.
⁵   Further and Higher Education Act 1992, ss 62 and 63. See IDI Dec 04, Ch 3, s 3.4.2.

9.34 *Bona fide private education institutions which maintain satisfactory records of enrolment and attendance*[1] are private colleges such as secretarial colleges, language schools and private 'crammers' which may be institutions of further or higher education, but are not under local authority control. They also include British campuses of US universities offering US degrees and qualifications.[2] Because private colleges are not publicly accountable in the same way as the previous category,[3] entry clearance officers and immigration officers are given latitude to check their bona fides and see that they keep satisfactory records of enrolment and attendance.[4] To become a registered education provider, the institution will have demonstrated that it meets the requirements of the immigration rules by satisfying the DfES that, in addition to maintaining satisfactory records it provides courses which involve a minimum of 15 hours organised daytime study per week; ensures that a suitably qualified tutor is present during the hours of study to offer teaching and instruction to the students; offers courses leading to qualifications recognised by appropriate accreditation bodies; employs suitably qualified staff to provide teaching, guidance and support to the students; provides adequate accommodation, facilities, staffing levels and equipment to support the numbers of students enrolled at the institution and complies with the latest IND guidance on notification of absent students.[5] In addition, students attending such colleges usually have to satisfy stringent requirements as to the number of hours studied each week.[6]

¹   HC 395, para 57(i)(b), For special classes of student see 9.59 below.
²   IDI Dec 04, Ch 3, s 3, para 3.4.2.1.1. Degrees awarded by American universities in the UK which are validated at honours level by the British Open University Validation Service would be considered 'recognised', but holders of unvalidated degrees from UK campuses of US universities will not be permitted to switch into work permit employment: Ch 3, s 3, para 3.4.2.1.1.
³   Private providers may apply to the BAC (British Accreditation Council for Independent Further and Higher Education) for accreditation. English language schools may be accredited by the British Council under the English in Britain Accreditation Scheme, run in conjunction with the Association of English Language Schools (ARELS) and the British Association of State English Language Teachers (BASELT), which recognises all such schools which are members of ARELS or BASELT as efficient. All these accredited and recognised institutions should be accepted as bona fide by the Secretary of State: see IDI Mar 02, Ch 3, Annex C, paras 3–4.
⁴   HC 395, para 57(i)(b). See eg *R v Immigration Appeal Tribunal, ex p Idiaro* [1991] Imm AR 546, QBD (investigations into London private college whose principal was eventually jailed for fraud).
⁵   IDI Dec 04, Ch 3, s 3, para 3.4.2.3.
⁶   HC 395, para 57(ii)(b); see 9.36 below.

9.35 *Independent fee-paying schools outside the maintained sector*[1] include preparatory and public schools. But again the more the precise meaning must derive from terms used in education law. According to this,[2] an 'independent school' is a school at which full-time education is provided for five or more pupils of compulsory school age, or at least one pupil of that age for whom a statement is maintained under the Education Act 1996, s 324 or who is looked after by a local authority under the Children Act 1989, s 22 (whether or not such education is also provided for pupils under or over that age), not being a school maintained by a local education authority or a special school not maintained by a local education authority.[3] City Technology Colleges, City Colleges for the Technology of the Arts and Academies are not defined as 'maintained'[4] but according to the Home Office,[5] are publicly funded and so not 'independent' for the purpose of the Rules. The IDI include in the 'maintained sector' all publicly-funded schools, including maintained schools, voluntary aided schools, sixth form colleges attached to maintained schools, special schools and nursery schools (as well as the City Technology Colleges, City Colleges for the Technology of the Arts) and Academies.[6] Independent schools must be registered[7] and an unregistered school will not be regarded as an independent school for the purposes of the Rules.[8] 'Fee paying' describes the school rather than the parent, and a pupil on a free scholarship could presumably qualify for admission as a student under the Immigration Rules.

1   HC 395, para 57(i)(c).
2   A 'maintained school' means: (a) a community school; (b) a foundation school; (c) a voluntary school (either voluntary aided or voluntary controlled); (d) a community special school and (e) a foundation special school: Schools Standards and Framework Act 1998, s 20. 'Special schools' are defined as schools which are specially organised to make special educational provision for pupils with special educational needs and which are community special schools, foundation special schools or special schools not maintained but for the time being approved by the Secretary of State as special schools: Education Act 1996, s 337 (as substituted by the Schools Standards and Framework Act 1998, s 140, Sch 30, para 80).
3   Education Act 1996, s 463 (as substituted by the Education Act 2002, s 172).
4   Education Act 1996, s 482 (as substituted by the Education Act 2002, s 65(1)).
5   IDI Dec 04, Ch 3, s 3, para 3.4.2.6.
6   IDI Dec 04, Ch 3, s 3, para 3.4.2.6.
7   Education Act 2002, s 157ff.
8   IDI Dec 04, Ch 3, s 3, para 3.4.2.5.

Course of study

9.36 Students must have been accepted for a course of study at one of the three types of educational institution above.[1] The course enrolled on may be a degree course or any other full-time course, but the detailed requirements differ according to the type of institution and course attended. Students enrolled on a full-time, recognised degree course at publicly funded institutions of further and higher education do not need to show that the course will involve any particular number of hours' study per week.[2] Similarly, students over 16 attending an independent fee-paying school may be enrolled on any full-time course of study,[3] but if the child is under 16, the course must meet the requirements of the Education Act 1996.[4] Children under five attending nursery or pre-school classes do not qualify for leave to enter or remain as students because the 1996 Act does not cover pre-school education.[5] Acceptance by a university on a full-time degree course or as a pupil at an independent fee-paying school will be sufficient to qualify, without any need to investigate the details of the particular course or the arrangements for attendance at lectures and tutorials. The IDI indicate that the same considerations apply to those following a degree course at a bona fide private education institution where the degree will be awarded by a recognised university, including the Open University.[6] All other students must meet the requirement to spend at least 15 hours per week in organised daytime study. Such students may not enrol on a collection of part-time courses at a number of establishments to make up their 15 hours. They must enrol at a single institution and study a single subject or directly related subjects.[7] Night-time or weekend study will not qualify,[8] but organised classes of less than 15 hours, supplemented by supervised private study which brings the total up to 15 hours, may do.[9] In *Entry Clearance Officer, Lagos v Amusu*[10] the Tribunal allowed an appeal by a journalism student whose course was primarily by correspondence but involved outside assignments, projects and tutorials estimated by the school to total 15 hours a week, primarily because of the appellant's proven interest in journalism and because a great deal of study was required to obtain the diploma at the end of the course. But in *Re SH (Pakistan)* the Tribunal held that a course involving 16 hours' study per week of which six hours was tuition, six hours independent study, three hours clinical practice and one hour of supervision did not meet the requirement of 15 hours.[11]

1   HC 395, para 57(i). A conditional acceptance may be insufficient: see *Chinwo v Secretary of State for the Home Department* [1985] Imm AR 74; *Yovsani* (3181).
2   HC 395, para 57(ii)(a). An Open University course with modules requiring 21 hours of study per week does not, however, constitute such a course: *Kagunya* (L36) [2000] 6 ILD No 1 at p 36.
3   HC 395, para 57(ii)(c).
4   HC 395, para 57(iii). The rules refer to the Education Act 1944, which was repealed by the 1996 Act. The Education (Independent School Standards) Regulations 2003, SI 2003/1910 (England) and SI 2003/3234 (Wales), made under the Education Act 2002, s 157, set out detailed standards for independent schools, and the Secretary of State for Education and Skills or the National Assembly for Wales can de-register a school which does not comply: Education Act 2002 s 165.
5   IDI Dec 04, Ch 3, s 3 para 3.19.1.
6   IDI Dec 04, Ch 3, s 3 para 3.11.1. But in *Kagunya* [2000] 6 ILD no 1 at p 36, an Open University course requiring 21 hours of study per week was not accepted as a full-time degree course. The DSP state at para 12.15 that correspondence courses at the OU do not qualify, but that certain postgraduate courses there do. The Tribunal held in *Re SH (Pakistan)* [2004] UKIAT 00211 that an MA course at a private university requiring considerable independent study did not qualify because the student was not required to attend for 15 hours per week.
7   HC 395, para 57(ii)(b). In *Koltaveesh* (19924) (29 November 1999, unreported), the Tribunal found that although the subjects were directly related, some were in reality evening classes, so the aggregate did not reach the requisite 15 hours of organised daytime study.
8   *R v Immigration Appeal Tribunal, ex p Idiaro* [1991] Imm AR 546, QBD. Classes starting at or after 6 pm, and weekend classes, will not be counted, although classes beginning in the afternoon and continuing after 6 pm may be acceptable: IDI, Ch 3, s 3, para 3.11.3.
9   *Awosika v Secretary of State for the Home Department* [1989] Imm AR 35; *Aguirre* (TH/3477/95) (7 January 2000, unreported).
10   [1974] Imm AR 16.
11   *Re SH (Pakistan)* fn 6 above.

9.37 Some arrangements for tuition are so vague that they do not qualify. In *Kpoma v Secretary of State for the Home Department*[1] it was suggested that to constitute a course of study, there must be something more than a coaching scheme, which is supplementary to some other main field of endeavour, and it must be a course which has a termination point and not one which could be of indefinite length. In *Ex p Kharrazi*[2] the Court of Appeal held that a 'full-time course of study' could include such full-time course of study as a boy of 12 might reasonably expect to follow through to its conclusion (ie the attainment of a degree), even though he had not at that stage been guaranteed a place at a university. It covered not only the course of study for which the prospective student had been accepted, but a coherent and definite educational proposal of more than one course of study which was reasonably capable of being carried out by him or her. Thus arrangements to go to a preparatory school followed by a public school might well be a full-time course of study, since although they would require separate arrangements they would be part of a coherent whole.

1   [1973] Imm AR 25.
2   *R v Chief Immigration Officer, Gatwick Airport, ex p Kharrazi* [1980] 3 All ER 373, [1981] 1 WLR 1396, CA.

Ability and intention

9.38 The immigration authority (the entry clearance officer or the immigration officer on arrival) may scrutinise the applicant's ability and intention to follow the course on which he or she is enrolled.[1] At the entry stage, an immigration officer may have regard to the adequacy of the applicant's qualifications,[2] and inability to converse in English may be relevant if the applicant is proposing immediate study of a complicated subject.[3] However, immigration officers should not normally attempt to second-guess decisions by colleges of enrolment as to the student's ability to follow the course.[4] Later on, it will become easier to assess ability, as students progress and pass or fail examinations.[5]

1   HC 395, para 57(ii).
2   *R v Secretary of State for the Home Department, ex p Bhambra* [1985] Imm AR 28, QBD.
3   *R v Secretary of State for the Home Department, ex p Ozkurtulus* [1986] Imm AR 80, QBD; *Entry Clearance Officer, Karachi v Ahmad (Zafar)* [1989] Imm AR 254.
4   The previous IDI (Dec 01, Ch 3, Annex A) indicated that where an immigration officer was doubtful about a student's ability to follow the course, the principal of the school or college should be contacted and asked to make an assessment. This guidance is not repeated in the current IDI, although immigration officers are still entitled to assess students' ability to follow their chosen course.
5   See 'Extensions of stay' 9.52 below.

Intention to leave

9.39 Those seeking entry for courses that lead to the award of a degree or equivalent, student nurses, postgraduate doctors and dentists in practice no longer have to demonstrate an intention to leave the UK on the completion of their studies,[1] although the immigration rules still require that they do so. For all other students however the requirement that they will only be admitted if they intend to leave the UK on completion of their studies is intended to emphasise that studying in the UK is not the stepping stone to a future career and settlement in this country. However, the 'intention to leave' clause is not the only way in which immigration law and the Immigration Rules attempt to effect this policy, since checks are made on the student's progress when leave has to be renewed,[2] and there are sanctions for any student who steps out of line. In terms of enforcing an effective immigration control the 'intention to leave' clause is unnecessary, ineffective (since the real evaders will keep quiet about their true intentions) and unfair, disqualifying merely the innocent or naïve.

[1]   Because they are eligible to switch into work permit employment (or in the case of science and engineering graduates) to remain to seek employment after qualification: HC 395 para 131A, 131B, 131C (inserted by Cm 5597, amended by HC 104 and Cm 6339): see IDI Dec 04, Ch 3, s 3, para 3.18.2; DSP 12.5, 12.6, 12.18.

[2]   Although the IDI Ch 3, s 3, para 3.18.3 state that after-entry inquiries as to intention need not be made except in cases where there is reason to believe the applicant does not intend to go home, eg if he or she is an unsuccessful asylum applicant, an applicant who has previously been refused in another capacity or one who appears to be moving from course to course without any intention of bringing his or her studies to a close. The DSP at 12.17 point out that for entry clearance, it is the student's intention on entry which is important.

9.40 The Rule is satisfied by an intention to leave at the end of the whole of the student's studies, and he or she does not have to intend to leave at the end of the particular course upon which the student is enrolled.[1] So an intention to progress from preparatory school to university does not fall foul of the Rule.[2] An intention to do vocational training or even an apprenticeship following academic studies may also be within the Rule.[3] An intention conditional upon there being no change of circumstances might also satisfy the Immigration Rules.[4] Harbouring a wish to gain work experience at the end of studies, if permitted to do so, does not necessarily disentitle the student from continuing his or her studies.[5] An application for settled status in another capacity is likely to result in refusal under the Rule, but it all depends on the facts.[6]

[1]   HC 395, para 57(iv); *R v Chief Immigration Officer, Gatwick Airport, ex p Kharrazi* [1980] 3 All ER 373, [1981] 1 WLR 1396, CA; *Fuller (Celie)* [2002] UKIAT 02814.

[2]   *Kharrazi* above.

[3]   *Patel v Immigration Appeal Tribunal* [1983] Imm AR 76, CA.

[4]   *R v Immigration Appeal Tribunal, ex p Perween Khan* [1972] 3 All ER 297, [1972] Imm AR 268, QBD.

[5]   *R v Immigration Appeal Tribunal, ex p Shaikh* [1981] 3 All ER 29, [1981] 1 WLR 1107, QBD.

[6]   *Patel v Immigration Appeal Tribunal* [1983] Imm AR 76. But in *Oduyemi* (17116) a refusal was quashed because the Home Office had wrongly relied on the existence of a relationship which had in fact broken down.

Proving intention

9.41 The importance attached to a student's intentions is matched by the difficulty in proving what a person's intention is. Statements of intention are not always reliable or to be taken at face value.[1] They may represent mere aspiration or wishful thinking rather than firm and settled intention,[2] a distinction recognised by the Tribunal and the High Court.[3] A conditional intention to return is not necessarily fatal.[4] In the absence of direct evidence of intention much will rest on the drawing of inferences. The Tribunal has been careful to warn that inferences must be drawn only from the evidence and that mere suspicion is not enough.[5] The IDI draw a distinction between on-entry and after-entry cases, indicating that in the former case, immigration officers may look carefully at the cost of the studies and availability of suitable courses in the country of residence to ascertain whether the enterprise is 'reasonable to a person of the applicant's family, social and education background'.[6] Where a student is undertaking short courses, the immigration and appellate authorities look for evidence of related employment prospects in the student's own country.[7]

1   The IDI, Dec 04, Ch 3, s 3, para 3.18.3, states that 'any student who expresses the wish to remain in the UK beyond his (sic) studies should not be refused without the opportunity to clarify his intentions'.
2   *Entry Clearance Officer, Lagos v Sobanjo* [1978] Imm AR 22, where, despite recognising the difficulties of deciding whether a young appellant's statements should be taken as firm and settled, the Tribunal refused the appeal of a 15-year-old Nigerian girl who had told the entry clearance officer that she wanted to study for eight years in this country and then stay on and work. Contrast *Nakawesa* (3043), where it was held that expressing a hope of remaining after the end of studies does not preclude an intention to leave.
3   *Entry Clearance Officer, Hong Kong v Lai* [1974] Imm AR 98; *R v Immigration Appeal Tribunal, ex p Shaikh* [1981] 3 All ER 29, [1981] 1 WLR 1107; in *Masood v Immigration Appeal Tribunal* [1992] Imm AR 69, CA Glidewell LJ said a wish only became an intention when there was some reasonable prospect of its being fulfilled (at 78).
4   *Sivasubramanian* (13174); *Mdawini* (G0039) IAS 1998 Vol 1 No 11.
5   *Entry Clearance Officer, New Delhi v Bhambra* [1973] Imm AR 14; *Murgai v Entry Clearance Officer, New Delhi* [1975] Imm AR 86.
6   IDI Dec 04, Ch 3, s 3, para 3.18.1.
7   'It would be appropriate to ask about his [sic] job opportunities in his country and the material benefits to be gained from the course and to weigh this against the cost of the course which may represent the expenditure of a large sum of money to a person or family of low income': IDI Dec 04, Ch 3, s 3, para 3.18.1. See also *Goffar v Entry Clearance Officer, Dacca* [1975] Imm AR 142; *Islam v Entry Clearance Officer, Dacca* [1974] Imm AR 83; *Ghosh v Entry Clearance Officer, Calcutta* [1976] Imm AR 60; *R v Secretary of State for the Home Department, ex p Mohotty* [1996] Imm AR 256, QBD. Guaranteed employment in the student's own country is not necessary: *Oni* (15886) IAS 1998 Vol 1 No 8. After entry inquiries into intention to leave are not generally necessary; see 9.39 fn 2 above.

Prospective students

9.42 Students who are not yet enrolled on a course can obtain entry clearance and admission as prospective students.[1] To obtain leave in this capacity, prospective students must be able to satisfy the immigration authorities that: (i) they have genuine and realistic intentions of studying in the UK[2] within six months of their date of entry; (ii) they intend to leave the UK on completion of their studies or on the expiry of their leave to enter if they do not qualify for further stay as an ordinary student or a student nurse; and (iii) they can, without working and without recourse to public funds, meet the costs of their intended course and of their own maintenance and accommodation and that of any dependants while making arrangements to study and during the course. They may then be admitted for a period not exceeding six months with a condition prohibiting employment.[3] Unless each of the three requirements is met, the prospective student's application will be refused.[4] If less than six months' leave is given, prospective students can obtain an extension to give them more time to find a college or school place, but six months is the maximum leave in this category and they cannot extend it beyond this time.[5]

At all times the prospective student must show 'genuine and realistic intentions' of studying, a phrase to which we shall return below.

1 HC 395, para 82.
2 On a course of study meeting the requirements of student or student nurse admission: HC 395, para 82.
3 HC 395, para 83.
4 HC 395, para 84.
5 HC 395, paras 85–87.

Genuine and realistic intentions

9.43 Satisfying an entry clearance officer or immigration officer about 'genuine and realistic' intentions is still necessary in those cases where a prospective student is unable to fulfil all the requirements for student admission.[1] An intention will not be 'realistic' if there is an obvious lack of correspondence between the student's previous attainments and the nature of the course proposed and its benefits to the student in terms of future job prospects are uncertain,[2] but will be realistic if the student shows that his or her educational qualifications are acceptable to the proposed college.[3] In *Alexander v Immigration Appeal Tribunal*[4] the House of Lords equated 'genuine and realistic' intentions with the requirement that the student applicant is able and intends to follow a full-time course of study. A student who was found not to be able to follow a course could not be said to have had realistic intentions of so doing.[5] Where an entry clearance officer has assessed these matters and granted a visa, it is not for the immigration officer to go over the same ground again at the point of entry.[6] There is even less cause to do so now that entry clearance stands as leave to enter.[7]

1 HC 395, para 82.
2 *Virdee v Secretary of State for the Home Department* [1972] Imm AR 215.
3 *Sharma* [1972] Imm AR 219n. See further *Puri v Secretary of State for the Home Department* [1972] Imm AR 21; *Entry Clearance Officer, New Delhi v Bhambra* [1973] Imm AR 14; *Islam v Entry Clearance Officer, Dacca* [1974] Imm AR 83; *R v Immigration Appeal Tribunal, ex p Khan* [1975] Imm AR 26, DC; *Khan (SGH) v Entry Clearance Officer, Karachi* [1975] Imm AR 64.
4 [1982] 2 All ER 766, [1982] 1 WLR 1076.
5 *R v Secretary of State for the Home Department, ex p Bhambra* [1985] Imm AR 28.
6 *Immigration Officer, Gatwick v Pattuwearachchi* [1991] Imm AR 341.
7 Immigration (Leave to Enter and Remain) Order 2000, SI 2000/1161, Art 4(3).

Student nurses

9.44 For the purpose of the Immigration Rules the term 'student nurse' means a person accepted for training as a student nurse or midwife leading to a registered nursing qualification; or an overseas nurse or midwife who has been accepted on an adaptation course leading to registration as a nurse within the UK Central Council for Nursing, Midwifery and Health Visiting.[1] To qualify for entry student nurses must fulfil six requirements.[2] First, they must come within the above definition of a student nurse. Secondly, they must have been accepted on a course of study in a recognised nursing educational establishment offering a recognised nursing training. Thirdly, acceptance must not have been obtained by misrepresentation. Fourthly, they must be able and intend to follow the course. Fifthly, they must not intend to engage in business or take employment except in connection with the training course. As a concession outside the Rules, however, before they start the course, student nurses and midwives may work at the hospitals where they are to be trained, for a maximum of eight weeks.[3] Sixthly, they must have sufficient funds to meet all their accommodation and maintenance expenses without engaging in business or taking employment (except in connection with the training course) or having recourse to public funds. Nursing students have now been brought into line with all other students in higher education, and are not eligible for an NHS bursary (save for students who started a course before November 2001), unless they have been ordinarily resident in the British Islands throughout the three years preceding the start date, are settled in the UK and are ordinarily resident in the UK.[4] As a result enquires will now be made to ensure that all student nurses have sufficient means to support and accommodate themselves and any dependants, where no bursary is held.[5] If one or more of these requirements cannot be met, the application to come as a student nurse will be refused.[6] When leave to enter is given this is usually for the duration of the training course with a restriction on the freedom to take employment.[7] Although the rules require an intention to leave the UK at the end of the studies, student nurses (including those on supervised practice) are now eligible to switch to work permit employment once they have qualified, and so intention to leave the UK should not be a consideration in their entry clearance applications.[8] However, nurses wishing to do post-registration courses will not be granted leave to remain as student nurses, but will need to obtain work permits or training and work experience (TWES) permits.[9]

[1] HC 395, para 63. The IDI Dec 04, Ch 3, s 5, para 5.10 gives details of nursing courses and qualifications. Note that the IDI in relation to student nurses are in the process of updating. An 'adaptation' course is now known as 'supervised practice', and generally lasts between 3–12 months: see DSP 12.5.
[2] HC 395, para 64.
[3] IDI Ch 3, s 5, para 5.6.
[4] IDI Ch 3, s 5, para 5.6, para 5.11; DSP 12.5.
[5] IDI Ch 3, s 5, para 5.6, para 5.11; DSP Ch 12.5.
[6] HC 395, para 66.
[7] HC 395, para 65.
[8] IDI Ch 3, s 5, para 5.6, 5.2.1; DSP 12.5. Switching to work permit employment is permitted by HC 395 para 131B (inserted by Cm 5597).
[9] IDI Ch 3, s 5, para 5.6, 5.10.3; DSP 12.5.

Postgraduate doctors and dentists

9.45 To become a fully registered doctor in the UK, a medical student must not only pass the necessary exams[1] but also have worked as a house officer or in approved medical practice for 12 months.[2] There is no similar requirement for dentists,[3] but graduate doctors and dentists may both wish to spend time training for further qualifications at basic or higher specialist level. Although both these situations are clearly in the nature of employment training, the Immigration Rules make provision for them under the student rules. There are two situations where a postgraduate doctor or a dentist may qualify for a period of training under the student rules. First there is the graduate from a medical school,[4] eligible for provisional or limited registration with the General Medical Council, who intends to undertake pre-registration house officer employment for up to 12 months, to be eligible for full registration.[5] He or she must not have spent more than 12 months in aggregate in such employment.[6] Secondly, there is the doctor or dentist, eligible for full or limited registration with the General Medical Council or the General Dental Council, who intends to undertake postgraduate training in a hospital, the community health services, or both.[7] In both cases the rules require that the graduate doctor or dentist must intend to leave the UK on completion of the training period, although, now that the rules permit switching to work permit employment, the 'intention to leave' requirement is in practice waived.[8] In addition they must be able to maintain and accommodate themselves and any dependants without recourse to public funds.[9] Doctors sponsored for postgraduate training under the Overseas Doctors' Training Scheme[10] or by the British Council, the World Health Organization or the Commonwealth Scholarship Foundation should be admitted without further inquiry on their training or registration.[11] Where the graduate doctor or dentist meets the requirements of the Immigration Rules leave will be granted for a period not exceeding 12 months (for pre-registration house officer employment)[12] or three years (for post-graduate training in hospital or community health services or both).[13] Unless each of the requirements is met the application will fail.[14] An extension of leave may be granted both to house officers and to those undergoing postgraduate training in a hospital or community health services.[15] In the latter (post-registration) category, an extension of leave is contingent on evidence of satisfactory progress, including the passing of any relevant examinations.[16] In the case of a pre-registration house officer, 12 months is the maximum time to be spent in such employment and no extension in this category beyond that period will be given.[17] In the case of postgraduate medical and dental hospital or community health service training, three years is the maximum period which will be given and no more than four years in aggregate may be spent in senior house officer basic specialist training, or equivalent.[18] Those engaged in higher specialist training (specialist registrar or equivalent grades) may be granted extensions of up to three years at a time without any maximum limit.[19] Graduates from medical schools abroad may enter the UK to take their Professional and Linguistic Assessment Board (PLAB) test, for a period of six months extendable on application to a maximum of 18 months, under the visitor rules (see 9.7 above), and if successful, may seek to remain in postgraduate training, or to undertake a clinical attachment, or as a work permit holder or under the highly skilled migrant programme.[20] A period of stay of up to 12 months is available under the rules for a clinical attachment or as a dental observer, for graduates from medical or dental schools.[21]

---

[1]   This means obtaining a primary UK qualification (the equivalent of a degree), and passing the qualifying examination Medical Act 1983, ss 3 (substituted by SI 1996/1591) and 4 (amended by SI 2000/1841).

[2]   The requirements are that the doctor must have been engaged for a period prescribed by regulations in employment in a resident medical capacity in one or more approved hospitals, approved institutions or approved medical practice, and have obtained an appropriate certificate from his or her examining body: Medical Act 1983 (as amended by SI 2002/3135, National Health Service (Primary Care) Act 1997, s 35), ss 10, 11. The Medical Act 1950 (Period of Employment as House Officers) Regulations Approval Order in Council 1952, SI 1952/2050 prescribes a period of 12 months. These regulations have

effect as if made under the Medical Act, 1983, ss 10 and 11. Special provision is made for eligible specialists and qualified general practitioners from abroad to be registered without fulfilling these requirements: see Medical Act 1983 s 21A (inserted by SI 2002/3135).

3   A person who is a graduate or licentiate in dentistry of one of the dental authorities is entitled to be registered in the dentists' register, subject to satisfying the registrar as to good character and so forth. See Dentists Act 1984, s 15; 30 *Halsbury's Laws* (4th edn) para 320ff.

4   The rules no longer require that it be a UK medical school. The IDI Aug 04, Ch 3 s 6, Annex J, give details of the General Medical Council requirements for provisional, limited and full registration. Graduates of EEA medical schools may be granted limited registration, and doctors qualifying at certain medical schools in Australia, Hong Kong, New Zealand, Singapore, South Africa and the West Indies may qualify for full registration (see fn 2 above).

5   HC 395, para 70(i)(a), substituted by HC 104, on 26 Nov 02.

6   HC 395, para 70(i)(a) (as substituted).

7   HC 395, para 70(i)(b) (as substituted). If there is doubt that a doctor or dentist is eligible for full or limited registration with the General Medical Council or General Dental Council but all other requirements are met, leave to enter should be granted for six months pending production of the registration certificate: IDI Ch 3, s 6, para 2.3.

8   HC 395, para 70(ii) as substituted. The IDI Ch 3, s 6 also emphasise this requirement, although the DSP indicate (at 12.6) that since postgraduate doctors, dentists and GPs could be eligible to switch to work permit employment (permitted by HC 395, para 131B, inserted by Cm 5597), intention to leave the UK should not be a consideration in their entry clearance applications.

9   HC 395, para 70(iii) as substituted. For the definition of public funds see para 6; see chapter 3 above.

10 Participating bodies include the Royal Colleges of Surgeons, Physicians, Anaesthetists and Psychiatrists.

11 IDI Ch 3, s 6, Annex J.

12 HC 395, para 71(a) as substituted.

13 HC 395, para 71(b) as substituted.

14 HC 395, para 72 as substituted.

15 HC 395, paras 73–75, as substituted.

16 HC 395, para 73(i)(b)(2) as substituted.

17 On rare occasions extensions beyond 12 months may be granted exceptionally: IDI Aug 04, Ch 3, s 6, Annex J.

18 Intervals for pregnancy, or sickness between training should normally be included in the four-year period, but time spent as a student, on clinical attachment or as a pre-registration house officer should be disregarded, as should periods abroad or GP training with a Training and Work Experience Permit (TWES): IDI Ch 3, Annex J para 3.

19 IDI Ch 3, s 6, Annex J.

20 HC 395, para 75A–F, inserted by HC 346 from 15 March 2005. See IDI Ch 3, s 7 (Mar 05). Transitional provisions allow doctors who entered the UK as visitors before that date specifically to take the test to be granted extensions up to the maximum of 18 months allowed under the rules and to benefit from the new switching provisions: IDI Ch 3, s 7), para 1.2.

21 HC 395, para 75G–M as inserted. The rule does not require the studies to have been undertaken in the UK. Clinical attachments may also be undertaken by successful PLAB examinees, and by doctors and dentists in the UK as work permit holders: para 75K. The post must be unpaid and involve observation only. The general requirements of the visit rules for visitors (see 9.7 above) must be complied with, except for the intention to leave, which is in the alternative to the grant of leave for further training or work as a doctor or dentist: para 75G(iii), 75K(iv). See also IDI Mar 05, Ch 3, s 8. Transitional arrangements benefit those admitted as visitors before the rule change for similar purposes: IDI Ch 3, s 8 para 1.2.

Spouses and children of students and prospective students

9.46 Spouses and children under 18 of a person admitted or allowed to remain as a student or prospective student[1] are to be given leave to enter in line, if they satisfy the requirements for leave to enter or remain. The rules do not currently require entry clearance (except for visa nationals and specified nationals).[2] A spouse may be admitted if the couple are married, the marriage is subsisting and the couple intend living with each other as husband and wife during the student's stay. There must be adequate provision for maintenance and accommodation of the couple and any dependants without recourse to public funds. The spouse may be permitted to take employment if the period of leave granted is 12 months or more,[3] but if not must not intend to seek it, and there must be an intention to leave the UK at the end of any period of leave granted.[4] An unmarried child of a student or prospective student qualifies for admission if he or she has not formed an independent family unit and is not leading an independent life, is under 18 or has leave to enter or remain in the same capacity,[5] can and will be maintained and accommodated adequately without recourse to public funds and will not stay in the UK beyond any period of leave granted to the child's parent.[6] The children of a student may work if admitted for 12 months or more. Where the student is on a short course and the period of leave granted is less than 12 months, the spouse and children will not be able to work. Clearly the ability of the spouse to work is a very important factor and may be crucial to the student's continued ability to study and to fulfil the maintenance and accommodation provisions of the Immigration Rules.[7]

[1] Under HC 395, paras 57–75 or 82–87: see paras 76–80. This includes spouses and children of student nurses and of postgraduate doctors and dentists.
[2] See 9.30 text and fn 8 above.
[3] Or if it would have been but for delay in the grant of leave because of queueing and processing times: IDI Dec 04, Ch 3, s 4, para 4.4.
[4] HC 395, paras 76–78, as amended by Cm 4851.
[5] This covers a student's child who was under 18 when first admitted with or joining the student, and is now over 18 but still lives with the family and should not be disqualified and required to leave the UK.
[6] HC 395, paras 79, 80, as amended by Cm 4851. Children may go to state schools while their parent is studying here, but will be expected to leave or to switch to private education when the parent's studies are complete. But children may be granted a short period of leave to finish a school year or take an important examination after a parent's studies are complete: IDI, Ch 3, s 4, paras 4.6–4.7.
[7] The IDI used to state that a spouse's income could be taken into account for this purpose on an application to extend student leave (Nov 00, Ch 3, Annex M) but the current version omits this. However, it seems a matter of common sense.

Registration with the police

9.47 Commonwealth students are not required to register with the police, but foreign nationals[1] admitted for more than six months, including the foreign spouse or child over 16 of such a student, will be required to register.[2]

[1] See Appendix 2 to HC 395.
[2] HC 395, para 325(ii) and (iii).

Students and work

9.48 Leave to enter or remain as a student is subject to a condition restricting employment,[1] which should be distinguished from the condition prohibiting employment imposed on prospective students.[2] Prospective students, in common with others subject to a condition prohibiting employment, may never work while they remain in this category. Students with a restriction on employment may take any part-time employment (up to 20 hours a week) in term-time, and full-time employment in vacations, without obtaining individual permission from a Job centre or the relevant government Department[3] Some may do full-time work, such as students doing sandwich courses (with a work placement approved by the institution providing the course) or internships, which last up to three months and are paid at a rate comparable with those for resident workers.[4] They may also work full-time on completion of the course, during extant student leave (for example, while waiting for examination results).[6] Graduates of medical schools may take up employment as pre-registration house officers for up to 12 months and doctors and dentists can do postgraduate training in hospitals or community health services for an aggregate of up to four years.[5] Nurses and midwives may accept employment in connection with their training.[6] Leave to enter or remain is only granted if the student or student nurse intends to abide by these Rules.[7]

1 HC 395, paras 58, 61. The stamp in the passport will now read '... work and any changes must be authorised'.
2 HC 395, paras 83 and 86.
3 HC 395, para 57(v) states that consent of the Secretary of State is needed, but this (misleadingly) can only refer to general and not individual consent. The official leaflet *International Students Working in the UK* states: 'You no longer require permission from a Job Centre to take work in the UK and you do not need individual permission from the Department for Education and Skills or Work Permits (UK) for a sandwich or internship placement.' See also DSP Ch 12.19. A student did not cease to be a student because his attendance fell below 15 hours per week, and the Secretary of State could not remove him for breach of conditions because he was in part-time work: *R (on the application of Zhou) v Secretary of State for the Home Department* [2003] EWCA Civ 51, [2003] INLR 211.
4 See IDI Dec 04, Ch 3, s 3, para 3.16.
5 HC 395, paras 70–75; see 9.33 above.
6 HC 395, para 64(v).
7 HC 395, paras 57(v), 64(v).

9.49 Students and student nurses may not engage in business,[1] but the question considered by the Court of Appeal in *Ayoola*,[2] whether students are permitted to transact business, is still open. Our view is that unless clearly prohibited from doing so by the Immigration Rules, they may. Conditions imposed by section 3(1) of the Immigration Act 1971 apply only to employment or occupation, and transacting business is not, in our view, an occupation until it crosses the dividing line into engaging in business.[3] In *Strasburger v Secretary of State for the Home Department*[4] the Tribunal held that the sale by a student of her artwork was not to be regarded as a breach of a condition not to engage in business. Provided a student complied with the requirements of the student rules, the fact that he or she sold the occasional picture, or indeed all that he or she produced, could be disregarded. Spouses and children of students are admitted without any employment restriction unless given less than 12 months' leave,[5] and may therefore obtain full-time year-round work without requiring anyone's consent.

1 HC 395, para 57(v), 64(v). This Rule confirms the Tribunal decision in *Durojaiye v Secretary of State for the Home Department* [1991] Imm AR 307.
2 *Ayoola v Secretary of State for the Home Department* [1992] Imm AR 170, CA.

³ See the distinction drawn in connection with the visitor rules, HC 395 para 40.
⁴ [1978] Imm AR 165.
⁵ HC 395, paras 77, 80.

Adequate means

9.50 Students must show that they have adequate means to pay for the course and their accommodation and maintenance costs. Applications may be lost simply because adequate documentary evidence of means has not been produced. Tribunals have indicated a willingness to accept post-decision evidence of means, particularly if this is the only outstanding issue on a student's entry.[1] Evidence of means should be substantiated by production of bank statements, wage slips, employers' letters or similar primary documentary evidence showing an ability to meet the necessary bills.[2] Vague, unsubstantiated assertions in letters are not acceptable. Evidence may also be necessary to show that funds abroad are transferable to the UK. The costs may be met by the student, a sponsoring government or international agency, a parent or close relative abroad, or a sponsor in this country. Occasionally a student may rely on a local education authority grant.[3] The Immigration Rules make it clear that throughout their studies, students must be able to meet the costs of their course and accommodation and the maintenance of themselves and any dependants without taking employment or engaging in business or having recourse to public funds.[4] This means that while there is provision for students to take employment during vacations or spare time (see 9.48 above), no account may be taken of any prospective earnings from that employment in assessing the ability of a student to meet the maintenance requirement except where the educational establishment with which the student has a place:

- is a publicly funded institution of further or higher education which is itself providing and guaranteeing the employment, and has provided details of how much the applicant will earn;
- (in the case of sandwich course students) is able to guarantee that there are jobs available and how much, if anything, the applicant will earn.[5]

The potential earnings of the spouse of a student may not be taken into account, but if he or she is already working, actual earnings may be.[6] Leave should not be refused on the ground of lack of funds alone where the student meets the other requirements of the Rules but is in temporary financial difficulties, for example, because of social or political upheaval at home leading to difficulty in arranging the transfer of funds or the continuance of sponsorship.[7] The Rules also state that students must not have recourse to public funds.[8] But students may receive the following without prejudice to their entry clearance applications:[9] educational grants; waiving of fees by institutions, funding councils or other government agencies; any scholarships or awards held by the student; NHS treatment (other than statutory charges for prescriptions, etc) for students accepted as ordinarily resident in England and Wales;[10] and free student accommodation at some colleges.

¹ *Murgai v Entry Clearance Officer, New Delhi* [1975] Imm AR 86; *Bhagat v Secretary of State for the Home Department* [1972] Imm AR 189.

2 *Ayetty v Secretary of State for the Home Department* [1972] Imm AR 261. Letters or receipts simply showing the balance in an account on a particular day are not sufficient; bank or building society statements should cover a period of approximately three months: IDI Ch 3, s 3, para 3.15.1.

3 Refusal should not be based on the grounds that the level of fees charged is low or that the student has a local education authority award: see IDI Ch 3, s 3, para 3.152–3.

4 HC 395, paras 57(vi), 60 (ii). Scholarships, bursaries, waiver of fees and provision of free accommodation do not breach the 'public funds' rule: IDI Ch 3, s 3, para 3.15; DSP 12.21.

5 IDI Ch 3, s 3, para 3.15.1; DSP Ch 12.21.1.

6 IDI Ch 3, s 3, para 3.15.4.

7 IDI Ch 3, s 3, para 3.15.7.

8 Defined in HC 395, para 6. Students are not liable to pay council tax: IDI Ch 3, s 3, para 3.15.9.

9 DSP Ch 12.21.

10 NB: Scotland offers free NHS treatment to all students regardless of the length of their course: DSP Ch 12.21.

Duration of leave

9.51 The student rules provide that ordinary students who meet the requirements of the rules should be granted leave to enter for an 'appropriate period'.[1] What is appropriate for various classes of student is set out in the IDI and DSI and in policy statements. Primary school children should be admitted for the duration of their course, ie up to age eleven; secondary students to age 16, and sixth-form students, to age 18.[2] Students taking GCSEs, 'A' levels, HNC, HND and degree courses should be given leave for the duration of their course plus four months or to the end of October after the exams, to enable them to decide and enrol on future studies.[3] Students on courses of 12 months or less at private educational institutions should be given leave for the duration of the course plus two months (or four months if the course is a precursor to a degree course, such as an English language course).[4] Students moving to or doing further degree and higher education courses should be given leave to remain for four months between courses (or exceptionally, six months).[5] Postgraduate students should be given leave for the duration of the degree course plus four months, or leave to the date of the submission of their thesis plus unspecified extra time.[6] Students doing re-sits should be given leave to the date of the re-sit plus two months, to allow time to receive the results.[7] It is important to ensure that the correct period of leave is given at the outset, to avoid costly extensions.[8] Students whose course is not due to start for some months may be granted leave if there is good reason for the delay and the person is currently engaged in studies, but an application by a student not currently engaged in studies for leave to remain for a course which is not due to start for four months or over will normally be refused.[9]

1 HC 395, para 58. Student nurses are given leave for the duration of their course: para 65, and postgraduate doctors, dentists and trainee general practitioners are given up to 12 months for pre-registration house officer employment, and up to three years for postgraduate training in a hospital or community health service: para 71 (substituted by HC 104).

2 IDI Dec 04 Ch 3 s 3, para 3.25.1; DSP 12.3.3.

3 IDI Ch 3, s 3, para 3.25.2.

4 IDI Ch 3, s 3, para 3.25.3–4.

5 IDI Ch 3, s 3, para 3.12.2.1.

6 IDI Ch 3, s 3, para 3.25.2. There is a separate policy for architectural students: see para 3.25.5.

7 See 9.52 below.

8　During a discussion on fee levels in the standing committee debate on the 2004 Bill, the minister of state pointed out that 'Students can apply for entry clearance outside the UK, cost £36, for the full period of their first course of study, whether one, two or three years, and would face no in-country charges': *Asylum and Immigration (Treatment of Claimants) Bill* Standing Committee, 10th sitting, col 385. For extensions and fees see below.
9　IDI Ch 3, s 3, para 3.12.2.

Extensions for students and student nurses

9.52 Those admitted as students can have their stay extended to continue a course or begin the next one, and prospective students may extend their stay to continue looking for a course (up to a six-month maximum)[1] and then as students. Non-visa nationals who entered as visitors or in some other temporary capacity can switch to degree student or student nurse status,[2] but no longer to courses below degree level;[3] visa nationals may not switch,[4] unless their application is for postgraduate medical or dental training.[5] To obtain an extension ordinary students must fulfil the following requirements:[6]

(i)　if visa nationals, they had a valid student or prospective entry clearance, when they were last admitted to the UK; if non-visa nationals, they must have had a similar entry clearance, when they were last admitted to the UK, if they are enrolled on a course below degree level.[7] These requirements are mandatory;[8]

(ii)　they meet all the requirements for the admission of a student;[9]

(iii)　they are enrolled for a full-time course of study which meets the requirements of paragraph 57 of the immigration rules;[10]

(iv)　they can produce satisfactory evidence of regular attendance during any course already begun or any other course for which they have been enrolled in the past.[11] Attendance is to be judged at the time of the decision on the application, and not by evidence showing that attendance has improved subsequent to the refusal;[12]

(v)　they can show evidence of satisfactory progress in their course of study,[13] including the taking and passing of any relevant exams.[14] A lack of success in exams[15] or a failure to sit them[16] can be taken into account. Where there are doubts as to progress but attendance is satisfactory and all other requirements are met, leave may be granted but with a warning that failure to produce evidence of satisfactory progress could result in a refusal of a further extension;[17]

(vi)　they would not, as a result of the extension of stay, spend more than two years on short courses below degree level (ie courses of less than a year's duration, or longer courses broken off before completion);[18]

(vii)　students whose studies are sponsored by a government or international scholarship agency must show that the sponsorship has not come to an end or, if it has, they have the written consent of their official sponsor for a further period of study and evidence that sufficient sponsorship funding is available.[19] The Rule enables students left stranded by a sponsoring government or agency, often because of a sudden change of government or civil war, to remain if they can find alternative funding and obtain the consent of the official sponsor.[20]

1　HC 395, para 85.

2 HC 395, para 60(i)(a), (b) (as amended by Cm 6339 from October 2004) and 67(i) (student nurses). The list of visa countries is set out in HC 395, Appendix 1.

3 HC 395, para 60(i)(b) requires acceptance for a course of study at degree level or above; otherwise admission with entry clearance as a student or prospective student is required: para 60(i)(c) as amended, in force 1 October 2004. Transitional provisions allow non-visa national visitors to switch to studies below degree level if they entered the UK before 22 July 2004, or applied for student leave before 30 September 2004: IDI Ch 3 s 3 para 3.10.2.

4 HC 395, para 60(i)(as amended). Nationals of countries recently added to the visa list are protected by transitional provisions if they did not require visas when they entered. See notes to para 60(i) in *Butterworths Immigration Law Service*, B[364].

5 HC 395, para 73.

6 HC 395, para 60. All relevant parts of the rule need to be satisfied: *Mohey-ud-Din* (15998) IAS 1998 Vol 1 No 6, IAT.

7 HC 395, para 60(i). See fn 3 above.

8 *R v Secretary of State for the Home Department, ex p Okello* [1995] Imm AR 269, CA.

9 HC 395, para 60(ii). On after-entry inquiries as to a student's intention to leave see 9.45 fn 1 above.

10 HC 395, para 60(iii). There are no transitional provisions enabling students to obtain extensions of leave after 1 January 2005 to continue studies at institutions which are not registered with the DfES: IDI Ch 3, s 3, para 3.4.

11 HC 395, para 60(iv). The IDI state that, since poor attendance is linked with progress and may signify a lack of funds and/or *bona fides*, checks on funds and progress should be made whenever attendance checks are made: IDI Dec 04, Ch 3, s 3, para 3.13. But students should be given an opportunity to explain any non-attendance: Ch 3, s 3, para 3.13. A person in the UK with student leave did not cease to be a student when his attendance fell below 15 hours per week, so as to enable the Secretary of State to remove him for breach of conditions (for working part-time): *R (on the application of Zhou) v Secretary of State for the Home Department* [2003] EWCA Civ 51, [2003] INLR 211.

12 *Juma v Secretary of State for the Home Department* [1974] Imm AR 96. This case may no longer be good law, because of the effect of s 85(4) Nationality, Immigration and Asylum Act 2002: see *DR (ECO post decision evidence) Morocco* [2005] UKIAT 00038 (starred); *LS (post decision evidence, direction, appealability) Gambia* [2005] UKIAT 00085; and see 18.63 below.

13 If after two years an English language student is seeking leave to remain to continue on a new course at the same level, of less than one year's duration, the application should normally be refused: IDI Ch 3, s 3, para 3.14.1.

14 HC 395, para 60(v). Students should provide evidence of all examinations attempted, and their results: IDI Ch 3, s 3, para 3.14.3. For accountancy and banking students the IDI para 3.6.3 describes the entry requirements, structure of courses and examinations of the five main bodies offering qualifications (CIMA, ACCA, AAT, ABE and CIB) against which to track a student's progress.

15 *R v Immigration Appeal Tribunal, ex p Gerami* [1981] Imm AR 187, DC; *Mahendran* [1988] Imm AR 492; *Amer v Secretary of State for the Home Department* [1979–80] Imm AR 87; *Blay* (18720) 23 June 1999. Passing exams is important, but it is not the only factor: *Sayeed* (G0068) IAS 1999 Vol 2 No 9, IAT.

16 *R v Secretary of State for the Home Department, ex p Adebodin* [1991] Imm AR 60. Dogged persistence over a lengthy period may not be enough to overcome repeated exam failure: *Ofori-Agyemang* (14323) IAS 1997 Vol 3 No 16. See below for rules on resits, para 69A.

17 IDI Ch 3, s 3, para 3.14.3. Refusing further leave without a warning might be premature in the light of the instruction. Account should be taken of the student's family's investment: *Ofoajoku* [1991] Imm AR 68. Students who have been unable successfully to complete an access course (a 12-month course providing access to a degree course for those without qualifications) will normally be refused on the basis that they are unlikely to be able to follow a degree course: IDI Ch 3, s 3, para 3.6.1.

18 HC 395, para 60(vi) as amended by Cm 6339 from 1 October 2004. The amendment reduced the total length of permissible short courses below degree level from four years to two and the length of each course to one year. It is not intended to prevent a person from taking short courses which form part of a planned course with a defined educational objective, but inquiries as to a student's educational plans should be considered where he or she has enrolled on a new course bearing no relation to previous studies, or is

re-enrolling on the same or similar course without apparently making progress, or breaks off mid-course for no good reason and seeks to commence another course, or where there is any reason to suspect that he or she is making the studies an excuse for remaining in the UK for some other purpose: IDI Dec 04, Ch 3, s 3, para 3.17. Previous short courses may not matter if the extension is for a long course: *Navarthinarajah* (14373) ILD 2000 Vol 6 No 1.

19 HC 395, para 60(vii), amended by Cm 4851, paras 11, 12 (by substituting 'official' sponsor for 'original' sponsor). Failure to obtain written consent may result in refusal: para 39A.

20 Thus an appellant such as *Salah* (20272) 2 February 2000, IAS 2000 Vol 3 No 10, IAT, whose father was willing to sponsor at the end of an official sponsorship, would no longer qualify unless the official sponsor gave written consent for the switch.

9.53 Nursing training will not be extended beyond four years.[1] But within this period student nurses may obtain extensions if they continue to meet all the requirements for admission and can produce satisfactory evidence of regular attendance.[2] If sponsored they must show continuing sponsorship or alternative funding with the official sponsor's written consent.[3]

1 HC 395, para 67(v).
2 HC 395, para 67(ii)–(iv).
3 HC 395, para 67(vi).

9.54 An application for an extension of leave should be made on the prescribed form, accompanied by the necessary documentation and other evidence,[1] and by the requisite fee.[2] If the Home Office requests further information, it must be provided promptly, since whatever the merits of the application, it is liable to be refused if there is unreasonable delay in producing the requested documents or evidence.[3] On appeal the Tribunal will consider the substantive merits of the case, but this may not be enough to overcome the adverse effect of the delay. Extensions may be refused if other general considerations apply, for example, if the student has taken full-time employment in breach of conditions.[4]

1 Immigration (Leave to Remain) (Prescribed Forms and Procedures) Regulations 2005, SI 2005/771; HC 395, para 32. The form for a student variation is FLR(S). See further 4.7–4.8 above.
2 The fee has doubled in two years. It is currently £250 for a postal application, and £500 for an application made in person: Immigration (Leave to Remain) (Fees) Regulations 2003, SI 2003/1711, as amended by SI 2005/564, from 1 April 2005. See further 4.10 above. A spouse and minor children may be included in the application with no extra fee.
3 HC 395, para 322(9).
4 HC 395, para 322(3); *Secretary of State for the Home Department v Thaker* [1976] Imm AR 114; but see *Strasburger v Secretary of State for the Home Department* [1978] Imm AR 165 where it was held that casual sales of a student's artwork were not employment which should be taken into account.

Re-sits, writing up a thesis, and sabbaticals

9.55 The Immigration Rules enable students to apply for leave to enter or remain to re-sit examinations provided that they meet the requirements for admission as a student, or, if no longer enrolled and following a course as required by sub-paragraphs 57(i) to (iii), that they met these requirements in the previous academic year and can still fulfil the general requirements in sub-paragraphs 57(iv) to (vi).[1] They must have written confirmation from the school or college concerned that they are required to re-sit an examination,[2] and evidence of regular attendance on any course currently or previously taken.[3] The sponsorship requirements apply,[4] and applicants will be refused if they have previously been granted leave to re-sit the examination.[5] The wording of this last Rule suggests that a re-sit leave may be available for each examination, although this will obviously be subject to the general student rules as to satisfactory progress.[6] The period of leave granted will be whatever is sufficient to enable the student to re-sit the exam at the first available opportunity, and will be subject to a condition restricting, but not prohibiting, employment.[7] Doctors may obtain extensions of leave for up to 18 months to re-sit the PLAB test.[8]

[1] HC 395, paras 69A(i), 69D, inserted by Cm 4851 on 20 September 2000.
[2] HC 395, paras 69A(ii), 69D.
[3] HC 395, paras 69A(iii), 69D.
[4] HC 395, paras 69A(iv), 69D; see 9.51 above.
[5] HC 395, paras 69A(v), 69D.
[6] HC 395, para 60(iv); see 9.51 above.
[7] HC 395, paras 69B, 69E. An additional two months is granted to allow time for the results to be received: IDI Ch 3 s 3, para 3.20.
[8] HC 395 para 75D(v), inserted by HC346 from 15 March 2005.

9.56 Similar rules apply to students seeking leave to enter or remain to write up a thesis.[1] They need to show that they meet the enrolment requirements, or met them in the previous academic year, and the general requirements (intention to leave and not to work, except part-time, and financial require-ments).[2] They must be postgraduate students enrolled as a full-time, part-time or writing-up student at an education institution,[3] which must support the application.[4] If sponsored, they must show continuing sponsorship or alter-native funding with the official sponsor's consent.[5] The maximum writing-up period is 12 months and they will be refused leave if they have already had this.[6]

[1] HC 395, paras 69G–69L, inserted by Cm 4851 on 20Sep/00.
[2] HC 395, paras 69G(i), 69J.
[3] HC 395, para 69G(ii).
[4] HC 395, para 69G(iii).
[5] HC 395, para 69G(iv).
[6] HC 395, paras 69H, 69I, 69G(v).

9.57 A student who has been elected as a students' union sabbatical officer may be granted leave to enter or remain for up to two years for the purpose, provided he or she is registered as a student at the establishment where the duties are to be performed and intends to complete a course of study already begun, take up a course which has been deferred for the duration of the sabbatical or leave the UK after the sabbatical.[1] He or she must not engage in business or take employment, except in connection with the post, and must satisfy the maintenance and accommodation and sponsorship criteria.

[1] HC 395, paras 87A–F, inserted by Cm 4851 on 20 September 2000.

Student exchange employment programme

9.58 As part of a reciprocal programme of student exchanges between the UK and the US, any American full-time college student may apply to come to the UK as part of a Work in Britain Programme. They get a BUNAC 'Blue Card', which is recognised by the Home Office and the Department for Education and Skills, which they present to immigration control on entry.[1] They can enter at any time of the year and stay for up to six months, working as little or as long as they wish. They have a condition restricting but not prohibiting employment. BUNAC students may transfer to student status but not to training or work experience.[2]

[1] See IDI, Ch 17, s 1. Further information may be obtained from the Council on International Exchange, 205 East 42nd Street, New York, NY 10017.
[2] IDI, Ch 17, s 1. See 10.31 below for other examples of special work cases.

Other special cases

9.59 The IDI on students give guidance on special classes of student or special courses. Postgraduate students working as researchers require a work permit even where their research will lead to the award of a higher degree, but higher degree students who will be awarded degrees by the university at which they are enrolled, and those enrolled at private colleges or research institutes, whose studies are validated by a university, should be admitted as students, as should junior research fellows.[1] Non-EEA national students aged 18 to 19 may come to the UK to work in schools during their 'gap year' (between secondary and tertiary education). They must have finished their secondary education less than 12 months ago; have an unconditional offer on a degree course overseas that will begin after leaving the UK; have a written offer of employment in a teaching or teaching assistant capacity in a school in the UK for three consecutive academic terms; have no intention of taking any other employment; have the means to pay for the outward journey; show that there will be no recourse to public funds; and have the intention to leave the UK and resume studying following completion of the 12 month period.[2] Exchange students, normally between the ages of 16 and 18, may be admitted for up to 12 months for attendance at state schools, on evidence that the local education authority has approved the exchange scheme and has assigned a school, and subject to suitable arrangements for support and accommodation (normally satisfied by provision of a host family) and the intention to leave requirement.[3] Music students enrolled at a reputable college of music or under a qualified private tutor may be admitted despite not meeting the general rule of 15 hours per week organised daytime study.[4] Similarly, Bar students accepted by an Inn of Court do not have to meet the 15 hours per week rule for admission.[5] Barristers who can demonstrate that they have been accepted on a pupillage scheme by a recognised chambers, may be treated as students under the immigration rules.[6] Articled clerks need a permit under the Training and Work Experience Scheme. Those who, having completed articles, wish to work for the Crown Prosecution Service may be referred to the Work Permits (UK) section.[7] Agricultural students undertaking practical training on a farm before beginning their course should be admitted as students for up to 12 months if the work is part of the curriculum and the student is supernumerary to the normal labour force.[8] There is also guidance in relation to children with learning disabilities who arrive for education at a special school without entry clearance,[9] riding school students, nautical students, students attending American Institute for Foreign Study programmes, students on Marshall scholarships, moral rearmament trainees, Pestalozzi children, students attending St George's University School of Medicine, Grenada programmes at affiliated UK teaching hospitals and students at Welbeck college (potential army officers).[10]

1   IDI Dec 04, Ch 3 s 3, para 3.24.9.
2   IDI Ch 17, s 11 (Jun 04). See 10.31 for other special cases.
3   IDI Ch 3, s 3, para 3.24.2 The exchange may be arranged by an organisation which runs such schemes or may be privately arranged.
4   IDI Ch 3, s 3, para 3.24.6.
5   IDI Ch 3, s 3, para 3.24.4.1.
6   IDI Ch 3, s 3, para 3.24.4.2.
7   IDI Ch 3, s 3, para 3.24.4.3.
8   IDI Ch 3, s 3, para 3.24.1.
9   IDI Ch 3, s 3, para 3.24.3.
10 IDI Ch 3, s 3, para 3.24.

Appeal rights

9.60 Students who arrive in the UK with a visa or entry clearance endorsed with its purpose and conditions are deemed to have leave to enter,[1] and if the leave is cancelled they have a right of appeal under section 82 of the Nationality, Immigration and Asylum Act 2002 and can remain here for the hearing of their appeal unless leave was cancelled or refused because they are seeking to enter for a different purpose.[2] Visa nationals and specified nationals who are refused entry on arrival in the UK without a visa, have no right of appeal (save on discrimination, human rights or asylum grounds).[3] Non-visa nationals who are refused entry on arrival in the UK without a visa, and students (whether visa nationals or not) who are refused entry clearance have a right of appeal against refusal[4] unless the proposed course is of not more than six months' duration[5] or they are potential students, intending to study but not yet accepted on any course.[6] Where leave to enter is refused and the student is not a holder of a current entry clearance, the appeal right cannot be exercised in-country.[7] A student who switches to an entirely different course after refusal of leave to enter or remain cannot expect to have the merits of a new course dealt with on appeal, since it should form part of a fresh application.[8]

1   Immigration (Leave to Enter and Remain) Order 2000, SI 2000/1161, Arts 3, 4(3).
2   Nationality, Immigration and Asylum Act 2002, s 92(3)–(3C) as substituted and inserted by Asylum and Immigration (Treatment of Claimants, etc) Act 2004, s 28 (from 1 October 2004); Immigration Act 1971, Sch 2, para 2A(9), inserted by Immigration and Asylum Act 1999, Sch 14, para 57, amended by NIAA 2002, s 114(3), Sch 7, para 2.
3   NIAA 2002, s 88(2)(b), (4).
4   NIAA 2002, s 82(1), (2)(a), (b).
5   NIAA 2002, ss 89(1)(b), (2), 91(1)(a). Dependants are also excluded from the right of appeal: ss 89(1)(d), 91(1)(c). An appeal may be brought on discrimination or human rights grounds: ss 89((3), 91(2), and on asylum grounds against refusal of leave to enter: s 89(3).

[6] NIAA 2002, ss 89(1)(c), (2), 91(1)(b). Dependants are also excluded from the right of appeal: ss 89(1)(d), 91(1)(c). An appeal may be brought on discrimination or human rights grounds: ss 89(3), 91(2), and on asylum grounds against refusal of leave to enter: s 89(3).

[7] NIAA 2002, s 92(1), (3) (as substituted by AI(TC)A 2004, s 28). A prospective student who was granted temporary admission and then refused leave to enter, but who had in the meantime enrolled on a full-time course of study, had become a student with a right of appeal from abroad against the refusal of leave: *Morikawa v Secretary of State for the Home Department* [1995] Imm AR 258, CA.

[8] *Secretary of State for the Home Department v Thaker* [1976] Imm AR 114 (switch from accountancy to economics); *Muthalakshmi v Secretary of State for the Home Department* [1972] Imm AR 231 (English language course substituted for dentistry).

Changing from student status

9.61 Students can switch from one course to another within the limits set out at 9.51 above. An ordinary student can become a student nurse.[1] On graduation, medical students can take employment as house officers and undertake postgraduate training.[2] Other students can switch to Home Office-approved training or work experience.[3] But the Immigration Rules do not allow the possibility of switching to other temporary categories, such as au pair[4] or working holidaymaker.[5] Graduates from British institutions,[6] student nurses, doctors and dentists and overseas doctors admitted for PLAB tests and clinical attachments or dental observation[7] may switch into work permit employment. Graduates and postgraduate doctors and dentists, and overseas doctors admitted for PLAB tests and clinical attachments or dental observation may additionally remain as highly skilled migrants.[8] Graduates may remain as innovators,[9] and maths, science and engineering graduates may remain in the UK for 12 months following graduation to seek and take work, without having to obtain a work permit, under the Science and Engineering Graduate Scheme (SEGS).[10] Other students (ie those who are not graduates from British institutions, student nurses or postgraduate doctors or dentists, and have not taken their PLAB test or had a clinical attachment in the UK) may not switch to business or employment (subject to rights under various Association Agreements: see 7.151 and 9.25 above). The only categories leading to settlement into which non-graduate and non-medical students may switch are: (i) Commonwealth citizens with a UK-born grandparent intending to take or seek employment;[11] (ii) close relatives, such as a student child of parents who decide to settle,[12] or a student wishing to remain as a dependent relative on compassionate grounds;[13] and (iii) students who marry someone settled here, or cohabit with an unmarried partner for two years, who may apply for leave to remain as a spouse or unmarried partner.[14]

[1] HC 395, para 67(i).
[2] HC 395, para 73. See above 9.34.
[3] HC 395, para 119(i) (substituted by Cmnd 5253).
[4] HC 395, para 92(i).
[5] HC 395, para 98(i).
[6] HC 395, para 131A (inserted by Cmnd 5597).
[7] HC 395, para 131B (as inserted), I31G, inserted by HC 346 from 15 March 2005.
[8] HC 395, paras 135DB, 135DC (as inserted), 135DG, inserted by HC 346 from 15 March 2005. Students with official sponsorship need the written consent of their official sponsor.
[9] HC 395, para 210DB (inserted by Cm 6339 from 1 October 2004).

10 HC 395, paras 135O, 135R (as inserted). To qualify, students must have obtained a second class honours or better degree, masters or PhD within the last 12 months in a subject approved by the DfES and satisfy maintenance and accommodation requirements. Those with official sponsorship need the written consent of their official sponsor.
11 HC 395, para 189.
12 HC 395, paras 298, 311 (adopted child).
13 HC 395, para 317.
14 HC 395, paras 284, 295D (inserted by Cm 4851). Certain students would require Home Office permission to marry: see 11.67 below.

AU PAIRS

Nature of the arrangement

9.62 According to the current Immigration Rules, an 'au pair' placement is an arrangement whereby a young person comes to the UK to learn English, lives for a time as a member of an English-speaking family with appropriate opportunities for study, and helps in the home for a maximum of five hours a day in return for a reasonable allowance and with two free days a week.[1] The arrangement is open to young men and women from European but non-EEA countries (nationals of EEA countries are dealt with exclusively under EC law and are excluded from the 'au pair' Rule). Apart from the reference to a 'reasonable allowance', the Rules are silent on pay[2] and there is no supervision by Work Permits (UK) or the Department of Work and Pensions, so the relationship is open to exploitation and abuse.[3]

1 HC 395, para 88.
2 The IDI Mar 04, Ch 4, s 1, Annex A refer (para 4) to an allowance of 'up to £55 a week. Any sum significantly in excess of this might suggest that the person is filling the position of domestic servant, or similar, which would require a work permit'.
3 Au pairs are not covered by minimum wage legislation. In a publication prepared by the Home Office in 1973 (when the arrangement was confined to young women) it was stated that an au pair 'receives her keep, entertainment and pocket money and is expected to help with the housework and take care of any children'. It referred to the relationship not as one between employer and employee but between 'the girl and her hostess'. 'Under a proper au pair arrangement the relationship between the hostess and the girl involves acceptance of social equality and is not founded on a mistress/servant basis': *Au pair in Britain* (1973) COI.

The requirements

9.63 The full requirements for entry to the UK as an au pair[1] are that the passenger:

(i) is seeking entry as an au pair within the definition in HC 395, paragraph 88;
(ii) is aged between 17 and 27 inclusive when first given leave to enter. Discretion may be exercised in the case of a young person who will be 17 within a few days, but discretion to admit new arrivals aged 28 or over will not be used unless arrival has been delayed by an unexpected domestic crisis, illness or completion of a long-term course of study. In such a case discretion may be exercised to admit someone up to six months over the age of 28;[2]

(iii) is unmarried;

(iv) is without dependants;

(v) is a national of Andorra, Bosnia-Herzegovina, Republic of Bulgaria, Croatia, The Faroes, Greenland, Macedonia, Monaco, Romania, San Marino, or Turkey;[3]

(vi) does not intend to stay in the UK for more than two years as an au pair;

(vii) intends to leave on completion of his or her stay as an au pair; and

(viii) if he or she has already been here as an au pair, is not seeking to remain beyond the two-year period from the date when leave to enter as an au pair was first given;

(ix) can maintain and accommodate him or herself without recourse to public funds[4]. Being maintained and accommodated by a third party (as will usually be the case) will suffice.[5]

If all these requirements are met, leave of up to two years may be given with a condition prohibiting employment except as an au pair.[6] Visa nationals require a visa, and non-visa nationals are advised to get one.[7] If all the requirements are not met, leave is to be refused.[8] An extension to the au pair arrangement can be obtained provided the person is working as an au pair, meets the main requirements of entry, and the extension would not take them beyond the two-year period, starting from the date of their first leave to enter as an au pair.[9] Previously, persons arriving on a visit could switch to 'au pair' but this is no longer possible under the new Rules.[10] An au pair may move to a new host family.[11]

---

[1] HC 395, para 89.
[2] IDI Ch 4, s 1, Annex A, para 1.
[3] HC 395, para 89(v), as amended by HC 523 (April 2004).
[4] HC 395, paras 89(ix), 92, as amended by HC 31.
[5] *Begum* (13489) (1996) 10 INLP 1; *Arman Ali* [2000] INLR 89.
[6] HC 395, para 90.
[7] HC 395, para 90.
[8] HC 395, para 91.
[9] HC 395, paras 92–94.
[10] HC 395, para 92 (i).
[11] IDI Ch 4, s 1, Annex A, para 3.

9.64 There is no need for an au pair to enrol on an educational course to learn English. He or she may improve linguistic skills simply by living in an English-speaking family.[1] Additional guidance is set out in the IDI.[2] The family with whom the au pair is placed should be resident in the UK, but not necessarily settled here.[3] It need not be a nuclear family but a person living alone is not a 'family' for the purposes of the au pair rules. There is nothing preventing a host family from having more than one au pair at a time. An au pair should be free to attend religious services as well as language classes and should have free board and lodging and the use of his or her own room. He or she may be expected to baby-sit for up to two nights a week. The 'reasonable allowance' should be in the region of £55.00 per week. A letter from the host family describing the duties, pocket money and arrangements for study should normally be requested.[4]

---

[1] *Soler* (4277), unreported.
[2] IDI Ch 4, s 1, Annex A.

³   IDI Ch 4, s 1, Annex A, para 2.
⁴   IDI Ch 4, s 1, Annex A, para 4.

WORKING HOLIDAYMAKERS

9.65 Young citizens of specified Commonwealth countries, BOCs, BOTCs and BNOs[1] aged 17 to 30 inclusive [2] may be admitted to the UK as working holidaymakers if they satisfy the immigration officer that they are coming to the UK for a working holiday and that they intend only to take employment incidental to a holiday, and do not intend to engage in business or professional sport, or to work for more than 12 months during their stay.[3] They must have the means to pay for their onward or return journey[4] and not need to have recourse to public funds,[5] and they must intend to leave the UK at the end of their working holiday.[6] They must not have spent time in the UK on a previous working holidaymaker entry clearance.[7] A working holidaymaker must be unmarried unless the spouse qualifies in his or her own right and the two are taking a working holiday together.[8] Working holidaymakers should be childless, except for children who will still be under five at the end of the working holiday.[9] Entry clearance is required and leave to enter will be refused without one.[10] A dependent child will only be admitted if both parents are making the trip, except where the working holidaymaker is a sole surviving parent, has sole responsibility for the child's upbringing, or there are serious and compelling family or other considerations and suitable arrangements for the child's care.[11] The child also needs entry clearance in this capacity.[12] If any of these conditions is not met, leave is to be refused.[13]

¹   HC 395, para 95(i), substituted by HC 302 from 8 February 2005. The specified Commonwealth countries are set out in Appendix 3 to the Immigration Rules. Although the Appendix currently contains nearly all Commonwealth countries and overseas territories, the Rules changes create the framework for bilateral agreements, contained in Memoranda of Understanding (MOU) with the country concerned. Each MOU will require a satisfactory returns agreement with the UK as a precondition to taking part in the scheme, and will contain provisions to suspend the bilateral scheme in the event of a sudden and unmanageable rise in applications: UK Visas to User Panel, 8 February 2005.
²   The relevant date for the age requirement is the date of application: HC 395, para 95(ii) as substituted.
³   HC 395, para 95(vi). The restrictions on business, professional sport and on the total period of employment during a working holidaymaker's stay are new. Although the Rules no longer specify the length for which a working holidaymaker visa will be granted, the IDI Ch 4 s 2 and Annex C, as amended to reflect the rule changes, indicate that the normal grant will still be two years. The changes do not include a transitional period for applications pending on 8 February 2005.
⁴   HC 395, para 95(iv).
⁵   HC 395, para 95(v). Money in a bank account is relevant to but not conclusive of means: *Tanveer* (L00008) IAS 2000 Vol 3 No 1, IAT.
⁶   HC 395, para 95(viii). See 9.67 below.
⁷   HC 395, para 95(ix) as substituted. This is a new provision. A working holiday visa is available only once. The IDI, Ch 4 s 2 and Annex C, indicate that the rule can be waived where the previous visa was not used, for good reason.
⁸   HC 395, para 95(iii).
⁹   HC 395, para 95(vii). See 9.66 below.
¹⁰   HC 395, paras 95(x), 97.
¹¹   HC 395, para 101(iv), substituted by HC 302 from 8 February 2005.
¹²   HC 395, para 101(v).
¹³   HC 395, para 103.

9.66 The rules on working holidaymakers have become considerably stricter over the years. Up until March 1980 working holidaymakers could be admitted for five years, not just two, and there were no age limits.[1] The present age limit matches those for 'au pairs',[2] although the two Rules otherwise bear no relation to each other. Entry clearance before travelling, not required for non-visa nationals prior to 1994,[3] is mandatory.[4] Not only must employment be only incidental to the holiday, but it must not total more than 12 months of the stay. On the other hand, working holidaymakers may now switch into some permanent employment and business categories. The most dramatic change is the ability to remove from the list of countries from which working holidaymakers come those which refuse to enter into strict readmission agreements regarding their nationals, which could significantly restrict the countries from which working holiday-makers come.[5]

[1] HC 79, para 28; HC 80, para 11. For earlier Rules and their effect, see *Clipsham v Secretary of State for the Home Department* [1972] Imm AR 35; *Ismail v Secretary of State for the Home Department* [1973] Imm AR 62.
[2] HC 395, para 89(ii).
[3] See HC 251, para 37.
[4] HC 395, paras 95(x), 97 and 101(v) as substituted.
[5] The scheme was temporarily suspended in Malaysia, Sri Lanka, Namibia and Botswana for six months in April 2005 (see 9.65 fn 1 above), and the High Commission in Pakistan was not accepting applications at the time of writing: UK Visas to User Panel, 8 February 2005, 4 April 2005.

Working holiday

9.67 Earlier rules referred to a working holiday as an extended holiday before the holidaymaker settled down in their own country.[1] A prospective working holidaymaker must intend to leave the United Kingdom on completion of his holiday.[2] The IDI accept, however, that in the course of a two-year stay plans may change, and a working holidaymaker may decide to apply for an extension of stay in another category. In such circumstances, an application for leave to remain in another capacity may be granted provided that the requirements of the Immigration Rules are met.[3] Working holidaymakers are permitted under the Immigration Rules to switch into work permit employment after they have spent more than 12 months in the United Kingdom in the category in total.[4] They may also seek leave to remain as highly skilled migrants,[5] or as innovators.[6]

[1] HC 251, para 37. See *Adejumoke v Secretary of State for the Home Department* [1993] Imm AR 265. Cf *Rani* (9987) [1993] INLP 140 where a bereaved Indian woman seeking to get over her husband's death and to get experience of the clothing trade was held to be eligible for working holidaymaker status because her job was incidental to her holiday. In *Lana v Secretary of State for the Home Department* [1997] Imm AR 17 the Court of Appeal preferred *Adejumoke* to *Rani* but pointed out that their decision had no relevance to the current Immigration Rules, since the requirement to come as a working holiday-maker 'before settling down in their own countries' had been sensibly dropped from the Rules.
[2] HC 395, para 95(viii).
[3] IDI Apr 04, Ch 4, Annex C, para 1.5.
[4] HC 395, para 131D, inserted by Cm 5949, August 2003.
[5] HC 395, para 135DD, inserted by Cm 6339, 1 October 2004.
[6] HC 395, para 210DCas inserted.

Employment incidental to holiday

9.68 Working holidaymakers are expected to intend only to take paid work in the United Kingdom which is incidental to their working holiday. If they do not intend working or have no reasonable prospect of obtaining the type of work envisaged then they will be unlikely to meet the requirements of the working holidaymaker rules.[1] However, in *Bari v Immigration Appeal Tribunal*[2] the Court of Appeal held that applicants are not disbarred if they intend only to get a job if they become bored or their financial arrangements go wrong. Having realistic proposals for work may be necessary for an applicant to establish the bona fides of the proposed working holiday, but it cannot be a criterion on its own, as it was treated by the Appeal Tribunal in that case. The category does not have specific requirements as to the type of work that working holidaymakers can do during their stay, save that they may not engage in professional sport or in business; entrants in the category may take any employment of their choice. But they may not engage in employment for longer than 12 months of the total stay. The changes in the rules emphasise the incidental nature of the work to the holiday, which should be their primary reason for being here[3]. In the interests of schools and their pupils the IDI provided for discretion in granting a short extension of leave to remain in the United Kingdom to a working holidaymaker who is already employed as a teacher, and whom the school wishes to retain, to enable them to complete the school term during which their leave to remain as a working holiday maker has expired.[4] A working holidaymaker may engage in some part-time study and short periods of full-time study, but may not engage in full-time study for the whole of his or her stay.[5]

1   IIDI Ch 4 Annex C (Apr 04), para 2.1.
2   [1987] Imm AR 13, CA. In *Acheampong* (18348) IAS 1999 Vol 2 No 6, the IAT came to the same conclusion notwithstanding that in HC 395, para 95 the word 'only' is omitted from the Rule. In *Singh (Surjit)* (14334) (1997, unreported), the IAT said that under the relevant rule in force then, intention to work is essential and *Bari* is no longer relevant.
3   IDI Ch 4, Annex C, para 2.2.
4   IDI Ch 17, s 12.
5   IDI Ch 4, s 2, Annex C, para 2.3.

Funds

9.69 Although the Immigration Rules require the working holidaymaker to be able to meet the cost of onward or return travel and fulfil the maintenance and accommodation self-sufficiency rule, the IDI state that 'the requirement to have the means to pay for the return or onward journey should be flexibly applied' where it is reasonably likely that the necessary funds will be earned within the two years.[1] To satisfy the 'no public funds' criterion for entry, the instructions state that working holidaymakers should show they can support themselves for at least the first two months after arrival, or at least one month if they have a job arranged in advance.[2]

1   IDI Apr 04, Ch 4, s 2, Annex C, para 1.4.
2   IDI Apr 04, Ch 4, s 2, Annex C, para 1.4.

Chapter 10

WORKING, BUSINESS, INVESTMENT AND RETIREMENT IN THE UK

INTRODUCTION

10.1 This chapter deals with admission for work and business purposes of non-EEA nationals, both Commonwealth and foreign.[1] It also covers the admission of those who intend not to work, but to invest in the UK, or to retire here. The rules for the admission of economic migrants are collectively referred to as 'commercial immigration law'. The chapter is mostly, but not exclusively, about admission in categories leading to settlement. It is in two parts; the first part deals with those coming to the UK to work for someone else in an employment relationship.[2] The second part deals with the other categories. In respect of each category, we give some indication whether an applicant may switch in-country to the category concerned (but see 10.57 for switching into work permit employment, and 10.121 for general discussion and specific policies on switching). We also identify any provision regarding the admission of family members. The whole scheme for admission for work, business and investor purposes is due for a big shake-up under the government's Five year strategy for asylum and immigration.[3] The intention is to introduce a 'transparent points system for all those who come to the UK to work', divided into four tiers;[4] to require sponsors for all but the most highly skilled and bonds where there has been evidence of abuse; and to phase out low skilled migration schemes, in the light of new labour available from the ten new Accession States in the European Union.[5]

1 The law governing admission to the UK for employment by EEA nationals and their families, including the new registration scheme for the eight new Central and Eastern European Member States (the 'A 8 Registration Scheme') and the general position under EC law of nationals of those eight Member States as regards free movement, is dealt with in chapter 7 above, as is the establishment of businesses by nationals of Bulgaria and Romania, with whom the EU has concluded Association Agreements (although this is outlined at 10.99 below).

2 For business visitors, au pairs and working holidaymakers see chapter 9.

3 *Controlling our borders: Making migration work for Britain – Five year strategy for asylum and immigration*, Cm 6472, Feb 05, paras 18–22.

4 The tiers are Tier 1 (highly skilled and will probably include investors and entrepreneurs); Tier 2 (skilled, such as nurses and teachers); Tier 3 (low skilled); and Tier 4 (students and specialists).

5 Additionally, the document explains that the government 'will introduce English language tests for everyone who wants to stay permanently in the UK ... only allow skilled workers to settle long-term in the UK; increase the period skilled workers have to be here before being allowed to stay permanently from four years to five years; [and] end chain migration – no immediate or automatic right for relatives to bring in more relatives' Executive Summary description of the document's Section 3.

Managed migration and rules v schemes

10.2 The government's framework policy within which commercial immigration law now falls is known as the managed migration policy. Managed migration is a concept that has emerged from developments in recent years and particularly from the 2002 Home Office White Paper *Secure Borders, Safe Haven: Integration with Diversity in Modern Britain*. Identifying the UK's precise needs, such as for short-term casual labour, and opening up new migration routes into the UK to satisfy those needs, are key aspects of the IND's managed migration policies, which are now dealt with by the managed migration team based in Work Permits (UK) in Sheffield. The February 2005 'Five year strategy for asylum and immigration' reverses much of the forward thinking underlying the 2002 White Paper.

10.3 Certain commercial immigration categories which have come into existence within the managed migration framework have reinforced the difference between two distinct approaches to the formulation of commercial immigration law. Historically, categories such as the businesspersons category, together with certain employment categories, have been contained within the Immigration Rules, administered by Home Office officials based in the IND at Croydon and subject to the statutory immigration appeals regime. By contrast, the work permit category was and is essentially a 'scheme' whose requirements were set out in easily amended guidance notes and administered, not by the Home Office, but by the department of state responsible for employment matters, whose offices were located in Sheffield. Refusals were and are not justiciable before the statutory immigration appellate authorities. Responsibility for the work permit scheme, and for processing work permit applications, shifted in 2001 from the Overseas Labour Section of the then Department for Education and Employment (now Department for Work and Pensions) to a new Home Office department, Work Permits (UK). The distinction between categories wholly within the Immigration Rules and 'scheme'-based categories was reinforced by the addition of new scheme-based categories. This is how the relevant categories now divide up:

Where the Immigration Rules set out all the requirements:

- au pairs;
- domestic workers in private and diplomatic households;
- airline staff;
- journalists, broadcasters, etc;
- sole representatives;
- overseas government employees, etc;
- ministers of religion, etc;
- working holidaymakers;
- UK ancestry;
- business persons (including under EC Association Agreements);
- investors;
- writers, composers and artists;
- retired persons of independent means.

Where the Immigration Rules defer to a separately administered scheme:

- seasonal workers (must have a valid Home Office work card issued by the operator of a scheme approved by the Secretary of State);
- exchange scheme teachers (an exchange scheme approved by the Education Departments or administered by the Central Bureau for Educational Visits and Exchanges or the League for the Exchange of Commonwealth Teachers);
- trainees and those on work experience (must have a valid TWES permit);
- work permit holders (must have a valid work permit or a valid Home Office immigration employment document);
- highly skilled migrant workers (must have a valid document issued by the Home Office confirming that they meet, at the time of the issue of that document, the criteria specified by the Secretary of State for entry to the United Kingdom under the Highly Skilled Migrant Programme 'HSMP');
- short-term work permit holders in sector specific employment (must have a valid Home Office immigration employment document issued under the Sectors-Based Scheme);
- multiple entry work permit holders (must hold a valid work permit);
- innovators (must be approved by the Home Office as a person who meets the criteria specified by the Secretary of State for entry under the innovator scheme at the time that approval is sought under that scheme);
- certain Graduate students may become participants in the Science and Engineering Graduates Scheme (SEGS).

Those seeking to enter or remain in the first group apply in the normal way, either to an entry clearance officer abroad or to the Immigration and Nationality Department (IND) of the Home Office. Those in the second category must first obtain separate written approval. Sometimes, this is in the form of a work permit, defined as '... a permit indicating, in accordance with the immigration rules, that a person named in it is eligible, though not a British citizen, for entry into the United Kingdom for the purpose of taking employment'.[1] The prior approval might be another type of 'immigration employment document'. An 'immigration employment document' (IED), introduced in 2002,[2] is defined to include work permits and any other document which relates to employment and is issued for a purpose of Immigration Rules or in connection with leave to enter or remain in the United Kingdom. It includes work permits, Multiple Entry work permits, TWES permits, Seasonal Agricultural Work Cards and approval under the Highly Skilled Migrants Programme (HSMP). It also includes, in the words of the 2002 Act's Explanatory Notes, 'letters of permission issued in-country, which give authority to work and which underpin employment-related leave to enter or remain'. It is the scheme, and not statute or even the Immigration Rules, that describes the principal requirements to be met for the issue of an immigration employment document (IED). While most IEDs, including those for highly skilled migrants, are issued by Work Permits (UK), not all IEDs are; seasonal agricultural workers apply direct to the approved operator, and Science and Engineering Graduates Scheme (SEGS) participants apply to IND in Croydon and not to Work Permits (UK). Innovators and exchange teachers also need approval under a scheme, but they do not need IEDs. It is thus important to establish, in relation to any applicant, not only whether he or she needs a work permit, but also whether he or she falls within the scope of any scheme which requires an IED, or some other form of approval, before an application for leave to enter or remain can be made.

[1]   Immigration Act 1971, s 33(1).
[2]   Nationality, Immigration and Asylum Act 2002, s 122.

10.4 The ad hoc development of the Rules is to blame for the multiplicity of schemes and the lack of coherence among them. However, it is not hard to see why the Home Office prefers schemes to traditional immigration Rules-based categories. Schemes are more flexible and refusals can be reviewed in-house as they fall beyond the reach of the statutory immigration appeals regime.[1] Overall, following the transfer of the Sheffield work permits bureaucracy to IND there is less and less cause to distinguish between Croydon and Sheffield – they are both within IND and their acts are the acts of the Secretary of State for the Home Department. But the distinction between Immigration Rules categories and the scheme-based categories – originally defined in terms of the two separate bureaucracies which administered them – is more sharp and significant than ever before.

[1]   Section 88 of the NIA Act 2002 extinguishes appeal rights in certain circumstances, one being where the person concerned does not have an 'immigration document' (s 88(2)(b)). Section 88(3) defines an 'immigration document' as including 'a work permit or other immigration employment document within the meaning of section 122'.

WORKERS (1): NON-WORK PERMIT EMPLOYEES

10.5 The main categories of non-work permit employment derived from both the Immigration Rules and Immigration Directorate Instructions (IDI) are:

- seasonal agricultural workers (who, however, need an immigration employment document (IED));[1]
- exchange teachers;
- overseas journalists and broadcasters;
- sole representatives;
- private servants in diplomatic households;
- domestic workers;
- overseas government employees;
- ministers of religion, missionaries and members of religious orders;
- operational ground staff of overseas airlines;
- Commonwealth citizens with grandparental connections;
- crew members.

Generally, these categories used to be described as the 'permit-free' categories[2] (meaning free of the need to obtain a work permit). Until 1985 the so-called permit-free categories used to include doctors and dentists coming to the UK to work, but this no longer applies.[3] The term 'permit-free' was abandoned in the current Immigration Rules [4] and in this text the categories concerned are referred to as non-work permit categories, simply to distinguish them as categories involving the immigration authorities alone, *not* Work Permits UK. Certain foreign nationals coming for non-work permit employment will be admitted, subject to a condition requiring registration with the police, unless they are ministers of religion, missionaries, members of religious orders or private servants in diplomatic households or their employment is for less than six months.[5] In all cases such persons need entry clearance in the appropriate category prior to arrival in the UK. Generally, switching is not allowed into these categories;[6] although there are exceptions, the Home Office is becoming less flexible in practice and so reference should be made to the specific categories discussed below. Apart from seasonal agricultural workers and crew members, persons in these capacities, may be accompanied or joined in the UK by their spouse or unmarried partner and children,[7] and in categories leading to settlement, these dependants will qualify for indefinite leave to remain at the same time as the principal.[8] There are no restrictions on the spouse or children taking employment.

[1] See 10.3 above.
[2] HC 251, paras 38–40.
[3] Their status is now regulated by the work permit scheme, the business provisions of the Immigration Rules, the Highly Skilled Migrant Programme (HSMP), and provisions relating to doctors and dentists in training: see 10.76, 10.107 and 9.45 respectively.
[4] HC 395, paras 136–199.
[5] HC 395, para 325(i).
[6] HC 395, paras 139(i), 147(i), 155(i), 164(i), 173 (i), 181(i).
[7] HC 395, paras 194–199 (spouses and children), 295J–K, inserted by Cm 4851 (unmarried partners); note that there is no provision for the admission of unmarried partners of exchange teachers.
[8] HC 395, paras 287, 295G, 298.

Seasonal farm work

10.6 The Seasonal Agricultural Workers Scheme (SAWS) was amended[1] in the light of the policy proposals set out in the 2002 Home Office white paper –

Secure Borders, Safe Haven: Integration with Diversity in Modern Britain.
The scheme which used to exist until late 2003 provided (under the then
Immigration Rules) that full time students aged between 18 and 25 could
come to do seasonal agricultural work in the UK. The idea was that they
would combine farm work with a short visit.[2] Leave was granted with a
condition restricting the freedom to take employment for a period not
exceeding three months, but extensions could be granted up to a total of six
months if further farm work was available. The category was strictly seasonal
and no leave extension was granted beyond 30 November in any year. A
student on the scheme could stay on as a visitor but could not switch to any
other category. The usual maintenance and accommodation provisions had to
be satisfied. Following the review of the Scheme, the upper age limit was
removed (although not the requirement that recruits be students), and SAWS is
now quota driven. The quota for 2003 and 2004 was 25,000 and is 16,250
for 2005. The reduction reflects the fact that many of those who participated
in the scheme in previous years were from countries which are now part of the
EEA, having joined on the 1 May 2004. Each quota will now run for a
calendar year from January to December. SAWS participants are permitted to
work for up to a maximum of six months.[3]

1   HC 395, paras 104–109 as amended by HC 538. For the inter-relationship between this
     scheme and the sector-based scheme work permit under HC 395 para 135I–K, see 10.63
     below.
2   Under HC 395, para 44 any period spent in farm work was and is still to be counted as a
     visit. Thus if four months is spent in farm work, up to two can be spent as a tourist.
3   HC 395, para 105.

10.7 The new SAWS continues to be run by selected Home Office-approved
operators who place applicant agricultural workers with farmers and growers.
They are then registered with those farmers or growers, who can then call on
the registered workers' services to meet their short term labour needs, using a
regulated system. The new scheme runs for the entire calendar year and an
applicant can enter at any time during that year and stay for the maximum
period of six months, provided he or she holds an immigration employment
document in the form of a valid Home Office work card issued by the
operator of the scheme[1] and intends to leave at the end of the period of leave
granted as a seasonal (agricultural) worker.[2] The work the applicant takes
must be that permitted by the work card.[3] It is not possible for applicants to
extend their leave to remain beyond the period of six months but the scheme
does permit multiple entries as a seasonal agricultural worker provided there
is a gap of 3 months from the last period of leave granted in that capacity.[4] In
addition, nationals of EC Association Agreement countries (Bulgaria and
Romania) may exceptionally be able to vary their leave to remain into self
employment, but mandatory entry clearance is now the general rule.[5] Participants are not entitled to bring dependants.

1   HC 395, para 104(ii). A fee of £12 is payable for the SAWS immigration employment
     document: Immigration Employment Document (Fees) Regulations 2003, SI 2003/541,
     reg 4C (amended by SI 2003/2447).
2   HC 395, para 104(iii).
3   HC 395, para 104(iv).
4   HC 395, para 104(v). The rationale behind the scheme is discussed and described on the
     Home Office website (www.workingintheuk.gov.uk).

5   HC 395, para 217, as amended in August 2004 by Cmd 6297; *Panayotova v Minister voor Vreemdelingenzaken en Integratie*. Case C-327/02(16 November 2004, unreported). See 10.99 below, and 7.170 above.

Exchange teachers

10.8 Ordinarily, teachers from abroad who are suitably qualified may only come to this country for full-time employment by obtaining a work permit. However, teachers and language assistants can come to the UK for up to two years on a number of different exchange schemes without work permits.[1] This category is steadily becoming redundant as the criteria for work permits for teachers are relaxed. Exchange teachers and language assistants must have prior entry clearance[2] and must be coming to a school or educational establishment in the UK under an exchange scheme approved by the Department for Education and Skills, the Scottish or Welsh Office of Education or the Department of Education, Northern Ireland, or administered by the British Council's Education and Training Group [3] or the League for the Exchange of Commonwealth Teachers.[4] They must be prepared to leave the UK at the end of the exchange period,[5] not to take employment except in the terms of this exchange scheme and be able to maintain and accommodate themselves and any dependants without recourse to public funds.[6] Normally leave is given for an initial 12 months,[7] and further extensions can be obtained provided this does not mean that the teacher remains in the UK for more than two years from the date when he or she was first given leave to enter.[8] The Immigration Rules do not allow exchange teachers to switch to ordinary employment. However, Work Permits UK currently considers teaching to be a shortage occupation and so the Home Office will exceptionally consider in-country applications to switch to work permit status on a case-by-case basis. Exchange teachers may be accompanied by spouses and children under 18.[9] There are no restrictions on the family members taking employment during the exchange period.

1   HC 395, paras 110–115.
2   HC 395, paras 110(v) and 122.
3   Formerly the Central Bureau for Educational Visits and Exchanges.
4   HC 395, para 110(i), as amended by Cmd 6339 on 1 October 2004.
5   HC 395, para 110(ii) and (iii).
6   HC 395, para 110(iv).
7   HC 395, para 111.
8   HC 395, para 113(v).
9   HC 395, paras 122–127. See 10.35 below. There is no provision for the admission of unmarried partners of exchange teachers.

Overseas journalists and broadcasters

10.9 Representatives of overseas newspapers, news agencies and broadcasting organisations on long-term assignment to the UK may qualify for an immigration status as such, and so will not require a work permit. But they must have been engaged by their organisation outside the UK before being posted here, intend to work full-time for the organisation and not to take any other kind of employment, and be able to satisfy the maintenance and accommodation provisions of the Immigration Rules.[1] According to the Home Office the term 'newspaper' is intended to cover not only daily newspapers but also other periodical publications concerned directly with news gathering and reporting.[2] Representatives of some overseas journals or magazines may, therefore, qualify for admission under these arrangements, but others will require work permits if they work for journals which are not directly concerned with news gathering and reporting. Employees other than journalists may be considered under this rule (for example, producers, news cameramen and front-of-camera personnel); secretaries and other administrative staff, however, need work permits.[3] At all times, the newspaper or broadcasting organisation must remain an 'overseas' organisation.[4] This is very much a question of fact. Although a newspaper or broadcasting organisation has its main office overseas, it may cease to be an 'overseas' organisation by having a branch or subsidiary in the UK if the UK activities mean that there is no real presence overseas. A journalist or broadcaster who does not qualify under this rule may qualify in the sole representative category if he or she is in fact the only representative.[5] Alternatively, if there is doubt whether the organisation is an 'overseas' one (because it already has a branch or a subsidiary here), it may be possible to apply for a work permit.

[1]   HC 395, paras 136–139.
[2]   Letter dated 9 April 1986 from the Home Office, printed in INLP 1(3) (October 1986).
[3]   IDI, Employment Ch 5, s 2, para 1.
[4]   HC 395, paras 136–143.
[5]   See 10.11 below.

10.10 Entry clearance is a mandatory requirement and admission is usually for up to 12 months initially.[1] Journalists and others admitted under this rule qualify for an extension of leave if they are still in the same employment for which they were admitted and their employer certifies that they are still required for the employment in question.[2] Normally the extension will be for three years, if the employer so certifies.[3] After four years they will qualify for settlement and removal of all restrictions.[4]

[1]   HC 395, para 136(v) and 137.
[2]   HC 395, para 139.
[3]   HC 395, para 140.
[4]   HC 395, para 142.

Sole representatives

10.11 Representatives of overseas firms which have no branch, subsidiary or other representative in the UK and have their headquarters and principal place of business outside the UK may qualify for an immigration status as such, and so will not require a work permit. They will need to demonstrate that they have been recruited and taken on as employees outside the UK; are senior employees with full authority to take operational decisions and can set up and operate a registered branch or wholly-owned subsidiary; will be employed full-time as sole representatives; do not intend to take employment except within the terms of the requirements for leave to enter as sole representatives;

are not majority shareholders in the overseas firm; and can satisfy the maintenance and accommodation provisions of the Immigration Rules.[1]

¹   HC 395, para 144.

10.12 Although entry clearance is mandatory,[1] one of the advantages of sole representative status is that there is no obligation on the entry clearance officer to refer the case to the Home Office, and very often the entry clearance officer will be prepared to deal with an applicant on the spot unless he or she has a complicated immigration history or the case raises difficult and unresolved legal points.[2] In practice, the rule is interpreted flexibly by entry clearance officers and the Home Office. It should be plain that the purpose of the application is the commercial benefit of the overseas business (which may be a sole trader, firm or company or even a trade union),[3] rather than the immigration convenience of the applicant. There must be an operating overseas business in existence, which must remain centred abroad. An employee of a 'brass plate' business will be regarded not as a sole representative but as someone coming to set up in business.[4] Moreover, the application will fail if an overseas business is a one-person business and there will be no one left to run it when the applicant arrives in the UK. The overseas business needs to be an active trading concern overseas apart from its proposed activities in the UK,[5] and a business which has been trading for less than 12 months will be required to justify the need to establish an overseas presence in the UK.[6] But the fact that the UK entity is likely to flourish so vigorously that it might eventually overshadow its parent does not mean that the application will fail.

¹   HC 395, paras 144(vii) and 145.
²   Diplomatic Service Procedures (DSP), Ch 18.8.
³   In the case of *Gurung* (TH/7895/98) it was held by an adjudicator that the overseas business is not limited to businesses in the form of companies as the Home Office had argued. The Home Office appears to accept this in practice.
⁴   *Certilan* (4689).
⁵   *Lokko v Secretary of State for the Home Department* [1990] Imm AR 539, QBD affirming the IAT decision at [1990] Imm AR 111.
⁶   IDI, Employment, Ch 5, Annex J, para 1.

10.13 The position of sole representatives who are owners of the overseas business either as shareholders or partners has always caused problems. If they own or partly own the overseas business, they may be considered as business persons seeking to expand their own business, unless they can show that they do not have a majority shareholding in the company or a majority share of the partnership. In *Lokko*[1] the Tribunal said that in principle there was nothing wrong with a majority shareholder or director becoming an overseas representative. However, majority shareholders are now expressly barred from qualifying as sole representatives under the current Immigration Rules.[2] If they wish to come to the UK, they must either divest themselves of control, apply under the business Rules or obtain a work permit.[3] The Home Office view is that where an applicant owns more than 30 per cent of the overseas business, the application should attract detailed scrutiny.[4] If it is evident that as well as owning a significant share, the applicant is also the driving force behind the overseas business, such that his or her presence in the UK is likely to mean that the centre of operations shifts to the UK, then the application will be refused.[5] However, there is now clear first-instance authority for the proposition that provided the applicant owns no more than 50 per cent of the overseas business he or she will not be a majority shareholder.[6]

1   *Lokko v Secretary of State for the Home Department* [1990] Imm AR 111, IAT.
2   HC 395, para 144(iv).
3   As a general rule it is not possible for a work permit to be issued if the intended worker holds more than 10% of the shares in the employing company or any connected business: Business and Commercial Work Permit Guidance Notes, para 24.
4   IDI, Employment Ch 5, Annex J, para 2.2.
5   IDI, Employment Ch 5, Annex J, para 2.2.
6   *Bakhsh v Entry Clearance Officer (Dubai)* (TH/7096/99); see also (2000) 3 IIEL 6.

10.14 An early Tribunal case ruled that a sole representative must have 'plenipotentiary' powers and not be a mere salesperson on commission.[1] The Immigration Rules now make it clear that sole representatives should be senior employees with full authority to take operational decisions, to set up and operate branches and subsidiaries and should be working full-time. Although sole representatives must have been recruited and taken on as employees outside the UK,[2] they do not have to have been employed by the overseas company for any minimum period. In practice, though, the Home Office prefers to see previous experience.[3] An applicant for entry clearance should be prepared to produce supporting documentation, including a contract of employment or letter of appointment, evidence that the overseas firm is functioning and trading, and an explanation why the firm wishes to appoint him or her and whether it has previously had a UK representative.[4] The application should make clear that decisions by the proposed sole representative generally will *not* have to be made with reference to the employer parent company. If the overseas business already has representation in the UK, the application should be to Work Permits UK for a work permit rather than a sole representative application.

1   *Hope* (832) (14 September 1976). The current IDI indicate that a remuneration package including commission is acceptable provided the salary element satisfies the maintenance and accommodation requirements: IDI Aug 01, Ch 5, s 3, Annex J, para 2.
2   HC 395, para 144(i); *Baydur* (5442); *Kongar* (5501); *Hope* (832).
3   IDI, Employment Ch 5, s 3, Annex J, para 2.
4   IDI Employment Ch 5, Annex K.

10.15 Leave will be granted for 12 months in the first instance, and during that time the sole representative must establish a registered branch or subsidiary (unless it is an overseas entity, such as a partnership, which is incapable of registering a branch).[1] An extension of stay will now only be granted if the sole representative has set up a registered branch or wholly owned subsidiary and is in charge of it.[2] The other requirements of the on-entry rule must continue to be satisfied. An extension is for three years, and at the end of this time the employee will qualify for indefinite leave to remain if he or she has met the sole representative requirements throughout the four-year period and is still needed for the employment in question.[3] Employees brought in from overseas to work in the newly established branch or subsidiary will need a work permit; this in itself will not affect the individual's sole representative status. The Home Office takes the view that every overseas company setting up a branch in the UK must apply to register with Companies House within one month of having opened the branch, or that a subsidiary must be incorporated within that time.[4] The Tribunal has rejected this view, deciding that branch registration or incorporation of a subsidiary need only take place within the first 12 months, and that the Home Office cannot refuse to grant a further three years leave to remain because of a failure to act more promptly, provided the applicant has in fact been employed by the overseas business for the purpose of representing it within the UK and managed to register a branch or incorporate a subsidiary by the end of the initial 12 months.[5] The one-month registration requirement is imposed by company law and not by the Immigration Rules.[6]

[1] See *Gurung* (TH/7895/98) at 10.12 fn 3 above.
[2] HC 395, para 147(iii).
[3] HC 395, para 150. For a discussion of the continuity requirement in this and other work-related Rules see 10.97 below.
[4] IDI, Employment Ch 5, Annex J, para 1.1.
[5] *Trivedi v Secretary of State for the Home Department* TH/8202/98 (00TH01059).
[6] Companies Act 1985, ss 690A, 691 and Sch 21A.

Private servants in diplomatic households[1]

10.16 Domestic workers hired by consular and diplomatic staff and members of their family to work in their households may qualify as 'private servants in diplomatic households' under the Immigration Rules.[2] They may undertake the work of a chauffeur, gardener, cook or nanny if they are providing a personal service relating to the running of the employer's household.[3] Previously, diplomatic servants could be recruited from the age of 16; now the minimum age is 18.[4] A diplomatic household means the household of a member of staff of a diplomatic or consular mission, who enjoys diplomatic privileges and immunity within the meaning of the Vienna Convention, or a member of the family forming part of the household of such a person.[5] Under earlier Rules employment could be part-time,[6] but now it must be full-time with no intention to work other than in this capacity.[7] To ensure that the maintenance and accommodation requirements of the Rules are met, the entry clearance officer will require the employer to sign a written undertaking to this effect. A separate bedroom must be provided. The employer must also complete and sign a statement of the main terms and conditions of the servant's employment.[8] The entry clearance officer will also interview the worker alone to ensure that he or she understands the terms or conditions, and if the application is successful will give him or her a leaflet (translated into several languages) explaining the worker's rights under UK law.[9] Initial leave is given for 12 months and extensions are given for 12 months at a time; after four years of continuous stay in this capacity, if the servant is still required for the employment in question, an application may be made for indefinite leave to remain, provided the relevant requirements have been met throughout the four-year period.[10] The Rules do not permit switching to this category,[11] though it is permissible for the servant of a diplomat to change diplomatic employers within the same Embassy. In those circumstances, the new employer will be required to sign a statement relating to the terms and conditions of the employment.[12]

1   The Home Office is currently reviewing these provisions by way of a public consultation
    process.
2   HC 395, paras 152–159.
3   IDI, Employment Ch 5, s 4, para 1.1.
4   HC 395, para 152(i), replacing HC 251, para 40(a).
5   HC 395, para 152(ii).
6   *Gunaben* (3475).
7   HC 395, para 152(iii) and (iv).
8   IDI, Employment Ch 5, s 4, Annex M, para 5.
9   IDI, Employment Ch 5, s 4, Annex M, paras 6 and 9.
10 HC 395, paras 156 and 158. For 'continuous', see 10.97 below.
11 HC 395, para 155.
12 IDI Employment Ch 5, s 4, Annex M, para 8.3.

10.17 Private servants in diplomatic households are to be distinguished from members of the service staff of a diplomatic mission, as the latter are exempt from immigration control.[1] In practice the distinction is a difficult one to make, as we have already seen.[2] Although not exempt from control, private servants in diplomatic households may enjoy limited immunity under the Vienna Convention.[3]

1   Immigration Act 1971, s 8(3). See *Kandiah* (2699) unreported. A servant of the head of
    mission employed at the official residence is employed at the mission; see Diplomatic
    Privileges Act 1964, Sch 1, para 1(i).
2   See 6.46 above.
3   Diplomatic Privileges Act 1964, Sch 1, para 37(4); *Diaz* (2584).

Domestic workers

10.18 The Rules regarding private servants in diplomatic households must also be distinguished from the former concessionary arrangements, which were outside the Immigration Rules, whereby visitors or those coming in a category which would lead to settlement could bring their domestic staff with them to the UK.[1] Under this former concession, from July 1998, domestic workers were permitted entry with their employer provided they had worked for that employer for 12 months before arrival and would be undertaking specific work at a level exceeding the International Labour Organisation's (ILO) basic definition of domestic work.[2] After various administrative changes in 2001, the concession was incorporated into the Immigration Rules with effect from 18 September 2002. Between 23 July 1998 and 23 October 1999, the Home Office operated a regularisation scheme for overstaying domestic workers, who had an initial entry clearance as a domestic worker and had fled their original employer. Subsequently, the Home Office confirmed that it would consider any application not made within the regularisation scheme deadline on a case by case basis.[3] They also indicated that a domestic worker who was granted an initial 12 months' leave under the regularisation programme and who subsequently applied for indefinite leave to remain, could count his or her continuous domestic employment prior to the date of regularisation as part of the four-year qualifying period.[4] Furthermore, within the regularisation process, where the worker had fled from a domestic household as a result of abuse or exploitation and had gone into other domestic work, but not in a private household, that other work could count towards the four years needed for indefinite leave, but only where the initial regularisation was on that basis.[5]

---

[1] For a potted history of the early scheme and the changes made to it in 1998 and 2001, see IDI Employment Ch 5, s 12, para 1.1, Dec 02.
[2] For details see 5th edition at 10.14.
[3] Letters from Home Office to CMS Cameron McKenna 1 February 2000.
[4] Two Home Office faxes of 15 January 2001 to Winstanley-Burgess.
[5] IDI Ch 5, s 2 Annex BB.

10.19 The Immigration Rules, HC 395, paragraphs 159A-H largely follow the terms of the previous concession, but also introduce an element of realism in laying down what sort of working relationship is required. Under the Rules, the domestic worker has to be aged between 18 and 65, and must have worked for the employer for one year or more immediately prior to the application for entry clearance under the same roof as the employer or in a household that the employer uses on a regular basis and where there is evidence that there is a connection between the employer and the domestic worker. The domestic worker must intend to travel to the United Kingdom in the company of the employer, the employer's spouse, or the employer's minor child. He or she must intend to work under the same roof as the employer or in a household used by the employer for him or herself on a regular basis and where there is evidence that there is a connection between the employer and the domestic worker. The domestic worker must satisfy the usual maintenance and accommodation requirements.[1] When an application is made, either for an entry clearance to work for an existing employer or for further leave to remain to work for a new employer, the employer is required to complete and sign a statement of the main terms and conditions of the domestic worker's employment. Domestic workers will usually be interviewed on their own, at least on their first application, to ensure that they understand the terms and conditions of their employment and are willing to go to the UK. If their application is successful, they will be given an information leaflet explaining their rights under United Kingdom criminal and employment laws. On arrival in the UK, they will initially be given leave in line with their employer, and, provided the employer is in a category leading to settlement, they will be able to apply for indefinite leave to remain at the same time as the employer.[2] The work which the domestic worker undertakes no longer needs to be at a level exceeding basic ILO standards. Domestic workers may include cleaners, chauffeurs, gardeners, cooks, those carrying out personal care for their employers or a member of their family, and nannies if they are providing a personal service relating to the running of the employer's household.[3]

---

[1] HC 395, para 159A, inserted by Cm 5597.
[2] IDI Employment Ch 5, s 12 (Dec 02) and Annex M, para 1.
[3] IDI Employment Ch 5, s 12, para 2.4.

10.20 Employers who employ domestic workers in breach of their landing conditions may be liable to prosecution under section 8 of the Asylum and Immigration Act 1996 (if the employment commenced on or after 27 January 1997). However, the Home Office indicated at the time of the regularisation scheme which operated between 1998 and 1999 (10.18 above) that despite the terms of the Act it was never envisaged that any action would be taken against an employer found to be employing a person illegally in his or her private household.[1] Whilst that position has not been formally withdrawn it related to employment which required regularisation under the scheme and may have no bearing on any other employment in a private household.

[1] IND to Kingsley Napley, 27.10.98; see also *Hansard* HC 23.7.98, col 611 (WA).

Overseas government employees

10.21 Overseas government employees are persons coming to the UK for employment by an overseas government or those employed by the UN or other international organisations of which the UK is a member,[1] but do not include diplomats, members of their service staff and others exempt from immigration control.[2] To obtain entry such employees must be able to produce either a valid entry clearance or satisfactory documentary evidence of their status as overseas government employees.[3] It must be their intention to work full-time and not to take employment in any other capacity, and they must be able to satisfy the maintenance and accommodation requirements of the Immigration Rules.[4] After 12 months, leave will be extended for a further three years if the employee is still in the same employment and the employer certifies that he or she is still needed.[5] If the same conditions are met after four years in the UK in this capacity, the employee qualifies for indefinite leave.[6] Employees should be posted from abroad and not recruited locally, as switching into this category is not allowed.[7] This group is also to be distinguished from private servants of diplomats.[8] The key here is that the employment contract should be with the overseas government and not the diplomat.

[1] HC 395, para 160, IDI, Sep 04, Ch 5, s 5; IDI, Sep 04 Ch 14, Annex B, which lists the relevant international organisations at para 5.
[2] See chapter 6 above. The IDI (IDI, Ch 14, Annex B) above also refers to governors, directors, alternates, officers and employees of the International Monetary Fund, the Commonwealth Secretariat, the International Bank for Reconstruction and Development, the International Development Association and similar organisations as partially exempt from control.
[3] HC 395, paras 161(i), 162 and 163. A visa is mandatory for visa nationals: IDI, Ch 5, s 5 para 1.
[4] HC 395, para 161(ii)–(iv).
[5] HC 395, paras 164 and 165.
[6] HC 395, para 167.
[7] HC 395, para 164 (i) and IDI, Ch 14, Annex B, para 4.1.
[8] *Hussain* (5035); see 10.16 above.

Ministers of religion, missionaries and members of religious orders

10.22 Ministers, missionaries and members of religious orders may be admitted for up to 12 months in the first instance if they hold a current entry clearance.[1] Under earlier Rules, the definitions of 'ministers of religion' and so forth were left largely to the appellate authorities and courts. Now such definitions, and the particular qualifications for entry to the UK, are set out in the Immigration Rules and amplified by the IDI.[2]

1   HC 395, paras 170(v) and 171.
2   HC 395, paras 170–177 and IDI Aug 04, Ch 5, s 6 and Annexes Q, R, S, T and U.

Minister of religion

10.23 A minister of religion is a religious functionary whose main regular duties comprise the leading of a congregation in performing the rites and rituals of the faith and in preaching the essentials of the creed.[1] To qualify for leave a minister must either have worked for at least one year as a minister of religion in any of the five years immediately prior to the date the application is made, or (where ordination is prescribed by a religious faith as the sole means of entering the ministry) have been ordained as a minister following at least one year's full-time or two years' part-time training for the ministry.[2] Whether a person is a minister of religion will depend on the structure of the religion in question and the extent to which it is divided into a priesthood and laity, and on the facts of any particular case.[3] Although the criteria for ministry appear to be objective, there is clearly room for discretion, and the IDI make it clear that the Church of Scientology and the Church of Unification (the 'Moonies') do not count as religions and their members do not qualify for admission as ministers of religion or missionaries,[4] although members of the International Society for Krishna Consciousness and Christian Scientists may do.[5] The IDI set out five 'core duties' which a minister of religion will be expected to perform: leading worship; providing religious education for children and adults by preaching and teaching; officiating at marriages, funerals, etc; offering counselling and welfare support to members of the congregation; and recruiting, training and co-ordinating the work of local volunteers and lay preachers.[6] They also contain a long list of additional duties which the minister might or might not be expected to perform.[7] From 23 August 2004 those seeking to be admitted as ministers of religion will be required to produce a certificate that they have passed an IELTS test in spoken English.[8]

1   HC 395, para 169(i).
2   HC 395, para 170(i)(a), as amended by Cmd 6297 on 23 Aug 04. An understanding of these definitions is assisted by reference to earlier Tribunal decisions, which held that ministers of religion could be defined either by their qualifications, eg ordination, or by their activities, eg leading prayers and responsibility for religious activity in the community: *Mobley* (5368); *Begum (Kalsoon) v Visa Officer, Islamabad* [1988] Imm AR 325. Both these elements of the former definition are contained in the Immigration Rules.
3   *Begum (Kalsoon)* above; *Singh (Piara) v Entry Clearance Officer, New Delhi* [1977] Imm AR 1; *Hamid v Entry Clearance Officer, Dhaka* [1986] Imm AR 469. IDI Nov 00, Ch 5, s 6, Annex T contains a summary of the beliefs, structures, etc of the major religions.
4   988 HC Official Report (5th series) written answers, col 123 (Scientology); IDI Aug 04, Ch 5, s 6, para 1. Moonies may only be admitted as visitors with a maximum stay of six months: IDI Sep 04, Ch 5, s 6, Annex U.
5   IDI, Ch 5, s 6, Annex U. The Home Office holds detailed files on a number of religions, which are frequently updated to provide a database to determine whether an employer or applicant qualifies under the Immigration Rules.
6   IDI, Ch 5, s 6, Annex Q.
7   IDI, Ch 5, s 6, Annex S.
8   International English Language Testing System: HC 395, para 170 (iva), as inserted by Cmd 6297; IDI Ch 5, s 6, Annex Q, para 2.

10.24 Following changes made to the Immigration Rules which came into force on 23 August 2004 it is now possible for someone who entered the

United Kingdom in some other temporary capacity to remain here as a minister of religion provided that he or she: [1]

- was admitted to the United Kingdom or given an extension of stay, except as a minister of religion or a visitor under paragraphs 40–56 of HC 395, which has resulted in him or her spending a continuous period of at least 12 months in the UK prior to the application being made; and

- has either been working for at least one year as a minister of religion in any of the five years immediately prior to the date on which the extension is sought or, where ordination is prescribed by a religious faith as the sole means of entering the ministry, has been ordained as a minister of religion following at least one year's full-time or two years part-time training for the ministry; and

- has obtained such experience of working, or has been ordained and received the specified period of training, either in the United Kingdom or abroad; and

- is imminently to be appointed, or has been appointed to a position as a minister of religion and is suitable for such a position, as certified by the leadership of his or her prospective congregation; and

- meets the requirements of paragraph 170(ii)–(iva).

An extension of stay not exceeding 12 months may be granted provided the minister continues to satisfy the requirements of the switching rule.[2] After four years the minister will qualify for settlement.[3]

[1]   HC 395, paras 174A and 174B, as amended by Cmd 6297; IDI Aug 04, Ch 5, s 6, Annex Q, para 7.
[2]   HC 395, para 174B, as amended by Cmd 6297.
[3]   HC 395, para 176, as amended by Cmd 6297.

Missionaries

10.25 Missionaries are persons who are directly engaged in spreading a religious doctrine and whose work is not in essence administrative or clerical.[1] To obtain entry as a missionary the person must have trained as a missionary or have worked as one and must be sent to the UK by an overseas organisation.[2] In *Kalsoon Begum v Visa Officer, Islamabad*[3] the Tribunal held that it was wrong to treat the applicant as a 'missionary' bearing in mind that she was seeking to work with committed Muslims rather than preach to prospective converts. On the other hand, a missionary is not restricted to a person engaged full-time in evangelical preaching or counselling, as the Tribunal decision in *Mobley*[4] indicates. There, the applicant wanted to work at the UK-based training centre of a Christian training and missionary society which operated in many countries. She was held to be a missionary even though her duties at the centre involved bookkeeping for 37 hours a week for the international office and 23 hours a week in evangelistic meetings, local church involvement, counselling, bible study and prayer meetings. Under the current Immigration Rules the main question of fact in such a case will be whether the bookkeeping duties make the work essentially administrative or clerical. The IDI give further definition to this rule and state that the duties of a missionary may include the organisation of missionary activity. Working full-time as a teacher in a school run by a Church or missionary organisation would not count as missionary work, but translating the Bible is missionary and not clerical work.[5] Thus a missionary may be doing field work but could be supervising staff and/or co-ordinating the organisation of ministry work or be in charge of a particular activity such as accounts/finance, personnel management or information technology. Those in support posts (clerical, secretarial, etc) should not be considered missionaries unless a substantial amount of time is spent in the UK in active field work. The IDI set out a number of organisations whose staff could be treated as missionaries.[6] Whilst the Rules do not permit switching into this category, the Home Office exercises its discretion in certain circumstances to permit visitors and students to remain as missionaries, but only where a general concession has been agreed with the Home Office on a religion-by-religion basis.[7]

[1] HC 395, para 169(ii).
[2] HC 395, para 170(i)(b).
[3] [1988] Imm AR 325.
[4] *Mobley* (5368).
[5] IDI Aug 04, Ch 5, s 6, Annex Q, para 8.
[6] IDI Sep 04, Ch 5, s 6, Annex U. Mormons, those working with Operation Mobilisation and with St Stephen's Society may be treated as missionaries.
[7] IDI Ch 5, s 6, Annex Q, para 10; IDI, Ch 5, s 6, Annex U.

Members of a religious order

10.26 Members of a religious order are persons who are coming to live in a community run by that order.[1] To qualify for admission they must be coming to live in a community maintained by the religious order of which they are members, and, if intending to teach, do not intend to do so save at an establishment maintained by their order.[2] According to the Tribunal in *Hamid*,[3] approved in *Kalsoon Begum v Visa Officer, Islamabad*,[4] a 'religious order' is a monastic order defined in the *codex juris canonici* (canon 487) as a 'stable mode of living in community in which the faithful bind themselves by vow to observe in addition to the precepts of the rule, the evangelical counsels of obedience, chastity and poverty'. The Tribunal believed this definition to be unduly narrow, but made it clear that the term could not extend to persons not in such an order who were simply fulfilling the role of a spiritual guide to a lay congregation. In practice this category is restricted to members of monastic communities, monks and nuns (usually Christian or Buddhist) and similar religious communities involving a permanent commitment.[5] Whilst most of the work undertaken by the member will be within the community itself, the Home Office accepts that some members may undertake outside work directed by their order which will permit teaching within their schools. Teaching in schools not maintained by the order will require a work permit. Novices whose training consists of taking part in the daily community life of an order should be treated as members of a religious order, although anyone taking on a formal course of study in a non-community maintained academic institution will be treated as a student.[6] Whilst the Immigration Rules do not permit switching into this category, the Home Office exercises its discretion in certain circumstances to permit switching exceptionally if the applicant entered the UK to visit or study under the auspices of the order and clearly meets the other requirements of the Rules.[7]

1   HC 395, para 169(iii).
2   HC 395, para 170(i)(c).
3   [1986] Imm AR 469.
4   [1988] Imm AR 325.
5   IDI Aug 04, Ch 5, s 6, Annex Q, para 11. This includes organisations such as the Bruderhof communities in the UK: Annex U.
6   IDI, Ch 5, s 6, Annex Q, para 12.
7   IDI, Ch 5, s 6, Annex Q, para 13.

Generally applicable requirements

10.27 Admission will only be given to ministers, missionaries and members of religious orders if they are coming to work full-time in their chosen calling,[1] do not intend to take employment other than in that calling,[2] and can maintain and accommodate themselves and any dependants without recourse to public funds.[3] Under the Immigration Rules employment must be full-time, but it is not the task of the entry clearance officer to consider whether the primary purpose of admission is to follow the particular religious calling, as was once held by the Tribunal.[4] But entry clearance officers may have to take into account the general public good,[5] in so far as it may be affected by the existence of a general prohibition such as the one which applies to Scientologists, or by the capacity of the religious work of the applicant to stir up inter-communal hatred, lead to public disorder, or incite violence.

1   HC 395, para 170(ii).
2   HC 395, para 170(iii).
3   HC 395, para 170(iv).
4   *Singh (Piara) v Entry Clearance Officer, New Delhi* [1977] Imm AR 1.
5   See HC 395, para 320(19).

10.28 Normally, ministers of religion are admitted for an initial period of 12 months.[1] At the end of this period extensions are usually for three years to continue their duties.[2] But they must obtain from the leadership of their congregation, their employer or the head of their religious order a certificate that their services are still required.[3] Thereafter they may apply for indefinite leave and removal of all restrictions on their stay.[4] They will need a further certificate that their services are still required.[5]

1   HC 395, para 171.
2   HC 395, para 174.
3   HC 395, para 173(iii).
4   HC 395, para 176, as amended by Cmd 6297.
5   HC 395, para 176(iii).

Concessionary arrangements

10.29 Various concessionary arrangements exist in relation to visiting preachers coming to the UK on a preaching tour, provided the visit is a temporary absence from permanent employment abroad and does not amount to disguised employment as a minister of religion in the UK.[1]

Religious musicians may be admitted without a work permit to perform at religious services in the UK.[2] Both these groups will be admitted as visitors for up to six months. Volunteers working for religious organisations are treated like any other charity worker; that is to say, they may be admitted in accordance with a concession which provides that the work must be for a listed [3] or registered charity, the work must be unpaid (save for subsistence, accommodation and expenses)[4] and directed towards a worthy cause closely related to the aims of the charity, and must be field work involving direct assistance to those the charity has been established to help.

1   IDI Aug 04, Ch 5, s 6, Annex Q, para 14.
2   IDI Ch 5, s 6, Annex Q, para 15 and IDI Jul 04 Ch 17, s 3 (entertainers).
3   IDI Ch 5, s 6, Annex Q, para 16 and IDI Jul 02, Ch 17, s 9, Annex B, which lists relevant charitable organisations.
4   IDI Jul 03, Ch 17, s 9.

Operational ground staff of overseas airlines

10.30 The provisions of the Immigration Rules allowing overseas airlines to send operational ground staff to the UK are first, that there must be a transfer to the UK to take up duties at an international airport as a station manager, security manager or technical manager.[1] Staff who are posted to work outside an airport are excluded, as are airport-based staff such as catering officers. These do not come within the category and will need a work permit.[2] The other conditions applying to operational ground staff of overseas airlines are that the individual must have an intention to work full-time for the airline concerned and not to take employment except within the terms of the requirements for leave to enter under this category; must satisfy a maintenance and accommodation requirement; and must hold a valid entry clearance.[3] Initial leave is normally for 12 months followed by a three-year extension and indefinite leave after four years, provided the employer certifies at each stage that the person is still required for the employment in question.[4]

1   HC 395, para 178(i). The rule does not apply to staff, whether operational or not, of British owned airlines. Unless they are otherwise admissible, they will need a work permit: see IDI Sep 04, Ch 5, s 7, paras 1 and 2.2.
2   See IDI, Ch 5, s 7, para 2.2; *Attivor v Secretary of State for the Home Department* [1988] Imm AR 109, CA;
3   HC 395, para 178(ii)–(v).
4   HC 395, paras 179–185.

Non-work permit categories outside the Immigration Rules

10.31 There are a number of other categories of persons who may be admitted for work without a work permit, which are listed in the IDI.[1] Most are temporary, such as research assistants to MPs (who are normally overseas students learning about government and politics before resuming studies or entering a career),[2] sportspersons,[3] entertainers,[4] film actors, producers, directors and technicians on location,[5] off-shore workers,[6] overseas insurance company representatives,[7] workers for the Jewish Agency[8] and certain exchange and placement students.[9] Temporary carers of a sick relative or friend are also listed in this miscellaneous category.[10] Workers qualified in

Rudolf Steiner educational methods coming to work at Camphill communities may be admitted with a view to settlement.[11]

1   Currently IDI, Ch 17. The section headings are as follows: Bunac students, carers, entertainers, off-shore workers, other permit free categories, research assistants to MPs, Rudolph Steiner establishments, sportsmen and women, voluntary workers from overseas, gap year entrants for work in schools, Japan Youth Exchange Scheme and concessionary leave outside the Rules for teachers with leave as working holidaymakers.
2   IDI Sep 04, Ch 17, s 6. They must satisfy the maintenance and accommodation requirement, with not more than reasonable expenses paid from the UK source. They may be granted up to 12 months' leave.
3   IDI Aug 01, Ch 17, s 8. The IDI are fairly complicated. A permit-free concession enables professional or amateur sportspersons to enter for sporting events such as tournaments and championships for up to six months, provided they satisfy the maintenance and accommodation requirements and can meet the cost of the onward or return journey. Polo grooms and personal coaches may be admitted with them for the same period. But sportspersons need work permits if they are based in the UK for a whole season or are coming to join a British professional team or to give regular coaching, or for over six months. See 10.43 below.
4   IDI Jul 04, Ch 17, s 3. Those coming for specific types of events, including charity concerts, Arts festivals and religious occasions may be admitted under the concession, provided they pose no threat to the domestic labour force, are not using the engagement to establish themselves here and do not intend to remain for more than six months. A definitive list of festivals and events covered by the concession can be found at IDI Jun 04 ch 17, s3, para 5.
5   IDI, Ch 17, s 3, para 12.
6   IDI Sep 04, Ch 17, s 4. Entry clearance is not mandatory and no work permit is required if no part of the work is on-shore. Switching is permitted but settlement should normally be refused.
7   IDI Oct 01, Ch 17, s 5, para 1 The processing of the policy must take place overseas. Leave may be granted for 12 months at a time up to three years.
8   IDI Ch 17, s 5, para 2. Leave may be granted for a maximum of 12 months.
9   IDI Ch 17, s 5, para 3 (International Association for Exchange of Students of Technical Experience): placements of up to three months with UK companies and local authorities; British Universities North America Club (BUNAC) (IDI Jun 02, Ch 17, s 1): see chapter 9 above.
10   IDI Jun 01, Ch 17, s 2.
11   IDI Sep 04, Ch 17, s 7. A list of some 70 establishments is given at Annex A. No work permit or entry clearance is required, and settlement may be achieved, but there is no switching into this category. Leave is granted for 12 months at a time. There is also provision made for trainees, either as volunteers or under TWES.

Crew members

10.32 Leave to enter may be given to crew members of ships, aircraft, hovercraft, hydrofoils or international train services to enable them to join their vessel, for hospital treatment, repatriation or transfer to another vessel, and so forth,[1] if the crew members concerned are not eligible for entry without leave.[2] The period of leave given will only be sufficient for the specific purpose and there is a presumption against extension,[3] unless the crew member is married to a person present and settled in the UK and meets the requirements for an extension of stay as a spouse under the Immigration Rules.[4]

1   IDI, Oct 03 Ch 16, s 1 (seamen); IDI, Sep 04 Ch 16, s 2 (aircrews).
2   See chapter 6 above.
3   IDI, Ch 16, s 1 (seamen); IDI, Ch 16, s 2 (aircrews).
4   HC 395, para 324.

Persons with UK ancestry

10.33 A Commonwealth citizen, one of whose grandparents was born in the UK, may come to the UK for the purpose of living and working here, but must have an entry clearance for that purpose.[1] Upon proof that one of his or her grandparents was born in the UK,[2] a Commonwealth citizen aged 17 or over who wishes to seek or take employment[3] in the UK and can satisfy the maintenance and accommodation requirements will be granted an entry clearance for that purpose. On arrival, such a person should be admitted for a period of four years.[4] There is no need to have a specific job to come to. An intention to seek employment and the ability to perform it[5] may suffice.[6] To prove UK ancestry it will usually be necessary to obtain a certified copy of the grandparent's birth certificate and all necessary marriage and birth certificates to show the connection.[7] An adoptive relationship qualifies under the rule.[8] The word 'grandparents' in HC 395, paragraph 186 refers to both maternal and paternal grandparents. The Immigration Rules expressly provide that the 'parent' of an illegitimate child is not just the mother but includes the father where he is proved to be the father,[9] reversing the practice that resulted from Tribunal and Court of Appeal authority to the contrary.[10]

[1]   HC 395, paras 186–193. The requirement of Commonwealth citizenship only needs to be satisfied as of the date of application under the UK ancestry category; compare Commonwealth citizens claiming the right of abode in the UK: see chapter 2 above.
[2]   Or the Channel Islands, the Isle of Man or (before 31 March 1922) the Republic of Ireland or on board a British registered ship or aircraft: IDI Dec 04, Ch 5, s 8, para 3.2.
[3]   Employment embraces self-employment: HC 395, para 6.
[4]   HC 395, para 187.
[5]   Ability in terms of health: IDI, Dec 04 Ch 5, s 8, para 3. 4
[6]   Entry clearance officers will only refuse an application if they have reason to believe that there is no realistic prospect of the applicant obtaining employment and that he or she may have recourse to public funds: IDI, Ch 5, s 8, para 3.4.
[7]   The word 'usually' permits an entry clearance officer to accept alternate evidence of the grandparent's birth in the UK, such as a baptismal certificate or other official records.
[8]   IDI, Ch 5, s 8, para 3.3.
[9]   HC 395, para 6.
[10]   *C (an infant) v Entry Clearance Officer, Hong Kong* [1976] Imm AR 165, IAT; *R v Secretary of State for the Home Department, ex p Crew* [1982] Imm AR 94, CA.

10.34 Earlier Rules provided for immediate settlement on arrival, but now a continuous period of four years in the UK in this capacity is required.[1] Continuous employment is not required, but a Commonwealth citizen with a poor or non-existent employment record is likely to be refused indefinite leave in the absence of a good reason.[2] The Home Office will wish to see evidence of the current employment position and an employer's confirmation that current employment will continue. If the Commonwealth citizen is not employed at the time of the application, evidence will be requested of the employment record throughout the four years and of attempts to find employment. It used to be possible to make an in-country switch into this category. This is no longer allowed.[3]

[1]   HC 395, para 192. For 'continuous', see 10.97.
[2]   IDI, Dec 04, Ch 5, s 8, para 4.3.
[3]   HC 395, para 190.

Family members

10.35 Spouses, unmarried partners and children under 18, but no other dependants, can accompany or join a principal in any of the above categories except seasonal agricultural workers and crew members coming to the UK. The requirements for spouses and children are that:

- the couple intend to cohabit during their stay and the marriage is subsisting;
- the spouse and children do not intend to stay beyond any period given to the non-work permit employee;
- the maintenance and accommodation provisions of HC 395, paragraph 194 are fulfilled; and
- the spouse and children have entry clearance.[1]

Unmarried partners additionally must show that any previous marriage or relationship has broken down; that they are not in a consanguineous relationship with each other, that a relationship akin to marriage has lasted for two years, and that each of the parties intends to live with the other as his or her partner during the applicant's stay.[2] A child is not to be admitted to join a principal if the worker's spouse or partner is not also admitted, unless that person is deceased, or the worker has had sole responsibility for the child's upbringing, or there are serious and compelling family or other considerations making exclusion undesirable, and suitable arrangements have been made for the child's care.[3] Children who have married, have formed an independent family unit or lead an independent life will not be admitted. Spouses, partners and children are usually free to take any employment without any need for Home Office approval. Persons here in a temporary capacity may not normally switch to family member of a non-work permit holder, but the no-switching rule may be waived for dependants, if *all* the other requirements of the Rule are met and *exceptional compassionate circumstances* prevail. For dependants of those with UK ancestry, caseworkers may waive the no-switching provision in the Rules if they are satisfied that *all* the other requirements are met. [4] Extensions and indefinite leave to remain are normally given to family members routinely if given to the principal, but children over 18 years old must still be truly dependent on their parents.[5] No provision is made for seasonal farm workers and crew members to bring to, or be joined in, the UK by any family member.

---

[1] HC 395, paras 194 and 197 (spouses and children); 295J (unmarried partners). Paras 122–127 deal with spouses and children of exchange teachers and of those under TWES; there is no provision for the admission of their unmarried partners.
[2] HC 395, para 295J (ii)–(v), inserted by Cm 4851 and amended by Cm 5949.
[3] HC 395, para 197(vi).
[4] IDI Sep 04, Ch 5, s 9, para 2.2.
[5] HC 395, paras 195, 198, 295K, 295A.

WORKERS (2): WORK PERMIT EMPLOYEES

Work permit origins and the different types of permit currently available

10.36 Prior to the Immigration Act 1971, work permits were issued only to foreign nationals (then known as aliens). Commonwealth citizens were issued employment vouchers, which gave them a right to immediate settlement. Under the 1971 Act the work permit regime was applied to Commonwealth citizens and foreign nationals alike. The current scheme came into force on 1 January 1980. Since then a number of administrative changes have taken place, but its central purpose has been to strike a balance between enabling employers to recruit or transfer skilled people from abroad and protecting job opportunities for resident workers.[1] The scheme applies to England, Wales, Northern Ireland and Scotland. It is operated by the Work Permits (UK) (formerly the Overseas Labour Section), part of the Home Office. The Channel Islands and the Isle of Man have a similar scheme designed to protect resident workers; details of those schemes can be obtained by contacting the relevant government departments in those places.

[1]   Business and Commercial notes. For the current version see the Work Permits (UK) website at www.workingintheuk.gov.uk The full set of application forms, guidance notes and other documents are as follows: guidance on applications for work permits (general); application forms and guidance notes WP1 (business and commercial) WPSI (student internship); WP3 (sportspeople and entertainers); SBI (sector based scheme); GATS A and GATS B (employees of GATS organisations in a service contract with a UK operator). The guidance notes are in English, Welsh, Bengali, Chinese, Gujarati, Hindi, Punjabi and Urdu. They describe detailed criteria for eligibility and set out how to apply (some applications can be made by e-mail) and what evidence to supply.

10.37   The work permit scheme is divided into two distinct sections:

A: *The main work permit scheme.* This is sub-divided into a number of parts:

  (i)   Business and commercial
      (a)   first tier
         ● Intra-company transfers (this used to include a sub-category, not leading to settlement, called 'career development')
         ● board-level positions
         ● inward investment positions
         ● shortage occupation positions
      (b)   second tier
         ● all other applications (this used to include a sub-category, not leading to settlement, called 'key workers')
  (ii)   Sportspersons and entertainers
  (iii)   Sectors based scheme
  (iv)   GATS permits
  (v)   student internships

B: *The training and work experience scheme*

The training part of the training and work experience scheme has already been transferred to the main part of the scheme, although it is still possible to make such an application provided the training is supernumerary: see below.

Discretionary basis of the work permit scheme

10.38 The work permit scheme is a manifestation of policy, similar to Home Office concessions outside the Immigration Rules.[1] This appreciation gives an insight into the sort of judicial challenges to which decisions under the scheme may be prone. Although there are references to work permits in the Immigration Acts, the work permit scheme is a creature of pure policy rather than statute. The Immigration Act 1971 defines a 'work permit'[2] as:

> 'a permit indicating, in accordance with the immigration rules, that a person named in it is eligible, though not a British citizen,[3] for entry into the United Kingdom for the purpose of taking employment.'

However, no immigration statute provides a power to establish a work permit scheme or stipulates how the scheme is to operate. The Immigration Rules (HC 395) include a work permit category[4] and training and work experience scheme category[5] but are similarly silent as to the legal basis for issuing permits and the operational criteria applied. They provide only that holding a valid work permit or training and work experience scheme permit is a requirement for leave to enter for employment or training or work experience, as the case may be.[6] Thus the scheme envisaged by the statute and the Rules is for Work Permits (UK) to devise, so as to identify those who may work here even though they are subject to immigration control.[7] The schemes that have been devised accordingly comprise pure policy and customarily are notified as guidance notes accompanying the various application forms. Those guidance notes are supplemented by the Work Permits (UK) website, *ad hoc* or seasonal statements of arrangements regarding particular sorts of permit, government evidence to parliamentary proceedings and Work Permits (UK) policy letters. The predominant policy on which the scheme is based is set out clearly at the start of the guidance notes:

> 'The work permit arrangements allow employers based in Great Britain to employ people who are ... not entitled to work in this country ... *We aim to strike the right balance between enabling employers to recruit or transfer skilled people from abroad and protecting job opportunities for resident workers.*' (emphasis supplied.)

[1] Like extra-Rules' policies and practices, the work permit scheme is outside the Immigration Rules and a decision to refuse a work permit does not count as an 'immigration decision', so as to give rise to an immigration appeal: see Nationality, Immigration and Asylum Act 2002, s 82.

[2] See Immigration Act 1971, s 33(1); Nationality, Immigration and Asylum Act 2002, s 122(6).

[3] To be construed as including a reference to anyone with the right of abode in the UK: Immigration Act 1971, s 2(2), as amended by the British Nationality Act 1981, s 39(2) and Immigration Act 1988, s 3(3).

[4] HC 395, paras 128–135.

[5] HC 395, paras 116–121.

[6] HC 395, paras 128(i) and 116(i) respectively.

[7] It should be noted that possession of a work permit is not conclusive of eligibility to enter: see 10.54 below.

Where no work permit is required

10.39 Not all persons who are subject to immigration control need a work permit or Work Permits UK approval in order to be able to work lawfully.

First, as we have seen, there are those who come to the UK for non-work permit employment. Secondly, there are those who in law cannot be made subject to any condition restricting or prohibiting their employment. These include persons with indefinite leave to enter or remain,[1] EEA nationals exercising free movement rights,[2] some persons arriving in the UK on a local journey from another part of the common travel area[3] and those exempted from immigration control.[4] Thirdly, there are those who under the Immigration Rules are given leave to enter without any condition restricting or prohibiting employment. This category can be altered at any time by changing the Rules. They consist of highly skilled migrants,[5] science and engineering graduate scheme (SEGS) participants,[6] innovators,[7] spouses and dependent children under 18 of students given leave to enter for 12 months or longer[8] and of teachers on exchange schemes and trainees;[9] spouses, unmarried partners and dependent children under 18 of work permit holders, persons in non-work permit employment, including Commonwealth citizens with a grandparent born in the UK, highly skilled migrants and SEGS participants[10] and of persons establishing themselves in business, investors, innovators, writers, composers and artists.[11] Fourthly, there are those allowed to enter under various concessions outside the Immigration Rules, such as charitable volunteers.[12] Fifthly, there are individuals who have claimed to be treated as refugees and have been granted permission to work ,[13] refugees and those given discretionary leave or humanitarian protection. None of these people requires a work permit, although often the only way to prove this to an employer is by production of a passport[14] and applying a detailed knowledge of the Immigration Rules and law.

1   Immigration Act 1971, s 3(1)(b) and (c).
2   Chapter 7 above.
3   IA 1971, s 1(3); chapter 6 above.
4   IA 1971, s 8; chapter 6 above.
5   HC 395, para 135B.
6   HC 395, para 135P.
7   HC 395, para 210B.
8   HC 395, paras 77 and 80. Students' dependants admitted for less than 12 months may now ask for and be given the freedom to work: letter from Home Office to UKCOSA, 16 December 1999.
9   HC 395, paras 123 and 126.
10   HC 395, paras 195, 198 and 295K.
11   HC 395, paras 241, 244 and 295K.
12   See 10.31 above.
13   For the policy on work for asylum seekers see 13.209 below.
14   See *Dhatt v McDonald's Hamburgers Ltd* [1991] 3 All ER 692.

The main work permit scheme

10.40 As explained above, 'the work permit scheme' refers to both the 'main' scheme (as it is popularly called) and 'the training and work experience scheme', as well as to the subsidiary schemes for student interns, GATS workers and specific sectors. We now focus on the main scheme for business, commercial, sporting and entertainment work permits, looking at the criteria for eligibility, the procedure for obtaining a work permit, for entering the UK with it, for extending it, for applying for leave to remain with it, for bringing in family members, and for challenging a refusal of a permit. The training and work experience scheme and the subsidiary schemes are discussed separately afterwards.

Who is eligible for a work permit?

10.41 Persons from overseas who are not in one of the 'non-work permit' categories need a work permit if they wish to come to the UK for employment. Work Permits UK previously only issued work permits for jobs needing relatively high-level skills, but the skills criteria were dramatically reduced on 2 October 2000. Prior to this date the criteria for business and commercial permits were that the job needed a degree-level qualification and two years' relevant post-qualification experience; had to be a senior executive or senior manager position which needed at least five years' relevant senior management experience; or one which needed high-level technical or similar skills and substantial relevant specialised experience. The new criteria for such permits are that the job requires a graduate or someone with an HND-level qualification in the specific field, or an HND (not relevant to the post on offer) with one year's relevant work experience. The employee must also be suitably skilled or experienced. Work permits are still not issued for jobs at manual, craft, clerical, secretarial or similar levels, or for resident domestic work such as nannies or housekeepers. The sectors based scheme does however allow permits to be issued for less skilled workers, currently limited to those working in the hospitality and food processing industries. There are also specialist work permits for top-class entertainers and international sportspersons. Work permits are not issued if the employee holds more than a 10 per cent share of the employing business. Shares up to this level may be held if they have been or are to be given to the employee as part of a pay package linked to their employment[1] and that this method of remuneration is of a size necessary to recruit the worker.

[1]   Business and Commercial (notes), para 24.

Where are the scheme's rules to be found?

10.42 Details of the main work permit scheme are contained in a number of guidance leaflets issued by Work Permits UK General Information notes: Business and Commercial (notes) are the general guide for employers on work permit applications and Sportspersons and entertainer (notes) deal with work permit applications for entertainers and sport persons. Each category requires an application form to be completed (WP1, WP3 for sportspersons, including professional footballers).[1] The work permit scheme is liable to be varied at any time with or without consultation, and care should be taken to ensure that fully up-to-date information on the scheme is obtained before making any work permit application.

[1]   These guidance notes and application forms are available from Work Permits UK Distribution Centre 08705 210 224 and Helpline 0114 259 4074 or by downloading them from its website at www.workingintheuk.gov.uk.

What qualifications/experience/skill must the employee have?

10.43 Within the main scheme there are a number of important requirements. First, an employee needs:

- a UK degree-level qualification; or
- an HND-level occupational qualification relevant to' the post on offer, eg medical laboratory technician; or
- an HND-level qualification (not relevant to the post of offer) plus one year's relevant work experience; or
- three years' experience using specialist skills acquired by doing the type of job for which the permit is sought. This type of job should be at NVQ level 3 or above. Those who would qualify include head or second chefs, specialist chefs with skills in preparing ethnic cuisine and those with occupational skills and language or cultural skills not readily available in the EEA.[1]

Entertainers only need to prove that they have performed at the highest level and have established a reputation in their profession and are engaged to perform or do work which only they can do. Cultural artists have to be skilled in foreign Arts which are rare or unavailable in the UK and must be able to make a contribution to the arts, cultural relations or cultural awareness. Sportspersons must be internationally established at the highest level in their sport and must be able to make a significant contribution to the development of that particular sport in the UK at the highest level.[2] Their coaches must be suitably qualified to the highest level. Each of the above groups may have technical/support people to accompany them, provided the work is directly related to the employment of an entertainer, cultural artist, sportsperson or a dramatic production in which that person should have proven technical or other specialist skills.[3] Experience gained through working illegally in the UK or through work done whilst the person was in this country as a working holidaymaker[4] or student will not normally be taken into account.[4]

[1]   Business and Commercial (notes) para 27, Those within the hotel and catering industry and those with occupational skills, language or cultural skills not readily available within the EEA used to be in a sub-scheme called 'the key workers' scheme (in which the maximum permitted stay was three years), but they have now been integrated into the main work permit scheme.
[2]   See 10.31 fn 3 above.
[3]   Sportspersons and entertainers (notes), para 20(d).
[4]   But see discussion on working holidaymakers, chapter 9 above, HC 395, para 131D.

Who should apply for a work permit?

10.44 In general, only an employer based in the UK who needs to employ a person to work in England, Scotland, Northern Ireland or Wales may apply. The employer makes an application for the named person to do a specific job, normally on a full-time basis (perceived by Work Permits UK to be a minimum of 30 hours per week or, if in teaching, 20 hours per week). A work permit is not transferable to a different employer without Work Permit UK being notified. It will decide whether a fresh work permit application has to be made, depending on how the change of employment is undertaken e.g. by a takeover or company re-structuring.[1] The person who is the subject of the application must be the employer's employee, though in certain circumstances such as temporary transfer, secondment or provision of services to a UK-based client under contract (other than simply the supply of staff) the employee may remain employed by the overseas employer.[2] This means that the relationship between the individual on a work permit and the UK employer need not be the only or primary employer/employee relationship in which the individual participates. In the context of employment for the purpose of the work permit scheme, a UK employer cannot avoid the requirements of UK laws, but subject to this, it stands to reason that the UK employer may be nominal in the case of an individual on secondment from an overseas company. Generally, employees employed by their own overseas companies or engaged through other third parties (including overseas companies) whose main involvement with the work is to hire their services to others (a recruitment or employment agency or other similar businesses) cannot obtain work permits.[3]

[1]   Business and Commercial (notes), paras 114 to 119.
[2]   Business and Commercial (notes), paras 8 and 9.
[3]   Business and Commercial (notes), para 13.

Advertising for the position

10.45 Since one of the central requirements of the scheme is to protect the resident labour force, for certain posts the employer must show that there is no resident labour capable of filling the position. The resident labour force for these purposes means the EEA labour market and those who are settled in the UK.[1] Of course, there are others who are part of the resident labour force, but Work Permits UK is only interested in responses to advertisements from EEA and settled applicants. Under the terms of the scheme not all positions need to be advertised. If they do not, only part 1 of the form WP1 needs completion. Those posts which do not need to be advertised are described in the guidance notes and are:

- intra-company transfers for employees of multinational companies who are transferring to a skilled post in Great Britain where the post needs an established employee who has essential company knowledge and experience and at least six months experience working with the overseas company;
- senior board-level posts or posts at an equivalent level for which there is no other suitable candidate. The person must have personal daily input into the directing of the company at a strategic level and substantial senior board-level experience;
- new posts essential to an inward investment project bringing in jobs and a minimum capital investment of normally £250,000;
- occupations which are acknowledged by Work Permits UK to be in very short supply.[2]

Posts which need specific skills, knowledge and experience that are rare will not be considered under this category if the occupation itself is not acknowledged by Work Permits UK to be in short supply.[3] In such cases, employers must complete both parts 1 and 2 of the application form and advertise the position. It is, of course, always open to an employer to ask for the advertising requirement exceptionally to be waived and Work Permits UK may comply if there are good commercial reasons for so doing. If there is real doubt about the merits of the argument in a particular case, employers should err on the side of caution and start the advertising process, which is time-consuming (the employer must wait for four weeks for the results of any advertising to be known before the application may proceed further).[4]

[1] Business and Commercial (notes), para 1.
[2] These categories change frequently and are available on the Work Permits (UK) website or via their dedicated telephone line 0114 259 4074.
[3] Business and Commercial (notes), para 54.
[4] Business and Commercial (notes), para 68 to 83.

10.46 Advertising, if required, must be undertaken in a particular way. Work Permits (UK) expects the advertisement to be placed in the most appropriate medium for reaching suitably qualified resident workers. This will normally be national newspapers or professional journals which are readily available throughout the EEA. It is also possible to advertise on the internet, if this is the most appropriate means of advertising the post. Work Permits (UK) is concerned that the advertisement display and prominence should reflect the level and nature of the post so that it truly attracts the broadest range of candidates. To ensure that the advertisement trawls the resident labour market effectively, it must give full details of the post, qualifications and experience needed, an indication of the salary or salary range and the closing date for the application. The employer must wait for four weeks from the date of the advertisement, but no later than six months, before making the application. The application must set out details of the responses received to the advertisement, the number of candidates shortlisted for interview and full reasons why any resident worker was not offered employment, with reference to the job requirements, as well as details of why the chosen candidate met the requirements.[1] Headhunters may be used [2] for certain senior level or specialist posts, where the headhunter has given advice on suitable candidates after considering candidates within a well-defined group. Evidence of the limited group and of the search undertaken by the headhunter would be of considerable importance.[3] There is no need to advertise the position of entertainers who are internationally established, able to perform in their own right or are cultural artists. The advertising requirement still applies to applications for residencies of one month or more at the same venue or a series of venues, where performers are not generally well known or unique.[4]

[1] Business and Commercial (notes), para 84.
[2] But not recruitment consultants or executive search services which find candidates only from persons registered with them. Business and Commercial (notes) para 77.
[3] Business and Commercial (notes), para 78.
[4] Sports and Entertainments (notes), paras 23–25.

Documents to be sent with the application

10.47 In the case of applications which do not require advertising because they relate to intra-company transfers, board-level positions and posts that are essential for inward investment, there is no need to send copies of the individual's academic or professional qualifications. In respect of all applications, Work Permits (UK) must be satisfied that the employer exists and is trading. If the employer is not known to Work Permits (UK) or no application has been made in the last five years, it will need to see:

- a copy of the employer's latest audited accounts, with the accountant's name clearly shown, or a copy of the latest annual report, both of which must be signed. If the employer has not been in existence for long enough to have accounts, other evidence must be provided to prove its existence, trading position and contracts. This might include a staff list, publicity material, a certificate of incorporation, and/or contracts entered into showing it is trading;[1] or
- in the case of professional partnerships, such as solicitors, veterinary surgeons, dentists and doctors, Work Permits (UK) will accept a copy of one of the partner's registration details with the appropriate professional body.

Where a position has been advertised or the candidate's relevant experience must be proved, the following additional documents are needed:

- copies of the candidate's academic and professional qualifications;
- statements from past employers on their headed notepaper verifying the candidate's relevant work experience in the last two years. These must be accompanied by a certified translation, if necessary. The statements must give start and finish dates of the employment and details of any work and experience making the person qualified to do the job. A general character reference does not prove a candidate's work record. In the case of entertainers and sportspersons, copy publicity material should be provided;[2]
- a copy of the advertisement (including any placed by a recruitment agency if one was used). The whole page should be sent, showing the name and date of the publication, with the advertisement clearly marked. If the advertisement is not available, the text of it can be sent with an invoice from the publication in which it was placed. If alternative means such as a headhunter were used, Work Permits (UK) will require details of the terms on which the search was commissioned and the methods used, with supporting evidence.[3] Work Permits (UK) will permit other forms of trawling the resident labour market but these will need to be justified. For example, if the job market is very narrow it might be possible to persuade Work Permits (UK) that all candidates for the position are known and they have been approached personally to fill it. Supporting evidence from those candidates would be essential to justify this approach;
- details of the responses to all methods of recruitment, including the total number of people who apply, the number shortlisted, full reasons why none of the candidates who are resident workers were employed.[4]

---

[1] Business and Commercial (notes), para 18. The website www.workingintheuk.gov.uk adds that as many as possible of the following documents should be sent to establish the existence of the employer: annual reports, employers' liability certificate, lease of premises and floor plan, copies of necessary registration documents, invoices, utility bills, VAT

returns, Inland Revenue accounts, P24NI from the Inland Revenue. If the employer is in the hotel and catering industry, evidence of registration with the local council should also be provided; if in education, a prospectus.
2   Sportspersons and Entertainers (notes), para 20 and Business and Commercial (notes), paras 60 to 61.
3   Business and Commercial (notes), para 78.
4   Business and Commercial (notes), para 84.

Fees

10.48 Section 122 of the Nationality, Immigration and Asylum Act 2002 gave the Secretary of State power to charge a fee for the issue of a work permit,[1] and section 42 of the Asylum and Immigration (Treatment of Claimants, etc) Act 2004 allows the fee to exceed the administrative costs of processing the application so as to reflect the benefits the Secretary of State thinks likely to accrue if an application is successful.[2] The fee set by regulations made under section 122 is £153.[3] A single fee is payable, even if the application is for a group of sportspersons or entertainers.[4] No fee is payable if the prospective work permit holder is a national of a state which has ratified the 1961 Council of Europe Social Charter or the Revised European Social Charter of 1996.[5] Fees in respect of teachers are subject to a special arrangement between the Home Office and the Department for Education and Skills.[6]

1   Or for any immigration employment document: see 10.3 above.
2   There is a power (but not a duty) to refund the part reflecting that benefit if the application is unsuccessful: s 42(4), (5).
3   Immigration Employment Document (Fees) Regulations 2003, SI 2003/541, reg 4 as amended by SI 2003/1277, 2003/2447, 2003/2626, 2004/1485, from July 2004 (ie, before the coming into force of s 42 of the 2004 Act, which came into force on 1 October 2004: SI 2004/2523.
4   See website. SI 2003/541 as amended, reg 4A provides that a single fee of £95 is payable for applications covering all members of a dance, theatre, circus or music group or orchestra coming to the UK to perform under a contract.
5   These are Bulgaria, Romania, Turkey, Moldova, Albania, Armenia and Croatia: SI 2003/541 as amended, reg 5, Schedule.
6   SI 2003/541 as amended, reg 7.

Timing of applications

10.49 Applications cannot be made more than six months before the employer wishes to engage the overseas national. In the case of someone already here in approved employment, an application should probably be made no earlier than three months and no later than one month before the person's leave to remain expires.[1] Once all necessary advertising procedures have been performed, the employer completes the appropriate application form for the position (WP1 and any annexes, or WP3 and any annexes) and forwards it to Work Permits UK Payment section in Doncaster for onward transmission to Sheffield. It aims to decide at least 70 per cent of applications within one week of receiving all relevant information, and straightforward applications are dealt with in days. If other government departments have to be consulted, a longer period should be allowed.

1   Business and Commercial (notes), paras 148–149.

Self-certification

10.50 There was a pilot scheme for multinational employers to self-certify that a named employee should be issued with a work permit rather than apply for a work permit for employees on intra-company transfers. This scheme, which ran for six months from 1 October 2000, permitted such employers to issue their own work permits, provided they meet the requirements' of the work permit scheme. It was discontinued.

Duration of work permits

10.51 Permits are in principle available for between one day and five years. Until 29 September 2000, work permits were limited to 36 months in respect of career development work permits and work permits for key workers who did not have the occupational skills to meet the criteria required by the work permit scheme. As this distinction has now been abolished, all work permits issued under the main scheme, save multiple entry work permits, now potentially lead to settlement. Entertainers and sportspersons are issued with short-term permits to cover the period of engagement, although in principle there is no reason why they may not apply for settlement if they manage to remain in approved employment for a continuous period of four years.[1]

1   IDI Aug 01, Ch 17, s 8, para 9 provides that indefinite leave to remain may be granted to sportspersons of international reputation who intend to make their home in the UK and have spent four of the last eight years on short-term work permits. For an analysis of the work permit scheme and other Immigration Rules relating to sportspersons and entertainers and their tax position see (2000) 3 IIEL 15–19. For a discussion on the meaning of 'continuous', see 10.97 below.

Who must pay the worker?

10.52 As a general rule the employer in the UK is responsible for the pay and national insurance and tax deductions of the work permit holder. This rule does not apply if the person is seconded to work for a UK employer from an overseas employer, when the overseas contract of employment may continue, but see Business and Commercial (notes), para 21(a), (b)[1] which effectively state that the UK employer cannot avoid the minimum requirements of UK law. Even where the individual will continue to be paid abroad, under his or her contract of employment there, the UK employer has to be at least a nominal employer – ie, an employer for the purpose of the work permit scheme – and Work Permits UK therefore requires the application form to be signed by the UK employer: see 10.44 above.[2]

1   See 10.44 above.
2   Business and Commercial (notes), para 9.

What happens when the work permit is issued?

10.53 Once issued, the work permit is sent to the employer or its representative. The permit is issued for a specified period starting on the date the employer wants the overseas national to enter the UK. If the work permit holder does not enter the UK within six months from the date of issue, the permit loses its validity and must be returned so a new one can be issued. Where the overseas national is already in the UK, whether in approved employment or not, the final decision on whether the individual may work rests with the IND, since it is only when the IND agrees to grant the necessary leave to enter or remain that the overseas worker is possessed of permission to work. This is endorsed in the overseas national's passport.[1]

[1]   Re Miah (Suruk) (1976) Times, 4 February, CA.

Entry to the UK with a work permit

10.54 To qualify for admission under the Immigration Rules, workers must hold a valid work permit; must not be of an age which puts them outside the limits for employment (though the work permit scheme itself no longer has any age limits); must be capable of undertaking the employment specified in the permit; must not intend to take employment except as specified in the permit; must, if the permit is valid for a period of 12 months or less, intend to leave the UK at the end of their approved employment; and must be able to maintain and accommodate themselves and any dependants adequately without recourse to public funds.[1] All those, whether they are visa nationals or not, who seek entry for work permit employment, must have an entry clearance for entry in this capacity prior to arrival, except where the work permit is valid for six months or less,[2] or the holder is a national of one of the eight new Member States of the European Union. Visa nationals with a work permit for six months or less will need a visa prior to entry. Normally the period of leave granted will be co-extensive with the period of validity of the work permit, which will not exceed five years.[3] A condition will be imposed restricting the work permit holder to employment approved by Work Permits UK though it is now possible to undertake supplementary employment without further permission.[4] If the worker has been issued with a work permit valid for four years or more and the employer wishes the job to continue, the worker will become eligible to seek indefinite leave to remain.[5] If the initial leave is less than four years, an extension of leave will only be granted if Work Permits UK gives written approval for the continuation of the employment for a further period.[6] The extension will be for a corresponding period.[7] Since extensions depend on the written approval of Work Permits UK, it is that department of the Home Office, which sets the policy for continued stay in the UK.

[1]   HC 395, para 128 (i)–(vi).
[2]   HC 395, para 128 (vii), inserted by HC 1224 on 12 Nov 03.
[3]   Business and Commercial (notes), paras 124 and 151–153.
[4]   Business and Commercial (notes), paras 126–127and Sports and Entertainments (notes), para 86–88.
[5]   HC 395, para 134.
[6]   HC 395, para 131.
[7]   HC 395, para 132.

10.55 Possession of a work permit is not conclusive evidence of eligibility for entry for employment. Under the Immigration Rules, immigration officers have a wide discretion to refuse entry. Leave to enter should normally be refused where 'whether or not to the holder's knowledge, the making of false representations or the failure to disclose any material fact for the purpose of obtaining an immigration employment document'[1] or 'whether or not to the applicant's knowledge, the submission of a false document in support of an application'.[2] An illustration of the way in which the immigration officers' refusal powers operate is provided by the case of *Caballero v Secretary of State for the Home Department*.[3] The appellant had a work permit as a domestic worker which had been sent to him in the Philippines. He was unaware that it was his employer's intention that he should be employed by more than one employer. But the immigration officer discovered this and refused him entry. The Tribunal upheld his decision: a work permit was for specific employment with a specific employer. Since this was not the employer's intention here, the permit had been obtained by false representations and the concealment of material facts. Leave to enter was, therefore, properly refused.[4]

1 HC 395, para 320(15). See *R v Secretary of State for the Home Department, ex p Wah Chun Wan* (LTA 96/5916/D) (31 October 1996, unreported) for a discussion of the difference between an invalid permit, as in *R v Immigration Officer, ex p Chan* [1992] 1 WLR 541, and a permit which is improperly issued but valid, as in *R v Secretary of State for the Home Department, ex p Ku* [1995] QB 364. Even an improperly issued rather than invalid permit is not conclusive evidence of eligibility: see *R v Secretary of State for Education and Employment, ex p Shu Sang Li* [1999] Imm AR 367.
2 HC 395, para 320 (21).
3 [1974] Imm AR 13.
4 For the effect of improperly issued work permits, see the cases cited in fn 1 above.

Extension of stay in approved employment

10.56 The employer must complete form WP1X or WP3X and have complied with any conditions set out in the letter approving the initial employment, which also details the information required for an extension. Advertising (if originally required) does not need to be repeated, provided the job remains the same.[1] If the application is for the same type of job with a different employer, no advertising needs to be undertaken; only a change of occupation will require fresh advertising If any advertising is undertaken, the same evidence of its results must be provided to Work Permits UK as for the initial application.[2] If the employer had not been trading for sufficient time to have audited accounts available at the time of the initial application, the work permit will have been limited to a period of 18 months, and Work Permits UK will expect to see the audited accounts of the business on the extension application. The same fee is payable for an extension of the work permit as for the original permit.[3] The employee may continue to work whilst the application is pending.[4] Once the written approval for the continuation of the employment has been obtained from Work Permits UK an application for an extension of leave can then be made to the IND.[5]

1 Business and Commercial (notes), para 100.
2 See 10.46–10.47 above.
3 See the definition of 'immigration employment document' which includes both a work permit and an extension: 10.3 above.
4 Business and Commercial (notes), para 102.

⁵   HC 395, para 131. The worker must continue to meet the requirements of entry set out in para 128 (ii) to (v). The application for further leave to remain for holders of an immigration employment document is also subject to a fee, this time £335, unless they are nationals of states which have ratified the Council of Europe Social Charter 1961 or the Revised Social Charter of 1996 (these states are Bulgaria, Romania, Turkey, Moldova, Albania, Armenia, Croatia): Immigration (Leave to Remain) (Fees) Regulations 2003, SI 2003/1711 (as amended by SI 2005/654 from 1 April 2005), reg 3A, 5(c). The fee is payable in respect of each applicant for leave to remain, but no additional fee is payable for dependants included in the application of the principal.

Switching to approved employment

10.57 The main work permit scheme is designed for workers who are abroad at the time the employer makes the application for a permit, or who are already here in approved employment. Those admitted as visitors or for temporary purposes other than degree-level study are not eligible for leave to remain as a work permit holder unless specific exceptional circumstances apply.[1] The current Immigration Rules make provision for switching, and although there is now more flexibility than previously, the cases in which this is routinely allowed are carefully circumscribed. The Rules permit switching to work permit employment for graduates from UK further or higher education institutions,[2] student nurses, post-graduate doctors or dentists, doctors admitted for the PLAB test or for clinical attachments and dentists admitted as dental observers,[3] participants in the Science and Engineering Graduates Scheme,[4] persons admitted as highly skilled migrants[5] or as innovators,[6] and working holidaymakers who have been over 12 months in the UK in that capacity and the employment is in an occupation listed on the Work Permits UK shortage occupation list.[7] If an overseas national already has leave in one of these capacities, an application is first made to Work Permits UK for approval of the proposed employment. Once that is approved by Work Permits UK (but in any event before leave expires), the prospective worker then makes a personal application on form FLR(IED) to the IND for further leave to remain, annexing to it the IED (immigration employment document) which will have been issued by Work Permits UK, and the required fee.[8] In other cases not specified in the Rules, it will be necessary to persuade Work Permits UK that in the circumstances it would be 'unduly harsh' to require the individual to return abroad rather than switch in-country – see 10.123 for the exact wording of this 'unduly harsh' policy, in force since 1 October 2004. Where the Immigration Rules do not provide for in-country switching and the 'unduly harsh' policy does not apply, the last resort is to seek wholly exceptional treatment, outside the Rules and policy, on the particular facts of the individual case. For example, difficulties may be encountered, under present policy, where the applicant is a refused refugee claimant, with special skills, and is here on temporary admission. Temporary admission means that the person has not yet entered the UK,[9] and, therefore requires leave to enter. In principle there is no reason why he or she should not qualify for entry under HC 395 paragraph 128, provided the work permit has been approved by Work Permits UK. IND do not like it, but have conceded where eligibility for employment is strong. Where refugee status has been granted, there is no restriction on taking employment and no work permit is needed.

1 Circumstances relating to the job, employment and the labour market will not be considered as exceptional circumstances. Only circumstances relating to the individual, making it 'unduly harsh' for him to return home to apply, may be considered: see 'Changing Immigration status while in the UK ("Switching")' quoted at 10.123 below.
2 HC 395, para 131A, inserted by Cmd 5597 on 27 Aug 2002 and HC 104 on 26 November 2002. For these purposes, an HND does not count as degree-level study: Work Permit Users Panel notes, 29 September 2004.
3 HC 395, para 131B, inserted by Cmd 5597 on 27 August 2002; 131DG, inserted by HC 346 from 15 March 2005. The WP(UK) leaflet says trainee GPs may switch, but the Immigration Rules do not provide for this.
4 HC 395, para 131C, (substituted by Cm 6339, September 2004). The previous para 131C allowed sector-based workers to switch into work permit employment, now no longer permitted.
5 HC 395, para 131E (inserted by Cm 6339).
6 HC 395, para 131F, inserted by Cm 6339.
7 HC 395, para 131D (iii), inserted by HC 302 on 7 Feb 2005.
8 The fee for further leave to remain in connection with an immigration employment document, FLR (IED), is £335: Immigration (Leave to Remain) (Fees) Regulations 2003, SI 2003/1711 (as amended by SI 2005/654) reg 3. See 10.56 fn 5 above.
9 Immigration Act 1971, s 11.

Appealing a work permit refusal

10.58 There is no provision in the Immigration Acts for an appeal either by the worker or the employer against the refusal of a work permit as such. This is because the refusal of a work permit is not an 'immigration decision' within section 82 of the Nationality, Immigration and Asylum Act 2002. Further, where the decision is prima facie appealable under section 82, because there is also a refusal of entry clearance or a refusal to vary leave and so forth, section 88 of the 2002 Act extinguishes the appeal right where the person concerned does not have an 'immigration document',[1] which is defined to include a work permit or other immigration employment document.[2] Work Permits UK does have its own internal appeals procedure which permits an employer to challenge a refusal. An appeal must be made (or an intention so to appeal must be stated) within 28 days. The procedure gives a review of the application by an official senior to the one who took the original decision.[3] A decision to refuse a work permit, or leave to remain for work, may also be challenged by judicial review, on the grounds of illegality, irrationality or procedural impropriety.[4]

1 NIA 2002, s 88(2)(b).
2 NIA 2002, s 88(3). For the definition of an immigration employment document see 10.3 above.
3 Business and Commercial (notes) para 203.
4 See *R v Department of Employment, ex p Allan* [1991] Imm AR 336, QBD.

Judicial challenges

10.59 A work permit scheme, comprising a complex of policies notified primarily by guidance notes, is not *per se* unlawful. However, in certain cases there may be scope for a public law challenge to the way in which a particular policy is applied, a refusal to depart from that policy or even to the legality of the policy itself.

10.60 Successful challenges to the legality of a policy are rare but possible; see, for example, *R v Immigration Appeal Tribunal, ex p Manshoora Begum*[1] where a provision of the Immigration Rules was struck down for illegality. There does not appear to be a reported case of a successful challenge to the legality of a provision of the work permit scheme, but that is not to say there has not been the scope for such a challenge. Arguably, for example, a policy to issue seasonal permits rather than back-to-back permits could be challenged if it were to prevent an ordinarily resident worker from ever being in the UK for a 'continuous' period of four years for the purposes of the settlement provisions of the Immigration Rules. There have been several successful challenges to the way in which the then Department for Education and Employment has applied its stated policies in a particular case. In *ex p Ying Fu Chan*[2] Harrison J found the Department had failed to apply its own policy because no account had been taken of experience gained in the UK, even though the relevant guidance notes did not require all such experience to be discounted. In *ex p Portsmouth FC*[3] McCullough J found, *inter alia*, that the then Department ought to have taken into account that but for injury a footballer would have been selected to play in 75 per cent of his country's competitive matches.

[1]   [1986] Imm AR 385 QBD.
[2]   *R v Secretary of State for Education and Employment, Secretary of State for the Home Department, ex p Ying Fu Chan* (CO/4079/97) (25 March 1999, unreported).
[3]   *R v Secretary of State for Education and Employment, ex p Portsmouth Football Club Ltd* [1998] COD 142, QBD.

10.61 Just as the Secretary of State for the Home Department may treat a person more (but not less) favourably than the Immigration Rules or a concession require, so too he or she may relax the terms of the work permit scheme. The refusal to depart from policy in such a way may be challenged, for example on grounds of unreasonableness, but such challenges are difficult to sustain. In *Ex p Kwok Shun Yee*[1] it was argued that although, contrary to overseas labour section requirements, no references were available to confirm a chef's expertise, that expertise could easily be confirmed by an examination board. Jowitt J found that:

> 'the Overseas Labour Service has a wide margin of appreciation within *Wednesbury* principles as to whether or not it regards the examination board approach as an acceptable way of demonstrating that Mr Kwok meets the requirements of a key worker and it does not seem to me that it can be faulted in the conclusion that it has reached'.

Overall, there are few work permit judicial reviews relative to the number of immigration judicial reviews, though this may be more a reflection of the reluctance of employers to litigate than of near-perfect Work Permits (UK) legality in formulating and applying its policies and administering the work permit scheme generally.

[1]   *R v Secretary of State for the Home Department, ex p Kwok Shun Yee* (CO/95/97) (25 June 1998, unreported).

Family members

10.62 Spouses, unmarried partners and children under 18, but no other dependants, can accompany or join a work permit holder [1] in the UK, provided the maintenance and accommodation provisions of the Immigration Rules are fulfilled.[2] The Home Office will by concession permit over-age dependent children to accompany their parent transferred into approved employment by way of intra-company transfer, provided they have remained part of the family unit. The concession also applies to dependent parents.[3] This is because employees, generally, move at the behest of their employers and not necessarily of their own volition.[4] Other dependent relatives may be admitted at the discretion of the entry clearance officer if there are exceptional compassionate circumstances.[5] Otherwise, the details are the same as those applying to family members of non-work permit employees at 10.35 above. Spouses, partners and children are free to take any employment without the need for Home Office approval.

[1]   The general rule does not apply to the dependants of holders of work permits under the multiple entry Sectors-Based Scheme or student internships.
[2]   HC 395, paras 194–199, and 295J.
[3]   IDI Sep 04, Ch 5, s 5, para 1.1.
[4]   Home Office letter to Bates, Wells and Braithwaite, 16 December 1999.
[5]   Home Office letter to Sturtivant and Co, 6 August 1996.

SECTORS-BASED SCHEME

10.63 The Sectors-Based Scheme (SBS) is a new part of the work permit scheme introduced on 30 May 2003 as part of the government's managed migration programme announced in the 2002 Home Office White Paper *Secure Borders, Safe Haven: Integration with Diversity in Modern Britain.* It provides for Work Permits UK to issue work permits for certain sector-specific employment.[1] The scheme is quota limited[2] and is available to non-European nationals aged between 18 and 30. Apart from the level of qualifications of the employee, the same criteria that apply to an employer applying for a main scheme work permit apply to an employer applying for a sector-based scheme work permit: the employer must be UK-based, the employee must be filling a genuine vacancy; pay and conditions must be equal to those given resident employees; the employment must be full-time; the employee must have no significant shareholding in the business or a connected business; there must be no suitable resident workers to do the work and there are similar advertising requirements.[3] In addition, the employer must make suitable arrangements for accommodating the worker under the scheme, and the employee must speak adequate English.[4] The maximum permission that can be gained in respect of each work permit is 12 months, at the end of which the worker is expected to leave the United Kingdom,[5] but may have a further sector-based scheme work permit after a gap of at least two months. This is to ensure that no-one with a succession of sector-based scheme work permits can ever apply for indefinite leave to remain. There is no provision for the admission of dependants. Sector-based workers may take supplementary employment in the same sector, not exceeding 20 hours per week.[6] Between 30 May 2003 and 1 October 2004 it was possible to extend the leave given by a sector-based scheme work permit into full employment provided the employee had obtained an immigration employment document other than one issued under the Sectors-Based Scheme and the main requirements of the work permit scheme were met.[7] After October 2004, that is no longer possible.[8]

1   Specifically in hospitality and food manufacture, the full details of which can be seen at www.workingintheuk.gov.uk
2   An intention to leave the UK at the end of approved employment has to be shown: HC 395, para 135I(vi).
3   See Sectors-based scheme notes, paras 11, 16, 24, 42–48. Jobs must be advertised for four weeks in a JobCentre, JobCentrePlus or Job and Employment Office and in EURES: para 43. The information required about responses is the same as for the main scheme, see 10.46–10.47 above.
4   Sectors-based scheme notes, para 24, 41.
5   HC 395, paras 135J, 135L, inserted by HC 464.
6   Sectors-based scheme notes, 'supplementary employment' para 71.
7   HC 395, para 131C, inserted by Cmd 5829 on 30 May/03.
8   See Cmd 6339 and see further on switching at 10.121, below.

GATS PERMITS

10.64 The GATS agreement scheme is a concessionary arrangement within the work permit rules, enabling those whose employer does not have a commercial presence within the EU to work in the UK on a service contract awarded to the employer by a UK-based organisation.[1] The scheme applies only to organisations based in signatory States to the World Trade Organisation (WTO).[2] Permits are available to workers on contracts for periods not exceeding three months, or for periods of three months in any one year, in the fields of legal services, accountancy, book keeping, tax advice services, architecture, engineering, urban planning, advertising, management consultancy, technical testing and analysis and site investigation.[3] Detailed guidance is contained in GATS A notes (for overseas employers) and GATS B notes (for UK contractors).

1   See GATS A notes, para 2
2   GATS A notes, para 4.
3   GATS A notes, paras 6, 8 and 17.

STUDENT INTERNSHIPS

10.65 There are now a number of different routes for trainees, depending on the field they are in,[1] the length of the training and whether they are filling a vacancy and training on the job or are additional to the employer's normal requirements. The main work permit scheme allows training work permits to be issued for jobs requiring advertisement: see 10.67 below. Student internships fall under a separate subsidiary scheme under the work permit scheme. They are available for companies with a significant trading presence in the UK and elsewhere,[2] to enable them to recruit as trainees overseas students on first or higher degree courses abroad, for a maximum of three months' training at N/SVQ level 3 or above,[3] and his or her payment should reflect normal trainee rates for the profession or sector.[4] Evidence to be submitted includes a copy of the internship programme.⁵ The intern should be abroad when the application is submitted. There is no provision for family members to accompany the intern.⁶

1   For student nurses etc see 9.44 above.
2   Student internship (notes) para 5.
3   Student internship (notes), paras 6 and 9.
4   Student internship (notes), para 8.
5   Student internship (notes), para 17. Other evidence relates to the existence of the employer (see 10.47 above).
6   Student internship (notes), para 37.

THE TRAINING AND WORK EXPERIENCE SCHEME (TWES)

Introduction and history

10.66 Previous incarnations of this part of the work permit scheme used to state that its aim was to assist businesses and organisations in their international development, and to help other countries by increasing the skills and experience of their citizens. The Department for Education and Employment (as it then was) had a special Eastern European Unit which was set up to deal with nationals from a defined list of countries, whose training in UK businesses was intended to promote the UK, and in particular UK businesses, as natural trading partners. The training and work experience scheme has gone through many superficial changes since then and recently has undergone a major review. The principal consequence of the review is that the availability of resident labour, which used to be irrelevant, becomes crucial. If the post can be filled by a resident worker, the application cannot be made under the training and work experience scheme, which is now only available for trainees who are additional to the normal staffing requirements of the employer.¹ Furthermore, as a result of the changes in skills thresholds in the main work permit scheme, elements of the old training and work experience scheme have been transferred to the main work permit scheme. Training and work experience scheme permits are available for employers based in the UK. Separate arrangements exist for, the Isle of Man and the Channel Islands.

1   Training and Work experience (TWES) (notes), para 21.

Who is eligible for a training and work experience scheme (TWES) permit?

10.67 Persons requiring Work Permits UK approval¹ need a training and work experience scheme (TWES) permit to enter the UK or to remain for training leading to a professional qualification or for work experience. Work Permits UK only issues TWES permits for work-based training for a professional or specialist qualification, or for a period of work experience where the individual will be additional to the employer's normal staffing requirements. Those individuals who are not surplus to labour needs, but are in fact filling a vacancy, must apply under the main work permit scheme which requires the position to be advertised.² So employees who used to be granted TWES permits as graduate trainees, those wishing to undertake on-the-job training for a professional or specialist qualification, or work experience which is filling a vacancy, must now apply under the main work permit scheme. Work Permits UK will not normally issue TWES permits in the sports and entertainment sectors.[3] This is a change from the previous terms of the scheme and there would be some room for making representations to Work Permits UK in special cases.

[1] See 10.39 above.
[2] TWES (notes), para 21.
[3] TWES (notes), para19.

Where are the scheme's rules to be found?

10.68 Details of the training and work experience scheme are contained in guidance leaflets issued by Work Permits UK. Training and Work Experience (notes) is the general guide for employers on TWES applications and Student internship (notes) deals with internship placements for overseas students who need to complete an internship programme with an employer which has a significant trading presence in the UK and abroad. The employer must be considering recruiting the student as a trainee on completion of his or her course. Each category requires an application form to be completed WP1for training and work experience and WPSI for internship programme students. The TWES is liable to change at any time with or without consultation, and care should be taken to ensure that fully up-to-date information on the scheme is obtained before making an application for a TWES permit.

Qualifications for TWES permit

10.69 The training and work experience scheme requirements for a permit to train for a professional qualification are as follows:

- an academic or vocational qualification at UK degree level or National or Scottish Vocational Qualification (NVQ or SVQ) level 3. This is defined by the National Vocational Qualification Board;
- the relevant qualifications necessary for the training;
- the training should be at least 30 hours per week (excluding associated study) and should lead to a recognised professional or specialist qualification at postgraduate level;
- the company and the person managing the training should be competent to provide it. This will normally involve being registered or approved by the relevant professional body;
- the training should be completed in the shortest possible time, interpreted by Work Permits UK as requiring the employee to take an exam at the earliest possible sitting. Two attempts or possible attempts can be made in respect of each exam. Each exam not taken is counted as a possible attempt;
- a TWES permit is not normally issued for training for a qualification which can be obtained by full-time study. If this is possible, the employee will have to apply to remain as a student and perhaps undertake part-time employment;

- applications are only approved for the employee to achieve one qualification, but if the employment ends before the qualification is obtained and the employee wishes to continue training with a new employer, a further application can be made on form WP1 within three months of the end of the previous training. If there is a gap of more than three months, the training will be deemed to have ceased;
- pay and other conditions should be comparable to those normally given to a resident worker doing this level of training and should reflect the person's experience.[1] The pay must meet the national minimum wage which came into effect on 1 April 1999.

[1] Training and Work Experience (notes), para 38.

10.70 The TWES requirements for a work experience permit are as follows:

- the employee should have previous relevant experience or appropriate academic or vocational qualifications to enable him or her to benefit from a work experience programme at this level. Those with neither relevant experience nor academic or vocational qualifications will not normally have their applications approved;
- the work experience should be at managerial level or at least N/SVQ level 3 or equivalent;
- the application should describe the type and level of experience to be gained and how this will be supervised. It should set out a detailed timetable for each stage of the programme, a description of the tasks to be undertaken and who will be supervising the work experience. The more detailed the programme the more likely the period requested will be granted;
- in general Work Permits UK expects that most work experience programmes will not exceed 12 months. If a longer period is requested, this should be explained in the initial application. As a matter of practice, if a 24-month period is requested and granted, a full 24-month permit is issued immediately. Extensions to a work experience permit are only approved where there are exceptional circumstances, up to a maximum of 24 months;[1]
- the pay and conditions should be no more than those given to a resident worker doing equivalent work experience, although persons coming under an exchange agreement or to be paid by an overseas employer or organisation may receive their normal salary. The pay must meet the national minimum wage which came into effect on 1 April 1999.

[1] Training and Work Experience (notes).

Procedures for obtaining a TWES permit

10.71 The UK employer applies for the TWES permit and normally pays the worker,[1] and the considerations set out in 10.44 above in relation to the main work permit scheme apply also in respect of the TWES.[2] The same type of documents should be sent with the TWES application to prove that the employer exists.[3] In respect of a training application the following should be sent:

- evidence of the person's degree-level qualification;
- evidence of any exemptions from exams;
- a copy of the training plan or programme agreed with the appropriate professional body (if applicable); and
- evidence from the appropriate professional body, where this has not previously been supplied, to show that the trainer is approved to provide the training;

In respect of a work experience application:

- the work experience programme;
- the person's academic or vocational qualifications;
- references from past employers; [4]

and in both cases:

the appropriate fee.[5]

The timing of the application is the same as for the main scheme.[6]

---

[1]   See 10.52 above and TWES (notes), para 19.
[2]   TWES (notes), paras 9–15.
[3]   See 10.47 above.
[4]   TWES (notes), paras 39 and 41–45.
[5]   The fee is the same as for a work permit under the main scheme, currently £153: see Immigration Employment Document (Fees) Regulations 2003, SI 2003/541, reg 4 (not payable if the permit is for a national of a state which has ratified the 1961 Council of Europe Social Charter or the 1996 Revised Social Charter (reg 5); see also payment guidance.
[6]   See 10.49 above.

Duration of the TWES permit

10.72 The TWES permit for approved training will be issued for the average period expected for the trainee to complete the training, up to a maximum of five years.[1] It will be issued for only six months initially if the employer is unable to provide evidence of the person's degree-level qualification. Further periods will be granted to allow the trainee to continue training, attempt examinations and complete the required practical experience leading to the qualification sought.[2] The period Work Permits UK will allow varies from profession to profession, and checks should be made with them to identify the appropriate period in a given case. The TWES permit for work experience is issued for an initial period of up to 12 months and, exceptionally, for a further 12-month period, taking the total to 24 months.[3]

---

[1]   TWES (notes) para 34.
[2]   TWES (notes), paras 33 to 35.
[3]   TWES (notes), para 45(c).

Entry to the UK with a TWES permit

10.73 The TWES permit, like the main work permit, is sent to the employer, unless the firm is using a solicitor or other representative.[1] Under the

Immigration Rules, a person seeking admission to the UK for training or work experience must hold a valid TWES permit;be capable of undertaking the training or work experience specified in the permit; intend to leave the UK on completion of the training or work experience; not intend to take any other employment; and be able to maintain and accommodate him or herself and any dependants adequately without recourse to public funds.[2] As with work permits, possession of a TWES permit is no guarantee of admission to the UK.[3] The period of leave may be extended if Work Permits UK have given written approval for an extension and the other conditions of admission are met.[4] Changes of employment need Work Permits UK permission.[5] Special provision is made for chartered accountants, to whom the Department will approve employment on qualification, usually for two years, to enable them to obtain a practising certificate.[6] For an extension of the permit, the employer must complete form WP1X and must have complied with any conditions set out in the letter approving the initial employment. That initial letter will also have explained what information needs to be sent with the application for an extension. If the employer had not been trading for sufficient time to have audited accounts available at the time of the initial application, audited accounts will be expected to accompany the extension application. A further fee is payable for an extension of the TWES permit.[7] Whilst the application is pending the trainee may continue working, provided the application was received by Work Permits (UK) before the trainee's initial leave expired.[8] Review rights for those refused TWES permits are the same as for the main work permit scheme.[9]

[1] See para 10.53 above and TWES (notes), para 96.
[2] HC 395, paras 116(i)–(vi).
[3] See para 10.55 above.
[4] HC 395, para 119(ii) and (iii).
[5] HC 395, paras 117 and 120.
[6] 979 HC official report (5th series) written answers col 18.
[7] See payment guidance, Oct 2004. The fee is currently £153: Immigration Employment Document (Fees) Regulations 2003, SI 2003/541 (amended by SI 2003/1277, 2003/2447, 2003/2626, 2004/1485).
[8] TWES (notes), para 55.
[9] See 10.58 above.

Switching into and out of TWES employment

10.74 Under earlier rules[1] visitors as well as students could switch to training under TWES, but under the current Immigration Rules only students may do so.[2] Switching from TWES employment to approved (main work permit) employment is prohibited both under the Rules[3] and under the terms of the training and work experience scheme unless there are exceptional circumstances,[4] both of which provide that trainees would not normally be allowed to transfer to work permit employment in Great Britain and must intend to return overseas at the end of the agreed period.

[1] HC 251, para 120.
[2] HC 395, paras 119(i) and 131A–G, 132 (substituted by HC 346 as from 15 March 2005).
[3] HC 395, para 116(iv)–(v).
[4] TWES (notes), para 22.

Admission of families

10.75 Those undergoing training or work experience may be joined by their spouses (not their unmarried partners) and their children under 18, provided they can meet the cost of maintenance and accommodation without recourse to public funds.[1] There are no restrictions on family members taking employment.

[1]   HC 395, paras 122–127.

BUSINESS AND THE SELF-EMPLOYED

Introduction and history

10.76 The Immigration Rules relating to business and self-employment have undergone many changes since 1973. Formerly, there was a broad discretion to admit persons wishing to start or join a business, and to permit visitors or others on a temporary stay in the UK to remain in that capacity.[1] There was no minimum investment required and the application was to be considered in the round, with no one factor being conclusive. This broad brush approach was first put forward by the Divisional Court in *R v Immigration Appeal Tribunal, ex p Joseph*[2] and was endorsed in the later case of *R v Immigration Appeal Tribunal, ex p Peikazadi*[3] and in the unreported Court of Appeal decision in *Mawji v Immigration Appeal Tribunal.*[4] The Rules in force in 1973 remain important for Turkish nationals, since the European Court of Justice held in *Savas*[5] that under the 'standstill clause' in Article 41 of the Additional Protocol to the EC-Turkey Association Agreement, the parties had agreed not to introduce additional barriers to establishment. Turkish nationals can, therefore, rely on the Rules as they were when the UK acceded to the EEC in January 1973, both in relation to switching from visitor to business status and in respect of the substantive requirements of the business Rules.[6]

[1]   See HC 510, para 21.
[2]   *R v Immigration Appeal Tribunal, ex p Joseph* [1977] Imm AR 70, QBD.
[3]   *R v Immigration Appeal Tribunal, ex p Peikazadi* [1979–80] Imm AR 191, QBD.
[4]   *Mawji v Immigration Appeal Tribunal* (29 October 1984, unreported), CA.
[5]   *R v Secretary of State for the Home Department, ex p Savas* [2000] INLR 398, C37/98. The Court of Appeal endorsed this in *R (on the application of Tum) v Secretary of State for the Home Department, R (on the application of Dari) v Secretary of State for the Home Department* [2004] EWCA Civ 788, [2004] INLR 442, but on appeal by the Secretary of State the House of Lords referred the issue to the ECJ. See chapter 7 above.
[6]   For more details see chapter 7, above.

10.77 Since 1980 the business person category of the Immigration Rules has become much more restrictive. The general formula that applications should be 'considered on merit' has been replaced by specific requirements with which the business applicant must comply. The broad brush approach, which overcame some of the 'astonishingly unattractive' results of a literal interpretation,[1] was rejected in *ex p Rahman*[2] by the majority of the Court of Appeal, who said that although a degree of latitude is allowed in construing the Rules, it does not extend to departing from the plain, ordinary, natural meaning of the language. Business applicants must therefore comply fully with each of the specific requirements of the Rules, however badly geared they may be to the needs of businesses. It is true that in particular cases the Home Office may be persuaded to waive requirements of the Rules, but there is no guarantee of this. So perhaps it is not surprising that prior to January 2002 business persons and their legal advisers tried to avoid the business provisions of the Rules and structure their investments so as to achieve the same result through the work permit scheme sole representative, investor or innovator categories. Since January 2002 business persons have had the additional option of making an application under the highly skilled migrant programme (HSMP). This flexible programme, which permits employment and self employment without any capital investment, is the most dramatic development in commercial immigration law for the past 30 years and has made many of the other commercial immigration categories effectively redundant. As we saw in 10.1, more shake-ups are expected under the government's proposed five year plan, including a swing to an HSMP-style 'transparent points system' for all those who come to the UK to work.

1   See *R v Immigration Appeal Tribunal, ex p Rahman* [1985] Imm AR 222, QBD, per Woolf J.
2   *R v Immigration Appeal Tribunal, ex p Rahman* [1987] Imm AR 313, CA. The first attack on the 'in the round' approach came from the Tribunal in *Patel v Entry Clearance Officer, Nairobi* [1987] Imm AR 116.

10.78 It should be noted that business status under the Immigration Rules only applies to those who wish to establish themselves in business. Persons who wish to make business visits to the UK without establishing a business here are free to do so, subject to the restrictions on business visitors already dealt with (chapter 9 above). Different considerations also apply to EEA nationals who wish to set up in business or self-employment in the UK and third country nationals exercising EC law rights (chapter 7 above). But below we deal to some extent with individuals and companies from the Central and Eastern European states with which the EC has concluded Association Agreements. We do so because in this regard EC law is being implemented in the UK by the incorporation of special business provision into the Immigration Rules. These special provisions are an adaptation of the normal business provisions and immediately follow them in HC 395. It is therefore appropriate at least to sketch them in here.

Business status

Requirements

10.79 HC 395, paragraphs 200–223 deal with the admission of those wishing to establish themselves in business; the standard provision is set out in paragraphs 200–210, while paragraphs 211–223 make special provision for business persons seeking admission under the EC Association Agreements. The text that follows focuses on the standard provision; for the position where the Association Agreements apply see 10.99 and chapter 7.

10.80 The first general rule is that a passenger seeking admission must hold a current entry clearance issued for that purpose.[1] All business applications must be referred by the overseas post to the Business Case Unit at the Home Office. Despite the unambiguous requirement for entry clearance, attempts are often made by those already in the UK to switch to business status by making an application direct to the Home Office.[2] Although such applications are to be refused under the Immigration Rules,[3] the entry clearance requirement is sometimes waived on an exceptional basis, for example, if there is no country to which the applicant can safely return; there is no British Embassy or other post issuing entry clearances in the particular country; or where it is apparent that the applicant meets all the relevant requirements of the Rules.[4] If a request is made to waive the no switching rule, IND would be bound to consider it,[5] but if no request is made, the application can be refused without any consideration of the merits, and there will be no right of appeal because of the provisions of section 88(2) (b) and (3) of the Nationality, Immigration and Asylum Act 2002.

[1] HC 395, para 201(xi).
[2] IDI Ch 6, s 1.
[3] HC 395, para 205.
[4] IDI Sep 04, Ch 6 s 1 para 4.2.
[5] See *Pearson v Immigration Appeal Tribunal* [1978] Imm AR 212, CA.

10.81 Under the Immigration Rules a business means an enterprise as a sole trader, or a partnership, or a company registered in the UK.[1] The purpose of the Rule is to identify the different forms a business enterprise may take without limiting its activities. For example, 'sole trader' is not intended to limit business activity to trading rather than manufacturing or a profession, but merely refers to persons who engage in business on their own account rather than in partnership or under the umbrella of a company. Where a company is used, it must be registered in the UK. Where the business investment is made through a company it is sometimes difficult to determine whether to apply for a work permit or seek business status. A business application is appropriate in the case of a shareholder with a controlling or equal interest in the business.

[1] HC 395, para 200; IDI Sep 04, Ch 6, s 1, Annex C.

10.82 The Immigration Rules have a long list of requirements which must be fulfilled by anyone wishing to set up in business in the UK or join or take over an existing business. They distinguish between new and existing businesses and lay down additional requirements for each. The common requirements are that all business applicants:[1]

- have not less than £200,000 to invest in the business and that this is their own money under their control and disposable in the UK;
- have sufficient additional funds to meet the maintenance and accommodation requirements of the Rules until their business starts to provide an income;
- will be actively involved full-time in the business;
- will maintain a level of financial investment proportional to their interests in the business;

- will have an equal or controlling interest in the business and that any partnership or directorship does not amount to disguised employment;
- will be able to bear their share of the liabilities;
- demonstrate a genuine need for their investment and services in the UK;
- demonstrate that their share of the profits will be sufficient to meet the maintenance and accommodation requirements of the Rules; and
- do not intend to supplement their business activities by taking or seeking employment in the UK other than their work for the business.

1   HC 395, para 201.

10.83 In addition to meeting these common requirements, where the business is already in existence, applicants who wish to take it over, join it or become a director must also produce:[1]

- a written statement of the terms on which they are to take over or join the business;
- audited accounts for the business for previous years; and
- evidence that their services and investment will result in a net increase in the employment provided by the business to persons settled here to the extent of creating at least two new full-time jobs.

Where the business is new, applicants must (in addition to meeting the common requirements) produce evidence that:[2]

- they will be bringing into the country sufficient funds of their own to establish a business; and
- the business will create full-time employment for at least two persons already settled in the UK.

1   HC 395, para 202.
2   HC 395, para 203.

10.84 The Immigration Rules establish a minimum financial requirement of £200,000.[1] Overseas lawyers are exempted from this requirement (and need not create two new jobs for persons settled in the UK). These are persons from abroad who have qualified here as solicitors or barristers or who qualified abroad and wish to practise here as consultants in that overseas law. They must be able to support themselves and their families and meet the costs of establishing themselves in practice (because they must be self-employed, and not employees, to come within the scope of business status).[2] In addition, they must satisfy certain regulatory requirements.[3]

1   HC 395, para 201(ii).
2   IDI Sep 04, Ch 6, s 1, Annex D.
3   IDI, Ch 6, s 1, Annex D.

Money of their own, disposable in the UK

10.85 The Rule requires the applicants' investment to be money of their own, which is held in their own name and under their control and disposable in the UK.[1] The purpose is threefold: first, to ensure that the applicant is the investor and not fronting for someone else;[2] secondly, to ensure that the investment is not going to be thwarted because a third party can stop payment or withdraw the funds; thirdly, to ensure that the monies are immediately available for the investment and not tied up elsewhere. The first of these aims is addressed by the requirement that the money must be in the investor's own name and not held in a trust fund or some other investment vehicle. Clearly there will be cases where the applicant's money is tied up, for example, in a trust or off-shore investment company prior to the business investment. What is required is that the money must be unequivocally released into the investor's own name and control in time for the decision on the application. For money to be disposable in the UK it must be immediately available for investment in the business. For this purpose money invested in a house will not usually count (although it may do in respect of the separate categories of retired persons of independent means and investors).[3]

₁   HC 395, para 201(ii).
₂   *R v Immigration Appeal Tribunal, ex p Peikazadi* [1979–80] Imm AR 191.
₃   *Entry Clearance Officer, Rome v Rahman (Hussain)* [1991] Imm AR 102. See 10.111–10.115 below.

10.86 The term 'under his control' was also used in previous Immigration Rules dealing with persons of independent means and is retained in the current Rules for retired persons of independent means, and additionally applied to investors. The earlier case law therefore remains relevant. In *Ex p Chiew*[1] the Court of Appeal held that 'control' in this context means a right which can be enforced in law against any person who might wish to interfere with it. Thus a wife's money from a legally enforceable separation agreement is money under her control.[2] A continued permission to use and spend family funds in accordance with Chinese family custom is not an enforceable right and will be insufficient.[3] On the other hand money coming from the applicant's family and at the applicant's unfettered disposition will suffice as his or her own money because it is a gift.[4] In the IDI it is suggested that a copy of an irrevocable Deed of Gift should be requested to ensure that the money is under the applicant's own control. [5] In the case of new businesses, the requirement that applicants will be bringing into the country sufficient funds of their own to establish a business[6] suggests the need for some kind of transfer of funds from overseas, but in practice this is not a substantive additional requirement.[7]

₁   *R v Immigration Appeal Tribunal, ex p Chiew* [1981] Imm AR 102, QBD; see also *R v Immigration Appeal Tribunal, ex p Mehra* [1983] Imm AR 156, QBD.
₂   *Secretary of State for the Home Department v Rohr* [1983] Imm AR 95.
₃   *R v Immigration Appeal Tribunal, ex p Chiew* above.
₄   *R v Immigration Appeal Tribunal, ex p Chiew* above; *R v Immigration Appeal Tribunal, ex p Kwok on Tong* [1981] Imm AR 214, QBD and IDI Nov 00, Ch 6, s 1, Annex A.
₅   IDI Sep 04, Ch 6, s 1, Annex A, para 1.2. This suggests that the dictum in *R v Immigration Appeal Tribunal, ex p Peikazadi* [1979–80] Imm AR 191, to the effect that family funds will suffice if they have been lent on a sufficiently long-term basis, is no longer applicable.
₆   HC 395, para 203(i).
₇   See *R v Immigration Appeal Tribunal, ex p Rahman* [1987] Imm AR 313 at 317, per Woolf J in QBD, and at 322, per Bingham LJ in CA.

10.87 The investment has to be 'put into the business' and it is, therefore, insufficient if part of the funds goes into the business and part into living accommodation for the applicant's family.[1] If the applicant proposes to buy premises which include residential accommodation for his or her family, the value of this part of the property should be deducted from the business investment.[2] Money already in the business is insufficient, as in,[3] where the applicant inherited the business as a going concern when his father died. Applicants may make their investment by a direct cash investment, share capital or a combination of the two. A director's loan (unless it is unsecured and fully subordinate to all third-party creditors) and an investment from or through an off-shore company are both unacceptable.[4] In practice the Home Office would expect the full amount to be invested by the time the applicant applies for a first extension of leave, ie within 12 months of the initial entry.[5]

1 *Patel v Entry Clearance Officer, Nairobi* [1987] Imm AR 116 at 126.
2 IDI Sep 04, Ch 6, s 1, Annex A.
3 *R v Immigration Appeal Tribunal, ex p Rahman* [1987] Imm AR 313, CA.
4 IDI, Ch 6, s 1, Annex A.
5 This is consistent with *Trivedi v Secretary of State for the Home Department* TH/8202/98 (00 TH 01059), a sole representative case in which the Tribunal held that the 'on entry' requirement need only be satisfied by the end of the initial 12-month period.

Full-time involvement in the business

10.88 The Immigration Rules require a business person to be involved full-time in the business.[1] This does not mean being in the UK full-time, since trips and possibly lengthy periods abroad may be a necessary part of promoting the business. But absences abroad have to be watched, since they may adversely affect a later application for settlement (see 10.96 below). A business which consists of separate and distinct activities may also qualify,[2] but the business applicant must intend to be involved full-time in their management or supervision. The actual wording of the Rules, however, is not quite so clear cut. 'Trading' and 'providing services' are broad and open terms which embrace a full range of business activity including manufacture and research. In the case of company directors, they must be involved in the full-time promotion or management of the company to comply with HC 395, paragraph 201(iv). 'Promotion and management' connote a degree of control and supervision over the aims and objects of the company and must be construed with the requirement of a controlling or equal interest in the business and the ban on disguised employment.[3] Where the business activity involves a lot of promotion or supervision of the company's operations, and in a small company where the director does most of the work and employs very few administrative staff, there is no problem. But where a director does not control but works under the direction of others, that work may be neither promotional nor managerial, and may risk being classified as 'disguised employment.[4] The immigration admission of the applicant must be necessary in the interest of the business, and the business not simply a convenient device for the applicant.[5] The Home Office looks at franchise arrangements particularly closely, to see whether the applicants work full-time and there is a genuine need for their services, as it takes the view that the franchisee often has little say in how the business is run and may not, therefore, have much input except for the investment.

1 HC 395, para 201(iv).

²   *Otani* (3234).
³   HC 395, para 201(vi).
⁴   An example of disguised employment is provided by *Singh (Pritpal) v Secretary of State for the Home Department* [1972] Imm AR 154 where the appellant was a director and secretary of the company with an annual salary. He had loaned money to the company and held £15 shares out of the company share capital of £100; he received no interest on his loan nor dividend on his shareholding. There was no agreement in writing as to his future in the company and he could be removed from the board of directors and from his secretarial duties at any time by the majority shareholders. It was held that he was in reality a paid employee.
⁵   IDI Sep 04, Ch 6, s 1, Annex A.

Proportionality of investment

10.89 The requirement that the level of financial investment is proportionate to the business investor's interest in it [1] is a further safeguard against the business Rules being used to evade the need to obtain a work permit. A business person who receives 50 per cent of the profits should have an equivalent shareholding or partnership stake in the enterprise. The IDI contend that a person who has a majority or equal financial interest in a business but who nevertheless clearly has no major say in running the business or setting its policy will not have an interest in the business proportional to his or her investment.[2]

¹   HC 395, para 201(v).
²   IDI Sep 04, Ch 6, s 1, Annex A.

Controlling or equal interest

10.90 Applicants need to show that they will have either a controlling or equal interest in the business and that any partnership or directorship does not amount to disguised employment.[1] The purpose of this is to ensure that an investment is not simply used as an entrée to the UK or a front for disguised employment. For example, an investment of £200,000 by a leading motor car designer coming to work for the Ford motor company with a promised seat on the Board would probably not qualify under this Rule, although he or she would be a prime candidate for a work permit.

¹   HC 395, para 201(iv) and IDI Sep 04, Ch 6, s 1, Annex A. See also *Singh (Pritpal) v Secretary of State for the Home Department* [1972] Imm AR 154, 10.88 above.

Able to bear share of liabilities

10.91 Business investors need to show that they will be able to bear their share of the liabilities.[1] If a business is a limited company, then its liabilities will be limited to the total of its assets and in that sense every promoter of such a business will be able to bear his or her share of liabilities. In *ex p Hirani*[2] it was held that 'liabilities' referred to those a business is reasonably expected to incur and it was wrong to require an applicant to show a 'capital reserve to cater for any unforeseen liabilities'. The structure of the business may affect an applicant's eventual liability. A sole trader receives all the profit and bears all the losses of the business, is personally responsible for all debts and can be made bankrupt and his or her belongings can be sold to pay creditors.[3] In a partnership each partner is liable without limit for the partnership debts. Creditors may sue an individual partner, a group of partners or the firm itself. A partner who is sued can be made bankrupt if he or she fails to pay the debts or obtain contributions from other partners even if the debts were incurred by another partner.[4]

1	HC 395, para 201(vii).
2	*R v Immigration Appeal Tribunal, ex p Hirani* (2 July 1981, unreported), QBD.
3	IDI Sep 04, Ch 6, s 1, Annex C.
4	IDI Ch 6, s 1, Annex C.

Genuine need for services and investment

10.92 There is uncertainty as to precisely what this provision means. It would be too restrictive to suggest that applicants must identify some market research on the need for their business before receiving entry clearance.[1] However, market research can be helpful to justify the applicant's financial projections.[2] Clearly a business that is wholly unwanted will fail, but this is taken care of by the rules on profitability. Part of the entrepreneurial ethic is to create needs where none existed before. The better meaning of these words, therefore, is that the business must need the service and investment. The needs are those of the business, not the local or national economy. It is no good investing £200,000 in a shop that does not require an investment of that amount. This view accords with the meaning of the phrase under earlier Rules, where it was confined to an existing business and clearly related back to the needs of that business and not to some wider economic interest.[3] Tribunal decisions are somewhat ambivalent and contradictory.[4] However, the IDI state that unless there is uncertainty about the *bona fides* of the applicant it will normally be sufficient to concentrate on evidence of funds and the requirement to provide employment.[5] It comes to this: the business must require an investment of at least £200,000, so if it only needs £1,000 for a phone and a desk and the remaining £199,000 will be placed on deposit, the application will fail for want of a 'genuine need' for the investment. But the Home Office is apparently content for only £190,000 to be required in this sense, leaving £10,000 for contingencies.

1	See *Patel* (4895), IAT.
2	IDI Sep 04, Ch 6, s 1, Annex A.
3	See the comment of the Tribunal in *Otani* (3234).
4	*Patel* above (market research); *Otani* above (no strict commercial test); *Seyed* (5006) (commercial test with an element of general public economic interest).
5	IDI Ch 6, s 1, Annex A.

Profitability

10.93 Applicants need to show that the business will be sufficiently profitable to support them and their families without recourse to employment or public funds.[1] If they intend to supplement their business activity by taking any employment other than their work in the company, sole tradership or partnership, their application will be refused.[2] The applicant must produce a detailed business plan showing the object of the business, the investment and employment involved and financial projections. The IDI set out a comprehensive list of the minimum information that the business plan should contain[3] and the formulae that the Home Office uses to assess the viability of the business.[4]

[1] HC 395, para 201(ix).
[2] HC 395, para 201(x).
[3] IDI Sep 04, Ch 6, s 1, Annex A.
[4] IDI Ch 6, s 1, Annex B.

Job creation

10.94 Whether the investment is into a new or existing business, it must lead to the creation of new, paid, full-time employment in the business for two persons already settled in the UK. Employment of part-time workers or temporary trainees would be insufficient.[1] The business plan must identify the number of new jobs expected to be created and the likely pay, hours and duties.[2] The new employees do not need to be in post at the outset or even during the early period of the business,[3] but they will be expected to be so by the end of the initial 12 months.[4] It is employment, not self-employment, which must be created and the use of self-employed contractors is, therefore, insufficient.[5]

[1] *Fanous v Secretary of State for the Home Department* [1993] Imm AR 200 and IDI Sep 04, Ch 6, s 1, Annex A.
[2] IDI Sep 04, Ch 6, s 1, Annex A.
[3] *Singh (Inderjit)* (4620).
[4] HC 395, para 206(viii), confirming *Jamnadas* (6597). See *Trivedi* TH/8202/98 (00 TH 01059) 10.87 fn 5 above.
[5] *Seyed v Secretary of State for the Home Department* [1987] Imm AR 303.

10.95 The Immigration Rules refer to employees being recruited from persons 'settled here' and 'already settled in the UK'[1] and are clearly intended to make inroads into UK, rather than continental, unemployment figures. However, where EEA nationals and others exercising EC law rights are in the UK, it is not clear whether they are to be regarded as 'settled' in the UK for these purposes unless they come within regulation 8 of the Immigration (European Economic Area) Regulations.[2] Where an existing business is taken over, the Rules now make it clear that there must be a net increase in employment.[3] Maintaining existing jobs is not enough.

[1] HC 395, paras 202(iii) and 203(ii).
[2] SI 2000/2326, defining certain categories of EEA nationals and their family members who are to be regarded as being in the UK without being subject to any restriction. They are retired workers and self-employed persons and their families, family members of deceased workers, and persons with indefinite leave to remain.
[3] HC 395, paras 202(iii) and 206(viii)(b), and IDI Sep 04, Ch 6, s 1, Annex A.

Extensions and settlement

10.96   Applications for extensions of stay by persons established in business will only be granted if the applicant continues to meet the requirements needed to obtain entry.[1] More particularly, applicants must be in a position to show:

- audited accounts proving the precise financial position of the business and confirming that the applicants have made a direct investment into the business of not less than £200,000 of their own money;
- that they are actively involved full-time in the business;
- that their level of financial investment is proportional to their interest in the business;
- that they have an equal or controlling interest in the business and that any partnership or directorship does not amount to disguised employment;
- that they are able to bear their share of liabilities;
- that there is a genuine need for their investment and services in the UK;
- that new full-time paid employment has been created in the business for at least two persons settled in the UK;
- that their share of profits will be sufficient to meet the maintenance and accommodation provisions of the Immigration Rules; and
- that they do not, and do not intend to, supplement their business activities by taking or seeking employment in the UK other than their work for the business.

These provisions suggest that the Home Office will be concerned to see how far the original business proposition has been carried out. The capital will have to have been invested fully and the planned employees will have to be in their posts.[2] The requirement to be able to show audited accounts is not insisted upon at the 12-month stage. At this stage, a business person who has taken over an existing business may be able to produce audited accounts, but in the case of a new enterprise, draft or management accounts will be sufficient.[3] Clearly some business projects will take longer than others to show a return on investment, and where profits appear low or non-existent, leave will be refused unless the slow take-off was anticipated in the original business plan and is covered by the additional funds needed at that time,[4] or there is a good explanation and a realistic expectation of profitability.

1   HC 395, para 206.
2   HC 395, paras 206(ii) and (viii) confirming *Jamnadas* (6597)
3   IDI Sep 04, Ch 6, s 1, para 4.3.
4   HC 395, para 201(iii).

10.97   The initial grant of leave is for 12 months, with a condition restricting freedom to take employment.[1] Where an application for an extension is successful, the applicant's stay will usually be extended for a further period of three years on the same condition.[2] If the Home Office is not satisfied that the requirements for a three-year extension have been met but an outright refusal would be inappropriate, it may grant a further 12 months, instead of three years, as a repeat of the initial 12 months.[3] This gives applicants an opportunity to satisfy the Rules next time. In these circumstances, they should be advised that they have re-started the four year period leading to settlement (since, in order to qualify for settlement they will need to have qualified under the Rules throughout the last four years).[4] If the business satisfies the Rules at the end of that 12 months and the businessperson is then given the normal three years leave, he or she would expect indefinite leave at five years. The rules now enable persons with leave to enter or remain in the UK for work permit employment, or as highly skilled migrants, or participants in the Science and Engineering Graduates Scheme, or as innovators, or as degree level students, or as working holidaymakers, to switch into the business category provided they meet the main requirements of the business Rules.[5] Business persons qualify for settlement if they have spent a continuous period of four years in the UK in the business capacity and are still engaged in the business in question.[6] They must have met all the requirements of the Immigration Rules 'throughout the 4-year period',[7] and produce audited accounts for the first three years and management accounts for the fourth year.[8] The Home Office approach is to construe 'continuous' as allowing for short absences abroad such as holidays or business trips consistent with maintaining employment or self-employment in the UK. Longer periods of absence may break the continuity. 'Continuous' must be given a commonsense rather than a literal meaning, with Home Office practice and nationality legislation as a guide to what is sensible. At the time of going to print, the Home Office is indicating that business persons (and others) will not normally be granted indefinite leave at the end of the four years if they have been absent for more than a total of six months over the entire four year period (12.5 per cent). Indefinite leave has already been refused in one case. If this policy is allowed to stand, it would effectively undermine the will of Parliament to allow access to British citizenship after five years in the UK with up to 25 per cent absences. It would also inevitably deter people from migrating to the UK in the first place.

1   HC 395, para 204.
2   HC 395, para 207, substituted by HC 346 with effect from 15 March 2005.
3   IDI Sep 04, Ch 6, s 1, para 4.6.
4   IDI Sep 04, Ch 6, s 1, para 4.6.
5   HC 395, paras 205A–206F, inserted by HC 346 with effect from 15 March 2005; paras 207 and 208 as substituted.
6   HC 395, para 209(i).
7   HC 395, para 209(ii). See *Fanous v Secretary of State for the Home Department* [1993] Imm AR 200 for an example of a failure to do this.
8   HC 395, para 209(iii).

10.98 Where the Home Office considers that a business person has been absent too long or too often to permit settlement to be granted, it may grant a further extension of 12 or 24 months instead. This corresponds with the practice of granting a repeat 12 months at the end of the initial 12 months set out in the previous paragraph, and the considerations there apply. An applicant must specifically apply for settlement at the end of four years; an application for further leave to remain will be treated as such and not as an application for indefinite leave.[1]

1   IDI Sep 04, Ch 6, s 1 para 5.

Business status under the EC Association Agreements

10.99 The Immigration Rules make special provision for those who wish to establish themselves in business in the UK under EC Association Agreements.[1] Business persons who can rely on the Agreements are not required to make the minimum investment of £200,000, as required under the normal business provisions, or to create new full-time employment, but they are required to obtain entry clearance[2] and to meet the requirements of the Immigration Rules. Detailed guidelines are set out in the IDIs, which were amended in August 2004.[3] We discuss these Agreements in chapter 7. The Rules cover nationals from Bulgaria and Romania.[4] Turkish nationals are in a special position.[5]

[1] HC 395, paras 211–223, as amended by Cm 4851 on 2 October 2000 and Cmd 6297 on 9 Aug 2004.
[2] IDI Aug 04, Ch 6, s 2. Doubts about whether it was possible to switch into this category without obtaining prior entry clearance have now been largely resolved by the immigration rule changes (HC 395, para 217, as amended by Cmd 6297 in August 2004) and mandatory prior entry clearance has won the seal of approval by the European Court of Justice in *Panayotova and Others v Minister voor Vreemdelingenzaken en Integratie* Case C-327/02 (16 November 2004, unreported). According to the IDI, switching will only be allowed if it would be disproportionate to require the person to go home for an entry clearance, and this will usually only happen where the viability of the application is 'clear and manifest' IDI Aug 04, Ch 6, s 2. See also 7.170 above.
[3] IDI Ch 6, s 2.
[4] For more detail of the applicable provisions of the Association Agreements see 7.166ff above.
[5] See 7.163 above.

Writers, composers and artists

10.100 Under the pre-1980 Immigration Rules, writers and artists were not distinguished from other self-employed persons and could be admitted if they were able to support themselves and any dependants without recourse to public funds.[1] From 1980 the self-employed (writers and artists apart) became grouped with, and treated similarly to, business persons. The current Immigration Rules continue this distinction. The category has been expanded to include composers. Writers, composers and artists qualify for admission[2] if they:

- have established themselves outside the UK as a writer, composer or artist primarily engaged in producing original work which has been published (other than exclusively in newspapers or magazines), performed or exhibited for its literary, musical or artistic merit;
- do not intend to work except as related to their self-employment as a writer, composer or artist;
- have been able to support themselves for the preceding year from their own resources without working except as a writer, composer or artist;[3]
- will be able to support themselves and their family from their own resources without working except as a writer, composer or artist and without recourse to public funds; and
- hold a valid entry clearance for entry in this capacity.

¹   HC 79, para 36 and HC 81, para 32. No reference was made in the Immigration Rules to support from private sources, but in *Secretary of State for the Home Department v Jones* [1978] Imm AR 161 the Tribunal held that the appellant did not meet the requirements of the Rules where he had received no money for his work as a playwright for 18 months and relied upon money sent by his family abroad to cover his living expenses. See now 10.102.
²   HC 395, para 232.
³   Writers, composers and artists therefore cannot qualify in this category straight from postgraduate studies.

10.101 Immigration law generally distinguishes between the self-employed, including writers, composers and artists, and those who require a work permit. This distinction, however, was fudged when it came to dealing with certain artists. In *Secretary of State for the Home Department v Stillwaggon*[1] one of the questions for the Tribunal was whether a singer required a work permit as an entertainer or could be treated as a self-employed performing 'artist'. The answer to such a question would surely depend on whether she was an employee or self-employed. The Tribunal, however, begged the question and held that she was an entertainer rather than an artist, since the Rule referred to painters or sculptors rather than to singers. This decision, which is still applied, means that singers of international repute who come to perform in the UK cannot qualify in the writers, composers and artists category. Nor can they qualify as business visitors, because they would be selling services direct to the public, contrary to the visitor requirements (see chapter 9). The only way to enter the UK is therefore via the work permit scheme, and for this there needs to be (a) an employer (usually the promoter) and (b) an entertainer who has performed at the highest level and established an international reputation.[2] The combination of these various requirements makes it virtually impossible for an unknown performer to perform in the UK, unless under a special dispensation from the work permit requirements for recognised festivals and charity concerts.[3] But it does not end there. The distinction between applications under the Immigration Rules and Work Permits may also be difficult to apply in the case of musicians who both compose and sing.[4] They face difficulties satisfying the requirements of the writers, composers and artists category since it is clear that (under the *Stillwaggon* doctrine) they intend to do work other than that related to their self-employment (ie sing).

¹   [1975] Imm AR 132.
²   Work Permits (UK) application form and WP3 Sports and Entertainments (notes) guidance, and see work permits (10.40 above).
³   See IDI Jul 03 Ch 17, s 3 for a list of such events.
⁴   Composers may conduct their work provided most of their income is derived from their composing. If they wish to play in a band they require authorisation from Work Permits UK, but the IDI suggest that subject to this permission, the activity is compatible with remaining in this capacity: IDI Sep 04, Ch 6, s 4, Annex J: guidance on persons who qualify as self-employed writers, composers and artists.

10.102 The Immigration Rules permit writers, composers and artists to meet the maintenance and accommodation requirements from their 'own resources without working except as a writer, composer or artist'.[1] This marks a change from earlier Rules which required maintenance and accommodation to come from 'their own resources *including the proceeds of self-employment* without recourse to public funds'.[2] In *Boehm-Bradley v Visa Officer, Washington*[3] the

Tribunal held that the phrase 'including the proceeds of self-employment' meant that an applicant had to be able to generate some income from his or her artistic activities. Now that these words have been removed from the Rules, it is arguable that this class of entrant may be self-supporting from savings, a pension or unearned income, without any need to show earnings from their artistic activities. The IDI state that such persons must support themselves mainly from the proceeds of their work, although they may supplement this with income from their own investments; and that in the calculation, funds sent from abroad are to be disregarded.[4] This suggests that it is only income earned otherwise than through the artistic activities which would give rise to problems.

1   HC 395, para 232(iii) and (iv).
2   HC 251, para 45 (emphasis supplied).
3   [1986] Imm AR 305.
4   IDI Sep 04, Ch 6, s 4, Annex J.

10.103 Extensions of stay in the writers, composers and artists category are granted if the person continues to meet the requirements for admission. Initial leave will usually be for up to 12 months with a restriction on taking employment,[1] and the subsequent extension will usually be for up to three years on the same conditions.[2] This leads to settlement once the person has spent a four-year continuous period in the UK in this capacity and has met all the requirements during that period.[3]

1   HC 395, para 233.
2   HC 395, para 236.
3   HC 395, para 238; for the meaning of 'continuous', see the discussion in the context of business persons at 10.97 above.

THE NEW BRAINS OF BRITAIN

Innovators

10.104 In July 2000 the government announced the launch of a two-year pilot scheme to attract entrepreneurs with innovative business ideas to the UK.[1] The pilot scheme commenced on 4 September 2000 and the category is now part of the Immigration Rules.[2] The key distinguishing features of the innovators scheme are that no minimum investment is required, third party funding is permitted and applications will be assessed in order to identify and select 'outstanding entrepreneurs who will bring exceptional economic benefits to the UK. The Innovator category is focused in particular on talented entrepreneurs in e-business and other new technology fields, although applicants operating in other fields may also apply. The category was introduced in response to government concern that overseas entrepreneurs were being deterred from establishing businesses in the UK by the rigidity of the existing Immigration Rules. Before the introduction of the pilot scheme some innovators were unable to meet the requirements of any existing immigration category; in particular, the size of their shareholding made them unsuitable for the work permit scheme and they may have had insufficient money of their own to meet the requirements of the businesspersons' Rules. In addition, they would typically not retain a controlling or equal interest in the venture which would be established. However, the expectations of the Scheme have not been met and it has become almost totally redundant since the introduction of the Highly Skilled Migrant Programme (HSMP), which we deal with below. For example, in 2003, when both schemes were fully operational, fewer than 20 applications were made in the Innovator category. It is thought that this category and the Sectors-based Scheme are earmarked for deletion when the current consolidation exercise is complete.

[1]   Immigration and Nationality Directorate website, 25 July 2000.
[2]   HC 395, para 210A, inserted by HC 538 on 31 March 2003.

10.105 Applications for innovator status must meet four main requirements:[1]

- the applicant is able to meet the criteria specified by the Home Secretary for entry under the innovator scheme at the time he or she seeks approval under that scheme;
- the proposed business must lead to the creation of full-time employment for at least two persons already settled in the UK;
- the applicant intends to maintain a minimum 5 per cent shareholding of the equity capital; and
- the applicant will be able to maintain and accommodate him or herself and any dependants adequately without recourse to public funds or other employment.

In order to see whether the applicant meets the specified criteria of the scheme, the application is assessed using a points system, which has some similarity to the system used by the Canadian immigration authorities in respect of an equivalent status.[2] In order to be successful, the applicant must achieve a minimum score in each of three separate areas, and a higher overall score. The three areas are:

(i)   personal characteristics (business experience, educational qualifications and proven entrepreneurial ability);
(ii)   the general business plan (including evidence of the technical, commercial and financial viability of the plan and proposals for the establishment of a management team); and
(iii) the economic benefits of the business plan (the number and skills level of the jobs which will be created and the innovative aspect of the proposals).

Each application must be supported by relevant documentation, including academic certificates, employers' references, research, financial and technical references, a full business plan, containing a marketing plan and evidence of the individual's shareholding in the proposed company.[3]

[1]   HC 359, para 210A (i)–(iv), as inserted by HC 538 on 31 Mar/03.
[2]   See the Canadian Citizenship and Immigration website at www.canada.org.uk/visa-info/immig/e_immig.htm and Canadian Immigration and refugee Protection Act 2001.
[3]   See 'Innovators: guide for applicants' on the Work Permits (UK) website: workingintheuk.gov.uk.

10.106 Applicants from overseas need to obtain entry clearance before travelling to the UK[1]. This is to be rigidly enforced, and people coming as visitors and for other temporary purposes will not normally be allowed to switch into this category. But for applicants already in the UK in certain other defined categories, provision is now made for switching. Provision is also made for switching in other cases in exceptional circumstances: see 10.121ff below. The Rules operating between March 2003 and September 2004 were extraordinarily wide. Anyone who was granted leave to enter or remain in the UK, other than as an ordinary visitor, could qualify for an extension of stay as an innovator.[2] Since October 2004 there is a much narrower but clearer policy to the Rules.[3] Extensions of stay may be granted to (i) those given leave to enter as such, who have established a viable trading business, by reference to the audited accounts and trading records of that business and meet the other requirements of the scheme;[4] (ii) work permit holders who meet the main requirements of the scheme;[5] (iii) students with a degree qualification from a recognised degree course, who, if necessary, have obtained written consent of their official sponsor and meet the main requirements of the scheme;[6] (iv) working holiday makers, who entered as such and meet the main requirements of the scheme;[7] (v) postgraduate doctors, dentists and trainee general practitioners who have the written consent of their official sponsor to remain in the innovator category (if government or international sponsorship is ongoing or recently ended) and meets the requirements of the scheme;[8] (vi) Science and Engineering Graduate Scheme participants who meet the requirements of the scheme;[9] (vii) highly skilled migrants who meet the requirements of the scheme;[10] and (viii) persons with leave to enter or remain in business, who meet the requirements of the scheme.[11] On acceptance into the scheme innovators are given leave to remain in the UK for an initial period of 18 months,[12] which can be extended a further 30 months, making a total of four years, on further application.[13] At the end of those four years innovators may apply for settlement.[14]

1   HC 395, para 210A(v).
2   HC 395, para 210D(i) and (ii)(b), as inserted by HC 538 on 31 March 2003.
3   See further on switching policy at 10.121 below.
4   HC 395, para 210D(i), as amended by Cmd 6339 on 1 October 2004.
5   HC 395, para 210DA, inserted by Cmd 6339.
6   HC 395, para 210DB, as inserted.
7   HC 395, para 210DC, as inserted.
8   HC 395, para 210DD, inserted by HC 1112 on 18 October 2004.
9   HC 395, para 210DE, as inserted.
10 HC 395, para 210DF, as inserted.
11 HC 395, para 210DG, inserted by HC 346 on 15 March 2005.
12 HC 395, para 210B.
13 HC 395, para 210E, substituted by HC 346.
14 HC 395, para 210G. Regarding absences during the four year period, see the discussion at 10.97.

THE HIGHLY SKILLED MIGRANT PROGRAMME (HSMP)

10.107 In January 2002 the Highly Skilled Migrant Programme ('HSMP') was launched. The programme represents a fundamental change in business immigration law and is key to the government's managed migration policy. The term 'highly skilled' is rather a misnomer and the scheme in its current guise attracts those with intermediate skills. Since 31 March 2004 entry and stay under the programme has been regulated by the Immigration Rules,[1] but the earlier IDI of March 2002 is still operative and contains detailed guidance notes on how to make applications and on the scheme generally.[2] The main requirements to be met by a person seeking leave to enter under the programme are that an applicant must (i) produce a valid document from the Home Office, confirming that he or she meets the current criteria for the programme; (ii) intend to make the UK his or her main home; and (iii) demonstrate an ability to support him- or herself and any dependants without resource to public funds.[3] Successful applicants are permitted to take any form of employment or self-employment. The scheme is based on a points system.[4] On 31 October 2003 there was a reduction of the point thresholds from 75 to 65, an introduction of a young person's assessment for those aged under 28, and the introduction of a 10 points allowance for those with a skilled partner.[5] Unlike the innovator scheme, points can be accumulated in various areas and an applicant does not have to have a specific number of points from any one area. Points are awarded for academic background, work experience, earnings during the past 12 months and achievement in their chosen filed.[6] HSMP priority applications are available for general practitioners and points are given to those with skilled spouses and long-term partners who can contribute to the UK economy.[7] At present there is a strong demand for admission under the programme, and it is possible that the Home Office may review this scheme and increase the number of points necessary. On 12 April 2005 the scheme was amended to enable applicants with an eligible MBA degree to meet the points criteria on the basis of their MBA alone.[8]

1 HC 395, paras 135A–135H, inserted by HC 538 on 31 March 2003.
2 IDI Mar 02, Ch 5, s 11 and Annexes Z1 to Z5. The IDI are out of date as regards some of the detailed criteria for admission, which are set out on the Work Permits UK website, workingintheuk.gov.uk.
3 HC 395, paras 135A(i) to (iii). Approval of an HSMP counts as an 'immigration employment document', and the fee for the application is currently £315 from 1 April 2005: Immigration Employment Document (Fees) Regulations 2003, SI 2003/541, as amended by SI 2003/541 and the Immigration Employment Document (Fees) (Amendment) Regulations 2005 SI 2005/627. There is no fee if the applicant is a national of a state which has ratified the 1961 European Social Charter or the 1996 Revised Social Charter: reg 5. The fee exemption applies to nationals of Bulgaria, Romania, Turkey, Moldova, Albania, Armenia and Croatia.
4 See 'Highly Skilled Migrant Programme' on workingintheuk.gov.uk.
5 See 'Highly Skilled Migrant Programme'.
6 See 'Highly Skilled Migrant Programme'.
7 See 'Highly Skilled Migrant Programme'.
8 IDI, Ch 5, s 12, para 1.

10.108 Applicants from overseas need to obtain entry clearance before travelling to the UK.[1] The procedure is that the application is made from abroad, the decision is then communicated to the applicant, and, if successful, he or she must then obtain entry clearance. This requirement is to be rigidly enforced, and people coming as visitors and for other temporary purposes will not normally be allowed to switch into this category. But for applicants already in the UK in certain other defined categories, provision is now made for switching. For others in the UK, there is provision in the current policy to switch in-country into the HSMP category in 'exceptional circumstances': see

10.121ff. The rules operating between March 2003 and September 2004 were extraordinarily wide. Anyone who was granted leave to enter or remain in the UK, other than as an ordinary visitor, could qualify for an extension of stay as a highly skilled migrant, if they met the main requirements for that category, as set out in the previous paragraph.[2] Since October 2004 there is a narrower but clearer policy to the Rules.[3] Extensions of stay may be granted to (i) those given leave to enter as highly skilled migrants, who have already taken all reasonable steps to become lawfully economically active in the UK and meet the other main requirements of the Programme;[4] (ii) work permit holders who meet the main requirements of the Programme;[5] (iii) students with a degree qualification from a recognised degree course, who, if necessary, have obtained written consent of their official sponsor and meet the main requirements of the Programme;[6] (iv) postgraduate doctors, dentists and trainee GPs, who were given leave to enter in this capacity, and have, if necessary, obtained written consent of their official sponsor, and meet the main requirements of the Programme;[7] (v) working holiday makers, who entered as such and meet the main requirements of the scheme,[8] (vi) Science and Engineering Graduate Scheme participants who meet the main requirements of the programme;[9] (vii) persons granted leave to enter or remain as innovators, who meet the main requirements of the programme;[10] and (viii) those granted leave to enter or remain to take a PLAB test or for a clinical attachment, who hold a valid document issued by the Home Office confirming that they meet the criteria for entry under the priority application process for general practitioners under the HSMP and meet the main requirements of the programme.[11] On acceptance into the programme, applicants are given an initial leave for 12 months,[12] which can then be renewed for a further three years.[13] Highly skilled migrants can qualify for indefinite leave by aggregating time spent under different kinds of leave. They can do so, if they have had a continuous period of at least four years as a highly skilled migrant or have had a continuous period of at least four years which includes periods of leave granted under paragraphs 128 to 319 of the Rules, [14] ie in work permit employment, in the Sectors-based scheme, as an overseas journalist, as a sole representative, private servant in a diplomatic household, domestic worker, overseas government employee, Minister of religion, missionary or member of a religious order, as airport based operational staff of an overseas airline, as a person with UK ancestry, as a business person, as innovator, as an EC Association Agreement business person, investor, writer, composer or artist, as a child resident in the UK, as EEA national, as retired person of independent means, as person of long residence in the UK, and as a family member or relative of any of the above. As a settlement provision this rule is unique. For the meaning of 'continuous', see the discussion at 10.97 above.

[1]   HC 395, para 135A (iv).
[2]   HC 395, para 135A (i)–(iii), as inserted by HC 538 on 31 Mar/03.
[3]   On switching policy see further 10.121 below.
[4]   HC 395, para 135D, as amended by Cmd 6339 on 1 Oct/04.
[5]   HC 395, para 135DA.
[6]   HC 395, para 135DB. An HND is not 'degree level' for these purposes: Work Permits (UK) User Panel meeting notes, 29 September 2004.
[7]   HC 395, para 135DC.
[8]   HC 395, para 135DD.
[9]   HC 395, para 135DE, inserted by HC 1112, in force 18 October 2004.
[10]   HC 395, para 135DF as inserted.

[11]   HC 395, para 135DG, inserted by HC 346 from 15 March 2005.
[12]   HC 395, para 135B.
[13]   HC 395, para 135E as substituted by HC 346, in force 15 March 2005. Those switching from one of the permitted categories would be granted three years' rather than 12 months' leave.
[14]   HC 395, para 135G.

SCIENCE AND ENGINEERING GRADUATE SCHEME

10.109   A new Science and Engineering Graduate Scheme (SEGS) has been introduced, no doubt, to tempt overseas graduates in those disciplines to come to the UK for an initial 12-month period with the idea of going into full-time employment at the end of that period. The requirements are set out in recent Immigration Rules which came into force on 25 October 2004.[1] To qualify for entry into the Scheme, applicants must (i) have obtained a second class or higher undergraduate degree, a masters degree or a PhD in a subject approved by the Department of Education and Skills;[2] (ii) intend to seek and take work during their stay in the UK; (iii) be able to maintain and accommodate themselves and any dependants during their stay without recourse to public funds; (iv) be recent graduates, having completed their degree or PhD in the last 12 months; (v) not be coming into the Scheme for more than 12 months; (vi) intend to leave the UK at the end of their initial 12 months' stay, unless they obtain leave under the work permit scheme, the HSMP, or as a business person or Innovator. The Home Office has indicated an intention to bring in a similar scheme for MBAs, to attract students from the top 50 business schools.[3]

[1]   HC 395, paras 135 to 135T, inserted by Cm 6339 on 25 October 2004
[2]   The DfES list of approved courses is available on the workingintheuk.gov.uk website as a link from 'Science and Engineering Graduate Students'. It does not include HNC, HND, DipHE or Foundation degree courses.
[3]   Work Permit UK user panel notes, 29 September 2004.

10.110   Graduates coming from overseas, other than specified British nationals,[1] need to obtain entry clearance before travelling to the UK.[2] British nationals already in the UK can apply in-country; so too may students on student visas, if they meet the requirements of the scheme, but no-one else.[3] The maximum stay is 12 months, but participants in the Scheme, whose terms of admission require them to seek and take work,[4] may take a wide range of employment at any time during their 12-month stint as participants. The requirements for an extension of stay to take employment are that applicants (i) have leave to enter or remain as participants in the Scheme; (ii) have been granted a valid Home Office immigration employment document;[5] and (iii) meet the main requirements for someone coming to the UK to work, as set out in HC 395, paragraph 128 (ii) to (vi).[6] The range of employment open to participants in the Scheme is a wide one and includes, for example, employment in the Sectors-based Scheme, which is no longer a stepping stone to mainstream employment.[7] So care needs to be exercised in the choice of employment, if the graduate wishes to fulfil long-term prospects in the UK.

[1]   British National (Overseas), British Overseas Territories citizen, British Overseas citizen, British Protected Person, and British subjects under the British Nationality Act 1981.

2   HC 395, para 135O(viii), inserted by Cmd 6339 on 25 October 2004.
3   See HC 395, para 135R(ii), as inserted.
4   HC 395, para 135O(ii), as inserted.
5   Ie, a work permit or any other document which relates to employment and is issued for the purpose of the Immigration Rules or in connection with the grant of leave to enter or remain: Nationality, Immigration and Asylum Act 2002, s 122. See 10.3 above.
6   HC 395, para 131C, as inserted.
7   See 10.63 above.

INVESTMENT AND SELF SUFFICIENCY

Investors

10.111 In October 1994 a new immigration category was introduced for investors.[1] Further changes were introduced on 13 January 2004. The investor category is aimed at people who wish to make the UK their main home and have substantial funds to invest here. The application will be refused if it appears that the investor does not intend to make his or her main home in the UK and intends only short visits. In those cases, it is more appropriate for the applicant to enter as a visitor.[2] An investor may not take employment but can engage full-time or part-time in business or self-employment, for example, as a consultant or non-executive director.[3]

1   HC 395, paras 224–23, as amended by HC 176.
2   IDI Jan 04 Ch 6, s 3, Annex G.
3   HC 395, para 224(iv).

10.112 To qualify, Investors must either (a) have money of their own under their control in the UK of not less than £1,000,000, or (b) own personal assets worth more than £2,000,000 net and have money under their control in the UK of not less than £1,000,000 which may have come from their own sources or have been loaned to them by a financial institution regulated by the Financial Services Authority.[1] Capital may be held in a husband and wife's joint names if one spouse is a principal applicant and will be accompanied by the other spouse as a dependant and they both apply for entry clearance at the same time.[2] Investors must intend to invest not less than £750,000 in the UK in the form of UK government bonds, share capital or loan capital in active and trading UK-registered companies (other than those principally engaged in property investment).[3] Investors cannot invest in property companies, banks, building societies or offshore companies.[4] 'Property companies' means companies whose main function is to own or manage land or buildings. It does not include companies principally engaged in construction or in other business areas such as retailing, which happen to own a substantial amount of property.[5] The investor can invest the £750,000 in a regulated collective investment scheme such as a unit trust, provided the funds are invested in companies which meet the requirements of the Immigration Rules. Many standard unit trusts which involve investments in a selection of different companies will include property companies in their portfolio. This investment will be acceptable provided the total value of the investment exceeds £750,000 and £750,000 of the investment can fairly be said to qualify under the Rules. Fund managers' prospectuses may be requested in order to check that a sufficient proportion of the investment qualifies under the Rules.[6] The £750,000 must not be invested through an off-shore company or trust. This is to ensure that maximum tax benefits accrue to the UK.

[1] HC 395, para 224 (i) (a) and (b), as amended by HC 176 on 12 January 2004.
[2] IDI Jan 04 Ch 6, s 3, Annex G.
[3] HC 395, para 224(ii).
[4] HC 395, para 224(ii) and IDI Ch 6, s 3, Annex G.
[5] IDI Ch 6, s 3, Annex G.
[6] IDI Ch 6, s 3, Annex G.

10.113 Once an investor has invested at least £750,000 as required under the Immigration Rules, he or she may invest the remaining £250,000 in the UK in property companies or any major durable assets situated here, such as an unmortgaged property or significant works of art. Personal effects such as jewellery and antique furniture do not count as major assets unless it is clear that such items are held for investment purposes.[1] Investors must fulfil the maintenance and accommodation requirements of the Rules and not have recourse to public funds.[2] The Home Office will consider carefully the investor's personal circumstances and level of financial commitment; for example, an investor with a number of children who are being privately educated is likely to require a larger disposable income than an investor without children. In the light of current rates of return on government bonds, investors may need substantially more than £1,000,000 to satisfy the Rules. Investors supplementing their investment income by earning money on a self-employed basis will be required to provide details of the intended work.

[1] IDI Jan 04, Ch 6, s 3, Annex G.
[2] HC 395, para 224(iv).

10.114 The Home Office is always concerned to establish the source of the applicant's funds and documentary evidence of this will assist the application. Entry clearance is mandatory,[1] but the current IDIs disclose the following in-country switching policy:[2]

> 'If an applicant with valid leave to remain in the UK in another capacity seeks to switch to investor status and he is able to produce documentary evidence that he fully meets the requirements of the Rules, the entry clearance requirement may be waived'.

We suggest that the 'valid leave to remain' requirement, properly construed, is a reference to valid leave, be it leave to enter or remain (see further 10.122 below). If so, the policy should benefit anyone lawfully in the country so long as the application is complete and meritorious, raising no unaddressed issues. However, in practice it seems that this policy is rarely applied, perhaps because most in-country applicants have leave to enter rather than leave to remain and the Home Office is relying on the distinction. In-country applicants should be ready to argue the construction point but also to argue the application individually, on its own merits. The rules permit switching for anyone with leave to enter or remain as a work permit holder, a highly skilled migrant, a business person or an innovator.[3] All investor applications are referred to the Business Case Unit of the Home Office. An investor does not have to bring any money to the UK before the application has been approved, but has to demonstrate that he or she has the requisite amount and the intention to invest in accordance with the Immigration Rules. The investor will normally be expected to have transferred capital and made the requisite investments within three months of the application being approved.[4] After the initial period of 12 months, investors may apply to extend leave for a further period of three years if they can demonstrate that no less than £1,000,000 of their own money is under their control in the UK, they have made the UK their main home and have invested not less than £750,000 in accordance with the Rules.[5] An investor who has suffered a major loss in his or her £750,000 portfolio, as a result of which he or she no longer has £1,000,000, may be granted leave to remain for one year only in order to keep the case under close review. After a continuous period of four years in the UK the investor may apply for settlement.[6]

[1] HC 395, para 224(v).
[2] IDI Jan 04 Ch 6, s 3, para 4.3; for further details, see 10.121 below.
[3] HC 395 para 227A–D, inserted and 228–229 substituted by HC 346, from 15 March 2005.
[4] IDI Ch 6, s 3, Annex G; but the legality of this Home Office expectation is not beyond doubt: see *Trivedi v Secretary of State for the Home Department* above at 10.87 fn 5.
[5] HC 395, para 227.
[6] HC 395, para 230; as to the meaning of 'continuous', see 10.97 above.

Retired persons of independent means

10.115 The current Immigration Rules greatly limit the ambit of the 'person of independent means' category. Prior to October 1994 there was no age limit,[1] but since that date applicants have had to be 60 or over.[2] An income of not less than £25,000 a year is required[3] (net of any overseas tax)[4] and there is no capital alternative.[5] There must also be an intention to make the UK the main home.[6] A verbal or written statement of such an intention is normally sufficient.[7] Applicants must demonstrate a close connection with the UK.[8] There is no longer an alternative requirement that the individual's admission be in the general interests of the UK (as was the case before October 1994).[9] However, the IDI specifically refer to a discretionary category of applicants who may exceptionally be granted leave on the basis that their presence will reflect well on the UK or their abilities are likely directly to benefit people in the UK other than by taking employment.[10] Persons of independent means must be able to support themselves and their families from their own resources with no assistance from any other person and without taking employment or having recourse to public funds.[11] Where applicants satisfy these conditions they will normally be admitted for an initial period of four years with a prohibition on the taking of employment.[12] For the position of British passport holders, see 10.119 below.

[1] HC 251, para 44.
[2] HC 395, para 263(i).
[3] HC 395, para 263(ii).
[4] IDI Sep 04, Ch 7, s 4, Annex G.
[5] Under earlier Rules, income of £20,000 or capital of £200,000 was required: HC 251, para 44.
[6] HC 395, para 263(v).
[7] IDI Sep 04, Ch 7, s 4, Annex H.

8   HC 395, para 263(iv) and IDI Dec 00, Ch 7, s 4, Annex H: see 10.108 below.
9   See HC 251, para 44. The meaning of this phrase was never certain. The suggestion in *Nasby* (3358) that simply being a good citizen was in the interests of the state was rejected in *Wasmouth v Visa Officer, Paris* [1984] Imm AR 151, and see *Mah* (3511); *Yuen* (4654); and *Sanji* (3524). Bringing in large investments was regarded as possibly sufficient in *Ahmadi* (2770); *Tong* (4960); *Nasnas* (4156); an intention to deploy the wealth in a manner beneficial to the UK was important in *Zandfani* (2945). In fact the Home Office operated a concession that the investment of £500,000 in the UK was prima facie in the general interests of the UK, which was withdrawn when the investor category was introduced.
10   IDI Sep 04, Ch 7, s 4, Annex I.
11   HC 395, para 263(iii).
12   HC 395, para 264.

Control of income

10.116 The availability of capital is no longer a consideration for admission as a person of independent means. Income alone is necessary and this must be under the person's control and disposable in the UK. The source of income does not have to be located in the UK provided the income itself is disposable here.[1] Thus problems arise if the income flow is blocked by exchange control regulations.[2] In the case of *Ex p Chiew*[3] the High Court held that the applicant must prove that he or she has a right to a supply of sufficient funds, legally enforceable against any person. Mere permission to use and spend is not control. Thus family funds from which contributions are made to an applicant will not generally count if it cannot be said that the applicant is able to control the advance of funds for the indefinite future.[4] In *Rohr*[5] a legally enforceable maintenance agreement was held to be sufficiently under the person's control for the purpose of the Immigration Rules. If the applicant and his or her spouse or partner are applying to come to the UK together, joint income or income from the spouse or partner can be counted.[6] The standard of proof in these matters is the normal civil one of a balance of probabilities and the Tribunal falls into error if it expresses itself in terms of not being convinced as to the source of funds.[7]

1   *Kotedia* (4977) unreported.
2   See *Entry Clearance Officer, Canberra v Ward* [1975] Imm AR 129 and IDI Sep 04, Ch 7, s 4, Annex G.
3   *R v Immigration Appeal Tribunal, ex p Chiew* [1981] Imm AR 102, QBD.
4   See *Gautam* (1891) (guaranteed regular payment from third parties); *Madanipoor* (1969) (voluntary payment from husband to wife).
5   *Secretary of State for the Home Department v Rohr* [1983] Imm AR 95.
6   IDI Sep 04, Ch 7, s 4, Annex G.
7   *R v Immigration Appeal Tribunal, ex p Mehra* [1983] Imm AR 156, QBD.

Retirement activity

10.117 Although the Immigration Rules refer to retired persons, the only express requirements suggesting retirement are that applicants must be at least 60 years of age and have sufficient resources without taking employment.[1] A condition prohibiting employment is also attached to leave until such time as settlement is attained.[2] Earlier Rules relating to persons of independent means contained the words 'without working' and Tribunal case law established that working covered remunerative activity including self-employment[3] inside or outside the UK.[4] It could be argued that the change of wording to 'without taking employment' is, therefore, significant and indicates that (a) there is no longer any need to make fine distinctions between establishing a business and making investments[5] and (b) there are now no restrictions on persons of independent means keeping their existing business interests going or engaging in new ventures. However, the IDI state that applicants will be expected to have relinquished all work commitments both in the UK and abroad and applications should be refused if an applicant intends to continue running a business abroad.[6] The IDI draw the distinction between overseeing 'business interests' and 'taking an active interest' in a business.[7]

1   HC 395, para 263(i) and (iii).
2   HC 395, para 264.
3   *Jahangard v Entry Clearance Officer, Vienna* [1985] Imm AR 69.
4   *Khan (Asadullah)* (2931); *Aalullum* (3056); *Jahangard* above; *Shikley* (4179).
5   See *Nasby* (3358) (a sleeping partner is an investor only); *Mah* (3511) (an exercise of talent as an artist or writer is not establishing a business, if it is not done for profit).
6   IDI Sep 04, Ch 7, s 4 and Annex G.
7   IDI Sep 04, Ch 7, s 4 and Annex G.

Close connection with the UK

10.118 These words are deliberately loose and fall to be interpreted in the light of the particular case. The examples given in earlier Rules ('presence of close relatives' and 'periods of previous residence')[1] were examples only and not an exhaustive list. Although the current provision gives no examples at all, undoubtedly those previously given are still relevant.[2] A close relative includes relatives of the blood and by affinity.[3] If a close relative is the eldest son, this may carry more weight than if it is a more distant relative.[4] A close relative present in the UK is not to be discounted simply because he or she is here in a temporary capacity, such as student or visitor, although obviously this will carry less weight.[5] A partner in a gay or lesbian relationship counts.[6] A period of previous residence by the applicant may on its own constitute a close connection,[7] and the quality of the previous residence may be more important than its duration.[8] Thus temporary residence counts. It does not have to constitute settlement to be taken into consideration, nor need it be of any particular duration.[9] The matter must be looked at in the round.[10] Prior British nationality of the applicant or a close relative may also count,[11] but not the constitutional link between the UK and an existing Crown Colony,[12] nor connections with a former UK-mandated territory.[13] It is not necessary to sever connections with another country in order to have close connections with the UK.[14] A strong sense of identity with and belonging to the UK is a significant factor,[15] and speaking or writing English fluently or 'without trace of accent' will help.[16] Property or business connections may be taken into account.[17]

1   HC 251, para 44.
2   See now IDI Sep 04, Ch 7, s 4, Annex H. Examples given are close relatives, periods of previous residence, or a combination of factors such as long-standing possession of substantial property, employment with a British company involving frequent business visits to Britain, or letters of support from eminent British citizens. The possession of British nationality (other than British citizenship) does not constitute a close connection.

3   *Mistry* (3039); *Fung v Entry Clearance Officer, Hong Kong* [1984] Imm AR 159; *Yuen* (4654).
4   *Fung* above.
5   *Bagherzadeh* (2898).
6   *Thong* TH/30896/87 (adjudicator), noted in Mungo Bovey 'UK Immigration Law and the Homosexual' (1984) INLP 8 at 62
7   *R v Immigration Appeal Tribunal, ex p Zandfani* [1984] Imm AR 213; in *Nasby* (3358) eight out of 50 years was insufficient; and see IDI Dec 00, Ch 7, s 4, Annex H.
8   See *Secretary of State for the Home Department, ex p Rohr* [1983] Imm AR 95; *Nasby* above.
9   *Zandfani* above; see also *Rohr* above, where residence as a student for six years was part of the reasons for holding that a close connection existed.
10 *Zandfani* above; and see IDI Dec 00, Ch 7, s 4, Annex H.
11 See *Rohr* above; *Fung* above; *Antiglevich* (4661); *Yuen* above. It is insufficient on its own to constitute a close connection: IDI Sep 04, Ch 7, s 4, Annex H.
12 *Chui* (4172); *Yuen* above.
13 *Nasnas* (4156).
14 *Fung* above.
15 *Bagherzadeh* (2898).
16 *Jambuserwara* (2852); *Wasmouth* (3426); *Antiglevich* (4661).
17 *Rohr* above, approved in *Nasnas* above, but not if the property is a purely speculative investment: see *Fung* above; *Sanji* (3524).

10.119 Retired persons of independent means are normally given up to four years' leave on entry.[1] However a British passport holder (British Overseas Territories citizen, British National (Overseas), British Overseas citizen, British subject under the British Nationality Act 1981 or British Protected Person) should be given indefinite leave to enter immediately.[2] If less than four years is given, an extension to take the person up to four years may be granted.[3] Indefinite leave to remain will then be granted on application,[4] provided the applicant has spent a continuous period of four years in the UK in this capacity and has met and continues to meet the requirements of the Immigration Rules.[5]

1   HC 395, para 264.
2   IDI Dec 00, Ch 7, s 4.
3   HC 395, para 267.
4   IDI Sep 04, Ch 7, s 4, and see 10.98 above.
5   HC 395, para 269; for the meaning of 'continuous' see 10.97 above.

Family members of business, self-employed, investors and retired people

10.120 The spouse, unmarried partner and children under 18 of persons in self-employment (as business persons, investors, innovators or writers, composers and artists), or of retired persons of independent means, may also be admitted to the UK.[1] In all cases they will need to satisfy the maintenance and accommodation provisions of the Immigration Rules which require accommodation which is owned or occupied exclusively by the applicant. In the case of spouses and partners it is essential that the marriage or relationship is subsisting. In the case of children leave will only be granted if they are unmarried, have not formed an independent family unit and are not leading an independent life. Normally, children must be accompanying or joining *both* parents but will be allowed to accompany or join just one parent if the other is deceased, if the parent has had sole responsibility for the child's upbringing, or if there are serious and compelling family or other considerations which make exclusion undesirable and suitable arrangements have been made in such cases for the child's care. As a general rule the spouse, partner and dependent children who have been given permission to accompany or join the principal applicant will be free to take employment or engage in business or other self-employment.[2] However, the spouse and any child of retired persons of independent means are not permitted to take any form of work,[3] though the Home Office may allow dependent children of retired persons of independent means to undertake training after the first year of residence in the UK.[4]

[1] HC 395, paras 240–245 (spouses and children of businesspersons, investors, writers, composers and artists), 271–276 (spouses and children of retired persons of independent means), 295J–K (unmarried partners), Immigration and Nationality Directorate website, 25 July 2000 (spouses and children of innovators).
[2] HC 395, paras 241, 244; IDI Sep 04, Ch 6, s 5.
[3] HC 395, paras 272, 275; IDI Sep 04, Ch 7, s 4, Annex J.
[4] IDI Sep 04, Ch 7, s 4, Annex J.

SWITCHING

10.121 As a general policy, ever since the introduction of mandatory prior entry clearance there have been restrictions on switching in-country to a status requiring such entry clearance. There are exceptions, but the general policy has been to move consideration of eligibility criteria to the posts abroad so as not to be left with the problem of getting rid of someone who does not qualify for the status in question. Whether or not switching is permitted to or from a particular status is governed by the Immigration Rules, the IDIs and/or the guidance notes relating to particular schemes, like the work permit scheme. There are no generalised provisions; in each category it is necessary to look up the Rules, IDIs or guidance concerned. These change frequently. For example, on 19 May 2004 a Written Ministerial Statement announced new restrictions on temporary low-skilled migration routes, such as the Sectors Based Scheme, including the prevention of those working in these schemes from switching into work permit employment.[1] The current rules permit a considerable degree of switching from degree courses and post-graduate medical and dental studies, training, clinical attachment and observation to work permit, innovator and highly skilled migrant categories; from working holidaymaker to career categories; and between the work permit, highly skilled migrant, innovator, investor, business and retired (independent means) categories.[2] Often there is inconsistency, such as between the IDIs and the guidance notes, in which case the more recent should prevail. Even if the Rules, IDI and guidance forbid switching, the Secretary of State always has a statutory discretion under section 4 of the Immigration Act 1971 to grant leave and that includes a discretion in the particular circumstances of an individual case to waive the entry clearance requirement.

[1] See 10.63 above.
[2] For rules on switching into employment etc for graduates see 9.61, for post-graduate medical students etc see 9.45 above; for working holidaymakers see 9.67 above.

10.122 Because such policies are so easily varied, it is not practicable to set them all out here; but to illustrate how different such policies may be, we set some brief details of those relating to (a) investor status (waiving entry clearance on-entry, after entry and in respect of dependants) and (b) HSMP status, where normally no switching is allowed if the person is given entry as a visitor or in other temporary capacities, but where switching from certain specified categories is now allowed. Switching to investor status is governed by provisions of the Immigration Rules and the IDIs. Switching to HSMP status is governed by provisions of the Rules, IDI and a Home Office (Work Permits UK) guidance document, in force since 1 October 2004, called *Changing Immigration Status While in the UK ('Switching')*. This document also sets out policies regarding switching to work permit employment and to Innovator status. Switching to work permit employment is discussed at 10.57, but for the sake of completion the quote, below, from the policy document includes the section on work permit switches. Dealing first with the published policy relating to switches to investor status, this is in the IDIs and states: [1]

'If an applicant with valid leave to remain in the UK in another capacity seeks to switch to investor status and he is able to produce documentary evidence that he fully meets the requirements of the Rules, the entry clearance requirement may be waived'.

We suggest that the requirement here should be interpreted as a requirement for the individual to have leave, not specifically leave to remain. This is because it would be arbitrary and irrational to require leave to remain as distinct from leave to enter, and in the few instances in which the Immigration Rules appear to specify leave to remain (as distinct from leave to enter) as a requirement, the corresponding IDI describe the requirement as one of leave (whether to enter or remain).[2] The policy as regards switching in respect of the dependent spouse or child of a prospective investor (or businessman, writer/composer/artist) states:[3]

'Entry clearance is mandatory for entry in this category. After-entry, however, where the applicant was not admitted as a spouse or child, caseworkers may waive the no-switching provision in the Rules if they are satisfied that all the other requirements are met. Any case which falls to be refused, however, should be refused on no-switching grounds.'

Then there is the position of a person who seeks entry at a port as an investor but who does not possess the requisite entry clearance:[4]

'Most people seeking leave to enter in this capacity are in possession of the required entry clearance ... An immigration officer may require further guidance where ... a person arrives without entry clearance but there are *exceptional compassionate circumstances* and discretionary treatment is being considered. It will be necessary for the immigration officer to examine the person thoroughly on arrival and make enquiries in order to determine if he is likely to satisfy the criteria in [the Rules relating to investors].' (emphasis added)

The position regarding HSMP status is dealt with quite differently in the IDI:[5]

'The presumption is that those seeking to enter will obtain prior entry clearance. In order to enforce this, applications by those in the United Kingdom as a visitor or other short term capacity will not be considered. Any applicants are to be informed that they must obtain prior entry clearance and applications must be refused without substantive consideration. The refusal will reflect the fact that those in UK as visitors or other short term capacity must return to their country of residence and seek entry clearance in order to enter under HSMP.

Those in the United Kingdom with current leave in [other specified categories] … can make an application to switch into the [HSMP] category and will be considered in the same way as those who apply for entry clearance.'

1   IDI Ch 6, s 3, para 4.3.
2   See for example paragraph 295D(i) of the Rules (requiring an unmarried partner seeking an extension to have 'leave to remain') and the IDI, Ch 8, s 7, para 3.1 (describing this as a requirement to be in the UK 'lawfully').
3   IDI Ch 6, s 5, para 2.2.
4   IDI Ch 6, s 3, para 3.2.
5   IDI Ch 6, s 3, para 4.1. Much of the policy quoted above has been omitted, as it has been overtaken by the later publication of HC 395, paras 135A to 135H, as inserted by HC 538 on 31 March 2003 and now further modified as regards para 135D by new paras 135D, 135DA, 135DB, 135DC and 135DD, inserted by Cmd 6339 on 1 October 2004, 135DE and 135DF, inserted by HC 1112 on 18 October 2004, and 135DG, and substituted paras 135E and 135F, by HC 346, in force 15 March 2005. Very similar switching Rules apply to innovators: HC359, paras 210A to 210H, as inserted by HC 538 on 31 March 2003 and now further modified by Cmd 6339 as from 1 October 2004, by HC 1112 as from 18 October 2004 and by HC 346 from 15 March 2005.

10.123 Switching policies at Immigration Rules level were revised in the summer of 2004, following an announcement on 22 July 2004 by the Home Secretary, David Blunkett, who stated that the new restrictions on switching were to help ensure that the separation of temporary and permanent migration routes, which was necessary for an effective immigration control, was preserved. Measures include:

- preventing switching into work permit employment and the highly skilled migrant programme except by those already permitted in the Rules such as doctors, dentists and graduates;[1]
- permitting foreign nationals who are in the UK on a temporary visa and wish to remain in the UK to study, to switch into degree level courses only,[2] to prevent visitors obtaining leave to remain as students by enrolling in lower level private sector and further education courses.
- permitting in-country switching to minister of religion status in certain circumstances (for example students and work permit holders), although visitors will not be allowed to switch.[3]

The changes were part of an ongoing programme of work to safeguard the government's policy of selective admission. Those who do not meet the government's strict criteria cannot come to the UK, but those with the skills needed to boost the British economy can be admitted.

Switching policies outside the Immigration Rules were unified, as regards switches to work permit employment and the HSMP and innovator categories, as of 1 October 2004 by the policy document *Changing Immigration Status While in the UK* ('*Switching*'),[4] the substance of which reads as follows:

Switching into Work Permit Employment

Nationals from non-EEA countries may apply to switch into work permit employment without leaving the UK provided they satisfy the work permits criteria and have existing leave as:

- A student and have successfully graduated at a UK higher or further education institute; or
- A postgraduate doctor or dentist or trainee general practitioner; or
- A student nurse; or
- A working holidaymaker who has been in the UK at least twelve months; or
- A participant on the Science and Engineering Graduate Scheme; or
- A Highly Skilled Migrant; or
- An Innovator.

Postgraduate doctors, dentists, trainee general practitioners and student nurses may only switch into work permit employment as a doctor, dentist, general practitioner and nurse respectively. The presumption will be that applications made from non-EEA nationals currently in the UK in any other capacity will be refused. Therefore, non-EEA nationals in the UK on a Sectors-Based Scheme permit will no longer be allowed to switch into work permit employment.

Switching into the Highly Skilled Migrant and Innovators categories

Nationals from non-EEA countries may apply to switch into the Highly Skilled Migrant and Innovators categories without leaving the UK provided they have existing leave as:

- A work permit holder; or
- A student who has graduated at a UK higher or further educational establishment; or
- A working holiday maker; or
- A postgraduate doctor or dentist or trainee general practitioner; or
- A participant on the Science and Engineering Graduate Scheme.

Participants on the Highly Skilled Migrant Programme may switch into the Innovators category. Similarly Innovators may switch into the Highly Skilled Migrant Programme.

What happens if an application is submitted where the non-EEA national is not a member of one of the designated switching categories?

Switching from categories other than those stated in this leaflet will not be allowed except in exceptional circumstances. These circumstances will be assessed by caseworkers on a case by case discretionary basis. Circumstances relating to the job, employment and labour market will not be accepted as exceptional circumstances. Only circumstances relating to the individual which would make it unduly harsh for them to return to their country of residence may be considered as exceptional.

The immigration rules have been updated in line with this policy document. Additionally, doctors who come to the UK to take the PLAB test, or on clinical attachment or as a dental observer, are permitted to switch into work permit employment, or as a highly skilled migrant,[5] and the rules now permit more switching between work permit, innovator, investor, business and retired (independent means) categories.[6] The policy to switch in-country outside the rules, where exceptional circumstances relating to the individual would make it unduly harsh to return to the country of residence, is certainly applied by the Home Office in practice and, therefore, may be very useful.

¹ HC 395, para 135DC, as inserted by Cmd 6339 on 1 October 2004. See 10.122 above.
² HC 395, para 60, as amended by Cmd 6339 on 1 October 2004. See chapter 9 above. Note that this does not affect visa nationals, who could not switch from visitor to student status before the rule change.
³ HC 395, paras 174A and 174B, as amended by Cmd 6297; IDI Aug 04, Ch 5, s 6, Annex Q, para 6. See 10.24 above.
⁴ Published at: http://www.workingintheuk.gov.uk/working_in_the_uk/en/homepage/news/announcements/Changing_Immigration_Status_While_in_the_UK_Switching_Maincontent.0002.file.tmp/Switching%20leaflet.pdf. How this policy is reconciled with the government's stated desire not to poach the most highly skilled and educated from third world countries is not clear.
⁵ HC 395 paras 131G, 135DG, inserted and 132, 133, 135E and 135F substituted by HC 346 paras 8–11, as from 15 March 2005.
⁶ HC 395 paras 132, 133, 135E, 135F, 210E, 210F, 228, 229, 267, 268 as substituted; paras 206A–F, 210DG, 227A–D, 266A–D as inserted.

Chapter 11

FAMILIES, PARTNERS AND CHILDREN

INTRODUCTION

11.1 This chapter examines how legislation, the Immigration Rules and current concessions and policies apply to families, partners and children. It will deal with immigration law related to marriage, engagement, unmarried partners and same sex relationships, family reunion, adoption and unaccompanied (or separated) children. It will also consider the interaction between family and immigration law and the relevant, applicable family law provisions on the validity of marriage, on overseas divorce, adoption and domicile.

11.2 It will be necessary to cross-refer to other chapters in this book for further information on how the law applies in certain more specific circumstances. For example, the law relating to family reunion for refugees is dealt with at 12.179ff and the law relating to family members of EEA nationals is considered at 7.86ff. It continues to be an absurd anomaly that the admission

11.2 Families, Partners and Children

of family members of British citizens who have travelled and worked elsewhere in the EC is governed by the generous provisions of EC law,[1] while restrictive domestic Immigration Rules continue to govern the family reunion rights of those who have stayed or worked in the UK. Practitioners should be astute to search for an EC law solution to family reunion difficulties.[2]

[1] See *R v Immigration Appeal Tribunal and Surinder Singh, ex p Secretary of State for the Home Department* [1992] Imm AR 565, [1992] 3 All ER 798 at 7.60 above.
[2] See *Carpenter v Secretary of State for the Home Department*: C-60/00 [2002] 2 CMLR 64, [2002] INLR 439.

11.3 The Immigration Rules were amended on the coming into force of the Human Rights Act 1998 on 2 October 2001 to bring them into line with ECHR obligations,[1] particularly those regarding the right to respect for family and private life. A number of extra-rules concessions affecting unmarried partners (heterosexual or same-sex),[2] bereaved spouses[3] and the children of fiancé(e)s[4] have been brought within the Rules, as has the admission of children for adoption.[5] The rules allowing former spouses to enter for access to children of a former marriage, which were heavily criticised in past editions, have been rewritten to allow for work and settlement rights for contact parents,[6] although there is still no right of entry for primary carers of settled children. The admission of spouses and children of refugees has been brought within the Rules.[7] The rules on public funds have been amended in line with the former policy, allowing the UK-settled party to claim in his or her own right so long as the arrival of the family member does not result in additional recourse to public funds.[8] However, other rule changes which require children to be supported by their sponsoring parent or relative[9] appear to entrench Home Office opposition to long-term third party support of children and other family members, attempting to reverse the effect of *Arman Ali*.[10] This limb of the relevant Rules, to be human rights-compliant, should be construed as not precluding third party support to parents, since the amended Rules do not require parental support of children to be from their own resources. Alternatively, it would have to be disapplied in cases involving, for example, disabled parents where support is provided by a third party, so as to avoid discrimination in the enjoyment of family life contrary to Articles 8 and 14 of the ECHR. In addition to these changes the government has introduced a number of restrictions preventing spouses of British citizens and residents from varying their leave to enter on grounds of marriage if on their last admission they were not granted leave for more than six months.[11] Persons who are not EEA citizens and who are subject to immigration control face severe restrictions on their rights to marry in the UK and may have to obtain permission from the Secretary of State before registering their intention to marry here.[12] We examine these changes below.

[1] By Cm 4851.
[2] HC 395, as amended, paras 295A–L.
[3] HC 395, as amended, para 287(b); bereaved unmarried partners are included at para 295M.
[4] HC 395, as amended, paras 303A–F.
[5] HC 395, as amended, paras 316A–C.
[6] HC 395, as amended, paras 246–248F.
[7] HC 395, as amended, paras 352A–F.
[8] HC 395, as amended, para 6A.

9   HC 395, as amended, paras 297(v), 298(v), 301(v), 310(v), 311(v), 314(v), 317(v).
10 *R v Secretary of State for the Home Department, ex p Ali* [2000] INLR 89.
11 HC 395, para 284(i) as amended by HC 538 from 31 March 2003, substituted by Cm 5949 from 25 August 2003. The rule change affects all in-country spouse applications made after 31 March 2003. See 11.66 below.
12 Asylum and Immigration (Treatment of Claimants, etc) Act 2004 ss19–25, in force 1 February 2005. See 11.66 below.

11.4 Concessions which operate outside the immigration rules to prevent the removal of unlawfully resident children, with long residence in the UK,[1] and unlawfully resident spouses or parents of British citizens or UK-settled persons,[2] are still outside the Immigration Rules. Recent government practice has been to apply these concessions strictly, and to require those, who have failed to obtain entry clearance prior to arrival, to return home to obtain one.[3] The former concession allowing the settlement of spouses and partners who have suffered domestic violence in their probationary period is now in the Rules. The former under 12s concession has been ended and has not been replaced.

1   DP69/99 (formerly DP5/96): *Butterworths Immigration Law Service* D[1121]. See 11.122 below.
2   DP3/96, DP4/96: *Butterworths Immigration Law Service* D[551] and D[601]. See 11.74 below.
3   See eg *R v Secretary of State for the Home Department, ex p Zighem* [1996] Imm AR 194; *R v Secretary of State for the Home Department, ex p Gangadeen* [1998] INLR 206; *R v Secretary of State for the Home Department, ex p Kebbeh* (CO 1269/98) (30 April 1999, unreported); *Patel v Secretary of State for the Home Department, Ahmed v Secretary of State for the Home Department* [1998] INLR 570, CA; *R (on the application of Isiko) v Secretary of State for the Home Department* [2001] 1 FCR 633, CA; *R (on the application of Mahmood) v Secretary of State for the Home Department* [2001] 1 WLR 840. See, on whether there are insurmountable obstacles to the making of an entry clearance application from abroad: *MS (inability to make entry clearance application) Somalia* [2005] UKIAT 00003 (17 January 2005, unreported), *AB and others (Risk, Return, Israel Check Points) Palestine CG* [2005] UKIAT 00046 (1 February 2005, unreported), *KJ (Entry Clearance Proportionality) Iraq CG* [2005] UKIAT 00066 (10 March 2005, unreported).

11.5 Since the last edition, the law relating to inter-country adoption has been radically reformed and the trafficking of women and children for the purposes of prostitution and domestic servitude has become an issue of international and domestic concern. There have been many changes to the way in which children's applications are processed, and further changes are proposed. As these changes mean that the Home Office will interview more child applicants, practitioners will need to be familiar with expert evaluations on the competence and veracity of children and safeguards and presumptions concerning young people's evidence. There are now more age dispute challenges involving young applicants. These disputes can involve the Home Office and social services departments. There is also growing concern at Home Office practices returning unaccompanied and trafficked children before, at, or soon after they become 18. Social services are increasingly involved with children and families at risk of removal. Chapter 13 deals with the support services for children and parents. There have also been a number of important cases defining the extent to which those wishing to remain in or enter the United Kingdom can rely upon Article 8 of the ECHR. These cases are noted in this chapter but are discussed in more detail in chapter 8.

THE INTER-RELATIONSHIP BETWEEN FAMILY AND IMMIGRATION LAW

11.6 Before considering the immigration rules concerning families, partners and children, it is useful to mention the significant interplay between family and immigration legislative arrangements and case loads. Questions which arise in an immigration context, over the admission, for example, of a child who has been adopted overseas, could equally arise in a family law context, where the same child has been seized on arrival in the UK by a local authority under an emergency protection order.[1] Family and immigration law both concern State and parental rights over children's travel and the international movements of families. Immigration and nationality law confer certain entitlements on the spouse and children of British citizens, and immigration lawyers therefore need a working knowledge of private international law on the validity of marriage, adoption and divorce. In 2000, foreign-born residents constituted nearly 8 per cent of the total UK population.[2] Furthermore there have been enormous changes in the social and religious life of the UK and profound changes in family life in recent decades. These and the great variety of forms taken by the family in a multicultural and pluralistic Britain, have been eloquently sketched out in the CA in *Singh v Entry Clearance Officer, New Delhi* by Munby J, who stressed the need for the law in the combined context of family, human rights and immigration to adapt itself to these new realities.[3] Caseloads in the family courts reflect both this social diversity and the general increase in family mobility. Parents or children in family cases may be British or foreign nationals, permanent or temporary residents, overstayers, claimants for asylum or the victims of trafficking or of domestic violence in their home countries. In certain cases the Home Office, immigration appellate authorities and family courts are simultaneously engaged with the same family, determining questions associated with parental/child contact, care and protection or residence.[4]

[1] See per Munby J in *Singh v Entry Clearance Officer, New Delhi* [2004] EWCA Civ 1075 [2004] INLR 515, at para 56.

[2] Secretary of State for the Home Department, *Secure Borders, Safe Haven: Integration with Diversity in Modern Britain*, February 2002, p 25.

[3] *Singh*, above; see per Munby J at paras 61–65, and note his emphasis at para 67 on the secularity and even handedness of the law: '… the starting point of the law is a tolerant indulgence to cultural and religious diversity and an essentially agnostic view of religious beliefs. A secular judge must be wary of straying across the well-recognised divide between church and state.'

[4] See *Re S (children) (abduction: asylum appeal)* [2002] EWCA Civ 843, [2002] All ER (D) 424 (Apr).

11.7 There are few reported cases dealing with intersecting family and immigration issues,[1] but family case practice exemplifies a wide variety of family situations where immigration issues are relevant. Such issues can arise from status questions. If the parties in family litigation have different nationalities, it can be important to consider the nationality or potential nationalities of their children, in order to facilitate family contact in a home country or to guard against the child's abduction.[2] Family litigation can concern children's contacts with parents in or outside the UK, their residence, care or protection or their removal or retention by parents in the UK. Family litigation frequently calls for evidence on the immigration status and nationalities of family members as the Court is required to consider where and with whom children should reside.

1   See *Re J (Adoption: Non-Patrial)* [1998] 1 FLR 225, CA.
2   Practitioners advising on nationality issues need to consider whether the acquisition of British nationality by a child can mean that the child's existing citizenship is lost or jeopardised because the home country does not allow dual nationality.

11.8 Immigration and nationality issues also arise in care and wardship cases. Some of these cases involve children privately fostered in the UK in arrangements which have exposed them to risk and exploitation, including as domestic or sex workers. Other care cases concern asylum seekers. Many such applicants have suffered severe trauma, affecting their parenting capacities. Their children too may have been traumatised, and may suffer severe disturbance and prove difficult to manage or to protect. Additionally unaccompanied children and young people may be at particular risk of harm, or if they are young, single parents, may need assistance caring for their babies. Their babies may be the focus of local authority concern both in the UK, and in the home country if the young person is to be removed without the requisite parenting skills or protective supports. It is probable that local authorities will have protection concerns in particular cases if the Secretary of State removes unaccompanied children before they become 18.

11.9 The intersection of family and immigration jurisdictions and the risk of conflicting outcomes in overlapping cases have persuaded courts and the Home Office of the need to share information in cases featured in both jurisdictions.[1] Statements filed in Children Act proceedings are confidential to those proceedings but if such statements and reports are relevant to immigration or asylum proceedings, the parties can apply for and secure their disclosure for those purposes.[2] Exchanges of information between the two jurisdictions are also facilitated by the protocol arrangements issued by the President of the Family Division. The protocols set down the arrangements for information requests or orders made concerning the Home or Passports Offices in family proceedings. A family court request or order for immigration information is made to the Home Office through the Family Division lawyer in the President's chambers who facilitates the exchange of information on status or seeks to acquire a case officer's views as to the likely effect of a family order or the likelihood of a party being granted leave to enter or remain.[3] Protocol interventions can be very helpful in securing information or Home Office co-operation in family cases where the immigration status of the child or carers are relevant factors.

1   See *Re S (children) (abduction: asylum appeal)* [2002] EWCA Civ 843, [2002] All ER (D) 424 (Apr), per Thorpe J at para 40. The Tribunal does not have the same concern about inconsistent outcomes from care and immigration jurisdictions. See *BE (Care Proceedings) Jamaica* [2005] UKIAT 00098 (28 February 2005) where Ouseley J held that 'the care and the immigration proceedings should be treated as concurrent and independent. Some of the considerations or evidence may overlap, but they are viewed from different perspectives. Each must proceed at its own timetable. If Care Orders override immigration decisions, then they can be invoked to prevent removal; and if not, not.'
2   *Re F (Child Case: Disclosure of Documents)* [1995] 1 FCR 589. See also: *Re B (a child) (disclosure)* [2004] EWHC 411(Fam); *In the matter of C (a minor)* [1996] EWCA Civ 560.

3   Protocols on 'Communicating with the Home Office and Passport Office', updated 4 June
     2004, Court Service Guides and notices, www.courtservice.gov.uk

11.10 Not only do family and immigration jurisdictions deal with the same families, they are also linked by their shared association with bilateral, European and international instruments governing the international movement of children in transnational adoptions, abductions and cross-jurisdictional family orders and contacts.[1] In the same way that states have sought to harmonise their immigration control arrangements, states have also made agreements for comity and mutual recognition and enforcement of family orders.[2] Recent examples include the immigration rules for adopted or prospective adoptive children, which incorporate the Hague Convention protections for transnational adoptions.[3] Arrangements to obtain passports, and immigration rules requiring appropriate parental or other consent for children's applications for entry clearance or for variation of leave, are framed to deter and prevent child abduction.[4] And to achieve consistency with family and human rights provisions favouring contact between children and their parents, the Immigration Rules now make provision for parents who may not be the main carers to remain in the UK for the purpose of contact and an active role in the child's upbringing.[5] One major potential difference between family and immigration law in the application of a relevant international human rights treaty arises out of the UN Convention on the Rights of the Child. As a result of a UK reservation, the Secretary of State is not bound by this Convention in immigration decision-making, but the Convention is binding in family law.[6]

1   For example: Brussels Convention on Jurisdiction and the Recognition and Enforcement of Judgements in Matrimonial Matters of 28 May 1998, European Convention on the Recognition and Enforcement of Decisions Concerning Custody of Children and on the Restoration of Custody of Children 1980, European Convention on the Exercise of Children's Rights 1996, Hague Convention on Jurisdiction, Applicable Law and Recognition of Decrees relating to Adoption 1965, Hague Convention on Protection of Children and Co-operation in Respect of Intercountry Adoption 1993, Hague Convention on the Civil Aspects of International Child Abduction 1980. See also: Lowe, Everall et al *International Movement of Children* (2004) Jordan Publishing.
2   See for example on international child contact, *Re G (Foreign Contact Order: Enforcement)* [2003] EWCA Civ 1607, [2004] 1 WLR 521; *Re A (Foreign Contact order: Jurisdiction)* [2003] EWHC 2911 (Fam), [2004] 1 All ER 912; Council Regulation (EC) No 1347/2000 (on jurisdiction and the recognition and enforcement of judgements in matrimonial matters and in matters of parental responsibility for children of both spouses) as well as the 1980 Hague Convention on the Civil Aspects of International Child Abduction and the 1980 Luxembourg Convention (commonly referred to as 'the European Convention'). The two Conventions were given effect in UK domestic law by the Child Abduction and Custody Act 1985. The government has recently consulted on whether the United Kingdom should sign and ratify the Council of Europe Convention on Contact Concerning Children. See Department for Constitutional Affairs *Consultation Paper on the Council of Europe Convention on Contact Concerning Children* CP 02/04, 28 May 2004.
3   The Hague Convention on Protection of Children and Co-operation in Respect of Intercountry Adoption 1993 is incorporated in The Adoption and Children Act 2002, the Adoption (Bringing Children into the United Kingdom) Regulations 2003 and the Immigration Rules HC 395, para 310.
4   See for example HC 395, para 320(16), 322(11), UK Passport Agency guidelines on passport issue to children, reproduced at [1994] Fam Law 651, and Diplomatic Service Procedures (DSP), Entry Clearance Vol 1, General Instructions Feb 04, Ch 14, para 14.5, stating that entry clearance officers should take care to ensure that the issue of a settlement entry clearance to the child will not contravene the terms of the custody order (at

www.ukvisas.gov.uk). See also *Hamilton Jones v David & Snape (a firm)* [2003] EWHC 3147, [2004] 1 All ER 657, a claim for damages against a solicitor's firm which negligently failed to re-register a child at risk of removal with the UK Passport Agency.

5   HC 395, para 246–248F.
6   When the UK ratified the Children's Convention it reserved the right to apply legislation relating to entry into, stay in and departure from the UK of those who did not have the right under the law of the UK to enter and remain in the UK and to the acquisition and possession of citizenship in a manner which did not necessarily comply with the Convention. See *R v Secretary of State for the Home Department, ex p Gangadeen and Jurawan, R v Secretary of State for the Home Department, ex p Khan* [1998] INLR 206, [1988] 1 FLR, [1998] Imm AR 106, [1997] EWCA Civ 2799; *Patel v Secretary of State for the Home Department, Ahmed v Secretary of State for the Home Department* [1998] EWHC Admin 453, [1999] Imm AR 22. Although the UK reservation covers entry, stay and removal decisions, the important Convention principles concerning representation and participation by children in judicial and administrative cases affecting them (Art 12) arguably apply in funding decisions by the Legal Services Commission in immigration cases involving children. Note that the Convention is incorporated in the Council Directive 2004/83 EC 29 April 2004 on minimum standards for the gualification and status of third country nationals or stateless persons as refugees or as persons who otherwise need international protection and the content of the protection granted, see 12.3 above.

11.11 In these intersecting family and immigration cases, courts and immigration authorities are required to evaluate varied family customs and arrangements when they have to decide on the validity of marriages, divorces or adoptions as well as whether there is established family life and grounds to remove or return children to another jurisdiction. These judgements are made by reference to 'the diversity of forms' that the family takes in 'our multicultural and pluralistic society'.[1] In recent judgements concerning the return and entry of children the courts have emphasised the need for sensitivity and respect to be shown to family arrangements in different cultures and jurisdictions.[2] In *Singh v Entry Clearance Officer, New Delhi*[3] the issue was whether there was a 'family life' between parents and their adoptive child where the adoption was valid under Indian law but not recognised in English law, the Court of Appeal noted:[4]

> 'it is important in this type of case, even if the adoption is not one that our law recognises, to have regard not merely to the fact of the adoption but also to all the personal, emotional and psychological, as well as the social, cultural and religious, consequences that flow from it.'

A similar approach was taken to the return to Sudan of Sudanese children wrongfully brought to England by their Sudanese mother. She had argued against their removal because under Sudanese law, as she had remarried she was not entitled to obtain custody of the children (although she could seek substantial access). Thorpe LJ noted that the number and diversity of States that have joined 'the Hague club' rendered it impossible to formulate minimum standard requirements of other family justice systems. He was extremely doubtful of a principle enabling a judge in England to criticise the standards or paramount principles applied by the family justice systems of a non-Convention State save in exceptional circumstances, such as where there was found to be persecution, or ethnic, sex or other discrimination. His Lordship considered that there was no absolute standard of the concept of paramountcy and that 'what constitutes the welfare of the child must be subject to the cultural background and expectations of the jurisdictions to achieve it'.[5] He drew attention to:

'the importance of according to each State liberty to determine the family justice system and principles that it deems appropriate to protect the child and to serve his best interests. There is an obvious threat to comity if a State whose system derives from Judaeo-Christian foundations condemns a system derived from an Islamic foundation when that system is conceived by its originators and operators to promote and protect the interests of children within that society and according to its traditions and values.'[6]

1   In *Singh v Entry Clearance Officer, New Delhi* [2004] EWCA Civ 1075, [2004] INLR 515 Munby J noted that 'the Strasbourg court has never sought to identify any minimum requirements that must be shown if family life is to be held to exist. That is because there are none. In my judgment there is no single factor whose existence is crucial to the existence of family life, either in the abstract or even in the context of any particular type of family relationship' (at para 72).
2   In *Re E (Abduction: Non-Convention Country)* [1999] 2 FLR 642 at 647 Thorpe LJ stated that States should respect the 'variety of concepts of child welfare derived from differing cultures and traditions' and 'a recognition of this reality must inform judicial policy'.
3   [2004] EWCA Civ 1075, [2004] INLR 615.
4   At para 86 per Munby J.
5   In *Re E (Abduction: Non-Convention Country)* [1999] 2 FLR 642 at 647.
6   [1999] 2 FLR 642 at 649. Pill LJ said much the same at 651: 'I have no difficulty in accepting the judge's conclusion that the application of Muslim law to this Muslim family is appropriate and acceptable.'

11.12 As *Re E (Abduction: Non-Convention Country)* intimates, State obligations under family and other human rights treaties are not always compatible. The notable example is in certain child abduction or wrongful retention cases. The family courts have considered, but have yet to rule on, whether they are obliged to take account of or comply with the non-*refoulement* obligation in the Refugee Convention as a freestanding instrument in cases where they are acting under the Hague Convention on international child abduction and could reach opposite conclusions, depending on which international rule they followed.[1] Subject to certain exceptions, the Hague Convention obliges the speedy return of unlawfully removed or retained children to their country of habitual residence. One such exception is where there is a grave risk that the child's return would expose him or her to physical or psychological harm or otherwise place the child in an intolerable situation.[2] The courts have interpreted this provision as requiring 'clear and compelling evidence' that there is a grave risk of harm or other intolerability to the child, which must be measured as 'substantial, not trivial'.[3] This test is not the same as that used in the Refugee Convention, where a much lower threshold of evaluation is required to succeed in a claim of the kind which might be made by an abducting parent, if she faced persecution from domestic violence in the home country and was seeking international protection for herself and her children on this ground. The core questions in such a case are whether the children's return should be delayed to await the outcome of the asylum claim and whether 'the physical or psychological harm' exception should still apply, if the parent is found to be a refugee on social group grounds.[4] These questions were raised but not answered in the case of *Re S (children) (abduction: asylum appeal)*.[5]

1   *Re S (children) (abduction: asylum appeal)* [2002] EWCA Civ 843 at para 25, *Re H (Child Abduction: Mother's Asylum)* [2003] EWHC 1820 (Fam), [2003] 2 FLR 1105. In both these cases, allegations of family violence were disputed in the family proceedings.
2   Convention on the Civil Aspects on International Child Abduction, Art 13(b).

³ *Re C (Abduction: Grave Risk of Psychological Harm)* [1999] 1 FLR 1145, *B v B (Child Abduction: Custody Rights)* [1993] Fam 32, 12 FLR 238. See as an example where the exception to return applied: *Re F (A Minor) (Abduction: Custody Rights Abroad)* [1995] Fam 224, sub nom *Re F (Child Abduction Risk if Returned)* [1995] 2 FLR 31.

⁴ Where the mother had been granted asylum status on domestic violence grounds, but the father, seeking the children's return, disputed such finding in the family jurisdiction, the Court ordered the return of the child to Pakistan upon undertakings by the father. *Re H (Child Abduction: Mother's Asylum)* [2003] EWHC 1820. See also: *Re E (Abduction, Non-Convention Country)* [1999] 2 FLR 642, [1999] Fam Law 610, *Re S (Children) (abduction: asylum appeal)*, sub nom *S v K* [2002] EWHC 816 (Fam), [2002] 2 FLR 437. Under the Hague Convention, courts determine Art 13(b) exceptions by reference to whether the home State has effective mechanisms for protection against domestic violence, whether the father provides undertakings to safeguard the parent and children or is able to care for the children if the mother refuses to return: Lowe, Everall et al *International Movement of Children* (2004) Jordan Publishing, pp 331–2.

⁵ [2002] EWCA Civ 843, [2002] 1 WLR 2548. See also *S v (1) B (2) Y (A Child)* 11 May 2005 (Lawtel notation) in which the President of the Family Division held that although an order that the mother return a child to her place of habitual residence might interfere with the human rights of the mother and her other child, the Hague Abduction Convention by its structure and terms accorded paramount importance to the rights and freedom of the child subject to the application (Family Division, 4 May 2005, per Sir Mark Potter).

11.13 In *Re S*, the mother, an Indian citizen, sought asylum in the UK on domestic violence/social group grounds. Her children were dependants in her asylum claim. The father disputed the allegations of violence and sought (and obtained) an order from the High Court for the children's summary return.[1] On appeal against this order, the Court of Appeal (per Laws LJ) stated that: 'Having regard to the rule as to the paramountcy of the child's interests arising under section 1 of the Children Act 1989 … a family judge would at the least pay very careful attention to any credible suggestion that a child might be persecuted if he were returned to his country of origin or habitual residence before making any order that such a return should be effected'.[2] The case of *S* is unlikely to be the last word on family and human rights treaty obligations, since the judge at first instance in that case (Bennett J) disbelieved the mother's account of family violence. A court has yet to grapple with these issues in a case where the risks of violence to the mother in the home jurisdiction are accepted by the Family Court.

¹ *Re S (Children)(abduction: asylum appeal)*, sub nom *S v K* [2002] EWHC 816 (Fam), [2002] 2 FLR 437, para 113.

² *Re S (children) (abduction: asylum appeal)* [2002] EWCA Civ 843, [2002] 1 WLR 2548 at para 25.

11.14 Immigration decision-makers and courts likewise have given little attention to the legal consequences of generic restrictions applicable to certain child removals or departures, which we set out below. These restrictions are not binding on the Secretary of State, but they do have consequences for parents and carers, who may have to decide whether they can voluntarily leave the UK to establish family life elsewhere. These statutory restrictions on child removals therefore are relevant matters to consider in the fair balance assessment under Article 8 ECHR or a public interest balance on a parent's deportation under UK domestic immigration law. These issues are most likely to arise where a partner of the person being removed has children from another relationship and the Home Office or immigration authority is considering whether the resident partner can be expected to leave the jurisdiction with his or her excluded partner. The removal of a habitually resident[1] child from the UK without the consent of a parent or carer, or permission of a court, can constitute a wrongful removal or abduction. The Hague Convention on the Civil Aspects of International Child Abduction applies to a child under 16 who, immediately before the retention or removal, was habitually resident in the UK and whose removal is in breach of rights of custody attributed to a person, institution or any other body, either jointly or alone.[2] Section 1 of the Child Abduction Act 1984 makes it an offence for a parent to take or send a child out of the UK without the consent of all those with parental responsibility.[3] Section 13 of the Children Act 1989 imposes a restraint on the international movement of children if there is a residence order in force and there is more than one holder of parental responsibility, except that the holder of a residence order can take the child out of the jurisdiction for periods up to a month at a time.[4]

[1]   Habitual residence is a question of fact. The authorities show that the question whether a person is habitually resident depends upon residence for an appreciable period of time and a settled intention. The status of children can depend upon the intentions which parents have for the children. *Nessa v Chief Adjudication Officer* [1999] 1 WLR 1937, *Al Habtoor v Fotheringham* [2001] EWCA 186, [2001] 1 FCR 385; *Re S (Custody: Habitual Residence)* [1998] AC 750.

[2]   Articles 3, 4, 5. Note also the prohibition on removal of wards and children in care. It is prohibited to remove a ward from the jurisdiction without leave of the Court: Family Law Act 1986, s 38. It is also an offence to remove a child in care from a place of safety or from the responsible person (Children Act 1989, s 49; Children and Young Persons Act 1969, s 32(3)) and their placement outside England and Wales requires leave from the Court, even if all persons with parental responsibility for the child have consented: Children Act 1989 Sch 2, para 19.

[3]   Under Children Act 1989, s 3(1) 'parental responsibility' is defined as 'all the rights, duties, powers, responsibilities and authority which by law a parent of a child has in relation to the child and his property'. Note that an unmarried father does not automatically have parental responsibility for his child: Children Act 1989, s 2(2). Some aspects of parental responsibility acknowledged by the courts include: determining a child's religion and education, consenting to their medical treatment, having physical possession or contact with the child, consenting to or arranging the child's emigration and protecting and maintaining the child. See Hershman & McFarlane *Children Law and Practice* Vol 1A 'parental responsibility'.

[4]   Where a residence order is in force with respect to a child, no person may remove the child from the United Kingdom without either the written consent of every person who has parental responsibility for the child or leave of the court: Children Act 1989, s 13(1). An unmarried father does not have parental responsibility in the absence of a parental responsibility agreement or a court order: Children Act 1989 s 4, but see *Re C (Child Abduction Unmarried Father: Rights of Custody)* [2002] EWHC 2219 (Fam), [2003] 1 WLR 493; *Re H (Child Abduction Unmarried Father: Rights of Custody)* [2003] EWHC 492 (Fam), [2003] 2 FLR 153.

11.15 Although the family and immigration jurisdictions overlap, courts have repeatedly emphasised that the functions of the court under the Children Act 1989 and of the Secretary of State under the Immigration Act 1971 and related legislation, are by and large separate and distinct.[1] When exercising their powers under the Children Act 1989, courts are not entitled to have regard to immigration policy.[2] Family courts must be guided by the interests of the child, and the interests of children are paramount. In the Secretary of State's decisions the child's interests are not paramount.[3]

[1] *Re Mohamed Arif (An Infant)* [1968] Ch 643 at 662D per Russell LJ; *Re F (A Minor) (Immigration: Wardship)* [1990] Fam 125, [1989] 1 FLR 233; *Re A (A Minor) (Wardship: Immigration)* [1992] 1 FLR 427; *Re K and S (Minors) (Wardship: Immigration)* [1992] 1 FLR 432; and *Re Matondo* [1993] 1 AC 541. See *BE (Care Proceedings) Jamaica* [2005] UKIAT 00098 (28 February 2005), where Ouseley J held that 'the care and the immigration proceedings should be treated as concurrent and independent.'
[2] *Re A (children) (care proceedings: asylum seekers)* [2003] EWHC 1086 (Fam), [2003] 2 FLR 921, where the continuation of care proceedings was held abusive in respect of children whose failed asylum seeker parents were to be removed but where the father (in a crisis response later disavowed) threatened to kill the family if removal were to occur. There were no protection concerns for the children at the date of the hearing.
[3] *R v Secretary of State for the Home Department, ex p Teame* [1995] 1 FLR 293.

11.16 UK family courts[1] generally have jurisdiction to determine applications in relation to any child who is habitually resident [2] or present within its geographical jurisdiction.[3] This is true even if the child in question is liable to removal or deportation.[4] Similarly, family courts can decide on applications for family court orders [5] from adults (parents or carers) who are liable to removal or deportation.[6] These family orders define the rights and obligations of parents in relation to their children in private law cases,[7] or, in the case of public law orders [8] or wardship,[9] operate to protect the child from significant harm at the hands of his parents or carers or resolve particular issues concerning children.

[1] Family proceedings courts, county courts, the Principal Registry and the Family Division of the High Court. Section 42(1) applies the Family Law Act 1986 to England and Wales, Scotland and Northern Ireland.
[2] See 11.14 fn 1 above; see also *Re R (Abduction: habitual residence)* [2003] EWHC 1968 (Fam) The status of children can depend upon the intentions which their parents (but not one parent acting unilaterally) have for them: *B v H (Habitual Residence: Wardship)* [2002] 1 FLR 388.
[3] Family Law Act 1986, s 2(2), (3), 3(1), *Re R (Care Proceedings: Jurisdiction)* [1995] 3 FCR 305, *Re Matondo* [1993] Imm AR 541 also known as *Re M (A Minor) (Immigration: Residence Order)* [1993] 2 FLR 858, *R v Home Secretary, ex p Khawaja* [1984] 1 AC 74. See for adoption jurisdiction, Adoption and Children Act 2002, s 49.
[4] *R v Secretary of State for the Home Department, ex p T* [1994] Imm AR 368, [1995] 1 FLR 293; *Re A (children) (care proceedings: asylum seekers)* [2003] EWHC 1086 (Fam), [2003] 2 FLR 921.
[5] For example, residence, contact, specific issues and prohibited steps orders under s 8 of the Children Act 1989 or care or supervision orders under s 31 of the Children Act 1989 or wardship under the High Court's inherent jurisdiction.
[6] *R v Secretary of State for the Home Department, ex p T* [1994] Imm AR 368, [1995] 1 FLE 293; *Re A (children) (care proceedings: asylum seekers)* [2003] EWHC 1086 (Fam), [2003] 2 FLR 921.
[7] Cases when there is a dispute between parents or other carers about whom the child should live with (residence order) or what contact the child should have with them (contact order) or whether the child should be removed from the jurisdiction (prohibited steps order) or, for example, enrolled at a certain type of school (specific issue order).
[8] Care orders which vest parental responsibility in the local authority and supervision orders which place the child under the supervision of a local authority whilst continuing to live with the carers.
[9] The inherent jurisdiction developed by the High Court deriving from what Lord Denning in *Re L (An Infant)* [1968] 1 All ER 20 at 24G termed the 'right and duty of the Crown as parens patriae to take care of those who are not able to take care of themselves.'

11.17 These family orders have no necessary or direct effect on the immigration status of any party to the application. The fact that an overstayer parent is granted contact to a British child or that a family court order prevents removal of the child from the jurisdiction does not deprive the Secretary of State of the power conferred by the immigration laws to remove the adult or child in question from the UK or deny them entry to the UK.[1] Family courts, whether exercising their private law powers under Part II of the 1989 Act, their public law powers under Part IV of the 1989 Act, the wardship jurisdiction, or the inherent jurisdiction in relation to children recognised and to an extent regulated by section 100 of the 1989 Act, cannot constrain or undercut the immigration powers of the Secretary of State.[2] Adoption proceedings apart,[3] whatever jurisdiction a judge of the Family Division, of the County Court or a Family Proceedings Court may be exercising, such judge cannot make an order which has the effect of depriving the Secretary of State of the power to remove a child or any other party to the proceedings.

1　See on Secretary of State's power to remove a ward, *Re Mohamed Arif (An Infant)* [1968] Ch 643 at 662D per Russell LJ, *Re F (A Minor) (Immigration: Wardship)* [1990] Fam 125, [1989] 1 FLR 233, *Re A (A Minor) (Wardship: Immigration)* [1992] 1 FLR 427, *Re K and S (Minors) (Wardship: Immigration)* [1992] 1 FLR 432 and *Re Matondo* [1993] 1 AC 541 and see on the 'different perspective' and separate timetables of care and immigration proceedings, *BE (Care Proceedings) Jamaica* [2005] UKIAT 00098 (28 February 2005, unreported).

2　*Re A (children) (care proceedings: asylum seekers)* [2003] 2 FLR 921 per Munby J at para 48.

3　Adoption proceedings are distinguished because under the British Nationality Act 1981 where a court in the UK makes an order authorising the adoption of a minor child who is not a British citizen, by an adopter or adopters, one of whom is a British citizen on that date, the child is a British citizen from the date of the adoption. This change in the child's nationality status resolves any irregularity in his/her previous immigration status and prevents the child's deportation or removal: *Re W (Adoption: Non-Patrial)* [1986] Fam 54, [1986] 1 FLR 179. There is no such analogy with Children Act orders, which do not affect status: *R v Secretary of State for the Home Department, ex p T* [1995] 1 FLR 293 per Hoffmann LJ at 297E.

11.18 The Court of Appeal has held that it was not a contempt of court for the Secretary of State to remove a person with whom a child had been ordered to live or even to remove the child before family proceedings had been completed.[1] However, as a matter of practice, and consistently with the Human Rights Act 1998, the Secretary of State does not remove or deport children or parents when family or other court proceedings are current and is usually prepared to grant short periods of discretionary leave or to extend temporary admission or release to await the outcome of family litigation.[2] In exercising his powers of removal or exclusion in such cases, the Secretary of State should have regard to any relevant family court order or finding.[3]

1　*Re T* [1994] Imm AR 368, CA.

2　*R v Secretary of State for Home Department, ex p Kebbeh* (CO/1269/98) (22 April 1999), *Re A (children) (care proceedings: asylum seekers)* [2003] EWHC 1086 (Fam). The fair trial rights protected by Art 6, and the procedural requirements of Art 8, are relevant in such cases: see eg *Ciliz v Netherlands* [2000] 2 FLR 469.

3　*R v Secretary of State for the Home Department, ex p T* [1994] Imm AR 368. For the analogous case concerning the Secretary of State's obligations to consider criminal court findings on Art 8 see *M v Secretary of State for the Home Department* [2003] EWCA Civ 146, [2003] 1 WLR 1980. See also IDI, Ch 8 'Family Members', Annex M 'Children General Guidance', s 3, para 9.

11.19 It is not just the Secretary of State who can 'trump' a family order. As *Re S* shows, the High Court can order the removal of a child, pursuant to its

Hague Convention obligations even though the Secretary of State's removal powers are constrained by sections 77 and 78 of the Nationality, Immigration and Asylum Act 2002 (preventing removal of persons awaiting an asylum or appeal determination). The Court of Appeal held that a statutory constraint on removal of this kind is directed to immigration authorities but was not intended 'to occupy any wider canvas', creating an exception to a family court's obligations arising under Article 12 of the Hague Convention or the duty and discretion of a judge exercising the wardship jurisdiction to order the speedy return of an abducted child'.[1]

[1]   *Re S (children) (abduction: asylum appeal)* [2002] EWCA Civ 843, [2002] All ER (D) 424 (May) (on the predecessor provisions to Nationality, Immigration and Asylum Act 2002, s 77).

11.20 Where there is no genuine dispute about the child's care or any need for ongoing protection, a family court will not allow itself to be used as a means of influencing the immigration decision to be made by the Secretary of State for the Home Department. Indeed, the use of the court's jurisdiction merely to attempt to influence the Secretary of State is an abuse of process.[1] In certain family cases where the immigration issues are contentious, the Secretary of State may seek to be joined as a party and make representations on the appropriate orders to be made.[2] The Family Division protocol arrangements help to ensure that the Home Office is alerted where there are immigration issues in family cases and that there is evidence of Home Office decisions or their attitude to outstanding immigration applications.[3]

[1]   *R v Secretary of State for the Home Department, ex p T* [1994] Imm AR 368, CA, *R v Secretary of State for the Home Department, ex p Teane* [1995] 1 FLR 293; *Re A (children) (care proceedings: asylum seekers)* [2003] EWHC 1086 (Fam), [2003] 2 FLR 921.
[2]   For example: *Re A (children) (care proceedings: asylum seekers)* [2003] EWHC 1086 (Fam), [2003] 2 FLR 921.
[3]   See 11.9 fn 3 above.

11.21 Notwithstanding such reservations on the interplay between the respective jurisdictional reaches of immigration and family law, in practice, family courts do make care orders when the appropriate Children Act tests have been met, notwithstanding that the parents or children have uncertain or irregular immigration status. Where the adult applicant is not settled in the United Kingdom the court will have to take this into account in terms of the child's future security and care. In care cases involving overstaying or temporarily resident children at risk of neglect or harm, the child's immigration status can often be resolved only after the family court proceedings. In such cases, it is appropriate to alert the Home Office to the circumstances of the parties prior to the family hearing.[1] In considering the child's best interests, the family courts frequently investigate the possibility of the child's return to his or her home country and family as well as care and residence arrangements in the UK. The child's immigration status will vary, depending on whether, at the conclusion of the family proceedings, the child is, for example, placed with a carer who has indefinite or temporary leave to remain or is subject to a full care order in local authority care. In certain circumstances the family order made might have practical effect only for a relatively short time. In one case a residence order was granted to a child's sister whilst the child's asylum application was being considered to ensure that someone in the UK had parental responsibility for her. The order was expressly designed to expire if the child decided voluntarily to leave the UK or the Secretary of State set directions for her removal.[2]

1   See 11.9 fn 3 above.
2   *Re E* [1995] Imm AR 475.

11.22 Where a family court has awarded residence or contact or determined the need for protection, the family court judgement concerning care, residence or contact can persuade the Secretary of State that removal or deportation of the child or carer is not appropriate. The Home Office instructions reflect this outcome. Officers are advised that particularly for younger children, welfare considerations may outweigh the immigration considerations and that: 'Decisions about the future of children in the care of the local authority should be left primarily in the hands of their social services department as they will be best placed to act in the child's best interests. ... If the social services advise that it would be appropriate for the child to remain in the United Kingdom, consideration should be given to granting the child leave to remain.'[1]

1   IDI, Ch 8, s 3, 'Children', Annex M, para 7. The instructions distinguish between children in care, whose welfare is primarily decided by social services, and those children where the social services are merely 'involved'. In the latter cases, social services' views 'should be taken into account'. However, the instructions state 'it will not always be right to act on their recommendation, particularly if there is independent evidence to justify proceeding with refusal and removal'. The term of stay to be granted to unaccompanied children is not mentioned (except for children born in the UK, who, under the Rules, are to be granted settlement under HC 395, paras 305(i)(c) and 308, if subject to a full care order). The Home Office often seeks to limit discretionary leave to end on the child's 18th birthday. Social services or a children's guardian may wish to make representations on the term of leave to be granted in appropriate cases. They may have a welfare interest in the child beyond the age of 18 under leaving care arrangements. Under the Children Act 1989, ss 22–24D, Sch 2, Part II, paras 19A–19C, as amended by the Children (Leaving Care) Act 2000, local authorities are required to advise, assist and befriend 'eligible' children, to take reasonable steps to stay in touch, continue the appointment of a personal adviser and provide and review a 'pathway' plan for their transition out of care. 'Eligible' children are those who have been 'looked after' for at least 13 weeks since they reached the age of 14 and who continue to be looked after.

RELEVANT PRINCIPLES OF PRIVATE INTERNATIONAL LAW

11.23 The intersection between family and immigration law also occurs in private international and domestic family law provisions concerning the validity of marriages, divorces and adoptions. These private international and domestic provisions can establish whether a child is able to establish entitlement to citizenship by descent, or whether a person qualifies for entry as a spouse or child of the sponsor. The previous text has shown the importance of a parent's or child's habitual residence in international family cases; the other key concept utilised in immigration and family status questions is domicile. To this we now turn.

DOMICILE

11.24 Domicile is an important concept in English law. It is a neutral rule for determining the system of personal law with which the individual has the appropriate connection, so that it shall govern his or her personal status and questions relating to personal transactions –marriage, divorce, the legitimacy of his or her children, adoptions, and rights of inheritance.[1] In private international law it is referred to as a connecting factor. Although it is a test for jurisdiction, it is also one of the key connecting factors for the choice of law (for example, English or French law) which is to apply to a particular case. A domicile may be acquired in England and Wales, Scotland or Northern Ireland, but not in the UK or Great Britain. It governs capacity to marry, the legitimacy of children, and succession after death to moveable property and it is one of the tests of the validity of a will.[2] Questions of domicile arise in immigration and nationality cases where it is disputed that an applicant is a spouse, is free to marry or that children are legitimate.[3] These can be decisive questions for entry or nationality.

1   See Dicey & Morris *The Conflict of Law* (13th edn, 2000, Sweet and Maxwell), Vol 1, ch 6.
2   See *Mark v Mark* [2004] EWCA Civ 168.
3   See *Akhtar (Ali)* [2002] UKIAT 02135; *Baig v Entry Clearance Officer, Islamabad* [2003] INLR 117.

11.25 Domicile is to be distinguished from other connecting or identifying factors, such as nationality, the place of celebration of a marriage, or habitual residence. Domicile and nationality are distinct and separate concepts. Nationality identifies the person's political status; domicile shows a person's civil status.[1] A person may have citizenship of one country and domicile in another as it is possible to acquire a domicile of choice irrespective of nationality.[2] A person also may change nationality without this necessarily affecting domicile,[3] although naturalisation in accordance with the requirements of the British Nationality Act 1981, Schedule 1, paragraph 1(1)(d)(i) (an intention that his or her principal home will be in the UK) may evidence a change in domicile.[4] A person may have dual nationality but only has one domicile at a time. If a new domicile is obtained by choice, the previous domicile is no longer applicable.[5]

1   *Udny v Udny* (1869) LR 1 Sc & Div 441, 1869 WL 7841.
2   *Boldrini v Boldrini and Martini* [1932] P 9, 1931 WL 7870.
3   *Wahl v A-G* (1932) 147 LT 382: a German national lived in England and became a naturalised British subject, and later returned to Germany to look after his father's estate. Held: although he changed his nationality he had retained his domicile of origin in Germany.
4   See *S (Yemen)* [2003] UKIAT 00008 (04 June 2003, unreported).
5   *Moorhouse Ltd v Lord* (1863) 10 HL Cas 272 at 285 per Lord Chelmsford.

11.26 Domicile can be acquired by origin, by choice or by dependence.[1] In *Udny* Lord Westbury stated:

'Domicile of choice is a conclusion or inference which the law derives from the fact of a man fixing voluntarily his sole or chief residence in a particular place with an intention of continuing to reside there for an unlimited time ... it must be a residence not for a limited period or particular purpose, but general and indefinite in its contemplation.'[2]

Where the intended residence is for a limited period, it is immaterial whether that limitation is expressed in terms of time or is made dependent on the happening of some event or the achievement of a particular task during the person's lifetime. The position was spelt out more clearly by Scarman J in *Re Fuld's Estate (No 3)*:[3]

'If a man intends to return to the land of his birth upon a clearly foreseen and reasonably anticipated contingency, the end of his job, the intention required by law is lacking; but, if he has in mind only a vague possibility, such as making a fortune (a modern example might be winning a football pool)... such a state of mind is consistent with the intention required by law.'

[1] See now Domicile and Matrimonial Proceedings Act 1973, ss 1–4.
[2] (1869) LR 1 Sc & Div 441 at 458.
[3] [1968] P 675 at 684–685. See also *Lawrence v Lawrence* [1985] Fam 106, [1985] 2 All ER 733, CA; *R v Immigration Appeal Tribunal, ex p Bibi (Rafika)* [1989] Imm AR 1, QBD. See also [2005] UKSSCSC CP_3108_2004 (25 April 2005), a case about entitlement to widow's pension.

11.27 There is a link between habitual residence and domicile, but residence in a particular place does not necessarily establish domicile there.[1] The requirement of an intention to remain permanently distinguishes domicile from mere residence and in particular from ordinary residence.[2] Although for immigration purposes a person is not to be treated as ordinarily resident in the United Kingdom at a time when he or she is there in breach of the Immigrations laws,[3] a person can be treated as having acquired a British domicile even if residing here unlawfully.[4] This concession derives from public policy. The Court of Appeal noted that there must be a very large number of extremely longstanding but unlawful residents in this and other countries whose only real links are with their adopted country and whose personal affairs should properly be governed by the laws of that country, whether to their advantage or disadvantage. Illegality may be relevant in showing that a person is not habitually resident or domiciled in the UK. The court declined a blanket assumption that a person was not domiciled if unlawfully resident because, amongst other considerations, such prescriptive rule would be at risk of infringing Article 6 ECHR.[5]

[1] See Domicile and Matrimonial Proceedings Act 1973, s 5(2).
[2] On 'ordinary residence' see *Shah v Barnet London Borough Council* [1983] 2 AC 309; see 5.5 above.
[3] Immigration Act 1971, s 33(2).
[4] *Mark v Mark* [2004] EWCA Civ 168, [2005] Fam 267.
[5] *Mark v Mark* [2004] EWCA Civ 168, [2005] Fam 267.

11.28 The distinction between a domicile of origin and domicile of choice is important. The domicile of origin is the domicile that everyone acquires at birth and is the country in which their parent (or if the parents are not married, the mother) is domiciled at the date of the birth.[1] A domicile of origin is never lost. It may be displaced by a domicile of choice but will revive if the domicile of choice is abandoned.[2] A person's capacity to acquire a domicile of choice arises at the age of 16, or if already married, at the date of marriage.[3] Until a child has this capacity, his/her domicile is dependent upon that of the parents and will change when the parent's domicile changes.[4]

[1] The Domicile and Matrimonial Proceedings Act 1973 abolished the domicile of dependence of married women. If the parents are separated the child will have the domicile of the parent with whom she or he lives.
[2] *Udny v Udny* (1869) LR 1 Sc & Div 441, 1869 WL 7841.
[3] Domicile and Matrimonial Proceedings Act 1973, s 3.
[4] Domicile and Matrimonial Proceedings Act 1973, s 4.

11.29 The legal rules may be summarised as follows:

(i)   'There is a strong presumption in favour of the continuance of the domicile of origin. As contrasted with the domicile of choice, "its character is more enduring, its hold stronger and less easily shaken off".'[1]

(ii)   The intention to settle permanently must be ascertained by objective criteria, and statements as to domicile by a testator in a will,[2] by a taxpayer on an Inland Revenue form,[3] or in an application for registration or naturalisation as a British citizen are not necessarily reliable.[4]

(iii)   The burden of proving that a domicile of choice has been acquired rests on the person who asserts that the domicile of origin has been lost.[5] If the burden of proving a change has not been discharged, the domicile of origin will remain.[6]

(iv)   The abandonment of a domicile of choice is easier than its acquisition, although there must be unequivocal evidence of abandonment.[7] One reason for the difference is that abandonment of a domicile of choice does not depend upon the acquisition of a new domicile. As stated, if no new domicile of choice is acquired, the domicile of origin revives.

[1] Per Lord MacNaughten in *Winans v A-G* [1904] AC 287 at 290. For modern examples see *Cramer v Cramer* [1986] Fam Law 333, CA; [2005] UKSSCSC CP_3108_2004 (25 April 2005) a case about entitlement to widow's pension.
[2] *Re Steer* (1858) 3 H & N 594; *A-G v Yule and Mercantile Bank of India* (1931) 145 LT 9.
[3] *Buswell v IRC* [1974] 2 All ER 520, [1974] 1 WLR 1631. Every fact, however trivial, is admissible for the purpose of proving an intention to acquire or discard a domicile: *Re Flynn, Flynn v Flynn* (1968)1 All ER 49.
[4] *Begum (Rokeya) v Entry Clearance Officer* [1983] Imm AR 163; *Khatun (Hamida) v Entry Clearance Officer, Dhaka* [1988] Imm AR 138, IAT.
[5] *Winans v A-G* [1904] AC 287 at 290 and 291. See also *R v Entry Clearance Officer, Islamabad, ex p Ali CO* (3585/97) (20 January 1999, unreported) per Turner J, concerning ambiguities and inferences from the questionnaire used by the Home Office to test domicile.
[6] *Scappaticci v A-G* [1955] P 47, [1955] 1 All ER 193. See also *Ahktar (Ali)* [2002] UKIAT 02135.
[7] *Re Lloyd Evans, National Provincial Bank v Evans* [1947] Ch 695 at 703; *Re Raffenel's Goods* (1863) 3 Sw & Tr 49.

11.30 In the case of *Ex p Miah*[1] the problems of domicile were well illustrated. A Bangladesh-born national came to the UK in 1963, where he had worked and lived ever since. He married his first wife in 1972 and a second wife in 1987. The second wife applied for entry clearance as a spouse. The entry clearance officer argued that the sponsor had acquired a domicile of choice in the UK, and therefore the second marriage was void. But the evidence that Miah intended to make his home in the UK was predicated on the ability of the second wife to come here, which was precisely what was excluded if he had a UK domicile. The paradox was to be resolved by the presumption in favour of the domicile of origin, unless it could be shown that the sponsor intended to live in the UK regardless of whether his second wife came.

1   *R v Immigration Appeal Tribunal, ex p Miah* (CO/2100/92) (14 June 1994, unreported). QBD. See also *Ahktar (Ali)* [2002] UKIAT 02135, and *Bibi* (12488), where a seaman in the UK since 1946, who registered as British in 1951, was held to have retained his domicile of origin in Bangladesh, where he maintained a matrimonial home with three wives and their children.

11.31 The Immigration Directorate Instructions (IDI)[1] set out the factors which will be taken into account in assessing whether someone has acquired a domicile of choice in the UK. They point out that length of residence is not conclusive, and neither is acquisition of nationality, although it is more important if the person has given up his or her former nationality. A statutory declaration made for naturalisation purposes, that an applicant intends to reside permanently in the UK, may be taken into account, as may possession of property, in particular the purchase of a burial plot. The nature and length of the person's employment in this country, registration as an elector, residence of other family members in the UK and the education of children in the UK are all relevant. The IDI also point out that the burden is on the Secretary of State to show that a polygamous marriage which took place abroad is invalid because at the time of a marriage one party had acquired a domicile of choice in the UK.[2] A domicile questionnaire to be completed by a sponsor who entered a polygamous marriage abroad is attached to the IDI. In *Ex p Ali* [3] the problems of domicile questionnaires were exposed. The sponsor, not understanding its purpose, had omitted all information which suggested continuing links with Pakistan, which he had left in the late 1960s to work in the UK. Only on the eve of an application for judicial review of the entry clearance officer's refusal of a certificate of entitlement to the children of his second (polygamous) marriage did the sponsor reveal evidence of land purchases, a bank account, frequent long visits and the procreation of more children with his first wife, all of which together negatived the impression given by his answers in the questionnaire that he had lost his domicile of origin in Pakistan and acquired a domicile of choice in the UK by the time of the second marriage. So long as sponsors believe that domicile questionnaires exist to test the sincerity of their desire to live in the UK rather than their domicile and therefore the validity of their second marriage, similar problems are likely to persist.

1   IDI, Ch 8 Family Members, Annex D, para 5. See also: *R v Immigration Appeal Tribunal, ex p Khalida Begum* (CO/4262/98) (12 March 1999, unreported).
2   IDI, Ch 8 Family Members, Annex E, para 7.
3   *R v Entry Clearance Officer Islamabad, ex p Ali* (CO/3585/97) (20 January 1999, unreported), QBD.

MARRIAGE

General problems of validity

11.32 In order to obtain admission as a spouse, the applicant must satisfy the entry clearance officer that the marriage is lawful and complies with the requirements of the Immigration Rules. A valid marriage requires that both parties had the necessary capacity to marry, and that the celebration was in a valid form. Capacity to marry is normally determined by the ante-nuptial domiciliary law of each party. The formal validity of the marriage is determined by the law of the place of celebration. The parties can apply to the courts for a declaration that a marriage was at its inception a valid marriage, or that it subsisted or did not subsist at a particular date, if one of the parties to the marriage is domiciled in the UK or on the date of application had been habitually resident in England and Wales for one year preceding the date of the application.[1] A detailed review of private international law relating to validity of marriages and divorces is beyond the scope of this work,[2] but we focus on the particular problems likely to be encountered in immigration cases, in particular the rules relating to polygamous marriages and the recognition of *talaq* divorces.

[1] Family Law Act 1986, s 55. If it is asserted that the marriage was void *ab initio*, the remedy lies in a petition of nullity. In deciding whether to grant recognition to a foreign marriage, the court will exercise 'common sense, good manners and reasonable tolerance': *Cheni v Cheni* [1965] P 85, recognising the marriage of an uncle and niece as valid under the law of their domicile but noting that an overseas marriage that would be 'offensive to the conscience of the English Court' may not be recognised even if it is valid under the foreign law. See on the presumption of validity of marriage: *FI (Bangladesh presumption marriage legitimacy)* [2005] UKIAT 00016

[2] The IDI, Ch 8 Annex B, Recognition of Marriage and Divorce, deals with several of the most common validity issues, namely polygamous, proxy and telephone marriages, as well as *talaq* and customary divorces and divorce in the Philippines. See on proxy phone marriage for the purpose of Art 8 ECHR, *J (Pakistan)* [2003] UKIAT 00167.

Polygamous marriages

11.33 Polygamous marriages are those where under the law of the place of the celebration of the marriage (*lex loci celebrationis*) the husband is permitted to marry more than one wife during the subsistence of the marriage, or the wife is permitted to take another husband.[1] A man or woman whose personal law does not allow polygamous marriage has no capacity to contract a valid polygamous marriage.[2] A marriage contracted in a place which permits polygamy may be actually or potentially polygamous. It is actually polygamous where either partner has more than one spouse, and potentially so if the couple have no other spouse but the husband or wife is entitled to take more than one spouse under the local law. A polygamous marriage entered into in England is always invalid.[3] The common law rule was that all marriages celebrated in the UK must be monogamous, whatever the form used.[4] A person with a domicile in England and Wales is not permitted to marry polygamously.[5] For marriages taking place after 31 July 1971, validity is dealt with by statute. The Matrimonial Causes Act 1973, section 11(d) provides that:

'A marriage celebrated after 31 July 1971 shall be void on the following grounds only, that is to say ...

(d)   in the case of a polygamous marriage entered into outside England and Wales, that either party was at the time of the marriage domiciled in England and Wales.

For the purposes of paragraph (d) of this subsection a marriage *is not* polygamous if at its inception neither party has any spouse additional to the other.'[6]

Thus under the Matrimonial Causes Act 1973, so long as neither party is already married, a couple, either of whom may be domiciled in England and Wales, may marry under a law where polygamy is permitted and will have that marriage accepted as valid under English law.[7] The effect of this provision is that if neither party is married to another at the time the marriage is celebrated then the marriage is not void on the ground that it is potentially polygamous.[8]

[1]   The system of marriage where the wife can take a second husband is polyandry. However the amended para 278 of HC 395 uses the word 'polygamous' in a gender-neutral way.
[2]   *Re Bethell, Bethell v Hildyard* (1888) 38 Ch D 220; *Ali v Ali* [1968] P 564, [1966] 1 All ER 664. Note that marriages which start off as polygamous may be converted into monogamous marriages by subsequent events: the spouses may change their religion; may subsequently marry in an English registry office; may obtain a domicile where polygamous marriage is not allowed; or the local law may change and prohibit polygamy: *Chetti v Chetti* [1909] P 67; *Mehta (otherwise Kohn) v Mehta* [1945] 2 All ER 690; *Sinha Peerage Claim* [1946] 1 All ER 348n, *Ohochuku v Ohochuku* [1960] 1 All ER 253, [1960] 1 WLR 183, *Parkasho v Singh* [1968] P 233, [1967] 1 All ER 737.
[3]   *R v Bham* [1966] 1 QB 159, [1965] 3 All ER 124, CCA; *R v Mohammed Ali* [1964] 2 QB 350n.
[4]   *Chetti v Chetti* [1909] P 67.
[5]   Matrimonial Causes Act 1973, s 11(b).
[6]   The words in italics were inserted by the Private International Law (Miscellaneous Provisions) Act 1995, s 8(2), Sch, para 2(1), (2) (in force January 1996). Prior to this, the sub-section provided that a marriage was polygamous even though at its inception neither party had any additional spouse.
[7]   Matrimonial Causes Act 1973, s 11(d).
[8]   This modification inserted into the Matrimonial Causes Act 1973, s 11(d) by the Private International Law (Miscellaneous Provisions) Act 1995 is generally retrospective. Private International Law (Miscellaneous Provisions) Act 1995, s 6. This resolves the anomaly exposed by *Hussain v Hussain* [1983] Fam 26. The husband in that case had an English domicile and was married in Pakistan which did not permit women to have more than one spouse. The marriage was therefore valid. Had the woman been domiciled in England and the husband domiciled in Pakistan, under the law then applying, the marriage would have been void in English law as potentially polygamous. The change resolved such problems. See also IDI, Ch 8, Family Members, Annex C: Polygamous and potentially polygamous marriages.

11.34 The fact that a marriage is void as polygamous will not necessarily make the children of the marriage illegitimate. Where one of the parties to the marriage is domiciled in the UK the Legitimacy Act 1976 may apply, which provides that if one of the parties to a marriage ceremony believed that the marriage was valid at the time of the child's conception, the child will be legitimate despite the invalidity of the marriage.[1] There may be difficulties in proving the belief at the relevant time.[2] Although illegitimacy is no bar to admission to join a father under the Immigration Rules,[3] citizenship by descent and acquisition of the right of abode through the father still depends on legitimacy –although this is set to change.[4] A child of a polygamous marriage who has the right of abode is not prevented from entry to the UK in the same way as a spouse,[5] but where a parent is to be refused entry or leave to remain for settlement on the ground of polygamy, the Rules are not to be construed as permitting the parent's child to be granted entry clearance, leave to enter or remain or a variation of leave.[6]

1 Legitimacy Act 1976, s 1. The belief must be in the validity of the marriage in the UK, not in the place of its celebration: *Azad v Entry Clearance Officer, Dhaka* [2001] INLR 109, [2001] Imm AR 318, CA.
2 See *Begum (Dilara)* (10108) where the children were born after a decision that the marriage was polygamous and so invalid, when neither party could have believed in its validity: *Begum (Minara)* (19500). See also *Azad (Misba)* (L00033) IAS 2000, Vol 3, No 8: the presumption of legitimacy introduced by Family Law Reform Act 1987, s 28 did not apply to children born before that Act came into force and the burden of proof was on the appellant.
3 HC 395, para 6 (definition of 'child' for immigration purposes).
4 British Nationality Act 1981, ss 50(9) and 47. The Nationality, Immigration and Asylum Act 2002, s 9 substitutes a new s 50(9) BNA 1981, which provides that the father of a child is the husband at the time of the child's birth of the woman who gives birth to the child or any person who satisfies prescribed proof of paternity. However at the time of writing this section is not yet in force. The Secretary of State may nevertheless register as a British citizen the illegitimate child of a British citizen father under general registration powers: British Nationality Act 1981, s 3(1).
5 For the rules on the admission of polygamous spouses see 11.60 below.
6 HC 395, para 296. It is doubtful whether this rule would prevent the admission of such a child under the 'exclusion undesirable' provisions (see 11.94 below) if abandoned or neglected by its parent abroad.

Recognition of talaq and other overseas divorces

11.35 The rules relating to recognition of foreign divorces and judicial separations are now to be found in sections 44 to 54 of the Family Law Act 1986[1] and are not set out comprehensively here. The recognition of Islamic *talaq* divorces is an issue which usually arises in the immigration context when considering whether the parties are married and a claimant can enter the UK as a spouse. Under Islamic sharia law, a husband is permitted to divorce a wife without recourse to court proceedings simply by declaring unequivocally his intention to repudiate the marriage in the presence of witnesses. This is a bare *talaq* and involves no proceedings at all. Most Islamic countries have modified religious law by requiring some additional formal registration of the *talaq* with a court or administrative body and/or that the parties undertake conciliation proceedings. Thus in Pakistan the Muslim Family Law Ordinance requires registration of the *talaq* with the Chairman of the Union District Council, and the *talaq* does not become effective until the elapse of a period for reconciliation.[2] A failure to comply with these formalities renders the husband liable to a penalty.[3] In Azad Kashmir, however, the Muslim Family Law Ordinance does not apply.[4]

1 In force 4 April 1988. If a divorce fails to be recognised under the provisions of the 1986 Act, s 52(4) and (5) of that Act allows 'stepping back' to the previous legislation, the Recognition of Divorce and Legal Separations Act 1971 (in force 1 January 1972), including amendments to that Act by the Domicile and Matrimonial Proceedings Act 1973 (the amendments commenced on 1 January 1974). See IDI, Ch 8, Annex B on the recognition of marriage and divorce.

2   Muslim Family Law Ordinance 1961. See discussion of Pakistani *talaq* requirements in
     Baig v Entry Clearance Officer, Islamabad [2003] INLR 117.
3   It may be that a divorce that fails to comply with these provisions is still a valid divorce
     recognised in Pakistan, and may therefore be recognised in the UK under the Immigration
     Rules where no proceedings have taken place; see below.
4   See *Bi (Maqsood)* (10144), and see below. The jurisdictional limits of Pakistan's legal
     jurisprudence were confirmed in *Khan (Sakhi Daler) v The State of Pakistan* PLD 1957
     Lahore 813 and in the Azad Jammu and Kashmir Interim Constitution Act 1974.

11.36 Formerly, English common law could give recognition to such a
divorce if it were recognised by the law of the parties' domicile, even if the
talaq had been pronounced in the UK.[1] The position is now governed by
statute, which applies to any divorce, whether obtained before or after 5 April
1988.[2] No *talaq* pronounced in the UK will be a valid divorce, even if
followed by proceedings overseas, because no divorce obtained in the United
Kingdom is effective unless it is granted by a court of civil jurisdiction.[3] This
rule cannot be evaded by divorcing in a foreign embassy, which is considered
to be in the UK.[4] Nor can it be evaded by obtaining a foreign court's
recognition of the extra-judicial English divorce and seeking to recognise the
foreign judgment.[5]

1   *Qureshi v Qureshi* [1972] Fam 173, [1971] 1 All ER 325. See also [2005] UKSSCSC
     CP_3108_2004 (25 April 2005), a case about entitlement to widow's pension.
2   Family Law Act 1986, ss 45 and 52; but the Act preserves, inter alia, s 6 of the Recognition
     of Divorces and Legal Separations Act 1971, for the survival of some common law rules on
     recognition.
3   Family Law Act 1986, Pt II s 44(1); *Re Fatima* [1986] AC 527, [1986] 2 All ER 32, HL;
     Hamid (14314) IAS 1996, Vol 4, No 1, *Sulaiman v Juffali* [2002] 1 FLR 479, [2002]
     2 FCR 427, [2002] Fam Law 97. See also on a transnational Israeli divorce, *Berkovits v
     Grinberg, (Attorney-General intervening)* [1995] Fam 142 (Fam Div).
4   *Radwan v Radwan* [1972] 3 All ER 967; IDI Dec 00, Ch 8, s 1, Annex B.
5   *Maples v Maples* [1988] Fam 14, [1987] 3 All ER 188.

11.37 Section 46 of the Family Law Act 1986 draws a distinction between a
divorce 'obtained by means of proceedings' and a divorce 'obtained otherwise
than by means of proceedings'.[1] A divorce 'obtained otherwise than by means
of proceedings' cannot be valid if either party to the marriage was habitually
resident in the United Kingdom during the period of one year immediately
preceding the date the divorce was obtained.[2] This particular provision is of
great importance in immigration cases, because, in an immigration context, it
very frequently happens that one of the parties to the claimed divorce was so
resident in the UK. Where the sponsor has at all material times been habitually
resident in the United Kingdom, the divorce is entitled to recognition in
English law only if it was 'obtained by means of proceedings'.[3] In the starred
determination *Baig v Entry Clearance Officer, Islamabad*, the Tribunal held
that an effective divorce must have been obtained under the law of the country
in which it was obtained and that the divorce be 'obtained by means of' the
proceedings – one must be able to say that if the proceedings had not taken
place, the divorce would not have been obtained.[4] Registration of a *talaq*
under the Muslim Family Law Ordinance amounts to proceedings,[5] but a bare
talaq does not,[6] nor does a *talaq al-hasan*, obtained by the required pronouncements, if it is not notified to the Chairman of the Union Council under
the Muslim Family Law Ordinance.[7]

1   Family Law Act 1986, s 46(1) and (2)
2   Family Law Act 1986, s 46(2). On the meaning of 'habitual residence' see 11.14 n1, above.
3   Family Law Act 1986, s 46(1), *Baig v Entry Clearance Officer, Islamabad* [2002] UKIAT
     04229, [2003] INLR 117 (starred).
4   [2002] UKIAT 04229, [2003] INLR 117. See also Family Law Act 1986, s 46(1); *Qureshi
     v Qureshi* [1972] Fam 173, [1971] 1 All ER 325; *R v Registrar General, ex p Minhas*
     [1977] QB 1, [1976] 2 All ER 246.
5   *Quazi v Quazi* [1980] AC 744, [1979] 3 All ER 897, HL.
6   *Bi (Maqsood)* (10144); *Nadeem* (00TH 00100) IAS 2000, Vol 3, No 8.
7   *Baig v Entry Clearance Officer, Islamabad* [2003] INLR 117.

11.38 As stated, some provision is made in UK law for recognising overseas divorces which are obtained without any proceedings at all.[1] The requirements are that the divorce is effective under the law of the country in which it was obtained; that either the two parties were domiciled in the country where the divorce was obtained at the time or one party was so domiciled and the divorce is recognised as valid in the law of the other party's domicile; and that neither party was habitually resident in the UK in the year before the divorce.[2] Thus a West African customary divorce may be recognised if evidence of either dissolution by a customary court or agreement by the heads of the parties' families is available by affidavit, accompanied by a document registering the divorce and a certificate of the Minister for Foreign Affairs.[3]

1   Family Law Act 1986, s 46. The IDI (Ch 8 Annex B) deal with Filipino divorces, which
     pose a particular problem for those who retain a Philippines domicile as at present it is
     only possible to obtain a divorce permitting remarriage in the Philippines if both parties are
     Muslims.
2   Family Law Act 1986, s 46(2).
3   See for example *Wicken v Wicken* [1999] Fam 224.

11.39 The above summary of the legal rules suffices for consideration of the validity of divorces for immigration purposes. It should be noted that where there is a dispute between parties, an overseas divorce, whether obtained by proceedings or not, may be refused recognition by the English courts in circumstances: (a) where notice of proceedings was not reasonably given or where a party to the marriage has not been given a reasonable opportunity to take part in the proceedings; (b) where, for divorces obtained otherwise than by means of proceedings, there is no official certificate or document certifying that the divorce is effective under the law of that country; or (c) where recognition would be manifestly contrary to public policy.[1] In *Chaudhary v Chaudhary* [2] an alternative ground for non-recognition of a bare *talaq* was that recognition would be contrary to public policy because the husband pronounced it to defeat the wife's claim to ancillary relief in the UK. Recognition will also be withheld if the foreign divorce conflicts with the judgment on the subsistence or validity of the marriage by a British court or a court whose judgment is entitled to be recognised in the UK.[3]

1   Family Law Act 1986, s 51(3).
2   [1985] Fam 19.
3   Family Law Act 1986, s 51(1)(b). See also *Tahir v Tahir* 1993 SLT 194, 1992 WL
     1349617.

Spouses under 16

11.40 The age at which a person can contract a valid marriage varies from country to country. An age requirement will usually be classified as a matter of capacity affecting the essential validity of the marriage. It will therefore fall, under English law, to be dealt with according to the law of the domicile of the particular person. A marriage contracted by a spouse domiciled in the UK is not valid if he or she is under 16.[1] However, in a number of countries marriage under the age of 16 is permitted and marriage by a spouse under this age, domiciled there, is regarded as valid. The immigration rules concerning young spouses are contained in HC 395, paragraph 277. The Rules do not permit entry for settlement or leave to remain as a spouse if either the applicant or sponsor is under 18 at the date of arrival or grant of leave.[2]

1   Matrimonial Causes Act 1973, s 11(a)(ii).
2   See 11.60 below. The government is considering raising the age for spouse leave to 21 'to prevent forced marriages': *Controlling our Borders: Making Migration Work for Britain: The Five year Strategy for Asylum and Immigration*, Cm 6472, February 2005, p 22.

Proving the validity of a marriage

11.41 Apart from the requirement of monogamy, marriages celebrated in the UK must comply with the requirements of the Marriage Acts 1949–94 and subordinate regulations, and are void if they do not comply. The marriage should have been celebrated in a building approved for civil marriage by the Marriage Act 1994,[1] and there should be a marriage certificate issued by a registrar or superintendent registrar, a clergyman of the Church of England or Wales, a synagogue, a non-conforming church or the Society of Friends.[2] An irregular ceremony *bona fide* entered into may benefit from the presumption of validity of marriage: thus in *Bath*[3] the Court of Appeal relied on the presumption to find that a long marriage preceded by an irregular ceremony in an unregistered Sikh temple was valid; but if there is deliberate or wilful disregard of the requirements the marriage is void.[4] If the marriage took place abroad, entry clearance officers are instructed to consider whether the marriage is one recognised in the country in which it took place and properly executed so as to satisfy the requirements of the law in the country in which it took place. If these conditions are satisfied and there is no impediment in the law of either party's country of domicile restricting the person's freedom to enter the marriage, then the marriage should be taken to be valid.[5] The onus is on the parties to prove the relationship as claimed but evidence of a marriage certificate and post-nuptial correspondence may shift the burden of persuasion to the Home Office to disprove the relationship. Previous findings of the appellate authorities carry substantial weight but are not conclusive in the face of fresh evidence.[6]

1   Marriage Act 1949, s 49. Many buildings, including hotels and foreign embassies may be registered for the purpose: Marriage Act 1949, ss 46, 69–73 (as amended); IDI May 03, Ch 8, s 1, Annex B. Note the requirement from 1 February 2005 for persons who are not EEA nationals and require leave to enter or remain (whether or not leave has been given) to register for their marriage at a designated registration centre: Asylum and Immigration (Treatment of Claimants, etc) Act 2004, s 19(2); The Immigration (Procedure for Marriage) Regulations 2005, SI 15/2005, Sch 1, and a marriage registered elsewhere may be void: s 20.

2   Marriage Act 1949, s 53.
3   *Chief Adjudication Officer v Bath* [2000] 1 FCR 419, CA, [1999] UKSSCSC
    CG_11331_1995 (21 October 1999), a case about entitlement to widow's pension. See also
    FI (Bangladesh, presumptions – marriage– legitimacy) Bangladesh [2005] UKIAT 00016
    (24 January 2005).
4   *Gereis v Yagoub* [1997] 1 FLR 854.
5   IDI May 03, Ch 8, s 1, Annex B.
6   *Ali (Momin) v Secretary of State for the Home Department* [1984] 1 All ER 1009, [1984]
    Imm AR 23; *R v Immigration Appeal Tribunal, ex p Miah (Lulu)* [1987] Imm AR 143.

11.42 Normally, the best proof of a marriage is a marriage certificate,[1] but this is not always available or there may be doubts as to its authenticity or accuracy and the general credibility of the parties,[2] and the existence of the marriage may have to be proved in other ways. The Immigration Appeal Tribunal has accepted presumptions which go to establish the existence of a marriage in the parties' country of origin. Thus in *Begum (Nazir)*[3] the Tribunal accepted as a presumption of Muslim law that:

> 'Marriage will be presumed in the absence of direct proof, from:
> (a)   prolonged and continued cohabitation as husband and wife; or
> (b)   the fact of the acknowledgment by the man of the child born to the
>   woman, provided all the conditions of a valid acknowledgement ... are
>   fulfilled; or
> (c)   the fact of the acknowledgment by the man of the woman as his wife.'[4]

1   Where a marriage certificate is produced, a party disputing the validity of the marriage has
    to prove to a high degree of probability that the marriage is not valid: *Babir* (16466) IAS
    2000, Vol 3, No 7.
2   *Ilyas* [2002] UKIAT 08345. See, on the validity of marriage where parties had a false tax
    family, *R v Immigration Appeal Tribunal, ex p Kaur (Kulbander)* [1991] Imm AR 107; *R v
    Immigration Appeal Tribunal, ex p Gondalia* [1991] Imm AR 519.
3   [1976] Imm AR 31.
4   From *Mulla's Principles of Mohamedan Law* (19th edn, 1990), s 268. See also *Ali (Syed
    Shanur)* (18900) (26 November 1998, unreported); *FI (Bangladesh, presumptions;
    marriage– legitimacy) Bangladesh* [2005] UKIAT 00016 (24 January 2005, unreported).

11.43 In *Akhtar*[1] the Tribunal accepted the view of experts on Islamic law that in that tradition the parties need not have met, and so a telephone marriage was valid even though the husband was not present at the marriage ceremony. In *Ur Rehman* the Tribunal held that if both parties are domiciled in a country where a telephone marriage is valid, the marriage is recognised under English law even if one of the parties was resident in the UK on the date of the marriage.[2] The IDI states that proxy marriages are valid, provided they are recognised in the country where they are celebrated.[3] The fact that a proxy may be appointed by telephone from England would not detract from recognition of the marriage celebrated elsewhere. However, by the time the application for entry clearance is determined, the couple must have met in order to comply with a specific requirement of the Immigration Rules aimed at arranged marriages.[4] A Pakistan Islamic marriage is complete even if the attendant traditional ceremonial such as the departure of the bride (ruksati) is dispensed with.[5]

1   (2166).

2   *Ur Rehman* (TH 5885/99) IAS 2000, Vol 3, No 15. The IDI however, say that a telephone marriage is not valid if one party is in the UK at the time: IDI May 03, Ch 8, s 1, Annex B, para 3.1. This advice, in our view, is wrong, unless of course the party who is in the UK has acquired a domicile in England and Wales, Scotland or Northern Ireland.
3   IDI May 03, Ch 8, s 1, Annex B, para 3.1.
4   HC 395, para 281(iii); see further 11.65 below.
5   *Hussain (Basharat) v Visa Officer, Islamabad* [1991] Imm AR 182.

11.44 It is trite law that if the evidence shows that the parties were indeed married it is not necessary to pinpoint the actual date of marriage.[1] But the date of the marriage may be relevant to questions concerning the age and nationality status of children. A marriage that is held to be invalid may nevertheless qualify the applicant for admission as a fiancé(e) if it is demonstrated that the applicant was willing and able to remarry at the date of the decision,[2] or as an unmarried partner if he or she was unable to do so,[3] but there is no jurisdiction to allow an appeal on the basis of the fiancé(e) or unmarried partner rules where the application had been made on the basis of a marriage held to be invalid.[4] The principle is that an applicant must make clear the facts that he or she relies on, but not necessarily all the different potentially applicable rules. When in doubt, therefore, simultaneous applications as a spouse or as a fiancé(e) or an unmarried partner may need to be made in the alternative.[5] A spouse application refused on invalidity grounds could attract an appeal on human rights grounds if the parties had cohabited and family life was established, and if the refusal constituted a failure of respect for family life (because the parties could not live together in the other spouse's country of residence) which was disproportionate to the legitimate aim pursued by the decision.

1   *Khanom v Entry Clearance Officer, Dacca* [1979–80] Imm AR 182.
2   *Ach-Charki v Entry Clearance Officer, Rabat* [1991] Imm AR 162.
3   HC 395, para 295A(iii). But parties legally unable to marry on grounds of consanguineous relationships or age may not seek admission as unmarried partners: HC 395, para 295A(ii) and see *R v Secretary of State for the Home Department, ex p Ozminnos* [1994] Imm AR 287, QBD; HC 395, para 295AA, amended by HC 164.
4   *Uddin v Immigration Appeal Tribunal* [1991] Imm AR 134, QBD. In the validity case of *Majid* (01TH01357) (26 September 2001, unreported) the Tribunal held that the fiancé rule contemplated the reasonable foreseeability that a marriage will take place in the United Kingdom within the period of limited leave granted for that purpose not the legal capacity to marry at the date of decision.
5   See comments in *Majid* (01TH01357) (26 September 2001, unreported), IAT.

ADMISSION OF FAMILY MEMBERS AND PARTNERS

11.45 In order for family members and partners to be admitted for entry or permitted to stay in the UK they must have a sponsor who is in the UK and who wants to bring in the family member or partner.[1] The sponsor may be a person with limited leave such as a student or work permit holder, or settled in the UK. Persons admitted as spouses or partners are dependent on the immigration status of their partner until they obtain settlement.[2] Although entry clearance to join family in the UK stands as leave to enter, a change of circumstances between issue of the entry clearance and arrival here may result in cancellation of leave by an immigration officer.[3] If the sponsor is found to have obtained entry unlawfully, or doubts are raised about the validity of the marriage or the relationship, or if the relationship breaks down, or the new arrival has recourse to public funds, an extension of stay may be refused or existing leave curtailed.[4] A decision to remove the person will normally follow. The Rules allow the grant of settlement to spouses and unmarried partners who have been victims of domestic violence by their sponsor or a member of his or her family during the probationary period.[5] Spouses and unmarried partners bereaved during their probationary period may now obtain settlement under the Immigration Rules.[6] Once spouses and unmarried partners have been granted settlement they may not normally be deprived of it, whether or not the marriage or relationship lasts,[7] and cannot be removed from the UK, unless the Home Office can demonstrate that deception was used in seeking (whether successfully or not) to obtain settlement,[8] or they are the subject of a deportation order.[9]

1   See next section for maintenance, accommodation and third-party support.
2   Note that the spouse and unmarried partner rules do permit the grant of indefinite leave to remain in circumstances where the sponsorship no longer exists, either because the spouse or partner has died or the relationship ended through domestic violence. These concessions are the exception to the ongoing sponsorship requirement.
3   HC 395, para 321(ii), 321A; Immigration (Leave to Enter and Remain) Order 2000, SI 2000/1161, Art 6. See chapter 3 above for refusal and cancellation of leave.
4   HC 395, paras 322, 323. See chapter 4 above for curtailment of leave.
5   HC 395, paras 289A, 289B, inserted by HC 104, HC 538.
6   HC 395, as amended by Cm 4851, paras 287(b) (spouses) and 295M (unmarried partners).
7   Indefinite leave to remain can only be revoked in one of the situations set out in the Nationality Immigration and Asylum Act 2002, s 76.
8   Immigration and Asylum Act 1999, s 10(1)(b).
9   A deportation order nullifies any leave to remain, including indefinite leave. Prior to the passage of s 10 of the Immigration and Asylum Act 1999 (fn 8 above), persons entering sham marriages to remain in the UK were deported on public good grounds: see *R v Immigration Appeal Tribunal, ex p Cheema* [1982] Imm AR 124, CA; *R v Immigration Appeal Tribunal, ex p Patel (Anilkumar Rabindrabhai)* [1988] AC 910, [1988] 2 All ER 378, [1988] 2 WLR 1165; *Patel (Yanus) v Immigration Appeal Tribunal* [1989] Imm AR 416, CA. See chapter 15 below.

11.46 Those with limited leave to enter or remain as students, workers or business people, have certain rights to sponsor family or partners. Generally the spouse or unmarried partner and children under 18 of work permit holders, the highly skilled, retired persons of independent means, those with UK ancestry, domestic servants, persons here in business, innovators, investors or EC Association categories can qualify for the same term of stay as the sponsor.[1] Minor children are permitted entry or stay where both parents are in the UK, the sponsor is the sole parent or has sole responsibility for the child or there are serious or compelling family considerations which make the child's exclusion undesirable.[2] Such applicants require entry clearance in that capacity, must satisfy maintenance and accommodation requirements and that they will not remain in the UK beyond the term of stay of their sponsor. The rules for family sponsorship by students, teachers and language assistants on approved exchanges and those on approved work experience or traineeships are slightly different. There is no requirement that the children of such sponsors be here with both parents or a single parent with sole responsibility.[3] As with the sponsor, such family members must show they intend to leave the UK at the expiry of their leave.[4] The family members of students are permitted to work only if the student has been granted leave of 12 months or more.[5] Under the Rules persons present and settled in the UK can sponsor a broader array of family members, including adopted children and dependent relatives.[6] Refugees can also sponsor family members,[7] as may persons with temporary protection,[8] but those with discretionary leave must still rely on policy concessions for family reunion rights.[9] On the family sponsorship of EEA nationals see 7.86ff above.

[1] Spouses and children are provided for in HC 395, as amended, paras 194–199 (for work permit holders, highly skilled, domestic servants, ministers of religion and UK ancestry holders) 240–245 (for business, investors, writers, composers and EC Association holders) 271–73 (for retirees). HC 395, para 295J–K covers unmarried partners of sponsors who qualified under Rules 128–193 (entry or remaining for employment), 200–239 (business, investor, self-employed, writer, composer, artist), 263–270 (retiree).

[2] HC 395, paras 123, 197, 243, 274. Note that under the terms of a policy concession work permit holders who are intra-company transferees can also sponsor their adult dependent children who are part of the family unit: IDI, Ch 5, s 9, para 1.1.

[3] HC 395, para 79 (students and prospective students), 125 (teachers and trainees). A working holiday maker can sponsor his/her child providing the child is under five and will leave the UK before reaching that age and either both parents are in the UK of the sponsor is the sole parent or has sole responsibility for the child. Or there are serious and compelling family circumstances making the child's exclusion undesirable: para 101–102, substituted by HC 302 from 8 February 2005.

[4] HC 395, paras 76, 122.

[5] HC 395, paras 77, 80.

[6] HC 395, paras 277–319.

[7] HC 395, as amended, paras 352A–F. See 12.179 below. Note that under the proposed Five Year Strategy for Asylum and Immigration (Cm 6472, Feb 2005), refugees and those granted humanitarian protection will both be granted five years limited leave and will both have family reunification rights from the date of grant. Under the current arrangements persons given humanitarian protection can sponsor their family only after three years.

[8] See 12.173 below.

[9] See 12.179ff below.

ENTRY CLEARANCE REQUIREMENTS

11.47 Persons who wish to enter the UK with a view to settlement with a family member, including a spouse or cohabitee, must obtain a prior entry clearance before doing so[1] unless they claim the right of abode. The exceptions are returning residents[2] and children born in the UK who are not British citizens.[3] This requirement is strictly applied. A person who marries while on temporary admission,[4] or having been granted leave to enter or remain in the UK for a period of six months or less [5] will be required to return home for entry clearance unless there are exceptional circumstances, which make this requirement disproportionate.[6] The inconvenience or expense of having to travel home to obtain a visa is not considered sufficient reason for waiver,[7] even where the Home Office is satisfied that all other requirements of the Immigration Rules (presence of sponsor; intention to live together; having met; maintenance and accommodation) are met.[8] Entry clearance as leave to enter may be cancelled if there has been a change of circumstance since its issue (such as the death of a partner or the breakdown of the marriage prior to entry) [9] or it was obtained through false representations or non-disclosure of material circumstances.[10] We have seen that entry clearances are issued in the country of residence and are valid as leave to enter.[11]

¹ HC 395, paras 281(vi) (spouses), 276R(vi) (spouses of discharged soldiers), 290(vii) (fiancé(e)s), 295A(viii), 295J (ix) (unmarried partners), 276X(iv), 297(vi), 301(vi), 310(xii), 314(xii) (children), 317(vi) (other dependent relatives). Leave to enter is to be refused if no such entry clearance is produced on arrival: paras 276T, 276Z, 283, 292, 295C, 300, 303, 303C, 313, 316, 316C, 316F, and 319.

² HC 395, para 18. See 4.25ff above.

³ HC 395, para 305.

⁴ Under Immigration Act 1971, Sch 2, para 21; for temporary admission see 17.11 below.

⁵ HC 395, para 284(i), amended by HC 538 and substituted by Cm 5949, as applied by para 286.

⁶ IDI Jul 03, Ch 8, s 1, para 2.4; Dec 00, Ch 8, Annex G, para 2. See *Dyfan (Musu) v Secretary of State for the Home Department* [1995] Imm AR 206, CA. See now requirement for permission to marry at 11.66 below.

⁷ See IDI May 03, Ch 8, s 2, para 3.2. This refers to the no switching rule for fiancé(e)s (see 11.67 below), but is also applicable to spouses on temporary admission. The Tribunal has considered whether it was feasible for spouse entry clearance applications to be made by Iraqi, Somali and Pakistani applicants in circumstances where there are no or limited entry clearance facilities in the home country and travel to a neighbouring entry clearance facility is dangerous. See *MS (Inability to make entry clearance application) Somalia* [2005] UKIAT 00003; *EH (Palestinian entry clearance proportionality) Iraq* [2005] UKIAT 00062; *KJ (entry clearance proportionality) Iraq* [2005] UKIAT 00066; *A (Pakistan)* [2004] UKIAT 00034.

⁸ *R v Secretary of State for the Home Department, ex p Mahmood* [2001] WLR 840, CA, disapproving *R v Secretary of State for the Home Department, ex p Hashim* (CO 2052/99) (12 June 2000, unreported); *Huang v Secretary of State for the Home Department* [2005] EWCA Civ 105.

⁹ HC 395, para 321(ii); para 286 referring to para 284(vi).

¹⁰ HC 395, para 321(i). Refusal would also be justified on the grounds of restricted returnability, medical grounds, or where the person is subject to a deportation order, exclusion would be conducive to the public good, or the person has a criminal record: para 321(iii).

¹¹ HC 395, para 28. Immigration (Leave to Enter and Remain) Order 2000, SI 2000/1161, Arts 3, 5. See further chapter 3.

11.48 *Certificates of entitlement.* Family members claiming the right of abode need a certificate of entitlement unless they have a UK passport describing them as a British citizen or a CUKC having the right of abode.[1] Certificates of entitlement can be issued abroad prior to travel or in the UK.[2] There is a duty on the entry clearance officer abroad properly to classify an application as either one for entry clearance or for a certificate of entitlement to the right to abode; this is not the responsibility of the applicant.[3] In *R v Secretary of State for the Home Department, ex p Phansopkar* [4] the Court of Appeal held that where there was considerable delay in processing certificates of entitlement, a person with the right of abode could travel without one and require his or her application to be determined in the UK by the Home Office without having to be removed first. However, the Immigration Act 1988 amended the Immigration Act 1971 to require a person claiming the right of abode to prove it by means of a certificate of entitlement if he or she did not have a British passport,[5] and those without one or other of these documents have no right of appeal against refusal of leave to enter.[6] Arrival without a certificate of entitlement, therefore, will be unwise. It will also be difficult for the person to board an airline to come to the UK without proper documentation.[7]

¹ Immigration Act 1971, s 3(9), inserted by Immigration Act 1988, s 3.

² HC 395, paras 12–14 do not prescribe where a certificate of entitlement must be applied for; see *R v Secretary of State for the Home Department, ex p Phansopkar* [1976] QB 606, [1975] 3 All ER 497, CA.

[3]   *Khatun (Kessori)* (4272) founded the long-established principle, upheld by the Immigration Appeal Tribunal in *Rahman* (00TH00307) (25 January 2000, unreported), that an applicant cannot be expected to know or understand the complexities of the immigration and nationality laws of the UK. Note that the UK Visas application forms for a certificate of entitlement (VAF4 2004) and for entry clearance for settlement (VAF2 2004) are now different, and the correct application is more easily ascertained.

[4]   [1976] QB 606, [1975] 3 All ER 497, CA.

[5]   IA 1971, s 3(9), as amended by IA 1988, s 3; HC 395, para 12. For further details on proof of entitlement to a right of abode, see 2.21–2.22.

[6]   Immigration and Asylum Act 1999, s 60(1).

[7]   See carriers' liability provisions IAA 1999, Pt II, ss 40ff, chapter 14 below.

11.49 *Family permits for family members of EEA nationals.* So far as concerns non-EEA family members coming to join EEA nationals other than British citizens in the UK, the imposition of a strict requirement that a family permit should be obtained prior to departure for the UK is, in our view, incompatible with the right of admission granted by EC law.[1] The rules now make provision for leave to enter as the primary carer or relative of an EEA national self-sufficient child, for which entry clearance is required.[2]

[1]   See 7.116 above.

[2]   HC 395, para 257C, inserted by HC 164 from 21 December 2004.

11.50 Persons given leave to enter as a visitor, student or in some other temporary capacity may apply to vary that leave to stay with their relatives or partners in the UK without having first to return to their country of origin.[1] However a person, who was granted leave to enter for six months or less in a capacity other than a fiancé(e), may not remain as a spouse, but must return home and obtain an entry clearance in that capacity.[2] Persons who intended to marry or join relatives here permanently when they arrived for a visit or other form of temporary stay run some risk of refusal or being treated as an illegal entrant on the basis that they deceived the immigration officer on entry.[3]

[1]   HC 395, paras 284, amended by HC 538, Cm 5949 (spouses, who may not switch from visitor status), 295D (unmarried partners), 298 (children), 311, 314 (adopted children) and 317(vi) (other dependants), where the distinction is made between the requirement of an entry clearance when seeking leave to enter and leave to remain. This does not apply to fiancé(e)s, who cannot 'switch' from another category.

[2]   HC 395, para 284 (i) as amended.

[3]   For illegal entry, see chapter 16 below. They may also be refused permission to marry in the UK. See 11.67 below.

PRESENCE OF SPONSOR

11.51 Family settlement claims require a sponsor who is present and settled in the UK, except in cases where all the relevant members of the family will be admitted for settlement at the same time.[1] These conditions are deemed to be satisfied in the case of a sponsor who is a member of the armed forces serving abroad but based in the UK, or a permanent member of the diplomatic service or a comparable UK-based staff member of the British Council, or a British staff member of the Department for International Development on a tour of duty abroad.[2] In cases of joint sponsorship, both sponsors must be present and settled.[3] 'Settled' means ordinarily resident in the UK without being subject to any restrictions on stay under the immigration laws.[4] When entry clearance officers are considering applications, they are entitled to consider whether these conditions will be met at the time of admission.[5] A fleeting visit will not be sufficient to establish ordinary residence in the UK,[6] but an intention to live here permanently is not required[7] and one can be ordinarily resident in two places at the same time.[8]

[1] HC 395, paras 281 (spouses), 290(i) (fiancé(e)s), 295A(i) (unmarried partners), 297(i), 301(i), 305(i), 310(i), 311(i), 314(i) (children), 317(i) (other dependants) and 276R–276AB spouse and children of Gurkha or foreign or Commonwealth citozens discharged from HM Forces and present and settled in UK). See 11.46 above for admission of family members of those not settled in the UK.
[2] HC 395, para 281 as amended by Cm 5597.
[3] *Shabir v Visa Officer, Islamabad* [1989] Imm AR 185.
[4] Immigration Act 1971, s 33(2A), as amended; HC 395, para 6. See further chapter 5 above. The residence must be lawful residence so if the sponsor is an illegal entrant who has obtained leave to remain in a false name, the dependants will not qualify: *Akhtar (Kalsoom)* (10755). An entitlement to reside without actual residence will not suffice: *Secretary of State for the Home Department v Wong* [1992] Imm AR 180. Those with exceptional leave to remain, humanitarian protection or discretionary leave are not eligible for settlement for four and six years respectively and so cannot obtain family reunion before then, save in compelling compassionate circumstances. The proposed Five Year Strategy for Asylum and Immigration (Cm 6472, Feb 2005) is expected to provide for refugees and those granted humanitarian leave to be given equivalent five-year terms of leave, and family reunification rights operative from the time of the grant. See 12.179 below.
[5] *Bibi (Rashida) v Immigration Appeal Tribunal* [1988] Imm AR 298, CA.
[6] *Bibi (Rashida) v Immigration Appeal Tribunal* [1988] Imm AR 298, CA.
[7] *R v Immigration Appeal Tribunal, ex p Rafique* [1990] Imm AR 235.
[8] *Shah v Barnet London Borough Council* [1983] 2 AC 309, [1983] 1 All ER 226, HL; *R v Secretary of State for the Home Department, ex p Chugtai* [1995] Imm AR 559.

11.52 The Immigration Rules do not stipulate where the sponsor should be at the time that the application is made. In the case of *R v Immigration Appeal Tribunal, ex p Manek*[1] (decided under earlier rules) the Court of Appeal suggested that a sponsor had to be physically present in the UK at the time of the application. It is now sufficient for the sponsor to be ordinarily resident with a right to return to the UK, rather than physically present here at the time of the application, provided that he or she will be present when the sponsored relative arrives.[2] This clarification is important in practice, given the length of time it takes for some applications to be processed and the hardship caused if families have to be divided. However, the sponsor's absence from the UK while the application is being processed may make it more difficult to satisfy maintenance and accommodation criteria at the date of the decision of the entry clearance officer.

[1] [1978] Imm AR 131, CA, interpreting HC 79, para 39.
[2] *Raheen* (2949), *Bibi (Mokbul)* (4954) (1987) 2 INLP 50.

MAINTENANCE AND ACCOMMODATION

11.53 Before granting entry clearance to family members to join a sponsor, the entry clearance officer will have to be satisfied that there is adequate maintenance and accommodation for them in the UK without recourse to public funds.[1] These rules apply to both accommodation and maintenance.

The spouses and children of refugees, of persons granted temporary protection and of discharged Gurkhas and foreign and Commonwealth soldiers from the British army are not subject to the maintenance and accommodation requirements.[2] The Home Office has also waived the requirement in particular cases for family members of those with exceptional leave to remain (now humanitarian protection or discretionary leave).[3] The IDI referring to spouses and partners, children and other dependent relatives state that care should be taken in refusing applications on this ground alone.[4] 'Public funds' are defined[5] as:

- income support or income-based jobseekers' allowance;
- housing and homelessness assistance;
- housing benefit and council tax benefit;
- state pension credit or child and working tax credit;[6]
- child benefit;[7]
- attendance allowance;
- severe disablement allowance;
- carers' allowance;
- disability living allowance;
- a social fund payment.

Neither NHS treatment nor state education counts as recourse to public funds for the purpose of the Rule.[8] There are a number of precise exceptions which qualify the scope of the public funds prohibition list, set out in the relevant instructions.[9] For example, working tax credit can be claimed by a foreign spouse or unmarried partner and it appears from the Immigration Directorate Instructions that is not considered recourse to public funds for the purposes of the rule.[10] A common question was whether the receipt of public funds by sponsors in their own right could disqualify relatives from joining them in circumstances where there would be no additional recourse to public funds, but where the relatives benefited indirectly. This was known as 'indirect reliance on public funds'. After years of divergence between Home Office policy as set out in correspondence[11] and the wording of the Rules, and of conflicting Tribunal and High Court decisions,[12] this issue was put to rest in 2000 by an Immigration Rule amendment stating that 'a person is not to be regarded as having (or potentially having) recourse to public funds merely because he is (or will be) reliant in whole or in part on public funds provided to his sponsor, unless, as a result of his presence in the UK, the sponsor is (or would be) entitled to increased or additional public funds'.[13]

1   See 11.47.
2   HC 395, as amended, paras 276R, 276X, 352A–F, 356.
3   For example, in a policy set out in a Home Office letter of 17 May 1990 and withdrawn on 15 January 1996, a policy specifically for Somali nationals was established which agreed to take a 'flexible approach and consider waiving the requirement in individual cases; in deciding whether to do this each case is considered on its individual merits, and the decision maker would look, inter alia, at the degree of difficulty continuing separation of the family is causing'. 'Somali Family Reunion Policy' [1993] Imm AR 40.
4   IDI Apr 04, Ch 8, s 1, Annex F. Such cases 'should be considered on their merits and any compassionate circumstances should be taken into account'.
5   HC 395, para 6. This rule is subject to frequent change and an up-to-date version should be consulted. See also IDI May 02, Ch 1, s 7 and IDI Apr 04, Ch 8, s 1.

6   The UK-settled sponsor may claim working credit and child benefit for his or her family if they are entitled to it under social security legislation (see chapter 13 below), and see fn 10 below.

7   See fn 6 above. According to the May 02 IDI (Ch 1, s 7, Annex W, 2.5), where the only extra benefit being claimed is child benefit and one partner is British or has permanent residence or is an EEA national, it should not be considered as additional recourse to public funds.

8   IDI May 02, Ch 1, s 7.

9   See HC 395, para 6B, inserted by HC 3546 in February 2005, which provides for exceptions by way of regulations under Immigration and Asylum Act 1999, s 115 and Tax Credits Act 2002, s 42. This more finely aligns the prohibition under the rules with exclusions from entitlement to the relevant benefits. See also IDI May 02, Ch 1, s 7.

10 IDI May 02, Ch 1, s 7, Annex W. The Apr 04 IDI is in slightly different terms: 'where a foreign wife (sic) is married to a person present and settled in the UK, she may claim working tax credit on behalf of her husband and family'. IDI Apr 04, Ch 8, s 1, Annex F, The Tax Credits (Immigration) Regulations 2003, SI 2003/653, provide that where one member of a couple is a person subject to immigration control and the other is not, or is in one of the excepted categories set out in the regulations, their entitlement to tax credit is determined as if neither is subject to control. See also HC 395, para 6B, fn 9 above.

11 See eg letter from Nicholas Baker to Sir Giles Shaw MP, October 1994, (1995) Legal Action (July) at 21; Nicholas Baker to Max Madden MP, set out in *Kausar v Entry Clearance Officer (Islamabad)* [1998] INLR 141 at 144. The relevant policy statements are also set out in *Butterworths Immigration Law Service* D[1021].

12 *R v Immigration Appeal Tribunal, ex p Singh* [1989] Imm AR 69; *R v Secretary of State for the Home Department, ex p Bibi (Islam)* [1995] Imm AR 157; *Entry Clearance Officer v Ahmed (Bashir)* [1991] Imm AR 130; *Yousaf* (9190); *Ramzan* (11185); *Scott (Clevon Marcus)* (13389); *Kausar v Entry Clearance Officer (Islamabad)* [1998] INLR 141; *Hussain (Gulam)* (20671); *Khan (Shamima Jaham)* (HX 00663).

13 HC 395, para 6A, inserted by Cm 4851 from 2 October 2000.

11.54 The maintenance and accommodation rules for the admission for settlement of spouses and unmarried partners are slightly different from those applying to children and other relatives. Spouses and unmarried partners need to show that there will be adequate accommodation for themselves and any dependants, without recourse to public funds, in accommodation which they own or occupy exclusively, and that they will be able to maintain themselves and any dependants adequately, without recourse to public funds.[1] Children must show that they can and will be accommodated adequately by the parent, parents or relative sponsoring the child, without recourse to public funds, in accommodation owned or occupied exclusively by the sponsor, and that they can and will be maintained adequately by the parent, parents or relative, without recourse to public funds.[2] Other dependent relatives must show that they can and will be accommodated adequately together with any dependants, without recourse to public funds, in accommodation owned or occupied exclusively by the sponsor, and that they can and will be maintained adequately, together with any dependants, without recourse to public funds.[3] The different wording reflects the Home Office view as to who should be responsible for maintaining and accommodating the particular relatives. In the case of spouses, the Rule appears to envisage that the spouses will provide for themselves; children may be accommodated and supported only by their parent or parents or other sponsoring relative; and other dependent relatives may be supported by anyone, but must join sponsors in accommodation provided by the sponsor. The October 2000 amendments to the Immigration Rules made by Cmd 4851 thus appear to have reopened the controversy as to whether and to what extent someone other than the sponsor can provide the support and accommodation necessary for family reunion, often referred to as 'third party support'. This used to be the subject of conflicting decisions in the Tribunal, with some divisions holding that the Rules precluded support from anyone other than the UK sponsor, others that third party support was acceptable so long as it was reliable.[4] After a number of restrictive Tribunal decisions were quashed by consent,[5] the issue seemed to have been resolved as a result of the decision in *Arman Ali*[6] which held that the maintenance and accommodation requirements of the Rules could be met by long-term third party support.[7] Collins J held that the Rules should be applied sensibly and purposively, to give effect to family life rights. The Rules neither limited third party assistance to family members nor precluded children from supporting themselves from their own resources.[8] However, although the Home Office did not appeal *Arman Ali*, the December 2000 IDI[9] and the October 2000 changes to the rules relating to the admission of children, suggest that it is unwilling to accept the good sense of the court's ruling in *Arman Ali* on third party support and child self-support. Family life considerations under Article 8 of ECHR mean that the liberal interpretation of the maintenance and accommodation rules, in which any form of support is permissible so long as the family member's arrival does not result in additional recourse to public funds, ought to prevail.[10]

---

[1]   HC 395, paras 281(iv) and (v) (spouses), 295A(v) and (vi) (unmarried partners). Fiancé(e)s may not work before the marriage, so that they must be adequately maintained and accommodated until that time, and thereafter the provisions mirror those for spouses: HC 395, para 290(iv)–(vi).

[2]   HC 395, paras 297(iv) and (v), 298(iv) and (v), 301(iv) and (iva), 303A(iv) (child of fiancée) 310(iv) and (v), 311(iv) and (v), 314(iv) and (iva) (amendments introduced by Cm 4851 in Oct 00), 316A (iv), 316D (v).

[3]   HC 395, para 317(iv) and (iva), as amended by Cm 4851 in Oct 00.

[4]   *Entry Clearance Officer, Islamabad v Hussain (Mohammed Jahangir)* [1991] Imm AR 476; *Neesa (Najmun)* (11545): third party support not acceptable; *Khan (Zamal)* (16392); *Nguyen (Thi B)* (18738) IAS 1999, Vol 2, No 9: third party support was acceptable for a very limited period; *Azad* (5993); *Khan* (6283); *Modi* (9714); *Kumar (Rajesh)* (18885) IAS 1999, Vol 2, No 21: acceptable in short to medium term; *Ahmed (Mukhtar)* (9028): long-term third party support acceptable in marriage case, *Njoku* (18520) IAS 1999, Vol 2, No 14: long-term third party support acceptable in principle both in marriage and children cases (sponsors were elderly grandparents who relied on support from relations).

[5]   Eg *Ahmed (Ishaque)* (12292); *Begum (Zabeda)* (16677), rejecting long-term third party support in principle. The consent orders quashing these decisions were not publicised, and so later Tribunals continued to rely on them.

[6]   *R v Secretary of State for the Home Department, ex p Arman Ali* [2000] INLR 89, QBD.

[7]   The decision in *Jabeen (Azra) v Visa Officer, Islamabad* [1991] Imm AR 178, that the maintenance rule could not be satisfied when the sponsor was serving a sentence of imprisonment, would not survive if the applicant could rely on third party support or his or her own earnings so as to prevent reliance on public funds.

[8]   The Tribunal had held in *Begum (Hasna)* (15629) and *Bibi (Sonor)* (19199), IAS 1999, Vol 2, No 17, that earnings of a dependent child could be taken into account in assessing whether there would be sufficient maintenance to avoid recourse to public funds under HC 395, paras 281(v) and (vi) and 297(iv).

[9]   The IDI relating to spouses say that an undertaking from members of a couple's families to support them until they are able to support themselves from their own resources 'is unacceptable as the Rules require the couple to be able to support themselves … from their own resources', although the arrangement may be accepted exceptionally for a limited period. This guidance, now contained in IDI Apr 04, Ch 8, s 1, Annex F (previously IDI Dec 00, Ch 8, s 1, Annex H) is wrong: the Immigration Rules do not require self-support from a couple's own resources.

10   The Tribunal did not have full representations on this issue in *GG (HC 395, para 317 Joint Sponsorship) Jamaica* [2004] UKIAT 00095 but nevertheless held in respect of a sponsorship under para 317(i)(f), that where there are a number of relatives who have severally undertaken the responsibilities of sponsorship, it is unlikely to matter much which of the sponsors provides the support for accommodation and maintenance. See also *Mahmood (Amjad) v Entry Clearance Officer, Islamabad* [2002] UKIAT 01819 concerning the application of the *Arman Ali* approach to maintenance and accommodation issues in a spouse claim.

11.55 The Immigration Rules do not require that adequate maintenance and accommodation are available at the date of the decision (which would preclude the entry of spouses and partners and other economically active family members whose own earning power is relied on to satisfy the Rule), but that it is reasonably foreseeable that the requirements will be met within six months (the currency of the visa).[1] A written undertaking of support may be required, save in the case of admission of spouses and children under 16, where there is a statutory obligation to support.[2] A refusal to provide such an undertaking may lead to a refusal of the application.[3] Copies of the undertaking are sent to the Department of Social Security, and failure to honour it may lead to a prosecution of the sponsor[4] and/or in certain cases a refusal to extend stay.[5] However, short-term and emergency recourse to public funds through no fault of the sponsor will not have adverse consequences.[6]

1   *Begum (Momotaz)* (18699), (1999) 5 ILD No 2; *Seen, Arif* (16167). However note (on admission of evidence of 'circumstances appertaining' at the date of the decision and matters 'arising' after that date in entry clearance and certificate of entitlement cases); *DR (ECO post decision evidence) Morocco* [2005] UKIAT 00038, *LS (post decision evidence, direction, appealability) Gambia* [2005] UKIAT 00085.
2   See National Assistance Act 1948, s 42, as amended by Family Law Reform Act 1987, Sch 2; Social Security Administration Act 1992, s 78 (liability to maintain as a result of an undertaking under the Immigration Act 1971). The undertaking does not need to be on any prescribed form and need only be a document expressing in reasonably clear language a future promise or agreement to maintain a sponsored immigrant: *R (on the application of Begum) v Social Services Commissioner* (2003) Times, 4 December; *Ahmed v Secretary of State for Work and Pensions* [2005] EWCA Civ 535.
3   HC 395, para 320(14).
4   Under National Assistance Act 1948, s 51, as amended, in the case of spouse and children, and Social Security Administration Act 1992, s 105 (sponsors who have given an undertaking under the Immigration Act 1971).
5   HC 395, para 322(6). Refusal of an extension is only possible in the case of spouses, partners and children who were granted limited leave to remain in the first instance (paras 287, 294, 295G, 298, 311). Admission on the basis of false representations as to availability of support and accommodation could result in the applicants being referred by the local authority to which they applied for support to the Home Office for consideration of whether the person is an illegal entrant: *R v Secretary of State for the Environment, ex p London Borough of Tower Hamlets* [1993] Imm AR 495.
6   IDI Apr 04,Ch 8, s 1, Annex F.

11.56 In determining whether parties or sponsors are able to support themselves and their dependants, information is obtained about their normal income and regular commitments and the case is then assessed to see whether the money available will be sufficient to support the dependants concerned.[1] Where someone is joining a sponsor in the UK, generally there would have to be evidence of an ability to maintain the immigrant from the sponsor's own earnings and savings. Fiancé(e)s are not permitted to work until their leave has been extended after marriage,[2] but persons admitted as spouses can take into account their own anticipated earnings.[3] Applicants' skills and qualifications may suffice without evidence of a job offer if they are of direct value to gaining employment in the UK, but those with few skills might need to show that there is a job open to them in the UK, or that relatives or friends can realistically offer an opening.[4] The IDI state that jobs that are unrealistic in the light of the applicant's skills, or jobs that appear to have been manufactured for the application, which lack any prospect of continuing, will not suffice. However, the instructions also state that 'care must be taken not to make assumptions'. The fact that unemployment in a certain area is high is not in itself enough to warrant refusal.[5] Adequacy of maintenance should take into account tax obligations,[6] and undeclared earnings may be disregarded.[7] Income support has been held an appropriate comparator to assess whether the income available to the sponsor and his or her family would be adequate.[8] The Tribunal has also accepted that account should be taken of the values and habits of the applicants' and sponsors' culture, which may be relatively frugal, with a willingness to assist each other in times of need.[9]

[1] In *Uvovo* (00TH01450) IAS 2000, Vol 3, No 15, the Tribunal held, disapproving *Osman* (16249), that evidence of a sponsor's regular outgoings was not essential.
[2] HC 395, para 291; IDI Apr 04, Ch 8, s 1, Annex F, Dec 00, Ch 8, s 1, Annex H.
[3] The IDI Apr 04, Ch 8, s 1, Annex F states that the earnings of either party whould be taken into equal account and, and evidence of sufficient independent means, employment or sufficient prospects of employment for one or both of the parties should be provided.
[4] IDI Apr 04, Ch 8, s 1, Annex F.
[5] IDI Apr 04, Ch 8, s 1, Annex F.
[6] *Keyani* (5662).
[7] *Tedeku* (6024).
[8] *Islam* (13183), *Begum (Momotaz)* (18699), (1999) 5 ILS No 2; *Uvovo* (00TH01450) IAS 2000, Vol 3, No 15. In the latter case the Tribunal said the sponsor's income must match income support net of accommodation costs and other items such as school meals and prescription charges, to which income support is a gateway. See *RB (Maintenance income support schedules) Morocco* [2004] UKIAT 00142, where voluntary payments from family members reduced the level of income support.
[9] *Khan (Deywan)* (00TH 02531); *Yasin (Mohammed)* (G0027). However in *Begum (Momotaz)* above, the Tribunal held that family members could not be admitted if their standard of living was going to fall below the minimum considered acceptable nationally. Without evidence of savings from benefits, it can be assumed that a person on disability requires the whole of those benefits for his/her own adequate maintenance: *Nisa (Munibun) v Entry Clearance Officer, Islamabad* [2002] UKIAT 01369. There is very little recent case law on these provisions, however.

11.57 The accommodation available for the family member must either be owned or occupied exclusively by the parties or the sponsor; these requirements are alternatives, not cumulative.[1] A freehold interest is not necessary to comply with the requirement of ownership, but there must be some interest in the house, such as a tenancy. Occupation of premises may be as a licensee or lodger. It is doubtful whether boarding children with a neighbour will suffice until the sponsor is the occupier in law,[2] but there is no requirement that the accommodation should be the sponsor's sole or main residence.[3] Exclusive occupation does not have to extend to the whole of premises; exclusive occupation of a bedroom will suffice, with shared use of the remainder of the premises.[4] There may be an issue as to whether the Rule is compliant with the ECHR; if durable accommodation is actually available to the family and there will in fact be no recourse to the local authority, then applying the approach in *Arman Ali*,[5] refusal on the basis that occupation is not exclusive may constitute a disproportionate interference with family life contrary to ECHR, Article 8, and if the Rule has disproportionately adverse effects on those from cultures where sleeping in shared accommodation in extended families is the norm, it could violate the anti-discrimination provisions of Article 14 combined with Article 8.

1   *Sokoya* (00TH 02272) IAS 2000, Vol 3, No 17.
2   *Entry Clearance Officer, New Delhi v Baidwan* [1975] Imm AR 126; *Jabeen (Musrat)* (4925).
3   *Sokoya*, fn 1 above.
4   *Zia v Secretary of State for the Home Department* [1993] Imm AR 404 at 412; *Kasuji v Entry Clearance Officer, Bombay* [1988] Imm AR 587; IDI Apr 04, Ch 8, s 1, Annex F.
5   [2000] INLR 89. See 11.53 above.

11.58 Like maintenance, accommodation does not have to be available at the time of the application or decision, but only when the family member arrives in the UK.[1] However, the Tribunal may not admit evidence of available accommodation at an appeal if the arrangement was not in existence or at least canvassed at the time of the decision.[2] The standard of adequacy of the accommodation is that the applicant may live there without breach of the public health laws or statutory overcrowding.[3] An applicant should not, however, be required to produce a report from a local authority as to the fitness of accommodation in every case, since in most cases the issue is not adequacy but availability of accommodation.[4] On an application for settlement, the fact that accommodation does not meet local authority standards does not allow refusal, if the applicant has not received emergency housing prior to the making of the decision, even if it appears likely that the family will require emergency housing in the near future.[5] Accommodation is not 'adequate' if it is shared with someone who has abused the child.[6]

1   *Jan (Munir)* (1517); *Begum (Sultan)* (3155). IDI Apr 04, Ch 8, s 1, Annex F accept that accommodation will often be prospective rather than available, and the test should be whether there is a reasonable prospect that adequate accommodation will be available.
2   *Kazmi* (5866); *Azad* (5993); generally for admissibility of evidence not before the decision taker see Nationality, Immigration and Asylum Act 2002, s 85(4), (5), *DR (Entry Clearance Officer post decision evidence) Morocco* [2005] UKIAT 00038, *R v Immigration Appeal Tribunal, ex p Hassanin* [1987] 1 All ER 74, [1986] 1 WLR 1448, CA.
3   *Thompson (Gayon)* (17926). Congestion is not the same as statutory overcrowding: *Sultana (Nighat)* (19228) IAS 1999, Vol 2, No 2. IDI Apr 04, Ch 8, s 1, Annex F set out guidance on overcrowding at para 6.3 and note that local authorities have the power to licence temporary overcrowding. But see *S (Pakistan)* [2004] UKIAT 00006 where a surveyor confirmed adequacy of accommodation in terms of Housing Act 1985 although accepting that the accommodation would be congested and the IAT held that on a 'practical' view it would not be adequate.
4   *Rehman v Entry Clearance Officer* [1998] INLR 500.
5   IDI Apr 04, Ch 8, s 1, Annex F.
6   See *M and A v Secretary of State for the Home Department* [2003] EWCA Civ 263, [2003] Imm AR 4, where the Court of Appeal held that It is not a misuse of the language to describe accommodation as inadequate for a child because it is occupied by a parent who has physically or sexually abused the child in the past, and is likely to do so in the future. In such a case, the accommodation is unsafe, and therefore inadequate.

WHICH SPOUSES QUALIFY FOR ENTRY AND STAY?

11.59 We have said that, in order to obtain admission as a spouse, an applicant must satisfy the entry clearance officer that the marriage is lawful or valid and that it complies with the requirements of the Immigration Rules. 11.32–11.44 above dealt with issues of validity. The following sections detail additional strictures or requirements for relationships imposed by the Immigration Rules, which for example restrict the entry of spouses even if the marriage is valid. These issues arise most commonly for young and polygamous spouses.

Spouse under 18

11.60 We showed at 11.40, that although marriages by spouses under 16 are not valid in the UK, in a number of countries marriage under the age of 16 is permitted and marriage by a spouse under this age, domiciled there, is regarded as valid. In the past, wives or husbands under 16 qualified for admission to the UK under the Immigration Rules. An amendment to the rules in 1986 required both parties to a marriage to be aged 16 or above on arrival in the UK before an entry certificate or leave to enter or remain was granted. The repeal of section 1(5) of the Immigration Act 1971 in 1988 meant that this Rule applied to all marriages.[1] But a spouse who married validly abroad when under the age of 16 was eligible to enter to join a spouse here on reaching that age, if the other requirements of the Rules were met. From 21 December 2004 the Rules have been amended again, to prevent the grant of entry clearance or leave to enter or remain if either the sponsor or applicant spouse is aged under 18 at the date of arrival or grant of leave in the UK.[2]

1   HC 395, para 277.
2   HC 395, para 277 as amended by HC 164. Between 31 March 2003 and 20 December 2004, the rule required the sponsor to have reached 18 and the applicant to have reached 16: para 277 as amended by HC 538. The minimum age requirements apply equally to fiancé(e)s and unmarried partners: HC 395, paras 289AA, 295AA, inserted by HC 164. See also 11.40 fn 2.

Polygamous marriages

11.61 Under immigration law a polygamous spouse can qualify for leave to enter or remain, providing the marriage is valid and another spouse has not been permitted entry to the UK.[1] Until 1988, entry could be given to a second wife of an actually polygamous marriage if that marriage was recognised as valid by the domiciliary law of the parties.[2] The Immigration Act 1988 provided that no entry clearance or certificate of entitlement would be issued to a woman married under a system of law that allows polygamy, if there was another wife alive who has been to the UK since the marriage or has been granted entry clearance or a certificate of entitlement.[3] The first marriage must be a valid one in order to disqualify the second wife.[4] Women who have the right of abode as Commonwealth citizens married to a CUKC before 1983 may therefore be prevented from exercising the right of abode. The disqualification only applies if the right of abode was obtained as a wife, and will not apply to women who are British citizens.[5] The provisions do not prevent a wife from returning to the UK if she previously came for settlement as a wife before 1 August 1988,[6] nor do they apply if the wife has been in the UK at any time since her marriage before there was a second wife.[7] Disqualifying presence in the UK by the other spouse will be disregarded if it was as a visitor, as a person on temporary admission or as an illegal entrant.[8] In these cases of actually polygamous marriages, a spouse cannot be admitted to the UK as such until divorce or death removes the other spouse. The IDI provide that entry clearance may not be withheld from a second wife where the husband has divorced the previous wife and the divorce is thought to be one of convenience, even if the husband is still living with the previous wife and to issue the entry clearance would lead to the formation of a polygamous household.[9] The Immigration Rules have now been amended to preclude the admission of a (so-called) polygamous husband of a woman in the same terms as the rules for men.[10] They apply to all applications made after 2 October 2000, regardless of the date of the marriage. The provisions do not prevent polygamous spouses entering the UK in any other capacity. In a recent case the Tribunal upheld the refusal of entry for settlement to the husband of a British citizen who was his second polygamous wife, on the grounds that the husband did not intend to live together permanently with the sponsor, as he intended to remain here with the wife for only six months each year and spend the remaining months with his other wife and family in Bangladesh.[11]

1   Immigration Act 1988, s 2; HC 395, paras 278–279.
2   *Entry Clearance Officer, Dhaka v Begum (Ranu)* [1986] Imm AR 461.
3   IA 1988, s 2(2); HC 395, para 278. The order in which polygamous spouses marry is not important but the order in which they come to the UK for settlement is. It is the spouse who applies for settlement second, rather than the one who marries second, who will be refused: IDI May 03, Ch 8, s 1, Annex C.
4   The burden of proving the invalidity of a second marriage on the grounds of the existence of a prior valid marriage falls on the party asserting the invalidity, usually in these cases the Home Office: *Mussarat (Rukshana)* (9610). See 11.41 above.
5   IA 1988, s 2(1).
6   IA 1988, s 2(4); HC 395, para 279(i).
7   IA 1988, s 2(4); HC 395, para 279(ii).
8   IA 1988, s 2(7) and HC 395, para 280.
9   IDI May 03, Ch 8, Annex C, para 8
10   HC 395, as amended by Cm 4851, para 278. Polyandry is in fact extremely rare.
11   *AB (Settlement – six months in UK) Bangladesh* [2004] UKIAT 00314. See 11.65 below.

Marriages of convenience and 'sham' marriages

11.62 A marriage is not invalid under the general law of England simply because it is entered for a purpose other than mutual cohabitation,[1] and the parties to such a marriage have the relationship of man and wife. But the Immigration Rules require parties to intend to live together permanently as husband and wife,[2] and the policy generally is only to permit admission as a spouse for the purpose of matrimonial cohabitation.[3] The old rule on marriages of convenience, in force between 1977 and 1979, gave no claim to admission to the UK where the authorities concluded that (a) the marriage was primarily entered into to obtain settlement and (b) there was no intention to live permanently together as husband and wife.[4] Women who had the right of abode under the original section 2 of the Immigration Act 1971 and those who were married to Commonwealth citizens settled here before 1973 could enter or remain notwithstanding that their marriages were ones of convenience.[5] The Immigration (European Economic Area) Regulations 2000,[6] like their predecessor the Immigration (EEA) Order 1994,[7] purport to exclude parties to marriages of convenience from the definition of spouse,[8] and there is some support for a similarly narrow view in a number of Tribunal decisions.[9] But the position is not quite so clear cut in Community law. We examine the position more fully at 7.88–7.90 above.

1   In *Vervaeke v Smith* [1983] 1 AC 145, [1982] 2 All ER 144, HL the House of Lords upheld the validity of an English marriage which the wife had contracted in 1954 solely in order to obtain British nationality and a British passport and to escape the possibility of deportation for being a prostitute. The validity of a marriage has also been upheld in other cases where it has been contracted with the object of evading immigration control: *Silver v Silver* [1955] 2 All ER 614, [1955] 1 WLR 728; see also *Martens v Martens* (1952) SA 771, approved by Karminski J in *H v H* [1954] P 258, [1953] 2 All ER 1229. See further *Szechter (otherwise Karsov) v Szechter* [1971] P 286, [1970] 3 All ER 905. But see *Puttick* below.
2   HC 395, para 281(iii).
3   *Patel (Yanus) v Immigration Appeal Tribunal* [1989] Imm AR 416, CA. See also *VK (marriage of Convenience) Kenya* [2004] UKIAT 00305.
4   HC 239, para 264, March 1977. See *R v Immigration Appeal Tribunal, ex p Khan (Mahmud)* [1983] QB 790, [1983] 2 All ER 420, CA.
5   *Secretary of State for the Home Department v Huseyin* [1988] Imm AR 129, CA; *R v Secretary of State for the Home Department, ex p Puttick* [1981] QB 767, [1981] 1 All ER 776.
6   SI 2000/2326, reg 2.
7   SI 2000/2326, reg 2(2).
8   For example, the Tribunal in *Yee-Kee Kwong* (106 61) held that a marriage entered into without any intention of living together as husband and wife did not qualify the partner for admission under community law. In *Lau* (10859) the Tribunal followed *Kwong* but pointed out that the burden of proof lay on the Home Office, and where a couple refused to answer questions about their marital intentions, there was insufficient evidence to discharge the burden of proof. This was applied in *Desmond* (15063) and *Yuen* (18283) IAS 1999, Vol 2, No 8. And see further *Wong (Pui-Yu)* (12602) 1996 2 ILD No 16; and *Chen v Immigration Officer* [1998] INLR 642 (not in accordance with EC law to examine on re-entry the marriage on which a residence permit had been granted to see if it was a marriage of convenience). See analysis of the case law in *VK (Marriage of Convenience) Kenya* [2004] UKIAT 00305 (24 November 2004).

11.63   The Immigration and Asylum Act 1999[1] imposes a duty on marriage registrars to whom a notice of marriage has been given to report to the Secretary of State for the Home Department suspicions on reasonable grounds that the marriage will be a sham marriage.[2] A 'sham' marriage is defined as:

'a marriage (whether or not void)
(a)   entered into between a person ('A') who is neither a British citizen nor a national of an EEA State other than the United Kingdom and another person (whether or not such a citizen or such a national); and
(b)   entered into by A for the purpose of avoiding the effect of one or more provisions of the United Kingdom immigration law or the immigration rules.'[3]

A further implicit requirement for a 'sham' marriage must be, we suggest, that the parties do not intend to live together as husband and wife; if it were otherwise there would be no sham, and the provision of the 1999 Act would be re-introducing, at least as regards the right to marry in a registry office in the UK, the reviled primary purpose rule, which was removed in June 1997. This required parties to a genuine marriage (one in which the parties intended to cohabit) to prove additionally that the primary purpose of the marriage was not the chance to obtain to obtain settlement in the UK for the applicant spouse.[4] Our interpretation of this section accords with the old rule on marriages of convenience.

[1] Immigration and Asylum Act 1999, s 24; Reporting of Suspicious Marriages and Registration of Marriages (Miscellaneous Amendments) Regulations 2000, SI 2000/3164. Similar provisions will apply to civil partnerships when the Civil Partnership Act 2004 is in force: IAA 1999, s 24A, in force from a date to be appointed (CPA 2004, s 261, Sch 27, para 162).

[2] These provisions are additional to the requirements of the Asylum and Immigration (Treatment of Claimants, etc) Act 2004, ss 19–25 which require permission for civil marriage to be obtained from the Home Office, for which see 11.67 below.

[3] IAA 1999, s 24(5).

[4] For detailed discussion of the primary purpose rule and the case law to which it gave rise, see the fourth edition of this work at 11.54–11.69 and *VK (Marriage of Convenience) Kenya* [2004] UKIAT 00305 (24 November 2004, unreported).

11.64 A marriage found to be a 'sham' on our interpretation would not give rise to any right to enter or remain, since the requirement of the Immigration Rules that the couple intend to live together would not be fulfilled. In *Choudhry v Metropolitan Police Comr*[1] the court went further, suggesting that a representation that a person is married implies that the parties intend to live together as man and wife, thus making the representor liable to prosecution if he or she knew that the parties did not intend to do so. This must be doubted. It would be extraordinary that a representation that was accurate in law should be held to be a misrepresentation in the absence of a specific intent to deceive.[2]

[1] *Choudhry v Metropolitan Police Comr* (24 November 1984, unreported), DC, cited in *Patel v Immigration Appeal Tribunal* [1989] Imm AR 416, CA.

[2] In *Vervaeke v Smith* [1983] 1 AC 145, [1982] 2 All ER 144, HL, Lord Hailsham suggested that an immigration marriage where payment was made to a stranger to undergo a ceremony of marriage was not what was normally considered a marriage of convenience. This is, however, exactly what a layman would understand by a 'sham' marriage. But note that payment is not required for a marriage to be regarded as a 'sham' for Immigration and Asylum Act 1999, s 24.

'Intention to live together'

11.65 As indicated above, admission of a spouse is conditional on an intention to live together permanently as husband and wife and the continuing subsistence of the marriage. The abolition of the primary purpose rule in June 1997 was intended to ensure that all those with genuine marriages would be able to live with UK-based spouses, and only those in sham marriages would be excluded. Practitioners have, however, seen an increase in refusals of entry clearance in cases where formerly the intention to live together was not doubted, although doubts might have been expressed about the primary purpose of the marriage. However, in the vast majority of cases, doubt as to intention to live together is unwarranted, and it should certainly not be inferred from the reluctance or refusal of the UK-based partner to move to the other partner's country.[1] The primary purpose rule should not be reintroduced through the back door by detailed questions as to where the parties intend to cohabit, and the fact that a marriage might have economic motivation is of little or no significance in assessing the intention of the parties to live together.[2] Previous cohabitation or the birth of a child would satisfy the requirements of the rule. The relevant date on which an intention to live together as man and wife used to be the date of the immigration authorities' decision, but the Tribunal may now hear evidence about matters arising after the date of the decision.[3] Fiancé(e)s must show that they intend to live together permanently after the marriage;[4] applicants who are already married must show this is their present intention.[5] On an application for settlement after the probationary period, delays in decision-making may mean that the marriage has broken down while the application is under consideration, even though it survived the probationary period under the rules on variation of leave. This will result in refusal under the variation rule.[6] However, it should be noted that the rule is directed at the permanent intentions of the parties rather than to any temporary quarrels between them which may have interrupted cohabitation.

[1]   *R v Immigration Appeal Tribunal, ex p Lunat* (6 October 1986, unreported), QBD; *R v Secretary of State for the Home Department, ex p Wali* [1989] Imm AR 86, QBD; *R v Immigration Appeal Tribunal, ex p Khatab* [1989] Imm AR 313, QBD; *Iqbal v Immigration Appeal Tribunal* [1988] Imm AR 469, CA; *Zia v Secretary of State for the Home Department* [1993] Imm AR 404. The dicta of Glidewell LJ in *Masood (Sumeina) v Immigration Appeal Tribunal* [1992] Imm AR 69, CA on conditional intention are to be seen in the factual context of the case, set out in the judgment of Simon Brown J in the DC at [1991] Imm AR 283. Also on conditional intention see Glidewell LJ's dicta in *R v Secretary of State for the Home Department, ex p Brakwah* [1989] Imm AR 366.
[2]   See eg *Saftar v Secretary of State for the Home Department* [1992] Imm AR 1, CA.
[3]   Nationality Immigration and Asylum Act 2002, s 85(4); however this does not apply to entry clearance appeals, but evidence of post-decision facts may cast a flood of light on the parties' intentions at the date of decision: *R v Secretary of State for the Home Department, ex p Hoque and Singh* [1988] 2 FLR 542, CA. See on admission of post-decision evidence *DR (Entry Clearance Officer post decision evidence) Morocco* [2005] UKIAT 00038, *LS (post-decision evidence; direction; appealability) Gambia* [2005] UKAIT 00085 (19 April 2005, unreported).
[4]   HC 395, para 290(iii).
[5]   HC 395, para 281(iii). A husband in a polygamous marriage who intended dividing his time between his British and Bangladeshi wives was held not to have an intention to live with the British wife permanently in *AB (Settlement six months in UK) Bangladesh* [2004] UKIAT 00314. The Tribunal's interpretation of 'intention to live together permanently ' involves the additional requirement that cohabitation should be full-time, which we suggest is wrong.
[6]   For an example of such a case see *R v Immigration Appeal Tribunal, ex p Idrish* (1984) Times, 14 July, CA; a subsequent appeal against deportation was however successful: *Idrish v Secretary of State for the Home Department* [1985] Imm AR 155.

The requirement that the parties have met

11.66 The rule that the parties have met appears to have been directed principally at arranged marriages. The Tribunal has interpreted the paragraph to exclude casual meetings when the parties were very young.[1] There must be a meeting to the extent that the parties recognise and know each other, but it does not have to be a meeting in the context of marriage. It may be sufficient for the parties to have seen each other and there does not have to have been a conversation between them.[2] Refusal on the grounds of not having met will be reconsidered if the parties meet after the original decision to refuse, and entry clearance will be issued if the decision was based solely on that ground.[3]

[1] *Raj (Rewal) v Entry Clearance Officer, New Delhi* [1985] Imm AR 151. See also IDI Sep 04, Ch 8, Annex J: 'if the parties had been childhood friends, it could be acceptable, although the meeting of two infants would not.'

[2] *Meharban Entry Clearance Officer, Islamabad* [1989] Imm AR 57. IDI Sep 04, Ch 8, Annex J says the parties should have made each other's acquaintance.

[3] IDI Sep 04, Ch 8, Annex J, para 2.2.

Marriage in the UK: restrictions

11.67 The government has invoked public concern at the problem of sham immigration marriages as justification for a number of strictures which prevent or limit the rights of persons subject to immigration control and their partners marrying in the UK or switching their short-term leave to remain to leave on spouse grounds.[1] These restrictions impact on the genuine as well as the sham marriage. We have referred at 11.63 above to the requirement for registrars to inform the Secretary of State of suspected 'sham' marriages. The most significant and onerous restrictions, however, are contained in the Asylum and Immigration (Treatment of Claimants) Act 2004 which requires 'persons who are subject to immigration control'[2] who wish to marry in the UK [3] before a marriage registrar[4] to meet an additional qualifying condition before the marriage registrar can enter notice of their proposed marriage in the marriage notice book.[5] From 1 February 2005 such a prospective spouse must satisfy the registrar that he or she has entry clearance as a fiancé(e) or marriage visitor,[6] or is settled in the UK, or has a Home Office certificate of approval for the marriage.[7] The Home Office guidance on the granting of certificates permitting marriage states that in order to qualify for a certificate of approval, there must be no legal impediment to the marriage[8] and the person must have valid leave to enter or remain in the UK, must have been granted over six months leave to enter or remain on the last occasion; and have at least three months of this leave remaining at the time of making the application.[9] According to the Instruction 'only if there are compelling and compassionate features, which would make it inappropriate for the person to be required to go abroad to obtain an entry clearance, will a certificate of approval be issued where the person does not have leave to enter or remain'.[10] There is no right of appeal against the Secretary of State's decision refusing permission to marry, although such a decision is susceptible to judicial review. These provisions impact adversely on both the British/European and foreign marriage partners, can have a differential impact depending on the religion or belief of one of the partners[11] and strike at fundamental human rights to marry. There is certain to be a legal challenge to their validity and effect.[12]

[1] The 'no switching' provision prevents persons from qualifying to vary their leave to remain as the spouse of a British citizen or resident if they have not been in the UK beyond six months from the date of last admission, unless admitted as a fiancé. (HC 395, para 284 as amended, applying to marriage applications from 1 April 2003).

[2] A person is 'subject to immigration control' for these purposes if he or she is not an EEA national and requires leave to enter or remain in the United Kingdom under the Immigration Act 1971 (whether or not leave has been given): Asylum and Immigration (Treatment of Claimants Act 2004, s 19(4)

[3] AI(TC)A 2004, ss19–20 (England and Wales), 21–22 (Scotland), 23–24 (Northern Ireland)

[4] The provisions in AI(TC)A 2004, s 19(1) apply to marriages solemnised on the authority of certificates issued by a superintendent registrar under Part III of the Marriage Act 1949 (ss 27, 31). This means that marriages according to the rites of the Church of England

solemnised after the publication of banns or on the authority of special or common licences are not affected by the new provision. This distinction appears clearly discriminatory, as marriages involving similar British and foreign partners who may be practising Anglican or Muslim or Jewish will be subject to different immigration requirements affecting their rights to marry. The Joint Committee on Human Rights held that the provisions would lead to a significant risk of discrimination on the grounds of religion or belief without necessary objective and reasonable justification. The Committee was concerned, amongst other matters, with the discrepancy between the 2251 reported 'sham' marriages in January to June 2004 and the 37 criminal charges brought for such abuse (14th report Session 2003–2004).

5   The entry in the marriage notice book enables the persons to marry in the UK before a registrar. The relevant prospective spouse must give their notice (see on form of prescribed notice the Registration of Marriages (Amendment) Regulations 2005, SI 2005/155) to designated registrars (listed in the Immigration (Procedure for Marriage) Regulations 2005, SI 2005/15), even if they intend marrying in a different registry office.

6   The marriage visitor requirements apply to persons subject to immigration control who intend coming to the UK for a short visit in order to marry. Such persons, even where the parties are non-visa nationals, require entry clearance granted expressly for the purpose of enabling them to marry in the UK: see HC 395, paras 56D–F, inserted by HC 346 from 15 March 2005. If both parties to the marriage are subject to immigration control they both need the certificate permitting their marriage. IDI Feb 05, Ch 1, s 15.

7   AI(TC)A 2004, s 19(3). The certificate is valid for three months from the date of the grant: IDI Feb 05, Ch 1, s 15.

8   Such as that one party is under 16 or has not been validly divorced from a former spouse. In a response to ILPA dated 9 March 2005, the Home Office has stated that only if there is 'clear evidence on the file that the person could not marry in the UK' will this provision be relied upon. The Home Office guidance appears to put its officers in the position of registrars who have statutory responsibility to ensure that there is no legal impediment to proposed marriages.

9   IDI Feb 05, Ch 1, s 15. In a letter to ILPA dated 28 January 2005 the Assistant Director of Managed Migration Strategy and Review stated that 'we have set a minimum of 3 months extant leave to remain for certificate of approval applications. This is simply because of the time it will take to apply for a certificate, for that application to be considered and a certificate issued, for notice of marriage to be given, for the waiting time until the marriage can take place and finally for an application for leave to remain on the basis of that marriage to be made'. Although three months may be reasonable as an estimate of the time required for such arrangements, the three months requirement has the effect of disentitling an even larger group of persons from marrying in the UK.

10 IDI Feb 05, Ch 1, s 15, Annex NN. The health grounds cited as compassionate and compelling include where either party is unfit to travel abroad to marry, including unfit due to pregnancy or has a medical condition which means that their life expectancy is less than 12 months. See cases cited at 11.47 fn 7 above.

11 See n 4 above.

12 See *Hamer v United Kingdom* (1979) 4 EHRR 139, EComHR (concerning a successful challenge to the denial of a prisoner's right to marry). The EComHR has held that rules intended to prevent marriages of convenience do not injure the substantive right to marry: *Sanders v France* 87B DR 160, *Klip and Kruger v Netherlands* 91A DR 66. However as the Joint Committee on Human Rights report (fn 4 above) held these provisions could prove excessively burdensome to genuine marriage partners and applies to more people than strictly necessary to meet the stated aims to prevent sham marriages. The marriage of convenience cases therefore are distinguishable.

Leave to enter and remain

11.68 As previously stated, fiancé(e)s and spouses seeking to enter must normally have entry clearance.[1] Fiancé(e)s are given up to six months leave to enter, with a prohibition on taking employment,[2] and spouses are given an initial period, which is often referred to as a probationary period, not exceeding two years, with no such prohibition (although they are granted indefinite leave to enter if they have been married and living together outside the UK for four years prior to the application).[3] If a fiancé(e) fails to marry during the initial period of leave, an explanation will have to be given to the Home Office, and an extension of leave for an appropriate period may be given if the explanation is acceptable and there is evidence that the marriage will take place soon.[4] Once the fiancé(e) has married and has obtained the initial probationary leave to remain as a spouse, the employment prohibition is lifted. A person admitted in another capacity (for a period greater than six months) who marries during his or her stay here[5] can apply for leave to remain as a spouse if, in addition to fulfilling the requirements for entry in that capacity (except for entry clearance), he or she has not remained in breach of the immigration laws and the marriage did not take place after a decision to deport or a recommendation for deportation had been made, or a preparatory notice served.[6] However, no 'switching' is permitted from another temporary capacity to that of fiancé(e), and an application to remain as a fiancé(e) from a person admitted in another capacity will be refused unless there are exceptional compassionate circumstances, such as a serious or terminal illness of one of the parties.[7] It should be noted that fiancé(e)s and spouses are not precluded from coming to the UK as visitors before or even during their settlement application, provided they intend to leave the UK at the end of the particular visit for which entry is sought. See 11.98 for entry of the children of fiancé(e)s.

[1] See 11.47 above; HC 395, paras 281(vi) (spouses) and 290(viii) (fiancé(e)s).
[2] HC 395, para 291. In cases where the applicant is not sure whether he or she will remain in the UK or return home after the wedding, he or she should be treated as a fiancé(e) rather than as a visitor: IDI May 03, Ch 8, s 2, Annex K.
[3] HC 395, para 282.
[4] HC 395, para 293 and 294.
[5] See 11.67 above on restrictions on the right to marry in the UK.
[6] HC 395, para 284 (i), (iv) and (v). The IDI appear to allow a 'grace' period after a limited leave has expired, for certain applications after entry for leave to remain as a spouse: IDI Oct 04, Ch 8, s 1, para 5.8.
[7] IDI May 03, Ch 8, s 2, para 3.2.

11.69 After what was a 12 months' and is now a two years' probationary leave as a spouse, an application can be made for indefinite leave to remain, which should be granted provided the maintenance and accommodation conditions are still met, the marriage is subsisting and each of the parties intends to live permanently with the other as his or her spouse.[1] The language of the rule is discretionary, allowing the Secretary of State to grant further limited leave rather than settlement. The IDI used to state that such leave could be granted only when there is reason to doubt the lasting nature of the marriage or where there is real prospect of reconciliation between separated spouses.[2] This has now been deleted. The IDI now indicate that detailed inquiries on the state of the marriage will normally only be made (i) where doubts exist as to whether the relationship is genuine and subsisting, (ii) there are real reasons to doubt the validity of the marriage, (iii) there is an allegation or other information that the marriage is not genuine, the marriage is a forced marriage or the parties are no longer living together, (iv) there is a poor immigration history; (v) it is suspected to be a marriage of convenience, (vi) there is a previous refusal of leave to enter or remain, (vii) the marriage took place during limited leave to a comparative stranger, (viii) information is received that the parties are no longer living together, or (ix) where the only evidence as to the continued subsistence of the marriage comes from the benefiting spouse.[3] Extensions of stay are subject to the general discretion to refuse on the ground of undesirable conduct,[4] but it is wrong for the Tribunal, when allowing an appeal, to direct that settlement not be given until four years have elapsed.[5] There is no discretion to grant leave to remain under the Immigration Rules in the case of marriage breakdown,[6] except for the purpose of access to children of the marriage who are remaining with the settled spouse (see 11.76 below), or because of domestic violence (see 11.70 below). Where a person leaves the UK during the currency of a temporary leave, that person may be re-examined as to the fulfilment of the marriage requirements on a re-entry to the UK during the currency of that leave, and leave may be cancelled if the marriage has broken down,[7] unless the person would qualify for settlement under the domestic violence rule. Where the settled spouse has died during the probationary period, indefinite leave will be granted provided that the marriage was still subsisting at the time of the death and the parties intended to continue cohabitation.[8]

1   HC 395, para 287(a).
2   IDI Oct 04, Ch 8, s 1, para 2.1. Further limited leave should not be granted where the requirements for settlement are met: *Tanweer* (3490).
3   IDI Oct 04, Ch 8, s 1, paras 3.2 and 4.2.
4   HC 395, paras 322, 323; *Al Saidi* (5324).
5   *Aslam* (6248). On the limits of the power to give directions, see *Sharif (Omeed)* [2002] UKIAT 00953, para 12.
6   *Patel v Secretary of State for the Home Department* [1986] Imm AR 440.
7   *R v Immigration Appeal Tribunal, ex p Chaudhry* [1983] Imm AR 208, QBD.
8   HC 395, para 287(b), inserted by Cm 4851. See also IDI Oct 04, Ch 8, s 1, para 6.

Domestic violence rule

11.70 An overseas national spouse or unmarried partner (see 11.71 below) may be granted indefinite leave to remain provided that there is proof that the applicant has been the victim of domestic violence during the probationary period while the marriage or relationship was subsisting and the applicant is able to produce evidence to establish that a permanent breakdown of the relationship was caused before the end of that period as a result of domestic violence.[1] The rule (formerly a concession outside the Rules) does not apply to persons admitted to the UK as the spouse or unmarried partner of a sponsor who had only limited leave to remain, or where the sponsor is an EEA national exercising free movement rights under EC law.[2] Nor does it apply to fiancé(e)s. The requirements of proof are less stringent than under the previous concession; however the rule requires the applicant to produce 'such evidence as may be required by the Secretary of State'. The IDI suggest the following:

(i)   an injunction, non-molestation order or other protection order made against the sponsor (but not an *ex parte* or interim order);[3]
(ii)   a relevant court conviction against the sponsor;[4] or
(iii) full details of a relevant police caution issued against the sponsor.[5]

In recognition of the fact that it is difficult for victims of domestic violence to produce such documentary evidence, the Secretary of State will instead accept more than one of the following:

(i)   a medical report from a hospital doctor confirming that the applicant has injuries consistent with being a victim of domestic violence;

(ii) a letter from a family practitioner who has examined the applicant and is satisfied that the injuries are consistent with being a victim of domestic violence;

(iii) an undertaking given to a court that the perpetrator of the violence will not approach the victim;

(iv) a police report confirming attendance at the home of the applicant as a result of a domestic violence incident;

(v)   a letter from a social services department confirming its involvement in connection with domestic violence;

(vi) a letter of support or report from a women's refuge.[6]

Where an applicant submits evidence to show that he or she has been subjected to domestic violence from persons other than the sponsor, they may still qualify under the concession if it is clear that this has been the reason for the marriage breakdown, for example, where those abusing the applicant are members of the sponsor's family against whom the sponsor offers no protection.[7] The application should be made while the applicant still has leave to remain as a spouse or partner, but applications made out of time will be considered sympathetically. Acceptable reasons for the delay should be given and may include the fact that the sponsor withheld the applicant's passport, or that the stress of the situation caused the applicant to overlook the need to regularise his or her status.[8]

[1]   HC 395, para 289A. See, on whether the proven domestic violence was the cause of the breakdown of the relationship, *R (on the application of Butler) v Secretary of State for the Home Department* [2002] EWHC 854 (Admin).

[2]   IDI Oct 04, Ch 8, s 1, para 5. The rationale is that 'such persons have not been admitted to the UK for the purpose of settlement'.

[3]   The original or a certified copy of the court order or memorandum of conviction is required, if produced ILR should be granted without further enquiry: IDI Oct 04, Ch 8, s 1, para 5.3.

[4]   Where a prosecution is pending, indefinite leave will not be granted, but the applicant will be granted further leave to remain for six months at a time until the outcome of the prosecution is known: IDI Oct 04, Ch 8, s 1, para 5.5.

[5]   Since there is no documentary evidence of this, the applicant must provide full details of the sponsor to enable inquiries to be carried out with the local police: IDI Oct 04, Ch 8, s 1, para 5.4.

[6]   IDI Oct 04, para 5.7.

[7]   IDI Oct 04, Ch 8, s 1, para 5.9. See also *Butler* (fn 1 above).

[8]   IDI Oct 04, Ch 8, s 1, para 5.8. The IDI provide that applications from long term overstayers who are unable to provide the evidence required should be refused; the implication is that even long term overstayers may be regularised on production of sufficient evidence.

ADMISSION OF UNMARRIED AND SAME-SEX PARTNERS

11.71 The Immigration Rules now make provision for the admission of people who are not married but have a permanent relationship.[1] The Rules replaced hard-won concessions concerning the admission of heterosexual cohabitees and same-sex partners, and were added in October 2000 to give effect to the right to family or private life under Article 8 of the ECHR.[2] The Rules allow for the admission of men and women aged 18 or over to join partners of the same or opposite sex aged 18 or over,[3] who are present and settled or being admitted for settlement in the UK,[4] or who are in the UK with limited leave for work, business or investment,[5] and with whom they have been living in a relationship akin to marriage for two years.[6] Short breaks apart would be acceptable for good reason, such as work commitments or looking after a relative which takes one partner away for a period of up to six months where it was not possible for the other partner to accompany him or her, and it can be seen that the relationship continued throughout that period.[7] The threshold cohabitation rule will not be satisfied by partners merely visiting each other as often as they can during the two years, but where they have been living together in a committed relationship for the two years (barring short breaks) but have divided their time between countries and have used the 'visitor' category to do this, this will be sufficient to meet the requirement.[8] Any previous marriage or similar relationship must have permanently broken down.[9] There is no longer any requirement that the parties are unable to marry, but they must not be involved in a consanguineous relationship.[10] They must intend to live together permanently[11] and be able to satisfy the maintenance and accommodation criteria.[12] On-entry applicants need entry clearance, just as spouses do.[13] Normally leave will be granted for a two-year probationary period, followed by settlement, if the relationship still subsists (see 11.72 below). But where an unmarried partner has lived abroad with their British citizen or settled partner for a period of four years, indefinite leave to enter will be granted straight away.[14] Applicants seeking to enter or remain as the partner of a person with limited leave for such purposes as work, business or investment must not intend to remain beyond the period of leave granted to their partner.[15] After-entry applicants (those switching from another category such as visitor or student) must not have remained in breach of the immigration laws, and the relationship must have pre-dated any enforcement action (decision to deport, recommendation for deportation or service of notice preparatory to recommendation, or directions for removal as an overstayer under section 10 of the Immigration and Asylum Act 1999).[16] We do not know if these rules will change when the Civil Partnership Act 2004 comes into force, but the provisions requiring registrars to notify the Secretary of State of suspected sham marriages are to apply to civil partnerships under that Act.[17] There is no policy for unmarried partners equivalent to DP3/96 (see 11.75 below), but a claim that a decision to remove constitutes an interference with private life rights under ECHR, Article 8 (for example, where homosexuality is illegal or socially unacceptable in the partner's country of nationality or residence, precluding the establishment of the couple there), could found an appeal on human rights grounds.[18]

1   HC 395, paras 295A–O, inserted by Cm 4851 on 2 October 2000.
2   See chapter 8 for cases on Art 8 in this context.
3   HC 395, para 295AA, inserted by HC 538 and amended by HC 164 from 21 December 2004.
4   HC 395, para 295A(i). A member of HM forces serving overseas, a permanent member of the diplomatic service or a UK-based staff member of the British Council on a tour of duty abroad, or a staff member of the Department for International Development who is a British citizen or settled in the UK, is to be regarded as 'present and settled' for this

purpose: para 295A as amended by Cm 5597. However, there is no provision as yet for the admission of unmarried partners of discharged Gurkhas or Commonwealth soldiers in HM Forces who are settled or admitted for settlement under HC 395, paras 276E–Q.

5 HC 395, para 295J, referring to partners present in the UK under HC 395, paras 128–193 (work permit and other employment), 200–239 (business, self-employment, investor, writer, composer or artist), or 263–270 (retired persons of independent means).

6 The policy formulated in October 1997 required four years' cohabitation as a threshold period, which made it very difficult for someone who began a relationship with a British citizen while here in a temporary capacity, eg as a student, to qualify. The minimum cohabitation period was reduced to two years as from 16 June 1999.

7 IDI May 03, Ch 8, s 7, Annex Z.

8 IDI May 03, Ch 8, s 7, Annex Z. Evidence of a committed relationship, such as joint commitments, correspondence or official records linking partners to the same address, or record of the births of children born to the relationship, will be required.

9 HC 395, paras 295A(ii), 295D (ii), and 295J(ii).

10 HC 395, paras 295A(iii), 295D(v), 295J(iii), inserted by Cm 5949. Para 295A(iv), which required inability to marry, was deleted by HC 538. The Rule gives statutory effect to the decision in *R v Secretary of State for the Home Department, ex p Ozminnos* [1994] Imm AR 287, QBD.

11 HC 395, paras 295A(vii), 295D(x); for those joining partners with limited leave to remain they must intend to live together during the partner's stay: para 295J(v).

12 HC 395, paras 295A(v) and (vi); 295D(viii) and (ix); and 295J(vi) and (vii).

13 HC 395, paras 295A(viii) and 295J(ix). In *R v an Immigration Officer, ex p Hashim* (CO 2052/1999) (12 June 2000, unreported), Jackson J quashed a refusal of leave to enter and a decision to remove the Malaysian homosexual partner of a British citizen who had no entry clearance, on the ground that the Home Office accepted that he fulfilled all the other requirements of the Immigration Rules and to require him to return to Malaysia served no useful purpose. The Court of Appeal disapproved this approach in *R (on the application of Mahmood) v Secretary of State for the Home Department* [2001] 1 WLR 840.

14 HC 395, para 295B as amended by HC 538 on 31 Mar 2003.

15 HC 395, para 295J(viii).

16 HC 395, para 295D(iv) and (vii).

17 Immigration and Asylum Act 1999, s 24A (not yet in force at the time of writing). It may be that the 'permission to marry' scheme referred to at 11.67 above will be extended to civil partnerships as well.

18 See chapter 8 above. The minister indicated in a written answer of 16 June 1999 that the arrangements for unmarried partners (then contained in a policy outside the rules) would be taken into account when deciding whether to initiate enforcement action (eg for overstaying); see *Butterworths Immigration Law Service* D[1031].

11.72 Leave to enter to join or accompany an unmarried partner settled in the UK, or leave to remain with such a partner, will normally be for two years in the first instance,[1] and indefinite leave may be granted at the end of the probationary period, provided the relationship is still subsisting, each of the parties intends to live permanently with the other as his or her partner and the maintenance and accommodation criteria are still met.[2] Indefinite leave may also be granted if the UK-settled partner dies during the probationary period and at the time of the death the relationship was subsisting and the parties intended to live together permanently.[3] The Rules as amended make it clear that for the purposes of admission of unmarried partners, a member of HM Forces serving overseas, a permanent member of HM Diplomatic Service or a comparable UK-based member of staff of the British Council on a tour of duty abroad or a staff member of the Department for International Development who is a British Citizen or is settled in the United Kingdom is to be regarded as present and settled in the UK. Unmarried partners may also benefit from the provisions of the rules relating to access to children,[4] and from the domestic violence rule, just like parties to a marriage.[5]

¹   HC 395, paras 295B, 295E (save for those referred to in 11.71, above who have been living together in a relationship outside the UK for four years or more, who will be granted indefinite leave to enter)
²   HC 395, paras 295G, 295H.
³   HC 395, paras 287(b) and 295M–295O, putting unmarried partners on a par with married couples.
⁴   HC 395, paras 246–248F, as amended by Cm 4851, see 11.76 below.
⁵   HC 395, para 289A; see 11.70 above.

11.73 Once settlement as a spouse or unmarried partner is achieved, readmission will be as a returning resident rather than a spouse, and thus subsequent marriage or relationship breakdown does not affect immigration status. However, if settlement has been obtained by means of a false representation made by the immigrant (for example as to the subsistence of the relationship), he or she may be subject to administrative removal.¹

¹   Immigration and Asylum Act 1999, s 10(1)(b), inserted by Nationality, Immigration and Asylum Act 2002, s 74. For details see 16.42 below.

MARRIAGE BY OVERSTAYERS AND ILLEGAL ENTRANTS

11.74 There remains the situation of those who marry or enter a relationship and one (or both) of the parties is or becomes liable to removal, because he or she is an overstayer or illegal entrant. As we have seen, the Immigration Rules provide that a person who entered in a temporary capacity and seeks leave to remain for marriage or to stay with a partner must be in the UK with limited leave and must not have remained in breach of the immigration laws.¹ Such persons may now not qualify for permission to marry in the UK.² However, to give effect to the UK's obligations under the ECHR,³ the Home Office has adopted policies to deal with these situations. Much time was spent in court debating the ambit and legality of the policy, DP 2/93, which operated between 1993 and 1996.⁴ This was replaced in 1996 by DP3/96, applying to marriages which came to the notice of the Home Office after 13 March 1996.⁵ The 1993 policy included common-law relationships,⁶ but they were expressly excluded from the 1996 policy.⁷ Neither policy dealt with same-sex relationships, which at that time were completely off the map. Under DP 3/96, which deals only with married couples, removal action will not normally be initiated if (a) the couple have been married and have cohabited for at least two years before the commencement of enforcement action and (b) it would be unreasonable to expect the settled spouse to accompany his or her spouse on removal.⁸ Although the policy uses the language of deportation to cover situations where administrative removal rather than deportation is now the order of the day, it still applies as before.⁹ It is not clear, however, whether, as in the case of children, these policies now apply to those who are neither illegal entrants nor overstayers, and whose marriage or cohabitation has occurred during temporary admission.¹⁰

¹   HC 395, para 284(i) and (iv) (spouses); 295D(iv), (vii) (unmarried partners).
²   See 11.67 above.
³   The policy was held to be compatible with ECHR, Art 8 in *Gangadeen v Secretary of State for the Home Department* sub nom *Khan v Secretary of State for the Home Department* [1998] Imm AR 106, CA.

4   Set out in *Butterworths Immigration Law Service* D[501]. See eg *R v Secretary of State for the Home Department, ex p Amankwah* [1994] Imm AR 240; *Lye v Secretary of State for the Home Department* [1994] Imm AR 63; *Secretary of State for the Home Department v Hastrup* [1996] Imm AR 616; *Mirza v Secretary of State for the Home Department* [1996] Imm AR 314.

5   Set out in *Butterworths Immigration Law Service* D[551]. Other policies published at about the same time dealt with children: see *Butterworths Immigration Law Service* D [600] and [601] and the Appendix to the judgments in *R (on the application of Dabrowski) v Secretary of State for the Home Department* [2003] EWCA Civ 580, [2003] INLR 411. See 11.122 below.

6   The instructions, DP2/93, provided that persons who had married or begun cohabitation with a partner before enforcement action began, and who had been married or cohabiting for two years before coming to attention, should not as a general rule be forced to leave the UK: *Butterworths Immigration Law Service* D[501], para 2.

7   Statement of policy made by former Home Office Minister of state, Mr Kirkhope, on 22 Feb 96, set out in *Butterworths Immigration Law Service* D[801].

8   DP3/96, set out in *Butterworths Immigration Law Service* D[551] para 5. 'Enforcement action' includes a specific instruction to leave with a warning of liability to deportation if the subject fails to do so, in addition to the service of a notice of intention to deport or illegal entry papers, or a recommendation for deportation: DP3/96, para 5.

9   See Appendix to judgements in *R (on the application of Dabrowski) v Secretary of State for the Home Department* [2003] EWCA Civ 580, [2003] INLR 411.

10   *Dabrowski* above at paras 12–17 (Sedley LJ) and para 28 (Laws LJ).

11.75   There may be cases in which a too-rigid application of the policy in DP 3/96 can give rise to a challenge using Article 8 of the ECHR. The exclusion of an unmarried or same sex partner who fulfilled policy criteria would almost certainly be held unlawful after the inclusion of unmarried and same sex partners into the Immigration Rules, especially in the light of Article 8 read with Article 14 ECHR.[1] A rigid insistence on marriage two years before enforcement action could be challengeable as a breach of Article 8, depending on the facts. However, when considering the impact of a marriage which took place before the commencement of enforcement action, it is a relevant question whether or not one spouse was aware that the immigration status of the other was precarious, since such knowledge militates against a finding that removal of the non-resident spouse violates Article 8.[2]

1   Further, the then Minister of State, Mike O'Brien, indicated in a written statement to parliament on 16 June 1999 that the then unmarried partners concession would be taken into account in the same way as the marriage policy in deciding whether to remove overstayers etc.

2   *R v (on the application of Mahmood) v Secretary of State for the Home Department* [2001] 1 WLR 840, CA, per Lord Phillips MR at paras 55 and 61, citing *Poku v United Kingdom* (1996) 22 EHRR CD 94.

ADMISSION OR STAY FOR THE PURPOSES OF CONTACT WITH RESIDENT CHILDREN

11.76   In 1994, the immigration rules made provision for the first time for parents to come to Britain for access visits to their UK resident children.[1] Although the rules were substantially amended and widened in October 2000 in order to ensure compliance with ECHR Article 8 obligations of respect for family life, as set out in the ECHR decision in *Berrehab*,[2] in one important respect the Rule was and is deficient. It provides for entry to a contact parent where the parent or carer with whom the child permanently resides is resident in the UK.[3] On the face of it, the rule appears not to afford entry where the applicant parent is the 'custodial' parent with whom the child permanently resides and that parent's entry and stay is designed to facilitate frequent contact between the British parent and the child. In our view, an interpretation that excluded entry or stay in such circumstances would be discriminatory and contrary to the ECHR jurisprudence the Rule is designed to incorporate.[4] Under the Rule entry is no longer confined to visits but could lead to settlement. Entry clearance is required for those already living abroad, but not for someone who still has leave to enter or remain as a spouse or unmarried partner but whose marriage or relationship has broken down.[5] The applicant must have a residence or contact order granting him or her access rights, or a certificate from a district judge confirming his or her intention to maintain contact with the child.[6] In the case of a variation application, the applicant may also provide a statement from the child's other parent or from a supervisor where access is supervised, confirming his or her intention to maintain contact with the child.[7] The applicant must intend in either case to take an active role in the child's upbringing [8] and satisfy the maintenance and accommodation requirements,[9] but the old prohibition on employment for this category has gone, and while leave is for 12 months in the first instance,[10] settlement in this category is now possible under the Immigration Rules,[11] provided the applicant has completed 12 months in this capacity, enjoys frequent and regular visiting or staying access[12] and continues to meet the other requirements of the Rules. In particular the parent must not have remained in breach of the immigration laws, either as an overstayer or illegal entrant. If applicants have done so, the Home Office will expect them to leave the UK and apply for entry clearance, in the absence of exceptional circumstances.[13] When deportation is being considered (on conducive grounds or after conviction of a criminal offence) the considerations of DP4/96[14] will continue to apply, since the effect of the order would be to prevent parental access in the UK for three years.

1   HC 395, paras 246–248, amended by Cm 4851 on 2 Oct 2000.
2   *Berrehab v Netherlands* (1988) 11 EHRR 322; see also *Ciliz v Netherlands* [2000] 2 FLR 469. Whether there is a breach of Art 8 of the ECHR will depend on the degree of contact between parent and child: see *Hlomodor v Secretary of State for the Home Department* [1993] Imm AR 534, CA above; *Lye v Secretary of State for the Home Department* [1994] Imm AR 63 and *R v Secretary of State for the Home Department, ex p Nijjar* [1994] Imm AR 50.
3   HC 395, para 246(ii).
4   See note 2 above.
5   HC 395, para 248A(vii), as amended. The rule does not require the relationship to have broken down, and would apply equally to an ongoing relationship which did not involve cohabitation by the parties.
6   HC 395, paras 246(iii) and 248A(iii).
7   HC 395, para 248(iii)(c). These provisions for consensual arrangements go some way to meeting the difficulties posed by the previous rule, which required a court order. In *R v Secretary of State for the Home Department, ex p Kebbeh* (CO 1269/98, 30 April 1998, unreported) a removal decision was quashed because, inter alia, it prevented the applicant obtaining the necessary order from the family court to enable him to comply with the rule.
8   HC 395, paras 246(iv) and 248A(iv).
9   HC 395, paras 246(ix), (x) and 248A(ix), (x).
10   HC 395, paras 247, 248B.
11   HC 395, paras 248D, 248E.
12   HC 395, para 248D(iii).

13 The combination of the much improved immigration rules and the abolition of deportation for overstayers by Immigration and Asylum Act 1999, s 10 (see chapter 15) means that any interruption of contact caused by the need to return for entry clearance is likely to be short and so (unless the child is very young or the delay disproportionate) compatible with Art 8 family life considerations.

14 DP4/96, *Butterworths Immigration Law Service* D[601], para 8, providing that 'it may be unreasonable to expect [the subject of a deportation order] to return abroad to apply for entry clearance ... in these cases it will be important to assess the quality and the regularity of access to the child in deciding how much weight should be attached to it as a compassionate factor'.

ADMISSION OF CHILDREN UNDER 18

Introduction

11.77 In this section we examine the rules relating to children under the age of 18 at the time of the application. The entry and stay of adult children is provided for in the immigration rules dealing with dependent relatives.[1] We examine in turn:

  (i)   children with the right of abode;

  (ii) the rules relating to children born in the UK who are not British citizens;

 (iii) the rules for admission of children born abroad who have at least one parent settled or intending to settle here;

  (iv) the sole responsibility and 'exclusion undesirable' rules;

  (v)   inter-country adoptions.

  (vi) unaccompanied minors

 (vii) removal of children.

1 HC 395, para 317: see 11.123ff below. Until 1994, unmarried dependent daughters between 18 and 21 could be admitted to join parents in the UK if they had been living as part of the family unit: HC 251, para 55. More generous age limits for children applied under the special voucher scheme, which has now been abolished. For details of the scheme see the 5th edition at 8.83 and *HG & RG* [2005] UKIAT 00062, *RM (Special Vouchers – representation) India* [2005] UKIAT 00067 'Reported'. For applicants who may still benefit from the under 12s concession withdrawn on 29 March 2003, see *KK (under 12 policy in-country) Jamaica* [2004] UKIAT 00268.

Meaning of 'parent'

11.78 HC 395 gave a new and more liberal definition of parent for the purpose of the application of the Immigration Rules generally. A 'parent' now includes both the mother and father of an illegitimate child if paternity is proved.[1] This contrasts with the position in British nationality law, where (until implementation of section 9 of the NIAA 2002) the father of an illegitimate child is still not able to pass on citizenship.[2] It is thus clear that, whatever the position in nationality law, illegitimate children will be treated the same as others for the purposes of all of the Immigration Rules, subject to proof of the relationship.[3]

1 HC 395, para 6.

2   British Nationality Act 1981, s 50(9). This has been substantially amended by NIAA 2002,
     s 9, but the provision is not in force at the time of writing. The Immigration and
     Nationality Directorate has a policy of discretionary registration of such children where
     there are no doubts as to paternity, no reasonable objection from either parent and no
     character objections: NI Ch 9, s 9. See 2.19, 2.52 (citizenship by descent), 2.42 (bar on
     British citizenship), 2.44 (no breach of Art 8 ECHR), 2.48 (discretion to register).
3   It was this factor which prevented the discrimination in nationality law from being held
     unlawful under Arts 8 and 14 of the ECHR in *R (on the application of Montana) v
     Secretary of State for the Home Department* [2001] 1 WLR 552, CA.

11.79 Other aspects of the definition of parent are more restrictive. First, the
previous rule is still retained whereby a step-parent will only qualify as a
parent when the natural parent whom the step-parent replaces is dead.[1]
Secondly, in the case of children born in the UK who are not British, 'parent' is
extended to mean a person to whom there has been a genuine transfer of
parental responsibility on the ground of the original parent or parents'
inability to care for the child.[2] This could include foster-parents, appointed by
local authorities for children in care, as well as other relatives. For the
purposes of all the rules, except those relating to children joining parents for
settlement, 'parent' includes an adoptive parent, but only where a child was
adopted in accordance with a decision taken by the competent administrative
authority or court in a country whose adoption orders are recognised by the
UK or is the subject of a *de facto* adoption which meets the requirements of
the relevant rule.[3] There are different hurdles to overcome to join adoptive
parents in the UK for settlement.[4] The rules have been amended to include *de
facto* adoptions in certain circumstances.[5] The rules also provide for a child to
come to the UK for the purpose of adoption.[6]

1   HC 395, para 6.
2   HC 395, para 6.
3   HC 395, para 6, as amended by HC 538. The requirements for recognition of a de facto
     adoption are dealt with at para 309A, as inserted.
4   HC 395, para 310(i)(a)–(g). See 11.99 below.
5   HC 395, paras 309A, 310(vi)(b), and see 11.112 below.
6   HC 395, paras 316A–F.

Disputes as to age or identity

11.80 The difficulties in establishing the relationship of parent and child have
been largely resolved by DNA testing,[1] although problems remain where the
parents are dead or a full blood comparison is not possible. Past disputed
relationships gave rise to the problem of re-applications by adult children who
were refused as minors, but later recognised as related as claimed to the parent
settled in the UK. The Immigration Rules make no provision for such cases,
and the policy outside the Rules is restrictive, requiring strong compassionate
circumstances and that the over-age child remains unmarried and fully
dependent on the UK parent.[2] The High Court held that the policy was not
unreasonable.[3] Other over-age applicants must comply with the dependent
relatives rules.[4] Another problem has arisen with children who are claimed as
the child of both parents, but after DNA analysis are discovered to be the
child of only one of them. In such cases admission should be possible under
either the 'exclusion undesirable' or '*de facto* adoption' rules, (see 11.94 and

11.112 below), particularly if the child has been brought up as a child of both parents. Evidence of age or relationship which was not available to the entry clearance officer has always been admissible on appeal, as it is not evidence of post-decision facts (which remains inadmissible in entry clearance appeals despite the liberalisation of the evidence requirements in relation to all other appeals),[5] but post-decision evidence of already existing facts.[6]

[1]   DNA Profiling in Immigration Casework: A Progress Report (February 1989) Home Office B2 Division where guidance for reliance on these tests is set out. Care is taken to prevent impersonation of donors. In 1990 the Government announced the scheme for publicly funded DNA-testing in cases of doubt; the costs were to be met by raising the fees for entry clearance applications: see HL Official Report (5th series) written answers col 55, 20 December 1990. See also Legal Action (December 1990) p 25. For the weight to be given to DNA tests see *Ali* (9717) (1993, unreported), IAT.

[2]   Ministerial statement, 14 June 1989. See *AA & NA (Concession on DNA testing) Bangladesh* [2004] UKIAT 00180.

[3]   *R v Immigration Appeal Tribunal, ex p Ali* [1990] Imm AR 531; *Miah (Hassan) v Secretary of State for the Home Department* [1991] Imm AR 437, CA. Depending on the circumstances, refusal of admission to an over-age child might be a breach of ECHR, Art 8.

[4]   HC 395, paras 317–319.

[5]   Nationality Immigration and Asylum Act 2002, s 85(4), (5). For the admission of evidence of post-decision facts in 2002 Act appeals see *DR (Entry Clearance Officer post decision evidence) Morocco* [2005] UKIAT 00038, *LS (post-decision evidence; direction; appealability) Gambia* [2005] UKAIT 00085 (19 April 2005, unreported). Evidence of post-decision facts is relevant only for the light it sheds on the position at the date of decision: *R v Secretary of State for the Home Department, ex p Hoque and Singh* [1988] Imm AR 216, CA.

[6]   *R v Immigration Appeal Tribunal, ex p Hassanin* [1987] 1 All ER 74, [1986] 1 WLR 1448, [1986] Imm AR 502; *R v Immigration Appeal Tribunal, ex p Nathwani* [1979–80] Imm AR 9; *R v Immigration Appeal Tribunal, ex p Kotecha* [1983] 1 WLR 487, [1982] Imm AR 88. See also *R v Immigration Appeal Tribunal, ex p Secretary of State for the Home Department* [1993] Imm AR 298, QBD, affirmed in the Court of Appeal under the name *Hussain (Dilowar and Iqbal) v Secretary of State for the Home Department* [1993] Imm AR 590. See 18.63 below.

11.81 Children will have to establish their age. The relevant age for the settlement rules is the age of the child when the application is made, rather than at the date of decision,[1] and entry clearance or leave to enter will not be refused merely because the child has become over-age since the application was made.[2] The child's date of birth will have to be established by reference to birth certificates, contemporaneous declarations, the date of marriage if applicable and return visits by sponsors or other credible testimony. Evidence obtained for the purpose of nullity and paternity proceedings is admissible in an immigration appeal if it was read into the record, unless the family court otherwise orders.[3] On age dispute questions in the context of asylum see 11.118 and 12.117 below.

[1]   HC 395, paras 27 and 321(ii). Equally a child who becomes over-age while the Home Office or the appellate authority is considering the application is not disadvantaged: para 298(i); *Mahmood (Fazal)* [1979–80] Imm AR 71n. A person admitted with a view to settlement will still be able to obtain indefinite leave to remain after entry despite becoming over age: see para 298(ii); but a child who enters in some other capacity and then seeks indefinite leave to remain as a dependent child must apply before his or her 18th birthday in order to comply with the Immigration Rules. Note that the relevant age for children accompanying or joining parents for purposes other than settlement is the age at the date of the decision: para 27. See also IDI Aug 03, Ch 8, s 3, Annex M.

2   HC 395, paras 27, 321(ii). An application is only made when any fee payable in respect of a specific application is paid: HC 395, para 30, reversing *Entry Clearance Officer, Port Louis v Ross* [1992] Imm AR 493. For the previous decisions on what is an application see also *Brown v Entry Clearance Officer, Kingston* [1976] Imm AR 119; *Prajapati v Immigration Appeal Tribunal* [1981] Imm AR 199, QBD; affd [1982] Imm AR 56, CA; *Soyemi v Secretary of State for the Home Department* [1990] Imm AR 564, IAT.
3   *Hussein* (R 15512) 29 August 1997; CPR 32.12.

Children with the right of abode

11.82 A child who has the right of abode must prove it by production of either a British passport or a certificate of entitlement.[1] On proof of the right of abode, such a child does not require leave to enter and is dealt with in the same way as any other British citizen. The child will acquire the right of abode if, after 1 January 1983, he or she has been registered as a British citizen, or was born in the UK to a parent who was settled in the UK at the time of birth; or was born abroad to a parent who was a British citizen otherwise than by descent, at the time of birth.

1   Immigration Act 1971, s 3(9). Without such documents the child may be unable to board an airline to get to the UK, or (if refused leave to enter on arrival) appeal before removal save on human rights grounds: see Nationality, Immigration and Asylum Act 2002, s 88(2), (6). See also *R v Secretary of State for the Home Department, ex p Bibi (Shorzan)* [1987] Imm AR 213. There is a right of appeal against a refusal of a certificate of entitlement: Nationality, Immigration and Asylum Act 2002, s 82(1), (2)(c).

Non-British children born in the UK

11.83 It has already been noted that children born in the UK after 1 January 1983 will not become British citizens by birth in the UK if neither parent was a British citizen or settled in the UK.[1] A child who remains in the UK continuously for the first ten years of his or her life (with limited provisions for short absences abroad) is entitled to registration as a British citizen.[2] A child under 18, one of whose parents becomes settled or acquires British nationality, will also be entitled to register as a British citizen.[3] Special immigration rules apply to children born in the UK after 1 January 1983 who do not become British citizens.[4] While they remain in the UK without leaving, they do not need leave to remain. Obtaining leave to remain is therefore optional, but advisable if it is expected that the child will travel and seek re-admission, when leave to enter will be required.[5]

1   British Nationality Act 1981, s 1(1). See 2.44 above.
2   BNA 1981, s 1(4).
3   BNA 1981, s 1(3).
4   HC 395, paras 304–309.
5   HC 395, para 304.

11.84 The Immigration Rules lay down similar requirements for non-British children born in the UK seeking leave to enter and leave to remain. Such children must be born in the UK, under 18, unmarried, not leading an independent life or having formed an independent family unit, and must not have been away from the UK for more than two years.[1] If the child is accompanied by or seeking to join a parent with limited leave, leave to enter is given for the same period as that of the parents, or the longer of the two periods if each parent has a different period of leave, save where the parents are separated, in which case leave is given for the same period as the parent who has day-to-day control.[2] If neither of the parents has a current leave, leave to enter or remain will normally be refused, unless it is unlikely that the parents will be removed in the immediate future and there is no other person outside the UK who could reasonably be expected to care for the child.[3] In such cases, three months' leave to enter may be given. If one of the parents is a British citizen or if the parental rights and duties in respect of the child are vested in a local authority, indefinite leave to enter or remain may be given.[4]

[1]   HC 395, para 305(ii)–(v).
[2]   HC 395, paras 305(i)(a) and 306.
[3]   HC 395, para 307.
[4]   HC 395, paras 305(i)(b) and (c) and 308.

11.85 The distinguishing feature of the Immigration Rules for these children compared with those applying to other children is that, provided they return to the UK within two years of leaving, they do not have to satisfy the normal requirements as regards maintenance, accommodation or the presence in the UK of both parents. They can obtain prior entry clearance, but do not have to do so, unless they are visa nationals. Children who return after an absence of over two years have to qualify under the ordinary rules, either as dependent children or in some other capacity, such as students.

Children under 18 with UK-settled parent, parents or relative

11.86 The Immigration Rules limit family reunion rights. Children who have no right of abode and were not born in the UK, who are seeking to enter or remain with a UK-settled parent, parents or a relative, must be under 18 at the date of application, unmarried, not leading an independent life[1] or part of an independent family unit,[2] but dependent on the parent, parents or relative in the UK,[3] and capable of being supported and accommodated by them without recourse to public funds.[4] A distinction is then drawn between children both of whose parents (or in the case of death, the surviving parent) live in the UK, and those who have only one such parent or are seeking to join a relative other than a parent.

[1]   The IDI indicate that the child should be unmarried and not be in or have previously formed a relationship equivalent to marriage, still living with parents and siblings unless at boarding school, and should not be employed full-time or for a significant number of hours per week, excluding Saturday and holiday jobs: IDI Aug 03, Ch 8, Annex M, para 3. But in *Luchow* (2004 unreported) the Tribunal accepted that a 17-year-old who had moved away from the family home to study, was staying with relatives and remained financially dependent on the sponsor, was not leading an independent life.
[2]   The IDI interpret this as not currently being in or having previously formed a relationship with another person (such as a common-law or homosexual relationship) which could be said to be the equivalent of being married, except for name and legal recognition: IDI Aug 03, Ch 8, Annex M, para 3. In *Tabassum v Entry Clearance Officer, Karachi* [2002] UKIAT 03749, siblings some of whom worked to support the others were held to be in an 'independent family unit'.

³   For both financial and emotional support, according to IDI Aug 03, Ch 8, Annex M,
    para 3.
⁴   HC 395, para 297(ii)–(vi). See 11.53–11.58 above for a discussion of the maintenance and
    accommodation requirements.

11.87 Children, both of whose natural parents are settled in the UK, and who
can comply with the general conditions, qualify for entry clearance, which will
operate as indefinite leave to enter¹ unless on arrival in the UK it transpires
there has been a change of circumstances since issue. The fact that a child has
become over 18 since the issue of the entry clearance does not constitute such
a change.² The same is true if both parents are being admitted for settlement
in the UK at the same time as the child,³ or one is coming to join the other,⁴ or
one natural parent is settled or will be admitted for settlement and the other
parent (including a parent of an illegitimate child) is dead.⁵ Where one natural
parent has died and the other parent has remarried, then the step-parent must
be settled or admitted for settlement as well as the natural parent,⁶ although
the relationship of step-parent would terminate on divorce of the parties. The
Immigration Rules are the same for adoptive children where the qualifying
conditions for adoption are met.⁷ A child who enters in some other capacity,
for example as a visitor or student, qualifies for the grant of indefinite leave to
remain if the same conditions are met after entry, including the fact that he or
she is under 18 at the time of application.⁸

¹   HC 395, paras 297(i)(a) and 299; Immigration (Leave to Enter and Remain) Order 2000,
    SI 2000/1161, Arts 2 and 3.
²   HC 395, para 321(ii).
³   HC 395, para 297(i)(b).
⁴   HC 395, para 297(i)(c).
⁵   HC 395, para 297(i)(d).
⁶   HC 395, para 6 (definition of parent); see also *Alam (Manzar) v Entry Clearance Officer,
    Lahore* [1973] Imm AR 79 and *McGillivary v Secretary of State for the Home Department*
    [1972] Imm AR 63.
⁷   HC 395, para 6 (definition of parent), and for adoptions not falling within that paragraph,
    paras 310 and 311. See below 11.99ff for detailed consideration of adopted children.
⁸   HC 395, para 298.

11.88 Where one parent is settled and the other parent is given a limited leave
to enter with a view to subsequent settlement, the child is given the same leave
as the non-settled parent¹ and must apply for indefinite leave at the same time
as that parent.² The fact that a child has become over 18 since arrival in the
UK does not matter if the child was previously admitted by the immigration
service with a view to settlement.³

¹   HC 395, para 302.
²   HC 395, para 298.
³   HC 395, para 298(ii)(b).

The sole responsibility rule

11.89 Where one parent (including a step-parent where a natural parent is
dead) is settled in the UK and the other parent is alive and is not coming to the
UK for settlement, their child applicant seeking entry clearance for settlement
generally must satisfy the entry clearance officer that the parent in the UK has

had sole responsibility for the child.[1] The same requirement must be satisfied where indefinite leave to remain is sought after entry in another capacity.[2] The phrase is intended to reflect a situation where the chief parental responsibility for the child's upbringing rests to all intents and purposes with one parent. The parent claiming sole responsibility must satisfactorily demonstrate that he or she has been the person exercising primary responsibility.[3] Where the sole responsibility test is not met, then the child may still qualify under the 'exclusion undesirable' rule considered below, which also permits a child to join a relative other than a parent settled here.[4]

1   HC 395, para 297(i)(e).
2   HC 395, para 298(i)(c).
3   IDI Aug 03, Ch 8, Annex M, para 4.1 (note the IDI states 'usually for a substantial period of time'; however see *Nmaju v Immigration Appeal Tribunal* [2001] INLR 26, CA; *Qui Zou* [2002] UKIAT 07463.
4   HC 395, paras 297(i)(f), 298(i)(d).

11.90 In any case where a parent comes to the UK and leaves the child behind, the person who is looking after the child clearly has some responsibility for the child's upbringing. A literal interpretation of 'sole responsibility' would defeat all claims. This was recognised in *Emmanuel v Secretary of State for the Home Department*[1] where the Tribunal found that literal or absolute sole responsibility of the parent in the UK could never be established and there must be, in nearly all such cases, some form of responsibility of the relative with whom the child lives. This does not prevent the parent in the UK having 'sole responsibility'. Sole responsibility is not the same as legal custody. The IDI state that where a residence order has been made (or a custody order exists)[2] giving responsibility for the child to the parent who is settled in the UK or being admitted for settlement, this should normally be accepted as evidence that the 'sole responsibility' requirement is met.[3] In *Nmaju*[4] the Court of Appeal stated that a parent's legal responsibility for the child under the appropriate legal system would be a relevant consideration in deciding sole responsibility, but would not be conclusive. It is necessary to look at what actually was done in relation to the child's upbringing, by whom and whether it had been done under the direction of the parent settled here. In *Sloley v Entry Clearance Officer, Kingston Jamaica*[5] the mother left her son with her mother but had sole financial responsibility and had been continuously consulted about the child's schooling, upbringing and activities. In holding that she had had sole responsibility, the Tribunal considered as relevant, inter alia, the source and degree of financial support of the child and whether there was cogent evidence of genuine interest in and affection for the child by the sponsoring parent in the UK. Where responsibility has not been delegated to a grandmother or other relative who is looking after the child, but has been abdicated, then the parent in the UK will not be treated as having sole responsibility.[6] A proper delegation involves a continuing financial and emotional commitment to the child.

1   [1972] Imm AR 69.
2   Under the Children Act 1989 custody orders have been replaced by residence orders. The Child Abduction and Custody Act 1985 makes provision for certain overseas custody orders to be recognised under UK law, provided they have been registered with the court. A list of countries whose 'custody' orders are recognised is contained in IDI Aug 03, Ch 8, s 3, Annex M, para 4.5.

3   IDI Aug 03, Ch 8, s 3, Annex M, para 4.4.
4   *Nmaju v Immigration Appeal Tribunal* [2001] INLR 26, CA. See also *Qui Zou* [2002] UKIAT 07463.
5   [1973] Imm AR 54.
6   *Martin v Secretary of State for the Home Department* [1972] Imm AR 71; *McGillivary v Secretary of State for the Home Department* [1972] Imm AR 63. In *Cenir v Entry Clearance Officer* [2003] EWCA Civ 572, [2003] All ER (D) 286 (Mar), the court stressed the importance of the parent with responsibility, albeit at a distance, having direction over or control of important decisions in the child's life.

11.91 The IDI[1] suggest that the following factors should be considered where the issue is not clear:

(i)   the period for which the parent in the UK has been separated from the child;

(ii)   what the arrangements were for the care of the child before that parent migrated to the UK;

(iii) who has been entrusted with day-to-day care and control of the child since the sponsor migrated here;

(iv)   who provides the financial support for the child's care and upbringing and in what proportion;

(v)   who takes the important decisions about the child's upbringing, such as where and with whom the child lives, the choice of school, religious practice, etc;

(vi)   the degree of contact that has been maintained between the child and the parent claiming responsibility; and

(vii) what part in the child's care and upbringing is played by the parent not in the UK and relatives.[2]

The courts have acknowledged as aspects of parental responsibility: determining and fostering the child's religion; determining and encouraging the child's education; consenting to the child's medical treatment; representing and assisting the child with respect to legal proceedings and agreeing to their interview; lawfully correcting a child; arranging the child's residence and emigration; protecting and maintaining a child and having contact with a child.[3]

1   IDI Aug 03, Ch 8 s 3, Annex M, para 4.3.
2   In *Dilliogu* (14045) IAS 1997, Vol 3, No 13, the Tribunal held that the adjudicator was entitled to take into account post-decision facts on these issues lending support to the finding of assumption of responsibility.
3   Hershman and McFarlane *Children Law and Practice*, vol 1 A[4].

11.92 In *Uddin*[1] the High Court stated that the sponsor did not need to have had responsibility for the upbringing of the child for the whole of his or her life, but for a 'not insubstantial period'. In *Nmaju*[2] the Court of Appeal deprecated the Tribunal's attempt to treat the phrase 'a not insubstantial period' as though it were incorporated into the Immigration Rules; time was a relevant, but not conclusive, factor. In that case it upheld the claim of a mother who had had the sole responsibility for her child for two-and-a-half months.

1   *R v Immigration Appeal Tribunal, ex p Uddin* [1986] Imm AR 203, QBD.
2   *Nmaju v Immigration Appeal Tribunal* [2001] INLR 26, CA. See 11.90 above.

11.93 Construing the meaning in the context of the Immigration Rules as a whole, it might be thought that the word 'sole' refers only to responsibility as between the two parents. It is irrelevant if a child has been left with grandparents during its formative years, if both parents are settled in the UK, so why should a child be disqualified merely because only one parent is so settled? But the Tribunal, the High Court and the Court of Appeal have endorsed the practice of having regard to persons other than parents with whom responsibility could be shared.[1] However, if the child has been living abroad with the other parent, or that parent's relatives, it will be more difficult to establish that the UK-settled parent had sole responsibility than if the child has been living with a relative of the UK-settled parent.[2] In earlier decisions it had been held that daily attention and care by the other natural parent would be fatal to the application of this rule, even though it may have been intermittent and insubstantial.[3] However, this is no longer the case. To disqualify a child for admission, the other parent's involvement needs to have amounted to an independent exercise of responsibility.[4] Certainly distant past responsibility by the other parent should not render the sponsoring parent's responsibility other than sole.[5]

[1] *R v Immigration Appeal Tribunal, ex p Mahmood* [1988] Imm AR 121, QBD; *Ramos v Immigration Appeal Tribunal* [1989] Imm AR 148, CA.
[2] IDI Aug 03, Ch 8, s 3, Annex M, para 4.1 and 4.2. Where two foreign nationals separate and the child remains with the parent abroad for several years and then wishes to join the UK parent to take advantage of the educational system, there is no reason why the child should not remain with the parent abroad, and the UK parent would not be considered to have sole responsibility.
[3] *Secretary of State for the Home Department v Pusey* [1972] Imm AR 240; see also *Eugene v Entry Clearance Officer* [1975] Imm AR 111.
[4] *Nmaju v Immigration Appeal Tribunal*, 11.89 fn 3 above; *Entry Clearance Officer, Manila v Acheampong* [2002] UKIAT 06687; *Qui Zou* [2002] UKIAT 07463. See also *Alagon* [1993] Imm AR 336 CS, Lord Prosser.
[5] See *Emmanuel v Secretary of State for the Home Department* [1972] Imm AR 69, EAT; *Rudolph v Entry Clearance Officer, Columbo* [1984] Imm AR 84.

The rule that family or other considerations make exclusion undesirable

11.94 Children who fail to qualify under the sole responsibility rule may qualify on the grounds that there are serious and compelling family or other reasons which make their exclusion from the UK undesirable and arrangements have been made for their care.[1] This rule permits such children to join either a parent or a relative other than a parent. 'Relative' is not defined and may be given a broad definition of those related by blood or marriage, including fairly distant relatives. It might include legal guardians.[2]

[1] HC 395, paras 297(i)(f) and 298(i)(d). Where a child is shown by DNA tests to be the child of only one of its claimed parents, he or she may nevertheless qualify under this paragraph: *R v Immigration Appeal Tribunal, ex p Ali (Iqbal)* [1994] Imm AR 295, CA. For the jurisdiction of the Tribunal to entertain a child's application under a different rule than first identified see *Hussain (Shabir) v Entry Clearance Officer, Islamabad* [1991] Imm AR 483. See 18.56 below.
[2] *Shamsuddin* (5366) IAT. HC 395, para 320(16) makes reference to legal guardians of children under 18.

11.95 The Immigration Rules make it clear that if family or other considerations are to make exclusion undesirable, they must be of a serious and compelling nature. The Rules do not amplify this expression, unlike earlier rules, which gave the example of the other parent's incapacity (physical or mental) to care for the child.[1] The IDI state that where the UK sponsor is a UK-settled parent, the circumstances may relate to the child or the parent, but where the sponsor is not settled or is not a parent, the factors to be considered must relate only to the child.[2] This test is harsher than Tribunal case law, which made no distinction between parents and others in considering the circumstances of the UK sponsor. In *Saluguo*[3] the fact that the child was living comfortably with her aunt and siblings in the Philippines was outweighed by the fact that her mother, a Filipina domestic worker who had worked under poor conditions for a number of years to provide her children with financial security and an education, had a strong desire to bring her youngest child to the UK.

[1]   HC 251, para 53(f).
[2]   IDI Aug 03, Ch 8, s 3, Annex M, para 1. It is questionable whether the attempt by the IND to limit those who may qualify under the rule is lawful.
[3]   *Saluguo* (18815). See also *WAAW (Somalia)* [2003] UKIAT 00174.

11.96 In *Secretary of State for the Home Department v Campbell*[1] it was said that when considering family or other considerations, the conditions under which the child is living in the home country are not to be weighed against the conditions available for the child in the UK. Conditions in this country are only to be considered if conditions in the overseas country show that exclusion is undesirable. In *Entry Clearance Officer, Kingston v Holmes*[2] these tests were satisfied where the child was living in poverty and overcrowded conditions and, importantly, her mother who had been looking after her was about to emigrate to Canada and would not be able to take the child with her. The Tribunal has also considered the death of the carer as being capable of amounting to a compelling and compassionate circumstance. The fact that there are far worse conditions elsewhere in the country is not relevant. Bad conditions are not made better by the existence of worse ones. However, it has also been held that if there is overcrowding it must be shown to be unavoidable.[3] Poverty on its own and unemployment are not enough[4] and the earning potential of the applicant child may be taken into account to relieve temporary difficulties.[5] Initially, the Tribunal set a high standard of 'intolerable' conditions[6] but in *Rudolph v Entry Clearance Officer, Columbo*[7] the Tribunal rejected the 'intolerable conditions' test, pointing out that the underlying purpose of the Immigration Rules is to unite families and not divide them and holding that where a father was incapable of caring for a child, that in itself would be grounds for deeming exclusion undesirable. In *Awuko*[8] a father's failure to care for a child was held to be evidence of his incapacity to do so. Voluntary abandonment may make the circumstances compelling.[9] Relevant factors to be weighed may include the willingness and ability of the overseas adult to look after the child; the living conditions available for the child, although to be able to qualify it is not necessary that these be shown to be intolerable; the greater vulnerability of small children; and the importance of family unity.[10] Contact with a parent overseas which is undesirable may be sufficient to render exclusion of the child from the UK undesirable.[11]

1   [1972] Imm AR 115.
2   [1975] Imm AR 20.
3   *Pinnock v Entry Clearance Officer, Kingston, Jamaica* [1974] Imm AR 22.
4   *Williams v Secretary of State for the Home Department* [1972] Imm AR 207.
5   *Needham v Entry Clearance Officer, Kingston* [1973] Imm AR 75.
6   *Howard v Secretary of State for the Home Department* [1972] Imm AR 93.
7   [1984] Imm AR 84.
8   *Awuko* (4220).
9   *Caballero* (4605); *Darko* (4697); *Anoth* (5954), *Haughton* (4889). This rule, unlike certain of the adoption rules, does not require inability to care for the child on the part of the parent or carer abroad, cf *Sharma v Entry Clearance Officer, New Delhi* [2005] EWCA Civ 89.
10 *Hardwood* (00TH01522), IAT unreported.
11 *Atenaga* (15932). See also *Buendia* (9488).

The 'under 12 concession'

11.97 The Home Office used to have a concession whereby, where the child seeking to join the UK single parent was under 12 but the sole responsibility rule was not satisfied, entry clearance for settlement was granted on a concessionary basis if there was adequate accommodation.[1] The IDI on this 'under 12s concession' stated that it might be appropriate to withhold the concession where the UK parent was so handicapped, according to professionally confirmed evidence, as to be incapable of properly caring for the child; or where there were older siblings, or if it was being used to get round the prohibition on the entry of certain children of polygamous marriages.[2] Unfortunately this useful concession was abolished on 29 March 2003. Applications after that date are not being accepted.[3] There will be cases in the appeal system where the policy remains applicable.[4]

1   IDI Dec 00, Ch 8, Annex M, para 12. In *Alecia* (15337) IAS 1998, Vol 1, No 14, the Tribunal held that the concession had discretionary elements and the adjudicator could not substitute his or her own discretion to allow an appeal outright. Since 2 October 2000 this restriction would not apply in a case such as this in relation to ECHR, Art 8 issues, where these are engaged.
2   IDI Dec 00, Ch 8, Annex M, para 12, The detailed guidance for the admission of children with older siblings provided that the numbers of children either side of the dividing line would be relevant, as would whether or not the children have been living together as a group, the arrangements for the care of the children in the UK and the hardship caused by leaving an older sibling alone at home. See on the reunion of separated siblings *Sen v Netherlands* (2003) 36 EHRR 7, ECtHR.
3   IDI Aug 03, Ch 8, s 3, Annex M.
4   *KK (under 12 policy in-country applications) Jamaica* [2004] UKIAT 00268.

Children of fiancé(e)s

11.98 The Immigration Rules were amended in October 2000 to provide for the admission of children of fiancé(e)s.[1] Such children will be granted limited leave to enter if they are accompanying or joining a person who is being or has been admitted in that capacity[2] if: they are under 18, unmarried and not leading an independent life;[3] they can be maintained and accommodated adequately with their parent; there are serious and compelling family or other considerations making their exclusion undesirable; suitable arrangements have been made for their care in the UK; and there is no one outside the UK who could reasonably be expected to care for them.[4] They must have entry clearance.[5]

1   HC 395, para 303A–F.
2   HC 395, para 303A(i).
3   HC 395, para 303A(ii) and (iii). See 11.86 above.
4   HC 395, para 303A(v).
5   HC 395, para 303A(vi).

INTER-COUNTRY ADOPTION

11.99 An inter-country adoption is one in which the prospective adoptive parent does not have the same nationality and/or habitual residence as the child he or she wishes to adopt. Such adoptions can involve a British citizen or person resident here who wishes to adopt a child who is a national of and resident in another country or citizens of another country who want to adopt a child who is, for example, a British citizen or a foreign national resident in the UK. These adoptions often involve the birth relatives of the children. Inter-country adoptions in Britain generally occur when relatives seek to assume responsibility for children after the death of the child's British parents, or the child's reception into local authority care. Until relatively recently inter-country adoptions were not subject to internationally agreed standards or procedures, and the children being adopted were vulnerable to exploitation and even trafficking for gain. This led to the formulation of the Hague Convention on Protection of Children and Co-operation in Respect of Intercountry Adoption (the Convention).[1] The United Kingdom ratified the Convention on 1 June 2003 and its provisions were extended to the Isle of Man on 1 November 2003. It has now come into force in 45 other states,[2] and five others have signed but not yet ratified it.[3] The Convention has three important objectives. It seeks to establish safeguards to ensure that inter-country adoptions take place in the best interests of the child and with respect for his or her fundamental rights. It aims to establish a system of co-operation amongst Contracting States to ensure that those safeguards are respected and the abduction, sale or trafficking of children for adoption prevented. Finally, it enables Contracting States to recognise adoptions made in other Contracting States, so preventing the need for children to be adopted for a second time in the receiving state. Inter-country adoptions involve the consideration of domestic and private international family law as well as immigration law. These principles and the associated arrangements to enforce them have become a feature of Convention and non-Convention inter-country adoptions in the UK.

1   The Convention was concluded on 29 May 1993 and its text can be found in Sch 1 to the Adoption (Intercountry Aspects) Act 1999.
2   These are Albania, Australia, Austria, Belarus, Brazil, Bulgaria, Canada, Chile, Cyprus, Czech Republic, Denmark, Estonia, Finland, France, Georgia, Germany, Hungary, Iceland, India, Israel, Italy, Latvia, Lithuania, Luxembourg, Malta, Mexico, Monaco, Netherlands, New Zealand, Norway, Panama, Peru, Poland, Portugal, Romania, Slovak Republic, Slovenia, South Africa, Spain, Sri Lanka, Sweden, Switzerland, Turkey, Uruguay and Venezuela. The Convention website regularly updates the list of states which have ratified the Convention. This is the position as at April 2005.
3   United States of America, Ireland, Belgium, Russian Federation and China.

11.100 The Adoption (Intercountry Aspects) Act 1999 was passed in order to give effect to the Convention in domestic law. The main provisions of the Act came into force on 1 June 2003, when the United Kingdom ratified the Convention. Local authorities are now obliged to provide home study reports for the purposes of an inter-country adoption.[1] It is also now a criminal offence for anyone but a local authority or a designated Voluntary Adoption Agency[2] to provide a home study report for an inter-country adoption.[3] The dangers posed to children by unscrupulous 'independent social workers' were exemplified in the case of *Re M (Adoption: International Adoption Trade)*[4] in which a private home study report did not reflect the true reality of the family into which the child was to be adopted or the fact that a child already in the family had been on the Child Protection Register and the mother had not been found suitable to be an adopter by either her local authority or Barnardos. Anyone wanting to adopt a child from abroad in the United Kingdom now has to obtain an official home study report and a Certificate of Eligibility and Suitability from the Secretary of State for Education and Skills before he or she brings the child to the United Kingdom.[5] When the child arrives in the United Kingdom, the prospective adopter must inform his or her local authority within 14 days of the child's arrival.[6] The Adoption and Children Act 2002, which was passed in November 2002, will reform domestic adoption law when it comes into force in its entirety. It incorporates much of the Adoption (Intercountry Aspects) Act 1999 and will replace much of the Adoption Act 1976.[7]

1   Adoption (Intercountry Aspects) Act 1999, ss 9,13.
2   As at 1 September 2004 these were Childlink, The Doncaster Adoption and Family Welfare Society Ltd, Norwood Jewish Adoption Society, Parents and Children Together, Nugent Care Society and SSAFA Forces Help.
3   Adoption (Intercountry Aspects) Act 1999, s 14, Adoption and Children Act 2002, s 94.
4   [2003] EWHC 219 (Fam), [2003] 3 FCR 193. See also Introduction to Department of Education and Skills, *Consultation on Draft Adoption Regulations* and *Guidance on Adoption Reports and Adoptions with a Foreign Element* (January 2004).
5   Adoption (Intercountry Aspects) Act 1999, s 14, the Intercountry Adoption (Hague Convention) Regulations 2003, SI 2003/118, para 3.
6   Adoption (Intercountry Aspects) Act 1999, s 14, the Intercountry Adoption (Hague Convention) Regulations 2003, SI 2003/118, para 15, Adoption (Bringing Children into the United Kingdom) Regualtions 2003 para 5. See on procedures for intercountry adoptions, Department of Health, Intercountry Adoption Guide, 24 May 2003.
7   The only sections of the Adoption (Intercountry Aspects) Act 1999 which will remain in force will be ss 1 and 2 which enabled the United Kingdom to ratify the Convention, s 7 which amended the British Nationality Act 1981, and Sch 1. Until the Adoption and Children Act is in force, inter-country adoption will be regulated by the Adoption (Intercountry Aspects) Act 1999. The government intends the 2002 Act to be fully in force by 30 December 2005. For adoption information see the government adoption site http://www.dfes.gov.uk/adoption/.

11.101 There are now seven different types of adoption, which may or will have inter-country aspects. These are: (i) a Convention adoption made in a court in the United Kingdom;(ii) a non-Convention adoption for a foreign child made by a court in the UK; (iii) a Convention adoption made in a court abroad in a country which has ratified the Hague Convention 1993 ;(iv) an overseas adoption in a country designated by the Secretary of State for the Home Department under the Adoptions (Designation of Overseas Adoptions) Order 1973; (v) a legal adoption in a non-designated country; (vi) a *de facto* adoption and (vii) an overseas adoption recognised at common law. It is important to understand the distinctions between these different types of adoptions. Adopters and prospective adopters may need advice concerning the legality and effect of an adoption that they have already undertaken or on the procedures they must follow in order to adopt a foreign child in the UK or abroad. All such adoptions require consideration of the adopter's capacity to adopt here and/or abroad. Depending on the law in the adopting and reception countries, the adopters may need to establish domicile, habitual or a specified term of residence or to have particular religious beliefs to obtain a legal adoption.[1] Some countries do not have formal adoption laws and any transfer of parental responsibility will be informal or *de facto*.[2] Those who have adopted or are considering an adoption need to know the validity and effect of their adoption in family and immigration law as well as the nationality consequences for the children. As the text below makes clear, certain children adopted informally whose adoptions are not valid or recognised as legal adoptions in the UK may nevertheless qualify for entry under the Immigration Rules. On the other hand children whose adoption is legal or capable of legal recognition in the UK may not qualify for entry as adopted children. In this complex area of law and practice, advisers need to be aware of both adoption and immigration law requirements.

[1]   On habitual residence see 11.14 fn 1 above, and 13.23 below, and on domicile 11.24–11.31 above. Several of the overseas adoptions which feature in immigration law are made in India. Persons who are British citizens or residents may have the capacity to obtain a legal adoption in India because the Hindu Adoptions and Maintenance Act 1956, ss 6–8 simply requires adults of sound mind to be Hindu.

[2]   See 11.112 below.

Convention adoption abroad

11.102 A British citizen or resident who has the legal capacity (that is, as noted above, the required domicile, residence or religion) to secure a Convention adoption abroad will have to meet certain British legal requirements for the Convention adoption before making that application abroad. The requirements comprise the assessment and home study obligations necessary for all Convention adoptions.[1] The adopter's first step is to apply to an adoption agency for a determination of eligibility, and an assessment of his/her suitability, to adopt.[2] The adoption agency, which will be a local authority or a designated Voluntary Adoption Agency,[3] will then undertake a home study report and consider whether the adopters are suited to adopting a child from abroad. Police checks[4] and medical reports are required. If the adoption agency considers that the adopters are suitable a report is presented to an Adoptions Panel,[5] which considers the report, can investigate further and can recommend or decline to approve the adopters and adoption arrangements. The adoption agency must have regard to the panel recommendation in making the final decision whether to approve or decline to approve the adopters.[6] The adoption agency is required to send notification of approvals and its reports to the Department of Health which will issue a Certificate of Eligibility and Suitability confirming that the prospective adopter has been assessed, approved as suitable to be an adoptive parent, is eligible to adopt, and that the child will be authorised to enter and reside permanently in the

United Kingdom if entry clearance and leave to enter or remain is granted and not revoked or curtailed and a Convention adoption order or Convention adoption is made.[7] The Department of Health is the British Central Authority responsible under the Convention for coordinating and supervising Convention adoption arrangements. The adopter's eligibility certificate is forwarded in turn to the Central Agency responsible for Convention adoptions in the child's home country, where it forms part of the evidence in the Convention adoption proceedings.[8] Where a child has been adopted overseas by means of a Convention adoption by an individual who is, or a married couple who are habitually resident in the United Kingdom,[9] there is no need for the child to be adopted again in the United Kingdom, as the overseas Convention adoption is recognised in the UK.[10] If the adopter or, in the case of a joint adoption, one of the adopters is a British citizen and the adopter, or if joint, both adopters are habitually resident in the UK, there is also no need for the child to apply for leave to enter the United Kingdom. The child adopted abroad via a Convention adoption will have acquired British citizenship by virtue of the Convention adoption[11] and the adoptive parents can apply for the child to be issued with a British passport at the appropriate post abroad. If neither parent is British but they are settled in the United Kingdom or if the parent(s) are British but not habitually resident here, the adopted child will have to qualify for leave to enter as their child under the Immigration Rules.[12]

[1] See The Intercountry Adoption (Hague Convention) Regulations 2003, SI 2003/118 which set out the requirements, procedure, recognition and effect of Convention adoptions where the UK is the receiving state or state of origin for the adopted child.
[2] SI 2003/118, reg 3. In order to be eligible, the person or persons (if a joint adoption) must be adult and resident in the UK for 12 months prior to their application to be approved as an adoptive parent. If it is a joint adoption both parents must fulfil the residence requirement (reg 4).
[3] See 11.100 fn 2.
[4] SI 2003/118, reg 6.
[5] SI 2003/118, regs 8 and 9.
[6] SI 2003/118, regs 7, 10. The agency is required to notify the adopters and give reasons for declining to approve adopters. Prospective adopters have the right to apply to an independent review panel for a review of the agency's qualifying determination. See Independent Review of Determinations (Hague Convention Adoptions and Miscellaneous Amendments) Regulations 2004 SI 2004/1868, in force 20 August 2004. See also Department for Education and Skills Local Authority Circular 2004/23.
[7] The IA(HC) Regulations 2003, reg 10.
[8] The IA(HC) Regulations 2003, reg 11.
[9] On the meaning of habitual residence see 11.14 fn1 above.
[10] The Adoption and Children Act 2002, s 66 defines an adoption as including a Convention adoption. The effect is to enable Convention adoptions to be recognised automatically by operation of law and the adopted person's status to be conferred by s 66 of the Act, obviating the need for a domestic adoption.
[11] British Nationality Act 1981, s 1(5), (5A), inserted by the Adoption (Intercountry Aspects) Act 1999, s 7, in force 1 June 2003.
[12] HC 395, para 6 (definition of 'parent'), 297, 310.

Convention and non-Convention adoptions in the UK

11.103 The Hague Convention arrangements apply both to adoptions in overseas Convention countries and to adoptions of children in the UK. The procedures to be followed in order to adopt a child under a Convention adoption abroad or in the United Kingdom are similar.[1] Thus a British couple seeking to adopt a child resident in a Convention signatory country, for example, Hungary, will have to complete the procedures and obtain approval as adopters as noted above, not simply to adopt in Hungary, but also to bring the child back into the UK and undertake their Convention adoption here. The same Convention procedures must also be followed if, for example, an Australian adopter comes to the UK to adopt a child resident here. In that case the adopter will have completed the Convention formalities above in Australia before initiating the adoption proceedings here. The regulations set down the further procedures for placement of the child with the prospective adopters and the grant of permission for the child to be removed from his/her home jurisdiction for the purpose of adoption.[2] There are additional requirements for notification and supervision when the child and the prospective adopters return to or are established in the UK, and to deal with possible breakdown of the adoptive placement and the refusal of a court to make the Convention adoption order.[3] If the child who is to be adopted in the UK is not from a Convention signatory country, or if the prospective adopters have not complied with Convention adoption procedures, or if the child has been adopted abroad and the adoption is not recognised in the UK, the Courts in the UK may still make an adoption order, but it will not be a Convention adoption.[4] As noted, the Adoption (Intercountry Aspects) Act 1999 seeks to impose home study and eligibility assessments for all inter-country adoptions in the UK. The court will have to balance the welfare benefits to the child of the adoption when deciding whether to waive those requirements.[5]

1   See the Intercountry Adoption (Hague Convention) Regulations 2003, SI 2003/118 which sets mirror criteria for adoption where the UK is the reception country or country of origin for the child. See on procedures for inter-country adoptions, Department of Health, Intercountry Adoption Guide, 24 May 2003,
2   SI 2003/118 regs 12–16, Adoption (Bringing Children into the United Kingdom) Regulations 2003, SI 2003/1173, regs 5–6.
3   SI 2003/118, regs 13–24.
4   Under s 24(2) of the Adoption Act 1976, the court could not make an adoption order if there had been a contravention of the s 57 prohibition on making certain payments for adoption. Section 57 has been replicated and expanded in section 95 of the Adoption and Children Act 2002 but the court is not precluded from making an adoption order in the event of contravention. Further, the 2002 Act gives greater emphasis to the paramount consideration of the child's welfare 'throughout his life'. It can be expected that the caselaw balancing welfare and public, including immigration, policy will continue to be important in such cases. See *Re H (a Minor) (Adoption Non-patrial)* [1983] 4 FLR 85; *Re H (Adoption: Non-patrial)* [1996] 2 FLR 187; *Re An Adoption Application* [1992] 1 FLR 341; *Re J (Adoption Non-patrial)* [1998] 1 FLR 225; *Re B (Adoption Order Nationality)* [1999] 1FLR 907; *Re R (Intercountry Adoptions: Practice)* [1999] 1 FLR 1042; *Re C (Adoption Legality)* [1999] 1 FLR 370.
5   See note above. See also *Re K (Adoption and Wardship)* [1997] 2 FLR 221 in which Butler-Sloss LJ set aside an adoption order relating to a Bosnian child in favour of British applicants due to numerous procedural irregularities.

11.104   When a child is adopted overseas via a Convention adoption, and one of the adoptive parents is a British citizen and one or both of them is habitually resident in the UK, the child will have acquired British citizenship, and will not need leave to enter,[1] In all other overseas Convention adoptions and where the child is adopted in a Designated Adoption, he or she does not become a British citizen and will need leave to enter. Under the Immigration rules a 'parent' is defined to include: 'an adoptive parent, where a child was adopted in accordance with a decision taken by the competent administrative authority or court[2] in a country whose adoption orders are recognised by the United Kingdom',[3] and as such will need to qualify for entry under the provisions of HC 295, paragraph 310, which contain much more onerous requirements than the very carefully thought out safeguards of the whole Convention regime. Is this because the Home Office want to be awkward or is it simply that they have not read the requirements of the Hague Convention regime? If the child has been placed with but not adopted by his or her British adopter parents, the child requires limited leave to enter the UK with a view to settlement as a child for adoption. Here it will be necessary to show that the child is seeking leave to accompany or join his or her prospective adopter or adopters who are habitually resident in the United Kingdom and who wish to adopt him or her under the Hague Convention, that he or she is the subject of an agreement under Article 17(c) of the Hague Convention and has been entrusted to the prospective parents by the competent administrative authorities of the country from which he or she is coming for adoption under the Hague Convention, is under 18 and can and will be maintained and accommodated adequately without recourse to public funds in accommodation which the prospective parent or parents own or occupy exclusively.[5] Children coming to be adopted by means of a Convention Adoption can be admitted for up 24 months initially.[6] The prospective adopters must inform their local authority of the child's arrival within 14 days[7] If the prospective adopter is the parent, step-parent or a relative of the child, he/she will have to have the child living with him or her for 13 weeks before an application for adoption can be made.[8] Other adopters who are not related to the child have to wait for six months before lodging the adoption application.[9] If an adoption order is subsequently made in the United Kingdom and the adopter, or if it is a joint adoption by a married couple, one of them, is a British citizen the child becomes a British citizen automatically.[10] If the adoption order is subsequently annulled, the child's citizenship will not be revoked.[11] However, this is not the case if the Home Office has successfully appealed against the making of the order in the first place.[12]

[1] British Nationality Act 1981, s 1(5), (5A), inserted by the Adoption (Intercountry Aspects) Act 1999, s 7. See 2.50, above.

[2] HC 395, para 6 defines parents of such adopted children as 'a parent', but expressly forbids an adopted children from applying for leave in order to accompany or join their parent or parents in the UK under HC 395, para 297–303 (entry of children joining or accompanying parents). Instead rhey must enter under para 310 (more onerous requirements for entry of adopted children).

[3] Convention and overseas designated adoption orders are recognised by the UK. The Adoption and Children Act 2002 s 66 defines an adoption as including a Convention adoption. The effect is to enable Convention adoptions to be recognised automatically by operation of law and the adopted person's status to be conferred by s 66 of the Act, obviating the need for a domestic adoption. Adoption. In the case of designated adoptions see Adoption (Designation of Overseas Adoptions) Order 1973.

[4] HC 395, para 316D as inserted, (i)–(vi).

[5] HC 395, para 316D as inserted, (i)–(vi).

[6] HC 395, para 316E as inserted.

[7] The Intercountry Adoptions (Hague Convention) Regulations 2003, SI 2003/118, para 15.

[8] Adoption Act 1976, s 13(1).

[9] Adoption Act 1976, s 13(1A).

[10] British Nationality Act 1981, s 1(5).

[11] BNA 1981, s 1(6).

[12] *Re K (A Minor)* [1994] 3 All ER 553.

Designated overseas adoptions

11.105 Where a child is legally adopted in a country[1] which has been designated for the purposes of the Adoption (Designation of Overseas Adoptions) Order 1973, the United Kingdom recognises that there has been a legal Overseas Adoption.[2] It is not necessary to adopt the child for a second time in the United Kingdom. However, where the adopters or any one of them are habitually resident[3] in the United Kingdom and the overseas adoption has taken place during the previous six months, they must comply with the requirements and conditions set out in the Adoption (Bringing Children into the United Kingdom) Regulations 2003[4] before bringing the child to the United Kingdom. These are family law requirements. The adopter(s) in a Designated Adoption, as with Convention adopters, must apply for and receive Agency approval and certification of their suitability to adopt in the United Kingdom.[5] A failure to comply with these requirements may render an adopter liable up to six months' imprisonment or a fine on summary conviction or up to 12 months' imprisonment or a fine on conviction on indictment.[6] Designated Adoptions are being phased out as more designated countries ratify the Convention. The intention is to provide all adopted children with the same high standard of child protection. There are also plans to introduce further legislation to prune the list of designated countries to remove those where adoption practices do not adhere to international standards. A Designated Adoption does not change the child's nationality in the way that a Convention Adoption does, and the child will require leave to enter the United Kingdom. as the child or dependant of his or her adopted parent or parents for settlement.[7] and meet the criteria listed in paragraph 310 of the Immigration Rules HC 395. These, as we indicated in the previous paragraph, are much more rigorous than the family law requirements for Convention adoptions. They include the requirements that there has been a genuine transfer of parental responsibility, that the child has lost or broken ties with his or her family of origin, and that the adoption is not one of convenience to facilitate admission to the United Kingdom. The adoptive parent(s) will also have to show that the child can be accommodated and maintained without recourse to public funds.

---

[1]   In March 2004, these were the Commonwealth countries of Anguilla, Australia, Bahamas, Barbados, Belize, Bermuda, Botswana, British Virgin Islands, Canada, Cayman Islands, Cyprus, Dominica, Fiji, Ghana, Gibraltar, Guyana, Hong Kong, Jamaica, Kenya, Lesotho, Malaysia, Malawi, Malta, Mauritius, Montserrat, Namibia, New Zealand, Nigeria, Pitcairn Island, St Christopher and Nevis, St Vincent, Seychelles, Singapore, South Africa, Sri Lanka, Swaziland, Tanzania, Tonga, Trinidad and Tobago, Uganda, Zambia and the non-Commonwealth countries of Austria, Belgium, China (but only where the child was adopted on or after 5 April 1993), Denmark (including Greenland and the Faroes), Finland and France (including Reunion, Martinique, Guadeloupe and French Guyana), Germany, Greece, Iceland, Ireland, Israel, Italy, Luxembourg, The Netherlands (including the Antilles), Norway, Portugal (including the Azores and Madeira), Spain (including the Balearic and Canary Islands), Surinam, Sweden, Switzerland, Turkey, the United States of America, (but none of the states which make up the former Yugoslavia) and Zimbabwe.

[2]   Adoption and Children Act 2002, s 66(1), Adoption (Designation of Overseas Adoptions) Order 1973.

[3]   See 11.14 fn1, above, and 13.23, below, for definition of habitual residence.

[4]   SI 2003/1173, which came into force on 1 June 2003. See also Adoption Act 1976, s 56A, The Adoption (Bringing Children into the United Kingdom) Regulations 2003, SI 2003/1173, reg 5.

'Genuine transfer of parental responsibility ...'

11.106 The requirement that the transfer of parental responsibility must be due to the original parents' or current carer's inability to care for the child is a more rigorous test than is applied in the domestic courts in adoption proceedings.[1] A similar immigration rule was criticised by the Court of Appeal in the past.[2] The rule has been applied literally; the Court of Appeal has held in *Sharma v Entry Clearance Officer (New Delhi)* that the original parents' rejection of the child because of her gender did not satisfy the requirement that the original parent was 'unable' to care for the child.[3] A more sensible interpretation has been given to the requirement that the child must have 'lost or broken his ties with his family of origin': Sir Andrew Collins held in *Boadi v Entry Clearance Officer, Ghana* that the rule referred to ties of responsibility, not ties of affection.[4] Thus, a child adopted in an intra-family adoption is not required to sever close relationships with his or her natural family to qualify for adoption.

1   Ie 'to safeguard and promote the child's welfare throughout his or her childhood'.
2   *Khan (Asif) v Immigration Appeal Tribunal* [1988] All ER 40, CA.
3   *Sharma v Entry Clearance Officer, New Delhi* [2005] EWCA Civ 89, (2002) Times, 23 February. The 'inability to care' requirement may, however, be waived where all the other requirements of the rule are met and the child has lived as a member of the adoptive family unit for more than 12 months: DSP 14.11 (Feb/05).
4   *Boadi v Entry Clearance Officer, Ghana* [2002] UKIAT 01323, [2003] INLR 54. The later case of *MF (Immigration, adoption, genuine transfer of parental responsibility) Philippines* [2004] UKIAT00094 cannot, we submit, stand with the earlier case.

11.107 Once the child is settled in the United Kingdom, the adoptive parent or parents can apply to register the child as a British citizen,[1] if the adoptive parent is a British citizen or if the adopters are a married couple and one of them is British. Alternatively, an application could be made at a British post abroad before the child comes to the United Kingdom[2] but this might lead to delay and consequently a separation from some members of the adoptive family.

1   British Nationality Act 1981, s 3(1).
2   Intercountry Adoption Guide, Department of Health, May 2003, ch 13, para 25.

11.108 The designation of countries from which Overseas Adoptions are accepted as legally valid is now under review as part of the process of implementing the Adoption and Children Act 2002. It is intended to create a new list based on criteria specified in regulations.[1] The draft Adoptions with a Foreign Element Regulations include four criteria:

(1)   that the child is treated as not being the child of any other person but the adopter;

(2)   that measures are in place to prevent the abduction, sale of, or traffic in children and to prevent improper financial or other gain;

(3)   that informed consent is given by those with parental responsibility and the consent of the mother is given not less than six weeks after the child's birth;

(4)   that the prospective adopter has been assessed and found to be eligible and suitable to adopt.

However, when fully in force, the Adoption and Children Act 2002 will make provision for the continued recognition of adoptions made in countries included on the designated list prior to the review.[2] It is presently Home Office policy to accept as valid an adoption order made in a designated country until such an order is revoked by a court in that country, even if it believes that deception may have been used to obtain the order.[3] This still leaves the possibility that the Home Office will refuse entry if it believes that the purported adoption order was not made or that a document being adduced is a forgery.

[1]   Regulations will be made under Adoption and Children Act 2002, s 87.
[2]   Adoption and Children Act 2002, s 87(2).
[3]   IDI Sep 01, Ch 8, Annex Q, para 9.2.

Legal adoption in or from a non-designated and non-convention country

11.109   If a child has not been adopted abroad by means of a Convention or an Overseas Adoption but has been legally adopted in a non-designated country, the adoption is not recognised for the purpose of domestic law.[1] The child will have to come to the United Kingdom to be adopted, and will require entry clearance for that purpose. The prospective adopter must comply with the requirements of section 56A of the Adoption Act 1976 and the Adoption (Bringing Children into the United Kingdom) Regulations 2003 which apply to overseas adoptions which have taken place during the six months prior to the adopted child's entry into the United Kingdom – that is they need to show they have been assessed and approved as adopters.[2] A single adopter, or, if the application is being made by a married couple, one of them, will have to show that he or she is domiciled in the United Kingdom in order to apply to adopt a child in the United Kingdom.[3] The child will need limited leave to enter the United Kingdom for adoption.[4] The requirements for leave to enter are that the prospective adoptive parent(s) are either being admitted for settlement or are present and settled in the United Kingdom, the child is under 18 and unmarried and not leading an independent life and that the prospective parent(s) can accommodate and maintain the child without recourse to public funds. It is also necessary to show that the child will have the same rights and obligations as any other child of the family, is being adopted due to the inability of the original parent(s) or carer(s) to care for him, that there is a genuine transfer of parental responsibility, that the child has lost or broken or intends to lose or break his or her ties with his family of origin and the proposed adoption is not one of convenience arranged to facilitate his or her admission to the United Kingdom.

[1]   Adoption and Children Act 2002, s 66(1),

2   See 11.105 above.
3   Adoption Act 1976, ss 14(2), 15(2). For domicile see 11.24ff above.
4   HC 395, para 316A.

11.110 Once the child has been admitted to the United Kingdom for the purposes of adoption and the requirements of the Adoption (Bringing Children in the United Kngdom) Regulations 2003 have been complied with, the usual procedures for adoption must be followed.[1] The question of whether a child's previous guardian has to give consent to the adoption may arise. The court should consider whether that person's duties, rights and responsibilities equated to those of a person with parental responsibility under the Children Act 1989. If they did, consent was needed.[2] However, if the child was in the care of a local authority or an orphanage, no individual or institution may have acquired parental responsibility and there will be no need for consent to be sort. This will depend on the particular fact of each case.[3] The Secretary of State for the Home Department is informed of intercountry adoption applications because adoption can confer British citizenship.[4] The Secretary of State must be put on notice of an adoption, where an adoption order would confer British citizenship on the child to be adopted.[5] The Secretary of State can apply under rule 15(3) of the Adoption Rules to be joined as a party to the application. It is his policy[6] to do so unless a child:

(1)   is being adopted by a couple one of whom is a natural parent;
(2)   was admitted in possession of an entry clearance endorsed 'for adoption';
(3)   has been granted or would qualify for indefinite leave to remain or leave in some other capacity where it is accepted that the child's original family is unable to care for him eg as a minor dependent relative or in the absence of parents;
(4)   has been granted or would qualify for leave to remain for the purpose of adoption.

Where one of the conditions (1) to (4) applies, the Secretary of State will write to the Court stating that he or she does not wish to intervene. The Secretary of State, if joined as a party, has a right of appeal, which is not excluded by section 1(6) of the British Nationality Act 1981.[7] The President of the Family Division's Guidelines[8] state that at the First Directions Hearing the judge should consider and give directions about notifying the Home Office that there has been an application for an intercountry adoption. Where the requirements of the Adoption (Intercountry Aspects) Act 1999 and the Adoption (Bringing Children into the United Kingdom) Regulations 2003 and the Intercountry Adoption (Hague Convention) Regulations 2003 have not been met, the case may need to be transferred to the High Court.

1   Adoption Rules 1984 as amended by the Adoption (Amendment) Rules 2003, SI 2003/183. See on whether, and whose consent to the adoption might be required: *Re J (Adoption Consent of Foreign public Authority)* [2002] EWHC 766 (Fam), *Re AGN (Adoption, Foreign Adoption)* [2000] 2 FLR 431, *Re D (Adoption Foreign Guardianship)* [1999] 2 FLR 865, *Re AMR (Adoption Procedure)* [1999] 2 FLR 807.
2   *Re AMR (Adoption: Procedure)* [1999] 2 FLR 807.
3   *Re J (Adoption: Consent of Foreign Public Authority* [2002] EWHC 766 (Fam), [2002] 3 FCR 635; *Re D (a minor) (Adoption: Foreign Guardianship)* [1999] 2 FLR 865.
4   British Nationality Act 1981, s 1(5).

5   *Re H (A minor) (Adoption: Non-patrial)* [1982] Fam 121, *Re W (A minor) (Adoption: Non-patrial)* [1986] Fam 54.
6   IDI Jul 01, Ch 8, Annex S, para 5.
7   *Re K (A Minor) (Adoption Order: Nationality)* [1994] 3 WLR 572, [1994] 2 FLR 557.
8   *President's Guidelines: Adoption Proceedings – A New Approach* in Hershman & Mc Farlane *Children Law and Practice* Vol 2, L239.

11.111 At one time, the family court considering intercountry adoptions gave greater weight to the need to maintain strict immigration controls when considering whether to grant an adoption which would facilitate a child's being granted British citizenship in order to be able to study and work in the United Kingdom.[1] Following *Re B (adoption order: nationality)*[2] the courts now consider whether, 'l the adoption will bring about a genuine transfer of parental responsibility and not only be motivated by a wish to assist the child to obtain a right of abode ?' and, 'taking into account all the child's circumstances, including the benefits of British citizenship' whether the adoption will confer real benefits on the child throughout his or her childhood?' The House of Lords went on to state' in that case that although the views of the Home Office should be taken into account, it was very unlikely that general concerns relating to the maintenance of immigration controls would justify the rejection of an order which met both the two tests outlined above. In *Re B*, the child in question was 16 years old and was being adopted by her grandparents. Her mother had returned to Jamaica to a life of destitution and her grandparents wanted to be able to provide the child with a secure home and educational opportunities. When a Court in the United Kingdom makes an adoption order, the adopted child becomes a British citizen automatically if his or her adopter is British or, in the case of a joint adoption, if one of the adopters is a British citizen.[3] If the adopters are not British citizens but are settled in the United Kingdom, the child is likely to be granted indefinite leave to remain as a dependant child.

1   *Re W (A Minor) (Adoption: Non-patrial)* [1986] Fam 54; *Re K (Adoption and Wardship)* [1997] 2 FLR 221.
2. [1999] 2 AC 136, HL. See 11.103 fn 4 case authorities.
3   British Nationality Act 1981, s 1(5).

De facto adoptions

11.112 Some countries, many of which are Muslim, have not enacted laws concerning adoption. In these countries, children cannot be formally adopted, although there is general social recognition of changed family relationships equivalent to adoption. It is generally accepted that these de facto, customary adoptions have real significance for the parties involved and should be given some legal effect. In certain circumstances, children who are the subject of de facto adoptions may be admitted to the United Kingdom for settlement with their adoptive parents[1]. These circumstances are where it can be shown that at the time immediately preceding the application for entry clearance the adoptive parent (or if it is joint adoption, both parents) had been living abroad for at least 18 months and that they had cared for the child for at least the 12 months immediately preceding the application for entry clearance. They must also have assumed the role of the child's parents since the beginning of the 18-month period, so that there has been a genuine transfer of parental responsibility.[2] Any child who is informally adopted needs to satisfy the requirements of paragraph 309A.[3] Where a child, who is the subject of a de facto adoption, arrives in the United Kingdom without prior entry clearance, immigration officers are instructed to inform the appropriate local authority, the Department of Health and the police.[4] This is to protect the child from possible trafficking and abduction.[5] Where a child is admitted for settlement on the basis of a de facto adoption, it is presumed that his or her de facto adopters will not later apply for an adoption order in the United Kingdom. If an application for adoption is later made in the United Kingdom and the adopter(s) is or are deemed to have been habitually resident in the United Kingdom[6] when the child was brought to the United Kingdom, an offence under section 56A of the Adoption Act 1976 may have been committed by bringing the child to the United Kingdom without complying with the requirements of this section and those of the Adoption (Bringing Children into the United Kingdom) Regulations 2003. After the child has entered the United Kingdom, the adopters, if one or both is British, can apply for him or her to be registered as a British citizen.[7]

1   HC 395, para 310(vi).
2   HC 395, para 309A, inserted by HC 538 from 31 March 2003. See 11.105–11.106 above. The IDI Sep 04, Ch 8, Annex R, which post-date the incorporation of de facto adoption into the rules, have been drafted in total ignorance of those rules and treat de facto adoption as outside the rules. The DSP refer to the relevant requirements.
3   HC 395, *para 6A 'a parent', 309A; R (on the application of Acan) v Immigration Appeal Tribunal* [2004] EWHC Admin 297.
4   IDI Sep 04, Ch 8, Annex Q, para 3.3; Annex R.
5   Note that entry clearance officers, citing such concerns, are putting obstacles in the way of the admission of de facto adopted children in the context of Somali refugee family reunion, demanding home study reports etc – an example of over-zealous bureaucrats defeating the object of benign provisions.
6   The question of habitual residence is one of fact and all the circumstances of the case will be taken into account. It must also be given its ordinary meaning: *Re G (Adoption: Ordinary Residence)* [2002] EWHC 2447 (Fam), [2003] 2 FLR 944. It is defined more by the quality of the residence than its length and requires an element of intention. Bringing possessions, doing everything necessary to establish residence before coming, having a right of abode, seeking to bring family, 'durable ties' with the country of residence or intended residence and many other factors may be taken into account: *Nessa v Chief Adjudication Officer* [1999] 4 All ER 677. The period of time can be short *Re S (A Minor) (Custody: Habitual Residence)* [1998] AC 750. It is also possible to be habitually resident in two countries at once. Factors such as location of the home, employment, financial arrangements and location of bank account and local connections are just some of the many factors which may be relevant.
7   British Nationality Act 1981, s 3 (1) The 'parents' may also wish to apply for a residence order in the family jurisdiction so as to clarify their responsibility for and status concerning the child.

Adoptions recognised at common law

11.113 The case of *Valentine*[1] concerns the common law redcognition of overseas adoptions. Lord Denning held that in order for an adoption to be recognised everywhere, in addition to the adoptive parents being both domiciled in the child's country of origin, the child must be ordinarily resident there. These requirements reflected English domestic law at the time. There is no requirement for both adopters to be domiciled here for an adoption to take place, and domicile has been superseded by habitual residence as a requirement for the purpose of Convention Adoptions. To that extent, the requirements for common law recognition of non-designated adoptions are likely to have been modified and relaxed. In any contemporary application for common law recognition the requirements contained in the Adoption (Bringing Children into the United Kingdom) Regulations 2003, and these regulations and the international Conventions may prove a disqualifying factor, and limit the scope for common law recognition of other overseas adoptions.[2]

1   *Re Valentine's Settlement, Valentine v Valentine* [1965] Ch 831.
2   Where the parents are of different nationality, and the adoption is valid by reference to one parent's domiciliary law but is not a Convention adoption, a court in the UK may decide that the common law allows such an adoption to be given recognition.

Adoptions by relatives

11.114 It is not uncommon for childless couples to adopt the children of close relatives. In the past these cases were often refused leave to enter on the grounds that the child has not broken all ties with his or her family of origin and, that parental responsibility had not been genuinely transferred to the prospective adoptive parents on the grounds of the parent's inability to care for the child.[1] Entry applications were more difficult if, as could often happen, the child was living with his or her family of origin at the date of the application.[2] However, the landmark decision of the Court of Appeal in *Singh v Entry Clearance Officer, Delhi*[3] has changed the discourse on these cases and focussed attention on the nature and significance of the relationship between the parties. The appellant was a seven-year-old boy who had been adopted in India by his uncle and aunt who lived in the UK. The adoption had been carried out within the family in accordance with a social, religious and cultural tradition which served a humane purpose. It had legal effect in India. Three things flowed from this: first, although the child was not living with his adoptive parents, there had been a genuine transfer of parental responsibility; secondly, the child had become a member of his adoptive parents' family for the purposes of Article 8 ECHR; and thirdly, the failure to grant him entry clearance to come to the UK was a violation of Article 8. The court found there was a family life established between the child and his adoptive parents even though their relationship had no formal recognition and they were not living together and upheld the Adjudicator's finding that his exclusion was disproportionate.

1   See HC 395, para 310.
2.   See 11.106 above.
3   [2004] EWCA Civ 1075 [2004] INLR 515. Clearly such cases are fact sensitive. Munby J compared this case favourably with *Re J (Adoption: Non-Patrial)* [1998] 1 FLR 225, [1998] INLR 424, CA, but contrasted it with a 'sordid intercountry adoption' in *Re M (Adoption: International Adoption Trade)* [2003] EWHC 219 (Fam), [2003] 1 FLR 1111.

Proposal for British child to be adopted abroad

11.115 If a child who is a British subject is taken into care or accommodated due to the death or inability of his or her parents to care for him or her, a local authority may wish to place the child abroad for adoption. In order to do so, the local authority will have to apply to the family court for permission to place the child abroad with relatives or family friends.[1] The prospective adopters must also apply for parental responsibility for the child in question under section 55 of the Adoption Act 1976.[2] An order under this section terminates any existing care orders and previous parents cease to have any parental responsibility.[3] In order to qualify for parental responsibility prospective adopters have to spend a period of 26 weeks resident in the United Kingdom.[4] If section 55 of the Adoption Act 1976? is not complied with the act of removing the child from the United Kingdom will amount to a criminal offence under section 56A.[5] This offence could be committed by the prospective adopters or a local authority.[6] However, where a child is subject to a care order, section 56 does not apply.[7] If a child is not subject to a care order but is being accommodated under section 20 of the Children Act 1989 (or assisted under section 17 of the Children Act 1989) as the result of a freeing order or otherwise, section 56 will still apply.[8]

1   Children Act 1989, Sch 2, para 19. See *Re S (Freeing for Adoption)* [2002] EWCA Civ 798.
2   Adoption Act 1976, s 55.
3   *Re G (Adoption: Ordinary Residence)* [2002] EWHC 2447 (Fam), [2003] 2 FLR 944.
4   Adoption Act 1976, ss 13(1) and 55.
5   Adoption Act 1976, s 56.
6   A person can include a body of persons corporate or incorporate: Interpretation Act 1978, s 1.
7   Children Act 1989, Sch 2, para 19(1), (6).
8   *B v Birmingham City Council* [2004] EWCA Civ 515, [2004] 2 FCR 129.

UNACCOMPANIED CHILDREN

11.116 Paragraph 349 of the Immigration Rules HC 395 defines a child as a person under 18 years of age or who, in the absence of documentary evidence establishing age, appears to be under that ageThe Home Office defines an unaccompanied minor as a person below the age of eighteen who arrives in the United Kingdom unaccompanied by an adult responsible for him whether by law or custom and makes a claim for asylum.[1] The definition currently used by the Immigration Service is 'passengers and asylum seekers who are under the age of 18, but who are neither accompanied by a suitable adult nor have a suitable adult sponsor within the United Kingdom'.[2] The Separated Children in Europe Programme[3] prefers the use of the term 'separated children' and defines them as 'children under 18 years of age who are outside their country of origin and separated from both parents or their previous legal/customary primary caregiver'. This definition better describes the fact that the vast majority of children who arrive here alone will have been separated from the adults who previously cared for them by some form of traumatic event whether it was war, persecution or trafficking.

1   Asylum Seekers (Reception Conditions) Regulations 2005, SI 2005/7, reg 6(3)(a).
2   UK Immigration Service *Best Practice: Unaccompanied Minors* Version 01.01.04.
3   A joint initiative of some members of the International Save the Children Alliance in Europe and the UNHCR.

11.117 Unaccompanied children may have arrived in the UK alone to claim asylum, have been abandoned by their parents or carers after arrival here or left with unsuitable private foster carers. They may have been trafficked here for the purposes of prostitution or domestic slavery. Whether they originally fled to the UK in order to claim asylum they can have protection needs. It is very difficult to estimate the total number of unaccompanied children who enter the United Kingdom every year, as many will have been brought in illegally and will remain without immigration status until some event brings them to the notice of social services, the police or the Immigration Service. However, figures do now exist for unaccompanied asylum seeking children, who have come to the notice of the Immigration and Nationality Department. The Department reported that in 2002, 6,200 unaccompanied asylum seeking children claimed asylum in the United Kingdom and in 2003 a further 2,800 claimed asylum. The number of applications fell very slightly to 2,755 in 2004.[1] The Refugee Council's Panel of Advisers statistics of unaccompanied asylum seeking children referred for their assistance showed 4,405 referrals in 1999, 4,118 in 2000, 5,005 in 2001, 6,513 in 2002 and 4,685 in 2003.[2] The discrepancies arise from the fact that Home Office statistics do not always include all enforcement offices and there are instances of late recording of applications by unaccompanied minors.

[1]   Home Office Research, Development and Statistics Directorate.
[2]   Figures collated by the Refugee Council (unpublished).

11.118 When an asylum applicant claims to be a child but his or her appearance strongly suggests that he or she is over 18, it is the IND's policy to treat the applicant as an adult until there is credible documentary evidence to demonstrate the age claimed.[1] It is only in borderline cases that it is said to be appropriate to give the minor the benefit of the doubt and treat him as a minor.[2] In relation to asylum seeking children, this reliance on physical appearance runs counter to the guidance given by UNHCR[3] where it states that any assessment should take into account not only the physical appearance of the child but also his or her psychological maturity. It also recommends that a child should be given the benefit of the doubt if his exact age is uncertain. Neither is it supported by the Royal College of Paediatricians and Child Health, who have stated[4] that a child's age cannot be determined by a medical examination alone but must be the result of a holistic assessment taking into account the child's physical, mental and social development and maturity. It also warns against making any cultural or other assumptions about the physical development of any child or of their life experiences.[5] This approach has now been approved by the Administrative Court.[6] When a professional social worker has already undertaken such an assessment, it is now IND policy to accept his or her assessment, and where the IND is unhappy about the assessment the applicant must continue to be treated as a minor whilst the Asylum Policy Unit undertakes any review.[7] However, where a professional social worker has not had the opportunity to make his or her own assessment, it is not presently IND policy to seek the advice of a professional social worker before concluding, on the basis of appearance alone, that he or she is over 18.[8] Furthermore, even in borderline cases, social services are only consulted if they are immediately available to give advice.[9] As the majority of unaccompanied children claim asylum after they have entered the United Kingdom it is

advisable to ensure that they have documentary proof or supporting evidence
of their age, wherever possible, when they make their application.

1   UK Immigration Service *Best Practice: Unaccompanied Minors* Version 01.01.04, para 1.1.
2   UK Immigration Service *Best Practice: Unaccompanied Minors* Version 01.01.04, para 1.2.
3   UNHCR Guidelines on Policies and Procedures in dealing with Unaccompanied Children Seeking Asylum para 5.11.
4   *The Health of Refugee Children: Guidelines for Paediatricians*, Royal College of Paediatricians and Child Health November 1999.
5   Starting in May 2002, the Association of the Directors of Social Services undertook a pilot project looking at the assessment of asylum seeking children's ages. This methodolody is now accepted throughout the United Kingdom, but the ADSS has yet to formally adopt the Practice Guidelines and pro forma used in the pilot project. They stress the need for a holistic assessment taking into account many of the same issues pinpointed by the Royal College of Paediatricians. See Practice Guidelines for Age Assessment of Young Unaccompanied Asylum Seekers, Association of Directors of Social Services, 2003.
6   *R (on the application of B) v London Borough of Merton* [2003] EWHC 1689 (Admin), [2003] 4 All ER 280. See also *ST (Minor) (Age Dispute) Afghan* [2005] UKIAT 00048.
7   UK Immigration Service *Best Practice: Unaccompanied Children* Version 01.01.04.
8   UK Immigration Service *Best Practice: Unaccompanied Children* Version 01.01.04, para 1.1.
9   UK Immigration Service *Best Practice: Unaccompanied Children* Version 01.01.04, para 1.2. However, this policy may change as the result of an Unaccompanied Asylum Seeking Children Pilot, which is being run by the Immigration Service in Dover and Kent Social Services. Unaccompanied children in the pilot are granted temporary admission for seven days, whilst Kent Social Services assesses their age. They return with a social worker at the end of that period for an interview and the social worker acts as the responsible adult. See *Best Practice* para 13.

11.119 There is a growing concern about the number of unaccompanied
children who are being trafficked into the United Kingdom for the purposes of
prostitution and domestic slavery. The Government has stated that it needs 'to
increase [its] capacity to support children who have been trafficked against
their will'.[1] It has also said that it will 'seek to invest more in training for
immigration officers to improve their identification of children at risk and
help them respond appropriately'[2] A Trafficking Toolkit[3] has been produced
and there have a number of joint initiatives between the Immigration Service,
local authority social services departments and child protection officers at
ports.[4] The IND has become more aware of the possible child protection
issues raised by the arrival of an unaccompanied child in the United Kingdom.
Immigration officers are now instructed to consider contacting their local
Child Protection Officer if they believe that an unaccompanied child is in need
of protection even if she or he has a 'sponsor' in the United Kingdom.[5] If a
sponsor does not come to meet a child and the immigration officer thinks that
she or he is vulnerable, the sponsor should be asked to attend and to provide
photographic identification of their identity.[6] A range of police checks should
also be undertaken and his or her address checked against the Electoral Roll.
If the Immigration Officer is not satisfied that the child would be safe with the
sponsor, social services and the local Child Protection Officer should be
contacted. If an unaccompanied child provides any information during an
asylum or immigration interview which may relate to criminal activity, for
example trafficking or abuse, the interview should be terminated and the
police called immediately.[7]

1   *Every Child Matters* CM 5860, September 2003, para 2.54.
2   CM 5860, September 2003, para 2.51.

3   Home Office Crime Prevention Unit Website.
4   For example, *Paladin Child: The Safeguarding Children Strand of Maxim funded by Reflex: A Partnership Study of Child Migration to the UK via London Heathrow*, UK Immigration Service (2004).
5   UK Immigration Service *Best Practice: Unaccompanied Children* Version 01.01.04, para 8.1.
6   UK Immigration Service *Best Practice: Unaccompanied Children* Version 01.01.04, para 9.1.
7   UK Immigration Service *Best Practice: Unaccompanied Children* Version 01.01.04, para 7.3.

11.120 It is IND policy only to detain unaccompanied children in exceptional circumstances, for example, where Social Services have declined to intervene but the IND is concerned about the suitability of the child's sponsor.[1] Even then they can only be detained overnight until alternative arrangements for their safety can be made. However, there has been concern about the increasing number of unaccompanied children who are being age-disputed and detained as adults. In the 12 months up until September 2003, the Refugee Council's Panel of Advisers received 192 referrals relating to unaccompanied children said to be wrongfully detained in removal centres.[2] The Chief Inspector of Prisons has recommended[3] that 'the detention of children [even if accompanied by their parents] should be avoided wherever possible, and only take place for the shortest possible time, in no case more than seven days'. She has also stated that 'there should be an independent assessment of the welfare, developmental and educational needs of each child, as soon as practicable after a decision to detain and repeated at regular intervals, to advise on the compatibility of detention with the welfare of the child and to inform decisions about the necessity of detention, or continued detention'.[4] The detrimental effect of detention is well documented in a number of pieces of research.[5]

1   UK Immigration Service *Best Practice: Unaccompanied Children* Version 01.01.04, para 4.1.
2   Refugee Council figures reported to Refugee Children's Consortium Meeting on 26 September 2003.
3   *Introduction and Summary of Findings: Inspection of Five Immigration Service Custodial Establishments*, HM Inspectorate of Prisons, April 2003, p 10.
4   *An Inspection of Dungavel Immigration Removal Centre*, HM Inspectorate of Prisons, October 2002, p 73.
5   *No place for a child: children in UK immigration detention*, Save The Children, Feb 2005; *A Few Families Too Many: Detention of Asylum-Seeking Families in the UK*, Emma Cole Bail for Immigration Detainees (London, March 2003), Sarah Cutler *Detention of asylum seeking children* (Childright, June 2002); Alison Harvey *Briefing on detention of asylum seeking children and young people* (Medical Foundation, September 2000); *A Second Exile: the Mental Health Implications of Detention of Asylum Seekers in the United Kingdom* (North Birmingham Mental Health NHS Trust, 1996), *Mothers in Exile: Maternity Experiences of Asylum Seekers in England* (Maternity Alliance, London).

11.121 In the past, if the IND refused an unaccompanied child asylum, it would grant him or her exceptional or discretionary leave to remain.[1] This policy has now changed, and the IND intends to start a programme of enforced returns of children to their countries of origin in 2005.[2] The actual process of return will be piloted with 16- to 17-year-olds from Albania. In preparation for this children from certain countries are only being granted discretionary leave for 12 months or less.[3] When unaccompanied children who have previously been granted exceptional or discretionary leave up until their eighteenth birthday without an interview apply for further leave to remain, they are likely to be interviewed.[4] The IND has also set up a 'Transitions Group' with the Association of Directors of Social Services and in particular the London Borough of Croydon and Kent County Council to look at the planned returns of these young people to their countries of origin. If a child has been accommodated by a local authority and it wishes to place the child abroad it will have to obtain the approval of a family court and show that such a placement would be in the child's best interests and that suitable arrangements will be made for his or her reception and welfare and that the child and every person with parental responsibility has consented.[5] The child's consent can be dispensed with if he or she does not have sufficient understanding to give or withhold consent. A parent's consent can be dispensed with if he or she cannot be found, is incapable of consenting or withholds his or her consent unreasonably.

1   Asylum Policy Unit Notice 1/2003. See 12.174 below.
2   *Controlling Our Borders: Making Migration Work for Britain: A Five Year Strategy for Asylum and Immigration* Cm 6472 February 2005.
3   Asylum Policy Unit Notice 5/2004.
4   Minutes of UASC Stakeholder Group 2 July 2003.
5   Children Act 1989, Sch 2, para 19.

REMOVAL OF CHILDREN

11.122 If a child has no claim to remain in the UK, the decision on their removal is to be made by reference to factors such as the age of the child, the length of his or her stay in the UK, the type of care he or she has had in the UK and the effect of disrupting it, the circumstances abroad and the child's feelings. Generally, the younger the child and the longer the stay, the less likely is removal. The Home Office has provided guidance to its enforcement section as to when removal of children would be inappropriate. It may be summarised:

(i)   children under 16 who are on their own in the UK should not be removed unless their voluntary departure cannot be arranged;[1]

(ii)   no unaccompanied child will be removed from the UK unless the Home Office is satisfied that adequate reception and care facilities are in place in the country to which he or she is to be removed, and where there is evidence that care arrangements are seriously defective or inadequate, exposing the child to a serious risk of harm, removal should not take place;[2]

(iii) enforcement action will not normally proceed against families with children born here and who have lived here continuously to the age of seven or over, or where, having come to the UK at an early age, children have accumulated seven years' or more continuous residence. Relevant considerations will include the length of the parents' residence without leave and whether removal has been delayed by protracted and repetitive representations or by parents going to ground, the age of the children, whether any of them were conceived when either parent had leave to remain, whether return to the parents' country would cause

659

extreme hardship to the children or put their health at risk, whether either parent has a history of criminal behaviour or deception;[3]

(iv)   in all cases involving potential removal of children, the requirements of ECHR, Article 8 (family and private life) will have to be complied with.[4]

In *Jagot*, the High Court quashed the decision to remove the applicant child, who had lived in the UK with his grandparents for over seven years while maintaining links with his parents and siblings in Malawi, holding that the policy DP069/99 contemplated that the requirements of a firm immigration control could not, without strong reason, justify the uprooting of a child who had spent a substantial and formative part of his life in the UK. Nor could disruption to existing family life caused by removal be justified by the possibility of a future effective family life abroad.[5] In *Jagot*, the court proceeded on the basis that the policy applied to 'port cases' ie, where the applicant had sought entry at the port and had remained on temporary admission ever since, just as it applied to cases of deportation and administrative removal for overstaying etc. In *Dabrowski*, the Court of Appeal indicated the principle behind this equivalence of treatment as being to prevent the lawful implementation of immigration and asylum policy after a certain period of time, from unnecessarily uprooting children or inducing family break-up.[6]

---

1   DP4/96, para 2 (*Butterworths Immigration Law Service* D [601]).

2   DP4/96, paras 2 and 3, *Re Sujon Miah* (CO 3391/1994) (6 December 1994, unreported): irrational to seek to remove child to abusive parents in Pakistan. The very harsh decision in *GP (return, minor, Roma) Romania CG* [2003] UKIAT 00212 was predicated on the Secretary of State's undertaking in accordance with this policy.

3   DP069/99 (formerly DP5/96); for wording of policy see appendix to *R (on the application of Dabrowski) v Secretary of State for the Home Department* [2003] EWCA Civ 580, [2003] Imm AR 454, [2003] INLR 411. A decision on proportionality (Art 8.2) which failed to have regard to the policy was reversed in *N (Kenya)* [2004] UKIAT 00008.

4   See chapter 8 above.

5   *R v Secretary of State for the Home Department, ex p Jagot* [2000] INLR 501.

6   *R (on the application of Dabrowski) v Secretary of State for the Home Department*, fn 3 above. However, an absence of three months broke continuity for the purposes of the 'seven-year rule' in that case. See also *MA (Seven Year Child Concession) Pakistan* [2005] UKIAT 00090.

PARENTS, GRANDPARENTS AND OTHER DEPENDENT RELATIVES

The classes of admissible dependent relatives

11.123   The Immigration Rules severely limit the range of dependent relatives other than spouses, fiancé(e)s, unmarried partners and minor children who may join their relatives in the UK, and the circumstances in which they may do so. All such relatives must be seeking to join or accompany a person who is present and settled in the UK or being admitted for settlement,[1] must be wholly or mainly financially dependent on the relative present and settled in the UK[2] and have no other close relatives in their own country to turn to for financial support.[3] Parents and grandparents of children settled in the UK are allowed to join them only if they are:

(i)   widows or widowers aged 65 or over;[4] or

(ii)   travelling together and at least one of them is aged 65 or over;[5] or

(iii)   aged 65 or over, remarried, but who cannot look to the spouse or children of the second marriage for financial support;[6] or

(iv)   under 65, mainly dependent financially on relatives settled in the UK and living alone in the most exceptional compassionate circumstances.[7]

In *Zanib Bibi*[8] it was held that a separated parent was to be equated with a widow and thus need not comply with the 'most exceptional compassionate circumstances' limb. However, the age requirements still have to be satisfied, and both widowed and separated spouses have to satisfy that limb if they are under 65. The Home Office issued guidance to caseworkers in the UK that all elderly dependent relatives over 65, for whom a sponsor has given an undertaking of support, should be granted indefinite leave to remain without detailed inquires.[9]

1   HC 395, para 317(ii).
2   HC 395, para 317(iii); see 11.127 below.
3   HC 395, para 317(v); see 11.130 below.
4   HC 395, para 317(i)(a) and (b). Previous rules allowed widowed mothers to be under 65, but the other requirements had to be complied with: *R v Immigration Appeal Tribunal, ex p Khan (Azam)* [1993] Imm AR 33, QBD. The rules were 'equalised' downwards in 1994.
5   HC 395, para 317(i)(c).
6   HC 395, para 317(i)(d).
7   HC 395, para 317(i)(e).
8   *R v Immigration Appeal Tribunal, ex p Zanib Bibi* [1987] Imm AR 392; see also *Rosario* (9600). We suggest that this would apply to divorced and single mothers too: see IDI Sep 04, Ch 8, Annex V.
9   Memo from B1 Management Unit, January 1994. This is now set out in IDI Oct 04, Ch 8, s 6.

11.124 Sons, daughters, sisters, brothers, uncles and aunts over 18 can qualify for admission to join a sponsor in the UK only if they are living alone outside the UK in the most exceptional compassionate circumstances and mainly financially dependent on relatives settled in the UK.[1] The Rule is apparently intended to be exhaustive of the categories of relative admissible for entry.[2]

1   HC 395, para 317(i)(f).
2   See DSP 15.1, which stipulates that 'nephews and nieces are not included'. The IDI Sep 04, Ch 8, Annex W, para 1 simply lists the relatives covered by the rule.

The requirement of entry clearance

11.125 Dependent relatives must always have an entry clearance if seeking leave to enter in that capacity.[1] The position remains that entry clearance is not required for applications for leave to remain as a relative; such applications are to be granted if the other conditions of the Immigration Rules are met.[2] Where the application comes post-entry from someone who entered as a visitor or a student, it may be sensible to enquire whether there has been a change of circumstances since entry, to deal with any allegation of deception on entry (ie, by failing to indicate an intention to remain as a dependent relative. But on such an application, the requirements of dependency, that the applicant has no close relatives to turn to at home and (if applicable) that he or she is living alone in the most exceptional compassionate circumstances (for which see below) are to be applied by assessing the notional condition of the applicant if he or she were in the home country at the date of decision, rather than seeking actual dependency etc before arrival.[3] On a repeated application for entry clearance by dependent relatives, the *Devaseelan* principles apply.[4]

[1]   HC 395, para 317(vi). Where a person arrives without entry clearance, the immigration officer will examine him or her to decide whether exceptional compassionate circumstances warrant the exercise of discretion: IDI Oct 04, Ch 8, s 6, para 2.2. Refusal will not give rise to an in-country appeal except on human rights grounds, and only if not certified clearly unfounded: Nationality, Immigration and Asylum Act 2002, ss 92, 94.

[2]   HC 395, paras 318 and 319; see also *R v Immigration Appeal Tribunal, ex p Kaur (Mohinder)* [1994] Imm AR 526, QBD confirming that after entry cases must still fulfil the on entry rules.

[3]   See TH/04414/2004 (21 January 2005, unreported) (drawn to our attention by Peter Wilkinson of 6 Kings Bench Walk).

[4]   *Devaseelan* [2003] Imm AR 1 (starred), above 8.108. See *B (Pakistan)* [2003] UKIAT 00053.

Maintenance and accommodation

11.126   There must be a sponsor who is present and settled in the UK (or will be on arrival of the relatives), and there must be adequate accommodation owned or occupied by the sponsor, and adequate maintenance for the new arrivals and any dependants of theirs.[1] The wording of the maintenance and accommodation rule suggests that the sponsor does not have to provide the maintenance and accommodation, which can be provided by a third party. This is in contrast to the wording of the rules for children, spouses and partners.[2] However, the IDI indicate that joint sponsorship is not acceptable.[3] Both the IDI and the DSP state that sponsors should be required to give formal sponsorship undertakings.[4]

[1]   HC 395, para 317(iv) and (iva) as amended by Cm 4851.

[2]   See discussion at 11.52ff above.

[3]   IDI Oct 04, Ch 8, s 6, para 3.2, but see *GG (HC 395 para 317: Joint Sponsorship) Jamaica* [2004] UKIAT 00095.

[4]   DSP 15.5 (Mar 03). The DSP also indicate that the UK sponsor of a parent who has remarried should be able to support any children of the second marriage, whether or not they are coming with the applicant.

Dependency

11.127   The relative must be wholly or mainly financially dependent on the sponsor.[1] It is not sufficient to demonstrate that the family with whom the relative lives is so dependent. In *Bibi*[2] the sponsor began to remit money to his brother, with whom the appellant mother lived, when the children's educational needs imposed an impossible burden on the family finances in Bangladesh. Prior to this, the sponsor had not remitted any money and the appellant was dependent upon the family in Bangladesh. It was argued that the family was dependent upon this remittance and therefore the appellant, as a member of the family, was financially dependent mainly on the sponsor. The Court of

Appeal, in finding that the appellant was not financially dependent, held that the focus of the examination must be upon the appellant. A connection must be shown between the money provided by the sponsor and the appellant's needs. 'Financially' in the words of the paragraph means money or money's worth, and someone whose needs for accommodation, clothing, food and other necessities, including social comfort and support in old age,[3] are met by another is financially dependent on that person.[4] The case law on dependency under the previous rules will continue to have relevance. Dependency refers to the needs of the applicants, which are not contrived[5] and which they are unable to meet by themselves.[6] Other types of dependency may tip the balance where there is a partial financial dependency; but without financial dependency, this requirement of the Immigration Rules cannot be met. Emotional dependency may turn into financial dependency if expenditure is involved to meet it.[7] There must be some element of material support and a history of close contact for emotional dependency to count.[8] In *Parekh*[9] the Tribunal held that a finding of dependency would normally follow when there was no close relative to turn to. The word 'mainly' is not apt to describe a mathematical calculation, although in some cases arithmetic may provide a useful approach; the phrase calls for a rounded appraisal.[10]

1   HC 395, para 317(iii). Relatives claiming admission because they live alone in the most exceptional compassionate circumstances have to show they are financially mainly dependent on relatives settled in the UK (not necessarily the sponsor): HC 395, para 317(i)(e) and (f); *Botan* (18175) (12 May 1999, unreported), IAT, but they are also required to be financially mainly dependent on the sponsor: para 317(iii). The IDI Oct 04, Ch 8, s 6, para 3.2 state that support from two or more relatives in the UK is unacceptable, and applicants in this situation must nominate one sponsor upon whom they have been financially mainly dependent and who will be 'singularly' responsible for their maintenance and accommodation in the UK. The wording of the rules does not necessitate this restrictive interpretation, which is, we suggest, wrong.
2   *Bibi v Entry Clearance Officer, Dhaka* [2000] Imm AR 385, CA.
3   *Immigration Appeal Tribunal v Swaran Singh* [1987] Imm AR 563, CA; *R v Immigration Appeal Tribunal, ex p Sayana Khatun* [1989] Imm AR 482, QBD.
4   *Bibi v Entry Clearance Officer Dhaka* above; *Desai v Entry Clearance Officer* [2000] INLR 10, CA.
5   *Chavda v Entry Clearance Officer, Bombay* [1978] Imm AR 40; *Zaman v Entry Clearance Officer, Lahore* [1973] Imm AR 71; *Musa (Hasan Bibi) v Entry Clearance Officer, Bombay* [1976] Imm AR 28; *Entry Clearance Officer, Port Louis v Grenade* [1978] Imm AR 143.
6   *Bhattacharjee* (3476); *R v Immigration Appeal Tribunal, ex p Patel* (1982) Times, 7 April; *George* (4184).
7   *Bi (Rehmat)* (16074) IAS 1998, Vol 1, No 5.
8   *R v Immigration Appeal Tribunal, ex p Bastiampillai* [1983] 2 All ER 844, [1983] Imm AR 1, QBD, where it was said that emotional dependence could tip the balance, but it must mean more than ordinary family affection. See *Dairion* (3356), *Keogh* (5868) and *Ting* (18735) (5 October 1998, unreported) for examples of emotional dependence. For a review of the authorities see *Entry Clearance Officer, Hong Kong v Cheng (Shen)* [1993] Imm AR 81. The DSP advise entry clearance officers to take emotional and physical dependency into account and that they may swing the balance: DSP 15.2 (Mar/03).
9   *Parekh (Hasmuklal)* (14016) IAS 1997, Vol 3, No 14.
10   *Desai v Entry Clearance Officer* above.

11.128 The dependency must be of necessity, not of choice. In *Zaman v Entry Clearance Officer, Lahore*[1] an elderly Pakistani farmer and his wife applied to join their son in the UK. The father owned two farms and the income from these was given away to three sons who were still resident in that country, in accordance with custom. This left the parents wholly dependent upon money sent to them by their son in the UK. Nevertheless, the Tribunal held that they were not wholly or mainly dependent, since their dependence was not necessary. This approach was confirmed in *Musa v Entry Clearance Officer, Bombay*[2] where two able-bodied teenage sons were held to be capable of supplementing their mother's earnings and it could not, therefore, be said that they were necessarily dependent on the eldest son in the UK. In another case, the Tribunal upheld a refusal of admission where a widowed mother had given up her job voluntarily and without explanation and become dependent on her son in the UK.[3] Where the sponsor's support was for the purposes of keeping up a particular lifestyle, there was no necessary dependency.[4] However, it should be noted that it is only a voluntary act done with intent to become dependent that creates a dependence that is not necessary. Where an act done bona fide for other purposes in fact results in dependence, it cannot be said to be a contrived or unnecessary dependence.[5] Where the alternative source of dependence is conditional on the ability of others to find work and support the applicant, dependence on a sponsor in the UK is still necessary.[6]

[1]   [1973] Imm AR 71. See also *Begum (Fazal)* (15920) IAS 1998, Vol 1, No 8, Immigration Appeal Tribunal. See also DSP 15.2 (Mar 03).
[2]   [1976] Imm AR 28.
[3]   *Entry Clearance Officer, Port Louis v Grenade* [1978] Imm AR 143; see also *R v Immigration Appeal Tribunal, ex p Coelho* (5 February 1986, unreported).
[4]   *Sithamparapillai* (15724) IAS 1998, Vol 1, No 6, Immigration Appeal Tribunal. This seems to be using 'necessity' in a different sense; see below.
[5]   *Bibi v Entry Clearance Officer Dhaka* [2000] Imm AR 385, CA; *George* (4184).
[6]   *Chavda v Entry Clearance Officer, Bombay* [1978] Imm AR 40.

11.129 Difficulties may also arise where the applicants have some assets of their own. Early Tribunal decisions were concerned with when the assets were likely to run out, and held that it was not necessary for applicants to use up all their resources before becoming necessarily dependent on remittances from the UK.[1] An alternative approach is that taken by the Department of Social Security in income support cases where an estimate is made of the income which could reasonably be derived from any capital. In *Bhattacharjee*[2] the Tribunal adopted the guidance of the High Court in *Ex p Patel*[3] and determined that the question was whether there was a deficiency in the applicant's own resources available to meet his or her needs. In *George*[4] the Tribunal applied this test to the value of a house owned in the UK and it was held that there was a deficiency, in that the proceeds would not provide a home and an income for the applicants without substantial recourse to the support of their children. We suggest that the true rationale of *Sithamparapillai*,[5] where the UK sponsor provided support because the pension of a retired government official was not sufficient for the life-style he wished to adopt, was that support which supplements an adequate income does not result in the relative being 'mainly' dependent on the sponsor. The IDI pose the test that 'the payments from the sponsor are essential to help the applicant achieve a reasonable life style'.[6]

[1]   *Sharma* (227) and *Patel* (506) unreported.
[2]   (3476) unreported.
[3]   *R v Immigration Appeal Tribunal, ex p Patel* (1982) Times, 7 April, QBD.
[4]   (4184) unreported
[5]   *Sithamparapillai* (15724) IAS 1998 Vol 1 No 6, Immigration Appeal Tribunal. The Tribunal found the dependence was not one of necessity; see 11.128 fn 4 above.

[6]   IDI Sep 04, Ch 8, Annex V, para 2. The support may be remittances, a house where the
applicant lives, or rent from land owned by the sponsor, which provides an income for the
applicant: ibid, see also DSP 15.2 (Mar 03).

Without close relatives to turn to

11.130 The present Immigration Rules require relatives seeking admission to
be without close relatives in their own country to whom to turn for financial
support.[1] Before the October 1994 change, the Rule simply required that there
were no close relatives there 'to turn to'. There are numerous decisions
interpreting the phrase in the previous rules. In *Bastiampillai*[2] the High Court
held that the Rules imply that the relatives must have the ability to provide
shelter or financial support to make it reasonable for the applicant to depend
on them rather than the sponsor. This was followed in *Ex p Dadibhai*,[3] where
it was held that the phrase implied a willingness to support by the alternative
relatives. Relatives who are hostile or indifferent to the applicant could not be
relied on. This is accepted by the Home Office.[4] The decisions in *Devshi*[5] and
Yip[6] are examples of how even close residence with other relatives does not
necessarily make them relatives to turn to in this context. The IDI and the DSP
make it clear that to disqualify an applicant on this ground there must be
sound evidence of both ability and willingness to provide support, which must
be long-term, not merely emergency support. But the support may be provided
by relatives acting jointly.[7] The relatives must be in the applicants' own
country and this has been interpreted as their country of residence rather than
that of nationality.[8]

[1]   HC 395, para 317(v).
[2]   *R v Immigration Appeal Tribunal, ex p Bastiampillai* [1983] 2 All ER 844, [1983] Imm AR
       1, QBD.
[3]   *R v Immigration Appeal Tribunal, ex p Dadibhai* (24 October 1983, unreported), QBD.
[4]   IDI Sep 04, Ch 8, Annex V.
[5]   *Devshi* (3163).
[6]   *Yip* (2894).
[7]   IDI Sep 04, Ch 8, Annex V, para 2, DSP 15.3 (Mar 03). Both sets of instructions indicate
       that ability of home-based relatives to support is partly cultural, and that a married
       daughter in the Indian sub-continent is unlikely to be able to provide support.
[8]   *Levy v Entry Clearance Officer, Kingston* [1978] Imm AR 119; *Patel* (20542) IAS 2000,
       Vol 3, No 2, IAT.

11.131 In *Immigration Appeal Tribunal v Singh*[1] the Court of Appeal
indicated that the correct approach to the previous rule was to recognise it as
a rule of broad humanity that had not previously been humanely administered. Thus, any kind of need of the appellant that was established by the
evidence that could not be met by relatives in the appellant's own country
would satisfy the requirements of the rule. Despite the authoritative terms of
this Court of Appeal decision, the Home Office sought to argue in *Entry
Clearance Officer, Dhaka v Khatun*[2] that the court had not meant to include
financial need. This viewpoint was rejected once again. It can thus be stated:
that before the applicant is disqualified, there must be close relatives in his or
her own country to turn to, who are able and willing to meet the needs of the
applicant, even if these are supplied by the sponsor in the UK.[3] *R v
Immigration Appeal Tribunal, ex p Khatun*[4] also provides an example of what

the unmet needs can include. Here the applicant had spent many years in the household of her daughter-in-law and grandchildren, and was used to living with them. The adjudicator decided that this fact made it reasonable not to turn to her elderly brothers who were willing to support and accommodate her. The Tribunal reversed the adjudicator, but their decision was in turn quashed by the High Court, which held that in the light of the adjudicator's findings there were emotional and social needs of the applicant that only the sponsor in the UK could satisfy. The rule was amended in 1994 to refer explicitly to financial needs. However, the DSP advise entry clearance officers to have regard to the distance between the applicant and the close relatives, particularly in countries where even short journeys are arduous, and the age and any illness or other vulnerability of the applicant – an indication that emotional and social needs remain relevant.[5]

1   *Immigration Appeal Tribunal v Swaran Singh* [1987] Imm AR 563, CA.
2   [1988] Imm AR 348, IAT; [1989] Imm AR 482, QBD.
3   *R v Immigration Appeal Tribunal, ex p Kara* [1989] Imm AR 120, QBD.
4   [1989] Imm AR 482, QBD.
5   DSP 15.3 (Mar 03).

Living alone in the most exceptional compassionate circumstances

11.132 The test for admission for those relatives who can only qualify by satisfying this supplementary requirement undoubtedly is a high one,[1] but it must not be interpreted in an unrealistically high way. The rule is intended to assist those who are unable to care for themselves, or suffer isolation and social stigma without the support of their family.[2] However, the financial support from UK-settled relatives, which is necessary for qualification, may mitigate the applicant's circumstances and so take them below the threshold,[3] and the rule is not to be construed as if the financial support was not there.[4] If an applicant is in the UK when an application is made, the rule should be construed as requiring an examination of what the position would have been at the date of decision had the applicant remained where he or she was and had not come here.[5] The Tribunal has held that one can be living alone without necessarily living on one's own.[6] The requirement to be 'living alone' is not restricted to physical isolation and can include those who have been so psychologically isolated as to cut themselves off from those around them.[7] The proper approach to deciding upon the existence of most exceptional compassionate circumstances is to take all the elements of hardship cumulatively,[8] and these have included the existence of a very close relationship between an appellant and her granddaughter;[9] the fact that in the appellant's community a young single woman living alone would be regarded as immoral[10] and the fact that on return to their country appellants would be new re-arrivals in an area of high crime and going to a house which had deteriorated during their absence.[11] The IDI refer to illness, incapacity, isolation and poverty as capable of constituting most exceptional compassionate circumstances for parents and grandparents under 65.[12] For other relatives, the IDI suggest that the circumstances will need to be such that the applicant is unable to function (due to illness or disability) without the held or support of friends or relatives, and no such help is available in the country where he or she is living, a test which we suggest is unnecessarily restrictive.[13]

1 See eg *AA and NA (Concession on DNA testing) Bangladesh* [2004] UKIAT 00180 (adult child wrongly refused as child); *SS (Entry Clearance Officer Article 8) Malaysia* [2004] UKIAT 00091; *S (Uganda)* [2004] UKIAT 00064; *RM (Special Vouchers Representation) India* [2005] 00067 (no legitimate expectation of entry under old rule), for examples of how rigorously it is applied. Most cases are argued in the alternative as Art 8 cases (for which see chapter 8 above).

2 *Begum (Iqbal)* (5580).

3 See *Bibi (Nessa)* (21162A) IAS, Vol 3, No 13, Immigration Appeal Tribunal.

4 *R v Immigration Appeal Tribunal, ex p Manshoora Begum* [1986] Imm AR 385, QBD; *Begum (Zohra) v Immigration Appeal Tribunal* [1994] Imm AR 381, CA.

5 See TH/04414/2004 (21 January 2005, unreported).

6 *Paw* (4328) unreported.

7 *Boshir* (10902).

8 *Agoro* (16078) IAS 1998, Vol 1, No 5, Immigration Appeal Tribunal. But see *Nessa (Sharijun)* (16391) IAS 1998, Vol 1, No 23: the factors of dependency and living alone are separate and not to be 'blurred' with the most exceptional compassionate circumstances test. See also *Husna Begum v Entry Clearance Officer, Dhaka* [2001] INLR 115, CA.

9 *Wu* (12359).

10 *Bayar* (12380). The IDI state that where the applicant is a young single or divorced woman living in a country where it is claimed that it is socially unacceptable for her to live there alone, this may be taken into account when considering whether the test is met, but that such a situation is not on its own sufficient: IDI Oct 04, Ch 8, s 6.

11 *Mohammed* (15454).

12 IDI Sep 04, Ch 8, Annex V.

13 IDI Sep 04, Ch 8, Annex W.

Chapter 12

REFUGEES, ASYLUM AND EXCEPTIONAL LEAVE

INTRODUCTION

Asylum

12.1 In layman's language, refugees are people seeking asylum in a foreign country because of war, civil war or other catastrophic events in their own. It is only in the artificial world of the 1951 Convention Relating to the Status of Refugees, now the major convention used throughout the world for the protection of refugees, with 145 State parties,[1] that generalised catastrophe disqualifies, rather than qualifies, a person from the status of refugee.[2] It is partly this mismatch between 'legal' or 'Convention' refugees and 'actual' or 'de facto' refugees which has allowed western European governments to enact ever more restrictive measures against refugees, often irresponsibly described as 'bogus' or 'abusive'.[3] Over the past decade the word 'asylum' has almost lost its meaning under the weight of political scaremongering to which it has been subject.

[1] UNHCR Note on International Protection, July 2003, para 43.
[2] The Convention concerning the Specific Aspects of Refugee Problems in Africa 1969 contains a broader definition of the term 'refugee' and one more in keeping with the word's natural meaning, embracing those compelled to leave their place of habitual residence through 'external aggression, occupation, foreign domination or events seriously disturbing public order in either part or the whole of the country' (Plender *Basic Documents on International Migration Law* (2nd revised edn, 1999), p 117).

668

[3] The recognition rate for refugees has less to do with merits than with politics. Thus between 1989 and 1998 Canada granted refugee status to over 80 per cent of applicants from Sri Lanka, France to 74 per cent, and the UK to 1 per cent: Refugee Council response to the Home Secretary's Lisbon Proposals, January 2001.

12.2 Asylum in its ordinary dictionary meaning is a refuge, shelter or protection. Article 14 of the Universal Declaration of Human Rights (UDHR) refers to a right to 'seek and enjoy asylum from persecution' but does not specify the meaning or grounds of persecution. The concept of territorial asylum[1] includes asylum for humanitarian reasons rather than specifically for particular types of refugees. In the UK, the law and the Immigration Rules used to distinguish between asylum and Convention refugee status; that distinction disappeared in 1993[2] and the words are now used synonymously.[3] Thus, in considering appeals against refusal of leave to enter or remain on asylum grounds, the appellate authorities' principal concern will be whether the applicant is a Convention refugee.[4] This chapter is predominantly concerned with the application of the rules relating to asylum, and so references to refugees, asylum and the Convention are references to the statutory definition. Convention refugees are those who seek to escape persecution for reasons of race, religion, nationality, membership of a social group, or political opinion. The scope of this Convention definition is examined in greater detail below (at 12.21ff).

[1] See the Declaration of the Committee of Ministers of the Council of Europe on Territorial Asylum 1977, the Caracas Convention on Territorial Asylum 1954, the Caracas Convention on Diplomatic Asylum 1954 and the Cartagena Declaration on Refugees 1984. See also Recommendation R (1981) 16 on the Harmonisation of National Procedures Relating to Asylum (Plender 12.1 fn 2 above, pp 140, 147).

[2] With the Asylum and Immigration Appeals Act 1993, s 1 of which (still in force) for the first time defined 'asylum' as meaning refugee status within the meaning of the Convention Relating to the Status of Refugees (Geneva, 1951) and its 1967 Protocol (collectively the Refugee Convention). See also the immigration rules HC 395, para 327, defining an asylum applicant as a person who claims that it would be contrary to the United Kingdom's obligations under the Refugee Convention for him to be removed from or required to leave the United Kingdom. However, for the purposes of 'asylum support' in Pt VI of the 1999 Act, a 'claim for asylum' is defined to include a claim that removal would be contrary to Art 3 ECHR: see s 94. A similar definition is used in Part 2 (Accommodation Centres) of the Nationality, Immigration and Asylum Act 2002: see s 18(3).

[3] See Home Office evidence to the House of Commons Home Affairs Committee Sub-Committee on Race and Immigration 1984–85, 72 HC Official Report (6th series) col iv, 17 December 1984. The Education (Mandatory Awards) Regulations 1991, SI 1991/1838 referred to 'refugees or others granted asylum', but the regulations made since 1993 no longer use this terminology.

[4] Nationality, Immigration and Asylum Act 2002, ss 82 and 84(1)(g). This does not preclude other matters, including human rights grounds, from being litigated in the same proceedings: see chapter 18 below.

12.3 However wide the definition of refugee, there will be those deserving protection under other international instruments who may fall outside it. People may be fleeing torture and inhuman or degrading treatment even though such treatment may not be on the grounds of race, religion, nationality, membership of a social group or political opinion.[1] Expulsion of such persons in circumstances where there are substantial grounds to conclude that they face such treatment would be contrary to other international obligations.[2] The distinction is recognised in EU law by the grant of a subsidiary status to those who cannot be expected to return to their country of origin for reasons not qualifying them for refugee status.[3] In the UK, such persons have historically been unrecognised in the Immigration Rules, although the Home Office may grant Humanitarian Protection or Discretionary Leave,[4] and the incompatibility of an immigration decision with rights protected under the Human Rights Convention has since 2 October 2000 been a statutorily recognised ground of appeal.[5] We examined the ECHR in chapter 8 above and will look at the grant of Humanitarian Protection and Discretionary Leave in 12.174 below.

[1]   See *Ameyaw v Secretary of State for the Home Department* [1992] Imm AR 206 (unfair trial); *R v Secretary of State for the Home Department, ex p Zibirila-Alassia* [1991] Imm AR 367, QBD (fear of being selected as victim of ritual sacrifice); *R v Immigration Appeal Tribunal, ex p Hernandez* [1994] Imm AR 506, QBD (retribution from guerilla groups); *Hamieh v Secretary of State for the Home Department* [1993] Imm AR 323 (pressure from extremist groups) for examples of possible persecution for non-Refugee Convention reasons.

[2]   Most notably Art 3 of the ECHR and Art 3 of the UN Convention Against Torture: see *R v Secretary of State for the Home Department, ex p Chahal* [1994] Imm AR 107, [1995] 1 All ER 658, CA; *Chahal v United Kingdom* (1996) 23 EHRR 413. See also *Mutombo v Switzerland* (1994) 15 HRJ 164; *Alan v Switzerland* [1997] INLR 29. See also Gorlick 'Refugee Protection and the Committee Against Torture' (1995) 7 IJRL 504.

[3]   In Art 63(2)(a) EC, inserted by Treaty of Amsterdam, signed on 2 October 1997 by 15 Member States, such persons are described as 'other persons in need of international protection'. See now the Council Directive 2004/83/EC on minimum standards for the qualification and status of third country nationals and stateless persons as refugees or as persons who otherwise need international protection, in force 20 October 2004 (2004 OJ L 304/12) (hereafter the 'EC Qualification Directive'). Arts 2(e) and 15 provide for 'subsidiary protection' for those in flight from the death penalty or execution, torture, inhuman or degrading treatment or punishment, and serious threats to life or person. It does not cover those in flight from poverty, famine or environmental degradation, leaving the grant of discretionary leave on compassionate grounds to national authorities. At the time of writing, Home Office policy is not to grant leave but to suspend removal of failed asylum seekers from particular countries, whether for political reasons (eg Iraq) or because of natural disasters (parts of Indonesia, India, Sri Lanka, Somalia and the Maldives affected by the tsunami of December 2004). Note also Council Directive 2001/55/EC of 20 July 2001 regarding the giving of temporary protection by Member States in the event of a mass influx of displaced persons (the 'EC Temporary Protection Directive', dealt with in Part 11A of the immigration rules, HC 395).

[4]   'Exceptional leave to remain' was abolished with effect from 1 April 2003 and replaced with the two types of leave mentioned, each of which would be 'more focussed than the ... exceptional leave provisions'. According to the Home Office Humanitarian Protection (but not Discretionary Leave) would be added to the Rules. At time of writing the rules have yet to incorporate Humanitarian protection.

[5]   Nationality, Immigration and Asylum Act 2002, ss 82 and 84. Decisions before 1 April 2003 attract appeal rights under the Immigration and Asylum Act 1999, s 65. Prior to 2 October 1999, the only remedy for refusal to give effect to ECHR obligations was judicial review. See the judgment of Sedley J in *R v Secretary of State for the Home Department, ex p McQuillan* [1995] 4 All ER 400 for a most coherent exposition of *R v Secretary of State for the Home Department, ex p Brind* [1991] 1 AC 696 and the court's jurisdiction to ensure that domestic standards of rationality do not fall out of line with international obligations.

12.4   The present UK practice is that all those who are granted asylum in the UK are recognised as refugees and the appropriate Refugee Convention travel document is given in recognition of this status.[1] But refugees present in the UK do not have to be given asylum here if there is a safe third country to which they can be removed.[2] Those who do not qualify as refugees may be granted a period of Humanitarian Protection or Discretionary Leave, which may be renewed on review, and may lead to settlement. They will not receive a Convention travel document, but may apply for a Home Office travel document.[3] Refugees enjoy family reunion rights with their pre-existing spouses and minor children who formed part of the family unit prior to the principal's departure,[4] and the refugee sponsor is not expected to meet the maintenance and accommodation requirements of the Immigration Rules. But someone with Humanitarian Protection or Discretionary Leave cannot exercise family reunion rights (in the absence of compelling, compassionate circumstances) until becoming eligible to apply for indefinite leave to remain after completing three or six years, and will be expected to satisfy the maintenance and accommodation requirements.[5]

[1]   As required by the Refugee Convention, Art 28, Schedule.
[2]   HC 395, paras 334, 345. We examine the UK's practice on safe third countries at 12.132 below.
[3]   For humanitarian protection and discretionary leave see 12.174 below. For travel documents see **12.178** below. The provisions have been substantially tightened with effect from 27 March 2003.
[4]   The position of the spouse and children of refugees is covered by the Immigration Rules (paras 352A–E of HC). The Asylum Policy Instrutions (API) also cover other family members. See 12.179 below.
[5]   See API. Those with exceptional leave to remain (ELR) (not granted since April 2003) must wait for four years before exercising family reunion rights. Family reunion for those with subsidiary protection is discussed at 12.179 below.

12.5 The general rule of customary international law is that no individual may assert a right to enter a state of which he or she is not a national, and this rule is normally accepted as applying to refugees as well as ordinary migrants.[1] In accordance with this rule the right of asylum is not a right accorded to an individual refugee (except vis-à-vis the country of origin),[2] but is a discretionary right of a state to grant or withhold asylum.[3] The importance of giving states the right to grant asylum was to emphasise that such a grant was not an unfriendly act against the state of which the refugee was a national. These provisions of customary international law are reflected in the international legal instruments that have come into being since 1948. Article 14 of the Universal Declaration of Human Rights 1948 (UDHR) recognised the fundamental right to 'seek and enjoy asylum', and although the Convention and Protocol studiously avoid creating any legal right to asylum or any duty to grant asylum or to give a refugee leave to enter a particular territory, the two provisions are not incompatible. First, if there is a right to seek asylum (as posited by Article 14 of UDHR), there is a corresponding duty on the country where it is sought at least to consider that application and in doing so to act fairly and consistently as between one asylum seeker and another.[4] Secondly, this implies a further obligation on that country, which is to offer asylum seekers at the very least temporary admission until the state has assured itself that their return to a third country or to their country of origin would not be in breach of Article 33. [5] Furthermore, it is a matter of contention whether over 50 years of state practice have modified this position in international customary law.[6]

[1]   Lauterpacht *Oppenheim's International Law* (7th edn, 1952) p 616; R Plender *International Migration Law* (2nd edn, 1988) p 394; see also F Morgenstern 'The Right of Asylum' (1949) 26 BYBIL 327 at 335; P Weis 'Legal Aspects of the Convention Relating to

the Status of Refugees' (1953) 30 BYBIL 478 at 481. See also Goodwin-Gill *The Refugee in International Law* (2nd edn, 1996); Goodwin-Gill's editorial comment 'Asylum: The Law and Politics of Change' (1995) 7 IJRL 1; and Roman Boed, 'The state of the right of asylum in international law', (1994) 5 Duke Journal of Comparative International Law 1.

2   UDHR, Art 13(2); International Covenant on Civil and Political Rights, Art 12(2).

3   The position in municipal law might be different: see Immigration Rules, HC 395, para 334; *R v Secretary of State for the Home Department, ex p Deniz Mersin* [2000] INLR 511, QBD, at 12.102, fn 8 below where Elias J held that an asylum seeker who had succeeded on appeal had a right to be granted refugee status and indefinite leave to remain.

4   The duty to consider has given rise to internationally applied practices and procedures, the key element of which can be found in the UNHCR Handbook Part 2 (see dicta in Court of Appeal in *Robinson v Secretary of State for the Home Department* [1997] Imm AR 568, at para 11, per Brooke LJ.

5   See UNHCR Handbook, para 192 (vii).

6   UNHCR refers to instances of denial of access to protection through closure of borders and non-admission to the territory or to asylum procedures as 'serious breaches of the internationally recognised rights of refugees and asylum seekers' in its *Note on International Protection*, ExCom 50th session, UN doc A/AC.96/914, 7 July 1999, (1999) 11(3) IJRL 557. The existence of an international law duty which is broader in its terms than the Geneva Convention obligation of non-refoulement was doubted in *European Roma Rights Centre v Immigration Officer at Prague Airport* [2004] UKHL 55, [2005] 2 WLR 1.

The Geneva Convention

12.6 The key international instrument is the Geneva Convention of 1951 Relating to the Status of Refugees, as amended by the Protocol to the Convention 1967 (collectively the Refugee Convention). The original Convention was concerned with the displacement of people as a result of the Second World War and its aftermath, and restricted the definition of refugees to those whose fear of persecution arose from events occurring before 1 January 1951. The Protocol removed this time limitation, but enabled parties who had imposed a geographic limitation on the application of the Convention to continue such limitations to post-1951 refugees. Some states made declarations limiting the application of the Convention to refugees fleeing their countries as a result of events occurring in Europe. In the past this included some European countries, but now all EU countries have ratified both Convention and Protocol without temporal or geographical limitations.[1] The Asylum and Immigration Appeals Act 1993 incorporated the Convention into UK law to the extent of providing that it would be unlawful for Immigration Rules to be made that are inconsistent with the Convention.[2]

1   Italy, in particular, used to have a geographical reservation. In 1990 the Member States of the EU formulated the Dublin Convention to prevent asylum seekers making multiple applications within the EU. In order to achieve this, signatory states were required to have ratified the Protocol. This first Dublin Convention, which came into force in September 1997, was substituted with effect from 1 September 2003 by Council Regulation (EC) No 343/2003 of 18 February 2003 establishing the criteria and mechanisms for determining the Member State responsible for examining an asylum application lodged in one of the Member States by a third-country national (known as Dublin II). See further 12.150 below.

2   Asylum and Immigration Appeals Act 1993, s 2; HC 395, para 334. The House of Lords in *R v Secretary of State for the Home Department, ex p Sivakumaran* [1988] AC 958 took the view that 'the UK having acceded to the Convention and Protocol, their provisions have for all practical purposes been incorporated into UK law'. In *R v Uxbridge Magistrates' Court, ex p Adimi* [1999] INLR 490 the Divisional Court held that refugees had a legitimate expectation that the provisions of the Convention would be followed. In *European Roma Rights Centre v Immigration Officer at Prague Airport* [2004] UKHL 55,

[2005] 2 WLR 1, the House of Lords confirmed that the Convention was incorporated into domestic law (per Lord Bingham at para 7, Lord Steyn at paras 41–42 and Lord Hope at para 50).

12.7 In broad terms the Refugee Convention provides a definition of refugees, creates exclusions from the definition and sets out circumstances when a person may cease to be a refugee,[1] and defines the duties owed to and by refugees vis-à-vis their host states. While the principal duty owed to refugees is that of *non-refoulement*,[2] it is clear from the decision in *Saad*[3] that this is not the only duty; as a party to the Refugee Convention the United Kingdom must afford all the Convention rights to anyone who is a refugee within the meaning of Article 1A to avoid a breach of the UK's international obligations. Where someone is recognised as a refugee and granted asylum, signatory states are under a duty to secure equal treatment with own nationals, or sometimes with other lawfully resident third country nationals, in respect of religion, personal status, property, freedom of association, gainful occupation, welfare, administrative measures and the issue of special travel documents to be used in place of the refugee's national passport.[4] It is important to note that refugees are recognised by states rather than created by them: an asylum claimant should thus be treated as a potential refugee unless and until a valid determination is made that he or she is not to be so recognised,[5] but this principle does not preclude the construction of the particular Articles of the Convention which refer to refugees 'lawfully on the territory' as referring to recognised refugees who have been granted leave to stay.[6]

1   Refugee Convention, Art 1.
2   See 12.8 below.
3   *Saad, Diriye and Osorio v Secretary of State for the Home Department* [2001] EWCA Civ 2008, [2002] Imm AR 471 [2002] INLR 34.
4   Refugee Convention, Arts 4–30.
5   See UNHCR *Handbook on Procedures and Criteria for Determining Refugee Status* (1979) para 28; *Khaboka v Secretary of State for the Home Department* [1993] Imm AR 484 at 487, CA, per Nolan LJ.
6   See For the meaning of 'lawfully in the territory' see *Bugdaycay v Secretary of State for the Home Department* [1987] AC 5114 at 526, per Lord Bridge. See also *R v Secretary of State for the Home Department, ex p Joint Council for the Welfare of Immigrants* [1996] 4 All ER 385, [1997] 1 WLR 275, where the Court of Appeal assumed that Art 23 of the Refugee Convention (the right of refugees lawfully staying on the territory to social security on the same basis as nationals) did not apply to asylum seekers.

12.8 The states that are signatories to the Refugee Convention did not surrender their discretionary power to grant or withhold asylum, but in practice the scope of this discretion is greatly narrowed by duties assumed by states signatory to the Convention and the other instruments, such as the UN Convention Against Torture and the regional human rights Treaties, such as the ECHR.[1] Signatory states agree to abide by Article 33 which prohibits *refoulement* (ie the expulsion or return of refugees in any manner whatsoever to the frontiers of territories where their lives or freedom would be threatened on account of their race, religion, nationality, membership of a particular social group or political opinion). If there is no safe third country to which a person can be sent, the principle of *non-refoulement* effectively requires a state to determine an asylum claim made by someone within its territory (including the border or transit zone at an airport).[2] In the UK, if a person is recognised as a refugee, asylum is granted. The immigration rules provide for a grant of limited leave, but Home Office policy is to grant indefinite leave to enter or remain.[3] The EC Qualification Directive 2004/83 sets out the residence rights which should be granted to recognised refugees and to other persons needing international protection throughout the Community.[4]

[1]   *T v Immigration Officer* [1996] AC 742, [1996] 2 WLR 766, [1996] Imm AR 443 at 446, per Lord Mustill. See also Joan Fitzpatrick 'Revitalising the 1951 Refugee Convention' (1996) 9 Harvard Human Rights Journal 229 at 251: 'The most enduring contribution of the Convention is its elevation of *non-refoulement* to the status of an international norm.'

[2]   The French attempt to circumvent domestic constraints on detention of asylum seekers by declaring the airport an 'international zone' was thwarted in *Amuur v France* (1996) 22 EHRR 533 where the detention was held to breach Art 5 of the ECHR.

[3]   See HC 395, para 335; see also *Asylum applications: a brief guide to procedures in the UK* (on Home Office website) p 87. The government proposes to grant refugees temporary leave in the first instance, with a review after five years: see *Controlling our borders: Making migration work for Britain: Five year strategy for asylum and immigration*, Cm 6472, Feb 2005, para 39.

[4]   EC Qualification Directive 2004/83/EC, 12.3 fn 3 above, Arts 20–30.

12.9 A big issue in contemporary refugee law is whether the Refugee Convention has extra-territorial effect. The question has assumed great importance as more and more states employ measures, ranging from carrier sanctions and visa controls to airline liaison officers, to prevent undocumented passengers boarding transport in countries of origin, physical interception and return of asylum seekers on the high seas, and increasingly, agreements with countries of origin and transit to prevent asylum seekers leaving for western countries. UNHCR takes the view that the obligation of *non-refoulement*, which is 'progressively acquiring the character of a peremptory rule of international law', extends to all government agents acting in an official capacity, whether within or outside national territory. 'Given the practice of States to intercept persons at a great distance from their own territory, the international refugee protection regime would be rendered ineffective if States' agents abroad were able to act at variance with their obligations under international refugee law and human rights law.'[1] Similarly, Goodwin-Gill has trenchant criticism of the US Supreme Court's decision in *Sale v Haitian Centers Council*[2] upholding the policy of extra-territorial interception and return of Haitian asylum seekers to Haiti by US coastguards without any determination of their claims,[3] and Lord Bingham expressly distinguished *Sale*, where the asylum seekers were outside the country of their nationality and so *prima facie* entitled to protection under the Convention, from the situation in *European Roma Rights,* where pre-entry controls were carried out in the country of origin of the would-be asylum claimants.[4] Their Lordships did not however expressly state that asylum claimants who were outside their country of nationality but not at the borders of the UK should be allowed to continue their journey, and their judgements make no inroads on the carriers' liability and other provisions which prevent travel to the UK. In an earlier case the High Court concluded that, where a Tamil seeking asylum had been detained in Oman for using false documents to board a plane to come to the UK to claim asylum, the international obligation only arose when the claimant reached the territory of the state where asylum was claimed.[5] The courts have recognised the effect that carrier sanctions have on refugees' ability to seek asylum, but have not declared them unlawful.[6]

¹ UNHCR ExCom Standing Committee, *Interception of asylum seekers and refugees*, 18th meeting, 9 June 2000, EC/50/SC/CRP.17, paras 21–23. See also UNHCR: *The trafficking and smuggling of refugees: the end game in European asylum policy?* July 2000; UNHCR ExCom 50th session, Note on International Protection, UN doc A/AC.96/914, 7 July 1999, in (1999) 11(3) IJRL 557.

² 113 S Ct 2549 (1993), in which in which the court by 8–1 held that the US Immigration Service had acted lawfully in intercepting a boatload of Haitian would-be asylum seekers in international waters and returning them to Haiti. Blackmun J, dissenting, found it 'extraordinary ... that the executive, in disregard of the law, would take to the seas to intercept fleeing refugees and force them back to their persecutors – and that the court would strain to sanction that conduct'. The Inter-American Commission for Human Rights in Report No 51/96 preferred Blackmun J's dissenting judgment but in *European Roma Rights Centre* (fn 4 below) Lord Hope considered that the majority had been correct. For the EU's own interception and return project, Operation Ulysses, see Institute of Race Relations website (www. irr.org.uk).

³ Goodwin-Gill 12.5 fn 1 above, pp 142–144. See also (1994) 6(1) IJRL 68–109.

⁴ *European Roma Rights Centre v Immigration Officer at Prague Airport (United Nations High Commissioner for Refugees intervening)* [2004] UKHL 55, [2005] 2 WLR 1. The appellants and UNHCR argued that the pre-entry clearance regime which prevented an asylum seeker from reaching the border was contrary to the good faith obligation interpreted in the light of the object and purpose of the Refugee Convention.

⁵ *R v Secretary of State for the Home Department, ex p Sritharan* [1992] Imm AR 184. It was held that there was no arguable case that the UK owed an obligation to issue a visa to enable him to continue his journey, despite the risk that Oman would return him to Sri Lanka without entertaining an asylum claim. For a discussion of diplomatic asylum and public international law see *R (on the application of B) v Secretary of State for Foreign and Commonwealth Affairs* [2004] EWCA Civ 1344, [2005] 2 WLR 618 (a challenge to the return to Australian custody of Afghan children who had escaped from detention in Australia and sought protection in the British embassy, decided with reference to the ECHR, not the Geneva Convention).

⁶ *European Roma Rights* (fn 4 above); *R v Secretary of State for the Home Department, ex p Yassine* [1990] Imm AR 354, QBD; *R v Uxbridge Magistrates' Court, ex p Adimi* [1999] INLR 490; *R v Secretary of State for the Home Department, ex p Hoverspeed* [1999] INLR 591, at 14.97 below. On the compatibility of carrier sanctions with international law see Erika Feller 'Carrier Sanctions and International Law' (1989) 1 IJRL 48; A Ruff 'The United Kingdom Immigration (Carriers Liability) Act 1987' (1989) 1 IJRL 481. For the background to the enactment of the first carrier sanctions see Nicholas Blake 'The Road to *Sivakumaran*' in (1989) 3 INLP 1 at 12. For detailed consideration of carrier sanctions see 14.88ff below.

12.10 Article 32 of the Refugee Convention gives refugees lawfully within the territory of a contracting state a right not to be expelled, save on grounds of national security or public order. Even then, expulsion is only possible following a decision reached in accordance with due process of law, and there must be a right of appeal and of representation before a competent authority. The UK provisions for deportation now give effect to this requirement, although only since 1998 in cases of removal on grounds relating to national security.¹ Article 32 does not apply to asylum seekers who claim asylum on arrival, since they cannot claim to be 'lawfully within the territory' until they have been given leave to enter.² It does not, therefore, prevent removal of potential refugees to safe third countries for determination of their claim elsewhere, or guarantee appeal rights to asylum seekers before removal.³

¹ Following the condemnation of the UK for lack of an effective remedy under Art 13 of the ECHR in *Chahal v United Kingdom* (1996) 23 EHRR 413, the government set up the Special Immigration Appeals Commission (Special Immigration Appeals Commission Act 1997) which hears all appeals, including asylum appeals, in which there is a national security element. See chapter 18 below.

2   *Bugdaycay v Secretary of State for the Home Department* [1987] AC 514 at 526, per Lord Bridge; see 12.7 text and fn 6 above.
3   See Nationality, Immigration and Asylum Act 2002, s 94 (and s 115 'transitional' provisions), 12.161 below.

12.11 Article 31(1) of the Refugee Convention precludes a state from imposing penalties on refugees coming directly from territories where they are persecuted on account of their illegal entry and presence, provided they report themselves to the authorities promptly.[1] A refugee is not an illegal entrant simply because he or she arrives without a passport or visa, or may have deceived the carrier in order to travel to the UK,[2] but lies told to the immigration officer on arrival are a different matter.[3] The meaning and application of Article 31(1) was considered by the Divisional Court in *R v Uxbridge Magistrates' Court, ex p Adimi*,[4] which concerned asylum seekers who had used false passports to enter the UK. Mr Adimi had claimed asylum after being refused leave to enter as a visitor on the basis of a false passport. He had come from Algeria via Italy and France (neither of which recognised persecution by non-state agents as giving rise to a Convention claim), and had spent several weeks in transit. He had been charged with a Forgery and Counterfeiting Act offence and sought judicial review of the magistrates' refusal to stay the proceedings because of Article 31(1) of the Refugee Convention. The other two applicants, Sorani and Kaziu, were Albanians who had entered the UK in transit to Canada, where they hoped to claim asylum. They had been apprehended boarding the onward flight with false passports and had been taken off. They had been similarly charged, convicted and sentenced to several months' imprisonment, which they had served. All three applicants were held to be covered by the protection of Article 31(1). The court held that where illegal entry or the use of false documents or delay can be attributed to a *bona fide* desire to seek asylum, whether here or elsewhere, that conduct should be covered by Article 31(1).[5] As to 'coming directly', some element of choice is, the court held, open to refugees as to where they may properly claim asylum. Any merely short-term stopover en route to such intended sanctuary cannot forfeit the protection of the Article. The main touchstones by which exclusion from protection should be judged are the length of stay in the intermediate country, the reasons for delaying there (even a substantial delay in an unsafe third country would be reasonable where the time was spent trying to acquire the means of travelling on), and whether or not the refugee sought or found there protection de jure or de facto from the persecution they were fleeing.[6] The requirement that the refugee presents himself or herself promptly does not require an asylum seeker to claim on arrival, so long as there is an intention to claim asylum within a short time of arrival having successfully secured entry on false documents.[7] The prohibition on penalties does not prevent the detention of asylum seekers,[8] nor does it prevent their being charged as long as they are not convicted.[9] There is now a statutory defence in section 31 of the Immigration and Asylum Act 1999 to protect asylum seekers against wrongful conviction of possession or use of false documents in breach of the Article: see 14.38, and in *Pepushi*[10] the Administrative Court, following the reconsideration of *Adimi* by the Court of Appeal in the *European Roma Rights Centre* case,[11] held that the prosecuting authority and the court were bound to apply the narrower provisions of section 31, even if this results in the UK being in breach of the Refugee

Convention. We find this reading very difficult to reconcile with the House of Lords' judgment in *European Roma Rights*.[12] Many *bona fide* asylum seekers are now being charged, convicted and imprisoned for the new offence of failing to produce a travel document at a post-arrival interview – in many cases, we suggest, in flagrant breach of Article 31, because of the mis-match between its provisions and the requirements of the statutory defence.[13] Article 31(2) does not prevent return of asylum seekers to countries through which they have travelled, in accordance with the 1999, 2002 and 2004 Acts and the Immigration Rules, or to consult with those countries to ensure that asylum will be offered there.[14]

[1]   On Art 31 of the Refugee Convention, see Hathaway and Neve 'Making International Refugee Law Relevant Again: A Proposal for Collectivized and Solution-Orientated Protection' (1997) 10 Harvard Human Rights J 115 at 161; Rodger Haines 'International Law and Refugees in New Zealand' [1999] NZLR 119 at 128–130.

[2]   *R v Naillie* [1993] AC 674; *Nzamba-Liloneo v Secretary of State for the Home Department* [1993] Imm AR 225, CA. For the offence under the Asylum and Immigration (Treatment of Claimants, etc) Act 2004, s 2 see text and fn 13 below, and see further 14.34.

[3]   See illegal entry through deceiving the immigration officer at 16.16 below.

[4]   *R v Uxbridge Magistrates' Court, ex p Adimi* [1999] INLR 490.

[5]   *Adimi* above at 496.

[6]   *Adimi* above at 497.

[7]   *Adimi* above at 498.

[8]   See *A-G v E* [2000] 3 NZLR 257; see also A Davidson 'Article 31(2) of the Refugee Convention and its implementation in New Zealand: Is detention defensible?'.

[9]   See further 14.37ff below.

[10] *R (on the application of Pepushi) v Crown Prosecution Service* [2004] EWHC 798 (Admin), [2004] All ER (D) 129 (May), Thomas LJ and Silber J, who also held that the proper course to follow for unexceptional challenges to decisions to prosecute was to take the point in the criminal courts rather than bringing an application before the High Court. See also *R (on the application of Hussain) v Secretary of State for the Home Department* [2001] EWHC Admin 555, holding that Immigration and Asylum Act 1999, s 31 represented the UK's incorporation of Art 31 and so should be followed.

[11] *European Roma Rights Centre v Immigration Officer at Prague Airport (United Nations' High Commissioner for Refugees Intervening* [2003] EWCA Civ 666, [2004] QB 811, [2003] 4 All ER 247, in which Simon Brown LJ doubted his decision in *Adimi* and Laws LJ denounced as constitutionally heretical the basis of the decision, ie incorporation by legitimate expectation of an international treaty.

[12] The House of Lords in *European Roma Rights Centre* [2004] UKHL 55, [2005] 2 WLR 1 confirmed that the Convention was incorporated; see 12.6 fn 2 above.

[13] Under the Asylum and Immigration (Treatment of Claimants, etc) Act 2004, s 2. Challenges to convictions under s 2 on the basis of Art 31 are in process. See further 14.33 below.

[14] Immigration and Asylum Act 1999, ss 11, 12; Nationality, Immigration and Asylum Act 2002, s 80; Asylum and Immigration (Treatment of Claimants, etc) Act 2004, s 33, Sch 3; HC 395, para 345.

United Nations High Commissioner for Refugees

12.12 The Office of the UN High Commissioner for Refugees (UNHCR) was established in 1951 pursuant to a UN General Assembly resolution.[1] The High Commissioner is called upon to provide international protection, under the auspices of the UN, to refugees falling within the competence of the Commissioner's office. This mandate covers all those who are outside their country of nationality or habitual residence and have or have had a well-founded fear of persecution for Refugee Convention reasons,[2] whether or not recognised as refugees. In some countries the determination of refugee status is performed by the UNHCR on behalf of the receiving state. This is not the case in the UK, save for a small number of 'quota' refugees,[3] but full account is taken of the views of the UK representative, particularly in respect of whether a third country is safe or not.

1 General Assembly Resolution 428, December 1950; Goodwin-Gill, 12.5 fn 1, p 241; Plender Documents 12.1 fn 2 above, p 81.
2 Statute of the Office of the UNHCR, Arts 6A and 6B (Plender above, 82–83). See also the UK government's paper and the UNHCR reply in (1995) 7(1) IJRL 2.
3 Under a scheme started in 2004, like that involving Vietnamese refugees in the 1960s and 70s, accepting for settlement a small number of refugees processed abroad by UNHCR. Although not all these will necessarily be Convention refugees, the government has expressed interest in developing this model in order to reduce the number of 'ad hoc' refugees. See House of Lords, EU Committee, 11th report 2003–4, 'Handling EU asylum claims: new approaches examined' (HL 74) for a critique of similar schemes involving extra-territorial processing.

12.13 The statute setting up the Office of the High Commissioner for Refugees provides that, in the exercise of his or her functions, the Commissioner shall request the opinion of an advisory committee on refugees in matters of difficulty.[1] The advisory committee is composed of representatives of states selected by the Economic and Social Council of the UN 'on the basis of their demonstrated interest in and devotion to the solution of the refugee problem'.[2] The advisory committee is called the Executive Committee of the Programme of the United Nations High Commissioner for Refugees, and is known as ExCom. Its recommendations, conclusions and reports provide valuable guidance on the interpretation of the Refugee Convention and the procedures to be adopted. The collected conclusions are published by the UNHCR. In 1979, at the request of Ex Com, a *Handbook on Procedures and Criteria for Determining Refugee Status* was produced. The *Handbook* is frequently referred to and approved by the UK appellate authorities and the courts,[3] and should form part of the equipment of any lawyer practising in this area of immigration law.[4] In addition, UNHCR periodically produces Guidelines on aspects of international protection which are giving rise to difficulty or controversy. Recent issues have covered internal relocation, religion and gender-based claims, the cessation and exclusion clauses and the meaning of 'particular social group' within the refugee definition.[5]

1 See Statute of the Office of UNHCR, Ch 1, para 1; Plender Documents, 12.1 fn 2 above, p 82.
2 Statute of the Office of the UNHCR, para 4.
3 See eg *T v Immigration Officer* [1996] AC 742, [1996] 2 All ER 865, [1996] 2 WLR 766, [1996] Imm AR 443, HL; *Adan v Secretary of State for the Home Department* [1999] 1 AC 293; *R v Secretary of State for the Home Department, ex p Adan* [2001] INLR 44, HL.
4 The *Handbook* is reproduced in *Butterworths Immigration Law Service*, 2C[73] and is available from the UNHCR (on its website, and see Appendix 2). ExCom's conclusions are published in booklet form; many of them are set out as appendices to Goodwin-Gill 12.5 fn 1 above and all are available on the UNHCR website.
5 Guidelines on international protection No 1: Gender-related persecution within the context of Article 1A(2) of the 1951 Convention and/or the 1967 Protocol relating to the status of refugees (HCR/GIP/02/01) 7 May 2002; No 2: 'Membership of a particular social group' within the context of Article 1A(2) of the 1951 Convention and/or the 1967 Protocol relating to the status of refugees (HCR/GIP/02/02) 7 May 2002; No 3: Cessation of refugee

status under Article 1C(5) and (6) of the 1951 Convention (the 'ceased circumstances' clauses) (HCR/GIP/003/03) 10 February 2003; No 4: 'Internal flight' or the 'internal relocation alternative' within the context of Article 1A(2) of the 1951 Convention and/or the 1967 Protocol relating to the status of refugees (HCR/GIP/03/04) 23 July 2003; No 5: The application of the exclusion clause, Article 1F of the 1951 Convention (HCR/GIP/03/05) 4 September 2003; No 6: Religion-based refugee claims under Article 1A(2) of the 1951 Convention and/or the 1967 Protocol relating to the status of refugees (HCR/GIP/04/06) 28 April 2004.

12.14 The UNHCR materials do not have the force of law or form part of the Refugee Convention. Neither the ExCom recommendations and conclusions nor the *Handbook* have been incorporated into UK Immigration Rules, and therefore, although they can provide guidance, they will not override express terms of the Immigration Acts or Rules, and will not be the subject of construction and application by the courts.[1] In *Robinson* the Court of Appeal described the *Handbook* as particularly helpful:

> 'as a guide to what is the international understanding of the Convention obligations, as worked out in practice, based on the knowledge accumulated by the High Commissioner's Office. This knowledge was derived, inter alia, from the practice of states in regard to the determination of refugee status, exchanges of views between the office and the competent authorities of contracting states, and the literature devoted to the subject over the previous quarter of a century.'[2]

The provisions are general rather than specific, and tend to be more exhortatory in tone than directive, although they are nonetheless an authoritative guide to the proper interpretation of the Refugee Convention.[3] The duty of co-operation with the UNHCR imposed by Article 35 of the Convention does not translate into a legally enforceable duty to comply with the recommendations of the High Commissioner and the Executive Committee.[4] The Secretary of State is entitled to have regard to them when deciding whether the UK is an appropriate country of asylum, and it is 'an important source of law, though not having the force of law',[5] but there is no requirement to follow them.[6] In short, the UNHCR materials are useful and authoritative aids to interpretation of the Convention and may be relevant to the exercise of a broad discretion, although not themselves the source of obligations and duties.

[1] See *Bugdaycay v Secretary of State for the Home Department* [1987] AC 514 at 524, per Lord Bridge. See also the arguments of the intervener in *R v Secretary of State for the Home Department, ex p Sivakumaran* [1988] AC 958, and at 1000–1001, per Lord Goff, and observations in *T v Immigration Officer* [1996] AC 742; *Adan v Secretary of State for the Home Department* [1999] 1 AC 293; *R v Immigration Appeal Tribunal, ex p Shah* [1999] 2 AC 629; *Danian v Secretary of State for the Home Department* [2000] Imm AR 96 at 120.

[2] *Robinson v Secretary of State for the Home Department* [1997] Imm AR 568, CA at 11. See also, to similar effect, *R v Secretary of State for the Home Department, ex p Adan, Subaskaran and Aitseguer* [1999] 3 WLR 1274 at 1296.

[3] See observations of Purchas LJ in *Alsawaf v Secretary of State for the Home Department* [1988] Imm AR 410 at 419, CA.

[4] This argument was advanced and rejected in *R v Secretary of State for the Home Department, ex p Mehari* [1994] QB 474, [1994] Imm AR 151.

[5] *T v Secretary of State for the Home Department* [1996] AC 742.

[6] See *Miller v Immigration Appeal Tribunal* [1988] Imm AR 358, CA; *R v Secretary of State for the Home Department, ex p Yassine* [1990] Imm AR 354, QBD. See further *Sepet v Secretary of State for the Home Department* [2001] EWCA Civ 681; [2003] UKHL 15, [2003] 3 All ER 304.

Determination of status

12.15 The Refugee Convention sets out no procedures for the determination of refugee status. It is left to contracting states to establish appropriate procedures having regard to their particular constitutional and administrative structures.[1] The wide variation in what was believed appropriate by different contracting states led the Executive Committee to formulate basic requirements for a fair procedure:[2]

(i) the official (immigration officer or border police) receiving the claim should have clear instructions on how to deal with cases engaging international obligations, must act in accordance with the principle of non-refoulement and refer the case to a higher authority;

(ii) the applicant should receive necessary guidance on procedure;

(iii) a clearly identified authority should have responsibility for examining requests and taking first-instance decisions;

(iv) the applicant should be given the necessary facilities, including a competent interpreter, for submitting the case, and should have the right to contact a UNHCR representative (and be informed of it);

(v) if recognised as a refugee, the applicant should be informed and issued with appropriate documentation;

(vi) if not, there should be a right to appeal either to the same or a different authority (administrative or judicial);

(vii) both the claim (unless established as clearly abusive) and the appeal should be suspensive.

The draft EU Council Directive on minimum standards on procedures in Member States for granting and withdrawing refugee status, which received political agreement at the April 2004 Council meeting, has been criticised for incorporating standards which fall short of those identified by the Executive Committee.[3]

[1] UNHCR *Handbook*, 12.13 above, para 189.
[2] At its 28th session in 1977: see UNHCR *Handbook* above, para 192. It may be that the demands of fairness are more rigorous a quarter of a century on.
[3] COM (2000) 578, 20 Sep. 2000; OJ 2001 C 62 E/231); amended proposal (COM (2002) 326, 18 June 2002; OJ 2002 C 291 E/143) (awaiting Parliamentary approval at time of writing).

Legislation relating to asylum in the UK

12.16 The UK had a long history of affording asylum before the 1951 Convention and its 1967 Protocol, and both the Extradition Act 1870 and the Aliens Act 1905 contained provisions exempting respectively political offences from extradition and political and religious refugees from refusal of entry.[1] The express enactment of these provisions in 1870 and 1905 meant that it was the UK courts rather than the Secretary of State who decided whether an offence was political or not. This has remained the practice in extradition cases.[2] However, when the Aliens Restriction Acts 1914 and 1919 replaced the 1905 Act, the exemption for refugees was not repeated, and subsequent immigration statutes followed this course until 1993. This omission gave rise to a body of jurisprudence that refugee status was not a matter for the courts but only the Secretary of State,[3] an attitude which passed into the modern decisions under more recent immigration laws.[4] In *Bugdaycay*[5] the House of Lords made it clear that in judicial review proceedings whether a person was a 'refugee' was a question for the Secretary of State and not a matter of jurisdictional fact or law for the courts. However, even before the Asylum and Immigration Appeals Act 1993 restored the statutory recognition of refugees, the appellate authorities could review the merits of certain decisions of the Secretary of State relating to asylum.[6]

[1] Extradition Act 1870, s 3(1); Aliens Act 1905, s 1(3); see also Fugitive Offenders Act 1967, s 5(1) and Extradition Act 1989, ss 6, 24. For a full history of policy in this respect see Dummett and Nicol *Subjects, Citizens, Aliens and Others* (1990), in particular, chapters 6 and 8.
[2] See *Cheng v Governor of Pentonville Prison* [1973] AC 931; *R v Governor of Brixton Prison, ex p Kolczynski* [1955] 1 QB 540 and 12.49 below.
[3] See eg *R v Chiswick Police Station Superintendent, ex p Sacksteder* [1918] 1 KB 578, CA; *R v Secretary of State for Home Affairs, ex p Duke of Chateau Thierry* [1917] 1 KB 922, CA; *R v Zausmer* (1911) 7 Cr App Rep 41; *R v Governor of Brixton, ex p Sarno* [1916] 2 KB 742.
[4] See *Ali v Immigration Appeal Tribunal* [1973] Imm AR 33 at 35, CA, following *R v Governor of Brixton Prison, ex p Soblen* [1963] 2 QB 243, [1962] 3 All ER 641, CA.
[5] *Bugdaycay v Secretary of State for the Home Department* [1987] AC 514.
[6] There was an in-country appeal against refusal of leave to enter (ie if the passenger held an entry clearance), or a variation or a deportation appeal under ss 13–15 of the Immigration Act 1971, if the appellant had claimed asylum.

12.17 The decade since the 1993 Act has seen a further four major Acts come onto the statute books dealing with asylum. The Asylum and Immigration Act 1996 removed in-country appeals against decisions to remove asylum seekers to 'safe third countries', and created a so-called 'white list' of 'safe' countries of origin, whose nationals had restricted appeal rights.[1] The Immigration and Asylum Act 1999 introduced human rights appeals and abolished the 'white list', but introduced a presumption of safety in the EU and in designated third countries.[2] The Nationality, Immigration and Asylum Act 2002 re-introduced a 'white list' of safe countries of origin and removed suspensive appeals from applicants whose claims the Secretary of State deemed 'clearly unfounded',[3] which, together with the presumption of safety, removed the possibility of appeal from thousands. The 1999 and 2002 Acts also removed asylum claimants from mainstream welfare benefits and, in many cases, from all support (see chapter 13), a process continued and extended by the Asylum and Immigration (Treatment of Claimants, etc) Act 2004. The 2004 Act also criminalised asylum claimants unable to produce a travel document and those refusing to cooperate with arrangements for their removal, and extended the 'safe third country' provisions to many more countries and parts of countries.[4]

[1] Asylum and Immigration Act 1996, ss 1, 2, referring to and amending Asylum and Immigration Appeals Act 1993, Sch 2, para 5.
[2] Immigration and Asylum Act 1999, s 11, reproduced in the Nationality, Immigration and Asylum Act 2002, s 80.
[3] Nationality, Immigration and Asylum Act 2002, s 94.
[4] Asylum and Immigration (Treatment of Claimants, etc) Act 2004, ss 2, 35, 33 and Sch 3.

12.18 During the 1960s the first Immigration Rules were published and, after representations from the UNHCR, these Rules made reference to asylum and refugees, although not to the 1951 Convention. Considerable advance was achieved in 1980 with the first reference in the Rules to the 1951 Convention and 1967 Protocol. But before 1993 there was tension between the provisions of the Rules giving primacy to the 1951 Convention and the Immigration Act 1971, which made no reference to the Convention and whose provisions were in some respects incompatible with it.[1] People who claimed asylum on arrival and who had no entry clearance had only an out-of-country appeal exercisable on return to the place of feared persecution, and so relied on judicial review for their remedy against removal.[2] The Asylum and Immigration Appeals Act 1993 gave statutory effect to the primacy of the Convention in the immigration rules,[3] and the rules made since the passing of the AIAA 1993 have attempted to provide a coherent structure in which asylum applications are considered and determined.[4] In addition, since 1998 the Asylum Directorate's instructions to caseworkers (ADI) (now Asylum Policy Instructions or API) have been published, providing a yet more detailed framework within which decisions are taken.[5]

[1] See *R v Immigration Appeal Tribunal, ex p Muruganandarajah* [1983] Imm AR 141, QBD, affirmed on appeal [1986] Imm AR 382, CA, for absence of rights of appeal in deportation cases following court recommendations.
[2] See *R v Secretary of State for the Home Department, ex p Sivakumaran* [1988] AC 958 where asylum seekers were unsuccessful in judicial review but succeeded on appeal to an adjudicator after removal to Sri Lanka where a number were tortured: *Secretary of State for the Home Department v Immigration Appeal Tribunal* [1990] Imm AR 492. In *Vilvarajah v United Kingdom* (1991) 14 EHRR 248 the ECtHR held, reversing the Commission, that judicial review was an effective remedy against the refusal of asylum for the purposes of Art 13 of the ECHR. The decision surprised the British government, which had decided to concede in-country appeal rights to asylum seekers in anticipation of losing on this point.
[3] Asylum and Immigration Appeals Act 1993, s 2.
[4] HC 395, paras 327–352; Asylum and Immigration Appeals Act 1993. Laws J in *R v Secretary of State for the Home Department, ex p Mehari* [1994] QB 474, [1994] Imm AR 151, QBD had regard to the Immigration Rules and the statutory instruments 'intended to dovetail with the new regime' in interpreting the 1993 Act.
[5] The API, which are regularly updated, are available on the Home Office website (www.ind.homeoffice.gov.uk/) and in hard copy at selected addresses (see Appendix 2).

12.19 People who have had an asylum claim turned down generally have a right of appeal prior to removal on the ground that to remove them would breach the UK's obligations under the Refugee Convention.[1] For third country cases, where the asylum claim is not entertained, see 12.132ff below. The appeal deals with the question of whether the appellant is a refugee. Where refugee status has been refused but the claimant has been granted leave to enter or remain, an appeal against the refusal of asylum is possible only where the leave granted exceeds one year in total.[2] Previously, appellants could appeal to an adjudicator and then to the Immigration Appeal Tribunal, but the Asylum and Immigration (Treatment of Claimants Etc) Act 2004 abolished the two-tier immigration appellate authority, replacing it with a single-tier Asylum and Immigration Tribunal.[3] Repeated applications for asylum on the same basis will not trigger a fresh right of appeal.[4] But the right of an asylum seeker to make a fresh application for asylum has been recognised by the Court of Appeal in *R v Secretary of State for the Home Department,* *ex p Onibiyo*[5] and is reflected in paragraph 353 of HC 395. The new rule no longer stipulates that the new material must have been previously unavailable, perhaps because if the material is sufficiently compelling it would clearly breach Convention obligations to refuse to look at it.[6]

[1] Under Nationality, Immigration and Asylum Act 2002, s 82 (in force 1 April 2003) the appeal lies against the immigration decision, and the Refugee Convention provides a ground of appeal. Those with leave to enter or remain in another capacity when they claim asylum will not have a right of appeal if their original leave is still extant at the date of decision: see s 82(2)(d), and will have to await a decision to remove them to have an appeal (under s 82(2)(g)). The in-country appeal is provided by s 92(4) (unless the Secretary of State has issued a third country certificate under Sch 3 to the AI(TC)A 2004 (or, more controversially, where the Secretary of State certifies that the claim is clearly unfounded under NIAA 2002, s 94 (as amended by Asylum and Immigration (Treatment of Claimants, etc) Act 2004, s 27): see 12.161 below).

[2] Nationality, Immigration and Asylum Act 2002, s 83. This will apply where, for example, a person is not recognised as a refugee but granted Humanitarian Protection or Discretionary Leave, for which see API 1.4.03 on Humanitarian Protection and Discretionary Leave and API on Discretionary Leave, para 5). The restriction on the right of appeal is difficult to justify in light of the importance of recognition of the status of refugee, and the advantages of refugee status over subsidiary protection: see e g *Adan v Secretary of State for the Home Department* [1997] Imm AR 251 at 256, CA per Simon Brown LJ; *Saad, Diriye and Osorio v Secretary of State for the Home Department* [2001] EWCA Civ 2008, [2002] INLR 34. See also EC Qualification Directive 2004/83/EC, 12.3 fn 3 above, Arts 20–30, where the gap between the two kinds of protection is fully exposed.

[3] Asylum and Immigration (Treatment of Claimants, etc) Act 2004, s 26.

[4] Nationality, Immigration and Asylum Act 2002, s 96, as amended by Asylum and Immigration (Treatment of Claimants, etc) Act 2004, s 30 from 1 October 2004. In *R v Secretary of State for the Home Department, ex p Kazmi* [1995] Imm AR 73, Dyson J held that *Kalunga (Lemba) v Secretary of State for the Home Department* [1994] Imm AR 585, CA bound him to apply a judicial review approach to the Secretary of State's decision as to whether a further decision could be made, generating a further right of appeal. An asylum application made after a prior refusal of leave to enter on some other ground must trigger a fresh refusal of leave to enter, however: HC 395, para 332 and *Kazmi* (above). On the judicial review approach to whether further representations constitute a fresh claim see also *Cakabay v Secretary of State for the Home Department (No 2)* [1999] Imm AR 176, [1998] INLR 623, CA. *Nassir v Secretary of State for the Home Department* [1999] Imm AR 250; *R v Secretary of State for the Home Department, ex p Bell* [2000] Imm AR 396.

[5] [1996] Imm AR 370, CA. The test for a fresh application is whether the claim advanced is significantly different from the material previously considered, ie if the content has not already been considered, and taken together with the previously considered material, create a realistic prospect of success: HC 395, para 353 (inserted by HC 1112, 18 October 2004, in place of para 346, which was deleted). The evidence must be apparently credible though not uncontrovertible: *R v Secretary of State for the Home Department v Boybeyi* [1997] Imm AR 491, CA. See 12.170 below

[6] A failure by advisers to obtain evidence earlier did not make the evidence 'previously unavailable' under the previous provision: *Kabala v Secretary of State for the Home Department* [1997] Imm AR 517. But 'unavailability' includes psychiatric inability to give evidence: *R v Secretary of State for the Home Department, ex p Molly Ejon* [1998] INLR 195. See also *Haile v Immigration Appeal Tribunal* [2001] EWCA Civ 663, [2002] Imm AR 170, [2002] INLR 283, and discussion of fresh evidence in *E v Secretary of State for the Home Department* [2004] EWCA Civ 49, [2004] QB 1044, [2004] 2 WLR 1351.

12.20 There may be an appeal against the decision to remove the appellant to a safe third country without considering the asylum claim,[1] although such appeals have become very rare; in most cases appeal is now precluded by statute.[2] Under the 1999 and 2002 Acts, EU Member States to which it was proposed to send an asylum seeker under standing arrangements benefitted from a statutory presumption that they were safe and would not return the appellant elsewhere save in accordance with the Refugee Convention.[3] These presumptions of safety are extended to other specified states, and to the Human Rights Convention, by the provisions of the 2004 Act, which dramatically reduces the possibilities for appeals (both in-country and out of country) in 'third country' cases.[4]

1   For 'safe third country' removals see 12.132ff below.
2   Asylum and Immigration (Treatment of Claimants, etc) Act 2004, Sch 3 (in force 1 October 2004 in respect of all claims certified on or after that date, SI 2004/2523 Art 3) removes appeal rights on asylum and quasi-asylum human rights grounds in respect of removals to states deemed safe for the purposes of the Refugee and/or Human Rights Conventions, and on non-asylum human rights grounds (eg grounds depending on illness or the presence of family members) where the Secretary of State certifies the claim clearly unfounded, which is the 'default position'; see 12.140ff.
3   Immigration and Asylum Act 1999, s 11 (as substituted by Nationality, Immigration and Asylum Act 2002, s 80), inserted after the Court of Appeal held, in *R v Secretary of State for the Home Department, ex p Adan, Aitseguer and Subaskaran* [1999] INLR 362, that the French and German interpretation of the Refugee Convention was unlawful in not recognising persecution from non-state agents. The decision has since been upheld by the House of Lords at [2001] INLR 44.
4   Asylum and Immigration (Treatment of Claimants, etc) Act 2004, s 33, Sch 3, repealing and replacing the previous 'third-country' regime as from 1 October 2004. The provisions preclude appeals inconsistent with the presumptions of safety (under the Refugee Convention, the Human Rights Convention or both) which apply to EU Member States, to other States specified by order of the Secretary of State and to states certified by him as safe for individuals. See further 12.140ff below.

THE DEFINITION OF REFUGEE

12.21 The definition of refugees for the purposes of the Refugee Convention is contained in Article 1A(2), as applied by the 1967 Protocol. A refugee is any person who:

> 'owing to a well-founded fear of being persecuted for reasons of race religion nationality membership of a particular social group or political opinion, is outside his country of nationality and is unable or, owing to such fear, is unwilling to avail himself of the protection of that country; or who, not having a nationality and being outside the country of his former habitual residence ... is unable or, owing to such fear, is unwilling to return to it.'[1]

We will now consider the various elements.[2]

1   Convention Relating to the Status of Refugees 1951, Art 1A(2), as applied by the 1967 Protocol. The New York Protocol of 1967 applies the 1951 Convention, for those (but only for those) countries that are parties to the Protocol (whether or not they also be parties to the Convention), as if the words in Art 1A(2) of the Convention, which impose a temporal limitation on refugee claims are omitted: see Art 1 of the Protocol. Thus the Protocol does not strictly amend the Convention but rather applies it in such a way as to allow for persons to be refugees as a result of events that have occurred since 1951: see *Minister for Immigration & Multicultural Affairs v Savvin* [2000] FCA 478 per Katz J in the Full Court of the Federal Court of Australia.
2   In *R v Secretary of State for the Home Department, ex p Adan, R v Secretary of State for the Home Department, ex p Aitseguer* [2001] 2 AC 477, the House of Lords emphasised the importance of attaching an autonomous meaning to each of the terms within the refugee definition, per Lord Slynn at 509: 'The phrase "otherwise than in accordance with the Convention" does not mean "otherwise than in accordance with the relevant state's possible reasonable, permissible or legitimate view of what the Convention means" '.

'Owing to a well-founded fear'

The fear

12.22 A genuine fear of persecution must be behind the asylum seeker's absence from his or her country of residence or nationality. This is referred to as the subjective element.[1] Even if objective conditions are such that a reasonable person would have reason to fear persecution, the claimant will not be a refugee unless he or she has such a fear. The use of the term 'fear' was intended to emphasise the forward-looking nature of the test, and not to ground refugee status in an assessment of the refugee claimant's state of mind.[2] The refugee does not have to have left the country because of such a fear, since a person can become a refugee by reason of events after their departure; such a person is referred to as a 'refugee *sur place*'.[3] There is no reason why the fear should not arise from the refugee's activities abroad, even if carried out in bad faith, although a claim based exclusively on such acts will be scrutinised with some scepticism as self-serving and lacking in credibility.[4] The fear must still exist at the date of determination; despite indications in the *travaux préparatoires* of the 1951 Convention which suggested that historic fear may be sufficient to ground refugee status if the refugee is currently unable to return,[5] this interpretation, accepted by the majority in the Court of Appeal,[6] was rejected by the House of Lords in *Adan*,[7] which held that while a historic fear may be relevant in providing evidence to establish a present fear, it is the existence or otherwise of a present fear which is determinative. Where objectively it is shown that there is a serious possibility of persecution, then it may well be difficult to refuse an application on the basis that the applicant does not believe the persecution will occur.[8]

---

[1] See UNHCR *Handbook*, 12.13 above, paras 37 and 38; *R v Secretary of State for the Home Department, ex p Singh* [1987] Imm AR 489, DC.

[2] James Hathaway *The Law of Refugee Status* (1991) pp 68–69. Hathaway gives one of the most authoritative and highly regarded accounts of the Convention, with particular reference to Canadian and US case law, and is regularly cited with approval in the higher courts. See also, on meaning of 'fear', *Asuming* (11530).

[3] UNHCR *Handbook*, 12.13 above, paras 94–96.

[4] *Danian v Secretary of State for the Home Department* [2000] Imm AR 96, [1999] INLR 533, CA; HC 395, para 341(vi). The EU Council Directive 2004/83/EC on minimum standards for the qualification and status of third country nationals and stateless persons as refugees or persons who otherwise need international protection (30.9.04 OJ L304/12, in force 30 October 2004), Art 20(6) provides that within the limits set out by the Refugee Convention, Member States may reduce the benefits granted to a refugee whose refugee status has been obtained on the basis of activities engaged in for the sole or main purpose of creating the necessary conditions for being recognised as a refugee.

[5] See UN Doc E/1818 containing Ecosoc Res 319 (X1 B): 'who has had, or has well founded fear ... and owing to such fear has had to leave, shall leave or remains outside the country of nationality.' The drafting group's explanatory note of the definition was 'that a person has either been actually a victim of persecution or can show good reason why he [or she] fears persecution'.

[6] *Adan v Secretary of State for the Home Department, Nooh v Secretary of State for the Home Department* [1997] Imm AR 251, CA.

[7] *Secretary of State for the Home Department v Adan* [1999] 1 AC 293, [1998] Imm AR 338, [1998] INLR 325, HL.

[8] *Radivojevic* (13372), followed in *Gashi v Secretary of State for the Home Department* [1997] INLR 96, IAT.

Well-founded

12.23   The fear of persecution must not only exist but must be well-founded. In *Sivakumaran*[1] the House of Lords, reversing the Court of Appeal, rejected the advice in paragraph 42 of the *Handbook*:

> 'In general the applicant's fear should be considered well-founded if he can establish, to a reasonable degree, that his continued stay in his country of origin has become intolerable to him for the reasons stated in the definition, or would for the same reasons be intolerable if he returned there.'[2]

It held that well-foundedness was an objective test, to be ascertained independently of the appellant's state of mind. But this does not mean that there must have been actual persecution in the past. It is sufficient if there is a well-founded fear of it occurring in the future.[3] Past persecution will always be of great significance. The *travaux* reveal that the drafting group's explanatory note of the Article 1A definition was that 'a person has either been an actual victim of persecution or can show good reason why he [or she] fears persecution'.[4] The House of Lords' decision in *Adan* means, however, that a refugee must have a current risk, as well as a current fear, of persecution.[5] But past persecution means that future persecution is more likely (and the fear of it more likely to be well-founded) unless there has been a significant change of circumstances.[6] The past persecution of an individual may be contrasted with a past generalised risk of violence in an area which has been diminished by government measures to prevent abuse. Thus in *Ravichandran*[7] the Court of Appeal distinguished the Canadian case of *Thirunavukkarasu*[8] on the safety of Tamils in Colombo, on the basis that it related to a different time.

1   *R v Secretary of State for the Home Department, ex p Sivakumaran* [1988] AC 958 at 996, per Lord Keith.
2   UNHCR *Handbook*, 12.13 above, para 195.
3   Hathaway 12.22 fn 2 above, paras 3.1, p 66, 3.2.3, p 87. See *Horvath v Secretary of State for the Home Department* [1999] INLR 7 at 18F, IAT, and *Kiani* [2002] UKIAT 01328 at para 7. See also *Appellant S395/2002 v Minister for Immigration and Multicultural Affairs; Appellant S396/2002 v Minister for Immigration and Multicultural Affairs* [2003] HCA 71 at para 58 per McHugh and Kirby JJ and at paras 72–77 per Gummow and Hayne JJ in the High Court of Australia for a recent and instructive restatement of some basic principles relating to the application of the refugee definition in respect of fear of future persecution.
4   Report of the Ad Hoc Committee, 17 February 1950, p 39. See the argument of the intervener in *R v Secretary of State for the Home Department, ex p Sivakumaran* [1988] AC 958 at 976–989 for the drafting history of Art 1 of the Refugee Convention and the admissibility of *travaux preparatoires* as an aid to the construction of international instruments. For the relevance of *travaux* in the construction of an international instrument see Vienna Convention on the Law of Treaties (1969), Art 32. And as noted at 12.12 above, UNHCR's jurisdiction extends to those who 'have had' a well-founded fear of persecution. Hathaway suggests that the final definition adopted by the drafters intended persecution to be prospective save for those who had suffered pre-1951 persecution and became refugees by reason of Art 1A(1) of the Refugee Convention and whose status is not now a matter of present debate: Hathaway above, para 3.1.1 p 66ff.
5   *Adan v Secretary of State for the Home Department* [1999] 1 AC 293, [1998] Imm AR 338, [1999] INLR 325. See also *R (on the application of Hoxha) v Secretary of State for the Home Department, R (on the application of B) v Secretary of State for the Home Department* [2005] UKHL 19, [2005] 1 WLR 1063, (2005) 149 Sol Jo LB 358.
6   See eg *Demirkaya v Secretary of State for the Home Department* [1999] INLR 441 at 449D, CA; *Avci v Secretary of State for the Home Department* [2002] EWCA Civ 977 at para 22; *S* (01/TH/00632) at para 9. Hathaway, above, concludes that 'individualised past

persecution is generally a sufficient, though not a mandatory means of establishing prospective risk' (p 88). The German Constitutional Court goes further, stating that where there has been past persecution the test for the determining authority is whether 'future persecution could be excluded with sufficient certainty': Case No 193 (1994) 6(2) IJRL 282. See also UNHCR Handbook at para 45.

7   *Ravichandran (Senathirajah) v Secretary of State for the Home Department* [1996] Imm AR 97.

8   *Thirunavukkarasu v Minister of Employment and Immigration* (1993) 109 DLR (4th) 682.

12.24 Problems can arise where a decision on refugee status has been delayed for several years, during which time the human rights environment has improved without there being some fundamental alteration in the factors giving rise to the fear. In *Arif*[1] the Court of Appeal decided to proceed by analogy with the cessation clause at Article 1C(5) of the Refugee Convention and held that, since the appellant would have qualified for refugee status had his application been dealt with expeditiously, it was now for the Home Office to demonstrate that a significant change of circumstances had removed the basis for the claim.[2] However, in *Hoxha and B*[3] the Court of Appeal held that the cessation clause in Article 1C(5) can itself only be relevant where a person has been formally recognised as a refugee, a conclusion upheld by the House of Lords.[4]

1   *Arif (Mohammed) v Secretary of State for the Home Department* [1999] INLR 327, where the appellant had been sentenced *in absentia* to a persecutory prison sentence, but by the date of the hearing, his own party had regained power. However, where there is no evidence that the applicant would have so qualified, the shifting evidential burden does not apply: *Salim v Secretary of State for the Home Department* [2000] Imm AR 503, CA. In *S* (01/TH/00632) at paras 8–9 the then President of the IAT, Collins J, criticised reliance on *Arif* as 'unhelpful ... if ... there is no significant change in the situation and the appellant was persecuted for a Convention reason before he left, it would be difficult to see how the decision could not be favourable to him.' See also *S v Secretary of State for the Home Department* [2002] EWCA Civ 539, [2002] INLR 416 at paras 13–15.

2   See 12.84 below for the cessation clause.

3   *R (on the application of Hoxha) v Secretary of State for the Home Department, R (on the application of B) v Secretary of State for the Home Department* [2002] EWCA Civ 1403, upheld at [2005] UKHL 19, [2005] 1 WLR 1063, (2005) 149 Sol Jo LB 358.

4   The Court of Appeal (and the House of Lords) also held that the proviso to Art 1C(5) only applies to statutory refugees falling under the definition in Art 1A(1) of the Convention – persons recognised as refugees under International Arrangements and Conventions pre-dating the 1951 Convention (and is therefore no longer of practical relevance). See 12.84 below.

The burden and standard of proof

12.25 The burden of establishing a well-founded fear is on the applicant. In *Sivakumaran*[1] the House of Lords held that for a fear to be well-founded, the question was whether there was a 'real and substantial risk' or a 'reasonable degree of likelihood' of persecution for a Refugee Convention reason. It is clear that showing a real likelihood of persecution is a lesser standard than proving that persecution will occur on the balance of probabilities, and the House of Lords approved the words of Lord Diplock in *Fernandez v Government of Singapore*[2] to this effect. Lord Diplock had suggested that the requisite degree of likelihood could be indicated by words such as 'a reasonable chance', 'substantial grounds for thinking', or 'a serious possibility'. In his speech in *Sivakumaran* Lord Keith[3] appeared to approve Stevens J's dictum in the US case of *Immigration and Naturalisation Service v Cardozo Fonseca*[4] that a one in ten chance of being persecuted could amount to a reasonable possibility of persecution.[5] In those circumstances the addition of the word 'substantial' to 'real' ('a real and substantial possibility ... of persecution') can only be intended to eliminate minimal or mere possibilities rather than to indicate something in the nature of a probability or a prediction. In *Adjei v Minister of Employment and Immigration*[6] a Canadian Court of Appeal preferred to follow the language of reasonable possibility rather than some of the alternative formulations mentioned in the speeches in *Sivakumaran*. The Canadian court indicated that use of the word 'would' instead of 'could' in determining the reality of persecution was evidence of a misdirection on burden of proof. This reflects the words of Lord Keith, who had succinctly stated the issue: 'if the examination shows that persecution might indeed take place then the fear is well-founded'. In the case of *Chan*[7] the Australian High Court adopted the test of 'real chance'. To avoid any possibility of confusion in the application of the *Sivakumaran* test, we prefer to state the test in terms of real risk rather than likelihood.[8]

1   *R v Secretary of State for the Home Department, ex p Sivakumaran* [1988] AC 958.
2   [1971] 2 All ER 691, [1971] 1 WLR 987, HL.
3   [1988] AC 958 at 994.
4   94 L ED 2d 434 (1987).
5   Sedley LJ, pointing out the danger of assimilating risk to probability in *Batayav v Secretary of State for the Home Department* [2003] EWCA Civ 1489, [2004] INLR 126, said: 'If a type of car has a defect which causes one vehicle in ten to crash, most people would say that it presents a real risk to anyone who drives it, albeit crashes are not generally or consistently happening' (at paras 38–9).
6   (1989) 57 DLR (4th) 153.
7   (1989) 63 ALR 561.
8   In *R v Gough* [1993] AC 646 at 670 Lord Goff noted in the context of the appropriate test for bias, 'for the avoidance of doubt I prefer to state the test in terms of real danger rather than real likelihood, to ensure that the court is thinking in terms of possibility rather than probability of bias'. In *Kacaj v Secretary of State for the Home Department* [2001] INLR 354 (starred) at para 12, the Tribunal held that it would now be better in both refugee asylum and human rights cases, for the phrase, 'real risk', to be adopted in preference to those of a 'serious possibility' or a 'reasonable degree of likelihood' – all of which in any case seek to convey the same meaning and are to be distinguished from 'beyond reasonable doubt' or 'on a balance of probabilities'. In *Ahmed (Hussain)* [2002] UKIAT 00841, Professor Jackson's Tribunal warned at paras 36–38 that the 'real risk' test should not be taken as amounting to more than a 'serious possibility' and that the phrase 'substantial grounds for believing' did not import another standard.

12.26 The general human rights background of the country in question is important in assessing the objective foundation for the fear.[1] Background human rights data should be collected from a broad cross-section of official and non-governmental sources in order to supplement the claimant's evidence. The Immigration and Nationality Directorate of the Home Office now has a Country Information Policy Unit (CIPU) which produces sourced country reports on the main refugee-producing countries.[2] The existence of a consistent pattern of gross, flagrant or mass violations of human rights in a country can in itself, but does not necessarily (it depends on all of the facts), constitute a sufficient ground for determining that a person would be in danger on return,[3] but where human rights reports substantiate that a real risk of

ill-treatment exists, a genuine fear of persecution in a country is likely to be
well-founded if it is for a Refugee Convention reason.[4] Where there is a doubt
after all the evidence has been placed before the Tribunal of fact, the benefit of
it should be given to the applicant.[5]

1　UNHCR *Handbook* 12.13 above, paras 196, 204; *Hathaway* 12.22 fn 2 above, pp 89–90.
　See also UN Convention Against Torture, Art 3(2); *Mutumbo v Switzerland* (1994) 15
　HRLJ 164.
2　See Home Office IND website under headings, 'Introduction'/'Country Information' for
　the up-to-date CIPU reports (produced generally twice a year in April and October) on the
　countries that generate the largest number of asylum applications in the UK. See further
　12.126.
3　See *Alan v Switzerland* [1997] INLR 29 (UNCAT); *Hariri v Secretary of State for the
　Home Department* [2003] EWCA Civ 807, (2003) 147 Sol Jo LB 659, [2003] All ER (D)
　340; *Batayav v Secretary of State for the Home Department* [2003] EWCA Civ 1489,
　[2003] All ER (D) 60 (Nov); *Iqbal (Muzafar)* [2002] UKIAT 02239.
4　*Hathaway* 12.22 fn 2 above cites the Federal Court of Appeal in *Attakora (Benjamin) v
　Minister for Employment and Immigration* (Decision A-1091–87) (19 May 1989, unre-
　ported), at para 3.2.1 (p 80) that 'persons who flee countries that are known to commit or
　acquiesce in persecutory behaviour should benefit from a rebuttable presumption that they
　have a genuine need for protection'. For an example of a situation where an appellant had
　not suffered persecution and relied wholly on evidence of country conditions see *Drrias v
　Secretary of State for the Home Department* [1997] Imm AR 346, CA.
5　UNHCR *Handbook* above, paras 196, 203. See also *Kaja v Secretary of State for the
　Home Department* [1995] Imm AR 1, below.

12.27　The correct approach to assessment of past events was authoritatively
set out by the Court of Appeal in *Karanakaran*.[1] The Tribunal had been
divided on what standard of proof to apply to evidence of past or present facts
before the necessary assessment of future risk is undertaken. In *Kaja*[2] the
minority had held that historic events should be proven on the normal civil
balance and the reduced burden of 'reasonable likelihood' should apply only
in respect of future events, while the majority had concluded that the
decision-maker should not omit from the assessment of future risk any
evidence of past events to which they were prepared to give some credence.
They referred to the 'positive role for doubt' in asylum, given the inability of
the asylum seeker to produce witnesses from the country of persecution, and
the general lack of documentary or other evidence proving either past or
future persecution.[3] The Court of Appeal endorsed this approach, which does
not lay down a standard of proof for past events but asks the decision-maker
to weigh everything for what it is worth in assessing the risk of persecution.
Sedley LJ warned that:

'the decision-maker must not, by a process of factual findings on particular
elements of the material which is provided, foreclose reasonable speculation on
the chances of persecution emerging from a consideration of the whole of the
material. Everything capable of having a bearing has to be given the weight,
great or little, due to it ... [The] facts, so far as they can be established, are
signposts on the road to a conclusion.'

Brooke LJ, relying on the Australian decision of *Wu Shan Liang*,[4] distinguished between civil litigation, where 'the court has to decide where, on the
balance of probabilities, the truth lies as between the evidence the parties to
the litigation have thought it in their respective interests to adduce at the trial',
and administrative decision-making, where 'a whole range of possible

approaches ... may be correct' and 'the use of such terms provides little assistance'. He reproduced with approval a number of principles derived from the Australian case law:[5]

'(1)   There may be circumstances in which a decision-maker must take into account the possibility that alleged past events occurred even though it finds that these events probably did not occur. The reason for this is that the ultimate question is whether the applicant has a real substantial basis for his fear of future persecution. The decision-maker must not foreclose reasonable speculation about the chances of the future hypothetical event occurring.

(2)   Although the civil standard of proof is not irrelevant to the fact-finding process, the decision-maker cannot simply apply that standard to all fact-finding. It frequently has to make its assessment on the basis of fragmented, incomplete and confused information. It has to assess the plausibility of accounts given by people who may be understandably bewildered, frightened and, perhaps, desperate, and who often do not understand either the process or the language spoken by the decision-maker/investigator. Even applicants with a genuine fear of persecution may not present as models of consistency or transparent veracity.

(3)   In this context, when the decision-maker is uncertain as to whether an alleged event occurred, or finds that although the probabilities are against it, the event may have occurred, it may be necessary to take into account the possibility that the event took place in deciding the ultimate question (for which see question 1 above)...

(4)   Although the "What if I am wrong?" terminology has gained currency, it is more accurate to see this requirement as simply an aspect of the obligation to apply correctly the principles for determining whether an applicant has a 'well-founded fear of being persecuted' for a Convention reason.

(5)   There is no reason in principle to support a general rule that a decision-maker must express findings as to whether alleged past events actually occurred in a manner that makes explicit its degree of conviction or confidence that its findings were correct ...

(6)   If a fair reading of the decision-maker's reasons as a whole shows that it "had no real doubt" that claimed events did not occur, then there is no warrant for holding that it should have considered the possibility that its findings were wrong.'

[1]   *Karanakaran v Secretary of State for the Home Department* [2000] 3 All ER 449, [2000] INLR 122, [2000] Imm AR 271. The Court of Appeal's evaluative approach to refugee status determination in *Karanakaran* was approved by the House of Lords in *R (on the application of Sivakumar) v Secretary of State for the Home Department* [2003] UKHL 14, [2003] 2 All ER 1097.
[2]   *Kaja v Secretary of State for the Home Department* [1995] Imm AR 1.
[3]   See UNHCR *Handbook* above, paras 196–197.
[4]   *Minister of Immigration and Ethnic Affair v Wu Shan Liang* (1996) 185 CLR 259.
[5]   *Rajalingam v Minister for Immigration and Multicultural Affairs* [1999] FCA 719, per Sackville J, conveniently summarised and quoted in [2000] Imm AR 271 at 290–292.

12.28   It is, however, for the applicant to establish his or her claim, albeit to a lower than normal civil standard.[1] Thus it is for him or her to establish statelessness, if it forms part of the claim.[2] However, in the context of asylum as elsewhere, where it is the Secretary of State who asserts something, such as that a document produced by an applicant is a forgery, the burden is on him or her to prove it.[3] *Karanakaran*[4] was a case about the 'internal relocation alternative', ie where it is accepted that the applicant faces persecution in part of the country and the issue is whether it would be unduly harsh for him or her to relocate to a safe area.[5] Again, different divisions of the Tribunal had differed on whether the applicant had to show on the balance of probabilities that it would be unduly harsh,[6] or only that it was a 'serious possibility'.[7] The court in *Karanakaran* held that it would be quite impracticable to maintain a regime in which there was one approach to the evidential material relating to historic or existing facts for the purpose of the first part of the definition of 'refugee' in the Convention, and a different approach to such material for the purpose of considering issues of protection and internal relocation.[8] The question was simply 'would it be unduly harsh', but in answering it, only evidence about which there was no doubt that it was not correct should be excluded. The guidance in *Karanakaran* does not, however, disturb the line of jurisprudence to the effect that where there is no real doubt that the whole story of the applicant is unworthy of belief, issues of standard of proof do not arise.[9]

[1]   The burden is not different or lower for someone with mental problems: *Bolat v Secretary of State for the Home Department* (99/6206/C) (23 February 2000, unreported), CA; *Singh v Secretary of State for the Home Department* [2000] Imm AR 340, CA.

[2]   *Tikhonov* [1998] INLR 737, IAT. In *Smith (Agartha)* (00/TH/02130) the Tribunal suggested that a more flexible approach to proof of nationality should be adopted in asylum cases (as they were not nationality arbitrations – a criticism of the approach in *Tikhonov*) and that in most cases the decision on nationality has to be made on the same basis as decisions on other elements of the refugee definition. 'If there is some valid evidence that can be weighed in the balance, even if meagre, then that may suffice to discharge the burden lying on the appellant to prove nationality (or statelessness)' (paras 54–55). In *Hamza* [2002] UKIAT 05185 (starred) Collins J (the then President) held that in the context of making findings in respect of nationality an adjudicator 'must bear in mind that if he is going to make a positive finding against the appellant, then he must do so not on the asylum standard, but on a higher standard which would be the balance of probabilities' (para 12).

[3]   *R v Immigration Appeal Tribunal, ex p Shen* [2000] INLR 389, QBD; *Makozo* (20003) 12 February 1999, IAT; *Escobar* (20553) 26 March 1999, IAT. But see *R v Immigration Appellare Authority, ex p Mohammed (Mukhtar)* [2001] Imm AR 162, QBD. In *Ahmed (Tanveer) v Secretary of State for the Home Department* [2002] UKIAT 00439, [2002] Imm AR 318, [2002] INLR 345, IAT, the IAT held that whether or not a document is a forgery is rarely the real issue and that the real, or indeed only, question is whether the document is one upon which reliance should properly be placed. This approach was approved in *Mungu v Secretary of State for the Home Department* [2003] EWCA Civ 360 at paras 18–19, [2003] All ER (D) 289 (Feb). See also *Zarandy v Secretary of State for the Home Department* [2002] EWCA Civ 153, [2002] All ER (D) 355 (Jan).

[4]   *Karanakaran v Secretary of State for the Home Department* [2000] 3 All ER 449, [2000] INLR 122, [2000] Imm AR 271.

[5]   *Robinson v Secretary of State for the Home Department* [1997] Imm AR 568; *AE and FE v Secretary of State for the Home Department* [2003] EWCA Civ 1032, [2004] QB 531, [2004] 2 WLR 123. See 12.43 below. Whether 'internal relocation/flight' is in issue at all should depend initially on the applicant's claim, and, just as for other aspects of the refugee claim, the responsibility for putting the factual basis and burden of establishing the case lies on the applicant: see *Aziz v Secretary of State for the Home Department* [2003] EWCA Civ 118; *R v Secretary of State for the Home Department, ex p Salim* [2000] Imm AR 6, [1999] INLR 628, QBD.

[6]   A school of thought exemplified by *Manoharan* [1998] Imm AR 455.

[7]   *Sachithananthan* [1999] INLR 205.

[8]   *Karanakaran v Secretary of State for the Home Department* [2000] Imm AR 271 at 293.

[9]   *R v Secretary of State for the Home Department, ex p Kingori (aka Mypanguli)* [1994] Imm AR 539, CA; *Bulut (Huseyin) v Secretary of State for the Home Department* [1999] Imm AR 210, CA.

Credibility

12.29 The debate about standard of proof is inextricably linked with issues of credibility. The issue of credibility is one which needs to be addressed seriously, in light of the widespread perception that adverse credibility findings are too easily reached, on too little material, both by the Secretary of State for the Home Department and by the appellate authorities.[1] For a fuller treatment of credibility in the context of asylum appeals see 12.163 below.

> [1] See (in a non-asylum context but equally applicable) *R v Immigration Appeal Tribunal, ex p Hussain* (CO 990/1995) (25 April 1996, unreported), QBD where Turner J said that 'Credibility is not in itself a valid end to the function of an adjudicator ... there is a risk ... that overemphasis on the issue of credibility may distort the findings of an adjudicator'. See also *Horvath v Secretary of State for the Home Department* [1999] INLR 7, [1999] Imm AR 121, IAT, and cases cited at 18.135 below. It has been largely left to organisations such as Asylum Aid to draw attention to the 'culture of disbelief' informing Home Office asylum decisions: see eg Asylum Aid *No reason at all* (1995) and Asylum Aid *Still no reason at all* (1999).

12.30 The principle of the benefit of the doubt operates once all the evidence is submitted. In order to benefit from it, the applicant should have co-operated with the investigating authorities and should not attempt to deceive them.[1] Section 8 of the Asylum and Immigration (Treatment of Claimants, etc) Act 2004, and paragraph 341 of the Immigration Rules, HC 395, as substituted by HC 164 from 1 January 2005, list different kinds of behaviour which must be taken into account as damaging the claimant's credibility. See 12.164 below.

> [1] UNHCR *Handbook* 12.13 above, para 205.

Inconsistent acts

12.31 Issues of credibility are also engaged where a person's claim to asylum is based solely on acts done since leaving the country of feared persecution and these are inconsistent with previous beliefs. In *Danian*[1] the Court of Appeal reviewed earlier authorities which had held that unreasonable activities, or activities performed in bad faith, could not be relied on by an asylum seeker in support of his or her claim.[2] It concluded that a refugee *sur place* who has acted in bad faith did not fall outside the protection of the Refugee Convention and could not be removed if the activities gave rise to a genuine and well-founded fear of persecution.[3] Brooke LJ, noting the decision in *Mbanza*[4] that a fraudulent claim could attract protection, emphasised that the credibility of such an application was likely to be low and would be rigorously scrutinised. Buxton LJ pointed out that the Convention had provided specific exceptions to refugee status (in Articles 1D–F) which should not be added to unless required by a clear international consensus or international practice. Neither criterion was fulfilled in the case of a 'bad faith' claim.[5] Part of the rationale for the decision was the recognition that the applicant would have an irresistible claim to protection under Article 3 of the ECHR.[6] It has been held in other cases that the mere fact of having claimed asylum in another state may put the person at risk for a Convention reason.[7]

¹   *Danian v Secretary of State for the Home Department* [2000] Imm AR 96.
²   *R v Immigration Appeal Tribunal, ex p B* [1989] Imm AR 166; *Gilgham (Mustapha) v Immigration Appeal Tribunal* [1995] Imm AR 129; *Re HB* (1995) 7 IJRL 332 (NZ).
³   *Danian* fn 1 above, at 122.
⁴   *Mbanza v Secretary of State for the Home Department* [1996] Imm AR 136.
⁵   *Danian* above, at 130.
⁶   *Chahal v United Kingdom* (1996) 23 EHRR 413, paras 79–80, cited at *Danian* above, at 118.
⁷   See observations of Laws J in *R v Immigration Appeal Tribunal, ex p Senga* (unreported, 9 March 1994); see also (1992) 4(3) IJRL 261, Case 111 (Polish asylum seeker held to have been prejudiced by information given in a claim made in Germany). The difficulties in establishing a Convention reason were demonstrated in the case of *Senga* itself when remitted to the Tribunal (12842) – see comment in [1998] 10(3) INLP 110. See also *L (DRC)* [2004] UKIAT 00007 at paras 32–33. However, in *Mohammed (Baheldin)* (13465) a Sudanese claim based on likely inquiries on return succeeded.

Refraining from acts exacerbating risk

12.32 Similarly, in *Ahmed (Iftikhar)*¹ the question of how far a refugee should voluntarily refrain from exercising fundamental human rights to avoid persecution was revisited. In the earlier cases of *Mendis*² and *Ahmad*,³ it was intimated that a person cannot generally found a claim for asylum solely on future activity he or she might engage in on return to the country of origin, where this might infringe the law. In both of those cases, the applicants had not so far done any acts which might lead to prosecution in their own countries, and the court rejected their asylum claims on the basis that they would not do in the future what they had not done in the past. The receiving state does not have to grant asylum if the full exercise of human rights cannot be permanently guaranteed in the country of origin, and is entitled to expect some degree of prudence in the activities of the applicant if returned to his or her own country. But, as Simon Brown LJ pointed out in *Ahmed (Iftikhar)*, while it may well be reasonable to require asylum seekers to refrain from certain political or even religious activities to avoid persecution on return, it is quite another thing to say that, if in fact it appears that the asylum seeker would not refrain from such activities – if in other words it is established that he or she would in fact act unreasonably – he or she is not entitled to refugee status.⁴ The appellant, a devout Ahmadi, would continue to proselytise, and however unreasonable that was, it entitled him to protection. This is in accordance with the suggestion in the *Handbook* that refugee status may be based on political opinion as yet unknown to the persecuting government which will become known if the asylum seeker is returned.⁵ Asylum seekers cannot be required to give up their religion, racial or sexual identity, or their political opinions, in order to avoid persecution in their own country.⁶ In *Ex p Jonah*⁷ it was held that to require a former trade union leader to give up his lifelong activities, live apart from his wife and family and withdraw to a remoter part of the country in order to avoid the attention of the authorities was unreasonable and those circumstances amounted to persecution.⁸

¹   *Ahmed (Iftikhar) v Secretary of State for the Home Department* [2000] INLR 1.
²   *Mendis v Immigration Appeal Tribunal and Secretary of State for the Home Department* [1989] Imm AR 6.
³   *Ahmad v Secretary of State for the Home Department* [1990] Imm AR 61; see also *Yavari v Secretary of State for the Home Department* [1987] Imm AR 138.
⁴   *Ahmed (Iftikhar)* above, at 7.

5   UNHCR Handbook 12.13 above, para 82.
6   Clearly there is tension between this proposition and the earlier proposition that the receiving state is not obliged to grant asylum where the full exercise of human rights cannot be guaranteed in the home country; there is, however, a distinction between freedom of conscience (an absolute right) and freedom to manifest beliefs and freedom of expression (both qualified ones). And as Simon Brown LJ said in *Ahmed (Iftikhar)*, the single question is whether the particular claimant has a well-founded fear of persecution. See also *Sokoto* (00/TH/2367) and *Kone* (16006) for IAT decisions that applicants cannot be expected to cease to express their political opinions so as to avoid risk of persecution if returned 'home'. See further 12.33 below.
7   *R v Immigration Appeal Tribunal, ex p Jonah* [1985] Imm AR 7.
8   In *R (on the application of Vallaj) v Secretary of State for the Home Department* [2001] EWCA Civ 782, [2001] INLR 342, at [19] Simon Brown LJ held that 'Sometimes ... it is sufficient to show that the asylum seeker himself can and should change his own ways so as to avoid future persecution. By the same token that it is reasonable to require someone to abstain from political action to avoid persecution – see Nolan J's judgment in *R v Immigration Appeal Tribunal, ex p Jonah* [1985] Imm AR 7, 12 – so it seems to me perfectly reasonable to require Mr Vallaj to take KFOR's advice and cease living in an isolated tent so as to be able to continue caring for his sheep.' In terms of the facts of the case, Simon Brown LJ is simply advising an individual to avoid serious harm by exercising some common sense (do not sleep in the woods if the woods are full of dangerous brigands, or wild animals for that matter) rather than requiring him to cease the exercise of fundamental human rights. Nonetheless his interpretation of Nolan J's judgment in *Jonah* sits somewhat uncomfortably with his own judgment in *Ahmed (Iftikhar)* (above).

12.33   We suggest that the best approach so far on this issue is that of the majority in the High Court of Australia in *Appellant S*.[1] McHugh and Kirby JJ held:[2]

'Persecution does not cease to be persecution for the purpose of the Convention because those persecuted can eliminate the harm by taking avoiding action within the country of nationality ... It would undermine the object of the Convention if the signatory countries required [claimants] to modify their beliefs or opinions or to hide their race, nationality or membership of particular social groups before those countries would give them protection under the Convention.'

They added that 'the notion that it is reasonable for a person to take action that will avoid persecutory harm invariably leads a tribunal of fact into a failure to consider properly whether there is a real chance of persecution if the person is returned to the country of nationality'.[3]

1   *Appellant S395/2002 v Minister for Immigration and Multicultural Affairs* [2003] HCA 71 (9 December 2003).
2   *Appellant S* at paras 40–41, where they cited with approval Simon Brown LJ in *Ahmed (Iftikhar)* (see 12.32 above), and para 43.
3   Gummow and Hayne JJ added at para 80 that 'to say to an applicant that he or she should be 'discreet' about such matters is simply to use gentler terms to convey the same meaning,' and pointed out that the question to be considered in assessing whether the applicant's fear of persecution is well founded is what may happen if the applicant returns to the country of nationality; it is not, could the applicant live in that country without attracting adverse consequences.' The New Zealand Refugee Status Appeals Authority developed the argument, anchoring it in principles of non-discrimination in the enjoyment of core human rights of dignity and privacy, in *Refugee Appeal No 74665/03* (NZRSAA) (7 July 2004, unreported).

'Outside the country of nationality ... residence'

12.34   It is fundamental to the definition of a Convention refugee that the person should be outside his or her country owing to the fear of persecution.[1]

A person sheltered in a foreign embassy in the country of persecution is outside that country's jurisdiction, but not its territory, and cannot be recognised as a Convention refugee.[2]

1   See UNHCR *Handbook* 12.13 above, para 88. For a discussion of this territorial limitation – the principle of 'alienage' – generally see Hathaway 12.22 fn 2 above, pp 29–33. In *European Roma Rights Centre v Immigration Officer at Prague Airport* [2004] UKHL 55, especially per Lord Bingham, the House of Lords held that measures specifically designed to prevent potential asylum seekers ever reaching a state's territory are not contrary to the Convention. Their Lordships also rejected arguments to the effect that measures designed to prevent asylum seekers even being able to reach UK territory in order to make a claim here, were unlawful in terms of customary international law as being contrary to the 'spirit' of the Convention. See also the Australian High Court in *Minister for Immigration and Multicultural Affairs v Ibrahim* [2000] HCA 55 and *Minister for Immigration and Multicultural Affairs v Khawar* [2002] HCA 14, and the US Supreme Court in *Sale, Acting Commissioner, INS v Haitian Centres Council Inc* (1993) 509 US 155, and see 12.9 above.
2   UNHCR *Handbook* above, para 88, fn. See the discussion of 'diplomatic asylum' in *R (on the application of B) v Secretary of State for the Foreign and Commonwealth Office* [2004] EWCA Civ 1344, [2005] 2 WLR 618, (2004) Times, 25 October.

12.35 It may be necessary to determine what the person's true nationality is, since, if it is not that of the country of feared persecution, the claimant can be returned to the country of nationality.[1] Similarly, a person who is a national of more than one country will be expected to satisfy the refugee definition in respect of each country, or seek protection of that country where persecution is not feared.[2] But the second nationality must be effective, not merely formal, before it disqualifies someone from refugee status vis-à-vis the country of persecution.[3] Where there is a dispute as to nationality, the decision of the country of purported nationality will be decisive, rather than the host country's conclusion as to what the nationality should be.[4] Possession of a passport issued by another state may not be evidence of nationality if it was issued as a travel document to enable the bearer to move elsewhere.[5] However, possession of such a travel document may be evidence that the person can be removed to a safe third country.[6] Arbitrary exclusion from the country of nationality, implying cutting off from the enjoyment of all the benefits and rights enjoyed by citizens, can itself amount to persecution.[7] The Convention definition applies to stateless persons as well as to those who have a nationality. Stateless persons[8] qualify if they flee from the country of former habitual residence[9] and cannot go back there because of a well-founded fear of persecution,[10] although if they are unable to return to the country of habitual residence, other international law obligations are engaged.[11]

1   *R v Special Adjudicator, ex p Abudine* [1995] Imm AR 60, QBD. In *Smith (Agartha)* (00/TH/02130) the IAT held that although a failure to make a positive finding as to nationality may be fatal to a determination of an asylum claim, it need not be in every case so long as a particular country is identified as being the one in which persecution is feared.
2   Refugee Convention, Art 1A(2); UNHCR *Handbook* 12.13 above, paras 106–107; *A-G of Canada v Ward* [1997] INLR 42, S Ct Can. In the particular context of cases involving possible Ethiopian and/or Eritrean nationality or neither, leading to statelessness, see *Tecle v Secretary of State for the Home Department* [2002] EWCA Civ 1358 (CA permission refusal); *R (on the application of Tewolde) v Immigration Appeal Tribunal* [2004] EWHC 162 (Admin); and *L (Ethiopia)* [2003] UKIAT 00016, to the effect that a claimant asserting statelessness should prove it, if necessary by applying for the relevant nationality.
3   *R (on the application of Milisavljevic) v Immigration Appeal Tribunal* [2001] EWHC Admin 203, [2001] Imm AR 580; and the Australian Federal Court cases of *Jong Kim Koe v Minister for Immigration and Multicultural Affairs* [1997] 306 FCA (Full Court) and *Al-Anezi v Minister for Immigration & Multicultural Affairs* [1999] FCA 355 (per Lehane J).

4   See *Oppenheimer v Cattermole* [1976] AC 249, [1975] 1 All ER 538, HL; *Stoeck v Public Trustee* [1921] 2 Ch 67; *Bibi (Mahaboob) v Secretary of State for the Home Department* [1987] Imm AR 340, CA. This also accords with the rule of public international law that in general each state may determine who are its nationals: see R Plender *International Migration Law* (2nd edn, 1998), pp 39ff. But the decision of the purported country of nationality may be ignored if it violates international humanitarian law: *Oppenheimer v Cattermole* [1976] AC 249, HL.
5   (1993) 5(3) IJRL 466, Case No 156.
6   *Alsawaf v Secretary of State for the Home Department* [1988] Imm AR 410, CA.
7   See the decision of the Court of Appeal in *Lazarevic v Secretary of State for the Home Department* [1997] Imm AR 251 at 270–272, per Hutchison LJ, CA. See also *Stula* (14622), though of course it remains for the applicant to establish a discriminatory Convention reason.
8   See *Samanter* (14520) for circumstances in which statelessness may arise.
9   A stateless applicant who has lived in more than one country before claiming asylum in yet another should only have to show that he is a refugee in relation to one of the former countries, or at least only in relation to the first of them: see UNHCR Handbook, para 104 and *Al-Anezi* (fn 3 above). This is because an applicant with only one nationality is not precluded from refugee status merely by the fact that he has lived in third countries, and as far as possible applicants with and those without nationality should be treated equally under the Convention. For the difference between a country in which a stateless applicant 'most recently lived' and one of former 'habitual residence', see *Zrilic* (17106). In *Dag* [2001] Imm AR 587 a starred Tribunal held, following the reasoning of *Thje Kwet Koe v MIEA* [1997] FCA 912, that the Turkish Republic of Northern Cyprus, which was not a state in international law, is not capable of being the country of a person's nationality (paras 30–33), and 'tentatively', that although the phrase 'country of former habitual residence' was wider, an area which formed part of an unrecognised state could not itself be a country of former habitual residence within the meaning of the Refugee Convention (para 39). On the related issue of 'protection', within the meaning of the refugee definition, in the context of de facto, non-internationally recognised, quasi-state entities, see 12.41 below.
10   *Revenko v Secretary of State for the Home Department* [2000] Imm AR 610, [2000] INLR 646, where the Court of Appeal rejected the argument that a stateless person needed only to show inability to return to qualify as a refugee – again, this conforms with the principle that as far as possible applicants with and those without nationality should be treated equally under the Convention (see fn 9 above).
11   UN Convention on the Status of Stateless Persons 1954: see 8.117 above. See also *Tjhe Kwet Koe v MIEA* [1997] FCA 912.

12.36 Before the British Nationality Act 1981 came into force in 1983, it was doubtful whether Commonwealth citizens could be afforded refugee status in the UK, because all were 'British subjects'.[1] As such, they might be said to be British nationals for the purposes of international law and thus under British protection. In the light of the restricted definition of British subject under the 1981 Act, citizens of independent Commonwealth countries ceased to be British subjects and, therefore, British nationals.[2] The problem, however, remained in respect of British Nationals (Overseas) and British Overseas citizens who found themselves persecuted in their country of habitual residence.[3] The problem has been resolved for the future by statutory provision for the grant of full British citizenship, carrying the right of abode, to all categories of British nationals, including British protected persons, who have no other nationality.[4]

1   For British nationality, see chapter 2 above.
2   British Nationality 1948 s 1(2) repealed and replaced by British Nationality Act 1981, s 37(4).
3   In *R v Chief Immigraion Officer, Gatwick Airport, ex p Singh* [1987] Imm AR 346, it was held that where a British Protected person had been rejected elsewhere, he or she could be treated as a person without nationality and issues were, therefore, raised under the Refugee

Convention – a very practical way of bypassing what otherwise might have been difficult questions of the UK's international obligations.

4   British Nationals (Overseas) with no other nationality may register as British citizens under the British Nationality (Hong Kong) Act 1997. British Overseas citizens, British subjects under the 1981 Act and British protected persons with no other nationality may register under s 4B of the 1981 Act as inserted by Nationality, Immigration and Asylum Act 2002, s 12: see 2.19 above.

12.37 Although refugees must first leave their own country in order to claim asylum, many of the countries from which refugees are fleeing are visa countries, ie their nationals require visas to enter the UK and other EU countries. While there is nothing in the Refugee Convention that would prevent a contracting state issuing a visa to enable a person to enter as a refugee, there is nothing that obliges them to do so.[1] UK practice, set out in the API, is that entry clearance officers have discretion to accept applications for entry clearance where applicants meet the requirements of the Convention and have close ties with the UK (family, or time spent there as a student) and the UK is the most appropriate country of refuge. The visa application form will be sent to the Home Office.[2] However, the applicant is still required to be outside his or her own country. If a visa is refused or not applied for, but the asylum seekers nevertheless reach the UK, the absence of a visa will not prevent their claims to asylum from being considered. However, the corollary to the imposition of a mandatory visa requirement for most refugee-producing countries has been the enactment of measures penalising the carriers of asylum seekers. This began with the Immigration (Carriers' Liability) Act 1987, which provided for the imposition of a penalty on carriers for each passenger brought into the UK without proper documentation.[3] During the parliamentary debate on the passage of the 1987 Act, amendments to exempt carriers from financial penalties in the case of refugees were rejected. Instead, policy guidelines on the exercise of discretion were adopted (making limited provision for the waiver of fines, inter alia, where a passenger was subsequently accepted as a genuine refugee or where the passenger was in 'imminent and self-evident danger of his life').[4] The 1987 Act was repealed by the Immigration and Asylum Act 1999,[5] and re-enacted in amended form in sections 40–43.[6] The 1999 Act also imposes civil penalties on carriers bringing 'clandestine entrants' into the country, whether by design or inadvertently, which force van and lorry drivers and rail freight operators to check their vehicles and containers for stowaways.[7] The Government has rejected demands for a waiver of penalties in respect of clandestine entrants recognised as refugees, although it has a policy of waiving penalties imposed on carriers for inadequately documented passengers.[8]

1   See *European Roma Rights Centre v Immigration Officer at Prague Airport* [2004] UKHL 55, [2005] 2 WLR 1.
2   API on 'Special Applications/Applications from abroad'. Reassuringly, caseworkers are told that an entry clearance issued in this capacity should 'not include any reference to asylum': para 3.2.
3   For the background to the passage of this Act see Nicholas Blake 'The Road to *Sivakumaran*' in (1989) 3 INLP 1 at 12. From 1991 the level of the fine per undocumented passenger was £2,000 (SI 1991/1497); Immigration and Asylum Act 1999, s 40(2) (as amended by the Nationality, Immigration and Asylum Act 2002) sets the fine at £2,000, or such other sum as may be substituted by order of the Secretary of State: 1999 Act, s 40(10) (as amended). For more detailed discussion of carrier sanctions see 14.88ff below.
4   See 14.94 below, where the guidance is set out in full.

12.37 *Refugees, Asylum and Exceptional Leave*

Immigration and Asylum Act 1999, Sch 16.
The 1999 Act, ss 40–43 were amended by the Nationality, Immigration and Asylum Act 2002, Sch 8 (such that new ss 40A and 40B were added and s 42 repealed). See fn 3 above and chapter 14 below.
See 14.89ff below.
326 HC Official Report (6th series) col 1032.

'Unable or ... unwilling to avail himself of the protection'

12.38 The failure of state protection is at the heart of refugee law. The refugee definition treats those with nationality and those who are stateless differently. To qualify as refugees, the former must be unable or unwilling to avail themselves of the protection of their country; the latter unable or unwilling to return to the country of habitual residence.[1] At the time of drafting the Refugee Convention it was envisaged that stateless persons, and nationals 'refused passport facilities or other protection by their own governments', would be the main categories qualifying through inability (as opposed to unwillingness) to obtain protection or to return.[2] But the category of refugees who have a nationality but are unable to secure the protection of their country is much wider than originally contemplated. It includes those who are unable through circumstances beyond the control of the state (for example, civil war or grave disturbance) as well as circumstances for which the state is directly responsible (for example, the refusal of passport facilities or denial of admission to the territory, which may itself in particular cases amount to persecution).[3] 'Inability' implies circumstances beyond the control of the person concerned, while 'unwillingness' implies his or her refusal to accept protection because of a fear of persecution.[4] For stateless persons, no question of availment of protection arises and the abandonment of the country of former habitual residence may in itself mean that the person is unable to return.[5] But all categories of refugees, including stateless persons, must demonstrate a current well-founded fear of Convention persecution to fulfil the definition requirements.[6]

[1] Refugee Convention, Art 1A(2): see 12.20 above. The meaning of 'country' in each phrase has been held to be different by the Tribunal in *Dag* [2001] Imm AR 587 at 12.35 fn 9 above. See also *Tjhe Kwet Koe v MIEA* [1997] FCA 912 (Aust); *Zalzali v Minister of Employment and Immigration* [1991] 3 CF 605, CA (Can). See also however 12.35, fnn 9 and 10 above for the principled approach to interpretation of the refugee definition that seeks, as far as possible, to minimise the differences in treatment between nationals and stateless persons.

[2] See Goodwin-Gill 12.5 fn 1 above, p 41 citing report of the *Ad Hoc* Committee: UN doc. E/1618, 39. In the High Court of Australia in *Minister for Immigration and Multicultural Affairs v Khawar* [2002] HCA 14, Gleeson CJ stated that the words 'the protection of that country', of which a refugee with nationality must be unable or, owing to his well-founded fear, unwilling to avail himself for the purposes of the Art 1A(2) definition, refer to diplomatic or consular protection abroad. Thus, where the country of nationality has a consular post in the country of refuge, a refugee will be unwilling to avail himself of his own country's protection there owing to his well-founded fear of being persecuted. Where there is no such consular post, the refugee will be unable to avail himself of any protection from his own country. McHugh and Gummow JJ agreed with Gleeson CJ on this issue.

[3] *Lazarevic v Secretary of State for the Home Department* [1997] Imm AR 251 at 272, per Hutchison LJ. The example in that case was the refusal of the Federal Republic of Yugoslavia to permit the return of its nationals who had fled the conflict in former Yugoslavia and sought asylum abroad. See 12.35, fn 7 above.

698

4   UNHCR *Handbook*, 12.13 above, paras 97–100. In *Svazas v Secretary of State for the Home Department* [2002] EWCA Civ 74, [2002] INLR 197 at para 22, Sedley LJ gave as an example of refugees who are unwilling to avail themselves of State protection, German Jews who had been attacked by Brownshirt thugs in 1938 at a time when the Nazi authorities were pretending that such attacks were beyond their control. Clearly the reality then was that the authorities were in fact able to protect the Jews and so the drafters of the 1951 Convention would have had this in mind when inserting the 'unwilling to avail' clause.

5   UNHCR *Handbook* above, para 101; *R v Secretary of State for the Home Department, ex p Adan* [1999] 1 AC 293.

6   *Revenko v Secretary of State for the Home Department* [2000] Imm AR 610, [2000] INLR 646, CA.

12.39 The mere possession of a valid national passport from the country where persecution is feared is not evidence that the person continues to seek protection from that country and is therefore no bar to refugee status; however, refugees who refuse to surrender their national passports to the host country without good reason may throw doubts on their unwillingness to avail themselves of the protection of their own country.[1]

1   UNHCR *Handbook* 12.13 above, paras 48–49, 97–101; *Refugee Appeal No 67/92 Re BR* (10 November 1992, unreported) (NZRSAA). See also *Minister for Immigration and Multicultural Affairs v Khawar* [2002] HCA 14, at 12.38 fn 2 above.

12.40 In *Adan*[1] the House of Lords considered whether a Somali national who had left his own country because of a well-founded fear of persecution, and who was unable to avail himself of the protection of that country because there was no effective state, was a refugee although he no longer had a well-founded fear of persecution. The Court of Appeal had held by a majority that as long as past persecution or fear of it was still a reason for the refugee's presence in the host country, it was unnecessary to show a current well-founded fear of persecution.[2] The House of Lords disagreed. Lord Lloyd, giving the leading judgment,[3] analysed the refugee definition as comprising a 'fear test' and a 'protection' test', both of which had to be satisfied.[4]

1   *R v Secretary of State for the Home Department, ex p Adan* [1999] 1 AC 293, [1998] INLR 325.

2   *Lazarevic v Secretary of State for the Home Department* [1997] 1 WLR 1107 at 1114–1115, [1997] INLR 1 at 8, [1997] Imm AR 251.

3   [1999] 1 AC 293 at 304–305; [1998] INLR 325, at 330–331. Lord Slynn reasoned that the use of the present tense in the definition, '*is* unable or, owing to such fear, unwilling to avail himself of the protection of that country' required a well-founded fear when refugee status was determined. Lords Goff, Nolan and Hope agreed with Lord Lloyd's reasoning. In *Sivakumaran* (18147) the IAT held that the same reasoning must apply to stateless applicants: see also *Revenko v Secretary of State for the Home Department* [2000] Imm AR 610, [2000] INLR 646, CA, at 12.38 above, text and fn 6.

4   Lord Lloyd's formulation was, however, significantly modified by the House of Lords in *Horvath v Secretary of State for the Home Department* [2000] INLR 329, HL, in the context of the meaning of 'persecution': see 12.52 below.

12.41 In *Vallaj*[1] the Administrative Court considered and rejected as 'narrowly linguistic' an argument that the protection available to someone to disqualify him or her from refugee status had necessarily to be provided by the authorities of the country of nationality. The issue arose in relation to ethnic Albanians in the Serbian province of Kosovo, in the Federal Republic of

12.41 *Refugees, Asylum and Exceptional Leave*

Yugoslavia, who were receiving protection not from the authorities of their own country but from a UN interim administration (known as UNMIK) and by NATO troops (known as KFOR) mandated by a UN security council resolution. An earlier starred Tribunal case, *Dyli*,[2] had held that the phrase 'the protection of the country' in the refugee definition referred to any protection available in the territory of the country of nationality, whatever its source. In *Vallaj* Dyson J held that the Refugee Convention should, as a living instrument, be interpreted in a way which takes account of the realities of the interventionist role that the UN Security Council now adopts when circumstances require it. Protection provided under lawful authority by a body to which all the powers and functions of the state (including the function of protection) have been transferred falls within the definition of 'protection of the country', and a person in receipt of such protection is not, subject to issues of adequacy of protection, a refugee.[3] On the other hand, in *Gardi*[4] the Court of Appeal acknowledged, obiter, the strength of the argument that the appellant – an Iraqi Kurd – could not avail himself of the 'protection of his country', for the purposes of the refugee definition, by seeking the protection of one of the two major Kurdish parties that had de facto control of northern Iraq. Unfortunately, for jurisdictional reasons, the Court of Appeal had to declare its judgment a nullity.[5] However, in *Saber*[6] the Inner House of the Scottish Court of Session (to which the appeal in *Gardi* had properly lain) fully adopted both the ratio and the obiter of the *Gardi* judgment and held that such de facto authorities were not capable of providing protection within the meaning of the refugee definition. But the EC Qualification Directive 2004/83[7] provides that protection 'can be provided by a state or by parties or organisations, including international organisations, controlling the state or a substantial part of the territory of the state' – a formulation which seems at odds with the refugee definition.[8]

---

[1] *R (on the application of Vallaj) v Immigration Appeal Tribunal* [2001] INLR 655, per Dyson J.

[2] *Dyli v Secretary of State for the Home Department* [2000] INLR 372, [2000] Imm AR 652.

[3] *Vallaj* above, paras 24–35. Leave to appeal was refused by the Court of Appeal on 24 May 2001 in a reasoned judgment fully upholding Dyson J's approach: *R (on the application of Vallaj) v Secretary of State for the Home Department* [2001] EWCA Civ 782, [2001] INLR 342, CA.

[4] *Gardi v Secretary of State for the Home Department* [2002] EWCA Civ 750, [2002] 1 WLR 2755, [2003] Imm AR 39.

[5] Because the adjudicator from whom the appeal emanated had sat in Scotland: see *Gardi v Secretary of State for the Home Department* [2002] EWCA Civ 1560, [2002] 1 WLR 3282.

[6] *Saber v Secretary of State for the Home Department* (Appeal No XA129/02) (13 November 2003, unreported), IHCS. See also *R (on the application of Mahmud) v Secretary of State for the Home Department* [2004] EWHC 148 (Admin), (2004) All ER (D) 102 (Feb) per Sullivan J.

[7] EC Qualification Directive 2004/83/EC, 12.3 fn 3 above, Art 7.

[8] The Tribunal in *GH (Iraq) CG* [2004] UKIAT 00248 referred obiter to a Canadian case, *Zatzoli v Minister of Employment and Immigration* [1991] 3 CF 605 in support of the proposition that it was practical protection that was relevant to refugee status rather than the protection of the official government in circumstances of civil war. The status of the Canadian court is not clear and the judgment cited appears to be one of impression rather than authority.

Internal relocation alternative

12.42 Because the principal concern of refugee law is the provision of international protection to persons unable to receive protection in their own country, a purely localised risk will generally be insufficient to make someone a refugee. International protection is not needed if the person can obtain protection by moving elsewhere in his or her own country.[1] But if, as the UNHCR *Handbook* points out, internal flight or internal relocation, to another part of the country is not reasonable or safe, it is not necessary to prove that persecution for a Convention reason extends to the whole of the country.[2] The EC Qualification Directive 2004/83 allows Member States to refuse asylum if there is a part of the country of origin where there is no well-founded fear of persecution or real risk of suffering serious harm, and where the applicant can reasonably be expected to stay.[3] These considerations are reflected in the Immigration Rules,[4] which provide that an asylum claim *may* be refused if there is a part of the country to which it would be reasonable to expect the applicant to go, where he or she does not have a well founded fear of persecution. The issue of internal relocation only arises if the asylum seeker has a well-founded fear of persecution in his or her home area, or if he or she cannot return there without a real risk of persecution on the way.[5] Academic opinion is that there is no possible internal relocation where persecution emanates from the state itself or its own agents;[6] UNHCR's view is that in such a case there should be a (rebuttable) presumption against there being a possible internal relocation alternative.[7]

---

1   See eg *R v Secretary of State for the Home Department, ex p Robinson* [1998] QB 929, [1997] INLR 182, [1997] Imm AR 568; *AE and FE v Secretary of State for the Home Department* [2003] EWCA Civ 1032, [2004] QB 531 (see further 12.44 below).

2   UNHCR *Handbook* 12.13 above, para 91. The previously preferred term, 'internal flight', is problematic in that it refers to the past (whether the applicant *could have* moved elsewhere) rather than to the crucial issue as to whether now, on return to the country, the applicant could internally relocate within it: see *AE and FE v Secretary of State for the Home Department* [2003] EWCA Civ 1032, [2004] QB 531 at [19]. The preferable concept is 'internal protection': see the Michigan Guidelines on the Internal Protection Alternative, April 1999, given 'outline approval' by the Court of Appeal in *R (on the application of Vallaj) v Secretary of State for the Home Department* [2001] EWCA Civ 782, [2001] INLR 342 at para 27. See also *Refugee Appeal No 71684/99* [2000] INLR 165, NZRSAA – although the Court of Appeal rejected the ratio of this New Zealand decision in *E v Secretary of State for the Home Department* [2003] EWCA Civ 1032, [2004] QB 531 at paras 47–48.

3   EC Qualification Directive 2004/83/EC, 12.3 fn 3 above, Art 8. This affords significantly weaker protection than its predecessor, the EU Joint Position (96/196/JHA) of 4 March 1996 on harmonised application of definition of the term 'refugee' (*Butterworths Immigration Law Service*, 2D[138]), which required 'effective protection' in the 'safe' part of the country in order to disqualify the claimant from international protection.

4   HC 395, para 343.

5   *Dyli* [2000] INLR 372, [2000] Imm AR 652, (starred IAT); *R (on the application of Vallaj) v A Special Adjudicator* [2001] INLR 655, QBD, per Dyson J; upheld as *R (on the application of Vallaj) v Secretary of State for the Home Department* [2001] EWCA Civ 782, [2001] INLR 342 (permission refusal) The alternative area must be reachable on return without the applicant having to land in or travel through an area in which he does have a well-founded fear of Convention persecution: see *Senga (Jouanna)* (11821) (UNITA supporter could not be safely returned to Luanda as she would be at risk of persecution there before she would be able to reach 'safe' UNITA held territory); see also *Ganeshan v Secretary of State for the Home Department* (SLJ 99/6274/3) (27 August 1999, unreported), CA, grant of permission per Schiemann LJ (it is arguably incumbent upon the UK

authorities to consider whether a claimant is likely to be persecuted or is at risk of being persecuted in the part of the country to which it is proposed to return him or her).

6   Expressed by specialists in refugee law including Hathaway in the Michigan Colloquium of April 1999: see the Michigan Guidelines on the internal protection alternative, April 1999, available at www:refugee.law.nz.

7   See the UNHCR 'Position Paper on Relocating Internally as Reasonable Alternative to Seeking Asylum', February 1999. See also UNHCR's 'Guidelines on International Protection No 4: Internal Flight or the Internal Relocation Alternative within the context of Art 1A(2) of the 1951 Convention and/or the 1967 Protocol relating to the status of refugees (HCR/GIP/03/04) 23 July 2003. This approach is adopted in New Zealand – see eg NZ Court of Appeal decision *No 181/97* (13 October 1997, unreported). In *R v Immigration Appeal Tribunal, ex p Chen Guang* [2000] INLR, QBD, Keene J accepted that internal relocation was less likely to be an option where the fear was of state authorities, but disliked elevating this idea into a presumption. The presumption against internal relocation in state agent cases may be rebutted where the fear is of a specific local police force (eg the Punjab police in India: see *Singh (Chinhu)* [1998] Imm AR 551; or the police in Zanzibar, where there is a possibility of relocation to mainland Tanzania: see *R v Secretary of State for the Home Department, ex p Salim* [1999] INLR 628, [2000] Imm AR 6, QBD and *Aziz v Secretary of State for the Home Department* [2003] EWCA Civ 118).

12.43 In *Robinson*[1] the Court of Appeal considered the appellate authorities' jurisdiction to decide on the reasonableness of relocation to an area of the country where there was no fear of persecution. The Tribunal had been divided on whether it could consider the issue, with one division holding that its jurisdiction was limited to the issue whether returning the appellant would breach the UK's obligations under the Refugee Convention[2] and that the wording of paragraph 343 of the Immigration Rules reflected an unreviewable discretion,[3] and another that the possibility of internal flight was part of the refugee definition.[4] The Court of Appeal, after reviewing Commonwealth jurisprudence and the views of academics, held that both the safety and the reasonableness of the 'internal flight alternative' went to ability and willingness to avail oneself of the protection of the country of persecution, and thus were within the appellate authorities' jurisdiction. As to what would be 'reasonable', the court emphasised that decision-makers must consider 'all relevant circumstances against the backcloth that the issue is whether the claimant is entitled to the status of refugee'. Such circumstances might include whether as a practical matter (for financial, logistical or other good reason) the 'safe' part of the country is reasonably accessible; whether the claimant is required to encounter great physical danger or to undergo undue hardship in travelling there or staying there, and whether the quality of the internal protection fails to meet basic norms of civil, political and socio-economic human rights.[5] The court approved the test by Linden JA in the Canadian Federal Court in *Thirunavukkarasu*:[6] 'Would it be unduly harsh to expect this person to move to another less hostile part of the country?'[7] In *Canaj*[8] the Court of Appeal suggested that *Robinson* should now be read together with the New Zealand decision in *Refugee Appeal No 71684/99*.[9]

1   *R v Secretary of State for the Home Department, ex p Robinson* [1998] QB 929, [1997] INLR 182, [1997] Imm AR 568.

2   Asylum and Immigration Appeals Act 1993, s 8 (now Nationality, Immigration and Asylum Act 2002, s 84(1)(g), (3)); *R v Secretary of State for the Home Department, ex p Mehari* [1994] QB 474.

3   *Dupovac* (11846); *Ahmed* (13371); *Nirmalan* (14361).

4   *Ikhlaq* (13679).

5   *Robinson* above, para 18, referring to the Preamble to the Refugee Convention.
6   *Thirunavukkarasu v Minister of Employment and Immigration* (1993) 109 DLR (4th) 682 per Linden JA at 687 (Can Fed Ct).
7   *Robinson* above, para 29.
8   *R (on the application of Vallaj) v Secretary of State for the Home Department* [2001] EWCA Civ 782, [2001] INLR 342 (but see 12.42 fn 2, above).
9   [2000] INLR 165.

12.44 The issue of what would make internal relocation 'unduly harsh' and thereby 'unreasonable', so that an applicant, who has a well-founded fear of persecution for a Convention reason in his home area, qualifies as a refugee, was revisited by the Court of Appeal in *AE*[1] in the light of the Human Rights Act 1998. The court drew a distinction between factors relevant to refugee status and those relevant to the grant of humanitarian leave, holding that in Refugee Convention cases, consideration of the reasonableness of internal relocation should focus on the consequences to the asylum seeker of settling in the place of relocation *instead of his or her previous home*:

> 'The comparison between the asylum seeker's situation in this country and what it will be in the place of relocation is not relevant for this purpose, though it may be very relevant when considering the impact of the Human Rights Convention, or the requirements of humanity.'[2]

In other words, for a person with a well-founded fear of persecution in his or her home area but not in the whole country to be granted refugee status, conditions in the place of internal relocation must be so bad as effectively to drive the applicant back to the place where he or she has a well-founded fear of persecution. Lesser levels of 'harshness' in a place of possible internal relocation may however engage the Human Rights Convention and warrant a grant of humanitarian protection or discretionary leave.[3]

1   *AE v Secretary of State for the Home Department* [2003] EWCA Civ 1032, [2004] QB 531, [2004] 2 WLR 123, [2003] INLR 475 (currently on appeal to the House of Lords).
2   *AE* at paras 64, 67.
3   The Secretary of State has been granted leave to appeal to the House of Lords in respect of this aspect of the Court of Appeal's judgment: see [2004] 1 WLR 1179.

12.45 A further difficulty with internal relocation, or flight, related to the burden and standard of proving whether internal relocation was reasonable or 'unduly harsh'. Who had to prove what, to which standard? In *Manoharan*[1] a tribunal had held that the burden was on the applicant to show on balance of probabilities that it would be unduly harsh to return him; in *Sachithananthan*[2] a tribunal held (following *Thirunavukkarasu*)[3] that the test was whether there was a serious possibility that it would be unduly harsh. The issue was resolved in *Karanakaran*[4] where the Court of Appeal decided that no 'standard of proof' as such applied; the question was simply whether, taking all relevant[5] matters into account, return of the claimant would be unduly harsh. This was a matter of evaluation and conscientious judgment.[6] Everything capable of having a bearing on the question was to be taken into account (which might include the need to consider the cumulative effect of a whole range of disparate considerations).[7] The court commended the methodology of the Tribunal in the case of *Sayandan* where, in considering whether return would be unduly harsh, it had set out some eleven disparate risks as matters worthy of attention and had evaluated both the likelihood of a risk eventuating and the seriousness of the consequences.[8] The burden remains on the applicant to demonstrate that it would not be reasonable to expect him to relocate internally within his country of origin.[9]

1   *Manoharan v Secretary of State for the Home Department* [1998] INLR 519.
2   *Sachitananthan* [1999] INLR 205.
3   *Thirunavukkarasu v Minister of Employment and Immigration* (1993) 109 DLR (4th) 682.
4   *Karanakaran v Secretary of State for the Home Department* [2000] 3 All ER 449, [2000] INLR 122, CA.
5   In *Gnanam v Secretary of State for the Home Department* [1999] INLR 219, CA Tuckey LJ emphasised that what may be relevant factors in one case would not necessarily be so in another, whether considered individually or cumulatively.
6   *Karanakaran v Secretary of State for the Home Department* above [2000] 3 All ER 449 at 477and 479, [2000] INLR 122 at 152 and 154, CA. This approach was expressly approved by Lord Steyn in *R (on the application of Sivakumar) v Immigration Appeal Tribunal* [2003] INLR 457, at para 19, HL. On this approach presumably it would be open to different countries to take different views about what was reasonable: see *R (on the application of Yogathas and Thangarasa) v Secretary of State for the Home Department* [2002] UKHL 36, [2003] 1 AC 920, [2002] INLR 620, at para 115, per Lord Scott.
7   *Gnanam* (above) and *Karanakaran* at INLR 145, per Brooke LJ. Sedley LJ observed at INLR 154–155 that the correct approach coincided with that advocated by Simon Brown LJ in *Ravichandran (Senathirajah) v Secretary of State for the Home Department* [1996] Imm AR 97 at 109, ie consideration of the 'single composite question' whether a person has a 'well-founded fear of being persecuted for Convention reasons' in the round and with all relevant circumstances brought into account. In Australia a similar wide-ranging approach to internal flight has been adopted: see eg *Randhawa v MILGEA* (1994) 52 FCR 437; *Franco-Buitrago v Minister for Immigration and Multicultural Affairs* [2000] FCA 1525.
8   *Sayandan* (16312) 5 March 1998. The risks identified in returning a Tamil to Colombo were arrest and return to the North East because of lack of documents; repeated arrest in round-ups; being subject to extortion; unduly harsh treatment before accessing judicial process; dreadful prison conditions if detained; not being able to find or retain accommodation; not being able to find employment because of discrimination; where the appellant could not speak Sinhalese; being subjected to a regime where racial discrimination was part of everyday life; having no real contacts or ties in Colombo; and previous ill-treatment in Sri Lanka by both the LTTE and the security forces.
9   See *Aziz v Secretary of State for the Home Department* [2003] EWCA Civ 118; *R v Secretary of State for the Home Department, ex p Salim* [1999] INLR 628, [2000] Imm AR 6, QBD.

Persecution for Convention reasons

Persecution

12.46 The Refugee Convention does not define persecution[1] and, although the term, like the entire refugee definition, has an autonomous meaning,[2] there is no universally accepted definition.[3] As we shall see in relation to persecution by non-state agents, its meaning is linked to the availability of state protection, at least so far as the UK is concerned.[4] The *Handbook* indicates that, while a threat to life or freedom for the relevant reason will always amount to persecution,[5] persecution does not have to involve threats to life or freedom; other serious violations of human rights will also qualify.[6] In *Jonah*[7] Nolan J ruled that the word must be given its ordinary dictionary definition 'to pursue with malignancy or injurious action, especially to oppress for holding a heretical opinion or belief'. The case law reveals a tension between (i) the approach which sees the issue solely as one of fact for the decision maker and the immigration judge, subject to challenge in the Administrative Court solely on *Wednesbury* principles,[8] and (ii) attempts to provide a coherent framework for persecution based on human rights law. The human rights approach dictated by the preamble of the Refugee Convention has been propounded by James Hathaway, who in his seminal book *The Law of Refugee Status* defined persecution as 'the sustained or systemic failure of state protection in relation to one of the core entitlements which has been recognised by the international community',[9] a definition endorsed by Lord Steyn in *Ullah*.[10] In the influential case of *Gashi*,[11] the Tribunal adopted UNHCR's analysis of persecution,[12] which drew heavily on Hathaway's definition,[13] in relation to three categories of human rights. Breaches of inviolable human rights such as the right of life and the prohibition against torture, cruel, inhuman or degrading treatment would always be persecution. Violation of rights whose limited derogation or curtailment by the state could be justified only in time of public emergency (freedom from arbitrary arrest and detention and freedom of expression) would be persecution if unjustified. The denial of rights reflecting goals for social, economic or cultural development, such as the right to a livelihood, could amount to persecution if it was systematic and discriminatory. More recently, Goodwin-Gill[14] has stated that the 'core meaning' of persecution 'readily includes the threat of deprivation of life or physical freedom' although 'less overt measures may suffice, such as the imposition of serious economic disadvantage, denial of access to employment, to the professions, or to education, or other restrictions on the freedoms traditionally guaranteed in a democratic society'.[15] In *Appellant S*[16] in the Australian High Court McHugh and Kirby JJ made the point that a *threat* of serious harm, with its 'menacing implications', can constitute persecution, especially when it causes a person to alter his or her behaviour.[17] Although mere discrimination is probably not enough, evidence of discrimination will make it easier to demonstrate persecution. And where discrimination is so severe, frequent or protracted that it inhibits freedom to exercise basic human rights such as the right to a livelihood or to practice a religion, it may amount to persecution[18] The disadvantage of linking the definition of persecution to core human rights is that if the asylum seeker cannot establish the existence of the core right, there will be no persecution.[19]

---

[1]   This section considers the meaning of 'persecution' at the hands of the state – the classic or paradigm case of persecution that would have been foremost in the minds of the drafters of the Refugee Convention in the aftermath of the Second World War and the defeat of the Nazi regime. Following *Horvath v Secretary of State for the Home Department* [2001] 1 AC 489, [2000] INLR 239, a modified meaning is required where the allegation relates to persecution by non-state agents: see *Persecution by non-state actors* at 12.51ff below. See also 12.42 above on the differing relevance of the 'internal relocation alternative' depending on whether the persecutor is a state or non-state actor.

[2]   See *R v Secretary of State for the Home Department, ex p Adan, R v Secretary of State for the Home Department, ex p Aitseguer* [2001] 2 AC 477, [2001] INLR 44.

[3]   In *Appellant S395/2002 v Minister for Immigration and Multicultural Affairs* [2003] HCA 71 at para 66, Aust High Ct, Gummow and Hayne JJ (in a joint judgment forming part of the majority) pointed out that 'It is not of great assistance and is apt to mislead to approach the matter by saying, as did an English court, that "persecution" is a "strong word".' The English case was *R v Secretary of State for the Home Department, ex p Binbasi* [1989] Imm AR 595 at 599 per Kennedy J. See also 12.47, fn 13 below.

[4]   *Horvath* fn 1 above, at 12.51ff.

5   This is clear from the 'non-refoulement' provision in Art 33, which prohibits the return of a refugee to the frontiers of territories where 'life or freedom would be threatened' for a Refugee Convention reason.

6   UNHCR *Handbook* 12.13 above, para 51; *R v Secretary of State for the Home Department, ex p Sivakumaran* [1988] AC 958, per Lord Goff; *Horvath* above, at 215H, per Lord Lloyd.

7   *R v Immigration Appeal Tribunal, ex p Jonah* [1985] Imm AR 7.

8   See *Kagema v Secretary of State for the Home Department* [1997] Imm AR 137; *Faraj v Secretary of State for the Home Department* [1999] INLR 451. In *Horvath* above Lord Lloyd described the proposition that persecution should be given its ordinary dictionary meaning as 'settled law' (at 251).

9   See 12.22 fn 2 above.

10 *R (on the application of Ullah) v Special Adjudicator* [2004] UKHL 26, [2004] 3 WLR 23, at para 32. See also Lord Hope in *Horvath v Secretary of State for the Home Department* [2000] 3 All ER 577, [2000] 3 WLR 379, HL; Lord Bingham in *Sepet v Secretary of State for the Home Department* [2003] 1 WLR 856 (para 7).

11 *Gashi v Secretary of State for the Home Department* [1997] INLR 96. See also Schiemann LJ in *Blanusa v Secretary of State for the Home Department* (IATRF 98/1495/4) (18 May 1998, unreported), CA.

12 UNHCR appeared as intervener in the case.

13 In Hathaway's formulation, the types of harm to be protected against include the breach of any right within the first category, a discriminatory or non-emergency abrogation of a right within the second category, or the failure to implement a right within the third category which is either discriminatory or not grounded in the absolute lack of resources: see *The Law of Refugee Status* (n 9 above) pp 101–116.

14 *The Refugee in International Law*, 12.5 fn 1 above, pp 66–68.

15 Whether such restrictions amount to persecution requires assessment of a complex of factors, including (1) the nature of the freedom threatened, (2) the nature and severity of the restriction, and (3) the likelihood of the restriction eventuating in the individual case: Goodwin-Gill fn 14 above. See *Chen Shi Hai v Minister for Immigration* [2000] INLR 455, Aust HC: adverse treatment which a 'black child' (one born in contravention of the 'one child' policy) is likely to receive in China – denial of access to food, education and health care – could amount to persecution. In *Chan v Minister for Immigration and Ethnic Affairs* (1989) 169 CLR 379, Aust HC, McHugh J considered that measures in disregard of human dignity may, in appropriate cases, constitute persecution (a proposition approved in the joint judgment of six members of the High Court in *Minister for Immigration and Ethnic Affairs v Guo* (1997) 191 CLR 559). See the judgment of Lady Hale in *R (on the application of Hoxha) v Secretary of State for the Home Department, R (on the application of B) v Secretary of State for the Home Department* [2005] UKHL 19, [2005] 1 WLR 1063, (2005) 149 Sol Jo LB 358.

16 See fn 3 above: Gummow and Hayne JJ and McHugh and Kirby JJ, each giving joint judgments, formed the majority.

17 Conversely however, in *R (on the application of Hoxha) v Secretary of State for the Home Department* [2002] EWCA Civ 1403, the Court of Appeal rejected an argument that the *sequelae* of past persecution can amount to persecution. However, the House of Lords did not rule this out; Lady Hale dealt in particular with the continuing punishment of stigma and ostracism likely to result from a public rape in the context of a deeply patriarchal society; see [2005] UKHL 19 at paras 30ff. She referred to this again in her judgment in *N v SSHD* [2005] UKHL 31, para 58.

18 UNHCR *Handbook* 12.13 above, paras 54–55; *Chen* above, at 24; *Ahmad v Secretary of State for the Home Department* [1990] Imm AR 61 at 66, per Farquarson LJ. Tribunal determinations in which findings of persecution have been made in 'third category' cases include *Padhu* (12318) (inability to work and deprivation of state benefits) and *Lucreteanu* (12126) (threatening phone calls in Romania). In *Kadham v Canada* IMM-652–97 (8 January 1998, unreported), FC Moulden J observed that harassment could constitute persecution if it was sufficiently serious or long-lasting as to threaten the claimant's physical or moral integrity.

19 *Sepet v Secretary of State for the Home Department* [2003] UKHL 15, [2003] 3 All ER 304, [2003] 1 WLR 856, [2003] Imm AR 428 (no right of conscientious objection to military service).

12.47 In *Ravichandran*[1] the Court of Appeal found Hathaway's human rights-based analysis of persecution instructive. In *Adan* [2] Hutchinson LJ saw no reason not to accept it. And in *Horvath*[3] it received the seal of approval from Lord Hope. *Ravichandran* held that the arbitrary detention of young Tamils for periods of a few days following terrorist atrocities did not amount to persecution, although long-term detention, or detention accompanied by ill-treatment, would have been a different matter.[4] The court held that the question whether an individual's fear is one of persecution for a Convention reason is a single composite question to be determined in the round with all relevant circumstances being taken into account.[5] Breaches of rights other than absolute rights probably require an element of persistence to constitute 'persecution'.[6] But the question of whether persistence is a necessary element of physical ill-treatment has been the subject of conflicting decisions. While the reference in Hathaway to 'sustained or systemic denial of core human rights' is meant to refer to country practices underlying individual claims, it was adopted in *Ravichandran*[7] as an individual requirement by Staughton LJ, who observed that 'persecution must at least be persistent and serious ill-treatment without just cause by the state, or from which the state can provide protection but chooses not to'. His remarks have become detached from their context (short-term but arbitrary and unlawful detention of Tamils as terrorist suspects) and wrongly applied as a rigid legal criterion regardless of the nature of the feared persecution.[8] It would, however, be absurd to deny refugee status to someone with a well-founded fear of life-threatening torture on the ground that the torture would not be repeated. Freedom from torture is an absolute right which can never be balanced or qualified, and its violation must always constitute persecution.[9] This was accepted by the Court of Appeal in *Demirkaya*,[10] although apparently not by a different division of the court in *Faraj*.[11] The Australian and New Zealand courts regard any requirement of systematic conduct aimed at the claimant as a misdirection.[12] Back in the UK, the higher courts have held that the threshold of 'serious harm' is a high one,[13] although regard should be had to the individual's characteristics and expectations in deciding what the refugee from a troubled part of the world ought to be able to put up with.[14] There is no requirement that a person be 'singled out' for persecution to be a refugee.[15] In *Katrinak*[16] Schiemann LJ considered that it is possible to persecute an individual by persecuting a close member of his or her family.

---

1   *Ravichandran (Senathirajah) v Secretary of State for the Home Department* [1996] Imm AR 97 at 107. It had already been accepted by La Forest J in the leading Canadian case of *A-G of Canada v Ward* [1993] 2 SCR 689 at 709.

2   *Adan v Secretary of State for the Home Department* [1997] 1 WLR 1107 at 1126E.

3   *Horvath v Secretary of State for the Home Department* [2001] 1 AC 489 at 498E–G.

4   'If there remained a practice of torturing those detained, I very much doubt whether a finding of persecution on Convention grounds would be precluded merely because the torture was intended to discourage terrorism or to persuade detainees to inform on their associates rather than inflicted for purposes of oppression': Simon Brown LJ at 109. See also *R (on the application of Sivakumar) v Secretary of State for the Home Department* [2003] UKHL 14, [2003] 2 All ER 1097, see 12.65 fn 4, below.

5   *Ravichandran* above; see also *Karanakaran v Secretary of State for the Home Department* [2000] INLR 122, CA.

6   See the reference to 'cumulative grounds' in UNHCR *Handbook* 12.13 above, para 53.

7   *Ravichandran (Senathirajah) v Secretary of State for the Home Department* [1996] Imm AR 97 at 114.

8 Simon Brown LJ understood this distinction; see his reference in *Ravichandran* above to a 'practice of torturing those detained' as opposed to an individual requirement of repetitive ill-treatment.

9 See UNHCR *Handbook* above, para 51. In *Sepet v Secretary of State for the Home Department* [2001] EWCA Civ 681, [2001] INLR 33, 403, Laws LJ stated at [63] that: 'There are some classes of case in which threatened conduct is of such a kind that it is universally condemned, by national and international law, and always constitutes persecution: torture, rape (though of course it is not necessarily persecution for a Convention reason) ... Torture is absolutely persecutory; imprisonment only conditionally so.'

10 *Demirkaya v Secretary of State for the Home Department* [1999] INLR 441. This accords with the EC Qualification Directive 2004/83/EC, 12.3 fn 3 above, Art 9(1)(a) which states that acts of persecution '... must be sufficiently serious, by their nature *or* their repetition' (our emphasis).

11 *Faraj v Secretary of State for the Home Department* [1999] INLR 451, CA. But on the analysis of Peter Gibson LJ, a claimant might be a refugee based on a single incident 'if there are other incidents affecting a group of which that person is a member' (at 456E). See also the obiter remark of Lord Clyde in *Horvath v Secretary of State for the Home Department* [2000] INLR 239, HL quoting Hathaway ('sustained or systemic') when stating that persecution appeared to carry with it 'some element of persistence' (at 261F).

12 See *Appellant S395/2002 v Minister for Immigration and Multicultural Affairs* [2003] HCA 71 at para 66; *Minister for Immigration and Multicultural Affairs v Ibrahim (Haji)* (2000) 204 CLR 1, [2001] INLR 228; *Chan v Minister for Immigration and Ethnic Affairs* (1989) 169 CLR 379, 430; *Abdalla v Minister for Immigration and Multicultural Affairs* (1998) 51 ALD 666 at 671–673; *Anjum v Minister for Immigration and Multicultural Affairs* (1998) 52 ALD 225 at 230–232; *Refugee Appeal No 71462/99* [2000] INLR 311, para 78 (NZRSAA). See also *Doymus* (00 TH 01748) (19 July 2000, unreported), IAT: 'persistence is usual but not universal'; *Foughali* (00 TH 01514) (2 June 2000, unreported), IAT.

13 See *Horvath v Secretary of State for the Home Department* [2000] INLR 15, CA, at 50, per Ward LJ: 'anything short of a really serious flouting of the citizen's human rights and dignities will not do'.

14 UNHCR *Handbook* above, para 52.

15 *R v Secretary of State for the Home Department, ex p Jeyakumaran* [1994] Imm AR 45.

16 *Katrinak v Secretary of State for the Home Department* [2001] EWCA Civ 832, [2001] INLR 499 at para 23 per Schiemann LJ: 'It is possible to persecute a husband or a member of a family by what you do to other members of his immediate family. The essential task for the decision taker ... is to consider what is reasonably likely to happen to the wife and whether that is reasonably likely to affect the husband in such a way as to amount to persecution of him.'

Prosecution

12.48 Persecution must be distinguished from prosecution, and the *Handbook* points out that fugitives from common law offences are unlikely to be refugees.[1] But prosecution is not always inconsistent with persecution and may be good evidence of it. The nature of the allegations against the applicant and procedural safeguards to ensure a fair trial will have to be examined with care. The conclusion of persecution may be drawn where a fair trial would be denied; where punishment is excessive; where a particular political viewpoint or religion is expressly prohibited or the state's laws prohibit other normal and reasonable human activity guaranteed by fundamental human rights; or where there is other reason to suspect that the prosecution is being conducted for political reasons.[2] In deciding whether arrangements in the country of origin breach the Refugee Convention, the principles of comity between nations have no place.[3] Of course, a persecutory prosecution must also relate to a Convention reason to found refugee status.[4] In *Iqbal*[5] the Tribunal summarised how asylum claims, based on a fear of prosecution amounting to persecution, should be dealt with: (1) although it is not the purpose of the asylum determination process to judge guilt or innocence, nonetheless a factual evaluation as to whether there is a real risk that the claimant faces injustice rather than justice must be made; (2) whether prosecution amounts to persecution is a question of fact, and all relevant circumstances must be considered on a case by case basis; (3) the criminal justice process in the county of origin must be looked at as a whole, with possible harms considered cumulatively and not separately; (4) whether prosecution amounts to persecution must be analysed by reference to international human rights norms; (5) prosecution does not amount to persecution unless likely failures in the fair trial process go beyond shortcomings and pose a threat to the very existence of the right to a fair trial; (6) when considering whether there is a general risk of persecution to any person subjected to the criminal law process in a given country, it is important to establish the scale of relevant human rights violations, particularly in relation to mistreatment in detention and the right to a fair trial, and, using Article 3 ECHR as a benchmark, it is useful to ask whether whether the level of human rights abuse rises to the level of a 'consistent pattern of gross, flagrant or mass violations of human rights.'[6] This approach of the Tribunal in *Iqbal* was approved by the Court of Appeal in *Hariri* [7] and again in *Batayav*[8] (with Sedley LJ sounding a note of caution to the effect that the need to show a 'consistent pattern' of human rights violations was 'intended to elucidate the jurisprudential concept of real risk, not to replace it.') [9]

[1]   UNHCR *Handbook* 12.13 above, paras 56–60; *R v Secretary of State for the Home Department, ex p Singh (Bilged)* [1994] Imm AR 42. See also Goodwin-Gill 12.5 fn 1 above, at 4.3.2.
[2]   Hathaway 12.22 fn 2 above, para 5.6.1, p 169. The EC Qualification Directive 2004/83/EC, 12.3 fn 3 above, Art 9(2) states that acts of persecution may include discriminatory legal or judicial measures (or measures implemented in a discriminatory way), discriminatory or disproportionate prosecution or punishment or denial of judicial redress. Prosecution for participation in a protest march is likely to be persecution: *R (on the application of Tientchu) v Immigration Appeal Tribunal* (C/00/6288) (18 October 2000, unreported), CA.
[3]   *Krotov v Secretary of State for the Home Department* [2004] EWCA Civ 69, [2004] 1 WLR 1825 at paras 43–51 per Potter LJ; *Zaitz v Secretary of State for the Home Department* [2000] INLR 346 at paras 39–41, per Buxton LJ; *Islam v Secretary of State for the Home Department* [1999] INLR 144 at 166B–C, per Lord Hoffmann.
[4]   Trials of smugglers before a Tribunal condemned as unfair did not give rise to a Refugee Convention claim in *Ameyaw v Secretary of State for the Home Department* [1992] Imm AR 206; but contrast 4(3) IJRL 261, Case 111 where the risk of prosecution for revealing state secrets was held to be Convention persecution.
[5]   *Iqbal (Muzafar)* [2002] UKIAT 02239. See also *Fazilat* [2002] UKIAT 00973 and *HD (Iran)* [2004] UKIAT 00209.
[6]   See *Drozd and Janousek v France and Spain* (Application 12747/87) (1992) 14 EHRR 745, ECtHR and *Devaseelan* [2002] UKIAT 00702 (starred).
[7]   *Hariri v Secretary of State for the Home Department* [2003] EWCA Civ 807, (2003) 147 Sol Jo LB 659.
[8]   *Batayav v Secretary of State for the Home Department* [2003] EWCA Civ 1489, [2003] All ER (D) 340 (May), CA.
[9]   *Batayav* at para 38: see also 12.25 fn 5 above.

12.49 The distinction between prosecution and persecution is also relevant to a consideration of the exclusion from protection of refugees who have committed serious non-political offences.[1] UK practice on extradition gave a generous interpretation to the political offence exemptions in the Extradition Act 1870 and Fugitive Offenders Act 1967, and the Extradition Act 2003 still enables a fugitive to demonstrate that 'the request for his extradition (though purporting to be made on account of the extradition offence) is in fact made for the purpose of prosecuting or punishing him on account of his race, religion, nationality, gender, sexual orientation or political opinions; or if extradited he might be prejudiced at his trial or punished, detained or restricted in his personal liberty by reason of his race, religion, nationality, gender, sexual orientation or political opinions'.[2] These considerations are equally relevant to the determination of refugee status.[3]

1   See *Re Castioni* [1891] 1 QB 149; *Re Meunier* [1894] 2 QB 415; *R v Governor of Brixton Prison, ex p Kolczynski* [1955] 1 QB 540; *Schtraks v Government of Israel* [1964] AC 556, [1962] 3 All ER 529, HL; *Re Gross* [1968] 3 All ER 804, [1969] 1 WLR 12; *Fernandez v Government of Singapore* [1971] 2 All ER 691, [1971] 1 WLR 987; *Cheng v Governor of Pentonville Prison* [1973] AC 931, [1973] 2 All ER 204, HL; *R v Governor of Winson Green Prison, ex p Littlejohn* [1975] 3 All ER 208, [1975] 1 WLR 893. But see *T v Immigration Officer* [1996] AC 742; see also 12.95 below.
2   Extradition Act 2003, ss 13 and 81.
3   Note that although the references to 'gender and sexual orientation' are not included in the refugee definition in Art 1A(2) of the Refugee Convention, they will often in practice be encompassed by 'membership of a particular social group': see 12.78ff below.

12.50 Prosecution for an offence which is political in itself (such as sedition) or for contravention of laws which themselves infringe human rights[1], will give rise to an inference of persecution more easily than common law offences which are committed for a relevant political purpose,[2] unless in the latter case the accused is likely to be prejudiced in the trial or during lawful punishment for a Convention reason.[3] Even where there is such a risk, the decision of the House of Lords in *T v Immigration Officer*[4] means that Convention protection can be lost if the crime is an atrocious one or the violence inflicted is considered too remote from an effective political objective to be said to be political, although the offender could be exempted from extradition because of the prohibition on extradition for a political offence. In these circumstances, the broader protection against torture and inhuman and degrading treatment offered by the ECHR and other international instruments will be very relevant.[5] A number of cases raise the question whether a prosecution under a law of general application amounts to persecution for a Convention reason. The question is posed in an acute way in cases of conscientious objection to military service. Why is a prosecution persecution? Is the person being prosecuted for merely breaking the law, or being persecuted for a Convention reason? The House of Lords held in *Sepet v Secretary of State for the Home Department* [6] that unless and until the right to conscientious objection to military service becomes a recognised human right, prosecution for refusing to bear arms does not amount to persecution. In Canada, the courts have adopted a test of looking at the intent of the law of general application to see whether it is 'neutral' or 'persecutory'.[7] For discussion of the problems raised by evasion of military service see 12.75 below.

1   *Jain v Secretary of State for the Home Department* [2000] Imm AR 76 at 84 per Evans LJ: 'If a state imposes or threatens punishment for what is regarded for the purposes of the Convention as legitimate sexual activity, then I wonder whether the actual or threatened

loss of liberty is not the relevant form of persecution ... It seems to me that under the Convention the individual enjoys the right not to be persecuted for his private legitimate behaviour.'

2   *O v Immigration Appeal Tribunal* [1995] Imm AR 494, where the Court of Appeal rejected a submission that prosecution for the offence of stockpiling arms to foment a tribal insurrection was in itself persecution for a political reason. But the court's reference to a latter-day Guy Fawkes confuses the issue, since a member of a persecuted religious minority who tried to end the persecution by eliminating the government would have a case for Convention status if he or she faced torture and execution in a prosecution for high treason.

3   Goodwin-Gill 12.5 fn 1 above, p 52; EC Qualification Directive 2004/83/EC (12.3 fn 3 above) Art 11(2).

4   [1996] AC 742, [1996] 2 WLR 766, sub nom *T v Secretary of State for the Home Department* [1996] Imm AR 443.

5   *Chahal v United Kingdom* (1996) 23 EHRR 413; see chapter 8 above.

6   *Sepet v Secretary of State for the Home Department* [2003] UKHL 15, [2003] 3 All ER 304, [2003] 1 WLR 856, [2003] Imm AR 428, affirming *Sepet v Secretary of State for the Home Department (UNHCR intervening)* [2001] EWCA Civ 681, [2001] INLR 376.

7   *Zolfagharkani v Canada* [1993] 3 FC 540 at 552, per MacGuigan JA; *Ciric v Canada* [1994] 2 CF 65.

Persecution by non-state actors

12.51 The *Handbook* states that although:

'persecution is normally related to action by the authorities of a country [it] may also emanate from sections of the population that do not respect the standards established by the laws of the country concerned ... where serious discriminatory or other offensive acts are committed by the local populace, they can be considered as persecution if they are knowingly tolerated by the authorities, or if the authorities refuse, or prove unable, to offer effective protection'.[1]

The authorities of a country here include regional or local government, or parties which in practice control the state.[2] Where legal authority is breaking down, anyone purporting to exercise government authority may be an agent of persecution, whether the state is legally recognised internationally or not. The security forces of a country do not cease to be agents of official persecution merely because it is not the policy of central government to persecute the victims in question.[3] It is equally persecution when the authorities condone, tolerate or fail to protect against persecution by one section of the population against another. In *Jeyakumaran*[4] Tamils resident in Colombo were the victims of reprisal by the local Sinhalese population and received no protection from the state. The High Court held it irrelevant to the merits of the claim that the victims were not 'singled out' for persecution by the government. The House of Lords in *Adan and Aitseguer*[5] affirmed the principle established in *Ward*[6] and *Adan v Secretary of State for the Home Department*[7] that the autonomous meaning of 'persecution' does not limit the concept to conduct which can be attributed to a state, but includes circumstances where the state is not complicit in the persecution, whether this is because it is unwilling or unable to afford protection.[8]

1   UNHCR *Handbook* 12.13 above, para 65.

2   Contrast the authorities able to provide the 'protection of the country' within the meaning of the refugee definition: see 12.42 above. (But note that the EC Qualification Directive 2004/83/EC (12.3 fn 3 above) Art 7 provides that parties or organisations controlling the

state or a substantial part of its territory may be providers of protection so as to disqualify those who can access such 'protection' from refugee status.)

³ Hathaway 12.22 fn 2 above, para 4.5.1; *R v Secretary of State for the Home Department, ex p Chahal* [1995] 1 WLR 526 at 536, per Staughton LJ.

⁴ *R v Secretary of State for the Home Department, ex p Jeyakumaran* [1994] Imm AR 45.

⁵ *R v Secretary of State for the Home Department, ex p Adan, R v Secretary of State for the Home Department, ex p Aitseguer* [2001] INLR 44, HL.

⁶ *A-G of Canada v Ward* (1993) 103 DLR (4th) 1, [1993] 2 SCR 689, [1997] INLR 42, Canada Sup Ct.

⁷ *Adan v Secretary of State for the Home Department* [1999] 1 AC 293 at 305–306: 'if for whatever reason the state is unable to afford protection against factions within the state, the qualifications for refugee status are complete'.

⁸ Traditionally there have been two approaches to the situation where the feared harm emanates not from the state itself but from individuals or groups within it – the 'attribution theory', in which a degree of state complicity in the persecution is required to ground refugee status, and the 'protection theory', where refugee status will be granted unless the state is both able and willing to protect against the persecutory acts of others. German and French adherence to the attribution theory caused the HL in *Adan and Aitseguer* to hold that the Secretary of State was wrong in law to certify that the applicants could be returned compatibly with Article 33 of the Convention to Germany (where a person cannot be a refugee from a country where there is no state authority) and France (where a person cannot be a refugee if the state is merely unable, as distinct from unwilling, to protect him) respectively. The EC Qualification Directive 2004/83/EC (12.3 fn 3 above) Art 6(c) adopts the 'protection theory', in line with UK practice.

12.52 The appellant in *Horvath*¹ was a Roma from Slovakia who feared persecution by skinheads against whom, he said, the Slovak police were unable to provide protection. He also alleged discrimination in the field of employment, the right to marry and education. The principal focus of the opinions in the House of Lords was on whether the word 'persecution' denotes merely sufficiently serious ill-treatment, or sufficiently severe ill-treatment against which the state fails to afford protection. The House of Lords upheld the Tribunal's conclusion that the fear of violence at the hands of non-state agents was not a fear of 'persecution', since the authorities were neither involved nor failed to provide a 'sufficiency of protection'.² In the leading judgment, Lord Hope pointed out that:

'the obligation to afford refugee status arises only if the person's own state is unable or unwilling to discharge its own duty to protect its own nationals ... to satisfy the 'fear' test in a non-state agent case, the applicant must show that the persecution which he fears consists of acts of violence or ill-treatment against which the state is unable or unwilling to provide protection. The applicant may have a well-founded fear of threats to his life due to famine or civil war or of isolated acts of violence *or of ill-treatment for a Convention reason which may be perpetrated against him*. But the risk, however severe, and the fear, however well-founded, do not entitle him to the status of refugee. The Convention has a more limited objective, the limits of which are identified by the list of Convention reasons and by the principle of surrogacy.'³

He thus assimilated ill-treatment for a Refugee Convention reason with famine and civil war, and concluded that ill-treatment for a Convention reason does not amount to persecution unless there is a failure of state protection. This was the majority view. Lord Lloyd disagreed with this approach, holding that the ordinary meaning of the word 'persecution' does not involve a failure of state protection. 'The text of the Convention does not suggest that anything other than the ordinary meaning should be used, nor is there any hint that the failure of state protection is an ingredient in the meaning of the word.'[4] We agree, and so in effect did the Australian High Court in *Khawar*,[5] in which, in a joint judgment, McHugh and GummowJJ criticised the House of Lords' approach to the issue of protection in *Horvath*, taking the view that the 'internal' protection and 'surrogacy' protection theories as a foundation for the construction of the Convention 'add a layer of complexity ... which is an unnecessary distraction'.[6] The court preferred the approach of the UNHCR.[7]

[1]   *Horvath v Secretary of State for the Home Department* [2000] INLR 239, HL.
[2]   [1999] INLR 7. There had been a line of Tribunal decisions on what was a 'sufficiency of protection' which would disqualify the victim of non-state persecution from international protection, e g *Jaworski* (17152); *Debrah v Secretary of State for the Home Department* [1998] INLR 383; *Singh (Chinder)* [1998] Imm AR 551; *Mojka* (18265); *Dymiter* (18467).
[3]   *Horvath* above, at 247–248. Our emphasis.
[4]   *Horvath* above at 251–252. On this analysis, the availability and efficacy of protection is relevant to the well-foundedness of the fear.
[5]   *Minister for Immigration and Multicultural Affairs v Khawar* [2002] HCA 14.
[6]   They identified the source as being the 'writings of a Canadian scholar, Professor Hathaway concerning "surrogate" or "substitute" protection': *Khawar* above, paras 66–73.
[7]   See Fortin, 'The Meaning of 'Protection' in the Refugee Definition', (2001) 12 IJRL 548 and 'Interpreting Article 1 of the 1951 Convention Relating to the Status of Refugees' (UNHCR, April 2001).

12.53 According to the majority in *Horvath*, the standard of protection which disqualifies victims of non-state violence from international protection is not one which would eliminate all risk; rather, it is a 'practical standard' taking proper account of the duty owed by the state to all its own nationals. Lord Clyde cited the ECHR case of *Osman*[1] to the effect that the obligation to protect must not be so interpreted as to impose an impossible or disproportionate burden on the authorities. For him, what was required was 'a system of domestic protection and machinery for the detection, prosecution and punishment of actings contrary to the purposes which the Convention requires to have protected', and 'more importantly ... an ability and a readiness to operate that machinery'.[2] He approved Stuart Smith LJ's formulation in the Court of Appeal:[3]

> 'There must be in force in the country in question a criminal law which makes the violent attacks by the persecutors punishable by sentences commensurate with the gravity of the crimes. The victims as a class must not be exempt from the protection of the law. There must be a reasonable willingness by the law enforcement agencies, that is to say the police and courts, to detect, prosecute and punish offenders ...'

Further, inefficiency and incompetence is not the same as unwillingness, there may be various sound reasons why criminals may not be brought to justice, and the corruption, sympathy or weakness of some individuals in the system of justice does not mean that the state is unwilling to afford protection. It will require cogent evidence that the state which is able to afford protection is unwilling to do so, especially in the case of a democracy.[4]

[1]   *Osman v United Kingdom* (1998) 29 EHRR 245.
[2]   *Horvath* 12.52 fn 1 above, at 259.
[3]   [2000] INLR 15, para 22.
[4]   *Horvath* 12.52 fn 1 above, at 260A–D.

12.54 A further question considered in *Horvath* concerned the phrase 'unwilling, owing to such fear, to avail himself of the protection' of the country of nationality, and its application to non-state cases. Lord Hope considered that the fear which prevented recourse to state protection in such cases had to be fear of reprisals from the persecutors. In other words, the fear had to be a well-founded fear of being persecuted *because* the claimant had sought the state's protection.[1] We believe a more realistic analysis was given in *Svazas*,[2] where Sedley LJ used, as an example of unwillingness, the situation of German Jews who had been attacked by Brownshirt thugs in 1938 at a time when the Nazi authorities were pretending that such attacks were beyond their control – an example the drafters of the 1951 Convention would have had in mind when inserting the 'unwilling to avail' clause. On this reading, unwillingness might be caused by a perception of collusion by the state with the perpetrators.

1   *Horvath* 12.52 fn 1 above. Lord Hope and Lord Clyde delivered the two main judgments. Lord Hobhouse agreed with Lord Hope (266G); Lord Browne-Wilkinson (249G) agreed with Lords Hope and Clyde. Lord Lloyd (249H–256D) disagreed with the majority on the first question.
2   *Svazas v Secretary of State for the Home Department* [2002] EWCA Civ 74, [2002] 1 WLR 1891 at para 22.

12.55 The majority in *Horvath* have, we believe, adopted a strained and difficult definition of 'persecution' in non-state cases which could lead to the rejection of cases deserving of international protection.[1] The test for sufficiency of protection has moved perilously close to the 'attribution' test rejected by the Lords in *Adan and Aitseguer*.[2] New Zealand's Refugee Status Appeals Authority has suggested that the House of Lords' decision in *Horvath* enables an individual to be returned to his or her country of origin notwithstanding a well-founded fear of persecution for a Convention reason, and has commented that:

'[T]his interpretation of the Refugee Convention is at odds with the fundamental obligation of non-refoulement ... [which] cannot be avoided by a process of interpretation which measures the sufficiency of state protection not against the absence of a real risk of persecution, but against the availability of a system for the protection of the citizen and a reasonable willingness by the state to operate that system. The point which emerges from *Ward* is that the refugee inquiry is not an inquiry into blame. Rather the purpose of refugee law is to identify those who have a well-founded fear of persecution for a Convention reason. If the net result of a state's 'reasonable willingness' to operate a system for the protection of the citizen is that it is incapable of preventing a real chance of persecution of a particular individual, refugee status cannot be denied that individual. The persecuted clearly do not enjoy the protection of their country of origin.'[3]

1   The House of Lords accepted that persons with a well-founded fear of serious harm for a Convention reason – like the Slovakian Roma family in the case before them – would not, on their formulation, be entitled to protection, because the state is 'reasonably willing' to operate the machinery of protection: see below; so what the family fears is not 'persecution'.
2   The attribution or accountability test confines persecution to conduct which can be attributed to a state. *R v Secretary of State for the Home Department, ex p Adan, R v Secretary of State for the Home Department, ex p Aitseguer* [2001] INLR 44, HL, see 12.51 above.
3   Refugee Appeal No 71427/99, [2000] INLR 608 (R P G Haines QC and L Tremewan), NZRSAA. See also the IAT's obiter view in *Kovac* (00/TH/00026).

12.56 The criticism of *Horvath* from New Zealand was specifically rejected by Auld LJ sitting in the Divisional court in *Dhima*,[1] and in *Bagdanavicius*[2] the Court of Appeal reviewed the jurisprudence on the question of state protection from feared harm at the hands of non-state agents, rejected all criticisms of the *Horvath* approach and concluded, in a summary set out at the beginning of the judgment, that:

'(1)   The threshold of risk is the same in both asylum and Article 3 ECHR claims; the main reason for introducing a human rights appeal was not to provide an alternative, lower threshold of risk and/or a higher level of protection, but to widen the reach of protection regardless of the motive giving rise to the persecution;

(2)   An asylum claimant is entitled to asylum if he or she can show a well-founded fear of persecution for a Refugee Convention reason *and* that there would be insufficiency of state protection to meet it: *Horvath*;

(3)   Fear of persecution is well-founded if there is a 'reasonable degree of likelihood' that it will materialise: *Sivakumaran*;

(4)   Sufficiency of state protection (whether from acts of state agents or of non-state actors) means a willingness *and* ability by the state to provide through its legal system a reasonable level of protection from ill-treatment of which the claimant for asylum has a well-founded fear: *Osman*,[3] *Horvath*, *Dhima*;

(5)   The effectiveness of the system is normally to be judged by its systemic ability to deter and/or prevent the form of persecution of which there is a risk, not just punishment of it after the event: *Horvath*, *Banomova*,[4] *McPherson*[5] and *Kinuthia*;[6]

(6)   Notwithstanding systemic sufficiency of state protection, a claimant may still have a well-founded fear of persecution if its authorities know or ought to know of circumstances particular to his or her case giving rise to the fear, but are unlikely to provide the additional protection the particular circumstances reasonably require: *Osman*.'

---

[1]   *Dhima v Immigration Appeal Tribunal* [2002] EWHC 80 (Admin), [2002] Imm AR 394, [2002] INLR 243. Auld LJ stated at [35] that the NZRSAA had misunderstood the ratio of the Lords' judgment in *Horvath*, which was that 'what is critical is a combination of a willingness and ability to provide protection to the level *that can reasonably be expected to meet and overcome the real risk of harm from non-state agents*. What is reasonable protection in any case depends, therefore, on the level of the risk, without that protection, for which it has to provide'. (Our emphasis)

[2]   *R (on the application of Bagdanavicius) v Secretary of State for the Home Department* [2003] EWCA Civ 1605, [2004] 1 WLR 1207 (leave to appeal to the HL granted: [2004] 1 WLR 2449).

[3]   *Osman v United Kingdom* (1998) 29 EHRR 245.

[4]   *Banomova v Secretary of State for the Home Department* [2001] EWCA Civ 807, [2001] All ER (D) 344 (May).

[5]   *McPherson v Secretary of State for the Home Department* [2001] EWCA Civ 1955, [2002] INLR 139.

[6]   *Kinuthia v Secretary of State for the Home Department* [2001] EWCA Civ 2100, [2002] INLR 133.

12.57 Thus, in post-*Horvath* cases, the courts and the Tribunal have made it clear that, while it will always be relevant to ask whether or not there is in general sufficiency of protection in a country, the crucial question remains whether there is a reasonable likelihood of Convention persecution in the individual case.[1] The axiom of refugee determination, that one examines both the general situation and the situation of the individual claimant, does not lose force simply because the focus of the examination is the protection issue.[2] In *Noune* the Court of Appeal held that if a decision-maker interpreted *Horvath* to mean that where the law enforcement agencies are doing their best and are not being either generally inefficient or incompetent, this was enough to disqualify a potential victim from being a refugee, this interpretation would be an error of law.[3] In *Kinuthia*[4] the Court of Appeal held that the possibility of recourse to remedies after ill-treatment has been suffered does not in itself provide adequate protection against such ill-treatment. The Tribunal has held that the crucial part of any case involving non-state agents is precisely where the general system of protection in force is tested against how it actually worked in the individual case.[5] Jews targeted by anti-Semites in Russia and Roma from the Czech and Slovak Republics and some areas of Poland have been held to be refugees.[6]

1   *Noune (Souad) v Secretary of State for the Home Department* [2001] INLR 526, CA (Algerian civil servant targeted by Islamists); *Koudriachov* (00TH02254) (Jews and their families in Russia).
2   Refugee Appeal No 71427/99, [2000] INLR 608, 12.55 fn 3, above.
3   *Noune (Souad)* above, at para 28, per Schiemann LJ. Similarly, in the context of obviating a real risk of mistreatment violating Art 3 ECHR (see chapter 8 above), in *McPherson v Secretary of State for the Home Department* [2002] INLR 139 at 147 (para 21) Sedley LJ stated that: 'What matters is that protection should be practical and effective, not that it should take a particular form.' Arden LJ at paras 31, 36, 37, 38 and 39 also made clear that in terms of domestic protection 'measures for the purposes of Art 3 must be those which attain an adequate degree of efficacy in practice as well as exist in theory' (see para 38 at 151).
4   *Kinuthia v Secretary of State for the Home Department* [2001] EWCA Civ 2100, [2002] INLR 133.
5   *Harangova* (00TH01325) (8 November 2000, unreported).
6   *Doudetski* (00TH01768); *Koudriachov* above; *Hinar* (00/TH/02407), *Franczak* (00TH02394), *Ferenc* [2002] UKIAT 00343 and *Havlicek* (00TH01448).

12.58 Of importance in this context is the degree to which an asylum claimant needs to have made efforts to avail him or herself of domestic protection before seeking 'surrogate' protection abroad. In *Canada v Ward* La Forest J stated:[1]

'Only in situations in which State protection "might reasonably have been forthcoming", will the claimant's failure to approach the State for protection defeat his claim ... the claimant will not meet the definition of 'Convention refugee' where it is objectively unreasonable for the claimant not to have sought the protection of his home authorities; otherwise, the claimant need not literally approach the State.

... clear and convincing confirmation of a State's inability to protect must be provided. For example, a claimant might advance testimony of similarly situated individuals let down by the State protection arrangement or the claimant's testimony of past personal incidents in which State protection did not materialise. Absent some evidence, the claim should fail, as nations should be presumed capable of protecting their citizens.'

In *Harakal*,[2] the Court of Appeal in the case of a Czech Roma, held that, on the particular facts, it was not necessary for the applicant to have exhausted all possible domestic remedies to demonstrate a failure of protection.[3]

1   *Canada v Ward* [1993] 2 SCR 689, [1997] INLR 42, Supreme Court of Canada (30 June
    1993). La Forest J's judgment (giving the judgment of the court) on this point at 60–61was
    effectively adopted by the IAT in *Horvath* [1999] INLR 7 at 33.
2   *R (on the application of Harakal) v Secretary of State for the Home Department* [2001] All
    ER (D) 139 (May), CA.
3   See also *R (on the application of Bagdanavicius) v Secretary of State for the Home
    Department* [2003] EWCA Civ 1605, [2004] 1 WLR 1207, proposition 6 (at 12.56
    above).

12.59 What of the situation where the feared harm emanates from state
agents acting 'unofficially' rather than from 'sections of the population'?[1] It
might seem that where mistreatment emanates from police officers, or other
state agents, the *Horvath* principle has no application and the very fact of the
mistreatment illustrates the lack of protection. After all, governments rarely if
ever formally sanction the use of torture or other serious harm by their
'agents' and no state is capable of persecuting anyone other than through the
actions of its agents. However, the Court of Appeal in *Svazas*[2] rejected the
argument that the *Horvath* principle had no part to play in this situation, and
the majority (Simon Brown LJ and Sir Murray Stuart-Smith) effectively held
that it was simply a question of degree.[3] Sedley LJ, on the other hand,
demanded a different and higher standard of domestic protection where the
feared mistreatment emanates from state agents misbehaving themselves,
holding that evidence of 'timely and effective rectification of the situation
which is allowing the misconduct to happen' would be necessary to disqualify
the victim from international protection.[4]

1   UNHCR *Handbook* 12.13 above, para 65 and 12.51 above.
2   *Svazas v Secretary of State for the Home Department* [2002] EWCA Civ 74, [2002]
    1 WLR 1891, which involved police officers in Lithuania physically mistreating detainees
    who were Communist Party members.
3   *Svazas* at paras 44–46 per Sir Murray Stuart-Smith and at [51]–[53] per Simon Brown LJ,
    who also held at para 54 that, in cases such as this, the seniority of the police officers
    involved in the misconduct is relevant to determining whether the system of protection is
    sufficient.
4   *Svazas* at para 37.

12.60 In *Fadli*[1] the Court of Appeal held that the risk to a soldier or
ex-soldier of being killed by a terrorist group was not a risk of persecution for
a Refugee Convention reason. The reasoning of the court was that the
Convention does not distinguish between soldiers engaged on the battlefield in
combat against others observing the rules of war and those engaged on
internal security duties against terrorists who breach the laws of war. It held
that to allow soldiers' claims for asylum based on the failure of the state to
provide practical protection to the soldiers would strengthen the terrorists'
hand and 'hinder the home state in providing the very protection for the
generality of its citizens which the definition of refugee in the Convention
assumes that the home state should provide'.

1   *R (on the application of Fadli) v Secretary of State for the Home Department*, [2001]
    02 LS Gaz R 40, CA.

Civil war

12.61 The House of Lords held in *Adan and Aitseguer*[1] that for someone to
qualify for refugee status, there need be no effective state authority and that

the state does not have to encourage or tolerate the feared persecution.[2] The inability of the state to provide protection against Convention persecution, for any reason, including civil war or internal armed conflict, founds refugee status. But in an earlier *Adan* case,[3] the House of Lords, reversing the Court of Appeal, held that:

'the language of the Convention did not apply to those caught up in a civil war where law and order had broken down and every group was fighting some other group or groups in an endeavour to gain power. What the members of each group may have is a well-founded fear not so much of persecution by other groups as of death or injury or loss of freedom due to the fighting between the groups. In such a situation the individual or group has to show a well-founded fear of persecution over and above the risk to life and liberty inherent in the civil war'.[4]

Lord Lloyd referred to it as 'differential impact'.[5]

[1]   *R v Secretary of State for the Home Department, ex p Adan, ex p Aitseguer* [2001] INLR 44, HL.
[2]   The former was the situation in Somalia in *Adan*, the latter in Algeria in *Aitseguer*: see 12.51 above.
[3]   *Secretary of State for the Home Department v Adan* [1999] 1 AC 293, [1998] Imm AR 338, [1998] INLR 325, HL.
[4]   *Adan* above [1998] INLR 325 at 327, per Lord Slynn.
[5]   *Adan* above [1998] INLR 325 at 336.

12.62   The decision in *Adan* is hard to comprehend where the basis of the civil war (and therefore the risk of persecution) is a Convention reason. In the Court of Appeal Simon Brown LJ appreciated the 'floodgates' consequences of holding that all who may be identified with the interests of either side are potential refugees, but considered that his conclusion more faithfully reflected the Convention and gave better effect to its broad humanitarian instincts.[1] We agree. If a refugee claimant from a civil war is at risk of persecution because of his or her race, it is not legitimate to ignore that fact simply because the source of the risk is a civil war, and to require a fear of something over and above 'the ordinary risks of clan warfare'. Once the claimant has shown a real risk of persecution for reasons of one of the five Convention reasons he or she is a refugee and nothing more can be required.[2] The danger inherent in the House of Lords' approach is that it reintroduces in a civil war situation the requirement of being 'singled out'.[3] The Canadian case of *Salibian* on which Lord Lloyd relied[4] supports this proposition.

[1]   [1997] Imm AR 251 at 264–265.
[2]   See decision of New Zealand Refugee Status Appeals Authority in Refugee Appeal No 71462/99 [2000] INLR 311, declining to follow *Adan* for these reasons (paras 67–86 at 328).
[3]   What the NZRSAA calls 'the old heresy ([2000] INLR 311, para 69), following Crawford and Hyndman 'Three heresies in the application of the Geneva Convention' (1989) 1 IJRL 155. The reasoning in *Adan* was also rejected by the full court of the Australian FCA in *Minister for Immigration and Multicultural Affairs v Abdi* (1999) 162 ALR 105; see also *Minister for Immigration and Multicultural Affairs v Ibrahim* [2000] HCA 55.
[4]   *Salibian v Minister of Employment and Immigration* [1990] 73 DLR (4th) 551.

12.63   It is important, however, to realise how limited the application of *Adan* is. Their Lordships were not concerned to exclude from the refugee definition those at risk of death, torture or imprisonment on suspicion of siding with one party in territory under the effective control of the other. They are concerned only with a situation where 'the fear is felt indiscriminately by all citizens as a consequence of the civil war', or where law and order have completely broken down[1] and state authority has ceased to exist, as in Somalia in the circumstances of that case.[2] Lord Lloyd, citing Goodwin-Gill,[3] contrasted the civil war in Somalia with that in Liberia 'on the ground that in the former country none of the competing clans has yet emerged as an authority in fact, controlling territory and possessing a minimum of organisation'.[4] The distinction reflects the rules of international law on the recognition of a government of a state.[5] *Adan* does not apply, for example, to Sri Lanka, Algeria or Angola, where, although engaged against insurrectionary movements, fully functioning states continue to exist.[6] Even where *Adan* does apply, however, the applicant will very likely be entitled to humanitarian protection.[7]

[1]   *Adan* above, at 327H–328A, per Lord Slynn (12.61 above).
[2]   In *R v Secretary of State for the Home Department, ex p Aitsegeur* at first instance, 18 December 1998, Sullivan J held *Adan* applicable in civil war situations 'where state authority had ceased to exist', and in *R v Secretary of State for the Home Department, ex p Adan (Lul)* [1999] INLR 84, the Secretary of State for the Home Department accepted that it applied to situations 'where civil war has destroyed state authority'.
[3]   Goodwin-Gill 12.5 fn 1 above, p 76.
[4]   *Adan* above at 336.
[5]   See *Somalia (Republic of) v Woodhouse, Drake & Carey (Suisse) SA* [1993] QB 54 where Hobhouse J held (at 67–68) that factors to be taken into account in recognition were (a) whether it is the constitutional government of the state; (b) the degree, nature and stability of administrative control, if any, that it exercises over the territory of the state; (c) whether Her Majesty's Government has any dealings with it and if so the nature of those dealings; and (d) in marginal cases, the extent of international recognition that it has as the government of the state.
[6]   See, for example, *Matondo v Secretary of State for the Home Department* (15 March 1999, unreported), where leave to appeal was granted against a Tribunal decision purporting to apply *Adan* to the situation in Angola, and the appeal was allowed by consent on the appellant being recognised as a refugee. See also *Yogarajah v Secretary of State for the Home Department* (14 January 1999, unreported), CA, where in a consent order, the Secretary of State accepted that the situation in Sri Lanka was not analogous to that in Somalia, where there had been a total breakdown of society, and that the test in *Adan* applied only to 'this type of extreme and widespread form of civil war'. In *SS (Burundi) CG* [2004] 00290 the IAT held that *Adan* could not apply in Burundi because the civil war there had ended. But see *Kibiti v Secretary of State for the Home Department* [2000] Imm AR 594, CA, where the Immigration Appeal Tribunal's application of *Adan* to Congo was upheld. See also Theodor Meron *Human Rights in Internal Strife* (1987); von Sternberg 'Political Asylum and the Law of Internal Armed Conflict' (1993) 5(2) IJRL 153; UNHCR Executive Committee Conclusion (October 1994) (1995) 7(1) IJRL 142; and decision of German Constitutional Court in a Bosnian case: (1995) 7(1) IJRL case 226.
[7]   See 12.3 above. The applicant Adan himself had been granted exceptional leave.

'For reasons of'

12.64 The definition of a refugee requires consideration of the reasons for the persecution. It is not enough to face persecution; it must be connected to one of the reasons assigned by the Refugee Convention.[1] In non-state agent cases (see above), the Convention reason may be the reason for the non-state agents' actions, with the state simply unable to protect the applicant, or it may be the reason for the state's unwillingness to protect the applicant against non-state agents however motivated; it need not be both.[2] Nonetheless, the issue of causation raises difficult questions. Should the proper focus of attention be the fear of the applicant or the motives of the persecutor? To what extent does the motivation of the persecutor need to be established? Persecutory conduct may have more than one motive, and it is established that so long as one motive is a Convention ground, the requirement is satisfied.[3] It is not necessary that the Convention ground is the sole reason for the fear.[4] The question of causation must be considered principally on the particular facts of the individual case, rather than on a 'group basis'.[5]

1   In recent years there has been a tendency for the courts to require discrimination on Convention grounds (as well as lack of sufficient protection: see 12.51ff above) before 'serious harm' can be held to constitute 'persecution' at all: see *R v Immigration Appeal Tribunal, Secretary of State for the Home Department, ex p Shah; Islam v Secretary of State for the Home Department* [1999] 2 AC 629, [1999] INLR 144 (see 12.67 below); *Horvath v Secretary of State for the Home Department* [2001] 1 AC 489, [2000] INLR 239; *Ravichandran (Senathirajah) v Secretary of State for the Home Department* [1996] Imm AR 97, CA; *R (on the application of Pedro) v Secretary of State for the Home Department* [2001] Imm AR 489, CA.

2   See *Shah and Islam* (above) and *Horvath v Secretary of State for the Home Department* [2000] Imm AR 205, CA, per Hale LJ. See also *Refugee Appeal No 71427/99* [2000] INLR 608 (NZRSAA) and *Minister for Immigration and Multicultural Affairs v Khawar* [2002] HCA 14 (Aust HC).

3   *Suarez v Secretary of State for the Home Department* [2002] EWCA Civ 722, [2002] 1 WLR 2663 per Potter LJ, approved in *R (on the application of Sivakumar) v Secretary of State for the Home Department* [2003] UKHL 14, [2003] 2 All ER 1097, by Lord Rodger, with whom Lord Hoffmann agreed. See also *Harpinder Singh v Ilchert* 63 F 3d at 1501 (US 9th Cir).

4   *Jahazi v Minister for Immigration and Ethnic Affairs* (1995) 133 ALR 437, 443 (French J); approved in *Minister for Immigration and Multicultural Affairs v Abdi* (1999) 162 ALR 105, 112 (FC). *Sivakumar, Suarez* (above).

5   See *Appellant S395/2002 v Minister for Immigration and Multicultural Affairs* [2003] HCA 71 per McHugh and Kirby JJ at para 58; the UNHCR *Guidelines on International Protection: 'Membership of a particular social group'* (7 May 2002) (HCR/GIP/02/02) point out at para 17 that not all members of a group must be at risk of being persecuted; see also *R v Immigration Appeal Tribunal, ex p Shah; Islam v Secretary of State for the Home Department* [1999] 2 AC 629, [1999] INLR 144, per Lords Steyn and Hoffmann.

12.65 The humanitarian obligation is to be interpreted broadly: a refugee may well not be aware of the reasons for the persecution, and it is not his or her duty to identify or analyse the reasons in detail.[1] The focus therefore is on the acts of the persecutors. Thus a person who is not in fact involved in any political opposition to the government may nevertheless be persecuted by the government for perceived or imputed opinions.[2] The Convention ground does not have to be the sole cause of the persecution,[3] and the fact that the persecutor may have some ulterior motive, such as suppression of disorder or terrorism, does not necessarily remove it from the realm of Convention persecution if acts of sufficient gravity are done against a person or group identified by race, religion, nationality, social group or political opinion.[4] The test of Canadian law is whether the applicant's personal status exposes him or her to heightened risk so that persecution would not arise *but for* race, religion or another Convention ground. Other international cases adopt the approach of whether the persecution is 'related' to Convention reasons.[5]

1   UNHCR *Handbook* 12.13 above, para 66.

2   In *Danian v Secretary of State for the Home Department* [1999] INLR 533 at 557H, Buxton LJ stated as being an elementary proposition that 'a political opinion may be one imputed to him by the authorities of the country in question, even if it is not in fact held by

him.' See also *Asante* [1991] Imm AR 78; *R v Secretary of State for the Home Department and Special Adjudicators, ex p Stefan, Chiper and Ionel* [1995] Imm AR 410 at 413; *Ward v A-G Canada* [1993] 2 SCR 689, [1997] INLR 42.

3   See 12.64, fns 3 and 4 above and see Hathaway 12.22 fn 2 above, p 140.

4   *Ravichandran (Senathirajah) v Secretary of State for the Home Department* [1996] Imm AR 97 at 109. See also (1993) 5(2) IJRL 154 (sexual abuse linked to political opinion or other characteristics); (1993) 5(3) IJRL, Case 161 *Veeravagu v Canada* (1992) FCJ No 468 where the Canadian Court of Appeal held that, irrespective of whether young Tamils constituted a social group, there was racial persecution if a person faced real risk of oppression because he belonged to a group one of whose defining characteristics was race. However in *R (on the application of Sivakumar) v Secretary of State for the Home Department* [2003] UKHL 14, [2003] 2 All ER 1097 the House of Lords rejected both the Secretary of State's argument that persecutory harm by state agents in the process of investigating suspected terrorism necessarily falls outside the protective net of Art 1A of the Refugee Convention, and the applicant's argument that it necessarily falls within Art 1A since terrorism involves matters of political opinion. They held that there could be no legal inference or presumption that severe mistreatment of someone of a particular social group, race or likely political opinion amounted to persecution for a Convention reason; the cumulative effect of all the relevant factors in the case had to be evaluated.

5   See (1992) 4(2) IJRL, Case 109, Case 110; (1993) 5(2) IJRL, Case 154.

12.66   The issue of causation had earlier been considered by the House of Lords in *Shah and Islam*[1] where Lord Hoffmann rejected the Canadian 'but for' test[2] as too simplistic and noted that the meaning of any statutory notion of causation depends on the context. He gave the example of women vulnerable to sexually motivated attacks by marauding men during a time of civil unrest. While the *but for* test would be satisfied (the women would not be subject to rape but for their gender), in a context where attacks and failure of protection alike were indiscriminate, their treatment was not *for reasons of their gender*. By contrast, a Jew in Germany in 1935 who was punished for contravening racial laws (by failing to wear a yellow star) was persecuted on ground of race; so was a Jewish shopkeeper attacked for reasons of commercial rivalry in a climate of impunity, because the authorities' failure to provide protection was based on race.[3]

1   *R v Immigration Appeal Tribunal, ex p Shah; Islam v Secretary of State for the Home Department* [1999] 2 AC 629, [1999] INLR 144. Such an analysis may well under-estimate the use of rape as a weapon as war: see Lady Hale in *R (on the application of Hoxha) v Secretary of State for the Home Department, R (on the application of B) v Secretary of State for the Home Department* [2005] UKHL 19, [2005] 1 WLR 1063, (2005) 149 Sol Jo LB 358, at paras 30ff, and in *N v Secretary of State for the Home Department* [2005] UKHL 31 at para 58. See 12.80 below.

2   Ie the women would not have feared persecution *but for* their gender: see above.

3   See further 12.64 above.

12.67   In *Shah and Islam* the House of Lords used the touchstone of discrimination in deciding that the persecution was for reasons of membership of a particular social group (Pakistani women). The House concluded that a fundamental purpose of the Refugee Convention was counteracting discrimination[1] and that the concept of discrimination was central to an understanding of the Convention.[2] It was concerned with persecution based on discrimination, or with making distinctions inconsistent with the right of every human being to equal treatment and respect. All Convention reasons are grounds upon which a person may be discriminated against by society.[3] Persecution must be discriminatory.[4] In the light of this formidable authority it is difficult to assert that discrimination is not usually necessary in establishing causation.[5] Where there is evidence of discrimination, it will not be difficult to establish the necessary causal link between the fear and the Convention reason. But it will not always be necessary to prove conscious discrimination by the persecutor. In *Omoruyi*[6] Simon Brown LJ suggested that some element of conscious discrimination, based on a Convention reason, is a necessary ingredient of Convention persecution. On the facts of the case, concerning the motives of a criminal gang, this was correct. But in cases of state persecution, conscious discrimination is not a prerequisite of Convention persecution, as his judgment went on to acknowledge.[7] An objective approach which looks at the discriminatory *impact* of persecutory laws or practices, is in line with UK domestic law in the context of the Race Relations and Sex Discrimination Acts.[8] In *Sepet*[9] the Court of Appeal held that conscious discrimination was not a necessary element of persecution for a Convention reason, although it would be strong evidence of it. In the House of Lords, Lord Hoffmann was inclined to agree,[10] while Lord Bingham accepted that in most cases decision makers were not concerned to explore the motives or purposes of the persecutors and that the application of the causation test called for the exercise of an objective judgment.[11] In *Sivakumar*, heard by the same constitution of the House, Lord Rodger noted that 'the law is concerned with the reasons of the persecution and not with the motives of the persecutor'.[12]

1   [1999] INLR 144 at 150E, per Lord Steyn.
2   [1999] INLR 144 at 161G–H, per Lord Hoffmann.
3   [1999] INLR 144, per Lord Hope.
4   [1999] INLR 144 at 170A, per Lord Millett. See 12.61 fn 1 above.
5   See Goodwin-Gill, in his commentary on *Shah and Islam* in (1999) 11 IJRL. In *Skenderaj v Secretary of State for the Home Department* [2002] EWCA Civ 567, [2002] 4 All ER 555, [2002] Imm AR 519 the CA doubted that discrimination plays a determinative role in defining a particular social group where the feared persecution emanates from non-state actors or agents. But see Lady Hale's judgment in *R (on the application of Hoxha) v Secretary of State for the Home Department, R (on the application of B) v Secretary of State for the Home Department* [2005] UKHL 19, [2005] 1 WLR 1063, (2005) 149 Sol Jo LB 358. See further 12.51 text and fn 2 above, 12.78ff below.
6   *Omoruyi v Secretary of State for the Home Department* [2001] Imm AR 175, CA.
7   'Discrimination, *at least in the sense that the substantive law or its enforcement in practice bears unequally upon different people or different groups*, is essential to the concept of persecution under the Convention' (Our emphasis).
8   These laws recognise direct and indirect discrimination, and the case law makes it clear that direct discrimination does not need to be conscious or intentional: *Nagarajan v London Regional Transport* [1999] IRLR 572, HL; *R v Birmingham City Council, ex p Equal Opportunities Commission* [1989] IRLR 173, HL; *James v Eastleigh Borough Council* [1990] IRLR 288, HL; *European Roma Rights Centre v Immigration Officer at Prague Airport & Secretary of State for the Home Department* [2003] EWCA Civ 666, CA per Laws LJ, [2004] UKHL 55, [2005] 2 WLR 1, per Lord Steyn and Baroness Hale; *Pereira v Civil Service* [1982] IRLR 147, EAT.
9   *Sepet v Secretary of State for the Home Department* [2001] EWCA Civ 681 per Laws LJ at para 93: 'The question is always whether the asylum claimant faces discrimination on a Convention ground. There will be, are, cases where that is made out by reference to the persecutor's motives. There will be, are, others where his motive matters not.'
10   *Sepet v Secretary of State for the Home Department* [2003] UKHL 15, [2003] 1 WLR 856, para 54.
11   [2003] UKHL 15, para 55. Lords Steyn and Hutton agreed with Lord Bingham, and Lord Rodger agreed with him about how a decision-maker should determine the reasons for the persecution feared.
12   *R (on the application of Sivakumar) v Secretary of State for the Home Department* [2003] UKHL 14, [2003] 2 All ER 1097 at para 41.

12.68 The House of Lords in *Sivakumar* and *Sepet* noted the Australian High Court case of *Chen Shi Hai*,[1] which also held that proof of the persecutor's motives is unnecessary. The case concerned a Chinese child born in contravention of the one-child policy and likely to be denied access to food, shelter, medical treatment and education under Chinese law. The Court decisively rejected any requirement of personal animus, enmity or malignancy to the Refugee Convention attribute as a necessary ingredient of causation.[2] Such attribution, it held, 'risks a fictitious personification of the abstract and the impersonal'. The court also took into account the extreme difficulty or impossibility of an inquiry into the motives and feelings of the alleged persecutors in a foreign country.[3] It rejected any formula, rule or principle which could be substituted for the Convention language. As Kirby J said, 'In the end it is necessary ... to return to the broad expression of the Convention ... the decision-maker must evaluate the postulated connection between the asserted fear of persecution and the ground suggested to give rise to the fear.'

[1]   *Chen Shi Hai v Minister for Immigration and Multicultural Affairs* [2000] INLR 455, Aust HC.
[2]   Goodwin-Gill does not accept that motivation is a necessary condition of persecution: *The Refugee in International Law* (2nd edn, 1996) pp 50–51.
[3]   *Chen Shi Hai v Minister for Immigration and Multicultural Affairs* [2000] INLR 455, Aust HC, para 64.

Race

12.69 A broad definition of race that includes membership of ethnic groups is to be adopted.[1] The EC Qualification Directive includes colour, descent and membership of an ethnic group in the Convention meaning of race.[2] Article 1 of the Convention on the Elimination of All Forms of Racial Discrimination 1965 (CERD) defines 'racial discrimination' as 'any distinction, exclusion, restriction or preference based on race, colour, descent, or national or ethnic origin'. The House of Lords in *Shah and Islam*[3] emphasised that counteracting discrimination was a fundamental purpose of the Convention. Racial discrimination represents an important element in determining the existence of racial persecution, and may be a sufficient foundation for recognition if it affects human dignity to the extent of incompatibility with inalienable or elementary rights.[4]

[1]   *King-Ansell v Police* [1979] 2 NZLR 531, 533; *Mandla (Sewa Singh) v Dowell Lee* [1983] 2 AC 548 at 563–564.
[2]   EC Qualification Directive 2004/83/EC, 12.3 fn 3 above, Art 10(1)(a). This supersedes the EU Joint Position (96/196/JHA), 4 March 1996, para 7.1, which stated that 'persecution should be deemed to be founded on racial grounds where the persecutor regards the victim of his persecution as belonging to a racial group other than his own, by reason of a real or supposed difference, and this forms the grounds for his action.'
[3]   *R v Immigration Appeal Tribunal, ex p Shah; Islam v Secretary of State for the Home Department* [1999] 2 AC 629, [1999] INLR 144 at 150, per Lord Steyn.
[4]   UNHCR *Handbook* 12.13 above, paras 68–69.

Religion

12.70 Persecution may take the form of a total ban on worship and religious instruction, or severe discrimination in the profession of a religion which renders life unbearable.[1] Apostate Muslims who convert to Christianity have in some cases been held to have a well-founded fear of persecution on account of the severity of the penalties for conversion.[2] Punishment for proselytising has created difficulties. The Universal Declaration of Human Rights proclaims the right to manifest a religion in public, but a state has some margin of appreciation that would preclude causing offence to others.[3] A number of cases concern the Ahmadi sect, regarded as heretical by orthodox Pakistani Muslims, whose members are subjected to severe punishments for proselytising.[4] In *Ahmed (Iftikhar)* the Court of Appeal held that if an Ahmadi would proselytise on return and would therefore be at risk of persecution, a claim for refugee status would not be defeated on the basis that the claimant is inviting persecution and should refrain.[5] In so holding, the court put to rest the suggestion found in *Mendis*[6] and *Ahmad*,[7] that a claim could not be founded on deliberate conduct inviting persecution (at least where the conduct is an exercise of fundamental rights of freedom of conscience).[8] Discriminatory punishment for conscientious objection to military service based on religious conviction could be Refugee Convention persecution.[9] Apostasy, without the adoption of another religion, has been accepted as founding a claim on the basis of fear of persecution for reason of religion,[10] and in *Omoruyi*[11] Simon Brown LJ held that:

'It is, therefore, plain (and hardly surprising) that, whether the harm is perpetrated by the religious upon the non-religious or vice versa (or indeed by one religious body upon another), and whether because of adherence (or a refusal to adhere) to a belief or because of behaviour, there will be persecution for reasons of religion provided always that the other ingredients are satisfied.'[12]

[1]   UNHCR *Handbook* 12.13 above, paras 71–73. In its *Guidelines on International Protection No 6:* Religion-based refugee claims under Art 1A(2) of the 1951 Convention and/or the 1967 Protocol relating to the status of refugees (HCR/GIP/04/06), 28 April 2004, UNHCR divides religion-based claims into those involving religion as belief (or non-belief); religion as identity; and religion as a way of life (para 5). The EC Qualification Directive 2004/83/EC (12.3 fn 3 above) Art 10(1)(b) defines 'religion' as including beliefs (theistic, non-theistic or atheistic); participation in or abstention from worship (private or public), or communal conduct based on or mandated by religious belief. Two German cases show that the link to religions need not be direct: in one, membership of a Christian social club was viewed with suspicion by the authorities (1993) 5 IJRL Case 164; in another, an Iranian Muslim would face measures for having married a Catholic Polish woman: (1993) 5 IJRL Case 165.

[2]   *R v Secretary of State for the Home Department, ex p Kazmi* [1994] Imm AR 94, QBD. More recently see *FS (Iran – Christian converts) CG* [2004] UKIAT 00303 for lengthy IAT guidance on the risk faced by Iranian converts from Islam to Christianity. See also *Bastanipour v INS* (1992) 980 F 2d 1129, USCA (7th Cir), a US decision that an Iranian convicted drug smuggler who converted to Christianity in prison had a well-founded fear. UK cases involving Iranian converts to Christianity have focussed on the 'genuineness' of the claimant's new-found faith (see eg *J (Iran)* [2004] UKIAT 00158 and *Ghodratzadeh* [2002] UKIAT 01867), a focus approved in relation to post-departure conversion cases in UNHCR's *Guidelines on International Protection:* Religion-based refugee claims (fn 1 above) para 34, whereas in Canada, the emphasis has been on the attitude of the authorities to the fact of conversion; see Rouleau J in the Federal Court in *Sadeghi v Minister of Citizenship and Immigration* [2002] FCT 1083 at para 18.

[3]   See the discussion of prosecution and persecution at 12.48 above. Religions which have proselytising as the essence of their witness will more easily lead to recognition *Ahmad v Secretary of State for the Home Department* [1990] Imm AR 61, CA, per Farquarson LJ. See also *Ahmed (Iftikhar)* below.

[4]   See inter alia *Khan* (18982); *R v Secretary of State for the Home Department, ex p Arshad* (C/2000/5154) (14 July 2000, unreported), QBD.

5   *Ahmed (Iftikhar) v Secretary of State for the Home Department* [2000] INLR 1, reinstating
     the decision of a Special Adjudicator, which had been reversed on appeal by the Tribunal
     on the grounds that the claimant should 'make some allowances for the situation in
     Pakistan and ... exercise a measure of discretion in his conduct and in the profession of his
     faith'. UNHCR's *Guidelines on International Protection:* Religion-based refugee claims (fn
     1 above) also indicate that religion 'can be seen as so fundamental to human identity that
     the individual should not be compelled to hide, change or renounce it in order to avoid
     persecution' (para 13).
6   *Mendis v Immigration Appeal Tribunal* [1989] Imm AR 6, CA.
7   *Ahmad* [1990] Imm AR 61.
8   See also *Danian v Secretary of State for the Home Department* [1999] INLR 533, CA.
9   *Kokkinakis v Greece* (1993) 17 EHRR 397; *Thrimmenos v Greece* (Application
     34369/97), see 8.66 fn 6 above. Cf *Sepet v Secretary of State for the Home Department*
     [2001] EWCA Civ 681; [2003] UKHL 15.
10   *Yaqub* (19569) – applicant from Pakistan lost his faith whilst in the UK and became an
     atheist.
11   *Omoruyi v Secretary of State for the Home Department* [2001] Imm AR 175.
12   See also *Hellman v Minister for Immigration and Multicultural Affairs* [2000] FCA 645;
     Dehlaghijadid [2002] UKIAT 06165: 'In the context of a state which persecutes many of
     those who reject the state religion, being perceived as against a religion can be as much a
     basis for persecution on account of religion as can being perceived as in favour of a
     different religion.' Whether harm arising from disapproval of the applicant's conduct by
     religious people can be said to be persecution for reasons of religion has received different
     answers in *Ameen* [2003] INLR 595 and *A (Iran)* [2003] UKIAT 00095. UNHCR's
     Guidelines on Religion-based refugee claims and the EC Qualification Directive
     2004/83/EC (both at fn 1 above) agree that it can.

Nationality

12.71 Like race, 'nationality' should be interpreted broadly to include a
specific cultural or linguistic minority identifying itself as such.[1] The persecution of Gypsies may be on grounds of race or nationality.[2] Denial of full
citizenship in a person's own country may ground refugee status if this puts
him or her at risk of persecution.[3] The right to return is one of the normal
incidents of 'nationality' and where citizens are arbitrarily deprived of their
right to return this can amount to persecution (although there may be overlap
with other Convention reasons in such cases).[4]

1   UNHCR *Handbook* 12.13 above, paras 74–76; EC Qualification Directive 2004/83/EC
     (12.3 fn 3 above) Art 10(1)(c), which defines 'nationality' as including membership of a
     cultural, ethnic or linguistic group, geographical or political origins, and relationship with
     the population of another state.
2   Nowadays it is more likely to be described as persecution on grounds of race or ethnicity.
     See eg *Harangova* (00TH 01325) (8 November 2000, unreported); *Franczak* CC-10255–
     00. See *Commission for Racial Equality v Dutton* [1989] QB 783, CA (Gypsies are an
     ethnic group for the purposes of the Race Relations Act 1976).
3   Hathaway 12.22 fn 2 above, p 144.
4   See *Adan, Lazarevic v Secretary of State for the Home Department* [1997] Imm AR
     251, CA where Hutchison LJ stated that 'if a state arbitrarily excludes one of its citizens,
     thereby cutting him off from enjoyment of all those benefits and rights enjoyed by citizens
     and duties owed by a state to its citizens, there is in my view no difficulty in accepting that
     such conduct *can* amount to persecution' (at 272). Certain nationals of the former
     Yugoslavia have been denied the right to return to the Federal Republic of Yugoslavia
     (Serbia) since 1994. See eg *Stula* (14622), where a Tribunal found persecution by reason of
     the Federal Republic of Yugoslavia's deprivation of citizenship and the denial of the refugee
     claimant's right to return. (The case was quashed by the CA on grounds not affecting the
     Tribunal's discussion of the principles.)

Political opinion

12.72 Freedom of expression is a core value of democratic societies,[1] and freedom of thought, conscience, opinion, expression, assembly and association are human rights protected by various international instruments.[2] These considerations, together with the need to adopt a broad purposive construction to all Refugee Convention grounds,[3] provide the context for the construction of the term 'political opinion'. For Goodwin-Gill, 'political opinion' covers 'any opinion on any matter in which the machinery of state, government and policy may be engaged',[4] while Hathaway defines political opinion as 'any action perceived to challenge governmental authority'.[5] The latter definition was approved by a 'starred' Tribunal in *Gomez*,[6] which involved a Colombian citizen who was threatened by guerrillas, after assisting a victim of extortion. At issue was whether, as a differently constituted tribunal had found in *Acero-Garces*,[7] persecution by non-state actors of persons obstructing their aims and activities was for reasons of political opinion.[8] In the Colombian context, this involved scrutiny of the relationship between political and criminal activity. The Tribunal held that this was not necessarily so, in a decision which reviewed international jurisprudence. Looking at the definition of political opinion, the Tribunal in *Gomez* observed that where non-state actors are involved, the phrase had to be given 'a more inclusive, multi-sided definition' than one limited by reference to party politics[9] or to government or governmental authority,[10] but doubted whether it would embrace power relationships at all levels of society. Save in very unusual circumstances political opinion would not be established 'at the purely domestic or interpersonal level'.[11]

[1] See *Handyside v United Kingdom* (1976) 1 EHRR 737.
[2] See UDHR, Arts 18–20; International Covenant on Civil and Political Rights, Arts 19, 20, 21, 22; ECHR, Arts 9–11.
[3] *R v, Immigration Appeal Tribunal, ex p Shah; Islam v Secretary of State for the Home Department* [1999] Imm AR 283 at 293, HL.
[4] Goodwin-Gill 12.5 fn 1 above, p 49. The starred Tribunal in *Gomez* (*Emila del Socorro Gutierrez*) [2000] INLR 549 doubted whether this definition was wide enough.
[5] Hathaway 12.22 fn 2 above, p 154, approved by the Federal Court of Australia in *V v Minister for Immigration and Multicultural Affairs* [1999] FCA 428 and cited with approval by Waller LJ in *Sepet v Secretary of State for the Home Department* [2001] EWCA Civ 681, [2001] INLR 376 at 433 at para 159.
[6] *Gomez* fn 4 above, endorsed by Keene LJ in *Suarez v Secretary of State for the Home Department* [2002] EWCA Civ 722, [2002] 1 WLR 2663.
[7] *Acero-Garces* [1999] INLR 460.
[8] *Gomez* above, para 4.
[9] As in the 'classical' definition of Lord Diplock in *Cheng v Governor of Pentonville Prison* [1973] AC 931; *Gomez* above, para 28.
[10] *Gomez* above, para 31ff, referring to *V v Minister for Immigration and Multicultural Affairs* [1999] FCA 428, Federal Court of Australia.
[11] To engage the Refugee Convention, power relationships must in some way link up to the major power transactions that take place in government or related sectors such as industry and the media. Politics at the 'micro' level must in some way relate to politics at the 'macro' level: *Gomez* above, para 38.

12.73 The Convention ground of political opinion refers both to the holding of the opinion and the expression of it.[1] Having an opinion implies the right to express it and persecution will not usually be alleged on the ground of having the opinion alone;[2] but political *action* or *activity*, although possibly an important indication of political opinion, is not necessary to found a claim.[3] Political opinion may be express, implied or imputed,[4] and in establishing an imputed political opinion it is not the persecutor's political opinions but those attributed, rightly or wrongly, to the victims which are considered.[5] Thus a civil servant accused of politically motivated sabotage may have been performing functions negligently rather than expressing a political opinion, but the imputation of such an opinion by persecutors would establish the Convention reason.[6] In *Ward* [7] the Supreme Court of Canada held that punishment of a former member of a terrorist political group for failing to execute hostages could amount to persecution for the political opinion that placed humanitarian obligation over the orders of the group.[8] In certain circumstances, as the Tribunal in *Gomez* recognised, neutrality may constitute a political opinion.[9] Trade union activists and those working against the power of organised cartels may have political opinions attributed to them in particular situations.[10] But there is no universal proposition that those on the side of law and order and justice who face persecution from non-state actors, be they guerrilla organisations or political or criminal gangs, will have a political opinion attributed to them.[11] All would depend on the relationship between crime and power in a particular country at a particular time.[12] While non-state actors might have political objectives, persecutors do not always attribute political opinions to victims or opponents,[13] and not all persecution by political groups is for political reasons; sometimes it is simple extortion of money or drugs.[14]

[1] UNHCR *Handbook* 12.13 above, para 80ff.
[2] UNHCR *Handbook* above, para 81. On the other hand, in terms of the relevance of the *right* to express a political opinion on return to the country of feared persecution and the effect of the likely exercise of this right on refugee status, see 12.32–12.33 above.
[3] *Minister of Immigration and Ethnic Affairs v Guo* (1997) 191 CLR 559, High Court of Australia; *Gomez (Emila del Socorro Gutierrez)* [2000] INLR 549, para 24; see also *Orlov* (18505).
[4] See eg *Adan v Secretary of State for the Home Department, Lazarevic v Secretary of State for the Home Department* [1997] Imm AR 251; *Danian v Secretary of State for the Home Department* [1999] INLR 533; *Sepet v Secretary of State for the Home Department* [2001] EWCA Civ 681, [2001] INLR 376; *Otchere* [1988] Imm AR 21; *Asante* [1991] Imm AR 78; *A-G (Canada) v Ward* [1993] 103 DLR (4th) 1, [1993] 2 SCR 689, [1997] INLR 42.
[5] *Danian v Secretary of State for the Home Department* [1999] INLR 533 at 557H, where Buxton LJ stated this as an elementary proposition. See also *Sanga v INS* 103 F 3d 1482 (9th Cir, 1997), US; *Allie* (14814); *Galvis* (22502).
[6] See *Asante* [1991] Imm AR 78.
[7] *A-G (Canada) v Ward* (1993) 103 DLR (4th) 1, [1993] 2 SCR 689, [1997] INLR 42.
[8] Cited, together with *Klinko v Canada (Minister of Citizenship and Immigration)* 22 February 2000, FCA, in *Gomez* above, para 32.
[9] *Sanga v INS* above.
[10] *Gomez* 12.72 fn 4 above, paras 48, 51; *R v Secretary of State for the Home Department, ex p Walteros-Castenada* (CO/2383/99) (27 June 2000, unreported), QBD.
[11] *Gomez* above, para 47. To this extent the starred Tribunal disapproved *Acero-Garces* (above).
[12] In *Storozhenko v Secretary of State for the Home Department* [2001] EWCA Civ 895, [2001] All ER (D) 160 (Jun) the Court of Appeal upheld the Tribunal's determination (19935) that those on the side of law and order in the Ukraine would not have a political opinion imputed to them.
[13] *Gomez* above, para 52.
[14] *Gomez* above, at para 54; *R v Secretary of State for the Home Department, ex p Hernandez* [1994] Imm AR 506; *R v Secretary of State for the Home Department, ex p Gedrimas* [1999] Imm AR 486; *R v Special Adjudicator, ex p Roznys (Sigitas)* [2000] Imm AR 57; *Quijano* (10699); *Re Jeah* (Refugee Appeal No 2507/95), NZRSAA; *INS v Elias-Zacarias* 112 S Ct 812 (1992) (US).

12.74 Thus the term 'political opinion' needs to be a flexible one, since the boundaries between the political and the non-political will change in historical time and place.[1] What makes an opinion political is the social structure and social context of the asylum seeker's country of origin.[2] There is little doubt that feminism qualifies as a political opinion,[3] and the Home Office Asylum Policy Instructions recognise that 'if a woman resists gender oppression, her resistance is political'.[4] Transgression of social roles and behaviour,[5] such as violation of dress codes in a fundamentalist Muslim country,[6] seeking exercise of a fundamental human right, as in the case of China's one-child policy, or unauthorised travel abroad, may establish a sufficient link with a political opinion, depending on all the circumstances.[7] Working in local government will not normally provide the basis of itself for the imputation of political opinions, although this may be the case where there is a major armed conflict between the authorities and guerrilla groups.[8] Similarly, there are no fixed distinctions between what is political and what is criminal,[9] nor between what is political and economic,[10] nor between actions motivated by personal interests and by political opinions.[11] A person who has not previously expressed his political dislike of the regime may be exposed by the very fact of flight and claiming asylum.[12] A claim may be based on the future expression of political opinion.[13]

[1]   The Refugee Convention is a living instrument constantly adapting to meet changing times: see Sedley J in *R v Immigration Appeal Tribunal, ex p Shah* [1997] Imm AR 145 at 152 and Schiemann LJ in *Jain v Secretary of State for the Home Department* [2000] INLR 71 at 77C.

[2]   Berkowitz and Jarvis *Immigration Appellate Authority Asylum Gender Guidelines* (Nov 2000) paras 3.18, 3.22ff.

[3]   *Fatin v INS* 12 F 3d 1233 (3rd Cir, 1993) (US).

[4]   API on 'assessing the claim', para 9.5. See also API on 'gender issues in the asylum claim'.

[5]   *Fathi and Ahmady* (14264).

[6]   *Re MN*, Refugee Appeal No 2039/93, 12 February 1996 (NZRSAA); *Gomez* 12.72 fn 4 above, para 40.

[7]   Canada: *Cheung v Minister of Employment and Immigration* (1993) 102 DLR (4th) 214; *Chan v Minister of Employment and Immigration* 128 DLR (4th) 213 SCJ; Australia: *Minister for Immigration and Ethnic Affairs v A* (24 February 1997, unreported); New Zealand: *Re ZWD Refugee Appeal 3/91* (20 October 1992, unreported). See also Goodwin-Gill 12.5 fn 1 above, pp 52–53, 359. Gender guidelines for the application of the Refugee Convention to women who face compulsory abortions have been established in Canada, US, Australia and New Zealand as well as in the UK, although the ambit of the protection has proved politically controversial in the US and Australia. See *Asylum Gender Guidelines* above, para 2A.17.

[8]   *Gomez* 12.72 fn 4 above, para 40. See *Doufani* (14798) and *Woldemichael* (17663).

[9]   *Gomez* above, paras 41–42 and cases there discussed. Participation in a banned demonstration is clearly political rather than criminal: *R (on the application of Tientchu) v Immigration Appeal Tribunal* (18 October 2000, unreported), CA.

[10]   *Gomez* above, para 43.

[11]   *Gomez* above, para 44

[12]   UNHCR *Handbook* 12.13 above, paras 82–83; Hathaway 12.22 fn 2 above, pp 149ff. See *M v Secretary of State for the Home Department* [1996] Imm AR 136, CA: where the act of claiming asylum is perceived by a regime as expressing hostile political opinions towards it, the act of putting forward a baseless claim for asylum (and thereby establishing risk on return) could itself found a claim based on imputed political opinion.

[13]   *Omar v Minister for Immigration and Multicultural Affairs* [2000] FCA 1430, drawing on *Ahmed (Iftikhar) v Secretary of State for the Home Department* [2000] INLR 1; *Danian v Secretary of State for the Home Department* [2000] Imm AR 96; *Minister for Immigration and Multicultural Affairs v Mohammed* [2000] FCA 576, Fed CA (Aust).

Refusal to perform military service

12.75 The UNHCR handbook makes it clear that those who claim refugee status on the basis of a refusal to perform military service[1] are not refugees per se, since a state may require compulsory military service of its nationals and prosecution and punishment arising from refusal may be seen not as persecution but as prosecution and punishment under a law of general application.[2] However, draft evaders and deserters are not excluded from refugee status either; the state's right to demand military service is not absolute and there are important exceptions to the general rule. According to the Handbook it is certainly open to states to regard prosecution and punishment as persecutory if they override a genuine and deeply held conviction on conscientious or other principled grounds,[3] and the UK courts may eventually follow suit, if and when they find that the right of conscientious objection to military service is recognised as a fundamental human right.

[1] See generally UNHCR *Handbook* 12.13 above, paras 167–170; Hathaway 12.22 fn 2 above, pp 179–185; Goodwin-Gill, *The Refugee in International Law* (2nd edn, 1996) pp 54–59.
[2] UNHCR *Handbook* above, para 167.
[3] UNHCR *Handbook* above, paras 168–172.

12.76 In *Foughali*[1] the Tribunal analysed the principles and identified four broad exceptions to the general rule that draft evasion or desertion does not ground refugee status:

(i)   persecution due to the conditions of life in the military service in question;

(ii) persecution due to the repugnant nature of military duty likely to be performed;

(iii) persecution due solely to genuine political, religious or moral convictions, or to valid reasons of conscience;[2] and

(iv) persecution due to likely disproportionate punishment.

Paragraphs (i), (ii) and (iv) are not in dispute. The area of contention is (iii), and in *Sepet*[3] the House of Lords upheld the judgment of the majority in the CA to the effect that there is as yet no recognised, codified human right to conscientious objection, so that punishment for draft evasion based on such an objection will not per se amount to persecution.[4] Nonetheless the Court of Appeal in *Sepet*[5] unanimously held that an objection to serve in the military is inherently an implied expression of political opinion, contrary to governmental authority, and that punishment for refusing to serve in circumstances where there was a likelihood of being forced to take part in the kind of actions condemned by the international community as contrary to human rights norms could amount to persecution for reason of political opinion. This was not disputed in the House of Lords. Accordingly, while the traditional conscientious objector (such as the pacifist Quaker) may not yet have a right to object based on freedom of conscience which takes priority over the state's right to require performance of military service,[6] others who object to fighting on principled grounds may have their fundamental rights violated by the requirement to perform military service. For example, they may object to the use of chemical weapons,[7] or to fighting an oppressed minority or their own people.[8] Domestically, *Sepet* is the last word – for the moment. It has, however, to be remembered that human rights are developing all the time and should a right to conscientious objection evolve in the meantime, perhaps in other jurisdictions, the domestic position could change. Internationally, there is uncertainty, however, as to whether the holding of a genuine and principled objection to the performance of military service can of itself substantiate a claim.[9] The language of the UNHCR *Handbook* is somewhat cautious, merely stating that it is open to contracting states to grant refugee status to 'persons who object to performing military service for genuine reasons of conscience'.[10]

[1] (00TH01513), para 9.
[2] See UNHCR *Handbook* 12.13 above, para 170. Note in this context that the listing of particular types of conscientious objection has given way to what the Tribunal in *Foughali* described as 'a more flexible "compelling reasons of conscience" ' definition. See eg Council of Europe Committee of Ministers Recommendation R(87)8; UN Commission on Human Rights report 2 March 1995, E/CN.4/1995/L.82, noting the general comment No 22(48) of the Human Rights Committee that 'there should be no differentiation between conscientious objectors on the basis of the nature of their particular beliefs'.
[3] *Sepet v Secretary of State for the Home Department* [2003] UKHL 15, [2003] 1 WLR 856.
[4] In *Sepet v Secretary of State for the Home Department* [2001] EWCA Civ 681, [2001] Imm AR 452 the Court of Appeal held that the apparent acceptance, without argument on the issue, of a human right to conscientious objection by the Court of Appeal in *Zaitz v Secretary of State for the Home Department* [2000] INLR 346 was not in any way authoritative and that the Tribunal in *Foughali* (above) had erred in treating it as such.
[5] *Sepet v Secretary of State for the Home Department* [2001] EWCA Civ 681, [2001] Imm AR 452.
[6] See ECHR Art 9, and the views of Commission members in *Thlimmenos v Greece* (App 34369/97) (2000) 31 EHRR 411, (2000) 9 BHRC 12, at paras 44–45.
[7] *Zolfagharkani v Canada* [1993] 3 FC 540.
[8] *Ciric v Canada* [1994] 2 CF 65. Note however that *Sepet* (above) involved Turkish Kurds who objected to performing military service because it was likely to involve fighting fellow Kurds; the Tribunal ([2000] Imm AR 445) had dismissed the appeals on the ground (not upheld by the Court of Appeal or the House of Lords) that the appellants' objection was partial and contained unacceptable discrimination against non-Kurds.
[9] See the speech of Lord Hoffmann in *Sepet* in the House of Lords (fn 3 above) at paras 39 and 52, and the judgments of Laws and Waller LJJ in the Court of Appeal (fn 5) at paras 20–81, 187–200.
[10] Note however that the Handbook was written in 1979. See also Goodwin-Gill *The Refugee in International Law* (2nd edn, 1996) at p 55ff.

12.77 In *Adan and Lazarevic*[1] the Court of Appeal held that a person who faces prosecution for a genuine objection to the performance of military service involving action contrary to basic rules of human conduct is expressing a political opinion and is a refugee.[2] Paragraph 171 of the UNHCR *Handbook* refers to military action 'condemned by the international community', and in *Krotov*[3] the Court of Appeal considered conflicting Tribunal decisions on when military action with which an asylum claimant does not wish to be associated, can properly be said to be condemned by the international community as contrary to the basic rules of human conduct, so that punishment for desertion or refusal to serve can itself amount to persecution.[4] Potter LJ held that where acts prohibited by the humanitarian norms expressed in the international law of armed conflict, such as genocide, the deliberate killing and targeting of the civilian population, rape, torture, the execution and ill-treatment of prisoners and the taking of civilian hostages,[5] 'are committed on a systemic basis as an aspect of deliberate policy, or as a result of official indifference to the widespread actions of a brutal military' they 'qualify as acts contrary to the basic rules of human conduct in respect of which punishment for a refusal to participate will constitute persecution within the ambit of the 1951 Convention'.[6] He emphasised that the individual asylum-seeker had to be at real risk of being 'required to participate' in such military actions, rather than merely being 'associated' with them, eg through wearing of the uniform.[7] In *Adan and Lazarevic*,[8] the issue was whether refugee status could be granted to draft evaders from an army engaged in an internationally condemned conflict, regardless of whether their objection to fighting was genuine or (as the adjudicator had found) opportunistic. Hutchison LJ held that the fact that they were opportunists and not genuine objectors was fatal to their claim. It will always be important for asylum seekers who base their claims on a wish to avoid the performance of military service to give detailed and cogent evidence.[9]

1 *Adan v Secretary of State for the Home Department, Lazarevic v Secretary of State for the Home Department* [1997] 1 WLR 1107. See further *Altun v Secretary of State for the Home Department* (1999/0845/C), 28 January 2000, where the Court of Appeal accepted that the interpretation of Art 1A(2) of the Refugee Convention required recognition in such circumstances. See also *Sepet*, CA (12.76 above).

2 UNHCR *Handbook* 12.13 above, para 171. See also (in the context of the *Yugoslavian* conflicts) *Azapovic* (13611) and *Drvis* (13129); *Tallah* [1998] INLR 258 and *Rieda* (14359) (Algeria); *Zolfagarkhani v Canada* [1993] 3 FC 540 (use of chemical weapons in Iran-Iraq war). For an attempt to argue that laying land mines in a civilian area falls within the ambit of repugnant military action, punishment for refusal to perform which gives rise to refugee status, see *BE (Iran)* [2004] UKIAT 00183 (awaiting rehearing following remittal from the Court of Appeal).

3 *Krotov v Secretary of State for the Home Department* [2004] EWCA Civ 69, [2004] 1 WLR 1825.

4 In *Foughali* (00TH01513) and again in *B (Russia)* [2003] Imm AR 591 the IAT held that the correct approach was to consider the nature of the military actions in question (as objectively evidenced by human rights reports on the given conflict) in the context of international human rights law and international law governing armed conflicts and determine whether such actions are contrary to the basic rules of human conduct. International condemnation, especially by the UN General Assembly, would merely be one indicator – albeit a strong one – that the military actions in question were contrary to the basic rules of human conduct. However in *Krotov* [2002] UKIAT 01325 the Tribunal held that some kind of formal condemnation by the international community of the military actions in question was a prerequisite for any asylum claim to succeed on the basis that punishment per se for refusal to serve in an army that committed such actions amounts to persecution. The Court of Appeal in *Krotov* held in favour of the *Foughali* and *B* approach.

5 See Annexes V and VI to the UNHCR Handbook for Article 6 of the Charter of the International Military Tribunal established to try and punish Axis war criminals; The Rome Statute of the International Criminal Court 1998, Arts 6–8 (defining genocide, war crimes and crimes against humanity); and for a useful summary of the international laws of armed conflict, see Ministry of Defence *Manual of the law of armed conflict* (July 2004, OUP): see also the list in *Krotov* [2004] EWCA Civ 69 (above) at para 30.

6 *Krotov* [2004] EWCA Civ 69 (above) at para 37. He concluded: 'If a court or tribunal is satisfied (a) that the level and nature of the conflict, and the attitude of the relevant governmental authority towards it, has reached a position where combatants are or may be required on a sufficiently widespread basis to act in breach of the basic rules of human conduct generally recognised by the international community, (b) that they will be punished for refusing to do so and (c) that disapproval of such methods and fear of such punishment is the genuine reason motivating the refusal of an asylum seeker to serve in the relevant conflict, then it should find that a Convention ground has been established.' [51].

7   *Krotov* [2004] EWCA Civ 69 (above) at para 40. Rix and Carnwath LJJ agreed. In Canada, the case of *Zolfagarkhani v Canada* [1993] 3 FC 540 is authority for the proposition that the applicant does not have to prove that he or she would be required to participate in acts contrary to Article 1F of the Refugee Convention, only that the army in question performed them.
8   *Adan, Lazarevic v Secretary of State for the Home Department*, fn 1 above.
9   See eg UNHCR *Handbook* 12.13 above, para 174, referring to the need for 'a thorough investigation of ... personality and background' to establish the genuineness of the objection. Immigration judges tend to draw adverse conclusions on credibility more readily where the appellant's views are not explained in detail. See also *Kulet* (00TH00391).

Membership of a particular social group

12.78 This last category has been the most litigated of all the Refugee Convention reasons and the one where the necessity to see the Convention as a living instrument, constant in motive but mutable in form,[1] is most apparent. The cases have raised controversial issues as to the limits of Convention protection. However, those limits can be stated with a far greater degree of certainty following *Shah and Islam*[2] in which the House of Lords held that women in Pakistan constituted a particular social group. Lord Steyn approved the following passage from the decision of the US Board of Immigration Appeals in *Acosta*:[3]

'We find the well-established doctrine of *ejusdem generis* ... to be most helpful in construing the phrase ... Each of [the other grounds] describes persecution aimed at an immutable characteristic: a characteristic that either is beyond the power of an individual to change or is so fundamental to individual identity or conscience that it ought not be required to be changed ...

Applying the doctrine of *ejusdem generis*, we interpret the phrase ... to mean persecution that is directed toward an individual who is a member of a group of persons all of whom share a common, immutable characteristic. The shared characteristic might be an innate one such as sex, colour, or kinship ties, or in some circumstances it might be a shared experience such as former military leadership or land ownership ... By construing [the phrase] in this manner we preserve the concept that refugee status is restricted to individuals who are either unable by their own actions, or as a matter of conscience should not be required, to avoid persecution.'[4]

Whether a number of people sharing particular characteristics constitute a 'particular social group' depends on the factual situation in the particular country. Westernised women may be seen as a distinct social group in some Middle Eastern countries but not in Israel, just as landowners were such a group in pre-revolutionary Russia but would not be in England today.[5] The following underlying principles emerge from the judgments:

(i)   interpretation of the phrase 'particular social group' must be seen in the context of the fundamental purpose of the Refugee Convention of counteracting discrimination;[6]

(ii)   the social group must exist independently of, and not be defined by, the persecution, otherwise anyone persecuted for whatever reason would qualify;[7]

(iii)   however, this does not mean that discrimination against members is irrelevant as a means of identifying the group.[8] On the contrary, women in Pakistan were held to be a particular social group precisely because as a group distinguished by gender, they were discriminated against and unprotected by the state;[9]

(iv) although cohesiveness may prove the existence of a particular social group, it is not a requirement for the existence of the group.[10]

In an attempt to unify the divergent approaches to the meaning of the phrase at the international level, the UNHCR gives the following definition:[11]

'a particular social group is a group of persons who share a common characteristic other than their risk of being persecuted, or who are perceived as a group by society. The characteristic will often be one which is innate, unchangeable, or which is otherwise fundamental to identity, conscience or the exercise of one's human rights.'

1   *R v Immigration Appeal Tribunal, ex p Shah* [1997] Imm AR 145 at 152, per Sedley J. His formulation was approved by the House of Lords.
2   *R v Immigration Appeal Tribunal, ex p Shah; Islam v Secretary of State for the Home Department* [1999] 2 AC 629, [1999] Imm AR 283, [1999] INLR 144.
3   (1985) 19 I & N 211.
4   See also LA Forest J's (similar) formulation in *A-G of Canada v Ward* (1993) 103 DLR (4th) 1, [1993] 2 SCR 689, [1997] INLR 42.
5   *Shah* and *Islam* above, per Lord Millett.
6   [1999] INLR 144 at 150A–F, 161E–162D, 167B–C. In *A v Minister for Immigration and Ethnic Affairs* [1998] INLR 1 at 15, Dawson J said that where a persecutory law or practice applies to all members of society, it cannot create a particular social group consisting of all who bring themselves within its terms (referring to China's one-child policy). Where the feared persecution emanates from non-state actors, it may be their discrimination or that of the state in failing to protect which constitutes the particular social group. But see *Skenderaj v Secretary of State for the Home Department* [2002] EWCA Civ 567, [2002] 4 All ER 555, [2002] Imm AR 519.
7   [1999] INLR 144 at 151A–151C, 156D–G, 167C. See also *Secretary of State for the Home Department v Savchenkov* [1996] Imm AR 28. But this does not mean that the actions of the persecutors cannot 'identify or even cause the creation of a particular social group in society': see Lord Steyn at 156D–G, endorsing McHugh J in *A v Minister for Immigration and Ethnic Affairs* [1998] INLR 1. Forgetting this may give rise to error of law: see *Liu v Secretary of State for the Home Department* [2005] EWCA Civ 249, (2005) All ER (D) 304 (Mar).
8   [1999] INLR 144 at 167E–F.
9   In the words of Lord Hoffmann, 'discrimination was the critical element in the persecution' ([1999] INLR 144 at 164H–165A). See also *R (on the application of Hoxha) v Secretary of State for the Home Department, R (on the application of B) v Secretary of State for the Home Department* [2005] UKHL 19, [2005] 1 WLR 1063, (2005) 149 Sol Jo LB 358 per Baroness Hale at paras 30ff.
10 Staughton LJ had held that cohesiveness (or interdependence or co-operation) was an essential prerequisite of a 'particular social group' in the Court of Appeal ([1998] INLR 97). Lord Steyn at 151D–154H and Lord Hoffmann at 162E–H rejected this ([1999] INLR 144), approving the decision of La Forest J in *Ward* (social group could include 'such bases as gender, linguistic background and sexual orientation' – none of which implied interdependence or co-operation).
11 UNHCR *Guidelines on International Protection: 'Membership of a particular social group'* (7 May 2002) (HCR/GIP/02/02) at para 11. The UNHCR guidelines, at para 15, also firmly reject any need for the group to be cohesive. See further Council Directive 2004/83/EC on minimum standards for the qualification and status of third country nationals and stateless persons as refugees or persons who otherwise need international protection (30.9.04 OJ L304/12, in force 20 October 2004), Art 10(1)(d).

12.79 Prior to *Shah and Islam* gender[1] had not been accepted in practice as the basis of a particular social group,[2] although it had been cited as one of the immutable characteristics which *could* found such a group in *Acosta* and *Ward.* Particular sub-groups defined partly by gender and partly by another characteristic (such as transgressing social mores) had been recognised.[3] Women who faced compulsory sterilisation or abortion because of China's one-child policy had been held to be refugees on the grounds of social group[4] or political opinion.[5] A divorced Somali woman who had no effective state protection from abuse by her husband and whose daughter might face mutilation was recognised as a refugee.[6] Western-educated Afghani,[7] Algerian[8] and Iranian[9] women had been held to have a well-founded fear of persecution arising from Islamic opposition to their identities and way of life.[10] A number of Canadian decisions had recognised as refugees women fleeing domestic violence,[11] forced marriage[12] or sexual exploitation[13] from which their state would or could not protect them. Rape and severe sexual harassment had been recognised in some cases as constituting Convention persecution,[14] and the Home Office had recognised that rape, forcible abortion, forcible sterilisation, acts involving genital mutilation or allied practices 'probably always' constitute torture.[15] But gender-based social groups had been rejected in a number of cases.[16]

1   See for discussion of gender persecution UNHCR *Guidelines on International Protection: Gender-Related Persecution* (7 May 2002) (HCR/GIP/02/01); Rodger Haines 'Gender-related persecution', in Feller, Turk and Nicholson *Refugee Protection in International Law, UNHCR's Global Consultations on International Protection* (2003); Heaven Crawley, *Refugees and Gender: Law and Process* (2001); Berkowitz and Jarvis *Immigration Appellate Authority Asylum Gender Guidelines* (Nov 2000). See also API on 'gender issues in the asylum claim'.

2   UNHCR's Executive Committee had issued a recommendation, No 39 of 1985, indicating that states *could* recognise women at risk for transgressing social mores as refugees; see also UNHCR *Guidelines on the Protection of Refugee Women* (1991) paras 54–57; Canadian Immigration and Refugee Board Guidelines above; US INS *Considerations for Asylum Officers Adjudicating Asylum Claims from Women* (May 1995); Australian Dept of Imm and Multicultural Affairs, Refugee and Humanitarian Visa applicants *Guidelines on Gender Issues for Decision Makers* (July 1996).

3   See UNHCR ExCom conclusion 39 (1985) above.

4   *Cheung v Minister of Immigration* (1993) FCJ No 309 digested in (1994) 6(1) 118, IJRL case 184. But contrast *Yu (Chang Zheng)* (15469) where a tribunal held that the one-child policy could not provide the basis of a social group. And see also *A v Minister for Immigration and Ethnic Affairs* [1997] 142 ALR 331, [1998] INLR 1, High Court of Australia: a husband and wife who feared forced sterilisation under the 'one-child policy' were not members of a social group. Lord Steyn in *Shah and Islam* ([1999] INLR 144 at 153B–D) said that the uniform application of the policy meant that there was 'no obvious element of discrimination'. On the other hand, children born in defiance of the one child policy, who then face official as well as societal discrimination for this reason, can constitute a particular social group for the purposes of the refugee definition: see *Chen Shi Hai v Minister for Immigration and Multicultural Affairs* (2000) 170 ALR 553, [2000] INLR 455, Aust HC.

5   *Guo v Carroll* 62 US Law Week 2473.

6   (1994) 6(4) IJRL 662 Case 207.

7   *Shaysta Ameer-Ali v Minister of Citizenship and Immigration* Imm-3404–95, 23 September 1996 (Can).

8   (1994) 6(4) IJRL Case 209.

9   (1993) 5(4) IJRL 611, Case 170.

10 See eg *Fatin v INS* 12 F 3d 1233; *Fisher v INS* 37 F 3d 1371.

11 *Mayers v Minister of Employment and Immigration* (1992) 97 DLR (4th) 729; *Narvaez v Canada* [1995] 2 CF 55; *Tahusi*, CRDD T9802494, 7 September 1999 (Georgia).

12 *Vidhani v Canada (Minister of Citizenship and Immigration)* TD Imm-3528–94, 8 June 1995.

13 *Cen v Canada (Minister of Citizenship and Immigration)* TD Imm-1023–95, 1995.

14 (1995) 5(4) IJRL 613 Case 173; (1994) 6(4) IJRL, Case 211; *Ransell (Eustaquio)* CRDD
    T98–04880, 20 October 1999 (Romania). See Laws LJ in *Sepet v Secretary of State for the
    Home Department* [2001] EWCA Civ 681, [2001] INLR 376 at 403, at para 63.
15 API Jul 98, Ch 3, para 2.1. Now see eg API on 'assessing the claim' at s 8.2 to the effect
    that 'rape and other serious sexual violence' amount to 'torture, cruel inhuman or
    degrading punishment or treatment'.
16 See eg *Khan (Nafees Parveen)* (15884) (unprotected Pakistani widow); *Safraz (Lubna)*
    (16179) (Pakistani woman at risk from husband); *Gomez v INS* 947 F 2d 660 (1991)
    (women previously raped by guerrillas).

12.80 Following *Shah and Islam* the Tribunal and the Court of Appeal
upheld a number of gender-based claims, including: an Iranian woman who
feared prosecution for adultery after leaving her violent husband;[1] a Pakistani
woman whose illegitimate children would be seen as evidence of sexual
immorality;[2] a single Pakistani woman without male protection at risk from
the Mohajirs;[3] educated Afghan women perceived as pro-western and anti-
Islamic;[4] a Ukrainian woman forced into prostitution[5] and an Albanian
woman trafficked for prostitution.[6] In the last two cases there was evidence
that the Ukraine and Albania were important source countries of girls and
women trafficked for sexual exploitation. On the other hand, attempts to
establish Jaffna Tamil women at risk of arrest and rape in Colombo as a social
group failed for lack of evidence of 'differential gender victimisation',[7] and a
deserted Kurdish wife who feared sexual exploitation and violence by neigh-
bours and in-laws was held not to belong to a particular social group in
Karakas,[8] because of lack of legal discrimination against women in Turkey.
The Tribunal and the Court of Appeal were until recently fairly reluctant to
allow gender-based claims. While forced marriage[9] and domestic violence[10]
grounded claims in the US,[11] women at risk of rape from soldiers in Uganda
were held not to constitute a particular social group in *R (on the application
of N) v Secretary of State for the Home Department*,[12] and women and girls
from various African countries who risk female genital mutilation were held
not to constitute a particular social group, on the basis that a group cannot be
defined by its persecution.[13] The Tribunal has repeatedly emphasised the need
to show a combination of legal and social discrimination of a particular level
of intensity.[14] However, recent cases suggest a more open approach. In *P and
M* the Court of Appeal castigated the Tribunal for reversing first instance
decisions that Kenyan women constituted a particular social group, and
accepted that domestic violence or female genital mutilation, against which
police would not provide protection despite central government initiatives,
were capable of giving rise to refugee status.[15] The Tribunal in *NS* held that a
first-instance finding that a rape was motivated by attraction was not based
on the evidence and constituted an error of law.[16] Lady Hale's discussion of
gender persecution in *B and Hoxha* took the analysis further, indicating that
stigmatisisation and marginalisation of women who have been rape victims,
and of their families, through deep-seated prejudices may ground a refugee
claim, if the state is unable to afford protection. Her judgment confirms that
state complicity, or state-anointed discrimination, is not a prerequisite to a
gender-based refugee claim.[17]

1 *Fatemeh (Miriam)* (00TH 00921) (for reasons mirroring those in *Shah and Islam*, given the
   similar position of women in Iran). See also *Hanif* [2002] UKIAT 07617 (Pakistani
   women). In *Davoodipanah v Secretary of State for the Home Department* [2004] EWCA
   Civ 106, the Court of Appeal held that the Secretary of State could not withdraw a

concession made before the adjudicator that 'adulterous wives in Iran' constitute a particular social group. In *ZH (Iran) CG* [2003] UKIAT 00207, the Tribunal held that institutional discrimination against women in Iran did not necessarily constitute them a particular social group, but in *TB (Iran)* [2005] UKIAT 00065, the Tribunal held that that case was based on insufficient evidence.

2   *Altaf (Robina)* (00TH 01370). Cf *Babalola (Olayinka Adebukola)* (00TH00926) where the social group contended for was divorced women in Nigeria. But since the claimant could establish no well-founded fear of persecution, the tribunal did not consider the evidence on the position of divorced women in Nigeria; see also *SN and HM (Divorced women: risk on return) Pakistan CG* [2004] UKIAT 283 Reported.

3   *Begum (Syeda)* (21257).

4   *Afghan cases 30, 27, 28* [2002] UKIAT 06500. The women in that case were additionally at risk for their family political connections.

5   *Dzhygun* (00TH00728). The particular social group was defined as 'women in the Ukraine forced into prostitution against their will', whose defining characteristics included gender and lack of state protection.

6   *SK (Albania) v Secretary of State for the Home Department* [2003] UKIAT 00023. The particular social group accepted by the Tribunal was 'women from the north-east of Albania'. In *VD (Albania) v Secretary of State for the Home Department* [2004] UKIAT 00115, the Tribunal rejected a wider group of 'Albanian women' but implicitly recognised that such women who had been sold and had escaped from their trafficker could be at risk of persecution (and could constitute a particular social group). But see the Tribunal's extraordinarily harsh decision in *JO (Nigeria)* [2004] UKIAT 00251, based on internal relocation for a victim of trafficking still under 18 at the date of hearing.

7   See eg *Thangarajah (Vathana)* (16414) where the Tribunal held that Tamil women from Jaffna were not a social group because it was not established that they were being raped or sexually assaulted as such, nor with impunity; *Muralitharali* (B20813).

8   [2002] UKIAT 06406. See fn 14 below.

9   A76–512-001, Imm Ct Chicago, 18 October 2000. See now *TB (Iran)* [2005] UKIAT 00065 (starred) for a UK forced marriage case.

10 *Aguirre-Cervantes v INS*, 21 March 2001, US CA (9th Cir). See now *P v Secretary of State for the Home Department* [2004] EWCA Civ 1640, [2004] All ER (D) 123 (Dec), discussed below.

11 See also the Canadian cases cited at 12.79 fn 11 and 12 above, and see the comprehensive treatment of gender issues in H Crawley *Refugees and gender: law and process* (2001).

12 *R (on the application of N) v Secretary of State for the Home Department* [2002] EWCA Civ 1082, dismissed on the objectionable grounds that what was feared was 'dreadful lust' rather than Convention persecution. See also *Castro (Rosa del Carmen)* [2002] UKIAT 00199 (women in Ecuador).

13 See *RM (Sierra Leone)* [2004] UKIAT 00108, where the Tribunal rejected 'Mendi women and girls who were intact' as a social group; see also *M (Kenya)* [2004] UKIAT 00022 (reversed by the Court of Appeal), disapproving *Yake* (00TH00493) and *Kasinga* (1996) US Bd Imm Appeals Int Dec 3278. The Tribunal in *M (Kenya)* also rejected the groups of 'Kenyan women', 'Kenyan women under 65' and 'Kikuyu women'. In *Hashim* [2002] UKIAT 02691, the Tribunal rejected the argument that young girls in Sudan constituted a particular social group because of their inability to escape FGM (they allowed the appeal on Art 3 ECHR grounds). The Tribunal's approach was criticised as over-technical in *P v Secretary of State for the Home Department* [2004] EWCA Civ 1640, [2004] All ER (D) 123 (Dec) and the appellant M granted status.

14 See *JO (Nigeria)* [2004] UKIAT 00251; *HM (Somalia) (CG)* [2005] UKIAT 40; *RA (Bangladesh)* [2005] UKIAT 70.

15 *P v Secretary of State for the Home Department* [2004] EWCA Civ 1640, [2004] All ER (D) 123 (Dec). The judgment, indicates the incorrectness of the Tribunal's analysis in *M (Albania)* [2004] UKIAT 00059 and *NA (Tajikistan)* [2004] UKIAT 00133, to the effect that clear discrimination against women enshrined in the law of the country concerned is an essential requirement of gender persecution.

16 *NS (Social group – women – forced marriage) Afghanistan CG* [2004] UKIAT 00328 'Reported', This analysis finally sets out the obvious truth underlying violence against women, locating sexual violence in power relations.

17 *R (on the application of Hoxha) v Secretary of State for the Home Department, R (on the application of B) v Secretary of State for the Home Department* [2005] UKHL 19, [2005] 1 WLR 1063, (2005) 149 Sol Jo LB 358, at paras 30ff. The judgment refers approvingly to

the UNHCR *Guidelines on International Protection: Gender-Related Persecution* (7 May 2002) and indicates that the source of the discrimination may be deep-seated patriarchal attitudes against which the state cannot contend. Lady Hale reinforced her observations about rape as a weapon of war in *N v Secretary of State for the Home Department* [2005] UKHL 31 at para 58.

12.81 The decision in *Shah and Islam* also made it clear that homosexuals may constitute a particular social group if, as a group defined by their sexuality (an immutable characteristic), they suffer discrimination.[1] There had been contradictory decisions of differently constituted Tribunals on this question.[2] In *Jain*[3] it was common ground before the Court of Appeal that homosexuals in India constitute a particular social group, since Indian law makes sodomy an offence, thus discriminating against the group on grounds of sexuality. Since *Shah and Islam*, homosexuals in various countries have been held to be members of a particular social group because of the combination of societal and legal discrimination against them.[4] However, being a member of a particular social group does not necessarily mean there is a well-founded fear of persecution, and even in relation to countries where homosexuality attracts severe penalties or is the subject of widespread discrimination, the Tribunal has been very reluctant to find a well-founded fear of persecution for homosexuals, at least for those who are discreet.[5] In *Appellant S*[6] the majority in the High Court of Australia warned against the dangers of this approach, since it is often the very fear of being persecuted that forces homosexuals to act more 'discreetly than they would otherwise choose to behave within the limits of exercising their legitimate human rights'.[7]

[1] [1999] INLR 144 per Lord Steyn at 154D–F; Lord Hoffmann at 162H; Lord Millett at 173F–H. Note Lord Steyn's express endorsement of the decision of the New Zealand Refugee Status Authority in *Re GJ* [1998] INLR 387. The UNHCR *Guidelines on International Protection: Gender-Related Persecution* (7 May 2002) at paras 16–17 and 30 also make clear that severely discriminatory policies or practices directed against homosexuals for reason of their sexuality can amount to persecution for reason of membership of a particular social group.

[2] See for example *Vraciu* (11559); *Golchin* (7623); *Jacques* (11580); *Saddegh* (13124): see also *R v Secretary of State for the Home Department, ex p Binbasi* [1989] Imm AR 595 where the court had assumed, without deciding, that homosexuals could form a social group.

[3] *Jain v Secretary of State for the Home Department* [2000] INLR 71. The court however found that there was no real risk of persecution.

[4] See *Beteringhe* (18120), in relation to Romania, where the claim succeeded, and *Dumitru* (00TH00945) where the claim failed on the facts, the Tribunal holding that the evidence fell short of establishing risk to homosexuals of a 'widespread and systematic pattern of abuses of their human rights'. In *Apostolov* (18547) a Tribunal accepted that a Bulgarian homosexual was a member of a social group, although dismissing the appeal on the facts. Ukrainian homosexuals were held to constitute a particular social group in *Bespalko* [2002] UKIAT 00135 (appeal allowed); Pakistani homosexuals in *Ali (Mohammed Asghar)* [2002] UKIAT 02153 (appeal allowed); Eritreans in *F (Eritrea)* [2003] UKIAT 00177, Ugandans in *K (Uganda)* [2004] UKIAT 00021 (appeals dismissed).

[5] See eg *Musavi* [2002] UKIAT 04050, relating to Iran; *MV (Ukraine)* [2003] UKIAT 00005; *SJ (Jamaica)* [2004] UKIAT 00202; *R (on the application of Dawkins) v Secretary of State for the Home Department* [2003] EWHC 373 Admin (Jamaica); *F (Eritrea)* and *K (Uganda)* fn 4 above.

[6] *Appellant S v Minister for Immigration and Multicultural Affairs* [2003] HCA 71. See also *Refugee Appeal No 74665/03* (7 July 2004), where the NZ Refugee Status Appeal Authority developed the argument based on core human rights of non-discrimination,

dignity and privacy, and see *Z v Secretary of State for the Home Department* [2004] EWCA Civ 1578, where the argument was accepted, but its application to the facts rejected.

7   See 12.33 above. The Tribunal in *K (Uganda)* [2004] UKIAT 00021 noted that the appellant had not engaged in homosexuality in Uganda for fear of the consequences, but held that this was evidence that he would not be persecuted as a homosexual in the future, rather than consider the impact of the threat of serious harm on his exercise of the fundamental right to be who he is.

12.82 Although *Shah and Islam* resolved many issues of principle on the particular social group, difficulties still occur in areas such as what characteristics are 'immutable', what is included in 'individual identity or conscience' and the relationship between persecution and the existence of the group. Previously, in *Savchenkov*,[1] the Court of Appeal had held that those refusing to join a Russian mafia were not a social group because they did not exist independently of the persecution feared.[2] Attempts since *Shah and Islam* to persuade Tribunals to reach a different conclusion and to identify groups by reference to risks from criminal gangs or corrupt officials have generally failed on the same basis: civic conscience is not, in most cases, enough to constitute a particular social group.[3] Linked to this is the important principle that it is far easier to establish membership of a particular social group on the basis of what one *is*, rather than on the basis of what one has *done*. Thus in *Morato v Minister for Immigration and Ethnic Affairs*[4] a citizen of Bolivia had claimed asylum on the grounds that he had been a police informer and as such a member of a group of police informers in fear of reprisals. The Australian Federal Court rejected the argument on the grounds that the applicant's problems resulted from his actions and not from his membership of any group.[5] In *Montoya*[6] the Tribunal summarised the jurisprudence on particular social groups, in the context of a claim by a landowner targeted by guerrillas in Colombia. In *Ouanes*[7] an Algerian government-employed midwife whose work involved giving advice on contraception (which put her at risk of persecution from fundamentalists) was held not to be employed in an occupation having 'that impact upon individual identities or conscience necessary to constitute employees a particular social group'. The court accepted that certain employments could reflect identity and conscience, citing membership of a religious order.[8] We suggest that this is an overly restrictive approach; many professions engage identity and conscience sufficiently to be capable of constituting a particular social group. Opportunist draft-evaders were held not to constitute a particular social group in *Lazarevic*.[9] Refugees[10] have been held not to constitute a social group, although it is hard to see why not, if they suffer marginalisation and discrimination as a group defined by the shared experience of exile.

1   [1996] Imm AR 28, CA.
2   But see *Chun Lan Liu v Secretary of State for the Home Department* [2005] EWCA Civ 249, where the Court of Appeal reminded the Tribunal that actions of the persecutors might serve to identify or even create a particular social group. See also *S v Minister for Immigration and Multicultural Affairs* [2004] HCA 25, where 'able-bodied young men' were accepted as a particular social group under theTaliban regime in Afghanistan.
3   See eg *Storozhenko v Secretary of State for the Home Department* [2001] EWCA Civ 895 (citizens of Ukraine conscientiously fulfilling their civic duty by seeking redress against the illegal actions of agents of the state are not a social group in the absence of discrimination or inability or unwillingness of the state to provide protection); *R v Immigration Appeal Tribunal, ex p Gedrimas* [1999] Imm AR 486 (Lithuanian businessmen at risk from Mafia

not arguably a social group); *Jegorovas* (00TH00724) (adjudicator's acceptance as social group 'Lithuanians who challenge the power of the Mafia' reversed on appeal as group identified by persecution – there was no evidence of an identifiable group); *Stankeviciute* (00TH01321) (attempts by embezzling ex-mayor to have Lithuanian claimant killed was a private vendetta); *Kayani* (19646) (informants in Pakistan about suspected crimes and drugs criminals not a social group because such group defined only by persecution). But see eg *Ermakova* [2002] UKIAT 07728 (member of a family of a political activist pursued by the state in collusion with the mafia), and *Gvarjaladze* [2002] UKIAT 07435 (members of a family opposing high-level corruption) for examples of positive decisions, which appear to depend on the involvement of high-level government figures in the corruption, thus making the persecution of the principal 'political'. See 12.72 above.

4   [1992] 106 ALR 367.
5   Similarly, parents who defy China's one child policy have been held not to be members of a particular social group (*A v MIEA* [1997] 142 ALR 331, [1998] INLR 1, Aust HC) while their children, born of that defiance, have been held to be members of such a group: *Chen Shi Hai v Minister for Immigration and Multicultural Affairs* (2000) 170 ALR 553, [2000] INLR 455, Aust HC): see 12.79 fn 4 above. (For an overview of the jurisprudence on refugee claims based on China's one child policy and membership of a particular social group, see *Chun Lan Liu v Secretary of State for the Home Department* [2005] EWCA Civ 249.) See also *E (Iran)* [2003] UKIAT 00166 (Iranian male adulterer not member of a particular social group); *Britton* [2002] 02514 (family of police informers in Jamaica). Cf *Osorio-Bonilla* (11451) (pre-*Shah and Islam*): those with criminal records *could* establish a social group if, because of their record, they were viewed by society in a particular way.
6   *Montoya v Secretary of State for the Home Department* (00TH00161), upheld and approved by the Court of Appeal at [2002] EWCA Civ 620, [2002] All ER (D) 130 (May). See also *Diallo* (00TH01231) (wealthy educated Sierra Leonean mine owner not member of social group where there were no immutable characteristics and risk was from generalised effects of civil war).
7   *Ouanes v Secretary of State for the Home Department* [1998] Imm AR 76.
8   *Ouanes* above, at 82.
9   *Lazarevic v Secretary of State for the Home Department* [1997] Imm AR 251, CA.
10 *R v Secretary of State for the Home Department, ex p Natando* Immigration Law Digest, Vol 1 no 4.

12.83 The family is the social group *par excellence*, and family membership may form the basis of a 'particular social group'.[1] The question which has emerged from the case law is whether it is enough to be persecuted because of membership of a family regardless of the reason for that family's original persecution, or whether another Convention reason must be behind the initial persecution. There are conflicting decisions. In *Ex p De Melo and De Arujo*[2] Laws J adopted the reasoning of the Tribunal in *Hernandez*[3] to the effect that although the murder of the head of the family by drug gangs might not be for a Convention reason, persecution of family members because of their family relationship to the dead man could be. He rejected the Secretary of State's argument that the non-Convention reason advanced against the principal continued to operate against the family, and concluded that membership of a social group was a distinct Convention reason and not a sub-group that had to be qualified by another Convention reason such as political opinion. The Court of Appeal in *Quijano*,[4] however, narrowed the application of the definition to exclude circumstances where ill-treatment of family members by a drug cartel was a fortuitous by-product of criminal activities, as likely to have been directed at employees as family members, and persecution was not therefore for reasons of membership of the family. Much depends on the reason for the targeting. Thus in *Jaramillo-Aponte*[5] (another case involving Colombian asylum seekers) a tribunal found Convention persecution because the claimants were at risk 'as members of the Escobar family'.[6] Although membership of a family is the basis of 'blood feuds', which specifically target adult male members of the target family, a blood feud was held in *Skenderaj* not to give rise to a refugee claim based on membership of a particular social group, because the family in question was not regarded as a distinct group by the claimant's society, while reliance on the attitude of the other party to the feud would be artificial.[7]

1 A kinship tie plainly is an immutable characteristic: see 12.78 above. A family as a social group was readily accepted by the Court of Appeal in *Quijano* below. See also *Kagedan*, CRDD A99–00215 (9 September 1999, unreported).
2 *R v Immigration Appeal Tribunal, ex p De Melo and De Arujo* [1997] Imm AR 43.
3 *Hernandez* (12773) was not followed by the IAT in *Quijano* (13693).
4 *Quijano v Secretary of State for the Home Department* [1997] Imm AR 227, upholding IAT (13693). See also *Obikwelu* (15343) where the claimant's child was at risk of sacrifice not as a member of the husband's family but for random and opportunistic reasons; *K v Secretary of State for the Home Department* [2004] EWCA Civ 986, [2004] All ER (D) 516.
5 *Jaramillo-Aponte and Ayala* (00TH00428).
6 But the Tribunal allowed appeals in *Gvarjaladze* [2002] UKIAT 07435 (members of a family opposing high-level corruption), and in *Ermakova* [2002] UKIAT 07728 (member of a family of a political activist pursued by the state in collusion with the mafia).
7 *Skenderaj v Secretary of State for the Home Department* [2002] EWCA Civ 567, [2003] INLR 323.

Cessation

12.84 The starting point is that refugee status, once granted, should not be reviewed or annulled except on the most substantial and clear grounds.[1] Formal recognition as a refugee carries the assurance of a secure future in the host country, and a legitimate expectation that he or she will not be stripped of this save for demonstrably good and sufficient reason.[2] A person who is a refugee may cease to qualify for international recognition if circumstances arise to bring about the operation of the cessation clauses of the Refugee Convention.[3] These are:

(i)   voluntary reavailment of the protection of the country of nationality;
(ii)   voluntary reacquisition of the refugee's old nationality;
(iii) acquisition of a new nationality and enjoyment of the protection of the country of the new nationality;
(iv)   voluntary reestablishment in the country where persecution was feared;
(v)   change of circumstances giving rise to recognition as a refugee.

The four 'voluntary' cessation clauses[4] are given direct domestic effect in the UK by the Nationality, Immigration and Asylum Act 2002, section 76(3),[5] under which the Secretary of State may revoke a refugee's indefinite leave to enter or remain in the UK (and that of his or her dependants) if the person ceases to be a refugee for any of the relevant four reasons. This power of revocation can be exercised in respect of leave granted before the provision comes into force but only in reliance on any action taken by the refugee after the provision came into force.[6] Furthermore, like anyone else settled in the UK, refugees can lose their indefinite leave if they remain outside the UK for more than two years continuously.[7] But holders of Refugee Convention travel documents are entitled to readmission at any time, so if the document is valid for more than two years, the holder cannot be denied admission even if absence has been for more than two years.[8]

1   *Babela* [2002] UKIAT 06124, citing UNHCR. See also *LW (Ethiopia – Cancellation of refugee status)* [2005] UKIAT 00042 and *KK (DRC – Recognition elsewhere as refugee)* [2005] UKIAT 00054.

2   *R (on the application of Hoxha) v Secretary of State for the Home Department, R (on the application of B) v Secretary of State for the Home Department* [2005] UKHL 19, [2005] 1 WLR 1063, (2005) 149 Sol Jo LB 358, per Lord Brown at para 65.

3   Refugee Convention, Art 1C. These provisions are 'mirrored' in the EC Qualification Directive 2004/83/EC, 12.3 fn 3 above, Art 11(1).

4   Ie (i)–(iv) above.

5   Nationality, Immigration and Asylum Act 2002, s 76(3) (in force from 10 February 2003: SI 2003/1). Art 1C(3) (acquiring a new nationality) is only relevant, in the domestic context, where the new nationality is other than British: see Nationality, Immigration and Asylum Act 2002, s 76(3)(c).

6   Nationality, Immigration and Asylum Act 2002, s 76(6). A right of appeal lies against the decision to revoke under ss 82(1), (2)(f); if no appeal is lodged, or if it is finally dismissed, a person whose indefinite leave is revoked under this provision can be removed from the UK as an overstayer under Immigration and Asylum Act 1999, s 10(1)(ba) (as inserted by 2002 Act, s 76(7) with effect 10 February 2003: SI 2003/1), with no right of appeal against removal. The API on 'revocation of indefinite leave', para 6 provide that three years or more spent in the UK since ILR was granted will normally constitute a compelling reason for not revoking it, except where other factors, such as an adverse criminal record or immigration history, are present. The API also state, at para 7, that revocation of indefinite leave under s 76(3) should always also be accompanied by revocation of refugee status (which may be relevant to the person elsewhere in the world).

7   See Immigration (Leave to Enter and Remain) Order 2000, SI 2000/1161, Art 13(4)(a) and HC 395, para 18; though also see HC 395, para 19, regarding persons who have lived in the UK for most of their lives.

8   *R v Secretary of State for the Home Department, ex p Shirreh* (CO 2194/97) (15 August 1997, unreported).

12.85 Refugees who apply for and obtain a fresh passport from the authorities from whom they feared persecution may be acting inconsistently with their fear and raise the question of voluntary reavailment. They will have been granted a Refugee Convention travel document with which to travel abroad. If they voluntarily obtain a fresh passport from the country from which they fled, or entry permits with a view to returning there, they will be presumed to intend to avail themselves of their country's protection in the absence of proof to the contrary.[1] But renewal of a national passport without more does not automatically give rise to such a presumption.[2] If the country of asylum instructs individuals to apply for a national passport, that will not be counted against them as it would not be a voluntary reavailment of protection.[3] There may be circumstances beyond their control which require them to have recourse to some measure of protection. This may particularly arise when the refugee is awaiting recognition and has not yet received a Convention travel document or any other document issued by the country where asylum is claimed. Obtaining other official documents such as marriage or birth certificates is less likely to give rise to a presumption of voluntary reacquisition of protection.[4] Acquisition of a new nationality means cessation of status.[5] But where the new nationality is lost, depending on the circumstances of the loss, refugee status may be revived.[6]

1   UNHCR *Handbook* 12.13 above, paras 120–124. See also *Thi Xuan Mai Phan*, Commission des recours des réfugiés, France, No 57165, 15 Sep 1989 (UNHCR Refworld) (obtaining national passport and using it for tourist visit was inconsistent with refugee

status). The API on 'revocation of indefinite leave' at para 3(a) give as an example of voluntary re-availment of protection, a refugee 'seek[ing] to obtain or renew a national passport *and us[ing] it in preference* to a refugee travel document.' (emphasis added).

2   *Thevarayan*, Conseil d'Etat, France, No 78.055, 13 Jan 1989 (UNHCR Refworld). The API on 'revocation of indefinite leave' at para 3(a) point out that: 'Where refugee status was granted on the grounds of non-state agent persecution, a person who seeks to obtain or renew a national passport would not necessarily be re-availing themselves of the protection of their country. It would depend on the circumstances of the case.'

3   UNHCR *Handbook* above, para 120.

4   UNHCR *Handbook* above, para 121; *Paramanathan (Sellathurai)*, Commission des recours des réfugiés No 247916, 7 July 1995 (going to Sri Lankan consulate in Singapore for documents in order to marry did not constitute 'reavailment of protection').

5   See Nationality, Immigration and Asylum Act 2002, s 76(3)(c), 12.84 fn 4 above.

6   UNHCR *Handbook* above, para 132.

12.86 Questions of voluntary re-establishment may arise if refugees visit their country of nationality on their Refugee Convention travel document. There clearly is a risk that the country of asylum will regard that as evidence that there is no longer a well-founded fear of persecution[1]. Where humanitarian protection (previously exceptional leave to remain for protection reasons) has been granted, holders of such a status are also vulnerable to a cancellation of such leave and refusal of readmission to the UK.[2] A temporary visit, however, usually falls far short of reestablishment,[3] and before any inference of voluntary re-acquisition of protection is drawn, regard should be had to the particular circumstances, such as the need to visit sick relatives or business associates.[4] The API allow for certain refugees to return 'home' for a brief visit, with prior approval from the Home Office, without risking their refugee status or indefinite leave to enter or remain in the UK.[5]

1   The API on 'revocation of indefinite leave' at para 3(d) state: 'The key question is whether the person has "re-established" themselves in that country and the purpose of the return to the country from which protection was sought will be relevant. Each case must be considered on its own facts.'

2   See *R v Secretary of State for the Home Department, ex p Zib* [1993] Imm AR 350; and see the API on 'humanitarian protection', para 7.1.

3   UNHCR *Handbook* 12.13 above, para 134; see also Decision A 1008308–479, 20 March 1992, Bundesamt für die Anerkennung ausländischer Flüchtlinge (brief visit to country of origin without notifying local authorities did not constitute reestablishment). The API on 'revocation of indefinite leave' at para 3(d) state: ' "Voluntary re-establishment" means a return to the country from which protection was sought, with a view to taking up permanent residence. A lengthy stay would be the most obvious indicator of re-establishment. A short visit to the former country of persecution would not necessarily constitute "re-establishment" but a series of visits might. A longer visit may not amount to re-establishment if the refugee is conducting an exploratory visit.'

4   UNHCR *Handbook* above, para 125. See also Goodwin-Gill 12.5 fn 1 above, para 3.1, pp 80–83; API on 'revocation of indefinite leave', para 3(d).

5   Exploratory visits to consider return, whether through an official 'Explore and Prepare' Programme or otherwise, are encouraged as an aid to resettlement, but the API envisage approval for other visits, for 'exceptional reasons': para 3(d).

12.87 If the circumstances in the country of nationality or, in the case of stateless persons, former habitual residence, have so changed that refugees can no longer refuse to avail themselves of the protection of that country, Refugee Convention refugee status will cease.[1] This rule is subject to an exception in the case of what the Convention terms 'statutory refugees' (essentially, pre-1939 refugees still recognised as such under Article 1A(1) of the Convention), who do not lose refugee status 'where there are compelling reasons arising out of previous persecution for refusing to avail themselves' of such protection.[2] The UNHCR *Handbook* suggests that similar considerations could also apply to post-1951 refugees on the general humanitarian principle that those who have suffered particularly atrocious forms of persecution should never be expected to repatriate.[3] However in *Hoxha*[4] the House of Lords, after reviewing the language of the proviso, the *travaux* and current State practice, held that the proviso to Article 1C(5) only applies to statutory refugees falling under the definition in Article 1A(1) of the Convention (and is therefore of no practical significance at all anymore). A cessation of circumstances refers to fundamental changes rather than merely transitory ones[5] and the UNHCR is of the view that refugee status should not be *lost* on the basis of a fundamental change of circumstances in part of the country of origin only, to which internal relocation would be possible such as would be enough to defeat an initial application.[6] A refugee's status should not be subject to frequent review since this would jeopardise a sense of security which the Convention was designed to provide.[7] Proof that the circumstances of persecution have ceased to exist would fall upon the receiving state.[8] In *Hoxha* the Court of Appeal held that the cessation clause in Article 1C(5) can only be relevant where a person has been formally recognised as a refugee, and this holding was upheld by the Lords.[9] However when an authority takes a long time to determine the claim of someone who would have been accepted as a refugee if the claim had been dealt with promptly, and circumstances change in the meantime, the Court of Appeal has also held that the situation is *analogous* to Refugee Convention, Article 1C(5) cessation such that the state bears an evidential burden to show that the change is sufficiently fundamental to deny status.[10] UNHCR and states parties to the Convention may issue formal declarations of general cessation of refugee status in respect of refugees from particular countries.[11] However, cessation of refugee status, whether on an individual or group basis, will not automatically mean repatriation, since many refugees will have acquired settlement rights in their country of refuge.[12] The legislation giving effect to the cessation provisions as grounds for revocation of indefinite leave to remain (see 12.84 above) does not include change of circumstances in the country of origin as a statutory ground for revocation, and Home Office policy is generally not to revoke refugee status on this ground.[13]

[1] Refugee Convention, Art 1C(5) and, for stateless persons, Art 1C(6). See generally the UNHCR *Guidelines on International Protection No 3: Cessation of Refugee Status under Article 1C(5) and (6)* (10 February 2003) (HCR/GIP/03/03). For a criticism of these UNHCR guidelines, on the grounds that they 'appear to go considerably beyond the Convention' in pursuit of wider humanitarian concerns, see *SB (Haiti – cessation and exclusion)* [2005] UKIAT 00036.

[2] Refugee Convention, Art 1C(5) and (6), second paras.

[3] UNHCR *Handbook* 12.13 above, para 136 and see UNHCR Guidelines (fn 1 above) at paras 20 and 21. The Refugee Status Appeals Authority in New Zealand in *Re RS* (135/92, 18 June 1993, unreported) held that although the strict wording of the proviso in Art 1C(5) refers only to those refugees falling within Art 1A(1), 'the validity of the underlying humanitarian principles do not depend upon their inclusion in any particular one Article.' However there was a certain degree of retraction from that earlier position by the same authority in *Refugee Appeal No 71684/94* [2000] INLR 165 and see now *Hoxha and B,* fn 4 below.

[4] *R (on the application of Hoxha) v Secretary of State for the Home Department, R (on the application of B) v Secretary of State for the Home Department* [2005] UKHL 19, [2005] 1 WLR 1063, (2005) 149 Sol Jo LB 358.

[5] UNHCR *Handbook* above, para 135 and UNHCR Guidelines (fn 1 above) paras 10–16. See eg *SB (Haiti)* (fn 1 above) and Decision V97/07790, 31 March 1998, Refugee Review Tribunal (Aus) (Austlii website: see Appendix 3). According to Art 11(2) of the EC Qualification Directive 2004/83/EC, 12.3 fn 3 above, a change of circumstances should be 'of a significant and non-temporary nature'.

[6] UNHCR Guidelines (fn 1 above) para 17 (and see 12.42–12.44 above).

[7] UNHCR *Handbook* above, para 135 and UNHCR Guidelines (fn 1 above) para 18. The UNHCR appears to take the view that Art 1C(5) and (6) should rarely if ever be used in individual cases, and should be reserved for group declarations, see fn 11 below.

[8] UNHCR Guidelines (fn 1 above) para 25(ii); Hathaway 12.22 fn 2 above, p 199. 'In the absence of compelling evidence to the contrary it should not be inferred that the grounds for fear had dissipated ... In the absence of facts indicating a material change in the state of affairs in the country of nationality, an applicant should not be compelled to provide justification for his continuing to possess a fear which he has established was well-founded at the time when he left the country of his nationality': *Chan v MIEA* (1989) 169 CLR 379 (Aus). In *SB (Haiti)* (fn 1 above) the Secretary of State conceded that he bore the burden of showing that Art 1C(5) applies.

[9] See fn 4 above. In *N (Kenya)* [2004] UKIAT 00009 the IAT had held that Art 1C(5) can be applied to a person who had previously been recognised as a refugee by an earlier Tribunal but never granted a status letter or ILR.

[10] *Arif v Secretary of State for the Home Department* [1999] INLR 327, CA. But see *Salim (Nabil) v Secretary of State for the Home Department* [2000] Imm AR 503, CA and *S v Secretary of State for the Home Department* [2002] EWCA Civ 539, [2002] INLR 416 at paras 13–15: this *only* applies where it is accepted (by the Secretary of State) that the applicant would have qualified as a refugee; see also *Hoxha and B* (above) and *Dyli* [2000] Imm AR 652, IAT. See the discussion in Goodwin-Gill 12.5 fn 1 above, pp 86–87 and *Yusuf v Canada* [1995] FCJ No 35: the issue of changed circumstances is in danger of being elevated in a question of law, when at bottom it is simply one of fact; the fundamental issue is the possibility or risk of persecution.

[11] UNHCR has such competence under Art 6A of the Statute of the Office of the High Commissioner for Refugees (see 12.12 and 12.13 above) in conjunction with Art 1C of the Refugee Convention: see UNHCR Guidelines (fn 1 above) at para 3.

[12] See two German cases reported in (1995) 7(1) IJRL, Cases 218 and 224. In the latter case the change of regime in Ethiopia removed the claim to Convention persecution but expulsion was not permitted because there was still fighting that made a compulsory return contrary to Art 3 ECHR. However, the applicant Thangarasa in the House of Lords 'third country case' of *R (on the application of Yogathas and Thangarasa) v Secretary of State for the Home Department* [2002] UKHL 36, [2003] 1 AC 920, [2002] INLR 620 (see 12.138 below) had had refugee status in Germany but appears to have lost it on Art 1C(5) cessation grounds.

[13] See Lord Bassam of Brighton, *Hansard* HL 17.7.02, col 1331. However, the EC Qualification Directive 2004/83/EC (12.3 fn 3 above), Art 14(1) states that in respect of applications for international protection filed after the entry into force of the Directive, Member States *shall* revoke, end or refuse to renew the refugee status of a person who has ceased to be a refugee as per the cessation provisions in art. 11 (see 12.84 fn 3 above). This is mandatory in tone and implies that the UK will have to revoke the refugee status (albeit not necessarily the indefinite leave, since the Directive is designed to impose *minimum* standards of protection) of persons who have ceased to be refugees in accordance with cessation clauses. The government proposes to grant refugees temporary leave in the first instance, with a review after five years: see *Controlling our borders: Making migration work for Britain: Five year strategy for asylum and immigration*, Cm 6472, Feb 2005.

Exclusion

12.88 The Refugee Convention will not apply to refugees in circumstances where protection of another state is unnecessary or the person is not deserving of protection. Article 1D of the Convention provides that refugees who are in receipt of assistance from a branch of the UN other than the UNHCR are outside the terms of the Convention until such assistance ceases.[1] In *El-Ali*[2] the Court of Appeal held that Article 1D only applies to those persons who, at the date of the signing of the Refugee Convention on 28 July 1951, were receiving protection from organs or agencies of the United Nations other than the High Commissioner for Refugees, so that in practice, only Palestinians who were alive and who were registered as receiving assistance from the United Nations Reliefs and Works Agency (UNRWA) at that date fall under the Article. All other persons, including Palestinians born after that date, even though receiving assistance from UNRWA, need to establish their status as refugees in the normal way under Article 1A(2) of the Convention.[3] However, Article 1D has been held not to be exhaustive of all the circumstances in which the role of international agencies is relevant for the purposes of the Convention definition.[4]

[1] Refugee Convention, Art 1D; UNHCR *Handbook* 12.13 above, paras 142–143.
[2] *El-Ali v Secretary of State for the Home Department* [2002] EWCA Civ 1103, [2003] 1 WLR 95; leave to appeal to the House of Lords refused: [2003] 1 WLR 1811.
[3] Laws LJ (with whom Lord Phillips MR and May LJ agreed) also held (obiter) that, for the purposes of the second sentence of Art 1D, the phrase 'such protection or assistance has ceased for any reason' refers to UNWRA ceasing to exist or ceasing to provide assistance and not to an individual Palestinian (who must now be over 53 years of age) ceasing for whatever reason to be assisted by UNRWA – although the potential difficulty this would present where such a person was prevented from re-availing him- or herself of UNRWA's assistance was acknowledged. The court also acknowledged that the phrase 'these persons shall *ipso facto* be entitled to the benefits of this Convention' means that if UNRWA ceases to provide assistance to those Palestinians who were registered with it on 28 July 1951 without their having been able to return to their original pre-1948 homes, they are automatically to be treated as refugees within the meaning of the 1951 Refugee Convention. Prior to *El-Ali*, a Palestinian registered with UNRWA in the Gaza strip had been held to qualify *ipso facto* as a refugee when he could not return there because of Israeli military occupation: (1992) 4(3) IJRL 387, case 120.
[4] See eg *R (on the application of Vallaj) v Secretary of State for the Home Department* [2001] EWCA Civ 782, [2001] INLR 342: see further 12.41 above.

12.89 People are not entitled to Refugee Convention protection if they do not need it because the authorities of the territory in which they have taken up residence recognise them as having the rights and obligations attached to the possession of nationality of that country.[1] This exception is of limited application. The person's status must be largely assimilated to that of a national of the receiving country for the exclusion to apply; for example, he or she must be fully protected against deportation or expulsion.[2] The UNHCR *Handbook* suggests that the drafters had in mind refugees of German extraction settling in Germany and recognised there as having the rights and obligations of Germans.[3] In UK terms this would suggest that a grant of settlement or of a subsidiary British nationality which did not confer full citizenship rights would not be enough to bring a person within the exception.[4]

[1] Refugee Convention, Art 1E; UNHCR *Handbook* 12.13 above, paras 144–146.
[2] In *Seare* (3853) unreported, refugee status in Sudan afforded to an Ethiopian national did not exclude the person from the Refugee Convention when he travelled to the UK. See also, in terms of the effect of a grant of asylum abroad on refugee status determination in the UK, *LW (Ethiopia – Cancellation of refugee status)* [2005] UKIAT 00042 (Ethiopian

granted asylum in Uganda – burden on Secretary of State to show 'the most substantial and clear grounds' for revisiting the earlier grant of asylum); *KK (DRC – Recognition elsewhere as refugee)* [2005] UKIAT 00054 (DRC citizen granted asylum in Zimbabwe under OAU Convention on refugees in Africa – not determinative of Geneva Convention refugee status); and *Babela* [2002] UKIAT 06124 (Congolese national with refugee status in South Africa – earlier grant of status should not be questioned unless there is a very good reason for doing so); Hathaway 12.22 fn 2 above, para 6.2.3.

3   UNHCR *Handbook* 12.13 above, para 144.
4   Interesting issues could arise where a former refugee is deprived of British citizenship under British Nationality Act 1981, s 40 (as substituted by Nationality, Immigration and Asylum Act 2002, s 4).

Exclusion for criminal activity

12.90 Article 1F of the Refugee Convention provides that the protection of the Convention does not apply where there are serious reasons for considering that a refugee has committed:

(a)   a war crime or a crime against humanity as defined in the relevant international instruments;[1]

(b)   a serious non-political crime committed outside the country of refuge prior to admission to that country as a refugee; or

(c)   an act contrary to the purposes and principles of the UN.[2]

The terms of Article 1F of the Convention are mandatory; the protective provisions of the Convention 'shall not' apply in these cases.[3] Whereas (b) has a geographical and temporal limit in respect of where and when the crime in question must have been committed, no such limits apply to the crimes and acts covered by Article 1F (a) and (c).[4] The intense focus of governments and international organisations on terrorism since September 2001 has brought wide discussion of these exclusion provisions in the Convention, but in the rush to judgment little notice has been taken of careful analysis in a growing body of literature.[5] In particular our own government has rushed into legislation which thrusts on to our courts and tribunals an order of working and a set of presumptions, which flout the spirit and aim of the Convention. We deal with these below.

1   These are listed in the UNHCR *Handbook* (12.13 above) at Annex VI and include the London Agreement 1945, the charter of the Nuremberg International Military Tribunal (extract in Annex V of the UNHCR *Handbook*), and the Geneva Conventions and additional Protocol relating to the protection of victims of war and international armed conflicts. The Rome Statute of the International Criminal Court 1998, Arts 7 and 8, provides updated definitions of war crimes and crimes against humanity.
2   Refugee Convention, Art 1F.
3   See *Gurung* [2002] UKIAT 04870 (starred) and *KK (Turkey)* [2004] UKIAT 00101.
4   In *KK* (above) the act relied on as contrary to the purposes and principles of the UN (arson attacks on Turkish businesses), occurred in the UK after the claimant had claimed asylum here: see 12.93 below.
5   See, for instance, Background Note on the Application of the Exclusion Clauses: Article 1F of the 1951 Convention relating to the Status of Refugees, UNHCR 2003 (hereinafter: UNHCR Background Note), UNHCR Executive Committee, Standing Committee sessions of 1997 (8th meeting) and 1998 (10th meeting); UNHCR Global Consultations on International Protection, Lisbon Expert Roundtable (May 2001), Summary Conclusions – Exclusion from Refugee Status, UNHCR Doc. EC/GC/01/2Track/1 (hereinafter UNHCR Lisbon Roundtable); UNHCR *Guidelines on International Protection No 5:* Application of the exclusion clauses: Article 1F (HCR/GIP/03/05) 4 September 2003; Lawyers Committee

for Human Rights, Research and Advocacy Project *Safeguarding the Rights of Refugees under the Exclusion Clauses* in IJRL Vol 12 Special Supplementary Issue 2000 Exclusion from Protection; and *Refugees, Rebels and the quest for justice, 2002;* PJ van Krieken (ed) *Refugee Law in Context: The Exclusion Clause* (The Hague 1999); ECRE, Position on the Interpretation of Article 1 of the Refugee Convention (September 2000); ECRE, Position on Exclusion from Refugee Status (March 2004).

12.91 The UNHCR *Handbook* points out that in view of the serious consequences of a decision to exclude from protection Article 1F must be interpreted restrictively.[1] The same point was made by the 1996 EU Joint Position, which stressed that the exclusion clause was to be applied only in very exceptional cases after thorough and careful consideration;[2] however the EC Qualification Directive 2004/83 makes no reference to a restrictive interpretation.[3] In asylum appeals before the Special Immigration Appeals Commission, legislation requires the Commission to decide whether the exclusion clause applies first, without considering whether the appellant would otherwise qualify for protection, and if it does, to dismiss the appeal.[4] In non-SIAC cases, the Tribunal has now followed this line, reversing previous jurisprudence to decide that in cases which appear to raise a possible exclusion issue, one should first determine whether the exclusion clause applies before considering whether the person is a refugee (and that if the exclusion clause does apply there is no need to determine whether the person is a refugee other than in borderline cases).[5] Serious reasons for a belief are not the same as proof of guilt beyond doubt; it is enough that 'there is sufficient proof warranting the assumption of the (claimant's) guilt of such a crime'.[6] The low standard of proof allows in the use of secret evidence and evidence of very doubtful reliability,[7] In the UK both legislation and the authorities are all against applying any principle of proportionality (balancing the harm that the claimant may suffer if denied protection against the harm that he or she has committed) to exclusion under Article 1F.[8] Where there is a real risk of severe harm, removal is in any case prohibited by virtue of Article 3 of the EHCR.[9]

[1]   UNHCR *Handbook* above, para 149 and see UNHCR *Guidelines on International Protection: Application of the Exclusion Clauses: Article 1F* (4 September 2003) (HCR/GIP/03/05) para 2. See also the Netherlands Council of State decision of *JMS v Staatsecretaris van Justitie* (17 December 1992) (NAV 1993, 1), digested in (1995) 7(1) IJRL 129.

[2]   Joint Position of 4 March 1996, para 13; see also *Minister for Immigration and Multicultural Affairs v Singh* [2002] HCA 7 (Aust HC).

[3]   EC Qualification Directive 2004/83/EC, 12.3 fn 3 above, Art 12.

[4]   Anti-terrorism, Crime and Security Act 2001 s 33(3), (4).

[5]   *Gurung* [2002] UKIAT 04870 (starred). For the previous contrary view see *Singh* (10860) and see also *JMS v Staatsecretaris van Justitie* fn 1 above. However the Canadian Federal Court of Appeal held it was not an error for the Tribunal to apply the exclusion clause without making any explicit finding on inclusion, in *Gonzalez v Minister of Employment and Immigration* [1994] FCJ 765. See Goodwin-Gill 12.5 fn 1 above, para 4.1.2, p 97.

[6]   See *Dhayakpa v Minister for Immigration and Ethnic Affairs* (1995) 62 FCR 556 (Aus): '"Serious reasons for considering" means it is unnecessary for the state to make a positive or concluded finding about the commission of the crime or the act of the class referred to.' See also Robinson 'Convention relating to the Status of Refugees' (1953) cited in Hathaway 12.22 fn 2 above, para 6.3, p 215. But the UNHCR *Guidelines* (fn 1 above) call for 'clear and credible evidence' which should be available to the individual concerned so that it can be challenged: paras 35, 36. Contrast the approach to evidence of the Special Immigration Appeals Commission (see chapter 18): see *Singh (Mukhtiar) and Singh (Paramjit) v Secretary of State for the Home Department* (SIAC, 31 July 2000).

7   In *A v Secretary of State for the Home Department* [2004] EWCA Civ 1123, [2005]
    1 WLR 414, [2004] NJLR 1291 (on certification as suspected international terrorists), the
    Court of Appeal held that neither the Secretary of State nor SIAC could be expected to
    investigate where the evidence came from and in particular, whether the circumstances in
    which the statement was obtained involved torture. The evidence relied on before SIAC for
    exclusion on terrorism grounds is likely to be similarly tainted. The case is on appeal to the
    House of Lords.
8   Anti-terrorism, Crime and Security Act 2001, s 34; *T v Immigration Officer* [1996] AC
    742, [1996] 2 WLR 766; *Singh (Mukhtiar) and Singh (Paramjit) v Secretary of State for the
    Home Department* (SIAC, 31 July 2000); *Gurung* [2002] UKIAT 04870 (starred) and *KK
    (Turkey)* [2004] UKIAT 00101. Contrast the UNHCR *Guidelines* (fn 1 above) para 24
    which, whilst acknowledging that a proportionality analysis would 'not normally be
    required in the case of crimes against peace, crimes against humanity, and acts falling
    under Article 1F(c), as the acts covered are so heinous', considers that proportionality is
    relevant to Art 1F(b) crimes and to less serious war crimes under Art 1F(a).
9   *Chahal v United Kingdom* (1996) 23 EHRR 413. Note that the EC Qualification Directive
    2004/83/EC (12.3 fn 3 above) Art 17 contains identical exclusion clauses for subsidiary
    protection.

12.92   The Canadian courts have held that the burden of establishing that the
exclusion clause applies rests on the state denying protection in reliance on
these provisions.[1] This accords with the view that determination of whether a
person is a refugee within Article 1A of the Refugee Convention must be
carried out in every case. As we have seen, the status determination approach
is now precluded in the UK by statute in cases before the Special Immigration
Appeals Commission.[2] In other cases (such as those involving the commission
of serious non-political crimes such as drug importation), the issue of the
burden of proof has not been authoritatively resolved beyond Tribunal level in
the UK;[3] it did not arise in the case of *T v Immigration Officer* since there
were undisputed admissions of participation in activity there.[4] The case of
Ramirez also considered the extent of participation required for an applicant
to be excluded under Article 1F of the Convention. It was held that some
personal activity must be shown, whether as a leader, organiser or accomplice
participating in the planning as well as the execution of the crime; mere
membership of a group which from time to time commits international
offences is not normally sufficient for exclusion from refugee status.[5] But
where an organisation is principally directed to a limited, brutal purpose, such
as a secret police activity, mere membership may by necessity involve personal
and knowing participation in persecutory acts.[6] The Dutch Council of State
has held that Article 1F of the Convention is to be interpreted restrictively and
primarily focused on persons who had acted as agents of the state. Private
persons would only come within the scope of the Article if they had
committed flagrant human rights violations.[7]

1   *Ramirez v Minister of Employment and Immigration* (1992) FCJ 109. See also UNHCR
    Guidelines on International Protection: Application of the Exclusion Clauses: Article 1F
    (4 September 2003) (HCR/GIP/03/05) para 34.
2   See 12.91 text and fn 4 above.
3   Though the IAT has taken this same approach in *Gurung* [2002] UKIAT 04870 (starred)
    (see 12.93 below) and *KK (Turkey)* [2004] UKIAT 00101.
4   *T v Immigration Officer* [1996] AC 742, [1996] 2 WLR 766.
5   This is highly relevant in the light of the proscription of 21 organisations to which exiles
    might belong, including the LTTE and the PKK, under the provisions of the Terrorism
    Act 2000. See *Gurung*, 12.93 below. The EC Qualification Directive 2004/83/EC, 12.3 fn
    3 above states that the exclusion clauses apply to persons who 'instigate or otherwise
    participate in the commission of the crimes or acts mentioned therein'.

[6] *Ramirez and Gurung* above; see also *Nantnakumar* (11619), IAT; W97/164, AAT No 12974 [1998] AATA 618, 10 June 1998 (Aus).
[7] *JMS v Staatsecretaris van Justitie* 12.91 fn 1 above.

12.93 In *Gurung*[1] the Tribunal gave the following guidance on the proper approach to exclusion under Article 1F (which applies equally to the Tribunal as it did to adjudicators):

(1)　the exclusion clauses are to be applied restrictively,[2] with the focus on the past (rather than, as with inclusion, on the future);

(2)　Article 1F is not to be equated simply with anti-terrorism; rather findings should be made about particular crimes or acts committed by the claimant and these should then be categorised as fitting within the particular sub-categories (a), (b) and/or (c) of Article 1F; the evidential burden of proving a claimant is excluded under Article 1F is on the Secretary of State but the standard is whether there are 'serious reasons for considering' and this is lower than a balance of probabilities;

(3)　the principles in *T v Secretary of State*[3] remain valid in considering Article 1F(b); but in deciding whether a claimant's membership in an organisation amounts to complicity sufficient for Article 1F purposes, all the circumstances must be taken into account, including not only the individual's role in that organisation but also that organisation's role in its society, so that the more an organisation makes terrorist acts its *modus operandi*, the harder it will be for the individual to show that his or her voluntary membership of it does not amount to complicity;

(4)　the exclusion clauses are in mandatory terms and so, although adjudicators should not go looking for reasons to exclude, where relevant issues arise they must be dealt with by adjudicators even if they have not been raised by the Secretary of State;

(5)　it is only necessary to consider exclusion in cases involving serious criminality as defined in Article 1F(a)–(c), but once such serious criminality is identified, there is nothing wrong with an adjudicator dealing with the exclusion issue first (before the inclusion issue);

(6)　only in very obvious exclusion cases should adjudicators direct the parties to confine their submissions to this issue; in less obvious cases the adjudicator should allow evidence and submissions on both inclusion and exclusion issues;

(7)　in determinations, adjudicators should deal with obvious exclusion issues first;

(8)　if the adjudicator finds that Article 1F does not apply he or she should immediately go on to determine the normal inclusion issue under Article 1A(2);

(9)　on the other hand if the adjudicator finds that Article 1F does apply, he or she should only go on to consider the inclusion issue if the decision on exclusion is seen as problematic or finely balanced;

(10)　but where the appeal also involves human rights grounds, the adjudicator must go on to consider whether removal would violate Article 3, ECHR, notwithstanding the finding on exclusion from the Refugee Convention;

(11)　the Secretary of State however, in cases where exclusion is in issue, should always address his or her mind in refusal letters to both inclusion and exclusion issues.

1   *Gurung* [2002] UKIAT 04870 (starred), [2003] INLR 133.
2   In *KK (Turkey)* [2004] UKIAT 00101 the Tribunal pointed out that the exclusion clauses,
    being mandatory, must be applied to anyone whose conduct came within their terms, so
    that the Tribunal in *Gurung* must have meant to state that the exclusion clauses are to be
    'interpreted', rather than 'applied', restrictively (see 12.91 above).
3   *T v Immigration Officer* [1996] AC 742, [1996] 2 WLR 766.

*War crimes, crimes against humanity and crimes against the purposes and
principles of the UN*

12.94

Until recently there were almost no UK cases concerned with war crimes,
crimes against humanity[1] or crimes against the purposes and principles of the
UN.[2] In *Amberber* the Tribunal, allowing an appeal of an Ethiopian accused
of 'wars of aggression' for participation in attacks by Ethiopian organisations,
said that Article 1F(a) of the Refugee Convention only applied to waging war
across international boundaries.[3] There is extensive Canadian and Australian
case law on both sub-paragraphs. The former has been applied to exclude
former government officials who have resorted to barbaric methods against
civilians in the repression of disorder.[4] The killing of civilians in the course of
internal conflict has been held not to engage the exclusion clause,[5] but torture,
genocide, and arbitrary reprisals do.[6] It is not sufficient that the act alleged
could be a crime against humanity; it must be established that it *would* be.[7] In
Pushpanathan[8] the Canadian Supreme Court held that narcotics trafficking
was not an act 'contrary to the purposes and principles of the UN'. It reasoned
that the rationale of Article 1F was that those responsible for the persecution
which creates refugees should not enjoy the benefits of the Convention
designed to protect those refugees. The purpose of Article 1F(c) was 'to
exclude those individuals responsible for serious, sustained or systemic violations of fundamental human rights which amount to persecution in a non-war
setting'. It may be applicable to non-state actors although it may be more
difficult for non-state actors to perpetrate human rights violations on a scale
amounting to persecution without the state thereby implicitly adopting the
acts.[9] In *Singh and Singh*[10] the Special Immigration Appeals Commission
(SIAC) rejected the appellants' contentions that (1) Article 1F(c) applied only
to those holding a position of authority in a state or acting on behalf of a state
and (2) acts could only fall within Article 1F(c) if they were committed other
than for political reasons or in pursuance of a right of self-determination.[11] In
Singh and Singh[12] and *KK*[13] the Special Immigration Appeals Commission and
the Tribunal respectively held that acts of terrorism are contrary to the
purposes and principles of the UN and accordingly come within the ambit of
Article 1F(c) wherever and whenever committed.[14] They came to this conclusion by considering not only Articles 1 and 2 of the 1945 Charter of the
United Nations (which set out the purposes and principles of the UN), but
also, in the light of Article 31 of the Vienna Convention on the Law of
Treaties (which sets out general rules of interpretation of treaties), subsequent
Security Council and General Assembly resolutions that unequivocally con-
demn terrorism and terrorist acts.[15] In interpreting the ambit of these
decisions, some care is needed, first, because of the very divergent definitions
of terrorism; and, secondly, because the exclusive focus of the UN Security

Council Resolutions after 11 September 2001 has been on Al Qaeda and a long list of named organisations and individuals allegedly associated with it, rather than on Turkish Kurds fighting for self-determination or Muslims in Gujerat, India, fighting against extremist communalism, but who have nevertheless been labelled as terrorists by the EU or under Indian anti-terrorist legislation.

1   Refugee Convention, Art 1F(a).
2   Refugee Convention, Art 1F(c).
3   *Amberber* (00TH 01570) (13 June 2000, unreported), IAT. The European jurisprudence on Art 1F(a) of the Refugee Convention is set out in Jean-Yves Carlier et al (eds) *Who is a Refugee?* (1997). In *PK (Sri Lanka)* [2004] UKIAT 00089 the Tribunal held that the adjudicator had erred in law in applying Art 1F(a) to a member of the LTTE who had admitted to having killed Sri Lankan soldiers in battle; the adjudicator had mistakenly assumed that the claimant had admitted to killing injured soldiers other than in the course of the battle itself.
4   See Article by Feisman (1996) 8 IJRL 111. Goodwin-Gill 12.5 fn 1 above, pp 95–100 suggests a somewhat narrower basis for exclusion under this head relying on the *travaux* and their reference to the principles established by the London Charter of the International Military Tribunal.
5   *Polyukhovich v Commonwealth of Australia* (1991) 172 CLR 501 at 669, per Toohey J.
6   *Gonzalez v Minister of Employment and Immigration* (1994) FCJ 765.
7   *Moreno v Minister of Employment and Immigration* (1993) 159 NR 210.
8   *Pushpanathan v MCI* [1998] 1 SCR 982, [1999] INLR 36. The refugee could not be excluded under Art 1F(b) of the Refugee Convention ('serious non-political crime') because the acts were committed inside Canada after recognition.
9   *Pushpanathan* above.
10   *Singh (Mukhtiar) and Singh (Paramjit) v Secretary of State for the Home Department* (SIAC, 31 July 2000).
11   As the SIAC rightly pointed out at para 65(b), there are no such caveats expressed in Art 1F(c), as distinct from the specified requirement that the 'serious crime' be 'non-political' in Art 1F(b) (below). Thus, Art 1F(c) is highly relevant to separatist groups who use violence in pursuit of their aims.
12   Fn 10 above.
13   *KK (Turkey)* [2004] UKIAT 00101.
14   See 12.90, fn 4 above.
15   Particularly SC Resolutions 1269 (1999) and 1373 (2001); and GA Resolutions 49/60 (1994), 51/210 (1996) and 54/164 (2000). The SIAC was content to use the definition of terrorism now contained in the Terrorism Act 2000, s 1, but the Tribunal in *KK (Turkey)* pointed out that use of such a domestic definition risked offending against the principle of applying an autonomous international meaning to the provisions of the Refugee Convention (see 12.21, fn 2 above). The Tribunal stated at para 74 that the question was 'what does the United Nations mean by "terrorism"?' However, it rejected UNHCR's opinion that the acts in question were not serious enough to found exclusion under Art 1F(c), reasoning that if the UN condemned terrorism and the acts were terrorist, the acts fell within the exclusion clause – an argument rejected as facile in relation to military actions condemned by the international community so as to found refugee status in *Krotov v Secretary of State for the Home Department* [2004] EWCA Civ 69, [2004] 1 WLR 1825 (12.77 above).

Serious non-political crime

12.95 It is only serious offences that will bring this limb of the exclusion clause into operation. The UNHCR *Handbook* suggests that they will have to be capital crimes or very grave punishable acts.[1] What constitutes a 'non-political offence' has given rise to difficulty. The drafters of the Refugee Convention intended a link with the international principles of extradition, and the extradition case law is likely to be relevant.[2] The fact that violence is used in support of a political objective does not render the case outside the political offence exception.[3] In the case of *T v Immigration Officer*[4] the House of Lords had to consider the exclusion clause in relation to someone who had been an organiser of a group which had planted a bomb at a civilian airport, killing a number of innocent people. Lord Lloyd, delivering the principal judgment, held that a crime is a political crime for the purposes of Article 1F(b) of the Refugee Convention if, and only if, it is committed for a political purpose (ie with the object of overthrowing or subverting or changing the government of a state or inducing it to change its policy),[5] and there is a sufficiently close and direct link between the crime and the alleged political purpose. In determining whether such a link exists, the court will bear in mind the means used to achieve the political end, the target (whether civilian or military) and whether it involved indiscriminate killing. The House disapproved observations in the *Handbook*[6] to the effect that a balance of the acts alleged against the consequences to the applicant was any part of deciding whether the acts constituted serious non-political crimes.[7]

1 UNHCR *Handbook* 12.13 above, para 155. See also Hathaway 12.22 fn 2 above, p 224; Goodwin-Gill 12.5 fn 1 above, para 4.2.1, pp 101–108. For a consideration of the application of the sub-paragraph to drugs offences see Martin Gottwald 'Asylum claims and drug offences: the seriousness threshold of Art 1F(b) of the 1951 Convention relating to the status of refugees and the UN Drug Conventions', UNHCR, 2004.
2 Hathaway above, pp 221–222. It was drawn on extensively in *T v Immigration Officer*; see below.
3 *Handbook* above, para 152. A hijacking was held not to fall under the exclusion clause in the Dutch case of *YYA v Staatsecretaris van Justitie* (R 02880417) (8 April 1991) (Council of State). On the other hand, rioting in which buses were burned, stones thrown and stores looted was held capable doing so in the US SC case of *INS v Aguirre-Aguirre* [2000] INLR 60, on the basis that the criminal outweighed the political aspect of the offence. The decision of the Board of Immigration Appeals (BIA), which had held the acts disproportionate to the aim (protest against government failure to investigate disappearances and rise in bus fares), was approved, and the court said it was not necessary for the acts to be atrocities for them to be disproportionate and so lose their political character.
4 [1996] AC 742, [1996] 2 WLR 766.
5 Notwithstanding the 'if and *only* if' formulation of Lord Lloyd, the House in *T* did not consider or reject Lord Diplock's conclusion in *R v Governor of Pentonville Prison, ex p Cheng* [1973] AC 931 (an extradition case, see text and fn 2 above) that an offence might be political if committed to '*enable [the offender] to escape from the jurisdiction of a government of whose political policies the offender disapproved but despaired of altering so long as he was there*' (emphasis added). See also *R v Governor of Brixton Prison, ex p Kolczynski* [1955] 1 QB 540 at 550 per Lord Goddard CJ: 'The revolt of the crew was to prevent themselves being prosecuted for a political offence and in my opinion, therefore, the offence had a political character.'
6 UNHCR *Handbook* above, para 156 and see UNHCR *Guidelines on International Protection: Application of the Exclusion Clauses: Article 1F* (4 September 2003) (HCR/GIP/03/05) para 24; see also Hathaway above, p 224; *SAM v BFF* (1994) 6(4) IJRL 672 Case 215.
7 [1996] 2 All ER 865 at 882. See 12.91, fn 8 above.

12.96 The courts have not decided whether the exclusion clause can apply if the offence has been the subject of an amnesty or is no longer capable of prosecution (other than because the claimant has already been convicted and served his sentence).[1] It can only apply to conduct committed before entry to the country of asylum.[2] Conduct arising after admission to the country of asylum is considered in the next paragraph.

1   For a view that it should not see Hathaway 12.22 fn 2 above, pp 222–223; see also *JMS v Staatsecretaris van Justitie* 12.91 fn 1 above. As to 'expiation', where the individual has already been punished for his crime, UNHCR suggest that the exclusion clause should not apply; see *Guidelines on International Protection: Application of the Exclusion Clauses: Article 1F* (4 September 2003) (HCR/GIP/03/05) para 23, but theTribunal in *KK (Turkey)* [2004] UKIAT 00101 rejected the argument (at para 91). The IAT in *Gurung* [2002] UKIAT 04870 (starred) at para 76 was undecided on this issue.
2   *Pushpanathan v MCI* [1998] 1 SCR 982, [1999] INLR 36 above.

EXPULSION OF REFUGEES

12.97 Article 33 of the Refugee Convention imposes an express duty on receiving states that may result in the grant of asylum. It provides:

'1.   No Contracting State shall expel or return (*"refouler"*) a refugee in any manner whatsoever to the frontiers of territories where his life or freedom would be threatened on account of his race, religion, nationality, membership of a particular social group or political opinion.

2.   The benefit of the present provision may not, however, be claimed by a refugee whom there are reasonable grounds for regarding as a danger to the security of the country in which he is, or who, having been convicted by a final judgment of a particularly serious crime, constitutes a danger to the community of that country.'

As far as the courts in the UK are concerned, the reference to 'would be threatened' does not import a higher standard of proof than under Article 1 of the Convention.[1] This is consistent with the purpose of the Convention, which is to prevent the removal of potential refugees to the place where they fear persecution. Unless there is a prior proper determination that a person is not a refugee, he or she may be one, and so removal without determination of refugee status can only be effected to a country where there is no risk of persecution or of onward removal to the country of persecution.[2]

1   See *R v Secretary of State for the Home Department, ex p Sivakumaran* [1988] AC 958, HL where Lord Keith distinguished *INS v Cardozo-Fonseca*, 480 US 421, a US case where the different standard of proof arose from the terms of the US statute.
2   *Re Musisi* [1987] AC 514 at 526.

12.98 The only exceptions to the prohibition on *refoulement* under the Refugee Convention[1] are (i) where there are reasonable grounds for regarding the refugee as a danger to the security of the country in which he or she is,[2] or (ii) the refugee constitutes a danger to the community in that country having been convicted of a particularly serious crime. The weight of international opinion is that these are two separate requirements, ie that the conviction of a particularly serious crime is not conclusive, and whether the commission of such a crime makes the refugee a danger to the community is a question of fact. The application of Article 33(2) of the Convention is not mechanistic, and will always involve a question of proportionality, with account taken of the consequences likely to befall the refugee on return.[3] The Canadian approach is to look both to the context of the crime and to the degree of persecution faced in the home country.[4] In *A v Minister for Immigration and Multicultural Affairs*[5] the Australian Federal Court of Appeal held that the provision was concerned with the perils represented by the refugee, and thus the nature of the crime committed was not conclusive.[6] Article 33(2) applies both to recognised refugees and to asylum seekers, but while the provisions of Article 1F above are mandatory, this is discretionary.

1   But even if Art 33(2) of the Refugee Convention applies, Art 3 of the ECHR prevents removal to torture or inhuman or degrading treatment or punishment, whatever the person has done and whatever threat he or she represents: *Chahal v United Kingdom* (1996) 23 EHRR 413. Also, as the Tribunal in *SB (cessation and exclusion) Haiti* [2005] UKIAT 00036 point out, a refugee (within the meaning of Art 1 of the Convention) who has lost the benefit of non-refoulement in terms of Art 33(2), but who cannot be removed due to ECHR Art 3 considerations, remains a refugee.
2   See 12.99 below.
3   *R v Secretary of State for the Home Department, ex p Chahal* [1994] Imm AR 107 at 113; *Raziastarie v Secretary of State for the Home Department* [1995] Imm AR 459 at 464. See Goodwin-Gill at 12.5 fn 1 above, para 3.2, p 140. However in *SB (cessation and exclusion) Haiti* [2005] UKIAT 00036 at para 81, a Tribunal chaired by the then President rejected the contention that a balance must be struck under Art 33(2) between the risk to the refugee on *refoulement* and the danger which his continued presence poses to the community. This meant that that the threshold for 'a particularly serious crime' and 'danger' must be higher than if there were a balance to be struck.
4   *Re Chu and MCI* 161 DLR 4th 499, 1 June 1998.
5   [1999] FCA 227, 16 March 1999, Australian Federal Court of Appeals.
6   See also *Betkoshabeh v Minister for Immigration and Multicultural Affairs* (1998) 157 ALR 95. This appears analogous to the EC provisions on deportation, where the criminal offences committed are not conclusive of deportation: see 7.133 above.

12.99   In the UK, conviction of an offence followed by a sentence of at least two years,[1] or conviction of a specified offence,[2] (whether in the UK or abroad)[3] carries a statutory presumption[4] that the person has been convicted by final judgment of a particularly serious crime and constitutes a danger to the community of the UK.[5] The presumption that the crime is particularly serious is not rebuttable, but the presumption that the person constitutes a danger to the community is.[6] In considering whether the presumption has been rebutted, no account is to be taken of the gravity or likelihood of risk of persecution.[7] On refusing a person asylum as a refugee, the Secretary of State may issue a certificate that a presumption under this provision applies to him or her[8] and on appeal, the appellate body must begin its substantive deliberation on the appeal by considering the certificate and, if accepting that the presumption applies, having given the appellant an opportunity for rebuttal, must dismiss the appeal insofar as it relies on refugee asylum grounds.[9] It seems unlikely that the drafters of the Refugee Convention envisaged two-year sentences marking a crime as particularly serious and the offender as a danger to the community so that the protection of the Refugee Convention may be withdrawn.[10]

1   Nationality, Immigration and Asylum Act 2002, s 72(2). The reference to a sentence of imprisonment of at least two years does not include reference to suspended sentences but does include references to sentences of detention in institutions other than prisons (in particular a hospital or a young offenders institution) and does include references to sentences of detention for indeterminate periods (provided that it may last for two years): 2002 Act, s 72(11). It is important to note that the presumption only applies if the sentence actually passed is two years or more, not merely on conviction of an offence carrying such a sentence.
2   NIAA 2002, s 72(4)(a). Such an order must be made by statutory instrument and shall be subject to annulment in pursuance of a resolution of either House of Parliament: NIAA 2002, s 72(5). The offences listed in the Nationality, Immigration and Asylum Act 2002 (Specification of Particularly Serious Crimes) Order 2004, SI 2004/1910, made under the

section range from undoubtedly serious crimes of violence or related to violence including manslaughter, kidnapping, possession of firearms with intent to endanger life or injure property; rape, indecent assault, importation, production or supply of Class A or Class B drugs; terrorism related offences including directing terrorism, terrorist fundraising, terrorist weapons training or membership of a proscribed organisation; other offences such as trafficking in prostitution, to minor offences of theft, criminal damage and public order offences. The inclusion of minor offences in the list means that a refugee who shoplifts, breaks a window or is caught up in an angry demonstration could have his or her ILR revoked, a result which makes a mockery of the 1951 Convention.

3   Where a person is convicted outside the UK, the rebuttable presumption applies if the offender could have been sentenced to two years on conviction in the UK: s 72(3), or the Secretary of State certifies that in his opinion the offence is similar to an offence specified in the order: s 72(4)(b). Whether or not the use of Art 33(2) is appropriate in the case of crimes committed abroad (and Art 1F(b) applies to offences committed abroad before arrival in the country of refuge), the person cannot be removed in any event by virtue of Art 3 of the ECHR.

4   NIAA 2002, s 72 (in force since 1 April 2003: SI 2003/754). Section 72(1) states that the section applies 'for the purpose of the construction and application of Article 33(2) of the Refugee Convention (exclusion from protection)'. In *N (Kenya)* [2004] UKIAT 00009 at para 21 the IAT was in no doubt (although their view was *obiter*) that, as an interpretative provision, the section has retrospective effect and can therefore apply to a person whose conviction and sentence occurred before the provision came into force. The Tribunal recognised that there are difficulties in interpreting the provision, especially with how the presumption is to be rebutted by evidence from the claimant. In *SB (cessation and exclusion) Haiti* [2005] UKIAT 00036 a Tribunal chaired by the President, sitting with the Deputy President (who had chaired in *N (Kenya)*), concluded that s 72 can only apply to *appeals* brought under the 2002 Act itself – and therefore only in respect of immigration decisions taken on or after 1 April 2003 (though clearly an immigration decision can be taken on the basis of a conviction that pre-dates it).

5   NIAA 2002, s 72(2), (3) and (4). The presumption does not apply while an appeal against conviction or sentence is pending or could be brought in time: NIAA 2002, s 72(7).

6   NIAA 2002, s 72(6).

7   NIAA 2002, s 72(8) (by applying Anti-terrorism, Crime and Security Act 2001, s 34: see 12.91 fn 5 above). The proportionality principle referred to at 12.98 (text and fn 3) above should, however, be given effect by the Secretary of State and/or the Tribunal in deciding whether the protection of the Refugee Convention should be withdrawn.

8   NIAA 2002, s 72(9)(b). The applicant must be notified of the certification and its effects along with the notice of any immigration decision: see Immigration (Notices) Regulations 2003, SI 2003/658, reg 5(5).

9   NIAA 2002, s 72(9) and (10). If the appellate body agrees with the Secretary of State's certificate to the effect that Art 33(2) applies, it does not go on to consider whether or not the appellant is a refugee under Art 1A(2) of the Refugee Convention.

10   UNHCR expressed concern that s 72 'suggests an approach to Article 33(2) of the 1951 Convention which is at odds with the Convention's objects and purposes' (Briefing on the Nationality, Immigration and Asylum Bill, see *Butterworths Immigration Law Service* at A[2671]).

12.100 A refugee who has already been recognised and granted admission to the UK can only be expelled to a country or territory other than that in which persecution is feared,[1] in accordance with the provisions of Article 32 of the Refugee Convention. First, this means that the only legitimate grounds of expulsion are national security or public order. Secondly, except where compelling reasons of national security otherwise require, 'the refugee shall be allowed to submit evidence to clear himself, and to appeal to and be represented before competent authority'. Previous UK practice provided an appeal only where the person was lawfully in the country at the date of the decision,[2] but following *Chahal*[3] there is always an appeal before expulsion, at least where asylum or human rights issues are raised, whether to the Asylum and Immigration Tribunal under section 82 of the Nationality, Immigration and Asylum Act 2002 as amended, or by virtue of section 2 of the Special Immigration Appeals Commission Act 1997. Where a receiving country intends to remove a refugee lawfully, an opportunity should be afforded for an alternative country of refuge to be found.[4]

1   As to which see Art 33 above.
2   *NSH v Secretary of State for the Home Department* [1988] Imm AR 389, CA.
3   *Chahal v United Kingdom* (1996) 23 EHRR 413, see below.
4   Refugee Convention, Art 32(3). An attempt to expel a leading Saudi dissident, Mohammed al-Masari, to Dominica failed in March 1996 when the appellate authority held that Dominica was not safe. The attempt was notorious for the exposure of the close links between diplomatic staff and arms salesmen (sometimes the same people), and by ministers' admission that the proposed expulsion was demanded by the Saudi authorities, and that the motivation for acceding to the demand was fear that billions of pounds' worth of arms contracts would be lost by Mr al-Masari's continued presence in the UK.

National security

12.101 National security can thus ground expulsion of asylum seekers and of recognised refugees by virtue of Articles 33(2) and 32 of the Refugee Convention. But the phrase is not defined in the Convention. In *Rehman*[1] the House of Lords gave an extremely broad meaning to the phrase 'national security' in the context of a non-asylum deportation; see 15.18 below. However, the ECHR in *Chahal v United Kingdom*[2] confirmed that even where there are national security grounds to expel an asylum claimant, Article 3 of the EHCR prohibits expulsion to a territory where there is a real risk of torture. And it is to *Chahal* that the edifice of the Special Immigration Appeals Commission is owed; the Strasbourg court roundly condemned the 'advisory panel' procedure in national security expulsions as not providing the necessary safeguards to the appellant – legal representation, information about the grounds for the expulsion decision, and not sufficiently independent or open, to constitute a court or an effective remedy for a potential breach of Article 3.[3] Now, section 2 of the Special Immigration Appeals Commission Act 1997 provides an appeal against expulsion, including on asylum and human rights grounds. The special procedure adopted there means that the refugee or asylum seeker does not hear all the evidence but his or her interests are represented in closed sessions by a special advocate. The system is certainly a vast improvement on the discredited advisory procedure, but still falls far short of the minimum requirements of fair trials set out in Article 6 ECHR.[4]

1   *Secretary of State for the Home Department v Rehman* [2001] UKHL 47, [2003] 1 AC 153, [2001] 3 WLR 877.
2   (1996) 23 EHRR 413.
3   (1996) 23 EHRR 413, para 130.
4   See 8.72ff above.

CONSEQUENCES OF RECOGNITION

12.102 Where the authorities recognise someone within their territory as a Convention refugee, they must issue identity papers or a travel document to enable the refugee to travel outside the country of asylum.[1] The charge for its issue must not exceed the lowest scale of fees for national passports.[2] Refugees must be readmitted to the state which issued the document at any time during its validity.[3] The Convention requires that refugees are granted the 'most favourable treatment accorded to nationals of a foreign country' as regards trade union membership (Article 15), entry to wage-earning employment (Article 17), self-employment (Article 18) and membership of the liberal professions (Article 19). They should be given 'treatment as favourable as possible' as regards housing (Article 21) and education (Article 22) and approximately the same treatment as nationals with respect to public relief and assistance (Article 23), labour legislation and social security (Article 24).[4] Their freedom of movement within the country of asylum is guaranteed by Article 26 and any state may, at the time of signing, ratifying or acceding to the Convention, declare that it shall extend to all or any territories for the international relations of which it is responsible (Article 40).[5] The policy of the Convention is that after asylum has been given, refugees shall as far as possible be integrated into their country of asylum and to that end contracting states are urged to expedite naturalisation procedures.[6] There has been a debate in the UK appellate authorities as to whether refugee status can be backdated on an appeal against refusal of asylum being allowed.[7] But the Divisional Court has condemned the delays in the grant of status following a successful appeal, which can be severely prejudicial to refugees.[8]

[1] Refugee Convention, Art 28.
[2] Refugee Convention, Sch, para 3.
[3] Refugee Convention, Sch, para 13. Thus a Somali refugee with indefinite leave to remain who had stayed in Ethiopia for over two years caring for a sick relative was wrongly refused re-entry as a returning resident since his refugee travel document was still valid: *R v Secretary of State for the Home Department, ex p Shirreh* (CO 2194/1997) (15 August 1997, unreported), QBD (permission; the case was conceded by the Home Office).
[4] In UK practice community support, housing, education (including language learning) access to health services, social security benefits and employment are perceived as the essential elements of refugee integration: Home Office Immigration and Nationality Directorate *The Integration of Recognised Refugees in the UK* (1999). Refugees are treated as own nationals for the purpose of health care, social security and housing, and as home students for education fees and grants purposes. There are no employment restrictions on recognised refugees.
[5] Under Art 40(2) extensions can be made after the Convention is in force by notifying the Secretary-General of the UN. The UK currently extends the Convention to the Channel Islands and the Isle of Man and to the Falkland Islands, St Helena and Montserrat (though a refugee recognised in the UK will be subject to the same restrictions on travelling to and staying in the Overseas Territories as would a British citizen – see Fransman *British Nationality Law*).
[6] Refugee Convention, Art 34.
[7] The Tribunal in *Haibe* [1997] INLR 119 held that because refugee status is not granted but recognised, in an appropriate case it is open to the appellate authority to declare that the status of refugee existed at the date of the decision or other appropriate date, and a direction can be given to that effect. Another Tribunal in *Altun* (16628) 17 July 1998 disapproved *Haibe*, saying that nothing in the Immigration Act 1971 allows directions of a retrospective nature and that it is no part of the appellate authorities' function, nor does the Refugee Convention require them to determine exactly when a person became a refugee. Any direction given by the Tribunal on allowing an appeal counts as part of its determination for appeal or review purposes: Nationality, Immigration and Asylum Act 2002, s 87(4).
[8] 'It would wholly undermine the rule of law if the Secretary of State could simply ignore a ruling without appealing it, nor could he deliberately delay giving effect to it': Elias J in *R v Secretary of State for the Home Department, ex p Mersin* [2000] INLR 511, QBD. A successful appellant has a right to be granted refugee status unless or until there was a change in the position. See also *R (on the application of Saribal) v Secretary of State for the*

Home Department [2002] EWHC 1542 Admin; *R (on the application of Boafo) v Secretary of State for the Home Department* [2002] EWCA Civ 44, [2002] 1 WLR 1919, [2002] Imm AR 383.

12.103 Where a refugee has left the country of refuge and entered another territory and lived there lawfully for a period of time, the Refugee Convention envisages that the responsibility for the issue of a further travel document may become that of the second country of residence.[1] The circumstances when this might happen are uncertain; a refugee has no right to have asylum transferred to a country in which he or she has temporary residence. In order to eliminate ambiguity, Member States of the Council of Europe drew up the European Agreement on Transfer of Responsibility for Refugees[2] which provides for the transfer of responsibility after two years' continuous lawful residence other than for the purposes of study, training, medical visit, or a period of imprisonment,[3] or if the refugee has been permitted to stay beyond the validity of his or her travel document from the first state (unless the extension beyond validity was for study or training, or the refugee is still re-admissible to the first state). The Agreement does not, however, assist in cases of unlawful residence, nor does it provide any mechanism or criteria for transfer of lawful residence.[4] Current Home Office policy is to consider cases falling outside the European Agreement on a case-by-case basis, accepting responsibility only where the UK clearly is the most appropriate place of long-term refuge. Factors which will be considered include the length of time spent in the first country, the strength of ties there compared with the UK and any compelling compassionate circumstances.[5] For short-term visa-free travel, the European Agreement on the Abolition of Visas for Refugees 1959[6] enables refugees resident in a contracting state and possessing a valid travel document issued under the Refugee Convention to travel without a visa to any other contracting state[7] for visits of up to three months.[8] The UK has suspended its obligations under the Agreement, and refugees living in contracting states now need visas to enter.[9]

1   Refugee Convention, Sch, para 11.
2   16 October 1980, European Treaty Series (ETS) 107, Cmnd 8127. Currently in force for: Denmark, Finland, Germany, Italy, Netherlands, Norway, Poland, Portugal, Romania, Spain, Sweden, Switzerland and UK. (The following Council of Europe Member States have signed but not yet ratified the Agreement: Belgium, Czech Republic, Greece and Luxembourg.)
3   European Agreement on Transfer of Responsibility for Refugees 1980 above, Art 2.
4   See *Rahman* [1989] Imm AR 325 for a case where the appellate authority exercised a broad discretion on a transfer of status case. An appeal on human rights grounds would be available where an immigration decision involved a refusal to transfer status and meant continued separation from close family members.
5   API on 'transfer of refugee status', s 3.
6   20 April 1959, UNTS 85, ETS 31, reproduced in *Butterworths Immigration Law Service*, 2D[1].
7   Belgium, Czech Republic, Denmark, Finland, France, Germany, Iceland, Ireland, Italy, Liechtenstein, Luxembourg, Malta, the Netherlands, Norway, Portugal, Romania, Spain, Sweden, Switzerland and the UK. Armenia, Cyprus, Poland and Slovakia have signed but not yet ratified the Agreement.
8   See also *Shramir v Secretary of State for the Home Department* [1992] Imm AR 542, IAT.
9   France suspended its obligations under the Agreement (in accordance with Art 7) in 1986, and the UK followed suit in February 2003. See Declaration of suspension contained in a letter from the Permanent Representative of the United Kingdom, dated 7 February 2003,

registered at the Secretariat General of the Council of Europe on 7 February 2003 and with effect from 11 February 2003. For the Secretary of State's justification for suspension see *Hansard* HC 7 February 2003, Col 31WS.

Refugees in the EU

12.104 Until refugees obtain the nationality of the country of refuge, they will not be entitled to freedom of movement rights as EC nationals. Article 39 (ex Art 48) of the EC Treaty dealing with the freedom of movement of workers does not apply to refugees. Apart from the European Agreements noted above, adopted within the framework of the Council of Europe in 1959 and 1980, the only other measure designed to give refugees rights within Europe was the 1964 EEC Council of Ministers' declaration that:

> 'the entry to their territories for the purpose of engaging in a paid activity there, of refugees recognised as such within the meaning of the Convention of 1951 and established in the territory of another Member State of the community should be examined with particular favour, particularly so as to afford to such refugees within their territories the most favourable treatment possible.'

Further to this declaration, Council Regulation (EEC) 1408/71[1] provided that refugees resident in the territory of a Member State are entitled to the same social security benefits as nationals of that state, a measure which did no more than Europeanise Article 24 of the Refugee Convention.

[1]   Article 2(3).

12.105 From the mid-1980s EU Member States' asylum policy was restricted to trying to stop 'irregular movements' – in practice, all movement of refugees into EU territory, by treating asylum seekers as essentially a policing problem. The early products of the work of the Ad Hoc Working Group in this field are described in the last edition of this work at 12.103. After 1993, when the Treaty on European Union institutionalised the inter-governmental character of immigration and asylum issues (apart from visa policy) in the Third Pillar of the Treaty, there was an attempt to harmonise criteria, procedures,[1] reception conditions[2] and refugees' rights[3] within the EU. The non-binding Joint Position of March 1996[4] was the main fruit of this process. It was the first attempt to reconcile the varying interpretations of the Convention by the Member States. Although welcomed in *Robinson*,[5] the Joint Position was dismissed in *Adan*[6] as no more than a political agreement which was not particularly useful.

[1]   See eg Resolution on minimum guarantees for asylum seekers and refugees, 21 June 1995, OJ 1996 C 274, 19 September 1996.
[2]   Draft Joint Action on the minimum conditions for the reception of asylum seekers, 17 August 1995, ASIM 223.
[3]   Draft Council Act adopting a common action on certain aspects on the status of refugees recognised by the Member States of the EU, 6784/95.
[4]   Joint Position of 4 March 1996 defined by the Council on the basis of Art K3 of the Treaty on European Union on the harmonised application of the term 'refugee' of Art 1 of the Convention relating to the status of refugees (Geneva, 28 July 1951), 96/196/JHA, reproduced in *Butterworths Immigration Law Service*, 2D[138].
[5]   *Robinson v Secretary of State for the Home Department* [1997] Imm AR 568.

6   On the issue of agents of persecution: *R v Secretary of State for the Home Department,
    ex p Adan* [1999] Imm AR 521, [1999] INLR 362, CA. See also Lord Steyn [2001] INLR
    44 at 57, HL.

12.106 In 1997 the Treaty of Amsterdam[1] brought immigration and asylum
policy as a whole being taken into Community competence. Title IV inserts
visas, asylum, immigration and other policies related to free movement of
persons into the EC Treaty. It contains the provisions previously dealt with
under Articles K1 to K3 and K6 of the Treaty on European Union. In
accordance with the Treaty of Amsterdam, the European Commission has
over the last five years drawn up proposals for new Regulations and Directives
for approval by the Council of Ministers (thereby giving them legislative
effect). So far, the Council of Ministers has approved a Directive on Family
Reunion;[2] a Directive laying down minimum standards for the reception of
asylum seekers;[3] a Directive on temporary protection,[4] and one setting out the
minimum standards for the qualification and status of third country nationals
and stateless persons as refugees or as persons who otherwise need international protection (the 'Qualification Directive');[5] two Regulations on Eurodac, the European fingerprint data and exchange system,[6] and a Council
Regulation 'establishing the criteria and mechanisms for determining the
Member State responsible for examining an asylum application lodged in one
of the Member States by a third-country national'.[7] Then there is the
Amended Proposal for a Council Directive on minimum standards on procedures in Member States for granting and withdrawing refugee status' (the
Procedures Directive).[8] This proposal in particular exemplifies the 'lowest
common denominator' approach to refugee protection in the EU.[9]

1   Signed on 2 October 1997 by 15 Member States.
2   Council Directive 2003/86/EC of 22 September 2003. The UK and Ireland and Denmark
    however have opted out.
3   Council Directive 2003/9/EC of 27 January 2003. Ireland and Denmark have opted out
    The UK government has amended the immigration rules to take account of this Directive,
    particularly the right of asylum seekers whose claim has not been dealt with to request
    permission to seek employment after a year: see HC 395, paras 357–361, making up
    Part 11B (as inserted by HC 194 from 4 February 2005).
4   Council Directive 2001/55 (OJ 2001 L212/12). See 12.173 below.
5   Council Directive 2004/83/EC on minimum standards for the qualification and status of
    third country nationals and stateless persons as refugees or persons who otherwise need
    international protection (30.9.04 OJ L304/12), which came into force on 20.10.04 and
    must be implemented by Member States in national measures by October 2006. Our view
    is that, while the Directive does not have direct effect under Community law until the
    expiry of the time for transposition into national law, it will then have direct effect, since
    the minimum standards it sets out are sufficiently precise; for direct effect see 7.43 above.
    Meanwhile, it is of persuasive value.
6   Council Regulation 2725/2000 (OJ 2000 L 316/1); Council Regulation 407/2002 imple-
    menting the Eurodac Regulation (OJ 2002 L 62/1).
7   Council Regulation (EC) No 343/2003 of 18 February 2003, the 'Dublin II Regulation'
    replacing the Dublin Convention. Denmark however has opted out (Regulation preamble,
    para 18) and accordingly the Dublin Convention will remain in force and will continue to
    apply as between Denmark and the other Member States (Regulation preamble, para 19).
    See also Commission Regulation (EC) No 1560/2003 of 2 September 2003 laying down
    detailed rules for the application of the 'Dublin II Regulation' and see further 12.150ff.
8   COM (2000) 578, 20 Sep. 2000; OJ 2001 C 62 E/231); amended proposal (COM (2002)
    326, 18 June 2002; OJ 2002 C 291 E/143), the subject of political agreement by the JHA
    Council on 21 April 2004.

[9] The proposed Procedure Directive has been strongly criticised as failing to give effect to minimum standards of protection by inter alia Amnesty International, etc see Statewatch *European Monitor (Semdoc) Leglislative Observatory* at www.statewatch.org for commentaries.

12.107 EU nationals are not prevented from applying for asylum in another Member State,[1] but their claims must be assessed against the presumption contained in the 1997 Protocol to the EC Treaty[2] that 'given the level of protection of fundamental rights and freedoms, Member States shall be regarded as constituting safe countries of origin in respect of each other for all legal and practical purposes in relation to asylum matters'. Applications may be considered or declared admissible only if the applicant's Member State has taken measures derogating from the ECHR, or the Council determines that the Member State in question is in serious and persistent breach of principles of liberty, democracy, respect for human rights and fundamental freedoms,[3] or if the procedure for such a determination has been initiated. If a Member State unilaterally decides to consider an asylum claim and none of these conditions apply, the Council must be immediately informed, and the application will be dealt with as manifestly unfounded. In accordance with the Treaty and Act providing for their accession to membership of the EU,[4] the 10 states (Cyprus, Czech Republic, Estonia, Hungary, Latvia, Lithuania, Malta, Poland, Slovakia and Slovenia) that joined the EU on 1 May 2004 became parties to the EU and EC Treaties.[5] The presumption in Protocol 29 therefore applies to asylum claims made by nationals of the accessions states and in practice, in the UK, such asylum claims will be refused and certified as 'clearly unfounded'.[6]

[1] However, Art 2 of the EU Procedures Directive (Amended Proposal for a Council Directive on Minimum Standards on Procedures in Member States for Granting and Withdrawing Refugee Status, 8415/04) approved in principle by the Justice and Home Affairs Council in April 2004 defines an asylum application in a way which excludes EU citizens. See also HC 395, para 357 (as inserted by HC 194 from 4 February 2005) which declares that Part 11B of the immigration rules, dealing with 'reception conditions for non-EU asylum applicants' (see 12.106, fn 3 above) only applies to asylum applicants who are not nationals of a Member State.

[2] Protocol 29 on asylum for nationals of Member States of the European Union, added by the Treaty of Amsterdam in 1997.

[3] Treaty on European Union, Arts 6 and 7 (ex F and F.1).

[4] See OJ L 236 of 23 September 2003. The Treaty was signed on 16 April 2003 and entered into force on 1 May 2004. The Act also came into force, in accordance with the Treaty, on 1 May 2004.

[5] See chapter 7 above.

[6] Currently under the Immigration (European Economic Area) Regulations 2000, SI 2000/2326, reg 33(1B)–(1D) (inserted by SI 2003/3188, substituted by SI 2004/1236 from 1 May 2004.

UK PRACTICE ON ASYLUM

The application

12.108 An asylum application is defined as a claim that it would be contrary to the UK's obligations under the Refugee Convention for the person to be removed from or required to leave the UK.[1] The asylum application will be determined in accordance with the UK's obligations under the Convention and will be granted if the applicant is in the UK or has arrived at a port of entry in the UK, is a Convention refugee, and refusing his or her application would result (whether immediately or after the expiry of leave) in *refoulement* contrary to the Convention.[2] In all other cases the application will be refused.[3] A spouse or minor child accompanying a principal applicant may be included in his application for asylum as a dependant,[4] or may make an asylum claim in his or her own right, which will be considered individually, and which should be made as soon as possible. If the principal applicant is granted asylum and leave to enter or remain, any spouse or minor child will be granted leave to enter or remain for the same duration.[5]

1   Asylum and Immigration Appeals Act 1993, s 1; HC 395, para 327.
2   HC 395, paras 328, 334.
3   HC 395, para 336.
4   The Amended Proposal for a Council Directive on minimum standards on procedures in Member States for granting and withdrawing refugee status COM (2000) 578, 20 Sep 2000; OJ 2001 C 62 E/231); amended proposal (COM (2002) 326, 18 June 2002; OJ 2002 C 291 E/143) (awaiting Parliamentary approval at time of writing), requires Member States to ensure that each dependent adult has consented to being included in the claim of the principal, and is aware of the right to make his or her own claim.
5   HC 395, para 349.

Applications at the port

12.109   A person arriving at a port of entry who intends to seek asylum will normally ask for it from an immigration officer on arrival. No particular form of words is required, and if a person expresses unwillingness to return to their country of nationality or habitual residence because they believe they would be in danger, it should be assumed that they are making an asylum application.[1] Arrangements whereby passengers without visas are prevented from leaving the aircraft and making a claim to an immigration officer are contrary to the UK's obligations under the Refugee Convention,[2] although the operation of pre-entry immigration controls by UK immigration officers abroad which prevent passengers embarking for the United Kingdom has been held not to violate the UK's obligations under the Refugee Convention.[3] Facilities at the port of entry must include an interpreter so that an applicant can make a claim. In the rare case where an entry clearance has been granted in order for a claim for asylum to be made, the immigration officer may grant leave to enter.[4] In all other cases, the claim will be referred to the Immigration and Nationality Directorate (IND) of the Home Office for determination.[5] Current practice in port cases is to conduct screening immediately (this will include taking identity details, fingerprinting[6] and, if the applicant is potentially returnable to a safe third country, questioning about the route of travel and any periods of stay in third countries).[7] The EC Reception Directive requires third-country and stateless asylum claimants to be given information and documentation reflecting their status and their right to remain in the country pending determination of their claim, and these requirements are reflected in the immigration rules.[8]

1   See API Handling Claims, s 1.2 (emphasising also that 'not all applicants know about the UN Convention so might not use the words "asylum" or "refugee" '). See also *R v Uxbridge Magistrates' Court, ex p Adimi* [1999] INLR 490 at 499, 506, and Art 2 of the proposed EC Procedures Directive (12.108 fn 4 above).

2   A number of cases of such practices came to light in 1990; judicial review proceedings were settled after the grant of permission. Similarly, cases have come to light of stowaways being removed without being able to make contact with an immigration officer. The proposed EC Procedures Directive (fn 1) contains no explicit obligation on Member States to ensure that asylum seekers arriving at the frontier are afforded an opportunity to lodge an asylum application, but such an obligation is implicit.

3   *European Roma Rights Centre v Immigration Officer at Prague Airport* [2004] UKHL 55, [2005] 2 WLR 1. See 12.9 above.

4   See 12.115 below.

5   HC 395, para 328.

6   Immigration and Asylum Act 1999 s 141 gives power to fingerprint asylum seekers: s 141(7)(e); their dependants: s 141(7)(f) and 141(14); and anyone else without a valid passport or a reasonable excuse: s 141(7)(a), (10). Home Office policy is to fingerprint all asylum seekers and their dependants who are over five: see Screening Best Practice for Operational Staff, Version 21.8.03. Children must be fingerprinted in the presence of a responsible adult: API 'Fingerprinting'. The High Court has held that a policy of fingerprinting unaccompanied children whose identity is in doubt is lawful: *R v Secretary of State for the Home Department, ex p Tabed* [1994] Imm AR 468. See 14.19 below.

7   The purpose of screening is to establish the claimant's identity and nationality, route to the UK, and previous travel history. There are four levels of screening. Screening may be concluded at level 1 if the claimed nationality, identity and route is supported by the documentation produced and there are no third country or Dublin convention considerations. Level 2 is used where the claimant holds no genuine travel document or there are doubts about the claimed nationality or identity. Level 3 provides an opportunity to challenge credibility if appropriate. Level 4 screening is used where it is considered that an immigration or criminal offence may have occurred, and is conducted by PACE-trained officers. Spouses are screened to the same level as the principal appellant. Minors under ten should not be interviewed. See Screening Best Practice for Operational Staff, Version 21.8.03.

8   EC Directive 2003/9 on reception conditions for asylum seekers (OJ 2003 L31/18); see HC 395, Part 11B (paras 357–361), inserted by HC 194, in effect from 4 February 2005, requiring the Secretary of State to provide information about the asylum procedure within 15 days of the claim, and a document indicating the asylum claimant's status within three days if possible.

12.110 After screening there are different procedures depending on the nationality of the applicant:[1]

(i)   single male applicants[2] from countries deemed safe by the Home Office[3] and considered to have straightforward claims may be sent to Harmondsworth or another Removal Centre and subjected to super 'fast-track' procedures (with induction on the day of arrival, a full asylum interview the next day, a decision the day after and an appeal within three days).[4] A challenge to the inherent unfairness of these procedures was dismissed by the Administrative Court in *R (on the application of the Refugee Legal Centre) v Secretary of State for the Home Department*.[5] Whilst Collins J recognised the real concerns of those working under the scheme that it had the potential for unfairness and that anything faster would be impossible to justify, he was satisfied that the scheme was flexible enough to cater for individual difficulties, and was not unlawful. The Court of Appeal upheld the decision, but told the Home Office it must formulate a policy setting out the criteria for departing from the three-day timetable, to ensure that the timetable was in truth 'guidance and not a straitjacket';[6]

(ii) asylum claimants from countries or territories deemed safe (principally those whose claims are presumptively clearly unfounded under section 94 of the Nationality, Immigration and Asylum Act 2002 and thus attract no in-country appeal)[7] may be detained at Oakington Reception Centre, where decisions were originally taken within seven to ten days, but since September 2004 have been subject to a 'target' time of between 10 and 14 days.[8] The Oakington detention regime was upheld as lawful by the House of Lords in *R (on the application of Saadi) v Secretary of State for the Home Department*,[9] and the procedures for deciding a claim 'clearly unfounded' were upheld as fair in *L*.[10]

(iii)   others may be sent to an induction centre,[11] or may simply be given a Statement of Evidence form to complete and return within 10 working days.[12] On return of the form, if asylum is not granted an interview will be fixed for five days ahead, and a decision will be taken immediately after that.

[1]   Procedures are subject to fairly regular change, as the IND frequently devises and runs pilot schemes.

[2]   The description of applicants going into the fast-track procedure as 'single males' did not preclude the use of the procedure to process those with family ties in the UK, although as a matter of policy, those with family members dependent on the claim would not be so processed: *R (on the application of Kpandang) v Secretary of State for the Home Department* [2004] EWHC 2130 (Admin), [2004] All ER (D) 555 (Jul). However, accommodation for asylum claimants must have regard to family unity, and to the special needs of vulnerable people: see the Asylum Seekers (Reception Conditions) Regulations 2005, SI 2005/7, made to comply with the EC Reception Directive 2003/9/EC (12.109 fn 8 above). Note Home Office plans for a fast track for women asylum claimants, who would be held at Yarls Wood: ILPA March 2005.

[3]   Discrimination by immigration officers in exercising immigration functions on the basis of nationality is exempted from the reach of the Race Relations Act 1976: see s 19D, inserted by Race Relations Amendment Act 2000. The countries or part countries appearing on the fast-track suitability list in November 2003 were: Afghanistan, Albania, Bangladesh, Benin, Bolivia, Botswana, Brazil, Bulgaria, Burkina Faso, Cameroon, Canada, Central African Republic, Chad, China, Congo, Djibouti, Ecuador, Equatorial Guinea, Gabon, Gambia, Ghana, Guinea-Bissau, Iraq, Ivory Coast, India, Jamaica, Kenya, Macedonia, Malaysia, Malawi, Mali, Mauritania, Mauritius, Moldova, Mongolia, Mozambique, Namibia, Niger, Pakistan, Romania, St Lucia, Serbia and Montenegro, Senegal, Somaliland, South Africa, Sri Lanka, Swaziland, Tanzania, Togo, Trinidad and Tobago, Turkey, Uganda, Zambia, Zimbabwe and the ten accession states (Cyprus, Czech Republic, Estonia, Hungary, Latvia, Lithuania, Malta, Poland, Slovakia, Slovenia). They are suitable for fast-tracking at Harmondsworth if single males (but see fn 2 above), or if not, at Oakington. Since the Harmondsworth procedure always carries an in-country appeal, nationals of countries listed in s 94 Nationality, Immigration and Asylum Act 2002 as amended are not sent there but to Oakington: see fn 7 below.

[4]   See Asylum and Immigration Tribunal (Fast Track Procedure) Rules 2005, SI 2005/560. The list of removal centres to which claimants assigned to the fast track may be sent is at Sch 2.

[5]   [2004] EWHC 684 (Admin), [2004] All ER (D) 580 (Mar).

[6]   [2004] EWCA Civ 1481, [2004] All ER (D) 201 (Nov).

[7]   Section 94 of the Nationality, Immigration and Asylum Act 2002 introduced a new certification regime in respect of the ten EU accession states, to which list the Asylum (Designated States) Order 2003, SI 2003/970, added Albania, Bulgaria; Serbia and Montenegro, Jamaica, Macedonia, Moldova and Romania (in respect of claims made on or after 1 April 2003) and the Asylum (Designated States) (No 2) Order 2003, SI 2003/1919, added Bangladesh (whose inclusion was however held unlawful in *R (on the application of Husain) (Zakir) v Secretary of State for the Home Department* [2005] EWHC 189 (Admin), Bolivia, Brazil, Ecuador, Sri Lanka, South Africa and Ukraine (in respect of claims made on or after 1 July 2003). The original ten states were removed from the list by the Asylum and Immigration (Treatment of Claimants, etc) Act 2004 s 47 and Sch 4, from 1 October 2004, after their accession to the EU on 1 May 2004. The section requires the Secretary of State to certify an asylum claim made by a person entitled to reside in such a state 'unless satisfied that it is not clearly unfounded'. On certification, the claimant cannot appeal in-country prior to removal: s 94(2). See further below 12.161.

8   See 'Fast track asylum and detention policy', Parliamentary Written answer of Desmond
    Browne MP, Minister for Citizenship and Immigration (16 September 2004, Column
    157WS). The announcement of a revised timescale followed the successful challenge to the
    detention at Oakington of an ailing 64-year-old detainee for five and a half weeks: see *R
    (Johnson) v SSHD* [2004] EWHC 1550 (Admin).
9   [2002] UKHL 41, [2002] 4 All ER 785, [2002] 1 WLR 3131.
10 *R (on the application of L) v Secretary of State for the Home Department* [2003] EWCA
    Civ 25, [2003] Imm AR 330, [2003] INLR 224.
11 See Nationality, Immigration and Asylum Act 2002, s 70. Screening, fingerprinting etc take
    place there. Once again, the aim is to speed up the asylum process. The North West Project
    (NWP) (effective since 6 December 2004) is an example of a new case management process
    which aims to deal with asylum applications made by claimants accommodated by NASS
    in 'induction service accommodation' within 17 working days.
12 The deadline is impossibly tight given that most asylum seekers who are not detained are
    dispersed all over the country for asylum support, with inadequate infrastructure of legal,
    linguistic or medical expertise to assist in completing the Statement of Evidence forms. The
    Home Office has refused to allow more time, however (although immigration officers have
    a discretion to extend time), and is adamant that the forms can be completed without legal
    assistance. They must be completed in full and in English, and returned with translations of
    all evidence relied on. See further API 'Non-compliance' and 12.127 below.

12.111 Port asylum claimants will either be detained[1] or granted temporary
admission[2] pending consideration of the claim. Temporary admission is given
by immigration officers at ports to allow applicants physically to enter the UK
while their application is being dealt with.[3] The Home Office guidelines on
detention[4] stress that this is used only where there is no alternative and there
are good grounds for believing that the person will not keep in touch
voluntarily. However, in *R (on the application of Saadi) v Secretary of State
for the Home Department*,[5] detention for seven to ten days of persons not
likely to abscond in order to determine their claims was upheld as lawful by
the House of Lords. For those not facing detention at such facilities, factors,
which will be considered when deciding whether or not to detain, include
whether there is a sponsor, satisfactory evidence of identity and past immigration history, and whether detention is available.[6] The 1994 instructions said
that the case for detaining an asylum seeker immediately on the claim being
made must be particularly strong;[7] the 2000 API went further, suggesting that
port applicants would only be detained if they were identified as illegal
entrants.[8] Detained persons have a right to apply to the Asylum and
Immigration Tribunal for bail if seven days have elapsed since arrival and no
decision has been taken.[9] For detailed consideration of detention, see chapter
17 below.

1   The power to detain is generally exercisable by immigration officers pursuant to Immigra-
    tion Act 1971, Sch 2, para 16, although the Secretary of State has wide detention powers
    pursuant to s 62 Nationality, Immigration and Asylum Act 2002 since 10 February 2003
    (SI 2003/1). To comply with Art 5 of the ECHR (right to liberty) the power must not be
    exercised arbitrarily and may only be exercised 'to prevent unauthorised entry into the
    country' or 'pending deportation', with rigorous judicial scrutiny: *Amuur v France* (1996)
    22 EHRR 533. But see *R (on the application of Saadi) v Secretary of State for the Home
    Department* below. See further Blake 'The international principles governing detention of
    asylum seekers' in Blake and Fransman (eds) *A guide to the Human Rights Act 1998*
    (1999); see chapter 17 below.
2   The power to grant temporary admission as an alternative to detention is governed by
    Immigration Act 1971, Sch 2, para 21.
3   Immigration Act 1971, s 11. This fiction means that a person can be refused 'leave to
    enter' after living in the UK for years, something which, in the context of EC law, was not
    acceptable: see *R (on the application of Yiadom) v Secretary of State for the Home
    Department* Case C-357/98 [2001] All ER (EC) 267, ECJ; see further 7.147 above.

4   API 'Handling claims', para 4.1 'Use of detention'. These coexist with the Immigration Service Instructions on Detention of 3 December 1991 and 20 September 1994 (reproduced in *Butterworths Immigration Law Service*, D[971]); see chapter 17 below.
5   [2002] UKHL 41, [2002] 4 All ER 785, [2002] 1 WLR 3131. The average time for processing Oakington claims has risen to 12–13 days: see HL EU Committee, 11th report 2003–4, 'Handling EU asylum claims: new approaches examined' (HL 74, Apr 04), Appendix 4; acknowledged by a new 'target time' of 10–14 days, see 12.110 fn 8 above.
6   API 'Handling claims' (fn 4 above).
7   Immigration Service Instruction on Detention 1994 above, para 2. See the UNHCR Guidelines on applicable criteria and standards relating to the detention of asylum seekers, 1995, reproduced in *Butterworths Immigration Law Service*, 2C[261]. Concern has been expressed by inter alia UNHCR, Amnesty International and the UN Committee Against Torture on the detention of asylum seekers, particularly children and torture victims. A number of children have been held in detention for over 100 days: see *Hansard* HL 27.4.04, col 711.
8   API Aug 00, Ch 1 s 1(4), now withdrawn.
9   Immigration Act 1971, Sch 2, para 22(1), (1A) amended by Asylum and Immigration (Treatment of Claimants, etc) Act 2004, Sch 2, para 1(2) from 4 April 2005 (SI 2005/565). Part III of the Immigration and Asylum Act 1999 (ss 44, 46) contained provisions for automatic bail hearings and a presumption in favour of bail, but these provisons were not implemented and were repealed by Sch 9 to the NIAA 2002.

12.112   The NIAA 2002 envisages that those not detained at Harmondsworth (or one of the other fast-track processing centres) or at Oakington will be required to attend at an induction centre, where they will be given an application registration card which may be used to access services provided for them as asylum seekers.[1] The Act sees the induction centres as part of a total system of control of asylum seekers, whose other elements were accommodation centres (see chapter 13), reporting centres to which asylum seekers will report regularly, and removal centres, to which they may be taken for removal at the end of the process, if not there throughout the process.[2] Temporary admission may be made subject to residence[3] and reporting[4] conditions, including two weeks in an induction centre.[5] Those granted temporary admission will be referred to the National Asylum Support Service (NASS) for assistance if they appear destitute. Home Office policy enabling asylum seekers to work if their claim remained outstanding for more than six months[6] was abolished in July 2002, in the belief that it encouraged economic migrants to come to the UK as asylum seekers.[7] The prohibition on employment was considered in *R(Q)*.[8] Pursuant to the provisions of the EC Reception Directive,[9] asylum claimants who are not EEA nationals may apply to work if the application is outstanding for more than a year.[10] Asylum claimants may not work without an application registration card (ARC) endorsed with permission to work[11] (unless they are accession state nationals, in which case they may work but must register their employment within a specified period).[12] Voluntary activity is permitted.[13]

1   Nationality, Immigration and Asylum Act 2002, s 70. For the application registration card (ARC) see 12.114 below. Proposals for induction centres at Saltdean (Brighton) and Sittingbourne have been dropped because of local opposition. One opened in Dover in January 2003. The North West Project has been operational since 6 December 2004: see 12.110 fn 11 above.
2   See Nationality, Immigration and Asylum Act 2002, Part 2 (accommodation centres), ss 69–71 (reporting and residence restrictions), 66 (removal centres). The Asylum and Immigration (Treatment of Claimants, etc) Act 2004 introduces electronic monitoring of those with residence restrictions: s 36 (in force 1 October 2004: SI 2004/2523, but no regulations have been made under the section, without which electronic monitoring remains unlawful).

3 Immigration Act 1971, Sch 2, para 21(2), (2B)ff; Asylum Support Regulations 2000, SI 2000/704. Asylum seekers may be prohibited from living in certain areas, as well as being directed to stay in particular accommodation. See further chapter 13 below.

4 Immigration Act 1971, Sch 2, para 21(2).

5 Nationality, Immigration and Asylum Act 2002, s 70 (fn 1 above).

6 The policy is set out in the decision of the Court of Appeal in *R v Secretary of State for the Home Department, ex p Jammeh* [1998] INLR 701 at 713H–714A.

7 The policy was abolished on 23 July 2002.

8 *R (on the application of Q) v Secretary of State for the Home Department* [2003] EWCA Civ 364, [2004] QB 36, [2003] All ER 905. Considering whether denial of support under s 55 of the 2002 Act constituted 'treatment' for Art 3 ECHR, the court held at para 57: 'The imposition by the legislature of a regime which prohibits asylum seekers from working and further prohibits the grant to them, when they are destitute, of support amounts to positive action directed against asylum seekers and not to mere inaction'.

9 Council Directive 2003/9 on minimum standards for the reception of asylum seekers, OJ 2003 L 31/18, Art 11.

10 HC 395, para 360, inserted by HC 194 from 4 February 2005.

11 API 'Application Registration Card' para 4.3.

12 Accession (Immigration and Worker Registration) Order 2004, SI 2004/1219.

13 Meals, travel and other costs may be reimbursed: API 'Guidance on undertaking voluntary activity', Feb 04.

Applications made in-country

12.113 Asylum applications may be made by applying for variation of a leave already granted (as a visitor or a student), or on apprehension as an illegal entrant,[1] or by someone facing removal for overstaying or breach of conditions. An in-country application must be made in person at a place designated by the Secretary of State.[2] In-country claims are screened at an ASU, sometimes immediately when the application is submitted.[3] Then, if the claimant is not detained for fast-track determination at Harmondsworth or Oakington,[4] he or she will be given a Statement of Evidence form to complete and return within ten working days.[5] Applicants are normally interviewed before a decision is taken on their application (unless it is refused on non-compliance grounds or unless there is already enough information on file to warrant a grant of refugee status).[6] There was previously no power to detain someone with leave to enter who applied for asylum, but since February 2003, the Secretary of State can impose restrictions on such asylum seekers as if they were on temporary admission, and can detain them for failure to comply with any such restrictions.[7] Moreover, an asylum claim made shortly after entry as a visitor or a student may result in an interview under caution and a decision to treat the applicant as an illegal entrant, who may be detained.[8] The previous provision for curtailment of leave on refusal of an asylum claim has been dropped.[9] The power to detain illegal entrants and those facing removal as overstayers or deportation is not affected by the making of an asylum claim which precludes immediate removal,[10] but must not be exercised capriciously, unreasonably or contrary to policy.[11] Since 1996 there has been a right to apply for bail pending removal.[12]

1 Those apprehended as illegal entrants at ports are generally treated as in-country applicants.

2 Under the Nationality, Immigration and Asylum Act 2002, this is not a requirement so much as part of the definition of an asylum seeker for different purposes: see s 18(1)(c) (accommodation centres), s 44(2) (amending definition in Immigration and Asylum Act 1999 s 94 (asylum support), 70(3) (induction centres), s 113(1) (appeals). No places

have yet been designated by statutory instrument, but the API provide that claims may be submitted in person at an Asylum Screening Unit (ASU) in Croydon, Liverpool or Birmingham or at a Public Enquiry Office (PEO) in Belfast or Glasgow): see API 'Handling Claims' para 2.1. Serious problems have arisen through the IND's refusal to register claims in local immigration offices in eg Manchester, East Midlands, Southampton, Bristol, Plymouth and at local police stations: see Statement from *Refugee Action*, 8.4.03 (ILPA). Home Office policy is to accept, register and screen claims other than those made in the ASU or PEOs from vulnerable asylum seekers such as unaccompanied children, visibly pregnant women, families with children and disabled or those with mental health difficulties. Claims from immigration offenders, those encountered on immigration raids or at the side of a road may be registered but not screened. Others who turn up at Immigration Service offices are directed to the nearest ASU, but basic details are taken for the decision on support: see Statement from Lynne Spiers, Asst Director UK Border Control Operations, 18.9.03.

3   This involves fingerprinting, giving details for the Application Registration Card, and perhaps being interviewed to establish why the claim was not made earlier, to decide whether support should be withheld, see Ch 13: see In-Country Screening: Best Practice for Operational Staff, Version 21.8.03.

4   See 12.110 above. Of those detained at Harmondsworth, 42% are in-country claimants (although many may have arrived as illegal entrants): see *R (on the application of the Refugee Legal Centre) v Secretary of State for the Home Department* [2004] EWHC 684 (Admin), [2004] All ER (D) 580 (Mar), para 3, per Collins J.

5   See 12.110 fn 10 above.

6   See API 'Handling Claims' at para 2.2.

7   By Nationality, Immigration and Asylum Act 2002, s 71 (in force on 10 February 2003: SI 2003/1).

8   Immigration Act 1971, Sch 2, para 16. Note the power to detain on suspicion of illegal entry in para 16(2). During the interview of known or suspected illegal entrants, questions will be asked to ascertain whether deception was used: API 'Illegal entrants'. There is nothing unfair about the same immigration officer conducting both an illegal entry interview and an asylum interview: *R v Secretary of State for the Home Department, ex p Range* [1991] Imm AR 505, QBD; see also *Odishu (Yousuf) v Secretary of State for the Home Department* [1994] Imm AR 475, CA. But in the Scottish case of *Kim v Secretary of State for the Home Department* 2000 SLT 249, OHCS, an asylum interview which turned into an illegal entry interview without a caution being administered was held inadmissible to prove illegal entry.

9   Asylum and Immigration Appeals Act 1993, s 7. The power remains to curtail leave by variation (Immigration Act 1971 s 3(3)(a)) where an asylum claim is inconsistent with the purpose for which leave was granted: see HC 395, para 323. See API, 'Curtailment of leave'.

10 *R v Secretary of State for the Home Department, ex p Khan* [1995] Imm AR 348, [1995] NLJR 216, CA.

11 *Vilvaraja (Nadarajah) v Secretary of State for the Home Department* (1987) Times, 31 October, [1990] Imm AR 457; see also *R v Governor of Haslar Prison, ex p Egbe* (1991) Times, 4 June. For current detention policy see *R (on the application of I) v Secretary of State for the Home Department* [2002] EWCA Civ 888, [2003] INLR 196, [2002] All ER (D) 243; *R (on the application of Amirthanathan) v Secretary of State for the Home Department* [2003] EWCA Civ 1768, [2004] INLR 139, at 8.61 above.

12 Immigration Act 1971, Sch 2, para 22(1)(b), as amended by Asylum and Immigration Act 1996, Sch 2, para 11.

Application registration card

12.114 The EC Reception Directive requires asylum claimants and their dependants (except for those in detention) to be issued within three working days with a document showing their status and identity.[1] Asylum claimants (except for EU nationals),[2] whether port or in-country, and their dependants,[3] are now issued with an application registration card (ARC), an electronic card which carries their personal details,[4] and is used to identify asylum-seekers, for access support, to prove entitlement to work (where applicable) and to facilitate reporting.[5] An ARC is issued after screening, from specified ports and reporting centres.[6] Detained asylum seekers are not issued with an ARC unless they are released.[7] The 2002 Act has created eight new criminal offences connected with forgery or possession of false regisration cards.[8]

[1] Council Directive 2003/9/EC of 27 January 2003 (12.109 fn 8 above), in force February 2005.
[2] API 'Application registration card', para 3.1. The ARC replaces the Standard Acknowledgement Letter (SAL). A SAL may still be used to acknowledge a claim for asylum where it is not possible to issue an ARC within three days of the claim being lodged, although any SAL issued will normally be valid for just two months from date of issue to enable arrangements to be made for the claimant and any dependants to be issued an ARC: see API 'Standard Acknowledgement Letters'.
[3] All dependants have their own ARCs, even children under five. Since they cannot be fingerprinted, their ARC is endorsed 'CUF' (in this context, 'child under five'): API para 3.3.2.
[4] The ARC fields are set out in Annex A to the API 'Application registration card'. Five fields are 'reserved' for unspecified information.
[5] See Immigration Act 1971, s 26A (inserted by Nationality, Immigration and Asylum Act 2002, s 148); API 'Application registration card' para 2.1, 4. The API suggest that the ARC will be the only approved means of proving entitlement to support. Production of the ARC may also be a formal requirement for reporting, and from 1 May 2004 the ARC endorsed with permission to work must be shown to prospective employers.
[6] API 'Application registration card para 3.1. The places of issue are set out in Annex 3 and include Dover East and Dover SEPST, Gatwick, Stansted, Heathrow (Terminals 1–4), Croydon (Lunar House), Liverpool (Reliance House), Oakington and the reporting centres at Croydon (Electric House), Glasgow, Leeds, Manchester, North Shields, Solihull and Folkestone.
[7] API ibid para 3.2.
[8] See Immigration Act 1971, s 26A(3), as inserted by NIAA 2002, s 148 and see 14.64 below.

Special cases

12.115 We have referred above to the possibility of making a claim for asylum abroad in exceptional circumstances,[1] and the criteria for the grant of entry clearance as a refugee. A recently introduced scheme is the quota refugee resettlement programme operated by IND with UNHCR.[2] The annual quota for admission under the scheme is set annually by ministers having considered the resources available, the need for resettlement globally, and the impact on local services in the UK.[3] In addition, mandate refugees (ie refugees recognised by UNHCR abroad) may be referred by the British Red Cross on nomination for resettlement by UNHCR.[4] Such cases attract priority, and should be granted if the UK is the most appropriate country of refuge. Applicants are required to demonstrate close ties with the UK, usually through close family, but sometimes through historical connections with the UK.[5] Another scheme run by the British Red Cross is the 'ten or more plan', established by UNHCR for the resettlement of disabled refugees in need of medical attention. Under it, host countries accept ten or more disabled refugees and their families annually. Again, refugee status has already been granted and entry for settlement should be granted if the severity of the disability and the applicant's circumstances in the present country of refuge warrant it, and if the UK is the most appropriate country of resettlement.[6] Applications for transfer of refugee status have been considered above.[7] Applications made in the UK from persons currently exempt from control (eg diplomats or consular staff) are dealt with as special cases,[8] as are claims by EU nationals.[9]

1   At 12.37 above.
2   The quota resettlement scheme puts into practice the government's belief that refugee processing should take place abroad rather than after arrival. Its proposal for regional protection zones, to be established in refugee-producing regions, were widely condemned as an attempt to withdraw from its obligations under the Refugee Convention. See HL, EU Committee, 11th report 2003–4, 'Handling EU asylum claims: new approaches examined (HL 74), April 2004. Applicants for resettlement under the programme have already been recognised as refugees by UNHCR.
3   No more than 500 people were to be resettled for the financial year 2003/04. See API 'Quota Refugee Resettlement Programme'. Government policy is to extend this scheme; see *Controlling our borders: Making migration work for Britain: Five year strategy for asylum and immigration*, Cm 6472, Feb 2005.
4   API 'Mandate Refugees'. In addition there is a policy in relation to stateless Palestinian refugees assisted by UNWRA under Art 1D of the Refugee Convention, who have family ties in the UK: see API 'UNWRA assisted Palestinians: Article 1D of the Refugee Convention'.
5   API 'Applications from abroad' and 'Mandate Refugees'.
6   API 'Ten or More Plan'.
7   See 12.103 above.
8   API 'Exempt Persons'.
9   Claims from EU nationals may be entertained, but will be presumed clearly unfounded: see API 'Claims from EU Nationals'; and 12.106 above.

Children

12.116 There are special provisions[1] for dealing with claims by children, both accompanied and unaccompanied.[2] A child is defined as a person who is under 18 or who, in the absence of documentary evidence, appears to be under that age.[3] An unaccompanied asylum seeking child is a person under 18 applying for asylum in his or her own right, who has no adult relative or guardian to turn to in this country.[4] When an unaccompanied child comes to the attention of immigration officers at the port or at the asylum unit at the Home Office, or where a child becomes unaccompanied during the asylum process (by being abandoned or taken into care, for example) Home Office staff are required to notify the Refugee Council's non-statutory Panel of Advisers,[5] whose members act as a 'friend' to the child in his or her dealings with the Home Office and other central and local government agencies. It is also IND's responsibility to ensure that all unaccompanied children who apply for asylum who are not already in the care of Social Services are referred to the responsible Social Services Department as soon as they have made their claim.[6] Where there are disputes over age, the Panel will be informed without prejudice, even if the application is proceeded with as for an adult.[7] Applications from children (accompanied or not) receive priority at all stages.[8] It will rarely be acceptable to hold an application from an unaccompanied child with no action on it for longer than six months.[9] Accompanied or unaccompanied children may be interviewed about the substance of their asylum claim or to determine their age and identity,[10] but children under ten years of age will not be interviewed.[11] Interviews must be conducted in the presence of an appropriate adult,[12] and the rules provide that interviewers must be sensitive to distress or tiredness, and if necessary stop the interview.[13] Particular care is needed in assessing the evidence of minors, and a more liberal interpretation of the benefit of the doubt is called for.[14] In assessing an application from a child (whether accompanied or not) more weight should be given to objective indications of risk than to the child's state of mind. An asylum application from or on behalf of a child should not be refused solely because the child is too young to understand his or her situation or to have formed a fear of persecution.[15] No unaccompanied child will be removed from the UK unless adequate reception and care arrangements are in place in the country to which he or she is to be removed.[16] In practice unaccompanied children are generally granted discretionary leave for periods up to their 18th birthday.[17] They are not generally subject to the non-suspensive appeal procedures, although they are not in principle excluded from them.[18]

[1] The API relating to children are being revised. Readers should refer to the current API and, in their absence, see 'Unaccompanied asylum seeking children: Home Office information note,' July 2002, which describes the Home Office's (then) policy in relation to asylum seeking children. See also 'Screening Best Practice for Operational Staff (at Ports)' (Version 210803) produced by the UK Immigration Service OASIS (Asylum Team) and 'Unaccompanied Minors Best Practice' (Version 010104), also produced by the UK Immigration Service OASIS (asylum team). For best practice as regards children see Heaven Crawley and others *Working with children and young people subject to immigration control – guidelines for best practice*, ILPA November 2004. See further chapter 11.

[2] HC 395, paras 349, 350–352; Unaccompanied Minors Best Practice, reflecting the concerns expressed in the UNHCR *Handbook* 12.13 above, paras 213–219.

[3] HC 395, para 349; API 'Dependants' para 3. For assessment of age see 12.117 below.

[4] Unaccompanied asylum seeking children (fn 1 above), para 1.

[5] API Aug 00, Ch 2, s 5, para 3.9. Ministers agreed to fund this panel on a non-statutory basis during the passage of the Asylum and Immigration Appeals Act 1993, to reflect the guidance in para 214 of the UNHCR Handbook.

[6] Unaccompanied asylum seeking children (fn 1 above), para 3. Unaccompanied children are referred to the Social Services Department covering the area of the address the child gives.

[7] API Aug 00, Ch 2, s 5, para 3.9 (no longer current: see fn 1 above).

[8] HC 395, para 350.

[9] API Aug 00, Ch 2, s 5, para 3.9 (no longer current).

[10] HC 395, para 352, as amended by Cm 5597 (27 August 2002). Previously, the rules leant against interviewing children unless it was imossible to obtain sufficient information to determine the claim from other sources; in *Orman* [1998] Imm AR 224 the Tribunal doubted the wisdom of this approach and suggested that a preferable course would be to allow the child to be interviewed with the Panel adviser.

[11] Screening Best practice (fn 1 above) para 4 (Unaccompanied Asylum Seeking Children).

[12] Not an immigration officer, a police officer or a Home Office civil servant: HC 395, para 352. There should be no adverse reliance on interviews conducted in the absence of a responsible adult, either in assessing the claim or on appeal: *Ehalaivan* (00TH01749) (3 August 2000, unreported), IAT; *Omotayo* (00TH00854) (12 April 2000, unreported), IAT.

[13] HC 395, para 352. The rules require close attention to be paid to the welfare of the child at all times: ibid para 351.

[14] UNHCR *Handbook* 12.13 above, para 219; *Jakitay* (12658) (15 November 1995, unreported), IAT.

[15] HC 395, para 351.

[16] *Re Sujon Miah* (CO 3391/1994) (6 December 1994, unreported); API Aug 00, Ch 2, s 5, para 3.5 (not current, see fn 1 above). See also the recommendation given by the Tribunal in *Afrifa* (18392) (24 March 2000, unreported), that before removal of the appellant whose asylum appeal it had rejected, International Social Services, International Red Cross and the British High Commission be asked to report on reception and care arrangements.

[17] See 12.175 below. This policy has now changed, and the IND is piloting return programmes with minors: see 11.121 above.

[18] API 'Application of non-suspensive appeals (NSA) process to asylum seeking children', which provides for unaccompanied children to be granted discretionary leave for 12 months or three years (depending on their country of origin), or until their 18th birthday (if sooner), where adequate reception arrangements cannot be established and there is no family to return to.

12.117 The determination of age is controversial. In principle the burden is on the applicant to demonstrate that he or she is a minor, but in practice it would normally be appropriate to give the applicant the benefit of the doubt unless his or her physical appearance strongly suggests that he or she is over 18.[1] The issue of age determination was thoroughly explored in *R (on the application of B) v Merton London Borough Council*,[2] where Stanley Burnton J noted that in the light of the five-year margin of error described by paediatricians, objectively verifiable determination of age for those between 16 and 20 was impossible.[3] He considered local authorities' guidelines for age assessment[4] and concluded that in general, in order to assess age it was important to elicit a history from the applicant, including family circumstances, education, activities and ethnic and cultural information. If the history is accepted as true and is consistent with an age below 18, the applicant will be accepted as a child, while an untrue history is not necessarily indicative of lies about age but would be relevant.[5] He held that the burden of proof was not helpful.[6] Reasons would always be required for a decision that an applicant was not a child, because of the consequences.[7]

[1] See 'Screening Best Practice for Operational Staff (at Ports)' (Version 210803) (12.116 fn 1 above), section 5, Age Dispute Cases: 'If ... there is any doubt over the applicant's age the applicant must be given the benefit of the doubt and treated as a minor'. The 'Unaccompanied Minors Best Practice' (Version 010104) (12.116 fn 1) states that where appearance strongly suggests the person to be over 18, Home Office policy is 'to treat the applicant as an adult unless there is credible documentary evidence to demonstrate the age claimed'. This policy 'must be applied robustly' (para 1.1). Stanley Burnton in *R (on the application of B) v Merton London Borough Council* [2003] EWHC 1689 (Admin), [2003] 4 All ER 280 held that except in clear cases, age could not be determined solely on the basis of appearance (para 37). See also 11.118 above.

[2] *R (on the application of B) v Merton London Borough Council* (fn 1 above), at paras 22, 28. See also *R (on the application of T) v Enfield London Borough Council* [2004] EWHC 2297 (Admin), in which the local authority's age assessment was held woefully defective, based as it was largely on the applicant's demeanour and appearance during an 'unfair and unduly hostile' interview.

[3] This case, and the evidence cited in it, should sound the death-knell for purely anthropometric assessments of age. There has been widespread concern over the reliability of such assessments, although in some cases it might still be appropriate as a purely voluntary matter, ancillary to the other methods of investigation. X-rays were held 'inappropriate' for use in age determination for immigration purposes only in July 1998 ADI (Ch 2, s 5, para 3.13); previously, 'bone-age testing' by X-ray was sometimes conducted at the behest of the immigration authorities in the context of family reunion applications from the Indian sub-continent.

[4] The issue has become relevant for local authorities since they have duties under the Children Act 1989 to under-18s, but not to adults (except those leaving care). See 13.118 below.

[5] *R (on the application of B) v Merton London Borough Council* (fn 1 above), at para 28.

[6] *R (on the application of B) v Merton London Borough Council* (fn 1 above) at para 38.

[7] *R (on the application of B) v Merton London Borough Council* (fn 1 above) at paras 45 et seq. The consequences vis-à-vis the Home Office might be the grant or withholding of discretionary leave; vis-à-vis the local authority, the grant or withholding of accommodation and support.

12.118 Any unaccompanied child who claims asylum must be referred either to the social services department for the area in which he or she lives or, if he or she has no address or local connection, to the department covering the area where the asylum claim was made.[1] The IND must also pass the child's details to the Refugee Council's Panel of Advisers within 24 hours of the claim being lodged, even if they are disputing that the person is a minor.[2] Despite what is said in the Government's White Paper *Every Child Matters*,[3] the Panel of Advisers is usually able to do no more than provide the child with the name and address of an immigration solicitor with an LSC contract and a referral to his or her local social services department. In addition, as the White Paper acknowledges, the Panel can only provide support to a minority of unaccompanied asylum seeking children.[4] This means that many unaccompanied minors are having to fend for themselves in relation to both the determination of their asylum or immigration application and their access to support. UNHCR has recommended that each country which has ratified the Refugee Convention should establish an independent and formally accredited organisation which would provide each unaccompanied child with a guardian, who would ensure that the interests of the child were safeguarded at each stage of the process and that his or her legal, social, medical and psychological needs are appropriately met during the refugee status determination process and until a durable solution for the child has been found and implemented.[5] There is a presumption that unaccompanied children will be accommodated by their local authority under section 20 of the Children Act 1989,[6] which has led to unaccompanied asylum seeking children making up approximately 6 per cent of all children looked after nationally by local authorities, many in London and the south east.[7]

[1] ADI Unaccompanied Asylum Seeking Children Information Note, para 3.
[2] UK Immigration Service Best Practice: Unaccompanied Children Version 01.01.04, para 2.1. The Panel is funded by the Home Office to give initial advice to unaccompanied asylum seeking children but has no statutory status and neither central or local government is obliged to follow its recommendations.
[3] *Every Child Matters* CM 5860 September 2003, para 2.53.
[4] In 2002/2003, of 6,404 such children referred to the Panel only 1,500 were allocated a named adviser: statistics from the Refugee Council 2003.
[5] UNHCR *Guidelines on Policies and Procedures in dealing with Unaccompanied Children Seeking Asylum* para 5.7. It also recommends that 'as an unaccompanied asylum seeking child is not legally independent they should be represented by an adult who is familiar with his or her background and whose role it is to protect his or her interests': para 8.3. This is in addition to being provided with a qualified legal representative.
[6] UK Immigration Service Best Practice: Unaccompanied Minors Version 01.01.04, para 12.2.
[7] In November 2002, there were 4,872 unaccompanied asylum seeking children being supported by London local authorities. This fell to 4,266 by November 2003: Report to Leaders' Committee of the Association of London Government, 10.02.2004. Due to pressure on resources a number of the unaccompanied children being initially accommodated by authorities in London and the south east of England were then being placed outside these areas on an ad-hoc basis, many hundreds of miles from the social workers who were supposed to be responsible for them.

12.119 The Immigration Rules HC 395, state that particular priority and care should be given to the determination of asylum applications from children.[1] When immigration service staff become aware of the presence of an unaccompanied minor or someone who may be an unaccompanied minor, they should be given immediate attention wherever possible.[2] If the child appears unwell, distressed or if the Immigration Officer has any concerns about the child's welfare, immediate medial assistance should be sought.[3] Currently each port has a nominated officer who is responsible for dealing with matters relating to unaccompanied children and ports are being encouraged to establish their own dedicated minors teams.[4] The IND has also admitted that it owes a duty of care to unaccompanied children who it is examining.[5] However, alongside the objective of minimising the welfare risks to unaccompanied minors seeking entry to the United Kingdom, there is the declared goal of assisting the development of robust controls on the travel to the United Kingdom of unaccompanied minors.[6] The proposed measures to achieve this objective include increasing sponsor checks and testing the credibility of unaccompanied children. It is in this context that all children over five years of age are fingerprinted.[7] Following a rule change in 2002, children can now also be interviewed about the substance of their claim and in order to determine their age or identity.[8] Minors arriving in the UK without a parent or guardian, who express a fear of return to their country of origin, are deemed to have made an asylum application as unaccompanied minors and if they are ten or over will be given a screening interview.[9] Where an unaccompanied child claims asylum (whether in person, through a representative or a sponsor or by post), he or she will be deemed to be a vulnerable person and will not be expected to travel to an Asylum Screening Unit for his or her screening interview if there is an enforcement office which is closer.[10] However, the child will have to attend either the local enforcement office or an Asylum Screening Unit to progress his or her claim. A child who is under ten will not usually be screened but the Immigration Service will attempt to obtain as much information as possible through a question and answer session.[11] Older minors will be screened to the appropriate level[12] and immigration officers can use their discretion and test the evidence if they feel that credibility is in question.[13] A training programme has been implemented to ensure that each port has a number of officers specially trained in interviewing children.[14]

1 HC 395, para 350.
2 UK Immigration Service *Best Practice: Unaccompanied Children* Version 01.01.04, para 10.1.
3 UK Immigration Service *Best Practice: Unaccompanied Children* Version 01.01.04, para 10.2.
4 UK Immigration Service *Best Practice: Unaccompanied Children* Version 01.01.04, para 11.6.
5 UK Immigration Service *Best Practice: Unaccompanied Children* Version 01.01.04, para 5.1.
6 UK Immigration Service *Best Practice: Unaccompanied Children* Version 01.01.04 – objectives.
7 UK Immigration Service *Best Practice: Unaccompanied Minors* Version 01.01.04, para 2.2.
8 Immigration Rules HC 395, para 352. In practice, they are also interviewed about their status and their mode of travel and route to the UK.
9 UK Immigration Service *Best Practice: Screening (Enforcement)*, Version 21.08.03, para 17.
10 UK Immigration Service *Best Practice: Screening (Enforcement)* Version 01.01.04, para 8.4.
11 UK Immigration Service *Best Practice: Screening (Enforcement)* Version 01.01.04, para 17.
12 There are four possible levels of screening and Level 4 is used when an immigration or criminal offence may have been committed.
13 UK Immigration Service OASIS (asylum team) *Best Practice: Screening (Enforcement)* Version 01.01.04, para 17.

[14] UK Immigration Service *Best Practice: Unaccompanied Children* Version 01.01.04, para 7.2 (IND plans to train about 10% of operational staff at bigger ports and at least 4% at smaller ones). See also 11.119 above.

12.120 Minors are issued with a Children's SEF (Statement of Evidence Form) for self-completion and return within a month. If the questionnaire is not completed, the child's application for asylum will be refused on non-compliance grounds.[1] The Children's SEF is almost identical to that used for adult asylum seekers, apart from the fact that the questions are usually split into a series of subsections. No mention is made on the form of child-specific forms of persecution.[2] The introduction of substantive asylum interviews for children was to address concerns that children should be allowed to make their claims in person, in their own words, and to combat alleged abuse of the asylum system by children and those claiming to be children.[3] A pilot project was undertaken in 2003,[4] which was inconclusive, but raised concerns about the ability of the Immigration and Nationality Directorate to meets its two-month deadline for initial decisions on asylum applications if children were interviewed, given the delay caused by the need to have a responsible adult at the interview. A futher pilot project is planned, and in practice unaccompanied minors are not generally being interviewed.[5] The Rules[6] state that when an interview is necessary it should be conducted in the presence of a parent, guardian, representative or another adult who for the time being takes responsibility for the child and is not an immigration officer, an officer of the Secretary of State or a police officer. The Statement of Evidence Form UASC SEF (Interview) states that a responsible adult can only intervene in the interview if it is clear that the child is becoming distressed or tired and a break is required. The rules also require the interviewer to have particular regard to the possibility that a child will feel inhibited or alarmed and state that the child should be allowed to express himself in his own way and at his own speed. It is not clear from the present policy, what action will be permitted within the interview process itself if these requirements of paragraph 352 are not complied with. As with the screening interview form, little or nothing has been done to make SEF interviews child friendly and transparent and comprehensible to the majority of children. The failure to do so, together with the difficulties faced by children in providing the consistent and coherent account of past persecution required by the Home Office and the Tribunal, raises the concern that interviews of children will result in many of them being returned to countries where they do have a well founded fear of persecution. Children who are from countries from which asylum claims can be certified as being 'clearly unfounded' are not given the right to an in-country appeal against any decision to refuse to grant them asylum. It is arguable that this breaches the United Kingdom's obligations under the Refugee Convention.[7]

[1] Immigration Rules HC 395, para 340 and APU Notice 2/2003 Application of Non Suspensive Appeal (NSA) Process to Asylum Seeking Children.
[2] It was designed by the IND's Asylum Processes and Procedures Unit in consultation with operational and policy colleagues and Home Office legal advisers and the IND later defended its decision not to simplify concepts such as 'membership of a social group' or 'cash subsistence' for the benefit of the children involved (Letter to ILPA, 22 December 2003, para 3).
[3] Letter to ILPA, 22 December 2003.

4 Between 6 October and 19 December 2003, 120 children, from the ages of 12 to 17 were interviewed from a variety of countries. A further 13 children failed to attend their interviews and three were refused on non-compliance grounds and were therefore not interviewed about the substance of their application. Evaluation of the NSA UASC Interview Pilot Asylum Casework Directorate, August 2004 (unpublished), sent to ILPA 13 January 2005).
5 IND planned to have trained 600 Immigration Service staff to interview children by March 2005 and did not intend to video or tape record these interviews: IND to ILPA 22 December 2003.
6 HC 395, para 352.
7 UNHCR Guidelines on Policies and Procedures in dealing with Unaccompanied Children Seeking Asylum, para 8.5.

Investigation of asylum claims

12.121 As a result of the particular difficulties experienced by those fleeing persecution, and the likely lack of documentary evidence in support of claims, the UNHCR *Handbook*[1] indicates that the duty to ascertain and evaluate all the relevant facts is shared between the applicant and the examiner. The applicant should tell the truth and assist the examiner to the full in establishing the facts of his or her case, make an effort to support his or her statements by any available evidence, give a satisfactory explanation for any lack of evidence, and if necessary make an effort to procure additional evidence. He or she should supply as much detail as is necessary about him- or herself and should answer any questions put. The examiner should ensure that the applicant presents his or her case as fully as possible, with all available evidence; assess his or her credibility and evaluate the evidence, if necessary giving the applicant the benefit of the doubt, in order to establish the objective and subjective elements of the claim, and relate the elements to the relevant criteria of the Refugee Convention to arrive at a correct conclusion on the applicant's refugee status.[2] This guidance would suggest that all asylum claimants should be interviewed. However, whilst substantive interviews are conducted for most asylum applications,[3] the Secretary of State is not obliged to interview a claimant for asylum; the duty is to inform himself sufficiently of the nature of the claim and the facts underlying it to enable the claim to be properly considered it on its merits.[4]

1 12.13 above, paras 195–205.
2 UNHCR *Handbook* above, Summary, para 205.
3 The API, ' Interviewing', state that interviewing may not be necessary where an applicant obviously falls to be granted refugee status, but indicate that caseworkers should always seek to interview before refusing an asylum application substantively (except where asylum seekers have failed to comply with directions regarding reporting or returning Statement of Evidence forms; for non-compliance cases: see 12.130 below).
4 See *R (on the application of Zaier) v Immigration Appeal Tribunal* [2003] EWCA Civ 937, [2003] All ER (D) 153 (Jul) at para 6, where Auld LJ held that if the Secretary of State reasonably considers that he can do that without an interview, 'he can dispense with it and rely, for example, on the claimant's response to a questionnaire or written statement and/or other relevant information'. The proposed EC Procedures Directive (12.108 fn 4 above), provides that adverse decisions may be taken without interview in a number of situations, including where the deciding authority considers the application unfounded because it is inconsistent, unlikely or implausible (Art 10(2)(b), (c)) – exactly the situations where an interview is essential.

12.122 The White Paper of July 1998[1] contained an undertaking to reduce the time taken on determination of asylum claims to a total of six months: two months for the initial determination and four months for the appeal. The commitment to reduce the time taken to determine asylum claims has been given even greater prominence in recent years by the fast-tracking of claims at both the Oakington Reception Centre and the Harmondswoth Removal Centre. Previous delays of several years were unjust; they denied refugees the prompt determination of status which they deserved, and created difficulties for those who were ultimately found not to need international protection. But the implementation of the commitment to reduce delays has caused its own problems. The conditions under which asylum determination is now carried out in the UK – in particular, the pernicious combination of an overly ambitious and over-rigid timetable for determining claims and the dispersal or detention of asylum seekers (neither of which is conducive to clarity of recollection or articulation) – make compliance with the duties set out in the *Handbook* extremely difficult, if not impossible, for both the applicant and the examiner. As we have seen above, in many port cases applicants are detained and interviewed within a day or two of arrival,[2] and have no effective opportunity to submit evidence in support of the claim.[3] Many other applicants are sent hundreds of miles to areas where legal, medical, social and linguistic support is scarce and living conditions squalid, and are given 14 days to complete evidence forms in full and in English, obtain all relevant documents and get them translated. The time limit will not be extended except in the rarest of cases.[4] Illness (evidenced by medical certificate) or a postal strike would constitute good reason for extension, but not the illness or absence of a representative or solicitor, since the view of the Home Office remains that applicants do not need legal assistance in filling the form.[5]

---

[1]   *Fairer, faster and firmer: a modern approach to immigration and asylum.*
[2]   A wealth of evidence has been presented to the Home Office showing how exhaustion, fear, linguistic difficulties, confusion and unfamiliarity all combine to render on-arrival interviews less than comprehensive or reliable: see 12.164 below. The Home Office does not generally conduct a substantive asylum interview on the day of arrival, but overnight detention compounds the difficulties. The UNHCR *Handbook* 12.13 above, para 198 points out that non-disclosure at a first interview should not be held against the asylum seeker; see further below. Sedley LJ in *R (on the application of the Refugee Legal Centre) v Secretary of State for the Home Department* [2004] EWCA Civ 1481, [2004] All ER (D) 201 (Nov) said that, whether or not an asylum claimant was entitled to an appeal, a fair initial hearing and decision must be provided. The question had to be: 'Does the system provide a fair opportunity for the asylum seeker to put his case?' and held that the three-day timetable at Harmondsworth, while not inherently unfair, had to be used as 'guidance, not a straitjacket'.
[3]   Fast-track claimants at Oakington are given two working days to submit post-interview representations. Harmondsworth claimants, those who have been through an induction centre, or issued with a SEF form before the interview was arranged, are given no post-interview period to submit further evidence, in the absence of exceptional circumstances such as awaiting a Medical Foundation report: see API 'Interviewing' para 6.6. Where such a period is given, it is normally limited to five days, with requests for further time frequently rejected on the grounds that the further evidence 'can be produced on appeal'. The API 'Medical Foundation', para 2.1 require written confirmation from the Medical Foundation that it has agreed to provide a report, before an extension of time can be given. See *R (on the application of the Refugee Legal Centre) v Secretary of State for the Home Department* above.
[4]   See fn 3 above and 12.130 below.

5 This attitude extends to legal assistance at interviews: see API 'Interviewing', para 3: 'We do not consider that it is necessary for an asylum applicant to be legally represented at the asylum interview, as it is a non-adversarial fact-finding exercise.' See below.

12.123 The Immigration Rules are silent on the procedural safeguards to be adopted during investigation, with the exception of specific provision for unaccompanied children.[1] Despite the absence of particular rules for adults, it is recognised that the procedures must be fair: there must be an opportunity for contact with the UNHCR or voluntary advice agencies such as the Refugee Legal Centre; there must be competent interpreters skilled in the applicant's language.[2] But the practice of interviewing on or shortly after arrival cuts across the principle that applicants may have access to a lawyer throughout the asylum procedures.[3] Legal assistance at the asylum interview has been recommended by UNHCR[4] and its importance recognised by (inter alia) the Lord Chancellor's Department and the Legal Services Commission.[5] There is no right to legal representation at interview, but the immigration officer's discretion to admit or exclude a legal representative must be exercised properly.[6] Morover, the importance of a representative at the asylum interview was recognised in *Dirshe*, to ensure the requisite standards of fairness by providing 'a real, practical safeguard against faulty interpreting or inadequate or inaccurate record keeping'.[7] But the Home Office view that lawyers are unnecessary has prevailed, and from 1 April 2004, public funding is generally not available for attending an interview conducted on behalf of the Secretary of State with a view to his reaching a decision on a claim for asylum.[8] Limited exceptions are made in the cases of unaccompanied minors; applicants going through fast-track initial decision processes and those suffering from a recognised and verifiable mental incapacity making it impractical to undergo an interview without support.[9] When funding was available for attendance, Pitchford J had held in *Mapah* that it was not procedurally unfair for the Secretary of State to refuse to allow representatives to tape record interviews.[10] But the Court of Appeal held in *Dirshe* that the absence of a legal representative from the interview, because of the withdrawal of funding for attendance, meant that tape recording of interviews provided the only safeguard for claimants.[11] The Asylum Policy Instructions contain a protocol governing the conduct of substantive interviews and the roles of interviewing officers, representatives and their interpreters.[12] The interviewer has a duty to elicit details of the claim, to enable the applicant to do justice to it.[13] Representatives (if present) are required to be almost entirely passive during the interview: they may not answer questions on behalf of the applicant and must wait until the end of the interview to comment (unless to draw attention to problems with the standard of interpretation or to request clarification of a question or comment by the interviewing officer.[14] A representative considered to be seriously disrupting the course of the interview may be excluded from an interview. If the claimant brings his or her own interpreter to the interview, he or she may comment only at the end of the interview (except where necessary to point out any serious discrepancy in translation, or to point out that a party may not have understood something, particularly alerting the parties to a possible missed cultural inference).[15] Previous Asylum Directorate Instructions emphasised the importance of agreeing the transcript of the interview with the applicant at the end of the interview,[16] which is clearly desirable in the interests of fairness and accuracy; in June 2000 however the Home Office announced the end of the 'read-over' procedure[17] except in cases involving illiterate or traumatised applicants, where the immigration officer retains a discretion.[18] The extent to which a failure to mention aspects of the claim at an initial screening interview should be allowed adversely to affect credibility remains controversial.[19]

1   As to which see 12.116ff above.
2   The API 'Interviewing' state that Home Office staff should not interview in a foreign language without departmental qualification and express authorisation (para 4). See Annex A: Protocol for conduct of interview including role of interpreter. The proposed EC Procedure Directive (12.108 fn 4) states that interviews need not be in the preferred language of the claimant if he or she can communicate in another language (Art 9).
3   The philosophy of the Home Office is that lawyers are not needed by asylum seekers at interviews. However, the API 'Interviewing' emphasise that the presence of a representative should not be objected to without specific reason and prior reference to a senior caseworker (para 3), and state that 'irrespective of the wishes of the applicant, the ACD should not seek to conduct a substantive interview straight after a Screening Interview where the applicant has engaged the services of a representative who is not present (para 6).
4   'The presence of a legal representative or other counsel who is familiar with the refugee criteria, local jurisprudence and the applicant's claim is helpful not only to the applicant but also to the interviewer': UNHCR Guidelines 1995, para 15.
5   ACLEC *Improving the quality of immigration advice and representation: A report* (1998), para 2.23. See also ILPA *Breaking down the barriers: a report on the conduct of asylum interviews at ports* (1999).
6   *R v Secretary of State for the Home Department, ex p Lawson* [1994] Imm AR 58.
7   *R (on the application of Dirshe) v Secretary of State for the Home Department* [2005] EWCA Civ 421, a judgment which is very important for its recognition of the difficulties faced by unrepresented applicants at interview.
8   Community Legal Service (Scope) Regulations 2004, SI 2004/1055, made under s 6(7) of the Access to Justice Act 1999 and amending Sch 2 to the Act. For the government's justification see Lord Filkin *Hansard* HL 31.3.04 Col 1411. There was vehement oppositon to these proposals in the House of Lords, see eg HL EU Committee 11th report 2003–4, HL 74, para 111: 'undue restrictions on legal aid and access to qualified legal representation are likely to lead to unfairness and more poor decisions'. See also to similar effect Second Report of the Constitutional Affairs Committee, 2003/4, on Asylum and Immigration Appeals, HC 211–1, February 2004. It remains to be seen whether the reforms prove to be a false economy; the absence of the fundamental safeguards of legal advisers and the opportunity to read back and correct the record of interview increases the likelihood of serious disputes arising about the accuracy of asylum interviews. But see text and fn 11 below.
9   See Lord Filkin, *Hansard* above; the exception is not reflected in legislation.
10   *Mapah v Secretary of State for the Home Department* [2003] EWHC 306 Admin, [2003] Imm AR 395.
11   The decision gives unrepresented applicants the right to have their asylum interview tape-recorded. A protocol and guidance (not available at time of writing) are expected to be put in place. Further funding arrangements are being discussed at time of writing (between the LSC, ILPA and others) to give representatives time to listen to and transcribe tapes.
12   API 'Interviewing' Annex A, which became binding on representatives from 1 January 2003. Representatives must carry and show identification and must be prepared at all times to carry and show confirmation of their authorisation to provide immigration advice or services. They may not make use of, or refer to any documents during the course of the interview, except for those disclosed to IND in support of the application.
13   *R v Secretary of State for the Home Department, ex p Akdogan* [1995] Imm AR 176, QBD (although see *R (on the application of Zaier) v Immigration Appeal Tribunal* [2003] EWCA Civ 937, [2003] All ER (D) 153 (Jul) at 12.118 above).
14   API 'Interviewing' Annex A.
15   API 'Interviewing' Annex A. See *R v Secretary of State for the Home Department, ex p Bostanci* [1999] Imm AR 411 on unfair exclusion of an interpreter.

16 ADI Jul/98, Ch 16, s 3, para 6.4, Annex A, para 4: 'The readback is an essential part of the interview.'

17 IND letter, 23 June 2000, stating that the SEF form lessens the scope for omissions and misunderstandings at interview, while in non-SEF cases the applicant has five days after interview to make representations. See now API 'Interviewing' para 6.4. A copy of the interview record should be handed to the applicant. The Tribunal in *Bilbil v Secretary of State for the Home Department* (01TH1603) (referred to by Pitchford J in *Mapah*, fn 10 above) described the change of policy as a regrettable step and one which failed implicitly to protect the interests of the interviewee and the interviewer.

18 API 'Interviewing' para 6.4. It will usually be appropriate to offer a readover where an applicant is visibly upset having recounted a torture claim: ibid.

19 In *Salim* (13202) and *Simsek* (13202) the Tribunal held that great care was needed in weighing discrepancies between the first, unsigned interview, at which 'basic details only' were sought, and the full asylum interview. See also *Mayisokele* (13039); *Vimaleswaran* (15493); *Jeevaponkalan* (17742). But failure to mention a central feature of the claim may affect credibility: *R v Secretary of State for the Home Department, ex p Agbonmenio* [1996] Imm AR 69. In *R (on the application of the Refugee Legal Centre) v Secretary of State for the Home Department* [2004] EWCA Civ 1481, [2004] All ER (D) 201 (Nov), Sedley LJ pointed out that 'if the record of interview which goes before the adjudicator has been obtained in unacceptably stressful or distressing circumstances so that it contains omissions and inconsistencies when compared with what the applicant later tells the adjudicator, the damage may not be curable' (para 15).

12.124 Since the elaboration of gender guidelines by the Refugee Women's Legal Group in 1998,[1] the Immigration and Nationality Directorate has begun to recognise the importance of gender-sensitive procedures and has elaborated its own gender guidelines for caseworkers.[2] They confirm that every effort will be made to provide same sex interviewing officers and interpreters where requested.[3] They also acknowledge that victims of sexual assault or abuse may need to be interviewed alone, may suffer trauma affecting their confidence, concentration and memory, and may be reluctant to talk in detail about their experiences,[4] a reluctance recognised by the High Court in *Ejon*.[5] The policy instructions on interviewing accept that victims of torture generally may face particular difficulties in recounting their experiences, both because of the nature of the experiences to be recounted and because of their previous experience of officialdom,[6] and that in extreme cases there may be compelling medical reasons for not interviewing at all.[7] The Home Office recognises the particular expertise of the Medical Foundation for the Care of Victims of Torture and endorses its 'Guidelines for the examination of survivors of torture' which describes medical and psychological effects of torture and their impact on asylum seekers' ability to present their case.[8] Instructions on interviewing state that it might be appropriate to read over the record of interview at the end (a practice otherwise largely abandoned) where an applicant is clearly traumatised.[9] Special arrangements have been agreed to allow requests for an extension of a period for post-interview representations to enable the Medical Foundation to prepare and submit a medical report.[10] Where such a report supports the claimant's account of torture, this conclusion should be accepted in the absence of significant reasons for rejecting it.[11]

1 Refugee Women's Legal Group *Gender Guidelines for the Determination of Asylum Claims in the United Kingdom* (July 1998). The guidelines were referred to with approval by Lord Hoffmann in *Islam v Secretary of State for the Home Department; R v Immigration Appeal Tribunal* [1999] 2 AC 629; [1999] INLR 144, HL. See now the Asylum Gender Guidelines issued by the IAA in November 2000, and see also H Crawley *Refugees and gender: law and process* (Jordans, 2001) chs 1 and 10.

2 API, 'Gender issues in the asylum claim'.

3 API, 'Gender issues' above, para 8. This is subject to operational requirements, and may not be possible when the request is made on the day of the interview.
4 Ibid. The API acknowledge that feelings of guilt and shame may inhibit full disclosure and that inability to provide information should not affect credibility. They also acknowledge that many forms of abuse do not leave physical signs. The API on gender issues should be read and re-read by Home Office caseworkers, presenting officers and by Asylum and Immigration Tribunal members, who are on occasion all too ready to disbelieve women's accounts of sexual abuse.
5 *R v Secretary of State for the Home Department, ex p Ejon (Molly)* [1998] INLR 195, QBD: psychiatric as much as physical injury may prevent early disclosure of evidence.
6 API 'Interviewing', para 7.3.
7 Ibid para 7.6. This applies not just to disturbed torture victims but to all claimants with medical or psychiatric problems making interview problematic.
8 API, 'Medical Foundation' para 1. Caseworkers are expected to be familiar with 'best practice' guidelines before interviewing possible torture victims and to appreciate that genuine victims of torture may not be prepared to go into much detail about the ill-treatment they have experienced (perhaps because of cultural barriers, or simply due to the traumatic or humiliating nature of the mistreatment they suffered, and that failure to do so should not affect credibility. See our comment at fn 4, which applies equally here. See also Kock and Winter, *The psychological sequelae of torture – use of evidence in the asylum procedure*, available from RLC database, and other research cited in Henderson: Best Practice Guide to asylum and human rights appeals (ILPA/RLG, 2003) at [26.13]. In a number of cases, the Tribunal has accepted psychiatric evidence as helping to explain discrepancies: see eg *Kaygisiz* [2002] UKIAT 03283; *Muhoro* (00TH01502).
9 API 'Interviewing' para 7.4 ('traumatised victims'). For read-overs see 12.123 text and fn 18 above.
10 API, 'Medical Foundation', para 2.1. Such requests should be refused only in exceptional circumstances. Although the Medical Foundation is the only organisation for which special arrangements have been made, there is no reason in principle why an extension should not be granted for the preparation and submission of a report from any reputable medical practitioner. Where, after an extension, no report is produced and no explanation offered for its non-production, the Home Office cannot demand a report, but the API allow an adverse inference to be drawn on the claimant's account of torture: para 2.2.
11 API, 'Medical Foundation', para 2.3.

12.125 There was previously no reflection in the Immigration Rules or the asylum policy instructions of the UNHCR *Handbook*'s guidance for investigation of the claims of mentally disturbed persons.[1] The Tribunal has held that it is totally wrong to conduct an interview by asking a series of leading questions, and especially so if the interviewee has a known mental condition; such claimants must be allowed to tell their story in their own way.[2] Policy instructions now treat mentally disturbed applicants, with 'traumatised victims' and 'other medical cases', as interviewees requiring 'particular care'.[3]

1 UNHCR *Handbook* 12.13 above, paras 206–212, which point out the necessity for different techniques of examination, with more emphasis on medical and objective evidence, and perhaps requiring a lighter burden of proof (para 210), but calling for a close examination of the applicant's past history and background, using whatever outside sources of information may be available. The Court of Appeal has rejected the idea that a mentally ill applicant enjoyed a lighter burden of proving her claim in *Bolat v Secretary of State for the Home Department* (permission) (499/66206/C) (23 February 2000, unreported); see also *Yesilyurt* (permission) (A99–7352-C) (2 March 2000, unreported). The particular difficulties where clients are unable to give instructions might make it appropriate for representatives to consider appointing a guardian.
2 *Ibrahim v Secretary of State for the Home Department* [1998] INLR 511, IAT. See also *Ermias* (HX00312) (11 August 1999, unreported), where the Tribunal agreed that an interview with an applicant who was not fit to be interviewed had no evidential value.

3   API, 'Interviewing' paras 7.4–7.6. Medical evidence should if possible be obtained setting
     out the nature and degree of mental illness and assessing an applicant's ability to be
     interviewed in connection with the claim. If interview is inappropriate or unworkable, the
     claim will be dealt with by other means such as written representations. If the claimant is
     interviewed, a read-back will probably be appropriate: see API 'Interviewing' para 7.4.

12.126 The UNHCR *Handbook*[1] indicates that in the light of the particular
evidential and practical difficulties faced by asylum seekers, the duty to
ascertain and evaluate all the relevant facts is shared between the applicant
and the examiner.[2] However, the Immigration Rules require claimants to make
prompt and full disclosure of material facts, and to assist the Secretary of State
in establishing the facts,[3] but are otherwise silent on the actual practice of
obtaining relevant information. In *Musisi* Lord Bridge found it 'strange that
such an important interview as this should be entrusted to an immigration
officer at a port of entry with no knowledge of conditions in the country of
origin of a claimant for asylum'.[4] Port interviews are still conducted by
Immigration Service staff and so his comments are still apposite. This
contrasts with asylum claims made after entry which are usually conducted by
specialist asylum staff. Claims are determined against the background of
information about countries of origin provided by the Country Information
Policy Unit (CIPU), which produces detailed, sourced and publicly available
assessments of the main refugee-producing countries,[5] and sometimes, information from the Foreign and Commonwealth Office. An Advisory Panel on
country information (APCI) has been set up under s 142 Nationality,
Immigration and Asylum Act 2002 to consider and make recommendations
about the content of country information.[6]

1   See 12.13 above. Paras195–205 deal with establishing the facts.
2   *Handbook* para 196, which continues that in some cases it might be for the examiner to
     use all the means at his (sic) disposal to produce the necessary evidence in support of the
     application. Para 200 requires the examiner to gain the confidence of the applicant to assist
     the latter in putting forward the case.
3   HC 395, para 340.
4   *Re Musisi* [1987] AC 514.
5   Currently 20 in number (not always the same 20). Twice-yearly reports are supplemented
     by bulletins issued throughout the year on these and other countries. These reports and
     bulletins are 'not widely accepted by parties as authoritative, credible and free from
     political or policy bias, as are the (Canadian) Immigration and Refugee Board's informa-
     tion products': HL EU Committee 11th report 2003–4, HL 74 at para 115; see also
     Immigration Advisory Service: 'Home Office country information dangerously inaccurate
     and misleading' (September 2003); 'Home Office country information remains flawed' (on
     CIPU's October 2003 assessments); 'Lack of objectivity in Home Office country reports'
     (on CIPU's April 2004 assessments); all available through IAS' website. It is important to
     check the sources cited to ensure that CIPU's summary is correct.
6   The Panel's terms of reference include reviewing and providing advice on the content of
     country information material produced by the Home Office, and on CIPU's sources,
     methods of research and quality control to help ensure that the material produced is as
     accurate, balanced, impartial and up to date as possible. The Panel welcomes observations
     on the CIPU material. Its assessments of specific CIPU reports, published on its website
     (acpi.org), bear out the criticisms of undue optimism, selectivity and partiality. It is hoped
     that the Panel's criticisms will make a real difference to the balance of CIPU assessments.

12.127 A significant development has been the Home Office practice of
giving full reasons for rejection of asylum claims.[1] It is now recognised

generally in administrative law that even in the absence of statutory obliga-tion, reasons are required for a decision which will have significant effects on the rights of individuals affected.[2] Once the giving of reasons became standard practice it was apparent that in a number of cases adverse inferences were being drawn on matters that were capable of reply and had never been canvassed in interview. In a series of cases the courts held that such an approach was a breach of the duty of fairness.[3] In *Thirukumar*[4] the Court of Appeal held that if an opportunity to make representations was to be meaningful an applicant should be informed of the matters to which his or her attention needed to be directed, and, where time had elapsed since the interview, to be reminded of what had been said. The introduction of a right of appeal in July 1993 put an end to the provisional decision to refuse which invited observations as to why a different course should be adopted. Now, if adverse inferences are wrongly drawn in a refusal letter, the remedy is to address them at the statutory appeal, and failure to do so will mean that they stand.[5] Where the appeal is non-suspensive,[6] there must be an opportunity to correct adverse inferences before implementation of the decision.[7] Now that there is power to serve refusal of leave to enter by post after adjourning examination of an applicant for further inquiries,[8] there is no longer an expectation of a final interview at which the refusal letter will be served and the applicant asked for comments.[9]

[1]   Since the case of *R v Secretary of State for the Home Department, ex p Singh (Gurmeet)* [1987] Imm AR 489 in which the Divisional Court indicated that the giving of reasons was highly desirable in asylum cases.

[2]   *R v Secretary of State for the Home Department, ex p Doody* [1994] 1 AC 531; *Stefan v General Medical Council* [1999] 1 WLR 1293; *R v Secretary of State for the Home Department, ex p Zighem* [1996] Imm AR 194. However, Dyson J held in *R (on the application of Vallaj) v Special Adjudicator* [2001] INLR 455 at [59]–[60], that the Secretary of State is not bound to give reasons for certifying a claim as manifestly unfounded.

[3]   *R v Secretary of State for the Home Department, ex p Yemoh* [1988] Imm AR 595; *Gaima v Secretary of State for the Home Department* [1989] Imm AR 205, CA; *R v Secretary of State, ex p Oran (Ayse)* [1991] Imm AR 290.

[4]   [1989] Imm AR 402, CA, upholding the QBD at [1989] Imm AR 270.

[5]   See 18.129 below.

[6]   Under s 94 Nationality, Immigration and Asylum Act 2002: see 12.160 below.

[7]   *R (on the application of L) v Secretary of State for the Home Department* [2003] EWCA Civ 25, [2003] Imm AR 330, [2003] INLR 224.

[8]   Immigration (Leave to Enter and Remain) Order 2000, SI 2000/1161, Art 12. Previously, the provisions of Immigration Act 1971, Sch 2, para 6(1) (six months' leave to enter deemed given where notice of decision not given within 24 hours of final examination) meant that, in port cases, immigration officers had to complete examination by calling the applicant to a final interview where the refusal letter was served. See 3.41 above.

[9]   See 18.83 for service of refusal decisions.

12.128 Refusal letters usually set out a summary of the applicant's claim and contain a number of standard paragraphs referring to credibility issues such as failure to claim in a country of transit or on arrival, and to conditions in the country of feared persecution. Following complaints about unsourced asser-tions and unfair credibility findings in refusal letters, the Immigration and Nationality Directorate promised in May 2000 that paragraphs on country conditions would be sourced by reference to the Country Immigration Policy Unit assessments, that credibility would not be given disproportionate weight and letters would set out clear findings on what was and was not accepted.[1]

Asylum Processes Stakeholders' Group meeting, May 2000. In its June 2004 response to the 2nd report of the Constitutional Affairs Committee on Immigration Appeals, the government proposed that UNHCR provide an external assessment of the quality of decisions (Cm 6236, para 3).

12.129 There is nothing in the Rules relating to confidentiality of asylum claims, but the Immigration and Nationality Directorate respects the principle of confidentiality in general in asylum claims,[1] and that principle is given added weight by the fact that respect for confidential information is a vital aspect of the right to respect for privacy under Article 8 of the ECHR.[2] It is not permissible for a decision to refer to information provided in confidence by another applicant, including a spouse, unless that information is already in the public domain.[3] Details from forgery reports relied on to discredit documents produced by an asylum claimant will not normally be disclosed.[4]

[1]   API, 'Disclosure and confidentiality' (and see also Chapter 24 of the IDI, in particular the section on Disclosure to Third Parties of Information Relating to Asylum Applications).
[2]   *Z v Finland* (1997) 25 EHRR 371. The API, 'Disclosure and confidentiality' para 3 give guidance on the circumstances when information about asylum seekers may be disclosed to other government departments or agencies, international organisations and other bodies in the exercise of their functions.
[3]   API, 'Disclosure and confidentiality', para 2.3. The API used to state that asylum claims enter the public domain once an appeal has been heard in public, but the relevant part (para 2.4) was being updated at the time of writing. The Procedure Rules enable directions to be given to secure the anonymity of a party (or a witness): Asylum and Immigration Tribunal (Procedure) Rules 2005, SI 2005/230, r 45(4)(i), whilst r 54 makes provision for the exclusion of members of the public from all or part of any hearing of an appeal.
[4]   API, 'Disclosure and confidentiality' para 2.11; see also Nationality, Immigration and Asylum Act 2002, s 108 and SI 2005/230, r 54(2).

Non-compliance refusal

12.130 HC 395, paragraph 340 provides that a failure without reasonable explanation to make a prompt disclosure of material facts or to assist the Secretary of State in establishing the facts of the case may lead to refusal. It includes failure to comply with a requirement to report for fingerprinting, failure to complete an asylum questionnaire and failure to attend for interview or to report for an immigration officer for examination.[1] The actions of an agent may be taken into account for these purposes.[2] Failure to return Statement of Evidence (SEF) forms in time[3] leads to refusal of the claim for non-compliance, even (in one case) where the asylum seeker concerned was in hospital having a baby when the form was due.[4] Late receipt of the form does not result in cancellation of the refusal decision or to interview on the claim, merely to 'consideration' of the material in the form.[5] Failure to attend or late attendance for either screening or substantive interview will also lead to non-compliance refusal unless exceptional circumstances prevented attendance.[6] In *Haddad*, a starred Tribunal held that an application may not be refused on non-compliance grounds alone; in each case the Home Office is obliged to decide the asylum claim, and the appellate authority the appeal, on the material available.[7] In *Busuulwa* the Tribunal lamented that the words of the statute forced the appellate authority to exercise original jurisdiction over asylum claims which have never been considered substantively,[8] although it was wrong in principle for the primary decision to be taken other than in accordance with the UNHCR guidelines. It called on the Secretary of State to withdraw non-compliance refusals which failed to review the merits of the asylum claim.[9] In *Nori* [10] the Tribunal reviewed flawed non-compliance refusals, ie, refusals on non-compliance grounds where the Statement of Evidence form was received in time, or where a claimant's failure to attend an interview was occasioned by error on the part of the Home Office.[11] It noted that once an incorrect decision had been withdrawn (which it had to be), there was nothing left to appeal against.[12] After *Nori*, the Home Office reviewed its procedures, and the policy instructions state that where the claim was made in-country, a flawed non-compliance decision refusing leave to remain will be withdrawn;[13] decisions regarding port claims will be cancelled.[14] Where an appeal has been lodged, the appellant is invited to withdraw the appeal.[15]

[1]   HC 395, para 340.
[2]   HC 395, para 342.
[3]   The Statement of Evidence form must be returned within ten working days. Requests to extend the time limit should be considered and discretion exercised reasonably where there are exceptional circumstances, but an extension will not be granted to enable the applicant to instruct a representative to complete the form: API 'Non-compliance', para 4.2. Note that non-compliance may also lead to withdrawal of asylum support: see Asylum Support Regulations 2000, SI 2000/704, reg 20 as amended by SI 2005/11 pursuant to the Reception Directive 2003/9/EC, from 5 February 2005.
[4]   Judicial review proceedings were lodged but were withdrawn when the Home Office accepted the late Statement of Evidence. There was a flood of non-compliance refusals during 2000, including many issued when forms had been returned either within or only just outside the period; it was widely believed that had more to do with political priorities (production of statistics showing vastly improved rate of decision-making) than with proper refugee determination.
[5]   See correspondence between ILPA and Barbara Roche, 24 October 2000.
[6]   HC 395, para 340. Caseworkers are advised to wait five working days for an explanation for the non-attendance before making the final decision on the claim. A reasonable explanation for failure to attend may include illness of the applicant (supported by acceptable medical evidence) or transport disruption; non-availability of the representative is not considered a reasonable explanation: API 'Non-Compliance' paras 3, 5.
[7]   *Haddad (Ali) v Secretary of State for the Home Department* [2000] INLR 117. Earlier cases such as *Davies (Sandra)* (17797), holding that the correct course for the appellate authority finding good reason for non-compliance was to allow the appeal and remit to the Secretary of State for substantive consideration of the asylum claim, were not referred to. In *Shreef* (01TH00476) another Tribunal held that the course adopted in *Davies* was correct. But the Court of Appeal approved *Haddad* in *R (on the application of Zaier) v Secretary of State for the Home Department* [2003] EWCA Civ 937, [2003] All ER (D) 153 (Jul) at paras 31 and 37 per Auld LJ. Since *Haddad*, refusal letters relying on non-compliance also refer to the Refugee Convention claim not being made out (HC 395, para 336).
[8]   *Busuulwa* (01TH00239). By March 2001, nearly one-third of all claims were refused without consideration of the merits, for alleged non-compliance with time limits. A fair proportion of these were erroneous, e g there was evidence that the Statement of Evidence form had been returned in time.
[9]   *Busuulwa* above.
[10]   *Nori (Rasheed)* [2002] UKIAT 01887.
[11]   See API 'Non-compliance' para 8.
[12]   *Nori* above, para 19. The Tribunal pointed out that once the decision to refuse asylum had been withdrawn, the refusal of leave to enter or remain (ie, the immigration decision against which the appeal was brought) could not stand.
[13]   API 'Non-compliance' para 8.4.
[14]   API 'Non-compliance' para 8.2, 8.5, advising that the refusal of leave to enter will be cancelled and the claimant advised that they are required to attend for further examination (to prevent the deemed six months' leave which would otherwise arise by statute: sch 2 para 6 Immigration Act 1971, see 3.41 above).

15 API 'Non-compliance' para 8.5. This is unnecessary: the appellate authority would no longer have jurisdiction as there is no longer an immigration decision, and so no extant appeal: Nationality, Immigration and Asylum Act 2002 s 82(1); see also *Nori* above para 19.

Asylum and the one-stop procedure

12.131 The aim of the one-stop procedure is to make applicants give all their reasons for wanting to enter or remain in the UK as early as possible. This is intended to allow the Home Office to deal with applications quickly, taking into account all the reasons why the person wish to remain.[1] The 'one-stop' procedures implemented by the Immigration and Asylum Act 1999[2] have been considerably simplified by the Nationality, Immigration and Asylum Act 2002 and the Asylum and Immigration (Treatment of Claimants, etc) Act 2004. Section 120 of the 2002 Act allows[3] the Secretary of State or an immigration officer to require[4] any person who has applied to enter or remain in the United Kingdom or in respect of whom an immigration decision[5] has been or may be taken, to state his or her reasons for wishing to enter or remain in the United Kingdom, any grounds on which he or she should be permitted to enter or remain and any grounds on which he or she should not be removed from or required to leave the United Kingdom.[6] Failure to set out all such grounds in response to a one-stop warning, or to use an earlier right of appeal to litigate them, may result in certification[7] of a later application, which precludes a further appeal.

1   API 'Appeals: one-stop procedure' para 1.
2   Immigration and Asylum Act 1999 ss 74–77. There were different procedures for in-country claimants on the one hand and for port claimants, illegal entrants and overstayers on the other. Relevant family members were also included in the procedure. For details see the last edition of this work, at 12.123 and 18.53.
3   There is no statutory obligation on the Secretary of State or the immigration officer to serve a one-stop warning at any particular time or at all: see API 'Appeals: one-stop procedure', para 1.
4   By notice in writing: Nationality, Immigration and Asylum Act 2002, s 120(2). In practice this is often done by a paragraph in a notice refusing leave, or in the reasons for refusal letter: see API 'Appeals: one-stop procedure' para 1. There is no time limit within which the applicant must return a statement of additional grounds.
5   Ie, a decision attracting a right of appeal under Nationality, Immigration and Asylum Act 2002, s 82(2). Note however that a one-stop notice may be served at any time, and is not dependent on such a decision; see API 'Appeals: one-stop procedure' para 1. A notice is not served where the decision is to grant humanitarian protection or discretionary leave: ibid.
6   Nationality, Immigration and Asylum Act 2002, s 120(2). The response to the one-stop warning need not repeat grounds already set out in the application: s 120(3).
7   Under Nationality, Immigration and Asylum Act 2002, s 96(1) as substituted by Asylum and Immigration (Treatment of Claimants, etc) Act 2004, s 30 from 1 October 2004, the Secretary of State or an immigration officer may, in refusing an application, certify that the new application relies on a ground which could have been raised on appeal earlier (whether or not the applicant used the earlier right of appeal, and whether or not he or she has been out of the country since); and under s 96(2) (as substituted), an application can be certified if it relates to a ground which the person should have included in a statement he was required to make under s 120 in relation to another immigration decision or application. In each case a reasonable explanation for the failure to raise the matter earlier should preclude certification. Certification prevents an appeal under s 82(1) from being brought. See 18.43 below.

REMOVAL TO SAFE THIRD COUNTRIES

Introduction

12.132 The Asylum and Immigration Appeals Act 1993 was the first statutory provision[1] incorporating and extending an international practice whereby claims for asylum made in one state could be refused without substantive consideration on the basis that the claimant could be removed to a country other than the country of feared persecution, which would be responsible for determining the asylum claim. The practice was based upon the 'first country of asylum' principle of international law whereby neighbouring countries were expected to take refugees fleeing a persecuting state.[2] In modern times, governments have turned the principle round so as to expect a refugee to find refuge locally wherever possible.[3] Removal to 'safe third countries' is a controversial practice[4] and one that resulted in substantial and protracted litigation during the 1990s, and consequential significant statutory amendment in the Asylum and Immigration Act 1996, the Immigration and Asylum Act 1999, the Nationality, Immigration and Asylum Act 2002 and the Asylum and Immigration (Treatment of Claimants, etc) Act 2004. This section examines briefly the third country regimes under the provisions of the 1993 and the 1996 Acts. The 1999 Act (amended by the 2002 and 2004 Acts) is considered in more detail because, although repealed with effect from 1 October 2004,[5] there is a transitional saving in respect of certificates issued before that date to which the 1999 Act regime will continue to apply. Therafter we set out the current regime contained in the 2004 Act.

[1] Prior to the Asylum and Immigration Appeals Act 1993, removal of an asylum seeker on third country grounds had been entirely a matter of administrative discretion subject only to the requirement in the Immigration Rules that the rules should lay down no practice which was not in accordance with the Refugee Convention. The landmark and foundation case of *Re Musisi* [1987] AC 514, in which the removal of a Ugandan to Kenya was quashed because of Kenya's practice of returning Ugandans home, had established that Art 33 of the Refugee Convention prevented indirect as well as direct *refoulement*: *Musisi* at 532C–E.

[2] See references in Goodwin-Gill 12.5 fn 1 above.

[3] See eg Preamble to Resolution on a harmonised approach to questions concerning host third countries, approved by EU ministers 30 November 1992 under Third Pillar.

[4] See UNHCR 'The "safe third country" policy in the light of the international obligations of countries vis-à-vis refugees and asylum seekers' London, July 1993. See also Amnesty International *Playing human pinball: Home Office practice in 'safe third country' asylum cases* (June 1995); ECRE *Safe third countries: myths and realities* (February 1995). In *R v Uxbridge Magistrates' Court, ex p Adimi* [1999] INLR 490, the Divisional Court held, rejecting the submission of the Home Office to the contrary, that asylum seekers had an element of choice as to where they might claim asylum: per Simon Brown LJ at 496H–497A–C and Newman J at 507C.

[5] Section 33(2) Asylum and Immigration (Treatment of Claimants, etc) Act 2004 and Asylum and Immigration (Treatment of Claimants, etc) Act 2004 (Commencement No 1) Order 2004, SI 2004/2523. However, Art 3 of the Commencement Order provides that IAA 1999, ss 11 and 12 and NIAA 2002, ss 80 and 93 shall continue to have effect in relation to a person who is subject to a certificate under IAA 1999, s 11(2) or s 12(2) or (5) which was issued by the Secretary of State before 1 October 2004. For a discussion of the relationship between the provisions of the 1999 and 2002 Acts see *ST (Sri Lanka)* [2005] UKIAT 00006.

12.133 A third country removal engages the UK's obligations under the Refugee Convention only if it exposes the claimant (directly or indirectly)[1] to a real risk of *refoulement*;[2] there is no breach if removal may be ineffective in the sense that the third country returns the applicant to the UK.[3] However, repeated ineffective removals would be oppressive and might constitute inhuman treatment[4] and in practice the Home Office normally only operates the third country procedure once, dealing with the claim substantively if the person is returned here. If the third state removes the claimant to a fourth state, that in itself would not breach the UK's obligations under the Convention if it were a safe country and a procedure was in place in the third state to assess the safety of the fourth state,[5] but where a removal by the UK instigated a real risk of *refoulement* via a chain of states then the UK's obligation would still be engaged.

1   *Re Musisi* at 12.132 fn 1 above.
2   Ie return to the borders of the territory where persecution is feared. See Goodwin-Gill 12.5 fn 1 above, ch 4.
3   *R v Secretary of State for the Home Department, ex p Dursun* [1991] Imm AR 297; *R v Secretary of State for the Home Department, ex p Mehari* [1994] QB 474; *Thavathev-athasan v Secretary of State for the Home Department* [1994] Imm AR 249; *Jafar v Secretary of State for the Home Department* [1994] Imm AR 497.
4   *Karali v Secretary of State for the Home Department* [1991] Imm AR 199.
5   *Martinas v Special Adjudicator and the Secretary of State for the Home Department* [1995] Imm AR 190, CA.

The 1993 and 1996 Acts

12.134 Section 6 of the Asylum and Immigration Appeals Act 1993[1] prohibited the removal of asylum seekers until their claims were determined, but asylum claims by those deemed removable to a third country[2] were determined by the Secretary of State without consideration of the merits and certified 'without foundation' as not engaging the UK's obligations under the Refugee Convention.[3] An in-country appeal against refusal on third country grounds was provided, with its own special procedures.[4] The procedure was predicated on speedy removals[5] and an underlying assumption that there would be little if any basis for challenging the certificates, since most third-country returns were to European, usually EU, states. But many certificates were overturned on appeal or on judicial review because of unsafe procedures in EU Member States and the risk of chain or direct *refoulement* from them.[6] The Asylum and Immigration Act 1996 removed the in-country right of appeal where the third country was an EU Member State or a designated country.[7] The 1996 Act expressly excluded asylum claimants removable to third countries from the protection from removal provided in section 6 of the Asylum and Immigration Appeals Act 1993[8] and put into statutory form the criteria for certification on 'third country' grounds previously only contained in the Immigration Rules.[9]

1   Re-enacted as Immigration and Asylum Act 1999, s 15.
2   Defined under the immigration rules, HC 395, para 345 (still in force), as those who had not arrived directly in the UK from the place where persecution is feared and had had an opportunity to make contact with the authorities of another country to seek their protection, or there was clear evidence of their admissibility to a third country, and who could be removed (a) to a country of which they were not a national or citizen, (b) where their life or freedom was not threatened contrary to Article 33 of the Refugee Convention and (c) from where they would not be sent elsewhere in a manner inconsistent with the Convention.

³ Asylum and Immigration Appeals Act 1993, Sch 2, para 5(2).
⁴ Asylum and Immigration Appeals Act 1993 s 8; Asylum Appeals (Procedure) Rules 1993, SI 1993/1661.
⁵ *R v Secretary of State for the Home Department, ex p Mehari* [1994] Imm AR 151, QBD; *Secretary of State for the Home Department v Abdi and Gawe* [1994] Imm AR 402, CA, [1996] Imm AR 288, HL.
⁶ Between 1993 and 1996, special adjudicators (designated under Asylum and Immigration Appeals Act 1993, s 8(5) to hear asylum appeals) consistently rejected certificates relating to removals to France and Belgium: see *Secretary of State for the Home Department, ex p Canbolat* [1997] Imm AR 442 at 454; *R v Special Adjudicator, ex p Bostem* [1996] Imm AR 388 at 393, and frequently rejected certificates relating to other Member States; and the Secretary of State ceased removing asylum seekers to Italy, Greece and Portugal following adverse decisions on their asylum procedures.
⁷ Asylum and Immigration Act 1996, s 3(2). The countries designated under s 2(3) as safe third countries were Canada, Norway, Switzerland and the US: Asylum (Designated Countries of Destination and Designated Safe Third Countries) Order 1996, SI 1996/2671, in force 1 October 1996. The same four countries are designated under the Asylum (Designated Safe Third Countries) Order 2000, SI 2000/2245. Following the coming into force of the 1996 Act the Secretary of State resumed third country removals to all EU Member States (see fn 6 above).
⁸ Asylum and Immigration Act 1996, s 2(2).
⁹ Asylum and Immigration Act 1996, s 2(2).

The 1999 and 2002 Acts

12.135 Sections 11,¹ 12² and 15³ of the Immigration and Asylum Act 1999 replaced the provisions of the 1993 and 1996 Acts in respect of all three categories of third-country cases: removals to EU Member States under standing arrangements,⁴ removals to Member States otherwise than under standing arrangements⁵and to designated countries,⁶ and removals to non-EU and non-designated countries.⁷ The Nationality, Immigration and Asylum Act 2002 amended these provisions, as well as replacing the appeals regime under the IAA 1999.⁸ The Asylum and Immigration (Treatment of Claimants, etc) Act 2004 repealed sections 11 and 12 of the 1999 Act with effect from 1 October 2004, ⁹ subject to transitional provisions.¹⁰

¹ As substituted by Nationality, Immigration and Asylum Act 2002, s 80.
² As amended by the Nationality, Immigration and Asylum Act 2002 (Consequential and Incidental Provisions) Order 2003, SI 2003/1016, Sch, para 11, to reflect its legal effect within the new appeals framework in Part 5 of the NIAA 2002.
³ Replaced by Nationality, Immigration and Asylum Act 2002, s 77.
⁴ Immigration and Asylum Act 1999, s 11 (as substituted).
⁵ IAA 1999, s 12(1)(a).
⁶ IAA 1999, s 12(1)(b). The countries designated under the 1999 Act are, as before, Canada, Norway, Switzerland and the US: Asylum (Designated Safe Third Countries) Order 2000, SI 2000/2245.
⁷ Immigration and Asylum Act 1999, s 12(4), (5) (as amended).
⁸ See Part V Nationality, Immigration and Asylum Act 2002 (ss 81–117).
⁹ Section 33(2) Asylum and Immigration (Treatment of Claimants, etc) Act 2004 and Asylum and Immigration (Treatment of Claimants, etc) Act 2004 (Commencement No 1) Order 2004, SI 2004/2523.
¹⁰ SI 2004/2523 para 3; see 12.133 above.

Removals to EU countries under standing arrangements under the 1999 and 2002 Acts

12.136 Section 11 of the Immigration and Asylum Act 1999 (as substituted)¹ allowed asylum seekers to be removed despite the statutory protection against removal[2] if the Secretary of State had certified that: (i) a Member State had accepted responsibility under standing arrangements for the asylum claim[3] and (ii) in his or her opinion, the claimant was not a national or citizen of the Member State to which he or she was to be sent[4] (unless a human rights claim had been made,[5] which had not been certified clearly unfounded,[6] and an appeal could be brought or was pending).[7] Section 11(1) contained the first statutory presumption of safety, providing that in determining whether the person would be removed under standing arrangements a Member State was to be regarded 'as a place where life and liberty is not threatened for Refugee Convention reasons and from which the person will not be sent to another country otherwise than in accordance with the Refugee Convention'.[8] As the Court of Appeal subsequently held in *Ibrahim*,[9] the statutory presumption of safety worked. Despite the wording of section 11(3) and (4), suggestive of in-country appeal possibilities, in the great majority of cases there was no in-country appeal right. This was because the Secretary of State certified the human rights claim as clearly unfounded in the vast majority of cases, and the issue of the certificate prevented an in-country appeal.[10]

---

[1]   By Nationality, Immigration and Asylum Act 2002, s 80 (with full effect from 1 April 2003 (see Nationality, Immigration and Asylum Act 2002 (Commencement No 4) Order 2003, SI 2003/754). For a discussion of the relationship between the provisions of the 1999 and 2002 Acts see *ST (Sri Lanka)* [2005] UKIAT 00006.

[2]   See NIAA 2002, s 77.

[3]   Immigration and Asylum Act 1999, s 11(2)(a) (as substituted). Standing arrangements were defined in s 11(5) as arrangements in force between two or more Member States for determining which State was responsible for considering applications for asylum. Although not specifically named, this meant the Dublin II regulation (Council Regulation (EC) No 343/2003 of 18 February 2003 establishing the criteria and mechanisms for determining the Member State responsible for examining an asylum application lodged in one of the Member States by a third-country national), which replaced the 1990 Dublin Convention with effect from 1 September 2003.

[4]   IAA 1999, s 11(2)(b) (as substituted).

[5]   NIAA 2002, s 113(1) defined a 'human rights claim' as 'a claim made by a person to the Secretary of State at a place designated by the Secretary of State that to remove the person from or require him to leave the United Kingdom would be unlawful under section 6 of the Human Rights Act 1998 (c 42) (public authority not to act contrary to Convention) as being incompatible with his Convention rights'.

[6]   NIAA 2002, s 93(2). Note the separate power to certify a third country 'safe' in human rights terms, under s 94(7). This human rights certification was developed under the 2004 Act, Sch 3: see 12.140ff below.

[7]   IAA 1999, s 11(4) (as substituted). No in-country appeal could be brought if the Secretary of State certified removability to a third country unless a human rights claim had been made which was not certified. Note that there were potentially two certificates in play here: (i) under IAA 1999, s 11(2) or 12(2) (as amended), allowing removal to the third country; (ii) under NIAA 2002, s 93(2)(b), that a human rights claim was clearly unfounded.

[8]   IAA 1999, s 11(1)(a) and (b). The presumption was inserted during the passage of the 1999 Act in direct response to the Court of Appeal's decision in *Adan* in order to meet and defeat challenges to removal without investigation by the courts into Member State's interpretation or application of the Convention (see *R v Secretary of State for the Home Department, ex p Adan* [1999] 4 All ER 774, subsequently upheld by the House of Lords in *R v Secretary of State for the Home Department v Adan, R v Secretary of State for the Home Department, ex p Aitseguer* [2001] INLR 44 and see 12.145 below). Announcing the amendment in July 2000, the minister explained that it was based on 'the principle that Member States trust each other to consider asylum claims in accordance with the 1951 Convention'. But the lesson of the litigation since 1993 is that trust alone cannot ensure compliance with the UK's obligations to refugees.

⁹ *R (on the application of Ibrahim) (Ayman) v Secretary of State for the Home Department* [2001] EWCA Civ 519, [2001] Imm AR 430; see also *R (on the application of Hatim) v Secretary of State for the Home Department* [2001] EWHC Admin 574, [2001] Imm AR 688. In Simon Brown LJ's words, 'Parliament has, it is clear, in unambiguous terms dictated that henceforth France, amongst other Member States, is to be regarded as a safe third country. Of course the Secretary of State is not bound to certify in every case, but where he chooses to do so, in my judgment that certificate cannot be impugned on grounds that France after all is not properly to be regarded as a safe third country.' Although the only challenge was to the section 11 certification, and no human rights claim had yet been made, both Simon Brown LJ and Tuckey LJ expressed the view that certification of any such claim would be difficult to challenge (at paras 26 and 30). See further 12.140ff below.

¹⁰ IAA 1999, s 11(4)(b) (as substituted).

Other removals under the 1999 and 2002 Acts

12.137 Section 12 of the Immigration and Asylum Act 1999 (as amended)[1] applied to removals to (i) EU Member States (or territories forming part of a Member State) otherwise than in accordance with standing arrangements,[2] (ii) designated countries[3] and (iii) countries which are neither Member States nor designated.[4] The conditions for certification on third-country grounds in such cases were that (a) the claimant was not a national or citizen of the country to which he or she was to be sent; (b) his or her life and liberty would not be threatened there by reason of his or her race, religion, nationality, membership of a particular social group, or political opinion; and (c) the government of that country would not send him or her to another country otherwise than in accordance with the Refugee Convention.[5] Unlike the positon where return to the third country was under standing arrangements, there was no statutory presumption of safety of the third state in these cases. Subsections (7A) and (7B) of section 12 replicated the provisons of subsection (3) and (4) of section 11.[6] Shortly stated, the effect was that persons being removed under third-country provisions to countries in categories (i) and (ii) above all had an in-country appeal if they made a human rights claim in the UK, unless the human rights claim was certified as clearly unfounded. In the event of certification the only remedy was judicial review, although without the difficulties caused by the statutory presumption of safety in IAA 1999, section 11(1). In cases involving non-Dublin removals to EU states, and all other removals, the full range of arguments on the third state's interpretation and application of the Convention, and the likelihood of *refoulement* or chain removal from there, were open (whether on appeal or judicial review, depending on whether the human rights claim has been certified). Finally, where removal was to a country falling within category (iii) above (neither EU Member States nor designated countries) there was always a suspensive in-country appeal right, irrespective of whether any human rights claim had been made).[7]

¹ By the Nationality, Immigration and Asylum Act 2002 (Consequential and Incidental Provisions) Order 2003, SI 2003/1016, para 11, Sch. For a discussion of the relationship between the provisions of the 1999 and 2002 Acts see *ST (Sri Lanka)* [2005] UKIAT 00006.

² Immigration and Asylum Act 1999, s 12(1)(a).

³ Currently Canada, Norway, Switzerland and the USA: Immigration and Asylum Act 1999, s 12(1)(b); Asylum (Designated Safe Third Countries) Order 2000, SI 2000/2245. See *R v Secretary of State for the Home Department, ex p Salas* [2001] Imm AR 105 in which

challenge was made to the safety of the USA as a third country, in particular as to that country's interpretation of Arts 1A(2) and 33 of the Refugee Convention.

4   IAA 1999, s 12(4).
5   IAA 1999, s 12(7). The conditions are the same as those contained in the immigration rules, HC 395, para 345.
6   See 12.136 above.
7   NIAA 2002, s 93(1) prevents in-country appeals where certificates are issued under IAA 1999, ss 11(2) and 12(2). Countries which are neither Member States nor designated are dealt with separately under IAA 1999, s 12(4). One significant change introduced by the appeals regime under the NIAA 2002 for third country appeals was the ability to appeal on the ground that a discretion conferred by the immigration rules should have been exercised differently (NIAA 2002, s 84(1)(f)). Under the previous appeals regime, a person facing return to a third country could not argue by reference to any such discretion, because the appeal was limited to consideration of the United Kingdom's obligations under the Refugee Convention (see *R v A Special Adjudicator, ex p Mehari* [1994] QB 474, [1994] 2 All ER 494, [1994] Imm AR 151). Since para 345 of the immigration rules sets out how the Secretary of State will 'normally' approach third country cases, the rule conferred a reviewable discretion.

Certification of human rights claims under the 2002 Act

12.138 As pointed out above,[1] the presumption of safety under section 11 of the IAA 1999 applied only as regards the Refugee Convention. A person facing removal to a third country (whether under standing arrangements or otherwise) might have raised various human rights claims against removal. The approach on judicial review to challenges to a 'third country' removal which is likely to lead to suicide or to interfere with the right to respect for family and private life is considered in chapter 8. Here, we consider the scope under the IAA 1999 regime for arguing that removal under standing arrangements to an EU Member State engages Article 3 ECHR because of the risk of *refoulement*. In the last edition we pointed out that since the presumption of EU Member States' safety is a statutory one, it could only be overridden by the appellate authority reading in the words 'unless the contrary is proved',[3] in accordance with the interpretative obligation of the Human Rights Act 1998[4] to interpret legislation in a way which gives effect to, rather than defeats, human rights. This would allow the asylum seeker to adduce evidence disproving the presumption in a particular case. Cogent evidence that the statutory presumption of safety was not justified in an individual case or category of case ought to have provided a basis for challenge to a certificate that the human rights claim is clearly unfounded.[5] It might have been thought that the decision in *Adan and Aitsegeur*[6] would provide the basis for such a challenge, in particular in light of the decision of the ECtHR in *TI v United Kingdom*,[7] where the court ruled both that removal through an intermediary country (also a contracting state) did not affect the UK's obligation to ensure that the claimant was not exposed to treatment contrary to Article 3 ECHR, and that the Dublin Convention, as an international agreement for attribution of responsibility between European countries for deciding claims in the related area of asylum, did not absolve the UK from its obligations under the ECHR.[8] In *Thangarasa*,[9] the Secretary of State certified as manifestly unfounded[10] the human rights claim of a Sri Lankan Tamil facing removal to Germany (based on the risk of chain removal to Sri Lanka), and a challenge to the certification of the human rights claim based on the decision of the ECtHR in *TI v United Kingdom* was rejected by the House of Lords.[11] There have to date been no successful challenges to certification on *refoulement* grounds. Thus in practical terms, even though the statutory presumption of safety under section 11(1) applied expressly only to the Refugee Convention, it defeated ECHR-based *refoulement* arguments as well. Nevertheless, as will be seen, under the Asylum and Immigration (Treatment of Claimants, etc) Act 2004, the statutory presumption of safety in repect of *refoulement* under the Refugee Convention is treated separately from any such presumption with reference to the Human Rights Convention, with some countries being deemed 'safe' in respect of both Conventions, while others are deemed safe only in respect of the former Convention.[12]

1   See 12.136 above.
2   See 12.136 above.
3   By analogy with the court's approach to an irrebuttable presumption of service contained in former procedural rules, in *R v Secretary of State for the Home Department, ex p Saleem* [2000] INLR 413, CA; see 5th edition at 12.156.
4   Human Rights Act 1998, s 3; see 8.13 above. Otherwise, the Divisional Court might have to make a declaration of incompatibility under s 4 of the Human Rights Act 1998, on the basis that preventing an asylum seeker from proving the existence of facts which make his or her removal potentially in breach of Art 3 of the ECHR is itself a breach of that Article together with Art 13 of the ECHR (the right to an effective remedy): see 8.15 above.
5   Ie, a certificate under Nationality, Immigration and Asylum Act 2002, s 93(2)(b), referred to in Immigration and Asylum Act 1999, s 11(4)(b) (as substituted by s 80 NIAA 2002).
6   *R v Secretary of State for the Home Department, ex p Adan, R v Secretary of State for the Home Department, ex p Aitseguer* [2001] INLR 44, HL, upholding the Court of Appeal's judgment in *R v Secretary of State for the Home Department, ex p Adan* [1999] 4 All ER 774 that French and German interpretations of the Refugee Convention were incorrect, see 12.145 below.
7   *TI v United Kingdom* [2000] INLR 211 (ECtHR).
8   *TI v United Kingdom* above, at 228–229. The ECtHR rejected the application as manifestly ill-founded on the facts, concluding that there was no real risk that Germany would expel the applicant to Sri Lanka in breach of Art 3 ECHR.
9   *R (on the application of Thangarasa) v Secretary of State for the Home Department* [2001] EWHC Admin 420 (Collins J), upheld by the Court of Appeal at [2001] EWCA Civ 1611, [2001] All ER (D) 121 (Sep) and by the House of Lords at [2002] UKHL 36, [2003] 1 AC 920, [2002] 4 All ER 800, [2002] 3 WLR 1276, [2002] INLR 620.
10 The 1999 Act certification regime was based on claims being 'manifestly unfounded'; the 2002 Act introduced the present formulation, clearly unfounded' (which has the same meaning: see *R (on the application of L) v Secretary of State for the Home Department* [2003] EWCA Civ 25, [2003] Imm AR 330, [2003] INLR 224).
11 The Court of Appeal accepted that in Germany the applicant would have a right of individual petition to the ECtHR, that Germany would scrupulously comply with any request from the court to suspend execution of any deportation order and that it was the universal practice of the German courts and executive to comply with ECtHR judgments (paras 65–66). Lord Hope in the House of Lords found these considerations 'conclusive of the issue as to whether his rights under Art 3 would be at risk of being violated if he were to be returned to Germany' (HL para 56).
12 Asylum and Immigration (Treatment of Claimants, etc) Act 2004, Sch 3; see below at 12.140.

Third country certification under section 94 of the 2002 Act

12.139 We have shown above that the third country regime was based on an interplay between sections 11 and 12 of the 1999 Act (as amended) and the appeals provisions of the NIAA 2002. The hallmarks of the regime were the certification procedures enabling the Secretary of State to effect removal of asylum seekers to third countries without substantive consideration of their claims and, in some cases, without suspensive appeal. Section 94 of the NIAA 2002 controversially extended the non-suspensive appeal regime in a number of ways.[1] First, section 94(7) is a discrete provision enabling any third-country case to be certified on the ground that there is 'no reason to believe that the person's rights under the Human Rights Convention will be breached' in the third country. Certification prevents the bringing of an in-country appeal against removal. Secondly, there is a statutory presumption of safety contained in section 94(8) in respect of countries which are the subject of section 94(7) certificates. This presumption of safety mirrors that contained in section 11(1) of the IAA 1999.[2] But whereas the section 11(1) presumption bit only in respect of removals under standing arrangements to EU Member States, certification and the statutory presumption of safety under section 94(8) can be applied to *any* country. This is reminiscent of the famous 'Humpty Dumpty' speech of Lord Atkin;[3] the Secretary of State can make any country 'safe' simply by certifying it so, and neither you nor I nor the vicar's dog may gainsay him. This is faith, not justice.

[1]   See Nationality, Immigration and Asylum Act 2002 s 94, and 8.102 above.
[2]   It provides that in determining whether a person in relation to whom a certificate has been issued under sub-s (7) may be removed from the United Kingdom, the country specified in the certificate is to be regarded both as a place where a person's life and liberty is not threatened by reason of his race, religion, nationality, membership of a particular social group, or political opinion, and a place from which a person will not be sent to another country otherwise than in accordance with the Refugee Convention: Nationality, Immigration and Asylum Act 2002, s 94(8). The provision is somewhat curious since the focus of sub-s (7) is on the *Refugee* Convention whereas certification arises in respect of third country removals where there is no reason to believe that the person's righs under the *Human Rights* Convention will be breached.
[3]   Dissenting in *Liversidge v Anderson* [1942] AC 206.

Asylum and Immigration (Treatment of Claimants, etc) Act 2004

12.140 The third country regime is substantially re-cast (again) by the provisons of the AI(TC)A 2004 which further develop the main ideas of the 1999 and 2002 Acts (a lava flow of presumptions of safety and relentless removal of in-country appeal rights). Sections 11 and 12 of the IAA 1999 (as amended) were repealed with effect from 1 October 2004 and replaced by the provisons in AI(TC)A 2004 Schedule 3, although the previous provisions continue to have effect in relation to those already subject to certificates under the 1999 Act regime.[1] Part 2 of the Schedule contains a list of 26 countries, the 'First List of Safe Countries (Refugee Convention and Human Rights)',which presently comprise the other 24 EU Member States (United Kingdom excepted) together with Iceland and Norway.[2] For the purposes of the determination by any person, tribunal or court whether an asylum or human rights claimant may be removed from the United Kingdom to a state of which he is not a national or citizen the First List countries are to be treated as places:

(i)   where a person's life and liberty are not threatened by reason of his race, religion, nationality, membership of a particular social group or political opinion;

(ii)   from which a person will not be sent to another State in contravention of his [Human Rights] Convention rights; and

(iii) from which a person will not be sent to another State otherwise than in accordance with the Refugee Convention.[3]

The prohibition on removal while a claim for asylum is pending under section 77 of the NIAA 2002 does not prevent removal from the United Kingdom to one of the First List countries, provided that the Secretay of State certifies that in his opinion the person is not a national or citizen of the destination state.[4] Further, a certificate to the same effect issued by the Secretary of State prevents an in-country appeal being brought on the basis that the country is not safe in refoulement terms as regards either the Refugee Convention or the Human Rights Act 1998, or at all.[5] As regards any other human rights claims, there is no in-country appeal where the Secretary of State certifies the claim 'clearly unfounded'.[6] What is new here is the requirement to certify unless satisfied that the claim is not clearly unfounded, extending the provisions of secton 94(3) of the NIAA 2002 to human rights claims in third country cases.[7] Moreover, even where a person appeals after removal, an appeal cannot be brought on any ground that is inconsistent with the presumptions of safety as regards First List countries – either asserting that life or liberty are threatened for Refugee Convention reasons in the country, or asserting a risk of *refoulement* under the Refugee Convention or engaging the Human Rights Act 1998.[8] Finally, although the position as regards suspensive appeals does not preclude a challenge by judicial review, it would still be necessary to contend with the statutory presumptions of safety and the position adopted by Simon Brown LJ in *Ibrahim*.[9] There is no reason to suppose that a different approach would be taken to the statutory presumption of safety now that it has been extended by Parliament as regards human rights claims.

[1] Asylum and Immigration (Treatment of Claimants, etc) Act 2004, s 33(2) repeals ss 11 and 12 of the IAA 1999, s 33(3) repeals ss 80 and 93 of the NIAA 2002, and s 33(1) refers to the detailed provisions of Sch 3. For commencement see SI 2004/2523. Article 3 of the Order provides that ss 11 and 12 of the 1999 Act and ss 80 and 93 of the Nationality, Immigration and Asylum Act 2002 continue to have effect in relation to a person who is subject to a certificate under s 11(2) or s 12(2) or (5) of the 1999 Act issued before 1 October 2004. See above at 12.135–12.138.

[2] The countries are those which are subject or have agreed to be bound by the Dublin arrangements. Additional countries joining the Dublin arrangements may be added by order: see Sch 3, Part 6, providing for amendment by statutory instrument of the Sch 3 para 2 list by addition of states. Curiously, unlike the position with the Second and Third Lists in Sch 3 paras 7 and 12, there is no power to remove a State from the First List.

[3] AI(TC)A 2004, Sch 3, para 3.

[4] AI(TC)A 2004, Sch 3, para 4.

[5] AI(TC)A 2004, Sch 3, para 5(2) precludes, any appeal which would otherwise be in-country under NIAA 2002, s 92(2) including a variation appeal, and a deportation appeal, or an appeal against refusal of leave to enter where the person concerned holds an entry clearance: AI(TC)A 2004, Sch 3, para 5(2). Sch 3, para 5(3) precludes an in-country appeal relying on s 84(1)(g) of the 2002 Act.

[6] AI(TC)A 2004, Sch 3 para 5(4), (5).

[7] See Explanatory Notes to the Asylum and Immigration (Treatment of Claimants, etc) Act 2004 at para 148.

[8] AI(TC)A 2004, Sch 3, para 6.

[9] *R (on the application of Ibrahim) (Ayman) v Secretary of State for the Home Department* [2001] EWCA Civ 519, [2001] Imm AR 430; see also *R (on the application of Hatim) v Secretary of State for the Home Department* [2001] EWHC Admin 574, [2001] Imm AR 688 and see above at 12.136 fn 9 above.

12.141 We set out below an example of how the provisions of the AI(TC)A 2004 would work in respect of the claim for asylum made by someone arriving in the United Kingdom from a First List country:

> A Somali national claims asylum at Dover having arrived by ferry from Calais. As well as claiming asylum based on her fear of return to Somalia, she claims that removal to France would result in France returning her to Somalia in breach of the Refugee Convention (because of France's application or interpretation of the Refugee Convention – thereby also breaching Article 3 ECHR), and that her removal would also breach her right to respect for family life (under Article 8 ECHR) based on the presence in the UK of family members.[1]
>
> (i)   France is a First List country. Unlike the position under the previous third country regimes it does not matter whether the French authorities accept that France is the State responsible for determining the asylum claim under Dublin arrangements.[2] The Secretary of State may refuse leave to enter and issue a certificate under Sch 3 paras 3 and 4 of the AI(TC)A 2004 to the effect that removal is to a First List country and that in his opinion the claimant is not a national or citizen of that State.
>
> (ii)   Since refusal of leave to enter is not an immigration decision against which an in-country right of appeal lies by virtue of section 92(2) of the Nationality, Immigration and Asylum Act 2002, the claimant cannot appeal in-country, nor could she do so even if, when refused leave to enter she had held either an entry clearance or work permit as provided for by section 92(3) of the 2002 Act.[3]
>
> (iii) Moreover, she cannot appeal by virtue of section 92(4)(a) (that is as a person who has made an asylum or human rights claim)[4] in reliance on any assertion that her removal to France would breach the United Kingdom's *Refugee Convention* obligations,[5] nor in reliance on an assertion that her removal to France would breach her human rights 'because of the possibility of removal from [France] to another state'. [6]
>
> (iv)   This leaves only the claimant's Article 8 claim based on the presence of family members in the United Kingdom, which will give rise to an in-country appeal unless the Secretary of State certifies the claim as clearly unfounded. But the Secretray of State is likely to certify the claim, since he or she is required to do so 'unless satisfied that the claim is not clearly unfounded'.[7]

The only remedy for the claimant is judicial review. As we have already observed, it is inevitable that the decision of the Court of Appeal in *Ibrahim* [8] on the statutory presumption of safety in section 11(1) of the 1999 Act would be applied to the statutory presumptions under the 2004 Act regime, as regards both the Refugee Convention and *refoulement* under the Human Rights Act 1998. We consider the possibility of challenge to the certification of human rights claims below. Finally, as regards any discrete judicial review challenge to the application of Dublin II, see the discussion at 12.150ff below.

---

[1]   *Refoulement* and family life issues are of course not the only possible human rights grounds that might be raised in a third country case. Factors relating to the health of the claimant if the impact of removal is sufficiently severe to engage Art 3 ECHR, *R (on the application of Soumahoro) v Secretary of State for the Home Department* [2003] EWCA Civ 840, [2003] Imm AR 529 or the moral and physical integrity of the person as an aspect of their private life protected by Art 8 may also be raised: see eg *R (on the application of Razgar) v Secretary of State for the Home Department* [2004] UKHL 27, [2004] 3 WLR 58; see further 8.53, 8.92 above.

2   Note that although the provisions of AI(TC)A 2004, Sch 3 make no reference to standing
     arrangements or acceptance of responsibility, the United Kingdom is party to Dublin II and
     judicial review might be available to challenge any irregularity in its appication: see further
     below at 12.150.
3   AI(TC)A 2004, Sch 3 para 5(2) which disapplies the provisions of s 92(2) and (3)
     Nationality, Immigration and Asylum Act 2002, which provide in-country appeal rights to
     persons refused a certificate of entitlement, variation (in certain circumstances), revocation
     of indefinite leave, persons facing deportation and to certain persons refused leave to enter
     when holding entry clearance or a work permit.
4   Generally, those making human rights claims in the UK may appeal in-country: National-
     ity, Immigration and Asylum Act 2002, s 92(4)(a).
5   AI(TC)A 2004, Sch 3, para 5(3)(a).
6   AI(TC)A 2004, Sch 3, para 5(3)(b).
7   AI(TC)A 2004, Sch 3, para 5(4).
8   *R (on the application of Ibrahim) (Ayman) v Secretary of State for the Home Department*
     [2001] EWCA Civ 519, [2001] Imm AR 430; *R (on the application of Hatim) v Secretary
     of State for the Home Department* [2001] EWHC Admin 574, [2001] Imm AR 688; see
     12.136 above.

12.142 The 'Second List of Safe Countries (Refugee Convention and Human
Rights)', the subject-matter of Part 3 of Schedule 3, are states which may be
specified by the Secretary of State by statutory instrument.[1] In third-country
proceedings, these specified states are to be treated as places (i) where a
person's life and liberty are not threatened by reason of his race, religion,
nationality, membership of a particular social group or political opinion; (ii)
from which a person will not be sent to another State otherwise than in
accordance with the Refugee Convention.[2] As with the First List countries in
Part 2 of Schedule 3, the presumption of safety precludes any appeal (in- or
out of country) which is inconsistent with it.[3] A certificate that an applicant is
not a national or citizen of the state will disapply the statutory protection
against removal to a specified state[4] and will prevent an in-country immigration appeal, including one relying on an asylum claim based on *refoulement*
arguments.[6] Human rights claims will not attract an in-country appeal if
certified as clearly unfounded, and certification is the 'default' position.[7]

1   At the time of writing, no statutory instrument has been made, so there are no states in this
     Part.
2   Asylum and Immigration (Treatment of Claimants, etc) Act 2004, Sch 3, para 7.
3   AI(TC)A 2004, Sch 3, para 11. Note that on an out-of-country appeal it is still possible to
     argue that removal to the specified state was likely to lead to a breach of Art 3 ECHR,
     whether direct or by *refoulement* from there to the country of origin, since unlike the
     limitation in para 6 on grounds which may be raised in relation to First List countries,
     there is nothing in Sch 3, para 11 to prevent the argument as regards removal contrary to
     the ECHR.
4   AI(TC)A 2004, Sch 3, para 9.
5   AI(TC)A 2004, Sch 3, para 10(2); see 12.140 fn 6 above.
6   AI(TC)A 2004, Sch 3, para 10(3).
7   AI(TC)A 2004, Sch 3, para 10(4). The effect of the two sub-paragraphs taken together is
     that in-country human rights appeals, whether relying on *refoulement* arguments (see
     12.136 above) or not, may be brought but are likely to be prevented by certification that
     the claim is clearly unfounded. In any event, s 94(7) Nationality, Immigration and Asylum
     Act 2002 remains in force, enabling the Secretary of State to certify that there is no reason
     to believe that the person's rights under the Human Rights Convention will be breached in
     the third country concerned, which also prevents an appeal: see 12.139 above.

12.143 The 'Third list of safe countries (Refugee Convention only)' referred
to in Part 4 of the Schedule,[1] are once again countries which are to be

specified by order of the Secretary of State. In relation to these countries, the same presumptions apply, with the same effects, as with the 'Second List' countries, save that an in-country human rights appeal may be brought unless the Secretary of State certifies it clearly unfounded, and there is no 'default position' that he or she will so certify.[2]

---

[1] Asylum and Immigration (Treatment of Claimants, etc) Act 2004, Sch 3, paras 12–16. As in relation to the second list, at the time of writing no statutory instrument has been made, so there are no states in this Part.

[2] AI(TC)A 2004, Sch 3, para 15(4), cf para 10(4).

12.144 Part 5 of the Schedule deals with 'Countries certified as safe for individuals'. As its title suggests, this Part enables the Secretary of State to certify any other third country as a place (i) where a person's life and liberty will not be threatened by reason of his race, religion, nationality, membership of a particular social group or political opinion; (ii) from which the person will not be sent to another State otherwise than in accordance with the Refugee Convention.[1] As with the Third List countries, certification under this part disapplies the statutory protection against removal,[2] prevents an in-country immigration appeal, including one relying on an asylum claim based on *refoulement* arguments,[3] and prevents out-of-country asylum appeals which challenge the presumption of safety.[4] Human rights claims will not attract an in-country appeal if certified clearly unfounded, but there is no 'default position' that such a claim is clearly unfounded, as with the first two lists.[5] The pernicious aspect of this Part (as with the power under section 94(7) of the 2002 Act, see 12.139 above) is that there is no Parliamentary scrutiny whatever of the Secretary of State's opinion that a particular country is safe for the individual, an opinion which results in a very serious loss of judicial protection for the individual. It is all part of a philosophy of creating a sheltered system of unchallengeable executive decisions which are kept as immune from judicial scrutiny as possible.

---

[1] Asylum and Immigration (Treatment of Claimants, etc) Act 2004, Sch 3, para 17(c).

[2] AI(TC)A 2004, Sch 3, para 18.

[3] AI(TC)A 2004, Sch 3, para 19(a), (b).

[4] AI(TC)A 2004, Sch 3, para 19(d).

[5] AI(TC)A 2004, Sch 3, para 19(c).

12.145 Until the introduction of the statutory presumption of safety under the 1999 Act, the principal issue in third country cases was the possibility that the third country would remove the claimant in a manner inconsistent with its Refugee Convention obligations. As we have seen, the presumption was reinforced by the 2002 Act, and the current 2004 Act regime for the first time extends the presumption as regards First List countries so as to preclude the possibility of raising *refoulement* arguments under the ECHR. Nevertheless, as we have sought to argue, the presumption of safety cannot be conclusive, and there will be some cases to which it is not applied. The fact that the country has signed the Refugee Convention or other relevant international agreements that reaffirm its Convention obligations, that it co-operates with the UNHCR and has procedures in place to give effect to its obligations, has been held to constitute some evidence on which the Secretary of State could rely to conclude that removal would not be contrary to the UK's obligations.

But these factors were held to create a rebuttable presumption of safety which could be displaced by examination of the actual practice and procedures of the country.[1] The difficulty, in the light of the statutory presumption, lies in being able to litigate such matters. However, the possibility of *refoulement* by the third country has been the subject matter of close scrutiny by the courts, and readers are referred for analysis to the last edition of this work.[2] Other issues that have arisen in third country cases and have been the subject matter of scrutiny by English courts have included different approaches taken to the Refugee Convention (which culminated in the decision of the House of Lords in *Adan and Aitsegeur* [3] rejecting the Secretary of State's argument that there is a permissible range of interpretations of the Refugee Convention);[4] chain removals; de facto protection;[5] and the relevance of previous refusals.

[1]   In *R v Secretary of State for the Home Department, ex p Gashi* [1999] INLR 276; revsd [1999] Imm AR 415, the Court of Appeal quashed a certificate in respect of the removal of two Kosovar Albanians to Germany on the basis that the Secretary of State could not demonstrate that adequate inquires had been made which would explain the gross disparity in outcome of claims from ethnic Albanians in the UK, where they were universally recognised as refugees, and Germany, where only a tiny per centage were given refugee status and many were returned to ethnic cleansing in the Federal Republic of Yugoslavia. The Secretary of State withdrew an appeal to the House of Lords, and *Gashi* remains good law on the standard of inquires expected of the Secretary of State in such cases. The change in conditions in Kosovo in 1999 after the UN-sanctioned intervention meant that after June 1999 the disparity in treatment as between Germany and the UK disappeared and the Secretary of State could resume the certification of Germany as safe in such cases: *R v Secretary of State for the Home Department, ex p Gjoka and Gashi (Shefki)* (15 June 2000, unreported), Collins J. More controversially the Secretary of State sought to re-certify in cases which had been stayed pending the resolution of the litigation in *Gashi*. In *R (on the application of Zeqiri) v Secretary of State for the Home Department* [2001] EWCA Civ 342, the House of Lords held that the decision of the Court of Appeal in *Besnik Gashi* did not create any legitimate expectation for applicants 'stacked up' behind him such as Mr Zeqiri (see [2002] UKHL 3, [2002] Imm AR 296, [2002] All ER (D) 184 (Jan)).

[2]   See 5th edition, 12.131–12.134.

[3]   *R v Secretary of State for the Home Department, ex p Adan, R v Secretary of State for the Home Department, ex p Aitseguer* [2001] INLR 44, HL, holding that the true meaning of Art 1A(2) did not require state complicity for harm inflicted by non-state agents to constitute persecution; the protection of the Convention extends to those persecuted by non-state agents where 'for whatever reason the state in question is unable to afford protection against factions within the state'. See also *R (on the application of Kerkeb) v Secretary of State for the Home Department* (22 May 2000, unreported), QBD, upheld in the Court of Appeal at [2001] EWCA Civ 747, [2001] Imm AR 614.

[4]   With the coming into force of the EC Qualification Directive 2004/83/EC (12.3 fn 3 above), great disparities in interpretation among EU Member States, such as formed the basis of the *Adan and Aitseguer* litigation, should disappear. It is important to note that the Directive lays down *minimum* standards, necessarily admitting of more favourable interpretation, and cannot override the terms of the Convention itself, which the courts must still be free to determine, although the Directive would be relevant to interpretation of the Convention as evidence of State practice: see Vienna Convention on the Law of Treaties, Arts 31, 32.

[5]   In *Adan and Aitsegeur* the House of Lords left open the question of whether the conditions for removal were satisfied by alternative forms of protection in the receiving state despite differences in interpretation which would exclude asylum seekers from recognition as refugees there. In the previous edition of this work, we suggested that any such alternative protection would have to be measured against the protection requirements of the Refugee Convention, so that to avoid a breach of Article 33, the Secretary of State would have to show that equivalent protection was available in the third country. The House of Lords considered and rejected this suggestion in *R (on the application of Yogathas and Thangarasa) v Secretary of State for the Home Department*, holding that 'the Convention is directed to a very important but very simple and very practical end, preventing the return

of applicants to places where they will or may suffer persecution. Legal niceties and refinements should not be allowed to obstruct that purpose' ([2002] UKHL 36, [2002] INLR 620, para 9, per Lord Bingham of Cornhill). If in practice *refoulement* from the third state is not likely, a lesser status in that state will not prevent removal there.

Opportunity to claim in the third state

12.146 The immigration rules indicate that the Secretary of State will not issue a certificate to remove an asylum claimant to a 'safe' third country in accordance with Schedule 3 to the AI(TC)A 2004 unless the asylum claimant has not arrived in the UK directly from the country in which she or he claims to fear persecution, and has had an opportunity at the border or within the third country to make contact with the authorities of that country or territory in order to seek their protection, or there is other clear evidence of the person's admissibility to a third country or territory.[1] In most cases, certification will proceed on the basis of clear evidence of admissibility (for which see below), but where that evidence is lacking or ambivalent, the issue of opportunity to claim in the third country will assume importance. In considering whether the asylum claimant had the opportunity to claim asylum in the third country or at its borders, opportunity is to be objectively assessed. It does not mean a knowing opportunity in the sense that the claimant was aware of the third country's procedures for receiving refugee applications and could form a judgment as to whether it was appropriate to apply there. The question is whether the claimant could have approached the authorities at the border or internally and could have had an asylum claim received.[2] Of course, opportunity is only relevant if the country is safe. The courts have held that the fact that an agent planned the journey and for all intents and purposes dictated the claimant's actions does not preclude the claimant from having an opportunity to make a claim *en route*.[3] But there will be no opportunity if the claimant was transported clandestinely through a country in a vehicle, or the method or duration of the transit is such that no immigration officials were met. The Rule does not import the concept of 'constructive opportunity': it must be the claimant who has the opportunity, not some third party over whom he or she has no control.

[1]   HC 395, para 345(2)(i), substituted by HC 1112, 18 October 2004.
[2]   *R v Special Adjudicator, ex p Kandasamy* [1994] Imm AR 333, QBD.
[3]   *Dursun v Secretary of State for the Home Department* [1993] Imm AR 169, CA; *R v Secretary of State for the Home Department, ex p Musa* [1993] Imm AR 210, QBD.

Clear evidence of admissibility

12.147 This is the alternative 'condition precedent' for third country removal, where the Secretary of State cannot prove that the asylum claimant had an opportunity to claim asylum in the third country to which removal is proposed.[1] 'Clear evidence of admissibility' is a higher threshold than 'reason to believe he would be admitted' which is the criterion for selecting removal destination in other refusal of entry cases,[2] but authorities on the latter test have some relevance. In *Alsawaf*[3] the court held that claimants do not have to be admitted for settlement in the third country for the test to be satisfied; it is enough if they are accepted for a temporary period while their asylum claim and other relevant circumstances are considered. This approach was followed and applied in *de Carvalho*.[4] In *Yassine*[5] Lebanese claimants with tourist visas for Brazil, who claimed asylum while in transit in the UK, were refused asylum on the assumption that they could travel on to Brazil; the decision was quashed as the Secretary of State had not demonstrated that the claimants would be admitted to Brazil. The visas had been obtained by misrepresentation: the claimants were refugees, not tourists, and they had no other connection with Brazil apart from the visa. However, in *Shah*[6] Collins J held that a Portuguese visa on a passport which had been obtained by deception and to which the holder was not entitled was a 'valid' visa for the purposes of the Dublin Convention, enabling the applicant to be returned to Portugal.

[1]   HC 395, para 345(2)(ii), substituted by HC 1112 from 18 October 2004.
[2]   Immigration Act 1971, Sch 2, para 8(1)(c)(iv).
[3]   *Alsawaf v Secretary of State for the Home Department* [1988] Imm AR 410, CA, at 422, per Staughton LJ.
[4]   *R v Secretary of State for the Home Department, ex p Carvalho* [1996] Imm AR 435.
[5]   *R v Secretary of State for the Home Department, ex p Yassine* [1990] Imm AR 354, QBD.
[6]   *R (on the application of Shah) v Secretary of State for the Home Department* [2001] EWHC Admin 197, para 31.

12.148 In most cases of removal to the EU, the terms of the Dublin Convention,[1] which came into force in September 1997, and its successor the EC Dublin II Regulation,[2] provide sufficient evidence of admissibility to another Member State, and for the most part it is no longer a live issue. Admissibility is relevant to cases of removal to non-designated countries. Other forms of re-admission agreements could provide evidence of admissibility, along with residence permits, a valid visa, or other evidence of a right of entry.[3]

[1]   See below 12.149.
[2]   See Council Regulation 2003/343/EC (OJ 2003 L 50/1, in force 1.9.03) and Regulation 2003/1560/EC (OJ 2003 L 222/3, in force 6.9.03), implementing Dublin II. These Regulations establish the criteria and mechanisms for determining the Member State responsible for examining an asylum application, lodged in one of the Member States by a third-country national (at 12.150 below).
[3]   *Miller v Immigration Appeal Tribunal* [1988] Imm AR 358, CA. An attempt to avoid removal to Belgium by withdrawing an asylum claim was rejected in *R (on the application of Zajmi) v Secretary of State for the Home Department*, 15 November 2000, CA.

Dublin Convention 1990

12.149 The Dublin Convention[1] was one of the first multilateral agreements between states to delineate responsibility for examining asylum applications. Its main purposes were on the one hand to prevent multiple claims and 'forum-shopping' by asylum seekers,[2] and on the other to prevent the situation of refugees 'in orbit', passed between states with no one state having responsibility for examining the asylum application, by guaranteeing a determination of the asylum claim in one country. A new EC Council Regulation [3] (referred to here as 'Dublin II') came into force on 1 September 2003, and applies to requests made by Member States in respect of asylum seekers from that date. Both the UK and Ireland have opted in to Dublin II.[4] Denmark, on the other hand, has opted out of it, [5] with the effect that the original Dublin Convention remains in force and continues to apply between Denmark and the Member States that are bound by Dublin II until such time as an agreement allowing Denmark's participation in Dublin II has been concluded.[6] For this reason, and because the structure of Dublin II reflects that of the original Convention, discussion of the provisions of the Dublin Convention in the last edition will remain of some relevance. In this edition however we focus on Dublin II, to which we now turn.

[1] The Convention Determining the State Responsible For Examining Applications For Asylum Lodged in One of the Member States of the European Community [1990] Imm AR 604. It came into force on 1 September 1997. See A Nicol and S Harrison 'The law and practice in the application of the Dublin Convention in the UK' (1999) 1 EJML 465. For detailed consideration of the Dublin Convention see the last edition of this work, 12.146–12.151.

[2] As has been pointed out repeatedly by non-governmental organisations since the Dublin Convention was signed, when the protection offered by contracting states varies, there is profound injustice if asylum claimants have no choice over their country of asylum. For discussion of this problem see Gregor Noll 'Formalism vs. empiricism: some reflections on the Dublin Convention on the occasion of recent European case law' ECRAN weekly update, 25 January 2001.

[3] Council Regulation 2003/343/EC of 18 February 2003 (OJ 2003 L 50/1, in force 1 September 2003), establishing the criteria and mechanisms for determining the Member State responsible for examining an asylum application lodged in one of the Member States by a third-country national, and see also Regulation 2003/1560/EC (OJ 2003 L 222/3, in force 6 September 2003), implementing Dublin II.

[4] Council Regulation 2003/343/EC, above, Preamble, para 17.

[5] Council Regulation 2003/343/EC, above, Preamble, para 18.

[6] Council Regulation 2003/343/EC, above, Preamble, para 19.

Dublin II

GENERAL PRINCIPLES

12.150 The obligation to examine an asylum application made by any third-country national at the border or in the territory of a Member State belongs to a single Member State which is to be identified by reference to the hierarchy of criteria' set out in Chapter III of the Regulation,[1] although Member States are free to examine any application, even if examination is not its responsibility.[2] Member States have the right to send an asylum seeker to a third country.[3] The responsibility for examining a claim includes responsibility for minors accompanying a parent or guardian asylum seeker.[4] Where an asylum seeker is present in one Member State but lodges an application with the authorities of a second Member State, the Member State in whose territory the applicant is present identifies the Member State responsible for examination of the claim.[5] Where an asylum seeker is present in a second Member State and lodges an application there after withdrawing his or her application made in a first Member State during the process of determining the responsible Member State, he or she must be taken back by the first Member State to complete the process of determining the responsible Member State.[6]

[1] Council Regulation 2003/343/EC, above, Art 3(1). The process of determining the Member State responsible is to commence 'as soon as an application for asylum is first lodged with a Member State' (which is deemed to be once an application form or a report prepared by the authorities has reached the competent authorities: Art 4(1), (2)). The

obligations include the requirement to inform asylum seekers in writing and in a language they may reasonably be expected to understand regarding the application of the Regulation, its time limits and its effects: Art 3(4).

2 Council Regulation 2003/343/EC Article 3(2); see also Preamble para 7, pointing out that Member States should be able to derogate from the responsibility criteria so as to make it possible to bring family members together where this is necessary on humanitarian grounds. In this case, the Member State should inform the state previously responsible, the one conducting a procedure for determining the Member State responsible or the one which has been requested to take charge of or take back the applicant. Cf *R v Secretary of State for the Home Department, ex p S* [1998] Imm AR 416, where Forbes J held that the UK had not assumed responsibility under Art 3(4) of the original Dublin Convention for examination of the claim, even though the claimant had been interviewed about the merits of the claim on two occasions for a total of nine hours. In the absence of some positive statement that the UK has accepted the unconditional or exclusive right to examine the claim, the actual examination of the claim was not sufficient.

3 Council Regulation 2003/343/EC, Art 3(3).

4 Council Regulation 2003/343/EC, Art 4(3). The same applies to children born after the asylum seeker arrives in the territory of a Member State, although without the need to initiate a new procedure.

5 Council Regulation 2003/343/EC, Art 4(4). The latter Member State must be informed without delay by the Member State which received the application and is then regarded as the state with which the application for asylum was lodged.

6 Council Regulation 2003/343/EC, Art 4(5). The obligation ceases if the asylum seeker has in the meantime left the EU for at least three months or has obtained a residence document from a Member State.

THE HIERARCHY OF CRITERIA

12.151 The criteria for determining which Member State is responsible for examining an asylum application are set out in Articles 5–14 (Chapter III). They must be applied in the order in which they are set out and on the basis of the factual situation when the application was first lodged with a Member State.[1] They are as follows:

- *Unaccompanied minors*: the Member State responsible for examining the application is the one where a member of his or her family is legally present, provided that this is in the best interest of the minor. In the absence of a family member, the responsible Member State is the one in which the application for asylum was lodged.[2]

- *Family members refugees*: the Member State responsible for examining the application (provided that the persons concerned so desire) is the one where a family member[3] of an asylum seeker has been allowed to reside as a refugee (regardless of whether the family was previously formed in the country of origin).[4]

- *Family members asylum seekers*: the Member State responsible for examining the application, provided that the persons concerned so desire, is the one where the asylum seeker has a family member whose asylum application remains undecided.[5]

- *Residence documents and visas*: Where the asylum seeker is in possession of a valid residence document the responsible state is the one which issued the document. The situation is the same in relation to a valid visa,[6] unless the visa was issued on behalf of or on the written authorisation of another Member State, in which case that other Member State is responsible.[7] Where the asylum seeker is in possession of more than one valid residence document or visa issued by different Member States, responsibility is assumed in the following order: (a) the Member State which issued the residence document conferring the right to the longest period of residency or, where the periods of validity are identical, the Member State which issued the residence document having the latest expiry date; (b) the Member State which issued the visa having the latest expiry date where the various visas are of the same type; (c) where visas are of different kinds, the Member State which issued the visa having the longest period of validity, or, where the periods are identical, which issued the visa having the latest expiry date.[8] Where the asylum seeker possesses one or more residence documents which have expired less than two years previously, or one or more visas which have expired less than six months previously and which enabled him or her actually to enter the territory of a Member State, then these provisions apply while the applicant remains in the territories of the Member States. But once over two years or six months respectively have elapsed since the expiry of the residence documents or visas, the responsible Member State is the one in which the application is lodged.[9]

- *Asylum seekers irregularly crossing borders*: the Member State into which an asylum seeker irregularly crosses the border by land, sea or air having come from a third country, is responsible for examining an application for asylum made within 12 months.[10] After that time, responsibility will lie with the Member State in which, at the time of lodging the application, the asylum seeker has been previously living for a continuous period of at least five months (or, where there is more than one such state, the one in which the asylum seeker has lived most recently).[11]
- *Waiver of visa requirement*: responsibility lies with the Member State which waived the requirement, although the principle does not apply if the third country national lodges an asylum application in another Member State in which the visa requirement is also waived, when the latter Member State is responsible.[12]
- *International transit areas:* Responsibility for an application made in an international transit area of an airport of a Member State will lie with that Member State.[13]
- *No Member State responsible*: Where these critieria do not identify a responsible Member State, then responsibility lies with the first Member State with which the application for asylum was lodged.[14]

The prominence given to family unity by the Regulation is reflected not only in the preamble and in Articles 5–8, but also in Article 14, which provides that where several family members submit applications simultaneously in the same Member State, or on dates close enough for the procedures for determining the responsible Member State to be conducted together, and application of the criteria would lead to separation, responsibility will lie with the Member State responsible under the criteria for the largest number of family members or (failing this) with the Member State responsible for examining the application of the oldest of them.

[1] Council Regulation 2003/343/EC, above, Art 5.

2   Council Regulation 2003/343/EC, Art 6.
3   'Family member' is defined in Article 2(i) (insofar as the family already existed in the country of origin) as (i) the spouse of the asylum seeker or his or her unmarried partner in a stable relationship, where the legislation or practice of the Member State concerned treats unmarried couples in a way comparable to married couples under its law relating to aliens; (ii) the minor children of couples referred to in (i) or of the applicant, on condition that they are unmarried and dependent and regardless of whether they were born in or out of wedlock or adopted as defined under the national law; and (iii) the father, mother or guardian when the applicant or refugee is a minor and unmarried.
4   Council Regulation 2003/343/EC, Art 7.
5   Council Regulation 2003/343/EC, Art 8.
6   The fact that a residence document or visa was issued on the basis of a false or assumed identity, or on submission of forged, counterfeit or invalid documents, does not prevent responsibility being allocated to the Member State which issued it, but if the fraud was committed after the document or visa had been issued, the issuing Member State is not responsible: Art 9(4). This principle is also reflected in *R (on the application of Shah) v Secretary of State for the Home Department* [2001] EWHC Admin 197, where Collins J held that a Portuguese visa on a passport obtained by deception to which the holder was not entitled was still a valid visa under the Dublin Convention.
7   Council Regulation 2003/343/EC, Art 9(1)–(2). Where however a Member State first consults the central authority of another Member State, in particular for security reasons, the latter's reply to the consultation shall not constitute written authorisation within the meaning of this provision.
8   Council Regulation 2003/343/EC, Art 9(3).
9   Council Regulation 2003/343/EC, Art 9(4).
10   Council Regulation 2003/343/EC, Art 10. Irregular border crossing is to be established on the basis of proof or circumstantial evidence as described in the two lists mentioned in Article 18(3), including the data referred to in Chapter III of Regulation (EC) 2725/2000.
11   Council Regulation 2003/343/EC, Art 10(2).
12   Council Regulation 2003/343/EC, Art 11.
13   Council Regulation 2003/343/EC, Art 12, reflecting Art 7(3) of the original Dublin Convention. Cf *R v Secretary of State for the Home Department, ex p Behluli* [1998] INLR 594, CA where a dispute arose between the UK and Italian governments as to the application of Art 7, when 53 Kosovo Albanians were held in transit in an Italian airport for over 24 hours while officials argued about whether they could travel on to the UK. The dispute centred on whether asylum claims had been made in Italy. The Italian government denied it was responsible under Art 7, but agreed to the Kosovans' return as a matter of discretion.
14   Council Regulation 2003/343/EC, Art 13.

THE HUMANITARIAN CLAUSE

12.152 The prominence given to family unity is reflected also by the 'humanitarian clause', Article 15, which provides that any Member State, even where not responsible under the criteria, may take on responsibility for examining a claim so as to bring together family members, as well as other dependent relatives, on humanitarian grounds based in particular on family or cultural considerations, and 'shall' do so when requested by another Member State (subject to the consent of the family member concerned).[1] The power should be exercised where the person concerned is dependent on the assistance of another on account of pregnancy or a new-born child, serious illness, severe handicap or old age (provided that family ties existed in the country of origin).[2] Moreovoer, where the asylum seeker is an unaccompanied minor who has a relative or relatives in another Member State who can take care of him or her, Member States shall if possible unite the minor with his or her relative or relatives, unless this is not in the best interests of the minor.[3]

1   Council Regulation 2003/343/EC, Art 15(3). The Article makes provision for conciliation
    mechanisms for settling differences between Member States on the need to unite family
    members or the place (ie, country) where it should be done. See 12.155 fn 5 below.
2   Council Regulation 2003/343/EC, Art 15(2).
3   Council Regulation 2003/343/EC, Art 15(3).

TAKING CHARGE AND TAKING BACK

12.153 Chapter V of the Regulation lays down detailed procedures to be
applied between Member States dealing with the 'taking charge and taking
back' of asylum seekers. We have seen that the process of determining the
Member State responsible is to commence 'as soon as an application for
asylum is first lodged with a Member State'.[1] Where a Member State considers
that responsibility for examination of the claim lies with another Member
State it has a maximum of three months within which to call upon the other
Member State to take charge of the applicant, failing which responsibility
remains with the Member State in which the application was lodged.[2] Once a
request is made, the requested state has two months to make the necessary
checks and give a decision on the request to take charge,[3] except where
urgency has been pleaded, in which case the reply should be given within the
time requested, or if this is not possible, in any case within one month. Failure
to act within the two-month or one-month period is tantamount to accepting
the request.[4] The asylum seeker must be notified of the decision by the
Member State in which the application was lodged.[5] Any appeal or review will
not suspend the implementation of the transfer unless the courts or competent
bodies of the Member State so decide.[6] The transfer of the asylum applicant
must be carried out as soon as practically possible, and at the latest within six
months of acceptance of the request (or of the decision on an appeal or review
where it is given suspensive effect).[7] Failure to comply with the six-month time
limit means that responsibility reverts to the Member State in which the
application for asylum was lodged.[8] Provision is made for the taking back of
an asylum applicant (i) who is in the territory of another Member State
without permission, or (ii) has withdrawn an application and made an
application in another Member State or (iii) goes to the territory of another
Member State without permission after rejection of an application.[9] The
Court of Appeal held in *Omar* that the Dublin Regulation drew a clear
distinction between criteria and mechanisms, and a breach of procedures did
not give rise to a right on the part of the asylum claimant to have his or her
claim dealt with in the UK.[10]

1   12.150 above.
2   Council Regulation 2003/343/EC, Art 17(1). Article 17(2) enables the requesting state to
    ask for an 'urgent reply' in cases where the asylum seeker's stay is irregular or where he or
    she is held in detention. Article 17(3) makes provision for the form in which such requests
    to take charge are to be made, including the evidence required to enable the requested state
    to check whether it is responsible.
3   Council Regulation 2003/343/EC, Art 18(1). Article 18(2)–(5) makes provision for the
    elements of proof and circumstantial evidence to be used.
4   Council Regulation 2003/343/EC, Art 18(7).
5   Council Regulation 2003/343/EC, Art 19(1).
6   Council Regulation 2003/343/EC, Art 19(2).
7   Council Regulation 2003/343/EC, Art 19(3).

8   Council Regulation 2003/343/EC, Art 19(4). This time limit may be extended up to a maximum of one year if the transfer could not be carried out due to imprisonment of the asylum seeker or up to a maximum of eighteen months if he or she absconds.
9   Council Regulation 2003/343/EC, Art 20.
10 *Omar (Mohammed Abdi) v Secretary of State for the Home Department* [2005] EWCA 285, upholding the Administrative Court at [2004] EWHC 1427.

ADMINISTRATIVE COOPERATION

12.154 In Chapter V of the Regulation, which deals with administrative cooperation, Member States agree (subject to specified limitations) to exchange information for the determination of the Member State responsible for examining the application for asylum, for the examination of the application for asylum and for the implmentation of any obligation arising under the Regulation.[1] An asylum seeker has the right to be informed, on request, of any data that is processed concerning him or her.[2] Provision is made also enabling bilateral administrative arrangements to be established between Member States concerning the practical details of the implementation of the Regulation, in order to facilitate its application and increase its effectiveness.[3]

1   Council Regulation 2003/343/EC, Art 21.
2   Council Regulation 2003/343/EC, Art 21(9). If information has been processed in breach of the Regulation or of Directive 95/46/EC of the European Parliament and the Council of 24 October 1995 on the protection of individuals with regard to the processing of personal data and on the free movement of such data, in particular because it is incomplete or inaccurate, the asylum applicant is entitled to have it corrected, erased or blocked: Art 21(8). Exchanged data shall be kept for a period not exceeding that which is necessary for the purposes for which it is exchanged: Article 21(11).
3   These may relate to the exchanges of liaison officers and the simplification of the procedures and shortening of the time limits relating to transmission and the examination of requests to take charge of or take back asylum seekers: Council Regulation 2003/343/EC, Art 23. The arrangements must be communicated to the Commission, which is obliged to check that they do not infringe the Regulation. See also Regulation 2003/1560/EC (OJ 2003 L 222/3, in force 6 September 2003), setting out more detailed provisions for the implementation of the Dublin II regulation.

12.155 The Dublin II Regulation was adopted under Article 63(1)(a) EC Treaty,[1] and has general application and is binding in its entirety and directly applicable in all Member States.[2] The Dublin II Regulation thus has *direct effect*. This should mean that individuals can in principle rely on its provisions before national courts where these conflict with any national law measures. As the Advocate General stated in his opinion in *Panayatova*, 'inherent in the recognition of direct effect is an idea of effectiveness and judicial protection of the individual rights granted to individuals'.[3] This makes Dublin II very different to the original Dublin Convention, which did not have direct effect and whose provisions could not be relied on in the courts.[4] However, the regulation is primarily aimed at determining responsibility between Member States, rather than conferring rights on individuals, and the potential practical impact of the difference may be limited. This was demonstrated by the decision of the Court of Appeal in *G*,[5] a claim by a Somali minor facing return to Italy on third country grounds, seeking judicial review of the certification of her human rights claim, based on Article 8 ECHR because of the presence in the United Kingdom of relatives, while in Italy she had no-one. Relying on

12.155 *Refugees, Asylum and Exceptional Leave*

Article 15 of Dublin II,[6] she argued that removal to Italy would not be 'in accordance with the law' given her status as an unaccompanied minor with relatives here. The Court held however that Article 15 did not confer a freestanding substantive right on individual applicants; rather its effect was 'to regulate the relationship between two or more Member States'.[7]

[1] Under Art 63(1)(a), the Council is to adopt measures on asylum on the criteria and mechanisms for determining which Member State is responsible for considering an application for asylum submitted by a national of a third country in one of the Member States. See further 7.34.

[2] Article 249 EC Treaty.

[3] *Panayatova v Minister voor Vreemdelingenzaken en Integratie* Case C-327/02 (19 February 2004, unreported), ECJ, para 36.

[4] See fifth edition of this work at 12.149 and cases cited there.

[5] *R (on the application of G) v Secretary of State for the Home Department* [2005] EWCA Civ 546.

[6] See 12.152 above.

[7] Maurice Kay LJ held that the two states, Italy and the UK, had agreed that Italy would process the claim, and it was open to the claimant to approach the Italian authorities, inviting them to request the UK authorities to process the application. It may be that advisers should consider approaching the authorities of the destination state in future. However, the Article 15 humanitarian clause is permissive (see below), unlike the other hierarchy criteria, on which it might be possible to rely in a future challenge to the legality of a removal purportedly made under Dublin II.

Discretionary cases

12.156 Articles 3(2) and 15 are important provisions of the Dublin II Regulation, in that they preserve Member States' sovereign discretion to consider asylum claims for which they are not responsible according to the other criteria, at claimants' request or with their agreement.[1] Article 3(2) is, of course, necessary in cases where a domestic court rules that the responsible state is not 'safe' and the asylum seeker may not be returned there. These provisions also appear to recognise the element of choice afforded to refugees in seeking international protection[2] and alleviate some of the hardship that third-country removals can cause. Although the Home Office, in common with its European counterparts, usually refuses to accept this, asylum seekers make rational choices (if they are able) about the country in which to seek asylum, most obviously on the basis of their perception of the safety of the country, but also because of family ties, for reasons of language and culture and other connections to the country. The ability to depart from the normal practice by reference to these factors also promotes a subsidiary purpose of the Refugee Convention, which is the integration of refugees into the host community – an aim more likely to be achieved if they have pre-existing connections with it.

[1] These Articles correspond to Arts 3(4) and 9 of the original Dublin Convention. The Art 15 humanitarian clause in particular is much stronger than its Art 9 counterpart.

[2] See *R v Uxbridge Magistrates' Court, ex p Adimi* [1999] INLR 490.

12.157 The Secretary of State's policy on the circumstances in which discretion would be exercised by considering an asylum claim substantively in the United Kingdom despite the person's arrival from a 'safe' third country was first set out in a written answer to a parliamentary question dated 25 July

1990. It required evidence of 'substantial links' with the United Kingdom making it reasonable for the claim exceptionally to be considered in the UK.[1] A restrictive approach to the exercise of discretion in this area has not always been approved by the courts.[2] In *Ex p Nicholas*[3] a decision to remove a claimant who had married after arrival, pursuant to a policy distinction between pre- and post-arrival marriage, was quashed as unreasonable where there was no issue as to the genuineness of the marriage. On 22 July 2002, the policy was restated.[4] It still required 'substantial links' with the UK and expressly excluded spouses where the marriage took place after arrival in the UK.[5] According to the 2002 policy, a claimant will not normally be removed on third-country grounds if (i) he or she has a spouse or unmarried minor children in the UK or (ii) he or she is an unmarried minor with a parent in the UK. Discretion may be execised if the minor is married, although this is more likely if the married minor is the applicant with a parent in the UK, than if the applicant is a parent with a married minor child in the UK. Discretion may also be exercised where the applicant is an elderly or otherwise dependent parent. Other family links may qualify but only where there is clear evidence that the applicant is wholly or mainly dependent on the relative in the UK and there is an absence of support elsewhere. Adult claimants with parents and/or siblings in the UK have rarely had discretion exercised in their favour.[6] The 2002 policy also limits the meaning of 'in the UK'.[7] In these and other respects, the Secretary of State 'substantive links' policy does not adequately reflect the considerations set out in Dublin II, and the policy will need to be reassessed generally and in particular cases to ensure conformity with Article 8 of the ECHR.[8]

[1] Written reply by then Minister David Waddington MP, *Hansard*, HC Official Reports, cols. 262–263. The reference to 'substantial links' was explained in a letter dated 21 March 1991 from IND to UKIAS, reproduced in *Butterworths Immigration Law Service*.

[2] In *R v Secretary of State for the Home Department, ex p B* (CO 1818/1998) (24 June 1999, unreported), removal of a minor was held 'cruel'. See also *R v Secretary of State for the Home Department, ex p Islam (Asif)* (CO 628/1999) (1 February 2000, unreported).

[3] *R v Secretary of State for the Home Department, ex p Nicholas* [2000] Imm AR 334.

[4] *Hansard*, HC Offical Reports, 22 July 2002, col 860W (Beverley Hughes MP).

[5] The July 2002 policy, depriving those who had married after arrival in the UK from the benefit of the policy, came after the grant of permission in *R (on the application of Nadarajah) v Secretary of State for the Home Department*, a Nicholas-type case (see fn 3 above), but at the full hearing the Home Office succeeded in the argument that the new rather than the old policy should apply, see [2002] EWHC 2595. An appeal to the Court of Appeal on the point of which policy should apply has been deferred.

[6] In *R v Secretary of State for the Home Department, ex p Raj (Reena)* (CO 2630/1998) (30 November 1999, unreported) the Secretary of State conceded a challenge to the removal of an Indian woman who, prior to her last entry into the UK, had been continuously resident for nine years in the UK, had been educated, employed and established a substantial network of supportive friends here and was vulnerable to mental illness if deprived of these support networks. However in *R v Secretary of State for the Home Department, ex p Ahmed (Marion)* (1 February 1999, unreported), the Court of Appeal held that the applicant could not rely on connections made during delays caused by her own representations or litigation against removal.

[7] 'In all cases "in the United Kingdom" is to be taken as meaning with leave to enter or remain or on temporary admission to this country as an asylum seeker prior to an initial decision on their application': *Hansard* (fn 4 above).

[8] Both the 1991 and 2002 policies have been found to be lawful and in conformity with Art 8 ECHR: see eg *R (on the application of Demiroglu) v Secretary of State for the Home Department* [2001] EWHC Admin 663, (Collins J); *R (on the application of Kozany) v Secretary of State for the Home Department* [2002] EWHC 2830 (Admin), [2002] All ER (D) 39 (Dec) (Gibbs J). The 2002 policy makes it clear that cases citing other family ties

and not displaying any of the features which engaged the exercise of discretion, would not normally be considered substantively. Thus 'a brother, who was not dependent on his sibling(s), would not normally have his case considered here, no matter how strong his cultural or linguistic links with the United Kingdom'.

ASYLUM APPEALS

12.158 The Nationality, Immigration and Asylum Act 2002 and the Asylum and Immigration (Treatment of Claimants, etc) Act 2004 have radically changed the appeals regime from that considered in the fifth edition of this work. The appeals regime is considered in detail in chapter 18. For present purposes we identify some of the principal differences. First, there is no longer a separate 'asylum' appeal provison (as there was under section 69 Immigration and Asylum Act 1999); section 82 of the 2002 Act gives a right of appeal in respect of specified 'immigration decisions', and section 84(1) enacts the permissible grounds of appeal, including an 'asylum' ground (namely that removal from the United Kingdom in consequence of the immigration decision would breach the United Kingdom's obligations under the Refugee Convention).[1] Secondly, the certification regime under the 1999 Act[2] was abolished by the 2002 Act.[3] Thirdly, the 2002 Act controversially introduced a new certification regime whereby claims considered to be clearly unfounded attract no suspensive appeal prior to removal.[4] Fourthly, the two-tiered immigration appellate authority of adjudicators and the Immigration Appeal Tribunal has been substituted by a new, single-tiered body called the Asylum and Immigration Tribunal, and appeal and review rights thereafter substantially modified.[5]

[1] The immigration decisions are set out in Nationality, Immigration and Asylum Act 2002, s 82(2)(a)–(k). There is no general right of appeal against refusal of asylum, when leave is granted on some other ground, unless the leave exceeds one year (or totals one year in aggregate): s 83. The 'asylum ground' is at s 84(1)(g).
[2] IAA 1999, Sch 4, para 9, inherited from the 1993 and 1996 Acts: see fifth edition at 12.163–12.174.
[3] Nationality, Immigration and Asylum Act 2002, Sch 9.
[4] NIAA 2002, s 94.
[5] Asylum and Immigration (Treatment of Claimants, etc) Act 2004, s 26.

12.159 The right of appeal given by section 82 of the 2002 Act is only exercisable while the person is in the United Kingdom if (inter alia) the appellant 'has made an asylum claim'.[1] Thus a claim for asylum is a pre-requisite for an in-country appeal on asylum grounds. But not every asylum claim necessarily gives rise to an appeal,[2] and certainly not every claim gives rise to an appeal on the merits, or even an in-country appeal. We have described above the 'safe third country' procedures under Schedule 3 to the Asylum and Immigration (Treatment of Claimants, etc) Act 2004, which preclude full investigation of an asylum claim in the UK, an in-country asylum appeal or an out-of-country appeal relying on *refoulement* arguments in respect of removal to any country on one of the lists in the Schedule, where the Secretary of State has issued a certificate.[3] Section 94 of the NIAA 2002 prevents in-country asylum appeals against direct removal to the country of feared persecution., We look at these 'safe country of origin' provisions below.

[1] Nationality, Immigration and Asylum Act 2002, s 92(4)(a).

2   For the impact of one-stop appeals on repeat claims for asylum, see 12.170 and 18.43 below.
3   Asylum and Immigration (Treatment of Claimants, etc) Act 2004, Sch 3, in force from 1 October 2004. Sch 4 to the 2004 Act repeals the previous equivalent provision, s 93 Nationality, Immigration and Asylum Act 2002. See 12.140ff above.

Safe countries of origin

12.160 Countries of origin were first designated 'safe' by provisions of the Asylum and Immigration Act 1996.[1] The countries designated in 1996 – the so-called 'white list' – were Bulgaria, Cyprus, Ghana, India, Pakistan, Poland and Romania.[2] The designation power was very controversial,[3] as was its use, particularly in relation to Pakistan in the light of the difficulties faced there by Christians, Ahmadis and women among others. A certified claim reduced (but did not remove) in-country appeal rights available to nationals of certified countries.[4] The measure was controversial, and was not replicated when the Immigration and Asylum Act 1999 replaced the appeals provisions of the 1993 and 1996 Acts.

1   Section 1 of the 1996 Act substituted a new para 5 of Sch 2 to the Asylum and Immigration Appeals Act 1993 which included (in sub-para (2)) the power to designate a country or territory as one in which it appeared to the Secretary of State that was 'in general no serious risk of persecution'. If the adjudicator accepted that the person was a national of a 'white list' country, the appellant could not appeal to the Immigration Appeal Tribunal (Sch 2, para 5(7)).
2   Asylum (Designated Countries of Destination and Designated Safe Third Countries) Order 1996, SI 1996/2671.
3   In that it tended to undermine the principle of individual determination of claims required by the Refugee Convention.
4   The adjudicator could not discharge the certificate (in the absence of evidence of torture), on the ground that the claim should not have been certified (*R v Special Adjudicator, ex p Mohammed Zaman* [2000] Imm AR 68; *Talat Bajwa v Secretary of State for the Home Department* [2000] Imm AR 364, CA). Any challenge to designation and to certification had to be by way of judicial review (*R v Special Adjudicator and Secretary of State for the Home Department, ex p Dhanoa* (1999/7535/C) (21 January 2000, unreported), CA). In *R (on the application of Javed) v Secretary of State for the Home Department* [2001] EWCA Civ 789, [2002] QB 129, the Court of Appeal held that the Secretary of State's decision to designate Pakistan as a country in which there was in general no risk of persecution was made on an erroneous view of the facts or the law. And in *R (on the application of Singh) (Balwinder) v Secretary of State for the Home Department* [2001] EWHC Admin 925, [2001] All ER (D) 235 (Nov), Burton J held that India too had been unlawfully designated.

12.161 The use of discredited 'white lists' returned with a vengeance in section 94 of the Nationality, Immigration and Asylum Act 2002, which makes provision for the certification of both refugee and human rights claims. Where a claimant who applied after 7 November 2002[1] is entitled to reside in a listed State,[2] including one (or part of one) designated by order of the Secretary of State as a State in which there is in general no serious risk of persecution and removal to which will not in general contravene the United Kingdom's obligations under the Human Rights Convention,[3] then the Secretary of State is obliged to certify such claim as clearly unfounded unless satisfied that it is not.[4] The difference between the 2002 Act regime and that contained in the 1996 Act however is dramatic. Whereas under the 1996 Act the scope of appeal was limited to appeals to adjudicators without the possibility of further appeal to the Immigration Appeal Tribunal, under the new regime those whose claims are certified as clearly unfounded have no suspensive in-country appeal.[5] The range of states whose nationals may have their asylum or human rights claims certified clearly unfounded was radically increased by section 27 of the Asylum and Immigration (Treatment of Claimants, etc) Act 2004, which provides that where the conditions in section 94(5) are met for a 'description of person' within a State or part of a State, then that State or part may be added to the list in in respect of that description of person.[6] The purpose of the provision is said to be 'to provide extra flexibility to identify groups of persons within a State or part for whom conditions are generally safe'.[7] The inclusion of Bangladesh on the list of designated States was successfully challenged in *Zakir Husan*,[8] and Pakistan (whose designation under the 1996 Act was successfully challenged in *Javed*,[9] has not been included, but India has been added to the list despite its having been the subject of a successful challenge.[10] However, further amendments to the 2002 Act mean that a claimant who is subject to extradition proceedings who would normally have a *non-suspensive* right of appeal will have a *suspensive* right of appeal against any refusal of an asylum or human rights claim.[11]

[1] Nationality, Immigration and Asylum Act 2002, s 94 did not come into force until 1 April 2003 (SI 2003/754, Art 2(1) and Sch 1), but transitional provisions under s 115, in identical terms, came into force on the passing of the Act: s 162(2)(w).

[2] The original version of s 94(4) listed the Acession States (the Republic of Cyprus, the Czech Republic, the Republic of Estonia, the Republic of Hungary, the Republic of Latvia, the Republic of Lithuania, the Republic of Malta, the Republic of Poland, the Slovak Republic, and the Republic of Slovenia) which joined the European Union on 1 May 2004. These states were removed from the list on 1 October 2004 by Asylum and Immigration (Treatment of Claimants, etc) Act 2004, s 27(4): SI 2004/2523. From that date, the appeal rights of asylum claimants from one of those states are governed by the Immigration (European Economic Area) Regulations 2000 as amended by SI 2003/549.

[3] NIAA 2002, s 94(5). States which have been added by statutory instrument are Albania, Bulgaria, Serbia and Montenegro, Jamaica, Macedonia, Moldova, Romania (from 1 April 2003, SI 2003/970); Bangladesh, Bolivia, Brazil, Ecuador, Sri Lanka, Ukraine (from 23 July 2003, save in relation to asylum or human rights claims before that date: SI 2003/1919); India (from 13 February 2005, save in relation to asylum or human rights claims before that date: SI 2005/330). Bangladesh was removed by SI 2005/1016.

[4] NIAA 2002, s 94(3). The Secretary of State may certify any other asylum or human rights claim clearly unfounded, but this is not the 'default' position, as it is in 'safe country of origin' and 'safe third country' cases; see s 94(2).

[5] NIAA 2002, ss 92(1), (4) (which provide for in-country appeals if an asylum or human rights claim has been made in the UK); s 94(1A), (2) (which remove it on certification). Where a certificate is issued under s 94, an appeal taking place outside the United Kingdom is to be considered as if the applicant had not been removed.

[6] NIAA 2002, s 94 (5A)–(5C), added by Asylum and Immigration (Treatment of Claimants, etc) Act 2004 s 27(5) from 1 October 2004: SI 2004/2523. The 'description of person' refers to Refugee Convention attributes and include additionally gender, language, or 'any other attribute or circumstance that the Secretary of State thinks appropriate': s 94(5C). States added to the 'safe list' under these provisions may be removed, or modified: s 94(6), as inserted.

[7] Asylum and Immigration (Treatment of Claimants, etc) Act 2004 Explanatory Notes, at para 129. This could apply to majority groups (defined by ethnicity, religion etc) in countries where minorities are persecuted.

8   R *(on the application of Husan) v Secretary of State for the Home Department* [2005] EWHC 189 (Admin), [2005] All ER (D) 371 (Feb), Wilson J, who held that no rational decision-maker could have been satisfied that the statutory presumptions of safety were met. Following the judgment, Bangladesh was removed from the list of safe countries under s 94(5): see fn 3 above.
9   R *(on the application of Javed) v Secretary of State for the Home Department* [2001] EWCA Civ 789, [2002] QB 129.
10 R *(on the application of Singh) v Secretary of State for the Home Department* [2001] EWHC Admin 925, [2001] All ER (D) 235 (Nov).
11 NIAA 2002, s 94(6A), inserted by Asylum and Immigration (Treatment of Claimants, etc) Act 2004, s 27(7) from 1 October 2004: SI 2004/2523.

Procedure on asylum appeals

12.162 Asylum appeals used to be subject to different time limits and procedures, and had their own procedure rules.[1] The procedure rules now embrace all immigration and asylum appeals,[2] except for those of detained claimants in the 'fast-track' procedure, who are single male asylum applicants considered to come from 'safe' countries and to have straightforward claims.[3] Their appeals are subject to special procedure rules, with very tight time limits and with restricted powers to extend time and to adjourn.[4] Details of appeal procedures are to be found at 18.76ff below. Although asylum appeals are subject to the same appeal procedures as other immigration appeals, the fundamental importance of what is at stake means that the courts are particularly concerned that the highest standards of fairness apply and that procedural and evidential requirements are not over-stringently applied. Thus, where a decision has potentially grave consequences for an asylum seeker, it may be proper to grant an adjournment for further evidence to be adduced,[5] and neither the *Ladd v Marshall*[6] principles governing the reception of fresh evidence, nor the rule in *Al-Mehdawi*[7] apply with their full rigour in asylum or human rights appeals.[8] The Tribunal's own obligations to prevent *refoulement* under the Refugee Convention meant that it must be alive to obvious points of Convention law even when these are not adverted to by the appellant.[9] In asylum cases where the most anxious scrutiny is required,[10] it would only be in an extreme case that a procedural error depriving the appellant of an opportunity to present the case in full could be treated as of no practical effect.[11]

1   Asylum Appeals (Procedure) Rules 1993, SI 1993/1661; Asylum Appeals (Procedure) Rules 1996, SI 1996/2070.
2   Asylum and Immigration Tribunal (Procedure) Rules 2005, SI 2005/230.
3   See 12.110 above.
4   See Asylum and Immigration Tribunal (Fast Track Procedure) Rules 2005, SI 2005/560; 18.80 below.
5   R *(on the application of F) v Special Adjudicator* [2002] EWHC Admin 777, [2002] Imm AR 407.
6   [1954] 3 All ER 745, [1954] 1 WLR 1489 (CA).
7   *Al-Mehdawi v Secretary of State for the Home Department* [1989] 3 All ER 843, [1990] 1 AC 876, [1989] 3 WLR 1294, HL, which established that a procedural failure caused by an appellant's own representative did not lead to an appeal hearing being in breach of the rules of natural justice so as to found a judicial review.
8   R *(on the application of Haile) v Immigration Appeal Tribunal* [2002] INLR 283, CA; R *(on the application of Azkhosravi) v Immigraion Appeal Tribunal* [2001] EWCA Civ 977, [2002] INLR 123 (failure to explain late submission of evidence, approving *R v Immigration Appeal Tribunal, ex p Aziz* [1999] INLR 355). The Court of Appeal gave

guidance on the admission of evidence demonstrating a mistake of fact and the role of the Tribunal in *E v Secretary of State for the Home Department, R v Secretary of State for the Home Department* [2003] EWCA Civ 49. See also *R (on the application of Tofik) v Immigration Appeal Tribunal* [2003] EWCA Cv 1138, [2003] INLR 623 (extension of time).

9   *R v Secretary of State for the Home Department, ex p Robinson* [1997] Imm AR 568, CA, applied in *R (on the application of Naing) v Immigration Appeal Tribunal, R (on the application of Eyaz) v Immigration Appeal Tribunal* [2003] EWHC 771 (Admin).

10 The 'most anxious scrutiny' is a quotation from Lord Bridge in *Bugdaycay v Secretary of State for the Home Department* [1987] AC 514, HL.

11 *Gardi v Secretary of State for the Home Department* [2002] EWCA Civ 750, [2003] Imm AR 39, [2002] INLR 499. The case was subsequently declared null for want of jurisdiction (it should have been heard by the Court of Session, not the English court), at [2002] EWCA Civ 1560, [2002] INLR 557, but the principle remains sound. However in *Secretary of State for the Home Department v Makke* [2005] EWCA Civ 1581, the CA observed that relief should not be granted unless the underlying claim has merit.

Credibility

12.163 English courts have not given the same assistance to appellate authorities dealing with credibility in the context of asylum claims[1] as has been given by the Canadian courts,[2] which have held that 'when an applicant swears to the truth of certain allegations, this creates a presumption that those allegations are true unless there be reason to doubt their truthfulness',[3] and that 'a reasonable margin of appreciation be applied to any perceived flaws in the claimant's testimony'.[4] But decisions based on adverse credibility have been subjected to careful scrutiny by the Tribunal and the Administrative Court to ensure that they are properly reasoned and take account of relevant evidence,[5] and appellate bodies' unsupported assertions that a witness is not credible are no longer acceptable. Questions of credibility are, however, matters for the tribunal of fact, which should be cautious in rejecting as incredible an account by an anxious and inexperienced asylum seeker, whose reasons for seeking asylum may well be expected to contain inconsistencies and omissions in the course of its revelation to the authorities and investigation on appeal.[6] The Tribunal has noted that 'It is perfectly possible for an adjudicator to believe that a witness is not telling the truth about some matters, has exaggerated the story to make his case better, or is simply uncertain about matters, but still to be persuaded that the centrepiece of the story stands'.[7] The API acknowledge this: 'Discrepancies, exaggerated accounts, and the addition of new claims of mistreatment may affect credibility. However, they may equally reflect a concern on the part of the applicant, or their advisers, to bolster a claim due to a very real fear of return. Applicants should be given the opportunity to explain any apparent discrepancies and the reasons for any changes in their accounts.'[8]

1   The Refugee Legal Centre has produced a useful training document: 'Issues arising from "credibility", procedure and evidence before the appellate authorities' containing references to Canadian, US, New Zealand and Australian case law to supplement that of the UK courts. See further Catriona Jarvis *The Judge as Juror revisited* [2003] Immigration Law Digest (Winter) p 7; Amanda Weston *A Witness of Truth – Credibility Findings in Asylum Appeals* (1998) INLP, vol 12, No 3; Dr Stuart Turner *Discrepancies and Delays in Histories Presented by asylum seekers: Implications for* Assessment, Traumatic Stress Clinic, 18 Dec/1996; Herlihy et al 'Discrepancies in autobiographical memories: implications for assessment of asylum claims', BMJ 2002, 324–7 (available on BMJ website); Regina Graycar *The Gender of Judgments: An Introduction,* in Feminist Legal debates, ed

Margaret Thornton, OUP 1995; Professor Patricia J Williams *The Obliging Shell (An informal Essay on Formal Equal Opportunity)* in After Identity, ed. Danielson and Engle, Routledge 1995; Sir Thomas Bingham *The Judge as Juror: Judicial Determination of Factual Issues 1985 Current Legal problems*; and the Canadian Guidelines, below.

2   The Immigration and Refugee Board has produced a useful guide 'Assessment of credibility in the context of CRDD hearings' (October 1999), setting out all relevant Federal Court of Appeal decisions on various aspects of credibility. It is available on the Immigration and Refugee Board website www.irb.gc.ca.

3   *Maldonado v Canada (Minister of Employment and Immigration)* [1980] 2 FC 302, CA, cited in Hathaway 12.22 fn 2 above, p 84.

4   *Attakora (Benjamin) v Minister of Employment and Immigration*, FCA Decision A-1091–87, 19 May 1989, cited in Hathaway above, p 85. The UN Committee Against Torture has made the same point, saying that 'complete accuracy is not to be expected from victims of torture', in *Alan v Switzerland* [1997] INLR 29. And in *Hrickova* (00TH 02034) (9 August 2000, unreported), IAT, inconsistencies in the account of a Slovak Roma of stabbing and gang rape were 'properly explained by the nature of human recollection, particularly dealing with traumatic incidents'.

5   See cases cited at 18.135ff below.

6   Hathaway above, pp 84–88; *Re SA*, NZRSAA 1/92 (NZ); *Matter of SMJ* Interim Decision 3303 (BIA) 1997 (US); *Kopalapillai v Minister for Immigration and Multicultural Affairs* [1997] 1510 FCA (24 December 1997) (Aus).

7   *Chiver* (10758); see also *Guo v Minister for Immigration and Ethnic Affairs* (1996) 64 FRC 151 at 194, a decision of the full court of the Federal Court of Australia. Elevation of peripheral matters into matters of determinative weight was held unlawful in *R (on the application of Choudrey) v Immigration Appeal Tribunal* [2001] EWHC Admin 613, [2001] All ER (D) 04 (Aug).

8   API on 'Assessing the Asylum Claim', section 11.

12.164 Since it is not in the nature of repressive regimes and societies to behave reasonably, the strange or unusual cannot be dismissed as incredible or improbable, particularly if there is supporting material of similar accounts in the relevant human rights literature, and decision-makers should constantly be on their guard to avoid implicitly recharacterising the nature of the risk based on their own perceptions of reasonability.[1] An assessment of credibility can only be made on the basis of a complete understanding of the entire picture.[2] The approach of the UN Committee on Torture emphasises the importance of a consistent pattern of gross, flagrant or mass violations of human rights in the assessment of risk.[3] There are also difficulties in drawing conclusions on credibility from the manner in which evidence is given, usually through an interpreter, by a person from a different society and cultural background.[4] Nonetheless decision-makers are generally encouraged to make definite findings on credibility before concluding on future risk – rather than approaching the matter by firstly determining whether a claim for refugee status could be made out on the basis that all that the applicant says is true before considering whether or not the evidence is credible.[5] Further judicial guidance on a cautious approach to questions of credibility was given in *Ex p Chunu Miah*.[6]

1   Hathaway 12.22 fn 2 above, p 81. See *Kasolo* (13190); *Mendes* (12183); and cases cited at 18.135ff below. A number of influential Canadian and Australian cases have held that adverse findings on plausibility should be made only in the clearest of cases: see eg *Divsalar v Canada* [2002] FCT 653, [2002] FCJ 875; *Shenoda v Canada* (2003) FCT 207; *WAIJ v Minister for Immigration and Multicultural Affairs* [2004] FCAFC 74. But the Tribunal prefers a more robust approach: see *MM (plausibility) (DRC)* [2005] UKIAT 00019 'IAT reported'.

2   *Horvath v Secretary of State for the Home Department* [1999] INLR 7, [1999] Imm AR 121, IAT; *R v Immigration Appeal Tribunal, ex p Ahmed (Sardar)* [1999] INLR 473. But this only applies where country conditions are relevant: see *R (on the application of*

Shokrollahy) v Immigration Appeal Authority [2000] Imm AR 580, QBD; *R v Secretary of State for the Home Department, ex p Befekadu* [1999] Imm AR 467, QBD. The API on assessing the claim, s 10(ii) and (iii) states that a decision on credibility should be based on an objective assessment of the conditions in the proposed country of return at the time of the decision, and that if there is no reason to doubt credibility and no country information contradicting the applicant's statement, he or she must be given the benefit of the doubt.

3   *Mutombo v Switzerland* (Communication No 13/93) unreported, UNCAT (cited in *Alan v Switzerland* [1997] INLR 29).

4   The observations of Webster J in *R v Secretary of State for the Home Department, ex p Patel* [1986] Imm AR 208, QBD are a salutary reminder of the dangers of adverse findings against a person from a different cultural background speaking through an interpreter. See the materials cited above at 12.160 fn 1, and see also 18.135 below.

5   See the approach of the CA in *Jin Tao He v Secretary of State for the Home Department* [2002] EWCA Civ 1150, [2002] Imm AR 590 and in *Mishto v Secretary of State for the Home Department* [2003] EWCA Civ 1978: contrast *Guine* (13868).

6   (CO 2318/1994) (12 October 1995, unreported), QBD, see *Butterworths Immigration Law Service*, IV[99]. The API also warn caseworkers against making 'irrational judgments' based on, for example, an applicant's family's continued presence in the country of feared persecution. See API on 'Assessing the Asylum Claim', section 10.1.

12.165 Before 1993, in the absence of a right of appeal a judicial approach had evolved of ensuring that conclusions founded on credibility were not made without an opportunity for the asylum seeker to comment on specific issues.[1] The introduction of in-country rights of appeal removed direct scrutiny of adverse findings in decision letters by the High Court. Instead, the appellant is required to deal with adverse findings by evidence on the appeal. The test laid down in *Musisi* of 'anxious scrutiny'[2] is now applied by the Administrative Court not so much to the Secretary of State's original decision as to the appellate process (except in cases where there is no in-country right of appeal).[3] There is a tension between the appellate function[4] and the prospective nature of the question at issue in asylum claims, which makes the appeal hearing part of the determination process.[5] This has surfaced in appeal hearings where credibility is challenged for the first time; if the facts have not been put in issue by the Home Office, the prospective nature of the question should not necessitate a review of those facts.[6] An opportunity to deal with matters of credibility must be given during the appeal hearing, and if fresh issues are to be raised, the appellant will need sufficient time to deal with them, which may require an adjournment.[7]

1   For the principles of fairness in cases where there was no right of appeal see *R v Secretary of State for the Home Department, ex p Thirukumar* [1989] Imm AR 402, CA; *Gaima v Secretary of State for the Home Department* [1989] Imm AR 205; *R v Immigration Appeal Tribunal, ex p Akdogan* [1995] Imm AR 176, per Brooke J.

2   [1987] AC 514 at 531.

3   *R v Immigration Appeal Tribunal, ex p Ali (Omar)* [1995] Imm AR 45, QBD. Where there is no suspensive right of appeal, the Administrative Court will be concerned with the Secretary of State's decision that the claim is clearly unfounded, and in that context, must treat the claimant's account as credible, regardless of adverse credibility findings by the Secretary of State, unless no reasonable decision-maker could believe it: *R (on the application of L) v Secretary of State for the Home Department* [2003] EWCA Civ 25, [2003] Imm AR 330, [2003] INLR 224.

4   The Tribunal is required to decide whether the decision under appeal was in accordance with the law or the rules: Nationality, Immigration and Asylum Act 2002, s 86(3)(a), The 1999 Act contained explicit jurisdiction to review the 'facts on which the decision or action is based': Immigration and Asylum Act 1999, Sch 4, para 21.

5   *Ravichandran (Senathirajah) v Secretary of State for the Home Department* [1996] Imm AR 97 at 112–113. This applies equally on appeals on human rights grounds: *R (on the application of Razgar) v Secretary of State for the Home Department* [2004] UKHL 27,

[2004] 3 WLR 58 at para 20. For this purpose, NIAA 2002, s 85(4) enables the Tribunal to consider any relevant evidence, including evidence about post-decision facts.

6   *Ad hoc* challenges to credibility also make a nonsense of the power to give pre-hearing directions to identify and limit the issues in the appeal, in r 45 of the Asylum and Immigration Tribunal (Procedure) Rules 2005, SI 2005/230. However, the Tribunal has held that the Secretary of State's representative at a hearing is entitled to cross-examine on issues not specifically raised in the refusal letter: see eg. *D (Iran)* [2003] UKIAT 00087: 'Unless there is a specific concession, the refusal letter does not fetter or limit the scope of the case to be pursued by the Secretary of State'. Where however the facts are agreed, or the Secretary of State makes a concession that an appellant is telling the truth about specific matters or generally, the Tribunal should not go behind it: *R (on the application of Ganidagli) v Immigration Appeal Tribunal*, [2001] EWHC Admin 70; *Carcabuk and Bla* (00TH01426) (18 May 2000, unreported), IAT. In *Davoodipanah v Secretary of State for the Home Department* [2004] EWCA Civ 106, [2004] All ER (D) 285 (Jan), the Court of Appeal held that a concession made by either party may be formally withdrawn on appeal if the appeal court considers that there is good reason to take that course, but otherwise, the appeal court should not revisit issues relevant to a concession clearly made to a first instance immigration judge who had relied on it.

7   The Privy Council affirmed the principle that new points originating from the court should not take the parties by surprise in *Hoecheong Products v Cargill Hong Kong Ltd* [1995] 1 WLR 404. See 18.129 below.

12.166 Section 8 of the Asylum and Immigration (Treatment of Claimants, etc) Act 2004 lists various behaviours which must be taken into account as damaging the claimant's credibility. These include:

(i)   behaviour which the deciding authority[1] thinks is designed or likely[2] to coneal information or to mislead, or to obstruct or delay the handling or resolution of the claim or the taking of a decision in relation to the claimant;[3]

(ii)   failure to take advantage of a reasonable opportunity to make an asylum or human rights claim[4] while in a safe country;[5]

(iii)   failure to make an asylum or human rights claim before notification of an immigration decision (unless the claim relies wholly on matters arising after the notification);[6]

(iv)   failure to make an asylum or human rights claim before arrest under an immigration provision (unless there was no reasonable opportunity to do so or the claim relies wholly on matters arising since the arrest).[7]

Failure without reasonable explanation to produce a passport on request to an immigration officer or to the Secretary of State, the production of a document which is not a valid passport as if it were, the destruction, alteration or disposal, without reasonable explanation, of a passport, ticket or other document connected with travel, and failure without reasonable explanation to answer a question asked by a deciding authority, are to be treated as designed or likely to conceal information or to mislead.[8]

1   Ie, an immigration officer, the Secretary of State, the Asylum and Immigration Tribunal (or, before the coming into force of s 26 of the Act, the adjudicator or Immigration Appeal Tribunal), or the Special Immigration Appeals Commission: s 8(7). The section came into force on 1 January 2005: SI 2004/3398. A determination which fails to indicate that the Tribunal has had regard to the statutory matters would be vulnerable to setting aside for error of law, although the weight to be attached to them is clearly for the Tribunal to assess.

2 This formulation is on its face objectionable, since behaviour not designed to deceive, mislead or obstruct, but merely having that effect, should not affect the credibility of the actor. We suggest that the section must be read subject to exceptions on reasonable grounds, in order to be compatible with basic requirements of fairness. See fn 1 above.

3 Asylum and Immigration (Treatment of Claimants, etc) Act 2004, s 8(2).

4 As defined by Nationality, Immigration and Asylum Act 2002, s 113(1): AI(TC)A 2004, s 8(7).

5 Ie, in a country of transit: AI(TC)A 2004, s 8(4). In *Ozmico* [2002] UKIAT 00484, the Tribunal held that failure to claim in any safe country passed through in the back of a lorry was not a realistic credibility point.

6 AI(TC)A 2004, s 8(5). An 'immigration decision' means refusal or grant of leave to enter or remain in the UK, a decision to remove the claimant under Immigration and Asylum Act 1999 s 10 (persons unlawfully in the UK) or Immigration Act 1971, Sch 2, paras 8–12 (persons refused leave to enter, illegal entrants, and their family members), a decision to make a deportation order or an extradition decision: s 8(7). 'Notification' is defined in the Immigration (Claimant's Credibility) Regulations 2004, SI 2004/3263 to include decisions given orally or by email, by hand or by fax, and provides that notification which would not be valid under the Notices Regulations is valid for the purposes of s 8(5). The regulations also contain presumptions about receipt of notice which is posted or sent to a representative. It is hard to relate these provisions rationally to claimants' credibility.

7 AI(TC)A 2004, s 8(6). An 'immigration provision' means Immigration Act 1971, ss 28A–28CA (immigration offences), Sch 2, para 17 (control of entry), s 14 of the 2004 Act (immigration officers' powers of arrest for offences of fraud etc) and the Extradition Act 1989: AI(TC)A 2004, s 8(7).

8 AI(TC)A 2004, s 8(3). A passport is valid if it relates to the person producing it, has not been altered except by or with the permission of the issuing authority, and was not obtained by deception: AI(TC)A 2004, s 8(8). In the asylum context, it can be extremely dangerous to treat the production of a passport obtained by deception as damaging the credibility of the person producing it, which reinforces the suggestion that the provision must be read as subject to a general exonerating clause on reasonable grounds.

12.167 The factors set out in section 8 are additional to those set out in the immigration rules (paragraph 341 of HC 395, as amended) which may damage an asylum applicant's credibility. These include:

(i)   reliance on manifestly false evidence or false representations in support of the application;

(ii) the lodging of concurrent applications for asylum in the United Kingdom or in another country.[1]

The statutory provision is extraordinarily draconian – coupled with the Credibility Regulations, which are almost surreal[2] – and is in mandatory terms. Only in cases of non-production, destruction or disposal of a passport or a travel document is there the possibility of the decision maker having regard to a reasonable explanation.[3] We suggest that a literal reading of section 8 would result in the deciding authority failing to have regard to relevant circumstances, and thus reaching unlawful decisions. For example, failure to claim asylum in a safe country of transit may be for a very good reason, such as the presence in the UK of all the close relatives of a vulnerable and traumatised claimant. The requirement in all cases to take such failure into account as damaging credibility makes no allowance for such good reasons and denies the element of choice held by the Divisional Court in *Adimi*[4] to be properly open to refugees as to where they may claim asylum.

1 HC 395, para 341 as substituted by HC 164, in effect 1 January 2005.
2 Immigration (Claimant's Credibility) Regulations 2004, SI 2004/3263.

³ In *R v Secretary of State for the Home Department, ex p Yassine* [1990] Imm AR 354, QBD, and *R v Uxbridge Magistrates' Court, ex p Adimi* [1999] INLR 490, the Divisional Court acknowledged that as a result of the carriers' liability legislation, asylum seekers frequently need the assistance of an agent to obtain false papers to smuggle them out of the country (see 12.9 and 12.11 above, and 14.88ff below), and are obliged to destroy the documents to prevent the escape route being closed down.

⁴ *R v Uxbridge Magistrates' Court, ex p Adimi* above.

12.168 Similarly, there are many valid reasons why people do not make their asylum claim immediately on arrival: lack of knowledge of the procedures, arrival in a confused and frightened state, language differences or fear of officialdom may all be insuperable barriers to making any kind of approach to the authorities at the port of entry.[1] Delay in making an application does not necessarily reflect the absence of a fear: asylum seekers who have permission to remain in some other capacity may well not wish to make an asylum claim, which connotes a definitive break with the country where they may have their family and many other loved associations, and with all the uncertainties as to eventual outcome, unless it is apparent that they have no other claim to remain and face removal. Further, a refugee may be acting reasonably when deferring making a claim until obtaining advice from relatives, friends or advice organisations. The API acknowledge that an application which contains demonstrably false claims should nevertheless be accepted if there is sufficient evidence to show a reasonable likelihood of future persecution for a Refugee Convention reason.[2] It is often unfair to make adverse credibility findings on the basis of the use of lies or evasion as to the means of escape, false documents or the destruction of documents, or failure to claim promptly.[3] Such actions have nothing to do with the merits of the asylum claim, and should not be used to diminish credibility – at least, not indiscriminately or without a careful assessment in relation to the facts of individual cases and the applicant's explanation.

¹ Report of Social Services Advisory Committee (Cm 3062, January 1996) para 38. See also UNHCR *Handbook* 12.13 above, para 198; *R v Uxbridge Magistrates' Court, ex p Adimi* [1999] INLR 490 at 497–498; UNHCR's *Guidelines on applicable Criteria and Standards relating to the Detention of Asylum Seekers* (Butterworths Immigration Law Service, 2C[261]); Atle Grahl-Madsen *The Status of Refugees in International Law* Vol II (1972) p 218.

² API on assessing the claim, s 10(i). See also UNHCR *Handbook* above, para 199.

³ See *R v Naillie* [1993] AC 674 ; *R v Secretary of State for the Home Department, ex p Sivakumaran* [1990] Imm AR 80, QBD; *Nzamba-Liloneo v Secretary of State for the Home Department* [1993] Imm AR 225, QBD.

Country Guideline cases

12.169 The increased volume of asylum appeals has led the Tribunal to issue a number of what are called 'country guidance' cases, which, although clearly not binding in the strict sense because of the ever-changing factual situation, purport to give guidance on the determination of claims from the particular country, with reference to a large amount of up to date expert and country evidence.[1] The Court of Appeal has approved the notion of 'factual precedent' cases as generally 'benign and practical',[2] but has advised the Tribunal that 'if the concept of a factual precedent is to have utility in the context of the

Tribunal's duty, safeguards must exist, principally the obligation to give reasons with particular vigour, and special care must be taken to see that the decision is effectively comprehensive, and that the Tribunal addresses all the issues in the case capable of having a real (as opposed to a fanciful) bearing on the result, and explains what it makes of the substantial evidence going to each issue.'[3] It is not open to the Tribunal to decide contrary to the evidence for the sake of consistency.[4] We deal with 'Country Guideline' cases further at 18.142 below.

[1]   Tribunals are required to follow 'Country guideline' cases in relation to country conditions, in the absence of new evidence or a change in circumstances, and failure to do so, or to explain a different approach, renders determinations vulnerable to reconsideration: see AIT Practice Direction, 4 April 2005, para 18.

[2]   See however the Immigration Advisory Service report, *Country Guideline cases: 'benign and practical'?* (Feb 2005), which expresses widespread concerns of practitioners about the abuse of such cases, often decided on incomplete evidence, to shut out meritorious claims.

[3]   *S v Secretary of State for the Home Department* [2002] EWCA Civ 539, [2002] INLR 416. See also *Shirazi v Secretary of State for the Home Department* [2003] EWCA Civ 1562, [2004] 2 All ER 602, [2004] INLR 92.

[4]   *Sajfudinov v Secretary of State for the Home Department* [2001] Imm AR 628 (CA).

12.170 A person who has previously been refused asylum in the UK will not normally have an appeal against refusal of a second application. There are two situations where a second application may generate a further appeal:

(i)   Under the Immigration Rules, the second application may be accepted as a fresh claim for asylum, as opposed to further representations on the old claim, in order to generate a further right of appeal.[1] Where an asylum applicant has previously been refused asylum in the UK, the Secretary of State will decide whether further representations should be treated as a fresh claim for asylum. Representations will be treated as a fresh claim if they are significantly different from the material that has previously been considered. The rule indicates that submissions will only be significantly different if the content has not already been considered, and taken together with the previously considered material, it creates a realistic prospect of success, notwithstanding its rejection.[2] It is for the Secretary of State to decide if a fresh claim has been made, subject to *Wednesbury* review,[3] although some authorities suggest that where evidence of a relevant and substantial change in circumstances, or new evidence is advanced which could not reasonably have been advanced earlier, the Secretary of State is obliged to entertain the new claim, whatever the reasons for rejecting the previous one, unless the new evidence is not credible or is not capable of producing a different outcome.[4] Cases under the old fresh claims provisions continue to be relevant. They indicate that the new evidence would need to have an important influence on the result of the case, although it need not be decisive, and it must be apparently credible, although it need not be incontrovertible.[5] The requirement that the claim be 'sufficiently different' from the old one does not require a change in the factual basis of the application; convincing fresh evidence of the same persecution previously alleged is capable of giving rise to a fresh claim,[6] since it will amount to 'content which has not already been considered'. The rule, unlike its predecessor, does not specify that the new material should have been previously unavailable.[7] The same criteria have been applied to second human rights claims.[8]

(ii) The Secretary of State has a policy as to when fairness requires a subsequent application to trigger further appeal rights even where the application is not regarded as a fresh one. It includes previous loss of appeal rights by error or a serious miscarriage in procedure.[9] The policy may be prayed in aid where there is no change in the nature of the application or the evidence adduced, but where it would be unjust not to give the applicant an opportunity to appeal. A request for the Secretary of State to issue a fresh refusal to give rise to a fresh appeal on *Kazmi* grounds should be made promptly after the claimed miscarriage of procedure.[10] The case law on section 21 of the Immigration Act 1971, now repealed, is also relevant. This allowed the Secretary of State to refer a dismissed appeal back to the appellate authority for an advisory opinion in certain circumstances.[11] If the statutory appeal route had failed because of an adverse decision following a full hearing or because the applicant had taken a calculated risk in not attending, nothing short of potentially decisive evidence, reasonably capable of acceptance, would be required to prompt further consideration of the claim. Where, however, it had or may have failed because of lack of notice for which the applicant bore no personal or imputed blame, that was a relevant, though not a decisive, consideration for the Secretary of State in deciding whether to exercise the power.[12]

[1] Unless and until the Secretary of State accepts the application as a fresh claim, no decision falls within the section and no right of appeal arises: *R v Immigration Appellate Authority, ex p Secretary of State for the Home Department* [1998] Imm AR 52. Nor is NASS support available until it has been accepted as a fresh claim: see chapter 13.

[2] HC 395, para 353, inserted by HC 1112 on 18 October 2004. The rule replaces para 346, deleted by HC 1112. The case of *R v Secretary of State for the Home Department, ex p Onibiyo* [1996] Imm AR 370, CA established that a second asylum claim could be made following the rejection of an earlier one, according to the test of 'a reasonable prospect that a favourable view could be taken of the new claim'.

[3] *R v Secretary of State for the Home Department, ex p Ravichandran (No 3)* [1997] Imm AR 74; *Cakabay v Secretary of State for the Home Department (No 3)* [1999] Imm AR 176, [1998] INLR 623, CA; *R v Secretary of State for the Home Department, ex p Bell* [2000] Imm AR 396.

[4] *R v Secretary of State for the Home Department, ex p Habibi* [1997] Imm AR 391, QBD.

[5] *R v Secretary of State for the Home Department, ex p Boybeyi* [1997] Imm AR 491, [1997] INLR 130, CA.

[6] *R v Secretary of State for the Home Department, ex p Ravichandran (No 2)* [1996] Imm AR 418; *Ward v Secretary of State for the Home Department* [1997] Imm AR 236; *R (on the application of Senkoy) v Secretary of State for the Home Department* [2001] EWCA Civ 328.

[7] The courts might imply such a condition, although it would need to be applied carefully, so as not to defeat good claims. Failure to adduce evidence earlier may be relevant in relation to certification of claims under s 96, for which see below. The failure of advisers to obtain evidence earlier does not make that evidence 'previously unavailable'; *Kabala v Secretary of State for the Home Department* [1997] Imm AR 517, CA, but evidence was not 'available' if the giver of it was physically or psychologically unable to give it: *R v Secretary of State for the Home Department, ex p Ejon* [1998] INLR 195 (traumatised rape victim); cf *R v Secretary of State for the Home Department, ex p Khan (Saleem)* (CO 647/1999) (17 May 1999, unreported), QBD (evidence of the applicant's homosexuality was 'previously available' despite the taboo in Muslim society preventing disclosure to family members who were helping him on his first claim); see also *R (on the application of Maci) v Secretary of State for the Home Department* [2003] EWHC 1123 Admin.

⁸ Jackson J in *R (on the application of Ratnam) (Savasoba) v Secretary of State* [2003]
EWHC 398 Admin held that although the relevant rule (then HC 395, para 346) applied
only to asylum applications, the same principles should be applied by analogy to a fresh
claim based on human rights issues. See also *Djebbar v Secretary of State for the Home
Department* [2004] EWCA Civ 804, [2004] 33 LS Gaz R 36.
⁹ Home Office letter, 22 July 1994, cited in *R v Secretary of State for the Home Department,
ex p Kazmi* [1995] Imm AR 73.
¹⁰ *R v Secretary of State for the Home Department, ex p Kone* [1998] Imm AR 291.
¹¹ See *R v Secretary of State for the Home Department, ex p Bello* [1995] Imm AR 537,
QBD; *Khaldoun v Secretary of State for the Home Department* [1996] Imm AR 200, CA.
¹² *R v Secretary of State for the Home Department, ex p Yousaf, Jamil* [2000] INLR 432, CA.

12.171 However, even if further representations are accepted as a fresh claim,
a further appeal may be prevented by the issue of a certificate from the
Secretary of State or an immigration officer under section 96 Nationality,
Immigration and Asylum Act 2002, as amended.[1] The criteria for certification
under section 96(1) are that there was a previous opportunity to raise the
matter now relied on in an appeal (whether or not the right of appeal was
exercised), and that there is no satisfactory reason for the failure to raise it
then. The section 96(2) criteria for certification are that the application relies
on a ground which should have been put forward in response to a one-stop
warning under section 120 of the 2002 Act.[2] We have considered these
provisions at 8.101 above. The API indicate that the Secretary of State first
decides whether representations made after the dismissal of an appeal amount
to a fresh claim, and then whether the claim should be certified under
section 96.[3] But where the Secretary of State has accepted that representations
amount to a fresh claim with a realistic prospect of success on appeal,
certification under section 96 which would prevent such an appeal would in
all probability be challengeable by way of judicial review.[4] However, a
certificate under section 96 is a more likely response where an applicant seeks
a further appeal on the ground of miscarriage of procedure.[5] If it is clear that
the failure was not the fault of the claimant, who has not had a proper
opportunity to have a meritorious claim reviewed by the Tribunal, the
certificate is unlikely to be upheld.[6]

¹ By Asylum and Immigration (Treatment of Claimants, etc) Act 2004, s 30.
² The statute refers to 'a matter' which could have been raised earlier. A 'matter' suggests a
ground or a claim, cf Mitting J in *R (on the application of Balamurali) v Secretary of State
for the Home Department* [2003] EWHC 1183 (Admin), [2003] All ER (D) 121 (May),
who likened a ground or claim to a cause of action. Thus, a 'matter' is not the same as
'evidence'. It is at least arguable that failure to adduce relevant evidence earlier which goes
to the same 'matter' (as opposed to a failure to raise the 'matter' at all) would not be a
valid ground for certification.
³ API 'One stop procedure' para 3.1, 3.2.
⁴ But see *R (on the application of Borak) v Secretary of State for the Home Department*
[2004] EWHC 1861 (Admin), upheld on very narrow grounds by the Court of Appeal
at [2005] EWCA Civ 110, [2005] All ER (D) 163 (Jan) where judicial review on just such
a basis was rejected because of the claimant's failure to advert in his previous appeal to
information which he did not then have.
⁵ See one-stop appeals, 18.43, 18.87 below.
⁶ By analogy with cases where the court has re-opened appeals for procedural irregularity
not caused either by the appellate authority or by the appellant: see eg *R (on the
application of Tataw) v Immigration Appeal Tribunal* [2003] EWCA Civ 925, [2003]
INLR 585; *R (on the application of Hasa) v Immigration Appeal Tribunal* [2003] EWHC
Admin 396. The API recognise that serious failure on the part of a representative can be a
satisfactory reason for failing to raise a matter on appeal or in response to a one-stop
notice: API 'One stop procedure' para 3.2.

Leave to remain

Refugees

12.172 Where concurrent applications are made for refugee status and in some other capacity, current policy states that both applications will have to be considered, although the non-asylum application should normally be considered first and where the applicant is granted leave in a category leading to settlement the applicant will be invited to withdraw any outstanding asylum application.[1] People accepted as refugees will normally be granted indefinite leave when first recognised or upon request. However, on rare occasions it might be appropriate to refuse indefinite leave if an applicant has been convicted of a serious offence. If indefinite leave is refused because a serious crime has been committed it may be decided to grant (further) leave to remain (eg 12 months) in order for further character checks to be made when the applicant next applies.[2] This policy contrasts with the previous grant of limited leave for four years with the possibility of applying for indefinite leave thereafter. The dependants of the claimant will be granted leave in line.[3] The current practice of the Secretary of State is not normally to review the status of refugees from particular countries or groups to assess whether the cessation clause in Article 1C(5) of the Refugee Convention applies, although there are indications that this is to change.[4] However, section 76(3) of the Nationality, Immigration and Asylum Act 2002, giving domestic effect to Article 1C(1)–(4) of the Refugee Convention, provides for the revocation of indefinite leave if a person, or someone on whom he or she is a dependant, ceases to be a refugee as a result of voluntary availment of the protection of the person's country of nationality, their voluntary re-acquisition of a lost nationality, the acquisition of the nationality of a country other than the United Kingdom and availment of its protection, or their voluntary establishment in a country in respect of which the person was a refugee.[5] While the indefinite leave of a refugee is not yet liable to be revoked by change of circumstance, a grant of humanitarian protection or discretionary leave will be actively reviewed, in order to assess whether circumstances continue to exist justifying a further grant of leave.[6]

[1]   See API 'Assessing the claim', Part II, para 17 (concurrent asylum and non-asylum applications). There may be occasions (eg a likely grant of asylum or difficulties in concluding the non-asylum application) where the asylum claim may be considered first.

[2]   See API Assessing the Claim, para 14(k). A refugee not granted indefinite leave ceases to be a refugee when the circumstances giving rise to the status cease to exist, and is not entitled to any leave: see *N (Kenya)* [2004] UKIAT 00009 (not appealed on this point). The practice of granting indefinite leave to refugees has been the subject of judicial comment: see *Saad, Diriye and Osorio v Secretary of State for the Home Department* [2002] EWCA Civ 2008; *Hassan (Ahmed Faraj)* [2002] UKIAT 00062; and the Home Office proposes in future to grant five years' leave in the first instance: see *Controlling our Borders: Making Migration Work for Britain; The Five year Strategy for Asylum and Immigration* (Cm 6472). For cessation of refugee status see 12.84 above.

[3]   HC 395, para 349. See below for family reunion.

[4]   Answers to questions put by the French delegation on the application of the cessation clause in Article 1C(5) of the Refugee Convention, Telex No 4480 of 14 October 1998, SN 5054/98, 17 November 1998. During the passage of the 2002 Act, Lord Bassam of Brighton confirmed that ILR, once granted, would not be removed from refugees simply because of a change of circumstances removing the risk of persecution. See however the proposal for a grant of limited leave of up to five years for refugees, followed by a review of the circumstances in the country, in *Controlling our borders: Making migration work for Britain: Five year strategy for asylum and immigration*, Cm 6472, Feb 2005.

5   See API 'Revocation of Indefinite Leave'. The power under s 76(3) to revoke the ILR of
     those who, as a result of their own actions, cease to be refugees applies to leave granted
     before s 76 came into force on 10 February 2003, but rests only on actions (eg travelling to
     the country from which they sought protection) taken *on or after* that date.
6   See API 'Humanitarian protection', which states that extensions or settlement will not be
     granted automatically, but only where the circumstances continue to justify further leave
     (and subject to the person not falling into the exclusion criteria). See also (in respect of
     exceptional leave to remain) *Arulanandam v Secretary of State for the Home Department*
     [1996] Imm AR 587, CA.

TEMPORARY PROTECTION

12.173 The immigration rules[1] provide for the grant of temporary protection
pursuant to the terms of Council Directive 2001/55/EC,[2] if the Secretary of
State is satisfied that the applicant is in the UK or has arrived at a port, is
entitled to temporary protection as defined by the Directive and in accordance
with it,[3] does not hold an extant grant of it entitling him or her to reside in
another EU Member State,[4] and is not excluded under provisions analogous to
Article 1F and Article 33(2) of the Refugee Convention.[5] Temporary protection may be granted whatever the immigration status of the person, and it will
consist of leave to enter or remain, not subject to a condition prohibiting
employment, for up to 12 months, renewable for further periods of six
months.[6] The rules provide for the recipient of temporary protection to be
allowed to return to the UK from another EEA Member State,[7] to be provided
with documentation,[8] to be registered by the Secretary of State[9] and to be
accompanied by a wide range of family members[10] – not just the spouse or
unmarried partner[11] and minor children who lived with the principal applicant as part of the family unit immediately prior to displacement, but also
parents, grandparents, unmarried adult children, unmarried siblings, uncles
and aunts who lived with the applicant and were wholly or mainly dependent
on him or her, provided that they would face extreme hardship if reunification
did not take place.[12] In considering an application by a dependent child, the
Secretary of State is (for the first time ever) required by the rules to take into
consideration the best interests of that child.[13] The grant of temporary
protection does not prejudice an asylum claim, but the Directive allows
Member States to provide that temporary protection may not be enjoyed
concurrently with the status of asylum seeker.[14]

1   HC 395, Part 11A (paras 354–356B), inserted by HC 164, in effect 1 January 2005.
2   Council Directive 2001/55/EC on minimum standards for giving temporary protection in
     the event of a mass influx of displaced persons and on measures promoting a balance of
     efforts between Member States in receiving such persons and bearing the consequences
     thereof (OJ 2001 L 212/12).
3   Under the terms of the Directive, the Council, acting on a proposal from the Commission,
     decides on the existence of a mass influx of displaced persons (defined as third country
     nationals or stateless persons who have had to leave their country or region of origin, and
     are unable to return in safe and durable conditions because of the situation prevailing
     there, who may fall within the scope of the Geneva convention or other instruments giving
     international protection, including persons fleeing armed conflict or endemic violence, or
     victims or potential victims of systematic and generalised violations of human rights:
     Art 2). The Council decision has the effect of introducing temporary protection for the
     displaced persons to whom it relates, in all the Member States (Art 5). Temporary
     protection comes to an end when the maximum duration has been reached (two years,
     extendable by the Council for a further year: Art 4) or on a Council decision that the

situation in the country of origin is such as to permit safe and durable return with due respect for human rights and *non-refoulement* obligatons: Art 6.

4   HC 395, para 355 as inserted.
5   HC 395, para 355A as inserted. Consideration of exclusion is to be based solely on the personal conduct of the applicant concerned and exclusion decisions or measures must be based on the principle of proportionality: ibid.
6   HC 395, para 355B, 355C as inserted. Articles 12 and 14 of the Directive require Member States to authorise work, self-employment, education etc, and Article 13 requires them to provide suitable accommodation and social and welfare assistance. The Directive limits temporary protection to two years in total, extendable for a further year on a decision of the Council.
7   HC 395, para 355D as inserted.
8   HC 395, para 355E as inserted.
9   HC 395, para 355F as inserted.
10   HC 395, para 356–356B as inserted, reflecting the provisions of Art 15 of the Directive.
11   Provided that the parties have been living together in a relationship akin to marriage which has subsisted for at least two years: para 356(a)(ii).
12   HC 395, para 356(b)(ii). We suggest that 'extreme hardship' is a less severe test than 'the most exceptional compassionate circumstances' for the purposes of the distressed relative provisions of para 317.
13   HC 395, para 356B, reflecting Art 15(4) of the Directive.
14   Directive Art 3(1), 19(1). HC 395, para 355G enables the Secretary of State to defer consideration of an asylum claim made by someone with temporary protection until he or she ceases to be entitled to it.

HUMANITARIAN PROTECTION AND DISCRETIONARY LEAVE

12.174 The Home Office abolished 'exceptional leave to remain' with effect from 1 April 2003, and replaced it with 'humanitarian protection' or 'discretionary leave', which may be granted for up to three years.[1] When an asylum claim is refused, consideration should be given to granting humanitarian protection; if ineligible a person may qualify for discretionary leave.[2] Humanitarian protection is leave granted to a person who would, if removed, face a serious risk to life or person arising from the death penalty, unlawful killing or torture or inhuman or degrading treatment or punishment in the country of return. Unlawful killing includes the risk of being killed in a war or internal conflict.[3] Non-return to the risk of torture or inhuman or degrading treatment or punishment reflects the UK's obligations under Article 3 ECHR.[4] The API contemplate two types of case where a Refugee Convention claim would fail but humanitarian protection would be indicated by virtue of the application of Article 3: where persecution is feared for a reason falling outside the Refugee Convention, and where feared ill-treatment is severe enough to breach Article 3 but does not amount to persecution.[5] Where humanitarian protection is not warranted, caseworkers must consider whether a grant of discretionary leave is appropriate.[6] Humanitarian protection is not afforded to those whose claim rests on the severity of a medical condition,[7] who may instead be eligible for discretionary leave.[8] A person who would be excluded under 1F(b) of the the Refugee Convention will similarly be excluded from humanitarian protection,[9] but would qualify for a grant of discretionary leave if his or her removal would breach the ECHR.[10] Discretionary leave is granted where removal would involve a direct breach of Article 8 ECHR (defined by the API as a breach of the right to a private or family life in the United Kingdom),[11] and is also appropriate in medical or other humanitarian cases where return would breach Article 3 (or 8) ECHR,[12] and for unaccompanied children who qualify for neither asylum nor humanitarian protection but for whom there are not adequate reception arrangements available in their own country.[13] Other cases which could warrant the grant of discretionary leave for unsuccessful asylum seekers would require facts 'so compelling that it is considered appropriate to grant some form of leave'.[14]

[1] See API 'Humanitarian Protection and Discretionary Leave'.
[2] However, the API state that in the context of an asylum, human rights or humanitarian protection claim, discretionary leave is intended to be used sparingly and to be granted only if a case falls within limited categories: API 'Discretionary Leave' para 1.
[3] Reflecting Art 2 and Protocols 6 and 13 ECHR; see 8.39 above, where the exceptions to 'unlawful killing' are also set out. The crieria for the grant of HP reflect those for the grant of subsidiary protection set out in the EC Qualification Directive, 2004/83 (12.3 fn 3 above), Art 15. Discretionary leave based on compassionate grounds is outside the scope of the Directive.
[4] See 8.50 above.
[5] The API 'Humanitarian Protection' give the example of where the actions feared do not have a sufficiently systemic character to amount to persecution. This implies a misguided view of the requisites of persecution: see 12.46 above.
[6] See API, 'Discretionary leave', para 2.1.
[7] The API, 'Humanitarian Protection', indicate that where an Art 3 claim does not rest on ill-treatment but on want of medical facilities in the home country, the claimant is not in need of international protection. This reflects a very narrow view of the concept of 'international protection'; see *D v United Kingdom* [1997] 24 EHRR 423.
[8] See API, 'Discretionary Leave', para 2.3 (claims based upon 'torture, inhuman or degrading treatment or punishment where Humanitarian Protection is not granted'). The API state that in medical cases, 'the United Kingdom's obligations would only be engaged where: (a) the United Kingdom can be regarded as having assumed responsibility for the individual's care; (b) there is credible evidence that return, due to complete absence of medical treatment in the country concerned, would significantly reduce the applicant's life expectancy; and (c) return would subject them to acute physical and mental suffering.' The API reflect the Home Office interpetation of the majority decision of the Court of Appeal in *N v Secretary of State for the Home Department* [2003] EWCA Civ 1369, [2004] 1 WLR 1182, upheld by the House of Lords at [2005] UKHL 31. Previous policy on exceptional leave to remain was that leave would be granted where there was credible medical evidence that return would reduce the life expectancy and subject an applicant to acute physical and mental suffering, in circumstances where the UK could be regarded as having assumed responsibility for the person's medical care. See also 8.53 above.
[9] The API refer to exclusion criteria which reflect, but are far broader than, those contained in Article 1F of the Refugee Convention. The API reflecting Article 1F(b) provide for exclusion where the person 'has committed a serious crime in the United Kingdom or overseas', while the Article refers to a serious *non-political* crime committed outside the country of refuge (see 12.95 above). Compare the exclusion provisions for those with subsidiary protection under the EC Qualification Directive, 2004/83/EC (12.3 fn 3 above). The API also exclude from humanitarian protection persons considered to be threaten national security, and those with undesirable character, conduct or associations. DL will be granted where deportation would expose the person to a risk of treatment contrary to Art 2 or 3 ECHR (see API, 'Discretionary leave' para 2.6).
[10] The same exclusion criteria are used in considering discretionary leave cases as are used in relation to humanitarian protection, but their application is different. In particular, a person whose removal would (notwithstanding their actions) breach the ECHR and who does not qualify for any other form of leave should normally be granted a limited period of discretionary leave even if they fall within the exclusion criteria (API 'Discretionary Leave' para 2.7) (unless the option of deferred removal is taken: see below). If the exclusion criteria apply, someone otherwise eligible by reason of Art 8 is unlikely to be granted DL at all (since Art 8 is a qualified right); where minors are involved the Asylum Policy Unit will be consulted.

[11] The category does not cover cases where it is alleged that there would be a breach of Art 8 rights 'in the country of return'. Policy on handling applications for leave to remain on the basis of marriage to a person settled in the UK from illegal entrants, persons liable to removal under section 10 of the 1999 Act and persons subject to deportation action is contained in DP3/96 (see 11.74 above).

[12] For medical cases see fn 8 above. Other humanitarian cases referred to in the API ('likely to be rare') include extreme cases of such poor conditions if returned (eg absence of water, food or basic shelter) that removal of the individual could breach the United Kingdom's Art 3 obligations.

[13] See API on discretionary leave, para 2.4. Where an unaccompanied child qualifies for discretionary leave on more than one ground (ie because of inadequate reception arrangements and under another ground) he or she should be granted leave on the basis of the ground that provides the longer period of stay.

[14] API, 'Discretionary leave', para 2.5.

Duration, revocation and settlement

12.175 Leave granted on humanitarian protection grounds should normally be for a period of three years.[1] The position as regards discretionary leave varies depending on the category under which the leave is granted.[2] In Article 3 cases, three years is given; unaccompanied minors are also given three years, or leave until the child is 18 (whichever is the shorter). In Article 8 cases two years leave is granted, in line with the 'probationary period' in the immigration rules on marriage. In other cases, three years is normally given, although non-standard periods of leave may be given where it is clear from the individual circumstances of the case that the factors leading to discretionary leave being granted will be short-lived.[3] Where there are factors meriting the grant of discretionary leave but it is considered that removal would be possible within six months, deferred removal applies, ie the claim will be refused outright, but the Home Office will undertake not to remove until the basis for not removing has ended.[4] In exclusion catgerories, leave is given for six months.[5] For those granted humanitarian protection, settlement may be granted if at the end of three years and following an active review, it is decided that further protection is needed.[6] If protection is no longer needed and persons have no other basis of stay in the UK, they will be expected to leave. For those granted discretionary leave, further leave may be granted after review, but eligibility to apply for settlement normally arises only after six years.[7] Those in one of the exclusion categories will not become eligible for consideration for settlement until completion of ten years of continuous discretionary leave. Any time spent in prison does not count towards the six- or ten- year qualifying period for settlement. The API make detailed provison for revocation of leave.[8]

[1] API, Humanitarian protection, para 6.

[2] API, Discretionary leave, para 5.

[3] An example given in the API is an Art 8 case where leave is granted because of the presence of a family member in the United Kingdom, where the family member will be able to leave the United Kingdom within, say, 12 months. See *R (on the application of Shahid) v Secretary of State for the Home Department* [2004] EWHC 2550 (Admin), [2004] All ER (D) 153 (Oct) (not unreasonable for Secretary of State to grant three years' discretionary leave to asylum claimant who succeeded on appeal on Art 8 grounds).

[4] API, Discretionary leave, para 5.4.

[5] API, Discretionary leave, para 5.4 makes clear that the grant period of six months applies to the first grant and any subsequent grants following an active review.

6   API, Humanitarian protection, para 8. The 'active review' policy, introduced on 1 April
    2003, is applicable only to those who seek to extend their leave following a grant of HP,
    DL or a period of less than four years' ELR. Those who were granted a four-year period of
    ELR in one block are not subject to active review when they apply for ILR: Home Office to
    Hackney Community Law Centre, 24 January 2005.

7   API, Discretionary leave, para 8.

8   The API, Humanitarian protection, para 7 refer to voluntary actions leading to revocation
    (by analogy with Art 1C of the Refugee Convention) and revocation on grounds of
    character or conduct, during the currency of leave. Changes in country conditions, on the
    other hand, should not normally prompt a review during the currency of a grant of
    humanitarian leave. The API, Discretionary leave, para 6, however makes clear that,
    because the basis of DL is not protection, it will not usually be appropriate to revoke a
    person's leave simply because they have returned to their own country or have travelled on
    their own national passport; in fact those granted discretionary leave will normally be
    expected to keep their own national passport valid. Similarly, a change in country
    circumstances is less likely to affect those with discretionary leave than those with
    humanitarian protection. Discretionary leave granted on the basis of marriage, however,
    may be revoked where the marriage is clearly no longer subsisting. Discretionary leave
    should normally be varied if a person becomes subject to any of the exclusion criteria.
    Discretionary leave obtained by deception may result in removal directions as an illegal
    entrant or under Immigration and Asylum Act 1999, s 10. Leave granted to an
    unaccompanied minor may be revoked if an adult family member becomes available to
    care for them in their own country.

12.176 Additionally, a number of policies have granted leave to remain to
categories of asylum seekers who have been waiting for a considerable period
for their claims to be assessed. In the last edition we referred to the general
policy to grant leave in cases outstanding for more than seven years, and the
backlog clearance policy announced in April 1999.[1] A concession announced
by the Home Secretary on 24 October 2003 allows asylum seeking families
who had been in the UK for three or more years to stay.[2] The applicant must
have applied for asylum before 2 October 2000 and have at least one minor
dependant who has been living in the UK with the applicant since then.
Families are eligible no matter what stage their application has reached,
provided the applicant has not been removed.[3] The whole family should be
granted indefinite leave to remain. There are exclusions: the concession will
not apply where the principal applicant or any of the dependants have a
criminal conviction; have or have had an anti-social behaviour order or sex
offender order; have made (or attempted to make) an application for asylum
in the UK in more than one identity; should have their asylum claim
considered by another country); present a risk to security; fall within the scope
of Article 1F of the Refugee Convention; or whose presence in the UK is
otherwise not conducive to the public good.

1   See fifth edition at 12.180.

2   See APU notice 4/2003 'One-off exercise to allow families who have been in the UK for
    three or more years to stay'.

3   Families are ineligible if after refusal of that initial claim they have been removed or have
    made a voluntary departure. The Secretary of State conceded, however, in *R (on the
    application of NQ) v Secretary of State for the Home Department* (CO 5162/2003)
    (18 February 2004, unreported), that this does not apply if the removal was unlawful

12.177 In deciding whether to grant leave to a refused asylum claimant, the
Secretary of State is bound by the factual findings made after hearing evidence
on the appeal, unless they are perverse or relate solely to country conditions

which he or she is in as good a position to judge as the Tribunal.[1] Thus in *Danaie*[2] the adjudicator had rejected an Iranian man's asylum appeal but had found the appellant to be an adulterer; this made him vulnerable to execution in Iran and the Court of Appeal held that the Secretary of State was bound by the finding.

[1] For cases on country conditions where the Secretary of State is not bound, see *R v Secretary of State for the Home Department, ex p Alakesan* [1997] Imm AR 315; *Elhasoglu v Secretary of State for the Home Department* [1997] Imm AR 380.

[2] *R v Secretary of State for the Home Department, ex p Danaie* [1998] Imm AR 84, [1998] INLR 124, CA. On the need for the Secretary of State to respect findings made on appeal, see also *R (on the application of Ivanauskiene) v Special Adjudicator* [2001] EWCA Civ 1271, [2002] INLR 1; *R (on the application of Saribal) v Secretary of State for the Home Department* [2002] EWHC 1542 (Admin), [2002] INLR 596.

TRAVEL DOCUMENTS

12.178 A refugee is entitled to a Convention travel document as evidence of his or her status under the Refugee Convention.[1] The holder is entitled to re-admission to the country of refuge at any time during the validity of the document, so if the document is valid for more than two years, the two-year rule for returning residents cannot be applied to refuse readmission.[2] A person granted humanitarian protection or discretionary leave is not entitled to such a document. Current policy[3] is that a Certificate of Identity (a Home Office travel document) may be issued on request and payment of the prescribed fee,[4] on production of a letter from the Embassy or High Commission showing a formal and unreasonable refusal to issue a passport or travel document.[5] Applicants must also specify the country or countries they wish to visit (including any countries they may need to pass through in transit)[6] and show that they need to travel for essential employment or business related reasons,[7] exceptional compassionate grounds,[8] study or religious reasons or for other important reasons of conscience.[9] Neither a Convention travel document nor a national travel document (certificate of identity) is generally valid for the country of origin.[10]

[1] Refugee Convention, Art 28 and Sch: see 12.102 above. The fee payable should not exceed the minimum payable for a national passport. From 1 April 2005, the fee payable for a Convention travel document is £42 (£25 for persons under 16): Travel Documents (Fees) (Amendment) Regulations 2005, SI 2005/653. Children can no longer be named as dependants on the travel document of a parent or guardian as from that date.

[2] *R v Secretary of State for the Home Department, ex p Shirreh* (CO 2194/1997) (15 August 1997, unreported), QBD (permission; the case was conceded by the Home Office).

[3] See 'Certificates of identity: policy change from 27 March 2003' in API.

[4] A form TD 112 must be completed (available on the Home Office website). The fee for a certificate of identity is £195 from 1 April 2005 (£115 for persons under 16): Travel Documents (Fees) (Amendment) Regulations 2005, SI 2005/653. Children can no longer be named as dependants on the travel document of a parent or guardian as from that date. The statutory foundation for charges is Immigration and Asylum Act 1999, s 27.

[5] At the time of writing, exceptions are made for Somali and Iraqi applicants, who have no access to consular facilities. The policy of requiring applicants to demonstrate that they could not obtain a passport from their national authorities or other exceptional circumstances was upheld as not irrational in the absence of evidence of feared danger in *R v Secretary of State for the Home Department, ex p Najem* [1999] Imm AR 107, QBD

[6] If issued, the documents will not be valid for travel to any other countries.

7 The 27 March 2003 change of policy imposes strict documentary requirements. Where for example essential business reasons are relied on, employees should provide a letter and payslip from their employer explaining why the trip is essential and why it is essential for the applicant to go rather than another employee. The self-employed must provide an up-to-date balance sheet and profit and loss account for their business, or other evidence that their business exists as a going concern.

8 Examples of exceptional compassionate grounds include (but are not limited to) the serious illness of a close relative (if the relative is not the applicant's parent, child or sibling, the applicant must should explain why the relative is considered close, and a serious illness is one posing an imminent threat to life for which written medical evidence from a doctor will be required); the funeral of a close relative (for which evidence of the death and, where possible, arrangements for the funeral will be required); and medical treatment (the need for which must be certified by a doctor recognised by the General Medical Council, who must explain why satisfactory treatment cannot be given in the UK and specify the country where it will be given). A holiday, unless requested on certified medical advice, is not a compassionate reason to travel.

9 27 March 2003 Change of policy.

10 See 12.86 above for application of cessation clause to refugees who return to their own country. Similar considerations apply to those granted exceptional leave to remain on a protection basis.

FAMILY REUNION

12.179 The Final Act of the Conference which adopted the 1951 Convention recommended that governments took measures to ensure the unity of the refugee's family.[1] 'Family' usually means spouse and unmarried dependent children,[2] unless special circumstances exist, such as recognition of a broader family unit in certain societies.[3] The Refugee Convention does not incorporate family unity in the definition of the refugee, and family unity is not an obligation of the UK under the Convention, but the Final Act of the UN Conference on the Status of Refugees recommended governments to take the necessary measures for the protection of the refugee's family,[4] and the UK, in common with most other signatory states, makes provision for family reunion in its practices. Since October 2000 the Immigration Rules have made provision for the admission of the pre-existing spouse and minor children of a refugee.[5] The normal maintenance and accommodation criteria are not applied to them. Family members of refugees will normally themselves be recognised or admitted as refugees.[6] The parents and minor siblings of children recognised as refugees may be admissible, but not under the Rules and only where there are compelling compassionate circumstances.[7] The family reunion rights of those granted exceptional leave to remain[8] are not set out in the Immigration Rules either, but under current Home Office policy they have to wait for four years before exercising them, unless there are compelling compassionate circumstances justifying waiver of the qualifying period,[9] and they have to satisfy the normal maintenance and accommodation requirements.[10] Where the sponsor has humanitarian protection, family members qualify for family reunion once the sponsor has been granted settlement in the UK (normally after three years of humanitarian protection), although if the family are already in the United Kingdom (whether port or in-country cases), normal policy is to grant them permission to remain in line with the sponsor. Applications may be considered before the sponsor is settled, although entry clearance in such cases will be granted only where there are compelling, compassionate circumstances. Again, sponsors must be able to maintain and accommodate their dependants.[11] Family reunion for those with discretionary leave must normally await the settlement of the sponsor, which in this case is six years.[12] The Home Office has proposed a change to immediate family reunion for all categories of persons granted protection.[13] All applicants for family reunion must apply for entry clearance.[14]

1 UNHCR *Handbook* 12.13 above, Annex I.
2 UNHCR *Handbook* above, Annex I.
3 See UNHCR *Handbook* above, para 185; Somali Family Reunion Policy, set out in [1993] Imm AR 40; *Butterworths Immigration Law Service*, 2B[4]. The UNHCR has formulated a very broad definition including anyone in fact dependent on the principal: see 'Family Protection Issues', ExCom Sub-Committee 15th meeting, para 3, in (1999) 11(3) IJRL 582. See also ExCom Conclusion No 88 (1999) 'The Protection of the Refugee's Family', which calls on states to consider 'liberal criteria in identifying those family members who can be admitted, with a view to promoting a comprehensive reunification of the family'.
4 The Final Act of the United Nations Conference of Plenipotentiaries on the Status of Refugees and Stateless Perons (set out in the UNHCR *Handbook* above). See *DS Abdi v Secretary of State for the Home Department* [1996] Imm AR 148, disapproving *Ali* (10520), where the Tribunal had held that refugee family reunion was an obligation under the Refugee Convention and therefore within the rules (HC 395, para 327). The debate is no longer so important now that refugee family reunion has been brought within the Immigration Rules.
5 HC 395, paras 352A–F. 'Spouse' means husband or wife, according to the API 'Family reunion' (thus excluding unmarried partners). However, Art 2 of the EC Qualification Directive 2004/83/EC (12.3 fn 3 above), includes unmarried partners where their rights are equivalent in the immigration law of the relevant Member State. For the direct effect of EC Directives see 7.41 above. Family reunion may be refused if family members fall within the terms of one of the exclusion clauses in the 1951 UN Convention: para 352A(iii), 352D(iv).
6 It may not always be possible to recognise the family as refugees: they may have a different nationality to the sponsor or they may not wish to be recognised as refugees. However, if they meet the criteria they will still be admitted to join the sponsor.
7 The parents and siblings of a minor who has been recognised as a refugee are not entitled to family reunion, but the family may be granted entry to the UK where there are compelling, compassionate circumstances. In such circumstances, the Home Offie may exceptionally allow other members of the family such as elderly parents to come to the UK: API on family reunion.
8 Even although the status was abolished with effect from 1 April 2003 many persons still have exceptional leave to remain, and will be seeking to exercise family reunion rights..
9 See *Warsame v Entry Clearance Officer, Nairobi* [2000] Imm AR 155.
10 API 'Family reunion' para 3.2. The API state that in all cases the sponsor will be expected to satisfy the maintenance and accommodation requirements as set out in the Immigration Rules (paragraphs 240 (iii) and (iv) of HC 395,), thus reversing the policy of discretionary waiver mentioned in the last edition at 12.183 fn 6 (referring to a 30 June 2000 letter from an immigration minister to Lord Archer).
11 API 'Family reunion' para 3.3.
12 API 'Family reunion' para 3.4. The dependants of those with exceptional leave to remain may not seek entry as dependants of those in the UK with a view to settlement under para 301 of the rules; 'settled' in the context of the rules means 'settled under the rules': *R (on the application of Acan) v Immigration Appeal Tribunal* [2004] EWHC 297.
13 Controlling our Borders: Making Migration Work for Britain; The Five year Strategy for Asylum and Immigration (Cmnd 6472), February 2005.
14 API 'Family reunion' para 4. The best known concessionary policy, the Somali Family Reunion Policy, enabled sponsors to apply informally to the Home Office in the UK, who would indicate how a formal application would be decided by the ECO. It was withdrawn in 1996. A similar concession allowed Vietnamese nationals who were refugees in the UK to apply direct to the Home Office by letter for relatives in Vietnam to join them. This concession was withdrawn on 1 November 1999. See API Aug 00, Ch 6, s 2, para 4.

12.180 In cases involving the admission of relatives other than pre-existing spouses and minor children of refugees, and the admission of any relatives of sponsors with exceptional leave to remain, humanitarian protection or discretionary leave,[1] the Tribunal has no jurisdiction to review refusals of entry clearances to family members outside the rules relating to settled family members (although they will of course have jurisdiction to consider an allegation that an immigration decision is in breach of a person's human rights,[2] which may come close to a full merits review). Where a refusal is inconsistent with a published policy on family unity, the appellate authorities used to be able to consider whether a failure to apply the policy is in accordance with the law,[3] and for that purpose could review the facts on which any refusal was based and decide whether on the true facts there had been a misapplication of any policy. The 2002 Act seeks to abolish this jurisdiction, providing that there is no right of appeal (save on human rights grounds) where a refusal is based on the fact that the person is seeking to enter for a purpose other than one for which entry is permitted in accordance with the immigration rules.[4] The extent of this exclusionary clause has yet to be tested in litigation.[5]

1   See *Hersi v Secretary of State for the Home Department* [1996] Imm AR 569; *Darbiye v Entry Clearance Officer, Nairobi* [1998] Imm AR 64, CA.
2   Nationality, Immigration and Asylum Act 2002, s 84(1)(c).
3   Under s 19(1)(a)(i) Immigration Act 1971, later Sch 4 para 21(1)(a) Immigration and Asylum Act 1999. See *Karshe* (18486), IAT (failure to consider relevant factors); *Abdi v Secretary of State for the Home Department* [1996] Imm AR 148, CA, on the Somali Family Reunion Policy, for which see the previous edition of this work at 12.185. For this purpose, the appellate authorities used to construe the relevant policies: see *Osman* (13757) applying *Paw* (4328) on 'living alone'; *Sabriye* (13673), *Munim* (HX00367) reaching contrary conclusions on 'dependent member of the refugee's immediate family unit'.
4   NIAA 2002, s 88(2)(d), (4).
5   We suggest however that a relative other than a spouse or minor child of a refugee is not excluded from appealing under s 88(2), since the purpose of the entry (family reunion for refugees) is within the rules and the appellant is not disqualified by age, nationality or citizenship (s 88(2)(a)), but by the nature of the relationship. There would be good grounds to appeal (or if an appeal is not available, for judicial review) where for example the excluded person is a pre-existing unmarried partner, whose rights to family reunion are recognised by the EC Qualification Directive, 2004/83/EC (see 12.179 fn 5).

12.181 In *Gasmelsid*[1] the Tribunal held that where a refugee married following recognition, the family reunion policy included his or her spouse, so that the normal rules did not apply. The couple in that case had been engaged before the refugee fled and the Tribunal emphasised that they had been unable to marry at that time through no fault of their own. A construction of the family reunion policy excluding such persons would 'give an artificial, strained and unjust construction to a rule the underlying purpose of which is to unite family members rather than keep them apart'. In *A (Somalia)* [2] the Tribunal held that, where a woman leaves the country of her nationality and marries a man in another country before seeking asylum in the UK, she is not precluded from having him join her in the United Kingdom after her recognition as a refugee by reason only of the fact that the country in which they married is not the country of her nationality in relation to which she was recognised by the United Kingdom as a refugee. In *Onen* the Tribunal by a majority held that it was unfair to rely on the prolonged separation of family members who had fled to different countries to hold that the relationship between spouses was no longer subsisting.[3]

¹   (13261) 29 April 1996, IAT.
²   [2004] UKIAT 00031 'Reported', for its interpretation of para 352A of the Immigration Rules.
³   *Onen* (22101) (8 October 1999, unreported), IAT.

12.182 In summary, where one member of a family is in the UK and wants to be joined by others, the following practices apply:

(i)   where a person is recognised as a refugee, immediate application for entry clearance can be made for other family members (as above) without any need for the maintenance and accommodation provisions of the Immigration Rules to be met;¹

(ii)   family members other than the pre-existing spouse and minor children of a refugee may not be admitted under the Rules. Refusal to admit them may be no longer appealable on the ground that refusal is not in accordance with the law, but only on human rights grounds (depending on the interpretation of the exclusionary provisions);²

(iii) a broad range of family members of persons with temporary protection are provided for in the immigration rules and may seek to join the principal immediately;³

(iv)   where a person has exceptional leave to enter or remain, an application for entry clearance for other family members will normally have to wait for four years (until the sponsor is settled) and will have to satisfy the maintenance and accommodation provisions. Refusal is appealable as in (ii) above;

(iv)   where a person has humanitarian protection, an application for entry clearance for other family members will normally have to wait for three years (until the sponsor is settled) and will have to satisfy the maintenance and accommodation provisions. Refusal is appealable as in (ii) above;

(v)   where a person has discretionary leave, an application for entry clearance for other family members normally will have to wait for six years (until the sponsor is settled) and will have to satisfy the maintenance and accommodation provisions. Refusal is appealable as in (ii) above;

(vi)   family members who arrive in the UK without entry clearance to claim asylum in their own right or as a dependant may be able to prevent removal to a safe third country under the Dublin II Regulation, the effect of Articles 6–8 of which is that that the UK will be responsible for examining the claims of (a) unaccompanied minors who have a family member legally present in the UK, (b) asylum seekers with a family member recognised as a refugee in the UK and (c) asylum seekers who have a family member in the UK with an outstanding asylum claim.⁴

¹   HC 395, paras 352A–F.
²   Nationality, Immigration and Asylum Act 2002 s 88(2)(d), 88(4).
³   HC 395, para 356–356B; see 12.170 above.
⁴   'Family member' is defined in Article 2(i) of the Dublin II Regulation (insofar as the family already existed in the country of origin) as (i) the spouse of the asylum seeker or his or her unmarried partner in a stable relationship, where the legislation or practice of the Member State concerned treats unmarried couples in a way comparable to married couples under its law relating to aliens; (ii) the minor children of couples referred to in (i) or of the applicant,

on condition that they are unmarried and dependent and regardless of whether they were born in or out of wedlock or adopted as defined under the national law; and (iii) the father, mother or guardian when the applicant or refugee is a minor and unmarried.

12.183 We referred (at 12.108 above) to asylum claims by dependent relatives of the principal claimant. A husband or wife or minor children accompanying a principal asylum applicant may be included in the application, and will be granted leave to enter or remain in line with the principal.[1] Family members may claim asylum in their own right, and if they have a separate claim and wish to do so, they should do so as soon as possible, as failure to claim promptly will be taken into account and may damage credibility.[2] Where the principal claimant is refused asylum and a dependant has already been refused in his or her own right, the dependant may be removed immediately, regardless of any right of that the principal asylum seeker wishes to exercise.[3]

1 HC 395, para 349. This is also applied to unmarried partners, where there is evidence of a stable pre-existing relationship.
2 HC 395, para 349. Unless there is a good reason, eg a couple have separated since arrival.
3 HC 395, para 349. Where serial asylum claims are made by a husband and wife, a decision to remove the husband after the dismissal of his appeal but before his wife's was held not to be *Wednesbury* unreasonable or a breach of Arts 6 or 8 of the ECHR in *R v Secretary of State for the Home Department, ex p Polat* (7 November 1996, unreported), QBD. See also *R v Secretary of State for the Home Department, ex p Uzun* [1998] Imm AR 314; *R v Secretary of State for the Home Department, ex p Yolamba* [1997] Imm AR 564, QBD.

Chapter 13

ASYLUM SUPPORT, COMMUNITY CARE AND WELFARE BENEFITS

INTRODUCTION

13.1 As a general rule, asylum seekers and those who are 'subject to immigration control' are not entitled to any form of welfare benefits from the Department of Work and Pensions, or to any accommodation or financial assistance from their local authority unless they fall within an exceptional class. They may fall within such a class and be entitled to welfare benefits if, for example, they have contributed to the UK's national insurance scheme in the past or are nationals of states which have ratified certain international agreements to which the UK is a party. Alternatively, they may be entitled to NASS support or community care provision. The overall trend since 1996 has been for successive governments to use legislation to reduce access to welfare benefits and local authority provision for asylum seekers and others who are subject to immigration control and place a more limited responsibility on the

Immigration and Nationality Department to provide support for asylum seekers. This has been done in a piecemeal fashion, which means that there are now a number of schemes currently providing different forms of support to individuals whose immigration status is the same but who entered the UK by different methods or became destitute at different times. This chapter will look at these different forms of benefit and support. The starting point will be a consideration of the position of the small minority who are subject to immigration control but are still entitled to welfare benefits.

13.2 Access to social security benefits by those subject to immigration control was radically restructured from 3 April 2000. Persons 'subject to immigration control' are excluded by statute from that date from access to most non-contributory social security benefits.[1] These social security benefits (some of which have changed since April 2000) are: attendance allowance, income-based jobseeker's allowance; severe disablement allowance; carer's allowance;[2] disability living allowance; income support; child tax credit;[3] working tax credit;[4] state pension credit;[5] social fund payments; child benefit; housing benefit; and council tax benefit. The non-contributory benefits which are not subject to the exclusion are industrial injuries benefits, category D retirement pensions and guardian's allowance. Prescribed categories of persons are, however, exempted by regulations,[6] which exempt different persons in respect of the different benefits[7] and also apply transitional protection. Certain benefits – income support, income-based jobseeker's allowance, housing benefit and council tax benefit – require claimants to satisfy the 'habitual residence' test as well, whether they are British citizens, EEA nationals or third country nationals.[8] We consider below first, who is 'subject to immigration control'; next, who is exempted from the test, and for which benefits, and who gets transitional protection; and finally, the habitual residence test and who is exempted from it.

---

1. The Immigration and Asylum Act 1999, s 115(1), (2), (9) as amended by the State Pension Credit Act and the Tax Credits Act 2002, excludes those subject to immigration control from benefits under the Social Security Contributions and Benefits Act 1992, Jobseekers Act 1995 and the Social Security Contributions and Benefits (Northern Ireland) Act 1992. The Tax Credit (Immigration) Regulations 2003, SI 2003/653, reg 3 excludes those subject to immigration control from child tax credit and working tax credit under the Tax Credit Act 2002.
2. Invalid care allowance was replaced by carer's allowance by The Regulatory Reform (Carer's Allowance) Order 2002, SI 2002/1457, Art 2, Sch, para 1, 3(c).
3. Child tax credit replaced children's tax credit from 6 April 2003: see Tax Credit Act 2002, s 1(1).
4. Working tax credit replaced working families' tax credit from 6 April 2003: see Tax Credit Act 2002, s 1(1).
5. Inserted by the State Pension Credit Act 2002, s 4(2) from 6 October 2003.
6. Social Security (Immigration and Asylum) Consequential Amendments Regulations 2000, SI 2000/636, made under the Immigration and Asylum Act 1999, s 115(3)–(8).
7. Immigration and Asylum Act 1999, s 115(4).
8. See 13.23 below.

Subject to immigration control

13.3 Those who fall within the definition of being 'subject to immigration control' are:

- non-EEA nationals who require leave to enter or remain in the UK but have no such leave;[1]
- non-EEA nationals whose leave is subject to a condition of no recourse to public funds;[2]
- those given leave as the result of a 'maintenance undertaking';[3]
- those with a statutory leave pending appeal under the Immigration and Asylum Act 1999.[4]

No British or EEA nationals[5] are 'subject to immigration control'. However nationals of eight of the ten accession countries which joined the EEA on 1 May 2004 will have restricted access to some benefits.[6] A mistaken grant of leave to enter to a person who does not require it will *not* render that person 'subject to immigration control'.[7]

[1] Immigration and Asylum Act 1999, s 115(9)(a).
[2] Immigration and Asylum Act 1999, s 115(9)(b). The Home Office's decision as to the conditions upon which leave is granted is conclusive: Commissioner's Decisions R(SB) 25/85 and R(SB) 2/85.
[3] Immigration and Asylum Act 1999, s 115(9)(c).
[4] Immigration and Asylum Act 1999, s 115(9)(d).
[5] Ie, nationals of the EU Member States (Austria, Belgium, Denmark, Finland, France, Germany, Greece, Republic of Ireland, Italy, Luxembourg, the Netherlands, Portugal, Spain, Sweden and the UK, and from 1 May 2004 Bulgaria, the Czech Republic, Cyprus, Estonia, Hungary, Latvia, Lithuania, Malta, Poland, Romania, Slovakia and Slovenia), together with Norway, Liechtenstein and Iceland: Immigration and Asylum Act 1999, s 167(1), European Union (Accessions) Act 2003.
[6] See 13.4 below
[7] Commissioner's Decision R(SB) 11/88 (under earlier regulations).

13.4 EEA nationals are excluded from the definition whether or not they are exercising Treaty rights. This contrasts with the previous benefits regime, which defined as 'persons from abroad' those EEA nationals who were 'required by the Secretary of State to leave the UK'.[1] From April 1993,[2] the Secretary of State for the Home Department issued letters to those in the UK not exercising Treaty rights,[3] for example, those who had been in the UK as work-seekers for over six months without finding work or any genuine chance of doing so,[4] requiring them to leave the UK, which had the effect of excluding them from entitlement to benefit. In the cases of *Remilien and Wolke*[5] the House of Lords held that the letters lacked the necessary degree of compulsion to amount to a 'requirement' to leave so as to exclude EEA nationals from entitlement to benefits. What the regulations envisaged was an order for removal.[6] Nationals of eight of the ten accession countries[8] who are Accession State workers requiring registration[9] are not entitled to income support, job seekers allowance, housing benefit, council tax benefit, state pension credit,[10] child benefit,[11] tax credits,[12] or housing benefit until they have worked in the UK for a registered employer for 12 months or more and have so obtained a right to reside. Neither are they eligible for public housing.[13]

[1] Income Support (General) Regulations 1987, SI 1987/1967, reg 21(1)(h).
[2] When the amendment to the regs came into force: Income-related Benefits Schemes (Miscellaneous Amendments) Regulations 1993, SI 1993/315, reg 4.
[3] See chapter 7 above.
[4] *R v Immigration Appeal Tribunal, ex p Antonissen* [1991] ECR I-745.
[5] *Remilien v Secretary of State for Social Security, Chief Adjudication Officer v Wolke* [1998] 1 All ER 129, HL.

6   Under Art 15(2) of the Immigration (European Economic Area) Order 1994, SI 1994/1895; see now Immigration (European Economic Area) Regulations 2000, SI 2000/2326, reg 21(3). A deportation order would also suffice.
7   For a treatment of EC law relating to the 'co-ordination' of social security benefits and the 'protection of social advantages', see CPAG's *Migration & Social Security Handbook* (3rd edn, 2001) (4th edn forthcoming).
8   Bulgaria, the Czech Republic, Estonia, Hungary, Latvia, Lithuania, Poland, Romania, Slovakia and Slovenia.
9   The Accession (Immigration and Worker Registration) Regulations 2004, SI 2004/1219, reg 2.
10   The Social Security (Habitual Residence) Amendment Regulations 2004, SI 2004/1232.
11   The Child Benefit (General) (Amendment) Regulations 2004, SI 2004/1244.
12   The Tax Credits (Residence) (Amendment) Regulations 2004, SI 2004/1243.
13   The Allocation of Housing and Homelessness (Amendment) (England) Regulations, SI 2004/1235.

Those who require but who are without leave to enter or remain

13.5 Most non-British and non-EEA citizens require leave to enter. Apart from British citizens, a small number of Commonwealth nationals have the right of abode.[1] There are other categories who are exempt from requiring leave to enter, including certain members of the crew of a ship or aircraft, certain diplomats and their families, members of certain visiting armed forces and of Her Majesty's forces.[2] When they cease to be exempt, most need leave but do not have it, but former diplomats are treated as having been granted leave for 90 days after their exemption expires[3] and will not be 'subject to immigration control' for benefits purposes during that period.

1   Immigration Act 1971, ss 1(1), (2), 2(1), (2), and see chapter 2 above.
2   Immigration Act 1971, ss 8(1), (3)–(6), 8A, 8B; see chapter 6 above.
3   Immigration Act 1971, s 8A, inserted by Immigration and Asylum Act 1999, s 7. Such leave is not subject to conditions (save as to duration) and is not caught by s 115(9)(b) or (c) of the 1999 Act. This also applies to the 28 days' concessionary leave granted to discharged foreign and Commonwealth soldiers from HM Forces. See 6.50–6.51 above.

Leave subject to a condition of no recourse to public funds

13.6 Those who have leave to enter or remain in the UK which is subject to a condition of no recourse to public funds are 'subject to immigration control' for benefits purposes.[1] Only someone whose leave is subject to this express condition is 'subject to immigration control' under this head. The definition of 'public funds' has expanded over the years and is contained in the Immigration Rules.[2] The Rules require persons seeking leave to enter or remain in the UK for most purposes to show that they can maintain and accommodate themselves and their dependants without recourse to public funds.[3] No such requirement is imposed on refugees and their dependants,[4] transit visitors,[5] returning residents,[6] bereaved spouses and unmarried partners of persons who were settled in the UK who are seeking indefinite leave to remain,[7] discharged Gurkha, foreign and Commonwealth soldiers from HM Forces and their dependants,[8] and non-British citizen children born in the UK and now seeking leave to enter or remain.[9] Showing there will be no recourse to public funds in order to gain entry is not the same as having leave subject to this condition, however. Since November 1996, the immigration authorities have been able to attach a condition to leave that the recipient will not have recourse to public funds.[10] There is no guidance as to when such a condition should be imposed. A person with indefinite leave cannot be 'subject to immigration control' on this basis, since this leave by definition has no conditions attached to it.[11] But someone with indefinite leave could be 'subject to immigration control' if their leave was give as the result of a maintenance undertaking (see below).

1   Immigration and Asylum Act 1999, s 115(9)(b).
2   HC 395, para 6. For discussion of the entries see 11.53ff above.
3   Eg for visits, study, work, family reunion. For the substantive requirements of these rules, see chapters 9–11 above.
4   HC 395, Pt XI.
5   HC 395, paras 47–50.
6   HC 395, paras 18–20, although the applicant must not have received assistance from public funds towards previous departure from the UK: para 18(iii).
7   HC 395, paras 287(b) and 295M, inserted by Cm 4851, paras 31 and 32.
8   HC 395, paras 276E–276AC, inserted by HC 1112 and HC 346.
9   HC 395, para 305–309.
10   Immigration Act 1971, s 3(1)(c); HC 395, para 8, as amended by Cm 3365, para 3.
11   IA 1971, s 3(1)(c), (3)(a).

Leave given as the result of a maintenance undertaking

13.7 A person given leave to enter or remain in the UK as the result of a maintenance undertaking is 'subject to immigration control'.[1] A maintenance undertaking for these purposes means a 'written undertaking given by another person in pursuance of the immigration rules to be responsible for that person's maintenance and accommodation'.[2] This wording is almost identical to that used under the regulations in force prior to 3 April 2000.[3] It used to be thought that only formal undertakings entered into under the Immigration Rules exclude a person from benefit entitlement, but the courts have now held that an undertaking does not need to be on any prescribed form and need only be a document expressing in reasonably clear language a future promise or agreement to maintain a sponsored immigrant.[4]

1   Immigration and Asylum Act 1999, s 115(9)(c).
2   Immigration and Asylum Act 1999, s 115(10).
3   See, inter alia, Income Support (General) Regulations 1987, SI 1987/1967, reg 21(3)(i); the change from the words 'upon' an undertaking being given to 'as a result of [an undertaking]' emphasises the requisite causal connection; see Commissioner's decision CIS/6608/1999.
4   *Shah v Secretary of State for Social Security* [2002] EWCA Civ 285 (the court must look at the substance, not the form of an undertaking, but the phrase 'I am able and willing' is insufficient for the purpose as it signifies current, not future ability and willingness); *R (Begum) v Social Services Commissioner* (2003) Times, 4 December; *Ahmed v Secretary of State for Work and Pensions* [2005] EWCA Civ 535. See HC 395, para 35.

Leave pending appeal

13.8 Persons who had leave only by statutory extension pending appeal under the 1999 Act under the IAA 1999 were 'subject to immigration control'.[1] This did not apply to those whose leave was extended by statute pending determination of an application.[2] Although the provisions of the IAA 1999 have been repealed and replaced with a new statutory leave which operates both pending determination of an application and pending appeal,[3] the definition of 'subject to immigration control' refers only to the old, repealed provisions. It is thus arguable that those with statutory leave under the new provisions are not subject to immigration control unless the original leave was subject to a public funds condition or was given as the result of a maintenance undertaking.[4]

1   Immigration and Asylum Act 1999, s 115(9)(d), with reference to Sch 4, para 17(1) (continuation of leave pending appeal). Although Sch 4 was repealed by Nationality, Immigration and Asylum Act 2002, s 114, Sch 9 with effect from 1 April 2003, s 115 has not been amended to reflect the change.
2   The exclusion under IAA 1999, s 115(9)(d) applied only to those who had leave 'only' as a result of Sch 4, para 17.
3   Immigration Act 1971, s 3C, inserted by IAA 1999, s 3, and substituted by s 118 NIAA 2002 from 1 April 2003 (SI 2003/754). The new s 3C covers both statutory leave pending determination of the application, reflecting the old s 3C, and also statutory leave pending appeal, reflecting the now repealed IAA 1999, Sch 4, para 17 (see fn 1 above).
4   See 13.6 and 13.7 above.

Exemptions from 'subject to immigration control' test

13.9 The exemptions from the 'subject to immigration control' test vary between the benefits, although there is some overlap, as appears below, and it is therefore convenient to consider the benefits in groups.

Income-based jobseeker's allowance, income support, social fund payments, housing benefit, council tax benefit

13.10 There are three groups of people who are exempted from the 'subject to immigration control' test and are therefore eligible to claim these benefits.[1] The first exemption applies to those who have been given leave within the Immigration Rules having satisfied a requirement that they will not have recourse to or be a charge on public funds[2] and who are temporarily without funds owing to the disruption of remittances from abroad.[3] There must, however, be a 'reasonable expectation' that the supply of funds will be resumed. The classic case is that of a student whose funds from their home sponsor have been disrupted by, for example, short-term banking problems in that country.

1   Social Security (Immigration and Asylum) Consequential Amendments Regulations 2000, SI 2000/636, reg 2(1) and Sch, Pt I.
2   SI 2000/636, Sch, para 1(a).
3   SI 2000/636, Sch, para 1(b).

13.11 The next exempt group consists of certain persons granted leave to enter or remain under a maintenance undertaking.[1] Such persons are exempt if either the sponsor who gave the undertaking has died[2] or the person has been resident in the UK for a period of five years since either the date of entry into the UK or the date of the undertaking (whichever date is later).[3]

1   Primarily excluded by Immigration and Asylum Act 1999, s 115(9)(c), (10): see 13.6 above.

2 Social Security (Immigration and Asylum) Consequential Amendments Regulations 2000, SI 2000/636, Sch, Pt I, para 2.
3 SI 2000/636, Sch, Pt I, para 3.

13.12 The final exempt group are nationals of states which have ratified either of two Treaties of the Council of Europe, the European Convention on Social and Medical Assistance (ECSMA)[1] or the Council of Europe Social Charter (CESC)[2] and who are 'lawfully present' in the UK.[3] Other than EEA Member States, Albania, Armenia, Moldova and Turkey have ratified the Revised Social Charter, and Turkey has in addition ratified the ECSMA. Their nationals must also be 'lawfully present' in the UK to benefit from this exemption. Those lawfully present for temporary purposes (visitors, students, au pairs, etc) are protected.[4] In *Kaya v Haringey London Borough Council*[5] the Court of Appeal held that asylum claimants on temporary admission were not 'lawfully present' for the purposes of ECSMA. The court relied principally upon the House of Lords' interpretation in *Musisi*[6] of the phrase 'lawfully in the territory' in Article 32(1) of the Refugee Convention, and noted that no material had been placed before the court to suggest that a different approach should be adopted for the purposes of ECSHA or CESC. Further materials were placed before the Court of Appeal in *Szoma v Secretary of State for Work and Pensions*[7] but the court upheld its decision in *Kaya*. It reasoned that a person who was subject to immigration control and who was on temporary admission could not be said to have entered the UK for the purposes of section 11(1) of the Immigration Act 1971[8] and therefore was not lawfully present.[9]

1 European Treaty Series (ETS) No 14, Paris, 11 December 1953.
2 ETS No 35, Turin, 18 October 1961.
3 Social Security (Immigration and Asylum) Consequential Amendments Regulations 2000, SI 2000/636, Sch, para 4.
4 See Lenia Samuel *Fundamental Social Rights: Case law of the European Social Charter* (1997) Council of Europe p 325 citing the Conclusions of the Committee of Experts at Conclusions XIII-2, p 142, Norway; Conclusions XIII-3, p 367, Finland.
5 [2001] EWCA Civ 677, [2001] All ER (D) 15 (May).
6 [1987] AC 514, HL at 522–526, [2003] All ER (D) 530 (Jul).
7 [2003] EWCA Civ 1131.
8 See 3.5 above.
9 The House of Lords granted leave to appeal in July 2004.

13.13 Transitional provisions protect certain claimants from the regime in force from 3 April 2000 and preserve eligibility for these benefits. There are provisions continuing existing transitional protection from previous changes made in 1996 and others preserving entitlement under the regime in force from 1996 to April 2000.

Those entitled to benefit before 5 February 1996

13.14 There are two categories of person who are exempt from the 'subject to immigration control' test for income support, social fund payments, housing and council tax benefits[1] as a result of previous transitional provisions in regulations in force from 5 February 1996.[2] First is a diminishing class of asylum seekers who claimed asylum, whether on arrival or not, prior to 5 February 1996 and who have not since then received the next decision on their claim (whether of the Secretary of State for the Home Department or of the appellate authorities on appeal).[3] To benefit from this protection, the claimant must have been entitled to benefit immediately before 5 February 1996.[4] For a long time there remained uncertainty as to whether a claimant remains protected following a break in entitlement after 5 February 1996 (for example, where the asylum seeker obtains and then loses work after that date).[5] The Court of Appeal decided in *Yildiz*[6] that entitlement continues in these circumstances. Members of an asylum seeker's family who were receiving the benefit concerned on 4 February 1996 who claim asylum in their own right after that date are also transitionally protected under this rule.[7] Also protected are persons in respect of whom a sponsor gave a maintenance undertaking before 5 February 1996 and who were receiving, or entitled to receive, income support, housing benefit or council tax benefit immediately[8] before that date.[9]

1   But not income-based jobseeker's allowance.
2   Social Security (Immigration and Asylum) Consequential Amendments Regulations 2000, SI 2000/636, reg 2(4).
3   SI 2000/636, regs 2(4)(a), 12(11)(b) applying Social Security (Persons from Abroad) Miscellaneous Amendments Regulations 1996, SI 1996/30, reg 12(1), and see CIS/3108/1997.
4   See *R v Secretary of State for Social Security, ex p Vijeikis, Zaheer and Okito* (10 July 1997, unreported), QBD, Dyson J, upheld 5 March 1998, CA; see also CIS/16992/96, CIS/2809/97, CFC/1580/97.
5   The Commissioner in CIS/1115/1999 held that protection ended in these circumstances, applying *R v Adjudication Officer, ex p B* (9 December 1998, unreported), CA (which dealt with different provisions); however in *R v Secretary of State for Social Security, ex p Markovic* (CO 3855/1999) (24 May 2000, unreported) it was conceded as arguable that a break in entitlement does not end transitional protection under SI 2000/636, reg 12(1). The application for permission was dismissed on other grounds.
6   *Yildiz v Secretary of State for Social Security* [2001] EWCA Civ 309, (2001) Independent, 9 March.
7   SI 1996/30, reg 12(1), as amended by Asylum and Immigration Act 1996, Sch 1, para 5.
8   Commissioner's Decision CIS/16992/96.
9   SI 2000/636, regs 2(4)(a), 12(11)(b); SI 1996/30, reg 21(2).

Those entitled to benefit before 3 April 2000

13.15 There is also transitional protection for persons entitled to income support, income-based jobseeker's allowance,[1] social fund payments, housing and council tax benefit before 3 April 2000. The first protected group are persons who submitted a claim for asylum 'on arrival in the UK' on or before 2 April 2000.[2] The claim must have been made to the Secretary of State for the Home Department, and 'recorded by the Secretary of State as having been made before that date.[3] A claim for asylum in this context means a claim under the Refugee Convention, not the ECHR. To be eligible for jobseeker's allowance as opposed to income support, the claimant must hold a work permit or have written authorisation to work in the UK from the Secretary of State.[4]

1   Both paid at the 'urgent cases' rate of 90% of the claimant's ordinary 'applicable amount' calculated under the Income Support (General) Regulations 1987, SI 1987/1967, reg 21, Jobseekers Allowance Regulations 1996, SI 1996/207, reg 128.

2   Social Security (Immigration and Asylum) Consequential Amendments Regulations 2000, SI 2000/636, regs 2(5), (6), 12(3), (7).
3   SI 2000/636, regs 2(5), (6), 12(3), (7). For what constitutes a 'claim' and a 'record' see 13.40–13.42 below.
4   SI 2000/636, reg 12(4)(c).

13.16 Before the Social Security (Immigration and Asylum) Consequential Amendments Regulations 2000,[1] the phrase 'on arrival' was used in the Social Security (Persons from Abroad) Miscellaneous Amendments Regulations 1996,[2] and led to considerable difficulty and divergent case law in the decisions of the Social Security Commissioners. During the passage of the 1996 legislation, an attempt was made in the House of Lords to incorporate a three-day period of grace in which a person might claim asylum without losing access to benefits.[3] The defeat of the amendment left open the question whether Parliament intended the somewhat elliptical phrase 'on arrival' to be sufficiently flexible to avoid injustice.[4] The Secretary of State interprets 'on arrival' as synonymous with 'clearing immigration control', and the issue is whether more flexibility was intended. Divergent views have been taken by different social security Commissioners. In the one reported decision, Commissioner Rowlands held that the term 'on arrival' was used deliberately, instead of a more precise term, in order to maintain a level of flexibility, the extent of which was to be considered on a case by case basis. He held that it was not a universal test that asylum should have been claimed before 'clearing immigration control'.[5] That approach was followed by other Commissioners where claimants sought to claim asylum after passing through controls but while still at the port[6] and where a claimant submitted a claim for asylum two or three days after entering, alleging that he had been too ill to claim at the immigration desk.[7] In the latter case, the Commissioner cited his own earlier dismissal of the appeal of a clandestine entrant who claimed asylum in Wales near his brother's home after being released from the back of a lorry in central London.[8] The Court of Appeal held in *Shire*[9] that 'there has to be a limit to the elasticity of the words 'on arrival', and that a person who employs an agent to obtain access to the UK is not in a comparable position to someone who is physically unable to claim asylum at an earlier stage, through illness or being locked in a container. Unless there is clear evidence of some form of physical duress, the asylum-seeker who employs an agent is deemed to be in control of the situation and can be held to have chosen not to claim asylum on arrival.

1   SI 2000/636.
2   SI 1996/30.
3   Referred to in Commissioner's Decisions *CIS/143/97*, para 7 and *CIS/4117/97*, para 19.
4   Bonner et al *Social Security: Legislation 2000* (Sweet & Maxwell, 2000).
5   *R(IS) 14/99*. The appeal was rejected on the facts (young female asylum seeker acting under the control of an agent at port, claiming asylum three days later), demonstrating the stringency of the test even applied with some flexibility. The same Commissioner allowed an appeal where a claim was submitted very shortly after the claimant came through immigration controls: *CIS/4439/98*. The Commissioner noted (paras 12–18) that to interpret 'on arrival' in the manner contended for by the respondent would be inconsistent with the UK's obligations under the Refugee Convention, Art 31, which precludes the imposition of penalties on refugees 'provided they present themselves without delay to the authorities and show good cause for their illegal entry or presence': see 12.11 above, 14.37ff below. The Commissioner accepted (para 16) that civil penalties as well as criminal penalties fell within Art 31, and that denial as well as removal of a right was a 'penalty'.

Thus, he reasoned, construing 'on his arrival' similarly to 'without delay' in Art 31 would render consistency between the provision and the UK's international obligations.

6   CIS/4341/98, paras 2, 13.
7   CIS/3803/98, para 5. The Commissioner remitted the matter to the appeal tribunal for a proper investigation of the facts.
8   CIS/3231/97, paras 3, 10. It is to be assumed that these two decisions of the same Commissioner are consistent and adhere to the somewhat clearer analysis of the Commissioner in CIS/3803/98.
9   *Shire (Amina Jama) v Secretary of State for Work and Pensions* [2003] EWCA Civ 1465, [2003] All ER (D) 211 (Oct).

13.17 Asylum seekers who claimed asylum in-country before 3 April 2000 and within three months of what has become known as a 'declaration of upheaval' are also transitionally protected for these benefits.[1] There have only been two declarations that a country 'is subject to such a fundamental change of circumstances that [the Secretary of State] would not normally order the return of a person to that country': in respect of former Zaire (now the Democratic Republic of Congo) on 17 May 1998, and in respect of Sierra Leone on 1 July 1997. Both these declarations expired after three months.[2] Claimants must have submitted a claim for asylum to the Secretary of State within three months of the date of the declaration and the claim must have been recorded by the Secretary of State as having been made.[3] Where a claimant arrived in the UK after the declaration had been made but was nevertheless present in the UK and claimed asylum within three months of it, the Commissioner dismissed an appeal, holding that it was necessary for the claimant actually to have been in the UK at the time of the declaration.[4]

1   Social Security (Immigration and Asylum) Consequential Amendments Regulations 2000, SI 2000/636, regs 2(5), 12(3), (4)(b), (6), (7)(b).
2   Written Answer to House of Commons by Mike O'Brien, Hansard 3 March 1999, col 757/758.
3   SI 2000/636, reg 12(4)(b)(ii), (iii), (6)(ii), (iii).
4   CIS/3864/98. Leave to appeal to the Court of Appeal was granted but the appeal was not pursued.

13.18 Both 'on arrival' and 'declaration of upheaval' claimants lose entitlement when the asylum claim is recorded as having been determined (by the Secretary of State, not on appeal), or is 'abandoned'.[1] In 2003 the House of Lords held in *Anufrijeva*[2] that a decision to refuse asylum does not become a determination until an asylum seeker has been properly notified of the refusal by the Home Office.[3] An asylum seeker who was in receipt of benefit and whose claim was recorded as determined prior to 25 September 2000 became eligible to apply for interim asylum support on refusal if he or she appealed or had a child living as part of the household. If the claim was recorded as determined after that date he or she would be similarly eligible for NASS support.[4]

1   Social Security (Immigration and Asylum) Consequential Amendments Regulations 2000, SI 2000/636, reg 12(5), (8).
2   *R (on the application of Anufrijeva) v Secretary of State for the Home Department* [2003] UKHL 6, [2004] 1 AC 604, [2003] 3 All ER 827.
3   The majority held that it was unconstitutional for a person to be adversely affected by a decision of which he or she had had no notice, and against which there was no possibility of appeal.
4   Immigration and Asylum Act 1999, s 94 and NASS Policy Bulletins 51–53.

Rates of benefit and dependants in respect of income support and jobseeker's allowance

13.19 The pre-3 April 2000 claimants benefiting from transitional benefits, having claimed on arrival or within three months of an upheaval declaration, are eligible for income support and income-based jobseeker's allowance, not at the full rate but at the 'urgent cases' rate of 90 per cent of a claimant's ordinary weekly applicable amount.[1] The reduced rate also applies to those exempted from the 'subject to immigration control' test on the basis that they are temporarily without funds or were granted leave under a sponsorship undertaking and the sponsor has died.[2] However, these groups may at least obtain benefit for their spouses and children, whether or not the latter are 'subject to immigration control',[3] whereas those entitled to these benefits at the ordinary rates may not obtain benefit in respect of their spouses who are subject to immigration control nor, if such a spouse is present, for any children who are subject to control. However, where the claimant is a single parent or the *spouse* is not subject to immigration control, additional benefit is due, regardless of their immigration status.[4]

[1]   Income Support (General) Regulations 1987, SI 1987/1967, reg 71; Jobseeker's Allowance Regulations 1996, SI 1996/207, reg 148.
[2]   SI 1987/1967, reg 70(1), (2), (2A); SI 1996/207, reg 147(1), (2), (2A).
[3]   SI 1987/1967, reg 71(1)(a)(i), (ii) with reference to Sch 2, paras 1, 2; SI 1996/207, reg 148(1)(a)(i), (ii) with reference to Sch 1, paras 1, 2.
[4]   SI 1987/1967, reg 21, Sch 7 para 16; SI 1996/207, reg 85, Sch 5, para 13A.

Attendance allowance, severe disablement allowance, carer's allowance, disability living allowance, social fund payments, child benefit

13.20 Three classes of people are exempted from the 'subject to immigration control' test for these benefits:[1]

(i)   Those given leave to enter or remain in the UK upon a maintenance undertaking.[2] This wide exemption re-includes that whole class of claimant primarily excluded by one of the limbs of section 115 of the Immigration and Asylum Act 1999;

(ii)   Family members of EEA nationals,[3] except for family members of nationals of Bulgaria, the Czech Republic, Estonia, Hungary, Latvia, Lithuania, Poland, Romania, Slovakia and Slovenia, who will not be entitled to child benefit unless they have a right to reside in the UK;[4]

(iii) Those nationals, and their family members who are living with them, of countries with which the EC has concluded an agreement[5] which provides for the equal treatment of workers who are nationals of the signatory state in the area of social security.[6] The exemption extends to association agreements and to Association Council decisions made under them.[7]

In addition, transitional protection applies to persons entitled to or receiving the benefits as a result of the transitional provisions of the February 1996 changes.[8] The claimant must have been entitled to the benefit in question prior to 5 February 1996,[9] and protection continues until *either* any claim to asylum is recorded as having been determined or is abandoned *or* entitlement to that benefit is revised or superseded by the social security determining authorities.[10] Unlike income support, protection only applies to the benefit award made before 5 February 1996 and not to renewal claims made after that date.[11] For child benefit, the claimant needs to have been paid the benefit immediately prior to 7 October 1996,[12] and the conditions for cessation of benefit are similar.[13]

1 Social Security (Immigration and Asylum) Consequential Amendments Regulations 2000, SI 2000/636, reg 2(2), Sch, Pt II.
2 SI 2000/636, Sch, Pt II, para 4. See 13.7 above.
3 Sch, Pt II, para 1. 'Family members' is not defined, but it is suggested that it should be understood to include at least those who are treated as family members under EC free movement provisions.
4 Child Benefit (General) (Amendment) Regulations 2004, SI 2004/1244 and the Accession (Immigration and Worker Registration) Regulations 2004, SI 2004/1219.
5 Under Art 310 EC (ex Art 238).
6 Social Security (Immigration and Asylum) Consequential Amendments Regulations 2000, SI 2000/636, Sch, Pt II, paras 2–3.
7 Commissioner's Decision CFC/2613/97. The exemption applies to nationals of Algeria, Morocco, Slovenia, Tunisia and Turkey.
8 SI 2000/636, regs 2(4), 12(10) and Social Security (Persons From Abroad) Miscellaneous Amendments Regulations 1996, SI 1996/30, reg 12(3).
9 *R v Secretary of State for Social Security, ex p Vijeikis, Zaheer and Okito* (10 July 1997, unreported), QBD, Dyson J, upheld by the Court of Appeal on 5 March 1998; for the need for entitlement immediately prior to 5 February 1996 see Commissioner's Decisions *CIS/16992/96, CIS/2809/97, CFC/1580/97*.
10 SI 2000/636, reg 12(10), Social Security Act 1998, ss 9–10.
11 *R v Chief Adjudication Officer, ex p B* (9 December 1998, unreported).
12 When the Asylum and Immigration Act 1996 removed entitlement from anyone 'subject to immigration control' by inserting s 146A into the Social Security Contributions and Benefits Act 1992.
13 SI 2000/636, regs 2(4)(b), 12(10), Child Benefit (General) Regulations 1976, SI 1976/965, reg 14B(g).

Tax credits

13.21 Certain classes of persons who are subject to immigration control are entitled to child tax credit.[1] These are persons who were given leave to enter or remain upon the undertaking of another person to be responsible for their maintenance and accommodation, who have been resident in the UK for a period of at least five years commencing on or after the date of their entry into the UK or the date on which the undertaking was given, whichever is the later. A person can also claim earlier if the person giving the undertaking dies. A person with limited leave to enter the UK subject to a condition of no recourse to public funds, who has complied with the condition, is entitled to claim child tax credit for up to 42 days in aggregate within the period of leave granted (including any extension) if he or she is temporarily without funds because remittances from abroad have been disrupted and there is a reasonable expectation that they will be resumed.[2] Nationals of a state which has ratified the European Convention on Social and Medical Assistance or the Council of Europe Social Charter[3] and who are lawfully present[4] may claim working tax credit, and child tax credit subject to further conditions.[5] Nationals of states with which the EEA has concluded a Co-operation Agreement and who are able to work lawfully in the UK may claim child tax credit.[6] However, tax credits can only be claimed if a person has a right to reside in the UK.[7] Where one member of a married or unmarried couple is subject to immigration control and the other is not, or is within one of the exempted classes described in the five cases above, the calculation of the amount due and the methods of applying the credit will be the same as for couples not subject to immigration control.[8] But where the exemption arises through being a national of a state which has ratified the European Convention on Social and Medical Assistance or the Council of Europe Social Charter or is a national of a state which is party to a Co-operation Agreement, the concession in relation to partners only applies if the partner is entitled to apply for a child tax credit him- or herself.[9] When a person is recognised as a refugee in the UK and claims child tax credit within three months of that recognition, he or she is treated as if the claim for tax credit for had been made on the date of the asylum claim and every year on 6 April in the intervening years, but deductions will be made for any asylum support received during that period.[10]

1   Tax Credits (Immigration) Regulations 2003, SI 2003/653, reg 3(1).
2   SI 2003/653, reg 3(1), Cases 1–3.
3   See 13.12 above.
4   See 13.12 text and fnn 5–9 above.
5   Child tax credit is available to this class only from 6 April 2004, and only if immediately before that date they were eligible for additional income support or income-related jobseekers' allowance in respect of the child: Tax Credits (Immigration) Regulations 2003 SI 2003/653, reg 3(1), Case 4.
6   SI 2003/653, reg 3(1), Case 5. Countries with which the EC has Cooperation Agreements in this field are Algeria, Morocco, Tunisia and Turkey, but the agreements confer no right to reside or to work in the UK, so to qualify, nationals would have to have leave to enter or remain in the UK which permitted them to work.
7   See the Tax Credits (Residence) (Amendment) Regulations 2004, SI 2004/1243; Accession (Immigration and Worker Registration) Regulations 2004, SI 2004/1219.
8   Tax Credits (Immigration) Regulations 2003, SI 2003/653, reg 3(2).
9   Tax Credits (Immigration) Regulations 2003, SI 2003/653, reg 3(3).
10 Tax Credits (Immigration) Regulations 2003, SI 2003/653, reg 3(5)–(9).

Child benefit, attendance allowance, disability living allowance

13.22 Attendance allowance, disability living allowance and child benefit are payable under another exemption from section 115 of the Immigration and Asylum Act 1999. The UK has certain reciprocal agreements with both EEA and non-EEA countries which are given effect by Orders in Council.[1] Where an agreement is in effect in respect of any of these benefits, nationals of (or in some cases, migrants coming from) the contracting state are exempted from the 'subject to immigration control test' and are eligible to claim benefit.[2] However, those claiming child benefit also need to show that they have a right to reside in the UK.[3]

1   Made under the Social Security Administration Act 1992, s 179. Among the non-EEA countries and territories which have concluded agreements in respect of any of these benefits are Australia, Barbados, Canada, Israel, Jersey and Guernsey, Mauritius, New Zealand, Switzerland, Federal Republic of Yugoslavia.
2   Social Security (Immigration and Asylum) Consequential Amendments Regulations 2000, SI 2000/636, reg 2(3). The provisions of the agreements are too detailed to set out here. See Cox et al *Migration and Social Security Benefits Handbook* CPAG (2nd edn, 1997) pp 372–378.
3   Child Benefit (General) (Amendment) Regulations 2004, SI 2004/1244.

Habitual residence

13.23 The 'habitual residence' test applies an additional obstacle to eligibility for income support, income-based jobseeker's allowance, housing benefit and council tax benefit[1] and State Pension Credit, subject to the exemptions below. It was introduced in August 1994 in order to combat what the then government viewed as 'benefit tourism'[2] on the part of EEA nationals and is retained in the regime applicable to these benefits from 3 April 2000. In principle it applies to nationals of all countries, including EEA nationals and British citizens, who must be habitually resident in the common travel area.[3] The test has been further refined: in order to be habitually resident a person must now also have a right to reside in the UK, the Channel Islands, the Isle of Man or the Republic of Ireland.[4] In other areas of law, the concept of habitual residence has been seen as synonymous with 'ordinary residence', ie the claimant must be lawfully resident for a settled purpose, which is a question of fact to be determined in the light of all the circumstances.[5] It is clearly distinct from that of domicile,[6] since it is possible to be habitually resident in more than one country at the same time.

[1]   Income Support (General) Regulations 1987, SI 1987/1967, reg 21(3); Jobseeker's Allowance Regulations 1996, SI 1996/207, reg 85(4); Housing Benefit (General) Regulations 1987, SI 1987/1971, reg 7A(4)(e); Council Tax Benefit (General) Regulations 1992, SI 1992/1814, reg 4A(4)(e); State Pension Credit Regulations 2002, SI 2002/1792.
[2]   See eg the speech of Rt Hon Peter Lilley MP, Secretary of State for Social Security, to Conservative Party annual conference, Autumn 1993.
[3]   Ie the UK, Channel Islands, Isle of Man, Republic of Ireland: see chapter 6 above.
[4]   The Social Security (Habitual Residence) Amendment Regulations 2004, SI 2004/1232.
[5]   *Shah v Barnet London Borough Council* [1983] 2 AC 309, followed in *Al-Habtoor v Fotheringham (sub nom AH v F)* [2001] EWCA Civ 256; *Ikimi v Ikimi* [2001] EWCA Civ 873, [2002] Fam 72; *Armstrong v Armstrong* [2003] EWHC 777 (Fam), [2003] Fam Law 559; *Mark v Mark* [2004] EWCA Civ 168, [2005] Fam 267; see chapter 5 above. The Social Security Commissioner has recognised that asylum seekers awaiting resolution of their claims may be habitually resident: *CIS/564/94*.
[6]   *R(U) 8/88*; see 11.27–11.33 above.

13.24 In *Nessa*,[1] the Commissioner endorsed the view of an earlier case[2] that an 'appreciable period' of residence by the claimant was required to establish habitual residence.[3] The Court of Appeal (by a majority) and the House of Lords agreed, although the Lords accepted that the 'appreciable period' may be as short as a month,[4] and that there may be 'special cases', such as resumption of earlier residence.[5] As long as a person can show that she or he has a right to reside in the UK, the Channel Islands, the Isle of Man or the Republic of Ireland,[6] it is a question of fact dependent upon the circumstances of each case. Bringing possessions, doing everything necessary to establish residence before coming, having a right of abode, seeking to bring family in, 'durable ties' with the country of residence or intended residence and many other factors have to be taken into account. A different meaning was given to the term by the ECJ in *Swaddling*,[7] where the court considered that no minimum period of residence in the Member State in which the claimant had applied for social security benefit was necessary to establish habitual residence there for the purposes of Council Regulation 1408/71 (EEC), although the reasons for a person's presence, its duration and the claimant's intentions were all relevant factors. The Court of Appeal has rejected the argument that habitual residence is an EU concept so that the meaning given in *Swaddling* should overrule *Nessa*.[8] It is arguable that if the required period of residence is too long, this will lead to a breach of Article 8 ECHR, as it applies to benefits of last resort.[9]

1   *R(IS)* 2/00, *Nessa v Chief Adjudication Officer* [1998] 2 All ER 728.
2   *R(IS)* 6/96.
3   Contrast, in another context, *Macrae v Macrae* [1949] 2 All ER 34.
4   By reference to *Re F (a minor)* [1994] FLR 548.
5   See further *CIS/1304/97* and, for retention of habitual residence during a period of absence, *CIS/14591/96*.
6   This requirement does not form part of the ratio of the case, but has been added by SI 2004/1232 (see 13.23 text and fn 4 above).
7   *Swaddling v Adjudication Officer* [1999] All ER (EC) 217, applied to an EU citizen in *R(IS)* 3/00.
8   *Gingi v Secretary of State for Work and Pensions* [2001] EWCA Civ 1685, [2002] 1 CMLR 587.
9   See *Ahmed v Austria* (Application 25964/94) (1996) 24 EHRR 278, [1998] INLR 65, ECtHR (at 8.85 above). For the human rights implications of denial of support (in the context of asylum support) see 13.57 below.

Exemptions from habitual residence test

13.25   The following persons are exempt from the habitual residence test:

- 'workers' within the meaning of Council Regulations 1612/68 (EEC) or 1251/70 (EEC) who have a right to reside in the UK, the Channel Islands, the Isle of Man or the Republic of Ireland;[1]
- persons with a right to reside in the UK pursuant to Council Directives 68/360 (EEC) or 73/148 (EEC);
- refugees within the meaning of Article 1A(2) of the Refugee Convention;
- persons who have been granted Humanitarian Protection or exceptional or discretionary leave to enter or remain.[2]

In addition, persons who are not 'subject to immigration control' for the purposes of the Immigration and Asylum Act 1999,[3] and who are in the UK as a result of their deportation, or other removal by compulsion from another country to the UK, are exempt from the habitual residence test for the purposes of income support and income-based jobseekers' allowance.[4] Once in *receipt* of income support or income-based jobseeker's allowance, such a claimant may receive housing benefit and council tax benefit regardless of the habitual residence test.[5]

1   The Social Security (Habitual Residence) Amendment Regulations 2004, SI 2004/1232 and the Accession (Immigration and Worker Registration) Regulations 2004, SI 2004/1219.
2   Income Support (General) Regulations 1987, SI 1987/1967, reg 21(3); Jobseeker's Allowance Regulations 1996, SI 1996/207, reg 85(4); Housing Benefit (General) Regulations 1987, SI 1987/1971, reg 7A(4)(e); Council Tax Benefit (General) Regulations 1992, SI 1992/1814, reg 4A(4)(e).
3   IAA 1999, s 115.
4   SI 1987/1967, reg 21(3); SI 1996/207, reg 85(4).
5   SI 1987/1971, reg 7A(4), (5); SI 1992/1814, reg 4A(4), (5).

Backdating of benefits for refugees

13.26   There are two regimes in force for the backdating of income support for asylum seekers subsequently granted refugee status:

(i)   Those who claimed asylum before 3 April 2000, provided they claim income support within 28 days of notification that they have been recorded as a refugee by the Secretary of State, are entitled to backdated payment of benefit *at the urgent case*s *rate* from the date that the claim to asylum was refused (if the asylum claim was made on arrival)[1] or from the date of the claim, or 5 February 1996 if that is later, if the claim was made in-country,[2] to the date they are recorded by the Secretary of State as a refugee;[3]

(ii)   Those who claimed asylum on or after 3 April 2000, and who claim income support within 28 days of notification of being recorded as a refugee, are entitled to backdated benefit paid at the *full rate* from the date of the claim for asylum.[4] However, for these claimants, as opposed to the pre-3 April 2000 claimants, the award of income support is subject to an express deduction representing asylum support received under either NASS or the interim scheme.[5] A deduction may also be made to cover support provided in an accommodation centre.[6] There is no provision to deduct the value of any support received under section 4 of the Immigration and Asylum Act 1999.[7]

Similar provisions apply in respect of the back-dating of awards of housing benefit and council tax benefit.[8] Since 6 April 2004, an asylum-seeker who is recognised as a refugee and granted indefinite leave to remain has also been able to claim backdated child benefit provided that the claim is made within three months of receiving notification of refugee status.[9]

1   This category were eligible for benefits until refusal of their claim.
2   This category lost eligibility on 5 February 1996, see above.
3   Income Support (General) Regulations 1987, SI 1987/1967, reg 21ZA, now superseded by Social Security (Immigration and Asylum) Consequential Amendments Regulations 2000, SI 2000/636, reg 3(5) but preserved for pre-3 April 2000 asylum applicants by reg 12(1), (2).
4   SI 1987/1967, reg 21ZB, inserted by SI 2000/636, reg 3(5).
5   Immigration and Asylum Act 1999, s 123(7); SI 1987/1967, reg 21ZB(3).
6   IAA 1999, s 123(7) as amended by the Nationality, Immigration and Asylum Act 2002, s 52.
7   Ie, 'hard cases support' for failed asylum seekers who cannot leave the UK. See 13.175 below.
8   Housing Benefit (General) Regulations 1987, SI 1987/1971, reg 7B, Sch A1; Council Tax Benefit (General) Regulations 1992, SI 1992/1814, reg 4D, Sch A1; as amended by SI 2000/636, regs 6(4)–(6), 7(4)–(6) respectively, with transitional arrangements for pre-3 April 2000 claimants contained in SI 2000/636, reg 12(2)(c), (d).
9   Child Benefit and Guardian's Allowance (Miscellaneous Amendments) Regulations 2004, SI 2004/761.

13.27   It is at least arguable that backdating of welfare benefits is an obligation under the 1951 Refugee Convention, since an asylum seeker is a refugee once he or she fulfils the criterion set out in Article 1 of the Convention. A successful asylum application or appeal merely recognises the refugee's true status. It does not create it, and Article 24(b) of the 1951 Convention entitles refugees to receive the same treatment in respect of social security as UK nationals. However, this view is not shared by the current government, and section 12 of the Asylum and Immigration (Treatment of Claimants, etc) Act 2004 provides for the abolition, as from a date to be appointed, of section 123 of the Immigration and Asylum Act 1999 and the benefit regulations which enable refugees to claim backdated benefits. After that date, anyone who is recognised as a refugee will be unable to claim backdated benefits.[1] The Act replaces the entitlement to backdated benefits with a power for the Secretary of State to set up a discretionary integration loan scheme for refugees,[2] in which the refugee's income and assets and his or her ability to repay any loan would be taken into account, and insolvent or under-age refugees would be ineligible.[3] Under the proposed scheme, few asylum seekers who have previously been supported due to destitution would qualify for an integration loan, and in our view the scheme represents a shabby derogation from international humanitarian responsibilities.[4]

[1]   Asylum and Immigration (Treatment of Claimants, etc) Act 2004, s 12(5) (not in force at the time of writing).
[2]   AI(TC)A 2004, s 13(1).
[3]   AI(TC)A 2004, s 13(3)(a).
[4]   AI(TC)A 2004, s 13(3)(c).

Further residence requirements and contributory benefits

13.28 Some of the benefits referred to above have additional residence tests, which cannot be set out within the scope of this text, which may require presence in the UK for a certain specified period of time and/or ordinary residence in the UK.[1] The benefits to which additional requirements are added are: attendance allowance, child benefit/guardian's allowance (for which the rules are most complex), disability living allowance, working tax credit, child tax credit, carer's allowance, category D retirement pension, severe disablement allowance. Access to the contributory benefits – contribution-based jobseeker's allowance, incapacity benefit, maternity allowance, bereavement payment, widowed parent's allowance, bereavement allowance, category A and B retirement pensions – does not depend upon immigration status, but they are payable only in those cases in which sufficient national insurance contributions have been paid. In practice, this may exclude many who are coming or who have recently come to the UK.

[1]   See CPAG's *Migration and Social Security Handbook* (3rd edn, 2001, revised October 2002; 4th edn forthcoming).

THE ASYLUM SUPPORT SCHEME

13.29 In July 1998 the government announced the introduction of a new national system of support for asylum seekers and their dependants.[1] The new system that was finally introduced took shape in the form of two distinct, although similar, structures for providing asylum support, both enacted through the provisions of the Immigration and Asylum Act 1999.[2] The stated aim of the government was to ensure that genuine asylum seekers were not left destitute while at the same time containing the cost to the public purse of providing for asylum seekers.[3] One means of achieving this was to provide 'incentives' to asylum seekers to look first to their own communities for support.[4] A key disincentive to applying for asylum support, and one of the most controversial aspects of the scheme, has been the provision of accommodation on a 'no-choice' basis outside the London and the south-east of England. This system of dispersing asylum seekers reflected the aim of the government to reduce both the costs of support – by using empty social housing in different parts of the country – and the perceived burden on authorities in London and the south-east. Equally controversial was the government's decision to implement a largely cashless system requiring asylum seekers to present vouchers redeemable for goods at participating retail outlets[5] – a system whose explicit policy aim was to reduce the 'incentive to economic migration'[6] and which was withdrawn in the light of widespread public concern about its effects. The basis on which this policy was formulated has since been called into question by research commissioned by the Home Office itself,[7] which revealed that where an asylum seeker had a choice of countries in which to seek asylum, the factors which shaped his or her decision were the presence of relatives or friends, a belief that the UK was a safe, tolerant and democratic country, previous links between the country of origin and the UK including colonialism, and ties of language. There was very little evidence that asylum seekers who had been interviewed for the study had a detailed knowledge of UK immigration and asylum procedures, entitlement to benefits or the availability of work in the UK.

1 See Home Office White Paper *Fairer, Faster, Firmer: A Modern Approach to Asylum and Immigration* (Cm 4018, July 1998).
2 Immigration and Asylum Act 1999, Pt VI and Schs 8–10.
3 White Paper above.
4 Asylum Seekers Support Project Team, Immigration Nationality Directorate *Asylum Seekers Support* (March 1999) para 1.1.
5 The main participating supermarket chains were Tesco, Sainsbury's, Asda and Somerfield.
6 *Asylum Seekers Support* above, paras 1.1, 1.4.
7 Vaughan Robinson and Jeremy Segrott *Understanding the decision making of asylum seekers* Home Office Research Study 243 (Home Office Research, Development and Statistics Department, July 2002).

13.30 These two features of the system, in particular, attracted persistent criticism both during the passage of the Immigration and Asylum Act 1999[1] and after its implementation.[2] In June 2000, the Audit Commission reported[3] that the lack of effective support for asylum seekers in the areas of dispersal could lead them to become trapped in a cycle of social exclusion and dependency in those areas, or to their drifting back to London (as did resettled Vietnamese refugees two decades earlier). The Commission's report highlighted, in particular, the absence outside the capital of sufficient legal support (less than half the law firms contracted by the Legal Services Commission to provide immigration advice were outside London),[4] mental health services, English language support and refugee community organisations. Also significant was the hostile media coverage given to asylum seekers, which inflamed public opinion and encouraged violent attack.[5] By the end of 2000, the warnings made by the Commission appeared to have been borne out. The dispersal system was reported to be in a state of collapse as large numbers of asylum seekers abandoned dispersed accommodation, where they were fearful of racial harassment and unable to access necessary support, for cramped accommodation with relatives in and around London.[6] Also in October 2000, in the face of mounting criticism of the voucher system,[7] the Government was forced to agree to review its operation,[8] and the Home Office Research, Development and Statistics Directorate undertook a fieldwork study of asylum seekers. The results of this study were published in March 2002,[9] and the following month the voucher scheme was finally scrapped and replaced by a system of cash vouchers redeemable at local post offices. In June 2004, cash vouchers were replaced by cash payments.[10]

[1]   See for example Memorandum from the African-Caribbean and Refugee Support Project on the 'distressing and humiliating' effect of vouchers, and evidence of the Hackney Churches Refugee Network, to the House of Commons Special Standing Committee on the 1999 Bill. The Local Government Association told the Committee that vouchers could be 'costly, bureaucratic and stigmatising' and that an unofficial market had developed by their being sold on at under face value by asylum seekers needing to buy essential non-food items.

[2]   For example, in October 2000 the report of the Commission on the Future of Multi-ethnic Britain, set up by the Runnymede Trust in January 1998 to propose ways of countering racial discrimination and disadvantage and to promote racial justice, proposed a return to a cash system of support for asylum seekers at no less than the basic level of income support and a choice of available housing. (The report was published by Profile Books.)

[3]   Audit Commission *Another Country: Implementing dispersal under the IAA 1999* (June 2000); the early difficulties faced by the dispersal scheme are further apparent from the 'Asylum Seekers' Voluntary Dispersal Scheme' Bulletins 1–6 (on the Local Government Association website www.lga.gov.uk).

[4]   By January 2004, there was only one solicitors' firm with a contract in Norwich, one in Ipswich, none in Canterbury and two in Hull plus a law centre. The changes to funding for public funded immigration and asylum work introduced in 2004 (see 18.124 below) have led many more immigration practitioners to close their doors.

[5]   The Commission found that only 6% of 161 local press articles analysed between October and November 1999 referred to the positive contribution made by asylum seekers and refugees.

[6]   See 'Refugees pour back to London', 'Nowhere left to run' *Observer*, 31 December 2000.

[7]   See eg Oxfam GB, the Refugee Council and the Transport and General Workers Union 'Token Gestures – the effects of the voucher scheme on asylum seekers and organisations in the UK' (December 2000). The difficulties encountered by asylum seekers using the voucher system have also been noted by the UNCHR: *Reception standards for asylum seekers in the European Union* (2000).

[8]   Parliamentary answer of Secretary of State for the Home Department, 355 HC Official Report (6th series) col 210W, 26 October 2000.

[9]   *Asylum seekers' experiences of the voucher scheme in the UK – fieldwork report* Home Office, Development and Statistics Directorate, March 2002. The report identified a wide range of problems: 60% of respondents stated that they were unable to buy everything they needed with their vouchers; over half said that a shop had refused to accept their vouchers; nearly three-quarters felt embarrassed using their vouchers; and four-fifths said that they were given insufficient cash to pay fares to appointments.

[10] Asylum Support (Amendment) (No 2) Regulations 2004, SI 2004/1313, in force 4 June 2004, amending reg 10(2) and 10A of the Asylum Support Regulations 2000, SI 2000/704. Vouchers are now being reintroduced as part of 'hard cases' support in some areas: see 13.175 below.

13.31 The Home Office's own statistics belie the proposition that restricting the right to financial support acts as a disincentive to asylum claims as had been predicted.[1] In 1999, there were 71,160 applications for asylum in the UK. In 2000, there were 80,315 and in 2001 there were 71,025. In 2002, the number of applications rose to 84,130.[2] The data provided by the Home Office on applications for asylum made by different nationalities reveals an ebb and flow of applications which closely mirrors the objective circumstances in the asylum seekers' countries of origin.[3] The clear inference to be drawn from both the research and the statistics is that the number of asylum seekers coming to the UK is more indicative of the level of conflict and human rights abuse prevalent in the world at any one time than the availability of asylum support in the UK.

[1] Home Office Research, Development and Statistics Directorate, Immigration and Nationality Directorate, Departments of Education and Employment, Health, Social Security: *Asylum Seeker Support: estimates of public expenditure*, at Appendix E, paras 5, 6, 11. A full breakdown of the Research Directorate's projection is cited in Asylum Seekers Support Project Team, IND *Asylum Seeker Support* (March 1999) chapter 2 and in the Home Office paper *Cluster Areas: Role of Local Organisations*.
[2] *Control of Immigration Statistics: United Kingdom 2002* Home Office, November 2003, Cm 6053.
[3] See Table 4.2 of statistics referred to in fn 2 above.

13.32 The low level of financial support and poor standard of the accommodation provided under the asylum support scheme was explained by the short period for which it would be needed. The White Paper[1] stated that by April 2001, asylum decisions would take two months on average and asylum appeals would be resolved within a further four months. In 2002/2003, over a quarter of asylum applicants waited over two months for the initial decision, with 16 per cent waiting over four months and 13 per cent over six months. Data produced by the IAA revealed that less than half of appeals received by the appellate authority in 2002/3 were determined within the target 17-week period.[2] This means that many asylum seekers and their dependants are having to stay for long periods in poor accommodation and with inadequate financial support. This was explicitly acknowledged by the government when it made provision for a one off payment where an asylum applicant had not been finally determined within six months.[3] However, this provision was abolished in June 2004.[4]

[1] Home Office White Paper *Fairer, Faster, Firmer: A Modern Approach to Asylum and Immigration* July 1998, Cm 4018.
[2] Asylum Statistics: 3rd Quarter 2003 United Kingdom Immigration Research, Development and Statistics Directorate of the Home Office.
[3] Asylum Support Regulations 2000, SI 2000/704, reg 11.
[4] Asylum Support (Amendment) (No 2) Regulations 2004, SI 2004/1313, revoking reg 11 from 4 June 2004.

Providing support

13.33 The Immigration and Asylum Act 1999 established two parallel schemes to provide support: a national one, which was designed to be permanent, and a local 'interim scheme' which was to provide support during the transitional period until the national scheme was fully operational. From 6 December 1999 an 'interim' support scheme for asylum seekers and their dependants, operated by local authorities, was introduced in England and Wales (but not in Scotland or Northern Ireland).[1] The introduction of the interim scheme coincided with the exclusion from many community care services of most asylum seekers and others 'subject to immigration control' within the meaning of section 115 of the Immigration and Asylum Act 1999.[2] Most asylum seekers who were in receipt of support under section 21 of the

National Assistance Act 1948 or section 17 of the Children Act 1989 did not notice or experience any change in their support with the introduction of the interim scheme, as they were deemed to have been accepted for support by the local authority under the interim provisions.[3] The Government's intention was to ensure that local authorities had a 'purpose-designed' statutory duty of support until its main scheme could be introduced, rather than the ill-fitting duties under the community care and Children Act legislation.[4]

[1] Immigration and Asylum Act 1999, Sch 9; Asylum Support (Interim Provisions) Regulations 1999, SI 1999/3056.
[2] IAA 1999, ss 116–117.
[3] SI 1999/3056, reg 11.
[4] NASS Director's circular to all Chief Executives of local authorities in England and Wales, 19 November 1999, para 6.

13.34 From 3 April 2000 the national scheme was introduced, administered by the National Asylum Support Service of the Home Office (the 'NASS scheme').[1] Although under this scheme NASS is charged with the responsibility for deciding whether a person is entitled to support and what forms of support are appropriate,[2] the Secretary of State may arrange for the actual delivery of the support by another agency.[3] In particular, although not exclusively, local authorities are empowered to provide support under such arrangements[4] and may form companies and enter into contracts with the Secretary of State, either alone or with other agencies such as registered social landlords, housing associations and the private and voluntary sectors, for the provision of support services to asylum seekers.[5] At present, accommodation is being provided by a mixture of local authorities, regional consortia, voluntary sector agencies and private landlords under contracts let by NASS. Many of these contracts expire in 2005, and NASS is presently developing a national accommodation strategy, which will be delivered regionally after that date.[6] NASS works closely with voluntary sector agencies[7] which assist asylum seekers to apply for NASS support and provide emergency full board accommodation whilst their applications are being determined.

[1] Immigration and Asylum Act 1999, Pt VI, and Schs 8, 10.
[2] See IAA 1999, ss 95(1), (5), (7), 96(2), (3), 97(1), (2), (4), (5), (7), 98(1) and the decision-making functions devolved to the Secretary of State in the Asylum Support Regulations 2000, SI 2000/704.
[3] IAA 1999, ss 95(1), 98(1).
[4] IAA 1999, s 99(1), (2), (3).
[5] IAA 1999, s 99(4), (5).
[6] NASS Information Sheet 1, *The 2005 Programme*, 23 December 2003.
[7] Refugee Arrivals Project, Migrants Helpline, Refugee Action, the Refugee Council, the Scottish and Welsh Refugee Councils, the North of England Refugee Service and the Northern Ireland Council for Ethnic Minorities.

13.35 The purpose of the NASS scheme is to provide support for asylum seekers who are not entitled to community care provisions or welfare benefits. NASS will eventually take over responsibility for all those currently supported under the interim scheme. The interim scheme was designed to end on 1 April 2002,[1] but was extended and is now due to end on 4 April 2006.[2] The IAA 1999 enabled the Secretary of State to give directions to local authorities to treat the interim period as ending for certain classes of asylum seekers on dates earlier than 1 April 2002,[3] whereupon the affected classes became ineligible for support under the interim scheme[4] and potentially eligible for NASS support.[5] Four such directions have been given, which had the general effect of rendering different classes of new asylum seekers and different classes of newly 'disbenefitted' asylum seekers[6] eligible for NASS rather than interim support between April and September 2000.[7] The directions brought new asylum seekers, and asylum seekers who had hitherto been entitled to social security, into the NASS scheme where responsibility would otherwise have lain with the local authorities under the interim scheme. They have not had the effect of literally 'moving' classes of asylum seeker already supported under the interim scheme, into the NASS scheme.

1 Immigration and Asylum Act 1999, Sch 9, para 15 and Asylum Support (Interim Provisions) Regulations 1999, SI 1999/3056, regs 1(1), 2(5).
2 Asylum Support (Interim Provisions) (Amendment) Regulations 2005, SI 2005/ 595.
3 The time span of the interim period was set by SI 1999/3056 and could be changed by amending regulations.
4 IAA 1999, Sch 15, para 14(1), (4); this provision enables the Secretary of State for the Home Department to direct local authorities to 'treat the interim period' as coming to an end earlier than 1 April 2002: for specified purposes; in relation to a specified area or locality; or in relation to persons of a specified description.
5 SI 1999/3056, reg 3(1) provides in terms that an authority '... must provide support during the interim period to eligible persons'.
6 Asylum Support Regulations 2000, SI 2000/704, reg 4(5)(a).
7 Ie those who have received a negative decision by the Secretary of State having up to that point been entitled to social security benefit.
8 Direction Nos 1, 2, 2A, 3 of the Secretary of State for the Home Department issued on 13 March, 10 April, 10 April and 11 July 2000 respectively, see 13.159ff below.

Further powers

13.36 The Secretary of State has powers to require local authorities, registered social landlords and housing associations to provide assistance in the provision of NASS accommodation.[1] This includes putting suitable spare accommodation at the Secretary of State's disposal in return for appropriate reimbursement[2] as well as providing the Secretary of State with information about their housing stock on request.[3] The Secretary of State also has powers to designate areas consisting of one or more local authorities as 'reception zones' in which local authorities may be directed to make available to NASS, or to another agency with which NASS has contracted to provide support, a specified amount of accommodation.[4] The Secretary of State has indicated that these powers will only be used if local authorities refuse to co-operate voluntarily in providing accommodation for asylum seekers.[5]

1 Immigration and Asylum Act 1999, s 100.
2 Explanatory Notes to the IAA 1999, para 310.
3 IAA 1999, s 100(4).
4 IAA 1999, s 101; if such powers are implemented, further regulations would be required dealing, inter alia, with the management of such housing accommodation; see s 101(10)–(14).
5 See Explanatory Notes to IAA 1999, para 312.

Other changes

13.37 The new system of asylum support must be seen in the context of simultaneous changes in provision of community care and social security benefits with particular ramifications for asylum seekers. From 6 December 1999 those who fall within the statutory definition of being 'subject to immigration control' were prima facie excluded from access to many community care services and, from 3 April 2000, from social security benefits.[1] In February 2005, the EC Reception Conditions Directive came into force.[2] Article 13 of the Directive requires that the material conditions provided to asylum seekers ensure a standard of living adequate for the health of applicants and their dependants, which is capable of ensuring their subsistence. Article 14 requires Member States to protect rights to family life in the provision of housing, and to ensure the possibility of contact with relatives, legal and other advisers, UNHCR and relevant NGOs. The Directive also requires Member States to provide asylum seekers with information about asylum procedures and support provision, to have regard to the special needs of vulnerable persons, including minors, elderly and disabled people, pregnant women, single parents and victims of torture, in carrying out asylum support functions, and to give access to the labour market to asylum seekers who have been waiting for over a year for the initial decision on their claim. Although the Directive allows Member States to reduce or withdraw support in specified situations, including failure to claim asylum as soon as reasonably practicable, measures of reduction or withdrawal of support must be proportionate. The principles of the Directive ought to make a significant change in the provision of asylum support, in particular in the areas of dispersal and in exclusion from, or suspension or discontinuance of support. The Asylum Seekers (Reception Conditions) Regulations 2005[3] reflect some of the Directive's principles, and the Asylum Support Regulations[4] and Immigration Rules[5] have been amended in line. However, the Directive has direct effect where the rights and obligations it sets out are sufficiently precise,[6] and so where domestic provisions and practice do not adequately reflect the Directive, its terms prevail.

[1]   Immigration and Asylum Act 1999, ss 115–117; see 13.3–13.22 (for social security) and 13.177–13.181 (for community care services).
[2]   Council Directive 2003/9/EC, OJ L 31/18, 6 February 2003.
[3]   SI 2005/7, in force 5 February 2005.
[4]   SI 2000/704 amended by the Asylum Support (Amendment) Regulations 2005, SI 2005/11. Note that the interim support regulations have not been reflected to give effect to the Directive; see 13.131ff below.
[5]   HC 395 Part 11B, paras 357–361, inserted by HC 194, in force 4 February 2005.
[6]   For direct effect see 7.42 above.

COMMON ASPECTS OF THE TWO SCHEMES FOR SUPPORT

13.38 Although the detail of the two schemes of support is provided for in separate secondary legislation,[1] important elements of the primary provision made for the two schemes in the Immigration and Asylum Act 1999 overlap so that many of the key conditions relating to entitlement are the same.[2] The general conditions of eligibility for support under the schemes are that the person is an 'asylum seeker' or the 'dependant of an asylum seeker' within the meaning of Part VI of the 1999 Act and is either destitute or likely to become destitute within a limited period.[3] We deal now with these common general conditions of eligibility.

13.38 *Asylum Support, Community Care and Welfare Benefits*

1   The Asylum Support (Interim Provisions) Regulations 1999, SI 1999/3056 as amended by
    SI 2002/471 regulate interim support and the Asylum Support Regulations 2000,
    SI 2000/704 as amended by SI 2002/472, SI 2002/3110, SI 2003/241, SI 2004/763 and
    SI 2004/1313 provide for the main scheme of support. Appeals are regulated by the
    Asylum Support Appeals (Procedure) Rules 2000, SI 2000/541 as amended by
    SI 2003/1735.
2   Immigration and Asylum Act 1999, ss 94, 95, Sch 9, paras 1, 3.
3   IAA 1999, ss 94(1), 95(1), Sch 9, paras 1–3; SI 1999/3056, regs 2(1), 3; SI 2000/704, reg 3.

'Asylum seekers' under the support schemes

13.39 An 'asylum seeker' for the purposes of the asylum support schemes is a
person aged 18 or over who has made a 'claim for asylum', which has been
'recorded' by the Secretary of State and which has not been 'determined'.[1]
When Section 44 of the Nationality, Immigration and Asylum Act 2002 comes
into force,[2] the asylum claim will have to be made at a place designated by the
Secretary of State.[3]

1   Immigration and Asylum Act 1999, ss 94(1), 95(1), Sch 9 para 1(1), (2); Asylum Support
    (Interim Provisions) Regulations 1999, SI 1999/3056, reg 2(1); SI 2000/704, reg 3(1).
2   No date has yet been appointed under s 162 of the Act.
3   See 13.41 below.

Claim for asylum

13.40 An asylum claim under the support regime is a claim by a person that
it would be a breach of the UK's obligations under the Refugee Convention or
Article 3 of the ECHR for him or her to be removed from or required to leave
the UK.[1] Unlike the Refugee Convention,[2] Article 3 of the ECHR contains no
express prohibition on returning persons to a country where they may face
ill-treatment, but a claim under Article 3 is nevertheless predicated on the
assumption that it will be a breach of the UK's obligations under the
Convention to remove a person to a country where they face a real risk of it.[3]
A claim under Article 3 may re-engage eligibility for asylum support after
entitlement has ceased by the final determination of a claim under the Refugee
Convention.[4] Similarly, a fresh claim for asylum may re-engage eligibility for
asylum support in such circumstances.[5] Until 1 December 2004, asylum
seekers with minor dependants were entitled to accommodation and support
up until the point at which the Secretary of State certified that their
applications have been finally determined, appeal rights exhausted and they
had failed to cooperate with removal directions issued in respect of them.[6]
However, under section 9 of the Asylum and Immigration (Treatment of
Claimants etc) Act 2004,[7] the withdrawal of support no longer awaits the
issue and non-compliance with removal directions; families with children lose
support if the Secretary of State certifies that, after their applications have
been finally determined and any appeal rights exhausted, they have failed to
take reasonable steps to leave the UK voluntarily, or to place themselves in a
position in which they will be able to do so. The only support which a local
authority will be permitted to provide in such a situation is accommodation
for any child who appears to be in need under section 20 of the Children
Act 1989.[8]

1   Immigration and Asylum Act 1999, s 94(1).
2   1951 Convention relating to the Status of Refugees, Arts 32, 33.
3   *Soering v United Kingdom* (1989) 11 EHRR 439; *D v United Kingdom* (1997) 24 EHRR 423.
4   In *R v London Borough of Lambeth, ex p Tekeste* (CO/77/00) (11 January 2000, unreported) Maurice Kay J granted interim relief to the asylum seeker in judicial review proceedings turning on this point, but the applicant was granted exceptional leave before the full hearing.
5   The jurisprudence on 'fresh claims' to asylum (*Singh (Manvinder) v Secretary of State for the Home Department* (8 December 1995, unreported), CA; *R v Secretary of State for the Home Department, ex p Onibiyo* [1996] Imm AR 370, CA; *R v Secretary of State for the Home Department, ex p Senkoy* [2001] EWCA Civ 328, [2001] Imm AR 399; *R (on the application of Sivaruban) v Secretary of State for the Home Department* [2002] EWHC 2005 (Admin), [2002] All ER (D) 390 Jul) is based on an analysis of the term 'claim to asylum' as defined in the Asylum and Immigration Appeals Act 1993, s 1, a definition in identical terms to that used in Immigration and Asylum Act 1999, s 94 (aside from the addition of ECHR, Art 3 claims). Thus, the same approach should govern the question of fresh claims for support purposes regardless of the lack of specific provision in the IAA 1999 or the regulations. A purportedly fresh asylum claim does not, however, automatically trigger continuing asylum support, as the Secretary of State must first determine whether or not the claim is in fact a fresh claim: *R (on the application of Nigatu) v Secretary of State for the Home Department* [2004] EWHC (Admin), (2004) Times, 30 July, Collins J. Hard cases support may, however, be available in these circumstances: see 13.175 below.
6   Nationality, Immigration and Asylum Act 2002, s 54, Sch 3, paras 1(1), 6, 17. See 13.43 below.
7   Inserting para 7A into Sch 3 (fn 6 above). The section came into force on 1 December 2004 (SI 2004/2599); at the time of writing, it is being implemented in Manchester, Leeds and central and east London on a pilot basis.
8   NIAA 2002, Sch 3 para 2. In addition, support may be provided if necessary to avoid a breach of human rights (ibid), for which see 13.57 below.

13.41 There is no particular form in which a claim for asylum must be made. The Home Office accepts that a claim has been made when a person asserts that it would be 'contrary to the Refugee Convention to require him (sic) to leave the UK,'[1] or 'where it appears to the immigration officer as a result of information given that he may be eligible for asylum.'[2] The Home Office advice to its own caseworkers is that an expression of unwillingness to return to the country of nationality or habitual residence as a result of some perceived danger is sufficient. The merits of a claim are irrelevant at that stage.[3] Case law of the Social Security Commissioners is to similar effect: there is no need for a person to have completed any particular forms[4] and 'an indication of a desire to claim asylum is itself a claim for asylum'.[5] Since 8 February 2003, postal applications for asylum are no longer acceptable from 'in country' applicants, who must apply in person at an Asylum Screening Unit[6] unless the claimant comes within a restricted number of vulnerable categories such as visibly pregnant women, families with children, asylum seekers who are not able-bodied and asylum seekers whose individual needs appear to require special consideration. Such applicants must also apply in person, but may do so at their nearest enforcement office.[7] Local enforcement offices may also accept applications from illegal entrants already known to them.[8]

1   The current Immigration Rules, HC 395, para 327.
2   The formulation under earlier Immigration Rules, HC 251, para 75, uncontroversially cited on this point in *R v Uxbridge Magistrates' Court, ex p Adimi* [1999] 4 All ER 520 at 530D–F.

3   API 'Assessing the Claim'.
4   Commissioner's Decision *CIS/4341/98*, para 10.
5   Commissioner's Decision *CIS/4439/98*, para 7; see also *CIS/3867/98*, para 9 and *CIS/259/99*, para 9.
6   UK Immigration Service *Best Practice: Screening: Enforcement* Version 01.01.04, para 8.1, 8.2, 8.4.
7   *Best Practice: Screening* above para 8.1.1.
8   *Best Practice: Screening* above para 8.1.1.

Claim for asylum has been 'recorded by the Secretary of State'

13.42 The claim to asylum must have been 'recorded by the Secretary of State'.[1] All that is necessary for a claim to have been recorded, we suggest, is that there is in the Home Office some note made by an officer of the Secretary of State which identifies the person making the claim and which is sufficient to indicate that a claim to asylum has been made by that person. Again, the case law of the Social Security Commissioners dealing with claims recorded as having been made for benefits purposes may be applicable in this context. In one case, a Commissioner held that there was no specified manner in which the record of the claim had to be made, and relied on a letter from the Secretary of State issued in response to a complaint as to how a person had been treated on entry to the UK as either a sufficient record of the claim in itself or as secondary evidence of a Home Office record.[2] There is no requirement that the asylum seeker be notified of the recording of the claim. From the language of the provision we suggest that it does not matter if the record of the claim is subsequently lost, for example, if the Home Office loses the relevant file, provided that it can be established that the claim was originally made and recorded.[3] The fact that an in-country asylum claim must be made in person at an Asylum Screening Unit or local enforcement office[4] as soon as reasonably practicable[5] is likely to reduce the uncertainty in relation to whether or not a claim has been recorded.

1   Immigration and Asylum Act 1999, s 94(1).
2   Commissioner's Decision *CIS/4439/98*, paras 3, 7, 8.
3   Section 94(1) of the IAA 1999 uses the perfect tense: 'a claim for asylum which has been recorded by the Secretary of State'.
4   See 13.41 text and fnn 6–8 above.
5   See Nationality, Immigration and Asylum Act 2002, s 55 (13.56 below).

Claim for asylum has not been determined

13.43 As a general rule, a person remains an 'asylum seeker' for support purposes until the claim for asylum 'has been determined'.[1] However if there is a dependent child in the asylum seeker's household, the person does not cease to be an asylum seeker for the purposes of asylum support under s 94 Immigration and Asylum Act 1999 while the child remains under 18 and both remain in the UK (unless the person is granted leave to remain).[2] The legislation is contradictory: under section 94, asylum support continues to be available to families with children after their claims are determined, while they remain in the UK. But the provisions of Schedule 3, paragraph 6 to the Nationality, Immigration and Asylum Act 2002, which remove support from 'failed asylum-seekers'[3] who fail to cooperate with removal directions, and their dependants, contain their own definition of 'asylum seeker', removing the special treatment of families with children.[4] Schedule 3, paragraph 7A to the NIAA 2002[5] also means that a failed asylum seeker accompanied by a dependent child will lose entitlement to any support, either from NASS or a local authority, 14 days after receiving notice that the Secretary of State for the Home Department has certified that in his opinion he or she is a person who has failed without reasonable excuse to take reasonable steps to leave the UK voluntarily or to place him- or herself in a position to be able to leave the UK voluntarily.[6] A failed asylum seeker will be able to appeal against such a certificate to an Asylum Support Adjudicator if NASS is providing the support, but not when the support comes from a local authority within the Interim Support Scheme.[7] A local authority will still have the power to provide accommodation for any dependent children (but not their parents) under section 20 of the Children Act 1989.[8] It will also still retain its child protection powers to provide alternative accommodation for the children if they were deemed to be at risk under section 31 of the Children Act 1989.[9]

[1] Immigration and Asylum Act 1999, s 94(1). Amendments made by Nationality, Immigration and Asylum Act 2002 s 44 (in force from a date to be appointed) do not materially affect this definition.
[2] IAA 1999, s 94(5). The section is replaced by a new s 94(3A), to the same effect, by s 44 NIAA 2002, as from a date to be appointed.
[3] Heading of NIAA 2002, Sch 3, para 6. The Schedule removes various classes of person from eligibility for housing, social services, community care and NASS support: Sch 3, para 1(1).
[4] See NIAA 2002, Sch 3, para 17 for the definition of 'asylum seeker' for the purpose of the Schedule. It is not clear how these two definitions interact, and whether the provisions of the Schedule condition the provision of support under the 1999 Act, although this is the assumption of the NASS Policy Bulletin No 77 *Failure to Comply with Removal Directions* Version 1.0 20 January 2003.
[5] Inserted by Asylum and Immigration (Treatment of Claimants, etc) Act 2004 s 9, in force 1 December 2004 (SI 2004/2999).
[6] New para 7A, 'failed asylum seeker with family', spells out its application to those treated as asylum seekers for the purpose of s 94(3A) of the IAA 1999 (see fn 2 above).
[7] Under IAA 1999, s 103: see AI(TC)A 2004, s 9(3)(b), (4), in force 1 December 2004 (SI 2004/2999).
[8] See NIAA 2002, Sch 3, para 2(1)(b).
[9] NIAA 2002, Sch 3, para 1 does not remove this power.

13.44 In cases where there are no dependent children, and cases to which the provisions of Schedule 3 to the NIAA 2002 apply,[1] a person ceases to be an asylum seeker 21 days after[2] either[3] the day on which the Secretary of State notifies him or her in writing[4] of the decision on the claim for asylum or, if there is an appeal against the decision, when the appeal is disposed of.[5] Thus a person remains an asylum seeker, for these purposes, throughout the period during which there is no decision on the asylum application and, if the Secretary of State's decision is negative, throughout the entire appeals process. If an asylum seeker fails to appeal within prescribed time limits and then makes an application for permission to appeal out of time, he or she is not an asylum seeker for the purposes of asylum support until permission has been granted to appeal out of time.[6]

[1] Ie Sch 3, para 7A (as inserted from 1 December 2004) and para 6 (see 13.43 above).

2   Asylum Support Regulations 2000, SI 2000/704, reg 2(2), (3), Asylum Support (Interim Provisions) Regulations 1999, SI 1999/3056, reg 2(6).
3   IAA 1999, s 93(3), (4) (s 94(3) amended by NIAA 2002, s 44 from a date to be appointed).
4   IAA 1999, s 94(8).
5   IAA 1999, ss 94(4), 167 (s 94(4) amended by NIAA 2002, s 44 from a date to be appointed), referring to NIAA 2002, s 104.
6   *R (on the application of Erdogan) (Sahsenem) v Secretary of State for the Home Department* [2004] EWCA Civ 1087, [2004] All ER (D) 421 (Jul).

13.45 Viewing the determination of an asylum claim as inclusive of the appeal process both accords with the case law[1] and avoids the situation which arose in 1996 where asylum seekers had, in theory, important appeal rights but were, in practice, unable to exercise them because of destitution.[2] Eligibility for social security benefits and community care services is restored when asylum seekers are successful on appeal and are recognised as refugees and granted indefinite leave to remain by the Home Office accordingly. There have, unfortunately, been very severe delays in the Home Office granting refugee status to successful appellants, which has caused prejudice in terms of access to conventional social security benefits and housing, naturalisation, travel documents and entitlement to work. The High Court has declared such delays unlawful,[3] and a duty of care may arise in such a situation so as to found a damages claim.[4] Financial and other loss caused by such delays is covered by a Home Office *ex gratia* compensation scheme.[5]

1   Which sees the asylum appellate process as an extension of the original asylum decision-making process: see *Ravichandran v Secretary of State for the Home Department* [1996] Imm AR 97, CA.
2   See observations in *R v Secretary of State for Social Security, ex p Joint Council for the Welfare of Immigrants* [1996] 4 All ER 385.
3   *R v Secretary of State for the Home Department, ex p Mersin (Deniz)* [2000] INLR 511, Elias J; timely notification of decisions was a further factor identified by the Audit Commission as critical for the proper and efficient functioning of the dispersal system in *Another Country: Implementing dispersal under the Immigration and Asylum Act 1999* June 2000.
4   *R (on the application of Kanidagli) v Secretary of State for the Home Department* [2004] EWHC 1585 (Admin), [2004] NLJR 1141.
5   Home Office *Framework: Consolatory Payments for Non-Financial Loss.*

Dependants of asylum seekers

13.46 Both schemes provide for support to be provided not only to asylum seekers but also to the dependants of asylum seekers.[1] There are some minor differences in the wording of the regulations defining dependants for the two schemes.[2] The general definition of dependants which applies to both NASS and the interim scheme is set out below, with the differences between the two schemes discussed immediately afterwards. A person is the 'dependant of an asylum seeker' if he or she is related or connected to the asylum seeker in one of the following ways:[3]

(a)   is the spouse of the asylum seeker (almost certainly in a marriage recognised by UK law);[4]
(b)   is the child of the asylum seeker *or* of his or her spouse, who is under 18 and dependent on the asylum seeker;

(c) is a member of the asylum seeker's or his or her spouse's 'close family'[5] who is under 18;

(d) has been living as part of the asylum seeker's household *either* for at least six of the 12 months before the day on which the claim for support was made or since birth and, in either case, is under 18;

(e) is in need of care and attention from the asylum seeker or a member of his or her household by reason of a disability *and is either* a member of the asylum seeker's or their spouse's close family *or* has been living as part of the asylum seeker's household for six of the 12 months before the date on which the claim to support was made *or* since birth;

(f) has been living with the asylum seeker as a member of an unmarried couple for at least two of the three years before the day on which the claim to support was made;

(g) is living with the asylum seeker as part of his or her household and was receiving assistance from a local authority under section 17 of the Children Act 1989 immediately before 6 December 1999;[6]

(h) has made a claim for leave to enter or remain in the UK, or to vary such leave, which is being considered on the basis that the person is the dependant of an asylum seeker. Under the Immigration Rules,[7] only the spouse and minor children of asylum seekers are to be considered as dependants on the asylum claim, but the Secretary of State may, as a matter of discretion, treat other family members as dependent on the asylum seeker for the purposes of the asylum claim;[8]

(i) is an asylum seeker, in circumstances where his or her dependant has claimed support.

[1] Immigration and Asylum Act 1999, ss 94(1)(a)–(c), 95(1), Sch 9, para 1(2); Asylum Support (Interim Provisions) Regulations 1999, SI 1999/3056, reg 2(1); Asylum Support Regulations 2000, SI 2000/704, reg 3(3).

[2] SI 2000/704, reg 2(9) prevents the definition of dependant under NASS from being applied to the interim scheme.

[3] SI 1999/3056, reg 2(1); SI 2000/704, reg 2(4).

[4] See 11.32ff above.

[5] 'Close family' remains undefined in the regulations.

[6] The date on which the interim regulations (Asylum Support, SI 1999/3056) came into force, and thus the beginning of the 'interim period' for SI 1999/3056, reg 1(1), 2(1)(g), 2(5); ASR, SI 2000/704, reg 2(4)(g).

[7] HC 395, para 349.

[8] The acceptance of the spouse and minor child is the 'minimum requirement' of the policy on family reunion of the United Nations High Commission for Refugees and the Final Act of the Conference which adopted the Refugee Convention, and this is Government policy, although other relatives will be admitted in compelling compassionate circumstances: see 12.181 above.

13.47 In addition to the categories referred to above, a person qualifies as a dependant under NASS if he or she is living as a part of the asylum seeker's household and, immediately before 3 April 2000, was receiving support from a local authority in Scotland or Northern Ireland under provisions equivalent to the Children Act 1989.[1] This category ensures that dependants in Scotland and Northern Ireland are provided for by NASS rather than by the social services, as the interim scheme has never applied in Scotland and Northern Ireland.[2]

[1] Asylum Support Regulations 2000, SI 2000/704, reg 2(4)(h).

[2] Asylum Support (Interim Provisions) Regulations 1999, SI 1999/3056, reg 1(2).

13.48 The regulations for the NASS scheme expressly provide that, in categories (b), (c) and (d) above, young people count as dependants if they were under 18 at the time that the application for support was made, or when they joined a supported asylum seeker in the UK,[1] and so will continue to receive support after their eighteenth birthday, provided all the other conditions continue to be met. The interim provisions contain no such express protection for dependants after they reach 18.

1   Asylum Support Regulations 2000, SI 2000/704, reg 2(4)(b), (c), (d), (6).

13.49 In category (f), under the NASS scheme, those joining a partner in the UK while the latter was being supported, must have lived with him or her as a couple for two of the three previous years.[1] The interim scheme makes no separate provision for this situation. Further, the NASS regulations define an 'unmarried couple' as a man and woman who, though not married to each other, are living together as if married,[2] in contrast to the interim regulations, which do not define 'unmarried couple'. In the interim scheme it could therefore be argued that a same-sex couple living together in a relationship akin to marriage are an 'unmarried couple' and that the non-asylum seeker partner qualifies as a dependant. This is not the case in relation to NASS support because of the explicit definition of unmarried couple.[3]

1   Asylum Support Regulations 2000, SI 2000/704, reg 2(4)(f), (6).
2   SI 2000/704, reg 2(1). See also paragraph 13 of ASA/03/06/6653.
3   ASA/03/06/6653.

'Destitute' or likely shortly to become 'destitute'

13.50 In order for asylum seekers to obtain support under either scheme, they must appear to be either destitute or likely to become destitute[1] within 14 days.[2] A person is destitute if he or she either[3] does not have 'adequate accommodation' or the means to secure it or has adequate accommodation or the means of getting it but cannot meet his or her other 'essential living needs'. Statutory rules set out what may and what may not be taken into account in determining this issue and they are different for the two schemes of support (they are therefore dealt with separately in the sections below).[4] The needs which are referred to in the asylum support provisions are generally current needs. The concept of 'entitlement' over a particular period, which exists in social security law, does not form part of the scheme of asylum support, so that asylum seekers may face difficulties in seeking to 'backdate' support.[5]

1   Immigration and Asylum Act 1999, s 95(1), Sch 9, para 1(2).
2   Asylum Support (Interim Provisions) Regulations 1999, SI 1999/3056, reg 2(1); Asylum Support Regulations 2000, SI 2000/704, reg 7(a).
3   IAA 1999, s 95(2), Sch 9, para 3.
4   IAA 1999, s 95(5), (6), as applied by Sch 9, para 3 (interim scheme); s 95(5)–(8) and SI 2000/704, regs 6, 8–9 (NASS scheme).
5   *R v Hammersmith London Borough Council, ex p Isik* (19 September 2000, unreported), CA. But see ASA 01/02/0202, paras 4 and 14 where an adjudicator held an asylum seeker legally entitled to amounts due from the date of the asylum support application to the date when he was granted indefinite leave to remain and became entitled to social security benefit, subject only to deduction for backdated income support (as to which see 13.26 above).

Differences between the two schemes

13.51 Despite their common features, there are many differences between the two schemes. The obvious difference is that under the interim scheme, local authorities are responsible for determining who is entitled to support and for making arrangements to provide it,[1] whereas under NASS, it is the Secretary of State for the Home Department who is responsible for determining eligibility and ensuring that support is provided.[2] There are also differences in the procedures for making applications for support, the operation of temporary support, what may be provided, decisions on dispersal of asylum seekers, rules excluding persons from support and the procedures for challenging decisions.

---

[1] Immigration and Asylum Act 1999, Sch 9, para 2(1); Asylum Support (Interim Provisions) Regulations 1999, SI 1999/3056, reg 3(2).
[2] IAA 1999, s 95(1); Asylum Support Regulations 2000, SI 2000/704, reg 5.

NATIONAL ASYLUM SUPPORT SCHEME (NASS)

13.52 The National Asylum Support Service (NASS) is a body established as part of the Home Office to be responsible for providing comprehensive support to destitute asylum seekers. It has been operational since 3 April 2000, when it took on responsibility for the support of certain new asylum applicants.[1] The intention is that, eventually, all destitute asylum seekers will have recourse to NASS rather than to the interim scheme.[2] By the end of August 2000, all new asylum seekers were eligible to apply for NASS support, and on 4 April 2006, when the interim scheme is set to end,[3] NASS should be responsible for all asylum seekers.[4] NASS has regional offices in Manchester, Leeds, Newcastle, Birmingham, Leicester, Cambridge, Bristol, Cardiff, Glasgow, Dover, Croydon and Belfast as well as its headquarters in Croydon. These regional offices deal with outreach work, investigations and housing contract management.[5]

---

[1] The system of support provided by NASS is set out in Immigration and Asylum Act 1999, Pt VI and Schs 8 and 10; the key provisions were brought into force from 3 April 2000 (Immigration and Asylum Act 1999 (Commencement No 3) Order 2000, SI 2000/464, Art 2 and Sch), on which date the regulations which set out the detailed machinery of the scheme also came into force: Asylum Support Regulations 2000, SI 2000/704, reg 1; Asylum Support Appeals (Procedure) Rules 2000, SI 2000/541, r 1.
[2] See 13.159ff below for a detailed description of which asylum seekers are eligible to apply NASS support and which for interim support.
[3] See Asylum Support (Interim Provisions) (Amendment) Regulations 2004, SI 2004/566.
[4] Asylum Support (Interim Provisions) Regulations 1999, SI 1999/3056, as amended, regs 1(1) and 2(5). Local authorities will retain community care responsibilities for those whose need for care and attention does not arise solely from destitution, however: *R (on the application of Westminster City Council) v Secretary of State for the Home Department* [2001] EWCA Civ 512, 33 HLR 938, [2001] All ER (D) 100 (Apr); see 13.177 below.
[5] *NASS in the Regions* on NASS website

Procedures under the NASS scheme

Applications for support

13.53 The NASS scheme, unlike the interim scheme, requires an application to NASS for support.[1] The application must be in a specified form, known as a NASS1. The application may not be entertained if it is not in the prescribed form, or if the Secretary of State is not satisfied that the information provided is complete or accurate or that the applicant is co-operating with enquiries.[2] Asylum seekers may receive assistance completing the form from the voluntary sector 'assistants' who help to identify and convey relevant information to NASS.[3] The application may be for a sole applicant or for the applicant and his or her dependants,[4] and a group application may be made on one application form. A new or newly arrived dependant of a person who is already being supported by NASS does not need to complete another application, and NASS will consider providing additional support when notified of his or her existence.[5] NASS may make further inquiries of the asylum seeker in connection with any of the details contained in the application form.[6] Those who apply for NASS support are screened to see if they have claimed asylum as soon as reasonably practicable after their arrival in the UK, before their application is considered further.[7] A person in detention who is awaiting the hearing of a bail application may make an application for support in anticipation of release.[8]

[1] Asylum Support Regulations 2000, SI 2000/704, reg 3 as amended by the Asylum Support (Amendment) (No 3) Regulations 2002, SI 2002/3110.
[2] Immigration and Asylum Act 1999, Sch 8, para 12, amended by Nationality, Immigration and Asylum Act 2002, s 57; Asylum Support (Amendment) (No 3) Regulations 2002, SI 2002/3110, reg 2. If the Secretary of State (ie, NASS) makes further enquiries in connection with the application, the applicant has five working days to respond unless he or she has a reasonable excuse for not doing so: ASR 2000, reg 3(5A) and 3(5B), inserted by SI 2005/11 reg 3. If the applicant does not comply, the application will not be entertained, and temporary support under IAA 1999 s 98 will be discontinued: reg 3(5C) as inserted.
[3] Refugees Arrival Project, Migrants Helpline, Refugee Action, the Refugee Council, Scottish and Welsh Refugee Councils, the North of England Refugee Service and the Northern Ireland Council for Ethnic Minorities.
[4] SI 2000/704, reg 3(2).
[5] SI 2000/704, reg 3(6).
[6] SI 2000/704, reg 3(5).
[7] NIAA 2002, s 55.
[8] SI 2000/704, notes to NASS1 Form 'Do you live in any other kind of accommodation?' NASS Policy Bulletin 64 *Applications for Support from People Detained under the Immigration Act 1971 or who have been Granted Immigration Bail.*

13.54 The Asylum Support Regulations 2000[1] contain no express time limits for making the decision on support, but we may infer that the process should be extremely speedy.[2] There is no requirement in the regulations that decisions must be in writing, but clearly it is intended that a written explanation will be provided of a decision refusing all support, with details of whether an appeal is available and if so, how to appeal.[3] Emergency support is provided if there is a delay in deciding whether an application for asylum was made as soon as reasonably practicable, and full reasons must be given for a decision that it was not and that NASS support will not be provided.[4]

1 SI 2000/704 as amended.
2 See the very strict and short time limits for appealing refusal of asylum support at 13.117 below.
3 SI 2000/704, Sch, Notes 'What happens next?'
4 *R (on the application of Q) v Secretary of State for the Home Department* [2003] EWCA Civ 364, [2004] QB 36, [2003] 2 All ER 905. See also Maurice Kay J's guidance for claimants seeking to challenge negative decisions under s 55 (for which no right of appeal to the ASA is available), which indicates that the Secretary of State should reach a decision on asylum support on the day of or the day following the application, in the same case, in the Administrative Court: [2003] EWHC 1195 (Admin).

Persons entitled to NASS support

13.55 In order to be entitled to NASS support a person must satisfy the general conditions of entitlement, ie, that a person is an asylum seeker or a dependant of an asylum seeker[1] and is destitute or likely to become so. From 8 January 2003, asylum seekers who are not accompanied by minor dependants[2] and are not themselves unaccompanied minors[3] have also had to establish that they claimed asylum as soon as reasonably practicable after their arrival in the UK.[4] Section 55 has lead to thousands of asylum seekers having to sleep on the streets or in parks with inadequate clothing and no food. The despair and degradation this has caused has been the subject of a number of reports and considerable litigation.[5] From February 2005, the entry into force of the EC Reception Conditions Directive, reduction or withdrawal of support for non-compliance with procedural requirements must comply with the principle of proportionality.[6]

1 For the definition of 'asylum seeker' see 13.39 above.
2 Nationality, Immigration and Asylum Act 2002, s 55(5)(c).
3 See definition of 'asylum seeker' in Immigration and Asylum Act 1999 s 94 (as amended by NIAA 2002, s 44 from a date to be appointed).
4 NIAA 2002, s 55(1), (2). NASS was entitled to withdraw asylum support previously given to an asylum seeker when it discovered that she had altered her documentation to make it appear that she had claimed on arrival, as she had never been entitled to support: *R (Secretary of State for the Home Department) v Chief Asylum Support Adjudicator* [2003] EWHC 269 (Admin), [2003] All ER (D) 116 (Feb), Toulson J.
5 See e g Inter-Agency Partnership Section 55 Report, February 2004; *Destitution by Design: Withdrawal of Support from In-country Asylum Applicants: An Impact Assessment for London,* Mayor of London, February 2004.
6 See 13.37 above.

'As soon as reasonably practicable'

13.56 The leading case of *Q* established that the test immigration officers should apply is whether 'on the premise that the purpose of coming to this country was to claim asylum and having regard both to the practical opportunity of claiming asylum and to the asylum seeker's personal circumstances, could the asylum seeker reasonably have been expected to claim earlier that he or she did?'[1] The Court of Appeal also accepted that in deciding whether an asylum seeker claimed asylum as soon as reasonably practicable, it was right to have regard to the effect of anything that the asylum seeker may have been told by his or her facilitator.[2] On 17 December 2003, following further litigation on what was 'reasonably practicable', the Secretary of State announced that as a matter of policy, anyone claiming asylum within three days of his or her arrival in the UK would not be refused support under section 55.[3] However, there remain severe evidential difficulties in proving the date of a clandestine arrival.[4]

[1]   *R (on the application of Q) v Secretary of State for the Home Department* [2003] EWCA Civ 364, [2004] QB 36, [2003] 2 All ER 905.
[2]   *R (on the application of Q)* above at para 43.
[3]   Letter to Tim Crowley, Inter-Agency Co-ordination Team, 12 January 2004.
[4]   See 13.58 below on procedures.

Avoiding a breach of a person's Convention rights

13.57 Section 55 should not disqualify an asylum seeker from support where a failure to provide support would give rise to any breach of the European Convention on Human Rights.[1] This provision has given rise to a huge volume of litigation. In *Q*, the Court of Appeal accepted that denial of support to an asylum seeker constituted 'treatment' for the purposes of Article 3 ECHR,[2] but held that 'destitution' as defined in the asylum support provisions does not necessarily amount to 'inhuman and degrading' treatment for the purposes of the Article.[3] The court declined to provide a simple test for claimants to satisfy in order to show that failing to support them would breach their human rights, but held that it was not unlawful for the Secretary of State to refuse support unless it was clear that charitable support had not been provided and that the individual was incapable of fending for him- or herself.[4] In *T*,[5] the court held that the condition of the destitute asylum seeker must verge on the degree of severity described in *Pretty v United Kingdom*,[6] where it was described as 'ill-treatment that attains a minimum level of severity and involves actual bodily injury or intense physical or mental suffering [or] treatment [which] humiliates or debases an individual showing lack of respect for, or diminishing his or her human dignity or arousing feelings of fear, anguish or inferiority capable of breaking an individual's moral or physical resistance'. Following these cases, Administrative Court judges continued to differ in their interpretation of the point at which an asylum seeker could be said to verge on the degree of severity needed to attract the protection of Article 3 ECHR (and thus s 55(5)).[7] The conflict was resolved when the Court of Appeal held in *Limbuela and others* that it was:

> 'not necessary ... to show the actual onset of severe illness or suffering. If the evidence establishes clearly that charitable support in practice is not available, and that [the asylum seeker] has no other means of "fending for himself", then the presumption will be that severe suffering will imminently follow. He has done enough to show that he is 'verging on' the necessary degree of severity, and that Article 3 is accordingly engaged'.[8]

[1]   Nationality, Immigration and Asylum Act 2002, s 55(5)(a).
[2]   For Art 3 ECHR see 8.47 above.
[3]   *R (on the application of Q) v Secretary of State for the Home Department* [2003] EWCA Civ 364, [2004] QB 36 at para 59.
[4]   *R (on the application of Q)* at paras 61, 63.
[5]   *R (on the application of T) v Secretary of State for the Home Department* [2003] EWCA Civ 1285, [2004] HLR 254, [2003] NLJR 1474. The claimant failed to establish a breach of his human rights, since although he was living rough at an airport, he had access to shelter, toilets and wash basins and some food.

6   (2002) 35 EHRR 1, [2002] 2 FCR 97.
7   See *R (on the application of Zardasht) v Secretary of State for the Home Department*
    [2004] EWHC Admin, [2004] All ER (D) 196 (Jan) (a hard-line decision); cf the first
    instance decisions in *R (on the application of Limbuela) v Secretary of State for the Home
    Department* [2004] EWHC 219 (Admin), [2004] All ER (D) 56 (Feb); *R (on the
    application of Tesema) v Secretary of State for the Home Department* [2004] EWHC 295
    (Admin), [2004] All ER (D) 247 (Feb), *R (on the application of Adam) v Secretary of State
    for the Home Department* [2004] EWHC 354 (Admin), [2004] All ER (D) 56 (Feb).
8   *R (on the application of Adam) v Secretary of State for the Home Department, R (on the
    application of Tesema) v Secretary of State for the Home Department, R (on the
    application of Limbuela) v Secretary of State for the Home Department* [2004] EWCA Civ
    540, [2004] QB 1440 – although the Court of Appeal's judgment is unlikely to be the last
    word; Laws LJ dissented, and at the time of writing an appeal by the Secretary of State was
    pending in the House of Lords.

13.58 The decision on whether the asylum claimant is disqualified from support by claiming too late is taken after an interview known as a RANS Screening interview.[1] If a decision cannot be made immediately, the claimant will be given a letter authorising time-limited emergency accommodation under section 98 of the Immigration and Asylum Act 1999.[2] If the decision is positive, the asylum seeker will then have to complete and submit a NASS1. If the decision is negative, the asylum seeker will have to vacate his or her emergency accommodation within seven days.[3] The claimant can ask the Secretary of State to reconsider a negative decision in the light of any subsequent evidence or a change in his or her circumstances, and the Secretary of State has undertaken to endeavour to complete this reconsideration within 24 hours.[4] In order to obtain emergency accommodation pending reconsideration, the asylum seeker will have to show a seriously arguable case that the provision of support is necessary for the purposes of avoiding a breach of his or her rights under the European Convention on Human Rights, or obtain an injunction.[5] Heavily pregnant women are unlikely to be refused under section 55 as NASS recognises that this is likely to give rise to a breach of Convention rights.[6] As a result of the Court of Appeal decision in *Q*,[7] which upheld first instance criticism of the system of decision-making on section 55 as unfair, the screening interview forms and the guidance provided to immigration officers undertaking these interviews were significantly revised.[8] There is no right of appeal against disqualification from asylum support under section 55,[9] with the result that the Administrative Court has been clogged with applications for judicial review.[10]

1   'RANS' means 'Restricted Access to NASS Support'. The interview is conducted by a NASS
    Eligibility Assessment Team (NEAT).
2   Letter to Tim Crowley, Inter-Agency Co-ordination Team, 18 November 2003.
3   Letter to Tim Crowley, above. See however Maurice Kay J's guidance in *R (on the
    application of Q) v Secretary of State for the Home Department* [2003] EWHC 2507
    (Admin), that the Secretary of State ought not to evict so precipitately, particularly when
    there is likely to be a challenge on human rights grounds.
4   Letter to Tim Crowley, above. See Maurice Kay J in *R (Q)* above.
5   Letter to Tim Crowley, above. See Maurice Kay J in *R (Q)* above.
6   *Section 55 of the NIAA 2002 – ECHR Reconsiderations – Update on Process.*
7   *R (on the application of Q) v Secretary of State for the Home Department* [2003] EWCA
    Civ 364, [2004] QB 36, [2003] 2 All ER 905.
8   NASS Policy Bulletin 75 *Section 55 (Late Claims) 2002 Act Guidance* Version 3.0,
    11 April 2003.
9   Nationality, Immigration and Asylum Act 2002, s 55(10).
10 See the figures cited by Maurice Kay in *R (Q)* above.

13.59 When unaccompanied minor asylum seekers become 18, they will be interviewed to see whether they claimed asylum as soon as reasonably practicable.[1] Similarly, as soon as an asylum seeker no longer has any minor dependants in his or her household, NASS will consider the timeliness of his or her application for asylum. This late consideration could lead to NASS support being terminated under section 55.[2] A person who makes an in-country application for asylum following a significant change in circumstances in his or her country of origin will be provided with NASS support as long as her or she makes his or her application at the earliest possible opportunity following that change of circumstances.[3]

[1]   All asylum seekers who claim to be under 18 are referred to the Refugee Council's Panel of Advisers whether NASS believes their claimed age or not. If a person claims to be under 18, his or her age will be assessed during the screening process, and a physical appearance strongly suggestive of an over 18-year-old is likely to result in the claimant being treated as an adult unless there is credible evidence to substantiate that he or she is not: NASS Policy Bulletin 75 *Section 55 (Late Claims) 2002 Act Guidance* Version 4.0, 11 February 2004, para 10.1–10.3. It is now Home Office policy to accept the views of a qualified social worker in relation to a claimant's age: see *Best Practice: Unaccompanied Asylum and Non-asylum Children*, the UK Immigration Service, Version 01.01.04, para 1.3. See also *R (on the application of B) v L B Merton* [2003] EWHC (Admin) 1689, [2003] 4 All ER 280 and 12.118 above.
[2]   Letter to Tim Crowley, 26 February 2004.
[3]   Policy Bulletin 75 *Section 55 (Late Claims) 2002 Act Guidance* Version 4.0 11 February 2004, para 5.8.

Deciding whether a person is destitute under NASS

13.60 To determine whether an applicant for support and any dependants are 'destitute' or 'likely to become destitute', NASS must consider whether they have 'adequate accommodation' or any means of obtaining it, and whether or not they can meet their other 'essential living needs'.[1] In relation to both accommodation and essential living needs, NASS must take into account any of the following in relation to the applicant *or* his or her dependants:[2]

- any income they have or which they may reasonably be expected to have;
- any other support which is available or which may reasonably be expected to be available;[3] and
- any of the following assets which might reasonably be expected to be available: cash, savings, investments, land, vehicles, goods for trade or business.

Assets which do not fall into these categories, NASS support or temporary support and items of jewellery, personal clothing, bedding and medical or optical items must be disregarded.[4] Applicants are, however, required to disclose items of jewellery or watches worth over £1,000 and to inform NASS immediately if they are sold and how much was received for them, so that the level of support may be adjusted accordingly.[5] NASS uses its own internal threshold tables, based loosely on what it would provide, a rule of thumb for the different categories of asylum seeker (below) to determine whether they are able to meet their essential living or accommodation requirements.[6] If the application for support relates to more than one person, NASS will consider whether the group taken as a whole is destitute or likely to become so.[7] NASS applies the same approach when considering whether to continue to provide support for those already supported, and their dependants who are already being supported or are being added to the application for support.[8]

[1] Immigration and Asylum Act 1999, s 95(1), (3).
[2] Asylum Support Regulations 2000, SI 2000/704, reg 6(4), (5).
[3] For example, the asylum support adjudicators have held that 'emergency money' provided by a relative and not returned may be taken into account (ASA 00/05/0011), as may money which the asylum seeker has had, if he or she cannot provide a reasonable explanation of its disposal (ASA 00/06/0017) (drawing on conventional social security law: Commissioner's Decision R(SB) 38/85); ASA 00/06/0020).
[4] SI 2000/704, reg 6(3), (6), Sch, Notes to NASS1 'Cash savings and assets'.
[5] SI 2000/704, Notes to NASS1 'Jewellery'.
[6] NASS Policy Bulletin No 4 V1.2 where the threshold tables are set out. Advice is also provided on when support should be suspended or discontinued when the claimant acquires capital or an income; see NASS Policy Bulletin 65 *Assessing Other Income or Capital that has Become Available to an Asylum Seeker Supported under the Immigration and Asylum Act 1999.*
[7] IAA 1999, s 95(4); SI 2000/704, reg 5(1).
[8] SI 2000/704, reg 5(2).

Determining whether a person can meet their 'essential living needs'

13.61 For the purposes of deciding whether a person can meet their essential living needs, certain items are treated as not essential. Inability to pay for sending or receiving faxes, photocopying, buying or using computer facilities and travelling expenses is not relevant to determining destitution[1] (although if a person is found to be destitute, these costs may be met by NASS either as expenses incurred in connection with the asylum claim or 'exceptional' circumstances). The regulations appear to exclude *any* travelling requirements which a person may have[2] except the costs of the initial journey to NASS accommodation, or to the applicant's notified address if he or she is not going to NASS accommodation.[3] The fact that any other need that a person may have is not expressly excluded does not automatically convert it into an 'essential living need' so as to oblige NASS to take into account an inability to meet it in deciding destitution;[4] NASS will decide for itself whether any claimed need is essential for the person's living. However, in *Ouji*,[5] Collins J held that 'essential living needs' were to be considered from the standpoint of an ordinary person without disabilities, and that individual disability was not a matter to be taken into account by NASS. This suggests a somewhat Procrustean approach to the issue, seemingly at odds with a human rights-based consideration of the legislation.

[1] Immigration and Asylum Act 1999, s 95(8), Asylum Support Regulations 2000, SI 2000/704, reg 9(3), (4).
[2] SI 2000/704, reg 9(4)(d).
[3] SI 2000/704, reg 9(4)(d), (5).
[4] SI 2000/704, reg 9(6).
[5] *R (on the application of Ouji) v Secretary of State for the Home Department* [2002] EWHC 1839 (Admin), [2003] Imm AR 88.

Clothing

13.62 In deciding whether a person can meet their essential living needs as regards clothing, NASS cannot take into account personal clothing preferences.[1] The rule is designed to prevent applications based on inability to buy clothing which is more expensive than that which is reasonably required, such as fashion items or designer wear. NASS must, however, take into account individual circumstances, including health or cultural needs and weather and hygiene requirements, in deciding whether a person can meet their clothing needs.[2]

[1] Immigration and Asylum Act 1999, s 95(7)(b); Asylum Support Regulations 2000, SI 2000/704, reg 9(1), (2).
[2] SI 2000/704, reg 9(2).

Determining whether a person has 'adequate' accommodation

13.63 If a person applies for support, including accommodation, but already has accommodation, NASS must decide whether the existing accommodation is 'adequate'. Similarly, if a person who is already being supported by NASS without the provision of accommodation, requests it, NASS will need to decide whether the accommodation available to the applicant is adequate or whether NASS should be providing accommodation. In deciding either of these questions,[1] NASS must have regard to whether:[2]

- it is 'reasonable' for the person to continue to occupy the accommodation;
- the person can afford to pay for the accommodation;
- the accommodation is provided as temporary support under NASS or on any other emergency basis while the claim for asylum support is being determined;
- entry to the accommodation may be gained by the asylum seeker;
- if the accommodation is a houseboat, caravan or some other moveable structure which may be lived in, there is somewhere where the person is able to place it and live in it;
- the person may live in the accommodation together with his or her dependants;
- the asylum seeker or a dependant is likely to suffer domestic violence if he or she continues to live in the accommodation.

NASS may ignore any of the above matters, except the affordability of the accommodation and whether it is temporary NASS or other emergency accommodation, if the asylum seeker wishes to stay there.[3] There are also certain matters which *cannot* be taken into account in determining whether a person has adequate accommodation,[4] namely: the fact that the person does not have a legal right to stay in the accommodation; that it is shared or temporary; and its location. However, the word 'adequate' in section 95 of the Immigration and Asylum Act 1999 should not be interpreted so as to imply that a lower standard of accommodation might be appropriate for a disabled child than accommodation that was suited to a disabled adult under section 21 of the National Assistance Act 1948.[5]

1   The regulations apply to either situation: Asylum Support Regulations 2000, SI 2000/704, reg 8(1)(a), (b).
2   Immigration and Asylum Act 1999, s 95(5)(a); SI 2000/704, reg 8(1)(a), (b), (3).
3   SI 2000/704, reg 8(2).
4   Immigration and Asylum Act 1999, s 95(5), (6).
5   *R (on the application of A) v National Asylum Support Service* [2003] EWCA Civ 1473, [2004] 1 All ER 15.

Reasonable to continue to occupy

13.64 In deciding whether it is reasonable for an asylum seeker to continue to occupy accommodation,[1] NASS may have regard to the general housing circumstances which exist in the district[2] of the local government housing authority in which the accommodation is situated.[3]

1   Asylum Support Regulations 2000, SI 2000/704, reg 8(3)(a).
2   By SI 2000/704, reg 8(6)(b), 'district' for these purposes is given the same meaning as in s 217(3) of the Housing Act 1996.
3   SI 2000/704, reg 8(4).

Affordability of the accommodation

13.65 In determining whether the asylum seeker can afford to pay for the accommodation,[1] NASS must take account of his or her assets and savings, the costs of the accommodation and other reasonable living expenses.[2]

1   Asylum Support Regulations 2000, SI 2000/704, reg 8(3)(b).
2   SI 2000/704, reg 8(5)(a), (b).

Domestic violence

13.66 The Home Office defines domestic violence as including 'any violence between current and former partners in an intimate relationship, wherever and whenever the violence occurs. The violence may include physical, sexual, emotional and financial abuse'.[1] The NASS Policy Bulletin also points out that, in family and housing law, domestic violence includes violence or threats from an 'associated person', a phrase covering a range of relatives including present and former spouses, cohabitees, fiancé(e)s and other people who live or have lived in the same household. Accommodation providers must give paramount importance to the safety of victims of abuse and their children, and ensure that victims and any children are transferred to alternative accommodation that is safe and secure immediately, and no prior consent from NASS is required if the victim feels unable safely to return to his or her previous address. If this is impracticable or the victim needs accommodation with support, an accommodation provider can refer the victim to a refuge and NASS wll pay for this accommodation. If a victim flees from NASS accommodation on account of domestic violence and finds alternative accommodation, NASS will pay the reasonable costs of such accommodation.[2] NASS will also provide the victim with interim support vouchers. Accommodation providers must warn offenders of the possible consequences of their abuse, which includes prosecution and loss of their accommodation and support.[3] Victims will eventually be re-housed in alternative NASS accommodation in either the same or another area. Whilst NASS is not allowed to have regard to a person's preference as to the locality of accommodation, victims will be consulted regarding the safety of the proposed area.[4]

1   NASS Policy Bulletin 70 *Domestic Violence* (replacing the references to domestic violence in NASS Policy Bulletin 18 *Dealing with Allegations of Racial Harassment, General Harassment and Domestic Violence* from 23 January 2004), para 2.2.
2   NASS Policy Bulletin 70 *Domestic Violence*, para 6.3.
3   Offenders may be evicted: NASS Policy Bulletin 70 *Domestic Violence* para 4.3. If an asylum seeker reports domestic violence to a one stop service or a one stop service suspects domestic violence is occurring, it should refer the victim to other appropriate agencies, such as the police and social services and, if the victim consents, it should also report the matter to the NASS Investigations team leader and the accommodation provider: It is preferable that a victim should not have to resort to NASS emergency accommodation, but if no alternative is immediately available, the one stop agency may admit the victim and any children to such accommodation in its own region. Voluntary organisations in other regions cannot admit the victim to emergency accommodation: Policy Bulletin, para 5. The NASS Investigations team leader should also convene a case conference usually within a week to decide on future accommodation and what action to take in relation to the abuser. He or she should also arrange for the victim to have a suitable interpreter at that conference: Policy Bulletin, para 8.
4   NASS Policy Bulletin 70, para 8.7.

Racist incidents

13.67 NASS policy involving racist incidents and harassment is contained in NASS Policy Bulletin 81. NASS adopts the definition of a racist incident contained in the report of the Stephen Lawrence Inquiry, ie 'any incident which is perceived to be racist by the victim or any other person'.[1] A racist incident may or may not be a crime in policing terms.[2] The safety and security of the victims of racist incidents must be ensured, and accommodation providers (with NASS agreement) must urgently arrange safe temporary housing where they have concerns for the victim's immediate safety.[3] A permanent transfer must be arranged if there is no prospect of a victim's safe return to the former address, or where, following a report to the police, the police support a transfer.[4] Emergency accommodation must be arranged by NASS regional staff where no safe temporary or permanent transfer can be arranged.[5] Accommodation which has become unsafe through racial harassment cannot be considered adequate.[6]

1   NASS Policy Bulletin 81 *Racist Incidents*, paras 2.1, 3.1. This Bulletin replaces Policy Bulletin 18 *Dealing with Allegations of Racial Harassment, General Harassment and Domestic Violence*. The Policy Bulletin requires accommodation providers to be aware of the Code of Practice for social landlords: 'Tacking Racial Harassment', published by the Office of the Deputy Prime Minister.
2   PB 81 above, paras 2.4, 3.2.
3   PB 81 para 8.1.
4   PB 81 para 8.2.
5   PB 81 para 8.4.
6   PB 81 para 9. See, however, *R (on the application of Gezer) v Secretary of State for the Home Department* [2003] EWHC Admin 860 (upheld at [2004] EWCA Civ 1730) for an example of 'worst practice' in responding to racist violence affecting a dispersed family. See 13.78 below.

EXCLUSION FROM SUPPORT

13.68 The following categories of people are excluded from NASS support:[1]

(1)   persons not excluded from obtaining social security benefits by their immigration status;

(2)   persons not treated by the Home Office as having claimed asylum or as the dependants of an asylum seeker;

(3)   persons eligible to obtain interim support;

(4)   persons who have been offered support under another provision of the 1999 or 2002 Act;[2]

(5)   persons who have not claimed asylum as soon as reasonably practicable, where provision of support is not necessary to avoid a breach of their human rights;[3]

(6)   persons who are citizens of other EEA States or who have been granted refugee status in these states;

(7)   failed asylum seekers who fail to cooperate with removal directions;

(8)   failed asylum seekers with dependent children who have without reasonable excuse failed to take reasonable steps to leave the UK voluntarily or to place themselves in a position where they can do so.[4]

Categories (1) to (4) are discussed in turn below, and category (5) has been dealt with at 13.56ff above. Categories (6) to (8) are dealt with under the rubric of community care provision at 13.177 below. All the categories except for category (5) are also excluded from temporary NASS support,[5] and *must* be excluded from NASS support;[6] since NASS has no power to provide support for people in these categories, support will be refused or brought to an end as soon as one of the conditions applies. Emergency accommodation may be provided by NASS for people in category (5) whilst it is reconsidering a refusal of support, if it believes that there is a seriously arguable case that a failure to provide NASS support will lead to a breach of the European Convention on Human Rights.[7] NASS support cannot be provided to a person in categories (6) to (8). The responsibility falls on the relevant local authority to provide temporary accommodation if this is necessary to prevent a breach of Convention rights. The local authority may make travel arrangements to return persons in category (6) to their country of origin or habitual residence (in the case of a refugee granted status in another EEA state) and to provide temporary accommodation until the arrangements have been made and they fail to comply with them.[8] Provision for persons in categories (7) and (8) is made in section IAA s 4, which is dealt with at 13.175 below.

[1]   Immigration and Asylum Act 1999, s 95(2); Asylum Support Regulations 2000, SI 2000/704, reg 4; Nationality, Immigration and Asylum Act 2002, ss 51, 55, Sch 3.

[2]   NIAA 2002, s 51, in force from a date to be appointed.

[3]   NIAA 2002, s 55.

[4]   NIAA 2002, Sch 3, paras 3–7A (para 7A inserted by AI(TC)A 2004 s 9).

[5]   SI 2000/704, reg 4(8), (9); NIAA 2002 s 51(2)(c) (not yet in force).

[6]   By exclusion from the provisions of the IAA 1999 require NASS to provide support: see IAA 1999, s 95(1), (2); Asylum Support (Interim Provisions) Regulations 1999, SI 1999/3056, reg 4(1); Asylum Seekers (Reception Conditions) Regulations 2005, SI 2005/7.

[7]   Letter to Tim Crowley, Inter-Agency Co-ordination Team, 18 November 2003; see 13.56 above.

8 NIAA 2002, Sch 3, paras 8, 9; Withholding and Withdrawal of Support (Travel Assistance and Temporary Accommodation) Regulations 2002, SI 2002/3078; *R (on the application of M) v London Borough of Islington* [2004] EWCA Civ 235, [2004] 4 All ER 709. A local authority could decide to pay for the person concerned to return home: *R (on the application of Kimani) v Lambeth LBC* [2004] 1 WLR 272. This option is not available to deal with other excluded categories, however: *R (on the application of Grant) v Lambeth LBC* [2004] EWHC 1524 (Admin).

Exclusions in group applications for support in categories 1–3

13.69 Persons applying for NASS support not for themselves alone but for others as well, or included in a joint application, are only excluded if every person who is included in that application is excluded from NASS support for any of the three reasons in categories (1)–(3).[1] On its face, the purpose of this provision appears to be to ensure that groups containing 'mixed' applicants are brought within NASS. However, households should in fact access all other available means of support before asylum support is made available,[2] and so asylum seekers whose spouses may claim social security benefit or interim support may apply for asylum support, but deductions will be made reflecting the amount of the benefit.[3] Accommodation will only be provided by NASS if what is otherwise available is inadequate (see 13.63 above).

1 Asylum Support Regulations 2000, SI 2000/704, reg 4(3), (4); in particular because reg 4(3)(c) refers to each person as falling within any of the categories in reg 4(4); this exclusion only applies to applications for support, not once support has been approved: ASA 00/06/0018.
2 See NASS Policy *Bulletin No 11*.
3 This is the approach which has been applied by the asylum support adjudicators: ASA 00/07/0039; 00/08/0033; 00/09/0054, ASA 01/02/0202, citing SI 2000/704, reg 6, which requires NASS to take into account any other support which is available to the principal or any dependant.

Exclusion where applicant is the dependant of a supported asylum seeker in categories 1–3

13.70 A person is not excluded under categories (1) to (3), whether applying for themselves alone or as part of a joint application, if, when the application is made, the person is the dependant of a person already receiving asylum support.[1]

1 Asylum Support Regulations 2000, SI 2000/704, reg 4(7). 'Dependant' for these purposes bears precisely the same meaning as dependant of asylum seeker: reg 2(4). See 13.46 above.

Persons not excluded from obtaining social security benefits by their immigration status

13.71 An asylum seeker is excluded from support if, as a sole applicant, he or she is not excluded from obtaining income-based jobseeker's allowance, income support, housing benefit or council tax benefit through his or her immigration status.[1] Those affected by this exclusion are asylum seekers who, for the purpose of these social security benefits, are exempted from the 'subject to immigration control' test. They are set out at 13.9ff above. The regulations do not exclude from access to asylum support all the possible categories of asylum seekers who might be able to obtain these benefits.[2] For example, they do not exclude persons who, although they have applied for asylum, still have leave to enter or remain in the UK which is not subject to a condition of not having recourse to public funds nor as the result of an undertaking, nor leave automatically granted by the law while an appeal is pending.[3] Thus, a person who claims asylum while in the UK as a student may be eligible for social security benefits and NASS support. Nor do the regulations exclude EEA nationals. However, nationals of the Czech Republic, Estonia, Hungary, Latvia, Lithuania, Poland, Slovakia and Slovenia, who are Accession State workers who are required to be registered and who have not worked for 12 months or more for a registered employer, will not have a right to reside in the UK and will therefore be deemed not be habitually resident for the purpose of claiming income support, job seeker's allowance, housing benefit, council tax benefit and state pension credit.[4] NASS may refuse support to persons who have access to social security benefits. It may also require proof from the Benefits Agency that benefit has been refused before providing support to asylum seekers who were previously entitled.[5]

[1] Asylum Support Regulations 2000, SI 2000/704, reg 4(2), (4)(b), (6)(a); by reg 4(6)(b), this also includes income-based jobseeker's allowance or income support, housing benefit in Northern Ireland provided under the Jobseekers (Northern Ireland) Order 1995, SI 1995/2705 and the Social Security Contributions and Benefits (Northern Ireland) Act 1992.

[2] These are persons who may be seeking asylum in the UK but are not excluded from benefit generally by s 115(9) of the Immigration and Asylum Act 1999.

[3] See Immigration Act 1971, s 3C (as substituted by s 118 Nationality, Immigration and Asylum Act 2002 from 1 April 2003 (SI 2003/754); 13.8 above.

[4] See Social Security (Habitual Residence) (Amendment) Regulations 2004, SI 2004/1232; Accession (Immigration and Worker Registration) Regulations 2004, SI 2004/1219.

[5] NASS Policy *Bulletin No 16* 4 August 2000.

Persons not treated by the Home Office as having claimed asylum or as the dependants of an asylum seeker[1]

13.72 Those excluded from NASS support under this provision are sole applicants who are not treated by the Home Office as 'an asylum seeker or dependent on an asylum seeker' for immigration purposes.[2] Since the definition of 'asylum seeker' under the asylum support provisions is wide, no asylum seeker should be excluded from support under this provision. But it might prevent support being provided, potentially, to a large group of persons who are 'dependants' for support purposes[3] but not for immigration purposes. A spouse and minor children who accompany an asylum seeker to the UK, or who are mentioned by the asylum seeker in interview or written application, are always considered by the Home Office as dependants of the asylum claim.[4] A dependent child who reaches 18 before a decision is made on the asylum seeker's application will continue to be treated as a dependant pending the decision and during the appeals process.[5] However, other relatives and those who do not arrive with the principal applicant may be treated as dependants on the asylum claim at the discretion of the Home Office, provided there has been no decision on the asylum application.[6]

1 This exclusion relates to people who have not made a 'claim for leave to enter or remain in the UK or for variation of any such leave' in which they are being considered an asylum seeker or dependent on one. A claim for asylum or as the dependant of an asylum seeker is simultaneously a claim for leave to enter or remain in that capacity: see HC 395, paras 327–328, 330, 335, 349.
2 Asylum Support Regulations 2000, SI 2000/704, reg 4(2), (4)(c).
3 SI 2000/704, reg 2(4) and see 13.46 above.
4 HC 395, para 349; API *Dependants*, para 2; in the latter case Home Office case-workers will assume that they are applying for leave to enter or remain in the UK as dependants of the asylum seeker, although confirmation will later be sought from him or her.
5 API *Dependants*, para 3.
6 API *Dependants*, para 2.

Persons eligible to obtain interim support

13.73 A person applying for NASS support as a sole applicant will be excluded if he or she is eligible to obtain support under the interim scheme from a local authority.[1] For obvious reasons, this exclusion extends to persons whose application to a local authority has been rejected or whose support has been discontinued or suspended on grounds other than qualification for NASS support.[2]

1 Asylum Support Regulations 2000, SI 2000/704, reg 4(2), (4)(a), (5).
2 SI 2000/704, reg 4(5)(b), (c); Asylum Support (Interim Provisions) Regulations 1999, SI 1999/3056, regs 7, 8.

Persons offered alternative form of support

13.74 The Secretary of State may refuse to provide support, including NASS support[1] or temporary support,[2] to a person who has been offered another form of support.[3] The section, which comes into force on a date to be appointed, provides that the form of support offered may be dictated by administrative or other matters not relating to a claimant's personal circumstances, and may include the importance of testing the operation of a particular provision. The purpose of the section is to enable the Home Office to try out other forms of support, in particular accommodation centres, which were controversial from the first.

1 Ie, under IAA 1999, s 95.
2 Under IAA 1999, s 98.
3 Ie, support under IAA 1999, s 4 (accommodation for persons temporarily admitted or released from detention) or under NIAA 2002, s 17 or 24 (accommodation centres; provisional accommodation): NIAA 2002, s 51, in force from a date to be appointed.

SUSPENSION OR DISCONTINUATION OF SUPPORT

13.75 The Asylum Support Regulations additionally provide eleven separate grounds for suspension or discontinuation of support, as follows:[1]

(1) reasonable grounds to believe the supported person or a dependant has committed a serious breach of the rules of collective accommodation;

(2) reasonable grounds to believe that the supported person or a dependant has committed an act of seriously violent behaviour;

(3)   commission of an offence in relation to asylum support;
(4)   reasonable grounds to believe the supported person or a supported dependant has abandoned the address without notification or permission;
(5)   non-compliance with request for information about eligibility for or receipt of support;
(6)   failure without reasonable excuse to attend an interview about eligibility for or receipt of support;
(7)   non-compliance with request for information about asylum claim;
(8)   reasonable grounds to believe the supported person or a supported dependant has concealed financial resources and has unduly benefited from receipt of support;
(9)   non-compliance with a reporting requirement;
(10) reasonable grounds to believe that the supported person or a supported dependant has made or sought to make a concurrent asylum claim in the same or a different name;
(11) failure without reasonable excuse to comply with a relevant condition.

The criteria for suspension or discontinuation of NASS support have been substantially amended by the 2005 Amendment Regulations, as a result of the entry into force in February 2005 of the EC Reception Directive,[2] with its restricted grounds on which support may be reduced or withdrawn. Some of the grounds are new; some revised. There must now be an actual breach of conditions, or an actual commission of a criminal offence, to justify suspension or discontinuation of support; reasonable suspicion of these matters is no longer enough. The 'intentional destitution' ground contained in the unamended regulation 20 of the ASR, has gone.[3] We consider the grounds for suspension and discontinuation of support in more detail in the following paragraphs.

[1]   Asylum Support Regulations 2000, SI 2000/704, reg 20, substituted by the Asylum Support (Amendment) Regulations 2005, SI 2005/11, from 5 February 2005.
[2]   For detailed analysis of the 'intentional destitution' ground in SI 2000/704 reg 20(1)(c) (before amendment) see previous edition at 13.71–13.78.
[3]   Council Directive 2003/9/EC laying down minimum standards for the reception of asylum seekers. See also the Asylum Seekers (Reception Conditions) Regulations 2005, SI 2005/7.

Procedural requirements for discontinuance of support

13.76 All the grounds for suspension or discontinuation of support under the new regulation 20 are discretionary.[1] Any decision to discontinue support must be taken individually, objectively and impartially, and reasons must be given.[2] Decisions must be based on the particular situation of the person concerned, and particular regard must be had to whether he or she is a vulnerable person, as described by Article 17 of the EC Reception Directive.[3] No one's asylum support may be withdrawn before a decision is made in accordance with the provisions.[4] The principle of proportionality must be applied to decisions on suspension or discontinuance of support.[5]

[1]   Asylum Support Regulations 2000, SI 2000/704, reg 20(1), substituted by the Asylum Support (Amendment) Regulations 2005, SI 2005/11, from 5 February 2005.
[2]   Council Directive 2003/9/EC, Art 16; SI 2004/704, reg 20(3) as substituted.

3   Council Directive 2003/9/EC, in force 5 February 2005; see also Asylum Seekers (Reception Conditions) Regulations 2005, SI 2005/7, reg 4. 'Vulnerable people' include (but are not limited to) minors, unaccompanied minors, disabled and elderly people, pregnant women, single parents with minor children, and persons who have been subjected to torture, rape or other serious forms of psychological, physical or sexual violence.
4   SI 2004/704, reg 20(4). The regulation appears on the face of it not to preclude suspension of support pending a reasoned decision, but the Directive prohibits withdrawal or reduction of support before a negative decision, which would preclude suspension: Council Directive 2003/9/EC Art 16.5.
5   Council Directive 2003/9/EC, Art 16.4.

Serious breach of rules of accommodation

13.77 Where support is being provided to the supported person or a dependant in collective accommodation, defined as accommodation which is shared with any other supported person,[1] it may be suspended or discontinued if the Secretary of State has reasonable grounds to believe that the supported person or dependant has committed a serious breach of the rules of that accommodation.[2] There is likely to be considerable overlap between this provision and (11) (non-compliance with conditions) (see 13.88 below), but since suspension or discontinuance under this head can be triggered by reasonable belief, the breach of rules would have to be such as to pose a significant risk to the health, safety or comfort of other supported persons, the accommodation provider or the public, to justify withdrawal of support.[3]

1   This can include accommodation in which only facilities (eg kitchen, bathroom) are shared: Asylum Support Regulations 2000, SI 2000/704, reg 20(6) (reg 20 substituted by SI 2005/11 reg 6 from 5 February 2005).
2   SI 2000/704 reg 20(1)(a) as substituted; Council Directive 2003/9/EC, Art 16.3.
3   See by analogy PB 71 (Version 2, 31 March 2005) para 8.2(i) on withdrawal of s 4 accommodation for acts of 'anti-social or violent' behaviour.

Seriously violent behaviour

13.78 Asylum support for a supported person and/or any dependants of such a person may be suspended or discontinued if the Secretary of State has reasonable grounds to believe that any of them has committed an act of seriously violent behaviour, whether or not the act occurs in accommodation provided by way of asylum support, at the authorised address[1] or elsewhere.[2] There is as yet no published guidance on what constitutes 'seriously violent' behaviour, but the use of the qualifying adverb, and the power to suspend support on reasonable belief, both support an interpretation which requires at least actual bodily harm and possibly even the use of a weapon. It should certainly exclude violence in lawful self-defence, and would apparently exclude minor brawls and punch-ups.

1   Defined for the purposes of the regulation as the accommodation provided by way of asylum support or, if none is provided, the address notified by the supported person to the Secretary of State in the application for asylum support or in any change of address notified under reg 15 or under the Immigration Rules: SI 2000/704, reg 20(6)(a) (reg 20 substituted by SI 2005/11 from 5 February 2005).
2   SI 2004/704, reg 20(1)(b) as substituted; Council Directive 2003/9/EC, Art 3.

Commission of an offence in relation to asylum support

13.79 Asylum support for a supported person and /or any dependants of such a person may be suspended or discontinued if any of them has committed a criminal offence under Part VI of the Immigration and Asylum Act 1999, which is connected to the provision of support.[1] This includes such as[2] making false representations or producing false documents or false information,[3] or failure to notify a relevant change of circumstances,[4] or obstructing a person administering support,[5] or refusal or failure to answer questions, give information or produce documents.[6] Before amendment by the Amendment Regulations 2005, it was not necessary for the supported person or dependant to have been convicted or even charged with an offence for this ground of exclusion to operate, as only 'reasonable grounds' for suspecting that an offence has been committed were required.[7] Now, however, the offence must actually have been committed, so NASS support should only be suspended or discontinued on conviction of a relevant offence.

1 Asylum Support Regulations 2000, SI 2000/704, reg 20(1)(c) (reg 20 substituted by SI 2005/11 from 5 February 2005).
2 All the relevant offences are contained in Immigration and Asylum Act 1999, Pt VI. See 14.73 below.
3 IAA 1999, ss 105(1)(a), (b), 106(1)(a), (b).
4 IAA 1999, ss 105(1)(c), (d), 106(1)(c), (d).
5 IAA 1999, s 107(1)(a).
6 IAA 1999, s 107(1); SI 2000/704, reg 3(2), (3), (5), Sch, requiring applicants for support to provide the information contained in the prescribed form and authorising the making of further inquiries into any matter 'connected with the application'.
7 See SI 2004/704 reg 20(1)(b) before amendment; see previous edition at **13.70**.

Abandonment of authorised address

13.80 The Secretary of State may suspend or discontinue support on reasonable grounds for believing that the supported person or any dependant being provided with support has abandoned the authorised address without first informing the Secretary of State or, if such a request was made, without permission.[1] The authorised address for these purposes is either the accommodation NASS is providing or, where it is not providing accommodation, the address notified to the Home Office or a change of address given to the Home Office or NASS since the person has been provided with support.[2] It is not necessary for the Home Office to have granted temporary admission on the basis that the asylum seeker will live at the notified address, although a notice of temporary admission with the address on it will constitute the clearest evidence of the address notified to the Home Office by the asylum seeker. Where the person is traced, or voluntarily reports to police, to the Secretary of State or to an immigration officer, the regulations require a 'duly motivated' (reasoned) decision to be taken as to reinstatement of support, in whole or part, based on the reasons for the person's disappearance.[3] Support could not, we suggest, lawfully be withheld if a reasonable excuse was forthcoming for the person's disappearance. The provision is couched in terms of 'reasonable belief' of the Secretary of State because of the difficulties inherent in knowing when absence from accommodation amounts to abandonment of it.

1   Council Directive 2003/9/EC, Art 16.1(a); Asylum Support Regulations 2000,
     SI 2000/704, reg 20(1)(d) (reg 20 substituted by SI 2005/11 from 5 February 2005). The
     domestic provision replaces two provisions in the unamended regulations; reg 20(1)(d)
     enabled support to be removed from persons who 'ceased to reside' at the authorised
     address, while reg 20(1)(e) did the same for absence from the address for for more than
     seven consecutive days and nights or a total of more than 14 days and nights in any
     six-month period, in either case without the permission of the Secretary of State.
2   SI 2004/704 reg 20(6) as substituted.
3   SI 2004/705 reg 20(5) as substituted.

Non-compliance with request for asylum support information

13.81 Support may be suspended or discontinued for non-compliance within
a reasonable period[1] with a request for information by the Secretary of State
relating to the eligibility for, or receipt of, asylum support on the part of the
supported person or a dependant.[2] The request may relate to a change of
circumstances under regulation 15 of the Asylum Support Regulations.[3] This
is a new provision. There is no 'reasonable excuse' exception, but failure to
have regard to a reasonable explanation for the failure would render the
removal of support unlawful. This and the following 'procedural non-
compliance' provisions are likely to be used for suspension of NASS support
to enforce compliance, and total discontinuance of support as punishment for
procedural non-compliance would, we suggest, be disproportionate and
incompatible with the standards of the EC Reception Directive.[4]

1   Defined as at least five working days beginning with the day on which the request was
     received: Asylum Support Regulations 2000, SI 2000/704, reg 20(1)(e) (reg 20 substituted
     by SI 2005/11 from 5 February 2005).
2   Council Directive 2003/9/EC, Art 16.1(a); SI 2004/704, reg 20(1)(e) as substituted.
3   For regulation 15 see 13.105 below.
4   Council Directive 2003/9/EC; see 13.75 above.

Failure to attend NASS interview

13.82 Support may be suspended or discontinued if the supported person
fails without reasonable excuse to attend an interview relating to the supported persons's or dependant's eligibility for or receipt of asylum support.[1]
See comments above.

1   Council Directive 2003/9/EC, Art 16.1(a); Asylum Support Regulations 2000,
     SI 2000/704, reg 20(1)(f) (reg 20 substituted by SI 2005/11 from 5 February 2005).

Non-compliance with request for information on asylum claim

13.83 Support may be suspended or discontinued if the supported person (or
his or her dependant, if that person is an asylum seeker) has not complied,
within a reasonable period,[1] with a request for information by the Secretary of
State relating to the asylum claim.[2] This is a new provision, and its purpose is
not altogether clear. There is provision within the asylum determination
procedure for claims to be determined adversely to claimants who fail to
return Statements of Evidence within a specified period.[3] Claimants who then

appeal against such non-compliance refusals remain asylum seekers for the purposes of asylum support;[4] the new provision appears to seek to use the asylum support provisions to deny support pending appeal in this situation. Once again, although the provision does not have a 'reasonable excuse' exception, this is implicit in the discretionary nature of the suspension and discontinuance provisions.

1.   Defined as at least ten working days beginning with the day on which the request was received: Asylum Support Regulations 2000, SI 2000/704, reg 20(1)(g) (reg 20 substituted by SI 2005/11 from 5 February 2005).
2.   Council Directive 2003/9/EC, Art 16.1(a); SI 2004/704, reg 20(1)(g) as substituted.
3.   For non-compliance refusals see 12.130 below.
4.   See definition of 'asylum seeker' in IAA 1999, s 94, 13.39 above.

Concealment of financial resources

13.84 Asylum support may be suspended or discontinued if the Secretary of State has reasonable grounds to believe that a supported person or a supported dependant has concealed financial resources and has therefore unduly benefited from the receipt of asylum support.[1] This provision is new, and it is hard to see under what circumstances it would be appropriate to discontinue support under it, although it could be used to suspend support where a criminal offence is reasonably suspected, or where charges have been brought, pending a criminal trial.[2]

1.   Council Directive 2003/9/EC, Art 16.1(b); Asylum Support Regulations 2000, SI 2000/704, reg 20(1)(h) (reg 20 substituted by SI 2005/11 from 5 February 2005).
2.   This is because reg 20(1)(c) now requires the commission of a criminal offence, rather than reasonable suspicion of one; see 13.79 above.

Non-compliance with a reporting requirement

13.85 Asylum support may be suspended or discontinued where the supported person, or a supported dependant, has failed to comply with a reporting requirement.[1] For these purposes, a reporting requirement is a condition or restriction requiring the person concerned to report to the police, an immigration officer or the Secretary of State, imposed as a condition of temporary admission[2] or release from detention[3] or as a condition of bail.[4] Where the person is traced, or voluntarily reports to police, to the Secretary of State or to an immigration officer, the regulations require a 'duly motivated' (reasoned) decision to be taken as to reinstatement of support, in whole or part, based on the reasons for the person's non-compliance.[5]

1.   Asylum Support Regulations 2000, SI 2000/704, reg 20(1)(i) (reg 20 substituted by SI 2005/11 from 5 February 2005).
2.   Ie, under IA 1971, Sch 2, para 21; see 17.11 below.
3.   Under IA 1971, Sch 2, para 21 or Sch 3, para 2; see 17.15 below.
4.   Under IA 1971, Sch 2, para 22, or Sch 3, para 5 (see 17.55 below): SI 2004/704, reg 20(6) as substituted.
5.   SI 2004/704, reg 20(5) as substituted.

Further asylum claim

13.86 Asylum support may be suspended or discontinued if the Secretary of State has reasonable grounds to believe that the supported person, or a supported dependant, has made a claim for asylum ('the first claim') and, before the first claim has been determined, makes or seeks to make a further claim for asylum, being part of the first claim, in the same or a different name.[1] This is another new provision, once again seeking to use the asylum support provisions to police the substantive asylum determination regime, but the circumstances in which it is likely to be deployed are unclear. An attempt to make a second claim in a different name (whether or not a first claim is still pending) is a criminal offence for which support may be discontinued in any event.[2] The one-stop provisions in the 2002 Act require asylum claimants to set out, on demand by the Secretary of State, any other reasons they have for seeking to remain in the UK,[3] and they could hardly have asylum support discontinued as a result of a response which raised further asylum or Article 3 issues.

1   Asylum Support Regulations 2000, SI 2000/704, reg 20(1)(j) (reg 20 substituted by SI 2005/11 from 5 February 2005).
2   See 13.79 above.
3   For the one-stop procedure see 18.40 below.

Failure without reasonable excuse to comply with a relevant condition

13.87 NASS may provide support subject to conditions.[1] Any conditions which are made must be set out in writing[2] and given to the person who is being supported.[3] However, relevant conditions whose breach may lead to suspension or discontinuance of support are narrowly defined as conditions which make the provision of asylum support subject to actual residence by the supported person or a dependant for whom support is being provided in a specified place or location.[4] Behaviour which breaches conditions of support will not otherwise lead to suspension or discontinuance of support if it does not fall within one of the categories set out above. For exclusion on grounds of breach of a relevant condition (ie for failure to go to or live at the specified place), the conditions must have been set out in writing and given to the asylum seeker;[5] even if it were possible in principle to remove from support an asylum seeker not given the conditions in writing, there will almost certainly be a 'reasonable excuse' for failure to comply in these circumstances.

1   Immigration and Asylum Act 1999, s 95(9). Breaches of conditions imposed under the sub-section which relate to the use of the support provided, or to compliance with a restriction imposed under Immigration Act 1971, Sch 2, para 21 or Sch 3, para 2 or 5 (temporary admission or release) (Immigration and Asylum Act 1999 s 95(9A) as inserted by Nationality, Immigration and Asylum Act 2002 s 50(1) from 7 November 2002) are dealt with separately above. In ASA 00/09/0063 the adjudicator found that an allegation of a physical attack on a fellow asylum seeker at the premises gave NASS 'reasonable grounds to suspect' a breach of conditions before criminal proceedings were resolved. See now SI 2004/704 reg 20(1)(a) and (b), substituted by SI 2005/11, at 13.77 and 13.78 above.
2   IAA 1999, s 95(1).
3   IAA 1999, s 95(11); ASA 00/10/1174 at para 14 and ASA 00/10/0077.

4   SI 2000/704, regs 19(2), 20(1)(k), as amended and substituted. Note too that, unlike the previous regulations, the provision requires actual breach of a relevant condition, not merely reasonable suspicion of breach.
5   IAA 1999, ss 95(1), (11).

Failure to travel

13.88 NASS has adopted a number of policies in relation to the failure to comply with dispersal arrangements, or to return to accommodation which has been left.[1] There have been a considerable number of decisions of asylum support adjudicators on the circumstances which constitute a reasonable excuse for breach of this condition.[2] Many have concerned previous racial harassment. Asylum support adjudicators have held the nature, degree, frequency, persistence and organisation of harassment and its effect on the asylum seeker all relevant,[3] and whether it has been reported to the police and if so, whether police action has been effective.[4] The 'sufficiency of protection' test of refugee status itself[5] has even been applied to deciding whether a refusal to return to the site of previous racist harassment was reasonable in the light of the police response.[6] These decisions suggest that there is such a thing as an acceptable level of racial harassment (or a level of harassment which asylum seekers must accept, which is the same thing). In our view, a 'sufficiency of protection' test has no place in this area of the law. Reasonable excuse may also derive from a combination of factors such as ill-health, single parenthood with young children, language difficulties and lack of proof that NASS had notified details of the travel arrangements.[7] Emotional trauma at the prospect of dispersal,[8] lack of awareness of the travel arrangements,[9] insufficient notice of dispersal decision[10] or finding alternative accommodation[11] have been held good reasons for not travelling to NASS accommodation. NASS caseworkers must minute their decisions and their reasons for reaching these decisions,[12] and failure to note claimants' reasons for not wishing to be dispersed led to appeals being allowed.[13] NASS Policy Bulletin 31: *Dispersal Guidelines* indicate situations in which asylum seekers should be allocated accommodation in London or the south-east of England, referring in particular to the need to continue medical treatment or be supported by family members.[14] The availability of specialist support from the Medical Foundation for the Care of Victims of Torture should also be taken into account.[15] The availability of treatment for those who are HIV positive is also a relevant factor.[16] The need to maintain regular contact with a child was also a reason for dispersal not to be reasonable in the light of Article 8 of the European Convention on Human Rights.[17]

1   See NASS Policy Bulletin 17 *Failure to Travel* and NASS Bulletin 57 *Changes in Failure to Travel Policy: Transitional Arrangements*.
2   However, the Court of Appeal held in *R (Secretary of State for the Home Department) v Chief Asylum Support Adjudicator and Ahmet Dogan)* [2003] EWCA Civ 1673) that no right of appeal existed against withdrawal of support offered on condition of dispersal; see further below 13.117.
3   ASA 00/08/0034; 00/08/0036; 00/09/0044. In ASA 00/09/0066 and 00/08/0036, verbal abuse and gesturing was held insufficient. Frequent racist taunts were held sufficient to constitute reasonable excuse in 00/07/0024. See now NASS Policy Bulletin 81, 'Racist Incidents', 13.67 above.
4   ASA 00/09/0044.
5   See *Horvath v Secretary of State for the Home Department* [2000] Imm AR 552.

6   ASA 00/09/0044.
7   ASA 00/09/0046.
8   ASA 00/09/0057.
9   ASA 00/09/0058.
10   ASA/01/04/0269.
11   ASA 00/09/0067.
12   Policy Bulletin 17: *Failure to Travel*, para 2.7–2.8.
13   ASA/02/02/1776; ASA/04/02/7597. But see fn 2 above.
14   See ASA/02/02/1829; ASA/03/06/6559; ASA/01/06/ 0365; ASA/02/02/2002;
     ASA/02/07/4305; ASA/03/03/6140; ASA/00/11/0095; ASA/01/08/0714; ASA/00/1/0095;
     ASA/01/11/1307; see also *R (on the application of Wanjugu) v National Asylum Support
     Service* [2003] All ER (D) 37 (Dec).
15   See ASA/00/09/047 and NASS Policy Bulletins 19 & 21.
16   See ASA/02/07/4305; ASA/03/10/7085.
17   See ASA/01/06/0369; ASA/04/01/7494.

PROVISION OF SUPPORT

The EC Reception Directive

13.89 Asylum support has since February 2005 been subject to the minimum requirements of Council Directive 2003/9/EC of 27 January 2003 laying down minimum standards for the reception of asylum seekers.[1] We have noted at 13.75–13.76 above the changes to the procedures and criteria for suspension and discontinuance of support necessitated by the coming into force of the Directive. The Directive also requires changes in the provision of asylum support. The Asylum Seekers (Reception Conditions) Regulations[2] transposes these requirements into domestic law. The power to provide asylum support to eligible persons becomes a duty.[3] In providing or arranging for the provision of accommodation for an asylum seeker and his or her family members under s 95 or s 98 of the Immigration and Asylum Act 1999, the Secretary of State must have regard to family unity and ensure, so far as reasonably practicable, that family members (spouse, partner in a stable relationship and unmarried dependent minor children of either) are accommodated together (subject to their consent).[4] The special needs of asylum seekers and/or family members who are vulnerable, ie those who are minors, disabled or elderly, pregnant, single parents with minor children, and victims of torture, rape or other forms of psychological, physical or sexual violence,[5] must be taken into account, and there are duties to trace family members of unaccompanied minors so as to protect the minors' best interests.[6]

1   OJ 2003 L 31/18.
2   SI 2005/7.
3   SI 2005/7, reg 5.
4   SI 2005/7, regs 2, 3. The duty does not apply when the Secretary of State is providing or
     arranging for the provision of accommodation of the child under Immigration and Asylum
     Act 1999 s 122: reg 3(3).
5   SI 2005/7, reg 4(1), (2). However, a person is only classified as vulnerable under the
     provision if they have had an individual evaluation of their situation which confirms that
     they have special needs: reg 4(3), and the Secretary of State is not obliged to carry out such
     an evaluation: reg 4(4). It will be for applicants' advisers to secure such assessments,
     whether through local authorities, by reference to their community care duties (see 13.177
     below) or otherwise.
6   SI 2005/7, reg 6.

Emergency NASS support

13.90 NASS must provide support or arrange for emergency accommodation to be provided to an asylum seeker or the dependant of an asylum seeker who it appears may be destitute.[1] Various voluntary agencies funded by NASS to provide this support employ 'reception assistants' who are responsible for placing asylum seekers in temporary accommodation. Emergency support is given where it appears to the Secretary of State that an asylum-seeker and any dependants may be destitute but no decision about providing asylum support has been made.[2] Where the asylum-seeker is not accompanied by minor dependants, emergency support may also be provided while the Secretary of State decides whether the application for support was made as soon as reasonably practicable or is reconsidering a decision to refuse support under section 55 of the Nationality, Immigration and Asylum Act 2002.[3] Emergency accommodation will also be provided to those asylum seekers who are no longer entitled to benefits,[4] and to those who have left NASS accommodation alleging racial harassment or other reasonable excuse.[5] If NASS refuses support, emergency accommodation ends immediately. As with full NASS support, emergency accommodation may be provided subject to conditions, which must be given in writing to the recipients of temporary support.[6] There are no rules governing what can and cannot be provided by way of emergency support,[7] but NASS has adopted a number of policies on eligibility and procedures for new applicants and for those formerly on cash only support or who have previously left accommodation to which they were dispersed.[8]

[1]   Immigration and Asylum Act 1999, s 98(1); Asylum Seekers (Reception Conditions) Regulations 2005, SI 2005/7, reg 5. The same definition of destitution applies as with full NASS support.
[2]   IAA 1999, s 98(2).
[3]   Nationality, Immigration and Asylum Act 2002, s 55(5)(c).
[4]   See NASS Policy Bulletin 53 *Temporary Support for NASS Eligible Disbenefited Singles or Childless Couples.*
[5]   See NASS Policy Bulletin 73 *Admittance to Emergency Accommodation*, para 5.1.
[6]   IAA 1999, s 98(3), applying s 95(11).
[7]   IAA 1999, ss 96–97 and Asylum Support Regulations 2000, SI 2000/704, deal with support provided under the full NASS scheme (Immigration and Asylum Act 1999, s 95) rather than support provided as a temporary measure (Immigration and Asylum Act 1999, s 98).
[8]   Policy Bulletin 73: *Admittance to Emergency Accommodation.*

Support provided under NASS

13.91 NASS may provide the following kinds of support to eligible asylum seekers and their dependants:[1]

- essential living needs; and/or
- accommodation which is adequate; and/or
- expenses, other than legal expenses, in connection with the asylum claim; and/or
- expenses in attending bail hearings where the asylum seeker or their dependants are detained for immigration purposes;
- services in the form of education, English language lessons, sporting or other developmental activities;[2]

- *if the circumstances of the particular case are exceptional,* any other form of support which NASS thinks necessary to enable the asylum seeker and their dependants to be supported.[3]

The Secretary of State may by order restrict the provision of support to those asylum-seekers who are also being provided with accommodation by NASS.[4] An order may relate to particular geographical locations or to asylum-seekers who made an application by or after a certain date.[5] No order has yet been made. Statistical data suggests that the majority of asylum-seekers who are in receipt of support only assistance are in London and the south-east of England. The Secretary of State can also make payments to an asylum-seeker in order to meet the expenses incurred in connection with his or her claim for asylum and to enable an asylum-seeker and his or her dependants to attend bail hearings.[6] Asylum-seekers who decide not to remain in NASS accommodation must supply NASS with their new address. They cannot use their emergency accommodation address or any other address provided by NASS.[7]

1   Immigration and Asylum Act 1999, s 96(1).
2   IAA 1999, Sch 8, para 4; Asylum Support Regulations 2000, SI 2000/704, reg 14.
3   IAA 1999, s 96(2).
4   NIAA 2002, s 43, in force 7 November 2002 (s 162).
5   NIAA 2002, s 43(2).
6   IAA 1999, s 96(1)(c), (d).
7   NASS Policy Bulletin 24: *Instructions about Asylum-seekers Deciding against Staying in NASS Accommodation and Choose to Find Their Own and Requesting a Change of Address* Version 1.1.

13.92 NASS may disregard any preference which an asylum seeker or dependant may have as to the way support is given.[1] In particular, the Secretary of State may in the future decide to provide NASS support by placing an asylum-seeker and any dependants in an accommodation centre.[2] In deciding on the level and kind of support to provide to an applicant and his or her dependants or to anyone already being provided with support, NASS must take into account income, support which may be reasonably expected to be available and any assets such as cash or savings.[3] It may take into account previous breach of any conditions on which the support has been or is being provided,[4] but must have regard to the seriousness or triviality of the breach in deciding whether to alter the level of support and by how much.[5]

1   Immigration and Asylum Act 1999, s 97(7).
2   Nationality, Immigration and Asylum Act 2002, s 22, in force from a date to be appointed.
3   Asylum Support Regulations 2000, SI 2000/704, reg 12(3).
4   SI 2000/704, reg 19(1).
5   SI 2000/704, reg 19(1) allows the Secretary of State to take into account the extent to which conditions have been complied with.

Providing essential living needs

13.93 Where NASS decides that a person needs support in relation to essential living needs, he or she will be provided with cash payments.[1] An additional single payment of £50, payable after every period of six months, has now been abolished.[2] A single, one-off 'maternity' payment of £300 may be provided to asylum seekers to assist with the costs of a newborn baby.[3] A written application must be lodged by the father or mother close to the date of the birth, and the child must generally have been born to a NASS-supported person. A maternity payment may also be made in respect of a baby under three months old who was born outside the UK to an asylum-seeker who subsequently qualified for NASS support. From 3 March 2003, an additional weekly payment has been provided to pregnant women and to children under the age of three.[4] There is provision for replacement of lost or stolen payments.[5]

1   Asylum Support Regulations 2000, SI 2000/704, reg 10(2), 10A as amended by SI 2004/1313, from 4 June 2004.
2   SI 2004/1313, revoking reg 11 of the Asylum Support Regulations 2000, SI 2000/704. The single payment acknowledged that the target period of six months for deciding the claim (including any appeal) had not been met, and that after that period the asylum seeker was likely to have needs which could not be met by the weekly payments.
3   NASS Policy Bulletin 37: *Maternity Payments* V1.1: October 2003.
4   Asylum Support (Amendment) Regulations 2003, SI 2003/ 241; Policy Bulletin 78 – *Additional Payments to Pregnant Women and Children Aged Under 3* Version 1.0 26 February 2003. Babies under one currently receive an additional £5 per week, while those under three and pregnant mothers receive £3.
5   See NASS Policy Bulletin 80: *Backpayment of Asylum Support.*

Amounts provided

13.94 Regulation 2 of the Asylum Support (Amendment) (No 2) Regulations 2005 sets out the current levels of support given to asylum seekers.[1] For the purposes of payment, to count as a married couple, the couple must be a man and a woman who are married to each other and who are members of the same household;[2] to count as an unmarried couple, the couple must be a man and a woman who, although not married, are living together as though they are married;[3] a 'lone parent' is a person who is not a part of a married or unmarried couple who is the parent of a child under 18 and support is being provided for the child;[4] a 'single person' is a person who is neither a member of a married or unmarried couple nor the parent of a child under 18 for whom support is being provided.[5] The amounts payable will be reduced where NASS provides accommodation as part of the support which includes some provision for essential living needs, such as bed and breakfast or full board.[6]

1   SI 2005/ 738, in force 11 April 2005, under which the rates are as follows:
    –   Married or unmarried couple at least one of whom is 18 or over but where neither is under 16: £61.71;
    –   Lone parent aged 18 or over, or single person aged 25 or over: £39.34;
    –   Single person aged 18–24: £31.15;
    –   Person aged 16–17 (except a member of a married or unmarried couple as referred to above): £ 33.85;
    –   Person aged under 16: £43.88. See 13.93 fn 4 above for additional payments for babies and pregnant mothers.
2   Asylum Support Regulations 2000, SI 2000/704, reg 2(1).
3   SI 2000/704, reg 2(1).
4   SI 2000/704, reg 10(4)(b), (d).
5   SI 2000/704, reg 10(4)(c).
6   SI 2000/704, reg 10(5).

13.95 The amounts payable are less than the 'applicable amounts' of income support which similarly situated persons would be entitled to if they qualified, reflecting approximately 70 per cent of the applicable amounts of income support.[1] This is partly in recognition of the fact that the support is to be temporary[2] and does not need to include the cost of service bills, replacement items of clothing and household items which are usually provided.[3] The rules on provision for essential living needs are, however, all rules of thumb[4] which set out what an asylum seeker can generally expect to receive. In appropriate cases, NASS may provide more, or less, or make provision in a different form. Where an asylum seeker is married to someone who is in receipt of benefits in his or her own right, NASS must consider whether the asylum seeker's essential needs could properly be met from his or her income as some of this may be unavailable to him or her due to the partner's needs and the needs of any of their dependants.[5]

[1]   Applicable amounts for income support are provided pursuant to the Social Security Contributions and Benefits Act 1992, s 124(4).
[2]   Immigration and Asylum Act 1999, s 97(5).
[3]   See para 305 of Explanatory Notes to the IAA 1999.
[4]   See Asylum Support Regulations 2000, SI 2000/704, regs 10(2), (6), 11(1).
[5]   *R (on the application of Secretary of State for the Home Department) (National Asylum Support Service) v Asylum Support Adjudicators* [2001] EWHC Admin 881, [2001] All ER (D) 13 (Nov). See also NASS Policy Bulletin 11 *Mixed Households*.

Providing accommodation

13.96 The system of 'dispersal' was one of the most controversial aspects of the Immigration and Asylum Act 1999.[1] In deciding upon the location and nature of the accommodation which a person will be given, NASS must have regard to the fact that support by way of accommodation is only being provided on a temporary basis until the claim to asylum (including any appeal) has been dealt with, and that it is desirable to provide accommodation for asylum seekers in those areas where there is a good supply of accommodation.[2] But NASS may not have regard to any preferences of the asylum seeker as to the area in which he or she wishes the accommodation to be located, the nature of the accommodation to be provided;[3] or the nature and standard of the fixtures and fittings in the accommodation.[4] It may, however, take into account the asylum seeker's and his or her dependants' individual circumstances as they relate to their accommodation needs.[5] The court has been fairly generous in its approach, holding in *ex p Mahida* that location close to a mosque was not merely a matter of preference, but was relevant to the applicant's religious and emotional needs and so to his or her welfare, in assessing adequacy of the accommodation.[6] NASS must also consider whether dispersal would amount to a breach of Article 8 of the European Convention on Human Rights.[7]

[1]   See above 13.29–13.30. For dispersal under the interim scheme see 13.153–13.157 below.
[2]   Immigration and Asylum Act 1999, s 97(1)(a) with reference to ss 94(3), (4), 97(1)(b).
[3]   Asylum Support Regulations 2000, SI 2000/704, reg 13(2)(a).
[4]   SI 2000/704, reg 13(2)(b).
[5]   SI 2000/704, reg 13(2), and see ASA 00/11/0110 at para 9, enabling consideration of the asylum seeker's family-related concerns.
[6]   *R v Islington London Borough Council, ex p Mahida* CO 2519/2000 (14 August 2000, unreported), QBD, on the similar provisions under interim support provisions (Asylum Support (Interim Provisions) Regulations 1999, SI 1999/3056, reg 6(2).

7   R *(on the application of Blackwood) v Secretary of State for the Home Department* [2003] EWHC 97 (Admin), [2003] HLR 638.

13.97 Applying the above statutory criteria, NASS general policy is to seek to disperse asylum seekers away from London and the south-east.[1] In allocating accommodation to someone who seeks to remain in that area, NASS will consider whether it is reasonable to disperse, whether such an allocation will meet the person's needs and whether the decision is compatible with the Human Rights Act 1998. In determining what is reasonable in a particular case, consideration should be given to medical treatment, special needs,[2] family ties, education, ethnic group, religion, employment, legal advice and language. Since the NASS1 application form seeks information in relation to all these factors, it is reasonable to assume that they are factors which NASS should take into account when considering where an asylum-seeker will be accommodated. In practice, however, dispersal has generally been dependent upon bed spaces becoming available.[3] The standard of accommodation has also often been less than adequate.

1   NASS Policy *Bulletin 31 Dispersal Guidelines* refers to s 97 of the Immigration and Asylum Act 1999, which requires NASS to have regard, in general, to the desirability of providing accommodation in areas in which there is a ready supply. Current policy, however, is that where an asylum seeker applies for asylum in a 'dispersal area' and asks to be accommodated in that area, the request will normally be met, subject to the availability of accommodation: *Bulletin 31* at para 2.3.
2   R *(on the application of Wanjugu) v Secretary of State for the Home Department* [2003] EWHC 3116 (Admin), where the court quashed a decision to disperse a claimant with post traumatic stress disorder. *See also 13.78 above.*
3   See fn 1 above.

13.98 Family ties are clearly a key factor in the light of Article 8 of the ECHR. Although the instruction recognises the need to consider each case on its merits, NASS is of the view that 'in the absence of exceptional circumstances' relating to this factor, dispersal will normally be appropriate.[1] So far as education is concerned, where an asylum seeker has children who are about to take GCSE A or AS level exams, dispersal should be deferred.[2] The existence of an ethnic community in the preferred area is normally insufficient to militate against dispersal, as NASS accommodation is all supposed to be in areas which boast an established ethnic minority community and are 'able to sustain a new ethnic group and voluntary and community infrastructures'.[3] If there is only one area where an asylum seeker can properly worship, then his or her request may be accommodated having regard to Article 9 ECHR (freedom of thought, conscience and religion).[4] In the case of new port and in-country applicants, where a referral[5] is made to the Medical Foundation for the Care of the Victims of Torture, NASS must give careful consideration to deferring dispersal from the south-east, and where, after initial assessment, the Medical Foundation accepts the applicant for treatment, NASS must give sympathetic consideration to providing local accommodation. The same applies to those already receiving treatment.[6] Sending a family to an inner city estate where racial abuse and hostility was prevalent did not breach Article 3 ECHR without evidence of a specific risk of the necessary ill-treatment.[7] In *Gezer* Moses J concluded that the Secretary of State was (1) under an obligation to provide protection against a risk of treatment falling within

Article 3 if he knew of ought to have known about it; (2) the level of protection he was required to provide was that which was reasonably available; (3) that level need not afford a guarantee against the danger but had to be reasonable, as a matter of practicality, common-sense and humanity, taking into account relevant policy considerations; (4) the measures to be taken are those which afford a real prospect of avoiding the danger; and (5) the extent of the risk will inform the extent to which protection should be offered.

1 NASS Policy *Bulletin 31 Dispersal Guidelines*, para 4.
2 NASS Policy *Bulletin 31*, para 6.3.
3 NASS Policy *Bulletin 31*, para 7.1.
4 NASS Policy *Bulletin 31*, para 7.2.
5 Normally the referral should be made by the reception assistant using the standard form at Annex A to NASS Policy *Bulletin 19 The Medical Foundation for the Care of Victims of Torture.*
6 NASS Policy *Bulletin 19*.
7 *R (on the application of Gezer) v Secretary of State for the Home Department* [2003] EWHC 860 (Admin), [2003] HLR 972 (upheld by the Court of Appeal at [2004] EWCA Civ 1730).

13.99 If, applying the above factors, a decision is made to disperse an asylum seeker, he or she is likely to be provided with a document providing details, and stating that the support is provided on condition that the asylum seeker travels there in accordance with the enclosed travel instructions. A warning letter advises the person that travel will only be rearranged where there are exceptional reasons for not travelling at the appointed time. Failure to travel to the accommodation without good reason is likely to result in the withdrawal of support and the refusal of any further application on the basis that support has previously been discontinued.[1]

1 Asylum Support Regulations 2000, SI 2000/704, regs 19–21, and see NASS Policy *Bulletin 17* (4 August 2000), a casework instruction on 'failure to travel' and NASS Policy *Bulletin 28* (26 September 2000) 'Travel'. See 13.78 above. Withdrawal of support which was conditional on failure to travel to dispersal accommodation does not generally give rise to a right of appeal: *R (Secretary of State for the Home Department) v Chief Asylum Support Adjudicator and Ahmet Dogan* [2003] EWCA Civ 1673.

Expenses in connection with asylum claim

13.100 NASS may meet expenses connected with the asylum claim,[1] excluding 'legal' expenses such as the costs of paying a lawyer for preparation or for representation. Included are travel expenses of the asylum seeker (or those of witnesses) in attending the appeal or interviews or examinations in connection with the claim.[2] Expenses in preparing and copying documents,[3] sending letters and faxes in order to obtain further evidence are also included. Travel expenses for a Medical Foundation assessment in connection with the asylum application or where referred by a GP should generally be met.[4] The Secretary of State also has power to pay for travel expenses incurred by an asylum-seeker needing to comply with reporting restrictions.[5]

1 Immigration and Asylum Act 1999, s 96(1)(c).

2   These are expressly included in the interim scheme (Asylum Support (Interim Provisions) Regulations 1999, SI 1999/3056, reg 5(3)), and it would be anomalous if they were to be left out for the purposes of NASS. See NASS Policy Bulletin 56: *Reimbursing Asylum Seekers their Essential Travel Costs.*

3   See Explanatory Notes to the Immigration and Asylum Act 1999, at para 300.

4   See NASS Policy *Bulletin 19 The Medical Founation for the Care of Victims of Torture* and NASS Policy *Bulletin 28 Travel*, Policy Bulletin 56 (fn 1 above) for the procedures for obtaining payment. This applies to those on temporary support: NASS Policy Bulletin 66: *Providing Travelling Expenses to Persons Supported under the Immigration and Asylum Act 1999 section 98.*

5   Nationality, Immigration and Asylum Act 2002, s 69, in force 7 November 2002.

Other services

13.101 NASS may provide education services (including English language classes) and sporting or other developmental activities to any person who is receiving NASS support.[1] These services are not provided automatically, but may only be provided in order to 'maintain good order' among supported asylum seekers.[2] This does not require that good order has broken down before these services are provided, but that without the stimulation of sport, education and developmental activities, and the access to and integration with the wider community these activities entail, morale and thus 'good order' could be jeopardised.

1   Immigration and Asylum Act 1999, Sch 8, para 4; Asylum Support Regulations 2000, SI 2000/704, reg 14.

2   SI 2000/704, reg 14(1).

Contributions to support

13.102 In deciding what level of support to provide to a destitute asylum seeker, NASS must take into account the income, support and assets which are available or might reasonably be expected to be available to him or her.[1] As an alternative to reducing the level of support, NASS may require that the asylum seeker makes a contribution from their own income or assets to the support being provided.[2] In these circumstances, the asylum seeker will be required to make payments directly to NASS.[3] Where support is provided with a requirement of a contribution by the asylum seeker, NASS may make it a condition of the provision of support that 'prompt payments' are made.[4]

1   Asylum Support Regulations 2000, SI 2000/704, reg 12(3).

2   SI 2000/704, reg 16(2).

3   SI 2000/704, reg 16(3).

4   SI 2000/704, reg 16(4).

National Health Service prescriptions/dental treatment/sight tests

13.103 When an application for asylum support is accepted, NASS will simultaneously issue the individual with an HC2 certificate entitling the holder to free NHS prescriptions, dental treatment, sight tests and wigs.[1] The asylum seeker may also be eligible for vouchers towards the costs of glasses, contact lenses and refunds on the costs of travel to and from hospital for NHS treatment.[2] Asylum seekers are currently entitled to the full range of NHS treatment free of charge.[3]

1   See NASS Policy *Bulletin 43 HC2 Certificates*.
2   See below, 13.198ff.
3   See below, 13.198ff.

Conditions

13.104 NASS may provide support subject to conditions.[1] Any conditions must be set out in writing[2] and given to the person who is being supported.[3] Breach of conditions upon which support is provided may be taken into account in deciding whether to provide or continue support and the level or kind of support provided.[4]

1   Immigration and Asylum Act 1999, s 95(9), see para 13.77 above.
2   IAA 1999, s 95(1).
3   IAA 1999, s 95(11).
4   Asylum Support Regulations 2000, SI 2000/704, reg 19.

Changes of circumstances

13.105 Supported persons are required to notify NASS of relevant changes in their circumstances.[1] NASS must be notified if the asylum seeker (or any dependant):[2]

- is joined in the UK by a dependant;
- receives or obtains access to any money or savings, investments, land, cars or other vehicles, or goods for the purposes of trade or other business which have not previously been declared to NASS;[3]
- becomes unemployed;
- changes his or her name;
- gets married;
- begins living with another person as if married to that person;
- gets divorced;
- separates from a spouse or from a person with whom they have been living as if married;
- becomes pregnant;
- has a child;
- leaves school;
- begins to share accommodation with another person;
- moves to a different address or otherwise leaves accommodation;
- goes into hospital;
- goes to prison or some other form of custody;
- leaves the UK; or
- dies.

Where, as a result of notification of a change in circumstances, NASS believes that asylum support should be provided for a person for whom it is not currently provided (for example a new dependant arriving or the birth of a child) or should not be provided for an existing recipient, or that asylum support is otherwise affected, it may make further inquiries to determine what support should now be provided.[4] It may change the nature or level of the existing support or provide or withdraw support.

1 Asylum Support Regulations 2000, SI 2000/704, reg 15(1).
2 SI 2000/704, reg 15(2).
3 See NASS Policy Bulletin 65 *Assessing Other Income or Capital that has Become Available to an Asylum-Seeker Supported under the Immigration and Asylum Act 1999 s 95.*
4 SI 2000/704, reg 15(3), (4).

Further applications for support

13.106 In most circumstances, there is nothing to prevent repeat claims for support and NASS must consider the application unless it is not made in the prescribed form,[1] or the person has previously had his or her support suspended or discontinued,[2] or the claim for asylum was not made as soon as reasonably practicable unless a failure to provide the claimant with NASS support would lead to a breach of the European Convention on Human Rights,[3] or a further application for support is made after an appeal to the Asylum Support Adjudicator is dismissed,[4] and there has been no 'material change in circumstances'.[5]

1 Asylum Support Regulations 2000, SI 2000/704, reg 3(3), (4).
2 SI 2000/704, reg 21.
3 Nationality, Immigration and Asylum Act 2002, s 55; *R (on the application of Q) v Secretary of State for the Home Department* [2003] EWCA Civ 364, [2004] QB 36.
4 Immigration and Asylum Act 1999, s 103(6).
5 SI 2000/704, reg 21; IAA 1999, s 103(6).

PREVENTING ABUSE

13.107 There are various safeguards to prevent abuse of the NASS scheme. First, there are the grounds on which people, although destitute, may be excluded from obtaining asylum support by their own conduct.[1] Secondly, criminal charges may be brought against persons who, in relation to asylum support, make false representations or produce false documents or information,[2] fail to notify a required change of circumstances,[3] delay or obstruct a person administering the support scheme,[4] fail to provide required information,[5] seek assistance or accommodation or further repatriation assistance under Schedule 3 to the NIAA 2002 without mentioning a previous claim for assistance or after repatriation by a local authority,[6] or fail, as a sponsor, to maintain a sponsored person who is then provided with asylum support.[7] Thirdly, there are ways to recover asylum support to which asylum seekers were not entitled.[8]

1 See 13.77ff above.
2 Immigration and Asylum Act 1999, ss 105(1)(a), (b), 106(1)(a), (b). For criminal offences relating to asylum support see 14.72 below.
3 IAA 1999, ss 105(1)(c), (d), 106(1)(c), (d).
4 IAA 1999, s 107(1)(a).
5 IAA 1999, s 107(1).
6 NIAA 2002, Sch 3, para 13(1), (2).

7   IAA 1999, s 108(1).
8   See para 13.110 below.

13.108 To detect and act on abuses of the system, NASS has a number of further powers. It may obtain a warrant from a justice of the peace (or, in Scotland, a sheriff) to enter premises provided as temporary or ordinary NASS support where there is reason to believe that the person/s who are supposed to be supported there are not in fact resident there or the accommodation is being used for other purposes, or other persons are residing there.[1] Reasonable force may be used to enter the accommodation with a warrant.[2] NASS may also require the owner or manager of property provided by way of ordinary NASS support[3] to provide information about the premises and those living there.[4] The power might be used to require landlords to notify the Secretary of State when an asylum seeker has left or is subletting property.[5] NASS may further require the Royal Mail, or others delivering post, to provide information about redirection requests.[6] Employers may be equired to provide information about employees. For further details on the Secretary of State's information-gathering powers, see 14.24–14.25 below. With the exception of the power to obtain information about the re-direction of mail, it is doubtful whether these powers apply to support under the interim scheme, and there is an argument that the criminal charges do not apply either,[7] although there may be other measures available in respect of interim support. The grounds on which persons may be excluded from interim support are described below, 13.133ff.

1   Immigration and Asylum Act 1999, s 125. See 14.17 below.
2   IAA 1999, s 125(3)(b).
3   This power does not extend to temporary NASS support because it relates only to accommodation which has been provided for 'supported persons' (IAA 1999, s 126(1)), defined in s 94(1) of the IAA 1999 as asylum seekers or their dependants in receipt of support under s 95.
4   IAA 1999, s 126. No regulations have been made under this section.
5   Explanatory Notes to the IAA 1999, para 126.
6   IAA 1999, s 127.
7   The criminal offences in ss 105–109 relate to support provided 'under Part VI' of the Immigration and Asylum Act 1999. Interim support is provided under Sch 9. Albeit certain of the key provisions of Part VI are applied to that support, it is not support which is provided 'under' Part VI. Similarly, the provisions relating to recovery, ss 112–114 IAA 1999, Sch 8, para 11(1) read with Asylum Support Regulations 2000, SI 2000/704, reg 17, refer to recovery of support under either or both s 95 and s 98 of the 1999 Act but not to interim support under Sch 9. Entry of premises (s 125) is only permitted in relation to support provided under s 95 or s 98, information from property owners may only be obtained in respect of persons who have been provided with ordinary NASS support (s 126(1) refers to 'supported persons' who are defined in s 94(1) as persons provided with support under s 95) but information about redirection relates to support under Part VI or for 'for any other purpose relating to the provision of support to asylum seekers' (see s 127(1)(c)), which may allow that power to be used in relation to interim support as well.

Eviction from accommodation

13.109 One of the government's aims was to ensure that the asylum support scheme is untrammelled by the procedural safeguards operating in the general law. So when the time comes for asylum support to be terminated, the legislation makes provision for tenancies or licences provided by way of asylum support to come to an end before they would have done in accordance with the general law. Thus, where asylum support is terminated for any reason, any tenancy or licence granted during the period of support is brought to an end at the end of the period specified in the 'notice to quit',[1] 'regardless of when it could otherwise be brought to an end'.[2] Notices to quit must be given in writing.[3]

[1] Seven days or less in the case of any termination of support other than due to the determination of the claim to asylum (Asylum Support Regulations 2000, SI 2000/704, reg 22(3)(a)); or where the termination of the support is due to the determination of the asylum claim, 14 days after the determination by the Secretary of State or 14 days after the time limit for further appeal expires (reg 22(3)(b)(i), (ii) read with Immigration and Asylum Act 1999, s 94(3), (4) and Sch 14, para 55 and SI 2000/704, regs 2(2), (3) and Asylum Support (Interim Provisions) Regulations 1999, SI 1999/3056, reg 2(6); or, in any case, less than seven days, when the 'circumstances of the case are such that that notice period is justified' (SI 2000/704, reg 22(4)).
[2] SI 2000/704, reg 22(1).
[3] SI 2000/704, reg 22(3), (4)(a).

Recovery of support

13.110 There are five circumstances in which support which has been provided may be recovered:

(1)   where a supported person is later able to realise assets held at the time of the support application;[1]
(2)   where a person was overpaid support as a result of an error;[2]
(3)   where a person obtained support as the result of a misrepresentation or failure to disclose a material fact;[3]
(4)   where it transpires that the supported person was not in fact destitute;[4]
(5)   recovery from a person who sponsored the stay in the UK of a person who subsequently resorted to asylum support.[5]

These circumstances are considered in more detail below, but the following general comments can be made. In the first two cases, the recovery is, at least initially, made directly by NASS, whereas in the last two cases NASS makes an application to the court (in the third case, to the county court and in the last, to the magistrates, or in Scotland, to the sheriff in either case).

[1] Asylum Support Regulations 2000, SI 2000/704, reg 17.
[2] Immigration and Asylum Act 1999, s 114.
[3] IAA 1999, s 112.
[4] SI 2004/704, reg 17A, inserted by SI 2005/11 from 5 February 2005.
[5] IAA 1999, s 113.

13.111 Overpayments made as a result of an error, misrepresentation or failure to disclose may be recovered under ordinary and temporary NASS support,[1] while recovery from realised assets or from a sponsor is available only under ordinary NASS support.[2] Where assets becoming realisable or where overpayment has been made in error, recovery may take the form of deductions from NASS support[3] or the sums may be recovered as a 'debt' due to NASS in ordinary court proceedings.[4] Where overpayment resulted from a misrepresentation or a failure to disclose or from a sponsor's default, recovery starts and ends with the courts.[5] NASS appears to have a discretion as to whether to pursue recovery of an overpayment in all cases.[6] A new sub-section of the Asylum Support Regulations makes provision for recovery of asylum support when it transpires that at any time during which asylum support was being provided, the recipient was not destitute. This is a catch-all category, obviating the necessity to apportion blame.[7]

[1] Immigration and Asylum Act 1999, ss 112(1)(b), 114(1).
[2] The former is referred to only in Asylum Support Regulations 2000, SI 2000/704, reg 17(3)(a), which does not refer to temporary support, and the enabling provisions refer solely to s 95: Sch 8, para 11(1); in the latter case, s 113(1)(b) refers only to s 95 (asylum support); cf ss 112(1)(b) and 114(1), which refer to both s 95 and s 98 (temporary asylum support). See also NASS Policy Bulletin 67 *Overpayments* V1.1
[3] The deductions themselves may only be made from NASS support: Immigration and Asylum Act 1999, s 114(4), Sch 8, para 11(2)(b), SI 2000/704, regs 17(4) and 18.
[4] IAA 1999, s 114(2), Sch 8, para 11(2)(a), (b); SI 2000/704, regs 17(4), 18.
[5] IAA 1999, ss 112–113.
[6] The discretion is explicit in IAA 1999, ss 113(2), 114(2) and SI 2000/704, reg 17(2), but must be inferred in respect of misrepresentation and failure to disclose in s 112.
[7] SI 2000/704, reg 17A, inserted by SI 2005/11 from 5 February 2005, reflecting Council Directive 2003/9/EC, Art 16.1(b).

Convertible assets

13.112 NASS may require the repayment of the value of any asylum support which has been provided if, at the time when the supported person applied for support, he or she had assets (in the UK or elsewhere) such as savings, investments, property or shares, which could not then be converted into money, but have become realisable since (even if they have not in fact been converted).[1] NASS may require repayment up to the total money value of the assets concerned or the total money value of all the support provided (whichever is less).[2]

[1] Immigration and Asylum Act 1999, Sch 8, para 11, Asylum Support Regulations 2000, SI 2000/704, reg 17(1). NASS has a discretion to recover less than the recoverable amount, see SI 2000/704, reg 17(2): '... a sum not exceeding'. It is unclear whether NASS can require a person who is no longer being supported to repay the value of the support, since these provisions contain no wording equivalent to s 114(2) (recovery of overpayments made in error from a person who is or has been a supported person).
[2] SI 2000/704, reg 17(2), (3), (5).

Recovery of overpayments of support as a result of error

13.113 NASS may require the repayment of any temporary support or asylum support which has been provided as a result of its own error,[1] up to the total money value of the overpayment.[2] For recovery of these overpayments (in contrast to the position with most social security benefits), there is no need for the supported person to be responsible for the overpayment or at fault in any way. The overpayment may be recovered even after support ends.[3]

[1] Immigration and Asylum Act 1999, s 114(1).
[2] IAA 1999, s 114(2).
[3] IAA 1999, s 114(2).

Recovery following misrepresentation or failure to disclose

13.114 If NASS determines that a person has received support (temporary or ordinary) as a result of a misrepresentation or failure to disclose a material fact, it may apply to a county court for an order that the person who made the misrepresentation or who was responsible for the failure to disclose, repay the amount.[1] Recovery may be made from any person who made the misrepresentation or failed to disclose, not only from the asylum seeker or dependant who received the support. The amount which the court can order repaid is the total money value of the support paid as a result of the misrepresentation or failure to disclose which would not otherwise have been provided.[2]

[1]   Immigration and Asylum Act 1999, s 112.
[2]   IAA 1999, s 112(2), (3).

Recovery from sponsor

13.115 Support may be recovered from a sponsor of a person in receipt of (ordinary) asylum support,[1] ie the person who gave a written undertaking for the purposes of the immigration rules to be responsible for the maintenance and accommodation of that person when he or she sought to enter or remain in the UK.[2] This form of recovery is intended to deal with the situation where a person obtains admission to the UK as a result of a sponsorship undertaking in a non-asylum capacity and then seeks to remain in the UK as a refugee and becomes entitled to asylum support during the process. The sponsor can only be made liable to make payments covering the period over which the undertaking has effect.[3] Thus, if a person is granted six months' visitor leave on the strength of an undertaking by a sponsor, and claims asylum (and obtains asylum support) after a month, the sponsor could be made liable to repay five months' support. If the same visitor claims asylum after five months, the liability of the sponsor would be limited to a month. If the visitor overstays and then claims asylum and support a year later, we suggest the sponsor is not liable, since no asylum support payment has been made over the period of the undertaking. The same applies if the visitor obtains leave to remain as a student (with no further undertaking) and then claims asylum and support; there would be no liability.

[1]   Immigration and Asylum Act 1999, s 113.
[2]   IAA 1999, s 113. For such undertakings see 13.7 above.
[3]   IAA 1999, s 113(1)(b).

13.116 The procedure for recovery is that NASS must make a complaint to a magistrates' court (in Scotland, a sheriff) for an order. The court may order the sponsor to make weekly payments to NASS of an amount which the court thinks appropriate having regard to all the circumstances of the case and, in particular, to the sponsor's own income.[1] The weekly sum must not be more than the weekly value of the support being provided to the asylum seeker.[2] The court may order repayment of support already paid before the date of the complaint but, if it does so, it must have regard to the sponsor's income during the period concerned rather than their current income.[3] The order can be enforced in the same way as a maintenance order.[4]

1   Immigration and Asylum Act 1999, s 113(3).
2   IAA 1999, s 113(4).
3   IAA 1999, s 113(5).
4   IAA 1999, s 113(6).

APPEALS UNDER THE NATIONAL ASYLUM SUPPORT SCHEME

Rights of appeal

13.117 There are rights of appeal against certain NASS decisions to an asylum support adjudicator, who is appointed by the Secretary of State.[1] The circumstances in which an asylum seeker or dependant may appeal are extremely limited. A person may only appeal if NASS decides that the person is not entitled to any support at all,[2] or terminates all support for reasons other than the person ceasing to be an asylum seeker.[3] An asylum seeker with minor dependants may also appeal against a decision by NASS to terminate his or her support following certification by the Secretary of State that he or she has failed to co-operate with steps to remove him or her from the United Kingdom.[4] The asylum support adjudicators have been at pains to stress that they have no jurisdiction to hear complaints about location of accommodation,[5] and the way the issue has come before them has been in appeals against termination of support for breach of conditions, where the breach is failing to attend or return to dispersed accommodation and appellants have argued that features of the location give rise to a reasonable excuse for the breach. However, the Court of Appeal has now held that as a matter of statutory construction, a right of appeal under section 103(2) of the 1999 Act only arises where the Secretary of State decides to stop providing support to an asylum seeker or his or her dependants, and not where a decision to provide support is conditional on the asylum claimant moving to a particular location, and the condition is not complied with.[6] This decision will affect families with children in particular, as NASS holds offers of accommodation open where there are minor dependants even if the family refuses to relocate to a dispersal area.[7] The Secretary of State has a power to introduce regulations permitting asylum seekers to appeal against a dispersal location,[8] but has not done so. See 13.78 above. There is no right of appeal against a decision that a person is not entitled to support by virtue of not having claimed asylum as soon as reasonably practicable.[9] The only means of challenging these decisions, or any decision relating to interim support, will be by way of judicial review.[10] It is accepted that in relation to appeals before an asylum support adjudicator the minimum standards of fairness set out in Article 6 ECHR apply.[11]

1   Immigration and Asylum Act 1999, s 103. Asylum support adjudicators constitute an independent tribunal for the purposes of Art 6 ECHR: *R (on the application of Husain) v Asylum Support Adjudicator* [2001] EWHC Admin 852, [2001] All ER (D) 107 (Oct); see 8.73 above.
2   IAA 1999, s 103(1). There is also an appeal against refusal of 'hard cases' support under s 4 (as to which see 13.175ff below): s 103(2A), inserted by the Asylum and Immigration (Treatment of Claimants, etc) Act 2004, s 10(4) from 31 March 2005 (SI 2005/372). Once accommodation centres (for which see 13.170ff below) are in use for asylum seekers, the appeals provisions will apply to refusal of support in an accommodation centre (NIAA 2002, s 17): s 103(1), (2) as substituted by the Nationality, Immigration and Asylum Act 2002, s 53 and AI(TC)A 2004, s 10(4) from a date to be appointed

3   IAA 1999, s 103(2), which becomes s 103(3) when the Nationality, Immigration and Asylum Act 2002, s 53 comes into force; where a decision is made to stop providing support the appeal may be made before support actually ends. These are referred to as qualification appeals and stoppage appeals respectively: see *Dogan* below.

4   Nationality, Immigration and Asylum Act 2002, Sch 3, para 7A, inserted by Asylum and Immigration (Treatment of Claimants etc) Act 2004, s 9. None of the other persons categorised in NIAA 2002, Sch 3 as being ineligible for support may appeal if the decision refusing support was made on or after 1 December 2004: AI(TC)A 2004 s 9(3), SI 2004/2999, Art 4 (transitional provisions).

5   ASA 00/09/0046; 00/09/0066; 00/10/0087; although adjudicators have directed NASS not to return asylum seekers to particular locations: ASA 00/07/0024, para 11.

6   *R (Secretary of State for the Home Department) v Chief Asylum Support Adjudicator and Dogan (Ahmet)* [2003] EWCA Civ 1673.

7   NASS Policy Bulletin 17 *Failure to Travel*, para 5.

8   Under IAA 1999, s 103(7) (which becomes new s 103A, and applies to location of support provided under s 4 ('hard cases support', when NIAA 2002, s 53 comes into force).

9   NIAA 2002, s 55(10).

10 The ECHR does not require that a merits appeal on the facts against all administrative decisions in respect of a person's civil rights: *Kaplan v United Kingdom* (1980) 4 EHRR 64 at para 61; *Bryan v United Kingdom* (1995) 21 EHRR 342, *W v United Kingdom* (1987) 10 EHRR 29. Concerns at the lack of appeal rights in s 55 cases were dismissed by the Court of Appeal in *R (on the application of Q) v Secretary of State for the Home Department* [2003] EWCA 364, [2004] QB 36, but the court indicated that the procedures for determining the claims were not Art 6-compliant. Since the judgment, procedures have been significantly revised.

11 *R (on the application of Husain) v Asylum Support Adjudicator* [2001] EWHC Admin 852, [2001] All ER (D) 107 (Nov); see also ASA 00/09/0063, ASA 00/10/0087 and ASA 00/10/0089. Concerns under Art 6 relate to the lack of legal aid for representation: *Airey v Ireland* (1979) 2 EHRR 305, ECtHR), particularly if appeals where an appellant's personal conduct are at issue are determined in the appellant's absence: *Muyldermans v Belgium* (1991) 15 EHRR 204, ECtHR at para 64.

Appeal procedures

13.118 The main emphasis in the rules on asylum support appeals is speed.[1] The appeal procedures set out in the rules are not detailed, but the adjudicator has a general power to give directions on matters connected with the appeal where he or she considers that it is in the interests of justice to do so.[2] In addition, a failure to comply with the rules does not automatically mean that the appeal or the decision on the appeal has no effect.[3] If, however, a party has been disadvantaged as a result of a failure to comply with the rules, the adjudicator must do whatever he or she can to reduce the disadvantage.[4] Appellants may be represented throughout the appeal procedure by any person whom they choose to represent them, whether legally qualified or not,[5] in which case, provided they are notified, relevant documents sent by NASS or the adjudicator to the appellant must be copied to the representative.[6]

1   See Immigration and Asylum Act 1999, s 104(3); Asylum Support Appeals (Procedure) (Amendment) Rules 2003, SI 2003/1735, Preamble.

2   SI 2000/541, r 14. The asylum support adjudicator has also used this power to direct NASS to expedite consideration of a second application for asylum support: ASA 00/06/0017.

3   SI 2000/541, r 19(1).

4   SI 2000/541, r 19(2). When an asylum seeker arrived too late for a hearing, having taken the specific train directed, the adjudicator used r 19, the interpretative provisions of s 3 of the Human Rights Act and fair hearing standards of ECHR, Art 6 to set aside the decision and re-list the appeal: ASA 00/11/0106.

5   SI 2000/541, r 2(2)(d), 15. The Housing and Immigration Group has now set up a 'duty solicitor' scheme, staffed by experienced volunteer solicitors and barristers, to assist claimants at hearings.
6   SI 2000/541, r 2(2)(c).

Notice of appeal

13.119 Any decision against which an appeal lies must be communicated by NASS by letter.[1] Notice of appeal must be sent so that it is received by the adjudicator no later than three days after the day on which the notice of the decision was received.[2] It is given by filling out the standard form which is issued by NASS or a self-made form substantially the same as the NASS form.[3] The standard form itself is attached to the Asylum Support Appeals (Procedure) (Amendment) Rules 2003.[4] The form must be signed by the appellant or his or her representative.[5] In particular, the form must contain details of the grounds of appeal and whether the appellant requires an oral hearing and if so, whether an interpreter would be required. The form must be completed in full and in English.[6] Any information or evidence which has not been submitted may be sent in with the form.[7]

1   The Asylum Support Regulations 2000, SI 2000/704, contain no express requirement that these decisions must be communicated by letter but the Asylum Support Appeals (Procedure) Rules 2000, SI 2000/541, assume that they will be: see definition of 'appeal bundle' and 'decision letter' in SI 2000/541, rr 2(1) and 3(3); see also NASS Policy Bulletin 23 *Asylum Support Appeals Process* V5.
2   SI 2000/541, r 3(3).
3   SI 2000/541, r 3(1), as amended by the Asylum Support Appeals (Procedure) (Amendment) Rules 2003, SI 2003/1735, reg 3.
4   SI 2003/1735, Sch. Any changes in the form require its re-issue as a new Schedule: SI 2000/541, r 3(1).
5   SI 2000/541, r 3(2).
6   SI 2000/541, r 3(1).
7   See form.

13.120 The adjudicator may be asked to extend the time limit for appealing, either before or after its expiry, but may only do so if: (i) it is in the interests of justice; and (ii) the asylum seeker or the representative could not comply with the time limit due to circumstances beyond their control.[1] The strength of the case is relevant to the question of whether it is in the interests of justice to extend time.[2] The second limb is more difficult to meet, as there needs to be some practical reason for the inability to submit a notice of appeal in time, for which the would-be appellant was not responsible. If an adjudicator refuses to extend time, the remedies will be either a new application for support or a judicial review of the refusal. It may or may not be possible in these circumstances to seek judicial review of the NASS decision.[3]

1   Asylum Support Appeals (Procedure) Rules 2000, SI 2000/541, rule 3(4). The asylum support adjudicators have so far applied a liberal approach to the extension of time, where an appellant appeared not to have had access to an interpreter (ASA 00/04/0003); where a notice of appeal was submitted with a page missing (ASA 00/06/0017); where NASS was unable to confirm that the decision had been sent by first class post (ASA 00/07/0021); where no reference to the right of appeal was contained in the decision letter, although the explanatory notes to the application forms said this would be the case (ASA 00/07/0030); and where there had been postal delays (ASA 00/08/0037).

2   See *R v Immigration Appeal Tribunal, ex p Mehta* [1976] Imm AR 38, CA, and 18.103
    below. In ASA 00/00/0056 no reasons for extending time were given, but the merits appear
    to have been relevant.
3   In judicial review proceedings, the court may refuse to interfere with the decision where an
    applicant has failed to exercise a statutory right of appeal. See chapter 18 below.

Preparation of the appeal bundle

13.121 On the same day that the adjudicator receives notice of appeal, or, if
that is not reasonably practicable, as soon as possible on the next day, the
adjudicator must fax a copy of the notice of appeal and any supporting
documents to NASS.[1] Two days after receipt of the notice of appeal, NASS
must deliver (by fax or hand) to the adjudicator and (by fax or first class post)
to the appellant, copies of the form on which support was claimed and any
supporting documentation which was attached to that form (where the appeal
is against a refusal as opposed to a withdrawal of support), the decision letter
refusing support, and any other evidence which NASS took into account in
refusing support.[2]

1   Asylum Support Appeals (Procedure) Rules 2000, SI 2000/541, r 4(1).
2   SI 2000/541, r 4(2), as amended by the Asylum Support Appeals (Procedure) (Amendment)
    Rules 2003, S1 2003/1735, para 4; see definition of 'appeal bundle' in r 2(1).

Decision of the adjudicator whether to hold a hearing of the appeal

13.122 On the day after NASS sends the documentation to the adjudicator,
the adjudicator must consider the documents, decide whether to hold an oral
hearing of the appeal or to determine it without a hearing and, in either case,
set a date for determination of the appeal.[1] If the adjudicator decides to hold
an oral hearing, he or she must, on the same day, notify NASS and the
appellant of the time, date and place of the hearing.[2] The adjudicator must
hold an oral hearing if it was requested in the notice of appeal, or if he or she
thinks it necessary to decide the appeal justly.[3] This would be the case where,
for example, the appellant disputed allegations about breach of conditions or
other conduct resulting in termination of support. The adjudicator may also
decide to hold an oral hearing of the appeal for any other reason.[4] Where an
oral hearing is decided upon, it must be held and the appeal determined within
five days of the decision to hold it.[5] If the adjudicator decides not to hold an
oral hearing, he or she must determine the appeal on the same day or 'as soon
as possible' thereafter and in any event within five days.[6]

1   Asylum Support Appeals (Procedure) Rules 2000, SI 2000/541, r 4(3)(a), (b), (4).
2   SI 2000/541, r 4(3)(c), (4), 7.
3   SI 2000/541, r 4(3), 5(1).
4   SI 2000/541, r 5(2).
5   SI 2000/541, r 6(1), as amended by the Asylum Support Appeals (Procedure) (Amendment)
    Rules 2003 SI 2003/1735, r 5.
6   SI 2000/541, r 6(2), as amended by the Asylum Support Appeals (Procedure) (Amendment)
    Rules 2003 SI 2003/1735, r 6.

Further evidence before determination of the appeal

13.123 If there is further evidence in support of the appeal, which was not submitted with the notice of appeal, it may be submitted subsequently for consideration by the adjudicator, within the extremely tight time limits above. The evidence must, at the same time, be sent to NASS.[1] If no oral hearing is to be held, the adjudicator will be determining the appeal, at most, five days after the notice of appeal was received. If NASS wishes to rely on any further evidence which was not submitted after it received the notice of appeal, it may submit it to the adjudicator before the appeal is determined, and must send it to the appellant at the same time.[2] The adjudicator may admit evidence showing a change in the appellant's circumstances since the NASS decision.[3]

[1]   Asylum Support Appeals (Procedure) Rules 2000, SI 2000/541, r 8(1), (2).
[2]   SI 2000/541, r 8(3), (4).
[3]   SI 2000/541, r 10(2).

Oral hearings

13.124 Oral hearings before the adjudicator generally take place in public,[1] although the adjudicator may exclude the public or particular persons from all or part of the hearing if he or she considers it in the public interest.[2] The appellant's interests or desire for the appeal to be heard in private is not decisive. There are no rules setting out the procedure to be adopted at the oral hearing, and the adjudicator has a broad discretion, but fairness requires that appellants are allowed to give oral evidence, call witnesses in support,[3] question any witnesses relied on by NASS, and address the adjudicator on the law and the facts (by themselves or their representatives). If witnesses are called, the adjudicator may require that their evidence is given under oath or affirmation.[4] NASS should meet an appellant's reasonable travelling expenses to attend the oral hearing.[5] If either party adduces new evidence at the hearing, the other party must be given the opportunity of looking at that evidence and photocopying it in order to comment on it.[6] If the appellant fails to attend despite notification of the date, time and place of the hearing, or indicated in the notice of appeal that he or she did not wish to attend or be represented at the hearing, the appeal may be heard in the absence of the appellant.[7] The appeal may also go ahead in the absence of a NASS representative.[8] The adjudicator must ensure that a written record is made of the proceedings.[9] Appellants may obtain a refund of their travel costs for attending an asylum support appeal.[10]

[1]   Asylum Support Appeals (Procedure) Rules 2000, SI 2000/541, r 12(1).
[2]   SI 2000/541, r 12(2).
[3]   SI 2000/541, r 10(5) assumes that witnesses may be called.
[4]   SI 2000/541, r 10(4).
[5]   Immigration and Asylum Act 1999, s 103(9).
[6]   Asylum Support Appeals (Procedure) Rules 2000, SI 2000/541, r 10(6).
[7]   SI 2000/541, r 9(1), (2).
[8]   SI 2000/541, r 9(3).
[9]   SI 2000/541, r 11.

¹⁰   NASS Policy Bulletin 56: *reimbursing asylum seekers' essential travel costs*, V 1.2; ASA 00/07/0027, para 3. NIAA 2002, s 103B inserted by NIAA 2002, s 53 in force from a date to be appointed, provides a statutory foundation for the Secretary of State's obligation to pay reasonable travelling expenses to enable an appellant to attend an asylum support appeal.

Decision and reasons

13.125 Whether an appeal is dealt with orally or without a hearing, the adjudicator must give reasons for his or her decision in writing.[1] On an oral hearing, the adjudicator must inform the parties of the decision at the end of the hearing.[2] If a party is neither present nor represented at the hearing, the adjudicator must send notice of the decision to that party on the day the appeal is heard.[3] Whether or not the parties attended, the adjudicator must send them a statement containing reasons for the decision no later than three days after the hearing.[4] If no oral hearing is held, the adjudicator must send notice of the decision, with a statement of reasons, on the day the appeal is determined.[5] Asylum support adjudicators are not bound by their own decisions.[6]

1   Immigration and Asylum Act 1999, s 103(4).
2   Asylum Support Appeals (Procedure) Rules 2000, SI 2000/541, r 13(1).
3   SI 2000/541, r 13(1)(b) and (d).
4   SI 2000/541, r 13(1)(d), (4), as amended by the Asylum Support Appeals (Procedure) (Amendment) Rules 2003, SI 2003/1735, r 7.
5   SI 2000/541, r 13(2), (4).
6   ASA 00/08/0034, para 14.

Evidence and burden of proof

13.126 In deciding the appeal, the adjudicator may take into account any changes of circumstances since the decision.[1] There are no rules on who bears the burden of proof in asylum support appeals but, applying ordinary legal principles, the person who makes a particular assertion must prove it. The burden may, therefore, rest with the person claiming support to establish matters such as destitution, but if NASS has sought to exclude someone from support despite prima facie entitlement, it should establish the ground of exclusion.[2] The asylum support adjudicators have generally applied the balance of probabilities as the appropriate standard of proof,[3] although arguably a higher civil standard applies where NASS alleges particularly egregious conduct in breach of conditions, or an offence under Part VI of the Immigration and Asylum Act 1999, in order to exclude a person from support.[4]

1   Asylum Support Appeals (Procedure) Rules 2000, SI 2000/541, r 10(2).
2   ASA/02/10/4566.
3   See eg ASA 00/04/0003.
4   Asylum Support Regulations 2000, SI 2000/704, regs 19, 20.

Adjudicators' powers

13.127 On deciding the appeal, the asylum support adjudicator may require NASS to reconsider the question of whether the appellant should be provided with support, replace the NASS decision with his or her own decision or dismiss the appeal so that the decision of NASS stands.[1] The extent of the asylum support adjudicators' powers is not specified in the 1999 Act, in contrast to ordinary immigration judges, but it is clear that they must apply the provisions of the Act and the asylum support regulations, and they have also shown themselves willing to consider whether decisions are in accordance with the Secretary of State's policy, as set out, inter alia, in the NASS Policy *Bulletins.*[2] Asylum support adjudicators have endeavoured to ensure that their decisions do not constitute or adopt a breach of the appellant's human rights, by, for example, considering whether the termination of support following breach of conditions will leave an appellant exposed to levels of suffering which would engage ECHR, Article 3, or breach rights to home and physical integrity under ECHR, Article 8.[3] In one case an adjudicator allowed an appeal with reference to ECHR, Article 3 (in the context of reasonable excuse for breach of conditions) where an appellant with heart trouble had to go without food if he missed the hostel meals which were provided at rigidly enforced times.[4]

[1] Immigration and Asylum Act 1999, s 103(3).
[2] ASA 00/09/0044; 00/09/0049; 00/11/0095.
[3] See eg ASA 00/10/0089.
[4] ASA 00/11/0106.

13.128 The adjudicator's decision is effective from the day on which it is made.[1] Therefore, where the parties are notified at the hearing that the appeal has been successful, NASS must, as far as possible, take immediate steps to implement the decision rather than wait for the written reasons. It is not apparent from the legislation whether the adjudicator should focus on the date of the NASS decision or the date of hearing. The power to require NASS to reconsider the decision suggests the latter.[2] There are no express rules as to the backdating of support or compensating an asylum seeker who has been without support as a result of an erroneous earlier decision.[3] The interim period will be very short but where no temporary support has been provided during that period, NASS should presumably take into account the effect of being without support for that period in meeting the asylum seeker's current needs.

[1] Asylum Support Appeals (Procedure) Rules 2000, SI 2000/541, r 13(3).
[2] See Immigration and Asylum Act 1999, s 103(3)(a). But see ASA 00/10/0071, where an adjudicator dismissed an appeal on destitution although by the time of the decision the appellant's capital would have diminished sufficiently to qualify. See also ASA 00/11/0105, paras 9 and 15.
[3] Although the asylum support adjudicator has held that an asylum seeker is legally entitled to amounts due from the date of the asylum application subject to deduction for backdated social security benefit: ASA 01/02/0202, paras 4 and 14; but see also *R v Hammersmith London Borough Council, ex p Isik* (19 September 2000, unreported), CA.

Procedures following an appeal

13.129 There is no further appeal against the decision of the asylum support adjudicator and no provision for a review by the adjudicator.[1] A party dissatisfied with a decision of an asylum support adjudicator must proceed by way of judicial review.[2] If the appeal is dismissed, NASS may not consider any further application for support from the appellant unless it thinks that there has been a 'material' change of circumstances.[3] Relevant changes would include, but are not limited to, those about which a supported asylum seeker must notify NASS.[4]

[1] Immigration and Asylum Act 1999, s 103(5).
[2] There have been a number of challenges on behalf of the Secretary of State to decisions by the asylum support adjudicator: see eg *R (on the application of the Secretary of State for the Home Department) v Chief Asylum Support Adjudicator* [2003] EWHC 269 (Admin), [2003] All ER (D) 116 (Feb); *R (on the application of the Secretary of State for the Home Department) (National Asylum Support Service) v Asylum Support Adjudicators* [2001] EWHC Admin 881, [2001] All ER (D) 13 (Nov); *R (Secretary of State for the Home Department) v Chief Asylum Support Adjudicator and Dogan (Ahmet)* [2003] EWCA Civ 1673.
[3] IAA 1999, s 103(6), to become s 103(7) when Nationality, Immigration and Asylum Act 2002, s 53 is in force, as amended by Asylum and Immigration (Treatment of Claimants, etc) Act 2004, s 10(4)(c) when in force to include support in accommodation centres).
[4] See Asylum Support Regulations 2000, SI 2000/704, reg 15. Other relevant changes might include disentitlement to social security benefits by refusal of an asylum claim.

Ending the appeal by withdrawal

13.130 An appellant may decide at any stage not to proceed with an appeal, in which case NASS and the adjudicator should be notified as soon as possible.[1] If NASS decides at any time to withdraw the decision against which the appeal is brought, it must notify the appellant and the adjudicator as soon as possible.[2] In either case, the appeal is treated as having come to an end.[3] On the face of the regulation, if NASS withdraws its decision, it is required to make a fresh decision on the application for support, which may be the subject of a further appeal. But in one case[4] the adjudicator treated the further decision as an amendment of the earlier one, so avoiding the delay created by the need to lodge a further appeal.[5]

[1] Asylum Support Appeals (Procedure) Rules 2000, SI 2000/541, r 16(2).
[2] SI 2000/541, r 16(1).
[3] SI 2000/541, r 16(3).
[4] ASA 00/11/0116.
[5] Such delay could deprive the appellant of the right to a hearing within a reasonable time required by ECHR, Art 6, read with Human Rights Act 1998, s 3.

INTERIM SUPPORT SCHEME

13.131 Designed as a temporary stop-gap, the interim scheme for the support of asylum seekers had effect from 6 December 1999[1] and operates during what has been called the 'interim period'[2] which now runs to 4 April 2006.[3] The Secretary of State for the Home Department took steps between April and

September 2000 to give responsibility to NASS for the support of asylum seekers who would otherwise have made initial applications for support to local authorities under the interim scheme.[4] The interim scheme does not extend to Scotland or Northern Ireland[5] and the community care provisions under which asylum seekers were supported continued in those countries until the introduction of the NASS scheme in April 2000. The local authorities which may owe duties under the interim scheme are, therefore,[6] in England: a county council, metropolitan district council, a district council, a London borough council, the Common Council of the City of London and the Council of the Isles of Scilly and, in Wales, a county council or a county borough council.

[1]   The provisions enabling the scheme came into force on 11 November 1999, the day the Immigration and Asylum Act 1999 received Royal Assent (see s 170(3)(g), (r)), the duty upon local authorities to provide support for destitute asylum seekers was introduced from 6 December 1999: see Immigration and Asylum Act 1999 (Commencement No 1) Order 1999, SI 1999/3190, Sch, Art 2, commencing s 95(3)–(8) of the 1999 Act for the purposes of the interim scheme and Asylum Support (Interim Provisions) Regulations 1999, SI 1999/3056, reg 1(1).
[2]   Immigration and Asylum Act 1999, Sch 9, paras 1(1), 15.
[3]   Asylum Support (Interim Provisions) (Amendment) Regulations 2005, SI 2005/.595
[4]   See 13.159ff below.
[5]   SI 1999/3056, reg 1(2).
[6]   SI 1999/3056, reg 2(1).

13.132 To be entitled to support under the interim scheme, an asylum seeker must satisfy the general conditions of entitlement,[1] be eligible for interim support as opposed to NASS support,[2] and must not be excluded from interim support.[3]

[1]   See 13.39–13.51 above.
[2]   See 13.159ff below.
[3]   See Asylum Support (Interim Provisions) Regulations 1999, SI 1999/3056, regs 7 and 8.

Exclusions from interim support

13.133 Overall, it is intended to exclude from interim support persons able to obtain other forms of support; persons who are, in truth, the responsibility of another authority; and persons whose conduct disqualifies them. An authority *must* refuse support to the following persons:[1]

- persons who are 'intentionally destitute';
- persons who have made a claim for support to another authority;
- persons who have made a claim for support to an authority other than one from which, in the previous year, they sought assistance under section 21 of the National Assistance Act 1948 or section 17 of the Children Act 1989;
- certain persons who are not prevented from getting income support because of their immigration status;
- persons whom the Home Office is not treating as asylum seekers or as dependent on the asylum claim of another for immigration purposes;
- Citizens of other EEA States and refugees who have been granted status in such states unless this would lead to a breach of their rights under the European Convention on Human Rights.[2]

An authority *may* suspend or discontinue support to the following:

- persons who fail, without reasonable excuse, to comply with the conditions on which the support is provided;
- persons who, without reasonable excuse, leave the accommodation in which support is granted for more than seven days.

Some of these exclusions mirror the exclusions from NASS set out at 13.68–13.89 above. The grounds for exclusion are dealt with separately below but some general comments can be made. The last two refer to people who have already been granted support by the local authority. In those cases withdrawal of support is discretionary[3] and may be temporary (suspension) or indefinite (discontinuance).[4] For example, an authority might suspend the provision of support until the asylum seeker has remedied the breach of conditions or returned to their accommodation. All the other categories of exclusion appear mandatory rather than discretionary in their operation. They provide that in such cases support must be refused, but they do not appear to allow support to be withdrawn once provided,[5] unless the authority then becomes aware of disqualifying circumstances which were unknown at the time of the decision to provide support.[6] The authority may not be able to rely on disqualifying circumstances which it knew, or perhaps which it ought with reasonable diligence to have known, nor on matters that arise after support has been provided.[7] For example, if the authority discovers, after providing support, that the asylum seeker had failed to take up a reasonable job offer and so was 'intentionally destitute' when he or she applied for support, it can rely on this to withdraw support, but if it knew this when it provided support, it should not be able to withdraw support later on that basis. If the asylum seeker fails to take a reasonable job offer after support is provided, the authority cannot withdraw support on the ground of intentional destitution.[8] Further, arguably a person cannot be declared intentionally destitute on the basis of conduct which took place before the interim scheme came into effect.[9]

1 Asylum Support (Interim Provisions) Regulations 1999, SI 1999/3056, regs 7(1), 8. These provisions have not been amended, as have the NASS regulations (SI 2000/704, reg 20) to secure their compliance with the EC Reception Conditions Directive.
2 Nationality, Immigration and Asylum Act 2002, Sch 3, paras 3–5.
3 Contrast SI 1999/3056, reg 8(2)(a) 'Support may be suspended or discontinued' with Reg 7(1)(a) 'support must be refused' where other exclusions apply.
4 SI 1999/3056, reg 8(2).
5 See the wording of SI 1999/3056, reg 7(1).
6 SI 1999/3056, regs 8(1) and 7(3).
7 SI 1999/3056, regs 8(1) and 7(3).
8 SI 1999/3056, regs 7(1), (3), 8(1), which do not admit of circumstances post-dating the granting of support forming the basis of exclusion of support, although the authority could argue that the person is no longer destitute, having the means of obtaining accommodation (Immigration and Asylum Act 1999, s 95(3)(a)) or support/assets reasonably expected to be available to them (SI 1999/3056, reg 6(1)(b)).
9 *Fetiti v Islington London Borough Council* (C/OO/2748) (19 October 2000, unreported), per Laws LJ, CA (permission hearing, case subsequently settled).

Intentional destitution

13.134 Where a person has intentionally made himself or herself and any dependants destitute, he or she is to be refused support.[1] The meaning of intentional destitution is that used in homelessness law. This is no longer a valid ground for suspension or discontinuance of support under the EC Reception Conditions Directive.[2] Refusal of interim support on this ground would therefore be unlawful, since the Directive takes direct effect in the UK.

[1]   Asylum Support (Interim Provisions) Regulations 1999, SI 1999/3056, reg 7(1)(a).
[2]   Council Directive 2003/9/EC, in force 5 February 2005.

A claim for support to another local authority

13.135 If a person claims support from one local authority and then makes a claim to another authority, the second authority must refuse support.[1] This rule is intended to prevent 'shopping around' between authorities. The exclusion rule clearly does not apply if one authority transfers a claim for support to another local authority.[2]

[1]   Asylum Support (Interim Provisions) Regulations 1999, SI 1999/3056, reg 7(1)(b).
[2]   SI 1999/3056, reg 9.

A previous National Assistance Act or Children Act claim to another authority

13.136 If in the 12 months before the claim for interim support, the asylum seeker has claimed assistance from a different local authority under either section 21 of the National Assistance Act 1948 or section 17 of the Children Act 1989, the second local authority must refuse the claim for interim support.[1] This does not mean that the asylum seeker will not be entitled to support at all, merely that the claim for interim support must be made instead to an authority from which the assistance was earlier claimed.

[1]   Asylum Support (Interim Provisions) Regulations 1999, SI 1999/3056, reg 7(1)(c).

Immigration status does not preclude income support

13.137 The purpose of this exclusion is apparently to prevent those who are asylum seekers for support purposes from getting interim support when they may obtain income support (and housing benefit and council tax benefit).[1] As with NASS, persons falling into this category could also be excluded on the basis that they are not 'destitute'.[2] The regulations do not exclude from access to interim support all the possible categories of asylum seekers who might be able to obtain these benefits. The situations not accounted for are set out at 13.73 above. The rules for exclusion from interim support on this basis[3] are more complicated than the equivalent rules under NASS support.[4]

[1]   See Social Security (Immigration and Asylum) Consequential Amendments Regulations 2000, SI 2000/636, regs 2(1), (4)(a), 12(6)–(8), Sch, Part 1, para 4 (formerly Housing Benefit (General) Regulations 1987, SI 1987/1971, reg 7A(3)(a), Council Tax Benefit (General) Regulations 1992, SI 1992/1814, reg 4A(3)(a).
[2]   Because they have the 'means of obtaining' adequate accommodation and essential living needs: Immigration and Asylum Act 1999, s 95(3); additionally, the authority must have regard to any income or assets which the asylum seeker 'might reasonably be expected to have': reg 6(1)(b).

3   SI 1999/3056, reg 7(1)(d).
4   Asylum Support Regulations 2000, SI 2000/704, reg 4(4), (6), see 13.73 above.

13.138 The regulations are poorly drafted. The intention is to exclude from interim support persons defined as 'asylum seekers' for benefit purposes who remain entitled to benefit, and nationals of states which have signed the European Convention on Social and Medical Assistance (ECSMA) or the Council of Europe Social Charter (CESC). These categories are dealt with separately below. Unhelpfully, the definitions used in the interim support regulations refer to welfare benefits regulations which have now been repealed.[1] A literal reading would mean that no-one could be excluded from interim support on this basis. But since the definitions have been repeated with minor modifications in more recent regulations, the interim support regulations must probably be read as referring to the definitions in the later regulations.[2] This is reasonable where there is only minor modification ('asylum seekers' refer to those who claimed prior to 2 April 2000 in the later regulations).[3] But for nationals of signatory states to ECSMA or CESC, the change is not so minor. To obtain income support (and so be excluded from interim support) their state must now not merely have signed but also ratified ECSMA or CESC,[4] and instead of having leave subject to a 'no recourse to public funds' condition, they need only be lawfully present in the UK.[5] The difficulty for these nationals is that, although they may not be excluded from income support by their *immigration status*, they may still be unable to access income support even though they are destitute,[6] and may access income-based jobseeker's allowance[7] instead only if, as asylum seekers, they have been given permission to work by the Home Office and so are available for and actively seeking employment.[8] These nationals could therefore find themselves excluded from both social security and interim support.

1   The Income Support (General) Regulations 1987, SI 1987/1967, reg 70 (definition of asylum seeker) has been repealed by Social Security (Immigration and Asylum) Consequential Amendments Regulations 2000, SI 2000/636, reg 3(7)(c), and SI 1987/1967, reg 21(3)(a) (exemption from the definition of 'persons from abroad' for certain nationals of states signatory to the European Convention on Social and Medical Assistance or the Council of Europe Social Charter) by SI 2000/636, reg 3(4)(b).
2   See Bennion *Statutory Interpretation* (3rd edn) at p 230, s 21; *Britnell v Secretary of State for Social Security* [1991] 2 All ER 726 as to the meaning of 'modification'.
3   SI 2000/636, reg 12(3)–(5) (transitional provisions).
4   For a list of non-EEA states which have ratified the Convention and the Charter see 13.12 above.
5   SI 1987/1967, reg 21(3)(a); SI 2000/636, Sch, para 4.
6   These nationals appear to be excluded from the 'prescribed categories' of people who may claim income support: Social Security Contributions and Benefits Act 1992, s 124(1)(e), SI 1987/1967, reg 4ZA(1) and para 21 (as amended), referring to the persons to whom SI 1987/1967, reg 70(2A) applies. Persons to whom SI 2000/636, Sch, Part 1, para 4 applies (nationals of ratifying states to the European Convention on Social and Medical Assistance or the Council of Europe Social Charter) are excluded.
7   SI 2000/636, reg 2(1), Sch, Part 1, para 4.
8   Jobseekers Act 1995, s 1(2).

Asylum seekers for benefit purposes

13.139 Persons who are 'asylum seekers' for the purposes of income support and therefore able to claim income support are not entitled to support under the interim scheme.[1] This can only apply to people who claimed asylum on or before 3 April 2000.[2] The definition of 'asylum seekers' for these purposes is identical to that in the NASS scheme and is set out at 13.39 above.

[1]   Asylum Support (Interim Provisions) Regulations 1999, SI 1999/3056, reg 7(1)(d).
[2]   This is because the Income Support (General) Regulations 1987, 1987/1967 have been amended so that the only persons who remain asylum seekers for income support purposes are those who were asylum seekers for those purposes before 3 April 2000; see Social Security (Immigration and Asylum) Consequential Amendments Regulations 2000, SI 2000/636, regs 2(4)(a), 3(7)(a)–(c), 12(4), (5); Social Security (Persons from Abroad) Miscellaneous Amendments Regulations 1996, SI 1996/30, reg 12(1).

Nationals of states signatories of the European Convention on Social and Medical Assistance or the Council of Europe Social Charter

13.140   The regulations exclude from interim support those able to access benefit by being exempted from the definition of 'persons from abroad' in the income support regulations.[1] These were defined as nationals of a state which has signed the European Convention on Social and Medical Assistance or the Council of Europe Social Charter, who have leave to enter or remain in the UK subject to a condition that they have no recourse to public funds.[2] The new exemption from the definition of 'persons from abroad' refers to nationals of states which have *ratified* ECSMA or CESC, not simply signed it, who are 'lawfully present' (broader than 'having leave to remain') in the UK.[3] It is not at all clear whether the regulations cover those who fall into the new or the old definition or whether they manage to cover persons falling into both.

[1]   Asylum Support (Interim Provisions) Regulations 1999, SI 1999/3056, reg 7(1)(d)(iii).
[2]   Income Support (General) Regulations 1987, SI 1987/1967, reg 21(3)(a).
[3]   Social Security (Immigration and Asylum) Consequential Amendments Regulations 2000, SI 2000/636, reg 2(1), Sch, para 4. See 13.139 above. Past asylum claimants on temporary admission have been held not to be lawfully present 'for this purpose': *Kaya v Haringey London Borough Council* [2001] EWCA Civ 677, [2001] All ER (D) 15 (May); *Szoma v Secretary of State for Work and Pensions* [2003] EWCA Civ 1131, [2003] All ER (D) 530 (Jul).

Persons the Home Office are not treating as asylum seekers or as dependants on a claim for asylum

13.141   Where the Home Office does not accept that a person is an asylum seeker or his or her dependant for the purpose of an asylum claim, the local authority must refuse interim support.[1] This exclusion is identical to that under the NASS scheme, set out at 13.74 above. It may well be important where a fresh claim is made which the Home Office does not accept as such,[2] as well as where the dependants for support purposes[3] do not match those accepted by the Home Office for the purposes of the asylum claim. An unmarried common-law partner who has been living with the asylum seeker for two of the last three years, for example, is a 'dependant' for support purposes[4] but not for the purposes of the asylum claim,[5] unless discretion is exercised in his or her favour.

[1]   Asylum Support (Interim Provisions) Regulations 1999, SI 1999/3056, reg 7(1)(e).
[2]   See 13.40 above.

3   See 13.46 above.
4   SI 1999/3056, reg 2(1)(f).
5   See HC 395, para 349.

Persons who fail to comply with conditions on which the support is provided

13.142 The local authority, like NASS, may provide support subject to conditions,[1] which similarly must be in writing[2] and given to the person who is being supported.[3] The regulations permit local authorities to suspend or discontinue support for breach of those conditions by the asylum seeker or a dependant.[4] However, although the regulations have not been amended in line with the EC Reception Conditions Directive, Council Directive 2003/9/EC, suspension or discontinuance of support for breach of conditions other than those set out in the Directive is unlawful, since the Directive has direct effect in domestic law even if not transposed. The only lawful grounds for suspension or discontinuance of support by local authorities are those set out in the Directive, which have been transposed into the NASS regulations. See 13.75ff above.

1   Asylum Support (Interim Provisions) Regulations 1999, SI 1999/3056, reg 5(6). Para 6A of Sch 9 to the IAA 1999 (inserted by Nationality, Immigration and Asylum Act 2002, s 50(2)) enables regulations to impose a condition of compliance with restrictions on temporary admission or release under Immigration Act 1971, Sch 2 or 3, but the regulations have not been amended to impose such a requirement.
2   SI 1999/3056, reg 5(7).
3   SI 1999/3056, reg 5(8).
4   SI 1999/3056, reg 8(2).

Persons who leave the accommodation on which support is granted for more than seven days

13.143 The Interim Support Regulations provide that support may be suspended or discontinued if an asylum seeker, or any dependant, leaves the accommodation provided as part of such support for more than seven consecutive days without reasonable excuse.[1] The regulations have not been amended to comply with Council Directive 2003/9/EC on reception conditions for asylum seekers. These permit the reduction or withdrawal of support only where an asylum seeker abandons the place of residence allotted, and absence for seven days is unlikely to constitute abandonment. Local authorities seeking to rely on the regulations rather than the Directive to discontinue support are likely to be acting unlawfully. See 13.80 above.

1   Asylum Support (Interim Provisions) Regulations 1999, SI 1999/3056, reg 8(2)(b).

Procedures for obtaining interim support

13.144 The regulations do not prescribe any particular procedures for applying for and obtaining interim support or for reviewing decisions relating to entitlement.

Claims and decision relating to interim support

13.145 The scheme requires a claim for support to be made to a local authority[1] but does not specify how. 'Claim' suggests an active process and it is unlikely that an authority has duties to persons who come to its attention otherwise than by making an application.[2] The authority has a responsibility to determine whether a person claiming support is an 'eligible person', namely he or she is an asylum seeker or the dependant of one and is destitute.[3]

[1]   See eg Immigration and Asylum Act 1999, Sch 9, paras 2(2), 9(6), 10(1), 12; Asylum Support (interim Provisions) Regulations 1999, SI 1999/3056, regs 3(3), 4(2), 9. The Secretary of State has not used the powers under the Immigration and Asylum Act 1999, Sch 9, para 12 to make rules about how to claim support and how claims for support will be determined.
[2]   SI 1999/3056, reg 3(3).
[3]   SI 1999/3056, reg 2(1), 3(2), (3).

13.146

If the asylum seeker is eligible for support and not excluded from support or entitled to apply for NASS rather than interim support, then, if the local authority cannot transfer the claim for support to another local authority, it must provide support.[1] If the authority transfers the claim for support to another local authority, it need not decide whether the person is eligible for support or not. That decision, and the duty to provide support if eligibility is determined,[2] become the responsibility of the authority to whom the claim for support has been transferred.[3] Pending a decision on eligibility for support or transfer to another authority, the local authority must provide temporary support.[4]

[1]   Asylum Support (Interim Provisions) Regulations 1999, SI 1999/3056, reg 3(1).
[2]   SI 1999/3056, reg 3(1).
[3]   SI 1999/3056, reg 3(1)–(3),
[4]   SI 1999/3056, reg 4, see 13.150 below.

13.147 There are no rights of appeal to an independent body against decisions concerning interim support.[1] Because the availability of adequate support is fundamental to the ability of asylum seekers to pursue their claims for asylum,[2] authorities must proceed with a high degree of care, thoroughness and with high standards of fairness in making their decisions.[3] In particular, if an authority conducting inquiries into the circumstances of applicants comes across matters of particular concern which will affect the decision whether and how to provide support, it should put them to the applicants or their advisers for their comments or explanations before taking a decision.[4] Procedural fairness is particularly important where the authority believes that the asylum seeker has more resources available than have been disclosed, and on matters such as suspected offences and breach of conditions. Although the regulations do not stipulate that reasons for a decision refusing support are required, it is likely that the courts will impose such a duty because of the nature and subject matter of the decision.[5]

[1]   This may raise issues as to whether the scheme complies with ECHR, Art 6, see 13.117 fnn 2 and 6 above.

² See *R v Secretary of State for Social Security, ex p Joint Council for the Welfare of Immigrants* [1997] 1 WLR 275, CA.
³ See *Secretary of State for the Home Department v Thirukumar* [1989] Imm AR 402, CA; *Re Musisi* [1987] AC 514.
⁴ The general legal principle that fair decision-making requires that a person must have a proper opportunity of being heard before a decision affecting their interests is made, has been applied in the field of social welfare law: see *R v Gravesham Borough Council, ex p Winchester* (1986) 18 HLR 207 at 214; *R v Wyre Borough Council, ex p Joyce* (1983) 11 HLR 73; *R v Nottingham City Council, ex p Edwards* (1999) 31 HLR 33.
⁵ See *R v Higher Education Funding Council, ex p Institute of Dental Surgery* [1994] 1 WLR 242.

Reviewing support

13.148 The regulations do not deal with how support decisions may be reviewed following a change in circumstances after the award of support. But since the authority is only required to provide support for an asylum seeker who is destitute or likely to become destitute within 14 days[1] and it is for the authority to determine this issue,[2] it is implicit that an authority may review the question of destitution if there is a relevant change of circumstances – if, for example, the asylum seeker finds work. The changes which are likely to be material will be similar to those which a person supported by NASS is required to notify.[3] Similarly, where the resources available to an asylum seeker have increased (or decreased) although he or she remains within the definition of destitution,[4] it is implicit that the authority may review the nature and the level of support provided.[5] The local authority may also review the support provided if it appears that there are grounds to discontinue or to suspend support, in accordance with the procedural guarantees provided by Council Directive 2003/9/EC on reception conditions for asylum seekers, see 13.76 above.

¹ Immigration and Asylum Act 1999, Sch 9, para 1(1), (2); Asylum Support (Interim Provisions) Regulations 1999, SI 1999/3056, regs 2(1), 3(1.)
² IAA 1999, Sch 9, para 2(1); SI 1999/3056, reg 3(2).
³ See 13.105 above.
⁴ IAA 1999, s 95(3), Sch 9, para 3; see 13.50, 13.60ff above.
⁵ This is also implicit from the wording of SI 1999/3056, reg 5(1)(a), (b).

Determining destitution

13.149 The general common criteria relating to destitution are set out at 13.50 above. Unlike the NASS scheme, no additional rules have been made under the interim scheme prescribing what may or may not be taken into account in deciding whether a person cannot meet their essential living needs.[1] However, under the statute, in determining whether a person has adequate accommodation, no account may be taken of the fact that the asylum seeker has no legal right to stay there, or that the accommodation or part of it is shared with other persons; or that it is temporary, or its location.[2]

¹ The Secretary of State has not used his rule-making powers for these purposes (Immigration and Asylum Act 1999, Sch 9, para 3). Contrast the NASS rules; see 13.60ff above.
² Immigration and Asylum Act 1999, s 95(5)(6), as applied to the interim scheme by Sch 9, para 3.

Temporary interim support

13.150 An authority to which a claim for support has been made[1] or transferred[2] is under a duty to provide temporary support pending its decision on transfer or eligibility for support. Temporary support must be adequate to meet the needs of the applicant and his or her dependants.[3] It may include accommodation, essential living needs and any other necessary support.[4]

[1] Asylum Support (Interim Provisions) Regulations 1999, SI 1999/3056, reg 4(2)(a).
[2] SI 1999/3056, reg 4(1), (2)(b).
[3] SI 1999/3056, reg 4(3); 'dependants' has the same meaning as in interim support: SI 1999/3056, reg 2(1).
[4] See below.

Provision of interim support

Forms of support provided

13.151 An authority is bound to provide to destitute asylum seekers[1] accommodation which appears to the local authority to be adequate for them and their dependants (if any), and support to meet what appear to be the essential living needs of the asylum seeker and their dependants and to meet reasonable travel expenses incurred in attending interviews with the Home Office concerning the asylum application and the hearing of an asylum appeal. The requirements of Council Directive 2003/9/EC on reception conditions for asylum seekers on the provision of support to families and vulnerable persons, at 13.89 above, apply to interim support. The interim support regulations require the local authority to provide both accommodation and support to meet essential living needs.[2] Thus a person who already has adequate accommodation but no means of meeting his or her needs for food and clothing, a fairly common situation,[3] must be given both. This provision, which replicates the case law under section 21 of the National Assistance Act that it was unlawful for an authority to provide food vouchers alone to an asylum seeker without also the provision of residential accommodation,[4] prejudices both the asylum seeker, who may face unnecessary and unwanted dispersal in order to meet essential living needs, and the public purse.[5] The motive for this indissoluble package is not unwonted generosity but a desire to force asylum seekers out of accommodation which is too big or too expensive (such as flats) and into hostels.

[1] Asylum Support (Interim Provisions) Regulations 1999, SI 1999/3056, reg 5(1), (3).
[2] SI 1999/3056, reg 5(1).
[3] Or vice versa, which is not at all common.
[4] *R v Newham London Borough Council, ex p Gorenkin* (1998) 1 CCL Rep 309.
[5] The apparently unnecessary cost implications were referred to by Hooper J in *R v Camden London Borough, ex p Dürshe* (CO/5069/99) (24 February 2000, unreported), para 8.

13.152 There are two exceptions to this unfortunate regime. First, accommodation may be separated from support where the asylum seeker's household includes a dependent child who is under 18.[1] The second exception is that, if the circumstances of a particular case are 'exceptional', support may be provided 'in such other ways as are necessary to enable the assisted person and his dependants ... to be supported'[2] – sufficiently wide words to enable the authority to split the package and offer support or accommodation only where appropriate.[3] In practice, if a person already has adequate accommodation, the authority may fulfil its statutory duty by providing essential living needs and making arrangements with the accommodation provider (including payment) to continue to provide it. Where essential living needs are already being met, the authority could fulfil its duty by taking over the support or by meeting any deficiency in it. There is, however, no power simply not to provide one or other form of support because it is not wanted.

1   Asylum Support (Interim Provisions) Regulations 1999, SI 1999/3056, reg 5(2); for definition of 'dependant' see reg 2(1) and 13.46 above. In *R v Camden London Borough, ex p Diirshe* (CO/5069/99) (24 February 2000, unreported) the court held that the child could fall within any of the listed categories of dependant in SI 1999/3056, reg 2(1), rejecting the local authority's argument that the child had to fall within the narrow definition in SI 1999/3056, reg 2(1)(b) ('a child of his ... who is under 18 and dependent on him'). The Administrative Court has held that even where there are dependants under 18, the authority is entitled to provide accommodation and essential living needs as a package, and is not obliged to provide solely essential living needs if the family reject the dispersal accommodation: *R v Hammersmith and Fulham London Borough Council, ex p Isik*, CO 1945/2000 (26 June 2000, unreported). Leave to appeal was granted but the matter became academic.
2   SI 1999/3056, reg 5(4).
3   This interpretation is supported by the Secretary of State's Guidance, in NASS letter to Chief Executives of Local Authorities in England and Wales, 1 December 1999, at para 9, and has generally been accepted by local authorities.

Level and nature of support

13.153 In deciding what to provide by way of accommodation and essential living needs, the local authority must have regard[1] to income or assets which the asylum seeker and his or her dependants have or might reasonably be expected to have,[2] the welfare of the asylum seeker and their dependants and the costs of providing support. But in providing accommodation, it must not have regard to the asylum seeker's preferences as to the locality in which the accommodation is provided, its nature or the nature and standard of fixtures and fittings in it.[3] There is a clear tension between the requirement to ignore a person's preferences on the location of the accommodation and the requirement to take into account the asylum seeker's welfare, since in most cases preference and welfare will coincide. For example, the welfare of the individual claimant may only be properly safeguarded by placing them near appropriate medical facilities, other family members or the children's school – all of which will be reflected in the person's preferences. The discretion as to locality is a further disguised form of dispersal which may be operated by local authorities in addition to the formal dispersal scheme, by way of transfer (below). In one case,[4] an authority was prevented from moving asylum seekers to whom it was already providing support, until it had at least consulted them. The authority must have regard to family unity and to the needs of vulnerable persons.[5]

1   Asylum Support (Interim Provisions) Regulations 1999, SI 1999/3056, reg 6(1).

2 An authority is entitled to take into account evidence (electronic entertainment and communication equipment) of other income from sub-letting in reducing support for essential living needs: *R v Camden London Borough, ex p Kwiek* (12 April 2000, unreported), QBD, upheld by the Court of Appeal on 12 October 2000 (C/00/1699; renewed permission).

3 SI 1999/3056, reg 6(2).

4 *R v Newham London Borough, ex p Ally* (21 January 2000, unreported); an injunction was granted, after which the authority consulted.

5 The requirements of Council Directive 2003/9/EC on reception conditions for asylum seekers on the provision of support to families and vulnerable persons, at 13.89 above, apply to interim support, although the Asylum Seekers (Reception Conditions) Regulations 2005, SI 2005/7, appear on their face to apply only to persons whose claim for asylum was recorded on or after 5 February 2005. Such persons would not be eligible for interim support.

13.154 The accommodation provided must be adequate.[1] In the context of the immigration rules, the Immigration Appeal Tribunal has held that, to be adequate, accommodation must not be statutorily overcrowded or unfit for human habitation.[2] We suggest that the standard of adequacy here is higher, as it is framed in terms which involve a subjective element of adequacy 'for the needs of the assisted person'.[3] To comply with the local authority's duty, it must meet any particular needs which the asylum seeker has. As for the provision of essential living needs, there are no 'rule of thumb' rates of support for those eligible, as in NASS.[4] It may be reasonable for local authorities to consider the rates paid by NASS. However, the Court of Appeal has held that as local authorities have been entrusted with the responsibility under regulation 5 of determining what appears to them to be adequate accommodation and provision for essential living needs, it can make its own assessment; 'the regulations setting up the NASS scheme do not apply to that assessment and nothing requires a local authority to apply the NASS rates'.[5]

1 Asylum Support (Interim Provisions) Regulations 1999, SI 1999/3056, reg 5(1)(a).

2 See 11.57 above. The risk of violence could be taken into account in assessing the adequacy of accommodation for a dependant under the immigration rules: *B v Secretary of State for the Home Department* [2003] EWCA Civ, 4 February 2003.

3 SI 1999/3056, reg 5(1)(a). See *R v Islington London Borough Council, ex p Mahida* (CO 2519/2000) (14 August 2000, unreported), QBD: location of accommodation near mosque was relevant to applicant's welfare and so to adequacy of accommodation.

4 See 13.94 above.

5 *R (Satu) v Hackney London Borough Council* [2002] EWCA Civ 1843.

Transferring claims for support

13.155 In certain circumstances, a local authority may transfer a claim for support to another local authority without deciding whether the applicant is eligible for interim support. The authority to which the claim is transferred then has the responsibility for determining whether the asylum seeker is eligible for support and for providing support accordingly.[1] These circumstances are not set out in the regulations; instead, local authorities may make their own arrangements.[2] The Secretary of State may make rules to force certain authorities to accept referrals and provide support where a claim is made to an authority which is already supporting a specified maximum number of asylum seekers,[3] or to prevent authorities from providing support in particular areas.[4] At the request of the local authorities, the Secretary of

State has so far refrained from making any such rules, in the hope that the agreed arrangements between the local authorities will work to relieve the pressure on the areas where most asylum seekers are concentrated, London and the south-east.[5] Authorities are able not only to transfer claims for support to another authority under their own agreements but may also transfer their duty to provide support or further support.[6]

¹ Asylum Support (Interim Provisions) Regulations 1999, SI 1999/3056, reg 3.
² SI 1999/3056, reg 9.
³ Immigration and Asylum Act 1999, Sch 9, paras 9(1)–(4).
⁴ IAA 1999, Sch 9, para 8.
⁵ Letter from Bob Eagle, Director of NASS, to Chief Executives of local authorities in England and Wales, 19 November 1999, para 20. An annex to the letter consists of a draft form of regulations to be brought in if the voluntary arrangements do not work.
⁶ IAA 1999, Sch 9, para 9(6), (7); SI 1999/3056, regs 9 and 3(1)(b) all make this clear.

13.156 The agreements between the local authorities developed out of a cooperative process between the local authorities, the Local Government Association, the Home Office and the Association of London Government. Transfer may take place in the following circumstances:[1]

- the applicant for support is aged 18 or over; and
- the claim for support has been made in London or Kent; and
- the asylum seeker has made an in-country asylum claim and is awaiting an initial Home Office appointment or is a port asylum applicant who has received a negative decision from the Home Office and is appealing against such decision; and
- the applicant is destitute in accordance with the standard applied by the relevant local authority;[2] and
- the claim for support discloses a need for the provision of accommodation, not just essential living needs; and
- neither the applicant nor his or her dependants have any 'exceptional reasons' for needing to be accommodated in London or Kent; and
- the asylum seeker was not in receipt of accommodation and help with essential living needs before 6 December 1999 (when the interim scheme came into force).[3]

In addition, where it is apparent that the applicant and his or her dependants have 'special needs', a comprehensive assessment and investigation must be completed before a decision is made as to whether transfer of the claim is appropriate.

¹ The details are set out (although very poorly) in the 'Guidance Note to Local Authorities in England and Wales: Interim Arrangements for Asylum Seeker Support' issued by the Home Office, ss 1 (final page), 2 (parts 3 and 4), and Annex 2.
² This criterion cuts across Asylum Support (Interim Provisions) Regulations 1999, SI 1999/3056, which does not require the transferring authority to determine eligibility: SI 1999/3056, reg 3(1)(a), (3).
³ In general, this excludes from transferral people who were supported under the National Assistance Act 1948, s 21 by a local social services department before 6 December 1999.

13.157 In transferring claims for support, local authorities must have regard to the guidance issued by the Secretary of State as to when claims can and cannot be transferred.[1] The Secretary of State's guidance[2] suggests that authorities should undertake an assessment to determine whether there are exceptional reasons why asylum seekers should remain in the authority where they claimed support. Exceptional reasons for remaining in London and Kent are expressed to include (but are not limited to) circumstances where the asylum seeker has particular medical needs which can only be met locally. The example given is access to the Medical Foundation for the Care of Victims of Torture, which provides specialist counselling and treatment, and prepares reports for use in asylum claims. The guidance also cites close family members already living in the area as exceptional reasons. It also sets out criteria for local authorities receiving transferred asylum seekers on where to place them,[3] which is intended to cohere with the approach to dispersal under the NASS scheme.[4] Local authorities placing transferred asylum seekers are required to take into account:

- the culture and language of the asylum seeker;
- his or her particular needs regarding the type of accommodation required (the examples given are accommodation suitable for families, those with special needs or disabilities);
- accessibility of other forms of services and support needed by asylum seekers;
- the possibilities for developing support provided by existing voluntary and community groups in the area;
- whether there is likely to be suitable accommodation available in the particular location;
- whether there is an existing multi-ethnic population or infrastructure able to assist asylum seekers there.

[1] Immigration and Asylum Act 1999, Sch 9, para 9(7).
[2] Letter of Judith Simpson, NASS to all Chief Executives of Local Authorities in England and Wales, 1 December 1999. Paragraphs 1 and 2 make it clear that the letter constitutes 'guidance' under the Immigration and Asylum Act 1999 to which the local authorities are legally obliged to have regard.
[3] See NASS Guidance, 1 December 1999, paras 1–6; but the legal force of this guidance is doubtful, since Immigration and Asylum Act 1999, Sch 9, para 9(7) requires authorities to have regard to it in exercising any 'power under the regulations to refer or transfer', not after transfer.
[4] Asylum seekers should not be placed in isolated surroundings but in 'cluster areas' where there already exists a multi-cultural population: see the Home Office document 'Cluster Areas: Role of local organisations', September 1999.

Challenges to interim support decisions

13.158 There are no rights of appeal against decisions on interim support, in contrast to the appeal rights under NASS against refusal or withdrawal of support.[1] The only means of challenging decisions on interim support (and decisions on NASS asylum support which are not susceptible to appeal), is by way of judicial review.[2]

[1] See 13.117ff above.
[2] The alternative remedy for maladministration (as opposed to an unlawful decision) is a complaint to the local government Ombudsman, but this would probably not be sufficiently speedy for cases concerning support. For a discussion of this possibility see *R v Lambeth London Borough Council, ex p Crookes* (1995) 29 HLR 28 at 35ff.

WHICH SUPPORT? ELIGIBILITY FOR INTERIM OR NASS SUPPORT

13.159 Since September 2000, no new asylum claimant, wherever he or she makes the application, has been eligible for interim support and all have been entitled to apply for NASS. However, many asylum claimants who previously obtained or were eligible for interim support, will continue to receive it or will remain eligible to apply for it. The important dates are not the dates on which support was claimed but the date of the asylum claim and (if applicable) its rejection or withdrawal. The interim support scheme came into force on 6 December 1999 and the scheme for NASS support on 3 April 2000. Between those two dates, all destitute asylum seekers who were without social security or community care provision were required to apply to their local authority for interim support. Those who, on 5 December 1999, were already receiving support under section 21 of the National Assistance Act or under the Children Act 1989 were generally transferred into the interim support scheme.[1] These forms of assistance are however different in scope and in their qualifying criteria. The effect of the 'transitional provision'[2] was not to require local authorities to make exactly the same provision as previously, but to assess asylum seekers under the terms of the interim provisions to determine the nature and level of support appropriate.[3] The situation became more complex on 3 April 2000, from which date the two schemes continued in tandem.

[1] Asylum Support (Interim Provisions) Regulations 1999, SI 1999/3056, reg 11. See also letter from Director of NASS, to all Chief Executives of local authorities in England and Wales, 19 November 1999.
[2] SI 1999/3056, reg 11.
[3] *R v Derby City Council, ex p Bajric* (CO/1139/00) (14 August 2000, unreported) per Newman J at paras 43–45.

13.160 On their face, the Interim Support Regulations appear to operate so that all destitute asylum seekers and their dependants are able to get interim support.[1] However, asylum seekers can only be provided with interim support during what is called the 'interim period',[2] which in general terms runs from 6 December 1999 to 4 April 2006.[3] But the Secretary of State may direct local authorities to treat the interim period as ending for certain classes of asylum seekers on an earlier date,[4] with the effect that interim support ends for them on that date[5] and they become eligible for NASS support.[6] The Secretary of State may specify different dates for the ending of the interim period for different classes of case.[7]

[1] Asylum Support (Interim Provisions) Regulations 1999, SI 1999/3056, reg 2(1).
[2] SI 1999/3056, reg 3(1); Immigration and Asylum Act 1999, Sch 9, paras 1(1) and 15.
[3] SI 1999/3056, regs 1(1), 2(5), Asylum Support (Interim Provisions) (Amendment) Regulations 2005, SI 2005/595
[4] Immigration and Asylum Act 1999, Sch 15, para 14(1) enables the Secretary of State to direct local authorities to 'treat the interim period' as coming to an end earlier than 1 April 2002: for specified purposes; in relation to a specified area or locality; or in relation to persons of a specified description. See below for such directions.
[5] SI 1999/3056, reg 3(1) provides that an authority '... must provide support during the interim period to eligible persons'.
[6] Asylum Support Regulations 2000, SI 2000/704, reg 4(5)(a), (b), (c).
[7] IAA 1999, Sch 15, para 14(1), read with para 14(4).

Those ineligible for interim support, but eligible for NASS support

13.161 The following groups of people are unable to get interim support and so able to apply for NASS support because the interim period is treated as having ended for them on the date given.

Post-2 April 2000 port/declaration asylum seekers/Oakington Reception Centre detainees/ cases in Scotland and Northern Ireland

13.162 From 3 April 2000, the following asylum seekers are ineligible for interim support and so able to apply for NASS support:

(a)   persons who apply for asylum after 3 April 2000 who *either* claim asylum on their arrival in the UK; *or* within three months of a declaration of upheaval by the Secretary of State;[1]

(b)   persons who make a claim for asylum in-country after 3 April 2000 and are, at any time after making that claim, detained at Oakington Reception Centre;[2]

(c)   persons who claim asylum after 3 April 2000 in Scotland or Northern Ireland.[3]

[1]   A declaration of upheaval is a declaration that the country from which the applicant is seeking asylum is subject to such a fundamental change of circumstances that the Secretary of State would not normally order the return of any person to that country. Direction No 1 of Secretary of State, March 2000, paras (a), (b).

[2]   Direction No 1 of Secretary of State, March 2000, para (d).

[3]   The interim scheme does not extend to Scotland or Northern Ireland: Asylum Support (Interim Provisions) Regulations 1999, SI 1999/3056, reg 1(2), and so asylum seekers in these areas are not people to whom interim support applies for the purposes of Asylum Support Regulations 2000, SI 2000/704, reg 4(5) (exclusion from NASS support).

Pre-3 April 2000 port/declaration asylum claimants after refusal ('disbenefitted' cases)

13.163 Persons who made claims for asylum before 3 April 2000 either on arrival or within three months of a declaration of upheaval and who either:

(a)   abandon their asylum claim after 25 September 2000; *or*

(b)   have their claim to asylum recorded as decided by the Secretary of State after 25 September

are no longer entitled to interim support from the date of abandonment or decision, but may instead apply for NASS support.[1] These asylum seekers would have received social security benefit, rather than interim support, both before and, as a result of the transitional provisions, after 1 April 2000. NASS provides local authorities with funding to assist disbenefitted families with dependent children in applying for NASS support and to provide emergency accommodation to them whilst a decision is being reached. If the children in the family have been in school in the area in which they are presently living, this period will be used by NASS to try and relocate them in that area. NASS may also fund a local authority to assist an asylum seeker who is single and pregnant or who has a pregnant dependant over 18 or where the asylum seeker or his or her dependant is vulnerable as the result of old age, mental illness or mental or physical disability.[2]

1   Direction No 3 of Secretary of State, 11 July 2000, para 5.
2   Policy Bulletin 52 *Disbenefitted Arrangements – Special Funding for Local Authorities for Dealing With Disbenefitted Families with Children.*

Kent and Medway asylum seekers

13.164 Special provisions were made for local authorities of Kent and Medway. Kent County Council and Medway District Council have no power to provide support for asylum seekers who claimed asylum in the circumstances above (on arrival or after an upheaval declaration) and who receive a notice of decision on the claim for asylum after 17 April 2000.[1] Asylum seekers who are refused asylum after 17 April 2000 while in Kent or Medway, cannot be provided with interim support from any other local authority either.[2] The Direction requires the 'Kent and Medway' asylum seekers to have received notice of the decision on the asylum claim, in contrast to the non-Kent or Medway cases, which only require a decision to have been recorded but not necessarily received.[3] These 'Kent and Medway' asylum seekers are also all eligible for NASS rather than for interim support from local authorities.

1   Direction No 2A of Secretary of State, 10 April 2000, para (b).
2   Direction No 2 of Secretary of State, 10 April 2000, para (b).
3   *R v Secretary of State for the Home Department, ex p Salem* [1999] QB 805.

In-country asylum seekers

13.165 Those who made in-country applications for asylum after certain dates shown below are not entitled to interim support from the authorities shown. They are entitled to apply for NASS support instead, as long as they are not excluded from support by section 55 of the Nationality, Immigration and Asylum Act 2002.[1] The directions, set out below, provide a cut-off date for interim support for all the local authorities in England and Wales.

(a)   Those who claim asylum in-country after 17 April 2000 may not obtain interim support from Kent County Council or Medway District Council.[2]

(b)   Those who claim asylum in-country after 24 July 2000 may not obtain interim support from a London borough council or the Common Council of the City of London.[3]

(c)   Those who claim asylum in-country after 31 July 2000 may not obtain interim support from a local authority in the North East, Yorkshire and Humberside or Wales.[4]

(d)   Those who claim asylum in-country after 14 August 2000 may not obtain interim support from a local authority in the North West, East Midlands, Eastern, South West or South Central England.[5]

(e)   Those who claim asylum in-country after 29 August 2000 may not obtain interim support from a local authority in the West Midlands or Sussex.[6]

The directions achieve this by stating that the relevant authority is to treat the interim period as having come to an end for those asylum seekers. If an asylum seeker applies in-country after the relevant cut-off date for the authority to which it later applies for interim support, the application must be refused by that authority,[7] and the asylum seeker would be able to apply for NASS support as there would be no local authority which must provide interim support.[8]

1 This affects those claiming on or after 8 January 2003: see 13.55 above.
2 Direction No 2A of Secretary of State, 10 April 2000, para (a).
3 Direction No 3 of the Secretary of State, 11 July 2000, para 1.
4 Direction No 3 of the Secretary of State, 11 July 2000, para 2 and Sch Part I.
5 Direction No 3 of the Secretary of State, 11 July 2000, para 3 and Sch Part II.
6 Direction No 3 of the Secretary of State, 11 July 2000, para 4 and Sch Part III.
7 Asylum Support (Interim Provisions) Regulations 1999, SI 1999/3056, reg 3(1).
8 Asylum Support Regulations 2000, SI 2000/704, reg 4(5).

Those eligible for interim support

13.166 It may be apparent from the above that all new asylum seekers after 29 August 2000, wherever they claim asylum, are now eligible to apply for NASS rather than interim support whether they claim on arrival, within three months of a declaration of upheaval or in-country. The persons who are still entitled to get interim support rather than social security benefits or NASS support are the following.

Port/declaration asylum seekers

13.167 Asylum seekers who, before 3 April 2000, claimed asylum at port or within three months of a declaration of upheaval and who were recorded as having their claim to asylum determined by the Secretary of State prior to 25 September 2000[1] unless they received notice of refusal of their asylum claim on or after 17 April 2000 while they were living in the area of Kent County Council or Medway District Council,[2] in which case they are eligible for NASS support.

1 Direction No 3 of Secretary of State, 11 July 2000, para 5, only ends interim support for those whose claim is abandoned or refused on or after 25 September 2000.
2 The combined effect of Direction No 2 of the Secretary of State of 10 April 2000, para (b) and Direction No 2A of Secretary of State of 10 April 2000, para (b) precludes any local authority from providing interim support for such asylum seekers. An asylum seeker in this group who receives notice of decision while living in Kent or Medway continues to be entitled to interim support after 17 April 2000 only if the notice was received before 17 April 2000.

In-country asylum seekers

13.168 Persons who claimed asylum in-country before the relevant cut-off date for the local authority to whom they apply for interim support. The cut-off date refers to claims for asylum, not for support.[1] It doesn't matter whether these in-country asylum seekers claimed asylum before or after

3 April 2000, the only relevant date is that which relates to in-country asylum claims for the local authority concerned.

¹ See ASA 00/11/0016 and ASA 00/11/0115 at para 9, where the adjudicator laments that the local authority may well have committed precisely this error.

13.169 Those entitled to interim support as a result of the above rules continue to be entitled after the relevant cut-off dates. Thus, a person in the first group above, who was entitled to interim support rather than NASS support when his or her pre-April 2000, port claim to asylum was recorded as being determined before 25 September 2000, remains entitled to interim support thereafter pending the hearing of any appeal. Similarly, a person in the second group who made an in-country asylum claim before the cut-off date for his or her local authority, remains entitled to receive, apply for and obtain interim support from that authority after the authority's cut-off date.¹

¹ The cut-off dates depend on the date of the asylum claim or its refusal or notification of refusal, not when asylum support was claimed: see Directions 2, 2A and 3 of the Secretary of State above. See also letter of NASS to all Chief Executives and Directors of Social Services in England and Wales, 10 July 2000, accompanying Direction No 3: 'Nothing in this letter or the Direction applies to asylum seekers being supported under the interim arrangements prior to the relevant date. They continue to be so supported.'

ACCOMMODATION CENTRES

13.170 Part II of the Nationality, Immigration and Asylum Act 2002¹ provides for the accommodation of destitute asylum seekers in accommodation centres. While asylum seekers will not be detained in these centres, the Act enables the Secretary of State to control the movements of asylum seekers and to streamline the asylum process.² The establishment of the centres is very controversial; the provisions excluding children from mainstream education are widely seen as particularly damaging to their welfare, and supporters and opponents of asylum seekers both see the centres as dumping grounds for asylum seekers. It did not help that one of the proposed sites had previously been used for the burial of millions of diseased cattle. An avowed intention of the Home Secretary in creating them was to make removal at the end of the process easier by hindering asylum seekers' integration with local communities.³ The process of establishing the centres, often in the teeth of local resistance, has met with varying success in the courts.⁴

¹ Ie, ss 16–42. Only s 16 and ss 40–42 (devolutionary obligations) are fully in force; s 18 (definition of asylum seeker) is in force for other purposes (s 55 and Sch 3 withdrawal of support: see SI 2003/1, Sch.)
² The government proposed to establish a number of large centres which would house around 3,000 asylum seekers from application through initial decision to any appeal: see White Paper, *Secure Borders, Safe Havens: Integration with Diversity in Modern Britain*, CM 5387, para 4.30.
³ See Rt Hon David Blunkett in *Hansard* HC, 24 April 2002, col 353.
⁴ See eg *R (on the application of Cherwell District Council) v First Secretary of State and Secretary of State for the Home Department* [2004] EWHC 724 (Admin), [2004] 16 EG 111 (CS), [2004] All ER (D) 94 (Apr) Collins J, upheld by the Court of Appeal on 8 July 2004, holding that the decision to approve the development of an accommodation centre in Bicester, Oxfordshire was lawful.

13.171 The Secretary of State has power to arrange for the provision of accommodation[1] for asylum seekers[2] (or their dependants),[3] who the Secretary of State thinks are destitute or likely to be destitute[4] within a prescribed period.[5] Regulations will prescribe the procedure to be followed in relation to the provision of accommodation in accommodation centres;[6] none have yet been made. The Secretary of State may provide facilities for both the immigration service and immigration adjudicators at or near an accommodation centre.[7] The point at which an asylum claim is treated as determined, the requirement to send a notice informing the asylum claimant of the decision, and the definition of a disposed appeal, for the purpose of support in an accommodation centre,[8] are in substance, the same as subsections 94(3), (4), (8) and (9) of the Immigration and Asylum Act 1999. Support under section 95 of the Immigration and Asylum Act 1999 may be provided by accommodation in an accommodation centre,[9] as may 'hard cases' support.[10] Support will not be available in an accommodation centre once any form of leave is granted.[11]

[1] Nationality, Immigration and Asylum Act 2002, s 16(1).
[2] Defined in NIAA 2002, s 18(1) (in force for the purpose of exclusion from support under s 55 of, and Sch 3 to, the Act: SI 2003/1), which adds to the definition in Immigration and Asylum Act 1999, s 94(1) the requirements that the asylum claim is made at a designated place and that the person is in the UK (see 13.39 above). Section 44 of the Act, when in force, will amend IAA 1999, s 94(1) so that its definition of asylum seeker matches that in s 18(1). A person shall continue to be treated as an asylum seeker while his or her household includes a dependent child under 18: s 18(2). This does not prevent the removal of support from failed asylum seekers with dependent children under Sch 3 para 7A, added by Asylum and Immigration (Treatment of Claimants, etc) Act 2004, s 9 (in force 1 December 2004: SI 2004/2999).
[3] Dependants of asylum seekers are those who are present in the UK, and who further, fall within a prescribed class: NIAA 2002, s 20(2). Section 44 of the Act, when in force, will amend IAA 1999, s 94(5) so that its definition of dependants matches that in s 20(2). The Secretary of State may inquire into and determine a person's age, by s 21(2).
[4] NIAA 2002, s 19(1). The definition of destitution is similar to that in IAA 1999, s 95. Section 44 of the Act, when in force, will amend IAA 1999, s 95(2) to (8) so that the definition of destitution, the matters to be considered when determining adequacy of accommodation, and regulations relating to destitution, will match exactly the provisions of s 19.
[5] NIAA 2002, s 17(1). This section mirrors the powers given to the Secretary of State to provide support under IAA 1999, s 95.
[6] NIAA 2002, s 17(2), (3).
[7] NIAA 2002, s 16(3) (not amended to take account of the abolition of immigration adjudicators on 4 April 2005). The hearing of appeals in or near the accommodation centre may adversely affect the perception of the fairness and independence of the appellate authority, as has happened in relation to Harmondsworth Removal Centre.
[8] NIAA 2002, s 21(3)–(5).
[9] NIAA 2002, s 22.
[10] NIAA 2002, s 23(5), referring to accommodation under IAA 1999, s 4 (including that section as amended, from 7 November 2002, by NIAA 2002, s 49). For 'hard cases' support see 13.175 below.
[11] This is because they no longer fall within the definition of 'asylum seeker': see NIAA 2002, s 18(2)(b).

13.172 A person who is granted temporary admission or release from detention by an immigration officer, or who is subject to deportation proceedings and has been granted temporary release by the Secretary of State, may be required to reside at an accommodation centre as a condition of temporary release.[1] If such a person commits one of the offences specified in section 35 of the Nationality, Immigration and Asylum Act 2002,[2] fails to comply with travel arrangements or breaches the conditions imposed on residents of the accommodation centre, and as a consequence is required to leave the centre,[3] then he or she will be treated as having broken his or her residence restriction.[4] A person may not spend more than six months in accommodation centres,[5] unless an agreement is reached between the person and the Secretary of State, however, if the Secretary of State thinks that it is appropriate because of the individual circumstances of an asylum seeker, he may extend the period of time from six months to nine months.[6] The Secretary of State may provide accommodation in an accommodation centre or elsewhere (including an arrangement with a local authority), if he thinks that an asylum seeker may be eligible for accommodation in an accommodation centre, but has not yet reached a decision on eligibility.[7]

[1]   Nationality, Immigration and Asylum Act 2002, s 23(1)–(2).
[2]   The section applies the provisions of the Immigration and Asylum Act 1999 which create criminal offences relating to asylum support (ss 105–109, see 13.107 above and 14.72 below), to obtaining support in an accommodation centre.
[3]   NIAA 2002, s 26: see below.
[4]   NIAA 2002, ss 23(4). Such a person will then be liable to arrest under para 24 of Sch 2 to the Immigration Act 1971 for breaching a condition of his or her bail or temporary admission or release.
[5]   NIAA 2002, s 25(1).
[6]   NIAA 2002, s 25(2)(a), (b).
[7]   NIAA 2002, s 24(1).

13.173 The Secretary of State may arrange for the provision of (inter alia) food and other essential items, money, transport, certain expenses, health facilities, education and training, facilities for religious observance and legal advice at an accommodation centre.[1] Conditions to be observed by residents of accommodation centres may be imposed, in particular requiring them to remain at the centre during certain hours and to report to an immigration officer.[2] They must be imposed in writing.[3] If a resident, or his or her dependant breaches a condition, they may be required to leave the accommodation centre.[4] Residents may be subject to a condition requiring them to contribute to the accommodation and support they receive at an accommodation centre.[5] The Secretary of State may terminate accommodation at an accommodation centre if a person or a dependant commits one of the offences specified in section 35 of the Nationality, Immigration and Asylum Act 2002 or fails to comply with travel arrangements,[6] subject to a right of appeal under section 103 of the Immigration and Asylum Act 1999.[7] Residents of an accommodation centre will not acquire a tenancy or any other legal right to occupy the accommodation centre, and any licence to occupy which is acquired will not prevent eviction.[8] All the measures contained within Part VI of the Immigration and Asylum Act 1999 which are designed to enforce compliance with the scheme of support under that Part of the Act, are applicable to support provided by way of accommodation in accommodation centres.[9] Each accommodation centre will have an Advisory Group who will hear residents' complaints, [10] and the Secretary of State will appoint a Monitor of Accommodation Centres who will report on the operation of accommodation centres, at least once a year.[11]

[1]   Nationality, Immigration and Asylum Act 2002 s 29.

² NIAA 2002, ss 30(1)–(3).
³ NIAA 2002, s 30(6).
⁴ NIAA 2002, ss 30(4)–(5).
⁵ NIAA 2002, s 31.
⁶ NIAA 2002, s 26(1).
⁷ NIAA 2002, s 26(4).
⁸ NIAA 2002, s 32.
⁹ NIAA 2002, s 35 (criminal offences, powers of recovery of expenditure and redirection of post).
¹⁰ NIAA 2002, s 33.
¹¹ NIAA 2002, s 34.

13.174 The most controversial aspect of Part II is that residents of accommodation centres are not, for the purposes of education, treated as part of the population of a local education authority's area.[1] This means that children who are resident in an accommodation centre may not be admitted to a maintained school or nursery,[2] unless they are subject to a statement of special educational needs, in which case they may be admitted to the school named in the statement.[3] Residents are precluded from a number of rights that parents of children have, such as stating a preference as to where their child is educated; appealing against a refusal to admit a child to a maintained school; having their child educated in an off-site educational facility; having special needs provision in a mainstream school; and stating a preference as to where a child with special educational needs will be educated.[4] Whoever is running the accommodation centre, or the local education authority, must ensure that a resident child with special educational needs receives appropriate support within the education facilities provided within the centre.[5] There is, however, no such responsibility if it is beyond their capability to comply because of the severity of the child's needs, the disruption it causes to the education of other resident children, or the cost of doing so.[6] However, any decision not to provide for a child with special educational needs will be subject to a reasonableness test.[7] The bar on admission into maintained schools and nurseries is not applicable in relation to resident children if education is not provided in the accommodation centre.[8] The provisions excluding children of asylum seekers from education in the community have been the subject of fierce criticism and may be susceptible to challenge under the Human Rights Act 1998 if they discriminate in relation to the right to education guaranteed by Protocol 1, Article 2 ECHR.[9]

¹ Nationality, Immigration and Asylum Act 2002, s 36(1).
² NIAA 2002, s 36(2). In special cases, an education provider in an accommodation centre can apply to the local education authority under s 37, asserting that it is not able to provide for a child within the accommodation centre due to his or her special circumstances, and the local education authority has a discretion to provide education for the child concerned (s 37(2)). In such a case, the local education authority can require a maintained school to admit the child, unless that admission would breach the statutory limit on infant class sizes: s 37(4), (5).
³ NIAA 2002, s 36(3).
⁴ NIAA 2002, s 36(5).
⁵ NIAA 2002, s 36(7).
⁶ NIAA 2002, s 36(7)(a)–(c).
⁷ NIAA 2002, s 36(8).
⁸ NIAA 2002, s 36(10).
⁹ Article 14 ECHR together with Protocol 1 Art 2.

HARD CASES

13.175 Another controversial area of the asylum support system is the complete termination of all support – interim or NASS under sections 95 or 98 of the Immigration and Asylum Act 1999 – to those without dependent children under 18, once all appeals have been exhausted,[1] and to failed asylum seekers with dependent children whose appeals have been exhausted and who fail without reasonable cause to take reasonable steps to leave the UK voluntarily or to place themselves in a position in which they are able to do so.[2] The Secretary of State has a reserve power under section 4 of the Immigration and Asylum Act 1999 to provide, or arrange for the provision of facilities for the accommodation of anyone who is temporarily admitted to the UK, released from detention by the immigration authorities or released on bail from immigration detention. Section 49 of the Nationality, Immigration and Asylum Act 2002 amended section 4 of the IAA 1999[3] to make explicit reference to a power to provide accommodation facilities for failed asylum seekers and their dependants. In practice this support is provided by NASS under its Hard Cases Fund. In order to qualify for support under this fund, failed asylum seekers must show that they are destitute and that one of a number of statutory conditions are met.[4] These are:

(a) they are taking all reasonable steps to leave the United Kingdom or place themselves in a position in which they are able to leave the United Kingdom, which may include complying with attempts to obtain a travel document to facilitate their departure;

(b) there is a physical impediment to travel or some other medical reason to prevent their leaving the UK;

(c) they are unable to leave the UK because in the opinion of the Secretary of State there is no viable route of return available;[5]

(d) they have obtained permission for judicial review of a decision in relation to their asylum claim,[6]

(e) provision of accommodation is necessary to avoid a breach of their Convention rights.[7]

The 'inability to leave the country' criterion was applied strictly in *Guveya*[8], where Moses J held that the fact that the Secretary of State had adopted a 'generous' policy of non-removal of failed asylum seekers to Zimbabwe did not mean that it was reasonable for the claimant to refuse to return voluntarily or that he was bound to be provided with accommodation. However, in *Nigatu*,[9] Collins J held that persons who had made representations which were not clearly unfounded in support of a fresh claim for asylum or under Article 3 ECHR were eligible, and in *Womba*,[10] an asylum support adjudicator held that only IND caseworkers, and not NASS workers, were able to decide that representations were clearly unfounded. Policy Bulletin 71 accepts that the submission of further representations seeking a fresh claim, or submission of a late appeal which is under consideration by the appellate authorities, are situations where the provision of hard cases support is necessary to avoid a breach of Convention rights.[11] An asylum seeker who is refused support under section 55 of the Nationality, Immigration and Asylum Act 2002 is not entitled to hard cases support.[12] Neither is an adult asylum seeker who has failed to comply with removal directions, or the adults in a family certified as having failed to take reasonable steps to leave voluntarily following final determination of their claim, save where support is necessary to avoid a breach of their Convention rights.[13] The regulations under section 4(5)[14] allow conditions to be imposed on the continued provision of section 4 support, including a condition that the person in question performs or participates in specified community activiites.[15] The AI(TC)A 2004 also provides a new right of appeal to an asylum support adjudicator in relation to refusal or termination of support under section 4.[16]

[1]   Since they cease to be asylum seekers within the statutory definition: see 13.39 above.
[2]   Asylum and Immigration (Treatment of Claimants, etc) Act 2004, s 9, inserting a new para 7A into the Nationality, Immigration and Asylum Act 2002, Sch 3.
[3]   The amended s 4 came into force on 7 November 2002.
[4]   Immigration and Asylum (Provision of Accommodation to Failed Asylum Seekers) Regulations 2005, SI 2005/930, reg 3, in force 31 March 2005. The criteria for eligibility were previously set out in NASS Policy Bulletin 71, which also gives details of the evidence needed to prove entitlement.
[5]   In *R (on the application of Abdullah) v Secretary of State for the Home Department* (CO/3709/04), Charles J granted permission to apply for judicial review of decisions to refuse hard cases support to failed Iraqi asylum seekers save on the basis that they return voluntarily to Iraq, there being arguably no safe route of return.
[6]   SI 2005/930, reg 3(1), 3(2)(d), which provides for the equivalents in Scotland and Northern Ireland. The 'permission for judicial review' test needs modification in the light of the changes to the asylum appeals system wrought by Nationality, Immigration and Asylum Act 2002, s 101 and Asylum and Immigration (Treatment of Claimants, etc) Act 2004, s 26. In *R v Immigration Appeal Tribunal, ex p Mohamed* [1999] Imm AR 48, Dyson J held that it was not unreasonable to use section 4 support for asylum seekers awaiting a test case on third country removals, whose asylum claims were not being decided substantively.
[7]   SI 2005/930, reg 3(1), 3(2)(a)–(e).
[8]   *R (on the application of Guveya) v National Asylum Support Service* [2004] EWHC 2371 (Admin), [2004] All ER (D) 594 (Jul), a case with serious implications for asylum seeking families deprived of support under NIAA 2002, Sch 3, para 7A (inserted by AI(TC)A 2004, s 9 from 1 December 2004) if they fail to leave the country voluntarily or put themselves in a position where they are able to do so.
[9]   *R (on the application of Nigatu) v Secretary of State for the Home Department* [2004] EWHC 1806 (Admin).
[10] ASA/05/04/9198.
[11] NASS Policy Bulletin 71, Version 2 (31.3.05), para 5.3.
[12] At least, not while he or she remains an asylum seeker (as opposed to a failed asylum seeker who cannot leave, when hard cases support might be available under SI 2005/930 reg 3.
[13] SI 2005/930 reg 3(1), (2)(a) above, unless they qualify under one of the other subparagraphs such as a medical condition precluding removal.
[14] SI 2005/930, in force 31 March 2005. Sub-sections (5)–(9) were inserted into the Immigration and Asylum Act 1999, s 4 by AI(TC)A 2004, s 10(1), in force 1 December 2004 (SI 2004/2999). Section 10(1), (2), (6) and (7) were brought into force on 1 December 2004 by the Asylum and Immigration (Treatment of Claimants etc) Act 2004 (Commencement No 2) Order 2004, SI 2004/2999 and s 10(3), (4) and (5) were brought into force on 31 March 2005 by the Asylum and Immigration (Treatment of Claimants etc) Act 2004 (Commencement No 4) Order 2005, SI 2005/372. The Immigration and Asylum (Provision of Accommodation to Failed Asylum-Seekers) Regulations 2005, SI 2005/930 also came into force on 31 March 2005.
[15] SI 2005/930, regs 4–6. The Joint Committee on Human Rights expressed concern that the performance of community service as a condition of subsistence support could violate Article 4 ECHR: 14th report Session 2003–2004: Asylum and Immigration (Treatment of Claimants) Bill, additional clauses, 5.7.04 (HL 130/HC 828. Other conditions which may be imposed include compliance with standards of behaviour, reporting and residence restrictions and with specified steps to facilitate removal: reg 6.
[16] AI(TC)A 2004, s 10(3), inserting s 103(2A) NIAA 2002, in force 31 March 2005: SI 2005/372.

13.176 The support which may be provided is primarily accommodation, but NASS has accepted that it will be 'full board'.[1] Meals rather than vouchers and cash will be provided.[2] At present, most of the accommodation provided under these powers is outside London. When Part II of the 2002 Act is in force, section 4 accommodation may be provided in an accommodation centre.[3] Even though section 4, as amended by section 49 of the 2002 Act, gives the Secretary of State a discretion to accommodate failed asylum seekers, in practice, for those who meet the criteria for its provision, it has become a right, and the Immigration and Nationality Department's policy of not informing failed asylum seekers of its existence was held to be unlawful.[4]

[1]   NASS letter 3 April 2000 to 'Assistant' voluntary sector organisations involved in administering NASS support scheme, Annex A.
[2]   NASS letter 3 April 2000 (see fn 3 above) para 3.
[3]   Nationality, Immigration and Asylum Act 2002 s 23(5).
[4]   *R (on the application of Salih) v Secretary of State for the Home Department* [2003] EWHC 2273 (Admin), [2003] All ER (D) 129 (Oct).

COMMUNITY CARE PROVISION FOR THOSE SUBJECT TO IMMIGRATION CONTROL

13.177 In *R v Westminster City Council, ex p M, P, A and X* [1] the Court of Appeal held that all destitute asylum seekers, able bodied as well as disabled, who were deprived of other support were entitled to assistance under section 21 of the National Assistance Act 1948. This led in part to the creation of the National Asylum Support Service, which was designed to relieve local authorities of the responsibility for providing support to such asylum seekers. One of the stated purposes behind the Immigration and Asylum Act 1999 was also to reduce the perceived incentive provided by the availability of welfare benefits and community care provision, which was thought to attract economic migrants, as opposed to asylum seekers, to make applications for asylum in the UK.[2] Section 116 of the IAA 1999 was designed to amend section 21 of the National Assistance Act 1948 in order to prevent local authorities giving assistance to destitute asylum seekers. or to anyone who was subject to immigration control if the need for assistance arose solely from destitution or because of the physical or anticipated physical effects of being destitute.[3] But an asylum seeker who has a need for care and attention which arises as the result of his or her age, illness, disability or other circumstances, which is not being met, is still entitled to assistance under the NAA 1948, if the need for care and attention is to any material extent made more acute by some circumstance other than mere lack of accommodation and funds.[4] In such a case, the House of Lords held in *Westminster v National Asylum Support Service* that NASS is relieved of any duty which would otherwise fall upon it to support that person under the asylum support provisions.[5] Their Lordships characterised the asylum support powers to provide under the Immigration and Asylum Act 1999 as residual powers, which could be exercised if no other support was available for an asylum seeker. A local authority has a duty to provide residential accommodation for a destitute asylum seeker who suffers from a disability even if the disability would not generally require the provision of residential accommodation,[6] since all destitute asylum seekers are entitled to assistance under section 21 of the NAA

1948 following the Court of Appeal's decision in *R v Westminster City Council, ex p M, P, A and X*[7] unless specifically excluded by the insertion of (1A) into that section by section 116 of the Immigration and Asylum Act 1999. Where a destitute asylum-seeking parent is entitled to support under section 21 of the National Assistance Act 1948 as a result of her need for care and attention as a person who is HIV positive, a local authority will have no power to provide care and assistance to her children, as its powers under section 21 are restricted to those who are aged 18 and over. In such a situation, as she and her dependants have additional needs which are not being met by section 21 and cannot be met by section 17 of the Children Act 1989 because of the provisions of s 122 of the 1999 Act,[8] NASS should make arrangements with the local authority to make a financial contribution to cover the costs of supporting her children.[9]

1 (1997) 1 CCLR 85.
2 'Basis of a Safety Net Scheme' in White Paper 'Fairer, Faster and Firmer – A Modern Approach to Immigration and Asylum', July 1998, chapter 8, p 39.
3 IAA 1999, s 116, inserting new ss 1A and 1B into National Assistance Act 1948, s 21.
4 *R v Wandsworth London Borough Council, ex p O, R v Leicester City Council, ex p Bhikha* [2000] 4 All ER 590, CA.
5 *R (on the application of Westminster City Council) v National Asylum Support Service* [2002] UKHL 38, [2002] 4 All ER 654, [2003] LGR 23.
6 *R (on the application of Mani) v London Borough of Lambeth and the Secretary of State for the Home Department* [2003] EWCA Civ 836, [2004] LGR 35.
7 At fn 1 above.
8 See discussion in para 13.168 below.
9 *R (on the application of O) v Haringey London Borough Council* [2004] EWCA Civ 535, [2004] LGR 672, [2004] 2 FCR 219.

13.178 Persons who are subject to immigration control and who are not asylum seekers may also be entitled to support under the National Assistance Act 1948 if their need arose for those same reasons and not merely because of an inability to access benefits or to obtain permission to work, or otherwise support themselves. For instance, where an overstayer was chronically ill as a result of being HIV positive, his needs arose from a combination of illness and destitution and he was held to be a person who was entitled to care and attention from his local authority under the Act.[1] A victim of domestic violence may also be entitled to care and attention under the Act.[2] Those who are unfit to return to their country of origin,[3] or who are prevented from returning home by factors outside their own control,[4] may also be entitled to care and attention. However, any entitlement is subject to the provisions of Schedule 3 to the Nationality, Immigration and Asylum Act 2002 and the Withholding and Withdrawal of Support (Travel Assistance and Temporary Accommodation) Regulations 2002.[5] Schedule 3 prevents a local authority from providing support to various categories of people defined by their nationality, their immigration status and whether they have failed to comply with removal directions or failed to take steps to leave the country,[6] save where the support is necessary to avoid a breach of either ECHR or EC rights.[7] The categories prima facie ineligible for support are: non-EEA nationals with refugee status abroad, and their dependants;[8] citizens of other EEA Member States and their dependants;[9] former asylum seekers who fail to cooperate with removal directions, and their dependants;[10] persons who are not asylum seekers and are in the UK in breach of the immigration laws;[11] and failed asylum seekers with families who fail to take reasonable steps to leave voluntarily, or to put themselves in a position to do so, after their appeals are finally determined.[12] No appeal lies against refusal or withdrawal of support, except in the last case.[13] At present a local authority can make arrangements to provide care and attention to a person accompanied by a dependent child who has not failed to comply with individual removal directions.[14] Where a woman with a dependent child had an outstanding appeal against removal and the local authority from whom she sought support had no power to make travel arrangements for her (as she was not an EEA national or a refugee in an EEA state) the local authority had the power to provide accommodation under Schedule 3 until such time as she failed to comply with any individual removal directions (which had not then been set).[15] However, a local authority could also choose to purchase tickets to return a parent and his or her children to his or her country of origin even if there was an outstanding application for leave to remain on the basis of the length of residence in the United Kingdom.[16] Pending determination of a claim for judicial review arising from a failure by a local authority to exercise its powers under section 21 National Assistance Act 1948, the Court can order that the local authority to provide the claimant with care and assistance.[17]

[1]   *R (on the application of M) v Slough Borough Council* [2004] EWHC 1109 (Admin), [2004] LGR 657, [2004] All ER (D) 283, Collins J. At the time of writing an appeal was pending to the Court of Appeal.

[2]   *R (on the application of Khan) v Oxfordshire County Council* [2004] EWCA Civ 309, [2004] HLR 706. On the facts of the case she was not found to be entitled to care and attention under s 21.

[3]   *R v Brent London Borough Council, ex p D* [1998] 1 CCL Rep 234.

[4]   *R v Lambeth London Borough Council, ex p Sarhangi* [1999] 2 CCL Rep 145.

[5]   SI 2002/3078.

[6]   Nationality, Immigration and Asylum Act 2002, Sch 3, paras 4–7A (para 7A inserted as from a date to be appointed by Asylum and Immigration (Treatment of Claimants, etc) Act 2004), s 10. The provisions disqualify affected persons from support or assistance under National Assistance Act, ss 21 and 28 (accommodation and welfare), Health Services and Public Health Act 1968, s 45 (welfare of elderly), National Health Service Act 1977, s 21 and Sch 8 (social service), Children Act 1989, ss 17, 23C, 24A and 24B (welfare powers which can be exercised in relation to adults), and their Scottish and Northern Irish equivalents: Sch 3, para 1(1).

[7]   NIAA 2002, Sch 3, para 3.

[8]   NIAA 2002, Sch 3, para 4.

[9]   NIAA 2002, Sch 3, para 5.

[10] NIAA 2002, Sch 3, para 6.

[11] NIAA 2002, Sch 3, para 7.

[12] NIAA 2002, Sch 3, para 7A (see fn 6 above). People in this category are liable to lose support 14 days after receipt of a certificate from the Secretary of State that in his opinion they have failed without reasonable excuse to take reasonable steps to leave the UK voluntarily or to place themselves in a position in which they can do so: 7A(1). It applies to their dependants: para 7A(2). An appeal may be brought against the decision under IAA 1999, s 103, and the asylum support adjudicator may annul the certificate or require the Secretary of State to reconsider: Asylum and Immigration (Treatment of Claimants, etc) Act 2004, s 9(3), (4).

[13] See AI(TC)A 2004, s 9(3), in force 1 December 2004: SI 2004/2999.

[14] NIAA 2002, Sch 3, para 10.

[15] *R (on the application of M) v Islington London Borough Council* [2004] EWCA Civ 235, [2004] 4 All ER 709, contradicting guidance previously give to local authorities by the Secretary of State in December 2002 which stated that support should be given for not more than 10 days.

[16] *London Borough of Lambeth v Grant* [2004] EWCA Civ 1711.

13.179 If a person has been given refugee status in another EEA state or is a
national of an EEA state or a dependant of such a person, local authorities can
make travel arrangements for him or her and his or her dependants to return
to the relevant EEA state, and may accommodate them pending their
departure.[1] There is no question here of having to wait for removal directions
to be issued, and it is envisaged that accommodation will only have to be
provided for a short period of time. In *R (on the application of K) v Lambeth
London Borough Council*,[2] Lambeth had terminated interim support to a
Kenyan woman with one child who was married to an Irish national from
whom she had separated, on the basis that she was the dependant of an EEA
national. She asserted that it was a breach of her rights under Articles 3 and 8
of the European Convention on Human Rights to refuse to support her whilst
she exercised her right of appeal against the decision of the Secretary of State
that her marriage was one of convenience giving rise to no EC rights. The
court accepted that she was a spouse but distinguished her case from that of
an asylum seeker with an outstanding appeal on the basis that there was
nothing to stop her from returning to Kenya pending her appeal and that the
state owed no duty under the Convention to a foreign national who had been
permitted to enter the state's territory but could return home.

1   Nationality, Immigration and Asylum Act 2002, Sch 3, paras 8 and 9, Withholding and
    Withdrawal of Support (Travel Assistance and Temporary Accommodation) Regula-
    tions 2002, SI 2002/3078, reg 3.
2   [2003] EWCA Civ 1150, [2004] 1 WLR 272, [2003] 3 FCR 222.

13.180 Section 117 of the Immigration and Asylum Act 1999 modifies and
partially removes the duties placed on local authorities which arise from
section 45 of the Health Services and Public Health Act 1968 (the duty to
promote the welfare of the elderly) and paragraph 2 of Schedule 8 to the
National Health Service Act 1977 (the duty to make arrangements to prevent
illness and to provide care and after-care), when the need arises solely from
destitution or the physical effects of such destitution. The extent of the
residual duties was not discussed in *R v Wandsworth London Borough
Council, ex p O*,[1] but it would be reasonable to assume that the same
principles will apply as in that case, ie that where the effects of destitution
were aggravated by illness or other vulnerability, the duty remains. Paragraph 341 of the Explanatory Notes to the IAA 1999 would also suggest that
this is the correct interpretation. A local authority has powers under section 2
of the Local Government Act 2000 to provide accommodation or assist
someone to secure accommodation but this power too is restricted to those
who are not in need of care and assistance solely by reason of destitution
caused by their not being entitled to welfare benefits and support.[2]

1   *R v Wandsworth London Borough Council, ex p O; R v Leicester City Council,
    ex p Bhikha* [2000] 4 All ER 590.
2   *R (on the application of Khan) v Oxfordshire County Council* [2004] EWCA Civ 309,
    [2004] HLR 706.

13.181 Where a person is entitled to assistance under the National Assistance Act 1948, existing case law relating to it will still be applicable. Therefore, local authorities will have no power to give assistance in cash.[1] Neither do they have the power to provide an individual with food vouchers, if they are not also providing accommodation. However, in that situation, the person could be in need of care and attention because he or she had no food (although there would have to be another reason, or no duty would arise) and the local authority should therefore consider whether it should secure residential accommodation for the person, even if he or she is not yet threatened with eviction.[2] The local authority does not have to provide residential accommodation within an institutional setting and can provide ancillary services, appropriate to the individual's needs, including board, as part of an overall package.[3] Neither is it restricted to providing bed and breakfast accommodation.[4] Health and social services authorities have a duty to provide residential accommodation free of charge to anyone who has been discharged from detention under section 3 of the Mental Health Act 1983.[5] Schedule 3 to the Nationality, Immigration and Asylum Act 2002 does not apply to or limit this power.[6] Where it is thought that a person has community care needs, the local authority is under a duty to undertake a needs assessment.[7]

[1]   *R v Secretary of State for Health, ex p Hammersmith and Fulham London Borough Council* [1999] 31 HLR 475, [1999] BLGR 354.
[2]   *R v Newham London Borough Council, ex p Gorenkin (Mikhail)* [1997–98] 1 CCL Rep 309.
[3]   *R v Newham London Borough Council, ex p Medical Foundation for the Care of Victims of Torture* [1997–98] 1 CCL Rep 227. For guidance on when the duty is discharged see *R v Royal Borough of Kensington and Chelsea, ex p Kujtim* (1999) 32 HLR 579, CA.
[4]   *R v Newham London Borough Council, ex p C* (1998) 31 HLR 567.
[5]   Mental Health Act 1983, s 117; *R v Richmond upon Thames London Borough Council, ex p Watson* [2001] QB 370, CA.
[6]   The provision is not listed in NIAA 2002, Sch 3, para 1(1).
[7]   National Health Service and Community Care Act 1990, s 47(1). See Council Directive 2003/9/EC, and the requirement to have regard to the needs of vulnerable persons; see 13.89 above.

CHILDREN ACT 1989

13.182 Before the Children Act 1989 came into force, the National Assistance Act 1948 contained a power to assist both adults and children in need of care and attention but the Children Act 1989 amended the 1948 Act to restrict its powers to those aged 18 or over.[1] The Children Act 1989 includes a general target duty for all local authorities to safeguard and promote the welfare of children within their area who are in need, to meet these needs by providing a range of appropriate services, and to promote the upbringing of such children by their families wherever that is consistent with promoting their welfare.[2] This duty may include the provision of accommodation and financial support to both the children and their families. Local authorities may owe a duty under section 17 to non-asylum seeking families who are subject to immigration control. However, section 17 does not place an absolute duty on a local authority to provide accommodation in accordance with a family's assessed need; neither does it impose a specific duty to meet the needs of each individual child. It only places a general duty on a local authority to maintain a level and range of services sufficient to enable it to discharge its functions under the Act. Its more specific duties are contained in other sections of the Act.[3] In cases covered by Schedule 3 to the Nationality, Immigration and Asylum Act 2002, the authority may provide accommodation and support only to the children, except in cases where this would lead to a breach of rights protected by the ECHR.[4] Local authorities are not permitted to exercise their powers to provide accommodation and essential living needs to asylum seekers and their minor dependants whilst NASS is either providing them with support or has the power to do so if they were to apply for support.[5] Responsibility for supporting the children of asylum seekers lies exclusively with NASS. So where an able-bodied asylum seeker had two disabled minor dependants, no duty arose under section 17 and NASS was held to be responsible for providing adequate accommodation to meet the children's needs. It was held that in such circumstances, NASS should use its powers to request local authorities and social landlords to assist it to find adequate accommodation for the family.[6]

1   Children Act 1989, Sch 13, para 11.
2   Children Act 1989, s 17.
3   *R (on the application of G) v Barnet London Borough Council* [2003] UKHL 57, [2004] 2 AC 208, [2003] 3 WLR 1194, [2004] 1 All ER 97.
4   See eg *R (on the application of Grant) v Lambeth London Borough Council* [2004] EWHC 1524 (Admin), [2004] 3 FCR 494.
5   Immigration and Asylum Act 1999, s 122 (to be substituted by Nationality, Immigration and Asylum Act 2002, s 47 from a date to be appointed).
6   *R (on the application of A) v National Asylum Support Service* [2003] EWCA Civ 1473, [2004] 1 All ER 15.

13.183 Where a local authority has 'looked after' unaccompanied minor asylum seekers between the ages of 14 and 18 prior to 7 November 2002 under section 17 or 20 of the Children Act 1989, it may owe those young persons an ongoing duty until the age of up to 24, to provide them with any necessary accommodation or support (in terms of travel expenses, money for books and equipment or perhaps even fees) to ensure that they can continue their education or enter the employment market.[1] Even if the local authority asserts that the child was only assisted under section 17 on or after 7 November 2002 when it had ceased to be classified as a power to 'look after' the child,[2] there is a rebuttable presumption that the local authority should have been looking after an unaccompanied child under section 20 of the Children Act 1989, and thus owes the continuing duty.[3] It is also under a duty to provide him or her with a pathway plan and a personal adviser.[4] If a young person who is over 18 has been granted refugee status, Humanitarian Protection or exceptional or discretionary leave, this support will be additional to any support he or she is entitled to from his or her local housing authority or from the Department for Work and Pensions. Sixteen- or seventeen-year-olds who were previously looked after by a local authority are not entitled to claim income-based jobseekers allowance, income support or housing benefit and should continue to be supported by their local authority.[5] If he or she is still an asylum seeker when he or she becomes eighteen, NASS will reimburse the local authority with the cost of his or her accommodation and support so that he or she can remain in that local authority's area.[6]

1   Children Act 1989, ss 24, 24A, 24B (as amended and inserted by the Children (Leaving Care) Act 2000 and the Adoption and Children Act 2002).
2   Ie, as a result of the Children Act 1989, s 22 being amended by the Adoption and Children Act 2002, s 116(2) on 7 November 2002.
3   Local Authority Circular LAC(2003) 13 *Guidance on Accommodating Children in Need and Their Families*, 2 June 2003; see also *R (on the application of Berhe) v London Borough of Hillingdon* [2003] EWHC 2075 (Admin), [2004] 1 FLR 439, followed in *R (on the application of W) v Essex County Council* [2003] EWHC 3175 (Admin), [2003] All ER (D) 402 (Dec).
4   Children Act 1989, s 23B, 23C, inserted by the Children (Leaving Care) Act 2000, ss 2, 4.
5   Children (Leaving Care) Act 2000, s 6.
6   See the *Children Leaving Care Act Regulation and Guidance*, paras 7–12; see also NASS Policy Bulletin 29 *Transition at the Age of 18*.

ACCESS TO HOUSING

13.184 A person who is subject to immigration control[1] has the right to own property in the UK and to enter into a private tenancy agreement. As a private sector tenant, he or she has the same rights to security of tenure, access to civil remedies in cases of disrepair or excessive rent rises as any other private tenant and may rely on the Protection from Eviction Act 1977.[2] He or she is also protected from discrimination on the basis of race, when seeking accommodation.[3] However, there is no eligibility for housing benefit[4] except for those who have been granted indefinite leave to remain as refugees, Humanitarian Protection or discretionary leave, and certain categories of asylum seeker. Those who claimed asylum on arrival before 3 April 2000 whose applications are not yet recorded by the Secretary of State as having been decided or abandoned, are still entitled to housing benefit[5] even if they did not apply for housing benefit on arrival. They are also entitled to housing benefit, if they are entitled to income support or income-based jobseeker's allowance for some other reason.[6] They will not generally be eligible for public sector housing.[7] Section 160A of the Housing Act 1996, inserted by the Homelessness Act 2002, prevents local housing authorities from allocating public sector housing to persons from abroad, including those subject to immigration control under the 1996 Act,[8] those excluded from housing benefit by section 115 of the 1999 Act[9] and other classes as prescribed. Regulations under section 160A prescribe categories of persons who are subject to immigration control but who may be allocated housing under the Act.[10] These are:

- refugees and persons with exceptional leave to remain (since they are not excluded from having recourse to public funds);
- persons who have indefinite leave to remain and are habitually resident in the common travel area (except for sponsored immigrants who have been here for less than five years and whose sponsor is still alive);
- persons over 18, who left Montserrat after 1 November 1995 because of the effect on that territory of a volcanic eruption; and
- nationals of a state which has ratified[11] the European Convention on Social and Medical Assistance or the Council of Europe Social Charter and who are lawfully present and habitually resident here.[12] Prior to 3 April 2000, nationals of states which had signed the Convention and Charter and who were habitually resident here were also entitled to join

the housing register, but this right has now been removed, unless they are owed an extant duty under Part III of the Housing Act 1985 (Housing the Homeless) or Part VII of the Housing Act 1996 (Homelessness).

Nationals of EEA states are ineligible for allocation of housing unless they are habitually resident in the common travel area and are also workers[13] or persons with the right to reside pursuant to the Immigration (European Economic Area) Regulations 2000 and the relevant Council directives.[14] This applies to accession state workers who are treated as qualified persons under the EEA Regulations.[15] Those entitled to housing accommodation may apply to a local housing authority for housing, and their entitlement will be considered in line with the usual procedures contained in the Housing Act 1996. If they are homeless, they may apply as a homeless person under that Act as amended by the Homelessness Act 2002. Those refused housing allocation on grounds of ineligibility have a right to written reasons for the refusal, but not to a review of the decision.[16]

1   Immigration and Asylum Act 1999, s 118(6).
2   *Akinbolu v Hackney London Borough Council* (1996) 29 HLR 259.
3   Race Relations Act 1976, ss 20–21.
4   IAA 1999, s 115(1)(j).
5   Social Security (Immigration and Asylum) Consequential Amendments Regulations 2000, SI 2000/636, regs 12(6), (7)(a), (8).
6   Housing Benefit (General) Regulations, 1987, SI 1987/1971, reg 7A(5)(f).
7   IAA 1999, s 118.
8   Housing Act 1996, s 160A(1), (3) (inserted by the Homelessness Act 2002, s 4 from 5 December 2002).
9   HA 1996, s 160A(4) as inserted.
10   Allocation of Housing (England) Regulations 2002, SI 2002/3264, as amended by SI 2004/1235, regs 4, 5(1) (for Wales see Allocation of Housing (Wales) Regulations 2003, SI 2003/239).
11   For non-EEA states which have ratified these agreements see 13.12 above.
12   Allocation of Housing (England) Regulations 2002, SI 2002/3264, reg 4. For 'lawfully present' see *Kaya v Haringey London Borough Council* [2001] EWCA Civ 677, [2001] All ER (D) 15 (May) 13.12 above.
13   Council Regulation (EEC) 1612/68 or 1251/70.
14   Council Directives (EEC) No 68/360 and 73/148 or 75/34/EEC. In *Sheich (Habiba) v Bristol County Council 5* BS 03394, HHJ Purcell held that an EEA national who was not employed and who was not a work seeker or otherwise a qualified person within the meaning of reg 5 of the Immigration (European Economic Area) Regulations 2000 was eligible for housing assistance under Part VII of the Housing Act 1996, because she was in receipt of income support and fell within Class 1 of reg 3 of the Homelessness (England) Regulations 2000.
15   SI 2000/2326. By the application of the Accession (Immigration and Worker Registration) Regulations 2004, SI 2004/1219, reg 5: Allocation of Housing (England) Regulations 2002, SI 2002/3264, as amended by SI 2004/2004, reg 5(2).
16   HA 1996, s 160A(9), (10) as inserted.

13.185 Section 118 of the Immigration and Asylum Act 1999, which re-enacts section 9(1) of the Asylum and Immigration Act 1996, requires housing authorities to ensure that, so far as is practicable, tenancies and licences are not granted under Part II of the Housing Act 1985 (provision of housing accommodation) to persons subject to immigration control, except for certain classes specified in regulations.[1] The regulations consolidate previous provisions made under section 9 of the AIA 1996. However, from

3 April 2000, regulations also permit housing authorities to use hard to let accommodation held under Part II of the Housing Act 1985 for overseas students, as long as they are not granted secure tenancies.[2] From 3 April 2000, nationals of states which have signed, but not ratified, the European Convention on Social and Medical Assistance or the Council of Europe Social Charter do not qualify for housing under Part II of the Housing Act 1985, and nationals of ratifying states must be lawfully present[3] in order to qualify. Section 118 does not apply to secure tenancies allocated under Part VI of the Housing Act 1996, but few persons subject to immigration control qualify for inclusion on the housing register in any event.[4]

1   Persons Subject to Immigration Control (Housing Authority Accommodation and Homelessness) Order 2000, SI 2000/706, Art 3.
2   SI 2000/706, reg 4(e). See also the Persons Subject to Immigration Control (Housing Authority Accommodation) (Wales) Order 2000, SI 2000/1036 (W67).
3   See 13.12 above.
4   See previous paragraph.

13.186 From 3 April 2000, asylum seekers are ineligible for housing authority accommodation if they are homeless, even if they are in priority need and not intentionally homeless.[1] They must instead apply to NASS for a decision on whether they are destitute.[2] If they have accommodation but it is in a very poor state of repair, it is unlikely to be deemed adequate so as to preclude a finding of destitution.[3] If they are facing eviction from previous accommodation, NASS will only deem them destitute if the actual eviction is due to take place in 14 days or less.[4] In order to provide accommodation for asylum seekers, NASS enters into contractual arrangements with local authorities, registered social landlords and private landlords and companies. It does not enter into a contract with the asylum seekers themselves. The accommodation provider does not provide them with a tenancy agreement, but enters into an occupation agreement. Asylum seekers provided with accommodation by NASS are, therefore, not secure tenants, unless their landlord expressly notifies them that they have been given a secure tenancy.[5] This is the case even if they are occupying local authority accommodation. Neither can they be assured tenants.[6] In addition, they will not benefit from the Protection against Eviction Act 1977.[7] Once an asylum application has been finally determined,[8] the asylum seeker is expected to leave the accommodation provided by NASS within a further seven days.[9] However, if NASS does evict a person from accommodation it has previously provided to him or her, it would be expected to act reasonably in doing so.[10]

1   Immigration and Asylum Act 1999, Sch 16, amending Housing Act 1996, s 183(2); Homelessness (England) Regulations 2000, SI 2000/701, reg 3(f); NASS Policy *Bulletin 10.* See also the Homelessness (Wales) Regulations 2000, SI 2000/1079 (W 72).
2   See above 13.60ff.
3   *Lismane v Hammersmith and Fulham London Borough Council* (1998) 31 HLR 427; see 13.63 above.
4   Asylum Support Regulations 2000, SI 2000/704, reg 7(a).
5   Housing Act 1985, Sch 1, para 4A; Housing (Scotland) Act 1987, Sch 2, para 5A.
6   Housing Act 1988, Sch 1, para 12A; Housing (Scotland) Act 1988, Sch 4, para 11B.
7   Immigration and Asylum Act 1999, Sch 14, para 73 excludes asylum seekers from security of tenure.
8   The claim is determined 28 days after a claim for asylum is accepted, or 21 days after a negative decision by the Secretary of State or (if there is an appeal) after the disposal of the appeal: Immigration and Asylum Act 1999 s 93(4), Asylum Support Regulations 2000,

SI 2000/704, reg 2(2), as amended by SI 2002/472, reg 3; Asylum Support (Interim Provisions) Regulations as amended by SI 2002/471. For final determination of a claim see further 13.43ff above.

9   Asylum Support Regulations 2000, SI 2000/704, reg 22. The total period after the final decision on the claim is thus 35 or 28 days (see fn 8 above), but a further two days is added for receipt of the relevant notices. See NASS Policy Bulletin *Grace Periods*.

10   See *R v Newham London Borough Council, ex p Ojuri (No 5)* (1998) 31 HLR 631 and *R v Secretary of State for the Environment, ex p Shelter and the Refugee Council* (23 August 1996, unreported), QBD.

13.187 If an asylum seeker has been granted refugee status, Humanitarian Protection, or exceptional or discretionary leave to remain and is homeless, eligible for assistance, in priority need and not intentionally homeless, he or she is entitled to local authority accommodation on the same basis as other homeless persons.[1] The local authority will also be under a duty to provide accommodation on a temporary basis whilst his or her entitlement to such accommodation is being assessed,[2] or pending a possible referral to another authority.[3] The House of Lords held that a successful asylum seeker was not obliged to seek assistance from the local authority to whose area he or she had formerly been dispersed, as dispersal accommodation provided by NASS on a no-choice basis could not give rise to residence of choice in that area for the purpose of establishing a local connection. Therefore, another local authority to whom the applicant may choose to apply for assistance under Part VII of the Housing Act 1996 could not seek to hold the 'dispersal' authority responsible for providing him or her with accommodation.[4] In response, the Government rushed through a new section 11 of the Asylum and Immigration (Treatment of Claimants, etc) Act 2004, which came into force on 4 January 2005, and effectively reverses their decision. It provides that a person has a local connection with the district of a local housing authoriity if he or she was (at any time) provided with accommodation in that district under section 95 of the Immigration and Asylum Act 1999 unless he or she was subsequently provided with accommodation in the district of another local housing authority.[5] Accommodation in an accommodation centre does not give rise to a local connection for housing purposes.[6] When the section comes into a force a homeless person, who was previously provided with accommodation in Scotland (otherwise than in an accommodation centre) under section 95 of the Immigration and Asylum Act 1999 at any time and has not been able to establish a local connection with a district of a local housing authority in either England and Wales or Scotland will be entitled only to temporary accommodation and advice and assistance from his or her local housing authority for the period needed to give him or her a reasonable opportunity of securing accommodation.[7] Refugees and others who have been granted leave to remain may be able to show an alternative local connection through their employment, family associations or as a result of special circumstances.[8] Family associations may give rise to a local connection if they involve parents, siblings or people who previously were part of the same household.[9] A young person who was formerly an unaccompanied minor asylum seeker and who was looked after by a local authority for more than 13 weeks after the age of 14 and before the age of 18, who subsequently becomes homeless when he or she is no longer looked after, will be deemed to be in priority need for rehousing (as long as he or she is otherwise eligible for public housing for

example as a refugee or as someone who has been granted Humanitarian
Protection or exceptional or discretionary leave).[10]

1   Housing Act 1996, s 193 (as amended by the Homelessness Act 2002, from 31 July 2002).
2   HA1996, s 188 as amended.
3   HA 1996, s 200, as amended.
4   *Al-Ameri v Kensington and Chelsea Royal London Borough Council; Osman v Harrow
    London Borough Council* [2004] UKHL 4, [2004] 2 AC 159, upholding [2003] EWCA
    Civ 235, [2003] 2 All ER 1.
5   HA 1996, s 199(6), inserted by Asylum and Immigration (Treatment of Claimants, etc)
    Act 2004 s 11(1), in force 4 January 2005: SI 2000/2999.
6   HA 1996, s 199(7)(b), as inserted.
7   Asylum and Immigration (Treatment of Claimants, etc) Act 2004, s 11(2), (3).
8   HA 1996, s 199(1) (as amended).
9   *R v Hammersmith and Fulham London Borough Council, ex p Avdic* (1996) 30 HLR 1;
    Munting v Hammersmith and Fulham London Borough Council [1998] CLY 3017.
10 Homelessness (Priority Need for Accommodation) (England) Order 2002, SI 2002/2051.

13.188 Accommodation provided by NASS should be adequate for the needs
of the asylum seeker.[1] Ministerial statements suggest that the adequacy of the
accommodation should be judged on the same basis as the suitability of
accommodation provided to homeless persons under housing legislation.[2] It is
likely that the need to access specialist hospital services, to ensure the safety,
welfare and protection of children and to protect public health will be taken
into account.[3] Other factors which may be taken into account are the location
of members of the same ethnic or religious group, health needs, disability and
dietary needs.[4] As asylum seekers do not hold the accommodation which they
occupy under a tenancy, they are not protected by any implied repairing
obligation if the property is in disrepair.[5] Occupation agreements drawn up by
accommodation providers are unlikely to include express repairing obligations. However, if the accommodation is in such a state of disrepair that it
could be said to be prejudicial to the health of asylum seekers or their
dependants, they can seek an abatement order in the county court against a
local authority, a registered social landlord or a private landlord.[6] If the
accommodation is provided by a registered social landlord or a private
landlord, they could also request inspection by an environmental health officer
and, if appropriate, ask the local authority to serve a statutory notice.[7] If there
is a significant risk of violence occurring to the asylum seeker or one of his or
her dependants, as a result of racial harassment directed towards them, NASS
should provide alternative accommodation.[8]

1   Immigration and Asylum Act 1999, s 96(1)(a).
2   Barbara Roche (Parliamentary Under-Secretary of State), Written Answer, 348 HC Official
    Report (6th series), col 593, 20 April 2000. See 13.96ff above.
3   Lord Williams of Mostyn, 605 HL Official Report (5th series), col 1163, 20 October 1999.
    See now the duty to have regard to family unity and the needs of vulnerable persons, in
    Council Directive 2003/9/EC, and the Asylum Seekers (Reception Conditions) Regula-
    tions 2005, SI 2005/7.
4   NASS Application Form, note 11.
5   Under Landlord and Tenant Act 1985, s 11.
6   Environmental Protection Act 1990, s 82.
7   EPA 1990, s 80.
8   NASS Policy *Bulletin 81: Racist Incidents;* see 13.67 above.

13.189 Those persons who claimed asylum on arrival in the UK before
3 April 2000 and whose applications are not yet recorded as having been

decided (other than on appeal) or abandoned, are still eligible for temporary accommodation as homeless persons under Part VII of the Housing Act 1996 if they are homeless, in priority need and not intentionally homeless.[1] They may also apply for housing benefit.[2] If they are homeless but not in priority need,[3] the local authority is not obliged to house them, but has a duty to provide advice and assistance in relation to finding alternative housing.[4] This may involve access to a rent deposit scheme, a hostel placement, a lodger scheme or fast tracking of housing benefit. An asylum seeker whose application is recorded as having been made within three months of a declaration of fundamental upheaval and whose claim is not yet recorded as having been decided (other than on appeal) or abandoned, will also be entitled to accommodation under homelessness legislation[5] and to housing benefit.[6] Such an asylum seeker will be deemed to be in priority need if he or she is vulnerable on grounds of age, illness, pregnancy or disability or has dependent children or a pregnant partner.[7] If a single asylum seeker, who was eligible for housing but for the fact that he or she was not in priority need, is joined by a dependant with such needs on or after 3 April 2000, he or she will become eligible, if they enter as his or her dependants and if his or her application has not yet been recorded as decided.[8]

1 Homelessness (England) Regulations 2000, SI 2000/701, reg 3(f); NASS Policy *Bulletin 10.* Persons who are ineligible for assistance are defined in reg 4 (as substituted by the Allocation of Housing and Homelessness (Amendment) (England) Regulations 2004, SI 2004/1235 from 1 May 2004.
2 Social Security (Immigration and Asylum) Consequential Amendments Regulations 2000, SI 2000/636, reg 12(6), (7)(a).
3 The most usual example of this is a single person in good health, with no dependants.
4 Housing Act 1996, s 192 as amended by the Homelessness Act 2002.
5 SI 2000/701, reg 3(g).
6 SI 2000/636, reg 12(6), (7)(b).
7 HA 1996, s 189 as amended.
8 SI 2000/701, reg 3(f).

13.190 Amendments to Part VII of the Housing Act 1996 (homelessness) have also been introduced to enable local authorities to disperse asylum seekers to areas outside London and the south-east and for the receiving local authorities to place them in housing authority accommodation.[1] These regulations came into force on 6 December 1999 and will continue in force whilst local authorities need to exercise such powers.[2]

1 The Homelessness (Asylum-Seekers) (Interim Period) (England) Order 1999, SI 1999/3126.
2 See 13.155ff above.

13.191 Persons who are subject to immigration control, but who qualify for public sector housing under housing legislation, will be allocated long-term accommodation by a local authority or a registered social landlord.[1] Their applications will be considered in accordance with the provisions of Part VI of the Housing Act 1996 or the equivalent parts of the appropriate housing legislation in Wales. Housing is allocated according to housing need and local authorities are required to draw up procedures by which they prioritise the allocation of their available housing stock.[2]

1 A housing association, trust or co-operative or limited company, which is registered with the Housing Corporation under Housing Act 1996, Part I.

² Housing Act 1996, s 167 (as amended by the Homelessness Act 2002); DoE/ DoH Code of Guidance on the Housing Act 1996, Parts VI and VII. For eligibility and ineligibility for housing under s 160A of the Act as amended, see 13.184 above.

ACCESS TO EDUCATIONAL PROVISION

Pre-school, primary and secondary education

13.192 Although children may not be admitted to the UK for the purpose of state education,[1] access to state education for children between the ages of four and 16 is not subject to any restriction in the immigration legislation. Even if an adult's leave to remain is subject to the condition that they do not rely on public funds or they are illegal entrants or overstayers, they are entitled to send their children to school. Similarly, unaccompanied asylum seeking children and children who have been granted asylum, humanitarian protection or discretionary or exceptional leave to remain are also entitled to free education in maintained schools.[2] Local authorities have a duty to provide school places to any child residing, temporarily or permanently, in their area.[3] If the child is from an asylum-seeking family, NASS should inform the relevant education authority that a child is being dispersed to its area.[4] From September 2000 to March 2003, schools in dispersal areas were eligible for a one -off grant of £500 for each pupil they admitted from an asylum-seeking family which was supported by NASS.[5] Since then education authorities have been expected to absorb the costs of educating these children within the Standard Spending Assessment System.[6] Local education authorities also receive funding to provide free early education places to the most needy three-year-olds in their area. It is up to the authorities to set their own criteria of social need, which may include providing places to children from asylum-seeking families. As a matter of policy, in the case of chidren of in-country or disbenefitted asylum seekers and unaccompanied minors, NASS caseworkers should consider exceptionally deferring dispersal if a child is in his or her final year at school or college and is about to take his or her final examinations at GCSE, AS or A level.[7]

1 HC 395, para 57; see chapter 9 above.
2 School Standards and Framework Act 1998, s 20(7).
3 Education Act 1996, s13.
4 NASS Policy Bulletin 63 *Education*.
5 See Ofsted report on The Education of Asylum-Seeking Pupils, HMI 453 (October 2003).
6 NASS Policy Bulletin 63 *Education*, para 6.
7 NASS Policy Bulletin *Dispersal Guidelines* para 6.3.

13.193 If Part 2 of the Nationality, Immigration and Asylum Act 2002 is brought into force and asylum seekers are housed in accommodation centres, local authorities will be deprived of the power to admit children accommodated there to maintained schools or nurseries[1] unless the child in question is admitted to a community or foundation special school which had been named in a statement of special educational needs under section 324 of the Education Act 1996[2] or there is no educational provision at the centre provided under section 29(1)(f) of the Nationality, Immigration and Asylum Act 2002.[3] Local authorities and governors of maintained schools are also required to admit children to the school of their parents' choice, subject to resource considerations,[4] unless the child in question is resident in an accommodation centre.[5] This also applies to children with special educational needs[6] unless they are resident in an accommodation centre.[7] Children with special educational needs also have the right to be educated in mainstream school if this is appropriate to their needs[8] unless they are resident in an accommodation centre.[9] Educational provision within accommodation centres will not be 'schools' as defined by section 4 of the Education Act 1996 but will be subject to school inspections[10] and reviews and assessments of educational needs.[11] Children of asylum seekers will also be entitled to free school meals.[12] Local education authorities also have a discretion to provide asylum seeking children with school uniform grants and bus passes.[13] Some schools have developed good models to assist the integration of children from asylum-seeking families into maintained schools.[14]

1   Nationality, Immigration and Asylum Act 2002, s 36(2).
2   NIAA 2002, s 36(3).
3   NIAA 2002, s 36(10).
4   School Standards and Framework Act 1998, ss 86 (1), (2), 94.
5   NIAA 2002, s 36(5).
6   Education Act 1996, Sch 27, paras 3, 8.
7   NIAA 2002, s 36(5)(e).
8   Education Act 1996, s 316(2), (3).
9   NIAA 2002, s 36(5)(d). Children with special educational needs who are resident in an accommodation centre will be provided with education there unless this is incompatible with receiving the special educational provision which his or her learning difficulty calls for, the provision of efficient education for other children who are resident in the accommodation centre or the efficient use of resources: s 36(7), (8). If so, the education provider at the accommodation centre will advise the local education authority in writing that that there are special circumstances which call for it to provide for the particular child's special educational needs and it will be able to disapply the provisions of NIAA 2002, s 36 which prevented it from making such provision: s 37(1), (2). The Secretary of State can provide guidance to local authorities in relation to such eventualities but has not done so yet: s 37(3), (6).
10   School Inspections Act 1996.
11   Education Act 1996, s 329A, Learning and Skills Act 2000, s 140.
12   Education Act 1996, s 512(3) as amended by the Immigration and Asylum Act 1999, Sch 14, para 117.
13   NASS Policy Bulletin 63 *Education* para 8.
14   See Ofsted report on The Education of Asylum-Seeking Children, HMI 453 (October 2003).

Further education

13.194 The Learning and Skills Council is responsible for determining whether to fund further education for asylum seekers. Colleges have a discretion as to whether they accept asylum seekers onto their courses and most colleges do. Once a college has accepted the asylum seeker onto a course it can apply to the Learning and Skills Council for funding for him or her.[1] Young people who were looked after by a local authority for more than 13 weeks after they reached the age of 14 and before they became 18 are entitled to additional assistance with the additional costs of travel, accommodation and books associated with attending further or higher education or training.[2] This will include assistance to pay for accommodation during vacations. Young people in these categories who were 'looked after' by a local authority before 1 October 2001 for at least three months and who are not entitled to support as a result of the Children (Leaving Care) Act 2000 can apply to their local education authority in England and Wales or to the Student Awards Agency for Scotland or the appropriate Education and Library Board in Northern Ireland for financial support.

¹ NASS Policy Bulletin 63 Education, para 8.
² Children Act 1989, ss 24, 24A, 24B, the Children (Leaving Care) (England) (Regulations) 2001, SI 2001/2874; see also *R (on the application of Berhe) v Hillingdon London Borough Council* [2003] EWHC 2075 (Admin), [2004] 1 FLR 439; Guidance on Accommodating Children in Need and Their Families, LAC(2003)13.

Higher Education

13.195 Publicly-funded educational institutions are permitted to charge higher fees for students of further¹ and higher² education, who do not qualify as 'home students'.³ For higher education courses, individual higher education institutions are responsible for classifying students for fees purposes.⁴ A student is likely to qualify as a 'home student' for the purposes of higher education courses if he or she falls within one of six categories:

(1)   British citizens, those with the right of abode in the UK or with indefinite leave to remain here, who have been ordinarily resident⁵ throughout the three-year period preceding the start of the course,⁶ and that ordinary residence must not have been wholly or mainly for the purpose of receiving full-time education;

(2)   EU nationals and their children who have been orginarily resident in the EEA for the three years prior to the start of their course where such residence must not have been wholly or mainly for the purpose of receiving full-time education. Nationals of EU Accession states⁷ will be able to qualify as 'home students' from the start of the 2004/2005 academic year and they will be deemed to have been resident for the necessary three-year period in the EEA;

(3)   EEA nationals,⁸ and Swiss nationals or residents, who are in the UK as 'migrant workers' and their spouses and children, who have been ordinarily resident in the EEA for the three years prior to the commencement of their course. A spouse of a migrant worker can only qualify if he or she is living with him or her in the UK;

(4)   People granted refugee status in the UK and their spouses and children, who have become or remained ordinarily resident in the UK since ther status was recognised. The UKCOSA Guidance states that if a person is granted refugee status part way through a course, he or she will be liable to pay 'home fees' on the next occasion that fees are due. However, as the grant of refugee status merely recognises the fact that the person is a refugee and does not create this status, it is arguable that a refugee is entitled to a repayment of any additional fees paid as an 'overseas' student' before his or her status was formally recognised;

(5)   Persons granted Humanitarian Protection or discretionary or exceptional leave to remain and their spouses and children following the refusal of asylum. They must also have been ordinarily resident in the

UK or the Channel Islands or the Isle of Man for the three years prior to the start of their course. However, any time spent as an asylum seeker counts towards this period;

(6) Students studying under a formal exchange programme where fees have to be paid. (It is usual under such programmes for the fees to be waived.)

1 GCSE, 'A' level and their equivalent, NVQ, GNVQ, BTEC and access courses.
2 Undergraduate, post-graduate, HND and HNC courses.
3 Education (Fees and Awards) Act 1983, s 1; Education (Fees and Awards) Regulations 1997, SI 1997/1972.
4 In line with the Education (Fees and Awards) Regulations 1997, as amended or the Education (Fees and Awards) (Scotland) Regulations 1997, SI 1997/93 as amended by SI 1997/2008.
5 Ordinary residence was defined by the House of Lords in *Shah v Barnet London Borough Council* [1983] 2 AC 309 as 'abode in a particular place or country which [the person] has adopted voluntarily and for a settled purpose as part of the regular order of his life for the time being, whether of short or long duration'. Reasons for the residence can include business or profession, employment, health, family or merely love of the place. If a person is not legally present in the UK he or she cannot be ordinarily resident.
6 This will be calculated as the date closest to 1 January, 1 April or 1 September.
7 Cyprus, the Czech Republic, Estonia, Hungary, Latvia, Lithuania, Malta, Poland, Slovakia and Slovenia.
8 Nationals of the EU plus Iceland, Liechtenstein and Norway.

13.196 Most institutions providing further education courses will charge 'home fees' or no fees at all to the following categories :

- people who have lived in the UK for the three years before the start of their course (but those who have come from outside the EEA as students may be excluded);
- asylum seekers in receipt of assistance from NASS or in receipt of any means tested benefit or in receipt of voucher or financial services from a Social Services department or who are between 16 and 18, unaccompanied and being 'looked after' by Social Services;
- people who became settled in the UK less than three years before the start of their course;
- a husband or wife who came to the UK to join a settled spouse and who has been living in the UK for more than 12 months and married for at least 12 months;
- people granted Humanitarian Protection or exceptional or discretionary leave to enter or remain, even if this is not as the result of an asylum application;
- 16–18 year olds who are British citizens or who have right of abode;
- Other exceptional circumstances.[1]

In Scotland, most institutions offering further education will charge 'home fees' if an asylum seeker is on a full-time or part-time English for Speakers of Other Languages ('ESOL') course or other part-time non-advanced courses funded by the Scottish Further Education Funding Council or anyone on a part time ESOL course. In Wales, most institutions offering further education will charge 'home fees' to asylum seekers receiving support from NASS, means tested benefits or voucher/financial support from Social Services or who are 16 to 18 years old and being 'looked after' by Social Services where the courses funded by Education and Learning Wales. 16–18-year-olds who are British citizens will also be charged 'home fees' No special arrangements exist in Northern Ireland.

¹ Guidance Notes for Students 2003 – 2004, UKCOSA and DfES website.

13.197 Local authorities may lawfully impose eligibility criteria for awards of Student Support in the form of a grant for tuition fees and a loan for living costs. Student Support is available for first degree courses (either full time or sandwich), a Higher National Diploma, a Diploma in Higher Education or a Postgraduate Certificate in Education or some part-time courses of initial teacher training. Students who fall within categories (1), (3), (4), and (5) above (13.196) are potentially eligible for a grant to cover tuition fees and a loan to meet maintenance costs subject to meeting financial criteria of need.¹ Those in (2) are only eligible for a grant to cover tuition fees or part of them but not for a student loan or any supplementary grants.² Student Support is administered by local authorities in England and Wales, the Student Awards Agency for Scotland and the appropriate Education and Library Board in Northern Ireland. However, EU nationals and their children should apply directly to the Department for Education and Skills. The Government also plans to provide Higher Education Grants to new full-time, sandwich and part-time initial teacher training courses starting in 2004/2005. Those who fall within categories (1), (3), (4) and (5) will qualify for such grants if they meet the relevant financial criteria.

¹ Education (Mandatory Awards) Regulations 1997, SI 1997/431, reg 13.
² Education (Student Support) (No 2) Regulations 2002, SI 2002/3200.

ACCESS TO THE NATIONAL HEALTH SERVICE

13.198 The founding principle of the National Health Service was the provision of treatment which was free at the point of delivery, comprehensive and provided on the basis of need.¹ But inroads were made into the principle of free treatment in the late 1980s, when the Secretary of State was empowered to make regulations imposing charges for non-emergency treatment on people who are not ordinarily resident in the UK.² The term 'overseas visitors' has been and is used in the relevant regulations to describe those who are not ordinarily resident.³ Subsequent regulations permitted charges to be made.⁴ These charges can be calculated at an appropriate commercial basis and the power to set these rates has been devolved to the Strategic Health Authorities, Primary Care Trusts, Foundation Trusts and NHS Trusts in England.⁵

¹ See now National Health Service Act 1977, s 1(1)(b).
² National Health Service Act 1977, s 121 as amended by ss 7(12) and (14) of the Health and Medicines Act 1988. For ordinary residence see chapter 5 above.
³ National Health Service (Charges to Overseas Visitors) Regulations 1989, SI 1989/306, reg 1.
⁴ National Health Service (Charges to Overseas Visitors) Regulations 1989, SI 1989/306, as amended by SI 1991/438 and SI 1994/1535 and the National Health Service (Charges to Overseas Visitors) (Amendment) Regulations 2004, SI 2004/614.
⁵ National Health Service (Charges to Overseas Visitors) Regulations 1989, SI 1989/306, reg 7, as amended by SI 2000/602, reg 2(d) and SI 2004/614, Sch 2.

Visits for the purpose of private medical treatment

13.199 Persons entering the UK as visitors for medical treatment are required to pay privately as a condition of entry and further leave to remain.[1] In such cases, the NHS can withhold treatment pending payment in advance for any treatment or an acceptable guarantee of the future payment for any such treatment.[2] In exceptional humanitarian circumstances where a person can satisfy the Secretary of State that the treatment which he or she needs is not available in his or her country of origin, that the necessary arrangements have been made to accommodate him and her and any authorised companion or child,[3] and that the necessary arrangements have been made for them to return home at the end of the treatment, no charge for that treatment will be made or recovered.[4]

[1] HC 395, paras 51–56; see chapter 9 above.
[2] *R v Hammersmith Hospitals NHS Trust, ex p Reffell* (2000) 55 BMLR 130.
[3] 'Authorised' in this context means granted leave to enter the UK with the person obtaining a course of treatment in respect of which no charges are payable: National Health Service (Charges to Overseas Visitors) Regulations 1989, SI 1989/306, as amended by SI 2004/614, reg 1(2).
[4] National Health Service (Charges to Overseas Visitors) Regulations 1989, SI 1989/306, as amended, reg 6A.

NHS hospital treatment

13.200 NHS hospital treatment is no longer free for all at the point of delivery. Free treatment is limited by reference to an individual's immigration status and/or nationality unless the treatment falls within one of the categories listed in 13.202 below. Since 1 April 2004, amendments to the regulations[1] mean that only individuals who come within certain specified categories will enjoy the same entitlement to free non-emergency NHS hospital treatment as Britiish citizens and those who have indefinite leave to remain in the UK. The categories include:

(1) those who have resided in the UK lawfully for more than one year immediately preceeding the time when the treatment is provided, unless this period of residence resulted from being granted leave to enter for purpose of undergoing private medical treatment or was the result of a decision by the Secretary of State to grant leave and exempt the visitor from any charges for his or her treatment in the light of exceptional humanitarian reasons;[2]

(2) those engaged in employment with an employer which has its principal place of business in the UK or which is registered in the UK as a branch of an overseas company;[3]

(3) self-employed persons whose principal place of business is the UK;[4]

(4) those pursuing a full time course of study which is substantially funded by the UK government or is of at least six months duration;[5]

(5) persons working on a ship registered in the UK;[6]

(6) persons in receipt of a UK war pension;[7]

(7) diplomats working in a foreign embassy;[8]

(8) members of HM armed forces;[9]

(9) persons recruited inthe UK to work abroad for the UK civil service, the British Council or the Commonwealth War Graves Commission or working abroad in a post financed in part by the UK government; [10]

(10) persons working abroad who previously lived in the UK lawfully for a continuous period of ten years and have been away for less than five years; [11]

(11) persons working in another EEA state or in Switzerland but who pay National Insurance contributions in the UK; [12]

(12) persons in receipt of a UK state pension living not less than six months a year in the UK who are not registered as a resident in another EEA country;[13]

(13) members of NATO armed forces where treatment cannot readily be obtained in their own country or from the UK armed forces medical service;[14]

(14) volunteers with a voluntary organisation that is providing a service similar to a relevant service as defined in sections 64 and 65 of the Health Services and Public Health Act 1968 or the service to which Article 71 of the Health and Personal Social Services (Northern Ireland) Order 1972 refers;[15]

(15) persons who are taking up permanent residence in the UK;[16]

(16) persons accepted as refugees or who have made a formal application for leave to remain as a refugee which has not yet been determined,[17]

(17) those granted Humanitarian Protection or exceptional or discretionary leave;[18]

(18) persons detained in prison or immigration detention centres.[19]

Dependants of those falling within these categories are also entitled to free NHS hospital treatment. An individual who is no longer eligible for free treatment on or after 1 April 2004 on the basis that he or she cannot establish lawful residence in the UK for a period of not less than 12 months, but who prior to that date was receiving free NHS hospital treatment, will be entitled to complete his or her course of treatment without being obliged to pay.[20] Nationals of EEA Member States and those who have been accepted as refugees or stateless persons in those states may also be entitled to free NHS hospital treatment as a result of European law. For example, nationals of EEA Member States who are temporarily working or studying in the UK and who are in possession of a form E128 are entitled to free NHS treatment of all types, as are their families.[21]

1 See reg 4 of the National Health Services (Treatment of Overseas Visitors) (Amendment) Regulations 2004, SI 2004/614.
2 National Health Service (Charges to Overseas Visitors) Regulations 1989, SI 1989/306, as amended by SI 2004/614, reg 4(1)(b).
3 SI 1989/306, as amended by SI 2004/614, reg 4(1)(a)(zi).
4 SI 1989/306, as amended by SI 2004/614, reg 4(1)(a)(i).
5 SI 1989/306, as amended by SI 2004/614, reg 4(1)(a)(iii).
6 SI 1989/306, as amended by SI 2004/614, reg 4(1)(d).
7 SI 1989/306, as amended by SI 2004/614, reg 4(1)(e).
8 SI 1989/306, as amended by SI 2004/614, reg 4(1)(f).
9 SI 1989/306, as amended by SI 2004/614, reg 4(1)(g).
10 SI 1989/306, as amended by SI 2004/614, reg 4(1)(h), (i).
11 SI 1989/306, as amended by SI 2004/614, reg 4(1)(k).
12 SI 1989/306, as amended by SI 2004/614, reg 4(1)(l).
13 SI 1989/306, as amended by SI 2004/614, reg 4A(1).

[14]   SI 1989/306, as amended by SI 2004/614, reg 6.
[15]   SI 1972/1265 (NI 14) as amended. SI 1989/306, as amended by SI 2004/614, reg 4(1)(a)(ii).
[16]   SI 1989/306, as amended by SI 2004/614, reg 4(1)(a)(iv).
[17]   SI 1989/306, as amended by SI 2004/614, reg 4(1)(c).
[18]   Department of Health *Entitlement to NHS Treatment* (correct at 1 April 2004).
[19]   SI 1989/306, as amended by SI 2004/614, reg 4(1)(n).
[20]   SI 1989/306, as amended by SI 2004/614, reg 4(2).
[21]   SI 1989/306, as amended by SI 2004/614, reg 4(1)(m); Council Regulation 1408/71, OJ L149/2, 5.7.71; Council Regulation 1390/81, OJ L143, 12.5.81.

13.201 Asylum seekers and refugees in particular suffer a high rate of medical problems, exacerbated by poverty, poor housing, and loss of status and family support.[1] The Department of Health has produced a resource pack to provide advice to local health and social care agencies in NASS dispersal areas.[2] Asylum seekers should also be provided with their own Patient Held Health Records which they can take with them as they are dispersed around the country.[3]

[1]   See Refugee Health Consortium *Promoting the Health of Refugees* (November 1998) published by ILPA. The incidence of mental illness is particularly high. See eg Brent and Harrow HA 'Brent and Harrow Refugee Survey' (1995); Carey Wood and others 'The settlement of refugees in Britain' HO Research Study No 1441 (HMSO, 1995); Health of Londoners Project 'Refugee Health in London – Key issues for public health' HOLP, c/o East London and City HA (1999); Home Office Online Report 13/03 *Asylum Seekers in Dispersal – Healthcare Issues* by Mark R D Johnson, The HARP Programme whose steering group is based at the University of East London can also provide a good source of information on current research and information at www.harpweb.org.uk.
[2]   *Caring for Dispersed Asylum Seekers: A Resource Pack*, Department of Health, 19 June 2003.
[3]   This was developed by the Department of Health's Asylum Seeker Co-ordination Team and is downloadable from the Department of Health's website at www.dh.gov.uk They also produce a regular Asylum Seeker Newsletter.

13.202 Other individuals have a more limited entitlement to free NHS hospital treatment for conditions which arose during a visit.[1]

(1)   Nationals of EEA Member States and those who reside in these states as refugees or stateless persons and their dependants are entitled to all necessary care for illness which develop during their time in the UK or to emergency treatment (whether or not they are in possession of a form E 111, as a visitor, a form E 119, as a job seeker, or a form E 128 as a posted worker or student or a new European Health Insurance Card);[2]

(2)   Individuals who reside in countries other than Israel which have a reciprocal agreement with the UK are entitled to immediately necessary treatment;[3]

(3)   A person who is without sufficient resources to pay, is lawfully present in the UK and who is a national of a country which is a contracting party to the European Convention on Social and Medical Assistance 1954 is entitled to similar treatment;[4]

(4)   Persons receiving a UK state pension who have either lived lawfully in the UK for ten continuous years or have been employed by the UK government for ten continuous years at some point, or their spouse or

school-age children,[5] individuals who have lived lawfully for 10 continuous years in the UK but who are now living in an EEA Member State, Switzerland or a non-EEA country (other than Israel) with which the UK has a reciprocal agreement[6] and their spouse and school-age children are also entitled to treatment the need for which arises during their visit.[7]

EEA or Swiss nationals in possession of a form E112 are eligible for treatment for the particular condition specified on the form and for which they have been referred to the UK. Oxygen therapy and renal dialysis are available free of charge to nationals of EEA states.[8] Waiting lists for organ transplants are organised according to immigration status.[9]

[1] National Health Service (Charges to Overseas Visitors) Regulations 1989, SI 1989/306, as amended by S1 2004/614, reg 5.
[2] SI 1989/306, as amended by S1 2004/614, reg 5(a).
[3] SI 1989/306, as amended by S1 2004/614, reg 5(c). The countries are set out in Sch 2 to the Regulations.
[4] SI 1989/306 as amended by S1 2004/614, reg 4(1)(p). The ECSMA (Cmd 9512 of 1955) entered into force on 1 July 1954. Article 1 provides that 'Each contracting state undertakes to ensure that nationals of other contracting states who are lawfully present and are without sufficient resources shall be entitled to the same social and medical assistance as their own nationals'. The only non-EEA contracting state is Turkey.
[5] SI 1989/306, as amended by S1 2004/614, reg 5(b).
[6] Ie, the countries set out in Sch 2 to the Regulations.
[7] SI 1989/306, as amended by S1 2004/614, reg 5(e).
[8] Regulation (EEC) 1408/71, Art 21(1)(a).
[9] NHS Directions on the Allocation of Human Organs for Transplantation, 12 February 1996.

13.203 Treatment in accident and emergency and casualty departments of NHS hospitals remains free of charge to anyone requiring such treatment regardless of their immigration status or nationality until the point at which he or she is admitted to the hospital as an in-patient or is referred to an out-patient clinic.[1] Also free is emergency treatment in an NHS walk-in centre.[2] The diagnosis and treatment of certain specified diseases such as TB, malaria, whooping cough, salmonella etc, which are notifiable and to which specific public health enactments apply, is also free.[3] Treatment of sexually transmitted diseases, except for Human Immunodeficiency Virus (HIV) and AIDS, at a special clinic for the treatment of sexually transmitted diseases or on referral from such a clinic is also free of charge to all. Free services in connections with HIV or AIDS are limited to a diagnostic test and any counselling associated with such a test and its result.[4] Family planning services are also free to all.[5] Anyone who is detained in a hospital or received into guardianship under the Mental Health Act 1983 or any similar enactment or subjected to treatment under section 3(1) of the Powers of the Criminal Courts Act 1973 is also entitled to free treatment.[6] Treatment other than hospital treatment remains free (see below).[7]

[1] National Health Service (Charges to Overseas Visitors) Regulations 1989, as amended by SI 1994/1535, reg 3.
[2] SI 1989/306, as amended by SI 2004/614, reg 3.
[3] SI 1989/306, as amended, reg 3, Sch 1.

⁴ SI 1989/306, as amended, reg 3(d). The exclusion from free treatment of overseas visitors suffering from HIV/AIDS has been widely condemned among public health professionals, not only on humanitarian grounds but also on public health grounds, and many doctors have indicated that they will not comply.
⁵ SI 1989/306, as amended by SI 1991/438, reg 3(bb).
⁶ SI 1989/306, reg 3(e), (f).
⁷ SI 1989/306, reg 3(b).

Primary care

13.204 At present primary health care in the NHS is provided by general practitioners under GMS (general medical services) or PMS (personal medical services) contracts with the NHS or by NHS Walk-In Centres, NHS Direct or by Primary Care Trusts through PCTMS (primary care trust medical services) or APMS (alternative provider medical services) usually provided by voluntary organisations. Anyone needing primary care can either approach his or her local Primary Care Trust who will direct him or her to a local practice or he or she can apply to register with a local practice directly. Local practices have a discretion to register anyone as a permanent patient, regardless of his or her immigration status or nationality.¹ They may register a person as a temporary patient if he or she has lived in the practice's area for more than 24 hours but less than three months. Local practices may refuse to register a particular patient, but from 1 April 2004, they must have reasonable grounds for doing so which do not relate to the applicant's race, gender, social class, age, religion, sexual orientation, appearance, disability or medical condition.² General practitioners are obliged to treat anyone whose need for treatment is immediately necessary, in the opinion of the clinician, or where there is a need for emergency treatment.³ This treatment must be provided for 14 days or until her or she can register elsewhere, even if the patient is not accepted onto the practice's permanent list and there is no agreement to treat the person as a temporary patient.

¹ National Health Service (General Medical Services) Regulations 1992, SI 1992/635, as amended, reg 6; National Health Service (General Medical Services) (Contracts) Regulations 2004 (SI 2004/291); General Medical Services and Private Medical Services Transitional and Consequential Provision Order 2004 (SI 2004/865).
² NHS (GMS) (Contracts) Regulations 2004, SI 2004/291, reg 17.
³ NHS (GMS) Regulations 1992, SI 1992/635, as amended, Sch 2 para 4(4).

13.205 Refugees and those who have been granted Humanitarian Protection, discretionary or exceptional leave are entitled to free primary care, as defined in the previous paragraph, and if under 18 or in receipt of benefits, will not have to pay any prescription charges. Asylum seekers who are supported by NASS are issued with an HC2 Certificate by NASS on behalf of the Department of Health. This will entitle them to free prescriptions, dental treatment, eye tests, wigs and fabric supports, travel costs to and from hospital and vouchers towards the cost of glasses.¹ Persons who are deemed to be ordinarily resident in the UK are similarly eligible.² At present, it is accepted that anyone who has been living in the UK for more than a year is ordinarily resident. This will include workers and students but can also include illegal entrants and overstayers. Temporary visitors from EEA states and Switzerland, who are nationals of those states or who have been accepted as refugees or stateless persons there, are entitled to all necessary care for conditions which develop while they are here, including problems arising from a chronic condition.[3] They may be in possession of a Form E111 or the new European Health Insurance Card but there is no legal requirement to produce such evidence of entitlement. International transport workers may have a Form E110 and EEA and Swiss job-seekers may have a Form E119. EEA and Swiss residents may also be entitled to treatment for specific conditions noted on a Form E112. A person or his or her dependants who has had, at any time, not less than ten years continuous residence in the UK or not less than ten years continuous service as a Crown servant and who is in receipt of a UK pension is also entitled to free treatment for any conditions which develop while he or she is here. A person who is resident in an EEA state and has had ten years prior continuous residence in the UK is also entitled to free NHS treatment for any condition which develops whilst he or she is in the UK. A Turkish national who is lawfully in the UK and who is without sufficient resources to obtain private treatment is entitled to free treatment as a national of a state which has ratified the European Convention on Social and Medical Assistance.[4] Once accepted as a patient, the person concerned will be entitled to free NHS Primary Care services and to Secondary Care services referred to above which are not limited by immigration status or nationality. Asylum seekers and refugees will be entitled to both free Primary and Secondary NHS care, as will other individuals who fall within the exceptions referred to above. Persons who are not entitled to free Secondary Care will not be able to access it even if a referral is made by their GP or other Primary Care provider. This means that patients registered with a GP who need treatment for cancer, AIDS and other very serious conditions will only receive more specialist treatment if they pay for it out of their own resources. They will remain entitled to treatment in accident and emergency and casualty departments, and it is likely that there will be a significant increase in admissions to these departments of those suffering from very serious chronic or terminal illness which have gone untreated.

[1] NASS Policy Bulletin 43 *HC2 Certificates*.
[2] *Shah v Barnet London Borough Council* [1983] 2 AC 309.
[3] These categories are similar to those exempt from NHS charges for hospital treatment, see 13.201–13.202 above.
[4] NHS (Charges to Overseas Visitors) Regulations 1989, SI 1989/306, as amended, reg 4.

13.206 General dental practitioners cannot accept a patient on to their list on a temporary basis, in the same way that GPs may.[1] Ophthalmic opticians have a discretion to provide free treatment, subject to certain eligibility criteria.[2] Persons accepted as eligible for NHS treatment will be entitled to a free eye test and, if eligible under further regulations,[3] will be issued with an optical voucher if required. Asylum seekers and those who have been granted Humanitarian Protection or discretionary or exceptional leave to remain who are on a low income may also qualify for free optical and dental treatment and free prescriptions, even when they are not in receipt of NASS or income support, by completing a form HCI, which can be obtained from the NHS, the Benefits Agency or the Health Benefits Division. Pharmacists cannot dispense medication free to those who are required to pay prescription charges, and the

NHS Counter Fraud and Security Management Services conduct random checks to see whether individuals have been falsely claiming to be exempt from charges.

1   Health Service Circular HSCV 1999/018, DoH 1 February 1999, para 31.
2   NHS (General Ophthalmic Services) Regulations 1986, SI 1986/975.
3   NHS (Optical Charges and Payment) Regulations 1997, SI 1997/818.

13.207 The Government conducted a consultation on *Proposals to Exclude Overseas Visitors from Eligibility to Free NHS Primary Care Services*. Its intention is to bring entitlement to primary care into line with entitlement to secondary care as outlined above. However, as GPs enjoy a certain independence as private practitioners, it has yet to be decided whether they will have to charge those not entitled to treatment as private patients or whether they will have to charge a NHS rate which is decided centrally. What seems certain, however, is that universal free health care at the point of need has succumbed to political pressure and is no longer a reality.

ACCESS TO EMPLOYMENT

13.208 The concession which permitted asylum seekers to obtain permission to work if their application for asylum had not been determined within six months was wthdrawn on 23 July 2002. Those who were already benefitting from the concession were permitted to continue to work until their application was finally determined. However Council Directive 2003/9/EC on the minimum standards for the reception of asylum seekers requires Member States to grant access to the labour market to asylum seekers who have waited for more than 12 months for their claim to be determined,[1] and the immigration rules have been amended to enable such persons to apply for permission to take employment (although not to become self-employed or engage in a business or professional activity.[2] Other exceptional circumstances may also justify the grant of permission to work.[3] Asylum seekers who do not have permission to work are encouraged to undertake voluntary activities.[4] Supported asylum seekers wishing to take up vocational training will need the conditions attached to their temporary admission amended to allow unpaid employment, and any training allowance may impact on their eligibility for NASS support.[5] Failed asylum seekers may be required to perform unpaid work as a condition of continued entitlement to support under s 4 Immigration and Asylum Act 1999.[6]

1   Directive 2003/9/EC, Art 11.2.
2   HC 395 para 360, inserted by HC 194 from 4 February 2005.
3   Letter from Beverley Hughes to Andrew Mackinlay MP, 22 July 2003.
4   NASS Policy Bulletin 72 *Employment and Voluntary Activity*, para 2.1.
5   NASS Policy Bulletin 72 *Employment and Voluntary Activity*, para 4.0.
6   Immigration and Asylum (Provision of Accommodation to Failed Asylum-Seekers) Regulations 2005, SI 2005/930, reg 4.

Chapter 14

PENAL AND CARRIER SANCTIONS

INTRODUCTION

14.1 Enforcement of immigration control has become the major policy issue preoccupying UK ministers and their EU counterparts. Immigration officers now have an array of powers which have transformed them into an immigration police force independent of the police. A welter of offences have been created, including offences designed to criminalise immigrants and asylum seekers in their attempts to enter the country and in their resistance to leaving it. There are a number of overlapping enforcement mechanisms. For example, in a case where leave to enter has been obtained by deception, an immigrant might be summarily removed as an illegal entrant by the immigration service,[1] deported on conducive to the public good grounds by the Secretary of State[2] or prosecuted in the courts by the police,[3] with a possibility of a recommendation for deportation as part of the sentence.[4] We deal with deportation in chapter 15 and removal in chapter 16. In this chapter we deal with arrests by police and immigration officers, the criminal sanctions aimed at immigrants and asylum seekers and those who assist them, and the burgeoning sanctions against employers and carriers.

[1]   Immigration Act 1971, Sch 2, para 9; See 16.2 below.
[2]   IA 1971, s 3(5)(a); *Immigration Appeal Tribunal v Patel* [1988] Imm AR 434, HL.
[3]   IA 1971, ss 24A (as amended by Immigration and Asylum Act 1999, s 2(8), 26(1)(c).
[4]   IA 1971, s 3(6).

14.2 From the immigrant's point of view, the existence of a parallel set of criminal and administrative sanctions means that there is no knowing which way they are going to be dealt with. Unlike other sections of the population, those subject to immigration control are always in double jeopardy. The fact that they have been arrested by the police and charged with a criminal offence is no guarantee that they will not be summarily removed as an illegal entrant under the administrative powers.[1] The principle of double jeopardy is enshrined in section 28(4) of the Immigration Act 1971, which provides that:

'Any powers exercisable under this Act in the case of any person may be exercised notwithstanding that proceedings for an offence under this Part of this Act have been taken against them.'

The criminal law has been used increasingly frequently against those using deception or false documents on arrival, as well as those obtaining leave to remain by deception. Draconian new offences to criminalise those arriving without documentation, contained in the Asylum and Immigration (Treatment of Claimants etc) Act 2004, are being enthusiastically deployed.[2] But the use of the criminal law against overstayers remains rare where immediate removal is a viable option;[3] and the IDI on overstayers, who come to notice while embarking, indicate that they 'should not be detained for prosecution'.[4] Although there has been a great increase in criminal sanctions in recent years, these are directed mainly at preventing the entry of immigrants and asylum seekers to the UK,[5] and at deterring employers from employing them.

[1] See *Anwar (Mohammed)* DC No 448/77 (19 January 1978, unreported), where the Divisional Court held that the abandonment of criminal proceedings for illegal entry in favour of administrative removal of a suspected impostor was not an unreasonable exercise of the Secretary of State's discretion.
[2] Asylum and Immigration (Treatment of Claimants, etc) Act 2004, s 2. The AI(TC)A 2004 also criminalises failure to cooperate with arrangements for removal, s 35.
[3] The use of criminal sanctions against overstayers virtually ceased when rights of appeal against deportation were restricted in 1988 by the Immigration Act 1988, s 5.
[4] IDI Ch 20 (Evasion of control), para 3.1. However, the IDI are silent on criteria for prosecution of those overstayers and illegal entrants discovered prior to embarkation. The detailed instructions from the Immigration Service Enforcement Directorate (ISED) covering evasion of control, illegal entry, deportation work, offences against the immigration laws and procedures for investigation, remain confidential.
[5] The geographical reach of offences relating to entry has been extended to continental ports by the Channel Tunnel (International Arrangements) Order 1993, the Channel Tunnel (Miscellaneous Provisions) Order 1994 and the Nationality, Immigration and Asylum Act 2002 (Juxtaposed Controls) Order 2003; see eg 14.31 fn 8, 14.40 fn 2 below.

14.3 In addition to the alternative procedures – criminal or administrative – for dealing with an offender against the immigration laws, immigrants also face the possibility of being held in detention under widely different powers. First there are the normal criminal law powers of detention in custody on suspicion of having committed an offence. These carry all the normal safeguards of the criminal law – the requirement to charge and bring before a court. But then there are the additional powers of detention contained in Schedules 2 and 3 to the Immigration Act 1971 pending a decision on whether the person is to be refused entry, or be removed as an illegal entrant or overstayer, or be made subject to a deportation order. Here there are few of the safeguards normally given to those suspected of a criminal offence, although detention must comply with common law and ECHR Article 5 standards. We deal with detention in chapter 17 below.

POLICE, IMMIGRATION OFFICERS' AND SECRETARY OF STATE'S POWERS

14.4 The police have a number of different functions relating to immigration which can be summarised as:

(i) investigating criminal offences;

(ii) performing duties given to them under the Immigration Act 1971 in connection with the administration of immigration control;

(iii) conducting civil inquiries for the Home Office;

(iv) intelligence gathering.

We have already referred to their general powers under immigration law in 1.66 above. Here we only deal with their arrest powers under the Immigration Act 1971. The Immigration and Asylum Act 1999, the Nationality, Immigration and Asylum Act 2002 and the Asylum and Immigration (Treatment of Claimants etc) Act 2004 have extended the powers of arrest of immigration officers considerably, and have given them powers of search, entry and seizure in respect of immigration offences equivalent to those of the police.[1] They have the power to use reasonable force if necessary in carrying out any of their functions.[2] The aim of the increase in their powers is to reduce dependency on the police, who previously carried out arrests and removals under the 1971 Act, by enabling immigration officers to perform these functions alone.[3] The Immigration Service is now a true immigration police force. The AI(TC)A 2004 bestows yet more powers on immigration officers to arrest for offences formerly the sole province of the police.[4] Detention custody officers, who are usually private sector employees, also have considerable powers, particularly search powers, although they have no independent powers of arrest.[5] And finally, the Secretary of State and immigration officers have extensive powers of coercive information gathering.[6]

[1] Immigration and Asylum Act 1999, ss 128–139.
[2] Immigration and Asylum Act 1999, s 146(1).
[3] Explanatory Note to Immigration and Asylum Act 1999, Pt VII; Mike O'Brien speech to Special Standing Committee, 13 May 1999.
[4] Asylum and Immigration (Treatment of Claimants etc) Act 2004, s 14.
[5] Immigration and Asylum Act 1999, Sch 11, paras 2–3, Sch 12, para 2–3; Detention Centre Rules 2001, SI 2001/238, made under Immigration and Asylum Act 1999, s 153.
[6] See 14.25 below.

14.5 Broadly, there are three types of arrest power under the Immigration Act 1971, as amended by the Immigration and Asylum Act 1999 and the Nationality, Immigration and Asylum Act 2002: (a) without a warrant on reasonable suspicion of certain immigration-related offences; (b) with a warrant on reasonable suspicion of immigration offences; and (c) administrative arrests for the purpose of detention and removal of persons refused leave to enter, absconders from temporary admission, illegal entrants, overstayers and persons in breach of conditions, persons awaiting deportation on conducive grounds or following a recommendation, or persons reasonably suspected of being in those categories.

14.6   *Penal and Carrier Sanctions*

Arrest without warrant

14.6   A police or immigration officer has a power of arrest without warrant in respect of offences under sections 24 and 24A of the Immigration Act 1971, such as illegal entry, overstaying and obtaining leave by deception;[1]; for various offences under sections 25, 25A and 25B of facilitating illegal entry into an EU Member State, or the arrival in the UK of asylum seekers and EU national deportees;[2] and for offences relating to false, altered or forged registration cards and possession of immigration stamps under section 26A and 26B.[3] The offences of facilitation and some of those relating to false registration cards are arrestable offences, because of the penalties they impose, and, therefore there is no need to have a specific statutory power of arrest, as there is in the case, for example, of illegal entry and obtaining leave by deception.[4] The power is exercisable on suspicion of an offence based on reasonable belief.[5] Immigration officers also have a power of arrest without warrant for the offence of obstruction, but only where it would be impracticable to proceed by way of summons.[6] Under the Asylum and Immigration (Treatment of Claimants etc) Act 2004 immigration officers now have arrest powers in relation to the most serious offences of trafficking under the Sexual Offences Act 2003 and the equivalent Scottish law, and trafficking for exploitation under the Act of 2004.[7] There is no power of arrest for offences (other than obstruction) connected with the administration of the 1971 Act, or by captains of ships or aircraft or operators of trains.[8]

[1]   Immigration Act 1971, s 28A(1), inserted by Immigration and Asylum Act 1999, s 128. The power of arrest only applies to s 24(1)(d) offences (failing to report for a medical examination), if the officer applies for a warrant: IA 1971, ss 28A(2) and 28AA; see fn 1 at 14.8 below.
[2]   IA 1971, s 28A(3) as amended by Nationality, Immigration and Asylum Act 2002, s144. The police power of arrest comes from Police and Criminal Evidence Act 1984, s 24(1)(b). Arrestable offences are those carrying a term of five years' imprisonment and offences listed in Sch 1A to the 1984 Act.
[3]   These offences were added by Nationality, Immigration and Asylum Act 2002, s 146; powers of arrest are under Immigration Act 1971, s 28A(9), inserted by s 150 of the NIAA 2002.
[4]   For arrestable offences under the Police and Criminal Evidence Act see fn 2 above.
[5]   'Reasonable grounds for suspicion' require the officer to have formed a genuine suspicion (subjective element), and there must be reasonable grounds for it (objective element): *O'Hara v Chief Constable of Royal Ulster Constabulary* [1997] AC 286, HL. It is curious and disturbing that para A1.7 of the PACE Code of Practice on Stop and Search, which says that reasonable suspicion can never be based on a person's colour or on stereotyped images of certain persons or groups as more likely to be committing offences, is disapplied to immigration officers by the Immigration (PACE Codes of Practice) Direction 2000.
[6]   Immigration Act 1971, s 26(1)(g); s 28A(5) of the IA 1971, inserted by s 128 of the Immigration and Asylum Act 1999. The provisions mirror the police' general power of arrest (PACE, s 25) requiring either reasonable doubts as to the identity or address of the person or the risk of physical injury or loss or damage to property, to justify arrest without warrant.
[7]   Under the Asylum and Immigration (Treatment of Claimants etc) Act 2004, s 14(2)(n)–(p) (from 1 December 2004: SI 2004/2999).
[8]   IA 1971, ss 26 and 27.

14.7 Under the Asylum and Immigration (Treatment of Claimants etc) Act 2004 police and immigration officers have powers of arrest without warrant of anyone reasonably suspected of not having an immigration document,[1] or of failing to comply with a requirement of the Secretary of State to enable removal.[2] In addition, immigration officers also have new and extensive powers of arrest without warrant for a large number of offences involving dishonesty, including conspiracy to defraud, bigamy, making false statements, offences under the Perjury Act, theft, obtaining by deception, false accounting, handling, forgery and the use and possession of false instruments, and equivalents in Scotland and Northern Ireland.[3] The power is available where an immigration officer is exercising a function under the Immigration Acts, such as conducting an interview or looking at seized documents, and forms a reasonable suspicion that the person has committed or attempted to commit one of the listed offences.[4]

[1] Asylum and Immigration (Treatment of Claimants etc) Act 2004, s 2(10) (in force 22 September 2004: s 48(1)).
[2] AI(TC)A 2004, s 35(5) (in force 22 September 2004: s 48(1)).
[3] AI(TC)A 2004, s 14(2) (in force 1 December 2004: SI 2004/2999).
[4] AI(TC)A 2004, s 14(1) (in force 1 December 2004: SI 2004/2999).

Arrest with a warrant

14.8 An immigration officer may arrest on a warrant from a JP (or a sheriff in Scotland) for failure to report to a medical officer,[1] or for the offence of employing someone not entitled to work in the UK.[2]

[1] Under Immigration Act 1971, s 24(1)(d); the power of arrest is created by IA 1971, s 28AA, inserted by Nationality, Immigration and Asylum Act 2002, s 152.
[2] Under Asylum and Immigration Act 1996, s 8; see fn 1 for the power of arrest.

Entry and search before arrest

14.9 Police and immigration officers have power to enter and search without a warrant any premises where they believe on reasonable grounds that a suspect is, in order to make an arrest for an offence of assisting a breach of immigration law or the arrival of asylum claimants under sections 25, 25A and 25B of the Immigration Act 1971.[1] Immigration officers' powers of entry and search without a warrant are vastly increased by the Asylum and Immigration (Treatment of Claimants, etc) Act 2004, to embrace offences such as fraud, bigamy, theft, handling stolen goods and perjury.[2] Police and immigration officers also have power to enter and search business premises without a warrant, and arrest any suspected illegal entrants, overstayers or persons who are in breach of conditions or who have used deception to remain.[3] With a warrant issued by a justice of the peace or sheriff, they may enter named premises, if need be by reasonable force, to search for and arrest a person suspected of an ever expanding list of offences,[4] such as illegal entry, overstaying, breach of conditions, failing to report for medical examination or to comply with conditions of temporary admission, unlawful disembarkation, entry or remaining by deception, and offences connected with registration cards and immigration stamps.[5] The offences of unlawful employment,[6] of not having an immigration document on arrival and of failure to cooperate with removal have now been added to the list of 'relevant offences' for the purpose of entry and search with a warrant.[7]

14.9 Penal and Carrier Sanctions

1   Police power comes from Police and Criminal Evidence Act 1984, s 17; immigration
    officers' from Immigration Act 1971, s 28C, inserted by Immigration and Asylum
    Act 1999, s 130, as amended by Nationality, Immigration and Asylum Act 2002, s 144.
2   Asylum and Immigration (Treatment of Claimants, etc) Act 2004, s 14(3), in force
    1 December 2004: SI 2004/2999. Police have these powers under PACE: see fn 1 above.
3   Immigration Act 1971, s 28CA, inserted by NIAA 2002, s 153. The power may be used for
    the purpose of making an arrest for the offences under s 24 or s 24A or under Sch 2,
    para 17 (the administrative provisions of the Act). The operation must be authorised by the
    Secretary of State (if performed by an immigration officer) or by a Chief Superintendent
    (for police), and the police or immigration officer must produce identity if the premises are
    occupied: IA 1971, s 28CA(2), (4). The authority expires after seven days: IA 1971,
    s 28CA (3).
4   Starting with the Asylum and Immigration Act 1996, s 7, which applied to offences under
    s 24(1)(a), (aa) and (b) (illegal entry, entry by deception and overstaying). This was
    repealed (Sch 14, para 14) and replaced (s 129) by the IAA 1999, which extended the
    power to s 24(1)(d), (e), and (f), s 24A and s 25(2). The NIAA 2002, s 150(2) extended it
    to ss 26A and 26B (new offences in relation to immigration or asylum documents). Now it
    has been further extended by the AI(TC)A 2004, as set out below.
5   IA 1971, s 28B, inserted by Immigration and Asylum Act 1999, s 129 as amended by
    NIAA 2002, ss 144 and 150.
6   AIA 1996 s 8(10) as amended by NIAA 2002, s 147(4).
7   AI(TC)A 2004, ss 2(11), 35(6), in force 22 September 2004: s 48(1).

Administrative arrest

14.10 Police and immigration officers also have extensive powers of arrest
under Schedules 2 and 3 to the Immigration Act 1971 in support of the
administration of the Act. The administrative powers under these provisions
are not concerned with the task of catching and prosecuting offenders, but to
facilitate examination of new arrivals and the removal of persons without
leave to enter (including illegal entrants and overstayers) and deportees. The
following may be arrested: persons who are required to submit to examination
by an immigration officer on arrival in the UK, those who have been refused
leave to enter the country or whose leave to enter is suspended, members of
the crew of a ship or aircraft who are suspected of deserting ship or
overstaying their leave, illegal entrants, overstayers, those awaiting deportation, and their family members.[1] Persons suspected of belonging to any of
these categories may all be detained under the authority of an immigration
officer or the Secretary of State for the purpose of examination, a decision on
removal or being given removal directions.[2] All these people may be arrested
without warrant by an immigration officer or a police officer.[3] If they cannot
be found, a justice of the peace or sheriff may issue a warrant to the police to
enter premises where any of them is reasonably believed to be for the purpose
of searching for and arresting that person. Reasonable force may be used in
the execution of the warrant.[4] There is also a power to arrest those who have
broken or are about to break bail conditions imposed by the appellate
authorities,[5] or restrictions imposed by a court on those recommended for
deportation.[6]

1   Immigration Act 1971, Sch 2, para 10A, inserted by Nationality, Immigration and Asylum
    Act 2002, s 73, assimilated the position of family members of groups covered by
    paras 8–10 of the Schedule (those refused leave to enter and illegal entrants), to family
    members of overstayers (Immigration and Asylum Act 1999, s 10(7)) who have always
    been liable to removal from the UK with the principal. The provision enables the removal

960

of British-born (but not British citizen) children of those remaining in the UK on temporary admission for lengthy periods before refusal of an asylum or human rights claim.

2   Immigration Act 1971, Sch 2, para 16(1), (1A) and (2), applied to the Secretary of State by NIAA 2002, s 62, applied to overstayers by IAA 1999, s 10(7) (save those falling within the transitional 'regularisation' provisions of s 9), and Sch 3, para 2 for deportees. Note Sch 2, para 16(2) which empowers detention on suspicion; previously, being in one of the categories, e g an illegal entrant, was a condition precedent for detention, and damages could be (and were) awarded for the detention of a person reasonably but incorrectly suspected of being an illegal entrant and detained under Sch 2.

3   IA 1971, Sch 2, para 17(1). A police or immigration officer may enter and search any business premises to arrest under para 17 without a warrant: IA 1971, s 28CA(1), inserted by NIAA 2002, s 153. See above.

4   IA 1971, Sch 2, para 17(2), as amended by IAA 1999, s 140(2), NIAA 2002, s 62.

5   IA 1971, Sch 2, paras 24(1), 33(1).

6   IA 1971, Sch 3, para 7.

Powers of arrest in control zones

14.11 Powers of arrest for arrestable offences, offences under the Immigration Acts and for administrative detention are exercisable by police in control zones in France and Belgium.[1] The control zones include Coquelles, Frethun, Paris Gare du Nord, Brussels Gare du Midi, Lille, Calais (ferryport and hoverport), Boulogne and Dunkirk.[2]

1   Channel Tunnel (International Arrangements) Order 1993, SI 1993/1813, Art 6, Sch 3, para 2; Channel Tunnel (Miscellaneous Provisions) Order 1994, SI 1994/1405, Arts 4–6, Sch 3; Nationality, Immigration and Asylum Act 2002 (Juxtaposed Controls) Order 2003, SI 2003/2818, Arts 11–13.

2   The control zones are not set out in the 1993 and 1994 Orders, but the control zones in the ports of Calais, Boulogne and Dunkirk are set out in SI 2003/2818, Sch 1.

Ancillary powers: search and seizure of evidence

Search for evidence of crime

14.12 Police and immigration officers may enter premises to search for and seize evidence on a warrant from a justice of the peace or sheriff[1] on reasonable grounds for belief that a 'relevant offence' has been committed, that material evidence of substantial value to the investigation of the offence is on the premises and it is not practicable to enter without a warrant.[2] On arrest, premises, where the suspect was arrested or had been immediately before arrest, may be searched for evidence relating to the offence[3] without any warrant or other authority. In the more serious offences under sections 25, 25A or 25B of the Immigration Act 1971 premises suspected of being occupied or controlled by a suspect can be entered and searched, after arrest, by immigration officers, if they obtain the authorisation of a chief immigration officer.[4] An arrested suspect may be searched, outside or in the police station, for weapons, escape tools, evidence and documents.[5] Immigration officers have these ancillary powers of entry and search[6] in respect of the criminal offences of fraud, perjury, bigamy etc which they uncover in the course of their immigration duties.[7]

14.12 Penal and Carrier Sanctions

1. The powers of entry and search in respect of serious arrestable offences (as defined in Police and Criminal Evidence Act 1984, s 116 and Sch 5, are applied to 'relevant offences' under Immigration Act 1971, s 28D(4) (inserted by Immigration and Asylum Act 1999, s 131) by PACE, s 8(6) as amended. Immigration officers' powers are contained in Immigration Act 1971, s 28D (as inserted).
2. IA 1971, s 28D(1)(a)–(e) and (2) as inserted. 'Relevant offences' include illegal entry, deception, overstaying and breach of conditions or restrictions, failure to report to a medical officer, unlawful disembarkation, assisting breaches of immigration law, helping asylum seekers to arrive, offences relating to registration cards and immigration stamps and employment offences: IA 1971, s 28D(4) as inserted by Nationality, Immigration and Asylum Act 2002, ss 144, 147(10), 150. They also include entry without a passport and failure to cooperate with removal: Asylum and Immigration (Treatment of Claimants, etc) Act 2004, ss 2(11), 35(6) (in force 22 September 2004: s 48(1)).
3. Police have power under Police and Criminal Evidence Act 1984, s 18; immigration officers under IA 1971, s 28E, inserted by Immigration and Asylum Act 1999, s 132(1). For immigration officers, the power covers all offences under Pt III of IA 1971.
4. IA 1971, s 28F, inserted by Immigration and Asylum Act 1999, s 133. Police have this power in respect of arrestable offences (including s 25 offences) by virtue of Police and Criminal Evidence Act 1984, s 18.
5. Police powers of search of persons derive from Police and Criminal Evidence Act 1984, ss 32, 54, 55; immigration officers are given equivalent powers under Immigration Act 1971, ss 28G and 28H, inserted by Immigration and Asylum Act 1999, ss 134(1) and 135(1). A gap of over two hours between arrest and search however meant that the power of search on arrest was no longer available: *R (on the application of Hewitson) v Chief Constable of Dorset Police* [2003] EWHC 3296 (Admin), [2003] All ER (D) 344 (Dec) (a case on PACE, s 32 but applicable to immigration officers' powers of search). Immigration officers have no powers to conduct intimate body searches.
5. Ie, under IA 1971, ss 28C (entry and search before arrest), 28E and 28F (entry and search following arrest), 28G (search of arrested person) and 28I (seizure of materials).
7. Asylum and Immigration (Treatment of Claimants, etc) Act 2004, s 14(3) (in force 1 December 2004: SI 2004/2999).

Search for evidence to assist immigration control

14.13 Similar powers as those described above exist on arrest or detention under the administrative provisions of Schedule 2 to the Immigration Act 1971. Thus there is power to search the person of the arrested person,[1] or (with the authority of a chief immigration officer) premises controlled or occupied by the arrested person, to look for such things as documents which might establish the person's identity, nationality, citizenship, his or her country of embarkation and of destination.[2] Additionally, but only for the purpose of examining new arrivals, immigration officers have the power to search a newly arrived ship or aircraft or anything on board it, or any vehicle taken off it, to find passengers.[3] They may search passengers and their luggage, their vehicle, and the ship, vehicle or aircraft on or in which they arrived, to check whether they have documents such as passports, other identity documents or any other documents immigration officers wish to see (which might, for example, be relevant to their intentions on entry).[4] Immigration officers also have extensive powers of examination and search under the Terrorism Act 2000.[5]

1. Immigration Act 1971, Sch 2, paras 25B and 25C, inserted by Immigration and Asylum Act 1999, ss 134(2) and 135(2). Immigration officers have no power to conduct an intimate body search.
2. IA 1971, Sch 2, para 25A, inserted by IAA 1999, s 132(2).
3. IA 1971, Sch 2, para 1(5). This power applies in control zones: see SI 1993/1813, Sch 4, para 1(11)(a).

4   IA 1971, Sch 2, para 4(3).
5   Terrorism Act 2000, s 53, Sch 7; see 6.29 above.

14.14 There are in addition powers to detain vehicles, small ships and aircraft, used or intended to be used in connection with offences of assisting a breach of immigration laws or the arrival of asylum seekers and trafficking for exploitation, and vehicles in which clandestine entrants have arrived, either pending a criminal prosecution,[1] or pending the payment of a civil penalty.[2] In criminal cases the vehicle may be forfeited on conviction, and in civil cases it may be sold if the penalty remains unpaid.[3]

1   Immigration Act 1971, s 25D, inserted by Immigration and Asylum Act 1999, s 38, renumbered and substituted by Nationality, Immigration and Asylum Act 2002, s 144, applied to offences of trafficking for exploitation by Asylum and Immigration (Treatment of Claimants, etc) Act 2004, s 5(4) and (5) as from 1 December 2004: SI 2004/2999.
2   See 14.93 below.
3   IA 1971, s 25C, substituted for the original provision in s 25 by NIAA 2002, s 143; IAA 1999, s 37(5A), inserted by the NIAA 2002, Sch 8, para 11, as from a date to be appointed.

14.15 The NIAA 2002 gave police and immigration officers extensive additional powers to search business premises with and without a warrant and seize employee records, where they suspect overstayers and illegal entrants are or have been unlawfully employed. In broad terms, the preconditions of a search without a warrant are (a) the presence or suspected presence on the premises of illegal entrants, overstayers or people committing related offences,[1] (b) a reasonable belief that they are working there illegally, and (c) a reasonable belief that employee records, or other evidence, which will be of substantial value in investigating the employment offence, will be found there. Records may also be seized for the investigation of asylum support fraud.[2] An additional power to enter and search business premises for personnel records may be exercised, with a warrant, on a reasonable belief that an employer has provided inaccurate or incomplete information in response to a demand by the Secretary of State,[3] that gaps in the information provided will be filled by seizing records kept on the premises, and that it is not practicable to proceed without a warrant.[4]

1   Ie, persons suspected of offences under Immigration Act 1971, ss 24(1) and s 24A, or suspected of being liable to removal, under Sch 2, para 17.
2   IA 1971, s 28FA, inserted by Nationality, Immigration and Asylum Act 2002, s 154.
3   For powers of coercive information gathering see 14.25 below.
4   IA 1971, s 28FB, as inserted. 'Business premises' are defined in NIAA 2002, s 155.

Detainee custody officers

14.16 Detention custody officers look after people in immigration detention. They have power to search any detained person for whose delivery or custody they are responsible[1] and anyone else seeking to enter the place where the detained person is held.[2] They are authorised to use reasonable force if necessary.[3] They may enter business[4] and other[5] premises to search persons detained there by police or immigration officers. They have powers under the Detention Centre Rules to measure and photograph detainees[6] and to test them for drugs or alcohol.[7]

¹   Immigration and Asylum Act 1999, Sch 11, Sch 13, para 2.
²   IAA 1999, Sch 11, Sch 13, para 2(2); the latter power does not authorise removal of clothing except for an outer coat, jacket or gloves.
³   IAA 1999, Sch 13, para 2(4).
⁴   IA 1971, s 28CA(5), (6) inserted by Nationality, Immigration and Asylum Act 2002, s 153.
⁵   IA 1971, Sch 2, para 17(3)–(5), inserted by NIAA 2002, s 64.
⁶   IAA 1999, Sch 12, para 1; Detention Centre Rules 2001, SI 2001/238, r 5.
⁷   IAA 1999, Sch 12, para 2; SI 2001/238, r 44.

Search powers under asylum support provisions

14.17   To enforce the draconian provisions on compulsory dispersal of asylum seekers and their dependants, the Immigration and Asylum Act 1999 contains powers of search of premises in which accommodation has been provided by 'a person authorised by the Secretary of State' (who could be a private hotel-owner) on a warrant, where there is reason to believe that the supported person or his or her dependants for whom the accommodation is provided are not living there, or the accommodation is being used for any other purpose, or any unauthorised person is living there.[1] This would presumably include putting up another family member or friend, running a small business (for example, as a mechanic or seamstress) from the room, as well as unauthorised sub-letting. Reasonable force may be used in entering premises under the warrant.[2]

¹   Immigration and Asylum Act 1999, s 125. See further 13.108 above.
²   IAA 1999, s 125(3)(b).

Immigration Service Commissioner

14.18   The Immigration Service Commissioner through his or her investigating officer has powers of entry of premises on a warrant where there are reasonable grounds for believing that immigration advice or services are provided by a registered person who is the subject of an investigation or complaint.[1] The Commissioner may require documents to be produced and remove computer data. A registered person who does not allow access, or otherwise obstructs or fails to cooperate, may have his or her registration cancelled.[2] The Commissioner also has powers of entry on a warrant to search for and seize material on the premises which is likely to be of substantial value to the investigation of an offence of unauthorised provision of immigration advice or services.[3]

¹   Immigration and Asylum Act 1999, Sch 5, para 7.
²   Immigration and Asylum Act 1999, Sch 5, para 7.
³   IAA 1999, s 92A, inserted by Asylum and Immigration (Treatment of Claimants etc) Act 2004, s 38, in force 1 October 2004: SI 2004/2523.

Fingerprinting and other biometrics

14.19 Police (but not immigration officers) have power to take fingerprints from those charged with criminal offences.[1] Police, immigration officers and anyone else so authorised may take fingerprints, photographs or other identification measures in respect of anyone detained under the administrative provisions of Schedule 2 or 3 to the Immigration Act 1971.[2] Immigration officers were given powers to fingerprint asylum seekers and their dependants (defined as spouse and children under 18) by the Asylum and Immigration Appeals Act 1993, with powers of arrest without warrant for those who fail to comply with a notice requiring their attendance for the purpose.[3] These powers were extended to other classes of person by the Immigration and Asylum Act 1999:

(i)   those who fail to produce a passport or other satisfactory evidence of identity when they are asked to do so by an immigration officer;

(ii)   those refused leave to enter, who have been granted temporary admission, who the immigration officer reasonably suspects will breach conditions of residence or reporting;

(iii)   those served with a notice to remove them as illegal entrants, overstayers, or after a deportation order;[4]

(iv)   those arrested under paragraph 17 of Schedule 2 (persons liable to be detained under paragraph 16);

(v)   asylum claimants;

(vi)   dependants of any of the above.[5]

The Secretary of State may serve written notice on any of the above persons requiring them to attend for fingerprinting at a specified place, on seven days' notice. Refusal to comply can be met with a number of responses. First, non-attenders can be arrested. Secondly, reasonable force can be used to take the prints.[6] Thirdly, according to Home Office guidance, refusal to cooperate may result in no registration card being issued to the recalcitrant asylum seeker, or in refusal of the asylum claim on non-compliance grounds, or in adverse credibility findings.[7] Once taken, fingerprints can be kept indefinitely,[8] except in the case of British citizens and those with a right of abode, and their dependants, where there is a statutory requirement to destroy them as soon as reasonably practicable.[9]

---

1   Police and Criminal Evidence Act 1984, ss 27, 61. They may be taken without consent at a police station in order to confirm or disprove involvement in an offence, on charge or after conviction of a recordable offence.

2   Immigration Act 1971, Sch 2, para 18(2); *Irawo-Osan v Secretary of State for the Home Department* [1992] Imm AR 337.

3   Asylum and Immigration Appeals Act 1993, s 3 (repealed by IAA 1999, s 169).

4   IAA 1999 s 141, amended by Asylum and Immigration (Treatment of Claimants etc) Act 2004, s 15 as from 1 October 2004: SI 2004/2523.

5   Immigration and Asylum Act 1999, s 141. Fingerprints may not be taken from a child under 16 except in the presence of a parent or carer: s 141(3). Children under five are not fingerprinted: API 'Fingerprinting' para 1.

6   IAA 1999, ss 142, 146, amended in relation to the use of force by Nationality, Immigration and Asylum Act 2002 s 153(2).

7   API 'Fingerprinting', para 3.

8   Detailed provisions for the destruction of fingerprints within specified periods, in the IAA 1999, s 143(3)–(8) and (14), were repealed by the Anti-terrorism, Crime and Security Act 2001, ss 36(1)(a), (2), 125 and Sch 8, Pt 3. The Immigration (PACE Codes of Practice

No 2 and Amendment) Directions 2000 provide for the destruction of fingerprints, if taken with consent, in ten years, and if taken under IA 1971, Sch 2, para 18, as soon as reasonably practicable after they have been used for identity purposes. The API 'Fingerprinting' state that fingerprints will normally be destroyed after ten years: para 2.3.
9   IAA 1999, s 143(2), (9).

14.20 The purposes of the broad fingerprinting powers in relation to asylum seekers include detection of those who have made a claim before, in another identity, or in another EU Member State, to enable them to be refused or returned to the other Member State under the provisions of the Dublin Convention and Regulation (Dublin II).[1] Under the EU Eurodac regulations,[2] the fingerprints of all asylum seekers over 14 and other third country nationals who are apprehended crossing borders irregularly or are found 'illegally present' in any Member State,[3] are sent to a central unit for matching,[4] so as to enable concerted expulsion measures.[5]

1   For the Dublin Conventions see **12.149**ff above.
2   Council Regulation (EC) 2725/2000 concerning the establishment of 'Eurodac' for the comparison of fingerprints for the effective application of the Dublin Convention; Council Regulation (EC) 407/2002 laying down certain rules implementing regulation (EC) 2725/2000 (OJ L 062).
3   Regulation (EC) 2725/2000, Arts 8, 11.
4   Regulation (EC) 2725/2000, Art 4.
5   Council Directive 2001/40/EC on mutual recognition of decisions on expulsion of third country nationals (OJ L 149/341).

14.21 The Secretary of State was empowered under the IAA 1999 to make regulations enabling data on other external physical characteristics to be collected. Under the Nationality, Immigration and Asylum Act 2002 the power to collect, store and exchange biometric data was taken further.[1] Biometric data can now be required from applicants other than asylum claimants, including visitors. Regulations can now be made requiring any applicant for entry clearance, leave to enter or leave to remain to provide 'information about external physical characteristics', including features of the iris or other parts of the eye.[2] So far, regulations have been limited to fingerprints.[3] The first non-asylum applicants to be required to give fingerprints were Sri Lankans in July 2003, followed by applicants seeking entry clearance in Djibouti, Eritrea, Ethiopia, Kenya, Rwanda, Tanzania and Uganda.[4] The regulations enable the Secretary of State to pass on biometric data to policing and other agencies.[5] The 2002 also enabled the Secretary of State to set up a voluntary scheme for the collection and storage of biometric data, to expedite the entry of frequent travellers.[6]

1   Nationality, Immigration and Asylum Act 2002, s 126.
2   NIAA 2002, s 126(9).
3   Immigration (Provision of Physical Data) Regulations 2003, SI 2003/1875. The government plans that all visa applicants will be required to give fingerprints by 2008: *Controlling our borders: Making migration work for Britain: Five year strategy for asylum and immigration*, Cm 6472, Feb 2005.
4   SI 2003/1875, Schedule, as amended by SI 2004/474 and 1834.
5   SI 2003/1875, para 6.
6   NIAA 2002, s 127, in force 10 December 2004: SI 2004/2998.

14.22 The Home Office planned to include biometric data in all new passports by the year 2005.[1] The requirement to provide physical data in advance of travelling to the UK, data which is then digitised, would enable the Home Office to achieve its ambition of 'e-borders', involving the automatic transmission of passenger information in real time at the point of departure (advanced passenger processing), with data-matching followed by the grant or refusal of authority to board the ship or aircraft.[2] Meanwhile, fingerprint information is stored in a microchip on asylum Application Registration Cards (ARC), together with a photographic image and information such as NASS status, languages spoken by the holder and family members, and employment status.[3] In November 2003, the Home Secretary announced the Government's decision to introduce compulsory identity cards, incorporating biometric data such as fingerprints or an iris scan, for all legal residents of the UK, to start in 2007/8. Biometric residence cards will then be mandatory for all foreign nationals staying in the UK for over three months.[4]

[1]   Asylum and Immigration (Treatment of Claimants) Bill Standing Committee (Commons), 11th sitting, col 401, 27.1.03.
[2]   Ibid. This plan features in the five-year strategy document *Controlling our borders: Making migration work for Britain: Five year strategy for asylum and immigration*, Cm 6472, Feb 2005.
[3]   Hansard HC, 6 February 2002, col 974W, Angela Eagle. See *Controlling our borders* above.
[4]   Hansard HC, 11 November 2003, col 171, David Blunkett.

Electronic monitoring

14.23   Under provisions contained in the Asylum and Immigration (Treatment of Claimants etc) Act 2004, adults who are liable to detention but released on temporary admission by an immigration officer or the Secretary of State, or on bail, may be required to submit to electronic monitoring, in accordance with regulations under the Act, to ensure compliance with residence conditions or as an alternative to physical reporting.[1] Electronic monitoring may be by way of voice recognition,[2] tagging[3] or use of tracking technology,[4] all of which the Home Office ihas piloted.[5] Electronic monitoring could only be used with the consent of the subject, as an alternative to detention.

[1]   Asylum and Immigration (Treatment of Claimants etc) Act 2004, s 36 (in force 1 October 2004: SI 2004/2523). No regulations had been made under the section at the time of writing.
[2]   Voice recognition technology uses biometric voice recognition software to facilitate reporting over a telephone from a fixed land line from a fixed address at a notified time. This could obviate the need for people to report physically to a centre on a weekly basis. They would be given a particular number to ring in, and have their voice and location checked: Asylum and Immigration (Treatment of Claimants) Bill Standing Committee (Commons) 10th sitting, 22.1.04, col 363–4, Beverley Hughes.
[3]   Tagging involves wearing a bracelet which emits a signal to a receiver at the subject's home address. The subject may be required to be at home for a particular hour in the week, or more frequently for people who present other kinds of risk, to confirm that they are complying with a residence restriction. That would often serve in lieu of physical reporting: ibid.
[4]   Tracking involves using global positioning satellite technology to pinpoint the whereabouts of a subject on a continuous basis. It is in its infancy: ibid.
[5]   Since electronic monitoring must, under the terms of the Act, comply with regulations which have not yet been promulgated, the legal basis for the pilot which started in October 2004 is unclear. The same goes for current attempts by Home Office presenting officers to seek to tag persons released on Immigration Act bail (see chapter 17 below).

Other information-gathering powers

14.24 The Immigration and Asylum Act 1999 created a wide information exchange network between the Secretary of State on the one hand and, on the other, a range of agencies including the police, the National Criminal Intelligence Service (NCIS), the National Crime Squad (NCS) and Customs and Excise. Information held by a chief officer of one of these agencies, a contractor or sub-contractor of the Home Office or 'any other specified person', may be supplied to the Secretary of State for immigration purposes, including the administration of control, the prevention, detection, investigation and prosecution of offences under the Immigration Acts, civil penalties (carrier sanctions), asylum support and other specified purposes.[1] Similarly, the Secretary of State is empowered to supply information held by him or her in connection with the exercise of immigration functions to chief officers of the same agencies.[2] The Secretary of State may also provide information (including fingerprints) to the authorities of a country to which he or she seeks to remove an undocumented person.[3] The 2002 Act added powers for the Commissioners of the Inland Revenue to supply information to enable the Secretary of State to locate someone reasonably suspected not to have leave to enter or permission to work.[4] Information may also be provided to determine whether a person is of good character (in connection with a naturalisation application) or for the purposes of the maintenance and accommodation requirements of the immigration rules.[5] Further, section 17 of the AI(TC)A 2004 enables the Secretary of State or an immigration officer to retain any document coming into their possession in the course of the exercise of an immigration function, while they suspect that a person to whom the document relates may be liable to removal from the UK and that retention of the document may facilitate the removal.[6]

[1]   Immigration and Asylum Act 1999, s 20.
[2]   IAA 1999, s 21.
[3]   IAA 1999, s 13. The transfer of information is deemed 'necessary for reasons of substantial public interest' for the purposes of the Data Protection Act 1998: IAA 1999, s 13(4).
[4]   Nationality, Immigration and Asylum Act 2002, s 130.
[5]   Nationality, Immigration and Asylum Act 2002, s 130.
[6]   Asylum and Immigration (Treatment of Claimants, etc) Act 2004, s 17. This power is so broad as to invite abuse.

Coercive information gathering

14.25 The Immigration and Asylum Act 1999 contained a number of coercive provisions allowing the Secretary of State to require information from various sources. Property owners and managers could be required to provide information about premises and their occupants, for asylum support purposes.[1] The post office and other carriers could be required to provide redirection information for use in the prevention, detection, investigation and prosecution of criminal offences relating to asylum support, to check the accuracy of the information given about support or for other purposes relating to asylum support.[2] Marriage registrars were fixed with a duty to report suspicious marriages.[3] The Nationality, Immigration and Asylum Act 2002 took these coercive information-gathering powers further. Local authorities can be compelled by the Secretary of State to supply information to help find someone who is or has been living in their area, if the person is reasonably suspected of an offence of illegal entry, overstaying, breach of conditions or restrictions on stay, unlawful disembarkation, obtaining leave to enter or remain by deception, making false representations or using or possessing a false document.[4] Employers can be similarly compelled to provide information on an employee or former employee reasonably suspected of these offences, or offences in relation to asylum support, if the information is needed to establish their whereabouts, earnings or employment history.[5] A bank or building society can be compelled to provide relevant financial information which the Secretary of State reasonably believes it possesses about an account holder reasonably suspected of an asylum support offence.[6] In the case of employers and financial institutions, the Act requires written notice to be served specifying the information required and the manner and period in which it is to be provided. Failure to comply without reasonable excuse is an offence.[7]

[1] Immigration and Asylum Act 1999, s 126. No regulations have been made under the section.
[2] IAA 1999, s 127. No regulations have been made under this section.
[3] IAA 1999, s 24; Reporting of Suspicious Marriages and Registration of Marriages (Miscellaneous Amendments) Regulations 2000, SI 2000/3164. The information required includes the names, dates of birth or ages of the parties, their marital status, address(es) and nationalities, the date, place and time of the marriage, the evidence produced of name, age, marital status and nationality, the reasons for the report and the full name of the reporting officer making the report. In the first year of its operation there were 700 reports. (Hansard HL, 24.6.02, col 1177, Lord Filkin). Note now Asylum and Immigration (Treatment of Claimants, etc) Act 2004, ss 19–25 which prevents marriage registrars from marrying non-EEA nationals who do not have entry clearance for the purpose of marriage, unless they have written permission from the Secretary of State to marry in the UK or fall within a specified class: see 11.66 below.
[4] Ie, offences under Immigration Act 1971, ss 24, 24A and 26(1)(c) and (d): Nationality, Immigration and Asylum Act 2002, s 129.
[5] NIAA 2002, s 134.
[6] NIAA 2002, s 135.
[7] NIAA 2002, s 136.

Passenger information

14.26 The powers under the IA 1971 for immigration officers to demand passenger and crew lists from captains of ships and aircraft[1] arriving in the UK were modified by regulations made under the 1999 Act[2] to enable immigration officers to require much more detailed information, including passengers' gender, date of birth, travel document number, visa expiry date, ticket number and date and place of issue, the identity of the person booking the ticket, the method of payment, the passenger's travel itinerary and the names of all other passengers on the reservation.[3] Immigration officers may demand the information in relation to ships and aircraft expected to arrive and those which have left or are expected to leave the UK.[4] A senior officer may also require information about the expected arrival of any craft expected to carry non-EEA nationals.[5] There is provision in the Asylum and Immigration (Treatment of Claimants etc) Act 2004 to allow immigration officers to demand copies of particular passengers' travel documents as well, a power which would be targeted as individuals, rather than applied in a blanket manner, because of the huge delays which copying all passengers' documents would entail.[6] When the authority to carry scheme in section 124 of the Nationality, Immigration and Asylum Act 2002 is brought into force, the passenger information may be required in advance of boarding, to enable a check to be made against Home Office databases so that, if a passenger is identified as a security or immigration risk, authority to carry him or her may be refused.[7] A request to a carrier continues in force until withdrawn, and can last up to six months, or longer if renewed. The data required is not restricted to foreign nationals but can cover all passengers, including British and European citizens. However, up to now the power has been used for specific flights or flights from specific destinations. Additional powers exist under the Terrorism Act 2000 to require passenger information.[8]

[1] Immigration Act 1971, Sch 2, para 27.
[2] IA 1971, Sch 2, para 27B, inserted by Immigration and Asylum Act 1999, s 18.
[3] Immigration (Passenger Information) Regulations 2000, SI 2000/912.
[4] IA 1971, Sch 2, para 27B(1)(a) and (b). The power is exercisable in respect of a particular passenger or craft, or all passengers and/or all craft of the carrier.
[5] IA 1971, Sch 2, para 27C, inserted by IAA 1999, s 19.
[6] Asylum and Immigration (Treatment of Claimants) Act 2004, s 16, amending IA 1971, Sch 2, para 27B as from a date to be appointed.
[7] See 14.100 below.
[8] Terrorism Act 2000, Sch 7, para 17.

Codes of Practice

14.27 The Codes of Practice issued under the Police and Criminal Evidence Act 1984 have always applied to persons who are not police officers who are investigating offences,[1] and have been held to apply to immigration officers exercising administrative powers in relation to illegal entrants and overstayers, at least if a criminal offence was potentially involved.[2] Now, in the exercise of powers of arrest, questioning, search, fingerprinting, entry and seizure – whether investigating criminal offences or in the course of their Immigration Act 1971, Schedule 2 functions – immigration officers are statutorily obliged to have regard to certain specified (but not all) provisions of the Codes of Practice.[3] Thus, when arresting a suspect without a warrant, whether for an immigration offence or for a related offence, immigration officers must have regard to all the provisions of Codes C, D and E.[4] When conducting interviews, they should not refuse access to solicitors, and questioning should be under caution and contemporaneously recorded.[5] But when arresting without warrant under the administrative provisions of the Schedule, none of the provisions of Code C relating to the conduct of interviews apply, according to the Codes of Practice Direction.[6] Where there is a Code breach, this does not necessarily mean that the immigration officer or Secretary of State cannot subsequently rely on what is said at an interview.[7] If it is not voluntary, has been obtained by force, inducement or oppression, or a statement has been made at a time of stress, it may be ruled out.[8] But if there is simply a failure to inform the applicant that his or her solicitor is available, all the court or Secretary of State need do is to be very careful to test the reliability of the answers.[9]

[1] Police and Criminal Evidence Act 1984, s 67(9).
[2] *R v Secretary of State for the Home Department, ex p Ibrahim* [1993] Imm AR 124, QBD.

3   Immigration and Asylum Act 1999, s 145, Immigration (PACE Codes of Practice) Direction 2000, Immigration (PACE Codes of Practice No 2 and Amendment) Direction 2000 (on taking, retention and destruction of fingerprints).

4   The Detention, Treatment and Questioning of Persons by Police Officers; The Identification of Persons by Police Officers; Tape Recording of Interviews with Suspects.

5   See PACE Code C as applied by the Immigration (PACE Codes of Practice) Direction 2000, paras 6, 10, 11, and 12. Illegal entry interviews where no caution was administered were held inadmissible in the Scottish cases of *Oghonoghor v Secretary of State for the Home Department* 1995 SLT 733, OHCS and *Kim (Sofia) v Secretary of State for the Home Department* 2000 SLT 249, OHCS.

6   Immigration (PACE Codes of Practice) Direction 2000, Sch 1. In practice, immigration officers are likely to adhere to the relevant Code, as (broadly speaking) they have done in the past.

7   But see *Oghonoghor v Secretary of State for the Home Department, Kim v Secretary of State for the Home Department*, fn 5 above.

8   Evidence of a police interview was excluded by an adjudicator in a deportation appeal (breach of conditions) in *Oyefuwa* (18035).

9   *Ibrahim*, above at 129. In addition it should be recalled that Police and Criminal Evidence Act 1984, ss 76 and 78 (exclusion of evidence obtained unfairly or by oppression) do not apply to civil proceedings.

14.28 Powers of entry and search of premises, seizure of documents and search of the person, and similarly intrusive measures including the taking, transmission and storage of fingerprints and other biometric data, all constitute interference with privacy under Article 8 of the ECHR. To conform with the Convention, the exercise of the powers must be not only in accordance with the law but also must have a legitimate aim and be proportionate to the aim pursued.[1] If they are not (an extreme example might be a midnight, intrusive search causing damage looking for someone who has failed to report to a medical officer) damages would be recoverable.[2] Breaches of Article 8 would also be relevant to admissibility of evidence in criminal proceedings.[3]

1   *Chappell v United Kingdom* (1989) 12 EHRR 1; *Niemietz v Germany* (1992) 16 EHRR 97; *R (on the application of S) v Chief Constable of South Yorkshire; R (on the application of Marper) v Chief Constable of South Yorkshire* [2002] EWCA Civ 1275, [2002] 1 WLR 3223, [2003] 1 All ER 148 (retention of fingerprints and DNA). See 8.93 above.

2   Human Rights Act 1998, s 8.

3   In *Attorney-General's Reference No 3 of 1999* [2001] 1 Cr App Rep 475, the House of Lords held that use of a DNA sample which should have been destroyed was fair bearing in mind the powers of discretionary exclusion of evidence under Police and Criminal Evidence Act 1984, s 78, lawful and necessary for the investigation and prosecution of serious crime.

14.29 Complaints about immigration officers' exercise of their powers of arrest, search and seizure under Part III of the Immigration Act 1971 are referred to the Immigration Service Complaints Unit for consideration of whether an investigation is required; investigations are supervised by a Complaints Audit Committee – an arrangement which the CAC has described as unsatisfactory.[1]

1   See Complaints Audit Committee Annual Report 2002–3, on IND website. There were 436 complaints in 2002, of which 128 were substantiated.

CRIMINAL OFFENCES

Illegal entry and deception

14.30 The criminal offence of illegal entry is defined in section 24(1)(a) of the Immigration Act 1971. The offence cannot be committed by a British citizen.[1] It occurs if contrary to the Act a person knowingly enters the UK without the leave of an immigration officer or in breach of a deportation order. It requires actual entry, and can only be committed on the day of entry.[2] It is a purely summary offence punishable with a fine on level 5 or imprisonment up to six months.[3] The extended time limit for prosecution applies.[4] Suspected offenders can be arrested without warrant.[5] Normally the burden of proving an illegal entry is on the prosecution, but an exception is made in cases brought within six months of the date of entry, where the defendant must prove that he or she had leave to enter.[6] Proof in such cases will be on the balance of probabilities, in accordance with the normal rule of criminal law where the burden of proof is reversed.[7] Whether the reverse burden would be held incompatible with the presumption of innocence in Article 6(2) of the ECHR, and read as an evidential rather than persuasive burden, has yet to be tested in this context.[8]

[1] Immigration Act 1971, s 24(1), as amended by British Nationality Act 1981, Sch 4, para 2(a).
[2] *Grant v Borg* [1982] 2 All ER 257, [1982] 1 WLR 638, HL.
[3] IA 1971, s 24(1), as amended by Criminal Justice Act 1982, ss 38 and 46, and by Asylum and Immigration Act 1996, s 6(a). A level 5 fine is presently £5,000 in England and Wales: Criminal Justice Act 1982, s 37 as amended by Criminal Justice Act 1991, s 17.
[4] IA 1971, ss 24(3), 28(1). See below **14.65**.
[5] IA 1971, s 28A, added by Immigration and Asylum Act 1999, s 128.
[6] IA 1971, s 24(4)(b).
[7] *R v Carr-Briant* [1943] KB 607, [1943] 2 All ER 156.
[8] See *R v DPP, ex p Kebilene* [2000] 2 AC 326; *R v Lambert* [2001] UKHL 37, [2001] 3 WLR 206 [2002] AC. In cases involving regulatory offences, and in some cases involving true criminal offences, a reverse persuasive burden has been held proportionate: *R v Matthews* [2003] EWCA Crim 813, [2004] QB 690; *Sliney v London Borough of Havering* [2002] EWCA Crim 2558, [2003] 1 Cr App R 602. See now on reverse burden of proof *R v Johnstone* [2003] UKHL 28; *A-G Reference No 2 of 2004, Sheldrake v DPP* [2004] UKHL 43.

14.31 The offence of using deception to enter or remain was added in 1996 and expanded in scope in 1999. It is set out in section 24A of the Immigration Act 1971. Again, it cannot be committed by a British citizen.[1] It occurs if, by means which include deception by him or her, a person:

(a) obtains or seeks to obtain leave to enter or remain in the United Kingdom;[2] or

(b) secures or seeks to secure the avoidance, postponement or revocation of enforcement action against him or her.[3]

The wording of the offence makes clear that the deception must be by the immigrant and not some third party. It must be material, ie instrumental in obtaining leave to enter, remain, etc,[4] although it does not have to be the sole effective means of obtaining entry, stay, etc. Deception can be carried out by conduct or conduct accompanied by silence as to a material fact, such as the silent presentation of a false passport.[5] 'Enforcement action' is defined to include removal directions, the making of a deportation order or removal in consequence of either. The offence is considerably broader in certain respects than the offence of illegal entry. It can be committed by seeking to enter, as well as by actually doing so. It extends to embrace action taken to remain in the UK, and to prevent or defer removal, as well as action taken to enter.[6] It has been used against failed asylum seekers who have sought asylum again under a different identity.[7] It can be committed in a control zone.[8] The offence is triable either way, with a fine up to the statutory maximum and/or up to six months' imprisonment on summary conviction, or a fine and/or up to two years' imprisonment on indictment.[9]

[1]   Immigration Act 1971, s 24A(1), inserted by Immigration and Asylum Act 1999, s 28.
[2]   This subsection was previously enacted as Immigration Act 1971, s 24(1)(aa), added by Asylum and Immigration Act 1996, s 4. It applies in a control zone as in the UK: Channel Tunnel (International Arrangements) Order 1993, Art 5; Channel Tunnel (Miscellaneous Provisions) Order 1994, Art 5; Nationality, Immigration and Asylum Act 2002 (Juxtaposed Controls) Order 2003, Art 12.
[3]   This sub-section was added by the Immigration and Asylum Act 1999.
[4]   See discussion in the House of Lords during passage of the Asylum and Immigration Act 1996, which created the offence: 571 HL Official Report (5th series) col 1633, 1996.
[5]   *Choudhry v Metropolitan Police Comr* (24 November 1984, unreported), QBD; *R v Secretary of State for the Home Department, ex p Patel* [1986] Imm AR 515, CA (cases relating to false representations under Immigration Act 1971, s 26(1)(c)). See 16.16 below.
[6]   Immigration Act 1971, s 24A(2).
[7]   *R v Nagmadeen* [2003] EWCA Crim 2004, [2003] All ER (D) 342 (Jun).
[8]   Nationality, Immigration and Asylum Act 2002 (Juxtaposed Controls) Order 2003, SI 2003/2818, Art 12.
[9]   Immigration Act 1971, s 24A(3). When the offence was created in 1996 it was summary only. In *R v Ali (Nasir)* [2001] EWCA Crim 2874, [2002] 2 Cr App R (S) 32 a sentence of 18 months was reduced to 12 months on appeal for a Pakistani national pleading guilty to seeking leave to enter by deception by posing as an Afghani asylum seeker. Twelve-month sentences were upheld in *R v Nagmadeen* (fn 7 above) for Iraqi Kurds claiming asylum a second time under false names after their original claims were rejected and their appeals dismissed. An 18-month sentence for using false documents to re-enter the UK was reduced to nine months in *R v Rehman (Asif)* [2003] EWCA Crim 2473, [2003] All ER (D) 197 (Sep) where the motivation was to visit his sick mother at home and to avoid the inevitability of an asylum appeal being dismissed by his leaving the country. In *R v Kishentine* [2004] EWCA Crim 3352, a nine-month sentence was upheld for an entry by deception ten weeks before an asylum claim was made, and the court held that where a defence under s 31 did not apply (see 14.38 below), the sentencing judge was not obliged to assess the strength of any asylum claim made by the defendant. However, a four-month detention and training order imposed by a youth court on a 17-year-old asylum claimant was quashed as wrong in principle, and a conditional discharge substituted, in *K v Croydon CC* [2005] EWHC 478 (Admin). The court emphasised the importance of the agent's role.

14.32   It is important to distinguish the offences of illegal entry and entry by deception from the status of an illegal entrant. The status of illegal entrant requires no intention, or even knowledge, of a breach of immigration law, and includes those who enter without realising that they require and have no leave to enter or are subject to a deportation order.[1] The criminal offence, on the other hand, is only committed if done knowingly. Illegal entrants also include those who have obtained leave by another person's deception,[2] but entry by means of another person's deception cannot ground a criminal prosecution. Thus, persons who do not realise that they have no leave, and those who were brought in (usually as children) by the deception of another person (usually a relative), or those wrongly believed to be British citizens and so not granted leave to enter, cannot be prosecuted, even though they can be removed summarily as illegal entrants.[3]

1   See *R v Governor of Ashford Remand Centre, ex p Bouzagou* [1983] Imm AR 69, CA; *R v Secretary of State for the Home Department, ex p Yeboah* [1986] Imm AR 52 at 59, QBD. See 16.7ff below.
2   Immigration Act 1971, s 33 as amended by Asylum and Immigration Act 1996, Sch 2, para 4). For the position under EC law, see 16.327 below.
3   *R v Governor of Ashford Remand Centre, ex p Bouzagou* above; *R v Secretary of State for the Home Department, ex p Khaled* [1987] Imm AR 67, QBD; *Mokuolo v Secretary of State for the Home Department* [1989] Imm AR 51, CA.

Non-production of passport

14.33 In the 1993 case of *Naillie*,[1] the House of Lords ridiculed the suggestion that the duty of passengers to produce a passport to an immigration officer on arrival[2] gave rise to criminal liability for non-production. Now, Parliament has provided that it does. A person commits a criminal offence punishable by up to two years' imprisonment if at a leave or asylum interview, he or she does not have a passport or other travel document which is in force and satisfactorily establishes his or her identity and nationality or citizenship. If the passenger is travelling with a dependent child, it is also an offence not to have such documentation in respect of the child.[3] On the plain wording of the Act, the offence may be committed by a child who is travelling alone.[4] No offence is committed, if the interview takes place after the passenger has entered the UK, and he or she is able to provide the correct documentation within three days of the interview.[5] It is a defence for the accused person to prove that (a) he or she, or the child for whom he or she is responsible, is an EEA national, (b) he or she or the child is a family member of an EEA national exercising a Treaty right, (c) he or she has a reasonable excuse for not being in possession of a 'document of the kind' needed at the interview to prove identity, or (d) to produce a false document and to prove that it was used for all purposes in connection with their journey to the UK, or (e) to prove that at no stage of the journey to the UK did he or she have a passport or similar immigration document.[6] Deliberate destruction or disposal of the document is deemed not to be a reasonable excuse for non-possession at the interview, unless the destruction or disposal was beyond the passenger's control or was done for a reasonable cause (which does not include delaying the handling or resolution of a claim or application, increasing its chances of success or complying with the instructions or advice of a facilitator or someone offering advice, unless it is unreasonable to expect non-compliance with those instructions or advice).[7]

1   *R v Naillie, R v Kanesarajah* [1993] AC 674, [1993] 2 All ER 782, [1993] 2 WLR 927, [1993] Imm AR 462, [1993] 27 LS Gaz R 34, [1993] NLJR 848, 137 Sol Jo LB 145.
2   Under Immigration Act 1971, Sch 2, para 4.
3   Asylum and Immigration (Treatment of Claimants etc) Act 2004, s 2(1) and (2). Failure to produce a document to an immigration officer on request gives rise to a presumption that the person does not have one: s 2(6). The penalty is six months or a fine up to the statutory maximum if tried summarily; two years or a fine on indictment: AI(TC)A 2004, s 2(7). 86 people had been convicted in the first three months of the section's operation (Asylum Process Stakeholders Group, January 2005). In *R v Wang (Bei Bei)* [2005] EWCA Crim 293, a guideline case, the Court of Appeal reduced a sentence of ten months imposed on an

18-year-old girl on a guilty plea, to two months and quashed a recommendation for deportation. In *R v Safari and Zanganeh* [2005] EWCA Crim 830 the court, applying *Wang*, reduced a sentence of nine months imposed on a husband and wife to three months. But in *R v Lu Zhu Ai* [2005] EWCA Crim 936 the court, reducing a nine-month sentence to five months, held that a deterrent message had to be sent to agents that their clients faced a real risk of a custodial sentence in the UK. Ironically, the role and authority of the agent were held to be strong mitigating factors justifying the quashing of a custodial sentence against a 17-year-old in *K v Croydon CC* [2005] EWHC 478 (Admin), a deception case: see 14.31 fn 9 above.

4   It is not the Home Office's intention that vulnerable people and in particular younger children should be convicted: Beverley Hughes (then Minister for Immigration, Citizenship and Counter-Terrorism), Asylum and Immigration (Treatment of Claimants) Bill Standing Committee (Commons) 8.1.04, col 15.

5   Asylum and Immigration (Treatment of Claimants etc) Act 2004, s 2(3).

6   Asylum and Immigration (Treatment of Claimants etc) Act 2004, s 2, (4), (5) and (6). For EEA nationals and family members see chapter 7.

7   Asylum and Immigration (Treatment of Claimants etc) Act 2004, s 2(7).

14.34 The criminalisation of arrival without travel documents is designed to address the large-scale destruction and disposal of documents before arrival, which creates problems in terms of tracing passengers back to particular carriers or ports of embarkation, and therefore delays their removal. It is based on the assumption that all passengers presenting themselves at immigration control must have had travel documents when they embarked, because carrier sanctions penalise carriers who bring undocumented passengers,[1] although the same assumption cannot be made in respect of clandestine entrants, who have left a container lorry during a ferry crossing or have been apprehended after the lorry has reached the UK. It is doubtful whether criminalising vulnerable people who have been forced to use unlawful methods to reach safety and who simply obey the instructions of agents bringing them in, is either lawful (having regard to the UK's Refugee Convention obligations)[2] or an efficient or humane way of dealing with the problem, which could be better addressed by administrative measures to ensure better tracking of passengers. The new offence raises additional problems. First, it is questionable whether the reverse burden of proof meets the requirements of Article 6(2) of ECHR. The essential feature of the offence is the presumed destruction or disposal of travel documents without reasonable excuse. If so, it is surely incumbent on the prosecution to prove at least these essential elements.[3] But, as enacted, all the prosecution has to prove is the absence of a current and valid identity document at an interview. Defendants who say 'I never had such a document' will almost certainly be disbelieved, even if their final means of arrival was in the back of a container lorry. Similarly, if they produce a poor forgery, they are almost certainly not going to be believed, because it will be said no self-respecting border official would be fooled. So we are back to the essential and underlying premise of the offence, which the prosecution does not have to prove. Conviction will occur on the unproved assumption that the accused did have a document and had no reasonable excuse for getting rid of it. Even when the 'reasonable excuse', or, indeed, the 'no documents' or 'forged documents' defence is run, there is every chance that the accused will be convicted, because he or she will be unable to prove the defence on a balance of probabilities; yet the judge or jury may still have a reasonable doubt about each or any of these matters.[4] We exclude from these propositions the defence that a person is an EEA national or family member of such a person, because this is arguably in the same category as the licence cases, where a reverse burden may well be justifiable.[5] Secondly, the criminal offence here is integral to the leave or asylum interview. Questions about how the refugee claimant travelled to the UK are an inevitable part of the asylum interview, for no other reason than that they go to credit.[6] But before that stage is reached, the refugee claimant will already be a suspect, because of the absence of the required identity documents. In that case it is incumbent on the interviewer to caution the person being interviewed, to offer him or her the services of a solicitor and the opportunity to seek consular assistance. The criminalisation of the asylum interview process surely drives a coach and four through the whole notion of the asylum interview as being a cooperative exercise carried out sensitively. Furthermore, if the refugee claimant is advised to make 'no comment', as would be his or her right, it would be quite wrong for the immigration official to draw any adverse inference for asylum purposes from the accused's silence. Poor thinking produces counterproductive law.

1 For carrier sanctions see 14.88ff below.
2 Both the Home Affairs Committee and the Joint Committee on Human Rights expressed concern at the risk that the UK would, as a result of the creation of the offence, fail to discharge its obligations under Article 31 of the Refugee Convention (as to which see 12.11 above and 14.37ff below) Home Affairs Committee, First Report of Session 2003–04, Asylum and Immigration (Treatment of Claimants) Bill, HC 109, paras 12–14; Joint Committee on Human Rights Fifth Report 2003–04, paras 11–14. It has been held at first instance that asylum seekers have no legitimate expectation that they will not be prosecuted on facts giving rise to the offence under s 2: *R v Chohan*, Isleworth CC, 3 February 2005 (HHJ McGregor-Johnson). But there should be no prosecution, or at least no conviction, where the actions are related to a bona fide quest for asylum: see *R v Uxbridge Magistrates' Court ex p Adimi* [1999] INLR 490 (at 14.37 below).
3 See *A-G Hong Kong v Lee Kwong Kut* [1993] AC 951, [1993] 3 All ER 939, PC.
4 See *R v Lambert* [2001] UKHL 37, [2001] 3 WLR 206 and Canadian cases cited therein.
5 See *R v Hunt* [1987] AC 352, [1987] 1 All ER 1, [1986] 3 WLR 1115.
6 See in particular Asylum and Immigration (Treatment of Claimants etc) Act 2004, s 8 which imposes an astonishing statutory direction on credibility, which incorporates the very subject matter of the s 2 offence. If such directions were incorporated into trials of murderers and other domestic miscreants there would be the most almighty outcry, but those fleeing persecution are apparently outside the elementary rules of fairness and fair game for statutory presumptions to suggest that they are unworthy of belief and should be pilloried as criminals.

14.35 The use of criminal sanctions against those entering the UK illegally, or unable to produce travel documents at interview after arrival, has given rise to issues relating to the UK's obligations under EC law and under international law relating to refugees.

EC nationals

14.36 The ECJ has ruled that illegal entry or a failure to report their presence to the authorities does not affect an EC national's right of residence under Community law. However, these rights do not prevent any Member State from prosecuting such persons, provided that the penalty imposed is not so disproportionate to the gravity of the infringement that it becomes an obstacle to the free movement of persons.[1] EU nationals exercising Community rights do not require leave to enter,[2] and will rarely be illegal entrants, although an EU national entering the UK after an exclusion order was made against him, which had not been set aside, was held to have been properly characterised as an illegal entrant in the *Shingara* case,[3] and an EU national entering the UK in breach of a deportation order is an illegal entrant.

[1]   Case 118/75 *Re Watson and Belmann* [1976] ECR 1185, ECJ (failure to report); *Royer* 48/75 [1976] ECR 497, ECJ (clandestine entry); *R v Pieck*: C-157/79 [1981] QB 571, ECJ.
[2]   By virtue of Immigration Act 1988, s 7.
[3]   *Shingara v Secretary of State for the Home Department* [1999] Imm AR 257, CA.

Refugees

14.37 The criminal sanctions laid down in the Immigration Act 1971 made no allowance for refugees who entered the UK illegally. But the combined effect of visa requirements and carrier sanctions has forced refugee claimants to adopt illegal methods in order to find safety. The growing use of false documents, either on entry to the UK or in transit via the UK to Canada and the US, led to numerous criminal prosecutions under the Forgery and Counterfeiting Act 1981 and under section 24A and 26(1)(d) of the 1971 Act (falsification of documents),[1] with custodial sentences of up to nine months being imposed (and upheld by the Court of Appeal).[2] In *Ex p Adimi*[3] the Divisional Court denounced this practice as contrary to Article 31(1) of the Refugee Convention. This provides that contracting states should not impose penalties on refugees who enter their territory illegally, provided they present themselves without delay to the authorities. The court recognised that 'the combined effect of visa regimes and carriers' liability has made it well-nigh impossible for refugees to travel to countries of refuge without false documents'.[4] The broad purpose sought to be achieved by Article 31(1), it held, was 'to provide immunity for genuine refugees whose quest for asylum reasonably involved them in breaching the law', so that 'where the illegal entry or use of false documents or delay can be attributed to a bona fide desire to seek asylum whether here or elsewhere, that conduct should be covered by Article 31'.[5] The protection of Article 31(1) applies not only to those ultimately recognised as refugees, but to those claiming asylum in good faith, and to those using false documents as well as clandestine entrants.[6] Since some element of choice is open to refugees as to where they may properly claim asylum, the phrase 'coming directly' should be interpreted in such a way that any merely short-term stopover en route to the intended sanctuary cannot forfeit the protection of the Article. The main touchstones by which exclusion from protection should be judged are the length of stay in the intermediate country, the reasons for delaying there (even a substantial delay in an unsafe third country would be reasonable were the time spent trying to acquire the means of travelling on), and whether or not the refugee sought or found there protection de jure or de facto from the persecution they were fleeing.[7] The requirement in the Article to 'present themselves without delay' was not necessarily breached by a failure to claim asylum on arrival.[8] Simon Brown LJ expressed the hope that prosecutions would be conducted only 'where the offence itself appears manifestly unrelated to a genuine quest for asylum'.[9] The court was divided on the issue of responsibility for ensuring compliance with Article 31; Newman J held that the Secretary of State for the Home

Department should determine entitlement to the protection of Article 31(1) since it was analogous to a pardon, which was an executive act;[10] Simon Brown LJ did not feel able to impose such an obligation on the executive and believed that the magistrates' abuse of process jurisdiction could be invoked.[11]

1   See 14.62 and 14.69 below.
2   A sentence of eight months was held appropriate in *R v Singh (Daljit)* [1999] 1 Cr App Rep (S) 490, a 'guideline case' involving a guilty plea to using a false instrument in respect of an attempt to travel to Canada using a false passport. The court said that cases involving the use of false passports will almost always merit a significant period of custody (six to nine months). See also cases cited at 14.31 fn 9 above. Evidence to the Home Affairs Committee in 2003 put the number of convictions at between 5,000 (JUSTICE) and under 1,000 (the government): First Report of Session 2003–04, Asylum and Immigration (Treatment of Claimants) Bill, HC 109, paras 12–14.
3   *R v Uxbridge Magistrates' Court, ex p Adimi; R v Crown Prosecution Service, ex p Sorani; R v Secretary of State for the Home Department, ex p Kaziu* [1999] INLR 490.
4   [1999] INLR 490 at 492G, per Simon Brown LJ. He held that Art 31 was justiciable in the UK courts through the doctrine of legitimate expectation, a conclusion he later described as 'suspect': see *European Roma Rights Centre v Immigration officer Prague Airport and Secretary of State for the Home Department* [2003] EWCA Civ 666, [2003] INLR 374, para 51. Laws LJ described it as a 'constitutional solecism'. See further 12.11 above.
5   [1999] INLR 490 at 496D–E.
6   [1999] INLR 490 at 496F.
7   [1999] INLR 490 at 497A–C.
8   [1999] INLR 490 at 498E.
9   [1999] INLR 490 at 504C.
10   [1999] INLR 490 at 513F.
11   [1999] INLR 490 at 503C.

14.38   After the judgment in *Adimi* a statutory defence was enacted to charges of deception under section 24A of the Immigration Act 1971 or falsification of documents under section 26(1)(d) of the Act, and to charges under the Forgery and Counterfeiting Act 1981 (forgery, use and possession of false instruments) by the Immigration and Asylum Act 1999, section 31. The statutory defence is significantly narrower in its scope than the protection afforded by Article 31(1) of the Refugee Convention according to *Adimi*. It applies only to those ultimately recognised as refugees;[1] requires refugees to have made a claim for asylum as soon as was reasonably practicable after arrival in the UK (in addition to presenting themselves to the authorities without delay);[2] and excludes the defence where refugees have stopped en route to the UK in another country, unless they could not reasonably have expected to be given protection in that country.[3] It provides that those wrongly convicted before the commencement of the section may apply to the Criminal Cases Review Commission for their cases to be referred to the Court of Appeal.[4] In practice section 31 of the 1999 Act removes much of the protection which the Divisional Court held was provided by Article 31(1) of the Refugee Convention. In line with the remarks of Simon Brown and Laws LJJ in the *ERRC* case[5] on the domestic justiciability of Article 31, the UK courts have shown themselves reluctant to accept the more generous criteria of Article 31 as expounded in *Adimi*. In *Hussain*[6] one judge in the Administrative Court declined to do so, saying that section 31 represented Parliament's interpretation of the UK's obligations under Article 31. A two-judge Divisional Court went further in *Pepushi*,[7] holding that section 31 was to be followed even if it put the UK in breach of the Refugee Convention. That asylum seekers can be deprived of the full benefit of such a fundamental aspect of refugee protection by a very restrictive interpretation is bad enough; that the UK courts can regard this situation with equanimity indicates an alarming return to the most narrowly traditional view of the constitutional role of Parliament and the courts in respect of international human rights law.[8]

1   Immigration and Asylum Act 1999, s 31(1), (6). A refused asylum seeker can seek to avail himself of the defence, but the burden of proof is on him or her to show that he or she is in fact a refugee: s 31(7).
2   IAA 1999, s 31(1)(a) and (c).
3   IAA 1999, s 31(2).
4   IAA 1999, s 31(8). In fact most convictions were in the magistrates' court, and could be reopened under Magistrates' Courts Act 1980, s 142(2), to enable the Crown to offer no evidence. Asylum seekers who were wrongly convicted and imprisoned have received compensation of up to £40,000: see *Abdi v Secretary of State for the Home Department* (2002) Legal Action, November. Home Office evidence to the Home Affairs Committee was that fewer than 20 people had successfully claimed compensation for wrongful conviction: Home Affairs Committee First Report of Session 2003–04, Asylum and Immigration (Treatment of Claimants) Bill, HC 109.
5   *European Roma Rights Centre v Immigration Officer Prague Airport (United Nations HIgh Comr for Refugees Intervening)* [2003] EWCA Civ 666, [2003] INLR 374; see 14.37 above at fn 4, although the House of Lords reaffirmed that the Refugee Convention was incorporated into domestic law, at [2004] UKHL 55, [2005] 2 WLR 1.
6   *R (Hussain) v Secretary of State for the Home Department* [2001] EWHC Admin 555.
7   *R (on the application of Pepushi) v CPS* [2004] EWHC 798 (Admin), [2004] All ER (D) 129 (May).
8   There is only one correct interpretation of the Convention, see *R v Secretary of State for the Home Department, ex p Adan* [2001] 1 All ER 593, [2001] 2 WLR 143, [2001] INLR 44. There is clearly tension between the courts' need to interpret an important safeguard of liberty contained in the Convention which has been incorporated into UK law and Parliament's rather à la carte approach to the implementation of the UK's international obligations, without having the benefit of a declaration of incompatibility or special interpretive tools, as under ss 3 and 4 of the Human Rights Act 1998, to deal with the constitutional supremacy of Parliament.

14.39   The Asylum Policy Instructions (API) on section 31 and Article 31 state that the *primary* focus for the CPS following the enactment of section 31 has to be upon the law to be found in the section and not the law on Article 31 to be found in the *Adimi* judgment.[1] The API state that where someone has not received a decision on their claim or has been refused and is appealing, it would normally be appropriate to await the outcome of the claim or appeal before proceeding to prosecution (if it was considered to be in the public interest to do so), but that persons granted humanitarian or discretionary leave on human rights grounds cannot claim the benefit of the defence, not being refugees.[2] The API provide guidance on the issues of 'good cause for illegal entry',[3] presenting oneself to the authorities 'without delay', claiming asylum 'as soon as reasonably practicable'[4] and the effect of stopping in another country outside.[5]

1   API 'Section 31 and Article 31', para 3. A joint Memorandum of Good Practice, drafted by representatives of the police, the Home Office, the Crown Prosecution Service and the Law Society in the wake of the *Adimi* judgment, indicated that immigration officers, police and prosecutors should apply both Article 31(1) of the Refugee Convention and the statutory defence in deciding whether to investigate, initiate or continue a prosecution, and stated that only in the clearest of cases (for example, where the suspect is a British citizen or says nothing to suggest any fear of persecution) should police proceed to charge. It was never formally published. For details see the previous edition of this work, at 14.26.
2   API 'Section 31 and Article 31', para 6.

3   The API (para 7) acknowledge that a refugee will *ipso facto* have good cause, although not a refugee *sur place* since the illegal entry was not necessitated by flight.

4   The API apply strict criteria to the issue of delay; 'Anyone who has completed their journey to the UK but not then made an immediate effort to regularise their stay should not benefit, save in the most exceptional circumstances.' The guidance normally expects anyone entering unlawfully to make a claim within 24 hours, adding that it is 'not reasonable to argue that they had to approach a lawyer or voluntary organisation first', although a delay to wait for family members to reach the UK might be acceptable: API ibid para 8. It is important to remember that this is merely the Home Office's interpretation, and that the criteria laid down by the court in *Adimi* should be applied unless the statutory defence prevents it.

5   The API recognise that an asylum seeker in transit through a third country 'might not have come into contact with immigration officials and might not therefore have had the opportunity to make an asylum claim' and that under these circumstances 'it may be considered reasonable' for the section 31 defence to apply: ibid para 9.

Offences of facilitating unlawful immigration and assisting asylum seekers

14.40 Sections 25, 25A and 25B of the Immigration Act 1971[1] widen and extend the old facilitation provisions, and cover any act facilitating a breach of immigration law by a non-EU citizen (including a breach of another Member State's immigration law, and acts covered by the old offence of harbouring), helping asylum seekers to arrive in the UK, or helping EU citizens to enter the UK in breach of a deportation order or an exclusion order. Actions performed in a control zone constitute the offence.[2] These are the most serious offences in the Act. On summary trial they carry a fine up to the statutory maximum[3] and imprisonment of up to six months, but it is rare for magistrates to accept jurisdiction, and on indictment a prison sentence of up to 14 years can be given.[4] They are arrestable offences within the meaning of the Police and Criminal Evidence Act 1984, s 24(1)(b).[5]

1   As substituted by Nationality, Immigration and Asylum Act 2002, s 143.
2   See the Channel Tunnel (International Arrangements) Order 1993, Art 5, Channel Tunnel (Miscellaneous Provisions) Order 1994, Nationality, Immigration and Asylum Act 2002 (Juxtaposed Controls) Order 2003, Art 12.
3   The statutory maximum is presently £5,000: Magistrates' Courts Act 1980, s 32(9); Criminal Justice Act 1991, s 17.
4   Immigration Act 1971, s 25(6), s 25A(4), s 25B(4) as substituted. The original offence of facilitating illegal entry attracted a seven-year sentence. The IAA 1999 increased the maximum sentence to ten years. Sentences of nine and 7½ years were reduced to seven and six years for a conspiracy straddling the commencement date of the 1999 provisions, on the basis of Art 7 ECHR, in *R v Hobbs* [2002] EWCA Crim 387, [2002] 2 Cr App Rep 324, [2002] 2 Cr App Rep (S) 425.
5   See 14.6 above.

14.41 Section 25 of the Immigration Act 1971 makes it an offence to do an act which facilitates the commission of a breach of immigration law by someone who is not an EU citizen, knowing or having reasonable cause to believe both that the act facilitates a breach of immigration law and that the individual assisted is not an EU citizen. 'Immigration law' includes the laws of any Member State regarding entitlement to enter, transit or be in a state[1], and the immigration laws of Member States are to be conclusively proved by a certificate from the government concerned.[2] The offence is defined broadly enough to encompass both the old offences of assisting illegal entry (whether by smuggling someone in in a vehicle or by providing false documents for presentation at a port), assisting someone to remain by deception (for example by entering into a sham marriage or by procuring false documents),[3] and other forms of assistance which facilitate a breach of the immigration laws. In *R v Naillie*,[4] decided under the old law, it was held that in a prosecution for facilitation it was necessary to determine whether the persons whose entry was assisted were illegal entrants; a distinction was to be drawn between arrival and entry, and mere disembarkation without a passport was not enough to make the asylum seekers illegal entrants; that they did not seek to enter the UK in breach of the laws until they presented a false passport to an immigration officer or tried to pass out of the immigration control area without submitting to examination at all; that by requesting asylum without any attempt to deceive, they did not seek to enter in breach, and were not illegal entrants. But the offence is committed if the intending immigrants are discovered before entry in circumstances indicating their intention to enter illegally.[5] The Crown no longer has to prove that those assisted are illegal entrants, but does have to prove that the acts facilitated a breach of the immigration laws, to the defendant's knowledge or reasonable belief. This could create prosecuting difficulties if the section is used (for example) against someone who provides support or accommodation to an overstayer or illegal entrant; there could be arguments as to mens rea if the person so helped has no other means of subsistence in the UK. It is to be hoped that, notwithstanding the potential breadth of the offence (said to be necessary for the purpose of compliance with EU law),[6] its outer limits will not be tested. The defence of necessity has been used at first instance when those smuggled in were refugees and smuggling was the only way to secure their safety from a threat of death or serious injury,[7] and an argument based on abuse of process succeeded in a case under the old provisions where a charge of helping asylum seekers was brought but dropped in favour of a facilitating illegal entry charge when the Crown realised it could not prove gain.[8] However, the defence afforded to refugees by Article 31 or section 31 (see 14.37–14.39 above) is not available to those smuggling refugees or otherwise helping them to arrive in breach of the immigration laws.[9]

---

1   *Immigration Act 1971, s 25(2) as substituted by the Nationality, Immigration and Asylum Act 2002, s 143.*

2   *IA 1971, s 25(3) as substituted. 'Member State' includes a state on a list of 'Schengen Acquis' states: s 25(7); see Immigration (Assisting Unlawful Immigration) (Section 25 List of Schengen Acquis States) Order 2004, SI 2004/2877, which lists Norway and Iceland.*

3   *Ie, offences previously covered by IA 1971, s 25(1)(c).*

4   *R v Naillie* [1993] AC 674, HL.

5   *R v Adams* [1996] Crim LR 593; *R v Eyck, R v Hadakoglu* [2000] INLR 277, CA.

6   European Directive and Framework Decision on the Facilitation of Unauthorised Entry, Transit and Residence, OJ 2002 L 328, OJ 2002 L 203/1. The UK has opted in to both provisions.

7   See *R v Martin* [1989] 1 All ER 652, [1989] 88 Cr App Rep 343, CA at 345–346, per Simon Brown J; *R v Pommell* [1995] 2 Cr App Rep 601, CA; *R v Abdul-Hussain* [1999] Crim LR 570; *R v Cairns* [1999] 2 Cr App Rep 137, CA.

8   *R v KS*, Middlesex Guildhall, 3 October 1999, HHJ Blacksall. See (2000) Legal Action February, p 21.

9   *R v Alps (Rudolph) (2 February 2001, unreported CA).*

14.42 The new section 25A of the Immigration Act 1971, inserted by the NIAA 2002,[1] is a reworking of the offence created in 1996 of facilitating the entry of asylum claimants. No element of smuggling is required to make out the offence; the asylum seekers do not need to be illegal entrants. The offence is aimed at those who, for gain, bring asylum seekers to the UK to enable them to claim asylum; it was intended to plug the gap disclosed by *R v Naillie*.[2] Since the right to seek and enjoy asylum is declared a fundamental human right by Article 14 of the UDHR, the criminalisation of those who assist asylum seekers to reach this country's shores for genuine humanitarian reasons was a controversial move on its introduction in 1996, and the Government was at pains to stress that it was aimed at 'illegal racketeering activity' of 'those who make profit by facilitating the entry of asylum seekers'.[3] The definition of the offence is knowingly and for gain facilitating the arrival in the UK of an individual known or reasonably believed to be an asylum seeker. An 'asylum seeker' is defined as a person who intends to claim that to remove him or her, or require him or her to leave the UK, would be contrary to the UK's obligations under the Refugee Convention or the Human Rights Convention.[4] The requirement of gain is now clearly part of the definition of the offence. The wording of the old section 25(1)(b), stating that the section did not apply to acts done 'otherwise than for gain', created confusion over the correct burden and standard of proof.[5] Section 25A exempts paid charity workers by asserting that the section does not apply to anything done by a person acting on behalf of an organisation which aims to assist asylum seekers and does not charge for its services.[6] A conspiracy to 'assist persons claiming asylum in the UK' is not an offence known to law.[7]

[1]   Nationality, Immigration and Asylum Act 2002, s 143, in force 10 February 2003.
[2]   14.41 fn 4 above. The case distinguished between 'arrival' and 'entry'. The old s 25(1)(b) ('facilitating the entry of asylum claimants') still used the word 'entry' in the definition of the offence, enabling defence lawyers to argue, following *R v Naillie* [1993] AC 674, HL that all their clients did was to facilitate arrival, not entry. The new section does not fall into this trap, using the word 'arrival' instead of the term of Art 'entry'. This change enabled the draftsman to do away with the sub-section exempting immigration lawyers from criminal responsibility for advising and assisting their clients (thereby facilitating the grant of leave to enter to them).
[3]   See HL Official Report (5th series); cols 570–574, 20 June 1996.
[4]   Immigration Act 1971, s 25A(2) as inserted.
[5]   See *R v Hunt* [1987] AC 352; *R v Duibi* (Harrow Crown Court, 30 March 1999, (2000) Legal Action February, p 21).
[6]   Immigration Act 1971, s 25A(3) as inserted.
[7]   *R v Hadi (Dawood)* [2001] EWCA Crim 2534, [2001] All ER (D) 450 (Oct).

14.43 The courts have been unwilling to apply the principle behind Article 31(1) of the Refugee Convention to allow those who smuggle in refugees for purely humanitarian reasons to escape penalty.[1] But in sentencing for the offence of facilitating illegal entry, the courts must have regard to whether, in particular, the motivation was commercial or humanitarian, as well as to whether the offence was an isolated act or repeated, the degree of organisation and the defendant's role. However, the Court of Appeal has deemed an immediate custodial sentence appropriate for all but the most minor offences.[2] Reported sentences range from six months for smuggling a husband[3] to six years for carrying large numbers in a specially adapted truck,[4] and eight years for conspiracy where 58 Chinese nationals suffocated to death in the lorry after the driver closed the air vents.[5] In addition to the penalties of fines and imprisonment, the Crown Court has very wide powers to order the forfeiture of any vehicle used or intended to be used for an offence under one of the sections, or a ship or aircraft carrying more than twenty entrants.[6] The vehicle or craft may be detained under the authority of a police or senior immigration officer pending prosecution, conviction and forfeiture.[7]

[1]   See 14.41 fn 9 above.
[2]   *R v Le, R v Stark* [1999] 1 Cr App Rep (S) 422. A suspended sentence of 18 months was imposed in *R v Belliki* [1998] 1 Cr App Rep (S) 135 (driving through immigration control with an illegal entrant concealed in van), because of exceptionally difficult domestic circumstances.
[3]   *R v Ozdemir* [1996] 2 Cr App Rep (S) 64. In *R v Toor* [2003] EWCA Crim 185, [2003] 2 Cr App Rep (S) 349 a sentence of 30 months was upheld for bringing in a brother on another brother's passport with a substituted photograph.
[4]   *R v Salem (Lofti ben) [2003] EWCA Crim 2172, [2003] All ER (D) 123 (Aug)*: a truck driver had 24 illegal entrants hidden in the truck, and holes had been drilled to enable them to breathe and to communicate with him.
[5]   *R v Wacker (Perry) [2002] EWCA Crim 1944, [2002] Crim LR 839, [2003] QB 1207, [2003] 4 All ER 295.*
[6]   Immigration Act 1971, s 25C as substituted by Nationality, Immigration and Asylum Act 2002, s 143.
[7]   Immigration Act 1971, s 25D, inserted by Immigration and Asylum Act 1999, s 38(2), and renumbered by Nationality, Immigration and Asylum Act 2002, s 144. See 14.14 above.

14.44 The new section 25B of the IA 1971[1] makes it an offence to assist the entry to the UK of an EU national in breach of a deportation or exclusion order. The section plugs the gap created by the new section 25, which excludes EU nationals from its remit. The offence is committed by doing an act which facilitates a breach of a deportation order in force against an EU citizen, knowing or having reasonable cause to believe that the act facilitates a breach of the order,[2] or, in a situation where the Secretary of State has personally excluded an EU citizen from the UK on public good grounds, doing an act which assists the person to arrive in, enter or remain in the UK, knowing or having reasonable cause to believe that the act has that effect and that the Secretary of State has made an exclusion order.[3]

[1]   Immigration Act 1971, s 25B, inserted by Nationality, Immigration and Asylum Act 2002, s 143.
[2]   IA 1971, s 25B(1).
[3]   IA 1971, s 25B(2).

14.45 Since a large part of the arrangements for assisting breaches of immigration laws, the illegal entry of EU nationals and for bringing asylum claimants will be made outside the UK, it is provided that acts committed abroad are triable in the UK, if committed by British citizens, British Overseas Territories citizens, British Overseas citizens, British Nationals (Overseas), British Protected Persons and British Subjects, and by companies incorporated in the UK.[1] As noted above, offences are triable in the UK if committed in control zones by persons of any nationality.[2]

[1]   Immigration Act 1971, ss 25(6), 25A(4), 25B(4) as substituted and inserted by Nationality, Immigration and Asylum Act 2002, s 143.
[2]   See 14.40 above, text and fn 2.

Trafficking offences

14.46 The Nationality, Immigration and Asylum Act 2002 created a new offence of trafficking in prostitution, making it an offence punishable by up to 14 years' imprisonment to arrange or facilitate a passenger's arrival in, travel within, or departure from the UK, (a) intending to exercise control over prostitution by the passenger in the UK or elsewhere, or (b) believing that another person would do so.[1] The Sexual Offences Act 2003 repeals these provisions and replaces them with an offence of trafficking for sexual exploitation, an offence much broader in its reach.[2] The offence is committed by intentionally arranging or facilitating the arrival in, travel within, or departure from the UK of a passenger, (a) intending to do anything to the passenger in any part of the world which involves the commission of a relevant offence, or (b) believing that another person is likely to do so.[3] A huge range of sexual offences is incorporated within the definition of 'relevant offence'.[4] As with the offences of facilitating arrival at or entry into the UK, the courts have jurisdiction in trafficking cases over acts done abroad, if committed by British nationals of all categories, British Protected Persons or UK-incorporated companies.[5] The placing of the new trafficking offence in an immigration statute and then removing it to a sexual offences one raises the question of why it was in the immigration statute in the first place. Although facilitating is an essential element of the offence, it is quite different from the raft of offences dealing with facilitating unlawful immigration, in that there is a clearly identified victim in trafficking. Exercise of control over the victim by the initial trafficker or by others is a key characteristic of the offence. While the victim is nearly always going to have an unlawful immigration status (reason enough for placing it in an immigration statute), it is surprising that domestic immigration law and practice is entirely silent on the measures which need and ought to be taken to protect the victim. Indeed initial experience of the operation of the new laws is that they give authority and justification for rounding up women engaged in prostitution and speedily deporting them, while doing very little against their exploiters. It seems the government has turned its back on the vibrant discussion at UN and EC level on the central question of the protection of victims, which is to give them renewable short term and, in some cases, permanent stay in the country to which they have been taken.[6] Passing the criminal laws is easy; tackling the exploitation and protecting the victims cannot properly be ignored.

---

1 Nationality, Immigration and Asylum Act 2002, s 145.
2 Sexual Offences Act 2003, ss 139, 140, 141(1), Sch 6, 7, in force 1 May 2004: SI 2004/874.
3 SOA 2003, ss 57–59.
4 SOA 2003, s 60. The definition includes offences under part I of the Act and under s 1(1)(a) Protection of Children Act 1978, equivalent offences in Northern Ireland, or anything done elsewhere which would be an offence in England, Wales or Northern Ireland.
5 NIAA 2002, s 146(1), (2); SOA 2003, s 60(2). The provisions regarding detention and forfeiture of vehicles echo more for facilitators (see 14.43 text and fn 6 above).
6 Proposal for a Council Directive on the short-term residence permit issued to victims of action to facilitate illegal immigration or trafficking in human beings who cooperate with the competent authorities COM (2002) 71 final. This Proposal corresponds to recommendations issued by different international organisations on the fight against trafficking in human beings, eg. the Protocol to Prevent, Suppress and Punish Trafficking in Persons, especially Women and Children, supplementing the United Nations Convention Against

Transnational Organized Crime, GA res 55/25, Annex II U.N. GAOR Supp (n° 49) at 60, UN Doc A/45/49 (Vol I) (2001). See further 'Integration of the human rights of women and the gender perspective violence against women', report of the Special Rapporteur on violence against women, its causes and consequences, Radhika Coomaraswamy, on trafficking in women, women's migration and violence against women, submitted in accordance with Commission on Human Rights Resolution 1997/44, Economic and Social Council, E/CN4/2000/68. See also Council of Europe, Parliamentary Assembly Recommendation 1545 (2002), 21.01.2002.

14.47 The Asylum and Immigration (Treatment of Claimants etc) Act 2004 creates the new offence of trafficking people for exploitation. The offence is designed to deal with the activities of 'snakeheads' and gangmasters who make vast profits bringing people in and making them work as debt slaves, or paying illegally low wages. The activities of these gangs came to public attention when 23 Chinese workers drowned collecting cockles on a Lancashire beach in February 2004. The offence is committed by arranging or facilitating the arrival, travel within the UK or departure of a passenger, intending to exploit the passenger in the UK or elsewhere or believing that another person is likely to do so.[1] 'Exploitation' is defined as: (i) behaviour contravening Article 4 ECHR (slavery and forced labour); (ii) encouraging, requiring or expecting the passenger to do anything which would amount to an offence under the Human Organ Transplants Act;[2] (iii) subjecting the passenger to force, threats or deception to induce him or her to provide services or benefits of any kind or to enable someone else to acquire benefits, or (iv) requiring or inducing someone to undertake an activity because they are mentally or physically ill or disabled, young or have a family relationship, when another person without those characteristics is likely to refuse or resist.[3] The offences carry maximum sentences of 14 years.[4] The UK courts have jurisdiction over acts done abroad by British nationals, BPPs and UK-incorporated companies,[5] and the provisions about detention and forfeiture of vehicles apply.[6] Once again, the government's resolve to catch the traffickers is regrettably not matched by concern for their victims. It has opted out of the proposed EU directive which would enable victims of trafficking to obtain residence permits, in line with the recommendations of the UN in its anti-trafficking Convention.[7]

[1] Asylum and Immigration (Treatment of Claimants, etc) Act 2004, s 4 (in force 1 December 2004: SI 2004/2999).
[2] Ie sale of organs.
[3] AI(CT)A 2004, s 4(1)–(3).
[4] AI(CT)A 2004, s 4(4).
[5] AI(CT)A 2004, s 5(1), (2), see 14.45 above.
[6] AI(CT)A 2004, s 5(4); see 14.43 text and fn 5 and 6 above.
[7] Proposal for a Directive on Residence Permits for the Victims of Trafficking (COM 2002 71), 14.46 fn 7 above.

Breach of conditions and overstaying

14.48 A person who is not a British citizen commits a criminal offence if, having only a limited leave to enter or remain in the UK, he or she knowingly either:

(i)   remains beyond the time limited by the leave; or

(ii)　fails to observe a condition of the leave.[1]

Both these offences are summary only. The maximum penalty is six months' imprisonment and a fine at level 5,[2] and police and immigration officers may arrest suspected offenders without warrant.[3]

1　Immigration Act 1971, s 24(1)(b), as amended by British Nationality Act 1981, Sch 4, para 2.
2　Set at £5,000: Criminal Justice Act 1982, s 37(2), as amended by Criminal Justice Act 1991, s 17.
3　Immigration Act 1971, s 28A, inserted by Immigration and Asylum Act 1999, s 128.

14.49 Overstaying used to be the most common immigration offence but since overstayers' rights of appeal against deportation were restricted in 1988,[1] it has rarely been used. The wording of the offence gives rise to difficulty: 'having' a limited leave does not readily fit an offence of remaining beyond the leave. It is entirely appropriate for the second limb of the offence, where there must be an extant leave in order for there to be a breach of conditions.[2] To make sense of the wording, 'having' has to be interpreted as meaning 'having had', although such an interpretation of identical words in section 14 of the Immigration Act 1971 was rejected by the House of Lords in the case of *Suthendran*.[3] The offence of overstaying is defined as a continuing offence which is committed at any time when the immigrant knows that the time limited by his or her leave has expired and nevertheless remains in the UK.[4] There is no need for any provision to extend the time limits for prosecution. But a person cannot be prosecuted more than once in respect of the same limited leave.[5]

1　By Immigration Act 1988, s 5. The Immigration and Asylum Act 1999, s 10 made overstayers and those in breach of conditions of leave liable to administrative removal rather than deportation and removed rights of appeal (except on asylum or human rights grounds).
2　*Singh (Gurdev) v R* [1974] 1 All ER 26, [1973] 1 WLR 1444, DC.
3　*Suthendran v Immigration Appeal Tribunal* [1977] AC 359, [1976] 3 All ER 611, HL.
4　Immigration Act 1971, s 24(1A), inserted by Immigration Act 1988, s 6, except in relation to persons whose leave had expired before 10 July 1988, for whom the offence could only be committed on the day following the expiry of their leave: *Grant v Borg* [1982] 2 All ER 257, [1982] 1 WLR 638, HL.
5　Immigration Act 1971, s 24(1A), as amended.

14.50 Persons who applied before the expiry of their leave for further leave and who remain awaiting a decision on their application are not overstayers because their leave is extended by statute until the end of the period allowed for the bringing of an appeal, and while any appeal is pending.[1] These considerations give rise to evidential difficulties in that the expiry date on the leave stamp in a passport is not conclusive evidence that the accused has overstayed.[2]

1　Immigration Act 1971, s 3C, substituted by Nationality, Immigration and Asylum Act 2002, s 118. The normal period allowed for the bringing of an appeal under ibid s 82(1) is ten days: Asylum and Immigration Tribunal (Procedure) Rules 2005, SI 2005/230, r 7.
2　See *Zoltak v Sussex Constabulary* [1983] CLY 1923 where a conviction for overstaying was quashed where the defendant had applied for an extension, and the application was date-stamped as received two days after his leave expired. The court held that since the

application was made when it was posted (following *Lubetkin v Secretary of State for the Home Department* [1979–80] Imm AR 162) the prosecutor had not established that on the date of the alleged offence the defendant did not have deemed leave under the provisions of the Immigration (Variation of Leave Order) 1976, the precursor of s 3C.

14.51 A conviction for overstaying requires proof of knowledge. A belief that one's leave expires on a different date is a mistake of fact; so also is the belief that another person – a friend or agent – has made an application for an extension when this is not the case. There may be cases of illiterate persons or persons whose comprehension of English is so poor that they do not appreciate that their leave has expired, or persons whose employer has retained their passport and has never shown the employee the endorsement. Sheer forgetfulness, and oversight owing to the stress caused by bereavement, may be capable of providing good defences.[1]

[1] *Immigration Appeal Tribunal v Chelliah* [1985] Imm AR 192, CA; *R v Bello* (1978) 67 Cr App Rep 288, [1978] Crim LR 551, CA (dismissed on the facts).

14.52 Since the right of entry and residence of EEA nationals flows directly from the provisions of EC law and is not subject to the requirements of the Immigration Act 1971 to obtain leave to enter or remain,[1] it is difficult to see how an EEA national covered by the free movement provisions of the EC Treaty can commit the offence of overstaying under section 24(1)(b) of the 1971 Act by remaining after his or her residence permit expires. The 'no visa' rule, however, does not apply to members of the EEA worker's family who are not EEA nationals. They are required to obtain a family permit confirming their rights of entry under EC law (see chapter 7 above). But their rights flow from EC law and provided they continue to qualify as members of the family, they should not be liable to criminal or administrative action for remaining beyond the time limited by their permit.

[1] *R v Pieck*: 157/79 [1981] QB 571, [1981] 3 All ER 46, ECJ; Immigration Act 1988, s 7.

14.53 Under section 8(1) of the Immigration Act 1971,[1] as we have seen, crews of ships, international trains and aircraft are allowed entry without leave until their ship, train or aircraft leaves the country again. Under section 24(1)(c) of the 1971 Act it is an offence if seamen or air or train crews stay longer than the temporary period of admission normally allowed under section 8(1) when their ship, train or aircraft docks, arrives or lands here. The extended time limit applies to such offences,[2] and they may be arrested without warrant by the police or immigration officers if with reasonable cause they are suspected of having committed such an offence.[3] This offence was intended in particular to catch seamen who deserted ship when it arrived in the UK, but it is a less effective way, from the authorities' point of view, than the extensive administrative powers of removal under Schedule 2 to the 1971 Act.

[1] Modified in relation to international trains by the Channel Tunnel (International Arrangements) Order 1993, SI 1993/1813, Art 7, Sch 4, para 1(7); Channel Tunnel (Miscellaneous Provisions) Order 1994, SI 1994/1405, Art 7.
[2] Immigration Act 1971, ss 24(3), 28.
[3] IA 1971, s 28A, inserted by Immigration and Asylum Act 1999, s 128.

14.54 Conditions can only be attached to a limited leave to remain, and the only conditions that can be attached to leave are a restriction on employment or occupation in the UK, a condition requiring an immigrant to maintain and accommodate him or herself and any dependants without recourse to public funds, or to register with the police, or all three.[1] Thus there is no power to attach conditions to an indefinite leave, and where a limited leave is extended to become an indefinite leave any conditions automatically cease.[2] Where a limited leave is subject to conditions, an automatic extension of leave under the statutory provisions also extends the conditions.[3] However, a person can only be guilty of the offence of a breach of conditions during a period in which the conditions apply; where the leave itself has run out and is not extended by statute (whether by an application or by an appeal) there is nothing for the conditions to attach to and the conditions will lapse.[4] Thereafter a person may be guilty of overstaying the leave but not of contravening restrictions attached to it.[5] Thus a person who takes employment after the expiry of leave is not committing any additional offence by doing so (although his or her employer is: see 14.82ff below). The same principles apply to persons who are required to register with the police; this requirement attaches to a leave and expires with the leave.[6] The offence is a continuing one in that the Crown is not confined to the first occasion of the breach of condition.[7] The extended time limit for prosecutions does not apply to an offence of breach of conditions, and a prosecution must, therefore, be brought within six months of the commission of the offence. Knowledge of the conditions is a prerequisite of the offence.

1   Immigration Act 1971, s 3(1)(c), as amended by Asylum and Immigration Act 1996, Sch 2, para 1(1).
2   Immigration Act 1971, s 3(3)(a).
3   Immigration Act 1971, s 3C, as substituted by Nationality, Immigration and Asylum Act 2002 s 118; *Ali (Shaukat) v Chief Adjudication Officer* (1985) Times, 24 December, CA; *Rajendran v Secretary of State for the Home Department* [1989] Imm AR 512.
4   *Suthendran v Immigration Appeal Tribunal* [1977] AC 359, [1976] 3 All ER 611, HL.
5   *Singh (Gurdev) v R* [1974] 1 All ER 26, [1973] 1 WLR 1444, DC.
6   *R v Naik* (1978) Times, 26 July, CA.
7   *Manickavsagar v Metropolitan Police Comr* [1987] Crim LR 50, DC. See further *Singh (Gurdev)* above.

14.55 Where a person is given temporary admission – either pending a further examination on entry, or pending removal as an illegal entrant, overstayer or deportee – it is an offence to fail to observe any requirements as to residence, employment or occupation, or reporting to the police, an immigration officer or the Secretary of State, without reasonable excuse.[1] A person who has been placed on board a train, ship or aircraft pursuant to removal directions commits an offence if he or she disembarks, as does a person who embarks in contravention of an Order in Council made under the provision of the Immigration Act 1971 to permit retaliatory measures or hostage orders.[2] The extended time limits do not apply to any of the offences considered in this section.

1   Immigration Act 1971, s 24(1)(e), as amended by Nationality, Immigration and Asylum Act 2002, s 62(9). The amendment reflects the fact that the Secretary of State (through Home Office civil servants) now has most of the powers of immigration officers in respect of entry. Failure to cooperate with electronic monitoring, once the requisite regulations are in force, will be treated for these purposes as failure to comply with a residence or

reporting condition: Asylum and Immigration (Treatment of Claimants) Act 2004,
s 36(2)(b), (3)(b). Immigration officers may arrest for this and the following offences
without a warrant: s 28B, 14.6 above.
2   Immigration Act 1971, s 24(1)(f) and (g), modified in its application to the Channel Tunnel
by the Channel Tunnel (International Arrangements) Order 1993, Art 7(1), Sch 4,
para 1(7).

Breach of immigration officers' directions

14.56 A variety of miscellaneous offences exist to back up the immigration
officer's powers on examination and removal, although they have rarely been
used in the past. Thus it is an offence to fail to comply with a direction to
report to a medical officer of health, as directed, or to fail to attend or to
submit to an examination required by such an officer.[1] There is a defence of
reasonable excuse, which might apply, for example, to a refusal to undergo an
examination which was not conducted by properly qualified medical staff.
There used to be no power of arrest for this offence, but a power of arrest on
warrant was created in 2002.[2] Immigration officers may search premises to
effect an arrest with a warrant.[3]

1   Immigration Act 1971, s 24(1)(d).
2   IA 1971, s 28AA, inserted by Nationality, Immigration and Asylum Act 2002, s 152.
3   IA 1971, s 28B, inserted by Immigration and Asylum Act 1999, s 129.

Failure to cooperate with arrangements for removal

14.57 The Asylum and Immigration (Treatment of Claimants, etc) Act 2004
creates the offence of failure without reasonable excuse to comply with a
requirement of the Secretary of State imposed to facilitate the obtaining of a
travel document and the person's deportation or removal.[1] The offence may
be committed by failing to comply with a requirement to:

- provide information or documents to the Secretary of State or anyone
  else;
- obtain information or documents;
- provide fingerprints and submit to the taking of a photograph;
- submit to a process for the recording of information about external
  physical characteristics such as the iris;
- make or consent or cooperate with making an application to the
  representative of another government;
- cooperate with a process designed to enable determination of an
  application;
- complete a form accurately and completely;
- attend an interview and answer questions accurately and completely;
- make an appointment.[2]

Failure to comply can result in imprisonment for up to two years on
indictment, or to six months or the statutory maximum fine on summary
conviction.[3] The offence carries a power of arrest without warrant.[4] As the
Joint Committee on Human Rights noted, the section would enable the
administration to abuse its power by demanding information and cooperation

which could then be used to facilitate the person's deportation later.[5] It could create grave dangers for those wrongly refused asylum and for any relatives in the home country.[6] Furthermore, if during the course of the interview there arises a suspicion that the detainee may have committed a criminal offence, the interview should immediately stop, the caution should be administered, and the suspect should be told of his or her right to a lawyer, and, in appropriate circumstances to consular access.

1 Asylum and Immigration (Treatment of Claimants etc) Act 2004, s 35(4). Home Office guidance indicates that once the defendant raises an excuse it is for the Crown to disprove it or show it was not reasonable. Examples of reasonable excuse given in the guidance are limited to medical emergencies or transport problems; but see fn 6 below. Home Office Guidance on section 35, para 7.3.
2 AI(TC)A 2004, s 35(1), (2)(a)–(h). The Home Office Guidance, above, does not rule out the prosecution of minors under the section, but acknowledges that 'special care' is needed.
3 AI(TC)A 2004, s 35(4).
4 AI(TC)A 2004, s 35(5).
5 Joint Committee on Human Rights 5th report session 2003–4, 10.2.04, para 79.
6 The court accepted in *R (on the application of Amirthanathan) v Secretary of State for the Home Department* (upheld in the Court of Appeal with no reference to this part of the judgment, as *Nadarajah v Secretary of State for the Home Department, R (on the application of Amirthanathan) v Secretary of State for the Home Department* [2003] EWCA Civ 1768, (2003) Sol Jo LB 24, [2003] All ER (D) 129 (Dec)) para 39, that 'once an appeal is lodged it is inappropriate to require a person to give an interview to the authorities of the destination country to facilitate the obtaining of a travel document, since the interview might lead to information being provided which might put the claimant or his family at risk'.

Offences in connection with the administration of the Immigration Acts

14.58 There are a number of summary offences which serve to emphasise the extensive powers of immigration officers when conducting an examination on entry. Persons who refuse or fail to submit to such an examination,[1] who refuse or fail to produce information in their possession, or documents under their control which they are required to produce, or fail to complete a landing card or embarkation card, commit offences if they have no reasonable excuse.[2] It is also an offence to fail without lawful excuse to comply with any regulations regarding registering with the police or keeping hotel records.[3]

1 Immigration Act 1971, s 26(1)(a). The maximum penalties are now six months' imprisonment or a level 5 fine. The offences are summary only.
2 IA 1971, s 26(1)(b). It is arguable that a reasonable excuse not to provide information would exist, if the examination interview involves asking certain questions, without administering the caution and informing the person of his or her right to a lawyer and possible consular access. These are questions about criminal offences, such as not having valid travel documents contrary to AI(TC)A 2004, s 2, of which the passenger has become a suspect. See 14.34 above.
3 IA 1971, s 26(1)(f).

14.59 Two of these offences bear closer examination. The first is that of making a false statement under section 26(1)(c) of the Immigration Act 1971. It is an offence to make a return, statement, or representation which is known to be false or not believed to be true to an immigration officer or other person acting in the execution of a 'relevant enactment', either on a 1971 Act, Schedule 2 examination or otherwise.[1] 'Otherwise' means otherwise acting in execution of the relevant Act. So the phrase qualifies both the person to whom the statement is made and the circumstances in which it is made. A great many people act in the course of their employment in functions which promote the purposes of the Acts, but they are not acting in the execution of the 'relevant enactments'.[2] The offence is committed where the false statement is addressed to a person pursuing a right or duty under one of the relevant Acts to receive information, such as immigration officers, perhaps entry clearance officers,[3] medical inspectors, police officers acting under the 1971 Act, Home Office officials who process applications to vary and the appellate authorities. The offence (along with all the other section 26 offences) may be committed in a control zone.[4] Prior to 1999, the offence could only be committed in relation to a person exercising functions under the 1971 Act. The amendments in 1999 and 2002 broadened the scope of the offence, which can now be committed by telling lies to a wider range of people – a detainee custody officer in a contracted-out detention centre[5] or to a NASS sub-contractor,[6] for instance, and can be committed by a much wider range of people in respect of a vastly wider range of functions. Lies told by a third party to an immigration officer who is searching a property for a person or for documents could be covered, since such a search is now a statutory function.

1 The phrase 'relevant enactments' was inserted and defined by Immigration and Asylum Act 1999, s 30, and amended by Nationality, Immigration and Asylum Act 2002, s 151. The 'relevant enactments' are defined as the Immigration Act 1971, the Immigration Act 1988, the Asylum and Immigration Appeals Act 1993, the Immigration and Asylum Act 1999 (apart from Part VI) or the Nationality, Immigration and Asylum Act 2002 (apart from Part 5).
2 *R v Clarke* [1985] AC 1037, [1985] 2 All ER 777, HL in which lies told to police investigating an offence under the Immigration Act 1971 were held not to constitute the offence since the officers were not acting 'in the execution of the Act'.
3 *R v Secretary of State for the Home Department, ex p Kwadwo Saffu-Mensah* [1991] Imm AR 43, QBD, affd on different grounds in the Court of Appeal [1992] Imm AR 185. Though made abroad, such representations may be prosecutable in the UK as an act done to obtain a benefit here, or having a real and substantial link with the UK: *R v Baxter* [1972] 1 QB 1, [1971] 2 All ER 359, CA; *DPP v Stonehouse* [1977] 2 All ER 909 at 913; *Somchai Liangsiriprasert v Government of the United States of America* [1991] 1 AC 225, PC – although the explicit territorial extensions elsewhere in the Act make such an implied extension unlikely, particularly in the penal context.
4 *Nationality, Immigration and Asylum Act 2002 (Juxtaposed Controls) Order 2003*, SI 2003/2818, Art 12.
5 In respect of the functions performed under Immigration and Asylum Act 1999, Pt VIII in contracted-out detention centres.
6 In respect of the provision of accommodation; however these would more likely be charged as asylum support offences, for which see **14.73** below.

14.60 According to *Khawaja v Secretary of State for the Home Department* the Crown needs to prove that the false representation concerned was 'effective' in obtaining leave to enter, but subsequent cases have suggested that the deception need only be 'material' in the sense that that it was likely to influence the decision to allow entry.[1] Nowadays, making false representations to immigration officers giving leave to enter, or to Home Office officials giving leave to remain or deciding on removal or deportation, is more likely to be charged as deception (if performed by the immigrant) or assisting a breach of immigration law or obstruction (if performed by third parties). These offences are committed if the means of entry, remaining, etc included deception.[2]

Charging deception also gets round the technical problems described in 14.59 above and discussed in *R v Clarke*[3] as to when a person was acting in the execution of the relevant Act.

[1] See 16.21 below. In *R v Secretary of State for the Home Department, ex p Castro* [1996] Imm AR 540, the court held that the deception of the mother was both effective and material in obtaining the leave for her children. The case was not a criminal case but a judicial review of a decision that the person was an illegal entrant, following *Khawaja v Secretary of State for the Home Department* [1984] AC 74, [1983] 1 All ER 765, [1983] 2 WLR 321, [1982] Imm AR 139, HL, which held that the offence was at the heart of illegal entry by deception. Perhaps, more importantly the court decided that a deceit by the mother could be imputed to her children under s 26(1)(c), following *R v Secretary of State for the Home Department, ex p Khan* [1977] 1 WLR 1466, CA and an *obiter* in *R v Secretary of State for the Home Department, ex p Salim* [1990] Imm AR 316 at 323–4, and distinguishing *R v Immigration Officer, ex p Chan* [1992] 1 WLR 541, CA and *R v Secretary of State for the Home Department, ex p Kuet* [1995] Imm AR 274, CA.
[2] See 14.31 above.
[3] [1985] AC 1037, [1985] 2 All ER 777, HL.

14.61 There is also an offence of obstructing an immigration officer or other person acting in execution of the Immigration Act 1971.[1] By analogy with the offence of obstructing a police officer, the offence would require some physical or other unlawful activity which prevents or impedes a person from carrying out some particular duty entrusted to them by the Act.[2] Where the obstruction consists of a refusal to do something requested by an immigration official, the offence will only be committed if there is a duty under the Act to do what is requested, such as permitting inspection of luggage by an immigration officer.[3] The offence can be committed in a control zone.[4] There is a restricted power of arrest without warrant for obstruction, on failure of the suspect to provide a reliable name or address.[5]

[1] Immigration Act 1971, s 26(1)(g).
[2] See *R v Clarke* [1985] AC 1037, [1985] 2 All ER 777, HL.
[3] Immigration Act 1971, Sch 2, para 4.
[4] Nationality, Immigration and Asylum Act 2002 (Juxtaposed Controls) Order 2003, SI 2003/2818, Art 12.
[5] Immigration Act 1971, s 28A(5), inserted by Immigration and Asylum Act 1999, s 128.

14.62 The final offences in connection with the administration of the Immigration Acts are in respect of documents and stamps. It is an offence to alter a certificate of entitlement, entry clearance, work permit or other document issued or made under or for the purposes of the IA 1971 or used for its purposes.[1] This might include police registration books. These are all documents emanating from the UK authorities. Furthermore it is an offence to use for the purposes of the 1971 Act, or to possess with intent to use, any passport, certificate of entitlement, entry clearance, work permit or other document which a person knows to be false or has reasonable cause to believe to be false.[2] The category of documents here is wider, and might include any document presented to an immigration officer or Home Office official for the purpose of obtaining leave to enter or remain. The reference to a document being false must be a reference to a false particular of a material kind to give the general character of falsity to the document.[3] The document concerned must actually be false for the offence to be committed;[4] the reasonable cause for belief in its falsity is necessary but not sufficient for the offence to be made out. It is likely that the defendant must actually believe the document to be false.[5] The penalties for this, as for the other 1971 Act, section 26 offences, are a fine on level 5 and up to six months' imprisonment.[6] If the possession or use of the false document is related to a bona fide quest for asylum, the section 31/Article 31(1) defence is available.[7]

[1]   Immigration Act 1971, s 26(1)(d).
[2]   Immigration Act 1971, s 26(1)(d).
[3]   See Webster J in *R v Secretary of State for the Home Department, ex p Patel* [1986] Imm AR 208, QBD; affd [1986] Imm AR 515, CA.
[4]   By analogy with the assisting offences of ss 25, 25A and 25B of the Immigration Act 1971, which have the same wording – those assisted must actually be illegal entrants or asylum claimants: see *R v Naillie* [1993] AC 674.
[5]   By analogy with 'reasonable grounds for suspicion', which requires actual suspicion: *O'Hara v Chief Constable of Royal Ulster Constabulary* [1997] AC 286, HL. See discussion in *R v Secretary of State for the Home Department, ex p Rouse* (1985) Times, 25 Noevember, QBD.
[6]   Immigration Act 1971, s 26. The fine is currently £5,000: Criminal Justice Act 1982, s 37, as amended by Criminal Justice Act 1991, s 17.
[7]   Immigration and Asylum Act 1999, s 31; Refugee Convention, Art 31(1): see 14.37–14.39 above.

14.63   All the offences discussed in this section can be committed by British as well as non-British citizens. There is no power of arrest without warrant, and the offences must be prosecuted within six months, save the offences of false statements and false documents, in respect of which the extended time limit applies.

14.64   The NIAA 2002 created new offences relating to registration cards and immigration stamps. It is an offence to make a false registration card, or to alter a registration card with intent to deceive, or to use or attempt to use a false or altered card with intent to deceive, or to make something designed to be used in making or altering a card, or to possess a false or altered card or a forgery tool without reasonable excuse.[1] The offences, unlike those in section 26(1)(d), are triable either way, and making, altering or using carry a sentence of up to ten years' imprisonment on indictment, while offences of possession carry up to two years on indictment.[2] The registration card is defined as a document which carries information about a person (whether or not electronic) and is used by the Secretary of State in connection with an asylum claim (whether or not by that person).[3] The offences of possession of an immigration stamp or a replica stamp without reasonable excuse[4] carry sentences up to two years on indictment.[5] Both offences carry powers of arrest without warrant[6] and the other ancillary powers of search of premises.[7]

[1]   Immigration Act 1971, s 26A, inserted by Nationality, Immigration and Asylum Act 2002, s 148.
[2]   IA 1971, s 26A (5), (6). On summary trial they carry six months' imprisonment and/or a fine up to the statutory maximum.
[3]   The asylum registration card carries a wealth of information, including biometric information: see **14.22** above. Applicants and their dependants each have a card, which serves as evidence of their status in the UK. The anomaly between the penalties for offences under s 26 (including deception) and s 26A is likely to result in prosecution under s 26A rather than s 26.
[4]   IA 1971, s 26B, inserted by Nationality, Immigration and Asylum Act 2002, s 148.

5 IA 1971, s 26B(4). On summary trial the penalties are as for the s 26A offences: see fn 2 above.
6 IA 1971, s 28A(9) inserted by NIAA 2002, s 150.
7 IA 1971, s 28B(5) and s 28D(4), as amended by NIAA 2002, s 150.

Extended time limit

14.65 Normally the time limit for bringing a prosecution for a summary offence is six months.[1] This normal time limit applies to most immigration offences, but, as already indicated, there are a number of offences to which the extended time limit, set out in section 28 of the Immigration Act 1971, applies. In particular, it applies to the offences of illegal entry, overstaying[2] and making a false statement or altering a document.[3] In England and Wales the extended time limit enables a magistrate's court to try an information if it is laid within three years after the commission of the offence and not more than two months after the date certified by a chief officer of police to be the date on which evidence sufficient to justify proceedings came to the notice of an officer of that police force.[4] In Scotland the certifying officer is the Lord Advocate[5] and in Northern Ireland, a police officer not below the rank of assistant chief constable.[6] The 'trial' of the information begins with the hearing of the information, not with the plea of not guilty, which only marks the need for a trial.[7] 'Evidence' means more than information given over the telephone, which would be inadmissible in proceedings.[8]

1 Magistrates' Courts Act 1980, s 127.
2 Immigration Act 1971, s 24(3).
3 IA 1971, s 26(2).
4 IA 1971, s 28(1)(a).
5 IA 1971, s 28(1)(b).
6 IA 1971, s 28(1)(c).
7 *Quazi v DPP* (1988) 152 JP 385.
8 *Enaas v Dovey* (1986) Times, 25 November

14.66 The operation of the extended time limit was illustrated in *Ex p Offei*,[1] where a certificate to enable an extended time limit to apply had been signed by the chief constable, but officers from the same force had interviewed the applicant in connection with his overstaying at least 18 months earlier than the two-month period to which the certificate related. As a result of the earlier interview, all the evidence needed to prosecute him for an offence against section 24(1)(b) of the Immigration Act 1971 was to hand. The Divisional Court quashed his conviction, holding that by reason of the earlier interview there was evidence sufficient to justify proceedings and the certificate was therefore a nullity. The court held that there would not have been sufficient evidence if the overstayer's whereabouts were unknown. It also held that the challenge to the validity of the certificate was for the High Court rather than the magistrates,[2] although a different view was taken in *Enaas v Dovey*,[3] which held that magistrates could go behind the certificate to see whether the decision of the chief of police was reasonable. Resolution of these conflicting views has not yet happened. The sufficiency of evidence is a matter for the chief of police's judgment, which can only be successfully challenged if it is unreasonable in a *Wednesbury*[4] sense. The extended time limit for prosecution is no longer of importance in relation to the offence of overstaying, since it can be prosecuted at any time until the person leaves the country (see 14.49 above), but it is still important in offences which are not continuing, such as illegal entry and using a false document.

1   *R v Clerk to Birmingham Justices, ex p Offei* (28 November 1985, unreported), QBD.
2   By analogy with the absence of the Director of Public Prosecutions' consent in *R v Angel* [1968] 2 All ER 607n, [1968] 1 WLR 669, CA.
3   (1986) Times, 25 November.
4   *Associated Provincial Picture Houses Ltd v Wednesbury Corpn* [1948] 1 KB 223, [1947] 2 All ER 680, CA.

Offences in relation to passports and acquisition of nationality

14.67 It is an offence punishable on summary conviction by a fine up to level 5[1] or up to three months' imprisonment, or both, for any person, for the purpose of procuring anything to be done or not to be done under the British Nationality Act 1981, knowingly or recklessly to make any statement which is false in a material particular.[2] The offence would be committed by a person lying about the length of his or her residence in the UK to obtain naturalisation, for example. The extended time limit for prosecution applies.[3]

1   Set at £5,000: Criminal Justice Act 1982, s 37(2), as amended by Criminal Justice Act 1991, s 17.
2   British Nationality Act 1981, s 46(1), as amended, penalty to be increased to 51 weeks by Criminal Justice Act 2003, s 280, Sch 26, para 29, as from a date to be appointed.
3   British Nationality Act 1981, s 46(3).

14.68 Making a statement which is to the person's knowledge untrue for the purpose of procuring a passport for him or herself or for any other person[1] is a more serious offence, triable either way and punishable on summary conviction by a fine up to the statutory maximum fine and/or up to six months' imprisonment, and on indictment by up to two years' imprisonment. Where a passport is actually obtained by a fraudulent application and used, it is more appropriate to charge an offence of obtaining property by deception;[2] the offence under this section is more appropriate where no passport is actually obtained.[3] A custodial sentence has been held appropriate for a first offence.[4]

1   Criminal Justice Act 1925, s 36. This has become an arrestable offence by s 3 Criminal Justice Act 2003 (in force 29 January 2004: SI 2004/81), by adding it to Sch 1A to the Police and Criminal Evidence Act 1984 (see 14.6 fn 2 above).
2   *R v Ashbee* [1989] 1 WLR 109, (1989) 88 Cr App R 357, CA.
3   *R v Bunche* (1993) 157 JP 780, CA.
4   *R v Walker* [1999] 1 Cr App Rep (S) 42, where an overstayer applied for a passport using a false name, date and place of birth. The sentence of 18 months was however reduced to nine months.

14.69 A passport is an 'instrument' for the purposes of 'relevant offences' under the Forgery and Counterfeiting Act 1981.[1] Relevant offences are forgery (making a false instrument),[2] using a false instrument,[3] possession of a false instrument with intent,[4] and possession of a false instrument without lawful authority or excuse.[5] All the offences are triable either way, punishable on summary conviction by a fine up to the statutory maximum or six months' imprisonment, and on indictment by a maximum of 10 years' imprisonment, save for possession without lawful authority when the maximum sentence on indictment is two years.[6] Persons presenting false passports at immigration control are frequently charged with the possession offences. The statutory defence under the Immigration and Asylum Act 1999, s 31, and Refugee Convention, Article 31 argument, apply to these offences.[7] The Asylum and Immigration (Treatment of Claimants etc) Act 2004 adds other 'immigration documents' to the definition of 'instrument' under the 1981 Act, including cards and adhesive labels carrying information about the person (which might be electronic), and about the leave granted, or given to confirm a right of residence under the Community Treaties.[8]

[1]   Forgery and Counterfeiting Act 1981, ss 8(1)(a), 5(5)(f).
[2]   FCA 1981, s 1.
[3]   FCA 1981, s 3.
[4]   FCA 1981, s 5(1).
[5]   FCA 1981, s 5(2).
[6]   FCA 1981, s 6; the statutory maximum is £5,000: Magistrates' Courts Act 1980, s 32(9). See *R v Kolawole* (2004) Times, 16 November: 12–18 months is an appropriate sentence for use of a false passport for a person of good character on a guilty plea. See also cases cited at 14.31 fn 9 above.
[7]   Immigration and Asylum Act 1999, s 31(3) and (4); see 14.37–14.39 above.
[8]   Asylum and Immigration (Treatment of Claimants etc) Act 2004, s 3, inserting FCA 1981, s 5(5)(fa), 5(9)–(11) as from a date to be appointed.

Offences by persons connected with ships, aircraft, ports or trains

14.70   Captains of ships or aircraft, and managers of Eurostar through trains and shuttle trains, commit an offence if they allow people to disembark or leave the transport when required to prevent it, or fail to provide passenger lists, particulars of crew members, and information on non-EEA arrivals as required, or fail without reasonable excuse to comply with directions for a person's removal.[1] In the last-mentioned case, the owner or agent is also liable. Whether a demonstration by anti-deportation protesters or a refusal by other passengers to travel on a flight with a deportee constitute 'reasonable excuse' for failure to comply with directions for a passenger's removal has yet to be tested in the courts. Additionally, an owner or agent who arranges for a ship or aircraft to call at an unauthorised port, or who without reasonable excuse fails to provide landing or embarkation cards, commits an offence. The offences may be committed in a control zone.[2] They are all summary only and punishable by a fine up to level 5 and/or six months' imprisonment.[3]

[1]   Immigration Act 1971, s 27, modified in relation to Channel Tunnel trains by the Channel Tunnel (International Arrangements) Order 1993, SI 1993/1813, Sch 4, para 1(9). The requirement to provide passenger lists and particulars of crew is contained in Immigration Act 1971, Sch 2 para 27(2); wider passenger information and times of arrival in Sch 2, paras 27B, and 27C, inserted by Immigration and Asylum Act 1999, ss 18 and 19 (modified in relation to Channel Tunnel trains by the Channel Tunnel (International Arrangements) (Amendment) Order 2000, SI 2000/913). The Asylum and Immigration (Treatment of Claimants etc) Act 2004 s 16 imposes a further duty on carriers to provide copies of travel documents requested by an immigration officer, breach of which will similarly be a criminal offence.
[2]   Nationality, Immigration and Asylum Act 2002 (Juxtaposed Controls) Order 2003, SI 2003/2818, Art 12. This does not apply to captains of aircraft.
[3]   IA 1971, s 27.

Failure to supply information by employers and financial institutions

14.71 An employer or financial institution which fails without reasonable excuse to comply with a requirement to supply information to the Secretary of State about a person commits an offence and may be sentenced to a maximum of three months' imprisonment or a fine on level 5 of the standard scale on summary conviction.[1] Where the offence is committed by a company, its director, manager, secretary or member may be criminally responsible.[2]

[1]   Nationality, Immigration and Asylum Act 2002, s 137, to be amended by increase of penalty to 51 weeks (from a date to be appointed) by Criminal Justice Act 2003, Sch 26, para 58.

[2]   NIAA 2002, s 138.

Offences in relation to detention

14.72 Assaulting a detainee custody officer (DCO), acting in accordance with escort arrangements or performing custodial functions, is an offence carrying a maximum sentence of six months' imprisonment and a fine at level 5.[1] Resistance to or wilful obstruction of a DCO in these circumstances carries a fine of up to level 3.[2] In addition, those detained at a removal centre and their visitors may be subject to a range of offences under Schedule 12 to the Immigration and Asylum Act 1999.[3] A detainee who fails to submit to a medical examination without reasonable excuse is guilty of an offence if there is an authorisation in force for the removal centre[4] and there are reasonable grounds to believe that the person is suffering from a specified disease.[5] Assisting detainees to escape, or bringing, sending or leaving anything at the centre with intent to facilitate an escape, carries a maximum sentence of two years on indictment.[6] Bringing or leaving alcohol to a centre is an offence, as is allowing alcohol to be sold or used (applied to DCOs and other staff.[7]) Bringing anything else into a centre, or taking something out, contrary to the rules, is a summary offence.[8]

[1]   Immigration and Asylum Act 1999, Sch 11, para 4.

[2]   IAA 1999, Sch 11, para 5.

[3]   IAA 1999, Sch 12 as amended by Nationality, Immigration and Asylum Act 2002, s 66.

[4]   Ie, under para 3(1) of the Schedule.

[5]   The Detention Centre (Specified Diseases) Order 2001, SI 2001/240 specifies 33 diseases including cholera, plague, measles and food poisoning. The penalties are up to six months' imprisonment or a fine on level 5: IAA 1999, Sch 12, para 3(5).

[6]   Or on summary conviction, six months or the maximum fine: IAA 1999, Sch 12, para 4.

[7]   The offences are summary only, carrying six months' imprisonment or a fine on level 3. IAA 1999, Sch 12, para 5.

[8]   The penalty is a fine up to level 3: IAA 1999, Sch 12, para 6.

Offences in relation to asylum support

14.73 The Immigration and Asylum Act 1999 removed virtually everyone subject to immigration control from mainstream social security benefits and created a new Home Office department, NASS, which provides limited subsistence support to destitute asylum seekers.[1] This support regime is enforced by a number of new offences modelled on offences relating to social security:[2] false representations; dishonest representations and obstruction; and failure by a sponsor to maintain. They can be committed by corporate bodies, whose officers and even members may be liable if they have consented to or connived at the offence, or it is attributable to neglect on their part.[3] In Scotland, partnerships and partners may be liable in corresponding circumstances.[4] All the offences can be committed in relation to the support to be provided in accommodation centres set up under the Nationality, Immigration and Asylum Act 2002[5] as they apply to NASS and interim support provided under the IAA 1999. The powers of entry and search on a warrant issued by a magistrate to check for the presence of unauthorised persons or the absence of authorised ones[6] are of relevance in relation to these offences. Separately, Schedule 3 to the NIAA 2002, which provides for EEA nationals, their family members and persons with refugee status abroad to be given temporary support while their departure from the UK is arranged,[7] makes it a criminal offence to come back and seek assistance or accommodation or further repatriation assistance.[8] Other categories of person for whom limited welfare provision may be made commit an offence by failing to mention a previous request for assistance.[9] Both offences carry a maximum penalty of six months' imprisonment on summary conviction.[10]

[1]   See chapter 13 above.
[2]   The new offences are in Immigration and Asylum Act 1999, ss 105–108, and are based on Social Security Administration Act 1992, ss 105 and 111–113.
[3]   IAA 1999, s 109(1).
[4]   IAA 1999, s 109(4).
[5]   Nationality, Immigration and Asylum Act 2002, s 35.
[6]   IAA 1999, s 125: see 14.16 above.
[7]   NIAA 2002, Sch 3, paras 1, 4, 5 and 8: see 13.179 above.
[8]   NIAA 2002, Sch 3, para 13(1).
[9]   NIAA 2002, Sch 3, para 13(2).
[10] NIAA 2002, Sch 3, para 13(3).

14.74 The offence of false representations is committed by a person who, with a view to obtaining support for him- or herself or for any other person, makes a statement or representation he or she knows to be false in a material particular,[1] gives a document or information he or she knows to be false to someone performing asylum support functions,[2] fails to notify a relevant change of circumstances[3] or without reasonable excuse, knowingly causes another person to fail to notify such a change.[4] It is a summary offence, punishable by up to a level 5 fine or three months' imprisonment, or both.[5] There is no power of arrest without warrant. The Secretary of State may require employers and financial institutions to provide information in connection with an offence under this section,[6] and may seize and retain employee records.[7]

[1]   Immigration and Asylum Act 1999, s 105(1)(a).
[2]   IAA 1999, s 105(1)(b). Persons performing functions under Pt VI of the Act include officers of NASS and of local authorities who process applications for support. They could also include officers of registered social landlords and housing associations by virtue of s 100, employees of sub-contractors providing accommodation and support, including private landlords, and asylum support adjudicators by virtue of ss 102–103.
[3]   IAA 1999, s 105(1)(c). The relevant changes are set out in the Asylum Support Regulations 2000, SI 2000/704, reg 15(2), and include being joined by a dependant, receiving or getting access to any previously undeclared money or other asset, becoming employed or unemployed, changing one's name, marrying, divorcing, separating, becoming

pregnant, having a child, leaving school, sharing, moving or leaving accommodation, going into hospital or prison, leaving the UK and dying.

4   IAA 1999, s 105(1(d).
5   IAA 1999, s 105(2), to be amended by increase in penalty to 51 weeks as from a date to be appointed by Criminal Justice Act 2003, s 280(3), Sch 26, para 53.
6   Under Nationality, Immigration and Asylum Act 2002, ss 134, 135: see **14.25** above.
7   IA 1971 ss 28FA, 28FB(5), inserted by NIAA 2002, s 154.

14.75 The offence of dishonest representations is committed by performing the same acts, but with a view to obtaining any benefit or advantage under Part VI of the Immigration and Asylum Act 1999 for him or herself or any other person. The acts must have been performed dishonestly.[1] The offence is a broad one and can be committed by landlords or providers of other services attempting to defraud NASS. The section is directed at cases of serious and calculated fraud, such as where a person makes a plan to extract as much from the Home Office as possible by deception.[2] This is evident from the penalties: it is triable either way, and punishable on summary conviction by a fine up to the statutory maximum or up to six months' imprisonment, or both, and on indictment by a fine and/or up to seven years' imprisonment,[3] making it an arrestable offence within the meaning of section 24(1)(b) of the Police and Criminal Evidence Act 1984. The Secretary of State may require employers and financial institutions to provide information in connection with an offence under this section,[4] and may seize and retain employee records.[5]

1   Immigration and Asylum Act 1999, s 106(1).
2   Explanatory notes to IAA 1999, s 106.
3   IAA 1999, s 106(2).
4   Under Nationality, Immigration and Asylum Act 2002, ss 134, 135: see **14.25** above.
5   IA 1971, ss 28FA, 28FB(5), inserted by NIAA 2002, s 154.

14.76 The offence of delay or obstruction is committed by intentionally delaying or obstructing someone exercising asylum support functions, or refusing or neglecting to answer a question, give information or produce a document when required to do so.[1] It is summary only and punishable by a fine up to level 3.[2] There is no power of arrest without warrant.

1   Immigration and Asylum Act 1999, s 107(1). For persons exercising functions under Pt VI of the Act see chapter 13 and 14.75 fn 2 above.
2   Immigration and Asylum Act 1999, s 107(2).

14.77 The offence of failure to maintain is committed by a sponsor (a person who has given a written undertaking under the Immigration Rules to be responsible for the maintenance and accommodation of another person) who, during the period covered by the undertaking, persistently refuses or neglects, without reasonable excuse, to maintain the person in accordance with the undertaking, with the result that support has to be provided under Part VI of the Immigration and Asylum Act 1999.[1] A sponsor is not to be taken to have refused or neglected to maintain another person by reason only of anything done or omitted in furtherance of a trade dispute.[2] The proviso that the refusal or neglect must be without reasonable excuse was added at Report stage, after the minister had made clear that 'it is not our intention to catch people who might become ill or unable to support the person for a genuine reason'.[3] Sponsored immigrants are not entitled to social security benefits for at least five years unless their sponsor dies,[4] and so the offence, which requires receipt of support in consequence of the failure to maintain, can, it appears, only be committed if the sponsored immigrant concerned applies for asylum as a refugee or under Article 3 of the ECHR[5] and receives asylum support because of the sponsor's failure. The offence is summary only and punishable by a fine up to level 4 or a maximum of three months' imprisonment, or both.[6] There is no power of arrest without warrant.

[1] Immigration and Asylum Act 1999, s 108(1).
[2] Immigration and Asylum Act 1999, s 108(3).
[3] HC Official Report, Special SC (Immigration and Asylum Bill), 21st sitting, 11 May 1999, col 1422; 606 HL Official Report (5th series) cols 839–842, 2 November 1999.
[4] By Immigration and Asylum Act 1999, s 115 and the Social Security (Immigration and Asylum) Consequential Amendments Regulations 2000, SI 2000/636, Sch, paras 2 and 3.
[5] See interpretation section, Immigration and Asylum Act 1999, s 94(1).
[6] Immigration and Asylum Act 1999, s 108(2). Level 4 is currently £2,500: Criminal Justice Act 1982, s 37(2), as amended by Criminal Justice Act 1991, s 17. The penalty is to be increased to 51 weeks as from a date to be appointed by Criminal Justice Act 2003, s 280(3), Sch 26 para 53.

Offences in relation to provision of immigration advice or services

14.78 The Immigration Acts police not just immigrants and asylum seekers, but also those who advise and represent them. In response to widespread disquiet at the abuse and exploitation of immigrants and asylum seekers by lawyers and by unqualified consultants, Part V of the Immigration and Asylum Act 1999 created a structure of authorisation or registration within which advice and services are to be provided.[1] Essentially, no one may provide immigration advice or services unless he or she is registered with the Immigration Services Commissioner[2] (or employed or supervised by such a person or body) or is authorised by a designated professional body, such as the Law Society or the Bar Council[3] (or employed or supervised by such a person),[4] or, like a student union, is exempt.[5] The Commissioner has a duty to investigate complaints regarding the competence or fitness of persons providing advice, or alleging breaches of Commissioners' rules and Code of Practice,[6] and may decline or cancel registration.[7] There is an Immigration Services Tribunal, which hears appeals and disciplinary charges arising from the Commissioner's decisions, or the disciplinary body with jurisdiction over the service provider (if he or she is a solicitor, legal executive or barrister). It may make restraining orders restricting, suspending or prohibiting the advice or services of the individual or firm concerned.[8] In the course of an investigation, the Commissioner has power to enter and search premises where it is believed on reasonable grounds that advice is being provided, and may require the production of documents or information held on a computer, which may be copied or removed.[9]

[1] Immigration and Asylum Act 1999, s 84.
[2] IAA 1999, s 84(2)(a) and (b). The Commissioner is created by s 83. Fees for initial registration are £1,700 for an organisation with up to four advisers, £1,900 for between five and nine, and £2,300 for ten or more. The fees for continued registration are £1,250, £1,550 and £2,050 respectively: Immigration Services Commissioner (Registration Fee) Orer 2002, SI 2002/2011. Applicants must demonstrate competence. The Commissioner believes that around 1,000 advisers have not applied for registration: ISC website: report of conference 30 October 2003.

3   The full list is set out in the Immigration and Asylum Act 1999, s 86(1) as the Law Society, the Law Society of Scotland, the Law Society of Northern Ireland, the Institute of Legal Executives, the General Council of the Bar, the Faculty of Advocates and the General Council of the Bar of Northern Ireland. There is provision to amend the list after consultation: s 86(2)–(7). A body can be removed from the list if it consistently fails to supervise its members properly. In response to the ISC's concerns, the Law Society has set up an accreditation scheme for immigration solicitors. The Bar Council's (voluntary) scheme appears to have fallen into desuetude.

4   IAA 1999, s 84(2)(c) and (f). Paras (d) and (e) deal with those registered or authorised in another EEA state.

5   Educational institutions, student unions and health sector bodies are exempt: Immigration and Asylum Act 1999 (Part V Exemption: Educational Institutions and Health Service Bodies) Order 2001, SI 2001/1403. Employers providing immigration advice or services free to (prospective) employees who have been granted work permits, for them and their families, are exempt: Immigration and Asylum Act 1999 (Part V Exemption: Relevant Employers) Order 2003, SI 2003/3214. Not for profit bodies providing immigration advice and services must apply for exemption, and will need a Legal Services Commission Quality Mark.

6   IAA 1999, Sch 5, para 5.

7   IAA 1999, Sch 5, para 6(3), Sch 6, paras 2 and 3.

8   IAA 1999, ss 89(8), 90(1), Sch 5, para 9(3).

9   IAA 1999, Sch 5, para 7, as amended by Nationality, Immigration and Asylum Act 2002, s 140, which extends the power of entry to investigations on the Commissioner's own initiative.

14.79 It is an offence for an unqualified person (one who is not registered, authorised or exempt), or for someone subject to a restraining order, to provide immigration advice or services.[1] The offence is triable either way, and is punishable on summary conviction with a fine up to the statutory maximum or up to six months' imprisonment, or both, and on indictment by a fine or up to two years' imprisonment, or both.[2] Where it is committed by a corporate body, the company's officers (director, manager, secretary, etc) or members may be liable if they are proved to have connived in the offence or it is attributable to neglect on their part.[3] In Scotland, partners are liable in corresponding circumstances where the offence is committed by a partnership.[4] By September 2003, 16 prosecutions had been brought, all resulting in conviction, and fines, community service and imprisonment had been imposed.[5]

1   Immigration and Asylum Act 1999, s 91(1).

2   IAA 1999, s 91(1).

3   IAA 1999, s 91(3)–(5).

4   IAA 1999, s 91(6)–(7).

5   Stephen Seymour 'Using complaints as a vehicle for raising quality', OISC Conference, 30 October 2003.

14.80 The Asylum and Immigration (Treatment of Claimants etc) Act 2004 creates a new offence, punishable by a fine on level 4, of offering or advertising immigration advice and services which would be unlawful.[1] An extended time limit of two years applies.[2] The AI(TC)A 2004 also creates new powers of entry, search and seizure of evidential material on a warrant, on reasonable grounds that an offence of unlawful provision of advice or services has been committed.[3] It will be an offence to obstruct the Immigration Services Commissioner in the exercise of these new powers of entry, search and seizure, punishable by up to six months' imprisonment and/or a fine on level 5.[4]

1   Immigration and Asylum Act 1999, s 92B, inserted by Asylum and Immigration (Treatment of Claimants etc) Act 2004, s 39 from a date to be appointed.
2   For extended time limits see 14.65 above.
3   Immigration and Asylum Act 1999, s 92A, as inserted.
4   Immigration and Asylum Act 1999, s 92A(5), (6), as inserted.

Offences of disclosure

14.81 There are two offences relating to disclosure of confidential information. First, someone, who is or has been the Immigration Services Commissioner, or an agent or staff member of a Commissioner, commits an offence if, without lawful authority, he or she knowingly or recklessly discloses information relating to an identified or identifiable individual or business which was obtained by the Commissioner for the purposes of the Immigration and Asylum Act 1999 and is not in the public domain.[1] The offence is triable either way and punishable by a fine. Secondly, it is an offence for a private sector employee at a detention centre or on escort duties to make unauthorised disclosure of information relating to a particular detainee acquired in the course of his or her employment.[2] The maximum penalty for this offence, also triable either way, is a fine up to the statutory maximum or six months' imprisonment or both on summary conviction, and on indictment, two years' imprisonment.

1   Immigration and Asylum Act 1999, s 93(4).
2   IAA 1999, s 158.

EMPLOYER SANCTIONS

14.82 The Asylum and Immigration Act 1996 created a new offence for employers who employ persons aged 16 or over, who are subject to immigration control and are not entitled to work in the UK or not free to take the particular employment. Employers (including individuals, partners,[1] companies, directors, managers and other officers)[2] commit an offence punishable by a fine[3] if they employ someone subject to immigration control[4] (i) who has not been granted leave to enter or remain in the UK, (ii) whose leave is not valid and subsisting, or is subject to a condition precluding that employment.[5] The first category includes illegal entrants who entered clandestinely and those on temporary admission. The second includes overstayers (although it cannot include those whose leave was obtained by deception),[6] those with leave to enter as visitors (the leave is subject to a condition prohibiting employment), and business people, persons of independent means, and work permit holders who need the permission of the Department for Work and Pensions to change jobs. There are certain statutory exceptions, which include employees with a pending appeal whose previous leave, extended by statute, did not preclude the employment,[7] and persons permitted to work by the immigration rules.[8]

1   Asylum and Immigration Act 1996, s 8(6A) (inserted by Nationality, Immigration and Asylum Act 2002, s 147 from 1 April 2003). Limited partnerships are treated like corporate bodies.
2   Asylum and Immigration Act 1996, s 8(5) covers officers of corporate bodies.

3   Asylum and Immigration Act 1996, s 8(4). The fine was set at level 5, but the new
    sub-s (4), substituted by s 6 of the Asylum and Immigration (Treatment of Claimants, etc)
    Act 2004 from 1 October 2004 (SI 2004/2523), makes the offence triable either way, with
    an unlimited fine on indictment and the maximum fine on summary conviction. The
    government proposes a fixed penalty of £2000 per employee: see *Controlling our borders:
    Making migration work for Britain: Five year strategy for asylum and immigration*,
    Cm 6472, Feb 2005.
4   Broadly speaking this means anyone except British citizens, Commonwealth citizens with
    the right of abode, EEA nationals and their non-EEA family members, and the family
    members of exempt persons such as diplomats.
5   Asylum and Immigration Act 1996, s 8(1). Since statutory leave (together with any
    conditions) continues pending a variation appeal, under Immigration Act 1971, s 3C as
    substituted by Nationality, Immigration and Asylum Act 2002, s 118, the offence can be
    committed by someone awaiting appeal if his or her previous leave was subject to a
    prohibition on employment.
6   Immigration Act 1971, Sch 2, para 9(2) provides that leave to enter obtained by deception
    is to be disregarded *for the purposes of the paragraph* (setting removal directions); but
    following *Khawaja v Secretary of State for the Home Department* [1984] AC 74, for other
    purposes leave is not nullified until discovery of the deception by the immigration
    authorities, and remains valid and subsisting. To expect an employer to know that an
    apparently valid leave was obtained by deception would in any event be absurd.
7   Immigration (Restrictions on Employment) Order 2004, SI 2004/755, Schedule, para 3.
8   SI 2004/755, para 3(3). This category must include asylum seekers with permission to
    work, and those whose bail conditions do not preclude work, since the rules do not
    prevent work by those on temporary admission. The EU Directive on Reception Arrange-
    ments, in force February 2005, provides that asylum seekers must be permitted to work if
    they have no decision on their claim after 12 months. The Home Office has modified its
    policy accordingly, having earlier clamped down on working by asylum claimants.

14.83   The offence is one of strict liability, so that proof of knowledge of the
employee's ineligibility to work is unnecessary to found a conviction. But there
is a statutory defence available[1] to employers which requires them to prove
that, before the employment began, they saw, and retained or copied, one
document from one list of specified documents[2] or a combination of specified
documents[3] from a second list.[4] The employer is required to copy or scan the
document or documents,[5] but that is all that is necessary; it is not, for
example, necessary for the employer to prove a positive belief that the
employee was entitled to work. Nor are employers obliged to check the
authenticity of the document or the employee's entitlement to it, provided the
document appears to relate to the employee and to be one of the listed
documents.[5] However, actual knowledge that the employee was not entitled to
work cancels out the statutory defence afforded by the provision and retention
of the specified document.[6]

1   Under Asylum and Immigration Act 1996, s 8(2) as amended and (2A) as inserted by
    Nationality, Immigration and Asylum Act 2002, s 147.
2   The 'Part I' list, only one of which the employer is required to see and copy, includes a UK
    passport describing the holder as a British citizen or having the right of abode, a passport
    containing a certificate of entitlement to the right of abode, an EEA passport, a UK
    residence permit issued to an EEA national, a passport, travel or residence document
    showing that the holder has the right of residence in the UK as the family member of an
    EEA national, a passport showing that the holder is exempt from immigration control, has
    indefinite leave to remain or has no time limit on his or her stay in the UK, a passport
    showing that the holder has current leave to remain and is permitted to take the
    employment, or a registration card indicating that the holder is entitled to work:
    Immigration (Restrictions on Employment) Order 2004, SI 2004/755, Schedule, Pt I.
3   The 'Part II' list requires an employer to see and copy (1) a document issued by a previous
    employer, Inland Revenue, DWP's Jobcentre Plus, the Employment Service or Northern
    Ireland equivalents, containing the national insurance number of the person named in the

document, AND either a birth certificate issued in the UK, specifying the names of the holder's parents, or an Islands birth certificate, or a registration or naturalisation certificate as a British citizen, or a Home Office letter or immigration status document confirming that the holder has ILR, or such a letter or document confirming that the holder has limited leave and is entitled to take the employment in question; or (2) a work permit or other approval issued by Work Permits UK, AND either a passport or a Home Office letter showing that the holder has current leave to remain and may take the employment in question: Immigration (Restrictions on Employment) Order 2004, SI 2004/755, Schedule, Pt 2.

4   AIA 1996, s 8(2) as amended and (2A) as inserted by Nationality, Immigration and Asylum Act 2002, s 147; Immigration (Restriction on Employment) Order 2004, Art 4(2). In relation to employees taken on before 1 May 2004 (when the new sub-sections and the SI came into force) employers were required to see and copy or retain only one document from a list.
5   AIA 1996, s 8(2A)(c) (as inserted by NIAA 2002, s 147), Immigration (Restrictions on Employment) Order 2004, SI 2004/755, Sch, Pt 3.
6   AIA 1996, s 8(3).

14.84 The offence is not retrospective, and it is therefore not an offence to continue to employ someone ineligible to work whom the employer has employed since before 27 January 1997, when section 8 of the Asylum and Immigration Act 1996 came into force. Nor do the more rigorous checks required for the statutory defence since 1 May 2004 apply to employees taken on before that date. Additionally, it does not cover using the services of a self-employed person under a contract for services.[1] Voluntary work is unlikely to constitute a contract of service, so organisations assisted by volunteers would have no liability. Only in cases of a legally binding obligation to work in exchange for remuneration would section 8 apply.[2] The offence is one to which the search, entry, arrest and seizure provisions of the IA 1971 apply.[3] By mid-2003, there had been 34 successful prosecutions covering some 140 offences.[4] In its report on gangmasters issued in September 2003, the Select Committee on the Environment, Fisheries and Food expressed itself 'appalled by the lack of priority given' to their illegal activities. Describing government enforcement in the area as 'perfunctory and un-coordinated', the Select Committee complained that 'no significant resources' were allocated, no targets set and no minister took overall responsibility.[5]

1   Asylum and Immigration Act 1996, s 8(8), Hansard (HL) 571, col 1849, 2 May 96. There could be difficulties over employment *versus* self-employment in marginal cases; also over agency staff, as to whether the agency or the employer to whom staff are sent is liable. See Berkowitz 'Employer sanctions and their impact on asylum seekers' in *United Kingdom Asylum law in its European context* (1999).
2   Letter from Immigration and Nationality Directorate to Commission for Racial Equality, 7 July 1997.
3   Asylum and Immigration Act 1996, s 8(10) as inserted by Nationality, Immigration and Asylum Act 2002, s 147 from 1 April 2003. Note that the 2002 Act also provided for the extended time limit under IA 1971, s 28(1) to apply to prosecutions under the section (see 14.65 above), but this is repealed as from 1 October 2004 (SI 2004/2523) by s 6 Asylum and Immigration (Treatment of Claimants, etc) Act 2004.
4   Home Office: 'Prevention of Illegal Working'.
5   Select Committee on the Environment, Fisheries and Rural Affairs: Gangmasters, report and minutes of evidence issued 18 September 2003. The report describes 'Operation Gangmaster' which was set up in 1998 to coordinate enforcement activity between the Department of Work and Pensions, the Inland Revenue, Customs & Excise, the IND and others including DEFRA as required. It notes that between 35% and 50% of a casual

workforce of around 70,000 in agriculture are supplied by gangmasters, of whom around 20% are committing a wide range of offences. See now the Gangmasters (Licensing) Act 2004.

14.85 The creation of the offence was deeply controversial, with many believing it would exacerbate and entrench racial discrimination in employment while not preventing illegal working but driving it further underground to yet more exploitative conditions. Section 8A of the Asylum and Immigration Act 1996, added by the Immigration and Asylum Act 1999,[1] obliges the Secretary of State to issue a Code of Practice for employers to avoid racial discrimination in complying with the requirements of the statutory defence under section 8(2).[2] Failure on the part of an employer to observe a provision of the code, while not itself creating liability for unlawful racial discrimination, is admissible in proceedings for race discrimination.[3] The Code of Practice states that there is no need to ask about an applicant's immigration status, apart from asking if he or she needs permission to work, and that to avoid race discrimination all applicants should be treated in the same way, for example, by a reminder that the successful applicant would be asked to produce one of the listed documents. Guidance issued to employers, 'Prevention of illegal working', states that the IND can only release information about a person's immigration status to an employer with the employee's or his or her representative's written authorisation.[4]

[1]   Immigration and Asylum Act 1999, s 22, in force 19 February 2001 for the purpose of laying a draft code before Parliament: Immigration and Asylum Act 1999 (Commencement No 9) Order 2001, SI 2001/239.
[2]   The Code of Practice came into force on 2 May 2001.
[3]   Asylum and Immigration Act 1996, s 8A(9), (10).
[4]   IDI, Ch 24, s 7. Elsewhere, the Home Office website states that its policy on requests for information from employers is to handle them according to the procedures set out in the 1997 Code of Practice on Access to Government Information, the Data Protection Act 1998, the Human Rights Act 1998 and the common-law duty of confidence.

14.86 The accession of 10 new members to the EU in May 2004 has created one further offence for employers. Eight of these new states do not have immediate rights of free movement for workers. Their nationals are subject to UK national law for a possible five-year period until 30 April 2009. Meanwhile the UK government has created a registration scheme, giving workers from these new Eastern European accession Member States very wide rights to work, provided they are registered and their employer is authorised. The scheme is described in detail at 7.12. It is now an offence for an employer to employ an accession worker requiring registration during a period when the employer is not an authorised employer in relation to the worker.[1] It is punishable on summary conviction to a fine not exceeding level 5. Employers who are bodies corporate or partnerships may be prosecuted.

[1]   The Accession (Immigration and Worker Registration) Regulations 2004, SI 2004/1219, reg 9.

14.87 As we have seen at 14.25 and 14.71 above, employers can be obliged to provide information to the Secretary of State about someone suspected of an immigration offence or irregularity, on pain of imprisonment. However, the information thus obtained cannot be used in a prosecution against the employer under section 8 of the 1996 Act.[1] Employers' premises may also be searched and employee records seized,[2] and there is no such constraint on the use of material seized.

[1] Nationality, Immigration and Asylum Act 2002, s 139.
[2] Immigration Act 1971, ss 28FA, 28FB, inserted by Nationality, Immigration and Asylum Act 2002, s 154. See 14.25 above.

CARRIERS' LIABILITY

14.88 Ever since the first carriers' liability legislation in the UK, passed in 1987 in a panic response to the arrival of a flight containing 58 Sri Lankan Tamils with no visas, carrier sanctions have been one of the favourite and well-used weapons in the armoury against illegal entrants and asylum seekers (too often seen as synonymous).[1] Despite concerns that they undermine the fundamental right to seek and enjoy asylum set out in Article 14 of the UDHR and the right to leave ones own country conferred by Article 12 of the International Covenant on Civil and Political Rights,[2] and despite overwhelming evidence that carrier sanctions do not deter immigration or the quest for asylum but merely drive up the price and the human cost,[3] the UK government, in common with its European partners, continues the restrictive policies which both make legal entry well-nigh impossible and penalise all those involved, however inadvertently, in illegal entry.[4] The latest turn of the screw is the penalties for carriers of clandestine entrants, introduced in 1999 to join the original penalties for carriers of inadequately documented passengers – themselves extended to cover almost all forms of transport. A formidable range of powers is deployed to enforce carrier sanctions. The provisions are all contained in Part II of the Immigration and Asylum Act 1999, as amended by the Nationality, Immigration and Asylum Act 2002.[5]

[1] See for example the Resolution on manifestly unfounded applications for asylum drafted by the Ad Hoc Group on Immigration and adopted at the Council of Ministers' meeting of 30 November 1992, which described as 'unlawful' the actions of asylum seekers who travelled to another continent rather than availing themselves of local protection.
[2] Among the vast critical literature see James Hathaway 'Harmonizing for Whom? The Devaluation of Refugee Protection in the Era of European Economic Integration' (1993) 26 Cornell International Law Journal 719; UNHCR Position on Conventions Recently Concluded in Europe (Dublin and Schengen Conventions), Aug 16 1991; International Law Association International Committee on the Status of Refugees, *Restrictive Measures in Europe* 21 (1992).
[3] On 31 July 2000 58 Chinese would-be asylum claimants were found dead in a lorry in Dover. Every year hundreds of would-be asylum claimants from sub-Saharan Africa, Iraq, Afghanistan and other refugee-producing areas of the world die attempting to cross the sea to Europe in small boats, or hiding in the holds of ships or in the undercarriages of aircraft or in lorries.
[4] See John Morrison *The trafficking and smuggling of refugees* UNHCR (July 2000).
[5] Nationality, Immigration and Asylum Act 2002 s 125, Sch 8.

Liability for clandestine entrants

14.89 The Immigration and Asylum Act 1999 imposed a fixed penalty of £2,000 for each clandestine entrant brought in by carriers, with no flexibility to reflect mitigating factors, no rights of appeal and a reverse burden of proof on the carrier to establish one of the statutory defences. It also gave the Secretary of State draconian powers of seizure and detention of vehicles. This combination of features was held by a majority of the Court of Appeal in *Roth*[1] to render the provisions incompatible with Article 6 and Article 1 of Protocol 1 of the ECHR. The provisions have been significantly modified as a result. Fixed penalties have been replaced by discretionary variable penalties, to be assessed with reference to a Code of Practice.[2] A right of appeal now exists against liability for a penalty and its amount.[3] Safeguards attend the seizure and detention of vehicles.[4]

1 *International Transport Roth GmbH v Secretary of State for the Home Department* [2002] EWCA Civ 158, [2002] 3 WLR 344.
2 Level of penalties: Code of Practice under Immigration and Asylum Act 1999, ss 32(2), 32A, inserted by Nationality, Immigration and Asylum Act 2002, Sch 8, para 3.
3 Immigration and Asylum Act 1999, s 35A, inserted by NIAA 2002, Sch 8, para 8.
4 IAA 1999, s 36A, inserted by NIAA 2002, Sch 8, para 10.

14.90 Section 32 of the Immigration and Asylum Act 1999 (as amended) allows the Secretary of State to impose a penalty on persons responsible for a clandestine entrant. A clandestine entrant is defined as someone who either claims or intends to claim asylum or evades or tries to evade immigration control, having arrived in the UK concealed in a vehicle, ship, aircraft or rail freight wagon, passed or tried to pass through immigration control concealed in a vehicle; or arrived in the UK on a ship or aircraft, after embarking outside the UK concealed in a vehicle.[1] Aircraft includes hovercraft and a vehicle includes a trailer, semi-trailer, caravan or anything else designed for towing.[2] The owner and captain of the ship or aircraft, the train operator and the owner, hirer and driver of the vehicle (or operator, if the vehicle was a trailer) in or on which the clandestine entrant was concealed, are all 'responsible persons'.[3] All 'responsible persons' are potentially liable for a penalty up to a prescribed maximum[4] in respect of each clandestine entrant or concealed person carried.[5] 'Immigration control' for the purposes of the section includes any UK immigration control operated in a prescribed control zone outside the UK, and carriers are liable for the arrival of clandestine entrants in such a control zone.[6]

1 Immigration and Asylum Act 1999, s 32(1) as amended by Nationality, Immigration and Asylum Act 2002, Sch 8, para 2.
2 IAA 1999, s 43.
3 IAA 1999, s 32(5), (5A) and (6), as amended by Nationality, Immigration and Asylum Act 2002, Sch 8, para 2(5)–(7). But the provisions are not yet in force in relation to ships and aircraft.
4 The maximum currently prescribed by the Carriers' Liability Regulations 2002, SI 2002/2817 reg 3(1) is £2,000, with a maximum aggregate penalty of £4,000. The Secretary of State must have regard to the provisions of a Code of Practice on the level of penalty in determining the amount of any penalty: IAA 1999, s 32A, inserted by NIAA 2002, Sch 8, para 3.
5 IAA 1999, s 32(2) and (4), as amended by NIAA 2002, Sch 8, para 2.
6 IAA 1999, s 32(10). The part of France situated at Coquelles, which is a control zone for international purposes, is prescribed by SI 2000/685, reg 5. The Nationality, Immigration and Asylum Act 2002 (Juxtaposed Controls) Order 2003, SI 2003/2818, Art 2, Sch 1 added Calais, Boulogne and Dunkirk.

14.91 The statutory definition of 'clandestine entrants' for whom responsible persons may incur penalties is far broader than its everyday usage. It includes not just those who try to enter without seeing (or being seen by) an immigration officer, but also those who present themselves at immigration control and claim asylum after stowing away on a ship or aircraft, or hidden in a lorry or rail freight wagon for the journey. In such a case the owner and captain of the ship or aircraft, or manager of the train in which they stowed away, or the owner, hirer and driver or operator of the lorry or trailer would all be potentially liable to pay a penalty. It also includes asylum seekers who present themselves at immigration control in, say, Dover having hidden in a vehicle in Ostend to embark on a cross-Channel ferry and got out of the vehicle during the crossing to leave the boat as a foot passenger. In such a situation, the owner, hirer or the driver of the vehicle in which they hid at Ostend would in theory be liable, although not the owner or captain of the ferry.[1] The provisions apply to private as well as public vehicles, so all car drivers must check that their vehicles are not concealing extra passengers, that windows are fully closed and doors and car boots fully locked before driving on to the cross-Channel ferry on their return from a continental holiday, to avoid liability. The provisions are not yet in force in relation to ships and aircraft, only in relation to vehicles (including buses, coaches, lorries and cars) and freight trains. They were held in *Roth*[2] not to amount to a restriction on free movement under EC law.

1 See Immigration and Asylum Act 1999, s 32(6). This would not apply if the ferry came from a designated port in a control zone (Calais, Boulogne or Dunkirk) because controls are carried out there: Nationality, Immigration and Asylum Act 2002 (Juxtaposed Controls) Order 2003, SI 2003/2818.
2 *International Transport Roth GmbH v Secretary of State for the Home Department* [2002] EWCA Civ 158 [2002] 3 WLR 344, CA.

14.92 When a carrier becomes potentially liable for a penalty under section 32 of the IAA 1999 as amended, there are three statutory defences, the burden of proof in each being on the carrier:

(i)   duress;[1] or
(ii)   that the carrier did not know and had no reasonable grounds for suspecting that a clandestine entrant might be concealed in the transporter; that an an effective system for preventing the carriage of clandestine entrants was in operation in relation to the transporter; and that system was properly operated on the occasion in question;[2] or
(iii) (for rail freight), that the carrier knew or suspected that a clandestine entrant was or might be concealed in a rail freight wagon but could not stop the train or the shuttle of which the wagon formed a part without endangering safety, and an efficient system was in operation for preventing the carriage of clandestine entrants and was operated properly on the occasion in question.[3]

If a defence of duress is successfully relied on, every other responsible person is entitled to the benefit of the defence.[4] Codes of Practice have been issued which detail the precautions which should be taken by owners, hirers, operators and drivers of road haulage and other commercial vehicles, buses and coaches and private vehicles;[5] and those operating rail freight transport.

Regard will be had to its provisions in determining whether the system in operation is effective for the purposes of the Immigration and Asylum Act 1999, section 34(3) defence.[6]

1 Immigration and Asylum Act 1999, s 34(2).
2 IAA 1999, s 34(3).
3 IAA 1999, s 34(3A), inserted by Nationality, Immigration and Asylum Act 2002, Sch 8, para 6.
4 IAA 1999, s 34(6) as amended by NIAA 2002, Sch 8, para 6.
5 The Prevention of Clandestine Entrants: Civil Penalty: Code of Practice for Vehicles was brought into force by the Carriers' Liability (Clandestine Entrants) (Code of Practice) Order 2000, SI 2000/684, on 3 April 2000. The Code of Practice for Rail Freight was brought into force by the Carriers' Liability (Clandestine Entrants) (Code of Practice for Rail Freight) Order 2001, SI 2001/312, on 1 March 2000; that for freight shuttle wagons by the Carriers' Liability (Clandestine Entrants) (Code of Practice for Freight Shuttle Wagons) Order 2001, SI 2001/3233. The Code of Practice for Vehicles is to be amended to apply to the control zones in Calais, Boulogne and Dunkirk, according to a Home Office consultation document of 12 September 2003.
6 Immigration and Asylum Act 1999, s 34(4).

14.93 Once the responsible persons are served with a penalty notice, payment must be made within 60 days[1] unless a notice of objection is served within 28 days,[2] in which case the Secretary of State decides whether to cancel, reduce, uphold or increase the penalty.[3] There is a right of appeal to a county court (or sheriff's court in Scotland)[4] against the imposition of a penalty or its amount, and the court may cancel or reduce the penalty or dismiss the appeal, which is by way of rehearing, having regard to the relevant Codes of Practice.[5] An appeal may be brought whether or not a notice of objection has been given or the penalty reduced or increased by the Secretary of State.[6] Now that the appeal system is in place, the Divisional Court's advice in *Balbo Auto Transporti*[7] to raise defences during enforcement proceedings is no longer appropriate, and is precluded by statute.[8] If a penalty notice has been given, a senior officer may detain a vehicle, small ship, small aircraft or rail freight wagon until all penalties and expenses are paid, but only if the driver is the owner or hirer or their employee or the penalty notice has been given to the owner or hirer,[9] and only if the officer believes there is a significant risk that the penalty will not be paid otherwise and no alternative security has been given.[10] Senior officers have the power to detain a relevant vehicle, small ship, small aircraft or rail freight wagon ('the transporter') pending (a) a decision whether to issue a penalty notice, or (b) its issue, or (c) a decision after issue of the penalty notice, whether to detain the the transporter until all penalties and expenses have been paid, but such a 'provisional' detention' may not be exercised in any case for longer than is necessary in the circumstances, and may not exceed 24 hours following the first search of the transporter by an immigration officer after it arrived in the UK.[11] Application may be made to the County Court for release of the transporter by anyone whose interests may be affected by detention.[12] On such an application, there is no longer any requirement to show a 'compelling need' to have the transporter released, as before, but the court is obliged to consider the extent of the hardship caused by its detention and the extent of the responsibility of the applicant, and any other relevant matter including the security provided and the risk of non-payment and doubts about liability.[13] The powers to detain transporters on non-payment of penalties are wider and the criteria for their release by a court more stringent.[14] Subject to any appeal or court order for release, the Secretary of State is empowered to sell the transporter after 12 weeks if the penalty is not paid.[15]

1   Period defined by the Carriers' Liability Regulations 2002, SI 2002/2817, reg 4.
2   Period defined by SI 2002/2817, reg 5.
3   Immigration and Asylum Act 1999, s 35 as amended by Nationality, Immigration and Asylum Act 2002, Sch 8, para 7. He must do so within 70 days of the issue of the penalty notice: SI 2002/2817, reg 7.
4   IAA 1999, s 43 as amended by NIAA 2002, Sch 8, para 15; the court may transfer the proceedings to the High Court or Court of Session.
5   IAA 1999, s 35A, added by NIAA 2002, Sch 8, para 8.
6   IAA 1999, s 35A(6).
7   *R (on the application of Balbo B&C Auto Transporti Internazionali) v Secretary of State for the Home Department* [2001] EWHC Admin 195, (2001) 145 Sol Jo LB 85, QBD.
8   IAA 1999, *s 35(11), inserted by NIAA 2002, Sch 8, para 7(5).*
9   IAA 1999, s 36(1), (2A) as amended by NIAA 2002, Sch 8, para 9.
10   IAA 1999, s 36(2), as inserted.
11   IAA 1999, s 36(2B), (2C) as inserted.
12   IAA 1999, s 37(2), (3), (3A), (3B) as amended and inserted. For 'court' see fn 4 above. In England, Wales and Northern Ireland; in Scotland, the sheriff or the Court of Session: IAA 1999, s 43.
13   IAA 1999, s 37(3B) as inserted.
14   IAA 1999, s 36A, inserted by NIAA 2002, Sch 8, para 10. The power is not to be exercised while an appeal against a penalty is pending or could be brought: s 36A(5). A court may release a transporter detained for non-payment of a penalty only if it considers that detention is unlawful or if the penalty notice was not issued to the owner or employee and the court considers release the right course: s 37(3A), (7) as amended and inserted.
15   IAA 1999, s 37(5A), inserted by NIAA 2002, Sch 8, para 11. The power of sale lapses if not exercised within a prescribed period, which is currently 60 days: s 37(5B) as inserted, SI 2002/2817, reg 11.

Liability for inadequately documented passengers

14.94   An EC Directive[1] requires Member States to enforce carriers' responsibility to check passengers' travel documents and to impose penalties on carriers which do not comply. The UK has had carriers' liability legislation to this effect in force since 1987,[2] but the provisions have been overhauled by the Nationality, Immigration and Asylum Act 2002. Section 40 of the Immigration and Asylum Act 1999, as substituted by the NIAA 2002,[3] imposes a fixed penalty of £2,000 on owners of ships or aircraft[4] on which passengers arrive who require leave to enter the UK [5] and fail, if required, to produce to an immigration officer an immigration document and a visa of the required kind [6] An 'immigration document' is a passport or a document relating to a non-British citizen serving the same purpose as a passport.[7] It must be in force and must satisfactorily establish the identity and nationality or citizenship of the holder, thus penalising carriers for passengers' possession of false documents, although carriers are entitled to regard a document as authentic and belonging to the holder unless the contrary is reasonably apparent.[8] No penalty is payable if the owner shows that the now undocumented passenger produced a document on embarkation.[9] Guidance has been issued to carriers on passport and visa requirements.[10]

1   Directive 2001/51/EC of 28 June 2001.
2   Immigration (Carriers' Liability) Act 1987, rushed through Parliament in response to the arrival of a group of 58 Tamil asylum seekers on one flight from Sri Lanka.

3   Nationality, Immigration and Asylum Act 2002, Sch 8, para 13.
4   Not vehicles or trains, although the section can be amended by order to include trains: IAA 1999, s 40(7), (8) as substituted.
5   Ie, excluding British nationals, those with the right of abode, EEA and Swiss nationals (who do not require leave to enter under IA 1988, s 7), and diplomats, who are exempt from immigration control: IAA 1999, s 40(1) as substituted.
6   IAA 1999, s 40(1), (2) as substituted. A visa might include a transit visa if one is required by passengers of that nationality: IAA 1999, s 40(6). The power to require transit passengers to hold a transit visa is now contained in s 41 (in force 8 December 2002). Persons requiring transit visas are set out in the Immigration (Passenger Transit Visas) Order 2003, SI 2003/1185, as amended by SI 2003/2628, SI 2004/1304 and SI 2005/492. They are currently nationals of Afghanistan, Albania, Algeria, Angola, Bangladesh, Belarus, Burma, Burundi, Cameroon, China, Colombia, Congo, Democratic Republic of Congo (formerly Zaire), Ecuador, Eritrea, Ethiopia, Former Yugoslav Republic of Macedonia (FYROM), Gambia, Ghana, Guinea, Guinea-Bissau, India, Iran, Iraq, Ivory Coast, Kenya, Lebanon, Liberia, Moldova, Mongolia, Nepal, Nigeria, Pakistan, Palestinian Territories, Rwanda, Senegal, Serbia and Montenegro, Somalia, Sri Lanka, Sudan, Tanzania, Turkey, Uganda, Vietnam and Zimbabwe. Many are countries from which refugees come. There is a limited exemption for passengers travelling via the UK to or from Canada, Australia, New Zealand and the US (SI 2005/492). The arrival without a visa of nationals of countries to whom the Transit Without a Visa (TWOV) concession does not apply, and of passengers accepted for transit under TWOV who are subsequently denied onward carriage by an airline while in the UK, will render the inward carrier liable: *Charging Procedures: A guide for carriers*, introduction, 2.2.
7   IAA 1999, s 40(9) as substituted.
8   IAA 1999, s 40(5) as substituted. One of the complaints in the *Hoverspeed* case (*R v Secretary of State for the Home Department, ex p Hoverspeed* [1999] INLR 591) was that under French law it is a criminal offence for unauthorised persons, including carriers, to conduct identity checks, as opposed to documentary checks, but this did not allow the company to claim the benefit of the defence under this subsection.
9   Immigration and Asylum Act 1999, s 40(4) as substituted.
10 *Passports and Visas: A Guide for Carriers* (1998 edn), known as the *Blue Guide*. See now the Visa Poster on the Home Office website.

14.95 If the Secretary of State decides to impose a penalty under section 40, he must notify the carrier of the reasons for doing so, specify the amount, set the date and manner of payment, and inform the carrier of the provisions for objecting to the imposition of a penalty. The notice must also explain the steps the Secretary of State may take to recover the charge.[1] If an objection is made in accordance with the procedure,[2] the Secretary of State may cancel the charge.[3] The time limits for making an objection and for the Secretary of State to make a decision in response are the same as for carriers of clandestine entrants.[4] There are also similar appeal rights to those operating in the case of clandestine entrants,[5] but the power to detain or sell transporters has been abolished, since liability no longer applies to vehicles.[6]

1   IAA1999, s 40A, inserted by Nationality, Immigration and Asylum Act 2002, Sch 8, para 13, in force 8 December 2002: SI 2002/2811.
2   IAA1999, s 40A(3), (4), Carriers' Liability Regulations 2002, SI 2002/2817, reg 6.
3   IAA1999, s 40A(5) as inserted.
4   IAA1999, s 40A as inserted; Carriers' Liability Regulations 2002, SI 2002/2817. See 14.93 above.
5   IAA 1999, s 40B as inserted. See 14.93 above.
6   IAA 1999, s 42 was repealed by NIAA 2002, Sch 8, para 14.

14.96 The Immigration and Nationality Directorate has issued guidance for carriers facing penalties under section 40[1] and has set out some of the situations in which immigration inspectors will normally be prepared to waive a charge:

- the passenger is a child travelling as part of an organised school group, in the care of a responsible adult;
- the passenger has arrived on a flight or ship which, following departure, has been diverted to the UK;[2]
- the passenger is a stowaway and the carrier has taken all reasonable security and searching measures to ensure that no unauthorised persons board (but a carrier regularly carrying stowaways may find the charge maintained);[3]
- the carrier has no realistic alternative to bringing the passenger to or via the UK, eg where the law or government of another country requires it (unless the carrier has taken the passenger there through the UK without the requisite documents);
- the carrier acted on the advice of a UK government representative and it was reasonable to rely on that advice;[4]
- the case is the first to arise in respect of the particular carrier from that port;[5]
- at the time of check-in the passenger was in imminent and self-evident danger of his or her life, and had no reasonable means of obtaining the necessary documents, and the UK was the only or clearly the most appropriate destination, and the carrier had no opportunity to verify his or her acceptability with the UK authorities;[6]
- there are exceptional compelling compassionate reasons or other compelling circumstances justifying waiver.[7]

In addition, it is the Government's policy to waive or refund the charge in respect of passengers ultimately granted full refugee status (a concession not extended to those admitted for any other reason).[8] Charges will also be waived for visa nationals arriving by air who qualified for a visa waiver under the Transit without Visa concession, where the passenger had the necessary documentation for his or her ultimate destination and the carrier genuinely believed that their sole purpose was to pass through the UK in onward passage. The waiver will not apply, if the passenger is subsequently denied onward carriage by the airline, while in the UK, owing to detection of inadequate documentation.[9] Carriers may also escape liability by achieving and retaining Approved Gate Check (AGC) Status, for which they have to fulfil stringent criteria for checking passengers' documentation prior to embarkation.[10] As of October 2003, two sea carriers and 58 air carriers had Approved Gate Check status at 252 stations.[11]

---

1   *Charging Procedures, a Guide for Carriers* (1996 edn, as revised); *Charging Procedures* (2004 draft).
2   The waiver will not apply where it was known prior to departure that the destination would be the UK: *Charging Procedures* ibid, Appendix A, 2004 draft.
3   The 2004 guidance has been updated to take account of new technology, including carbon dioxide detectors, passive millimetre wave imagers and heartbeat detectors, which the Immigration Service lends to ferry operators to check containers for stowaways, and to be consistent with the International Maritime Organisations' International Ship and Port Facilities' Security Code (ISPS) adopted by contracting governments in December 2002 and in force July 2004, which requires port authorities and shipping companies to introduce measures for the security of ships and port facilities. It states that inspectors will take account of the carrier's previous record and history of cooperation with the Immigration Service, and in particular whether the carrier has acted on advice or made proper use of equipment offered by the Service: *Charging Procedures* ibid, Appendix A, 2004 draft.

4 A number of ports and airports overseas now have UK liaison immigration officers (LIOs) or airline liaison officers (ALOs) permanently based there, advising carriers on passengers' eligibility to travel and authenticity of their documentation. They are responsible for preventing many hundreds of passengers, including refugees, from embarking on journeys to the UK. See *European Roma Rights Centre v Immigration Officer at Prague Airport* [2003] EWCA Civ 666, [2003] INLR 374, rvsd [2004] UKHL 55, [2005] 2 WLR 1. See also Morrison *The Trafficking and Smuggling of Refugees* (July 2000), UNHCR p 40; UNHCR *Interception of Asylum seekers and Refugees: The international framework and recommendations for a comprehensive approach* Standing Committee, 9 June 2000 [EC/50/SC/CRP.17].

5 Again, any relevant history of the carrier will be taken into account in deciding whether to waive a charge, and a waiver under this paragraph is unlikely to be granted more than once: *Charging Procedures* ibid, Appendix A (2004 draft).

6 The advised course of action under the guidance is to contact the nearest UNHCR office or UK representative: Charging Procedures ibid, Appendix A (2004 draft).

7 Carriers are advised to ascertain whether a waiver is likely to be given pre-embarkation if possible: *Charging Procedures, a Guide for Carriers* above, Appendix A (2004 draft).

8 *Charging Procedures* ibid, Appendix B (2004 draft).

9 See *Charging Procedures, a Guide for Carriers* para 2.2 for detailed requirements of this concession. See 14.94 fn 6 above for a list of countries whose nationals require transit visas.

10 The criteria for Advanced Gate Check status are an audited high standard of document checking and security procedures at the port of embarkation, a good level of cooperation from the carrier and a satisfactory record in relation to carriers' liability responsibilities: Charging Procedures, a Guide for Carriers above, para 8.

11 Ibid; Home Office consultation document on charging procedures, October 2003.

14.97 In the *Hoverspeed* case[1] the company, which had incurred (disputed) liabilities of almost £500,000 for carrying inadequately documented passengers, mostly passengers without a valid or current visa, sought declarations that the carriers' liability legislation offended against EC law in two distinct ways: (i) it constituted an unlawful restriction on the company's right to provide services, contrary to Article 49 EC (ex Article 59); (ii) it constituted an unlawful interference with the free movement rights of EEA nationals and their families who were subjected to documentary checks, an interference which the company was entitled to rely on. The Divisional Court rejected both arguments. Simon Brown LJ made the point that the Schengen Convention,[2] incorporated into EU law via the Amsterdam Treaty, obliged Member States (except the UK, Ireland and Denmark, which have opted out) to impose carrier sanctions, making it realistic to assume that it was compatible with EC law,[3] and held that the legislation did not impose measures so disproportionate as to thwart the central purpose of the EC Treaty, the free movement of persons, and so did not constitute a restriction for the purposes of Article 49 EC (ex Article 59).[4] If it did amount to a restriction, it was justified on public policy grounds, in the interests of immigration control, as an essential adjunct to the effective operation of the visa system.[5] Nor did it impede free movement of EEA nationals, who suffered only a brief though careful documentary check which had no perceptible effect on their freedom to travel.[6] In the course of his judgment he accepted implicitly that carrier sanctions deprived asylum seekers of any choice as to the country of asylum,[7] a choice which he held in the later *Adimi* case[8] to be open to asylum seekers on a limited basis as part of the international obligations towards refugees.

1 *R v Secretary of State for the Home Department, ex p Hoverspeed* [1999] INLR 591.
2 Article 26(2) of the Schengen Convention.
3 *Hoverspeed* above, at 603A.

⁴   *Hoverspeed* above, at 607H.
⁵   *Hoverspeed* above, at 608D. In *International Transport Roth GmbH v Secretary of State
    for the Home Department* [2002] EWCA Civ 158 [2002] 3 WLR 344) the CA held that
    the scheme penalising carriers of clandestine entrants did not breach EC law either.
⁶   *Hoverspeed* above, at 612H.
⁷   *Hoverspeed* above, at 599H.
⁸   *R v Uxbridge Magistrates' Court, ex p Adimi* [1999] INLR 490 at 496H–497F; see **14.37**
    text and fn 4 above.

14.98   It is clear from the terms of the Immigration and Asylum Act 1999, as
amended, and the guidance, that imposing a penalty on carriers is a matter of
both jurisdiction and discretion. Under section 1 of the original Immigration
(Carriers' Liability) Act 1987, liability was imposed where undocumented
passengers arrived in the UK or did not possess the necessary visas, but the
carriers had a defence if the passenger had shown them travel documents at
the port of departure, whose falsity was not reasonably apparent. In the
Hoverspeed case Simon Brown LJ appears to have treated this as a jurisdictional threshold, which it was for the court, not the Home Office, to decide.[1]
If correct, this suggests that the power to impose a penalty depends upon the
establishment of jurisdictional or precedent facts. But once the jurisdictional
basis is established, then there is room for a further challenge to the exercise of
the Secretary of State's discretion, for example, in setting the standards of
scrutiny he or she would expect from carriers, before deciding to enforce the
penalty. As Simon Brown LJ said, 'it is ultimately for the court to decide, in
any given case, whether the Secretary of State is, by his officials, setting
impermissibly high standards for the detection of forged or otherwise inadequate travel documents'[2] This puts the carrier regime on the same basis as
immigration detention, which can give rise to a jurisdictional challenge as well
as a challenge on traditional public law principles to a particular policy of
detention. The distinction is important, but is unlikely to be tested in the
higher courts, given the newly established rights of appeal.

¹   *R v Secretary of State for the Home Department, ex p Hoverspeed* [1999] INLR 591,
    QBD, at 602A. On precedent fact cases, see *R v Governor of Pentonville Prison,
    ex p Ahsan* [1969] 2 QB 222, QBD (proof that arrest took place within 24 hours of A's
    entry into the UK); *Khawaja v Secretary of State for the Home Department* [1984] AC 74,
    at 97E (Lord Fraser), 110E and111E (Lord Scarman), 122–124 (Lord Bridge) (proof of
    illegal entry);*Tan Te Lam v Superintendent of Tai A Chau Detention Centre* [1997] AC 97,
    111B–E and 113E–D, PC (proof that detention is 'pending removal').
²   *Hoverspeed* above, at 602C. Contrast *R v Governor of Durham Prison ex p Singh* [1984]
    1 WLR 704, QBD and *Tan Te Lam v Superintendent of Tai A Chau Detention Centre*
    [1997] AC 97, at 113E–D, PC (probably both jurisdictional challenges according to
    Mance LJ in *R (on the application of Khadir) v Secretary of State for the Home
    Department* [2003] INLR 426, at para 72) with *Nadarajah v Secretary of State for the
    Home Department* [2004] INLR 139, CA (challenge to policy not to treat removal as
    imminent, when judicial proceedings have been initiated). See further chapter 17 below.

14.99   The carrier sanction regime imposes on carriers the duty of trying to
apply the correct visa requirements on its passengers, and, inevitably, they will
get it wrong. Does this make them liable for refusing to carry someone,
because they wrongly believe that they do not have the correct travel
documents? In *Naraine v Hoverspeed*[1] a British citizen of Asian/Caribbean
origin holding a British visitor's passport (BVP), who was refused access to a
hovercraft to France on a day trip, lost his claim against Hoverspeed on the

ground that the company's action was dictated by French insistence on visas for BVP holders and the need to follow its carrier sanction regime, which was not in breach of EC law, and there was no racial discrimination since all BVP holders were treated in the same way. But in *Farah v British Airways and Home Office*,[2] an appeal against the striking out of a negligence claim, Somali nationals, who had been refused access to a British Airways flight in Cairo on the advice of an airline liaison officer and were subsequently deported to Ethiopia, were held entitled to pursue a claim against the Home Office for the wrong advice, since loss, including non-economic loss, was eminently foreseeable and it was arguable that the airline liaison officer owes a duty of care to passengers to give correct and accurate advice to airlines as to the validity of documents issued at a British diplomatic post overseas.

1   (1999) Independent, 18 November; [1999] CLY 2273.
2   *Farah v British Airways and Home Office* (2000) Times, 26 January, CA.

The future

14.100 The combined effects of September 11 and the 'war on terror', and the crackdown on asylum and illegal entry have led to a vastly increased array of duties, responsibilities and penalties for carriers and vastly increased powers for the immigration and policing authorities. The Secretary of State has power under the NIAA 2002 Act[1] to set up an 'authority to carry' scheme, requiring carriers to seek authority for carrying passengers prior to their journey, on pain of penalties for failing to seek such authority or for carrying passengers in disregard of refusal. As noted above, the Asylum and Immigration (Treatment of Claimants etc) Act 2004 empowers the Secretary of State to demand copies of passengers' travel documents from the carriers.[2] An agreement between the EU and US authorities enables the US to demand passenger information on all passengers travelling to the US – transfers of data which the EU Data Protection Working Party have condemned as illegal.[3] A proposed directive under Title IV of the Treaty of the European Community (TEA) (visas, asylum and immigration) for the collection and vetting of passenger data, currently before the EC Council, incorporates the UK's proposal on advance passenger information (API), which would be available to police and customs authorities as well as to immigration officers.[4] These developments will result in a European-wide system of advance authorisation for boarding, with severe penalties for failing to transmit information or for boarding 'inadmissible' passengers, which has serious data protection and privacy implications as well as spelling the end for many asylum seekers' hopes of reaching safety. Meanwhile, a new Schengen Information System, SIS II, to which the UK has opted in, will allow the UK and Ireland and the ten Accession states to participate in a vast intelligence and information exchange system which by March 2003 embraced 125,000 terminals across 13 Member States, Norway and Iceland, and had records on 877,655 people.[5] SIS II will extend the range of persons who can be entered on the system, but more importantly, will transform SIS from an information system into an investigating system, allowing for interlinking, access by new authorities, and storage and transmission of biometric data.[6] Together with a new visa information system (VIS) and with exchange of passenger data, SIS II will bring about the surveillance of the movements of everyone in the EU – citizens, legally resident third country nationals, visa entrants and irregular migrants – and storage of their data on an unprecedented scale.[7]

1   Nationality, Immigration and Asylum Act 2002, s 124, not yet in force.
2   Asylum and Immigration (Treatment of Claimants etc) Act 2004, s 16, amending Immigration Act 1971, Sch 2, para 27B.
3   Opinion 4/2003 on the level of protection ensured in the US for the transfer of passenger data, 11070/03/EN WP 78. The EU Data Protection working party is set up under the Data Protection Directive and comprises the information commissioners of Member States.
4   The proposed directive was condemned by the House of Lords Select Committee as 'seriously flawed': EU Committee 5th report session 2003–4, HL 29, 12 February 04.
5   See Statewatch: From the Schengen Information System to SIS II and the Visa Information (VIS): the proposals explained, Feb 2004.
6   Under the Schengen Information System, personal data are stored in the central computer in Strasbourg and simultaneously on linked-up national systems for searches with a view to arrest, remand in custody, tracing people, discreet surveillance, or with a view to returning a person to the external borders of the contracting states, or introducing measures to terminate residence and expel persons apprehended on the territory of a contracting state. This will enable persons sought for immigration offences to be arrested in any EU Member State. See Eur Comm: COM 2001 720, 18.12.01; Regulation 2421/2001/EC. The proposals are draft Council decision and draft regulations, 10054/03 and 10055/03.
7   Statewatch: From the Schengen Information System to SIS II and the Visa Information (VIS): the proposals explained, Feb 2004.

Chapter 15

DEPORTATION AND REPATRIATION

15.1   Deportation
15.54   Repatriation

DEPORTATION

Introduction

15.1 Deportation is the process whereby a non-British citizen can be compulsorily removed from the UK and prevented from returning unless the deportation order is revoked.[1] There is no power to deport a person who has already left the UK. A deportation order operates to cancel leave to remain.[2] But deportation has an effect long after the removal. A deportation order continues in force until revoked. Deportation is thus to be distinguished from other forms of compulsory removal which only bring a particular application or entry to an end, although they may create difficulties for an immigrant seeking to enter in the future. These various powers are not mutually exclusive: being an illegal entrant or a psychiatric patient does not prevent the exercise of the power to deport, provided the conditions for deportation exist.[3]

---

[1]   Immigration Act 1971, s 5(1) and (2).
[2]   Immigration Act 1971, s 5(1).
[3]   See *Patel (Yanus) v Immigration Appeal Tribunal* [1989] Imm AR 416, CA. As to the alternative use of deportation or Mental Health Act 1983 powers see *R v Immigration Appeal Tribunal, ex p Alghali* [1986] Imm AR 376; *X v Secretary of State for the Home Department* [2001] 1 WLR 740, [2001] INLR 205, CA, and see 16.68 below.

15.2 Deportation and Repatriation

History of the power to deport

15.2 Deportation was a power originally confined to aliens,[1] or foreign nationals. Its origins were in the prerogative powers of the Crown relating to aliens, but it came to be regulated by statute. For example, there was power under the Aliens Order 1953 to deport aliens on the ground that to do so was conducive to the public good.[2] In 1962 the first provisions enabling the deportation of Commonwealth citizens were introduced. But at first deportation was only available on the recommendation of a criminal court following a conviction, including convictions for immigration offences under the Commonwealth Immigrants Act 1962.[3] In 1969 the Secretary of State for the Home Department was given the power to initiate deportation proceedings against Commonwealth citizens who were in breach of their conditions of admission.[4] With the coming into force of the Immigration Act 1971 in 1973, the position of Commonwealth immigrants and aliens was made broadly the same. Anyone (except exempt persons including certain Commonwealth citizens, see below) could be deported for overstaying or breaching conditions of leave; on grounds that it was conducive to the public good; for belonging to the family of someone being deported on these grounds; or on a recommendation in a criminal case.[5]

[1] Ie not Commonwealth citizens. Defined in British Nationality Act 1981, s 50(1).
[2] Aliens Order 1953, Art 20(2)(b), now repealed.
[3] Commonwealth Immigrants Act 1962 and 1968, s 6, now repealed.
[4] Immigration Appeals Act 1969, s 16, now repealed.
[5] Immigration Act 1971, unamended, s 3(5), (6).

15.3 The law distinguished between illegal entrants, who (like those refused leave to enter) could be removed without further ado,[1] and those who had entered lawfully but had breached conditions or overstayed. The latter were made subject to deportation (connoting not just removal but prohibition on re-entry), but had the protection of an in-country appeal right before this was done. In one of its more dramatic reforms, the Immigration and Asylum Act 1999 removed this distinction. From 2 October 2000, overstayers, those breaching conditions of their leave and persons obtaining leave by deception, together with their families, became subject to administrative removal procedures identical to those applying to illegal entrants.[2] Only those protected by transitional provisions and those participating in a regularisation programme are excepted.[3]

[1] Immigration Act 1971, Sch 2, para 9.
[2] Immigration and Asylum Act 1999, s 10. See chapter 16 below.
[3] Immigration and Asylum Act 1999, s 9, Sch 15, para 12.

Liability to be deported

Non-British citizens

15.4 A British citizen cannot be deported.[1] If someone becomes a citizen (or acquires the right of abode and is therefore deemed to be a citizen for the purposes of the Immigration Acts) any deportation order ceases to have effect.[2] The term 'British citizen' includes a Commonwealth citizen who had the right of abode in the UK before 1983.[3] Thus a Commonwealth woman married to a British citizen before 1983 is not liable to be deported.[4] There is no legal bar in UK domestic law to deporting a British Overseas Territories citizen or a British Overseas citizen,[5] and in the case of British Overseas citizen visitors there can be no legitimate expectation that they will not be deported.[6] In practice, however, it is extremely difficult as there appears to be little obligation on the country of former residence to receive them back.[7] Equally, there is no bar on the deportation of EEA nationals, but special rules apply, as we have seen in chapter 7 above.[8] There is no statutory bar on the deportation of Convention refugees, although the Immigration Rules preclude the making of a deportation order against anyone whose removal would breach the UK's obligations under the Refugee Convention or the ECHR.[9]

[1]   Immigration Act 1971, ss 3(5), 6(2).
[2]   Immigration Act 1971, s 5(2). This contrasts with the position under the old law of an alien who became a British subject after the making of a deportation order: see *C v E* (1946) 62 TLR 326.
[3]   Immigration Act 1971, s 2, as amended by British Nationality Act 1981.
[4]   Immigration Act 1971, ss 2(2) and 5(2). But if the marriage took place after a deportation order had been signed, then she would not be deemed to be a British citizen.
[5]   See *R v Immigration Appeal Tribunal, ex p Sunsara* [1995] Imm AR 15.
[6]   *Patel v Secretary of State for the Home Department* [1993] Imm AR 392, CA.
[7]   See *R v Chief Immigration Officer, Gatwick Airport, ex p Harjendar Singh* [1987] Imm AR 346, QBD. The absence of evidence that the country specified in the removal direction would accept a person did not remove the Secretary of State's power to deport: *Sunsara* above.
[8]   See also 15.44 below.
[9]   HC 395, para 380, as amended by Cm 4851. See *Raziastaraie v Secretary of State for the Home Department* [1995] Imm AR 459, CA.

Exemption from deportation

Diplomatic exemption

15.5 Under section 8(3) of the Immigration Act 1971 and the Immigration (Exemption from Control) Order 1972[1] made under section 8(2), as we have seen in chapter 6 above, exemption from immigration control is given to diplomats and international functionaries. In some cases full immunity is given, including immunity from deportation, but in other cases the exempted category of person can still be deported on grounds conducive to the public good. Where someone is subject to an exemption, normally the exemption will extend to members of their family who form part of their household.[2] Whether someone falls within this category sometimes can be difficult to determine.[3] Diplomats who are the subject of a *demarche* under Article 9(1) of the Vienna Convention on Diplomatic Relations are probably not deportable, even though they cease to have diplomatic exemption, because they normally leave before the 'expiry of a reasonable period in which to do so', and because Article 39(2) and (4), which are part of UK law,[4] provide that their privileges and immunities continue until that time or until they leave the country.

[1]   SI 1972/1613.
[2]   See chapter 6 above.

15.5 Deportation and Repatriation

3   Gupta v Secretary of State for the Home Department [1979–80] Imm AR 52 at 57; R v
    Secretary of State for the Home Department, ex p Bagga [1990] Imm AR 413, CA.
4   Diplomatic Privileges Act 1964.

Five-year rule for Irish and Commonwealth citizens

15.6 Certain Commonwealth[1] and Irish citizens, who were ordinarily resident in the UK when the Immigration Act 1971 came into force, are exempted
from liability for deportation.[2] Under earlier laws, Commonwealth or Irish
citizens could not be deported if they had completed five years ordinary
residence, excluding any long periods spent in prison.[3] At the same time, no
Commonwealth or Irish citizen could be deported on conducive to the public
good grounds. These exemptions were continued in the circumstances set out
in section 7 of the 1971 Act for Commonwealth and Irish citizens who became
ordinarily resident in the UK on or before 1 January 1973, when the 1971 Act
came into force, and were Commonwealth or Irish citizens at that time.[4] The
burden of proving entitlement to the exemption is on the proposed deportee,
and not the authorities.[5] Essentially this means showing that they have been
'ordinarily resident' for the requisite period.

1   For Commonwealth citizens see British Nationality Act 1981, s 37, Sch 3. For nationals of
    Pakistan and South Africa see 15.10 below.
2   Immigration Act 1971, s 7(1)(b). The subsection was modified by Immigration and Asylum
    Act 1999, Sch 14, para 46, applying the exemption to those who would formerly have
    been deported but are now subject to administrative removal by virtue of s 10.
3   Commonwealth Immigrants Act 1962, s 7(2), now repealed, and see R v Edgehill [1963]
    1 QB 593, [1963] 1 All ER 181, CCA.
4   Immigration Act 1971, s 7(1), as amended by Immigration and Asylum Act 1999, Sch 14,
    para 46.
5   Immigration Act 1971, s 7(5).

15.7 Commonwealth and Irish citizens cannot be deported on any ground, or
recommended for deportation by a criminal court) if they were ordinarily
resident at 1 January 1973 and have been so for the five years prior to the
decision or conviction.[1] The five years must have been completed at the time
of the decision or conviction, not the date of the actual making of the order.[2]
The date on which a decision to deport is made is a matter of fact, not law,
and is not necessarily the date when notice of it is given to or reaches the
potential deportee.[3]

1   Immigration Act 1971, s 7(1)(b), substituted by the Nationality, Immigration and Asylum
    Act 2002 s 75, and (c). Section 7(1)(a) (which exempted Commonwealth and Irish citizens
    from deportation on public good grounds if they were ordinarily resident on 1 January
    1973 and at all times until the date of the decision) was repealed as redundant (NIAA
    2002, s 75). See R v Secretary of State for the Home Department, ex p Olashehinde [1992]
    Imm AR 443, QBD.
2   Mehmet v Secretary of State for the Home Department [1977] Imm AR 68, CA.
3   Rehman v Secretary of State for the Home Department [1978] Imm AR 80. Contrast Rafiq
    v Secretary of State for the Home Department [1998] Imm AR 193, CA: a grant of leave is
    not effective until communicated. See also on the communication of decisions R (on the
    application of Anufrijeva) v Secretary of State for the Home Department [2003] UKHL 36,
    [2003] Imm AR 570, [2003] INLR 521. The practice of serving deportation decisions on
    the file when the person's whereabouts were unknown, prevalent until 1986 when it was

abandoned as unfair, meant that many long-term overstayers were not aware of deportation decisions, and even deportation orders, against them for many years. The 2003 Notices Regulations (SI 2003/658) revive the power. See 18.85 below.

15.8 Normally a person is not to be treated as ordinarily resident at a time when he or she is in this country 'in breach of the immigration laws'.[1] But for the purposes of this exemption from deportation, the position is different. Section 7(2) of the Immigration Act 1971 provides that a person who has at any time become ordinarily resident is not to be treated for the purposes of the exemption as having ceased to be so by reason only of having remained in breach of the immigration laws. Deserting seamen[2] and illegal entrants[3] will not gain exemption, only those who entered lawfully and subsequently overstayed. For example, in the case of *R v Immigration Appeal Tribunal, ex p Perdikos*[4] the applicant returned to this country while he was still subject to a deportation order. Woolf J held that he never acquired ordinary residence, and so could not benefit from the deportation exemption.

[1]   Immigration Act 1971, s 33(1); see chapter 5 above.
[2]   *Re Abdul Manan* [1971] 2 All ER 1016, [1971] 1 WLR 859, CA: a deserting seaman had never become ordinarily resident since he was guilty of an offence when he deserted ship, and continued to be so during the whole period of his stay in this country.
[3]   *R v Bangoo* [1977] Imm AR 33n, CA; *R v Immigration Appeal Tribunal, ex p Perdikos* (1981) 131 NLJ 477.
[4]   (1981) 131 NLJ 477, following *Manan* above. See further *R v Secretary of State for the Home Department, ex p Margueritte* [1983] QB 180, [1982] 3 All ER 909, CA; *Immigration Appeal Tribunal v Chelliah* [1985] Imm AR 192, CA; *R v Secretary of State for the Home Department, ex p Oni* (CO 2863/1998) (25 October 1999, unreported).

Section 1(5) cases

15.9 Until August 1988, a Commonwealth woman married to a Commonwealth man settled here before 1 January 1973 was not liable to be deported, even if the marriage was a sham one.[1] Children under 16 at the time of the decision to deport also benefitted.[2] This exemption disappeared with the repeal of section 1(5) of the Immigration Act 1971 by the Immigration Act 1988,[3] and it is doubtful if any privilege or right under section 1(5) was preserved by section 16 of the 1988 Act after the repeal.[4]

[1]   This was because of the saving provision of s 1(5) of the Immigration Act 1971 combined with provisions allowing such women to register as British on marriage. See *Secretary of State for the Home Department v Huseyin* [1988] Imm AR 129, CA; this did not apply to alien wives of Commonwealth citizens: see *O'Shea v Secretary of State for the Home Department* [1988] Imm AR 484, CA. It did not apply if the marriage took place after the deportation order had been signed: *R v Secretary of State for the Home Department, ex p Hayden* [1988] Imm AR 555, QBD. Nor did it apply to husbands of women settled here: *Singh v Immigration Appeal Tribunal* [1988] Imm AR 582.
[2]   *Menn v Secretary of State for the Home Department* [1992] Imm AR 245, CA.
[3]   Immigration Act 1988, s 1.
[4]   *Menn* above; *R v Secretary of State for the Home Department, ex p Delpratt* [1991] Imm AR 5n, QBD; see also *R v Secretary of State for the Home Department, ex p Ovakkouche* [1991] Imm AR 5, QBD.

Application to citizens of Pakistan and South Africa

15.10 Pakistan withdrew from the Commonwealth on 30 January 1972. Section 1 of the Pakistan Act 1973, passed on 25 July 1973 and in force on 1 September 1973, enacted that citizens of Pakistan ceased to be Commonwealth citizens at commencement. But transitional provisions enabled citizens of Pakistan to retain some of their rights as Commonwealth citizens for long enough to register as citizens of the UK and colonies (CUKC).[1] In 1989 Pakistan rejoined the Commonwealth.[2] Thus from 1 October 1989 its citizens have been able to claim exemption again if they fulfilled the residence conditions set out above.[3] In 1994 South Africa rejoined the Commonwealth, and its citizens became able to claim exemption if they fulfilled the residence conditions set out above.[4]

1   By deeming them Commonwealth citizens until 31 August 1974, giving one year to apply for registration as a CUKC. If such an application was made, deemed Commonwealth citizenship continued pending its determination. Those not applying in time lost eligibility for the exemption.
2   British Nationality (Pakistan) Order 1989, SI 1989/1331.
3   In *Siddique* (16050) (7 January 1998, unreported), IAT, a Pakistan national relied on the transitional provisions to found exemption from deportation on the ground of ordinary residence on 1 January 1973 and for five years preceding the decision.
4   See British Nationality (South Africa) Order 1994, SI 1994/1634, which came into force on 26 July 1994.

Grounds of deportation

15.11 A person who is not a British citizen and not exempt is liable to deportation from the UK in the following circumstances:

(i)   the Secretary of State deems his or her deportation to be conducive to the public good;[1]
(ii)   another member of the family to which he or she belongs is to be deported;[2]
(iii) a court recommends deportation after conviction of an offence punishable by imprisonment.[3]

1   Immigration Act 1971, s 3(5)(a), as amended by Immigration and Asylum Act 1999, Sch 14, para 44(2).
2   Immigration Act 1971, s 3(5)(b), as amended.
3   Immigration Act 1971, s 3(6).

Deportation conducive to public good

15.12 The power to deport on public good grounds has existed in the case of foreign nationals for most of the last century, and probably before, under the prerogative powers of the Crown. There was no right of appeal until 1969 and the decided cases in the High Court all favoured the executive, although the judges proclaimed their ability to protect the liberty of the subject.[1] The power is now contained in section 3(5)(a) of the Immigration Act 1971, as amended. A special regime applies to political cases, as we shall see.[2] The most frequent use of the power is against convicted criminals who have not been recommended for deportation by the court which sentenced them,[3] as the section 3(5)(a) power does not need a prior court recommendation.[4]

[1] *R v Governor of Brixton Prison, ex p Sarno* [1916] 2 KB 742 at 749 and 752 ('if it was clear that an act was done by the executive with the intention of misusing those powers, this court would have jurisdiction to deal with the matter'); *R v Chiswick Police Station Supt, ex p Sacksteder* [1918] 1 KB 578 at 586–587, CA ('if that order is ... practically a sham ... it seems to me the court can go behind it'); cf *R v Governor of Brixton Prison, ex p Bloom* (1920) 85 JP 87 at 88. See further *R v Secretary of State for Home Affairs, ex p Duke of Chateau Thierry* [1917] 1 KB 922; *R v Home Secretary, ex p Bressler* (1924) 88 JP 89; see *C v E* (1946) 62 TLR 326; *R v Governor of Brixton Prison, ex p Soblen* [1963] 2 QB 243, [1962] 3 All ER 641. See A W Brian Simpson *In the Highest Degree Odious* (1994) for an illuminating review of the treatment of aliens under wartime and emergency regulations.
[2] See 15.18 below.
[3] The failure or even the reasoned refusal of a criminal court to make a recommendation does not prevent the minister initiating deportation proceedings under s 3(5)(a): see *Martin* [1993] Imm AR 161, IAT; *R v Secretary of State for the Home Department, ex p Figueiredo* [1993] Imm AR 606, QBD; *M v Secretary of State for the Home Department* [2003] EWCA Civ 146, [2003] INLR 306; *Jaroudy* [2002] UKIAT 06653.
[4] The 1971 Act retained the criminal courts' power to make recommendations for deportation, which could then be acted on without an appeal in the immigration system. There was some procedural unfairness in retaining both avenues, mitigated to an extent by the regime of asylum appeals introduced by the Asylum and Immigration Appeals Act 1993, s 8, and by the human rights appeal introduced by the Immigration and Asylum Act 1999, s 65; but now the Nationality, Immigration and Asylum Act 2002, s 82(2)(j) provides a right of appeal against any decision to deport, whether made under s 3(5) or s 3(6), thus removing the anomaly.

Criminal conviction

15.13 The existence of the power to deport on public good grounds based on a past criminal conviction is not in doubt.[1] It has been suggested that the power should only be exercised on specific and positive grounds,[2] and the Court of Appeal has on occasion suggested that the provisions of Council Directive 64/221 (EEC), which prevent deportation based on the mere fact of conviction, made good sense and were equally applicable in UK domestic law.[3] It has elsewhere adopted a more insular view, confining such dicta to recommendations by the criminal courts[4] and underlining the differences between the Immigration Act 1971, section 3(5)(a) regime and the EC public policy directive.[5]

[1] *R v Immigration Appeal Tribunal, ex p Florent* [1985] Imm AR 141, CA.
[2] *Khawaja v Secretary of State for the Home Department* [1984] AC 74, per Lord Bridge.
[3] *R v Secretary of State for the Home Department, ex p Santillo* [1981] QB 778, [1981] 2 All ER 897, CA, *R v Immigration Appeal Tribunal, ex p Ullah* [1982] Imm AR 124, CA (cited in *Goremsandu v Secretary of State for the Home Department* [1996] Imm AR 250 at 254, where the Court of Appeal assimilated the EC approach to the municipal law but adopted the ECJ's statement in *R v Bouchereau* [1978] QB 732, para 29 that while generally a present threat to public policy requires a propensity to reoffend, exceptionally, past conduct alone may constitute a threat to public policy).
[4] *R v Escauriaza* (1987) 87 Cr App Rep 344, CA; *R v Spura* (1988) 10 Cr App Rep (S) 376, CA.
[5] *R v Secretary of State for the Home Department, ex p Al-Sabah* [1992] Imm AR 223, CA; *R v Secretary of State for the Home Department, ex p Samaroo* (CO 4973/1999) (20 December 2000, unreported), para 56 (the point was not dealt with in the Court of

Appeal's judgment at [2001] EWCA Civ 1139, [2001] UKHRR 1150, [2002] INLR 55, although the accompanying appeal of *Sezek* was dismissed on the basis that he did not have the protection of EC law).

15.14 Nevertheless, it is not every conviction that could legitimately result in a deportation decision being taken. The acts proved must impinge on the public domain in a real sense.[1] There must be some public interest at stake in favour of removal. The power is not meant to be merely a supplement to punishment. It is not the label attached to an offence but its factual circumstances that best indicate the nature of the conduct and its repercussions on the public domain.[2] Although recidivism and a propensity to commit further offences are not essential preconditions to the exercise of the power to deport under section 3(5)(a) of the Immigration Act 1971,[3] they are generally material considerations when considering the merits of a decision.[4] However, cases do arise, exceptionally, where the personal conduct of a proposed deportee has been such that, whilst not necessarily evincing any clear propensity to re-offend, it causes such deep public revulsion that public policy requires deportation.[5] Convictions for importing or supplying dangerous drugs[6] for example, or for rape,[7] incest,[8] violent robbery[9] and arson[10] have been held to be in themselves a sufficient threat to public order as to give rise to the exercise of the power, although human rights, compassionate or other relevant circumstances may outweigh the public good.[11]

[1] Per Woolf J in *R v Immigration Appeal Tribunal, ex p Ullah* (19 February 1982, unreported), QBD; affd [1982] Imm AR 124, CA.
[2] *R v Immigration Appeal Tribunal, ex p Florent* [1985] Imm AR 141, CA.
[3] *Said v Immigration Appeal Tribunal* [1989] Imm AR 372, CA; *Martinez-Tobon v Immigration Appeal Tribunal* [1988] Imm AR 319, CA; *R (on the application of Samaroo) v Secretary of State for the Home Department* [2001] EWCA Civ 1139, [2002] INLR 55.
[4] Andrews (Joseph) [2002] UKIAT 07598: 'propensity to re-offend is a significant factor in determining whether deportation is correct'. Where the deportee is an EU national, propensity to re-offend is generally (although not invariably) necessary to the exercise of the deportation power: *R v Bouchereau* [1978] 1 QB 732 para 29 and see 7.133ff above.
[5] *Ex p Florent* fn 2 above; *Said v Immigration Appeal Tribunal* [1989] Imm AR 372, CA; *Goremsandu v Secretary of State for the Home Department* [1996] Imm AR 250.
[6] *R v Secretary of State for the Home Department, ex p Marchon* [1993] Imm AR 384, CA; *R (on the application of Samaroo) v Secretary of State for the Home Department* (CO 4973/1999) (20 December 2000, unreported), affd [2001] EWCA Civ 1139, [2001] UKHRR 1150, [2002] INLR 55. But see below.
[7] *Galoo* (00TH0009): 'rape strikes at the roots of society, including the sanctity of the family'. See also *N (Kenya)* [2004] UKIAT 00009 (upheld by the Court of Appeal at [2004] EWCA Civ 1094, [2004] INLR 612); *Ayodele v Secretary of State for the Home Department* [2003] EWCA Civ 5 (perm).
[8] *Goremsandu v Secretary of State for the Home Department* [1996] Imm AR 250, CA.
[9] *Florent* above; *R (on the application of Schmelz) v Immigration Appeal Tribunal* [2004] EWCA Civ 29, [2004] All ER (D) 87 (Jan) (EU national).
[10] *Escudero* (20525) (8 March 1999, unreported).
[11] *R v Bouchereau* [1978] QB 732, particularly AG Warner at 742b–c; but see *Calfa (Criminal Proceedings against)*: C-348/96 [1999] ECR I-11.

Criminal conviction – some conclusions

15.15 Many of those facing deportation on conducive grounds after being convicted of serious criminal offences, particularly drug offences, claim the protection of Article 8 ECHR for family reasons (15.36 below). To justify these deportations and defeat the Article 8 claims, the Secretary of State has been obliged to explain the policy being followed in these cases. It was set out with some clarity in an affidavit in *Samaroo and Sezek*.[1] First, deportation is necessary to protect the interests of UK residents from (in that case) the harmful effects of drugs and in the interests of preventing disorder and crime. In other words it is a protective measure: deport and the residents of the UK will be protected from the effects of the deportee's future criminal conduct. Clearly, this first limb of the policy is only relevant or effective, if the deportee is likely to reoffend on release from his or her custodial sentence. Secondly, deportation is a valuable deterrent to actual or prospective drug traffickers (and presumably any other class of criminal). This second limb to the policy deals with deportees who may have been rehabilitated and are fit once more to lead 'a good and useful life', posing no risk of reoffending. Their deportation is necessary as an example to other actual or potential criminals. In his dissenting judgment in *N*[2] Sedley LJ said that, in the absence of evidence of the deterrent effect of deportation in such cases, the Secretary of State's policy was better described as a judgment.[3] We know of no such evidence, and the policy of deterrence appears to be untested but protected from court scrutiny, because it is in the Minister's 'discretionary area of judgement' – in our view not a satisfactory basis for any penal policy.

1   *R (on the application of Samaroo) v Secretary of State for the Home Department* [2001] EWCA Civ 1139, [2002] INLR 55, paras 8–10, CA.
2   *R (on the application of N) v Secretary of State for the Home Department* [2004] EWCA Civ 1094, [2004] INLR 612.
3   *R (on the application of N)* at paras 69, 75, in which he (alone of the judges) upheld the adjudicator's right to a different judgment on the weight to be attached to evidence of rehabilitation.

15.16 The position under the Human Rights Act and in Europe under the case law of the European Court of Human Rights at Strasbourg is harsh indeed. In none of the cases is the sentence of imprisonment ever taken into account. In domestic penal policy, the courts are required to consider the totality of the sentence, where a convicted person is being sentenced for a number of different offences committed at different times or places.[1] But with non-British citizens the totality principle is never applied to the extra punishment of deportation. Nor is the sentence undergone by the deportee ever considered in the case law as part of the legitimate and necessary means of combatting crime – which is an enormous and rather extraordinary omission. Failure to have regard to the sentence already undergone seriously distorts the balancing exercise performed in Article 8 cases, and means that for foreigners, there is little or no room for rehabilitation or the chance of 'a good and useful life'.[2] And on the other side it has been said that 'the right to respect for family life is not regarded as a right which requires a high degree of constitutional protection'.[3]

1   See *Archbold Criminal Evidence Pleading and Practice* 2004, para 5.165. The totality principle has been expressly preserved by the Powers of Criminal Courts (Sentencing) Act 2000, s 158(2)(b).
2   In *Samaroo* the applicant was described as a model prisoner with an exemplary prison record: *R (on the application of Samaroo) v Secretary of State for the Home Department* [2001] EWCA Civ 1139, [2002] INLR 55, para 4(k).
3   [2001] EWCA Civ 1139 per Dyson LJ at para 36.

15.17 It does not end there. The policy adumbrated in *Samaroo*,[1] justifying deportation as a proportionate response to criminal conduct, applies to nationals of some countries but not of others. It cannot be applied in its full extent to nationals of EEA countries or, for example, to certain Turkish nationals, who have been convicted and sentenced for serious crimes in the UK. Under EC law they cannot be deported solely in order to deter others from crime, because Directive 64/221 (EEC), as interpreted by the European Court of Justice, will not allow it.[2] Finally, so far as UK domestic law is concerned, the case law suggests a somewhat ambiguous and unsatisfactory position. First, it is said that when a court has to consider whether to recommend deportation as part of the sentencing exercise, it applies the same rules that operate under EC law regardless of the nationality of the defendant,[3] even though it will generally be impossible at that stage to judge whether he or she is likely to reoffend. Later, when it is possible to assess the risk of reoffending, the Secretary of State can ignore the rules of EC law and apply entirely different standards to those operating under Directive 64/221.[4]

[1]   [2001] EWCA Civ 1139, [2002] INLR 55, CA.
[2]   *Bonsignore v Oberstadt direktor der Stadt, Köln* Case 67/74 [1975] ECR 297, [1975] 1 CMLR 472, ECJ; Case C-348/96 *Calfa* [1999] ECR I-11; as regards Turkey, Art 14 of Commission Decision (ECSC) 1/80 under the Ankara Agreement means that Directive 64/221 applies to Turkish workers who have achieved free movement rights in a particular Member State: see C-340/97 *Nazli v Stadt Nürnberg* [2000] ECR I-957, para 63.
[3]   See 15.29 below.
[4]   See 15.13 above.

Political cases

15.18 Deportation may be deemed conducive to the public good as being in the interests of national security or of the relations between the UK and another country, or for other reasons of a political nature. In *Rehman*[1] the House of Lords, endorsing the Court of Appeal's judgment, held that 'national security', 'international relations' and 'other political reasons' may overlap, and gave an extremely broad meaning to the phrase 'national security'. Rejecting the approach of the Special Immigration Appeals Commission, which had held that endangering national security required engagement in, promotion or encouragement of violent activity targeted at the UK, its system of government or its people,[2] their Lordships agreed with the Court of Appeal that the promotion of terrorism against any state is capable of being a threat to the UK's national security, since increasingly the security of one country is dependent upon the security of others, so that any activity likely to create a risk of adverse repercussions, including conduct which could have an adverse effect on the UK's relationship with a friendly state, could threaten the UK's national security. Thus planning and organisation in the UK of terrorist acts abroad could found deportation,[3] although the Secretary of State would have to show that there was a real possibility of adverse repercussions in terrorist cases.[4] Not since the majority decision in *Liversidge v Anderson* has the executive been given such deference; one can hear the Secretary of State saying 'I can make national security mean anything I want it to mean.'[5] The House also endorsed the Court of Appeal's distinction between proof and evaluation; the Secretary of State's reasons are not counts on an indictment, and the task is evaluative and predictive, using a global approach to assess whether the subject is a danger to national security.[6] Nevertheless, the assertions on which the Secretary of State bases his evaluation of danger must be reliable, and suspicious circumstances do not necessarily make for a reasonable suspicion so as to justify deportation.[7] Public good grounds for deportation may also include assisting the proliferation of another country's nuclear capability contrary to international treaty.[8]

1   *Secretary of State for the Home Department v Rehman* [2001] UKHL 47, [2001] 3 WLR 877, [2002] INLR 92, [2002] Imm AR 98, affirming *Secretary of State for the Home Department v Rehman (Shafiq ur)* [2000] INLR 531.
2   *Rehman (Shafiq ur) v Secretary of State for the Home Department* [1999] INLR 517 (SIAC).
3   See *Rehman* above, per Lord Slynn at para 18, Lord Steyn (para 28), Lord Hoffmann (para 49). See also *Singh (Raghbir) v Secretary of State for the Home Department* [1996] Imm AR 507 at 510, CA.
4   *Rehman* above, para 16.
5   [1942] AC 206, HL. The limits of deference were set by the judgments of the majority in *A v Secretary of State for the Home Department* [2004] UKHL 56, [2005] 2 WLR 87, which held that while the assessment of threats to national security was primarily for the executive, restrictions on liberty required intense scrutiny by the courts: see 17.39 below.
6   *Rehman* above, para 29 (Lord Steyn), 49 (Lord Hoffmann).
7   *M v Secretary of State for the Home Department* [2004] EWCA Civ 324, [2004] 2 All ER 263 (permission), where SIAC's decision to quash a deportation order and a certificate under Anti-terrorism, Crime and Security Act 2001, s 21 was upheld: see 15.43 below.
8   *R v Secretary of State for the Home Department, ex p Saleem* (23 July 1996, unreported), QBD.

Other conducive grounds

15.19 The circumstances other than criminal behaviour (apart from political cases) where the public good power can be exercised are not defined. Whatever they are, it is for the Secretary of State to prove the detrimental conduct complained of and to demonstrate that it impinges on the public domain. It has been held that a sham marriage qualifies because it undermines a fundamental institution of society,[1] though the appellate body must be careful that all the elements of a sham marriage are proved.[2] Criminal associations which have not led to a conviction might be a further basis, but here, although the Secretary of State may rely on inferences,[3] there may be difficulty in proving the acts complained of. The standard is the civil burden of proof, but flexibly applied, so that the graver the allegation the more certain the proof required.[4] The commission of offences abroad might be a ground for a public good deportation,[5] so long as it is not disguised extradition[6] and does not engage human rights considerations.[7]

1   *R v Immigration Appeal Tribunal, ex p Cheema* [1982] Imm AR 134. See below.
2   *R v Immigration Appeal Tribunal, ex p Khan* [1983] QB 790.
3   *Martinez-Tobon v Immigration Appeal Tribunal* [1988] Imm AR 319, CA.
4   *Khawaja v Secretary of State for the Home Department* [1984] AC 74.
5   *El-Awam* (12807) (14 December 1995, unreported).
6   A decision to deport on conducive grounds for a conspiracy triable abroad is lawful provided the purpose is not to surrender the deportee without the benefit of extradition safeguards, but if during the process an extradition request is received, there are powerful reasons of comity for giving it priority: *Caddoux, Re* [2004] EWHC 642 (Admin), [2004] All ER (D) 498 (Mar), para 6. Using deportation to bypass the safeguards of extradition could also amount to an abuse of process: *R v Mullen* [2000] QB 520, CA; *R v Horseferry*

15.19 *Deportation and Repatriation*

Road Magistrates' Court, ex p Bennett [1994] 1 AC 42, HL; *R v Bow Street Magistrates, ex p Mackeson* (1981) 75 Cr App Rep 24, Div Ct.
7   See 15.36 below.

Deception of the Home Office

15.20 Where the Home Office has been misled into granting an indefinite leave to remain, it can base a decision to deport under section 3(5)(a) of the Immigration Act 1971 on that ground.[1] This may involve false allegations as to marital status, or as to the continued existence of cohabitation at a time when the parties are living separately, or a fabricated claim to refugee status. Whether there has been a deception is a matter of fact to be proved to the satisfaction of the Tribunal on a civil balance of proof, flexibly applied to take into account the gravity of the allegation.[2] Fraud must be 'clear and manifest' to justify deportation of someone granted indefinite leave to remain as a refugee.[3] In *Patel*[4] Lord Bridge reconsidered and withdrew his dictum in *Khawaja*[5] that the power could not be used to deport someone who told lies on entry if his or her conduct thereafter was perfectly satisfactory, and lies on entry may form the basis of a later deportation on conducive grounds,[6] although administrative removal as an illegal entrant is easier[7] and therefore far more likely.

1   *Re Owusu-Sekyere* [1987] Imm AR 425, CA. However, administrative removal under s 10 Immigration and Asylum Act 1999 (as now amended by Nationality, Immigration and Asylum Act 2002, s 74) is also available for anyone who uses deception in seeking (whether successfully or not) leave to remain, and Home Office policy is not to deport but to use administrative removal in respect of any deception to obtain settlement which took place after 1 October 1996: Operational Enforcement Manual 'Deportation' para 13.3; IDI Sep 01, Ch 13 s 1.
2   *Tahir v Immigration Appeal Tribunal* [1989] Imm AR 98, CA.
3   *R (on the application of Saribal) v Secretary of State for the Home Department* [2002] EWHC 1542 (Admin), [2002] All ER (D) 379 (Jul).
4   *R v Immigration Appeal Tribunal, ex p Patel (Anilkumar Ravindrabhai)* [1988] AC 910, [1988] Imm AR 434; see also *R v Immigration Appeal Tribunal, ex p Karim* [1986] Imm AR 428 (use of a false identity).
5   *Khawaja v Secretary of State for the Home Department* [1984] AC 74, [1983] 1 All ER 765, HL.
6   *R v Secretary of State for the Home Department, ex p Chaumun* [1999] INLR 479.
7   Immigration Act 1971, Sch 2, para 9; see chapter 16 below.

Deportation of family members

15.21 The power to deport on public good grounds has applied to members of a family for the best part of a century.[1] Under section 3(5)(b) of the Immigration Act 1971,[2] the Secretary of State possesses the power to deport the dependent spouse and dependent children of an immigrant where the spouse or parent respectively (hereafter called the principal deportee) has been deported or is ordered to be deported. In the past this power was only likely to be used where the family were all settled in the UK; where the family had a limited leave in consequence of the principal's status, then an extension of that leave would normally be refused on a decision to deport the principal deportee. But current Home Office policy is to use the family deportation

1028

provisions 'to avoid a possible Article 8 challenge'.[3] Under a family deportation, not only a spouse but also any children under 18 may be deported, even where they are the children of the dependent spouse and not the principal's own.[4] Adopted[5] and illegitimate children may also be deported, but not natural children who have been adopted by someone else.[6] For the purposes of this section, 'wife' includes each of two or more wives.[7] A dependent spouse who is separated from the principal remains a member of the family of the principal deportee until divorce and would still be liable to family deportation. However, the Immigration Rules make plain that the Secretary of State will not deport a dependent spouse who has qualified for settlement in his or her own right or has been living apart from the principal deportee.[8] Children will not normally be considered for deportation where they are living apart from the deportee or have left home and established themselves on an independent basis, or married before deportation came into prospect.[9]

1   Aliens Restriction Act 1914, s 1(1); *R v Home Secretary, ex p Bressler* (1924) 88 JP 89, where the courts upheld the decision of the Secretary of State to deport Mrs Bressler because of her husband's deportation following a criminal conviction.
2   As substituted by Immigration and Asylum Act 1999, Sch 14, para 46.
3   ECHR, Art 8. The policy applies where the principal is liable to deportation and the rest of the family to administrative removal: Operational Enforcement Manual 'Deportation' para 14. The idea appears to be to keep the family together.
4   Immigration Act 1971, s 5(4)(a), (b). Children born in the UK may be deported prior to their gaining entitlement to British citizenship through length of residence: OEM 'Deportation' para 14.
5   'Adopted' children for this purpose includes those adopted legally or de facto: Immigration Act 1971, s 5(4).
6   Immigration Act 1971, s 5(4).
7   Immigration Act 1971, s 5(4).
8   HC 395, para 365.
9   HC 395, para 366.

15.22 The power can be exercised where a decision to deport has been taken against the head of the family. No actual deportation order is necessary.[1] But a decision to deport family members must be taken independently and considered on its merits rather than following as a matter of course.[2] Further, there are limits on family deportation. If a principal deportee leaves the country after the deportation order and eight weeks elapse, no family deportation order can be made against any family members.[3] Similarly, if someone ceases to belong to the family of the deportee (because a marriage is dissolved or a child reaches 18), a family deportation order ceases to have effect against him or her.[4] If the deportation order against the principal deportee ceases to have effect, for example, because it is revoked, any family deportation order also lapses.[5]

1   *Ibrahim v Immigration Appeal Tribunal* [1989] Imm AR 111, CA, reversing the earlier case of *R v Immigration Appeal Tribunal, ex p Mehmet (Ekrem)* [1977] Imm AR 56.
2   *Wah (Yau Yak) v Home Office* [1982] Imm AR 16, CA.
3   Immigration Act 1971, s 5(3).
4   Immigration Act 1971, s 5(3). For separated spouses see HC 395, para 365, 15.21 text and fn 8 above.
5   Immigration Act 1971, s 5(3).

Deportation recommended by court

15.23 The third head of deportation arises where a non-citizen over 17 years of age[1] is convicted[2] of an offence punishable with imprisonment[3] and is recommended for deportation by the court.[4] The recommendation may be made by any court having power to sentence him or her for the offence, unless the court commits the person to be sentenced or further dealt with for that offence by another court.[5] Thus, the recommendation may be made by the magistrates' court, a Crown Court, or the Court of Appeal.[6] There is no statutory restriction on the combination of a recommendation with other any other sentence;[7] it may be made in respect of an offender who is sentenced to imprisonment for life[8] or one who is sentenced to a fine, although it is unlikely a non-custodial sentence would reach the entry-point criteria for demonstrating 'potential detriment'. A recommendation may also be made in respect of youth custody, although such a sentence, intended to rehabilitate and train, may mean that it is not a proper case for a recommendation.[9]

[1]   A person is deemed to have attained the age of 17 if, on consideration of any available evidence, he or she appears to the court to have done so: Immigration Act 1971, s 6(3)(a).
[2]   A person is convicted of an offence for deportation purposes if he or she is found to have committed it, notwithstanding any enactment to the contrary and notwithstanding that the court does not proceed to conviction: Immigration Act 1971, s 6(3).
[3]   Whether an offence is punishable with imprisonment is to be determined without regard to any enactment restricting imprisonment of young offenders, or first offenders: Immigration Act 1971, s 6(3)(b).
[4]   Immigration Act 1971, s 3(6).
[5]   Immigration Act 1971, s 6(1), in which special provision is made for Scotland.
[6]   In Scotland a recommendation may be made by a Sheriff or the High Court of Justiciary (subject to provisos): see Immigration Act 1971, s 6(1). The Court of Appeal's jurisdiction is conferred by Criminal Appeal Act 1968, ss 11(3), 50.
[7]   Notwithstanding any rule of practice restricting the matters which ought to be taken into account in dealing with an offender sentenced to imprisonment: Immigration Act 1971, s 6(4) and see *R v Assa Singh* [1965] 2 QB 312, [1965] 1 All ER 938, CCA.
[8]   *R v Akan* [1973] QB 491.
[9]   See *R v Flynn* [1963] Crim LR 647.

15.24 A recommendation is to be treated as a sentence for the purposes of appealing against sentence.[1] In England an appeal may be made to the Crown Court or the Court of Appeal against a recommendation for deportation, even if this is the only part of the sentence against which an appeal is made.[2] But in those cases in which no appeal lies to the Court of Appeal from a sentence of a lower court, no appeal can be made to that court against a recommendation.[3] Until the 2002 Act, there was no appeal to the immigration appellate authorities[4] if the Secretary of State decides to follow the recommendation, except on asylum, human rights or race discrimination grounds,[5] but that decision now attracts a right of appeal on the merits under section 82 of the Nationality, Immigration and Asylum Act 2002.[6]

[1]   Immigration Act 1971, s 6(5)(a), as amended by Race Relations Amendment Act 2000.
[2]   See *R v Edgehill* [1963] 1 QB 593, [1963] 1 All ER 181, CCA on a similar provision in the repealed Commonwealth Immigrants Act 1962.
[3]   *R v Lynch* [1965] 3 All ER 925, [1966] 1 WLR 92, CCA.
[4]   Under Immigration and Asylum Act 1999, s 63.
[5]   The right of appeal on asylum grounds attached to the Secretary of State's refusal to revoke a deportation order made on the criminal court's recommendation, under Immigration and Asylum Act 1999, s 69(4). The human rights and race discrimination appeal was conferred

by Immigration and Asylum Act 1999, s 65, a wide, free-standing right of appeal against any decision relating to entitlement to enter or remain in the UK.
6   Section 82(2)(j).

15.25 No court may recommend a person for deportation unless he or she has been given seven days' notice in writing.[1] If the notice has not been served in time, the hearing may be adjourned, even after conviction, to enable the notice to be served.[2] The court needs a 'full inquiry into all the circumstances' and counsel should be invited to address the court specifically on the issue of a recommendation.[3] Where a court decides to make a recommendation, full reasons for the decision should be given, in fairness to the offender and in order to assist the Secretary of State with the ultimate decision as to whether to proceed with deportation.[4] A failure by the sentencing court to provide any, or any adequate, reasoning does not automatically lead to a recommendation being quashed, however, since the Court of Appeal has the power to give its own reasons where it considers deportation appropriate.[5]

1   Immigration Act 1971, s 6(2). The proper course is to attach the acknowledgment of service of the notice to the case file, to avoid later disputes: *R v Edgehill* [1963] 1 QB 593, [1963] 1 All ER 181, but this is not essential, and service may be inferred from strong circumstantial evidence: *R v Rodney* [1996] 2 Cr App Rep (S) 230; *R v Adomako* [1998] EWCA Crim 3019.
2   Immigration Act 1971, s 6(2).
3   *R v Nazari* (1980) 71 Cr App Rep 87; *R v Escauriaza* (1987) 9 Cr App Rep (S) 542; *R v Omojudi* (1992)13 Cr App Rep (S) 346; *R v Frank* (1991) 13 Cr App Rep (S) 500.
4   *R v Nazari* above; *R v Rodney* [1998] INLR 118, [1996] 2 Cr App Rep (S) 230; *R v Bozat* [1997] 1 Cr App Rep (S) 270; *R v Dosso* [1998] EWCA Crim 3180; *R v Ntua* [1999] EWCA Crim 1520.
5   *R v Bozat* above; *R v Green (Steven)* [1997] EWCA Crim 2661; *R v Dudeye* [1998] 2 Cr App Rep (S) 430.

Guidelines for criminal courts

15.26 The power to make a recommendation must be exercised judicially and is concerned with criminal behaviour rather than the enforcement of an immigration policy.[1] The court is not under an obligation to recommend deportation in serious cases concerning evasion of immigration controls (such as forging passports or organising illegal entry)[2] and the question whether to recommend deportation should be decided quite independently of the immigration status of the offender.[3] The basic statement of principle to guide the criminal courts was set out in the decision in *R v Caird*.[4] In quashing a recommendation for deportation against one of the defendants, the court stated that it wished to emphasise:

> 'that the courts when considering a recommendation for deportation are normally concerned simply with crime committed and the individual's past record and the question as to what is their effect on the question of potential detriment to this country of the appellant remaining here. It does not embark, and indeed is in no position to embark, upon the issue as to what is likely to be his life if he goes back to his country of origin. That is a matter for the Home Secretary.'

Caird was cited with approval and amplified in the leading case of *R v Nazari*,[5] where the widely differing cases of four appellants were dealt with

15.26 *Deportation and Repatriation*

together and the Court of Appeal set out a series of guidelines for courts. The criminal courts are concerned with potential detriment to the UK, and assessing potential detriment is a question of fact in each case, involving consideration of matters other than the gravity of the offence. Detriment refers to the potential harm caused by the defendant's criminal behaviour, and not such matters as receipt of welfare benefits[6] or immigration status.[7] A comparatively minor offence will not make continued presence a detriment;[8] the important issue is the defendant's likely future conduct.[9] The likelihood of re-offending is usually relevant; indeed the EC criteria have to all intents and purposes been assimilated into domestic criminal law.[10]

[1] See Arthur Rogerson 'Deportation' [1963] PL 305 at 309; Graham Zellick 'The Power of The Courts To Recommend Deportation' [1973] Crim LR 612; the Wilson Committee on Immigration Appeals (1967) Cmnd 2739, para 94.

[2] *R v Akan* (1972) 56 Cr App Rep 716, CA; *R v Anno-Firempong* [1997] EWCA Crim 1054 (possession of a false passport boarding an aircraft for Canada); *R v Dosso* [1998] EWCA Crim 3180 (assisting illegal entry).

[3] The relevant considerations were the offender's history, particularly criminal history, and the gravity of the offence: *R v Khandri*, 24 April 1979, Bridge LJ. A similar view was expressed in *Miller v Lenton* (1981) 3 Cr App Rep (S) 171; *R v Nunu* (1991) 12 Cr App Rep (S) 752, CA. See also *R v Stefanski, R v Kwiek* [2002] EWCA Crim 1810.

[4] (1970) 54 Cr App Rep 499, CA.

[5] [1980] 3 All ER 880 at 885–886, 71 Cr App Rep 87.

[6] *R v Serry* (1980) 2 Cr App Rep (S) 336, [1980] LS Gaz R 1181, CA.

[7] See fn 3 above.

[8] *R v Kraus* (1982) 4 Cr App Rep (S) 113, CA; *R v Compassi* (1987) 9 Cr App Rep (S) 270, CA; *R v Okelola* (1992) 13 Cr App Rep (S) 560, CA. In *R v Williams (Vivian)* [1996] EWCA Crim 354, the Court of Appeal treated sexual abuse on and impregnation of a 12-year-old stepdaughter as a relatively minor offence not meriting deportation, although such offences are deemed to merit at least ten years' absence from the UK by the Home Office: see IDI Dec 00, Ch 13, Annex A, 'Period normally appropriate for revocation', and such a decision is, one hopes, inconceivable today. However, a conspiracy to defraud (cashing giros) was deemed sufficiently serious in *R v Lembo, R v Mobonda, R v Mukwete* [2003] EWCA Crim 3246. In *R v Tangestani-Najad* [1998] EWCA Crim 1970, assault occasioning actual bodily harm on a tenant by a landlord with previous convictions was deemed not serious enough to merit deportation.

[9] *R v David* (1980) 2 Cr App Rep (S) 362, CA; *R v Tshuma* (1981) 3 Cr App Rep (S) 97; *R v Altawel* (1981) 3 Cr App Rep (S) 281 and other cases cited in Thomas *Current Sentencing Practice* Part K.

[10] *R v Escauriaza* (1987) 87 Cr App Rep 344, CA; *R v Spura* (1988) 10 Cr App Rep (S) 376, CA. Note the different approach under Immigration Act 1971, s 3(5)(a), for which see *R)on the application of Samaroo) v Secretary of State for the Home Department* (CO 4973/1999) (20 December 2000, unreported) (affd [2001] EWCA Civ 1139, [2001] UKHRR 1150, [2002] INLR 55).

15.27 The second guideline from *Nazari* and *Caird* is that the (criminal) courts are not concerned with the political system in the offender's home country, or with what is likely to be the offender's life there.[1] The guidance was adopted because of the difficulties and undesirability of their making such an assessment, particularly if there may be a long period of imprisonment between the conviction and the execution of the deportation order, during which time there may be a change of circumstances.[2] In the previous edition of this work[3] we suggested that this policy would need to be modified in the light of the court's primary obligation under the Human Rights Act 1998.[4] The Court of Appeal has taken a different view, generally refusing to embark on investigation into conditions awaiting proposed deportees in the home country and leaving these matters to the Secretary of State.[5] Given the introduction of a right of appeal against the subsequent decision of the Secretary of State,[6] this arrangement is compatible with the UK's obligations under Article 13 of the ECHR.[7]

1   *R v Caird* (1970) 54 Cr App Rep 499, CA; *R v Nazari* [1980] 3 All ER 880, 71 Cr App Rep 87. The policy was subject to exceptions, where there was cogent evidence of the consequences of deportation, and where the anticipated deportation was reasonably proximate to the decision: see eg *R v Dudeye (Said)* [1998] 2 Cr App Rep (S) 430 (recommendation against young Somali refugee for robbery quashed in light of circumstances in Somalia).
2   *R v Uddin* [1971] Crim LR 663, CA; *R v Caird* above.
3   Fifth edition, 15.27.
4   As a public authority under Human Rights Act 1998, s 6: see 8.16 above.
5   See *R v Chen (Ling)* [2001] EWCA Crim 885; *R v Lembo, R v Mobonda, R v Mukwete* [2003] EWCA Crim 3246.
6   Nationality, Immigration and Asylum Act 2002, s 82(2)(j) (from 1 April 2003); previously (from 2 October 2000) a decision to act on a recommendation was appealable on human rights grounds under Immigration and Asylum Act 1999, s 65, and on asylum grounds by seeking revocation of a deportation order and appealing refusal under s 69(4).
7   Before 2 October 2000 the Secretary of State's decision to act on a recommendation could be judicially reviewed as *Wednesbury* unreasonable if it violated fundamental rights: see *R v Secretary of State for the Home Department, ex p M* [1999] Imm AR 548 (decision to deport AIDS sufferer following court recommendation). For the effect of Art 13 of ECHR see 8.100 above.

15.28   The third *Nazari* guideline[1] is that the criminal courts will have regard to the effect of any recommendation on innocent third parties. The courts have no desire to break up families and force spouses to choose between the interests of their children or the future of their marriage.[2] The guideline reflects the need for compliance with Article 8 ECHR; the courts will consider whether deportation would result in interference with family or private life (ie whether the proposed deportee has family or other ties in the UK which would be interfered with by deportation, eg if family members could not reasonably be expected to accompany the deportee abroad) and if such interference would result, whether it is proportionate to the legitimate aim of preventing crime or disorder – which requires balancing matters such as the prevalence and gravity of the crime and its impact on society against the family or private life considerations. The reported cases show that the Court of Appeal has generally applied this guideline with care and in a more generous spirit than have the appellate authorities in 'conducive to the public good' deportations.[3] The Court has however held that in certain circumstances the sheer gravity of an offence, absent the propensity to repeat it, can override family or private life interests under Article 8(2) of the ECHR.[4]

1   [1980] 3 All ER 880 at 886, 71 Cr App Rep 87.
2   *R v Craviato* (1990) 12 Cr App Rep (S) 71; *R v Odendaal* (1991) 13 Cr App Rep (S) 341; *R v Shittu* (1992) 14 Cr App Rep (S) 283.
3   See eg *R v Ifekwe* [1997] EWCA Crim 1691; *R v Mounganga* [1999] EWCA Crim 1706; *R v Zand-Lashami* [1999] EWCA Crim 1723; *R v Stefanski, Kwiek* [2002] EWCA Crim 1810; and 15.15–15.17 above.
4   *R (on the application of Samaroo) v Secretary of State for the Home Department* [2001] EWCA Civ 1139, [2002] INLR 55, a judgment by the civil division of the court, reviewing the Secretary of State's decision rather than hearing an appeal against a Crown Court judge's recommendation.

15.29   *Nazari* did not deal with the position of EC nationals and others deriving rights from EC law,[1] and the restrictions on the court's powers to recommend deportation (see chapter 7 above). But the courts have remedied this by indicating that British law provides the same standards as EC law and so there has to be a continuing threat to some identifiable element of public interest that requires deportation.[2] Thus a recommendation for deportation may be made against a person protected by the EC Treaty, provided the conditions set down in Articles 3 and 9 of Council Directive (EEC) 64/221 have been met.[3]

1   Such as Turkish nationals enjoying rights under the Ankara Agreement: Case C-340/97 *Nazli v Stadt Nürnberg* [2000] ECR I-957.
2   *R v Escauriaza* (1987) 87 Cr App Rep 344, CA; *R v Spura* (1988) 10 Cr App Rep (S) 376, CA.
3   Article 3 of Council Directive (EEC) 64/221 provides that measures of expulsion taken on grounds of public policy or public security must be based exclusively on the personal conduct of the individual, and that previous criminal convictions should not in themselves constitute grounds for taking such measures. See *Bonsignore v Oberstadt-direktor der Stadt, Köln* Case 67/74 [1975] ECR 297, [1975] 1 CMLR 472, ECJ; Case C-348/96 *Calfa (Criminal proceedings against)* [1999] ECR I-11; Case C-340/97 *Nazli v Stadt Nürnberg* [2000] ECR I-957, ECJ. Article 9 provides for review by an independent competent authority before expulsion. See further 7.145 above.

The decision to deport: consideration of merits

15.30 Whether or not a criminal court recommends deportation, the decision to deport is one for the Secretary of State. The general rule for deportations is contained in HC 395, para 364. It applies to all decisions to deport. It reads:

'In considering whether deportation is the right course on the merits, the public interest will be balanced against any compassionate circumstances of the case. While each case will be considered in the light of the particular circumstances, the aim is the exercise of the power of deportation that is consistent and fair as between one person and another, although one case will rarely be identical with another in all material respects. In cases to which [the transitional provisions] apply,[1] deportation will normally be the proper course for a person who has failed to comply with or has contravened a condition or has remained without authority. Before a decision to deport is reached the Secretary of State will take into account all relevant factors known to him including:
  (i)   age;
  (ii)   length of residence in the UK;
  (iii) strength of connections with the UK;
  (iv)   personal history, including character, conduct and employment record;
  (v)   domestic circumstances;
  (vi)   previous criminal record and the nature of any offence of which the person has been convicted;
  (vii) compassionate circumstances;
  (viii) any representations received on the person's behalf.'

1   HC 395, para 363A, inserted by Cm 4851 (transitional deportation of overstayers): see 15.42 below.

Consistent and fair

15.31 This rule indicates that the task in a deportation case is one of discretion rather than the application of a precise code having mandatory effect. Secondly, in exercising discretion, the task of the decision maker is essentially one of reaching a fair balance between the public interest in the proper exercise of immigration control and the personal interests of the proposed deportee. The aim is an exercise of power which is proportionate and fair. Thirdly, although the paragraph is phrased in terms of interests rather than rights, many of the relevant factors, especially those pertaining to the deportee, are likely to comprise justiciable human rights. Fourthly, the assessment of the factors to be taken into account in gauging the strength or weakness of the public interest, is a not dissimilar exercise to that involved under Article 8(2) of the ECHR. The same goes for the determination of proportionality under paragraph 364. Fifthly, this jurisdiction has existed since 1969 and no question of deference to the Secretary of State arose prior to the coming into force of the Human Rights Act 1998 in October 2000.[1] The paragraph characterises the essential issue in most cases but it is not intended to be exhaustive or comprehensive. It is not designed to restrict what are relevant factors or to limit the consideration of factors simply to compassionate ones.[2] In *Idrish*[3] the Tribunal held that the strength of the public interest in deporting could and should be assessed in the light of all circumstances. The reference to the power being exercised consistently and fairly as between one person and another is more than a mere requirement that the Home Office apply the Immigration Rules to all deportees,[4] and means that they must be even-handed between a particular applicant and others, and disparate treatment may found a successful appeal.[5] Where one party who has played the principal part in some criminal enterprise is allowed to stay, it would be inconsistent and unfair to allow another whose involvement is minor to be deported, unless there is some other weighty or distinguishing feature in their two cases.[6] Such comparisons of individual cases will occur relatively rarely because, as the rule says, one case is rarely identical with another. But where the minister makes general statements as to how the power will be exercised, such statements can be relied on by an appellant. The Secretary of State has published policies precluding enforcement action against nationals of countries which are active war zones;[7] indicating when indefinite leave will be granted to failed asylum seeking families;[8] and setting out when marriage to a British citizen, or the birth of children, or a period of residence in the UK, will normally prevent enforcement action.[9] In judicial review terms the publication of a policy will no doubt give rise to a legitimate expectation that it will be applied consistently as between all applicants who apply to regularise their position,[10] and in any event unexplained departure from it would be inconsistent and unfair, and therefore irrational.[11]

1 Compare *Singh (Bakhtaur) v Immigration Appeal Tribunal* [1986] 2 All ER 721, [1986] 1 WLR 910, [1986] Imm AR 352, HL, with *R (on the application of N) v Secretary of State for the Home Department* [2004] EWCA Civ 1094, [2004] INLR 612.
2 *Singh (Bakhtaur) v Immigration Appeal Tribunal*, above.
3 *Idrish* [1985] Imm AR 155, IAT.
4 *Alsawaf v Secretary of State for the Home Department* [1988] Imm AR 410, CA.
5 See *R v Secretary of State for the Home Department, ex p Sheikh (Shafat Ahmed)*, (DC/260/81) (4 February 1982), QBD, in which the inconsistent treatment of two brothers, both innocent beneficiaries of corruptly obtained leave, founded a successful challenge.

6 *R v Immigration Appeal Tribunal, ex p Alavi-Veighoe* (CO 1431/1988) (20 July 1989, unreported), QBD; *Secretary of State for the Home Department v Yasin* [1995] Imm AR 118, CA; *Arshad* (9888), IAT; *Cardona* (14949), IAT.
7 Operational Enforcement Manual 'Deportation' para 12.3.
8 'One-off exercise to allow families who have been in the UK for three or more years to stay', 24 October 2003, APU Notice 4/2003. The concession does not apply to a family where the principal applicant or any of the dependants has a criminal conviction, an anti-social behaviour order or sex offender order; has made or attempted to make an asylum claim in the UK in more than one identity, presents a security risk or falls within the scope of Art 1F of the Refugee Convention (see 12.88 above), or whose presence in the UK is otherwise not conducive to the public good: ibid.
9 DP2/93, DP4/95, DP3/96, DP5/96, DP069/99. The application of the wrong policy on the effect of marriage (DP3/96 instead of the more generous DP2/93) led to a successful appeal in *Aramide v Secretary of State for the Home Department* (C/2000/0288) (24 July 2000, unreported). See 11.74 above.
10 *Khan v Immigration Appeal Tribunal* [1984] Imm AR 68, CA (refusal of entry clearance); *Gyeabour* [1989] Imm AR 94, IAT; *Hussain and Begum v Immigration Appeal Tribunal* [1991] Imm AR 413, CA; *Andrews (Joseph)* [2002] UKIAT 07598. Many previous concessionary policies are now incorporated into the immigration rules (eg unmarried partners, domestic violence, access to children, long residence); many (but not all) are published in the IDI on the Home Office website.
11 *R v Secretary of State for the Home Department, ex p Amankwah* [1994] Imm AR 240; *R v Secretary of State for the Home Department, ex p Urmaza* [1996] COD 479, (1996) Times, 23 July; See 11.74 above. However a policy is not a rule, and need not be followed rigidly, provided reasons are given for not following it in a particular case: *Secretary of State for the Home Department v Hastrup* [1996] Imm AR 616, CA.

All relevant circumstances

15.32 The listed circumstances in paragraph 364 include everything that is properly persuasive for or against deportation, including the background situation in the country to which deportees are to be deported.[1] The impact of the proposed deportation on third parties, whether family,[2] work colleagues, employees,[3] police[4] or members of a local community, is always a relevant circumstance and it does not have to be squeezed into the category of compassionate circumstances.[5] Only what is irrelevant to a decision to deport should be excluded (such as the threat of industrial action or other forms of unrest either in support of or against deportation, matters to which it would be improper for the minister to have regard).[6] Thus, the listed circumstances which may militate against deportation are far broader than simple compassionate circumstances; many go to the public interest side of the balancing exercise involved in every decision to deport under paragraph 364, suggesting that the public interest in removal and exclusion in the exercise of immigration control is a much more flexible concept than the case-law under Article 8(2) of ECHR would suggest. In domestic law there has long since been a policy to remove overstayers and those who breach their conditions of entry; but in carrying out the balancing exercise, decision makers and any reviewing appellate authority have to gauge the strength or weakness of the public interest in applying the policy against all the relevant circumstances. The exercise they perform is a more sophisticated one than just putting the policy on one side of the scales like a sack of potatoes and demanding to the appellant 'match that with your compassionate circumstances, if you can'. The contrast with human rights law under Article 8(2) of ECHR is often quite stark. There, the need for immigration control and the different policies embodied in the legislation and the Rules is often cast uncritically into the scales as the constitutionally unassailable work of the elected government, which the courts can only peer at timidly from under the long skirts of deference, citing the need for constitutional propriety, better expertise and so forth.[7] In fact the assessment of expulsion under immigration control is rarely, if ever, to do with a challenge to policy, but whether a statutory discretion has been exercised too harshly in the particular circumstances of the case. The framer of paragraph 364, for all the jumbled structure of the paragraph, has understood the position well and has attempted to direct the minds of the immigration official and of the appellate judges to the proper fulfilment of their task.[8] Perhaps those grappling with justification of human rights breaches in immigration expulsion cases might do the same.

[1] *Kamara (Elizabeth)* (20155); *Kamara (Mohammed)* (21814); *Kapusnik* (00TH01897).
[2] *Tantono* [2002] UKIAT 00356, where the effect of deportation on the children of a long-term resident convicted of manslaughter and false imprisonment in exceptional circumstances prevented his deportation.
[3] *Leong* (5055), IAT where deportation would have resulted in a loss of employment for persons settled here.
[4] But the desire of police officers to retain the services of a valuable informer was held not decisive against deportation in *CM v Secretary of State for the Home Department* [1997] Imm AR 336.
[5] *Singh (Bakhtaur) v Immigration Appeal Tribunal* [1986] 2 All ER 721, [1986] 1 WLR 910, [1986] Imm AR 352, HL.
[6] *Singh (Bakhtaur)* fn 5 above; *CM* fn 4 above.
[7] See chapter 8 above.
[8] Aided by the interpretations given by the courts: see per Lord Bridge in *Singh (Bakhtaur)* (fn 5 above).

15.33 Where representations have been made, the minister must have regard to them.[1] The representations may be ones made during the course of an interview (although provided there is an opportunity to put forward compassionate or other relevant factors, fairness will not generally require such an interview),[2] or may take the form of letters from members of Parliament or members of the public, or petitions.[3] If there is no opportunity to make representations before the decision is taken, this is not fatal since on appeal, the appellate authorities can hear evidence of any factor in existence at the date of the decision even though unknown to the Home Office.[4]

[1] HC 395, para 364. But the desire of police officers to retain the services of an informer cannot be decisive: *CM* [1997] Imm AR 336.
[2] In *Afful* [1986] Imm AR 230, the Tribunal held that an interview was required; in *Agyemang* [1988] Imm AR 519 that it was not. Even the opportunity to rebut any adverse conclusions of fact before a decision is reached is not essential provided there is a right of appeal.
[3] Such representations may be of great value, see eg *Singh (Bakhtaur) v Immigration Appeal Tribunal* [1986] 2 All ER 721, [1986] Imm AR 352, HL above.
[4] *R v Immigration Appeal Tribunal, ex p Hassanin* [1987] 1 All ER 74, [1986] 1 WLR 1448, CA.

Age and length of residence in the UK

15.34 Generally speaking, Home Office policy is to consider persons for deportation in their own right (as opposed to family members) if they are aged

15.34 *Deportation and Repatriation*

between 16 and 65.[1] Strength of connections with the UK and length of residence are matters of degree. Past UK citizenship (being a former UK and Colonies citizen) would be of little significance as it would not necessarily amount to a connection with the UK as opposed to a former colony. But a past claim to the right of abode may be of weight.[2] Length of residence is a stronger factor if the residence has been lawful, but the fact that a proposed deportee has or had no claim to remain in the country under the Rules does not mean that he or she must be deported,[3] and a marriage or other relationship which has not satisfied the Immigration Rules for the purposes of settlement may nevertheless give rise to compassionate factors or family life considerations militating against deportation.[4] In *Aramide*,[5] the Court of Appeal held that thirteen years' lawful residence as a visitor, a student, a spouse and with indefinite leave, a British wife and three British citizen children could not rationally be described as 'minimal ties to the UK'.[6] The Home Office policy on long residence, sometimes known as the 'ten year rule' and the 'fourteen year rule', is now incorporated into the immigration rules,[7] but itself includes a public interest proviso in which all the listed factors relevant to deportation (15.30 above) must be considered. See 16.47 below.

1   IDI Sep 01, Ch 13, s 1, para 3.1.
2   *Lawrence* (3171).
3   *Idrish* [1985] Imm AR 155; *Singh (Bakhtaur) v Immigration Appeal Tribunal* [1986] 2 All ER 721, [1986] Imm AR 352, HL.
4   *R v Secretary of State for the Home Department, ex p Arora* [1990] Imm AR 89, QBD.
5   *Aramide v Secretary of State for the Home Department* (C/2000/0288) (24 July 2000, unreported), CA.
6   For an example of a successful appeal on grounds of length of residence and private and family life, see *Antwi* [2002] UKIAT 06668 (an overstayer case).
7   HC 395 para 276A–D. The IDI state that generally speaking, deportation will be considered where the person has been in the UK for less than 14 years, or where residence is more than 14 years but there is a poor immigration history, e g concerted efforts to avoid detection, or conviction of a serious criminal offence: IDI Sep 01, Ch 13, s 1, para 3.2.

Recommendations by criminal court

15.35 In considering whether to deport an offender in respect of whom a recommendation has been made by the courts,[1] the factors to be taken into account by the Secretary of State in exercising his or her discretion are the same as in conducive to the public good cases.[2] Although a recommendation by a sentencing judge carries weight and may afford a presumption in favour of deportation, and although the reasoning of the sentencing judge is a material factor for the Secretary of State, the recommendation simply initiates the Secretary of State's task; it is essentially dealing with an assessment made, when the offender is sentenced, of the potential detriment to the UK of the offender's criminal behaviour and, in particular, his or her likely future conduct.[3] By the time the Secretary of State makes a decision, the offender will be near the end of his or her sentence, and may be rehabilitated and at little or no risk of re-offending. Clearly the sentencing judge's reasons and decision should not be substituted for what the Secretary of State has to decide.[4] But the fact that the sentencing judge made no reference to a recommendation when sentencing should not lead to the inference that he or she decided deportation was inappropriate;[5] and even a reasoned refusal of a recommendation, or a decision by the Criminal Division of the Court of Appeal to quash a recommendation made by the sentencing judge, does not create a presumption that the Secretary of State must follow, because of the wider range of factors considered by him or her. In this situation, however, the Secretary of State must apply the principle of proportionality. The court's judgment is a relevant matter, and reasons must be given for taking a different view.[6] Convictions which are reported to the Home Office by police include those where a recommendation for deportation is made, convictions for an offence under the Immigration Act 1971,[7] convictions for violence against the person or drugs resulting in a custodial sentence (including a suspended sentence) or hospital order; convictions for any offence resulting in a custodial sentence of 12 months or more.[8] A decision to deport should not usually be based on spent convictions.[9]

1   See 15.23–15.29 above.
2   HC 395, para 364.
3   *R v Caird* (1970) 54 Cr App Rep 499, CA.
4   *R v Secretary of State for the Home Department, ex p Dinc* [1999] Imm AR 380, [1999] INLR 256, CA.
5   *Jaroudy* [2002] UKIAT 06653.
6   *M v Secretary of State for the Home Department* [2003] EWCA Civ 146, [2003] INLR 306.
7   For such offences, see 14.30ff above.
8   IDI, Ch 13, s 4, para 2. Police also have discretion to report any other conviction in exceptional circumstances.
9   IDI, Ch 13, s 4, para 5.4. The IDI sets out the relevant provisions of the Rehabilitation of Offenders Act 1974. The exception to non-reliance on spent convictions is where justice cannot otherwise be done, e g where the person has delayed enforcement action by going to ground.

Human rights considerations

15.36 The Immigration Rules expressly provide that a deportation order will not be made against a person with a well-founded fear of persecution,[1] or a person whose removal would be in breach of the UK's obligations under the ECHR.[2] Deportation will not take place where the consequences of return would be disproportionately severe,[3] although the Secretary of State may revoke indefinite leave to remain where the person would be liable to deportation but cannot be deported for legal reasons (ie, because deportation would be in breach of the Human Rights Convention).[4] Previously, the Convention had been held not to be part of the relevant circumstances to be taken into account in considering whether deportation is the right course on the merits,[5] but in practice it had become so in cases involving the deportation of spouses and parents of persons settled in the UK, through the policy adopted in purported compliance with the ECHR after *Berrehab*.[6] Although the Secretary of State now routinely refers directly to Article 8 ECHR,[7] on which the policies DP2/93 and its successors DP4/95, DP3/96 and DP5/96 (as amended) were based, the policies themselves are still relevant to a decision to deport.[8]

1   HC 395, para 380. This does not prevent the deportation of a refugee, simply because he or she has in the past been granted refugee status, if by his or her criminal activities the protection of the Refugee Convention has been lost: *Raziastaraie v Secretary of State for the Home Department* [1995] Imm AR 459, CA, or if leave to remain was never granted

and the circumstances in which he or she was recognised as a refugee have ceased to exist: *N (Kenya)* [2004] UKIAT 00009. But no removal could take place if a real risk engaging the ECHR exists.

2   HC 395 para 380.
3   Home Office policy is not to take enforcement action against nationals of countries which are active war zones: Operational Enforcement Manual 'Deportation' para 12.3. See also *Kim* (11041) (Korean national convicted of several homicides, appeal allowed on basis of double jeopardy and possibility of execution); *Oyedeji* (19618) (drugs, serious possibility of arrest and charge on return, which would be double jeopardy, and life-threatening detention conditions); *Tantono* [2002] UKIAT 00356 (human rights situation in Indonesia); and see cases on Art 3 ECHR at 8.50ff above and on Art 8 at 8.79ff.
4   Nationality, Immigration and Asylum Act 2002, s 76(1).
5   *Chundawadra v Immigration Appeal Tribunal* [1988] Imm AR 161, CA.
6   *Berrehab v Netherlands* (1988) 11 EHRR 322, ECHR where the expulsion of a Moroccan father enjoying regular contact with his Dutch child was held a disproportionate interference with the parties' rights to respect for family life. See also *Ciliz v Netherlands* [2000] 2 FLR 469, ECtHR. DP2/93 was held compliant with Art 8 ECHR in *R v Secretary of State for the Home Department, ex p Gangadeen and Khan* [1998] INLR 206, CA. See further 8.79, 11.74 and 15.31 above.
7   The leading case on Art 8 in the context of deportation on conducive grounds (for criminal convictions) is *R (on the application of Samaroo) v Secretary of State for the Home Department* [2001] EWCA Civ 1139, [2002] INLR 55 (see 15.15–15.17 above). The earlier case of *B v Secretary of State for the Home Department* [2000] Imm AR 478, [2000] INLR 361, in which the Court of Appeal held disproportionate the deportation of a long resident EU national for sexual offences against his children, held that it was for the courts to determine as a matter of law whether the decision was proportionate. B was disapproved in subsequent Court of Appeal and Immigration Appeal Tribunal jurisprudence, which held that the courts' function was to determine whether the decision of the Secretary of State on proportionality was 'within a range of reasonable responses'. But the House of Lords, recognising the appellate authorities' fact-finding function, restored to them the task of deciding the issue of proportionality for themselves on all the evidence in *R (on the application of Razgar) v Secretary of State for the Home Department* [2004] UKHL 27, [2004] 3 WLR 58, at paras 20 (per Lord Bingham) and 60 (per Lady Hale), and their decision was followed by the Court of Appeal in *Huang, Abu-Qulbain, Kashmiri v Secretary of State for the Home Department* [2005] EWCA Civ 105. See 8.18–8.21 above. For a careful analysis of the private life issues engaged by deportation on conducive grounds (criminal conduct) of someone with long residence in the UK see *Tadesse* [2002] UKIAT 06378; see also *Oviasogie* [2002] UKIAT; *N (Kenya)* [2004] UKIAT 00009 (upheld by the Court of Appeal at [2004] EWCA Civ 1094, [2004] INLR 612).
8   See eg *K (Russia)* [2003] UKIAT 82 (March 2004, unreported), where the Tribunal held that Home Office policies were 'in accordance with the law' for the purpose of Art 8(2) (false asylum claim deprived appellant of the benefit of the concession). See also *Aramide v Secretary of State for the Home Department* (C/2000/0288) (24 July 2000, unreported).

Family deportations

15.37 The decision to deport family members[1] must be taken independently and considered on its merits rather than following as a matter of course.[2] Apart from the usual considerations which apply to all deportations, the following additional considerations apply to family deportations:

(i)   the ability of the spouse to maintain himself or herself and any children in the UK, or to be maintained by relatives or friends without charge to public funds for the foreseeable future;

(ii)   in the case of a child of school age, the effect of removal on his or her education;[3]

(iii) the practicability of any plans for a child's care and maintenance in this country if one or both of the child's parents were deported; and

(iv) any representations made by or on behalf of the spouse or child.[4]

Where a decision is made to deport someone as a member of the principal deportee's family, the right of appeal will be notified and at the same time the procedure of voluntary departure will be explained.[5] Deported family members may be able to seek re-admission to the UK under the Immigration Rules when a child reaches 18, when the marriage to the principal deportee comes to an end;[6] or when the deportation order against the principal deportee is revoked.

[1] See 15.21 above.
[2] *Wah (Yau Yak) v Home Office* [1982] Imm AR 16
[3] *Ozter* [1978] Imm AR 137, IAT; *Mustafa* [1979–80] Imm AR 33, IAT. See now ECHR, Protocol 1, Art 2, and see *R (on the application of Holub) v Secretary of State for the Home Department* [2001] Imm AR 282, CA (no breach of right to education to remove child to Poland, which had a well-established education system).
[4] HC 395, para 367.
[5] HC 395, para 368.
[6] HC 395, para 389.

Procedure and appeals

Making and notifying a decision

15.38 In two of the three cases where a person is liable to deportation, the initiative is taken by the Secretary of State for the Home Department. Save where a decision is required by statute to be taken by the Secretary of State personally,[1] administrative arrangements can be made for departmental officers to exercise these powers. The Secretary of State is entitled to act through departmental civil servants, pursuant to the *Carltona* principles,[2] including immigration officers.[3] Decisions to deport on the grounds of public good other than political cases, and decisions to deport family members, are taken by the officials at the enforcement section of the Home Office at Croydon. A deportation order may not be made on the recommendation of a court while an appeal against the recommendation, or against conviction, is pending or can be brought (or in Scotland, for 28 days after the recommendation),[4] but subject to this the Secretary of State may choose when to act on the recommendation.[5] Now that Parliament has given all proposed deportees a right of appeal against the Secretary of State's decision,[6] the practice in relation to those recommended for deportation and those not recommended is likely to converge. In all criminal cases, the Secretary of State waits until near the end of the sentence,[7] and then reviews the case in the light of any changed circumstances (which might include evidence of rehabilitation as well as changed domestic circumstances and changes in the situation in the country of destination). For this purpose representations are normally sought from the proposed deportee before the decision is reached.[8]

[1] Under eg Nationality, Immigration and Asylum Act 2002 s 97. The decision need not be signed personally: *Re Khan (Amanullah)* [1986] Imm AR 485.
[2] *Carltona Ltd v Works Comrs* [1943] 2 All ER 560, CA.
[3] *R v Secretary of State for the Home Department, ex p Oladehinde* [1991] 1 AC 254, [1990] 3 All ER 393, [1990] 3 WLR 797, HL.
[4] Immigration Act 1971, s 6(6).

5 R (on the application of Sezek) v Secretary of State for the Home Department [2001] EWCA Civ 1139, [2001] UKHRR 1150, [2002] INLR 55.
6 Nationality, Immigration and Asylum Act 2002, s 82(2)(j).
7 This is because in most cases, the risk of re-offending, which is generally assessed by prison staff with reference to evidence of the proposed deportee's performance in rehabilitation programmes etc, is relevant to the balancing exercise. For the effect of lapse of time, see Case 131/79 R v Secretary of State for the Home Department, ex p Santillo [1980] ECR 1585, [1980] 2 CMLR 308.
8 Ayo v Immigration Appeal Tribunal [1990] Imm AR 461, CA. Inviting further representations from a deportee does not mean that the original decision is flawed: R v Secretary of State for the Home Department, ex p Amoa [1992] Imm AR 218, QBD.

15.39 A decision to deport must be notified in accordance with the Immigration (Notices) Regulations 2003,[1] and the notice must include or be accompanied by a statement of the reasons for the decision, indicate the country or territory to which it is proposed to remove the person, and indicate the right of appeal and how it may be exercised.[2] Amplification of the reasons for a decision to deport is permissible consequent to notification,[3] although a decision-maker may not switch to a different statutory category.[4] The appellate authority may not allow an appeal solely on the basis of a defect in the notice, if the decision itself was in accordance with the law and the rules.[5] The Regulations allow service of the notice either at an address provided for correspondence by the person or his or her representative, or (where there is no such correspondence address) at the last known or usual home or business address of either the proposed deportee *or* the representative.[6] Service may be achieved by fax transmission in addition to the traditional methods of hand and post (recorded delivery).[7] Under the old rules, if the Secretary of State or his officers had no knowledge of the whereabouts or place of abode of a prospective deportee, service could be dispensed with altogether, and there was no necessity for re-service of the notice if the deportee was subsequently located.[8] Although deemed intra vires by the courts,[9] the power was abandoned in 1986 as unfair and ineffective.[10] It has been revived in the 2003 Regulations; where the person's whereabouts are unknown and the decision-maker has no address or only a defective, false or out-of-date address for him or her, and no representative appears to be acting, notice is deemed given when it is put on the file with a note of the circumstances.[11] When the subject of the notice is located, he or she is to be given a copy notice, but this will not generate the right to an in-time appeal.[12] See 18.83 below.

1 SI 2003/658, reg 4. The Regulations apply to deportation appeals generated under s 15 of the Immigration Act 1971 which have arisen as a result of the regularisation procedures under s 9 of the Immigration and Asylum Act 1999: see reg 3. A decision to deport following a recommendation by a judge (s 3(6) Immigration Act 1971) has been appealable only since 1 April 2003 (by Nationality, Immigration and Asylum Act 2002, s 82(2)(j), and prior to that date, notice of the decision was not required under the corresponding notices regulations (SI 2000/2246) unless an asylum claim or human rights allegation was made.
2 SI 2003/658, reg 5.
3 R v Immigration Appeal Tribunal, ex p Hubbard [1985] Imm AR 110; R v Immigration Appeal Tribunal, ex p Dukobo [1990] Imm AR 390.
4 Wah (Yau Yak) v Home Office [1982] Imm AR 16, CA; R v Immigration Appeal Tribunal, ex p Mehmet (Ekrem) [1977] Imm AR 56, QBD; Parsaiyan v Visa Officer, Karachi [1986] Imm AR 155. For further discussion see 18.111 below.
5 R v Immigration Appeal Tribunal, ex p Jeyeanthan [2000] 1 WLR 354, [1999] Imm AR 10, [1999] INLR 241, CA.

6   SI 2003/658, reg 7(1)(c)(ii). The election is that of the Secretary of State, so a notice may be
     sent to the deportee's last known address even if it is known that he or she no longer lives
     there: *Singh (Pargan) v Secretary of State for the Home Department* [1993] Imm AR 112,
     (although in such a case, there is the option of 'service on the file' in accordance with
     reg 7(2): see below). Service at the last known address has been held valid under previous
     regulations despite the person's request that notices be served on the representative: *Tongo
     v Secretary of State for the Home Department* [1995] Imm AR 109, CA, but this decision
     would be unlikely under the current regulations and in the light of the importance given to
     actual notice of adverse decisions in cases such as *R v Secretary of State for the Home
     Department ex p Saleem (Asifa)* [2000] Imm AR 529, [2000] INLR 413, CA and *R (on the
     application of Anufrijeva) v Secretary of State for the Home Department* [2003] UKHL 36,
     [2003] Imm AR 570, [2003] INLR 521.
7   SI 2003/658, reg 7(1). A notice sent by post is deemed to have been received two business
     days after posting: reg 7(4)–(6).
8   SI 1984/2040, reg 3(4); *Singh (Pargan)* above at 117; *R v Secretary of State for the Home
     Department, ex p Brew* [1988] Imm AR 93, QBD.
9   *Singh (Pargan)* above; *Rhemtulla v Immigration Appeal Tribunal* [1979–80] Imm AR
     168, CA.
10   Under a policy DP5/86; see *R v Secretary of State for the Home Department, ex p Popatia
     and Chew* [2000] INLR 587, 16.47 below.
11   SI 2003/658, reg 7(2).
12   The time for appealing would run from the date the notice was placed on the file:
     SI 2003/658, reg 7(3). Immigration service caseworkers are advised not to re-serve
     decisions to deport on missing overstayers who are found, presumably since such re-service
     would be likely to generate an in-time appeal (Operational Enforcement Manual Ch 16,
     'Service of notice of intention to deport'). Query whether this advice is good in the light of
     the landmark decision of the House of Lords in *R (on the application of Anufrijeva) v
     Secretary of State for the Home Department* [2003] UKHL 36, [2003] Imm AR 570,
     [2003] INLR 521.

Right of appeal

15.40 When a decision to deport is taken, whether on conducive grounds
(other than political cases) or on family grounds, or following a recommendation by a criminal court, there is a right of appeal to the Asylum and
Immigration Tribunal under section 82(2)(j) of the Nationality, Immigration
and Asylum Act 2002.[1] Notice of appeal should be served within ten working
days of the decision being notified[2] (or within five working days if the person
is in detention),[3] though there is provision for an extension of time where
'special circumstances' can be demonstrated.[4] The right of appeal comes after
the decision to deport, but before the making of a deportation order. The
sequence is thus decision, appeal, deportation order. The clear distinction
between a 'decision to deport' and a 'deportation order' should be noted. Both
the decision to deport and a refusal to revoke a deportation order are
'immigration decisions' for the purposes of the appeal provisions of the 2002
Act.[5] However, while the appeal against a decision to deport is in-country,[6] an
appeal against refusal to revoke a deportation order cannot be exercised while
the appellant is in the UK, unless he or she is an EEA national or a member of
the family of an EEA national relying on Community rights, or has made an
asylum or human rights claim in the UK.[7] In such a case, however, the
in-country appeal is not limited to those grounds.[8]

1   The right to appeal against a decision taken after a recommendation by a criminal court is
     new. Any remaining overstayers who applied, prior to 9 October 2000, to regularise their
     position under the Immigration and Asylum Act 1999, s 9 and are still awaiting a decision,
     may also appeal under this section, if their application is rejected. Section 82(2) embraces

all decisions to deport under Immigration Act 1971, s 5. In political cases the appeal is to the Special Immigration Appeals Commission: Nationality, Immigration and Asylum Act 2002, s 97, Special Immigration Appeals Commission Act 1997, s 2 (as amended).

2 Asylum and Immigration Tribunal (Procedure) Rules 2005, SI 2005/230, r 7(1)(b) read with r 57(1)(b) (calculation of time).

3 Asylum and Immigration Tribunal (Procedure) Rules 2005, r 7(1)(a).

4 SI 2005/230, r 10. See also 18.94ff below.

5 Nationality, Immigration and Asylum Act 2002, s 82(1), (2)(j) and (k).

6 NIAA 2002, s 92(1), (2).

7 NIAA 2002, s 92(4); however an in-country appeal under s 92(4) may not be brought if the Secretary of State certifies that the asylum or human rights claim concerned is clearly unfounded: s 94(2); see 18.24ff below.

8 This is clear from the wording of ss 82, 84 (grounds of appeal), 85(1) (matters to be considered) and 92(4) (in-country appeals). Appeal rights under the 2002 Act are thus wider than under the provisions of either the 1999 or the 1971 Acts. But in a family deportation, the appeal of the family member (a UK-born child of the person subject to a deportation order) is predicated on the deportation of the principal and cannot be used as a lever to re-open the issue of the principal's deportation: *N v Secretary of State for the Home Department* [2001] EWCA Civ 688, [2001] All ER (D) 220.

15.41 While an appeal against the decision to deport may be brought or is pending, a deportation order cannot be made against a person under section 5(1) of the Immigration Act 1971.[1] An appeal is pending until it is either 'finally determined' or has been withdrawn or treated as abandoned.[2] Where a decision is being challenged on judicial review the appeal is no longer pending, but the Home Office will usually stay its hand pending the determination of the Administrative Court, although the practice does not of itself give rise to a legitimate expectation that a deportation order will not be made.[3] The decision to deport enables the immigrant to be detained in custody or subjected to restrictions.[4] If it has been served on the deportee, it stops the clock for the purpose of the long residence rule.[5] Although a deportation order will not be signed without further consideration of whether to maintain enforcement action by the Home Office, many people used to leave voluntarily before this happened, and a number were removed because they waived their appeal rights and did not wish to be detained in custody.[6] Those with in-country appeal rights used to have the right to challenge the destination to which it was proposed to remove them,[7] but there is no longer an explicit right of appeal on this ground, although proposed deportation to an impermissible destination would seem to be 'not in accordance with the law'.[8]

1 Nationality, Immigration and Asylum Act 2002, s 79. However, a deportation order may be made (although not implemented) while any other appeal is pending, e g against refusal of leave to enter or certificate of entitlement, refusal to vary leave or revocation of ILR: s 78(3); and if it is made while the appeal is pending, the appeal lapses: s 104(5), with reference to s 82(2)(a), (c), (d), (e) or (f). It is hard to see how these provisions will bite, given the right of appeal against all deportation decisions including those following a court recommendation (s 82(2)(j)). A deportation order may also be made (but not implemented) while an asylum claim is pending: s 77(4)(b). This is likely to apply to those who have made a very late asylum claim following dismissal of an earlier deportation appeal, or following apprehension after a period of disappearance during which appeal rights have been lost. Refusal of an asylum claim in these circumstances would attract an appeal against refusal to revoke the order: see 15.40 text and fns 7 and 8 above.

2 Nationality, Immigration and Asylum Act 2002 s 104; see also Sch 7, amending Immigration Act 1971, s 33(4).

3 *R v Secretary of State for the Home Department, ex p Yesufu* [1987] Imm AR 366, QBD.

4 Immigration Act 1971, Sch 3, para 2(2).

[5] *Musah v Secretary of State for the Home Department* [1995] Imm AR 236, CA; *R v Secretary of State for the Home Department, ex p Popatia and Chew* [2000] INLR 587, cases decided under the pre-rule policy. See now HC 395 para 276B (inserted by HC 538). The rule does not indicate that service must have been effective to bring the decision to the attention of the proposed deportee (cf *Popatia and Chew*), and the 2003 Notices Regulations permit 'service on the file' (see 15.39 text and fn 11) but we would argue that the rule should be so construed in line with ECHR jurisprudence on Art 8 private and family life.

[6] Voluntary departure avoids the prohibition on re-entry: see 15.47 below.

[7] Immigration and Asylum Act 1999, s 63(3)–(4).

[8] Nationality, Immigration and Asylum Act 2002 s 84(1)(e). Only deportation to the country of nationality or a country to which it is reasonable to believe the person would be admitted is permissible: Immigration Act 1971, Sch 3, para 1, See further 16.56ff below.

Transitional provisions and regularisation scheme

15.42 Where a decision to deport was made before 2 October 2000, the old appeal regime continued to operate; appeals would be made under section 15 of the Immigration Act 1971 or section 5 of the Immigration Act 1988, and the appeal continued to have effect notwithstanding the repeal of those sections.[1] Then, section 9 of the Immigration and Asylum Act 1999 gave overstayers a short window between 1 February 2000 and 2 October 2000 to apply for regularisation of their status.[2] If their application is refused, they are deported rather than summarily removed, and have the right of appeal against deportation accorded to all other proposed deportees.[3] If they last entered the UK within seven years of the date of the decision, the appeal is limited to the ground that the Secretary of State does not possess 'power in law' to make an order;[4] otherwise they have a full appeal on the merits of the decision.[5] The appeals, if there are any left, are governed by the current procedure rules and notices regulations.[6]

[1] Immigration and Asylum Act 1999, Sch 15, para 11; Commencement Order No 6 (SI 2000/444), Sch 2, para 1(2).

[2] Immigration and Asylum Act 1999, s 9, and Immigration (Regularisation Period for Overstayers) Order 2000, SI 2000/265.

[3] Immigration and Asylum Act 1999, Sch 15, para 12; Nationality, Immigration and Asylum Act 2002, s 82(2)(j). According to the Minister, a total of 17,120 applications for regularisation were made by the closing date (2 October 2000). By November 2002, just under 3000 had been granted, 425 refused and nearly 12,000 were awaiting consideration: *Hansard* HC 28 November 2002, col 424W. No later figures have been provided.

[4] Immigration and Asylum Act 1999, Sch 15, para 12; Immigration Act 1988, s 5; Immigration (Restricted Right of Appeal against Deportation) (Exemption) Order 1993, SI 1993/1656.

[5] For an example of an appeal against deportation for overstaying where the Tribunal held deportation disproportionate on private and family life grounds, see *Antwi* [2002] UKIAT 06668.

[6] Asylum and Immigration Tribunal (Procedure) Rules 2005, SI 2005/230, r 62; Immigration (Notices) Regulations 2003, SI 2003/658, reg 3.

Political cases

15.43 There is no appeal to the Tribunal against a decision certified by the Secretary of State personally or in accordance with his or her direction identifying the appellant, as resting wholly or partly on the ground that the appellant's removal is in the interests of national security or the relationship between the UK and another country,[1] or if the Secretary of State personally certifies a decision as taken wholly or partly on information which he or she believes should not be made public for similar or other public interest reasons.[2] In each case the right of appeal is to the Special Immigration Appeals Commission (SIAC), under section 2 of the Special Immigration Appeals Commission Act 1997.[3] The history of the Commission and its procedures are set out at 18.160ff below. For the previous procedures involving an advisory panel, see the last edition of this work at 15.52–15.56. The House of Lords described in *Rehman*[4] the functions of SIAC on a deportation appeal. Lord Hoffmann said that SIAC's role was to review the facts, to assess whether the Secretary of State's decision was *Wednesbury* unreasonable on those facts, and to assess the risk of Article 3 ill-treatment.[5] It was 'not entitled to differ from the opinion of the Secretary of State on the question of whether the promotion of terrorism in a foreign country by a UK resident would be contrary to the interests of national security'.[6] The other members of the panel agreed that considerable deference was due to the Secretary of State's view of the requirements of national security, but Lord Steyn and Lord Slynn used the language of proportionality rather than *Wednesbury* as the yardstick against which SIAC should test the decision.[7]

1 Nationality, Immigration and Asylum Act 2002, s 97(1) and (2). This applies both to a decision to deport and a refusal to revoke a deportation order already made on other grounds.
2 Nationality, Immigration and Asylum Act 2002, s 97(3).
3 As substituted from 1 April 2003 by Nationality, Immigration and Asylum Act 2002, s 114, Sch 7 (SI 2003/754).
4 *Rehman v Secretary of State for the Home Department* [2001] UKHL 47, [2001] 3 WLR 877, [2002] INLR 92, [2002] Imm AR 98, upholding the Court of Appeal's decision at [2000] INLR 531. SIAC's original decision allowing Mr Rehman's appeal is at [1999] INLR 517.
5 *Rehman*, HL, above, para 54. This has been followed up by the proscription of 21 organisations under the provisions of the Terrorism Act 2000, s 3, the logic being that membership of, or even support for any of them (including the PKK and the LTTE), in itself justifies national security expulsion.
6 *Rehman*, HL, above, para 53.
7 At para 11 (Lord Slynn), 30–31 (Lord Steyn). Lord Clyde agreed with Lord Hoffmann; Lord Hutton with all three. The degree of deference to be accorded to the Secretary of State's assessment of national security requirements is thus unclear. Only once has SIAC's reversal of a decision on national security been upheld by the Court of Appeal: *M v Secretary of State for the Home Department* [2004] EWCA Civ 324, [2004] 2 All ER 863, a case in which the Court of Appeal was at pains to emphasise the importance of the SIAC appeal in testing the Secretary of State's evidence. The Secretary of State did not challenge SIAC's decision to allow the appeals of Mukhtiar and Paramjit Singh on human rights grounds. However, it may be that *Rehman* was the high water-mark of deference; the House took back considerable ground in *A v Secretary of State for the Home Department* [2004] UKHL 56, [2005] 2 WLR 87, holding the provisions of the Anti-terrorism, Crime and Security Act 2001 permitting indefinite detention of foreign terrorist suspects disproportionate, discriminatory and incompatible with Arts 5 and 14 ECHR: see 8.15 fn 3 above and 17.19 below.

Deportation of EEA nationals

15.44 The deportation of EEA nationals exercising Treaty rights is subject to special rules which provide both procedural safeguards and more rigorous justification for deportation. This is dealt with in detail at 7.127ff above. The most important points are first, that the decision to deport must be reviewed by an independent competent authority before it is implemented.[1] This reviewing body may be the court making a recommendation or the Asylum and Immigration Tribunal or Special Immigration Appeals Commission. Secondly, a measure interfering with EC freedom of movement rights must be taken only on grounds of public policy, public security or public health,[2] must be based exclusively on the personal conduct of the individual concerned, which must constitute a present threat to the requirements of public policy;[3] and the measure must be a proportionate response to the risk posed by the person's conduct. This means that there can be no automatic deportation based simply on the gravity of an offence[4] without consideration of propensity to re-offend and all the individual's circumstances.[5]

1   Council Directive (EEC) 64/221, Art 9; *Adoui and Cornuaille v Belgium* [1982] ECR 1665, [1982] 3 CMLR 631.
2   Article 39(3) EC (ex Art 48(3)); Art 46 EC (ex Art 56).
3   Council Directive 64/221, Art 3. See *Bonsignore v Oberstadt direktor der Stadt Köln* Case 67/74 [1975] ECR 297, [1975] 1 CMLR 472, ECJ; Case C-348/96 *Calfa (Criminal proceedings against)* [1999] ECR I-11; Case C-340/97 *Nazli v Stadt Nürnberg* [2000] ECR I-957, ECJ.
4   Case C-348/96 *Calfa (Criminal proceedings against)* [1999] ECR I-11.
5   *B v Secretary of State for the Home Department* [2000] Imm AR 478, [2000] INLR 361, CA; see 7.138–139 above

Successful appeals

15.45 If the appeal is allowed, the decision is reversed but the Asylum and Immigration Tribunal has no power to direct the grant of leave to remain in non-human rights cases.[1] It may direct that appropriate leave be granted, where there has been a finding that deportation would be in breach of human rights.[2] If the proposed deportee's leave has expired, and the Home Office has not renewed it pending appeal, leave to remain will normally be granted in order to regularise the position. But this does not follow as a matter of course. Immigrants who succeed in an appeal should not, therefore, leave the country for a celebratory holiday until leave has been obtained.[3] If they do they have no right to be treated as a returning resident and would have no other claim to re-enter. The Tribunal has no power to grant a stay of deportation, for example because of the political situation then pertaining in a country,[4] but a determination that deportation is not currently the right course on the merits could be properly made without prejudice to a future exercise of the power if the person's behaviour merits deportation. In one case an adjudicator allowed the appeal on the grounds that the applicant was a genuine student who should be given a further opportunity to progress with his studies.[5] But where an appeal was unsuccessful, a period of grace, to allow the appellant to finish his course and make a voluntary departure, did not constitute fresh leave, and the Secretary of State was entitled to sign a deportation order when he did not leave.[6]

1   *R v Immigration Appeal Tribunal, ex p Singh (Mahendra)* [1984] Imm AR 1, QBD. See 18.69 below. The Tribunal may recommend this course, however.
2   *Sharif (Omeed)* [2002] UKIAT 00953.
3   *R v Secretary of State for the Home Department, ex p Botta* [1987] Imm AR 80, QBD.

4   *Yuksel* [1976] Imm AR 91, IAT.
5   *Youssef* (TH114300 Adjudicator); see also *Dexter* (4980) unreported.
6   *R v Secretary of State for the Home Department, ex p Smith* [1996] Imm AR 331. For a
    similar categorisation of 'packing up time', see *R v Secretary of State for the Home
    Department, ex p Banji* [1977] Imm AR 89, CA; but c f Lord Russell in *Suthendran v
    Immigration Appeal Tribunal* [1977] AC 359 at 372 and *Halil v Davidson* [1979–80] Imm
    AR 164, HL. *Ex p Smith* was decided before administrative removal replaced deportation
    for overstaying; Home Office practice now would be to sign the order but defer its
    implementation for the relevant period.

Signing and revocation of deportation orders

Detaining deportees

15.46   The power to detain deportees arises at three stages; first when a court recommends deportation;[1] secondly when the decision to deport is made,[2] and thirdly when the deportation order is signed.[3] At all three stages there is also the option of bail or release on temporary admission, subject to requirements as to residence and so forth.[4] The position is dealt with more fully in the chapter on detention (chapter 17 below).

1   Immigration Act 1971 Sch 3, para 2(1). For the legality of detention pending the
    implementation of a recommendation to deport, see *Re Nwafor* [1994] Imm AR 91, QBD.
2   Immigration Act 1971, Sch 3, para 2(2); HC 395, para 382.
3   Immigration Act 1971 Sch 3, para 2(3).
4   Immigration Act 1971 Sch 3, para 2 as amended by Immigration and Asylum Act 1999,
    s 54, from 10 February 2003 (Immigration and Asylum Act 1999 (Commencement Order
    No 12) 2003, SI 2003/2).

Voluntary or supervised departure

15.47   Persons liable to deportation who are not detained may leave the UK voluntarily, paying for their own passage and leaving under their own auspices, at any time before a deportation order is signed.[1] This may require liaison with the port if travel documents are held. The advantage of this option is that it does not preclude a future return under the Immigration Rules, since the power to sign a deportation order can only be exercised when the person is in the UK.[2] If it is known that a person has embarked, enforcement action will cease.[3] For this reason it may be unfair to reject representations to remain on compassionate grounds and sign a deportation order before giving the opportunity for a voluntary departure.[4] However, the benefits of voluntary departure can easily be lost, if the reasons for the decision to deport are used to exclude the person from the UK on an attempt to re-enter.[5] Voluntary departure is not the same thing as supervised departure. Reference to supervised departure has been deleted from the current Immigration Rules, but it remains in the IDI, which suggest that it would be appropriate where a person agrees to leave immediately and signs a waiver regarding appeal rights.[6] Supervised departure may be at the individual's or the Secretary of State's expense.[7] Like other voluntary departures, supervised departure does not debar the subject from re-entering.[8]

1   Voluntary departure is not to be confused with being deported in travel arranged and paid
     for by the deportee, so as to make it less stressful and saving public funds: *Babalola*
     (00ᵀᴴ00926), IAT (unreported).
2   Immigration Act 1971, s 5(1).
3   IDI Ch 13, s 1, para 9.3.
4   The argument was unsuccessful on its facts in *R v Secretary of State for the Home
     Department, ex p Brew* [1988] Imm AR 93.
5   See HC 395, para 320(18), (19).
6   IDI Ch 13, s 1, para 9.
7   Section 5(6) of the Immigration Act 1971 refers to persons liable to deportation who leave
     the UK to live permanently abroad and enables the Secretary of State to meet their
     expenses. Undoubtedly such funding will be a relevant consideration if the person seeks to
     return.
8   IDI Ch 13, s 1, para 9.3.

Signing the deportation order

15.48 In criminal cases, where a recommendation has been made by the
courts, the Secretary of State may not make a deportation order until the
convicted person has exhausted all rights of appeal or until the time for
bringing an appeal has expired (in Scotland, until the expiry of 28 days from
the date of the recommendation).[1] In all cases, where no appeal is lodged or if
the appeal is dismissed, the order for deportation is submitted to the minister
for signature.[2] Earlier Immigration Rules stated that the submission would
include a summary of the facts of the case, written confirmation of the
dismissal of any appeal, and a note of any other relevant information, whether
or not it was available to the courts or the appellate authorities.[3] It is believed
that the practice remains the same. In *Sanusi*[4] the Court of Appeal held that
the Secretary of State could not make a deportation order between the making
of an asylum application and the notification of a decision on it, because of
the statutory prohibition on removal (then section 6 of the Asylum and
Immigration Appeals Act 1993). The case was reversed by statute.[5] Hitherto,
it has been assumed that the signing of the deportation order by the Secretary
of State is what made it effective. Thus it could be said if the order is signed
while the proposed deportee is in the UK but he or she leaves without
becoming aware of it, it is still effective; and in one case it was held that a
failure to serve the order and the return of the person's passport with an
uncancelled indefinite leave stamp did not give rise to a legitimate expectation
that the order would not be enforced.[6] But since the important decision of the
House of Lords in *R (on the application of Anufrijeva) v Secretary of State for
the Home Department*[7] it is strongly arguable that the order, even if properly
signed, is not effective, unless and until it is notified.

1   Immigration Act 1971, s 6(6). Now that there is a right of appeal to the Tribunal against
    the decision of the Secretary of State to follow a court recommendation under NIAA 2002,
    s 82(2), (2)(j), no order may be submitted to the minister until appeal rights are exhausted.
2   Normally the order is signed by the Home Office immigration minister, but contentious
    cases may be referred to the Secretary of State for the Home Department for signature: IDI
    Ch 13, s 1.
3   HC 251, para 157.
4   *R v Secretary of State for the Home Department, ex p Sanusi* [1999] INLR 198, [1999]
    Imm AR 334.
5   Immigration and Asylum Act 1999, s 15, Sch 4, para 20; see now Nationality, Immigration
    and Asylum Act 2002, s 77(4)(b).

⁶   *Dey (Sri Kumar) v Secretary of State for the Home Department* [1996] Imm AR 521, CA.
⁷   [2003] UKHL 36, [2003] Imm AR 570, [2003] INLR 521.

Removal of deportees

15.49 Following the making of a deportation order, removal directions will be set.¹ Removal must be to the country of nationality, or to any other country to which there is reason to believe the deportee will be admitted.² Where the person is serving a prison sentence, arrangements for removal will be made to coincide with his or her release wherever possible.³ The costs of removal are always defrayed by the Secretary of State rather than the carrier.⁴ For removal see chapter 16 below. Under EC Directive 2001/40 on the mutual recognition of expulsion decisions a decision on expulsion issued in one Member State is enforceable in another; so a deportee from the UK could find him or herself deported from any other EU country he or she attempted to enter while the deportation order is still in force.⁵

1   The subject of a deportation order who disappears may be removed in pursuance of the order if he or she comes to light within three months, provided the circumstances are unchanged and no undertaking was given to review the case; otherwise the case is to be referred for further consideration: Operational Enforcement Manual 'Deportation', para 18.6.
2   Immigration Act 1971, Sch 3, para 1.
3   IDI Ch 13, s 1, para 6. The practice of the Parole Board in refusing early release to prisoners subject to deportation action was held to violate Art 14 with Art 5 in *R (on the application of Hindawi), R (Headley) v Secretary of State for the Home Department* [2004] EWHC Admin 78. Sections 259–260 of the Criminal Justice Act 2003 (not yet in force) provides for early release for prisoners liable for deportation or administrative removal. (They can be returned to prison if they return to the UK before the expiry of their sentence: s 261.)
4   Operational Enforcement Manual, 'Deportation', para 19.1 (unless a deportation order is made in respect of someone refused at the port, eg a drugs courier, in which case removal is the responsibility of the refusing port: ibid).
5   OJ 2001 L 150/47, which was supposed to have been implemented by 2 December 2002.

Revocation of deportation orders

15.50 The effect of a deportation order is to invalidate any leave to enter or remain in the UK given before the order is made or while it is in force.¹ A deportation order comes into force on the day it is signed rather than when it is served.² There are statutory provisions for when it ceases to apply. The order ceases to have effect automatically:

(1)   if the deportee becomes a British citizen;³
(2)   if a spouse, deported under a family order, is divorced from the principal deportee;⁴
(3)   in the case of children deported under a family order, as soon as they reach the age of 18.⁵

An order may also become invalid if the deportee has become a family member of an EEA national exercising Treaty rights in the UK.⁶ In all other circumstances a deportation order continues in force until it is revoked by a further order of the Secretary of State.⁷ Revocation of a deportation order, however, does not entitle the person to re-enter the UK, but merely to qualify for admission under the Immigration Rules.[8] Application for revocation can be made to the entry clearance officer or the Home Office.[9] Normally, three years must have elapsed.[10] Time runs from the date the order was signed, not the date of removal, although time spent out of the UK is relevant.[11]

1 Immigration Act 1971, s 5(1).
2 *Peerbocus* [1987] Imm AR 331; *Dey (Sri Kumar) v Secretary of State for the Home Department* [1996] Imm AR 521, CA.
3 Immigration Act 1971, s 5(2). But an order is not revoked merely because a Commonwealth citizen marries a British citizen after the order is signed: *R v Secretary of State for the Home Department, ex p Hayden* [1988] Imm AR 555, QBD.
4 Immigration Act 1971, s 5(3), (4).
5 Immigration Act 1971, s 5(3), (4).
6 IDI Ch 13, s 5, para 2; see chapter 7 above.
7 Immigration Act 1971, s 5(2). A deportation order cannot be impliedly revoked and the grant of entry clearance while the order is in existence does not have this effect: *Watson* [1986] Imm AR 75.
8 HC 395, para 392.
9 HC 395, para 392.
10 HC 395, para 391; but since the question of revocation is a matter of the minister's discretion, shorter or longer periods are possible: *Udoh* [1972] Imm AR 89, where it was held that one year was a sufficient time for atonement; and see further *Dervish* [1972] Imm AR 48 where it was felt that 12 months was too soon to revoke the order, but a further seven months led the Tribunal to recommend an early consideration of revocation. See now IDI, Ch 13 Annex A, 'Periods normally appropriate for revocation'.
11 *Peerbocus* [1987] Imm AR 331, IAT.

15.51 An application for revocation of a deportation order will be considered in the light of all the circumstances, including the grounds on which the order was made, any representations in support of revocation, the interests of the community, including the maintenance of an effective immigration control, and the interests of the applicant including any compassionate circumstances.[1] The Immigration Rules lay down a practice that in the case of an applicant with a serious criminal record, continued exclusion for a long term of years will normally be the proper course.[2] Where the order was founded on a criminal conviction which has become spent under the Rehabilitation of Offenders Act 1974, revocation should normally be granted.[3] In other cases, revocation of the order will not normally be authorised unless the situation has been materially altered, either by a change of circumstances since the order was made, or by fresh information coming to light.[4] In an old case, failure by counsel to advise of the possibility of an appeal against a recommendation for deportation was held not to be such a circumstance,[5] but clearly this depends on whether the original order was made in the knowledge of all the relevant circumstances. The passage of time since the person was deported may also, in itself, amount to such a change of circumstances as to warrant revocation of the order.[6] The IDI indicate that revocation would normally be appropriate three years after departure in cases involving over-stayers deported under the earlier provisions, and family members, while serious offences (violence against the person including murder, attempted murder, conspiracy or threats to kill, manslaughter, grievous bodily harm or actual bodily harm; sexual offences including offences against children, rape, indecent assault, procurement, pornography; armed robbery; persistent or large-scale burglary or theft; blackmail; counterfeiting or forgery including

15.51 *Deportation and Repatriation*

trafficking false passports; trafficking drugs; and public order, including riot or affray) would normally require a ten-year wait before revocation.[7]

1 HC 395, para 390.
2 HC 395, para 391.
3 IDI Ch 13, s 5 'Revocation', para 3.3. The IDI set out in detail the Rehabilitation of Offenders Act and when convictions become spent: see 15.35 fn 9 above.
4 The IDI state that cases should be decided on their known circumstances, but further inquiries might be appropriate where further offences may have been committed abroad or, in a case where less than three years have elapsed since the order was enforced, where there appears to have been a material change, such as marriage after deportation or the sickness of a relative in the UK.
5 *Osu* (4851), IAT.
6 HC 395, para 391. See *Sanusi* [1975] Imm AR 114.
7 IDI, Ch 13, Annex A.

15.52 If an application for revocation is refused there is a right of appeal against the refusal.[1] Where the Secretary of State certifies that the appellant's continued exclusion is in the interests of national security or the relationship between the UK and another country, or that the decision to refuse revocation was taken wholly or partly on information which he or she believes should not be made public for similar or other public interest reasons, the appeal lies to the Special Immigration Appeals Commission.[2] No revocation appeal is possible so long as the person is in the UK (either because they have not left or because they have returned illegally),[3] unless the subject of the order has made an asylum or human rights claim[4] which is not certified clearly unfounded by the Secretary of State,[5] or asserts that the decision breaches his or her Community law rights, in which case the appeal is in-country.[6]

1 Nationality, Immigration and Asylum Act 2002, s 82(2)(k).
2 Nationality, Immigration and Asylum Act 2002, s 97; Special Immigration Appeals Commission Act 1997, s 2 (as amended by s 114 and NIAA 2002, Sch 7).
3 Nationality, Immigration and Asylum Act 2002, s 92(1).
4 Nationality, Immigration and Asylum Act 2002, s 92(4)(a).
5 Nationality, Immigration and Asylum Act 2002, s 94(1), (2).
6 Nationality, Immigration and Asylum Act 2002, s 92(4). There is no provision for certifying clearly unfounded a revocation appeal resting on Community law.

Returned deportees

15.53 Where someone returns to the UK in breach of a deportation order, he or she may lawfully be deported under the original order.[1] But every case should be considered in the light of all the relevant circumstances.[2] A person who enters in breach of a deportation order is an illegal entrant[3] and a person who does so knowingly is, in addition, guilty of a criminal offence.[4]

1 Immigration Act 1971, s 5(5).
2 HC 395, para 388; *Alsawaf v Secretary of State for the Home Department* [1988] Imm AR 410, where the country of proposed destination refused to accept the deportee. The IDI state (Sep 01, Ch 13, s 1, para 7.1) that returned deportees who are not Irish are generally treated as illegal entrants, while Irish nationals are removed under the original order. See also OEM 'Deportation' para 18.5.

3   Immigration Act 1971, s 33(1): see 16.12 below. A decision to remove an illegal entrant
     attracts an appeal under s 82(2)(h) of the Nationality, Immigration and Asylum Act 2002,
     but it does not suspend removal unless an asylum or human rights claim has been made
     which is not certified as clearly unfounded, or the subject asserts a right under the
     Community Treaties: s 92(1), (4), s 94.
4   Immigration Act 1971, s 24(1)(a); *R v Secretary of State for the Home Department,
     ex p Yeboah* [1986] Imm AR 52, QBD.

REPATRIATION

Voluntary repatriation

15.54 As noted above, section 5(6) of the 1971 Act empowers the Secretary
of State to meet the expenses (including travelling expenses for members of the
family or household) of someone liable for deportation, who leaves the UK
voluntarily to live permanently abroad.[1] Similar, but broader provision is
made for others who wish to live abroad. In November 2002, section 58 of
the 2002 Act repealed the voluntary repatriation scheme under the Immigration Act 1971,[2] and replaced it with a new scheme to assist 'voluntary
leavers'.[3] The section provides arrangements to help those (not British citizens
or EEA nationals) who are leaving the UK for a place where they hope to take
up permanent residence, where the Secretary of State thinks it is in their
interests to leave and they wish to do so. The help they may be given includes
resettlement expenses and expenses of 'explore and prepare' trips to help
people decide whether they wish to leave and if so, to make preparations for
leaving.[4] The scheme is not meant to provide a facility for repatriating visitors
or those subject to a deportation order.[5] A person settled in this country who
makes use of public funds for resettlement will not be able to claim re-entry as
a returning resident, but are not required to sign an undertaking not to return,
and may be admitted if they otherwise qualify under the rules.[6] The 2002 Act
also enables financial support to be given to international organisations
working in the field of international migration, including resettlement of
refugees overseas.[7]

1   Immigration Act 1971 s 5(6); see 15.47 fn 7 above.
2   The old 'voluntary repatriation' scheme was under s 29 Immigration Act 1971. It was
     administered by the International Social Services of the UK, and was intended to help those
     persons who have failed to settle satisfactorily in the UK and who wished to leave but
     lacked the means to do so. Only travel costs, and no resettlement expenses, could be
     provided. 2,545 individuals were assisted between 1972 and 1995: *Hansard* (HC)
     5 February 1996, col 48.
3   'Voluntary leavers' are defined in Nationality, Immigration and Asylum Act 2002, s 58(1).
4   Nationality, Immigration and Asylum Act 2002, s 58(2), (3). See also the explanatory notes
     to the Act.
5   IDI May 04, Ch 19, s 6, 'Voluntary repatriation' para 1.
6   HC 395, para 18(iii); IDI above para 3.
7   Nationality, Immigration and Asylum Act 2002, s 59. The organisations to be funded
     under this section are the International Organisation for Migration, which is heavily
     involved in 'voluntary return' programmes for failed asylum seekers (including unaccom-
     panied minors), and UNHCR.

Prison repatriation

15.55 The Council of Europe Convention on the Transfer of Sentences
Persons 1983 provided for repatriation to enable prisoners sentenced abroad

to serve their sentences in their home country, with the consent of the prisoner and the agreement of the two countries concerned. Under the Convention the prisoner must have at least six months of his or her sentence left to serve and be a national of the state to which he or she is to be transferred. There should be no outstanding appeal to a higher court against sentence or conviction. The Repatriation of Prisoners Act 1984 was enacted to give effect to the Convention in UK law. British prisoners convicted overseas may be repatriated to complete their sentence in a British jail or other institution, and overseas prisoners in UK jails may be sent back to their own countries to complete their sentences. Under the 1984 Act any repatriation must take place under an international arrangement, such as the Council of Europe Convention or some bilateral arrangement between the UK and another government,[1] and consent must be given by the prisoner and the two countries concerned.[2] Transfer in and out is effected at the British end by a warrant issued by the Secretary of State for the Home Department. In outward transfers this authorises the taking of a prisoner to any place in any part of the UK, his or her delivery at a place of departure to the custody of an agent of the transfer country and the removal of the prisoner from the UK.[3] In inward transfers the 1984 Act authorises the return of prisoners to the UK and their subsequent detention in a prison, hospital or other institution as authorised by the Secretary of State's warrant.[4] A prisoner who is in the UK or on board a British ship, aircraft or hovercraft is deemed to be in the legal custody of the Secretary of State.[5] A prisoner who escapes can be arrested by the police without warrant.[6] The provisions of the 1984 Act do not apply to anyone who is detained in pursuance of a sentence of the International Criminal Court.[7]

[1] Repatriation of Prisoners Act 1984, ss 1(1) and 8(1).
[2] Repatriation of Prisoners Act 1984, s 1(1)(b) and (c). The Habeas Corpus Act of 1679, s 11 forbids the sending of any person as a prisoner out of the realm (ie, without his or her consent) and imposes the penalty of life imprisonment upon anyone taking part in such illegal repatriation or deportation. But s 12 exempts from this prohibition any persons, who 'by contract in writing agree with ... any merchant or owner of any plantation, or other persons whatsoever, to be transported to any parts beyond the seas'.
[3] Repatriation of Prisoners Act 1984, s 2.
[4] Repatriation of Prisoners Act 1984, s 3.
[5] Repatriation of Prisoners Act 1984, s 5(2).
[6] Repatriation of Prisoners Act 1984, s 5(5).
[7] International Criminal Court Act 2001, s 42(5)(a).

Inducements to depart

15.56 A person liable to be sentenced by a criminal court or punished for contempt of court may be encouraged to avoid punishment by agreeing to a voluntary departure and not to return to the UK. This inducement was used in the nineteenth century for convicted prisoners, who were offered free pardons if they left the UK.[1] There were a number of contempt cases where the application to commit was adjourned *sine die* on the agreement to depart.[2] The more frequent technique of persuasion has been the use of a bind-over at common law to come up for judgment when called on to do so upon terms that the person leaves the UK within a specified time and does not return within a specified number of years.[3] There is no power to make such a condition under the Justices of the Peace Act 1361[4] or a probation order,[5] and it can only be made in lieu of and not in addition to a sentence of the court.[6] The Court of Appeal has held that consent remains free even though given in the face of the alternative of imprisonment.[7] The making of such a bind-over was considered to be a purely internal situation and therefore not contrary to community law in the case of *R v Saunders*.[8] But it is unlikely to survive litigation under the Human Rights Act 1998.[9]

1   O Higgins 'Voluntary Deportation' [1963] Crim LR 680.
2   *Yager v Musa* [1962] Crim LR 240; *Smith v Smith* (1963) Times, 23 August.
3   See D Williams 'Suspended Sentence at Common Law' [1963] PL 441; Supreme Court Act 1981, s 79.
4   *R v Ayu* [1958] 3 All ER 636, [1958] 1 WLR 1264.
5   *R v McCartan* [1958] 3 All ER 140, [1958] 1 WLR 933.
6   *R v Ayu* above; *R v Governor of Brixton Prison, ex p Havilde* [1969] 1 All ER 109, [1969] 1 WLR 42.
7   *R v Williams)* [1982] 3 All ER 1092, [1982] 1 WLR 1398.
8   Case C-175/78 [1980] QB 72.
9   On bind-overs see *Steel v United Kingdom* (1998) 28 EHRR 603. On the prohibition of exile in international law see Nuala Mole 'Constructive deportation' (1995) EHRLR 64.

Chapter 16

REMOVAL AND OTHER EXPULSION

INTRODUCTION

16.1 In this chapter we examine the grounds for administrative removal from the UK and the means by which it is achieved. In contrast to removal by deportation, which we dealt with in the last chapter, there is no formal ban on return in cases of summary administrative removal, although the removal is often a blot on the person's immigration record, making return to the UK at a later date more difficult. Immigrants who are liable to removal are those refused leave to enter; illegal entrants; overstayers, and those in breach of their conditions of stay; those using deception to remain; former refugees; family members of those liable to removal, and crew members remaining unlawfully. The Nationality, Immigration and Asylum Act 2002 made it possible for the first time to remove persons who attempted but failed to obtain leave to remain using deception;[1] former refugees[2] and the UK-born children of all those liable to removal including illegal entrants and persons refused leave to enter.[3] The powers of removal are by and large unchanged save for these extensions; removal of those refused leave to enter, illegal entrants, their family members and sea and air crews is dealt with in Schedule 2 to the

1056

Immigration Act 1971,[4] and of the other groups in section 10 of the Immigration and Asylum Act 1999 and the Immigration (Removal Directions) Regulations 2000.[5] Removal of asylum claimants to 'safe third countries' under sections 11 and 12 of the 1999 Act is dealt with in chapter 12 above. In addition, there are provisions for the summary removal of sea, air and train crews who are in the UK illegally, and for detained psychiatric patients and members of visiting forces. We examine each of these categories in turn. Although the arrangements differ slightly according to the category of person being removed, the Immigration and Asylum Act 1999 introduced greater uniformity, in particular in subjecting overstayers, persons in breach of conditions of leave and others formerly eligible for deportation, to administrative removal procedures without the process of deportation. The most complicated arrangements remain the removal of persons refused entry, for reasons mainly to do with cost.[6]

[1] Immigration and Asylum Act 1999, s 10(1)(b), substituted by Nationality, Immigration and Asylum Act 2002, s 74, from 10 February 2003: SI 2003/1, Art 2.
[2] Immigration and Asylum Act 1999, s 10(1)(ba), inserted by Nationality, Immigration and Asylum Act 2002, s 76(7), from 10 February 2003: SI 2003/1.
[3] Immigration Act 1971, Sch 2, para 10A, inserted by Nationality, Immigration and Asylum Act 2002, s 73(1), from 10 February 2003: SI 2003/1.
[4] Immigration Act 1971, Sch 2, paras 8–15 as amended.
[5] SI 2000/2243.
[6] See 16.50 below.

REMOVAL OF ILLEGAL ENTRANTS AND OVERSTAYERS

16.2 Historically the treatment of illegal entrants liable to summary removal[1] was in stark contrast to the position of those who had entered lawfully but breached conditions or remained beyond the time limited by their leave. Prior to 2 October 2000 (the coming into force of the relevant provisions of the Immigration and Asylum Act 1999), overstayers and those in breach of conditions were liable to deportation,[2] but had an in-country right of appeal, which allowed the appellate authority to look at the merits of their case, if they had been here for more than seven years or if the decision to deport followed a curtailment decision.[3] Illegal entrants had no in-country right of appeal and could only challenge the decision to treat them as illegal entrants by way of judicial review.[4] Yet both might have long-established roots in the community. Section 10 of the Immigration and Asylum Act 1999 levelled down the treatment of the two groups by making overstayers subject to the same summary removal process as illegal entrants. The safeguard of an in-country right of appeal, which has the effect of suspending removal during the appeal process, is still available to persons presenting a claim on asylum and human rights grounds, but in a decreasing proportion of cases.[5]

[1] Immigration Act 1971, Sch 2, para 9 as amended by Asylum and Immigration Act 1996, Sch 2, para 6; see Lord Bridge in *Khawaja v Secretary of State for the Home Department* [1984] AC 74.
[2] Immigration Act 1971, s 3(5)(a) as originally enacted, s 5: see chapter 15 above.
[3] Immigration Act 1971, s 15, as amended by Immigration Act 1988, s 5; see also Immigration (Restricted Right of Appeal Against Deportation) (Exemption) Order 1993, SI 1993/1656.

4   The only suspensive appeal against removal was on asylum grounds. The right of appeal against removal directions under s 16 of the Immigration Act 1971, and subsequently s 66 of the Immigration and Asylum Act 1999, was exercisable only after removal, and jurisdiction was limited to whether the power in law exists. See now Nationality, Immigration and Asylum Act 2002, s 82(2)(g)–(i) (at 16.60 below).

5   See Nationality, Immigration and Asylum Act 2002 s 82(2)(g)–(ia) (previously there were separate appeals under the Immigration and Asylum Act 1999, s 69(5) for asylum applicants, and s 65 for human rights claimants). The suspensive effect of such appeals is provided by s 92(4)(a) of the Nationality Immigration and Asylum Act 2002, but can be avoided by a certificate that the claim is clearly unfounded under s 94: see 8.102 above and 18.23 below.

Definition of illegal entry

16.3 An illegal entrant is defined in section 33(1) of the Immigration Act 1971 as:[1]

'a person:
   (a)   unlawfully entering or seeking to enter in breach of a deportation order or of the immigration laws; or
   (b)   entering or seeking to enter to enter by means which include deception by another person,

and includes also a person who has entered as mentioned in paragraph (a) or (b) above.'

The definition of 'illegal entrants' thus covers three stages:

● those who enter;
● those who seek to enter;
● those who have entered.

1   As amended by Asylum and Immigration Act 1996, Sch 2, para 4. See also Immigration and Asylum Act 1999, s 167(2), which provides that 'illegal entrant' has the same meaning as in the Immigration Act 1971.

16.4 By section 11(1) of the Immigration Act 1971 'entry' is distinguished from 'arrival'.[1] Usually passengers 'arriving' at a port or airport are deemed not to 'enter' the UK until they have (1) disembarked from their ship, aircraft or Channel Tunnel train;[2] and (2) left the areas reserved for immigration control.[3] If detained or temporarily admitted or released while liable to detention,[4] they are deemed not to have 'entered'. By contrast, those who arrive at a remote beach or private landing strip or away from a designated port or airport are treated as 'entering' as soon as they leave their ship or aircraft.[5] These statutory distinctions between 'arriving' and 'entering' may help distinguish between someone seeking to enter and someone who has entered.

1   See also 3.5 above.
2   In relation to Channel Tunnel trains, which are designated control areas while passing through control zones in France and Belgium, passengers 'enter' the UK by remaining on the train after it ceases to be a control area: Immigration Act 1971, s 11 modified in relation to Channel Tunnel by SI 1993/1813, Art 7(1), Sch 4, para 1(5), and in relation to frontier controls between the UK, France and Belgium by SI 1994/1405, Art 7.

3   The area is defined by s 11(1) of the Immigration Act 1971 as such area at the port 'as may be approved for this purpose by an immigration officer'. Thus, stowaways who claimed asylum before the ferry bringing them to the UK docked were not illegal entrants: *Ex p Karakoc, ex p Karatas* (CO 694, 695/2000) (16 May 2000, unreported), and stowaways in a lorry on the Eurostar shuttle who took steps to alert the immigration service of their presence and to make an asylum claim immediately on entering the UK, and before leaving the designated control area, were not illegal entrants: *Ex p Uzun, ex p Karadag* (CO 2089, 2090/2000) (10 July 2000, unreported), (permission granted, Home Office conceded that such persons could not be treated as having entered or having sought to enter illegally).

4   Immigration Act 1971, s 11(1) as amended, inserting references to Immigration and Asylum Act 1999, Part III, Nationality, Immigration and Asylum Act 2002, ss 62, 68, all of which provide for temporary admission or release on bail, which displaces the presumption of entry by leaving immigration control.

5   Thus, asylum seekers hidden in a lorry who sought asylum on arrival at the freight port of Immingham were illegal entrants because the port is not a designated port for immigration purposes: *R (Uluyol and Cakmak) v Immigration Officer* [2001] INLR 194.

16.5 The provisions of the Immigration and Asylum Act 1999 and Orders made under it to grant or refuse leave to enter 'before arrival in the United Kingdom', and for entry clearance 'to have effect as leave to enter the United Kingdom',[1] mean that a person who has obtained leave to enter by deception, becomes an illegal entrant before leaving his or her own country. He or she would then be liable to removal on arrival in the UK.[2]

1   Immigration Act 1971, s 3A, inserted by Immigration and Asylum Act 1999, s 1 makes 'further provision as to leave to enter'. See Immigration (Leave to Enter and Remain) Order 2000, SI 2000/1161, Art 2; and 3.22 above.
2   Immigration Act 1971, Sch 2, para 9(1), (2).

16.6 It is not entirely clear why those seeking to enter should be treated as illegal entrants (unless it is facilitate the prosecution of those assisting them under section 25 or 25B of the Immigration Act 1971).[1] For if they are caught before they succeed in entering, they can be examined by immigration officers and, if necessary, refused entry and removed without being classified as illegal entrants.[2] Home Office policy is to do exactly that in most cases.[3] However, there are two differences which may follow from classifying someone seeking to enter as an illegal entrant:

(i)   the safeguards given to those seeking to enter lawfully do not apply; an illegal entrant is not entitled to a notice of refusal of entry within 24 hours of examination or further examination and a deemed leave to enter if this provision is not fulfilled;[4]

(ii)   an illegal entrant has no right of appeal on the merits under section 82 of the Nationality Immigration and Asylum Act 2002 against a refusal of leave to enter,[5] although illegal entrants and their dependants may appeal against a decision to remove them, and unlike their predecessors, the appeal provisions of the 2002 Act do not limit the appellant to a contention that the decision was not in accordance with the law.[6] The appeal rights are not ordinarily exercisable in-country however.[7]

A person who arrives at immigration control without a valid passport (whether an asylum seeker or not) is not seeking to enter in breach of the immigration laws unless he or she intends to deceive the immigration officer,

1059

and so cannot be treated as an illegal entrant,[8] despite the enactment of the criminal offence of having no immigration document.[9]

1   Those who assist the arrival of asylum seekers may be prosecuted even though their entry or proposed entry is not unlawful, but only if they do so for gain: Immigration Act 1971, s 25A, inserted by Nationality, Immigration and Asylum Act 2002, s 143, replacing s 25(1)(b) of the IA 1971, which was itself added by Asylum and Immigration Act 1996, s 5.
2   Immigration Act 1971, Sch 2, para 8. See below 16.54.
3   'People who seek leave to enter at arrivals in breach of a deportation order or by verbal deception or misrepresentation should normally be refused leave to enter at on-entry control and dealt with as a passenger refusal. The same applies to clandestines, including stowaways, who bring themselves voluntarily to the notice of the immigration officer at or before control. But a person detected after control should be dealt with as an illegal entrant (except at Cheriton): IDI, Ch 20, para 2.4.
4   Immigration Act 1971, Sch 2, para 6(1), as amended by Immigration Act 1988. In *Re Maqbool Hussain* (4 May 1976, unreported), DC the Divisional Court said that the time limit in this para does not apply to an illegal entrant; but this was a case of someone who had entered illegally rather than someone seeking to enter. But see 3.40 above.
5   An illegal entrant who seeks leave to enter is unlikely to fulfil the eligibility criteria outlined in Nationality Immigration and Asylum Act 2002, s 88(1)–(2). But there is a right of appeal against removal: see text and fnn 6, 7 below.
6   Under Nationality, Immigration and Asylum Act 2002, s 82(g)–(i); there is no restriction in Part V of the 2002 Act prohibiting illegal entrants from invoking any of the grounds of appeal set out in s 84 of the Act.
7   Nationality, Immigration and Asylum Act 2002, s 92(1), (2). But the appeal rights of illegal entrants who raise EC Treaty, asylum or human rights grounds in support (s 84(1)(d), 84(1)(g)) are suspensive unless (in the case of asylum or human rights grounds) certified unfounded under s 94(2) as amended by s 27 Asylum and Immigration (Treatment of Claimants, etc) Act 2004: s 92(4); see 18.23 below. Suspensive asylum and human rights appeals were formerly provided by Immigration and Asylum Act 1999, ss 65, 69(5).
8   *R v Naillie* [1993] AC 674, [1993] 2 All ER 782, [1993] Imm AR 462, HL.
9   Asylum and Immigration (Treatment of Claimants) Act 2004, s 2; see 16.23 below.

16.7 As we have seen, an illegal entrant is a person (a) unlawfully entering or seeking to enter the UK in breach of a deportation order or of the immigration laws, or (b) entering or seeking to enter by means which include deception by another person. The 'immigration laws' means the Immigration Act 1971 and any law for purposes similar to this Act.[1] In order to sustain an allegation of illegal entry, it is therefore necessary to show that the person has entered in breach of some statutory provision. To enter clandestinely without leave is, of course, such a case, if entry is in breach of the requirement of section 3(1) of the IA 1971 that a person 'shall not enter unless given leave to do so in accordance with the Act'. Entry in breach of the immigration laws is a wider concept than entry in breach of section 3(1), and will include not only the offence of illegal entry under IA 1971, section 24(1)(a) but also (most commonly) entry by deception in breach of sections 24A and 26(1)(c) of the Act.[2] The use of the word 'unlawfully' in the definition does not appear to add anything, since it is difficult to envisage any entry in breach of the immigration laws which would be regarded as lawful. In *Ex p Bouzagou*,[3] which concerned a man who had entered the UK from the Republic of Ireland without knowing that he was entering in breach of the immigration law, the court held that the word 'unlawfully' did not import a requirement of mens rea (ie an awareness of illegality) into the definition. Thus it would appear that the only possible entry in breach of the immigration laws which is not unlawful is an involuntary act or one compelled by necessity,[4] as where an aircraft develops a fault and is forced to land or a boat is forced ashore by bad weather.

[1] Immigration Act 1971, s 33(1). See also the Nationality, Immigration and Asylum Act 2002, s 158, and now the Asylum and Immigration (Treatment of Claimants) Act 2004, s 44, defining 'the Immigration Acts' as meaning the 1971 Act, the Immigration Act 1988, the Asylum and Immigration Appeals Act 1993, the Asylum and Immigration Act 1996, the Immigration and Asylum Act 1999, the Nationality, Immigration and Asylum Act 2002 and the 2004 Act.

[2] For the criminal offences of illegal entry, deception etc see 14.30 above.

[3] *R v Governor of Ashford Remand Centre, ex p Bouzagou* [1983] Imm AR 69, CA. See also *Ali (Ifzal) v Secretary of State for the Home Department* [1994] Imm AR 69. Normally 'unlawfully' means 'without lawful justification or excuse', and does not connote a mental element: see *Archbold Criminal Pleading, Evidence and Practice* (Sweet & Maxwell, 2005) para 17.44.

[4] See *R v Conway* [1989] QB 290, [1989] 88 Crim App Rep 159, CA; *R v Martin* (1989) 88 Cr App Rep 343, CA; *R v Hussain (Abdul)* [1999] Crim LR 570, CA (hijacking an aircraft and bringing it to the UK); *R v Safi (Ali Ahmed)* [2004] 1 Cr App Rep 14, CA (Afghanistan hijacking case).

16.8 There are four kinds of possible illegal entry under the Immigration Act 1971:

* entry without leave;
* entry in breach of a deportation order;
* entry through the common travel area; and
* entry by deception, use of false documents and corruption.

Effectively, the first three are 'no leave' cases and in the fourth leave is granted but deception is involved. The entry without leave and subsequent overstay of crew members is dealt with at 16.45 below.[1]

[1] For the history of the powers of removal of illegal entrants see the fourth edition at 16.1–16.6.

NO LEAVE CASES

16.9 Entry to the UK without leave normally constitutes a breach of section 3(1)(a) of the Immigration Act 1971, which requires that, unless otherwise provided, a person who is not a British citizen shall not enter the UK unless given leave to enter in accordance with the Act. Such persons will be illegal entrants within the statutory definition (having entered the UK in breach of the immigration laws). However, the spectrum of persons who are illegal entrants on this basis varies greatly. At one end are clandestine entrants, who evade immigration control and knowingly enter without leave; at the other end are the entirely blameless victims of someone else's fraud or mistake. Clandestine entrants who enter without leave will include those who go through immigration control hidden in the back of container lorries,[1] slip through the airport terminal,[2] or land on a remote beach at night.[3] There are also those the circumstances of whose entry are unknown, but who cannot show that leave was granted,[4] or can only point to a leave which is forged.[5]

[1] See 16.4 fnn 3 and 5, above.

2 See *Re Hassan* [1976] 2 All ER 123, DC.
3 See *R v Governor of Brixton Prison, ex p Ahsan* [1969] 2 QB 222, [1969] 2 All ER 347, DC.
4 Leave no longer has to be in writing in every case: Immigration (Leave to Enter and Remain) Order 2000, SI 2000/1161, Art 8. But the burden of proof as to the date and manner of entry is on the entrant: see SI 2000/1161, Art 11. See 3.40 above.
5 *R v Secretary of State for the Home Department, ex p Musawwir* [1989] Imm AR 297, QB.

16.10 Particular problems arise over mistakes or ignorance of the law. There are considerable numbers of people who do not need leave to enter, in view of their citizenship, the common travel area, EEA, diplomatic exemptions and so forth.[1] Because of the complexity of the law and the Immigration Rules, it is easy for both travellers and immigration officers to make mistakes. For example, people come from Ireland not knowing that their particular group needs leave to enter; others are wrongly allowed through immigration control by immigration officers who mistakenly think that they do not need leave. The law is harsh. They are all illegal entrants.[2] It was formerly thought that people who submitted to immigration control and were mistakenly passed through by the immigration service had been examined and were the beneficiaries of a deemed leave under the Immigration Act 1971, Schedule 2, paragraph 6.[3] But the case law makes it clear that such a deemed leave only arises where an immigration officer carries out an examination intending to give a limited leave or to refuse leave, but fails to record the decision within the appropriate time limits.[4] Thus persons who are wrongly assumed to be British citizens may later find themselves being treated as illegal entrants through no fault of their own.[5] Yet others become illegal entrants even though they have been examined and an open date stamp has been placed in their passport, indicating exemption from control.[6] Again the law is harsh, since here it is the immigration officer's mistake in allowing them entry without leave which founds the illegality.[7] These cases are to be contrasted with the case where the immigration officer's mistaken grant of leave is valid.[8]

1 The list of exemptions from leave is at 3.4 above. See *R v Secretary of State for the Home Department, ex p Wuan* [1989] Imm AR 501.
2 *R v Governor of Ashford Remand Centre, ex p Bouzagou* [1983] Imm AR 69, CA; *R v Secretary of State for the Home Department, ex p Mohan* [1989] Imm AR 436.
3 *R v Secretary of State for the Home Department, ex p Malik* (2 October 1987, unreported), QBD. See 3.40ff above.
4 *Secretary of State for the Home Department v Thirukumar* [1989] Imm AR 402, CA; *Rehal v Secretary of State for the Home Department* [1989] Imm AR 576, CA; *R v Secretary of State for the Home Department, ex p Kumar* [1990] Imm AR 265.
5 *Rehal* above; *R v Secretary of State for the Home Department, ex p Khaled* [1987] Imm AR 67; *Mokuolo v Secretary of State for the Home Department, Ogunbiyi v Secretary of State for the Home Department* [1989] Imm AR 51, CA.
6 *Mokuolo* above; *R v Secretary of State for the Home Department v Bagga* [1990] Imm AR 413, CA. See 3.47 above.
7 In view of the more relaxed requirements for notice of leave under the Immigration and Asylum Act 1999, there is doubt whether these decisions remain relevant: see 3.40 above.
8 *R v Secretary of State for the Home Department, ex p Ram* [1979] 1 All ER 687, [1979] 1 WLR 148, DC. See 3.43 above.

16.11 The case of *Noor Nawal Khan*[1] illustrates the absurdities of this doctrine. At the time of his birth in Pakistan in 1971, Mr Khan was a citizen of the UK and colonies by descent. He became a British Dependent Territories citizen on the coming into force of the British Nationality Act 1981. On arrival in the UK in 1992, he presented his passport describing him (correctly) as a British Dependent Territories citizen, although he believed himself entitled to enter and depart from the UK freely by reason of his father's registration as a CUKC in 1965 at the British Sovereign Base in Cyprus. Initially granted temporary admission whilst his claim was investigated, he later received a letter from a chief immigration officer informing him that his 'British nationality had been resolved', that he was 'deemed to be a British citizen' and that he could apply for a British passport describing him as such. His subsequent application for registration as a British citizen, however, was rejected and the letter from the chief immigration officer was held to be incorrect, although he was told he could re-apply for registration later. When he applied for leave to remain as a working holidaymaker, the Home Office responded by informing him that he was an illegal entrant with no claim to remain and that he should 'now make arrangements to return to Pakistan'. Fortunately, on judicial review McCullough J held that the decision declaring Mr Khan to be an illegal entrant and telling him that he should 'now' leave the country was 'altogether excessive and out of proportion to the occasion'. Once it had been decided that he was not going to be allowed to remain to enable him to apply again for British citizenship, 'fairness demanded that he should have been invited to make representations to argue the contrary'.

[1] *R v Secretary of State for the Home Department, ex p Khan (Noor Nawal)* (9 May 1997, unreported) (McCullough J).

Breach of deportation order

16.12 A deportation order is defined by section 5(1) of the Immigration Act 1971 as an order requiring a person to leave and prohibiting him or her from entering the UK (see chapter 15) The section provides that a deportation order against a person invalidates any leave to enter or remain in the UK given before the order was made or while it is in force. What this means is that if someone subject to a deportation order still in force manages to obtain leave to enter, this will be invalidated by section 5(1). Questions of deception do not arise. The statutory invalidation of leave operates whether the deportee obtained it by deception or through the immigration officer's mistake.[1] The immigration authorities can make arrangements for the removal of deportees under the existing deportation order.[2] The only gain from removing them as illegal entrants is that sometimes the airline or shipping company can be made to pay their return fare, whereas in a deportation it is the British government which pays.[3]

[1] *R v Secretary of State for the Home Department, ex p Yeboah* [1986] Imm AR 52.
[2] Immigration Act 1971, Sch 3, para 1; on procedure see Immigration Rules, HC 395, para 388. For appeal rights see 16.60 below.
[3] See 16.52 and 16.54 below for arrangements for removal of illegal entrants and deportees respectively.

16.13 Most returning deportees will be illegal entrants because they have no leave.[1] They would still be illegal entrants if the words 'in breach of a deportation order' were omitted from the definition of illegal entrants in section 33(1) of the Immigration Act 1971. But these words are essential for those who do not need leave to enter the UK, such as Irish citizens and deportees of other nationalities who return through Ireland, or EEA nationals exercising free movement rights.[2] The operation of the deportation order is unaffected by the leave-free travel provisions of the EEA or common travel area.[3] Deportees of other nationalities who return to the UK on a local journey from Ireland do not need leave to enter, but are illegal entrants because their return is in breach of the deportation order. Where someone has been deported from the Channel Islands or the Isle of Man the order has the same effect as if it was a UK deportation order,[4] and the person who tries to enter the UK in breach of it would be an illegal entrant.

1 Immigration Act 1971, s 5(1).
2 See eg *Shingara v Secretary of State for the Home Department* [1999] Imm AR 257, CA.
3 Immigration Act 1971, ss 1(3) and 9(4).
4 Immigration Act 1971, Sch 4, para 3(1).

Entry through the common travel area

16.14 Those who arrive in this country after a local journey[1] from Ireland, the Channel Islands or Isle of Man – all parts of the common travel area – do not normally require leave to enter[2] and so unless they have arrived in breach of a deportation order they will not usually be illegal entrants.[3] But there are a number of exceptions. Those arriving from the Channel Islands or the Isle of Man will be illegal entrants if:

- their presence there was unlawful;[4] or
- they have previously been refused entry to the UK and have not been given a later leave to enter or remain.[5]

1 For the definition of a local journey, see Immigration Act 1971, s 11(4).
2 IA 1971, s 1(3). Generally on the common travel area see chapter 6 above.
3 By IA 1971, s 9(4) leave-free travel within the common travel area under s 1(3) does not affect the operation of a deportation order.
4 IA 1971, Sch 4, para 4.
5 IA 1971, s 9(4)(b).

16.15 For arrivals from Ireland the position is more complicated. A distinction has to be made between citizens of the Republic and other nationals who come via Ireland. Citizens of the Republic will only be illegal entrants if: (1) they are returning deportees; or (2) they return after being refused entry for national security reasons.[1] Other nationals who come via Ireland will be illegal entrants if they need leave to enter the UK under the Immigration (Control of Entry through Republic of Ireland) Order 1972[2] and enter without it.[3] Even if they are unaware that they ought to have obtained leave,[4] they can nevertheless be treated as illegal entrants in the following circumstances:[5]

(i)   they have previously been refused entry to the UK and have not been given later leave to enter or remain;[6]
(ii) although arriving on an aircraft which began its flight in the Republic they entered the Republic in transit from another country and did not obtain leave to land;[7]

(iii) they are visa nationals who have no valid visa to enter the UK;[8]

(iv) they entered the Republic unlawfully from a place outside the common travel area;[9]

(v) they entered the Republic from the UK or Northern Ireland when they were illegal entrants or overstayers there;[10]

(vi) directions have been given to exclude them from the UK on the ground that their exclusion is conducive to the public good.[11]

[1] Immigration Act 1971, s 9(4)(a). Here, the EC law public policy derogation will apply: see 7.131ff above.

[2] SI 1972/1610 (as amended by SI 1979/730, SI 1982/1028, SI 1985/1854, SI 1987/2092, SI 2000/1776); see chapter 6 above.

[3] They 'enter' the UK as soon as they leave their ship or plane (unless they have been examined by an immigration officer on board, and immigration officers do not usually travel on board): see Immigration Act 1971, s 11(1) and (2). So unless they obtain leave before leaving Ireland, they will already have become illegal entrants by the time they find an immigration officer on arrival.

[4] *R v Governor of Ashford Remand Centre, ex p Bouzagou* [1983] Imm AR 69, CA; *R v Secretary of State for the Home Department, ex p Mohan* [1989] Imm AR 436.

[5] See further 6.24 above.

[6] IA 1971, s 9(4)(b).

[7] SI 1972/1610 as amended, Art 3(1)(a).

[8] SI 1972/1610 as amended, Art 3(1)(b)(i).

[9] SI 1972/1610 as amended, Art 3(1)(b)(ii).

[10] SI 1972/1610 as amended, Art 3(1)(b)(iii). In *R v Secretary of State for the Home Department, ex p Wuan* [1989] Imm AR 501 a British Dependent Territories citizen from Hong Kong entered the UK when exempt from control as a member of the armed forces; he left for the Republic of Ireland after he ceased to be exempt; it was held that he was not excluded from the common travel area as an overstayer and had accordingly been given a deemed leave on his re-entry to the UK.

[11] SI 1972/1610 as amended, Art 3(1)(b)(iv).

DECEPTION, FALSE DOCUMENTS AND CORRUPTION

16.16 The amended definition of 'illegal entrant' in section 33 of the Immigration Act 1971 (16.7 above) is incomplete and still does not provide a satisfactory basis for illegal entry by deception, except where the deception is by a third party. Instead we have to look to the criminal provisions of the Act in much the same way as did the House of Lords in *Khawaja*.[1] Entry by deception occurs where the entrant: (i) makes or causes to be made a false representation contrary to section 26(1)(c) of the Immigration Act 1971 and such deception is the effective means of entry;[2] (ii) enters the UK by means including deception, contrary to section 24A of the 1971 Act;[3] or (iii) enters or seeks to enter by means which include deception by another person.[4] The decision in *Khawaja*[5] established that leave to enter is obtained in breach of the Act if the effective means of obtaining it is the commission of the offence of making a false representation under section 26(1)(c) of the 1971 Act.[6] The court held that the entrant had no duty of candour,[7] and is not deemed to be aware of all the Immigration Rules and conditions for entry. They doubted whether a person who was personally innocent of any fraud could be removed as an illegal entrant by reference to section 26(1)(c).[8] This part of the judgment has been superseded by the extension of the definition of illegal entry to include entry by means of deception by a third party.[9] The creation of a new criminal offence of obtaining or seeking to obtain leave to enter by deception[10] provides a clear statutory foundation for illegal entry by deception.

1 *Khawaja v Secretary of State for the Home Department* [1984] AC 74, [1984] 1 All ER 765, HL.
2 For ingredients of offence see 14.58 above.
3 For ingredients of offence see 14.30 above.
4 See definition of illegal entrant, Immigration Act 1971, s 33(1)(b).
5 *Khawaja v Secretary of State for the Home Department* [1984] AC 74, [1984] 1 All ER 765, HL.
6 *Khawaja* above at 118–119, per Lord Bridge.
7 Imposed on immigrants in the 1979 case of *Zamir v Secretary of State for the Home Department* [1980] AC 930, [1980] 2 All ER 768, HL.
8 *Khawaja* above at 199, per Lord Bridge.
9 Immigration Act 1971, s 33(1) as amended by Asylum and Immigration Act 1996, Sch 2, para 4. This statutory creation put an end to 20 years' debate in the courts: see *Khan v Secretary of State for the Home Department* [1977] 3 All ER 538, [1977] 1 WLR 1466, CA; *Khawaja v Secretary of State for the Home Department* [1984] AC 74, [1984] 1 All ER 765, HL; *Chan v Secretary of State for the Home Department* [1992] Imm AR 233, CA; *Hamid v Secretary of State for the Home Department* [1993] Imm AR 216, CA; *Kuet v Secretary of State for the Home Department* [1995] Imm AR 274, CA.
10 IA 1971, s 24A, inserted by Asylum and Immigration Act 1996, s 4 and amended by Immigration and Asylum Act 1999, s 28.

16.17 Deception in illegal entry cases involves representations made to the immigration officer at the port of entry and to an entry clearance officer at an overseas post.[1] Knowledge of falsehood is a key element. The deception may take a variety of forms. It may involve landing cards filled out on the plane, answers given to questions by an immigration officer, an entry clearance officer or medical inspector, as well as a whole host of representations which the courts have implied from the mere presentation of a passport, and representations by conduct.[2]

1 *R v Secretary of State for the Home Department, ex p Saffu-Mensah* [1991] Imm AR 43, QBD.
2 See *Akinde v Secretary of State for the Home Department* [1993] Imm AR 512, CA; *Al-Zahrany v Secretary of State for the Home Department* [1995] Imm AR 510, CA; *R v Secretary of State for the Home Department, ex p Awan* [1996] Imm AR 354, QBD; *R v Secretary of State for the Home Department, ex p Kuteesa* [1997] Imm AR 194, QBD.

16.18 The fact that leave no longer lapses when the holder leaves the common travel area[1] means that, if leave was obtained by deception, the holder enters illegally each time he or she enters the UK using it. What of the situation where leave obtained by deception lapses and fresh leave is sought on entry? For example, a returning resident seeking entry after more than two years away presents a passport endorsed with a previous indefinite leave to enter; strictly, the representation of indefinite leave, and thus eligibility as a returning resident, is accurate, as leave is not vitiated or rendered non-existent by deception; but if the presenter of the passport knows that the previous leave was improperly obtained, the judges will infer an implied representation that the leave was a lawful one.[2] Offering a passport containing a student leave implies a representation that the holder had validly been granted leave as a student.[3]

1   Immigration (Leave to Enter and Remain) Order 2000, SI 2000/1161, Art 13: see 4.4 above.

2   *R v Secretary of State for the Home Department, ex p Patel* [1986] Imm AR 515, CA; *R v Secretary of State for the Home Department, ex p Salim* [1990] Imm AR 316, QBD.

3   *Durojaiye v Secretary of State for the Home Department* [1991] Imm AR 307, CA.

16.19 Where the passport contains an entry clearance, a representation is implied: (i) that entry clearance was validly obtained; and (ii) that the person seeks entry for that purpose and no other.[1] The representation may be a silent one; although the duty of candour has gone, judicial enthusiasm for implying representations from the silent presentation of a passport has almost plugged the gap.[2] Each case will depend on its own facts, however, and an entrant who has reason to believe that a previous irregularity has been cured or pardoned will not be guilty of misrepresentation as to the nature of a previous leave.[3] Where there has been no contact at all between the immigrant and the immigration officer or entry clearance officer, there is no representation of any kind.[4] In *Doldur*[5] (where between the grant of a settlement visa as a dependent son and entry the applicant had married) the Court of Appeal held (by majority) that it was not an irresistible inference that he failed to reveal his marriage because he knew that to do so would affect his chances of entry. Rather, it was a reasonable inference that the applicant believed his marriage did not alter the fact that he entered as his father's dependant and would remain so until he found a job and could provide for his wife himself. The applicant had been asked no questions on arrival by the immigration officer and (in the words of Evans LJ) seeking to rely on his failure to volunteer information as a positive misrepresentation came very close to contending that he owed a duty of candour.[6] In *James* two adult twins who were mentally impaired were brought to the UK as visitors by their aunt, who subsequently died. The twins' admission that they had always wanted to live in the UK did not make them illegal entrants, because there was no evidence that this was the aunt's intention and they themselves had had no dealings with the immigration officer.[7]

1   *R v Secretary of State for the Home Department, ex p Saffu-Mensah* [1991] Imm AR 43, QBD (husband intending to join wife permanently if she would have him obtains entry clearance as visitor). See also *AL Zahrany v Secretary of State for the Home Department* [1995] Imm AR 510, CA; *R v Secretary of State for the Home Department, ex p Awan* [1996] Imm AR 354, QBD. Note that Immigration Act 1971, Sch 2, para 2A(2A), inserted by Asylum and Immigration (Treatment of Claimants) Act 2004, s 18 (in force 1 October 2004: SI 2004/2523), provides for examination of passengers with entry clearance for the express purpose of cancelling their leave if their purpose on entry is not that for which the entry clearance was issued.

2   See cases referred to at 16.17 fn 2 above. Silent presentation of a passport showing an earlier leave to enter obtained by false representations amounts to a fresh false representation: *R v Secretary of State for the Home Department, ex p Patel* [1986] Imm AR 515, CA. Re-entry on the basis of leave to enter obtained by a false representation is a fresh false representation which carries forward from one trip to the next *ad infinitum*: see *Khatun (Layla)* [1993] Imm AR 616, IAT (false representation made in 1969 still effective in 1992).

3   *R v Secretary of State for the Home Department, ex p Addo* (1985) Times, 18 April, QBD, followed in *R v Secretary of State for the Home Department, ex p Okunbowa* (19 November 1985, unreported), QBD.

4   *R v Secretary of State for the Home Department, ex p Dordas* [1992] Imm AR 99, QBD (ill-treated domestic servant, who decided before she left Kuwait to run away in the UK if the opportunity arose, was not an illegal entrant where her entry clearance was obtained by her employer and at the port her passport was also presented by him).

5   *Doldur v Secretary of State for the Home Department* [1998] Imm AR 352. For a case on
    the other side of the line see *Jahangir v Secretary of State for the Home Department*
    (11 December 1996, unreported), CA.
6   See also *R (Wilson) v Secretary of State for the Home Department* [2001] EWHC Admin
    115, in which visit leave was held not to have been obtained by deception, although an
    intention to remain with a settled spouse existed, because there were no questions on the
    length of the visit and the applicant was unaware of the visa requirement for family
    reunion.
7   *R v Secretary of State for the Home Department, ex p James* (CO 1955, 1956/92) (27 May
    1994, unreported), QBD (Sedley J).

16.20 In *Choudhry v Metropolitan Police*[1] the Divisional Court found that
an application to the Home Office to remain on the ground of marriage
carried with it an implied representation that it was a 'genuine' marriage and
not a marriage of convenience entered into solely to persuade the Home Office
to grant leave. The judgment was given on the basis that the implied
representation was of general application and not confined to the particular
defendant, with his particular knowledge of the Immigration Rules relating to
husbands. Unfortunately, the court did not refer to older cases dealing with
marriages of convenience.[2] A marriage solely for immigration and nationality
purposes is nevertheless a valid one; it is for the Home Office to consider
whether it also complies with the Rules.[3] The decision in *Choudhry* turns a
perfectly accurate statement of the law into a deception. The fact of marriage
is by no means conclusive of immigration and nationality status; such matters
as the parties' intention to cohabit and their financial security are further
criteria which may need to be satisfied.[4] To import into a statement that the
parties are married further representations that the marriage has qualities
required to give the spouse admission under the Rules is to turn application
and investigation upside down. It is strongly arguable that the decision in
Choudhry was wrong. Too great a readiness to find false representations risks
bringing back the duty of candour via the back door. It is to be hoped that the
issue may fall for reconsideration.

1   (24 November 1984, unreported), QBD.
2   *Silver (otherwise Kraft) v Silver* [1955] 2 All ER 614, [1955] 1 WLR 728; *Vervaeke v Smith*
    [1983] 1 AC 145, [1982] 2 All ER 144, HL; *Puttick v A-G* [1980] Fam 1, [1979] 3 All ER
    463.
3   Until the British Nationality Act 1981 came into force on 1 January 1983, Commonwealth
    citizens marrying patrial men automatically became patrial, no matter what the purpose of
    the marriage, provided merely that it was a valid one. If, however, fraud had been used, the
    courts might refuse to grant any relief: see *Puttick v A-G* above
4   The further criterion that the 'primary purpose' of the marriage should not be settlement
    was withdrawn from 5 June 1997 (one of the first acts of the new Labour government in
    honouring a manifesto commitment): see HC 26, amending Pt 8 of HC 395.

Effective deception

16.21 In *Khawaja* the House of Lords held that deception or fraud must be
the effective, or one of the effective means, of obtaining leave to enter, so as to
make the contravention of the Immigration Act 1971 and the obtaining of
leave two inseparable elements in the single process of entry.[1] This was further
explained in *Bugdaycay*,[2] where the House of Lords held that the question of
whether a fraud was effective in obtaining entry could only be considered in

the light of the application actually made and it was irrelevant that the person might have been admitted in some other capacity. In *Khawaja, Lord Bridge* thought that useful guidance as to what constituted effective means was given in the earlier case of *Jayakody*.[3] There the Court of Appeal held that the fraud must be decisive of the application, *ie* in all probability the leave would have been refused but for the deception. Thus a failure to reveal one of the purposes of an otherwise genuine visit, or to tell the immigration officer that a spouse was resident in the UK, might not be decisive of the grant or refusal of leave to enter. But the binding effect of *Jayakody* has been watered down by subsequent cases, which have moved the focus away from 'effective means' to mere 'materiality'. First, in *Durojaiye v Secretary of State for the Home Department*[4] Staughton LJ said that false answers to questions about a student's hours of attendance at college plainly were 'material in the sense it was likely to influence the decision'. This was followed by Laws J in *Ex p Ming*,[5] holding that a representation was material if, on revelation of the truth, 'at the very least further inquiries would have been made'. And in *Kaur v Secretary of State for the Home Department*[6] (an appeal against refusal of leave to enter on the ground that material facts were not disclosed for the purpose of obtaining a visa) Ward LJ stated that the time had come 'to put the *Jayakody* test to rest' as being 'quite inconsistent' with *Bugdaycay*[7] and *Durojaiye*.[8] He agreed expressly with Staughton LJ's analysis in *Durojaiye* as being the 'appropriate test'. However, *Khawaja* is still binding authority, and, by bedding *Jayakody*, the Court in *Kaur* cannot have intended to substitute 'mere materiality' for 'effective means' as the proper test for establishing the causal connection between the deception practised and the leave to enter granted by the immigration officer. That would be too much of a watering down. What is clear, however, is that the wording of the section 24A offence, inserted into the IA 1971 in 1999,[9] endorses the view put forward in *Khawaja* that the deception employed need only have been one of the factors leading to the grant of leave to enter, an effective but not necessarily decisive one.

[1]   *Khawaja v Secretary of State for the Home Department* [1984] AC 74 at 118E, per Lord Bridge.
[2]   *Bugdaycay v Secretary of State for the Home Department* [1987] AC 514, where a visitor failed to disclose his intention of applying for asylum. He was held to be an illegal entrant despite the fact that he would not have been removable had he claimed asylum.
[3]   *R v Secretary of State for the Home Department, ex p Jayakody* [1982] 1 All ER 461, [1982] 1 WLR 405, CA.
[4]   [1991] Imm AR 307, CA.
[5]   *R v Secretary of State for the Home Department, ex p Ming* [1994] Imm AR 216, Laws J. See also *R v Secretary of State for the Home Department, ex p Castro* [1996] Imm AR 540 where Dyson J was satisfied that deception was the effective means of obtaining leave to enter, but thought it 'may' have been sufficient for the Secretary of State to show that deception was material in the sense of being likely to influence the decision.
[6]   [1998] Imm AR 1, CA.
[7]   [1987] 1 AC 514, see fn 2 above.
[8]   [1991] Imm AR 307, CA.
[9]   Immigration and Asylum Act 1999, s 28.

16.22   There is substantial case law on the existence and effect of deception.[1] In the past particular problems were created where the Immigration Rules allowed a switch in categories from visitor to student or dependent relative status.[2] It was not permissible to come in with leave in one category with a fixed intention of applying to vary to another.[3] Although it was acknowledged by authority that there was a difference between a wish and an intention,[4] the courts are prepared to draw the inference of deception where all the circumstances warrant it.[5]

1   See, for example, *Re Olusanya* [1988] Imm AR 117, QBD (intending student gained entry as visitor); *R v Secretary of State for the Home Department, ex p Mahoney* [1992] Imm AR 275, QBD (visitor, always intended to study); *Tadimi v Secretary of State for the Home Department* [1993] Imm AR 90, CA (doing work inconsistent with student status); *R v Secretary of State for the Home Department, ex p Ahmed* [1993] Imm AR 242, QBD and *R v Secretary of State for the Home Department, ex p Miah* [1994] Imm AR 279, QBD (son pretending to be single when in fact married); *R v Secretary of State for the Home Department, ex p Zeenat Bibi* [1994] Imm AR 326, QBD (spouse posing as unmarried visitor). For instances where a deception was immaterial, see *R v Secretary of State for the Home Department, ex p Miah* [1989] Imm AR 559, CA; *R v Secretary of State for the Home Department, ex p Khan (Hiram)* [1990] Imm AR 327, CA.

2   Immigration Rules HC 395, para 60, 298. The introduction of mandatory entry clearance for all categories of entry over six months will eventually mean the end of post-entry switching from visitor to settlement categories, and therefore the end of this line of cases.

3   *Adesina v Secretary of State for the Home Department* [1988] Imm AR 442, CA; *Ex p Mahoney* above. Cf *R v Immigration Appeal Tribunal, ex p Coomasaru* [1983] 1 All ER 208, [1982] Imm AR 77 (returning residents entering as visitors, fixed intention to settle qualifies them as returning residents rather than as illegal entrants). This scenario is much less likely in any event since the Immigration (Leave to Enter and Remain) Order 2000, SI 2000/1161, Art 13.

4   See *Masood v Immigration Appeal Tribunal* [1992] Imm AR 69, per Glidewell LJ.

5   *R v Secretary of State for the Home Department, ex p Brakwah* [1989] Imm AR 366, QBD; *R v Secretary of State for the Home Department, ex p Nwanurue* [1992] Imm AR 39, QBD.

Invalid documents and third party deception

16.23 Although section 24A of the Immigration Act 1971 gives a firmer jurisprudential basis for illegal entry by deception, it only deals with deception by the person seeking to enter or remain, not deception by third parties. However, the amendment of the statutory definition of illegal entrant in section 33(1) in 1996[1] put to rest the question of third party deception, left open by the House of Lords in *Khawaja*,[2] and made it clear beyond doubt that the innocent proffering of false documents now makes the person proffering them an illegal entrant. The use of a false document, the falsity of which is unknown to the entrant, will now be dealt with as 'means which include deception by another'. But the person must have entered or be seeking to enter by means of the false documents; so where someone travels on forged documents but claims asylum at the immigration desk without seeking entry on the basis of the documents, the person is not an illegal entrant.[3] The need for a causal nexus between the offence and the entry makes it unlikely that the mere failure to produce a valid immigration document at a leave or asylum interview – although an offence under section 2 of the Asylum and Immigration (Treatment of Claimants etc) Act 2004 – could make the person an illegal entrant by entry in breach of the immigration laws.[4]

1   Asylum and Immigration Act 1996, Sch 2, para 4.
2   *Khawaja v Secretary of State for the Home Department* [1984] AC 74.

³ *R v Naillie* [1993] AC 674, [1993] 2 All ER 782, HL. However, intending immigrants discovered before entry in circumstances indicating an intention to enter illegally have been treated as illegal entrants for the purpose of convicting a facilitator in *R v Eyck, R v Hadakoglu* [2000] INLR 277.
⁴ For discussion of this offence see 14.33 above.

Breaking conditions of temporary admission

16.24 Where a person's examination is left unfinished for further inquiries to be made, he or she is normally given temporary admission under paragraph 21 of Schedule 2 to the Immigration Act 1971. Under section 11 of the Act persons on temporary admission are not deemed to have 'entered' the UK unless they have 'otherwise entered'. Absconders and those in breach of conditions of temporary admission may be detained, refused leave and summarily removed,[1] but, according to the Court of Appeal in *Akhtar v Governor of Pentonville Prison*,[2] they may also be treated as illegal entrants either on the basis that they were seeking entry by deception or that by breaking conditions of temporary admission they have 'otherwise entered' the UK without obtaining leave to enter.[3] But not every breach of temporary admission will make a person an illegal entrant, or at least liable to removal, unless, according to Evans LJ, the breach is sufficiently serious and deliberate to amount to an entry or an attempt to enter without leave.[4] This decision seems an unnecessary complication, which stretches the already fictional concept of 'entry' created by section 11. There are already adequate ways of dealing with those in breach of the conditions of their temporary admission (see 17.11 below), without the introduction of this kind of legal sophistry. In any event the test suggested by Evans LJ may well be unworkable, because the subjective intention of the absconder, almost certainly unaware of the conceptual subtleties imposed on us by section 11, will be an intention to remain, not to enter.

¹ Immigration Act 1971, Sch 2, paras 6, 8 and 21(1) and (4).
² *Akhtar v Governor of Pentonville Prison* [1993] Imm AR 424, CA; see also *R v Secretary of State for the Home Department, ex p Khan (Taj)* [1985] Imm AR 104, CA. See 16.29 below.
³ See *Akhtar* above at 431, per Sir Thomas Bingham MR.
⁴ *Akhtar* above at 431, per Evans LJ. We suggest that only absconding, and not breach of employment restrictions or of the draconian residence conditions which are envisaged in Immigration Act 1971, Sch 2, para 21(2B), would constitute illegal entry, since the latter does not indicate an intention to 'enter'. Escape from a removal centre would probably constitute illegal entry.

Leave to enter obtained by corruption or forgery

16.25 A forged leave to enter is clearly no leave at all.[1] A leave to enter obtained in knowing reliance on an entry clearance or a work permit itself obtained by corruption would be a leave obtained by fraud (because the proffering of such a permit or endorsement carries a representation that it was duly obtained).[2] But what if the entrant was unaware of the corruption? In previous editions of this work[3] we raised the possibility of an innocent entrant (not party to any false or corrupt procurement of leave to enter) being able to rely on such leave if it was issued by someone who had the authority to do so, particularly since an immigrant is not to be penalised for the errors or dishonesty of public officials.[4] If an innocent immigrant presents an entry clearance or work permit obtained by corruption to which he or she has not been a party, it is hard to see why such document, issued by a person with authority to do so, cannot be relied on, since neither it nor any leave obtained in reliance on it has been obtained by deception on anyone's part – unless it could be said that the endorsement of the passport by the corrupt official constitutes third-party deception just as forgery of a visa does.

1   *R v Secretary of State for the Home Department, ex p Musawwir* [1989] Imm AR 297.
2   See 16.19 above.
3   Fourth edition at para 16.34.
4   *R v Secretary of State for the Home Department, ex p Kuet* [1995] 2 All ER 891 (sub nom *Ku*), [1995] Imm AR 274, CA, observations of Sir Thomas Bingham MR.

Persons claiming to be British citizens

16.26 Persons who are British citizens cannot be removed as illegal entrants, even if they entered under some other nationality.[1] The difficulty may lie in proving the entitlement. The burden of proof rests on the immigrant concerned.[2] Section 3(9) of the Immigration Act 1971 requires proof of the right of abode by means either of a UK passport describing the holder as a British citizen (or a CUKC with the right of abode), or a certificate of entitlement certifying such right of abode. This will satisfy the initial burden and it will then be for the Home Office to demonstrate that the documents were improperly obtained or that the holder was not entitled to them.[3] In *Obi*[4] the burden of proof was everything (since it was accepted that if it lay on the Secretary of State it was not one he could discharge). The applicant had produced a UK passport describing him as a British citizen. The Secretary of State accepted that the passport described Mr Obi as a British citizen, but contended that until the applicant proved that he was Mr Obi, the passport was not one describing 'him' as a British citizen. The physical possession of a UK passport alone would not satisfy the section 3(9) test (for example, if it was believed to be stolen or forged the burden could not be discharged until the bearer could show him- or herself to be the person described in the passport). But here it was undisputed both that the person described in the passport as a British citizen had applied for it in Liverpool and that that person was the applicant (the photograph being indisputably his). Sedley J held that no further burden lay on the applicant. Where such an allegation is made in the course of illegal entry proceedings, the case is one within *Khawaja* principles. It should be noted that production of a birth certificate in the name of the applicant[5] or an identity document is not proof of British citizenship so as to shift the burden of proof on to the Secretary of State.[6] For disputed citizenship and deprivation of citizenship obtained by fraud see 2.61–2.62 above.

1   Immigration Act 1971, s 1(1).
2   Immigration Act 1971, s 3(8); see *Re Bamgbose* [1990] Imm AR 135, CA where a birth certificate did not discharge the burden as there was a dispute as to whether it truly related to the applicant. In *Mokuolo v Secretary of State for the Home Department* [1989] Imm AR 51, CA a statement as to birth in the UK in a Nigerian passport was similarly not sufficient.

3 A passport or certificate of entitlement are the means specified in the Immigration Act 1971 for proving citizenship: see s 3(9); Sch 2, para 3.
4 *R v Secretary of State for the Home Department, ex p Obi* [1997] Imm AR 420 QBD.
5 *Re Bamgbose* [1990] Imm AR 135, CA.
6 *Minta v Secretary of State for the Home Department* [1992] Imm AR 380, CA (British visitors passport (BVP), now discontinued).

Nationals of EEA and Association Agreement States

16.27 Similar considerations apply to EEA nationals. Under the Immigration (European Economic Area) Regulations 2000[1] EEA nationals must be admitted to the UK if, on arrival, they produce a valid national identity card or passport issued by another EEA state,[2] unless there are public policy reasons for their exclusion.[3] Community rights, as we have seen, flow from EC law and do not need any grant of leave under the Immigration Act 1971.[4] Add the removal of internal frontiers, and entry in breach of the immigration laws will be a rare and exceptional thing. It could occur if someone enters clandestinely without any intention of exercising free movement rights, for example, to land a consignment of drugs, or if someone enters in breach of a deportation order. The Court of Appeal held in *Shingara*[5] that it occurred when an EEA national entered after being excluded pursuant to a validly imposed exclusion order which complied with Council Directive (EEC) 64/221. Where an EEA national has entered illegally, removal can only take place in accordance with the public policy provisions of Council Directive (EEC) 64/221 and must not be discriminatory or disproportionate to the limited rights of Member States to impose penalties for infringements of their national procedures.[6] On the other hand, nationals of EC Association Agreement states seeking to establish themselves in business or self employment require leave to enter and may be required to obtain a visa,[7] and those who have established themselves in business or self-employment after entering unlawfully may be required to leave and seek entry in the proper way.[8]

1 SI 2000/2326.
2 SI 2000/2326, reg 12.
3 SI 2000/2326, reg 21.
4 *R v Pieck* [1981] QB 571; Immigration Act 1988, s 7(1); see chapter 7 above.
5 *Shingara v Secretary of the State Department* [1999] Imm AR 257, CA.
6 *EC Commission v Belgium* [1990] 2 CMLR 492, ECJ; *Re Royer* [1976] 2 CMLR 619, ECJ; *Re Watson and Belmann* [1976] 2 CMLR 552, ECJ.
7 *R (on the application of Barkoci) v Secretary of State for the Home Department* (C-257/99) [2001] ECR I-6357, ECJ.
8 *R v Secretary of State for the Home Department, ex p Gloszczuk* Case C-63/99 [2001] ECR I-6369; *R v Secretary of State for the Home Department, ex p Kondova* (C-63/99, C-235/99) [2000] ECR I-6427; *R (on the application of Krzysztofik) v Secretary of State for the Home Department* [2002] EWHC 744 (Admin), [2002] Imm AR 434. See further 7.169 above.

Refugees

16.28 Illegal entrants who are refugees cannot be removed to a country where they have a well-founded fear of persecution,[1] unless they are excluded from the protection of the Refugee Convention consequent to the commission of a particularly serious crime and constitute a danger to the community of the

UK,[2] and even then they cannot be removed if substantial grounds exist for believing that they face a real risk of treatment contrary to Article 3 ECHR: see 8.50 above. It is not contrary to the Immigration Acts or the UK's international obligations to treat asylum claimants who obtained leave to enter by deception (eg by presenting themselves as visitors) as illegal entrants.[3]

1   See chapter 12 above; Refugee Convention, Art 33.
2   Nationality Immigration and Asylum Act 2002, s 72; 12.97 above. Former refugees may be removed: see 16.43 below.
3   *Bugdaycay v Secretary of State for the Home Department* [1987] AC 514, [1987] 1 All ER 940, HL.

Treating someone as an illegal entrant

16.29 Although the immigration officer is the official responsible under statute for the decision that a person is to be treated as an illegal entrant and removed,[1] in practice it will often be made by the Home Office, either because of instructions given to the immigration officer or because the main decision is whether or not to grant leave to remain, and that decision is for the Secretary of State for the Home Department under section 4(1) of the Immigration Act 1971. Where the authorities decide to remove someone as an illegal entrant, despite an earlier grant of leave to enter, the burden of proving there was an illegal entry falls on the Home Office, and in any judicial proceedings the court inquires whether the facts precedent to the exercise of the administrative power have been proven.[2] However, the fact that a person has entered illegally does not oblige the Secretary of State to proceed to summary removal, as there is always a discretion to allow the person to stay.[3] In the previous edition, we discussed the difficulty caused by the fact that a number of policy statements[4] have conferred benefits on illegal entrants and overstayers which did not on their face apply to those seeking leave to enter, who might nevertheless have physically been in the country (on temporary admission), forming relationships and ties with the country, for many years, making it, paradoxically, necessary for persons to be 'recognised'[5] as illegal entrants rather than 'mere' port applicants to obtain the benefit of policies on family life.[6] This anomaly has now, we hope, been laid to rest by the Home Office acceptance in *Dabrowski*[7] that it was illogical and unfair not to give port claimants the benefit of such policies. Thus it should no longer be necessary for illegal entrants to insist on being treated as such, thereby laying themselves open to the charge of seeking to benefit from their own wrongdoing.[8] In any event, since the policies were designed to meet human rights concerns, the right of appeal on human rights grounds will normally enable the policy issues to be considered before removal.[9]

1   Immigration Act 1971, Sch 2, para 9. Modifications to Sch 2 made by the Immigration (Entry Otherwise than by Sea or Air) Order 2002, SI 2002/1832 give the same power to the Secretary of State when the illegal entrant arrives from Ireland.
2   *Khawaja v Secretary of State for the Home Department* [1984] AC 74, HL. See *R (on the application of Ullah) v Secretary of State for the Home Department* [2003] EWHC 679 (Admin), where the court rejected the argument that an allegation of illegal entry was a 'criminal charge' for Art 6 ECHR purposes, adding that the court could give leave to cross-examine where necessary.
3   See *Afunyah v Secretary of State for the Home Department* [1998] Imm AR 201, fn 8 below. Contrast *R v Secretary of State for the Home Department, ex p Urmaza* [1996] COD 479 (seaman deserter was illegal entrant and it was not open to Secretary of State not

to treat him as one). See further, on the need for an immigration official to exercise discretion whether or not to treat a person who is an illegal entrant as such, *R (Uluyol and Cakmak) v An Immigration Officer* [2001] INLR 194. The Home Office policy on when to treat port cases as illegal entrants is set out in IDI Ch 20 para 2.4.

⁴ See for example the marriage policy (DP/3/96) and the policies on children (DP/4/95 and DP 5/96), for which see *Butterworths Immigration Law Service*, D[551].

⁵ *Shahed (Abu) v Secretary of State for the Home Department* [1995] Imm AR 303; *Jackson (Magdalena) v Secretary of State for the Home Department* [1996] Imm AR 243; *Kadi v Secretary of State for the Home Department* [2001] EWHC Admin 375, [2001] All ER (D) 154 (May); cf *R v Secretary of State for the Home Department ex p Jagot (Mobin)* [2000] INLR 501.

⁶ See the previous edition of this work, 16.29. The relevant policies are set out in an addendum to *Dabrowski* (fn 7 below).

⁷ *R (on the application of Dabrowski) v Secretary of State for the Home Department* [2003] EWCA Civ 580 [2003] Imm AR 454 [2003] INLR 411. See para 17. The distinction between 'on-entry' and 'enforcement' cases is described in a Home Office witness statement reproduced as an addendum.

⁸ See *Afunyah v Secretary of State for the Home Department* [1998] Imm AR 201, CA followed in *R v Secretary of State for the Home Department, ex p Olawole* (FC3/000/6002/C) (18 April 2000, unreported), CA; *R (Ahmed) (Khalid) v Immigration Appeal Tribunal* [2002] EWHC Admin 624, [2002] Imm AR 427; contrast decision of Sedley J in *R v Secretary of State for the Home Department, ex p Urmaza* [1996] COD 479 (fn 3 above).

⁹ Nationality, Immigration and Asylum Act 2002, s 82, applying to immigration decisions generated on or after 1 April 2003. For pre-1 April 2003 decisions see Immigration and Asylum Act 1999, s 65. See further 16.60 below and 8.101ff above.

16.30 Once it is established that the person is an illegal entrant and that the immigration officer or Secretary of State is going to treat the person as such, the practice is to serve an IS 151A notice. There is no statutory requirement to do so, since it is not a decision to give or refuse leave, nor a notice of an immigration decision,¹ since it is not a decision to remove.² The service of such notice is significant in its own right, however, in that it dates the 'commencement of enforcement action' for the purposes of rules, policies and concessions based on long residence, marriage or other ties which the person may seek to rely on to argue that he or she should not be removed.³

¹ Ie, one of the decisions listed in Nationality, Immigration and Asylum Act 2002, s 82(2).
² In practice the IS 151A notice is now generally served together with the IS 151A part 2: See Operational Guidance Notes Ch 7, Service of notice of illegal entry: procedures. The notice of decision to remove gives rise to appeal rights and so attracts the provisions of the Notices Regulations: see Immigration (Notices) Regulations 2003, SI 2003/658, reg 4.
³ See 11.74 above for the policies relating to marriage; 11.122 for those relating to children, and 16.47 below for the long-residence rule. A marriage post-dating the commencement of enforcement action will not benefit from the Home Office policy on marriage, and makes an Art 8 family life claim difficult, see *R (on the application of Mahmood) v Secretary of State for the Home Department* [2001] 1 WLR 840.

Later leave to enter or remain

16.31 Under paragraph 9 of Schedule 2 to the Immigration Act 1971 the power of removal only arises where the illegal entrant has not been given 'leave to enter or remain':¹

'(1)   Where an illegal entrant is not given leave to enter or remain in the United Kingdom, an immigration officer may give any such directions in respect of him as in a case within paragraph 8 above as are authorised by paragraph 8(1);

(2)   any leave to enter the United Kingdom which is obtained by deception shall be disregarded for the purposes of this paragraph.'

This reflects the discretion of the immigration officer or Secretary of State to decide whether or not to allow an illegal entrant to remain in the UK. Section 9(2) was added to resolve the difficulty caused by the decision in *Khawaja*[2] to the effect that leave obtained by deception remained valid.[3] However, leave granted on a completely different basis (eg as a refugee) in ignorance of initial illegal entry (as, say, a visitor) cannot be disregarded, and would prevent removal, since the initial deception played no role in the grant of the new leave. The paragraph does not, however, cover the position of those who entered lawfully, but who subsequently obtained leave to remain by deception. Persons in this category who have left the UK and re-entered are clearly illegal entrants on re-entry with their original leave. Those who have obtained leave to remain by deception and have not left the country since are not illegal entrants, but may be summarily removed under section 10 of the Immigration and Asylum Act 1999.[4]

1   Immigration Act 1971, Sch 2, para 9(1), as amended by Asylum and Immigration Act 1996, Sch 2, para 6.
2   *Khawaja v Secretary of State for the Home Department* [1984] AC 74, HL.
3   The section gives statutory effect to the Court of Appeal decision in *R v Secretary of State for the Home Department, ex p Lapinid* [1984] 3 All ER 257, [1984] 1 WLR 1269, that Sch 2 para 9 to the Immigration Act 1971 must exclude leave obtained by deception, or any extension of it. Following *Azam v Secretary of State for the Home Department* [1974] AC 18, HL, an extension of leave granted by the Home Office prevented removal under para 9 even if based on the initial deception – a construction now excluded by para 9(2).
4   See 16.42 below. Prior to the 1999 Act such persons had to be deported on 'conducive to the public good' grounds (Immigration Act 1971, s 3(5)(b), as originally enacted).

16.32 Section 73 of the Nationality, Immigration and Asylum Act 2002 provides for the removal of the family members of illegal entrants.[1] Previously, the UK-born children of illegal entrants could not be removed, although young children would normally be taken by their departing parent at public expense. But it was up to the family whether they were taken or left in the care of friends or family in the UK, and they were not removable.[2]

1   Inserting a new para 10A into Sch 2 to the Immigration Act 1971.
2   Children born in the UK do not need leave to remain, so long as they do not leave the country, but they need leave to return: HC 395, para 304; see 11.83 above.

OVERSTAYERS AND OTHERS

16.33 From 2 October 2000 the following categories of individual who were formerly subject to deportation action became subject to administrative removal procedures identical to those which apply to illegal entrants and those refused leave to enter:

●   persons overstaying their limited leave;

- persons breaching a condition of their limited leave;
- those whose continued stay was obtained by deception; and
- family members of any of the above.[1]

Of these, only overstayers and those in breach who applied before 2 October 2000 for leave to remain in accordance with a specially constituted regularisation scheme were excluded from these procedures.[2] Those who qualified under the scheme, together with their dependants, remain subject to pre-existing arrangements.[3] The 2002 Act added two further categories of persons who may be administratively removed:

- those unsuccessfully using deception in seeking leave to remain;[4]
- persons ceasing to be refugees, whose indefinite leave to remain has been revoked.[5]

Under the removal provisions for the categories listed above, the person to be removed will be given written notice of the decision,[6] following which the immigration officer may authorise detention or make an order restricting residence, employment or occupation, or imposing reporting conditions pending removal.[7]

[1] Immigration and Asylum Act 1999, s 10(1); HC 395, para 395B as amended by Cm 4851. The first two categories were formerly liable to deportation under old s 3(5)(a) of the Immigration Act 1971, the third under s 3(5)(aa) and the last under s 3(5)(c).
[2] IAA 1999, s 10(2). The regularisation scheme is set out in s 9 of the IAA 1999. It closed on 2 October 2000. The Home Office said it had completed the exercise of processing all applications in August 2003. By November 2002 (the latest figure for which statistics are available), 2,954 applications under the scheme had been granted and 425 refused (WA 28.11.02, col 424W).
[3] Ie, they are subject to deportation action under former Immigration Act 1971, s 3(5)(a): Immigration and Asylum Act 1999, s 10(2), Nationality, Immigration and Asylum Act 2002 (Commencement No 4) Order 2003, SI 2003/754, Sch 2, para 6(2).
[4] IAA 1999 s 10(1)(b) as amended by Nationality, Immigration and Asylum Act 2002, s 74, from 10 February 2003 (SI 2003/1).
[5] IAA 1999 s 10(1)(ba), inserted by Nationality, Immigration and Asylum Act 2002, s 76(7), from 10 February 2003: SI 2003/1.
[6] HC 395, para 395E inserted by Cm 4851.
[7] HC 395, para 395F as inserted. See also Home Office Operational Guidance Notes Ch 11, Administrative removal procedures.

Exemption from administrative removal

16.34 Since administrative removal powers only apply to those who have had leave to enter the UK, British citizens and those with the right of abode, EEA nationals and their dependants, and persons exempt from control under section 8 of the Immigration Act 1971 are all exempt from administrative removal, since none of them needs leave to enter. Additionally, Commonwealth and Irish citizens who are exempt from deportation because they were ordinarily resident in the UK on 1 January 1973 and have been ordinarily resident for the five years immediately preceding the decision,[1] are also exempt from removal under section 10 of the IAA 1999.[2]

[1] For exemption from deportation see 15.5; for ordinary residence in this context see 15.8 above.

Overstaying and breach of conditions

16.35

Leave to enter the UK may be given for a limited period, and may be subject to a condition restricting employment or occupation, precluding recourse to public funds in maintenance or accommodation, or requiring registration with the police.[1] Failing to observe any of these conditions or remaining beyond the time limited by the leave makes a person liable to removal under section 10 of the Immigration and Asylum Act 1999. Thereafter, there needs to be a decision to remove, which involves the exercise of a discretion; see 16.46 below. The burden of proving overstaying or breach of conditions is on the Home Office. The Secretary of State must establish the facts which give rise to the power to remove, although reasonable suspicion is enough to justify detention. There are, however, one or two areas of difficulty. What are the ingredients of overstaying and breach of conditions which need to be proved in order to justify removal under section 10 of the 1999 Act?

1   Immigration Act 1971, s 3(1)(c): see 3.7 above.

16.36 The words in section 10(1)(a) of the Immigration and Asylum Act 1999 referring to persons 'having only a limited leave to remain' suggest the existence of a current leave either at the time of the breach or of the decision to remove, but this would make the provision inoperative as far as overstaying is concerned. The words are confusing, and in the context of overstaying the established view is that they need to be read as 'having had' leave.[1] To establish overstaying, the date of the expiry of leave will clearly need to be proved. Normally this can be done by looking at the passport, but where the passport is not available, or where leave was granted by other means, such as orally or by e-mail, no assumption may be made as to the date and duration of any leave granted. While the Home Office must prove overstaying as a precedent fact to the exercise of the power to remove, the provisions of the Immigration (Leave to Enter and Remain) Order 2000[2] impose a burden on the recipient of an oral leave, or a leave granted through a responsible third party, to establish the manner and date of his or her entry into the UK. The date of expiry of leave is not conclusive on the issue of overstaying, since if a valid in-time application for a variation was made prior to the expiry of limited leave, that leave is extended by statute while the decision on the variation application is pending and, if the decision is negative, while an in-time appeal could be brought and while any appeal is pending.[3]

1   See *Suthendran v Immigration Appeal Tribunal* [1977] AC 359, [1977] Imm AR 44, HL where this argument failed in relation to the similar construction of appeal rights under s 14 of the Immigration Act 1971. See further *Sabbagh* [1986] Imm AR 244.
2   SI 2000/1161, Art 11.
3   Immigration Act 1971, s 3C, as substituted by the Nationality Immigration and Asylum Act 2002, s 118 from 1 April 2003 (Nationality Immigration and Asylum Act 2002 (Commencement No 4) Order 2003, SI 2003/754), replacing s 3 and Sch 4, para 17(1) Immigration and Asylum Act 1999. Transitional provisions in SI 2003/754, Art 3, Sch 2,

para 2 provide that the terms of the amended s 3C shall apply to all decisions made on or after 1 April 2003 whenever the application to vary was submitted. Statutory leave lapses if the applicant or appellant leaves the UK: Immigration Act 1971, s 3C(3) as amended.

16.37 An issue which arose in the earlier case law on deportation was whether past overstaying or breach of conditions justifies removal. Past breaches of conditions were held to found liability for deportation in *Sabir*,[1] but different considerations may arise now that the response is summary removal in respect of which there is generally no suspensive merits appeal.[2] The use of the present tense in the reference to not observing a condition of leave or remaining beyond the time limited suggests that only current overstaying and breach of conditions founds liability to removal, not an historical breach, so that someone who has been granted further leave to remain after overstaying cannot be removed. In our view this is the only sensible construction; it is inconceivable that the grant of a fresh leave after overstaying could leave a residual liability to summary removal under section 10 of the Immigration and Asylum Act 1999 because of a past overstay or breach of conditions. It would be different if there were further overstaying or breaches. If a fresh leave was granted in ignorance of past overstay or breach, liability for summary removal would in any event result, if it were shown that the failure to refer to the past breaches constituted deception. If no deception was employed to obtain the fresh leave, and the past breaches were sufficiently severe to warrant enforcement action, we suggest the right course would be to make a decision to deport under section 3(5)(a) of the Immigration Act 1971 (deportation conducive to the public good). This would at least give rise to an appeal on the merits.

1   *Sabir* [1993] Imm AR 477. The Tribunal failed in that case to address the question as to whether liability to removal for breach of conditions continues once fresh leave is granted, which is not subject to the relevant condition.
2   For appeal against removal see 16.60 and 18.37 below.

16.38 If there is no extant leave, no conditions attach to it, so there can be no liability to removal for breach of conditions where the alleged breach occurs after leave expires. But leave extended under section 3C of the Immigration Act 1971 will be subject to the same conditions as the original leave. Thus, if a person who had leave with a condition prohibiting employment, works while an appeal against refusal of an extension is pending, he or she becomes liable to removal for breach of conditions under section 10 of the Immigration and Asylum Act 1999.[1]

1   Statutory leave pending appeal under IAA 1999, Sch 4, para 17(1) (repealed by Nationality Immigration and Asylum Act 2002, Sch 9 with effect from 1 April 2003) made this explicit, but the NIAA 2002 provisions are no less clear in intention and effect.

16.39 What happens if someone overstays or breaches conditions and then becomes exempt from immigration control under section 8(1) of the Immigration Act 1971? Cases under the old law established that exemption simply removed the person from control for the period of the exemption, so that liability to removal arising before the exemption continued to exist after the exemption ended.[1] But if leave was still current on termination of the exemption there was no continuing liability to enforcement action.[2] The position is not clear now that statutory leave of 90 days operates automatically at the end of the exemption if the person requires leave and does not have it.[3] One view is that removal could be enforced in this situation, since removal directions under section 10 of the Immigration and Asylum Act 1999 invalidate any leave granted before they were made, or while they are in force.[4] Another view is that the pre-1999 Act position still holds. Alternatively, since the 90-day leave is statutory, it is unaffected by what happened pre-exemption.

1   See *Sabbagh* [1986] Imm AR 244; *Noorhu* [1984] Imm AR 190, IAT.
2   *Ashiwaju* [1994] Imm AR 233, IAT.
3   Immigration Act 1971, s 8A(2), inserted by Immigration and Asylum Act 1999, s 7.
4   Immigration and Asylum Act 1999, s 10(8).

16.40 In cases of breach of conditions, the Home Office must show that the conditions are ones which may be lawfully imposed – there are only three conditions which may be lawfully imposed on a grant of leave: restrictions on employment or occupation; no recourse to public funds; and registration with police[1] – and that they have been properly notified.[2] This is particularly important with visit leave, which may be granted orally, and normally will be subject to conditions restricting working and precluding recourse to public funds. However, a person does not need to be knowingly an overstayer or in breach of conditions to be liable to removal (knowledge founds liability to criminal prosecution),[3] although in considering whether removal is justified by reference to the factors set out in the Immigration Rules, lack of knowledge will be highly relevant.[4]

1   Immigration Act 1971, s 3(1)(c). Thus, failure by a student to maintain 15 hours a week attendance on a course would not place him or her in breach of a condition attached to the leave to enter, so as to render that person liable to removal under section 10 of the IAA 1999, although it could give rise to curtailment of student leave under Immigration Act 1971, s 3(3)(a), or refusal of an extension (HC 395 para 323): *R (on the application of Zhou) v Secretary of State for the Home Department* [2003] EWCA Civ 51, [2003] 12 LS Gaz R 30.
2   IA 1971, s 4(1). Conditions are an integral part of leave and must be notified in writing along with the leave, unless the leave is visit leave granted orally by Immigration (Leave to Enter and Remain) Order 2000, SI 2000/1161, Art 8(3).
3   IA 1971, s 24(1)(b).
4   HC 395, para 395C, inserted by Cmd 4851; see *Hanif* [1985] Imm AR 57, IAT.

16.41 Another issue is whether every overstay or breach of conditions, however trivial, gives rise to liability to removal under section 10 of the Immigration and Asylum Act 1999. The likely answer is that all breaches give rise to liability, but trivial breaches are likely to be condoned.[1] A decision to remove always involves the exercise of a discretion, and could be challenged where, for example, Home Office policy is to overlook a minor breach or a short overstay, since it would be inconsistent with good administration and unfair to remove someone on that basis. For example, anyone whose leave is subject to a condition of no recourse to public funds may be liable to summary removal if he or she claims any welfare or social security benefits or homeless persons housing.[2] However, Home Office policy in relation to extension of stay is not to refuse in the case of strictly temporary recourse to public funds;[3]

it would thus be unreasonable to remove someone on this basis. Similar considerations apply to an overstay of a few weeks.

1   See *R v Secretary of State for the Home Department, ex p Amoa* [1992] Imm AR 218, QBD; *R v Secretary of State for the Home Department, ex p Ajayi* (1994) 28 HLR 25 (deportation). Home Office instructions state that working in breach must be recent (within the past six months), and of sufficient gravity to warrant removal: Operational Enforcement Manual Section B, Ch 10, para 10.6.4. Action may be appropriate where it appears that a student's main purpose in being here is work rather than study: para 10.6.5, and persons who have overstayed for only a short period may be removed if there is reason to believe that they have no intention of leaving the UK: ibid 10.6.3.
2   For the definition of public funds see HC 395, para 6, 6A (at 11.53 above).
3   See eg IDI Dec 04, Ch 8, Annex F, para 8.

Use of deception in seeking leave to remain

16.42   A person who obtained leave to remain by deception was for the first time rendered liable to removal (as opposed to deportation) by section 10 of the Immigration and Asylum Act 1999.[1] Section 74 of the Nationality Immigration and Asylum Act 2002 has substantially extended liability to removal in this category, which is now triggered by any use of deception by a person seeking leave to remain, 'whether successful or not.[2] The amendment appears to render irrelevant the proposition that any deception must have been 'effective' in order to permit initiation of enforcement action.[3] The wording of the section indicates that the deception must be that of the applicant him- or herself rather than that of a third party, although it can clearly include the use of false documents as well as the making of false representations. Leave granted on the basis of such deception would be invalidated by the issue of removal directions,[4] but deception must be proved to a high degree of probability.[5]

1   Immigration and Asylum Act 1999, s 10(1)(b).
2   Immigration and Asylum Act 1999, s 10(1)(b) as amended by Nationality, Immigration and Asylum Act 2002, s 74. Section 76 of the Nationality Immigration and Asylum Act 2002 enables the Secretary of State to revoke ILR granted by deception even where the person cannot be removed for legal or practical reasons (eg Art 3 ECHR, or no direct flights to the country or territory concerned). See 5.11 above.
3   See the discussion at 16.16–16.22 above on what constitutes deception, and what is a material deception in leave to enter cases.
4   Immigration and Asylum Act 1999, s 10(8).
5   *Khawaja v Secretary of State for the Home Department* [1984] AC 74.

Persons ceasing to be refugees

16.43   The Nationality Immigration and Asylum Act 2002 provides that refugees may have their indefinite leave to remain revoked if they voluntarily avail themselves of the protection of their country of nationality, voluntarily re-acquire a lost nationality, acquire the nationality or avail themselves of the protection of a country other than the UK, or voluntarily establish themselves in the country in respect of which they were granted refugee status.[1] Once indefinite leave is revoked, they are liable to removal.[2] There is a right of appeal against revocation of indefinite leave, but no separate right of appeal against removal after revocation.[3]

16.43 *Removal and other Expulsion*

1   Nationality Immigration and Asylum Act 2002, s 76(3)(a)–(d), reflecting the provisions of the Refugee Convention, Art 1C(1)–(4). The Act does not provide for revocation of the indefinite leave of refugees where the circumstances in their country of origin have changed fundamentally (Art 1C(5) of the Convention), reflecting the Secretary of State's policy only to withdraw ILR on the basis of a voluntary act by a refugee incompatible with continuing refugee status: Lord Bassam of Brighton, *Hansard* (HL) 17July 2002, col 1331. See further: *Secretary of State for the Home Department v MW (National passport: re-availment of protection) Pakistan* [2004] UKIAT 0013, a significant case in that the Tribunal applied the principle of re-availment of national protection to humanitarian protection. See further 12.84ff above.

2   Immigration and Asylum Act 1999, s 10(1)(ba), inserted by Nationality, Immigration and Asylum Act 2002, s 76(7).

3   Nationality, Immigration and Asylum Act 2002, s 82(2)(f) (right of appeal against revocation), see s 82(2)(g) which omits this category from those liable to removal under Immigration and Asylum Act 1999, s 10 who may appeal against removal.

Family members

16.44 Where directions have been given for the removal of a person under section 10 of the Immigration and Asylum Act 1999, his or her family members are also liable to removal under section 10 provided those family members were notified no more than eight weeks after the departure of the first person.[1] The detailed criteria for removal of family members mirror those for deportation of family members, at 15.21 and 15.37, to which reference should be made.

1   Immigration and Asylum Act 1999, ss 10(1)(c), (3), as amended by Nationality Immigration and Asylum Act 2002, s 73.

SEA, AIR AND TRAIN CREWS

16.45 Seamen and air and train crews are a special category, as we have seen.[1] Section 8(1) of the Immigration Act 1971 provides that they may enter the UK without leave, and remain until the departure of the ship, aircraft or train in which they are required by their engagement to leave. This concession is subject to exceptions, and means that crew members can be treated as illegal entrants if they require leave to enter and enter without it. They also become illegal entrants if they desert their ship, plane or train and remain in this country. This is because of the provisions of section 11(5) of the Act which provide that someone who enters the UK lawfully under section 8(1) and seeks to remain beyond the section 8(1) time limit is to be treated as 'seeking to enter the UK'.[2] However, these distinctions are somewhat academic, because Schedule 2 to the Act gives immigration officers powers to order the removal of crew members who overstay, or who the immigration officer reasonably suspects of intending to do so.[3] In view of these draconian powers there is perhaps no need to declare seamen or air or train crews illegal entrants and to treat them as such.

1   See 6.30 above.

2   See *R v Secretary of State for the Home Department, ex p Urmaza* [1996] COD 479 where Sedley J held that a seaman deserter was an illegal entrant on this analysis. DP/2/93 applied to 'all illegal entry cases' and on the plain and ordinary meaning of such words it was not open to the Secretary of State to contend that it did not apply to the applicant as a seaman

deserter. Contrast this approach with *Afunyah v Secretary of State for the Home Department* [1998] Imm AR 201, CA (16.29 fn 8 above).
3   Immigration Act 1971, Sch 2, paras 12 and 13, modified in relation to Channel Tunnel trains by SI 1993/1813, Sch 4, para 1(11)(n).

USE OF DISCRETION IN REMOVAL CASES

16.46 The fact that a person is liable to be removed as an illegal entrant, or an overstayer and so on, does not always mean that he or she should be removed. In relation to those who are liable to removal as illegal entrants, the Immigration Rules are silent on how the discretion is to be exercised. But in the case of those liable to removal under section 10, the rules set out factors which the Secretary of State must take into account, which are identical to the factors required to be considered in deportation cases.[1] This requires consideration of all relevant circumstances, including: age; length of residence and strength of connections with the UK; personal history, including character, conduct and employment record; domestic circumstances; criminal record; compassionate circumstances; and representations made on the person's behalf. They are discussed in detail at 15.30ff above. In the case of family members, the factors listed in HC 395, paras 365–368 will also be taken into account.[2] In addition, there are policies to which the Secretary of State must have regard in deciding whether to remove illegal entrants and overstayers – in particular, those relating to marriage and children,[3] which are described at 11.74 and 11.122 above. No one may be removed as an illegal entrant or as an overstayer, etc if removal would be contrary to the Refugee Convention or the ECHR.[4]

1   See HC 395, para 395A–D, as amended by Cmd 4851.
2   HC 395, para 395C. These relate to the degree of independence of the principal of the family members the Secretary of State proposes to remove.
3   See e g *R v Secretary of State for the Home Department, ex p Amankwah* [1994] Imm AR 240, QBD; *R v Secretary of State for the Home Department, ex p Ahmed, R v Secretary of State for the Home Department, ex p Patel* [1998] Imm AR 375, [1998] INLR 546, QBD; on appeal [1998] INLR 570, CA; *R (on the application of Dabrowski) v Secretary of State for the Home Department* [2003] EWCA Civ 580, [2003] Imm AR 454, [2003] INLR 411.
4   HC 395, para 395D as amended. For the Refugee Convention see chapter 12 above, for ECHR see chapter 8.

The long residence rule

16.47 The 'long residence' rule incorporated into the immigration rules on 1 April 2003,[1] which was formerly a Home Office concession, originated in the UK's ratification in 1969 of the European Convention on Establishment. Article 3(3) of the Convention provided that nationals of any contracting state who had been lawfully resident for over ten years in the territory of another party could only be expelled for reasons of national security or for particularly serious reasons relating to public order, public health or morality. The Home Office, when implementing this Article, extended it in three respects:

- to include all foreign nationals;
- to grant indefinite leave rather than simply refrain from removal; and
- to allow those who have been in the UK illegally to benefit.

16.47 *Removal and other Expulsion*

The rule perpetuates the distinction between lawful residence, which confers eligibility for settlement after ten years,[2] and residence partly or wholly unlawful, conferring eligibility only after 14 years.[3] In either case, it must be continuous. Continuity of residence will not be broken by short absences of six months or less at any one time during periods of leave, but will be broken by removal, deportation or departure after refusal of leave to enter; departure from the UK with a clear intention not to return or in circumstances where there was no reasonable prospect of lawful return; by a custodial sentence or hospital order; or by a total of 18 months outside the UK.[4] The grant of indefinite leave under the rules on the grounds of long residence is discretionary, and ILR will only be granted, if there are no reasons, having regard to the public interest, making it undesirable to do so, taking into account a list of factors almost identical to those the Secretary of State is required to consider when contemplating deportation action. These include: age, strength of connections in the UK, personal history including character, conduct, associations and employment record, domestic and compassionate circumstances, criminal convictions and representations from third parties.[5]

1 HC 395, para 276A–E, inserted by HC 538.
2 Lawful residence means residence with leave to enter or remain, on temporary admission where leave is subsequently granted, or an exemption from control: HC 395, para 276A(b). The IDI (Ch 18) para 7 assert that a person who is still exempt from control cannot apply for ILR, but the rule does not require an applicant to have current leave to remain in order to qualify, and on the face of it would not preclude an application from someone whose exemption from control was extant but about to end.
3 The distinction was first made in 1987; see previous edition 16.43. The 14 years' residence under the rule excludes any period spent in the UK following service of notice of liability to removal, of removal directions under Sch 2 to the IA 1971 or s 10 of the IAA 1999, or of a notice of intention to deport: HC 395 para 276B(i)(b) as amended by Cmd 6339 on 24 Sep 2004. This reflects the case law under the previous policy: see *R v Secretary of State for the Home Department, ex p Ofori* [1994] Imm AR 34, CA; *Musah v Secretary of State for the Home Department* [1995] Imm AR 236, *Hussain v Immigration Appeal Tribunal and Secretary of State for the Home Department* [1991] Imm AR 413, although this was held only to apply when the person became aware of the notice: *R v Secretary of State for the Home Department, ex p Popatia and Chew* [2000] INLR 587.
4 HC 395, para 276A(a) as inserted. For cases on continuity of residence under the old policy see the previous edition of this work, 16.43 text and fn 4.
5 HC 395, para 276B(ii) as inserted.

16.48 Policies which have not found their way into the rules include the policy against removal of unaccompanied minors, which applies where there is no evidence of suitable reception and care arrangements available in the home country,[1] and the 'seven year rule', a concession embodying a general presumption against removal of families with children who have put down roots in the UK. The policy benefits families otherwise liable to be removed, with children who were born in the UK and have lived here continuously to the age of seven or over, or who, having come to the UK at an early age, have accumulated seven years' or more continuous residence.[2] There may be circumstances where enforcement action is still considered appropriate, for example, where the parents have a particularly poor immigration history and have deliberately caused serious delay to the consideration of their case. Relevant factors will include the length of the parents' residence without leave, whether removal has been delayed through protracted and repetitive representations, or by going to ground; the age of the children; whether they were

1084

conceived when either parent had leave to remain; whether return to the parents' country of origin would cause extreme hardship for the children or put their health seriously at risk; and whether either parent has a history of criminal behaviour or deception.[3] Additionally, a one-off exercise announced in October 2003 benefited asylum seeking families with children, where an application for asylum had been made before 2 October 2000 and a dependent child aged under 18 at the date of the announcement was living in the UK since 2 October 2000.[4]

[1] DP4/96, see 11.122 above.
[2] DP069/99, previously known as DP5/96, modified on 24 February 1999, see *Butterworths Immigration Law Service*, D[1121]. It does not apply where the child is over 18 at the time the case is considered; these cases will be considered on their merits. See also 11.122 above. At the time of writing there are indications that this policy is to be abolished or modified.
[3] Policy DP069/99.
[4] One-off exercise to allow families who have been here for at least three years to stay, Home Office press release 24 October 2003, amended August 2004. Families where the principal applicant or a dependant had a criminal conviction, an anti-social behaviour order (ASBO) or a sex offender order, had made or attempted to make an asylum claim in more than one identity, or was the subject of a possible third country removal, were excluded from the exercise, as were those presenting a security risk, or falling within Article 1F of the Refugee Convention (exclusion from refugee protection) or whose presence in the UK was deemed otherwise not conducive to the public good). The deadline for applications under the concession was 31 December 2004.

REMOVAL DIRECTIONS

16.49 Removal can only take place if directions are properly given in accordance with paragraphs 8–10 of Schedule 2 to the IA 1971. The statutory provisions for making removal directions have a coherent structure: the various powers to give directions comprise a progression in which each envisages directions less specific than the last. The first stage is directions for removal in the very vessel (ship or aircraft) in which the person arrived (para 8(1)(a)). The second is directions for removal in any specified vessel owned or operated by the same carrier as brought the person to the UK (para 8(1)(b)). The third is directions to that carrier to remove the person in any specified or indicated vessel (even if the carrier is not the vessel's owner or agent) to a specified country or territory (para 10(1)). The last is directions for removal 'in accordance with arrangements to be made by the Secretary of State' to any country or territory to which he could have been removed under the previous two powers paragraph 10(2).[1] Directions may be given, a deportation order may be signed, and any other preparatory steps to facilitate removal may be undertaken, at any time while a claim for asylum or a suspensive appeal is pending.[2] Actual removal cannot, however, be effected until a decision on the asylum claim is notified and any in-country rights of appeal are exhausted.[3] Removal directions are not mere notifications to the carrier of its obligations, but are part of the machinery for removal. An immigrant affected by a direction is therefore entitled, in appropriate circumstances, to challenge its validity.[4] In *DJ v Secretary of State for the Home Department* the Tribunal considered the effect of removal directions which were defective in that there was no indication on their face whether the Secretary of State was removing the person as an illegal entrant, an overstayer or other 'immigration offender', as required by the Notice Regulations,[5] and held that where reasons had been provided in a separate letter there was substantial compliance.[6]

1   *Jazayeri v Secretary of State for the Home Department* [2001] INLR 489, para 15.
2   Nationality Immigration and Asylum Appeals Act 2002, ss 77(4) and 78(3), subject to ss 79 and 92. It used to be thought that a direction was only valid if it indicated clearly that the immigrant was then, and not at some future unspecified date, required to be removed: see *R v Immigration Officer, ex p Shah* [1982] 2 All ER 264, [1982] 1 WLR 544, DC (a direction to the airline to remove the applicant to India 'as soon as his application to enter the UK is finally resolved' was held invalid); *R (on the application of Khadir) v Secretary of State for the Home Department* [2003] EWCA Civ 475, [2003] INLR 426, para 46 (dictum by Chadwick LJ that, at a time when there were no flights to the Kurdish Autonomous Zone and no possibility of return to Baghdad, it was difficult to see how directions for the removal of an Iraqi Kurd 'by scheduled airline to Iraq at a time and date to be notified' could have been thought appropriate or to be an effective exercise of the power conferred by Sch 2 to the Immigration Act 1971); contrast *Jayazeri v Secretary of State for the Home Department* [2001] INLR 489 IAT (immigration officers directions for removal 'at a time and date to be notified' upheld); *Hussain* [2002] UKIAT 03419; *Messar* [2002] UKIAT 00846. In *Hashemi* [2002] UKIAT 02975 the Tribunal thought such a notice could well be invalid, but that the defect could be remedied by amendment prior to determination of an appeal.
3   Nationality, Immigration and Asylum Act 2002, ss 77(1) and 78(1).
4   *R v Immigration Officer, ex p Shah* [1982] 2 All ER 264, [1982] 1 WLR 544; *Singh (Parshotam) v Secretary of State for the Home Department* [1989] Imm AR 469, CA.
5   See 18.83 below.
6   *DJ v Secretary of State for the Home Department (Defective Notice of Decision) Iraq* [2004] UKIAT 00194.

Removal after refusal of leave to enter

16.50 Where passengers arriving in the UK are refused leave to enter, an immigration officer may arrange for their removal by the owners or agents of the aircraft or ship which brought them in.[1] If such arrangements are made within two months the carriers must bear the costs of removal, and they are also liable if removal is not effected within this timescale but the immigration officer has given them written notice of the intention to remove.[2] In calculating the period of two months, any period during which an appeal is pending under the Immigration Acts is to be disregarded.[3] As indicated above, enforcement action cannot be effected whilst a suspensive right of appeal under section 82(1) of the Nationality Immigration and Asylum Act 2002 is pending. However, as we saw in the last paragraph, there is no longer a statutory prohibition on the giving of removal directions (or the initiation of other preparatory steps to facilitate removal) whilst a claim for asylum or appeal proceedings are outstanding.[4] Where directions are issued in respect of a principal applicant, directions may also be given in respect of family members.[5] The failure to remove a person refused leave to enter within two months, or to make arrangements or give notice to the carriers of proposed removal, does not prevent later removal.[6] But after two months the Secretary of State for the Home Department takes responsibility for the removal and must pay for it.[7] The government will pay the cost of removal when removal under the normal procedure is 'not practicable' or would be 'ineffective' and special arrangements have to be made.[8] A captain of a ship or airline who is told to remove someone and fails, without reasonable excuse, to comply, commits a criminal offence and is liable to a fine or imprisonment.[9] In this context it is also material to note that the IAA 1999 for the first time provided that directions for removal may include provision that the person being removed have an escort, which the carrier may be required to pay for.[10]

1 Immigration Act 1971, Sch 2, para 8(1). There is no specific provision for the removal of persons whose advance leave to enter is cancelled under Sch 2, para 2A(8), who are left in limbo, unable to enter the UK without leave but apparently irremovable until a further decision to refuse leave to enter.

2 IA 1971, Sch 2, para 8(2), as amended by Immigration Act 1988, Sch, para 9. The modification of para 8 by the Immigration (Entry otherwise than by Sea or Air) Order 2002, SI 2002/1832, provides for the Secretary of State to defray the costs of returning persons entering or seeking to enter via the land border through the Republic of Ireland.

3 IA 1971, Sch 2, para 8(2), as amended by Nationality Immigration and Asylum Act 2002, Sch 7, para 4.

4 Nationality Immigration and Asylum Act 2002, ss 77 and 78. Sch 9 to the Act repealed the Immigration and Asylum Act 1999, Sch 4, Pt II, para 10 which precluded the making of removal directions and provided that directions previously issued ceased to have effect while an appeal was pending, from 1 April 2003.

5 IA 1971, Sch 2, para 10A, inserted by Nationality Immigration and Asylum Act 2002, s 73 from 10 February 2003 (SI 2003/1). Read literally, the amendment would allow immigration officers to remove UK-based family members of a visitor refused leave to enter, which would clearly be absurd. The Explanatory Notes to the 2002 Act state that its purpose is to remove UK-born children of those who have been on temporary admission for some time, and of illegal entrants.

6 IA 1971, Sch 2, para 10(1)(b). See *Rahman (Mohammed) v Secretary of State for the Home Department* [1995] Imm AR 488, CA; *Al Zahrany v Secretary of State for the Home Department* [1995] Imm AR 283.

7 IA 1971, Sch 2, para 10(3).

8 IA 1971, Sch 2, para 10(1)(a). In *Jayazeri v Secretary of State for the Home Department* [2001] INLR 489 (starred), a starred Tribunal held that an immigration officer could issue directions under this paragraph without express delegation from the Secretary of State.

9 IA 1971, s 27(a). This measure forms part of the range of measures, including carriers' liability, penalties for inadvertent carriage of stowaways and employer sanctions, which implicate private companies and individuals in the enforcement of immigration control.

10 Immigration and Asylum Act 1999, s 14. Regulations may require the carrier to arrange for the escort's return to the UK and for his or her remuneration. No regulations have yet been made under the section.

16.51 Apart from the time limit which determines who is to pay for removal, there is no express requirement on the part of the authorities to act quickly. In *Rafiq*[1] the Divisional Court had held that it was entirely reasonable to delay for six weeks the giving of directions for removal, until the Home Office had discovered whether or not the applicant would be admitted to Pakistan. The alternative course would have been to direct his removal without establishing whether the directions would be effective. But where a person is in custody pending removal, there is a requirement to act reasonably promptly; otherwise detention may become unlawful.[2] The Nationality, Immigration and Asylum Act 2002[3] allows persons in respect of whom removal directions have been or might be set, but who cannot be removed for practical or legal reasons, to be treated as 'liable to detention' for the purpose of granting temporary admission, even though they cannot actually be detained.[4]

1 *R v Secretary of State for the Home Department, ex p Rafiq* [1970] 3 All ER 821.

2 *R v Governor of Durham Prison, ex p Singh* [1984] 1 All ER 983, [1984] 1 WLR 704, [1983] Imm AR 198, QBD: see 17.41 below.

3 Nationality Immigration and Asylum Act 2002, s 67.

⁴ *R (on the application of Khadir) v Secretary of State for the Home Department* [2003] EWCA Civ 475, [2003] INLR 426, on appeal to the House of Lords at the time of writing.

Removal of illegal entrants

16.52 Precisely the same removal procedure operates in the case of illegal entrants (assuming of course that the illegal entrant can in fact be removed),¹ save that the two-month time limit for immigration officers' directions does not apply.² Illegal entrants who are discovered as stowaways coming off a particular ferry may clearly be the subject of directions to the captain, but in the case of illegal entrants who are not detected at the port, it will rarely be 'practicable' or 'effective' to identify or issue directions to the company which brought them in, in which case responsibility falls on the Secretary of State, who bears the costs.³ Where directions are issued for the removal of an illegal entrant, directions may also be given for the removal of family members.⁴

¹ See *R v Secretary of State for the Home Department, ex p Yu and Lin* (CO 393/1999, CO 4621/1999) where permission was granted for judicial review of the failure to remove or to regularise Chinese illegal entrants for over four years while travel documents were awaited from the Chinese authorities. The matter never reached full hearing because the travel documents were finally issued and removal was effected.
² Immigration Act 1971, Sch 2, para 9, referring to para 8(1). See *Rahman v Secretary of State for the Home Department* [1995] Imm AR 488, CA. The modification of para 9(1) by the Immigration (Entry otherwise than by Sea or Air) Order 2002, SI 2002/1832, provides for the Secretary of State to defray the costs of returning persons entering or seeking to enter illegally via the land border through the Republic of Ireland.
³ IA 1971, Sch 2, para 10(1)(a), 10(3).
⁴ Immigration Act 1971, Sch 2, para 10A, inserted by Nationality, Immigration and Asylum Act 2002, s 73(1). This allows UK-born children of illegal entrants to be removed, although the breadth of the power would need to be limited by reasonable criteria such as age, length of residence in the UK etc.

Removal under section 10 of the Immigration and Asylum Act 1999

16.53 For persons subject to administrative removal, including those whose indefinite leave to remain has been revoked under section 76(3) of the Nationality Immigration and Asylum Act 2002,¹ but excluding those overstayers subject to the deportation procedure under transitional provisions² and those who would be exempt from deportation,³ directions are set by the Secretary of State as if after refusal of leave or illegal entry.⁴ Issue of removal directions immediately invalidates any extant leave.⁵ The costs of removal, so far as reasonably incurred, will be borne by the Secretary of State.⁶ Family members may be removed if directions have been issued in respect of the person to whose family they belong, provided the Secretary of State has given written notice of the intention to remove.⁷ If removal as a dependant is proposed then directions must be given within eight weeks of the departure of the principal to whose family they belong.⁸

¹ Ie, those ceasing to be refugees: Immigration and Asylum Act 1999, s 10(1)(ba), inserted by Nationality Immigration and Asylum Act 2002, s 76(7).

2   Ie, overstayers or those in breach of conditions served with a notice of intention to deport before 2 October 2000, or who applied for regularisation under s 9 of the IAA 1999 and have been served with a notice of intention to deport since: Nationality, Immigration and Asylum Act 2002 (Commencement No 4) Order 2003, SI 2003/754, Art 3 and Sch 2, para 6(2): see 16.33 above.

3   Immigration and Asylum Act 1999, s 10(10), inserted by Nationality, Immigration and Asylum Act 2002, s 75.

4   IAA 1999, s 10(7); see the Immigration (Removal Directions) Regulations 2000, SI 2000/2243.

5   IAA 1999, s 10(8). Leave may be extant although obtained by deception, or in cases of breach of conditions.

6   IAA 1999, s 10(9).

7   IAA 1999, s 10(1)(c) and 10(3) (s 10(3) substituted by Nationality Immigration and Asylum Act 2002, s 73(2) from 10 February 2003 (SI 2003/1). Directions for the removal of family members cannot take effect if they cease to be family members (eg by divorce, leaving home or turning 18): s 10(5A) as inserted.

8   IAA 1999, s 10(4), as substituted.

Removal of deportees

16.54 For persons subject to deportation action, the arrangements for removal are set out in Schedule 3 to the Immigration Act 1971.[1] The cost again falls on the Secretary of State for the Home Department, except where the deportees are made to pay for their own removal.[2] A deportation order may not be made whilst an appeal against deportation under section 82(1) of the Nationality Immigration and Asylum Act 2002 may be brought or is pending,[3] but may be made in respect of a person who has a claim for asylum pending.[4] Thus a person who does not claim asylum until a deportation appeal has been dismissed may have an order made against him or her, though plainly it cannot be effected while the claim is being determined.[5]

1   Immigration Act 1971, Sch 3, para 1.

2   IA 1971, Sch 3, para 1(4).

3   Nationality Immigration and Asylum Act 2002, s 79, in force 1 April 2003 (SI 2003/754 Art 2, Sch 1), applied to appeals under the old appeals provisions by Art 3 and Sch 2, para 1(4).

4   Nationality Immigration and Asylum Act 2002, s 77(4), applying to claims pending both before and after 31 March 2003 (SI 2003/754 Arts 2, 3, Sch 1, Sch 2, para 1(2)).

5   Nationality Immigration and Asylum Act 2002, s 77(1).

Removal of sea, air and train crews

16.55 Here the removal arrangements are very similar to those of persons refused entry. Initially, responsibility for removal and its costs are borne by the owners or agents of the ship or aircraft or train manager of whose crew the person to be removed is a member, but if this is not practicable or would be ineffective the alternative removal arrangements are paid for by the government.[1] In the case of *Ex p Urmaza*,[2] Sedley J had to consider when enforcement action began against a deserting seaman who had married and resided in this country. He concluded that it was when removal directions were given and not when the exemption from obtaining leave to enter was revoked, and thus the enforcement policy applied in the same way as other cases.

1 Immigration Act 1971, Sch 2, paras 12–14.
2 *R v Secretary of State for the Home Department, ex p Urmaza* [1996] COD 479, (1996) Times, 23 July.

COUNTRIES TO WHICH REMOVAL IS POSSIBLE

16.56 The range of countries to which removal may be effected varies according to the immigration status of the person being removed. Overstayers etc and deportees may only be removed to a country:

- of which they are nationals or citizens; or
- to which there is reason to believe they will be admitted.[1]

Illegal entrants and those refused entry can be removed to a wider range of countries:

- of which they are nationals or citizens;
- in which they obtained a passport or identity documents;[2]
- from which they embarked for the UK; or
- to which there is reason to believe they will be admitted.[3]

The power to return those refused leave to enter to the country of embarkation or any country to which there is reason to believe that they will be admitted provides the statutory basis for the removal of asylum claimants to 'safe' third countries without determining their claim under section 33 of and Schedule 3 to the Asylum and Immigration (Treatment of Claimants, etc) Act 2004. Members of a ship or aircrew may additionally be removed to the country where they were engaged.[4]

1 Immigration (Removal Directions) Regulations 2000, SI 2000/2243, reg 4(2); Immigration Act 1971, Sch 3, para 1.
2 The Tribunal in *Matanoviq* [2002] UKIAT 01874 was of the view that 'other document of identity' in Sch 2, para 8(1)(c)(ii) of the IA 1971 has to be read *ejusdem generis* as 'passport' – the provision appears to require some document of identity issued at some stage by the state authorities of the country in question, which will at least raise an inference that the holder has a right to be there.
3 Immigration Act 1971, Sch 2, paras 8(1)(c)(i)–(iv) and 10(1). 'Admitted' does not mean admitted for an indefinite period: *Alsawaf v Secretary of State for the Home Department* [1988] Imm AR 410, CA.
4 IA 1971, Sch 2, para 12(2)(c)(iv).

16.57 The country of nationality or citizenship may under the rules of international law be bound to receive its own nationals.[1] There is, therefore, usually no problem about admission.[2] But where persons are being removed to other countries, there may be difficulties. There is nothing in any of the legislation which suggests that the immigration authorities must check on whether a person will be admitted before directing their removal to that country. But it is not enough for the Secretary of State to conclude that a person ought to be admitted to a country which is not obliged to accept him or her if there is no evidence that admission is likely to be granted.[3]

1 See chapter 8 above.

2   This is subject to proof of nationality: see discussion at 16.65 below on measures related to the provision of travel documents for removal.
3   *R v Secretary of State for the Home Department, ex p Yassine* [1990] Imm AR 354.

16.58 The country of destination specified in removal directions has been the subject of extensive scrutiny by the courts. Removal directions which fail to specify a country of destination at all are invalid and do not give rise to a right of appeal.[1] This does not apply where a part of a country or a city is named so as to leave no doubt as to the country to which removal is intended.[2] The naming of the wrong country in the removal directions has been held not to affect an asylum appeal, but to require reconsideration and amendment of the directions.[3] A starred Tribunal in *Zeqaj v Secretary of State for the Home Department* laid down detailed guidance on the proper approach to dealing with cases of this type, indicating that any apparent defects as to destination in the removal directions should be raised at the preliminary hearing stage in appeal proceedings.[4] They indicated that where the error had prejudiced the appellant, the directions should be withdrawn and fresh directions served, giving rise to a fresh appeal, but where the appellant was not so prejudiced, irregularities should be waived.

1   *Makambo* [2002] UKIAT 06619, 19 February 2003 (a legal tribunal headed by Deputy President Ockleton). The earlier decision of *No 19* (01/TH/0093), in which a Tribunal of Collins P, Ockleton DP and Moulden VP held a notice valid for appeal purposes even though no destination was specified, cannot in our view stand.
2   *Sula and Demaj* (01/TH/00504), where removal directions for 'Kosovo' and 'Pristina' were held sufficiently unambiguous as to the country of destination to be valid.
3   *Ertan* (19510) 5 July 1999. See also *Wolde v Secretary of State for the Home Department* [2002] UKIAT 01068 (10 April 2002, unreported).
4   *Zeqaj* [2002] UKIAT 00232 (4 February 2002, unreported) (starred). Although the Court of Appeal reversed the Tribunal's decision, see *Zeqaj v Secretary of State for the Home Department* [2002] EWCA Civ 1919, [2003] Imm AR 298, [2003] INLR 109, the point on appeal was the scope of an appeal under the Immigration and Asylum Act 1999, s 66 and does not affect this guidance.

16.59 The situation is more complex where nationality is disputed. In cases where the Secretary of State does not accept the claimed nationality of an asylum seeker, the issue of which country to specify in removal directions has caused many problems for the appellate authorities dealing with an asylum appeal.[1] The Secretary of State's current practice is to specify removal to the applicant's claimed country of nationality, for appeal purposes, a practice which received the endorsement of a starred Tribunal in *MY (Somalia)*,[2] and the Tribunal and the High Court have made it clear that an applicant who claims to be of a specified nationality for the purposes of an asylum claim cannot be heard to deny that nationality when it comes to removal directions.[3] It is not the function of the appellate authority to ascertain an alternative nationality.[4] However, where the Secretary of State asserts that the applicant has more than one nationality, and issues directions specifying one destination country, so that the issues on an asylum appeal are limited to that country, he cannot subsequently switch and issue directions to the second country without allowing the applicant a further appeal.[5]

1   See eg *Abubakar* (01TH02477) (6 December 2001, unreported), where an adjudicator upheld the Secretary of State's decision that the asylum seeker was not Somali and then held that the removal directions specifying Somalia were invalid and that there was no

valid appeal. The Tribunal allowed the Secretary of State's appeal but remitted the case to the Secretary of State to reconsider nationality and to issue directions accordingly.

2 [2004] UKIAT 00174, in which the President (Ouseley J) said that it was difficult to see how an applicant could challenge the rejection of nationality and its consequences without any removal being proposed.

3 *Khan (Asif)* [2002] UKIAT 04412 (where the claimant's contention that he was from Afghanistan was rejected, and before the Tribunal he sought to challenge the removal directions specifying Afghanistan on the ground that the adjudicator had found he was not of that nationality); *Hamza* [2002] UKIAT 05185; *R (on the application of Tu) v Secretary of State for the Home Department* [2002] EWHC 2678 Admin, [2003] Imm AR 288, a similar scenario involving a disputed Indonesian nationality, where the Administrative Court exercised its inherent jurisdiction to refuse relief.

4 *Khan (Asif)* above. The Secretary of State accepts that, where the adjudicator upholds his decision on an appellant's nationality, he must undertake further investigations to seek to ascertain the true nationality to effect lawful removal (unless removal can be effected to another lawful destination under Immigration Act 1971, Sch 2, para 8(1)(c) such as the country of embarkation). The court in *Tu* (fn 3 above) left open the possibility that a challenge to the legality of removal directions may be feasible on the grounds that risk on return had not been assessed in relation to the new destination. However in *MY (Somalia)* (fn 2 above) the Tribunal made it clear that an applicant who had lied about his or her nationality would not be able to put forward a fresh, inconsistent story in response to removal directions to a different country.

5 *Wolde v Secretary of State for the Home Department* [2002] UKIAT 01068.

CHALLENGING DECISIONS TO REMOVE

Appeal rights

16.60 The complicated and fragmented structure of appeals against removal and against destination provided for in the 1971 and 1999 Acts has been swept away by the Nationality, Immigration and Asylum Act 2002.[1] A decision to remove someone as an overstayer, for breach of conditions or for obtaining or seeking to obtain leave to remain by deception, is an immigration decision which gives rise to a right of appeal under section 82 of the NIAA 2002.[2] A decision to remove a person as an illegal entrant[3] is likewise an immigration decision, as is a decision to remove someone as a family member of a person in either group, and a decision to remove a member of a crew.[4] It is the decision which attracts the right of appeal, and not its implementation by removal directions. All the potential grounds of appeal set out in section 84 are available, including the argument that the decision is 'not in accordance with the law',[5] enabling arguments about both whether the condition prec- edent for removal in each case is met (ie whether the person is in fact liable to removal as a member of the particular category), and whether the specified country of destination is a lawful one.[6] Appeals against the decision to remove are not suspensive of removal and are out-of-country, unless there is an EEA issue[7] or the person has made an asylum or human rights claim in the UK, which has not been certified clearly unfounded,[8] but an appeal which is in-country by virtue of such a claim is not limited to asylum or human rights grounds, and the difficulties encountered in the previous regime by the Court of Appeal in *Zeqaj*[9] should no longer deter the Tribunal from addressing the lawfulness of a proposed destination. An issue which arose in the context of asylum appeals under the Asylum and Immigration Appeals Act 1993 and human rights appeals under the Immigration and Asylum Act 1999 was whether, in the frequent case where removal directions are set, deferred or cancelled and then re-set, the second set gave rise to a second right of appeal.[10] The Court of Appeal held this to be the case in *Kariharan*,[11] but section 82 of the NIAA 2002 reversed the effect of the decision by tying appeal rights to the decision to issue removal directions, rather than the directions themselves.[12]

[1]   Immigration and Asylum Act 1999, s 66 provided an appeal against removal directions to an illegal entrant or overstayer, limited to arguing that there was no power in law to make them on the ground stated. This effectively limited appellants to arguing that they were not in fact illegal entrants etc, and prevented arguments on issues such as the lawfulness of the country of destination: *Zeqaj v Secretary of State for the Home Department* [2002] EWCA Civ 1919, [2003] Imm AR 298, [2003] INLR 109. In addition, certain categories of person had an appeal against destination under s 67 of the Act, but they had to be able to proffer an alternative destination which would take them: see the previous edition of this work, at 16.64–16.66.

[2]   Nationality, Immigration and Asylum Act 2002, s 82(2)(g).

[3]   Nationality Immigration and Asylum Act 2002, s 82(2)(h).

[4]   Nationality Immigration and Asylum Act 2002, s 82(2)(i), (ia).

[5]   Nationality Immigration and Asylum Act 2002, s 84(1)(e).

[6]   Ie, under Immigration Act 1971, Sch 2, para 8(1)(c); Sch 3, para 1; Immigration (Removal Directions) Regulations 2000, SI 2000/2243, reg 4(2). See 16.58 above.

[7]   EEA nationals and their family members may appeal in-country if they claim that the decision breaches their rights under the Community Treaties: Nationality Immigration and Asylum Act 2002, s 92(4)(b); Immigration (EEA) Regulations 2000 SI 2000/2326 (as amended), regs 29(1) and 30 and Immigration (Swiss Freedom of Movement) (No 3) Regulations 2002, SI 2002/1241, reg 2(1) which equates Swiss nationals with EEA nationals for free movement purposes.

[8]   Nationality Immigration and Asylum Act 2002, s 92(4)(a) read with s 94(2); for clearly unfounded claims see 8.102 above.

[9]   *Zeqaj v Secretary of State for the Home Department* [2002] EWCA Civ 1919, [2003] Imm AR 298, [2003] INLR 109; fn 1 above. For a discussion about lawful destinations see 16.56 above.

[10]   The Asylum and Immigration Appeals Act 1993, s 8(4), and Immigration and Asylum Act 1999, s 69 attached the right of appeal to the issue of directions. Section 65 of the IAA 1999 gave an appeal on human rights grounds against any decision relating to the appellant's entitlement to enter or remain in the UK', a formulation broad enough to encompass the setting of removal directions: see below.

[11]   *R (on the application of Kariharan, Kumarakuruparan and Koneswaran) v Secretary of State for the Home Department* [2002] EWCA Civ 1102, [2002] 3 WLR 1783, where the Court held that the setting of removal directions was a 'decision relating to entitlement to enter or remain' under IAA 1999, s 65.

[12]   Section 82(2)(g)–(i) (appeal against decision to remove by directions: overstayers etc, illegal entrants and family members). Transitional provisions protect appeal rights under IAA 1999, s 65 against decisions taken before 1 April 2003, where an allegation was made prior to 1 July 2003 that the decision violated the appellant's human rights: SI 2003/754 Sch 2, para 7(5).

Judicial review

16.61 An appeal against a decision to remove someone alleged to be unlawfully in the country cannot, as we have indicated above, be brought in-country unless there is an EEA, human rights or asylum issue, and there is no separate appeal against the removal directions themselves (as opposed to the decision to issue them). In cases which do not raise such issues, and where the validity or appropriateness of removal directions is contended, judicial review will continue to be the principal means of challenge. Before 1999, habeas corpus could be brought to challenge the detention for removal of a person believed to be an illegal entrant, and the court was bound to ensure that the jurisdictional facts (that the applicant was in fact an illegal entrant) had been established. But the 1999 amendments to the powers of detention mean that anyone may now be detained if he or she is *reasonably suspected* of being someone in respect of whom removal directions may be given.[1] Those suspected of being illegal entrants, overstayers, in breach of conditions, or guilty of remaining by deception may be detained under the amended provisions of the Immigration Act 1971, as may members of their families and crew members, and a *habeas corpus* application to secure their release would fail, provided reasonable suspicion could be made out, such suspicion being the only condition precedent to lawful detention. Effectively, this change sounded the death-knell for *habeas corpus* in removal cases, save where there is no reasonable suspicion (ie *mala fides* is alleged) or where detention is excessively lengthy (the *Singh* situation).[2]

[1] Immigration Act 1971, Sch 2, para 16(2), as amended by Immigration and Asylum Act 1999, s 140(1).
[2] *R v Governors of Durham Prison, ex p Singh* [1984] 1 All ER 983, QBD. See 17.41 below.

16.62 However, on a plain reading of the Immigration 1971 and Immigration and Asylum Act 1999, the power to *remove* illegal entrants, overstayers, and so forth is still contingent on their actually being such, and not on reasonable suspicion.[1] On any challenge to proposed removal, whether by way of judicial review or on a statutory appeal, the Secretary of State must establish the factual basis for the jurisdiction to remove, ie, that the person to be removed is an illegal entrant, or is someone who had a limited leave and overstayed, or breached conditions of stay, sought or obtained leave to remain by deception, is a former refugee whose indefinite leave to remain has been revoked, or is a family member of a person liable to removal. The court must arrive at its own conclusion on the evidence before it.[2] Once the party seeking relief has discharged the initial burden of showing that he or she has a case fit to be considered by the court (in illegal entry cases a burden discharged by a leave stamp in the person's passport or other evidence that leave was granted,[3] or by the production of a British passport),[4] the burden of proving the necessary facts lies on the immigration officer or Secretary of State.[5]

[1] Immigration Act 1971, Sch 2, para 9; Immigration and Asylum Act 1999, s 10(1). Contrast IA 1971, Sch 2, para 12(2), which allows removal of those reasonably suspected of being overstaying sea or air crew members.
[2] *Khawaja v Secretary of State for the Home Department* [1984] AC 74, [1983] 1 All ER 765.
[3] Immigration (Leave to Enter and Remain) Order 2000, SI 2000/1161, Art 8.
[4] Immigration Act 1971, s 3(8), *R v Secretary of State for the Home Department, ex p Obi* [1997] INLR 173.
[5] *Khawaja, Obi* above.

Standard of proof and evidential issues

16.63 If the Secretary of State for the Home Department must discharge the burden of showing that an applicant is an illegal entrant, an overstayer, etc if removal directions are challenged, how and to what standard is it done? In *Khawaja* Lords Bridge and Scarman concluded that the civil standard of proof applied, but that where fraud was alleged 'the court should not be satisfied with anything less than probability of a high degree'.[1] The Court of Appeal followed this in *Rahman*.[2] Where the immigration appellate authority has decided a disputed issue of identity or relationship after hearing oral evidence, and the Secretary of State later treats the person as an illegal entrant on new information on the disputed issue, the starting point is the binding decision of an appropriate Tribunal in favour of the applicant, so the standard of proof to establish illegality is even higher.[3] However, on judicial review or post-removal appeal, the facts may (and in the vast majority of cases will) be established by way of written statements, although in judicial review, cross-examination may be permitted by a judge when justice so demands.[4] In *Ex p Patel*[5] Webster J thought that very little assistance would be gained from the cross-examination of witnesses who could only give their evidence through an interpreter or in English as their second or third language. He considered at length the difficulties of assessing the demeanour and credibility of such witnesses – reflections which should be borne in mind by the appellate authority. In *Doldur v Secretary of State for the Home Department*[6] Thorpe LJ commented that it was incumbent on the Secretary of State to face the applicant with the challenge of cross-examination where the allegation of deceit was based on failure to volunteer information, since, following *Khawaja*, there was no duty of candour, and deception could not be irresistibly inferred. The court should examine all the evidence, including hearsay evidence, on which the Secretary of State or the immigration officer relied in reaching the decision, to decide whether the conclusion of illegal entry, overstay, etc was justified.[7] Because of the erratic and haphazard way illegal entry interviews were recorded by Home Office officials, Woolf J recommended[8] proper safeguards such as making contemporaneous notes and reading them over to the person being interviewed; in fact most, if not, all illegal entry interviews are now tape-recorded. In England and Wales an allegation that a caution was not properly administered does not render an interview inadmissible, but goes to the weight to be attached to any admissions contained in it.[9] But the Scottish courts have held that interviews not conducted under caution may not be relied on to establish illegal entry by deception.[10]

---

1   *Khawaja v Secretary of State for the Home Department* [1984] AC 74 (per Lords Bridgeand Scarman).
2   *R v Secretary of State for the Home Department, ex p Rahman* [1997] Imm AR 197, CA.
3   *R v Secretary of State for the Home Department, ex p Miah* [1983] Imm AR 91; *Ali v Secretary of State for the Home Department* [1984] 1 All ER 1009, [1984] Imm AR 23.
4   *Khawaja v Secretary of State for the Home Department* [1984] AC 74 at 124. See also *R v Secretary of State for the Home Department, ex p Rouse and Shrimpton* (13 November 1985, unreported), DC where Woolf J said that cross-examination should not be used to shore up a weak case.
5   *R v Secretary of State for the Home Department, ex p Patel* [1986] Imm AR 208, affirmed at [1986] Imm AR 515, CA.
6   [1998] Imm AR 352.
7   *Khawaja* above, per Lord Templeman [1983] 1 All ER 765 at 794–795 and [1984] AC 74 at 128; *ex p Rahman* [1996] 4 All ER 945, QBD; affd [1997] Imm AR 197, CA. More recently in *R (on the application of Ullah) v Secretary of State for the Home Department* [2003] EWCA Civ 1366, [2003] All ER (D) 179 (Oct), a case concerning an assertion by a UK settled spouse (the complainant) that a marriage was not genuine and subsisting at the time when leave to enter was granted, the Court of Appeal held that the production of a witness statement from the complainant was not a prerequisite to founding an allegation of illegal entry and that hearsay evidence from the complainant recorded in an interview with an immigration officer was evidence which could be relied on to found the allegation, was

admissible in judicial review proceedings and was evidence to which a judge was entitled to have regard for the purpose of forming his own conclusion, although its weight was a matter for the court.

8   In *R v Secretary of State for the Home Department, ex p Govinden* (1985) Times, 12 July.
9   *Yasin v Secretary of State for the Home Department* [1997] Imm AR 97, CA.
10 *Oghonoghor v Secretary of State for the Home Department* 1995 SLT 733, OACS; *Kim (Sofia) v Secretary of State for the Home Department* 2000 SLT 249.

Challenging the exercise of discretion in judicial review

16.64 As indicated above, most decisions to remove will be appealable in-country if human rights grounds are raised,[1] so judicial review of the exercise of discretion, where liability for removal is accepted, will be limited to cases where the Secretary of State certifies that a human rights or asylum claim is clearly unfounded or repetitive or tardy, and so does not attract in-country appeal rights (dealt with at 8.102 and 12.171 above) or cases raising issues other than asylum or human rights grounds. For those cases, challenges in respect of this exercise of discretion will be based on normal judicial review principles.[2] It may, for example, be possible to establish a legitimate expectation that someone should have the benefit of one of the Home Office policies.[3] Where it is accepted that the person is innocent of any irregularity, this is a relevant consideration in deciding whether removal should follow;[4] this remains the position even though 'innocent' entrants may be illegal entrants on the basis of third-party deception.[5] For an illustrative example of a successful challenge of this exercise of discretion see the decision of McCullough J in *Noor Nawal Khan*.[6]

1   See 16.60 above. Note that pursuant to the Immigration (Notices) Regulations 2003, SI 2003/658, reg 5(6) the refusal notice will not have indicated that such an appeal was available unless the person concerned claims that the decision is unlawful under the Race Relations Act or the ECHR or the Refugee Convention, in which case the notice must be re-served with the relevant appeal information.
2   For judicial review see 18.183 below.
3   See eg *Gyeabour* [1989] Imm AR 94, IAT; *Zeriba* (1999) 5 ILD 2, IAT.
4   Donaldson J in *R v Secretary of State for the Home Department, ex p Hassan* (1981) Times, 22 July, CA; see also *R v Secretary of State for the Home Department, ex p Sheikh* (4 February 1982, unreported), DC; Sir Thomas Bingham MR in *Ex p Kuet* [1995] Imm AR 274; *Rehal v Secretary of State for the Home Department* [1989] Imm AR 576, CA, but the court will not necessarily grant permission for the issue of innocence to be judicially resolved.
5   Immigration Act 1971, s 33(1), as amended by Asylum and Immigration Act 1996, Sch 2, para 4; 16.19 above.
6   *R v Secretary of State for the Home Department, ex p Khan (Noor Nawal)* (9 May 1997, unreported); see 16.11 above.

CARRYING OUT REMOVAL

16.65 Those liable to be removed from the UK, particularly illegal entrants, will often possess no valid travel documents (or none at all) and no proof of identity or nationality. The authorities of the state to which removal is proposed may, not unreasonably, require production of identification data to enable them to confirm the person's nationality before issuing a travel document. Although under the Immigration Act 1971 wide powers existed to deal with this situation,[1] the process usually required the co-operation of the proposed returnee, which was not always forthcoming. Rejected asylum seekers in particular resisted giving information which they feared might endanger families at home. In the first instance judgment in *Amirthanathan*, the Administrative Court recognised this fear as well-founded in cases where an appeal had been lodged:

> 'It is inappropriate to require a person to give an interview to the authorities of the destination country to facilitate obtaining a travel document, since the interview might lead to information being provided which might put the claimant or his family at risk'.[2]

The IAA 1999 empowered the Secretary of State to release to the authorities of the proposed country of removal identification data on the returnee, such as fingerprints.[3] Provisions of the Data Protection Act 1988 forbidding transfer of personal data to states outside the EEA were avoided by deeming the transfer of such personal data 'necessary for reasons of substantial public interest'.[4] Finally, the AI(TC)A 2004 forces returnees to cooperate in their own removal, by making it a criminal offence punishable by two years' imprisonment to fail without reasonable excuse to cooperate in endeavours to obtain travel documents.[5] The Act also enables the Secretary of State or an immigration officer to retain any document which comes into their possession in the exercise of an immigration function, while there is a suspicion that the person to whom it relates may be liable to removal and that retention of the document might facilitate the removal.[6]

[1]   Immigration Act 1971, Sch 2, para 18(2) and (2A), allowing immigration officers, police, prison officers and anyone else authorised by the Secretary of State to photograph, measure, fingerprint and otherwise identify detainees, and para 18(3), allowing them to take detainees anywhere necessary to establish their citizenship, and to make arrangements for their admission to another country.

[2]   *R (on the application of Amirthanathan) v Secretary of State for the Home Department* [2003] EWHC Admin 1107, [2003] All ER (D) 29 (May) at para 39. This aspect of the judgment was not dealt with by the Court of Appeal at [2003] EWCA Civ 1768, [2003] All ER (D) 129 (Dec). However, in *R v Secretary of State for the Home Department, ex p Z* [1998] Imm AR 516, Moses J had held that the power to make removal directions implied a power to obtain the information required to implement the directions, and failure to co-operate would empower the Secretary of State to detain under Immigration Act 1971, Sch 2, para 18(2).

[3]   Immigration and Asylum Act 1999, s 13. At present the data concerned is confined to fingerprints, but s 13(5)(b) empowers the Secretary of State to make regulations permitting collation of data on other external physical characteristics which may also be released under s 144 of the Act.

[4]   Immigration and Asylum Act 1999, s 13(4), which renders inapplicable the eighth principle of Sch 1 to the Data Protection Act 1998, prohibiting transfer of personal data to countries outside the EEA unless an adequate level of protection in relation to its processing is guaranteed. The only express limitation is that the Secretary of State must not disclose whether or not an asylum claim has been made (s 13(3)). This miserable sole safeguard is wholly inadequate to protect those whose national authorities are made aware by the transfer of identification data that they are in the UK without travel documents and that they are shortly to be returned home.

[5]   Asylum and Immigration (Treatment of Claimants, etc) Act 2004, s 35, in force 22 July 2004 (s 48(1)).

[6]   AI(TC)A 2004, s 17, in force 1 December 2004 (SI 2004/2999).

16.66 To ensure that directions for removal are effective against the captain of a ship or airline or against the owners or agents, it is made a criminal offence for them to disobey directions without reasonable excuse.[1] Where directions for removal have been given, the person to be removed may be placed, under the authority of an immigration officer or the Secretary of State, on board any ship or aircraft in which that person is to be removed in accordance with those directions.[2] Detainee custody officers are empowered to use force in the exercise of their functions,[3] and force has certainly been used, on occasion with fatal effects.[4] Once the person is on board, it becomes the responsibility of the captain of the ship or aircraft to prevent them escaping. For this purpose they may be detained until removal is fulfilled.[5] A captain who knowingly lets such persons disembark, commits a criminal offence and is liable to a fine or imprisonment.[6] Where a person who is being removed threatens suicide, or gives any indication that he or she may attempt suicide, immigration officers are under instruction to seek the port medical inspector's opinion of the person's state of mind and not to pursue removal without reference to the passenger casework section of the Immigration Service.[7] The Immigration and Asylum Act 1999 has provision for escorts to accompany the removed person, to be specified in the removal directions.[8] The section empowers the Secretary of State to make regulations regarding the costs of such escorts.[9] A person's removal under the provisions of section 5, Schedule 2 or Schedule 3 to the IA 1971 is not precluded by a travel restriction order under the Criminal Justice and Police Act 2001.[10]

1   Immigration Act 1971, s 27(a)(ii) and (b)(iii).
2   IA 1971, Sch 2, paras 11 and 15; Sch 3, para 1(3) (modifed in relation to the Channel Tunnel by SI 1993/1813, Art 7(1), Sch 4, para 1(11); in relation to controls between the UK, France and Belgium by SI 1994/1405, Art 7, and in relation to certain persons entering or seeking to enter through the Republic of Ireland by SI 2002/1832).
3   Immigration and Asylum Act 1999, Sch 11, Sch 13, para 2(4).
4   In the case of Joy Gardner, who died after being gagged with 13 feet of tape in addition to being manacled and handcuffed in August 1993. Other deportees have been seriously injured by the use of inappropriate restraint, and protests by passengers at excessive physical restraint of deportees on aircraft became increasingly common. The government now regularly uses special charter flights. See eg Amnesty International *Cruel, inhuman or degrading treatment during forcible deportation* (July 1994); Medical Foundation *Harm on removal: Excessive force against failed asylum seekers* (October 2004).
5   IA 1971, Sch 2, para 16(4) – this is a very clumsily worded paragraph and our interpretation involves placing the words 'or before the directions for his removal have been fulfilled ...' after 'an immigration officer'.
6   IA 1971, s 27(a)(i). This is an absolute offence with no room for 'reasonable excuse'. Where the condition of a deportee or other compelling factors such as an on-board protest dictate removal of the deportee from the aircraft, the captain would have to obtain the permission of the immigration officer or the Secretary of State to avoid criminal liability.
7   IDI Sep 04, Ch 9, s 6, para 5.
8   IAA 1999, s 14.
9   No regulations have been made under this section.
10   Ie, under Criminal Justice and Police Act 2001, s 33 (travel restriction order against certain persons convicted of drug trafficking offences). Section 37 provides that an order under the Act does not prevent removal under prescribed powers, and the removal powers are set out in the Travel Restriction Order (Prescribed Removal Powers) Order 2002, SI 2002/313, Sch.

EUROPEAN CO-OPERATION

16.67 Removal of illegal entrants and overstayers is a major preoccupation of immigration authorities, not just of the UK government but throughout the

European Union. Several measures have been adopted to facilitate cooperation on expulsion, including Council Directive 2001/40 on the mutual recognition of decisions on expulsion of third country nationals,[1] which the UK has opted into and which was required to be implemented in national law by 2 December 2002. The Directive enables expulsion decisions made against third country nationals in one Member State to be enforced in another. The expulsion decisions concerned must be based on conviction of an offence punishable by 12 months' or more imprisonment, serious grounds for believing that the person has committed or intends to commit a serious criminal offence, or failure to comply with national rules on the entry or residence of aliens.[2] The UK has also opted into implementation measures such as the Decision on joint expulsion flights.[3]

[1] Directive 2001/40, OJ 2001 L 150/47. See further 7.36 above.
[2] Directive 2001/40 Art 3. The provisions do not apply to family members of EU nationals: Art 1.
[3] OJ 2004 L 261/28.

COMPULSORY REMOVAL OF PSYCHIATRIC PATIENTS

16.68 Section 86 of the Mental Health Act 1983 empowers the Secretary of State for the Home Department to authorise the removal to any country abroad of certain detained patients who have been given leave to enter or remain, but do not have a right of abode in the UK and who are receiving in-patient treatment for psychiatric illness. The power originated with the Lunacy Act 1890, under which aliens detained as persons of unsound mind could be returned to their own country at the request of their family or friends, a right of initiative removed by the Mental Health Act 1959. The Secretary of State's powers of removal of mental patients were increased by the Immigration Act 1971[1] and the British Nationality Act 1981[2] to embrace all patients without the right of abode. The main purpose of the power, according to the government, is to 'enable patients who are either irrationally opposed to their removal, or are unable to express a view, to be compulsorily removed to another country when this is judged to be in their best interests. It is also used to enable patients to be kept under escort on their journey home if this is necessary'.[3] Before exercising these powers the Secretary of State must have obtained the approval of a Mental Health Review Tribunal[4] and must be satisfied that proper arrangements have been made for the removal of patients and for their care or treatment, and that removal is in their interests.[5] Where a psychiatric patient is liable to removal under some other provision of the IA 1971, for example because he or she is on temporary admission, the Secretary of State is not obliged to use this procedure for removal of psychiatric patients, so the safeguard of the Mental Health Review Tribunal does not apply.[6] As removal under section 30 is not an 'immigration decision' within the meaning of section 82 of the Nationality, Immigration and Asylum Act 2002, there is no right of appeal, and a challenge would have to be by way of judicial review.[7] Removal under this section is not prevented by a travel restriction order.[8] On arrival at their destination, any orders or directions made in respect of them will cease to have effect,[9] and there is nothing to prevent patients who have been removed from applying for re-admission to the UK at any time.[10] The removal powers are, however, draconian and need very rigorous adherence to the safeguards to avoid non-compliance with due process and private life requirements of the ECHR.

1   Immigration Act 1971, s 30(1).
2   British Nationality Act 1981, s 39(7).
3   White Paper *The Review of the Mental Health Act 1959* (Cmd 7320) para 8.26. Powers of escort are now expressly contained in Immigration and Asylum Act 1999, s 14, and are not confined to psychiatric patients.
4   Mental Health Act 1983, s 86(3).
5   Mental Health Act 1983, s 86(2).
6   *X v Secretary of State for the Home Department* [2001] 1 WLR 740, [2001] INLR 205, CA.
7   See (under the old appeal provisions) *R v Immigration Appeal Tribunal and the Secretary of State for the Home Department, ex p Alghali* [1986] Imm AR 376, QBD.
8   Ie, under Criminal Justice and Police Act 2001, s 33 (travel restriction order against certain persons convicted of drug trafficking offences). Section 37 provides that an order under the Act does not prevent removal under prescribed powers, and removal under Mental Health Act 1983, s 86 is among the prescribed removal powers set out in the Travel Restriction Order (Prescribed Removal Powers) Order 2002, SI 2002/313, Sch.
9   Mental Health Act 1983, s 91.
10 But a compulsory order under s 37 of the Mental Health Act 1983 takes effect on a patient's return.

REMOVAL OF DESERTERS FROM FRIENDLY FORCES

16.69 The position of deserters or absentees without leave in the UK from friendly foreign forces is governed by the Visiting Forces Act 1952, under which deserters can be arrested, detained and removed from the UK.[1] Arrest must be by warrant granted either to the police or army personnel. The person is then brought before a court which decides whether they should be handed over for trial as a deserter to the country concerned. Court proceedings can be dispensed with if the deserter surrenders voluntarily at a police station. As in extradition proceedings the magistrates courts' powers are subject to *habeas corpus* proceedings or judicial review. This is how the provisions work.

1   The Visiting Forces Act 1952 applies to the forces of Antigua and Barbuda, Australia, Bahamas, Bangladesh, Barbados, Belize, Bermuda, Botswana, Brunei, Cameroon, Canada, Republic of Cyprus, Dominica, Fiji, The Gambia, Ghana, Grenada, Guyana, India, Jamaica, Kenya, Kiribati, Lesotho, Malawi, Malaysia, Maldives, Malta, Mauritius, Mozambique, Namibia, Nauru, the New Hebrides, New Zealand, Nigeria, Pakistan, Papua New Guinea, Saint Christopher and Nevis, Saint Lucia, Saint Vincent and the Grenadines, Seychelles, Sierra Leone, Singapore, Solomon Islands, South Africa, Sri Lanka, Swaziland, Tanzania, Tonga, Trinidad and Tobago, Tuvalu, Uganda, Vanuatu, Western Samoa, Zambia, Zanzibar and Zimbabwe: see Visiting Forces Act s 1(1) as amended; Visiting Forces Act (Application to Bermuda) Order 2001, SI 2001/3922. It also applies under designation orders made under s 1(2) of the 1952 Act to Albania, Armenia, Austria, Azerbaijan, Belarus, Belgium, Bulgaria, Czech Republic, Denmark, Estonia, Finland, France, Georgia, Germany, Greece, Hungary, Italy, Latvia, Lithuania, Luxembourg, Kazakhstan, Kyrgystan, Former Yugoslav Republic of Macedonia, Moldova, Netherlands, Norway, Poland, Portugal, Romania, Russia, Slovakia, Slovenia, Spain, Sweden, Switzerland, Turkey, Turkmenistan, Ukraine, United States of America and Uzbekistan (see SI 1999/1736, Sch 1, See 3 *Halsbury's Laws* (4th edn) p 936. The Act also applies, with adaptations, to any headquarters or organisation set up in pursuance of arrangements for defence (International Headquarters And Defence Organisations Act 1964, s 5); SI 1999/1736, Art 3(2).

16.70 Section 13(1) of the Visiting Forces Act 1952 (as substituted)[1] applies the Army Act 1955, sections 186–188[2] and 190 (which allows for the apprehension, detention and delivery into military custody of deserters and absentees without leave from the regular forces)[3] to deserters and absentees from forces of any country to which the section applies. But first there must be a request (either specific or general) of the appropriate authority of the country to which the person belongs and a certificate that he or she is a deserter or absentee. Section 13(3) states that references in the sections of the 1955 Act to the delivery of a person into military custody shall be construed as references to the handing over of that person to such authority of the country to which he or she belongs, at such place in the UK as may be designated by the appropriate authority of that country.

[1] Section 13(1)–(3) substituted by the Revision of Army and Air Force Acts (Transitional Provisions) Act 1955, s 3, Sch 2, para 17(1).
[2] Section 186 of the Army Act 1955 gives power to arrest suspected deserters/absentees to a constable, or if none is available, any officer, warrant officer, NCO or soldier of the regular forces. A warrant for the arrest of a suspect as aforesaid can be issued by anyone having authority to issue warrants for arrest of persons charged with crime. A person in custody by virtue of s 186 shall be brought before a court of summary jurisdiction as soon as practicable. If the person admits being a deserter and the court is satisfied with the truth of the admission, or if he denies it but the court is satisfied that (a) he is under military law and (b) that there is sufficient evidence for him to be tried for desertion, the court shall deliver him into military custody, but otherwise discharge him (s 187). If a person surrenders himself to the police as a deserter and it appears to the police that he is telling the truth, the police may deliver him into military custody without taking him to court (s 188). Governors of police stations and persons in charge of prisons are under a duty to receive deserters and detain them until they can be delivered into military custody (s 190).
[3] Visiting Forces Act 1952, s 13(2) as substituted. Under s 14 (as amended by SI 1964/488) the magistrates' court will require two certificates: (1) stating that the country concerned has made a request for the exercise of the 1952 Act (this is signed by the Secretary of the Defence Council); and (2) stating that the person is a deserter or an absentee without leave (this is signed by the officer commanding a unit or detachment of any of the forces of the country concerned).

16.71 Section 13 of the Visiting Forces Act 1952 does not apply just to deserters from visiting forces (ie those stationed in the UK) but also to all the forces of a country to which the section applies. In *R v Thames Justices, ex p Brindle*[1] an American citizen resident in England returned to the US, joined the army and was posted to Germany, deserted and came to England where he was arrested for other offences and ordered by the magistrate to be handed into the custody of the US military authorities on completion of his sentence. The Court of Appeal held that although Part I of the 1952 Act (ss 1–12) applied just to visiting forces as defined in section 12(1), section 13 applied to deserters from the 'forces of any designated country' without a limitation to visiting forces.

[1] [1975] 3 All ER 941, [1975] 1 WLR 1400, CA.

16.72 The procedure and standard of proof to be applied by a magistrates' court in such cases was spelt out by the Divisional Court in *R v Tottenham Magistrates' Court, ex p Williams*.[1] Mr W, a Nigerian lawfully settled in the UK, was arrested as a deserter from the Nigerian airforce, but claimed that his engagement had terminated before he came to the UK. The magistrate had ordered his surrender on the basis that he was the person named in a certificate signed by an officer commanding a unit of the Nigerian forces who stated that Mr W was a deserter. She did not take into account the evidence and statement of Mr W. The Divisional Court quashed the decision. Donaldson LJ pointed out that there was a very heavy onus and that no one was to be imprisoned or delivered into the custody of any authority, whether British or Nigerian, save in strict compliance with the law. As Mr W did not admit he was legally absent, two things had to be proved under the Visiting Forces Act 1952 procedure:

- that Mr W was subject to Nigerian military law. The magistrates had to be satisfied beyond reasonable doubt – the criminal standard of proof; and

- if so, that there was sufficient evidence to justify his being tried in Nigeria for desertion.

This is the less onerous test applied to committal proceedings. In deciding both questions magistrates had to consider all the evidence tendered and not just that of the prosecution. In *Re Virdee*[2] the Divisional Court held that proceedings under the Visiting Forces Act 1952 were quasi-criminal, like the exercise of extradition powers, and so not affected by Article 48 EC (now Art 39), since the purpose both of extradition and of handover under section 13 was a trial by a foreign court with a view to punishment, rather than exclusion from the UK.

1   [1982] 2 All ER 705, DC.
2   [1980] 1 CMLR 709, DC.

EXTRADITION

16.73 Extradition is another form of compulsory removal from this country and is a topic beyond the scope of this work.[1] There may be an overlapping of extradition and immigration law where a fugitive offender is refused leave to enter the country and enters unlawfully, or resists extradition on the ground of being a refugee. The Extradition Act 2003[2] provides for 'fast-track' extradition procedures to EU Member States without consideration of evidence, and simplifies procedures under the previous legislation. For the first time, the 2003 Act deals with asylum claims by persons in respect of whom extradition warrants are issued. It provides that a person must not be extradited in pursuance of the warrant before the asylum claim is finally determined.[3] These provisions are in addition to the ban on extradition where a prosecution is brought for a Refugee Convention reason or where the offender is likely to be prejudiced at trial for a Convention reason, which have been carried forward into the 2003 Act.[3] Finally, once an extradition judge has decided that the offence is an extradition offence and that there is no statutory bar to extradition, he or she must decide if extradition is compatible with the person's rights under the Human Rights Convention, and if not, must discharge the offender.[4] Administrative removal should not be used in order to circumvent extradition safeguards, but provided immigration powers are used lawfully and bona fide, removal may be ordered to any destination permitted under the statute, including the country requesting extradition.[5]

¹ See Sambel and Jones *Extradition Law Handbook* (2004); Stanbrook and Stanbrook *Extradition Law and Practice* (2000).

² In force 1 January 2004, except for cases where a request was received on or before 31 December 2003 (which will be dealt with under the Extradition Act 1989).

³ Extradition Act 2003, ss 39 (Category 1 territories), 121 (Category 2 territories). The Category 1 territories are defined as the EU Member States by the Extradition Act 2003 (Designation of Part 1 territories) Order 2003, SI 2003/3333, amended by SI 2004/1898), No state which retains the death penalty can be included in Category 1: Extradition Act 2003, s 1(3). The Category 2 territories are set out in the Extradition Act 2003 (Designation of Part 2 territories) Order 2003, SI 2003/3334, amended by SI 2004/1898). The ban on extradition before an asylum claim is 'finally determined' (defined for this purpose to include appeals) is lifted where extradition is to an EU Member State which has accepted responsibility under standing arrangements for determining the asylum claim, or where the person's life and liberty will not be threatened in that state, which will not *refoule* the person in breach of the Refugee Convention, and the person is not a national or citizen.

⁴ Extradition Act 2003, ss 21 (Category 1 territories); 87 (Category 2 territories).

⁵ *Re Caddoux* [2004] EWHC 642 (Admin), [2004] All ER (D) 498 (Mar); *R v Mullen* [2000] QB 520, CA; *R v Horseferry Road Magistrates' Court, ex p Bennett* [1994] 1 AC 42, HL; *R v Bow Street Magistrates, ex p Mackeson* (1981) 75 Cr App Rep 24, Div Ct. For permitted destination countries, see 16.56 above.

Chapter 17

DETENTION AND BAIL

INTRODUCTION

17.1 The use of detention for immigrants and asylum seekers has increased since the last edition of this book and detention has become a central focus of government policy as the key to fast tracking of asylum cases and enforcement.[1] A policy intention behind the Nationality, Immigration and Asylum Act 2002, with its reception, accommodation and removal centres,[2] was to normalise the use of detention as an inevitable part of the examination process, to be used in part as a matter of administrative convenience for processing claims quickly by placing the Oakington process on a statutory footing.[2] In the 2002 White Paper *Secure Borders, Safe Haven,* the Oakington facility was described as 'a central plank of asylum policy'.[3] 250 applicants can be held in the centre and their claims processed within one week. The government estimated that up to 13,000 applicants could be processed in any one year.[4] In March 2003 the Home Office extended this procedure to Harmondsworth Removal Centre and introduced a scheme which has as its cornerstone detention throughout the entire process of the asylum claim, including any appellate remedies, which is intended to be completed within five weeks.[5]

---

[1] Nationality, Immigration and Asylum Act 2002, s 66.
[2] Oakington is a reception centre where asylum seekers have been detained since 2000 for what was supposed to be seven days, but is now sometimes measured in weeks, to enable their claim for asylum to be determined within that period; see below at 17.32. The legality

of the policy was upheld by the House of Lords in *R (on the application of Saadi) v Secretary of State for the Home Department* [2002] 1 WLR 3131. See 12.113 above.
3 White Paper *Secure Borders, Safe Haven* (2002 Cm 5387), at para 4.69.
4 Cm 5387, para 4.72.
5 In *R (on the application of Refugee Legal Centre) v Secretary of State for the Home Department* [2004] EWCA (Civ) 1481, [2004] All ER (D) 201 (Nov) the Court of Appeal concluded that the procedure provided a fair opportunity for asylum seekers to put their case provided that a policy was formulated to enable the strict timetable for processing the claim to be adapted in individual cases.

17.2 The actual use of the power to detain is still very much restricted by the availability of accommodation space[1] and the need for a rational policy for determining who is to be detained and in what circumstances. Detention, therefore, remains in principle and in practice for the vast majority of cases a measure of last resort to be utilised at the end of the determination process immediately prior to removal. The broad powers of administrative detention are also limited in a number of important ways by implied statutory restrictions, Home Office policy and human rights law, and are subject to increasing judicial scrutiny, particularly in the Administrative Court on judicial review. These limitations and safeguards were, however, suspended for certain foreign nationals suspected of involvement in international terrorism linked to Al Qaeda with the enactment of Part 4 of the Anti-terrorism Crime and Security Act 2001, which sanctioned indeterminate detention without trial, requiring derogation from Article 5 of the ECHR and ousting the jurisdiction of the High Court on habeas corpus or judicial review.[2] In *A and X v Secretary of State for the Home Department*,[3] the House of Lords ruled that the derogation from Article 5 of ECHR was discriminatory and disproportionate, quashed the Derogation Order,[4] and made a declaration that the provisions of the 2001 Act which allowed indefinite detention were incompatible with Articles 5 and 14 ECHR. In a potential constitutional stand-off the government refused to release the detainees, and the Special Immigration Appeals Commission granted the detainees bail in March 2005, while the Lords and the Commons were locked in marathon combat over the provisions for control orders designed to replace them, which apply to British and foreign nationals alike.[5]

1 As of November 2004, 1,438 cases had been placed on the Harmondsworth fast track. 151 of these were removed from the fast track before an initial decision was taken. Of 1,207 initial decisions, all but 5 were refusals of asylum. A further 270 were removed from the fast track pending appeal. Of 995 appeals decided by adjudicators, 19 were allowed; and of 16 further appeals to the IAT, one succeeded. Three of the 57 applications for statutory review also succeeded: see of *R (on the application of Refugee Legal Centre) v Secretary of State for the Home Department* [2004] EWCA (Civ) 1481, [2004] All ER (D) 201 (Nov), para 3.
2 The Special Immigration Appeal Commission (SIAC) had exclusive jurisdiction in respect of challenges to the derogation: Anti-Terrorism Crime and Security Act 2001, s 30. Part IV of the ATCSA 2001 (ss 21–32) was repealed by PTA 2005, s 16 on 14 April 2005.
3 *A and X v Secretary of State for the Home Department* [2004] UKHL 56, [2005] 2 WLR 87.
4 Human Rights Act 1998 (Designated Derogation) Order 2001, SI 2001/3644, quashed by the House of Lords in *A*, above.
5 Hansard HC (2005) 25 January, Statement by Home Secretary; Prevention of Terrorism Act 2005, s 1. To date nine control orders have been issued against foreign nationals previously held under ATCSA 2001, placing severe restrictions on their liberty including a 12-hour curfew, electronic tagging, restrictions on visitors and on use of phones and electronic equipment, etc.

17.3 Detention and Bail

17.3 We will examine in this chapter the limits to the power to detain under the Immigration Acts and the special provisions in national security cases; the power to grant bail by immigration officers, the Asylum and Immigration Tribunal, the Special Immigration Appeals Commission (SIAC) and by the Administrative Court while proceedings are pending before it, as well as the availability of habeas corpus and judicial review to challenge the lawfulness of the detention itself. For the first time an overview will be given of the available remedies in cases of unlawful detention.

17.4 The original powers of detention are to be found in Schedule 2, paragraph 16 and Schedule 3 to the Immigration Act 1971, as later amended by the 1999 and the 2002 Acts. Historically the exercise of those powers to detain immigrants was made ancillary to other immigration measures; essentially they were holding powers pending administrative acts of examination, removal or deportation. Section 62 of the NIAA 2002 not only gave the Secretary of State the power to detain, where previously this had been the preserve of immigration officers,[1] but also extended those powers, first, by linking them to the taking of putative decisions rather than just administrative action, so that a person can be detained, for example, *pending* a decision whether or not to give directions for his or her removal as an overstayer or illegal entrant.[2] Secondly, detention is now possible where the Secretary of State has a reasonable, albeit mistaken, belief that he or she has the power to detain or release someone in any of the situations covered by the new statutory powers.[3] In principle, therefore, the Secretary of State has acquired more open-ended powers of detention, although as we shall see, in practice, stated policy significantly restricts and refines this broaden discretion.

[1] Previously the Secretary of State only had powers under Immigration Act 1971, Sch 3 to detain or release a person against whom deportation action was being taken, and to grant temporary admission to (but not detain) a person claiming asylum (including a claim that removal would be in breach of the person's human rights) on arrival at a port (Immigration (Leave to Enter) Order 2001, SI 2001/2590, Art 3).

[2] Nationality, Immigration and Asylum Act 2002, s 62(1)(a); Immigration Act 1971, Sch 2, para 16(2), as amended by Immigration and Asylum Act 1999, s 140(1) and Sch 14, para 60 and by NIAA 2002, s 73(5).

[3] NIAA 2002, s 62(7); IA 1971, Sch 2, para 16(2) as amended.

17.5 Detention in connection with immigration is a lawful purpose under Article 5(1)(f) of the ECHR, if used to prevent someone effecting an unauthorised entry into the country or with a view to removal, but the power to detain is still (both under the ECHR and at common law) circumscribed and limited to the stated statutory purpose which is a condition precedent for the exercise of the discretion.[1] Thus excessive delay, or detention pending removal when there is no practical prospect of removal, will render the use of the power unlawful.[2] Under the Immigration Act 1971 there was strict liability – either the person was detained for the stated purpose or they were not. However section 140 of the Immigration and Asylum Act 1999 amended the 1971 Act, requiring only that the detainor had 'reasonable grounds for suspecting' that the person is someone in respect of whom removal directions may be given because, for example, the person is an illegal entrant, or has been refused leave to enter.[3] This does not affect the Administrative Court's jurisdiction on judicial review in a challenge to the lawfulness of the removal directions: whether the detainee is actually removable or an illegal entrant is still a precedent fact question for the Court. Moreover, it would follow that if the objective facts of, for example, illegal entry could not be established, there would be no lawful power to continue to detain after a reasonable period for investigation of the facts, however reasonable the suspicion. Having reasonable grounds for suspecting the relevant precedent fact is, however, as we shall see, a potential defence to a claim for false imprisonment; the detention is authorised if the relevant suspicion is established and objective and rational grounds for the suspicion exist.

¹   *Tan Te Lam v Superintendent of Tai A Chau Detention Centre* [1997] AC 97, [1996] All ER 256, [1996] 2 WLR 865, 140 Sol Jo LB 106, PC, approving *R v Governor of Durham Prison, ex p Singh* [1983] Imm AR 198; followed in *Re Mahmood* [1995] Imm AR 311, QBD, where Laws J said: 'While of course Parliament is entitled to confer power of administrative detention without trial, the courts will see to it that ... the statute that confers it will be strictly and narrowly construed and its operation and effect will be supervised by the court according to high standards.'
²   *Khawaja v Secretary of State for the Home Department* [1984] AC 74 (illegal entry), *Tan Te Lam*, above (removal).
³   Immigration Act 1971, Sch 2, para 16(2), amended by Immigration and Asylum Act 1999, s 140(2); for the Secretary of State's equivalent power to detain on suspicion see NIAA 2002, s 62(7).

17.6 Nevertheless, what constitutes reasonable grounds in this context has yet to be defined and its compatibility with Article 5 ECHR determined. In Article 5(1)(f) cases, removal is only authorised for the purposes of preventing unauthorised entry and where action is being taken with a view to deportation, and not in circumstances where there is a reasonable suspicion to that effect. Reasonable suspicion for this purpose is not necessarily the same as that required to constitute a suspicion of commission of a criminal offence justifying a simple arrest and limited detention for further investigation. The context, circumstances and the consequences to the individual, particularly in respect of the length of detention, are relevant to the test to be applied.[1] Moreover the question of whether or not the grounds are reasonable itself requires an assessment of objective circumstances which is to be determined by the court[2] and can be challenged on ordinary administrative law principles.[3] An error of law on the part of the detainor, even if entirely understandable, would not constitute reasonable grounds for the relevant suspicion.[4] An example in the immigration context is derived from the unreported case of *N v Home Office*[5] where an immigration officer entirely misconstrued an application under the regularisation scheme for overstayers under s 9 of the Immigration and Asylum Act 1999 as simply a long residence application, thereby failing to determine the application under the scheme. The officer then issued removal directions under s 10 of the IAA 1999 for administrative removal and proceeded to detain the person on the basis that she had no in-country rights of appeal and could be subject to administrative removal. The immigration officer's errors, even if based upon understandable mistake as to the nature of the application, meant that the detention was not authorised. Deportation, not administrative removal was the issue, and this was for the Secretary of State to deal with under section 3(5)(a)[6] and Schedule 3, paragraph 2(2) to the 1971 Act. The immigration officer failed to take into account this procedure and her entitlement, if a deportation decision was made, to a right of appeal under section 15 of the 1971 Act.[7] The detention was unlawful because there was no power in law to detain her under Schedule 2, paragraph 16 to the 1971 Act and relevant considerations had not been taken into account, namely, her right of appeal and the policy consideration relating to outstanding legal proceedings.

1   In *Hogg v Ward* (1858) 3 H & N 417 per Watson B at 423, it was long ago stated that reasonable suspicion requires that 'every case must be governed by its own circumstances, and the charge must be reasonable as regards the subject matter and the person making it'. This is because, as underlined in *O'Hara v Chief Constable of the Royal Ulster Constabulary* [1977] AC 286 per Lord Hope at 297H, where Parliament has provided powers which interfere with liberty on the basis of suspicion alone: 'The protection of the subject lies in the nature of the test which has to be applied in order to determine the requirement that there be reasonable grounds that the suspicion is satisfied'. This approach is consistent with that adopted by the European Court of Human Rights in *Fox, Campbell & Hartley v United Kingdom* (1990) 13 EHRR 157: 'the reasonableness of the suspicion on which arrest must be based form an essential part of the safeguard against arbitrary arrest and detention which is laid down in Art 5(1)(c). The court agrees with the Commission and the government that having a 'reasonable suspicion' presupposes the existence of facts or information which would satisfy an objective observer that the person concerned may have committed the offence. What may be regarded as reasonable will however depend upon all the circumstances'. See also *Murray v United Kingdom* [1994] 18 EHRR CD 1 at para 56.
2   *Chapman v DPP* (1989) 89 Cr App Rep 190.
3   *Holgate-Mohammed v Duke* [1984] AC 437.
4   *Walker v Lovell* [1975] 1 WLR 1141 per Lord Diplock at 115E–F, and see *R v Governor of Brockhurst Prison, ex p Evans (No 2)* [2001] 2 AC 19, [2000] 3 WLR 843, where the House of Lords ruled that an error of law in respect of computation of sentence by a prison governor who was applying the law as pronounced by the Court of Appeal but which was subsequently overruled by the House of Lords, did not have a defence of justification in a claim for false imprisonment relating to the extra days served by the prisoner.
5   The case was resolved on mediation in 2004 and the claimant received £30,000 in compensation for 69 days' detention. Likewise in *I v Home Office* (June 2004) the case was settled after issue of the proceedings for £10,000 for 6 days detention on the mistaken belief that the claimant had exhausted all remedies and faced imminent removal, when in fact the IAT had allowed an appeal and remitted the case.
6   Ie, the original s 3(5)(a), before amendment by Immigration and Asylum Act 1999, Sch 14, para 44.
7   Preserved in respect of overstayers who applied for regularisation before 2 October 2000 by Immigration and Asylum Act 1999, Sch 15, paras 11 and 12.

17.7 On arrival in the UK detention is used pending examination or further examination, pending a decision to grant, cancel or refuse leave to enter, and after refusal or cancellation of leave pending removal. At this stage it is likely to take place in the immigration control areas of sea and airports and its duration is likely to be short, except for those detained pending consideration of asylum claims, who may be detained for a limited period during the processing and determination of their application for asylum, under the Oakington process (designed as a 7–10 day period)[1] or the fast track procedure[2]—but many others may be detained for much longer periods and often in inappropriate conditions.[3] In overstaying and illegal entry cases detention is quite likely to start in a police station and end in prison awaiting removal. In deportation cases, where public good grounds are relied on or a recommendation for deportation is made by a criminal court, the same thing may happen. But where the person has a stable address and family in the UK, there may be little or no detention throughout the whole process.

1 The 'target time' for Oakington claims has increased to ten to 14 days: see 'Fast track asylum and detention policy', Parliamentary Written answer of Desmond Browne MP, Minister for Citizenship and Immigration (Hansard 16 September 2004, Column 157WS). See 12.111 above.
2 See 12.111 above and 18.80 below.
3 For criticisms of the exercise of the power to detain asylum seekers and migrants in the UK, see inter alia Amore *Immigration detention in the UK: submission to the UN Working Group on Arbitrary Detention* (Bail for Immigration Detainees, 2002); HM Inspectorate of Prisons *Introduction and Summary of Findings: Inspection of Five Immigration Service Custodial Establishments* (April 2003); HM Inspectorate of Prisons *An Inspection of Dungavel Immigration Removal Centre* (October 2002); Emma Cole *A Few Families Too Many: Detention of Asylum-Seeking Families in the UK* (Bail for Immigration Detainees, London, March 2003); North Birmingham Mental Health NHS Trust *A Second Exile: the Mental Health Implications of Detention of Asylum Seekers in the United Kingdom* (1996); Amnesty International: *Cell Culture: detention and imprisonment of Asylum Seekers in the UK* (1997).

17.8 There is no doubt that the power to detain is wide and the safeguards, while significantly enhanced by the requirement to apply stated policy and as a result of the incorporation of Article 5 ECHR, are often inadequate in practice.[1] The government's decision not to implement sections 44–52 of the IAA 1999, which provided for automatic bail hearings, and to repeal them in section 68 of the NIAA 2002,[2] is to be regretted as a lost opportunity to provide greater access to scrutiny of decisions to detain, particularly for those held in long-term detention, many of whom are inadequately represented. We shall deal with bail, temporary admission and release on conditions, and note that, while a statutory presumption in favour of release is a new feature of the English and Welsh system (although of much older vintage in Scotland), there is still no statutory time limit on the period of examination pending a decision on whether or not to grant leave to enter (nor on the period of detention itself.[3] The IAA 1999[4] and detention rules made under it[5] for the first time regulate immigration detention centres and the powers and duties of custodians, and provide a statutory basis (albeit not in primary legislation) for the giving of written reasons for detention.[6]

1 *R v Secretary of State for the Home Department, ex p Thirakumar* [1989] Imm AR 402.
2 Nationality, Immigration and Asylum Act 2002, s 68(6), in force 10 February 2003: Nationality, Immigration and Asylum Act 2002 (Commencement No 2) Order 2003, SI 2003/1.
3 A statutory time limit on Immigration Act detention was considered and rejected during the passage of the Immigration and Asylum Act 1999: see 603 HL Official Report (5th series) col 220, 29 June 1999; 605 HL Official Report (5th series) col 1248, 20 October 1999.
4 See Pt VIII of the Immigration and Asylum Act 1999 (ss 147–159).
5 The Detention Centre Rules 2001, SI 2001/238. Note that detention centres' name was changed to removal centres by NIAA 2002, s 66(4).
6 SI 2001/238, r 9.

IMMIGRATION OFFICERS' POWERS TO DETAIN

17.9 The code for regulating the examination and admission of non-nationals to UK territory is contained within the Immigration Acts 1971 to 2004. Incidental to the power to examine or remove a non-national is the ancillary power to detain pending the conclusion of such examination or removal.

17.9 Detention and Bail

Under paragraph 16 of Schedule 2 to the Immigration Act 1971, immigration officers are authorised to detain in the following situations:

(i) persons arriving in the UK may be detained pending examination by an immigration officer to establish whether they need or should be granted leave to enter.[1] There is no equivalent power to detain those who are seeking to leave the UK, even though such persons may be examined in order to establish whether they are British citizens or to check their identity;[2]

(ii) those who, on arrival in the UK with leave to enter granted prior to arrival, have been examined under paragraph 2A of Schedule 2 to the IA 1971[3] and had their leave suspended, may be detained pending completion of the examination and a decision on whether to cancel leave;[4]

(iii) those refused leave to enter and those reasonably suspected of having been refused leave to enter[5] may be detained pending the giving of directions for their removal from the UK;[6]

(iv) illegal entrants and those reasonably suspected of being illegal entrants may be detained, pending a decision on whether to issue removal directions and pending removal in pursuance of directions;[7]

(v) those who, having limited leave to enter or remain, do not observe a condition attached to their leave or remain beyond their leave or who have sought or obtained leave to remain by deception, or whose indefinite leave to remain has been revoked, or are reasonably suspected of being such persons, may be detained pending a decision to remove them or pending removal;[8]

(vi) members of the family of someone who has been given removal directions as described in the previous four paragraphs;[9]

(vii) members of the crew of a ship, aircraft or train who remain beyond the leave granted to enable them to join their ship, aircraft or train, or abscond having lawfully entered without leave, or are reasonably suspected of doing so, may also be detained.[10]

Persons may be detained under Schedule 2, paragraph 16 anywhere the Secretary of State directs.[11]

---

1 Immigration Act 1971, Sch 2, para 16(1).
2 IA 1971, Sch 2, para 3(1).
3 IA 1971, Sch 2, para 2A (inserted by Immigration and Asylum Act 1999, Sch 14, para 57) allows examination on entry of those granted leave prior to entry, to establish (i) if there has been a change circumstances since that leave was given; (ii) whether that leave was obtained as a result of false information or a failure to disclose material facts; (iii) if there are medical grounds on which that leave should be cancelled; (iv) if it would be conducive to the public good for that leave to be cancelled. Para 2A(2A), inserted by Asylum and Immigration (Treatment of Claimants, etc) Act 2004, s 18, adds a further ground for holders of entry clearance, and (v) whether the person's purpose in arriving in the UK is different from that specified in the entry clearance.
4 IA 1971, Sch 2, para 16(1A), inserted by Immigration and Asylum Act 1999, Sch 14, para 60.
5 Ie, suspected of having absconded from temporary admission having been refused leave to enter.
6 IA 1971, Sch 2, paras 8, 16(2), as amended by IAA 1999, s 140(1); and NIAA 2002, s 73(5).

1110

7   IA 1971, paras 9, and 16(2), as amended. Note that the amended wording of para 16(2) allows detention of suspected illegal entrants as well as those who actually are illegal entrants, although actual illegal entry will still be a precedent fact founding the power to remove: see 17.6 above.
8   IAA 1999, s 10(1)(a), (b), (ba) and (7). The latter applies the provisions of IA 1971, Sch 2, para 16.
9   IA 1971, Sch 2, para 10A, 16(2) inserted and amended by NIAA 2002, s 73(1) and 73(5) respectively; IAA 1999, s 10(1)(c) and (7).
10 IA 1971, Sch 2, paras 12–14, 16(2), modified in relation to Channel Tunnel train crews by the Channel Tunnel (International Arrangements) Order 1993, SI 1993/1813, Sch 4, para 1(11)(n) and (p).
11 IA 1971, Sch 2, para 18(1): see 17.21 below.

17.10 In the case of a port or illegal entrant asylum claimant, the examination referred to in Schedule 2 to the Immigration Act 1971, pending a decision on leave to enter, may embrace the whole asylum determination procedure, impliedly limited only by a period reasonably necessary to conduct the examination and come to the relevant decision.[1] The exercise of this power need not have regard to the individual's propensity to abscond, as ruled by the House of Lords, who in the Oakington Case, upheld the immigration officer's power to detain for up to ten days in order to facilitate speedy decision making by ensuring the claimant's availability for interview at any time.[2] Whilst section 77 of the Nationality Immigration and Asylum Act 2002 reproduces the protection against removal pending the determination of an asylum claim formerly contained in section 15 of the Asylum and Immigration Act 1999,[3] section 77 also provides that directions for removal may be given, preparatory steps to facilitate removal may be taken, and a deportation order may be served during that period.[4] The amended provisions of paragraph 16(2) of the 1971 Act ensure that the prohibition on removal does not preclude the power to detain and prevents a claim for unlawful detention on the basis that there is no power of removal and therefore no lawful purpose for the detention.[5]

1   *R (on the application of Saadi) v Secretary of State for the Home Department* [2002] UKHL 41, [2002] 1 WLR 3131, [2002] INLR 523.
2   *R (on the application of Saadi) v Secretary of State for the Home Department* above.
3   Ministers confirmed however, during the passage of the 1999 Act, that no directions or deportation order would be served until a negative determination: Lord Williams of Mostyn, 605 HL Official Report (5th series) col 785; 606 HL Official Report (5th series) cols 766–767.
4   Nationality Immigration and Asylum Act 2002, s 77(4).
5   *Secretary of State for the Home Department v Khan* [1995] Imm AR 348, CA.

Temporary admission

17.11 For those liable to be detained pending removal under any of the Schedule 2 powers in the Immigration Act 1971, the main alternative to incarceration is the grant of temporary admission to the UK. The power can be exercised by both immigration officers and the Secretary of State[1] by giving written notice.[2] Those temporarily admitted are deemed not to have entered the UK.[3] The status may be subject to significant restrictions as to residence, employment or occupation, and may require reporting to the police or an immigration officer. The restrictions may be varied by either an immigration officer or the Secretary of State, who may each vary conditions imposed by the other.[4] The grant of temporary admission is without prejudice to the exercise of the power to detain. A failure to observe any restriction imposed under these provisions can be grounds for detaining or re-detaining and, in the absence of any reasonable excuse may also constitute a criminal offence under section 24(1)(e) of the IA 1971. On the other hand the power to re-detain does not require breach of conditions of temporary admission, although it might be condemned as arbitrary if there was no actual or anticipated breach.[5] The residence restrictions may include prohibitions on residence in a specified area, or a condition requiring residence in specified accommodation provided under section 4 of the Immigration and Asylum Act 1999,[6] and prohibiting absence from it, in accordance with regulations.[7] An additional residence restriction may be imposed on asylum seekers and their dependants, requiring them to reside at a specified location for a period not exceeding 14 days in order to attend an induction programme being held nearby.[8] An employment restriction will ordinarily be imposed on asylum seekers, but it may be lifted on request if the asylum application is not dealt with (including appeal) within six months.[9] Illegal entrants and overstayers who are granted temporary release may not be made subject to an employment restriction if consideration of their case is likely to be protracted and the person is supporting his or her family by employment.[10] Reporting to the police or the immigration service should not normally be required more than once a month, and if a case remains unresolved for three years, should be lifted.[11] The Secretary of State may make a payment to cover travel expenses incurred in complying with a reporting restriction.[12] Section 71 of the NIAA 2002 permits similar restrictions to be imposed on those who have extant leave to enter or remain at the time of making a claim for asylum as can be imposed on other asylum seekers who are given temporary admission under paragraph 21 of Schedule 2 to the Immigration Act 1971, and similar powers of detention for breach of restrictions.[13]

---

1   Immigration Act 1971, Sch 2, para 21 (immigration officers); Nationality Immigration and Asylum Act 2002, s 62(3)(b) (Secretary of State).
2   IA 1971, Sch 2, para 21(1), (2), as amended by Immigration Act 1988, Sch, para 10.
3   IA 1971, s 11(1), referred to as a fictional status by Chadwick LJ in *R (on the application of Khadir) v Secretary of State for the Home Department* [2003] EWCA Civ 475, [2003] INLR 426 at para 57.
4   IA 1971 Sch 2 para 21(2); NIAA 2002, s 62(4)(a), (b).
5   Persons liable to be detained under IA 1971, Sch 2, para 16, who may be arrested under para 17, include those on temporary admission: *R (on the application of Khadir) v Secretary of State* above.
6   Section 4 of the Immigration and Asylum Act 1999 empowers the Secretary of State to provide accommodation for persons temporarily admitted or released from detention, the immigration equivalent of bail hostels. Amendments made by NIAA 2002, s 49 extends the provision of such temporary accommodation to failed asylum seekers. See the Immigration and Asylum (Provision of Accommodation to Failed Asylum Seekers) Regulations 2005, SI 2005/930.
7   IA 1971, Sch 2, para 21(2A)–(2E), inserted by IAA 1999, Sch 14, para 62. No regulations have been made under these paragraphs, although the provision of accommodation under s 4 IAA 1999 is regulated by SI 2005/930, see above.
8   NIAA 2002, s 70(1). A programme of induction means education about the nature of the asylum process: NIAA 2002, s 70(3).
9   See 12.113 above.
10   Operational Enforcement Manual (21 December 2000) para 38.19.
11   Operational Enforcement Manual above, para 38.19.
12   Nationality Immigration and Asylum Act 2002, s 69(1).
13   Ie, under IA 1971, Sch 2, para 16: NIAA 2002, s 71(3)(b).

17.12 Those on temporary admission are excluded from income support and related benefits, but if they are asylum claimants, may be eligible for NASS support whilst their application or appeal is outstanding. Thereafter they only have access to hard cases support, with the qualification, introduced in 2003, that those who can leave the jurisdiction, but choose not to, are excluded even from this minimal support. See chapter 13. This state of affairs was the subject of litigation in the case of *Khadir*,[1] where the Administrative Court held that under the 1971 Act, temporary admission was not available when the power to detain no longer exists, and consideration had to be given to the grant of leave to remain. The case concerned Iraqi Kurds who could not safely be returned to Iraq because of the practical impossibility of return directly to the Kurdish Autonomous Region, and it could not, therefore be said that removal was 'pending' for the purpose of paragraph 16 of Schedule 2 to the IA 1971. If removal was not pending then the person was not liable to be detained and consequently there was no power to grant temporary admission, with its associated reporting, residence and employment restrictions.

1 *R (Khadir) v Secretary of State for the Home Department* (CO/5118/2001) (29 July 2002, unreported), Crane J. This part of the judgment was upheld at [2003] EWCA Civ 475, [2003] INLR 426, per Chadwick LJ at paras 52–53.

17.13 However, by the time *Khadir* had reached the Court of Appeal,[1] section 67 of the NIAA 2002 had come into force with retrospective effect.[2] It provides a revised definition of 'person liable to detention'. Persons are included within the definition, if the only reason why they cannot be detained is that (a) they cannot presently be removed from the United Kingdom, because of a legal impediment connected with the United Kingdom's obligations under an international agreement,[3] (b) there are practical difficulties impeding or delaying the making of arrangements for their removal from the United Kingdom, or (c) practical difficulties, or demands on administrative resources, are impeding or delaying the taking of decisions in respect of them.[4] Section 67 does not authorise detention in those circumstances, but does authorise temporary admission to be granted. This allows conditions and restrictions to be imposed on those in the situation of the applicants in *Khadir*. But what happens if they breach their conditions? If the rationale for this section is that such persons cannot be detained, then breach of conditions or restrictions cannot be backed by the threat of detention, unless the criminal law is brought into effect. That would be one way of getting over the 'legal impediment' of giving asylum seekers human rights. The Court of Appeal held that, given the clear retrospective application of the section, it applied in that case.[5] The decision has been appealed to the House of Lords, and judgment is awaited.

1 *R (on the application of Khadir) v Secretary of State for the Home Department* [2003] EWCA Civ 475, [2003] INLR 426.
2 NIAA 2002, s 67(3).
3 NIAA 2002, s 67(2). The description of legal obligations under the Human Rights Act as a 'legal impediment' to the exercise of the power of removal is an extraordinary example of the mind-set of the government towards asylum seekers' rights.
4 It is to be noted that s 67(2) is not exhaustive and there may be situations where it does not apply, for example, the policy of non-removal adopted by the Home Office in respect of Zimbabwean nationals, which does not appear to fall within the ambit of s 67(2), because the Secretary of State has expressly disavowed human rights considerations as the rationale

for it. Instead he says it 'is based on political rather than legal grounds. It is not in place because it is considered unsafe for failed asylum seekers to return to Zimbabwe': see the statement produced in *Dowu v Secretary of State for the Home Department* [2003] EWCA Civ 753.

5   *R (on the application of Khadir) v Secretary of State for the Home Department* fn 1 above.

SECRETARY OF STATE'S POWERS TO DETAIN

17.14 The Nationality Immigration and Asylum Act 2002 gave the Secretary of State the following powers to detain:

(i)   the power to detain pending a decision whether to direct removal pursuant to the Secretary of State's powers under Schedule 2 to the 1971 Act, and pending removal;[1]

(ii)   the power to detain persons seeking leave to enter the UK[2] who have made an asylum or human rights claim or who have sought departure from the immigration rules, pending the Secretary of State's examination, decision whether to grant or refuse leave to enter, decision whether to remove following refusal, and removal;[3]

(iii)   the power to detain where the Secretary of State has reasonable grounds to suspect that he or she may make one of the specified decisions above;[4]

(iv)   the power to detain persons who make a claim for asylum when they have leave to enter or remain and who fail to comply with restrictions imposed on them.[5]

In addition to these new powers, the Secretary of State has always had wide powers to detain persons liable to deportation, contained in Schedule 3 to the IA 1971. Detention may occur in the following situations:

(i)   *Court recommendation.* Where a recommendation for deportation made by a court is in force and the person is not detained pursuant to the sentence or order of any court, he or she must be detained pending the making of a deportation order,[6] unless *either* the court by which the recommendation is made, or an appeal court[7] otherwise directs, *or* the Secretary of State directs that the person be released pending further consideration of the case, *or* he or she is released on bail.[8]

(ii)   *Decision to deport.* Where notice has been given to a person of a decision to make a deportation order under section 3(5) of the IA 1971,[9] and that person is not detained pursuant to the sentence or order of a court, he or she may be detained under the authority of the Secretary of State pending the making of the deportation order.[10]

(iii)   *Deportation order made.* Persons against whom a deportation order is in force may be detained under the authority of the Secretary of State pending their removal or departure from the UK. If they are already detained under either of the previous provisions they shall continue to be detained unless the Secretary of State directs otherwise or they are released on bail.[11]

In cases (ii) and (iii) above, the powers of arrest, entry, search and seizure possessed by immigration officers under Schedule 2 to the Immigration

Act 1971 in relation to persons detained pending removal also apply to detained deportees.[12] Detained deportees may also benefit from the bail provisions in paragraphs 22 to 23 of Schedule 2 to the IA 1971.[13]

[1] Ie, directions to remove persons refused leave to enter, illegal entrants and members of their families, and overstaying crew members in the situations described at Immigration Act 1971, Sch 2, paras 10, 10A and 14: Nationality Immigration and Asylum Act 2002, s 62(1)(a), (b).

[2] Ie, port claimants or illegal entrants.

[3] NIAA 2002, s 62(2), (3)(a). The powers on which the power to detain is contingent are set out in the Immigration (Leave to Enter) Order 2001, SI 2001/2590, Art 2, made under IA 1971, s 3A (inserted by Immigration and Asylum Act 1999, s 1).

[4] NIAA 2002, s 62(7).

[5] NIAA 2002, s 71(1)–(3).

[6] IA 1971, Sch 3, para 2(1), as amended by Asylum and Immigration (Treatment of Claimants etc) Act 2004, s 34(1). Before amendment by the AI(TC)A 2004, the paragraph allowed (or arguably required) the release of a person recommended for deportation who was on bail from the criminal court. See explanatory Notes to the AI(TC) Bill (HL), para 109.

[7] The appeal court may direct release while upholding the recommendation: IA 1971, Sch 3, para 2(1A), inserted by the Criminal Justice Act 1982, s 64, Sch 10.

[8] IA 1971, Sch 3, para 2(1), as amended by Immigration and Asylum Act 1999, s 54(3) which finally came into force on 10 February 2003: SI 2003/2. The paragraph has no application where the person is serving a sentence or on remand to a criminal court: see *Re Nwafor* [1994] Imm AR 91, QBD.

[9] Deportation deemed conducive to the public good, and of family members of deportees: IA 1971, s 3(5), as substituted by IAA 1999, s 169 and Sch 14, para 44(2).

[10] IA 1971, Sch 3, para 2(2), as amended the Asylum and Immigration (Treatment of Claimants etc) Act 2004, s 34(2).

[11] IA 1971, Sch 3, para 2(3), as amended by Immigration and Asylum Act 1999, s 54(3) (in force 10 February 2003: SI 2003/2).

[12] These powers do not apply to those detained by the Secretary of State following a recommendation for deportation: IA 1971 Sch 3, para 2(4) as amended by IAA 1999.

[13] IA 1971, Sch 3, para 2(4A), inserted by IAA 1999.

Restriction orders

17.15 In each of these cases, including the case of recommendations by the courts, an alternative to detention is provided. On the Secretary of State's direction, the person may instead be subjected to a restriction order which places him or her under such restrictions as to residence, employment or occupation and a requirement to report to the police or immigration officer, as the Secretary of State may from time to time notify in writing.[1] The restrictions mirror those which an immigration officer may impose on temporary admission, for which see 17.6 above.

[1] Immigration Act 1971, Sch 3, para 2(5) and (6), as substituted by CJA 1982, s 64, Sch 10 and amended by IA 1988, Sch, para 10; Asylum and Immigration Act 1996, Sch 2, para 13.

Accommodation centres

17.16 Section 16 of the Nationality Immigration and Asylum Act 2002 gave the Home Secretary power to set up accommodation centres to house destitute asylum seekers and their dependants.[1] The 2002 White Paper makes clear that the use of accommodation centres is also closely linked to the speedy processing of an asylum claim and is said to contribute to the efficient management of the asylum system.[2] It further suggests that asylum seekers will not be 'detained' in accommodation centres and they will be able to come and go. Accommodation centres have not yet come into use, but in practice they may well constitute a deprivation of liberty attracting the protection of Article 5 of the ECHR. First, it is inevitable that allocation to an accommodation centre, as with dispersal, will involve a strong element of compulsion, with withdrawal of support and destitution as the penalty for refusal.[3] Secondly, section 23 of the 2002 Act provides for the imposition of a residence restriction to enforce residence at a centre and residents may be required to observe other conditions of residence.[4] Breach of the residence condition will be treated as a breach of the conditions of temporary admission and may constitute an immigration offence.[5] Other breaches will be sanctioned with expulsion from the accommodation centre and the threat of destitution.

[1]   Nationality Immigration and Asylum Act 2002, ss 17–22. There is a duplication of powers with those under Immigration and Asylum Act 1999, s 95, although there is no difference in the primary legislation between the tests imposed by ss 17–21 of the NIAA 2002 and those under s 95 of the IAA 1999. See chapter 13 above.
[2]   *Fairer Faster and Firmer – A Modern Approach to Immigration and Asylum* (Cm 4018, July 1998), para 4.28–4.29.
[3]   NIAA 2002, s 26; see *Al-Ameri v. Chelsea and Kensington Royal London Borough Council* [2004] UKHL 4, [2004] 2 WLR 354.
[4]   NIAA 2002, s 30, not yet in force. A breach of the residence regulations resulting in expulsion from a centre will be treated as a breach of a s 23 residence condition to reside there.
[5]   NIAA 2002, s 23(2).

Prisoners recommended for deportation

17.17 The qualified requirement to detain those recommended for deportation pending the decision of the Secretary of State was the subject of considerable criticism, as long ago as 1978, on the grounds that it resulted in unnecessary detention in custody of such persons, either at the end of a prison sentence or immediately, where a non-custodial sentence had been given. In July 1978, partly in response to these criticisms, the Home Office issued a circular to the courts[1] reminding them that because of appeal rights, a person recommended for deportation may spend at least five weeks in detention; that the Secretary of State would not necessarily be in a position to decide whether to exercise his or her discretion to release the person if the court had not already done so; and that courts might wish to bear in mind, when considering whether or not to release, the principal grounds for withholding bail in criminal proceedings under the Bail Act 1976. The circular also reminded the courts of the importance of submitting a certificate of recommendation without delay to the Home Office. The clear intention of the circular was to make release the rule rather than the exception. It became clear, however, that this guidance was not being followed by the Secretary of State, and instead, up until 2001 the Home Office proceeded on the basis that Schedule 3 created a presumption in favour of detention, at the end of a prison sentence, to enable a decision to be reached whether or not to deport. This presumption would only be displaced by exceptional circumstances. In *Sedrati*[2] the government conceded that this approach was wrong in law, and the Court made a declaration that there is no presumption under paragraph 2 of Schedule 3 to the IA 1971 in favour of detention after the end of the deportee's prison sentence. The same case also revealed the absence of any effective procedural safeguards for those detained at the completion of criminal sentences. Now section 54 of the Immigration and Asylum Act 1999, which is finally in force, assimilates the position of persons detained for deportation (whether after a recommendation, a notice of intention to deport or a deportation order) to that of persons detained by immigration officers, and they can apply for release on immigration officer or Tribunal bail.[3]

1   Home Office Circular No 113/1978 'Immigration Act 1971: Detention Pending Deportation'.
2   *R (Sedrati) v Secretary of State for the Home Department* [2001] EWHC Admin 418.
3   Immigration Act 1971, Sch 3, para 2(4A), inserted by Immigration and Asylum Act 1999, s 54(4) in force 20 February 2003. For bail under the IA 1971, Sch 2, para 22 see 17.56 below.

17.18 The Secretary of State has also adopted policies with regard to prisoners subject to possible deportation. Firstly, they are not permitted to be held in Category D open prison conditions whilst serving their prison sentences. This is a highly questionable policy which is unlikely to withstand review if, as appears to be the case, it is applied on a blanket basis without any or any proper reference to the individual circumstances of the prisoner, the prisoner's conduct during sentence, family ties and the prospects for resisting deportation. Secondly, detainees subject to deportation after the completion of a criminal sentence of 12 months or more are not eligible for transfer to immigration facilities at the end of their sentence, but have to remain within the prison system on conditions which are substantially inferior to those of a sentenced prisoner or an immigration detainee.[1] After the *Sedrati* litigation a consent order between the parties made clear that this policy would be revised so that transfer would depend on the individual circumstances of the prisoner.[2] Thirdly, there are the provisions of the Criminal Justice Act 1991, ss 35(1) and 46(1), (introduced following the 1988 Carlisle Committee report) which leave entirely to the Secretary of State the decision whether long term prisoners who are liable to removal should be released on licence. Prisoners not liable to be removed have a right to have their cases referred to the Parole Board. In *Hindawi*[3] the Court of Appeal overruled a decision of the Administrative Court which had ruled that this situation constituted discrimination on the grounds of nationality contrary to Article 14 read together with Article 5 of ECHR. The Court of Appeal somewhat surprisingly concluded that the case fell outside of the ambit of Article 5 ECHR on the basis that detention pursuant to the criminal sentence was lawful and that procedures for release did not engage questions of liberty.[4] The court also held that any material difference in treatment was objectively justified – a conclusion which appears to fall foul of the House of Lords' judgment in the derogation case, *A v Secretary of State for the Home Department*.[5]

1   Operation Enforcement Manual (OEM), para 38.8.
2   *R (on the application of Sedrati) v Secretary of State for the Home Department* [2001] EWHC Admin 418. The information comes from counsel and is not referred to in the very short judgment of the court.

3   *R (on the application of Hindawi) v Secretary of State for the Home Department* [2004] EWCA Civ 1309, [2004] EWHC 78 (Admin) at para 30.
4   This conclusion appears to run contrary to the Strasbourg jurisprudence, which does not require a breach of a substantive Art of the ECHR, merely discrimination in the enjoyment of the rights protected by the Article, in order to fall within the ambit of Art 14. See 8.98 above.
5   [2004] UKHL 56, [2005] 2 WLR 87.

National security

17.19 There is (at the time of writing) no power to detain simply on national security grounds. Persons whose deportation is deemed to be conducive to the public good on grounds of national security[1] can be detained under the provisions of Schedule 3 to the Immigration Act 1971, which apply to all deportations, pending a decision to make a deportation order[2] and, where a deportation order is in force, pending removal or departure from the UK.[3] National security concerns are of course relevant to the lawfulness of continued detention and would justify continued detention while deportation is pending.[4] This includes cases based upon allegations of involvement in terrorism.[5] Special provision was made in Part IV of the Anti-Terrorism Crime and Security Act 2001 (ATCSA) for the indefinite detention of those foreign nationals, who could not be safely removed or deported from the UK, if the Secretary of State certified that he or she (a) reasonably believed that the person's presence in the UK was a risk to national security and (b) reasonably suspected that the person was an international terrorist.[6] However, in *A (FC)*,[7] the House of Lords ruled that the derogation from Article 5 of ECHR was discriminatory and disproportionate, quashed the Derogation Order,[8] and made a declaration that s 23 of the 2001 Act, which allowed indefinite detention was incompatible with Articles 5 and 14 of ECHR. The government refused to release the detainees, and threatened to renew the legislation, until new laws were enacted introducing control orders, allowing the men to be placed under conditions of 'house arrest' and other restrictions on liberty.[9]

1   Immigration Act 1971, s 3(5)(a).
2   IA 1971, Sch 3, para 2(2): see 17.14 above.
3   IA 1971, Sch 3, para 2(3).
4   Such considerations could also be relevant to the period of time which the Court would consider reasonable for the Secretary of State to arrange removal, by parity of reasoning with Simon Brown LJ's observations in *R (I) v Secretary of State for the Home Department* [2003] INLR 196, [2002] EWCA Civ 888 (para 29) to the effect that a substantially longer period of time would be afforded if there was clear evidence that the person would abscond or re-offend.
5   Terrorism under the anti-terrorist legislation is defined in s 1 of the Terrorism Act 2000. It has an exceptionally wide meaning, covering the use or threat of action to advance a political, religious or ideological cause and either involves the use of firearms and explosives or is designed to influence government or to intimidate the public or a section of the public. Action means serious violence against he person or endangering someone's life, serious damage to property, serious risk to health and safety of the public or a section of the public or designed to seriously interfere with or seriously disrupt an electronic system.
6   Anti-Terrorism Crime and Security Act 2001, s 21.
7   *A and X v Secretary of State for the Home Department* [2004] UKHL 56, [2005] 2 WLR 87.
8   Human Rights Act 1998 (Designated Derogation) Order 2001, quashed by the House of Lords *A and X*, above.

⁹   Hansard HC (2005) 25 January, Statement by Home Secretary; see now Prevention of Terrorism Act 2005, s 1. The provisions of the new Act apply to British and foreign nationals alike, and are outside the scope of this work.

Power of arrest

17.20 In cases where persons are liable to detention either under the authority of the Secretary of State or of an immigration officer, they may be arrested without warrant by a police or immigration officer.¹ The power of arrest without warrant applies to persons released on bail by immigration officers or by the Tribunal, for reasonable cause; see 17.57 and 17.58 below. In addition, warrants may be issued to the police for the purpose of searching for and arresting such persons.²

1   Immigration Act 1971, Sch 2, para 17(1) and Sch 3, para 2(4). This does not, however, apply to those recommended for deportation by a court, presumably because if they are not detained, it is by direction of the Secretary of State or because they have been released on bail; see 17.14 fn 12 above. The powers of arrest are additional to the power to arrest those in breach of release or bail conditions under Sch 2, para 24 and Sch 3, para 7: see 17.57ff below.
2   IA 1971, Sch 2, para 17(2), para 24(1)(b) and Sch 3, para 2(4). Note that immigration officers may not obtain search warrants for persons liable to detention for removal, although the Immigration and Asylum Act 1999 gave them considerable new powers to search premises for immigration offenders: see chapter 14 above.

WHY, WHERE AND HOW DETAINED

Place of detention

17.21 Under the Immigration (Places of Detention) Direction 2001 it is permissible for detention to be in police cells (albeit briefly),¹ detention accommodation, local prisons or discrete accommodation provided by the Prison Service.² The vast majority of those detained are held in immigration service detention, which consists of dedicated immigration facilities run by private security firms and subject to the Detention Centre Rules.³ The Operational Enforcement Manual has identified certain persons who are not normally considered suitable for immigration service detention because they require particular security, care and control, and it is contemplated that they may be detained in prison hospitals or prisons with immigration detention units. They are:

(i)   the physically violent or emotionally disturbed;
(ii)   those with suicidal tendencies;
(iii) determined absconders;
(iv)   those with a violent or serious criminal background.

For those who face deportation on national security grounds and are detained, the use of criminal prisons in high security conditions has been the norm. For 'ordinary' detainees who find themselves detained in criminal prisons, there is no provision or policy in the pubic domain governing decisions to transfer detainees from immigration accommodation to mainstream prison. Reasons for the transfer are rarely given, even if based upon the conduct of the person, and there is no mechanism for review or challenge of any decision to transfer to a prison. In the course of the criminal proceedings arising from the disturbance at Campsfield evidence was given of a practice in respect of this matter but it is not to be found anywhere in written form in the public domain. The radical change in regime occasioned by such transfer and the lack of any identified criteria for transfer and effective procedural safeguards may render such a transfer unfair and/or a violation of Article 8 and/or Article 5(4) of the ECHR.

1   The Immigration (Places of Detention) Directions are not accessible on the Home Office website, although the five-day maximum period of detention in police cells, which was set out in the 1996 and 1999 Direction, is referred to in the Operational Enforcement Manual written in 2001. In its response to the Metropolitan Police Authority on 29 July 2004 the Home Office stated that although the Direction permitted detention in police cells of up to five days, and seven days if the person is being removed, it has an informal two-day target for getting detainees out, and in the majority of cases, they are moved out after 24 hours (paras 11, 12: on Metropolitan Police website).

2   SI 2001/238. The use of mainstream prison for the detention of immigrants and asylum seekers has been controversial and the Home Office is committed to stop its use. At para 4.78 of the 2002 White Paper (*Fairer Faster and Firmer – A Modern Approach to Immigration and Asylum* (Cm 4018, July 1998)) the government repeated that their strategy was to 'eliminate ... reliance on this accommodation, subject to limited exceptions'. Those exceptions have not been defined beyond para 4.79 which refers to 'reasons of security' and includes those held under Part IV Anti-terrorism, Crime and Security Act 2001 as suspected international terrorists (now lapsed). Use of local prisons was withdrawn, including use of dedicated accommodation at HMP Rochester, and the Home Office adopted a policy of redesignation of immigration facilities within mainstream prisons at HMP Haslar, HMP Lindholme and HMYOI Dover as removal centres subject to the Detention Centre Rules UNHCR has stated that in its view asylum seekers and refugees should never be placed with common criminals: UNHCR *Guidelines on applicable Criteria and Standards relating to the Detention of Asylum Seekers* (February 1999) set out in *Butterworths Immigration Law Service*, 2C[261], *Guideline 10*.

3   To date Oakington, outside Cambridge, is the only functioning reception centre. There are several removal centres with varying capacities: Campsfield House (184), Dover Harbour (20), Dungavel (150), Harmondsworth (550), Manchester Airport (16), Queens Building (15), Tinsley House (137) and Yarlswood (200); and three dedicated immigration facilities in prisons, run by the prison service and called removal prisons: Dover Young offenders Institute (316), Lindholme (112) and Haslar (160) (Home Office Research and Statistics Directorate).

17.22 Rule 11 of the Detention Centre Rules sets out the conditions of detention for families and minors[1] and provides that family members are entitled to enjoy family life save to the extent necessary in the interests of security and safety.[2] The accommodation must be suitable to meet the needs of minors and families and everything reasonably necessary for the protection, safety and well being and the maintenance and care of infants and children shall be provided. Minors, if not detained in an immigration facility, may only be detained in a place of safety which includes any home provided by a local authority, any remand home or police station or any hospital, surgery or other suitable place the occupier of which is willing temporarily to receive the child.[3]

1   Detention Centre Rules 2001, SI 2001/238.
2   SI 2001/238, r 11.
3   Operational Enforcement Manual para 38.7.3. See the regular HM Inspectorate reports on immigration removal centres (IRCs), for observations on conditions of immigration detention, particularly as they impact on children and other vulnerable persons. Child welfare safeguards were found lacking in recent reports on Tinsley House and Dungavel IRCs; see 17.30 fn 11 below.

17.23 Detainees can be, and are, transferred from England to Scotland to be held at Dungavel Detention Centre. This has repercussions for legal representation and access to the courts because of Scotland's separate legal jurisdiction.[1] It can lead to complexity and confusion, with lawyers acting in both jurisdictions on different aspects of the individuals case. It can also cause delay in seeking bail. This was a feature of the *Konan* case which was observed to have 'created real difficulties for the claimant's in pursuing their legal remedies'.[2] This would amount to a legitimate reason for objecting to a proposed transfer to Dungavel. Consideration should also be given to the impact on any family ties if detainees are moved many miles from their family's home. Frequent transfers, which are a feature of prolonged detention, also present difficulties for access to legal representatives and there is inefficiency in coordinating the location of bail applications with the removal centre.

1   See *Gardi v Secretary of State for the Home Department* [2002] EWCA Civ 1560, [2002] INLR 557, for the complications that can arise in the case (Court of Appeal's judgment nullified because of lack of jurisdiction, first instance appeal having been heard in Scotland).
2   *R (on the application of Konan) v Secretary of State for the Home Department* [2004] EWHC 22 (Admin), [2004] All ER (D) 151 (Jan) at para 13.

Conditions of detention

17.24 The Detention Centre Rules make provision for minimum conditions of detention by requiring that the detention facilities (i) have been certified as having lighting, heating, ventilation and fittings adequate for health;[1] (ii) the detainee is provided with clothing adequate for warmth and health;[2] and the detainee is provided with toilet Articles necessary for health and cleanliness.[3] Rule 40 provides for segregation of detainees and solitary confinement which requires authorisation by a removal centre manager for the first 24 hours (r 40(1) and thereafter by the Secretary of State).[4] Written reasons must be given to the detainee within two hours of removal to the segregation unit, and notice of what has happened must be provided to the visiting community, a medical practitioner and the manager of religious affairs without delay.[5] Detainees must be visited at least once a day during their segregation by the Removal Centre Manager, a medical practitioner and an Officer of the Secretary of State.[6] There are no published criteria for segregation, and there is no available procedure, unlike in criminal prisons, to challenge a decision to segregate a detainee. This gives rise to potential challenge under Article 8 and/or Article 5(4) of the ECHR.[7] The European Committee for the Prevention of Torture places particular emphasis on three fundamental rights, namely the right of detained persons to inform a close relative or another third party of their choice of their situation, to have access to a lawyer, and to have access to a doctor.[8] The UN Working Group on Arbitrary Detention, visiting in 1998, found that the main problem for detainees was in access to lawyers, and obtaining information about their case.[9]

1   Detention Centre Rules 2001, SI 2001/238, r 15(3). The centres are subject to inspection by HM Prisons Inspectorate, and the inspection reports are all available online from the Home Office website.
2   SI 2001/238, r 12(2).

3 SI 2001/238 r 16(2), (3).
4 SI 2001/238, r 40(3), where the manager is directly managed. Where it is contracted out, solitary confinement always requires authorisation (although the centre manager may assume the Secretary of State's responsibility in cases of urgency, provided the Secretary of State is notified as soon as possible: r 40(1), (2).
5 SI 2001/238, r 40(5), (6).
6 SI 2001/238, r 40(9).
7 But see *R (on the application of Munjaz) v Merseycare NHS Trust* [2003] EWCA Civ 1036, [2004] QB 395.
8 Report on visit to UK and Isle of Man by the Committee for the Prevention of Torture and Inhuman or Degrading Treatment or Punishment, March 2005 (CPT Inf/2005 1).
9 UN Working Group on Arbitrary Detention *Report on a visit to the UK on the issue of immigrants and asylum seekers,* E/CN.4/1999/63/Add.3 (1998).

17.25 It is also important to note that place and conditions of detention are relevant to the lawfulness of the deprivation of liberty under Article 5 of ECHR because there must be 'some relationship between the ground of permitted deprivation of liberty relied upon and the place and conditions of detention'.[1] Thus the detention of a mentally ill man accused of a criminal offence on remand in an ordinary criminal prison was held to be unlawful because it should have been effected in a hospital, clinic or other appropriate institution consistent with the provisions of Article 5(1)(e).[2] Likewise a juvenile in need of educational supervision should not be detained in a prison where no education is available.[3] By analogy a mentally ill immigrant detained in a detention centre or mainstream prison as opposed to a hospital may be unlawfully detained in breach of Article 5.

1 See further 8.64–8.66 above.
2 *Aerts v Belgium* (2000) 29 EHRR 50, at para 46.
3 See *Bouamar v Belgium* (1998) 11 EHRR 1.

Reasons for detention

17.26 There is no requirement in primary legislation for reasons to be given for detention, despite the obligation in Article 5(2) ECHR.[1] The 1998 White Paper contained a commitment for written reasons to be given on initial detention and at monthly intervals thereafter, or shorter periods in cases involving families.[2] Since October 1999 immigration officers have served written reasons in the IS 91 in the form of a checklist.[3] They are instructed to ensure that the contents of the checklist are interpreted into the detainee's language.[4] Rule 9 of the Detention Centre Rules 2001[5] represents the first statutory requirement for written reasons for detention, and incorporates the commitment that reasons be given monthly and not just on first detention. The Operational Enforcement Manual requires regular reviews of detention, in order to determine whether continued detention is essential.[6] One of the consistent defaults of the immigration service, even where they have carried out the review, is a failure to serve the reasons for continued detention on the detainee, even where there have been significant changes in circumstances between the reviews. In, *ex p B*[7] the failure of the Secretary of State to consider 'carefully and urgently' new circumstances that had emerged, relating to the merits of the claim for asylum and the availability of sureties, led the court to rule that the continued detention of the claimant was unlawful. The need for such a review was described by Kay J as 'imperative'. Human rights implications should be considered as part of the regular review.[8]

[1]   See 8.67 above.
[2]   *Fairer, Faster and Firmer – a Modern Approach to Immigration and Asylum* (Cm 4018, July 1998).
[3]   The use of a checklist has been criticised as contrary to UNHCR's requirements of individualised written reasons, and there are indications that the checklist often masks the real reasons for detention: see Leanne Weber *Deciding to detain* (University of Cambridge Institute of Criminology, 2000).
[4]   *Operational Enforcement Manual* (OEM), 21 December 2000, para 38.5.2.
[5]   SI 2001/238.
[6]   OEM, para 38(6), requiring a review after 24 hours, and thereafter as directed, usually weekly and then monthly.
[7]   *R v Special Adjudicator and Secretary of State for the Home Department, ex p B* [1998] INLR 315, QBD. See also *R v Secretary of State for the Home Department, ex p Brezinski and Glowacka* (19 July 1996, unreported) QBD.
[8]   OEM, para 38.6.

POLICY AND CRITERIA FOR DETENTION

17.27 The criteria for detention are based on a series of policy statements set out in Immigration Service Instructions to staff on detention dated 3 December 1991 and 20 September 1994,[1] factors set out in two White Papers of 1998 and 2002,[2] and now incorporated in a single detailed document, the Operation Enforcement Manual (OEM).[3] The 1991 and 1994 criteria were previously confidential and only came to the attention of practitioners through accidental disclosure. The general policy is set out in chapter 38(1) of the OEM, and can be summarised as follows:

(i)   detention is only to be used as a last resort;

(ii)   detention will usually only be appropriate to effect removal, establish identity or the true basis of the claim, or prevent absconding;

(iii) detention at Oakington (and now under the fast track asylum procedure at Campsfield House, Colnbrook House, Harmondsworth and Yarls Wood Immigration Removal Centres)[4] will only be used where it appears that the claim can be decided quickly;

(iv)   people should not be detained for lengthy periods if it would be practical to effect detention later in the process once appeal rights have been exhausted.[5]

Section 38.3 of the Manual reiterates that 'there is a presumption in favour of temporary admission or temporary release. There must be strong grounds for believing that a person will not comply with conditions of temporary admission or release for detention to be justified. All reasonable alternatives to detention must be considered before detention is authorised. Once detention has been authorised, it must be kept under close review to ensure that it continues to be justified.' The factors identified in the policy statements as relevant to the exercise of the power to detain are as follows:

(i)   the likelihood of the person being removed and after what timescale;

(ii)   previous absconding from detention;

(iii) previous failure to comply with conditions of temporary admission or bail;

(iv) evidence of previous disregard for the immigration laws (eg entry in breach of a deportation order, attempted or actual clandestine entry);

(v) previous attempts to gain entry by presenting falsified documentation;

(vi) history of compliance with the requirements of immigration control – eg by applying for a visa, further leave, etc;

(vii) the ties with the UK evidenced by a settled address, employment, close relatives (including dependants) in the country;

(viii) the individual's expectations about the outcome of the case and any factors which would provide an incentive to keep in contact with the department, such as an outstanding application for judicial review, representations or an appeal;

(ix) a history of torture,

(x) the physical or mental health of the subject;[6]

(xi) the duration of the detention – the longer a person has been detained, particularly if it is the result of a failure on the part of the Home Office to resolve the case, the greater the onus on the Secretary of State to justify continuation of detention.[7]

1 Cited in *R v Secretary of State for the Home Department, ex p Brezinski and Glowacka* (CO 4251/1995) and (CO 4237/1995) (19 July 1996, unreported), Kay J.

2 *Fairer, Faster and Firmer – a Modern Approach to Immigration and Asylum* (Cm 4018, July 1998); *Secure Borders, Safe Havens: Integration with Diversity in Modern Britain* (Cm 5387, February 2002).

3 Operational Enforcement Manual relevant paragraphs of which are referred to below. Section 38, which deals with detention, is not posted on the IND website, but the December 2000 version is available on the website of Advice for Immigration Detainees (AVID), at Aviddetention.org.uk.

4 The removal centres specified for fast track asylum applicants (see 12.111) under SI 2005/560, Sch 2.

5 For the way in which decisions to detain are actually taken see Leanne Weber's valuable study *Deciding to detain* (17.26 fn 3 above).

6 These factors are all set out in the 1991 policy, ISC 26/1991: see *Butterworths Immigration Law Service*, D[971].

7 The additional factor set out in the 1994 statement, which deals largely (but not exclusively) with detention of asylum seekers.

17.28 The Immigration Service has designed a form, the IS91R, which identified six justifications for detention and which is intended to inform the detainee of the reasons for their detention. It is an important part of the published policy.[1] The specified reasons are as follows:

(1) You are likely to abscond if given temporary admission or release.

(2) There is insufficient reliable information to decide on whether to grant you temporary admission or release.

(3) Your removal from the United Kingdom is imminent.

(4) You need to be detained whilst alternative arrangements are made for your care.

(5) Your release is not considered conducive to the public good.

(6) I am satisfied that your application may be decided quickly using the fast track procedure at Oakington/Harmondsworth etc Reception/ Removal Centre.

The most significant issues in the application of the policy are normally (i) the assessment of the timescale for removal and whether removal can said to be *imminent* – the criteria adopted by the Home Office as the touchstone for detention at the end of the process; and (ii) the effect of outstanding legal obstacles to removal, including outstanding applications, representations, and, in particular, legal proceedings by way of appeals and judicial review, each of which is accepted as providing an incentive to comply with conditions of release[2] and meaning that removal is not imminent. In *Nadarajah and Amirthanathan*[3] N was detained, although the immigration officer knew that judicial review proceedings were about to be issued. In A's case, he was detained after his human rights claim was rejected, even though the immigration officer knew he had a right of appeal, which he intended to exercise. The detention policy was described by a senior executive officer in the Home Office, who explained that 'an application for judicial review suspends removal of the claimant and it would be most unlikely that detention would be maintained throughout protracted judicial review proceedings', and that 'removal will not be treated as imminent once proceedings which challenge the right to remove have been initiated'.[4] The court upheld the finding in the Administrative court that it was not realistic to say that removal was imminent in either case and dismissed the Secretary of State's appeals.

1.   *R (on the application of Amirthanathan) v Secretary of State for the Home Department* [2004] EWCA Civ 1768, [2004] INLR 139, at para 55.
2.   IS 91R at para 38.3.
3.   *R (on the application of Amirthanathan) v Secretary of State for the Home Department* [2004] EWCA Civ 1768, [2004] INLR 139.
4.   [2004] EWCA Civ 1768 at para 58. The court summarised the policy as follows (para 28): 'Where proceedings have been initiated which challenge the right to remove an immigrant, it is not the policy of the Secretary of State to detain an immigrant on the ground that his removal is imminent. Normally, in such circumstances he will be granted temporary admission pending the result of those proceedings'.

17.29 The policy is clear in cases where proceedings, either judicial review or appeals, have been lodged.[1] The question which arose in *Amirthanathan* was the effect of solicitors indicating a genuine intention to initiate proceedings. The published policy was silent as to this matter, but solicitors acting on behalf of the claimants proceeded on the basis that such an indication meant detention would not normally take place. The Secretary of State, however, revealed that, although not publicly disclosed, the actual policy of the immigration service when considering the imminence of removal was to ' disregard information from those acting for asylum seekers that proceedings were about to be initiated, however credible that information might be'. The Court held that it was unlawful to rely upon this undisclosed policy[2] which was at odds with the published statements, because it was not accessible, and a detention based on factors at odds with the Home Office's published policy was arbitrary and, therefore, in breach of Article 5(1)(f) ECHR. At the heart of this important decision is the bugbear that properly prepared notices by solicitors that they intend to challenge decisions to remove are often ignored and clients are placed in detention for a matter of days until the proceedings are lodged and then have to be released because removal is not imminent. In *Amirthanathan* the Court of Appeal considered that if such a practice was part of an accessible and published policy it would be neither arbitrary nor irrational,[3] but did not go into the matter fully. The distress, disruption and cost of such a practice hardly seems sensible and it does not, on its face, appear consistent with the general policy of using detention as a last resort to deal with cases of imminent removal or high risk of absconding. The long-standing policy of suspending removal for only five working days if the person is not detained (three days if they are) was referred to in *Amirthanathan*, with the Home Office explaining that the policy does not carry with it the implication that detention will not take place during the five-day period, only that removal will not be effected, in order to permit access to the court.[4] The Court of Appeal's endorsement of this approach is a general one only and does not prevent challenge to its application in any individual case, particularly where there may be other factors such as health or family ties to consider in detaining the individual. In *Amirthanathan* the Secretary of State made clear that it is not his policy 'to detain whenever removal is imminent, but only where there is some additional reason for detaining,'[5] for example if detention is necessary for an orderly removal.[6] This was explained by the court on the basis that imminence of removal is a *reason* for detention but the risk of a failure to comply is the *justification*.[7] The Secretary of State also indicated that the categories set out in IS91 are not exhaustive and there may be other reasons not specifically set out justifying the decision to detain.[8]

[1] *R (on the application of Konan) v Secretary of State for the Home Department* [2004] EWHC 22 (Admin), [2004] All ER (D) 151 (Jan) where appeal rights had been exhausted but removal was challenged on the basis of a fresh claim for asylum and on human rights grounds. The Administrative Court held that the detention was unlawful from the date that judicial review proceedings were lodged, because it was inconsistent with stated policy.

[2] There is a worrying pattern of cases emerging where the Secretary of State fails to act consistently with stated policy, but instead, gets to court and then pulls out of the hat the white rabbit of a different and undisclosed understanding of policy, which is at odds with the plain terms of the published criteria. See *R (on the application of Amirthanathan) v Secretary of State for the Home Department* [2004] EWCA Civ 1768, [2004] INLR 139; *R (on the application of Gashi) v Secretary of State for the Home Department* [2003] EWHC 1198; *R v Secretary of State of the Home Department, ex p Nicholas* [2000] Imm AR 334, QBD. We hope the *Amirthanathan* judgment will put an end to this practice.

[3] *Amirthanathan* above, para 63.

[4] *Amirthanathan* para 59; see also *R (on the application of Ben Pharis) v Secretary of State for the Home Department* [2004] EWCA Civ 654 para 15, [2004] 3 All ER 316, where the Court of Appeal referred to the consequential arrangements between the Treasury Solicitor and the IND and the High Court known as the concordat, whereby it was agreed that removal directions would not be implemented following the lodging of an application for judicial review pending the decision of the court on the papers, as to whether to grant permission and if renewed, until the judicial review process was exhausted. The court stated at para 17 that the practice need not continue, citing abuse of the system as the justification and indicated that an express application for a stay should be made in accordance with CPR 52.7 which states that, unless the appeal court or the lower court orders otherwise, an appeal should not operate as a stay of any order or decision of the lower court. Appeals from the IAT were, however, excepted and did act as a stay: see CPR 52.7(b).

[5] Secretary of State's submission at para 42 and the Court of Appeal's summary at para 56.

[6] [2004] EWCA Civ 654, at para 57.

[7] [2004] EWCA Civ 654, para 56.

[8] [2004] EWCA Civ 654, para 43.

Special categories of detainee

17.30 In its 1998 White Paper,[1] the government set out certain special categories of asylum seeker whose detention would not normally be appropriate. This includes cases where there is evidence of torture, which should weigh strongly in favour of temporary admission. It referred to the need to exercise particular care in considering a person's physical or mental health in deciding whether to detain.[2] It stated that unaccompanied minors should never be detained other than in the most exceptional circumstances, and then only overnight.[3] In all cases, children under the age of 18 are to be referred to the Refugee Council Children's Panel. Where reliable medical evidence indicates that a person is under 18 years of age he or she will be treated as a minor and should not be detained. Detention of families should be effected (if at all) as close to removal as possible so as to ensure that families are normally not detained for more than a few days.[4] The Operational Enforcement Manual (OEM) chapter 38 incorporated these intentions and identified the following special cases:

(i) *Women:* due to the limited amount of detention space suitable for women, detention requires authorisation by an inspector and review by an Assistant Director;[5]

(ii) *Spouses of British or EEA nationals:* this also requires authorization by an inspector and review by an Assistant Director; 38.7.2;

(iii) *Unaccompanied minors and those under 18 years of age* should only ever be detained in the most exceptional circumstances and then only overnight whilst alternative arrangements are made. In the absence of responsible family or friends, unaccompanied minors and those under 18 will be placed in the care of the local authority. Where age is disputed, Home Office policy is to treat as adults those whose appearance strongly suggests that they are such, particularly (but not only) where they initially claimed to be adult, until credible documentary or medical evidence is produced to the contrary,[6] although the policy states that the benefit of the doubt should be given in borderline cases.[7]

(iv) *Families:* the OEM states that families may only be detained to effect removal, and detention should be as close to removal as possible so that families are not normally detained for more than a few days. Exceptions to this policy were made by including families in the categories of those who may be detained under the Oakington process.[8] The policy stresses that its aim is to keep the family as a single unit and to have proper regard to Article 8 of the ECHR although separation of parent and child is contemplated if it is in the best interests of the child to be accommodated elsewhere and in the care of the local authority.[9]

In addition, other groups considered unsuitable for detention, who should be detained only in very exceptional circumstances are:

(i) the elderly, especially were supervision is required;

(ii) pregnant women;

(iii) those suffering from serious medical conditions;

(iv) those who are mentally ill, although they may be detained somewhere other than an immigration removal centre;

(v) those where there is independent evidence that they have been tortured;

(vi) people with serious disabilities.

[1] *Fairer Faster and Firmer – A Modern Approach to Immigration and Asylum* (Cm 4018, July 1998).

2 These factors are reflected in the Operational Enforcement Manual, which indicates that persons who are elderly, or pregnant, who suffer serious physical or mental ill-health or a serious disability, or who have independent evidence of torture, should not be detained: Manual 21 December 2000, para 38. However at 38.8 it says that emotionally disturbed or suicidal detainees should be sent to prison!

3 The Manual (above) also indicates that minors should be detained only in a 'place of safety' as defined in the Children and Young Persons Act 1933, the Social Work (Scotland) Act 1958 or the Children and Young Persons (Northern Ireland) Act 1968. In England and Wales this includes local authority accommodation, a remand home, a police station, a hospital, a surgery or an 'other suitable place'. In Scotland and Northern Ireland the statutory definition is narrower.

4 For detention of families see *A Few Families Too Many: Detention of Asylum-Seeking Families in the UK* Emma Cole, Bail for Immigration Detainees, London, March 2003.

5 For the experiences of women in detention see Sarah Culter and Sophia Ceneda *They took me away: women's experiences of immigration detention in the UK* (BID and Refugee Women's Project, 2004).

6 For age assessment see 11.118 and 12.117 above. The leading case on age assessment, *R (on the application of B) v Merton London Borough Council* [2003] EWHC Admin 1689 (12.117 above) was followed and applied in *R (on the application of C) v Enfield London Borough Council* [2004] EWHC 2297 (Admin). Significant numbers of young people spend substantial periods of time in detention before their acceptance as minors by the Home Office or the appellate authority, and there is increasing litigation both by judicial review and in civil actions. In *R (on the application of A) v Secretary of State for the Home Department* (CO/2858/2004) (8 October 2004, unreported) the Secretary of State conceded that a cursory assessment carried out by a social worker was not a proper basis to detain the claimant. *R (Igor Ivan) v Secretary of State for the Home Department* (C0/352/2005) (judgment awaited) is a challenge to decisions to continue to detain claimants whose claims to be minors are supported by paediatric evidence.

7 OEM at 38.7.3; policy on Unaccompanied asylum seeker children July 2002 para 6.1.

8 In an answer to a Parliamentary question on detention of children the then Minister Barbara Roche MP announced that family accommodation had been made available at Oakington and 'that families may be held together for around seven days if it appears that their applications can be decided quickly' Hansard, HC report, 18 July 2000, Col 165W. In October 2001 it was indicated that detention of families may take place in circumstances other than pre-removal where, for example there is risk of absconding, or identities and claims need clarification: letter from Kevan Brewar, Director of Immigration Services to BID, confirmed in the 2002 White Paper, Cm 5387 at para 4.77.

9 OEM 38.7.3.2. Concerns relating to the detention of children were expressed by the official Solicitor presented to the Standing Committee on the 1999 Act and have been consistently expressed by the Refugee Children's Consortium, the Medical Foundation for Victims of Torture and Bail for Immigration Detainees. it is important to stress that the policy with regard to the detention of minors, including where they are part of the family, remains essentially the same: where detention is to effect removal, which will be the majority of cases, it should be done as close to the date for removal as possible and should only be for a few days. This was the approach of Collins J in *R (on the application of Konan) v Secretary of State for the Home Department* [2004] EWHC 22 (Admin), [2004] All ER (D) 151 (Jan), having heard full argument on the effect of changes to policy indicated by the correspondence and the 2002 White Paper. See on detention of children HM Chief Inspector of Prisons: *Report of Announced Inspection at Tinsley House Immigration Removal Centre*, 18 May 2005; HM Chief Inspector of Prisons: *Report of Unannounced Inspection at Dungavel IRC*, 18 May 2005; see also Save The Children *No place for a child: children in UK immigration detention* (Feb 2005); Sarah Cutler *Detention of asylum seeking children* (Childright, June 2002); Alison Harvey *Briefing on detention of asylum seeking children and young people* (Medical Foundation, Sept 2000).

17.31 The Detention Centre Rules[1] provide for medical examination of all immigration detainees within 24 hours of admission to the removal centre, and oblige the medical practitioner to report to the centre manager, who must send a copy of the report to the Secretary of State, any case where the detainee may have been the victim of torture, or is potentially suicidal, or whose health is likely to be injuriously affected by detention or detention conditions, or who becomes seriously ill, is injured or is removed to hospital on account of mental disorder.[2] These are essential requirements which must be observed if the policy is to be properly applied, since it provides the only effective opportunity at an early stage of detention to obtain relevant information about the person's history and the state of his or her physical and mental health. If the policy is to be effective to avoid detention of those categories of persons deemed unsuitable for detention, it is necessary for the immigration service themselves to have screening interviews intended to elicit relevant information before they decide whether or not to detain the person. This does not take place at present, and the policy is routinely breached. In practice this wrongly places the onus on detainees to provide the material to demonstrate that they ought not, in accordance with the policy, to be detained.

[1] The Detention Centre Rules 2001, SI 2001/238.
[2] SI 2001/238, rr 34–36. A number of reputable organisations including the Medical Foundation for the Care of Victims of Torture and Bail for Immigration Detainees report that torture victims are still being detained too frequently. See eg Alison Harvey 'The detention of asylum seekers', a conference paper given at the University of Cambridge Institute of Criminology, 20 March 2001. See also Leanne Weber *Deciding to detain* above.

Oakington and Harmondsworth – fast track detention

17.32 In March 2000 a much wider use of detention was sanctioned by the government in a parliamentary answer[1] amending the White Paper[2] criteria in respect of detention at Oakington, a detention centre for holding asylum seekers whose claims are expected to be processed swiftly.[3] Later in *Saadi*, as we have seen in 17.10, above, the House of Lords upheld the legality of this kind of detention.[4] Asylum applicants can now be detained at Oakington if it appears their applications can be decided quickly and if they do not present an absconding risk. People are detained for a week[5] whilst their asylum claims are considered. The vast majority are then given temporary admission or release and others are moved to a longer term detention centre. The Enforcement Manual[6] set out criteria for those unsuitable for detention at Oakington, including persons not belonging to a specified nationality;[7] those whose claims raise complicating factors making it unlikely that they can be resolved quickly, unaccompanied minors, disabled applicants and those with special needs; and likely absconders.

[1] 346 HC Official Report (6th series) written answers col 263N, 16 March 2000, Barbara Roche.
[2] Cm 4018, above.
[3] Detention there was to be for a period of seven days, while applicants are interviewed and an initial decision made. If a decision has not been taken, the applicant will be granted temporary admission or transferred to longer-term detention; if refused, a decision about further detention will be made in accordance with normal criteria: ibid; see *R (on the application of Saadi) v Secretary of State for the Home Department* [2002] UKHL 41, [2002] INLR 523.
[4] *R (on the application of Saadi) v Secretary of State for the Home Department* [2002] UKHL 41, [2002] INLR 523.
[5] In practice, the period of detention has stretched and some claimants are now detained for a fortnight or more. The 'target time' has been increased in line: see 17.7 fn 1 above.
[6] Operational Enforcement Manual (21 December 2000) para 38.3.1.

7   For the latest list of specified nationalities see 7.34 below. The Race Relations Act 1976, s 19D (inserted by the Race Relations (Amendment) Act 2000) makes discrimination based on nationality, or ethnic or national origin, lawful in respect of immigration functions in specified situations. See 1.28 above.

17.33 The Harmondsworth scheme,[1] first piloted in March 2003, extended the Oakington fast track procedure to single male asylum applicants who were considered to have straight orward claims and were from countries believed by the Secretary of State to raise in general no serious risk of persecution. A screening process identifies those suitable for the fast track, who are then taken to the removal centre and assigned a legal representative, who sees them the next morning. They are interviewed in the afternoon and a decision is made the next day (usually a refusal). Their claims are not certified and in each case they have a right of appeal. Notice of appeal is to be lodged within two days, and the appeal heard the next day with a determination to follow the day after that. The appeal process is also greatly curtailed, with the whole process, including any onward appeal or reconsideration, intended to take no more than five weeks.[2] Significantly, however the applicant remains detained throughout the entire period. In *R (on the application of Refugee Legal Centre)* the Court of Appeal held that the scheme was just flexible enough to be lawful.[3] The scheme is, however limited in general to single males with no dependants on their asylum claims.[4] Applicants are also excluded from the scheme if their claim, despite being from a designated country, is complex, or if factors such as age or medical condition make it inappropriate for them to be detained.[5]

1   Originally, fast track claimants were detained only at Harmondsworth, although there is now provision for their detention at Campsfield, Colnbrook and Yarl's Wood too: see the Asylum and Immigration Tribunal (Fast Track Procedure) Rules 2005, SI 2005/560, Sch 2. Unlike Oakington detainees, Harmondsworth fast track claimants all have an in-country right of appeal, under the fast track procedure rules: see 18.79 below.
2   For the fast track appeal process see chapter 18, and particularly 18.79.
3   *R (on the application of Refugee Legal Centre) v Secretary of State for the Home Department* [2004] EWCA Civ 1481, [2004] All ER (D) 201 (Nov), upholding Collins J at [2004] EWHC 684 (Admin), [2004] Imm AR 142.
4   In *R (on the application of Kpandang) v Secretary of State for the Home Department* [2004] EWHC 2130 (Admin), [2004] All ER (D) 555 (Jul) the policy was explained as meaning that the accommodation is only suitable for men on their own, and is not intended to relate to the marital or relationship status of claimants: see para 48.
5   *R v Refugee Legal Centre* [2004] Imm AR 142 at para 11; see 18.80 fn 2 below.

17.34 In April 2003, following the introduction of the Harmondsworth scheme, the Home Office introduced revised criteria for detention in claims identified as suitable for the fast track process at either Oakington or Harmondsworth.[1] They replace the Oakington criteria set out above in the Enforcement Manual. The policy has since been revised on a number of occasions, most recently in November 2004.[2] The current policy states that 'any claim may be fast tracked where it appears after screening to be one that may be decided quickly, whatever the nationality of the claimant.[3] A list of countries with qualifications similar to the Oakington list is then set out.[4] The following people have been identified as unsuitable for the fast track processes:

• pregnant females[5] of 24 weeks and above;

- anyone with a medical condition which requires 24-hour nursing or medical intervention;
- disabled applicants, except the most easily manageable;
- anybody identified as having infectious/contagious disease;
- anybody presenting with acute psychosis, eg schizophrenia and requiring hospitalisation;
- anybody presenting with physical and/or learning disabilities requiring 24-hour nursing care;
- unaccompanied minors;
- age disputed possible minors where the applicant's appearance does not strongly suggest that he/she is over 18;
- any case which does not appear to be one in which a quick decision can be made.

The Home Office have also indicated that the non-fast track list should include those who have confirmation of an appointment with the Medical Foundation prior to the asylum interview.[6] Those with mental health problems other than acute psychosis, and torture victims, are not expressly included in the list, but in both cases they are unlikely to satisfy the criteria of claims which are straightforward and can be quickly decided.

[1] Provision has been made within the policy for transfer from Oakington to Harmondsworth for claimants from the 24 designated countries on the non-suspensive appeals list under s 94(4) of the Nationality Immigration and Asylum Act 2002, if it is thought that they are unlikely to be certified as clearly unfounded. Transfer is subject to approval by a senior case manager at Oakington.

[2] Letter from Ian Martin, IND to lSC, IAS and RLC, 17 November 2004.

[3] The shift from lists of designated countries to any nationality was first announced by letter to the LSC, IAS and RLC on 22 April 2004.

[4] The November 2004 list of countries whose nationals may be 'fast tracked' contains Afghanistan, Albania (non-suspensive appeal, or NSA), Bangladesh (NSA), Benin, Bolivia (NSA), Botswana, Brazil (NSA), Bulgaria (NSA), Burkina FASO, Cameroon, Canada, Central African Republic, Chad, China (not female claims based on the one-child policy with possible forced abortion/sterilisation), Congo (Brazzaville), Djibouti, Ecuador (NSA), Equatorial Guinea, Gabon, Gambia, Ghana (not female claims based on female genital mutilation), Guinea-Bissau, Iraq (not currently accepted), Ivory Coast, India (NSA), Jamaica (NSA), Kenya (not female claims based on female genital mutilation), Macedonia (NSA), Malaysia, Malawi, Mali. Mauritius, Mauritania, Mauritius, Moldova (NSA), Mongolia, Mozambique, Namibia, Niger, Nigeria (not female claims based on female genital mutilation), Pakistan (not Christian or female), Romania (NSA), St Lucia, Serbia & Montenegro (NSA) including Kosovo, Senegal, Somaliland (Not Somalia), South Africa (NSA), Sri Lanka (NSA), Swaziland, Tanzania, Togo, Trinidad and Tobago, Turkey (claims must be based on the following: Ethnic Kurdish origin; Military Service/draft evader; involvement of a family member in an illegal organisation; Membership of HADEP, religious grounds), Uganda, Ukraine (NSA), Zambia, Zimbabwe (not currently accepted. Not claims based on membership of an ethnic minority ie no one who claims to be a member of the Ndebele tribe, since they have been deemed to constitute a minority in Zimbabwe. This will also apply to most other tribes in Zimbabwe other than the majority Shona). But under the new policy, nationals of other countries may also be 'fast tracked' if they satisfy the general criteria of straightforwardness and likely speed of resolution.

[5] The use of the word 'females' rather than 'women' tends to dehumanise.

[6] Letter from John Bowers to Vicki Crook of RLC at Oakington, 8 August 2004.

17.35 The difficulty in practice is that, prior to detention, there is no effective screening (apart from determining the person's nationality), to find out if Oakington is suitable or if any of the general policy considerations militating against detention apply. In particular, there is no effective screening to see whether the person is a torture victim, has mental health problems or other special medical needs. The lack of any adequate investigation on arrival creates the real possibility, in our view, of arbitrary detention based on nationality and in breach of stated policy. The case of *Renford Johnson*[1] is indicative. Mr Johnson, a Jamaican national in his sixties, was detained at Oakington in circumstances where his claim could not be determined within the seven-day period but nevertheless, and despite the requirement for reviews, remained detained at Oakington pending a decision on his claim for over five weeks. Jack J held that the detention became unlawful after six days, when it was clear that the claim could not be determined speedily, and roundly rejected the surprising submission on behalf of the Secretary of State that seven days 'was merely a target' on the basis that it was 'wholly contrary' to the Department's submissions in *Saadi* and the basis on which the lawfulness of such detention was upheld by the House of Lords in that case.[2] He also held unlawful the period of Oakington detention after the decision on the claim, as it was contrary to the general policy, there being no basis for concluding that Mr Johnson would not co-operate or that he might abscond.[3] Following this case the Home Office revised the fast track detention policy, stating that the timetable for processing claims was only a guide and that if the timetable could not be adhered to, detention would continue beyond the 10 to 14-day timescale which was the subject of the litigation in *Saadi*, if ' the indications are that we can make and serve a decision within a reasonable timescale'. The revised policy also states that detention may be prolonged, if merited according to the general detention criteria, and could continue after service of a decision.[4] Application of the fast track procedures have proved particularly controversial in disputed minors cases, where expert reports necessary to displace assumptions of adulthood[5] cannot normally be performed within the usual 7-day period, leading to delays and/or the reconsideration of cases where interviews have taken place, during which period claimants remain in detention. We suggest that detention and fast-tracking is patently unsuitable in such cases.[6]

[1] R *(Johnson Renford) v Secretary of State for the Home Department* [2004] EWHC 1550 (Admin).
[2] R *(Johnson)* above at para 32.
[3] R *(Johnson)* above at para 34.
[4] Desmond Browne (Minister for Citizenship and Immigration) Hansard HC, 16 Sept 2004, Column 157–158 WS.
[5] See 17.30 text and fn 8, above.
[6] For a challenge to the practice of detention while age disputes are resolved see R *(Igor Ivan) v Secretary of State for the Home Department* (C0/352/2005) (judgment awaited), 17.30 fn 8 above.

UNHCR Guidelines for detention of asylum seekers

17.36 The UNHCR has issued guidelines relating to the detention of asylum seekers.[1] These guidelines include the general principle that it is inherently undesirable to detain asylum seekers and there should be a presumption against detention.[2] The only permissible exceptions, according to UNHCR,[3] are:

(i)   for the purposes of a preliminary interview to verify identity where this is undetermined or in dispute or to determine the elements on which the claim for refugee status or asylum is based;

(ii) where an individual has destroyed or used fraudulent travel or identity documents in order to mislead the authorities of the receiving country;

(iii) to protect national security and public order.

Unaccompanied minors should not be detained,[4] and unaccompanied elderly persons, torture or trauma victims, or persons with mental or physical disabilities should only be detained on the certification of a qualified medical practitioner that detention will not adversely affect their health and well being.[5] The Guidelines also refer to the UN Body of Principles for the Protection of all Persons under any form of Detention or Imprisonment 1988,[6] which set out indispensable procedural safeguards for detainees. These include reasons for detention in a language the detainee can understand; medical screening to identify trauma or torture victims; the segregation of asylum seekers from criminal prisoners; the segregation of men and women, and children from adults, unless they are part of a family group; rights to communicate with the outside world, with family, friends and consular officials; the right to challenge detention, with appropriate legal advice and assistance; the right to prompt medical attention; and educational, social, religious and cultural rights. The UN Working Group on Arbitrary Detention has also observed that it is 'inherently unjust' to detain people who have been in the UK for 10 or 12 years and have put down roots.[7]

1   UNHCR *Guidelines on applicable Criteria and Standards relating to the Detention of Asylum Seekers* (February 1999) set out in *Butterworths Immigration Law Service*, 2C[261].
2   UNHCR *Guidelines* above, Introduction and Guideline 3.
3   Set out in UNHCR *Guidelines* above, Guideline 3.
4   UNHCR *Guidelines* above, Guideline 6. The UN Working Group on Arbitrary Detention, in its report on detention of immigrants and asylum seekers, states that unaccompanied minors should never be detained: Commission on Human Rights, 55th Session, 18 December 1998, E/CN.4/1999/63 Add 3, para 37.
5   UNHCR *Guidelines* above, Guideline 7. See now Detention Centre Rules 2001, SI 2001/238, rr 35 and 36, 17.31 above.
6   UNGA 43/173, 1988.
7   UN Commission on Human Rights, 55th Session, 18 December 1998, E/CN.4/1999/Add.3, paras 22–23.

Children

17.37 Specific guidance has also been issued by UNHCR in respect of refugee children. 'Because detention can be very harmful to refugee children,' it says, 'it must be used only as a measure of last resort and for the shortest appropriate period of time'. This wording is derived from Article 37 of the UN Convention on the Rights of the Child (CRC) which also expressly requires humane conditions, protection from physical abuse, the need to keep a family together, and access to education and play. Reference is also made to the UN General Assembly's detailed standards which apply whenever juveniles are deprived of their liberty.[1] Article 2 of these standards reiterates that deprivation of the liberty of a juvenile should be a measure of last resort and for the minimum necessary period and should be limited to exceptional cases. The European Union has also adopted similar recommendations, stating in Articles 24(1) and 24(2) of the European Charter of Fundamental Rights that:

'Children shall have the right to such protection and care as is necessary for their well-being ... In all actions relating to children, whether taken by public authorities or private institutions, the child's best interests must be a primary consideration.'

1   UN Rules for the Protection of Juveniles Deprived of Liberty (1990) (UN General Assembly Resolution 45/113, 14 December 1990).
2   Charter of Fundamental Rights of the European Union, OJ 2000 C 364/1, December 2000.

17.38 The legal relevance of these international materials, particularly the UN Convention on the Rights of the Child and the requirement to treat the best interests of the child as a paramount consideration, has had a vexed history, with the Secretary of State succeeding in the past in persuading the courts that they had no relevance to the exercise of discretion, as unincorporated treaties.[1] However, the position has changed with the incorporation of the European Convention on Human Rights into domestic law and the requirement to interpret its provisions consistently with other human rights instruments.[2] In *Singh v Entry Clearance Officer, New Delhi*,[3] the Secretary of State submitted, and the Court accepted, that Article 8 of the ECHR had to be interpreted consistently with other principles of international law of which it forms part including the UN Convention on the Rights of the Child (CRC),[4] this despite the UK's derogation from the CRC in respect of immigration matters. The ECtHR has itself ruled to that effect in the recent case of *Pini v France*.[5] The position of British children detained in Young Offenders' Institutions[6] or accommodated with a parent serving a criminal sentence[7] has been the subject of litigation, which has established their rights (i) to be treated as other children, (ii) subject to the protection of the Children Act 1989 and (iii) for their best interests to be the paramount consideration consistent with international norms. There can be no justifiable distinction in respect of children who are foreign nationals and who find themselves in detention under the Immigration Acts.[8]

1   *R v Secretary of State for the Home Department, ex p Gangadeen* [1998] INLR 206.
2   *Golder v United Kingdom* (1975) 1 EHRR 524; *V v United Kingdom* (1999) 30 EHRR 121 at para 76; *Pini et al v Romania* (78028/01) (22 June 2004, unreported), para 138–139. For a review of some of the other relevant authorities see *R (on the application of the Howard League for Penal Reform) v Secretary of State for the Home Department* [2002] EWHC 2497 (Admin), [2003] 1 FLR 484, per Munby J at paras 51–52.
3   *Singh v Entry Clearance Officer, New Delhi* [2004] EWCA Civ 1075, [2004] INLR 515.
4   *Singh v Entry Clearance Officer, New Delhi* at paras 30, 32, per Dyson LJ.
5   (22 June 2004, unreported).
6   *R (on the application of the Howard League for Penal Reform) v Secretary of State for the Home Department* [2002] EWHC 2497 (Admin), [2003] 1 FLR 484.
7   *R (on the application of P) v Secretary of State for the Home Department* [2001] EWCA Civ 1151, [2001] 1 WLR 2002.
8   See also the EC Qualification Directive 2004/83/EC, and the Reception Conditions Directive 2003/9/EC, both now in force, and both of which require Member States to make the best interests of children a primary consideration. On detention of children see materials cited at 17.30 fn 11 above.

LIMITS TO THE POWER TO DETAIN

General principles

17.39 The right to liberty is a fundamental right and in the domestic common law there is a presumption of liberty which flows from the Magna Carta.[1] It is a pre-eminent right and a foundation stone of freedom in a democracy. According to Lord Bingham of Cornhill:[2] 'Freedom from executive detention is arguably the most fundamental and probably the oldest, the most hard won and the most universally recognised of human rights ...' It means no person within the jurisdiction can be deprived of his or her liberty without cause, irrespective of their immigration status or nationality.[3] This right was reflected in the Immigration Service Instructions to staff on detention issued in 1991 and 1994 and repeated in the Operational Enforcement Manual, which the courts have confirmed embodies a presumption in favour of release.[4]

1 The right to personal liberty is described by Blackstone as an 'absolute right inherent in every Englishman' see Clayton & Tomlinson *The Law of Human Rights* (OUP, 2000) p 449; *Re S-C (Mental Patient): Habeas Corpus* [1996] QB 599, 603. The right is no longer confined to Englishmen; it now extends to women and foreign nationals: see fn 3, below. Control Orders under the new Prevention of Terrorism Act have turned the adage that every Englishman's home is his castle into:' every Englishman's home is his prison.'
2 Lord Bingham 'Personal Freedom and the Dilemma of Democracies' (2003) 52 ICLQ 841–858.
3 *Khawaja v Secretary of State for the Home Department* [1984] AC 74, per Lord Scarman at 110–112; *R (on the application of Abbassi) v Secretary of State for Foreign and Commonwealth Affairs* [2002] EWCA Civ 1598, [2003] UKHRR 76, paras 59–60; *A and X v Secretary of State for the Home Department* [2004] UKHL 56, [2005] 2 WLR 87.
4 *Minteh (Lamin) v Secretary of State for the Home Department* (8 March 1996, unreported), CA, ILD 1996 Vol 3. The stated policy was to ' grant temporary admission/release whenever possible and to authorise detention only where there is no alternative. The aim is to free detention space for all those who have shown a real disregard for the immigration laws and whom we expect to remove within a realistic timetable'. The presumption of release was confirmed in the 1998 White Paper: *Fairer, Faster, Firmer – A Modern Approach to Immigration and Asylum* (Cmd 4018, July 1998).

17.40 The courts will jealously guard the liberty of the person and will require clear words in a statute to take away liberty and to interfere with fundamental rights.[1] Broad statutory discretions to detain will be construed narrowly and strictly ensuring that they are only exercised for the proper statutory purpose.[2] There is no statutory time limit placed on administrative detention but the power is impliedly limited to a duration and circumstances consistent with that statutory purpose and which are reasonable.[3] The lawfulness of a detention therefore depends on a number of considerations:

(i) whether it is or continues to be for the statutory purpose for which the power is given;

(ii) whether the detention has gone on for longer than is reasonably necessary for the purpose for which it is authorised;

(iii) whether the exercise or continued exercise of the power is in accordance with administrative law principles of rationality, fairness and reasonableness, and in particular, whether the exercise of discretion is consistent with stated policy;[4]

(v) as an overriding consideration embracing some of the above factors, whether the detention is for a lawful purpose, is prescribed by law and is proportionate to its legitimate aim under Article 5(1)(f) of the ECHR.

1   *Tan Te Lam v Superintendent of Tai A Chau Detention Centre* [1997] AC 97; *R v Secretary of State for the Home Department, ex p Simms* [1999] 3 WLR 328, 341F.
2   In *Re Mahmod (Wasfi)* [1995] Imm AR 311 Laws J stated the position as follows 'While of course Parliament is entitled to confer power of administrative detention without trial, the courts will see to it that ... the statute that confers it will b e strictly and narrowly construed and its operation and effect will be supervised by the court according to high standards'.
3   *R v Governor of Durham Prison, ex p Singh* [1984] 1 WLR 704 approved by the PC in *Tan Te Lam* and applied in *Re Mahmod (Wasfi)* [1995] Imm AR 311.
4   *R (on the application of Amirthanathan) v Secretary of State for the Home Department* [2003] EWCA Civ 1768, [2004] INLR 139; *R v Special Adjudicator and Secretary of State for the Home Department, ex p B* [1998] INLR 315, *R (on the application of Konan) v Secretary of State for the Home Department* [2004] EWHC 22 (Admin), [2004] All ER (D) 151 (Jan).

The purpose and length of detention

17.41 The purpose for which detention is authorised is spelt out in the immigration Acts. As we have seen above, administrative detention under the Immigration Act 1971 is authorised pending examination or further examination, a decision on the grant, refusal or cancellation of leave, pending the making of a deportation order, the giving of removal directions and pending the removal of the person from the UK. Detention is not authorised for any other purpose.[1] Thus, detention as a deterrent to would-be asylum claimants[2] or a practice of routine detention of particular nationalities, of heads of households or of undocumented passengers which was not for one of the above purposes would be unlawful in domestic law as well as under Article 5 of the ECHR.[3] In *Saadi* [4] the House of Lords held that detaining recently arrived asylum seekers in order to process their claims quickly and efficiently was lawful both under domestic and ECHR law, even although there was no risk of any of the applicants absconding. Thus the power to detain pending examination is not subject to any need to show that detention is necessary to prevent the applicants running away, nor is it limited to those who cannot appropriately be granted temporary admission.[5]

1   See Immigration Act 1971, Sch 2, paras 2, 2A and 16; Sch 3, para 2, Nationality, Immigration and Asylum Act 2002, s 62: 17.9–17.14 above.
2   See *Amuur v France* (1996) 22 EHRR 533, para 43.
3   Police have no power to detain an asylum seeker not carrying identity documents to check immigration status, and a four-hour detention sounded in damages of £2,000 in *Okot v Metropolitan Police Comr*, 1 September 1995, Central London Trial Centre (reported in (1996) Legal Action, February, p 12).
4   *R (on the application of Saadi) v Secretary of State for the Home Department* [2002] UKHL 41, [2002] 1 WLR 3131; [2002] INLR 523, followed in *ID v Home Office* [2005] EWCA Civ 38, [2005] All ER (D) 253 (Jan) (a civil claim for damages).
5   *Saadi*, above at paras 22–24; *ID v Home Office* [2005] EWCA Civ 38, at para 24.

17.42 The limits of the power to detain in domestic law were spelt out in the seminal case of *Ex p Singh*.[1] The case concerned the power given to the Secretary of State authorising the detention of a person against whom a

1136

deportation order had been made. The principles set out in the case apply to all administrative detentions.[2] It was held that this particular power authorised the detention of the applicant only pending his removal and could not be used for any other purpose. Secondly, the power of detention was thereby implicitly limited to the period reasonably necessary for the purpose. Thirdly, it was implicit that the Secretary of State should exercise all reasonable expedition to ensure that all necessary steps were taken for the removal of the applicant within a reasonable time. A failure by the immigration authority responsible for detention to take the action it should take, or to take it sufficiently promptly, renders the detention unlawful.[3] Singh had been detained for five and a half months whilst the Home Office were seeking the necessary travel documents to return him to India. *Singh* was followed by the High Court in the case of *Mahmod*,[4] where a 10-month detention to obtain travel documents to effect removal was held to be excessive, and was approved by the Privy Council when reviewing the lengthy detention of Vietnamese asylum seekers in Hong Kong.[5] Prolongation of detention pending exhaustion of the judicial process is not necessarily unlawful,[6] but in *R (I) v Secretary of State for the Home Department* the Court of Appeal held that whilst a detained asylum seeker cannot invoke the delay necessarily occasioned by his own claim for asylum to contend that removal is not going to be possible within a reasonable period of time, this does not preclude a person who for other reasons of practicality or politics cannot be removed asserting that he is unlawfully detained within the Singh principles whilst a claim for protection is being determined.[7] Dyson LJ provided a useful though not exhaustive list of the circumstances relevant to the question of reasonableness of the period of detention:

> 'the length of the period of detention; the nature of the obstacles which stand in the path of the Secretary of State preventing a deportation; the diligence, speed and effectiveness of the steps taken ...to surmount such obstacles; the conditions in which the detained person is being kept; the effect of detention on him and is family; the risk that if he is released from detention he will abscond; and the danger that, if released, he will commit criminal offences'. [para 48]

Where there had been lengthy detention, the court warned that there must be cogent evidence of a risk of re-offending and not merely a risk of absconding to justify further indeterminate detention,[8] but also warned against detention simply to prevent the commission of crime, which would be incompatible with Article 5(1)(f) ECHR. An undertaking to 'take no steps to remove' an applicant once judicial review proceedings had been issued was held not to preclude detention.[9]

---

1   *R v Governor of Durham Prison, ex p Singh* [1984] 1 All ER 983, [1984] 1 WLR 704, [1983] Imm AR 198, QBD approved by the Privy Council in *Tan Te Lam v Superintendent of Tai A Chau Detention Centre* [1997] AC 97, [1996] 4 All ER 256, PC, and applied by the House of Lords in *R (on the application of Saadi) v Secretary of State for the Home Department* [2002] UKHL 41, [2002] 1 WLR 3131, [2002] INLR 523 to detention pending examination of a claim as well as removal.

2   *R (on the application of Saadi) v Secretary of State for the Home Department* [2002] UK HL 41, [2002] 1 WLR 3131, [2002] INLR 523.

3   In *R v Special Adjudicator and Secretary of State for the Home Department, ex p B* [1998] INLR 315 continued detention after an asylum seeker had established his identity was held unlawful on the basis, *inter alia*, that the Home Office had had long enough to check the information he provided.

4   *Re Mahmod (Wasfi)* [1995] Imm AR 311.
5   *Tan Te Lam v Superintendent of Tai A Chau Detention Centre* [1997] AC 97, [1996] 4 All ER 256, PC.
6   *R v Secretary of State for the Home Department, ex p Chahal* [1996] Imm AR 205. A 30-month detention of a long-term overstayer which appeared 'inordinate and inexcusable' was held not unreasonable in *R v Secretary of State for the Home Department, ex p Ghaly* (CO 4303/1997) (11 November 1997) because it was largely due to the applicant's applications to adjourn his hearing before the appellate authorities. This case would now be arguable in the context of the Home Office policy not to treat removal as imminent when there are outstanding proceedings. Prolonged detention caused by failure to cooperate in obtaining travel documents for removal is relevant to the length of detention which is reasonable for removal, see *I v Secretary of State for the Home Department* below; such non-cooperation is now a criminal offence under the AI(TC)A 2004 s 35.
7   [2002] EWCA Civ 888, [2003] INLR 196. On the facts, the length of detention already undergone by the claimant, who had served a criminal sentence, and had been in immigration detention for 16 months with no realistic prospect of speedy removal, led the court to rule that detention was beyond the legal limits of the power to detain: para 35, per Simon Brown LJ and para 56, per Dyson LJ, Mummery J dissenting at para 44.
8   *I v Secretary of State for the Home Department* above, per Simon Brown LJ at para 37. The relevance of a risk of absconding should not be overstated. It cannot be treated a trump card irrespective of other factors in the case, not least the length of the period of detention (per Dyson LJ para 35); such a result would be 'a wholly unacceptable outcome where human liberty is at stake'.
9   *R v Secretary of State for the Home Department, ex p Singh (Jaswinder)* [1997] Imm AR 166, OHCS.

17.43 On the other hand a continued detention may be inherently unreasonable having regard to the circumstances of the case or it may be so because of the absence of any material distinction between the case in hand and those 'normal' cases in which conditional release is granted.[1] In *Sokha*[2] Lord Prosser highlighted the difference between the Scottish courts' approach to detention and that in England. In Scotland the risk of absconding, which is an inevitable concomitant of liberty, was, he said, not normally regarded by the Secretary of State as justifying continued detention, so that for such detention to be reasonable there had to be some feature in the particular case which indicated that there was a greater risk of absconding than usual. The decision was followed in *Rafaqat Ali*[3] where the Outer House of the Court of Session found detention lawful on the basis that the particular applicant had not employed a 'normal' degree of deception, but a 'degree and duration going far beyond the normal case of illegal immigration'. Since then, the English courts have asserted the presumption of liberty at common law, through the application of Home Office policy and through the provisions of the ECHR, which should lead to a convergence of approach in the two jurisdictions. Cases, however, are awaited.

1   For an unreasonable exercise of the discretion to detain in the English courts in another context, see *Holgate-Mohammed v Duke* [1984] AC 437 at 444, 446 where Lord Diplock's comments on the unreasonable exercise by a police officer of a lawful power of arrest could also apply to immigration officers. See also *R v Special Adjudicator and Secretary of State for the Home Department, ex p B* [1998] INLR 315.
2   *Sokha v Secretary of State for the Home Department* [1992] Imm AR 14, CS.
3   *Rafaqat Ali v Secretary of State for the Home Department* [1999] SCLR 555, OHCS.
4   See eg *R v Special Adjudicator and Secretary of State for the Home Department, ex p B* [1998] INLR 315, 17.45 fn 4 below.

17.44 In cases where the detention is not for one of the statutory purposes, either because it is for an extraneous reason unauthorised by the provisions, or because of unreasonable delay in effecting the statutory purpose, the challenge goes to the power to detain. In other cases, where there is no dispute about whether the power to detain exists, the question is whether or not the decision to detain or to continue detention is consistent with administrative law requirements of rationality, fairness and reasonableness. This will apply especially in the policy cases, to which we now turn. However, policy which embodies a presumption in favour of release, or even a presumption against detention as in the case of those who have completed their prison sentence following a recommendation for deportation,[1] may also affect the vires of a detention, particularly, where the allegation is that detention has gone on too long.

[1]   In *R (Sedrati) v Secretary of State for the Home Department* [2001] EWHC 415 a declaration was made that the terms of Immigration Act 1971, Sch 3, para 2 do not create a presumption in favour of detention upon completion of a sentence of imprisonment.

Policy cases

17.45 It is well established and accepted that a failure by the Secretary of State to follow his own policy constitutes an error of law[1] which entitles the court to quash the decision or grant some other appropriate remedy.[2] This was confirmed by the Court of Appeal in *Amirthanathan*.[3] An earlier example was, *ex p B*[4] where Kay J held it was unlawful to detain an asylum seeker for two months after his identity had been established and sureties had been offered because there had been a failure to apply the relevant policy criteria and in particular a failure, following a change of circumstances in the claimant's case, to reconsider detention in accordance with the criteria.[5] It follows from these cases that detention of torture victims, those who are mentally ill, or unaccompanied minors, for example, would normally be unlawful, because the policy of the Home Office is not to detain these categories of person. It would be incumbent on the Home Office officials to set out fully the reasons for departing from stated policy in any given case.[6] Furthermore, if the decision maker is to show that the policy has been properly applied, he or she must give detailed reasons explaining why the detention has taken place and on what basis considerations within the policy pointing for and against detention have been taken into account. These reasons are then open to scrutiny by the courts.

[1]   *R v Secretary of State for the Home Department, ex p Khan (Asif Mahmood)* [1984] 1 WLR 1337.
[2]   *R (on the application of Amirthanathan) v Secretary of State for the Home Department* [2003] EWHC 1107 (Admin) at para 36 records the Secretary of State's concession to that effect; see *R (on the application of Amirthanathan) v Secretary of State for the Home Department* [2003] EWCA Civ 1768, [2004] INLR 139,CA; *R (on the application of Konan) v Secretary of State for the Home Department* [2004] EWHC 22 (Admin), [2004] All ER (D) 151 (Jan).
[3]   *R (on the application of Amirthanathan) v Secretary of State for the Home Department* [2003] EWCA Civ 1768, [2004] INLR 139.
[4]   *R v Special Adjudicator and Secretary of State for the Home Department, ex p B* [1998] INLR 315.
[5]   See also *R v Secretary of the State for the Home Department, ex p Brezinski and Glowacka* (CO 4251/95) (19 July 1996, unreported) cited in *ex p B* [1998] INLR 315 at 317–318, *R (on the application of Konan) v Secretary of State for the Home Department* [2004] EWHC 22 Admin, *R (on the application of Johnson) v Secretary of State for the Home Department* [2004] EWHC 1550 (Admin).

6   *R v Secretary of State for the Home Department, ex p Amankwah* [1994] Imm AR 240, QBD (decision quashed for unfairness).

17.46 If there is an issue as to what precisely the policy is, this will be resolved by the court. In *Ali Gashi* Maurice Kay J said that the true meaning of the policy is to be found in its language, purpose and context.[1] He first determined the true construction of the policy according to the plain and natural meaning of the words in the context of the relevant statutory materials. Then he asked himself whether in light of the true construction it can nevertheless be said that the alternative interpretation placed upon it by the Secretary of State is reasonably open to him.[2] The extent to which the Secretary of State has a margin of discretion in interpretation of his policy is not conclusively decided and it is important to distinguish between cases concerned with interpretation or construction of the policy, which is a matter of law for the judge, and its application where the Secretary of State is exercising a discretion.[3] This issue will no doubt be revisited in the context of the stricter requirements of legal certainty and forseeability required by Convention legality.[4] In practice it is unlikely that there will be many cases in which the Secretary of State will have wrongly but reasonably construed his own policy. It should also be noted that it will not be reasonable for the Secretary of State to rely upon any alternative interpretation of the policy that was not reasonably foreseeable even if there is a sensible justification for the Secretary of State's approach.[5] This is in line with the requirements of Convention law that a policy must also be sufficiently clear and certain to ensure fairness and be sufficiently accessible and precise to meet the standards of Convention legality.[6] The clear message from the cases in this area is that the Secretary of State will be acting unlawfully in detaining some one in circumstances that are inconsistent with the plain meaning of a policy and that any alternative approach requires a clear public statement and a reformulation of the policy.[7]

1   *R (on the application of Gashi) v Secretary of State for the Home Department* [2003] EWHC 1198 (Admin), [2003] All ER (D) 338 (May), paras 11–12, see also *R (on the application of Amirthanathan) v Secretary of State for the Home Department* [2003] EWCA Civ 1768, [2004] INLR 139 at para 25.
2   In three cases relating to the policy of not sending asylum seekers to safe third countries if they had family ties in the UK the court has found in favour of the claimant's claim as to the disputed terms of the policy: *Gashi* above (the correct approach to the term 'claim for asylum'); *R (Amirthanathan)* above, (the term 'asylum seeker'); and *R v Secretary of State for the Home Department, ex p Nicholas* [2000] Imm AR 334 (whether the policy was limited to spouses only where the marriage took place before flight to the UK).
3   See the discussion in *R (Amirthanathan)*, above at para 21–22 and contrast *R v Secretary of State for the Home Department, ex p Urmaza* [1996] COD 479 and summary in Craig *Administrative Law* (4th edn) with *Gangadeen v Secretary of State for the Home Department* [1998] INLR 206, [1998] COD 216, CA and *R v Secretary of State for the Home Department, ex p Ozminnos* [1994] Imm AR 287.
4   *R v Governor of Brockhill Prison, ex p Evans (No 2)* [2001] 2 AC 19 at 47, per Lord Hobhouse; *ID v Home Office* [2005] EWCA Civ 38, [2005] All ER (D) 253 (Jan).
5   *Amirthanathan* above at para 67.
6   *Amirthanathan* above at paras 64–67.
7   *Nicholas* above, per Harrison J at para 25.

EUROPEAN CONVENTION ON HUMAN RIGHTS

17.47 Detention must also be compatible with Article 5 of the ECHR to be lawful. We deal with this Article in detail in chapter 8. Here we simply remind readers that the central purpose of the Article is to prevent arbitrary interference with the personal liberty of the individual, which is both a substantive and procedural right. Article 5 consists of specific provisions, contained in Article 5(1)(a)–(f), restricting the circumstances in which persons can be lawfully denied their liberty. This list is exhaustive of the grounds for lawful detention.[1] Article 5(4) entitles anyone detained to have access to a speedy review by a court of the legality of the detention, and Article 5(5) uniquely gives detainees an enforceable right to compensation for any breach. In any action to test the legality of detention, it is for the decision maker to establish that detention is authorised by a competent authority,[2] and that authority has the burden of establishing the lawful basis and justification for the detention,[3] by showing that:

(i) it is to prevent unauthorised entry or to remove a person liable to expulsion, or for another purpose expressly permitted by Article 5 of the ECHR (such as prevention of the commission of crime,[4] lawful detention for non-compliance with an order of a court,[5] lawful detention of a minor for educational supervision[6] or lawful detention of persons of unsound mind)[7];

(ii) it is in accordance with domestic law[8] and with the requirements of precision and predictability;[9]

(iii) it is proportionate to its aim.[10]

---

[1] See *Ireland v United Kingdom* (1978) 2 EHRR 25 para 194.
[2] *Grauslys v Lithuania* (36743/97), 10 October 2000, ECtHR.
[3] *Zamir v United Kingdom* (1985) 40 DR 42, para 102.
[4] ECHR, Art 5(1)(c).
[5] ECHR, Art 5(1)(b).
[6] ECHR, Art 5(1)(d).
[7] ECHR, Art 5(1)(e).
[8] *Raninen v Finland* (1997) 26 EHRR 563, para 46; *R v Governor of Brockhill Prison, ex p Evans (No 2)* [2001] 2 AC 19, [2000] 3 WLR 843.
[9] The three requirements of Convention legality have been formulated by the ECtHR as follows: (i) the interference in question must have some basis in domestic law; and (ii) the law must be accessible; and (iii) the law must be formulated so that it is sufficiently foreseeable: *Sunday Times v United Kingdom (No 1)* (1979) 2 EHRR 245; *Silver v United Kingdom* (1983) 5 EHRR 347; *Malone v United Kingdom* (1984) 7 EHRR 14. See further Lord Hope in *R v Governor of Brockhill Prison, ex p Evans (No 2)* [2001] 2 AC 19 at 38C–E, [2000] 3 WLR 843.
[10] Per Lord Hope in *R v Governor of Brockhill Prison, ex p Evans (No 2)*, above. Conditions of detention are also relevant to proportionality: see 8.64 above.

17.48 Detention for purposes which are plainly not within Article 5(1)(f), such as detaining heads of household so as to deter other family members from absconding, is not lawful, unless based on reasonable apprehension that person is otherwise likely to abscond.[1] Similar considerations apply to detention of particular nationalities. The so-called 'special exercises', involving detention of nationals of particular countries,[2] and the nationality criteria for detention at Oakington,[3] give rise to concern that detention is not justified by the facts of the particular case but by reference to a policy decision on the approach to claimants of a particular nationality, often appearing to be motivated by the numbers arriving rather than the context of the claim. The *Saadi* litigation[4] involved Iraqi Kurds who had been arriving in the UK in increasing numbers, whose claims were said to be suitable for fast tracking despite presenting complex issues of law.[5] Other concerns about UK practice on detention on arrival include the very wide disparities in the proportion of those detained on arrival at different ports. A survey in 2000 showed that 32 per cent of all arrivals at Manchester airport's Terminal 2 are detained overnight, compared with 1.5 per cent of arrivals at London Heathrow's Terminal 1. Stansted airport detains 18 per cent of arrivals for over five days; Felixstowe only 1.5 per cent.[6]

1   *R v Secretary of State for the Home Department, ex p Ferko* (CO 4205/1997) (11 December 1997, unreported), Kay J The *Operational Enforcement Manual* (21 December 2000) para 38.1.1.1 acknowledges that 'detention for purposes such as deterrence to others where detention is not necessary for the purposes of removal of the individual is not compatible with Article 5'. It also accepts that such detention may offend Art 8 of the ECHR by separating families, although it may be justifiable to enforce immigration control, and that it would be disproportionate to detain whole families: para 38.1.1.2.
2   See exchange of correspondence between Bail for Immigration Detainees and the Immigration Service Enforcement Directorate, 26 and 30 October 2000.
3   *Operational Enforcement Manual* para 38.3.1. See 17.32 above.
4   *R (on the application of Saadi) v Secretary of State for the Home Department* [2002] UKHL 41, [2002] 1 WLR 3131, [2002] INLR 523.
5   See *Gardi v Secretary of State for the Home Department* [2002] 1 WLR 2755, [2002] INLR 499 (decision annulled at [2002] INLR 557, for want of jurisdiction, the adjudicator having sat in Glasgow, and has no value other than as an interesting opinion of a Lord Justice, sitting without jurisdiction) This decision records the undertaking of the Home secretary that no-one from the Kurdish autonomous region would be returned there via other parts of Iraq until it was safe to do so; and this froze the position, so that in practice none had been removed: *R (on the application of Khadir) v Secretary of State for the Home Department* [2003] EWCA Civ 475, [2003] INLR 426.
6   Leanne Weber *Deciding to Detain* (2000); see 17.26 fn 3 above. The UN Human Rights Commission's Working Group on Arbitrary Detention, which visited the UK in 1998, was concerned, firstly, at the fact that availability of detention accommodation was a criterion, making detention somewhat arbitrary. Secondly, it was troubled, inter alia, at the length of detention, the lack of written grounds or judicial supervision, and that the decision to detain an asylum seeker is made by an immigration officer, who may not have sufficient training in refugee law or the human rights situation in refugee-producing countries: See Report of the visit of the Working Group to the UK on the issue of immigrants and asylum seekers EC/CN.4/1999/Add.3, 18 December 1998, para 18(h).

CHALLENGING DETENTION IN THE HIGH COURT

Habeas corpus and judical review

17.49 A challenge to detention in the High Court may be made either by *habeas corpus* or judicial review. Although many of the technical and procedural complexities of the parallel jurisdictions that have concerned the courts in the past no longer apply,[1] the distinction between the two remedies is that habeas corpus goes to the power to detain and judicial review to the broader exercise of the discretion to detain (although the latter clearly also includes the former). *Singh*[2] was a habeas corpus application where the lawful power to detain was impliedly limited to a period reasonably necessary to enable enforcement of a decision to remove to be carried out. In *Ex p*

Muboyayi[3] the Court of Appeal made it clear that *habeas corpus* is not available if the real challenge is to an underlying administrative decision, such as a refusal of entry, which involves making a judgment after consideration of a number of circumstances and factors. The appropriate remedy in such a case is judicial review. It is also not appropriate to use *habeas corpus* to challenge an immigration judge's conclusion that he or she had no jurisdiction to grant bail pending an appeal.[4] A *habeas corpus* application, while appropriate where the challenge is to the jurisdiction to detain, may also be used to challenge the compatibility of detention with ECHR, Article 5, including the requirements of proportionality.[5]

---

1   In *Barker v Barking, Havering and Brentwood Community Health Care NHS Trust* [1999] 1 FLR 106, Lord Woolf (then MR) expressed his wish to combine the two remedies and to make an order for *habeas corpus* on an application for judicial review, to avoid two sets of proceedings, and added that until that time every effort should be made to harmonise the proceedings. Extra-judicial comments to the same effect were made by Simon Brown LJ in a 1999 lecture to the Administrative Bar Association.

2   *R v Governor of Durham Prison, ex p Singh* [1984] 1 WLR 704.

3   *R v Secretary of State for the Home Department, ex p Muboyayi* [1991] 3 WLR 442 at 448F. See also *R v Secretary of State for the Home Department, ex p Cheblak* [1991] 2 All ER 319, CA.

4   *Re Maybasan* [1991] Imm AR 89, QBD. Habeas corpus was granted where the immigration service had instructed the police to detain an asylum seeker who was on bail to the immigration judge under IA 1971, Sch 2, para 22, to effect her removal, in purported exercise of the power to detain for this purpose under para 16(2) of the Schedule. The court held that once bail had been granted by an immigration judge, it was for him or her to determine whether re-detention was appropriate by reference to the strict conditions of para 24 of the Schedule: *R (Nawpeno) v Secretary of State for the Home Department* [2005] EWHC (Admin).

5   Proportionality is, as has been seen, central to the legality of the detention under ECHR, but on *habeas corpus* applications the High Court is used to examining the duration and purpose of detention and the reasonableness of the period of detention as part of the Secretary of State's domestic jurisdiction to detain: see *Re Mahmod* [1995] Imm AR 311.

17.50 The main substantive advantage of *habeas corpus* is that, once illegality is established, the writ must be issued and there is no discretion to withhold relief as in the judicial review jurisdiction. In the past there were also some clear procedural advantages in seeking *habeas corpus*, though these are now largely historical.[1] Although there are no time limits for a *habeas* application, delay may be fatal to the application. In *Sheikh*[2] the Court of Appeal held that a *habeas corpus* application seeking to challenge a determination of illegal entry which founded a past detention, made some time after the failure of a renewed application for judicial review, itself years out of time, undermined the principle of finality in litigation and was an abuse of process. Where there is a challenge to the legality of a detention governed by paragraph 16 of Schedule 2 to the Immigration Act 1971, it is no answer to an application for *habeas corpus* to rely on the provision of paragraph 18(4) of that Schedule, which provides that 'a person shall be deemed to be in legal custody at any time when he is detained under paragraph 16'. Criticism of views to the contrary expressed in a number of cases[3] was accepted 'unreservedly' in *Ex p Muboyayi*.[4] The object of paragraph 18 is to provide that once an order of detention is made the person named in that order may be kept in custody anywhere the Secretary of State directs.[5] The bail jurisdiction of the

17.50 *Detention and Bail*

Special Immigration Appeals Commission (SIAC) does not oust the *habeas corpus* jurisdiction of the High Court,[6] except in the now defunct anti-terrorist detention cases.[7]

Judicial review is the more widely used and effective remedy available to challenge unlawful detention. Unlike habeas corpus, it covers cases where the detention is authorised by the statutory provisions but where the exercise of the discretion to detain is challenged on public law grounds. The most common ground for judicial review in detention cases in recent years has been a failure by the Home office to apply its stated policy for detention.[8]

[1] See Woolf MR in *Barker v Barking, Havering and Brentwood Community Health Care NHS Trust* [1999] 1 FLR 106.
[2] *R v Secretary of State for the Home Department, ex p Sheikh* [2001] INLR 98, CA. See also *R v Governor of Pentonville Prison, ex p Tarling* [1979] 1 WLR 1417; *R v Secretary of State for the Home Department, ex p Ali (Momin)* [1984] 1 WLR 663.
[3] *R v Secretary of State for the Home Department, ex p Cheblak* [1991] 2 All ER 319, CA; *Re Olusanya* [1988] Imm AR 117, DC.
[4] *R v Secretary of State for the Home Department, ex p Muboyayi* [1991] 3 WLR 442.
[5] *R v Secretary of State for the Home Department, ex p Greene* [1942] 1 KB 87 at 117, per Goddard LJ.
[6] *In the matter of Yousseff* (CO 706/1999) (2 March 1999), QBD [2000] 6 (1) ILD.
[7] The Anti-Terrorism Crime and Security Act 2001 gave exclusive jurisdiction to the Special Immigration Appeals Commission (SIAC) in respect of all matters relating to detention of suspected international terrorists under s 23 of the Act, including the derogation from Art 5 ECHR, and for these purposes gives SIAC all the powers of the High Court: s 30(3)(c), with a a right of appeal to the Court of Appeal in respect of a refusal or grant of bail by SIAC: ATCSA 2001, s 24(4), (5), inserted by Asylum and Immigration (Treatment of Claimants, etc) Act 2004, s 32. Part IV of the ATCSA 2001 (ss 21–32) was repealed by the PTA 2005, s 16 on 14 April 2005.
[8] See 17.45 above.

17.51 In both *habeas corpus* and judicial review, the Secretary of State has the burden of demonstrating that the power to detain exists and that the detention is for a purpose authorised by the statute.[1] Since the issues involve liberty, the burden on the Secretary of State is a heavy one.[2] In judicial review, as in *habeas corpus* cases, the court will determine as a precedent fact whether the power to detain exists, for example, whether or not the person is an illegal entrant.[3] In other words the conditions for lawful detention must be established on a precedent fact basis and it is for the court to decide for itself whether the power to detain has been lawfully exercised. This includes the *Singh* question of whether the detention is for a period which is reasonably necessary to effect the statutory purpose.[4] In *Youssef v Home Office*[5] the judge rejected the contrary submission of the Home Office that in assessing the legality of the detention, the standard is a *Wednesbury* standard.[6] Although the case was a civil action for damages for false imprisonment, the court applied the same principles as in public law proceedings. The issues were whether there had been a failure to exercise all reasonable expedition to ensure removal took place within a reasonable period of time. Although this involved determining difficult questions of fact, including whether there was any realistic chance of the government obtaining workable guarantees from the Egyptian government that the plaintiff would not be subjected to torture or ill treatment if returned, the judge held that the court was entitled to come to its own judgment on these matters.[7] In so doing 'the court would have regard to all of the circumstances and in so doing make allowance for the way that the government functions and be slow to second-guess the Executive's assessment of diplomatic negotiations'.[8]

1   *Hicks v Faulkner* (1881) 8 QBD 167 affirmed (1882) 46 LT 127, CA; *Tan Te Lam v Superintendent of Tai A Chau Detention Centre* [1997] AC 97, [1996] 4 All ER 256, PC.
2   *Khawaja v Secretary of State for the Home Department* [1984] AC 74.
3   *Khawaja* above.
4   See 17.46 above.
5   *Youssef v Home Office* [2004] EWHC 1884, [2004] NLJR 1452, QBD at paras 62–63.
6   Ie, that the decision to treat the person as liable to detention is one which could reasonably be reached: *Associated Provincial Picture Houses Ltd v Wednesbury Corpn* [1948] 1 KB 223.
7   *Youssef v Home Office* above, at para 62.
8   *Youssef v Home Office* above, at para 63. In the event it was held that the claimant had been unlawfully detained for a two week period prior to his release, when it should have been apparent to the Home Secretary that there was no realistic prospect of removing the claimant in compliance with Art 3 ECHR. The case provides a unique and extraordinary insight into the political, bureaucratic and diplomatic machinations involved in such cases, and illustrates the significant advantages of civil claims in terms of disclosure of documents in comparison with disclosure in *habeas* or judicial review proceedings (as to which see below).

Damages, judicial review and county court actions

17.52 Although CPR Part 54 now permits the Administrative Court to award damages in addition to other relief on an application for judicial review,[1] it has no jurisdiction to entertain a claim for damages alone.[2] Further, there are no facilities whereby a jury may be empanelled in the Administrative Court to try an action for damages for false imprisonment,[3] and contested actions involving a human rights element often require cross-examination which is more conveniently provided for outside the Administrative Court list. In *R (on the application of Wilkinson) v Responsible Medical Officer, Broadmoor Hospital Authority*[4] Hale LJ said that it should not matter whether proceedings in respect of forcible treatment of detained patients were brought by way of an ordinary action in tort, an action under section 7(1) of the Human Rights Act 1998, or judicial review.[5] In *ID v Home Office*[6] the Court of Appeal expressed the hope that claims of procedural exclusivity might fall away under the CPR regime,[7] and held that if proceedings are viable, they can be properly brought as a private law action in the county court or begun as a judicial review challenge in the Administrative Court.[8] Where a claim for damages for false imprisonment is made ancillary to a public law challenge in the Administrative Court, the damages claim survives even if the underlying immigration decision is quashed or settled and thereby falls away and/or the person is released from detention. It often happens that the person has been released from detention before the conclusion of proceedings challenging the detention, but this does not prevent the Administrative Court determining the issue and where appropriate awarding damages. Damages, however, can only be awarded if the claimant is be able to establish a private law cause of action which in the ordinary case will be a claim for false imprisonment[10] and/or possibly misfeasance in public office[11] or a claim under the Human Rights Act 1998.[12]

1   Supreme Court Act 1981, s 31(4); CPR 54.1(2).

2 CPR 54.3(2).
3 See County Courts Act 1984, s 66(3)(b) and Supreme Court Act 1981, s 69(1)(b).
4 [2001] EWCA Civ 1545, [2002] 1 WLR 419.
5 *R (on the application of Wilkinson) v Responsible Medical Officer, Broadmoor Hospital Authority* [2001] EWCA Civ 1545, [2002] 1 WLR 419 at para 62. See also Simon Brown LJ at para 24, and *R (on the application of Q) v Home Secretary* [2001] EWCA Civ 1151 at [20], [2001] 1 WLR 2002, 2037.
6 [2005] EWCA Civ 38, [2005] All ER (D) 253 (Jan).
7 The court referred to Lord Woolf MR in *Clark v University of Lincolnshire and Humberside* [2000] 1 WLR 1988 at paras 25–27 and 32–39, who said that the relevant question was not whether 'the right procedure' had been adopted, but whether the protection provided by (then) RSC Order 53 had been flouted in circumstances which were inconsistent with the proceedings being able to be conducted justly in accordance with the general principles contained in CPR Part 1. 'These principles are central to determining what is now due process,' (para 39).
8 'To restrict access to justice by insisting on proceeding by way of CPR Part 54 in a damages claim would in such circumstances amount to the antithesis of the overriding objective in CPR Part 1' (para 106, per Brooke LJ).
9 In *R (on the application of Konan) v Secretary of State for the Home Department* [2004] EWHC 22 (Admin), [2004] All ER (D) 151 (Jan) the claimant had been on adjudicator bail for several months and had been given a limited leave to remain by the time of the hearing of the challenge to the lawfulness of the detention.
10 In *R v Secretary of State for the Home Department, ex p Honegan* (13 March 1995, unreported), QBD, a settlement of £17,000 was agreed for four days' detention over Christmas, following a judgment that the refusal of leave to enter on which the detention depended was irrational. £17,000 was awarded for detention of a British citizen and her infant child for approximately five days following a successful judicial review of her detention in *R v Secretary of State for the Home Department, ex p Ejaz* [1994] Imm AR 300, CA. In *ex p AKB* [1998] INLR 315 the damages claim was transferred to the Queens Bench Division for assessment by a Master, who awarded £10,000 for 63 days of unlawful detention (which followed a substantial period of lawful detention) and £8,000 for damages for exacerbation of a psychiatric condition. In *Konan* (fn 9 above), £60,000 was awarded to the claimant mother and child for six months' detention, including a sum for deterioration in the mother's mental health and the stress of caring for a sick infant in difficult circumstances. In *R (on the application of Q) v Secretary of State for the Home Department* (CO/5162/2003), a claim for unlawful detention and removal of a Kosovan family was resolved by consent on 28 January 2004, with £7,500 each for the father and children's claims for a day's detention prior to removal and a further six days' detention on return. The mother obtained damages of £18,500, reflecting the exacerbation of her psychiatric condition. See also *R (on the application of Johnson) v Secretary of State for the Home Department* [2004] EWHC 1550 (Admin), where £15,000 was agreed in settlement of Mr Johnson's claim for 32 days of unlawful detention after it became apparent that his claim was not suitable for fast tracking at Oakington.
11 See, eg *R (on the application of Bernard) v Enfield London Borough Council* [2002] EWHC 2282 (Admin), [2003] UKHRR 148; *Anufrijeva v Southwark London Borough Council* [2003] EWCA Civ 1406, [2004] 1 All ER 833.
12 The principles of misfeasance are beyond the scope of this book; see *Bourgoin SA v Ministry of Agriculture* [1986] QB 716; *Three Rivers District Council v Bank of England (No 3)* [2003] 2 AC 1, [2000] 2 WLR 1220. Detention and forcible removal from the jurisdiction without any or any adequate notice to the claimant and in particular his or her legal representative, with refusal to stay removal for legal proceedings to be initiated or even after their initiation, could found a misfeasance claim; see *R (Changuizi) v Secretary of State for the Home Department* [2002] EWHC 25; *R (Q) v Secretary of State for the Home Department* (CO/5162/2003). See *Conka v Belgium* 34 EHRR 54 1298.

17.53 In *ID v Home Office*[1] a Czech Roma family consisting of parents and two young daughters were detained in Oakington, Yarlswood and Campsfield detention centres and were all suffering from post-traumatic stress disorder and depression as a result of their experiences. The detentions resulted from decisions of immigration officers, purportedly exercising their powers under

Schedule 2 to the Immigration Act 1971. The claimants started actions for declarations and damages in the county court, which were struck out at the instigation of the Home Office. They appealed to the Court of Appeal. The Home Office argued on two main fronts. First, they said that the immigration officers were immune from suit. Secondly, they argued that the complainants' remedy was limited to a declaration that the act was unlawful and/or a quashing order, by way of judicial review and not an action in the county court. They lost on each of these arguments. First, the court rejected the argument that foreign nationals who have not been granted leave to enter this country fall into a very special category.[2] The court held that by 1924 it was clear that aliens lawfully within this country in time of peace were accorded the same civil rights as British citizens,[3] and that in *Khawaja* Lord Scarman put it beyond doubt that the rule of law extended to aliens subject to administrative detention.[4] Secondly, the court held that immigration officers were not immune from being sued.[5] Thirdly, they held that, following (i) the Human Rights Act and the need to read domestic law in the light of Article 5 of ECHR and (ii) the House of Lords decision in *Evans*,[6] Home Office officials could be sued for false imprisonment on a strict liability basis, and that a complainant was not confined to seeking a declaration or quashing order[7] through judicial review or *habeas corpus* proceedings in the Administrative Court. This landmark decision clears away obstacles previously blocking the path of the would-be claimant who has been wrongfully imprisoned without trial. In his judgment Brooke LJ set out the background to this growing area of litigation:

'The evidence of the interveners showed, however, that when the Home Office determined to embark on the policy of using powers of administrative detention on a far larger scale than hitherto, the practical implementation of that policy threw up very understandable concerns in individual cases. The transition from a world where decisions affecting personal liberty are made by officials of the executive who operate according to unpublished criteria, and where there is no way of compensating those who lose their liberty through administrative muddles and misfiling, to a world where the relevant criteria have to be published and where those officials are obliged to ensure that their decisions are proportionate and to justify them accordingly, is bound to be an uneasy one in the early years, and mistakes are bound to be made. But so long as detention, which may cause significant suffering, can be directed by executive decision and an order of a court (or court-like body) is not required, the language and the philosophy of human rights law, and the common law's emphatic reassertion in recent years of the importance of constitutional rights, drive inexorably, in my judgment, to the conclusion I have reached.'[8]

1   *ID v Home Office* [2005] EWCA Civ 38, [2005] All ER (D) 253 (Jan).
2   Counsel argued that the power of a state to control immigration is well recognised in international law and under the ECHR (see Lord Slynn in *Saadi* at para 31), and that this right extends beyond the simple control of entry to encompass the treatment of aliens and the control of their activities whilst they are present or resident in the state, citing *Nishimura Ekiu v United States* 142 US 651, 659 (1892); *Musgrove v Chun Teong Toy* [1891] AC 272, 283; and *Attorney-General for Canada v Cain* [1906] AC 542, 546; and Lord Denning MR in *R v Governor of Brixton Prison, ex p Soblen* [1963] 2 QB 243 at 300, citing Sir William Blackstone's *Commentaries* (Vol 1, 1765) at pp 259–260 to the effect that strangers who came spontaneously were liable to be sent home whenever the king saw occasion.
3   *Johnstone v Pedlar* [1921] 2 AC 262.

4   *Khawaja v Secretary of State for the Home Department* [1984] AC 74 per Lord Scarman at
    111–112, who said that this principle had been in the law at least since Lord Mansfield
    freed 'the black' in *Sommersett's Case* (1772) 20 State Tr 1.
5   The court cited well known authority, including *Eleko (Eshugbayi) v Government of
    Nigeria* [1931] AC 662 per Lord Atkin at 670); '[I]n English law every imprisonment is
    prima facie unlawful and ... it is for a person directing imprisonment to justify his act. The
    only exception is in respect of imprisonment ordered by a judge, who from the nature of
    his office cannot be sued, and the validity of whose judicial decisions cannot in such
    proceedings as the present be questioned' (*Liversidge v Anderson* [1942] AC 206, per
    Lord Atkin at 245). 'The law attaches supreme importance to the liberty of the individual
    and if he suffers a wrongful interference with that liberty it should remain actionable even
    without proof of special damage': *Murray v Ministry of Defence* [1988] 1 WLR 692, per
    Lord Griffiths at 703–3).
6   *R v Governor of Brockhill Prison, ex p Evans (No 2)* [2001] 2 AC 19, where Lord Steyn
    relied on the first of Lord Atkin's dicta (above) as the traditional common law view,
    supporting an entitlement to compensation on the ground of false imprisonment where the
    executive can no longer support the lawfulness of the detention (at 28).
7   In so ruling the court distinguished (almost to the point of overruling, which they cannot
    do because of the doctrine of binding precedent) *W v Home Office* [1997] Imm AR 302,
    309 and 311 and *Ullah (Mohammed) v Home Secretary* [1995] Imm AR 166.
8   *ID v Home Office* [2005] EWCA Civ 38, [2005] All ER (D) 253 (Jan) at para 130. There
    is no specific guidance on the courts' approach to the assessment of damages in claims
    arising in the immigration context. The relevant principles, particularly in relation to false
    imprisonment claims, have been most developed in the context of civil actions against the
    police, and as a general rule the approach of the courts to the quantum of damages in these
    cases is followed, for which see *Thompson v Metropolitan Police Comr* [1998] QB 498,
    [1997] 3 WLR 403; *Lunt v Liverpool City Justices* (5 March 1991, unreported), CA. For
    recent damages awards see 17.52 fn 10 above.

PAYING FOR DETENTION

17.54 The expense of detention will normally be the responsibility of the
immigration authorities. However, carriers may be required to pay the
detention costs (up to a maximum of 14 days) of those who are removed after
being refused leave to enter,[1] except those passengers holding a certificate of
entitlement, entry clearance or work permit,[2] or any person who successfully
appeals.[3] Carriers may also be required to pay the detention costs of illegal
entrants[4] or absconding or overstaying crew members who are facing
removal.[5] No liability arises in the case of those held to be illegal entrants by
deception whose leave was not cancelled within 24 hours of its grant.[6] A
person facing deportation may find his or her money used to defray the costs
of detention.[7]

1   Immigration Act 1971, Sch 2, para 19(1). The 14-day limitation was inserted by the
    Asylum and Immigration Act 1996, Sch 2, para 8.
2   IA 1971, Sch 2, para 19(2).
3   IA 1971, Sch 2, para 19(3).
4   IA 1971, Sch 2, para 20(1)(a).
5   IA 1971, Sch 2, para 20(1)(b).
6   IA 1971, Sch 2, para 20(1A) (inserted by Asylum and Immigration Act 1996, Sch 2,
    para 9), referring to para 6(2) (cancellation of leave within 24 hours of grant by
    immigration officer).
7   IA 1971, Sch 3, para 1(4).

PROVISIONS FOR RELEASE OR BAIL

17.55 In all cases where the Secretary of State or immigration officer have a
power to detain, they also have a power to release. The power to grant

temporary admission or a restriction order as an alternative to detention has been described in 17.11 and 17.15 above. In addition, everyone detained under the Immigration Act 1971 may seek bail from the immigration authorities or the Asylum and Immigration Tribunal under paragraphs 22 and 34 of Schedule 2 to the IA 1971. Those awaiting appeal may apply for bail to the Asylum and Immigration Tribunal under paragraph 29 of Schedule 2, and there are in addition possibilities of obtaining bail in judicial review or *habeas corpus* proceedings. The grant of bail is distinct from the issue of the lawfulness of the detention[2] (although the issues of eligibility for bail and lawfulness of detention are sometimes difficult to separate).[3] Bail is, therefore, not an alternative remedy that must be exhausted before proceedings for judicial review challenging the legality of detention can be sought, and refusal of bail is irrelevant to the question of the legality of the decision to detain, so that such a challenge cannot be properly characterised as a collateral challenge to the refusal of bail. Moreover, in practice immigration judges are not always provided with accurate reasons and information by the Home Office in bail summaries and they may well have refused bail on an erroneous basis.[4] We describe below the provisions for release on bail under the IA 1971 and in *habeas corpus* and judicial review proceedings.

1   As amended by Asylum and Immigration Act 1996, Sch 2, para 11, Immigration and Asylum Act 1999, Sch 14, para 63, Asylum and Immigration (Treatment of Claimants, etc) Act 2004, s 26(7), Sch 2, Pt 1. The bail provisions apply to those detained by the Secretary of State under Nationality, Immigration and Asylum Act 2002, s 62: s 62(3).
2   See *In the matter of Yousseff* (CO 706/1999) (2 March 1999), QBD [2000] 6 (1) ILD.
3   In *R (on the application of Konan) v Secretary of State for the Home Department* [2004] EWHC 22 (Admin), [2004] All ER (D) 151 (Jan) the court rejected the Secretary of State's submissions that bail was an alternative remedy to judicial review challenging the legality of the detention. The distinction between the two remedies was clear and the court confirmed that when an immigration judge is considering bail he or she is not determining the lawfulness of the detention. See para 30.
4   *R (on the application of Konan)* above, at para 26 and *R (on the application of Johnson) v Secretary of State for the Home Department* [2004] EWHC 1550 (Admin), para 36.

New arrivals and those detained for removal: bail under the Immigration Act 1971

17.56 The right to apply for bail has been achieved through the accretion of amendments to Schedule 2 to the Immigration Act 1971 by the Asylum and Immigration Act 1996, the Immigration and Asylum Act 1999 and the Nationality, Immigration and Asylum Act 2002. It applies to new arrivals detained for more than seven days pending examination,[1] and anyone detained pending a decision on cancellation of leave to enter,[2] or after refusal of leave to enter pending removal directions,[3] or as a suspected illegal entrant or overstayer detained pending the giving of directions,[4] or persons detained following a decision to deport or a recommendation for deportation or a deportation order. Bail may be granted by a chief immigration officer[6] or police officer not below the rank of inspector[7] or by the Asylum and Immigration Tribunal,[8] on the person's own recogisance (or bail bond in Scotland), with a condition to appear before an immigration officer at a time and place notified in writing,[9] and other conditions may be imposed to secure the appearance of the person bailed at the requisite time and place.[10]

Immigration officers and police may arrest those in breach of bail or those they reasonably believe will breach, are breaching or have breached conditions,[11] or on notice in writing of a surety that the released person is likely to breach a condition and that the surety wishes to withdraw.[12] A person arrested under these circumstances must be brought before an immigration judge or a justice of the peace as soon as reasonably practicable and in any event within 24 hours to decide whether detention or release should be ordered.[13] There is provision for the forfeiture of the recognisance or bail bond in case of breach of bail.[14] Bail may also be granted to persons against whom removal directions have been set.[15]

1   Immigration Act 1971, Sch 2, para 22(1)(a), (1B), as amended by Asylum and Immigration Act 1996, Sch 2, para 11(1)–(3). The bail provisions apply to those detained by the Secretary of State under Nationality, Immigration and Asylum Act 2002, s 62 by virtue of s 62(3).
2   IA 1971, Sch 2, para 22(1)(aa), inserted by Immigration and Asylum Act 1999, Sch 14, para 63. There is no seven-day waiting requirement in relation to this category, or indeed to anyone except new arrivals seeking leave to enter.
3   IA 1971, Sch 2, para 22(1)(b), applied to persons detained by the Secretary of State under NIAA 2002, s 62 by NIAA 2002, s 62(3).
4   IA 1971, Sch 2, para 22(1)(b) applied as above by the NIAA 2002.
5   Immigration and Asylum Act 1999, s 54, extending paras 22–25 of Sch 2 to the IA 1971 to those detained under the relevant provisions of Sch 3, para 2. The sentencing court or the appeal court, may also release on bail: *R v Governor of Holloway Prison, ex p Giambi* [1982] 1 All ER 434. The appeal court may grant bail pending an appeal against a recommendation, under Criminal Appeal Act 1968, s 19: *R v Ofori and Tackie* (1993) 99 Cr App Rep 219, and may direct release while upholding the recommendation: IA 1971, Sch 3, para 2(1A), inserted by Criminal Justice Act 1982 s 64, Sch 10, paras 1–2.
6   The *Operational Enforcement Manual* (21 December 2000) para 39 sets out criteria for CIO bail including the likelihood of absconding, the likely delay pending a decision or disposal of an appeal, any special reasons for detention, the reliability and standing of sureties and (in deportation cases) the views of the caseworker. It stipulates that normally two sureties will be required, and professional sureties suspected of acting for financial gain, or with a view to evasion, will be rejected. It expects sureties to have a personal connection with the applicant or to be acting on behalf of a reputable organisation with an interest in the detainee's welfare. The 'normal' requirement for two sureties may be unlawful if applied without proper regard to its necessity in individual cases: see 17.35 below.
7   IA 1971, Sch 2, para 22(1A).
8   IA 1971, Sch 2, para 22(1A), as amended by Asylum and Immigration (Treatment of Claimants, etc) Act 2004, s 26(7), Sch 2, Pt 1.
9   IA 1971, Sch 2, para 22(1A).
10   IA 1971, Sch 2, para 22(2).
11   IA 1971, Sch 2, para 24(1)(a), without a warrant, and para 17(2), with a warrant for entry into premises.
12   IA 1971, Sch 2, para 24(1)(b).
13   IA 1971, Sch 2, para 24(2).
14   IA 1971, Sch 2, para 23.
15   IA 1971, Sch 2, para 34, applying the provisions of para 22 as to release on bail, and paras 23–25 relating to arrest, forfeiture of recognisance and bail procedures, to persons detained for removal. The paragraph is applied to those detained by the Secretary of State under NIAA 2002, s 62 by NI 2002, s 62(3).

Bail pending appeal

17.57 Persons detained under Schedules 2 and 3 to the Immigration Act 1971 are eligible for bail if they have an in-country appeal pending before the

Asylum and Immigration Tribunal.[1] As with bail pending examination, bail on appeal may be granted by a chief immigration officer or police inspector[2] as well as by the Tribunal.[3] The grant of bail is discretionary, and may be withheld on grounds of previous non-compliance, prevention of crime, public health and protection for appellants vulnerable through mental disorder or youth.[4] It may be subject to the giving of sureties or recognisance and to conditions.[5] The Schedule provides that where removal directions are in force or the power to give directions is exercisable, the consent of the Secretary of State to bail must be obtained.[6] In *Ex p Alghali*[7] the court held that, since directions for removal are of no effect while an appeal is pending, the consent of the Secretary of State is not needed. However, the Nationality, Immigration and Asylum Act 2002 provides that, although a person may not be removed from the UK under the Immigration Acts pending an appeal under section 82, removal directions may be given.[8] The effect of this provision, read literally, would be to make all bail pending appeal subject to the Secretary of State's consent. Such an interpretation would be an unwarranted restriction on the powers of the appellate authorities to grant bail, and would in all likelihood offend against Article 5(4) of the ECHR. We suggest that the better interpretation of the provision is to limit its effect to those cases where, prior to the appeal being lodged, directions for removal had actually been set.[9] Immigration officers and police officers may arrest persons released on bail pending appeal on reasonable grounds for believing that the person is likely to break the conditions of bail, or is breaking or has broken such conditions,[10] or on written notice by a surety that he or she no longer wishes to stand surety because of a belief that the person on bail will not appear.[11] There are powers for the Tribunal to forfeit any recognisance in whole or in part,[12] in which case a magistrates' court is specified to recover the sum.[13]

1 Immigration Act 1971, Sch 2, para 29(1), as amended by Nationality, Immigration and Asylum Act 2002, Sch 7 from 1 April 2003 (SI 2003/754) to provide for bail pending all appeals under Part 5 of the 2002 Act (see 18.15).
2 IA 1971, Sch 2, para 29(2) as amended by Asylum and Immigration (Treatment of Claimants, etc) Act 2004, s 26(7), Sch 2, Pt 1.
3 IA 1971, Sch 2, para 29(3) as amended.
4 IA 1971, Sch 2, para 30(2) as amended.
5 IA 1971, Sch 2, para 29(3), (5), 30(2) as amended.
6 IA 1971, Sch 2, para 30(1).
7 *R v Immigration Appeal Tribunal, ex p Alghali* [1984] Imm AR 106, QBD.
8 Nationality, Immigration and Asylum Act 2002, s 78(1)(a), (3)(a).
9 In such a situation, however, the appellant could rely on paras 22 and 34 of Sch 2 (grant of bail pending removal), which is not subject to the Secretary of State's consent. We believe that the effect of s 78 of the 2002 Act on the provisions of Sch 2 to the IA 1971 was simply not thought through, and that para 30(1) ought to be repealed.
10 IA 1971, Sch 2, para 33(1)(a). Even this could offend against the requirements of Art 5(4) of the EHCR; see above.
11 IA 1971, Sch 2, para 33(1)(b).
12 IA 1971, Sch 2, para 31(1).
13 IA 1971, Sch 2, para 31(2)–(5).

17.58 Bail pending appeal to the Court of Appeal from the Tribunal[1] was provided for in section 9A of the Asylum and Immigration Appeals Act 1993. Bail could be granted by a chief immigration officer, a police inspector or the Tribunal pending an appeal or an application for leave to appeal.[2] There was a statutory right to bail where leave to appeal has been granted or where the immigrant or asylum seeker is the respondent to the Secretary of State's appeal,[3] subject to statutory exceptions,[4] and the provisions for arrest for breach of bail and for forfeiture of recognisances also applied.[5] The section is prospectively repealed by the Asylum and Immigration (Treatment of Claimants, etc) Act 2004,[6] and it is not clear whether the Tribunal has power to grant bail pending reconsideration or appeal to the Court of Appeal under the amended provisions of Schedule 2 to the 1971 Act, or whether an intending applicant or appellant would have to seek bail from the High Court or Court of Appeal in their inherent jurisdiction.[7]

[1]   Under Asylum and Immigration Appeals Act 1993, s 9A, inserted by Asylum and Immigration Act 1996, amended by Immigration Act 1999, made subject to the NIAA 2002 in respect of appeals lodged after 4 April 2003 (SI 2003/1016) and prospectively repealed by the AI(TC)A 2004, s 47 and Sch 4.
[2]   AIAA 1993, s 9A(1), (2), (3).
[3]   AIAA 1993, s 9A(3)(a) and (b).
[4]   AIAA 1993, s 9A(4) applies the relevant provisions of Immigration Act 1971, Sch 2, paras 29 and 30(2) to bail pending appeal to the Court of Appeal.
[5]   AIAA 1993, s 9A(5), applying the provisions of Immigration Act 1971, Sch 2, paras 31–33 (see 17.31 above).
[6]   Asylum and Immigration (Treatment of Claimants, etc) Act 2004, s 47 and Sch 4, see also Sch 2, para 9.
[7]   Immigration Act 1971 Sch 2 para 29, as amended by Asylum and Immigration (Treatment of Claimants, etc) Act 2004, Sch 2, para 1. Whether the Tribunal has jurisdiction depends on the interpretation of 'appeals under Part 5 of the 2002 Act'; for interpretation of a similar provision of the 1999 Act (in the different context of statutory abandonment of appeals) see *Shirazi v Secretary of State for the Home Department* [2003] EWCA Civ 1562, [2004] 2 All ER 602, [2004] INLR 92.

Bail before the Special Immigration Appeals Commission

17.59 The provisions of the Immigration Act 1971 in relation to bail are modified in respect of the following persons:

(i)   those detained under provisions of the Immigration Act 1971 or the Nationality, Immigration and Asylum Act 2002 whose detention has been certified by the Secretary of State as necessary in the interests of national security;[1]

(ii)   those detained under either Act following a decision to refuse leave to enter on the ground that exclusion is in the interests of national security;[2]

(iii) those detained following a decision to deport on national security grounds.[3]

The modifications are set out in Schedule 3 to the Special Immigration Appeals Commission Act 1997. In all national security cases it is the Special Immigration Appeals Commission which has the power to grant bail, not immigration or police officers or the Tribunal.[4] This applies both to new arrivals and to appellants.[5] Provisions as to arrest for breach of bail and forfeiture of recognisances are modified accordingly.[6]

[1]   Special Immigration and Appeals Commission Act 1997, s 3(1) (as amended by SI 2003/1016 Art 3, Sch, para 10(2)(a). Until March 2005 the list included those detained under s 23 of the Anti-terrorism, Crime and Security Act 2001 who were certified as suspected international terrorists under s 21 of the Act: ATCSA 2001, s 24(2).

2   SIACA 1997, s 3(2)(b).
3   SIACA 1997, s 3(2)(c).
4   SIACA 1997, Sch 3, para 1, as amended by Asylum and Immigration (Treatment of Claimants, etc) Act 2004, s 26(7), Sch 2, Pt 1.
5   SIACA 1997, Sch 3, para 4 as amended, substituting references to the Tribunal with references to the Commission.
6   SIACA 1997, Sch 3, paras 2–8 as amended.

Bail procedure before Asylum and Immigration Tribunal

17.60 The procedure governing bail applications before the immigration appellate authority is governed by Part 4 of the Asylum and Immigration Tribunal (Procedure) Rules 2005.[1] A bail application must be made by filing an application notice in the prescribed form with the Tribunal.[2] The notice must contain the full name, date of birth and date of arrival in the UK of the applicant; the address where he or she is detained; whether an appeal is pending; a bail address (or reason why no such address is given); the amount of any recognisance offered; the names, addresses, occupations and dates of birth of any persons who have agreed to stand as sureties and the amounts offered by them; the grounds of the application and if a previous application has been refused, full details of any change in circumstances. If an interpreter is required for the hearing this must also be stated.[3] The application must be signed by the applicant or a representative or (if the detainee is a minor or for some other reason is incapable of acting) by a person acting on his or her behalf.[4] Where an application for bail is filed, the appellate authority must as soon as reasonably practicable serve a copy on the Secretary of State and fix a hearing.[5] The Secretary of State must file a written statement of reasons for contesting the application (if it is contested) not later than 2.00 pm before the day of the hearing, or where notice was received less than 24 hours before that time, as soon as reasonably practicable.[6] Bail applications are to be listed within three working days of the Tribunal's receipt of the notice of application.[7] The Tribunal must serve written notice of its decision on the parties and the person having custody of the applicant.[8] If bail is granted the notice must include the conditions of bail, and the amount in which the applicant and any sureties are to be bound.[9] Where bail is refused, the notice must include reasons for the refusal.[10] Applicants must be released once the person in whose custody they are has received a copy of a decision to grant bail and is satisfied that any recognisances have been entered into.[11] There are some minor variations in form to rules 38 to 41 for applications for bail made in Scotland, where cautioners replace sureties and deposits are given by both applicants and cautioners, and rule 40 does not apply.[12]

1   SI 2005/230, applied to applicants on fast track appeals by the Asylum and Immigration Tribunal (Fast Track Procedure) Rules 2005, SI 2005/560, r 4(2)(b). A person in the fast track who is granted bail must be transferred out of the fast track under r 31. The rules came into force on 4 April 2005 and apply to any application pending on 3 April 2005 before an adjudicator or the Tribunal. See Emily Burnham *Challenging immigration detention: best practice guide* (ILPA/BID, 2003) for procedure in bail applications before the appellate authority.
2   SI 2005/230, r 38(1). The relevant form, B1, is attached in the Schedule to the Procedure Rules.
3   SI 2005/230, r 38(2)(a)–(i).

4   SI 2005/230, r 38(3). If bail is granted subject to a recognisance or surety, the recognisance or surety must also be in writing and must state the amount agreed and that the applicant or surety has read and understood the bail decision and agrees to pay that amount of money if the applicant fails to comply with the conditions set out in the bail decision: SI 2005/230, r 40(1). The recognisance must be signed by the applicant or surety and filed with the Tribunal: r 40(2).
5   SI 2005/230, r 39(1).
6   SI 2005/230, r 39(2).
7   Practice Direction 2005/1, 19.1.
8   SI 2005/230, r 39(3).
9   SI 2005/230, r 39(4).
10 SI 2005/230, r 39(5).
11 SI 2005/230, r 41.
12 SI 2005/230, r 42.

17.61   Until the Tribunal formulates its own guidelines, the Practice Direction advises that the Guidance Notes for Adjudicators from the Chief Adjudicator on applications for bail[1] should continue to be followed. The Guidance notes refer to a 'common law presumption in favour of bail'.[2] The burden of proof that detention is necessary therefore lies on the Secretary of State, to the standard of balance of probabilities.[3] The notes request immigration judges to have regard to the Immigration Service Instructions, the White Papers,[4] the UNHCR guidelines on detention[5] and other relevant policies.[6] The Guidance stresses that 'sureties are only required if [the Tribunal] cannot otherwise be satisfied that the applicant will comply with any conditions imposed and a sense of obligation would reinforce them'.[7] Where sureties are considered necessary then the assessment of the amount of recognisance to be taken from a surety should be based upon the means of that surety.[8] In *Lamin Minteh* the Court of Appeal held unlawful the declared practice of an adjudicator not to grant bail if there were no sureties regardless of whether there was evidence that the applicant was likely to abscond.[9] In *AKB* it was held that an adjudicator had to justify his decision to refuse bail; it was not good enough to say merely that there was a chance the applicant might abscond.[10] The Guidance Notes advise immigration judges to consider bail in three stages: whether bail should be granted in principle, subject to satisfactory conditions; whether sureties are necessary; and whether those offered are satisfactory.[11] The applicant should attend the hearing if there is a dispute over issues of fact.[12] The applicant should attend all hearings for renewal of bail, but sureties need not do so if they have been given permission not to attend and have written indicating their willingness to continue.[13] A failure to comply with a residence or reporting condition is not a reason for instituting forfeiture proceedings, but the Tribunal may take such a failure into account in renewing bail.[14] A failure to apply these guidelines, or action which is inconsistent with them, may be a ground for judicial review of a refusal of bail.

1   *Bail: Guidance notes for Adjudicators from the Chief Adjudicator* (3rd edn, 2003) (available at http://www.iaa.gov.uk/1497.htm)
2   Guidance notes above, para 1.4.
3   Guidance notes above, para 2.6.1.
4   See 17.27ff above.
5   See 17.36 above.
6   See 17.27–17.38 above.
7   Guidance notes above, para 2.2.2.
8   Guidance notes above, para 2.3.2.

⁹ *R v Secretary of State for the Home Department, ex p Minteh (Lamin)* (396/5400/D) (8 March 1996, unreported), CA.
¹⁰ *R v Secretary of State for the Home Department, ex p AKB* [1996] 3 (2) ILD, QBD.
¹¹ Guidance notes above, para 2.7.3.
¹² Guidance notes, para 2.1.2.
¹³ Guidance notes above, para 3.1.
¹⁴ Guidance notes above, para 3.2.

Procedures before the Special Immigration Appeals Commission

17.62 Procedures for bail hearings before the Special Immigration Appeals Commission are more formal than other bail hearings, and are contained in the Commission's Procedure Rules.[1] A bail application must be in writing and must contain particulars of the full name of the applicant, his or her date of birth, date of arrival in the UK, the address where he or she is detained, whether there are any proceedings pending before the Commission to which the applicant is a party, a bail address, the amount of any recognisance offered, the names, addresses and occupations of any potential sureties and the amounts they might offer, the grounds of the application and any change in circumstances since a previous unsuccessful application.[2] Where an application for bail is filed the Commission must as soon as reasonably practicable serve a copy on the Secretary of State and fix a hearing.[3] The Secretary of State must file a written statement of his reasons for contesting he application not later than 2.00 pm before the day of the hearing or, where he has received notice less than 24 hours before that time, as soon as reasonably practicable.[4] The Secretary of State can object to the written statement being disclosed to the applicant or his representatives and a closed hearing may be held [5] for the Commission to decide whether the objection to disclosure should be upheld.[6] The applicant's interests are represented by a Special Advocate during the closed session.[7] To date all those with appeals before the Special Immigration Appeals Commission have been detained except for the appellant Rehman,[8] who was on temporary admission for the entire period of the proceedings, and in only one case so far has bail been granted.[9] The Commission has made it plain that it will be the rare case where bail will be appropriate for those whom the Secretary of State believes to be a risk to national security. This has raised question marks about the effectiveness of bail as a review mechanism under Article 5(4) ECHR.

1 Special Immigration Appeals Commission (Procedure) Rules 2003, SI 2003/1034, Part 6, rr 28–31.
2 SI 2003/1034, r 29(1), (2)(a)–(h). The application must also state whether the applicant requires an interpreter at the hearing and if so, for what language and dialect, and must be signed by the applicant or his or her representative or (for those incapable of acting by childhood or other reason) someone acting on his or her behalf. These rules are virtually identical to the bail provisions before the Tribunal, at 17.61 above.
3 SI 2003/1034, r 30(1).
4 SI 2003/1034, r 30(2).
5 SI 2003/1034, r 37.
6 SI 2003/1034, r 38.
7 SI 2003/1034, r 38(2).
8 *Secretary of State for the Home Department v Rehman* [2002] Imm AR 98, HL.
9 In *G v Secretary of State for the Home Department* [2004] EWCA Civ 265, [2004] 1 WLR 1349, the Commission granted bail despite upholding the Secretary of State's certificate under Anti-terrorism, Crime and Security Act 2001, s 21 (suspected international terrorist),

on health grounds. The Court of Appeal held it had no statutory jurisdiction to hear the Secretary of State's appeal (this lacuna led to the enactment of Asylum and Immigration (Treatment of Claimants, etc) Act 2004, s 32, providing an appeal to the Court of Appeal against the grant or refusal of bail by SIAC) but reconstituted itself into a Divisional Court to hear a judicial review of the grant of bail. G was released on house arrest, under draconian conditions described by the House of Lords in *A and X v Secretary of State for the Home Department* [2004] UKHL 56, [2005] 2 WLR 87 at para 35. The ATCSA detention and bail provisions lapsed in April 2005.

17.63 The Immigration and Asylum Act 1999 enables the Secretary of State by regulation to make new provisions in relation to bail applications for those detained under the Immigration Act 1971 or section 62 of the Nationality, Immigration and Asylum Act 2002.[1] The regulations may confer a right to bail in prescribed circumstances,[2] may create or transfer jurisdiction for bail hearings,[3] provide where bail applications may be held,[4] the procedure to be followed[5] and the circumstances and conditions where an applicant may be released on bail.[6] They may amend or repeal any enactment relating to bail.[7] Any such regulations must provide that the authority which hears the bail application is the same one as hears the appeal.[8] The Lord Chancellor must approve the regulations.[9] None have been made to date since the coming into force of this provision in February 2003.

[1] Immigration and Asylum Act 1999, s 53(1) in force since 10 February 2003 (SI 2003/2), as amended by Nationality, Immigration and Asylum Act 2002, s 62(13).
[2] IAA 1999, s 53(2).
[3] IAA 1999, s 53(3)(a) as amended.
[4] IAA 1999, s 53(3)(b).
[5] IAA 1999, s 53(3)(c).
[6] IAA 1999, s 53(3)(d).
[7] IAA 1999, s 53(3)(e).
[8] Ie, a bail hearing must be heard by the Special Immigration Appeals Commission if the appeal is to that body: Immigration and Asylum Act 1999, s 53(4), amended by NIAA 2002, Sch 7, para 28.
[9] IAA 1999, s 53(6). In Scotland the consent of the Scottish Ministers must be obtained: s 53(7).

Bail pending judicial review or habeas corpus

17.64 The statutory scheme for release on bail is, as has been seen above, is now comprehensive, The remaining notable *lacuna*, is the inability to apply for bail for new arrivals until seven days have elapsed.[1] In this context the only available remedy is by way of judicial review of the refusal to release.[2] The Higher Courts will entertain bail applications pursuant to their inherent jurisdiction pending the hearing of an application for judicial review, notwithstanding the availability of bail from the appellate authority.[3] In *Ex p Turkoglu*[4] the Court of Appeal reviewed the position regarding bail in judicial review cases and held that the High Court has jurisdiction to grant bail on an application for permission to apply for judicial review or a substantive application as part of the power to grant ancillary orders. Where the High Court judge refuses bail in such a case, an appeal lies to the Court of Appeal.[5] But bail in this context is ancillary to some other substantive proceeding, and if the High Court refuses permission for judicial review it is *functus officio* and therefore has no jurisdiction to grant bail. The Court of Appeal has its own inherent jurisdiction on a renewed application for permission. Where there is a statutory right to apply for bail, it should generally be sought from the appellate authority, but in *Ex p Kelso*,[6] Collins J held that, where such an application could result in a further application for judicial review if returned to an adjudicator who refused bail or imposed unsatisfactory conditions, and were the matter can be dealt with expeditiously, it was appropriate for the High Court to entertain the application.[7]

1   Immigration Act 1971, Sch 2, para 22(1B).
2   *Vilvarajah v Secretary of State for the Home Department* [1990] Imm AR 457.
3   Supreme Court Act 1981 s 15(3) and see *R (on the application of Sezek) v Secretary of State* [2001] INLR 675 and *R (on the application of Doku) v Secretary of State for the Home Department* (C/2000/3360) (30 November 2000, unreported), CA.
4   *R v Secretary of State for the Home Department, ex p Turkoglu* [1988] QB 398, [1987] 2 All ER 823.
5   *Turkoglu above.*
6   *R v Secretary of State for the Home Department, ex p Kelso* [1998] INLR 603, QBD.
7   See also *R v Secretary of State for the Home Department, ex p Taher* (CO 3106/99) (24 September 1999, unreported), HC.

17.65 In *Kelso*[1] Collins J also retrieved the High Court's original jurisdiction to grant bail on the merits (as opposed to a jurisdiction to determine the reasonableness of detention on *Wednesbury* grounds), by adverting to the distinction drawn in *Vilvarajah*[2] between detention in respect of which statutory bail was not available and detention in respect of which it was. Only in the former case, where it was in effect the discretion to grant temporary admission that was in issue, was the jurisdiction limited to a *Wednesbury* review. In the latter case, the court's inherent jurisdiction allowed it to decide for itself on the material before it whether bail should be granted as an adjunct to the proceedings, and virtually all immigration detention now falls within that category.[3] *Kelso* was approved by the Court of Appeal in *Doku*,[4] a case involving detention pursuant to a recommendation for deportation. However, in *Sezek*[5] the Court of Appeal emphasised that significant weight had to be given to the fact that the Secretary of State had decided that the person should be detained and to the reasons why he had opposed release of that person. Reference was also made to the need for consideration to be given to the detention policy. The incorporation of Article 5 of the ECHR, as the court observed in *Sezek* at para 15, means that the distinction between the judicial review and the bail jurisdiction is less significant since the standards of the court scrutiny and the requirements that the Secretary of State demonstrate that the decision is justified and proportionate are the same. Judicial review is available to challenge a refusal of bail by an adjudicator.[6] In *ex p B*[7] the challenge was initially to both the refusal of bail and the Secretary of State's underlying decision to detain. Bail is not an alternative remedy where the decision of the Secretary of State to detain is unlawful, and the grant or refusal of bail is irrelevant to a judicial review of the legality of detention.[8] Even if the detainee is released on bail any previous period of detention, which is unlawful, can be the subject of judicial review proceedings seeking a declaration and damages under the common law and/or Article 5(5) of ECHR. In *ex p B* the claimant had been released by the Secretary of State following the grant of permission in the judicial review and in *Konan*[8] the claimant had been released on bail by an Adjudicator prior to the grant of permission in a judicial review challenging substantive decision in the case as well as a challenge to the lawfulness of the detention.

1   *R v Secretary of State for the Home Department, ex p Kelso* [1998] INLR 603, QBD.
2   *Vilvarajah v Secretary of State for the Home Department* [1990] Imm AR 457, CA.
3   *Kelso* above, at 606.
4   *R (on the application of Doku) v Secretary of State for the Home Department* (C/2000/3360) (30 November 2000, unreported), CA.
5   *R (on the application of Sezek) v Secretary of State* [2001] INLR 675.
6   *R v Secretary of State for the Home Department, ex p Brezinski and Glowacka* (19 July 1996, unreported) QBD.
7   *R v Special Adjudicator and Secretary of State for the Home Department, ex p B* [1998] INLR 315.
8   See also *R (on the application of Konan) v Secretary of State for the Home Department* [2004] EWHC 22 (Admin), [2004] All ER (D) 151 (Jan).

Chapter 18

IMMIGRATION APPEALS

BACKGROUND AND STRUCTURE OF THE APPEALS SYSTEM

Background

18.1 'The right of access to justice ... is a fundamental and constitutional principle of a legal system.'[1] Rights of appeal against immigration and asylum decisions have undergone great changes since the last edition of this work. The biggest change has been the abolition of the two-tier appellate system, which had been in existence since the Immigration Appeals Act 1969, and its replacement by the single-tier Asylum and Immigration Tribunal (AIT) by the Asylum and Immigration (Treatment of Claimants) Act 2004.[2] An attempt during the passage of that Act to remove rights of appeal to the higher courts by a draconian ouster clause was successfully fought off with the assistance of senior judges, who expressed outrage at the trespass on the courts' constitutional area of sovereignty.[3] What we are left with is a somewhat complicated and cumbersome system of one-tier appeals by one- to three-judge panels, review and onward appeal which will require very careful calibration to achieve the desired combination of efficiency and fairness.

---

[1]   R (on the application of Anufrijeva) v Secretary of State for the Home Department [2003] UKHL 36, [2004] 1 AC 604, per Lord Steyn at para 26.
[2]   Section 26(1), which repeals and replaces Nationality, Immigration and Asylum Act 2002, s 81.
[3]   For the constitutional position of the courts see eg Lord Bridge in X Ltd v Morgan-Grampian Ltd [1991] 1 AC 1 at 48E, cited in Michael Fordham 'The common-law illegality of ousting judicial review', January 2004.

1159

18.2 Immigration Appeals

18.2 The 1969 Immigration Appeals Act, passed in response to the Wilson Committee report,[1] had provided Commonwealth citizens (but not aliens) with appeals against exclusion, removal and other decisions affecting immigrants. The appellate system thus set up was not intended in any way to undermine an effective immigration control. It was calculated to ease the fears of racial discrimination that immigration restrictions, imposed on Commonwealth immigrants for the first time only seven years previously in 1962, had provoked by seeing that the controls were imposed fairly; to provide 'a sense of protection against oppression and injustice, and ... reassurance against fears of arbitrary action on the part of the Immigration Service',[2] and to ensure a more consistent and rational decision-making process. It was intended to be informal and largely inquisitorial; legal representation was not envisaged as necessary; it was for Commonwealth citizens only; and it did not provide appeals against deportation or other restrictive action 'on grounds which are primarily of a political nature'.[3] The Immigration Act 1971 adopted the scheme of the IAA 1969 and extended it to aliens, who had hitherto had no appeal rights. There were, however, important gaps in the scheme. Those who were refused leave to enter and had no entry clearance could exercise their rights of appeal only from abroad – a devastating disadvantage in asylum cases. There was no appeal against a proposed deportation where the decision had been made following a recommendation of a criminal court, nor against a decision to remove those deemed illegal entrants. Persons excluded, refused leave to enter or remain or subjected to deportation action on national security or political grounds had no right of appeal, only a right to an extra-statutory advisory procedure involving no disclosure of the grounds of proposed exclusion.[4]

[1] Committee on Immigration Appeals, set up in 1966, chaired by Sir Roy Wilson QC (Cmnd 3387, 1967).
[2] Cmnd 3387, para 85.
[3] Cmnd 3387, para 191.
[4] See the fourth edition of this book 15.52–15.57.

18.3 The Immigration Act 1971 provided suspensive appeal rights to everyone who was subject to deportation as an overstayer or for breaching conditions of stay, in acknowledgment of the fact that, unlike illegal entrants, they had been admitted to the UK lawfully and so had a right to be heard before removal. The undermining of that distinction began in 1988, with the introduction of restricted rights of appeal for those whose last entry to the UK was within seven years of the decision to deport.[1] Adjudicators were henceforth precluded from reviewing the merits of the deportation decision in such cases.[2]

[1] Immigration Act 1988, s 5; exceptions to the seven-year rule were laid by statutory instrument, but resulted in arbitrary distinctions between those who had a right of appeal and those who did not.
[2] For a salutary case of the exercise of such discretion, see *Idrish* [1985] Imm AR 155. The removal of a right of appeal immediately led to harsher decisions being taken: see observations of Lord Griffiths in *R v Secretary of State for the Home Department, ex p Oladehinde* [1991] 1 AC 254, [1990] 3 All ER 393, [1990] 3 WLR 797.

18.4 By 1993 the big issue in immigration law was asylum. The lack of suspensive appeal rights for refused asylum seekers who claimed on arrival had led to litigation at the European Court of Human Rights.[1] The Asylum and Immigration Appeals Act 1993 introduced rights of appeal before removal for nearly all asylum seekers, including those who were to be removed to an EU Member State through which they had travelled to get to the UK, but removed the appeal rights of rejected visitors, short-term students and all applicants who did not possess either the requisite documents or the necessary age or nationality qualifications.

[1] *Vilvarajah v United Kingdom* (1991) 14 EHRR 248. The judgment, which appeared after the 1993 Bill was published, in fact upheld the government's submission that judicial review of an adverse asylum decision was an effective remedy for the purposes of Art 13 to prevent a breach of Art 3 (exposure to torture or inhuman or degrading treatment by return to Sri Lanka), reversing the Commission on this point.

18.5 The accelerating integration of the UK into Europe marked in 1993 by the Treaty of European Union, and by proliferating inter-governmental measures on immigration and more particularly on asylum, had its impact on immigration appeals. The Immigration (EEA) Order 1994, SI 1994/1895 partially resolved the problem of EEA nationals and their families who, by virtue of the fact of not requiring leave to enter under the Immigration Act 1971, had found themselves deprived of appeal rights against exclusion, removal and deportation. The embarrassing number of successful appeals against the removal of asylum seekers to the 'safe' countries of the EU,[1] on the grounds that *refoulement* from these countries to the country of persecution could not be ruled out, led to the abolition of the in-country appeal for this group of asylum seekers in the Asylum and Immigration Act 1996.[2] That Act, the first product of a co-ordinated European approach to asylum,[3] also curtailed the appeal rights of others, whose appeals were 'certified' for a variety of reasons, including the country they fled from, the timing of their claim and its nature.[4] The latter group of claimants had a first instance appeal but none to the Immigration Appeal Tribunal. Neither the 1993 nor the 1996 Act brought appeal rights to persons who could not claim to be refugees but whose removal arguably breached fundamental human rights, an omission which led to the proliferation of challenges to removal by judicial review, with particular reference to Article 3 and Article 8 of the ECHR.[5]

[1] Under ad hoc arrangements preceding the Dublin Convention, which came into force in 1997: see 12.149ff.
[2] Sections 2–3.
[3] See eg the Resolution on manifestly unfounded applications for asylum, anticipating the coming into force of the Dublin Convention, produced by the EU Member States' Ad hoc Group on Immigration and agreed at the immigration ministers' meeting of 30 November 1992, whose principles were reflected in Asylum and Immigration Act 1996, s 1 (now Asylum and Immigration (Treatment of Claimants, etc) Act 2004, s 33 and Sch 3).
[4] Asylum and Immigration Act 1996, s 1, amending Asylum and Immigration Appeals Act 1993, Sch 2, para 5.
[5] See eg *R v Secretary of State for the Home Department, ex p Kebbeh* (30 April 1998, Hidden J) on removal of disabled applicant to destitution and despair in Gambia (Art 3); *Ahmed and Patel v Secretary of State for the Home Department* [1998] INLR 570; *R v Secretary of State for the Home Department, ex p Gangadeen* [1998] Imm AR 106; *R v Secretary of State for the Home Department, ex p Ali (Arman)* [1999] INLR 89 (Art 8).

18.6 In response to the European Court of Human Rights' condemnation in *Chahal*[1] of the lack of judicial scrutiny of national security-based deportation and detention, and similar criticisms by the European Court of Justice in *Shingara and Radiom*,[2] an appeal against exclusion, refusal of leave to enter or remain, or deportation on political or security grounds was introduced by the Special Immigration Appeals Commission Act 1997.[3] The intention was specifically to protect the UK against further findings of violations of ECHR Article 3 in such cases – although the machinery for a direct human rights appeal (as opposed to an asylum appeal) was not provided until the Human Rights Act 1998 and the human rights appeal of the Immigration and Asylum Act 1999 came simultaneously into force on 2 October 2000.

1   *Chahal v United Kingdom* (1996) 23 EHRR 413.
2   C-65/95, C-111/95, [1997] 3 CMLR 703.
3   See 18.160 below.

18.7 The Immigration and Asylum Act 1999 completed the process, begun in 1988, of removing the distinction between illegal entrants on the one hand, and overstayers and those in breach of conditions on the other, by taking the latter out of the deportation process altogether, in the process removing rights of appeal.[1] But the IAA 1999 introduced a free-standing appeal, suspensive of removal, which could be resorted to by anyone who asserted that the effect of any decision affecting his or her entitlement to enter or remain in the UK would be to breach the appellant's human rights or was racially discriminatory.[2] The appeal bridged the gap in international protection by ensuring that (subject to procedural requirements) human rights or discrimination arguments could be aired in all cases prior to removal. The only exception to the suspensive appeal was where an asylum claimant was to be removed to an EU Member State or another designated third country,[3] and the Secretary of State certified as manifestly unfounded a claim that such removal would breach the person's human rights.[4] To prevent what were seen as abusive and repetitious applications and multiple appeals, the IAA 1999 introduced the one-stop appeal system.[5] Its rationale was simple – that all issues relating to a person's right to stay in the UK, and that of his or her family, should wherever possible be dealt with in one appeal, but the procedures designed to effect it were needlessly obscure and complex.

1   Immigration and Asylum Act 1999, s 10.
2   IAA 1999, s 65 as amended by the Race Relations (Amendment) Act 2000.
3   Under IAA 1999, s 11 or 12; for designated countries see Asylum (Designated Safe Third countries) Order 2000, SI 2000/2245.
4   IAA 1999, ss 11(3), 12(5) and (6), 72(2)(a) as amended by the Race Relations (Amendment) Act 2000.
5   IAA 1999, ss 73–76; the Immigration and Asylum Appeals (One-stop Procedure) Regulations 2000, SI 2000/2244.

18.8 The appeal provisions of the Nationality, Immigration and Asylum Act 2002 attempted to simplify appeal rights, by replacing disparate rights of appeal against various immigration decisions with a generic right of appeal against an 'immigration decision',[1] and by defining and bringing together the grounds of appeal which may be deployed.[2] Certain little-used appeal rights, such as the right of appeal against destination and the right of appeal against the decision that a person requires leave to enter, were abolished (although the lawfulness of a destination, and a requirement for leave, may be the subject of argument in the new appeals).[3] The one-stop procedure was simplified.[4] More controversially, the NIAA 2002 removed suspensive rights of appeal from anyone, and not only those being removed to third countries, whose asylum or human rights claim was certified clearly unfounded,[5] and created a quasi-presumption in favour of certification in respect of listed countries,[6] which meant that for the first time since 1993, a person could be returned to the country where he or she asserted a fear of persecution before being able to appeal against the removal. Another controversial curtailment of rights of access to the courts was the replacement of judicial review[7] of an Immigration Appeal Tribunal's refusal of permission to appeal by statutory review, a purely paper review, and one subject to much stricter time limits than judicial review.[8] The jurisdiction of the Tribunal, historically embracing both fact and law, was reduced to points of law only.[9] The NIAA 2002 also contained provision for costs awards to be made, and for public funding to be withheld in unmeritorious cases in the Tribunal.[10]

[1] Nationality, Immigration and Asylum Act 2002, s 82(1), (2).
[2] NIAA 2002, s 84(1).
[3] On the ground that the decision is 'not in accordance with the law' under s 84(1)(e).
[4] NIAA 2002, ss 96, 120.
[5] NIAA 2002, s 94.
[6] When the appeals provisions came into force (1 April 2003) and for the transitional provisions (from November 2002), the listed countries were the ten EU accession states; these states were removed from the list on 1 May 2004 when they joined the EU. Other states were added by statutory instrument. See 18.82 below.
[7] Although it was accepted in *R (on the application of S) v Immigration Appeal Tribunal, R (on the application of H) v Immigration Appeal Tribunal* [2004] EWCA Civ 1731, [2005] 2 All ER 165 (upholding the Administrative Court's judgment at [2004] EWHC 588 (Admin)) that the 2002 did not oust judicial review, either expressly or by implication, the Court of Appeal held that statutory review provided an adequate and proportionate protection of the rights of asylum seekers, so that the court could decline to hear an application for judicial review of issues which had been or could have been the subject of a statutory review. The court observed that the fact that immigrants and asylum claimants have no vested right to remain in the UK provides objective justification for any discrimination involved in the restriction of review rights.
[8] NIAA 2002 (before amendment), s 101(2).
[9] NIAA 2002, s 101(1).
[10] NIAA 2002, s 101(3)(d) in relation to statutory review, and s 106(3) at Tribunal level (providing a rule-making power. See Immigration and Asylum (Procedure) Rules 2003, rr 24 (certificate of no merit), 25 (costs of statutory review application), see now SI 2005/230, r 33 (costs of reconsideration); 18.177 below.

18.9 Representation on immigration and asylum appeals was severely affected by restrictions in public funding which came into effect on 1 April 2004. While the Legal Services Commission seemingly succumbed to the 'culture of refusal' which practitioners had for years complained of in the appellate authority, forcing practitioners to spend more time on (frequently fruitless) appeals against negative funding decisions, new rules dramatically curtailed the amount of work on applications and appeals which the Commission would fund, required firms to provide minute justifications for funding, and made switching representatives virtually impossible.[1] The funding restrictions were modified after strong condemnation by the House of Commons Committee on Constitutional Affairs,[2] but even in their modified form, they have created an extremely hostile climate for practitioners, matching that facing their clients in and outside the appeals system.[3]

18.9 Immigration Appeals

1 Legal Services Commission: Immigration Specification, April 2004. The accreditation scheme introduced for solicitors has been welcomed, but the rewards for accreditation are insufficient to prevent a stream of practitioners leaving the field.
2 Immigration and Asylum: the Government's proposed changes to publicly funded immigration and asylum work, Fourth Report of Session 2002–03, HC 1171.
3 Many firms have been forced to close down, or have stopped taking publicly funded immigration cases in order to survive. See David Burgess's Response to the LSC proposals, delivered at the ILPA 2003 Annual AGM (November 2003) and subsequently published by ILPA.

18.10 The main change effected by the Asylum and Immigration (Treatment of Claimants, etc) Act 2004 is the merger of adjudicators and the Immigration Appeal Tribunal into a single-tier appellate authority. By amendment to the NIAA 2002,[1] the Act created the Asylum and Immigration Tribunal (AIT), which hears all immigration and asylum appeals (save those involving national security, which continue to be heard by the Special Immigration Appeals Commission). The Act envisages that appeals may be heard by a single member or by a group of members, or by specified members or groups of members, according to the discretion of the President.[2] The passage of the 2004 Act was marked by an unprecedented attempt by the Secretary of State and the Lord Chancellor's Department to oust the jurisdiction of the higher courts in immigration and asylum matters. The AIT's decision was not to be the subject of any appeal or review (save for allegations of bad faith), except on a reference from the AIT itself.[3] The ouster clause was condemned by the Select Committee on Constitutional Affairs[4] and did not survive the wrath of the House of Lords. The replacement review provisions are not too far removed from those of the NIAA 2002 before amendment (see below).

1 Nationality, Immigration and Asylum Act 2002, s 81, substituted by Asylum and Immigration (Treatment of Claimants, etc) Act 2004, s 26(1), in force 4 April 2005.
2 NIAA 2002, Sch 4, para 7, substituted by Asylum and Immigration (Treatment of Claimants, etc) Act 2004, Sch 1. See AIT Practice Direction 1/2005.
3 Asylum and Immigration (Treatment of Claimants, etc) Bill, cl 11.
4 Select Committee on Constitutional Affairs, Second Report (2003–04 session), March 2004. The report quotes evidence from (inter alia) Hugh Tomlinson QC, Nicholas Blake QC (on behalf of the Bar Council), Ouseley J and Collins J on the constitutional impropriety of the ouster clause.

Structure of the appeal system

18.11 In ordinary cases (those not involving national security), after the coming into force of the appeal provisions of the 2004 Act, all appeals go to the Asylum and Immigration Tribunal.[1] Thereafter, in all cases except those heard by three or more legally qualified members,[2] there is the possibility of a review for error of law by either party to the High Court (or the Outer House of the Court of Session in Scotland),[3] which may order the Tribunal to reconsider the decision, or refer it to the appropriate appeal court (the Court of Appeal in England, the Court of Session in Scotland and the Northern Ireland Court of Appeal in Northern Ireland),[4] for decision.[5] There is also an appeal on a point of law to the appropriate appeal court following the Tribunal's reconsideration of the appeal[6] or from a decision of the Tribunal sitting as a panel of three legally qualified members.[7]

1 Nationality, Immigration and Asylum Act 2002, s 81 (as substituted by Asylum and Immigration (Treatment of Claimants, etc) Act 2004, s 26. For transitional provisions see 18.78 below.
2 NIAA 2002, s 103A(8) inserted by Asylum and Immigration (Treatment of Claimants, etc) Act 2004, s 26.
3 NIAA 2002, s 103A as inserted.
4 NIAA 2002, ss 103C(4), 103B(5) as inserted.
5 NIAA 2002, s 103A(1), 103C(1) as inserted.
6 NIAA 2002, s 103B as inserted.
7 NIAA 2002, s 103E as inserted.

Asylum and Immigration Tribunal

18.12 Members of the Asylum and Immigration Tribunal are appointed by the Lord Chancellor.[1] They are required to be barristers, advocates or solicitors of seven years' standing, or to have appropriate legal or lay experience.[2] Members may work until the age of 70.[3] The President, appointed by the Lord Chancellor, must be someone who holds or has held high judicial office.[4] Deputy Presidents are also appointed by the Lord Chancellor.[5] The President may direct how many members exercise the jurisdiction of the Tribunal, although a three-member Tribunal is the default position under the Act.[6] The directions may relate to the whole or part of proceedings, may specify different proceedings, may enable jurisdiction to be exercised by a single member, and may require or permit the transfer of proceedings (in whole or part) from one member to another, or from a member to a group of members or vice versa.[7] The President is empowered to make arrangements for the allocation of cases, but another member of the Tribunal may perform the allocation if the President's directions permit this.[8]

1 Adjudicators were originally appointed by the Home Office, leading to concerns about their independence. The Lord Chancellor's Department took over the appointments in 1987 (Transfer of Functions (Immigration Appeals) Order 1987, SI 1987/465).
2 NIAA 2002, Sch 4 (substituted by Asylum and Immigration (Treatment of Claimants, etc) Act 2004, Sch 1) para 2. This provision does not quite end the involvement of lay persons in the appellate authority, although lay adjudicators were abolished by the IAA 1999 (in practice only legally qualified adjudicators had been appointed since 1987). It is unlikely that further lay members will be appointed.
3 Extendable to 75: see NIAA 2002, Sch 4 (as substituted) para 3(1)(b), (2).
4 Ie in the Court of Appeal or High Court (or Scottish or Northern Irish equivalents), see Administration of Justice Act 1876: NIAA 2002, Sch 4 (as substituted), para 5(1)(a).
5 NIAA 2002, Sch 4 (as substituted), para 5(1)(b).
6 NIAA 2002, Sch 4 (as substituted), para 7(1). Unless a specific direction is given, appeals and reconsideration hearings are to be heard by a legally qualified member or two members at least one of whom is legally qualified. Appeals which must be reheard because members disagree require at least three members; appeals to be determined without a hearing require a legally qualified member: Practice Direction 1/2005 para 2.2.
7 NIAA 2002, Sch 4 (as substituted), para 7(1).
8 NIAA 2002, Sch 4, para 8.

The Special Appeals Commission

18.13 The Lord Chancellor also appoints members of the Special Immigration Appeals Commission, established in 1997 to hear appeals involving national security.[1] It is 'duly constituted' by three members, of whom one holds or has held high judicial office,[2] and one is or has been a member of the Asylum and Immigration Tribunal.[3] The third member of the Commission needs no particular qualification by statute, but during the passage of the Bill the minister indicated that the third member would 'have some experience of national security matters and will be familiar with the evidence that is likely to be presented to the commission'.[4]

[1] Special Immigration Appeals Commission Act 1997, Sch 1, para 1.
[2] SIACA 1997, Sch 1, para 5(a). This means a High Court or Court of Appeal judge. The current incumbent is Ouseley J.
[3] SIACA 1997, Sch 1, para 5(b) as amended by Asylum and Immigration (Treatment of Claimants, etc) Act 2004, Sch 2, para 12(1).
[4] 301 HC Official Report (6th series) col 1033, 26 November 1997.

RIGHTS OF APPEAL

18.14 The circumstances in which an appeal may be brought are set out in sections 82 and 83 of the Nationality, Immigration and Asylum Act 2002,[1] regulations 29–31 of the Immigration (European Economic Area) Regulations 2000, as substituted by Immigration (European Economic Area) (Amendment) Regulations 2003[2] and in national security cases, the Special Immigration Appeals Commission Act 1997, sections 2 and 2B. The rules of procedure for the Tribunal are contained in the Asylum and Immigration Tribunal (Procedure) Rules 2005 and the Asylum and Immigration Tribunal (Fast Track Procedure) Rules 2005.[3] Rules regarding the service of notices are contained in the Immigration (Notices) Regulations 2003.[4] Appeals to the Special Immigration Appeals Commission have their own special procedure rules.[5] Subject to the exceptions and qualifications discussed below, appeals can be brought:

(1) against an 'immigration decision' as defined under section 82 of the Nationality Immigration and Asylum Act 2002;

(2) against the refusal of an asylum claim if leave to enter or remain for a period exceeding one year has been granted, or if periods of leave to enter or remain exceeding one year in aggregate have been granted;[6]

(3) against an 'EEA decision';[7]

(4) against a decision by the Secretary of State to make an order depriving a person of his or her citizenship.[8]

[1] As amended by Asylum and Immigration (Treatment of Claimants, etc) Act 2004, s 26(2), (3).
[2] SI 2000/2326, as substituted by SI 2003/549 and amended by SI 2005/671.
[3] SI 2005/230 and SI 2005/560 respectively.
[4] SI 2003/658.
[5] Special Immigration Appeals Commission (Procedure) Rules 2003, SI 2003/1034.
[6] Nationality, Immigration and Asylum Act 2002, s 83.
[7] Defined by reg 2(1) of the Immigration (European Economic Area) Regulations 2000, SI 2000/2326, as amended by SI 2003/549.
[8] British Nationality Act 1981, s 40A inserted by NIAA 2002, s 4.

Immigration decisions

18.15 The following are 'immigration decisions' against which a person may appeal under section 82 of the Nationality, Immigration and Asylum Act 2002:

(a)   refusal of leave to enter the United Kingdom;[1]

(b)   refusal of entry clearance;[2]

(c)   refusal of a certificate of entitlement to the right of abode under section 10 of the Nationality, Immigration and Asylum Act 2002;[3]

(d)   refusal to vary a person's leave to enter or remain in the United Kingdom if the result of the refusal is that the person has no leave to enter or remain;[4]

(e)   variation of a person's leave to enter or remain in the United Kingdom if when the variation takes effect the person has no leave to enter or remain;[5]

(f)   revocation under section 76 of the Nationality, Immigration and Asylum Act of indefinite leave to enter or remain;[6]

(g)   a decision that a person is to be removed from the United Kingdom by way of directions under section 10(1)(a), (b), (ba) or (c) of the Immigration and Asylum Act 1999 (ie as an overstayer, a person who has breached a condition of his or her leave to enter or remain; as a person who has obtained leave to remain by deception or as the family member of someone being removed on these grounds);[7]

(h)   a decision that an illegal entrant is to be removed from the United Kingdom;[8]

(i)   a decision that a person is to be removed from the United Kingdom by way of directions under paragraph 10A of Schedule 2 to the Immigration Act 1971 (ie as the family member of a person being removed as an illegal entrant or after refusal of leave to enter);[9]

(j)   a decision to make a deportation order under section 5(1) of the 1971 Immigration Act, either following a recommendation to deport by a Court under s 3(6) or on the ground that the person's deportation, or that of a family member, is deemed conducive to the public good under section 3(5);[10]

(k)   a refusal to revoke a deportation order;[11]

(l)   a decision to give directions for the removal of an overstaying member of the crew of an aircraft or ship under paragraph 12 of Schedule 2 to the Immigration Act 1971.[12]

Decisions which are not 'immigration decisions' for the purposes of section 82(1) and which do not therefore give rise to a right of appeal include:

- refusal of asylum;[13]
- refusal to grant a work permit;[14]
- the imposition of conditions of leave or refusal to revoke conditions;[15]
- the grant of a lesser period of leave than that sought;[16]
- refusal to grant leave to a person who had no leave at the date of the application.

The cancellation of leave when the holder is outside the common travel area, which did not previously attract a right of appeal, now does so because of the changed wording of the appeals provisions of s 82.[17]

---

1   Nationality, Immigration and Asylum Act 2002, s 82(2)(a).
2   NIAA 2002, s 82(2)(b).
3   NIAA 2002, s 82(2)(c).
4   NIAA 2002, s 82(2)(d).
5   NIAA 2002, s 82(2)(e).

6   Ie revocation of indefinite leave to enter or remain because the person (i) is liable to deportation but cannot be deported for legal reasons (eg because deportation would breach Art 3 ECHR), (ii) obtained the leave by deception and would be liable to removal as a result but cannot be removed for legal or practical reasons, (iii) obtained the leave as a refugee but ceases to be a refugee as a result of a voluntary acquisition of nationality, establishment or availment of protection of his or her own or another country, or (iv) is a dependant of a person to whom (iii) applies: see 12.84 above. NIAA 2002, s 82(2)(f).

7   NIAA 2002, s 82(2)(g).

8   NIAA 2002, s 82(2)(h).

9   NIAA 2002, s 82(2)(i).

10   NIAA 2002, s 82(2)(j). A decision to make a deportation order following a recommendation by a court has never previously been an appealable decision. The Immigration Rules (HC 395, para 378 as substituted from 2 October 2000 by HC 4851) have not been brought up to date to reflect the new appeal right against a decision to make a deportation order following the recommendation of a court. The distinction made by para 381 of the rules (as substituted) is no longer lawful following the change in the law.

11   NIAA 2002, s 82(2)(k).

12   NIAA 2002, s 82(2)(ia) as inserted by Asylum and Immigration (Treatment of Claimants etc) Act 2004, s 31, thereby restoring the old right of appeal which disappeared when the NIAA 2002 was originally enacted.

13   The refusal of asylum is not an 'immigration decision' for the purposes of s 82, although it may be appealable under s 83: see below.

14   Work permit decisions were until 2001 the province of the Department of Work and Pensions or its previous incarnations, and although they were brought under the umbrella of the Home Office in 2001 there is still no appeal right, although there is now a right to internal review: see 10.58.

15   Conditions imposed under s 3(1)(c) of the IA 1971 were appealable under that Act, but were excluded under the IAA 1999, and their continued exclusion is achieved by the definition of 'immigration decision' in NIAA 2002, s 82.

16   Curtailment of leave is however appealable as an immigration decision if it results in the person having no leave: s 82(2)(e).

17   Under Immigration (Leave to Enter and Remain) Order 2000, SI 2000/1161, Art 13(2): NIAA 2002, s 82(2)(d). The wording of the appeals provisions of the 1999 Act (Immigration and Asylum Act 1999, s 61), couched in terms of being 'required to leave the UK within 28 days', manifestly precluded appeals against variation or refusal to vary leave while the holder was abroad. This wording was not repeated in the 2002 Act.

Refusal of asylum

18.16 A refusal of a claim for asylum is an appealable decision per se only if the person refused asylum has been granted leave to enter or remain for a period exceeding one year or for periods exceeding one year in aggregate[1] (or if he or she has a right to reside in the UK under the EEA Regulations).[2] The refusal of an asylum claim does not otherwise attract a right of appeal. A person refused asylum without being granted leave to enter or remain for more than a year may only appeal if, as well as being refused asylum, he or she is the subject of an 'immigration decision' within the meaning of section 82(2) of the Nationality, Immigration and Asylum Act 2002. So, for example, if an overstayer or an illegal entrant made a claim for asylum and that claim was refused, the refusal of asylum would not be an appealable immigration decision. The person would only be able to appeal if an immigration decision was made to give directions for his or her removal from the United Kingdom. An appeal could then be brought against the immigration decision on the ground that removal would be contrary to the Refugee Convention. Circumstances in which a refusal of asylum will not attract a right of appeal include: where a person with extant leave to enter or remain makes an asylum claim and, when asylum is refused, the person still has leave but the leave was for one year or less;[3] where a person with extant leave to enter or remain is refused asylum but granted leave in some other capacity but the total period of leave is one year or less;[4] where an overstayer or illegal entrant makes a claim for asylum and, although asylum is refused, no decision to remove the person is made.[5] In such circumstances the asylum seeker's only remedy against the refusal of asylum would be judicial review (which, however, will not decide the merits of the claim; see 18.183 below).

[1]   Nationality, Immigration and Asylum Act 2002, s 83. It is not clear whether the requirement is met only by leave granted following the refusal of asylum or includes any leave that the person may have had before the refusal of asylum.

[2]   Immigration (European Economic Area) Regulations 2000, SI 2000/2326 as amended by SI 2003/549, SI 2003/3188 and SI 2004/1236, reg 33(1B). The right of appeal does not apply if the Secretary of State certifies that the claim is clearly unfounded: reg 33(1C), and it will be certified unless the Secretary of State is satisfied that it is not: reg 33(1D). For asylum claims from EEA nationals see 12.107 above.

[3]   This situation might have attracted an appeal under Immigration and Asylum Act 1999, s 69(3), but not under the NIAA 2002, s 82(2)(d) because the applicant still has leave to enter or remain (see 18.15 below), or under s 83, because the leave was for a year or less.

[4]   This situation attracted an appeal under Immigration and Asylum Act 1999, s 69(3) but not under the NIAA 2002, s 82(2)(e) because the applicant has leave when the variation takes effect, nor under s 83, because the leave is for a year or less.

[5]   There is no right of appeal in the absence of an 'immigration decision' under s 82(2)(g)–(i).

EEA decisions

18.17   Since EEA nationals and their family members[1] do not require leave to enter, and must be admitted unless there are good reasons based on public policy, public security or public health for their exclusion, the appeals regime which applies to them is a modified one. An EEA national or a family member of an EEA national (or a person claiming to be an EEA national or a family member) may appeal to the Asylum and Immigration Tribunal or, in appropriate cases, to the Special Immigration Appeals Commission against an 'EEA decision'.[2] An EEA decision is a decision made under the Immigration (European Economic Area) Regulations 2000 ('the Regulations') or under EC Regulation 1251/70 concerning a person's removal from the United Kingdom, his or her entitlement to be admitted to the United Kingdom or his or her entitlement to be issued with, have renewed or not to have revoked a residence permit or residence document.[3] However, a person claiming to be an EEA national may not appeal under the Regulations unless he or she produces a valid national identity card or passport issued by an EEA State,[4] and someone claiming to be a family member of an EEA national may not appeal under the Regulations unless he or she can produce an EEA family permit or other proof of the relationship.[5] A national of a country with an EC Association Agreement which confers rights of entry or residence is equated with an EEA national for the purpose of appealing on Community law grounds against an immigration decision.[6]

[1]   As defined in reg 6 of the EEA Regulations SI 2000/2326 as amended by SI 2001/865, SI 2003/549 and SI 2003/3188.

² SI 2000/2326 as amended, reg 29. Any appeal made on or after 1 April 2003 is treated as an appeal under Nationality, Immigration and Asylum Act 2002, s 82 and an 'EEA decision' is treated as an immigration decision for the purposes of the one-stop provisions of s 96 of that Act: reg 33(3).
³ SI 2000/2326 as amended, reg 2.
⁴ SI 2000/2326, as amended, reg 29(2).
⁵ SI 2000/2326, as amended, reg 29(3).
⁶ SI 2000/2326 as amended, reg 33(2). The precise scope of this provision is unclear; it would appear to apply to nationals of Bulgaria and Romania, who benefit from specific rights of establishment, but the position of Turkish nationals relying on rights under the Ankara Agreement is less straightforward. See 7.150ff above.

Deprivation of citizenship

18.18 The Secretary of State may by order deprive a person of his or her citizenship for actions seriously prejudicial to the vital interests of the United Kingdom or a British overseas territory[1] or for obtaining citizenship by registration or naturalisation by fraud, false representation or concealment of a material fact.[2] The Secretary of State must give the person notice of the decision to make the order[3] and the person given that notice may appeal against the decision before the order is made.[4] Under the old provisions for deprivation of citizenship in the 1981 Act,[5] there was no right of appeal against a decision to deprive a person of his or her British citizenship, although there was a right to appear before a specially appointed committee of inquiry. The 1981 Act provisions were never in fact invoked, and have been abolished and replaced by an appeal to the Asylum and Immigration Tribunal[6] or, if the decision was taken wholly or partly in reliance on information which the Secretary of State believes should not be made public for national security, political or other public interest reasons, to the Special Immigration Appeals Commission.[7]

¹ British Nationality Act 1981, s 40(2) as substituted by Nationality, Immigration and Asylum Act 2002, s 4.
² BNA 1981, s 40(3) and (6) as substituted.
³ BNA 1981, s 40(5) as substituted.
⁴ BNA 1981, s 40A, inserted by NIAA 2002, s 4.
⁵ BNA 1981, s 40(6)–(9) (before amendment).
⁶ Under BNA 1981, s 40A(1) as inserted and amended by Asylum and Immigration (Treatment of Claimants, etc) Act 2004, Sch 2, para 4.
⁷ BNA 1981, s 40A(2) as inserted; Special Immigration Appeals Commission Act 1997, s 2B (inserted by NIAA 2002, s 4(2)).

Human rights and race discrimination

18.19 With the repeal of section 65 of the Immigration and Asylum Act 1999 [1] there is no longer a freestanding right of appeal against the rejection of an allegation that a decision breaches a person's human rights or would be racially discriminatory.[2] Only decisions of the kind set out above attract a right of appeal. Human rights grounds can be relied on in appeals against immigration decisions,[3] including EEA decisions.[4]

¹ By Nationality, Immigration and Asylum Act 2002, s 114(1).

2 Thus (reversing *R (on the application of Kariharan) v Secretary of State for the Home Department, R (on the application of Kumarakuruparan) v Secretary of State for the Home Department* [2002] EWCA Civ 1102, [2003] Imm AR 163) decisions such as the rejection of representations making a human rights claim to enter or remain in the UK, or the setting of removal directions (as opposed to the decision to make removal directions) are no longer appealable as they were under Immigration and Asylum Act 1999, s 65. This is subject to the issue of 'fresh claims' generating new immigration decisions: see 12.170 above.

3 Under Nationality, Immigration and Asylum Act 2002, s 84(1)(c) and (g).

4 Immigration (European Economic Area) Regulations 2000, SI 2000/2326 as amended, reg 29(7) and Sch 2.

Venue

18.20 Appeals against 'immigration decisions', 'EEA decisions', refusals of asylum and deprivation of citizenship are normally made to the Asylum and Immigration Tribunal.[1] However, a small number of people are excluded from the normal system of appeals because of the political or national security grounds of the decision, and must instead appeal to the Special Immigration Appeals Commission The excluded decisions are:[2]

(1) a personal decision of the the Secretary of State taken wholly or partly on the ground that the person's removal or exclusion from the United Kingdom is in the interests of national security or in the interests of the relationship between the United Kingdom and another country;[3]

(2) a decision taken in accordance with a personal direction from the Secretary of State, identifying the person to whom the decision relates and wholly or partly on national security or diplomatic grounds;[4]

(3) a decision taken wholly or partly in reliance on information which the Secretary of State personally certifies should not be made public for national security, diplomatic or other public interest reasons;[5]

(4) a decision to deprive a person of his or her citizenship taken wholly or partly in reliance on information which the Secretary of State certifies should not be made public for national security, diplomatic or other public interest reasons.[6]

1 Nationality, Immigration and Asylum Act 2002, ss 82(1) (against immigration decisions) and 83(1) (against refusal of asylum); Immigration (European Economic Area) Regulations SI 2000/2326 as amended by SI 2003/549, SI 2005/671, reg 29(6) (against EEA decisions) and British Nationality Act 1981, s 40A(1) (inserted by s 4 NIAA 2002) (against deprivation of citizenship).

2 Special Immigration Appeals Commission Act 1997, ss 2(1)(a) (in respect of immigration decisions and refusals of asylum), s 2B (inserted by NIAA 2002, s 4(2) (in respect of deprivation of citizenship); Immigration (European Economic Area) Regulations 2000, SI 2000/2326 as amended by SI 2003/549, reg 31(1) (in respect of EEA decisions).

3 NIAA 2002, s 97(1)(a), (2) and (4) in the case of immigration decisions and refusals of asylum; in the case of EEA decisions, the Immigration (European Economic Area) Regulations 2000, SI 2000/2326 (as amended), reg 31(2)(a), (3) and (5).

4 NIAA 2002, s 97(1)(b), (2) and (4) in the case of immigration decisions and refusals of asylum; in the case of EEA decisions, the Immigration (European Economic Area) Regulations 2000, SI 2000/2326 (as amended, reg 31(2)(b), (3) and (5).

5 NIAA 2002, s 97(3) and (4) in the case of immigration decisions and refusals of asylum; in the case of EEA decisions, the Immigration (European Economic Area) Regulations 2000, SI 2000/2326 (as amended) reg 31(4) and (5).

6 British Nationality Act 1981, s 40A(2) as inserted by NIAA 2002, s 4.

Exclusion of the right of appeal

18.21 The right of appeal is excluded in the following cases:

(1) against a refusal of leave to enter, refusal of entry clearance, refusal to vary a leave to enter or remain, or a variation of leave to enter or remain taken on the ground that the person

    (i) does not satisfy a requirement as to age, nationality or citizenship specified in the immigration rules.[1] This would mean, for example, that a person refused leave to enter as an au pair would not be able to appeal against the refusal if he or she was younger than 17 or older than 27 or was not a national of one of the countries specified in the applicable rule;[2]

    (ii) does not have an immigration document, ie an entry clearance, a passport, a work permit or other immigration employment document;[3]

    (iii) is seeking to be in the United Kingdom for a period greater than that permitted by the immigration rules,[4] for example, an au pair seeking to remain in the UK for more than two years[5] or a visitor seeking to enter the UK for more than six months;[6]

    (iv) is seeking to enter or remain in the United Kingdom for a purpose other than one permitted by the immigration rules;[7] or

    (v) is a dependant of a person in (i)–(v);[8]

except that such a person may bring an appeal on human rights grounds, race discrimination grounds or asylum grounds.[9] The exclusion of the right of appeal in the above cases is characterised as 'ineligibility' in the Nationality, Immigration and Asylum Act 2002;[10]

(2) against refusal of entry clearance, if the decision to refuse is taken on grounds which relate to a provision of the immigration rules specified for that purpose in a statutory instrument. No provisions have yet been specified by statutory instrument. There is an appeal on race discrimination or human rights grounds;[11]

(3) against refusal of leave to enter as a visitor,[12] a short-term[13] or prospective student,[14] or a dependant of such,[15] unless the person holds an entry clearance at the time of the refusal.[16] There is an appeal on asylum, human rights or race discrimination grounds;[17]

(4) against refusal of entry clearance as a short-term or prospective student or their dependant,[18] or as a visitor (except to visit family members),[19] save on race discrimination or human rights grounds;[20]

(5) against a second immigration decision where there has been an earlier right of appeal, if the Secretary of State issues a certificate under section 96 of the Nationality, Immigration and Asylum Act 2002 (as to which, see below);

(6) against a refusal of leave to enter the United Kingdom or a refusal of entry clearance taken by the Secretary of State personally on public good grounds.[21] There is an appeal on human rights, race discrimination and (in the case of a refusal of leave to enter) asylum grounds;[22]

(7) against an EEA decision, where the appellant cannot produce proof of EEA nationality or membership of an EEA national's family.[23]

[1] Nationality, Immigration and Asylum Act 2002, s 88(1) and (2)(a).
[2] See HC 395, para 89(ii) (age), (v) (nationality).

³ NIAA 2002, s 88(1), (2)(b) and (3). Clearly, this means the 'required' immigration document; entry clearance for visa nationals, work permits for those coming to work etc. The Immigration Act 1971, Sch 2, para 4, and the Immigration Rules, HC 395, para 11, require persons arriving in the UK to produce a valid national passport or other document satisfactorily establishing their identity and nationality. Note that s 88 applies not only to refusal of leave to enter but also to refusal of variation. Thus, a visitor seeking to remain for a purpose for which entry clearance is required would not get a right of appeal against refusal, for want of the relevant entry clearance: *R v Secretary of State for the Home Department, ex p Ahmed* [1995] Imm AR 590; on appeal [1996] Imm AR 260, CA.
⁴ NIAA 2002, s 88(1) and (2)(c).
⁵ See HC 395, para 92(iv).
⁶ See HC 395, para 41(i).
⁷ NIAA 2002, s 88(1) and (2)(d). This is new; previously someone seeking to enter or remain for a purpose outside the Rules could appeal on the merits, since where there was no rule, there was no request to the Secretary of State to depart from the rules: see *Rahman (Jinnah)* [1989] Imm AR 325 (a refugee recognised elsewhere seeking to transfer his status to the UK), see 5th edn, 18.75. There is however an appeal on human rights grounds; see text and fn 9.
⁸ NIAA 2002, s 88(1) and (2).
⁹ NIAA 2002, s 88(4).
¹⁰ See headnote to NIAA 2002, s 88.
¹¹ NIAA 2002, s 88A, inserted by Asylum and Immigration (Treatment of Claimants, etc) Act 2004, s 29, in force 1 October 2004: SI 2004/2523.
¹² NIAA 2002, s 89(1)(a).
¹³ NIAA 2002, s 89(1)(b).
¹⁴ NIAA 2002, s 89(1)(c).
¹⁵ NIAA 2002, s 89(1)(d).
¹⁶ NIAA 2002, s 89(2). This applies whether or not the person requires entry clearance under the rules (for which see chapter 3 above).
¹⁷ NIAA 2002, s 89(3).
¹⁸ NIAA 2002, s 91.
¹⁹ NIAA 2002, s 90(1), (2). For this purpose, family members are defined by the Immigration Appeals (Family Visitor) Regulations 2003, SI 2003/518, reg 2 as the applicant's spouse, parent, child, sibling, grandparent, grandchild, uncle, aunt, nephew, niece, first cousin; the applicant's spouse's parent, sibling or child; the applicant's stepfather, stepmother, stepson, stepdaughter, stepbrother or stepsister or a person with whom the applicant has lived as a member of an unmarried couple for at least two of the three years before the date of the application.
²⁰ NIAA 2002, s 90. There is no appeal on asylum grounds in entry clearance cases.
²¹ NIAA 2002, s 98(1)–(3).
²² NIAA 2002, s 98(4), (5).
²³ EEA nationals must produce a valid national ID card or passport issued by an EEA Member State, and family members must produce an EEA family permit or other proof of the relationship: Immigration (European Economic Area) Regulations 2000, SI 2000/2326, as amended by SI 2003/549, reg 29(2), (3).

Other restrictions on scope or subject-matter of appeals

18.22 The restrictions imposed by the 1999¹ and 2002 Acts² on an asylum or human rights claimant's right of appeal against a decision to remove him or her to a third country have been extended by the 2004 Act which replaces the earlier provisions. Under Schedule 3 to the Asylum and Immigration (Treatment of Claimants, etc) Act 2004, presumptions of safety apply to varying degrees depending on the destination country. If it is an EU Member State, Norway, or another specified state,³ the statutory presumption is that that state is deemed safe (ie a place where the claimant's life or liberty is not under threat by reason of race, religion, nationality, membership of a particular social group or political opinion, and which will not send the claimant elsewhere in contravention of the ECHR or otherwise than in accordance with the Refugee Convention).[4] Other specified states are deemed safe in respect of the Refugee Convention, but there is no statutory presumption that they will not remove the claimant in contravention of the Human Rights Convention.[5] Yet other specified states are deemed safe vis-à-vis Refugee Convention obligations for the particular individual.[6] In each case, the statutory presumption of safety, however cast, precludes an appeal on grounds which are inconsistent with it. This restriction is discussed at 12.140ff above.

[1]   Immigration and Asylum Act 1999, ss 11 and 12.
[2]   Nationality, Immigration and Asylum Act 2002, s 80 (repealing and replacing Immigration and Asylum Act 1999, s 11).
[3]   Asylum and Immigration (Treatment of Claimants, etc) Act 2004, Sch 3, Part 2 (paras 2–6), entitled 'First list of safe countries (Refugee Convention and Human Rights)' deal with EU Member States and Norway; Part 3 (paras 7–11), entitled 'Second list of safe countries (Refugee Convention and Human Rights)' with states to be specified (none are so specified at time of writing).
[4]   AI(TC)A 2004, Sch 3, para 3(2)(a)–(c).
[5]   AI(TC)A 2004, Sch 3, paras 14–16, entitled 'Third list of safe countries: Refugee Convention only', para 13(2)(a)–(b). No states have yet been specified under this Part.
[6]   AI(TC)A 2004, Sch 3, Part 5, paras 17–19, entitled 'Countries certified as safe for individuals'. This Part does not contain a statutory presumption of safety, but precludes appeal on a ground which is inconsistent with the Secretary of State's opinion.

Presence of appellants in the UK

18.23 Appellants may not appeal to the tribunal or to the Special Immigration Appeals Commission[1] whilst in the United Kingdom and may only bring their appeals from outside the United Kingdom in the following circumstances:

(1)   where the appeal is against refusal of entry clearance;[2]
(2)   where the appeal is against refusal of leave to enter, unless the person is in the UK with entry clearance,[3] or is a British national[4] who holds a work permit and is in the UK,[5] or has made an asylum or human rights claim in the UK (which has not been certified as clearly unfounded)[6] or a claim that the refusal is in breach of Community law rights.[7] But possession of entry clearance (or non-lapsing leave) does not give in-country appeal rights if the ground for refusal or cancellation of leave is that the passenger's purpose in coming to the UK is not that specified in the entry clearance or leave;[8]
(3)   where the appeal is against a decision to remove the person as an overstayer, for breach of conditions, for deception in obtaining or seeking to obtain leave to remain, or as a family member of such a person,[9] unless he or she has made an asylum or human rights claim (which has not been certified 'clearly unfounded')[10] or a claim that removal breaches Community law rights;[11]
(4)   where the appeal is against a decision to remove a person as an illegal entrant,[12] subject to the same exceptions;[13]
(5)   where the appeal is against a decision to remove a person as the family member of a person who has been refused leave to enter or an illegal entrant,[14] subject to the same exceptions;[15]

(6) where the appeal is against a refusal to revoke a deportation order,[16] subject to the same exceptions;[17]

(7) where an asylum or human rights claim has been certified clearly unfounded,[18] unless the immigration decision is to revoke indefinite leave under section 76 of the NIAA 2002 or to make a deportation order under section 5(1) of the IA 1971;[19]

(8) where the decision is an EEA decision to refuse admission, to remove consequent to refusal of admission, refusal to revoke a deportation order, or refusal to issue an EEA family permit,[20] unless (a) the person held an EEA residence permit or document or an EEA family permit on arrival in the UK, or (b) the ground of appeal is that the decision breaches the appellant's rights under the ECHR or the Refugee Convention or (c) the appeal is to the Special Immigration Appeals Commission (ie the decision is on national security or public interest grounds).[21]

(9) where the Secretary of State certified before 1 October 2004 that an asylum seeker was being removed to a safe third country under section 11(2) or 12(2) Immigration and Asylum Act 1999,[22] (ie to countries which are members of the European Community or otherwise designated as a safe countries), unless the person makes a human rights claim which is not certified clearly unfounded;[23]

(10) where the Secretary of State certifies after 1 October 2004 that an asylum or human rights claimant is to be removed to a safe third country under Schedule 3 to the 2004 Act, and certifies the human rights claim clearly unfounded.[24]

1   Special Immigration Appeals Commission Act 1997, s 2(5).
2   Nationality, Immigration and Asylum Act 2002, s 92. Refusal of entry clearance is an immigration decision under s 82(2)(b). Under previous legislation there was nothing in principle to stop an appellant from obtaining entry clearance to come to the UK in order to participate in his or her appeal. Section 92 provides that appellants must be outside the UK to appeal unless their appeal is of a particular kind. In relation to refusal of entry clearance, only EEA nationals or members of their family, who claim that the refusal breaches their rights under Community law, may be in the UK for the appeal: s 92(4).
3   NIAA 2002, s 92(3)(b) (substituted by Asylum and Immigration (Treatment of Claimants, etc) Act 2004, s 28). Refusal of leave to enter is an immigration decision under NIAA 2002, s 82(2)(a). 'Entry clearance' includes leave to enter or remain which does not lapse when the holder leaves the UK under Immigration (Leave to Enter and Remain) Order 2000, SI 2000/1161, Art 13 (see 3.22 above) and is cancelled on return to the UK: Immigration Act 1971, Sch 2, para 2A(9). But see text and fn 8 below.
4   Ie a British Overseas Territories citizen, a British Overseas citizen, a British National (Overseas), a British Protected person or a British subject: NIAA 2002, s 92(3D)(c), inserted by Asylum and Immigration (Treatment of Claimants, etc) Act 2004, s 28.
5   NIAA 2002, s 92(3D), as inserted. Before the 2004 Act amendment, possession of a work permit was by itself sufficient to confer an in-country right of appeal against refusal of leave to enter.
6   NIAA 2002, ss 92(2), (4)(a), 94(2).
7   NIAA 2002, s 92(2), (4)(b).
8   NIAA 2002, s 92(3B) and (3C), inserted by Asylum and Immigration (Treatment of Claimants, etc) Act 2004, s 28 (in force 1 October 2004: SI 2004/2523). AI(TC)A 2004, s 18 inserted new paras 2A(8) and 2A(2A) into Sch 2 to the IA 1971, allowing entry clearance or non-lapsing leave to be cancelled at the port if the passenger seeks entry for a purpose other than that specified in the entry clearance or leave.
9   By virtue of Immigration and Asylum Act 1999, s 10: removal is an immigration decision under NIAA 2002, s 82(2)(g) which is not in the list of decisions appealable within the UK in s 92(2).
10 NIAA 2002, ss 92(4)(a), 94(2) (as amended by Asylum and Immigration (Treatment of Claimants, etc) Act 2004, s 27(3), in force 1 October 2004).

11 NIAA 2002, s 92(4)(b).
12 Ie under Immigration Act 1971, Sch 2, para 9. Such a decision is an immigration decision under NIAA 2002, s 82(2)(h).
13 Ie an asylum or human rights claim not certified clearly unfounded, or a claim that the decision breaches Community law rights: see fnn 10 and 11 above.
14 Ie under Immigration Act 1971, Sch 2, para 10A, inserted by NIAA 2002, s 73(1), which is an immigration decision under NIAA 2002, s 82(2)(i).
15 See fn 13 above.
16 Ie an immigration decision under NIAA 2002, s 82(2)(k).
17 See fn 13 above.
18 NIAA 2002, s 94 (as amended by Asylum and Immigration (Treatment of Claimants, etc) Act 2004, s 27 from 1 October 2004). This applies to variation appeals (ie immigration decisions under NIAA 2002, s 82(d) and (e), as well as to refusal of certificate of entitlement (s 82(2)(c)), meaning that someone in the UK as a visitor or student, who seeks to remain on asylum or human rights grounds, may be forced to leave the UK before appealing against a negative decision, if the claim is certified clearly unfounded.
19 These decisions, which are immigration decisions under NIAA 2002, s 82(2)(f) (revocation of ILR), (j) (decision to deport), attract an in-country appeal under s 92(2), which is not subject to s 94(1A) (inserted by s 27 Asylum and Immigration (Treatment of Claimants, etc) Act 2004, in force 1 October 2004: SI 2004/2523).
20 Immigration (European Economic Area) Regulations 2000, SI 2000/2326, as amended by SI 2003/549, reg 30(1), (2).
21 SI 2000/2326 as amended, reg 30(3). These restrictions on in-country appeal rights may be incompatible with Community law. The ECJ held in *R (on the application of Yiadom) v Secretary of State for the Home Department* Case C-357/98 [2001] All ER (EC) 267 that where a Community national has been physically present in the UK on temporary admission for a period of several months pending refusal of leave to enter, the refusal constitutes a decision concerning expulsion rather than entry, and so must attract a right of appeal or review before implementation by removal. See also *R v Secretary of State for the Home Department, ex p Darwiche* (CO 413/98).
22 NIAA 2002, s 93, repealed by the Asylum and Immigration (Treatment of Claimants, etc) Act 2004, ss 33(3)(b), 47, Sch 4 from 1 October 2004. For the transitional provisions see SI 2004/2523, Art 3. By the Asylum (Designated Safe Third Countries) Order 2000 SI 2000/2245, Canada, Norway, Switzerland and the United States of America are designated safe third countries. Immigration and Asylum Act 1999, ss 11 and 12 were substituted by NIAA 2002, s 80, also repealed by AI(TC)A 2004, s 33(2).
23 NIAA 2002, s 93(2), repealed as above.
24 Asylum and Immigration (Treatment of Claimants, etc) Act 2004, Sch 3, paras 5, 10, 15, 19.

Suspensory effect of an appeal

18.24 If some appeal rights may be exercised only from outside the UK, others are exercisable only from within the UK.[1] Once an appeal against an 'immigration decision' under section 82(1) of the Nationality, Immigration and Asylum Act 2002 is pending, then the appellant cannot be removed from or required to leave the United Kingdom.[2] However, removal directions can be given, or a deportation order made, while the appeal is pending.[3] An appeal is 'pending' once it is 'instituted',[4] ie by giving notice of appeal in accordance with the Asylum and Immigration Tribunal (Procedure) Rules 2005.[5] An appeal remains 'pending' until it is finally determined, withdrawn or abandoned or until it lapses.[6] An appeal is not finally determined while an application for an order requiring the tribunal to reconsider its decision could be made or is awaiting determination; reconsideration of an appeal has been ordered; an appeal has been remitted to the tribunal and is awaiting determination; an application for permission to appeal to the Court of Appeal (or Court of Session in Scotland) could be or has been made; an appeal to the Court of Appeal or Court of Session is awaiting determination, or a reference by the tribunal to the Court of Appeal or Court of Session is awaiting determination.[7] However, an appeal is not pending where an application for reconsideration or for permission to appeal has been or could be made outside the time limits provided under the Procedure Rules.[8]

1. Nationality, Immigration and Asylum Act 2002, s 104(4)(b), which provides that an appeal under s 82(1) shall be treated as abandoned if the appellant leaves the country. The Court of Appeal doubted, obiter, that this provision should be applied literally, without consideration of the length and purpose of the absence from the country, in *Shirazi v Secretary of State for the Home Department* [2003] EWCA Civ 1562, [2004] 2 All ER 602, [2004] INLR 92.

2. NIAA 2002, s 78(1)(a), (b). This provision also applies to appeals under 'the old appeals provisions' (eg appeals under the 1971 Act against deportation as an overstayer under the transitional provisions): see the Nationality, Immigration and Asylum Act 2002 (Commencement No 4) Order 2003 SI 2003/754, Sch 2, para 1(3).

3. NIAA 2002, s 78(3).

4. NIAA 2002, s 104(1)(a).

5. *R (on the application of Erdogan) v Secretary of State for the Home Department* [2004] EWCA Civ 1087, [2004] All ER (D) 421 (Jul); Asylum and Immigration Tribunal (Procedure) Rules 2005, SI 2005/ 230, r 6(1).

6. NIAA 2002, s 104(1)(b). An appeal 'lapses' by virtue of s 99 of the NIAA 2002 when a certificate is issued under s 97 or 98 (national security or other public good grounds). The section also provides for appeals to lapse following certification under s 96 (earlier appeal raising similar grounds), but following its amendment by Asylum and Immigration (Treatment of Claimants, etc) Act 2004, as from 1 October 2004 (SI 2004/2523), s 96 cannot be applied to appeals in progress: s 96(7).

7. NIAA 2002, s 104(2) (substituted by Asylum and Immigration (Treatment of Claimants, etc) Act 2004, Sch 2, para 20 from 4 April 2005).

8. NIAA 2002, s 104(2)(a), (d) as subsituted; see *R (on the application of Erdogan) v Secretary of State for the Home Department* [2004] EWCA Civ 1087, [2004] All ER (D) 421 (Jul), decided under the unamended provisions of s 104, where the Court of Appeal reversed the Administrative Court's decision that an asylum claimant had an appeal 'pending' (and so did not lose asylum support) when what he had pending was an application for permission to appeal out of time. However, the court (and the Secretary of State) agreed that once permission has been given to appeal out of time, the appeal has been (re)-instituted and is again pending: para 13. For out of time appeals see further 18.94 below.

18.25 In cases where there is a dispute as to whether the right of appeal is in-country or out-of-country (eg a dispute as to whether the appellant had a current entry clearance when refused leave to enter, or sought leave to enter for a different purpose), can the appellant seek to have the issue determined by the appellate authority, or does he or she have to bring judicial review proceedings to determine whether the appeal is in-country? Under earlier rules, where a notice of appeal is lodged from within the UK, removal could only be effected once the dispute is finally determined against the appellant by the appellate authority.[1] The 2005 Procedure Rules make provision for the Tribunal to determine the timeliness of an appeal as a preliminary issue,[2] but not for any wider issues of validity to be determined as such. To the contrary, they provide that where a person has given notice of appeal but there is no relevant decision (defined as a decision against which there is an exercisable right of appeal to the Tribunal), the Tribunal must not accept the notice of appeal, but must notify the person who gave the notice, and the respondent, and take no further action.[3] This provides no mechanism for resolving the dispute as to whether an in-country appeal exists (an 'exercisable' right of appeal) within the Tribunal itself, leaving the only remedy judicial review.

1 See *Lokko* [1990] Imm AR 111, decided under the Immigration Appeals (Procedure) Rules 1984.
2 Asylum and Immigration Tribunal (Procedure) Rules 2005, SI 2005/230, r 10.
3 SI 2005/230, r 9.

18.26 Where the appeal suspends removal, the ban on removal pending appeal does not however prevent detention under the administrative provisions of Schedules 2 and 3 to the Immigration Act 1971. The powers to give directions for a person's removal or to make a deportation order against him or her whilst an appeal is pending enable those powers of detention to be exercised.[1] For the exercise of detention powers under these provisions see chapter 17 above.

1 Nationality, Immigration and Asylum Act 2002, s 78(3).

18.27 An appeal against the refusal to vary leave has similar effect. A person's leave is extended whilst any appeal against the refusal to vary the leave could be brought or is pending,[1] as long as the application for leave to remain was made before the original leave expired and the decision on the application to vary leave was made after the original leave expired.[2] Similarly, a decision to curtail or revoke a person's leave to enter or remain is not to have effect whilst an appeal against the decision to curtail or revoke the leave is pending or could be brought.[3] A deportation order may not be made against a person whilst an appeal against the decision to make a deportation order could be brought or is pending.[4] A section 82 appeal is to be treated as abandoned if the appellant leaves the UK[5] or is granted leave to enter or remain.[6]

1 Immigration Act 1971, s 3C(2)(b) and (c) (inserted by Immigration and Asylum Act 1999, s 3; substituted by Nationality, Immigration and Asylum Act 2002, s 118).
2 IA 1971, s 3C(1); see discussion at 18.32 below.
3 Nationality, Immigration and Asylum Act 2002, s 82(3).
4 NIAA 2002, s 79.
5 NIAA 2002, s 104(4)(a); see 18.106 below.
6 NIAA 2002, s 104(4)(b). An attempt to argue that an appeal on asylum grounds under s 69 of the IAA 1999 could be 'converted' into an appeal against the refusal of refugee status under s 69(3) (now s 83 of the NIAA 2002) failed in *Kanyenkiko v Secretary of State for the Home Department* [2003] EWCA Civ 542 [2003] INLR 296.

18.28 An appeal against an EEA decision to refuse to admit a person to the UK, or to remove the person, prevents his or her removal from the United Kingdom. Any removal directions previously given cease to have effect and no directions may be given while an appeal against exclusion is pending.[1] Similarly, any directions for the removal of the appellant after revocation of the residence permit or in situations analogous with section 10 of the Immigration and Asylum Act 1999 or Schedule 3 to the Immigration Act 1971, are not to take effect while the appeal is pending.[2] This means that in deportation cases, and in cases analogous to overstayer removal, directions may be given during the period while the appeal is pending so long as they are not acted on. The detention powers contained in Schedules 2 and 3 to the

Immigration Act 1971 continue to apply despite the freezing of removal directions.[3] No deportation order is to be made against an EEA national while the deportation appeal is pending.[4]

1 Immigration (European Economic Area) Regulations 2000, SI 2000/2326, reg 32(1) (substituted by SI 2003/549).
2 SI 2000/2326, reg 32(2) as substituted.
3 SI 2000/2326, reg 32(3) as substituted.
4 SI 2000/2326, reg 32(5) as substituted. For EEA deportations, see 18.36 below.

Issues arising on particular appeals

18.29 Although section 82 of the Nationality, Immigration and Asylum Act 2002 creates a single appeal against an immigration decision, particular issues arise in relation to appeals in specific situations. We dealt above with exclusion of appeal rights; in this section we look at difficulties which have arisen in respect of particular types of appeal.

Entry clearance appeals

18.30 We noted above (18.21) the situations where a refusal of entry clearance gives rise to no right of appeal. The list of unappealable entry clearance decisions grows ever longer: to the frustrated visitors (except family visitors), short-term or prospective students, those who are too old or young, or hold the wrong nationality or citizenship, the AI(TC)A 2004 adds another group, whose boundaries are as yet undefined.[1] The Secretary of State has been given carte blanche to decide who can appeal against a refusal of entry clearance. Will the proposed regulations remove appeal rights from all who entry clearance officers decide do not qualify under the rules? Such a removal of rights should certainly not take place except by explicit legislation. We remain in the dark about the purpose of the amendment.

1 Nationality, Immigration and Asylum Act 2002, s 88A, inserted by Asylum and Immigration (Treatment of Claimants, etc) Act 2004, s 29(1) from 1 October 2004, which prevents an appeal (except on discrimination or human rights grounds) against refusal of entry clearance taken on grounds which relate to a provision of the immigration rules specified by order of the Secretary of State. No regulations have yet been made under this section.

Refusal of leave to enter

18.31 We have set out (at 18.21 above) the main situations where there is no right of appeal (except on asylum or human rights grounds) against refusal of leave to enter. The main issue in relation to refusal of leave to enter is whether the appeal is in-country or appellants must leave in order to exercise appeal rights.[1] In-country appeals against the refusal of leave to enter have always been the exception, limited in the past to those holding entry clearance or work permits.[2] Now, holding either of these documents does not necessarily ensure an in-country appeal. The holder of a work permit but no entry clearance who is refused entry to the UK can only appeal in-country if he is a

British national.[3] Surely there is scope here for a race discrimination argument;[4] it is hard to see the rationale for such a distinction in the deprivation of in-country appeal rights. So far as holders of entry clearance are concerned, if the entry clearance was issued for a different purpose than that for which the passenger seeks entry, refusal or cancellation of leave on this ground does not attract in-country appeal rights.[5] This provision does not preclude in-country appeals by those with visitor entry clearance refused asylum after a port claim, unless the claim is certified clearly unfounded, since asylum and human rights appeals against refusal of leave to enter, or decisions to remove, must always be in-country unless so certified.[6] However, it might unfairly prevent an in-country appeal by a returning resident who the immigration officer asserts is returning for a visit rather than to resume settlement.[7] In such a case, the remedy would have to be judicial review of the refusal.

1   See 18.23 above.
2   Immigration Act 1971, s 13(3); Immigration and Asylum Act 1999, s 60(3).
3   Nationality, Immigration and Asylum Act 2002, s 92(3D), inserted by Asylum and Immigration (Treatment of Claimants, etc) Act 2004, s 28 from 1 October 2004.
4   See the House of Lords' analysis in *A v Secretary of State for the Home Department* [2004] UKHL 56, [2005] 2 WLR 87 and in *European Roma Rights Centre v Immigration Officer at Prague Airport* [2004] UKHL 55, [2005] 2 WLR 1. This argument could however only be made in-country by way of a human rights claim (NIAA 2002, s 92(4)(a)), or by judicial review; an appeal based on a pure discrimination argument under s 84(1)(b) would have to be conducted from abroad.
5   NIAA 2002, s 92(3) provides the in-country appeal right for entry clearance holders; s 92(3A)–(3C), inserted by Asylum and Immigration (Treatment of Claimants, etc) Act 2004, s 28, remove it. Subsection (3B) applies to cancellation of advance leave and sub-s (3C) to refusal of leave to someone with entry clearance.
6   See NIAA 2002, s 92(4)(a) read with s 94(2) as amended by Asylum and Immigration (Treatment of Claimants, etc) Act 2004, s 27.
7   For returning residents see 5.30ff above.

Variation or refusal to vary leave

18.32 An appeal against a variation or refusal to vary a person's leave to enter or remain may only be brought if, as a result of the variation or refusal to vary the person has no leave to enter or remain.[1] This contrasts with the predecessor 'variation appeal' under the IAA 1999,[2] where an appeal could be brought if the person's leave would expire within 28 days of being notified of the decision.[3] The Home Office frequently prevents people from acquiring a right of appeal by notifying refusal to vary leave before the expiry of current leave. In order to obtain a right of appeal, the recipient of such a decision would have to make a further application for the leave to be varied, including payment of the prescribed fee, before it expired.

1   Nationality, Immigration and Asylum Act 2002, s 82(2)(d).
2   Asylum and Immigration Act 1999, s 61.
3   That in turn contrasted with its predecessor, the 'variation appeal' under Immigration Act 1971, s 14, which provided appeal rights against any variation or refusal to vary leave. It was these provisions which enabled appeals to be brought against unwelcome conditions or a lesser leave than that sought.

18.33 Under the 1971 Immigration Act the right of appeal against a refusal to vary leave was limited to situations where there was an existing leave at the time of the lodging of the appeal.[1] In *Subramaniam* in the Court of Appeal[2] and in *Suthendran* in the House of Lords[3] it was decided by a majority of the judges that on its true construction the Immigration Act 1971, section 14(1), the precursor of section 61 of the Immigration and Asylum Act 1999, and in similar terms, gave a right of appeal to 'a person who has a limited leave under this Act' and not to 'a person who has had' such limited leave. Thus there was no right of appeal under section 61 of the IAA 1999 for a person whose limited leave to remain in the UK had expired at the time of applying for a variation.[4] The successor provisions of the NIAA 2002 are materially different to their predecessors under both the 1971 and 1999 Acts because of the omission of the words 'which he has' in respect of the leave of which variation had been sought.[5] This suggests that the question of whether there is a right of appeal against a refusal to vary a leave which a person had, but which expired by the time of the application to vary, may need to be revisited.[6] The interpretation adopted by the majority in the House of Lords in *Suthendran* also meant that someone whose application was made in time, but whose limited leave expired before the Home Office reached a decision, would have no right of appeal. The majority of the House of Lords realised this, but said that the injustice could be cured by administrative means. The 'leave gap' was closed by the Variation of Leave Order 1976;[7] it is now dealt with by section 3C of the 1971 Act.[8] This provides that if a person with limited leave to enter or remain applies before the expiry of the leave for variation and when it expires no decision has been taken, the leave is to be treated as continuing until the end of the period allowed for appealing the decision and, if an appeal is brought, pending the appeal.[9] The section also provides that during this period of statutory leave, no further application for variation may be made, although the original application, which gave rise to the statutory leave, may be varied.[10] This may be done by means of a statement of additional grounds,[11] submitted after the original application, which would then have to be considered by the adjudicator hearing the appeal.[12] Statutory leave lapses if the applicant leaves the UK.[13]

[1]   *Akhtar v Secretary of State for the Home Department* [1991] Imm AR 232, CA; see also *Wa-Selo v Secretary of State for the Home Department* [1990] Imm AR 76, CA.

[2]   *R v Immigration Appeal Tribunal, ex p Subramaniam* [1977] QB 190, [1976] 3 All ER 604.

[3]   *Suthendran v Immigration Appeal Tribunal* [1977] AC 359, [1976] 3 All ER 611.

[4]   Since all applications (with some exceptions such as EEA, asylum and human rights or discrimination ones) must be on prescribed forms, which must be completed in full and sent with all requisite documents and fees to constitute a valid application, the effect of a letter seeking further leave, or (previously a common practice among students) the mere sending in of a passport to the Home Office for further endorsement, will be that no valid application has been made prior to expiry of leave, and so no right of appeal will accrue: see HC 395, para 32 as amended by HC 329 and HC 704. See further 4.7–4.8 above.

[5]   Nationality, Immigration and Asylum Act 2002, s 82(2)(d) which provides that refusal to vary leave to enter or remain in the UK is an immigration decision if the result of the refusal is that the person has no leave to enter or remain.

[6]   The probable answer, however, is that no right of appeal accrues if leave had already expired before the application to vary was made, since (i) the term 'variation' suggests that there must be an extant leave to vary, and (ii) if leave had already expired by the date of the application, the absence of leave is not the result of the refusal, which the section requires.

[7]   SI 1976/1572, as amended by SI 1989/1005, known as 'VOLO', and deemed leave under the Order was known as VOLO leave.

[8]   Inserted by Immigration and Asylum Act 1999, s 3, substituted by Nationality, Immigration and Asylum Act 2002, s 118.

18.33 *Immigration Appeals*

9   Immigration Act 1971, s 3C(2) (as substituted). For 'finally determined', 'withdrawn' and 'abandoned' see 18.104–18.106 below. Statutory leave under the section is subject to the same conditions as the original leave.
10 IA 1971, s 3C(4) and (5) (as substituted).
11 Under NIAA 2002, s 120.
12 By virtue of NIAA 2002, s 85(2).
13 IA 1971, s 3C(3) (as substituted).

Appeals by EEA nationals: refusal to issue or to renew, or revocation of residence documents

18.34 Refusal to issue or to renew a residence permit or document to an EEA national or family member in the UK, or revocation of such a document, is the EEA equivalent of variation or refusal to vary leave to enter or remain. The refusal to issue a residence permit to an EEA national (which is proof of entitlement to be in the UK),[1] or to a family member producing a family permit or other proof of eligibility,[2] may be grounded on public policy, public security or public health; the refusal to renew the permit, or a decision to revoke it, may additionally be grounded on a dispute as to whether the applicant is (or has ceased to be) a qualified person, the family member of such a person or satisfies conditions of dependency.[3] There is a right of appeal to the tribunal against a refusal or revocation, exercisable in the UK. If the decision is on conducive grounds relating to national security, diplomatic or political reasons and is followed by a decision to remove, there is a right of appeal to the Special Immigration Appeals Commission instead.[4] In *Boukssid v Secretary of State for the Home Department*, the Court of Appeal held that an EEA national or family member, seeking indefinite leave to remain but granted a five-year residence permit instead, has no right of appeal under the domestic law, because that depends on having limited leave under UK law, and there is no refusal of a residence permit so as to bring into play the appeal provisions of the Regulations. The only remedy in this situation is judicial review.[5] However, in *Baumbast* the Tribunal accepted an argument based on paragraph 255 of HC 395 that the only method of granting indefinite leave under paragraph 255 was to endorse the residence permit to show permission to remain in the UK indefinitely and therefore by necessary inference, to grant a permit. If that endorsement was refused, that amounted to a refusal of a residence permit, against which there was a right of appeal.[6]

1   Immigration (European Economic Area) Regulations 2000, SI 2000/2326, reg 15(1).
2   SI 2000/2326, reg 15(2).
3   SI 2000/2326, regs 10(3), 22.
4   SI 2000/2326, regs 29, 31.
5   *Boukssid v Secretary of State for the Home Department* [1998] INLR 275, CA, decided under equivalent provisions of the IA 1971 and the Immigration (European Economic Area) Order 1994, SI 1994/1895.
6   *Baumbast* (21263) (8 June 1999, unreported), IAT, also decided under the IA 1971 and the Immigration (European Economic Area) Order 1994 (fn 5 above).

Deportation appeals

18.35 Since overstayers and those in breach of conditions of leave are no longer deported but removed from the UK,[1] subject to transitional provisions affecting those served with a deportation notice or who applied to regularise their stay before 2 October 2000,[2] the range of people who are deported, and so enjoy a right of appeal before removal, is limited. Now only persons recommended for deportation by a criminal court, those whose deportation the Secretary of State deems to be conducive to the public good, and their family members, are to be deported and have corresponding appeal rights.[3] The appeal is to the tribunal,[4] and no order is to be made while such an appeal may be brought[5] or while it is pending.[6] However, once a deportation order is made, any pending appeal against refusal of leave to enter, refusal of a certificate of entitlement, refusal to vary, variation of or revocation of leave to enter or remain under section 82 of the Nationality, Immigration and Asylum Act 2002 is to be treated as finally determined.[7] The provisions of Schedule 3 to the Immigration Act 1971 apply to proposed deportees, who may be detained or granted temporary release or bail pending appeal.[8] If the grounds for the decision to deport are national security, diplomatic or political, the appeal is not to the tribunal[9] but to the Special Immigration Appeals Commission.[10] There is a right of appeal against a refusal to revoke a deportation order[11] but it may not be exercised from within the United Kingdom unless an asylum or human rights claim has been made and has not been certified clearly unfounded,[12] or an EEA national or family member of an EEA national claims that the decision breaches rights under Community law.[13] A refusal to revoke based on a personal decision by the Secretary of State that the applicant's exclusion from the UK would be conducive to the public good is not appealable to the tribunal but may be appealed to the Special Immigration Appeals Commission.[14]

[1]   Immigration and Asylum Act 1999, s 10.
[2]   Immigration and Asylum Act 1999, s 9 and Sch 15, paras 11 and 12, Immigration (Regularisation Period for Overstayers) Regulations 2000, SI 2000/265. The transitional provisions of Sch 15 enable these people to have a deportation appeal on the merits if they had been in the UK for seven years by the date of decision, and an appeal limited to whether the precedent conditions for deportation have been made out, if not, under Immigration Act 1971, s 15, Immigration Act 1988, s 5 and Immigration (Restricted Right of Appeal against Deportation) (Exemption) Order 1993, which are to continue to have effect in relation to this class of person notwithstanding their repeal.
[3]   Immigration Act 1971, s 3(5) and (6) as amended by Immigration and Asylum Act 1999, Sch 15, para 44(2). For the factors to be considered in deportation appeals, see 15.30 above.
[4]   Nationality, Immigration and Asylum Act 2002, s 81 (substituted by s 26 Asylum and Immigration (Treatment of Claimants, etc) Act 2004), s 82(1) as amended, s 82(2)(j).
[5]   NIAA 2002, s 79(1)(a).
[6]   NIAA 2002, 79(1)(b).
[7]   NIAA 2002, s 104(5).
[8]   For detention pending deportation, and bail pending appeal, see chapter 17 above.
[9]   NIAA 2002, s 97.
[10] Special Immigration Appeals Commission Act 1997, s 2(1), as amended; Immigration (European Economic Area) Regulations 2000, SI 2000/2326 (amended by SI 2003/549), reg 31.
[11] NIAA 2002, s 82(2)(k).
[12] NIAA 2002, ss 92(4)(a), 94(2) as amended by Asylum and Immigration (Treatment of Claimants, etc) Act 2004, s 27 (from 1 October 2004).
[13] NIAA 2002, s 92(4).
[14] See fn 10 above.

EEA public policy decisions to remove

18.36   Removal of an EEA national or family member on public policy, public security or public health grounds[1] is equivalent to a deportation on conducive grounds, and section 5 of and Schedule 3 to the Immigration Act 1971 apply.[2] Where national security, diplomatic or political reasons underlie the decision, the appeal is to the Special Immigration Appeals Commission,[3] otherwise, it is to the Tribunal.[4] The appeal is in-country and suspends removal.[5] An appeal against a refusal to revoke a deportation order is, however, out-of-country under the regulations.[6]

[1]   Immigration (European Economic Area) Regulations 2000, SI 2000/2326, reg 21(3)(b).
[2]   SI 2000/2326, reg 26(3).
[3]   SI 2000/2326, reg 31(2), substituted by SI 2003/549.
[4]   SI 2000/2326, reg 29(6) as substituted and amended by SI 2005/671; reg 29(7) applies the relevant sections of the NIAA 2002.
[5]   SI 2000/2326, reg 32 (as substituted) for suspensive effect. It is in-country by virtue of its omission from the list of out-of-country appeals at SI 2000/2326, reg 30 as substituted.
[6]   SI 2000/2326, reg 30(1)(b) as substituted. The exceptions in reg 30(3) do not apply to revocation appeals.

Appeals against removal: overstayers, illegal entrants, ship and aircrews

18.37   Illegal entrants,[1] overstayers (including overstaying crew members),[2] those in breach of conditions, persons who have remained in the UK by deception and their family members may be summarily removed by directions given by an immigration officer.[3] They have an unrestricted right of appeal against the decision to remove them[4] (by contrast to the right of appeal that existed under the IAA 1999, which was limited to challenging the existence of the power to remove on the grounds stated in the notice).[5] However, the right of appeal may only be exercised after removal[6] unless the person has made an asylum or human rights claim, which has not been certified clearly unfounded[7] or a claim that the decision breaches Community law, whilst in the UK.[8]

[1]   See 16.3 above.
[2]   See 6.36 above.
[3]   Under Immigration Act 1971, Sch 2, paras 9, 10, 12(2), 13(2), and Immigration and Asylum Act 1999, s 10; see chapter 16.
[4]   Nationality, Immigration and Asylum Act 2002, s 82(2)(g),(h), (i) and (ia) (s 82(2)(ia) inserted by Asylum and Immigration (Treatment of Claimants, etc) Act 2004, s 31 from 1 October 2004.
[5]   Immigration and Asylum Act 1999, s 66; see 5th edn at 18.25–18.26.
[6]   NIAA 2002, s 92(1).
[7]   NIAA 2002, s 92(4)(a) and 94(2) as amended by Asylum and Immigration (Treatment of Claimants, etc) Act 2004, s 27 from 1 October 2004 (SI 2004/2523).
[8]   NIAA 2002, s 92(4)(b).

EEA decisions to remove on grounds of non-qualification

18.38   A person may be removed from the UK if he or she is not, or has ceased to be, a qualified person or a family member of such a person.[1]

Removal of this group is equivalent to removal of overstayers under section 10(1)(a) of the Immigration and Asylum Act 1999, which is to apply.[2]
There is no right of appeal on the ground that the person is an EEA national
unless the appellant produces a valid national identity card or passport issued
by an EEA state.[3] A person claiming to be a family member for the purposes
of an appeal must produce a family permit or other proof of relationship.[4] An
appeal against removal may rely on asylum, human rights or race discrimination grounds.[5]

1   Immigration (European Economic Area) Regulations 2000, SI 2000/2326, reg 21(3)(a).
2   SI 2000/2326, reg 26(2).
3   SI 2000/2326, reg 29(2) (substituted by SI 2003/549). The requirement to provide this
    proof of qualification as an EEA national (or family member, see below) would, we
    suggest, apply to appeals under the Nationality, Immigration and Asylum Act 2002 against
    immigration decisions on EEA grounds, since the EEA regulations are made under s 109 of
    the Act. The documents provided are to be accepted as authentic unless their falsity is
    reasonably apparent: reg 29(4) as substituted.
4   SI 2000/2326, reg 29(3) as substituted. See fn 3 above.
5   SI 2000/2326, Sch 2 (substituted by SI 2003/3188), applying Nationality, Immigration and
    Asylum Act, s 84(1)(b)–(e), (g) to appeals under the Regulations.

Appeals objecting to destination

18.39 The previous legislation provided a right of appeal to an adjudicator
on the ground of an objection to the country or territory to which the
appellant was to be removed.[1] That right of appeal has not been reproduced
by the NIAA 2002, but since one of the statutory grounds of appeal is that
'the decision is … not in accordance with the law', this allows an appellant to
allege that there is no power in law to remove the person to the destination
specified in the notice.[2]

1   Immigration and Asylum Act 1999, s 67. The destination appeal, which was not founded
    on legal arguments about the Secretary of State's power to remove to the particular
    destination, but on the appellant's preference, was rarely used, largely because it was
    necessary to stipulate an alternative destination and show by evidence that the appellant
    was likely to be accepted there: see 5th edn at 18.52.
2   Nationality, Immigration and Asylum Act 2002, s 84(1)(e). For a discussion of legal
    objections to destination, see 16.56 above.

One-stop appeals

18.40 The one-stop appeal was introduced by the Immigration and Asylum
Act 1999[1] and is now in its third incarnation.[2] It applies only to in-country
appeals. The basic idea, as its name suggests, is that all the grounds relied on
to remain in the UK should be considered in the course of a single appeal, so
as to avoid delay and abuse. The positive aspect of the one-stop appeal,
therefore, is that the Asylum and Immigration Tribunal is obliged to consider
all matters which have been raised by the appellant, whether on the original
application or in response to a 'one-stop' notice.[3] The negative aspect of the
procedure is that service of such a notice, or an earlier right of appeal, will
generally preclude an appeal against a second immigration decision which
relies on a matter which should have been, but was not raised earlier.[4]

1   Sections 73–76; see 5th edn, 18.20ff.
2   The Nationality, Immigration and Asylum Act 2002, ss 96 and 120 simplified the procedure. Amendments by the Asylum and Immigration (Treatment of Claimants, etc) Act 2004, s 30 (from 1 October 2004) simplify the s 96 provisions further.
3   NIAA 2002, s 85(2), (3).
4   NIAA 2002, s 96(1), (2) as substituted by Asylum and Immigration (Treatment of Claimants, etc) Act 2004, s 30.

18.41 The Secretary of State or an immigration officer may serve a one-stop notice under section 120 of the Nationality, Immigration and Asylum Act 2002 on an applicant for leave to enter or remain, or the subject of an immigration decision (such as deportation or removal),[1] at any time, whether before or after the decision.[2] The notice requires the person to state reasons for wishing to enter or remain, for being permitted to do so, or why he or she should not be removed or required to leave (other than those forming the basis of the application, or already relied on to resist the decision).[3] The response to the one-stop warning is the 'Statement of Additional Grounds'. There is no statutory time limit for the service of the Statement, and the API state that the obligation to state additional grounds in response to the warning is a continuing one.[4] There is no statutory requirement for the Secretary of State or immigration officer to respond to a statement of additional grounds,[5] but any further grounds relied on in such a statement served in response to a one-stop warning must be considered in the appeal against the immigration decision.[6] The additional grounds could be further grounds for leave to enter or remain under the immigration rules, under a relevant Home Office policy, asylum or human rights or discrimination grounds. So for example, a person refused leave to enter as a visitor at the port, served with a section 120 notice, might claim asylum or adduce human rights grounds for seeking to enter, which would then give rise to an in-country appeal (unless certified as clearly unfounded);[7] an asylum claimant waiting for his or her claim to be processed might marry or enter a relationship which could form the basis of a human rights claim under Article 8 ECHR; or a person seeking leave to remain under the student rules, who has been living with someone settled in the UK for two years, may seek to rely on the unmarried partners' rule, and on Article 8 ECHR, in the statement of additional grounds, asserting that the decision is not in accordance with the law[8] and immigration rules[9] and is incompatible with the appellant's Convention rights.[10] It is not clear whether the Tribunal would be required to consider additional grounds raised by an appellant where no section 120 notice has been served, but we suggest that an attempt should be made to raise such grounds on appeal; the Secretary of State could not later complain of a failure to raise the matters on an earlier appeal (see below).

1   Nationality, Immigration and Asylum Act 2002, s 120(1)(a), (b). These provisions replace the complicated procedures under ss 74 and 75 of the IAA 1999, which provided for different one-stop procedures and notices in respect of specified applicants and appellants.
2   NIAA 2002, s 120(2). The flexibility provided by the section contrasts with the previous provisions (fn 1 above), which required the notice to be served at a particular point in the procedure which differed according to the application and the status of the applicant. Service of a notice under the section is not obligatory, but the Asylum Policy Instructions (API) indicate that it would be appropriate where an application is unlikely to be successful and it would be helpful to establish whether the applicant intended to put forward any other matters on appeal or to resist enforcement, and particularly where it is believed that an asylum or human rights claim may be made; or where a decision to remove or deport is

going to be made or a person who has not previously had a one-stop warning is being considered for removal (API: Appeals: the One-Stop Procedure Warnings and Certificates), para 2.1. Most refusal decisions now incorporate one-stop warnings as a final or penultimate paragraph.

³ NIAA 2002, s 120(2), (3).

⁴ API (fn 2 above), para 2.2. The IAA 1999 procedures contained strict time limits for compliance with the requirement to state additional grounds.

⁵ Under the previous scheme, procedure rules required the Secretary of State to respond to statements of additional grounds by supplementary refusal notices; this requirement was rarely observed, leading to problems for adjudicators who were unsure whether they were required to deal with all the issues notwithstanding the Secretary of State's failure (following *Haddad* [2000] INLR 117), or whether to insist on their role as an appellate body rather than a first-instance decision maker. The API (fn 2 above) state that if the Statement is served before the decision on the original application, the Secretary of State will treat it as a variation of the application and address it in the decision notice; if it is served before an appeal is heard it should be addressed in a letter supplementing the notice of decision.

⁶ NIAA 2002, s 85(2), (3). The section does not confer broader jurisdiction than the Tribunal has under s 84(1), so the additional grounds relied on must relate to one or other of the appeal grounds under that section.

⁷ Ie under NIAA 2002, s 94(2). In this example, there would have been no appeal if the asylum or human rights grounds had not been raised, because of s 88: see 18.21 above.

⁸ NIAA 2002, s 84(1)(e).

⁹ NIAA 2002, s 84(1)(a).

¹⁰ NIAA 2002, s 84(1)(c) and/or (g).

18.42 The certification procedure under section 96[1] precludes an appeal against a second immigration decision in two situations:

(i) where the Secretary of State or an immigration officer certifies that the person was notified of a right of appeal against an earlier immigration decision (regardless of whether an appeal was brought or has been determined), where the new claim or application relates to a matter which could have been raised in an appeal against the old decision, and there is no satisfactory reason for the failure to raise it;[2]

(ii) Where the Secretary of State or an immigration officer certifies that the person received a s 120 notice in respect of an earlier application or decision, should have raised the matter on which he or she now seeks to rely in a statement made in response to the notice, and there is no satisfactory reason for the failure to raise it.[3]

Thus, the one-stop procedure now rests simply on a failure to raise the matter now relied on earlier – either on appeal, if there was an opportunity to appeal at an earlier stage, or in a statement of additional grounds in response to a one-stop notice. The certification procedure only comes into play to block an appeal, in a situation where otherwise, there would have been one, ie where a further immigration decision under section 82 of the Nationality, Immigration and Asylum Act 2002 is taken in respect of someone who has previously made an application or been the subject of an earlier immigration decision. It does not apply where there is no such further immigration decision. Thus, it might apply to prevent a human rights appeal against a decision to remove an overstayer who had previously appealed against refusal to vary leave but had not raised human rights grounds on that appeal,[4] or to block an asylum claim, put forward late, after refusal of leave to enter on other grounds, and not referred to in response to a one-stop notice.[5] A further asylum or human rights claim made after the rejection of an earlier claim would not give rise to an 'immigration decision' unless it met the requirements of a fresh claim contained in the immigration rules,[6] and certification under section 96 is only considered once the Secretary of State has accepted further representations as a fresh claim for this purpose.[7] The simplified provisions thus make a much better fit with these 'fresh claims' provisions. The only issue for the Secretary of State or the immigration officer under section 96 is whether the reasons for the failure to put forward the new matter are satisfactory. The API indicate that a significant change of circumstances in the country of origin since an asylum appeal would be a satisfactory reason for failure to raise those circumstances on the appeal, as would the establishment of an appropriate relationship since the appeal which attracts the guarantees of Article 8 ECHR.[8] A serious failure by a representative to put forward a vital issue which would have had a significant impact on the outcome of the appeal might also be a satisfactory reason for the applicant's failure, provided that there is evidence to support the allegation and the matter is serious enough to justify a formal complaint to the representative's regulatory body or to the OISC.[9]

[1] Nationality, Immigration and Asylum Act 2002, s 96(1), (2), substituted by Asylum and Immigration (Treatment of Claimants, etc) Act 2004, s 30 from 1 October 2004.

[2] NIAA 2002, s 96(1) as substituted. This limb applies to earlier appeals under the IAA 1999 as well as the NIAA 2002: NIAA 2002, Sch 6, para 4(a). It does not require a s 120 notice to have been served, provided the earlier immigration decision gave rise to a right of appeal where the new matter could have been raised. It does not matter whether the applicant chose not to appeal, or withdrew or abandoned the appeal. However, if the new matter could not be raised on the appeal (eg because the Tribunal refused to allow it to be, or because it arose after the appeal), that would be a satisfactory reason for its not having been raised: see API Appeals: the One-Stop Procedure Warnings and Certificates), para 3.2. If the appeal could only have been exercised from abroad, and was not, the claim should not be certified, but it may be certified if the appeal from abroad was exercised and the matter not raised: ibid.

[3] NIAA 2002, s 96(2) as substituted. This limb does not require the applicant to have had an earlier right of appeal, but would apply where for example, a one-stop notice was issued in respect of an earlier immigration decision and had the applicant responded, relying on the human rights or asylum claim he or she now seeks to raise, that would have generated a right of appeal: see API (fn 2 above) para 3.2. It applies where a one-stop notice was served under earlier legislation: see NIAA 2002, Sch 6, para 4(b), (c).

[4] Ie someone who had already had a right of appeal under NIAA 2002, s 82(2)(d) or its predecessor, and who now seeks to appeal in-country under s 82(2)(g) by the application of s 92(4)(a). However, for s 96(1) to bite, the person must, we suggest, have been notified of the obligation to disclose additional grounds before the earlier appeal, whether by service of a one-stop notice or otherwise.

[5] NIAA 2002, s 96(2) as substituted. In this scenario, the claimant could have had an earlier appeal, relying on s 92(4)(a), had he or she made the asylum claim in response to the one-stop warning.

[6] HC 395, para 353: see 12.170 above.

[7] See API (fn 2 above), para 3.1.

[8] API (fn 2 above), para 3.2.

[9] API (fn 2 above), para 3.2.

18.43 Under the NIAA 2002 provisions, unlike the IAA 1999 provisions, an asylum or human rights claimant does not forfeit appeal rights solely because he or she is a family member of someone who had appeal rights earlier; the applicant him- or herself must have been an applicant or prospective appellant.[1] Other differences between the old and new regimes include the fact that the new provisions apply in respect of new applications made after the subject has left the country and returned, thus preventing a failed and expelled asylum seeker from being able to appeal against a new decision to refuse leave to enter, in the absence of a satisfactory reason for failing to refer to the new grounds on the previous occasion.[2] Another major difference is that certification under section 96 as amended cannot operate to block an appeal once it is lodged.[3] The one-stop procedure applies equally to appeals in the Special Immigration Appeals Commission[4] and to EEA appeals.[5]

[1]   Under the IAA 1999, one-stop notices were served not only on applicants and appellants but on their relevant family members too, who were thus precluded from making their own asylum or human rights claims later. Notices under s 120, and notices of appeal, are served only on applicants or subjects of immigration decisions.
[2]   Nationality, Immigration and Asylum Act 2002, s 96(5).
[3]   NIAA 2002, s 96(1) and (2) amended by, and (7) inserted by Asylum and Immigration (Treatment of Claimants, etc) Act 2004, s 30.
[4]   NIAA 2002, s 96(6).
[5]   Immigration (European Economic Area) Regulations 2000, reg 33(3), (4) (substituted by SI 2003/549, amended by SI 2005/671).

Transitional provisions

18.44   The rapid changes in legislation and rules regarding appeals make it necessary to know which provisions apply in any given case. It is particularly important to check which procedure rules apply in a 'transitional' situation.[1] Sometimes the legislation or the rules themselves contain clear and comprehensive transitional provisions.[2] When they do not, or a gap in the provisions is identified, there are a number of principles to bear in mind. First, Parliament can be assumed not to intend to produce unfair results,[3] so that a construction of a statute which appears retrospectively to remove rights of appeal is unlikely to be upheld, and if no specific provision is made, appeals pending under previous legislation proceed. Secondly, however, a right of appeal does not crystallise until a decision is made, so the restriction of rights of appeal in a statute is not unfair to those who have not yet received adverse decisions.[4] We deal with the transitional provisions under the 2004 Act at 18.78 below. The Tribunal has been scathing on occasion about transitional provisions contained in Commencement Orders: in *Pardeepan* it expressed dismay at the restriction of appeals on human rights grounds to events post-dating 1 October 2000,[5] and in *ZA (Ethiopia)*[6] it complained that the transitional provisions made in a commencement order under the NIAA 2002 regulating appeals submitted before that Act came into force[7] had 'some claim to be the worst drafted ... order ever passed by Parliament.'[8] *ZA (Ethiopia)* related to an asylum appeal under the IAA 1999 which was dismissed in November 2003 (after the NIAA 2002 came into force). A human rights appeal was allowed. Following the grant of permission to appeal to the Tribunal, the Secretary of State granted three years' humanitarian protection. The question for the Tribunal was whether this led to deemed abandonment of the appeal under the IAA 1999, or whether, as the appellant argued, the gap in the transitional provisions enabled her to proceed with her appeal. The Tribunal held that the old appeal provisions applied.[9] A case pending in the Administrative Court involves a certificate written before and received after the third-country provisions of the 2004 Act came into force.[10]

1   See for example *R (on the application of Ebadi) v Immigration Appeal Tribunal* [2004] EWHC 1645 (Admin), [2004] All ER (D) 228 (Jun), where the Tribunal had applied the wrong procedure rules in demanding good reason for the submission of late evidence (see below at 18.78).

2   Eg, Asylum and Immigration Act 1996, s 1, inserting into the Asylum and Immigration Appeals Act 1993 provisions restricting appeal rights in respect of designated countries, which stated that its provisions applied to all appeals after the Act came into force 'irrespective of the date of the asylum claim': see *R v Secretary of State for the Home Department and Special Adjudicator, ex p Chowdry (Nargis)* (QBCOF 97/1715/D) (2 February 1998, unreported), CA.

3   See eg *R (on the application of Kariharan)* [2002] EWCA Civ 1102, [2003] QB 933, construing 'decision relating to entitlement to enter and remain' (Immigration and Asylum Act 1999, s 65) to determine whether removal directions issued after the coming into force of that Act following a notice to an illegal entrant and an asylum appeal attracted a right of appeal under s 65.

4   *R v Secretary of State for the Home Department, ex p Mundowa* [1992] 3 All ER 606 (overstayer who expected to have right of appeal on merits against deportation, but had not been served with notice of intention to deport before Immigration Act 1988, s 5, restricting right of appeal, came into force, held not to be prejudiced as he had no right of appeal until service of notice).

5   *Pardeepan v Secretary of State for the Home Department* [2000] INLR 447.

6   [2004] UKIAT 00241, [2004] Imm AR 538.

7   Nationality, Immigration and Asylum Act 2002 (Commencement No 4) Order 2003, SI 2003/754 (amended by SI 2003/1040 and SI 2003/1339) Sch 2, paras 3, 4.

8   [2004] UKIAT 00241, [2004] Imm AR 538, para 17.

9   [2004] UKIAT 00241, [2004] Imm AR 538, at paras 18–19.

10 For discussion of transitional provisions in the different context of exclusion from *non-refoulement* protection, see *SB (Haiti)* [2005] UKIAT 00036; see 12.99 above.

POWERS OF THE TRIBUNAL

18.45 On an appeal, the power of the Tribunal to decide the appeal one way or the other is contained in section 86 of the Nationality, Immigration and Asylum Act 2002.[1] It also has a jurisdiction to determine as a preliminary issue whether a notice of appeal is out of time, and if so, whether the appeal should be allowed to proceed.[2] We deal with this preliminary issue jurisdiction at 18.113 below. The Tribunal has powers to make directions consequent on its determinations,[3] and in certain circumstances may reconsider its decisions.[4]

1   As amended by Asylum and Immigration (Treatment of Claimants, etc) Act 2004, Sch 2, para 18 from 4 April 2005. The section is in similar, although not identical terms, to its predecessors, Immigration and Asylum Act 1999, Sch 4, para 21 and Immigration Act 1971, s 19, the old jurisdiction provisions.

2   Asylum and Immigration Tribunal (Procedure) Rules 2005, SI 2005/230, r 10 (late notice of appeal).

3   Nationality, Immigration and Asylum Act 2002, s 87 (as amended by Asylum and Immigration (Treatment of Claimants, etc) Act 2004, Sch 2, paras 18, 19 from 4 April 2005).

4   NIAA 2002, s 103A(1) (inserted by Asylum and Immigration (Treatment of Claimants, etc) Act 2004, s 26) as amended by AI(TC)A 2004, Sch 2, para 30(2): see 18.169 below.

18.46 Section 86(3) of the Nationality, Immigration and Asylum Act 2002 provides that the Tribunal must allow the appeal if it thinks that:

(1)   a decision against which the appeal is brought or is treated as being brought was not in accordance with the law (including immigration rules);[1] or

(2)   a discretion exercised in making a decision against which the appeal is brought or is treated as being brought should have been exercised differently.[2]

Otherwise, the Tribunal must dismiss the appeal.[3] A decision to remove someone from the UK is not to be regarded as unlawful if it could have lawfully been made by reference to another provision.[4] A decision by the Secretary of State not to depart from the rules may not be reviewed on the merits, but may be reviewed to see whether it is in accordance with the law.[5]

[1]   Nationality, Immigration and Asylum Act 2002, s 86(3)(a), amended by Asylum and Immigration (Treatment of Claimants, etc) Act 2004, Sch 2, para 18.
[2]   NIAA 2002, s 86(3)(b) as amended. On the issue of discretion see *Pearson v Immigration Appeal Tribunal* [1978] Imm AR 212, CA.
[3]   NIAA 2002, s 86(5) as amended.
[4]   NIAA 2002, s 86(4), which prevents technical appeals brought solely on the basis that, for example, an illegal entrant has been served with directions to an overstayer. Earlier statutory provisions in Immigration and Asylum Act 1999, Sch 4, para 24, which compelled the appellate authorities to dismiss appeals brought by illegal entrants and those against whom a deportation order is extant, needed modification to bring them into line with the Human Rights Act 1998.
[5]   NIAA 2002, s 86(6). See 18.49ff below.

18.47 The powers of the Tribunal need to be read in the context of the statutory grounds of appeal, set out in section 84 of the NIAA 2002, and the matters which the Tribunal is obliged to consider under section 85 of the Act. An appeal against an immigration decision under section 82(1) must be brought on one or more of the statutory grounds. These are:

(a)   the decision is not in accordance with immigration rules;[1]
(b)   the decision is unlawful under section 19B Race Relations Act 1976 (discrimination by public authorities);[2]
(c)   the decision is unlawful under section 6 Human Rights Act 1998 (public authority not to act contrary to Human Rights Convention) as being incompatible with the appellant's Convention rights;[3]
(d)   the appellant is an EEA national or a member of the family of an EEA national and the decision breaches the appellant's rights under the Community Treaties in respect of entry to or residence in the UK;[4]
(e)   the decision is otherwise not in accordance with the law;[5]
(f)   the person taking the decision should have exercised differently a discretion conferred by immigration rules;[6]
(g)   removal in consequence of the decision would breach the UK's obligations under the Refugee Convention or would be unlawful under section 6 Human Rights Act 1998 as being incompatible with the appellant's Convention rights.[7]

An appeal under section 83 of the Act must be brought on the ground that removal of the appellant would breach the UK's obligations under the Refugee Convention.[8] The rationale for the appeal under section 83 is the right of refugees to have their status recognised[9] and the corresponding rights recognition brings under the Refugee Convention.[10] Attempts to argue human rights grounds in section 83 appeals have failed because of the wording of the section and of section 84(3), and because appellants have leave to remain in the UK, and will be able to argue human rights grounds if and when that leave is not renewed, bringing removal into prospect.[11]

1   Nationality, Immigration and Asylum Act 2002, s 84(1)(a). The NIAA 2002 is the first to define and delimit exhaustively the permitted grounds of appeal, but s 84 merely makes explicit what were previously implicit limitations drawn by the scope of appellate jurisdiction. A useful definition of a 'ground' is 'the application of particular legal rules to a set of facts to produce a legal result in the case in question': *R (on the application of Borak) v Secretary of State for the Home Department* [2005] EWCA Civ 110 (in the context of NIAA 2002, s 96 before amendment).
2   NIAA 2002, s 84(1)(b); see for example *European Roma Rights Centre v Immigration Officer at Prague Airport* [2004] UKHL 55, [2005] 2 WLR 1, where the House of Lords upheld a claim of race discrimination in the operation of pre-entry screening at Prague Airport.
3   NIAA 2002, s 84(1)(c). This ground is most apt in appeals against refusal of entry clearance, where this is said to breach the positive obligation to respect family life (Art 8 ECHR).
4   NIAA 2002, s 84(1)(d).
5   NIAA 2002, s 84(1)(e).
6   NIAA 2002, s 84(1)(f).
7   NIAA 2002, s 84(1)(g). Note that this ground embraces both Refugee and Human Rights Convention grounds, unlike ground (c); that is because in situations other than removal there is no question of the Refugee Convention's *non-refoulement* obligation being breached; see fn 3.
8   NIAA 2002, s 84(3).
9   For the duty to determine claims, see *Robinson v Secretary of State for the Home Department* [1997] Imm AR 568; *Saad v Secretary of State for the Home Department, Diriye v Secretary of State for the Home Department, Osorio v Secretary of State for the Home Department* [2001] EWCA Civ 2008, [2002] Imm AR 471, [2002] INLR 34.
10   See in particular Convention Relating to the Status of Refugees, Arts 17–30, 12.102 above.
11   See *P (Yugoslavia)* [2003] UKIAT 00017; *LA (Eritrea)* [2004] UKIAT 00113.

Scope of appeal

18.48 In accordance with the principle of 'one-stop' appeals (see 18.40 above), an appeal under section 82(1) is to be treated by the Tribunal as including an appeal against any decision in respect of which the appellant has a right of appeal under the section.[1] This simply means that it is not necessary for an appellant to lodge separate appeals in respect of different immigration decisions.[2] It is hard to think of a situation where an immigrant would receive more than one immigration decision simultaneously, which would necessitate two separate appeals if this section were not enacted; an example might be refusal of further leave to remain and a decision to deport on conducive grounds or following a recommendation for deportation. Section 85(2) obliges the Tribunal to consider additional grounds raised by the statement of additional grounds served in response to a one-stop notice, whether those grounds were served before or after the appeal was lodged,[3] if they fall within the scope of section 84(1). Section 86(2) re-emphasises the duty of the Tribunal to determine any matter raised as a ground of appeal or which section 85 obliges them to consider. The wording of section 86(3), requiring the Tribunal to allow appeals against decisions against which 'the appeal is brought *or is treated as being brought*',[4] brings these additional grounds within the scope of the appeal.

1 Nationality, Immigration and Asylum Act 2002, s 85(1). This section does not oblige the Tribunal to consider issues not raised by the appellant, subject to Refugee Convention obligations (*Robinson v Secretary of State for the Home Department* [1997] Imm AR 568).
2 Explanatory notes to NIAA 2002, para 224.
3 NIAA 2002, s 85(2), (3). Note that there is no statutory requirement for the Secretary of State to respond to a statement of additional grounds, and if there is no response, the Tribunal would effectively be a first-instance decision-maker in relation to these grounds. Although the language of a statement of additional grounds does not have to be legalistic, and complaints in Home Office refusal letters that the appellant has failed to specify which Articles of the Convention are relied on are unjustified, the Tribunal need consider only assertions which can be construed as grounds of appeal within s 84(1)(a)–(g). 'I fear torture' or 'I will be separated from my family' would obviously fall within their scope.
4 NIAA 2002, s 86(3)(a) and (b).

'In accordance with the law'

18.49 The Tribunal must allow an appeal if the decision which is the subject of the appeal was not in accordance with the law, including immigration rules. Legal incompatibility of decisions with the immigration rules is dealt with below. What does this limb of the appeal jurisdiction cover? This question has given rise to much litigation. The law is clearly something distinct from and much wider than the immigration rules or the 'immigration laws', both of which are terms of Art used and defined in the Immigration Act 1971.[1] Little difficulty is encountered where the Tribunal is called upon to construe and interpret the immigration or nationality laws, or some other applicable statutory provision, or to refer to the common law for the meaning of such terms as domicile, ordinary residence and the like. Clearly, the Tribunal is also required to ensure that the respondent's decision was not incompatible with EC law and the refugee and human rights Conventions.[2] The scope of this duty has given rise to some difficulty. In *SS (Malaysia)*,[3] a starred Tribunal held that the phrase 'not in accordance with the law' in the appeal provisions of the IAA 1999 did not extend to incompatibility with the Convention rights of the appellant's UK-resident mother, and that the invocation of the general jurisdiction attempted to subvert the express limitation of the scope of the appeal to the appellant's human rights. The differences in wording between the 1999 and 2002 Act provisions provide more scope for a successful argument now.[4] Another potential difficulty arises from the historic focus of the section: the Tribunal is required to allow the appeal if the decision 'was' not in accordance with the law, whereas the focus of appeals on asylum and human rights grounds is the future. Can it be said that a historic decision was not in accordance with the law because of unforeseeable events which have happened since – whether a coup at home or a marriage in the UK? The provisions of section 85 and 86(2) expressly require consideration of such events,[5] and we suggest that section 86(3) must be read, in appeals depending on asylum or human rights grounds, as if it required an appeal to be allowed if the decision 'would not be in accordance with the law if implemented now'.[6]

1 Immigration Act 1971, s 33. The definition covers all the immigration acts, a phrase itself defined by Asylum and Immigration (Treatment of Claimants, etc) Act 2004, s 44. If the intention of parliament had been to confine the appellate jurisdiction to checking whether the decision or action was in accordance with the immigration laws, the use of that phrase would have been entirely apt.

2   In asylum appeals, the Tribunal will be required to ensure that its decisions comply with the European Council Directive 2004/83/EC on minimum standards for the qualification and status of third country nationals and stateless persons as refugees or persons who otherwise need international protection (30.9.04, OJ L304/12), ie are no less favourable than the provisions of the Directive, although they may be more favourable. It is also necessary to ensure that decisions make the best interests of a child a primary consideration, a requirement incorporated in the Qualification Directive Art 18.5; Council Directive 2003/9/EC on minimum standards for the reception of asylum seekers, OJ 2003 L 31/18 Art 18. A similar requirement in the temporary protection directive is incorporated in the immigration rules, HC 395, para 356B, inserted by HC 164.

3   [2004] UKIAT 00091, [2004] Imm AR 153 (starred). The Immigration and Asylum Act 1999, Sch 4, para 21, required an adjudicator to allow an appeal against a decision which was not in accordance with the law, 'subject to any restrictions on the grounds of appeal'. SS, an adult son who sought to join his mother in the UK, could not succeed on his s 59 appeal against refusal of entry clearance under the immigration rules, para 317 (distressed relatives) since the exceptional compassionate circumstances related to his mother and not himself, so he was forced to rely on s 65 (human rights appeal), which referred to a breach of 'his human rights'.

4   Although s 84(1)(c) and (g) refer to 'the appellant's human rights', s 84(1)(e) refers to a decision being 'otherwise not in accordance with the law', and contains no restriction, unlike Immigration and Asylum Act 1999, Sch 4, para 21 (see fn 3 above). The Tribunal has held that because of the similarity of NIAA 2002, s 84(1)(g) and Immigration and Asylum Act 1999, s 65, SS *(Malaysia)* above applies also to an appeal under the 2002 Act: NS *(Sri Lanka)* [2005] UKIAT 00081. This means that the Tribunal is not concerned with possible breaches of non-appellants' human rights resulting from an immigration decision, save to the extent that such breaches impact on the appellant's human rights. As the law presently stands, and as the Tribunal itself has expressly stated (see *Kehinde v Secretary of State for the Home Department* (2001) (01TH 02668) (starred); SS *(Malaysia)*; AC *(Turkey)* [2004] UKIAT 00122) the remedy for non-appellants in respect of an immigration decision said to affect their human rights is judicial review.

5   For consideration of s 85 see 18.48 above and 18.63 below.

6   The Tribunal appears to have accepted that this is the correct interpretation of the phrase in an appeal raising asylum grounds, in OB *(Somalia)* [2005] UKIAT 'Reported'.

18.50 Another difficult issue, which has dogged the appellate authorities and the courts for decades, has been the question of how far the appellate authorities can and must have regard to the general principles of administrative law when considering the actions and decisions of the Secretary of State or an immigration officer, where these involve the exercise of a discretion. In the case of *Singh*[1] the House of Lords held that the appellate authorities were not precluded from examining any aspect of the Secretary of State's broad discretion in deportation cases. Lord Bridge reasoned that the appellate jurisdiction to determine whether a decision was in accordance with the law had to embrace the general requirements of administrative law and so an appeal would be allowed if the Secretary of State had failed to have regard to all relevant circumstances.[2] He equated the adjudicator's jurisdiction with the supervisory jurisdiction of the High Court in such circumstances. The judgment in *Singh* gave rise to almost two decades of litigation on the scope of appellate jurisdiction.[3] Much of it was concerned with appeals against decisions taken outside the immigration rules, where appellants argued that refusal, while in accordance with immigration rules, failed to have regard to relevant policies (such as the Somali family reunion policy which operated in the 1980s and 1990s, the various marriage and cohabitation policies and the long residence policy), and thus breached the general principles of administrative law referred to by Lord Bridge in *Singh*. In *Abdi*,[4] the Court of Appeal, while observing that 'it is not obvious that Parliament intended adjudicators to have the power to examine the validity of the Home Secretary's decision by reference to all the matters that would be relevant for a judicial review of that decision', went on to 'proceed on the footing that if it can be shown that the Home Secretary failed to act in accordance with established principles of administrative or common law, for example if he did not take account of or give effect to his own published policy, that was 'not in accordance with the law'.⁵ The Court of Appeal's endorsement of this principle in *Abdi* was followed in *Hersi*.⁶ The court in *Abdi* held that the exercise of discretion outside the rules was flawed if refusal was predicated on misapprehension of material facts, which was held to be a further head of illegality.⁷ Beyond that, however, the courts have been reluctant to go, and (with some notable exceptions such as Professor Jackson's embrace of legitimate expectation as falling within appellate jurisdiction⁸) the Tribunal has generally disavowed a broader jurisdiction, embracing for example procedural unfairness or appeals based on reasons challenges,⁹ mindful still of the warning of the Divisional Court in *Mumin's case* (where the Tribunal had held a decision outside the rules to be unlawful for procedural unfairness), that 'it would be prudent of chairmen of tribunals to leave such matters to this court, which is accustomed to dealing with them'.¹⁰

1 *Singh v Immigration Appeal Tribunal* [1986] 2 All ER 721, [1986] Imm AR 352, HL.
2 *Associated Provincial Picture Houses Ltd v Wednesbury Corpn* [1948] 1 KB 223, [1948] 2 All ER 680 – the origin of the '*Wednesbury* unreasonable' test in administrative law.
3 For a detailed exposition see 5th edn, 18.64–18.87.
4 *Abdi (Dhudi Saleban) v Secretary of State for the Home Department* [1996] Imm AR 148, CA.
5 *Abdi* above at 157.
6 *Hersi v Secretary of State for the Home Department* [1996] Imm AR 569, CA.
7 *Abdi*, fn 4 above; see now, on material mistake of fact, *E v Secretary of State for the Home Department* [2004] EWCA Civ 49, [2004] 2 WLR 1351. In such cases, the normal approach was for the Tribunal to find the relevant facts and to state that the issue remained outstanding, for determination on those facts, by the decision-maker. For the impact of human rights jurisdiction see 18.52 below.
8 Legitimate expectation was the basis of the decision in *Odozi* (9582), *Gyeabour* [1989] Imm AR 94, *Dave* (11313) (6 September 1994, unreported); *Suleman* (16371) (11 August 1998, unreported), IAT. In the context of tribunal jurisdiction, it is perhaps better expressed in terms of consistency and fairness (a stated aim of the rules), or having regard to relevant policies. But in *Entry Clearance Officer, Tehran v Arezi* [2002] UKIAT 07694, the Tribunal held that explicit assurances by the ECO gave rise to a substantive legitimate expectation of the grant of entry clearance under the family reunion policy; cf *K (Russia)* [2004] UKIAT 00082, where the Tribunal held that the 'October exercise' (for which see 12.178 above) gave rise to no substantive expectation since it required the exercise of discretion.
9 See e g *Duzgun v Entry Clearance Officer Istanbul* (00TH00754) (5 June 2000, unreported), where the Tribunal (Mr Freeman) succinctly rejected an appeal against refusal of entry clearance outside the rules based on a reasons challenge, on the ground that the Tribunal's task was to decide the appeal on the merits, and the decision, although inadequately reasoned, was not patently wrong.
10 *R v Immigration Appeal Tribunal, ex p Secretary of State for the Home Department* [1992] Imm AR 554, QBD, known as *Mumin's case* after the original appellant, whose application to switch (outside the rules) from visitor to student was refused in a decision held by the Tribunal to be flawed for unfairness (a conclusion rejected by the Divisional Court). The clear implication of the Divisional Court's warning was that the appellate authorities should stick to merits appeals; *Abdi* and *Hersi* are, on this reading, limited exceptions by reference to published policy.

18.51 The issue has lost some of its relevance, now that no right of appeal attaches against refusal to allow someone to remain for a purpose other than one for which entry or stay is permitted under the rules.[1] There is still room for an argument that the decision is 'not in accordance with the law' under section 86(3)(a), in cases where the *purpose* of stay is recognised by the rules, although waiver of part of the rule's requirements, or an extension of its application, is sought, in accordance with Home Office policy, and section 86(6) precludes argument on the merits of the extra-statutory discretion.[2] This might apply, for example, to cases involving family reunion (a purpose recognised by the rules) where the sponsor has discretionary leave (a status which does not provide for immediate family reunion). Another factor limiting the relevance of these old arguments on jurisdiction is that many of the policies which formed the basis of extra-rules appeals have now been incorporated into the rules,[3] and even where they have not, since policies are generally based on human rights considerations, many of the old arguments can be recast to better effect in human rights terms.[4] This has the added benefit that the Tribunal can decide the issue, allow the appeal and where appropriate issue directions for the grant of leave or entry clearance, rather than leaving it for the Secretary of State to decide on the proper basis – the limit of what could generally[5] be achieved in appeals relating to extra-rules discretion before the Human Rights Act.[6] Nevertheless, in appeals against removal in particular, it is still possible to argue that a decision is not in accordance with the law because it fails to have regard to a relevant policy (such as that on expulsion of families with children),[7] and this can be a free-standing ground of appeal; although the prerequisite of an in-country appeal against removal is an asylum or human rights claim in the UK, the appeal is not limited purely to human rights grounds.[8]

1   Nationality, Immigration and Asylum Act 2002, s 88(2)(d), although it is arguable that once an appeal is brought under s 88(4) on human rights grounds, the Tribunal would be obliged to allow it if the decision is not in accordance with the law; in other words the human rights ground acts as a gateway to all the statutory grounds of appeal under s 84(1).

2   An example from earlier times would be the Somali Family Reunion Policy, which (inter alia) extended the scope of family reunion to all family members living as part of the family unit before the sponsor's departure. The purpose of the stay, family reunion, was clearly recognised under the rules, but its extension to relatives other than spouse and minor children required extra-statutory discretion, not appealable on the merits but appealable by reference to the terms of the policy itself.

3   For example, former policies on long residence, unmarried partners, domestic violence, access to UK-based children are now all within the rules.

4   Policies on expulsion (eg of children, partners or spouses) may be used in human rights arguments, for example, to show that there is no public interest in removal under Art 8(2) (because the Secretary of State recognises the situation as one in which removal should not take place), as well as making the decision not in accordance with the law (for failure to apply the policy).

5   In some of the legitimate expectation line of cases (18.50 fn 8 above) the Tribunal held it could give effect to a substantive legitimate expectation. Where the application of a policy depends solely on a particular factual situation, without any element of discretion by the Secretary of State, the Tribunal held that the appellate authority could determine the matter itself, see *Umujakporne* (12448) (18 August 1995, unreported), IAT; but this was rare: see *Abdi (Dhudi Saleban)* [1996] Imm AR 148, CA.

6   The Tribunal cannot exercise the Secretary of State's discretion: NIAA 2002, s 86(6), *Kausar* [1998] INLR 141.

7   DP5/96 as amended (sometimes known as DP069/99), see *R (on the application of Dabrowski) v Secretary of State for the Home Department* [2003] EWCA Civ 580, [2003] Imm AR 454, [2003] INLR 411. However, policy considerations must be raised at the appropriate time, and the Tribunal has held that it is premature to argue that the Secretary

of State has failed to have regard to a policy before he or she is required to consider it: *BV (Vietnam)* [2004] UKIAT 00148, on application of policy on unaccompanied asylum seeking children.
8   See NIAA 2002, s 92(4)(a).

18.52 It used to be a general rule that, if an application called for the exercise of a discretion which had not in fact been exercised, the decision was not in accordance with the law, and an appeal would be allowed to the extent that the Secretary of State should reconsider the case.[1] This was based on the principle that the appellate authority was not an original decision taker and, therefore, could not determine an application which had been made to the Secretary of State but not determined prior to appeal.[2] The rule has undergone modification in the asylum and human rights context, given the different nature of the appellate jurisdiction in these fields, where it has been held to be more of an extension of the original decision-making function.[3] The Tribunal held in *Haddad*,[4] an appeal against a refusal of asylum on 'non-compliance' grounds,[5] that the adjudicator had no power to remit an unconsidered claim to the Secretary of State for reconsideration, and should deal with the asylum claim on the merits, if necessary as a primary decision maker. The Court of Appeal endorsed this conclusion in *Zaier*,[6] holding that the adjudicator had no power to remit claims to the Secretary of State for reconsideration.[7] It is thus not uncommon, and certainly not unlawful, for a Tribunal to decide an asylum or human rights claim raised for the first time in a statement of additional grounds served with the notice of appeal and not considered by the Secretary of State, or indeed, raised for the first time by way of a late amendment to the grounds of appeal, and as indicated above, the wording of sections 85 and 86 of the NIAA 2002 now suggests that the Tribunal could not lawfully decline to do so. However, outside the asylum and human rights context, the principle that failure to consider all aspects of the application renders the decision 'not in accordance with the law' probably still holds good. Thus, where the Secretary of State misinterprets the application and fails to apply the correct rule to it, or applies only one of the applicable rules,[8] the appeal may be allowed to the extent that the application remains outstanding before the Secretary of State for consideration under the proper rule, although we suggest that it would not be unlawful for the Tribunal to deal with the case itself on the basis of the correct rule, provided the Secretary of State had been given the opportunity to deal with it by way of submissions.[9] In *Yau Yak Wah*[10] the Court of Appeal held that a decision was not in accordance with the law where the Secretary of State had failed to give separate consideration to the case of each appellant in a case involving different members of a family, and thus failed to exercise discretion.

1   Sometimes this was expressed as the matter remaining outstanding before the decision-maker: see eg *Ibeakanma* (18632) (25 September 1998, unreported), IAT; *Adeyemi* (17115) (20 May 1998, unreported), IAT. See *H (Somalia)* [2004] UKIAT 00027.
2   *R v Immigration Appeal Tribunal, ex p Malik* (1981) Times, 16 November, Forbes J.
3   *Ravichandran v Secretary of State for the Home Department* [1996] Imm AR 97 (asylum); *R (on the application of Razgar) v Secretary of State for the Home Department* [2004] UKHL 27, [2004] 3 WLR 58, (human rights).
4   [2000] INLR 117, IAT.
5   For 'non-compliance' refusals of asylum under HC 395, para 340 see 12.130 above.
6   *R (on the application of Zaier) v Secretary of State for the Home Department* [2003] EWCA Civ 937, [2003] All ER (D) 153 (Jul).

7   However, *Zaier* was an appeal under the Asylum and Immigration Appeals Act 1993, s 8, in which the jurisdiction of the adjudicator was limited to consideration of whether the removal of the appellant would breach the UK's Refugee Convention obligations. In that context, the Court held that there was no power to do anything other than to determine the appeal, and that the direction to the Secretary of State to reconsider the asylum claim on its merits was not a procedural direction relating to the just, timely and effective disposal of the appeal, but related to a substantive issue. Following *Mwanza* [2001] Imm AR 557, CA, the court held the direction *ultra vires* the procedure rules. The court did not consider whether the 'not in accordance with the law' jurisdiction (then contained in the Immigration and Asylum Act 1999, Sch 4, para 21) would allow an adjudicator to allow an appeal against the non-compliance decision to the extent of holding that the claim remained outstanding before the Secretary of State.

8   *R v Secretary of State for the Home Department, ex p Ali* [1987] Imm AR 189.

9   This may be derived from Nationality, Immigration and Asylum Act 2002, s 86(2)(a), or from the lack of statutory powers of remittal from the Tribunal to the Secretary of State.

10 *Wah (Yau Yak) v Home Office* [1982] Imm AR 16, CA.

18.53 The Court of Appeal held in *Manshoora Begum*[1] that an immigration rule requiring certain classes of dependent relatives seeking entry to the UK to show (inter alia) that they enjoyed a standard of living substantially below that of their own country, was irrational and *ultra vires* the Immigration Act 1971 under which it was promulgated. The question whether the Tribunal itself has the power to hold rules *ultra vires* and invalid, rendering decisions made under them 'not in accordance with the law', has been answered in the negative by the Tribunal itself.[2] A starred Tribunal in *Pardeepan*[3] suggested without deciding that the *vires* of a commencement order under the IAA 1999 were a matter for the High Court, and in *Koprinov*[4] a Tribunal chaired by the President held it had no jurisdiction to decide whether a rule was *ultra vires*. However, the argument has shifted since the Human Rights Act to the question of compatibility with Convention rights, and the usual approach is for the Tribunal simply to disapply rules whose application in the particular case would result in a disproportionate interference with family or private life rights.[5]

1   *R v Immigration Appeal Tribunal, ex p Begum (Manshoora)* [1986] Imm AR 385.

2   The Court of Appeal in *Begum* assumed that the Tribunal did not possess this power, although in the later case of *Chief Adjudication Officer v Foster* [1993] AC 754, [1993] 1 All ER 705 the House of Lords, considering an analogous power possessed by the Chief Adjudication Officer on an appeal from a Social Security Appeal Tribunal, ruled that the Social Security Commissioner could determine the *vires* of a regulation under his or her 'erroneous in point of law' jurisdiction.

3   *Pardeepan v Secretary of State for the Home Department* [2000] INLR 447. The Tribunal proceeded on the basis that the order was *intra vires*. See also *Singh (Pawandeep)* (18465) (16 March 1999, unreported), IAT, where the Tribunal held that it had no power to determine whether the rules on adoption ran counter to the statutory scheme of the Adoption Act. In refusing leave to appeal, however, Buxton LJ was prepared to accept, without deciding, that the tribunal would have jurisdiction to enter upon that inquiry in an appropriate case, although in this case the rule was not *ultra vires*: SLJ 99/6917/4, 2 December 1999.

4   (01TH 00091) (5 February 2001, unreported).

5   See eg *R v Secretary of State for the Home Department, ex p Ali (Arman)* [2000] Imm AR 134, [2000] INLR 89; *Begum (Husna) v Entry Clearance Officer, Dhaka* [2001] INLR 115, *Boadi v Entry Clearance Officer, Ghana* [2002] UKIAT 01323, [2003] INLR 54 for discussions on interpretation and application of rules so as to give effect to human rights. See 8.13 above. The Tribunal is not given power to strike down legislation which is incompatible with the Convention, or to give a declaration of incompatibility: see 8.14 above.

Scottish or English law

18.54 The Immigration Acts and Rules apply throughout the UK and there is a unified appellate authority. This should mean that the law is the same in both Scotland and England. There are divergences in higher court decisions, particularly in areas such as detention,[1] in the exclusion of unfairly obtained evidence in illegal entry decisions,[2] and over the issue of delay in judicial review,[3] but in asylum cases at least, the distinctions between Scottish and English decisions are more apparent than real. Two questions arise. The first is a choice of law and the second a choice of jurisdiction. First, if there is a conflict between the Scottish and English decisions, which law should the Tribunal apply? In *Akbar*[4] the Tribunal suggested that if the judicial approach differs in any material way, it will be for the appellate authority to decide with which legal system the case is most closely connected. Secondly, can appellants choose whether to litigate in Scotland or England? At Tribunal level, the matter does not arise, since there is no distinct appellate unit in either jurisdiction. In applications for review and in appeals from determinations by the Tribunal the choice of jurisdiction is determined by statute. The appeal goes to the Court of Session where the determination of the Tribunal is made in Scotland and in all other cases to the Court of Appeal;[5] the application for review of a Tribunal decision made in Scotland goes to the Outer House of the Court of Session, and otherwise, to the Administrative Court.[6] Decisions of the Tribunal in Northern Ireland go on appeal to the Northern Ireland Court of Appeal and on review to the High Court in Northern Ireland.[7]

[1]   *Sokha v Secretary of State for the Home Department* [1992] Imm AR 14, CS.
[2]   *Oghonoghor v Secretary of State for the Home Department* 1995 SLT 733; *Kim (Sofia) v Secretary of State for the Home Department* 2000 SLT 249, OHCS, Lord Abernethy.
[3]   *Singh (Gurjit)* (14 March 2000, unreported), OH CS, Lord Nimmo Smith.
[4]   (8670) IAT.
[5]   Nationality, Immigration and Asylum Act 2002, s 103B(5), (6) (inserted by Asylum and Immigration (Treatment of Claimants, etc) Act 2004, s 26). The Court of Appeal's decision in *Gardi v Secretary of State for the Home Department* [2002] EWCA Civ 750 [2003] Imm AR 39, [2002] INLR 499 was nullified (see *Gardi v Secretary of State for the Home Department (No 2)* [2002] EWCA Civ 1560, [2002] INLR 557) because it transpired that the decision on appeal emanated from an adjudicator sitting in Scotland, and so should have gone to the Court of Session under the previous provisions, Immigration and Asylum Act 1999, Sch 4, para 23(3).
[6]   NIAA 2002, s 103A(9), (10) as inserted. Although prior to the NIAA 2002 there was no statutory jurisdictional bar on the High Court hearing applications for review of decisions from adjudicators in Scotland, Jackson J declined jurisdiction in *R (on the application of Majead) v Secretary of State for the Home Department* [2002] EWHC 2299 (Admin), citing by analogy the provisions of the IAA 1999 (above). See the Court of Appeal's judgment at [2003] EWCA Civ 615.
[7]   NIAA 2002, s 103A(9)(c).

18.55 In applications for judicial review of decisions of the Secretary of State, the question is not so easily determined: the English Administrative Court or the Scottish Court of Session may each have or claim jurisdiction. In *Sokha*[1] the Court of Session resolved the matter by the application of the doctrine of *forum non conveniens*, and rejected jurisdiction in a case with no Scottish connection. Although strong preference should be given to the forum chosen by the applicant, particularly where the alternative jurisdiction is another part of the UK, rather than a wholly foreign country, this preference may be overcome if the respondent can 'establish that there is another available forum which is clearly and distinctly more appropriate', although less advantageous.[2]

1   *Sokha v Secretary of State for the Home Department* [1992] Imm AR 14, Ct of Sess.
2   *Spiliada Maritime Corpn v Cansulex Ltd, The Spiliada* [1987] AC 460, per Lord Goff; *Trendtex Trading Corpn v Crédit Suisse* [1982] AC 679; *Abidin Daver, The* [1984] AC 398 at 411. The Court of Appeal held in *Majead* [2003] EWCA Civ 615 that judicial review should be brought in the country where the appeal was heard.

'Including immigration rules'

18.56 For the purposes of section 86(3)(a), 'the law' includes 'immigration rules' but is not synonymous with them. We have considered above situations where it is argued that the immigration rules themselves do not adequately reflect the relevant law.[1] But in many if not most cases, the Tribunal's first port of call, if not its last, will be the immigration rules. If a decision is not in accordance with immigration rules, the appeal should be allowed, subject to the proviso already referred to (that a removal decision will not be invalid because the wrong provision is cited, if the person is removable under another provision).[2] Thus, where the wrong rule is applied, and the decision is based on grounds which are inapplicable to the applicant, the decision is not in accordance with rules[3]; nor is it in accordance with immigration rules where the evidence before the Tribunal establishes the appellant's eligibility for entry under the relevant rule.[4] Because of this provision the immigration rules have the force of law for the purposes of appeals, though not for other purposes.[5] The case law reflects some conflict between two principles: on the one hand, the appellate authority must ensure that the decision is in accordance with immigration rules generally, implying a broad jurisdiction;[6] on the other, it is only entitled to determine that which is before it for determination.[7] The position may be summarised as follows:

(1)   The Tribunal is not restricted to the particular rule or part of a rule relied on in the notice of decision or explanatory statement, but, having found the facts, is entitled to apply the immigration rules applicable to the case having regard to those facts, subject to giving the parties a fair opportunity to deal with the issue.[8] This applies whether the new rule involves mandatory refusal or the exercise of discretion;[9]

(2)   The Tribunal is not entitled, however, to go behind a finding of fact of the Secretary of State favourable to the appellant;[10]

(3)   Similarly, the respondent may seek to rely on a new rule applicable to the facts, subject to providing the appellant with a fair opportunity to deal with the new rule, by amendment of the refusal decision or the issue of a new explanatory statement;[11]

(4)   The respondent may not, however, seek to alter the statutory basis of its decision, eg by relying on a wholly different deportation power in the Immigration Act 1971 from that originally exercised;[12]

(5)   The principle for appellants is that if they make clear the facts that they rely on when making their application, they are not required to set out all the different potentially applicable immigration rules.[13] They must be permitted to ventilate on appeal eligibility under rules other than those previously considered by the respondent, provided the fact found

forms part of the basis of the decision, since to hold otherwise would mean that the scope of the right of appeal would be confined to the basis on which the respondent chose to frame it.[14] The pre-2002 Act cases suggest that there is no jurisdiction to allow an appeal against a decision on the basis that if the application had been made on another ground it might have qualified under another section of the rules,[15] particularly if the grounds are mutually exclusive, but this restriction may no longer apply, given the one-stop principle and its draconian enforcement by NIAA 2002, s 96 on the one hand, and on the other, the new broad jurisdiction of the AIT;[16]

(6) The Tribunal may on its own initiative have regard to any particular rule that bears on the case put forward by the appellant with regard to the decision or action appealed against,[17] but it is not required to conduct a roving inquiry into whether the facts could fit any conceivable rule in the absence of submissions to that effect;[18]

(7) The appellant may raise wholly new matters on appeal, in response to a one-stop warning, by providing a statement of additional grounds.[19] Where no one-stop warning has been issued, we suggest that he or she may raise new matters by amendment to the grounds of appeal (subject to the consent of the Tribunal, which ought to give consent, provided the respondent is given a fair opportunity to deal with the new issues) otherwise, once more the scope of the appeal would be determined by the respondent, in this case by its failure to serve a one-stop notice.[20]

---

1   See also *M & A v Secretary of State for the Home Department* [2003] EWCA Civ 263, [2003] Imm AR 4, where the Court of Appeal emphasised that the rules must be given a purposive construction, so that the requirement that there be 'adequate accommodation' for children seeking to join parents would not be met when there were serious welfare concerns about the children living with their parents.

2   Nationality, Immigration and Asylum Act 2002, s 86(4).

3   *R v Immigration Appeal Tribunal, ex p Khan* [1975] Imm AR 26. This happens most frequently in cases involving family settlement, where for example the 'living alone in the most exceptional compassionate circumstances' test is wrongly applied to an appellant. This does not, of course, mean that the appellant would succeed on the merits under the correct rule, and there would be no point in allowing the appeal to the extent of holding that the issue remains outstanding before the Secretary of State or ECO for reconsideration under the correct rule, if it would make no difference to the result. That is why the Tribunal may – and perhaps should – instead consider the appeal under the correct rule, subject to giving the appellant a fair opportunity to deal with the issue; see below.

4   For a case which illustrates both the 'law' and 'rules' jurisdiction neatly, see *Ibeakanma* (18632) (25 September 1998, unreported).

5   *Pearson v Immigration Appeal Tribunal* [1978] Imm AR 212; *R v Secretary of State for the Home Department, ex p Hosenball* [1977] 3 All ER 452, [1977] 1 WLR 766, CA; *Singh v Immigration Appeal Tribunal* [1986] 2 All ER 721, [1986] Imm AR 352, HL.

6   *R v Immigration Appeal Tribunal, ex p Khan* [1975] Imm AR 26; *R v Immigration Appeal Tribunal, ex p Hubbard* [1985] Imm AR 110, QBD.

7   *R v Immigration Appeal Tribunal, ex p Akhtar* (1982) 126 Sol Jo 430, QBD. The Tribunal leant towards this approach in *Immigration Officer (Nigeria)* [2004] UKIAT 00179, holding that applicants for entry clearance 'are entitled to assume that their ability to satisfy particular requirements of the rules has not been put in issue unless the entry clearance officer unequivocally puts it in issue'. Although the Tribunal recognised that the immigration judge could give the appellant express notice that another requirement of the rules is being put in issue, it went on to observe that the injustice to the appellant caused by the delay inherent in such a procedure was likely to outweigh that caused by assuming that requirements not put in issue were in fact met.

8 *R v Immigration Appeal Tribunal, ex p Hubbard* [1985] Imm AR 110; *R v Immigration Appeal Tribunal, ex p Malik* (1981) Times, 16 November, QBD; *Agyen-Frempong v Immigration Appeal Tribunal* [1988] Imm AR 262, CA; see also *Entry Clearance Officer, Manila v Brey* [2002] UKIAT 06655.
9 *Tahir (Nadeem) v Immigration Appeal Tribunal* [1989] Imm AR 98, CA.
10 *R v Immigration Appeal Tribunal, ex p Hubbard* [1985] Imm AR 110. There is a distinction between a positive finding of fact or credibility by the Secretary of State, which the Tribunal should not seek to subvert, and a mere failure to take the point by the Secretary of State, which leaves the Tribunal free to do so: *Carcabuk and Bla* (00TH01426) (18 May 2000, unreported), IAT. But see *Immigration Officer (Nigeria)* [2004] UKIAT 00179 (fn 7 above).
11 *R v Immigration Appeal Tribunal, ex p Hubbard* [1985] Imm AR 110; *Parsaiyan* [1986] Imm AR 155, IAT; *Uddin v Immigration Appeal Tribunal* [1991] Imm AR 134, CA.
12 *R v Immigration Appeal Tribunal, ex p Mehmet* [1978] Imm AR 46; *Secretary of State for the Home Department v Ziar (Salah)* [1997] Imm AR 456, [1997] INLR 221 (grounds for certification of claim).
13 *Khatun (Kessori)* (4272).
14 *Rahman (Aklakur)* (00TH00307) (10 March 2000).
15 *Uddin (Hawa Bibi) v Immigration Appeal Tribunal* [1991] Imm AR 134, CA (application on the basis of marriage which was found invalid; appeal raised issue of common law relationship).
16 In particular, the omission of the definite article in s 84(1)(a) and the breadth of the matters to be considered in s 86(2)(b) and s 85(2), (4). For the position under the old law see *Hussain (Shabir)* [1991] Imm AR 483 (IAT).
17 *Uddin (Hawa Bibi) v Immigration Appeal Tribunal* [1991] Imm AR 134, CA; *R v Immigration Appeal Tribunal, ex p Ali (Tohur)* [1987] Imm AR 189, QBD; whether the appellate authority ought to do so was reserved in Court of Appeal [1988] Imm AR 237. In *Seymour (Selwyn)* [2002] UKIAT 00594 the Tribunal accepted that the adjudicator could have dealt with the appeal on the alternative basis put forward by the appellant.
18 *Ali (Mohammed Frazor) v Secretary of State for the Home Department* [1988] Imm AR 274, CA; *R v Immigration Appeal Tribunal, ex p Uddin (Hawa)* [1990] Imm AR 309, QBD; on appeal [1991] Imm AR 134, CA; *Robinson v Immigration Appeal Tribunal* [1997] Imm AR 568, CA. But see text and fn 16 above.
19 See 18.48ff above.
20 Cf *Rahman (Aklakur)*, fn 13 above. See discussion at 18.52 above.

18.57 Where a requirement of a rule has been waived by the Secretary of State, whether in the individual case or in the class of case to which the appellant belongs, it cannot be applied to the appellant without good cause, and a decision which did so would not be in accordance with the law. See 18.61 below.

Discretion should be exercised differently

18.58 Where persons are subject to immigration control, the Secretary of State for the Home Department and immigration officers have a general discretion as to who should be admitted and in what circumstances. Section 4(1) of the Immigration Act 1971 gives the responsibility to immigration officers of granting leave to enter and that of leave to remain to the Secretary of State. Under section 3(2) of the IA 1971, the Secretary of State is empowered to make immigration rules as to the practice to be followed in the administration of the Act for regulating the entry into and stay in the UK of persons required by the Act to have leave to enter. Thus, it is clear that under the IA 1971 the Secretary of State has a general and wide discretion to determine who can be admitted to the UK and in what circumstances, both through the guidelines set out in the immigration rules and in particular cases or situations not covered by the rules.[1] The Immigration Directorate Instructions (IDI) and the Asylum Policy Instructions (API), and other published material such as ministerial statements and parliamentary answers, provide detailed guidelines as to the exercise of discretion both inside and outside the immigration rules. Although many published policies have been brought within the immigration rules following the coming into force of the Human Rights Act 1998, dealing with matters such as the admission of children for adoption, the admission and stay of domestic workers, the treatment of spouses who have suffered domestic violence during their 'probationary period' in the UK and the 'long residence' rule,[2] other policies, dealing with the bringing of enforcement action against family members of those with residence rights in the UK,[3] or the grant of indefinite leave and family reunion rights to those with humanitarian protection or exceptional or discretionary leave to remain,[4] have not. There are also cases where the Secretary of State will allow someone to remain exceptionally, in the exercise of his or her general discretion, although the immigration rules expressly say that they should not qualify.

[1]   In *R v Secretary of State for the Home Department, ex p Ahmed and Patel* [1998] INLR 570 there was an inconclusive discussion on whether the extra-rules discretion in relation to the admission of aliens was derived from the statute or the prerogative. See *R v Immigration Appeal Tribunal and Immigration Appeal Adjudicator, ex p Secretary of State for the Home Department* [1990] Imm AR 166. The issue remains unresolved, but of little importance given the equal reviewability of both types of discretion following the GCHQ case, *Council of Civil Service Unions v Minister for the Civil Service* [1985] 1 AC 374.
[2]   See HC 395, paras 316A (admission of children for adoption, see 11.111 above); 159A (domestic workers, see 10.18 above); 289A (domestic violence, see 11.70 above); 276A (long residence, see 16.47 above).
[3]   For these policies see 11.74, 11.122 and 16.48 above.
[4]   For family reunion for those with these forms of leave see 12.182 above.

Discretion under the rules

18.59 In cases where the application of an immigration rule involves the exercise of a discretion, section 86(3)(b) of the Nationality, Immigration and Asylum Act 2002 empowers the appellate authorities to review the exercise of the discretion on the merits. In other words the Tribunal is not limited to determining whether the original decision was in accordance with the law, including immigration rules, but is required to consider whether the discretion should be exercised differently.[1] Whether there has been fresh evidence or not,[2] whether the evidence discloses a different factual situation to that before the original decision-maker or not, the Tribunal may exercise discretion differently and allow the appeal, or may uphold the decision on different grounds.[3] Where the focus of the decision-making process has been on how the discretion should be exercised, the Tribunal can go straight to this aspect of the case without being bound to make a finding on the lawfulness of the decision under section 86(3)(a) of the NIAA 2002.[4] This is a very wide power, particularly in the context of a deportation appeal, which is a balancing exercise in which all relevant factors are weighed.[5] However, the Court of Appeal in *N (Kenya)*, while acknowledging the breadth of the power, nonetheless set limits which appear to require deference to the policy reasons for the Secretary of State's decision.[6]

1   *R v Immigration Appeal Tribunal, ex p Desai* [1987] Imm AR 18.
2   *Begum (Zakia) v Visa Officer, Islamabad* [1988] Imm AR 465.
3   *Tahir (Nadeem) v Immigration Appeal Tribunal* [1989] Imm AR 98, CA.
4   *R v Immigration Appeal Tribunal, ex p Razaque* [1989] Imm AR 451, QBD.
5   *R v Immigration Appeal Tribunal, ex p Bakhtaur Singh* [1986] Imm AR 352 at 361; *R v Immigration Appeal Tribunal, ex p Dhaliwal* [1994] Imm AR 387 at 391.
6   *R (on the application of N) v Secretary of State for the Home Department* [2004] EWCA Civ 1094, [2004] INLR 612, para 64, but see Sedley LJ's dissenting remarks, at para 74, 77, with which we respectfully agree.

18.60 As we have seen, section 86(6) of the Nationality, Immigration and Asylum Act 2002 imposes limits on the use of the power to exercise discretion differently. This provides that refusal to depart from or to authorise departure from the immigration rules is not an exercise of discretion for the purposes of section 86(3)(b). The Tribunal's jurisdiction to review the decision in such a case is limited to deciding whether it is not in accordance with the law, which has been considered above.[1]

1   See 18.49 above. This was held in *Singh v Secretary of State for the Home Department* [1991] Imm AR 195 to apply to an application for further exceptional leave to remain, following the grant of a period of exceptional leave to remain: the Secretary of State was entitled to refuse under the rules, limiting the adjudicator's jurisdiction on appeal. Now, there would be no appeal against such a refusal of an application to remain 'for a purpose outside the rules' (Nationality, Immigration and Asylum Act 2002, s 88(2)(d)), except on human rights or discrimination grounds, ie compatibility with the Race Relations Act or with the Human Rights Convention, under s 84(1)(b), (c) or (g).

18.61 A request to depart from the rules arises where there is a rule requiring mandatory refusal of the application. This applies even where the Secretary of State has a policy outside the rules, thereby indicating that the discretion will normally be exercised within the terms of the policy and not the rules. A discretion exercised under the rules instead of the policy will, in such a situation, be 'not in accordance with the law' but the appellate authority cannot substitute its own decision on the merits. In *Abdi*[1] the Court of Appeal rejected the argument that a policy constituted a revised legal framework whereby the Secretary of State has agreed to depart from the rules. In *Kausar*[2] the Tribunal agreed that the policy of the Secretary of State – in applying the maintenance and accommodation criteria in family reunion cases so as to exclude only those whose arrival would cause additional recourse to public funds – appeared a de facto amendment to the rules by way of concession, but insisted that, while the adjudicator should make formal findings on the evidence, it could not take the decision itself on the basis of the concession. However, in *Scott*[3] the Tribunal exercised a full merits review on the exercise of discretion under the rule as de facto amended.

1   *Abdi (Dhudi Saleban) v Secretary of State for the Home Department* [1996] Imm AR 148, CA.
2   *Kausar v Entry Clearance Officer, Islamabad* [1998] INLR 141, IAT, followed in *Bi (Sakina)* [2002] UKIAT 01092, IAT.
3   (13389), IAT.

18.62 Where on appeal it has been determined that a discretion outside the rules has not been exercised properly, or at all, so that the decision is 'not in accordance with the law', the appellate authorities may not substitute their own discretion. They may substitute their own decision only where the correct legal framework gives rise to no possibility of an adverse decision – the opposite of a discretionary situation.[1] Their proper role is to make relevant factual findings and allow the appeal, remitting it to the primary decision-maker for decision in accordance with those facts and the correct legal framework.[2]

[1] See above.
[2] *Kausar v Entry Clearance Officer, Islamabad* [1998] INLR 141, IAT; *Bi (Sakina)* [2002] UKIAT 01092, IAT.

Reviewing questions of fact

18.63 In the exercise of its appellate jurisdiction under the Nationality, Immigration and Asylum Act 2002, section 86(3), the Tribunal can review the facts on which the decision under appeal was based. This power of review is no longer explicit, as it was under the 1971 and 1999 Acts,[1] but is to be implied by the provisions concerning evidence, and by the case law. In all appeals except appeals under section 82(1) against refusal of entry clearance or certificate of entitlement, the Tribunal 'may consider evidence about any matter which it thinks relevant to the substance of the decision, including evidence which concerns a matter arising after the date of the decision'.[2] In entry clearance and certificate of entitlement appeals, the Tribunal is limited to considering 'only the *circumstances appertaining* at the time of the decision to refuse'.[3] If Parliament intended to reverse a long line of case law and limit the Tribunal to *evidence* which was before the decision-maker at the time of the decision to refuse, it would have said so. This means that as far as questions of fact are concerned the Tribunal is not confined to the evidence which was before the immigration authority when they reached their decision or took action, but can consider all the evidence, including any further evidence found since the decision was taken, and in non-entry clearance or certificate of entitlement cases, evidence of facts which have arisen since, too. The Tribunal's fact-finding powers give it a different function from that of the Administrative Court on judicial review or statutory review, or the Court of Appeal, where the court is generally confined to the material which the minister or other body had before them.[4] In immigration appeals the Tribunal goes into the facts again,[5] and can correct factual errors made by the immigration authority,[6] and hear of facts which were unknown to the decision-maker.[7] By reason of this jurisdiction, and the power to determine exercises of discretion, the appellate authority can correct irrationality (eg failures to take into account important and relevant facts) and procedural unfairness (eg a failure to interview) without having to classify them as errors of law. But can it go further than that? Has the 2002 Act extended the appellate jurisdiction to make the Tribunal an extension of the decision-making process in all appeals (except those dealing with entry clearance or certificate of entitlement), as it has been hitherto in asylum and human rights appeals?[8] This would appear to be the effect of s 85(4), which requires anything relevant to the substance of the decision (rather than its particular justification) to be considered. The argument for a radical change in the Tribunal's jurisdiction gains support from the new one-stop provisions which require everything relevant to a right to remain to be considered by the Tribunal at one hearing; the breadth of the matters to be considered by s 85(2), which cannot be limited to matters in existence at the date of the original decision; the change from past to present tense in the statutory appeal grounds in s 84 (so that the Tribunal must allow the appeal if a decision 'is' unlawful).[9] However, in appeals against refusal of entry clearance and certificates of entitlement, any fresh evidence must relate to facts in existence at the time of the decision. The statute does not preclude consideration of post-decision facts (such as the birth of a child to a spouse or partner in a family reunion case), but the evidence is only relevant to the circumstances appertaining at the date of decision, ie whether at that date the couple intended to live together. Thirdly, the Tribunal must pay respect to the views of the entry clearance officer who has interviewed the appellant,[10] although it does not need to have fresh evidence before reversing the entry clearance officer.[11]

[1]   Immigration Act 1971, s 19(2); Immigration and Asylum Act 1999, Sch 4, para 21(3).
[2]   Nationality, Immigration and Asylum Act 2002, s 86(4), amended by Asylum and Immigration (Treatment of Claimants, etc) Act 2004, Sch 2, para 18.
[3]   NIAA 2002, s 86(5) as amended.
[4]   See *Ashbridge Investments Ltd v Minister of Housing* [1965] 3 All ER 371 at 374, CA. See 8.19 below for the role of the courts in human rights cases.
[5]   *R v Immigration Appeal Tribunal, ex p Hubbard* [1985] Imm AR 110, QBD.
[6]   *R v Secretary of State for the Home Department, ex p Husbadak* [1982] Imm AR 8.
[7]   *R v Immigration Appeal Tribunal, ex p Hassanin* [1987] 1 All ER 74, [1986] 1 WLR 1448, CA.
[8]   See *Ravichandran v Secretary of State for the Home Department* [1996] Imm AR 97 at 112; *R (on the application of Razgar) v Secretary of State for the Home Department* [2004] UKHL 27, [2004] 3 WLR 58, para 15.
[9]   See now *LS (Gambia)* [2005] UKIAT 00085, which supports this analysis.
[10] See *R v Immigration Appeal Tribunal, ex p Kwok On Tong* [1981] Imm AR 214, DC; *R v Immigration Appeal Tribunal, ex p Singh (Mahendra)* [1984] Imm AR 1, QBD. But the degree of deference due should not be exaggerated: *R (on the application of Hamfi) v Immigration Appeal Tribunal, Secretary of State for the Home Department* [2004] EWHC 939 (Admin), Collins J.
[11] *Begum (Zakia) v Visa Officer, Islamabad* [1988] Imm AR 465; *Entry Clearance Officer, Karachi v Ahmad (Zafar)* [1989] Imm AR 254.

18.64   A redetermination of facts on appeal after hearing oral evidence binds the Secretary of State unless the Tribunal's factual findings are perverse.[1] It used to be held that factual findings which related solely to the conditions in a particular country could not be binding.[2] The development by the Immigration Appeal Tribunal of 'country guidance' cases has modified the position, but not by as much as some immigration judges perhaps believe. In *S*,[3] Laws LJ held that such cases were 'intended in effect to be binding on the appellate authorities as to the factual state of affairs in [a particular country] absent a demonstrable change',[4] although appellants would 'of course be heard on any facts particular to his case, and ... evidence as to any deterioration in [the country] would be listened to'.[5] He held the notion of such cases in principle 'benign and practical' in attaining consistency of approach to the conditions in a particular country, but emphasised the importance of safeguards, and particularly a heightened duty on the Tribunal to give reasons for its conclusions in such cases.[6] There are difficulties and tensions inherent in the 'country guidelines' approach to bind immigration judges,[7] and it would certainly be an error of law for a Tribunal to adopt a cursory approach to its fact-finding function merely because of the existence of a country guidance case adverse to the appellant.

1 *R v Secretary of State for the Home Department, ex p Danaie* [1998] INLR 124, [1998] Imm AR 84, CA; *Onen* (14501) (2 February 1997, unreported) (ruling), (22101) (8 October 1999, unreported).
2 *Elhasoglu v Secretary of State for the Home Department* [1997] Imm AR 380; *Kamara v Secretary of State for the Home Department* [1997] Imm AR 105, CA.
3 *S v Secretary of State for the Home Department* [2002] EWCA Civ 539, [2002] INLR 416.
4 *S v Secretary of State for the Home Department* above, para 27.
5 Ibid.
6 *S v Secretary of State for the Home Department* above, para 29.
7 See Immigration Advisory Service *Country Guidelines cases: benign and practical?* (February 2005), which finds an inherent conflict in creating 'factual precedents' of cases in an adversarial context which not only turn on their particular facts, but also depend on the evidence put in by the parties. The study also found inadequate referencing of evidence in Tribunal decisions, obscure reasoning, expert evidence routinely rejected and relevant and up to date evidence ignored. We deal with *Country Guidelines* cases further at 18.142 below.

Determining liability for removal

18.65 Section 86(4) provides that for the purposes of subsection (3), a decision that a person should be removed from the UK under a provision is not to be regarded as unlawful if it could have been lawfully made by reference to removal under another provision. Thus, if the Tribunal determines that a person appealing against a decision to remove as an overstayer is an illegal entrant, or vice versa, the error in categorisation does not per se make the decision unlawful.[1] This does not mean that the appeal must be dismissed,[2] only that it should not be allowed on that basis. In the majority of appeals, it makes no difference at all whether the person is to be removed under one power or another, since the issue is whether removal would breach Refugee Convention or human rights obligations. This does not mean that illegal entry should be conceded in the absence of evidence; it still carries a stigma greater than overstaying an initial lawful stay, and could result in differential treatment on an application to return. In *Khawaja*[3] the House of Lords held that a person only became an illegal entrant by deception when the Home Office declared them to be such, and thus, in cases where the Secretary of State did not assert illegal entry, Tribunals should not attempt to usurp this function.[4] Section 86(4) does not give the Secretary of State the right to remove a person to a destination other than that permitted by the terms of Schedule 2, paragraph 8(1)(c) to the Immigration Act 1971.[5]

1 Nationality, Immigration and Asylum Act 2002, s 86(4).
2 This was previously the position if an appellant was held to be an illegal entrant: see Immigration and Asylum Act 1999, Sch 4, para 24(1) and (3).
3 *Khawaja v Secretary of State for the Home Department* [1984] AC 74, [1983] 1 All ER 765, HL.
4 *Watson v Immigration Officer, Gatwick* [1986] Imm AR 75, IAT. See also *R v Secretary of State for the Home Department, ex p Jayakody* [1982] 1 All ER 461, [1982] 1 WLR 405, CA; *R v Immigration Appeal Tribunal, ex p Akhtar* (1982) 126 Sol Jo 430, QBD.
5 See 16.56ff above.

The appellate jurisdiction in asylum and human rights appeals

18.66 While the jurisdiction of the Tribunal set out in section 86(3) of the Nationality, Immigration and Asylum Act 2002 applies equally to an appeal on asylum or human rights grounds under section 84(1)(g), in cases where no other appeal grounds are available, the ground of appeal is that the appellant's removal in consequence of the decision would breach the UK's obligations under the Refugee Convention or would be unlawful under section 6 of the Human Rights Act 1998 as incompatible with the Human Rights Convention.[1] This has positive and negative consequences for the Tribunal's jurisdiction on appeal. One the one hand, even where the Secretary of State has failed to consider a claim substantively but has refused an application for failure to attend an interview or complete a statement of evidence form, the Tribunal on appeal must decide whether the appellant's removal is in breach of the Refugee Convention (and, we suggest, the Human Rights Convention too).[2] An appeal on asylum grounds requires the Tribunal to decide whether, if returned, the appellant would face a real risk of persecution, even if for practical, political or other reasons the Home Office is not at that time removing persons to the country concerned.[3] On the other hand, the Tribunal has held that the limitation on the appellate jurisdiction precludes consideration of a human rights appeal where removal is not imminent.[4] This applies where, for example, an unaccompanied minor has been refused asylum but has been granted a period of humanitarian protection.[5] Because the statutory ground of appeal in such a situation is limited to asylum, ie Refugee Convention grounds,[6] and there is no longer an appeal against the grant of a lesser period of leave than that sought,[7] the effect on private life of being left in a state of uncertainty about the future, which was held capable of engagement of Article 8 ECHR in a concurring judgment in *HLR v France*,[8] cannot be litigated on appeal. An appeal under section 82 which suspends removal because the person has made an asylum or human rights claim in the UK which has not been certified clearly unfounded[9] (or a claim under Community law, for that matter),[10] is not limited to those grounds, however, but may include any or all of the statutory grounds under section 84(1). Such an appeal might encompass the lawfulness of the proposed removal destination, or arguably the lawfulness of the asylum procedure applied to a minor.[11] However, this does not apply to an appeal against refusal of leave to enter or refusal to vary leave where a ground of refusal is ineligibility; in such a case, any appeal may be brought only on discrimination, human rights or asylum grounds.[12] For the appellate jurisdiction in human rights and asylum appeals see 8.101ff and 12.158ff above.

1   Nationality, Immigration and Asylum Act 2002, s 86(3) read with s 84(1)(g), see also s 84(1)(c).
2   *Haddad (Ali)* [2000] INLR 117, *Busuulwa* (01TH 00239) IAT; see fn 1. Para 340 (non-compliance refusals) applies to asylum claims, while para 322(10) is an equivalent in non-asylum cases; and the principles of *Haddad* apply to removal which would breach either Convention. For a discussion of the wording of s 86(3) in relation to appeals on asylum and human rights grounds see 18.49 above.
3   *Saad v Secretary of State for the Home Department, Diriye v Secretary of State for the Home Department, Osorio v Secretary of State for the Home Department* [2001] EWCA Civ 2008, [2002] Imm AR 471, [2002] INLR 34; *R (Secretary of State for the Home Department) v Immigration Appeal Tribunal; R (on the application of Hwez) v Secretary of State for the Home Department* [2001] EWHC 1597 (Admin), [2002] Imm AR 116.

The difference between the Refugee and Human Rights Convention is that recognition under the Refugee Convention confers a particular status in international law: *L (Ethiopia)* [2003] UKIAT 00016, paras 62–63.

4   A risk is not imminent if the appellant has available a further effective remedy: *Vijayanathan and Pushpanajah v France* (1993)15 EHRR 62. The Tribunal held the risk of removal 'imminent' where an appellant no longer had leave to remain, in *P (Yugoslavia)* [2003] UKIAT 00017. In *L (Ethiopia)* [2003] UKIAT 00016 the Tribunal held that the risk of removal was not imminent where the Secretary of State had a policy of not removing those whom the destination country would not accept, so precluding a successful appeal on human rights grounds. See also *A (Eritrea)* [2003] 00063 'Reported'; *JC Ethiopia* [2005] UKIAT 00030.

5   *P (Yugoslavia)*. An appeal on asylum grounds only accrues once a person refused asylum has had leave to remain in the UK for over 12 months: NIAA 2002, s 83.

6   Under NIAA 2002, s 83.

7   NIAA 2002, s 82(2)(d); see 18.15 above.

8   (1997) 26 EHRR 29.

9   Ie under NIAA 2002, s 94.

10 NIAA 2002, s 92(4).

11 NIAA 2002, s 84(1)(e); see *Shaqiri* [2002] UKIAT 04159; *Melikli* [2002] UKIAT 07428.

12 NIAA 2002, s 88; see 18.21 above. Arguably, once an appeal has been brought on asylum or human rights grounds, ss 85 and 86 oblige the Tribunal to consider all the issues as set out there.

Discrimination appeals

18.67 Section 84(1)(b) of the NIAA 2002 provides that a person may appeal against an immigration decision on the ground that it is unlawful by virtue of section 19B of the Race Relations Act 1976.[1] However, an allegation of racial discrimination in (for example) refusal of leave to enter, does not make an appeal suspensive of removal, as it does if a human rights or asylum claim is made. In many cases, this would not present a problem, since the two grounds – race discrimination and human rights – would be likely to co-exist (for example, where the allegation related to refusal of leave to enter to visit family members).[2] But where the allegation related to refusal of leave to enter as a business visitor, and there were no relevant human rights grounds, the discrimination appeal would (in the absence of entry clearance) have to be conducted from abroad.

1   As amended by the Race Relations (Amendment) Act 2000: discrimination by public authorities. See 1.30 above.

2   This might breach Art 14 ECHR together with Art 8, and so be appealable under Nationality, Immigration and Asylum Act 2002, s 84(1)(c) and/or (g), as well as on race discrimination grounds s 84(1)(b).

Restricted jurisdiction in pre-October 2000 deportation appeals

18.68 On appeal against a decision to remove a person as an illegal entrant, an overstayer, a person who had breached conditions or remained by deception, or a family member of such a person, and in restricted deportation appeals under the Immigration Act 1988, the jurisdiction of the appellate authority used to be limited to deciding whether the Secretary of State had power in law to make the order for the reasons stated in the notice. The restriction no longer applies to those with appeals under the NIAA 2002. However, it still applies to the very small class of overstayers who applied before October 2000 for regularisation under the provisions of section 9 of the Immigration and Asylum Act 1999, who are refused regularisation and served with a decision to deport them, and who at the date of the decision have been in the UK for less than seven years.[1] The restriction on appellate jurisdiction does not allow a review of the merits of the decision to deport, nor does it allow the Tribunal to decide that the decision was 'not in accordance with the law'[2] for failure to comply with the ordinary principles of administrative law.[3] On such an appeal the Tribunal cannot claim a jurisdiction to protect the individual from the unfettered power of the executive.[4]

1   See 15.42 above.
2   See 18.49ff above.
3   The principle was settled in *R v Secretary of State for the Home Department, ex p Malhi* [1990] Imm AR 275, CA and *R v Secretary of State for the Home Department, ex p Oladehinde* [1991] 1 AC 254, [1990] 3 All ER 393, HL, and following *Chief Adjudication Officer v Foster* [1993] AC 754, [1993] 1 All ER 705, HL, was upheld by the Tribunal in *Singh (Dharam)* [1998] INLR 747.
4   *Rafiq (Robina) v Secretary of State for the Home Department* [1998] Imm AR 193, CA.

Giving directions where an appeal is allowed

18.69 Under section 87(1) of the Nationality, Immigration and Asylum Act 2002, where an appeal is allowed, the Tribunal may give a direction for the purpose of giving effect to the decision.[1] A direction is part of the Tribunal's decision on appeal, for the purposes of an application for review.[2] The person responsible for making the immigration decision must act in accordance with any relevant direction,[3] but directions have no effect while an in-time onward appeal or application for review may be brought, or has been brought and has not been finally determined, or where the Tribunal has made a reference under section 103C of the Act which is awaiting determination.[4] The power to make directions under this section is a completely separate power from the power of the Tribunal to give procedural directions for the conduct of the appeal, which is contained in the Procedure Rules.[5] Directions under the section (i) can only be given where an appeal is allowed, (ii) to give effect to the decision.[6] The difficulty is in defining when it is necessary to give directions. Where an application for entry clearance is made for settlement and an appeal against a refusal is allowed, there is little difficulty in directing that entry clearance should be issued in the capacity sought. This is because all relevant issues will now have been determined in favour of an appellant. The entry clearance officer will be bound by this direction in the absence of an appeal. But where the appeal is against a refusal of entry in some limited capacity, as a family visitor, an au pair or a student, it is likely that the passage of time since the decision will have led to a change of circumstances. The Tribunal has suggested that entry clearance should not generally be directed in these cases.[7] If the immigrant still seeks entry, the matter should be remitted for reconsideration by the entry clearance officer in the light of the decision.[8] In such circumstances the entry clearance officer would be bound by the positive findings in favour of the appellant unless it can be proved to a high civil standard that the findings were obtained by fraud,[9] but other issues such as *present* intentions or ability to maintain may be considered.[10] The direction given for the grant of entry clearance on a successful appeal is spent when such entry clearance is granted, and the failure of an appellant to use it does not oblige an entry clearance officer to grant another years later without a further decision.[11]

1   Nationality, Immigration and Asylum Act 2002, s 87. The power to make directions was formerly contained in Immigration and Asylum Act 1999, Sch 4, para 21(5) and para 22(5)–(7). The statutory power to make recommendations when allowing an appeal was rarely used and has been abolished.
2   NIAA 2002, s 87(4), amended by Asylum and Immigration (Treatment of Claimants, etc) Act 2004, Sch 2, para 19(b).
3   NIAA 2002, s 87(2).
4   NIAA 2002, s 87(3), amended by Asylum and Immigration (Treatment of Claimants, etc) Act 2004, Sch 2, para 19(a).
5   See Asylum and Immigration Tribunal (Procedure) Rules 2005, r 45.
6   Thus, the Secretary of State cannot be directed to issue a fresh refusal letter as a condition of defending a decision on appeal. The asylum rules are procedural, not substantive: *Mwanza v Secretary of State for the Home Department* [2001] Imm AR 557, [2001] INLR 616, CA; followed in *R (on the application of Emlik) v Immigration Appeal Tribunal* [2002] EWHC 1279 (Admin), [2002] All ER (D) 209 (Jun); *R (on the application of Zaier) v Immigration Appeal Tribunal* [2003] EWCA Civ 937, [2003] All ER (D) 153 (Jul), holding further that there was no power under the IAA 1999 to remit an asylum claim to the Secretary of State for redetermination. Directions issued for a purpose other than that of giving effect to the decision on appeal are of no effect: *Secretary of State for the Home Department v Fardy* [1972] Imm AR 192; *R v Immigration Appeal Tribunal, ex p Singh* [1984] Imm AR 1, QBD.
7   *MG (Jamaica)* [2004] UKIAT 00140, [2004] Imm AR 377, following *Immigration Officer, Heathrow v Obeid* [1986] Imm AR 341.
8   An alternative approach might be to direct entry clearance conditional on the production of up to date documents; *Visa Officer, Aden v Thabel* [1977] Imm AR 75. However, in *S (Yemen)* [2003] UKIAT 00008, the Tribunal held directions to an ECO to investigate the sponsor's property and domestic circumstances inappropriate, they were not direction for giving effect to a decision to allow a family visitor appeal, but for *not* giving effect to it unless satisfied on matters relevant to the genuineness of the visit..
9   *R v Immigration Appeal Tribunal, ex p Miah* [1987] Imm AR 143, QBD; *R v Secretary of State for the Home Department, ex p Yousuf* [1989] Imm AR 554; *R (on the application of Saribal) v Secretary of State for the Home Department* [2002] EWHC 1542 (Admin), [2002] INLR 596, [2002] All ER (D) 379 (Jul).
10   However, in the absence of an appeal, the failure to give directions to give effect to a determination relating to the subsistence of a marriage did not entitle the Secretary of State to issue a fresh decision after the marriage had broken down, and the applicant was entitled to the benefit of the positive determination: *R (on the application of Boafo) v Secretary of State for the Home Department* [2002] EWCA Civ 44, [2002] Imm AR 383, [2002] INLR 231.
11   *R v Secretary of State for the Home Department, ex p Moon* [1997] INLR 165, QBD. See also *Hashim* (6421), where directions were quashed by consent because there had been a change of circumstances and a fresh application for entry between the original decision and the appeal.

18.70 If on appeal the Tribunal finds that an appellant is a British citizen, directions may be given to the respondent for the issue of a certificate of entitlement to the right of abode.[1] In deportation cases, the question whether indefinite leave to remain or limited leave should be given following a successful appeal is one for the Secretary of State.[2] Similarly, following a successful appeal on human rights grounds, it is for the Secretary of State to decide on the length of leave to be granted.[3] The question of what directions it is lawful or appropriate to give on allowing an asylum appeal is unresolved, with divisions of the Tribunal holding on the one hand that the appellate authorities are entitled to give directions declaring that the appellant was a refugee at the date of decision, as well as the date of hearing,[4] and on the other, that it is not necessary for giving effect to the decision to direct the grant of status or its backdating, since the only direction required is leave to enter.[5] In our view, the latter view cannot be correct given that the withholding of refugee status would be contrary to the Convention, and effect is given to a successful asylum appeal not merely by the grant of leave, but specifically by granting recognition, whether or not that recognition must be backdated.[6] Where an asylum appeal was allowed but the appellant had by then been returned to the country of persecution (in a pre-1993 case where an appeal was not suspensive), the question arose whether directions should order his return to the UK.[7] The Tribunal decided that in view of the time that had passed since his removal and the lack of current knowledge of his circumstances, the appropriate direction was that, should he apply to a British post abroad, consideration should be given to the application as if he were in the UK. Clearly in such a case the entry clearance officer would be bound by the factual findings as to the past treatment of the appellant. The same reasoning should apply where an asylum seeker leaves the UK voluntarily before promulgation of the determination of his or her appeal.[8] We suggest that where a non-suspensive appeal takes place fairly speedily on removal, and is successful, there is no reason why directions should not be issued for the Secretary of State or his officers to use their best endeavours to facilitate the return of the appellant to the UK by the issue of an appropriate entry clearance.

1   *Rahman and Akhter* (00307) (10 March 2000, unreported), IAT.
2   *R v Secretary of State for the Home Department, ex p Botta* [1987] Imm AR 80; *Rathiesh* (14648) 14 March 1997, IAT.
3   *Sharif (Omeed)* [2002] UKIAT 00953. For the Secretary of State's policy on the period of discretionary leave granted, see 8.109 and 12.175 above.
4   *Haibe* [1997] INLR 119, IAT; *Belvue* (11834a), in accordance with the fact that refugees are recognised, not created, by the grant of refugee status: *Khaboka v Secretary of State for the Home Department* [1993] Imm AR 484, CA.
5   *Merzouk* [1999] INLR 468, IAT.
6   In *Altun (Guluzar)* (16628) (17 July 1998, unreported), the Tribunal held that 'there is nothing in the 1951 Convention which requires the determination of a notional point at which [an appellant] became a refugee', but accepted that the adjudicator could declare the appellant to be one.
7   *Kondo* (10413). There are as yet no reported determinations regarding the issue of directions to give effect to successful non-suspensive asylum or human rights appeals under the NIAA 2002.
8   Pending in-country appeals lapse by departure from the UK.

18.71 Directions may be given in extra-rules cases. Thus appropriate directions where the Secretary of State has failed to give effect to a policy will be that the respondent give consideration to the case in accordance with the relevant policy and in the light of the evidence available to him or her and the facts found by the Tribunal. It may well be right to add, as part of the direction, that the respondent give that consideration as an extended part of the original decision on the application, so that the appellant has no new fee to pay and the date of the application remains unchanged. It would not be appropriate for the Tribunal to direct the grant of entry clearance: the appellant's right is for the case to be considered in accordance with the policy, not an eventual decision in his or her favour.[1]

1   *Kausar v Entry Clearance Officer, Islamabad* [1998] INLR 141. See also *Antonipillai* (16588) (12 May 1998, unreported), IAT; *H (Somalia)* [2004] UKIAT 00027.

18.72   Directions should not be given without the parties having an opportunity to make submissions,[1] and if necessary to call evidence.[2] Directions need not be given at the same time as the decision allowing the appeal.[3] This is sensible as most decisions are delivered by post when there is no opportunity for oral argument on what directions are necessary. Thus a successful appellant can return to the appellate authority within a reasonable time after the appeal has been allowed to seek directions. This may provide some sanction against an obdurate entry clearance officer or immigration officer. The most prudent course is for the question of directions to be reserved in cases of anticipated difficulty, so a hearing can be reconvened for argument before there is any question of the authority becoming *functus*. Directions to give effect to a decision under section 86 of the Nationality, Immigration and Asylum Act 2002 (which are matters of substance) should not be confused with procedural directions under the Procedure Rules.[4] These are matters of procedure to which we turn below. Equally, they should not be confused with recommendations made to the Secretary of State when the Tribunal dismisses an appeal. These are purely gratuitous and have no basis in the Act or procedure rules.

1   *Immigration Officer, Heathrow v Adac-Bosompra* [1992] Imm AR 579. The old rule that directions could only be given at the request of a party, expressed in *Yousuf, ex p* [1990] Imm AR 191, has been superseded by the coming into force of the Human Rights Act 1998: *Hamad* [2002] UKIAT 07240.
2   The Court of Appeal in *R (on the application of Boafo) v Secretary of State for the Home Department* [2002] EWCA Civ 44, [2002] Imm AR 383, [2002] INLR 231 agreed with the Tribunal's observations in *Yousuf, ex p* [1990] Imm AR 191.
3   *Yousuf, ex p* [1990] Imm AR 191, approved in *Boafo* above.
4   Asylum and Immigration Tribunal (Procedure) Rules 2005, SI, 2005/230, r 45.

18.73   Directions are to be treated as part of the determination of the appeal for the purposes of section 103A of the NIAA 2002,[1] enabling the parties to seek reconsideration from the Tribunal or the Administrative Court, of a direction or of a refusal to make one. However, directions are probably not appealable to the Court of Appeal,[2] although a Tribunal's determination that it has no power to give directions would be appealable for error of law.

1   Nationality, Immigration and Asylum Act 2002, s 87(4), amended by Asylum and Immigration (Treatment of Claimants, etc) Act 2004, Sch 2, para 19.
2   The wording of s 87(4) strongly indicates that directions are *not* part of the decision for the purposes of the provisions of s 103 apart from s 103A.

Recommendations when an appeal is dismissed

18.74   There is no statutory power to make a recommendation when a case is dismissed, and a recommendation forms no part of the Tribunal's determination.[1] Although the Tribunal has a practically unfettered discretion to make extra-statutory comments as to any appropriate future course of action if it thinks fit, the ability to succeed on appeal on human rights grounds has reduced the necessity and utility of extra-statutory recommendations in most cases. Indeed, the Tribunal has repeatedly held that in the light of its human rights jurisdiction, such extra-statutory recommendations are not only unnecessary but positively undesirable.[2] However, the Administrative Court in *Shillova* referred to their continuing utility in situations where no asylum or human rights issues are engaged but it might be proper to draw to the Secretary of State's attention considerations of fairness, or the appellant's value to the community of the UK, or other considerations[3] Tribunals have made or endorsed extra-statutory recommendations in a variety of situations, either in general terms or limited to a specific objective.[4] Tribunals can hear evidence which is relevant only to a hoped-for recommendation, but if they decline to do so, or to adjourn the case so that such evidence can be called at a later date, or refuse to consider making a recommendation, or refuse to make one on the basis of the evidence which they have already heard, the High Court will not intervene.[5] This is so even where the refusal to make a recommendation is based on a material misapprehension of the facts, since the remedy lies against the Secretary of State if he or she adopts flawed findings of fact.[6]

[1]   *R v Immigration Appeal Tribunal, ex p Chavrimootoo* [1995] Imm AR 267, QBD; *R v Immigration Appeal Tribunal, ex p Anderson* (CO 1048/99) (14 March 2000, unreported), QBD; *Khatib-Shahidi v Immigration Appeal Tribunal* [2001] Imm AR 124, [2000] INLR 491, CA.

[2]   *Berisha* (HR/8328/01); *Gokteke* [2002] UKIAT 06608; *AM (Angola)* [2004] UKIAT 00146, where the adjudicator, dismissing a human rights appeal, made a recommendation on the basis that it would be 'entirely lacking in humanity' to return the appellant's pregnant wife to 'that terrible place'. The difficulty in such cases is not, as the Tribunal held, that the appellate authorities did not have access to all the information informing the Secretary of State's decision, but the encroachments on their human rights jurisdiction, first by cases such as *Edore v Secretary of State for the Home Department* [2003] EWCA Civ 716, [2003] Imm AR 516, [2003] INLR 361, *DM (Croatia)* [2004] UKIAT 24 (starred), which prevented Tribunals deciding the proportionality of removal for themselves, and now by *Huang v Secretary of State for the Home Department* [2005] EWCA Civ 105 which introduces an unwarranted presumption regarding the immigration rules and rigid and over-restrictive criteria: see 8.20–8.22 above.

[3]   See *R (on the application of Shillova) v Secretary of State for the Home Department* [2002] EWHC 1468 (Admin), [2002] INLR 611. Where a student had been very depressed as a result of criminal injuries but had improved in attendance and achievements since the decision, a recommendation might be appropriate: *S (India)* [2003] UKIAT 00043.

[4]   Thus in *Secretary of State for the Home Department v Okoth* [2002] UKIAT 06750, the Tribunal made a recommendation to enable the claimant to remain for his final nursing exams.

[5]   *R v Immigration Appeal Tribunal, ex p Chavrimootoo* [1995] Imm AR 267, QBD; *R v Immigration Appeal Tribunal, ex p Nalongo* [1994] Imm AR 536; *Wadia v Secretary of State for the Home Department* [1977] Imm AR 92; *Gillegao v Secretary of State for the Home Department* [1989] Imm AR 174; *R v Secretary of State for the Home Department, ex p Kumar* [1993] Imm AR 401, QBD; *R v Immigration Appeal Tribunal, ex p Anderson* (CO 1048/99) (14 March 2000, unreported); *Khatib-Shahidi v Immigration Appeal Tribunal* [2001] Imm AR 124, CA.

[6]   *Khatib-Shahidi v Immigration Appeal Tribunal* [2001] Imm AR 124, CA.

18.75   The policy of the Secretary of State is to accept an extra-statutory recommendation in dismissed or withdrawn appeals 'only where the written determination discloses clear exceptional compassionate circumstances which have not been previously considered and which would merit the exercise of my discretion outside the immigration rules'.[1] A failure to follow a recommendation did not betray any promise made on behalf of the Department.[2] In considering any recommendation or further application, the Secretary of State is bound by factual findings of the Tribunal after oral evidence,[3] unless these factual findings are themselves unsustainable.[4]

1   42 HC Official Report (6th series) col 173, 23 July 1996. For the former policy on recommendations see fourth edition of this book at 18.117.
2   *R v Secretary of State for the Home Department, ex p Sakala* [1994] Imm AR 143, CA; *R v Secretary of State, ex p Alakesan* [1997] Imm AR 315, QBD; *R v Secretary of State for the Home Department, ex p Gardian* (1996) Times, 1 April, CA; *R v Secretary of State for the Home Department, ex p Banu* [1999] Imm AR 161.
3   The Secretary of State was not in the past bound by the Tribunal's assessment of country conditions: see eg *Elhasoglu v Secretary of State for the Home Department* [1997] Imm AR 380; *Kamara v Secretary of State for the Home Department* [1997] Imm AR 105, CA. With the advent of Country Guidance cases, it is arguable that the Secretary of State could not reject a recommendation on the basis of its assessment of country conditions which wholly disregarded a recent Country Guidance case, particularly if the case contained criticism of its CIPU assessment.
4   *R v Secretary of State for the Home Department, ex p Danaie* [1998] Imm AR 84, [1998] INLR 124, CA; *R (on the application of Saribal) v Secretary of State for the Home Department* [2002] EWHC 1542 (Admin), [2002] INLR 596, [2002] All ER (D) 379 (Jul).

PROCEDURE ON APPEALS

18.76 Proceedings before the Asylum and Immigration Tribunal and the Special Immigration Appeals Commission are civil proceedings, and save where special provision is made, must be regarded as governed by the ordinary principles and practice relating to civil proceedings.[1] These appellate bodies are public authorities under the Human Rights Act 1998, and are therefore subject to an overriding duty to ensure compliance with the rights guaranteed by the Human Rights Convention.[2] However, the European Court of Human Rights (ECtHR) has repeatedly held that 'the right of an alien to reside in a country is a matter of public law' and is thus not a 'civil right' for the purposes of ECHR, Article 6 (fair trial in determination of civil rights and obligations),[3] and the Tribunal has simultaneously held that its procedures are Article 6 compliant, and that Article 6 does not apply to its procedures or to procedural provisions of the relevant Acts.[4] The duty of fairness imposed on the Tribunal is thus more likely to be derived from the high common law standards of fairness applied by the higher courts to immigration appeals of all kinds, and particularly to those raising issues of international protection.[5]

1   *Prendi* (01LS00060) (8 August 2001, unreported), IAT.
2   See Human Rights Act 1998, s 6(3); *MNM* (00TH02423); *SK* [2002] UKIAT 05613 (starred); 8.16 above.
3   *Agee v United Kingdom* (1977) 7 DR 164; *P v United Kingdom* (13162/87) (1987) 54 DR 211, *Bozano v France* (1984) 39 DR 119; *Maaouia v France* (Application 39652/98) (5 October 2000, unreported); *Ilic v Croatia* (Application 42389/98) (19 September 2000, unreported); *Mamatkulov and Abdurasulovic v Turkey* (Application 46827/99, 46951/99) (6 February 2003). Procedural safeguards have been held by the ECtHR to be vital ingredients of substantive Convention rights: see eg *Chahal v United Kingdom* (1996) 23 EHRR 413; *McCann v United Kingdom* (1995) 21 EHRR 97; *Kaya v Turkey* (1998) 28 EHRR 1; see 8.46 above. The European Court has also emphasised the importance of effective remedies under ECHR, Art 13 (deemed incorporated in practice and so not set out in the schedules to the Human Rights Act).
4   See *AM ('Upgrade' appeals) (Afghanistan)* [2004] UKIAT 186.
5   See eg *R v Secretary of State for the Home Department, ex p Fayed* [1998] 1 WLR 763; *R v Secretary of State for the Home Department, ex p Saleem (Asifa)* [2000] Imm AR 529, [2000] INLR 413, CA; *Ravichandran v Secretary of State for the Home Department*

[2000] Imm AR 10, CA; *R (on the application of the Refugee Legal Centre) v Secretary of State for the Home Department* [2004] EWCA Civ 1481, [2004] All ER (D) 201 (Nov); *R (on the application of Anufrijeva) v Secretary of State for the Home Department* [2003] UKHL 36, [2003] Imm AR 570, [2003] INLR 521.

18.77 Subject to that overriding duty, the procedure on appeals is governed by the Immigration (Notices) Regulations 2003,[1] the Asylum and Immigration Tribunal (Procedure) Rules 2005 (hereafter 'Procedure Rules'),[2] and where applicable, the Asylum and Immigration Tribunal (Fast Track Procedure) Rules 2005 (hereafter 'Fast Track Rules').[3] Separate consideration will be given to the procedures of the Special Immigration Appeals Commission.[4] The overriding objective of the Procedure Rules is to secure that proceedings before the Tribunal are handled as fairly, quickly and efficiently as possible; and, where appropriate, that members of the Tribunal have responsibility for ensuring this, in the interests of the parties to the proceedings and in the wider public interest.[5]

[1] SI 2003/658, made under Nationality, Immigration and Asylum Act 2002, s 105
[2] SI 2005/230, made under Nationality, Immigration and Asylum Act 2002, s 106 and 112, and British Nationality Act 1981 s 40A(3). The 2005 Rules came into force on 4 April 2005, replacing the Immigration and Asylum Appeals (Procedure) Rules 2003, SI 2003/652. For transitional provisions see below.
[3] SI 2005/560; see 18.80 below.
[4] See 18.160ff below.
[5] SI 2005/230, r 4. The overriding objective of the principal Procedure Rules is applied (together with other provisions of those Rules) to the Fast Track Rules by SI 2005/560, r 4.

Transitional provisions

18.78 On 3 April 2005, there were appeals (normal and fast track) pending before the adjudicator; applications for permission awaiting determination before the Immigration Appeal Tribunal; appeals pending before the Tribunal; applications for statutory review pending before the Administrative Court, applications for permission to appeal and appeals to the Court of Appeal pending. Some of these appeals and applications will relate to first-instance appeals under the Nationality, Immigration and Asylum Act 2002, heard under the 2003 Procedure Rules;[1] some, to appeals under the Immigration and Asylum Act 1999, or even the Immigration Act 1971, heard under the 2000 Procedure Rules.[2] What happens to all these appeals and applications? The 2005 Procedure Rules and Fast Track Procedure Rules apply, with minor modifications, to any appeal or application which was pending before an adjudicator or the Immigration Appeal Tribunal immediately before 4 April 2005 and which continues by virtue of transitional provisions made under the 2004 Act.[3] Transitional provisions deal with the change from service of the notice of appeal on the respondent to service direct on the Tribunal under the 2005 rules. Where notice of appeal had been served on the respondent before 4 April 2005, or a decision served on an applicant telling him or her to send notice of appeal to the respondent, the 2003 Procedure Rules continue to apply until the respondent has filed the appeal papers with the Tribunal,[4] when the 2005 rules apply.[5] Time limits imposed on the Tribunal by the 2005 rules do not apply to these transitional situations.[6] The Asylum and Immigration (Treatment of Claimants, etc) Act 2004 (Commencement No 5 and

Transitional Provisions) Order 2005[7] sets out the transitional provisions designed to deal with any outstanding cases in the system prior to 4 April 2005:

- An appeal or application which is pending before an adjudicator on 4 April 2005 continues as an appeal or application to the AIT.[8]
- An appeal pending before the IAT or a case remitted by the IAT to an adjudicator before 4 April 2005 continues as a reconsideration appeal before the AIT, and will not attract an application for reconsideration under section 103A when determined but an appeal to the Court of Appeal under s 103B.[9]
- Where an adjudicator or the IAT has heard but not determined an appeal by 4 April or the determination has been written but not served, it continues as an appeal before the adjudicator or the IAT until the determination is served.[10]
- An application for permission to appeal to the IAT which is pending before the Tribunal on 4 April 2005 is treated as an application for reconsideration.[11] Thus, if the application is refused after 4 April 2005, the applicant must renew the application to the High Court under section 103A, within five days of receipt of the Tribunal's decision.[12]
- Where an adjudicator has determined an appeal before 4 April 2005 but no application for permission has yet been lodged, the applicant could apply for reconsideration under s103A. Where time had started to run before 4 April the time limits were those under the old regime (five days if detained, ten days if applicant is in the UK, and 28 days if the applicant is abroad, extended for special circumstances,[13] and the retrospective funding provisions of section 103D will not apply.[14]
- An application for statutory review pending on 4 April 2005 continues as if the statutory review provisions of section 101 NIAA 2002 had not been repealed.[15]
- If the applicant was entitled to apply for statutory review before 4 April 2005 he or she could do so after that date as if section 101 was not repealed. The judge may affirm the IAT's refusal of permission to appeal, or on the application of the party who was successful before the adjudicator reverse a grant of permission, or make an order for reconsideration.[16] It is not clear whether this provision applies where a decision refusing permission to appeal to the Tribunal is made before but served after 4 April 2005.
- An appeal or application for permission to appeal to the Court of Appeal pending before the Court of Appeal on 4 April 2005 continues under the new provisions.
- An application pending before the IAT on 4 April 2005 for permission to appeal to the Court of Appeal is to be determined by the AIT under section 103 of the NIA Act 2002 as if it was not repealed.
- If the applicant was entitled to apply to the IAT for permission to appeal to the Court of Appeal under section 103 immediately before 4 April, he or she could do so afterwards under that section.[17]

A new funding regime came into force on 4 April 2005, and applies to funding for applications for reconsideration made in respect of Asylum and Immigration Tribunal determinations after that date (although it does not apply to fast track proceedings).[18] The new funding provisions do not apply to applications for reconsideration of adjudicator determinations.[19] See further 18.177 below.

1 Immigration and Asylum (Procedure) Rules 2003, SI 2003/652.
2 Immigration and Asylum (Procedure) Rules 2000, SI 2000/2333. It is impossible within the space of this volume to set out all the various appeal provisions and procedure rules which have come and gone with such speed. For the IAA 1999 and the 2000 Procedure Rules the reader can refer to the last edition of this work; for the 2003 Procedure Rules to Phelan (3rd edn) or to the rules themselves, available on the government statutory instrument website.
3 Asylum and Immigration Tribunal (Procedure) Rules 2005, SI 2005/230, r 62(1)(b); Asylum and Immigration Tribunal (Fast Track Procedure) Rules 2005, SI 2005/560, r 33(1).
4 Under r 9(1) of the 2003 Procedure Rules SI 2003/652 and r 6(3) of the Fast Track Rules SI 2003/801: SI 2005/230, r 62(2)(a), (b), (3); SI 2005/560, r 33(2), (3). The transitional provisions of the principal rules require the respondent to serve the appeal bundle on the appellant as soon as practicable: r 62(3)(b).
5 The provisions of the 2003 rules relating to late notices of appeal and variation of grounds of appeal (SI 2003/652, rr 10, 11) continue to apply to such appeals: SI 2005/230, r 62(3)(c). In fast track appeals, the provisions of the 2003 Rules relating to the appeal hearing (SI 2003/801, r 8) apply.
6 SI 2005/230, r 62(5). This provision does not apply to fast track appeals.
7 SI 2005/565.
8 SI 2005/565, Art 4.
9 SI 2005/565, Art 5.
10 SI 2005/565, Art 3.
11 SI 2005/565, Art 6(1). See also the Procedure Rules SI 2005/230, r 62(4). The corresponding transitional provision for the fast track procedure is SI 2005/560, r 33(6).
12 NIAA 2002, s 103A(a); see 18.168 below.
13 SI 2003/652 r 16.
14 SI 2005/565 Art 6(2)–(5).
15 SI 2005/565, Art 7(1).
16 SI 2005/565, Art 7(2)–(3).
17 SI 2005/565, Art 8.
18 SI 2005/966, reg 4(2).
19 SI 2005/565, Art 6(5).

Normal and fast track appeals

18.79 Appeals against immigration decisions, other than those dealing with national security, all come to the Asylum and Immigration Tribunal. But there are different procedures and, above all, different timescales, depending on whether the appeal is in the normal track, to which the principal Procedure Rules apply, or the fast track. We discussed earlier, at 12.111, the detention of single male asylum claimants from countries deemed 'safe' by the Home Office, and their subjection to fast track processing of their claim, in procedures which the Court of Appeal in the *Refugee Legal Centre* case held at the edge of illegality for unfairness, but just flexible enough to avoid it.[1] Those on the fast track have an in-country appeal, regulated by the Asylum and Immigration Tribunal (Fast Track Procedure) Rules 2005.[2] The fast track rules apply where the person giving notice of appeal was in detention under the Immigration Acts[3] in a specified removal centre when served with the notice of the immigration decision which is the subject of the appeal, and has been continuously in detention since.[4]

1 R *(on the application of the Refugee Legal Centre) v Secretary of State for the Home
   Department* [2004] EWCA Civ 1481, [2004] All ER (D) 580 (Mar), upholding Collins J
   at [2004] EWHC 684 (Admin). The court required the Secretary of State to formulate a
   written policy stating when the normal timescales would be adapted to the individual
   claimant's needs. Fast track claimants did not have to be single; it was physical constraints,
   not policy, which precluded the admission of partners and children to the fast track
   accommodation: R *(on the application of Kpandang) v Secretary of State for the Home
   Department* [2004] EWHC 2130 (Admin), [2004] All ER (D) 555 (Jul).
2 Asylum and Immigration Tribunal (Fast Track Procedure) Rules 2005, SI 2005/560, in
   force 4 April 2005 (formerly the Immigration and Asylum (Fast Track Procedure)
   Rules 2003, SI 2003/801). This group is to be distinguished from the 'NSA' or non-
   suspensive appeal group, who are also asylum claimants coming from countries deemed
   safe, but including families with children. The latter group, generally coming from
   countries listed in the Nationality, Immigration and Asylum Act 2002, s 94(4), are also
   detained and subject to speedy determination of their asylum claims, but refusal generally
   leads to immediate removal, and the right of appeal against the immigration decision may
   only be exercised from abroad. The normal procedure rules apply to non-suspensive
   appeals.
3 Defined in Asylum and Immigration (Treatment of Claimants, etc) Act 2004, s 44.
   Specified places of detention for rr 5 and 15 are Campsfield House, Colnbrook House,
   Harmondsworth and Yarlswood Immigration Removal Centres: SI 2005/560, Sch 2.
4 Asylum and Immigration Tribunal (Fast Track Procedure) Rules 2005, SI 2005/560, r 5
   (appeals to the Tribunal), r 15 (reconsideration).

18.80

Rule 31 of the fast track rules regulates transfer of cases out of the fast track
into the normal appeal procedures, and applies both to first appeals and to
reconsideration proceedings. It provides that the Tribunal must transfer cases
out of the fast track if all parties consent;[1] and may do so if satisfied by
evidence that there are exceptional circumstances meaning that the appeal or
application cannot otherwise be justly determined.[2] Additionally, the Tribunal
may order transfer out if the respondent fails to comply with a provision of
the rules or with a direction of the Tribunal, and the failure would prejudice
the appellant if the appeal or application remained in the fast track.[3]
Additionally, the fast track rules cease to apply if the appellant is released
from detention.[4] When the Tribunal orders transfer out of the fast track, it has
power to adjourn a hearing and give directions.[5] Once the fast track rules
cease to apply, the principal procedure rules apply, with their time limits.[6]

1 SI 2005/560, r 31(1)(a).
2 SI 2005/560, r 31(1)(b). In the *Refugee Legal Centre* case (18.79 fn 1above), the Home
   Office acknowledged that complex cases, those with medical issues or requiring expert
   evidence were not suitable for the fast track. The evidence before the Court in that case
   was that of 1438 claimants on the fast track, 151 were taken off the fast track before a
   decision and a further 270 pending appeal. But in K *(Côte d'Ivoire)* [2004] UKIAT 00061,
   the Tribunal rejected the argument that a case with complex facts, which necessitated a
   two-day hearing and an adjournment, should have been transferred out.
3 SI 2005/560, r 31(1)(c).
4 This is evident from rr 5 and 15.
5 SI 2005/560, r 31(2). If the Tribunal adjourns, it must fix a new date, time and place for
   the hearing: r 31(3)(a).
6 SI 2005/560, r 32.

18.81 In the *Refugee Legal Centre* case, the Court of Appeal acknowledged
that in some cases, transfer out of the fast track process at the appeal stage is
too late; the appeal would be flawed by the fundamental unfairness of the

determination process which has resulted in an interview which should not be relied on, still less be used as the basis of arguments about discrepancies and credibility.[1] Collins J observed at first instance that he could not believe that any competent representative would let his or her client be treated unfairly without intervening,[2] and it is clearly vital that representatives make vigorous representations in writing about any unfairness, including that arising by refusal to remove a case from the fast track at the initial determination stage. However, if representations are rejected, should the representative seek transfer at the appeal stage, or should he or she seek judicial review of the refusal of the Secretary of State to transfer out of the fast track at the earlier stage? In *Sunalla*,[3] Moses J agreed that an asylum determination procedure in the course of which the claimant had been interviewed for a total of 23 hours was likely to be unfair, and that such unfairness could not be cured on appeal, but refused permission for judicial review, because the claimant had not waited for an asylum decision. Thus, where the Secretary of State has refused to transfer an asylum claimant out of the fast track procedure, the proper course would seem to be to await initial decision to see whether the refusal has led to prejudice, and if so, to seek judicial review of the unfair procedure, with reference to the prejudice caused, while at the same time lodging a protective appeal.

[1] *R (on the application of the Refugee Legal Centre) v Secretary of State for the Home Department* [2004] EWCA Civ 1481, [2004] All ER (D) 580 (Mar).
[2] *R (Refugee Legal Centre) v Secretary of State for the Home Department* [2004] EWHC 684 (Admin).
[3] *R v Secretary of State for the Home Department, ex p Sunalla* (CO/2362/98).

Non-suspensive appeals

18.82 Non-suspensive appeals are appeals from decisions taken when the claimant is in the UK but which have to be conducted from abroad. The term is usually applied to appeals on asylum or human rights grounds which have been certified clearly unfounded under section 94 of the Nationality, Immigration and Asylum Act 2002.[1] Such appeals are not subject to special procedure rules, as fast track appeals are, but time for lodging the appeal runs from the date of departure rather than the date of service of the decision,[2] and non-standard directions may be given.[3] For example, after the High Court ruled that the Ahmadi family, who had sought sanctuary in a mosque, had been unlawfully removed to Germany, the Secretary of State persuaded the court not to order their return by pointing to the ability of the appellate authority to expedite a hearing of their appeal, with video link facilities to enable them and their medical witnesses to give evidence.[4]

[1] As amended by Asylum and Immigration (Treatment of Claimants, etc) Act 2004, s 27, in force 1 October 2004.
[2] Asylum and Immigration Tribunal (Procedure) Rules 2005, SI 2005/230, r 7(2)(a).
[3] SI 2005/230, r 45. For directions see 18.116 below.
[4] *R (on the application of Ahmadi) v Secretary of State for the Home Department* [2002] EWHC 1897 (Admin), [2002] All ER (D) 52 (Sep). It would not be in every case that the Secretary of State would offer to pay for an appellant's legal representative to be with the appellant to offer advice and assistance, however, as happened in that case.

Notices of action or decision

18.83 The first stage in the appeal procedure is for notice of the decision or action of the immigration authority in question to be given to the immigrant. Under the Notices Regulations,[1] a written notice of any appealable immigration decision or EEA decision must be served on the person in respect of whom the decision or action is taken.[2] In addition, a person who has been refused asylum but is granted leave to enter or remain for a period (or periods in aggregate) exceeding one year must be given notice of the right of appeal against refusal of asylum.[3] A decision may be given by hand or sent by recorded delivery post or fax[4] to the applicant or his or her representative[5] (either the last known or usual address or a correspondence address), and if no address is known, the decision may be 'served on the file'.[6] A refusal of leave to enter or variation of leave complying with section 4(1) of the Immigration Act 1971 will be deemed to comply with the regulations if accompanied by the prescribed information,[7] which must otherwise be contained in the notice. The notice, or a statement accompanying the notice, must contain the following information:

(1) the reasons for the decision;[8]
(2) the country or territory to which the person is to be removed, where the notice refers to the giving of directions for removal from the UK;[9]
(3) details of the person's right of appeal and the statutory provision on which the right of appeal is based;[10]
(4) whether or not the appeal may be brought whilst in the United Kingdom;[11]
(5) the grounds on which the appeal may be brought;[12]
(6) the facilities available for advice and assistance in connection with the appeal;[13]
(7) the time limit for bringing the appeal, the address to which the notice of appeal should be sent or taken by hand, or a fax number to which it may be sent;[14]
(8) reference to any provision under Part 5 of the Nationality, Immigration and Asylum Act 2002 that limits or restricts the right of appeal.[15]

The notice must also be accompanied by a notice of appeal. The notice of decision need not contain the information about appeal rights, or be accompanied by a notice of appeal, if the decision would not be appealable other than on race discrimination, asylum or human rights grounds. However, if a person is served with notice of such a decision and then makes an asylum, human rights or race discrimination claim, the decision maker must, as soon as practicable, re-serve the notice of decision including the requisite appeal information and forms.[16]

1   Immigration (Notices) Regulations 2003, SI 2003/658
2   SI 2003/658, reg 4(1).
3   SI 2003/658, reg 4(2).
4   SI 2003/658, reg 7(1); Immigration (Leave to Enter and Remain) Order 2000, SI 2000/1161, Art 8(2), 10(1).
5   SI 2003/658, reg 7(1)(c)(i), (ii).
6   SI 2003/658 reg 7(2). For service, including 'service on the file', see 18.85–18.86 below.
7   *R (on the application of Hashmi) v Secretary of State for the Home Department* [2002] EWCA Civ 728, [2002] INLR 377. A letter to an MP serves as notice for the purposes of Immigration Act 1971, s 4(1).

8   SI 2003/658, reg 5(1)(a). If the decision is the grant of leave and refusal of asylum, the notice must contain the reasons for the refusal of asylum: reg 5(2). A letter setting out the reasons for refusal is generally served with (or ahead of) the formal notice of decision, and such an arrangement meets the reasons requirement.

9   Ie a refusal of leave to enter, a decision to remove or to deport (under Nationality, Immigration and Asylum Act 2002, s 82(2)(a), (g)–(j)): SI 2003/658, reg 5(1)(b). For the validity of a decision notice containing no destination country, or one which appears not to comply with the requirements of Immigration Act 1971, Sch 2, para 8(1)(c) or Sch 3, para 1, see 16.58–59 above.

10   SI 2003/658, reg 5(3)(a).

11   SI 2003/658, reg 5(3)(b).

12   SI 2003/658, reg 5(3)(c).

13   SI 2003/658, reg 5(3)(d).

14   SI 2003/658, reg 5(4).

15   Eg, a statement under Asylum and Immigration (Treatment of Claimants, etc) Act 2004, Sch 3, paras 15(3), 19 (prohibited grounds of appeal): SI 2003/658, reg 5(5).

16   SI 2003/658, reg 5(6), (7). Time for appealing runs from re-service: reg 5(8).

18.84 Where a notice fails to comply with any of these requirements, do the defects invalidate the notice, or is the notice still good? Guidance on this question was given by the Court of Appeal in *Jeyeanthan*,[1] a case about a notice of appeal lacking the necessary declaration. The Master of the Rolls said that:

> 'the important question [is] what the legislator should be judged to have intended should be the consequence of non-compliance. This has to be assessed on a consideration of the language of the legislation against the factual circumstances of the non-compliance. In the majority of cases it provides limited, if any, assistance to inquire whether the requirement is mandatory or directory ... Procedural requirements are designed to further the interests of justice and any consequence which would achieve a result contrary to those interests should be treated with considerable reservation.'

He suggested that three questions were likely to arise:

(a)   Is the statutory requirement fulfilled if there has been substantial compliance with the requirement and, if so, has there been substantial compliance in the case in issue even though there has not been strict compliance? (The substantial compliance question.)

(b)   Is the non-compliance capable of being waived, and if so, has it been, or can it and should it be waived in this particular case? (The discretionary question.)

(c)   If it is not capable of being waived or is not waived then what is the consequence of the non-compliance? (The consequences question.)[2]

These considerations were expressed to apply to procedural requirements for both sides and at all stages of the appeal process. A notice which fails to tell an appellant of a right of appeal is likely to be held invalid, so that time would not begin to run for the purposes of appealing.[3]

Under the Immigration and Asylum Act 1999 this careful judicial solution to the non-compliance problem was precluded in the case of appellants' notices. Section 72(3) of that Act prevented the bringing of an appeal if the appellant had failed to comply with procedural requirements connected with the making of an application. That provision was repealed by the Nationality, Immigration and Asylum Act 2002, although failure by an applicant to comply with various procedural requirements (eg the use of a prescribed form, the provision of supporting documents) for the making of an application may result in the application being treated as invalid,[4] thus excluding the right of appeal (because no 'immigration decision' giving rise to a right of appeal need be made in response to an invalid application).

¹ *R v Immigration Appeal Tribunal, ex p Jeyeanthan; Ravichandran v Secretary of State for the Home Department* [2000] 1 WLR 354, [2000] Imm AR 10, [2000] INLR 241.
² *Jeyeanthan* above [2000] INLR 241 at 247. The court held that the Secretary of State's failure to make a declaration of truth on the form meant there was not substantial compliance (disapproving *R v Immigration Appeal Tribunal, ex p Nicholapillai* [1998] Imm AR 232) but that the non-compliance had in one case been waived and in the other had had no adverse consequences. See also *Hussain (Halgurd)* [2002] UKIAT 03419.
³ See *Akhuemonkhan v Secretary of State for the Home Department* [1998] INLR 265, where an appeal was allowed against a notice from the appellate authority of 'abandonment of appeal' with no indication of appeal rights. See also *Odomusu* (17109) 22 May 1998, IAT, a decision involving failure to serve notices on the children of a proposed deportee including rights of voluntary departure and of appeal. In *Mohamed (Omar) v Secretary of State for the Home Department* [2002] UKIAT 04634 the tribunal held that notice of a decision giving exceptional leave to remain was a valid grant of leave, in spite of its failure to comply with the requirement in the Notices Regulations to inform the recipient of the statutory provisions under which he could appeal. However, that failure would prevent the Secretary of State from taking any point as to the timeliness of any appeal brought against that decision. See also *ZA (Ethiopia)* [2004] UKIAT 00241, [2004] Imm AR 538, where an appellant was granted humanitarian protection after refusal of asylum but not advised of her appeal rights; time was not held to run against the appellant until she received a proper notice informing her of her right to appeal.
⁴ By Immigration Act 1971, s 31A (inserted by Immigration and Asylum Act 1999, s 165 and amended by Nationality, Immigration and Asylum Act 2002, s 121; Immigration (Leave to Remain) (Prescribed Forms and Procedures) Regulations SI 2005/771. The circumstances in which failure to comply with the regulations invalidates an application are set out in reg 14; see 4.7ff above.

Service of notice of decision

18.85 Elementary fairness supports the principle that a decision takes effect only on communication.[1] As we shall see, the Notices Regulations[2] do not always give effect to this principle, sometimes prioritising firm immigration control over fairness. The regulations contain no requirement that notice be served 'as soon as practicable' after a decision is taken. Cases under previous regulations[3] indicated that the notice could be sent to the last-known or usual place of abode even when the Home Office knew that the appellant was not there,[4] or had been asked to send it to the appellant's legal representative.[5] In *ex p Yeboah and Draz*,[6] where a letter was sent by post but not received by its intended recipient, the Court of Appeal held that the Interpretation Act 1978, section 7 did not enable the appellant to disprove the presumption of receipt by evidence of actual non-receipt. This harsh decision was reversed by statute,[7] following another Court of Appeal decision, *Saleem*,[8] which made it clear that such irrebuttable presumptions which deprived appellants of appeal rights were no longer acceptable in the new climate. The 2000 Procedure Rules required the notice of the decision to be 'received' in most cases before time limits for appealing started to run.[9] The 2003 Rules that replaced them, required notice to be 'served', and the 2005 Rules repeat that language.[10] A validly served notice starts time running even if not actually received, although non-receipt would be relevant to the discretion to extend time under rule 9(6) of the Procedure Rules.[11] There is deemed service of a notice of a decision which was sent by first class recorded delivery post, on the second day after it is posted if sent to a place within the UK, unless the contrary is proved.[12] Notices sent abroad are deemed to have been served on the 28th day after the day of posting unless the contrary is proved.[13] The Immigration Appeal Tribunal held, in a decision under the previous procedure rules, that evidence of sending a notice to a prison was insufficient to establish that a proposed deportee, an inmate, was served, in the absence of evidence of personal service on him. The decision emphasised the harsh consequences of non-compliance with the strict requirements of service of refusal or deportation decisions.[14] A notice which was not properly served could not give rise to a valid dismissal of an appeal on the ground that it was out of time or that the appellant did not appear.[15]

1　*R (on the application of Anufrijeva) v Secretary of State for the Home Department* [2003] UKHL 36, [2003] Imm AR 570, [2003] INLR 521, per Lord Steyn at para 30. The individual concerned must, he ruled, be in a position to challenge the decision in the courts (para 26). Lord Millett held that the presumption that notice of a decision must be given to the person adversely affected by it before it can have legal effect is a strong one (at para 43).

2　Immigration (Notices) Regulations 2003, SI 2003/658, made under Nationality, Immigration and Asylum Act 2002, s 105.

3　Immigration Appeals (Notices) Regulations 1984, SI 1984/2040.

4　*Singh (Pargat) v Secretary of State for the Home Department* [1993] Imm AR 112 at 118, HL.

5　*Tongo v Secretary of State for the Home Department* [1995] Imm AR 109, CA.

6　*R v Secretary of State for the Home Department, ex p Yeboah, R v Secretary of State for the Home Department, ex p Draz* [1987] Imm AR 414, CA.

7　Immigration and Asylum Act 1999, Sch 4, para 2; see also Immigration and Asylum Appeals (Procedure) Rules 2000, SI 2000/2333, r 48(2), succeeded by the Immigration (Notices) Regulations 2003, SI 2003/658, reg 7(4); Immigration and Asylum Appeals (Procedure) Rules 2003 SI 2003/652, rule 54(5).

8　*R v Secretary of State for the Home Department, ex p Saleem (Asifa)* [2000] Imm AR 529, [2000] INLR 413.

9　SI 2000/2333, r 6.

10　Asylum and Immigration Tribunal (Procedure) Rules 2005, SI 2005/230, r 7(1) (replacing the Immigration and Asylum Appeals (Procedure) Rules 2003, SI 2003/652, r 7); Asylum and Immigration Tribunal (Fast Track Procedure) Rules 2005, SI 2005/560, r 8.

11　The equivalent provision in the Fast Track rules is r 8(2).

12　Immigration (Notices) Regulations 2003, SI 2003/658, reg 7(4)(a). Proof to the contrary needs to be proof of non-service, not of non-receipt.

13　Immigration (Notices) Regulations 2003, SI 2003/658, reg 7(4)(b).

14　*Jaroudy* (20063) 9 February 1999, IAT.

15　*R v Secretary of State for the Home Department, ex p Kondo* [1992] Imm AR 326; *Babar* (18302) (2 October 1998, unreported), IAT, where *R v Secretary of State for the Home Department, ex p Lateef* [1991] Imm AR 334 was distinguished. In *R (on the application of Tataw) v Secretary of State for the Home Department* [2003] EWCA Civ 925, [2003] INLR 585, decided under the 2000 procedure rules, the fact that a determination was not received by an appellant meant that an appeal against it to the Immigration Appeal Tribunal was actually in time, although it appeared out of time. See also cases on service of notice of hearing, at 18.120 below.

18.86 The 1984 Notices Regulations permitted the decision maker to dispense with service altogether if the decision-maker had no knowledge of the whereabouts of the person who was the subject of the decision.[1] The decision could, in those circumstances, be 'served on the file'. This provision, which gave rise to considerable litigation,[2] was not reproduced in the 2000 Notices Regulations but has reappeared in the 2003 Notices Regulations, which provide that, where a person's whereabouts are unknown and there is no correspondence address or the address provided is defective, false or no longer in use by the person and no representative appears to be acting for the person, the notice is deemed to have been given if placed on the relevant file.[3] Where the person is subsequently located, he or she must be given a copy of the notice as soon as practicable, together with details of how and when it was served.[4] But the time for appealing does not start again, since the notice is not re-served. In deportation cases involving overstaying, the practice of dispensing with service was abandoned as unfair in 1986,[5] and the High Court has held that 'service on the file' of a deportation decision did not 'stop the clock' for the purpose of the long residence concession, since actual knowledge of such a decision was required to do this.[6] The rule is unlikely to be compatible with the requirements of elementary fairness referred to by the House of Lords in *Anufrijeva*,[7] particularly in the context of dispersal of and denial of support to asylum claimants, both of which make losing touch with the Home Office more likely, and given the legendary inefficiency of the Home Office, it is likely to give rise to serious miscarriages of justice.

[1] Immigration Appeals (Notices) Regulations 1984, SI 1984/2040.
[2] For cases under the regulation see the 4th edition of this work, 18.62 fn 2.
[3] Immigration (Notices) Regulations, SI 2003/658, reg 7(2).
[4] SI 2003/658, reg 7(3).
[5] By a little-known Home Office policy, DP5/86, quoted in *R v Secretary of State for the Home Department, ex p Chew, R v Secretary of State for the Home Department, ex p Popatia* [2000] INLR 587, QBD.
[6] *R v Secretary of State for the Home Department, ex p Chew, R v Secretary of State for the Home Department, ex p Popatia* [2000] INLR 587, QBD.
[7] *R (on the application of Anufrijeva) v Secretary of State for the Home Department*, 18.85 fn 1 above.

One-stop notice

18.87 A notice under section 120 of the Nationality, Immigration and Asylum Act 2002 can be served by the Secretary of State or an immigration officer at any time during the course of an application or on refusal, or before, on or after a decision to remove or deport is made.[1] The notice requires the person to state his or her reasons for wishing to enter or remain in the UK, any grounds on which he or she should be permitted to enter or remain in the UK and any grounds on which he or she should not be removed from or required to leave the UK.[2] There is no time limit within which the applicant must return a statement of additional grounds, and no obligation for IND to wait for a statement before making a decision, or to issue a supplementary decision relating to the matters raised in the statement. The effect of serving the section 120 notice is to give jurisdiction to the appellate authority to consider anything contained in the statement of additional grounds,[3] and to deprive the appellant of a second appeal on any grounds which should have been contained in the statement and/or considered on appeal, but were not.[4]

1   Nationality, Immigration and Asylum Act 2002, s 120(1). The API 'Appeals: One-stop Procedure' state that in asylum cases, the one-stop warning would normally be given during induction (see 12.114).
2   NIAA 2002, s 120(2). The statement in response need not repeat reasons or grounds set out in any application which has already been made: s 120(3).
3   By virtue of NIAA 2002, s 85(2). This applies whether the statement under s 120 was made before or after the appeal was commenced: s 85(3).
4   NIAA 2002, amended by Asylum and Immigration (Treatment of Claimants, etc) Act 2004, ss 30, 96(1), (2). This applies whether the appellant has been outside the UK since the requirement under s 120 arose: s 96(5). See 18.42–18.43 above.

Grounds for decision

18.88 Under the Immigration Act 1971 and the Immigration and Asylum Act 1999, where a statement of the reasons for the decision or action is included in a notice, it was 'conclusive of the person by whom and of the ground on which any decision or action was taken'.[1] This gave rise to considerable litigation. Although the NIAA 2002 contains no such provision rendering the grounds of a decision conclusive, the distinction drawn by the old case law still holds good. That case law established that where the grounds given reflected the immigration rules, the statutory finality did not prevent the immigration officer or Secretary of State amending the notice by varying or amplifying the reasons for the decision,[2] but if a decision was based on a statutory ground, the notice was in reality 'conclusive'. The principle is illustrated in the old case law on deportation. There used to be various statutory grounds for deportation: overstaying; breach of conditions; conducive to the public good; being a family member of a proposed deportee. A decision-maker could not switch between these statutory categories,[3] and we believe that an attempt to amend the grounds of a deportation decision from conducive grounds to being the family member of a proposed deportee,[4] or vice versa, without service of a fresh notice of decision, would still be held impermissible.[5]

1   Immigration Act 1971, s 18(2) and Immigration and Asylum Act 1999, Sch 4, para 1(2).
2   Grounds for a decision must always be contained in the notice, but not always reasons. A ground for a decision to deport is that deportation is conducive to the public good; reasons, which might relate to criminal, political or other anti-social behaviour, would need to be stipulated. A ground for refusal of leave to enter as a visitor is that the person is not genuinely seeking leave to enter for the period sought; further reasons have been held unnecessary for the purposes of the notice requirements. In *R v Immigration Appeal Tribunal, ex p Hubbard* [1985] Imm AR 110 Woolf J doubted whether it was right or sensible to draw a distinction between grounds and reasons and held that the appellate authorities were not restricted on an appeal to the grounds or reasons specified in the notice of refusal. See 18.56 above. An adjudicator's refusal to allow the respondent entry clearance officer to amend a notice to include consideration of para 317 of the immigration rules was criticised by the Tribunal in *Entry Clearance Officer, Manila v Brey* [2002] UKIAT 06655. The Tribunal's 2005 Practice Direction envisages that the respondent may amend the notice of decision, at 6.4.
3   *R v Immigration Appeal Tribunal, ex p Mehmet (Ekrem)* [1977] Imm AR 56, QBD; *Parsaiyan v Visa Officer, Karachi* [1986] Imm AR 155. See also *R v Secretary of State for the Home Department, ex p Cheblak* [1991] 2 All ER 319.
4   Ie from deportation under s 3(5)(a) Immigration Act 1971 to deportation under s 3(5)(b).
5   The distinction was particularly important where the appellate jurisdiction was confined to deciding whether there was power to implement the decision for the reason stated in the notice: in such a case the Secretary of State could not amend the notice so as to increase the jurisdiction of the appellate authority to take into account reasons not initially stated in the

grounds of decision; *Egbale v Secretary of State for the Home Department* [1997] INLR 88, IAT. See also *Secretary of State for the Home Department v Ziar (Salah)* [1997] Imm AR 456, [1997] INLR 221, IAT, a case on the statutory certification of an appeal. Since the effect of certification was to preclude a further appeal (from the adjudicator to the Immigration Appeal Tribunal), certification had to be based on the appropriate statutory ground and could not be amended in the course of the appeal.

Notice of appeal

18.89 A notice of appeal has to be in the appropriate prescribed form.[1] The notice must set out the name and address of the appellant and of his or her representative (if any), the grounds for the appeal and reasons in support of those grounds,[2] and must, so far as practicable, list any documents the appellant intends to rely on as evidence in support of the appeal.[3] The notice must be signed by the appellant or the appellant's representative and dated.[4] If the appellant's representative signs the notice, he or she must certify in the notice of appeal that it has been completed in accordance with the appellant's instructions.[5] The notice must, if reasonably practicable, be accompanied by a copy of the notice of decision which is the subject of the appeal.[6] The form requires other particulars, including details of the appellant's age, citizenship or nationality and of previous appeals. The same provisions apply to appeals under the fast track procedure.[7] Any notice of appeal or application notice filed with the Tribunal must be completed in English.[8] Cases under the old rules suggest that many of the requirements in the notice are not mandatory, and failure to include some of the information would not invalidate an appeal.[9] The guidance provided by the Court of Appeal case of *Jeyeanthan*[10] has resonance here, although the language of the Procedure Rules is very strict.[11]

1   Asylum and Immigration Tribunal (Procedure) Rules 2005, SI 2005/230, r 8(1). 'Appropriate prescribed form' means the appropriate form in the Schedule to the rules, or that form with any variations that the circumstances may require: r 2. The Schedule contains distinct forms for UK and overseas appeals, and for rights of appeal that can only be exercised on leaving the UK.
2   SI 2005/230, r 8(1)(a)–(d), see below.
3   SI 2005/230, r 8(1)(e). This requirement is new, and reflects the fact that the notice goes to the Tribunal, not (as before) to the respondent: see 18.91 below.
4   SI 2005/230, r 8(3).
5   SI 2005/230, r 8(4).
6   SI 2005/230, r 8(2). This requirement is new, and reflects the fact that the notice goes to the Tribunal, not (as before) to the respondent: see 18.91 below.
7   The Asylum and Immigration Tribunal (Fast Track Procedure) Rules 2005, SI 2005/560, r 6(b).
8   SI 2005/230, r 52(1)(a). It may be in Welsh, if the appeal is in or has a connection with Wales: r 52(2). The Tribunal is under no duty to consider a document which is not in English (or if appropriate, in Welsh): r 52(3), (2). Other documents filed with the Tribunal must be accompanied by a certified translation, if not in English or Welsh: r 52(1)(b), (2).
9   *Jarvis* [1994] Imm AR 102; *R v Immigration Appeal Tribunal, ex p Begum (Hamida)* [1988] Imm AR 199, QBD; *Re Sogunle* [1994] Imm AR 554. The intention is not to sanction appellants who, through no fault of their own, have failed to complete the form fully or correctly, but to encourage them to do so in order for their appeal to be handled promptly: DCA document following consultation on procedure rules, 8 February 2005.
10 *R v Immigration Appeal Tribunal, ex p Jeyeanthan; Ravichandran v Secretary of State for the Home Department* [2000] 1 WLR 354, [2000] Imm AR 10, [2000] INLR 241. See 18.84 above.

¹¹ Under the 2005 Procedure Rules r 2, a person is not an appellant unless he or she has given a notice of appeal to the Tribunal in accordance with the rules. Too strict an interpretation would be inconsistent with human rights obligations.

Grounds of appeal

18.90 The requirement to state grounds of appeal clearly refers to one or more of the statutory grounds under Nationality, Immigration and Asylum Act 2002, section 84(1) see 18.47 above.

The procedure rules also require reasons in support of the grounds. The reasons do not need to be lengthy, but require some application of the statutory grounds to the appellant's circumstances, eg which immigration rule or Home Office policy, is engaged, or how the appellant's human rights are affected by the decision, or the basis on which he or she claims the protection of the Refugee Convention, or how the decision is otherwise not in accordance with the law or the rules, or discretion should have been exercised. The grounds of appeal should refer to any procedural irregularity relied on. If it is clear that the refusal is based on a mistake of fact, the error should be referred to in the grounds.¹ If a one-stop warning has been given with the refusal decision,² any additional grounds relied on should be set out (these are most likely to be human rights or asylum grounds not originally relied on). However, the Court of Appeal recognised in *Zenovics*³ that elementary fairness would require the Tribunal to give more latitude to grounds drafted by appellants without legal representation.

¹ See also Henderson, M: Best practice guide to asylum and human rights appeals, ILPA, 2003, para 4.5ff.
² Under Nationality, Immigration and Asylum Act 2002, s 120.
³ *R (on the application of Zenovics) v Secretary of State for the Home Department* [2002] EWCA Civ 273, [2002] INLR 219; see 18.114 below. See also the Tribunal's duty to consider matters not raised in the grounds of appeal: Nationality, Immigration and Asylum Act 2002, s 85, 18.48 above.

18.91 Procedure rules historically required appellants to serve notice of appeal on the respondent, who then forwarded the notice, together with relevant documents, to the appellate authority.¹ This arrangement caused lengthy delays in the appeal process, as not infrequently, the Home Office would not forward the notice for months, and entry clearance officers frequently took even longer. The delays in entry clearance appeals were clearly prejudicial to appellants abroad, but Home Office delays in respect of in-country appeals were frequently prejudicial to appellants as well, leaving them in a state of chronic uncertainty. Practical problems abounded; appellants were obliged to notify the appellate authority of changes of address and representative, but until the respondent forwarded the appeal documents, the IAA had no file to which to attach the information. Appeals were lost because the IAA would send notices of hearing to the wrong address.² The 2005 Rules seek to remedy these problems by requiring appellants to serve the notice of appeal on the Tribunal in most cases.³ A person detained under the Immigration Acts may, as an alternative, serve the notice of appeal on the person who has custody of him or her, who must within two days (or if the appeal is in the fast track, immediately) forward it to the Tribunal, after endorsing it with the date on which it was served.[4] A person outside the UK who wishes to appeal against a decision of an entry clearance officer may serve the notice on the ECO as an alternative to sending it to the Tribunal, in which case the ECO must forward it to the Tribunal as soon as reasonably practicable and in any event within ten days, after endorsing it with the date on which it was served.[5] The notice and its accompanying documents may be delivered (presumably by hand), or sent by post, document exchange or by fax or by email, to an address, DX number, fax number or email address specified by the Tribunal or the person to whom the document is directed.[6] A notice of appeal served on a custodian or on the entry clearance officer is treated as being served on the day on which it is received;[7] otherwise, the rules are silent on when the notice of appeal is deemed received by the Tribunal.[8] The provisions apply, with modifications, to the fast track procedure.[9]

1   See eg Immigration Appeals (Procedure) Rules 1972, r 6; Immigration Appeals (Procedure) Rules 1984, r 6(2); Immigration and Asylum Appeals (Procedure) Rules 2003, SI 2003/652, r 6(1), (2).
2   See eg *R (on the application of Hasa) v Immigration Appeal Tribunal* [2003] EWHC 396 (Admin), [2003] All ER (D) 232 (Feb).
3   SI 2005/230, r 6(2).
4   SI 2005/230, r 6(3)(b), 6(5); Fast Track rules SI 2005/560, r 7. However, the detainee may send the notice direct to the Tribunal: r 6(3)(a), (2).
5   SI 2005/230, r 6(4)(b), (6). If practicable within this time, the ECO must send relevant documents relating to the appeal (see 18.100 below) with the notice: r 6(6)(c). The person abroad may send the notice direct to the Tribunal instead of giving it to the ECO: r 6(4)(a).
6   SI 2005/230, r 55(1). If it is sent to the wrong address and cannot be traced, the Tribunal is entitled to conclude that no valid appeal has been lodged: *Adeniyi v Secretary of State for the Home Department* [1995] Imm AR 123, CA; *Shaffi v Secretary of State for the Home Department* [1990] Imm AR 468.
7   SI 2005/230, r 55(6).
8   SI 2005/230, r 55(5) deems service on *a person* effected (unless the contrary is proved), if by post or DX from and to a place within the UK, on the second day after it was sent, if by post or DX from or to a place outside the UK, on the 28th day after sending, and in any other case, on the day in which it was sent or delivered to or left with the person. This refers to notices sent by the Tribunal to the parties. But r 55(1) distinguishes between filing with the *Tribunal* and service on *a person*. In the absence of a deeming provision for filing the notice of appeal, the notice is filed on actual receipt, and the appeal must be with the Asylum and Immigration Tribunal at the end of the period specified for filing it.
9   Rules 6(1)–(3) of the principal rules are applied to fast track appeals by the Asylum and Immigration Tribunal (Fast Track Procedure) Rules 2005, SI 2005/560, r 6.

Time limits for appealing

18.92 The time for appealing against any decision or action of an immigration authority varies according to whether the appellant is in the UK or abroad when served with notice of the decision and, if the appellant is in the UK, whether he or she is detained under the Immigration Acts and if so, whether under the fast track procedure. Where the appeal is in-country and the appellant is not detained, notice of appeal must be given no later than ten working days after being served with the notice of decision.[1] If the appellant is detained under the Immigration Acts, notice of appeal must be given no later than five working days after being served with the decision.[2] If the appellant is detained under the fast track provisions,[3] then the notice of appeal must be given not later than two days after being served with the decision.[4] Where the appellant was in the UK at the date of the decision but the appeal is out-of-country, the notice of appeal must be given not later than 28 days after departure from the UK.[5] Where the appellant was not in the UK when the decision was made, the notice of appeal must be given no later than 28 days after the decision was served.[6] Where a person is served with notice of a decision refusing asylum and does not yet satisfy the ground for appealing, but does later, the time for giving notice of appeal against the refusal of asylum begins to run from the date of service of the decision qualifying him or her to appeal.[7] Notices of appeal served on a custodian or on the entry clearance officer are deemed to have been given when received by them;[8] there are no deeming provisions in the 2005 rules relating to filing the notice with the Tribunal.[9] It is important to ensure that appeal notices have actually arrived at the Tribunal, and recorded delivery post is the best way to ensure this. When time *runs out*, the notice of appeal should have *reached* the respondent. It is no good if it has merely been posted by that time.[10] For in-country appeals, weekends and public holidays, the period from 25 to 31 December and Good Friday are not included in the time for appealing;[11] for all appeals, where time for serving notice runs out on a weekend or a public holiday, an appeal lodged on the next working day is in time.[12]

1   Asylum and Immigration Tribunal (Procedure) Rules 2005, SI 2005/230, r 7(1)(b) 57(1)(b), 57(3). The period is to be calculated so as to exclude the day on which the notice of decision was served: r 57(1)(a). The notice of decision is deemed served two business days after the decision was posted, or immediately if it was faxed or delivered in person: Immigration (Notices) Regulations 2003, SI 2003/658, reg 7(4), (5).
2   SI 2005/230, rr 7(1)(a), 57(1)(b).
3   Ie detained at the Immigration Removal Centres at Campsfield, Colnbrook House, Harmondsworth or Yarlswood: Asylum and Immigration Tribunal (Fast Track Procedure) Rules 2005, SI 2005/560, Sch 2.
4   SI 2005/560, r 8(1), which applies where an immigration decision was made on or after 4 April 2005 and the appellant was detained at a place specified in Sch 2 when the decision was served and continuously thereafter (r 5). Transitional provisions apply the 2003 Fast Track Procedure Rules, SI 2003/801, rr 6(1) and (3) to notices of appeal served in response to decisions prior to 4 April 2005: see 18.78 above. However, the time limit for service of the notice of appeal is the same under the old and new rules.
5   SI 2005/230, r 7(2)(a). Note that the 28 days is not 28 working days: r 57(1)(b), although the 28 days excludes the date of service of the decision: r 57(1)(a).
6   SI 2005/230, r 7(2)(b).
7   SI 2005 /230, r 7(3). A right of appeal against the refusal of asylum only accrues once the person has been granted leave to enter or remain in the UK for a period or periods in aggregate of a year or more: Nationality, Immigration and Asylum Act 2002, s 83(1)(b).
8   SI 2005/230, r 55(6), applied to the fast track procedures by SI 2005/560, r 27.
9   See 18.91 fn 7 above
10   *R v Immigration Appeal Tribunal, ex p Rocha* [1982] Imm AR 12, QBD.
11   SI 2005/230, r 57(1)(b), r 2 (definition of 'business day'). Note that for the purposes of the Fast Track rules, the definition of a 'business day' also excludes 24 December, Maundy Thursday and the Tuesday after the last Monday in May: SI 2005/560, r 2(3).
12   SI 2005/230, r 57(2), applied to the fast track procedures by SI 2005/560, r 27.

18.93 The existence of a time limit for appealing against the actions or decisions of the immigration authorities can mislead would-be appellants into thinking that if they merely adhere to the time limit they will be able to enjoy their full right of appeal. There are, however, situations where this may not be the case. For example, persons refused entry generally have a right of appeal without having to leave the UK if they had an entry clearance on arrival.[1] But the existence of a right of appeal does not in itself operate as a stay on removal. It is only once an appeal is 'pending', ie once notice of appeal has been given, that a person otherwise removable may not be removed from the United Kingdom.[2] Thus if such appellants delay giving notice of appeal they may in fact find themselves being removed from the UK. They still have a right of appeal, but can only exercise it from abroad,[3] whereas if they had given notice of appeal before their departure they would have been allowed to remain until their appeal was heard.

[1] Nationality, Immigration and Asylum Act 2002, s 82(2)(a) and s 92(3) (as amended by s 28 Asylum and Immigration (Treatment of Claimants, etc) Act 2004); see 18.23 above.
[2] NIAA 2002, ss 78(1), 104(1).
[3] Note that in this situation, notice of appeal must be served 28 days after being served with the notice of decision, not 28 days after departure: Asylum and Immigration Tribunal (Procedure) Rules 2005, SI 2005/230, r 7(2)(b).

Late notice of appeal

18.94 The Procedure Rules used to provide two routes for out-of-time appeals to be entertained: by consent of the responsible immigration authority; or at the discretion of the appellate authority.[1] Now that the notice of appeal is sent to the Tribunal, the first route to extend time – consent – has gone. The proposed respondent to the appeal now has no role in the issues of establishment of the timeliness of appeals, and extension of time. Where a notice of appeal is given outside the applicable time limit, it must include an application for an extension of time for appealing, which must state the reasons for failing to give the notice in time, attaching any written evidence in support of those reasons.[2] The rules contain provision for disputes as to whether the notice was served in time or not. If the notice appears to the Tribunal to have been given late, but does not include an application for an extension of time, then, unless it decides on its own initiative to extend time, the Tribunal must notify the person giving notice of appeal that it proposes to treat the appeal as out of time.[3] If the intending appellant contends that the notice of appeal was in fact given in time, or that special circumstances prevented giving the notice in time, which could not reasonably have been set out in the notice, he or she may file written evidence in support of that contention within three days (ten days if he or she is abroad) after receiving the Tribunal's allegation of lateness.[4] The Tribunal must then decide as a preliminary issue, without a hearing, whether the notice of appeal was in fact given in time and, if it was not, whether there are special circumstances by reason of which it would be unjust not to extend time for appealing,[5] and must serve written notice of its decision on the parties.[6] If the out-of-time notice of appeal is under section 82 of the NIAA 2002, and relates (wholly or partly) to an asylum claim where the intending appellant is in the UK, the Tribunal must, if it refuses to extend time for appealing, serve the notice of its decision on the respondent, who must serve it on the intending appellant within 28 days of receiving it.[7] The fast-track rules contain similar procedures for determining timeliness,[8] but the test for extension of time under the fast track procedure is stricter: the Tribunal must be satisfied that, because of circumstances outside the control of the intending appellant or his or her representative, it was not practicable for notice of appeal to be given within the time limit.[9]

1 See Immigration and Asylum Appeals (Procedure) Rules 2003, SI 2003/652, r 6(2).
2 SI 2005/230, r 10(1).
3 SI 2005/230, r 10(2). This rule does not refer to 'appellants' but to 'persons giving notice of appeal'; they do not become 'appellants', with all the protections that word entails, until or unless the appeal has been accepted as timely or an extension of time has been given. This reasoning accords with that of the Tribunal in *B (Zimbabwe)* [2004] UKIAT 00076. See also 18.98 below.
4 SI 2005/230, r 10(3), (4). Reasons for not acknowledging lateness or seeking an extension of time in the notice of appeal itself would clearly include postal strikes or other reasons for lateness occurring after timely dispatch of a notice, and possibly also simple miscalculation of time (if the appeal was only a day or so late and the explanation plausible). Note however that mere miscalculation of a time limit did not justify an extension of time where the appellant was the Secretary of State: *AK (Bulgaria)* [2004] UKIAT 00201 (starred); see below. Where an application which is in time is refused as out of time, without fault by the Tribunal, the refusal is based on mistake of fact and justice demands its quashing: *R (on the application of Tataw) v Secretary of State for the Home Department* [2003] EWCA Civ 925, [2003] INLR 585.
5 SI 2005/230, r 10(5), (6). It may 'only' take into account the matters stated in the notice of appeal, any evidence filed by the intending appellant, and 'any other relevant matters of fact within the knowledge of the Tribunal' – a vague formulation which presumably could include information about postal strikes or the inefficiency of particular firms of solicitors, against which to measure the explanation. There are dangers of unfairness in such a loose formulation. For 'special circumstances' justifying an extension of time see below.
6 SI 2005/230, r 10(7).
7 SI 2005/230, r 10(9). The respondent must notify the Tribunal as soon as practicable after serving the decision, the date and means of service, and if the Tribunal has had no notification from the respondent 29 days after service of the decision on it, the Tribunal must serve the decision on the person as soon as reasonably practicable thereafter: r 10(8)(ii), (9). The purpose of this rule, and its precursors and companion rules allowing service by the respondent, is to enable the immigration authorities to take failed claimants by surprise and to give them no opportunity to 'go to ground' following an unfavourable decision. The abiding danger is that of wrongful removal without giving such persons a real opportunity to take legal advice, or to challenge the decision – another procedure drafted for abuse, which penalises all asylum claimants. At least this rule contains safeguards against Home Office inefficiency.
8 See SI 2005/560, r 12. The fast track rules do not specify the procedure for disputing timeliness or for applying for an extension, however.
9 SI 2005/560, r 8(2).

18.95 The criterion for extending time for appealing in an ordinary case is the existence of special circumstances making it unjust not to do so, which is identical to the test under the 2003 Rules, and not too different from that under the 2000 Procedure Rules, which was whether it was 'just' to do so, or the test under the 1984 and 1972 Procedure Rules, which was whether it was 'just and right' to extend time.[1] Thus, the case law under the previous rules is still relevant. The leading Court of Appeal decision under the old rules held that the rule should be liberally interpreted so as not to let an appellant suffer unfairly.[2] There was no reason in law why the appellate authority should not take into account the substantive merits of the case, or the fact that the failure was due to a mistake by the applicant's legal advisers, or that the applicant had been lulled into a false sense of security. However, in a later case[3] the court emphasised that, although all these matters might be taken into account, it was still a matter of discretion whether to allow a late appeal to proceed and, therefore, the appellate authority should decide in each case what weight (if any) should be given to such factors. The later case attempted to explain more clearly what appellate authorities should do in assessing the substantive merits of an appeal and stated that this could only mean making, at best, a provisional assessment of the chances of success of the appeal.[4] The Immigration Appeal Tribunal followed the liberal line of authority, particularly in asylum appeals,[5] despite the more restrictive wording that obtained until October 2000, where it had to be shown that the failure was due to circumstances beyond the appellant's control.[6] Lord Denning's principle in, *ex p Mehta*[7] that the court 'would never let a party suffer because his solicitors had made a mistake and are a day or two late' has been held to extend to cases where the delay was longer, in the context of a leisurely decision-making process where an applicant could not be expected to make constant inquiries about the progress of the application.[8] The danger of pre-judging the merits in refusing an extension has been emphasised,[9] as has the fact that there was no requirement to show 'exceptional' circumstances.[10]

---

[1] Immigration and Asylum (Procedure) Rules 2003, SI 2003/652; Immigration and Asylum Appeals (Procedure) Rules, 2000, SI 2000/2333, r 12(5); Immigration Appeals (Procedure) Rules 1984, SI 1984/2041, r 11(4), Immigration Appeals (Procedure Rules) 1972, SI 1972/1684, r 11(4).

[2] *R v Immigration Appeal Tribunal, ex p Mehta* [1976] Imm AR 38, CA. Different considerations apply to onward appeals, where permission to appeal out of time will not be granted, even if an appellant is blameless, unless the appeal itself has a real prospect of success: *R (on the application of Makke) v Immigration Appeal Tribunal and Secretary of State for the Home Department* [2005] EWCA Civ 176, reversing the decision at [2004] EWHC 1523 (Admin).

[3] *R v Immigration Appeal Tribunal, ex p Mehta (VM)* [1976] Imm AR 174 at 184–185 CA, per Browne LJ. See also *AK (Bulgaria)* [2004] UKIAT 00201 (starred), fn 8 below.

[4] It should be noted that this part of the test is similar to that used for late appeals under the Sex Discrimination Act 1975 and the Race Relations Act 1976: see *Hutchison v Westward Television Ltd* [1977] ICR 279, EAT.

[5] But the tribunal has held that the imposition of a time limit for giving notice of appeal against a decision said to breach a person's rights protected by Art 3 ECHR is not incompatible with Art 3: *Kucaj* [2002] UKIAT 08396.

[6] Advisers' negligence or simple mistakes was usually grounds to allow an out-of-time appeal to proceed: see cases cited in previous edition, 18.104 fn 5, see also *Liaquat* (2001) 01TH03260 (appellant's representative overlooked the notice of appeal which had been left on the file); *R (on the application of Aouissi) v Immigration Appeal Tribunal* [2002] EWHC 3006 (Admin). See also *Mohammadi v Advocate-General for Scotland* [2003] Scot CS 129, where refusal to entertain an out-of-time appeal was quashed because the Tribunal had failed to explain why a two-day delay caused by representatives' error did not amount to special circumstances. Note that under the fast track procedure, a late appeal will only be entertained if the circumstances were outside the control of the appellant 'or his representative' (SI 2005/560, r 8(2)). Advisers' mistakes may not suffice, but the issue remains unlitigated.

[7] [1976] Imm AR 38 at 42, CA.

[8] *Abaci* (16605) 2 December 1998, where a long delay in lodging an asylum appeal because of a solicitor's mistake was seen in the context of a six-year delay in making the asylum decision. See, however, *AK (Bulgaria)* [2004] UKIAT 00201 (starred), where the Tribunal ruled that a one-day delay was not *de minimis* where time limits where intended to be short. The Tribunal noted in that case that it was impossible to provide a list of what might be regarded as 'special circumstances', but the strength of the grounds of appeal could not by itself justify extending time, nor could a simple miscalculation of a time limit.

[9] *Oremnle* (15844) (24 November 1997, unreported) where the Tribunal allowed an appeal against the refusal of an extension of time on a student appeal, lodged a day late, because the student had not passed many exams.

[10] *McNulty* (14204) (22 November 1996, unreported).

18.96 The Procedure Rules indicate that both decisions on timeliness of a notice of appeal, and whether to extend time, are preliminary decisions.[1] Because of this, there is no possibility of appeal[2] or review[3] under the NIAA 2002 as amended, of the Tribunal's decision that a notice of appeal was filed out of time and so that there is no valid appeal before it. A decision on the validity of a purported appeal is treated the same as an exercise of discretion not to extend time, although the two decisions could not be more different, as the Tribunal in *B (Zimbabwe)* explained.[4] After 4 April 2005, it appears that the only remedy for an unlawful decision that an appeal was lodged out of time is judicial review.

1   Asylum and Immigration Tribunal (Procedure) Rules 2005, SI 2005/230, r 10(6). See also the definition of 'determination' (excluding procedural, ancillary and preliminary decisions) in r 2. Rules 9–11 of the Procedure Rules also make it clear that a person giving notice of appeal is not thereby an 'appellant', also defined restrictively in r 2 as a person giving notice of appeal 'in accordance with these Rules'. For the fast track equivalents see Asylum and Immigration Tribunal (Fast Track Procedure) Rules 2005, SI 2005/560, rr 2(2), 12(1).
2   Under Nationality, Immigration and Asylum Act 2002, s 103E, inserted by Asylum and Immigration (Treatment of Claimants, etc) Act 2004, s 26. A preliminary decision is not a 'decision on an appeal' for the purpose of an onward appeal: s 103E(7)(a).
3   Under NIAA 2002, s 103A as inserted. A preliminary decision is not a 'decision on an appeal' for the purpose of review: s 103A(7)(a).
4   A decision on the preliminary issue of time was held to be a determination under the 1971 Act (making it appealable) in *Jaayeola* (14819) (2 April 1997). The definition of 'determination' under the 2000 Procedure Rules as a decision to allow or dismiss an appeal, excluded a decision on time, with the Tribunal holding in *B (Zimbabwe)* [2004] UKIAT 76 that once it had been established that a notice of appeal was out of time and an extension of time was refused, there was no valid appeal for the purpose of any onward appeal. However, in *MM (Burundi)* [2004] UKIAT 00182 the Immigration Appeal Tribunal held that however 'determination' was defined, it had jurisdiction to hear an appeal on a point of law relating to an adjudicator's decision that an appeal was invalid, which included the issue of timeliness (although not the exercise of discretion). The omission of any definition of 'determination' in the relevant part of the NIAA 2002 and the 2003 Rules enabled the Tribunal to reinstate a decision on timeliness as a 'determination', holding that a decision on time determined the appeal by bringing it to an end.

18.97 The rules do not specify a maximum period by which time for appealing may be extended; neither is a maximum imposed by statute.[1] However, once the time limit imposed by the Procedure Rules is past, any statutory leave which a person had as a result of an in-time application for an extension of leave ends, leaving the person vulnerable to removal.[2] Similarly, an appeal is no longer 'pending' for the purposes of asylum support etc.[3] However, if an extension of time for appealing is granted, the appeal reverts to 'pending' status, any statutory leave the person held resumes,[4] and the person cannot be removed.[5]

1   In variation appeals, there used to be a maximum delay of 14 days, beyond which time for lodging an appeal could not be extended, because of the complexities to which s 14 of the Immigration Act 1971 gave rise, for which see 5th edn at 18.105.
2   Immigration Act 1971, s 3C(2)(b) as substituted by Nationality, Immigration and Asylum Act 2002, s 118 (s 3C inserted by Immigration and Asylum Act 1999, s 3), which extends leave during the period while (inter alia) an appeal under s 82 could be brought (ignoring any possibility of an appeal out of time with permission).
3   NIAA 2002, amended by Asylum and Immigration (Treatment of Claimants, etc) Act 2004 Sch 2 para 20, s 104(2)(a), (d). See *R (on the application of Erdogan) v Secretary of State for the Home Department* [2004] EWCA Civ 1087, [2004] All ER (D) 421 (Jul), where the

Court of Appeal reversed the Administrative Court's decision that an asylum claimant had an appeal 'pending' for the purposes of s 104 (and so did not lose asylum support) when what he had pending was an application for permission to appeal out of time. However, the court (and the Secretary of State) agreed that once permission has been given to appeal out of time, the appeal has been (re)-instituted and is again pending.

4   Immigration Act 1971, s 3C(2)(c) as inserted and substituted.
5   NIAA 2002, s 78.

Invalid notice of appeal

18.98 The rules address one other situation where a person gives notice of appeal to the Tribunal which is not accepted as valid, and that is where there is no relevant decision.[1] In such a situation, the Tribunal 'shall not accept' the notice of appeal, and must notify the person giving notice of appeal, and the respondent, accordingly.[2] It is difficult to see how the Tribunal will be in a position to know whether there is a relevant decision without any involvement on the part of the respondent, for which there is no provision in the rule. However, appeal rights cannot be created by mistake or even by consent, and it is clear that if in fact no relevant decision has been taken (because, to take the most obvious example, further representations on asylum or human rights grounds following the dismissal of an earlier claim have not been accepted as amounting to a fresh claim which would generate a new immigration decision), there will be no valid appeal. It hardly needs a procedure rule to deal with that.

1   Defined in the Asylum and Immigration Tribunal (Procedure) Rules 2005, SI 2005/230, r 2 as a decision against which there is an exercisable right of appeal to the Tribunal. For a discussion in the context of in-country and out-of-country appeals, see 18.25 above.
2   SI 2005/230, r 9. The draft rules gave the Tribunal jurisdiction to decide as a preliminary issue whether there was a valid appeal before it, ie whether the person has a right of appeal against the decision, and if not, to strike out the notice of appeal. Presumably it was decided that the Tribunal's jurisdiction to decide there was no valid appeal before it was self-evident.

Imminent removal cases

18.99 As we have seen, the determination of the timeliness of an appeal or whether to extend time is a preliminary issue decided without reference to the immigration authorities. Rule 11 of the principal procedure rules assumes a situation where (presumably in ignorance of the pending proceedings) removal directions have been issued against an appellant and it is proposed to remove him or her within five calendar days of the date on which the notice of appeal was given. On notification of this by the respondent, the Tribunal must, if reasonably practicable, make a preliminary decision under rule 10 before the proposed date and time of removal,[1] and may notify the appellant orally, including by telephone, that it believes the appeal is out of time;[2] shorten the time for the appellant to give evidence in support of a contention that the appeal notice was filed in time;[3] and direct that such evidence be given orally, including by telephone, and hold a hearing or telephone hearing to receive the evidence.[4] This provision does not extend to the fast-track procedure.[5] Whether the intending appellant is protected from removal if the decision on the timeliness or validity of the appeal is not made before the projected removal is due to take place is not spelt out by the rules. Clearly, while an appeal is 'pending' for the purposes of section 78 of the NIAA 2002, removal would be unlawful.[6] Where there is a dispute about timeliness, we suggest that until it is resolved, the appeal must be treated as pending; the intending appellant must be protected from removal pending the Tribunal's decision on the issue, to give effect to elementary considerations of fairness (particularly where fundamental rights are engaged).[7] Somewhat different considerations apply where the appeal is self-confessedly out of time and the Tribunal is being asked to exercise discretion to extend time, since in such a situation, the appeal is no longer 'pending',[8] although given the importance of the appeal, it would arguably be unfair to remove, particularly where there was a good reason for the failure to file the appeal in time.[9]

1   Asylum and Immigration Tribunal (Procedure) Rules 2005, SI 2005/230, r 11(1), (2). Applications in imminent removal cases will normally be dealt with by senior immigration judges on a rota basis, who may have regard to matters including whether the person concerned is able to give evidence by telephone and, where the person is represented, to the practicability of receiving submissions from the representative: Practice Direction 1/2005, 5.3.
2   SI 2005/230, r 11(3)(a).
3   SI 2005/230, r 11(3)(b).
4   SI 2005/230, r 11(3)(c).
5   Presumably because there is far more coordination between the immigration authorities and the Tribunal in the case of fast track claimants (who are all detained), than in the case of other claimants, who may have lost touch with the Home Office and not responded to a decision notice. It is these claimants who might become subject to removal directions without the Home Office realising that they have lodged an (out of time) appeal.
6   Ie the prohibition on removal of appellants pending appeal: see 18.24 above. Previously, the submission of a notice of appeal was enough to halt removal: *Secretary of State for the Home Department v Omishore* [1990] Imm AR 582; *Secretary of State for the Home Department v Ibrahim* [1994] Imm AR 1.
7   See the observations of Sedley LJ on the balance between administrative convenience and fairness in *R (on the application of the Refugee Legal Centre) v Secretary of State for the Home Department* [2004] EWCA Civ 1481, [2004] All ER (D) 580 (Mar), para 6, and see *R v Secretary of State for the Home Department, ex p Fayed* [1998] 1 WLR 763 at 777. Premature removal which wrongly prevented the appellant from putting human rights arguments could well breach procedural requirements inherent in the relevant rights, cf *Ciliz v Netherlands* [2000] 2 FLR 469; *Conka v Belgium* (51564/99) (5 February 2002, unreported), ECtHR.
8   *R (on the application of Erdogan) v Secretary of State for the Home Department* [2004] EWCA Civ 1087, [2004] All ER (D) 421 (Jul).
9   Cf the situation of the appellant MM in the case of that name, *MM (Burundi)* [2004] UKIAT 00182 (starred), where the appellant's house had burned down at the crucial time, or even, less dramatically, that of the appellant in *Erdogan* (above), whose appeal was lodged out of time because of a postal strike. The court in *Erdogan* (para 20) remarked that the power of the Secretary of State to remove a person who was seeking an extension of time to appeal to the Tribunal would be subject to the supervisory role of the Administrative Court in judicial review to give protection where necessary.

Respondent's duty to file appeal papers

18.100 Once the notice of appeal has been filed with the Tribunal, it must serve a copy on the respondent as soon as reasonably practicable (unless the appellant served notice of appeal on the entry clearance officer),[1] or immediately, if the appeal is in the fast track.[2] The respondent must then (unless it has already done so) file the notice of the decision to which the notice of appeal relates, any other document giving reasons for that decision, any statement of evidence form completed by the appellant and record of interview with the appellant relating to the decision under appeal, any unpublished document referred to in the decision notice or reasons for refusal letter, and notice of any other decision made in relation to the appellant in respect of which he or she has a right of appeal under section 82 of the NIAA 2002.[3] Under the fast track procedure, the respondent is required to do this not later than two days after being sent the copy appeal notice.[4] In ordinary appeals, the respondent must lodge the documents in accordance with any directions given by the Tribunal, and if none are given, as soon as reasonably practicable, and in any event no later than 2pm on the day before the first hearing of the appeal.[5] A copy of all the documents lodged with the Tribunal must be served on the appellant at the same time.[6] Such is the measure of disenchantment with the Home Office, based on previous experience of its procedural non-compliance,[7] that no-one connected with immigration appeals expects the appeal documents to be made available to the Tribunal or to appellants earlier than 2pm on the day before the first hearing, and the adjournment provisions may have to be utilised if this duty proves too onerous.[8]

[1] Asylum and Immigration Tribunal (Procedure) Rules 2005, SI 2005/230, r 12.
[2] Asylum and Immigration Tribunal (Fast Track Procedure) Rules 2005, SI 2005/560, r 9.
[3] SI 2005/230, r 13(1). For the difficulties caused by the previous procedure see *R (on the application of Hasa) v Immigration Appeal Tribunal* [2003] EWHC 396 (Admin), [2003] All ER (D) 232 (Feb); 18.91 above.
[4] SI 2005/560, r 10. Otherwise the procedure in the principal rules applies: r 2.
[5] SI 2005/230, r 13(2). Similar provisions apply when the Tribunal has allowed an appeal to proceed following a decision on the timeliness or validity of the notice of appeal: r 13(3).
[6] SI 2005/230, r 13(4).
[7] See for example the cases at 18.117 below ('Non-compliance with directions').
[8] The Department for Constitutional Affairs has said, in response to a consultation on the new procedure rules, that 'where the Home Office fail to provide documents before the case management review hearing, the immigration judge will make a decision whether to proceed with the main hearing date or adjourn ... on the basis of the interests of the appellant not the Home Office.' DCA preliminary response to consultation, by email 8 February 2005. See SI 2005/230, r 21.

18.101 After a notice of appeal has been filed and forwarded to the respondent, and the appeal documents have been sent in, a number of further steps may be taken before the appeal comes on for a hearing or is determined. The Tribunal may hold a case management review hearing, and may issue directions relating to the conduct of the appeal, to determine the form of the appeal, whether there is to be a hearing, whether it is to be before a single immigration judge or a panel, the time it will take, the evidence, documentary and oral, that will be given and the issues to be addressed.[1] There is provision to allow the grounds of appeal to be varied during the course of the appeal.[2] The immigration authorities may reverse, withdraw or vary their decision – which will lead to the appeal being treated as abandoned[3] (other than in the case of an appeal against refusal of asylum under section 83 of the Nationality, Immigration and Asylum Act 2002).[4] The Tribunal may decide to determine an appeal without a hearing.[5] Special procedures and time limits must be observed in appeals relating to asylum.[6] Some of these steps will now be examined more closely.

1 Asylum and Immigration Tribunal (Procedure) Rules 2005, SI 2005/230, rr 43, 45, applied to fast track appeals by the Asylum and Immigration Tribunal (Fast Track Procedure) Rules 2005, SI 2005/560, r 27. For case management review hearings see 18.116 below.
2 SI 2005/230, r 14, applied to fast track appeals by SI 2005/560, r 6.
3 Nationality, Immigration and Asylum Act 2002, s 104(4).
4 The appeal against refusal of asylum is only available once leave exceeding a year in total has been granted; thus the grant of further leave will not affect a pending s 83 appeal.
5 SI 2005/230, r 15(2); SI 2005/560, r 13(2).
6 SI 2005/230, r 23.

Parties to an appeal

18.102 The parties to an appeal will be the appellant (ie the person who has given a notice of appeal to the Tribunal against a relevant decision in accordance with the Procedure Rules),[1] and the respondent (ie the decision maker specified in the notice of decision against which the appeal is brought).[2] In asylum appeals, the Tribunal must permit the UK representative of the United Nations High Commissioner for Refugees (UNHCR) to make representations in the proceedings, if he or she gives notice to the Tribunal that he wishes to participate in any proceedings where the appellant has made an asylum claim.[3] The 2005 Rules do not, as previous rules did,[4] permit the UK representative to become a party to the proceedings, but do entitle him or her to to be served with any documents served on the parties,[5] including notice of the time and place of the hearing,[6] written directions relating to the conduct of the appeal [7] and the determination of the appeal,[8] and to attend the hearing[9] and be represented.[10]

1 Note that a person who submits a notice of appeal is not an appellant; that condition is only met if (i) the notice is against a relevant decision, defined as a decision against which there is an exercisable right of appeal to the Tribunal, and (ii) the notice is served 'in accordance with these Rules': Asylum and Immigration Tribunal (Procedure) Rules 2005, SI 2005/230, r 2, applied to fast track appeals by the Asylum and Immigration Tribunal (Fast Track Procedure) Rules 2005, SI 2005/560, r 6. To hammer the point home, r 6 of the principal rules provides that an appeal *may only* be instituted by giving notice of appeal against a relevant decision in accordance with these Rules. For timeliness and compliance with other requirements relating to the notice of appeal see 18.94 and 18.98 above.
2 Asylum and Immigration Tribunal (Procedure) Rules 2005, SI 2005/230, r 2, applied to fast track appeals by the Asylum and Immigration Tribunal (Fast Track Procedure) Rules 2005, SI 2005/560, r 6.
3 SI 2005/230, r 49, applied to fast track appeals by SI 2005/560, r 27.
4 Immigration and Asylum (Procedure) Rules 2003, SI 2003/652, r 2.
5 SI 2005/230, r 55(7).
6 Under SI 2005/230, r 46(1).
7 Under SI 2005/230, r 45(3).
8 Under SI 2005/230, r 22(1).
9 SI 2005/230, r 54(6).
10 SI 2005/230, r 48(2).

Certification of pending appeal

18.103 The Secretary of State or an immigration officer may, while an appeal to the Tribunal under section 82 or 83 of the Nationality, Immigration and Asylum Act 2002 is pending, issue a certificate under section 97 or 98 (national security, diplomatic or public interest issues justifying exclusion or removal from the UK). In each case, the certificate has the effect of putting an end to the proceedings before the Tribunal.[1] The Procedure Rules require the Secretary of State to notify the Tribunal of any such certification, whereupon the Tribunal must notify the parties, and take no further action on the appeal.[2] There is no longer any power for the Secretary of State or an immigration officer to certify a pending appeal under section 96 (earlier right of appeal); although an appeal can be prevented by a certificate under the section, it cannot be aborted once lodged.[3]

1   See Nationality, Immigration and Asylum Act 2002, s 99, amended by Asylum and Immigration (Treatment of Claimants, etc) Act 2004.
2   Asylum and Immigration Tribunal (Procedure) Rules 2005, SI 2005/230, r 16. This provision does not apply to fast track appeals.
3   NIAA 2002, s 96(7), as amended. Note however that s 99 has not been amended, leading to a contradiction between s 96(7): 'A certificate shall have no effect in relation to an appeal instituted before the certificate is issued', and s 99, stating that an appeal 'shall lapse' where a certificate is issued under s 96(1) or (2) in respect of a pending appeal.

Withdrawal of appeals

18.104   All appeals may be withdrawn or abandoned. What are the distinctions between withdrawal and abandonment, and what are the consequences? Withdrawal of an appeal implies a positive act, while abandonment suggests a passive failure to prosecute the appeal, or an action incompatible with pursuing it whereby it is deemed abandoned by statute. In the case of a deemed withdrawal, which happens when the decision appealed against is withdrawn,[1] the positive act is that of the respondent rather than the appellant, but the distinction between withdrawal and abandonment vanishes with the concept of 'deemed abandonment' when the appellant is granted leave to enter or remain in the UK.[2] Much of the case law deals with the issue of who decides whether an appeal has been withdrawn, how the decision is made, and whether a decision that an appeal has been withdrawn is itself challengeable. An appellant may withdraw his or her appeal orally, at a hearing (including a preliminary hearing),[3] or at any time, by filing written notice with the appellate authority.[4] An appeal is treated as withdrawn if the respondent notifies the Tribunal that he or she has withdrawn the decision (or, if the appeal relates to more than one decision, all the decisions) to which the appeal relates.[5] If an appeal is withdrawn or treated as withdrawn, the Tribunal must serve on the parties a notice that the appeal has been recorded as having been withdrawn.[6] Such a notice is not a 'determination' within the meaning of the Procedure Rules,[7] or a 'decision on the appeal' for the purposes of appeal or statutory review,[8] and could be challenged only by judicial review. It is clear that whether an appeal has been withdrawn is a matter for the Tribunal and the courts, not for the Secretary of State.[9] Under the previous procedure rules, when notice of appeal was served on the respondent, giving notice of withdrawal to the respondent was not effective to withdraw an appeal, and the respondent was still obliged to forward appeal papers to the appellate authority even if the appellant notified the respondent of an intention to withdraw the appeal.[10] A withdrawal letter to the Home Office could be superseded by subsequent actions inconsistent with withdrawal, provided the Tribunal had not made a decision to accept the withdrawal.[11] Now that appeal notices go direct to the Tribunal, there is no reason for withdrawal of appeals to go through immigration authorities. Where an appeal is validly withdrawn prior to the hearing, and the withdrawal accepted by the Tribunal, the appeal does not go into a state of suspended animation but ceases to exist,[12] and any determination of the appeal (on the merits) is a nullity.[13]

1 Asylum and Immigration Tribunal (Procedure) Rules 2005, SI 2005/230, r 17(2). Rule 17 is applied to fast track appeals by SI 2005/560, r 6.
2 Nationality, Immigration and Asylum Act 2002, s 104(4)(a).
3 SI 2005/230, r 17(1)(a). See *Rahman (Akikur) v Immigration Appeal Tribunal* [1995] Imm AR 372, CA, for an analysis of the position under the Immigration Act 1971 (in similar terms to NIAA 2002, s 104(1).
4 SI 2005/230, r 17(1)(b).
5 SI 2005/230, r 17(2).
6 SI 2005/230, r 17(3).
7 SI 2005/230, r 2 (applied to fast track appeals by SI 2005/560 r 6), defining 'determination' as a decision by the Tribunal in writing to allow or dismiss the appeal, taken upon consideration of its merits, and excluding a procedural, ancillary or preliminary decision.
8 NIAA 2002, ss 103A(7)(a) (review), 103E(7)(a) (appeals from panel), exclude procedural, ancillary or preliminary decisions.
9 *Entry Clearance Officer v Hughes* (01TH01147) (22 May 2001, unreported), IAT, see fn 11 below.
10 See API, Appeals: withdrawal, para 2.1. The API states that inviting an appellant to withdraw an appeal should only be done 'with great care'. We suggest that the immigration authorities should not do it at all.
11 *El-Tuyeb* (12643), where the letter of withdrawal did not reach the appellate authority until the hearing, which the appellant attended to pursue the appeal. The case emphasised the importance of allowing the appellant to argue against withdrawal.
12 *Adewole* (18538) (22 September 1998, unreported), IAT; *Singh (Nachtar) v Secretary of State for the Home Department* [1991] Imm AR 195; *Osman (Ayse)* [1993] Imm AR 417.
13 *Kirungi* (13111) (20 March 1996, unreported), IAT. But see *Entry Clearance Officer v Hughes* (01TH01147) (22 May 2001, unreported), where the Tribunal dismissed (albeit on technical grounds) an ECO appeal against an adjudicator's decision allowing an appeal which had apparently been withdrawn, although the Tribunal had doubts about the circumstances of the withdrawal.

18.105 The main difficulty in practice has been whether the person withdrawing has the necessary instructions and authority to do so.[1] The general rule that a retainer of a solicitor includes authority to compromise an action or withdraw unless contrary instructions are expressly given,[2] does not appear to apply in immigration appeals,[3] and a solicitor without instructions has been held to have no authority to withdraw an appeal.[4] Where there is authority, withdrawal will be effective.[5] The old case law indicates that an employer or someone who has no right of audience at the appeal may validly withdraw an appeal,[6] even if that person is not registered or exempt under Part V of the IAA 1999.[7] The issue in all cases however is likely to be whether it is clear that the appellant intended to withdraw the appeal. If appellants have signed a letter of withdrawal, the burden is on them to show that they instructed their representative not to present it, or to withdraw it.[8]

1 See *R v Diggines, ex p Rahmani* [1985] QB 1109, [1986] Imm AR 195; *R v Immigration Appeal Tribunal, ex p Pollicino* [1989] Imm AR 531, QBD; *Nessa v Secretary of State for the Home Department* [1985] Imm AR 131, CA.
2 44 *Halsbury's Laws* (4th edn) para 121.
3 See *R v Diggines, ex p Rahmani* [1985] QB 1109, [1986] Imm AR 195.
4 *Singh v Secretary of State for the Home Department* [1991] Imm AR 195.

5   *Attivor v Secretary of State for the Home Department* [1988] Imm AR 109. The API
    (Appeals: Withdrawal, para 2.3) state that if the representatives who submitted the appeal
    write to withdraw it, it would normally be appropriate to accept subsequent correspond-
    ence from them stating that the appeal is to be withdrawn, but that care should be taken
    when the appellant has instructed a number of representatives during the course of an
    application; where there is doubt about a withdrawal by a representative, the appellant
    should be asked to confirm the withdrawal personally in writing. The API continue that
    the final decision to accept or reject a withdrawal by a representative rests with the
    Tribunal. The instructions are likely to be amended to reflect the loss of the immigration
    authorities' role in receiving appeal notices.
6   *Tanakloe v Secretary of State for the Home Department* [1991] Imm AR 611.
7   See Asylum and Immigration Tribunal (Procedure) Rules 2005, SI 2005/230, r 48(3),
    applied to fast track appeals by SI 2005/560, r 27.
8   *Adewole* (18538) (22 September 1998), IAT.

Abandonment of appeal

18.106 The 2005 Procedure Rules, unlike earlier rules, do not make specific
provision for abandonment by an appellant in the sense of simple failure to
prosecute his or her appeal.[1] They provide only for statutory abandonment of
the appeal.[2] An appeal against an immigration decision under section 82 of
the Nationality, Immigration and Asylum Act 2002 is deemed abandoned by
statute in two specific situations: (i) leaving the UK;[3] (ii) being granted leave to
enter or remain[4] (or, in an EEA appeal, a residence permit or a residence
document).[5] If any party to a pending appeal becomes aware of either of these
events, they must notify the Tribunal, which must, in turn, serve notice on the
parties informing them that the appeal is being treated as abandoned and
thereafter take no further action in relation to the appeal.[6] The same
procedure applies to an appeal which is treated as 'finally determined' when a
deportation order is made against the appellant.[7] The Court of Appeal held in
Shirazi [8] that statutory abandonment provisions in the IAA 1999 [9] did not
apply to appeals to itself, so that someone leaving the UK (and returning)
while an appeal to the Court of Appeal was pending was not deprived of that
appeal by statute.[10] Deemed abandonment on departure from the United
Kingdom does not apply to cases involving EEA nationals or their family
members.[11] A pending appeal is deemed abandoned by operation of statute as
soon as leave to enter or remain is granted, so that there is no longer an appeal
before the appellate authority,[12] but only an actual grant of leave by way of
notice in writing has this effect; an undertaking by the respondent to grant
leave does not result in the appeal being abandoned.[13] Where an asylum
seeker's appeal under Nationality, Immigration and Asylum Act 2002, s 82 is
treated as abandoned as a result of a grant of leave to enter or remain, he or
she acquires a new right of appeal under section 83(1), if the leave granted or
the aggregate of that and any previous leave exceeds one year. However, a new
notice of appeal must be filed in order to exercise that right of appeal; an
abandoned section 82 appeal cannot be varied so as to become a section 83
appeal, because there is no appeal left to vary.[14]

1   For example, the Immigration and Asylum Appeals (Procedure) Rules 2000, SI 2000/2333,
    r 32 provided that the appellate authorities could treat failure to attend a hearing or to
    comply with directions as tantamount to abandonment of the appeal: see *Gremesty* [2001]
    INLR 132, IAT.
2   Asylum and Immigration Tribunal (Procedure) Rules 2005, SI 2005/230, r 18, applied to
    fast track appeals by SI 2005/560, r 6.

3   Nationality, Immigration and Asylum Act 2002, s 104(4)(b): *Dupovac v Secretary of State for the Home Department* [2000] Imm AR 265 (referring to equivalent provisions in s 33(4) Immigration Act 1971, inserted by the Asylum and Immigration Act 1996). However, the appeal is not to be treated as abandoned by operation of that provision if the appellant 'leaves the United Kingdom' as a result of being illegally removed by the Secretary of State: *Muja* [2002] UKIAT 05107. The Court of Appeal cast further doubt on the applicability of the section to all cases of 'leaving' the UK in *Shirazi v Secretary of State for the Home Department* [2003] EWCA Civ 1562, [2004] 2 All ER 602, doubting whether a mere day trip to Calais would activate the abandonment provision, but did not decide the issue.

4   NIAA 2002, s 104(4)(a). A third 'deemed abandonment' of an appeal, under s 58(10) Immigration and Asylum Act 1999, applied where a deportation order was made against an appellant; under the NIAA 2002, however, appeals are to be treated as finally determined, rather than abandoned, in this situation: NIAA 2002, s 104(5): see fn 7 below.

5   Immigration (European Economic Area) Regulations 2000, reg 33(1A), inserted by SI 2003/549.

6   Asylum and Immigration Tribunal (Procedure) Rules 2005, SI 2005/230, r 18(1), (2).

7   Under NIAA 2002, s 104(5): see SI 2005/230, r 18.

8   *Shirazi v Secretary of State for the Home Department* [2003] EWCA Civ 1562, [2004] INLR 92.

9   Under Immigration and Asylum Act 1999, s 58.

10   The decision depended partly on the distinction in the Act itself (reproduced in the NIAA 2002 provisions) between appeals under the relevant Part of the Act, and 'further appeals', and partly on the inherent jurisdiction of the Court of Appeal. The same logic would apply to deemed abandonment by grant of leave to enter or remain. Any other interpretation of the abandonment provisions would deprive the Court of Appeal of its inherent discretion to consider appeals involving important legal or policy issues even though the grant of leave has made the issue academic in the particular case.

11   See *Baumbast* (21263) (8 June 1999, unreported), IAT and the Immigration (European Economic Area) Regulations 2000, SI 2000/2326 (as amended by SI 2003/549), reg 27(4).

12   NIAA 2002, s 104(4)(a); *Kanyenkiko v Secretary of State for the Home Department* [2003] EWCA Civ 542, [2003] All ER (D) 348 (Feb) (on the equivalent provisions under Immigration and Asylum Act 1999, s 58(9)). For the effect of transitional provisions, where leave to remain was granted after the coming into force of the appeal provisions of the NIAA 2002 but the appeal was brought under the IAA 1999, see *ZA (Ethiopia)* [2004] UKIAT 00241, [2004] Imm AR 538.

13   *Mohamed (Omar) v Secretary of State for the Home Department* [2002] UKIAT 04634. Note that the Home Office representative may concede a case at any time, and are instructed to do so where a change in the law since the date of decision fundamentally affects the appeal in the appellant's favour, or the decision maker clearly misapplied the law and a correct application would have led to a grant; where the Country Information Policy Unit has advised of significant developments in a particular country meaning that the appellant would be persecuted for a Convention reason on return; where further credible evidence is produced before or at the hearing which clearly meets the requirements of the rules; and where the circumstances of the case clearly fall within a published Home Office policy. The presenting officer is instructed to seek approval from a senior caseworker before conceding (Home Office to South Manchester Law Centre 12 November 2003). Conceding a case is not the same as granting leave, and should lead to the Tribunal allowing the appeal, not treating it as abandoned.

14   *Kanyenkiko v Secretary of State for the Home Department* (fn 12 above).

18.107 The Procedure rules about certification, withdrawal and abandonment are drafted in very similar terms.[1] In each case, the Tribunal apparently acknowledges a state of affairs which means there is no longer an appeal before it, by notifying the parties. It was doubtless the draftsman's intention to assimilate the situations, so that notices of withdrawal and abandonment were no different from certification. But in fact there are profound differences. The Secretary of State's certification is final and decisive in a way that an appellant's withdrawal of an appeal, even deemed withdrawal and deemed abandonment, is not. We have referred earlier to the substantial case law on withdrawal and on deemed abandonment.[2] It is a moot point as to whether the notice of the Tribunal that the appeal is treated as withdrawn, abandoned or finally determined is a 'determination' within the definition in rule 2 of the Procedure rules, or a 'decision on the appeal' under the review and onward appeal provisions of the NIAA 2002.[3] It is not obviously a decision to allow or dismiss the appeal under rule 2, but neither is it obviously procedural, ancillary or preliminary, so as to exclude it from review or onward appeal.[4] The Tribunal in *Gremesty*[5] held that an adjudicator's decision to treat an appeal as abandoned for the appellant's failure to prosecute it amounted to a 'determination' no less than a dismissal of the appeal on the merits, and in *MM (Burundi)*[6] referred to the 'error of law' jurisdiction as encompassing the issue of the validity of an appeal. On that basis it is likely that a decision to treat an appeal as abandoned would be susceptible to review or appeal.

1 SI 2005/230, rr 16–18. Rules 17 and 18 apply to fast track appeals, but not r 16: see SI 2005/560, r 6.
2 See 18.104–106 above.
3 See definition of 'determination' in SI 2005/230, r 2 and of 'decision on the appeal' in Nationality, Immigration and Asylum Act 2002, ss 103A(7)(a), 103E(7)(a), inserted by Asylum and Immigration (Treatment of Claimants, etc) Act 2004, s 26.
4 See discussion in *MM (Burundi)* (starred) (fn 6 below).
5 [2001] INLR 132, IAT. See also, under previous rules, *Akhuemonkhan* [1998] INLR 265, IAT; *Secretary of State for the Home Department v Ibrahim* [1994] Imm AR 1; *Secretary of State for the Home Department v Munchula* [1996] Imm AR 344; *R v Immigration Appeal Tribunal, ex p Lila* [1978] Imm AR 50.
6 *MM (Burundi)* [2004] UKIAT 00182, [2004] Imm AR 515, [2004] INLR 327 (starred).

Defining the issues pre-hearing

18.108 Under previous procedure rules, the respondent to an appeal was required to produce an explanatory statement of the facts relating to the decision and the reasons for it.[1] Although the 'explanatory statement' is no longer a requirement, the respondent is, as we have seen, required to file with the Tribunal and serve on the appellant the notice of the decision or decisions appealed against, any other document served on the appellant giving reasons for the decision, and evidence which has come into being during the decision process, such as statement of evidence forms, records of interview and any unpublished material referred to in the decision or reasons, or otherwise relied on by the respondent.[2] The respondent's duty to produce 'any unpublished material ... otherwise relied on by the respondent' is wider than before, and is designed to ensure that appellants are not taken by surprise. However, there may well be other evidence or information which the appellant requires from the Home Office.[3] There is, surprisingly, no power of discovery of documents in the Procedure rules,[4] but there are other ways of achieving the same result. In the exercise of its powers to give directions the Tribunal may require a party to provide further details of his or her case or any other information which appears to be necessary for the determination of the appeal or application,[5] as well as requiring statements of evidence,[6] chronologies[7] and bundles of all documents to be relied on[8] to be filed and served on all other parties.[9] The list of possible directions is not exhaustive.[10] However, directions may only be given in relation to procedural matters; they may not require the

Secretary of State to take a substantive step, such as issuing a fresh refusal letter,[11] interviewing an appellant [12] or reconsideration of an asylum claim (even where asylum had wrongly been refused on grounds of non-compliance with procedure).[13] But a direction could properly be made requiring the Secretary of State to provide reasons for refusing asylum on the merits where the only reasons given were that the appellant had failed to submit a statement or attend for interview.[14] While the main use of directions has been to control appellants' cases, they are apt to extract from the respondent in advance all evidence on which it seeks to rely, and also evidence in its possession which might assist the appellant. The new Tribunal is determined to impose some order on appeals under the new one-tier regime, and Practice Directions require both parties to provide to the Tribunal and to the other party any amendments, proposed amendments or applications to vary grounds of appeal or notices of decision at the case management review hearing. At the end of the hearing, the Tribunal is to give written confirmation to the parties of any issues that have been agreed at the CMR hearing as being relevant to the determination of the appeal, and any concessions made by a party at the CMR hearing (although it is unlikely that these concessions would be irrevocable, particularly if they are made before all the evidence is available).[15]

1   Immigration Appeals (Procedure) Rules 1984, SI 1984/2041. The explanatory statement was held to be evidence, not merely assertion: *R v Immigration Appeal Tribunal, ex p Weerasuriya* [1983] 1 All ER 195, QBD; *R v Immigration Appeal Tribunal, ex p Hassanin* [1987] 1 All ER 74, [1986] 1 WLR 1448, CA, *Manjit Singh v Entry Clearance Officer, New Delhi* [1986] Imm AR 219; but it is doubtful that these cases represent the law in the age of scepticism and procedural fairness.
2   Asylum and Immigration Tribunal (Procedure) Rules 2005, SI 2005/230, r 13; see 18.100 above.
3   It may, for example, be necessary to seek further particulars relating to an anonymous allegation. In an asylum case involving a person who had been suspected of support for terrorism by British police, it would be very important to find out whether any information about the appellant had passed between the British authorities and those of the appellant's country.
4   *R v Adjudicator (RG Care), ex p Secretary of State for the Home Department* [1989] Imm AR 423, QBD.
5   SI 2005/230, r 45(4)(d)(iii).
6   SI 2005/230, r 45(4)(e)(i).
7   SI 2005/230, r 45(4)(e)(vi).
8   SI 2005/230, r 45(4)(e)(ii).
9   SI 2005/230, r 45(4)(e).
10 This is apparent from the words 'in particular' in SI 2005/230, r 45(4).
11 *Mwanza v Secretary of State for the Home Department* [2001] INLR 616.
12 *R (on the application of Zaier) v Immigration Appeal Tribunal* [2002] EWHC 2215 (Admin), [2002] AIL ER (D) 70 (Oct).
13 *R (on the application of Emlik) v Immigration Appeal Tribunal* [2002] EWHC 1279 (Admin), [2002] All ER (D) 209 (Jan).
14 *Secretary of State for the Home Department v Razi* (2001) 01TH1836; *Secretary of State for the Home Department v Tekle* [2002] UKIAT 00704.
15 Practice Direction 1/2005, 6.3–4, 6.9.

18.109 An application for a direction requiring the provision of further information is particularly important in cases where the Secretary of State makes a positive assertion, eg that the unauthorised disclosure of an asylum claim to the authorities of the appellant's country will not affect his or her safety on return,[1] or that a particular practice operates at the airport of a particular country, or that a document is not genuine. In addition, the appellate authority is not to take account of evidence that has not been made available to the parties[2] unless it is alleged that the document relied on is forged and disclosure to that party of a matter relating to the detection of the forgery would be contrary to the public interest. In such a case the appellate authority must investigate the allegation in private and must proceed in private so far as necessary to prevent disclosure of the method of detection of the forgery.[3] It is also possible to obtain information or documents by summoning a witness to answer questions or to produce documents,[4] subject only to the limitation that a party or witness may not be compelled to give evidence or produce a document that he or she could not be compelled to give or produce in civil proceedings.[5] Where the respondent is asserting some matter, such as fraud or forgery of documents, the burden of proof is on the respondent, and the more serious the allegation, the clearer and more direct the proof should be.[6] In such cases a failure to produce or call evidence in support of the allegations should result in the respondent's allegations remaining unproven or of very little weight.[7]

[1] *R v Immigration Appeal Tribunal, ex p Agbenyenu* [1999] Imm AR 460, QBD. However, in *FZ* [2003] UKIAT00315, [2003] Imm AR 633, the Tribunal held that the Secretary of State was under no duty to embark on an investigation to identify evidence not in his hands, and that any duty of disclosure on the Secretary of State would generally be discharged by production of a relevant CIPU report.
[2] Asylum and Immigration Tribunal (Procedure) Rules 2005, SI 2005/230, r 51(7).
[3] Nationality, Immigration and Asylum Act 2002, s 108.
[4] SI 2005/230, r 50(1)(b).
[5] SI 2005/230, r 51(2).
[6] *Ali v Secretary of State for the Home Department* [1984] 1 All ER 1009, [1984] Imm AR 23, CA. See 18.146 below.
[7] See *R v Immigration Appeal Tribunal, ex p Cheema* [1982] Imm AR 124 at 133, CA.

18.110 Quite apart from these means of obtaining information, an individual is entitled to a copy of any information about him or her [1] that is held by any 'data controller' [2] such as the Immigration Service or Home Office or other government department.[3] Such information (for example, a copy of the individual's Home Office file) is to be provided when the individual makes a request in writing to the data controller and pays such a fee as may be required.[4] To obtain a copy of his or her Home Office file, an individual should write to the 'Subject Access Bureau' at the Home Office in Lunar House, Croydon, enclosing a cheque for £10 payable to 'the Accounting Officer, Home Office'. The request for information must be complied with within 40 days.[5] The obligation to disclose information is subject to exemptions relating, inter alia, to the safeguarding of national security,[6] the prevention and detection of crime and the prosecution of criminals.[7]

[1] Data Protection Act 1998, s 7(1)(c)(i) and s 8(2).
[2] DPA 1998, s 1(1).
[3] DPA 1998, s 63.
[4] DPA 1998, s 7(2). The fee that may be required is up to a maximum of £10. See Data Protection (Subject Access) (Fees and Miscellaneous Provisions) Regulations 2000, SI 2000/191, reg 3.
[5] DPA 1998, s 7(8) and (10).
[6] DPA 1998, s 28.
[7] DPA 1998, s 29.

Reasons for the decision or action appealed

18.111 The giving of reasons is a substantial matter. The Notices Regulations[1] require that reasons should be given when the decision or action is notified to the appellant, as seen above. The giving of reasons for an administrative decision adversely affecting rights of residence, family life, and even more fundamental rights protected by the Refugee Convention, is increasingly seen as vital for compliance with standards of fairness at common law,[2] and for compatibility with the Human Rights Convention.[3] It is for this reason thought that unless the notice of refusal is amended, it is not possible for the immigration authority to rely upon an entirely different reason for refusal at the hearing. The extent to which the reasons may be amended to reflect the true reasons for the decision and the extent to which the Tribunal is tied to the reasons contained in the notice and decision letter, when it comes to the hearing of the appeal, have already been considered.[4] The position under the Immigration Act 1971 was that the notice of decision and explanatory statement were preliminary definitions of the issues between the parties on appeal, but with the probable exception of statutory grounds (eg for deportation), not necessarily conclusive.[5] Certainly, the jurisdiction of the Tribunal is wide enough, at least in cases where the Refugee Convention is engaged,oblige it to measure its view of the facts[6] against the applicable statutes, rules, policies, Convention and administrative law standards, whether or not these have been expressly referred to, with the Court of Appeal decision in *Robinson*[7] providing the parameters of this duty.[8] So, where an asylum claim has been refused for reasons of non-compliance with the asylum determination procedure (eg failure to attend an interview), the Tribunal has held that the appellate authority has an obligation to decide for itself whether the appellant's removal would be contrary to the Refugee Convention.[9] A fair hearing demands a proper opportunity to meet the case made. In this connection it is important to recall that the Tribunal has power to limit the issues on appeal.[10] This provides an opportunity to agree facts and legal issues which once agreed, should not be reopened unless patently wrong.[11]

[1]   Immigration (Notices) Regulations 2003, SI 2003/658, reg 5(1)(a).
[2]   See eg *Stefan v General Medical Council* [1999] 1 WLR 1293; *R v Secretary of State for the Home Department, ex p Zighem* [1996] Imm AR 194.
[3]   *Stefan v General Medical Council* [1999] 1 WLR 1293; *R v Higher Education Funding Council, ex p Institute of Dental Surgery* [1994] 1 WLR 242.
[4]   See 18.56 and 18.88 above.
[5]   Woolf J in *R v Immigration Appeal Tribunal, ex p Hubbard* [1985] Imm AR 110.
[6]   Nationality, Immigration and Asylum Act 2002, s 85(4).
[7]   *Robinson v Secretary of State for the Home Department* [1997] Imm AR 568, CA.
[8]   *Rahman and Akhter* (00307) (10 March 2000, unreported), IAT; *Kaur (Sukhinder) v Secretary of State for the Home Department* [1998] Imm AR 1, CA; *R (on the application of Naing) v Immigration Appeal Tribunal, R (on the application of Eyaz) v Immigration Appeal Tribunal* [2003] EWHC 771 (Admin), [2003] All ER (D) 337 (Mar).
[9]   *Haddad (Ali)* [2000] INLR 117, IAT.
[10]   Asylum and Immigration Tribunal (Procedure) Rules 2005, SI 2005/230, r 45(4)(f)(iv).
[11]   See *R v Immigration Appeal Tribunal, ex p Akhtar and Bowen* (1982) 126 Sol Jo 430, QBD.

18.112 Where a question of fact (eg the credibility of an appellant's evidence) is conceded by the immigration authority, either in its decision letter or at a hearing, through the Home Office Presenting Officer, the concession must be accepted by the Tribunal.[1] But a concession is a positive act; mere failure to put a fact in issue in a refusal letter or to cross-examine on a fact or even to cross-examine at all, does not amount to a concession.[2] A concession may be withdrawn before the tribunal, but it is for the tribunal to decide whether to permit withdrawal of the concession taking account of all the circumstances, including whether the appellant would be prejudiced by the withdrawal.[3] Whether a concession was actually made may subsequently become a disputed question of fact[4] underlining the desirability of the parties reducing to writing any concession that is made.[5]

1 *R (on the application of Ganidagli) v Secretary of State for the Home Department* [2001] INLR 479; see also *Carcabuk and Bla v Secretary of State for the Home Department* (00TH01426) (although not starred because the tribunal consisted of only two members, this decision is to be regarded as binding).
2 *Carcabuk and Bla* above.
3 *Davoodipanah v Secretary of State for the Home Department* [2004] EWCA Civ 106, [2004] INLR 341; *R (on the application of Ivanauskiene) v Special Adjudicator* [2001] EWCA Civ 1271, [2002] INLR 1 (relating to a concession on the law, based on the law at the time of the appeal hearing); *Secretary of State for the Home Department v Abdalla* [2002] UKIAT 01900.
4 See eg *R (on the application of Kantharajah) v Secretary of State for the Home Department* [2002] EWHC 1456 (Admin.
5 *R (on the application of Ganidagli) v Secretary of State for the Home Department* [2001] INLR 479.

Preliminary issues

18.113 Previous Procedure Rules [1] provided for a preliminary issue jurisdiction for the resolution of allegations by the respondent immigration authority either that the appellant is not entitled to appeal or the notice of appeal was out of time. The current Procedure Rules [2] include a procedure for determination by the Tribunal of whether an appeal which appears to have been made out of time, was actually given in time or should be allowed to proceed even though given out of time.[3] However, express provision is no longer made for the Tribunal to determine as a preliminary issue an allegation by the immigration authority that the appellant is not entitled to appeal,[4] although the 2005 Procedure Rules continue to make provision for 'a particular matter to be dealt with as a preliminary issue'.[5] The change in the rules enabling notice of appeal to be lodged with the Tribunal, instead of with the respondent, means that it is no longer possible for the respondent unilaterally to decide that the appellant has no right of appeal, once a notice of appeal has been lodged. Subject to any issues of timeliness, discussed above, the person lodging a notice of appeal should be considered an appellant for all purposes, and specifically, the giving of notice of appeal should be sufficient (a) to institute an appeal which is then pending until determined, withdrawn or abandoned or lapsed;[6] ((b) to confer jurisdiction on the appellate authority to determine the appeal,[7] including the question of whether the appellant actually has a right of appeal;[8] (c) for the suspensive effects of a pending appeal to apply, including the prohibition on removal from the UK[9] and that a variation or revocation of leave should not have effect.[10]

1 Immigration and Asylum Appeals (Procedure) Rules 2000, SI 2000/2333, Immigration Appeals (Procedure) Rules 1984, SI 1984/2041.

2   Asylum and Immigration Tribunal (Procedure) Rules 2005, SI 2005/230 (for fast track appeals, SI 2005/560).
3   SI 2005/230, r 10; SI 2005/560, r 12; see 18.102 above.
4   SI 2000/2333, r 12 expressly provided for the adjudicator to determine the respondent's allegation that, for example, the appellant had no right of appeal because of a particular statutory provision or because an immigration document relied on was a forgery or because the notice of appeal had not been signed.
5   SI 2005/230, r 45(4)(d)(i), applied to fast track appeals by SI 2005/560, r 27.
6   Nationality, Immigration and Asylum Act 2002, s 104(1)(a).
7   *Lokko v Secretary of State for the Home Department* [1990] Imm AR 111.
8   *B (Zimbabwe)* [2004] UKIAT 00076; *MM (Burundi)* [2004] UKIAT 00182 (starred); see 18.96 above.
9   NIAA 2002, s 78.
10 NIAA 2002, s 82(3).

Amending the grounds of appeal

18.114 'The formulation of grounds of appeal is done rapidly, often by people with no mastery of either English law or the English language. All this in an area where the law is riddled with obscurities and regularly amended by primary or secondary legislation and by rules'. The Court of Appeal's observation in *Zenovics*[1] explains the need for appellants to be able to amend their grounds of appeal. Further, the real scope of an appellant's case often does not become clear until much of the preparatory work on an appeal has been done and certainly long after notice of appeal has been given. A wide discretion to allow grounds of appeal to be varied in asylum and human rights appeals is particularly necessary, bearing in mind the serious consequences of a wrong decision[2] and the principle that all possible grounds for seeking to remain should be dealt with in a single appeal. The 2005 Procedure Rules provide that the appellant may vary his or her grounds only with its permission.[3] Permission is of course not required to serve a statement in response to a one-stop notice under Nationality, Immigration and Asylum Act 2002, section 120.[4] There is no limitation to the power to permit the grounds of appeal to be varied under the 2005 Procedure Rules, other than the overriding objective to secure that proceedings before the Tribunal are handled as fairly, quickly and efficiently as possible, and the Tribunal members' responsibility for ensuring this. In the interests of the parties and the wider public interest;[5] and there are likely to be few, if any, circumstances where it would be right for permission to be refused.[6] Were the application to vary the grounds to be refused, the appellant could not, we suggest, reasonably be prevented by certification from relying on the new grounds in a future appeal.[7] Practice Directions require appellants to notify the Tribunal and the respondent at the case management review hearing of any application to amend the grounds of appeal, and any amendments to the reasons in support of the grounds.[8]

1   *R (on the application of Zenovics) v Secretary of State for the Home Department* [2002] EWCA Civ 273, [2002] INLR 219.
2   *Dyli v Secretary of State for the Home Department (No 2)* (01TH1010).
3   Asylum and Immigration Tribunal (Procedure) Rules 2005, SI 2005/230, r 14, applied to fast track appeals by SI 2005/560, r 6.
4   SI 2005/230, r 14, with reference to Nationality, Immigration and Asylum Act 2002, s 85(2) (duty of Tribunal to consider additional grounds responding to one-stop notice).

5   SI 2005/230, r 4, applied to fast track appeals by SI 2005/560, r 6. See case management review, below.
6   Cases such as *FF (Iran)* [2004] UKIAT 00192, where a late application to vary grounds of appeal to the Immigration Appeal Tribunal from an adjudicator's determination, have no application to first instance appeals, where both law and factual issues are at large. But note the observation of the Tribunal that outline submissions do not amount to varied grounds of appeal or an application to vary.
7   Ie under Nationality, Immigration and Asylum Act 2002, s 96(1), (as substituted by Asylum and Immigration (Treatment of Claimants, etc) Act 2004, s 30), which permits a second claim to be certified, thereby precluding appeal, if it relies on a matter which could have been raised on an earlier appeal. That condition cannot be satisfied if the Tribunal prevented an appellant from raising the matter on the earlier appeal by refusing to permit a variation of the grounds of appeal.
8   Practice Direction 1/2005, 6.3.

Notice of hearing

18.115 When the Tribunal fixes a hearing, it must serve on every party and on any representative acting for any party, notice of the date, time and place fixed for the hearing.[1] It may vary the date of the hearing, but must serve notice of any new date, time and place for the hearing.[2] In an appeal relating, in whole or in part, to an asylum claim, where the appellant is in the UK, the hearing must be fixed for a date not more than 28 days after the Tribunal receives the notice of appeal (or, where it has made a preliminary decision on time, after it has served the decision on the appellant).[3] However, this time limit does not apply if the respondent has failed to file the appeal documents in time, and if a hearing date has been fixed, it may be varied in such a situation if it would be unfair to the appellant to proceed on the fixed date.[4] The procedure under the old appeals regime[5] was for the appellate authority to issue a notice containing two dates: the 'first hearing' and the substantive hearing. The first hearing was a case management hearing, which did not require the attendance of the appellant or representative provided the information requested in the notice was submitted in time, indicating that the appellant was ready to proceed.[6] Practice Directions provide that a case management review (CMR) hearing will be held in respect of all in-country appeals except fast track and reconsideration appeals, and emphasise that the CMR is a hearing in the appeal, and that the appeal may be determined without a hearing, or in the absence of a party, if a party does not appear and is not represented at the CMR hearing.[7] The President has the power to extend the time limits set out in the rules, both in individual cases and in particular classes of case, and we would be surprised if this power is not frequently used.[8]

1   Asylum and Immigration Tribunal (Procedure) Rules 2005, SI 2005/230, r 46(1), applied to fast track appeals by the Asylum and Immigration Tribunal (Fast Track Procedure) Rules 2005, SI 2005/560, r 27.
2   SI 2005/230, r 46(2).
3   SI 2005/230, r 23(1), (2). This is a new provision which is likely to cause severe difficulties to appellants and their representatives, particularly since the respondent's documents will only arrive the day before the first hearing.
4   SI 2005/230, r 23(3). There is separate provision for adjournments of appeals in r 21 (see 18.125 below).
5   Under the Immigration and Asylum (Procedure) Rules 2003, SI 2003/652, which made provision for pre-hearing review, at r 38(5)(d)(ii).

6   Where a reply to the notice of first hearing was served late, the representative or the appellant should have attended, but in *K (Afghanistan)* [2004] UKIAT 00043, the Tribunal accepted that an appellant who was not personally at fault should not lose the right to a hearing of his appeal.
7   Practice Direction 1/2005, 6.2.
8   SI 2005/230, r 45(6).

Case management and directions

18.116 As we have seen, the Tribunal may (subject to the procedure rules) decide the procedure to be followed in relation to any appeal.[1] Case management includes decisions about whether the case should be heard by an immigration judge or a panel of judges; defining the issues, including any preliminary issues;[2] whether the appeal is to be determined without a hearing,[3] or joined with another appeal in one hearing;[4] readiness for the full hearing of the appeal; and the preparation and presentation of evidence. We have dealt with defining the issues at 18.108 above. Now, we turn our attention to other aspects of case management. Decisions relating to the constitution of the Tribunal (ie whether the appeal should be heard by one immigration judge or by a panel) are for the Tribunal itself, which is not required to consider representations by any party.[5] Unless the President's direction specifies otherwise, a single immigration judge may conduct a case management review hearing, give directions to the parties and deal with other preliminary or incidental matters.[6] The Tribunal may give directions orally or in writing relating to the conduct of any appeal or application, but must give them to every party.[7] The Tribunal must not direct an unrepresented party to do something unless it is satisfied that he or she is able to comply with the direction.[8] There may be a direction as to the witnesses to be heard, if any,[9] and how the evidence is to be given, eg by directing that witness statements stand as evidence in chief.[10] The power to direct that witness statements stand as evidence in chief is not subject to the appellant's consent, although this does not mean that at the hearing the appellant should not have the opportunity of adding to the witness statement anything necessarily supplementary to it to bring it to life.[11] Directions may also require parties to file and serve, within specified time limits,[12] statements of the evidence to be called, skeleton arguments, chronologies, paginated and indexed bundles of the documentary evidence to be relied on, time estimates, lists of witnesses, a chronology and details of any interpreter required.[13] Directions may limit the number or length of documents a party may rely on (particularly useful in asylum appeals where 'standard bundles' of over 300 pages are frequently served), the length of oral submissions, the time allowed for examination and cross examination of witnesses and the issues to be addressed at a hearing.[14] Directions may provide for a hearing to be conducted or evidence given or representations made by video link or by other electronic means.[15] They may make provision to secure the anonymity of a party.[16] But directions under the procedure rules must relate to the procedure to be followed by the parties for determination of the appeal and may not, for example, require the Secretary of State to re-interview an appellant or to make a fresh decision.[17]

1   Asylum and Immigration Tribunal (Procedure) Rules 2005, SI 2005/230, r 43, applied to fast track appeals by the Asylum and Immigration Tribunal (Fast Track Procedure) Rules 2005, SI 2005/560, r 27.

² SI 2005/230, r 45(4)(d)(i); see 18.113 above.

³ SI 2005/230, r 15(2)(a); see 18.118 below.

⁴ SI 2005/230, r 45(4)(g). This might happen where the appeals raise some common question of fact or law, relate to decisions in respect of members of the same family or where it is desirable for some other reason that they be heard together: r 20; see 18.149 below.

⁵ SI 2005/230, r 44(1). The Tribunal may give a direction at the case management review hearing that the appeal is to be heard by a group of members: Practice Direction 1/2005, 6.8.

⁶ This appplies where the appeal is to be heard by a panel: SI 2005/230, r 44(2).

⁷ SI 2005/230, r 45(1), (3).

⁸ SI 2005/230, r 45(5).

⁹ SI 2005/230, r 45(4)(d)(iv).

¹⁰ SI 2005/230, r 45(4)(d)(v). See Practice Direction 1/2005, 6.7, 7.2.

¹¹ *R v Secretary of State for the Home Department, ex p Singh* [1998] INLR 608, CA (permission). The Practice Direction 1/2005 insists (para 6.7) that 'in normal circumstances a witness statement should stand as evidence in chief', although it concedes that 'there may be cases where it will be appropriate' for appellants or witnesses to add to their statements. It is a rare case where it is *not* necessary to give such opportunity, at least to appellants.

¹² SI 2005/230, r 45(4)(b). Standard directions require the service by the appellant, seven days before the full hearing, of witness statements, a paginated and indexed bundle of all documents to be relied on, with a schedule identifying the essential passages, a skeleton argument identifying all relevant issues (including human rights claims) and citing all the authorities relied on; and a chronology of events. The respondent must serve a paginated and indexed bundle and schedule: Practice Direction 1/2005, 6.6. For non-compliance see below.

¹³ SI 2005/230, r 45(e)(i)–(vii).

¹⁴ SI 2005/230, r 45(f)(i)–(iv). Best practice for preparation of bundles includes typed translations of documents not in English, signed by the translator to certify accuracy, with details of that person's qualifications; highlighting of relevant passages of long documents; index; and cross-reference to the documents, with pagination, in the skeleton argument: Practice Direction 1/2005, para 8.2. The parties should not rely on the Tribunal having judicial knowledge of any country information or background reports: 8.6. The limit on issues to be addressed at the hearing must be read in the light of Nationality, Immigration and Asylum Act 2002, s 85 and in the light of the Tribunal's duty set out in *Robinson v Secretary of State for the Home Department* [1997] Imm AR 568; see 18.48 above.

¹⁵ SI 2005/230, r 45(4)(h). This provision is routinely used for hearings before the tribunal where the tribunal sits in Field House in London and where the parties appear by means of a video link in another hearing centre. It has been used to enable appellants to give evidence from outside the United Kingdom: see eg *R (on the application of Ahmadi) v Secretary of State for the Home Department* [2002] EWHC 1897 (Admin), [2002] All ER (D) 52 (Sep) at 1926.

¹⁶ SI 2005/230, r 45(4)(i). Anonymity for appellants is now provided by the Tribunal as a matter of course by the use of initials in published determinations, but the power is wider, and can be used to protect the anonymity of witnesses.

¹⁷ See 18.108 above.

18.117 What effect does non-compliance with a direction or a provision of the Procedure Rules have on the appeal? The Tribunal may determine the appeal without a hearing. However, it may follow that course only if satisfied that it is appropriate in all the circumstances, including the extent of the failure to comply with the rules or a direction and any reasons for the failure.¹ Consideration of 'all the circumstances' would require the Tribunal to take account of whether there was evidence of previous failure by the party to comply with a direction or rule.² It is no longer possible for the Tribunal to dismiss the appeal without consideration of the merits where the party failing to comply with the procedure rule or the direction is the appellant, a power contained in previous procedure rules which gave rise to considerable unfairness and litigation.³ Failure to file and serve evidence in accordance with time limits set out in the rules or in a direction will result in the Tribunal refusing to consider the evidence unless it is satisfied that there are good reasons for considering the evidence,[4] but 'as a general principle, the requirement to ensure that justice is done in appeals requiring the most anxious scrutiny will in most cases outweigh the understandable desire on the part of the appellate authority to ensure that its directions and the provisions of the procedure rules are not flouted with impunity'.[5] The power to determine an appeal without a hearing for non-compliance with directions should be exercised with extreme caution and will rarely if ever be appropriate if the party in default is present.[6]

[1] Asylum and Immigration Tribunal (Procedure) Rules 2005, SI 2005/230, r 15(2)(c); Asylum and Immigration Tribunal (Fast Track Procedure) Rules 2005, SI 2005/560, r 13(2)(b).

[2] *R (on the application of Karagoz) v Immigration Appeal Tribunal* [2002] EWHC 1228 (Admin): see 18.118 below. Since determination without a hearing generally prejudices the appellant and not the respondent, it is the appellant's default which will lead to the invocation of the rule. The respondent can flout the procedure rules with impunity in the knowledge that the only power the Tribunal has is that of adjourning hearings to ensure fairness to the appellant (SI 2005/230, rr 21, 23(3)).

[3] Immigration and Asylum Appeals (Procedure) Rules 2003, SI 2003/652, r 45(2). *Muhammad* (01/TH/1233); *Jamil* (01/TH/1863). The 2000 Procedure Rules, SI 2000/2333, r 33(2)(a) empowered the appellate authorities to allow appeals without consideration of the merits where the failure to comply was the respondent's, but the Court of Appeal in *R (on the application of Zaier) v Immigration Appeal Tribunal* [2003] EWCA Civ 937, [2003] All ER (D) 153 (Jul) and *Benkaddouri v Secretary of State for the Home Department* [2003] EWCA Civ 1250, [2004] INLR 1 held that the rules were there to regulate the conduct of appeals, and the power should only be used where repeated non-compliance made a fair hearing of the appeal impossible. That was the case in *Secretary of State for the Home Department v Razi* (01TH01836) and *Zand* [2002] UKIAT 04885.

[4] SI 2005/230, r 51(4), applied to fast track appeals by SI 2005/560, r 27. The immigration judge must not automatically exclude late evidence but must apply the 'good reason' test and consider whether the appeal should be adjourned to avoid prejudice to the other side: *MD (Pakistan)* [2004] UKIAT 00197 'Reported'. The 'good reason' applies to the admission of the evidence, and not to the reason for its lateness: *SA (Sri Lanka)* [2005] UKIAT 00028.

[5] *AK (Iran)* [2004] UKIAT 00103. See also *KK (Afghanistan)* [2004] UKIAT 00258. But see *Basnet v Secretary of State for the Home Department* [2002] EWCA Civ 1893, [2003] Imm AR 265 (permission), where the Court of Appeal held (in respect of a 'manifestly not credible' claim) that failure to comply with directions to file fresh evidence before the IAT, in an appeal from an adjudicator, entitled the Tribunal to disregard the evidence. The duty of anxious scrutiny does not apply in entry clearance appeals, where the 'good reasons' requirement is applied more rigorously: *EA (Ghana)* [2004] UKIAT 0022.

[6] *Meflah v Secretary of State for the Home Department* [1997] Imm AR 555, IAT; *R v Immigration Appeal Tribunal, ex p S* [1998] Imm AR 252, [1998] INLR 168. Although these cases were decided before an express power existed to dispense with a hearing, the overriding objective, and so the framework within which the appellate authority must exercise its discretion, remains the same.

TRIBUNAL HEARINGS

Dispensing with a hearing

18.118 The Tribunal has separate powers to determine an appeal without a hearing,[1] and to determine the appeal following a hearing in the absence of a party.[2] Here we consider determination of an appeal without a hearing at all. Under the 2005 Procedure Rules, every appeal must be considered by the Tribunal at a hearing except where:

(1)   the appeal lapses pursuant to section 99 of the Nationality, Immigration and Asylum Act 2002, ie where the appeal has been certified under section 97 (certification on national security grounds) or section 98 (certification on other grounds of public good) of the Act;[3]

(2)   the appeal is treated as abandoned pursuant to section 104(4) of the Nationality, Immigration and Asylum Act 2002, ie as a consequence of the appellant being granted leave to enter or remain or leaving the United Kingdom;[4]

(3)   on a deportation order being made with the result that an appeal against refusal of leave to enter, refusal of a certificate of entitlement to the right of abode, variation or refusal to vary a person's leave or revocation of a person's indefinite leave is treated as finally determined, by operation of Nationality, Immigration and Asylum Act 2002, section 104(5);[5]

(4)   the appeal is withdrawn, or is treated as withdrawn by virtue of rule 17, on the respondent withdrawing the decision;[6]

(5)   all the parties to the appeal consent;[7]

(6)   the appellant is unrepresented and is outside the United Kingdom or it is impracticable to give him or her notice of a hearing;[8]

(7)   a party has failed to comply with a provision of the Procedure Rules or a direction of the Tribunal, and the Tribunal is satisfied that in all the circumstances, including the extent of the failure and any reasons for it, it is appropriate to determine the appeal without a hearing;[9]

(8)   the Tribunal is satisfied, having regard to the material before it and the nature of the issues raised, that the appeal can justly be determined without a hearing, and the parties have had notice of its intention and an opportunity to make written representations in support of a hearing.[10]

The power to dispense with a hearing must be exercised by the Tribunal personally rather than a member of the administrative staff.[11] The Tribunal cannot decide to determine an appeal without a hearing and then receive submissions from counsel.[12] Where an in-country asylum appeal is to be determined without a hearing, the Tribunal must determine it no later than 28 days after its receipt of the notice of appeal, or its decision on timeliness (if applicable).[13]

---

[1]   Asylum and Immigration Tribunal (Procedure) Rules 2005, SI 2005/230, r 15; Asylum and Immigration Tribunal (Fast Track Procedure) Rules 2005, SI 2005/560, r 13.

[2]   SI 2005/230, r 19, applied (so far as applicable) to fast track appeals by SI 2005/560, r 6(f). The Tribunal should be clear to distinguish between the two situations and should make it clear which procedure it is adopting: *Abali* (15543) (6 October 1997, unreported), IAT; *JZ (Ivory Coast)* [2004] UKIAT 00102.

[3]   SI 2005/230, r 15(1)(a)(i); SI 2005/560, r 13(1)(b)(i). Note that the Secretary of State can no longer certify under Nationality, Immigration and Asylum Act 2002, s 96 to bring an end to an appeal: see s 96(7), amended by Asylum and Immigration (Treatment of Claimants, etc) Act 2004, s 30, although s 99 has not been amended to reflect this.

[4]   SI 2005/230, r 15(1)(a)(ii); SI 2005/560, r 13(1)(b)(ii). For abandonment of appeals see 18.106 above.

[5]   SI 2005/230, r 15(1)(a)(iii); SI 2005/560, r 13(1)(b)(iii).

6   SI 2005/230, r 15(1)(a)(iv); SI 2005/560, r 13(1)(b)(iv). For withdrawal of appeals see 18.104 above.
7   SI 2005/230, r 15(2)(a); SI 2005/560, r 13(2)(a).
8   SI 2005/230, r 15(2)(b) (there is no equivalent in the fast-track procedure, since appellants will always be in the UK). Before proceeding without a hearing under the rule, the Tribunal must notify both parties and give them an opportunity to make further representations: *Entry Clearance Officer v TMG (Turkey, South Africa, Colombia)* [2004] UKIAT 00028; *PP (India)* [2004] UKIAT 00128. On unrepresented appellants see *R v Diggines, ex p Rahmani* [1985] QB 1109, [1986] Imm AR 195, HL, where it was held that UKIAS had not ceased to act for the appellant, although they had lost her new address; before proceeding under this rule, the adjudicator should have required an unambiguous declaration from UKIAS either that their instructions had been withdrawn or that they had no instructions.
9   SI 2005/230, r 15(2)(c); SI 2005/560, r 13(2)(b). The power to dispense with a hearing for non-compliance with directions should be used very sparingly, and probably not at all when parties have appeared for the hearing: *MD (Pakistan)* [2004] UKIAT 00197. Where the appellant was not personally at fault when the representative filed the reply to the notice of hearing late, the appeal should not have been determined without a hearing: *K (Afghanistan)* [2004] UKIAT 00043. While it may be legitimate for an immigration judge to decide to proceed without a hearing, or a further hearing, after a failure to comply with directions, and even to decide to pass the case to another immigration judge, the second immigration judge must not determine the case as if he or she was the original immigration judge: *JZ (Ivory Coast)* [2004] UKIAT 00102, 'Reported'.
10   SI 2005/230, r 15(2)(d), (3); SI 2005/560, r 13(2)(c). Where both parties want a hearing, it would rarely be appropriate to dispense with one: *MD (Pakistan)* [2004] UKIAT 00197, and never when credibility is in issue: *Federation of Canadian Sikh Societies v Canadian Council of Churches* [1985] 1 SCR 178 (cited in *R v Immigration Appeal Tribunal, ex p S* [1998] Imm AR 252 at 267 and *R v Secretary of State for the Home Department, ex p Yousaf* [2000] INLR 432). Note that in the fast track procedure, the power is not subject to any opportunity to make representations.
11   *Singh (Piara)* (7069), IAT.
12   *Sivayokam* (16015) (8 January 1998), IAT.
13   SI 2005/230, r 23(1), (2)(b). This time limit does not apply if the respondent has failed to comply with directions regarding service of appeal documents: r 23(3).

The hearing

18.119 Every appeal must be considered at a hearing before an immigration judge or a panel of immigration judges unless a provision of the Procedure Rules or any other enactment permits or requires the Tribunal to dispose of an appeal without a hearing.[1] There is provision in the rules for hearings to be conducted, evidence given or representations made by video link or other electronic means,[2] opening up for the first time the possibility of appellants giving evidence in their own out-of-country appeals.[3] Time limits for the hearing of the appeal depend on the nature of the case. In-country asylum appeals must be heard within 28 days of the Tribunal's receipt of the notice of appeal, or of the date of service on the appellant of a decision allowing the appeal to proceed, where there was an issue about time.[4] The Asylum and Immigration Tribunal (Fast Track Procedure) Rules 2005 provide for even faster hearing and determination of some appeals.[5] They apply to persons who were, at the time of being served with an immigration decision, and thereafter, detained under the Immigration Acts at a specified Immigration Removal Centre.[6] The time limits may be extended by direction of the President,[7] and determinations are not invalidated by the Tribunal's failure to comply with the time limits for holding the hearing.[8] There is nothing in the procedure rules as to where hearings may take place. The Tribunal is not required to list an appeal at the hearing centre which is closest or most convenient for the appellant, but should transfer an appeal where there is a good reason.[9] An appellant has no legitimate expectation that the date of the hearing will not be brought forward, only that it will not be changed without reasonable notice.[10]

1   Asylum and Immigration Tribunal (Procedure) Rules 2005, SI 2005/230, r 15(1); Asylum and Immigration Tribunal (Fast Track Procedure) Rules 2005, SI 2005/560, r 13.
2   SI 2005/230, r 45(4)(i).
3   See by way of example, *R (on the application of Ahmadi) v Secretary of State for the Home Department* [2002] EWHC 1897 (Admin), [2002] All ER (D) 52 (Sep).
4   SI 2005/230, r 23(1), (2).
5   SI 2005/560, r 7 has a two-day time limit for appealing to the Tribunal; by r 9 the Tribunal serves a copy of the notice of appeal on the respondent immediately; r 10 requires the respondent to file the appeal documents within two days thereafter; and r 11 provides for the Tribunal to fix a hearing date which is no later than two days after the respondent files the documents, meaning that the appeal should be heard within five days of the appellant's filing of notice of appeal. Rule 11(2) allows some flexibility; if the Tribunal cannot arrange a hearing within the time it must do so as soon as practicable thereafter. For the fairness of the fast track procedure see *R (on the application of the Refugee Legal Centre) v Secretary of State for the Home Department* [2004] EWCA Civ 1481, [2004] All ER (D) 580 (Mar); see 18.79 above.
6   Currently Campsfield House, Colnbrook House, Harmondsworth and Yarlswood: SI 2005/560, Sch 2.
7   SI 2005/230, r 45(6), applied to fast track appeals by SI 2005/560, r 27.
8   SI 2005/230, r 59(2), applied to fast track appeals by SI 2005/560, r 27.
9   *Ahmad* (12033) (21 April 1995, unreported); *Kaur* (13052) (1 March 1996, unreported), IAT. In *R v Secretary of State for the Home Department, ex p Semaane* [1998] Imm AR 48, the High Court held that the listing of an appeal in Birmingham necessitating travel from London was not unreasonable where the appellant had some means and had sought a transfer from Glasgow, from where he had lived, distinguishing *Adedayo* (14940), where the Tribunal allowed an appeal after an adjudicator decided a transferred case in the absence of an appellant with no means who had been unable to travel. An unpublished instruction, the 'Marylebone Directive', issued in 1993 or 1994, required appeals of appellants with an address north of Marylebone Road in London to be listed in Birmingham to alleviate pressure on the lists, 'where judicial capacity at London hearing centres is fully committed'.
10 SI 2005/230, r 46; *R v Immigration Appeal Tribunal, ex p Shandar* [2000] Imm AR 181.

Proceeding in a party's absence

18.120 The 2005 Procedure Rules require the Tribunal to hear an appeal in the absence of a party or a party's representative if satisfied that notice of the date, time and place of the hearing was given but that the party or his or her representative has given no satisfactory explanation for his or her absence.[1] This is a mandatory requirement and applies equally to both parties: an adjudicator may not adjourn for the respondent to be present if there is no explanation for a Home Office presenting officer's absence.[2] In addition, the appellate authority may hear an appeal in the absence of a party if satisfied that one of the following conditions is satisfied: a representative of the party is present at the hearing;[3] the party is not in the UK;[4] he or she is suffering from a communicable disease or there is a risk of him or her behaving in a violent or disorderly manner;[5] the party cannot attend because of accident or illness or some other good reason;[6] the party is unrepresented and it is impracticable to give him or her notice of the hearing;[7] or the party has notified the appellate authority that he or she does not wish to attend the hearing.[8] This provision does not entitle the Tribunal to proceed as if the appellant were absent when he or she is present but the representative is absent.[9] The Tribunal has set out guidelines for immigration judges on how to proceed where the Home Office is not represented, attached to the starred case of *MNM*.[10]

1   Asylum and Immigration Tribunal (Procedure) Rules 2005, SI 2005/230, r 19(1). The Tribunal is not entitled to proceed under this rule without checking the correctness of the address of the representative, particularly where the address for the appellant is apparently incorrect: *Alabi* (12975) (6 February 1996). The mandatory rule applies if an application for an adjournment is not granted and a party fails to attend the hearing (since the rejection of the adjournment application will normally mean that there is no satisfactory explanation for absence), and it should never be assumed that the party need not attend if such an application has been made: see Practice Direction 1/2005, para 9.7.
2   *R v Special Adjudicator, ex p Demeter* [2000] Imm AR 424, QBD: 'To give the impression of allowing special favours to the Home Office by allowing an adjournment without an explanation for absence is dangerous.'
3   SI 2005/230, r 19(2)(a).
4   SI 2005/230, r 19(2)(b).
5   SI 2005/230, r 19(2)(c).
6   SI 2005/230, r 19(2)(d).
7   SI 2005/230, r 19(2)(e).
8   SI 2005/230, r 19(2)(f).
9   *Singh (Santokh)* (13002) (22 February 1996), IAT.
10 (00TH 02423) (starred) (1 November 2000), IAT ('the *Surendran* guidelines').

18.121 Most of the case law concerns allegations of non-receipt of notices of hearing, leading to hearings in the absence of appellants. Parties and representatives are obliged to notify the Tribunal in writing of a postal address for service of documents, and until change of address is notified, documents sent to that address are deemed to have been properly served on the appellant.[1] They also have a duty to maintain contact with representatives until the appeal is finally determined, and to notify them of any change of address.[2] Representatives have a duty to notify the Tribunal and the other party when they begin to act for a party,[3] and if they cease to act, both the representative and the party must notify the Tribunal and the other party, and give them the name and address of any new representative, if known.[4] The Tribunal is entitled to continue to treat a representative as acting for a party until there has been strict compliance with the Procedure Rules for notifying a change of representative, even where the party has withdrawn instructions from that representative.[5] Notice given to the immigration authorities of a change is not enough;[6] the respondent is under no duty to notify the Tribunal of an appellant's change of address or representative.[7] But all deemed service must arguably be subject to a proviso, whether or not expressly stated, allowing proof of non-receipt.[8] Procedural requirements are designed to further the interests of justice.[9] The Tribunal is obliged to consider an allegation of non-receipt of the notice of hearing in an application for reconsideration.[10] It would be a 'strong step' not to accept the assertion of any professional person that a notice sent otherwise than by recorded delivery had not been received.[11] Service of a notice of hearing is not legally adequate if the name on the envelope is incorrect.[12] Earlier decisions on judicial review suggest that where a direction requires a certificate of readiness to be submitted, failing which the party is to appear on the date in the notice, and a certificate of 'unreadiness' is sent in, the Tribunal is entitled to proceed in the absence of the appellant and the representative,[13] but most reported cases indicate that a failure by a representative to comply with procedural requirements should not prejudice the appellant to the extent of preventing his or her attendance to give oral evidence, where this is necessary for the just disposal of the appeal.[14] There is a clear tension between the mandatory terms of the rule where no satisfactory reason has been given for absence, and the need for substantive justice.

1 Asylum and Immigration Tribunal (Procedure) Rules 2005, SI 2005/230, r 56. For the difficulties this rule caused when appeals were lodged with the respondent rather than the appellate authority, so that the appellate authority had no file to which to attach notices of changes of address, see *R (on the application of Hasa) v Immigration Appeal Tribunal* [2003] EWHC 396 (Admin), [2003] All ER (D) 232 (Feb).

2 SI 2005/230, r 48(6).

3 SI 2005/230, r 48(4).

4 SI 2005/230, r 48(7).

5 SI 2005/230, r 48(9); *R (on the application of Ahmed) v Immigration Appeal Tribunal* [2004] EWCA Civ 399, [2004] All ER (D) 594 (Mar), where the Tribunal was held to have waived the strict requirement of the rules, by corresponding with the second representative.

6 *R v Secretary of State for the Home Department, ex p Hannach* [1997] Imm AR 162, QBD.

7 *R v Secretary of State for the Home Department, ex p Hannach* [1997] Imm AR 162, QBD, and see *Lapido v Secretary of State for the Home Department* [1997] Imm AR 51, CA.

8 Following *R v Secretary of State for the Home Department, ex p Saleem*, [2000] Imm AR 529, [2000] INLR 413, upholding Hooper J at [1999] INLR 621. See also *R (on the application of Hasa) v Immigration Appeal Tribunal* [2003] EWHC 396 (Admin), [2003] All ER (D) 232 (Feb).

9 *Ravichandran v Secretary of State for the Home Department* [2000] 1 WLR 354 at 359, per Lord Woolf MR.

10 *R v Immigration Appeal Tribunal, ex p Susikanth* [1998] INLR 185, CA, and grounds explaining non-attendance at a hearing as caused by solicitor error gave an explanation for non-attendance: *R (on the application of Habyl) v Immigration Appeal Tribunal* [2002] EWHC 2313 (Admin), [2002] All ER (D) 237 (Oct). The old case of *Al-Mehdawi v Secretary of State for the Home Department* [1990] 1 AC 876, in which the House of Lords held that a representative's failure to send the notice of hearing to the appellant did not ground an allegation of procedural impropriety in the subsequent hearing, where the appellant was absent and unrepresented, has been held inapplicable to cases in which human rights or asylum issues are engaged: *Haile v Immigration Appeal Tribunal* [2001] EWCA Civ 663, [2002] Imm AR 170, [2002] INLR 283; cf *E v Secretary of State for the Home Department* [2004] EWCA Civ 49, [2004] 2 WLR 1351.

11 *R (on the application of Karagoz) v Immigration Appeal Tribunal* [2003] EWHC 1228 (Admin); *R (on the application of Simeer) v Immigration Appeal Tribunal* [2003] EWHC 2683 (Admin), [2003] All ER (D) 419 (Oct), holding that it was irrational for the IAT to reject as without foundation the assertion made in grounds of appeal to the IAT that notice of hearing had not been received. But see *R (on the application of Maqsood) v Special Adjudicator and Secretary of State for the Home Department* [2002] Imm AR 268 where the claimant's solicitor's evidence of non-receipt of the notice of hearing was rejected.

12 *Choudhry* (15911) (7 January 1998, unreported), IAT. See also *Idrissi v Immigration Appeal Tribunal* [2001] EWCA Civ 235, where a decision was quashed on the basis that the Tribunal proceeded on a mistaken view of the facts (ie a belief that the appellant had been properly served), when an administrative mistake led to a notice of hearing going to the wrong representative.

13 *R v Secretary of State for the Home Department, ex p Butt* [1999] Imm AR 341, QBD; *R v Special Adjudicator, ex p Arshad* (CO 1145/97) (15 April 1997, unreported), QBD.

14 *K (on the application of Afghanistan)* [2004] UKIAT 00043; see also cases cited at fnn 8–10 above.

18.122 In exercising the power to proceed in a party's absence, or in deciding whether that there is no satisfactory explanation for absence, the condition precedent to the duty to proceed, the Tribunal must act fairly[1]. It would be wise for an immigration judge to take the precaution of trying to find out why a party was absent, eg by making a telephone call to his or her representative before deciding to proceed in the party's absence.[2] However, the Tribunal is not obliged to accept any excuse for non-attendance at face value. In particular, the Tribunal is not obliged to accept a medical certificate which does not explain why a party is unable to attend.[3] The Tribunal must specify precisely why it is proceeding in the absence of a party, ie which particular provision of the rule it is relying on.[4] If it proceeds, it must allow or dismiss the appeal.[5]

1   *Singh (Reshan) and Kaur v Secretary of State for the Home Department* [1993] Imm AR 382 (if hearing is described as pre-hearing review, it is unfair to proceed in the absence of appellant, as if it was the final hearing). But see *R (on the application of Maqsood) v Special Adjudicator and Secretary of State for the Home Department* [2002] Imm AR 268; and see Practice Direction 1/2005, para 9.7.
2   *R (on the application of Karagoz) v Immigration Appeal Tribunal* [2003] EWHC 1228 (Admin) and *R (Simeer) v IAT* [2003] EWHC 2683 (Admin), [2003] All ER (D) 419 (Oct).
3   *R v Immigration Appeal Tribunal, ex p Baira* [1994] Imm AR 487, QBD; *Deen-Koroma v Immigration Appeal Tribunal* [1997] Imm AR 242, CA; *R v Secretary of State for the Home Department, ex p Lal Singh* [1998] Imm AR 320, QBD.
4   *Jan* (7063), IAT; *Deb* [1990] Imm AR 14.
5   *Ali (Shaharia)* [1999] INLR 108, IAT. Additionally, if the immigration judge accepts material from the party in whose absence he or she is proceeding, that is tantamount to reopening the hearing, obliging the immigration judge to reconsider whether it is appropriate to proceed in the party's absence: *Feghali* (16602) (25 November 1998, unreported), IAT.

Representation

18.123 Appellants and bail applicants may appear in person or be represented by any person not prohibited from acting by section 84 of the Immigration and Asylum Act 1999;[1] the respondent, the Secretary of State or the UK Representative of the UN High Commissioner for Refugees may be represented by any person authorised to act on their behalf.[2] A representative has all the powers of the party he or she is representing, such as the giving or receipt of notices.[3] The appellant has a duty to maintain contact with his or her representative until the appeal is finally determined, and to notify the representative of changes of address.[4] Both the party and his or her representative have a duty to notify the Tribunal of changes in representation.[5] Until such notification, documents served on the first representative are deemed properly served on the party he or she was representing.[6]

1   Asylum and Immigration Tribunal (Procedure) Rules 2005, SI 2005/230, r 48(1). This includes qualified lawyers or registered or exempted immigration service providers: see 1.58 above.
2   SI 2005/230, r 48(2).
3   SI 2005/230, r 48(5). Whether a representative's purported withdrawal of an appeal can bind the appellant is discussed at 18.105 above. On the issue of whether representatives' failure to comply with procedural requirements such as time limits for appealing, responses to directions etc should deprive personally blameless appellants of appeal rights, the courts have tended towards greater leniency in recent years, at least where human rights or asylum issues are engaged: see 18.121 above.
4   SI 2005/230, r 48(6).

⁵ SI 2005/230, r 48(4), (7). Notification of acting or ceasing to act may be given orally at a hearing to the Tribunal and any other party present at the hearing, but otherwise must be given in writing: r 48(8).

⁶ SI 2005/230, r 48(9). See *R (on the application of Ahmed) v Immigration Appeal Tribunal* [2004] EWCA Civ 399, [2004] All ER (D) 594 (Mar), where the appellant changed representatives and the first representative failed to notify the Tribunal, and submitted grounds of appeal. The second representative also submitted grounds, which were not considered. The Tribunal was held to have waived the strict requirement of the rules, by corresponding with the second representative, and so should have considered the second representative's grounds.

Controlled legal representation (CLR)

18.124 Funding for immigration and asylum appeals has been available since 1 January 2000, for representatives who are contracted with the Legal Services Commission to provide funded immigration services.[1] Funding is restricted within very tight limits,[2] which may be raised if representation is carried out by members of the LSC's accreditation scheme who are accredited to level 3,[3] and lifted for cases raising exceptionally novel or complex points of law, or with significant potential to produce real benefits for others.[4] Fast track proceedings are funded separately.[5]

1 Community Legal Service (Funding) Order 2000, SI 2000/627, amended by SI 2001/831, SI 2003/651, SI 2004/597, SI 2004/2900, SI 2005/571.
2 SI 2000/627 as amended. In addition to the level of payment, reforms instituted include to prevent abuse include strict financial thresholds of five hours' funded work, which can be exceeded only with the prior authority of the LSC, the unique client number imposing a financial limit on the work done in respect of each client irrespective of changes of representative, the LSC's assumption of responsibility for the Immigration Advisory Service and the Refugee Legal Centre, and the compulsory accreditation scheme for solicitors.
3 SI 2000/627 as amended, Art 5(7B), (7C).
4 SI 2000/627 as amended, Art 5(4B).
5 There are exclusive contracts with the LSC for provision of assistance and representation in the fast track.

Adjournments

18.125 The Tribunal has power to adjourn a hearing, but may not do so on the application of a party unless satisfied that the appeal cannot otherwise justly be determined.[1] The power to grant adjournments is more circumscribed for fast track appeals, as to which, see below. A party seeking an adjournment must if practicable, notify all other parties of the application, show good reason why the adjournment is necessary, and produce evidence of any fact or matter relied on in support of the application.[2] Where adjournments are sought on the grounds of health, the higher courts have generally been content to leave it to the immigration judge's judgment,[3] so long as he or she has given an adequate opportunity to respond to objections to medical evidence.[4] In such a case, the Tribunal is obliged to make a conscientious judgment as to whether justice calls for an adjournment, taking into account the nature of the appellant's condition and the evidence about when, if ever, the appellant would be able to give evidence.[5] Where adjournments have been sought on grounds of the appellant's need to find representation, the higher courts have frowned upon what was a more liberal approach by the tribunal,[6] which in asylum appeals such as *Ajeh*[7] had said that 'whether or not an appellant is articulate, the need for representation at the hearing ... appears almost axiomatic given the obligation to give the most anxious scrutiny to cases of this kind'.[8] However, in, *ex p Ghaly*[9] Sedley J issued a reminder that 'the question of adjournment ... frequently throws up fundamental issues of fairness. If the maxim 'both sides are to be fairly heard' is to have any effect, it means that each side has to have a fair opportunity of preparing to deal with what the other side is going to say'.[10] In *Okiji*[11] the Tribunal deprecated the refusal of an adjournment when counsel was taken ill and the adjudicator had, in refusing, referred to the 'normal practice of the Bar' in sending a replacement 'even at one moment's notice'. It observed that the traditions of the Bar were 'not always consistent with the interests of the appellant'.[12] The withdrawal of a representative at a hearing (other than when an appellant withdraws instructions) has been held a good reason to adjourn.[13] An adjournment to enable the appellate authority to provide an interpreter of the kind that the appellant had originally requested should not have been refused.[14] However, there is doubt as to whether an adjournment should be granted if the appellant requests it, where there is evidence that a refusal on non-compliance grounds was erroneous.[15]

1   Asylum and Immigration Tribunal (Procedure) Rules 2005, SI 2005/230, rr 47, 21(2).
2   SI 2005/230, r 21(1).
3   See eg *R v Secretary of State for the Home Department, ex p Odubanjo* [1996] Imm AR 504, QBD (adjudicator entitled to use common sense regarding a pregnant appellant who felt unwell at the hearing); *R v Immigration Appeal Tribunal, ex p Choudhury (Kawsar)* (1999/6451/C) (2 November 1999, unreported), CA (adjudicator entitled to refuse adjournment having regard to medical evidence and appellant's demeanour and ability to answer questions at the hearing).
4   *Chisthi* (14953) (12 May 1997, unreported); *Awadh* (12783) (7 December 1995, unreported); *Gheorghiu* (12850) (28 December 1995, unreported). See also *WT (Ethiopia)* [2004] UKIAT 00176, where the Tribunal held that obtaining an appointment with the Medical Foundation did not (on the particular facts) justify granting an adjournment (but note the comments indicating that in such a case the Secretary of State might be more receptive to a fresh claim). For adjournments to obtain evidence see below.
5   *Ramirez v Secretary of State for the Home Department* [2001] EWCA Civ 1365, [2002] Imm AR 240.
6   In *R (on the application of Bogou) v Secretary of State for the Home Department and Immigration Appeal Tribunal* [2000] Imm AR 494, Maurice Kay J pointed to the tightening of the criteria for adjourning between the Asylum Appeals (Procedure) Rules 1993 and 1996, SI 1993/1661 and SI 1996/2070 and to the failure of Tribunal jurisprudence to reflect that change. In *R v Special Adjudicator, ex p Nitcheu* (00/5158/C) (7 March 2000), CA (renewed permission application) a refusal to adjourn for legal representation for an appellant who had lost his representation through compulsory dispersal was upheld. See also *R v Special Adjudicator, ex p Kotovas* [2000] Imm AR 26; *R v Immigration Appeal Tribunal, ex p Adrees* (95/5564/D) (18 April 1996, unreported), CA; *R v Secretary of State for the Home Department, ex p Janneh* [1997] Imm AR 154; *R v Secretary of State for the Home Department, ex p Twaha* (CO/4073/98) (1 December 1999), QBD.
7   (13853) (30 August 1996, unreported), IAT, followed in *(inter alia) Cabrera* (17123) (21 May 1998, unreported); *Kyeyune* (18153) (25 November 1998, unreported). The liberal approach is not evident in entry clearance cases, see eg *Musa (Ibne)* [2002] UKIAT 07625.
8   The Tribunal's view of the importance of representation in asylum and human rights appeals reflected those of the Genn Report *Representation before Tribunals* (1989) Hazel and Yvette Genn, the Legal Aid Board (now Legal Services Commission), *Access to quality services in the immigration category* (May 1999), and of the Lord Chancellor's Advisory Committee on Legal Education and Conduct *Improving the quality of immigration advice and representation: A report*, ACLEC (July 1998).

[9] *R v Secretary of State for the Home Department, ex p Ghaly* (27 June 1996, unreported), QBD.

[10] See also the guidance in *R v Kingston-upon-Thames Justices, ex p Martin* [1994] Imm AR 172, DC, which was held to apply, together with that in *Macharia* [2000] Imm AR 190, 196 to adjournments in human rights cases, so that refusal to await a psychiatric report on a rape victim, due in days and likely to assist in a human rights appeal, was held *Wednesbury* unreasonable in *R (on the application of Fana) v Special Adjudicator* [2002] EWHC 777 (Admin), [2002] Imm AR 407.

[11] (13079) (7 March 1996), IAT.

[12] See also *Bozkurt* (11783) (19 January 1995, unreported); *Muia* (17223) (29 May 1998, unreportd), IAT.

[13] *Kandeepan* (15124), IAT; particularly where the claimant had been ill-served by that representative: *R (on the application of Dirisu) v Immigration Appeal Tribunal* [2001] EWHC 970 (Admin), [2001] All ER (D) 449 (Nov). But see *AD (Algeria)* [2004] UKIAT 00155, where the Tribunal held that it would be wrong to adjourn an appeal merely because of the withdrawal or threatened withdrawal of a representative, where otherwise there was no merit in an adjournment request.

[14] *AT* [2002] UKIAT 02883.

[15] In *R (on the application of Habyl) v Immigration Appeal Tribunal* [2002] EWHC 2313 (Admin), [2002] All ER (D) 237 (Oct) the Administrative Court doubted that adjournment was the correct course, given the obligation identified in *Haddad;* see also *AA (Afghanistan)* [2004] UKIAT 00109. In *Busuulwa* (01TH00239), the Tribunal indicated that the proper course was for the respondent to withdraw the decision; otherwise the only remedy was judicial review.

18.126 For the first time, the 2005 Procedure Rules introduce additional criteria for adjourning in order to allow a party more time to produce evidence. The rules provide that the Tribunal must not adjourn on the application of the party in such a situation, unless satisfied that the evidence relates to a matter in dispute in the appeal; that it would be unjust to determine the appeal without permitting the party a further opportunity to produce the evidence; and where the party has failed to comply with directions for the production of the evidence, there is a satisfactory explanation for the failure.[1] Under the previous rules, an adjournment to obtain additional evidence might be refused where steps could have been, but were not taken earlier to obtain the evidence,[2] but where the evidence was not reasonably available at the hearing, an adjournment to adduce it was appropriate.[3] The appellate authority could not both refuse an adjournment, sought to enable an appellant to produce medical evidence of having been tortured, on the ground that the refusal did not prevent just disposal of the appeal, and at the same time reject the account of being tortured because of the absence of medical evidence.[4] Where the Tribunal permits a party to adduce evidence not previously sent to the other party, there must be an adjournment if necessary to avoid prejudice.[5] The Procedure Rules also give the Tribunal power to adjourn, or vary a hearing date, where the respondent has failed to lodge the appeal documents timeously.[6] An adjournment need not be granted to await an imminent and binding decision on the point at issue, under the current Procedure Rules which are 'hostile to adjournments in general'.[7] In *Kimbesa*,[8] a refusal to adjourn was quashed where, shortly before an asylum appeal hearing, the appellant's brothers, whose claims rested on the same facts, had arrived in the UK. Ognall J held that it was unfair to expect the brothers to have their accounts tested in an appeal hearing before they had been interviewed on their claim. In *Rajan*,[9] a starred Tribunal case, Collins J distinguished *Kimbesa*, and held that it was not authority for the proposition that wherever there was a concurrent application by a relative an adjournment was in the interests of justice, although the existence of concurrent applications by family members was a relevant consideration which may point to an adjournment in an appropriate case. A refusal to adjourn a hearing is clearly a procedural decision which is not per se susceptible to appeal or review,[10] but a wrongful refusal would give a ground for appeal or review of the subsequent decision on the appeal.[11]

1 Asylum and Immigration Tribunal (Procedure) Rules 2005, SI 2005/230, r 21(3).
2 *A (Afghanistan)* [2003] UKIAT 00165.
3 *R v Medical Appeal Tribunal, ex p Corrarini* [1966] 1 WLR 883; *Kondo* (10413) (12 November 1993, unreported), IAT; *Sarica* (15363) (21 August 1997, unreported), IAT; or to obtain a translation: *Getener* (14799), IAT. *R (Fana) v Special Adjudicator* [2002] EWHC 777 (Admin), [2002] Imm AR 407: it was irrational for the adjudicator both to refuse to adjourn the appeal to enable production of a psychological report and to refuse to agree to receive the report after the hearing, bearing in mind the possible consequences in a human rights case of preventing reliance on potentially cogent evidence.
4 *Ntoya* [2002] UKIAT 00155.
5 *Macharia v Immigration Appeal Tribunal* [2000] INLR 156, CA. The principle applies to any other situation in which the other party risks being taken by surprise, eg by a new ground of decision, or a new ground of appeal, or by the Tribunal taking a point not raised by the parties.
6 SI 2005/230, r 23(3).
7 *Secretary of State for the Home Department v DD (Croatia)* [2004] UKIAT 00032 (starred). The position contrasts with that under earlier rules: see *Glowacki* (R16139) (19 January 1998), IAT.
8 *R v Secretary of State for the Home Department, ex p Kimbesa* (29 January 1997, unreported), Ognall J.
9 *Rajan (Munigesu)* (01TH00244) (8 February 2001, unreported).
10 Nationality, Immigration and Asylum Act 2002, ss 103A(7)(a) (review), 103E(7)(a) (appeal).
11 On an application for reconsideration of, or for permission to appeal against, a decision on an appeal, where a ground is refusal to adjourn to produce evidence, the relevant evidence should be produced for the review or appeal court, to demonstrate that it would or might have made a difference: see *R (on the application of Bosombanguwa) v Immigration Appeal Tribunal* [2004] EWHC 1656 (Admin), [2004] All ER (D) 260 (Jul).

18.127

The Practice Direction requires an application for an adjournment to be made not later than 4pm one clear working day before the date of the hearing. Otherwise, the application must be made at the hearing, and requires the attendance of the party or representative.[1] Parties must not assume that an application will be successful, and must check with the Tribunal, since if the application is not granted and they fail to attend, the Tribunal is required to proceed in their absence if there is no satisfactory explanation for their non-attendance.[2] If the hearing of an appeal is adjourned, a new hearing date must be fixed for not more than 28 days after the original hearing date, unless the Tribunal is satisfied that because of exceptional circumstances, the appeal cannot justly be heard within that time, and in any event, no later than is strictly required by the circumstances necessitating the adjournment.[3] Thus, a party seeking an adjournment for more than 28 days will need to jump two hurdles: first, to show that the appeal cannot be justly determined without adjourning, and second, to demonstrate the exceptional circumstances which would make it unjust not to adjourn beyond the maximum period.[4]

1   Practice Direction 1/2005, paras 9.1, 9.2, 9.4. Full reasons must be submitted: para 9.3. Only in exceptional circumstances will a late application be considered without the attendance of a party or representative: 9.5.
2   Practice Direction above, paras 9.6, 9.7.
3   Asylum and Immigration Tribunal (Procedure) Rules 2005, SI 2005/230, r 21(4).
4   The previous Procedure Rules, SI 2003/652, had a 'closure date' of six weeks after the adjourned hearing (r 13), with a similarly high threshold for adjourning beyond the closure date. See *WT (Ethiopia)* [2004] UKIAT 00176.

18.128 Hearings of fast track appeals may only be adjourned if there is insufficient time to hear the appeal or application; if a party has not been served with notice of the hearing in accordance with the Rules; if the Tribunal is satisfied by evidence filed or given by a party that the appeal cannot be justly determined on the date on which it is listed for hearing but that it can justly be determined by an identifiable future date no more than 10 days after the date on which it was listed; or if it makes a transfer order under rule 31 of the Fast Track Procedure Rules.[1] A transfer order under rule 31 is an order that the Fast Track Procedure Rules for Tribunal appeals no longer apply so that only the principal rules [2] apply. Such an order must be made if all the parties consent,[3] and may be made if the Tribunal is satisfied that there are exceptional circumstances which mean that the appeal cannot otherwise be justly determined, or if the respondent has failed to comply with a provision of the Rules or a direction and the appellant would as a result be prejudiced if the appeal continued under the Fast Track Rules.[4] If an appeal is adjourned because the adjudicator has made a transfer order, the provisions of the principal rules concerning time limits apply.[5]

1   Asylum and Immigration Tribunal (Fast Track Procedure) Rules 2005, SI 2005/560, r 28.
2   Ie the Asylum and Immigration Tribunal (Procedure) Rules 2005, SI 2005/230.
3   SI 2005/560, r 31(1)(a).
4   SI 2005/560, r 31(1)(b)–(c).
5   SI 2005/560, r 32(2), (3).

Procedure at the hearing

18.129 There is extensive jurisprudence from the Tribunal and the higher courts on the scope of the duty of fairness in immigration appeals. At the hearing, each party may address the Tribunal, give evidence and call witnesses, and put questions to any witness. Each party should also be given an opportunity to make representations on the evidence (if any) and on the subject matter of the appeal generally. Where evidence is taken, the representations are normally made after the evidence is completed. The issues addressed, the oral and documentary evidence received and the submissions entertained may be limited in accordance with directions previously given and with the time estimate put in by the parties.[1] However, the Tribunal should not prevent an advocate from developing his or her submissions.[2] The Tribunal has power to conduct the proceedings in the manner it considers appropriate in the circumstances for ascertaining the matters in dispute and determining the appeal.[3] In doing so it must act fairly,[4] and should give an appellant a chance to comment on any adverse material in the evidence.[5] However, fairness does not require that every point that may be decided against an appellant should first of all be put to him or her; whether this is necessary depends on the circumstances of the particular case.[6] The Tribunal is not obliged to accept an improbable account simply because it has not been tested.[7] The Tribunal should not refuse to allow cross-examination of any witness who has been called to give oral evidence.[8] In cross-examining an appellant, the respondent is not limited to the issues raised in the 'reasons for refusal letter'.[9] The Tribunal's provisional conclusions should not be indicated at the outset of the hearing.[10] If an immigration judge has particular knowledge or experience relevant to the facts in issue, that should be made known to the parties and they should be invited to state whether they have any objection to that immigration judge hearing the appeal.[11] An immigration judge's personal knowledge should not be taken into account in a manner that may suggest bias.[12] If the Tribunal has access to relevant evidence not produced by the parties, their attention should be drawn to it.[13] A Tribunal may take into account material that comes to light after the hearing, but must inform the parties of its intention to do so and afford them an opportunity to comment on it.[14] If, having heard the evidence, the Tribunal expresses a positive view as to the credibility of the appellant, the hearing should be reconvened and submissions invited if the Tribunal subsequently changes its mind.[15] Similarly, if at the end of the hearing, the Tribunal indicates that the appeal is to be allowed, it may change its mind when giving a written determination, but only after inviting the parties to make further representations.[16] The parties should be given an opportunity to deal with any case they have not referred to which appears to be determinative or call for argument,[17] although immigration judges are entitled to take account of well-known Tribunal decisions, meaning those given under the Tribunal's reporting system, even if neither party has cited them.[18] In an asylum appeal, the Tribunal may introduce the issue of internal flight even if the Secretary of State has not, but should be cautious about doing so and must give the parties an opportunity to deal with it.[19] All representatives, including respondents', are under a duty to assist the Tribunal by presenting it with all relevant case law, including that contrary to the argument put forward.[20] The respondent must put to a witness any matter said to undermine the witness' credibility,[21] and must not knowingly mislead the court by not disclosing material which detracts from its case.[22] Further, the respondent is under an obligation to produce any evidence about which he or she knows or ought to know and which shows that an 'authoritative' tribunal decision does not accurately describe material conditions in the appellant's country.[23] It may be that asylum and human rights is a field where, since the court has an overriding obligation to ensure the highest standards of fairness, litigation privilege would not allow a party to refuse production of an expert report.[24] There is a need to be especially vigilant in fast track appeals, where each stage in the appeal process follows very swiftly, and the Tribunal must take care not to allow itself to be misdirected by the Secretary of State on the objective evidence.[25]

1   See 18.116 above and *R v Secretary of State for the Home Department, ex p Singh* [1998] INLR 608, CA, upholding an adjudicator's refusal to allow a witness to add orally to her statement, which was the subject of a direction that it stand as evidence in chief.
2   *Katrinak v Secretary of State for the Home Department* [2001] EWCA Civ 832, [2001] INLR 499.
3   Asylum and Immigration Tribunal (Procedure) Rules 2005, SI 2005/230, r 43(1), applied to fast track appeals by Asylum and Immigration Tribunal (Fast Track Procedure) Rules 2005, SI 2005/560, r 27.

4   So, for example, where an appellant put in a report from Amnesty International concerning the dangers facing failed asylum seekers from Algeria, which was unchallenged by the presenting officer, the adjudicator should not have rejected the evidence without allowing the appellant to adduce further evidence to confirm it: *Kriba v Secretary of State for the Home Department* 1998 SLT 1113, OHCS (Scot). And after an appellant had given evidence in the absence of the respondent's representative, whose inability to attend the hearing was the fault of the appellate authority, the hearing should not have proceeded, in fairness to the respondent, but should have been transferred: *Secretary of State for the Home Department v I (Somalia)* [2004] UKIAT 00062.

5   *Ahmed v Secretary of State for the Home Department* [1994] Imm AR 457, CA; *R v Immigration Appeal Tribunal, ex p Seri* (CO/2135/99) (27 June 2000, unreported); *R v Immigration Appeal Tribunal, ex p Gunn* (22 January 1998, unreported), QBD. This obligation does not extend to obvious discrepancies on matters central to the appellant's case and already drawn to the appellant's attention in the refusal letter: *R v Immigration Appeal Tribunal, ex p Williams* [1995] Imm AR 518; *Sahota v Immigration Appeal Tribunal* [1995] Imm AR 500, nor must the Tribunal foresee and put at the hearing every aspect of the evidence which goes into its findings on the facts: *R v Immigration Appeal Tribunal, ex p Hansford* [1992] Imm AR 407; *AA (Sudan)* [2004] UKIAT 00152. The Tribunal will not generally make findings of fact based on an allegation against former representatives unless they have had an opportunity to respond to the allegation and the tribunal is shown the response or correspondence revealing that there has been no response: *BT (Nepal)* [2004] UKIAT 00311.

6   *R (on the application of Maheshwaran) v Secretary of State for the Home Department* [2002] EWCA Civ 173, [2004] Imm AR 176. An appellant should, for example, be told if the Tribunal does not believe his or her claim to have scars and should be given an opportunity to show them: *Sabouhi* [2002] UKIAT 06662; if the Tribunal is dissatisfied with the extent of the appellant's knowledge about the political party he or she claimed to belong to, where the inadequacy of his or her knowledge is not self-evident: *Kucher* [2002] UKIAT 7439; or if the Tribunal considers the evidence to be 'vague' *B (DR Congo)* [2003] UKIAT 00012.

7   *R (on the application of Hyseni) v Immigration Appeal Tribunal* [2002] EWHC 1239 (Admin), [2002] All ER (D) 561 (May).

8   *GY (Iran)* [2004] UKIAT 00264.

9   *Secretary of State for the Home Department v D (Iran)* [2003] UKIAT 00087.

10 *Rajah* (15159) (24 June 1997, unreported), IAT. In *Gashi v Secretary of State for the Home Department* [2002] UKIAT 03935 an appeal was allowed against an adjudicator's dismissal of a Kosovan appeal where, at the beginning of the appeal hearing, he indicated that in his view Kosovan cases lacked merit.

11 *Secretary of State for the Home Department v MM* (2001) (01TH00994) IAT.

12 *Muse* [2002] UKIAT 01957 where the adjudicator rejected the appellant's complaint that she was ill served by her previous solicitors because of her personal knowledge of two partners in that firm. cf *BA (Israel)* [2004] UKIAT 00118, where the adjudicator's personal knowledge of the Gaza strip had not affected the decision.

13 *R v Secretary of State for the Home Department, ex p Fortunato* [1996] Imm AR 366, QBD; *Ghana Varathan and Norbert v Special Adjudicator* [1995] Imm AR 64, CA; *R v Immigration Appeal Tribunal, ex p Kang* (CO 497/2000) (6 October 2000, unreported), QBD; *Junaid* (01TH02540) IAT. Reaching adverse conclusions on credibility on the basis of material which formed the basis of the presenting officer's cross-examination of the appellant but which was not disclosed was unfair: *Ozmico* [2002] UKIAT 00484.

14 *Laci* (2001) (01/TH/01348), IAT.

15 *Paudel* [2002] UKIAT 06868.

16 *R v Special Adjudicator, ex p Bashir* [2002] Imm AR 1, AC; *K (Rwanda)* [2003] UKIAT 00047.

17 *R v Immigration Appeal Tribunal, ex p Sui Rong Suen* [1997] Imm AR 355.

18 *M (Afghanistan)* [2004] UKIAT 0004.

19 *He (Bai Hai)* (00TH00744), IAT; *Mehta* (17861), IAT.

20 *Choudhury* (10646) (11 February 1994, unreported), IAT.

21 *Ezzi* (G0003A) (29 May 1997, unreported), IAT.

22 *Kerrouche v Secretary of State for the Home Department* [1997] Imm AR 610, CA; *Konan v Secretary of State for the Home Department* (IATRF 00/0020/C) (20 March 2000, unreported), CA. The majority conclusion in *R v Secretary of State for the Home*

Department, ex p Gawe, Abdi v Secretary of State for the Home Department [1996] Imm AR 288, HL, of no general disclosure duty of country information, does not undermine this principle.

23 R (on the application of Cindo) v Immigration Appeal Tribunal [2002] EWHC 246 (Admin), [2002] All ER (D) 181 (Feb). Failure to produce such evidence would make the Tribunal's decision, made in reliance on the 'authoritative' tribunal decision, procedurally unfair or founded on a 'wrong factual basis'.

24 R v Secretary of State for the Home Department, ex p Gashi [1999] Imm AR 415, CA.

25 G (Turkey) [2004] UKIAT 00070.

18.130 In the context of the duty of fairness, the Tribunal has a reasonable inquisitorial function to make its own inquiries in the context of full disclosure and discussion of all relevant issues at the hearing, and is entitled to control the hearing by making interventions,[1] but should exercise the power sparingly.[2] Thus, the Tribunal is entitled to put questions to a witness in order to clarify issues that it will need to deal with in the determination. The Tribunal may ask questions intended to seek an explanation for inconsistencies or to address points of concern, even if they have not been raised in the refusal letter or by the parties.[3] Whilst in general, the Tribunal's questions should be asked after the witness has been examined and cross-examined, in some cases it might be more appropriate for the questions to be asked as they arise; interruptions by the Tribunal will not necessarily cause injustice.[4] What Tribunals should not do is to develop a different case to that being pursued by the parties, ask leading questions or questions that conceal their purpose or ask questions in a hostile manner or in a way that suggests that their mind is made up.[5] Where the respondent to an appeal is unrepresented, the Tribunal should ask, either directly or through the appellant's representative, such questions as are necessary to address the issues of credibility raised in the refusal letter and those that are apparent on reading the papers; the Tribunal is not limited to issues of credibility that are raised in the reasons for refusal letter but can put questions on any issue that is not the subject of a clear and unequivocal concession.[6] The propriety of questioning by the Tribunal does not depend upon compliance or non-compliance with the *Surendran Guidelines*[7] but on whether, in all of the circumstances of the case, its questions disclose apparent bias[8] or unfairness.[9] The parties should always be permitted to put any further questions to a witness after questioning by the Tribunal.[10]

1 R v Immigration Appeal Tribunal and Special Adjudicator, ex p Kumar (CO 5073/98) (17 April 2000, unreported), QBD; Moala (16409) (29 June 1999, unreported), IAT; Gimedhin (14019) (21 October 1996, unreported), IAT.

2 There is a fine line between legitimate inquiry and stepping into the respondent's shoes; see eg Bahar v Immigration Officer, Heathrow [1988] Imm AR 534; Muwyngyi (00052) IAT; R v Special Adjudicator, ex p Demeter [2000] Imm AR 424, QBD. Hostile questioning led to the appearance of bias in XS (Kosovo – adjudicator's conduct – psychiatric report) Serbia and Montenegro [2005] UKIAT 00093.

3 Yildizhan [2002] UKIAT 08315; K (Côte d'Ivoire) [2004] UKIAT 00061; SW (Somalia) [2005] UKIAT 00037.

4 Oyono [2002] UKIAT 02034, Ali (Shafqat) [2002] UKIAT 05944; SW (Somalia) [2005] UKIAT 00037.

5 K (Cote d'Ivoire) [2004] UKIAT 00061. A comment during the respondent's submissions that the appellant's account was 'like a Hollywood movie' would not lead an independent minded observer to perceive a risk of bias or unfairness: KR (Iraq) [2004] UKIAT 00117.

6 Surendran (21679); MNM (00/TH/02423) (31 October 2000), (starred) IAT and appended 'Surendran Guidelines'; WN (DRC) [2004] UKIAT 00213. In SW (Somalia) [2005] UKIAT 00037, the President ruled that Surendran and MNM should not be cited without WN,

which represented an 'evolution' of the guidelines. See also *T (Algeria) v Secretary of State for the Home Department* [2003] UKIAT 00128. The Tribunal is not subject to the same obligation to ask questions about issues of credibility that do not arise from perusal of the papers but only in the course of the hearing: *R (on the application of Hyseni) v Immigration Appeal Tribunal* [2002] EWHC 1239 (Admin), [2002] All ER (D) 561 (May).

7   See fn 6 above.

8   *T (Algeria) v Secretary of State for the Home Department* [2003] UKIAT 00128 applying *Porter v Magill* [2001] UKHL 67, [2002] 2 AC 357. For examples of inappropriate questioning by the adjudicator, see *Mohammadiani-Abolvardi v Secretary of State for the Home Department* (01TH02112) (11 October 2001) and *H (Iraq)* [2003] UKIAT 00048.

9   *R (on the application of Maheshwaran) v Secretary of State for the Home Department* [2002] EWCA Civ 173, [2002] All ER (D) 184 (Feb); *SW (Somalia)* [2005] UKIAT 00037; *Ahmed* [2002] UKIAT 07468, *Yildizhan* [2002] UKIAT 08315. See also *IS (Belarus)* [2004] UKIAT 114.

10 *Secretary of State for the Home Department v Yogalingam* (01TH02671) (4 January 2002), IAT.

18.131 Refusal to hear a witness, or other procedural impropriety by the Tribunal, amounts to a point of law for the purpose of an application for reconsideration or onward appeal against the decision on the appeal.[1] If on such an application an allegation is made of procedural impropriety in the conduct of a hearing before the Tribunal, it is likely to be perceived as wholly unsubstantiated if made in vague and general terms, and would only be considered arguable if it is sufficiently particularised, and is apparently made or supported by someone in a position to know what happened. Although a witness statement from a representative or a party to the proceedings would not necessarily be required at the permission stage, the application should show that such evidence would be available on the appeal.[2]

1   *YB (Jamaica)* [2005] 00029.

2   *YB (Jamaica)* above; *WN (DRC)* [2004] UKIAT 00213; see also *H (Iraq)* [2003] UKIAT 00048; *Fadhul* [2002] UKIAT 06186; *Yildizhan* [2002] UKIAT 08315. Where an application for permission to appeal is based on an assertion of fact as to what happened before the Tribunal which is at odds with what is said in the determination, the allegation should be supported by evidence: *R (on the application of Bosombanguwa) v Immigration Appeal Tribunal* [2004] EWHC 1656 (Admin).

18.132 The tribunal should not dictate to representatives which witnesses to call,[1] prevent cross-examination of a witness (although he or she may intervene to prevent unfairness).[2] or stop re-examination on the basis that a matter had been dealt with in chief.[3] At appeal hearings it is the usual practice to exclude witnesses (other than parties) from the hearing room until they give their evidence, a practice which it has been said tribunals are entitled to follow by virtue of the general control over proceedings given to them by the Procedure Rules,[4] but which is not a rule of law.[5] In the vast majority of cases the decision whether an interpreter should be used is for the appellant and his or her advisers, and it is not the function of the Tribunal to disagree or express any view on the matter.[6] Where an interpreter of the kind requested by an appellant is not provided, with the result that the appellant is inhibited in giving evidence, the Tribunal's adverse assessment of credibility is likely to be unsustainable.[7] The Tribunal should immediately address any dissatisfaction about the quality of the interpretation raised by a responsible legal representative.[8] If the Tribunal begins to hear evidence but has to adjourn the hearing owing to problems with the interpreter, it should not continue to hear the case with a new interpreter unless the parties expressly consent owing to the danger of being influenced by the tainted evidence.[9] It would be unfair for the Tribunal to permit the respondent to call the court interpreter to give opinion evidence about the appellant's language or accent.[10] The Tribunal must ensure that unrepresented appellants are aware of their entitlement to give evidence.[11] Women appellants alleging sexual abuse ought to be allowed an all-female Tribunal if requested.[12]

1 *Nabhani* (13195) (17 April 1996, unreported), IAT; *Petre* (12998) (13 February 1996, unreported), IAT; *Riasat* (13256) (17 April 1996, unreported), IAT; *Biley* (11579) (22 November 1994, unreported), IAT.
2 *GY (Iran)* [2004] UKIAT 00264.
3 *Kamara* (11984) (3 April 1996, unreported), IAT.
4 Asylum and Immigration Tribunal (Procedure) Rules 2005, SI 2005/230, r 43(1), applied to fast track appeals by SI 2005/560 r 27; *Wadia v Secretary of State for the Home Department* [1977] Imm AR 92.
5 *Moore v Registrar Lambeth county court* [1969] 1 All ER 782 at 783–784, DC; *R v Immigration Appeal Tribunal, ex p Patel (Jebunisha)* [1996] Imm AR 161, QBD.
6 *Cavusoglu* (15357) (28 May 1997, unreported). But there is no absolute right to an interpreter wholly irrespective of need: *R v Special Adjudicator, ex p Naqvi* (23 February 2000, unreported), CA.
7 *AT* [2002] UKIAT 02883. But an allegation of incompetence or inaccurate interpretation must be made at the hearing: *AW (Somalia)* [2004] UKIAT 00093.
8 *Perera (Jude) v Secretary of State for the Home Department* [2004] EWCA Civ 1002; *Y (Afghanistan)* [2003] UKIAT 00100. It was an error of law to permit an interpreter who had been criticised by the appellant's interpreter to lower his voice so that he could not be heard: *SJ (Iran)* [2004] UKIAT 00131.
9 *A (Ethiopia)* [2003] UKIAT 00103. The power to transfer proceedings, contained in the 2003 Procedure Rules, SI 2003/652, r 52, which was held to be an appropriate way of dealing with this situation (and others where a part-heard hearing could not be completed: see *I (Somalia)* [2004] UKIAT 00062), is absent from the 2005 Rules.
10 *Hydir* [2002] UKIAT 01132.
11 *Singh (Santokh)* (13002) (22 February 1996, unreported); *Tamba* (13525) (12 June 1996, unreported).
12 *Tiganov* (11193) (29 July 1994, unreported); *Akyol* (14745) (25 March 1997, unreported), IAT. See Berkowitz and Jarvis *Asylum Gender Guidelines* (IAA, November 2000); H Crawley *Refugees and gender: law and process* (2001).

Evidence

18.133 The Tribunal may issue a witness summons for the purposes of any appeal to require anyone in the UK to attend the hearing to answer questions or to produce relevant documents.[1] If a witness has important evidence to give but neither party wishes to call him or her, the Tribunal has the power to do so, although it should hesitate long before using it.[2] Where witnesses are called they may be required to give evidence on oath or affirmation,[3] and no witness can be compelled to give any evidence or produce any document which that witness could not be compelled to give or produce in a court of law.[4] Furthermore, except where the method of detecting forgeries might be disclosed, the Tribunal must not take account of any evidence that has not been made available to the parties.[5]

1 Asylum and Immigration Tribunal (Procedure) Rules 2005, SI 2005/230, r 50(1), applied to fast track appeals by SI 2005/560, r 27. A witness need not attend unless the summons is served on him or her, and the necessary expenses of attending are paid or tendered: r 50(2), by the party (if any) at whose request the witness summons was issued: r 50(3).

² *Kesse v Secretary of State for the Home Department* [2001] EWCA Civ 177, [2001] Imm
AR 366, CA, differing from *Jamali* (TH/131186/84) (25 April 1986, unreported), in which
the Immigration Appeal Tribunal held that the appellate authority could only call witnesses
if the parties assented.
³ SI 2005/230, r 51(3). This is left to Tribunals' discretion and is fairly rare.
⁴ SI 2005/230, r 51(2).
⁵ SI 2005/230, r 51(7) See *Odusanwo v Secretary of State for the Home Department* [1992]
Imm AR 430; *Hettierarachchi v Secretary of State for the Home Department* [1991] Imm
AR 499, CA.

18.134 In appeal hearings the rules of evidence applicable in a court of law
are relaxed. Rule 51(1) of the Procedure Rules provides that the Tribunal may
receive oral, documentary or other evidence of any fact which appears to be
relevant to the appeal, notwithstanding that it would be inadmissible in a
court of law.¹ Explanatory statements² and refusal letters³ have been held to
be evidence. The judge's sentencing remarks in a criminal trial are admissible
in a deportation appeal, along with social work, medical and probation
reports prepared for the criminal courts.⁴ Where the respondent asserts a fact,
little if any weight can be given to such assertion without evidence in support.⁵
It is for the respondent to make good an allegation of forgery with evidence.⁶
But a Home Office presenting officer cannot give evidence in the case he or
she is presenting⁷ and it would be wrong for the Tribunal to take account of
such evidence in making an adverse assessment of credibility.⁸ An entry
clearance officer who is trying to establish the truth as to a claimed
relationship is entitled to take into account information obtained from
villagers selected at random on a visit to the sponsor's village.⁹ Evidence in
rebuttal may be admitted from a witness who has carried out a village visit on
behalf of an appellant.¹⁰ In cases where the Tribunal may not receive evidence
of post-decision facts, as will be seen, evidence of facts not known to the
decision-maker is admissible.¹¹ The weight to be attached to such evidence is,
within reasonable limits, a matter for the Tribunal.¹² But a witness's evidence
supporting an appellant's case must be addressed¹³ and given properly
reasoned consideration.¹⁴ Written evidence need not be considered unless it is
either in English (or, where appropriate, Welsh) or is accompanied by a
certified translation.¹⁵

¹ SI 2005/230. Ie hearsay evidence is admissible: *R v Immigration Appeal Tribunal,
ex p Miah* [1987] Imm AR 143, QBD.
² *R v Immigration Appeal Tribunal, ex p Weerasuriya* [1983] 1 All ER 195, QBD.
³ *R v Secretary of State for the Home Department, ex p Gawe, Abdi v Secretary of State for
the Home Department* [1996] Imm AR 288, HL, in the context of the accelerated
procedure for certified appeals. These were third country appeals and it is arguable that the
majority were swayed by the need for particular speed in such cases. It is unlikely that the
decision would be followed today, with the far greater awareness both of the requirements
of fairness and of the incidence of mistaken and misleading assertions in decision letters (as
to which see 12.125 above). The respondent routinely submits evidence of country
conditions in asylum appeals.
⁴ *Ayo v Immigration Appeal Tribunal* [1990] Imm AR 461, CA; *N (Kenya)* [2004] UKIAT 9,
upheld [2004] EWCA Civ 1094, [2004] INLR 612.
⁵ *Gebretensae* (14794) (27 March 1997, unreported); *Lakew* (13214) (17 April 1996,
unreported); *Oni* (15886) (2 December 1997, unreported), IAT.
⁶ *R v Immigration Appeal Tribunal, ex p Shen* [2000] INLR 389, QBD; *Chowdhury (Ahmed
Hafiz)* (11721) (30 December 1994, unreported); *Findik* (17029) (12 May 1998, unreported); *Escobar* (20553) (26 March 1999, unreported); *A, B, C and D* (R17367, R21180,
R16463, R21181) (3 August 1999, unreported), IAT. See, however, *Kongo-Kongo* (0064)
(3 March 2000, unreported); *Waimatha* (16575) (18 August 1998, unreported), IAT; *R v*

Immigration Appeal Authority, ex p Mohammed (Mukhtar) [2001] Imm AR 162, QBD, where documentary evidence was patently not genuine on its face.

7   *Aitsaid* (11391).

8   *Ozmico* [2002] UKIAT 00484, where the Home Office presenting officer cross-examined the appellant on the basis of an undisclosed file note.

9   *Visa Officer, Islamabad v Altaf (Mohammed)* [1979–80] Imm AR 141. A previous grant of entry clearance to a woman as wife of the sponsor, although not an estoppel, is evidence relevant to the claimed relationship when another woman later applies for admission in the same capacity: *Visa Officer, Islamabad v Bi (Channo)* [1978] Imm AR 182. Where affidavit evidence about an event is tendered by an applicant or sponsor and is disputed by the Home Office, the matter should be tested in cross-examination and evidence in rebuttal should be tendered: *Kassam v Secretary of State for the Home Department* [1976] Imm AR 20.

10   *R v Immigration Appeal Tribunal, ex p Hussain* [1982] Imm AR 74, QBD.

11   *R v Immigration Appeal Tribunal, ex p Hassanin* [1987] 1 All ER 74, [1986] 1 WLR 1448, CA.

12   *R v Immigration Appeal Tribunal, ex p Kandiya* [1989] Imm AR 491, QBD; *R v Immigration Appeal Tribunal, ex p Khan (Aurangzeb)* [1989] Imm AR 524, QBD.

13   *R (on the application of Sugur) v Secretary of State for the Home Department* (CO 279/2000) (1 November 2000, unreported), CA.

14   *R (on the application of Arzpeyma) v Immigration Appeal Tribunal* [2002] EWHC 2395 (Admin), [2002] All ER (D) 21 (Nov) (dismissed on the facts, dismissal upheld at [2004] EWCA Civ 1101, [2004] All ER (D) 340 (Jul)); *AK (Turkey)* [2004] UKIAT 00230.

15   Asylum and Immigration Tribunal (Procedure) Rules 2005, SI 2005/230, r 52(1)(b), (2), (3), applied to fast track appeals by SI 2005/560, r 27.

Credibility of witnesses

18.135 Credibility is not in itself a valid end to the function of an immigration judge, and over-emphasis on the issue may distort his or her findings.[1] An adverse credibility finding should not be based solely on the fact that no oral evidence was called at the hearing.[2] However, credibility findings are one of the primary functions of the immigration judge, and in some cases may be the fulcrum of the decision.[3] The appellant must make a case,[4] and where credibility has been put in issue by the respondent, an appellant who does not give evidence cannot complain of an adverse credibility finding.[5] On the other hand, if there is an agreement between the parties as to the facts or a concession as to credibility it would be an error of law for the Tribunal to go behind the agreement.[6] It is an error of law to require corroboration for an appellant's evidence.[7] However, the Tribunal may take account of an unexplained failure to produce supporting evidence that should have been available to the appellant.[8] Where there is corroboration, it should be taken into account.[9] Supporting evidence should not be dismissed out of hand as 'self-serving'.[10] Prejudicial evidence of little probative value should not be the basis of an adverse credibility finding.[11] Caution should be exercised in relying on past deception,[12] or on the demeanour of a witness whose language and culture is different.[13] It is perfectly possible for a witness not to be telling the truth or to be exaggerating about certain matters, but for the centre-piece of his or her story to stand.[14] Late disclosure of a material fact may result from an asylum seeker's inhibition due to fear of his or her authorities[15] or cultural taboos[16] rather than indicating recent fabrication. Whether the Tribunal is entitled to make an adverse finding on the credibility of a witness whose evidence was not challenged at the hearing appears to depend on how obvious the discrepancies giving rise to the adverse finding are, or whether (in the case of an appellant) the respondent had already referred to them in the refusal letter.[17] The absence of specific challenge to a document[18] or a relationship[19] relied by an appellant might render rejection of the document or relationship unfair. In assessing credibility, the interview record should be approached with caution where there have been breaches of PACE codes[20] or defective[21] or confrontational questioning,[22] or where the record of interview was written substantially later,[23] or where the interview was a preliminary one[24] or where the applicant had felt unwell or tired,[25] or could not be represented at the interview because of the lack of LSC funding and the interview was not tape recoreded.[26] Failure to give reasoned consideration to a complaint about the interpretation of the appellant's evidence at the hearing would vitiate the decision.[27] It is inherently dangerous to place too much weight on 'plausibility' when assessing credibility because an immigration judge's judgment as to what is plausible is bound to be influenced by his or her own values and environment.[28] Decisions on credibility must be reasoned, just as decisions on other aspects of the case.[29] An assessment of credibility should be made on the basis of a holistic assessment of all of the evidence in which supporting evidence is weighed in favour a positive finding on credibility; it is an error of approach for the Tribunal first to come to a negative assessment of credibility and then on the basis of that assessment, to reject the potentially supporting evidence.[30] For credibility in the context of the burden of proof in asylum appeals, see 12.29 and 12.163ff above.

[1] *R v Immigration Appeal Tribunal, ex p Hussain* (CO/990/95) (25 April 1996, unreported), QBD; *Guine* (13868) (9 September 1996, unreported); *Jawaid* (17159) (20 May 1998, unreported), IAT.

[2] *Ahmed (Kaleem)* (12774) (8 November 1995, unreported), IAT; *Gok* (15971) (7 January 1998, unreported); *Coskuner* (16769) (23 July 1998, unreported); *Sad-Chaouche* (17423) (19 June 1998, unreported), IAT; *Secretary of State for the Home Department v Kacaj* [2001] INLR 354 (starred), IAT. Contra when potential witness who could have given highly relevant evidence was sitting in court but was not called: *R v Secretary of State for the Home Department, ex p Kajenthra* [1998] Imm AR 158, QBD.

[3] *SW (Somalia)* [2005] UKIAT 00037, where the Tribunal ruled that the extract from *Guine* (fn 1 above) that 'a decision which concentrates primarily on findings of credibility for its outcome is in general more likely to be found to be flawed' was always quoted out of context and should no longer be cited.

[4] *Singh v Secretary of State for the Home Department* [2000] Imm AR 340, CA; *Adebola* (16731) (19 August 1998, unreported), IAT; *Nderitu* [2002] UKIAT 01058.

[5] *Nassir v Secretary of State for the Home Department* (1999/5682/4) [1999] Imm AR 250, CA (permission). See also *Carcabuk and Bla* (00TH0146), distinguishing between a concession or agreement on the facts, which the Tribunal should not disturb, and mere failure to challenge, which does not bind it.

[6] *Carcabuk and Bla* above; *R (on the application of Ganidagli) v Secretary of State for the Home Department* [2001] EWHC 70 (Admin), [2001] INLR 479. So, for example, when at the end of cross-examination the Secretary of State's representative indicated that 'credibility was not an issue', it should not have been questioned: *Kabanda* (2001) (01TH01401), IAT.

[7] *Saspo* (14759) (24 March 1997, unreported); *Ozer (Nazim)* (14698) (13 March 1997, unreported), IAT; *Otkay* (01TH00722) (April 2001, unreported), IAT; *Yildirim* (01TH02606) (14 November 2001, unreported), IAT; *Ates* [2002] UKIAT 06221.

[8] *Jeichandrapalan* (01TH00512) (10 May 2001, unreported), IAT; *Jeyabalan* [2002] UKIAT 05992 (para 7); *Khan (Rashid)* [2002] UKIAT 06026.

[9] *Immigration Officer, Heathrow v Mirani* [1990] Imm AR 132; *Atwal* (13948) (7 October 1996, unreported), IAT, *AK (Turkey)* [2004] UKIAT 00230.

[10]   *Quijano* (13693) (16 July 1996, unreported); *Malakar* (16540) (23 September 1998, unreported), IAT. See also the useful remarks in *Re RS*, 135/92, New Zealand Refugee Status Appeals Authority (27 August 1991, unreported); *John Meadows v Minister for Immigraion and Multicultural Affairs* [1998] 1706 FCA (23 December 1998), Canada; *R (on the application of Shire) v Secretary of State for the Home Department* [2004] EWHC 874 (Admin).

[11]   *Iqbal v Immigration Appeal Tribunal* [1988] Imm AR 469, CA; *Ozmico* [2002] UKIAT 00484.

[12]   *R v Immigration Appeal Tribunal, ex p Miah* (12 October 1995, unreported), QBD; *Mahmood* (10629) (3 February 1994, unreported); *Majri* (12406) (9 August 1995, unreported); *Fernando* (11878) (23 February 1995, unreported); *Ibrahim* (17270) (17 June 1998, unreported); *Achiou* (2001) (01TH00159) para 10.

[13]   *Daniel* (13623) (2 July 1996, unreported); *Guarichico and Sarabia-Molina* (20230) (25 November 1999, unreported), IAT; *Luwuzi* [2002] UKIAT 07186. The Tribunal in *Khan (Rashid)* [2002] UKIAT 06026 accepted that it would be grossly unfair to judge credibility from demeanour where this might be affected by the medication taken by an appellant.

[14]   *Chiver* [1997] INLR 212, IAT.

[15]   The Tribunal accepted this explanation in *Sharafi* [2002] UKIAT 08115

[16]   *R (on the application of S) v Secretary of State for the Home Department* [2003] EWHC 352 (Admin), para 6; see also *R v Secretary of State for the Home Department, ex p Ejon* [1998] INLR 195.

[17]   See cases cited at 18.129–18.131 above; see also *Gaima v Secretary of State for the Home Department* [1989] Imm AR 65; *R v Special Adjudicator, ex p John* [1999] Imm AR 432; *R v Special Adjudicator, ex p Hassan* [2001] Imm AR 83.

[18]   *Secretary of State for the Home Department v Oleed* [2002] EWCA Civ 1906; [2003] INLR 179; *Luwuzi* [2002] UKIAT 07186.

[19]   *R (on the application of Kolcak) v Secretary of State for the Home Department* [2001] Imm AR 666, para 25.

[20]   *Ziraret* (12024) (19 April 1995, unreported), IAT.

[21]   *R v Secretary of State for the Home Department, ex p Akdogan* [1995] Imm AR 176; *Risan* (12551) (26 September 1995, unreported), IAT.

[22]   *Uruthiran* (21813) (8 March 2000, unreported), IAT; see also the Tribunal's comments in *Kara* [2002] UKIAT 01083, paras 16–17.

[23]   *Singh (Daya Pal)* (14829) (3 April 1997, unreported), IAT. But it was wrong to disregard interview notes merely because they were not read back to the claimant or signed by him or her: *DA (Turkey)* [2004] UKIAT 00104.

[24]   *Salim* (13202) (17 April 1996, unreported); *Mayisokele* (13039) (23 February 1996, unreported); *Vimaleswaran* (15493) (26 August 1997, unreported); *Jeevaponkalan* (17742) (24 July 1998, unreported); *Adong* (20404) (15 November 1999, unreported), IAT. Failure to mention a matter of great importance at the initial interview may, however, be taken into account: *R v Secretary of State for the Home Department, ex p Agbonmenio* [1996] Imm AR 69, QBD (leave).

[25]   *Velasco* (HX00476) (11 October 1999, unreported), IAT.

[26]   *R (on the application of Dirshe) v Secretary of State for the Home Department* [2005] EWCA Civ 421. See 12.123 above.

[27]   *Y (Afghanistan)* [2003] UKIAT 00100

[28]   *Kasolo* (13190) (1 April 1996, unreported); *Ali (Ibrahim)* [2002] UKIAT 07001, and see cases cited at 12.164 fn 1 above; but see too the Tribunal's approach in *MM (plausibility) (DRC)* [2005] UKIAT 00019.

[29]   *R v Immigration Appeal Tribunal, ex p Adin (Senol)* (CO 4533/98) (13 July 2000, unreported), QBD; *R v Secretary of State for the Home Department, ex p Chugtai* [1995] Imm AR 559; *Mecheti v Secretary of State for the Home Department* [1999] SCLR 998.

[30]   *R (on the application of Beqaraj) v Special Adjudicator* [2002] EWHC 1469 (Admin), [2002] All ER (D) 99 (Jun); *R (on the application of Perbalathan) v Immigration Appeal Tribunal* [2002] Imm AR 200; *R (on the application of Gautam) v Adjudicator* [2003] EWHC 1160 (Admin); *FZ (Afghanistan)* [2004] UKIAT 00304; see also below. See the Court of Appeal's guidance in *Karanakaran v Secretary of State for the Home Department* [2000] Imm AR 271.

18.136 All documentary evidence in support of the claim must be considered,[1] unless it is not in English or Welsh or accompanied by a certified translation.[2] The burden is on the individual relying on the document to establish that it supports his or her case and it is open to the Tribunal to find, in the context of the evidence as a whole, that the document cannot be relied on; there is no obligation on the respondent to make detailed inquiries about the document or to show that it is a forgery,[3] or necessary for the Tribunal to identify any evidence, either intrinsic or extrinsic to the document, showing it to be unreliable.[4] On the other hand, where the Secretary of State asserts that a document is a forgery, he bears the burden of proving it.[5] A document should not be found to be inauthentic without a challenge to its authenticity being made or without a warning to the appellant and absent a finding that a document is inauthentic, cogent reasons need to be given as to why the document does not support the appellant's case.[6] Late production of documents is not by itself a good reason for regarding them as unreliable,[7] nor by itself is the fact that what is produced is a poor photocopy.[8]

[1] *Okwu* (14518) (6 March 1997, unreported); *Yilmaz* (11896) (13 March 1995, unreported); *Karanakaran v Secretary of State for the Home Department* [2000] Imm AR 271.
[2] Asylum and Immigration Tribunal (Procedure) Rules 2005, SI 2005/230, r 52(1)(b), (2), (3), applied to fast track appeals by SI 2005/560, r 27.
[3] *Ahmed (Tanveer) v Secretary of State for the Home Department* [2002] UKIAT 00439; [2002] Imm AR 318; [2002] INLR 345 (starred).
[4] *R (on the application of Davila-Puga) v Immigration Appeal Tribunal* [2001] EWCA Civ 931, [2001] All ER (D) 393 (May); *Zarandy v Secretary of State for the Home Department* [2002] EWCA Civ 153, [2002] All ER (D) 355 (Jan); *Mungu v Secretary of State for the Home Department* [2003] EWCA Civ 360, [2003] All ER (D) 289 (Feb).
[5] *R v Immigration Appeal Tribunal, ex p Shen* [2000] INLR 389. Immigration judges are not forensic experts and should not make findings that documents have been forged on their own initiative, unless forgery is obvious: *Luwuzi* [2002] UKIAT 07186.
[6] *Secretary of State for the Home Department v Oleed* [2002] EWCA Civ 1906, [2003] INLR 179, [2003] Imm AR 499; *M (Peru) v Secretary of State for the Home Department* [2003] UKIAT 00029.
[7] *M (Peru) v Secretary of State for the Home Department* above.
[8] *O (Turkey) v Secretary of State for the Home Department* [2003] UKIAT 00006.

18.137 In asylum and human rights appeals, medical and psychiatric evidence capable of supporting an appellant's claim deserves careful and specific consideration,[1] and Tribunals should not make credibility findings in isolation from it.[2] An experienced immigration judge must have regard to the possibility that the quality of a witness' evidence may be affected by his or her mental state, which might explain inconsistency and forgetfulness.[3] A lay person cannot express a view on a medical matter without the benefit of medical evidence and should not reject a doctor's prognosis, without contrary medical evidence or without giving adequate reasons for doing so.[4] However, experienced Tribunals are entitled to assess the weight to be given to a medical report,[5] taking into account the doctor's qualifications, specialisation and experience,[6] the quality of the doctor's reasoning[7] and the extent to which any conclusion is related to established diagnostic criteria,[8] and the material on which the opinion is based.[9] The Tribunal should not regard the account given to the doctor as being unreliable without first of all deciding whether the doctor's opinion supports a positive finding as to the credibility of the appellant,[10] but a negative inference may be drawn from inconsistencies between the history given to a doctor and the evidence given to the Secretary of State or the Tribunal.[11]

1 *Mohammed (Swaleh)* (12412) (4 August 1995, unreported); *Ibrahim v Secretary of State for the Home Department* [1998] INLR 511, IAT; *Guney* (19159) (4 August 1999, unreported); *Sivakarathas* (01056) (12 May 2000, unreported), IAT.
2 *Kitshi* (11920) (23 March 1995, unreported). It is putting the cart before the horse to make an adverse assessment of credibility, based on the appellant's oral evidence, and then reject the medical evidence he or she has produced in support: *R (on the application of Beqaraj) v Special Adjudicator* [2002] EWHC 1469 (Admin), [2002] All ER (D) 99 (Jun); *MT (Syria)* [2004] UKIAT 00307.
3 *Mageto v Immigration Appeal Tribunal* [1996] Imm AR 56, CA; *Yahiaoui* [2002] UKIAT 03504; *Khan (Rashid)* [2002] UKIAT 06026. However, in *Singh (Amrik) v Secretary of State for the Home Department* [2000] Imm AR 340 the Court of Appeal held that psychiatric evidence of the effect of an appellant's mental state on his ability to recall reliably entitled the Tribunal to find his evidence unreliable and so reject his claim – an illustration of the double-edged nature of such evidence. The UNHCR Handbook recommends reliance on other sources of evidence in the case of mentally disturbed asylum claimants (paras 206–212).
4 *R v Secretary of State for the Home Department, ex p Khaira* [1998] INLR 731. See also *SP (Yugoslavia)* [2003] UKIAT 00017; *Secretary of State for the Home Department v S (Georgia)* [2003] UKIAT 00082; *Januzi v Secretary of State for the Home Department* [2003] EWCA Civ 1188; *R (on the application of Minani) v Immigration Appeal Tribunal* [2004] EWHC 582 (Admin), [2004] All ER (D) 410 (Feb).
5 *SP (Yugoslavia)* [2003] UKIAT 00017.
6 *Demaku* [2002] UKIAT 06001; *SP (Yugoslavia)* above.
7 *Jeyarajasingham* (2001) (01TH00845), IAT, para 16 (reasoning to be expected in medical reports dealing with scars). Expert psychiatrists exercise their critical faculties and experience, and should not be treated as accepting claimants' accounts uncritically: *R (on the application of Minani) v Immigration Appeal Tribunal* [2004] EWHC 582 (Admin), [2004] All ER (D) 410 (Feb); *Ademaj* [2002] UKIAT 00979.
8 *Demaku* above; *Secretary of State for the Home Department v Lama* [2002] UKIAT 07554; *M (DRC)* [2003] UKIAT 00054.
9 *Secretary of State for the Home Department v AE and FE* [2002] UKIAT 05237 [2003] Imm AR 152. This might include consideration how many times the psychiatrist met the subject of the report and for how long, what if any medical records were seen, and the extent to which the psychiatrist relied on the subject's untested account: *Cinar* [2002] UKIAT 06624; see also *SP (Yugoslavia)* [2003] UKIAT 00017. In *HE (DRC)* [2004] UKIAT 00321 'Reported', the Tribunal urged advocates seeking to support credibility by reference to medical reports to show that the support it provides is independent of what the claimant has told the psychiatrist.
10 *R (on the application of Gautam) v Special Adjudicator* [2003] EWHC 1160 (Admin), [2003] All ER (D) 81 (May); *R (on the application of Beqaraj) v Special Adjudicator* [2002] EWHC 1469 (Admin), [2002] All ER (D) 99 (Jun); *M (DRC)* [2003] UKIAT 00054.
11 *Basak* [2002] UKIAT 03570.

18.138 Credibility findings can only really be made on the basis of a complete understanding of the entire picture, placing a claim into the context of the background information regarding the country of origin,[1] although going into detail about the background circumstances will not always be necessary or fruitful,[2] and the Tribunal is not required to set out in detail all the background evidence it has read.[3] Where the background evidence is in conflict, the Tribunal and the courts have expressed a preference for independent, sourced reports,[4] but where there are divergent opinions from reputable human rights organisations about the conditions in a country, there should be an in-depth examination to see if the evidence can be reconciled,[5] and a real attempt to balance them.[6] If they cannot be reconciled, the Tribunal should give reasons for preferring one report over another.[7] The Tribunal need not invite oral evidence from an expert witness whose report he or she is minded to reject,[8] but expert evidence should not be rejected merely because it has not been tested in cross-examination,[9] or because it does not identify its sources,[10] nor should it be rejected as 'mere speculation'.[11] The Court of Appeal has been critical of the cursory and at times contemptuous way the appellate authorities have treated the evidence of reputable experts, and has pointed out that such evidence should not be lightly rejected[12] and that the Tribunal is 'bound to place heavy reliance on the views of experts and specialists'.[13] The Tribunal should not reject the opinion of an expert on grounds of the expert's 'partiality' without explaining why that label is applied to that expert.[14] In its reasoning it should clearly indicate what it has accepted from expert reports.[15] But expert witnesses' duty is to the court and it is important that they appreciate that, comply with it, believe in the truth of the facts in the report and the accuracy of the opinion given, cover all relevant matters and set out any matters affecting its validity.[16] In *Slimani*,[17] a starred Tribunal approved the guidance given in *The Ikarian Reefer*[18] that to be relied on, the expert needs to provide independent assistance to the tribunal, must not assume the role of an advocate, and needs to specify the facts on which his or her opinion is based. The Tribunal deprecated the practice of putting in evidence in one case expert reports prepared for a different case, unless the report is specified as a general one or the author has given his consent.[19] Foreign law is a question of fact which should be determined, in the absence of agreement between the parties, by expert evidence,[20] but in the absence of such evidence the appellate authority may review questions of foreign law for itself.[21]

1 UNHCR Handbook paras 42–43; *R v Immigration Appeal Tribunal, ex p Ahmed (Sardar)* [1999] INLR 473 (QBD); *Horvath v Secretary of State for the Home Department* [1999] Imm AR 121, [1999] INLR 7 (IAT); *Suleyman* (16242) (11 February 1998, unreported); *Tharunalingam* (18452); *Gurung v Secretary of State for the Home Department* [2003] EWCA Civ 654, [2003] All ER (D) 14 (May). For an example of the danger of assessing credibility in isolation, see *R v Immigration Appeal Tribunal, ex p Pratheepan* (CO 1102/98) (27 April 1999, unreported), QBD (adjudicator dismissed advocate's letter on basis of ignorance of legal procedures in Sri Lanka). See also *R (on the application of Gulbudek) v Immigration Appeal Tribunal* (CO 2174/2000) (21 November 2000, unreported), where an adjudicator's conclusion that the Turkish authorities would investigate rape and torture allegations was quashed as perverse; and *R (on the application of Vuckovic) v Special Adjudicator* (CO 3021/2000) (18 December 2000, unreported) (adjudicator unfair to determine case without Home Office country assessment which lent support to appellant's case).

2 *R v Secretary of State for the Home Department, ex p Befekadu* [1999] Imm AR 467, QBD.

3 *R (on the application of Shokrollahy) v Immigration Appellate Authority* [2000] Imm AR 580, QBD.

4 *Mario v Secretary of State for the Home Department* [1998] Imm AR 281, [1998] INLR 306, IAT; *Drrias v Secretary of State for the Home Department* [1997] Imm AR 346, CA (value of 'bland' FCO letter questioned); *X* (98/0474/4) 24 July 1998, CA (UNHCR report might deserve more weight than that of a national immigration authority). UNHCR reports have been seen as the most reliable: see *Ragavan* (15350) (21 August 1997, unreported); *Teshome* (15693).

5 *Hassen* (15558) (3 October 1997, unreported); see also *Lahori* (G0062) (7 October 1998, unreported), IAT.

6 *Mulumba* (14760) (24 March 1997, unreported).

7 *Thillarajah* (14606) (10 March 1997, unreported); *Vasikaran* (15241) (4 July 1997, unreported), IAT.

8 *R v Secretary of State for the Home Department, ex p Khanafer* [1996] Imm AR 212.

9   *Singh (Tarlochan) v Secretary of State for the Home Department* [2000] Imm AR 36. The
    written evidence of an expert, even if untested in cross-examination, is entitled to the
    respect due to persons who possess the relevant expertise: *Kilic* [2002] UKIAT 02714. But
    the testimony of an expert witness who did attend court would be highly important: *Zheng*
    (20271) (1 April 1999, unreported).

10 It is in the nature of an expert report that the expert is the source, although reference to
    sources would add weight to the expert's opinion: *Secretary of State for the Home
    Department v Markos* [2002] UKIAT 08313. But see *Slimani* (01TH00092) (12 February
    2001, unreported), (starred) IAT.

11 *Karanakaran v Secretary of State for the Home Department* [2000] Imm AR 271, CA. See
    also *Gomez* [2000] INLR 549; *Kapela v Secretary of State for the Home Department*
    [1998] Imm AR 294.

12 *Karanakaran* above; see also the Court of Appeal's observations in granting permission to
    appeal in *R v Immigration Appeal Tribunal, ex p Es-Eldin* (C/00/2681) (29 November
    2000, unreported), subsequently allowing by consent the appeal against the QBD decision
    reported in [2001] Imm AR 98. See also *Singh (Tarlochan) v Secretary of State for the
    Home Department* [2000] Imm AR 36.

13 *S v Secretary of State for the Home Department* [2002] EWCA Civ 539; [2002] INLR 416.
    The Tribunal has also emphasised the importance of giving proper consideration to expert
    reports: see e g *Misrak (Habteselassie)* (00308) (28 February 2000, unreported).

14 *Cherbal* [2002] UKIAT 02014.

15 *Djebari v Secretary of State for the Home Department* [2002] EWCA Civ 813, [2002] All
    ER (D) 184 (May). But equally, the Tribunal should not accept expert evidence uncritically,
    without explaining why it is preferred to a body of reputable evidence which contradicts it:
    Djebbar v Secretary of State for the Home Department [2004] EWCA Civ 804, [2004]
    33 LS Gaz R 36.

16 *Thambiah* (01372) (10 May 2000, unreported), IAT. Expert reports should show the status
    of their author and be specifically relevant to the case: *R v Immigration Appeal Tribunal,
    ex p Kilinc* [1999] Imm AR 588.

17 *Slimani* (01TH00092) (starred) (12 February 2001, unreported), IAT.

18 *National Justice Compania Naviera SA v Prudential Assurance Co Ltd* ('The Ikarian
    Reefer') [1993] 2 Lloyd's Rep 68 at 81–2.

19 *Slimani* (01TH00092) (starred) (1 February 2001), IAT; *Singh (Armardeep)* (00943)
    (28 April 2000); *Zheng* (20271) (1 April 1999, unreported), IAT.

20 *R v Secretary of State for the Home Department, ex p Bradshaw* [1994] Imm AR 359;
    Tikhonov [1998] INLR 737, IAT.

21 *R v Special Adjudicator, ex p Turus* [1996] Imm AR 388, QBD.

Evidence of post-decision facts

18.139 When determining an appeal under the pre-2002 Act legislation
(except one on asylum or human rights grounds),the appellate authorities
were restricted to consideration of facts in existence at the date of the decision
appealed against.[1] It was emphasised on a number of occasions that the
appellate authorities were not some kind of super entry clearance or immigration officers, or an extension of the original decision-making function, but a
process for enabling the decision to be reviewed. Evidence that was not before
the original decision maker could only be considered for the purpose of
determining the facts that were in existence at the time the decision was
made.[2] The exception was asylum and human rights cases. In *Ravichandran*[3]
the Court of Appeal held that in asylum cases, the appellate authority is an
extension of the decision-making process because of the nature of the question
to be asked, ie whether projected removal would bring a real risk of harm
contrary to the Refugee Convention, rather than fixing on a past situation.
This meant that evidence of facts which came into existence after the decision
on appeal was relevant and admissible. That decision was given statutory

effect in the IAA 1999,[4] and was extended to cases where it was asserted that removal would breach Article 3 ECHR.[5] The Tribunal applied the principle to Art 8 cases in *S&K*[6] and in *Razgar*[7] the House of Lords upheld this approach to all cases in which it was asserted that human rights would be breached by removal. The Nationality, Immigration and Asylum Act 2002 extends the admissibility of evidence of post-decision facts to non-asylum or human rights appeals. With the exception of appeals against refusal of entry clearance or refusal of a certificate of entitlement,[8] on an appeal under section 82 or 83 the Tribunal may consider evidence about any matter which it thinks relevant to the substance of the decision, including evidence which concerns a matter arising after the date of the decision.[9] This means that the focus of the Tribunal's scrutiny in all immigration appeals other than those challenging refusal of entry clearance or certificate of entitlement (not just those engaging the Refugee or Human Rights Convention) has shifted from the date of decision to the date of hearing.[10] The statutory changes mean, in our view, that the appellate process really does become, in all cases, an extension of the decision-making process. Thus, evidence of facts which were unforeseeable at the date of decision can now found a successful appeal.[11] Where the appeal is against refusal of entry clearance or refusal of a certificate of entitlement to the right of abode, the rule remains as it was before the NIAA 2002, with the Tribunal able to consider 'only the circumstances appertaining at the time of the decision'.[12] In respect of those appeals, the earlier authoritieson evidence of post-decision facts remain of relevance.[13] An amended decision notice has been held to give rise to a new date of decision, thus extending the scope for factual investigation on appeal.[14] But the submission of fresh evidence to the decision-maker post-decision, and the review of that evidence in a supplementary refusal letter, has been held not to give rise to a new date of decision, so that the evidence, on an entry clearance appeal, would not lose its quality of inadmissible post-decision evidence.[15] However, a number of decisions relating to entry clearance under the rules involve predictions: whether a business will succeed,[16] whether a couple will live together as man and wife,[17] whether the parties will have accommodation available,[18] whether a student will be able to pursue a course with reasonable success.[19] In these cases, evidence of post-decision facts that throw light on the decision was admissible[20] if the events were foreseeable at the time of the decision.[21] The Tribunal has held in the starred decision of *DR (Morocco)*[22] that section 85(5) now precludes the admission of evidence showing that something which was likely at the date of decision has actually happened. We believe its interpretation of the section to be unduly restrictive.[23] For fresh evidence on appeal or reconsideration, see 18.170 below.

1   *R v Immigration Appeal Tribunal, ex p Weerasuriya* [1983] 1 All ER 195, [1982] Imm AR 23, DC; *Sae-Heng v Visa Officer, Bangkok* [1979–80] Imm AR 69; *R v Secretary of State for the Home Department, ex p Miah* [1998] Imm AR 44, QBD.
2   *R v Immigration Appeal Tribunal, ex p Hassanin* [1987] 1 All ER 74, [1986] 1 WLR 1448, CA, per Dillon LJ.
3   *Ravichandran v Secretary of State for the Home Department* [1996] Imm AR 97, CA.
4   Immigration and Asylum Act 1999, s 77(3).
5   IAA 1999, s 77(4).
6   *Secretary of State for the Home Department v SK* [2002] UKIAT 05613 (starred).
7   *R (on the application of Razgar) v Secretary of State for the Home Department* [2004] UKHL 27, [2004] 3 WLR 58.
8   Nationality, Immigration and Asylum Act 2002, s 85(5).

9   NIAA 2002, s 85(4).
10 The explanatory notes to the Act do not assist in divining the purpose of the change, which may, contrary to our argument in the text, be simply a reflection of the fact that asylum and human rights issues no longer give rise to special appeals but form grounds of appeal against in-country immigration decisions: see ss 82, 84. Read this way, in relation to non-asylum or human rights issues, s 85(4) does no more than put in statutory form the recognition in *R v Immigration Appeal Tribunal, ex p Hoque and Singh* [1988] Imm AR 216, CA that evidence of post-decision facts (such as the birth of a child in a marriage case) may cast a flood of light on the intentions of the parties at the date of decision. This remains the position for entry clearance appeals.
11 *CA (Nigeria)* [2004] UKIAT 00243, where evidence of acquittal of criminal charges of using a false passport was held admissible in an appeal against cancellation of leave on the ground of possession of a false passport, to show that the immigration officer's discretion should have been exercised differently. See 18.63 above.
12 NIAA 2002, s 85(5).
13 See cases at fn 1 above, and *R v Secretary of State for the Home Department, ex p Husbadak* [1982] Imm AR 8, QBD.
14 *Rajendran v Secretary of State for the Home Department* [1989] Imm AR 512 at 519.
15 *R v Immigration Appeal Tribunal and Secretary of State for the Home Department, ex p Banu* [1999] Imm AR 161, [1999] INLR 226, QBD.
16 *R v Immigration Appeal Tribunal, ex p Amir Beaggi* (1982) Times, 25 May, QBD; *Secretary of State for the Home Department v Thaker* [1976] Imm AR 114.
17 *Patel v Secretary of State for the Home Department* [1986] Imm AR 440, IAT.
18 *Azad* (5993), IAT.
19 *Rajendran* [1989] Imm AR 512.
20 *R v Immigration Appeal Tribunal, ex p Kwok On Tong* [1981] Imm AR 214; *R v Immigration Appeal Tribunal, ex p Amir Beaggi* fn 16 above. The admission of post-decision evidence in these cases is, however, strictly limited to that purpose and still looks back to the date of decision.
21 *Adesegun v Entry Clearance Officer* [2002] UKIAT 02132: the sponsor becoming unable to work due to sickle cell anaemia, being unforeseeable at the time of the decision, should not have been taken into account. Post-decision evidence of existing facts is always admissible, however, to show that the situation was not what the entry clearance officer believed it to be: *Hassanin* (fn 2 above).
22 [2005] UKIAT 00038 (starred).
23 The Tribunal held that the rationale for the practise of admitting evidence of post-decision facts which were foreseeable at the date of decision has gone now that entry clearance stands as leave to enter. But with respect, that does not alter anything. The issue of entry clearance in those cases still depends on a prediction, and it is wholly unrealistic to exclude evidence that the predicted event (the sponsor obtaining a job or accommodation) took place. The restrictive interpretation amounts to a rewriting of the rules, which we do not believe was Parliament's intention.

Evidence and findings in other appeals

18.140 There are a number of circumstances in which factual findings made by other tribunals may be taken into account by a Tribunal including (1) findings of fact about conditions in a particular country made in an unrelated appeal; (2) findings of fact about conditions in a particular country made by the tribunal in a 'Country Guideline' case; (3) findings of fact made by a Tribunal where there has been an order for reconsideration; (4) findings of fact made in the appeal of a family member or relative; (5) findings of fact made in an earlier, unchallenged determination of an appeal by the same appellant. Each of these will be considered below.

EVIDENCE OF LIKE FACTS IN OTHER APPEALS

18.141 In asylum appeals evidence of the situation in a particular country may be common to a number of appeals and there may exist a number of determinations, for example, on whether in a particular country, members of a particular minority face persecution. The Tribunal has instituted a system of 'Country Guidance' cases, as to which see below, but if there is no relevant Country Guidance case relating to the appellant's country, is the Tribunal entitled, or obliged, to have regard to other decisions relating to that country? In *Gnanavarathan*,[1] the Court of Appeal held that adjudicators were arguably under an obligation to give full reasons, if they came to conclusions different to other adjudicators regarding country conditions. That decision is no longer apt in the light of the restrictions imposed on citation of cases before the appellate authority. In May 2003, the tribunal stopped publishing all of its decisions and introduced a distinction between 'reported ' and 'unreported' decisions. Whether a decision is to be reported or not is determined by the tribunal. A Practice Direction[2] stipulates that from 16 May 2003, no unreported decision of the tribunal (and no adjudicator determination) may be cited before the tribunal without its consent, unless the claimant or a family member was a party to the appeal. From 1 May 2004, decisions of the tribunal published in 2002 and previous years may not be cited unless the party citing the decision is able to certify that the matter or proposition for which the determination is cited has not been the subject of a more recent, reported tribunal decision. The Tribunal's present view is that decisions which are not 'Country Guidance' cases should not be cited as evidence of the general background situation of the appellant's country,[3] and if they are relied on, they should not be treated as a substitute for making proper reasoned conclusions on the material in the appeal.[4] The importance of the Tribunal reaching its own conclusion has been emphasised over the need for consistent treatment of those emanating from a particular country.[5] If an immigration judge chooses to rely on any determination not cited at the hearing, he or she should draw the parties' attention to it and invite submissions. This is also the practice where an immigration judge wishes to draw upon information obtained in the course of his or her experience or from data available generally to immigration judges.[6] The problem of the respondent's failure to provide the parties or the Tribunal with all the information available to it,[7] has been resolved to a large extent by the introduction of Home Office 'country bundles' which are produced on most asylum appeals,[8] and by the availability, albeit restricted, of legal aid for immigration and asylum appeals,[9] enabling some appellants to be properly represented by persons who have access to the material the Home Office sees.

1   [1995] Imm AR 64.
2   Practice Direction CA3 of 2003, 16 May 2003, [2003] INLR 358.
3   *Eshete* [2002] UKIAT 01963.
4   *Secretary of State for the Home Department v Jerjis* [2002] UKIAT 03272.
5   *Pasupathipillai* (14115) (11 November 1996, unreported); *Avtar Singh* (14191) (25 November 1996, unreported); *Kelecha* (15038) (15 May 1997, unreported); *Kapela* (16283) (29 April 1998, unreported); *Secretary of State for the Home Department v Jerjis* above. See the Court of Appeal's discussion in *S v Secretary of State for the Home Department* [2002] EWCA Civ 539, [2002] INLR 416 on the tension between consistency and individual justice.
6   See 18.129ff above.

7   See *Macdonald* (4th edn) and Supplement at 18.104; *R v Secretary of State for the Home Department, ex p Gawe, Abdi v Secretary of State for the Home Department* [1996] Imm AR 288.

8   From the Country Information and Policy Unit of the IND, CIPU. The reports are sourced and rely mainly on UNHCR, US State Department, Amnesty International and Europa World Year Book. The sources should always be inspected, to check the accuracy of the summaries in the CIPU reports. The Immigration Advisory Service (IAS) reports regularly on the CIPU assessments: see Immigration Advisory Service: *Home Office country information dangerously inaccurate and misleading* (September 2003); *Home Office country information remains flawed* (on the October 2003 CIPU assessments), *Lack of objectivity in Home Office country reports* (on April 2004 CIPU reports), all available on the IAS website. See also the website of the Advisory Panel on Country Information, set up by the Home Office, which has also criticised CIPU reports for their selectivity.

9   Controlled legal representation, from 1 January 2000: see 18.124 above.

COUNTRY GUIDELINE DETERMINATIONS

18.142   With the increase in asylum appeals, greater emphasis has been placed upon the importance of consistency of decision making, at least as far as the impact on individual cases of general conditions in asylum seekers' countries of origin is concerned.[1] In 1997, the Court of Appeal referred to the Tribunal's expertise in the assessment of material relating to country conditions and held that careful attention had to be paid to the tribunal's findings, although they are not findings of law to be treated as binding authority.[2] In 2002, the Court of Appeal went further, approving as 'benign and practical' the notion of a 'factual precedent' where the Tribunal decides to make an authoritative determination of some general question of fact with the intention that it should be binding as to the conditions then existing.[3] The Immigration Appellate Authority website now provides access to what the tribunal regards as 'Country Guideline determinations'.[4] Unless presented with new material that had not been before the Tribunal, an immigration judge or panel in a subsequent case dealing with the same country would have to have a valid reason for departing from the Tribunal's view expressed in such a decision,[5] although the continuing reliability of that view should always be checked against up to date country information.[6] The tribunal held in a starred decision, *DD (Croatia)*,[7] that it would be an error of law to make a decision that was incompatible with a decision of the IAT giving 'authoritative guidance' on a particular issue, even if the immigration judge was unaware of and had not been shown that tribunal decision. We believe this went too far, misinterpreting the Court of Appeal's decision in *Shirazi*,[8] and creates the potential for dangerous miscarriages of justice where, as happens, the 'Country Guidelines' case to be followed is not comprehensive or clearly reasoned,[9] and where the procedure and criteria for deciding that a case is to be a 'country guidelines' case are unknown, and therefore arguably unfair.[10] Even when hearing a case where there is a relevant 'factual precedent', the Tribunal is obliged to consider and determine the facts of the individual case and to consider any evidence showing a change of circumstances since the 'factual precedent' was decided.[11]

1   Eg *Gurung v Secretary of State for the Home Department* [2003] EWCA Civ 654, [2003] All ER (D) 14 (May); *Shirazi v Secretary of State for the Home Department* [2003] EWCA Civ 1562, [2004] 2 All ER 602, where the court held that the Tribunal should have had regard to inconsistent decisions. The court did not, however, hold that inconsistency per se is an error of law; see text and fn 8 below.

2   [1997] Imm AR 524, CA.
3   *S v Secretary of State for the Home Department* [2002] EWCA Civ 539, [2002] INLR 416; *Krotov v Secretary of State for the Home Department* [2004] EWCA Civ 69, [2004] 1 WLR 1825. *S* concerned an early example of a Tribunal determination which was meant to be authoritative as regards the country situation for particular groups, such as Croatian Serbs, which it involved, or Roma in the Czech Republic: see also *Puzova* (01/TH/0416). Buxton LJ questioned the viability of a 'Country Guideline' system where the Tribunal's jurisdiction was limited to error of law (as it was as a second-instance Tribunal under the NIAA 2002 before 4 April 2005) in *Batayav v Secretary of State for the Home Department (No 2)* [2005] EWCA Civ 366 (para 23).
4   www.iaa.gov.uk.
5   *Alamalikuyu* [2002] UKIAT 00749, IAT.
6   *Kokularamanan* [2002] UKIAT 00985.
7   *Secretary of State for the Home Department v DD (Croatia)* [2004] UKIAT 00032 (starred). Note that this was a decision under the appeal provisions of the Immigration and Asylum Act 1999, which did not require error of law to found an appeal.
8   Fn 1 above. See *Otshudi v Secretary of State for the Home Department* [2004] EWCA Civ 893, [2004] All ER (D) 12 (Jul) where Sedley LJ held that two conscientious decision makers could reach opposite or divergent conclusions on the same evidence, without affecting the legal soundness of the decisions.
9   The Immigration Advisory Service has criticised the Country Guidelines system as 'inimical to individual justice', finding many cases inadequately referenced, not based on comprehensive country information, obscurely reasoned and displaying the customary hostility towards expert opinion, rejecting rather than seeking to incorporate it: see *Country Guideline cases: 'benign and practical'?* (Feb 2005).
10 See *Dib v Secretary of State for the Home Department* [2004] EWCA Civ 1645 (permission) (case posted as 'Country Guidance' without warning to appellant). It is clear that there are far too many 'CG' cases, many of which are anything but, turning on particular facts and even on credibility, and the system urgently needs overhaul.
11 *S v Secretary of State for the Home Department* [2002] EWCA Civ 539, [2002] INLR 416; *Secretary of State for the Home Department v DD (Croatia)* [2004] UKIAT 00032 (starred); *DK (Croatia)* [2003] UKIAT 00153 (starred).

Evidence on reconsideration

18.143 On reconsideration pursuant to an order, the Tribunal can hear further evidence. The extent to which this power is exercisable will depend on the terms of the order for reconsideration. The Practice Direction states that where a fresh decision is to be substituted on reconsideration, the Tribunal carrying out the reconsideration will usually be required to hear evidence afresh and to make its own findings as to the credibility of the claimant and any witnesses, although it will have read the credibility findings in the original determination (since it will have had to determine whether the original Tribunal made an error of law). It is therefore inappropriate to seek to argue that the Tribunal should not have regard to the previous determination, or to seek a direction that oral evidence should be heard by a differently constituted Tribunal.[1] See further 18.171 and 18.174–175 below.

1   Practice Direction 1/2005, para 14.6. Unless specifically directed otherwise, a party preparing for a reconsideration hearing must make arrangements to attend, together with any witnesses and interpreters, in case the Tribunal decides to hear oral evidence: para 14.7. See 18.174ff below for procedure and evidence on reconsideration.

Evidence of facts found in appeals by family members

18.144 In *Chicaiza*,[1] the Tribunal held that an adjudicator hearing the appeal of one member of a family should in certain circumstances, where their claims are closely associated with each other, take into account the determinations of appeals by other family members, although the weight to be given to the findings of fact made in the other appeals is a matter for the adjudicator. In the same case, the Tribunal pointed out that where one member of a family was granted asylum on the basis of similar considerations to those raised by the appellant, dismissal of the asylum appeal would have to be very carefully reasoned. But it is important that Tribunals do not treat earlier determinations of other family members' appeals as determinative of the particular appeal before them. In *Otshudi*,[2] Sedley LJ upheld the importance of individual justice over consistency of determinations, and mere disparity of outcomes between family members does not amount to error of law.[3] But where a family member whose evidence had been disbelieved on his own appeal gave identical evidence on his wife's appeal, and her claim depended on his, in the absence of the respondent the immigration judge was entitled not only to have regard to the determination on his appeal but also to accept it as determinative of his credibility, although not determinative of the whole appeal.[4]

1 *Chicaiza* [2002] UKIAT 01200.
2 *Otshudi v Secretary of State for the Home Department* [2004] EWCA Civ 893, [2004] All ER (D) 12 (Jul).
3 *S (Sri Lanka)* [2004] UKIAT 00039.
4 *TK (Georgia)* [2004] UKIAT 00149.

Previous findings of fact in respect of the same person

18.145 Circumstances may arise, although less and less frequently under the one-stop system, where an individual who has had an unsuccessful appeal against an earlier decision acquires another right of appeal against a new decision. The tribunal set out guidelines in a starred decision, *Devaseelan*, about the approach to be taken in hearing the second appeal, to the factual findings made in the first.[1] The *Devaseelan* guidelines were approved in *Djebbar*, where the Court of Appeal said that the provision of guidance on how appellate bodies should deal with the fact of an earlier unsuccessful application when deciding a later one was 'essential to ensure consistency of approach'.[2] The Court emphasised that the most important feature of the guidance is that the fundamental obligation of every immigration judge independently to decide each new application on its own individual merits was preserved; the guidelines were not written in the language of *res judicata* or estoppel.[3] The *Devaseelan* guidelines state that matters arising since the first appellate decision, and facts that were not relevant to the issues before the first immigration judge or panel can be determined by the second.[4] However the first determination is generally to be regarded by the second immigration judge or panel as an authoritative determination of the issues of fact that were before the first appellate body. Generally, the second immigration judge or panel should not revisit findings of fact made by the first on the basis of evidence that was available to the appellant at the time of the first hearing. The findings of fact made by the first appellate body may be revisited in the light of evidence that was not available to the appellant at the time of the first appeal, and they may be revisited where the circumstances of the first appeal were such that it would be right for the second appellate body to treat the first determination as if it had never been made.[5] It may also be appropriate for the second appellate body to revisit earlier credibility findings if the issue of credibility remains arguably live.[6] If the second appeal contains asylum or human rights grounds, the second appellate body in applying the *Devaseelan* guidelines would have to be mindful of the obligations to take account of all relevant material[7] and to consider the case with 'the most anxious scrutiny'.[8] A 'factual finding' announced at the conclusion of a preliminary hearing does not bind the immigration judge or panel who hears the substantive appeal.[9]

1   *Devaseelan* [2003] Imm AR 1. The guidelines apply not only to asylum and human rights appeals but also to successive appeals against entry clearance decisions: *Entry Clearance Officer, Islamabad v B (Pakistan)* [2003] UKIAT 00053. However, the *Devaseelan* guidelines apply only to successive appeals by the same individual and it would be wrong to regard them as applicable to appeals by different members of the same family: *Diyenli* [2002] UKIAT 07173. But see *TK (Georgia)* [2004] UKIAT 00149.
2   *Djebbar v Secretary of State for the Home Department* [2004] EWCA Civ 804, [2004] 33 LS Gaz R 36, para 14.
3   *Djebbar* above, para 15.
4   The first tribunal who heard an asylum appeal may not have made findings of fact that were relevant to the later human rights appeal: *Ayella* [2002] UKIAT 06721
5   *Devaseelan*, fn 1 above.
6   *Ayella*, fn 2 above. Credibility findings might remain live where, for example, there was no appeal against an earlier decision dismissing an asylum appeal because of an unassailable finding that there was no Refugee Convention reason, rather than because adverse credibility findings were correct.
7   *Karanakaran v Secretary of State for the Home Department* [2000] 3 All ER 449, [2000] INLR 122, [2000] Imm AR 271 CA.
8   Dyson LJ in *R (on the application of Sivakumar) v Immigration Appeal Tribunal* [2001] EWCA Civ 1196, [2002] INLR 310 (upheld at [2003] UKHL 14, [2003] 2 All ER 1097) reminded decision makers in asylum cases that 'that is not a mantra to which only lip service should be paid. It recognises the fact that what is at stake in these cases is fundamental human rights, including the right to life itself'.
9   *L (Ethiopia)* [2003] UKIAT 00016 (adjudicator's conclusion on the 'preliminary issue' of the appellant's nationality, announced at a preliminary hearing, not binding on the adjudicator subsequently hearing the appeal).

Burden and standard of proof

18.146 The rules relating to the burden of proof in appeals may be summarised as follows:

(1)   The burden of proving British citizenship or any exemption from statutory provisions is on the person who makes the assertion.[1] Usually this will be the applicant, but not always.[2]

(2)   In an appeal, an appellant who wishes to assert that he or she has a right of abode or is exempt and, therefore, that the decision or action should not have been taken, must prove it.[3]

(3)   Most claims to enter or remain will depend on the applicant satisfying the entry clearance officer, immigration officer or Home Office of the necessary facts which will qualify them in the appropriate category, and consequently in an appeal the burden of proving such a claim is on the party making it.[4]

(4)   This applies equally to asylum and human rights or discrimination claims, where the burden of proof is on the applicant to make his or her case.[5]

(5)   But where it is accepted that at the date of the decision on the claim an asylum seeker did in fact qualify for refugee status, but the Secretary of State contends that by the date of the hearing the circumstances have changed, then by analogy with Article 1C(5) of the Refugee Convention (where proof that the circumstances of persecution have ceased to exist falls on the receiving state) there is an evidential burden on the Secretary of State to establish that the appellant can safely return home.[6]

(6)   Where an internal flight option is alleged by the Secretary of State, no question of burden or standard of proof arises; the question is simply whether, taking all relevant matters into account, it would be unduly harsh to expect the applicant to relocate.[7]

(7)   Where an applicant falls into a class of persons who are acknowledged to face particular treatment, it is for the respondent to show why the applicant faces no real risk of such treatment.[8]

(8)   Where the Secretary of State seeks to deport someone under section 3(5) of the IA 1971, the Secretary of State must prove the facts necessary to establish a ground for deporting. This will also be the case where the Home Office are relying on non-disclosure of material facts to justify the refusal of entry,[9] or on one of the general grounds for refusal, such as character, conduct, associations, criminal convictions and so forth. It falls on the party who asserts to prove.

(9)   There will also be a heavy burden on the Secretary of State if it is sought to contradict a finding as to relationship made in a previous appeal, although the concept of *res judicata* does not apply to the determination of the immigration appellate authorities.[10]

(9)   Where the respondent asserts that documents relied on by an appellant are false, it is for him or her to prove it.[11] However, possession of an apparently genuine national passport must raise an inference that the holder possesses the corresponding nationality, which it is for him or her to rebut.[12]

---

1   Immigration Act 1971, s 3(8).
2   An example would be where the applicant wishes to rely on a stamp on his or her passport giving indefinite leave, but the Home Office asserts that the stamp does not apply because the applicant had a diplomatic exemption at the time.
3   Asylum and Immigration Tribunal (Procedure) Rules 2005, SI 2005/230, r 53(1), applied to fast track appeals by SI 2005/560, r 27, reflecting Immigration Act 1971, s 3(8). The rule would also include an assertion of exemption from deportation under s 7 Immigration Act 1971.
4   SI 2005/230, r 53(2). See *R v Secretary of State for the Home Department, ex p Mughal* [1974] QB 313, [1974] 3 All ER 796, CA. See also *Visa Officer, Islamabad v Bi (Channo)* [1978] Imm AR 182 where, although the appellant had previously been granted entry clearance as the wife of the sponsor, she still had the burden of proving she was his wife on a later occasion when she sought readmission.
5   *Adebola* (16731) (19 August 1998, unreported), IAT. So in an onward appeal, the fact that the Secretary of State, as the appellant, has to show an error of law in the decision below is quite separate from proof by an asylum seeker of the basic elements needed to satisfy the criteria of a refugee claim: *Tikhonov* [1998] INLR 737, IAT. For burden and standard of proof in asylum appeals see 12.25ff above.
6   *Arif v Secretary of State for the Home Department* [1999] INLR 327, CA, distinguished in *Salim v Secretary of State for the Home Department* [2000] Imm AR 503, CA and *Dyli v Secretary of State for the Home Department* [2000] Imm AR 652 (starred). In *Sijakovic* (01TH 00632) the Tribunal said it was unhelpful to talk of a burden, whether legal or evidential, on the Secretary of State: the issue was whether there was a well-founded fear of

persecution. However, in *Saad v Secretary of State for the Home Department, Diriye v Secretary of State for the Home Department, Osorio v Secretary of State for the Home Department* [2001] EWCA Civ 2008, [2002] Imm AR 471, [2002] INLR 34 the Court of Appeal referred approvingly to *Arif*. Where a person has been recognised as a refugee by another government, the burden is on the Secretary of State to show that he is no longer a refugee: *Babela* [2002] UKIAT 06214.

7 *Karanakaran v Secretary of State for the Home Department* [2000] Imm AR 271 at 305. Previously, the question had been approached on the basis that the Secretary of State must show that it would be reasonable to expect an applicant to go to another part of the country, but that the applicant had an evidential burden to put forward matters indicating that it would be unduly harsh to expect him or her to do so: *R v Immigration Appeal Tribunal, ex p Tharumakulasingham* [1997] Imm AR 550, QBD Jowitt J. But there was some confusion about this; see *R v Secretary of State for the Home Department, ex p Salim* [1999] INLR 628, QBD, where the burden was held to be on the appellant to show that internal flight did not apply.

8 Thus, where a Country Assessment produced by the Home Office sets out the penalties that may be imposed for draft evasion, it is for the Secretary of State to show that there was no real risk that they would be enforced against a draft-evading asylum seeker: *Adam v Secretary of State for the Home Department* [2003] EWCA Civ 265.

9 *Ghati* (19707) (27 July 1999, unreported), IAT.

10 *Ali (Momin) v Secretary of State for the Home Department* [1984] 1 All ER 1009, [1984] Imm AR 23, CA; *R v Immigration Appeal Tribunal, ex p Miah (Lulu)* [1987] Imm AR 143; *R v Secretary of State for the Home Department, ex p Danaie* [1998] Imm AR 84; [1998] INLE 124.

11 *R v Immigration Appeal Tribunal, ex p Shen* [2000] INLR 389, QBD; *Makozo* (20033) (12 February 1999, unreported), IAT; *Escobar* (20553) (26 March 1999, unreported), IAT. But since the overall burden of proof is on the appellant, it is not necessary for the Secretary of State to prove forgery in order for a claim resting on documentary evidence to be dismissed: see cases cited at fn 6 above.

12 *MW (Pakistan)* [2004] UKIAT 00136.

18.147 Where the burden of proof lies on a party, he or she may adduce sufficient *prima facie* evidence to discharge that burden in the absence of reasons to the contrary or evidence in rebuttal. What is sufficient *prima facie* evidence will vary from case to case; the quality of documentation relied on as proof of events may be variable; for example later birth certificates will be less weighty than contemporaneous ones. In an asylum or Article 3 case, the Handbook indicates that evidence of past maltreatment is an excellent indicator of the fate that may await an applicant on return.[1] The Secretary of State is under no obligation to investigate unproven allegations of risk; such a duty would dilute the already lowered standard of proof.[2]

1 Handbook para 45; see also *Demirkaya v Secretary of State for the Home Department* [1999] Imm AR 498, [1999] INLR 441, CA; *R v Secretary of State for the Home Department, ex p Dahmas* (17 November 1999), CA (overturning [2000] Imm AR 151). See also Council Directive 2004/83/EC on minimum standards for the qualification and status of third country nationals and stateless persons as refugees or persons who otherwise need international protection (30.9.04 OJ L304/12), the Qualification Directive, Art 7(4). The court in *Demirkaya* also pointed out that the Tribunal's statement that it was 'reasonably likely that the appellant would be released after one or two days' was an incorrect application of the burden of proof. The proper question was whether there was a real risk that he would *not* be released.

2 *RK (DRC)* [2004] UKIAT 129, where the Tribunal rejected the argument that, since Art 3 ECHR contained an obligation to investigate, the appellant's return without investigating her allegation that failed asylum seekers were subjected to persecutory harm would breach Art 3. In this connection, the Tribunal distinguished between the State's duty to investigate alleged breaches by its own agents (*Aksoy v Turkey* (1996) 23 EHRR 553) and its much more limited duty to investigate conditions in the destination country, which were met by its production of CIPU and FCO reports. See also *S (Serbia and Montenegro)* [2003]

UKIAT 00031; *R v Secretary of State for the Home Department, ex p Gawe, Abdi v Secretary of State for the Home Department* [1996] Imm AR 288, HL: the Secretary of State was not obliged to embark on an investigation of evidence not in his hands, to assist appellants in making their cases.

Standard of proof

18.148 The standard of proof is generally that which applies in all civil proceedings – proof on balance of probabilities. This is so even when questions of citizenship and right of abode are at stake. So where the Tribunal stated that they were not 'convinced' of the appellant's means, this indicated that they were applying too high a standard of proof, more akin to that in criminal cases, and their determination was quashed.[1] The civil standard is, however, flexible and has regard to the nature of the allegation and its consequences. Where the allegation is fraud or corruption and the consequences for the appellant are correspondingly serious, proof to a high degree of probability is required.[2] So where the allegation is conduct leading to deportation, a very high standard is required.[3] Where there has already been a binding decision of an appropriate tribunal in favour of the applicant the standard is even higher.[4] In asylum cases where the onus is to show a well-founded fear of persecution, it is inappropriate to apply a test of balance of probabilities to what is likely to happen in the future and it will be sufficient if a reasonable likelihood of persecution is established.[5] The Court of Appeal gave guidance in *Karanakaran*[6] on how to apply this lower standard of proof, in the process illuminating the meaning of the decision in *Kaja*, in which the majority of the Tribunal had held that the lower standard applies to all aspects of proving that a person is a Convention refugee, including the assessment of accounts of past events.[7] This is dealt with in detail at 12.26ff above. Similar considerations apply in ECHR, Article 3 cases where the onus is to show a serious risk of the relevant harm.[8] But in the absence of personal risk, it will be difficult for an appellant to show that removal would breach Article 3 unless the evidence shows a consistent pattern of gross and sysematic violation of human rights in the country of return.[9] The burden is the same for someone with mental or psychological problems.[10]

1   *R v Immigration Appeal Tribunal, ex p Mehra* [1983] Imm AR 156 at 162.
2   *Khawaja v Secretary of State for the Home Department* [1984] AC 74, [1983] 1 All ER 765, HL.
3   *Offeh* (9662), unreported.
4   *Ali (Momin) v Secretary of State for the Home Department* [1984] 1 All ER 1009, [1984] Imm AR 23, CA; *R (on the application of Saribal) v Secretary of State for the Home Department* [2002] EWHC 1542 (Admin), [2002] INLR 596, [2002] All ER (D) 379 (Jul).
5   *R v Secretary of State for the Home Department, ex p Sivakumaran* [1988] AC 958. Expressions such as the 'balance of probabilities' have no place in asylum determination: *R (on the application of Xhelollari) v Immigration Appeal Tribunal* [2002] EWHC 2451 (Admin), [2002] All ER (D) 49 (Nov) (dismissed on facts).
6   *Karanakaran v Secretary of State for the Home Department* [2000] 3 All ER 449, [2000] INLR 122, [2000] Imm AR 271, CA.
7   *Kaja v Secretary of State for the Home Department* [1995] Imm AR 1, a majority decision of the Tribunal
8   *Kacaj v Secretary of State for the Home Department* (starred) (CC/23044/2000) (21 May 2001, unreported). See 12.25 above.

⁹ *Batayav v Secretary of State for the Home Department* [2003] EWCA Civ 1489, [2004] INLR 126, explaining *Hariri v Secretary of State for the Home Department* [2003] EWCA Civ 807, [2003] All ER (D) 340 (May); *Iqbal (Muzafar)* [2002] UKIAT 02239.

¹⁰ *Bolat v Secretary of State for the Home Department* (99/6206/C) (23 February 2000, unreported), CA (leave to appeal).

Combined hearings

18.149 The Procedure Rules¹ provide for the possibility of a combined hearing of two or more pending appeals. The Tribunal may hear appeals together if a common question of law or fact arises in them, or they relate to decisions or actions taken against members of the same family,² or for some other reason it is desirable to hear them together.³ The rules no longer require the parties to be given the opportunity to make representations before the tribunal determines the appeals together.⁴ In hearing a combined appeal, it is crucial that the Tribunal give separate consideration to the case for each appellant.⁵ Appellants' appeals should not fail solely because they differ in their testimony at a combined hearing.⁶ It is inappropriate to exclude any appellant from the hearing room from any part of the combined appeal.⁷ If two or more appeals are heard together it is preferable to issue separate determinations, unless the appeals are interdependent.⁸ Neither the Procedure Rules nor considerations of fairness require the Tribunal to adjourn the hearing of an appeal pending the determination of a family member's claim, nor is it unfair for a person whose claim has not yet been determined to give evidence in someone else's appeal.⁹

¹ Asylum and Immigration Tribunal (Procedure) Rules 2005, SI 2005/230, r 20.
² SI 2005/230, r 20(a), (b). It is inappropriate to list the principal's appeal with that of a divorced spouse who had no knowledge of the welfare of the child: *Aderibgbe* (16659) (12 May 1998, unreported), IAT.
³ SI 2005/230, r 20(c). The Tribunal has in the past made use of this power particularly in bringing together cases from a single country displaying a range of facts, in order to issue 'Country Guideline' determinations (see 18.142 above).
⁴ The previous procedure rules, SI 2003/652, made such provision in r 51(2). The Tribunal has power to give directions requiring the parties to take any steps to enable two or more appeals to be heard together: SI 2005/230, r 45(4)(g). An appellant who believed him- or herself prejudiced by a combined hearing would be able to raise this as a preliminary issue under r 45(4)(d)(i).
⁵ *Wah (Yau Yak) v Home Office* [1982] Imm AR 16, CA; *R v Immigration Appeal Tribunal, ex p Begum (Hamida)* [1988] Imm AR 199.
⁶ *Tabores and Munoz* (17819) (24 July 1998, unreported), IAT, where dismissal on the basis that they 'cannot both be telling the truth' was set aside.
⁷ *Tabores and Munoz* (17819) (24 July 1998, unreported), IAT.
⁸ *Twum v Immigration Officer, Heathrow* [1986] Imm AR 316; *Ahmed* (7903), unreported.
⁹ *Rajan* (01TH00244) (starred); *S (Sri Lanka)* [2004] UKIAT 00039, declining to follow *R v Secretary of State for the Home Department, ex p Kimbesa* (29 January 1997, unreported). See 18.126 above.

Hearings in public

18.150 Reflecting the principle of open justice enshrined in ECHR, Article 6,¹ the general rule for immigration and asylum appeals is that hearings take place in public.² The exceptions to the rule set out in rule 54 of the Procedure

Rules[3] mirror those permitted by ECHR, Article 6(1). There is a discretion to exclude a particular member of the public, or the public generally, from a hearing or part of a hearing, where:

(1)   it is necessary in the interests of public order or national security;

(2)   it is necessary to protect the private life of a party or the interests of a minor; or

(3)   in exceptional circumstances to ensure that publicity does not prejudice the interests of justice, but only if and to the extent that it is strictly necessary to do so.

There is no power to hold a hearing in private merely because a party requests it, and it will therefore be for an appellant to justify a closed hearing by reference to one of these public interest criteria. The exceptions are likely to be invoked by asylum seekers who will argue that a public hearing prejudices the interests of justice in inhibiting them from giving a full account of their claim, or indeed proceeding with the hearing at all, for shame, or fear of reprisals, and those who have psychological conditions which could be exacerbated by giving evidence in open court.[4] Regrettably, many asylum seekers are not aware that the cloak of confidentiality which surrounds their claim is lifted for the appeal unless they make a case for retaining it. The Tribunal's practice of reporting asylum cases by initial only provides retrospective protection, which can be extended by direction to other witnesses, and the Tribunal may make other directions necessary for preserving confidentiality.[5]

1   'A fair and public hearing': see eg *R v Secretary of State for Health, ex p Associated Newspapers* [2001] 1 WLR 292, CA.

2   Asylum and Immigration Tribunal (Procedure) Rules 2005, SI 2005/230, r 54(1), applied to fast track appeals by SI 2005/560, r 27.

3   SI 2005/230, r 54(3), (4), expressed to be without prejudice to the right of members of the Council of Tribunals or its Scottish Committee from attending appeals (r 54(5)). The UK representative of UNHCR is also entitled to attend any hearing

4   See *R v Legal Aid Board, ex p Kaim Todner* [1999] QB 966. For general principles underlying withholding of identity, see *A-G v Leveller Magazine Ltd* [1979] AC 440; see also *R v Westminster City Council, ex p Castelli* (1995) 7 Admin LR at 845.

5   SI 2005/230, rr 43, 45, which give wide powers to regulate the conduct of hearings; see in particular r 45(4)(i).

18.151 In addition to these circumstances, there is a duty to exclude the public (and a power to exclude the appellant and his or her representative, and the UNHCR representative) where evidence is being given of the method of detection of a forgery of a document relied on by a party to an appeal (such as a passport, other travel document or work permit) and it is alleged that it would be contrary to the public interest to disclose the methods of detection.[1] This is a very wide power (although rarely if ever used) and it is difficult to see why it has been retained. Such evidence is given in the presence of the parties in a criminal trial, and should also be given in an immigration matter, particularly when the burden of proving such an allegation falls on the Home Office and it will be impossible to challenge it, if the appellant does not know how the Home Office are proving it.

1   Asylum and Immigration Tribunal (Procedure) Rules 2005, SI 2005/230, r 54(2), referring to Nationality, Immigration and Asylum Act 2002, s 108.

Transfer of proceedings

18.152 Under previous procedure rules, specific powers were given to a senior adjudicator to transfer an appeal which an adjudicator had started to hear, where it was not practicable for the original adjudicator to complete the hearing or give a determination justly or without undue delay.[1] This power was used where an appeal was part-heard and events conspired to prevent its return to the adjudicator who started hearing the case within a reasonable time[2] or at all. Although such specific power no longer exists, it is inherent in the general power to decide the procedure to be followed in relation to any appeal,[3] in accordance with the overriding objectives of fairness, speed and efficiency,[4] and it is dealt with in the Tribunal's Practice Direction.[5] The cases under previous rules remain relevant. Where an appeal is adjourned because of interpretation problems, the appeal should be transferred to another Tribunal unless the original Tribunal is satisfied that he or she can properly continue to hear the appeal and both of the parties expressly consent to that Tribunal continuing to hear the appeal.[6] Failure by an adjudicator to obtain a transfer order to remedy a listing error by the appellate authority which prevented the Home Office Presenting Officer from appearing before the adjudicator rendered the hearing that took place unfair.[7] Transfer was held not unfair and justified when there had been a delay of ten months in a part-heard appeal, although the effect was that the appellant lost the benefit of provisional positive credibility findings.[8] On transfer the new Tribunal stands in the shoes of the first Tribunal.[9]

[1] Immigration and Asylum Appeals (Procedure) Rules 2003, r 52(1).
[2] A delay of four months between hearings led to the determination being ruled unsafe in *Kissi* (11873) (27 February 1995, unreported), IAT, and five months in *Jeyanthan* (11975) (30 March 1995, unreported), IAT.
[3] SI 2005/230, r 43, applied to fast track appeals by SI 2005/560, r 27.
[4] SI 2005/230, r 4, applied to fast track appeals by SI 2005/560, r 4.
[5] Practice Direction 1/2005, para 12.1, which enables a senior or designated immigration judge to direct transfer on the same basis as before.
[6] *A (Ethiopia)* [2003] UKIAT 00103.
[7] *Secretary of State for the Home Department v I (Somalia)* [2004] UKIAT 00062.
[8] *R v Special Adjudicator, ex p Akdogan (Hasan)* (CO 1357/99) (11 February 2000, unreported), QBD.
[9] Practice Direction 1/2005, para 12.2.

After the hearing

18.153 The Tribunal may indicate during the hearing that it is prepared to receive further evidence and/or submissions within a specified time, in order to do justice between the parties and ensure that all issues are not only ventilated but that all the requisite evidence and arguments are deployed in their support. The first guiding rule is equality of treatment; if an appellant is given extra time to submit a document which has not arrived in time for the hearing, the respondent must be afforded an opportunity to deal with it, in writing or even, if necessary, by reconvening the hearing. The course to be adopted will depend on the circumstances of the case, the approach of the parties and the Tribunal to the hearing itself.[1] The second guiding rule is that if theTribunal has allowed time for further submissions, they must not be ignored if they are sent within the specified time.[2] If the Tribunal gives an indication at the end of the hearing that it intends to allow the appeal, it is obliged to allow further evidence or submissions if it changes its mind.[3] The Tribunal remains seised of the appeal, and so able to take account of new evidence, up until the time when its decision is formally notified to the parties.[4]

[1] *Bwamiki* (17710) (10 July 1998, unreported), IAT.
[2] *Singh (Billa)* (G0071) (21 January 1999, unreported), IAT. The admission of fresh evidence would not depend on an indication by the Tribunal at the hearing, however; if further relevant evidence becomes available between the hearing and the promulgation of the determination, it should be submitted to the Tribunal and to the other party, and if not taken into account could form the basis of an application for appeal or review (see 18.166 below): *E v Secretary of State for the Home Department, R v Secretary of State for the Home Department* [2004] EWCA Civ 49, [2004] INLR 268.
[3] *R v Special Adjudicator, ex p Bashir* [2002] Imm AR 1, AC; *K (Rwanda)* [2003] UKIAT 00047. The same applies where the Tribunal reconsiders a positive finding on credibility which has been communicated to the parties: *Paudel* [2002] UKIAT 06868.
[4] *E v Secretary of State for the Home Department, R v Secretary of State for the Home Department* (fn 2 above), paras 27, 92.

Errors or irregularities in procedure

18.154 An error of procedure such as a failure to comply with a rule does not invalidate any step taken in the proceedings unless the Tribunal so orders. Further, prior to determining an appeal, the Tribunal may make an order or take any other step that it considers appropriate to remedy the error.[1] This would normally be done either by amendment of documents or the giving of any notice, but it is not confined to such steps. The procedure rules specifically provide that determinations retain their validity even if the hearing did not take place within the time specified under the rules, or the determination was not made or served within the specified time.[2] But this rule cannot be used to extend time limits or to give jurisdiction where none exists.[3] Procedural irregularities (other than late service of the determination) discovered after the Tribunal's determination can normally only be dealt with by way of an order for reconsideration or appeal.[4] The Tribunal also has power to correct clerical or other accidental errors, slips and omissions by amendment of orders, notices and determination.[5] It must serve the amended document on the parties on whom the original document was served,[6] except in fast track appeals, and if the error was contained in the determination of the appeal, time for appealing or applying for reconsideration runs from the date of service of the amended determination.[7]

[1] Asylum and Immigration Tribunal (Procedure) Rules 2005, SI 2005/230, r 59(1), applied to fast track appeals by SI 2005/560, r 27.
[2] SI 2005/230, r 59(2).
[3] *R v Immigration Appeal Tribunal, ex p Secretary of State for the Home Department* [1990] Imm AR 166; *Wa-Selo v Secretary of State for the Home Department* [1990] Imm AR 76, CA.
[4] Ie under Nationality, Immigration and Asylum Act 2002, s 103A or 103E.
[5] SI 2005/230, r 60(1), applied to fast track appeals by SI 2005/560, r 27.
[6] SI 2005/230, r 60(2), disapplied in respect of fast track appeals, see SI 2005/560 r 27.
[7] SI 2005/230, r 60(3).

Keeping a record of proceedings

18.155 Although the procedure rules are silent on the issue, Practice Directions require the Tribunal to keep a proper record of proceedings of any hearing.[1] There is a rebuttable presumption that it is accurate.[2] A party's note of the evidence is evidence of what was said by a witness in the proceedings.[3] Where an application for permission to appeal is based on an assertion of fact as to what happened before the Tribunal which is at odds with the record, the allegation should be supported by evidence.[4]

[1] Practice Direction 1/2005, para 11.
[2] *Ning* (9863), IAT.
[3] *Secretary of State for the Home Department v A (Somalia)* [2003] UKIAT 143.
[4] *R (on the application of Bosombanguwa) v Immigration Appeal Tribunal and Secretary of State for the Home Department* [2004] EWHC 1656 (Admin), [2004] All ER (D) 260 (Jul). See 18.131 above.

Making a determination

18.156 The determination is the decision by the Tribunal in writing to allow or dismiss the appeal, and does not include a procedural, ancillary or preliminary decision.[1] Written notice of the determination must be sent to every party,[2] and on the appellant's representative, if any,[3] in ordinary cases not later than ten days after the hearing finishes or the appeal is determined without a hearing,[4] This rule does not apply to determinations of in-country appeals on asylum grounds, where service of the determination is on the respondent, who then serves it on the appellant.[5] In such a case, the time limits for the Tribunal's service on the respondent are the same, but the respondent has 28 days to serve the appellant unless the respondent applies for permission to appeal or for review, in which case the appellant must be served no later than the date of such an application.[6] The Tribunal must allow or dismiss an appeal,[7] and cannot allow it on a conditional basis,[8] but an appeal may be allowed to the extent that the matter is remitted to the Secretary of State for consideration in accordance with the law and the correct facts as found by the Tribunal.[9] The question as to whether the definition of 'determination' in the Procedure Rules excludes a decision that there is no right of appeal or that an appeal had been abandoned has been considered at 18.107 above. The Tribunal is obliged to make a formal determination in every case where he or she purports to dispose of the appeal.[10] The Tribunal has indicated in a Practice Direction that where its jurisdiction is exercised by more than one member, there will be no indication whether its decision was unanimous, and dissenting views will not be included in it or otherwise communicated.[11] Although the freedom to express a dissenting view was rarely exercised in the old Immigration Appeal Tribunal, it was not banned, and this direction causes some concern in that it prevents the appellant from knowing what every defendant in a criminal case tried by a jury has the right to know, and offends the principle of open justice.

[1] Asylum and Immigration Tribunal (Procedure) Rules 2005, SI 2005/230, r 2, applied to fast track appeals by SI 2005/560, r 2.
[2] SI 2005/230, r 22(1). The fact that pages were missing from a determination could not ground an appeal where no steps had been taken to obtain the missing pages: *Secretary of State for the Home Department v W (Ethiopia)* [2004] UKIAT 00074.

3 SI 2005/230, r 55(3).
4 SI 2005/230, r 22(2). The new rules contain no express power to promulgate a determination orally at the end of the hearing, although it would clearly be within the power of the Tribunal to give the decision, while reserving the reasons, and some immigration judges routinely deliver the entire determination orally, sending a copy in writing as required by the rules. Where a written determination contradicted the oral decision to allow the appeal issued at the end of the hearing, the remedy was not a mandatory order to compel a written decision in accordance with the oral one, but an order to quash the written determination for the whole matter to be reconsidered de novo: *R v Special Adjudicator, ex p Bashir* (CO 4643/98) (6 December 1999, unreported), QBD. See also *K (Rwanda)* [2003] UKIAT 00047, and cases cited at 18.153 above.
5 SI 2005/230, r 22(1), 23(1), (4), (5)(a). The purpose of this provision, introduced by SI 2001/4014 in January 2002, is to prevent unsuccessful claimants from disappearing on receipt of unfavourable determinations. The idea was that they would be detained and removed shortly thereafter. In fact, in most cases nothing further is done to remove unsuccessful claimants, apart from removing entitlement to asylum support: see chapter 13 above. The rule for the service of the decision on the Secretary of State was held not to be *ultra vires* in *R (on the application of Bubaker) v Lord Chancellor* [2002] EWCA Civ 1107, [2002] Imm AR 552 (permission).
6 The respondent must notify the Tribunal as soon as practicable of its service of the determination on the appellant, and if the Tribunal has not received notice of service within 29 days, it must serve the determination on the appellant itself, as soon as reasonably practicable: r 23(5)(b), (6).
7 *Hamdan* (12338) (24 July 1995, unreported), IAT: there is no power to remit to the Secretary of State as an alternative to allowing or dismissing an appeal, although the Tribunal may adjourn to enable the respondent to deal with an issue arising in the course of a hearing: see 18.126 above.
8 *Secretary of State for the Home Department v Khalil* [1993] Imm AR 481; *Aryee* (8707), IAT.
9 *Kanahalashmi* (10007), IAT.
10 *Kouchalieva* (10259) (2 September 1993, unreported), IAT, where the adjudicator on a spouse entry clearance appeal decided that the appellant was a British citizen and made no formal determination.
11 Practice Direction 1/2005, para 10.

18.157 Determinations of the Tribunal must not only get the law right and keep within the proper sphere of the appellate jurisdiction, but they must also be properly reasoned. Inadequate reasons may form the basis for a successful appeal or review under the NIAA 2002. The adequacy of reasons has been dealt with in a number of decisions of the higher courts dealing with a variety of jurisdictions, including planning appeals and employment tribunals as well as immigration appellate authorities. A determination must state what the issues are, the Tribunal's decision on them, and the evidence by which it comes to that conclusion.[1] On a reasons challenge the applicant will need to show substantial prejudice, which can arise through ignorance as to the real basis of the decision.[2] In immigration appeals, as in other appeals,[3] the degree of particularity will vary according to the issues. In a deportation appeal the deportee should be able to follow the basis of the conclusion, and the determination should show that the Tribunal has taken account of all the relevant factors and carried out the balancing act required by the rules.[4] In family reunion, asylum and human rights appeals, and in other appeals where much may turn on credibility, the *locus classicus* of the Tribunal's obligation is *Mohammed Amin*:[5] 'An adjudicator should set out with some clarity what evidence was accepted, what rejected, on what evidence no conclusion could be reached and what evidence was irrelevant.' When assessing the adequacy of the Tribunal's reasons, the determination should be read as a whole and in a common-sense way,[6] but avoiding any temptation to rewrite the decision,[7] to see whether sufficient reasons, commensurate with the obligation of 'anxious scrutiny' have been given.[8] The reasons given should be sufficient to show why a claimant lost on a particular issue.[9] Findings must be consistent[10] and adequate.[11] Material facts must be the subject of clear findings.[12] A general statement that the appellant is not credible is insufficient.[13] In asylum and Article 3 appeals the Tribunal must make a clear statement as to the standard of proof to be applied.[14] A mechanical recitation of a certain formula to show matters have been taken into account may also be inadequate.[15]

---

[1] *R v Immigration Appeal Tribunal, ex p Khan (Mahmud)* [1983] QB 790, [1983] 2 All ER 420, CA. But the Tribunal need not give reasons for each conclusion reached in the course of the decision: *R v Criminal Injuries Compensation Board, ex p Cook* [1996] 1 WLR 1037; *Bolton Metropolitan District Council v Secretary of State for the Environment* (1995) 71 P & CR 309; *Arulanandam v Secretary of State for the Home Department* [1996] Imm AR 587, CA.

[2] *Save Britain's Heritage v Secretary of State for the Home Department* [1991] 1 WLR 153, HL, per Lord Bridge.

[3] *Union of Construction Allied Trades and Technicians v Brain* [1981] ICR 542, CA, per Lord Denning MR.

[4] *R v Immigration Appeal Tribunal, ex p Dhaliwal* [1994] Imm AR 387, QBD.

[5] *R v Immigration Appeal Tribunal, ex p Amin* [1992] Imm AR 367, QBD; see also *Singh (Jaswinder) v Secretary of State for the Home Department* 1998 SLT 1370; *Mecheti v Secretary of State for the Home Department* [1996] SCLR 998; *Senthuran v Secretary of State for the Home Department* [2004] EWCA Civ 950, [2004] 4 All ER 365; *AK (Turkey)* [2004] UKIAT 00230.

[6] *R (on the application of Bouchaal) v Immigration Appeal Tribunal* [2002] EWHC 1517 (Admin), [2002] All ER (D) 264 (Jun); *R (on the application of Kolcak) v Secretary of State for the Home Department* [2001] Imm AR 666; *R (on the application of Mohamad) v Special Adjudicator* [2002] EWHC 2496 (Admin).

[7] *R (on the application of Bahrami) v Immigration Appeal Tribunal* [2003] EWHC 1453 (Admin), [2003] All ER (D) 24 (Jun); see also Davis J in *R (on the application of Tesfaye) v Immigration Appeal Tribunal* [2004] EWHC 460 (Admin), [2004] All ER (D) 377 (Feb): 'This Court is entitled to have the reasons from the adjudicator and the tribunal and not from [counsel for the Secretary of State]'.

[8] *R (on the application of Kurecaj) v Special Adjudicator* [2001] EWHC 1199 (Admin), [2001] All ER (D) 278 (Dec); *Mohammadi v Advocate-General for Scotland* 2004 SCLR 612, OH.

[9] *Senthuran v Secretary of State for the Home Department* [2004] EWCA Civ 950; *R (on the application of Bahrami) v Immigration Appeal Tribunal* [2003] EWHC 1453 (Admin), [2003] All ER (D) 24 (Jun); *Krayem v Secretary of State for the Home Department* [2003] EWCA Civ 649, [2003] All ER (D) 80 (Apr) (reasons inadequate to show why a finding of persecution did not follow from evidence as to general conditions for Palestinian refugees in Lebanon). See also *Tezgel v Secretary of State for the Home Department* [2004] EWCA Civ 1766.

[10] *Singh (Avtar)* (12547) (26 September 1995, unreported), IAT; *Tadesse* (15079) (19 May 1997, unreported), IAT.

[11] In *R v Secretary of State for the Home Department, ex p Atputharajah* [2001] Imm AR 566, Elias J posed two tests for adequacy of reasons: (1) do the alleged defects create a genuine (as opposed to forensic) doubt whether a significant issue in dispute was properly addressed; (2) if so, is there any real doubt as to whether the decision would have been the same? See also *Januzi v Secretary of State for the Home Department* [2003] EWCA Civ 1188 (conclusion that return to Kosovo would not lead to deterioration of the claimant's mental health inadequately reasoned given that the only medical evidence showed such a deterioration would occur); *R (on the application of Kurecaj) v Secretary of State for the Home Department* [2001] EWHC 1199 (Admin), [2001] All ER (D) 278 (Dec); *R (on the application of Arzpeyma) v Immigration Appeal Tribunal* [2002] EWHC 2395, [2002] All ER (D) 21 (Nov) (no finding on weight, if any, attached to the evidence of a supporting witness).

12 Although not every single point in dispute need be the subject of a separate finding (*Rai* (00TH00048), all material aspects of a claim should be the subject of clear findings: *Habtegiorgis* (14446) (13 January 1997, unreported); *R (on the application of Orlenko) v Immigration Appeal Tribunal* [2002] EWHC 1960 (Admin), [2002] All ER (D) 270 (Jul) (no clear finding on risk of suffering conditions shown by background evidence to be prevalent and whether conditions breached Art 3); *Yelocagi v Secretary of State for the Home Department* (16 May 2000, unreported), CA; *R (Hussein) v Immigration Appeal Tribunal* [2003] EWHC 769 (Admin) (unclear whether claimant's evidence about being tortured whilst in detention was accepted or not).; *El-Rifai v Secretary of State for the Home Department* [2005] EWCA Civ 385, [2005] All ER (D) 263 (Feb).

13 *Nicu* (11615) (7 December 1994, unreported); *Gharbi* (11791) (23 January 1995, unreported); *Ayinde* (13015) (20 February 1996, unreported); *Muthengi* (13571) (24 June 1996, unreported); *Aboud* (15127) (23 June 1997, unreported), IAT; *Kaffash* [2002] UKIAT 00549 (use of the term 'a very low credibility assessment' not sufficiently clear finding of fact).

14 *Banica* (10789) (5 April 1994, unreported), IAT; *Krnic* (01TH02683) (burden of proof applied unclear).

15 *R v Immigration Appeal Tribunal, ex p Iqbal (Iram)* [1993] Imm AR 270, QBD; *Entry Clearance Officer v Khan (Ajaib)* [1993] Imm AR 68; *Saini v Secretary of State for the Home Department* [1993] Imm AR 96.

18.158 A material misdirection of fact in the determination will ground an appeal if it affects the general conclusion,[1] although a factual error on one issue does not necessarily vitiate the determination.[2] There is nothing objectionable in the Tribunal adopting the Secretary of State's decision letter, but there is a risk that any error in the letter will infect the decision,[3] and Tribunals must reach independent decisions following their own assessment of the evidence,[4] not simply ask themselves whether there was a proper basis for disagreeing with the decision maker.[5] It is incumbent on Tribunals to deal with all the issues before them.[6] The Court of Appeal has indicated that where an appeal is allowed on one ground, it is desirable that the Tribunal should decide all the other issues before it, particularly where findings of fact are involved, since they might become important on a subsequent appeal.[7] A starred Tribunal gave the opposite guidance.[8] It is clearly both wise and in accordance with the overriding objective of appeals for findings to be made on all disputed issues of fact and decisions reached on all issues raised.

1 *Manzeke v Secretary of State for the Home Department* [1997] Imm AR 524, CA; *R (on the application of Judes) v Secretary of State for the Home Department* [2001] EWCA Civ 825, [2001] All ER (D) 168 (May) (permission to appeal refused on erroneous basis that adjudicator had seen medical report); *Haile v Immigration Appeal Tribunal* [2001] EWCA Civ 663, [2002] Imm AR 170, [2002] INLR 283 (finding of credibility dependent on a mistaken view of the story told by the appellant). See also *Abdi (Dhudi Saleban) v Secretary of State for the Home Department* [1996] Imm AR 148.

2 *R v Secretary of State for the Home Department, ex p Yasun* [1998] Imm AR 215, QBD; *Wahome* (12755) (21 November 1995, unreported). Where the decision depended on the accuracy and reliability of the conclusions on credibility of the fact-finding tribunal, and that tribunal had made strange errors of fact such as describing a Pakistani asylum seeker as 'Egyptian' as well as giving inadequate reasons for disbelieving the appellant, the decision was unsafe: *R (on the application of Ahmed) v Secretary of State for the Home Department* [2004] EWCA Civ 552, [2004] All ER (D) 154 (Jan).

3 *R v Immigration Appeal Tribunal, ex p Peranantham* (20 June 1996), QBD; remitted *de novo* by IAT at (13752) (29 July 1996, unreported).

4 *Xie* (14644) (14 March 1997, unreported) (adoption of Secretary of State letter rendered decision flawed); *Al-Musshadi* (11254) (15 August 1994, unreported); *Randhawa* (11514) (3 November 1994, unreported); *Atwal* (12229) (27 June 1995, unreported) (adoption of

previous determination of same appeal rendered decision flawed); *Oyeleye v Entry Clearance Officer, Lagos* (01TH02325) IAT; *Iqbal v Entry Clearance Officer, Islamabad* [2002] UKIAT 01860

5   *A (Nigeria) v Entry Clearance Officer* [2004] UKIAT 00019
6   *Stefanescu* (11491); *Sakota* (13576) (24 June 1996, unreported), IAT.
7   *McPherson v Secretary of State for the Home Department* [2001] EWCA Civ 1955; [2002] INLR 139. The Tribunal held in the context of 'mixed' appeals (the precursor of 'one-stop' appeals, that it was an error of law to omit consideration of one limb of the appeal: *Angus* (17706) (8 July 1998, unreported); *Dragica* (13288) (29 April 1996, unreported), IAT.
8   *Hassan (Ahmed Faraj)* [2002] UKIAT 00062.

18.159 We have set out at **18.156** above the time limits within which the Tribunal should promulgate its determination. Case law under the previous procedure rules, which imposed no such time limits, held that delay in the promulgation of the determination did not by itself render a determination unsafe; it is necessary to show prejudice attributable to the delay.[1] The Tribunal has said that normally, a period of over three months between the date of hearing and promulgation is unacceptable where credibility is in issue,[2] although this is only a guide and it is not applicable where there is no prejudice, for example where the delay is administrative or where credibility findings were contemporaneously recorded, or where the decision was justified on grounds which did not depend on recollection and assessment of oral evidence[3] or where, because the nature of the evidence or other material before the Tribunal made its falsehood or absurdity plain.[4] Where there has been delay in promulgating a determination, the inference that something has been overlooked or forgotten by the Tribunal will be more readily drawn, particularly if there is no specific mention of it in the determination.[5] It is unlikely that the new time limits will have much effect on this case law regarding the effect of a late determination, in the absence of prejudice. There was a practice, which was given the blessing of the Tribunal, of repromulgating a determination when it appeared to have gone astray or where it was otherwise in the interests of justice to do so,[6] but the practice may have been unlawful.[7] But a determination not properly served and never received has not been promulgated, and on proof of non-receipt should be sent again.[8]

1   *R (on the application of Ghorbani) v Immigration Appeal Tribunal* [2004] EWHC 510 (Admin), [2004] All ER (D) 83 (Mar); *Cobham v Frett* [2001] 1 WLR 1775 (PC).
2   Memorandum to Tribunal chairs, referred to in *Waiganjo* (R15717) (17 October 1997, unreported), IAT. See *Mario v Secretary of State for the Home Department* [1998] Imm AR 281; *Omonijo* [2002] UKIAT 02643.
3   *Chaouche* (17423), IAT; *Behre v Secretary of State for the Home Department* [2000] Imm AR 463, CA (11-month delay before promulgation did not cause prejudice as case turned on issues of law, although it brought the appellate authority into disrepute); see also *B (Albania)* [2003] UKIAT 00028.
4   *Sambasivan v Secretary of State for the Home Department* [2000] Imm AR 85, [2000] INLR 105, CA. So a delay of nine months did not give rise to concern since it did not depend on oral evidence, there had been no material change, and nothing else had been put forward suggesting prejudice to the appellant: *R v Immigration Appeal Tribunal, ex p Shandar* [2000] Imm AR 181, QB; *Berhe* above. But in *Ehalaivan* (4275/99) 14 June 2000, CA, a delay of two months before dictating a determination should have been addressed by the Tribunal in considering leave to appeal.
5   *R (on the application of Ghorbani) v Immigration Appeal Tribunal* [2004] EWHC 510 (Admin), [2004] All ER (D) 83 (Mar).
6   *Raza (Hushard)* (16238); *Ahmed* (00TH00485); *Korsak and Pawlowska* (15855), IAT. The purpose of the practice was to mitigate the harshness of the non-extendable time-limit for applying to the Tribunal for leave to appeal, which was resolved by allowing the Tribunal to extend time for good reason: see SI 2000/2333, r 18(3).

7   *Akewushola v Secretary of State for the Home Department* [1999] Imm AR 594, CA. The
    assumption that the practice was unlawful formed the basis of a consent order in *R v
    Immigration Appeal Tribunal, ex p Nicoue* (CO 654/2000) (15 May 2000, unreported).
8   See *Korsak and Pawlowska* (15855) IAT; *R v Secretary of State for the Home Department,
    ex p Saleem (Asifa)* [2000] Imm AR 529, [2000] INLR 413.

APPEALS TO THE SPECIAL IMMIGRATION APPEALS COMMISSION

18.160 There is no appeal to the Tribunal if the grounds for an immigration
decision (refusal of entry or of leave to remain, a decision to curtail leave, to
remove or to deport), or refusal of asylum, are national security or political
grounds. The list of matters excluded from the normal appeals system is set
out at 18.20 above. In such cases, before 1998 the only recourse for those thus
fingered for exclusion was an extra-statutory advisory procedure known as
the 'three wise men', whose outstanding feature was the disregard for
elementary rules of natural justice. There were no particulars about the case to
be met, not even the names of witnesses, there was no right to representation,
no right even to know the advice tendered to the Secretary of State at the end
of the procedure.[1] In *Chahal v United Kingdom*[2] the European Court of
Human Rights concluded that the advisory panel was not a 'court' within the
meaning of ECHR, Article 5(4) (which guarantees the right to have the
lawfulness of detention decided speedily by a court). The Court deprecated the
use of the shibboleth of 'national security' by the executive to attempt to free
itself from effective control by the domestic courts and commended the
arrangements in Canada which 'both accommodate legitimate security concerns ... and yet accord the individual a substantial measure of protection'.[3]

1   The procedure is set out in detail in the fourth edition of this book, at 15.55–15.56.
2   (1996) 23 EHRR 413.
3   (1996) 23 EHRR 413, para 130.

18.161 The Special Immigration Appeals Commission Act 1997 was the
government's response. It provides a right of appeal against any immigration
decision under section 82, or against a refusal of asylum under section 83 of
the Nationality, Immigration and Asylum Act 2002, which would have been
available had the Secretary of State not certified the appeal under section 97.[1]
There is also an appeal to the Commission against a decision to deprive a
British citizen of his or her citizenship under section 40 of the British
Nationality Act 1981, if the Secretary of State certifies that the decision was
taken wholly or partly on information which should not become public on
national security or political grounds, so preventing an appeal to the Asylum
and Immigration Tribunal.[2] Many of the statutory provisions which apply in
respect of appeals before the Asylum and Immigration Tribunal also apply in
respect of appeals to the Special Immigration Appeals Commission, including
the statutory extension of leave pending a variation decision and pending an
appeal,[3] the prohibition of removal while an appeal is pending,[4] the suspensive effect of an appeal in relation to deportation, and variation or revocation
of leave,[5] the statutory grounds on which an appeal may be brought[6] and on
which the appeal may be allowed,[7] the matters and evidence which must and
may be considered on the appeal,[8] the power to give directions to give effect to
the decision,[9] exclusion of a second appeal in respect of matters which should

have been raised in an earlier appeal,[10] the definition of a 'pending appeal',[11] the obligation to give notice of the decision[12] and the grant-making power of the Secretary of State to bodies providing assistance.[13] Appellants to the Special Immigration Appeals Commission are now entitled to a grant of controlled legal representation.

[1] Special Immigration Appeals Commission Act 1997, s 2(1)(a). The certificate under s 97 of the NIAA 2002 may be issued on the ground that the person's removal from the UK is in the interests of national security or diplomatic relations, or on the ground that the immigration or asylum decision has been taken wholly or partly on information which should not be made public on national security, diplomatic or other public interest grounds. See 18.20 above. A certificate under s 97 may cause an extant appeal under s 82 or 83 to lapse: Nationality, Immigration and Asylum Act 2002, s 99, and in that case too, SIACA 1997 s 2 provides for an appeal to the Commission.

[2] Under British Nationality Act 1981 s 40A(2): Special Immigration Appeals Commission Act 1997, s 2B.

[3] Under s 3C Immigration Act 1971, see 18.32 above: Special Immigration Appeals Commission Act 1997, s 2(2)(a).

[4] Under Nationality, Immigration and Asylum Act 2002, s 78, see 18.24 above: Special Immigration Appeals Commission Act 1997, s 2(2)(b).

[5] Under NIAA 2002, ss 79, 82(3), see 18.24 and 18.35 above: Special Immigration Appeals Commission Act 1997, s 2(2)(c), (d).

[6] Under NIAA 2002, s 84, see 18.47 above: Special Immigration Appeals Commission Act 1997, s 2(2)(e).

[7] Under NIAA 2002, s 86, see 18.46 above: Special Immigration Appeals Commission Act 1997, s 2(2)(g).

[8] Under NIAA 2002, s 85, see 18.48 above: Special Immigration Appeals Commission Act 1997, s 2(2)(f).

[9] Under NIAA 2002, s 87, see 18.69 above: Special Immigration Appeals Commission Act 1997, s 2(2)(h).

[10] Under NIAA 2002, s 96, see 18.42 above: Special Immigration Appeals Commission Act 1997, s 2(2)(i).

[11] Under NIAA 2002, s 104 (as amended by Asylum and Immigration (Treatment of Claimants, etc) Act 2004 Sch 2 para 19), Special Immigration Appeals Commission Act 1997, s 2(2)(j).

[12] Under NIAA 2002, s 105, see 18.83 above.

[13] Under NIAA 2002, s 110.

18.162 The Special Immigration Appeals Commission also heard appeals[1] and reviews[2] under the Anti-terrorism, Crime and Security Act 2001 against the certification of a foreign national as a suspected international terrorist,[3] and against indefinite detention of such persons by derogation from Article 5 ECHR.[4] In *A* the House of Lords held that the provisions of the 2001 Act which allowed the indefinite detention of foreign nationals were disproportionate, discriminatory and unlawful.[5] The provisions expired in March 2005.

[1] Anti-terrorism, Crime and Security Act 2001, s 25.

[2] ACSA 2001, s 26.

[3] Ie under s 21 of that Act. The Commission must cancel the certificate if it believes that the Secretary of State did not have reasonable grounds for the belief or suspicion relied on in issuing the certificate, or for some other reason the certificate should not have been issued.

[4] ACSA 2001, s 30. A derogation order was made in the exercise of the Secretary of State's power under s 14 of the Human Rights Act 1998 on 11 November 2001. The order was upheld by the House of Lords in *A v Secretary of State for the Home Department* [2004] UKHL 56, [2005] 2 WLR 87.

[5] *A* fn 4 above.

Jurisdiction, procedure and evidence before the Special Immigration Appeals Commission

18.163 As noted above, the Commission's jurisdiction on an appeal against an immigration decision or a decision to refuse asylum is the same as that of the Asylum and Immigration Tribunal, in that it must allow the appeal if the decision was not in accordance with the law, including the immigration rules, or a discretion conferred by the rules should have been exercised differently, but otherwise it must dismiss the appeal.[1] The Court of Appeal in *Rehman*[2] agreed with the Commission that its role was a full merits review including reviewing the facts. However on appeal or review of certification that a person is a suspected international terrorist, its jurisdiction is limited to ascertaining whether reasonable grounds exist for the belief or suspicion.[3] The Commission may hear evidence which is not admissible in a court of law,[4] and the Commission and the Court of Appeal have unpardonably held that in an appeal under the 2001 Act, this may include evidence obtained through torture.[5] The balancing exercise which has to be performed, and to which the Lord Chancellor is obliged to have regard in making procedural rules, is between the need for a proper review of an executive decision and the need to secure that information is not disclosed contrary to the public interest.[6] This is reflected in the Special Immigration Appeals Commission (Procedure) Rules 2003, which set out the Commission's general duties in similar terms (but in reverse order).[7] To that end the special advocate system has been devised. In order to protect national security, there is evidence which even the appellant and his or her representative may not hear.[8] When the Secretary of State is served with a notice of appeal or application under the 1997 or the 2001 Act, then, unless it is intended to concede the appeal or not to object to the disclosure of any material on which the decision is based, the relevant law officer[9] must be notified,[10] with a view to appointing a special advocate, a security-vetted lawyer who represents the appellant's interests on the appeal but is not instructed by or responsible to the appellant,[11] and cannot have any direct contract with him or her after seeing the 'closed' material, without the leave of the court.[12] The procedure in a nutshell is thus: a national security decision is made or a certificate issued; the appellant appeals;[13] if the Secretary of State intends to rely on 'closed material' on the appeal he or she informs the appropriate law officer, who appoints a special advocate;[14] the appellant and his or her representative are served with the 'open' material and the special advocate with the material which the Secretary of State does not wish to disclose to the appellant (the 'closed material').[15] The Commission must test the Secretary of State's assertion that material should not be disclosed.[16] On the hearing of the appeal the appellant and his or her representative are excluded while that evidence is given[17] and the special advocate stays in the hearing to represent the appellant's interests by cross-examination, submissions and representations.[18] But none of that cross-examination or submissions is on instructions, since as soon as the special advocate receives the 'closed material' his or her contact with the appellant is at an end.[19] The procedure rules contain provision for representation, the giving of directions, the filing and service of documents, notification of hearings, adjournments, summoning of witnesses and combined hearings, in similar terms to those rules governing appeals to the Asylum and Immigration Tribunal.[20] On an asylum appeal UNHCR is entitled to be treated as a party, but on the same terms as the appellant as regards access to closed material.[21]

1 Nationality, Immigration and Asylum Act 2002, s 86(3), Special Immigration Appeals Commission Act 1997, s 2(2)(g).

2 *Secretary of State for the Home Department v Rehman (Shafiq Ur)* [2000] INLR 531, CA, upheld by the House of Lords at [2003] 1 AC 153. For the Commission decision see [1999] INLR 517.

3 Anti-terrorism, Crime and Security Act 2001 s 25(2)(a) (appeal), s 26(5)(a) (review); *M v Secretary of State for the Home Department* [2004] EWCA Civ 324, [2004] 2 All ER 863.

4 Special Immigration Appeals Procedure Rules 2003, SI 2003/1034, r 44(3). Section 5(7) provided that the exclusionary rule of evidence in the Interception of Communications Act 1985, s 9 did not apply in proceedings before the Commission, but this section was repealed by the Regulation of Investigatory Powers Act 2000, s 82.

5 *A, B, C, D v Secretary of State for the Home Department* (SC/1, 6, 7, 9, 10/2002) (2 October 2003) upheld in CA as *A and 9 others v Secretary of State for the Home Department* [2004] EWCA Civ 1123. The Court of Appeal held that evidence obtained by torture was admissible before the Special Immigration Appeals Commission, provided the torture was not that of the Secretary of State or his officers. We suggest that the ruling is unlawful by reference to the UN and European Conventions Against Torture, morally abhorrent and capable of inflicting immense damage on the reputation of the UK's judicial process. A ruling by the House of Lords is awaited.

6 Special Immigration Appeals Commission Act 1997, s 5(6).

7 SI 2003/1034, r 3.

8 Special Immigration Appeals Commission Act 1997, s 5(3)(a).

9 The Attorney-General in England and Wales, the Lord Advocate in Scotland and the Attorney General for Northern Ireland in Northern Ireland: Special Immigration Appeals Commission Act 1997, s 6(2).

10 SI 2003/1034, r 34.

11 Special Immigration Appeals Commission Act 1997, s 6, applied to certification appeals by the Anti-terrorism, Crime and Security Act 2001 s 27. See the comments of Lord Williams during the passage of the Act, 580 HL Official Report (5th series) col 1437.

12 SI 2003/1034, r 36.

13 SI 2003/1034, rr 7–9 (national security appeals), 14–15 (certification appeals). The time limit for appealing under the 1997 Act is five days if the appellant is in detention, otherwise ten days in-country, 28 if overseas: r 8. The time limit for appealing under the 2001 Act is three months, which may be extended with leave, if before the first six-monthly review of certification under s 26 of the Act: r 15. The notice of appeal is not in a prescribed form but must contain the appellant's name, address, representative and grounds, and must be signed by the appellant or representative, and dated: rr 9(2), (3), 14(6), (7). In addition, a notice of appeal under the 1997 Act must contain reasons in support of the grounds, and if signed by the representative, must certify that the notice has been completed in accordance with the appellant's instructions, and must attach a copy of the decision appealed: r 9(1), (4).

14 SI 2003/1034, r 34.

15 SI 2003/1034, rr 10(2), 16(2), 37.

16 SI 2003/1034, r 38. The Commission must fix a hearing to decide on whether the closed material should be disclosed (which is, of course, held in the absence of the appellant and his or her representative: r 38(5)) unless the special advocate and the Secretary of State consent to the issue being decided without a hearing, or the special advocate does not challenge the Secretary of State's objection to disclosing the material, or the Commission has previously upheld the Secretary of State's objection in respect of the same or substantially the same material: r 38(2). If the Commission rules against the Secretary of State, the material may not be relied on if it is not disclosed to the appellant: r 38(7).

17 SI 2003/1034, r 43.

18 SI 2003/1034, r 35.

19 SI 2003/1034, r 36. There is power to seek directions from the Commission authorising the special advocate to obtain information from the appellant after receipt of the 'closed material' but the Secretary of State must be notified of the application and may object: r 36(5)(b). The Commission deals with that issue in the same way as it deals with the Secretary of State's objection to disclosure of evidence to the appellant: r 38. The appellant may communicate with the special advocate, but only through a legal representative in

writing, and the special advocate may not reply, apart from sending a written acknowledgement, without a direction from the Commission: r 36(6).
20 See SI 2003/1034, rr 32–3 (parties and representation), 39–40 (directions; on noncompliance the Commission may issue an 'unless' order requiring compliance with a stated period, in default of which the appeal proceeds without the relevant evidence), 41 (notification of hearing), 42 (adjournments), 44–5 (evidence and summoning of witnesses), 46 (combined hearings), 49–50 (filing and service of documents), 51 (calculation of time), 52 (signature of documents), 53 (procedural errors), 54 (correction of slips).
21 SI 2003/1034 r 32(2), (3).

18.164 The Commission must record its decision and the reasons for it. It must serve its determination on the parties,[1] but its duty to give reasons is circumscribed once more by public interest considerations. The determination must contain reasons 'to the extent that it is possible to do so without disclosing information contrary to the public interest', and where the determination does not include the full reasons for the decision, the Commission must serve a separate determination, including those full reasons, on the Secretary of State and the special advocate.[2] The rules provide that the Secretary of State must be served with notice of the proposed determination before the appellant, to enable him to apply to the Commission to review the determination if he considers that it contains information which it would be contrary to the public interest to disclose.[3]

1 Special Immigration Appeals Commission (Procedure) Rules 2003, SI 2003/1034, r 47(1).
2 SI 2003/1034, r 47(2), (3). This raises questions as to the duty of a special advocate to put forward grounds of appeal based on closed material (see 18.166 below). In one case, in which the senior editor was special advocate, his junior is seeking to put forward grounds of appeal based entirely on closed material, which will presumably have to be heard behind closed doors andwhere the judgment, which may have a generall bearing on the law, will have to remain a secret for ever and a day unless the Commission decides otherwise – not a very satisfactory situation, in our view. The Court of Appeal in *Secretary of State for the Home Department v Shafiq ur Rehman* [2000] INLR 531 had expressed itself against two separate determinations.
3 SI 2003/1034, r 48. The Secretary of State has five days to apply to the Commission. The same procedure applies to service of any order or direction made or given in the Secretary of State's absence in the course of the proceedings.

ONWARD APPEALS AND REVIEW

18.165 From 4 April 2005, the two-tier appellate structure, involving an appeal to the adjudicator and then (with leave) to the Immigration Appeal Tribunal, in place since 1969 is no more. There is thus no further appeal within the appellate authority itself. So how is an Asylum and Immigration Tribunal decision to be challenged? The first answer, in the original version of the Bill[1] which became the Asylum and Immigration (Treatment of Claimants, etc) Act 2004, was: not at all. Only the Tribunal itself was to have the power to review its own decision or to refer a point to the Court of Appeal for an advisory opinion. There was to be no opportunity for the parties to appeal further or to challenge the Tribunal's decision by way of judicial review, for error of law, irrationality, procedural impropriety or unfairness short of bias. Lawyers, advisers and judges united in outrage, and after a high profile campaign the ouster was dropped in favour of a new appeals structure which retains some of the features of its predecessors.[2] The new provisions give two avenues of challenge to Asylum and Immigration Tribunal decisions: an application to the High Court (or the Outer House of the Court of Session, in Scotland), and for an unknown transitional period, to the Tribunal itself, for an order that the Tribunal reconsider its decision,[3] and an appeal to the Court of Appeal (or Court of Session).[4] The avenue which is used depends on the composition of the Tribunal and the stage of the proceedings (ie whether the decision has already been the subject of reconsideration). The reconsideration order procedure resembles its predecessor, statutory review, introduced by the NIAA 2002 to replace judicial review of the Immigration Appeal Tribunal's refusal of permission to appeal.[5] In each case, the jurisdiction rests on error of law.

[1] Asylum and Immigration (Treatment of Claimants, etc) Bill 2003, cl 11.
[2] See eg Constitutional Affairs Committee, 2nd report, session 2003–4, Asylum and Immigration Appeals, HC 211–1; Joint Committee on Human Rights 5th report of 2003–4, HL 35/HC 304.
[3] Nationality, Immigration and Asylum Act 2002, s 103A, inserted by s 26 Asylum and Immigration (Treatment of Claimants, etc) Act 2004, and modified by Sch 2, para 30.
[4] NIAA 2002, s 103B, 103E (as inserted).
[5] NIAA 2002, s 101(2), repealed by the Asylum and Immigration (Treatment of Claimants, etc) Act 2004, s 26(5) from 4 April 2005.

Error of law

18.166 An order for reconsideration may not be made unless the immigration judge or the reviewing court thinks that the Tribunal may have made an error of law. An appeal from the Tribunal can only be made on a point of law. What do these phrases encompass? According to the government, the 'error of law' formulation is 'sufficient to cover all the grounds that might otherwise form the basis of an application for judicial review of the Tribunal's decision on the appeal'.[1] Clearly the term includes legal misdirection, and in *Ivanauskiene* this was held to include the situation where all parties below acted on a mistaken view of the law.[2] What may constitute an error of law was reviewed by the Court of Appeal in *E v Secretary of State for the Home Department*, where the court held that it was generally a safe working rule that the substantive grounds for intervention were the same in the Court of Appeal on appeal and the High Court on review.[3] The court accepted that the term could include both material breach of the rules of natural justice,[4] and error of fact based on misunderstanding or ignorance of established and relevant facts.[5] The court acknowledged that 'the time has come to accept that mistake of fact leading to unfairness is a separate head of challenge in an appeal on a point of law, at least in statutory contexts where the parties share an interest in cooperating to achieve the correct result'.[6] Asylum law, they added, was undoubtedly such an area. *E v Secretary of State for the Home Department* dealt with the situation in which the mistake arose because relevant material was not before the fact-finding Tribunal. Where the fact-finding Tribunal was in possession of all material facts, a failure to have regard to relevant evidence is an error of law,[7] and a failure to make findings on relevant facts may vitiate the decision.[8] Facts are material if in the circumstances of a particular case the decision turns on their existence.[9] Although it cannot be said to be an error of law to adopt one of a number of differing points of view of the facts, each of which may be reasonably held,[10] error may occur in the weighing of evidence, in particular, in relation to plausibility findings in asylum cases.[11]

1 Government response to the 2nd Report of the Constitutional Affairs Committee 2003/4, on Asylum and Immigration Appeals, 9.6.04, Cm 6236, p 2. In the 'GCHQ' case, *Council of Civil Service Unions v Minister for the Civil Service* [1985] AC 374, these grounds were described as illegality, irrationality, and procedural impropriety. The grounds for intervention for error of law are the same whether the proceedings are by way of statutory appeal or judicial review: *Preston v Inland Revenue Commissioners* [1985] AC 835 at 862, and see the discussion in *E v Secretary of State for the Home Department, R v Secretary of State for the Home Department* [2004] EWCA Civ 49, [2004] INLR 264, at [40]–[43]. mistake of fact leading to unfairness is a separate head of challenge in an appeal on a point of law.

2 The appellant conceded that she could not in law qualify as a member of a particular social group following the Court of Appeal judgment in *R v Secretary of State for the Home Department, ex p Shah; Islam v Immigration Appeal Tribunal* [1998] 4 All ER 30, [1998] 1 WLR 74, reversed by the House of Lords on appeal: *R (on the application of Ivanauskiene) v Special Adjudicator* [2001] EWCA Civ 1271, [2002] INLR 1.

3 *E v Secretary of State for the Home Department, R v Secretary of State for the Home Department* [2004] EWCA Civ 49, [2004] INLR 264 per Carnwath LJ at [42], referring to *Railtrack plc (in Railway Administration) v Guinness Ltd* [2003] EWCA Civ 188, [2003] RVR 280; De Smith, Woolf and Jowell *Judicial Review* (5th edn), para 15–076).

4 *E v Secretary of State for the Home Department* at [38]; *Council of Civil Service Unions* at fn 1 above; *Gardi v Secretary of State for the Home Department* [2002] EWCA Civ 750, [2003] Imm AR 39 (annulled for want of jurisdiction at [2002] EWCA Civ 1560, [2002] INLR 557; *MNM* [2000] INLR 576, IAT; *R (on the application of Tataw) v Secretary of State for the Home Department* [2003] EWCA Civ 925, [2003] INLR 585.

5 *E v Secretary of State for the Home Department* at [38]; *R (on the application of Alconbury Developments Ltd) v Secretary of State for the Environment, Transport and the Regions* [2001] UKHL 23, [2003] 2 AC 295 [53] per Lord Slynn; *Secretary of State for Education and Science v Tameside Metropolitan Borough Council* [1977] AC 1014 at 1030; *Edwards (Inspector of Taxes) v Bairstow* [1956] AC 14.

6 *E v Secretary of State for the Home Department* at [66], following and explaining *R v Criminal Injuries Compensation Board, ex p A* [1999] 2 AC 330, [1999] 2 WLR 974.

7 *S v Secretary of State for the Home Department* [2002] EWCA Civ 539, [2002] INLR 416; *R v Secretary of State for the Home Department, ex p Parmak* (CO 702/90), (21 January 1992, unreported).

8 See eg *Minister for Immigration and Multicultural Affairs v Yusuf* [2001] HCA 30, 75 ALJR 1105; *Dhillon v Canada (Minister of Citizenship and Immigration)* [2001] FCT 1194, and cases cited at fn 6 above.

9 *R v Independent Television Commission, ex p Virgin Television Ltd* [1966] EMLR 318, cited in Demetriou and Houseman 'Review for error of fact: a brief guide' [1997] JR 27; *Minister for Immigration and Multicultural Affairs v Singh* (2000) 98 FCR 469.

10 See eg *Ndlova v Secretary of State for the Home Department* [2004] EWCA Civ; *C v Secretary of State for the Home Department* [2004] EWCA Civ 1165, [2004] 34 LS Gaz R 30; *Aung (Win) v Secretary of State for the Home Department* [2004] EWCA Civ 425: in each case, the Court of Appeal held that the Tribunal's disagreement with the first-instance decision of the adjudicator should not have resulted in its allowing the Secretary of State's appeal.

11 *Choudhury v Immigration Appeal Tribunal* [2001] EWHC 613. The Canadian courts have held that plausibility findings should be made only in the clearest of cases, where the facts presented are outside the realm of what could reasonably be expected or documentary evidence demonstrates that the events could not have happened in the manner described by the claimant: *Shenoda v Canada (Minister for Citizenship and Immigration* [2003] FCT 207; *Divsalar v Canada* [2000] FCJ 875; but see *MM (plausibility) (DRC)* [2005] UKIAT 00019.

Application for reconsideration

18.167 A party to an appeal under section 82[1] or 83[2] of the NIAA 2002 may apply to the appropriate court[3] for an order requiring the Tribunal to reconsider its decision, on the ground that the Tribunal has made an error of law.[4] No application for reconsideration can be made where the decision is by a Tribunal of three or more legally qualified members; in such a case, there will be the possibility of an appeal to the Court of Appeal instead.[5] Only one application for reconsideration may be made; once the Tribunal has reconsidered its decision, only an appeal to the Court of Appeal is possible[6] The application is on the papers only; the applicant has no right to an oral hearing,[7] and the statute indicates that the court's decision is final.[8] This wording does not oust the High Court's inherent jurisdiction in judicial review, but in *G and M*[9] the Court of Appeal held that the previous statutory review procedure provided 'adequate and proportionate' protection of the rights of asylum claimants, so that the court may decline to hear an application for judicial review of issues which had been or could have been the subject of statutory review. Only a substantive decision of the Tribunal can be the subject of an application for consideration; the 'Tribunal's decision on appeal' does not include a procedural, ancillary or preliminary decision,[10] or a decision following remittal.[11] The courts have historically had some difficulty in deciding the limits of a procedural or preliminary decision – is a decision that an appellant has abandoned his or her appeal preliminary or substantive?[12] Or a decision declining jurisdiction?[13] Both these decisions effectively dispose of an appeal, and in *R (Secretary of State for the Home Department) v Immigration Appeal Tribunal*[14] Collins J held that a refusal to extend time was an appealable determination under the now repealed provisions of the NIAA 2002;[15] however, the wording of the new section, with its explicit exclusion of procedural, ancillary and preliminary decisions, indicates that these types of decision would not now be the subject of an application for reconsideration, and so would be challengeable by judicial review.[16]

[1]   Ie an appeal against an immigration decision as there defined.

[2]   Ie an appeal against the refusal of asylum to a person who has been granted leave to enter or remain for more than one year.

[3]   Defined as the High Court in respect of an appeal decided in England and Wales, the Outer House of the Court of Session in respect of an appeal decided in Scotland, and the High Court in Northern Ireland, in respect of an appeal decided in Northern Ireland: Nationality, Immigration and Asylum Act 2002, s 103A(9), (10), inserted by Asylum and Immigration (Treatment of Claimants, etc) Act 2004, s 26. This puts into statutory form the Court of Appeal decision in *R (on the application of Majead) v Immigration Appeal Tribunal* [2003] EWCA Civ 615, [2003] 23 LS Gaz R 38, which held that a challenge to a decision of the Immigration Appeal Tribunal about an adjudicator's decision in Scotland should go to the Court of Session, not the Administrative Court, except in a 'real emergency'. It remains to be seen whether this exception survives the statutory codification.

[4]   Nationality, Immigration and Asylum Act 2002, s 103A(1), as inserted.

[5]   NIAA 2002, s 103A(8) as inserted. For appeals to the Court of Appeal see 18.178 below.

[6]   NIAA 2002, s 103A(2)(b) as inserted. For appeals to the Court of Appeal see 18.178 below.

[7]   NIAA 2002, s 103A(5) as inserted. The requirements of fairness embodied in Article 6 ECHR do not necessarily demand an oral hearing: see 8.72 above.

[8]   NIAA 2002, s 103A(6) as inserted.

[9]   *R (on the application of G) v Immigration Appeal Tribunal, R (on the application of M) v Immigration Appeal Tribunal* [2004] EWCA Civ 1731, [2005] 2 All ER 165, upholding Collins J at [2004] EWHC 588 (Admin). However, judicial review might be appropriate where, for example, a procedural irregularity constituted a denial of the claimant's right to a fair hearing below: see also *R (on the application of Sivasubramaniam) v Wandsworth County Court (Lord Chancellor's Department intervening)* [2002] EWCA Civ 1738, [2003] 2 All ER 160. So for example, where fast-track procedures were inappropriately

used for an asylum claimant, severely prejudicing him in his appeal (as Sedley LJ accepted might be the case in *R (on the application of the Refugee Legal Centre) v Secretary of State for the Home Department* [2004] EWCA Civ 1481, [2004] All ER (D) 201 (Nov)), judicial review of the decision to allocate to the fast-track might be brought where an application for reconsideration would not necessarily be appropriate, or even in parallel with such an application.

10   NIAA 2002, s 103A(7)(a) as inserted. Clearly, a Tribunal's ruling allowing amendment of a notice of decision or of grounds of appeal is a procedural decision: *Egbale v Secretary of State for the Home Department* [1997] INLR 88, but the ruling may have rendered the appeal hearing procedurally unfair, which could ground an appeal against the substantive decision on the appeal for error of law. Judicial review was traditionally available for interlocutory decisions: *R v Immigration Appeal Tribunal, ex p Lila* [1978] Imm AR 50, QBD. But see text and fn 9 above. The giving of directions to give effect to the decision is part of the decision on appeal: s 87(4) as substituted and could therefore be the subject of an application for reconsideration.

11   Ie remittal following appeal to the Court of Appeal or Court of Session: see 18.181 below: NIAA 2002, s 103A(7)(b) as inserted.

12   The Immigration Appeal Tribunal held in the starred case of *Gremesty* [2001] INLR 132 that such a decision was a determination of the appeal for the purposes of the IAA 1999 and the 2000 Procedure rules; see also (under earlier provisions) *Akhuemonkhan v Secretary of State for the Home Department* [1998] INLR 265, IAT.

13   The question of jurisdiction is clearly a preliminary issue, see eg *Secretary of State for the Home Department v Khan* [1999] INLR 309 (decided under IA 1971, s 20).

14   [2004] EWHC (Admin), 15 December 2004.

15   NIAA 2002, s 101, providing that a party to an appeal could appeal to the Immigration Appeal Tribunal against an adjudicator's determination on a point of law. Collins J rejected the Secretary of State's argument that until an extension of time to appeal was granted, the applicant was not a 'party to an appeal', distinguishing *R (on the application of Erdogan) v Secretary of State for the Home Department* [2004] EWCA Civ 1087, [2004] All ER (D) 421 (Jul), which held that where an application for permission to appeal had been made out of time, no second instance appeal was pending until an extension of time had been granted. Note that the Asylum and Immigration Tribunal (Procedure) Rules 2005, SI 2005/230, now explicitly distinguish between an 'appellant' and a 'person who has lodged notice of appeal (rr 2, 9–11). Thus, someone refused an extension of time is not an appellant and the decision is not a decision on the appeal for the purpose of review or appeal.

16   See 18.183 below for judicial review.

Application for reconsideration: procedure

18.168 The Act provides that an application for reconsideration is made by applying in writing to the appropriate court[1] within five days beginning with the date when the applicant is treated as receiving notice of the Tribunal's decision,[2] if the applicant is the appellant and is in the UK, or if the application is made by a party other than the appellant (ie by the Secretary of State).[3] If the applicant is made by an appellant who is outside the UK, the time limit is 28 days.[4] These time limits may be varied by order, and are dramatically reduced for reconsideration in the fast track.[5] The reviewing court has a discretion to permit the application to be made outside the specified period, but only where it thinks the application could not reasonably practicably have been made within the period.[6] This is a much stricter formulation than that for extending time to appeal to the Tribunal, who must be 'satisfied that by reason of special circumstances it would be unjust not to do so'.[7] In the different context of denial of asylum support for failing to make an asylum claim as soon as reasonably practicable, the Court of Appeal in *Q*[8] held that the question implied by the phrase was 'having regard both to practical opportunity and the personal circumstances of the applicant, could the applicant reasonably have been expected to make the application earlier than he or she did?' The merits of the appeal will need to be addressed on any application for permission to apply out of time.[9] An appeal remains pending under section 104 of the NIAA 2002 while an application under section 103A(1) can be made or is awaiting determination, other than an application out of time with permission, and if an order for reconsideration is made.[10] The effect of this is that a person who applies for reconsideration out of time is vulnerable to removal and (if applicable) to withdrawal of asylum support, even if permission is given to proceed with the application (meaning that the judge or immigration judge has accepted that it was not reasonably practicable to make the application within the time limit), and remains vulnerable until an order for reconsideration is made. It would therefore be advisable to apply for a stay on removal while applying for permission to proceed out of time.

1 See 18.167 above.
2 Ie under Asylum and Immigration Tribunal (Procedure) Rules 2005, SI 2005/230, rr 55–57; see 18.83 above for presumptions as to service. Service of asylum determinations on in-country appellants by the Secretary of State was introduced at the end of 2001 by amendment to the then procedure rules: see SI 2001/4014, and is continued by r 23 of the current rules.
3 Nationality, Immigration and Asylum Act 2002, s 103A(3)(a), (c), inserted by s 26 Asylum and Immigration (Treatment of Claimants, etc) Act 2004. Rules of court may specify days to be disregarded for this purpose: s 103A(4)(a) as inserted.
4 NIAA 2002, s 103A(3)(b) as inserted. Rules of court may specify days to be disregarded for this purpose: s 103A(4)(a) as inserted.
5 Asylum and Immigration (Treatment of Claimants, etc) Act 2004, s 26(8). The time limit for lodging an application for reconsideration in a fast track appeal is two days: see Asylum and Immigration (Fast Track Time Limits) Order 2005, SI 2005/561.
6 NIAA 2002, s 103A(4)(b) as inserted.
7 Asylum and Immigration Tribunal (Procedure) Rules 2005, SI 2005/230, r 10(5).
8 *R (on the application of Q) v Secretary of State for the Home Department* [2003] EWCA Civ 364, [2004] QB 36. The meaning depends to some extent on the context. A local authority decision which should have been recorded as soon as reasonably practicable and was not recorded for three months was quashed when no reason was given for the delay, in *R v Caerphilly County Council, ex p Jones* (1 February 1999, unreported), QBD; see also *R (on the application of Fuller) v Chief Constable of Dorset Police* [2003] QB 480.
9 *R (on the application of Makke) v Immigration Appeal Tribunal* [2005] EWCA Civ 176, (2005) Times, 5 April: a party seeking a substantial extension of time must show a real prospect of success on the appeal and it is not enough to rely on procedural points.
10 NIAA 2002, s 104(2), as substituted by the Asylum and Immigration (Treatment of Claimants, etc) Act 2004, Sch 2, para 20.

The filter

18.169 To meet concerns about the potential volume of cases reaching the High Court,[1] for an unknown transitional period all applications for reconsideration are to go through the filter process set out in Schedule 2, paragraph 30 to the 2004 Act. The filter system combines aspects of permission to appeal to the Tribunal and statutory review from the old regime. The application goes, not immediately to the High Court or Court of Session, but to a member of the Tribunal who is authorised by the President to deal with such applications.[2] The immigration judge may make an order for reconsideration under section 103A(1), or grant permission for the application to proceed out of time,[3] or may instead inform the applicant and the appropriate court that neither order is proposed.[4] He or she is required to decide the application within ten days of receiving the application notice,[5] unless the application is within the fast track appeal system, where the procedure is somewhat different. In the fast track, the immigration judge must serve the other party with the application, and give that party a day to make submissions in response to it, before deciding the application within a further day.[6] If the immigration judge decides to make no order on the application, the applicant may renew the application for reconsideration and/or for permission to apply out of time to the appropriate court.[7] The time limit for this is five days from deemed receipt of the immigration judge's notice.[8] There is scope for an extension of time for the renewal of the application, if it was not reasonably practicable for the applicant to give notice within the period.[9]

[1] See Government's response to the Constitutional Affairs Committee, 'Asylum and Immigration Appeals' June 2004, Cm 6236.
[2] Asylum and Immigration (Treatment of Claimants, etc) Act 2004, Sch 2, para 30(2); Asylum and Immigration Tribunal (Procedure) Rules 2005, SI 2005/230, r 26(1), applied to fast track appeals by SI 2005/560, r 16. The rules specifying days to be disregarded in calculating the time limit are those of the High Court, not the Tribunal: AITCA 2004, Sch 2, para 30(3)(b); SI 2005/230, r 25 as applied.
[3] Ie under Nationality, Immigration and Asylum Act 2002, s 103A(4)(b), inserted by Asylum and Immigration (Treatment of Claimants, etc) Act 2004, s 26.
[4] Asylum and Immigration (Treatment of Claimants, etc) Act 2004, Sch 2, para 30(4); SI 2005/230, r 26(5), applied to fast track appeals by SI 2005/560, r 16.
[5] SI 2005/230, r 26(4).
[6] SI 2005/560, r 17, 19(1).
[7] AITCA 2004, Sch 2, para 30(5).
[8] AITCA 2004, Sch 2, para 30(5)(b).
[9] AITCA 2004, Sch 2, para 30(5)(c)(ii); see 18.167 text and fn 8 above.

18.170 The immigration judge deals with the application without a hearing, by reference only to the written submissions and documents filed with the application notice[1] and, in fast track appeals, the submissions filed in response.[2] He or she is not required to consider any grounds other than those set out in the notice.[3] However, this provision, which echoes the old provisions on applications to the Tribunal for permission to appeal,[4] does not remove the obligation outlined in *Robinson*[5] to reflect the paramount need to seek the fulfilment of rights under the Refugee or Human Rights Convention, by ordering reconsideration if an obvious point of Convention jurisprudence has arguably been overlooked, even if the point is not raised in the application.[6] In asylum and human rights appeals, this means that the Tribunal should be astute to pick up plain errors of construction of a statute or misunderstanding of the immigration rules in the original determination, obvious unfairness or failure of proper procedures, and clear self-contradiction on the facts on the face of the determination. The immigration judge may order reconsideration only if satisfied both (i) that the Tribunal may have made an error of law[7] and (ii) that there is a real prospect that the Tribunal would decide the appeal differently on reconsideration.[8] The first question the immigration judge will have to consider and form a view on is whether the allegation of error of law is arguably correct, and if so, whether the error arguably made a material difference to the outcome. If so, then the application should be granted, for the prospects of success on appeal are good.

If, however, the immigration judge concludes that the Tribunal would inevitably have come to the same determination despite the error, then the application would be refused,[9] unless there is compelling new evidence or some other reason giving rise to a real possibility that the Tribunal would decide the appeal differently on reconsideration.[10] The rule does not require that the Tribunal 'would have decided' the appeal differently, but 'would decide' the appeal differently; this formulation allows the flexibility which lets in fresh evidence.

[1]   Asylum and Immigration Tribunal (Procedure) Rules 2005, SI 2005/230, r 26(2).

[2]   SI 2005/560, r 18.

[3]   SI 2005/230, r 26(3), applied to fast track appeals by SI 2005/560, r 16. There is no obligation to consider more than one set out grounds: *R (on the application of Nuredini) v Secretary of State for the Home Department* [2002] EWHC 1582 (Admin), [2002] Imm AR 577, [2003] INLR 61; *R (on the application of Hossein) v Immigration Appeal Tribunal* [2003] EWHC 2556 (Admin), [2003] All ER (D) 129 (Oct); *R (on the application of Kalombo) v Immigration Appeal Tribunal* [2004] EWHC 353 (Admin), [2004] All ER (D) 350 (Feb). But where there was a change of representation which was acknowledged by the Tribunal, it should have considered the grounds submitted by the second representative: *R (on the application of Ahmed) v Immigration Appeal Tribunal* [2004] EWHC Civ 399.

[4]   Immigration and Asylum Appeals (Procedure) Rules 2003, r 18(2).

[5]   *Robinson v Secretary of State for the Home Department* [1997] Imm AR 568, CA; *R v Secretary of State for the Home Department, ex p Kerrouche* [1998] INLR 88; *Taore v Secretary of State for the Home Department* [1998] Imm AR 450.

[6]   In *R (on the application of Nuredini) v Secretary of State for the Home Department* [2002] EWHC 1582 (Admin), [2002] Imm AR 577, [2003] INLR 61, the High Court indicated that r 18(6) of the 2000 Procedure Rules (in similar terms as r 18(2) of the 2003 rules and r 26(3) of the 2005 rules) was 'intended to relieve the Tribunal of the obligation to consider grounds not raised in the notice of appeal, and to restrict the scope of the obligation identified in *Robinson*, by preventing objection being taken to a refusal to consider grounds. In *R (on the application of Naing) v Immigration Appeal Tribunal, R (on the application of Eyaz) v Immigration Appeal Tribunal* [2003] EWHC 771 (Admin), the court accepted that the obligation in *Robinson* remained. Any new ground 'must have a strong prospect of success and be readily discernible'. In *R v Immigration Appeal Tribunal, ex p Kang* (CO 497/2000), the Court of Appeal held that extraneous considerations not referred to by the parties clearly flawed the determination, and the refusal of leave was quashed despite the failure of the grounds of appeal to raise the point.

[7]   A material error of fact will ground an application, where it would make a difference: *Manzeke v Secretary of State for the Home Department* [1997] Imm AR 524, CA; *E v Secretary of State for the Home Department, R v Secretary of State for the Home Department* [2004] EWCA Civ 49, [2004] 2 WLR 1351; see 18.166 above.

[8]   SI 2005/230, r 26(6), applied to fast track appeals by SI 2005/560, r 16. Procedural unfairness which deprived an appellant of a hearing will not therefore ground an order for reconsideration unless there is a real prospect of success, but reconsideration should be ordered where the case turns on credibility in such a situation, unless it could be said that no reasonable Tribunal could believe the appellant: cf *R (on the application of L) v Secretary of State for the Home Department* [2003] EWCA Civ 25, [2003] Imm AR 330, [2003] INLR 224.

[9]   SI 2005/230, r 26(6)(b), applied to fast track appeals by SI 2005/560, r 16. The draft rules allowed an order for reconsideration to be made where there was a compelling reason for re-hearing the appeal, regardless of the prospects of success, but that alternative ground was deleted from the final version.

[10] See by analogy *CA v Secretary of State for the Home Department* [2004] EWCA Civ 1165, [2004] INLR 453, holding that error of law had to be established before further evidence could be adduced on appeal from an adjudicator to the Immigration Appeal Tribunal under s 101 Nationality, Immigration and Asylum Act 2002 (now repealed: appeal on point of law). However, it would be necessary not only to submit the evidence but also a statement explaining why it was not previously available and how it would achieve a different result: see SI 2005/230, r 32.

Fresh evidence

18.171 Old procedure rules contained specific provision for the submission in support of an application for permission to appeal of evidence which was not before the adjudicator. Although the current rules contain no such express provision, where the appellant asserts error of law caused by ignorance or understanding of material facts, such as *E v Secretary of State for the Home Department*,[1] in order to make good the ground, the appellant will be required to submit evidence of the established factual situation, to demonstrate the misunderstanding or ignorance which had given rise to the error. The court in *E v Secretary of State for the Home Department* reviewed a large number of authorities[2] in order to deal exhaustively with the vexed question of when fresh evidence is admissible on an application for appeal or review, and held that there was a distinction between judicial review of the Secretary of State, who has a continuing public responsibility such that the court will not shut out evidence relevant to the issues,[3] and review or appeal from the Tribunal, which had a limited appellate function. In the latter case, the *Ladd v Marshall* principles, whereby the court would not normally admit fresh evidence unless it could not have been previously obtained with due diligence for use at the trial, would probably have had an important influence on the result, and was apparently credible,[4] remain the starting point, applied with additional flexibility in public law cases, but may be departed from in exceptional circumstances where the interests of justice so require.[5] The Tribunal is obliged to investigate an allegation of unfairness or procedural irregularity before refusing reconsideration.[6]

1   *E v Secretary of State for the Home Department, R v Secretary of State for the Home Department* [2004] EWCA Civ 49, [2004] INLR 268.
2   Cases involving submission of fresh evidence reviewed by the Court include *A v Secretary of State for the Home Department* [2003] EWCA Civ 175, [2003] INLR 249; *R v Criminal Injuries Compensation Board, ex p A* [1999] 2 AC 330, [1999] 2 WLR 974; *R (on the application of Cindo) v Secretary of State for the Home Department* [2002] EWHC 246 (Admin), [2002] All ER (D) 181 (Feb); *E v Secretary of State for the Home Department* [2003] EWCA Civ 1032, [2004] QB 531, [2004] 2 WLR 123, [2003] INLR 475, [2003] Imm AR 609; *Haile v Immigration Appeal Tribunal* [2001] EWCA Civ 664, [2002] INLR 283, [2002] Imm AR 170; *Khan v Secretary of State for the Home Department* [2003] EWCA Civ 530, [2003] All ER (D) 34 (Apr); *Kibiti v Secretary of State for the Home Department* [2000] Imm AR 594, CA; *Ali v Secretary of State for the Home Department* [1984] 1 WLR 663, [1984] 1 All ER 1009, [1984] Imm AR 23; *R v Secretary of State for the Environment, ex p Powis* [1981] 1 WLR 584, [1981] 1 All ER 788; *R v Secretary of State for the Home Department, ex p Turgut* [2000] INLR 292, [2000] UKHRR 403, [2001] 1 All ER 719, [2000] Imm AR 306.
3   See *R v Secretary of State for the Home Department, ex p Turgut* (fn 2 above); *E v Secretary of State for the Home Department* [2004] EWCA Civ 49, [2004] 2 WLR 1351, para [77].
4   *Ladd v Marshall* [1954] 1 WLR 1489, [1954] 3 All ER 745, (1954) FLR Rep 422, CA.
5   *E v Secretary of State for the Home Department*, at para 91.
6   *R v Immigration Appeal Tribunal, ex p Susikanth* [1998] INLR 185, CA; *R (on the application of Koncek) v Immigration Appeal Tribunal* (CO 1109/2000) (20 November 2000, unreported), QBD.

18.172 The immigration judge must give written notice of the decision on the application, including reasons, which may be in summary form.[1] The law relating to adequacy of reasons applies to this decision.[2] Where he or she makes an order for reconsideration, the notice of decision must state the grounds on which the Tribunal is ordered to reconsider its decision on the appeal, and may give directions for the reconsideration, including specifying the type of Tribunal which is to hear the appeal (whether a single judge, a panel or a full legal panel) and any other directions.[3] In non-fast track appeals, a copy of the decision and directions must be served on every party, and a copy of the application and supporting documents must be sent with the decision to the party which did not make the application.[4] However, where the appeal relates to an asylum claim and the appellant is in the UK, the decision, directions and other documents are instead served on the Secretary of State for service on the appellant, as before.[5] The respondent has 28 days to serve the appellant, and must notify the Tribunal as soon as practicable of service; in the absence of such notification within 29 days, the Tribunal must serve the documents on the appellant as soon as reasonably practicable thereafter.[6] In the fast track, only the respondent is served with the decision, for onward service on the appellant on the same day.[7] In either case, the appropriate court must be sent copies of the notice of decision, the application notice and any attached documents, on request.[8]

[1] SI 2005/230, r 27(1), applied to fast track appeals by SI 2005/560, r 16.
[2] See 18.157–158 above. Standard form reasons may be acceptable where an appeal truly depended on its own facts and on the immigration judge or panel's assessment of the evidence, which has been carried out carefully and reasonably: *Sahota v Immigration Appeal Tribunal* [1995] Imm AR 500, CA; *R v Secretary of State for the Home Department, ex p Thiruchchelvam* [1999] Imm AR 217, but the Tribunal should give clear reasons for refusing leave when unusual points have been put to it: *Robinson v Secretary of State for the Home Department* [1997] Imm AR 568 at 582, and should address specific arguments on legal issues and procedural irregularities in the decision, as well as fresh evidence adduced: *R v Immigration Appeal Tribunal, ex p Ehalaivan* (CO 4275/99) (14 June 2000, unreported), CA. See also *R v Immigration Appeal Tribunal, ex p Clavijo-Quintero* [2002] Imm AR 68. Where no reasons are given for refusing to extend time, relief should be refused only if there is no possibility on any view that the Tribunal would agree to do so: *R (on the application of Tofik) v Immigration Appeal Tribunal* [2003] EWCA Civ 1138, [2003] INLR 623.
[3] SI 2005/230, r 27(1), (2), applied to fast track appeals by SI 2005/560, r 16.
[4] SI 2005/230, r 27(3).
[5] SI 2005/230, r 27(4). See 18.156 above for service on the appellant via the respondent.
[6] SI 2005/230, r 27(5).
[7] SI 2005/560, r 19(1), (2)(a). The respondent must notify the Tribunal within a day of the date and means of service, failing which the Tribunal must serve the appellant itself: r 19(2)(b), (3).
[8] SI 2005/230, r 28, applied to fast track appeals by SI 2005/560, r 16.

Renewal

18.173 If the Tribunal records that it does not propose to make an order for reconsideration, or to grant permission to apply for reconsideration out of time, the applicant may renew the application to the appropriate court, ie the High Court or the Outer House of the Court of Session (see 18.167 above), and the time limits set out in the Act, and the Civil Procedure Rules and Practice Directions apply. The court determines the application on the papers, by reference only to the written submissions of the applicant.[1] There is no distinction here between applications emanating from the normal and fast track, although in the fast track, immigration judges will have considered respondents' submissions too.[2] Instead of making an order for reconsideration, the Court may refer the appeal to the appropriate appellate court, ie the Court of Appeal or the Court of Session, if it thinks that the appeal raises a question of law of such importance that it should be decided by that court.[3] In such a case, the appeal court has all its normal powers (as to which see below), but in addition, if it disagrees, it may restore the application under section 103A to the referring court.[4] The 2004 Act introduces retrospective public funding of applications for reconsideration. On making an order for reconsideration, or a reference to the appeal court, in England, Wales or Northern Ireland, the Court may order that the appellant's costs be paid out of the Community Legal Service Fund, pursuant to regulations to be made by the Secretary of State.[5] We consider funding in detail at 18.177 below.

[1] Nationality, Immigration and Asylum Act 2002, s 103A(5), inserted by Asylum and Immigration (Treatment of Claimants, etc) Act 2004, s 26.
[2] See 18.169 above.
[3] NIAA 2002, s 103C(1) as inserted.
[4] NIAA 2002, s 103C(2) as inserted.
[5] NIAA 2002, s 103D(1), (2), (5)–(9); see 18.177 below.

The reconsideration hearing

18.174 How does the Tribunal go about its reconsideration of an appeal? As we have seen, if the immigration judge orders reconsideration, he or she must state the grounds on which the Tribunal is ordered to reconsider, and may make directions under rule 45 at the same time.[1] The rules relating to the method of determining the appeal (ie with or without a hearing), withdrawal, abandonment and hearing the appeal in the absence of a party all apply to a reconsideration, as do the rules on combined appeals, adjournments and the giving of determinations,[2] and the general provisions (relating to directions, documents, service, representation, evidence, calculation of time etc).[3] But there are also special rules relating to reconsideration. First, there is provision for a respondent's notice, called a 'reply' in the principal rules, which must be served on the applicant by the other party if he or she contends that the Tribunal should uphold the initial determination for reasons different from or additional to those given in the determination.[4] The most common example might be where the Tribunal allowed the appeal on a human rights ground but rejected the asylum ground, and on reconsideration the claimant wishes to argue that the Tribunal was wrong to reject the asylum ground.[5] On reconsideration, which must take place as soon as reasonably practicable after the order has been served on the parties[6] (within two days, if possible, in the fast track),[7] the Tribunal must first decide whether the original Tribunal made a material error of law, and if it decides this question in the negative, it must order that the original determination of the appeal stands.[8] Otherwise, it must substitute a fresh decision to allow or dismiss the appeal.[9] In doing so, it must have regard to any directions given by the immigration judge or the court which ordered reconsideration, and may limit submissions or evidence to specified issues.[10] The reconsideration hearing might take place before a sole immigration judge or a panel of two or three.[11] It is unlikely to be before a full 'legal' tribunal unless there is a difficult legal issue requiring guidance. The Tribunal is under no duty to consider the parties' representations about the number or class of members to hear the appeal on reconsideration,[12] but it would clearly be inappropriate for a member who has previously made adverse credibility findings on the appellant to sit on the panel hearing his or her appeal on reconsideration.[13]

[1] Asylum and Immigration Tribunal (Procedure) Rules 2005, SI 2005/230, r 27(2)(a) and (b), applied to fast track appeals by SI 2005/560, r 16.

[2] SI 2005/230, r 29, applying rules 15 to 23, save for the special time limits in in-country asylum appeals (r 23(2)). In the fast track, the rules relating to withdrawal, abandonment and hearing the appeal in the absence of a party apply: SI 2005/560, r 20, applying rr 17–19 of the principal rules. In addition, some of the rules on evidence, SI 2005/230 rr 31(2)–(5) and 32(1) (see below), apply to reconsideration in the fast track.

[3] SI 2005/230 Part V (rr 43–60), applied with necessary modifications to fast track appeals by SI 2005/560, r 20.

[4] SI 2005/230, r 30. There is no such provision in the fast track, but the respondent to an application for reconsideration in respect of an appeal in the fast track has already had the opportunity to comment in response to the application itself: SI 2005/560, r 17(b).

[5] This most commonly happens when the original Tribunal accepts that the claimant will be mistreated on return but denies that such ill-treatment will be for a Refugee Convention reason (as to which see 12.64–12.83 above).

[6] SI 2005/230, r 31(1).

[7] SI 2005/560, r 21(1). The parties must be served with notice of the date, time and place of the reconsideration hearing no later than noon on the business day before the hearing. It is hard to see how (*pace* the Court of Appeal in *R (on the application of the Refugee Legal Centre) v Secretary of State for the Home Department* [2004] EWCA Civ 1481, [2004] All ER (D) 201 (Nov)) these time limits can conceivably allow adequate preparation time for reconsideration. Surely an order for reconsideration ought to merit transfer out of the fast track?

[8] SI 2005/230, r 31(2), applied to fast track appeals by SI 2005/560, r 20. A material error is an error of law which affected the Tribunal's decision on the appeal: r 31(5). This provision does not prevent an appeal succeeding on fresh evidence (see discussion of *E v Secretary of State for the Home Department* [2004] EWCA Civ 49, [2004] 2 WLR 1351 at 18.166 above) but it does prevent an appeal succeeding on a change of circumstances since the original determination.

[9] SI 2005/230, r 31(3), applied to fast track appeals by SI 2005/560, r 20. Thus, once error of law is shown, the Tribunal may allow (or dismiss) the appeal by reference to completely different matters, including a change of circumstance, evidence of which would be admissible under Nationality, Immigration and Asylum Act 2002, s 85(4) (subject to the procedure rules, see below). For evidence on reconsideration hearings see below.

[10] SI 2005/230, r 31(4), as applied. Any limitations directed would reflect the reasons given by the immigration judge or judge for making the order: see *RS (Sri Lanka)* [2004] UKIAT 00234 'Reported'. The power to allow a variation of grounds of appeal (r 14) does not apply on reconsideration.

[11] In accordance with directions given by the President: Nationality, Immigration and Asylum Act 2002, Sch 4, paras 7, 8 (as substituted by Asylum and Immigration (Treatment of Claimants, etc) Act 2004).

[12] SI 2005/230, r 44(1), applied to reconsideration hearings by r 29, and to fast track reconsideration hearings by SI 2005/560, r 20(2).

[13] *Huang* (14058) 4 November 1996. But it would not be improper for the immigration judge who refused reconsideration to sit on the appeal after the High Court ordered reconsideration: cf *Mwakulna v Secretary of State for the Home Department* (98/7306/4) (4 March 1999, unreported), CA.

Evidence

18.175 Any note or record made by the Tribunal of any previous hearing may be considered as evidence at the reconsideration hearing.[1] Other than that, the Tribunal may consider evidence which was not before the previous Tribunal, on application by a party. A party wishing to call additional evidence before the Tribunal must give written notice to this effect and indicate the nature of the evidence, and explain why it was not submitted before.[2] This must be done 'as soon as practicable' after the parties have been served with the order for reconsideration.[3] The Court of Appeal held in *Bashir* that only in exceptional circumstances should the Tribunal consider fresh material despite the appellant's failure to serve written notice of intention to adduce the evidence,[4] but on the other hand, the Court in *Azkhosravi* has emphasised the importance of substantive justice over procedural concerns, and in particular the necessity of evaluating the impact of the fresh evidence on the case.[5] The Tribunal can direct how any fresh evidence is to be given and by when it is to be filed.[6] The Procedure Rules which deal with the summoning of witnesses and the admission of evidence, also apply to reconsideration hearings.[7] At the time of writing, there is no guidance through case-law on the new provisions as to how the admission of fresh evidence will be dealt with in reconsideration hearings, but the same principles would seem to apply as to statutory review under the 2002 Act before amendment. A starred Tribunal held in *MA (Sri Lanka)*[8] that the principles set out in *E v Secretary of State for the Home Department*[9] regarding the admission of fresh evidence apply more widely, and would apply to appeals remitted from the Court of Appeal; the Tribunal is thus likely to hold that the same principles apply on a reconsideration hearing. If the fresh evidence did not go to the issue of whether the original Tribunal erred in law, it would not be admitted, regardless of its cogency, unless that issue was decided in favour of the appellant, but would then be admissible at the Tribunal's discretion.[10]

1   SI 2005/230, r 32(1), applied to fast track appeals by SI 2005/560, r 20.
2   SI 2005/230, r 32(2). Fresh evidence on fast track reconsideration is governed by SI 2005/560, r 22(1).
3   SI 2005/230, r 32(3). On the fast track, the rules require notification of fresh evidence to be given 'wherever practicable' before the date of the reconsideration hearing: SI 2005/560, r 22(2).
4   *Bashir v Secretary of State for the Home Department* [2004] EWCA Civ 696 [2004] 23 LS Gaz R 32, decided under the 2003 Procedure Rules.
5   *R (on the application of Azkhosravi) v Immigration Appeal Tribunal* [2001] EWCA Civ 977, [2002] INLR 123, where a lack of a proper explanation for failure to adduce evidence before was held not to justify its automatic exclusion.
6   SI 2005/230, r 32(4) (not applicable to the fast track).
7   SI 2005/230, rr 50, 51, applied to normal appeals by r 29 and to fast track appeals (with necessary modifications) by SI 2005/560, r 20(2).
8   [2004] UKIAT 00161.
9   *E v Secretary of State for the Home Department, R v Secretary of State for the Home Department* [2004] EWCA Civ 49, [2004] INLR 268; see 18.171 above.
10 Most of the cases under the earlier rules illustrate the principles that (i) the court will want to know why the evidence was not submitted before: *R (on the application of Sahin) v Immigration Appeal Tribunal* [2003] EWHC 107 (Admin), [2003] AlL ER (D) 97 (Jan); *R (on the application of Ucar) v Immigration Appeal Tribunal* [2003] EWHC 1330 (Admin), [2003] AlL ER (D) 278 (May), and (ii) will consider the impact of the evidence on the case: *Shehu v Immigration Appeal Tribunal* [2004] EWCA Civ 854, [2004] 28 LS Gaz R 34; *R (on the application of Shkambi) v Immigration Appeal Tribunal* [2004] EWHC 1044 (Admin), [2004] All ER (D) 245 (Apr); *R (on the application of Azkhosravi) v Immigration Appeal Tribunal* [2001] EWCA Civ 977, [2002] INLR 123. A failure to adduce evidence by previous representatives provides an excuse allowing its admission in extreme cases: *AG Turkey* [2005] UKIAT 00014. See also *AI (Somalia)* [2005] UKIAT 00063, a hard-line decision from the President's Tribunal which suggested that fresh evidence to 'improve' the case would 'almost never' be admitted. But see below. Updated evidence of country conditions and of changes in personal circumstances is clearly admissible.

The decision

18.176 We have seen above that the Tribunal may not make a fresh decision on the appeal unless it decides that the original Tribunal made an error of law, and that an error of law embraces not only legal misdirection and procedural irregularity but also failure to have regard to, misunderstanding or ignorance of material facts. Once the Tribunal concludes that there has been error of law, it makes a fresh decision of its own, to allow or dismiss the appeal.[1] The extent to which the Tribunal, in making a fresh decision, may review the facts found by the original Tribunal has been the subject of considerable litigation. The Court of Appeal has ruled in a number of cases that the Tribunal should be most reluctant to interfere with a finding of primary fact which was dependent on an assessment of the credibility of a witness who had given oral evidence,[2] and in principle there is no reason why credibility findings untouched by the error of law identified by the Tribunal should not stand. However, the Tribunal's Practice Direction indicates that once error of law has been found, it will decide everything *de novo* including credibility issues.[3] On reconsideration, the Tribunal is in as good a position as the original Tribunal to review documentary evidence of country conditions and draw its own inferences, subject to guidance given in 'country guideline' cases.[4] It is also open to the Tribunal to reverse the original decision on the basis of further evidence, and the Practice Direction indicates that in most cases it will expect to hear further oral evidence.[5] On reconsideration, the Tribunal must give sufficient and adequate reasons for its determination.

[1] SI 2005/230, r 31(3), applied to fast track reconsideration by SI 2005/560, r 20.
[2] *Borissov v Secretary of State for the Home Department* [1996] Imm AR 524; *Assah v Immigration Appeal Tribunal* [1994] Imm AR 519; *Ikhlaq v Secretary of State for the Home Department* [1997] Imm AR 404. The principle was approved in *Subesh v Secretary of State for the Home Department* [2004] EWCA Civ 56, [2004] INLR 417 (although the court was there considering the Tribunal's jurisdiction under the IAA 1999, which did not require the 'condition precedent' of error of law in order to reach a fresh decision). The Court of Appeal warned in *Arshad v Secretary of State for the Home Department* [2001] EWCA Civ 587, [2001] All ER (D) 240 (Apr) about the importance of even-handedness in the Tribunal's approach to earlier factual findings.
[3] Practice Direction 1/2005 indicates that the claimant and his or her witnesses should attend, with interpreters, to give oral evidence in the event that the Tribunal is satisfied that an error of law occurs and so needs to redetermine the appeal *de novo*. But this implies a great deal of preparation by claimants and their representatives, on a purely contingent basis, which wastes a great deal of both time and money. It seems to us, with respect, that the reconsideration process requires two distinct stages, so that once error of law has been established, directions can be given for the future conduct of the hearing, including the reception of fresh evidence, along the same lines as the case management review hearings for 'first' appeals.
[4] *R v Immigration Appeal Tribunal, ex p Balendran, Katheeskumaran* [1998] Imm AR 162, QBD; *Sarker v Secretary of State for the Home Department* (9 November 2000), CA. For 'country guidelines' cases see 18.142 above.
[5] In *Sachitananthan* (16860) the Tribunal held that, in an asylum appeal, following *Ravichandran v Secretary of State for the Home Department* [1996] Imm AR 97, CA, it had to look at the position at the date of the appeal before it. Now, the *Ravichandran* rule has been put into statutory form and broadened to all appeals except those relating to entry clearance by Nationality, Immigration and Asylum Act 2002, s 85(4), and there is nothing limiting the admission of evidence of post-decision facts in the subsection to first appeals; therefore this provision must apply to reconsideration too. In reconsideration of entry clearance appeals, fresh evidence going to the position at the date of decision would be admissible. See 18.139 above.

Funding of reconsideration

18.177 A new statutory scheme makes public funding of appellants on applications for reconsideration, and of reconsideration hearings, conditional on authorisation by the appropriate court or Tribunal. The scheme does not apply in relation to appeals decided in Scotland,[1] or to applications in the fast track.[2] Section 103D of the Nationality, Immigration and Asylum Act 2002 (inserted by the 2004 Act)[3] provides that where an order for reconsideration has been made, or where instead the court has referred the case to the Court of Appeal, on the application of an appellant, the court may order the appellant's costs to be paid out of the Community Legal Service fund.[4] Where the Tribunal has decided an appeal following an order for reconsideration which was made on the application of the appellant, the Tribunal may make a similar order, covering both the application for reconsideration and the reconsideration itself.[5] The draft Community Legal Services (Asylum and Immigration Appeals) Regulations 2005 provide that it should be the Tribunal which makes a funding order at the end of a reconsideration hearing, and that an immigration judge or the High Court should not normally make a funding order on making an order for reconsideration,[6] although the High Court should make a funding order if it refers the case to the Court of Appeal.[7] If the application for an order for reconsideration is refused, a funding order may be made only if there has been a change in the relevant circumstances or in the law since the application was made and when it was made, there was a significant prospect that the appeal would be allowed on reconsideration.[8] This is a very stringent test for funding failed applications and is, we believe, highly inimical to the development of the law and to the protection of claimants alike.[9] On a reconsideration pursuant to an order, the Tribunal must order funding of the appellant's costs of the application and of the reconsideration if it allows the appeal, but if it does not, it may make a funding order only if, when the application was made, there was a significant prospect that the appeal would be allowed on reconsideration.[10] We would expect it to be only in the rarest of cases that funding is refused on reconsideration following an order. In such cases, reasons must be given for the refusal.[11] The Tribunal's funding determination must be separate from its decision on reconsideration, and must be send to the appellant's representative and (where funding has been ordered) to the relevant funding body.[12] Where the Tribunal's substantive determination is served via the respondent, the Tribunal must not send out the funding determination until it has been notified that the respondent has completed service or the Tribunal has served the substantive decision itself.[13] The representative may apply in writing[14] for a review of the decision, which must be conducted by a senior immigration judge who has not been involved in the decision, and may be oral on the applicant's request, or otherwise on the papers. The senior immigration judge must give reasons for the decision to make the order or to confirm the Tribunal's decision not to fund.[15] The criteria for the Legal Services Commission's funding of legal representation in immigration review proceedings are modified to take account of these retrospective authorisation provisions.[16]

---

[1]   Nationality, Immigration and Asylum Act 2002, s 103D(9) (inserted by Asylum and Immigration (Treatment of Claimants, etc) Act 2004, s 26).

2   Community Legal Service (Asylum and Immigration Appeals) Regulations 2005, SI 2005/966, reg 4(2). The exclusion applies to proceedings for review in which, pursuant to an order under Asylum and Immigration (Treatment of Claimants, etc) Act 2004, s 26(8), the period for lodging an application for reconsideration under s 103A is varied to under five days.

3   Asylum and Immigration (Treatment of Claimants, etc) Act 2004, s 26.

4   NIAA 2002, s 103D(1), (2) as inserted. In Northern Ireland, funding is under the Access to Justice (Northern Ireland) Order 2003, SI 2003/435 (NI 10): s 103D(10).

5   NIAA 2002, s 103D(3), (4) as inserted.

6   SI 2005/966, reg 5(2). The High Court or immigration judge may make a funding order on the written application of the solicitor or counsel, if an order for reconsideration is made but no reconsideration takes place (because, for example, the Secretary of State grants the appellant leave to remain, and the appeal is deemed abandoned): reg 5(5).

7   SI 2005/966, reg 5(3).

8   SI 2005/966, reg 5(4).

9   The Constitutional Affairs Committee condemned the combination of retrospective funding and higher than normal threshold as unprecedented, unnecessary and bringing with it a significant risk that legitimate appeals would be wrongly restricted. See Legal Aid in Asylum Appeals: Fifth report 2004/5, HC 276.

10 SI 2005/966, reg 6(2), (3). Lord Falconer gave his understanding of the 'significant prospects of success' test in a letter to ILPA and the Bar Council of 23 February 2005: 'the intention is that if a supplier acts in good faith and pursues a case through to the reconsideration stage they can expect to be paid'. He continued, somewhat less helpfully, that 'success at the review stage is not in itself sufficient to secure funding'.

11 SI 2005/966, reg 6(4).

12 Asylum and Immigration Tribunal (Procedure) Rules 2005, SI 2005/230, r 33(1)–(3).

13 SI 2005/230, r 33(4).

14 SI 2005/966, reg 7(1). The application must be filed within ten business days of service of the funding determination, or longer as the Tribunal may permit: reg 7(2). 'Business days' are defined in reg 3.

15 SI 2005/966, reg 7(3)–(6).

16 SI 2005/966 reg 9(1), which disapplies the standard criteria for legal representation and support funding in the funding code (s 5) and those for prospects of success and cost benefit (s13). The remuneration limits are lifted by the Community Legal Service (Funding) Amendment Regulations 2005, SI 2005/571 in respect of applications for reconsideration. The effect of the LSC's grant of legal representation in immigration review proceedings (ie applications for reconsideration and subsequent reconsideration proceedings) is to cover advising on the merits of an application, and disbursements except for counsel's fees, but otherwise, payment is conditional on the making of a funding order by the High Court or the Tribunal: reg 9(2).

Appeal to the Court of Appeal or Court of Session

18.178 There can be only one reconsideration of an appeal.[1] If the appellant believes that the Tribunal has fallen into error in its reconsideration, he or she must appeal the decision to the Court of Appeal.[2] Additionally, there is no reconsideration if the original decision is taken by a panel of three or more legally qualified immigration judges.[3] In such a case, the appellant may appeal to the Court of Appeal.[4] The other way in which a case might go to the Court of Appeal is on referral by the High Court (or Outer House of the Court of Session), where an application for reconsideration is made but the Court thinks that the appeal raises a question of law of such importance that it should be decided by the appeal court instead of being reconsidered by the Tribunal.[5] This route is a short cut to authoritative determination by the Court of Appeal of vexed legal issues which might be the subject of differing Tribunal decisions. In all cases, the appeal to the Court of Appeal is on a point of law.[6] We considered the scope of this jurisdiction at 18.166 above. The

Court of Appeal is also the appellate court for the Special Immigration Appeals Commission (see 18.182 below).

1　Nationality, Immigration and Asylum Act 2002, s 103A(2)(b), inserted by Asylum and Immigration (Treatment of Claimants, etc) Act 2004, s 26(6).
2　Under s 103B(1) as inserted. An appeal under this section is also available against a Tribunal's determination of a remitted appeal (whether remitted under this section or under s 103C or 103E; see below).
3　NIAA 2002, s 103A(8) as inserted.
4　NIAA 2002, s 103E as inserted. In Scotland, appeals go to the Court of Session: s 103B(5), and 'Court of Appeal' is to be read in this section as including appeals to the Court of Session and, in Northern Ireland, to the Court of Appeal in Northern Ireland.
5　NIAA 2002, s 103C as inserted.
6　NIAA 2002, ss 103B(1), 103C(1), 103E(2).

18.179 An appeal against a reconsidered decision or a decision by a legal panel of the Tribunal may only be brought with the permission of the Tribunal, or if it is refused, with the permission of the appropriate appellate court.[1] An application to the Tribunal for permission to appeal must be made within five days of receipt of the Tribunal's written determination, if the applicant is in detention,[2] and in any other case, within 10 days.[3] The Tribunal has no power to extend the time limit.[4] The application must be in the appropriate prescribed form, must state the grounds of appeal and must be signed by the appellant or representative, and dated.[5] The other party to the appeal must be notified as soon as practicable that the application for permission has been filed.[6] The application is determined by a senior immigration judge without a hearing.[7] The Tribunal must serve written notice on the parties of its decision, including its reasons (which may be in summary form).[8] The senior immigration judge has the additional power at this stage of setting aside the Tribunal's decision if he or she intends to grant permission and thinks that the Tribunal has made an administrative error in relation to the proceedings.[9] If permission is refused by the Tribunal, the applicant can go direct to the Court of Appeal or Court of Session for permission. In England and Wales the procedure is governed by Civil Procedure Rules, part 52. The notice of appeal, including the application for permission if required, must be lodged with the Court of Appeal within 14 days of the decision appealed against.[10] The court may extend time for the application in its inherent discretion.[11] The application is dealt with by a single judge on the papers in the first instance with a renewal to the full court.[12] The single judge might issue a preliminary 'minded to refuse' decision and list the matter for hearing before him or herself. If so, the applicant should address the reasons for the judge being 'minded to refuse'.[13] The court will only grant permission if it considers that the appeal has a real prospect of success, or there is some other compelling reason for the appeal to be heard.[14] It may limit the issues to be argued and impose conditions on the grant of permission.[15] Once an appeal to the Court of Appeal is pending, the appellant may not be removed from the UK, but an application for permission lodged out of time would not prevent removal until permission was granted, so in such circumstances a stay should be sought from the court.[16] An appeal to the Court of Appeal is not deemed abandoned if the appellant leaves the UK.[17]

1　Nationality, Immigration and Asylum Act 2002, ss 103B(3), 103E(3), inserted by Asylum and Immigration (Treatment of Claimants, etc) Act 2004, s 26(6).

2   Asylum and Immigration Tribunal (Procedure) Rules 2005, SI 2005/230, r 35(1)(a). For fast track appeals, the time limit is two days after the appellant is served with the Tribunal's determination: SI 2005/560, r 25(1).

3   SI 2005/230, r 35(1)(b). This does not apply in the fast track, since all appellants there are detained.

4   SI 2005/230, r 35(2); for fast track appeals, the equivalent provision is SI 2005/560, r 25(2).

5   SI 2005/230, r 34(2). If the notice is signed by a representative, he or she must certify in the notice that it has been completed in accordance with the applicant's instructions: r 34(3). These rules are applied to fast track appeals by SI 2005/560, r 24. For the effects of minor non-compliance see *R v Immigration Appeal Tribunal, ex p Jeyeanthan; Ravichandran v Secretary of State for the Home Department* [2000] 1 WLR 354, [2000] Imm AR 10, [2000] INLR 241; 18.84 above.

6   SI 2005/230, r 34(4). The fast track rules require the other party to be notified immediately: SI 2005/560, r 25(3).

7   SI 2005/230, r 36(1), applied to the fast track by SI 2005/560, r 24.

8   SI 2005/230, r 36(4) as applied. In the fast track, the Tribunal must determine the application for permission to appeal, and serve its determination on every party, within a day of receipt of the application: r 26.

9   SI 2005/230, r 36(3) as applied. This provision echoes the review powers of the Tribunal under previous procedure rules, and provides a sensible short cut where the point of law relates to a procedural irregularity by the Tribunal which resulted in serious prejudice to the appellant.

10 Civil Procedure Rules (CPR) r 52.4(2)(b). The appellant's notice, including the permission appilcation, must be served on the respondent within seven days of its being lodged with the court: r 52.4(3).

11 CPR rr 3.1(2)(a); 52.6; *A v Secretary of State for the Home Department* [2003] EWCA Civ 175, [2003] INLR 249. For an example of refusal to extend, where no good reason was proffered and no extension of time sought before the time limit, see *R v Secretary of State for the Home Department, ex p Harris (Darrel)* [2002] EWCA Civ 100 (appeal in judicial review).

12 CPR r 52.3(3).

13 *Sad-Chaouche v Secretary of State for the Home Department* (29 March 2000, CA perm).

14 CPR r 52.3(6).

15 CPR r 52.3(7).

16 CPR r 52.7(b), not updated at the time of writing, indicates that an appeal to the Court of Appeal, other than from the Immigration Appeal Tribunal, does not operate as a stay of the order or decision under appeal, but this wording does not necessarily mean that an out of time appeal from the Tribunal automatically stays the decision. See Nationality, Immigration and Asylum Act 2002, ss 78, 104 (the latter substituted by Asylum and Immigration (Treatment of Claimants, etc) Act 2004, Sch 2, para 20) (at 18.24 above).

17 *Shirazi v Secretary of State for the Home Department* [2003] EWCA Civ 1562, [2004] INLR 92. Although the case was decided under the IAA 1999 appeals regime, the appeals provisions under the NIAA 2002 are not materially different for these purposes.

18.180 As with reconsideration under section 103A, only the Tribunal's 'decision on an appeal' goes to the Court of Appeal or Court of Session, not a procedural, ancillary or preliminary decision.[1] Thus, a decision to grant or refuse bail, a decision that an appeal is out of time and a refusal to extend time, may not be appealed to the Court of Appeal.[2] However, directions to give effect to a decision, which would appear to be ancillary to the decision, are by statute deemed to be part of the decision on the appeal, and so may apparently be the subject of appeal or review.[3] Where there is doubt as to whether the decision is a 'decision on the appeal' for the purpose of the section, it may be necessary first to renew the application for permission to appeal to the Court of Appeal or the Court of Session before judicial review is taken.[4] The scope of the court's jurisdiction was said in *E v Secretary of State for the Home Department*[5] to be the same as that of the Administrative Court in judicial review, and was considered at 18.166 above. The principles governing the admission of fresh evidence on appeal have been considered at 18.171 above. The court may, on agreed facts, decide that an asylum claimant fulfils the criteria for refugee status, as an alternative to remitting a successful appeal to the Tribunal.[6] The court will not hear academic appeals (ie where a respondent has abandoned a claim, as happened in *Dahir*,[7] or an appellant cannot be found, having been unlawfully removed from the country, as happened in *Re M*),[8] unless there is a good reason in the public interest for doing so, for example, the case raises questions of general importance which can be decided irrespective of the facts of individual appeals and would affect a large number of similar cases.[9] Nor will it hear an appeal on a point not argued before the Tribunal by agreement but raised before it in order to obtain a remittal to the Tribunal.[10] The doctrine of binding precedent applies to the Court of Appeal.[11]

[1] Nationality, Immigration and Asylum Act 2002, ss 103A(7), 103E(7).
[2] A decision on bail is ancillary, a decision that an appeal is out of time is preliminary, and a refusal to extend time is procedural. The Court of Appeal decided in *Abdi and Dahir* [1995] Imm AR 570 that there was no right of appeal to it against a ruling on a preliminary issue. The Tribunal has however held that decisions as to abandonment are decisions on the appeal, since they put an end to the appeal, and litigation may be necessary on this issue: see 18.96 and 18.167 above.
[3] NIAA 2002, s 87(4), amended by Asylum and Immigration (Treatment of Claimants, etc) Act 2004, Sch 2, para 19.
[4] *R v Immigration Appeal Tribunal, ex p Mukendi* (CO06694) (1994, unreported), QBD.
[5] *E v Secretary of State for the Home Department, R v Secretary of State for the Home Department* [2004] EWCA Civ 49, [2004] INLR 264. The distinction formerly drawn in cases such as *Macharia v Immigration Appeal Tribunal* [2000] Imm AR 190, between administrative law grounds, including procedural impropriety, and questions of law, which were believed to be narrower, has become obsolete, as procedural and evidential matters are seen as errors of law potentially vitiating decisions.
[6] As the House of Lords did in *Islam v Immigration Appeal Tribunal* [1999] 2 AC 629.
[7] *Secretary of State for the Home Department v Abdi and Dahir* [1995] Imm AR 570, CA. But an appeal to the Court of Appeal is not deemed abandoned if the appellant leaves the UK: *Shirazi v Secretary of State for the Home Department* [2003] EWCA Civ 1562, [2004] INLR 92, 18.179 fn 17 above.
[8] *Re M* [1994] 1 AC 377, where the issue was whether the Secretary of State was in contempt of court for removing and failing to return to the jurisdiction an asylum seeker in respect of whom an undertaking had been given not to remove him.
[9] *R v Secretary of State for the Home Department, ex p Salem* [1999] 1 AC 450, HL.
[10] *Srimanoharan v Secretary of State for the Home Department* (13 June 2000, unreported); *Zaitz v Secretary of State for the Home Department* [2000] INLR 346.
[11] See *HM v Secretary of State for the Home Department* [2003] EWCA Civ 583, [2003] Imm AR 470.

18.181 If the Tribunal has allowed an appeal and given directions for giving effect to the decision,[1] these have no effect while an application for reconsideration, or for permission to appeal (other than an application out of time) could be made or is awaiting determination, while reconsideration of an appeal has been ordered and has not been completed or an appeal or reference to the Court of Appeal[2] is awaiting determination, or an appeal which has been remitted to the Tribunal is awaiting determination.[3] Since directions are part of the Tribunal's decision on the appeal,[4] it follows that on reconsideration or remittal, the Tribunal may alter or add to any directions already given, or cancel or replace them.

1 Under Nationality, Immigration and Asylum Act 2002, s 87(1) as amended by Asylum and Immigration (Treatment of Claimants, etc) Act 2004, Sch 2, para 18; see 18.69ff above.
2 Or Court of Session, in Scotland: Nationality, Immigration and Asylum Act 2002, s 103B(5), inserted by Asylum and Immigration (Treatment of Claimants, etc) Act 2004, s 26.
3 NIAA 2002, s 87(3), as substituted by Asylum and Immigration (Treatment of Claimants, etc) Act 2004, Sch 2, para 19.
4 NIAA 2002, s 87(4) as substituted.

Appeal to the Court of Appeal from the Special Immigration Appeals Commission

18.182 An appeal lies from the Commission's decision to the Court of Appeal or Court of Session, with the leave of the Commission or of the court.[1] On an appeal from the Commission, the Court of Appeal will only accept a departure from the normal appellate procedure if it is necessary in the interests of justice with regard to the issues before the court. If there is such a departure the interests of the individual will be protected to the best of the court's ability.[2]

1 Special Immigration Appeals Commission Act 1997, s 7, applied to appeals under the Anti-terrorism, Crime and Security Act 2001 by s 27.
2 *Secretary of State for the Home Department v Shafiq ur Rehman* [2000] INLR 531, CA, directions hearing.

Judicial review

18.183 Judicial review is the High Court procedure to challenge the validity of a decision of a body exercising public law administrative functions. The branch of the High Court dealing with it is, since November 2000, known as the Administrative Court. An application for judicial review can only be started with the permission of the court (in immigration cases usually a single High Court judge). The procedure is set out in Part 54 of the CPR. Immigration cases used to take up a very large proportion of all applications for judicial review. In 2000, immigration cases, at 2119, made up half the total number of judicial review applications for permission.[1] Legislative changes have been directed towards a dramatic reduction of that number. This is not a book about judicial review and we merely flag up points pertinent to immigration law.[2]

1 Figures from the Administrative Court. See the Bowman report. For a historical account of the growth of immigration judicial review see Law Commission *Administrative Law: Judicial Review and Statutory Appeals* (HC669) p 12; Sunlin, Bridges and Meszaros *Judicial Review in Perspective* (1993) p 52.
2 See further de Smith, Woolf and Jowell *Judicial Review of Administrative Action* (2005); Fordham *Judicial Review Handbook* (4th edn, 2004); Wade and Forsyth *Administrative Law* (9th edn, 2004).

18.184 Most immigration decisions are potentially subject to judicial review, whether those of an entry clearance officer, an immigration officer, the Secretary of State or a criminal court dealing with immigration offences.[1] In *Javed* the Court of Appeal confirmed that a statutory instrument which had been approved by both Houses of Parliament was vulnerable to judicial review.[2] Decisions of the Secretary of State are reviewable, including prerogative acts such as the grant or refusal of a passport,[3] and even where statute makes express provision to the contrary.[4] Equally, failures and delays by administrative bodies are challengeable by judicial review.[5] In recent years, judicial review has increasingly been used to challenge policies and procedures, such as service of adverse decisions on appellants via the Secretary of State,[6] the removal of benefits from categories of asylum claimants,[7] the system in place to penalise unwitting carriers of clandestine entrants,[8] the failure of the Secretary of State to publicise a policy providing support to rejected asylum claimants,[9] detention of asylum claimants to process their claims,[10] the use of fast track procedures at Oakington and Harmondsworth removal centres,[11] racially discriminatory procedures[12] etc. Judicial review has become an important tool for seeking to ensure minimum standards of fairness and consistency in decision-making.[13] The rules of standing in judicial review are much more generous than those in (for example) the European Court of Human Rights,[14] enabling organisations with a legitimate interest in the subject matter, such as the Joint Council for the Welfare of Immigrants, the Immigration Law Practitioners' Association, the Refugee Legal Centre and Amnesty International among others to bring actions.

1   *R v Uxbridge Magistrates, ex p Adimi* [1999] 4 All ER 520 challenge to the conviction of asylum claimants as contrary to the Refugee Convention.
2   *R (on the application of Javed) v Secretary of State for the Home Department* [2001] EWCA Civ 789, [2002] QB 129, [2001] 3 WLR 323, followed in *R (on the application of Husain) v Secretary of State for the Home Department* [2005] EWHC 189 (Admin), [2005] All ER (D) 371 (Feb) in respect of the designation of Bangladesh as a safe country for the purpose of Nationality, Immigration and Asylum Act 2002, s 94 by statutory instrument.
3   *R v Secretary of State for Foreign and Commonwealth Affairs, ex p Everett* [1989] QB 811, [1989] 1 All ER 655, CA. In *R (on the application of Abbasi) v Secretary of State for Foreign and Commonwealth Affairs* [2002] EWCA Civ 1598, (2002) Times, 8 November, the Court of Appeal re-emphasised that 'it is no answer to a judicial review claim to say that the source of power ... is the prerogative. It is the subject matter that is determinative.' However, the court will not rule on questions of international law which affect foreign sovereign states, or questions of foreign policy: *R (on the application of Campaign for Nuclear Disarmament) v Prime Minister* [2002] EWHC 2712.
4   *R v Secretary of State for the Home Department, ex p Ejaz* [1994] QB 496; *R v Secretary of State for the Home Department, ex p Fayed* [1997] 1 All ER 228, [1997] INLR 138, CA (statutory exclusion of judicial review of decisions on grant or withholding of nationality under former legislation did not oust court's jurisdiction where decision was unlawful on administrative law grounds). See further G *and* M below.
5   See eg *R v Secretary of State for the Home Department, ex p Phansopkar* [1976] QB 606; *Cheng Poh v Public Prosecutor of Malaysia* [1980] AC 458, PC; *Engineers and Managers' Association v Advisory, Conciliation and Arbitration Service* [1980] 1 WLR 302; *R v Secretary of State for the Home Department, ex p Mersin (Deniz)* [2000] INLR 511; *R (on the application of Anufrijeva) v Secretary of State for the Home Department* [2003] UKHL 36, [2003] Imm AR 570, [2003] INLR 521.
6   *R (on the application of Bubaker) v Lord Chancellor* [2002] EWCA Civ 1107, [2002] Imm AR 552 (permission).
7   *R v Secretary of State for Social Security, ex p Joint Council for the Welfare of Immigrants* [1996] 4 All ER 385, [1997] 1 WLR 275.
8   *International Transport Roth GmbH v Secretary of State for the Home Department* [2002] EWCA Civ 158, [2002] 3 WLR 344.
9   *R (on the application of Salih) v Secretary of State for the Home Department* [2003] EWHC 2273 (Admin).
10 *R (on the application of Saadi) v Secretary of State for the Home Department* [2002] UKHL 41, [2002] 1 WLR 3131, [2002] INLR 523.

[11] R (on the application of the Refugee Legal Centre) v Secretary of State for the Home Department [2004] EWCA Civ 1481, [2004] All ER (D) 580 (Mar).

[12] R (on the application of Tamil Information Centre) v Secretary of State for the Home Department [2002] EWHC 2155 (Admin); European Roma Rights Centre v Immigration Officer at Prague Airport [2003] EWCA Civ 666, [2003] INLR 374, rvsd [2004] UKHL 55, [2005] 2 WLR 1.

[13] See R (on the application of the Refugee Legal Centre) v Secretary of State for the Home Department [2004] EWCA Civ 1481, [2004] All ER (D) 580 (Mar) (fn 11 above); Mapah v Secretary of State for the Home Department [2003] EWHC 306 (Admin), [2003] Imm AR 395.

[14] The restrictive rules on standing in claims under the Human Rights Act 1998 have not proved an obstacle to bringing public interest claims, as had been feared; see 8.26 above.

18.185 Judicial review has been used in a number of cases to explore the competing demands of consistency and fairness, sometimes articulated through the doctrine of legitimate expectation, against the principles of refugee determination,[1] in considering the effect of policies of the Secretary of State and of decisions in lead cases. In *Secretary of State v Zeqiri*,[2] the House of Lords held that ethnic Albanians from Kosovo whose claims had been deferred to await a lead decision had not thereby acquired a legitimate expectation that the outcome would be the same in their cases. The decision, and that of *Gashi and Kiche*,[3] prioritised the principle of individual and up to date refugee determination over issues of consistency and fairness. In *Joseph*,[4] a policy to grant four years' leave to remain exceptionally to Sierra Leonean asylum claimants in force at the date of the claimant's asylum claim was held not to give rise to a legitimate expectation where a flawed refusal was subsequently reconsidered after that policy had ended. But in *Rashid*,[5] the Administrative Court held that the claims of consistency and fairness trumped those of up to date refugee determination, where an unwarranted failure to adhere to the Secretary of State's policy on returns to the Kurdish Autonomous Zone in Iraq gave rise to inequality of treatment and outcome (because by the time the existence of the policy was made known to the appellant, and the claim reconsidered, the war in Iraq had overtaken it).[6] It is not easy to reconcile the authorities, but in *Rashid*, following consideration of all the case law, Davies J held that in any case involving an allegation of a wrongful breach of a policy, it was necessary to ask two questions: (i) do the terms of the policy admit of exceptions and room for departure, or is it universally applicable? and (ii) why has it not been applied in the particular case?[7] In order to found a legitimate expectation in cases not involving policy, a clear and unambiguous assurance given by a person empowered to take the relevant decision has been held necessary.[8]

[1] In particular, the principles of individual determination and of determination of risk at the date of the hearing rather than at the date of the original decision: see chapter 12 above.

[2] [2002] UKHL 3, [2002] Imm AR 296.

[3] R (on the application of Gashi) v Secretary of State for the Home Department [2001] EWCA Civ 1850, [2002] Imm AR 351 (refusal of leave to appeal from [2002] Imm AR 82, QBD).

[4] R (on the application of Joseph) v Secretary of State for the Home Department [2002] EWHC 758 (Admin). In R v Department of Education and Employment, ex p Begbie [2000] 1 WLR 1115, Laws LJ held that changes of policy fuelled by broad conceptions of the public interest could readily be accepted as taking precedence over the interests of groups who enjoyed expectations generated by an earlier policy, while Sedley LJ observed

that where government had made it known how it intended to exercise powers which affected the public at large, it may be held to its word, irrespective of whether a particular claimant had relied specifically on it.

5 *R (on the application of Rashid) v Secretary of State for the Home Department* [2004] EWHC 2465 (Admin).

6 In this case, the Secretary of State was seeking to rely on his own wrong, leaving the claimant without any proper redress. See also *R (on the application of Bibi) v Newham London Borough Council* [2003] 1 WLR 237, where Schiemann LJ approved a passage from Craig's *Administrative Law* which stated that 'consistency of treatment and equality are ... values [which] should be protected'.

7 He observed that in most cases, either the policy would admit of exceptions, or there will be a sufficient justification for failure to adhere to it in the particular case. In the case before him, there was neither, and he found 'moral detriment' (following *Bibi* above).

8 See *R v Secretary of State for the Home Department, ex p Mapere* [2001] Imm AR 89, [2001] INLR 159; *R (on the application of Hashmi) v Secretary of State for the Home Department* [2002] EWCA Civ 728, [2002] All ER (D) 48 (May); see also *Bibi* (fn 6 above), where the court asked (i) has the public authority committed itself, by practice or promise; (ii) is it acting or proposing to act unlawfully in relation to that commitment; (iii) what should the court do?

Statutory appeals, reconsideration and judicial review

18.186 Until 2003, judicial review was available to challenge a refusal of permission to appeal by the Immigration Appeal Tribunal (the second-instance appellate body now abolished by the 2004 Act).[1] The Nationality, Immigration and Asylum Act 2002 sought to replace judicial review with statutory review,[2] a review on the papers alone which has now been succeeded by the very similar reconsideration procedure in the 2004 amendments to the Act.[3] While judicial review of Tribunal decisions cannot be abolished by statute, the Court of Appeal held in *G and M*[4] that statutory review provides adequate and proportionate protection of the rights of asylum claimants, so that a court may decline to hear an application for judicial review of issues which had been or could be the subject of a statutory review. The court justified any less favourable legal procedures for immigrants and asylum-seekers on the curious basis that they had no vested right to enter or remain – perhaps an echo of the archaic definition in Article 6 ECHR of 'civil rights and obligations', which also excludes immigration status and asylum.[5] We hope that the House of Lords will reverse this judgment, and ensure that non-nationals are not consigned to a lower level of judicial protection, just as their Lordships have outlawed discrimination against non-nationals in the matter of detention.[6] For now, judicial review following a 'final' decision to refuse reconsideration is effectively ruled out,[7] and the only Tribunal decisions which may uncontroversially be challenged by way of judicial review are likely to be ancillary, procedural and preliminary decisions,[8] including a decision that no valid appeal has been lodged, refusal to extend time for appealing, and refusal or grant of bail.

1 In addition, in *Macharia v Immigration Appeal Tribunal* [2000] INLR 156 at 165, Sedley LJ expressed the view that the Administrative Court was the natural forum for questions of natural justice arising from tribunal proceedings, so that allegations of procedural impropriety or unfairness in any Tribunal hearing should be the subject of an application for judicial review of the Tribunal's final determination, rather than statutory appeal. For the convergence of jurisdiction on these issues see *E v Secretary of State for the Home Department, R v Secretary of State for the Home Department* [2004] EWCA Civ 49, [2004] INLR 264; 18.166 above.

2   Nationality, Immigration and Asylum Act 2002, s 101(2), in force from 1 April 2003 (SI 2003/754 and repealed from 4 April 2005.
3   Nationality, Immigration and Asylum Act 2002, s 103A, inserted by Asylum and Immigration (Treatment of Claimants, etc) Act 2004, s 26(6); see 18.167 above.
4   *R (on the application of G) v Immigration Appeal Tribunal, R (on the application of M) v Immigration Appeal Tribunal* [2004] EWCA Civ 1731, [2005] 2 All ER 165.
5   See *Maaouia v France* (2001) 33 EHRR 42 at 8.72 above.
6   In *A v Secretary of State for the Home Department* [2004] UKHL 56, [2005] 2 WLR 87.
7   Ie by an Administrative Court judge on the papers, on renewal of the application from a refusal by an immigration judge: see 18.169 above.
8   However it would be extremely rare for a procedural decision to be challenged in the course of ongoing proceedings (eg a refusal to adjourn); the normal course would be to wait until the determination and then use the statutory scheme of reconsideration or appeal to challenge the decision on the appeal on the basis that it was flawed by the procedural failure or error.

18.187 As we have indicated above, the scope of the appellate courts' review of Tribunal decisions has been held to be co-extensive with that of the Administrative Court on judicial review.[1] The issue of whether a challenge may be pursued by way of appeal or review now depends entirely on the availability of a statutory remedy. If such a remedy exists, it must be used. If not, the remedy, if any, lies in judicial review. So for example, a Tribunal's refusal to transfer a fast track appellant to the normal appeal track may ground a statutory reconsideration application if the appellant can show that the refusal prejudiced his or her substantive appeal under the fast track, so judicial review of the decision of the Tribunal would not lie. But the Secretary of State's refusal to transfer the person out of the fast track at the refugee determination stage could ground judicial review proceedings, since no statutory remedy exists except an appeal on asylum grounds, which, as the Court of Appeal recognised in *Refugee Legal Centre*, could be irrevocably flawed from the outset by the unfairness of the circumstances of the initial interview.[2] Where a statutory right of appeal exists against an immigration decision, judicial review cannot be used instead merely because the right can only be exercised out-of-country or is otherwise less convenient,[3] but where the appeal right is defective, eg a decision that a human rights or asylum claim is clearly unfounded, so that an appeal does not suspend removal to a country alleged by the claimant to be unsafe), judicial review is available.[4] We list below the main categories of decisions where judicial review is likely to be the appropriate challenge:

(1)   decisions of the Tribunal which are not 'decisions on the appeal' and are not subsumed in that decision, eg a ruling on a preliminary issue[5] such as timeliness, or a refusal to extend time;
(2)   decisions of the Tribunal on issues such as whether an appeal has been withdrawn or abandoned;[5]
(3)   decisions of the Secretary of State within the one-stop system that a claim is repetitive or should have been made earlier, with the result that no appeal lies, or an appeal in relation to that claim is to be treated as finally determined;[6]
(4)   decisions of the Secretary of State that an asylum or human rights claim is clearly unfounded;[7]
(5)   other decisions of the Secretary of State which give rise to no appeal rights, such as refusal to grant a work permit, imposition of conditions

on the grant of leave, or (where the basis of challenge does not engage human rights and so there is no right of appeal) refusal of leave to enter of a visitor who is not a family visitor;[8]

(6) decisions of the Secretary of State to detain, or of the Tribunal to refuse bail. But the appropriate course is *habeas corpus* where it is alleged that the detention is unlawful.[9]

[1] See 18.166 above.
[2] *R (on the application of the Refugee Legal Centre) v Secretary of State for the Home Department* [2004] EWCA Civ 1481, [2004] All ER (D) 580 (Mar); see 18.81 above.
[3] *R v Secretary of State for the Home Department, ex p Swati* [1986] 1 All ER 717, [1986] Imm AR 88, *Rehman v Secretary of State for the Home Department* [1987] Imm AR 602, CA; *R v Secretary of State for the Home Department, ex p Ozkurtulus* [1986] Imm AR 80, QBD; *R v Secretary of State for the Home Department, ex p Fernando* [1987] Imm AR 377, QBD; *R (on the application of Sivasubramaniam) v Wandworth County Court* [2002] EWCA Civ 1738, [2003] 2 All ER 160 (perm). But the court held judicial review appropriate to quash a decision to deport a claimant, despite the availability of a statutory appeal, where the decision was reached improperly, without regard to the determination by the Tribunal that the claimant was a refugee, the high threshold required to establish fraud and the absence of cogent evidence of fraud in *R (on the application of Saribal) v Secretary of State for the Home Department* [2002] EWHC 1542 (Admin), [2002] INLR 596.
[4] *IR v Secretary of State for the Home Department, ex p Canbolat* [1997] Imm AR 442, CA; *R (on the application of L) v Secretary of State for the Home Department* [2003] EWCA Civ 25, [2003] Imm AR 330, [2003] INLR 224.
[4] See 18.167 and 18.180 above.
[5] See 18.104–106 above.
[6] By reference to the immigration rules, HC 395, para 353 (inserted by HC 1112), and Nationality, Immigration and Asylum Act 2002, s 96 as amended by Asylum and Immigration (Treatment of Claimants, etc) Act 2004, s 30 (from 1 October 2004).
[7] By reference to Nationality, Immigration and Asylum Act 2002, s 94 as amended by Asylum and Immigration (Treatment of Claimants, etc) Act 2004, s 27.
[8] See 18.14 and 18.21 above.
[9] It may be an abuse of process to bring two separate proceedings (ie judicial review and *habeas corpus*) directed at the same issue: *R v Secretary of State for the Home Department, ex p Sheikh* [2001] INLR 98, CA.

Procedure

18.188 An application for judicial review must be made promptly[1] and in any event within three months of the decision complained of.[2] The time limit cannot be artificially extended by making further representations which contain no new material in order to generate a fresh formal decision; time starts to run at the date of the operative decision.[3] On the other hand, Lord Woolf said in *Ahmad and Simba*[4] that in the case of asylum claimants the court would normally be circumspect about being too rigorous in relation to delay, appreciating that to refuse an application solely on the ground of delay may have very grave consequences. This would apply equally to human rights claims. A late applicant for judicial review cannot rely on matters that have occurred during the period of delay, however.[5] The Civil Procedure Rules now require all applications for permission to be considered on the papers initially.[6] A pre-action protocol should normally be complied with, involving a letter of claim to a proposed defendant, and reasons must be given for failure to comply.[7] A copy of the claim form and supporting documents must be served on the defendant,[8] who must be given an opportunity to respond, by filing an acknowledgement of service, before permission is granted.[9] In urgent cases, time limits may be abridged and in cases of exceptional urgency, interim relief may be granted, on telephone application if necessary, pending lodging of the acknowledgment and sometimes on an undertaking to lodge the application.[10] The defendant may not apply to be set aside permission once granted.[11] Permission may be limited to one or more of the grounds, and if it is so limited, the claimant should not seek to re-open the refusal of permission on those grounds at the substantive hearing.[12] Refusal of permission may be appealed to the Court of Appeal, and if that court gives permission for the application but dismisses the appeal, to the House of Lords.[13]

[1] Civil Procedure Rules (CPR) r 54.5, a requirement which was held proportionate and lawful, and not restrictive of rights of access to a court in *Lam v United Kingdom* (Appn 41671/98), ECtHR. See also *R (on the application of Burkett) v Hammersmith London Borough Council* [2002] 1 WLR 1593. In *R (on the application of Agnello) v Hounslow LBC* [2003] EWHC 3112 (Admin) the court held that a claim brought within the three month time limit benefitted from a rebuttable presumption that it was brought promptly, in the absence of evidence of prejudice to the defendant or a third party. However in *R v Secretary of State for the Home Department, ex p Ondiek* (CO 4/2000) (25 February 2000, unreported), QBD, Owen J discharged an injunction preventing the applicant's removal when he failed to seek judicial review promptly of the Tribunal's decision that his appeal was out of time but had let a month go by, despite previous proceedings being compromised on the basis that he would not be removed while the appeal was pending. The applicant had a history of delays in making applications.

[2] CPR r 54.5. A five-year delay in challenging a decision to treat the claimant as an illegal entrant was held fatal to the application in *R v Secretary of State for the Home Department, ex p Ullah* [2002] Imm AR 62 (perm). Once permission has been granted without any objection based on delay, it is too late for the respondent to seek to argue on the substantive hearing that the application should not be allowed to proceed, although delay may be relevant to the issue of relief: *R v Criminal Injuries Compensation Board, ex p A* [1999] 2 AC 330; [1999] 2 WLR 974, HL.

[3] *R v Secretary of State for the Home Department, ex p Foster* (13 October 1998, unreported), QBD.

[4] *Ahmad and Simba v Secretary of State for the Home Department* [1999] Imm AR 356, CA.

[5] *Almad and Simba* above.

[6] CPR r 54.12. If permission is refused, or limited to certain grounds only, the application may be renewed orally, or the judge may adjourn the permission hearing to an oral hearing: r 54.12(3). Neither the defendant nor any interested party need attend a permission hearing unless directed to by the judge, and in the absence of such a direction the court will not generally make a costs order against the claimant: Practice Direction 54, 8.5–8.6.

[7] The protocol is inappropriate where the defendant does not have the legal power to change the decision being challenged, eg decisions issued by a court or tribunal, nor is it appropriate in urgent cases, eg where directions have been set, or are in force, for the claimant's removal from the UK, or where there is an urgent need for an interim order to compel a public body to act where it has unlawfully refused to do so (eg the refusal of NASS to provide support or accommodation to an asylum claimant): see 'Pre-Action Protocol for Judicial Review', on DCA website.

[8] CPR r 54.7–9. Any interested party should also be served; if the defendant is the Tribunal, the Secretary of State should always be served as an interested party.

[9] *R (on the application of Webb) v Bristol City Council* [2001] EWHC 696 (Admin). Where a claimant was on his fourth application seeking to judicially review his proposed removal, it was appropriate to direct an urgent oral hearing of the permission application rather than adopting the usual, longer procedure: *Dahmani v Secretary of State for the Home Department* [2003] EWHC 882, [2003] Imm AR 479.

[10] *R (on the application of Webb) v Bristol City Council* above. The claim form now includes a section to be completed if urgent consideration of the application is required.

[11] CPR r 54.13.

12 The right course is to appeal to the Court of Appeal against refusal of permission on the rejected grounds: *R (on the application of Opoku) v Principal of Southwark College* [2002] EWHC 2092 (Admin), [2003] 1 WLR 234.
13 *R (on the application of Burkett) v Hammersmith and Fulham LBC* [2002] UKHL 23, [2002] 1 WLR 1593.

18.189 When, following the issue of proceedings, the Secretary of State withdraws the decision under review, or other events supervene, should the court continue to hear the application? In *Canbolat*[1] and in *Abdi and Dahir*[2] the Court of Appeal heard the applications although in the former case there was no longer any question of the applicant's removal and in the latter, one of the persons who was the object of the application had disappeared, because of the general importance of the issues and the number of other cases affected by the legal point at issue. The principles are set out in *Salem*,[3] and apply equally to statutory reconsideration, appeals to the Court of Appeal and to judicial review applications. Whether judicial review of a refusal of leave to enter as a visitor should be pursued after the applicant has returned home and the Home Office has undertaken to decide any further application on its merits has been the subject of conflicting decisions,[4] but in *Zhou* the Court of Appeal allowed an application by a student to proceed although it had become academic in that he had been able through issue of the proceedings to remain beyond the period for which he had been granted leave to enter, on the basis that success would strengthen his position in applying for further leave to remain to complete the studies.[5] In *Alabi* the Court of Appeal dealt with an agreement to reconsider the decision under review. Simon Brown LJ held that it would be inappropriate in all but the rarest of cases involving a point of general importance and wide application to proceed to a substantive hearing while the decision-maker is undertaking to consider a decision afresh. Generally, such an agreement would exhaust whatever rights an applicant had in the challenge and bring an end to proceedings. But, he continued, where a *Wednesbury* irrationality challenge may lie against any future adverse decision however it comes to be reasoned, the right course is to put the judicial review on hold, with no further evidence and no steps to bring to substantive hearing, and a fresh decision should be reached as soon as possible, so that the future course of proceedings can be reviewed. If the parties cannot agree that the applicant may use the leave already obtained to advance a challenge the respondent thinks impossible, the respondent should apply to set aside the leave and strike out the proceedings.[6] Following that decision, it has been held that where the decision-maker agrees to reconsider during judicial review proceedings, he or she should make it clear what material has been considered and the reasons for rejecting it.[7]

1 *IR v Secretary of State for the Home Department, ex p Canbolat* [1997] Imm AR 442, CA
2 *Secretary of State for the Home Department v Abdi and Dahir* [1995] Imm AR 570, CA.
3 *R v Secretary of State, ex p Salem* [1999] 1 AC 450, HL. In *R (on the application of Yaseetharan) v Secretary of State for the Home Department and CIO Stansted* [2002] EWHC 1467 (Admin), [2003] Imm AR 62, a change of policy midway through the proceedings to allow legal representatives to be present for screening interviews at Stansted meant that pursuit of a challenge to the previous policy, which was now academic, was not justified.
4 In *R v Secretary of State for the Home Department, ex p Kekana* [1998] Imm AR 136, the judge refused to hear the application. In the earlier case of *R v Immigration Officer, ex p Honegan* (13 March 1995), QBD, the application was heard, the refusal of leave to

enter quashed and subsequently, damages of £17,000 awarded for the detention arising from the unlawful refusal. We suggest that wherever a decision has potentially prejudicial implications for future applications, a challenge cannot reasonably be pre-emptively rejected as academic.

5 *R (on the application of Zhou) v Secretary of State for the Home Department* [2003] EWCA Civ 51, [2003] INLR 211, para 3.

6 *R v Secretary of State for the Home Department, ex p Alabi* [1997] INLR 124, CA. Following the revision of the Civil Procedure Rules, the course of applying to set aside the permission is no longer appropriate, but the defendant could return to court to seek to have the claim dismissed.

7 *R v FCO, ex p Nwanya* (CO 1772/99) (17 February 2000, unreported), QBD.

Evidence

18.190 In removal cases the High Court can investigate the truth of an allegation that entry was obtained by deception or was otherwise illegal, because illegal entry is a precedent fact to the exercise of the power to remove[1] (although no longer to the exercise of the power to detain).[2] This has already been dealt with in chapter 16. Where the claimant seeks a declaration that he or she is a British citizen, the court will investigate that issue in its precedent fact jurisdiction.[3] In other cases the court's role is not a fact-finding one, although evidence will be carefully scrutinised in asylum and human rights cases.[4] Where the Secretary of State must establish the existence of precedent facts, the court will hear oral evidence and cross-examination if necessary,[5] but hearsay evidence is admissible.[6] So interviews in relation to variation of leave, for entry clearance and at the port may be admitted, as may confidential medical records which resolve the issue of whether someone is an impostor.[7] Discovery should be unnecessary in an application for judicial review, since it is the obligation of the respondent public body in its evidence to make frank disclosure to the court of the decision-making process. The absence of a requirement to give reasons cannot be prayed in aid to avoid discovery or the usual 'cards on the table' approach.[8]

1 *Khawaja v Secretary of State for the Home Department* [1984] AC 74, [1983] 1 All ER 765, HL.

2 Immigration Act 1971, Sch 2, para 16(2), as amended by Immigration and Asylum Act 1999, s 140.

3 *R (on the application of Harrison) v Secretary of State for the Home Department* [2003] EWCA Civ 432, [2003] INLR 284.

4 *Bugdaycay v Secretary of State for the Home Department* [1987] AC 514; *IR v Secretary of State for the Home Department, ex p Turgot* [2000] Imm AR 306, [2000] INLR 292, CA.

5 *Khawaja v Secretary of State for the Home Department* [1984] AC 74; *R v Secretary of State for the Home Department, ex p Yasmeen* (CO 2930/99) (29 September 1999, unreported), QBD. The reviewing court has the power to direct cross-examination where it is necessary to do justice, although the CPR gives no express power: *R (on the application of G) v London Borough of Ealing* [2002] EWHC 230 (Admin), [2002] ACD 298; *R (on the application of Wilkinson) v Broadmoor Hospital Authority* [2001] EWCA Civ 1345, [2002] 1 WLR 419. But the case of *Wilkinson* is not a charter for routine applications for oral evidence in human rights cases: *R (on the application of N) v M* [2002] EWCA Civ 1789, [2003] 1 WLR 562.

6 *R v Secretary of State for the Home Department, ex p Yilmaz* [1993] Imm AR 359; *R v Secretary of State for the Home Department, ex p Rahman* [1997] Imm AR 197, CA.

7 *R v Secretary of State for the Home Department, ex p Taj* (CO 1084/99) (20 October 1999, unreported), QBD. This clearly engages ECHR, Art 8 privacy issues, see *Z v Finland* (1997) 25 EHRR 371, and there would have to be a balancing exercise to see whether the interference was necessary in the circumstances.

8 *R v Secretary of State for the Home Department, ex p Fayed* [1997] INLR 138, CA. But
   see *R v Secretary of State for the Home Department, ex p BH* [1990] COD 445, where
   Roch J ordered discovery of documents relevant to an operation at Istanbul airport in
   which the claimant was prevented from boarding a flight to London, where the judge was
   satisfied that the defendant's affidavits did not disclose the whole story.

18.191 In *R v Secretary of State for the Home Department, ex p Turgot*,[1] a
case decided before the coming into force of the Human Rights Act 1998, the
Court of Appeal examined the standard of review and the correct approach to
the evidence required in a human rights case. It held that on an ECHR,
Article 3 challenge the court had an obligation to subject the Secretary of
State's decision to rigorous examination by reference to the underlying factual
material on which the decision was based. Although the court's role was still
supervisory, it would pay no special deference to the Secretary of State's
conclusions on the facts, since the right involved is absolute and fundamental.
The court was hardly less well placed than the decision-maker to evaluate the
risk once the relevant material was before it, and the discretionary area of
judgment of the Secretary of State was decidedly narrow. Since the material
date for the assessment of risk is the time of the court's consideration of the
case (following *Chahal*),[2] the Secretary of State had to reconsider the decision
repeatedly, and the High Court would not shut out evidence, might order
disclosure of evidence, and was not limited to the evidence before the
Secretary of State at the time of the decision.[3] And in *Daly*[4] the House of
Lords affirmed that the *Wednesbury* test of irrationality has no place in cases
engaging fundamental human rights, a view reaffirmed in the Court of Appeal
in *Huang*.[5]

1 [2000] Imm AR 306, CA.
2 *Chahal v United Kingdom* (1996) 23 EHRR 413, para 97: 'the notion of an effective
   remedy under Article 13 requires independent scrutiny of the claim that there exist
   substantial grounds for fearing a real risk of treatment contrary to Article 3.'
3 In *E v Secretary of State for the Home Department, R v Secretary of State for the Home
   Department* [2004] EWCA Civ 49, [2004] 2 WLR 1351 the Court of Appeal contrasted
   the Secretary of State's position, as someone with a continuing responsibility up to the
   point of removal, with that of the Tribunal, whose task was to make one discrete decision
   on the evidence before it at the time, in order to explain why on an application for judicial
   review of a decision to remove, post-decision material could continue to be submitted to
   the Secretary of State and considered by the Court.
4 *R (on the application of Daly) v Secretary of State for the Home Department* [2001]
   UKHL 26, [2001] 2 WLR 1622.
5 *Huang v Secretary of State for the Home Department* [2005] EWCA Civ 105, (2005) 149
   Sol Jo LB 297.

Relief

18.192 The most common order sought in the immigration context in judicial
review is a quashing order to quash a decision or removal directions, but
orders may be sought requiring the performance of a duty (such as an order to
provide NASS support to a claimant), or restraining the defendant from doing
something (such as an injunction preventing the defendant from removing the
claimant).[1] Interim relief may be sought in urgent cases, including an order to
return someone to the jurisdiction who has been wrongfully removed from it.[2]
A declaration may be sought (for example, that the claimant is a British

citizen[3] or even a refugee.[4] But it is not the function of the court to make orders as to how the Secretary of State should run his department, and the court refused to make a declaration about the general position regarding delays in granting asylum in *Arbab*.[5] The court has jurisdiction to grant relief in the form of an advisory declaration, but will not do so save for demonstrably good reasons.[6] Damages are also available in judicial review proceedings, if they have been specifically sought on the claim form.[7]

1   See CPR r 54.2.
2   The order is expressed in terms such as 'the Secretary of State to take all reasonable steps' or 'to use his best endeavours' to secure the return of the claimant to the UK. In *R (on the application of Changuizi) v Secretary of State for the Home Department* [2002] EWHC 2569, [2003] Imm AR 355, an undertaking not to remove the claimant from the jurisdiction was breached, and the judge concluded that the claimant should be returned. An application by the Secretary of State to be relieved of the undertaking to return the claimant pending an appeal to the Court of Appeal was rejected at [2003] EWCA Civ 165. See also *R v Secretary of State for the Home Department, ex p Shanmuganathan* (11 March 1999, unreported), CA.
3   CPR r 54.2; *R (on the application of Harrison) v Secretary of State for the Home Department* [2003] EWCA Civ 432, [2003] INLR 284.
4   *R (on the application of Rashid) v Secretary of State for the Home Department* [2004] EWHC 2465 (Admin), (2004) Times, 17 November.
5   *R (on the application of Arbab) v Secretary of State for the Home Department* [2002] EWHC 1249 (Admin), [2002] Imm AR 536, following *R v Secretary of State for the Home Department, ex p Fire Brigades Union* [1995] 2 WLR 464; see also *R v Secretary of State for the Home Department, Secretary of State for Social Security, ex p Paulo* [2001] Imm AR 645, to similar effect.
6   *R (on the application of Campaign for Nuclear Disarmament) v Prime Minister* [2002] EWHC 27177 (Admin), para 47.
7   CPR r 54.3; for damages in human rights cases see 8.28 above. In cases involving judicial review of detention, a prayer for damages in the claim form will prevent the application from being dismissed as academic if the claimant is released: see e g *AFP Nadarajah* [2002] EWHC 748 (Admin). But the Court of Appeal held in *Anufrijeva v Southwark London Borough Council* [2003] EWCA Civ 1406, [2004] 1 All ER 833 that permission to apply for judicial review would be granted in respect of damages for maladministration affecting human rights only if persuaded that a complaint procedure, e g through the Ombudsman, was not more appropriate.

18.193 Costs normally follow the event on a judicial review which goes to full hearing. In cases where a non-governmental organisation brings a claim in the public interest, pre-emptive or protective costs orders may be sought, limiting or even preventing a costs order against the claimant in the event of dismissal of the claim.[1] Save in exceptional circumstances, the costs of the defendant or interested party's attendance at an oral permission hearing should not be awarded against an unsuccessful claimant.[2] The most common problem is where the Secretary of State concedes after the grant of permission or, as frequently happens, before the permission hearing, once a claim has been lodged after a number of letters before action. The court has held that if the concession was made for administrative convenience, costs should not be awarded, while if the decision under challenge was withdrawn in recognition of the inevitability of final defeat, a costs order would be appropriate.[3] The court will not be persuaded that the concession represented a bowing to the inevitable unless the defendant admits it or there is clear and unequivocal evidence that this is the case; otherwise no order for costs will be made. The claimant's representatives have a duty to the court not to pursue hopeless applications and may be penalised in wasted costs orders if they ignore this duty.[4] A similar duty rests on the Secretary of State's representative, who is likewise concerned with the spending of public funds, not to continue to defend indefensible decisions.

1 In *R (on the application of Campaign for Nuclear Disarmament) v Prime Minister* [2002] EWHC 2712 (Admin), (2002) Times, 27 December, the court made a pre-emptive costs order capping the claimant's liability; in the light of the genuine public importance of the issues, it was right to give CND the certainty required to pursue them. In *R (on the application of the Refugee Legal Centre) v Secretary of State for the Home Department* [2004] EWCA Civ 1481, the Court of Appeal made a protective costs order protecting the claimant from paying the defendant's costs on appeal from dismissal of its judicial review claim.

2 CPR PD 54 (JR) 8.6; *R (on the application of Mount Cook Land Ltd) v Westminster City Council* [2003] EWCA Civ 1346, (2003) 43 EG 137, where the court held there was no good reason not to follow the guidance in the Practice Direction in the absence of exceptional circumstances, such as a hopeless case or abuse of judicial review for collateral ends, although a successful defendant at the permission stage who has complied with the pre-action protocol and has filed an acknowledgement of service should generally recover the costs of doing so from the claimant, approving *R (on the application of Leach) v Commissioner for Local Administration* [2001] EWHC 455 (Admin), [2001] 4 PRL 28.

3 *R v Kensington and Chelsea, ex p Ghebregiorgis* [1994] COD 502; *R v Liverpool City Council, ex p Newman* [1993] COD 65.

4 *R v Secretary of State for the Home Department, ex p Yeboah (Samuel)* (CO 3166/99) (8 September 1999, unreported), QBD.

Appendix 1

LEGISLATION AND MATERIALS

CONTENTS

Contents

UK IMMIGRATION STATUTES

IMMIGRATION ACT 1971

1971 CHAPTER 77

An Act to amend and replace the present immigration laws, to make certain related changes in the citizenship law and enable help to be given to those wishing to return abroad, and for purposes connected therewith

[28th October 1971]

BE IT ENACTED by the Queen's most Excellent Majesty, by and with the advice and consent of the Lords Spiritual and Temporal, and Commons, in this present Parliament assembled, and by the authority of the same, as follows:–

PART I
REGULATION OF ENTRY INTO AND STAY IN UNITED KINGDOM

1   General principles

(1)   All those who are in this Act expressed to have the right of abode in the United Kingdom shall be free to live in, and to come and go into and from, the United Kingdom without let or hindrance except such as may be required under and in accordance with this Act to enable their right to be established or as may be otherwise lawfully imposed on any person.

(2)   Those not having that right may live, work and settle in the United Kingdom by permission and subject to such regulation and control of their entry into, stay in and departure from the United Kingdom as is imposed by this Act; and indefinite leave to enter or remain in the United Kingdom shall, by virtue of this provision be treated as having been given under this Act to those in the United Kingdom at its coming into force, if they are then settled there (and not exempt under this Act from the provisions relating to leave to enter or remain).

(3)   Arrival in and departure from the United Kingdom on a local journey from or to any of the Islands (that is to say, the Channel Islands and Isle of Man) or the Republic of Ireland shall not be subject to control under this Act, nor shall a person require leave to enter the United Kingdom on so arriving, except in so far as any of those places is for any purpose excluded from this subsection under the powers conferred by this Act; and in this Act the United Kingdom and those places, or such of them as are not so excluded, are collectively referred to as "the common travel area".

(4)   The rules laid down by the Secretary of State as to the practice to be followed in the administration of this Act for regulating the entry into and stay in the United Kingdom of persons not having the right of abode shall include provision for admitting (in such cases and subject to such restrictions as may be provided by the rules, and subject or not to conditions as to length of stay or otherwise) persons coming for the purpose of taking employment, or for purposes of study, or as visitors, or as dependants of persons lawfully in or entering the United Kingdom.

(5)   ...

Appointment
Appointment: 1 January 1973: see SI 1972/1514, art 2.

Amendment
Sub-s (5): repealed by the Immigration Act 1988, s 1.

2   Statement of right of abode in United Kingdom

(1)   A person is under this Act to have the right of abode in the United Kingdom if—

(a)   he is a citizen of the United Kingdom and Colonies who has that citizenship by his birth, adoption, naturalisation or (except as mentioned below) registration in the United Kingdom or in any of the Islands; or

(b)   he is a citizen of the United Kingdom and Colonies born to or legally adopted by a parent who had that citizenship at the time of the birth or adoption, and the parent either—

    (i)   then had that citizenship by his birth, adoption, naturalisation or (except as mentioned below) registration in the United Kingdom or in any of the Islands; or

    (ii)   had been born to or legally adopted by a parent who at the time of that birth or adoption so had it; or

(c)   he is a citizen of the United Kingdom and Colonies who has at any time been settled in the United Kingdom and Islands and had at that time (and while such a citizen) been ordinarily resident there for the last five years or more; or

(d)   he is a Commonwealth citizen born to or legally adopted by a parent who at the time of the birth or adoption had citizenship of the United Kingdom and Colonies by his birth in the United Kingdom or in any of the Islands.

(2)   A woman is under this Act also to have the right of abode in the United Kingdom if she is a Commonwealth citizen and either—

(a)   is the wife of any such citizen of the United Kingdom and Colonies as is mentioned in subsection (1)(a), (b) or (c) above or any such Commonwealth citizen as is mentioned in subsection (1)(d); or

(b)   has at any time been the wife—

    (i)   of a person then being such a citizen of the United Kingdom and Colonies or Commonwealth citizen; or

    (ii)   of a British subject who but for his death would on the date of commencement of the British Nationality Act 1948 have been such a citizen of the United Kingdom and Colonies as is mentioned in subsection (1)(a) or (b);

but in subsection (1)(a) and (b) above references to registration as a citizen of the United Kingdom and Colonies shall not, in the case of a woman, include registration after the passing of this Act under or by virtue of section 6(2) (wives) of the British Nationality Act 1948 unless she is so registered by virtue of her marriage to a citizen of the United Kingdom and Colonies before the passing of this Act.

(3)   In relation to the parent of a child born after the parent's death, references in subsection (1) above to the time of the child's birth shall be replaced by references to the time of the parent's death; and for purposes of that subsection—

(a)   "parent" includes the mother of an illegitimate child; and

(b)   references to birth in the United Kingdom shall include birth on a ship or aircraft registered in the United Kingdom, or on an unregistered ship or aircraft of the Government of the United Kingdom, and similarly with references to birth in any of the Islands; and

(c)   references to citizenship of the United Kingdom and Colonies shall, in relation to a time before the year 1949, be construed as references to British nationality and, in relation to British nationality and to a time before the 31st March 1922. "the United Kingdom" shall mean Great Britain and Ireland; and

(d)   subject to section 8(5) below, references to a person being settled in the United Kingdom and Islands are references to his being ordinarily resident there without being subject under the immigration laws to any restriction on the period for which he may remain.

(4) In subsection (1) above, any reference to registration in the United Kingdom shall extend also to registration under arrangements made by virtue of section 8(2) of the British Nationality Act 1948 (registration in independent Commonwealth country by United Kingdom High Commissioner), but, in the case of a registration by virtue of section 7 (children) of that Act, only if the registration was effected before the passing of this Act.

(5) The law with respect to registration as a citizen of the United Kingdom and Colonies shall be modified as provided by Schedule 1 to this Act.

(6) In the following provisions of this Act the word "patrial" is used of persons having the right of abode in the United Kingdom.

Note
This is the text of section 2 *before* it was amended by the British Nationality Act 1981. The post-BNA 1981 amended text is set out below.

[2   Statement of right of abode in United Kingdom]

[(1) A person is under this Act to have the right of abode in the United Kingdom if—
- (a) he is a British citizen; or
- (b) he is a Commonwealth citizen who—
    - (i) immediately before the commencement of the British Nationality Act 1981 was a Commonwealth citizen having the right of abode in the United Kingdom by virtue of section 2(1)(d) or section 2(2) of this Act as then in force; and
    - (ii) has not ceased to be a Commonwealth citizen in the meanwhile.

(2) In relation to Commonwealth citizens who have the right of abode in the United Kingdom by virtue of subsection (1)(b) above, this Act, except this section and [section 5(2)], shall apply as if they were British citizens; and in this Act (except as aforesaid) "British citizen" shall be construed accordingly.]

Note
This is the text of section 2 *after* it was amended by the British Nationality Act 1981. The pre-BNA 1981 amended text is set out above.

Amendment
Substituted by the British Nationality Act 1981, s 39(2).
Sub-s (2): words in square brackets substituted by the Immigration Act 1988, s 3(3).

3   General provisions for regulation and control

(1) Except as otherwise provided by or under this Act, where a person is not [a British citizen]—
- (a) he shall not enter the United Kingdom unless given leave to do so in accordance [the provisions of, or made under,] with this Act;
- (b) he may be given leave to enter the United Kingdom (or, when already there, leave to remain in the United Kingdom) either for a limited or for an indefinite period;
- [(c) if he is given limited leave to enter or remain in the United Kingdom, it may be given subject to all or any of the following conditions, namely—
    - (i) a condition restricting his employment or occupation in the United Kingdom;
    - (ii) a condition requiring him to maintain and accommodate himself, and any dependants of his, without recourse to public funds; and
    - (iii) a condition requiring him to register with the police.]

(2)   The Secretary of State shall from time to time (and as soon as may be) lay before Parliament statements of the rules, or of any changes in the rules, laid down by him as to the practice to be followed in the administration of this Act for regulating the entry into and stay in the United Kingdom of persons required by this Act to have leave to enter, including any rules as to the period for which leave is to be given and the conditions to be attached in different circumstances; and section 1(4) above shall not be taken to require uniform provision to be made by the rules as regards admission of persons for a purpose or in a capacity specified in section 1(4) (and in particular, for this as well as other purposes of this Act, account may be taken of citizenship or nationality).

If a statement laid before either House of Parliament under this subsection is disapproved by a resolution of that House passed within the period of forty days beginning with the date of laying (and exclusive of any period during which Parliament is dissolved or prorogued or during which both Houses are adjourned for more than four days), then the Secretary of State shall as soon as may be make such changes or further changes in the rules as appear to him to be required in the circumstances, so that the statement of those changes be laid before Parliament at latest by the end of the period of forty days beginning with the date of the resolution (but exclusive as aforesaid).

(3)   In the case of a limited leave to enter or remain in the United Kingdom,—

(a)   a person's leave may be varied, whether by restricting, enlarging or removing the limit on its duration, or by adding, varying or revoking conditions, but if the limit on its duration is removed, any conditions attached to the leave shall cease to apply; and

(b)   the limitation on and any conditions attached to a person's leave [(whether imposed originally or on a variation) shall], if not superseded, apply also to any subsequent leave he may obtain after an absence from the United Kingdom within the period limited for the duration of the earlier leave.

(4)   A person's leave to enter or remain in the United Kingdom shall lapse on his going to a country or territory outside the common travel area (whether or not he lands there), unless within the period for which he had leave he returns to the United Kingdom in circumstances in which he is not required to obtain leave to enter; but, if he does so return, his previous leave (and any limitation on it or conditions attached to it) shall continue to apply.

[(5)   A person who is not a British citizen is liable to deportation from the United Kingdom if—

(a)   the Secretary of State deems his deportation to be conducive to the public good; or

(b)   another person to whose family he belongs is or has been ordered to be deported.]

(6)   Without prejudice to the operation of subsection (5) above, a person who is not [a British citizen] shall also be liable to deportation from the United Kingdom if, after he has attained the age of seventeen, he is convicted of an offence for which he is punishable with imprisonment and on his conviction is recommended for deportation by a court empowered by this Act to do so.

(7)   Where it appears to Her Majesty proper so to do by reason of restrictions or conditions imposed on [British citizens, [British overseas territories citizens] or British Overseas citizens] when leaving or seeking to leave any country or the territory subject to the government of any country, Her Majesty may by Order in Council make provision for prohibiting persons who are nationals or citizens of that country and are not [British citizens] from embarking in the United Kingdom, or from doing so elsewhere than at a port of exit, or for imposing restrictions or conditions on them

when embarking or about to embark in the United Kingdom; and Her Majesty may also make provision by Order in Council to enable those who are not [British citizens] to be, in such cases as may be prescribed by the Order, prohibited in the interests of safety from so embarking on a ship or aircraft specified or indicated in the prohibition.

Any Order in Council under this subsection shall be subject to annulment in pursuance of a resolution of either House of Parliament.

(8) When any question arises under this Act whether or not a person is [a British citizen], or is entitled to any exemption under this Act, it shall lie on the person asserting it to prove that he is.

[(9) A person seeking to enter the United Kingdom and claiming to have the right of abode there shall prove that he has that right by means of either—

(a) a United Kingdom passport describing him as a British citizen or as a citizen of the United Kingdom and Colonies having the right of abode in the United Kingdom; or

(b) a certificate of entitlement ...]

Appointment
Appointment: 1 January 1973: see SI 1972/1514, art 2.

Amendment
Sub-s (1): words "a British citizen" in square brackets substituted by the British Nationality Act 1981, s 39(6), Sch 4, paras 2, 4.
Sub-s (1): in para (a) words "the provisions of, or made under," in square brackets inserted by the Immigration and Asylum Act 1999, s 169(1), Sch 14, paras 43, 44(1). Date in force: 14 February 2000: see SI 2000/168, art 2, Schedule.
Sub-s (1): para (c) substituted by the Asylum and Immigration Act 1996, s 12(1), Sch 2, para 1(1).
Sub-s (3): words in square brackets substituted by the Immigration Act 1988, s 10, Schedule, para 1.
Sub-s (5): substituted by the Immigration and Asylum Act 1999, s 169(1), Sch 14, paras 43, 44(2). Date in force: 2 October 2000: see SI 2000/2444, art 2, Sch 1.
Sub-s (6): words "a British citizen" in square brackets substituted by the British Nationality Act 1981, s 39(6), Sch 4, paras 2, 4.
Sub-s (7): words from "British citizens," to "British Overseas citizens" in square brackets and words "British citizens" in square brackets in both places they occur substituted by the British Nationality Act 1981, s 39(6), Sch 4, paras 2, 4.
Sub-s (7): words "British overseas territories citizens" in square brackets substituted by virtue of the British Overseas Territories Act 2002, s 2(3). Date in force: this amendment came into force on 26 February 2002 (date of Royal Assent of the British Overseas Territories Act 2002) in the absence of any specific commencement provision.
Sub-s (8): words "a British citizen" in square brackets substituted by the British Nationality Act 1981, s 39(6), Sch 4, paras 2, 4.
Sub-s (9): substituted for existing sub-ss (9), (9A) by the Immigration Act 1988, s 3(1).
Sub-s (9): in para (b) words omitted repealed by the Nationality, Immigration and Asylum Act 2002, ss 10(5)(a), 161, Sch 9. Date in force: 1 April 2003: see SI 2003/754, art 2(1), Sch 1.

Modification
Modified, in relation to its application to frontier controls between the United Kingdom, France and Belgium, by the Channel Tunnel (Miscellaneous Provisions) Order 1994, SI 1994/1405, art 7.
Modified, in its application to the Channel Tunnel, by the Channel Tunnel (International Arrangements) Order 1993, SI 1993/1813, art 7(1), Sch 4, para 1(2).

Subordinate Legislation
Immigration (Revocation of Employment Restrictions) Order 1972, SI 1972/1647 (made under sub-s (3)).
Immigration (Variation of Leave) Order 1976, SI 1976/1572 (made under sub-s (3)).
Immigration (Variation of Leave) (Amendment) Order 1989, SI 1989/1005 (made under sub-s (3)(a)).

Immigration (Variation of Leave) (Revocation) Order 1991, SI 1991/980 (made under sub-s (3)(a)).
Immigration (Variation of Leave) (No 2) Order 1991, SI 1991/1083 (made under sub-s (3)(a)).
Immigration (Variation of Leave) (Amendment) Order 1993, SI 1993/1657 (made under sub-s (3)(a)).
Immigration (Variation of Leave) (Amendment) Order 2000, SI 2000/2445 (made under sub-s (3)(a)).

[3A   Further provision as to leave to enter]

[(1)   The Secretary of State may by order make further provision with respect to the giving, refusing or varying of leave to enter the United Kingdom.

(2)   An order under subsection (1) may, in particular, provide for—

(a)   leave to be given or refused before the person concerned arrives in the United Kingdom;
(b)   the form or manner in which leave may be given, refused or varied;
(c)   the imposition of conditions;
(d)   a person's leave to enter not to lapse on his leaving the common travel area.

(3)   The Secretary of State may by order provide that, in such circumstances as may be prescribed—

(a)   an entry visa, or
(b)   such other form of entry clearance as may be prescribed,

is to have effect as leave to enter the United Kingdom.

(4)   An order under subsection (3) may, in particular—

(a)   provide for a clearance to have effect as leave to enter—
    (i)   on a prescribed number of occasions during the period for which the clearance has effect;
    (ii)   on an unlimited number of occasions during that period;
    (iii)   subject to prescribed conditions; and
(b)   provide for a clearance which has the effect referred to in paragraph (a)(i) or (ii) to be varied by the Secretary of State or an immigration officer so that it ceases to have that effect.

(5)   Only conditions of a kind that could be imposed on leave to enter given under section 3 may be prescribed.

(6)   In subsections (3), (4) and (5) "prescribed" means prescribed in an order made under subsection (3).

(7)   The Secretary of State may, in such circumstances as may be prescribed in an order made by him, give or refuse leave to enter the United Kingdom.

(8)   An order under subsection (7) may provide that, in such circumstances as may be prescribed by the order, paragraphs 2, 4, 6, 7, 8, 9 and 21 of Part I of Schedule 2 to this Act are to be read, in relation to the exercise by the Secretary of State of functions which he has as a result of the order, as if references to an immigration officer included references to the Secretary of State.

(9)   Subsection (8) is not to be read as affecting any power conferred by subsection (10).

(10)   An order under this section may—

(a)   contain such incidental, supplemental, consequential and transitional provision as the Secretary of State considers appropriate; and
(b)   make different provision for different cases.

(11)   This Act and any provision made under it has effect subject to any order made under this section.

(12)   An order under this section must be made by statutory instrument.

(13)   But no such order is to be made unless a draft of the order has been laid before Parliament and approved by a resolution of each House.]

Amendment
Inserted by the Immigration and Asylum Act 1999, s 1; for transitional provisions see Sch 15, para 1(1). Date in force: 14 February 2000: see SI 2000/168, art 2, Schedule.

Subordinate Legislation
Immigration (Leave to Enter and Remain) Order 2000, SI 2000/1161 (made under sub-ss (1)–(4), (6), (10)).
Immigration (Leave to Enter) Order 2001, SI 2001/2590 (made under sub-ss (1), (7), (8), (10)).
Immigration (Leave to Enter and Remain) (Amendment) Order 2004, SI 2004/475 (made under sub-ss (1), (3), (6), (10)).

[3B   Further provision as to leave to remain]

[(1)   The Secretary of State may by order make provision as to further provision with respect to the giving, refusing or varying of leave to remain in the United Kingdom.

(2)   An order under subsection (1) may, in particular, provide for—

    (a)   the form or manner in which leave may be given, refused or varied;
    (b)   the imposition of conditions;
    (c)   a person's leave to remain in the United Kingdom not to lapse on his leaving the common travel area.

(3)   An order under this section may—

    (a)   contain such incidental, supplemental, consequential and transitional provision as the Secretary of State considers appropriate; and
    (b)   make different provision for different cases.

(4)   This Act and any provision made under it has effect subject to any order made under this section.

(5)   An order under this section must be made by statutory instrument.

(6)   But no such order is to be made unless a draft of the order has been laid before Parliament and approved by a resolution of each House.]

Amendment
Inserted by the Immigration and Asylum Act 1999, s 2; for transitional provisions see Sch 15, para 1(2). Date in force: 14 February 2000: see SI 2000/168, art 2, Schedule.

Subordinate Legislation
Immigration (Leave to Enter and Remain) Order 2000, SI 2000/1161 (made under sub-ss (2)(a), (c), (3)(a)).

[3C   Continuation of leave pending variation decision]

[(1)   This section applies if—

    (a)   a person who has limited leave to enter or remain in the United Kingdom applies to the Secretary of State for variation of the leave,
    (b)   the application for variation is made before the leave expires, and
    (c)   the leave expires without the application for variation having been decided.

(2)   The leave is extended by virtue of this section during any period when—

   (a)   the application for variation is neither decided nor withdrawn,

   (b)   an appeal under section 82(1) of the Nationality, Asylum and Immigration Act 2002 could be brought against the decision on the application for variation (ignoring any possibility of an appeal out of time with permission), or

   (c)   an appeal under that section against that decision is pending (within the meaning of section 104 of that Act).

(3)   Leave extended by virtue of this section shall lapse if the applicant leaves the United Kingdom.

(4)   A person may not make an application for variation of his leave to enter or remain in the United Kingdom while that leave is extended by virtue of this section.

(5)   But subsection (4) does not prevent the variation of the application mentioned in subsection (1)(a).

(6)   In this section a reference to an application being decided is a reference to notice of the decision being given in accordance with regulations under section 105 of that Act (notice of immigration decision).]

Amendment
Substituted (for this section as inserted by the Immigration and Asylum Act 1999, s 3) by the Nationality, Immigration and Asylum Act 2002, s 118. Date in force: 1 April 2003: see SI 2003/754, art 2(1), Sch 1; for transitional provisions in relation to applications made before that date, in respect of which no decision has been made on or before that date, see art 3(2), Sch 2, para 2(2) thereto (as amended by SI 2003/1040, art 2).

4   Administration of control

(1)   The power under this Act to give or refuse leave to enter the United Kingdom shall be exercised by immigration officers, and the power to give leave to remain in the United Kingdom, or to vary any leave under section 3(3)(a) (whether as regards duration or conditions), shall be exercised by the Secretary of State; and, unless otherwise [allowed by or under] this Act, those powers should be exercised by notice in writing given to the person affected, except that the powers under section 3(3)(a) may be exercised generally in respect of any class of persons by order made by statutory instrument.

(2)   The provisions of Schedule 2 to this Act shall have effect with respect to—

   (a)   the appointment and powers of immigration officers and medical inspectors for purposes of this Act;

   (b)   the examination of persons arriving in or leaving the United Kingdom by ship or aircraft [...], and the special powers exercisable in the case of those who arrive as, or with a view to becoming, members of the crews of ships and aircraft; and

   (c)   the exercise by immigration officers of their powers in relation to entry into the United Kingdom, and the removal from the United Kingdom of persons refused leave to enter or entering or remaining unlawfully; and

   (d)   the detention of persons pending examination or pending removal from the United Kingdom;

and for other purposes supplementary to the foregoing provisions of this Act.

(3)   The Secretary of State may by regulations made by statutory instrument, which shall be subject to annulment in pursuance of a resolution of either House of Parliament, make provision as to the effect of a condition under this Act requiring a person to register with the police; and the regulations may include provision—

(a) as to the officers of police by whom registers are to be maintained, and as to the form and content of the registers;

(b) as to the place and manner in which anyone is to register and as to the documents and information to be furnished by him, whether on registration or on any change of circumstances;

(c) as to the issue of certificates of registration and as to the payment of fees for certificates of registration;

and the regulations may require anyone who is for the time being subject to such a condition to produce a certificate of registration to such persons and in such circumstances as may be prescribed by the regulations.

(4) The Secretary of State may by order made by statutory instrument, which shall be subject to annulment in pursuance of a resolution of either House of Parliament, make such provision as appears to him to be expedient in connection with this Act for records to be made and kept of persons staying at hotels and other premises where lodging or sleeping accommodation is provided, and for persons (whether [British citizens] or not) who stay at any such premises to supply the necessary information.

Appointment
Appointment: 1 January 1973: see SI 1972/1514, art 2.

Amendment
Sub-s (1): words "allowed by or under" in square brackets substituted by the Immigration and Asylum Act 1999, s 169(1), Sch 14, paras 43, 45. Date in force: 14 February 2000: see SI 2000/168, art 2, Schedule.
Sub-s (2): words omitted, originally inserted by SI 1990/2227, art 3, Sch 1, Part I, para 1, repealed by SI 1993/1813, art 9, Sch 6, Part I.
Sub-s (4): words in square brackets substituted by the British Nationality Act, s 39(6), Sch 4, para 2.

Modification
Modified, in its application to the Channel Tunnel, by the Channel Tunnel (International Arrangements) Order 1993, SI 1993/1813, art 7(1), Sch 4, para 1(3).
Modified, in relation to its application to frontier controls between the United Kingdom, France and Belgium, by the Channel Tunnel (Miscellaneous Provisions) Order 1994, SI 1994/1405, art 7.

Subordinate Legislation
Immigration (Revocation of Employment Restrictions) Order 1972, SI 1972/1647 (made under sub-s (1)).
Immigration (Hotel Records) Order 1972, SI 1972/1689 (made under sub-s (4)).
Immigration (Registration with Police) Regulations 1972, SI 1972/1758 (made under sub-s (3)).
Immigration (Variation of Leave) Order 1976, SI 1976/1572 (made under sub-s (1)).
Immigration (Registration with Police) (Amendment) (No 2) Regulations 1982, SI 1982/1024 (made under sub-s (3)).
Immigration (Hotel Records) (Amendment) Order 1982, SI 1982/1025 (made under sub-s (4)).
Immigration (Variation of Leave) (Amendment) Order 1989, SI 1989/1005 (made under sub-s (1)).
Immigration (Registration with Police) (Amendment) Regulations 1990, SI 1990/400 (made under sub-s (3)).
Immigration (Variation of Leave) (Revocation) Order 1991, SI 1991/980 (made under sub-s (1)).
Immigration (Variation of Leave) (No 2) Order 1991, SI 1991/1083 (made under sub-s (1)).
Immigration (Variation of Leave) (Amendment) Order 1993, SI 1993/1657 (made under sub-s (1)).
Immigration (Registration with Police) (Amendment) Regulations 1995, SI 1995/2928 (made under sub-s (3)).
Immigration (Variation of Leave) (Amendment) Order 2000, SI 2000/2445 (made under sub-s (1)).

5 Procedure for, and further provisions as to, deportation

(1) Where a person is under section 3(5) or (6) above liable to deportation, then subject to the following provisions of this Act the Secretary of State may make a deportation order against him, that is to say an order requiring him to leave and prohibiting him from entering the United Kingdom; and a deportation order against a person shall invalidate any leave to enter or remain in the United Kingdom given him before the order is made or while it is in force.

(2) A deportation order against a person may at any time be revoked by a further order of the Secretary of State, and shall cease to have effect if he becomes [a British citizen].

(3) A deportation order shall not be made against a person as belonging to the family of another person if more than eight weeks have elapsed since the other person left the United Kingdom after the making of the deportation order against him; and a deportation order made against a person on that ground shall cease to have effect if he ceases to belong to the family of the other person, or if the deportation order made against the other person ceases to have effect.

(4) For purposes of deportation the following shall be those who are regarded as belonging to another person's family—

    (a) where that other person is a man, his wife [or civil partner,] and his or her children under the age of eighteen; and

    [(b) where that other person is a woman, her husband [or civil partner,] and her or his children under the age of eighteen;]

and for purposes of this subsection an adopted child, whether legally adopted or not, may be treated as the child of the adopter and, if legally adopted, shall be regarded as the child only of the adopter; an illegitimate child (subject to the foregoing rule as to adoptions) shall be regarded as the child of the mother; and "wife" includes each of two or more wives.

(5) The provisions of Schedule 3 to this Act shall have effect with respect to the removal from the United Kingdom of persons against whom deportation orders are in force and with respect to the detention or control of persons in connection with deportation.

(6) Where a person is liable to deportation under section [3(5)] or (6) above but, without a deportation order being made against him, leaves the United Kingdom to live permanently abroad, the Secretary of State may make payments of such amounts as he may determine to meet that person's expenses in so leaving the United Kingdom, including travelling expenses for members of his family or household.

Appointment
Appointment: 1 January 1973: see SI 1972/1514, art 2.

Amendment
Sub-s (2): words in square brackets substituted by the British Nationality Act 1981, s 39(6), Sch 4, para 2.
Sub-s (4): in para (a) words "or civil partner," in square brackets inserted by the Civil Partnership Act 2004, s 261(1), Sch 27, para 37(a). Date in force: to be appointed: see the Civil Partnership Act 2004, s 263(10)(b).
Sub-s (4): para (b) substituted by the Asylum and Immigration Act 1996, s 12(1), Sch 2, para 2.
Sub-s (4): in para (b) words "or civil partner," in square brackets inserted by the Civil Partnership Act 2004, s 261(1), Sch 27, para 37(b). Date in force: to be appointed: see the Civil Partnership Act 2004, s 263(10)(b).
Sub-s (6): reference to "3(5)" in square brackets substituted by the Immigration Act 1988, s 10, Schedule, para 2.

See Further
See further, in relation to the continued application of this section in relation to certain persons who, for the purposes of this section, are taken to be liable to deportation under s 3(5) hereof: the Nationality, Immigration and Asylum Act 2002 (Commencement No 4) Order 2003, SI 2003/754, art 3(2), Sch 2, para 2(3).

Subordinate Legislation
Pensions Increase (Speakers' Pensions) Regulations 1972, SI 1972/1653 (made under sub-ss (3), (4)).
Pensions Increase (Parliamentary Pensions) Regulations 1972, SI 1972/1655 (made under sub-s (3)).
Pensions (Increase) Act 1971 (Modification) (Teachers) Regulations 1972, SI 1972/1676 (made under sub-s (3)).
Increase of Pensions (Teachers' Family Benefits) Regulations 1972, SI 1972/1905 (made under sub-s (3)).

6 Recommendations by court for deportation

(1) Where under section 3(6) above a person convicted of an offence is liable to deportation on the recommendation of a court, he may be recommended for deportation by any court having power to sentence him for the offence unless the court commits him to be sentenced or further dealt with for that offence by another court:

Provided that in Scotland the power to recommend a person for deportation shall be exercisable only by the sheriff or the High Court of Justiciary, and shall not be exercisable by the latter on an appeal unless the appeal is against a conviction on indictment or against a sentence upon such a conviction.

(2) A court shall not recommend a person for deportation unless he has been given not less than seven days notice in writing stating that a person is not liable to deportation if he is [a British citizen], describing the persons who are [British citizens] and stating (so far as material) the effect of section 3(8) above and section 7 below; but the powers of adjournment conferred by [section 10(3) of the Magistrates' Courts Act 1980], [section 179 or 380 of the Criminal Procedure (Scotland) Act 1975] or any corresponding enactment for the time being in force in Northern Ireland shall include power to adjourn, after convicting an offender, for the purpose of enabling a notice to be given to him under this subsection or, if a notice was so given to him less than seven days previously, for the purpose of enabling the necessary seven days to elapse.

(3) For purposes of section 3(6) above—

(a) a person shall be deemed to have attained the age of seventeen at the time of his conviction if, on consideration of any available evidence, he appears to have done so to the court making or considering a recommendation for deportation; and

(b) the question whether an offence is one for which a person is punishable with imprisonment shall be determined without regard to any enactment restricting the imprisonment of young offenders or [persons who have not previously been sentenced to imprisonment];

and for purposes of deportation a person who on being charged with an offence is found to have committed it shall, notwithstanding any enactment to the contrary and notwithstanding that the court does not proceed to conviction, be regarded as a person convicted of the offence, and references to conviction shall be construed accordingly.

(4) Notwithstanding any rule of practice restricting the matters which ought to be taken into account in dealing with an offender who is sentenced to imprisonment, a recommendation for deportation may be made in respect of an offender who is sentenced to imprisonment for life.

(5) Where a court recommends or purports to recommend a person for deportation, the validity of the recommendation shall not be called in question except on an appeal against the recommendation or against the conviction on which it is made; but—

    (a)   ... the recommendation shall be treated as a sentence for the purpose of any enactment providing an appeal against sentence; ...

    (b)   ...

(6) A deportation order shall not be made on the recommendation of a court so long as an appeal or further appeal is pending against the recommendation or against the conviction on which it was made; and for this purpose an appeal or further appeal shall be treated as pending (where one is competent but has not been brought) until the expiration of the time for bringing that appeal or, in Scotland, until the expiration of twenty-eight days from the date of the recommendation.

(7) For the purpose of giving effect to any of the provisions of this section in its application to Scotland, the High Court of Justiciary shall have power to make rules by act of adjournal.

Appointment
Appointment: 1 January 1973: see SI 1972/1514, art 2.

Amendment
Sub-s (2): first and second words in square brackets substituted by the British Nationality Act 1981, s 39(6), Sch 4, para 2; third words in square brackets substituted by the Magistrates' Courts Act 1980, s 154, Sch 7, para 105; final words in square brackets substituted by the Criminal Procedure (Scotland) Act 1975, s 461(1), Sch 9, para 47.
Sub-s (3): words in square brackets substituted by the Criminal Justice Act 1972, s 64(1), Sch 5, and the Criminal Justice Act 1982, s 77, Sch 15.
Sub-s (5): words omitted repealed by the Criminal Justice (Scotland) Act 1980, s 83(3), Sch 8, and the Criminal Justice Act 1982, ss 77, 78, Sch 15, para 15, Sch 16.

7   Exemption from deportation for certain existing residents

(1) Notwithstanding anything in section 3(5) or (6) above but subject to the provisions of this section, a Commonwealth citizen or citizen of the Republic of Ireland who was such a citizen at the coming into force of this Act and was then ordinarily resident in the United Kingdom—

    (a)   ...
    [(b)   shall not be liable to deportation under section 3(5) if at the time of the Secretary of State's decision he had for the last five years been ordinarily resident in the United Kingdom and Islands;] and
    (c)   shall not on conviction of an offence be recommended for deportation under section 3(6) if at the time of the conviction he had for the last five years been ordinarily resident in the United Kingdom and Islands.

(2) A person who has at any time become ordinarily resident in the United Kingdom or in any of the Islands shall not be treated for the purposes of this section as having ceased to be so by reason only of his having remained there in breach of the immigration laws.

(3) The "last five years" before the material time under subsection (1)(b) or (c) above is to be taken as a period amounting in total to five years exclusive of any time during which the person claiming exemption under this section was undergoing imprisonment or detention by virtue of a sentence passed for an offence on a conviction in the United Kingdom and Islands, and the period for which he was imprisoned or detained by virtue of the sentence amounted to six months or more.

(4) For purposes of subsection (3) above—

(a) "sentence" includes any order made on conviction of an offence; and
(b) two or more sentences for consecutive (or partly consecutive) terms shall be treated as a single sentence; and
(c) a person shall be deemed to be detained by virtue of a sentence—
   (i) at any time when he is liable to imprisonment or detention by virtue of the sentence, but is unlawfully at large; and
   (ii) (unless the sentence is passed after the material time) during any period of custody by which under any relevant enactment the term to be served under the sentence is reduced.

In paragraph (c)(ii) above "relevant enactment" means [section 240 of the Criminal Justice Act 2003] (or, before that section operated, section 17(2) of the Criminal Justice Administration Act 1962) and any similar enactment which is for the time being or has (before or after the passing of this Act) been in force in any part of the United Kingdom and Islands.

(5) Nothing in this section shall be taken to exclude the operation of section 3(8) above in relation to an exemption under this section.

Appointment
Appointment: 1 January 1973: see SI 1972/1514, art 2.

Amendment
Sub-s (1): para (a) repealed by the Nationality, Immigration and Asylum Act 2002, ss 75(1), (2), 161, Sch 9. Date in force: 10 February 2003: see SI 2003/1, art 2, Schedule.
Sub-s (1): para (b) substituted by the Nationality, Immigration and Asylum Act 2002, s 75(1), (3). Date in force: 10 February 2003: see SI 2003/1, art 2, Schedule.
Sub-s (4): words "section 240 of the Criminal Justice Act 2003" in square brackets substituted by the Criminal Justice Act 2003, s 304, Sch 32, Pt 1, para 16. Date in force: 4 April 2005: see SI 2005/950, art 2(1), Sch 1, para 42(1), (10).

8   Exceptions for seamen, aircrews and other special cases

(1) Where a person arrives at a place in the United Kingdom as a member of the crew of a ship or aircraft under an engagement requiring him to leave on that ship as a member of the crew, or to leave within seven days on that or another aircraft as a member of its crew, then unless either—

(a) there is in force a deportation order made against him; or
(b) he has at any time been refused leave to enter the United Kingdom and has not since then been given leave to enter or remain in the United Kingdom; or
(c) an immigration officer requires him to submit to examination in accordance with Schedule 2 to this Act;

he may without leave enter the United Kingdom at that place and remain until the departure of the ship or aircraft on which he is required by his engagement to leave.

(2) The Secretary of State may by order exempt any person or class of persons, either unconditionally or subject to such conditions as may be imposed by or under the order, from all or any of the provisions of this Act relating to those who are not [British citizens].

An order under this subsection, if made with respect to a class of persons, shall be made by statutory instrument, which shall be subject to annulment in pursuance of a resolution of either House of Parliament.

(3) [Subject to subsection (3A) below,] the provisions of this Act relating to those who are not [British citizens] shall not apply to any person so long as he is a member of a mission (within the meaning of the Diplomatic Privileges Act 1964), a person who is

a member of the family and forms part of the household of such a member, or a person otherwise entitled to the like immunity from jurisdiction as is conferred by that Act on a diplomatic agent.

[(3A) For the purposes of subsection (3), a member of a mission other than a diplomatic agent (as defined by the 1964 Act) is not to count as a member of a mission unless—

    (a) he was resident outside the United Kingdom, and was not in the United Kingdom, when he was offered a post as such a member; and

    (b) he has not ceased to be such a member after having taken up the post.]

(4) The provisions of this Act relating to those who are not [British citizens], other than the provisions relating to deportation, shall also not apply to any person so long as either—

    (a) he is subject, as a member of the home forces, to service law; or

    (b) being a member of a Commonwealth force or of a force raised under the law of any ... colony, protectorate or protected state, is undergoing or about to undergo training in the United Kingdom with any body, contingent or detachment of the home forces; or

    (c) he is serving or posted for service in the United Kingdom as a member of a visiting force or of any force raised as aforesaid or as a member of an international headquarters or defence organisation designated for the time being by an Order in Council under section 1 of the International Headquarters and Defence Organisations Act 1964.

(5) Where a person having a limited leave to enter or remain in the United Kingdom becomes entitled to an exemption under this section, that leave shall continue to apply after he ceases to be entitled to the exemption, unless it has by then expired; and a person is not to be regarded for purposes of this Act as having been [settled in the United Kingdom at any time when he was entitled under the former immigration laws to any exemption corresponding to any of those afforded by subsection (3) or (4)(b) or (c) above or by any order under subsection (2) above.]

[(5A) An order under subsection (2) above may, as regards any person or class of persons to whom it applies, provide for that person or class to be in specified circumstances regarded (notwithstanding the order) as settled in the United Kingdom for the purposes of section 1(1) of the British Nationality Act 1981.]

(6) In this section "the home forces" means any of Her Majesty's forces other than a Commonwealth force or a force raised under the law of any associated state, colony, protectorate or protected state; "Commonwealth force" means a force of any country to which provisions of the Visiting Forces Act 1952 apply without an Order in Council under section 1 of the Act; and "visiting force" means a body, contingent or detachment of the forces of a country to which any of those provisions apply, being a body, contingent or detachment for the time being present in the United Kingdom on the invitation of Her Majesty's Government in the United Kingdom.

Appointment
Appointment: 1 January 1973: see SI 1972/1514, art 2.

Amendment
Sub-ss (2), (5): words in square brackets substituted by the British Nationality Act 1981, s 39(6), Sch 4, paras 2, 5.
Sub-s (3): first words in square brackets inserted by the Immigration Act 1988, s 4; second words in square brackets substituted by the British Nationality Act 1981, s 39(6), Sch 4, para 2.
Sub-s (3A) (as originally inserted by the Immigration Act 1988, s 4, except in relation to a person who has taken up the post before 1 August 1988): substituted by the Immigration and Asylum Act 1999, s 6. Date in force: 1 March 2000: see SI 2000/168, art 2, Schedule.

Sub-s (4): words in square brackets substituted by the British Nationality Act 1981, s 39(6), Sch 4, paras 2, 5; in para (b) words omitted repealed by the Statute Law (Repeals) Act 1995.
Sub-s (5A): inserted by the British Nationality Act 1981, s 39(4).

Modification
Modified, in its application to the Channel Tunnel, by the Channel Tunnel (International Arrangements) Order 1993, SI 1993/1813, art 7(1), Sch 4, para 1(4).
Modified, in relation to its application to frontier controls between the United Kingdom, France and Belgium, by the Channel Tunnel (Miscellaneous Provisions) Order 1994, SI 1994/1405, art 7.

Subordinate Legislation
Immigration (Exemption from Control) Order 1972, SI 1972/1613 (made under sub-s (2)).
Immigration (Exemption from Control) (Amendment) Order 1982, SI 1982/1649 (made under sub-ss (2), (5A)).
Immigration (Exemption from Control) (Amendment) Order 1985, SI 1985/1809 (made under sub-s (2)).
Immigration (Exemption from Control) (Amendment) Order 1997, SI 1997/1402 (made under sub-s (2)).
Immigration (Exemption from Control) (Amendment) (No 2) Order 1997, SI 1997/2207 (made under sub-s (2)).
Immigration (Exemption from Control) (Amendment) Order 2004, SI 2004/3171 (made under sub-s (2)).

[8A   Persons ceasing to be exempt]

[(1)   A person is exempt for the purposes of this section if he is exempt from provisions of this Act as a result of section 8(2) or (3).

(2)   If a person who is exempt—

  (a)   ceases to be exempt, and
  (b)   requires leave to enter or remain in the United Kingdom as a result,

he is to be treated as if he had been given leave to remain in the United Kingdom for a period of 90 days beginning on the day on which he ceased to be exempt.

(3)   If—

  (a)   a person who is exempt ceases to be exempt, and
  (b)   there is in force in respect of him leave for him to enter or remain in the United Kingdom which expires before the end of the period mentioned in subsection (2),

his leave is to be treated as expiring at the end of that period.]

Amendment
Inserted by the Immigration and Asylum Act 1999, s 7. Date in force: 1 March 2000: see SI 2000/168, art 2, Schedule.

[8B   Persons excluded from the United Kingdom under international obligations]

[(1)   An excluded person must be refused—

  (a)   leave to enter the United Kingdom;
  (b)   leave to remain in the United Kingdom.

(2)   A person's leave to enter or remain in the United Kingdom is cancelled on his becoming an excluded person.

(3)   A person's exemption from the provisions of this Act as a result of section 8(1), (2) or (3) ceases on his becoming an excluded person.

(4)   "Excluded person" means a person—

(a) named by or under, or

(b) of a description specified in,

a designated instrument.

(5) The Secretary of State may by order designate an instrument if it is a resolution of the Security Council of the United Nations or an instrument made by the Council of the European Union and it—

(a) requires that a person is not to be admitted to the United Kingdom (however that requirement is expressed); or

(b) recommends that a person should not be admitted to the United Kingdom (however that recommendation is expressed).

(6) Subsections (1) to (3) are subject to such exceptions (if any) as may specified in the order designating the instrument in question.

(7) An order under this section must be made by statutory instrument.

(8) Such a statutory instrument shall be laid before Parliament without delay.]

Amendment
Inserted by the Immigration and Asylum Act 1999, s 8. Date in force: 1 March 2000: see SI 2000/168, art 2, Schedule.

Subordinate Legislation
Immigration (Designation of Travel Bans) Order 2000, SI 2000/2724 (made under sub-ss (5), (6)).
Immigration (Designation of Travel Bans) (Amendment No 2) Order 2003, SI 2003/3285 (made under sub-s (5)).
Immigration (Designation of Travel Bans) (Amendment) Order 2004, SI 2004/3316 (made under sub-s (5)).

9   Further provisions as to common travel area

(1) Subject to subsection (5) below, the provisions of Schedule 4 to this Act shall have effect for the purpose of taking account in the United Kingdom of the operation in any of the Islands of the immigration laws there.

(2) Persons who lawfully enter the United Kingdom on a local journey from a place in the common travel area after having either—

(a) entered any of the Islands or the Republic of Ireland on coming from a place outside the common travel area; or

(b) left the United Kingdom while having a limited leave to enter or remain which has since expired;

if they are not [British citizens] (and are not to be regarded under Schedule 4 to this Act as having leave to enter the United Kingdom), shall be subject in the United Kingdom to such restrictions on the period for which they may remain, and such conditions restricting their employment or occupation or requiring them to register with the police or both, as may be imposed by an order of the Secretary of State and may be applicable to them.

(3) Any provision of this Act applying to a limited leave or to conditions attached to a limited leave shall, unless otherwise provided, have effect in relation to a person subject to any restriction or condition by virtue of an order under subsection (2) above as if the provisions of the order applicable to him were terms on which he had been given leave under this Act to enter the United Kingdom.

(4) Section 1(3) above shall not be taken to affect the operation of a deportation order; and, subject to Schedule 4 to this Act, a person who is not [a British citizen] may

not by virtue of section 1(3) enter the United Kingdom without leave on a local journey from a place in the common travel area if either—

    (a)   he is on arrival in the United Kingdom given written notice by an immigration officer stating that, the Secretary of State having issued directions for him not to be given entry to the United Kingdom on the ground that his exclusion is conducive to the public good as being in the interests of national security, he is accordingly refused leave to enter the United Kingdom; or

    (b)   he has at any time been refused leave to enter the United Kingdom and has not since then been given leave to enter or remain in the United Kingdom.

(5)   If it appears to the Secretary of State necessary so to do by reason of differences between the immigration laws of the United Kingdom and any of the Islands, he may by order exclude that island from section 1(3) above for such purposes as may be specified in the order, and references in this Act to the Islands ... shall apply to an island so excluded so far only as may be provided by order of the Secretary of State.

(6)   The Secretary of State shall also have power by order to exclude the Republic of Ireland from section 1(3) for such purposes as may be specified in the order.

(7)   An order of the Secretary of State under this section shall be made by statutory instrument, which shall be subject to annulment in pursuance of a resolution of either House of Parliament.

Appointment
Appointment: 1 January 1973: see SI 1972/1514, art 2.

Amendment
Sub-ss (2), (4): words in square brackets substituted by the British Nationality Act 1981, s 39(6), Sch 4, para 2.
Sub-s (5): words omitted repealed by the British Nationality Act 1981, s 52(8), Sch 9.

Subordinate Legislation
Immigration (Control of Entry through Republic of Ireland) Order 1972, SI 1972/1610 (made under sub-ss (2), (6)).
Immigration (Control of Entry through Republic of Ireland) (Amendment) Order 1982, SI 1982/1028 (made under sub-s (2)).
Immigration (Control of Entry through Republic of Ireland) (Amendment) Order 1985, SI 1985/1854 (made under sub-s (1)).
Immigration (Control of Entry through Republic of Ireland) (Amendment) Order 1987, SI 1987/2092 (made under sub-s (2)).
Immigration (Control of Entry through Republic of Ireland) (Amendment) Order 2000, SI 2000/1776 (made under sub-s (2)).

10   Entry otherwise than by sea or air

(1)   Her Majesty may by Order in Council direct that any of the provisions of this Act shall have effect in relation to persons entering or seeking to enter the United Kingdom on arrival otherwise than by ship or aircraft [...] as they have effect in the case of a person arriving by ship or aircraft [...]; *and any such Order may make such adaptations or modifications of those provisions, and such provisions supplementary thereto, as appear to Her Majesty to be necessary or expedient for the purposes of the Order.*

[(1A)   Her Majesty may by Order in Council direct that paragraph 27B or 27C of Schedule 2 shall have effect in relation to trains or vehicles as it has effect in relation to ships or aircraft.]

(1B)   Any Order in Council under this section may make—

    (a)   such adaptations or modifications of the provisions concerned, and

(b)   such supplementary provisions,

as appear to Her Majesty to be necessary or expedient for the purposes of the Order.]

(2)   The provision made by an Order in Council under *this section* [subsection (1)] may include provision for excluding the Republic of Ireland from section 1(3) of this Act either generally or for any specified purposes.

(3)   No recommendation shall be made to Her Majesty to make an Order in Council under this section unless a draft of the Order has been laid before Parliament and approved by a resolution of each House of Parliament.

Appointment
Appointment: 1 January 1973: see SI 1972/1514, art 2.

Amendment
Sub-s (1): words omitted inserted by SI 1990/2227, art 3, Sch 1, Part I, para 2, repealed by SI 1993/1813, art 9, Sch 6.
Sub-s (1): words from "any such order" to "of the Order" in italics repealed by the Immigration and Asylum Act 1999, s 169(1), (3), Sch 14, paras 43, 47(1), (2), Sch 16. Date in force: to be appointed: see the Immigration and Asylum Act 1999, s 170(4).
Sub-ss (1A), (1B): inserted by the Immigration and Asylum Act 1999, s 169(1), Sch 14, paras 43, 47(1), (3). Date in force: to be appointed: see the Immigration and Asylum Act 1999, s 170(4).
Sub-s (2): words "this section" in italics repealed and subsequent words in square brackets substituted by the Immigration and Asylum Act 1999, s 169(1), Sch 14, paras 43, 47(1), (4). Date in force: to be appointed: see the Immigration and Asylum Act 1999, s 170(4).

Subordinate Legislation
Immigration (Entry Otherwise than by Sea or Air) Order 2002, SI 2002/1832 (made under sub-s (1)).

11   Construction of references to entry, and other phrases relating to travel

(1)   A person arriving in the United Kingdom by ship or aircraft shall for purposes of this Act be deemed not to enter the United Kingdom unless and until he disembarks, and on disembarkation at a port shall further be deemed not to enter the United Kingdom so long as he remains in such area (if any) at the port as may be approved for this purpose by an immigration officer; and a person who has not otherwise entered the United Kingdom shall be deemed not to do so as long as he is detained, or temporarily admitted or released while liable to detention, under the powers conferred by Schedule 2 to this Act [or by Part III of the Immigration and Asylum Act 1999] [or section 62 of the Nationality, Immigration and Asylum Act 2002] [or by section 68 of the Nationality, Immigration and Asylum Act 2002].

[(1A)   ...]

(2)   In this Act "disembark" means disembark from a ship or aircraft, and "embark" means embark in a ship or aircraft; and, except in subsection (1) above,—

    (a)   references to disembarking in the United Kingdom do not apply to disembarking after a local journey from a place in the United Kingdom or elsewhere in the common travel area; and

    (b)   references to embarking in the United Kingdom do not apply to embarking for a local journey to a place in the United Kingdom or elsewhere in the common travel area.

(3)   Except in so far as the context otherwise requires, references in this Act to arriving in the United Kingdom by ship shall extend to arrival by any floating structure, and "disembark" shall be construed accordingly; but the provisions of this Act specially relating to members of the crew of a ship shall not by virtue of this provision apply in relation to any floating structure not being a ship.

(4)   For purposes of this Act "common travel area" has the meaning given by section 1(3), and a journey is, in relation to the common travel area, a local journey if but only if it begins and ends in the common travel area and is not made by a ship or aircraft which—

    (a)   in the case of a journey to a place in the United Kingdom, began its voyage from, or has during its voyage called at, a place not in the common travel area; or

    (b)   in the case of a journey from a place in the United Kingdom, is due to end its voyage in, or call in the course of its voyage at, a place not in the common travel area.

(5)   A person who enters the United Kingdom lawfully by virtue of section 8(1) above, and seeks to remain beyond the time limited by section 8(1), shall be treated for purposes of this Act as seeking to enter the United Kingdom.

Appointment
Appointment: 1 January 1973: see SI 1972/1514, art 2.

Amendment
Sub-s (1): words "or by Part III of the Immigration and Asylum Act 1999" in square brackets inserted by the Immigration and Asylum Act 1999, s 169(1), Sch 14, paras 43, 48. Date in force: to be appointed: see the Immigration and Asylum Act 1999, s 170(4).
Sub-s (1): words "or section 62 of the Nationality, Immigration and Asylum Act 2002" in square brackets inserted by the Nationality, Immigration and Asylum Act 2002, s 62(8). Date in force: 10 February 2003: see SI 2003/1, art 2, Schedule.
Sub-s (1): words "or by section 68 of the Nationality, Immigration and Asylum Act 2002" in square brackets inserted by SI 2003/1016, art 3, Schedule, para 1. Date in force: 4 April 2003: see SI 2003/1016, art 2(2).
Sub-s (1A): inserted by SI 1990/2227, art 3, Sch 1, Part I, para 3; repealed by SI 1993/1813, art 9, Sch 6.

Modification
Modified, in its application to the Channel Tunnel, by the Channel Tunnel (International Arrangements) Order 1993, SI 1993/1813, art 7(1), Sch 4, para 1(5).
Modified, in relation to its application to frontier controls between the United Kingdom, France and Belgium, by the Channel Tunnel (Miscellaneous Provisions) Order 1994, SI 1994/1405, art 7.

PART II
APPEALS

12   ...

...

Amendment
Repealed by the Immigration and Asylum Act 1999, s 169(1), (3), Sch 14, paras 43, 49, Sch 16. Date in force: 14 February 2000: see SI 2000/168, art 2, Schedule.

13   ...

...

Amendment
Repealed by the Immigration and Asylum Act 1999, s 169(1), (3), Sch 14, paras 43, 49, Sch 16. Date in force: 2 October 2000 (except in relation to events which took place before that date): see SI 2000/2444, art 2, Sch 1; for transitional provisions see art 3, Sch 2, para 2(4) thereof and SI 2003/754, art 3, Sch 2, para 2(4).

14 ...

...

Amendment
Repealed by the Immigration and Asylum Act 1999, s 169(1), (3), Sch 14, paras 43, 49, Sch 16.
Date in force: 2 October 2000 (except in relation to events which took place before that date): see
SI 2000/2444, art 2, Sch 1; for transitional provisions see art 3, Sch 2, para 2 thereof and
SI 2003/754, art 3, Sch 2, para 2(5), and SI 2000/3099, art 5.

15 ...

...

Amendment
Repealed by the Immigration and Asylum Act 1999, s 169(1), (3), Sch 14, paras 43, 49, Sch 16.
Date in force: 2 October 2000 (except in relation to events which took place before that date): see
SI 2000/2444, art 2, Sch 1; for transitional provisions see art 3, Sch 2, para 2(6) thereof and
SI 2003/754, art 3, Sch 2, para 2(6).

16 ...

...

Amendment
Repealed by the Immigration and Asylum Act 1999, s 169(1), (3), Sch 14, paras 43, 49, Sch 16.
Date in force: 2 October 2000 (except in relation to events which took place before that date): see
SI 2000/2444, art 2, Sch 1; for transitional provisions see art 3, Sch 2, para 2(7) thereof and
SI 2003/754, art 3, Sch 2, para 2(7).

17 ...

...

Amendment
Repealed by the Immigration and Asylum Act 1999, s 169(1), (3), Sch 14, paras 43, 49, Sch 16.
Date in force: 2 October 2000 (except in relation to events which took place before that date): see
SI 2000/2444, art 2, Sch 1; for transitional provisions see art 3, Sch 2, para 2(8) thereof and
SI 2003/754, art 3, Sch 2, para 2(8).

18 ...

...

Amendment
Repealed by the Immigration and Asylum Act 1999, s 169(1), (3), Sch 14, paras 43, 49, Sch 16.
Date in force: 2 October 2000 (except in relation to events which took place before that date): see
SI 2000/2444, art 2, Sch 1; for transitional provisions see art 3, Sch 2 thereto.

19 ...

...

Amendment
Repealed by the Immigration and Asylum Act 1999, s 169(1), (3), Sch 14, paras 43, 49, Sch 16.
Date in force: 2 October 2000 (except in relation to events which took place before that date): see
SI 2000/2444, art 2, Sch 1; for transitional provisions see art 3, Sch 2 thereto.

20 ...

...

Amendment
Repealed by the Immigration and Asylum Act 1999, s 169(1), (3), Sch 14, paras 43, 49, Sch 16.
Date in force: 2 October 2000 (except in relation to events which took place before that date): see
SI 2000/2444, art 2, Sch 1; for transitional provisions see art 3, Sch 2 thereto.

21 ...

...

Amendment
Repealed by the Immigration and Asylum Act 1999, s 169(1), (3), Sch 14, paras 43, 49, Sch 16.
Date in force: 2 October 2000 (except in relation to events which took place before that date): see
SI 2000/2444, art 2, Sch 1; for transitional provisions see art 3, Sch 2, para 2(9) thereof and
SI 2003/754, art 3, Sch 2, para 2(9).

Supplementary

22 Procedure

*(1) The [Lord Chancellor] may make rules (in this Act referred to as "rules of
procedure")—*

   *(a) for regulating the exercise of the rights of appeal conferred by this Part of this
       Act;*
   *(b) for prescribing the practice and procedure to be followed on or in connection
       with appeals thereunder, including the mode and burden of proof and
       admissibility of evidence on such an appeal; and*
   *(c) for other matters preliminary or incidental to or arising out of such appeals,
       including proof of the decisions of adjudicators or the Appeal Tribunal.*

(2) Rules of procedure may include provision—

   *(a) enabling the Tribunal, on an appeal from an adjudicator, to remit the appeal
       to an adjudicator for determination by him in accordance with any directions
       of the Tribunal, or for further evidence to be obtained with a view to
       determination by the Tribunal; or*
   *(b) enabling any functions of the Tribunal which relate to matters preliminary or
       incidental to an appeal, or which are conferred by Part II of Schedule 2 to this
       Act, to be performed by a single member of the Tribunal; or*
   *(c) conferring on adjudicators or the Tribunal such ancillary powers as the
       [Lord Chancellor] thinks necessary for the purposes of the exercise of their
       functions.*

*(3) The rules of procedure shall provide that any appellant shall have the right to be
legally represented.*

(4) Where on an appeal under this Part of this Act it is alleged—

   *(a) that a passport or other travel document, [certificate of entitlement], entry
       clearance or work permit (or any part thereof or entry therein) on which a
       party relies is a forgery; and*
   *(b) that the disclosure to that party of any matters relating to the method of
       detection would be contrary to the public interest;*

*then (without prejudice to the generality of the power to make rules of procedure) the
adjudicator or Tribunal shall arrange for the proceedings to take place in the absence
of that party and his representatives while the allegation at (b) above is inquired into
by the adjudicator or Tribunal and, if it appears to the adjudicator or Tribunal that the
allegation is made out, for such further period as appears necessary in order to ensure
that those matters can be presented to the adjudicator or Tribunal without any
disclosure being directly or indirectly made contrary to the public interest.*

(5)   *If under the rules of procedure leave to appeal to the Tribunal is required in cases where an adjudicator dismisses an appeal under section 13 above, then the authority having power to grant leave to appeal shall grant it—*

(a)   *in any case where the appeal was against a decision that the appellant required leave to enter the United Kingdom, and the authority is satisfied that at the time of the decision he held a [certificate of entitlement]; and*

(b)   *in any case where the appeal was against a refusal of leave to enter, and the authority is satisfied that at the time of the refusal the appellant held an entry clearance and that the dismissal of the appeal was not required by section 13(4).*

(6)   *A person who is required under or in accordance with rules of procedure to attend and give evidence or produce documents before an adjudicator or the Tribunal, and fails without reasonable excuse to comply with the requirement, shall be guilty of an offence and liable on summary conviction to a fine not exceeding [level 3 on the standard scale].*

(7)   *The power to make rules of procedure shall be exercisable by statutory instrument, which shall be subject to annulment in pursuance of a resolution of either House of Parliament.*

Appointment
Appointment: 1 January 1973: see SI 1972/1514, art 2.

Amendment
Repealed by the Immigration and Asylum Act 1999, s 169(1), (3), Sch 14, paras 43, 49, Sch 16. Date in force: 2 October 2000 (for certain purposes): see SI 2000/2444, art 2, Sch 1; for transitional provisions see art 3, Sch 2 thereto. Date in force (for remaining purposes): to be appointed: see the Immigration and Asylum Act 1999, s 170(4).
Sub-ss (1), (2): words in square brackets substituted by SI 1987/465, art 3.
Sub-ss (4), (5): words in square brackets substituted by the British Nationality Act 1981, s 39(6), Sch 4, para 3(1).
Sub-s (6): maximum fine increased and converted to a level on the standard scale by virtue of the Criminal Justice Act 1982, ss 37, 38, 46.

Modification
This section has effect as if the Asylum and Immigration Appeals Act 1993, s 8, were contained in this Part: see the Asylum and Immigration Appeals Act 1993, s 8(6), Sch 2.
Sub-ss (1)–(4), (6), (7) have effect as if the Asylum and Immigration Act 1996, s 3, were contained in this Part: see the Asylum and Immigration Act 1996, s 3(4).

23   ...

...

Amendment
Repealed by the Immigration and Asylum Act 1999, s 169(1), (3), Sch 14, paras 43, 49, Sch 16. Date in force: 2 October 2000 (except in relation to events which took place before that date): see SI 2000/2444, art 2, Sch 1; for transitional provisions see art 3, Sch 2 thereto.

PART III
CRIMINAL PROCEEDINGS

24   Illegal entry and similar offences

(1)   A person who is not [a British citizen] shall be guilty of an offence punishable on summary conviction with a fine of not more than [[level 5] on the standard scale] or with imprisonment for not more than six months, or with both, in any of the following cases:—

(a) if contrary to this Act he knowingly enters the United Kingdom in breach of a deportation order or without leave;

[(aa) ...]

(b) if, having only a limited leave to enter or remain in the United Kingdom, he knowingly either—
  (i) remains beyond the time limited by the leave; or
  (ii) fails to observe a condition of the leave;

(c) if, having lawfully entered the United Kingdom without leave by virtue of section 8(1) above, he remains without leave beyond the time allowed by section 8(1);

(d) if, without reasonable excuse, he fails to comply with any requirement imposed on him under Schedule 2 to this Act to report to a medical officer of health, or to attend, or submit to a test or examination, as required by such an officer;

(e) if, without reasonable excuse, he fails to observe any restriction imposed on him under Schedule 2 or 3 to this Act as to residence[, as to his employment or occupation] or as to reporting to the police[, to an immigration officer or to the Secretary of State];

(f) if he disembarks in the United Kingdom from a ship or aircraft after being placed on board under Schedule 2 or 3 to this Act with a view to his removal from the United Kingdom;

(g) if he embarks in contravention of a restriction imposed by or under an Order in Council under section 3(7) of this Act.

[(1A) A person commits an offence under subsection (1)(b)(i) above on the day when he first knows that the time limited by his leave has expired and continues to commit it throughout any period during which he is in the United Kingdom thereafter; but a person shall not be prosecuted under that provision more than once in respect of the same limited leave.]

(2) ...

(3) The extended time limit for prosecutions which is provided for by section 28 below shall apply to offences under [subsection (1)(a) and (c)] above.

(4) In proceedings for an offence against subsection (1)(a) above of entering the United Kingdom without leave,—

(a) any stamp purporting to have been imprinted on a passport or other travel document by an immigration officer on a particular date for the purpose of giving leave shall be presumed to have been duly so imprinted, unless the contrary is proved;

(b) proof that a person had leave to enter the United Kingdom shall lie on the defence if, but only if, he is shown to have entered within six months before the date when the proceedings were commenced.

Appointment
Appointment: 1 January 1973: see SI 1972/1514, art 2.

Amendment
Sub-s (1): words "a British citizen" in square brackets substituted by the British Nationality Act 1981, s 39(6), Sch 4, para 2.
Sub-s (1): words "level 5" in square brackets substituted by the Asylum and Immigration Act 1996, s 6.
Sub-s (1): words ending with the words "on the standard scale" in square brackets substituted by virtue of the Criminal Justice Act 1982, ss 37, 38, 46.
Sub-s (1): para (aa) (as originally inserted by the Asylum and Immigration Act 1996, s 4) repealed by the Immigration and Asylum Act 1999, s 169(1), (3), Sch 14, paras 43, 50, Sch 16. Date in force: 14 February 2000: see SI 2000/168, art 2, Schedule.

Sub-s (1): in para (e) words ", as to his employment or occupation" in square brackets inserted by the Immigration Act 1988, s 10, Schedule, para 10(3), (4).

Sub-s (1): in para (e) words ", to an immigration officer or to the Secretary of State" in square brackets substituted by the Nationality, Immigration and Asylum Act 2002, s 62(9). Date in force: 10 February 2003: see SI 2003/1, art 2, Schedule.

Sub-s (1A): inserted by the Immigration Act 1988, s 6(1), except in relation to a person whose leave expired before 10 July 1988.

Sub-s (2): repealed by the Immigration and Asylum Act 1999, s 169(1), (3), Sch 14, paras 43, 50, Sch 16. Date in force: 14 February 2000: see SI 2000/168, art 2, Schedule.

Sub-s (3): words in square brackets substituted by the Immigration Act 1988, s 6(2), except in relation to a person whose leave expired before 10 July 1988.

Modification
Modified, in its application to the Channel Tunnel, by the Channel Tunnel (International Arrangements) Order 1993, SI 1993/1813, art 7(1), Sch 4, para 1(7).
Modified, in relation to its application to frontier controls between the United Kingdom, France and Belgium, by the Channel Tunnel (Miscellaneous Provisions) Order 1994, SI 1994/1405, art 7.

[24A   Deception]

[(1)   A person who is not a British citizen is guilty of an offence if, by means which include deception by him—

    (a)   he obtains or seeks to obtain leave to enter or remain in the United Kingdom; or

    (b)   he secures or seeks to secure the avoidance, postponement or revocation of enforcement action against him.

(2)   "Enforcement action", in relation to a person, means—

    (a)   the giving of directions for his removal from the United Kingdom ("directions") under Schedule 2 to this Act or section 10 of the Immigration and Asylum Act 1999;

    (b)   the making of a deportation order against him under section 5 of this Act; or

    (c)   his removal from the United Kingdom in consequence of directions or a deportation order.

(3)   A person guilty of an offence under this section is liable—

    (a)   on summary conviction, to imprisonment for a term not exceeding six months or to a fine not exceeding the statutory maximum, or to both; or

    (b)   on conviction on indictment, to imprisonment for a term not exceeding two years or to a fine, or to both.

(4)   ...]

Amendment
Inserted by the Immigration and Asylum Act 1999, s 28. Date in force: 14 February 2000: see SI 2000/168, art 2, Schedule.
Sub-s (4): repealed by the Nationality, Immigration and Asylum Act 2002, ss 156(2), 161, Sch 9. Date in force: 10 February 2003: see SI 2003/1, art 2, Schedule.

[25   Assisting unlawful immigration to member State]

[(1)   A person commits an offence if he—

    (a)   does an act which facilitates the commission of a breach of immigration law by an individual who is not a citizen of the European Union,

    (b)   knows or has reasonable cause for believing that the act facilitates the commission of a breach of immigration law by the individual, and

    (c)   knows or has reasonable cause for believing that the individual is not a citizen of the European Union.

(2)   In subsection (1) "immigration law" means a law which has effect in a member State and which controls, in respect of some or all persons who are not nationals of the State, entitlement to—

(a)   enter the State,
(b)   transit across the State, or
(c)   be in the State.

(3)   A document issued by the government of a member State certifying a matter of law in that State—

(a)   shall be admissible in proceedings for an offence under this section, and
(b)   shall be conclusive as to the matter certified.

(4)   Subsection (1) applies to anything done—

(a)   in the United Kingdom,
(b)   outside the United Kingdom by an individual to whom subsection (5) applies, or
(c)   outside the United Kingdom by a body incorporated under the law of a part of the United Kingdom.

(5)   This subsection applies to—

(a)   a British citizen,
(b)   a British overseas territories citizen,
(c)   a British National (Overseas),
(d)   a British Overseas citizen,
(e)   a person who is a British subject under the British Nationality Act 1981 (c 61), and
(f)   a British protected person within the meaning of that Act.

(6)   A person guilty of an offence under this section shall be liable—

(a)   on conviction on indictment, to imprisonment for a term not exceeding 14 years, to a fine or to both, or
(b)   on summary conviction, to imprisonment for a term not exceeding six months, to a fine not exceeding the statutory maximum or to both.

[(7)   In this section—

(a)   a reference to a member State includes a reference to a State on a list prescribed for the purposes of this section by order of the Secretary of State (to be known as the "Section 25 List of Schengen Acquis States"), and
(b)   a reference to a citizen of the European Union includes a reference to a person who is a national of a State on that list.

(8)   An order under subsection (7)(a)—

(a)   may be made only if the Secretary of State thinks it necessary for the purpose of complying with the United Kingdom's obligations under the Community Treaties,
(b)   may include transitional, consequential or incidental provision,
(c)   shall be made by statutory instrument, and
(d)   shall be subject to annulment in pursuance of a resolution of either House of Parliament.]]

Amendment

Substituted, together with ss 25A–25C for this section as originally enacted, by the Nationality, Immigration and Asylum Act 2002, s 143. Date in force: 10 February 2003: see SI 2003/1, art 2, Schedule.

Sub-ss (7), (8): inserted by the Asylum and Immigration (Treatment of Claimants, etc) Act 2004, s 1(1). Date in force: 1 October 2004: see SI 2004/2523, art 2, Schedule.

Modification
Modified, in its application to the Channel Tunnel, by the Channel Tunnel (International Arrangements) Order 1993, SI 1993/1813, art 7(1), Sch 4, para 1(8).
Modified, in relation to its application to frontier controls between the United Kingdom, France and Belgium, by the Channel Tunnel (Miscellaneous Provisions) Order 1994, SI 1994/1405, art 7.

Subordinate Legislation
Immigration (Assisting Unlawful Immigration) (Section 25 List of Schengen Acquis States) Order 2004, SI 2004/2877 (made under sub-s (7)(a)).

[25A   Helping asylum-seeker to enter United Kingdom]

[(1)   A person commits an offence if—

(a)   he knowingly and for gain facilitates the arrival in the United Kingdom of an individual, and
(b)   he knows or has reasonable cause to believe that the individual is an asylum-seeker.

(2)   In this section "asylum-seeker" means a person who intends to claim that to remove him from or require him to leave the United Kingdom would be contrary to the United Kingdom's obligations under—

(a)   the Refugee Convention (within the meaning given by section 167(1) of the Immigration and Asylum Act 1999 (c 33) (interpretation)), or
(b)   the Human Rights Convention (within the meaning given by that section).

(3)   Subsection (1) does not apply to anything done by a person acting on behalf of an organisation which—

(a)   aims to assist asylum-seekers, and
(b)   does not charge for its services.

(4)   Subsections (4) to (6) of section 25 apply for the purpose of the offence in subsection (1) of this section as they apply for the purpose of the offence in subsection (1) of that section.]

Amendment
Substituted, together with ss 25, 25B, 25C for s 25 as originally enacted, by the Nationality, Immigration and Asylum Act 2002, s 143. Date in force: 10 February 2003: see SI 2003/1, art 2, Schedule.

[25B   Assisting entry to United Kingdom in breach of deportation or exclusion order]

[(1)   A person commits an offence if he—

(a)   does an act which facilitates a breach of a deportation order in force against an individual who is a citizen of the European Union, and
(b)   knows or has reasonable cause for believing that the act facilitates a breach of the deportation order.

(2)   Subsection (3) applies where the Secretary of State personally directs that the exclusion from the United Kingdom of an individual who is a citizen of the European Union is conducive to the public good.

(3)   A person commits an offence if he—

(a)   does an act which assists the individual to arrive in, enter or remain in the United Kingdom,
(b)   knows or has reasonable cause for believing that the act assists the individual to arrive in, enter or remain in the United Kingdom, and

(c) knows or has reasonable cause for believing that the Secretary of State has personally directed that the individual's exclusion from the United Kingdom is conducive to the public good.

(4) Subsections (4) to (6) of section 25 apply for the purpose of an offence under this section as they apply for the purpose of an offence under that section.]

Amendment
Substituted, together with ss 25, 25A, 25C for s 25 as originally enacted, by the Nationality, Immigration and Asylum Act 2002, s 143. Date in force: 10 February 2003: see SI 2003/1, art 2, Schedule.

[**25C** **Forfeiture of vehicle, ship or aircraft**]

[(1) This section applies where a person is convicted on indictment of an offence under section 25, 25A or 25B.

(2) The court may order the forfeiture of a vehicle used or intended to be used in connection with the offence if the convicted person—

(a) owned the vehicle at the time the offence was committed,

(b) was at that time a director, secretary or manager of a company which owned the vehicle,

(c) was at that time in possession of the vehicle under a hire-purchase agreement,

(d) was at that time a director, secretary or manager of a company which was in possession of the vehicle under a hire-purchase agreement, or

(e) was driving the vehicle in the course of the commission of the offence.

(3) The court may order the forfeiture of a ship or aircraft used or intended to be used in connection with the offence if the convicted person—

(a) owned the ship or aircraft at the time the offence was committed,

(b) was at that time a director, secretary or manager of a company which owned the ship or aircraft,

(c) was at that time in possession of the ship or aircraft under a hire-purchase agreement,

(d) was at that time a director, secretary or manager of a company which was in possession of the ship or aircraft under a hire-purchase agreement,

(e) was at that time a charterer of the ship or aircraft, or

(f) committed the offence while acting as captain of the ship or aircraft.

(4) But in a case to which subsection (3)(a) or (b) does not apply, forfeiture may be ordered only—

(a) in the case of a ship, if subsection (5) or (6) applies;

(b) in the case of an aircraft, if subsection (5) or (7) applies.

(5) This subsection applies where—

(a) in the course of the commission of the offence, the ship or aircraft carried more than 20 illegal entrants, and

(b) a person who, at the time the offence was committed, owned the ship or aircraft or was a director, secretary or manager of a company which owned it, knew or ought to have known of the intention to use it in the course of the commission of an offence under section 25, 25A or 25B.

(6) This subsection applies where a ship's gross tonnage is less than 500 tons.

(7) This subsection applies where the maximum weight at which an aircraft (which is not a hovercraft) may take off in accordance with its certificate of airworthiness is less than 5,700 kilogrammes.

(8)   Where a person who claims to have an interest in a vehicle, ship or aircraft applies to a court to make representations on the question of forfeiture, the court may not make an order under this section in respect of the ship, aircraft or vehicle unless the person has been given an opportunity to make representations.

(9)   In the case of an offence under section 25, the reference in subsection (5)(a) to an illegal entrant shall be taken to include a reference to—

(a)   an individual who seeks to enter a member State in breach of immigration law [(for which purpose "member State" and "immigration law" have the meanings given by section 25(2) and (7))], and

(b)   an individual who is a passenger for the purpose of section 145 of the Nationality, Immigration and Asylum Act 2002 (traffic in prostitution) [or section 4 of the Asylum and Immigration (Treatment of Claimants, etc) Act 2004 (trafficking people for exploitation)].

(10)   In the case of an offence under section 25A, the reference in subsection (5)(a) to an illegal entrant shall be taken to include a reference to—

(a)   an asylum-seeker (within the meaning of that section), and

(b)   an individual who is a passenger for the purpose of section 145(1) of the Nationality, Immigration and Asylum Act 2002 [or section 4 of the Asylum and Immigration (Treatment of Claimants, etc) Act 2004 (trafficking people for exploitation)].

(11)   In the case of an offence under section 25B, the reference in subsection (5)(a) to an illegal entrant shall be taken to include a reference to an individual who is a passenger for the purpose of section 145(1) of the Nationality, Immigration and Asylum Act 2002] [or section 4 of the Asylum and Immigration (Treatment of Claimants, etc) Act 2004 (trafficking people for exploitation)].

Amendment
Substituted, together with ss 25, 25A, 25B for s 25 as originally enacted, by the Nationality, Immigration and Asylum Act 2002, s 143. Date in force: 10 February 2003: see SI 2003/1, art 2, Schedule.
Sub-s (9): in para (a) words "(for which purpose "member State" and "immigration law" have the meanings given by section 25(2) and (7))" in square brackets substituted by the Asylum and Immigration (Treatment of Claimants, etc) Act 2004, s 1(2). Date in force: 1 October 2004: see SI 2004/2523, art 2, Schedule.
Sub-s (9): in para (b) words "or section 4 of the Asylum and Immigration (Treatment of Claimants, etc) Act 2004 (trafficking people for exploitation)" in square brackets inserted by the Asylum and Immigration (Treatment of Claimants, etc) Act 2004, s 5(5). Date in force (in relation to Scotland): 1 December 2004: see SSI 2004/494, art 2. Date in force (in relation to England, Wales and Northern Ireland): 1 December 2004: see SI 2004/2999, art 2, Schedule.
Sub-s (10): in para (b) words "or section 4 of the Asylum and Immigration (Treatment of Claimants, etc) Act 2004 (trafficking people for exploitation)" in square brackets inserted by the Asylum and Immigration (Treatment of Claimants, etc) Act 2004, s 5(5). Date in force (in relation to Scotland): 1 December 2004: see SSI 2004/494, art 2. Date in force (in relation to England, Wales and Northern Ireland): 1 December 2004: see SI 2004/2999, art 2, Schedule.
Sub-s (11): words "or section 4 of the Asylum and Immigration (Treatment of Claimants, etc) Act 2004 (trafficking people for exploitation)" in square brackets inserted by the Asylum and Immigration (Treatment of Claimants, etc) Act 2004, s 5(5). Date in force (in relation to Scotland): 1 December 2004: see SSI 2004/494, art 2. Date in force (in relation to England, Wales and Northern Ireland): 1 December 2004: see SI 2004/2999, art 2, Schedule.

[25D   Detention of ship, aircraft or vehicle]

[(1)   If a person has been arrested for an offence under [section 25, 25A or 25B], a senior officer or a constable may detain a relevant ship, aircraft or vehicle—

(a)   until a decision is taken as to whether or not to charge the arrested person with that offence; or

(b)   if the arrested person has been charged—

   (i)   until he is acquitted, the charge against him is dismissed or the proceedings are discontinued; or

   (ii)   if he has been convicted, until the court decides whether or not to order forfeiture of the ship, aircraft or vehicle.

(2)   A ship, aircraft or vehicle is a relevant ship, aircraft or vehicle, in relation to an arrested person, if it is one which the officer or constable concerned has reasonable grounds for believing could, on conviction of the arrested person for the offence for which he was arrested, be the subject of an order for forfeiture made under [section 25C].

[(3)   A person (other than the arrested person) may apply to the court for the release of a ship, aircraft or vehicle on the grounds that—

(a)   he owns the ship, aircraft or vehicle,

(b)   he was, immediately before the detention of the ship, aircraft or vehicle, in possession of it under a hire-purchase agreement, or

(c)   he is a charterer of the ship or aircraft.]

(4)   The court to which an application is made under subsection (3) may, on such security or surety being tendered as it considers satisfactory, release the ship, aircraft or vehicle on condition that it is made available to the court if—

(a)   the arrested person is convicted; and

(b)   an order for its forfeiture is made under [section 25C].

(5)   In the application to Scotland of subsection (1), for paragraphs (a) and (b) substitute—

"(a)   until a decision is taken as to whether or not to institute criminal proceedings against the arrested person for that offence; or

(b)   if criminal proceedings have been instituted against the arrested person—

   (i)   until he is acquitted or, under section 65 or 147 of the Criminal Procedure (Scotland) Act 1995, discharged or liberated or the trial diet is deserted simpliciter;

   (ii)   if he has been convicted, until the court decides whether or not to order forfeiture of the ship, aircraft or vehicle,

and for the purposes of this subsection, criminal proceedings are instituted against a person at whichever is the earliest of his first appearance before the sheriff on petition, or the service on him of an indictment or complaint."

(6)   "Court" means—

(a)   in England and Wales—

   [(ia)   if the arrested person has not been charged, or he has been charged but proceedings for the offence have not begun to be heard, a magistrates' court;]

   (iii)   if he has been charged and proceedings for the offence are being heard, the court hearing the proceedings;

(b)   in Scotland, the sheriff; and

(c)   in Northern Ireland—

   (i)   if the arrested person has not been charged, the magistrates' court for the county court division in which he was arrested;

   (ii)   if he has been charged but proceedings for the offence have not begun to be heard, the magistrates' court for the county court division in which he was charged;

1365

(iii) if he has been charged and proceedings for the offence are being heard, the court hearing the proceedings.

(7)   ...

(8)   "Senior officer" means an immigration officer not below the rank of chief immigration officer.]

Amendment
Section heading: renumbered and substituted by the Nationality, Immigration and Asylum Act 2002, s 144(1), (2). Date in force: 10 February 2003: see SI 2003/1, art 2, Schedule.
Inserted by the Immigration and Asylum Act 1999, s 38(2), (4). Date in force: 3 April 2000 (in relation to persons arrested for offences alleged to have been committed after that date): see SI 2000/464, art 2, Schedule.
Sub-s (1): words "section 25, 25A or 25B" in square brackets substituted by the Nationality, Immigration and Asylum Act 2002, s 144(1), (2)(a). Date in force: 10 February 2003: see SI 2003/1, art 2, Schedule.
Sub-s (2): words "section 25C" in square brackets substituted by the Nationality, Immigration and Asylum Act 2002, s 144(1), (2)(b). Date in force: 10 February 2003: see SI 2003/1, art 2, Schedule.
Sub-s (3): substituted by the Nationality, Immigration and Asylum Act 2002, s 144(1), (2)(c). Date in force: 10 February 2003: see SI 2003/1, art 2, Schedule.
Sub-s (4): in para (b) words "section 25C" in square brackets substituted by the Nationality, Immigration and Asylum Act 2002, s 144(1), (2)(b). Date in force: 10 February 2003: see SI 2003/1, art 2, Schedule.
Sub-s (6): para (a)(ia) substituted, for paras (a)(i), (ii) as originally enacted, by the Courts Act 2003, s 109(1), Sch 8, para 147.
Sub-s (7): repealed by the Nationality, Immigration and Asylum Act 2002, ss 144(1), (2)(d), 161, Sch 9. Date in force: 10 February 2003: see SI 2003/1, art 2, Schedule.

26   General offences in connection with administration of Act

(1)   A person shall be guilty of an offence punishable on summary conviction with a fine of not more than [[level 5] on the standard scale] or with imprisonment for not more than six months, or with both, in any of the following cases—

(a) if, without reasonable excuse, he refuses or fails to submit to examination under Schedule 2 to this Act;
(b) if, without reasonable excuse, he refuses or fails to furnish or produce any information in his possession, or any documents in his possession or control, which he is on an examination under that Schedule required to furnish or produce;
(c) if on any such examination or otherwise he makes or causes to be made to an immigration officer or other person lawfully acting in the execution of [a relevant enactment] a return, statement or representation which he knows to be false or does not believe to be true;
(d) if, without lawful authority, he alters any [certificate of entitlement], entry clearance, work permit or other document issued or made under or for the purposes of this Act, or uses for the purposes of this Act, or has in his possession for such use, any passport, [certificate of entitlement], entry clearance, work permit or other document which he knows or has reasonable cause to believe to be false;
(e) if, without reasonable excuse, he fails to complete and produce a landing or embarkation card in accordance with any order under Schedule 2 to this Act;
(f) if, without reasonable excuse, he fails to comply with any requirement or regulations under section 4(3) or of an order under section 4(4) above;
(g) if, without reasonable excuse, he obstructs an immigration officer or other person lawfully acting in the execution of this Act.

(2)   The extended time limit for prosecutions which is provided for by section 28 below shall apply to offences under subsection (1)(c) and (d) above.

[(3)   "Relevant enactment" means—

   (a)   this Act;
   (b)   the Immigration Act 1988;
   (c)   the Asylum and Immigration Appeals Act 1993 (apart from section 4 or 5); ...
   (d)   the Immigration and Asylum Act 1999 (apart from Part VI)[; or
   (e)   the Nationality, Immigration and Asylum Act 2002 (apart from Part 5)].]

Appointment
Appointment: 1 January 1973: see SI 1972/1514, art 2.

Amendment
Sub-s (1): words ending with "on the standard scale" in square brackets substituted by virtue of the Criminal Justice Act 1982, ss 37, 38, 46.
Sub-s (1): words "level 5" in square brackets substituted by the Asylum and Immigration Act 1996, s 6.
Sub-s (1): in para (c) words "a relevant enactment" in square brackets substituted by the Immigration and Asylum Act 1999, s 30(1), (2). Date in force: 14 February 2000: see SI 2000/168, art 2, Schedule.
Sub-s (1): in para (d) words "certificate of entitlement" in square brackets, in both places they occur, substituted by the British Nationality Act 1981, s 39(6), Sch 4, para 3(1).
Sub-s (3): inserted by the Immigration and Asylum Act 1999, s 30(1), (3). Date in force: 14 February 2000: see SI 2000/168, art 2, Schedule.
Sub-s (3): in para (c) word omitted repealed by the Nationality, Immigration and Asylum Act 2002, ss 151(a), 161, Sch 9. Date in force: 10 February 2003: see SI 2003/1, art 2, Schedule.
Sub-s (3): para (e) and word "; or" immediately preceding it inserted by the Nationality, Immigration and Asylum Act 2002, s 151(b). Date in force: 10 February 2003: see SI 2003/1, art 2, Schedule.

[**26A**   **Registration card**]

[(1)   In this section "registration card" means a document which—

   (a)   carries information about a person (whether or not wholly or partly electroni-cally), and
   (b)   is issued by the Secretary of State to the person wholly or partly in connection with a claim for asylum (whether or not made by that person).

(2)   In subsection (1) "claim for asylum" has the meaning given by section 18 of the Nationality, Immigration and Asylum Act 2002.

(3)   A person commits an offence if he—

   (a)   makes a false registration card,
   (b)   alters a registration card with intent to deceive or to enable another to deceive,
   (c)   has a false or altered registration card in his possession without reasonable excuse,
   (d)   uses or attempts to use a false registration card for a purpose for which a registration card is issued,
   (e)   uses or attempts to use an altered registration card with intent to deceive,
   (f)   makes an article designed to be used in making a false registration card,
   (g)   makes an article designed to be used in altering a registration card with intent to deceive or to enable another to deceive, or
   (h)   has an article within paragraph (f) or (g) in his possession without reasonable excuse.

(4)   In subsection (3) "false registration card" means a document which is designed to appear to be a registration card.

(5)   A person who is guilty of an offence under subsection (3)(a), (b), (d), (e), (f) or (g) shall be liable—

    (a)   on conviction on indictment, to imprisonment for a term not exceeding ten years, to a fine or to both, or

    (b)   on summary conviction, to imprisonment for a term not exceeding six months, to a fine not exceeding the statutory maximum or to both.

(6)   A person who is guilty of an offence under subsection (3)(c) or (h) shall be liable—

    (a)   on conviction on indictment, to imprisonment for a term not exceeding two years, to a fine or to both, or

    (b)   on summary conviction, to imprisonment for a term not exceeding six months, to a fine not exceeding the statutory maximum or to both.

(7)   The Secretary of State may by order—

    (a)   amend the definition of "registration card" in subsection (1);

    (b)   make consequential amendment of this section.

(8)   An order under subsection (7)—

    (a)   must be made by statutory instrument, and

    (b)   may not be made unless a draft has been laid before and approved by resolution of each House of Parliament.]

Amendment
Inserted by the Nationality, Immigration and Asylum Act 2002, s 148. Date in force: 10 February 2003: see SI 2003/1, art 2, Schedule.

[26B   Possession of immigration stamp]

[(1)   A person commits an offence if he has an immigration stamp in his possession without reasonable excuse.

(2)   A person commits an offence if he has a replica immigration stamp in his possession without reasonable excuse.

(3)   In this section—

    (a)   "immigration stamp" means a device which is designed for the purpose of stamping documents in the exercise of an immigration function,

    (b)   "replica immigration stamp" means a device which is designed for the purpose of stamping a document so that it appears to have been stamped in the exercise of an immigration function, and

    (c)   "immigration function" means a function of an immigration officer or the Secretary of State under the Immigration Acts.

(4)   A person who is guilty of an offence under this section shall be liable—

    (a)   on conviction on indictment, to imprisonment for a term not exceeding two years, to a fine or to both, or

    (b)   on summary conviction, to imprisonment for a term not exceeding six months, to a fine not exceeding the statutory maximum or to both.]

Amendment
Inserted by the Nationality, Immigration and Asylum Act 2002, s 149. Date in force: 10 February 2003: see SI 2003/1, art 2, Schedule.

27   Offences by persons connected with ships or aircraft or with ports

A person shall be guilty of an offence punishable on summary conviction with a fine of not more than [[level 5] on the standard scale] or with imprisonment for not more than six months, or with both, in any of the following cases—

(a)   if, being the captain of a ship or aircraft,—

    (i)   he knowingly permits a person to disembark in the United Kingdom when required under Schedule 2 or 3 to this Act to prevent it, or fails without reasonable excuse to take any steps he is required by or under Schedule 2 to take in connection with the disembarkation or examination of passengers or for furnishing a passenger list or particulars of members of the crew; or

    (ii)   he fails, without reasonable excuse, to comply with any directions given him under Schedule 2 or 3 [or under the Immigration and Asylum Act 1999] with respect to the removal of a person from the United Kingdom;

(b)   if, as owner or agent of a ship or aircraft,—

    (i)   he arranges, or is knowingly concerned in any arrangements, for the ship or aircraft to call at a port other than a port of entry contrary to any provision of Schedule 2 to this Act; or

    (ii)   he fails, without reasonable excuse, to take any steps required by an order under Schedule 2 for the supply to passengers of landing or embarkation cards; or

    (iii)   he fails, without reasonable excuse, to make arrangements for [or in connection with] the removal of a person from the United Kingdom when required to do so by directions given under Schedule 2 or 3 to this Act [or under the Immigration and Asylum Act 1999; or

    (iv)   he fails, without reasonable excuse, to comply with the requirements of paragraph 27B or 27C of Schedule 2];

(c)   if, as owner or agent of a ship or aircraft or as a person concerned in the management of a port, he fails, without reasonable excuse, to take any steps required by Schedule 2 in relation to the embarkation or disembarkation of passengers where a control area is designated.

[(d)   ...]

Appointment
Appointment: 1 January 1973: see SI 1972/1514, art 2.

Amendment
Words "level 5" in square brackets substituted by the Asylum and Immigration Act 1996, s 6.
Words ending with the words "on the standard scale" in square brackets substituted by virtue of the Criminal Justice Act 1982, ss 37, 38, 46.
Para (a): in sub-para (ii) words "or under the Immigration and Asylum Act 1999" in square brackets inserted by the Immigration and Asylum Act 1999, s 169(1), Sch 14, paras 43, 52(1), (2). Date in force: 2 October 2000: see SI 2000/2444, art 2, Sch 1.
Para (b): in sub-para (iii) words "or in connection with" in square brackets inserted by the Immigration and Asylum Act 1999, s 169(1), Sch 14, paras 43, 52(1), (3)(a). Date in force: 1 March 2000: see SI 2000/464, art 2, Schedule.
Para (b): words "or under the Immigration and Asylum Act 1999; or" in square brackets and sub-para (iv) inserted by the Immigration and Asylum Act 1999, s 169(1), Sch 14, paras 43, 52(1), (3)(b). Date in force: 3 April 2000: see SI 2000/464, art 2, Schedule.
Para (d): inserted by SI 1990/2227, art 3, Sch 1, Pt I, para 4, repealed by SI 1993/1813, art 9, Sch 6.

Modification
Modified, in its application to the Channel Tunnel, by the Channel Tunnel (International Arrangements) Order 1993, SI 1993/1813, art 7(1), Sch 4, para 1(9).

Modified, in relation to its application to frontier controls between the United Kingdom, France and Belgium, by the Channel Tunnel (Miscellaneous Provisions) Order 1994, SI 1994/1405, art 7.

28   Proceedings

(1)   Where the offence is one to which, under section 24... or 26 above, an extended time limit for prosecutions is to apply, then—

    (a) an information relating to the offence may in England and Wales be tried by a magistrates' court if it is laid within six months after the commission of the offence, or if it is laid within three years after the commission of the offence and not more than two months after the date certified by [an officer of police above the rank of chief superintendent] to be the date on which evidence sufficient to justify proceedings came to the notice of an officer of [the police force to which he belongs]; and

    (b) summary proceedings for the offence may in Scotland be commenced within six months after the commission of the offence, or within three years after the commission of the offence and not more than two months after the date on which evidence sufficient in the opinion of the Lord Advocate to justify proceedings came to his knowledge; and

    (c) a complaint charging the commission of the offence may in Northern Ireland be heard and determined by a magistrates' court if it is made within six months after the commission of the offence, or if it is made within three years after the commission of the offence and not more than two months after the date certified by an officer of police not below the rank of assistant chief constable to be the date on which evidence sufficient to justify the proceedings came to the notice of the police in Northern Ireland.

(2)   For purposes of subsection (1)(b) above proceedings shall be deemed to be commenced on the date on which a warrant to apprehend or to cite the accused is granted, if such warrant is executed without undue delay; and a certificate of the Lord Advocate as to the date on which such evidence as is mentioned in subsection (1)(b) came to his knowledge shall be conclusive evidence.

(3)   For the purposes of the trial of a person for an offence under this Part of this Act, the offence shall be deemed to have been committed either at the place at which it actually was committed or at any place at which he may be.

(4)   Any powers exercisable under this Act in the case of any person may be exercised notwithstanding that proceedings for an offence under this Part of this Act have been taken against him.

Appointment
Appointment (remaining purposes): 1 January 1973: see SI 1972/1514, art 2.

Amendment
Sub-s (1): references omitted repealed by the Nationality, Immigration and Asylum Act 2002, ss 156(1), 161, Sch 9. Date in force: 10 February 2003: see SI 2003/1, art 2, Schedule.
Sub-s (1): in para (a) words "an officer of police above the rank of chief superintendent" and "the police force to which he belongs" in square brackets substituted by the Immigration Act 1988, s 10, Schedule, para 4.

[28A   Arrest without warrant]

[(1)   A constable or immigration officer may arrest without warrant a person—

    (a) who has committed or attempted to commit an offence under section 24 or 24A; or

    (b) whom he has reasonable grounds for suspecting has committed or attempted to commit such an offence.

(2) But subsection (1) does not apply in relation to an offence under section 24(1)(d).

(3) An immigration officer may arrest without warrant a person—

(a) who has committed an offence under [section 25, 25A or 25B]; or
(b) whom he has reasonable grounds for suspecting has committed that offence.

(4) ...

(5) An immigration officer may arrest without warrant a person ("the suspect") who, or whom he has reasonable grounds for suspecting—

(a) has committed or attempted to commit an offence under section 26(1)(g); or
(b) is committing or attempting to commit that offence.

(6) The power conferred by subsection (5) is exercisable only if either the first or the second condition is satisfied.

(7) The first condition is that it appears to the officer that service of a summons (or, in Scotland, a copy complaint) is impracticable or inappropriate because—

(a) he does not know, and cannot readily discover, the suspect's name;
(b) he has reasonable grounds for doubting whether a name given by the suspect as his name is his real name;
(c) the suspect has failed to give him a satisfactory address for service; or
(d) he has reasonable grounds for doubting whether an address given by the suspect is a satisfactory address for service.

(8) The second condition is that the officer has reasonable grounds for believing that arrest is necessary to prevent the suspect—

(a) causing physical injury to himself or another person;
(b) suffering physical injury; or
(c) causing loss of or damage to property.

(9) For the purposes of subsection (7), an address is a satisfactory address for service if it appears to the officer—

(a) that the suspect will be at that address for a sufficiently long period for it to be possible to serve him with a summons (or copy complaint); or
(b) that some other person specified by the suspect will accept service of a summons (or copy complaint) for the suspect at that address.

[(9A) A constable or immigration officer may arrest without warrant a person—

(a) who has committed an offence under section 26A or 26B; or
(b) whom he has reasonable grounds for suspecting has committed an offence under section 26A or 26B.]

(10) In relation to the exercise of the powers conferred by subsections (3)(b)... and (5), it is immaterial that no offence has been committed.

(11) In Scotland the powers conferred by subsections (3)... and (5) may also be exercised by a constable.]

Amendment

Inserted by the Immigration and Asylum Act 1999, s 128. Date in force: 14 February 2000: see SI 2000/168, art 2, Schedule.
Sub-s (3): in para (a) words "section 25, 25A or 25B" in square brackets substituted by the Nationality, Immigration and Asylum Act 2002, s 144(1), (3)(a). Date in force: 10 February 2003: see SI 2003/1, art 2, Schedule.
Sub-s (4): repealed by the Nationality, Immigration and Asylum Act 2002, ss 144(1), (3)(b), 161, Sch 9. Date in force: 10 February 2003: see SI 2003/1, art 2, Schedule.

Sub-s (9A): inserted by the Nationality, Immigration and Asylum Act 2002, s 150(1). Date in force: 10 February 2003: see SI 2003/1, art 2, Schedule.
Sub-s (10): reference omitted repealed by the Nationality, Immigration and Asylum Act 2002, ss 144(1), (3)(c), 161, Sch 9. Date in force: 10 February 2003: see SI 2003/1, art 2, Schedule.
Sub-s (11): reference omitted repealed by the Nationality, Immigration and Asylum Act 2002, ss 144(1), (3)(d), 161, Sch 9. Date in force: 10 February 2003: see SI 2003/1, art 2, Schedule.

Modification
Sub-s (3) modified, in its application to the Channel Tunnel, by the Channel Tunnel (International Arrangements) Order 1993, SI 1993/1813, art 7(1), Sch 4, para 1(9A).

[28AA   Arrest with warrant]

[(1)   This section applies if on an application by an immigration officer a justice of the peace is satisfied that there are reasonable grounds for suspecting that a person has committed an offence under—

(a)   section 24(1)(d), or
(b)   section 8 of the Asylum and Immigration Act 1996 (c 49) (employment: offence).

(2)   The justice of the peace may grant a warrant authorising any immigration officer to arrest the person.

(3)   In the application of this section to Scotland a reference to a justice of the peace shall be treated as a reference to the sheriff or a justice of the peace.]

Amendment
Inserted by the Nationality, Immigration and Asylum Act 2002, s 152. Date in force: 8 January 2003: see SI 2002/2811, art 2, Schedule.

[28B   Search and arrest by warrant]

[(1)   Subsection (2) applies if a justice of the peace is, by written information on oath, satisfied that there are reasonable grounds for suspecting that a person ("the suspect") who is liable to be arrested for a relevant offence is to be found on any premises.

(2)   The justice may grant a warrant authorising any immigration officer or constable to enter, if need be by force, the premises named in the warrant for the purpose of searching for and arresting the suspect.

(3)   Subsection (4) applies if in Scotland the sheriff or a justice of the peace is by evidence on oath satisfied as mentioned in subsection (1).

(4)   The sheriff or justice may grant a warrant authorising any immigration officer or constable to enter, if need be by force, the premises named in the warrant for the purpose of searching for and arresting the suspect.

(5)   "Relevant offence" means an offence under section 24(1)(a), (b), (c), (d), (e) or (f)[, 24A][, 26A or 26B].]

Amendment
Inserted by the Immigration and Asylum Act 1999, s 129. Date in force: 14 February 2000: see SI 2000/168, art 2, Schedule.
Sub-s (5): reference to ", 24A" in square brackets substituted by the Nationality, Immigration and Asylum Act 2002, s 144(1), (4). Date in force: 10 February 2003: see SI 2003/1, art 2, Schedule.
Sub-s (5): words ", 26A or 26B" in square brackets inserted by the Nationality, Immigration and Asylum Act 2002, s 150(2). Date in force: 10 February 2003: see SI 2003/1, art 2, Schedule.

[28C Search and arrest without warrant]

[(1) An immigration officer may enter and search any premises for the purpose of arresting a person for an offence under [section 25, 25A or 25B].

(2) The power may be exercised—

(a) only to the extent that it is reasonably required for that purpose; and

(b) only if the officer has reasonable grounds for believing that the person whom he is seeking is on the premises.

(3) In relation to premises consisting of two or more separate dwellings, the power is limited to entering and searching—

(a) any parts of the premises which the occupiers of any dwelling comprised in the premises use in common with the occupiers of any such other dwelling; and

(b) any such dwelling in which the officer has reasonable grounds for believing that the person whom he is seeking may be.

(4) The power may be exercised only if the officer produces identification showing that he is an immigration officer (whether or not he is asked to do so).]

Amendment
Inserted by the Immigration and Asylum Act 1999, s 130. Date in force: 14 February 2000: see SI 2000/168, art 2, Schedule.
Sub-s (1): words "section 25, 25A or 25B" in square brackets substituted by the Nationality, Immigration and Asylum Act 2002, s 144(1), (5). Date in force: 10 February 2003: see SI 2003/1, art 2, Schedule.

[28CA Business premises: entry to arrest]

[(1) A constable or immigration officer may enter and search any business premises for the purpose of arresting a person—

(a) for an offence under section 24,

(b) for an offence under section 24A, or

(c) under paragraph 17 of Schedule 2.

(2) The power under subsection (1) may be exercised only—

(a) to the extent that it is reasonably required for a purpose specified in subsection (1),

(b) if the constable or immigration officer has reasonable grounds for believing that the person whom he is seeking is on the premises,

(c) with the authority of the Secretary of State (in the case of an immigration officer) or a Chief Superintendent (in the case of a constable), and

(d) if the constable or immigration officer produces identification showing his status.

(3) Authority for the purposes of subsection (2)(c)—

(a) may be given on behalf of the Secretary of State only by a civil servant of the rank of at least Assistant Director, and

(b) shall expire at the end of the period of seven days beginning with the day on which it is given.

(4) Subsection (2)(d) applies—

(a) whether or not a constable or immigration officer is asked to produce identification, but

(b) only where premises are occupied.

(5) Subsection (6) applies where a constable or immigration officer—

   (a)   enters premises in reliance on this section, and
   (b)   detains a person on the premises.

(6)   A detainee custody officer may enter the premises for the purpose of carrying out a search.

(7)   In subsection (6)—

"detainee custody officer" means a person in respect of whom a certificate of authorisation is in force under section 154 of the Immigration and Asylum Act 1999 (c 33) (detained persons: escort and custody), and
"search" means a search under paragraph 2(1)(a) of Schedule 13 to that Act (escort arrangements: power to search detained person).]

Amendment
Inserted by the Nationality, Immigration and Asylum Act 2002, s 153(1). Date in force: 8 January 2003: see SI 2002/2811, art 2, Schedule.

[28D   Entry and search of premises]

[(1)   If, on an application made by an immigration officer, a justice of the peace is satisfied that there are reasonable grounds for believing that—

   (a)   a relevant offence has been committed,
   (b)   there is material on premises specified in the application which is likely to be of substantial value (whether by itself or together with other material) to the investigation of the offence,
   (c)   the material is likely to be relevant evidence,
   (d)   the material does not consist of or include items subject to legal privilege, excluded material or special procedure material, and
   (e)   any of the conditions specified in subsection (2) applies,

he may issue a warrant authorising an immigration officer to enter and search the premises.

(2)   The conditions are that—

   (a)   it is not practicable to communicate with any person entitled to grant entry to the premises;
   (b)   it is practicable to communicate with a person entitled to grant entry to the premises but it is not practicable to communicate with any person entitled to grant access to the evidence;
   (c)   entry to the premises will not be granted unless a warrant is produced;
   (d)   the purpose of a search may be frustrated or seriously prejudiced unless an immigration officer arriving at the premises can secure immediate entry to them.

(3)   An immigration officer may seize and retain anything for which a search has been authorised under subsection (1).

(4)   "Relevant offence" means an offence under section 24(1)(a), (b), (c), (d), (e) or (f), [24A, 25, 25A, 25B][, 26A or 26B].

(5)   In relation to England and Wales, expressions which are given a meaning by the Police and Criminal Evidence Act 1984 have the same meaning when used in this section.

(6)   In relation to Northern Ireland, expressions which are given a meaning by the Police and Criminal Evidence (Northern Ireland) Order 1989 have the same meaning when used in this section

(7)   In the application of subsection (1) to Scotland—

(a) read the reference to a justice of the peace as a reference to the sheriff or a justice of the peace; and

(b) in paragraph (b), omit the reference to excluded material and special procedure material.]

Amendment

Inserted by the Immigration and Asylum Act 1999, s 131. Date in force: 14 February 2000: see SI 2000/168, art 2, Schedule.

Sub-s (4): reference to "24A, 25, 25A or 25B" in square brackets substituted by the Nationality, Immigration and Asylum Act 2002, s 144(1), (6). Date in force: 10 February 2003: see SI 2003/1, art 2, Schedule.

Sub-s (4): words ", 26A or 26B" in square brackets inserted by the Nationality, Immigration and Asylum Act 2002, s 150(3). Date in force: 10 February 2003: see SI 2003/1, art 2, Schedule.

See Further

See further, in relation to additional powers of seizure from premises and the obligation to return excluded and special procedure material: the Criminal Justice and Police Act 2001, ss 50, 55, Sch 1, Pt 1, para 15, Pt 3, para 95.

[28E   Entry and search of premises following arrest]

[[(1)   This section applies if a person is arrested for an offence under this Part at a place other than a police station.

(2)   An immigration officer may enter and search any premises—

(a) in which the person was when arrested, or

(b) in which he was immediately before he was arrested,

for evidence relating to the offence for which the arrest was made ("relevant evidence").

(3)   The power may be exercised—

(a) only if the officer has reasonable grounds for believing that there is relevant evidence on the premises; and

(b) only to the extent that it is reasonably required for the purpose of discovering relevant evidence.

(4)   In relation to premises consisting of two or more separate dwellings, the power is limited to entering and searching—

(a) any dwelling in which the arrest took place or in which the arrested person was immediately before his arrest; and]

(b) any parts of the premises which the occupier of any such dwelling uses in common with the occupiers of any other dwellings comprised in the premises.

(5)   An officer searching premises under subsection (2) may seize and retain anything he finds which he has reasonable grounds for believing is relevant evidence.

(6)   Subsection (5) does not apply to items which the officer has reasonable grounds for believing are items subject to legal privilege.]]

Amendment

Inserted by the Immigration and Asylum Act 1999, s 132(1). Date in force: 14 February 2000: see SI 2000/168, art 2, Schedule.

See Further

See further, in relation to additional powers of seizure from premises: the Criminal Justice and Police Act 2001, s 50, Sch 1, Pt 1, para 15.

[**28F**   *Entry and search of premises following arrest under section 25(1)* [<u>Entry and search of premises following arrest under section 25, 25A or 25B</u>]]

[(1)   An immigration officer may enter and search any premises occupied or controlled by a person arrested for an offence under [section 25, 25A, 25B].

(2)   The power may be exercised—

(a)   only if the officer has reasonable grounds for suspecting that there is relevant evidence on the premises;

(b)   only to the extent that it is reasonably required for the purpose of discovering relevant evidence; and

(c)   subject to subsection (3), only if a senior officer has authorised it in writing.

(3)   The power may be exercised—

(a)   before taking the arrested person to a place where he is to be detained; and

(b)   without obtaining an authorisation under subsection (2)(c),

if the presence of that person at a place other than one where he is to be detained is necessary for the effective investigation of the offence.

(4)   An officer who has relied on subsection (3) must inform a senior officer as soon as is practicable.

(5)   The officer authorising a search, or who is informed of one under subsection (4), must make a record in writing of—

(a)   the grounds for the search; and

(b)   the nature of the evidence that was sought.

(6)   An officer searching premises under this section may seize and retain anything he finds which he has reasonable grounds for suspecting is relevant evidence.

(7)   "Relevant evidence" means evidence, other than items subject to legal privilege, that relates to the offence in question.

(8)   "Senior officer" means an immigration officer not below the rank of chief immigration officer.]

Amendment
Section heading: words "Entry and search of premises following arrest under section 25(1)" in italics repealed and subsequent words in square brackets substituted by the Nationality, Immigration and Asylum Act 2002, s 144(1), (7). Date in force: to be appointed: see the Nationality, Immigration and Asylum Act 2002, s 162(1).
Inserted by the Immigration and Asylum Act 1999, s 133. Date in force: 14 February 2000: see SI 2000/168, art 2, Schedule.
Sub-s (1): words "section 25, 25A, 25B" in square brackets substituted by the Nationality, Immigration and Asylum Act 2002, s 144(1), (7). Date in force: 10 February 2003: see SI 2003/1, art 2, Schedule.

See Further
See further, in relation to additional powers of seizure from premises: the Criminal Justice and Police Act 2001, s 50, Sch 1, Pt 1, para 15.

[**28FA**   **Search for personnel records: warrant unnecessary**]

[(1)   This section applies where—

(a)   a person has been arrested for an offence under section 24(1) or 24A(1),

(b)   a person has been arrested under paragraph 17 of Schedule 2,

(c)   a constable or immigration officer reasonably believes that a person is liable to arrest for an offence under section 24(1) or 24A(1), or

(d) a constable or immigration officer reasonably believes that a person is liable to arrest under paragraph 17 of Schedule 2.

(2) A constable or immigration officer may search business premises where the arrest was made or where the person liable to arrest is if the constable or immigration officer reasonably believes—

(a) that a person has committed an immigration employment offence in relation to the person arrested or liable to arrest, and

(b) that employee records, other than items subject to legal privilege, will be found on the premises and will be of substantial value (whether on their own or together with other material) in the investigation of the immigration employment offence.

(3) A constable or officer searching premises under subsection (2) may seize and retain employee records, other than items subject to legal privilege, which he reasonably suspects will be of substantial value (whether on their own or together with other material) in the investigation of—

(a) an immigration employment offence, or

(b) an offence under section 105 or 106 of the Immigration and Asylum Act 1999 (c 33) (support for asylum-seeker: fraud).

(4) The power under subsection (2) may be exercised only—

(a) to the extent that it is reasonably required for the purpose of discovering employee records other than items subject to legal privilege,

(b) if the constable or immigration officer produces identification showing his status, and

(c) if the constable or immigration officer reasonably believes that at least one of the conditions in subsection (5) applies.

(5) Those conditions are—

(a) that it is not practicable to communicate with a person entitled to grant access to the records,

(b) that permission to search has been refused,

(c) that permission to search would be refused if requested, and

(d) that the purpose of a search may be frustrated or seriously prejudiced if it is not carried out in reliance on subsection (2).

(6) Subsection (4)(b) applies—

(a) whether or not a constable or immigration officer is asked to produce identification, but

(b) only where premises are occupied.

(7) In this section "immigration employment offence" means an offence under section 8 of the Asylum and Immigration Act 1996 (c 49) (employment).]

Amendment
Inserted by the Nationality, Immigration and Asylum Act 2002, s 154. Date in force: 8 January 2003: see SI 2002/2811, art 2, Schedule.

[28FB Search for personnel records: with warrant]

[(1) This section applies where on an application made by an immigration officer in respect of business premises a justice of the peace is satisfied that there are reasonable grounds for believing—

  (a) that an employer has provided inaccurate or incomplete information under section 134 of the Nationality, Immigration and Asylum Act 2002 (compulsory disclosure by employer),
  (b) that employee records, other than items subject to legal privilege, will be found on the premises and will enable deduction of some or all of the information which the employer was required to provide, and
  (c) that at least one of the conditions in subsection (2) is satisfied.

(2) Those conditions are—

  (a) that it is not practicable to communicate with a person entitled to grant access to the premises,
  (b) that it is not practicable to communicate with a person entitled to grant access to the records,
  (c) that entry to the premises or access to the records will not be granted unless a warrant is produced, and
  (d) that the purpose of a search may be frustrated or seriously prejudiced unless an immigration officer arriving at the premises can secure immediate entry.

(3) The justice of the peace may issue a warrant authorising an immigration officer to enter and search the premises.

(4) Subsection (7)(a) of section 28D shall have effect for the purposes of this section as it has effect for the purposes of that section.

(5) An immigration officer searching premises under a warrant issued under this section may seize and retain employee records, other than items subject to legal privilege, which he reasonably suspects will be of substantial value (whether on their own or together with other material) in the investigation of—

  (a) an offence under section 137 of the Nationality, Immigration and Asylum Act 2002 (disclosure of information: offences) in respect of a requirement under section 134 of that Act, or
  (b) an offence under section 105 or 106 of the Immigration and Asylum Act 1999 (c 33) (support for asylum-seeker: fraud).]

Amendment
Inserted by the Nationality, Immigration and Asylum Act 2002, s 154. Date in force: 30 July 2003 (being the day on which the Nationality, Immigration and Asylum Act 2002, s 134 came into force): see SI 2003/1747, art 2(b) and SI 2002/2811, arts 2, 6.

[28G Searching arrested persons]

[(1) This section applies if a person is arrested for an offence under this Part at a place other than a police station.

(2) An immigration officer may search the arrested person if he has reasonable grounds for believing that the arrested person may present a danger to himself or others.

(3) The officer may search the arrested person for—

  (a) anything which he might use to assist his escape from lawful custody; or
  (b) anything which might be evidence relating to the offence for which he has been arrested.

(4) The power conferred by subsection (3) may be exercised—

  (a) only if the officer has reasonable grounds for believing that the arrested person may have concealed on him anything of a kind mentioned in that subsection; and

(b) only to the extent that it is reasonably required for the purpose of discovering any such thing.

(5) A power conferred by this section to search a person is not to be read as authorising an officer to require a person to remove any of his clothing in public other than an outer coat, jacket or glove; but it does authorise the search of a person's mouth.

(6) An officer searching a person under subsection (2) may seize and retain anything he finds, if he has reasonable grounds for believing that that person might use it to cause physical injury to himself or to another person.

(7) An officer searching a person under subsection (3) may seize and retain anything he finds, if he has reasonable grounds for believing—

(a) that that person might use it to assist his escape from lawful custody; or
(b) that it is evidence which relates to the offence in question.

(8) Subsection (7)(b) does not apply to an item subject to legal privilege.]

Amendment
Inserted by the Immigration and Asylum Act 1999, s 134(1). Date in force: 14 February 2000: see SI 2000/168, art 2, Schedule.

See Further
See further, in relation to additional powers of seizure from the person: the Criminal Justice and Police Act 2001, s 51, Sch 1, Pt 2, para 78.

[28H   Searching persons in police custody]

[(1) This section applies if a person—

(a) has been arrested for an offence under this Part; and
(b) is in custody at a police station or in police detention at a place other than a police station.

(2) An immigration officer may, at any time, search the arrested person in order to see whether he has with him anything—

(a) which he might use to—
    (i) cause physical injury to himself or others;
    (ii) damage property;
    (iii) interfere with evidence; or
    (iv) assist his escape; or
(b) which the officer has reasonable grounds for believing is evidence relating to the offence in question.

(3) The power may be exercised only to the extent that the custody officer concerned considers it to be necessary for the purpose of discovering anything of a kind mentioned in subsection (2).

(4) An officer searching a person under this section may seize anything he finds, if he has reasonable grounds for believing that—

(a) that person might use it for one or more of the purposes mentioned in subsection (2)(a); or
(b) it is evidence relating to the offence in question.

(5) Anything seized under subsection (4)(a) may be retained by the police.

(6) Anything seized under subsection (4)(b) may be retained by an immigration officer.

(7)   The person from whom something is seized must be told the reason for the seizure unless he is—

    (a) violent or appears likely to become violent; or
    (b) incapable of understanding what is said to him.

(8)   An intimate search may not be conducted under this section.

(9)   The person carrying out a search under this section must be of the same sex as the person searched.

(10)   "Custody officer"—

    (a) in relation to England and Wales, has the same meaning as in the Police and Criminal Evidence Act 1984;
    (b) in relation to Scotland, means the officer in charge of a police station; and
    (c) in relation to Northern Ireland, has the same meaning as in the Police and Criminal Evidence (Northern Ireland) Order 1989.

(11)   "Intimate search"—

    (a) in relation to England and Wales, has the meaning given by section 65 of the Act of 1984;
    (b) in relation to Scotland, means a search which consists of the physical examination of a person's body orifices other than the mouth; and
    (c) in relation to Northern Ireland, has the same meaning as in the 1989 Order.

(12)   "Police detention"—

    (a) in relation to England and Wales, has the meaning given by section 118(2) of the 1984 Act; and
    (b) in relation to Northern Ireland, has the meaning given by Article 2 of the 1989 Order.

(13)   In relation to Scotland, a person is in police detention if—

    (a) he has been taken to a police station after being arrested for an offence; or
    (b) he is arrested at a police station after attending voluntarily at the station, accompanying a constable to it or being detained under section 14 of the Criminal Procedure (Scotland) Act 1995,

and is detained there or is detained elsewhere in the charge of a constable, but is not in police detention if he is in court after being charged.]

Amendment
Inserted by the Immigration and Asylum Act 1999, s 135(1). Date in force: 14 February 2000: see SI 2000/168, art 2, Schedule.

See Further
See further, references to a person being detained by a member of the Constabulary in the exercise of any of the powers or privileges conferred on him by the Energy Act 2004, s 56 and a person's accompanying a member of the Constabulary: the Energy Act 2004, s 68(7).

[28I   Seized material: access and copying]

[(1)   If a person showing himself—

    (a) to be the occupier of the premises on which seized material was seized, or
    (b) to have had custody or control of the material immediately before it was seized,

asks the immigration officer who seized the material for a record of what he seized, the officer must provide the record to that person within a reasonable time.

(2)   If a relevant person asks an immigration officer for permission to be granted access to seized material, the officer must arrange for him to have access to the material under the supervision—

(a)   in the case of seized material within subsection (8)(a), of an immigration officer;

(b)   in the case of seized material within subsection (8)(b), of a constable.

(3)   An immigration officer may photograph or copy, or have photographed or copied, seized material.

(4)   If a relevant person asks an immigration officer for a photograph or copy of seized material, the officer must arrange for—

(a)   that person to have access to the material for the purpose of photographing or copying it under the supervision—
   (i)   in the case of seized material within subsection (8)(a), of an immigration officer;
   (ii)   in the case of seized material within subsection (8)(b), of a constable; or
(b)   the material to be photographed or copied.

(5)   A photograph or copy made under subsection (4)(b) must be supplied within a reasonable time.

(6)   There is no duty under this section to arrange for access to, or the supply of a photograph or copy of, any material if there are reasonable grounds for believing that to do so would prejudice—

(a)   the exercise of any functions in connection with which the material was seized; or

(b)   an investigation which is being conducted under this Act, or any criminal proceedings which may be brought as a result.

(7)   "Relevant person" means—

(a)   a person who had custody or control of seized material immediately before it was seized, or

(b)   someone acting on behalf of such a person.

(8)   "Seized material" means anything—

(a)   seized and retained by an immigration officer, or

(b)   seized by an immigration officer and retained by the police,

under this Part.]

Amendment
Inserted by the Immigration and Asylum Act 1999, s 136(1). Date in force: 14 February 2000: see SI 2000/168, art 2, Schedule.

[28J   Search warrants: safeguards]

[(1)   The entry or search of premises under a warrant is unlawful unless it complies with this section and section 28K.

(2)   If an immigration officer applies for a warrant, he must—

(a)   state the ground on which he makes the application and the provision of this Act under which the warrant would be issued;

(b)   specify the premises which it is desired to enter and search; and

(c)   identify, so far as is practicable, the persons or articles to be sought.

(3)   In Northern Ireland, an application for a warrant is to be supported by a complaint in writing and substantiated on oath.

(4)   Otherwise, an application for a warrant is to be made ex parte and supported by an information in writing or, in Scotland, evidence on oath.

(5)   The officer must answer on oath any question that the justice of the peace or sheriff hearing the application asks him.

(6)   A warrant shall authorise an entry on one occasion only.

(7)   A warrant must specify—

(a)   the name of the person applying for it;
(b)   the date on which it is issued;
(c)   the premises to be searched; and
(d)   the provision of this Act under which it is issued.

(8)   A warrant must identify, so far as is practicable, the persons or articles to be sought.

(9)   Two copies of a warrant must be made.

(10)   The copies must be clearly certified as copies.

(11)   "Warrant" means a warrant to enter and search premises issued to an immigration officer under this Part or under paragraph 17(2) of Schedule 2.]

Amendment
Inserted by the Immigration and Asylum Act 1999, s 137. Date in force: 14 February 2000: see SI 2000/168, art 2, Schedule.

[28K   Execution of warrants]

[[(1)   A warrant may be executed by any immigration officer.

(2)   A warrant may authorise persons to accompany the officer executing it.

(3)   Entry and search under a warrant must be—

(a)   within one month from the date of its issue; and
(b)   at a reasonable hour, unless it appears to the officer executing it that the purpose of a search might be frustrated.

(4)   If the occupier of premises which are to be entered and searched is present at the time when an immigration officer seeks to execute a warrant, the officer must—

(a)   identify himself to the occupier and produce identification showing that he is an immigration officer;
(b)   show the occupier the warrant; and
(c)   supply him with a copy of it.]

(5)   If—

(a)   the occupier is not present, but
(b)   some other person who appears to the officer to be in charge of the premises is present,

subsection (4) has effect as if each reference to the occupier were a reference to that other person.

(6)   If there is no person present who appears to the officer to be in charge of the premises, the officer must leave a copy of the warrant in a prominent place on the premises.

(7)   A search under a warrant may only be a search to the extent required for the purpose for which the warrant was issued.

(8)   An officer executing a warrant must make an endorsement on it stating—

(a) whether the persons or articles sought were found; and
(b) whether any articles, other than articles which were sought, were seized.

(9) A warrant which has been executed, or has not been executed within the time authorised for its execution, must be returned—

[(a) if issued by a justice of the peace in England and Wales, to the designated officer for the local justice area in which the justice was acting when he issued the warrant;]
(b) if issued by a justice of the peace in Northern Ireland, to the clerk of petty sessions for the petty sessions district in which the premises are situated;
(c) if issued by a justice of the peace in Scotland, to the clerk of the district court for the commission area for which the justice of the peace was appointed;
(d) if issued by the sheriff, to the sheriff clerk.

(10) A warrant returned under subsection (9)(a) must be retained for 12 months by the [designated officer].

(11) A warrant issued under subsection (9)(b) or (c) must be retained for 12 months by the clerk.

(12) A warrant returned under subsection (9)(d) must be retained for 12 months by the sheriff clerk.

(13) If during that 12 month period the occupier of the premises to which it relates asks to inspect it, he must be allowed to do so.

(14) "Warrant" means a warrant to enter and search premises issued to an immigration officer under this Part or under paragraph 17(2) of Schedule 2.]

Amendment
Inserted by the Immigration and Asylum Act 1999, s 138; for transitional provisions see Sch 15, para 4(b) thereto. Date in force: 14 February 2000: see SI 2000/168, art 2, Schedule.
Sub-s (9): para (a) substituted by the Courts Act 2003, s 109(1), Sch 8, para 148(1), (2).
Sub-s (10): words "designated officer" in square brackets substituted by the Courts Act 2003, s 109(1), Sch 8, para 148(1), (3).

[28L   Interpretation of Part III]

[[(1)] In this Part, "premises" and "items subject to legal privilege" have the same meaning—

(a) in relation to England and Wales, as in the Police and Criminal Evidence Act 1984;
(b) in relation to Northern Ireland, as in the Police and Criminal Evidence (Northern Ireland) Order 1989"; and
(c) in relation to Scotland, as in section [412 of the Proceeds of Crime Act 2002].

[(2) In this Part "business premises" means premises (or any part of premises) not used as a dwelling.

(3) In this Part "employee records" means records which show an employee's—

(a) name,
(b) date of birth,
(c) address,
(d) length of service,
(e) rate of pay, or
(f) nationality or citizenship.

(4) The Secretary of State may by order amend section 28CA(3)(a) to reflect a change in nomenclature.

(5)   An order under subsection (4)—

    (a)   must be made by statutory instrument, and

    (b)   shall be subject to annulment in pursuance of a resolution of either House of Parliament.]]

Amendment
Sub-s (1): numbered as such by the Nationality, Immigration and Asylum Act 2002, s 155. Date in force: 8 January 2003: see SI 2002/2811, art 2, Schedule.
Inserted by the Immigration and Asylum Act 1999, s 139(1). Date in force: 14 February 2000: see SI 2000/168, art 2, Schedule.
Sub-s (1): in para (c) words "412 of the Proceeds of Crime Act 2002" in square brackets substituted by the Proceeds of Crime Act 2002, s 456, Sch 11, paras 1, 6. Date in force: 24 February 2003: see SI 2003/120, art 2, Schedule.
Sub-ss (2)–(5): inserted by the Nationality, Immigration and Asylum Act 2002, s 155. Date in force: 8 January 2003: see SI 2002/2811, art 2, Schedule.

PART IV
SUPPLEMENTARY

29   ...

...

Amendment
Repealed by the Nationality, Immigration and Asylum Act 2002, ss 58(5)(a), 161, Sch 9. Date in force: 7 November 2002: see the Nationality, Immigration and Asylum Act 2002, s 162(2)(q).

30   ...

...

Amendment
Repealed by the British Nationality Act 1981, s 52(8), Sch 9, and the Mental Health (Scotland) Act 1984, s 127(2), Sch 5.

31   Expenses

There shall be defrayed out of moneys provided by Parliament any expenses incurred [by the Lord Chancellor under Schedule 5 to this Act or] by a Secretary of State under or by virtue of this Act—

    (a)   by way of administrative expenses ... ; or

    (b)   in connection with the removal of any person from the United Kingdom under Schedule 2 or 3 to this Act or the departure with him of his dependants, or his or their maintenance pending departure; or

    (c)   ...

    (d)   ...

Initial Commencement
Royal Assent: 28 October 1971: (no specific commencement provision).

Amendment
Words "by the Lord Chancellor under Schedule 5 to this Act or" in square brackets inserted by SI 1987/465, art 3(4).
In para (a) words omitted repealed by the British Nationality Act 1981, s 52(8), Sch 9.
Para (c) repealed by SI 1987/465, art 3(4).
Para (d) repealed by the Nationality, Immigration and Asylum Act 2002, ss 58(5)(b), 161, Sch 9. Date in force: 7 November 2002: see the Nationality, Immigration and Asylum Act 2002, s 162(2)(q).

[31A   Procedural requirements as to applications]

[(1)   If a form is prescribed for a particular kind of application under this Act, any application of that kind must be made in the prescribed form.

(2)   If procedural or other steps are prescribed in relation to a particular kind of application under this Act, those steps must be taken in respect of any application of that kind.

(3)   "Prescribed" means prescribed in regulations made by the Secretary of State.

[(3A)   Regulations under this section may provide that a failure to comply with a specified requirement of the regulations—

(a)   invalidates an application,
(b)   does not invalidate an application, or
(c)   invalidates an application in specified circumstances (which may be described wholly or partly by reference to action by the applicant, the Secretary of State, an immigration officer or another person).]

(4)   The power to make regulations under this section is exercisable by statutory instrument.

(5)   Any such statutory instrument shall be subject to annulment in pursuance of a resolution of either House of Parliament.]

Amendment

Inserted by the Immigration and Asylum Act 1999, s 165. Date in force (for the purpose of enabling subordinate legislation to be made): 22 May 2000: see SI 2000/1282, art 2, Schedule. Date in force (for remaining purposes): 1 August 2003: see SI 2003/1862, art 2.
Sub-s (3A): inserted by the Nationality, Immigration and Asylum Act 2002, s 121. Date in force: 10 February 2003: see SI 2003/1, art 2, Schedule.

Subordinate Legislation

Immigration (Leave to Remain) (Prescribed Forms and Procedures) Regulations 2005, SI 2005/771.

32   General provisions as to Orders in Council, etc

(1)   Any power conferred by Part I of this Act to make an Order in Council or order (other than a deportation order) or to give any directions includes power to revoke or vary the Order in Council, order or directions.

(2)   Any document purporting to be an order, notice or direction made or given by the Secretary of State for the purposes of [the Immigration Acts] and to be signed by him or on his behalf, and any document purporting to be a certificate of the Secretary of State so given and to be signed by him [or on his behalf], shall be received in evidence, and shall, until the contrary is proved, be deemed to be made or issued by him.

(3)   Prima facie evidence of any such order, notice, direction or certificate as aforesaid may, in any legal proceedings or [other proceedings under the Immigration Acts], be given by the production of a document bearing a certificate purporting to be signed by or on behalf of the Secretary of State and stating that the document is a true copy of the order, notice, direction or certificate.

(4)   Where an order under section 8(2) above applies to persons specified in a schedule to the order, or any directions of the Secretary of State given for the purposes of [the Immigration Acts] apply to persons specified in a schedule to the directions, prima facie evidence of the provisions of the order or directions other than the prima facie evidence of the provisions of the order or directions other than the schedule and of any entry contained in the schedule may, in any legal proceedings or [other proceedings under the Immigration Acts], be given by the production of a document

purporting to be signed by or on behalf of the Secretary of State and stating that the document is a true copy of the said provisions and of the relevant entry.

[(5)   In subsection (4) "the Immigration Acts" has the meaning given by [s]ection 44 of the Asylum and Immigration (Treatment of Claimants, etc) Act 2004].

Initial Commencement
Royal Assent: 28 October 1971: (no specific commencement provision).

Amendment
Sub-s (2): words "the Immigration Acts" in square brackets substituted by the Immigration and Asylum Act 1999, s 169(1), Sch 14, paras 43, 54(1), (2)(a); for the application of this amendment see para 54(6) thereto. Date in force: 6 December 1999: see SI 1999/3190, art 2, Schedule.
Sub-s (2): words "or on his behalf" in square brackets inserted by the Immigration and Asylum Act 1999, s 169(1), Sch 14, paras 43, 54(1), (2)(b). Date in force: 6 December 1999: see SI 1999/3190, art 2, Schedule.
Sub-s (3): words "other proceedings under the Immigration Acts" in square brackets substituted by the Immigration and Asylum Act 1999, s 169(1), Sch 14, paras 43, 54(1), (3). Date in force: 6 December 1999: see SI 1999/3190, art 2, Schedule.
Sub-s (4): words "the Immigration Acts" and "other proceedings under the Immigration Acts" in square brackets substituted by the Immigration and Asylum Act 1999, s 169(1), Sch 14, paras 43, 54(1), (4). Date in force: 6 December 1999: see SI 1999/3190, art 2, Schedule.
Sub-s (5) (as inserted by the Immigration and Asylum Act 1999, s 169(1), Sch 14, paras 43, 54(1), (5)): substituted by the Nationality, Immigration and Asylum Act 2002, s 158(3). Date in force: 10 February 2003: see SI 2003/1, art 2, Schedule.
Sub-s (5): words "section 44 of the Asylum and Immigration (Treatment of Claimants, etc) Act 2004" in square brackets substituted by the Asylum and Immigration (Treatment of Claimants, etc) Act 2004, s 44(4)(a). Date in force: 1 October 2004: see SI 2004/2523, art 2, Schedule.

33   Interpretation

(1)   For purposes of this Act, except in so far as the context otherwise requires—

"aircraft" includes hovercraft, "airport" includes hoverport and "port" includes airport;
"captain" means master (of a ship) or commander (of an aircraft);
"certificate of [entitlement]" means such a certificate as is referred to in section 3(9) above;
["certificate of entitlement" means a certificate under section 10 of the Nationality, Immigration and Asylum Act 2002 that a person has the right of abode in the United Kingdom;]
["Convention adoption" has the same meaning as in the Adoption Act 1976 and the Adoption (Scotland) Act 1978 [or in the Adoption and Children Act 2002];]
[...]
"crew", in relation to a ship or aircraft, means all persons actually employed in the working or service of the ship or aircraft, including the captain, and "member of the crew" shall be construed accordingly;
["entrant" means a person entering or seeking to enter the United Kingdom and "illegal entrant" means a person—
  (a)   unlawfully entering or seeking to enter in breach of a deportation order or of the immigration laws, or
  (b)   entering or seeking to enter by means which include deception by another person,
and includes also a person who has entered as mentioned in paragraph (a) or (b) above;]
"entry clearance" means a visa, entry certificate or other document which, in accordance with the immigration rules, is to be taken as evidence [or the requisite evidence] of a person's eligibility, though not [a British citizen], for entry into the United Kingdom (but does not include a work permit);

"immigration laws" means this Act and any law for purposes similar to this Act which is for the time being or has (before or after the passing of this Act) been in force in any part of the United Kingdom and Islands;

"immigration rules" means the rules for the time being laid down as mentioned in section 3(2) above;

"the Islands" means the Channel Islands and the Isle of Man, and "the United Kingdom and Islands" means the United Kingdom and the Islands taken together;

"legally adopted" means adopted in pursuance of an order made by any court in the United Kingdom and Islands[, under a Convention adoption] or by any adoption specified as an overseas adoption by order of the Secretary of State under *[section 72(2) of the Adoption Act 1976]* [section 87 of the Adoption and Children Act 2002];

"limited leave" and "indefinite leave" mean respectively leave under this Act to enter or remain in the United Kingdom which is, and one which is not, limited as to duration;

"settled" shall be construed in accordance [with subsection (2A) below];

"ship" includes every description of vessel used in navigation;

[...]

["United Kingdom passport" means a current passport issued by the Government of the United Kingdom, or by the Lieutenant-Governor of any of the Islands or by the Government of any territory which is for the time being a [British overseas territory] within the meaning of the British Nationality Act 1981;]

"work permit" means a permit indicating, in accordance with the immigration rules, that a person named in it is eligible, though not [a British citizen], for entry into the United Kingdom for the purpose of taking employment.

[(1A) A reference to being an owner of a vehicle, ship or aircraft includes a reference to being any of a number of persons who jointly own it.]

(2) It is hereby declared that, except as otherwise provided in this Act, a person is not to be treated for the purposes of any provision of this Act as ordinarily resident in the United Kingdom or in any of the Islands at a time when he is there in breach of the immigration laws.

[(2A) Subject to section 8(5) above, references to a person being settled in the United Kingdom are references to his being ordinarily resident there without being subject under the immigration laws to any restriction on the period for which he may remain.]

(3) The ports of entry for purposes of this Act, and the ports of exit for purposes of any Order in Council under section 3(7) above, shall be such ports as may from time to time be designated for the purpose by order of the Secretary of State made by statutory instrument.

[(4) For the purposes of this Act, the question of whether an appeal is pending shall be determined [in accordance with section 104 of the Nationality, Immigration and Asylum Act 2002 (pending appeals)].]

(5) This Act shall not be taken to supersede or impair any power exercisable by Her Majesty in relation to aliens by virtue of Her prerogative.

Initial Commencement
Royal Assent: 28 October 1971: (no specific commencement provision).

Amendment
Sub-s (1): definition "certificate of entitlement" substituted by the Nationality, Immigration and Asylum Act 2002, s 10(5)(b). Date in force: to be appointed: see the Nationality, Immigration and Asylum Act 2002, s 162(1).

Sub-s (1): in definition "certificate of entitlement" word "entitlement" in square brackets substituted by the British Nationality Act 1981, s 39(6), Sch 4, para 2.

Sub-s (1): definition "Convention adoption" inserted by the Adoption (Intercountry Aspects) Act 1999, s 15(1), Sch 2, para 2(a). Date in force: 1 June 2003: see SI 2003/362, art 2(b).

Sub-s (1): in the definition "convention adoption" words "or in the Adoption and Children Act 2002" in square brackets inserted by the Adoption and Children Act 2002, s 139(1), Sch 3, para 15(a). Date in force: to be appointed: see the Adoption and Children Act 2002, s 148(1), (2).

Sub-s (1): definitions omitted inserted by SI 1990/2227, art 3, Sch 1, Pt I, repealed by SI 1993/1813, art 9, Sch 6.

Sub-s (1): definitions "entrant" and "illegal entrant" substituted by the Asylum and Immigration Act 1996, s 12(1), Sch 2, para 4(1).

Sub-s (1): in definition "entry clearance" words "or the requisite evidence" in square brackets inserted by the Immigration Act 1988, s 10, Schedule, para 5.

Sub-s (1): in definition "entry clearance" words "a British citizen" in square brackets substituted by the British Nationality Act 1981, s 39(6), Sch 4, para 2.

Sub-s (1): in definition "legally adopted" words ", under a Convention adoption" in square brackets inserted by the Adoption (Intercountry Aspects) Act 1999, s 15(1), Sch 2, para 2(b). Date in force: 1 June 2003: see SI 2003/362, art 2(b).

Sub-s (1): in definition "legally adopted" words "section 72(2) of the Adoption Act 1976" in square brackets substituted by the Adoption Act 1976, s 73(2), Sch 6, para 17.

Sub-s (1): in definition "legally adopted" words "section 72(2) of the Adoption Act 1976" in italics repealed and subsequent words in square brackets substituted by the Adoption and Children Act 2002, s 139(1), Sch 3, para 15(b). Date in force: to be appointed: see the Adoption and Children Act 2002, s 148(1), (2).

Sub-s (1): in definition "settled" words "with subsection (2A) below" in square brackets substituted by the British Nationality Act 1981, s 39(6), Sch 4, para 3.

Sub-s (1): definition "United Kingdom passport" inserted by the British Nationality Act 1981, s 39(6), Sch 4, para 7.

Sub-s (1): in definition "United Kingdom passport" words "British overseas territory" in square brackets substituted by virtue of the British Overseas Territories Act 2002, s 1(2). Date in force: this amendment came into force on 26 February 2002 (date of Royal Assent of the British Overseas Territories Act 2002) in the absence of any specific commencement provision.

Sub-s (1): in definition "work permit" words "a British citizen" in square brackets substituted by the British Nationality Act 1981, s 39(6), Sch 4, para 7.

Sub-s (1A): inserted by the Nationality, Immigration and Asylum Act 2002, s 144(1), (8). Date in force: 10 February 2003: see SI 2003/1, art 2, Schedule.

Sub-s (2A): inserted by the British Nationality Act 1981, s 39(6), Sch 4, para 7.

Sub-s (4): substituted by the Immigration and Asylum Act 1999, s 169(1), Sch 14, paras 43, 55. Date in force: 2 October 2000: see SI 2000/2444, art 2, Sch 1.

Sub-s (4): words "in accordance with section 104 of the Nationality, Immigration and Asylum Act 2002 (pending appeals)" in square brackets substituted by the Nationality, Immigration and Asylum Act 2002, s 114(3), Sch 7, para 1. Date in force: 1 April 2003: see SI 2003/754, art 2(1), Sch 1.

Modification
Modified, in its application to the Channel Tunnel, by the Channel Tunnel (International Arrangements) Order 1993, SI 1993/1813, art 7(1), Sch 4, para 1(10).
Modified, in relation to its application to frontier controls between the United Kingdom, France and Belgium, by the Channel Tunnel (Miscellaneous Provisions) Order 1994, SI 1994/1405, art 7.

Subordinate Legislation
Immigration (Ports of Entry) Order 1987, SI 1987/177 (made under sub-s (3)).

34   Repeal, transitional and temporary

(1)   Subject to the following provisions of this section, the enactments mentioned in Schedule 6 to this Act are hereby repealed, as from the coming into force of this Act, to the extent mentioned in column 3 of the Schedule; and—

  (a)   this Act, as from its coming into force, shall apply in relation to entrants or others arriving in the United Kingdom at whatever date before or after it comes into force; and

(b) after this Act comes into force anything done under or for the purposes of the former immigration laws shall have effect, in so far as any corresponding action could be taken under or for the purposes of this Act, as if done by way of action so taken, and in relation to anything so done this Act shall apply accordingly.

(2) Without prejudice to the generality of subsection (1)(a) and (b) above, a person refused leave to land by virtue of the Aliens Restriction Act 1914 shall be treated as having been refused leave to enter under this Act, and a person given leave to land by virtue of that Act shall be treated as having been given leave to enter under this Act; and similarly with the Commonwealth Immigrants Acts 1962 and 1968.

(3) A person treated in accordance with subsection (2) above as having leave to enter the United Kingdom—

(a) shall be treated as having an indefinite leave, if he is not at the coming into force of this Act subject to a condition limiting his stay in the United Kingdom; and

(b) shall be treated, if he is then subject to such a condition, as having a limited leave of such duration, and subject to such conditions (capable of being attached to leave under this Act), as correspond to the conditions to which he is then subject, but not to conditions not capable of being so attached.

This subsection shall have effect in relation to any restriction or requirement imposed by Order in Council under the Aliens Restriction Act 1914 as if it had been imposed by way of a landing condition.

(4) Notwithstanding anything in the foregoing provisions of this Act, the former immigration laws shall continue to apply, and this Act shall not apply,—

(a) in relation to the making of deportation orders and matters connected therewith in any case where a decision to make the order has been notified to the person concerned before the coming into force of this Act;

(b) in relation to removal from the United Kingdom and matters connected therewith (including detention pending removal or pending the giving of directions for removal) in any case where a person is to be removed in pursuance of a decision taken before the coming into force of this Act or in pursuance of a deportation order to the making of which paragraph (a) above applies;

(c) in relation to appeals against any decision taken or other thing done under the former immigration laws, whether taken or done before the coming into force of this Act or by virtue of this subsection.

(5) Subsection (1) above shall not be taken as empowering a court on appeal to recommend for deportation a person whom the court below could not recommend for deportation, or as affecting any right of appeal in respect of a recommendation for deportation made before this Act comes into force, or as enabling a notice given before this Act comes into force and not complying with section 6(2) to take the place of the notice required by section 6(2) to be given before a person is recommended for deportation.

(6) ...

Initial Commencement
Royal Assent: 28 October 1971: (no specific commencement provision).

Amendment
Sub-s (6): repealed by the Statute Law (Repeals) Act 1993.

35   Commencement, and interim provisions

(1)   Except as otherwise provided by this Act, Parts I to III of this Act shall come into force on such day as the Secretary of State may appoint by order made by statutory instrument; and references to the coming into force of this Act shall be construed as references to the beginning of the day so appointed.

(2)   Section 25 above, except section 25(2), and section 28 in its application to offences under section 25(1) shall come into force at the end of one month beginning with the date this Act is passed.

(3)–(5)   ...

Initial Commencement
Royal Assent: 28 October 1971: (no specific commencement provision).

Amendment
Sub-ss (3)–(5): repealed by the Statute Law (Repeals) Act 1986.

Subordinate Legislation
Immigration Act 1971 (Commencement) Order 1972, SI 1972/1514 (made under sub-s (1)).

36   Power to extend to Islands

Her Majesty may by Order in Council direct that any of the provisions of this Act shall extend, with such exceptions, adaptations and modifications, if any, as may be specified in the Order, to any of the Islands; and any Order in Council under this subsection may be varied or revoked by a further Order in Council.

Initial Commencement
Royal Assent: 28 October 1971: (no specific commencement provision).

Subordinate Legislation
Criminal Justice Act 1982 (Isle of Man) Order 1983, SI 1983/1898.
Immigration (Isle of Man) Order 1991, SI 1991/2630.
Immigration (Guernsey) Order 1993, SI 1993/1796.
Immigration (Jersey) Order 1993, SI 1993/1797.
Immigration (Isle of Man) Order 1997, SI 1997/275.
Immigration and Asylum Act 1999 (Jersey) Order 2003, SI 2003/1252.

37   Short title and extent

(1)   This Act may be cited as the Immigration Act 1971.

(2)   It is hereby declared that this Act extends to Northern Ireland, and (without prejudice to any provision of Schedule 1 to this Act as to the extent of that Schedule) where an enactment repealed by this Act extends outside the United Kingdom, the repeal shall be of like extent.

Initial Commencement
Royal Assent: 28 October 1971: (no specific commencement provision).

SCHEDULE 1
...

Amendment
Repealed by the British Nationality Act 1981, s 52(8), Sch 9.

SCHEDULE 2

ADMINISTRATIVE PROVISIONS AS TO CONTROL ON ENTRY ETC

Section 4

PART I
GENERAL PROVISIONS

Immigration officers and medical inspectors

1 (1) Immigration officers for the purposes of this Act shall be appointed by the Secretary of State, and he may arrange with the Commissioners of Customs and Excise for the employment of officers of customs and excise as immigration officers under this Act.

(2) Medical inspectors for the purposes of this Act may be appointed by the Secretary of State or, in Northern Ireland, by the Minister of Health and Social Services or other appropriate Minister of the Government of Northern Ireland in pursuance of arrangements made between that Minister and the Secretary of State, and shall be fully qualified medical practitioners.

[(2A) The Secretary of State may direct that his function of appointing medical inspectors under sub-paragraph (2) is also to be exercisable by such persons specified in the direction who exercise functions relating to health in England or Wales.]

(3) In the exercise of their functions under this Act immigration officers shall act in accordance with such instructions (not inconsistent with the immigration rules) as may be given them by the Secretary of State, and medical inspectors shall act in accordance with such instructions as may be given them by the Secretary of State or, in Northern Ireland, as may be given in pursuance of the arrangements mentioned in sub-paragraph (2) above by the Minister making appointments of medical inspectors in Northern Ireland.

(4) An immigration officer or medical inspector may board any ship [or aircraft] for the purpose of exercising his functions under this Act.

(5) An immigration officer, for the purpose of satisfying himself whether there are persons he may wish to examine under paragraph 2 below, may search any ship [or aircraft] and anything on board it, or any vehicle taken off a ship or aircraft in which it has been brought to the United Kingdom.

Examination by immigration officers, and medical examination

2 (1) An immigration officer may examine any persons who have arrived in the United Kingdom by ship [or aircraft] (including transit passengers, members of the crew and others not seeking to enter the United Kingdom) for the purpose of determining—

(a) whether any of them is or is not [a British citizen]; and
(b) whether, if he is not, he may or may not enter the United Kingdom without leave; and
[(c) whether, if he may not—
    (i) he has been given leave which is still in force,
    (ii) he should be given leave and for what period or on what conditions (if any), or
    (iii) he should be refused leave].

(2) Any such person, if he is seeking to enter the United Kingdom, may be examined also by a medical inspector or by any qualified person carrying out a test or examination required by a medical inspector.

(3)   A person, on being examined under this paragraph by an immigration officer or medical inspector, may be required in writing by him to submit to further examination; but a requirement under this sub-paragraph shall not prevent a person who arrives as a transit passenger, or as a member of the crew of a ship or aircraft, or for the purpose of joining a ship or aircraft as a member of the crew, from leaving by his intended ship or aircraft.

[Examination of persons who arrive with continuing leave

2A   (1)   This paragraph applies to a person who has arrived in the United Kingdom with leave to enter which is in force but which was given to him before his arrival.

(2)   He may be examined by an immigration officer for the purpose of establishing—

  (a)   whether there has been such a change in the circumstances of his case, since that leave was given, that it should be cancelled;
  (b)   whether that leave was obtained as a result of false information given by him or his failure to disclose material facts; or
  (c)   whether there are medical grounds on which that leave should be cancelled.

[(2A)   Where the person's leave to enter derives, by virtue of section 3A(3), from an entry clearance, he may also be examined by an immigration officer for the purpose of establishing whether the leave should be cancelled on the grounds that the person's purpose in arriving in the United Kingdom is different from the purpose specified in the entry clearance.]

(3)   He may also be examined by an immigration officer for the purpose of determining whether it would be conducive to the public good for that leave to be cancelled.

(4)   He may also be examined by a medical inspector or by any qualified person carrying out a test or examination required by a medical inspector.

(5)   A person examined under this paragraph may be required by the officer or inspector to submit to further examination.

(6)   A requirement under sub-paragraph (5) does not prevent a person who arrives—

  (a)   as a transit passenger,
  (b)   as a member of the crew of a ship or aircraft, or
  (c)   for the purpose of joining a ship or aircraft as a member of the crew,

from leaving by his intended ship or aircraft.

(7)   An immigration officer examining a person under this paragraph may by notice suspend his leave to enter until the examination is completed.

(8)   An immigration officer may, on the completion of any examination of a person under this paragraph, cancel his leave to enter.

(9)   Cancellation of a person's leave under sub-paragraph (8) is to be treated for the purposes of this Act and [Part 5 of the Nationality, Immigration and Asylum Act 2002 (immigration and asylum appeals)] as if he had been refused leave to enter at a time when he had a current entry clearance.

(10)   A requirement imposed under sub-paragraph (5) and a notice given under sub-paragraph (7) must be in writing.]

3   (1)   An immigration officer may examine any person who is embarking or seeking to embark in the United Kingdom [...] for the purpose of determining whether he is [a British citizen] and, if he is not, for the purpose of establishing his identity.

(2)   So long as any Order in Council is in force under section 3(7) of this Act, an immigration officer may examine any person who is embarking or seeking to embark in the United Kingdom [...] for the purpose of determining—

    (a)   whether any of the provisions of the Order apply to him; and
    (b)   whether, if so, any power conferred by the Order should be exercised in relation to him and in what way.

Information and documents

4   (1)   It shall be the duty of any person examined under paragraph 2[, 2A] or 3 above to furnish to the person carrying out the examination all such information in his possession as that person may require for the purpose of his functions under that paragraph.

(2)   A person on his examination under paragraph 2[, 2A] or 3 above by an immigration officer shall, if so required by the immigration officer—

    (a)   produce either a valid passport with photograph or some other document satisfactorily establishing his identity and nationality or citizenship; and
    (b)   declare whether or not he is carrying or conveying[, or has carried or conveyed,] documents of any relevant description specified by the immigration officer, and produce any documents of that description which he is carrying or conveying.
  In paragraph (b), "relevant description" means any description appearing to the immigration officer to be relevant for the purposes of the examination.

[(2A)   An immigration officer may detain any passport or other document produced pursuant to sub-paragraph (2)(a) above until the person concerned is given leave to enter the United Kingdom or is about to depart or be removed following refusal of leave.]

(3)   Where under sub-paragraph (2)(b) above a person has been required to declare whether or not he is carrying or conveying[, or has carried or conveyed,] documents of any description—

    [(a)   he and any baggage or vehicle belonging to him or under his control; and
    (b)   any ship, aircraft or vehicle in which he arrived in the United Kingdom,]

may be searched with a view to ascertaining whether he is doing [or, as the case may be, has done] so by the immigration officer or a person acting under the directions of that officer:
  Provided that no woman or girl shall be searched except by a woman.

(4)   An immigration officer may examine any documents produced pursuant to sub-paragraph (2)(b) above or found on a search under sub-paragraph (3), and may for that purpose detain them for any period not exceeding seven days; and if on examination of any document so produced or found the immigration officer is of the opinion that it may be needed in connection with proceedings on [an appeal under the Nationality, Immigration and Asylum Act 2002] or for an offence, he may detain it until he is satisfied that it will not be so needed.

5   The Secretary of State may by order made by statutory instrument make provision for requiring passengers disembarking or embarking in the United Kingdom, or any class of such passengers, to produce to an immigration officer, if so required, landing or embarkation cards in such form as the Secretary of State may direct, and for requiring the owners or agents of ships and aircraft to supply such cards to those passengers.

Notice of leave to enter or of refusal of leave

6   (1)   Subject to sub-paragraph (3) below, where a person examined by an immigration officer under paragraph 2 above is to be given a limited leave to enter the United Kingdom or is to be refused leave, the notice giving or refusing leave shall be given not later than [twenty-four hours] after the conclusion of his examination (including any further examination) in pursuance of that paragraph; and if notice giving or refusing leave is not given him before the end of those [twenty-four hours], he shall (if not [a British citizen]) be deemed to have been given [leave to enter the United Kingdom for a period of six months subject to a condition prohibiting his taking employment] and the immigration officer shall as soon as may be give him written notice of that leave.

(2)   Where on a person's examination under paragraph 2 above he is given notice of leave to enter the United Kingdom, then at any time before the end of [twenty-four hours] from the conclusion of the examination he may be given a further notice in writing by an immigration officer cancelling the earlier notice and refusing him leave to enter.

(3)   Where in accordance with this paragraph a person is given notice refusing him leave to enter the United Kingdom, that notice may at any time be cancelled by notice in writing given by an immigration officer; and where a person is given a notice of cancellation under this sub-paragraph, [and the immigration officer does not at the same time give him indefinite or limited leave to enter [or require him to submit to further examination], he shall be deemed to have been given leave to enter for a period of six months subject to a condition prohibiting his taking employment and the immigration officer shall as soon as may be give him written notice of that leave.]

(4)   Where an entrant is a member of a party in charge of a person appearing to the immigration officer to be a responsible person, any notice to be given in relation to that entrant in accordance with this paragraph shall be duly given if delivered to the person in charge of the party.

[Power to require medical examination after entry

7   (1)   This paragraph applies if an immigration officer examining a person under paragraph 2 decides—

  (a)   that he may be given leave to enter the United Kingdom; but
  (b)   that a further medical test or examination may be required in the interests of public health.

(2)   This paragraph also applies if an immigration officer examining a person under paragraph 2A decides—

  (a)   that his leave to enter the United Kingdom should not be cancelled; but
  (b)   that a further medical test or examination may be required in the interests of public health.

(3)   The immigration officer may give the person concerned notice in writing requiring him—

  (a)   to report his arrival to such medical officer of health as may be specified in the notice; and
  (b)   to attend at such place and time and submit to such test or examination (if any), as that medical officer of health may require.

(4)   In reaching a decision under paragraph (b) of sub-paragraph (1) or (2), the immigration officer must act on the advice of—

  (a)   a medical inspector; or

(b) if no medical inspector is available, a fully qualified medical practitioner.]

Removal of persons refused leave to enter and illegal entrants

8   (1) Where a person arriving in the United Kingdom is refused leave to enter, an immigration officer may, subject to sub-paragraph (2) below—

(a) give the captain of the ship or aircraft in which he arrives directions requiring the captain to remove him from the United Kingdom in that ship or aircraft; or

(b) give the owners or agents of that ship or aircraft directions requiring them to remove him from the United Kingdom in any ship or aircraft specified or indicated in the directions, being a ship or aircraft of which they are the owners or agents; or

(c) give those owners or agents [...] directions requiring them to make arrangements for his removal from the United Kingdom in any ship or aircraft specified or indicated in the direction to a country or territory so specified being either—

    (i) a country of which he is a national or citizen; or

    (ii) a country or territory in which he has obtained a passport or other document of identity; or

    (iii) a country or territory in which he embarked for the United Kingdom; or

    (iv) a country or territory to which there is reason to believe that he will be admitted.

(2) No directions shall be given under this paragraph in respect of anyone after the expiration of two months beginning with the date on which he was refused leave to enter the United Kingdom [(ignoring any period during which an appeal by him under the Immigration Acts is pending)] [except that directions may be given under sub-paragraph (1)(b) or (c) after the end of that period if the immigration officer has within that period given written notice to the owners or agents in question of his intention to give directions to them in respect of that person].

9   [(1)] Where an illegal entrant is not given leave to enter or remain in the United Kingdom, an immigration officer may give any such directions in respect of him as in a case within paragraph 8 above are authorised by paragraph 8(1).

[(2) Any leave to enter the United Kingdom which is obtained by deception shall be disregarded for the purposes of this paragraph.]

10   (1) Where it appears to the Secretary of State either—

(a) that directions might be given in respect of a person under paragraph 8 or 9 above, but that it is not practicable for them to be given or that, if given, they would be ineffective; or

(b) that directions might have been given in respect of a person under paragraph 8 above [but that the requirements of paragraph 8(2) have not been complied with];

then the Secretary of State may give to the owners or agents of any ship or aircraft any such directions in respect of that person as are authorised by paragraph 8(1)(c).

(2) Where the Secretary of State may give directions for a person's removal in accordance with sub-paragraph (1) above, he may instead give directions for his removal in accordance with arrangements to be made by the Secretary of State to any country or territory to which he could be removed under sub-paragraph (1).

(3) The costs of complying with any directions given under this paragraph shall be defrayed by the Secretary of State.

Appendix 1   Legislation and materials

[**10A**   Where directions are given in respect of a person under any of paragraphs 8 to 10 above, directions to the same effect may be given under that paragraph in respect of a member of the person's family.]

11   A person in respect of whom directions are given under any of paragraphs 8 to 10 above may be placed, under the authority of an immigration officer, on board any ship or aircraft in which he is to be removed in accordance with the directions.

Seamen and aircrews

12   (1)   If, on a person's examination by an immigration officer under paragraph 2 above, the immigration officer is satisfied that he has come to the United Kingdom for the purpose of joining a ship or aircraft as a member of the crew, then the immigration officer may limit the duration of any leave he gives that person to enter the United Kingdom by requiring him to leave the United Kingdom in a ship or aircraft specified or indicated by the notice giving leave.

(2)   Where a person (not being [a British citizen]) arrives in the United Kingdom for the purpose of joining a ship or aircraft as a member of a crew and, having been given leave to enter as mentioned in sub-paragraph (1) above, remains beyond the time limited by that leave, or is reasonably suspected by an immigration officer of intending to do so, an immigration officer may—

(a)   give the captain of that ship or aircraft directions requiring the captain to remove him from the United Kingdom in that ship or aircraft; or

(b)   give the owners or agents of that ship or aircraft directions requiring them to remove him from the United Kingdom in any ship or aircraft specified or indicated in the directions, being a ship or aircraft of which they are the owners or agents; or

(c)   give those owners or agents directions requiring them to make arrangements for his removal from the United Kingdom in any ship or aircraft specified or indicated in the directions to a country or territory so specified, being either—

(i)   a country of which he is a national or citizen; or

(ii)   a country or territory in which he has obtained a passport or other document of identity; or

(iii)   a country or territory in which he embarked for the United Kingdom; or

(iv)   a country or territory where he was engaged as a member of the crew of the ship or aircraft which he arrived in the United Kingdom to join; or

(v)   a country or territory to which there is reason to believe that he will be admitted.

13   (1)   Where a person being a member of the crew of a ship or aircraft is examined by an immigration officer under paragraph 2 above, the immigration officer may limit the duration of any leave he gives that person to enter the United Kingdom—

(a)   in the manner authorised by paragraph 12(1) above; or

(b)   if that person is to be allowed to enter the United Kingdom in order to receive hospital treatment, by requiring him, on completion of that treatment, to leave the United Kingdom in accordance with arrangements to be made for his repatriation; or

(c)   by requiring him to leave the United Kingdom within a specified period in accordance with arrangements to be made for his repatriation.

(2)   Where a person (not being [a British citizen]) arrives in the United Kingdom as a member of the crew of a ship or aircraft, and either—

(A)   having lawfully entered the United Kingdom without leave by virtue of section 8(1) of this Act, he remains without leave beyond the time allowed by section 8(1), or is reasonably suspected by an immigration officer of intending to do so; or

(B) having been given leave limited as mentioned in sub-paragraph (1) above, he remains beyond the time limited by that leave, or is reasonably suspected by an immigration officer of intending to do so;

an immigration officer may—

(a) give the captain of the ship or aircraft in which he arrived directions requiring the captain to remove him from the United Kingdom in that ship or aircraft; or

(b) give the owners or agents of that ship or aircraft directions requiring them to remove him from the United Kingdom, being a ship or aircraft specified or indicated in the directions, being a ship or aircraft of which they are the owners or agents; or

(c) give those owners or agents directions requiring them to make arrangements for his removal from the United Kingdom in any ship or aircraft specified or indicated in the directions to a country or territory so specified, being either—

    (i) a country of which he is a national or citizen; or

    (ii) a country or territory in which he has obtained a passport or other document of identity; or

    (iii) a country in which he embarked for the United Kingdom; or

    (iv) a country or territory in which he was engaged as a member of the crew of the ship or aircraft in which he arrived in the United Kingdom; or

    (v) a country or territory to which there is reason to believe that he will be admitted.

14 (1) Where it appears to the Secretary of State that directions might be given in respect of a person under paragraph 12 or 13 above, but that it is not practicable for them to be given or that, if given, they would be ineffective, then the Secretary of State may give to the owners or agents of any ship or aircraft any such directions in respect of that person as are authorised by paragraph 12(2)(c) or 13(2)(c).

(2) Where the Secretary of State may give directions for a person's removal in accordance with sub-paragraph (1) above, he may instead give directions for his removal in accordance with arrangements to be made by the Secretary of State to any country or territory to which he could be removed under sub-paragraph (1).

(3) The costs of complying with any directions given under this paragraph shall be defrayed by the Secretary of State.

15 A person in respect of whom directions are given under any of paragraphs 12 to 14 above may be placed, under the authority of an immigration officer, on board any ship or aircraft in which he is to be removed in accordance with the directions.

Detention of persons liable to examination or removal

16 (1) A person who may be required to submit to examination under paragraph 2 above may be detained under the authority of an immigration officer pending his examination and pending a decision to give or refuse him leave to enter.

[(1A) A person whose leave to enter has been suspended under paragraph 2A may be detained under the authority of an immigration officer pending—

(a) completion of his examination under that paragraph; and

(b) a decision on whether to cancel his leave to enter.]

[(2) If there are reasonable grounds for suspecting that a person is someone in respect of whom directions may be given under any of paragraphs [8 to 10A] or 12 to 14, that person may be detained under the authority of an immigration officer pending—

(a) a decision whether or not to give such directions;

(b) his removal in pursuance of such directions.]

(3)   A person on board a ship or aircraft may, under the authority of an immigration officer, be removed from the ship or aircraft for detention under this paragraph; but if an immigration officer so requires the captain of a ship or aircraft shall prevent from disembarking in the United Kingdom any person who has arrived in the United Kingdom in the ship or aircraft and been refused leave to enter, and the captain may for that purpose detain him in custody on board the ship or aircraft.

(4)   The captain of a ship or aircraft, if so required by an immigration officer, shall prevent from disembarking in the United Kingdom or before the directions for his removal have been fulfilled any person placed on board the ship or aircraft under paragraph 11 or 15 above, and the captain may for that purpose detain him in custody on board the ship or aircraft.

[(4A)   ...]

17   (1)   A person liable to be detained under paragraph 16 above may be arrested without warrant by a constable or by an immigration officer.

(2)   If—

    (a)   a justice of the peace is by written information on oath satisfied that there is reasonable ground for suspecting that a person liable to be arrested under this paragraph is to be found on any premises; or

    (b)   in Scotland, a sheriff, or a ... justice of the peace, having jurisdiction in the place where the premises are situated is by evidence on oath so satisfied;

he may grant a warrant [authorising any immigration officer or constable to enter,] [if need be by reasonable force], the premises named in the warrant for the purposes of searching for and arresting that person.

[(3)   Sub-paragraph (4) applies where an immigration officer or constable—

    (a)   enters premises in reliance on a warrant under sub-paragraph (2), and

    (b)   detains a person on the premises.

(4)   A detainee custody officer may enter the premises, if need be by reasonable force, for the purpose of carrying out a search.

(5)   In sub-paragraph (4)—

    "detainee custody officer" means a person in respect of whom a certificate of authorisation is in force under section 154 of the Immigration and Asylum Act 1999 (c 33) (detained persons: escort and custody), and

    "search" means a search under paragraph 2(1)(a) of Schedule 13 to that Act (escort arrangements: power to search detained person).]

18   (1)   Persons may be detained under paragraph 16 above in such places as the Secretary of State may direct (when not detained in accordance with paragraph 16 on board a ship or aircraft).

(2)   Where a person is detained under paragraph 16, any immigration officer, constable or prison officer, or any other person authorised by the Secretary of State, may take all such steps as may be reasonably necessary for photographing, measuring or otherwise identifying him.

[(2A)   The power conferred by sub-paragraph (2) includes power to take fingerprints.]

(3)   Any person detained under paragraph 16 may be taken in the custody of a constable, or of any person acting under the authority of an immigration officer, to and from any place where his attendance is required for the purpose of ascertaining his citizenship or nationality or of making arrangements for his admission to a country or territory other than the United Kingdom, or where he is required to be for any other purpose connected with the operation of this Act.

(4)   A person shall be deemed to be in legal custody at any time when he is detained under paragraph 16 or is being removed in pursuance of sub-paragraph (3) above.

19   (1)   Where a person is refused leave to enter the United Kingdom and directions are given in respect of him under paragraph 8 or 10 above, then subject to the provisions of this paragraph the owners or agents of the ship or aircraft in which he arrived [...] shall be liable to pay the Secretary of State on demand any expenses incurred by the latter in respect of the custody, accommodation or maintenance of that person [for any period (not exceeding 14 days)] after his arrival while he was detained or liable to be detained under paragraph 16 above.

(2)   Sub-paragraph (1) above shall not apply to expenses in respect of a person who, when he arrived in the United Kingdom, held a [certificate of entitlement] or a current entry clearance or was the person named in a current work permit; and for this purpose a document purporting to be a [certificate of entitlement], entry clearance or work permit is to be regarded as being one unless its falsity is reasonably apparent.

(3)   If, before the directions for a person's removal under paragraph 8 or 10 above have been carried out, he is given leave to enter the United Kingdom, or if he is afterwards given that leave in consequence of the determination in his favour of an appeal under this Act (being an appeal against a refusal of leave to enter by virtue of which the directions were given), or it is determined on an appeal under this Act that he does not require leave to enter (being an appeal occasioned by such a refusal), no sum shall be demanded under sub-paragraph (1) above for expenses incurred in respect of that person and any sum already demanded and paid shall be refunded.

(4)   Sub-paragraph (1) above shall not have effect in relation to directions which, in consequence of an appeal under this Act, have ceased to have effect or are for the time being of no effect; and the expenses to which that sub-paragraph applies include expenses in conveying the person in question to and from the place where he is detained or accommodated unless the journey is made for the purpose of attending an appeal by him under this Act.

20   (1)   Subject to the provisions of this paragraph, in either of the following cases, that is to say,—

   (a)   where directions are given in respect of an illegal entrant under paragraph 9 or 10 above; and
   (b)   where a person has lawfully entered the United Kingdom without leave by virtue of section 8(1) of this Act, but directions are given in respect of him under paragraph 13(2)(A) above or, in a case within paragraph 13(2)(A), under paragraph 14;

the owners or agents of the ship or aircraft in which he arrived in the United Kingdom [...] shall be liable to pay the Secretary of State on demand any expenses incurred by the latter in respect of the custody, accommodation or maintenance of that person [for any period (not exceeding 14 days)] after his arrival while he was detained or liable to be detained under paragraph 16 above.

[(1A)   Sub-paragraph (1) above shall not apply to expenses in respect of an illegal entrant if he obtained leave to enter by deception and the leave has not been cancelled under paragraph 6(2) above.]

(2)   If, before the directions for a person's removal from the United Kingdom have been carried out, he is given leave to remain in the United Kingdom, no sum shall be demanded under sub-paragraph (1) above for expenses incurred in respect of that person and any sum already demanded and paid shall be refunded.

(3)   Sub-paragraph (1) above shall not have effect in relation to directions which, in consequence of an appeal under this Act, are for the time being of no effect; and the

expenses to which that sub-paragraph applies include expenses in conveying the person in question to and from the place where he is detained or accommodated unless the journey is made for the purpose of attending an appeal by him under this Act.

Temporary admission or release of persons liable to detention

21   (1)   A person liable to detention or detained under paragraph 16 above may, under the written authority of an immigration officer, be temporarily admitted to the United Kingdom without being detained or be released from detention; but this shall not prejudice a later exercise of the power to detain him.

(2)   So long as a person is at large in the United Kingdom by virtue of this paragraph, he shall be subject to such restrictions as to residence[, as to his employment or occupation] and as to reporting to the police or an immigration officer as may from time to time be notified to him in writing by an immigration officer.

[(2A)   The provisions that may be included in restrictions as to residence imposed under sub-paragraph (2) include provisions of such a description as may be prescribed by regulations made by the Secretary of State.

(2B)   The regulations may, among other things, provide for the inclusion of provisions—

    (a)   prohibiting residence in one or more particular areas;

    (b)   requiring the person concerned to reside in accommodation provided under section 4 of the Immigration and Asylum Act 1999 and prohibiting him from being absent from that accommodation except in accordance with the restrictions imposed on him.

(2C)   The regulations may provide that a particular description of provision may be imposed only for prescribed purposes.

(2D)   The power to make regulations conferred by this paragraph is exercisable by statutory instrument and includes a power to make different provision for different cases.

(2E)   But no regulations under this paragraph are to be made unless a draft of the regulations has been laid before Parliament and approved by a resolution of each House.]

[(3)   Sub-paragraph (4) below applies where a person who is at large in the United Kingdom by virtue of this paragraph is subject to a restriction as to reporting to an immigration officer with a view to the conclusion of his examination under paragraph 2 [or 2A] above.

(4)   If the person fails at any time to comply with that restriction—

    (a)   an immigration officer may direct that the person's examination … shall be treated as concluded at that time; but

    (b)   nothing in paragraph 6 above shall require the notice giving or refusing him leave to enter the United Kingdom to be given within twenty-four hours after that time.]

22   [(1)   The following, namely—

    (a)   a person detained under paragraph 16(1) above pending examination;

    [(aa) a person detained under paragraph 16(1A) above pending completion of his examination or a decision on whether to cancel his leave to enter;] and

    (b)   a person detained under paragraph 16(2) above pending the giving of directions,

may be released on bail in accordance with this paragraph.

(1A) An immigration officer not below the rank of chief immigration officer or [the Asylum and Immigration Tribunal] may release a person so detained on his entering into a recognizance or, in Scotland, bail bond conditioned for his appearance before an immigration officer at a time and place named in the recognizance or bail bond or at such other time and place as may in the meantime be notified to him in writing by an immigration officer.

(1B) Sub-paragraph (1)(a) above shall not apply unless seven days have elapsed since the date of the person's arrival in the United Kingdom.]

(2) The conditions of a recognizance or bail bond taken under this paragraph may include conditions appearing to the [immigration officer or [the Asylum and Immigration Tribunal]] to be likely to result in the appearance of the person bailed at the required time and place; and any recognizance shall be with or without sureties as the [officer or [the Asylum and Immigration Tribunal]] may determine.

(3) In any case in which an [immigration officer or [the Asylum and Immigration Tribunal]] has power under this paragraph to release a person on bail, the [officer or [the Asylum and Immigration Tribunal]] may, instead of taking the bail, fix the amount and conditions of the bail (including the amount in which any sureties are to be bound) with a view to its being taken subsequently by any such person as may be specified by [the Asylum and Immigration Tribunal]; and on the recognizance or bail bond being so taken the person to be bailed shall be released.

23 (1) Where a recognizance entered into under paragraph 22 above appears to [the Asylum and Immigration Tribunal] to be forfeited, [the Asylum and Immigration Tribunal] may by order declare it to be forfeited and adjudge the persons bound thereby, whether as principal or sureties, or any of them, to pay the sum in which they are respectively bound or such part of it, if any, as [the Asylum and Immigration Tribunal] thinks fit; and an order under this sub-paragraph shall specify a magistrates' court or, in Northern Ireland court of summary jurisdiction, and—

(a) the recognizance shall be treated for the purposes of collection, enforcement and remission of the sum forfeited as having been forfeited by the court so specified; and

(b) [the Asylum and Immigration Tribunal] shall, as soon as practicable, give particulars of the recognizance to the [proper officer] of that court.

[(1A) In sub-paragraph (1) "proper officer" means—

(a) in relation to a magistrates' court in England and Wales, the [designated officer] for the court; and

(b) in relation to a court of summary jurisdiction in Northern Ireland, the clerk of the court.]

(2) Where a person released on bail under paragraph 22 above as it applies in Scotland fails to comply with the terms of his bail bond, [the Asylum and Immigration Tribunal] may declare the bail to be forfeited, and any bail so forfeited shall be transmitted by [the Asylum and Immigration Tribunal] to the sheriff court having jurisdiction in the area where the proceedings took place, and shall be treated as having been forfeited by that court.

(3) Any sum the payment of which is enforceable by a magistrates' court in England and Wales by virtue of this paragraph shall be treated for the [purposes of section 38 of the Courts Act 2003 (application of receipts of designated officers) as being] due under a recognizance forfeited by such a court ...

(4) Any sum the payment of which is enforceable by virtue of this paragraph by a court of summary jurisdiction in Northern Ireland shall, for the purposes of section 20(5) of the Administration of Justice Act (Northern Ireland) 1954, be treated as a forfeited recognizance.

24 (1) An immigration officer or constable may arrest without warrant a person who has been released by virtue of paragraph 22 above—

(a) if he has reasonable grounds for believing that that person is likely to break the condition of his recognizance or bail bond that he will appear at the time and place required or to break any other condition of it, or has reasonable grounds to suspect that that person is breaking or has broken any such other condition; or

(b) if, a recognizance with sureties having been taken, he is notified in writing by any sureties of the surety's belief that that person is likely to break the first-mentioned condition, and of the surety's wish for that reason to be relieved of his obligation as a surety;

and paragraph 17(2) above shall apply for the arrest of a person under this paragraph as it applies for the arrest of a person under paragraph 17.

(2) A person arrested under this paragraph—

(a) if not required by a condition on which he was released to appear before an immigration officer within twenty-four hours after the time of his arrest, shall as soon as practicable be brought before [the Asylum and Immigration Tribunal] or, if that is not practicable within those twenty-four hours, before [in England and Wales, a justice of the peace, in Northern Ireland,] a justice of the peace acting for the petty sessions area in which he is arrested or, in Scotland, the sheriff; and

(b) if required by such a condition to appear within those twenty-four hours before an immigration officer, shall be brought before that officer.

(3) [Where a person is brought before the Asylum and Immigration Tribunal, a justice of the peace or the sheriff by virtue of sub-paragraph (2)(a), the Tribunal, justice of the peace or sheriff]—

(a) if of the opinion that that person has broken or is likely to break any condition on which he was released, may either—
(i) direct that he be detained under the authority of the person by whom he was arrested; or
(ii) release him, on his original recognizance or on a new recognizance, with or without sureties, or, in Scotland, on his original bail or on new bail; and

(b) if not of that opinion, shall release him on his original recognizance or bail.

25 The power to make rules of procedure conferred by [section 106 of the Nationality, Immigration and Asylum Act 2002 (appeals)] shall include power to make rules with respect to applications to [the Asylum and Immigration Tribunal] under paragraphs 22 to 24 above and matters arising out of such applications.

[Entry and search of premises

25A (1) This paragraph applies if—

(a) a person is arrested under this Schedule; or
(b) a person who was arrested by a constable (other than under this Schedule) is detained by an immigration officer under this Schedule.

(2) An immigration officer may enter and search any premises—

(a) occupied or controlled by the arrested person, or
(b) in which that person was when he was arrested, or immediately before he was arrested,

for relevant documents.

(3)   The power may be exercised—

(a)   only if the officer has reasonable grounds for believing that there are relevant documents on the premises;

(b)   only to the extent that it is reasonably required for the purpose of discovering relevant documents; and

(c)   subject to sub-paragraph (4), only if a senior officer has authorised its exercise in writing.

(4)   An immigration officer may conduct a search under sub-paragraph (2)—

(a)   before taking the arrested person to a place where he is to be detained; and

(b)   without obtaining an authorisation under sub-paragraph (3)(c),

if the presence of that person at a place other than one where he is to be detained is necessary to make an effective search for any relevant documents.

(5)   An officer who has conducted a search under sub-paragraph (4) must inform a senior officer as soon as is practicable.

(6)   The officer authorising a search, or who is informed of one under sub-paragraph (5), must make a record in writing of—

(a)   the grounds for the search; and

(b)   the nature of the documents that were sought.

(7)   An officer searching premises under sub-paragraph (2)—

(a)   may seize and retain any documents he finds which he has reasonable grounds for believing are relevant documents; but

(b)   may not retain any such document for longer than is necessary in view of the purpose for which the person was arrested.

(8)   But sub-paragraph (7)(a) does not apply to documents which the officer has reasonable grounds for believing are items subject to legal privilege.

(9)   "Relevant documents" means any documents which might—

(a)   establish the arrested person's identity, nationality or citizenship; or

(b)   indicate the place from which he has travelled to the United Kingdom or to which he is proposing to go.

(10)   "Senior officer" means an immigration officer not below the rank of chief immigration officer.]

[Searching persons arrested by immigration officers

25B   (1)   This paragraph applies if a person is arrested under this Schedule.

(2)   An immigration officer may search the arrested person if he has reasonable grounds for believing that the arrested person may present a danger to himself or others.

(3)   The officer may search the arrested person for—

(a)   anything which he might use to assist his escape from lawful custody; or

(b)   any document which might—

(i)   establish his identity, nationality or citizenship; or

(ii)   indicate the place from which he has travelled to the United Kingdom or to which he is proposing to go.

(4)   The power conferred by sub-paragraph (3) may be exercised—

    (a)   only if the officer has reasonable grounds for believing that the arrested person may have concealed on him anything of a kind mentioned in that sub-paragraph; and

    (b)   only to the extent that it is reasonably required for the purpose of discovering any such thing.

(5)   A power conferred by this paragraph to search a person is not to be read as authorising an officer to require a person to remove any of his clothing in public other than an outer coat, jacket or glove; but it does authorise the search of a person's mouth.

(6)   An officer searching a person under sub-paragraph (2) may seize and retain anything he finds, if he has reasonable grounds for believing that the person searched might use it to cause physical injury to himself or to another person.

(7)   An officer searching a person under sub-paragraph (3)(a) may seize and retain anything he finds, if he has reasonable grounds for believing that he might use it to assist his escape from lawful custody.

(8)   An officer searching a person under sub-paragraph (3)(b) may seize and retain anything he finds, other than an item subject to legal privilege, if he has reasonable grounds for believing that it might be a document falling within that sub-paragraph.

(9)   Nothing seized under sub-paragraph (6) or (7) may be retained when the person from whom it was seized—

    (a)   is no longer in custody, or

    (b)   is in the custody of a court but has been released on bail.]

[Searching persons in police custody

25C   (1)   This paragraph applies if a person—

    (a)   has been arrested under this Schedule; and

    (b)   is in custody at a police station.

(2)   An immigration officer may, at any time, search the arrested person in order to ascertain whether he has with him—

    (a)   anything which he might use to—
        (i)   cause physical injury to himself or others;
        (ii)   damage property;
        (iii)   interfere with evidence; or
        (iv)   assist his escape; or
    (b)   any document which might—
        (i)   establish his identity, nationality or citizenship; or
        (ii)   indicate the place from which he has travelled to the United Kingdom or to which he is proposing to go.

(3)   The power may be exercised only to the extent that the officer considers it to be necessary for the purpose of discovering anything of a kind mentioned in sub-paragraph (2).

(4)   An officer searching a person under this paragraph may seize and retain anything he finds, if he has reasonable grounds for believing that—

    (a)   that person might use it for one or more of the purposes mentioned in sub-paragraph (2)(a); or

    (b)   it might be a document falling within sub-paragraph (2)(b).

(5)   But the officer may not retain anything seized under sub-paragraph (2)(a)—

(a) for longer than is necessary in view of the purpose for which the search was carried out; or

(b) when the person from whom it was seized is no longer in custody or is in the custody of a court but has been released on bail.

(6) The person from whom something is seized must be told the reason for the seizure unless he is—

(a) violent or appears likely to become violent; or

(b) incapable of understanding what is said to him.

(7) An intimate search may not be conducted under this paragraph.

(8) The person carrying out a search under this paragraph must be of the same sex as the person searched.

(9) "Intimate search" has the same meaning as in section 28H(11).]

[Access and copying

25D (1) If a person showing himself—

(a) to be the occupier of the premises on which seized material was seized, or

(b) to have had custody or control of the material immediately before it was seized,

asks the immigration officer who seized the material for a record of what he seized, the officer must provide the record to that person within a reasonable time.

(2) If a relevant person asks an immigration officer for permission to be granted access to seized material, the officer must arrange for that person to have access to the material under the supervision of an immigration officer.

(3) An immigration officer may photograph or copy, or have photographed or copied, seized material.

(4) If a relevant person asks an immigration officer for a photograph or copy of seized material, the officer must arrange for—

(a) that person to have access to the material under the supervision of an immigration officer for the purpose of photographing or copying it; or

(b) the material to be photographed or copied.

(5) A photograph or copy made under sub-paragraph (4)(b) must be supplied within a reasonable time.

(6) There is no duty under this paragraph to arrange for access to, or the supply of a photograph or copy of, any material if there are reasonable grounds for believing that to do so would prejudice—

(a) the exercise of any functions in connection with which the material was seized; or

(b) an investigation which is being conducted under this Act, or any criminal proceedings which may be brought as a result.

(7) "Relevant person" means—

(a) a person who had custody or control of seized material immediately before it was seized, or

(b) someone acting on behalf of such a person.

(8) "Seized material" means anything which has been seized and retained under this Schedule.]

[25E   Section 28L applies for the purposes of this Schedule as it applies for the purposes of Part III.]

Supplementary duties of those connected with ships or aircraft or with ports

26   (1)   The owners or agents of a ship or aircraft employed to carry passengers for reward shall not, without the approval of the Secretary of State, arrange for the ship or aircraft to call at a port in the United Kingdom other than a port of entry for the purpose of disembarking passengers, if any of the passengers on board may not enter the United Kingdom without leave ..., or for the purpose of embarking passengers unless the owners or agents have reasonable cause to believe all of them to be [British citizens].

[(1A)   Sub-paragraph (1) does not apply in such circumstances, if any, as the Secretary of State may by order prescribe.]

(2)   The Secretary of State may from time to time give written notice to the owners or agents of any ships or aircraft designating control areas for the embarkation or disembarkation of passengers in any port in the United Kingdom and specifying the conditions and restrictions (if any) to be observed in any control area; and where by notice given to any owners or agents a control area is for the time being designated for the embarkation or disembarkation of passengers at any port, the owners or agents shall take all reasonable steps to secure that, in the case of their ships or aircraft, passengers do not embark or disembark, as the case may be, at the port outside the control area and that any conditions or restrictions notified to them are observed.

(3)   The Secretary of State may also from time to time give to any persons concerned with the management of a port in the United Kingdom written notice designating control areas in the port and specifying conditions or restrictions to be observed in any control area; and any such person shall take all reasonable steps to secure that any conditions or restrictions as notified to him are observed.

[(3A)   The power conferred by sub-paragraph (1A) is exercisable by statutory instrument; and any such instrument shall be subject to annulment by a resolution of either House of Parliament.]

27   (1)   The captain of a ship or aircraft arriving in the United Kingdom—

  (a)   shall take such steps as may be necessary to secure that persons on board do not disembark there unless either they have been examined by an immigration officer, or they disembark in accordance with arrangements approved by an immigration officer, or they are members of the crew who may lawfully enter the United Kingdom without leave by virtue of section 8(1) of this Act; and

  (b)   where the examination of persons on board is to be carried out on the ship or aircraft, shall take such steps as may be necessary to secure that those to be examined are presented for the purpose in an orderly manner.

(2)   The Secretary of State may by order made by statutory instrument make provision for requiring captains of ships or aircraft arriving in the United Kingdom or of such of them as arrive from or by way of countries or places specified in the order, to furnish to immigration officers—

  (a)   a passenger list showing the names and nationality or citizenship of passengers arriving on board the ship or aircraft;

  (b)   particulars of members of the crew of the ship or aircraft;

and for enabling an immigration officer to dispense with the furnishing of any such list or particulars.

[27A   ...]

[Passenger information

27B (1) This paragraph applies to ships or aircraft—

    (a) which have arrived, or are expected to arrive, in the United Kingdom; or

    (b) which have left, or are expected to leave, the United Kingdom.

(2) If an immigration officer asks the owner or agent ("the carrier") of a ship or aircraft for passenger information, the carrier must provide that information to the officer.

(3) The officer may ask for passenger information relating to—

    (a) a particular ship or particular aircraft of the carrier;

    (b) particular ships or aircraft (however described) of the carrier; or

    (c) all of the carrier's ships or aircraft.

(4) The officer may ask for—

    (a) all passenger information in relation to the ship or aircraft concerned; or

    (b) particular passenger information in relation to that ship or aircraft.

[(4A) The officer may ask the carrier to provide a copy of all or part of a document that relates to a passenger and contains passenger information.]

(5) A request under sub-paragraph (2)—

    (a) must be in writing;

    (b) must state the date on which it ceases to have effect; and

    (c) continues in force until that date, unless withdrawn earlier by written notice by an immigration officer.

(6) The date may not be later than six months after the request is made.

(7) The fact that a request under sub-paragraph (2) has ceased to have effect as a result of sub-paragraph (5) does not prevent the request from being renewed.

(8) The information must be provided—

    (a) in such form and manner as the Secretary of State may direct; and

    (b) at such time as may be stated in the request.

(9) "Passenger information" means such information relating to the passengers carried, or expected to be carried, by the ship or aircraft as may be specified.

(10) "Specified" means specified in an order made by statutory instrument by the Secretary of State.

(11) Such an instrument shall be subject to annulment in pursuance of a resolution of either House of Parliament.]

[Notification of non-EEA arrivals

27C (1) If a senior officer, or an immigration officer authorised by a senior officer, gives written notice to the owner or agent ("the carrier") of a ship or aircraft, the carrier must inform a relevant officer of the expected arrival in the United Kingdom of any ship or aircraft—

    (a) of which he is the owner or agent; and

    (b) which he expects to carry a person who is not an EEA national.

(2) The notice may relate to—

    (a) a particular ship or particular aircraft of the carrier;

    (b) particular ships or aircraft (however described) of the carrier; or

    (c) all of the carrier's ships or aircraft.

(3)   The notice—

  (a)   must state the date on which it ceases to have effect; and
  (b)   continues in force until that date, unless withdrawn earlier by written notice given by a senior officer.

(4)   The date may not be later than six months after the notice is given.

(5)   The fact that a notice under sub-paragraph (1) has ceased to have effect as a result of sub-paragraph (3) does not prevent the notice from being renewed.

(6)   The information must be provided—

  (a)   in such form and manner as the notice may require; and
  (b)   before the ship or aircraft concerned departs for the United Kingdom.

(7)   If a ship or aircraft travelling to the United Kingdom stops at one or more places before arriving in the United Kingdom, it is to be treated as departing for the United Kingdom when it leaves the last of those places.

(8)   "Senior officer" means an immigration officer not below the rank of chief immigration officer.

(9)   "Relevant officer" means—

  (a)   the officer who gave the notice under sub-paragraph (1); or
  (b)   any immigration officer at the port at which the ship or aircraft concerned is expected to arrive.

(10)   "EEA national" means a national of a State which is a Contracting Party to the Agreement on the European Economic Area signed at Oporto on 2nd May 1992 as it has effect for the time being.]

Appointment
Appointment: 1 January 1973: see SI 1972/1514, art 2.

Amendment
Para 1: sub-para (2A) inserted by the Health Protection Agency Act 2004, s 11(1), Sch 3, para 3. Date in force: 22 September 2004: see the Health Protection Agency Act 2004, s 12(3).
Para 1: in sub-paras (4), (5) words "or aircraft" in square brackets substituted by SI 1993/1813, art 8, Sch 5, Pt I, para 1(a).
Para 2: in sub-para (1) words "or aircraft" in square brackets substituted by SI 1993/1813, art 8, Sch 5, Pt I, para 1(b).
Para 2: in sub-para (1)(a) words "a British citizen" in square brackets substituted by the British Nationality Act 1981, s 39(6), Sch 4, para 2.
Para 2: sub-para (1)(c) substituted by the Immigration and Asylum Act 1999, s 169(1), Sch 14, paras 43, 56. Date in force: 14 February 2000: see SI 2000/168, art 2, Schedule.
Para 2A: inserted by the Immigration and Asylum Act 1999, s 169(1), Sch 14, paras 43, 57. Date in force: 14 February 2000: see SI 2000/168, art 2, Schedule.
Para 2A: sub-para (2A) inserted by the Asylum and Immigration (Treatment of Claimants, etc) Act 2004, s 18. Date in force: 1 October 2004: see SI 2004/2523, art 2, Schedule.
Para 2A: in sub-para (9) words "Part 5 of the Nationality, Immigration and Asylum Act 2002 (immigration and asylum appeals)" in square brackets substituted by the Nationality, Immigration and Asylum Act 2002, s 114(3), Sch 7, para 2. Date in force: 1 April 2003 (except in relation to events which took place before that date): see SI 2003/754, arts 2(1), 3(1), Sch 1.
Para 3: words omitted, originally inserted by SI 1990/2227, art 3, Sch 1, Part I, para 8, repealed by SI 1993/1813, art 9, Sch 6, Part I.
Para 3: second words in square brackets substituted by the British Nationality Act 1981, s 39(6), Sch 4, para 2.
Para 4: in sub-para (1) reference to ", 2A" in square brackets inserted by the Immigration and Asylum Act 1999, s 169(1), Sch 14, paras 43, 58. Date in force: 14 February 2000: see SI 2000/168, art 2, Schedule.

Para 4: in sub-para (2) reference to ", 2A" in square brackets inserted by the Immigration and Asylum Act 1999, s 169(1), Sch 14, paras 43, 58. Date in force: 14 February 2000: see SI 2000/168, art 2, Schedule.

Para 4: in sub-para (2)(b) words ", or has carried or conveyed," in square brackets inserted by the Asylum and Immigration Act 1996, s 12(1), Sch 2, para 5(1).

Para 4: sub-para (2A) inserted by the Immigration Act 1988, s 10, Schedule, paras 6, 10.

Para 4: in sub-para (3) words ", or has carried or conveyed," in square brackets inserted by the Asylum and Immigration Act 1996, s 12(1), Sch 2, para 5(2)(a).

Para 4: sub-para (3)(a), (b) substituted by the Asylum and Immigration Act 1996, s 12(1), Sch 2, para 5(2)(b).

Para 4: in sub-para (3) words "or, as the case may be, has done" in square brackets inserted by the Asylum and Immigration Act 1996, s 12(1), Sch 2, para 5(2)(c).

Para 4: in sub-para (4) words "an appeal under the Nationality, Immigration and Asylum Act 2002" in square brackets substituted by the Nationality, Immigration and Asylum Act 2002, s 114(3), Sch 7, para 3. Date in force: 1 April 2003 (except in relation to events which took place before that date): see SI 2003/754, arts 2(1), 3(1), Sch 1.

Para 6: in sub-para (1) words "twenty-four hours" in both places they occur in square brackets substituted by the Immigration Act 1988, s 10, Schedule, paras 7, 8.

Para 6: in sub-para (1) words "a British citizen" in square brackets substituted by the British Nationality Act 1981, s 39, Sch 4, para 2.

Para 6: in sub-para (1) words from "leave to enter" to "his taking employment" in square brackets substituted by the Immigration Act 1988, s 10, Schedule, paras 7, 8.

Para 6: in sub-para (2) words "twenty-four hours" in square brackets substituted by the Immigration Act 1988, s 10, Schedule, paras 7, 8.

Para 6: in sub-para (3) words from "and the immigration officer" to "of that leave." in square brackets substituted by the Immigration Act 1988, s 10, Schedule, paras 7, 8.

Para 6: in sub-para (3) words "or require him to submit to further examination" in square brackets inserted by the Nationality, Immigration and Asylum Act 2002, s 119. Date in force: 8 January 2003: see SI 2002/2811, art 2, Schedule.

Para 7: substituted by the Immigration and Asylum Act 1999, s 169(1), Sch 14, paras 43, 59. Date in force: 14 February 2000: see SI 2000/168, art 2, Schedule.

Para 8: words omitted from sub-para (1), originally inserted by SI 1990/2227, art 3, Sch 1, Part I, para 9, repealed by SI 1993/1813, art 9, Sch 6, Part I.

Para 8: in sub-para (2) words "(ignoring any period during which an appeal by him under the Immigration Acts is pending)" in square brackets inserted by the Nationality, Immigration and Asylum Act 2002, s 114(3), Sch 7, para 4. Date in force: 1 April 2003 (except in relation to events which took place before that date): see SI 2003/754, arts 2(1), 3(1), Sch 1.

Para 8: in sub-para (2) words from "except that directions" to "of that person" in square brackets inserted by the Immigration Act 1988, s 10, Schedule, para 9.

Para 9: sub-para (1) numbered as such, and sub-para (2) inserted, by the Asylum and Immigration Act 1996, s 12(1), Sch 2, para 6.

Para 10: words in square brackets in sub-para (1) substituted by the Immigration Act 1988, s 10, Schedule, para 9.

Para 10A: inserted by the Nationality, Immigration and Asylum Act 2002, s 73(1). Date in force: 10 February 2003: see SI 2003/1, art 2, Schedule.

Paras 12, 13: words "a British citizen" in square brackets substituted by the British Nationality Act 1981, s 39(6), Sch 4, para 2.

Para 16: sub-para (1A) inserted by the Immigration and Asylum Act 1999, s 169(1), Sch 14, paras 43, 60. Date in force: 14 February 2000: see SI 2000/168, art 2, Schedule.

Para 16: sub-para (2) substituted by the Immigration and Asylum Act 1999, s 140(1). Date in force: 11 November 1999: see the Immigration and Asylum Act 1999, s 170(3)(m).

Para 16: in sub-para (2) words "8 to 10A" in square brackets substituted by the Nationality, Immigration and Asylum Act 2002, s 73(5). Date in force: 10 February 2003: see SI 2003/1, art 2, Schedule.

Para 16: sub-para (4A) inserted by SI 1990/2227, art 3, Sch 1, Part I, para 10, repealed by SI 1993/1813, art 9, Sch 6, Part I.

Para 17: first words omitted apply to Scotland only, repealed in part by the Asylum and Immigration Act 1996, ss 12(1), (3), Sch 2, para 7, Sch 4.

Para 17: in sub-para (2)(b) words omitted repealed by the Asylum and Immigration Act 1996, s 12(3), Sch 4.

Para 17: in sub-para (2) words in square brackets beginning with the words "authorising any" substituted by the Immigration and Asylum Act 1999, s 140(2). Date in force: 11 November 1999: see the Immigration and Asylum Act 1999, s 170(3)(m).

Para 17: in sub-para (2) words "if need be by reasonable force" in square brackets substituted by the Nationality, Immigration and Asylum Act 2002, s 63. Date in force: 10 February 2003: see SI 2003/1, art 2, Schedule.

Para 17: sub-paras (3)–(5) inserted by the Nationality, Immigration and Asylum Act 2002, s 64. Date in force: 10 February 2003: see SI 2003/1, art 2, Schedule.

Para 18: sub-para (2A) inserted by the Immigration and Asylum Act 1999, s 169(1), Sch 14, paras 43, 61. Date in force: 11 December 2000: see SI 2000/3099, art 3, Schedule.

Para 19: words omitted from sub-para (1) inserted by SI 1990/2227, Sch 1, Part I, para 11, repealed by SI 1993/1813, art 9, Sch 6, Part I.

Para 19: words in square brackets in sub-para (1) substituted by the Asylum and Immigration Act 1996, s 12(1), Sch 2, para 8.

Para 19: words in square brackets in sub-para (2) substituted by the British Nationality Act 1981, s 39(6), Sch 4, para 3(1).

Para 20: words omitted from sub-para (1) inserted by SI 1990/2227, Sch 1, Part I, para 12, repealed by SI 1993/1813, art 9, Sch 6, Part I.

Para 20: words in square brackets in sub-para (1) substituted by the Asylum and Immigration Act 1996, s 12(1), Sch 2, para 9(1).

Para 20: sub-para (1A) inserted by the Asylum and Immigration Act 1996, s 12(1), Sch 2, para 9(2).

Para 21: words in square brackets in sub-para (2) inserted by the Immigration Act 1988, s 10, Schedule, paras 6, 10.

Para 21: sub-paras (2A)–(2E) inserted by the Immigration and Asylum Act 1999, s 169(1), Sch 14, paras 43, 62(1), (2). Date in force: 11 November 1999: see the Immigration and Asylum Act 1999, s 170(3)(s).

Para 21: sub-paras (3), (4) inserted by the Asylum and Immigration Act 1996, s 12(1), Sch 2, para 10.

Para 21: in sub-para (3) words "or 2A" in square brackets inserted by the Immigration and Asylum Act 1999, s 169(1), Sch 14, paras 43, 62(1), (3). Date in force: 14 February 2000: see SI 2000/168, art 2, Schedule.

Para 21: in sub-para (4)(a) words omitted repealed by the Immigration and Asylum Act 1999, s 169(1), (3), Sch 14, paras 43, 62(1), (4), Sch 16. Date in force: 14 February 2000: see SI 2000/168, art 2, Schedule.

Para 22: sub-paras (1), (1A), (1B) substituted, for sub-para (1) as originally enacted, by the Asylum and Immigration Act 1996, s 12(1), Sch 2, para 11(1).

Para 22: sub-para (1)(aa) inserted by the Immigration and Asylum Act 1999, s 169(1), Sch 14, paras 43, 63. Date in force: 14 February 2000: see SI 2000/168, art 2, Schedule.

Para 22: in sub-para (1A) words "the Asylum and Immigration Tribunal" in square brackets substituted by the Asylum and Immigration (Treatment of Claimants, etc) Act 2004, s 26(7), Sch 2, Pt 1, para 1(1), (2)(a). Date in force: 4 April 2005: see SI 2005/565, art 2(d); for transitional provisions in relation to pending appeals which were made to an adjudicator before 4 April 2005 and in relation to further appeals and applications in such cases see arts 3–9 thereof.

Para 22: in sub-paras (2), (3) words in square brackets beginning with the words "immigration officer or" and "office or" substituted by the Asylum and Immigration Act 1996, s 12(1), Sch 2, para 11(2).

Para 22: in sub-paras (2), (3) words "the Asylum and Immigration Tribunal" in square brackets in each place they occur substituted by the Asylum and Immigration (Treatment of Claimants, etc) Act 2004, s 26(7), Sch 2, Pt 1, para 1(1), (2)(a). Date in force: 4 April 2005: see SI 2005/565, art 2(d); for transitional provisions in relation to pending appeals which were made to an adjudicator before 4 April 2005 and in relation to further appeals and applications in such cases see arts 3–9 thereof.

Para 22: sub-para (3) words "the Asylum and Immigration Tribunal" in square brackets in the final place they occur substituted by the Asylum and Immigration (Treatment of Claimants, etc) Act 2004, s 26(7), Sch 2, Pt 1, para 1(1), (2)(a). Date in force: 4 April 2005: see SI 2005/565, art 2(d); for transitional provisions in relation to pending appeals which were made to an adjudicator before 4 April 2005 and in relation to further appeals and applications in such cases see arts 3–9 thereof.

Para 23: in sub-para (1) words "the Asylum and Immigration Tribunal" in square brackets in the first place they occur substituted by the Asylum and Immigration (Treatment of Claimants, etc) Act 2004, s 26(7), Sch 2, Pt 1, para 1(1), (2)(b). Date in force: 4 April 2005: see SI 2005/565, art 2(d); for transitional provisions in relation to pending appeals which were made to an adjudicator before 4 April 2005 and in relation to further appeals and applications in such cases see arts 3–9 thereof.

Para 23: in sub-para (1) words "the Asylum and Immigration Tribunal" in square brackets, in the second, third and final places they occur, substituted by the Asylum and Immigration (Treatment of Claimants, etc) Act 2004, s 26(7), Sch 2, Pt 1, para 1(1), (2)(b). Date in force: 4 April 2005: see SI 2005/565, art 2(d); for transitional provisions in relation to pending appeals which were made to an adjudicator before 4 April 2005 and in relation to further appeals and applications in such cases see arts 3–9 thereof.

Para 23: in sub-para (1)(b) words "proper officer" in square brackets substituted by the Access to Justice Act 1999, s 90(1), Sch 13, para 70(1), (2). Date in force: 1 April 2001: see SI 2001/916, art 2(a)(ii).

Para 23: sub-para (1A) inserted by the Access to Justice Act 1999, s 90(1), Sch 13, para 70(1), (3). Date in force: 1 April 2001: see SI 2001/916, art 2(a)(ii).

Para 23: in sub-para (1A)(a) words "designated officer" in square brackets substituted by the Courts Act 2003, s 109(1), Sch 8, para 149(1), (2).

Para 23: in sub-para (2) words "the Asylum and Immigration Tribunal" in square brackets in the first place they occur substituted by the Asylum and Immigration (Treatment of Claimants, etc) Act 2004, s 26(7), Sch 2, Pt 1, para 1(1), (2)(b). Date in force: 4 April 2005: see SI 2005/565, art 2(d); for transitional provisions in relation to pending appeals which were made to an adjudicator before 4 April 2005 and in relation to further appeals and applications in such cases see arts 3–9 thereof.

Para 23: in sub-para (2) words "the Asylum and Immigration Tribunal" in square brackets in the final place they occur substituted by the Asylum and Immigration (Treatment of Claimants, etc) Act 2004, s 26(7), Sch 2, Pt 1, para 1(1), (2)(b). Date in force: 4 April 2005: see SI 2005/565, art 2(d); for transitional provisions in relation to pending appeals which were made to an adjudicator before 4 April 2005 and in relation to further appeals and applications in such cases see arts 3–9 thereof.

Para 23: in sub-para (3) words "purposes of section 38 of the Courts Act 2003 (application of receipts of designated officers) as being" in square brackets substituted by the Courts Act 2003, s 109(1), Sch 8, para 149(1), (3).

Para 23: in sub-para (3) words omitted repealed by the Criminal Justice Act 1972, ss 64(2), 66(7), Sch 6, Pt II.

Para 24: in sub-para (2)(a) words "the Asylum and Immigration Tribunal" in square brackets substituted by the Asylum and Immigration (Treatment of Claimants, etc) Act 2004, s 26(7), Sch 2, Pt 1, para 1(1), (2)(c). Date in force: 4 April 2005: see SI 2005/565, art 2(d); for transitional provisions in relation to pending appeals which were made to an adjudicator before 4 April 2005 and in relation to further appeals and applications in such cases see arts 3–9 thereof.

Para 24: in sub-para (2)(a) words "in England and Wales, a justice of the peace, in Northern Ireland," in square brackets inserted by the Courts Act 2003, s 109(1), Sch 8, para 149(1), (4).

Para 24: in sub-para (3) words from "Where a person" to "or sheriff" in square brackets substituted by the Asylum and Immigration (Treatment of Claimants, etc) Act 2004, s 26(7), Sch 2, Pt 1, para 1(1), (3). Date in force: 4 April 2005: see SI 2005/565, art 2(d); for transitional provisions in relation to pending appeals which were made to an adjudicator before 4 April 2005 and in relation to further appeals and applications in such cases see arts 3–9 thereof.

Para 25: words "section 106 of the Nationality, Immigration and Asylum Act 2002 (appeals)" in square brackets substituted by the Nationality, Immigration and Asylum Act 2002, s 114(3), Sch 7, para 5. Date in force: 1 April 2003: see SI 2003/754, art 2(1), Sch 1.

Para 25: words "the Asylum and Immigration Tribunal" in square brackets substituted by the Asylum and Immigration (Treatment of Claimants, etc) Act 2004, s 26(7), Sch 2, Pt 1, para 1(1), (2)(d). Date in force: 4 April 2005: see SI 2005/565, art 2(d); for transitional provisions in relation to pending appeals which were made to an adjudicator before 4 April 2005 and in relation to further appeals and applications in such cases see arts 3–9 thereof.

Para 25A: inserted by the Immigration and Asylum Act 1999, s 132(2). Date in force: 14 February 2000: see SI 2000/168, art 2, Schedule.

Para 25B: inserted by the Immigration and Asylum Act 1999, s 134(2). Date in force: 14 February 2000: see SI 2000/168, art 2, Schedule.

Para 25C: inserted by the Immigration and Asylum Act 1999, s 135(2). Date in force: 14 February 2000: see SI 2000/168, art 2, Schedule.

Para 25D: inserted by the Immigration and Asylum Act 1999, s 136(2). Date in force: 14 February 2000: see SI 2000/168, art 2, Schedule.

Para 25E: inserted by the Immigration and Asylum Act 1999, s 139(2). Date in force: 14 February 2000: see SI 2000/168, art 2, Schedule.

Para 26: in sub-para (1) words omitted repealed by the Immigration and Asylum Act 1999, s 169(1), (3), Sch 14, paras 43, 64(1), (2), Sch 16. Date in force: 14 February 2000: see SI 2000/168, art 2, Schedule.

Para 26: in sub-para (1) words "British citizens" in square brackets substituted by the British Nationality Act 1981, s 39(6), Sch 4, para 2.

Para 26: sub-para (1A) inserted by the Immigration and Asylum Act 1999, s 169(1), Sch 14, paras 43, 64(1), (3). Date in force: 14 February 2000: see SI 2000/168, art 2, Schedule.

Para 26: sub-para (3A) inserted by the Immigration and Asylum Act 1999, s 169(1), Sch 14, paras 43, 64(1), (4). Date in force: 14 February 2000: see SI 2000/168, art 2, Schedule.

Para 27A: inserted by SI 1990/2227, art 3, Sch 1, Part I, para 13; repealed by SI 1993/1813, art 9, Sch 6, Part I.

Para 27B: inserted by the Immigration and Asylum Act 1999, s 18. Date in force (for certain purposes): 1 March 2000: see SI 2000/464, art 2, Schedule. Date in force (for remaining purposes): 3 April 2000: see SI 2000/464, art 2, Schedule.

Para 27B: sub-para (4A) inserted by the Asylum and Immigration (Treatment of Claimants, etc) Act 2004, s 16. Date in force: to be appointed: see the Asylum and Immigration (Treatment of Claimants, etc) Act 2004, s 48(3)–(6).

Para 27C: inserted by the Immigration and Asylum Act 1999, s 19. Date in force: 3 April 2000: see SI 2000/464, art 2, Schedule.

Modification
Modified, in its application to the Channel Tunnel, by the Channel Tunnel (International Arrangements) Order 1993, SI 1993/1813, art 7(1), Sch 4, para 1(11).

Modified, in relation to its application to frontier controls between the United Kingdom, France and Belgium, by the Channel Tunnel (Miscellaneous Provisions) Order 1994, SI 1994/1405, art 7.

Paras 22–24 modified, in relation to a person detained on certain grounds relating to national security, by the Special Immigration Appeals Commission Act 1997, Sch 3, paras 1–3 (as amended by the Asylum and Immigration (Treatment of Claimants, etc) Act 2004, s 26, Sch 2, Pt I, paras 10, 13).

The Northern Ireland Act 1998 makes new provision for the government of Northern Ireland for the purpose of implementing the Belfast Agreement (the agreement reached at multi-party talks on Northern Ireland and set out in Command Paper 3883). As a consequence of that Act, any reference in this Schedule to the Parliament of Northern Ireland or the Assembly established under the Northern Ireland Assembly Act 1973, s 1, certain office-holders and Ministers, and any legislative act and certain financial dealings thereof, shall, for the period specified, be construed in accordance with Sch 12, paras 1–11 to the 1998 Act.

Transfer of Functions
Functions under this section: certain functions under para 1 are transferred, in so far as they are exercisable in or as regards Scotland, to the Scottish Ministers, by the Scotland Act 1998 (Transfer of Functions to the Scottish Ministers etc) Order 1999, SI 1999/1750, art 2, Sch 1.

Subordinate Legislation
Immigration (Particulars of Passengers and Crew) Order 1972, SI 1972/1667 (made under para 27(2)).

Immigration (Landing and Embarkation Cards) Order 1975, SI 1975/65 (made under para 5).

Immigration (Passenger Information) Order 2000, SI 2000/912 (made under para 27B(9), (10)).

PART II

EFFECT OF APPEALS

...

28   ...

Grant of bail pending appeal

29   (1)   Where a person (in the following provisions of this Schedule referred to as "an appellant") has an appeal pending under [Part 5 of the Nationality, Immigration

and Asylum Act 2002] and is for the time being detained under Part I of this Schedule, he may be released on bail in accordance with this paragraph.

(2)   An immigration officer not below the rank of chief immigration officer or a police officer not below the rank of inspector may release an appellant on his entering into a recognizance or, in Scotland, bail bond conditioned for his appearance before [the Asylum and Immigration Tribunal] at a time and place named in the recognizance or bail bond.

(3)   [The Asylum and Immigration Tribunal] may release an appellant on his entering into a recognizance or, in Scotland, bail bond conditioned for his appearance before [the Tribunal], or the [Immigration Appeal Tribunal] at a time and place named in the recognizance or bail bond; ...

(4)   ...

(5)   The conditions of a recognizance or bail bond taken under this paragraph may include conditions appearing to the person fixing the bail to be likely to result in the appearance of the appellant at the time and place named; and any recognizance shall be with or without sureties as that person may determine.

(6)   In any case in which [the Asylum and Immigration Tribunal] has power or is required by this paragraph to release an appellant on bail, [the Tribunal] may, instead of taking the bail, fix the amount and conditions of the bail (including the amount in which any sureties are to be bound) with a view to its being taken subsequently by any such person as may be specified by [the Tribunal]; and on the recognizance or bail bond so taken the appellant shall be released.

Restrictions on grant of bail

30   (1)   An appellant shall not be released under paragraph 29 above without the consent of the Secretary of State if directions for the removal of the appellant from the United Kingdom are for the time being in force, or the power to give such directions is for the time being exercisable.

(2)   Notwithstanding paragraph 29(3) or (4) above, [the Tribunal] shall not be obliged to release an appellant unless the appellant enters into a proper recognizance, with sufficient and satisfactory sureties if required, or in Scotland sufficient and satisfactory bail is found if so required; and [the Tribunal] shall not be obliged to release an appellant if it appears to [the Tribunal]—

(a)   that the appellant, having on any previous occasion been released on bail (whether under paragraph 24 or under any other provision), has failed to comply with the conditions of any recognizance or bail bond entered into by him on that occasion;

(b)   that the appellant is likely to commit an offence unless he is retained in detention;

(c)   that the release of the appellant is likely to cause danger to public health;

(d)   that the appellant is suffering from mental disorder and that his continued detention is necessary in his own interests or for the protection of any other person; or

(e)   that the appellant is under the age of seventeen, that arrangements ought to be made for his care in the event of his release and that no satisfactory arrangements for that purpose have been made.

Forfeiture of recognizances

31   (1)   Where under paragraph 29 above (as it applies in England and Wales or in Northern Ireland) a recognizance is entered into conditioned for the appearance of an appellant before [the Tribunal], and it appears to [the Tribunal], to be forfeited, [the

Tribunal] may by order declare it to be forfeited and adjudge the persons bound thereby, whether as principal or sureties, or any of them, to pay the sum in which they are respectively bound or such part of it, if any, as [the Tribunal] thinks fit.

(2)   An order under this paragraph shall, for the purposes of this sub-paragraph, specify a magistrates' court or, in Northern Ireland, court of summary jurisdiction; and the recognizance shall be treated for the purposes of collection, enforcement and remission of the sum forfeited as having been forfeited by the court so specified.

(3)   Where [the Tribunal] makes an order under this paragraph [the Tribunal] shall, as soon as practicable, give particulars of the recognizance to the [proper officer] of the court specified in the order in pursuance of sub-paragraph (2) above.

[(3A)   In sub-paragraph (3) "proper officer" means—

(a)   in relation to a magistrates' court in England and Wales, the [designated officer] for the court; and

(b)   in relation to a court of summary jurisdiction in Northern Ireland, the clerk of the court.]

(4)   Any sum the payment of which is enforceable by a magistrates' court in England or Wales by virtue of this paragraph shall be treated for the [purposes of section 38 of the Courts Act 2003 (application of receipts of designated officers) as being] due under a recognizance forfeited by such a court ...

(5)   Any sum the payment of which is enforceable by virtue of this paragraph by a court of summary jurisdiction in Northern Ireland shall, for the purposes of section 20(5) of the Administration of Justice Act (Northern Ireland) 1954, be treated as a forfeited recognizance.

32   Where under paragraph 29 above (as it applies in Scotland) a person released on bail fails to comply with the terms of a bail bond conditioned for his appearance before [the Tribunal], [the Tribunal] may declare the bail to be forfeited, and any bail so forfeited shall be transmitted by [the Tribunal] to the sheriff court having jurisdiction in the area where the proceedings took place, and shall be treated as having been forfeited by that court.

Arrest of appellants released on bail

33   (1)   An immigration officer or constable may arrest without warrant a person who has been released by virtue of this Part of this Schedule—

(a)   if he has reasonable grounds for believing that that person is likely to break the condition of his recognizance or bail bond that he will appear at the time and place required or to break any other condition of it, or has reasonable ground to suspect that that person is breaking or has broken any such other condition; or

(b)   if, a recognizance with sureties having been taken, he is notified in writing by any surety of the surety's belief that that person is likely to break the first-mentioned condition, and of the surety's wish for that reason to be relieved of his obligations as a surety;

and paragraph 17(2) above shall apply for the arrest of a person under this paragraph as it applies for the arrest of a person under paragraph 17.

(2)   A person arrested under this paragraph—

(a)   if not required by a condition on which he was released to appear before [the Tribunal] within twenty-four hours after the time of his arrest, shall as soon as practicable be brought [before the Tribunal] or, if that is not practicable within those twenty-four hours, before [in England and Wales, a justice of the peace, in Northern Ireland,] a justice of the peace acting for the petty sessions area in which he is arrested or, in Scotland, the sheriff; and

(b) if required by such a condition to appear within those twenty-four hours [before the Tribunal], shall be brought [before it].

(3) [Where a person is brought before the Asylum and Immigration Tribunal, a justice of the peace or the sheriff by virtue of sub-paragraph (2)(a), the Tribunal, justice of the peace or sheriff]—

(a) if of the opinion that that person has broken or is likely to break any condition on which he was released, may either—
   (i) direct that he be detained under the authority of the person by whom he was arrested; or
   (ii) release him on his original recognizance or on a new recognizance, with or without sureties, or, in Scotland, on his original bail or on new bail; and

(b) if not of that opinion, shall release him on his original recognizance or bail.

[Grant of bail pending removal

34 (1) Paragraph 22 above shall apply in relation to a person—

(a) directions for whose removal from the United Kingdom are for the time being in force; and

(b) who is for the time being detained under Part I of this Schedule,

as it applies in relation to a person detained under paragraph 16(1) above pending examination[, detained under paragraph 16(1A) above pending completion of his examination or a decision on whether to cancel his leave to enter] or detained under paragraph 16(2) above pending the giving of directions.

(2) Paragraphs 23 to 25 above shall apply as if any reference to paragraph 22 above included a reference to that paragraph as it applies by virtue of this paragraph.]

Appointment
Appointment: 1 January 1973: see SI 1972/1514, art 2.

Amendment
Para 28: repealed by the Immigration and Asylum Act 1999, s 169(1), (3), Sch 14, paras 43, 65, Sch 16. Date in force: 2 October 2000 (except in relation to an event which took place before that date): see SI 2000/2444, art 2, Sch 1; for transitional provisions see art 3, Sch 2, para 2(10) thereof and SI 2003/754, art 3, Sch 2, para 2(10)(a).
Para 29: in sub-para (1) words "Part 5 of the Nationality, Immigration and Asylum Act 2002" in square brackets substituted by the Nationality, Immigration and Asylum Act 2002, s 114(3), Sch 7, para 6(a). Date in force: 1 April 2003 (except in relation to events which took place before that date): see SI 2003/754, arts 2(1), 3(1), Sch 1.
Para 29: in sub-para (2) words "the Asylum and Immigration Tribunal" in square brackets substituted by the Asylum and Immigration (Treatment of Claimants, etc) Act 2004, s 26(7), Sch 2, Pt 1, para 1(1), (4)(a). Date in force: 4 April 2005: see SI 2005/565, art 2(d); for transitional provisions in relation to pending appeals which were made to an adjudicator before 4 April 2005 and in relation to further appeals and applications in such cases see arts 3–9 thereof.
Para 29: in sub-para (3) words "The Asylum and Immigration Tribunal" in square brackets substituted by the Asylum and Immigration (Treatment of Claimants, etc) Act 2004, s 26(7), Sch 2, Pt 1, para 1(1), (4)(b)(i). Date in force: 4 April 2005: see SI 2005/565, art 2(d); for transitional provisions in relation to pending appeals which were made to an adjudicator before 4 April 2005 and in relation to further appeals and applications in such cases see arts 3–9 thereof.
Para 29: in sub-para (3) words "the Tribunal" in square brackets substituted by the Asylum and Immigration (Treatment of Claimants, etc) Act 2004, s 26(7), Sch 2, Pt 1, para 1(1), (4)(b)(ii). Date in force: 4 April 2005: see SI 2005/565, art 2(d); for transitional provisions in relation to pending appeals which were made to an adjudicator before 4 April 2005 and in relation to further appeals and applications in such cases see arts 3–9 thereof.

Para 29: in sub-para (3) words "Immigration Appeal Tribunal" in square brackets substituted by the Nationality, Immigration and Asylum Act 2002, s 114(3), Sch 7, para 6(b). Date in force: 1 April 2003 (except in relation to events which took place before that date): see SI 2003/754, arts 2(1), 3(1), Sch 1.

Para 29: in sub-para (3) words omitted repealed by the Asylum and Immigration (Treatment of Claimants, etc) Act 2004, ss 26(7), 47, Sch 2, Pt 1, para 1(1), (4)(b)(iii), Sch 4. Date in force: 4 April 2005: see SI 2005/565, art 2(d); for transitional provisions in relation to pending appeals which were made to an adjudicator before 4 April 2005 and in relation to further appeals and applications in such cases see arts 3–9 thereof.

Para 29: sub-para (4) repealed by the Asylum and Immigration (Treatment of Claimants, etc) Act 2004, ss 26(7), 47, Sch 2, Pt 1, para 1(1), (4)(c), Sch 4. Date in force: 4 April 2005: see SI 2005/565, art 2(d); for transitional provisions in relation to pending appeals which were made to an adjudicator before 4 April 2005 and in relation to further appeals and applications in such cases see arts 3–9 thereof.

Para 29: in sub-para (6) words "the Asylum and Immigration Tribunal" in square brackets substituted by the Asylum and Immigration (Treatment of Claimants, etc) Act 2004, s 26(7), Sch 2, Pt 1, para 1(1), (4)(d)(i). Date in force: 4 April 2005: see SI 2005/565, art 2(d); for transitional provisions in relation to pending appeals which were made to an adjudicator before 4 April 2005 and in relation to further appeals and applications in such cases see arts 3–9 thereof.

Para 29: in sub-para (6) words "the Tribunal" in square brackets in the first place they occur substituted by the Asylum and Immigration (Treatment of Claimants, etc) Act 2004, s 26(7), Sch 2, Pt 1, para 1(1), (4)(d)(ii). Date in force: 4 April 2005: see SI 2005/565, art 2(d); for transitional provisions in relation to pending appeals which were made to an adjudicator before 4 April 2005 and in relation to further appeals and applications in such cases see arts 3–9 thereof.

Para 29: in sub-para (6) words "the Tribunal" in square brackets in the final place they occur substituted by the Asylum and Immigration (Treatment of Claimants, etc) Act 2004, s 26(7), Sch 2, Pt 1, para 1(1), (4)(d)(iii). Date in force: 4 April 2005: see SI 2005/565, art 2(d); for transitional provisions in relation to pending appeals which were made to an adjudicator before 4 April 2005 and in relation to further appeals and applications in such cases see arts 3–9 thereof.

Para 30: in sub-para (2) words "the Tribunal" in square brackets in the first and second places they occur substituted by the Asylum and Immigration (Treatment of Claimants, etc) Act 2004, s 26(7), Sch 2, Pt 1, para 1(1), (5)(a); for transitional provisions see s 26(7), Sch 2, Pt 2 thereto. Date in force: 4 April 2005: see SI 2005/565, art 2(d); for transitional provisions in relation to pending appeals which were made to an adjudicator before 4 April 2005 and in relation to further appeals and applications in such cases see arts 3–9 thereof.

Para 30: in sub-para (2) words "the Tribunal" in square brackets in the final place they occur substituted by the Asylum and Immigration (Treatment of Claimants, etc) Act 2004, s 26(7), Sch 2, Pt 1, para 1(1), (5)(c); for transitional provisions see s 26(7), Sch 2, Pt 2 thereto. Date in force: 4 April 2005: see SI 2005/565, art 2(d); for transitional provisions in relation to pending appeals which were made to an adjudicator before 4 April 2005 and in relation to further appeals and applications in such cases see arts 3–9 thereof.

Para 31: words "the Tribunal" in square brackets in first and fifth places they occur substituted by the Asylum and Immigration (Treatment of Claimants, etc) Act 2004, s 26(7), Sch 2, Pt 1, para 1(1), (5)(b); for transitional provisions see s 26(7), Sch 2, Pt 2 thereto. Date in force: 4 April 2005: see SI 2005/565, art 2(d); for transitional provisions in relation to pending appeals which were made to an adjudicator before 4 April 2005 and in relation to further appeals and applications in such cases see arts 3–9 thereof.

Para 31: in sub-para (1) words "the Tribunal" in square brackets in the second place they occur substituted by the Asylum and Immigration (Treatment of Claimants, etc) Act 2004, s 26(7), Sch 2, Pt 1, para 1(1), (5)(c); for transitional provisions see s 26(7), Sch 2, Pt 2 thereto. Date in force: 4 April 2005: see SI 2005/565, art 2(d); for transitional provisions in relation to pending appeals which were made to an adjudicator before 4 April 2005 and in relation to further appeals and applications in such cases see arts 3–9 thereof.

Para 31: words "the Tribunal" in square brackets in the third, fourth and final places they occur substituted by the Asylum and Immigration (Treatment of Claimants, etc) Act 2004, s 26(7), Sch 2, Pt 1, para 1(1), (5)(d); for transitional provisions see s 26(7), Sch 2, Pt 2 thereto. Date in force: 4 April 2005: see SI 2005/565, art 2(d); for transitional provisions in relation to pending appeals which were made to an adjudicator before 4 April 2005 and in relation to further appeals and applications in such cases see arts 3–9 thereof.

Para 31: in sub-para (3) words "proper officer" in square brackets substituted by the Access to Justice Act 1999, s 90(1), Sch 13, para 70(1), (4). Date in force: 1 April 2001: see SI 2001/916, art 2(a)(ii).

Para 31: sub-para (3A) inserted by the Access to Justice Act 1999, s 90(1), Sch 13, para 70(1), (5). Date in force: 1 April 2001: see SI 2001/916, art 2(a)(ii).

Para 31: in sub-para (3A)(a) words "designated officer" in square brackets substituted by the Courts Act 2003, s 109(1), Sch 8, para 149(1), (2).

Para 31: in sub-para (4) words "purposes of section 38 of the Courts Act 2003 (application of receipts of designated officers) as being" in square brackets substituted by the Courts Act 2003, s 109(1), Sch 8, para 149(1), (3).

Para 31: in sub-para (4) words omitted repealed by the Criminal Justice Act 1972, s 64(2), Sch 6, Pt II.

Para 32: words "the Tribunal" in square brackets in the first place they occur substituted by the Asylum and Immigration (Treatment of Claimants, etc) Act 2004, s 26(7), Sch 2, Pt 1, para 1(1), (5)(b); for transitional provisions see s 26(7), Sch 2, Pt 2 thereto. Date in force: 4 April 2005: see SI 2005/565, art 2(d); for transitional provisions in relation to pending appeals which were made to an adjudicator before 4 April 2005 and in relation to further appeals and applications in such cases see arts 3–9 thereof.

Para 32: words "the Tribunal" in square brackets in the second place they occur substituted by the Asylum and Immigration (Treatment of Claimants, etc) Act 2004, s 26(7), Sch 2, Pt 1, para 1(1), (5)(d); for transitional provisions see s 26(7), Sch 2, Pt 2 thereto. Date in force: 4 April 2005: see SI 2005/565, art 2(d); for transitional provisions in relation to pending appeals which were made to an adjudicator before 4 April 2005 and in relation to further appeals and applications in such cases see arts 3–9 thereof.

Para 32: words "the Tribunal" in square brackets in the final place they occur substituted by the Asylum and Immigration (Treatment of Claimants, etc) Act 2004, s 26(7), Sch 2, Pt 1, para 1(1), (5)(e); for transitional provisions see s 26(7), Sch 2, Pt 2 thereto. Date in force: 4 April 2005: see SI 2005/565, art 2(d); for transitional provisions in relation to pending appeals which were made to an adjudicator before 4 April 2005 and in relation to further appeals and applications in such cases see arts 3–9 thereof.

Para 33: in sub-para (2)(a) words "the Tribunal" in square brackets substituted by the Asylum and Immigration (Treatment of Claimants, etc) Act 2004, s 26(7), Sch 2, Pt 1, para 1(1), (5)(f); for transitional provisions see s 26(7), Sch 2, Pt 2 thereto. Date in force: 4 April 2005: see SI 2005/565, art 2(d); for transitional provisions in relation to pending appeals which were made to an adjudicator before 4 April 2005 and in relation to further appeals and applications in such cases see arts 3–9 thereof.

Para 33: in sub-para (2)(a) words "before the Tribunal" in square brackets substituted by the Asylum and Immigration (Treatment of Claimants, etc) Act 2004, s 26(7), Sch 2, Pt 1, para 1(1), (6)(a); for transitional provisions see s 26(7), Sch 2, Pt 2 thereto. Date in force: 4 April 2005: see SI 2005/565, art 2(d); for transitional provisions in relation to pending appeals which were made to an adjudicator before 4 April 2005 and in relation to further appeals and applications in such cases see arts 3–9 thereof.

Para 33: in sub-para (2)(a) words "in England and Wales, a justice of the peace, in Northern Ireland," in square brackets inserted by the Courts Act 2003, s 109(1), Sch 8, para 149(1), (4).

Para 33: in sub-para (2)(b) words "before the Tribunal" in square brackets substituted by the Asylum and Immigration (Treatment of Claimants, etc) Act 2004, s 26(7), Sch 2, Pt 1, para 1(1), (5)(g); for transitional provisions see s 26(7), Sch 2, Pt 2 thereto. Date in force: 4 April 2005: see SI 2005/565, art 2(d); for transitional provisions in relation to pending appeals which were made to an adjudicator before 4 April 2005 and in relation to further appeals and applications in such cases see arts 3–9 thereof.

Para 33: in sub-para (2)(b) words "before it" in square brackets substituted by the Asylum and Immigration (Treatment of Claimants, etc) Act 2004, s 26(7), Sch 2, Pt 1, para 1(1), (6)(b); for transitional provisions see s 26(7), Sch 2, Pt 2 thereto. Date in force: 4 April 2005: see SI 2005/565, art 2(d); for transitional provisions in relation to pending appeals which were made to an adjudicator before 4 April 2005 and in relation to further appeals and applications in such cases see arts 3–9 thereof.

Para 33: in sub-para (3) words from "Where a person" to "peace or sherriff" in square brackets substituted by the Asylum and Immigration (Treatment of Claimants, etc) Act 2004, s 26(7), Sch 2, Pt 1, para 1(1), (6)(c); for transitional provisions see s 26(7), Sch 2, Pt 2 thereto. Date in force: 4 April 2005: see SI 2005/565, art 2(d); for transitional provisions in relation to pending appeals which were made to an adjudicator before 4 April 2005 and in relation to further appeals and applications in such cases see arts 3–9 thereof.

Para 34: inserted by the Asylum and Immigration Act 1996, s 12(1), Sch 12, para 12.

Para 34: in para (1) words from ", detained under" to "leave to enter" in square brackets inserted by the Immigration and Asylum Act 1999, s 169(1), Sch 14, paras 43, 67. Date in force: 14 February 2000: see SI 2000/168, art 2, Schedule.

Modification
Paras 29–33 modified, in relation to a person detained on certain grounds relating to national security, by the Special Immigration Appeals Commission Act 1997, Sch 3, paras 4–8.

See Further
See further, in relation to the disapplication of para 29(1) above (as amended), where an appeal is made under Pt II hereof: the Nationality, Immigration and Asylum Act 2002 (Commencement No 4) Order 2003, SI 2003/754, art 3, Sch 2, para 2(10)(b)(i).

SCHEDULE 3
SUPPLEMENTARY PROVISIONS AS TO DEPORTATION

Section 5

Removal of persons liable to deportation

1   (1)   Where a deportation order is in force against any person, the Secretary of State may give directions for his removal to a country or territory specified in the directions being either—

(a)   a country of which he is a national or citizen; or

(b)   a country or territory to which there is reason to believe that he will be admitted.

(2)   The directions under sub-paragraph (1) above may be either—

(a)   directions given to the captain of a ship or aircraft about to leave the United Kingdom requiring him to remove the person in question in that ship or aircraft; or

(b)   directions given to the owners or agents of any ship or aircraft requiring them to make arrangements for his removal in a ship or aircraft specified or indicated in the directions; or

(c)   directions for his removal in accordance with arrangements to be made by the Secretary of State.

(3)   In relation to directions given under this paragraph, paragraphs 11 and 16(4) of Schedule 2 to this Act shall apply, with the substitution of references to the Secretary of State for references to an immigration officer, as they apply in relation to directions for removal given under paragraph 8 of that Schedule.

(4)   The Secretary of State, if he thinks fit, may apply in or towards payment of the expenses of or incidental to the voyage from the United Kingdom of a person against whom a deportation order is in force, or the maintenance until departure of such a person and his dependants, if any, any money belonging to that person; and except so far as they are paid as aforesaid, those expenses shall be defrayed by the Secretary of State.

Detention or control pending deportation

2   (1)   Where a recommendation for deportation made by a court is in force in respect of any person, [and that person is not detained in pursuance of the sentence or order of any court], he shall, unless the court by which the recommendation is made otherwise directs, [or a direction is given under sub-paragraph (1A) below,] be detained pending the making of a deportation order in pursuance of the recommendation, unless the Secretary of State directs him to be released pending further consideration of his case [or he is released on bail].

[(1A)   Where—

(a)   a recommendation for deportation made by a court on conviction of a person is in force in respect of him; and

(b)   he appeals against his conviction or against that recommendation,

the powers that the court determining the appeal may exercise include power to direct him to be released without setting aside the recommendation.]

(2)   Where notice has been given to a person in accordance with regulations under [section 105 of the Nationality, Immigration and Asylum Act 2002 (notice of decision)] of a decision to make a deportation order against him, [and he is not detained in pursuance of the sentence or order of a court], he may be detained under the authority of the Secretary of State pending the making of the deportation order.

(3)   Where a deportation order is in force against any person, he may be detained under the authority of the Secretary of State pending his removal or departure from the United Kingdom (and if already detained by virtue of sub-paragraph (1) or (2) above when the order is made, shall continue to be detained unless [he is released on bail or] the Secretary of State directs otherwise).

(4)   In relation to detention under sub-paragraph (2) or (3) above, paragraphs 17[, 18 and 25A to 25E] of Schedule 2 to this Act shall apply as they apply in relation to detention under paragraph 16 of that Schedule.

[(4A)   Paragraphs 22 to 25 of Schedule 2 to this Act apply in relation to a person detained under sub-paragraph (1), (2) or (3) as they apply in relation to a person detained under paragraph 16 of that Schedule.]

[(5)   A person to whom this sub-paragraph applies shall be subject to such restrictions as to residence[, as to his employment or occupation] and as to reporting to the police [or an immigration officer] as may from time to time be notified to him in writing by the Secretary of State.]

[(6)   The persons to whom sub-paragraph (5) above applies are—

(a)   a person liable to be detained under sub-paragraph (1) above, while by virtue of a direction of the Secretary of State he is not so detained; and

(b)   a person liable to be detained under sub-paragraph (2) or (3) above, while he is not so detained.]

Effect of appeals

[3   So far as they relate to an appeal under section 82(1) of the Nationality, Immigration and Asylum Act 2002 against a decision of the kind referred to in section 82(2)(j) or (k) of that Act (decision to make deportation order and refusal to revoke deportation order), paragraphs 29 to 33 of Schedule 2 to this Act shall apply for the purposes of this Schedule as if the reference in paragraph 29(1) to Part I of that Schedule were a reference to this Schedule.]

[*Powers of courts pending deportation*

4   Where the release of a person recommended for deportation is directed by a court, he shall be subject to such restrictions as to residence[, as to his employment or occupation] and as to reporting to the police as the court may direct.

5   (1)   On an application made—

(a)   by or on behalf of a person recommended for deportation whose release was so directed; or

(b)   by a constable; or

(c)   by an immigration order,

the appropriate court shall have the powers specified in sub-paragraph (2) below.

(2)   The powers mentioned in sub-paragraph (1) above are—

    (a)   if the person to whom the application relates is not subject to any such restrictions imposed by a court as are mentioned in paragraph 4 above, to order that he shall be subject to any such restrictions as the court may direct; and

    (b)   if he is subject to such restrictions imposed by a court by virtue of that paragraph or this paragraph—

        (i)   to direct that any of them shall be varied or shall cease to have effect; or

        (ii)   to give further directions as to his residence and reporting.

6   (1)   In this Schedule "the appropriate court" means except in a case to which sub-paragraph (2) below applies, the court which directed release.

(2)   This sub-paragraph applies where the court which directed release was—

    (a)   the Crown Court;

    (b)   the Court of Appeal;

    (c)   the High Court of Justiciary;

    (d)   the Crown Court in Northern Ireland; or

    (e)   the Court of Appeal in Northern Ireland.

[(2A)   Where the Crown Court directed release, the appropriate court is that court or a magistrates' court.]

(3)   Where ... the Crown Court in Northern Ireland directed release, the appropriate court is—

    (a)   the court that directed release; or

    (b)   a magistrates' court acting for the ... county court division where the person to whom the application relates resides.

(4)   Where the Court of Appeal or the Court of Appeal in Northern Ireland gave the direction, the appropriate court is the Crown Court or the Crown Court in Northern Ireland, as the case may be.

(5)   Where the High Court of Justiciary directed release, the appropriate court is—

    (a)   that court; or

    (b)   in a case where release was directed by that court on appeal, the court from which the appeal was made.

7   (1)   A constable or immigration officer may arrest without warrant any person who is subject to restrictions imposed by a court under this Schedule and who at the time of the arrest is in the relevant part of the United Kingdom—

    (a)   if he has reasonable grounds to suspect that that person is contravening or has contravened any of those restrictions; or

    (b)   if he has reasonable grounds for believing that that person is likely to contravene any of them.

(2)   In sub-paragraph (1) above "the relevant part of the United Kingdom" means—

    (a)   England and Wales, in a case where a court with jurisdiction in England or Wales imposed the restrictions;

    (b)   Scotland, in a case where a court with jurisdiction in Scotland imposed them; and

    (c)   Northern Ireland, in a case where a court in Northern Ireland imposed them.

8   (1)   A person arrested in [England or Wales in pursuance of paragraph 7 above shall be brought as soon as practicable and in any event within twenty-four hours after

his arrest before a justice of the peace in England or Wales, and a person arrested in] Northern Ireland in pursuance of paragraph 7 above shall be brought as soon as practicable and in any event within 24 hours after his arrest before a justice of the peace for the petty sessions ... district in which he was arrested.

(2) In reckoning for the purposes of this paragraph any period of 24 hours, no account shall be taken of Christmas Day, Good Friday or any Sunday.

9 (1) A person arrested in Scotland in pursuance of paragraph 7 above shall wherever practicable be brought before the appropriate court not later than in the course of the first day after his arrest, such day not being a Saturday, a Sunday or a court holiday prescribed for that court under section 10 of the Bail etc (Scotland) Act 1980.

(2) Nothing in this paragraph shall prevent a person arrested in Scotland being brought before a court on a Saturday, a Sunday or such a court holiday as is mentioned in sub-paragraph (1) above where the court is, in pursuance of section 10 of the said Act of 1980, sitting on such day for the disposal of criminal business.

10 Any justice of the peace or court before whom a person is brought by virtue of paragraph 8 or 9 above—

(a) if of the opinion that that person is contravening, has contravened or is likely to contravene any restriction imposed on him by a court under this Schedule, may direct—
    (i) that he be detained; or
    (ii) that he be released subject to such restrictions as to his residence and reporting to the police as the court may direct; and
(b) if not of that opinion, shall release him without altering the restrictions as to his residence and his reporting to the police.]

Appointment
Appointment: 1 January 1973: see SI 1972/1514, art 2.

Amendment
Para 2: in sub-para (1) words "and that person is not detained in pursuance of the sentence or order of any court" in square brackets substituted by the Asylum and Immigration (Treatment of Claimants, etc) Act 2004, s 34(1). Date in force: 1 October 2004: see SI 2004/2523, art 2, Schedule.
Para 2: in sub-para (1) words "or a direction is given under sub-paragraph (1A) below," in square brackets substituted by the Criminal Justice Act 1982, s 64, Sch 10.
Para 2: in sub-para (1) words "or he is released on bail" in square brackets inserted by the Immigration and Asylum Act 1999, s 54(1), (2). Date in force: 10 February 2003: see SI 2003/2, art 2, Schedule.
Para 2: sub-paras (1A), (6) inserted by the Criminal Justice Act 1982, s 64, Sch 10.
Para 2: in sub-para (2) words "section 105 of the Nationality, Immigration and Asylum Act 2002" in square brackets substituted by the Nationality, Immigration and Asylum Act 2002, s 114(3), Sch 7, para 7. Date in force: 1 April 2003 (except in relation to events which took place before that date): see SI 2003/754, arts 2(1), 3(1), Sch 1.
Para 2: in sub-para (2) words "and he is not detained in pursuance of the sentence or order of a court" in square brackets substituted by the Asylum and Immigration (Treatment of Claimants, etc) Act 2004, s 34(2). Date in force: 1 October 2004: see SI 2004/2523, art 2, Schedule.
Para 2: in sub-para (3) words "he is released on bail or" in square brackets inserted by the Immigration and Asylum Act 1999, s 54(1), (3). Date in force: 10 February 2003: see SI 2003/2, art 2, Schedule.
Para 2: in sub-para (4) words ", 18 and 25A to 25E" in square brackets substituted by the Immigration and Asylum Act 1999, s 169(1), Sch 14, paras 43, 68. Date in force: 14 February 2000: see SI 2000/168, art 2, Schedule.
Para 2: sub-para (4A) inserted by the Immigration and Asylum Act 1999, s 54(1), (4). Date in force: 10 February 2003: see SI 2003/2, art 2, Schedule.
Para 2: sub-para (5) substituted by the Criminal Justice Act 1982, s 64, Sch 10.

Para 2: in sub-para (5) words ", as to his employment or occupation" in square brackets inserted by the Immigration Act 1988, s 10, Schedule.

Para 2: in sub-para (5) words "or an immigration officer" in square brackets inserted by the Asylum and Immigration Act 1996, s 12(1), Sch 2, para 13.

Para 3: substituted by the Nationality, Immigration and Asylum Act 2002, s 114(3), Sch 7, para 8. Date in force: 1 April 2003 (except in relation to events which took place before that date): see SI 2003/754, arts 2(1), 3(1), Sch 1.

Para 4: inserted, together with paras 5–10, by the Criminal Justice Act 1982, s 64, Sch 10, para 2.

Para 4: words in square brackets inserted by the Immigration Act 1988, s 10, Schedule, para 10.

Paras 5–10: inserted, together with para 4, by the Criminal Justice Act 1982, s 64, Sch 10, para 2.

Para 6: sub-para (2A) inserted by the Courts Act 2003, s 109(1), Sch 8, para 150(1), (2).

Para 6: in sub-para (3) words omitted repealed by the Courts Act 2003, s 109(1), (3), Sch 8, para 150(1), (3), Sch 10.

Para 6: in sub-para (3)(b) words omitted repealed by the Courts Act 2003, s 109(1), (3), Sch 8, para 150(1), (3), Sch 10.

Para 8: in sub-para (1) words from "England or Wales" to "person arrested in" in square brackets substituted by the Courts Act 2003, s 109(1), Sch 8, para 150(1), (4)(a).

Para 8: in sub-para (1) words omitted repealed by the Courts Act 2003, s 150(1), (3), Sch 8, para 150(1), (4)(b), Sch 10.

Modification
Para 1 modified, in its application to the Channel Tunnel, by the Channel Tunnel (International Arrangements) Order 1993, SI 1993/1813, art 7(1), Sch 4, para 1(12).

Modified, in relation to its application to frontier controls between the United Kingdom, France and Belgium, by the Channel Tunnel (Miscellaneous Provisions) Order 1994, SI 1994/1405, art 7.

See Further
See further, in relation to the disapplication of para 3 above, where an appeal is made under Pt II hereof: SI 2003/754, art 3(2), Sch 2, para 2(10)(b)(ii).

SCHEDULE 4
INTEGRATION WITH UNITED KINGDOM LAW OF IMMIGRATION LAW OF ISLANDS

Section 9

Leave to enter

1   (1)   Where under the immigration laws of any of the Islands a person is or has been given leave to enter or remain in the island, or is or has been refused leave, this Act shall have effect in relation to him, if he is not [a British citizen], as if the leave were leave (of like duration) given under this Act to enter or remain the United Kingdom, or, as the case may be, as if he had under this Act been refused leave to enter the United Kingdom.

(2)   Where under the immigration laws of any of the Islands a person has a limited leave to enter or remain in the Island subject to any such conditions as are authorised in the United Kingdom by section 3(1) of this Act (being conditions imposed by notice given to him, whether the notice of leave or a subsequent notice), then on his coming to the United Kingdom this Act shall apply, if he is not [a British citizen], as if those conditions related to his stay in the United Kingdom and had been imposed by notice under this Act.

(3)   Without prejudice to the generality of sub-paragraphs (1) and (2) above, anything having effect in the United Kingdom by virtue of either of those sub-paragraphs may in relation to the United Kingdom be varied or revoked under this Act in like manner, and subject to the like appeal (if any), as if it had originated under this Act as mentioned in that sub-paragraph.

(4)   Where anything having effect in the United Kingdom by virtue of sub-paragraph (1) or (2) above ceases to have effect or is altered in effect as mentioned in

sub-paragraph (3) or otherwise by anything done under this Act, sub-paragraph (1) or (2) shall not thereafter apply to it or, as the case may be, shall apply to it as so altered in effect.

(5) Nothing in this paragraph shall be taken as conferring on a person a right of appeal under this Act against any decision or action taken in any of the Islands.

2   Notwithstanding section 3(4) of this Act, leave given to a person under this Act to enter or remain in the United Kingdom shall not continue to apply on his return to the United Kingdom after an absence if he has during that absence entered any of the Islands in circumstances in which he is required under the immigration laws of that island to obtain leave to enter.

Deportation

[3   (1)   This Act has effect in relation to a person who is subject to an Islands deportation order as if the order were a deportation order made against him under this Act.

(2)   Sub-paragraph (1) does not apply if the person concerned is—

(a)   a British citizen;
(b)   an EEA national;
(c)   a member of the family of an EEA national; or
(d)   a member of the family of a British citizen who is neither such a citizen nor an EEA national.

(3)   The Secretary of State does not, as a result of sub-paragraph (1), have power to revoke an Islands deportation order.

(4)   In any particular case, the Secretary of State may direct that paragraph (b), (c) or (d) of sub-paragraph (2) is not to apply in relation to the Islands deportation order.

(5)   Nothing in this paragraph makes it unlawful for a person in respect of whom an Islands deportation order is in force in any of the Islands to enter the United Kingdom on his way from that island to a place outside the United Kingdom.

(6)   "Islands deportation order" means an order made under the immigration laws of any of the Islands under which a person is, or has been, ordered to leave the island and forbidden to return.

(7)   Subsections (10) and (12) to (14) of section 80 of the Immigration and Asylum Act 1999 apply for the purposes of this section as they apply for the purposes of that section.]

Illegal entrants

4   Notwithstanding anything in section 1(3) of this Act, it shall not be lawful for a person who is not [a British citizen] to enter the United Kingdom from any of the Islands where his presence was unlawful under the immigration laws of that island, unless he is given leave to enter.

Appointment
Appointment: 1 January 1973: see SI 1972/1514, art 2.

Amendment
Para 1: in sub-paras (1), (2) words "a British Citizen" in square brackets substituted by the British Nationality Act 1981, s 39(6), Sch 4, para 2.
Para 3: substituted by the Immigration and Asylum Act 1999, s 169(1), Sch 14, paras 43, 70. Date in force: 2 October 2000: see SI 2000/2444, art 2, Sch 1.
Para 4: words "a British Citizen" in square brackets substituted by the British Nationality Act 1981, s 39(6), Sch 4, para 2.

SCHEDULE 5

...

Amendment

Repealed by the Immigration and Asylum Act 1999, s 169(3), Sch 16. Date in force: 14 February 2000: see SI 2000/168, art 2, Schedule.

SCHEDULE 6
REPEALS

Section 34

[Text omitted]

IMMIGRATION ACT 1988

1988 CHAPTER 14

An Act to make further provision for the regulation of immigration into the United Kingdom; and for connected purposes

[10th May 1988]

BE IT ENACTED by the Queen's most Excellent Majesty, by and with the advice and consent of the Lords Spiritual and Temporal, and Commons, in this present Parliament assembled, and by the authority of the same, as follows:–

1 Termination of saving in respect of Commonwealth citizens settled before 1973

[This section repeals the Immigration Act 1971, s 1(5).]

Appointment

Appointment: 1 August 1988 (except in relation to a wife or child of a Commonwealth citizen settled in the United Kingdom on 1 January 1973 where the application of the wife or child for an entry clearance was made before that date): see SI 1988/1133, arts 2, 3(1), Schedule.

Amendment

This section repeals the Immigration Act 1971, s 1(5).

2 Restriction on exercise of right of abode in cases of polygamy

(1) This section applies to any woman who—

    (a) has the right of abode in the United Kingdom under section 2(1)(b) of the principal Act as, or as having been, the wife of a man ("the husband")—

        (i) to whom she is or was polygamously married; and

        (ii) who is or was such a citizen of the United Kingdom and Colonies, Commonwealth citizen or British subject as is mentioned in section 2(2)(a) or (b) of that Act as in force immediately before the commencement of the British Nationality Act 1981; and

    (b) has not before the coming into force of this section and since her marriage to the husband been in the United Kingdom.

(2) A woman to whom this section applies shall not be entitled to enter the United Kingdom in the exercise of the right of abode mentioned in subsection (1)(a) above or

to be granted a certificate of entitlement in respect of that right if there is another woman living (whether or not one to whom this section applies) who is the wife or widow of the husband and who—

(a) is, or at any time since her marriage to the husband has been, in the United Kingdom; or

(b) has been granted a certificate of entitlement in respect of the right of abode mentioned in subsection (1)(a) above or an entry clearance to enter the United Kingdom as the wife of the husband.

(3) So long as a woman is precluded by subsection (2) above from entering the United Kingdom in the exercise of her right of abode or being granted a certificate of entitlement in respect of that right the principal Act shall apply to her as it applies to a person not having a right of abode.

(4) Subsection (2) above shall not preclude a woman from re-entering the United Kingdom if since her marriage to the husband she has at any time previously been in the United Kingdom and there was at that time no such other woman living as is mentioned in that subsection.

(5) Where a woman claims that this section does not apply to her because she had been in the United Kingdom before the coming into force of this section and since her marriage to the husband it shall be for her to prove that fact.

(6) For the purposes of this section a marriage may be polygamous although at its inception neither party has any spouse additional to the other.

(7) For the purposes of subsections (1)(b), (2)(a), (4) and (5) above there shall be disregarded presence in the United Kingdom as a visitor or an illegal entrant and presence in circumstances in which a person is deemed by section 11(1) of the principal Act not to have entered the United Kingdom.

(8) In subsection (2)(b) above the reference to a certificate of entitlement includes a reference to a certificate treated as such a certificate by virtue of section 39(8) of the British Nationality Act 1981.

(9) No application by a woman for a certificate of entitlement in respect of such a right of abode as is mentioned in subsection (1)(a) above or for an entry clearance shall be granted if another application for such a certificate or clearance is pending and that application is made by a woman as the wife or widow of the same husband.

(10) For the purposes of subsection (9) above an application shall be regarded as pending so long as it and any appeal proceedings relating to it have not been finally determined.

Appointment
Appointment: 1 August 1988 (except in relation to a woman who has made an application for a certificate of entitlement in respect of the right of abode mentioned in sub-s (1)(a) above before that date): see SI 1988/1133, arts 2, 3(2), Schedule.

3 Proof of right of abode

[This section amends the Immigration Act 1971, ss 2, 3, 13, and the British Nationality Act 1981, s 39.]

Appointment
Appointment: 1 August 1988: see SI 1988/1133, art 2, Schedule.

Amendment
This section amends the Immigration Act 1971, ss 2, 3, 13, and the British Nationality Act 1981, s 39.

Appendix 1   Legislation and materials

4   Members of diplomatic missions

[This section amends the Immigration Act 1971, s 8.]

Appointment
Appointment: 1 August 1988 (except in relation to a person who has taken up the post referred to in the Immigration Act 1971, s 8(3A) before that date): see SI 1988/1133, arts 2, 3(3), Schedule.

Amendment
This section amends the Immigration Act 1971, s 8.

5   ...

...

Amendment
Repealed by the Immigration and Asylum Act 1999, s 169(1), (3), Sch 14, paras 83, 84, Sch 16. Date in force: 2 October 2000 (except where directions for a person's removal from the United Kingdom were given, or the notice specifying the destination of his removal was served, before that date): see SI 2000/2444, art 2, Sch 1 and SI 2003/754, art 3, Sch 2, para 3(a); for further transitional provisions see art 3, Sch 2, para 3(b) thereto.

6   Knowingly overstaying limited leave

(1), (2)   ...

(3)   These amendments do not apply in relation to a person whose leave has expired before the coming into force of this section.

Initial Commencement
Specified date: 10 July 1988: see s 12(3).

Amendment
Sub-ss (1), (2): amend the Immigration Act 1971, s 24.

7   Persons exercising Community rights and nationals of member States

(1)   A person shall not under the principal Act require leave to enter or remain in the United Kingdom in any case in which he is entitled to do so by virtue of an enforceable Community right or of any provision made under section 2(2) of the European Communities Act 1972.

(2)   The Secretary of State may by order made by statutory instrument give leave to enter the United Kingdom for a limited period to any class of persons who are nationals of member States but who are not entitled to enter the United Kingdom as mentioned in subsection (1) above; and any such order may give leave subject to such conditions as may be imposed by the order.

(3)   References in the principal Act to limited leave shall include references to leave given by an order under subsection (2) above and a person having leave by virtue of such an order shall be treated as having been given that leave by a notice given to him by an immigration officer within the period specified in paragraph 6(1) of Schedule 2 to that Act.

Initial Commencement
Sub-ss (2), (3): Specified date: 10 July 1988: see s 12(3).

Appointment
Sub-s (1): Appointment: 20 July 1994: see SI 1994/1923, art 2.

8   Examination of passengers prior to arrival

(1)   This section applies to a person who arrives in the United Kingdom with a passport or other travel document bearing a stamp which—

(a)   has been placed there by an immigration officer before that person's departure on his journey to the United Kingdom or in the course of that journey; and

(b)   states that the person may enter the United Kingdom either for an indefinite or a limited period and, if for a limited period, subject to specified conditions.

(2)   A person to whom this section applies shall for the purposes of the principal Act be deemed to have been given on arrival in the United Kingdom indefinite or, as the case may be, limited leave in terms corresponding to those of the stamp.

(3)   A person who is deemed to have leave by virtue of this section shall be treated as having been given it by a notice given to him by an immigration officer within the period specified in paragraph 6(1) of Schedule 2 to the principal Act.

(4)   A person deemed to have leave by virtue of this section shall not on his arrival in the United Kingdom be subject to examination under paragraph 2 of Schedule 2 to the principal Act but may be examined by an immigration officer for the purpose of establishing that he is such a person.

(5)   The leave which a person is deemed to have by virtue of this section may, at any time before the end of the period of twenty-four hours from his arrival at the port at which he seeks to enter the United Kingdom or, if he has been examined under subsection (4) above, from the conclusion of that examination, be cancelled by an immigration officer by giving him a notice in writing refusing him leave to enter.

(6)   Sub-paragraphs (3) and (4) of paragraph 6 of Schedule 2 to the principal Act shall have effect as if any notice under subsection (5) above were a notice under that paragraph.

(7)   References in this section to a person's arrival in the United Kingdom are to the first occasion on which he arrives after the time when the stamp in question was placed in his passport or travel document, being an occasion not later than seven days after that time.

[(8)   ...]

Initial Commencement
Specified date: 10 July 1988: see s 12(3).

Amendment
Repealed by the Immigration and Asylum Act 1999, s 169(1), (3), Sch 14, paras 83, 85, Sch 16.
Date in force: to be appointed: see the Immigration and Asylum Act 1999, s 170(4).
Sub-s (8): inserted by SI 1990/2227, art 3, Sch 1, Part II; repealed by SI 1993/1813, art 9, Sch 6, Part I.

9   ...

...

Amendment
Repealed by the Immigration and Asylum Act 1999, s 169(1), (3), Sch 14, paras 83, 86, Sch 16.
Date in force: 30 June 2003: see SI 2003/1469, art 2, Schedule.

10   Miscellaneous minor amendments

The principal Act shall have effect with the amendments specified in the Schedule to this Act.

Initial Commencement
Specified date: 10 July 1988: see s 12(3).

11   Expenses and receipts

(1)   There shall be paid out of money provided by Parliament any expenses incurred by the Secretary of State in consequence of this Act.

(2)   Any sums received by the Secretary of State by virtue of this Act shall be paid into the Consolidated Fund.

Initial Commencement
Specified date: 10 July 1988: see s 12(3).

12   Short title, interpretation, commencement and extent

(1)   This Act may be cited as the Immigration Act 1988.

(2)   In this Act "the principal Act" means the Immigration Act 1971 and any expression which is also used in that Act has the same meaning as in that Act.

(3)   Except as provided in subsection (4) below this Act shall come into force at the end of the period of two months beginning with the day on which it is passed.

(4)   Sections 1, 2, 3, 4, 5 and 7(1) and paragraph 1 of the Schedule shall come into force on such day as may be appointed by the Secretary of State by an order made by statutory instrument; and such an order may appoint different days for different provisions and contain such transitional provisions and savings as the Secretary of State thinks necessary or expedient in connection with any provision brought into force.

(5)   This Act extends to Northern Ireland and section 36 of the principal Act (power to extend any of its provisions to the Channel Islands or the Isle of Man) shall apply also to the provisions of this Act.

Initial Commencement
Specified date: 10 July 1988: see para (3) above.

SCHEDULE
MINOR AMENDMENTS

Section 10

1–5   ...

Power to detain passport etc

6   (1)   ...

(2)   This amendment does not apply in relation to any person whose examination under paragraph 2 or 3 of Schedule 2 began before the coming into force of this paragraph.

Time-limit for giving, refusing or cancelling leave to enter

7   (1)   ...

(2)   This amendment does not apply in relation to any person whose examination under paragraph 2 began before the coming into force of this paragraph.

Leave in default of notice giving or refusing leave or cancelling refusal

8   (1), (2)   ...

(3) The amendment in sub-paragraph (1) above does not apply in relation to any person in whose case the time-limit in paragraph 6(1) of Schedule 2 has expired before the coming into force of this paragraph; and the amendment in sub-paragraph (2) above does not apply in relation to a person given a notice of cancellation under paragraph 6(3) of Schedule 2 before the coming into force of this paragraph.

Time-limit for removal directions

9   (1)–(3) ...

(4)   These amendments do not apply in relation to any person refused leave to enter the United Kingdom before the coming into force of this paragraph.

Restriction on work in case of persons temporarily admitted etc

10   (1)–(3) ...

(4)   These amendments apply in relation to persons granted temporary admission or released from detention under paragraph 21 of Schedule 2, becoming liable to detention under paragraph 2(2) or (3) of Schedule 3, or directed to be released as mentioned in paragraph 4 of that Schedule, as the case may be, before as well as after the coming into force of this paragraph.

Initial Commencement
Specified date
Paras 2–10: Specified date: 10 July 1988: see s 12(3).

Appointment
Para 1: Appointment: 16 May 1991: see SI 1991/1001, art 2.

Amendment
Paras 1–5: amend the Immigration Act 1971, ss 3(3)(b), 5(6), 14, 28(1)(a), 33(1).
Para 6: sub-para (1) amends the Immigration Act 1971, Sch 2, para 4.
Para 7: sub-para (1) amends the Immigration Act 1971, Sch 2, para 6(1), (2).
Para 8: sub-paras (1), (2) amend the Immigration Act 1971, Sch 2, para 6(1), (3).
Para 9: sub-paras (1)–(3) amend the Immigration Act 1971, Sch 2, paras 8(2), 10(1)(b), 28(4).
Para 10: sub-paras (1)–(3) amend the Immigration Act 1971, s 24(1)(e), Sch 2, para 21(2), Sch 3, paras 2(5), 4.

ASYLUM AND IMMIGRATION APPEALS ACT 1993

1993 CHAPTER 23

An Act to make provision about persons who claim asylum in the United Kingdom and their dependants; to amend the law with respect to certain rights of appeal under the Immigration Act 1971; and to extend the provisions of the Immigration (Carriers' Liability) Act 1987 to transit passengers

[1st July 1993]

BE IT ENACTED by the Queen's most Excellent Majesty, by and with the advice and consent of the Lords Spiritual and Temporal, and Commons, in this present Parliament assembled, and by the authority of the same, as follows

Introductory

1   Interpretation

In this Act—

"the 1971 Act" means the Immigration Act 1971;

"claim for asylum" means a claim made by a person (whether before or after the coming into force of this section) that it would be contrary to the United Kingdom's obligations under the Convention for him to be removed from, or required to leave, the United Kingdom; and

"the Convention" means the Convention relating to the Status of Refugees done at Geneva on 28th July 1951 and the Protocol to that Convention.

Initial Commencement
Royal Assent (for certain purposes): 1 July 1993: (no specific commencement provision).

Appointment
Appointment (for remaining purposes): 26 July 1993: see SI 1993/1655, art 2.

2   Primacy of Convention

Nothing in the immigration rules (within the meaning of the 1971 Act) shall lay down any practice which would be contrary to the Convention.

Initial Commencement
Royal Assent: 1 July 1993: (no specific commencement provision).

Treatment of persons who claim asylum

3   ...

...

Amendment
Repealed by the Immigration and Asylum Act 1999, s 169(1), (3), Sch 14, paras 99, 100, Sch 16.
Date in force: 11 December 2000: see SI 2000/3099, art 3, Schedule.

4   ...

...

Amendment

Repealed, in relation to England and Wales, by the Housing Act 1996, s 227, Sch 19, Part VIII. Repealed, in relation to Scotland and Northern Ireland, by the Immigration and Asylum Act 1999, ss 120(6), 121(3), 169(1), (3), Sch 14, paras 99, 101, Sch 16. Date in force: 3 April 2000: see SI 2000/464, art 2, Schedule.

5 ...

...

Amendment

Repealed, in relation to England and Wales, by the Housing Act 1996, s 227, Sch 19, Part VIII. Repealed, in relation to Scotland and Northern Ireland, by the Immigration and Asylum Act 1999, ss 120(6), 121(3), 169(1), (3), Sch 14, paras 99, 101, Sch 16. Date in force: 3 April 2000: see SI 2000/464, art 2, Schedule.

6 ...

...

Amendment

Repealed by the Immigration and Asylum Act 1999, Sch 14, paras 99, 102. Date in force: 26 July 1993, with retrospective effect: see the Immigration and Asylum Act 1999, ss 169(1), (3), 170(3)(s), Sch 14, para 102(2), Sch 16.

7 ...

...

Amendment

Repealed by the Immigration and Asylum Act 1999, s 169(1), (3), Sch 14, paras 99, 103, Sch 16. Date in force: 2 October 2000: see SI 2000/2444, art 2, Sch 1; for transitional provisions see art 3, Sch 2, para 3 thereof.

Rights of appeal

8 ...

...

Amendment

Repealed by the Immigration and Asylum Act 1999, s 169(1), (3), Sch 14, paras 99, 104, Sch 16. Date in force: 2 October 2000 (except in relation to events which took place before that date): see SI 2000/2444, art 2, Sch 1; for transitional provisions see art 3, Sch 2, para 3 thereof and SI 2003/754, art 3, Sch 2, para 4(2).

9 ...

...

Amendment

Repealed by the Immigration and Asylum Act 1999, s 169(1), (3), Sch 14, paras 99, 104, Sch 16. Date in force: 2 October 2000 (except in relation to events which took place before that date): see SI 2000/2444, art 2, Sch 1; for transitional provisions see art 3, Sch 2, para 3 thereof.

[9A ...]

...

Amendment

Inserted by the Asylum and Immigration Act 1996, s 12(2), Sch 3, para 3.

Repealed by the Asylum and Immigration (Treatment of Claimants, etc) Act 2004, ss 26(7), 47, Sch 2, Pt 1, para 9, Sch 4. Date in force: 4 April 2005: see SI 2005/565, art 2(d); for transitional provisions in relation to pending appeals which were made to an adjudicator before 4 April 2005 and in relation to further appeals and applications in such cases see arts 3–9 thereof.

10   ...

...

Amendment
Repealed by the Immigration and Asylum Act 1999, s 169(1), (3), Sch 14, paras 99, 104, Sch 16. Date in force: 2 October 2000 (except in relation to events which took place before that date): see SI 2000/2444, art 2, Sch 1; for transitional provisions see art 3, Sch 2, para 3 thereof.

11   ...

...

Amendment
Repealed by the Immigration and Asylum Act 1999, s 169(1), (3), Sch 14, paras 99, 104, Sch 16. Date in force: 2 October 2000 (except in relation to events which took place before that date): see SI 2000/2444, art 2, Sch 1; for transitional provisions see art 3, Sch 2, para 3 thereof.

12   ...

...

Amendment
Repealed by the Immigration and Asylum Act 1999, s 169(1), (3), Sch 14, paras 99, 107, Sch 16. Date in force: 8 December 2002: see SI 2002/2815, art 2, Schedule.

Supplementary

13   Financial provision

(1)   There shall be paid out of money provided by Parliament—

    (a)   any expenditure incurred by the Secretary of State under this Act; and

    (b)   any increase attributable to this Act in the sums payable out of such money under any other enactment.

(2)   Any sums received by the Secretary of State by virtue of this Act shall be paid into the Consolidated Fund.

Initial Commencement
Royal Assent: 1 July 1993: (no specific commencement provision).

14   Commencement

(1)   Sections 4 to 11 above (and section 1 above so far as it relates to those sections) shall not come into force until such day as the Secretary of State may by order appoint, and different days may be appointed for different provisions or for different purposes.

(2)   An order under subsection (1) above—

    (a)   shall be made by statutory instrument; and

    (b)   may contain such transitional and supplemental provisions as the Secretary of State thinks necessary or expedient.

(3)   Without prejudice to the generality of subsections (1) and (2) above, with respect to any provision of section 4 above an order under subsection (1) above may appoint different days in relation to different descriptions of asylum-seekers and dependants of

asylum-seekers; and any such descriptions may be framed by reference to nationality, citizenship, origin or other connection with any particular country or territory, but not by reference to race, colour or religion.

Initial Commencement
Royal Assent: 1 July 1993: (no specific commencement provision).

Subordinate Legislation
Asylum and Immigration Appeals Act 1993 (Commencement and Transitional Provisions) Order 1993, SI 1993/1655 (made under sub-ss (1), (2)(b)).

15   Extent

(1)   Her Majesty may by Order in Council direct that any of the provisions of this Act shall extend, with such modifications as appear to Her Majesty to be appropriate, to any of the Channel Islands or the Isle of Man.

(2)   This Act extends to Northern Ireland.

Initial Commencement
Royal Assent: 1 July 1993: (no specific commencement provision).

Subordinate Legislation
Immigration (Isle of Man) Order 1997, SI 1997/275 (made under sub-s (1)).

16   Short title

This Act may be cited as the Asylum and Immigration Appeals Act 1993.

Initial Commencement
Royal Assent: 1 July 1993: (no specific commencement provision).

SCHEDULE 1

...

Amendment
Repealed by the Immigration and Asylum Act 1999, s 169(1), (3), Sch 14, paras 99, 101, Sch 16. Date in force: 3 April 2000: see SI 2000/464, art 2, Schedule.

SCHEDULE 2

...

...

Amendment
Repealed by the Immigration and Asylum Act 1999, s 169(1), (3), Sch 14, paras 99, 104, Sch 16. Date in force: 2 October 2000 (except in relation to events which took place before that date): see SI 2000/2444, art 2, Sch 1; for transitional provisions see art 3, Sch 2, para 3 thereto and SI 2003/754, art 3, Sch 2, para 4(2), (4), (5) thereto, and SI 2000/3099, art 5.

See Further
See further, in relation to an appeal made under s 8 hereof: the Nationality, Immigration and Asylum Act 2002 (Commencement No 4) Order 2003, SI 2003/754, art 3(2), Sch 2, para 4(6).

ASYLUM AND IMMIGRATION ACT 1996

1996 CHAPTER 49

An Act to amend and supplement the Immigration Act 1971 and the Asylum and Immigration Appeals Act 1993; to make further provision with respect to persons subject to immigration control and the employment of such persons; and for connected purposes

[24th July 1996]

BE IT ENACTED by the Queen's most Excellent Majesty, by and with the advice and consent of the Lords Spiritual and Temporal, and Commons, in this present Parliament assembled, and by the authority of the same, as follows:–

Asylum claims

1   ...

...

Amendment

Repealed by the Immigration and Asylum Act 1999, s 169(3), Sch 16. Date in force: 2 October 2000: see SI 2000/2444, art 2, Sch 1.

2   Removal etc of asylum claimants to safe third countries

(1)   *Nothing in section 6 of the 1993 Act (protection of claimants from deportation etc.) shall prevent a person who has made a claim for asylum being removed from the United Kingdom if-*

  (a)   *the Secretary of State has certified that, in his opinion, the conditions mentioned in subsection (2) below are fulfilled;*

  (b)   *the certificate has not been set aside on an appeal under section 3 below; and*

  (c)   *except in the case of a person who is to be sent to a country or territory to which subsection (3) below applies, the time for giving notice of such an appeal has expired and no such appeal is pending.*

(2)   *The conditions are-*

  (a)   *that the person is not a national or citizen of the country or territory to which he is to be sent;*

  (b)   *that his life and liberty would not be threatened in that country or territory by reason of his race, religion, nationality, membership of a particular social group, or political opinion; and*

  (c)   *that the government of that country or territory would not send him to another country or territory otherwise than in accordance with the Convention.*

(3)   *This subsection applies to any country or territory which is or forms part of a member State, or is designated for the purposes of this subsection in an order made by the Secretary of State by statutory instrument.*

(4)   *The first order under this section shall not be made unless a draft of the order has been laid before and approved by a resolution of each House of Parliament.*

(5)   *A statutory instrument containing a subsequent order under this section shall be subject to annulment in pursuance of a resolution of either House of Parliament.*

(6) For the purposes of this section, an appeal under section 3 below is pending during the period beginning when notice of appeal is duly given and ending when the appeal is finally determined or withdrawn.

(7) In this section 'claim for asylum' and 'the Convention' have the same meanings as in the 1993 Act.

Amendment
Repealed by the Immigration and Asylum Act 1999, s 169(3), Sch 16. Date in force: 2 October 2000 (except in relation to events which took place before that date): see SI 2000/2444, art 2, Sch 1; for transitional provisions see art 3, Sch 2, para 4 thereof.

3   Appeals against certificates under section 2

(1) Where a certificate has been issued under section 2(1) above in respect of any person–

(a)   that person may appeal against the certificate to a special adjudicator on the ground that any of the conditions mentioned in section 2(2) above was not fulfilled when the certificate was issued, or has since ceased to be fulfilled; but
(b)   unless and until the certificate is set aside on such an appeal, he shall not be entitled to bring or pursue any appeal under-
 (i)   Part II of the 1971 Act (appeals: general); or
 (ii)   section 8 of the 1993 Act (appeals to special adjudicator on Convention grounds),

as respects matters arising before his removal from the United Kingdom.

(2) A person who has been, or is to be, sent to a country or territory to which section 2(3) above applies shall not be entitled to bring or pursue an appeal under this section so long as he is in the United Kingdom.

(3) The Lord Chancellor shall designate such number of the adjudicators appointed for the purposes of Part II of the 1971 Act as he thinks necessary to act as special adjudicators for the purposes of this section and may from time to time vary that number and the persons who are so designated.

(4) Subject to subsection (5) below, the following provisions of the 1971 Act, namely–

(a)   section 18 (notice of decisions appealable under that Part and statement of appeal rights etc.);
(b)   section 19 (determination of appeals under that Part by adjudicators);
(c)   section 21 (references of cases by Secretary of State for further consideration);
(d)   section 22(1) to (4), (6) and (7) (rules of procedure for appeals);
(e)   section 23 (grants to voluntary organisations helping persons with rights of appeal); and
(f)   Schedule 5 (provisions about adjudicators and Immigration Appeal Tribunal),

shall have effect as if this section were contained in Part II of that Act.

(5) Rules of procedure under section 22 of the 1971 Act–

(a)   may make special provision in relation to appeals under this section; and
(b)   may make different provision in relation to appeals by persons who have been, or are to be, sent to countries or territories of different descriptions;

and so much of paragraph 5 of Schedule 5 to that Act as relates to the allocation of duties among the adjudicators shall have effect subject to subsection (3) above.

(6)   Paragraph 29 of Schedule 2 to the 1971 Act (grant of bail pending appeal) shall have effect as if the references to appeals under sections 13(1), 15(1)(a) and 16 of that Act included references to appeals under this section.

Amendment
Repealed by the Immigration and Asylum Act 1999, s 169(3), Sch 16. Date in force: 2 October 2000 (except in relation to events which took place before that date): see SI 2000/2444, art 2, Sch 1; for transitional provisions see art 3, Sch 2, para 4 thereof.

Immigration offences

4   Obtaining leave by deception

[This section adds the Immigration Act 1971, s 24(1)(aa).]

Appointment
Appointment: 1 October 1996: see SI 1996/2053, art 2, Schedule, Pt III.

Amendment
This section adds the Immigration Act 1971, s 24(1)(aa).
Repealed by the Immigration and Asylum Act 1999, s 169(3), Sch 16. Date in force: to be appointed: see the Immigration and Asylum Act 1999, s 170(4).

5   Assisting asylum claimants, and persons seeking to obtain leave by deception

[This section amends the Immigration Act 1971, s 25(1), (5), (6) and adds s 25(1A).]

Appointment
Appointment: 1 October 1996: see SI 1996/2053, art 2, Schedule, Pt III.

Amendment
This section amends the Immigration Act 1971, s 25(1), (5), (6) and adds s 25(1A).
Repealed by the Nationality, Immigration and Asylum Act 2002, s 161, Sch 9. Date in force: to be appointed: see the Nationality, Immigration and Asylum Act 2002, s 162(1).

6   Increased penalties

[This section amends the Immigration Act 1971, ss 24(1), 26(1), 27.]

Appointment
Appointment: 1 October 1996: see SI 1996/2053, art 2, Schedule, Pt III.

Amendment
This section amends the Immigration Act 1971, ss 24(1), 26(1), 27.

7   ...

...

Amendment
Repealed by the Immigration and Asylum Act 1999, s 169(1), (3), Sch 14, paras 108, 109, Sch 16. Date in force: 14 February 2000: see SI 2000/168, art 2, Schedule.

Persons subject to immigration control

8   Restrictions on employment

(1)   Subject to subsection (2) below, if any person ("the employer") employs a person subject to immigration control ("the employee") who has attained the age of 16, the employer shall be guilty of an offence if—

(a) the employee has not been granted leave to enter or remain in the United Kingdom; or

(b) the employee's leave is not valid and subsisting, or is subject to a condition precluding him from taking up the employment,

and (in either case) the employee does not satisfy such conditions as may be specified in an order made by the Secretary of State.

[(2) It is a defence for a person charged with an offence under this section to prove that before the employment began any relevant requirement of an order of the Secretary of State under subsection (2A) was complied with.

(2A) An order under this subsection may—

(a) require the production to an employer of a document of a specified description;

(b) require the production to an employer of one document of each of a number of specified descriptions;

(c) require an employer to take specified steps to retain, copy or record the content of a document produced to him in accordance with the order;

(d) make provision which applies generally or only in specified circumstances;

(e) make different provision for different circumstances.]

(3) The defence afforded by subsection (2) above shall not be available in any case where the employer knew that his employment of the employee would constitute an offence under this section.

[(4) A person guilty of an offence under this section shall be liable—

(a) on conviction on indictment, to a fine, or

(b) on summary conviction, to a fine not exceeding the statutory maximum.]

(5) Where an offence under this section committed by a body corporate is proved to have been committed with the consent or connivance of, or to be attributable to any neglect on the part of—

(a) any director, manager, secretary or other similar officer of the body corporate; or

(b) any person who was purporting to act in any such capacity,

he as well as the body corporate shall be guilty of the offence and shall be liable to be proceeded against and punished accordingly.

(6) Where the affairs of a body corporate are managed by its members, subsection (5) above shall apply in relation to the acts and defaults of a member in connection with his functions of management as if he were a director of the body corporate.

[(6A) Where an offence under this section is committed by a partnership (other than a limited partnership) each partner shall be guilty of the offence and shall be liable to be proceeded against and punished accordingly.

(6B) Subsection (5) shall have effect in relation to a limited partnership as if—

(a) a reference to a body corporate were a reference to a limited partnership, and

(b) a reference to an officer of the body were a reference to a partner.]

(7) An order under this section shall be made by statutory instrument which shall be subject to annulment in pursuance of a resolution of either House of Parliament.

(8) In this section—

"contract of employment" means a contract of service or apprenticeship, whether express or implied, and (if it is express) whether it is oral or in writing;

1437

"employ" means employ under a contract of employment and "employment" shall be construed accordingly.

[(9) ...

(10)   An offence under this section shall be treated as—

    (a)   a relevant offence for the purpose of sections 28B and 28D of that Act (search, entry and arrest), and

    (b)   an offence under Part III of that Act (criminal proceedings) for the purposes of sections 28E, 28G and 28H (search after arrest).]

Appointment
Sub-ss (1), (2): Appointment (for the purpose of making orders): 1 December 1996 (except in relation to employment which began before 27 January 1997): see SI 1996/2970, art 2(2), (3).
Sub-ss (1), (2): Appointment (for remaining purposes): 27 January 1997 (except in relation to employment which began before that date): see SI 1996/2970, art 2(1), (2).
Sub-ss (3)–(8): Appointment: 27 January 1997 (except in relation to employment which began before that date): see SI 1996/2970, art 2(1), (2).

Amendment
Sub-ss (2), (2A): substituted, for sub-s (2) as originally enacted, by the Nationality, Immigration and Asylum Act 2002, s 147(1), (2). Date in force (for the purpose of enabling subordinate legislation to be made): 1 April 2003: see SI 2003/754, art 2(1), Sch 1. Date in force (for remaining purposes): 1 May 2004: see SI 2004/1201, art 2.
Sub-s (4): substituted by the Asylum and Immigration (Treatment of Claimants, etc) Act 2004, s 6(1). Date in force: 1 October 2004: see SI 2004/2523, art 2, Schedule.
Sub-ss (6A), (6B): inserted by the Nationality, Immigration and Asylum Act 2002, s 147(1), (3). Date in force: 1 April 2003: see SI 2003/754, art 2(1), Sch 1.
Sub-ss (9), (10): inserted by the Nationality, Immigration and Asylum Act 2002, s 147(1), (4). Date in force: 1 April 2003: see SI 2003/754, art 2(1), Sch 1.
Sub-s (9): repealed by the Asylum and Immigration (Treatment of Claimants, etc) Act 2004, ss 6(2), 47, Sch 4. Date in force: 1 October 2004: see SI 2004/2523, art 2, Schedule.

Subordinate Legislation
Immigration (Restrictions on Employment) Order 2004, SI 2004/755 (made under sub-ss (1), (2A)).

[8A   Code of practice]

[(1)   The Secretary of State must issue a code of practice as to the measures which an employer is to be expected to take, or not to take, with a view to securing that, while avoiding the commission of an offence under section 8, he also avoids unlawful discrimination.

(2)   "Unlawful discrimination" means—

    (a)   discrimination in contravention of section 4(1) of the Race Relations Act 1976 ("the 1976 Act"); or

    (b)   in relation to Northern Ireland, discrimination in contravention of Article 6(1) of the Race Relations (Northern Ireland) Order 1997 ("the 1997 Order").

(3)   Before issuing the code, the Secretary of State must—

    (a)   prepare and publish a draft of the proposed code; and

    (b)   consider any representations about it which are made to him.

(4)   In preparing the draft, the Secretary of State must consult—

    (a)   the Commission for Racial Equality;

    (b)   the Equality Commission for Northern Ireland; and

(c) such organisations and bodies (including organisations or associations of organisations representative of employers or of workers) as he considers appropriate.

(5) If the Secretary of State decides to proceed with the code, he must lay a draft of the code before both Houses of Parliament.

(6) The draft code may contain modifications to the original proposals made in the light of representations to the Secretary of State.

(7) After laying the draft code before Parliament, the Secretary of State may bring the code into operation by an order made by statutory instrument.

(8) An order under subsection (7)—

(a) shall be subject to annulment in pursuance of a resolution of either House of Parliament;
(b) may contain such transitional provisions or savings as appear to the Secretary of State to be necessary or expedient in connection with the code.

(9) A failure on the part of any person to observe a provision of the code does not of itself make him liable to any proceedings.

(10) But the code is admissible in evidence—

(a) in proceedings under the 1976 Act before an employment tribunal;
(b) in proceedings under the 1997 Order before an industrial tribunal.

(11) If any provision of the code appears to the tribunal to be relevant to any question arising in such proceedings, that provision is to be taken into account in determining the question.

(12) The Secretary of State may from time to time revise the whole or any part of the code and issue the code as revised.

(13) The provisions of this section also apply (with appropriate modifications) to any revision, or proposed revision, of the code.]

Amendment
Inserted by the Immigration and Asylum Act 1999, s 22. Date in force (for certain purposes): 19 February 2001: see SI 2001/239, art 2, Schedule. Date in force (for remaining purposes): 2 May 2001: see SI 2001/1394, art 2, Schedule.

Subordinate Legislation
Immigration (Restrictions on Employment) (Code of Practice) Order 2001, SI 2001/1436.

9 ...

...

Amendment
Repealed by the Immigration and Asylum Act 1999, s 169(1), (3), Sch 14, paras 108, 110, Sch 16. Date in force: 1 March 2000: see SI 2000/464, art 2, Schedule.

10 ...

...

Amendment
Repealed by the Immigration and Asylum Act 1999, s 169(1), (3), Sch 14, paras 108, 111, Sch 16. Date in force: 3 April 2000: see SI 2000/464, art 2, Schedule.

11 ...

...

Amendment

Repealed by the Immigration and Asylum Act 1999, s 169(1), (3), Sch 14, paras 108, 112, Sch 16.
Date in force: 3 April 2000: see SI 2000/464, art 2, Schedule.

Miscellaneous and supplemental

12   Other amendments and repeals

(1)   Schedule 2 to this Act (which contains amendments of the 1971 Act and a related amendment of the Immigration Act 1988) shall have effect.

(2)   Schedule 3 to this Act (which contains amendments of the 1993 Act) shall have effect.

(3)   The enactments specified in Schedule 4 to this Act are hereby repealed to the extent specified in the third column of that Schedule.

Appointment

Appointment (for certain purposes): 1 September 1996: see SI 1996/2053, art 2, Schedule, Pt II.
Sub-ss (1), (3): Appointment (for certain purposes): 1 October 1996: see SI 1996/2053, art 2, Schedule, Pt III.

13   Short title, interpretation, commencement and extent

(1)   This Act may be cited as the Asylum and Immigration Act 1996.

(2)   In this Act—

"the 1971 Act" means the Immigration Act 1971;
"the 1993 Act" means the Asylum and Immigration Appeals Act 1993;
"person subject to immigration control" means a person who under the 1971 Act requires leave to enter or remain in the United Kingdom (whether or not such leave has been given).

(3)   This Act, except section 11 and Schedule 1, shall come into force on such day as the Secretary of State may by order made by statutory instrument appoint, and different days may be appointed for different purposes.

(4)   An order under subsection (3) above may make such transitional and supplemental provision as the Secretary of State thinks necessary or expedient.

(5)   Her Majesty may by Order in Council direct that any of the provisions of this Act shall extend, with such modifications as appear to Her Majesty to be appropriate, to any of the Channel Islands or the Isle of Man.

(6)   This Act extends to Northern Ireland.

Appointment

Appointment: 26 July 1996: see SI 1996/2053, art 2, Schedule, Pt I.

Subordinate Legislation

Asylum and Immigration Act 1996 (Commencement No 1) Order 1996, SI 1996/2053 (made under sub-s (3)).
Asylum and Immigration Act 1996 (Commencement No 2) Order 1996, SI 1996/2127 (made under sub-s (3)).
Asylum and Immigration Act 1996 (Commencement No 3 and Transitional Provisions) Order 1996, SI 1996/2970 (made under sub-ss (3), (4)).
Asylum and Immigration Act 1996 (Jersey) Order 1998, SI 1998/1070 (made under sub-s (5)).
Asylum and Immigration Act 1996 (Guernsey) Order 1998, SI 1998/1264 (made under sub-s (5)).

SCHEDULE 1

...

Amendment

Repealed by the Immigration and Asylum Act 1999, s 169(1), (3), Sch 14, paras 108, 113. Date in force: 3 April 2000: see SI 2000/464, art 2, Schedule.

...

SCHEDULE 2
AMENDMENTS OF THE 1971 ACT AND THE IMMIGRATION ACT 1988

Section 12(1)

[This Schedule amends the Immigration Act 1988, s 5(1), the Immigration Act 1971, ss 3(1), (5), 5(4), 14, 33(1), (4), Sch 2, paras 4, 9, 17, 19–22, Sch 3, para 2, and adds Sch 2, para 34.]

Appointment

Paras 1(1), 3(1): Appointment: 1 November 1996: see SI 1996/2127, art 2, Schedule, Pt IV.
Paras 1(2), (3), 2, 4–7, 13: Appointment: 1 October 1996: see SI 1996/2053, art 2, Schedule, Pt III.
Paras 3(2), 8–12: Appointment: 1 September 1996: see SI 1996/2053, art 2, Schedule, Pt II.

Amendment

This Schedule amends the Immigration Act 1988, s 5(1), the Immigration Act 1971, ss 3(1), (5), 5(4), 14, 33(1), (4), Sch 2, paras 4, 9, 17, 19–22, Sch 3, para 2, and adds Sch 2, para 34.
Repealed in part by the Immigration and Asylum Act 1999, s 169(1), (3), Sch 14, paras 108, 114, Sch 16. Date in force: 2 October 2000: see SI 2000/2444, art 2, Sch 1.

SCHEDULE 3
AMENDMENTS OF THE 1993 ACT

Section 12(2)

1–5 *[This Schedule amends the Asylum and Immigration Appeals Act 1993, ss 7, 8, Sch 1, para 6, Sch 2, para 4(2) and adds s 9A.]*

Appointment

Paras 1–3, 5: Appointment: 1 September 1996: see SI 1996/2053, art 2, Schedule, Pt II.

Amendment

This Schedule amends the Asylum and Immigration Appeals Act 1993, ss 7, 8, Sch 1, para 6, Sch 2, para 4(2) and adds s 9A.
Paras 1, 2, 5: repealed by the Immigration and Asylum Act 1999, s 169(1), (3), Sch 14, paras 99, 115, Sch 16. Date in force: 2 October 2000: see SI 2000/2444, art 2, Sch 1.

SCHEDULE 4
REPEALS

Chapter	Short title	Extent of repeal
1971 c 77.	Immigration Act 1971.	In Schedule 2, in paragraph 17(2)(b), the words "magistrate or".
1993 c 23.	Asylum and Immigration Appeals Act 1993.	In section 8(3), the words from "but a person" to the end.

Appointment

Appointment (remainder): 1 October 1996: see SI 1996/2053, art 2, Schedule, Pt III.
Appointment (in part): 1 September 1996: see SI 1996/2053, art 2, Schedule, Pt II.

SPECIAL IMMIGRATION APPEALS COMMISSION ACT 1997

1997 CHAPTER 68

An Act to establish the Special Immigration Appeals Commission; to make provision with respect to its jurisdiction; and for connected purposes.

[17th December 1997]

BE IT ENACTED by the Queen's most Excellent Majesty, by and with the advice and consent of the Lords Spiritual and Temporal, and Commons, in this present Parliament assembled, and by the authority of the same, as follows:—

1   Establishment of the Commission

(1) There shall be a commission, known as the Special Immigration Appeals Commission, for the purpose of exercising the jurisdiction conferred by this Act.

(2) Schedule 1 to this Act shall have effect in relation to the Commission.

[(3) The Commission shall be a superior court of record.

(4) A decision of the Commission shall be questioned in legal proceedings only in accordance with—

    (a) section 7, ...

    (b) ...]

Appointment
Appointment: 3 August 1998: see SI 1998/1892, art 2.

Amendment
Sub-ss (3), (4): inserted by the Anti-terrorism, Crime and Security Act 2001, s 35. Date in force: 14 December 2001: see the Anti-terrorism, Crime and Security Act 2001, s 127(2)(a).
Sub-s (4): para (b) and word omitted immediately preceding it repealed by the Prevention of Terrorism Act 2005, s 16(2)(b). Date in force: 14 March 2005: see the Prevention of Terrorism Act 2005, s 16(3).

[2   Jurisdiction: appeals]

[(1) A person may appeal to the Special Immigration Appeals Commission against a decision if—

    (a) he would be able to appeal against the decision under section 82(1) or 83(2) of the Nationality, Immigration and Asylum Act 2002 but for a certificate of the Secretary of State under section 97 of that Act (national security, &c), or

    (b) an appeal against the decision under section 82(1) or 83(2) of that Act lapsed under section 99 of that Act by virtue of a certificate of the Secretary of State under section 97 of that Act.

(2) The following provisions shall apply, with any necessary modifications, in relation to an appeal against an immigration decision under this section as they apply in relation to an appeal under section 82(1) of the Nationality, Immigration and Asylum Act 2002—

    (a) section 3C of the Immigration Act 1971 (c 77) (continuation of leave pending variation decision),

(b)   section 78 of the Nationality, Immigration and Asylum Act 2002 (no removal while appeal pending),
(c)   section 79 of that Act (deportation order: appeal),
(d)   section 82(3) of that Act (variation or revocation of leave to enter or remain: appeal),
(e)   section 84 of that Act (grounds of appeal),
(f)   section 85 of that Act (matters to be considered),
(g)   section 86 of that Act (determination of appeal),
(h)   section 87 of that Act (successful appeal: direction),
(i)   section 96 of that Act (earlier right of appeal),
(j)   section 104 of that Act (pending appeal),
(k)   section 105 of that Act (notice of immigration decision), and
(l)   section 110 of that Act (grants).

(3)   The following provisions shall apply, with any necessary modifications, in relation to an appeal against the rejection of a claim for asylum under this section as they apply in relation to an appeal under section 83(2) of the Nationality, Immigration and Asylum Act 2002—

(a)   section 85(4) of that Act (matters to be considered),
(b)   section 86 of that Act (determination of appeal),
(c)   section 87 of that Act (successful appeal: direction), and
(d)   section 110 of that Act (grants).

(4)   An appeal against the rejection of a claim for asylum under this section shall be treated as abandoned if the appellant leaves the United Kingdom.

(5)   A person may bring or continue an appeal against an immigration decision under this section while he is in the United Kingdom only if he would be able to bring or continue the appeal while he was in the United Kingdom if it were an appeal under section 82(1) of that Act.

(6)   In this section "immigration decision" has the meaning given by section 82(2) of the Nationality, Immigration and Asylum Act 2002.]

Amendment
Substituted by the Nationality, Immigration and Asylum Act 2002, s 114(3), Sch 7, para 20. Date in force: 1 April 2003 (except in relation to an appeal which is pending, by virtue of s 7A hereof, on that date): see SI 2003/754, arts 2(1), 3, Sch 1, Sch 2, para 5.

[2A   ...]
[...]

Amendment
Inserted by the Immigration and Asylum Act 1999, s 169(1), Sch 14, paras 118, 121. Date in force (in so far as it relates to sub-ss (1)–(6)): 2 October 2000 (except in relation to events which took place before that date): see SI 2000/2444, art 2, Sch 1; for transitional provisions see art 3, Sch 2, para 5 thereof.
Repealed by the Nationality, Immigration and Asylum Act 2002, ss 114(3), 161, Sch 7, para 21, Sch 9. Date in force: 1 April 2003 (except in relation to an appeal which is pending, by virtue of s 7A hereof, on that date): see SI 2003/754, arts 2(1), 3, Sch 1, Sch 2, para 5.

[2B

[A person may appeal to the Special Immigration Appeals Commission against a decision to make an order under section 40 of the British Nationality Act 1981 (c 61) (deprivation of citizenship) if he is not entitled to appeal under section 40A(1) of that Act because of a certificate under section 40A(2) [(and section 40A(3)(a) shall have effect in relation to appeals under this section)].]

Amendment
Inserted by the Nationality, Immigration and Asylum Act 2002, s 4(2). Date in force: 1 April 2003 (except in relation to an appeal which is pending, by virtue of s 7A hereof, on that date): see SI 2003/754, arts 2(1), 3(2), Sch 1, Sch 2, para 5.
Words "(and section 40A(3)(a) shall have effect in relation to appeals under this section)" in square brackets inserted by the Asylum and Immigration (Treatment of Claimants, etc) Act 2004, s 26(7), Sch 2, Pt 1, paras 10, 11. Date in force: 4 April 2005: see SI 2005/565, art 2(d); for transitional provisions in relation to pending appeals which were made to an adjudicator before 4 April 2005 and in relation to further appeals and applications in such cases see arts 3–9 thereof.

3 Jurisdiction: bail

(1) In the case of a person to whom subsection (2) below applies, the provisions of Schedule 2 to the Immigration Act 1971 specified in Schedule 3 to this Act shall have effect with the modifications set out there.

(2) This subsection applies to a person who is detained under the Immigration Act 1971 [or the Nationality, Immigration and Asylum Act 2002] if—

    (a) the Secretary of State certifies that his detention is necessary in the interests of national security,

    (b) he is detained following a decision to refuse him leave to enter the United Kingdom on the ground that his exclusion is in the interests of national security, or

    (c) he is detained following a decision to make a deportation order against him on the ground that his deportation is in the interests of national security.

Appointment
Appointment: 3 August 1998: see SI 1998/1892, art 2.

Amendment
Sub-s (2): words "or the Nationality, Immigration and Asylum Act 2002" in square brackets inserted by SI 2003/1016, art 3, Schedule, para 10. Date in force: 4 April 2003: see SI 2003/1016, art 2(2).

4 ...

...

Amendment
Repealed by the Nationality, Immigration and Asylum Act 2002, ss 114(3), 161 Sch 7, para 22, Sch 9. Date in force: 1 April 2003 (except in relation to an appeal which is pending, by virtue of s 7A hereof, on that date): see SI 2003/754, arts 2(1), 3, Sch 1, Sch 2, para 5.

5 Procedure in relation to jurisdiction under sections 2 and 3

(1) The Lord Chancellor may make rules—

    (a) for regulating the exercise of the rights of appeal conferred by section 2 [...] [or 2B] above,

    (b) for prescribing the practice and procedure to be followed on or in connection with appeals under [section 2 ...[or 2B] above], including the mode and burden of proof and admissibility of evidence on such appeals, and

    (c) for other matters preliminary or incidental to or arising out of such appeals, including proof of the decisions of the Special Immigration Appeals Commission.

(2) Rules under this section shall provide that an appellant has the right to be legally represented in any proceedings before the Commission on an appeal under section 2 [...] [or 2B] above, subject to any power conferred on the Commission by such rules.

[(2A)   Rules under this section may, in particular, do anything which may be done by rules under section 106 of the Nationality, Immigration and Asylum Act 2002 (appeals: rules).]

(3)   Rules under this section may, in particular—

(a)   make provision enabling proceedings before the Commission to take place without the appellant being given full particulars of the reasons for the decision which is the subject of the appeal,

(b)   make provision enabling the Commission to hold proceedings in the absence of any person, including the appellant and any legal representative appointed by him,

(c)   make provision about the functions in proceedings before the Commission of persons appointed under section 6 below, and

(d)   make provision enabling the Commission to give the appellant a summary of any evidence taken in his absence.

(4)   Rules under this section may also include provision—

(a)   enabling any functions of the Commission which relate to matters preliminary or incidental to an appeal, or which are conferred by Part II of Schedule 2 to the Immigration Act 1971, to be performed by a single member of the Commission, or

(b)   conferring on the Commission such ancillary powers as the Lord Chancellor thinks necessary for the purposes of the exercise of its functions.

(5)   The power to make rules under this section shall include power to make rules with respect to applications to the Commission under paragraphs 22 to 24 of Schedule 2 to the Immigration Act 1971 and matters arising out of such applications.

(6)   In making rules under this section, the Lord Chancellor shall have regard, in particular, to—

(a)   the need to secure that decisions which are the subject of appeals are properly reviewed, and

(b)   the need to secure that information is not disclosed contrary to the public interest.

(7)   ...

(8)   The power to make rules under this section shall be exercisable by statutory instrument.

(9)   No rules shall be made under this section unless a draft of them has been laid before and approved by resolution of each House of Parliament.

Appointment
Appointment: 11 June 1998: see SI 1998/1336, art 2.

Amendment
Sub-s (1): in para (a) words omitted repealed by the Nationality, Immigration and Asylum Act 2002, ss 114(3), 161, Sch 7, para 23(a), Sch 9. Date in force: 1 April 2003 (except in relation to an appeal which is pending, by virtue of s 7A hereof, on that date): see SI 2003/754, arts 2(1), 3, Sch 1, Sch 2, para 5.
Sub-s (1): in para (a) words omitted inserted by the Race Relations (Amendment) Act 2000, s 9(1), Sch 2, para 28(a). Date in force: 2 April 2001: see SI 2001/566, art 2(1).
Sub-s (1): in para (a) words "or 2B" in square brackets inserted by the Nationality, Immigration and Asylum Act 2002, s 4(3). Date in force: 1 April 2003 (except in relation to an appeal which is pending, by virtue of s 7A hereof, on that date): see SI 2003/754, arts 2(1), 3(2), Sch 1, Sch 2, para 5.

Sub-s (1): in para (b) words in square brackets beginning with the words "section 2" substituted by the Race Relations (Amendment) Act 2000, s 9(1), Sch 2, para 28(b). Date in force: 2 April 2001: see SI 2001/566, art 2(1).

Sub-s (1): in para (b) words omitted repealed by the Nationality, Immigration and Asylum Act 2002, ss 114(3), 161, Sch 7, para 23(a), Sch 9. Date in force: 1 April 2003 (except in relation to an appeal which is pending, by virtue of s 7A hereof, on that date): see SI 2003/754, arts 2(1), 3(2), Sch 1, Sch 2, para 5.

Sub-s (1): in para (b) words "or 2B" in square brackets inserted by the Nationality, Immigration and Asylum Act 2002, s 4(3). Date in force: 1 April 2003 (except in relation to an appeal which is pending, by virtue of s 7A hereof, on that date): see SI 2003/754, arts 2(1), 3(2), Sch 1, Sch 2, para 5.

Sub-s (2): words omitted inserted by the Race Relations (Amendment) Act 2000, s 9(1), Sch 2, para 28(c). Date in force: 2 April 2001: see SI 2001/566, art 2(1).

Sub-s (2): words omitted repealed by the Nationality, Immigration and Asylum Act 2002, ss 114(3), 161, Sch 7, para 23(a), Sch 9. Date in force: 1 April 2003 (except in relation to an appeal which is pending, by virtue of s 7A hereof, on that date): see SI 2003/754, arts 2(1), 3(2), Sch 1, Sch 2, para 5.

Sub-s (2): words "or 2B" in square brackets inserted by the Nationality, Immigration and Asylum Act 2002, s 4(3). Date in force: 1 April 2003 (except in relation to an appeal which is pending, by virtue of s 7A hereof, on that date): see SI 2003/754, arts 2(1), 3(2), Sch 1, Sch 2, para 5.

Sub-s (2A): inserted by the Nationality, Immigration and Asylum Act 2002, s 114(3), Sch 7, para 23(b). Date in force: 1 April 2003 (except in relation to an appeal which is pending, by virtue of s 7A hereof, on that date): see SI 2003/754, arts 2(1), 3(2), Sch 1, Sch 2, para 5.

Sub-s (7): repealed by the Regulation of Investigatory Powers Act 2000, s 82(2), Sch 5. Date in force: 2 October 2000: see SI 2000/2543, art 3.

Subordinate Legislation
Special Immigration Appeals Commission (Procedure) Rules 2003, SI 2003/1034.

6   Appointment of person to represent the appellant's interests

(1)   The relevant law officer may appoint a person to represent the interests of an appellant in any proceedings before the Special Immigration Appeals Commission from which the appellant and any legal representative of his are excluded.

(2)   For the purposes of subsection (1) above, the relevant law officer is—

   (a)   in relation to proceedings before the Commission in England and Wales, the Attorney General,
   (b)   in relation to proceedings before the Commission in Scotland, the Lord Advocate, and
   (c)   in relation to proceedings before the Commission in Northern Ireland, the Attorney General for Northern Ireland.

(3)   A person appointed under subsection (1) above—

   (a)   if appointed for the purposes of proceedings in England and Wales, shall have a general qualification for the purposes of section 71 of the Courts and Legal Services Act 1990,
   (b)   if appointed for the purposes of proceedings in Scotland, shall be—
      (i)   an advocate, or
      (ii)   a solicitor who has by virtue of section 25A of the Solicitors (Scotland) Act 1980 rights of audience in the Court of Session and the High Court of Justiciary, and
   (c)   if appointed for the purposes of proceedings in Northern Ireland, shall be a member of the Bar of Northern Ireland.

(4)   A person appointed under subsection (1) above shall not be responsible to the person whose interests he is appointed to represent.

Appointment
Appointment: 3 August 1998: see SI 1998/1892, art 2.

Transfer of Functions
By virtue of the Scotland Act 1998, s 44(1)(c), the Lord Advocate ceased, on 20 May 1999 (see SI 1998/3178), to be a Minister of the Crown and became a member of the Scottish Executive. Accordingly, certain functions of the Lord Advocate are transferred to the Secretary of State (or as the case may be the Secretary of State for Scotland), or the Advocate General for Scotland: see the Transfer of Functions (Lord Advocate and Secretary of State) Order 1999, SI 1999/678 and the Transfer of Functions (Lord Advocate and Advocate General for Scotland) Order 1999, SI 1999/679.

7 Appeals from the Commission

(1) Where the Special Immigration Appeals Commission has made a final determination of an appeal, any party to the appeal may bring a further appeal to the appropriate appeal court on any question of law material to that determination.

(2) An appeal under this section may be brought only with the leave of the Commission or, if such leave is refused, with the leave of the appropriate appeal court.

(3) In this section "the appropriate appeal court" means—

  (a) in relation to a determination made by the Commission in England and Wales, the Court of Appeal,

  (b) in relation to a determination made by the Commission in Scotland, the Court of Session, and

  (c) in relation to a determination made by the Commission in Northern Ireland, the Court of Appeal in Northern Ireland.

(4) ...

Appointment
Appointment: 3 August 1998: see SI 1998/1892, art 2.

Amendment
Sub-s (4): repealed by the Immigration and Asylum Act 1999, s 169(1), (3), Sch 14, paras 118, 123, Sch 16. Date in force: 2 October 2000: see SI 2000/2444, art 2, Sch 1.

[7A ...]
[...]

Amendment
Repealed by the Nationality, Immigration and Asylum Act 2002, ss 114(3), 161, Sch 7, para 24, Sch 9. Date in force: 1 April 2003 (except in relation to an appeal which is pending, by virtue of this section, on that date): see SI 2003/754, arts 2(1), 3, Sch 1, Sch 2, para 5.
Inserted by the Immigration and Asylum Act 1999, s 169(1), Sch 14, paras 118, 124. Date in force: 2 October 2000: see SI 2000/2444, art 2, Sch 1.

8 Procedure on applications to the Commission for leave to appeal

(1) The Lord Chancellor may make rules regulating, and prescribing the procedure to be followed on, applications to the Special Immigration Appeals Commission for leave to appeal under section 7 above.

(2) Rules under this section may include provision enabling an application for leave to appeal to be heard by a single member of the Commission.

(3) The power to make rules under this section shall be exercisable by statutory instrument.

(4) No rules shall be made under this section unless a draft of them has been laid before and approved by resolution of each House of Parliament.

Appointment
Appointment: 11 June 1998: see SI 1998/1336, art 2.

9   Short title, commencement and extent

(1) This Act may be cited as the Special Immigration Appeals Commission Act 1997.

(2) This Act, except for this section, shall come into force on such day as the Secretary of State may by order made by statutory instrument appoint; and different days may be so appointed for different purposes.

(3) Her Majesty may by Order in Council direct that any of the provisions of this Act shall extend, with such modifications as appear to Her Majesty to be appropriate, to any of the Channel Islands or the Isle of Man.

(4) This Act extends to Northern Ireland.

Initial Commencement
Royal Assent: 17 December 1997: (no specific commencement provision).

Subordinate Legislation
Special Immigration Appeals Commission Act 1997 (Commencement No 1) Order 1998, SI 1998/1336 (made under sub-s (2)).
Special Immigration Appeals Commission Act 1997 (Commencement No 2) Order 1998, SI 1998/1892 (made under sub-s (2)).

SCHEDULE 1
THE COMMISSION

Section 1

Members

1   (1) The Special Immigration Appeals Commission shall consist of such number of members appointed by the Lord Chancellor as he may determine.

(2) A member of the Commission shall hold and vacate office in accordance with the terms of his appointment and shall, on ceasing to hold office, be eligible for re-appointment.

(3) A member of the Commission may resign his office at any time by notice in writing to the Lord Chancellor.

Chairman

2   The Lord Chancellor shall appoint one of the members of the Commission to be its chairman.

Payments to members

3   (1) The Lord Chancellor may pay to the members of the Commission such remuneration and allowances as he may determine.

(2) The Lord Chancellor may, if he thinks fit in the case of any member of the Commission pay such pension, allowance or gratuity to or in respect of the member, or such sums towards the provision of such pension, allowance or gratuity, as he may determine.

(3) If a person ceases to be a member of the Commission and it appears to the Lord Chancellor that there are special circumstances which make it right that the person should receive compensation, he may pay to that person a sum of such amount as he may determine.

Proceedings

4 The Commission shall sit at such times and in such places as the Lord Chancellor may direct and may sit in two or more divisions.

5 The Commission shall be deemed to be duly constituted if it consists of three members of whom—

(a) at least one holds or has held high judicial office (within the meaning of the Appellate Jurisdiction Act 1876), and

[(b) at least one is or has been a legally qualified member of the Asylum and Immigration Tribunal].

6 The chairman or, in his absence, such other member of the Commission as he may nominate, shall preside at sittings of the Commission and report its decisions.

Staff

7 The Lord Chancellor may appoint such officers and servants for the Commission as he thinks fit.

Expenses

8 The Lord Chancellor shall defray the remuneration of persons appointed under paragraph 7 above and such expenses of the Commission as he thinks fit.

Appointment
Appointment: 3 August 1998: see SI 1998/1892, art 2.

Amendment
Para 5: sub-para (b) substituted by the Asylum and Immigration (Treatment of Claimants, etc) Act 2004, s 26(7), Sch 2, Pt 1, paras 10, 12; for transitional provisions see s 26(7), Sch 2, Pt 2 thereto. Date in force: 4 April 2005: see SI 2005/565, art 2(d); for transitional provisions in relation to pending appeals which were made to an adjudicator before 4 April 2005 and in relation to further appeals and applications in such cases see arts 3–9 thereof.

SCHEDULE 2
...

...

Amendment
Repealed by the Nationality, Immigration and Asylum Act 2002, ss 114(3), 161, Sch 7, para 26, Sch 9. Date in force: 1 April 2003 (except in relation to an appeal which is pending, by virtue of s 7A hereof, on that date): see SI 2003/754, arts 2(1), 3, Sch 1, Sch 2, para 5.

SCHEDULE 3
BAIL: MODIFICATIONS OF SCHEDULE 2 TO THE IMMIGRATION ACT 1971

Section 3

1 (1) Paragraph 22 shall be amended as follows.

(2) In sub-paragraph (1A), for the words from the beginning to ["Tribunal"] there shall be substituted "The Special Immigration Appeals Commission .

(3) In sub-paragraph (2)—

(a)   for the words "immigration officer or [the Asylum and Immigration Tribunal"] there shall be substituted "Special Immigration Appeals Commission", and

(b)   for the words "officer or [the Asylum and Immigration Tribunal"] there shall be substituted "Commission".

(4)   In sub-paragraph (3)—

(a)   for "an immigration officer or [the Asylum and Immigration Tribunal"] there shall be substituted "the Special Immigration Appeals Commission", and

(b)   for "officer or [the Asylum and Immigration Tribunal"], in both places, there shall be substituted "Commission".

2   (1)   Paragraph 23 shall be amended as follows.

(2)   In sub-paragraph (1)—

(a)   for ["the Asylum and Immigration Tribunal"] there shall be substituted "the Special Immigration Appeals Commission", and

(b)   for ["the Asylum and Immigration Tribunal"], in each place, there shall be substituted "the Commission".

(3)   In sub-paragraph (2)—

(a)   for ["the Asylum and Immigration Tribunal"] there shall be substituted "the Special Immigration Appeals Commission", and

(b)   for ["the Asylum and Immigration Tribunal"] there shall be substituted "the Commission".

3   (1)   Paragraph 24 shall be amended as follows.

(2)   For sub-paragraph (2), there shall be substituted—

"(2)   A person arrested under this paragraph shall be brought before the Special Immigration Appeals Commission within twenty-four hours."

(3)   In sub-paragraph (3), for the words from the beginning to "above" there shall be substituted "Where a person is brought before the Special Immigration Appeals Commission by virtue of sub-paragraph (2) above, the Commission—"

4   (1)   Paragraph 29 shall be amended as follows.

(2)   For sub-paragraphs (2) to (4) there shall be substituted—

"(2)   The Special Immigration Appeals Commission may release an appellant on his entering into a recognizance or, in Scotland, bail bond conditioned for his appearance before the Commission at a time and place named in the recognizance or bail bond."

(3)   For sub-paragraph (6) there shall be substituted—

"(6)   In any case in which the Special Immigration Appeals Commission has power to release an appellant on bail, the Commission may, instead of taking the bail, fix the amount and conditions of the bail (including the amount in which any sureties are to be bound) with a view to its being taken subsequently by any such person as may be specified by the Commission; and on the recognizance or bail bond being so taken the appellant shall be released."

5   Paragraph 30(2) shall be omitted.

6   (1)   Paragraph 31 shall be amended as follows.

(2)   In sub-paragraph (1)—

(a)   for ["the Tribunal"] there shall be substituted "the Special Immigration Appeals Commission",

(b) for ["the Tribunal"] there shall be substituted "the Commission", and

(c) for ["the Tribunal"], in both places, there shall be substituted "the Commission".

(3) In sub-paragraph (3)—

(a) for ["the Tribunal"] there shall be substituted "the Special Immigration Appeals Commission", and

(b) for ["the Tribunal"] there shall be substituted "it".

7 Paragraph 32 shall be amended as follows—

(a) for ["the Tribunal"] there shall be substituted "the Special Immigration Appeals Commission",

(b) for ["the Tribunal"] there shall be substituted "the Commission", and

(c) for ["the Tribunal"] there shall be substituted "the Commission".

8 (1) Paragraph 33 shall be amended as follows.

(2) For sub-paragraph (2), there shall be substituted—

"(2) A person arrested under this paragraph shall be brought before the Special Immigration Appeals Commission within twenty-four hours."

(3) In sub-paragraph (3), for the words from the beginning to "above" there shall be substituted "Where a person is brought before the Special Immigration Appeals Commission by virtue of sub-paragraph (2) above, the Commission—".

Appointment
Appointment: 3 August 1998: see SI 1998/1892, art 2.

Amendment
Para 1: in sub-para (2) word ""Tribunal"" in square brackets substituted by the Asylum and Immigration (Treatment of Claimants, etc) Act 2004, s 26(7), Sch 2, Pt 1, paras 10, 13(1), (2); for transitional provisions see s 26(7), Sch 2, Pt 2 thereto. Date in force: 4 April 2005: see SI 2005/565, art 2(d); for transitional provisions in relation to pending appeals which were made to an adjudicator before 4 April 2005 and in relation to further appeals and applications in such cases see arts 3–9 thereof.
Para 1: in sub-para (3)(a) words "the Asylum and Immigration Tribunal"" in square brackets substituted by the Asylum and Immigration (Treatment of Claimants, etc) Act 2004, s 26(7), Sch 2, Pt 1, paras 10, 13(1), (3); for transitional provisions see s 26(7), Sch 2, Pt 2 thereto. Date in force: 4 April 2005: see SI 2005/565, art 2(d); for transitional provisions in relation to pending appeals which were made to an adjudicator before 4 April 2005 and in relation to further appeals and applications in such cases see arts 3–9 thereof.
Para 1: in sub-para (3)(b) words "the Asylum and Immigration Tribunal"" in square brackets substituted by the Asylum and Immigration (Treatment of Claimants, etc) Act 2004, s 26(7), Sch 2, Pt 1, paras 10, 13(1), (4); for transitional provisions see s 26(7), Sch 2, Pt 2 thereto. Date in force: 4 April 2005: see SI 2005/565, art 2(d); for transitional provisions in relation to pending appeals which were made to an adjudicator before 4 April 2005 and in relation to further appeals and applications in such cases see arts 3–9 thereof.
Para 1: in sub-para (4) words "the Asylum and Immigration Tribunal"" in square brackets in both places they occur substituted by the Asylum and Immigration (Treatment of Claimants, etc) Act 2004, s 26(7), Sch 2, Pt 1, paras 10, 13(1), (5); for transitional provisions see s 26(7), Sch 2, Pt 2 thereto. Date in force: 4 April 2005: see SI 2005/565, art 2(d); for transitional provisions in relation to pending appeals which were made to an adjudicator before 4 April 2005 and in relation to further appeals and applications in such cases see arts 3–9 thereof.
Para 2: in sub-para (2)(a) words ""the Asylum and Immigration Tribunal"" in square brackets substituted by the Asylum and Immigration (Treatment of Claimants, etc) Act 2004, s 26(7), Sch 2, Pt 1, paras 10, 13(1), (6); for transitional provisions see s 26(7), Sch 2, Pt 2 thereto. Date in force: 4 April 2005: see SI 2005/565, art 2(d); for transitional provisions in relation to pending appeals which were made to an adjudicator before 4 April 2005 and in relation to further appeals and applications in such cases see arts 3–9 thereof.

Para 2: in sub-para (2)(b) words ""the Asylum and Immigration Tribunal"" in square brackets substituted by the Asylum and Immigration (Treatment of Claimants, etc) Act 2004, s 26(7), Sch 2, Pt 1, paras 10, 13(1), (7); for transitional provisions see s 26(7), Sch 2, Pt 2 thereto. Date in force: 4 April 2005: see SI 2005/565, art 2(d); for transitional provisions in relation to pending appeals which were made to an adjudicator before 4 April 2005 and in relation to further appeals and applications in such cases see arts 3–9 thereof.

Para 2: in sub-para (3)(a) words ""the Asylum and Immigration Tribunal"" in square brackets substituted by the Asylum and Immigration (Treatment of Claimants, etc) Act 2004, s 26(7), Sch 2, Pt 1, paras 10, 13(1), (8); for transitional provisions see s 26(7), Sch 2, Pt 2 thereto. Date in force: 4 April 2005: see SI 2005/565, art 2(d); for transitional provisions in relation to pending appeals which were made to an adjudicator before 4 April 2005 and in relation to further appeals and applications in such cases see arts 3–9 thereof.

Para 2: in sub-para (3)(b) words ""the Asylum and Immigration Tribunal"" in square brackets substituted by the Asylum and Immigration (Treatment of Claimants, etc) Act 2004, s 26(7), Sch 2, Pt 1, paras 10, 13(1), (9); for transitional provisions see s 26(7), Sch 2, Pt 2 thereto. Date in force: 4 April 2005: see SI 2005/565, art 2(d); for transitional provisions in relation to pending appeals which were made to an adjudicator before 4 April 2005 and in relation to further appeals and applications in such cases see arts 3–9 thereof.

Para 6: in sub-para (2)(a) words ""the Tribunal"" in square brackets substituted by the Asylum and Immigration (Treatment of Claimants, etc) Act 2004, s 26(7), Sch 2, Pt 1, paras 10, 13(1), (10); for transitional provisions see s 26(7), Sch 2, Pt 2 thereto. Date in force: 4 April 2005: see SI 2005/565, art 2(d); for transitional provisions in relation to pending appeals which were made to an adjudicator before 4 April 2005 and in relation to further appeals and applications in such cases see arts 3–9 thereof.

Para 6: in sub-para (2)(b) words ""the Tribunal"" in square brackets substituted by the Asylum and Immigration (Treatment of Claimants, etc) Act 2004, s 26(7), Sch 2, Pt 1, paras 10, 13(1), (11); for transitional provisions see s 26(7), Sch 2, Pt 2 thereto. Date in force: 4 April 2005: see SI 2005/565, art 2(d); for transitional provisions in relation to pending appeals which were made to an adjudicator before 4 April 2005 and in relation to further appeals and applications in such cases see arts 3–9 thereof.

Para 6: in sub-para (2)(c) words ""the Tribunal"" in square brackets substituted by the Asylum and Immigration (Treatment of Claimants, etc) Act 2004, s 26(7), Sch 2, Pt 1, paras 10, 13(1), (12); for transitional provisions see s 26(7), Sch 2, Pt 2 thereto. Date in force: 4 April 2005: see SI 2005/565, art 2(d); for transitional provisions in relation to pending appeals which were made to an adjudicator before 4 April 2005 and in relation to further appeals and applications in such cases see arts 3–9 thereof.

Para 6: in sub-para (3)(a) words ""the Tribunal"" in square brackets substituted by the Asylum and Immigration (Treatment of Claimants, etc) Act 2004, s 26(7), Sch 2, Pt 1, paras 10, 13(1), (13); for transitional provisions see s 26(7), Sch 2, Pt 2 thereto. Date in force: 4 April 2005: see SI 2005/565, art 2(d); for transitional provisions in relation to pending appeals which were made to an adjudicator before 4 April 2005 and in relation to further appeals and applications in such cases see arts 3–9 thereof.

Para 6: in sub-para (3)(b) words ""the Tribunal"" in square brackets substituted by the Asylum and Immigration (Treatment of Claimants, etc) Act 2004, s 26(7), Sch 2, Pt 1, paras 10, 13(1), (14); for transitional provisions see s 26(7), Sch 2, Pt 2 thereto. Date in force: 4 April 2005: see SI 2005/565, art 2(d); for transitional provisions in relation to pending appeals which were made to an adjudicator before 4 April 2005 and in relation to further appeals and applications in such cases see arts 3–9 thereof.

Para 7: in sub-para (a) words ""the Tribunal"" in square brackets substituted by the Asylum and Immigration (Treatment of Claimants, etc) Act 2004, s 26(7), Sch 2, Pt 1, paras 10, 13(1), (15); for transitional provisions see s 26(7), Sch 2, Pt 2 thereto. Date in force: 4 April 2005: see SI 2005/565, art 2(d); for transitional provisions in relation to pending appeals which were made to an adjudicator before 4 April 2005 and in relation to further appeals and applications in such cases see arts 3–9 thereof.

Para 7: in sub-para (b) words ""the Tribunal"" in square brackets substituted by the Asylum and Immigration (Treatment of Claimants, etc) Act 2004, s 26(7), Sch 2, Pt 1, paras 10, 13(1), (16); for transitional provisions see s 26(7), Sch 2, Pt 2 thereto. Date in force: 4 April 2005: see SI 2005/565, art 2(d); for transitional provisions in relation to pending appeals which were made to an adjudicator before 4 April 2005 and in relation to further appeals and applications in such cases see arts 3–9 thereof.

Para 7: in sub-para (c) words ""the Tribunal"" in square brackets substituted by the Asylum and Immigration (Treatment of Claimants, etc) Act 2004, s 26(7), Sch 2, Pt 1, paras 10, 13(1), (17);

for transitional provisions see s 26(7), Sch 2, Pt 2 thereto. Date in force: 4 April 2005: see SI 2005/565, art 2(d); for transitional provisions in relation to pending appeals which were made to an adjudicator before 4 April 2005 and in relation to further appeals and applications in such 'cases see arts 3–9 thereof.

IMMIGRATION AND ASYLUM ACT 1999

1999 CHAPTER 33

An Act to make provision about immigration and asylum; to make provision about procedures in connection with marriage on superintendent registrar's certificate; and for connected purposes.

[11th November 1999]

BE IT ENACTED by the Queen's most Excellent Majesty, by and with the advice and consent of the Lords Spiritual and Temporal, and Commons, in this present Parliament assembled, and by the authority of the same, as follows:—

PART I

IMMIGRATION: GENERAL

Leave to enter, or remain in, the United Kingdom

1 Leave to enter

[Amends the Immigration Act 1971.]

Appointment
Appointment: 14 February 2000: see SI 2000/168, art 2, Schedule.

2 Leave to remain

[Amends the Immigration Act 1971.]

Appointment
Appointment: 14 February 2000: see SI 2000/168, art 2, Schedule.

3 Continuation of leave pending decision

[Amends the Immigration Act 1971.]

Appointment
Appointment: 2 October 2000: see SI 2000/2444, art 2, Sch 1.

4 [Accommodation]

[(1)] The Secretary of State may provide, or arrange for the provision of, facilities for the accommodation of persons—

(a) temporarily admitted to the United Kingdom under paragraph 21 of Schedule 2 to the 1971 Act;
(b) released from detention under that paragraph; or
(c) released on bail from detention under any provision of the Immigration Acts.

[(2)   The Secretary of State may provide, or arrange for the provision of, facilities for the accommodation of a person if—

   (a)   he was (but is no longer) an asylum-seeker, and
   (b)   his claim for asylum was rejected.

(3)   The Secretary of State may provide, or arrange for the provision of, facilities for the accommodation of a dependant of a person for whom facilities may be provided under subsection (2).

(4)   The following expressions have the same meaning in this section as in Part VI of this Act (as defined in section 94)—

   (a)   asylum-seeker,
   (b)   claim for asylum, and
   (c)   dependant.]

[(5)   The Secretary of State may make regulations specifying criteria to be used in determining—

   (a)   whether or not to provide accommodation, or arrange for the provision of accommodation, for a person under this section;
   (b)   whether or not to continue to provide accommodation, or arrange for the provision of accommodation, for a person under this section.

(6)   The regulations may, in particular—

   (a)   provide for the continuation of the provision of accommodation for a person to be conditional upon his performance of or participation in community activities in accordance with arrangements made by the Secretary of State;
   (b)   provide for the continuation of the provision of accommodation to be subject to other conditions;
   (c)   provide for the provision of accommodation (or the continuation of the provision of accommodation) to be a matter for the Secretary of State's discretion to a specified extent or in a specified class of case.

(7)   For the purposes of subsection (6)(a)—

   (a)   "community activities" means activities that appear to the Secretary of State to be beneficial to the public or a section of the public, and
   (b)   the Secretary of State may, in particular—
      (i)   appoint one person to supervise or manage the performance of or participation in activities by another person;
      (ii)   enter into a contract (with a local authority or any other person) for the provision of services by way of making arrangements for community activities in accordance with this section;
      (iii) pay, or arrange for the payment of, allowances to a person performing or participating in community activities in accordance with arrangements under this section.

(8)   Regulations by virtue of subsection (6)(a) may, in particular, provide for a condition requiring the performance of or participation in community activities to apply to a person only if the Secretary of State has made arrangements for community activities in an area that includes the place where accommodation is provided for the person.

(9)   A local authority or other person may undertake to manage or participate in arrangements for community activities in accordance with this section.]

Initial Commencement
Royal Assent: 11 November 1999: see s 170(3)(a).

Amendment
Section heading: substituted by the Nationality, Immigration and Asylum Act 2002, s 49(2). Date in force: 7 November 2002: see the Nationality, Immigration and Asylum Act 2002, s 162(2)(n). Sub-s (1): numbered as such by the Nationality, Immigration and Asylum Act 2002, s 49(2). Date in force: 7 November 2002: see the Nationality, Immigration and Asylum Act 2002, s 162(2)(n). Sub-ss (2)–(4): inserted by the Nationality, Immigration and Asylum Act 2002, s 49(1). Date in force: 7 November 2002: see the Nationality, Immigration and Asylum Act 2002, s 162(2)(n). Sub-ss (5)–(9): inserted by the Asylum and Immigration (Treatment of Claimants, etc) Act 2004, s 10(1), (6); for further effect in relation to regulations made under the new sub-s (5)(b), see s 10(7) thereof. Date in force: 1 December 2004: see SI 2004/2999, art 2, Schedule.

Subordinate Legislation
Immigration and Asylum (Provision of Accommodation to Failed Asylum-Seekers) Regulations 2005, SI 2005/930 (made under sub-s (5)).

5 Charges

(1) The Secretary of State may, with the approval of the Treasury, make regulations prescribing fees to be paid in connection with applications for—

(a) leave to remain in the United Kingdom;
(b) the variation of leave to enter, or remain in, the United Kingdom;
[(c) the fixing of a limited leave stamp or indefinite leave stamp on a passport or other document issued to the applicant where the stamp was previously fixed on another passport or document issued to the applicant].

(2) If a fee prescribed in connection with an application of a particular kind is payable, no such application is to be entertained by the Secretary of State unless the fee has been paid in accordance with the regulations.

(3) But—

(a) a fee prescribed in connection with such an application is not payable if the basis on which the application is made is that the applicant is—
  (i) a person making a claim for asylum which claim either has not been determined or has been granted; or
  (ii) a dependant of such a person; and
(b) the regulations may provide for no fee to be payable in prescribed circumstances.

(4) If no fee is payable in respect of some part of the application, the Secretary of State must entertain that part of the application.

[(5) In this section—

(a) "limited leave stamp" means a stamp, sticker or other attachment which indicates that a person has been granted limited leave to enter or remain in the United Kingdom, and
(b) "indefinite leave stamp" means a stamp, sticker or other attachment which indicates that a person has been granted indefinite leave to enter or remain in the United Kingdom.]

(6) "Claim for asylum" has the meaning given in subsection (1) of section 94; and subsection (3) of that section applies for the purposes of this section as it applies for the purposes of Part VI.

(7) "Dependant" has such meaning as may be prescribed.

Appointment
Appointment: 1 April 2003: see SI 2003/758, art 2.

Amendment
Sub-s (1): para (c) substituted by the Asylum and Immigration (Treatment of Claimants, etc)
Act 2004, s 43(1), (2). Date in force: 1 October 2004: see SI 2004/2523, art 2, Schedule.
Sub-s (5): substituted by the Asylum and Immigration (Treatment of Claimants, etc) Act 2004,
s 43(1), (3). Date in force: 1 October 2004: see SI 2004/2523, art 2, Schedule.

Subordinate Legislation
Immigration (Leave to Remain) (Fees) Regulations 2003, SI 2003/1711 (made under sub-ss (1),
(3)(b), (7)).
Immigration (Leave to Remain) (Fees) (Amendment) Regulations 2004, SI 2004/580 (made under
sub-ss (1), (3)(b)).
Immigration (Leave to Remain) (Fees) (Amendment No 2) Regulations 2004, SI 2004/3105 (made
under sub-ss (1), (3)(b)).
Immigration (Leave to Remain) (Fees) (Amendment) Regulations 2005, SI 2005/654 (made under
sub-ss (1), (3)(b)).

Exemption from immigration control

6   Members of missions other than diplomatic agents

In the 1971 Act, in section 8 (exceptions for certain categories of person), for
subsection (3A) (members of diplomatic missions) substitute—

"(3A)   For the purposes of subsection (3), a member of a mission other than a
diplomatic agent (as defined by the 1964 Act) is not to count as a member of a mission
unless—

   (a)   he was resident outside the United Kingdom, and was not in the United
         Kingdom, when he was offered a post as such a member; and
   (b)   he has not ceased to be such a member after having taken up the post."

Appointment
Appointment: 1 March 2000: see SI 2000/168, art 2, Schedule.

7   Persons ceasing to be exempt

[Inserts s 8A of the Immigration Act 1971]

Appointment
Appointment: 1 March 2000: see SI 2000/168, art 2, Schedule.

8   Persons excluded from the United Kingdom under international obligations

[Inserts s 8B of the Immigration Act 1971]

Appointment
Appointment: 1 March 2000: see SI 2000/168, art 2, Schedule.

Removal from the United Kingdom

9   Treatment of certain overstayers

(1)   During the regularisation period overstayers may apply, in the prescribed manner,
for leave to remain in the United Kingdom.

(2)   The regularisation period begins on the day prescribed for the purposes of this
subsection and is not to be less than three months.

(3)   The regularisation period ends—

   (a)   on the day prescribed for the purposes of this subsection; or
   (b)   if later, on the day before that on which section 65 comes into force.

(4) Section 10 and paragraph 12 of Schedule 15 come into force on the day after that on which the regularisation period ends.

(5) The Secretary of State must publicise the effect of this section in the way appearing to him to be best calculated to bring it to the attention of those affected.

(6) "Overstayer" means a person who, having only limited leave to enter or remain in the United Kingdom, remains beyond the time limited by the leave.

Initial Commencement
Royal Assent: 11 November 1999: see s 170(3)(b).

Subordinate Legislation
Immigration (Regularisation Period for Overstayers) Regulations 2000, SI 2000/265 (made under sub-ss (1), (2), (3)).

10   Removal of certain persons unlawfully in the United Kingdom

(1) A person who is not a British citizen may be removed from the United Kingdom, in accordance with directions given by an immigration officer, if—

  (a) having only a limited leave to enter or remain, he does not observe a condition attached to the leave or remains beyond the time limited by the leave;
  [(b) he uses deception in seeking (whether successfully or not) leave to remain;] or
  [(ba) his indefinite leave to enter or remain has been revoked under section 76(3) of the Nationality, Immigration and Asylum Act 2002 (person ceasing to be refugee);]
  (c) directions ... have been given for the removal, under this section, of a person ... to whose family he belongs.

(2) Directions may not be given under subsection (1)(a) if the person concerned has made an application for leave to remain in accordance with regulations made under section 9.

[(3) Directions for the removal of a person may not be given under subsection (1)(c) unless the Secretary of State has given the person written notice of the intention to remove him.

(4) A notice under subsection (3) may not be given if—

  (a) the person whose removal under subsection (1)(a) or (b) is the cause of the proposed directions under subsection (1)(c) has left the United Kingdom, and
  (b) more than eight weeks have elapsed since that person's departure.

(5) If a notice under subsection (3) is sent by first class post to a person's last known address, that subsection shall be taken to be satisfied at the end of the second day after the day of posting.

(5A) Directions for the removal of a person under subsection (1)(c) cease to have effect if he ceases to belong to the family of the person whose removal under subsection (1)(a) or (b) is the cause of the directions under subsection (1)(c).]

(6) Directions under this section—

  (a) may be given only to persons falling within a prescribed class;
  (b) may impose any requirements of a prescribed kind.

(7) In relation to any such directions, paragraphs 10, 11, 16 to 18, 21 and 22 to 24 of Schedule 2 to the 1971 Act (administrative provisions as to control of entry), apply as they apply in relation to directions given under paragraph 8 of that Schedule.

(8) Directions for the removal of a person given under this section invalidate any leave to enter or remain in the United Kingdom given to him before the directions are given or while they are in force.

(9) The costs of complying with a direction given under this section (so far as reasonably incurred) must be met by the Secretary of State.

[(10)   A person shall not be liable to removal from the United Kingdom under this section at a time when section 7(1)(b) of the Immigration Act 1971 (Commonwealth and Irish citizens ordinarily resident in United Kingdom) would prevent a decision to deport him.]

Appointment
Sub-ss (1)–(5), (7)–(9): Appointment: 2 October 2000: see SI 2000/2444, art 2, Sch 1; for transitional provisions see art 3, Sch 2, para 1(2), thereof.
Sub-s (6): Appointment: 22 May 2000: see SI 2000/1282, art 2, Schedule.

Amendment
Sub-s (1): para (b) substituted by the Nationality, Immigration and Asylum Act 2002, s 74. Date in force: 10 February 2003: see SI 2003/1, art 2, Schedule.
Sub-s (1): para (ba) inserted by the Nationality, Immigration and Asylum Act 2002, s 76(7). Date in force: 10 February 2003: see SI 2003/1, art 2, Schedule.
Sub-s (1): in para (c) words omitted repealed by the Nationality, Immigration and Asylum Act 2002, ss 73(2), (3), 161, Sch 9. Date in force: 10 February 2003: see SI 2003/1, art 2, Schedule.
Sub-ss (3)–(5), (5A): substituted, for sub-ss (3)–(5) as originally enacted, by the Nationality, Immigration Asylum Act 2002, s 73(2), (4). Date in force: 10 February 2003: see SI 2003/1, art 2, Schedule.
Sub-s (10): inserted by the Nationality, Immigration and Asylum Act 2002, s 75(4). Date in force: 10 February 2003: see SI 2003/1, art 2, Schedule.

See Further
See further, in relation to disapplication of this section in relation to certain persons who, for the purposes of section 5 hereof, are taken to be liable to deportation under s 3(5) hereof: the Nationality, Immigration and Asylum Act 2002 (Commencement No 4) Order 2003, SI 2003/754, art 3(2), Sch 2, para 6(2).

Subordinate Legislation
Immigration (Removal Directions) Regulations 2000, SI 2000/2243.

11   ...

...

Amendment
Repealed by the Asylum and Immigration (Treatment of Claimants, etc) Act 2004, ss 33(2), 47, Sch 4. Date in force: 1 October 2004 (except in relation to a person subject to a certificate under this section or s 12 hereof issued by the Secretary of State before that date): see SI 2004/2523, arts 2, 3, Schedule.

12   ...

...

Amendment
Repealed by the Asylum and Immigration (Treatment of Claimants, etc) Act 2004, ss 33(2), 47, Sch 4. Date in force: 1 October 2004 (except in relation to a person subject to a certificate under this section or s 11 hereof issued by the Secretary of State before that date): see SI 2004/2523, arts 2, 3, Schedule.

13   Proof of identity of persons to be removed or deported

(1)   This section applies if a person—

(a)   is to be removed from the United Kingdom to a country of which he is a national or citizen; but

(b)   does not have a valid passport or other document establishing his identity and nationality or citizenship and permitting him to travel.

(2)   If the country to which the person is to be removed indicates that he will not be admitted to it unless identification data relating to him are provided by the Secretary of State, he may provide them with such data.

(3)   In providing identification data, the Secretary of State must not disclose whether the person concerned has made a claim for asylum.

(4)   For the purposes of paragraph 4(1) of Schedule 4 to the Data Protection Act 1998, the provision under this section of identification data is a transfer of personal data which is necessary for reasons of substantial public interest.

(5)   "Identification data" means—

(a)   fingerprints taken under section 141; or

(b)   data collected in accordance with regulations made under section 144.

(6)   "Removed" means removed as a result of directions given under section 10 or under Schedule 2 or 3 to the 1971 Act.

Appointment
Appointment: 11 December 2000: see SI 2000/3099, art 3, Schedule.

14   Escorts for persons removed from the United Kingdom under directions

(1)   Directions for, or requiring arrangements to be made for, the removal of a person from the United Kingdom may include or be amended to include provision for the person who is to be removed to be accompanied by an escort consisting of one or more persons specified in the directions.

(2)   The Secretary of State may by regulations make further provision supplementing subsection (1).

(3)   The regulations may, in particular, include provision—

(a)   requiring the person to whom the directions are given to provide for the return of the escort to the United Kingdom;

(b)   requiring him to bear such costs in connection with the escort (including, in particular, remuneration) as may be prescribed;

(c)   as to the cases in which the Secretary of State is to bear those costs;

(d)   prescribing the kinds of expenditure which are to count in calculating the costs incurred in connection with escorts.

Appointment
Appointment: 1 March 2000: see SI 2000/168, art 2, Schedule.

15   ...

...

Amendment
Repealed by the Nationality, Immigration and Asylum Act 2002, ss 77(5), 161, Sch 9. Date in force: 1 April 2003: see SI 2003/754, art 2(1), Sch 1.

Provision of financial security

16   Security on grant of entry clearance

(1)   In such circumstances as may be specified, the Secretary of State may require security to be given, with respect to a person applying for entry clearance, before clearance is given.

(2)   In such circumstances as may be specified—

  (a)   the Secretary of State may accept security with respect to a person who is applying for entry clearance but for whom security is not required; and

  (b)   in determining whether to give clearance, account may be taken of any security so provided.

(3)   "Security" means—

  (a)   the deposit of a sum of money by the applicant, his agent or any other person, or

  (b)   the provision by the applicant, his agent or any other person of a financial guarantee of a specified kind,

with a view to securing that the applicant will, if given leave to enter the United Kingdom for a limited period, leave the United Kingdom at the end of that period.

(4)   Immigration rules must make provision as to the circumstances in which a security provided under this section—

  (a)   is to be repaid, released or otherwise cancelled; or

  (b)   is to be forfeited or otherwise realised by the Secretary of State.

(5)   No security provided under this section may be forfeited or otherwise realised unless the person providing it has been given an opportunity, in accordance with immigration rules, to make representations to the Secretary of State.

(6)   Immigration rules may, in particular—

  (a)   fix the maximum amount that may be required, or accepted, by way of security provided under this section;

  (b)   specify the form and manner in which such a security is to be given or may be accepted;

  (c)   make provision, where such a security has been forfeited or otherwise realised, for the person providing it to be reimbursed in such circumstances as may be specified;

  (d)   make different provision for different cases or descriptions of case.

(7)   "Specified" means specified by immigration rules.

(8)   Any security forfeited or otherwise realised by the Secretary of State under this section must be paid into the Consolidated Fund.

Initial Commencement
To be appointed: see s 170(4).

17   Provision of further security on extension of leave

(1)   This section applies if security has been provided under section 16(1) or (2) with respect to a person who, having entered the United Kingdom (with leave to do so), applies—

  (a)   to extend his leave to enter the United Kingdom; or

  (b)   for leave to remain in the United Kingdom for a limited period.

(2) The Secretary of State may refuse the application if security of such kind as the Secretary of State considers appropriate is not provided, or continued, with respect to the applicant.

(3) Immigration rules must make provision as to the circumstances in which a security provided under this section—

(a) is to be repaid, released or otherwise cancelled; or

(b) is to be forfeited or otherwise realised by the Secretary of State.

(4) No security provided under this section may be forfeited or otherwise realised unless the person providing it has been given an opportunity, in accordance with immigration rules, to make representations to the Secretary of State.

(5) Subsection (7) of section 16 applies in relation to this section as it applies in relation to that section.

(6) Any security forfeited or otherwise realised by the Secretary of State under this section must be paid into the Consolidated Fund.

Initial Commencement
To be appointed: see s 170(4).

Information

18   Passenger information

[Amends Sch 2 to the Immigration Act 1971]

Appointment
Appointment (for the purpose of enabling subordinate legislation to be made): 1 March 2000: see SI 2000/464, art 2, Schedule.
Appointment (for remaining purposes): 3 April 2000: see SI 2000/464, art 2, Schedule.

19   Notification of non-EEA arrivals

[Amends Sch 2 to the Immigration Act 1971]

Appointment
Appointment: 3 April 2000: see SI 2000/464, art 2, Schedule.

20   Supply of information to Secretary of State

(1) This section applies to information held by—

(a) a chief officer of police;

(b) *the Director General of the National Criminal Intelligence Service;*

(c) *the Director General of the National Crime Squad;*

[(b) the Serious Organised Crime Agency;]

(d) the Commissioners of Customs and Excise, or a person providing services to them in connection with the provision of those services;

(e) a person with whom the Secretary of State has made a contract or other arrangements under section 95 or 98 or a sub-contractor of such a person; or

(f) any specified person, for purposes specified in relation to that person.

[(1A) This section also applies to a document or article which—

(a) comes into the possession of a person listed in subsection (1) or someone acting on his behalf, or

(b) is discovered by a person listed in subsection (1) or someone acting on his behalf.]

(2)   The information[, document or article] may be supplied to the Secretary of State for use for immigration purposes.

[(2A)   The Secretary of State may—

    (a)   retain for immigration purposes a document or article supplied to him under subsection (2), and

    (b)   dispose of a document or article supplied to him under subsection (2) in such manner as he thinks appropriate (and the reference to use in subsection (2) includes a reference to disposal).]

(3)   "Immigration purposes" means any of the following—

    (a)   the administration of immigration control under the Immigration Acts;

    (b)   the prevention, detection, investigation or prosecution of criminal offences under those Acts;

    (c)   the imposition of penalties or charges under Part II;

    (d)   the provision of support for asylum-seekers and their dependants under Part VI;

    (e)   such other purposes as may be specified.

(4)   "Chief officer of police" means—

    (a)   the chief officer of police for a police area in England and Wales;

    (b)   the chief constable of a police force maintained under the Police (Scotland) Act 1967;

    (c)   the [Chief Constable of the Police Service of Northern Ireland].

(5)   "Specified" means specified in an order made by the Secretary of State.

(6)   This section does not limit the circumstances in which information[, documents or articles] may be supplied apart from this section.

Appointment
Appointment: 1 January 2000: see SI 1999/3190, art 2, Schedule.

Amendment
Sub-s (1): paras (b), (c) substituted, by subsequent para (b), by the Serious Organised Crime and Police Act 2005, s 59, Sch 4, paras 122, 123. Date in force: to be appointed: see the Serious Organised Crime and Police Act 2005, s 178(8).
Sub-s (1A): inserted by the Nationality, Immigration and Asylum Act 2002, s 132(1), (2). Date in force: 10 February 2003: see SI 2003/1, art 2, Schedule.
Sub-s (2): words ", document or article" in square brackets inserted by the Nationality, Immigration and Asylum Act 2002, s 132(1), (3). Date in force: 10 February 2003: see SI 2003/1, art 2, Schedule.
Sub-s (2A): inserted by the Nationality, Immigration and Asylum Act 2002, s 132(1), (4). Date in force: 10 February 2003: see SI 2003/1, art 2, Schedule.
Sub-s (4): in para (c) words "Chief Constable of the Police Service of Northern Ireland" in square brackets substituted by the Police (Northern Ireland) Act 2000, s 78(2)(a). Date in force: 4 November 2001: see the Police (Northern Ireland) Act 2000 (Commencement No 3 and Transitional Provisions) Order 2001, SR 2001/396, art 2, Schedule.
Sub-s (6): words ", documents or articles" in square brackets inserted by the Nationality, Immigration and Asylum Act 2002, s 132(1), (5). Date in force: 10 February 2003: see SI 2003/1, art 2, Schedule.

21   Supply of information by Secretary of State

(1)   This section applies to information held by the Secretary of State in connection with the exercise of functions under any of the Immigration Acts.

(2)   The information may be supplied to—

    (a)   a chief officer of police, for use for police purposes;

(b)   the Director General of the National Criminal Intelligence Service, for use for NCIS purposes;

(c)   the Director General of the National Crime Squad, for use for NCS purposes;

[(b) the Serious Organised Crime Agency, for use for SOCA purposes;]

(d)   the Commissioners of Customs and Excise, or a person providing services to them, for use for customs purposes; or

(e)   any specified person, for use for purposes specified in relation to that person.

(3)   "Police purposes" means any of the following—

(a)   the prevention, detection, investigation or prosecution of criminal offences;

(b)   safeguarding national security;

(c)   such other purposes as may be specified.

(4)   *"NCIS purposes" means any of the functions of the National Criminal Intelligence Service mentioned in section 2 of the Police Act 1997.*

(5)   *"NCS purposes" means any of the functions of the National Crime Squad mentioned in section 48 of that Act.*

[(4) "SOCA purposes" means any of the functions of the Serious Organised Crime Agency mentioned in section 2, 3 or 5 of the Serious Organised Crime and Police Act 2005.]

(6)   "Customs purposes" means any of the Commissioners' functions in relation to—

(a)   the prevention, detection, investigation or prosecution of criminal offences;

(b)   the prevention, detection or investigation of conduct in respect of which penalties which are not criminal penalties are provided for by or under any enactment;

(c)   the assessment or determination of penalties which are not criminal penalties;

(d)   checking the accuracy of information relating to, or provided for purposes connected with, any matter under the care and management of the Commissioners or any assigned matter (as defined by section 1(1) of the Customs and Excise Management Act 1979);

(e)   amending or supplementing any such information (where appropriate);

(f)   legal or other proceedings relating to anything mentioned in paragraphs (a) to (e);

(g)   safeguarding national security; and

(h)   such other purposes as may be specified.

(7)   "Chief officer of police" and "specified" have the same meaning as in section 20.

(8)   This section does not limit the circumstances in which information may be supplied apart from this section.

Appointment
Appointment: 1 January 2000: see SI 1999/3190, art 2, Schedule.

Amendment
Sub-s (2): paras (b), (c) substituted, by subsequent para (b), by virtue of the Serious Organised Crime and Police Act 2005, s 59, Sch 4, paras 122, 124(1), (2). Date in force: to be appointed: see the Serious Organised Crime and Police Act 2005, s 178(8).
Sub-ss (4), (5): substituted, by subsequent sub-s (4), by the Serious Organised Crime and Police Act 2005, s 59, Sch 4, paras 122, 124(1), (3). Date in force: to be appointed: see the Serious Organised Crime and Police Act 2005, s 178(8).

Employment: code of practice

22   Restrictions on employment: code of practice

[Inserts s 8A of the Asylum and Immigration Act 1996]

Appendix 1 Legislation and materials

Appointment
Appointment (for the purpose of laying a draft code before Parliament and the making of subordinate legislation under the Asylum and Immigration Act 1996, s 8A): 19 February 2001: see SI 2001/239, art 2, Schedule.
Appointment (for remaining purposes): 2 May 2001: see SI 2001/1394, art 2, Schedule.

Monitoring entry clearance

23 Monitoring refusals of entry clearance

(1) The Secretary of State must appoint a person to monitor, in such a manner as the Secretary of State may determine, refusals of entry clearance in cases where there is, as a result of [section 90 or 91 of the Nationality, Immigration and Asylum Act 2002], no right of appeal.

(2) But the Secretary of State may not appoint a member of his staff.

(3) The monitor must make an annual report on the discharge of his functions to the Secretary of State.

(4) The Secretary of State must lay a copy of any report made to him under subsection (3) before each House of Parliament.

(5) The Secretary of State may pay to the monitor such fees and allowances as he may determine.

Appointment
Appointment: 2 October 2000: see SI 2000/2444, art 2, Sch 1.

Amendment
Sub-s (1): words "section 90 or 91 of the Nationality, Immigration and Asylum Act 2002" in square brackets substituted by the Nationality, Immigration and Asylum Act 2002, s 114(3), Sch 7, para 27. Date in force: 1 April 2003 (except in relation to events which took place before that date): see SI 2003/754, arts 2(1), 3(1), Sch 1.

Reporting suspicious marriages

24 Duty to report suspicious marriages

(1) Subsection (3) applies if—

    (a) a superintendent registrar to whom a notice of marriage has been given under section 27 of the Marriage Act 1949,

    (b) any other person who, under section 28(2) of that Act, has attested a declaration accompanying such a notice,

    (c) a district registrar to whom a marriage notice or an approved certificate has been submitted under section 3 of the Marriage (Scotland) Act 1977, or

    (d) a registrar or deputy registrar to whom notice has been given under section 13 of the Marriages (Ireland) Act 1844 or section 4 of the Marriage Law (Ireland) Amendment Act 1863,

has reasonable grounds for suspecting that the marriage will be a sham marriage.

(2) Subsection (3) also applies if—

    (a) a marriage is solemnized in the presence of a registrar of marriages or, in relation to Scotland, an authorised registrar (within the meaning of the Act of 1977); and

    (b) before, during or immediately after solemnization of the marriage, the registrar has reasonable grounds for suspecting that the marriage will be, or is, a sham marriage.

(3)   The person concerned must report his suspicion to the Secretary of State without delay and in such form and manner as may be prescribed by regulations.

(4)   The regulations are to be made—

(a)   in relation to England and Wales, by the Registrar General for England and Wales with the approval of the Chancellor of the Exchequer;

(b)   in relation to Scotland, by the Secretary of State after consulting the Registrar General of Births, Deaths and Marriages for Scotland;

(c)   in relation to Northern Ireland, by the Secretary of State after consulting the Registrar General in Northern Ireland.

(5)   "Sham marriage" means a marriage (whether or not void)—

(a)   entered into between a person ("A") who is neither a British citizen nor a national of an EEA State other than the United Kingdom and another person (whether or not such a citizen or such a national); and

(b)   entered into by A for the purpose of avoiding the effect of one or more provisions of United Kingdom immigration law or the immigration rules.

Appointment
Appointment: 1 January 2001: see SI 2000/2698, art 2, Schedule.

Subordinate Legislation
Reporting of Suspicious Marriages and Registration of Marriages (Miscellaneous Amendments) Regulations 2000, SI 2000/3164 (made under sub-s (3)).
Reporting of Suspicious Marriages (Northern Ireland) Regulations 2000, SI 2000/3233 (made under sub-s (3)).

[24A   Duty to report suspicious civil partnerships]

[(1)   Subsection (3) applies if—

(a)   a registration authority to whom a notice of proposed civil partnership has been given under section 8 of the Civil Partnership Act 2004,

(b)   any person who, under section 8 of the 2004 Act, has attested a declaration accompanying such a notice,

(c)   a district registrar to whom a notice of proposed civil partnership has been given under section 88 of the 2004 Act, or

(d)   a registrar to whom a civil partnership notice has been given under section 139 of the 2004 Act,

has reasonable grounds for suspecting that the civil partnership will be a sham civil partnership.

(2)   Subsection (3) also applies if—

(a)   two people register as civil partners of each other under Part 2, 3 or 4 of the 2004 Act in the presence of the registrar, and

(b)   before, during or immediately after they do so, the registrar has reasonable grounds for suspecting that the civil partnership will be, or is, a sham civil partnership.

(3)   The person concerned must report his suspicion to the Secretary of State without delay and in such form and manner as may be prescribed by regulations.

(4)   The regulations are to be made—

(a)   in relation to England and Wales, by the Registrar General for England and Wales with the approval of the Chancellor of the Exchequer;

(b)   in relation to Scotland, by the Secretary of State after consulting the Registrar General of Births, Deaths and Marriages for Scotland;

    (c) in relation to Northern Ireland, by the Secretary of State after consulting the Registrar General in Northern Ireland.

(5) "Sham civil partnership" means a civil partnership (whether or not void)—

    (a) formed between a person ("A") who is neither a British citizen nor a national of an EEA State other than the United Kingdom and another person (whether or not such a citizen or such a national), and

    (b) formed by A for the purpose of avoiding the effect of one or more provisions of United Kingdom immigration law or the immigration rules.

(6) "The registrar" means—

    (a) in relation to England and Wales, the civil partnership registrar acting under Part 2 of the 2004 Act;

    (b) in relation to Scotland, the authorised registrar acting under Part 3 of the 2004 Act;

    (c) in relation to Northern Ireland, the registrar acting under Part 4 of the 2004 Act.]

Amendment
Inserted by the Civil Partnership Act 2004, s 261(1), Sch 27, para 162. Date in force (for the purpose of the power to make regulations): 15 April 2005: see SI 2005/1112, art 2, Sch 1. Date in force (for remaining purposes): to be appointed: see the Civil Partnership Act 2004, s 263(10)(b).

Immigration control: facilities and charges

25   Provision of facilities for immigration control at ports

(1) The person responsible for the management of a control port ("the manager") must provide the Secretary of State free of charge with such facilities at the port as the Secretary of State may direct as being reasonably necessary for, or in connection with, the operation of immigration control there.

(2) Before giving such a direction, the Secretary of State must consult such persons likely to be affected by it as he considers appropriate.

(3) If the Secretary of State gives such a direction, he must send a copy of it to the person appearing to him to be the manager.

(4) If the manager persistently fails to comply with the direction (or part of it), the Secretary of State may—

    (a) in the case of a control port which is not a port of entry, revoke any approval in relation to the port given under paragraph 26(1) of Schedule 2 to the 1971 Act;

    (b) in the case of a control port which is a port of entry, by order revoke its designation as a port of entry.

(5) A direction under this section is enforceable, on the application of the Secretary of State—

    (a) by injunction granted by a county court; or

    (b) in Scotland, by an order under section 45 of the Court of Session Act 1988.

(6) "Control port" means a port in which a control area is designated under paragraph 26(3) of Schedule 2 to the 1971 Act.

(7) "Facilities" means accommodation, facilities, equipment and services of a class or description specified in an order made by the Secretary of State.

Appointment
Appointment (for the purpose of enabling the Secretary of State to exercise the power to make subordinate legislation): 17 February 2003: see SI 2003/2, art 2, Schedule.
Appointment (for remaining purposes): 1 April 2003: see SI 2003/2, art 2, Schedule.

Subordinate Legislation
Immigration Control (Provision of Facilities at Ports) Order 2003, SI 2003/612 (made under sub-s (7)).

26 Charges: immigration control

(1) The Secretary of State may, at the request of any person and in consideration of such charges as he may determine, make arrangements—

    (a) for the provision at any control port of immigration officers or facilities in addition to those (if any) needed to provide a basic service at the port;

    (b) for the provision of immigration officers or facilities for dealing with passengers of a particular description or in particular circumstances.

(2) "Control port" has the same meaning as in section 25.

(3) "Facilities" includes equipment.

(4) "Basic service" has such meaning as may be prescribed.

Appointment
Appointment (for remaining purposes): 30 June 2003: see SI 2003/1469, art 2, Schedule.
Appointment (for the purpose of enabling the Secretary of State to exercise the power to make subordinate legislation): 5 June 2003: see SI 2003/1469, art 2, Schedule.

Subordinate Legislation
Immigration Control (Charges) (Basic Service) Regulations 2003, SI 2003/1502 (made under sub-s (4)).

Charges: travel documents

27 Charges: travel documents

(1) The Secretary of State may, with the approval of the Treasury, make regulations prescribing fees to be paid in connection with applications to him for travel documents.

(2) If a fee is prescribed in connection with an application of a particular kind, no such application is to be entertained by the Secretary of State unless the fee has been paid in accordance with the regulations.

(3) In respect of any period before the coming into force of this section, the Secretary of State is to be deemed always to have had power to impose charges in connection with—

    (a) applications to him for travel documents; or

    (b) the issue by him of travel documents.

(4) "Travel document" does not include a passport.

Initial Commencement
Royal Assent: 11 November 1999: see s 170(3)(d).

Subordinate Legislation
Travel Documents (Fees) Regulations 1999, SI 1999/3339.
Travel Documents (Fees) (Amendments) Regulations 2002, SI 2002/2155 (made under sub-s (1)).
Travel Documents (Fees) (Amendment) Regulations 2005, SI 2005/653 (made under sub-s (1)).

Offences

28   Deception

[Inserts s 24A of the Immigration Act 1971]

Appointment
Appointment: 14 February 2000: see SI 2000/168, art 2, Schedule.

29   Facilitation of entry

(1)   Section 25 of the 1971 Act (assisting illegal entry) is amended as follows.

(2)   In subsection (1), for "seven" substitute "ten".

(3)   For subsection (1A) substitute—

"(1A)   Nothing in subsection (1)(b) applies to anything done in relation to a person who—

(a)   has been detained under paragraph 16 of Schedule 2 to this Act; or
(b)   has been granted temporary admission under paragraph 21 of that Schedule.

(1B)   Nothing in subsection (1)(b) applies to anything done by a person otherwise than for gain.

(1C)   Nothing in subsection (1)(b) applies to anything done to assist an asylum claimant by a person in the course of his employment by a bona fide organisation, if the purposes of that organisation include assistance to persons in the position of the asylum claimant.

(1D)   "Asylum claimant" means a person who intends to make a claim that it would be contrary to the United Kingdom's obligations under the Refugee Convention or the Human Rights Convention for him to be removed from, or required to leave, the United Kingdom.

(1E)   "Refugee Convention" and "Human Rights Convention" have the meaning given in the Immigration and Asylum Act 1999."

(4)   *In subsection (5), for "Subsection (1)(a)" substitute "Paragraphs (a) and (b) of subsection (1)".*

Appointment
Sub-s (1): Appointment (for remaining purposes): 2 October 2000: see SI 2000/2444, art 2, Sch 1.
Sub-s (1): Appointment (for certain purposes): 14 February 2000: see SI 2000/168, art 2, Schedule.
Sub-ss (2), (4): Appointment: 14 February 2000: see SI 2000/168, art 2, Schedule.
Sub-s (3): Appointment: 2 October 2000: see SI 2000/2444, art 2, Sch 1.

Amendment
Repealed by the Nationality, Immigration and Asylum Act 2002, s 161, Sch 9. Date in force: to be appointed: see the Nationality, Immigration and Asylum Act 2002, s 162(1).

30   False statements etc

(1)   Section 26 of the 1971 Act (general offences in connection with administration of the Act) is amended as follows.

(2)   In subsection (1)(c), for "this Act" substitute "a relevant enactment".

(3)   After subsection (2), insert—

"(3)   "Relevant enactment" means—

(a)   this Act;

(b)   the Immigration Act 1988;
(c)   the Asylum and Immigration Appeals Act 1993 (apart from section 4 or 5); or
(d)   the Immigration and Asylum Act 1999 (apart from Part VI)."

Appointment
Appointment: 14 February 2000: see SI 2000/168, art 2, Schedule.

31   Defences based on Article 31(1) of the Refugee Convention

(1)   It is a defence for a refugee charged with an offence to which this section applies to show that, having come to the United Kingdom directly from a country where his life or freedom was threatened (within the meaning of the Refugee Convention), he—

(a)   presented himself to the authorities in the United Kingdom without delay;
(b)   showed good cause for his illegal entry or presence; and
(c)   made a claim for asylum as soon as was reasonably practicable after his arrival in the United Kingdom.

(2)   If, in coming from the country where his life or freedom was threatened, the refugee stopped in another country outside the United Kingdom, subsection (1) applies only if he shows that he could not reasonably have expected to be given protection under the Refugee Convention in that other country.

(3)   In England and Wales and Northern Ireland the offences to which this section applies are any offence, and any attempt to commit an offence, under—

(a)   Part I of the Forgery and Counterfeiting Act 1981 (forgery and connected offences);
(b)   section 24A of the 1971 Act (deception); or
(c)   section 26(1)(d) of the 1971 Act (falsification of documents).

(4)   In Scotland, the offences to which this section applies are those—

(a)   of fraud,
(b)   of uttering a forged document,
(c)   under section 24A of the 1971 Act (deception), or
(d)   under section 26(1)(d) of the 1971 Act (falsification of documents),

and any attempt to commit any of those offences.

(5)   A refugee who has made a claim for asylum is not entitled to the defence provided by subsection (1) in relation to any offence committed by him after making that claim.

(6)   "Refugee" has the same meaning as it has for the purposes of the Refugee Convention.

(7)   If the Secretary of State has refused to grant a claim for asylum made by a person who claims that he has a defence under subsection (1), that person is to be taken not to be a refugee unless he shows that he is.

(8)   A person who—

(a)   was convicted in England and Wales or Northern Ireland of an offence to which this section applies before the commencement of this section, but
(b)   at no time during the proceedings for that offence argued that he had a defence based on Article 31(1),

may apply to the Criminal Cases Review Commission with a view to his case being referred to the Court of Appeal by the Commission on the ground that he would have had a defence under this section had it been in force at the material time.

(9)   A person who—

(a) was convicted in Scotland of an offence to which this section applies before the commencement of this section, but

(b) at no time during the proceedings for that offence argued that he had a defence based on Article 31(1),

may apply to the Scottish Criminal Cases Review Commission with a view to his case being referred to the High Court of Justiciary by the Commission on the ground that he would have had a defence under this section had it been in force at the material time.

(10) The Secretary of State may by order amend—

(a) subsection (3), or
(b) subsection (4),

by adding offences to those for the time being listed there.

(11) Before making an order under subsection (10)(b), the Secretary of State must consult the Scottish Ministers.

Initial Commencement
Royal Assent: 11 November 1999: see s 170(3)(e).

PART II
CARRIERS' LIABILITY

Clandestine entrants

32   Penalty for carrying clandestine entrants

(1) A person is a clandestine entrant if—

(a) he arrives in the United Kingdom concealed in a vehicle, ship or aircraft,
[(aa) he arrives in the United Kingdom concealed in a rail freight wagon,]
(b) he passes, or attempts to pass, through immigration control concealed in a vehicle, or
(c) he arrives in the United Kingdom on a ship or aircraft, having embarked—
　　(i) concealed in a vehicle; and
　　(ii) at a time when the ship or aircraft was outside the United Kingdom,

and claims, or indicates that he intends to seek, asylum in the United Kingdom or evades, or attempts to evade, immigration control.

(2) *The person (or persons) responsible for a clandestine entrant is (or are together) liable to—*

(a) *a penalty of the prescribed amount in respect of the clandestine entrant; and*
(b) *an additional penalty of that amount in respect of each person who was concealed with the clandestine entrant in the same transporter.*

[(2) The Secretary of State may require a person who is responsible for a clandestine entrant to pay—

(a) a penalty in respect of the clandestine entrant;
(b) a penalty in respect of any person who was concealed with the clandestine entrant in the same transporter.

(2A) In imposing a penalty under subsection (2) the Secretary of State—

(a) must specify an amount which does not exceed the maximum prescribed for the purpose of this paragraph,

   (b)   may, in respect of a clandestine entrant or a concealed person, impose separate penalties on more than one of the persons responsible for the clandestine entrant, and

   (c)   may not impose penalties in respect of a clandestine entrant or a concealed person which amount in aggregate to more than the maximum prescribed for the purpose of this paragraph.]

(3)   A penalty imposed under this section must be paid to the Secretary of State before the end of the prescribed period.

(4)   *Payment of the full amount of a penalty by one or more of the persons responsible for the clandestine entrant discharges the liability of each of the persons responsible for that entrant.*

[(4)   Where a penalty is imposed under subsection (2) on the driver of a vehicle who is an employee of the vehicle's owner or hirer—

   (a)   the employee and the employer shall be jointly and severally liable for the penalty imposed on the driver (irrespective of whether a penalty is also imposed on the employer), and

   (b)   a provision of this Part about notification, objection or appeal shall have effect as if the penalty imposed on the driver were also imposed on the employer (irrespective of whether a penalty is also imposed on the employer in his capacity as the owner or hirer of the vehicle).

(4A)   In the case of a detached trailer, subsection (4) shall have effect as if a reference to the driver were a reference to the operator.]

(5)   In the case of a clandestine entrant to whom subsection (1)(a) applies, each of the following is a responsible person—

   (a)   if the transporter is a ship or aircraft, the owner *or* [and] captain;

   (b)   if it is a vehicle (but not a detached trailer), the owner, hirer *or* [and] driver of the vehicle;

   (c)   if it is a detached trailer, the owner, hirer *or* [and] operator of the trailer.

[(5A)   In the case of a clandestine entrant to whom subsection (1)(aa) applies, the responsible person is—

   (a)   where the entrant arrived concealed in a freight train, the train operator who, at the train's last scheduled stop before arrival in the United Kingdom, was responsible for certifying it as fit to travel to the United Kingdom, or

   (b)   where the entrant arrived concealed in a freight shuttle wagon, the operator of the shuttle-train of which the wagon formed part.]

(6)   In the case of a clandestine entrant to whom subsection (1)(b) or (c) applies, each of the following is a responsible person—

   (a)   if the transporter is a detached trailer, the owner, hirer *or* [and] operator of the trailer;

   (b)   if it is not, the owner, hirer *or* [and] driver of the vehicle.

[(6A)   Where a person falls within the definition of responsible person in more than one capacity, a separate penalty may be imposed on him under subsection (2) in respect of each capacity.]

(7)   Subject to any defence provided by section 34, it is immaterial whether a responsible person knew or suspected—

   (a)   that the clandestine entrant was concealed in the transporter; or

   (b)   that there were one or more other persons concealed with the clandestine entrant in the same transporter.

(8)   Subsection (9) applies if a transporter ("the carried transporter") is itself being carried in or on another transporter.

(9)   If a person is concealed in the carried transporter, the question whether any other person is concealed with that person in the same transporter is to be determined by reference to the carried transporter and not by reference to the transporter in or on which it is carried.

(10)   "Immigration control" means United Kingdom immigration control and includes any United Kingdom immigration control operated in a prescribed control zone outside the United Kingdom.

Appointment
Appointment (for certain purposes): 3 April 2000: see SI 2000/464, art 2, Schedule.
Appointment (for certain purposes): 18 September 2000: see SI 2000/2444, art 2, Sch 1.
Appointment (for certain purposes): 8 December 2002: see SI 2002/2815, art 2, Schedule.
Sub-ss (2)(a), (3), (10): Appointment (for the purpose of enabling subordinate legislation to be made): 6 December 1999: see SI 1999/3190, art 2, Schedule.

Amendment
Sub-s (1): para (aa) inserted by the Nationality, Immigration and Asylum Act 2002, s 125, Sch 8, paras 1, 2(1), (2). Date in force: 8 December 2002 (except in relation to a penalty notice issued to a person before that date): see SI 2002/2811, arts 2, 4, Schedule.
Sub-s (2): substituted, by subsequent sub-ss (2), (2A), by the Nationality, Immigration and Asylum Act 2002, s 125, Sch 8, paras 1, 2(1), (3). Date in force (for the purpose of enabling the Secretary of State to exercise the power to make subordinate legislation under sub-s (2A) above): 14 November 2002 (except in relation to a penalty notice issued to a person before that date): see SI 2002/2811, arts 2, 4, Schedule. Date in force (for the purposes of clandestine entrants who arrive in the United Kingdom concealed in a vehicle or a rail freight wagon): 8 December 2002 (except in relation to a penalty notice issued to a person before that date): see SI 2002/2811, arts 2, 4, Schedule. Date in force (for remaining purposes): to be appointed: see the Nationality, Immigration and Asylum Act 2002, s 162(1).
Sub-s (4): substituted, by subsequent sub-ss (4), (4A), by the Nationality, Immigration and Asylum Act 2002, s 125, Sch 8, paras 1, 2(1), (4). Date in force (for the purposes of clandestine entrants who arrive in the United Kingdom concealed in a vehicle or a rail freight wagon): 8 December 2002 (except in relation to a penalty notice issued to a person before that date): see SI 2002/2811, arts 2, 4, Schedule. Date in force (for remaining purposes): to be appointed: see the Nationality, Immigration and Asylum Act 2002, s 162(1).
Sub-s (5): in para (a) word "or" in italics repealed and subsequent word in square brackets substituted by the Nationality, Immigration and Asylum Act 2002, s 125, Sch 8, paras 1, 2(1), (5)(a). Date in force (for the purposes of clandestine entrants who arrive in the United Kingdom concealed in a vehicle): 8 December 2002 (except in relation to a penalty notice issued to a person before that date): see SI 2002/2811, arts 2,4, Schedule. Date in force (for remaining purposes): to be appointed: see the Nationality, Immigration and Asylum Act 2002, s 162(1).
Sub-s (5): in paras (b), (c) word "or" in italics repealed and subsequent word in square brackets substituted by the Nationality, Immigration and Asylum Act 2002, s 125, Sch 8, paras 1, 2(1), (5)(b). Date in force (for the purposes of clandestine entrants who arrive in the United Kingdom concealed in a vehicle): 8 December 2002 (except in relation to a penalty notice issued to a person before that date): see SI 2002/2811, arts 2, 4, Schedule. Date in force (for remaining purposes): to be appointed: see the Nationality, Immigration and Asylum Act 2002, s 162(1).
Sub-s (5A): inserted by the Nationality, Immigration and Asylum Act 2002, s 125, Sch 8, paras 1, 2(1), (6). Date in force: 8 December 2002 (except in relation to a penalty notice issued to a person before that date): see SI 2002/2811, arts 2, 4, Schedule.
Sub-s (6): in paras (a), (b) word "or" in italics repealed and subsequent words in square brackets substituted by the Nationality, Immigration and Asylum Act 2002, s 125, Sch 8, paras 1, 2(1), (7). Date in force (for the purposes of clandestine entrants who arrive in the United Kingdom concealed in a vehicle): 8 December 2002 (except in relation to a penalty notice issued to a person before that date): see SI 2002/2811, arts 2, 4, Schedule. Date in force (for remaining purposes): to be appointed: see the Nationality, Immigration and Asylum Act 2002, s 162(1).
Sub-s (6A): inserted by the Nationality, Immigration and Asylum Act 2002, s 125, Sch 8, paras 1, 2(1), (8). Date in force (for the purposes of clandestine entrants who arrive in the United Kingdom

concealed in a vehicle or a rail freight wagon): 8 December 2002 (except in relation to a penalty notice issued to a person before that date): see SI 2002/2811, arts 2, 4, Schedule. Date in force (for remaining purposes): to be appointed: see the Nationality, Immigration and Asylum Act 2002, s 162(1).

Subordinate Legislation
Carriers' Liability Regulations 2002, SI 2002/2817 (made under sub-ss (2A), (3), (10)).
Carriers' Liability (Amendment) Regulations 2004, SI 2004/244 (made under sub-s (10)).

[32A   Level of penalty: code of practice]

[(1)   The Secretary of State shall issue a code of practice specifying matters to be considered in determining the amount of a penalty under section 32.

(2)   The Secretary of State shall have regard to the code (in addition to any other matters he thinks relevant)—

    (a)   when imposing a penalty under section 32, and
    (b)   when considering a notice of objection under section 35(4).

(3)   Before issuing the code the Secretary of State shall lay a draft before Parliament.

(4)   After laying the draft code before Parliament the Secretary of State may bring the code into operation by order.

(5)   The Secretary of State may from time to time revise the whole or any part of the code and issue the code as revised.

(6)   Subsections (3) and (4) also apply to a revision or proposed revision of the code.]

Amendment
Inserted by the Nationality, Immigration and Asylum Act 2002, s 125, Sch 8, paras 1, 3. Date in force (for the purpose of enabling the Secretary of State to exercise the power under sub-ss (1), (3) and (4) above to lay a draft code of practice before Parliament and bring the code of practice into force): 14 November 2002 (except in relation to a penalty notice issued to a person before that date): see SI 2002/2811, arts 2, 4, Schedule. Date in force (for the purposes of clandestine entrants who arrive in the United Kingdom concealed in a vehicle or a rail freight wagon): 8 December 2002 (except in relation to a penalty notice issued to a person before that date): see SI 2002/2811, arts 2, 4, Schedule. Date in force (for remaining purposes): to be appointed: see the Nationality, Immigration and Asylum Act 2002, s 162(1).

Subordinate Legislation
Carriers' Liability (Clandestine Entrants) (Level of Penalty: Revised Code of Practice) Order 2004, SI 2004/251 (made under sub-ss (4), (6)).

33   *Code of practice* [Prevention of clandestine entrants: code of practice]

(1)   The Secretary of State must issue a code of practice to be followed by any person operating a system for preventing the carriage of clandestine entrants.

(2)   Before issuing the code, the Secretary of State must—

    (a)   consult such persons as he considers appropriate; and
    (b)   lay a draft before *both Houses of* Parliament.

(3)   The requirement of subsection (2)(a) may be satisfied by consultation before the passing of this Act.

(4)   After laying the draft code before Parliament, the Secretary of State may bring the code into operation by an order.

(5)   The Secretary of State may from time to time revise the whole or any part of the code and issue the code as revised.

(6) Subsections (2) and (4) also apply to any revision, or proposed revision, of the code.

Appointment
Appointment: 6 December 1999: see SI 1999/3190, art 2, Schedule.

Amendment
Section heading: substituted by the Nationality, Immigration and Asylum Act 2002, s 125, Sch 8, paras 1, 4. Date in force (for the purposes of clandestine entrants who arrive in the United Kingdom concealed in a vehicle or a rail freight wagon): 8 December 2002 (except in relation to a penalty notice issued to a person before that date): see SI 2002/2811, arts 2, 4, Schedule. Date in force (for remaining purposes): to be appointed: see the Nationality, Immigration and Asylum Act 2002, s 162(1).
Sub-s (2): in para (b) words "both Houses of" in italics repealed by the Nationality, Immigration and Asylum Act 2002, ss 125, 161, Sch 8, paras 1, 5, Sch 9. Date in force (for the purposes of clandestine entrants who arrive in the United Kingdom concealed in a vehicle or a rail freight wagon): 8 December 2002 (except in relation to a penalty notice issued to a person before that date): see SI 2002/2811, arts 2, 4, Schedule. Date in force (for remaining purposes): to be appointed: see the Nationality, Immigration and Asylum Act 2002, s 162(1).

See Further
See further, in relation to certain codes of practice which have effect by virtue of this section and s 39 hereof: the Nationality, Immigration and Asylum Act 2002, Sch 8, para 17.

Subordinate Legislation
Carriers' Liability (Clandestine Entrants) (Code of Practice) Order 2000, SI 2000/684.
Carriers' Liability (Clandestine Entrants) (Code of Practice for Rail Freight) Order 2001, SI 2001/312.
Carriers' Liability (Clandestine Entrants) (Code of Practice for Freight Shuttle Wagons) Order 2001, SI 2001/3233.
Carriers' Liability (Clandestine Entrants) (Revised Code of Practice for Vehicles) Order 2004, SI 2004/250 (made under sub-ss (4), (6)).

34   Defences to claim that penalty is due under section 32

(1) *This section applies if it is alleged that a person ("the carrier") is liable to a penalty under section 32.*

[(1) A person ("the carrier") shall not be liable to the imposition of a penalty under section 32(2) if he has a defence under this section.]

(2) It is a defence for the carrier to show that he, or an employee of his who was directly responsible for allowing the clandestine entrant to be concealed, was acting under duress.

(3) It is also a defence for the carrier to show that—

    (a) he did not know, and had no reasonable grounds for suspecting, that a clandestine entrant was, or might be, concealed in the transporter;
    (b) an effective system for preventing the carriage of clandestine entrants was in operation in relation to the transporter; and
    (c) *that* on the occasion in question the person or persons responsible for operating that system did so properly.

[(3A) It is also a defence for the carrier to show that—

    (a) he knew or suspected that a clandestine entrant was or might be concealed in a rail freight wagon, having boarded after the wagon began its journey to the United Kingdom;
    (b) he could not stop the train or shuttle-train of which the wagon formed part without endangering safety;

(c) an effective system for preventing the carriage of clandestine entrants was in operation in relation to the train or shuttle-train; and

(d) on the occasion in question the person or persons responsible for operating the system did so properly.]

(4) In determining, for the purposes of this section, whether a particular system is effective, regard is to be had to the code of practice issued by the Secretary of State under section 33.

(5) *If there are two or more persons responsible for a clandestine entrant, the fact that one or more of them has a defence under subsection (3) does not affect the liability of the others.*

(6) *But if a person responsible for a clandestine entrant has a defence under subsection (2), the liability of any other person responsible for that entrant is discharged.*

[(6) Where a person has a defence under subsection (2) in respect of a clandestine entrant, every other responsible person in respect of the clandestine entrant is also entitled to the benefit of the defence.]

Appointment
Appointment (for certain purposes): 8 December 2002: see SI 2002/2815, art 2, Schedule.
Appointment (for certain purposes): 3 April 2000: see SI 2000/464, art 2, Schedule.
Appointment (for certain purposes): 18 September 2000: see SI 2000/2444, art 2, Sch 1.

Amendment
Sub-s (1): substituted by the Nationality, Immigration and Asylum Act 2002, s 125, Sch 8, paras 1, 6(1), (2). Date in force (for the purposes of clandestine entrants who arrive in the United Kingdom concealed in a vehicle or a rail freight wagon): 8 December 2002 (except in relation to a penalty notice issued to a person before that date): see SI 2002/2811, arts 2, 4, Schedule. Date in force (for remaining purposes): to be appointed: see the Nationality, Immigration and Asylum Act 2002, s 162(1).
Sub-s (3): in para (c) word "that" in italics repealed by the Nationality, Immigration and Asylum Act 2002, ss 125, 161, Sch 8, paras 1, 6(1), (3), Sch 9. Date in force (for the purposes of clandestine entrants who arrive in the United Kingdom concealed in a vehicle or a rail freight wagon): 8 December 2002 (except in relation to a penalty notice issued to a person before that date): see SI 2002/2811, arts 2, 4, Schedule. Date in force (for remaining purposes): to be appointed: see the Nationality, Immigration and Asylum Act 2002, s 162(1).
Sub-s (3A): inserted by the Nationality, Immigration and Asylum Act 2002, s 125, Sch 8, paras 1, 6(1), (4). Date in force (for the purposes of clandestine entrants who arrive in the United Kingdom concealed in a vehicle or a rail freight wagon): 8 December 2002 (except in relation to a penalty notice issued to a person before that date): see SI 2002/2811, arts 2, 4, Schedule. Date in force (for remaining purposes): to be appointed: see the Nationality, Immigration and Asylum Act 2002, s 162(1).
Sub-s (5): repealed by the Nationality, Immigration and Asylum Act 2002, ss 125, 161, Sch 8, paras 1, 6(1), (5), Sch 9. Date in force (for the purposes of clandestine entrants who arrive in the United Kingdom concealed in a vehicle or a rail freight wagon): 8 December 2002 (except in relation to a penalty notice issued to a person before that date): see SI 2002/2811, arts 2, 4, Schedule. Date in force (for remaining purposes): to be appointed: see the Nationality, Immigration and Asylum Act 2002, s 162(1).
Sub-s (6): substituted by the Nationality, Immigration and Asylum Act 2002, s 125, Sch 8, paras 1, 6(1), (6). Date in force (for the purposes of clandestine entrants who arrive in the United Kingdom concealed in a vehicle or a rail freight wagon): 8 December 2002 (except in relation to a penalty notice issued to a person before that date): see SI 2002/2811, arts 2, 4, Schedule. Date in force (for remaining purposes): to be appointed: see the Nationality, Immigration and Asylum Act 2002, s 162(1).

35 Procedure

(1) If the Secretary of State decides that a person ("P") is liable to one or more penalties under section 32, he must notify P of his decision.

(2)   A notice under subsection (1) (a "penalty notice") must—

  (a)   state the Secretary of State's reasons for deciding that P is liable to the penalty (or penalties);
  (b)   state the amount of the penalty (or penalties) to which P is liable;
  (c)   specify the date before which, and the manner in which, the penalty (or penalties) must be paid; and
  (d)   include an explanation of the steps—
      (i)   that P *must* [may] take if he objects to the penalty;
      (ii)   that the Secretary of State may take under this Part to recover any unpaid penalty.

(3)   Subsection (4) applies if more than one person is responsible for a clandestine entrant.

(4)   If a penalty notice is served on one of the responsible persons, the Secretary of State is to be taken to have served the required penalty notice on each of them.

(5)   The Secretary of State must nevertheless take reasonable steps, while the penalty remains unpaid, to secure that the penalty notice is actually served on each of those responsible persons.

(6)   If a person on whom a penalty notice is served, or who is treated as having had a penalty notice served on him, alleges that he is not liable for one or more, or all, of the penalties specified in the penalty notice, he may give written notice of his allegation to the Secretary of State.

(7)   Notice under subsection (6) ("a notice of objection") must—

  (a)   give reasons for the allegation; and
  (b)   be given before the end of such period as may be prescribed.

(8)   If a notice of objection is given before the end of the prescribed period, the Secretary of State must consider it and determine whether or not any penalty to which it relates is payable.

[(3)   Subsection (4) applies where a person to whom a penalty notice is issued objects on the ground that—

  (a)   he is not liable to the imposition of a penalty, or
  (b)   the amount of the penalty is too high.

(4)   The person may give a notice of objection to the Secretary of State.

(5)   A notice of objection must—

  (a)   be in writing,
  (b)   give the objector's reasons, and
  (c)   be given before the end of such period as may be prescribed.

(6)   Where the Secretary of State receives a notice of objection to a penalty in accordance with this section he shall consider it and—

  (a)   cancel the penalty,
  (b)   reduce the penalty,
  (c)   increase the penalty, or
  (d)   determine to take no action under paragraphs (a) to (c).

(7)   Where the Secretary of State considers a notice of objection under subsection (6) he shall—

  (a)   inform the objector of his decision before the end of such period as may be prescribed or such longer period as he may agree with the objector,

(b)   if he increases the penalty, issue a new penalty notice under subsection (1), and

(c)   if he reduces the penalty, notify the objector of the reduced amount.]

(9)   The Secretary of State may by regulations provide, in relation to detached trailers, for a penalty notice which is *served* [issued] in such manner as may be prescribed to have effect as a penalty notice properly *served on* [issued to] the responsible person or persons concerned under this section.

(10)   Any sum payable to the Secretary of State as a penalty under section 32 may be recovered by the Secretary of State as a debt due to him.

[(11)   In proceedings for enforcement of a penalty under subsection (10) no question may be raised as to—

(a)   liability to the imposition of the penalty, or

(b)   its amount.

(12)   A document which is to be issued to or served on a person outside the United Kingdom for the purpose of subsection (1) or (7) or in the course of proceedings under subsection (10) may be issued or served—

(a)   in person,

(b)   by post,

(c)   by facsimile transmission, or

(d)   in another prescribed manner.

(13)   The Secretary of State may by regulations provide that a document issued or served in a manner listed in subsection (12) in accordance with the regulations is to be taken to have been received at a time specified by or determined in accordance with the regulations.]

Appointment
Appointment (for certain purposes): 3 April 2000: see SI 2000/464, art 2, Schedule.
Appointment (for certain purposes): 18 September 2000: see SI 2000/2444, art 2, Sch 1.
Appointment (for certain purposes): 8 December 2002: see SI 2002/2815, art 2, Schedule.
Sub-ss (7)–(9): Appointment (for the purpose of enabling subordinate legislation to be made): 6 December 1999: see SI 1999/3190, art 2, Schedule.

Amendment
Sub-s (2): in para (d)(i) word "must" in italics repealed and subsequent word in square brackets substituted by the Nationality, Immigration and Asylum Act 2002, s 125, Sch 8, paras 1, 7(1), (2). Date in force (for the purposes of clandestine entrants who arrive in the United Kingdom concealed in a vehicle or a rail freight wagon): 8 December 2002 (except in relation to a penalty notice issued to a person before that date): see SI 2002/2811, arts 2, 4, Schedule. Date in force (for remaining purposes): to be appointed: see the Nationality, Immigration and Asylum Act 2002, s 162(1).
Sub-ss (3)–(8): substituted, by subsequent sub-ss (3)–(7), by the Nationality, Immigration and Asylum Act 2002, s 125, Sch 8, paras 1, 7(1), (3). Date in force (for the purpose of enabling the Secretary of State to exercise the power to make subordinate legislation under sub-ss (5) and (7) above): 14 November 2002 (except in relation to a penalty notice issued to a person before that date): see SI 2002/2811, arts 2, 4, Schedule. Date in force (for the purposes of clandestine entrants who arrive in the United Kingdom concealed in a vehicle or a rail freight wagon): 8 December 2002 (except in relation to a penalty notice issued to a person before that date): see SI 2002/2811, arts, 2, 4, Schedule. Date in force (for remaining purposes): to be appointed: see the Nationality, Immigration and Asylum Act 2002, s 162(1).
Sub-s (9): word "served" in italics repealed and subsequent word in square brackets substituted by the Nationality, Immigration and Asylum Act 2002, s 125, Sch 8, paras 1, 7(1), (4)(a). Date in force (for the purpose of enabling the Secretary of State to exercise the power to make subordinate legislation): 14 November 2002 (except in relation to a penalty notice issued to a person before that date): see SI 2002/2811, arts 2, 4, Schedule. Date in force (for the purposes of clandestine entrants who arrive in the United Kingdom concealed in a vehicle or a rail freight

wagon): 8 December 2002 (except in relation to a penalty notice issued to a person before that date): see SI 2002/2811, arts 2, 4, Schedule. Date in force (for remaining purposes): to be appointed: see the Nationality, Immigration and Asylum Act 2002, s 162(1).

Sub-s (9): words "served on" in italics repealed and subsequent words in square brackets substituted by the Nationality, Immigration and Asylum Act 2002, s 125, Sch 8, paras 1, 7(1), (4)(b). Date in force (for the purpose of enabling the Secretary of State to exercise the power to make subordinate legislation): 14 November 2002 (except in relation to a penalty notice issued to a person before that date): see SI 2002/2811, arts 2, 4, Schedule. Date in force (for the purposes of clandestine entrants who arrive in the United Kingdom concealed in a vehicle or a rail freight wagon): 8 December 2002 (except in relation to a penalty notice issued to a person before that date): see SI 2002/2811, arts 2, 4, Schedule. Date in force (for remaining purposes): to be appointed: see the Nationality, Immigration and Asylum Act 2002, s 162(1).

Sub-ss (11)–(13): inserted by the Nationality, Immigration and Asylum Act 2002, s 125, Sch 8, paras 1, 7(1), (5). Date in force (for the purpose of enabling the Secretary of State to exercise the power to make subordinate legislation under sub-ss (12) and (13) above): 14 November 2002 (except in relation to a penalty notice issued to a person before that date): see SI 2002/2811, arts 2, 4, Schedule. Date in force (for the purposes of clandestine entrants who arrive in the United Kingdom concealed in a vehicle or a rail freight wagon): 8 December 2002 (except in relation to a penalty notice issued to a person before that date): see SI 2002/2811, arts 2, 4, Schedule. Date in force (for remaining purposes): to be appointed: see the Nationality, Immigration and Asylum Act 2002, s 162(1).

Subordinate Legislation
Carriers' Liability Regulations 2002, SI 2002/2817 (made under sub-ss (5), (7), (9), (12), (13)).

[35A   Appeal]

[(1)   A person may appeal to the court against a penalty imposed on him under section 32 on the ground that—

(a)   he is not liable to the imposition of a penalty, or
(b)   the amount of the penalty is too high.

(2)   On an appeal under this section the court may—

(a)   allow the appeal and cancel the penalty,
(b)   allow the appeal and reduce the penalty, or
(c)   dismiss the appeal.

(3)   An appeal under this section shall be a re-hearing of the Secretary of State's decision to impose a penalty and shall be determined having regard to—

(a)   any code of practice under section 32A which has effect at the time of the appeal,
(b)   the code of practice under section 33 which had effect at the time of the events to which the penalty relates, and
(c)   any other matters which the court thinks relevant (which may include matters of which the Secretary of State was unaware).

(4)   Subsection (3) has effect despite any provision of Civil Procedure Rules.

(5)   An appeal may be brought by a person under this section against a penalty whether or not—

(a)   he has given notice of objection under section 35(4);
(b)   the penalty has been increased or reduced under section 35(6).]

Amendment
Inserted by the Nationality, Immigration and Asylum Act 2002, s 125, Sch 8, paras 1, 8. Date in force (for the purposes of clandestine entrants who arrive in the United Kingdom concealed in a vehicle or a rail freight wagon): 8 December 2002 (except in relation to a penalty notice issued to a person before that date): see SI 2002/2811, arts 2, 4, Schedule. Date in force (for remaining purposes): to be appointed: see the Nationality, Immigration and Asylum Act 2002, s 162(1).

36   Power to detain vehicles etc in connection with penalties under section 32

(1)   If a penalty notice has been *given* [issued] under section 35, a senior officer may detain any relevant—

(a)   vehicle,
(b)   small ship, ...
(c)   small aircraft, [or
(d)   rail freight wagon,]

until all penalties to which the notice relates, and any expenses reasonably incurred by the Secretary of State in connection with the detention, have been paid.

(2)   That power—

(a)   may be exercised only if, in the opinion of the senior officer concerned, there is a significant risk that the penalty (or one or more of the penalties) will not be paid before the end of the prescribed period if the transporter is not detained; and

(b)   may not be exercised if alternative security which the Secretary of State considers is satisfactory, has been given.

[(2A)   A vehicle may be detained under subsection (1) only if—

(a)   the driver of the vehicle is an employee of its owner or hirer,
(b)   the driver of the vehicle is its owner or hirer, or
(c)   a penalty notice is issued to the owner or hirer of the vehicle.

(2B)   A senior officer may detain a relevant vehicle, small ship, small aircraft or rail freight wagon pending—

(a)   a decision whether to issue a penalty notice,
(b)   the issue of a penalty notice, or
(c)   a decision whether to detain under subsection (1).

(2C)   That power may not be exercised in any case—

(a)   for longer than is necessary in the circumstances of the case, or
(b)   after the expiry of the period of 24 hours beginning with the conclusion of the first search of the vehicle, ship, aircraft or wagon by an immigration officer after it arrived in the United Kingdom.]

(3)   If a transporter is detained under this section, the owner, consignor or any other person who has an interest in any freight or other thing carried in or on the transporter may remove it, or arrange for it to be removed, at such time and in such way as is reasonable.

(4)   The detention of a transporter under this section is lawful even though it is subsequently established that the penalty notice on which the detention was based was ill-founded in respect of all or any of the penalties to which it related.

(5)   But subsection (4) does not apply if the Secretary of State was acting unreasonably in issuing the penalty notice.

Initial Commencement
To be appointed: see s 170(4).

Appointment
Appointment (for certain purposes): 3 April 2000: see SI 2000/464, art 2, Schedule.
Appointment (for certain purposes): 18 September 2000: see SI 2000/2444, art 2, Sch 1.
Appointment (for certain purposes): 8 December 2002: see SI 2002/2815, art 2, Schedule.
Sub-s (2)(a): Appointment (for the purpose of enabling subordinate legislation to be made): 6 December 1999: see SI 1999/3190, art 2, Schedule.

Appendix 1   Legislation and materials

Amendment

Sub-s (1): word "given" in italics repealed and subsequent word in square brackets substituted by the Nationality, Immigration and Asylum Act 2002, s 125, Sch 8, paras 1, 9(1), (2)(a). Date in force (for the purposes of clandestine entrants who arrive in the United Kingdom concealed in a vehicle or a rail freight wagon): 8 December 2002 (except in relation to a penalty notice issued to a person before that date): see SI 2002/2811, arts 2, 4, Schedule. Date in force (for remaining purposes): to be appointed: see the Nationality, Immigration and Asylum Act 2002, s 162(1).

Sub-s (1): in para (b) word omitted repealed by the Nationality, Immigration and Asylum Act 2002, ss 125, 161, Sch 8, paras 1, 9(1), (2)(b), Sch 9. Date in force: 8 December 2002 (except in relation to a penalty notice issued to a person before that date): see SI 2002/2811, arts 2, 4, Schedule.

Sub-s (1): para (d) and word "or" immediately preceding it inserted by the Nationality, Immigration and Asylum Act 2002, s 125, Sch 8, paras 1, 9(1), (2)(c). Date in force: 8 December 2002 (except in relation to a penalty notice issued to a person before that date): see SI 2002/2811, arts 2, 4, Schedule.

Sub-ss (2A)–(2C): inserted by the Nationality, Immigration and Asylum Act 2002, s 125, Sch 8, paras 1, 9(1), (3). Date in force (for the purposes of clandestine entrants who arrive in the United Kingdom concealed in a vehicle or a rail freight wagon): 8 December 2002 (except in relation to a penalty notice issued to a person before that date): see SI 2002/2811, arts 2, 4, Schedule. Date in force (for remaining purposes): to be appointed: see the Nationality, Immigration and Asylum Act 2002, s 162(1).

Subordinate Legislation

Carriers' Liability Regulations 2002, SI 2002/2817 (made under sub-s (2)).

[36A   Detention in default of payment]

[(1)   This section applies where a person to whom a penalty notice has been issued under section 35 fails to pay the penalty before the date specified in accordance with section 35(2)(c).

(2)   The Secretary of State may make arrangements for the detention of any vehicle, small ship, small aircraft or rail freight wagon which the person to whom the penalty notice was issued uses in the course of a business.

(3)   A vehicle, ship, aircraft or wagon may be detained under subsection (2) whether or not the person to whom the penalty notice was issued owns it.

(4)   But a vehicle may be detained under subsection (2) only if the person to whom the penalty notice was issued—

    (a)   is the owner or hirer of the vehicle, or

    (b)   was an employee of the owner or hirer of the vehicle when the penalty notice was issued.

(5)   The power under subsection (2) may not be exercised while an appeal against the penalty under section 35A is pending or could be brought (ignoring the possibility of an appeal out of time with permission).

(6)   The Secretary of State shall arrange for the release of a vehicle, ship, aircraft or wagon detained under this section if the person to whom the penalty notice was issued pays—

    (a)   the penalty, and

    (b)   expenses reasonably incurred in connection with the detention.]

Amendment

Inserted by the Nationality, Immigration and Asylum Act 2002, s 125, Sch 8, paras 1, 10. Date in force (for the purposes of clandestine entrants who arrive in the United Kingdom concealed in a vehicle or a rail freight wagon): 8 December 2002 (except in relation to a penalty notice issued to a person before that date): see SI 2002/2811, arts 2, 4, Schedule. Date in force (for remaining purposes): to be appointed: see the Nationality, Immigration and Asylum Act 2002, s 162(1).

37   Effect of detention

(1)   This section applies if a transporter is detained under *section 36* [section 36(1)].

(2)   The person to whom the penalty notice was addressed, or the owner or any other person *claiming an interest in the transporter,* [whose interests may be affected by detention of the transporter,] may apply to the court for the transporter to be released.

(3)   The court may release the transporter if it considers that—

- (a)   satisfactory security has been tendered in place of the transporter for the payment of the penalty alleged to be due and connected expenses;
- (b)   there is no significant risk that the penalty (or one or more of the penalties) and any connected expenses will not be paid; or
- (c)   there is a significant doubt as to whether the penalty is payable *and the applicant has a compelling need to have the transporter released.*

[(3A)   The court may also release the transporter on the application of the owner of the transporter under subsection (2) if—

- (a)   a penalty notice was not issued to the owner or an employee of his, and
- (b)   the court considers it right to release the transporter.

(3B)   In determining whether to release a transporter under subsection (3A) the court shall consider—

- (a)   the extent of any hardship caused by detention,
- (b)   the extent (if any) to which the owner is responsible for the matters in respect of which the penalty notice was issued, and
- (c)   any other matter which appears to the court to be relevant (whether specific to the circumstances of the case or of a general nature).]

(4)   If the court has not ordered the release of the transporter, the Secretary of State may sell it if the penalty in question and connected expenses are not paid before the end of the period of 84 days beginning with the date on which the detention began.

(5)   "Connected expenses" means expenses reasonably incurred by the Secretary of State in connection with the detention.

[(5A)   The power of sale under subsection (4) may be exercised only when no appeal against the imposition of the penalty is pending or can be brought (ignoring the possibility of an appeal out of time with permission).

(5B)   The power of sale under subsection (4) shall lapse if not exercised within a prescribed period.]

(6)   Schedule 1 applies to the sale of transporters under this section.

[(7)   This section applies to a transporter detained under section 36A as it applies to a transporter detained under section 36(1); but for that purpose—

- (a)   the court may release the transporter only if the court considers that the detention was unlawful or under subsection (3A) (and subsection (3) shall not apply), and
- (b)   the reference in subsection (4) to the period of 84 days shall be taken as a reference to a period prescribed for the purpose of this paragraph.]

Appointment
Appointment (for certain purposes): 3 April 2000: see SI 2000/464, art 2, Schedule.
Appointment (for certain purposes): 18 September 2000: see SI 2000/2444, art 2, Sch 1.
Appointment (for certain purposes): 8 December 2002: see SI 2002/2815, art 2, Schedule.
Sub-s (6): Appointment (for certain purposes): 6 December 1999: see SI 1999/3190, art 2, Schedule.

Amendment
Sub-s (1): words "section 36" in italics repealed and subsequent words in square brackets substituted by the Nationality, Immigration and Asylum Act 2002, s 125, Sch 8, paras 1, 11(1), (2). Date in force (for the purposes of clandestine entrants who arrive in the United Kingdom concealed in a vehicle or a rail freight wagon): 8 December 2002 (except in relation to a penalty notice issued to a person before that date): see SI 2002/2811, arts 2, 4, Schedule. Date in force (for remaining purposes): to be appointed: see the Nationality, Immigration and Asylum Act 2002, s 162(1).
Sub-s (2): words "claiming an interest in the transporter," in italics repealed and subsequent words in square brackets substituted by the Nationality, Immigration and Asylum Act 2002, s 125, Sch 8, paras 1, 11(1), (3). Date in force (for the purposes of clandestine entrants who arrive in the United Kingdom concealed in a vehicle or a rail freight wagon): 8 December 2002 (except in relation to a penalty notice issued to a person before that date): see SI 2002/2811, arts 2, 4, Schedule. Date in force (for remaining purposes): to be appointed: see the Nationality, Immigration and Asylum Act 2002, s 162(1).
Sub-s (3): in para (c) words "and the applicant has a compelling need to have the transporter released" in italics repealed by the Nationality, Immigration and Asylum Act 2002, ss 125, 161, Sch 8, paras 1, 11(1), (4), Sch 9. Date in force (for the purposes of clandestine entrants who arrive in the United Kingdom concealed in a vehicle or a rail freight wagon): 8 December 2002 (except in relation to a penalty notice issued to a person before that date): see SI 2002/2811, arts 2, 4, Schedule. Date in force (for remaining purposes): to be appointed: see the Nationality, Immigration and Asylum Act 2002, s 162(1).
Sub-ss (3A), (3B): inserted by the Nationality, Immigration and Asylum Act 2002, s 125, Sch 8, paras 1, 11(1), (5). Date in force (for the purposes of clandestine entrants who arrive in the United Kingdom concealed in a vehicle or a rail freight wagon): 8 December 2002 (except in relation to a penalty notice issued to a person before that date): see SI 2002/2811, arts 2, 4, Schedule. Date in force (for remaining purposes): to be appointed: see the Nationality, Immigration and Asylum Act 2002, s 162(1).
Sub-ss (5A), (5B): inserted by the Nationality, Immigration and Asylum Act 2002, s 125, Sch 8, paras 1, 11(1), (6). Date in force (for the purpose of enabling the Secretary of State to exercise the power to make subordinate legislation under sub-s (5B) above): 14 November 2002 (except in relation to a penalty notice issued to a person before that date): see SI 2002/2811, arts 2, 4, Schedule. Date in force (for the purposes of clandestine entrants who arrive in the United Kingdom concealed in a vehicle or a rail freight wagon): 8 December 2002 (except in relation to a penalty notice issued to a person before that date): see SI 2002/2811, arts 2, 4, Schedule. Date in force (for remaining purposes): to be appointed: see the Nationality, Immigration and Asylum Act 2002, s 162(1).
Sub-s (7): inserted by the Nationality, Immigration and Asylum Act 2002, s 125, Sch 8, paras 1, 11(1), (7). Date in force (for the purpose of enabling the Secretary of State to exercise the power to make subordinate legislation): 14 November 2002 (except in relation to a penalty notice issued to a person before that date): see SI 2002/2811, arts 2, 4, Schedule. Date in force (for the purposes of clandestine entrants who arrive in the United Kingdom concealed in a vehicle or a rail freight wagon): 8 December 2002 (except in relation to a penalty notice issued to a person before that date): see SI 2002/2811, arts 2, 4, Schedule. Date in force (for remaining purposes): to be appointed: see the Nationality, Immigration and Asylum Act 2002, s 162(1).

Subordinate Legislation
Carriers' Liability Regulations 2002, SI 2002/2817 (made under sub-ss (5B), (7)).

38   Assisting illegal entry and harbouring

(1) *In section 25 of the 1971 Act (assisting illegal entry and harbouring), at the end of paragraph (c) of subsection (6), insert—*

  "*or*
  (d) *the driver of any such vehicle;".*

(2) After section 25, insert—

"25A   Detention of ships, aircraft and vehicles in connection with offences under section 25(1)

(1) If a person has been arrested for an offence under section 25(1)(a) or (b), a senior officer or a constable may detain a relevant ship, aircraft or vehicle—

(a) until a decision is taken as to whether or not to charge the arrested person with that offence; or

(b) if the arrested person has been charged—

    (i) until he is acquitted, the charge against him is dismissed or the proceedings are discontinued; or

    (ii) if he has been convicted, until the court decides whether or not to order forfeiture of the ship, aircraft or vehicle.

(2) A ship, aircraft or vehicle is a relevant ship, aircraft or vehicle, in relation to an arrested person, if it is one which the officer or constable concerned has reasonable grounds for believing could, on conviction of the arrested person for the offence for which he was arrested, be the subject of an order for forfeiture made under section 25(6).

(3) A person (other than the arrested person) who claims to be the owner of a ship, aircraft or vehicle which has been detained under this section may apply to the court for its release.

(4) The court to which an application is made under subsection (3) may, on such security or surety being tendered as it considers satisfactory, release the ship, aircraft or vehicle on condition that it is made available to the court if—

(a) the arrested person is convicted; and

(b) an order for its forfeiture is made under section 25(6).

(5) In the application to Scotland of subsection (1), for paragraphs (a) and (b) substitute—

"(a) until a decision is taken as to whether or not to institute criminal proceedings against the arrested person for that offence; or

(b) if criminal proceedings have been instituted against the arrested person—

    (i) until he is acquitted or, under section 65 or 147 of the Criminal Procedure (Scotland) Act 1995, discharged or liberated or the trial diet is deserted *simpliciter*;

    (ii) if he has been convicted, until the court decides whether or not to order forfeiture of the ship, aircraft or vehicle,

and for the purposes of this subsection, criminal proceedings are instituted against a person at whichever is the earliest of his first appearance before the sheriff on petition, or the service on him of an indictment or complaint."

(6) "Court" means—

(a) in England and Wales—

    (i) if the arrested person has not been charged, the magistrates' court for the petty sessions area in which he was arrested;

    (ii) if he has been charged but proceedings for the offence have not begun to be heard, the magistrates' court for the petty sessions area in which he was charged;

    (iii) if he has been charged and proceedings for the offence are being heard, the court hearing the proceedings;

(b) in Scotland, the sheriff; and

(c) in Northern Ireland—

    (i) if the arrested person has not been charged, the magistrates' court for the county court division in which he was arrested;

    (ii) if he has been charged but proceedings for the offence have not begun to be heard, the magistrates' court for the county court division in which he was charged;

    (iii) if he has been charged and proceedings for the offence are being heard, the court hearing the proceedings.

(7)   "Owner" has the same meaning as it has in section 25(6).

(8)   "Senior officer" means an immigration officer not below the rank of chief immigration officer."

(3)   *Subsection (1) has effect in relation to offences committed after the coming into force of that subsection.*

(4)   Subsection (2) has effect in relation to persons arrested for offences alleged to have been committed after the coming into force of that subsection.

Appointment
Appointment: 3 April 2000: see SI 2000/464, art 2, Schedule.

Amendment
Sub-ss (1), (3): repealed by the Nationality, Immigration and Asylum Act 2002, s 161, Sch 9. Date in force: to be appointed: see the Nationality, Immigration and Asylum Act 2002, s 162(1).

39   ...

...

Amendment
Repealed with savings by the Nationality, Immigration and Asylum Act 2002, ss 125, 161, Sch 8, paras 1, 12, Sch 9; for savings in relation to certain codes of practice which have effect by virtue of this section and s 33 hereof, see Sch 8, para 17 thereto. Date in force: 8 December 2002 (except in relation to a penalty notice issued to a person before that date): see SI 2002/2811, arts 2, 4, Schedule.

Passengers without proper documents

[40   Charge in respect of passenger without proper documents]

[(1)   This section applies if an individual requiring leave to enter the United Kingdom arrives in the United Kingdom by ship or aircraft and, on being required to do so by an immigration officer, fails to produce—

(a)   an immigration document which is in force and which satisfactorily establishes his identity and his nationality or citizenship, and
(b)   if the individual requires a visa, a visa of the required kind.

(2)   The Secretary of State may charge the owner of the ship or aircraft, in respect of the individual, the sum of £2,000.

(3)   The charge shall be payable to the Secretary of State on demand.

(4)   No charge shall be payable in respect of any individual who is shown by the owner to have produced the required document or documents to the owner or his employee or agent when embarking on the ship or aircraft for the voyage or flight to the United Kingdom.

(5)   For the purpose of subsection (4) an owner shall be entitled to regard a document as—

(a)   being what it purports to be unless its falsity is reasonably apparent, and
(b)   relating to the individual producing it unless it is reasonably apparent that it does not relate to him.

(6)   For the purposes of this section an individual requires a visa if—

(a)   under the immigration rules he requires a visa for entry into the United Kingdom, or

(b)   as a result of section 41 he requires a visa for passing through the United Kingdom.

(7)   The Secretary of State may by order amend this section for the purpose of applying it in relation to an individual who—

(a)   requires leave to enter the United Kingdom, and
(b)   arrives in the United Kingdom by train.

(8)   An order under subsection (7) may provide for the application of this section—

(a)   except in cases of a specified kind;
(b)   subject to a specified defence.

(9)   In this section "immigration document" means—

(a)   a passport, and
(b)   a document which relates to a national of a country other than the United Kingdom and which is designed to serve the same purpose as a passport.

(10)   The Secretary of State may by order substitute a sum for the sum in subsection (2).]

Amendment
Substituted, together with ss 40A, 40B for this section as originally enacted, by the Nationality, Immigration and Asylum Act 2002, s 125, Sch 8, paras 1, 13. Date in force: 8 December 2002: see SI 2002/2811, art 2, Schedule.

[40A   Notification and objection]

[(1)   If the Secretary of State decides to charge a person under section 40, the Secretary of State must notify the person of his decision.

(2)   A notice under subsection (1) (a "charge notice") must—

(a)   state the Secretary of State's reasons for deciding to charge the person,
(b)   state the amount of the charge,
(c)   specify the date before which, and the manner in which, the charge must be paid,
(d)   include an explanation of the steps that the person may take if he objects to the charge, and
(e)   include an explanation of the steps that the Secretary of State may take under this Part to recover any unpaid charge.

(3)   Where a person on whom a charge notice is served objects to the imposition of the charge on him, he may give a notice of objection to the Secretary of State.

(4)   A notice of objection must—

(a)   be in writing,
(b)   give the objector's reasons, and
(c)   be given before the end of such period as may be prescribed.

(5)   Where the Secretary of State receives a notice of objection to a charge in accordance with this section, he shall—

(a)   consider it, and
(b)   determine whether or not to cancel the charge.

(6)   Where the Secretary of State considers a notice of objection, he shall inform the objector of his decision before the end of—

(a)   such period as may be prescribed, or
(b)   such longer period as he may agree with the objector.

(7)   Any sum payable to the Secretary of State as a charge under section 40 may be recovered by the Secretary of State as a debt due to him.

(8)   In proceedings for enforcement of a charge under subsection (7) no question may be raised as to the validity of the charge.

(9)   Subsections (12) and (13) of section 35 shall have effect for the purpose of this section as they have effect for the purpose of section 35(1), (7) and (10).]

Amendment
Substituted, together with ss 40, 40B for s 40 as originally enacted, by the Nationality, Immigration and Asylum Act 2002, s 125, Sch 8, paras 1, 13. Date in force (for the purpose of enabling the Secretary of State to exercise the power to make subordinate legislation under sub-ss (4) and (6) above): 14 November 2002: see SI 2002/2811, art 2, Schedule. Date in force (for remaining purposes): 8 December 2002: see SI 2002/2811, art 2, Schedule.

Subordinate Legislation
Carriers' Liability Regulations 2002, SI 2002/2817 (made under sub-ss (4), (6)).

[40B   Appeal]

[(1)   A person may appeal to the court against a decision to charge him under section 40.

(2)   On an appeal under this section the court may—

(a)   allow the appeal and cancel the charge, or
(b)   dismiss the appeal.

(3)   An appeal under this section—

(a)   shall be a re-hearing of the Secretary of State's decision to impose a charge, and
(b)   may be determined having regard to matters of which the Secretary of State was unaware.

(4)   Subsection (3)(a) has effect despite any provision of Civil Procedure Rules.

(5)   An appeal may be brought by a person under this section against a decision to charge him whether or not he has given notice of objection under section 40A(3).]

Amendment
Substituted, together with ss 40, 40A for s 40 as originally enacted, by the Nationality, Immigration and Asylum Act 2002, s 125, Sch 8, paras 1, 13. Date in force: 8 December 2002: see SI 2002/2811, art 2, Schedule.

41   Visas for transit passengers

(1)   The Secretary of State may by order require transit passengers to hold a transit visa.

(2)   "Transit passengers" means persons of any description specified in the order who on arrival in the United Kingdom pass through to another country without entering the United Kingdom; and "transit visa" means a visa for that purpose.

(3)   The order—

(a)   may specify a description of persons by reference to nationality, citizenship, origin or other connection with any particular country but not by reference to race, colour or religion;
(b)   may not provide for the requirement imposed by the order to apply to any person who under the 1971 Act has the right of abode in the United Kingdom;

(c)   may provide for any category of persons of a description specified in the order to be exempt from the requirement imposed by the order;

(d)   may make provision about the method of application for visas required by the order.

Appointment
Appointment: 8 December 2002: see SI 2002/2815, art 2, Schedule.

Subordinate Legislation
Immigration (Passenger Transit Visa) Order 2003, SI 2003/1185.
Immigration (Passenger Transit Visa) (Amendment No 2) Order 2003, SI 2003/2628.
Immigration (Passenger Transit Visa) (Amendment) Order 2004, SI 2004/1304.
Immigration (Passenger Transit Visa) (Amendment) Order 2005, SI 2005/492.

42   ...

...

Amendment
Repealed by the Nationality, Immigration and Asylum Act 2002, ss 125, 161, Sch 8, paras 1, 14, Sch 9. Date in force: 8 December 2002: see SI 2002/2811, art 2, Schedule.

Interpretation

43   Interpretation of Part II

[(1)]   In this Part—

"aircraft" includes hovercraft;

"captain" means the master of a ship or commander of an aircraft;

"concealed" includes being concealed in any freight, stores or other thing carried in or on the vehicle, ship[, aircraft or rail freight wagon] concerned;

...

"detached trailer" means a trailer, semi-trailer, caravan or any other thing which is designed or adapted for towing by a vehicle but which has been detached for transport—

(a)   in or on the vehicle concerned; or

(b)   in the ship or aircraft concerned (whether separately or in or on a vehicle);

"equipment", in relation to an aircraft, includes—

(a)   any certificate of registration, maintenance or airworthiness of the aircraft;

(b)   any log book relating to the use of the aircraft; and

(c)   any similar document;

["freight shuttle wagon" means a wagon which—

(a)   forms part of a shuttle-train, and

(b)   is designed to carry commercial goods vehicles;

"freight train" means any train other than—

(a)   a train engaged on a service for the carriage of passengers, or

(b)   a shuttle-train;]

"hirer", in relation to a vehicle, means any person who has hired the vehicle from another person;

"operating weight", in relation to an aircraft, means the maximum total weight of the aircraft and its contents at which the aircraft may take off anywhere in the world, in the most favourable circumstances, in accordance with the certificate of airworthiness in force in respect of the aircraft;

"owner" includes—

    (a)   in relation to a ship or aircraft, the agent or operator of the ship or aircraft; ...

    (b)   ... and

in relation to a transporter which is the subject of a hire-purchase agreement, includes the person in possession of it under that agreement;

"penalty notice" has the meaning given in section 35(2);

["rail freight wagon" means—

    (a)   any rolling stock, other than a locomotive, which forms part of a freight train, or

    (b)   a freight shuttle wagon,

and for the purpose of this definition, "rolling stock" and "locomotive" have the meanings given by section 83 of the Railways Act 1993 (c 43);]

"senior officer" means an immigration officer not below the rank of chief immigration officer;

"ship" includes every description of vessel used in navigation;

["shuttle-train" has the meaning given by section 1(9) of the Channel Tunnel Act 1987 (c 53);]

"small aircraft" means an aircraft which has an operating weight of less than 5,700 kilogrammes;

"small ship" means a ship which has a gross tonnage of less than 500 tonnes;

"train" means a train which—

    (a)   is engaged on an international service as defined by section 13(6) of the Channel Tunnel Act 1987; but

    (b)   is not a shuttle train as defined by section 1(9) of that Act;

"train operator", in relation to a person arriving in the United Kingdom on a train, means the operator of trains who embarked that person on that train for the journey to the United Kingdom;

"transporter" means a vehicle, ship[, aircraft or rail freight wagon] together with—

    (a)   its equipment; and

    (b)   any stores for use in connection with its operation;

"vehicle" includes a trailer, semi-trailer, caravan or other thing which is designed or adapted to be towed by another vehicle.

[(2)   A reference in this Part to "the court" is a reference—

    (a)   in England and Wales, to a county court,

    (b)   in Scotland, to the sheriff, and

    (c)   in Northern Ireland, to a county court.

(3)   But—

    (a)   a county court may transfer proceedings under this Part to the High Court, and

    (b)   the sheriff may transfer proceedings under this Part to the Court of Session.]

Appointment
Appointment: 6 December 1999: see SI 1999/3190, art 2, Schedule.

Amendment
Sub-s (1): numbered as such by the Nationality, Immigration and Asylum Act 2002, s 125, Sch 8, paras 1, 15. Date in force: 8 December 2002 (except in relation to a penalty notice issued to a person before that date): see SI 2002/2811, arts 2, 4, Schedule.
Sub-s (1): in definition "concealed" words ", aircraft or rail freight wagon" in square brackets substituted by the Nationality, Immigration and Asylum Act 2002, s 125, Sch 8, paras 1, 15(a). Date in force: 8 December 2002 (except in relation to a penalty notice issued to a person before that date): see SI 2002/2811, arts 2, 4, Schedule.
Sub-s (1): definition "court" (omitted) repealed by the Nationality, Immigration and Asylum Act 2002, s 125, Sch 8, paras 1, 15(b). Date in force: 8 December 2002 (except in relation to a penalty notice issued to a person before that date): see SI 2002/2811, arts 2, 4, Schedule.

Sub-s (1): definitions "freight shuttle wagon" and "freight train" inserted by the Nationality, Immigration and Asylum Act 2002, s 125, Sch 8, paras 1, 15(c). Date in force: 8 December 2002 (except in relation to a penalty notice issued to a person before that date): see SI 2002/2811, arts 2, 4, Schedule.
Sub-s (1): in definition "owner" para (b) and word omitted immediately preceding it repealed by the Nationality, Immigration and Asylum Act 2002, ss 125, 161, Sch 8, paras 1, 15(d), Sch 9. Date in force: 8 December 2002 (except in relation to a penalty notice issued to a person before that date): see SI 2002/2811, arts 2, 4, Schedule.
Sub-s (1): definition "rail freight wagon" substituted by the Nationality, Immigration and Asylum Act 2002, s 125, Sch 8, paras 1, 15(e). Date in force: 8 December 2002 (except in relation to a penalty notice issued to a person before that date): see SI 2002/2811, arts 2, 4, Schedule.
Sub-s (1): definition "shuttle-train" inserted by the Nationality, Immigration and Asylum Act 2002, s 125, Sch 8, paras 1, 15(f). Date in force: 8 December 2002 (except in relation to a penalty notice issued to a person before that date): see SI 2002/2811, arts 2, 4, Schedule.
Sub-s (1): in definition "transporter" words ", aircraft or rail freight wagon" in square brackets substituted by the Nationality, Immigration and Asylum Act 2002, s 125, Sch 8, paras 1, 15(g). Date in force: 8 December 2002 (except in relation to a penalty notice issued to a person before that date): see SI 2002/2811, arts 2, 4, Schedule.
Sub-ss (2), (3): inserted by the Nationality, Immigration and Asylum Act 2002, s 124, Sch 8, paras 1, 15(h). Date in force: 8 December 2002 (except in relation to a penalty notice issued to a person before that date): see SI 2002/2811, arts 2, 4, Schedule.

PART III
BAIL

...

44 –52

...

Amendment
Repealed by the Nationality, Immigration and Asylum Act 2002, ss 68(6)(a), 161, Sch 9. Date in force: 10 February 2003: see SI 2003/1, art 2, Schedule.

Bail hearings under other enactments

53 Applications for bail in immigration cases

(1) The Secretary of State may by regulations make new provision in relation to applications for bail by persons detained under the 1971 Act [or under section 62 of the Nationality, Immigration and Asylum Act 2002].

(2) The regulations may confer a right to be released on bail in prescribed circumstances.

(3) The regulations may, in particular, make provision—

(a) creating or transferring jurisdiction to hear an application for bail by a person detained under the 1971 Act [or under section 62 of the Nationality, Immigration and Asylum Act 2002];
(b) as to the places in which such an application may be held;
(c) as to the procedure to be followed on, or in connection with, such an application;
(d) as to circumstances in which, and conditions (including financial conditions) on which, an applicant may be released on bail;
(e) amending or repealing any enactment so far as it relates to such an application.

(4) The regulations must include provision for securing that an application for bail made by a person who has brought an appeal under any provision of [the Nationality,

1489

Immigration and Asylum Act 2002] or the Special Immigration Appeals Commission Act 1997 is heard by the appellate authority hearing that appeal.

(5)   ...

(6)   Regulations under this section require the approval of the Lord Chancellor.

(7)   In so far as regulations under this section relate to the sheriff or the Court of Session, the Lord Chancellor must obtain the consent of the Scottish Ministers before giving his approval.

Appointment
Sub-ss (1)–(4), (6), (7): Appointment: 10 February 2003: see SI 2003/2, art 2, Schedule.

Amendment
Sub-s (1): words "or under section 62 of the Nationality, Immigration and Asylum Act 2002" in square brackets inserted by the Nationality, Immigration and Asylum Act 2002, s 62(13)(a). Date in force: 10 February 2003: see SI 2003/1, art 2, Schedule.
Sub-s (3): in para (a) words "or under section 62 of the Nationality, Immigration and Asylum Act 2002" in square brackets inserted by the Nationality, Immigration and Asylum Act 2002, s 62(13)(b). Date in force: 10 February 2003: see SI 2003/1, art 2, Schedule.
Sub-s (4): words "the Nationality, Immigration and Asylum Act 2002" in square brackets substituted by the Nationality, Immigration and Asylum Act 2002, s 114(3), Sch 7, para 28. Date in force: 1 April 2003 (except in relation to events which took place before that date): see SI 2003/754, arts 2(1), 3(1), Sch 1.
Sub-s (5): repealed by the Nationality, Immigration and Asylum Act 2002, ss 68(6)(b), 161, Sch 9. Date in force: 10 February 2003: see SI 2003/1, art 2, Schedule.

54   Extension of right to apply for bail in deportation cases

(1)   Paragraph 2 of Schedule 3 to the 1971 Act (detention or control pending deportation) is amended as follows,

(2)   In sub-paragraph (1), at the end insert "or he is released on bail".

(3)   In sub-paragraph (3), after "unless" insert "he is released on bail or".

(4)   After sub-paragraph (4) insert—

"(4A)   Paragraphs 22 to 25 of Schedule 2 to this Act apply in relation to a person detained under sub-paragraph (1), (2) or (3) as they apply in relation to a person detained under paragraph 16 of that Schedule."

Appointment
Appointment: 10 February 2003: see SI 2003/2, art 2, Schedule.

55   ...

...

Amendment
Repealed by the Nationality, Immigration and Asylum Act 2002, ss 68(6)(c), 161, Sch 9. Date in force: 10 February 2003: see SI 2003/1, art 2, Schedule.

PART IV

...

56   –81

...

Amendment
Repealed by the Nationality, Immigration and Asylum Act 2002, ss 114(1), (2), 161, Sch 9; for transitional provisions see Sch 6 thereto. Date in force: 1 April 2003 (except in relation to events which took place before that date): see SI 2003/754, arts 2(1), 3(1), Sch 1.

PART V
IMMIGRATION ADVISERS AND IMMIGRATION SERVICE PROVIDERS

Interpretation

82   Interpretation of Part V

(1)   In this Part—

"claim for asylum" means a claim that it would be contrary to the United Kingdom's obligations under—
  (a)   the Refugee Convention, or
  (b)   Article 3 of the Human Rights Convention,
for the claimant to be removed from, or required to leave, the United Kingdom;
"the Commissioner" means the Immigration Services Commissioner;
"the complaints scheme" means the scheme established under paragraph 5(1) of Schedule 5;
"designated judge" has the same meaning as in section 119(1) of the Courts and Legal Services Act 1990;
"designated professional body" has the meaning given by section 86;
"immigration advice" means advice which—
  (a)   relates to a particular individual;
  (b)   is given in connection with one or more relevant matters;
  (c)   is given by a person who knows that he is giving it in relation to a particular individual and in connection with one or more relevant matters; and
  (d)   is not given in connection with representing an individual before a court in criminal proceedings or matters ancillary to criminal proceedings;
"immigration services" means the making of representations on behalf of a particular individual—
  (a)   in civil proceedings before a court, tribunal or adjudicator in the United Kingdom, or
  (b)   in correspondence with a Minister of the Crown or government department,
in connection with one or more relevant matters;
"Minister of the Crown" has the same meaning as in the Ministers of the Crown Act 1975;
"qualified person" means a person who is qualified for the purposes of section 84;
"registered person" means a person who is registered with the Commissioner under section 85;
"relevant matters" means any of the following—
  (a)   a claim for asylum;
  (b)   an application for, or for the variation of, entry clearance or leave to enter or remain in the United Kingdom;
  [(ba) an application for an immigration employment document;]
  (c)   unlawful entry into the United Kingdom;
  (d)   nationality and citizenship under the law of the United Kingdom;
  (e)   citizenship of the European Union;
  (f)   admission to Member States under Community law;
  (g)   residence in a Member State in accordance with rights conferred by or under Community law;
  (h)   removal or deportation from the United Kingdom;

    (i)   an application for bail under the Immigration Acts or under the Special Immigration Appeals Commission Act 1997;

    (j)   an appeal against, or an application for judicial review in relation to, any decision taken in connection with a matter referred to in paragraphs (a) to (i); and

"the Tribunal" means the Immigration Services Tribunal.

(2)   In this Part, references to the provision of immigration advice or immigration services are to the provision of such advice or services by a person—

    (a)   in the United Kingdom (regardless of whether the persons to whom they are provided are in the United Kingdom or elsewhere); and

    (b)   in the course of a business carried on (whether or not for profit) by him or by another person.

[(3)   In the definition of "relevant matters" in subsection (1) "immigration employment document" means—

    (a)   a work permit (within the meaning of section 33(1) of the Immigration Act 1971 (interpretation)), and

    (b)   any other document which relates to employment and is issued for a purpose of immigration rules or in connection with leave to enter or remain in the United Kingdom.]

Appointment
Appointment: 22 May 2000: see SI 2000/1282, art 2, Schedule.

Amendment
Sub-s (1): in definition "relevant matters" para (ba) inserted by the Nationality, Immigration and Asylum Act 2002, s 123(1), (2). Date in force: 1 April 2004: see SI 2003/754, art 2, Sch 1 (as amended by SI 2003/1339, art 3 and SI 2003/2993, art 3).
Sub-s (3): inserted by the Nationality, Immigration and Asylum Act 2002, s 123(1), (3). Date in force: 1 April 2004: see SI 2003/754, art 2, Sch 1 (as amended by SI 2003/1339, art 3 and SI 2003/2993, art 3).

The Immigration Services Commissioner

83   The Commissioner

(1)   There is to be an Immigration Services Commissioner (referred to in this Part as "the Commissioner").

(2)   The Commissioner is to be appointed by the Secretary of State after consulting the Lord Chancellor and the Scottish Ministers.

(3)   It is to be the general duty of the Commissioner to promote good practice by those who provide immigration advice or immigration services.

(4)   In addition to any other functions conferred on him by this Part, the Commissioner is to have the regulatory functions set out in Part I of Schedule 5.

(5)   The Commissioner must exercise his functions so as to secure, so far as is reasonably practicable, that those who provide immigration advice or immigration services—

    (a)   are fit and competent to do so;
    (b)   act in the best interests of their clients;
    (c)   do not knowingly mislead any court, tribunal or adjudicator in the United Kingdom;

  (d) do not seek to abuse any procedure operating in the United Kingdom in connection with immigration or asylum (including any appellate or other judicial procedure);

  (e) do not advise any person to do something which would amount to such an abuse.

(6) The Commissioner—

  (a) must arrange for the publication, in such form and manner and to such extent as he considers appropriate, of information about his functions and about matters falling within the scope of his functions; and

  (b) may give advice about his functions and about such matters.

(7) Part II of Schedule 5 makes further provision with respect to the Commissioner.

Appointment

Sub-ss (1)–(3), (6), (7): Appointment: 22 May 2000: see SI 2000/1282, art 2, Schedule.

Sub-ss (4), (5): Appointment (for certain purposes): 22 May 2000: see SI 2000/1282, art 2, Schedule.

Sub-ss (4), (5): Appointment (for remaining purposes): 30 October 2000: see SI 2000/1985, art 2, Schedule.

The general prohibition

84   Provision of immigration services

(1) No person may provide immigration advice or immigration services unless he is a qualified person.

[(2) A person is a qualified person if he is—

  (a) a registered person,

  (b) authorised by a designated professional body to practise as a member of the profession whose members the body regulates,

  (c) the equivalent in an EEA State of—

    (i) a registered person, or

    (ii) a person within paragraph (b),

  (d) a person permitted, by virtue of exemption from a prohibition, to provide in an EEA State advice or services equivalent to immigration advice or services, or

  (e) acting on behalf of, and under the supervision of, a person within any of paragraphs (a) to (d) (whether or not under a contract of employment).

(3) Subsection (2)(a) and (e) are subject to any limitation on the effect of a person's registration imposed under paragraph 2(2) of Schedule 6.]

(4) Subsection (1) does not apply to a person who—

  (a) is certified by the Commissioner as exempt ("an exempt person");

  (b) is employed by an exempt person;

  (c) works under the supervision of an exempt person or an employee of an exempt person; or

  (d) who falls within a category of person specified in an order made by the Secretary of State for the purposes of this subsection.

(5) A certificate under subsection (4)(a) may relate only to a specified description of immigration advice or immigration services.

(6) Subsection (1) does not apply to a person—

  (a) holding an office under the Crown, when acting in that capacity;

(b)   employed by, or for the purposes of, a government department, when acting in that capacity;
(c)   acting under the control of a government department; or
(d)   otherwise exercising functions on behalf of the Crown.

(7)   An exemption given under subsection (4) may be withdrawn by the Commissioner.

Appointment
Sub-s (1): Appointment: 30 April 2001: see SI 2001/1394, art 2, Schedule.
Sub-s (4)(a): Appointment (for certain purposes): 30 October 2000: see SI 2000/1985, art 2, Schedule.
Sub-s (4)(a): Appointment (for remaining purposes): 30 April 2001: see SI 2001/1394, art 2, Schedule.
Sub-s (4)(b), (c): Appointment: 30 April 2001: see SI 2001/1394, art 2, Schedule.
Sub-s (4)(d): Appointment (for the purposes of enabling subordinate legislation to be made): 30 October 2000: see SI 2000/1985, art 2, Schedule.
Sub-s (4)(d): Appointment (for remaining purposes): 30 April 2001: see SI 2001/1394, art 2, Schedule.
Sub-ss (5), (7): Appointment: 30 October 2000: see SI 2000/1985, art 2, Schedule.
Sub-s (6): Appointment: 30 April 2001: see SI 2001/1394, art 2, Schedule.

Amendment
Sub-ss (2), (3): substituted by the Asylum and Immigration (Treatment of Claimants, etc) Act 2004, s 37(1). Date in force: 1 October 2004: see SI 2004/2523, art 2, Schedule.

Subordinate Legislation
Immigration and Asylum Act 1999 (Part V Exemption: Educational Institutions and Health Sector Bodies) Order 2001, SI 2001/1403 (made under sub-s (4)(d)).
Immigration and Asylum Act 1999 (Part V Exemption: Relevant Employers) Order 2003, SI 2003/3214 (made under sub-s (4)(d)).

85   Registration exemption by the Commissioner

(1)   The Commissioner must prepare and maintain a register for and the purposes of section 84(2)(a) ...

(2)   The Commissioner must keep a record of the persons to whom he has issued a certificate of exemption under section 84(4)(a).

(3)   Schedule 6 makes further provision with respect to registration.

Appointment
Sub-ss (1), (2): Appointment: 30 October 2000: see SI 2000/1985, art 2, Schedule.
Sub-s (3): Appointment (for certain purposes): 1 August 2000: see SI 2000/1985, art 2, Schedule.
Sub-s (3): Appointment (for remaining purposes): 30 October 2000: see SI 2000/1985, art 2, Schedule.

Amendment
Sub-s (1): words omitted repealed by the Asylum and Immigration (Treatment of Claimants, etc) Act 2004, ss 37(2), 47, Sch 4. Date in force: 1 October 2004: see SI 2004/2523, art 2, Schedule.

86   Designated professional bodies

(1)   "Designated professional body" means—

(a)   The Law Society;
(b)   The Law Society of Scotland;
(c)   The Law Society of Northern Ireland;
(d)   The Institute of Legal Executives;
(e)   The General Council of the Bar;

(f)   The Faculty of Advocates; or
(g)   The General Council of the Bar of Northern Ireland.

[(2)   The Secretary of State may by order remove a body from the list in subsection (1) if he considers that the body—

(a)   has failed to provide effective regulation of its members in their provision of immigration advice or immigration services, or
(b)   has failed to comply with a request of the Commissioner for the provision of information (whether general or in relation to a particular case or matter).]

(3)   If a designated professional body asks the Secretary of State to amend subsection (1) so as to remove its name, the Secretary of State may by order do so.

(4)   If the Secretary of State is proposing to act under subsection (2) he must, before doing so—

(a)   consult the Commissioner;
(b)   consult the Legal Services Ombudsman, if the proposed order would affect a designated professional body in England and Wales;
(c)   consult the Scottish Legal Services Ombudsman, if the proposed order would affect a designated professional body in Scotland;
(d)   consult the lay observers appointed under Article 42 of the Solicitors (Northern Ireland) Order 1976, if the proposed order would affect a designated professional body in Northern Ireland;
(e)   notify the body concerned of his proposal and give it a reasonable period within which to make representations; and
(f)   consider any representations so made.

(5)   An order under subsection (2) requires the approval of—

(a)   the Lord Chancellor, if it affects a designated professional body in England and Wales or Northern Ireland;
(b)   the Scottish Ministers, if it affects a designated professional body in Scotland.

(6)   Before deciding whether or not to give his approval under subsection (5)(a), the Lord Chancellor must consult—

(a)   the designated judges, if the order affects a designated professional body in England and Wales;
(b)   the Lord Chief Justice of Northern Ireland, if it affects a designated professional body in Northern Ireland.

(7)   Before deciding whether or not to give their approval under subsection (5)(b), the Scottish Ministers must consult the Lord President of the Court of Session.

(8)   If the Secretary of State considers that a body which—

(a)   is concerned (whether wholly or in part) with regulating the legal profession, or a branch of it, in an EEA State,
(b)   is not a designated professional body, and
(c)   is capable of providing effective regulation of its members in their provision of immigration advice or immigration services,

ought to be designated, he may by order amend subsection (1) to include the name of that body.

(9)   The Commissioner must—

(a)   keep under review the list of designated professional bodies set out in subsection (1); and
[(b)   report to the Secretary of State if the Commissioner considers that a designated professional body—

    (i) is failing to provide effective regulation of its members in their provision of immigration advice or immigration services, or

    (ii) has failed to comply with a request of the Commissioner for the provision of information (whether general or in relation to a particular case or matter)].

[(9A) A designated professional body shall comply with a request of the Commissioner for the provision of information (whether general or in relation to a specified case or matter).]

(10) For the purpose of meeting the costs incurred by the Commissioner in discharging his functions under this Part, each designated professional body must pay to the Commissioner, in each year and on such date as may be specified, such fee as may be specified.

(11) Any unpaid fee for which a designated professional body is liable under subsection (10) may be recovered from that body as a debt due to the Commissioner.

(12) "Specified" means specified by an order made by the Secretary of State.

Appointment
Sub-ss (1)–(9): Appointment: 22 May 2000: see SI 2000/1282, art 2, Schedule.
Sub-ss (10)–(12): Appointment (for remaining purposes): 30 April 2001: see SI 2001/1394, art 2, Schedule.
Sub-ss (10)–(12): Appointment (for the purposes of enabling subordinate legislation to be made): 30 October 2000: see SI 2000/1985, art 2, Schedule.

Amendment
Sub-s (2): substituted by the Asylum and Immigration (Treatment of Claimants, etc) Act 2004, s 41(1), (2). Date in force: 1 October 2004: see SI 2004/2523, art 2, Schedule.
Sub-s (9): para (b) substituted by the Asylum and Immigration (Treatment of Claimants, etc) Act 2004, s 41(1), (3). Date in force: 1 October 2004: see SI 2004/2523, art 2, Schedule.
Sub-s (9A): inserted by the Asylum and Immigration (Treatment of Claimants, etc) Act 2004, s 41(1), (4). Date in force: 1 October 2004: see SI 2004/2523, art 2, Schedule.

Subordinate Legislation
Immigration Services Commissioner (Designated Professional Body) (Fees) Order 2004, SI 2004/801 (made under sub-ss (10), (12)).
Immigration Services Commissioner (Designated Professional Body) (Fees) Order 2005, SI 2005/348 (made under sub-ss (10), (12)).

The Immigration Services Tribunal

87   The Tribunal

(1) There is to be a tribunal known as the Immigration Services Tribunal (referred to in this Part as "the Tribunal").

(2) Any person aggrieved by a relevant decision of the Commissioner may appeal to the Tribunal against the decision.

(3) "Relevant decision" means a decision—

    (a) to refuse an application for registration made under paragraph 1 of Schedule 6;
    (b) to withdraw an exemption given under section 84(4)(a);
    (c) under paragraph 2(2) of that Schedule to register with limited effect;
    (d) to refuse an application for continued registration made under paragraph 3 of that Schedule;
    (e) to vary a registration on an application under paragraph 3 of that Schedule;
    [(ea) to vary a registration under paragraph 3A of that Schedule;] or

(f) ...

(4) The Tribunal is also to have the function of hearing disciplinary charges laid by the Commissioner under paragraph 9(1)(e) of Schedule 5.

(5) Schedule 7 makes further provision with respect to the Tribunal and its constitution and functions.

Appointment
Sub-ss (1)–(4): Appointment: 30 October 2000: see SI 2000/1985, art 2, Schedule.
Sub-s (5): Appointment (for certain purposes): 1 August 2000: see SI 2000/1985, art 2, Schedule.
Sub-s (5): Appointment (for remaining purposes): 30 October 2000: see SI 2000/1985, art 2, Schedule.

Amendment
Sub-s (3): para (ea) inserted by the Nationality, Immigration and Asylum Act 2002, s 140(3). Date in force: 8 January 2003: see SI 2002/2811, art 2, Schedule.
Sub-s (3): para (f) repealed by the Asylum and Immigration (Treatment of Claimants, etc) Act 2004, ss 40, 47, Sch 4. Date in force: 1 October 2004: see SI 2004/2523, art 2, Schedule.

88 Appeal upheld by the Tribunal

(1) This section applies if the Tribunal allows an appeal under section 87.

(2) If the Tribunal considers it appropriate, it may direct the Commissioner—

(a) to register the applicant or to continue the applicant's registration;
(b) to make or vary the applicant's registration so as to have limited effect in any of the ways mentioned in paragraph 2(2) of Schedule 6;
(c) to restore an exemption granted under section 84(4)(a); or
(d) to quash a decision recorded under paragraph 9(1)(a) of Schedule 5 and the record of that decision.

Appointment
Appointment: 30 October 2000: see SI 2000/1985, art 2, Schedule.

89 Disciplinary charge upheld by the Tribunal

(1) This section applies if the Tribunal upholds a disciplinary charge laid by the Commissioner under paragraph 9(1)(e) of Schedule 5 against a person ("the person charged").

[(2) If the person charged is a registered person or acts on behalf of a registered person, the Tribunal may—

(a) direct the Commissioner to record the charge and the Tribunal's decision for consideration in connection with the registered person's next application for continued registration;
(b) direct the registered person to apply for continued registration as soon as is reasonably practicable.]

(4) If the person charged is certified by the Commissioner as exempt under section 84(4)(a), the Tribunal may direct the Commissioner to consider whether to withdraw his exemption.

(5) If the person charged is found to have charged unreasonable fees for immigration advice or immigration services, the Tribunal may direct him to repay to the clients concerned such portion of those fees as it may determine.

(6) The Tribunal may direct the person charged to pay a penalty to the Commissioner of such sum as it considers appropriate.

(7)   A direction given by the Tribunal under subsection (5) (or under subsection (6)) may be enforced by the clients concerned (or by the Commissioner)—

   (a)   as if it were an order of a county court; or
   (b)   in Scotland, as if it were an extract registered decree arbitral bearing a warrant for execution issued by the sheriff court of any sheriffdom in Scotland.

(8)   The Tribunal may direct that the person charged or any person [acting on his behalf or] under his supervision is to be—

   (a)   subject to such restrictions on the provision of immigration advice or immigration services as the Tribunal considers appropriate;
   (b)   suspended from providing immigration advice or immigration services for such period as the Tribunal may determine; or
   (c)   prohibited from providing immigration advice or immigration services indefinitely.

(9)   The Commissioner must keep a record of the persons against whom there is in force a direction given by the Tribunal under subsection (8).

Appointment
Appointment: 30 October 2000: see SI 2000/1985, art 2, Schedule.

Amendment
Sub-s (2): substituted, for sub-ss (2), (3) as originally enacted, by the Asylum and Immigration (Treatment of Claimants, etc) Act 2004, s 37(3)(a). Date in force: 1 October 2004: see SI 2004/2523, art 2, Schedule.
Sub-s (8): words "acting on his behalf or" in square brackets substituted by the Asylum and Immigration (Treatment of Claimants, etc) Act 2004, s 37(3)(b). Date in force: 1 October 2004: see SI 2004/2523, art 2, Schedule.

90   Orders by disciplinary bodies

(1)   A disciplinary body may make an order directing that a person subject to its jurisdiction is to be—

   (a)   subject to such restrictions on the provision of immigration advice or immigration services as the body considers appropriate;
   (b)   suspended from providing immigration advice or immigration services for such period as the body may determine; or
   (c)   prohibited from providing immigration advice or immigration services indefinitely.

(2)   "Disciplinary body" means any body—

   (a)   appearing to the Secretary of State to be established for the purpose of hearing disciplinary charges against members of a designated professional body; and
   (b)   specified in an order made by the Secretary of State.

(3)   The Secretary of State must consult the designated professional body concerned before making an order under subsection (2)(b).

(4)   For the purposes of this section, a person is subject to the jurisdiction of a disciplinary body if he is an authorised person or [is acting on behalf of] an authorised person.

(5)   "Authorised person" means a person who is authorised by the designated professional body concerned to practise as a member of the profession whose members are regulated by that body.

Appointment
Appointment (for the purposes of enabling subordinate legislation to be made): 1 August 2000: see SI 2000/1985, art 2, Schedule.
Appointment (for remaining purposes): 30 April 2001: see SI 2001/1394, art 2, Schedule.

Amendment
Sub-s (4): words "is acting on behalf of" in square brackets substituted by the Asylum and Immigration (Treatment of Claimants, etc) Act 2004, s 37(4). Date in force: 1 October 2004: see SI 2004/2523, art 2, Schedule.

Enforcement

91 Offences

(1) A person who provides immigration advice or immigration services in contravention of section 84 or of a restraining order is guilty of an offence and liable—

    (a) on summary conviction, to imprisonment for a term not exceeding six months or to a fine not exceeding the statutory maximum, or to both; or

    (b) on conviction on indictment, to imprisonment for a term not exceeding two years or to a fine, or to both.

(2) "Restraining order" means—

    (a) a direction given by the Tribunal under section 89(8) or paragraph 9(3) of Schedule 5; or

    (b) an order made by a disciplinary body under section 90(1).

(3) If an offence under this section committed by a body corporate is proved—

    (a) to have been committed with the consent or connivance of an officer, or

    (b) to be attributable to neglect on his part,

the officer as well as the body corporate is guilty of the offence and liable to be proceeded against and punished accordingly.

(4) "Officer", in relation to a body corporate, means a director, manager, secretary or other similar officer of the body, or a person purporting to act in such a capacity.

(5) If the affairs of a body corporate are managed by its members, subsection (3) applies in relation to the acts and defaults of a member in connection with his functions of management as if he were a director of the body corporate.

(6) If an offence under this section committed by a partnership in Scotland is proved—

    (a) to have been committed with the consent or connivance of a partner, or

    (b) to be attributable to neglect on his part,

the partner as well as the partnership is guilty of the offence and liable to be proceeded against and punished accordingly.

(7) "Partner" includes a person purporting to act as a partner.

Appointment
Appointment: 30 April 2001: see SI 2001/1394, art 2, Schedule.

92 Enforcement

(1) If it appears to the Commissioner that a person—

    (a) is providing immigration advice or immigration services in contravention of section 84 or of a restraining order, and

    (b) is likely to continue to do so unless restrained,

the Commissioner may apply to a county court for an injunction, or to the sheriff for an interdict, restraining him from doing so.

(2)   If the court is satisfied that the application is well-founded, it may grant the injunction or interdict in the terms applied for or in more limited terms.

(3)   "Restraining order" has the meaning given by section 91.

Appointment
Appointment: 30 April 2001: see SI 2001/1394, art 2, Schedule.

[92A   Investigation of offence: power of entry]

[(1)   On an application made by the Commissioner a justice of the peace may issue a warrant authorising the Commissioner to enter and search premises.

(2)   A justice of the peace may issue a warrant in respect of premises only if satisfied that there are reasonable grounds for believing that—

   (a)   an offence under section 91 has been committed,
   (b)   there is material on the premises which is likely to be of substantial value (whether by itself or together with other material) to the investigation of the offence, and
   (c)   any of the conditions specified in subsection (3) is satisfied.

(3)   Those conditions are—

   (a)   that it is not practicable to communicate with a person entitled to grant entry to the premises,
   (b)   that it is not practicable to communicate with a person entitled to grant access to the evidence,
   (c)   that entry to the premises will be prevented unless a warrant is produced, and
   (d)   that the purpose of a search may be frustrated or seriously prejudiced unless the Commissioner can secure immediate entry on arrival at the premises.

(4)   The Commissioner may seize and retain anything for which a search is authorised under this section.

(5)   A person commits an offence if without reasonable excuse he obstructs the Commissioner in the exercise of a power by virtue of this section.

(6)   A person guilty of an offence under subsection (5) shall be liable on summary conviction to—

   (a)   imprisonment for a term not exceeding six months,
   (b)   a fine not exceeding level 5 on the standard scale, or
   (c)   both.

(7)   In this section—

   (a)   a reference to the Commissioner includes a reference to a member of his staff authorised in writing by him,
   (b)   a reference to premises includes a reference to premises used wholly or partly as a dwelling, and
   (c)   a reference to material—
      (i)   includes material subject to legal privilege within the meaning of the Police and Criminal Evidence Act 1984 (c 60),
      (ii)   does not include excluded material or special procedure material within the meaning of that Act, and
      (iii)   includes material whether or not it would be admissible in evidence at a trial.

(8)   In the application of this section to Scotland—

(a) a reference to a justice of the peace shall be taken as a reference to the sheriff,
(b) for sub-paragraph (i) of subsection (7)(c) there is substituted—
"(i) includes material comprising items subject to legal privilege (as defined by section 412 of the Proceeds of Crime Act 2002 (c 29))," and
(c) sub-paragraph (ii) of subsection (7)(c) shall be ignored.

(9) In the application of this section to Northern Ireland the reference to the Police and Criminal Evidence Act 1984 shall be taken as a reference to the Police and Criminal Evidence (Northern Ireland) Order 1989 (SI 1989/1341 (NI 12)).]

Amendment
Inserted by the Asylum and Immigration (Treatment of Claimants, etc) Act 2004, s 38(1). Date in force: 1 October 2004: see SI 2004/2523, art 2, Schedule.

[92B Advertising]

[(1) A person commits an offence if—

(a) he offers to provide immigration advice or immigration services, and
(b) provision by him of the advice or services would constitute an offence under section 91.

(2) For the purpose of subsection (1) a person offers to provide advice or services if he—

(a) makes an offer to a particular person or class of person,
(b) makes arrangements for an advertisement in which he offers to provide advice or services, or
(c) makes arrangements for an advertisement in which he is described or presented as competent to provide advice or services.

(3) A person guilty of an offence under this section shall be liable on summary conviction to a fine not exceeding level 4 on the standard scale.

(4) Subsections (3) to (7) of section 91 shall have effect for the purposes of this section as they have effect for the purposes of that section.

(5) An information relating to an offence under this section may in England and Wales be tried by a magistrates' court if—

(a) it is laid within the period of six months beginning with the date (or first date) on which the offence is alleged to have been committed, or
(b) it is laid—
(i) within the period of two years beginning with that date, and
(ii) within the period of six months beginning with a date certified by the Immigration Services Commissioner as the date on which the commission of the offence came to his notice.

(6) In Scotland, proceedings for an offence under this section may be commenced—

(a) at any time within the period of six months beginning with the date (or first date) on which the offence is alleged to have been committed, or
(b) at any time within both—
(i) the period of two years beginning with that date, and
(ii) the period of six months beginning with a date specified, in a certificate signed by or on behalf of the procurator fiscal, as the date on which evidence sufficient in his opinion to warrant such proceedings came to his knowledge,

and any such certificate purporting to be so signed shall be deemed so signed unless the contrary is proved and be conclusive as to the facts stated in it.

(7)   Subsection (3) of section 136 of the Criminal Procedure (Scotland) Act 1995 (c 46) (date on which proceedings are deemed commenced) has effect to the purposes of subsection (6) as it has effect for the purposes of that section.

(8)   A complaint charging the commission of an offence under this section may in Northern Ireland be heard and determined by a magistrates' court if—

   (a)   it is made within the period of six months beginning with the date (or first date) on which the offence is alleged to have been committed, or

   (b)   it is made—

      (i)   within the period of two years beginning with that date, and

      (ii)   within the period of six months beginning with a date certified by the Immigration Services Commissioner as the date on which the commission of the offence came to his notice.]

Amendment
Inserted by the Asylum and Immigration (Treatment of Claimants, etc) Act 2004, s 39. Date in force: 1 October 2004: see SI 2004/2523, art 2, Schedule.

Miscellaneous

93   Information

(1)   No enactment or rule of law prohibiting or restricting the disclosure of information prevents a person from—

   (a)   giving the Commissioner information which is necessary for the discharge of his functions; or

   (b)   giving the Tribunal information which is necessary for the discharge of its functions.

(2)   No relevant person may at any time disclose information which—

   (a)   has been obtained by, or given to, the Commissioner under or for purposes of this Act,

   (b)   relates to an identified or identifiable individual or business, and

   (c)   is not at that time, and has not previously been, available to the public from other sources,

unless the disclosure is made with lawful authority.

(3)   For the purposes of subsection (2), a disclosure is made with lawful authority only if, and to the extent that—

   (a)   it is made with the consent of the individual or of the person for the time being carrying on the business;

   (b)   it is made for the purposes of, and is necessary for, the discharge of any of the Commissioner's functions under this Act or any Community obligation of the Commissioner;

   (c)   it is made for the purposes of any civil or criminal proceedings arising under or by virtue of this Part, or otherwise; or

   (d)   having regard to the rights and freedoms or legitimate interests of any person, the disclosure is necessary in the public interest.

(4)   A person who knowingly or recklessly discloses information in contravention of subsection (2) is guilty of an offence and liable—

   (a)   on summary conviction, to a fine not exceeding the statutory maximum; or

   (b)   on conviction on indictment, to a fine.

(5)   "Relevant person" means a person who is or has been—

(a) the Commissioner;
(b) a member of the Commissioner's staff; or
(c) an agent of the Commissioner.

Appointment
Appointment: 22 May 2000: see SI 2000/1282, art 2, Schedule.

PART VI
SUPPORT FOR ASYLUM-SEEKERS
Interpretation

94   Interpretation of Part VI

(1) In this Part—

"adjudicator" has the meaning given in section 102(2);

"asylum-seeker" means a person who is not under 18 and has made a claim for asylum which has been recorded by the Secretary of State but which has not been determined;

["asylum-seeker" means a person—
  (a) who is at least 18 years old,
  (b) who is in the United Kingdom,
  (c) who has made a claim for asylum at a place designated by the Secretary of State,
  (d) whose claim has been recorded by the Secretary of State, and
  (e) whose claim has not been determined;]

"claim for asylum" means a claim that it would be contrary to the United Kingdom's obligations under the Refugee Convention, or under Article 3 of the Human Rights Convention, for the claimant to be removed from, or required to leave, the United Kingdom;

"the Department" means the Department of Health and Social Services for Northern Ireland;

"dependant", in relation to an asylum-seeker or a supported person, means a person in the United Kingdom who—
  (a) is his spouse;
  (b) is a child of his, or of his spouse, who is under 18 and dependent on him; or
  (c) falls within such additional category, if any, as may be prescribed;

["dependant" in relation to an asylum-seeker or a supported person means a person who—
  (a) is in the United Kingdom, and
  (b) is within a prescribed class;]

"the Executive" means the Northern Ireland Housing Executive;

"housing accommodation" includes flats, lodging houses and hostels;

"local authority" means—
  (a) in England and Wales, a county council, a county borough council, a district council, a London borough council, the Common Council of the City of London or the Council of the Isles of Scilly;
  (b) in Scotland, a council constituted under section 2 of the Local Government etc (Scotland) Act 1994;

["Northern Ireland authority" has the meaning given by section 110(9);]

"supported person" means—
  (a) an asylum-seeker, or
  (b) a dependant of an asylum-seeker,
who has applied for support and for whom support is provided under section 95.

1503

(2)   References in this Part to support provided under section 95 include references to support which is provided under arrangements made by the Secretary of State under that section.

(3)   *For the purposes of this Part, a claim for asylum is determined at the end of such period beginning—*

   (a)   *on the day on which the Secretary of State notifies the claimant of his decision on the claim, or*
   (b)   *if the claimant has appealed against the Secretary of State's decision, on the day on which the appeal is disposed of,*

as may be prescribed.

[(3)   A claim for asylum shall be treated as determined for the purposes of subsection (1) at the end of such period as may be prescribed beginning with—

   (a)   the date on which the Secretary of State notifies the claimant of his decision on the claim, or
   (b)   if the claimant appeals against the Secretary of State's decision, the date on which the appeal is disposed of.

(3A)   A person shall continue to be treated as an asylum-seeker despite paragraph (e) of the definition of "asylum-seeker" in subsection (1) while—

   (a)   his household includes a dependant child who is under 18, and
   (b)   he does not have leave to enter or remain in the United Kingdom.]

(4)   An appeal is disposed of when it is no longer pending for the purposes of the Immigration Acts or the Special Immigration Appeals Commission Act 1997.

(5)   *If an asylum-seeker's household includes a child who is under 18 and a dependant of his, he is to be treated (for the purposes of this Part) as continuing to be an asylum-seeker while—*

   (a)   *the child is under 18; and*
   (b)   *he and the child remain in the United Kingdom.*

(6)   *Subsection (5) does not apply if, on or after the determination of his claim for asylum, the asylum-seeker is granted leave to enter or remain in the United Kingdom (whether or not as a result of that claim).*

(7)   For the purposes of this Part, the Secretary of State may inquire into, and decide, the age of any person.

(8)   A notice under subsection (3) must be given in writing.

(9)   If such a notice is sent by the Secretary of State by first class post, addressed—

   (a)   to the asylum-seeker's representative, or
   (b)   to the asylum-seeker's last known address,

it is to be taken to have been received by the asylum-seeker on the second day after the day on which it was posted.

Initial Commencement
Royal Assent: 11 November 1999: see s 170(3)(f).

Amendment
Sub-s (1): definition "asylum-seeker" substituted by the Nationality, Immigration and Asylum Act 2002, s 44(1), (2). Date in force: to be appointed: see the Nationality, Immigration and Asylum Act 2002, s 162(1).

1504

Sub-s (1): definition "dependant" substituted by the Nationality, Immigration and Asylum Act 2002, s 44(1), (3). Date in force: to be appointed: see the Nationality, Immigration and Asylum Act 2002, s 162(1).

Sub-s (1): definition "Northern Ireland authority" inserted by the Nationality, Immigration and Asylum Act 2002, s 60(2). Date in force: 10 February 2003: see SI 2003/1, art 2, Schedule.

Sub-s (3): substituted, by subsequent sub-ss (3), (3A), by the Nationality, Immigration and Asylum Act 2002, s 44(1), (4). Date in force: to be appointed: see the Nationality, Immigration and Asylum Act 2002, s 162(1).

Sub-ss (5), (6): repealed by the Nationality, Immigration and Asylum Act 2002, ss 44(1), (5), 161, Sch 9. Date in force: to be appointed: see the Nationality, Immigration and Asylum Act 2002, s 162(1).

Subordinate Legislation

Asylum Support (Interim Provisions) Regulations 1999, SI 1999/3056.

Asylum Support Regulations 2000, SI 2000/704.

Asylum Support (Interim Provisions) (Amendment) Regulations 2002, SI 2002/471 (made under sub-s (3)).

Asylum Support (Amendment) Regulations 2002, SI 2002472 (made under sub-s (3)).

Provision of support

95 Persons for whom support may be provided

(1) The Secretary of State may provide, or arrange for the provision of, support for—

   (a)   asylum-seekers, or
   (b)   dependants of asylum-seekers,

who appear to the Secretary of State to be destitute or to be likely to become destitute within such period as may be prescribed.

(2) *In prescribed circumstances, a person who would otherwise fall within subsection (1) is excluded.*

(3) *For the purposes of this section, a person is destitute if—*

   (a)   *he does not have adequate accommodation or any means of obtaining it (whether or not his other essential living needs are met); or*
   (b)   *he has adequate accommodation or the means of obtaining it, but cannot meet his other essential living needs.*

(4) *If a person has dependants, subsection (3) is to be read as if the references to him were references to him and his dependants taken together.*

(5) *In determining, for the purposes of this section, whether a person's accommodation is adequate, the Secretary of State—*

   (a)   *must have regard to such matters as may be prescribed for the purposes of this paragraph; but*
   (b)   *may not have regard to such matters as may be prescribed for the purposes of this paragraph or to any of the matters mentioned in subsection (6).*

(6) *Those matters are—*

   (a)   *the fact that the person concerned has no enforceable right to occupy the accommodation;*
   (b)   *the fact that he shares the accommodation, or any part of the accommodation, with one or more other persons;*
   (c)   *the fact that the accommodation is temporary;*
   (d)   *the location of the accommodation.*

(7) *In determining, for the purposes of this section, whether a person's other essential living needs are met, the Secretary of State—*

(*a*) *must have regard to such matters as may be prescribed for the purposes of this paragraph; but*

(*b*) *may not have regard to such matters as may be prescribed for the purposes of this paragraph.*

(8) *The Secretary of State may by regulations provide that items or expenses of such a description as may be prescribed are, or are not, to be treated as being an essential living need of a person for the purposes of this Part.*

[(2) Where a person has dependants, he and his dependants are destitute for the purpose of this section if they do not have and cannot obtain both—

(a) adequate accommodation, and

(b) food and other essential items.

(3) Where a person does not have dependants, he is destitute for the purpose of this section if he does not have and cannot obtain both—

(a) adequate accommodation, and

(b) food and other essential items.

(4) In determining whether accommodation is adequate for the purposes of subsection (2) or (3) the Secretary of State must have regard to any matter prescribed for the purposes of this subsection.

(5) In determining whether accommodation is adequate for the purposes of subsection (2) or (3) the Secretary of State may not have regard to—

(a) whether a person has an enforceable right to occupy accommodation,

(b) whether a person shares all or part of accommodation,

(c) whether accommodation is temporary or permanent,

(d) the location of accommodation, or

(e) any other matter prescribed for the purposes of this subsection.

(6) The Secretary of State may by regulations specify items which are or are not to be treated as essential items for the purposes of subsections (2) and (3).

(7) The Secretary of State may by regulations—

(a) provide that a person is not to be treated as destitute for the purposes of this Part in specified circumstances;

(b) enable or require the Secretary of State in deciding whether a person is destitute to have regard to income which he or a dependant of his might reasonably be expected to have;

(c) enable or require the Secretary of State in deciding whether a person is destitute to have regard to support which is or might reasonably be expected to be available to the person or a dependant of his;

(d) enable or require the Secretary of State in deciding whether a person is destitute to have regard to assets of a prescribed kind which he or a dependant of his has or might reasonably be expected to have;

(e) make provision as to the valuation of assets.]

(9) Support may be provided subject to conditions.

[(9A) A condition imposed under subsection (9) may, in particular, relate to—

(a) any matter relating to the use of the support provided, or

(b) compliance with a restriction imposed under paragraph 21 of Schedule 2 to the 1971 Act (temporary admission or release from detention) or paragraph 2 or 5 of Schedule 3 to that Act (restriction pending deportation).]

(10) The conditions must be set out in writing.

(11)   A copy of the conditions must be given to the supported person.

(12)   Schedule 8 gives the Secretary of State power to make regulations supplementing this section.

(13)   Schedule 9 makes temporary provision for support in the period before the coming into force of this section.

Initial Commencement
Sub-s (13): Royal Assent: 11 November 1999: see s 170(3)(g).
Sub-ss (1)–(12): To be appointed: see s 170(4).

Appointment
Sub-ss (1)–(11): Appointment (for the purposes of enabling subordinate legislation to be made): 1 January 2000: see SI 1999/3190, art 2, Schedule.
Sub-ss (1)–(11): Appointment (for remaining purposes): 3 April 2000: see SI 2000/464, art 2, Schedule.
Sub-ss (3)–(8): Appointment (for certain purposes): 6 December 1999: see SI 1999/3190, art 2, Schedule.
Sub-s (12): Appointment: 1 January 2000: see SI 1999/3190, art 2, Schedule.

Amendment
Sub-ss (2)–(8): substituted, by subsequent sub-ss (2)–(7), by the Nationality, Immigration and Asylum Act 2002, s 44(1), (6). Date in force: to be appointed: see the Nationality, Immigration and Asylum Act 2002, s 162(1).
Sub-s (9A): inserted by the Nationality, Immigration and Asylum Act 2002, s 50(1). Date in force: 7 November 2002: see the Nationality, Immigration and Asylum Act 2002, s 162(2)(o).

Subordinate Legislation
Asylum Support Regulations 2000, SI 2000/704.
Asylum Support (Amendment) (No 3) Regulations 2002, SI 2002/3110 (made under sub-s (12)).

96   Ways in which support may be provided

(1)   Support may be provided under section 95—

   (a)   by providing accommodation appearing to the Secretary of State to be adequate for the needs of the supported person and his dependants (if any);
   (b)   *by providing what appear to the Secretary of State to be essential living needs of the supported person and his dependants (if any);*
   [(b)   by providing the supported person and his dependants (if any) with food and other essential items;]
   (c)   to enable the supported person (if he is the asylum-seeker) to meet what appear to the Secretary of State to be expenses (other than legal expenses or other expenses of a prescribed description) incurred in connection with his claim for asylum;
   (d)   to enable the asylum-seeker and his dependants to attend bail proceedings in connection with his detention under any provision of the Immigration Acts; or
   (e)   to enable the asylum-seeker and his dependants to attend bail proceedings in connection with the detention of a dependant of his under any such provision.

(2)   If the Secretary of State considers that the circumstances of a particular case are exceptional, he may provide support under section 95 in such other ways as he considers necessary to enable the supported person and his dependants (if any) to be supported.

(3)   ...

(4)   ...

(5)   ...

(6)   ...

Appointment
Appointment: 3 April 2000: see SI 2000/464, art 2, Schedule.

Amendment
Sub-s (1): para (b) substituted by the Nationality, Immigration and Asylum Act 2002, s 45(1).
Date in force: to be appointed: see the Nationality, Immigration and Asylum Act 2002, s 162(1).
Sub-s (3): repealed by SI 2002/782, art 2. Date in force: 8 April 2002: see SI 2002/782, art 1.
Sub-ss (4)–(6): repealed by the Nationality, Immigration and Asylum Act 2002, ss 61(a), 161, Sch 9. Date in force: 7 November 2002: see the Nationality, Immigration and Asylum Act 2002, s 162(2)(s).

97   Supplemental

(1)   When exercising his power under section 95 to provide accommodation, the Secretary of State must have regard to—

    (a)   the fact that the accommodation is to be temporary pending determination of the asylum-seeker's claim;

    (b)   the desirability, in general, of providing accommodation in areas in which there is a ready supply of accommodation; and

    (c)   such other matters (if any) as may be prescribed.

(2)   But he may not have regard to—

    (a)   any preference that the supported person or his dependants (if any) may have as to the locality in which the accommodation is to be provided; or

    (b)   such other matters (if any) as may be prescribed.

(3)   The Secretary of State may by order repeal all or any of the following—

    (a)   subsection (1)(a);
    (b)   subsection (1)(b);
    (c)   subsection (2)(a).

(4)   When exercising his power under section 95 to provide *essential living needs* [food and other essential items], the Secretary of State—

    (a)   must have regard to such matters as may be prescribed for the purposes of this paragraph; but

    (b)   may not have regard to such other matters as may be prescribed for the purposes of this paragraph.

(5)   In addition, when exercising his power under section 95 to provide *essential living needs* [food and other essential items], the Secretary of State may limit the overall amount of the expenditure which he incurs in connection with a particular supported person—

    (a)   to such portion of the income support applicable amount provided under section 124 of the Social Security Contributions and Benefits Act 1992, or

    (b)   to such portion of any components of that amount,

as he considers appropriate having regard to the temporary nature of the support that he is providing.

(6)   For the purposes of subsection (5), any support of a kind falling within section 96(1)(c) is to be treated as if it were the provision of essential *living needs* [items].

(7)   In determining how to provide, or arrange for the provision of, support under section 95, the Secretary of State may disregard any preference which the supported person or his dependants (if any) may have as to the way in which the support is to be given.

Appointment
Appointment (for remaining purposes): 3 April 2000: see SI 2000/464, art 2, Schedule.
Appointment (for the purpose of enabling subordinate legislation to be made): 1 January 2000: see SI 1999/3190, art 2, Schedule.

Amendment
Sub-s (4): words "essential living needs" in italics repealed and subsequent words in square brackets substituted by the Nationality, Immigration and Asylum Act 2002, s 45(2)(a). Date in force: to be appointed: see the Nationality, Immigration and Asylum Act 2002, s 162(1).
Sub-s (5): words "essential living needs" in italics repealed and subsequent words in square brackets substituted by the Nationality, Immigration and Asylum Act 2002, s 45(2)(b). Date in force: to be appointed: see the Nationality, Immigration and Asylum Act 2002, s 162(1).
Sub-s (6): words "living needs" in italics repealed and subsequent word in square brackets substituted by the Nationality, Immigration and Asylum Act 2002, s 45(2)(c). Date in force: to be appointed: see the Nationality, Immigration and Asylum Act 2002, s 162(1).

Subordinate Legislation
Asylum Support Regulations 2000, SI 2000/704.

98   Temporary support

(1)   The Secretary of State may provide, or arrange for the provision of, support for—

(a)   asylum-seekers, or
(b)   dependants of asylum-seekers,

who it appears to the Secretary of State may be destitute.

(2)   Support may be provided under this section only until the Secretary of State is able to determine whether support may be provided under section 95.

(3)   Subsections (2) to (11) of section 95 apply for the purposes of this section as they apply for the purposes of that section.

Appointment
Sub-ss (1), (2): Appointment: 3 April 2000: see SI 2000/464, art 2, Schedule.
Sub-s (3): Appointment (for remaining purposes): 3 April 2000: see SI 2000/464, art 2, Schedule.
Sub-s (3): Appointment (for the purpose of enabling subordinate legislation to be made under s 95 as applied by this subsection): 1 March 2000: see SI 2000/464, art 2, Schedule.

Support and assistance by local authorities etc

99   Provision of support by local authorities

(1)   A local authority [or Northern Ireland authority] may provide support for asylum-seekers and their dependants (if any) in accordance with arrangements made by the Secretary of State under section 95 [or 98].

[(2)   Support may be provided by an authority in accordance with arrangements made with the authority or with another person.

(3)   Support may be provided by an authority in accordance with arrangements made under section 95 only in one or more of the ways mentioned in section 96(1) and (2).]

(4)   [An authority] may incur reasonable expenditure in connection with the preparation of proposals for entering into arrangements under section 95 [or 98].

(5)   The powers conferred on [an authority] by this section include power to—

(a) provide services outside their area;
(b) provide services jointly with one or more [other bodies];
(c) form a company for the purpose of providing services;
(d) tender for contracts (whether alone or with any other person).

Initial Commencement
Sub-ss (4), (5): Royal Assent: 11 November 1999: see s 170(3)(h).

Appointment
Sub-ss (1)–(3): Appointment: 3 April 2000: see SI 2000/464, art 2, Schedule.

Amendment
Sub-s (1): words "or Northern Ireland authority" in square brackets inserted by the Nationality, Immigration and Asylum Act 2002, s 56(1), (2)(a). Date in force: 7 November 2002: see the Nationality, Immigration and Asylum Act 2002, s 162(2)(p).
Sub-s (1): words "or 98" in square brackets inserted by the Nationality, Immigration and Asylum Act 2002, s 56(1), (2)(b). Date in force: 7 November 2002: see the Nationality, Immigration and Asylum Act 2002, s 162(2)(p).
Sub-ss (2), (3): substituted by the Nationality, Immigration and Asylum Act 2002, s 56(1), (3). Date in force: 7 November 2002: see the Nationality, Immigration and Asylum Act 2002, s 162(2)(p).
Sub-s (4): words "An authority" in square brackets substituted by the Nationality, Immigration and Asylum Act 2002, s 56(1), (4)(a). Date in force: 7 November 2002: see the Nationality, Immigration and Asylum Act 2002, s 162(2)(p).
Sub-s (4): words "or 98" in square brackets inserted by the Nationality, Immigration and Asylum Act 2002, s 56(1), (4)(b). Date in force: 7 November 2002: see the Nationality, Immigration and Asylum Act 2002, s 162(2)(p).
Sub-s (5): words "an authority" in square brackets substituted by the Nationality, Immigration and Asylum Act 2002, s 56(1), (5)(a). Date in force: 7 November 2002: see the Nationality, Immigration and Asylum Act 2002, s 162(2)(p).
Sub-s (5): in para (b) words "other bodies" in square brackets substituted by the Nationality, Immigration and Asylum Act 2002, s 56(1), (5)(b). Date in force: 7 November 2002: see the Nationality, Immigration and Asylum Act 2002, s 162(2)(p).

100   Local authority and other assistance for Secretary of State

(1) This section applies if the Secretary of State asks—

(a) a local authority,
(b) a registered social landlord,
(c) a registered housing association in Scotland or Northern Ireland, or
(d) the Executive,

to assist him to exercise his power under section 95 to provide accommodation.

(2) The person to whom the request is made must co-operate in giving the Secretary of State such assistance in the exercise of that power as is reasonable in the circumstances.

(3) Subsection (2) does not require a registered social landlord to act beyond its powers.

(4) A local authority must supply to the Secretary of State such information about their housing accommodation (whether or not occupied) as he may from time to time request.

(5) The information must be provided in such form and manner as the Secretary of State may direct.

(6) "Registered social landlord" has the same meaning as in Part I of the Housing Act 1996.

(7) "Registered housing association" has the same meaning—

(a) in relation to Scotland, as in the Housing Associations Act 1985; and
(b) in relation to Northern Ireland, as in Part II of the Housing (Northern Ireland) Order 1992.

Appointment
Appointment: 3 April 2000: see SI 2000/464, art 2, Schedule.

101 Reception zones

(1) The Secretary of State may by order designate as reception zones—

(a) areas in England and Wales consisting of the areas of one or more local authorities;
(b) areas in Scotland consisting of the areas of one or more local authorities;
(c) Northern Ireland.

(2) Subsection (3) applies if the Secretary of State considers that—

(a) a local authority whose area is within a reception zone has suitable housing accommodation within that zone; or
(b) the Executive has suitable housing accommodation.

(3) The Secretary of State may direct the local authority or the Executive to make available such of the accommodation as may be specified in the direction for a period so specified—

(a) to him for the purpose of providing support under section 95; or
(b) to a person with whom the Secretary of State has made arrangements under section 95.

(4) A period specified in a direction under subsection (3)—

(a) begins on a date so specified; and
(b) must not exceed five years.

(5) A direction under subsection (3) is enforceable, on an application made on behalf of the Secretary of State, by injunction or in Scotland an order under section 45(b) of the Court of Session Act 1988.

(6) The Secretary of State's power to give a direction under subsection (3) in respect of a particular reception zone must be exercised by reference to criteria specified for the purposes of this subsection in the order designating that zone.

(7) The Secretary of State may not give a direction under subsection (3) in respect of a local authority in Scotland unless the Scottish Ministers have confirmed to him that the criteria specified in the designation order concerned are in their opinion met in relation to that authority.

(8) Housing accommodation is suitable for the purposes of subsection (2) if it—

(a) is unoccupied;
(b) would be likely to remain unoccupied for the foreseeable future if not made available; and
(c) is appropriate for the accommodation of persons supported under this Part or capable of being made so with minor work.

(9) If housing accommodation for which a direction under this section is, for the time being, in force—

(a) is not appropriate for the accommodation of persons supported under this Part, but
(b) is capable of being made so with minor work,

the direction may require the body to whom it is given to secure that that work is done without delay.

(10)   The Secretary of State must make regulations with respect to the general management of any housing accommodation for which a direction under subsection (3) is, for the time being, in force.

(11)   Regulations under subsection (10) must include provision—

(a)   as to the method to be used in determining the amount of rent or other charges to be payable in relation to the accommodation;

(b)   as to the times at which payments of rent or other charges are to be made;

(c)   as to the responsibility for maintenance of, and repairs to, the accommodation;

(d)   enabling the accommodation to be inspected, in such circumstances as may be prescribed, by the body to which the direction was given;

(e)   with respect to the condition in which the accommodation is to be returned when the direction ceases to have effect.

(12)   Regulations under subsection (10) may, in particular, include provision—

(a)   for the cost, or part of the cost, of minor work required by a direction under this section to be met by the Secretary of State in prescribed circumstances;

(b)   as to the maximum amount of expenditure which a body may be required to incur as a result of a direction under this section.

(13)   The Secretary of State must by regulations make provision ("the dispute resolution procedure") for resolving disputes arising in connection with the operation of any regulations made under subsection (10).

(14)   Regulations under subsection (13) must include provision—

(a)   requiring a dispute to be resolved in accordance with the dispute resolution procedure;

(b)   requiring the parties to a dispute to comply with obligations imposed on them by the procedure; and

(c)   for the decision of the person resolving a dispute in accordance with the procedure to be final and binding on the parties.

(15)   Before—

(a)   designating a reception zone in Great Britain,

(b)   determining the criteria to be included in the order designating the zone, or

(c)   making regulations under subsection (13),

the Secretary of State must consult such local authorities, local authority associations and other persons as he thinks appropriate.

(16)   Before—

(a)   designating Northern Ireland as a reception zone, or

(b)   determining the criteria to be included in the order designating Northern Ireland,

the Secretary of State must consult the Executive and such other persons as he thinks appropriate.

(17)   Before making regulations under subsection (10) which extend only to Northern Ireland, the Secretary of State must consult the Executive and such other persons as he thinks appropriate.

(18)   Before making any other regulations under subsection (10), the Secretary of State must consult—

(a) such local authorities, local authority associations and other persons as he thinks appropriate; and

(b) if the regulations extend to Northern Ireland, the Executive.

Appointment
Appointment: 3 April 2000: see SI 2000/464, art 2, Schedule.

Appeals

102 Asylum Support Adjudicators

(1) There are to be adjudicators to hear appeals under this Part.

(2) A person appointed as an adjudicator under this Part is to be known as an Asylum Support Adjudicator (but is referred to in this Part as "an adjudicator").

(3) Schedule 10 makes further provision with respect to adjudicators.

Appointment
Appointment: 3 April 2000: see SI 2000/464, art 2, Schedule.

103   *Appeals* [**103 Appeals: general**]

(1) If, on an application for support under section 95, the Secretary of State decides that the applicant does not qualify for support under that section, the applicant may appeal to an adjudicator.

(2) If the Secretary of State decides to stop providing support for a person under section 95 before that support would otherwise have come to an end, that person may appeal to an adjudicator.

[(2A) If the Secretary of State decides not to provide accommodation for a person under section 4, or not to continue to provide accommodation for a person under section 4, the person may appeal to an adjudicator.]

(3) On an appeal under this section, the adjudicator may—

(a) require the Secretary of State to reconsider the matter;
(b) substitute his decision for the decision appealed against; or
(c) dismiss the appeal.

(4) The adjudicator must give his reasons in writing.

(5) The decision of the adjudicator is final.

(6) If an appeal is dismissed, no further application by the appellant for support under [section 4 or 95] is to be entertained unless the Secretary of State is satisfied that there has been a material change in the circumstances.

(7) The Secretary of State may by regulations provide for decisions as to where support provided under [section 4 or 95] is to be provided to be appealable to an adjudicator under this Part.

(8) Regulations under subsection (7) may provide for any provision of this section to have effect, in relation to an appeal brought by virtue of the regulations, subject to such modifications as may be prescribed.

(9) The Secretary of State may pay any reasonable travelling expenses incurred by an appellant in connection with attendance at any place for the purposes of an appeal under this section.

[[(1) This section applies where a person has applied for support under all or any of the following provisions—

(a)   section 4,
(b)   section 95, and
(c)   section 17 of the Nationality, Immigration and Asylum Act 2002.]

(2)   The person may appeal to an adjudicator against a decision that the person is not qualified to receive the support for which he has applied.

(3)   The person may also appeal to an adjudicator against a decision to stop providing support under a provision mentioned in subsection (1).

(4)   But subsection (3) does not apply—

(a)   to a decision to stop providing support under one of the provisions mentioned in subsection (1) if it is to be replaced immediately by support under [another of those provisions], or
(b)   to a decision taken on the ground that the person is no longer an asylum-seeker or the dependant of an asylum-seeker.

(5)   On an appeal under this section an adjudicator may—

(a)   require the Secretary of State to reconsider a matter;
(b)   substitute his decision for the decision against which the appeal is brought;
(c)   dismiss the appeal.

(6)   An adjudicator must give his reasons in writing.

(7)   If an appeal under this section is dismissed the Secretary of State shall not consider any further application by the appellant for support under a provision mentioned in [subsection (1)] unless the Secretary of State thinks there has been a material change in circumstances.

(8)   An appeal under this section may not be brought or continued by a person who is outside the United Kingdom.]

Appointment
Appointment: 3 April 2000: see SI 2000/464, art 2, Schedule.

Amendment
Substituted, together with ss 103A, 103B for this section as originally enacted, by the Nationality, Immigration and Asylum Act 2002, s 53. Date in force: to be appointed: see the Nationality, Immigration and Asylum Act 2002, s 162(1).
Sub-s (2A): inserted by the Asylum and Immigration (Treatment of Claimants, etc) Act 2004, s 10(3)(a), (6). Date in force: 31 March 2005: see SI 2005/372, art 2.
Sub-ss (6), (7): words "section 4 or 95" in square brackets substituted by the Asylum and Immigration (Treatment of Claimants, etc) Act 2004, s 10(3)(b), (6). Date in force: 31 March 2005: see SI 2005/372, art 2.
Sub-s (1) (as substituted by the Nationality, Immigration and Asylum Act 2002, s 53): substituted by the Asylum and Immigration (Treatment of Claimants, etc) Act 2004, s 10(4)(a), (6). Date in force: 31 March 2005: see SI 2005/372, art 2.
Sub-s (4)(a) (as substituted by the Nationality, Immigration and Asylum Act 2002, s 53): words "another of those provisions" in square brackets substituted by the Asylum and Immigration (Treatment of Claimants, etc) Act 2004, s 10(b), (6). Date in force: 31 March 2005: see SI 2005/372, art 2.
Sub-s (7) (as substituted by the Nationality, Immigration and Asylum Act 2002, s 53): words "subsection (1)" in square brackets substituted by the Asylum and Immigration (Treatment of Claimants, etc) Act 2004, s 10(4)(c), (6). Date in force: 31 March 2005: see SI 2005/372, art 2.

[103A   Appeals: location of support under] [section 4 or 95]

[(1)   The Secretary of State may by regulations provide for a decision as to where support provided under [section 4 or 95] is to be provided to be appealable to an adjudicator under this Part.

(2)   Regulations under this section may provide for a provision of section 103 to have effect in relation to an appeal under the regulations with specified modifications.]

Amendment
Section heading: words "section 4 or 95" in square brackets substituted by the Asylum and Immigration (Treatment of Claimants, etc) Act 2004, s 10(5), (6). Date in force: 31 March 2005: see SI 2005/372, art 2.
Substituted, together with ss 103, 103B for s 103 as originally enacted, by the Nationality, Immigration and Asylum Act 2002, s 53. Date in force: to be appointed: see the Nationality, Immigration and Asylum Act 2002, s 162(1).
Sub-s (1): words "section 4 or 95" in square brackets substituted by the Asylum and Immigration (Treatment of Claimants, etc) Act 2004, s 10(5), (6). Date in force: 31 March 2005: see SI 2005/372, art 2.

[103B   Appeals: travelling expenses]

[The Secretary of State may pay reasonable travelling expenses incurred by an appellant in connection with attendance for the purposes of an appeal under or by virtue of section 103 or 103A.]

Amendment
Substituted, together with ss 103, 103A for s 103 as originally enacted, by the Nationality, Immigration and Asylum Act 2002, s 53. Date in force: to be appointed: see the Nationality, Immigration and Asylum Act 2002, s 162(1).

104   Secretary of State's rules

(1)   The Secretary of State may make rules regulating—

   (a)   the bringing of appeals under this Part; and
   (b)   the practice and procedure of the adjudicators.

(2)   The rules may, in particular, make provision—

   (a)   for the period within which an appeal must be brought;
   (b)   as to the burden of proof on an appeal;
   (c)   as to the giving and admissibility of evidence;
   (d)   for summoning witnesses;
   (e)   for an appeal to be heard in the absence of the appellant;
   (f)   for determining an appeal without a hearing;
   (g)   requiring reports of decisions of adjudicators to be published;
   (h)   conferring such ancillary powers on adjudicators as the Secretary of State considers necessary for the proper discharge of their functions.

(3)   In making the rules, the Secretary of State must have regard to the desirability of securing, so far as is reasonably practicable, that appeals are brought and disposed of with the minimum of delay.

Appointment
Appointment: 1 January 2000: see SI 1999/3190, art 2, Schedule.

Subordinate Legislation
Asylum Support Appeals (Procedure) Rules 2000, SI 2000/541.
Asylum Support Appeals (Procedure) (Amendment) Rules 2003, SI 2003/1735.

Offences

105   False representations

(1)   A person is guilty of an offence if, with a view to obtaining support for himself or any other person under any provision made by or under this Part, he—

(a) makes a statement or representation which he knows is false in a material particular;

(b) produces or gives to a person exercising functions under this Part, or knowingly causes or allows to be produced or given to such a person, any document or information which he knows is false in a material particular;

(c) fails, without reasonable excuse, to notify a change of circumstances when required to do so in accordance with any provision made by or under this Part; or

(d) without reasonable excuse, knowingly causes another person to fail to notify a change of circumstances which that other person was required to notify in accordance with any provision made by or under this Part.

(2) A person guilty of an offence under this section is liable on summary conviction to imprisonment for a term not exceeding *three months* [51 weeks] or to a fine not exceeding level 5 on the standard scale, or to both.

Initial Commencement
Royal Assent: 11 November 1999: see s 170(3)(i).

Amendment
Sub-s (2): words "three months" in italics repealed and subsequent words in square brackets substituted by the Criminal Justice Act 2003, s 280(2), (3), Sch 26, para 53(1), (2). Date in force: to be appointed: see the Criminal Justice Act 2003, s 336(3).

106   Dishonest representations

(1) A person is guilty of an offence if, with a view to obtaining any benefit or other payment or advantage under this Part for himself or any other person, he dishonestly—

(a) makes a statement or representation which is false in a material particular;

(b) produces or gives to a person exercising functions under this Part, or causes or allows to be produced or given to such a person, any document or information which is false in a material particular;

(c) fails to notify a change of circumstances when required to do so in accordance with any provision made by or under this Part; or

(d) causes another person to fail to notify a change of circumstances which that other person was required to notify in accordance with any provision made by or under this Part.

(2) A person guilty of an offence under this section is liable—

(a) on summary conviction, to imprisonment for a term not exceeding six months or to a fine not exceeding the statutory maximum, or to both; or

(b) on conviction on indictment, to imprisonment for a term not exceeding seven years or to a fine, or to both.

(3) In the application of this section to Scotland, in subsection (1) for "dishonestly" substitute "knowingly".

Initial Commencement
Royal Assent: 11 November 1999: see s 170(3)(i).

107   Delay or obstruction

(1) A person is guilty of an offence if, without reasonable excuse, he—

(a) intentionally delays or obstructs a person exercising functions conferred by or under this Part; or

(b)   refuses or neglects to answer a question, give any information or produce a document when required to do so in accordance with any provision made by or under this Part.

(2)   A person guilty of an offence under subsection (1) is liable on summary conviction to a fine not exceeding level 3 on the standard scale.

Initial Commencement
Royal Assent: 11 November 1999: see s 170(3)(i).

108   Failure of sponsor to maintain

(1)   A person is guilty of an offence if, during any period in respect of which he has given a written undertaking in pursuance of the immigration rules to be responsible for the maintenance and accommodation of another person—

(a)   he persistently refuses or neglects, without reasonable excuse, to maintain that person in accordance with the undertaking; and

(b)   in consequence of his refusal or neglect, support under any provision made by or under this Part is provided for or in respect of that person.

(2)   A person guilty of an offence under this section is liable on summary conviction to imprisonment for a term not exceeding *3 months* [51 weeks] or to a fine not exceeding level 4 on the standard scale, or to both.

(3)   For the purposes of this section, a person is not to be taken to have refused or neglected to maintain another person by reason only of anything done or omitted in furtherance of a trade dispute.

Initial Commencement
Royal Assent: 11 November 1999: see s 170(3)(i).

Amendment
Sub-s (2): words "3 months" in italics repealed and subsequent words in square brackets substituted by the Criminal Justice Act 2003, s 280(2), (3), Sch 26, para 53(1), (3). Date in force: to be appointed: see the Criminal Justice Act 2003, s 336(3).

109   Supplemental

(1)   If an offence under section 105, 106, 107 or 108 committed by a body corporate is proved—

(a)   to have been committed with the consent or connivance of an officer, or
(b)   to be attributable to neglect on his part,

the officer as well as the body corporate is guilty of the offence and liable to be proceeded against and punished accordingly.

(2)   "Officer", in relation to a body corporate, means a director, manager, secretary or other similar officer of the body, or a person purporting to act in such a capacity.

(3)   If the affairs of a body corporate are managed by its members, subsection (1) applies in relation to the acts and defaults of a member in connection with his functions of management as if he were a director of the body corporate.

(4)   If an offence under section 105, 106, 107 or 108 committed by a partnership in Scotland is proved—

(a)   to have been committed with the consent or connivance of a partner, or
(b)   to be attributable to neglect on his part,

the partner as well as the partnership is guilty of the offence and liable to be proceeded against and punished accordingly.

(5) "Partner" includes a person purporting to act as a partner.

Initial Commencement
Royal Assent: 11 November 1999: see s 170(3)(i).

Expenditure

110   Payments to local authorities

(1) The Secretary of State may from time to time pay to any local authority or Northern Ireland authority such sums as he considers appropriate in respect of expenditure incurred, or to be incurred, by the authority in connection with—

    (a) persons who are, or have been, asylum-seekers; and
    (b) their dependants.

(2) The Secretary of State may from time to time pay to any—

    (a) local authority,
    (b) local authority association, or
    (c) Northern Ireland authority,

such sums as he considers appropriate in respect of services provided by the authority or association in connection with the discharge of functions under this Part.

(3) The Secretary of State may make payments to any local authority towards the discharge of any liability of supported persons or their dependants in respect of council tax payable to that authority.

(4) The Secretary of State must pay to a body to which a direction under section 101(3) is given such sums as he considers represent the reasonable costs to that body of complying with the direction.

(5) The Secretary of State must pay to a directed body sums determined to be payable in relation to accommodation made available by that body under section 101(3)(a).

(6) The Secretary of State may pay to a directed body sums determined to be payable in relation to accommodation made available by that body under section 101(3)(b).

(7) In subsections (5) and (6)—

    "determined" means determined in accordance with regulations made by virtue of subsection (11)(a) of section 101, and
    "directed body" means a body to which a direction under subsection (3) of section 101 is given.

(8) Payments under subsection (1), (2) or (3) may be made on such terms, and subject to such conditions, as the Secretary of State may determine.

(9) "Northern Ireland authority" means—

    (a) the Executive; or
    (b) a Health and Social Services Board established under Article 16 of the Health and Personal Social Services (Northern Ireland) Order 1972[; or
    (c) a Health and Social Services trust established under the Health and Personal Social Services (Northern Ireland) Order 1991 (SI 1991/194 (NI 1)].

Initial Commencement
Sub-ss (1), (2): Royal Assent: 11 November 1999: see s 170(3)(j).
Sub-s (8): Royal Assent (for certain purposes): 11 November 1999: see s 170(3)(j).
Sub-ss (3)–(7), (9): To be appointed: see s 170(4).
Sub-s (8): To be appointed (for remaining purposes): see s 170(4).

Appointment
Sub-ss (3)–(7): Appointment: 3 April 2000: see SI 2000/464, art 2, Schedule.
Sub-s (8): Appointment (for remaining purposes): 3 April 2000: see SI 2000/464, art 2, Schedule.
Sub-s (9): Appointment: 6 December 1999: see SI 1999/3190, art 2, Schedule.

Amendment
Sub-s (9): para (c) and word "; or" immediately preceding it inserted by the Nationality, Immigration and Asylum Act 2002, s 60(1). Date in force: 10 February 2003: see SI 2003/1, art 2, Schedule.

See Further
See further, in relation to the modification of this section in so far as it applies to the definition of asylum-seeker (as set out in s 94(1) hereof): the Nationality, Immigration and Asylum Act 2002, s 48.

111 Grants to voluntary organisations

(1) The Secretary of State may make grants of such amounts as he thinks appropriate to voluntary organisations in connection with—

(a) the provision by them of support (of whatever nature) to persons who are, or have been, asylum-seekers and to their dependants; and
(b) connected matters.

(2) Grants may be made on such terms, and subject to such conditions, as the Secretary of State may determine.

Initial Commencement
Royal Assent: 11 November 1999: see s 170(3)(k).

See Further
See further, in relation to the modification of this section in so far as it applies to the definition of asylum-seeker (as set out in s 94(1) hereof): the Nationality, Immigration and Asylum Act 2002, s 48.

112 Recovery of expenditure on support: misrepresentation etc

(1) This section applies if, on an application made by the Secretary of State, the court determines that—

(a) a person ("A") has misrepresented or failed to disclose a material fact (whether fraudulently or otherwise); and
(b) as a consequence of the misrepresentation or failure, support has been provided under section 95 or 98 (whether or not to A).

(2) If the support was provided by the Secretary of State, the court may order A to pay to the Secretary of State an amount representing the monetary value of the support which would not have been provided but for A's misrepresentation or failure.

(3) If the support was provided by another person ("B") in accordance with arrangements made with the Secretary of State under section 95 or 98, the court may order A to pay to the Secretary of State an amount representing the payment to B which would not have been made but for A's misrepresentation or failure.

(4) "Court" means a county court or, in Scotland, the sheriff.

Appointment
Appointment: 3 April 2000: see SI 2000/464, art 2, Schedule.

113 Recovery of expenditure on support from sponsor

(1) This section applies if—

(a) a person ("the sponsor") has given a written undertaking in pursuance of the immigration rules to be responsible for the maintenance and accommodation of another person; and

(b) during any period in relation to which the undertaking applies, support under section 95 is provided to or in respect of that other person.

(2) The Secretary of State may make a complaint against the sponsor to a magistrates' court for an order under this section.

(3) The court—

(a) must have regard to all the circumstances (and in particular to the sponsor's income); and

(b) may order him to pay to the Secretary of State such sum (weekly or otherwise) as it considers appropriate.

(4) But such a sum is not to include any amount attributable otherwise than to support provided under section 95.

(5) In determining—

(a) whether to order any payments to be made in respect of support provided under section 95 for any period before the complaint was made, or

(b) the amount of any such payments,

the court must disregard any amount by which the sponsor's current income exceeds his income during that period.

(6) An order under this section is enforceable as a magistrates' court maintenance order within the meaning of section 150(1) of the Magistrates' Courts Act 1980.

(7) In the application of this section to Scotland—

(a) omit subsection (6);

(b) for references to a complaint substitute references to an application; and

(c) for references to a magistrates' court substitute references to the sheriff.

(8) In the application of this section to Northern Ireland, for references to a magistrates' court substitute references to a court of summary jurisdiction and for subsection (6) substitute—

"(6) An order under this section is an order to which Article 98(11) of the Magistrates' Courts (Northern Ireland) Order 1981 applies."

Appointment
Appointment: 3 April 2000: see SI 2000/464, art 2, Schedule.

114   Overpayments

(1) Subsection (2) applies if, as a result of an error on the part of the Secretary of State, support has been provided to a person under section 95 or 98.

(2) The Secretary of State may recover from a person who is, or has been, a supported person an amount representing the monetary value of support provided to him as a result of the error.

(3) An amount recoverable under subsection (2) may be recovered as if it were a debt due to the Secretary of State.

(4) The Secretary of State may by regulations make provision for other methods of recovery, including deductions from support provided under section 95.

Appointment

Appointment (for the purpose of enabling subordinate legislation to be made): 1 January 2000: see SI 1999/3190, art 2, Schedule.

Appointment (for remaining purposes): 3 April 2000: see SI 2000/464, art 2, Schedule.

Subordinate Legislation

Asylum Support Regulations 2000, SI 2000/704.

Exclusions

115   Exclusion from benefits

(1)   No person is entitled to income-based jobseeker's allowance under the Jobseekers Act 1995 [or to state pension credit under the State Pension Credit Act 2002] or to—

(a)   attendance allowance,
(b)   severe disablement allowance,
(c)   [carer's allowance],
(d)   disability living allowance,
(e)   income support,
(f)   ...
(g)   ...
(h)   a social fund payment,
(i)   child benefit,
(j)   housing benefit, or
(k)   council tax benefit,

under the Social Security Contributions and Benefits Act 1992 while he is a person to whom this section applies.

(2)   No person in Northern Ireland is entitled to—

(a)   income-based jobseeker's allowance under the Jobseekers (Northern Ireland) Order 1995, or
(b)   any of the benefits mentioned in paragraphs (a) to (j) of subsection (1),

under the Social Security Contributions and Benefits (Northern Ireland) Act 1992 while he is a person to whom this section applies.

(3)   This section applies to a person subject to immigration control unless he falls within such category or description, or satisfies such conditions, as may be prescribed.

(4)   Regulations under subsection (3) may provide for a person to be treated for prescribed purposes only as not being a person to whom this section applies.

(5)   In relation to [child benefit], "prescribed" means prescribed by regulations made by the Treasury.

(6)   In relation to the matters mentioned in subsection (2) (except so far as it relates to [child benefit]), "prescribed" means prescribed by regulations made by the Department.

(7)   Section 175(3) to (5) of the Social Security Contributions and Benefits Act 1992 (supplemental powers in relation to regulations) applies to regulations made by the Secretary of State or the Treasury under subsection (3) as it applies to regulations made under that Act.

(8)   Sections 133(2), 171(2) and 172(4) of the Social Security Contributions and Benefits (Northern Ireland) Act 1992 apply to regulations made by the Department under subsection (3) as they apply to regulations made by the Department under that Act.

(9)   "A person subject to immigration control" means a person who is not a national of an EEA State and who—

  (a)   requires leave to enter or remain in the United Kingdom but does not have it;
  (b)   has leave to enter or remain in the United Kingdom which is subject to a condition that he does not have recourse to public funds;
  (c)   has leave to enter or remain in the United Kingdom given as a result of a maintenance undertaking; or
  (d)   has leave to enter or remain in the United Kingdom only as a result of paragraph 17 of Schedule 4.

(10)   "Maintenance undertaking", in relation to any person, means a written undertaking given by another person in pursuance of the immigration rules to be responsible for that person's maintenance and accommodation.

Initial Commencement
Sub-ss (1), (2): To be appointed (in accordance with the first regulations made under Sch 8): see s 170(2), (4).
Sub-ss (3)–(10): To be appointed: see s 170(4).

Appointment
Sub-ss (1), (2): Appointment: 3 April 2000 (in accordance with SI 2000/704, the first regulations made under Sch 8): see s 170(2), (4).
Sub-ss (3)–(10): Appointment (for the purpose of enabling subordinate legislation to be made): 1 January 2000: see SI 1999/3190, art 2, Schedule.
Sub-ss (3)–(10): Appointment (for remaining purposes): 3 April 2000: see SI 2000/464, art 2, Schedule.

Amendment
Sub-s (1): words "or to state pension credit under the State Pension Credit Act 2002" in square brackets inserted by the State Pension Credit Act 2002, s 4(2). Date in force (for the purpose only of exercising any power to make regulations or orders): 2 July 2002: see SI 2002/1691, art 2(d). Date in force (for remaining purposes): 6 October 2003: see SI 2003/1766, art 2(a).
Sub-s (1): in para (c) words "carer's allowance" in square brackets substituted by SI 2002/1457, art 2, Schedule, paras 1, 3(c). Date in force (for certain purposes): 1 September 2002: see SI 2002/1457, art 1(1)(b)(i). Date in force (for remaining purposes): 1 April 2003: see SI 2002/1457, art 1(1)(b)(ii).
Sub-s (1): paras (f), (g) repealed by the Tax Credits Act 2002, s 60, Sch 6. Date in force: 8 April 2003: see SI 2003/962, art 2(1), (4)(c), (e), Sch 2; for savings and transitional provisions see arts 3–5 thereof.
Sub-s (5): words "child benefit" in square brackets substituted by the Tax Credits Act 2002, s 51, Sch 4, paras 20, 21. Date in force (for the purpose of making regulations): 26 February 2003: see SI 2003/392, art 2. Date in force (for the purpose of transfer of functions etc and minor amendments): 1 April 2003: see SI 2003/392, art 2. Date in force (for remaining purposes): 7 April 2003: see SI 2003/392, art 2.
Sub-s (6): words "child benefit" in square brackets substituted by the Tax Credits Act 2002, s 51, Sch 4, paras 20, 21. Date in force (for the purpose of making regulations): 26 February 2003: see SI 2003/392, art 2. Date in force (for the purpose of transfer of functions etc and minor amendments): 1 April 2003: see SI 2003/392, art 2. Date in force (for remaining purposes): 7 April 2003: see SI 2003/392, art 2.

Subordinate Legislation
Social Security (Immigration and Asylum) Consequential Amendments Regulations 2000, SI 2000/636 (made under sub-ss (3), (4), (7)).
Immigration (Eligibility for Assistance) (Scotland and Northern Ireland) Regulations 2000, SI 2000/705 (made under sub-ss (3), (4)).
Social Security Amendment (Carer's Allowance) Regulations 2002, SI 2002/2497 (made under sub-ss (3)–(5)).
State Pension Credit (Transitional and Miscellaneous Provisions) Amendment Regulations 2003, SI 2003/2274 (made under sub-ss (3), (4)).

116   Amendment of section 21 of the National Assistance Act 1948

In section 21 of the National Assistance Act 1948 (duty of local authorities to provide accommodation), after subsection (1), insert—

"(1A)   A person to whom section 115 of the Immigration and Asylum Act 1999 (exclusion from benefits) applies may not be provided with residential accommodation under subsection (1)(a) if his need for care and attention has arisen solely—

(a)   because he is destitute; or

(b)   because of the physical effects, or anticipated physical effects, of his being destitute.

(1B)   Subsections (3) and (5) to (8) of section 95 of the Immigration and Asylum Act 1999, and paragraph 2 of Schedule 8 to that Act, apply for the purposes of subsection (1A) as they apply for the purposes of that section, but for the references in subsections (5) and (7) of that section and in that paragraph to the Secretary of State substitute references to a local authority."

Appointment
Appointment: 6 December 1999: see SI 1999/3190, art 2, Schedule.

117   Other restrictions on assistance: England and Wales

(1)   In section 45 of the Health Services and Public Health Act 1968 (promotion by local authorities of the welfare of old people), after subsection (4), insert—

"(4A)   No arrangements under this section may be given effect to in relation to a person to whom section 115 of the Immigration and Asylum Act 1999 (exclusion from benefits) applies solely—

(a)   because he is destitute; or

(b)   because of the physical effects, or anticipated physical effects, of his being destitute.

(4B)   Subsections (3) and (5) to (8) of section 95 of the Immigration and Asylum Act 1999, and paragraph 2 of Schedule 8 to that Act, apply for the purposes of subsection (4A) as they apply for the purposes of that section, but for the references in subsections (5) and (7) of that section and in that paragraph to the Secretary of State substitute references to a local authority."

(2)   In paragraph 2 of Schedule 8 to the National Health Service Act 1977 (arrangements by local authorities for the prevention of illness and for care and after-care), after sub-paragraph (2), insert—

"(2A)   No arrangements under this paragraph may be given effect to in relation to a person to whom section 115 of the Immigration and Asylum Act 1999 (exclusion from benefits) applies solely—

(a)   because he is destitute; or

(b)   because of the physical effects, or anticipated physical effects, of his being destitute.

(2B)   Subsections (3) and (5) to (8) of section 95 of the Immigration and Asylum Act 1999, and paragraph 2 of Schedule 8 to that Act, apply for the purposes of subsection (2A) as they apply for the purposes of that section, but for the references in subsections (5) and (7) of that section and in that paragraph to the Secretary of State substitute references to a local social services authority."

(3)   ...

(4)   ...

(5)   In the 1996 Act, omit section 186 (asylum-seekers and their dependants).

(6)   In section 187(1) of the 1996 Act (provision of information by Secretary of State), in paragraph (a), for "or has become an asylum-seeker, or a dependant of an asylum-seeker" substitute "a person to whom section 115 of the Immigration and Asylum Act 1999 (exclusion from benefits) applies".

Appointment
Sub-ss (1), (2): Appointment: 6 December 1999: see SI 1999/3190, art 2, Schedule.
Sub-ss (3), (4), (6): Appointment: 3 April 2000: see SI 2000/464, art 2, Schedule.

Amendment
Sub-s (3): repealed by the Homelessness Act 2002, s 18(2), Sch 2. Date in force (in relation to England): 31 July 2002: see SI 2002/1799, art 2. Date in force (in relation to Wales): 27 January 2003: see SI 2002/1736, art 2(2), Schedule, Pt 2.
Sub-s (4): repealed by the Homelessness Act 2002, s 18(2), Sch 2. Date in force (in relation to England): 31 July 2002: see SI 2002/1799, art 2. Date in force (in relation to Wales): 30 September 2002: see SI 2002/1736, art 2(1), Schedule, Pt 1.

118   Housing authority accommodation

(1)   Each housing authority must secure that, so far as practicable, a tenancy of, or licence to occupy, housing accommodation provided under the accommodation provisions is not granted to a person subject to immigration control unless—

(a)   he is of a class specified in an order made by the Secretary of State; or
(b)   the tenancy of, or licence to occupy, such accommodation is granted in accordance with arrangements made under section 95.

(2)   "Housing authority" means—

(a)   in relation to England and Wales, a local housing authority within the meaning of the Housing Act 1985;
(b)   in relation to Scotland, a local authority within the meaning of the Housing (Scotland) Act 1987; and
(c)   in relation to Northern Ireland, the Executive.

(3)   "Accommodation provisions" means—

(a)   in relation to England and Wales, Part II of the Housing Act 1985;
(b)   in relation to Scotland, Part I of the Housing (Scotland) Act 1987;
(c)   in relation to Northern Ireland, Part II of the Housing (Northern Ireland) Order 1981.

(4)   "Licence to occupy", in relation to Scotland, means a permission or right to occupy.

(5)   "Tenancy", in relation to England and Wales, has the same meaning as in the Housing Act 1985.

(6)   "Person subject to immigration control" means a person who under the 1971 Act requires leave to enter or remain in the United Kingdom (whether or not such leave has been given).

(7)   This section does not apply in relation to any allocation of housing to which Part VI of the Housing Act 1996 (allocation of housing accommodation) applies.

Appointment
Appointment (for the purpose of enabling subordinate legislation to be made): 1 January 2000: see SI 1999/3190, art 2, Schedule.
Appointment (for remaining purposes): 1 March 2000: see SI 2000/464, art 2, Schedule.

Subordinate Legislation
Persons subject to Immigration Control (Housing Authority Accommodation and Homelessness) Order 2000, SI 2000/706.
Persons Subject to Immigration Control (Housing Authority Accommodation) (Wales) Order 2000, SI 2000/1036.

119   Homelessness: Scotland and Northern Ireland

(1) A person subject to immigration control—

(a) is not eligible for accommodation or assistance under the homelessness provisions, and

(b) is to be disregarded in determining for the purposes of those provisions, whether another person—

(i) is homeless or is threatened with homelessness, or

(ii) has a priority need for accommodation,

unless he is of a class specified in an order made by the Secretary of State.

(2) An order under subsection (1) may not be made so as to include in a specified class any person to whom section 115 applies.

(3) "The homelessness provisions" means—

(a) in relation to Scotland, Part II of the Housing (Scotland) Act 1987; and

(b) in relation to Northern Ireland, Part II of the Housing (Northern Ireland) Order 1988.

(4) "Person subject to immigration control" has the same meaning as in section 118.

Appointment
Appointment (for the purpose of enabling subordinate legislation to be made): 1 January 2000: see SI 1999/3190, art 2, Schedule.
Appointment (for remaining purposes): 1 March 2000: see SI 2000/464, art 2, Schedule.

Subordinate Legislation
Persons subject to Immigration Control (Housing Authority Accommodation and Homelessness) Order 2000, SI 2000/706.

120   Other restrictions on assistance: Scotland

(1) In section 12 of the Social Work (Scotland) Act 1968 (general social welfare services of local authorities), after subsection (2) insert—

"(2A) A person to whom section 115 of the Immigration and Asylum Act 1999 (exclusion from benefits) applies is not to receive assistance under subsection (1) of this section (whether by way of residential accommodation or otherwise) if his need for assistance has arisen solely—

(a) because he is destitute; or

(b) because of the physical effects, or anticipated physical effects, of his being destitute.

(2B) Subsections (3) and (5) to (8) of section 95 of the Immigration and Asylum Act 1999, and paragraph 2 of Schedule 8 to that Act, apply for the purposes of subsection (2A) as they apply for the purposes of that section, but for the references in subsections (5) and (7) of that section and in that paragraph to the Secretary of State substitute references to a local authority."

(2) In section 13A of that Act (provision of residential accommodation with nursing), after subsection (3) insert—

1525

"(4)   No arrangements under subsection (1) above may be given effect to in relation to a person to whom section 115 of the Immigration and Asylum Act 1999 (exclusion from benefits) applies solely—

    (a)   because he is destitute; or
    (b)   because of the physical effects, or anticipated physical effects, of his being destitute.

(5)   Subsections (3) and (5) to (8) of section 95 of the Immigration and Asylum Act 1999, and paragraph 2 of Schedule 8 to that Act, apply for the purposes of subsection (4) above as they apply for the purposes of that section, but for the references in subsections (5) and (7) of that section and in that paragraph to the Secretary of State substitute references to a local authority."

(3)   In section 13B of that Act (provision of care and after-care), after subsection (2) insert—

"(3)   No arrangements under subsection (1) above may be given effect to in relation to a person to whom section 115 of the Immigration and Asylum Act 1999 (exclusion from benefits) applies solely—

    (a)   because he is destitute; or
    (b)   because of the physical effects, or anticipated physical effects, of his being destitute.

(4)   Subsections (3) and (5) to (8) of section 95 of the Immigration and Asylum Act 1999, and paragraph 2 of Schedule 8 to that Act, apply for the purposes of subsection (3) above as they apply for the purposes of that section, but for the references in subsections (5) and (7) of that section and in that paragraph to the Secretary of State substitute references to a local authority."

(4)   *In section 7 of the Mental Health (Scotland) Act 1984 (functions of local authorities), after subsection (2) insert—*

"(3)   *No arrangements under paragraph (a) or (c) of subsection (1) above may be given effect to in relation to a person to whom section 115 of the Immigration and Asylum Act 1999 (exclusion from benefits) applies solely—*

    (a)   *because he is destitute; or*
    (b)   *because of the physical effects, or anticipated physical effects, of his being destitute.*

(4)   *Subsections (3) and (5) to (8) of section 95 of the Immigration and Asylum Act 1999, and paragraph 2 of Schedule 8 to that Act, apply for the purposes of subsection (3) above as they apply for the purposes of that section, but for the references in subsection (5) and (7) of that section and in that paragraph to the Secretary of State substitute references to a local authority."*

(5)   *In section 8 of that Act (provision of after-care services), after subsection (3) insert—*

"(4)   *After care services may not be provided under subsection (1) above in respect of any person to whom section 115 of the Immigration and Asylum Act 1999 (exclusion from benefits) applies solely—*

    (a)   *because he is destitute; or*
    (b)   *because of the physical effects, or anticipated physical effects, of his being destitute.*

(5)   *Subsections (3) and (5) to (8) of section 95 of the Immigration and Asylum Act 1999, and paragraph 2 of Schedule 8 to that Act, apply for the purposes of subsection (4) above as they apply for the purposes of that section, but for the*

references in subsection (5) and (7) of that section and in that paragraph to the Secretary of State substitute references to a local authority."

(6) In the Asylum and Immigration Appeals Act 1993, omit sections 4 and 5 and Schedule 1 (provisions relating to housing of asylum-seekers).

Appointment
Appointment (for remaining purposes): 3 April 2000: see SI 2000/464, art 2, Schedule.
Appointment (for the purpose of enabling subordinate legislation to be made under s 95 as applied by any provision inserted by this section): 1 March 2000: see SI 2000/464, art 2, Schedule.

Amendment
Sub-ss (4), (5): repealed by the Mental Health (Care and Treatment) (Scotland) Act 2003, s 331(2), Sch 5, Pt 1. Date in force: 5 October 2005: see SSI 2005/161, art 3.

121   Other restrictions on assistance: Northern Ireland

(1) In Article 7 of the Health and Personal Social Services (Northern Ireland) Order 1972 (prevention of illness, care and after-care), after paragraph (2) insert—

"(3) No arrangements made under paragraph (1) may be given effect to in relation to a person to whom section 115 of the Immigration and Asylum Act 1999 applies solely—

(a)   because he is destitute; or
(b)   because of the physical effects, or anticipated physical effects, of his being destitute.

(3A) Subsections (3) and (5) to (8) of section 95 of the Immigration and Asylum Act 1999, and paragraph 2 of Schedule 8 to that Act, apply for the purposes of paragraph (3) as they apply for the purposes of that section, but for the references in subsections (5) and (7) of that section and in paragraph 2 of that Schedule to the Secretary of State substitute references to the Department."

(2) In Article 15 of that Order (general social welfare), after paragraph (5) insert—

"(6) Assistance may not be provided under paragraph (1) in respect of any person to whom section 115 of the Immigration and Asylum Act 1999 applies if his need for assistance has arisen solely—

(a)   because he is destitute, or
(b)   because of the physical effects, or anticipated physical effects, of his being destitute.

(7) Subsections (3) to (8) of section 95 of the Immigration and Asylum Act 1999, and paragraph 2 of Schedule 8 to that Act, apply for the purposes of paragraph (6) as they apply for the purposes of that section, but for references to the Secretary of State in subsections (5) and (7) of that section and in paragraph 2 of that Schedule substitute references to the Department."

(3) In the Asylum and Immigration Appeals Act 1993, omit sections 4 and 5 and Schedule 1 (provisions relating to housing of asylum-seekers).

Appointment
Appointment (for the purpose of enabling subordinate legislation to be made under s 95 as applied by any provision inserted by this section): 1 March 2000: see SI 2000/464, art 2, Schedule.
Appointment (for remaining purposes): 3 April 2000: see SI 2000/464, art 2, Schedule.

122   *Support for children* [Family with children]

(1)   In this section "eligible person" means a person who appears to the Secretary of State to be a person for whom support may be provided under section 95.

(2)   Subsections (3) and (4) apply if an application for support under section 95 has been made by an eligible person whose household includes a dependant under the age of 18 ("the child").

(3)   If it appears to the Secretary of State that adequate accommodation is not being provided for the child, he must exercise his powers under section 95 by offering, and if his offer is accepted by providing or arranging for the provision of, adequate accommodation for the child as part of the eligible person's household.

(4)   If it appears to the Secretary of State that essential living needs of the child are not being met, he must exercise his powers under section 95 by offering, and if his offer is accepted by providing or arranging for the provision of, essential living needs for the child as part of the eligible person's household.

(5)   No local authority may provide assistance under any of the child welfare provisions in respect of a dependant under the age of 18, or any member of his family, at any time when—

    (a)   the Secretary of State is complying with this section in relation to him; or
    (b)   there are reasonable grounds for believing that—
        (i)   the person concerned is a person for whom support may be provided under section 95; and
        (ii)   the Secretary of State would be required to comply with this section if that person had made an application under section 95.

(6)   "Assistance" means the provision of accommodation or of any essential living needs.

(7)   "The child welfare provisions" means—

    (a)   section 17 of the Children Act 1989 (local authority support for children and their families);
    (b)   section 22 of the Children (Scotland) Act 1995 (equivalent provision for Scotland); and
    (c)   Article 18 of the Children (Northern Ireland) Order 1995 (equivalent provision for Northern Ireland).

(8)   Subsection (9) applies if accommodation provided in the discharge of the duty imposed by subsection (3) has been withdrawn.

(9)   Only the relevant authority may provide assistance under any of the child welfare provisions in respect of the child concerned.

(10)   "Relevant authority" means—

    (a)   in relation to Northern Ireland, the authority within whose area the withdrawn accommodation was provided;
    (b)   in any other case, the local authority within whose area the withdrawn accommodation was provided.

(11)   In such circumstances as may be prescribed, subsection (5) does not apply.

[(1)   This section applies where a person ("the asylum-seeker") applies for support under section 95 of this Act or section 17 of the Nationality, Immigration and Asylum Act 2002 (accommodation centres) if—

    (a)   the Secretary of State thinks that the asylum-seeker is eligible for support under either or both of those sections, and

(b)   the asylum-seeker's household includes a dependant child who is under 18.

(2)   The Secretary of State must offer the provision of support for the child, as part of the asylum-seeker's household, under one of the sections mentioned in subsection (1).

(3)   A local authority (or, in Northern Ireland, an authority) may not provide assistance for a child if—

   (a)   the Secretary of State is providing support for the child in accordance with an offer under subsection (2),
   (b)   an offer by the Secretary of State under subsection (2) remains open in respect of the child, or
   (c)   the Secretary of State has agreed that he would make an offer in respect of the child under subsection (2) if an application were made as described in subsection (1).

(4)   In subsection (3) "assistance" means assistance under—

   (a)   section 17 of the Children Act 1989 (c 41) (local authority support),
   (b)   section 22 of the Children (Scotland) Act 1995 (c 36) (similar provision for Scotland), or
   (c)   Article 18 of the Children (Northern Ireland) Order 1995 (SI 1995/755 (NI 2)) (similar provision for Northern Ireland).

(5)   The Secretary of State may by order disapply subsection (3) in specified circumstances.

(6)   Where subsection (3) ceases to apply to a child because the Secretary of State stops providing support, no local authority may provide assistance for the child except the authority for the area within which the support was provided.]

Appointment
Appointment (for the purpose of enabling subordinate legislation to be made): 1 March 2000: see SI 2000/464, art 2, Schedule.
Appointment (for remaining purposes): 3 April 2000: see SI 2000/464, art 2, Schedule.

Amendment
Substituted by the Nationality, Immigration and Asylum Act 2002, s 47. Date in force: to be appointed: see the Nationality, Immigration and Asylum Act 2002, s 162(1).

Subordinate Legislation
Immigration (Eligibility for Assistance) (Scotland and Northern Ireland) Regulations 2000, SI 2000/705 (made under sub-s (11)).

123   Back-dating of benefits where person recorded as refugee

(1)   *This section applies if—*

   (a)   *a person is recorded by the Secretary of State as a refugee within the meaning of the Refugee Convention; and*
   (b)   *before the refugee was so recorded, he or his dependant was a person to whom section 115 applied.*

(2)   *Regulations may provide that a person mentioned in subsection (1)(b) may, within a prescribed period, claim the whole, or any prescribed proportion, of any benefit to which he would have been entitled had the refugee been so recorded when he made his claim for asylum.*

(3)   *Subsections (5) and (6) apply if the refugee has resided in the areas of two or more local authorities and he or his dependant makes a claim under the regulations in relation to housing benefit.*

(4)   *Subsections (5) and (6) also apply if the refugee has resided in the areas of two or more local authorities in Great Britain and he or his dependant makes a claim under the regulations in relation to council tax benefit.*

(5)   *The claim must be investigated and determined, and any benefit awarded must be paid or allowed, by such one of those authorities as may be prescribed by the regulations ("the prescribed authority").*

(6)   *The regulations may make provision requiring a local authority who are not the prescribed authority to supply that authority with such information as they may reasonably require in connection with the exercise of their functions under the regulations.*

(7)   *The regulations may make provision in relation to a person who has received support under this Part [or Part 2 of the Nationality, Immigration and Asylum Act 2002 (accommodation centres)] or who is a dependant of such a person—*

    (a)   *for the determination, or for criteria for the calculation, of the value of that support; and*
    (b)   *for the sum which he would be entitled to claim under the regulations to be reduced by the whole, or any prescribed proportion, of that valuation.*

(8)   *The reductions permitted by subsection (7) must not exceed the amount of the valuation.*

(9)   *"Regulations" means—*

    (a)   *in relation to jobseeker's allowance under the Jobseekers Act 1995, regulations made by the Secretary of State under that Act or the Social Security Administration Act 1992;*
    (b)   *in relation to jobseeker's allowance under the Jobseekers (Northern Ireland) Order 1995, regulations made by the Department under that Order or the Social Security Administration (Northern Ireland) Act 1992;*
    [(ba) *in relation to child benefit (and guardian's allowance), regulations made by the Treasury;]*
    (c)   *in relation to a benefit [(apart from child benefit and guardian's allowance)] under the Social Security Contributions and Benefits Act 1992 [or state pension credit], regulations made by the Secretary of State under that Act[, the Social Security Administration Act 1992 (c 5) or the State Pension Credit Act 2002];*
    (d)   *in relation to a benefit [(apart from child benefit and guardian's allowance)] under the Social Security Contributions and Benefits (Northern Ireland) Act 1992, regulations made by the Department under that Act or the Social Security Administration (Northern Ireland) Act 1992.*

Appointment
Appointment (for the purpose of enabling subordinate legislation to be made): 1 January 2000: see SI 1999/3190, art 2, Schedule.
Appointment (for remaining purposes): 3 April 2000: see SI 2000/464, art 2, Schedule.

Amendment
Repealed by the Asylum and Immigration (Treatment of Claimants, etc) Act 2004, ss 12(1), 47, Sch 4. Date in force: to be appointed: see the Asylum and Immigration (Treatment of Claimants, etc) Act 2004, s 48(3)–(6).
Sub-s (7): words "or Part 2 of the Nationality, Immigration and Asylum Act 2002 (accommodation centres)" in square brackets inserted by the Nationality, Immigration and Asylum Act 2002, s 52. Date in force: to be appointed: see the Nationality, Immigration and Asylum Act 2002, s 162(1).
Sub-s (9): para (ba) inserted by the Tax Credits Act 2002, s 51, Sch 4, paras 20, 22(1), (2). Date in force (for the purpose of making regulations): 26 February 2003: see SI 2003/392, art 2. Date

in force (for the purpose of transfer of functions etc and minor amendments): 1 April 2003: see SI 2003/392, art 2. Date in force (for remaining purposes): 7 April 2003: see SI 2003/392, art 2. Sub-s (9): in paras (c), (d) words "(apart from child benefit and guardian's allowance)" in square brackets inserted by the Tax Credits Act 2002, s 51, Sch 4, paras 20, 22(1), (3). Date in force (for the purpose of making regulations): 26 February 2003: see SI 2003/392, art 2. Date in force (for the purpose of transfer of functions etc and minor amendments): 1 April 2003: see SI 2003/392, art 2. Date in force (for remaining purposes): 7 April 2003: see SI 2003/392, art 2.

Sub-s (9): in para (c) words "or state pension credit" in square brackets inserted by the State Pension Credit Act 2002, s 14, Sch 2, Pt 3, para 42(a). Date in force (for the purpose only of exercising any power to make regulations or orders): 2 July 2002: see SI 2002/1691, art 2(l). Date in force (for remaining purposes): 6 October 2003: see SI 2003/1766, art 2(a).

Sub-s (9): in para (c) words ", the Social Security Administration Act 1992 (c 5) or the State Pension Credit Act 2002" in square brackets substituted by the State Pension Credit Act 2002, s 14, Sch 2, Pt 3, para 42(b). Date in force (for the purpose only of exercising any power to make regulations or orders): 2 July 2002: see SI 2002/1691, art 2(l). Date in force (for remaining purposes): 6 October 2003: see SI 2003/1766, art 2(a).

Subordinate Legislation
Social Security (Immigration and Asylum) Consequential Amendments Regulations 2000, SI 2000/636 (made under sub-ss (5), (6)).

Miscellaneous

124   Secretary of State to be corporation sole for purposes Part VI

(1)   For the purpose of exercising his functions under this Part, the Secretary of State is a corporation sole.

(2)   Any instrument in connection with the acquisition, management or of disposal of property, real or personal, heritable or moveable, by the Secretary of State under this Part may be executed on his behalf by a person authorised by him for that purpose.

(3)   Any instrument purporting to have been so executed on behalf of the Secretary of State is to be treated, until the contrary is proved, to have been so executed on his behalf.

Initial Commencement
Royal Assent: 11 November 1999: see s 170(3)(l).

125   Entry of premises

(1)   This section applies in relation to premises in which accommodation has been provided under section 95 or 98 for a supported person.

(2)   If, on an application made by a person authorised in writing by the Secretary of State, a justice of the peace is satisfied that there is reason to believe that—

(a)   the supported person or any dependants of his for whom the accommodation is provided is not resident in it,

(b)   the accommodation is being used for any purpose other than the accommodation of the asylum-seeker or any dependant of his, or

(c)   any person other than the supported person and his dependants (if any) is residing in the accommodation,

he may grant a warrant to enter the premises to the person making the application.

(3)   A warrant granted under subsection (2) may be executed—

(a)   at any reasonable time;

(b)   using reasonable force.

(4)   In the application of subsection (2) to Scotland, read the reference to a justice of the peace as a reference to the sheriff or a justice of the peace.

Appendix 1   Legislation and materials

Appointment
Appointment: 3 April 2000: see SI 2000/464, art 2, Schedule.

126   Information from property owners

(1)   The power conferred by this section is to be exercised with a view to obtaining information about premises in which accommodation is or has been provided for supported persons.

(2)   The Secretary of State may require any person appearing to him—

(a)   to have any interest in, or

(b)   to be involved in any way in the management or control of,

such premises, or any building which includes such premises, to provide him with such information with respect to the premises and the persons occupying them as he may specify.

(3)   A person who is required to provide information under this section must do so in accordance with such requirements as may be prescribed.

(4)   Information provided to the Secretary of State under this section may be used by him only in the exercise of his functions under this Part.

Appointment
Appointment: 3 April 2000: see SI 2000/464, art 2, Schedule.

127   Requirement to supply information about redirection of post

(1)   The Secretary of State may require any person conveying postal packets to supply redirection information to the Secretary of State—

(a)   for use in the prevention, detection, investigation or prosecution of criminal offences under this Part;

(b)   for use in checking the accuracy of information relating to support provided under this Part; or

(c)   for any other purpose relating to the provision of support to asylum-seekers.

(2)   The information must be supplied in such manner and form, and in accordance with such requirements, as may be prescribed.

(3)   The Secretary of State must make payments of such amount as he considers reasonable in respect of the supply of information under this section.

(4)   "Postal packet" has the same meaning as in the [Postal Services Act 2000].

(5)   "Redirection information" means information relating to arrangements made with any person conveying postal packets for the delivery of postal packets to addresses other than those indicated by senders on the packets.

Appointment
Appointment: 3 April 2000: see SI 2000/464, art 2, Schedule.

Amendment
Sub-s (4): words "Postal Services Act 2000" in square brackets substituted by SI 2001/1149, art 3(1), Sch 1, para 124. Date in force: 26 March 2001: see SI 2001/1149, art 1(2).

PART VII
POWER TO ARREST, SEARCH AND FINGERPRINT

Power to arrest

128   –139

[Amend the Immigration Act 1971]

1532

Appointment

Appointment: 14 February 2000: see SI 2000/168, art 2, Schedule.

Detention

140   Detention of persons liable to examination or removal

(1)   In paragraph 16 of Schedule 2 to the 1971 Act, for sub-paragraph (2) substitute—

"(2)   If there are reasonable grounds for suspecting that a person is someone in respect of whom directions may be given under any of paragraphs 8 to 10 or 12 to 14, that person may be detained under the authority of an immigration officer pending—

(a)   a decision whether or not to give such directions;
(b)   his removal in pursuance of such directions."

(2)   In paragraph 17(2) of that Schedule (power to grant constable a warrant to search and arrest), for the words from "authorising any constable" to "if need be" substitute "authorising any immigration officer or constable to enter, if need be".

Initial Commencement
Royal Assent: 11 November 1999: see s 170(3)(m).

Fingerprinting

141   Fingerprinting

(1)   Fingerprints may be taken by an authorised person from a person to whom this section applies.

(2)   Fingerprints may be taken under this section only during the relevant period.

(3)   Fingerprints may not be taken under this section from a person under the age of sixteen ("the child") except in the presence of a person of full age who is—

(a)   the child's parent or guardian; or
(b)   a person who for the time being takes responsibility for the child.

(4)   The person mentioned in subsection (3)(b) may not be—

(a)   an officer of the Secretary of State who is not an authorised person;
(b)   an authorised person.

(5)   "Authorised person" means—

(a)   a constable;
(b)   an immigration officer;
(c)   a prison officer;
(d)   an officer of the Secretary of State authorised for the purpose; or
(e)   a person who is employed by a contractor in connection with the discharge of the contractor's duties under a [removal centre] contract.

(6)   In subsection (5)(e) "contractor" and "[removal centre] contract" have the same meaning as in Part VIII.

(7)   This section applies to—

(a)   any person ("A") who, on being required to do so by an immigration officer on his arrival in the United Kingdom, fails to produce a valid passport with photograph or some other document satisfactorily establishing his identity and nationality or citizenship;
(b)   any person ("B") who has been refused leave to enter the United Kingdom but has been temporarily admitted under paragraph 21 of Schedule 2 to the 1971

Act if an immigration officer reasonably suspects that B might break any condition imposed on him relating to residence or as to reporting to the police or an immigration officer;

[(c) any person ("C") in respect of whom a relevant immigration decision has been made;]

(d) any person ("D") who has been arrested under paragraph 17 of Schedule 2 to the 1971 Act;

(e) any person ("E") who has made a claim for asylum;

(f) any person ("F") who is a dependant of any of those persons.

(8) "The relevant period" begins—

(a) for A, on his failure to produce the passport or other document;

(b) for B, on the decision to admit him temporarily;

[(c) for C, on the service on him of notice of the relevant immigration decision by virtue of section 105 of the Nationality, Immigration and Asylum Act 2002 (c 41);]

(d) for D, on his arrest;

(e) for E, on the making of his claim for asylum; and

(f) for F, at the same time as for the person whose dependant he is.

(9) "The relevant period" ends on the earliest of the following—

(a) the grant of leave to enter or remain in the United Kingdom;

(b) for A, B, C or D, his removal or deportation from the United Kingdom;

[(c) for C—

  (i) the time when the relevant immigration decision ceases to have effect, whether as a result of an appeal or otherwise, or

  (ii) if a deportation order has been made against him, its revocation or its otherwise ceasing to have effect;]

(d) for D, his release if he is no longer liable to be detained under paragraph 16 of Schedule 2 to the 1971 Act;

(e) for E, the final determination or abandonment of his claim for asylum; and

(f) for F, at the same time as for the person whose dependant he is.

(10) No fingerprints may be taken from A if the immigration officer considers that A has a reasonable excuse for the failure concerned.

(11) No fingerprints may be taken from B unless the decision to take them has been confirmed by a chief immigration officer.

(12) An authorised person may not take fingerprints from a person under the age of sixteen unless his decision to take them has been confirmed—

(a) if he is a constable, by a person designated for the purpose by the chief constable of his police force;

(b) if he is a person mentioned in subsection (5)(b) or (e), by a chief immigration officer;

(c) if he is a prison officer, by a person designated for the purpose by the governor of the prison;

(d) if he is an officer of the Secretary of State, by a person designated for the purpose by the Secretary of State.

(13) Neither subsection (3) nor subsection (12) prevents an authorised person from taking fingerprints if he reasonably believes that the person from whom they are to be taken is aged sixteen or over.

(14) For the purposes of subsection (7)(f), a person is a dependant of another person if—

(a) he is that person's spouse or child under the age of eighteen; and

(b)   he does not have a right of abode in the United Kingdom or indefinite leave to enter or remain in the United Kingdom.

(15)   "Claim for asylum" has the same meaning as in Part VI.

[(16)   "Relevant immigration decision" means a decision of the kind mentioned in section 82(2)(g), (h), (i), (j) or (k) of the Nationality, Immigration and Asylum Act 2002 (c 41).]

Appointment
Appointment: 11 December 2000: see SI 2000/3099, art 3, Schedule.

Amendment
Sub-s (5): in para (e) words "removal centre" in square brackets substituted by the Nationality, Immigration and Asylum Act 2002, s 66(2)(a), (3)(n). Date in force: 10 February 2003: see SI 2003/1, art 2, Schedule.
Sub-s (6): words "removal centre" in square brackets substituted by the Nationality, Immigration and Asylum Act 2002, s 66(2)(a), (3)(n). Date in force: 10 February 2003: see SI 2003/1, art 2, Schedule.
Sub-s (7): para (c) substituted by the Asylum and Immigration (Treatment of Claimants, etc) Act 2004, s 15(1), (2). Date in force: 1 October 2004: see SI 2004/2523, art 2, Schedule.
Sub-s (8): para (c) substituted by the Asylum and Immigration (Treatment of Claimants, etc) Act 2004, s 15(1), (3). Date in force: 1 October 2004: see SI 2004/2523, art 2, Schedule.
Sub-s (9): para (c) substituted by the Asylum and Immigration (Treatment of Claimants, etc) Act 2004, s 15(1), (4). Date in force: 1 October 2004: see SI 2004/2523, art 2, Schedule.
Sub-s (16): inserted by the Asylum and Immigration (Treatment of Claimants, etc) Act 2004, s 15(1), (5). Date in force: 1 October 2004: see SI 2004/2523, art 2, Schedule.

142   Attendance for fingerprinting

(1)   The Secretary of State may, by notice in writing, require a person to whom section 141 applies to attend at a specified place for fingerprinting.

(2)   The notice—

(a)   must give the person concerned a period of at least seven days within which to attend, beginning not earlier than seven days after the date of the notice; and
(b)   may require him to attend at a specified time of day or during specified hours.

(3)   A constable or immigration officer may arrest without warrant a person who has failed to comply with a requirement imposed on him under this section (unless the requirement has ceased to have effect).

(4)   Before a person arrested under subsection (3) is released—

(a)   he may be removed to a place where his fingerprints may conveniently be taken; and
(b)   his fingerprints may be taken (whether or not he is so removed).

(5)   A requirement imposed under subsection (1) ceases to have effect at the end of the relevant period (as defined by section 141).

Appointment
Appointment: 11 December 2000: see SI 2000/3099, art 3, Schedule.

143   Destruction of fingerprints

(1)   If they have not already been destroyed, fingerprints must be destroyed before the end of the specified period beginning with the day on which they were taken.

(2)   If a person from whom fingerprints were taken proves that he is—

(a)   a British citizen, or

(b)   a Commonwealth citizen who has a right of abode in the United Kingdom as a result of section 2(1)(b) of the 1971 Act,

the fingerprints must be destroyed as soon as reasonably practicable.

(3)   ...

(4)   ...

(5)   ...

(6)   ...

(7)   ...

(8)   ...

(9)   Fingerprints taken from F [(within the meaning of section 141(7))] must be destroyed when fingerprints taken from the person whose dependant he is have to be destroyed.

(10)   The obligation to destroy fingerprints under this section applies also to copies of fingerprints.

(11)   The Secretary of State must take all reasonably practicable steps to secure—

(a)   that data which are held in electronic form and which relate to fingerprints which have to be destroyed as a result of this section are destroyed or erased; or

(b)   that access to such data is blocked.

(12)   The person to whom the data relate is entitled, on request, to a certificate issued by the Secretary of State to the effect that he has taken the steps required by subsection (11).

(13)   A certificate under subsection (12) must be issued within three months of the date of the request for it.

(14)   ...

(15)   "Specified period" means—

(a)   such period as the Secretary of State may specify by order;

(b)   if no period is so specified, ten years.

Appointment
Appointment: 11 December 2000: see SI 2000/3099, art 3, Schedule.

Amendment
Sub-ss (3)–(8): repealed by the Anti-terrorism, Crime and Security Act 2001, ss 36(1)(a), (2), 125, Sch 8, Pt 3. Date in force: 14 December 2001: see the Anti-terrorism, Crime and Security Act 2001, s 127(2)(a).
Sub-s (9): words "(within the meaning of section 141(7))" in square brackets inserted by the Anti-terrorism, Crime and Security Act 2001, s 36(1)(b), (2). Date in force: 14 December 2001: see the Anti-terrorism, Crime and Security Act 2001, s 127(2)(a).
Sub-s (14): repealed by the Anti-terrorism, Crime and Security Act 2001, ss 36(1)(c), (2), 125, Sch 8, Pt 3. Date in force: 14 December 2001: see the Anti-terrorism, Crime and Security Act 2001, s 127(2)(a).

144   Other methods of collecting data about physical characteristics

[(1)]   The Secretary of State may make regulations containing provisions equivalent to sections 141, 142 and 143 in relation to such other methods of collecting data about external physical characteristics as may be prescribed.

[(2) In subsection (1) "external physical characteristics" includes, in particular, features of the iris or any other part of the eye.]

Appointment
Appointment: 11 December 2000: see SI 2000/3099, art 3, Schedule.

Amendment
Sub-s (1): numbered as such by the Nationality, Immigration and Asylum Act 2002, s 128(1). Date in force: 10 February 2003: see SI 2003/1, art 2, Schedule.
Sub-s (2): inserted by the Nationality, Immigration and Asylum Act 2002, s 128(1). Date in force: 10 February 2003: see SI 2003/1, art 2, Schedule.

Codes of practice

145   Codes of practice

(1)   An immigration officer exercising any specified power to—

(a)   arrest, question, search or take fingerprints from a person,
(b)   enter and search premises, or
(c)   seize property found on persons or premises,

must have regard to such provisions of a code as may be specified.

(2)   Subsection (1) also applies to an authorised person exercising the power to take fingerprints conferred by section 141.

[(2A)   A person exercising a power under regulations made by virtue of section 144 must have regard to such provisions of a code as may be specified.]

(3)   Any specified provision of a code may have effect for the purposes of this section subject to such modifications as may be specified.

(4)   "Specified" means specified in a direction given by the Secretary of State.

(5)   "Authorised person" has the same meaning as in section 141.

(6)   "Code" means—

(a)   in relation to England and Wales, any code of practice for the time being in force under the Police and Criminal Evidence Act 1984;
(b)   in relation to Northern Ireland, any code of practice for the time being in force under the Police and Criminal Evidence (Northern Ireland) Order 1989.

(7)   This section does not apply to any person exercising powers in Scotland.

Initial Commencement
Royal Assent: 11 November 1999: see s 170(3)(n).

Amendment
Sub-s (2A): inserted by the Nationality, Immigration and Asylum Act 2002, s 128(2). Date in force: 10 February 2003: see SI 2003/1, art 2, Schedule.

Use of force

146   Use of force

(1)   An immigration officer exercising any power conferred on him by the 1971 Act or this Act may, if necessary, use reasonable force.

[(2)   A person exercising a power under any of the following may if necessary use reasonable force—

(a)   section 28CA, 28FA or 28FB of the 1971 Act (business premises: entry to arrest or search),

(b)   section 141 or 142 of this Act, and

(c)   regulations under section 144 of this Act.]

Initial Commencement

Sub-s (1): Royal Assent: 11 November 1999: see s 170(3)(o).

Amendment

Sub-s (2): substituted by the Nationality, Immigration and Asylum Act 2002, s 153(2). Date in force: 8 January 2003: see SI 2002/2811, art 2, Schedule.

PART VIII

[REMOVAL CENTRES] AND DETAINED PERSONS

Interpretation

147   Interpretation of Part VIII

In this Part—

"certificate of authorisation" means a certificate issued by the Secretary of State under section 154;

"certified prisoner custody officer" means a prisoner custody officer certified under section 89 of the Criminal Justice Act 1991, or section 114 of the Criminal Justice and Public Order Act 1994, to perform custodial duties;

"contract monitor" means a person appointed by the Secretary of State under section 149(4);

"contracted out [removal centre]" means a [removal centre] in relation to which a [removal centre] contract is in force;

"contractor", in relation to a [removal centre] which is being run in accordance with a [removal centre] contract, means the person who has contracted to run it;

"custodial functions" means custodial functions at a [removal centre];

"detained persons" means persons detained or required to be detained under the 1971 Act [or under section 62 of the Nationality, Immigration and Asylum Act 2002 (detention by Secretary of State)];

"detainee custody officer" means a person in respect of whom a certificate of authorisation is in force;

...

"[removal centre] contract" means a contract entered into by the Secretary of State under section 149;

"[removal centre] rules" means rules made by the Secretary of State under section 153;

"directly managed [removal centre]" means a [removal centre] which is not a contracted out [removal centre];

"escort arrangements" means arrangements made by the Secretary of State under section 156;

"escort functions" means functions under escort arrangements;

"escort monitor" means a person appointed under paragraph 1 of Schedule 13;

"prisoner custody officer"—

(a)   in relation to England and Wales, has the same meaning as in the Criminal Justice Act 1991;

(b)   in relation to Scotland, has the meaning given in section 114(1) of the Criminal Justice and Public Order Act 1994;

(c)   in relation to Northern Ireland, has the meaning given in section 122(1) of that Act of 1994;

["removal centre" means a place which is used solely for the detention of detained persons but which is not a short-term holding facility, a prison or part of a prison;]

"short-term holding facility" means a place used solely for the detention of detained persons for a period of not more than seven days or for such other period as may be prescribed.

Appointment

Appointment: 1 August 2000: see SI 2000/1985, art 2, Schedule.

Amendment

In definition "contracted out removal centre" words "removal centre" in square brackets in each place they occur substituted by the Nationality, Immigration and Asylum Act 2002, s 66(2)(a), (3)(a). Date in force: 10 February 2003: see SI 2003/1, art 2, Schedule.

In definition "contractor" words "removal centre" in square brackets in both places they occur substituted by the Nationality, Immigration and Asylum Act 2002, s 66(2)(a), (3)(a). Date in force: 10 February 2003: see SI 2003/1, art 2, Schedule.

In definition "custodial functions" words "removal centre" in square brackets substituted by the Nationality, Immigration and Asylum Act 2002, s 66(2)(a), (3)(a). Date in force: 10 February 2003: see SI 2003/1, art 2, Schedule.

In definition "detained person" words "or under section 62 of the Nationality, Immigration and Asylum Act 2002 (detention by Secretary of State)" in square brackets inserted by the Nationality, Immigration and Asylum Act 2002, s 62(14). Date in force: 10 February 2003: see SI 2003/1, art 2, Schedule.

Definition "detention centre" (omitted) repealed by the Nationality, Immigration and Asylum Act 2002, ss 66(1)(a), 161, Sch 9. Date in force: 10 February 2003: see SI 2003/1, art 2, Schedule.

In definition "removal centre contract" words "removal centre" in square brackets substituted by the Nationality, Immigration and Asylum Act 2002, s 66(2)(a), (3)(a). Date in force: 10 February 2003: see SI 2003/1, art 2, Schedule.

In definition "removal centre rules" words "removal centre" in square brackets substituted by the Nationality, Immigration and Asylum Act 2002, s 66(2)(a), (3)(a). Date in force: 10 February 2003: see SI 2003/1, art 2, Schedule.

In definition "directly managed removal centre" words "removal centre" in square brackets in each place they occur substituted by the Nationality, Immigration and Asylum Act 2002, s 66(2)(a), (3)(a). Date in force: 10 February 2003: see SI 2003/1, art 2, Schedule.

Definition "removal centre" inserted by the Nationality, Immigration and Asylum Act 2002, s 66(1)(b). Date in force: 10 February 2003: see SI 2003/1, art 2, Schedule.

[Removal centres]

148   Management of [removal centres]

(1)   A manager must be appointed for every [removal centre].

(2)   In the case of a contracted out [removal centre], the person appointed as manager must be a detainee custody officer whose appointment is approved by the Secretary of State.

(3)   The manager of a [removal centre] is to have such functions as are conferred on him by [removal centre] rules.

(4)   The manager of a contracted out [removal centre] may not—

(a)   enquire into a disciplinary charge laid against a detained person;
(b)   conduct the hearing of such a charge; or
(c)   make, remit or mitigate an award in respect of such a charge.

(5)   The manager of a contracted out [removal centre] may not, except in cases of urgency, order—

(a)   the removal of a detained person from association with other detained persons;

(b) the temporary confinement of a detained person in special accommodation; or

(c) the application to a detained person of any other special control or restraint (other than handcuffs).

Appointment
Sub-ss (1), (2), (4), (5): Appointment: 2 April 2001: see SI 2001/239, art 2, Schedule.
Sub-s (3): Appointment (for the purposes of enabling subordinate legislation to be made): 1 August 2000: see SI 2000/1985, art 2, Schedule.
Sub-s (3): Appointment (for remaining purposes): 2 April 2001: see SI 2001/239, art 2, Schedule.

Amendment
Section heading: words "removal centres" in square brackets substituted by the Nationality, Immigration and Asylum Act 2002, s 66(2)(b), (3)(b). Date in force: 10 February 2003: see SI 2003/1, art 2, Schedule.
Sub-s (1): words "removal centre" in square brackets substituted by the Nationality, Immigration and Asylum Act 2002, s 66(2)(a), (3)(b). Date in force: 10 February 2003: see SI 2003/1, art 2, Schedule.
Sub-s (2): words "removal centre" in square brackets substituted by the Nationality, Immigration and Asylum Act 2002, s 66(2)(a), (3)(b). Date in force: 10 February 2003: see SI 2003/1, art 2, Schedule.
Sub-s (3): words "removal centre" in square brackets in both places they occur substituted by the Nationality, Immigration and Asylum Act 2002, s 66(2)(a), (3)(b). Date in force: 10 February 2003: see SI 2003/1, art 2, Schedule.
Sub-s (4): words "removal centre" in square brackets substituted by the Nationality, Immigration and Asylum Act 2002, s 66(2)(a), (3)(b). Date in force: 10 February 2003: see SI 2003/1, art 2, Schedule.
Sub-s (5): words "removal centre" in square brackets substituted by the Nationality, Immigration and Asylum Act 2002, s 66(2)(a), (3)(b). Date in force: 10 February 2003: see SI 2003/1, art 2, Schedule.

Subordinate Legislation
Detention Centre Rules 2001, SI 2001/238 (made under sub-s (3)).

149   Contracting out of certain [removal centres]

(1) The Secretary of State may enter into a contract with another person for the provision or running (or the provision and running) by him, or (if the contract so provides) for the running by sub-contractors of his, of any [removal centre] or part of a [removal centre].

(2) While a [removal centre] contract for the running of a [removal centre] or part of a [removal centre] is in force—

(a) the [removal centre] or part is to be run subject to and in accordance with the provisions of or made under this Part; and

(b) in the case of a part, that part and the remaining part are to be treated for the purposes of those provisions as if they were separate [removal centres].

(3) If the Secretary of State grants a lease or tenancy of land for the purposes of a [removal centre] contract, none of the following enactments applies to the lease or tenancy—

(a) Part II of the Landlord and Tenant Act 1954 (security of tenure);

(b) section 146 of the Law of Property Act 1925 (restrictions on and relief against forfeiture);

(c) section 19(1), (2) and (3) of the Landlord and Tenant Act 1927 and the Landlord and Tenant Act 1988 (covenants not to assign etc);

(d) the Agricultural Holdings Act 1986;

(e) sections 4 to 7 of the Law Reform (Miscellaneous Provisions) (Scotland) Act 1985 (irritancy clauses);

(f) the Agricultural Holdings (Scotland) Act 1991 [and the Agricultural Holdings (Scotland) Act 2003 (asp 11)];

(g) section 14 of the Conveyancing Act 1881;

(h) the Conveyancing and Law of Property Act 1892;

(i) the Business Tenancies (Northern Ireland) Order 1996.

(4) The Secretary of State must appoint a contract monitor for every contracted out [removal centre].

(5) A person may be appointed as the contract monitor for more than one [removal centre].

(6) The contract monitor is to have—

(a) such functions as may be conferred on him by [removal centre] rules;

(b) the status of a Crown servant.

(7) The contract monitor must—

(a) keep under review, and report to the Secretary of State on, the running of a [removal centre] for which he is appointed; and

(b) investigate, and report to the Secretary of State on, any allegations made against any person performing custodial functions at that centre.

(8) The contractor, and any sub-contractor of his, must do all that he reasonably can (whether by giving directions to the officers of the [removal centre] or otherwise) to facilitate the exercise by the contract monitor of his functions.

(9) "Lease or tenancy" includes an underlease, sublease or sub-tenancy.

(10) In relation to a [removal centre] contract entered into by the Secretary of State before the commencement of this section, this section is to be treated as having been in force at that time.

Appointment
Sub-ss (1), (3), (6)(a), (9): Appointment: 1 August 2000: see SI 2000/1985, art 2, Schedule.
Sub-ss (2), (4), (5), (6)(b), (7), (8), (10): Appointment: 2 April 2001: see SI 2001/239, art 2, Schedule.

Amendment
Section heading: words "removal centres" in square brackets substituted by the Nationality, Immigration and Asylum Act 2002, s 66(2)(b), (3)(c). Date in force: 10 February 2003: see SI 2003/1, art 2, Schedule.
Sub-s (1): words "removal centre" in square brackets in both places they occur substituted by the Nationality, Immigration and Asylum Act 2002, s 66(2)(a), (3)(c). Date in force: 10 February 2003: see SI 2003/1, art 2, Schedule.
Sub-s (2): words "removal centre" and "removal centres" in square brackets in each place they occur substituted by the Nationality, Immigration and Asylum Act 2002, s 66(2), (3)(c). Date in force: 10 February 2003: see SI 2003/1, art 2, Schedule.
Sub-s (3): words "removal centre" in square brackets substituted by the Nationality, Immigration and Asylum Act 2002, s 66(2)(a), (3)(c). Date in force: 10 February 2003: see SI 2003/1, art 2, Schedule.
Sub-s (3): in para (f) words "and the Agricultural Holdings (Scotland) Act 2003 (asp 11)" in square brackets inserted by the Agricultural Holdings (Scotland) Act 2003, s 94, Schedule, para 52. Date in force: 27 November 2003: see SSI 2003/548, art 2(h), (i).
Sub-s (4): words "removal centre" in square brackets substituted by the Nationality, Immigration and Asylum Act 2002, s 66(2)(a), (3)(c). Date in force: 10 February 2003: see SI 2003/1, art 2, Schedule.
Sub-s (5): words "removal centre" in square brackets substituted by the Nationality, Immigration and Asylum Act 2002, s 66(2)(a), (3)(c). Date in force: 10 February 2003: see SI 2003/1, art 2, Schedule.

Sub-s (6): in para (a) words "removal centre" in square brackets substituted by the Nationality, Immigration and Asylum Act 2002, s 66(2)(a), (3)(c). Date in force: 10 February 2003: see SI 2003/1, art 2, Schedule.

Sub-s (7): in para (a) words "removal centre" in square brackets substituted by the Nationality, Immigration and Asylum Act 2002, s 66(2)(a), (3)(c). Date in force: 10 February 2003: see SI 2003/1, art 2, Schedule.

Sub-s (8): words "removal centre" in square brackets substituted by the Nationality, Immigration and Asylum Act 2002, s 66(2)(a), (3)(c). Date in force: 10 February 2003: see SI 2003/1, art 2, Schedule.

Sub-s (10): words "removal centre" in square brackets substituted by the Nationality, Immigration and Asylum Act 2002, s 66(2)(a), (3)(c). Date in force: 10 February 2003: see SI 2003/1, art 2, Schedule.

Subordinate Legislation
Detention Centre Rules 2001, SI 2001/238 (made under sub-s (6)).

150   Contracted out functions at directly managed [removal centres]

(1)   The Secretary of State may enter into a contract with another person—

  (a)   for functions at, or connected with, a directly managed [removal centre] to be performed by detainee custody officers provided by that person; or

  (b)   for such functions to be performed by certified prisoner custody officers who are provided by that person.

(2)   For the purposes of this section "[removal centre]" includes a short-term holding facility.

Appointment
Appointment: 2 April 2001: see SI 2001/239, art 2, Schedule.

Amendment
Section heading: words "removal centres" in square brackets substituted by the Nationality, Immigration and Asylum Act 2002, s 66(2)(b), (3)(c). Date in force: 10 February 2003: see SI 2003/1, art 2, Schedule.

Sub-s (1): in para (a) words "removal centre" in square brackets substituted by the Nationality, Immigration and Asylum Act 2002, s 66(2)(a), (3)(c). Date in force: 10 February 2003: see SI 2003/1, art 2, Schedule.

Sub-s (2): words "removal centre" in square brackets substituted by the Nationality, Immigration and Asylum Act 2002, s 66(2)(a), (3)(c). Date in force: 10 February 2003: see SI 2003/1, art 2, Schedule.

151   Intervention by Secretary of State

(1)   The Secretary of State may exercise the powers conferred by this section if it appears to him that—

  (a)   the manager of a contracted out [removal centre] has lost, or is likely to lose, effective control of the centre or of any part of it; or

  (b)   it is necessary to do so in the interests of preserving the safety of any person, or of preventing serious damage to any property.

(2)   The Secretary of State may appoint a person (to be known as the Controller) to act as manager of the [removal centre] for the period—

  (a)   beginning with the time specified in the appointment; and

  (b)   ending with the time specified in the notice of termination under subsection (5).

(3)   During that period—

  (a)   all the functions which would otherwise be exercisable by the manager or the contract monitor are to be exercisable by the Controller;

(b)   the contractor and any sub-contractor of his must do all that he reasonably can to facilitate the exercise by the Controller of his functions; and

(c)   the staff of the [removal centre] must comply with any directions given by the Controller in the exercise of his functions.

(4)   The Controller is to have the status of a Crown servant.

(5)   If the Secretary of State is satisfied that a Controller is no longer needed for a particular [removal centre], he must (by giving notice to the Controller) terminate his appointment at a time specified in the notice.

(6)   As soon as practicable after making an appointment under this section, the Secretary of State must give notice of the appointment to those entitled to notice.

(7)   As soon as practicable after terminating an appointment under this section, the Secretary of State must give a copy of the notice of termination to those entitled to notice.

(8)   Those entitled to notice are the contractor, the manager, the contract monitor and the Controller.

Appointment
Appointment: 2 April 2001: see SI 2001/239, art 2, Schedule.

Amendment
Sub-s (1): in para (a) words "removal centre" in square brackets substituted by the Nationality, Immigration and Asylum Act 2002, s 66(2)(a), (3)(d). Date in force: 10 February 2003: see SI 2003/1, art 2, Schedule.
Sub-s (2): words "removal centre" in square brackets substituted by the Nationality, Immigration and Asylum Act 2002, s 66(2)(a), (3)(d). Date in force: 10 February 2003: see SI 2003/1, art 2, Schedule.
Sub-s (3): in para (c) words "removal centre" in square brackets substituted by the Nationality, Immigration and Asylum Act 2002, s 66(2)(a), (3)(d). Date in force: 10 February 2003: see SI 2003/1, art 2, Schedule.
Sub-s (5): words "removal centre" in square brackets substituted by the Nationality, Immigration and Asylum Act 2002, s 66(2)(a), (3)(d). Date in force: 10 February 2003: see SI 2003/1, art 2, Schedule.

152   Visiting Committees and inspections

(1)   The Secretary of State must appoint a committee (to be known as the Visiting Committee) for each [removal centre].

(2)   The functions of the Visiting Committee for a [removal centre] are to be such as may be prescribed by the [removal centre] rules.

(3)   Those rules must include provision—

(a)   as to the making of visits to the centre by members of the Visiting Committee;
(b)   for the hearing of complaints made by persons detained in the centre;
(c)   requiring the making of reports by the Visiting Committee to the Secretary of State.

(4)   Every member of the Visiting Committee for a [removal centre] may at any time enter the centre and have free access to every part of it and to every person detained there.

(5)   In section 5A of the Prison Act 1952 (which deals with the appointment and functions of Her Majesty's Chief Inspector of Prisons), after subsection (5), insert—

"(5A)   Subsections (2) to (5) apply to [removal centres] (as defined by section 147 of the Immigration and Asylum Act 1999 and including any in Scotland) and persons detained in such [removal centres] as they apply to prisons and prisoners."

Appendix 1   Legislation and materials

Appointment
Sub-ss (1), (4), (5): Appointment: 2 April 2001: see SI 2001/239, art 2, Schedule.
Sub-ss (2), (3): Appointment (for the purposes of enabling subordinate legislation to be made): 1 August 2000: see SI 2000/1985, art 2, Schedule.
Sub-ss (2), (3): Appointment (for remaining purposes): 2 April 2001: see SI 2001/239, art 2, Schedule.

Amendment
Sub-s (1): words "removal centre" in square brackets substituted by the Nationality, Immigration and Asylum Act 2002, s 66(2)(a), (3)(e). Date in force: 10 February 2003: see SI 2003/1, art 2, Schedule.
Sub-s (2): words "removal centre" in square brackets in both places they occur substituted by the Nationality, Immigration and Asylum Act 2002, s 66(2)(a), (3)(e). Date in force: 10 February 2003: see SI 2003/1, art 2, Schedule.
Sub-s (4): words "removal centre" in square brackets substituted by the Nationality, Immigration and Asylum Act 2002, s 66(2)(a), (3)(e). Date in force: 10 February 2003: see SI 2003/1, art 2, Schedule.
Sub-s (5): in the Prison Act 1952, s 5A (as set out) words "removal centres" in square brackets in both places they occur substituted by the Nationality, Immigration and Asylum Act 2002, s 66(2)(b), (3)(e). Date in force: 10 February 2003: see SI 2003/1, art 2, Schedule.

Subordinate Legislation
Detention Centre Rules 2001, SI 2001/238 (made under sub-ss (2), (3)).

153   [Removal centre] rules

(1)   The Secretary of State must make rules for the regulation and management of [removal centres].

(2)   [Removal centre] rules may, among other things, make provision with respect to the safety, care, activities, discipline and control of detained persons.

Appointment
Appointment (for the purposes of enabling subordinate legislation to be made): 1 August 2000: see SI 2000/1985, art 2, Schedule.
Appointment (for remaining purposes): 2 April 2001: see SI 2001/239, art 2, Schedule.

Amendment
Section heading: words "Removal centre" in square brackets substituted by the Nationality, Immigration and Asylum Act 2002, s 66(2)(a), (3)(f). Date in force: 10 February 2003: see SI 2003/1, art 2, Schedule.
Sub-s (1): words "removal centres" in square brackets substituted by the Nationality, Immigration and Asylum Act 2002, s 66(2)(b), (3)(f). Date in force: 10 February 2003: see SI 2003/1, art 2, Schedule.
Sub-s (2): words "Removal centre" in square brackets substituted by the Nationality, Immigration and Asylum Act 2002, s 66(2)(a), (3)(f). Date in force: 10 February 2003: see SI 2003/1, art 2, Schedule.

Subordinate Legislation
Detention Centre Rules 2001, SI 2001/238.
Detention Centre (Amendment) Rules 2005, SI 2005/673.

Custody and movement of detained persons

154   Detainee custody officers

(1)   On an application made to him under this section, the Secretary of State may certify that the applicant—

(a)   is authorised to perform escort functions; or
(b)   is authorised to perform both escort functions and custodial functions.

1544

(2) The Secretary of State may not issue a certificate of authorisation unless he is satisfied that the applicant—

(a) is a fit and proper person to perform the functions to be authorised; and
(b) has received training to such standard as the Secretary of State considers appropriate for the performance of those functions.

(3) A certificate of authorisation continues in force until such date, or the occurrence of such event, as may be specified in the certificate but may be suspended or revoked under paragraph 7 of Schedule 11.

(4) A certificate which authorises the performance of both escort functions and custodial functions may specify one date or event for one of those functions and a different date or event for the other.

[(5) The Secretary of State may confer functions of detainee custody officers on prison officers or prisoner custody officers.]

(6) A prison officer acting under arrangements made under subsection (5) has all the powers, authority, protection and privileges of a constable.

(7) Schedule 11 makes further provision about detainee custody officers.

Appointment
Sub-ss (1)–(6): Appointment: 2 April 2001: see SI 2001/239, art 2, Schedule.
Sub-s (7): Appointment (for certain purposes): 3 April 2000: see SI 2000/464, art 2, Schedule.
Sub-s (7): Appointment (for certain purposes): 1 August 2000: see SI 2000/1985, art 2, Schedule.
Sub-s (7): Appointment (for remaining purposes): 2 April 2001: see SI 2001/239, art 2, Schedule.

Amendment
Sub-s (5): substituted by the Nationality, Immigration and Asylum Act 2002, s 65(1). Date in force: 10 February 2003: see SI 2003/1, art 2, Schedule.

155 Custodial functions and discipline etc at [removal centres]

(1) Custodial functions may be discharged at a [removal centre] only by—

(a) a detainee custody officer authorised, in accordance with section 154(1), to perform such functions; or
(b) a prison officer, or a certified prisoner custody officer, exercising functions in relation to the [removal centre]—
(i) in accordance with arrangements made under section 154(5); or
(ii) as a result of a contract entered into under section 150(1)(b).

(2) Schedule 12 makes provision with respect to discipline and other matters at [removal centres] and short-term holding facilities.

Appointment
Sub-s (1): Appointment: 2 April 2001: see SI 2001/239, art 2, Schedule.
Sub-s (2): Appointment (for certain purposes): 1 August 2000: see SI 2000/1985, art 2, Schedule.
Sub-s (2): Appointment (for remaining purposes): 2 April 2001: see SI 2001/239, art 2, Schedule.

Amendment
Section heading: words "removal centres" in square brackets substituted by the Nationality, Immigration and Asylum Act 2002, s 66(2)(b), (3)(g). Date in force: 10 February 2003: see SI 2003/1, art 2, Schedule.
Sub-s (1): words "removal centre" in square brackets in both places they occur substituted by the Nationality, Immigration and Asylum Act 2002, s 66(2)(a), (3)(g). Date in force: 10 February 2003: see SI 2003/1, art 2, Schedule.
Sub-s (2): words "removal centres" in square brackets substituted by the Nationality, Immigration and Asylum Act 2002, s 66(2)(b), (3)(g). Date in force: 10 February 2003: see SI 2003/1, art 2, Schedule.

156 Arrangements for the provision of escorts and custody

(1) The Secretary of State may make arrangements for—

  (a) the delivery of detained persons to premises in which they may lawfully be detained;

  (b) the delivery of persons from any such premises for the purposes of their removal from the United Kingdom in accordance with directions given under the 1971 Act or this Act;

  (c) the custody of detained persons who are temporarily outside such premises;

  (d) the custody of detained persons held on the premises of any court.

(2) Escort arrangements may provide for functions under the arrangements to be performed, in such cases as may be determined by or under the arrangements, by detainee custody officers.

(3) "Court" includes—

  [(a) the Asylum and Immigration Tribunal;]

  (c) the Commission.

(4) Escort arrangements may include entering into contracts with other persons for the provision by them of—

  (a) detainee custody officers; or

  (b) prisoner custody officers who are certified under section 89 of the Criminal Justice Act 1991, or section 114 or 122 of the Criminal Justice and Public Order Act 1994, to perform escort functions.

(5) Schedule 13 makes further provision about escort arrangements.

(6) A person responsible for performing a function of a kind mentioned in subsection (1), in accordance with a transfer direction, complies with the direction if he does all that he reasonably can to secure that the function is performed by a person acting in accordance with escort arrangements.

(7) "Transfer direction" means a transfer direction given under—

  (a) section 48 of the Mental Health Act 1983 or section 71 of the Mental Health (Scotland) Act 1984 (removal to hospital of, among others, persons detained under the 1971 Act); or

  (b) in Northern Ireland, article 54 of the Mental Health (Northern Ireland) Order 1986 (provision corresponding to section 48 of the 1983 Act).

Appointment
Sub-ss (1)–(4), (6), (7): Appointment: 2 April 2001: see SI 2001/239, art 2, Schedule.
Sub-s (5): Appointment (for certain purposes): 1 August 2000: see SI 2000/1985, art 2, Schedule.
Sub-s (5): Appointment (for remaining purposes): 2 April 2001: see SI 2001/239, art 2, Schedule.

Amendment
Sub-s (3): para (a) substituted, for paras (a), (b) as originally enacted, by the Asylum and Immigration (Treatment of Claimants, etc) Act 2004, s 26(7), Sch 2, Pt 1, para 15; for transitional provisions see s 26(7), Sch 2, Pt 2 thereto. Date in force: 4 April 2005: see SI 2005/565, art 2(d); for transitional provisions in relation to pending appeals which were made to an adjudicator before 4 April 2005 and in relation to further appeals and applications in such cases see arts 3–9 thereof.

157 Short-term holding facilities

(1) The Secretary of State may by regulations extend any provision made by or under this Part in relation to [removal centres] (other than one mentioned in subsection (2)) to short-term holding facilities.

(2) Subsection (1) does not apply to section 150.

(3) The Secretary of State may make rules for the regulation and management of short-term holding facilities.

Appointment

Appointment (for the purposes of enabling subordinate legislation to be made): 1 August 2000: see SI 2000/1985, art 2, Schedule.
Appointment (for remaining purposes): 2 April 2001: see SI 2001/239, art 2, Schedule.

Amendment

Sub-s (1): words "removal centres" in square brackets substituted by the Nationality, Immigration and Asylum Act 2002, s 66(2)(b), (3)(h). Date in force: 10 February 2003: see SI 2003/1, art 2, Schedule.

Subordinate Legislation

Immigration (Short-term Holding Facilities) Regulations 2002, SI 2002/2538 (made under sub-s (1)).

Miscellaneous

158   Wrongful disclosure of information

(1) A person who is or has been employed (whether as a detainee custody officer, prisoner custody officer or otherwise)—

    (a)   in accordance with escort arrangements,

    (b)   at a contracted out [removal centre], or

    (c)   to perform contracted out functions at a directly managed [removal centre],

is guilty of an offence if he discloses, otherwise than in the course of his duty or as authorised by the Secretary of State, any information which he acquired in the course of his employment and which relates to a particular detained person.

(2) A person guilty of such an offence is liable—

    (a)   on conviction on indictment, to imprisonment for a term not exceeding two years or to a fine or to both;

    (b)   on summary conviction, to imprisonment for a term not exceeding six months or to a fine not exceeding the statutory maximum or to both.

(3) "Contracted out functions" means functions which, as the result of a contract entered into under section 150, fall to be performed by detainee custody officers or certified prisoner custody officers.

Appointment

Appointment: 2 April 2001: see SI 2001/239, art 2, Schedule.

Amendment

Sub-s (1): in paras (b), (c) words "removal centre" in square brackets substituted by the Nationality, Immigration and Asylum Act 2002, s 66(2)(a), (3)(i). Date in force: 10 February 2003: see SI 2003/1, art 2, Schedule.

159   Power of constable to act outside his jurisdiction

(1) For the purpose of taking a person to or from a [removal centre] under the order of any authority competent to give the order, a constable may act outside the area of his jurisdiction.

(2) When acting under this section, the constable concerned retains all the powers, authority, protection and privileges of his office.

Appointment
Appointment: 2 April 2001: see SI 2001/239, art 2, Schedule.

Amendment
Sub-s (1): words "removal centre" in square brackets substituted by the Nationality, Immigration and Asylum Act 2002, s 66(2)(a), (3)(j). Date in force: 10 February 2003: see SI 2003/1, art 2, Schedule.

PART IX
REGISTRAR'S CERTIFICATES: PROCEDURE

160   Abolition of certificate by licence

(1)   In the Marriage Act 1949, in section 26, omit subsection (2) (marriage under superintendent registrar's certificate to be by licence issued by the registrar or without licence).

(2)   In section 27 of the 1949 Act—

    (a)   in subsection (1), omit "without licence";
    (b)   omit subsection (2);
    (c)   in subsection (3), in paragraph (a), omit "in the case of a marriage intended to be solemnized without licence,";
    (d)   in subsection (3), omit paragraph (b).

(3)   Section 32 of the 1949 Act (marriage under certificate by licence) shall cease to have effect.

(4)   In section 31 of the 1949 Act (marriage under certificate without licence requiring 21 days' notice)—

    (a)   in subsection (1), omit "without licence" and for "twenty-one" substitute "15";
    (b)   in subsection (2), for "twenty-one" substitute "15";
    (c)   in subsection (4), omit "without licence" and for "said period of twenty-one days" substitute "waiting period in relation to each notice of marriage".

(5)   In section 31 of the 1949 Act, after subsection (4) insert—

"(4A)   "The waiting period", in relation to a notice of marriage, means—

    (a)   the period of 15 days, or
    (b)   such shorter period as may be determined by the Registrar General under subsection (5A) or by a superintendent registrar under any provision of regulations made under subsection (5D),

after the day on which the notice of marriage was entered in the marriage notice book."

(6)   In section 31 of the 1949 Act, insert at the end—

"(5A)   If, on an application made to the Registrar General, he is satisfied that there are compelling reasons for reducing the 15 day period because of the exceptional circumstances of the case, he may reduce that period to such shorter period as he considers appropriate.

(5B)   "The 15 day period" means the period of 15 days mentioned in subsections (1) and (2).

(5C)   If the Registrar General reduces the 15 day period in a particular case, the reference to 15 days in section 75(3)(a) is to be treated, in relation to that case, as a reference to the reduced period.

(5D)   The Registrar General may by regulations make provision with respect to the making, and granting, of applications under subsection (5A).

(5E)   The regulations—

(a)   may provide for the power conferred by subsection (5A) to be exercised by a superintendent registrar on behalf of the Registrar General in cases falling within a category prescribed in the regulations;

(b)   may provide for the making of an appeal to the Registrar General against a decision taken by a superintendent registrar in accordance with regulations made by virtue of paragraph (a);

(c)   may make different provision in relation to different cases;

(d)   require the approval of the Chancellor of the Exchequer.

(5F)   The Chancellor of the Exchequer may by order provide for a fee, of such an amount as may be specified in the order, to be payable on an application under subsection (5A).

(5G)   The order may make different provision in relation to different cases.

(5H)   The power to make regulations under subsection (5D) or an order under subsection (5F) is exercisable by statutory instrument.

(5I)   Any statutory instrument made under subsection (5F) shall be subject to annulment in pursuance of a resolution of either House of Parliament."

Appointment
Appointment: 1 January 2001: see SI 2000/2698, art 2, Schedule.

161   Notice of marriage

(1)   In the Marriage Act 1949, in section 27(1) (persons by whom notice of marriage must be given)—

(a)   in paragraph (a), for "either" substitute "each";

(b)   in paragraph (b), for "either" substitute "each" and for "each registration district in which one of them has resided" substitute "the registration district in which he or she has resided".

(2)   In section 27 of the 1949 Act, in subsection (3) (matters to be stated in notice of marriage), for "and place of residence" substitute ", place of residence and nationality".

(3)   In the 1949 Act, in section 26(1) (marriages which may be solemnized on authority of a certificate of a superintendent registrar), for "a certificate" substitute "two certificates".

(4)   ...

Appointment
Appointment: 1 January 2001: see SI 2000/2698, art 2, Schedule.

Amendment
Sub-s (4): repealed by SI 2003/413, art 40, Schedule. Date in force: 1 January 2004: see the Marriage (2003 Order) (Commencement) Order (Northern Ireland) 2003, SR 2003/466, art 2(b).

162   Power to require evidence

(1)   In the Marriage Act 1949, after section 28, insert—

"28A   Power to require evidence

(1)   A superintendent registrar to whom a notice of marriage is given under section 27, or any other person attesting a declaration accompanying such a notice, may require the person giving the notice to provide him with specified evidence—

    (a)   relating to that person; or

    (b)   if the superintendent registrar considers that the circumstances are exceptional, relating to each of the persons to be married.

(2)   Such a requirement may be imposed at any time—

    (a)   on or after the giving of the notice of marriage; but

    (b)   before the superintendent registrar issues his certificate under section 31.

(3)   "Specified evidence", in relation to a person, means such evidence of that person's—

    (a)   name and surname,

    (b)   age,

    (c)   marital status, and

    (d)   nationality,

as may be specified in guidance issued by the Registrar General."

(2)   ...

Appointment
Appointment: 1 January 2001: see SI 2000/2698, art 2, Schedule.

Amendment
Sub-s (2): repealed by SI 2003/413, art 40, Schedule. Date in force: 1 January 2004: see the Marriage (2003 Order) (Commencement) Order (Northern Ireland) 2003, SR 2003/466, art 2(b).

163   Refusal to issue certificate

(1)   In the Marriage Act 1949, in section 31(2) (issue of marriage certificate), for paragraph (a) substitute—

    "(a)   the superintendent registrar is not satisfied that there is no lawful impediment to the issue of the certificate; or".

(2)   In the 1949 Act, after section 31, insert—

"31A   Appeal on refusal under section 31(2)(a)

(1)   If, relying on section 31(2)(a), a superintendent registrar refuses to issue a certificate, the person applying for it may appeal to the Registrar General.

(2)   On such an appeal, the Registrar General must—

    (a)   confirm the refusal; or

    (b)   direct that a certificate be issued.

(3)   If—

    (a)   relying on section 31(2)(a), a superintendent registrar refuses to issue a certificate as a result of a representation made to him, and

    (b)   on an appeal against the refusal, the Registrar General declares the representation to have been frivolous and to be such that it ought not to obstruct the issue of a certificate,

the person making the representation is liable for the costs of the proceedings before the Registrar General and for damages recoverable by the applicant for the certificate.

(4) For the purpose of enabling a person to recover any such costs and damages, a copy of the declaration of the Registrar General purporting to be sealed with the seal of the General Register Office is evidence that the Registrar General has declared the representation to have been frivolous and to be such that it ought not to obstruct the issue of a certificate."

(3) ...

(4) ...

Appointment
Appointment: 1 January 2001: see SI 2000/2698, art 2, Schedule.

Amendment
Sub-ss (3), (4): repealed by SI 2003/413, art 40, Schedule. Date in force: 1 January 2004: see the Marriage (2003 Order) (Commencement) Order (Northern Ireland) 2003, SR 2003/466, art 2(b).

PART X
MISCELLANEOUS AND SUPPLEMENTAL

164 Institution of proceedings

In section 3(2) of the Prosecution of Offences Act 1985 (proceedings which must be conducted by the Director of Public Prosecutions), after paragraph (a) insert—

"(aa)to take over the conduct of any criminal proceedings instituted by an immigration officer (as defined for the purposes of the Immigration Act 1971) acting in his capacity as such an officer;".

Appointment
Appointment: 1 December 2004: see SI 2004/2997, art 2.

165 Procedural requirements as to applications

[Inserts s 31A of the Immigration Act 1971]

Appointment
Appointment (for certain purposes): 22 May 2000: see SI 2000/1282, art 2, Schedule.
Appointment (for remaining purposes): 1 August 2003: see SI 2003/1862, art 2.

166 Regulations and orders

(1) Any power to make rules, regulations or orders conferred by this Act is exercisable by statutory instrument.

(2) But subsection (1) does not apply in relation to [orders made under section 90(1),] rules made under paragraph 1 of Schedule 5 or immigration rules.

(3) Any statutory instrument made as a result of subsection (1) may—

(a) contain such incidental, supplemental, consequential and transitional provision as the person making it considers appropriate;
(b) make different provision for different cases or descriptions of case; and
(c) make different provision for different areas.

(4) No order is to be made under—

(a) section 20,
(b) section 21,
(c) section 31(10),
(d) section 86(2),
(e) ...

(f)   section 97(3),
(g)   section 143(15), or
(h)   paragraph 4 of Schedule 5,

unless a draft of the order has been laid before Parliament and approved by a resolution of each House.

(5)   No regulations are to be made under—

[(za) section 4(5),]
(a)   section 9,
(b)   section 46(8),
(c)   section 53, or
(d)   section 144,

unless a draft of the regulations has been laid before Parliament and approved by a resolution of each House.

(6)   Any statutory instrument made under this Act, apart from one made—

(a)   under any of the provisions mentioned in subsection (4) or (5), or
(b)   under section 24(3)[, 24A(3)] or 170(4) or (7),

shall be subject to annulment by a resolution of either House of Parliament.

Initial Commencement
Royal Assent: 11 November 1999: see s 170(3)(p).

Amendment
Sub-s (2): words "orders made under section 90(1)," in square brackets inserted by the Asylum and Immigration (Treatment of Claimants, etc) Act 2004, s 41(5). Date in force: 1 October 2004: see SI 2004/2523, art 2, Schedule.
Sub-s (4): para (e) repealed by the Nationality, Immigration and Asylum Act 2002, ss 61(b), 161, Sch 9. Date in force: 7 November 2002: see the Nationality, Immigration and Asylum Act 2002, s 162(2)(s).
Sub-s (5): para (za) inserted by the Asylum and Immigration (Treatment of Claimants, etc) Act 2004, s 10(2), (6). Date in force: 1 December 2004: see SI 2004/2999, art 2, Schedule.
Sub-s (6): in para (b) reference to ", 24A(3)" in square brackets inserted by the Civil Partnership Act 2004, s 261(1), Sch 27, para 163. Date in force: 15 April 2005: see SI 2005/1112, art 2, Sch 1.

167   Interpretation

(1)   In this Act—

"the 1971 Act" means the Immigration Act 1971;
"adjudicator" (except in Part VI) means an adjudicator appointed under section 57;
"Chief Adjudicator" means the person appointed as Chief Adjudicator under section 57(2);
"claim for asylum" (except in Parts V and VI and section 141) means a claim that it would be contrary to the United Kingdom's obligations under the Refugee Convention for the claimant to be removed from, or required to leave, the United Kingdom;
"the Commission" means the Special Immigration Appeals Commission;
"country" includes any territory;
"EEA State" means a State which is a Contracting Party to the Agreement on the European Economic Area signed at Oporto on 2nd May 1992 as it has effect for the time being;

"the Human Rights Convention" means the Convention for the Protection of Human Rights and Fundamental Freedoms, agreed by the Council of Europe at Rome on 4th November 1950 as it has effect for the time being in relation to the United Kingdom;

["the Immigration Acts" has the meaning given by [section 44 of the Asylum and Immigration (Treatment of Claimants, etc) Act 2004];]

"prescribed" means prescribed by regulations made by the Secretary of State;

"the Refugee Convention" means the Convention relating to the Status of Refugees done at Geneva on 28 July 1951 and the Protocol to the Convention;

"voluntary organisations" means bodies (other than public or local authorities) whose activities are not carried on for profit.

(2) The following expressions have the same meaning as in the 1971 Act—

"certificate of entitlement";
"entry clearance";
"illegal entrant";
"immigration officer";
"immigration rules";
"port";
"United Kingdom passport";
"work permit".

Initial Commencement
Royal Assent: 11 November 1999: see s 170(3)(p).

Amendment
Sub-s (1): definition "the Immigration Acts" substituted by the Nationality, Immigration and Asylum Act 2002, s 158(4). Date in force: 10 February 2003: see SI 2003/1, art 2, Schedule.
Sub-s (1): in definition "the Immigration Acts" words "section 44 of the Asylum and Immigration (Treatment of Claimants, etc) Act 2004" in square brackets substituted by the Asylum and Immigration (Treatment of Claimants, etc) Act 2004, s 44(4)(b). Date in force: 1 October 2004: see SI 2004/2523, art 2, Schedule.

168 Expenditure and receipts

(1) There is to be paid out of money provided by Parliament—

(a) any expenditure incurred by the Secretary of State or the Lord Chancellor in consequence of this Act; and

(b) any increase attributable to this Act in the sums so payable by virtue of any other Act.

(2) Sums received by the Secretary of State under section 5, 32, 40, 112 or 113 or by the Lord Chancellor under section 48(4) or 49(4) must be paid into the Consolidated Fund.

Initial Commencement
Royal Assent: 11 November 1999: see s 170(3)(p).

169 Minor and consequential amendments, transitional provisions and repeals

(1) Schedule 14 makes minor and consequential amendments.

(2) Schedule 15 contains transitional provisions and savings.

(3) The enactments set out in Schedule 16 are repealed.

Appointment
Sub-ss (1), (2): Appointment (for certain purposes): 6 December 1999: see SI 1999/3190, art 2, Schedule.

Sub-ss (1)–(3): Appointment (for certain purposes): 14 February 2000: see SI 2000/168, art 2, Schedule.
Sub-ss (1), (3): Appointment (for certain purposes): 1 March 2000: see SI 2000/464, art 2, Schedule.
Sub-ss (1), (3): Appointment (for certain purposes): 3 April 2000: see SI 2000/464, art 2, Schedule.
Sub-s (1): Appointment (for certain purposes): 1 August 2000: see SI 2000/1985, art 2, Schedule.
Sub-s (1): Appointment (for certain purposes): 2 October 2000: see SI 2000/2444, art 2, Sch 1.
Sub-ss (1), (3): Appointment (for certain purposes): 11 December 2000: see SI 2000/3099, art 3, Schedule.
Sub-ss (1), (3): Appointment (for certain purposes): 1 January 2001: see SI 2000/2698, art 2, Schedule.
Sub-ss (1), (3): Appointment (for certain purposes): 30 June 2003: see SI 2003/1469, art 2, Schedule.
Sub-s (2): Appointment (for certain purposes): 2 October 2000: see SI 2000/2444, art 2, Sch 1.
Sub-s (3): Appointment (for certain purposes): 2 October 2000: see SI 2000/2444, art 2, Sch 1.

170   Short title, commencement and extent

(1)   This Act may be cited as the Immigration and Asylum Act 1999.

(2)   Subsections (1) and (2) of section 115 come into force on the day on which the first regulations made under Schedule 8 come into force.

(3)   The following provisions come into force on the passing of this Act—

    (a)   section 4;
    (b)   section 9;
    (c)   section 15;
    (d)   section 27;
    (e)   section 31;
    (f)   section 94;
    (g)   section 95(13);
    (h)   section 99(4) and (5);
    (i)   sections 105 to 109;
    (j)   section 110(1), (2) and (8) (so far as relating to subsections (1) and (2));
    (k)   section 111;
    (l)   section 124;
    (m)   section 140;
    (n)   section 145;
    (o)   section 146(1);
    (p)   sections 166 to 168;
    (q)   this section;
    (r)   Schedule 9;
    (s)   paragraphs 62(2), 73, 78, 79, 81, 82, 87, 88 and 102 of Schedule 14;
    (t)   paragraphs 2 and 13 of Schedule 15.

(4)   The other provisions of this Act, except section 10 and paragraph 12 of Schedule 15 (which come into force in accordance with section 9), come into force on such day as the Secretary of State may by order appoint.

(5)   Different days may be appointed for different purposes.

(6)   This Act extends to Northern Ireland.

(7)   Her Majesty may by Order in Council direct that any of the provisions of this Act are to extend, with such modifications (if any) as appear to Her Majesty to be appropriate, to any of the Channel Islands or the Isle of Man.

Initial Commencement
Royal Assent: 11 November 1999: see sub-s (3)(q) above.

Subordinate Legislation

Immigration and Asylum Act 1999 (Commencement No 1) Order 1999, SI 1999/3190 (made under sub-ss (4), (5)).

Immigration and Asylum Act 1999 (Commencement No 2 and Transitional Provisions) Order 2000, SI 2000/168 (made under sub-ss (4), (5)).

Immigration and Asylum Act 1999 (Commencement No 3) Order 2000, SI 2000/464 (made under sub-ss (4), (5)).

Immigration and Asylum Act 1999 (Commencement No 4) Order 2000, SI 2000/1282 (made under sub-ss (4), (5)).

Immigration and Asylum Act 1999 (Commencement No 5 and Transitional Provisions) Order 2000, SI 2000/1985 (made under sub-ss (4), (5)).

Immigration and Asylum Act 1999 (Commencement No 9) Order 2001, SI 2001/239 (made under sub-ss (4), (5)).

Immigration and Asylum Act 1999 (Commencement No 10) Order 2001, SI 2001/1394 (made under sub-ss (4), (5)).

Immigration and Asylum Act 1999 (Commencement No 11) Order 2002, SI 2002/2815 (made under sub-s (4)).

Immigration and Asylum Act 1999 (Commencement No 12) Order 2003, SI 2003/2 (made under sub-s (4)).

Immigration and Asylum Act 1999 (Commencement No 13) Order 2003, SI 2003/758 (made under sub-s (4)).

Immigration and Asylum Act 1999 (Jersey) Order 2003, SI 2003/1252 (made under sub-s (7)).

Immigration and Asylum Act 1999 (Commencement No 14) Order 2003, SI 2003/1469 (made under sub-s (4)).

Immigration and Asylum Act 1999 (Commencement No 15) Order 2003, SI 2003/1862 (made under sub-s (4)).

Immigration and Asylum Act 1999 (Guernsey) Order 2003, SI 2003/2900 (made under sub-s (7)).

Immigration and Asylum Act 1999 (Commencement No 16) Order 2004, SI 2004/2997 (made under sub-s (4)).

SCHEDULE 1
SALE OF TRANSPORTERS

Sections 37(6) and 42(8)

Leave of court required

1 (1) The sale of a transporter requires the leave of the court.

(2) The court is not to give its leave except on proof—

- (a) that the penalty *or charge* is or was due;
- (b) that the person liable to pay it or any connected expenses has failed to do so; and
- (c) that the transporter which the Secretary of State seeks leave to sell is liable to sale.

Notice of proposed sale

2 Before applying for leave to sell a transporter, the Secretary of State must take such steps as may be prescribed—

- (a) for bringing the proposed sale to the notice of persons whose interests may be affected by a decision of the court to grant leave; and
- (b) for affording to any such person an opportunity of becoming a party to the proceedings if the Secretary of State applies for leave.

[2A Where the owner of a transporter is a party to an application for leave to sell it, in determining whether to give leave the court shall consider—

- (a) the extent of any hardship likely to be caused by sale,

1555

    (b)   the extent (if any) to which the owner is responsible for the matters in respect of which the penalty notice was issued, and

    (c)   any other matter which appears to the court to be relevant (whether specific to the circumstances of the case or of a general nature).]

Duty to obtain best price

3   If leave for sale is given, the Secretary of State must secure that the transporter is sold for the best price that can reasonably be obtained.

Effect of failure to comply with paragraph 2 or 3

4   Failure to comply with any requirement of paragraph 2 or 3 in respect of any sale—

    (a)   is actionable against the Secretary of State at the suit of any person suffering loss in consequence of the sale; but

    (b)   after the sale has taken place, does not affect its validity.

Application of proceeds of sale

5   (1) Any proceeds of sale arising from a sale under section 37 *or 42* must be applied—

    (a)   in making prescribed payments; and

    (b)   in accordance with such provision as to priority of payments as may be prescribed.

(2) The regulations may, in particular, provide for proceeds of sale to be applied in payment—

    (a)   of customs or excise duty,

    (b)   of value added tax,

    (c)   of expenses incurred by the Secretary of State,

    (d)   of any penalty *or charge* which the court has found to be due,

    (e)   in the case of the sale of an aircraft, of charges due as a result of regulations made under section 73 of the Civil Aviation Act 1982,

    (f)   of any surplus to or among the person or persons whose interests in the transporter have been divested as a result of the sale,

but not necessarily in that order of priority.

Appointment

Paras 1, 3, 4: Appointment (for certain purposes): 3 April 2000: see SI 2000/464, art 2, Schedule.
Paras 2, 5: Appointment: 6 December 1999: see SI 1999/3190, art 2, Schedule.

Amendment

Para 1: in sub-para (2)(a) words "or charge" in italics repealed by the Nationality, Immigration and Asylum Act 2002, ss 125, 161, Sch 8, paras 1, 16(1), (2), Sch 9. Date in force (for the purposes of clandestine entrants who arrive in the United Kingdom concealed in a vehicle or a rail freight wagon): 8 December 2002 (except in relation to a penalty notice issued to a person before that date): see SI 2002/2811, arts 2, 4, Schedule. Date in force (for remaining purposes): to be appointed: see the Nationality, Immigration and Asylum Act 2002, s 162(1).
Para 2A: inserted by the Nationality, Immigration and Asylum Act 2002, s 125, Sch 8, paras 1, 16(1), (3). Date in force (for the purposes of clandestine entrants who arrive in the United Kingdom concealed in a vehicle or a rail freight wagon): 8 December 2002 (except in relation to a penalty notice issued to a person before that date): see SI 2002/2811, arts 2, 4, Schedule. Date in force (for remaining purposes): to be appointed: see the Nationality, Immigration and Asylum Act 2002, s 162(1).
Para 5: in sub-para (1) words "or 42" in italics repealed by the Nationality, Immigration and Asylum Act 2002, ss 125, 161 Sch 8, paras 1, 16(1), (4), Sch 9. Date in force (for the purposes of

clandestine entrants who arrive in the United Kingdom concealed in a vehicle or a rail freight wagon): 8 December 2002 (except in relation to a penalty notice issued to a person before that date): see SI 2002/2811, arts 2, 4, Schedule. Date in force (for remaining purposes): to be appointed: see the Nationality, Immigration and Asylum Act 2002, s 162(1).

Para 5: in sub-para (2)(d) words "or charge" in italics repealed by the Nationality, Immigration and Asylum Act 2002, ss 125, 161, Sch 8, paras 1, 16(1), (5), Sch 9. Date in force (for the purposes of clandestine entrants who arrive in the United Kingdom concealed in a vehicle or a rail freight wagon): 8 December 2002 (except in relation to a penalty notice issued to a person before that date): see SI 2002/2811, arts 2, 4, Schedule. Date in force (for remaining purposes): to be appointed: see the Nationality, Immigration and Asylum Act 2002, s 162(1).

Subordinate Legislation
Carriers' Liability Regulations 2002, SI 2002/2817 (made under paras 2, 5).

SCHEDULE 2
...

...

Amendment
Repealed by the Nationality, Immigration and Asylum Act 2002, ss 114(1), (2), 161, Sch 9; for transitional provisions see Sch 6 thereto. Date in force: 1 April 2003 (except in relation to events which took place before that date): see SI 2003/754, arts 2(1), 3, Sch 1, Sch 2, para 6(4).

SCHEDULE 3
...

...

Amendment
Repealed by the Nationality, Immigration and Asylum Act 2002, ss 114(1), (2), 161, Sch 9; for transitional provisions see Sch 6 thereto. Date in force: 1 April 2003 (except in relation to events which took place before that date): see SI 2003/754, arts 2(1), 3, Sch 1, Sch 2, para 6(4).

SCHEDULE 4
...

...

Amendment
Repealed by the Nationality, Immigration and Asylum Act 2002, ss 114(1), (2), 161, Sch 9; for transitional provisions see Sch 6 thereto. Date in force: 1 April 2003 (except in relation to events which took place before that date): see SI 2003/754, arts 2(1), 3, Sch 1, Sch 2, para 6(4).

SCHEDULE 5
THE IMMIGRATION SERVICES COMMISSIONER

Section 83

PART I
REGULATORY FUNCTIONS

The Commissioner's rules

1 (1) The Commissioner may make rules regulating any aspect of the professional practice, conduct or discipline of—

(a) registered persons, and
[(b) those acting on behalf of registered persons,]

in connection with the provision of immigration advice or immigration services.

1557

(2)   Before making or altering any rules, the Commissioner must consult such persons appearing to him to represent the views of persons engaged in the provision of immigration advice or immigration services as he considers appropriate.

(3)   In determining whether a registered person is competent or otherwise fit to provide immigration advice or immigration services, the Commissioner may take into account any breach of the rules by—

    (a)   that person; and
    [(b) any person acting on behalf of that person].

(4)   The rules may, among other things, make provision requiring the keeping of accounts or the obtaining of indemnity insurance.

2   (1)   The Commissioner's rules must be made or altered by an instrument in writing.

(2)   Such an instrument must specify that it is made under this Schedule.

(3)   Immediately after such an instrument is made, it must be printed and made available to the public.

(4)   The Commissioner may charge a reasonable fee for providing a person with a copy of the instrument.

(5)   A person is not to be taken to have contravened a rule made by the Commissioner if he shows that at the time of the alleged contravention the instrument containing the rule had not been made available in accordance with this paragraph.

(6)   The production of a printed copy of an instrument purporting to be made by the Commissioner on which is endorsed a certificate signed by an officer of the Commissioner authorised by him for that purpose and stating—

    (a)   that the instrument was made by the Commissioner,
    (b)   that the copy is a true copy of the instrument, and
    (c)   that on a specified date the instrument was made available to the public in accordance with this paragraph,

is evidence (or in Scotland sufficient evidence) of the facts stated in the certificate.

(7)   A certificate purporting to be signed as mentioned in sub-paragraph (6) is to be treated as having been properly signed unless the contrary is shown.

(8)   A person who wishes in any legal proceedings to rely on an instrument containing the Commissioner's rules may require him to endorse a copy of the instrument with a certificate of the kind mentioned in sub-paragraph (6).

Code of Standards

3   (1)   The Commissioner must prepare and issue a code setting standards of conduct which those to whom the code applies are expected to meet.

(2)   The code is to be known as the Code of Standards but is referred to in this Schedule as "the Code".

(3)   The Code is to apply to any person providing immigration advice or immigration services other than—

    (a)   a person who is authorised by a designated professional body to practise as a member of the profession whose members are regulated by that body;
    [(b) a person who is acting on behalf of a person who is within paragraph (a);]
    (c)   a person mentioned in section 84(6).

(4) It is the duty of any person to whom the Code applies to comply with its provisions in providing immigration advice or immigration services.

(5) If the Commissioner alters the Code, he must re-issue it.

(6) Before issuing the Code or altering it, the Commissioner must consult—

(a) each of the designated professional bodies;
(b) the designated judges;
(c) the Lord President of the Court of Session;
(d) the Lord Chief Justice of Northern Ireland; and
(e) such other persons appearing to him to represent the views of persons engaged in the provision of immigration advice or immigration services as he considers appropriate.

(7) The Commissioner must publish the Code in such form and manner as the Secretary of State may direct.

Extension of scope of the Code

4 (1) The Secretary of State may by order provide for the provisions of the Code, or such provisions of the Code as may be specified by the order, to apply to—

(a) persons authorised by any designated professional body to practise as a member of the profession whose members are regulated by that body; and
[(b) persons acting on behalf of persons who are within paragraph (a)].

(2) If the Secretary of State is proposing to act under sub-paragraph (1) he must, before doing so, consult—

(a) the Commissioner;
(b) the Legal Services Ombudsman, if the proposed order would affect a designated professional body in England and Wales;
(c) the Scottish Legal Services Ombudsman, if the proposed order would affect a designated professional body in Scotland;
(d) the lay observers appointed under Article 42 of the Solicitors (Northern Ireland) Order 1976, if the proposed order would affect a designated professional body in Northern Ireland.

(3) An order under sub-paragraph (1) requires the approval of—

(a) the Lord Chancellor, if it affects a designated professional body in England and Wales or Northern Ireland;
(b) the Scottish Ministers, if it affects a designated professional body in Scotland.

(4) Before deciding whether or not to give his approval under sub-paragraph (3)(a), the Lord Chancellor must consult—

(a) the designated judges, if the order affects a designated professional body in England and Wales;
(b) the Lord Chief Justice of Northern Ireland, if it affects a designated professional body in Northern Ireland.

(5) Before deciding whether or not to give their approval under sub-paragraph (3)(b), the Scottish Ministers must consult the Lord President of the Court of Session.

Investigation of complaints

5 (1) The Commissioner must establish a scheme ("the complaints scheme") for the investigation by him of relevant complaints made to him in accordance with the provisions of the scheme.

(2) Before establishing the scheme or altering it, the Commissioner must consult—

1559

(a)   each of the designated professional bodies; and
(b)   such other persons appearing to him to represent the views of persons engaged in the provision of immigration advice or immigration services as he considers appropriate.

(3)   A complaint is a relevant complaint if it relates to—

(a)   the competence or fitness of a person to provide immigration advice or Immigration services,
(b)   the competence or fitness of a person [acting on behalf of] a person providing immigration advice or immigration services,
(c)   an alleged breach of the Code,
(d)   an alleged breach of one or more of the Commissioner's rules by a person to whom they apply, or
[(e)   an alleged breach of a rule of a relevant regulatory body,]

but not if it relates to a person who is excluded from the application of subsection (1) of section 84 by subsection (6) of that section.

(4)   The Commissioner may, on his own initiative, investigate any matter which he would have power to investigate on a complaint made under the complaints scheme.

(5)   In investigating any such matter on his own initiative, the Commissioner must proceed as if his investigation were being conducted in response to a complaint made under the scheme.

6   (1)   The complaints scheme must provide for a person who is the subject of an investigation under the scheme to be given a reasonable opportunity to make representations to the Commissioner.

(2)   Any person who is the subject of an investigation under the scheme must—

(a)   take such steps as are reasonably required to assist the Commissioner in his investigation; and
(b)   comply with any reasonable requirement imposed on him by the Commissioner.

(3)   If a person fails to comply with sub-paragraph (2)(a) or with a requirement imposed under sub-paragraph (2)(b) the Commissioner may—

(a)   in the case of a registered person, cancel his registration;
(b)   in the case of a person certified by the Commissioner as exempt under section 84(4)(a), withdraw his exemption; or
[(c)   in any other case, refer the matter to any relevant regulatory body].

Power to enter premises

7   (1)   This paragraph applies if—

(a)   the Commissioner is investigating a complaint under the complaints scheme;
(b)   the complaint falls within paragraph 5(3)(a), (b)[, (c)] or (d); and
(c)   there are reasonable grounds for believing that particular premises are being used in connection with the provision of immigration advice or immigration services by a [registered or exempt person].

[(1A)   This paragraph also applies if the Commissioner is investigating a matter under paragraph 5(5) and—

(a)   the matter is of a kind described in paragraph 5(3)(a), (b)[, (c)] or (d) (for which purpose a reference to an allegation shall be treated as a reference to a suspicion of the Commissioner), and

(b) there are reasonable grounds for believing that particular premises are being used in connection with the provision of immigration advice or immigration services by a [registered or exempt person].]

(2) The Commissioner, or a member of his staff authorised in writing by him, may enter the premises at reasonable hours.

(3) Sub-paragraph (2) does not apply to premises to the extent to which they constitute a private residence.

(4) A person exercising the power given by sub-paragraph (2) ("the investigating officer") may—

(a) take with him such equipment as appears to him to be necessary;
(b) require any person on the premises—
 (i) to produce any document which he considers relates to any matter relevant to the investigation; and
 (ii) if the document is produced, to provide an explanation of it;
(c) require any person to state, to the best of his knowledge and belief, where any such document is to be found;
(d) take copies of, or extracts from, any document which is produced;
(e) require any information which is held in a computer and is accessible from the premises and which the investigating officer considers relates to any matter relevant to the investigation, to be produced in a form—
 (i) in which it can be taken away; and
 (ii) in which it is visible and legible.

(5) Instead of exercising the power under sub-paragraph (2), the Commissioner may require such person as he may determine ("his agent") to make a report on the provision of immigration advice or immigration services from the premises.

(6) If the Commissioner so determines, his agent may exercise the power conferred by sub-paragraph (2) as if he were a member of the Commissioner's staff appropriately authorised.

(7) If a registered person fails without reasonable excuse to allow access under sub-paragraph (2) or (6) to any premises under his occupation or control, the Commissioner may cancel his registration.

(8) The Commissioner may also cancel the registration of a registered person who—

(a) without reasonable excuse fails to comply with a requirement imposed on him under sub-paragraph (4);
(b) intentionally delays or obstructs any person exercising functions under this paragraph; or
(c) fails to take reasonable steps to prevent an employee of his from obstructing any person exercising such functions.

[(9) Sub-paragraphs (7) and (8) shall apply to an exempt person as they apply to a registered person, but with a reference to cancellation of registration being treated as a reference to withdrawal of exemption.

(10) In this paragraph "exempt person" means a person certified by the Commissioner as exempt under section 84(4)(a).]

Determination of complaints

8 (1) On determining a complaint under the complaints scheme, the Commissioner must give his decision in a written statement.

(2) The statement must include the Commissioner's reasons for his decision.

(3)   A copy of the statement must be given by the Commissioner to—

  (a)   the person who made the complaint; and
  (b)   the person who is the subject of the complaint.

9   (1)   On determining a complaint under the complaints scheme, the Commissioner may—

  (a)   if the person to whom the complaint relates is a registered person [or is acting on behalf of] a registered person, record the complaint and the decision on it for consideration when that registered person next applies for his registration to be continued;
  (b)   if the person to whom the complaint relates is a registered person [or is acting on behalf of] a registered person and the Commissioner considers the matter sufficiently serious to require immediate action, require that registered person to apply for continued registration without delay;
  [(c)   refer the complaint and his decision on it to a relevant regulatory body;]
  (d)   if the person to whom the complaint relates is certified by the Commissioner as exempt under section 84(4)(a) or is employed by, or working under the supervision of, such a person, consider whether to withdraw that person's exemption;
  (e)   lay before the Tribunal a disciplinary charge against a relevant person.

(2)   Sub-paragraph (3) applies if—

  (a)   the Tribunal is considering a disciplinary charge against a relevant person; and
  (b)   the Commissioner asks it to exercise its powers under that sub-paragraph.

(3)   The Tribunal may give directions (which are to have effect while it is dealing with the charge)—

  [(a)   imposing restrictions on the provision of immigration advice or immigration services by the relevant person or by a person acting on his behalf or under his supervision;
  (b)   prohibiting the provision of immigration advice or immigration services by the relevant person or a person acting on his behalf or under his supervision].

(4)   "Relevant person" means a person providing immigration advice or immigration services who is—

  (a)   a registered person;
  [(b)   a person acting on behalf of a registered person;]
  (e)   a person certified by the Commissioner as exempt under section 84(4)(a);
  (f)   a person to whom section 84(4)(d) applies; or
  (g)   a person employed by, or working under the supervision of, a person to whom paragraph (e) or (f) applies.

Complaints referred to designated professional bodies

10   (1)   This paragraph applies if the Commissioner refers a complaint to a designated professional body under paragraph 9(1)(c).

(2)   The Commissioner may give directions setting a timetable to be followed by the designated professional body—

  (a)   in considering the complaint; and
  (b)   if appropriate, in taking disciplinary proceedings in connection with the complaint.

(3)   In making his annual report to the Secretary of State under paragraph 21, the Commissioner must take into account any failure of a designated professional body to comply (whether wholly or in part) with directions given to it under this paragraph.

(4) Sub-paragraph (5) applies if the Commissioner or the Secretary of State considers that a designated professional body has persistently failed to comply with directions given to it under this paragraph.

(5) The Commissioner must take the failure into account in determining whether to make a report under section 86(9)(b) and the Secretary of State must take it into account in determining whether to make an order under section 86(2).

Appointment

Paras 1(1), (2), (4), 2(1)–(4), (6)–(8), 3(1)–(3), (5)–(7), 4, 5(1)–(3), 6(1): Appointment: 22 May 2000: see SI 2000/1282, art 2, Schedule.
Paras 1(3), 2(5), 3(4), 5(4), (5), 6(2), (3), 7–10: Appointment: 30 October 2000: see SI 2000/1985, art 2, Schedule.

Amendment

Para 1: sub-para (1)(b) substituted by the Asylum and Immigration (Treatment of Claimants, etc) Act 2004, s 37(5)(a). Date in force: 1 October 2004: see SI 2004/2523, art 2, Schedule.
Para 1: sub-para (3)(b) substituted by the Asylum and Immigration (Treatment of Claimants, etc) Act 2004, s 37(5)(b). Date in force: 1 October 2004: see SI 2004/2523, art 2, Schedule.
Para 3: sub-para (3)(b) substituted by the Asylum and Immigration (Treatment of Claimants, etc) Act 2004, s 37(5)(c). Date in force: 1 October 2004: see SI 2004/2523, art 2, Schedule.
Para 4: sub-para (1)(b) substituted by the Asylum and Immigration (Treatment of Claimants, etc) Act 2004, s 37(5)(d). Date in force: 1 October 2004: see SI 2004/2523, art 2, Schedule.
Para 5: in sub-para (3)(b) words "acting on behalf of" in square brackets substituted by the Asylum and Immigration (Treatment of Claimants, etc) Act 2004, s 37(5)(e). Date in force: 1 October 2004: see SI 2004/2523, art 2, Schedule.
Para 5: sub-para (3)(e) substituted by the Asylum and Immigration (Treatment of Claimants, etc) Act 2004, s 37(5)(f). Date in force: 1 October 2004: see SI 2004/2523, art 2, Schedule.
Para 6: sub-para (3)(c) substituted by the Asylum and Immigration (Treatment of Claimants, etc) Act 2004, s 37(5)(g). Date in force: 1 October 2004: see SI 2004/2523, art 2, Schedule.
Para 7: in sub-para (1)(b) reference to ", (c)" in square brackets inserted by the Asylum and Immigration (Treatment of Claimants, etc) Act 2004, s 38(2)(a). Date in force: 1 October 2004: see SI 2004/2523, art 2, Schedule.
Para 7: in sub-para (1)(c) words "registered or exempt person" in square brackets substituted by the Asylum and Immigration (Treatment of Claimants, etc) Act 2004, s 38(2)(b). Date in force: 1 October 2004: see SI 2004/2523, art 2, Schedule.
Para 7: sub-para (1A) inserted by the Nationality, Immigration and Asylum Act 2002, s 140(1). Date in force: 8 January 2003 (except in relation to an investigation begun by the Commissioner under paragraph 5(5) above before that date): see SI 2002/2811, arts 2, 5, Schedule.
Para 7: in sub-para (1A)(a) reference to ", (c)" in square brackets inserted by the Asylum and Immigration (Treatment of Claimants, etc) Act 2004, s 38(2)(c). Date in force: 1 October 2004: see SI 2004/2523, art 2, Schedule.
Para 7: in sub-para (1A)(b) words "registered or exempt person" in square brackets substituted by the Asylum and Immigration (Treatment of Claimants, etc) Act 2004, s 38(2)(d). Date in force: 1 October 2004: see SI 2004/2523, art 2, Schedule.
Para 7: sub-paras (9), (10) inserted by the Asylum and Immigration (Treatment of Claimants, etc) Act 2004, s 38(2)(e). Date in force: 1 October 2004: see SI 2004/2523, art 2, Schedule.
Para 9: in sub-paras (1)(a), (b) words "or is acting on behalf of" in square brackets substituted by the Asylum and Immigration (Treatment of Claimants, etc) Act 2004, s 37(5)(h). Date in force: 1 October 2004: see SI 2004/2523, art 2, Schedule.
Para 9: sub-para (1)(c) substituted by the Asylum and Immigration (Treatment of Claimants, etc) Act 2004, s 37(5)(i). Date in force: 1 October 2004: see SI 2004/2523, art 2, Schedule.
Para 9: sub-paras (3)(a), (b) substituted by the Asylum and Immigration (Treatment of Claimants, etc) Act 2004, s 37(5)(j). Date in force: 1 October 2004: see SI 2004/2523, art 2, Schedule.
Para 9: sub-para (4)(d) substituted, for sub-para (4)(b)–(d) as originally enacted, by the Asylum and Immigration (Treatment of Claimants, etc) Act 2004, s 37(5)(k). Date in force: 1 October 2004: see SI 2004/2523, art 2, Schedule.

PART II
COMMISSIONER'S STATUS, REMUNERATION AND STAFF ETC

Status

11 (1)   The Commissioner is to be a corporation sole.

(2)   The Commissioner and the members of the Commissioner's staff are not to be regarded as the servants or agents of the Crown or as having any status, privilege or immunity of the Crown.

Period of office

12 (1)   The Commissioner—

(a)   is to hold office for a term of five years; but
(b)   may resign at any time by notice in writing given to the Secretary of State.

(2)   The Secretary of State may dismiss the Commissioner—

(a)   on the ground of incapacity or misconduct; or
(b)   if he is satisfied—
   (i)   that he has been convicted of a criminal offence; or
   (ii)   that a bankruptcy order has been made against him, or his estate has been sequestrated, or he has made a composition or arrangement with, or granted a trust deed for, his creditors.

(3)   The Commissioner is eligible for re-appointment when his term of office ends.

Terms and conditions of appointment

13   Subject to the provisions of this Schedule, the Commissioner is to hold office on such terms and conditions as the Secretary of State may determine.

Remuneration, expenses and pensions

14 (1)   There is to be paid to the Commissioner such remuneration and expenses as the Secretary of State may determine.

(2)   The Secretary of State may pay, or provide for the payment of, such pensions, allowances or gratuities to or in respect of the Commissioner as he may determine.

Compensation

15   If a person ceases to be the Commissioner, otherwise than when his term of office ends, and it appears to the Secretary of State that there are special circumstances which make it right for him to receive compensation, the Secretary of State may make a payment to him of such amount as the Secretary of State may determine.

Deputy Commissioner

16 (1)   The Secretary of State must appoint a person to act as Deputy Commissioner.

(2)   During any vacancy in the office of Commissioner, or at any time when he is unable to discharge his functions, the Deputy Commissioner may act in his place.

(3)   Paragraphs 11(2) and 12 to 15 apply to the Deputy Commissioner as they apply to the Commissioner.

Staff

17 (1) Subject to obtaining the approval of the Secretary of State as to numbers and terms and conditions of service, the Commissioner may appoint such staff as he considers appropriate.

(2) Subject to obtaining the approval of the Secretary of State, the Commissioner may pay, or provide for the payment of, such pensions, allowances or gratuities (including by way of compensation for loss of office or employment) to or in respect of his staff as he considers appropriate.

(3) Any functions of the Commissioner may, to the extent authorised by him, be performed by the Deputy Commissioner or any of his staff.

(4) The Employers' Liability (Compulsory Insurance) Act 1969 is not to require insurance to be effected by the Commissioner.

Expenditure

18 The Secretary of State may pay to the Commissioner—

(a) any expenses incurred or to be incurred by the Commissioner in respect of his staff; and

(b) with the approval of the Treasury, such other sums for enabling the Commissioner to perform his functions as the Secretary of State thinks fit.

Receipts

19 (1) Subject to any general or specific directions given to him by the Secretary of State, sums received by the Commissioner in the exercise of his functions must be paid to the Secretary of State.

(2) Sums received by the Secretary of State under this paragraph must be paid into the Consolidated Fund.

(3) The approval of the Treasury is required for any direction given under this paragraph.

Accounts and records

20 (1) The Commissioner must—

(a) keep proper accounts and proper records in relation to his accounts;

(b) prepare a statement of accounts for each financial year; and

(c) send copies of the statement to the Secretary of State and to the Comptroller and Auditor General on or before the specified date.

(2) The statement of accounts must be in such form as the Secretary of State may, with the approval of the Treasury, direct.

(3) The Comptroller and Auditor General must—

(a) examine, certify and report on each statement received by him under this paragraph; and

(b) lay copies of each statement and of his report before each House of Parliament.

(4) "Financial year" means the period of 12 months beginning with 1st April.

(5) "Specified date" means—

(a) 31st August next following the end of the year to which the statement relates; or

(b) such earlier date after the end of that year as the Treasury may direct.

Annual report

21 (1) The Commissioner must, as soon as is practicable after the end of each financial year, report to the Secretary of State on the performance of his functions in that year.

[(2) The report must, in particular, set out the Commissioner's opinion as to the extent to which each designated professional body has—

(a) provided effective regulation of its members in their provision of immigration advice or immigration services, and

(b) complied with requests of the Commissioner for the provision of information.]

(3) The Secretary of State must lay a copy of the report before each House of Parliament.

(4) "Financial year" has the same meaning as in paragraph 20.

Proof of instruments

22 A document purporting to be an instrument issued by the Commissioner and to be signed by or on behalf of the Commissioner is to be received in evidence and treated as such an instrument unless the contrary is shown.

Disqualification for House of Commons

23 In Part III of Schedule 1 to the House of Commons Disqualification Act 1975 (offices disqualifying for membership), insert at the appropriate place—

"The Immigration Services Commissioner

The Deputy Immigration Services Commissioner".

Disqualification for Northern Ireland Assembly

24 In Part III of Schedule 1 to the Northern Ireland Assembly Disqualification Act 1975 (offices disqualifying for membership), insert at the appropriate place—

"The Immigration Services Commissioner

The Deputy Immigration Services Commissioner".

The Parliamentary Commissioner Act 1967 (c 13)

25 In Schedule 2 of the Parliamentary Commissioner Act 1967 (departments and authorities subject to investigation) insert, at the appropriate place, "The Immigration Services Commissioner".

Appointment
Appointment: 22 May 2000: see SI 2000/1282, art 2, Schedule.

Amendment
Para 21: sub-para (2) substituted by the Asylum and Immigration (Treatment of Claimants, etc) Act 2004, s 41(6). Date in force: 1 October 2004: see SI 2004/2523, art 2, Schedule.

SCHEDULE 6
REGISTRATION

Section 85(3)

Applications for registration

1 (1) An application for registration under section 84(2)(a) ... must—

    (a) be made to the Commissioner in such form and manner, and
    (b) be accompanied by such information and supporting evidence,

as the Commissioner may from time to time determine.

(2) When considering an application for registration, the Commissioner may require the applicant to provide him with such further information or supporting evidence as the Commissioner may reasonably require.

Registration

2   (1) If the Commissioner considers that an applicant for registration is competent and otherwise fit to provide immigration advice and immigration services, he must register the applicant.

(2) Registration may be made so as to have effect—

    (a) only in relation to a specified field of advice or services;
    (b) only in relation to the provision of advice or services to a specified category of person;
    (c) only in relation to the provision of advice or services to a member of a specified category of person; or
    (d) only in specified circumstances.

Review of qualifications

3   (1) At such intervals as the Commissioner may determine, each registered person must submit an application for his registration to be continued.

(2) Different intervals may be fixed by the Commissioner in relation to different registered persons or descriptions of registered person.

(3) An application for continued registration must—

    (a) be made to the Commissioner in such form and manner, and
    (b) be accompanied by such information and supporting evidence,

as the Commissioner may from time to time determine.

(4) When considering an application for continued registration, the Commissioner may require the applicant to provide him with such further information or supporting evidence as the Commissioner may reasonably require.

(5) If the Commissioner considers that an applicant for continued registration is no longer competent or is otherwise unfit to provide immigration advice or immigration services, he must cancel the applicant's registration.

(6) Otherwise, the Commissioner must continue the applicant's registration but may, in doing so, vary the registration—

    (a) so as to make it have limited effect in any of the ways mentioned in paragraph 2(2); or
    (b) so as to make it have full effect.

(7) If a registered person fails, without reasonable excuse—

    (a) to make an application for continued registration as required by sub-paragraph (1) or by a direction given by the Tribunal under [section 89(2)(b)], or
    (b) to provide further information or evidence under sub-paragraph (4),

the Commissioner may cancel the person's registration as from such date as he may determine.

[Variation of registration

3A   The Commissioner may vary a person's registration—

(a) so as to make it have limited effect in any of the ways mentioned in paragraph 2(2); or

(b) so as to make it have full effect.]

Disqualification of certain persons

4   A person convicted of an offence under section 25 or 26(1)(d) or (g) of the 1971 Act is disqualified for registration under paragraph 2 or for continued registration under paragraph 3.

Fees

5   (1)   The Secretary of State may by order specify fees for the registration or continued registration of persons on the register.

(2)   No application under paragraph 1 or 3 is to be entertained by the Commissioner unless it is accompanied by the specified fee.

Open registers

6   (1)   The register must be made available for inspection by members of the public in a legible form at reasonable hours.

(2)   A copy of the register or of any entry in the register must be provided—

(a) on payment of a reasonable fee;

(b) in written or electronic form; and

(c) in a legible form.

(3)   Sub-paragraphs (1) and (2) also apply to—

(a) the record kept by the Commissioner of the persons to whom he has issued a certificate of exemption under section 84(4)(a); and

(b) the record kept by the Commissioner of the persons against whom there is in force a direction given by the Tribunal under section 89(8).

Appointment
Paras 1–4, 5(2), 6: Appointment: 30 October 2000: see SI 2000/1985, art 2, Schedule.
Para 5(1): Appointment (for the purposes of enabling subordinate legislation to be made): 1 August 2000: see SI 2000/1985, art 2, Schedule.
Para 5(1): Appointment (for remaining purposes): 30 October 2000: see SI 2000/1985, art 2, Schedule.

Amendment
Para 1: in sub-para (1) words omitted repealed by the Asylum and Immigration (Treatment of Claimants, etc) Act 2004, ss 37(6)(a), 47, Sch 4. Date in force: 1 October 2004: see SI 2004/2523, art 2, Schedule.
Para 3: in sub-para (7)(a) words "section 89(2)(b)" in square brackets substituted by the Asylum and Immigration (Treatment of Claimants, etc) Act 2004, s 37(6)(b). Date in force: 1 October 2004: see SI 2004/2523, art 2, Schedule.
Para 3A: inserted by the Nationality, Immigration and Asylum Act 2002, s 140(2). Date in force: 8 January 2003: see SI 2002/2811, art 2, Schedule.

Subordinate Legislation
Immigration Services Commissioner (Registration Fee) Order 2004, SI 2004/802 (made under para 5(1)).

SCHEDULE 7
THE IMMIGRATION SERVICES TRIBUNAL

Section 87(5)

Members

1 (1) The Tribunal is to consist of such number of members as the Lord Chancellor may determine.

(2) The members are to be appointed by the Lord Chancellor.

(3) A person may be appointed as a member only if—

(a) he is legally qualified; or

(b) he appears to the Lord Chancellor to have had substantial experience in immigration services or in the law and procedure relating to immigration.

The President

2 The Tribunal is to have a President appointed by the Lord Chancellor from among those of its members who are legally qualified.

Terms and conditions of appointment

3 (1) Each member is to hold and vacate office in accordance with the terms of his appointment.

(2) A member is eligible for re-appointment when his term of office ends.

(3) A member may resign at any time by notice in writing given to the Lord Chancellor.

(4) The Lord Chancellor may dismiss a member on the ground of incapacity or misconduct.

Remuneration and expenses

4 The Lord Chancellor may pay to any member such remuneration and expenses as he may determine.

Proceedings

5 The Tribunal is to sit at such times and in such places as the Lord Chancellor may direct.

6 (1) The Commissioner is entitled to be represented before the Tribunal, in relation to the hearing of appeals or disciplinary charges, by such persons as he may authorise.

(2) The Commissioner may authorise a person to represent him before the Tribunal in relation to—

(a) specified proceedings; or

(b) all or specified categories of proceedings.

(3) "Specified" means specified by the Commissioner.

Rules of procedure

7 (1) The Lord Chancellor may make rules as to the procedure and practice to be followed in relation to the exercise of the Tribunal's functions.

1569

(2)   Before making or altering any such rules, the Lord Chancellor must consult the Scottish Ministers.

(3)   Subject to the provisions of this Schedule and the rules, the Tribunal may determine its own procedure.

(4)   The rules must make provision for any person appealing to the Tribunal or otherwise subject to its jurisdiction to be entitled to be legally represented.

(5)   The rules may, in particular, make provision—

    (a)   as to the mode and burden of proof and the giving and admissibility of evidence;

    (b)   for proceedings before the Tribunal to be capable of being determined in the absence of any party to the proceedings if that party has failed, without reasonable excuse, to appear before the Tribunal or has failed to comply with any reasonable directions given by the Tribunal as to the conduct of the proceedings;

    (c)   with respect to other matters preliminary or incidental to, or arising out of, any matter with respect to which the Tribunal is or may be exercising functions;

    (d)   as to the period within which an appeal against a decision of the Commissioner can be brought;

    (e)   authorising such functions of the Tribunal as may be specified in the rules to be exercised by a single member.

Suspending the effect of a relevant decision

8   (1)   A relevant decision of the Commissioner is not to have effect while the period within which an appeal may be brought against the decision is running.

(2)   If the appellant applies to the Tribunal under this paragraph, the Tribunal may direct that while the appeal is being dealt with—

    (a)   no effect is to be given to the decision appealed against; or

    (b)   only such limited effect is to be given to it as may be specified in the direction.

(3)   Rules under paragraph 7 must include provision requiring the Tribunal to consider applications by the Commissioner for the cancellation or variation of directions given under this paragraph.

Staff

9   (1)   The Lord Chancellor may appoint such staff for the Tribunal as he considers appropriate.

(2)   The Lord Chancellor may pay, or provide for the payment of, such pensions, allowances or gratuities (including by way of compensation for loss of office or employment) to or in respect of the Tribunal's staff as he considers appropriate.

Expenditure

10   The Lord Chancellor may pay such other expenses of the Tribunal as he considers appropriate.

Meaning of "legally qualified"

11   A person is legally qualified for the purposes of this Schedule if—

    (a)   he has a 7 year general qualification, within the meaning of section 71 of the Courts and Legal Services Act 1990;

    (b)   he is an advocate or solicitor in Scotland of at least 7 years' standing; or

(c)   he is a member of the Bar of Northern Ireland or solicitor of the Supreme Court of Northern Ireland of at least 7 years' standing.

Disqualification for House of Commons

12   In Part I of Schedule 1 to the House of Commons Disqualification Act 1975 (offices disqualifying for membership), insert at the appropriate place—

"Member of the Immigration Services Tribunal".

Disqualification for Northern Ireland Assembly

13   In Part I of Schedule 1 to the Northern Ireland Assembly Disqualification Act 1975 (offices disqualifying for membership), insert at the appropriate place—

"Member of the Immigration Services Tribunal".

Appointment
Paras 1–6, 8(1), (2), 9–13: Appointment: 30 October 2000: see SI 2000/1985, art 2, Schedule.
Paras 7, 8(3): Appointment: 1 August 2000: see SI 2000/1985, art 2, Schedule.

Subordinate Legislation
Immigration Services Tribunal Rules 2000, SI 2000/2739 (made under paras 7, 8(3)).
Immigration Services Tribunal (Amendment) Rules 2002, SI 2002/1716 (made under para 7).

SCHEDULE 8
PROVISION OF SUPPORT: REGULATIONS

Section 95(12)

General regulation-making power

1   The Secretary of State may by regulations make such further provision with respect to the powers conferred on him by section 95 as he considers appropriate.

Determining whether a person is destitute

2   *(1)   The regulations may provide, in connection with determining whether a person is destitute, for the Secretary of State to take into account, except in such circumstances (if any) as may be prescribed—*

(a)   *income which the person concerned, or any dependant of his, has or might reasonably be expected to have, and*

(b)   *support which is, or assets of a prescribed kind which are, or might reasonably be expected to be, available to him or to any dependant of his,*

otherwise than by way of support provided under section 95.

(2)   The regulations may provide that in such circumstances (if any) as may be prescribed, a person is not to be treated as destitute for the purposes of section 95.

Prescribed levels of support

3   The regulations may make provision—

(a)   as to the circumstances in which the Secretary of State may, as a general rule, be expected to provide support in accordance with prescribed levels or of a prescribed kind;

(b)   as to the circumstances in which the Secretary of State may, as a general rule, be expected to provide support otherwise than in accordance with the prescribed levels.

Provision of items and services

4   The regulations may make provision for prescribed items or services to be provided or made available to persons receiving support under section 95 for such purposes and in such circumstances as may be prescribed.

Support and assets to be taken into account

5   The regulations may make provision requiring the Secretary of State, except in such circumstances (if any) as may be prescribed, to take into account, when deciding the level or kind of support to be provided—

  (a) income which the person concerned, or any dependant of his, has or might reasonably be expected to have, and
  (b) support which is, or assets of a prescribed kind which are, or might reasonably be expected to be, available to him or to any dependant of his,

otherwise than by way of support provided under section 95.

Valuation of assets

6   *The regulations may make provision as to the valuation of assets.*

Breach of conditions

7   The regulations may make provision for the Secretary of State to take into account, when deciding—

  (a) whether to provide, or to continue to provide, support under section 95, or
  (b) the level or kind of support to be provided,

the extent to which any condition on which support is being, or has previously been, provided has been complied with.

Suspension or discontinuation of support

8   (1)   The regulations may make provision for the suspension or discontinuance of support under section 95 in prescribed circumstances (including circumstances in which the Secretary of State would otherwise be under a duty to provide support).

(2)   The circumstances which may be prescribed include the cessation of residence—

  (a) in accommodation provided under section 95; or
  (b) at an address notified to the Secretary of State in accordance with the regulations.

Notice to quit

9   (1)   The regulations may provide that if—

  (a) as a result of support provided under section 95, a person has a tenancy or a licence to occupy accommodation,
  (b) one or more of the conditions mentioned in sub-paragraph (2) are satisfied, and
  (c) he is given such notice to quit as may be prescribed by the regulations,

his tenancy or licence is to be treated as ending with the period specified in that notice, regardless of when it could otherwise be brought to an end.

(2)   The conditions are that—

  (a) the support provided under section 95 is suspended or discontinued as a result of any provision of a kind mentioned in paragraph 8;

(b) the relevant claim for asylum has been determined;
(c) the supported person has ceased to be destitute;
(d) he is to be moved to other accommodation.

Contributions to support

10 The regulations may make provision requiring a supported person to make payments to the Secretary of State, in prescribed circumstances, by way of contributions to the cost of the provision of that support.

Recovery of sums by Secretary of State

11 (1) The regulations may provide for the recovery by the Secretary of State of sums representing the whole or part of the monetary value of support provided to a person under section 95 where it appears to the Secretary of State—

(a) that that person had, at the time when he applied for support, assets of any kind in the United Kingdom or elsewhere which were not capable of being realised; but
(b) that those assets have subsequently become, and remain, capable of being realised.

(2) An amount recoverable under regulations made by virtue of sub-paragraph (1) may be recovered—

(a) as if it were a debt due to the Secretary of State; or
(b) by such other method of recovery, including by deduction from support provided under section 95 as may be prescribed.

Procedure

12 The regulations may make provision with respect to procedural requirements including, in particular, provision as to—

(a) the procedure to be followed in making an application for support;
(b) the information which must be provided by the applicant;
(c) the circumstances in which an application may not be entertained [(which may, in particular, provide for an application not to be entertained where the Secretary of State is not satisfied that the information provided is complete or accurate or that the applicant is co-operating with enquiries under paragraph (d))];
(d) the making of further enquiries by the Secretary of State;
(e) the circumstances in which, and person by whom, a change of circumstances of a prescribed description must be notified to the Secretary of State.

Appointment
Appointment: 1 January 2000: see SI 1999/3190, art 2, Schedule.

Amendment
Paras 2, 6: repealed by the Nationality, Immigration and Asylum Act 2002, ss 45(3), 161, Sch 9. Date in force: to be appointed: see the Nationality, Immigration and Asylum Act 2002, s 162(1). Para 12: in sub-para (c) words from "(which may, in" to "under paragraph (d))" in square brackets inserted by the Nationality, Immigration and Asylum Act 2002, s 57. Date in force: 8 December 2002: see SI 2002/2811, art 2, Schedule.

Subordinate Legislation
Asylum Support Regulations 2000, SI 2000/704.
Asylum Support (Amendment) Regulations 2002, SI 2002/472 (made under paras 3(a), 4).
Asylum Support (Amendment) (No 3) Regulations 2002, SI 2002/3110 (made under para 12).
Asylum Support (Amendment) Regulations 2003, SI 2003/241 (made under paras 1, 3).

Asylum Support (Amendment) (No 2) Regulations 2004, SI 2004/1313 (made under paras 1, 3(a), 4, 12).
Asylum Support (Amendment) Regulations 2005, SI 2005/11.
Asylum Support (Amendment) (No 2) Regulations 2005, SI 2005/738 (made under paras 1, 3(a)).

SCHEDULE 9
ASYLUM SUPPORT: INTERIM PROVISIONS

Section 95(13)

1   (1)   The Secretary of State may by regulations make provision requiring prescribed local authorities or local authorities falling within a prescribed description of authority to provide support, during the interim period, to eligible persons.

(2)   "Eligible persons" means—

  (a)   asylum-seekers, or
  (b)   their dependants,

who appear to be destitute or to be likely to become destitute within such period as may be prescribed.

(3)   For the purposes of sub-paragraph (1), in Northern Ireland, a Health and Social Services Board established under Article 16 of the Health and Personal Social Services (Northern Ireland) Order 1972 is to be treated as a local authority.

2   (1)   The regulations must provide for the question whether a person is an eligible person to be determined by the local authority concerned.

(2)   The regulations may make provision for support to be provided, before the determination of that question, to a person making a claim for support under the regulations by the Secretary of State or such local authority as may be prescribed.

(3)   "The local authority concerned" has such meaning as may be prescribed.

3   *Subsections (3) to (8) of section 95* [Subsections (2) to (6) of section 95] apply for the purposes of the regulations as they apply for the purposes of that section, but for the references in *subsections (5) and (7)* [subsections (4) and (5)] to the Secretary of State substitute references to the local authority concerned.

4   The regulations may prescribe circumstances in which support for an eligible person—

  (a)   must be provided;
  (b)   must or may be refused; or
  (c)   must or may be suspended or discontinued.

5   The regulations may provide that support—

  (a)   is to be provided in prescribed ways;
  (b)   is not to be provided in prescribed ways.

6   The regulations may include provision—

  (a)   as to the level of support that is to be provided;
  (b)   for support to be provided subject to conditions;
  (c)   requiring any such conditions to be set out in writing;
  (d)   requiring a copy of any such conditions to be given to such person as may be prescribed.

[**6A**   The regulations may, in particular, require support to be provided subject to a condition of compliance with any restriction imposed under paragraph 21 of Schedule 2 to the 1971 Act (temporary admission or release from detention) or paragraph 2 or 5 of Schedule 3 to that Act (restriction pending deportation).]

7 The regulations may make provision that, in providing support, a local authority—

(a) are to have regard to such matters as may be prescribed;
(b) are not to have regard to such matters as may be prescribed.

8 The regulations may include provision—

(a) prescribing particular areas, or descriptions of area, (which may include a locality within their own area) in which a local authority may not place asylum-seekers while providing support for them;
(b) prescribing circumstances in which a particular area, or description of area, (which may include a locality within their own area) is to be one in which a local authority may not place asylum-seekers while providing support for them;
(c) as to the circumstances (if any) in which any such provision is not to apply.

9 (1) The regulations may make provision for the referral by one local authority to another of a claim for support made under the regulations if the local authority to whom the claim is made consider that it is not manifestly unfounded but—

(a) they are providing support for a number of asylum-seekers equal to, or greater than, the maximum number of asylum-seekers applicable to them; or
(b) they are providing support for a number of eligible persons equal to, or greater than, the maximum number of eligible persons applicable to them.

(2) For the purposes of any provision made as a result of sub-paragraph (1), the regulations may make provision for the determination by the Secretary of State of—

(a) the applicable maximum number of asylum-seekers;
(b) the applicable maximum number of eligible persons.

(3) The regulations may make provision for any such determination to be made—

(a) for local authorities generally;
(b) for prescribed descriptions of local authority; or
(c) for particular local authorities.

(4) The regulations may provide that a referral may not be made—

(a) to a prescribed local authority;
(b) to local authorities of a prescribed description; or
(c) in prescribed circumstances.

(5) The regulations may make provision for the payment by a local authority of any reasonable travel or subsistence expenses incurred as a result of a referral made by them.

(6) The regulations may make provision for the transfer of a claim for support, or responsibility for providing support, under the regulations from one local authority to another on such terms as may be agreed between them.

(7) In exercising any power under the regulations to refer or transfer, a local authority must have regard to such guidance as may be issued by the Secretary of State with respect to the exercise of the power.

10 (1) The regulations may make provision for the referral of claims for support made to the Secretary of State to prescribed local authorities or local authorities of a prescribed description.

(2) The regulations may make provision for the payment by the Secretary of State of any reasonable travel or subsistence expenses incurred as a result of a referral made by him as a result of provision made by virtue of sub-paragraph (1).

11 The regulations may make provision requiring prescribed local authorities or other prescribed bodies to give reasonable assistance to local authorities providing support under the regulations.

12 The regulations may make provision for the procedure for making and determining claims for support.

13 The regulations may make provision for an asylum-seeker or a dependant of an asylum-seeker who has received, or is receiving, any prescribed description of support from a local authority to be taken to have been accepted for support under the regulations by a prescribed local authority.

14 A person entitled to support under the regulations is not entitled to any prescribed description of support, except to such extent (if any) as may be prescribed.

15 "The interim period" means the period—

(a) beginning on such day as may be prescribed for the purposes of this paragraph; and

(b) ending on such day as may be so prescribed.

Initial Commencement
Royal Assent: 11 November 1999: see s 170(3)(r).

Amendment
Para 3: words "Subsections (3) to (8) of section 95" in italics repealed and subsequent words in square brackets substituted by the Nationality, Immigration and Asylum Act 2002, s 45(4)(a). Date in force: to be appointed: see the Nationality, Immigration and Asylum Act 2002, s 162(1).
Para 3: words "subsections (5) and (7)" in italics repealed and subsequent words in square brackets substituted by the Nationality, Immigration and Asylum Act 2002, s 45(4)(b). Date in force: to be appointed: see the Nationality, Immigration and Asylum Act 2002, s 162(1).
Para 6A: inserted by the Nationality, Immigration and Asylum Act 2002, s 50(2). Date in force: 7 November 2002: see the Nationality, Immigration and Asylum Act 2002, s 162(2)(o).

Subordinate Legislation
Asylum Support (Interim Provisions) Regulations 1999, SI 1999/3056 (made under paras 1, 2, 4–7, 9, 11, 13–15).
Asylum Support (Interim Provisions) (Amendment) Regulations 2002, SI 2002/471 (made under paras 5, 6, 15).
Asylum Support (Interim Provisions) (Amendment) Regulations 2004, SI 2004/566 (made under para 15).
Asylum Support (Interim Provisions) (Amendment) Regulations 2005, SI 2005/595 (made under para 15).

SCHEDULE 10
ASYLUM SUPPORT ADJUDICATORS

Section 102(3)

Adjudicators

1 (1) The Secretary of State must—

(a) appoint such number of adjudicators as he considers necessary;

(b) appoint one of the adjudicators to be the Chief Asylum Support Adjudicator; and

(c) appoint one of the adjudicators to be the Deputy Chief Asylum Support Adjudicator ("the Deputy").

(2) The adjudicators are to exercise their functions under the direction of the Chief Asylum Support Adjudicator.

(3)   The Chief Asylum Support Adjudicator is to have such other functions as the Secretary of State may from time to time direct.

(4)   During any vacancy in the office of Chief Asylum Support Adjudicator, or at any time when he is unable to discharge his functions, the Deputy may act in his place.

Terms and conditions of appointment

2   (1)   Each adjudicator is to hold and vacate office in accordance with the terms of his appointment.

(2)   An adjudicator is eligible for re-appointment when his term of office ends.

(3)   An adjudicator may resign at any time by notice in writing given to the Secretary of State.

Remuneration, expenses and pensions

3   (1)   The Secretary of State may pay to any adjudicator such remuneration and expenses as he may determine.

(2)   The Secretary of State may pay, or provide for the payment of, such pensions, allowances or gratuities to or in respect of any adjudicator as he may determine.

Compensation

4   If a person ceases to be an adjudicator, otherwise than when his term of office ends, and it appears to the Secretary of State that there are special circumstances which make it right for him to receive compensation, the Secretary of State may make a payment to him of such amount as the Secretary of State may determine.

Staff

5   (1)   The Secretary of State may appoint such staff for the adjudicators as he considers appropriate.

(2)   The Secretary of State may pay, or provide for the payment of, such pensions, allowances or gratuities (including by way of compensation for loss of office or employment) to or in respect of the adjudicators' staff as he considers appropriate.

Expenditure

6   The Secretary of State may pay such other expenses of the adjudicators as he considers appropriate.

Proceedings

7   For the purpose of discharging their functions, adjudicators are to sit at such times and in such places as the Secretary of State may direct.

Initial Commencement
To be appointed: see s 170(4).

SCHEDULE 11
DETAINEE CUSTODY OFFICERS

Section 154(7)

Obtaining certificates of authorisation by false pretences

1   A person who, for the purpose of obtaining a certificate of authorisation for himself or for any other person—

(a)   makes a statement which he knows to be false in a material particular, or
(b)   recklessly makes a statement which is false in a material particular,

is guilty of an offence and liable on summary conviction to a fine not exceeding level 4 on the standard scale.

Powers and duties of detainee custody officers

2   (1)   A detainee custody officer exercising custodial functions has power—

(a)   to search (in accordance with rules made by the Secretary of State) any detained person in relation to whom the officer is exercising custodial functions; and
(b)   to search any other person who is in, or is seeking to enter, any place where any such detained person is or is to be held, and any article in the possession of such a person.

(2)   The power conferred by sub-paragraph (1)(b) does not authorise requiring a person to remove any of his clothing other than an outer coat, jacket or glove.

(3)   As respects a detained person in relation to whom he is exercising custodial functions, it is the duty of a detainee custody officer—

(a)   to prevent that person's escape from lawful custody;
(b)   to prevent, or detect and report on, the commission or attempted commission by him of other unlawful acts;
(c)   to ensure good order and discipline on his part; and
(d)   to attend to his wellbeing.

(4)   The powers conferred by sub-paragraph (1), and the powers arising by virtue of sub-paragraph (3), include power to use reasonable force where necessary.

Short-term holding facilities

3   (1)   A detainee custody officer may perform functions of a custodial nature at a short-term holding facility (whether or not he is authorised to perform custodial functions at a [removal centre]).

(2)   When doing so, he is to have the same powers and duties in relation to the facility and persons detained there as he would have if the facility were a [removal centre].

Assaulting a detainee custody officer

4   A person who assaults a detainee custody officer who is—

(a)   acting in accordance with escort arrangements,
(b)   performing custodial functions, or
(c)   performing functions of a custodial nature at a short-term holding facility,

is guilty of an offence and liable on summary conviction to a fine not exceeding level 5 on the standard scale or to imprisonment for a term not exceeding six months or to both.

Obstructing detainee custody officers

5   A person who resists or wilfully obstructs a detainee custody officer who is—

(a)   acting in accordance with escort arrangements,
(b)   performing custodial functions, or
(c)   performing functions of a custodial nature at a short-term holding facility,

is guilty of an offence and liable on summary conviction to a fine not exceeding level 3 on the standard scale.

Uniforms and badges

6 For the purposes of paragraphs 4 and 5, a detainee custody officer is not to be regarded as acting in accordance with escort arrangements at any time when he is not readily identifiable as such an officer (whether by means of a uniform or badge which he is wearing or otherwise).

Suspension and revocation of certificates of authorisation

7 (1) If it appears to the Secretary of State that a detainee custody officer is not a fit and proper person to perform escort functions or custodial functions, he may revoke that officer's certificate so far as it authorises the performance of those functions.

(2) If it appears to the escort monitor that a detainee custody officer is not a fit and proper person to perform escort functions, he may—

(a) refer the matter to the Secretary of State; or
(b) in such circumstances as may be prescribed, suspend the officer's certificate pending a decision by the Secretary of State as to whether to revoke it.

(3) If it appears to the contract monitor for the [removal centre] concerned that a detainee custody officer is not a fit and proper person to perform custodial functions, he may—

(a) refer the matter to the Secretary of State; or
(b) in such circumstances as may be prescribed, suspend the officer's certificate pending a decision by the Secretary of State as to whether to revoke it.

[Prison officers and prisoner custody officers

8 A reference in this Schedule to a detainee custody officer includes a reference to a prison officer or prisoner custody officer exercising custodial functions.]

Appointment
Paras 1, 7(1): Appointment: 3 April 2000: see SI 2000/464, art 2, Schedule.
Paras 2(1)(a), 7(2), (3): Appointment (for the purposes of enabling subordinate legislation to be made): 1 August 2000: see SI 2000/1985, art 2, Schedule.
Paras 2(1)(a), 7(2), (3): Appointment (for remaining purposes): 2 April 2001: see SI 2001/239, art 2, Schedule.
Paras 2(1)(b), (2)–(4), 3–6: Appointment: 2 April 2001: see SI 2001/239, art 2, Schedule.

Amendment
Para 3: in sub-paras (1), (2) words "removal centre" in square brackets substituted by the Nationality, Immigration and Asylum Act 2002, s 66(2)(a), (3)(k). Date in force: 10 February 2003: see SI 2003/1, art 2, Schedule.
Para 7: in sub-para (3) words "removal centre" in square brackets substituted by the Nationality, Immigration and Asylum Act 2002, s 66(2)(a), (3)(k). Date in force: 10 February 2003: see SI 2003/1, art 2, Schedule.
Para 8: inserted by the Nationality, Immigration and Asylum Act 2002, s 65(2). Date in force: 10 February 2003: see SI 2003/1, art 2, Schedule.

Subordinate Legislation
Detention Centre Rules 2001, SI 2001/238 (made under para 2).
Immigration (Suspension of Detainee Custody Officer Certificate) Regulations 2001, SI 2001/241 (made under para 7(2), (3)).

SCHEDULE 12
DISCIPLINE ETC AT [REMOVAL CENTRES]

Section 155(2)

Measuring and photographing detained persons

1 (1) [Removal centre] rules may (among other things) provide for detained persons to be measured and photographed.

(2) The rules may, in particular, prescribe—

    (a) the time or times at which detained persons are to be measured and photographed;

    (b) the manner and dress in which they are to be measured and photographed; and

    (c) the numbers of copies of measurements or photographs that are to be made and the persons to whom they are to be sent.

Testing for drugs or alcohol

2 (1) If an authorisation is in force, a detainee custody officer may, at the centre to which the authorisation applies and in accordance with [removal centre] rules, require a detained person who is confined in the centre to provide a sample for the purpose of ascertaining—

    (a) whether he has a drug in his body; or

    (b) whether he has alcohol in his body.

(2) The sample required may be one or more of the following—

    (a) a sample of urine;

    (b) a sample of breath;

    (c) a sample of a specified description.

(3) Sub-paragraph (2)(c)—

    (a) applies only if the authorisation so provides; and

    (b) does not authorise the taking of an intimate sample.

(4) "Authorisation" means an authorisation given by the Secretary of State for the purposes of this paragraph in respect of a particular [removal centre].

(5) "Drug" means a drug which is a controlled drug for the purposes of the Misuse of Drugs Act 1971.

(6) "Specified" means specified in the authorisation.

(7) "Intimate sample"—

    (a) in relation to England and Wales, has the same meaning as in Part V of the Police and Criminal Evidence Act 1984;

    (b) in relation to Scotland, means—

        (i) a sample of blood, semen or any other tissue fluid, urine or pubic hair;

        (ii) a dental impression;

        (iii) a swab taken from a person's body orifice other than the mouth; and

    (c) in relation to Northern Ireland, has the same meaning as in Part VI of the Police and Criminal Evidence (Northern Ireland) Order 1989.

Medical examinations

3 (1) This paragraph applies if—

    (a) an authorisation is in force for a [removal centre]; and

(b) there are reasonable grounds for believing that a person detained in the centre is suffering from a disease which is specified in an order in force under sub-paragraph (7).

(2) A detainee custody officer may require the detained person to submit to a medical examination at the centre.

(3) The medical examination must be conducted in accordance with [removal centre] rules.

(4) A detained person who fails, without reasonable excuse, to submit to a medical examination required under this paragraph is guilty of an offence.

(5) A person guilty of an offence under sub-paragraph (4) is liable on summary conviction to imprisonment for a term not exceeding six months or to a fine not exceeding level 5 on the standard scale.

(6) "Authorisation" means an authorisation given by the manager of the [removal centre] for the purpose of this paragraph.

(7) The Secretary of State may by order specify any disease which he considers might, if a person detained in a [removal centre] were to suffer from it, endanger the health of others there.

Assisting detained persons to escape

4 (1) A person who aids any detained person in escaping or attempting to escape from a [removal centre] or short-term holding facility is guilty of an offence.

(2) A person who, with intent to facilitate the escape of any detained person from a [removal centre] or short-term holding facility—

  (a) conveys any thing into the centre or facility or to a detained person,
  (b) sends any thing (by post or otherwise) into the centre or facility or to a person detained there,
  (c) places any thing anywhere outside the centre or facility with a view to its coming into the possession of a person detained there,

is guilty of an offence.

(3) A person guilty of an offence under this section is liable—

  (a) on summary conviction, to imprisonment for a term not exceeding six months or to a fine not exceeding the statutory maximum or to both; or
  (b) on conviction on indictment, to imprisonment for a term not exceeding two years or to a fine or to both.

Alcohol

5 (1) A person who, contrary to [removal centre] rules, brings or attempts to bring any alcohol into a [removal centre], or to a detained person, is guilty of an offence.

(2) A person who places alcohol anywhere outside a [removal centre], intending that it should come into the possession of a detained person there, is guilty of an offence.

(3) A detainee custody officer or any other person on the staff of a [removal centre] who, contrary to [removal centre] rules, allows alcohol to be sold or used in the centre is guilty of an offence.

(4) A person guilty of an offence under this paragraph is liable on summary conviction to imprisonment for a term not exceeding six months or to a fine not exceeding level 3 on the standard scale or to both.

(5) "Alcohol" means any spirituous or fermented liquor.

Introduction of other articles

6   (1)   A person who—

(a)   conveys or attempts to convey any thing into or out of a [removal centre] or to a detained person, contrary to [removal centre] rules, and

(b)   is not as a result guilty of an offence under paragraph 4 or 5,

is guilty of an offence under this paragraph.

(2)   A person who—

(a)   places any thing anywhere outside a [removal centre], intending it to come into the possession of a detained person, and

(b)   is not as a result guilty of an offence under paragraph 4 or 5,

is guilty of an offence under this paragraph.

(3)   A person guilty of an offence under this paragraph is liable on summary conviction to a fine not exceeding level 3 on the standard scale.

Notice of penalties

7   (1)   In the case of a contracted out [removal centre], the contractor must cause a notice setting out the penalty to which a person committing an offence under paragraph 4, 5 or 6 is liable to be fixed outside the centre in a conspicuous place.

(2)   In the case of any other [removal centre], the Secretary of State must cause such a notice to be fixed outside the centre in a conspicuous place.

8   (1)   In the case of a contracted out short-term holding facility, the contractor must cause a notice setting out the penalty to which a person committing an offence under paragraph 4 is liable to be fixed outside the facility in a conspicuous place.

(2)   In the case of any other short-term holding facility, the Secretary of State must cause such a notice to be fixed outside the facility in a conspicuous place.

[Prison officers and prisoner custody officers

9   A reference in this Schedule to a detainee custody officer includes a reference to a prison officer or prisoner custody officer exercising custodial functions.]

Appointment
Paras 1, 2, 3(7): Appointment (for the purposes of enabling subordinate legislation to be made): 1 August 2000: see SI 2000/1985, art 2, Schedule.
Paras 1, 2, 3(7): Appointment (for remaining purposes): 2 April 2001: see SI 2001/239, art 2, Schedule.
Paras 3(1)–(6), 4–8: Appointment: 2 April 2001: see SI 2001/239, art 2, Schedule.

Amendment
Para 1: in sub-para (1) words "Removal centre" in square brackets substituted by the Nationality, Immigration and Asylum Act 2002, s 66(2)(a), (3)(l). Date in force: 10 February 2003: see SI 2003/1, art 2, Schedule.
Para 2: in sub-paras (1), (4) words "removal centre" in square brackets substituted by the Nationality, Immigration and Asylum Act 2002, s 66(2)(a), (3)(l). Date in force: 10 February 2003: see SI 2003/1, art 2, Schedule.
Para 3: in sub-paras (1)(a), (3), (6), (7) words "removal centre" in square brackets substituted by the Nationality, Immigration and Asylum Act 2002, s 66(2)(a), (3)(l). Date in force: 10 February 2003: see SI 2003/1, art 2, Schedule.
Para 4: in sub-paras (1), (2) words "removal centre" in square brackets substituted by the Nationality, Immigration and Asylum Act 2002, s 66(2)(a), (3)(l). Date in force: 10 February 2003: see SI 2003/1, art 2, Schedule.

Para 5: in sub-paras (1)–(3) words "removal centre" in square brackets in each place they occur substituted by the Nationality, Immigration and Asylum Act 2002, s 66(2)(a), (3)(l). Date in force: 10 February 2003: see SI 2003/1, art 2, Schedule.

Para 6: in sub-paras (1)(a), (2)(a) words "removal centre" in square brackets in each place they occur substituted by the Nationality, Immigration and Asylum Act 2002, s 66(2)(a), (3)(l). Date in force: 10 February 2003: see SI 2003/1, art 2, Schedule.

Para 7: in sub-paras (1), (2) words "removal centre" in square brackets substituted by the Nationality, Immigration and Asylum Act 2002, s 66(2)(a), (3)(l). Date in force: 10 February 2003: see SI 2003/1, art 2, Schedule.

Para 9: inserted by the Nationality, Immigration and Asylum Act 2002, s 65(3). Date in force: 10 February 2003: see SI 2003/1, art 2, Schedule.

Subordinate Legislation
Detention Centre Rules 2001, SI 2001/238 (made under paras 1–3).
Detention Centre (Specified Diseases) Order 2001, SI 2001/240 (made under para 3(7)).

SCHEDULE 13
ESCORT ARRANGEMENTS

Section 156(5)

Monitoring of escort arrangements

1 (1) Escort arrangements must include provision for the appointment of a Crown servant as escort monitor.

(2) The escort monitor must—

(a) keep the escort arrangements under review and report on them to the Secretary of State as required in accordance with the arrangements;

(b) from time to time inspect the conditions in which detained persons are transported or held in accordance with the escort arrangements;

(c) make recommendations to the Secretary of State, with a view to improving those conditions, whenever he considers it appropriate to do so;

(d) investigate, and report to the Secretary of State on, any allegation made against a detainee custody officer or prisoner custody officer in respect of any act done, or failure to act, when carrying out functions under the arrangements;

(3) Paragraph (d) of sub-paragraph (2) does not apply in relation to—

(a) detainee custody officers employed as part of the Secretary of State's staff; or

(b) an act or omission of a prisoner custody officer so far as it falls to be investigated by a prisoner escort monitor under section 81 of the Criminal Justice Act 1991 or under section 103 or 119 of the Criminal Justice and Public Order Act 1994.

Powers and duties of detainee custody officers

2 (1) A detainee custody officer acting in accordance with escort arrangements has power—

(a) to search (in accordance with rules made by the Secretary of State) any detained person for whose delivery or custody the officer is responsible in accordance with the arrangements; and

(b) to search any other person who is in, or is seeking to enter, any place where any such detained person is or is to be held, and any article in the possession of such a person.

(2) The power conferred by sub-paragraph (1)(b) does not authorise requiring a person to remove any of his clothing other than an outer coat, jacket or glove.

(3)   As respects a detained person for whose delivery or custody he is responsible in accordance with escort arrangements, it is the duty of a detainee custody officer—

    (a)   to prevent that person's escape from lawful custody;
    (b)   to prevent, or detect and report on, the commission or attempted commission by him of other unlawful acts;
    (c)   to ensure good order and discipline on his part; and
    (d)   to attend to his wellbeing.

(4)   The Secretary of State may make rules with respect to the performance by detainee custody officers of their duty under sub-paragraph (3)(d).

(5)   The powers conferred by sub-paragraph (1), and the powers arising by virtue of sub-paragraph (3), include power to use reasonable force where necessary.

Breaches of discipline

3   (1)   Sub-paragraph (2) applies if a detained person for whose delivery or custody a person ("A") has been responsible in accordance with escort arrangements is delivered to a [removal centre].

(2)   The detained person is to be treated, for the purposes of such [removal centre] rules as relate to disciplinary offences, as if he had been in the custody of the director of the [removal centre] at all times while A was so responsible.

(3)   Sub-paragraph (4) applies if a detained person for whose delivery or custody a person ("B") has been responsible in accordance with escort arrangements is delivered to a prison.

(4)   The detained person is to be treated, for the purposes of such prison rules as relate to disciplinary offences, as if he had been in the custody of the governor or controller of the prison at all times while B was so responsible.

(5)   "Director" means—

    (a)   in the case of a contracted out [removal centre], the person appointed by the Secretary of State in relation to the centre under section 149 or such other person as the Secretary of State may appoint for the purposes of this paragraph;
    (b)   in the case of any other [removal centre], the manager of the [removal centre].

(6)   This paragraph does not authorise the punishment of a detained person under [removal centre] rules or prison rules in respect of any act or omission of his for which he has already been punished by a court.

(7)   "Prison rules" means—

    (a)   rules made under section 47 of the Prison Act 1952;
    (b)   rules made under section 19 of the Prisons (Scotland) Act 1989;
    (c)   rules made under section 13 of the Prison Act (Northern Ireland) 1953.

Appointment
Paras 1, 2(1)(b), (2), (3), (5), 3: Appointment: 2 April 2001: see SI 2001/239, art 2, Schedule.
Para 2(1)(a), (4): Appointment (for the purposes of enabling subordinate legislation to be made): 1 August 2000: see SI 2000/1985, art 2, Schedule.
Para 2(1)(a), (4): Appointment (for remaining purposes): 2 April 2001: see SI 2001/239, art 2, Schedule.

Amendment
Para 3: in sub-paras (1), (2), (5)(a), (b), (6) words "removal centre" in square brackets in each place they occur substituted by the Nationality, Immigration and Asylum Act 2002, s 66(2)(a), (3)(m). Date in force: 10 February 2003: see SI 2003/1, art 2, Schedule.

Subordinate Legislation
Detention Centre Rules 2001, SI 2001/238 (made under para 2).

SCHEDULE 14
CONSEQUENTIAL AMENDMENTS

Section 169(1)

...

1 ...

2 ...

The Marriage Act 1949 (c 76)

3 The Marriage Act 1949 is amended as follows.

4 In section 3(1) (marriages of persons under 21)—

(a) for "a certificate" substitute "certificates"; and
(b) omit "whether by licence or without licence,".

5 In section 5 (methods of authorising marriages), in paragraph (d), for "a certificate" substitute "certificates".

6 In section 17 (marriage under superintendent registrar's certificate)—

(a) for "a certificate" substitute "certificates"; and
(b) for "notice of marriage and certificate" substitute "notices of marriage and certificates".

7 In section 25 (void marriages)—

(a) in paragraph (b), for "a certificate" substitute "certificates";
(b) in paragraph (c), for "a certificate of a superintendent registrar which is" substitute "certificates of a superintendent registrar which are"; and
(c) in paragraph (d), for "a certificate" substitute "certificates" and for "notice of marriage and certificate" substitute "notices of marriage and certificates".

8 In section 27(1) (notice of marriage), for "a certificate" substitute "certificates".

9 In section 27A (additional information required in certain cases)—

(a) in subsections (2) and (3), for the first "the notice" substitute "each notice";
(b) in subsection (4), for the first "The person" substitute "Each person"; and
(c) in subsection (6), for "either" substitute "each".

10 In section 27B (provisions relating to section 1(3) marriages)—

(a) in subsection (1), for "a certificate" substitute "certificates";
(b) in subsections (4) and (6), omit "or licence"; and
(c) in subsection (5), omit ", or certificate and licence,".

11 In section 28(1) (declaration to accompany notice of marriage), omit "or licence" and for paragraph (b) substitute—

"(b) that the persons to be married have for the period of 7 days immediately before the giving of the notice had their usual places of residence within the registration district or registration districts in which notice is given;".

12 In section 29 (caveat against issue of certificate or licence), omit every "or licence".

13 In section 30 (provision for issue of certificate to be forbidden) for first "a certificate" substitute "certificates".

14   In section 31 (marriage certificates)—

(a)   in subsections (1) and (4), for "a certificate" substitute "certificates"; and
(b)   in subsection (5), for "one of the persons to be married" substitute "the person by whom notice of marriage was given".

15   For section 33 substitute—

"33   Period of validity of certificate

(1)   A marriage may be solemnized on the authority of certificates of a superintendent registrar at any time within the period which is the applicable period in relation to that marriage.

(2)   If the marriage is not solemnized within the applicable period—

(a)   the notices of marriage and the certificates are void; and
(b)   no person may solemnize the marriage on the authority of those certificates.

(3)   The applicable period, in relation to a marriage, is the period beginning with the day on which the notice of marriage was entered in the marriage notice book and ending—

(a)   in the case of a marriage which is to be solemnized in pursuance of section 26(1)(dd), 37 or 38, on the expiry of three months; and
(b)   in the case of any other marriage, on the expiry of twelve months.

(4)   If the notices of marriage given by each person to be married are not given on the same date, the applicable period is to be calculated by reference to the earlier of the two dates."

16   For section 34 substitute—

"34   Marriages normally to be solemnized in registration district in which one party resides

Subject to section 35, a superintendent registrar may not issue a certificate for the solemnization of a marriage elsewhere in than within a registration district in which one of the persons to be married has resided for 7 days immediately before the giving of the notice of marriage."

17   (1)   Section 35 (marriages in registration district in which neither party resides) is amended as follows.

(2)   In subsection (1)—

(a)   omit ", or if the marriage is to be by licence, a certificate and a licence,"; and
(b)   for "or certificate and licence is issued" substitute "is issued in respect of each of the persons to be married".

(3)   In subsections (2) and (4), omit "or, if the marriage is to be by licence, a certificate and a licence,".

(4)   In subsections (2A) and (2B), omit "or, if the marriage is to be by licence, a certificate and licence,".

(5)   In subsection (5)—

(a)   for "a certificate" substitute "certificates";
(b)   for "the notice" substitute "each notice"; and
(c)   for "the certificate" substitute "each certificate".

18   Omit section 36 (superintendent registrar not normally to issue licences for marriages in registered buildings outside his district).

19   In section 37(1) (one party resident in Scotland)—

(a)   for first "a certificate" substitute "certificates"; and

(b)   omit "without licence".

20   (1)   Section 38 (one party resident in Northern Ireland) is amended as follows.

(2)   In subsection (1)—

(a)   for "a certificate" substitute "certificates"; and

(b)   omit "without licence".

(3)   In subsection (2), for "and place of residence" substitute ", place of residence and nationality".

(4)   In subsection (3), for "twenty-one" substitute "15".

21   In section 39(1) (issue of certificates on board Her Majesty's ships)—

(a)   for first "a certificate" substitute "certificates"; and

(b)   omit "without licence".

22   In section 40 (forms of certificates for marriage), omit subsection (2).

23   In section 44(1) (solemnization of marriage in registered buildings), for "a notice of marriage and certificate" substitute "the notices of marriage and certificates".

24   In section 45(1) (solemnization of marriage in register office)—

(a)   for "a certificate" substitute "certificates";

(b)   for first "notice" substitute "notices";

(c)   for "notice has" substitute "notices have"; and

(d)   for "certificate or certificate and licence, as the case may be, has or" substitute "certificates".

25   In section 47(2) (marriages according to usages of Society of Friends), in paragraph (a), for "the person" substitute "each person".

26   In section 48(1) (proof of certain matters not necessary to validity of marriages), in paragraph (a), for "notice" substitute "notices".

27   In section 49 (void marriages)—

(a)   in paragraph (b), after "issued" insert ", in respect of each of the persons to be married,";

(b)   omit paragraph (c);

(c)   in paragraph (d), for "a certificate which is" substitute "certificates which are"; and

(d)   in paragraph (e), for "notice" substitute "notices" and for "certificate" substitute "certificates".

28   In section 50 (person to whom certificate to be delivered)—

(a)   in subsection (1), for "a certificate" substitute "certificates" and omit "the certificate or, if notice of marriage has been given to more than one superintendent registrar,";

(b)   omit subsection (2); and

(c)   in subsection (3), for "certificate or certificate and licence, as the case may be," substitute "certificates".

29   In section 51(1) (fees of registrars for attending marriages), omit from first "the sum" to "case,".

30   (1)   Section 75 (offences relating to solemnization of marriages) is amended as follows.

(2)   In subsection (1)(b), for "a certificate" substitute "certificates".

(3)   In subsection (2)—

   (a)   in paragraph (a)(ii), for "notice of marriage and certificate" substitute "notices of marriage and certificates";
   (b)   in paragraph (d), for "a certificate" substitute "certificates" and for from "(not being" to "book" substitute "before the expiry of the waiting period in relation to each notice of marriage"; and
   (c)   in paragraph (e), for "a certificate" substitute "certificates".

(4)   After subsection (2), insert—

"(2A)   In subsection (2)(d) "the waiting period" has the same meaning as in section 31(4A)."

(5)   In subsection (3), for paragraph (a) substitute—

"(a)   issues any certificate for marriage before the expiry of 15 days from the day on which the notice of marriage was entered in the marriage notice book;".

(6)   In subsection (3), in paragraph (b), omit "or licence".

31   In section 78(3) (interpretation), in paragraph (a), for "the notice" substitute "each notice".

32   In Schedule 4 (provisions of Act which are excluded or modified in their application to naval, military and air force chapels), in Part III (exclusion of provisions relating to marriages otherwise than according to the rites of the Church of England), omit "The proviso to subsection (2) of section twenty-six".

The Prison Act 1952 (c 52)

33   In section 55 of the Prison Act 1952 (provisions extending to Scotland) at the end insert—

"(4A)   Subsections (2) to (5) of section 5A, as applied by subsection (5A) of that section, extend to Scotland."

The Firearms Act 1968 (c 27)

34   The Firearms Act 1968 is amended as follows.

35   In Schedule 1 (offences for which there is an additional penalty if committed when in possession of a firearm), after paragraph 5B insert—

"5C   An offence under paragraph 4 of Schedule 11 to the Immigration and Asylum Act 1999 (assaulting a detainee custody officer)."

36   In Schedule 2 (which lists corresponding Scottish offences), after paragraph 13A insert—

"13B   An offence under paragraph 4 of Schedule 11 to the Immigration and Asylum Act 1999 (assaulting a detainee custody officer)."

The Family Law Reform Act 1969 (c 46)

37   In section 2(3) (provisions relating to marriage), omit "or licence" in both cases.

The Marriage (Registrar General's Licence) Act 1970 (c 34)

38   The Marriage (Registrar General's Licence) Act 1970 is amended as follows.

39   In section 1(1) (marriages which may be solemnised by Registrar General's licence), for "a certificate" substitute "certificates".

40 In section 5 (caveat against issue of Registrar General's licence), omit "or licence".

41 In section 6 (marriage of persons under 18), for "a certificate" substitute "certificates".

42 In section 13 (void marriages)—

(a) in paragraph (a), for ""certificate" substitute ""certificates" and for ""Registrar" substitute ""a Registrar"; and
(b) omit paragraph (b).

The Immigration Act 1971 (c 77)

43 The 1971 Act is amended as follows.

44 (1) In section 3 (general provisions for regulation and control), in subsection (1)(a), after "in accordance with" insert "the provisions of, or made under,".

(2) In section 3, for subsection (5) substitute—

"(5) A person who is not a British citizen is liable to deportation from the United Kingdom if—

(a) the Secretary of State deems his deportation to be conducive to the public good; or
(b) another person to whose family he belongs is or has been ordered to be deported."

45 In section 4(1) (giving or refusal of leave to enter or remain to be in writing except where allowed by the Act) for "allowed by" substitute "allowed by or under".

46 In section 7(1) (exemption of certain residents from deportation)—

(a) ...
(b) in paragraph (b), for ", (b) or (c)" substitute "or (b) or 10 of the Immigration and Asylum Act 1999".

47 (1) Section 10 (entry otherwise than by sea or air) is amended as follows.

(2) In subsection (1), omit from "and any such Order" to the end.

(3) After subsection (1), insert—

"(1A) Her Majesty may by Order in Council direct that paragraph 27B or 27C of Schedule 2 shall have effect in relation to trains or vehicles as it has effect in relation to ships or aircraft.

(1B) Any Order in Council under this section may make—

(a) such adaptations or modifications of the provisions concerned, and
(b) such supplementary provisions,

as appear to Her Majesty to be necessary or expedient for the purposes of the Order."

(4) In subsection (2), for "this section" substitute "subsection (1)".

48 In section 11(1) (entry to the United Kingdom), at the end insert "or by Part III of the Immigration and Asylum Act 1999".

49 Omit Part II.

50 In section 24 (illegal entry and similar offences), omit subsections (1)(aa) and (2).

51 ...

52 (1)   Section 27 (offences by persons connected with ships or aircraft) is amended as follows.

(2)   In paragraph (a)(ii), after "Schedule 2 or 3" insert "or under the Immigration and Asylum Act 1999".

(3)   In paragraph (b)(iii)—

    (a)   after "arrangements for" insert "or in connection with"; and
    (b)   at the end insert—
"or under the Immigration and Asylum Act 1999; or
    (iv)   he fails, without reasonable excuse, to comply with the requirements of paragraph 27B or 27C of Schedule 2;".

53   ...

54 (1)   Section 32 (proof of documents) is amended as follows.

(2)   In subsection (2)—

    (a)   for "this Act" substitute "the Immigration Acts"; and
    (b)   after second "by him" insert "or on his behalf".

(3)   In subsection (3), for "proceedings under Part II of this Act" substitute "other proceedings under the Immigration Acts".

(4)   In subsection (4)—

    (a)   for first "this Act" substitute "the Immigration Acts"; and
    (b)   for "proceedings under Part II of this Act" substitute "other proceedings under the Immigration Acts".

(5)   After subsection (4) insert—

"(5)   "Immigration Acts" has the same meaning as in the Immigration and Asylum Act 1999."

(6)   The amendments made by sub-paragraphs (2)(a) and (5) apply whenever the document in question was made or issued.

55   In section 33 (interpretation), for subsection (4) substitute—

"(4)   For the purposes of this Act, the question of whether an appeal is pending shall be determined—

    (a)   in relation to an appeal to the Special Immigration Appeals Commission, in accordance with section 7A of the Special Immigration Appeals Commission Act 1997;
    (b)   in any other case, in accordance with section 58(5) to (10) of the Immigration and Asylum Act 1999".

56   In Schedule 2 (administrative provisions as to control on entry), in paragraph 2(1) (purposes for which persons arriving in the United Kingdom may be examined), for paragraph (c) substitute—

"(c)   whether, if he may not—
    (i)   he has been given leave which is still in force,
    (ii)   he should be given leave and for what period or on what conditions (if any), or
    (iii)   he should be refused leave."

57   In Schedule 2, after paragraph 2, insert—

"Examination of persons who arrive with continuing leave

2A (1) This paragraph applies to a person who has arrived in the United Kingdom with leave to enter which is in force but which was given to him before his arrival.

(2) He may be examined by an immigration officer for the purpose of establishing—

(a) whether there has been such a change in the circumstances of his case, since that leave was given, that it should be cancelled;

(b) whether that leave was obtained as a result of false information given by him or his failure to disclose material facts; or

(c) whether there are medical grounds on which that leave should be cancelled.

(3) He may also be examined by an immigration officer for the purpose of determining whether it would be conducive to the public good for that leave to be cancelled.

(4) He may also be examined by a medical inspector or by any qualified person carrying out a test or examination required by a medical inspector.

(5) A person examined under this paragraph may be required by the officer or inspector to submit to further examination.

(6) A requirement under sub-paragraph (5) does not prevent a person who arrives—

(a) as a transit passenger,

(b) as a member of the crew of a ship or aircraft, or

(c) for the purpose of joining a ship or aircraft as a member of the crew,

from leaving by his intended ship or aircraft.

(7) An immigration officer examining a person under this paragraph may by notice suspend his leave to enter until the examination is completed.

(8) An immigration officer may, on the completion of any examination of a person under this paragraph, cancel his leave to enter.

(9) Cancellation of a person's leave under sub-paragraph (8) is to be treated for the purposes of this Act and Part IV of the Immigration and Asylum Act 1999 as if he had been refused leave to enter at a time when he had a current entry clearance.

(10) A requirement imposed under sub-paragraph (5) and a notice given under sub-paragraph (7) must be in writing."

58 In Schedule 2, in paragraph 4(1) and (2) (production of information and documents in connection with examinations), after "paragraph 2" insert ", 2A".

59 In Schedule 2, for paragraph 7 substitute—

"Power to require medical examination after entry

7 (1) This paragraph applies if an immigration officer examining a person under paragraph 2 decides—

(a) that he may be given leave to enter the United Kingdom; but

(b) that a further medical test or examination may be required in the interests of public health.

(2) This paragraph also applies if an immigration officer examining a person under paragraph 2A decides—

(a) that his leave to enter the United Kingdom should not be cancelled; but

(b) that a further medical test or examination may be required in the interests of public health.

(3)   The immigration officer may give the person concerned notice in writing requiring him—

- (a)   to report his arrival to such medical officer of health as may be specified in the notice; and
- (b)   to attend at such place and time and submit to such test or examination (if any), as that medical officer of health may require.

(4)   In reaching a decision under paragraph (b) of sub-paragraph (1) or (2), the immigration officer must act on the advice of—

- (a)   a medical inspector; or
- (b)   if no medical inspector is available, a fully qualified medical practitioner."

60   In Schedule 2, in paragraph 16 (detention of persons liable to examination), after sub-paragraph (1), insert—

"(1A)   A person whose leave to enter has been suspended under paragraph 2A may be detained under the authority of an immigration officer pending—

- (a)   completion of his examination under that paragraph; and
- (b)   a decision on whether to cancel his leave to enter."

61   In Schedule 2, in paragraph 18 (treatment of persons detained), after sub-paragraph (2) insert—

"(2A)   The power conferred by sub-paragraph (2) includes power to take finger-prints."

62   (1)   In Schedule 2, paragraph 21 (temporary admission of persons liable to detention) is amended as follows.

(2)   After sub-paragraph (2) insert—

"(2A)   The provisions that may be included in restrictions as to residence imposed under sub-paragraph (2) include provisions of such a description as may be prescribed by regulations made by the Secretary of State.

(2B)   The regulations may, among other things, provide for the inclusion of provisions—

- (a)   prohibiting residence in one or more particular areas;
- (b)   requiring the person concerned to reside in accommodation provided under section 4 of the Immigration and Asylum Act 1999 and prohibiting him from being absent from that accommodation except in accordance with the restrictions imposed on him.

(2C)   The regulations may provide that a particular description of provision may be imposed only for prescribed purposes.

(2D)   The power to make regulations conferred by this paragraph is exercisable by statutory instrument and includes a power to make different provision for different cases.

(2E)   But no regulations under this paragraph are to be made unless a draft of the regulations has been laid before Parliament and approved by a resolution of each House."

(3)   In sub-paragraph (3), after "2" insert "or 2A".

(4)   In sub-paragraph (4)(a), omit "under paragraph 2 above".

63   In Schedule 2, in paragraph 22 (temporary release of persons liable to detention), in sub-paragraph (1)(a), after "examination;" insert—

"(aa)a person detained under paragraph 16(1A) above pending completion of his examination or a decision on whether to cancel his leave to enter;".

64 (1) In Schedule 2, paragraph 26 (supplementary duties of those connected with ships or aircraft or with ports) is amended as follows.

(2) In sub-paragraph (1), omit "and have not been given leave".

(3) After sub-paragraph (1) insert—

"(1A) Sub-paragraph (1) does not apply in such circumstances, if any, as the Secretary of State may by order prescribe."

(4) After sub-paragraph (3) insert—

"(3A) The power conferred by sub-paragraph (1A) is exercisable by statutory instrument; and any such instrument shall be subject to annulment by a resolution of either House of Parliament."

65 In Schedule 2, omit paragraph 28.

66 ...

67 In Schedule 2, in paragraph 34 (grant of bail pending removal), in sub-paragraph (1), after "examination" insert ", detained under paragraph 16(1A) above pending completion of his examination or a decision on whether to cancel his leave to enter".

68 In Schedule 3, in paragraph 2(4) (application of certain provisions if person detained under Schedule 3), for "and 18" substitute ", 18 and 25A to 25E".

69 In Schedule 3 (supplementary provision as to deportation), in paragraph 3—

(a) for "16 or 17" substitute "66 or 67 of the Immigration and Asylum Act 1999";
(b) omit "in paragraph 28(2), (3) and (6) and"; and
(c) for "15(1)(a)" substitute "63(1)(a) or 69(4)(a) of the Immigration and Asylum Act 1999".

70 In Schedule 4 (integration of United Kingdom and Islands immigration law), for paragraph 3 (deportation) substitute—

"**3** (1) This Act has effect in relation to a person who is subject to an Islands deportation order as if the order were a deportation order made against him under this Act.

(2) Sub-paragraph (1) does not apply if the person concerned is—

(a) a British citizen;
(b) an EEA national;
(c) a member of the family of an EEA national; or
(d) a member of the family of a British citizen who is neither such a citizen nor an EEA national.

(3) The Secretary of State does not, as a result of sub-paragraph (1), have power to revoke an Islands deportation order.

(4) In any particular case, the Secretary of State may direct that paragraph (b), (c) or (d) of sub-paragraph (2) is not to apply in relation to the Islands deportation order.

(5) Nothing in this paragraph makes it unlawful for a person in respect of whom an Islands deportation order is in force in any of the Islands to enter the United Kingdom on his way from that island to a place outside the United Kingdom.

(6)   "Islands deportation order" means an order made under the immigration laws of any of the Islands under which a person is, or has been, ordered to leave the island and forbidden to return.

(7)   Subsections (10) and (12) to (14) of section 80 of the Immigration and Asylum Act 1999 apply for the purposes of this section as they apply for the purposes of that section."

The House of Commons Disqualification Act 1975 (c 24)

71   In Part III of Schedule 1 to the House of Commons Disqualification Act 1975 (disqualifying offices)—

(a)   omit—

"Adjudicator appointed for the purposes of the Immigration Act 1971";
and

(b)   at the appropriate places, insert—

"Adjudicator appointed for the purposes of the Immigration and Asylum Act 1999";
and

"Asylum Support Adjudicator".

The Northern Ireland Assembly Disqualification Act 1975 (c 25)

72   In Part III of Schedule 1 to the Northern Ireland Assembly Disqualification Act 1975 (disqualifying offices)—

(a)   omit—

"Adjudicator appointed for the purposes of the Immigration Act 1971";
and

(b)   at the appropriate places, insert—

"Adjudicator appointed for the purposes of the Immigration and Asylum Act 1999";
and

"Asylum Support Adjudicator".

The Protection from Eviction Act 1977 (c 43)

73   In section 3A of the Protection from Eviction Act 1977 (excluded tenancies and licences), after subsection (7), insert—

"(7A)   A tenancy or licence is excluded if it is granted in order to provide accommodation under Part VI of the Immigration and Asylum Act 1999."

The Education (Scotland) Act 1980 (c 44)

74   Section 53 of the Education (Scotland) Act 1980 (requirement to provide school meals etc) is amended as follows—

(a)   in subsection (3)—
 (i)   for the words from the beginning to "an", where it occurs for the second time, substitute—

"(3)   Subsection (3AA) below applies in relation to a pupil—

(a)   whose parents are in receipt of—
 (i)   income support;
 (ii)   an income-based jobseeker's allowance (payable under the Jobseekers Act 1995); or

(iii) support provided under Part VI of the Immigration and Asylum Act 1999; or
(b) who is himself in receipt of income support or an income-based jobseeker's allowance.
(3AA) An";
and
(ii) for "him", where it occurs for the first time, substitute "the pupil"; and
(b) in subsection (3A), for "Subsections (1), (2) and (3)" substitute "Subsections (1) to (3AA)".

The Firearms (Northern Ireland) Order 1981 (SI 1981/155 (NI 2))

75 In Schedule 1 to the Firearms (Northern Ireland) Order 1981 (offences for which there is an additional penalty if committed when in possession of a firearm), after paragraph 4 insert—

"4A An offence under paragraph 4 of Schedule 11 to the Immigration and Asylum Act 1999 (assaulting a detainee custody officer)."

The Magistrates' Courts (Northern Ireland) Order 1981 (SI 1981/1675 (NI 26))

76 In Article 98(11) of the Magistrates' Courts (Northern Ireland) Order 1981 (enforcement of orders for periodical payment of money), at the end, insert—

"(k) section 113 of the Immigration and Asylum Act 1999."

The Marriage Act 1983 (c 32)

77 In section 1 of the Marriage Act 1983 (marriages of house-bound and detained persons in England and Wales)—

(a) in subsection (1), for "a superintendent registrar's certificate" substitute "certificates of a superintendent registrar"; and
(b) in subsection (2)(a), for "the notice" substitute "each notice".

The Housing (Northern Ireland) Order 1983 (SI 1983/1118 (NI 15))

78 In Schedule 2 to the Housing (Northern Ireland) Order 1983 (tenancies which are not secure tenancies), after paragraph 3, insert—

"Accommodation for asylum-seekers

3A (1) A tenancy is not a secure tenancy if it is granted in order to provide accommodation under Part VI of the Immigration and Asylum Act 1999.

(2) A tenancy mentioned in sub-paragraph (1) becomes a secure tenancy if the landlord notifies the tenant that it is to be regarded as a secure tenancy."

The Rent (Scotland) Act 1984 (c 58)

79 In section 23A of the Rent (Scotland) Act 1984 (excluded tenancies and occupancy rights), after subsection (5) insert—

"(5A) Nothing in section 23 of this Act applies to a tenancy or right of occupancy if it is granted in order to provide accommodation under Part VI of the Immigration and Asylum Act 1999."

The Police and Criminal Evidence Act 1984 (c 60)

80 (1) The Police and Criminal Evidence Act 1984 is amended as follows.

(2) In section 8 (power of justice to authorise entry and search of premises), at the end insert—

"(6) This section applies in relation to a relevant offence (as defined in section 28D(4) of the Immigration Act 1971) as it applies in relation to a serious arrestable offence."

(3) In section 22 (retention), at the end insert—

"(6) This section also applies to anything retained by the police under section 28H(5) of the Immigration Act 1971."

(4) In section 61 (fingerprints), in subsection (9)(a), after "1971" insert ", section 141 of the Immigration and Asylum Act 1999 or regulations made under section 144 of that Act".

The Housing Act 1985 (c 68)

81 In Schedule 1 to the Housing Act 1985 (tenancies which cannot be secure tenancies), after paragraph 4, insert—

"Accommodation for asylum-seekers

4A (1) A tenancy is not a secure tenancy if it is granted in order to provide accommodation under Part VI of the Immigration and Asylum Act 1999.

(2) A tenancy mentioned in sub-paragraph (1) becomes a secure tenancy if the landlord notifies the tenant that it is to be regarded as a secure tenancy."

The Housing (Scotland) Act 1987 (c 26)

82 In Schedule 2 to the Housing (Scotland) Act 1987 (tenancies which cannot be secure tenancies), after paragraph 5 insert—

"Accommodation for asylum-seekers

5A (1) A tenancy shall not be a secure tenancy if it is granted in order to provide accommodation under Part VI of the Immigration and Asylum Act 1999.

(2) A tenancy mentioned in sub-paragraph (1) becomes a secure tenancy if the landlord notifies the tenant that it is to be regarded as a secure tenancy."

The Immigration Act 1988 (c 14)

83 The Immigration Act 1988 is amended as follows.

84 Omit section 5 (restricted right of appeal against deportation in cases of breach of limited leave).

85 Omit section 8 (examination of passengers before arrival).

86 Omit section 9 (charges).

The Housing (Scotland) Act 1988 (c 43)

87 In Schedule 4 to the Housing (Scotland) Act 1988 (tenancies which cannot be assured tenancies), after paragraph 11A insert—

"Accommodation for asylum-seekers

11B A tenancy granted under arrangements for the provision of support for asylum-seekers or dependants of asylum-seekers made under Part VI of the Immigration and Asylum Act 1999."

The Housing Act 1988 (c 50)

88   In Schedule 1 to the Housing Act 1988 (tenancies which are not assured tenancies), after paragraph 12, insert—

"Accommodation for asylum-seekers

12A   (1)   tenancy granted by a private landlord under arrangements for the provision of support for asylum-seekers or dependants of asylum-seekers made under Part VI of the Immigration and Asylum Act 1999.

(2)   "Private landlord" means a landlord who is not within section 80(1) of the Housing Act 1985."

...

89   ...

The Police and Criminal Evidence (Northern Ireland) Order 1989 (SI 1989/1341 (NI 12))

90   (1)   The Police and Criminal Evidence (Northern Ireland) Order 1989 is amended as follows.

(2)   In Article 10 (provision for Northern Ireland corresponding to section 8 of the 1984 Act), at the end insert—

"(6)   This Article applies in relation to a relevant offence (as defined in section 28D(4) of the Immigration Act 1971) as it applies in relation to a serious arrestable offence."

(3)   In Article 24 (provision for Northern Ireland corresponding to section 22 of the 1984 Act), at the end insert—

"(6)   This Article also applies to anything retained by the police under section 28H(5) of the Immigration Act 1971."

(4)   In Article 61 (fingerprints) in paragraph (9)(a), after "1971" insert ", section 141 of the Immigration and Asylum Act 1999 or regulations made under section 144 of that Act".

The Courts and Legal Services Act 1990 (c 41)

91   (1)   The Courts and Legal Services Act 1990 is amended as follows.

(2)   In Schedule 10 (judicial and other appointments), omit paragraph 34.

(3)   In Schedule 11 (judges etc barred from legal practice), in the entry relating to the Immigration Appeal Tribunal, omit "appointed under Schedule 5 to the Immigration Act 1971" and after that entry insert—

"Adjudicator for the purposes of the Immigration and Asylum Act 1999 (other than Asylum Support Adjudicator)".

The Social Security Contributions and Benefits Act 1992 (c 4)

92   In the Social Security Contributions and Benefits Act 1992, omit section 146A (persons subject to immigration control).

The Social Security Contributions and Benefits (Northern Ireland) Act 1992 (c 7)

93   In the Social Security Contributions and Benefits (Northern Ireland) Act 1992, omit section 142A (persons subject to immigration control).

The Tribunals and Inquiries Act 1992 (c 53)

94   The Tribunals and Inquiries Act 1992 is amended as follows.

95   In Schedule 1 (tribunals under the supervision of the Council on Tribunals), after paragraph 2 insert—

"Asylum-seekers support	2A Asylum Support Adjudicators established under section 102 of the Immigration and Asylum Act 1999."

96   …

97   In Schedule 1, after paragraph 22, insert—

"Asylum-seekers support	2A Asylum Support Adjudicators established under section 102 of the Immigration and Asylum Act 1999."

The Judicial Pensions and Retirement Act 1993 (c 8)

98   (1)   The Judicial Pensions and Retirement Act 1993 is amended as follows.

(2)   …

(3)   …

(4)   In Schedule 6 (retirement date for certain judicial offices), omit paragraphs 37 and 38.

The Asylum and Immigration Appeals Act 1993 (c 23)

99   The Asylum and Immigration Appeals Act 1993 is amended as follows.

100   Omit section 3 (fingerprinting).

101   Omit sections 4 and 5 and Schedule 1 (housing of asylum-seekers and their dependants).

102   (1)   Omit section 6 (protection of asylum claimants from deportation etc).

(2)   This paragraph is to be treated as having come into force on 26th July 1993.

103   Omit section 7 (curtailment of leave).

104   Omit sections 8, 9, 10 and 11 and Schedule 2 (which relate to appeals).

105   For paragraph (a) of section 9A(1) (bail pending appeal from Immigration Appeal Tribunal), substitute—

"(a) has an appeal under Part IV of the Immigration and Asylum Act 1999 which is pending by reason of an appeal, or an application for leave to appeal;".

106   In section 9A(6), for "section 9 above" substitute "paragraph 23 of Schedule 4 of the Immigration and Asylum Act 1999".

107   Omit section 12 (carriers' liability).

The Asylum and Immigration Act 1996 (c 49)

108   The Asylum and Immigration Act 1996 is amended as follows.

109   Omit section 7 (power of arrest and search warrants).

110   Omit section 9 (entitlement to housing accommodation and assistance).

111   Omit section 10 (entitlement to child benefit).

112   Omit section 11 (saving for social security regulations).

113   Omit Schedule 1 (modifications of social security regulations).

114   In Schedule 2, omit sub-paragraphs (2) and (3) of paragraph 1, paragraph 3 and paragraph 4(2) (which are spent as a result of this Act).

115   In Schedule 3, omit paragraphs 1, 2 and 5 (which are spent as a result of this Act).

The Housing Act 1996 (c 52)

116   In section 183(2) of the Housing Act 1996 (interpretation of expressions related to assistance), in the definition of "eligible for assistance", omit "or section 186 (asylum seekers and their dependants)".

...

117   ...

The Special Immigration Appeals Commission Act 1997 (c 68)

118   The Special Immigration Appeals Commission Act 1997 is amended as follows.

119   ...

120   ...

121   ...

122   In section 4 (determination of appeals), after subsection (1) insert—

"(1A)   If a certificate under section 70(4)(b) of the Immigration and Asylum Act 1999 has been issued, the Commission on an appeal to it under this Act may, instead of determining the appeal, quash the certificate and remit the appeal to an adjudicator."

123   In section 7 (appeals from Commission), omit subsection (4).

124   After section 7, insert—

"**7A   Pending appeals**

(1)   For the purposes of this Act, an appeal to the Commission is to be treated as pending during the period beginning when notice of appeal is given and ending when the appeal is finally determined, withdrawn or abandoned.

(2)   An appeal is not to be treated as finally determined while a further appeal may be brought.

(3)   If a further appeal is brought, the original appeal is not to be treated as finally determined until the further appeal is determined, withdrawn or abandoned.

(4)   A pending appeal to the Commission is to be treated as abandoned if the appellant leaves the United Kingdom.

(5)   A pending appeal to the Commission is to be treated as abandoned if the appellant is granted leave to enter or remain in the United Kingdom.

(6)   But subsection (5) does not apply to an appeal brought under section 2(1) as a result of section 70(4) of the Immigration and Asylum Act 1999.

(7) A pending appeal brought under section 2(1) as a result of section 62(3) of that Act is to be treated as abandoned if a deportation order is made against the appellant."

125 In Schedule 1 (supplementary provision as to Commission), in paragraph 5(b)—

(a) in sub-paragraph (i), for "paragraph 1 of Schedule 5 to the Immigration Act 1971" substitute "section 57(2) of the Immigration and Asylum Act 1999"; and

(b) in sub-paragraph (ii), for "paragraph 7 of that Schedule" substitute "paragraph 1(3) of Schedule 2 to that Act".

126 ...

127 ...

128 ...

129 ...

Initial Commencement
Paras 62(2), 73, 78, 79, 81, 82, 87, 88, 102: Royal Assent: 11 November 1999: see s 170(3)(s).
Paras 1–61, 62(1), (3), (4), 63–72, 74–77, 80, 83–86, 89–101, 103–129: To be appointed: see s 170(4).

Appointment
Paras 1–32, 37–42, 77: Appointment: 1 January 2001: see SI 2000/2698, art 2, Schedule.
Para 43: Appointment (for certain purposes) by virtue of the appointment of para 54: 6 December 1999: see SI 1999/3190, art 2, Schedule.
Paras 43, 49, 80(1), 90(1), 94, 108, 118: Appointment (for certain purposes): 14 February 2000: see SI 2000/168, art 2, Schedule.
Paras 43, 52(1), 108: Appointment (for certain purposes): 1 March 2000: see SI 2000/464, art 2, Schedule.
Paras 43, 52(1), 99, 108: Appointment (for certain purposes): 3 April 2000: see SI 2000/464, art 2, Schedule.
Paras 43, 83, 99, 118: Appointment (for certain purposes): 2 October 2000: see SI 2000/2444, art 2, Sch 1; for transitional provisions see art 3, Sch 2 thereof.
Paras 44(1), 45, 50, 51, 53, 56–60, 62(1), (3), (4), 63, 64, 67, 68, 80(2), (3), 90(2), (3), 95, 96, 109, 125: Appointment: 14 February 2000: see SI 2000/168, art 2, Schedule.
Paras 44(2), 46, 55, 65, 66, 69, 70, 84, 103–106, 114, 115, 120, 122–124, 126–128: Appointment: 2 October 2000: see SI 2000/2444, art 2, Sch 1; for transitional provisions see art 3, Sch 2 thereto.
Paras 49, 121: Appointment (for certain purposes): 2 October 2000: see SI 2000/2444, art 2, Sch 1; for transitional provisions see art 3, Sch 2, para 2 thereto.
Paras 52(1), 108: Appointment (for remaining purposes): 2 October 2000: see SI 2000/2444, art 2, Sch 1.
Paras 52(3)(a), 110: Appointment: 1 March 2000: see SI 2000/464, art 2, Schedule.
Paras 52(3)(b), 74, 76, 92, 93, 101, 111–113: Appointment: 3 April 2000: see SI 2000/464, art 2, Schedule.
Paras 54, 117: Appointment: 6 December 1999: see SI 1999/3190, art 2, Schedule.
Para 61: Appointment: 11 December 2000: see SI 2000/3099, art 3, Schedule.
Paras 71, 72, 91, 98: Appointment: 14 February 2000: see SI 2000/168, art 2, Schedule; for transitional provisions see art 3 thereof.
Para 83: Appointment (for certain purposes): 30 June 2003: see SI 2003/1469, art 2, Schedule.
Para 86: Appointment: 30 June 2003: see SI 2003/1469, art 2, Schedule.
Para 118: Appointment (for certain purposes): 1 August 2000: see SI 2000/1985, art 2, Schedule.
Para 129: Appointment: 1 August 2000: see SI 2000/1985, art 2, Schedule.

Amendment
Paras 1, 2: repealed by SI 2003/413, art 40, Schedule. Date in force: 1 January 2004: see the Marriage (2003 Order) (Commencement) Order (Northern Ireland) 2003, SR 2003/466, art 2(b).
Paras 46(a), 51, 53, 66, 96, 98(2), (3), 120, 121, 126–129: repealed by the Nationality, Immigration and Asylum Act 2002, s 161, Sch 9. Date in force: 1 April 2003: see SI 2003/754, art 2(1), Sch 1.

Para 89: repealed by the Terrorism Act 2000, s 125(2), Sch 16, Pt I. Date in force: 19 February 2001: see SI 2001/421, art 2.

Para 117: repealed by the Education Act 2002, s 215(2), Sch 22, Pt 3. Date in force (in relation to Wales): 31 March 2003: see SI 2002/3185, art 5, Schedule, Pt II. Date in force (in relation to England): 6 April 2003: see SI 2003/124, art 5.

Para 119: repealed by SI 2000/2326, reg 32(4)(a). Date in force: 2 October 2000: see SI 2000/2326, reg 1(1).

SCHEDULE 15
TRANSITIONAL PROVISIONS AND SAVINGS

Section 169(2)

Leave to enter or remain

1 (1)   An order made under section 3A of the 1971 Act may make provision with respect to leave given before the commencement of section 1.

(2)   An order made under section 3B of the 1971 Act may make provision with respect to leave given before the commencement of section 2.

Section 2 of the Asylum and Immigration Act 1996

2 (1)   This paragraph applies in relation to any time before the commencement of the repeal by this Act of section 2 of the Asylum and Immigration Act 1996.

(2)   That section has effect, and is to be deemed always to have had effect, as if the reference to section 6 of the Asylum and Immigration Appeals Act 1993 were a reference to section 15, and any certificate issued under that section is to be read accordingly.

Adjudicators and the Tribunal

3 (1)   Each existing member of the Tribunal is to continue as a member of the Tribunal as if he had been duly appointed by the Lord Chancellor under Schedule 2.

(2)   Each existing adjudicator is to continue as an adjudicator as if he had been duly appointed by the Lord Chancellor under Schedule 3.

(3)   The terms and conditions for a person to whom sub-paragraph (1) or (2) applies remain those on which he held office immediately before the appropriate date.

(4)   The provisions of Schedule 7 to the Judicial Pensions and Retirement Act 1993 (transitional provisions for retirement dates), so far as applicable in relation to an existing member or adjudicator immediately before the appropriate date, continue to have effect.

(5)   The repeal by this Act of Schedule 5 to the 1971 Act (provisions with respect to adjudicators and the Tribunal) does not affect any entitlement which an existing member or adjudicator had immediately before the appropriate date as a result of a determination made under paragraph 3(1)(b) or 9(1)(b) of that Schedule.

(6)   "The appropriate date" means—

    (a)   in relation to existing members of the Tribunal, the date on which section 56 comes into force; and

    (b)   in relation to existing adjudicators, the date on which section 57 comes into force.

(7)   "Existing member" means a person who is a member of the Tribunal immediately before the appropriate date.

(8)   "Existing adjudicator" means a person who is an adjudicator immediately before the appropriate date.

References to justices' chief executive

4   At any time before the coming into force of section 90 of the Access to Justice Act 1999—

(a)   the reference in section 48(3)(b) to the justices' chief executive appointed by the magistrates' court committee whose area includes the petty sessions area for which the specified court acts is to be read as a reference to the clerk of that court; and

(b)   the reference in section 28K(9)(a) and (10) of the 1971 Act (inserted by section 138) to the justices' chief executive appointed by the magistrates' court committee whose area includes the petty sessions area for which the justice acts is to be read as a reference to the clerk to the justices for the petty sessions area for which the justice acts.

Duties under National Assistance Act 1948

5   Section 116 has effect, in relation to any time before section 115 is brought into force, as if section 115 came into force on the passing of this Act.

Duties under Health Services and Public Health Act 1968

6   Section 117(1) has effect, in relation to any time before section 115 is brought into force, as if section 115 came into force on the passing of this Act.

Duties under Social Work (Scotland) Act 1968

7   Subsections (1) to (3) of section 120 have effect, in relation to any time before section 115 is brought into force, as if section 115 came into force on the passing of this Act.

Duties under Health and Personal Social Services (Northern Ireland) Order 1972

8   Subsections (1) and (2) of section 121 have effect, in relation to any time before section 115 is brought into force, as if section 115 came into force on the passing of this Act.

Duties under National Health Service Act 1977

9   Section 117(2) has effect, in relation to any time before section 115 is brought into force, as if section 115 came into force on the passing of this Act.

Duties under Mental Health (Scotland) Act 1984

10   *Subsections (4) and (5) of section 120 have effect, in relation to any time before section 115 is brought into force, as if section 115 came into force on the passing of this Act.*

Appeals relating to deportation orders

11   Section 15 of the 1971 Act, section 5 of the Immigration Act 1988 and the Immigration (Restricted Right of Appeal against Deportation) (Exemption) Order 1993 are to continue to have effect in relation to any person on whom the Secretary of State has, before the commencement of the repeal of those sections, served a notice of his decision to make a deportation order.

12 (1) Sub-paragraph (2) applies if, on the coming into force of section 10, sections 15 of the 1971 Act and 5 of the Immigration Act 1988 have been repealed by this Act.

(2) Those sections are to continue to have effect in relation to any person—

    (a) who applied during the regularisation period fixed by section 9, in accordance with the regulations made under that section, for leave to remain in the United Kingdom, and

    (b) on whom the Secretary of State has since served a notice of his decision to make a deportation order.

Assistance under Part VII of the Housing Act 1996

13 (1) The Secretary of State may by order provide for any provision of Part VII of the Housing Act 1996 (homelessness) to have effect in relation to section 185(2) persons, during the interim period, with such modifications as may be specified in the order.

(2) An order under this paragraph may, in particular, include provision—

    (a) for the referral of section 185(2) persons by one local housing authority to another by agreement between the authorities;

    (b) as to the suitability of accommodation for such persons;

    (c) as to out-of-area placements of such persons.

(3) "Interim period" means the period beginning with the passing of this Act and ending on the coming into force of the repeal of section 186 of the Act of 1996 (asylum-seekers and their dependants) by this Act (as to which see section 117(5)).

(4) "Local housing authority" has the same meaning as in the Act of 1996.

(5) "Section 185(2) person" means a person who—

    (a) is eligible for housing assistance under Part VII of the Act of 1996 as a result of regulations made under section 185(2) of that Act; and

    (b) is not made ineligible by section 186 (or any other provision) of that Act.

(6) The fact that an order may be made under this paragraph only in respect of the interim period does not prevent it from containing provisions of a kind authorised under section 166(3)(a) which are to have continuing effect after the end of that period.

Provision of support

14 (1) The Secretary of State may, by directions given to a local authority to whom Schedule 9 applies, require the authority to treat the interim period fixed for the purposes of that Schedule as coming to an end—

    (a) for specified purposes,

    (b) in relation to a specified area or locality, or

    (c) in relation to persons of a specified description,

on such earlier day as may be specified.

(2) The Secretary of State may, by directions given to an authority to whom an amended provision applies, provide for specified descriptions of person to be treated—

    (a) for specified purposes, or

    (b) in relation to a specified area or locality,

as being persons to whom section 115 applies during such period as may be specified.

(3) Directions given under this paragraph may—

   (a)   make such consequential, supplemental or transitional provision as the Secretary of State considers appropriate; and

   (b)   make different provision for different cases or descriptions of case.

(4)   "Specified" means specified in the directions.

(5)   "Amended provision" means any provision amended by—

   (a)   section 116;

   (b)   section 117(1) or (2);

   (c)   section 120; or

   (d)   section 121.

Initial Commencement
Paras 2, 13: Royal Assent: 11 November 1999: see s 170(3)(t).
Paras 1, 3–11, 14: To be appointed: see s 170(4).
Para 12: To be appointed (in accordance with s 9): see s 170(4).

Appointment
Paras 1, 3, 4(b), 14: Appointment: 14 February 2000: see SI 2000/168, art 2, Schedule.
Paras 5, 6, 9: Appointment: 6 December 1999: see SI 1999/3190, art 2, Schedule.
Paras 11, 12: Appointment: 2 October 2000: see SI 2000/2444, art 2, Sch 1.

Amendment
Para 10: repealed by the Mental Health (Care and Treatment) (Scotland) Act 2003, s 331(2), Sch 5, Pt 1. Date in force: 5 October 2005: see SSI 2005/161, art 3.

Subordinate Legislation
Homelessness (Asylum-Seekers) (Interim Period) (England) Order 1999, SI 1999/3126 (made under para 13).

SCHEDULE 16
REPEALS

Section 169(3)

Chapter	Short title	Extent of repeal
1949 c 76	The Marriage Act 1949	In section 3(1), "whether by licence or without licence,".
		Section 26(2).
		In section 27, in subsection (1) "without licence", subsection (2), in subsection (3)(a) "in the case of a marriage intended to be solemnized without licence,", and subsection (3)(b).
		In section 27B, in subsections (4) and (6) "or licence", and in subsection (5) "or certificate and licence,".
		In section 28(1), "or licence".
		In section 29, every "or licence".

Chapter	Short title	Extent of repeal
		In section 31, in subsection (1) "without licence", and in subsection (4) "without licence".
		Section 32.
		In section 35, in subsection (1) ", or if the marriage is to be by licence, a certificate and a licence," in subsections (2) and (4) "or, if the marriage is to be by licence, a certificate and a licence,", and in subsections (2A) and (2B) "or, if the marriage is to be by licence, a certificate and licence,".
		Section 36.
		In section 37(1), "without licence".
		In section 38(1), "without licence".
		In section 39(1), "without licence".
		Section 40(2).
		Section 49(c).
		In section 50, in subsection (1) "the certificate or, if notice of marriage has been given to more than one superintendent registrar", and subsection (2).
		In section 51(1), from first "the sum" to "case,".
		In section 75(3), in paragraph (b) "or licence".
		In Schedule 4, in Part III, "The proviso to subsection (2) of section twenty-six".
1969 c 46	The Family Law Reform Act 1969	In section 2(3), "or licence" in both cases.
1970 c 34	The Marriage (Registrar General's Licence) Act 1970	In section 5, "or licence".
		Section 13(b).
1971 c 77	The Immigration Act 1971	In section 10(1), from "and any such Order" to the end.
		Part II.

Appendix 1   Legislation and materials

Chapter	Short title	Extent of repeal
		In section 24, subsections (1)(aa) and (2).
		Section 25(3).
		In Schedule 2, in paragraph 21(4)(a) "under paragraph 2 above", in paragraph 26(1) "and have not been given leave" and paragraph 28.
		In Schedule 3, in paragraph3, "in paragraph 28(2), (3) and (6) and".
		Schedule 5.
1975 c 24	The House of Commons Disqualification Act 1975	In Schedule 1, in Part III, "Adjudicator appointed for the purposes of the Immigration Act 1971".
1975 c 25	The Northern Ireland Assembly Disqualification Act 1975	In Schedule 1, in Part III, "Adjudicator appointed for the purposes of the Immigration Act 1971".
1987 c 24	The Immigration (Carriers' Liability) Act 1987	The whole Act.
1988 c 14	The Immigration Act 1988	Section 5.
		Section 8.
		Section 9.
1990 c 41	The Courts and Legal Services Act 1990	In Schedule 10, paragraph 34.
		In Schedule 11, in the entry relating to the Immigration Appeal Tribunal, "appointed under Schedule 5 to the Immigration Act 1971".
1992 c 4	The Social Security and Benefits Act Contributions 1992	Section 146A.
1992 c 7	The Social Security Contributions and Benefits (Northern Ireland) Act 1992	Section 142A.
1993 c 8	The Judicial Pensions and Retirement Act 1993	In Schedule 6, paragraphs 37 and 38.

Chapter	Short title	Extent of repeal
1993 c 23	The Asylum and Immigration Appeals Act 1993	Section 3.
		Section 4.
		Section 5.
		Section 6.
		Section 7.
		Section 8.
		Section 9.
		Section 10.
		Section 11.
		Section 12.
		Schedule 1.
		Schedule 2.
1996 c 49	The Asylum and Immigration Act 1996	Section 1.
		Section 2.
		Section 3.
		Section 4.
		Section 7.
		Section 9.
		Section 10.
		Section 11.
		In Schedule 2, paragraphs 1(2) and (3), 3 and 4(2).
		In Schedule 3, paragraphs 1, 2 and 5.
1996 c 52	The Housing Act 1996	In section 183(2), in the definition "eligible for assistance", "or section 186 (asylum seekers and their dependants)".
		Section 186.
		In Schedule 16, paragraph 3.
1997 c 68	The Special Immigration Appeals Commission Act 1997	Section 7(4).
		In Schedule 2, paragraph 5.

Appointment
Appointment (in part): 14 February 2000: see SI 2000/168, art 2, Schedule.
Appointment (in part): 1 March 2000: see SI 2000/464, art 2, Schedule.
Appointment (in part): 3 April 2000: see SI 2000/464,art 2, Schedule.
Appointment (in part): 2 October 2000: see SI 2000/2444, art 2, Sch 1; for transitional provisions see art 3, Sch 2 thereto.
Appointment (in part): 1 January 2001: see SI 2000/2698, art 2, Schedule.
Appointment (in part): 11 December 2000: see SI 2000/3099, art 3, Schedule.
Appointment (in part): 8 December 2002: see SI 2002/2815, art 2, Schedule.
Appointment (in part): 30 June 2003: see SI 2003/1469, art 2, Schedule.

NATIONALITY, IMMIGRATION AND ASYLUM ACT 2002

2002 CHAPTER 41

An Act to make provision about nationality, immigration and asylum; to create offences in connection with international traffic in prostitution; to make provision about international projects connected with migration; and for connected purposes.

[7th November 2002]

BE IT ENACTED by the Queen's most Excellent Majesty, by and with the advice and consent of the Lords Spiritual and Temporal, and Commons, in this present Parliament assembled, and by the authority of the same, as follows:—

PART 1
NATIONALITY

1   Naturalisation: knowledge of language and society

(1)   The following shall be inserted after the word "and" after paragraph 1(1)(c) of Schedule 1 to the British Nationality Act 1981 (c 61) (requirements for naturalisation)—

"(ca)that he has sufficient knowledge about life in the United Kingdom; and".

(2)   In paragraph 2(e) of that Schedule (waiver)—

(a)   for "the requirement specified in paragraph 1(1)(c)" there shall be substituted "either or both of the requirements specified in paragraph 1(1)(c) and (ca)", and

(b)   for "expect him to fulfil it" there shall be substituted "expect him to fulfil that requirement or those requirements".

(3)   The following shall be inserted after section 41(1)(b) of that Act (regulations)—

"(ba)for determining whether a person has sufficient knowledge of a language for the purpose of an application for naturalisation;
(bb) for determining whether a person has sufficient knowledge about life in the United Kingdom for the purpose of an application for naturalisation;".

(4)   The following shall be inserted after section 41(1) of that Act—

"(1A)   Regulations under subsection (1)(ba) or (bb) may, in particular—

(a) make provision by reference to possession of a specified qualification;
(b) make provision by reference to possession of a qualification of a specified kind;
(c) make provision by reference to attendance on a specified course;
(d) make provision by reference to attendance on a course of a specified kind;
(e) make provision by reference to a specified level of achievement;
(f) enable a person designated by the Secretary of State to determine sufficiency of knowledge in specified circumstances;
(g) enable the Secretary of State to accept a qualification of a specified kind as evidence of sufficient knowledge of a language."

Appointment

Sub-ss (3), (4): Appointment: 6 July 2004: see SI 2004/1707, art 2.

2 Naturalisation: spouse of citizen

(1) Paragraphs 3 and 4 of Schedule 1 to the British Nationality Act 1981 (c 61) (requirements for naturalisation as British citizen: spouse of citizen) shall be amended as follows—

(a) in paragraph 3(e) for "requirement specified in paragraph 1(1)(b)" substitute "requirements specified in paragraph 1(1)(b), (c) and (ca)", and
(b) in paragraph 4(c) omit "and (e)".

(2) Paragraphs 7 and 8 of that Schedule (requirements for naturalisation as British overseas territories citizen: spouse of citizen) shall be amended as follows—

(a) in paragraph 7(e) for "requirement specified in paragraph 5(1)(b)" substitute "requirements specified in paragraph 5(1)(b) and (c)", and
(b) in paragraph 8(c) omit "and (e)".

Appointment

Appointment: 28 July 2004: see SI 2004/1707, art 3.

3 Citizenship ceremony, oath and pledge

Schedule 1 (which makes provision about citizenship ceremonies, oaths and pledges) shall have effect.

Appointment

Appointment: 1 January 2004 (except in relation to any application for registration or naturalisation made before that date): see SI 2003/3156, arts 2(a), 3, 4.

4 Deprivation of citizenship

(1) The following shall be substituted for section 40 of the British Nationality Act 1981 (deprivation of citizenship)—

"40 Deprivation of citizenship

(1) In this section a reference to a person's "citizenship status" is a reference to his status as—

(a) a British citizen,
(b) a British overseas territories citizen,
(c) a British Overseas citizen,
(d) a British National (Overseas),
(e) a British protected person, or
(f) a British subject.

(2)   The Secretary of State may by order deprive a person of a citizenship status if the Secretary of State is satisfied that the person has done anything seriously prejudicial to the vital interests of—

    (a)   the United Kingdom, or
    (b)   a British overseas territory.

(3)   The Secretary of State may by order deprive a person of a citizenship status which results from his registration or naturalisation if the Secretary of State is satisfied that the registration or naturalisation was obtained by means of—

    (a)   fraud,
    (b)   false representation, or
    (c)   concealment of a material fact.

(4)   The Secretary of State may not make an order under subsection (2) if he is satisfied that the order would make a person stateless.

(5)   Before making an order under this section in respect of a person the Secretary of State must give the person written notice specifying—

    (a)   that the Secretary of State has decided to make an order,
    (b)   the reasons for the order, and
    (c)   the person's right of appeal under section 40A(1) or under section 2B of the Special Immigration Appeals Commission Act 1997 (c 68).

(6)   Where a person acquired a citizenship status by the operation of a law which applied to him because of his registration or naturalisation under an enactment having effect before commencement, the Secretary of State may by order deprive the person of the citizenship status if the Secretary of State is satisfied that the registration or naturalisation was obtained by means of—

    (a)   fraud,
    (b)   false representation, or
    (c)   concealment of a material fact.

40A   Deprivation of citizenship: appeal

(1)   A person who is given notice under section 40(5) of a decision to make an order in respect of him under section 40 may appeal against the decision to an adjudicator appointed under section 81 of the Nationality, Immigration and Asylum Act 2002 (immigration appeal).

(2)   Subsection (1) shall not apply to a decision if the Secretary of State certifies that it was taken wholly or partly in reliance on information which in his opinion should not be made public—

    (a)   in the interests of national security,
    (b)   in the interests of the relationship between the United Kingdom and another country, or
    (c)   otherwise in the public interest.

(3)   A party to an appeal to an adjudicator under subsection (1) may, with the permission of the Immigration Appeal Tribunal, appeal to the Tribunal against the adjudicator's determination on a point of law.

(4)   A party to an appeal to the Immigration Appeal Tribunal under subsection (3) may bring a further appeal on a point of law—

    (a)   where the decision of the adjudicator was made in Scotland, to the Court of Session, or
    (b)   in any other case, to the Court of Appeal.

(5) An appeal under subsection (4) may be brought only with the permission of—

(a) the Tribunal, or

(b) if the Tribunal refuses permission, the court referred to in subsection (4)(a) or (b).

(6) An order under section 40 may not be made in respect of a person while an appeal under this section or section 2B of the Special Immigration Appeals Commission Act 1997 (c 68)—

(a) has been instituted and has not yet been finally determined, withdrawn or abandoned, or

(b) could be brought (ignoring any possibility of an appeal out of time with permission).

(7) Rules under section 106 of the Nationality, Immigration and Asylum Act 2002 (immigration appeal: rules) may make provision about an appeal under this section.

(8) Directions under section 107 of that Act (practice directions) may make provision about an appeal under this section."

(2) The following shall be inserted before section 3 of the Special Immigration Appeals Commission Act 1997 (jurisdiction: bail)—

"2B A person may appeal to the Special Immigration Appeals Commission against a decision to make an order under section 40 of the British Nationality Act 1981 (c 61) (deprivation of citizenship) if he is not entitled to appeal under section 40A(1) of that Act because of a certificate under section 40A(2)."

(3) In section 5(1)(a) and (b) and (2) of that Act (procedure) after "section 2" there shall be inserted "or 2B".

(4) In exercising a power under section 40 of the British Nationality Act 1981 after the commencement of subsection (1) above the Secretary of State may have regard to anything which—

(a) occurred before commencement, and

(b) he could have relied on (whether on its own or with other matters) in making an order under section 40 before commencement.

Appointment
Appointment: 1 April 2003: see SI 2003/754, art 2(1), Sch 1; for transitional provisions in relation to sub-ss (2), (3) above, see art 3(2), Sch 2, para 5 thereto.

5   Resumption of citizenship

In the following provisions of the British Nationality Act 1981 (c 61) the words ", if a woman," shall cease to have effect—

(a) section 10(1) and (2) (registration as British citizen following renunciation of citizenship), and

(b) section 22(1) and (2) (registration as British overseas territories citizen following renunciation of citizenship).

Initial Commencement
Royal Assent: 7 November 2002: for effect see s 162(3).

6   Nationality decision: discrimination

(1) Section 19D of the Race Relations Act 1976 (c 74) (discrimination by public authority: permitted cases) shall be amended as follows.

(2) In subsection (1) for "immigration and nationality functions" substitute "immigration functions".

(3) For subsections (4) and (5) substitute—

"(4) In subsection (1) "immigration functions" means functions exercisable by virtue of any of the enactments mentioned in subsection (5).

(5) Those enactments are—

(a) the Immigration Acts (within the meaning of section 158 of the Nationality, Immigration and Asylum Act 2002) excluding sections 28A to 28K of the Immigration Act 1971 (c 77) so far as they relate to offences under Part III of that Act;

(b) the Special Immigration Appeals Commission Act 1997 (c 68);

(c) provision made under section 2(2) of the European Communities Act 1972 (c 68) which relates to immigration or asylum; and

(d) any provision of Community law which relates to immigration or asylum."

(4) Section 19E of the Race Relations Act 1976 (monitoring of use of section 19D) shall be amended as follows—

(a) in subsection (3)(a) for "immigration and nationality functions" substitute "immigration functions", and

(b) omit subsection (7).

(5) In section 71A of that Act (general statutory duty: special cases)—

(a) in subsection (1) the words "(within the meaning of section 19D(1))" shall be omitted, and

(b) the following shall be inserted after subsection (1)—

"(1A) In subsection (1) "immigration and nationality functions" means functions exercisable by virtue of—

(a) the Immigration Acts (within the meaning of section 158 of the Nationality, Immigration and Asylum Act 2002) excluding sections 28A to 28K of the Immigration Act 1971 so far as they relate to offences under Part III of that Act;

(b) the British Nationality Act 1981;

(c) the British Nationality (Falkland Islands) Act 1983 (c 6);

(d) the British Nationality (Hong Kong) Act 1990 (c 34);

(e) the Hong Kong (War Wives and Widows) Act 1996 (c 41);

(f) the British Nationality (Hong Kong) Act 1997 (c 20);

(g) the Special Immigration Appeals Commission Act 1997 (c 68);

(h) provision made under section 2(2) of the European Communities Act 1972 (c 68) which relates to the subject matter of an enactment within any of paragraphs (a) to (g); or

(i) any provision of Community law which relates to the subject matter of an enactment within any of those paragraphs."

Initial Commencement
Royal Assent: 7 November 2002: see s 162(2)(a).

7   Nationality decision: reasons and review

(1) Section 44(2) and (3) of the British Nationality Act 1981 (c 61) (no requirement to give reasons for discretionary decision, and no right of appeal) shall cease to have effect.

(2) Section 1(5) of the British Nationality (Hong Kong) Act 1990 (c 34) (no requirement to give reasons for discretionary decision, and no right of appeal) shall cease to have effect.

Initial Commencement
Royal Assent: 7 November 2002: see s 162(2)(b).

8 Citizenship: registration

In paragraph 3(1)(b) of Schedule 2 to the British Nationality Act 1981 (application by person born in United Kingdom or overseas territory for registration as citizen: age requirement) the words "had attained the age of ten but" shall cease to have effect.

Appointment
Appointment: 1 April 2003: see s 162(4) hereof and SI 2003/754, art 2(2).

9 Legitimacy of child

(1) The following shall be substituted for section 50(9) of the British Nationality Act 1981 (interpretation: child)—

"(9) For the purposes of this Act a child's mother is the woman who gives birth to the child.

(9A) For the purposes of this Act a child's father is—

  (a) the husband, at the time of the child's birth, of the woman who gives birth to the child, or
  (b) where a person is treated as the father of the child under section 28 of the Human Fertilisation and Embryology Act 1990 (c 37) (father), that person, or
  (c) where neither paragraph (a) nor paragraph (b) applies, any person who satisfies prescribed requirements as to proof of paternity.

(9B) In subsection (9A)(c) "prescribed" means prescribed by regulations of the Secretary of State; and the regulations—

  (a) may confer a function (which may be a discretionary function) on the Secretary of State or another person,
  (b) may make provision which applies generally or only in specified circumstances,
  (c) may make different provision for different circumstances,
  (d) must be made by statutory instrument, and
  (e) shall be subject to annulment in pursuance of a resolution of either House of Parliament.

(9C) The expressions "parent", "child" and "descended" shall be construed in accordance with subsections (9) and (9A)."

(2) In section 3(6) of that Act (registration of minor as British citizen)—

  (a) after paragraph (a) insert "and",
  (b) the word "and" after paragraph (b) shall cease to have effect, and
  (c) paragraph (c) (illegitimate child) shall cease to have effect.

(3) In section 17(6) of that Act (registration of minor as British overseas territories citizen)—

  (a) after paragraph (a) insert "and",
  (b) the word "and" after paragraph (b) shall cease to have effect, and
  (c) paragraph (c) (illegitimate child) shall cease to have effect.

(4) Section 47 of that Act (legitimated children) shall cease to have effect.

(5)   In Schedule 2 to that Act (persons otherwise stateless)—

  (a)   in paragraph 1(1)(b) (person born in United Kingdom), the words "he is born legitimate and" shall cease to have effect, and
  (b)   in paragraph 2(1)(b) (person born in British overseas territory), the words "he is born legitimate and" shall cease to have effect.

Initial Commencement
To be appointed: see s 162(1); for effect see s 162(5).

10   Right of abode: certificate of entitlement

(1)   The Secretary of State may by regulations make provision for the issue to a person of a certificate that he has the right of abode in the United Kingdom.

(2)   The regulations may, in particular—

  (a)   specify to whom an application must be made;
  (b)   specify the place (which may be outside the United Kingdom) to which an application must be sent;
  (c)   provide that an application must be made in a specified form;
  (d)   provide that an application must be accompanied by specified documents;
  (e)   require the payment of a fee on the making of an application;
  (f)   specify the consequences of failure to comply with a requirement under any of paragraphs (a) to (e) above;
  (g)   provide for a certificate to cease to have effect after a period of time specified in or determined in accordance with the regulations;
  (h)   make provision about the revocation of a certificate.

(3)   The regulations may—

  (a)   make provision which applies generally or only in specified cases or circumstances;
  (b)   make different provision for different purposes;
  (c)   include consequential, incidental or transitional provision.

(4)   The regulations—

  (a)   must be made by statutory instrument, and
  (b)   shall be subject to annulment in pursuance of a resolution of either House of Parliament.

(5)   The Immigration Act 1971 (c 77) shall be amended as follows—

  (a)   in section 3(9)(b) (proof of entitlement to right of abode) the words "issued by or on behalf of the Government of the United Kingdom certifying that he has such a right of abode" shall cease to have effect, and
  (b)   in section 33(1) for the definition of "certificate of entitlement" substitute—
""certificate of entitlement" means a certificate under section 10 of the Nationality, Immigration and Asylum Act 2002 that a person has the right of abode in the United Kingdom;".

(6)   Regulations under this section may, in particular, include provision saving, with or without modification, the effect of a certificate which—

  (a)   is issued before the regulations come into force, and
  (b)   is a certificate of entitlement for the purposes of sections 3(9) and 33(1) of the Immigration Act 1971 as those sections have effect before the commencement of subsection (5) above.

Initial Commencement
Sub-ss (1)–(4), (6): Royal Assent: 7 November 2002: see s 162(2)(c).
Sub-s (5): To be appointed: see s 162(1).

11 Unlawful presence in United Kingdom

(1) This section applies for the construction of a reference to being in the United Kingdom "in breach of the immigration laws" in section 4(2) or (4) or 50(5) of, or Schedule 1 to, the British Nationality Act 1981 (c 61).

(2) A person is in the United Kingdom in breach of the immigration laws if (and only if) he—

(a) is in the United Kingdom,

(b) does not have the right of abode in the United Kingdom within the meaning of section 2 of the Immigration Act 1971,

(c) does not have leave to enter or remain in the United Kingdom (whether or not he previously had leave),

(d) is not a qualified person within the meaning of the Immigration (European Economic Area) Regulations 2000 (SI 2000/2326) (person entitled to reside in United Kingdom without leave) (whether or not he was previously a qualified person),

(e) is not a family member of a qualified person within the meaning of those regulations (whether or not he was previously a family member of a qualified person),

(f) is not entitled to enter and remain in the United Kingdom by virtue of section 8(1) of the Immigration Act 1971 (crew) (whether or not he was previously entitled), and

(g) does not have the benefit of an exemption under section 8(2) to (4) of that Act (diplomats, soldiers and other special cases) (whether or not he previously had the benefit of an exemption).

(3) Section 11(1) of the Immigration Act 1971 (person deemed not to be in United Kingdom before disembarkation, while in controlled area or while under immigration control) shall apply for the purposes of this section as it applies for the purposes of that Act.

(4) This section shall be treated as always having had effect except in relation to a person who on the commencement of this section is, or has been at any time since he last entered the United Kingdom—

(a) a qualified person within the meaning of the regulations referred to in subsection (2)(d), or

(b) a family member of a qualified person within the meaning of those regulations.

(5) This section is without prejudice to the generality of—

(a) a reference to being in a place outside the United Kingdom in breach of immigration laws, and

(b) a reference in a provision other than one specified in subsection (1) to being in the United Kingdom in breach of immigration laws.

Initial Commencement
Royal Assent: 7 November 2002: see s 162(2)(d); for effect see sub-s (4) above.

12 British citizenship: registration of certain persons without other citizenship

(1) The following shall be inserted after section 4A of the British Nationality Act 1981 (c 61) (registration as British citizen)—

"4B   Acquisition by registration: certain persons without other citizenship

(1)   This section applies to a person who has the status of—

    (a)   British Overseas citizen,

    (b)   British subject under this Act, or

    (c)   British protected person.

(2)   A person to whom this section applies shall be entitled to be registered as a British citizen if—

    (a)   he applies for registration under this section,

    (b)   the Secretary of State is satisfied that the person does not have, apart from the status mentioned in subsection (1), any citizenship or nationality, and

    (c)   the Secretary of State is satisfied that the person has not after 4th July 2002 renounced, voluntarily relinquished or lost through action or inaction any citizenship or nationality."

(2)   In section 14(1) of that Act (meaning of British citizen "by descent"), in paragraph (d) for "section 5" there shall be substituted "section 4B or 5".

Appointment
Appointment: 30 April 2003: see SI 2003/754, art 2(1), Sch 1.

13   British citizenship: registration of certain persons born between 1961 and 1983

(1)   The following shall be inserted after section 4B of the British Nationality Act 1981 (registration as British citizen)—

"4C   Acquisition by registration: certain persons born between 1961 and 1983

(1)   A person is entitled to be registered as a British citizen if—

    (a)   he applies for registration under this section, and

    (b)   he satisfies each of the following conditions.

(2)   The first condition is that the applicant was born after 7th February 1961 and before 1st January 1983.

(3)   The second condition is that the applicant would at some time before 1st January 1983 have become a citizen of the United Kingdom and Colonies by virtue of section 5 of the British Nationality Act 1948 (c 56) if that section had provided for citizenship by descent from a mother in the same terms as it provided for citizenship by descent from a father.

(4)   The third condition is that immediately before 1st January 1983 the applicant would have had the right of abode in the United Kingdom by virtue of section 2 of the Immigration Act 1971 (c 77) had he become a citizen of the United Kingdom and Colonies as described in subsection (3) above."

(2)   In section 14(1) of that Act (meaning of British citizen "by descent"), in paragraph (d) after the words "section 4B" (as substituted by section 12(2) of this Act) there shall be inserted ", 4C".

Appointment
Appointment: 30 April 2003: see SI 2003/754, art 2(1), Sch 1.

14   Hong Kong

A person may not be registered as a British overseas territories citizen under a provision of the British Nationality Act 1981 (c 61) by virtue of a connection with Hong Kong.

Appointment

Appointment: 1 January 2004 (except in relation to any application for registration or naturalisation made before that date): see SI 2003/3156, arts 2(b), 3, 4.

15 Repeal of spent provisions

Schedule 2 (which repeals spent provisions) shall have effect.

Initial Commencement

Royal Assent: 7 November 2002: see s 162(2)(e).

PART 2
ACCOMMODATION CENTRES

Establishment

16 Establishment of centres

(1) The Secretary of State may arrange for the provision of premises for the accommodation of persons in accordance with this Part.

(2) A set of premises provided under this section is referred to in this Act as an "accommodation centre".

(3) The Secretary of State may arrange for—

(a) the provision of facilities at or near an accommodation centre for sittings of adjudicators appointed for the purpose of Part 5 in accordance with a determination of the Lord Chancellor under paragraph 2 of Schedule 4;

(b) the provision of facilities at an accommodation centre for the taking of steps in connection with the determination of claims for asylum (within the meaning of section 18(3)).

Initial Commencement

Royal Assent: 7 November 2002: see s 162(2)(f).

Use of centres

17 Support for destitute asylum-seeker

(1) The Secretary of State may arrange for the provision of accommodation for a person in an accommodation centre if—

(a) the person is an asylum-seeker or the dependant of an asylum-seeker, and

(b) the Secretary of State thinks that the person is destitute or is likely to become destitute within a prescribed period.

(2) The Secretary of State may make regulations about procedure to be followed in respect of the provision of accommodation under this section.

(3) The regulations may, in particular, make provision—

(a) specifying procedure to be followed in applying for accommodation in an accommodation centre;

(b) providing for an application to be combined with an application under or in respect of another enactment;

(c) requiring an applicant to provide information;

(d) specifying circumstances in which an application may not be considered (which provision may, in particular, provide for an application not to be considered where the Secretary of State is not satisfied that the information provided is complete or accurate or that the applicant is co-operating with enquiries under paragraph (e));

(e) about the making of enquiries by the Secretary of State;

(f) requiring a person to notify the Secretary of State of a change in circumstances.

(4) Sections 18 to 20 define the following expressions for the purpose of this Part—

(a) asylum-seeker,

(b) dependant, and

(c) destitute.

Initial Commencement
To be appointed: see s 162(1).

18 Asylum-seeker: definition

(1) For the purposes of this Part a person is an "asylum-seeker" if—

(a) he is at least 18 years old,

(b) he is in the United Kingdom,

(c) a claim for asylum has been made by him at a place designated by the Secretary of State,

(d) the Secretary of State has recorded the claim, and

(e) the claim has not been determined.

(2) A person shall continue to be treated as an asylum-seeker despite subsection (1)(e) while—

(a) his household includes a dependent child who is under 18, and

(b) he does not have leave to enter or remain in the United Kingdom.

(3) A claim for asylum is a claim by a person that to remove him from or require him to leave the United Kingdom would be contrary to the United Kingdom's obligations under—

(a) the Convention relating to the Status of Refugees done at Geneva on 28th July 1951 and its Protocol, or

(b) Article 3 of the Convention for the Protection of Human Rights and Fundamental Freedoms agreed by the Council of Europe at Rome on 4th November 1950.

Appointment
Appointment (for certain purposes): 8 January 2003: see SI 2003/1, art 2, Schedule.
Appointment (for certain purposes): 10 February 2003: see SI 2003/1, art 2, Schedule.

19 Destitution: definition

(1) Where a person has dependants, he and his dependants are destitute for the purpose of this Part if they do not have and cannot obtain both—

(a) adequate accommodation, and

(b) food and other essential items.

(2) Where a person does not have dependants, he is destitute for the purpose of this Part if he does not have and cannot obtain both—

(a) adequate accommodation, and

(b) food and other essential items.

(3) In determining whether accommodation is adequate for the purposes of subsection (1) or (2) the Secretary of State must have regard to any matter prescribed for the purposes of this subsection.

(4)   In determining whether accommodation is adequate for the purposes of subsection (1) or (2) the Secretary of State may not have regard to—

(a)   whether a person has an enforceable right to occupy accommodation,
(b)   whether a person shares all or part of accommodation,
(c)   whether accommodation is temporary or permanent,
(d)   the location of accommodation, or
(e)   any other matter prescribed for the purposes of this subsection.

(5)   The Secretary of State may by regulations specify items which are or are not to be treated as essential items for the purposes of subsections (1) and (2).

(6)   The Secretary of State may by regulations—

(a)   provide that a person is not to be treated as destitute for the purposes of this Part in specified circumstances;
(b)   enable or require the Secretary of State in deciding whether a person is destitute to have regard to income which he or a dependant of his might reasonably be expected to have;
(c)   enable or require the Secretary of State in deciding whether a person is destitute to have regard to support which is or might reasonably be expected to be available to the person or a dependant of his;
(d)   enable or require the Secretary of State in deciding whether a person is destitute to have regard to assets of a prescribed kind which he or a dependant of his has or might reasonably be expected to have;
(e)   make provision as to the valuation of assets.

Initial Commencement
To be appointed: see s 162(1).

20   Dependant: definition

For the purposes of this Part a person is a "dependant" of an asylum-seeker if (and only if) that person—

(a)   is in the United Kingdom, and
(b)   is within a prescribed class.

Initial Commencement
To be appointed: see s 162(1).

21   Sections 17 to 20: supplementary

(1)   This section applies for the purposes of sections 17 to 20.

(2)   The Secretary of State may inquire into and decide a person's age.

(3)   A claim for asylum shall be treated as determined at the end of such period as may be prescribed beginning with—

(a)   the date on which the Secretary of State notifies the claimant of his decision on the claim, or
(b)   if the claimant appeals against the Secretary of State's decision, the date on which the appeal is disposed of.

(4)   A notice under subsection (3)(a)—

(a)   must be in writing, and
(b)   if sent by first class post to the claimant's last known address or to the claimant's representative, shall be treated as being received by the claimant on the second day after the day of posting.

(5)   An appeal is disposed of when it is no longer pending for the purpose of—

    (a)   Part 5 of this Act, or

    (b)   the Special Immigration Appeals Commission Act 1997 (c 68).

Initial Commencement
To be appointed: see s 162(1).

22   Immigration and Asylum Act 1999, s 95

The Secretary of State may provide support under section 95 of the Immigration and Asylum Act 1999 (c 33) (destitute asylum-seeker) by arranging for the provision of accommodation in an accommodation centre.

Initial Commencement
To be appointed: see s 162(1).

23   Person subject to United Kingdom entrance control

(1)   A residence restriction may include a requirement to reside at an accommodation centre.

(2)   In subsection (1) "residence restriction" means a restriction imposed under—

    (a)   paragraph 21 of Schedule 2 to the Immigration Act 1971 (c 77) (temporary admission or release from detention), or

    (b)   paragraph 2(5) of Schedule 3 to that Act (control pending deportation).

(3)   Where a person is required to reside in an accommodation centre by virtue of subsection (1) the Secretary of State must arrange for the provision of accommodation for the person in an accommodation centre.

(4)   But if the person is required to leave an accommodation centre by virtue of section 26 or 30 he shall be treated as having broken the residence restriction referred to in subsection (1).

(5)   The Secretary of State may provide support under section 4 of the Immigration and Asylum Act 1999 (persons subject to entrance control) (including that section as amended by section 49 of this Act) by arranging for the provision of accommodation in an accommodation centre.

Initial Commencement
To be appointed: see s 162(1).

24   Provisional assistance

(1)   If the Secretary of State thinks that a person may be eligible for the provision of accommodation in an accommodation centre under section 17, he may arrange for the provision for the person, pending a decision about eligibility, of—

    (a)   accommodation in an accommodation centre, or

    (b)   other support or assistance (of any kind).

(2)   Section 99 of the Immigration and Asylum Act 1999 (c 33) (provision of support by local authority) shall have effect in relation to the provision of support for persons under subsection (1) above as it has effect in relation to the provision of support for asylum-seekers under sections 95 and 98 of that Act.

Initial Commencement
To be appointed: see s 162(1).

25 Length of stay

(1) The Secretary of State may not arrange for the provision of accommodation for a person in an accommodation centre if he has been a resident of an accommodation centre for a continuous period of six months.

(2) But—

(a) subsection (1) may be disapplied in respect of a person, generally or to a specified extent, by agreement between the Secretary of State and the person, and

(b) if the Secretary of State thinks it appropriate in relation to a person because of the circumstances of his case, the Secretary of State may direct that subsection (1) shall have effect in relation to the person as if the period specified in that subsection were the period of nine months.

(3) Section 51 is subject to this section.

(4) The Secretary of State may by order amend subsection (1) or (2)(b) so as to substitute a shorter period for a period specified.

Initial Commencement
To be appointed: see s 162(1).

26 Withdrawal of support

(1) The Secretary of State may stop providing support for a person under section 17 or 24 if—

(a) the Secretary of State suspects that the person or a dependant of his has committed an offence by virtue of section 35, or

(b) the person or a dependant of his has failed to comply with directions of the Secretary of State as to the time or manner of travel to accommodation provided under section 17 or 24.

(2) The Secretary of State may by regulations specify other circumstances in which he may stop providing support for a person under section 17 or 24.

(3) In determining whether or not to provide a person with support or assistance under section 17 or 24 of this Act or section 4, 95 or 98 of the Immigration and Asylum Act 1999 (asylum-seeker) the Secretary of State may take into account the fact that—

(a) he has withdrawn support from the person by virtue of this section or section 30(4) or (5), or

(b) circumstances exist which would have enabled the Secretary of State to withdraw support from the person by virtue of this section had he been receiving support.

(4) This section is without prejudice to section 103 of the Immigration and Asylum Act 1999 (c 33) (appeal against refusal to support).

Initial Commencement
To be appointed: see s 162(1).

Operation of centres

27 Resident of centre

A reference in this Part to a resident of an accommodation centre is a reference to a person for whom accommodation in the centre is provided—

(a) under section 17,
(b) by virtue of section 22,
(c) by virtue of section 23, or
(d) under section 24.

Initial Commencement
To be appointed: see s 162(1).

28 Manager of centre

A reference in this Part to the manager of an accommodation centre is a reference to a person who agrees with the Secretary of State to be wholly or partly responsible for the management of the centre.

Initial Commencement
To be appointed: see s 162(1).

29 Facilities

(1) The Secretary of State may arrange for the following to be provided to a resident of an accommodation centre—

(a) food and other essential items;
(b) money;
(c) assistance with transport for the purpose of proceedings under the Immigration Acts or in connection with a claim for asylum;
(d) transport to and from the centre;
(e) assistance with expenses incurred in connection with carrying out voluntary work or other activities;
(f) education and training;
(g) facilities relating to health;
(h) facilities for religious observance;
(i) anything which the Secretary of State thinks ought to be provided for the purpose of providing a resident with proper occupation and for the purpose of maintaining good order;
(j) anything which the Secretary of State thinks ought to be provided for a person because of his exceptional circumstances.

(2) The Secretary of State may make regulations specifying the amount or maximum amount of money to be provided under subsection (1)(b).

(3) The Secretary of State may arrange for the provision of facilities in an accommodation centre for the use of a person in providing legal advice to a resident of the centre.

(4) The Secretary of State shall take reasonable steps to ensure that a resident of an accommodation centre has an opportunity to obtain legal advice before any appointment made by an immigration officer or an official of the Secretary of State for the purpose of obtaining information from the resident to be used in determining his claim for asylum.

(5) The Secretary of State may by order amend subsection (1) so as to add a reference to facilities which may be provided.

Initial Commencement
To be appointed: see s 162(1).

30 Conditions of residence

(1) The Secretary of State may make regulations about conditions to be observed by residents of an accommodation centre.

(2) Regulations under subsection (1) may, in particular, enable a condition to be imposed in accordance with the regulations by—

    (a)   the Secretary of State, or

    (b)   the manager of an accommodation centre.

(3) A condition imposed by virtue of this section may, in particular—

    (a)   require a person not to be absent from the centre during specified hours without the permission of the Secretary of State or the manager;

    (b)   require a person to report to an immigration officer or the Secretary of State.

(4) If a resident of an accommodation centre breaches a condition imposed by virtue of this section, the Secretary of State may—

    (a)   require the resident and any dependant of his to leave the centre;

    (b)   authorise the manager of the centre to require the resident and any dependant of his to leave the centre.

(5) If a dependant of a resident of an accommodation centre breaches a condition imposed by virtue of this section, the Secretary of State may—

    (a)   require the resident and any dependant of his to leave the centre;

    (b)   authorise the manager of the centre to require the resident and any dependant of his to leave the centre.

(6) Regulations under this section must include provision for ensuring that a person subject to a condition is notified of the condition in writing.

(7) A condition imposed by virtue of this section is in addition to any restriction imposed under paragraph 21 of Schedule 2 to the Immigration Act 1971 (c 77) (control of entry to United Kingdom) or under paragraph 2(5) of Schedule 3 to that Act (control pending deportation).

(8) A reference in this Part to a condition of residence is a reference to a condition imposed by virtue of this section.

Initial Commencement
To be appointed: see s 162(1).

31 Financial contribution by resident

(1) A condition of residence may, in particular, require a resident of an accommodation centre to make payments to—

    (a)   the Secretary of State, or

    (b)   the manager of the centre.

(2) The Secretary of State may make regulations enabling him to recover sums representing the whole or part of the value of accommodation and other facilities provided to a resident of an accommodation centre if—

    (a)   accommodation is provided for the resident in response to an application by him for support,

    (b)   when the application was made the applicant had assets which were not capable of being realised, and

    (c)   the assets have become realisable.

(3) In subsection (2) "assets" includes assets outside the United Kingdom.

(4) An amount recoverable by virtue of regulations made under subsection (2) may be recovered—

    (a)   as a debt due to the Secretary of State;

    (b) by another prescribed method (which may include the imposition or variation of a residence condition).

Initial Commencement
To be appointed: see s 162(1).

32   Tenure

(1) A resident of an accommodation centre shall not be treated as acquiring a tenancy of or other interest in any part of the centre (whether by virtue of an agreement between the resident and another person or otherwise).

(2) Subsection (3) applies where—

    (a) the Secretary of State decides to stop arranging for the provision of accommodation in an accommodation centre for a resident of the centre, or

    (b) a resident of an accommodation centre is required to leave the centre in accordance with section 30.

(3) Where this subsection applies—

    (a) the Secretary of State or the manager of the centre may recover possession of the premises occupied by the resident, and

    (b) the right under paragraph (a) shall be enforceable in accordance with procedure prescribed by regulations made by the Secretary of State.

(4) Any licence which a resident of an accommodation centre has to occupy premises in the centre shall be an excluded licence for the purposes of the Protection from Eviction Act 1977 (c 43).

(5) The following shall be inserted after section 3A(7A) of the Protection from Eviction Act 1977 (disapplication of section 3: Part VI of Immigration and Asylum Act 1999 (c 33))—

"(7B) Section 32 of the Nationality, Immigration and Asylum Act 2002 (accommodation centre: tenure) provides for a resident's licence to occupy an accommodation centre to be an excluded licence."

(6) The following shall be inserted after section 23A(5A) of the Rent (Scotland) Act 1984 (c 58) (excluded tenancies and occupancy rights)—

"(5B) Nothing in section 23 of this Act applies to a resident's occupancy of an accommodation centre provided under section 16 or 24(1)(b) of the Nationality, Immigration and Asylum Act 2002 ("resident" being construed in accordance with section 27 of that Act)."

(7) In this section a reference to an accommodation centre includes a reference to premises in which accommodation is provided under section 24(1)(b).

Initial Commencement
To be appointed: see s 162(1).

33   Advisory Groups

(1) The Secretary of State shall appoint a group (to be known as an Accommodation Centre Advisory Group) for each accommodation centre.

(2) The Secretary of State may by regulations—

    (a) confer functions on Advisory Groups;

    (b) make provision about the constitution and proceedings of Advisory Groups.

(3)   Regulations under subsection (2)(a) must, in particular, provide for members of an accommodation centre's Advisory Group—

   (a)   to visit the centre;
   (b)   to hear complaints made by residents of the centre;
   (c)   to report to the Secretary of State.

(4)   The manager of an accommodation centre must permit a member of the centre's Advisory Group on request—

   (a)   to visit the centre at any time;
   (b)   to visit any resident of the centre at any time, provided that the resident consents.

(5)   A member of an Advisory Group shall hold and vacate office in accordance with the terms of his appointment (which may include provision about retirement, resignation or dismissal).

(6)   The Secretary of State may—

   (a)   defray expenses of members of an Advisory Group;
   (b)   make facilities available to members of an Advisory Group.

Initial Commencement
To be appointed: see s 162(1).

General

34   The Monitor of Accommodation Centres

(1)   The Secretary of State shall appoint a person as Monitor of Accommodation Centres.

(2)   The Monitor shall monitor the operation of this Part of this Act and shall, in particular, consider—

   (a)   the quality and effectiveness of accommodation and other facilities provided in accommodation centres,
   (b)   the nature and enforcement of conditions of residence,
   (c)   the treatment of residents, and
   (d)   whether, in the case of any accommodation centre, its location prevents a need of its residents from being met.

(3)   In exercising his functions the Monitor shall consult—

   (a)   the Secretary of State, and
   (b)   such other persons as he considers appropriate.

(4)   The Monitor shall report to the Secretary of State about the matters considered by the Monitor in the course of the exercise of his functions—

   (a)   at least once in each calendar year, and
   (b)   on such occasions as the Secretary of State may request.

(5)   Where the Secretary of State receives a report under subsection (4)(a) he shall lay a copy before Parliament as soon as is reasonably practicable.

(6)   The Monitor shall hold and vacate office in accordance with the terms of his appointment (which may include provision about retirement, resignation or dismissal).

(7)   The Secretary of State may—

   (a)   pay fees and allowances to the Monitor;
   (b)   defray expenses of the Monitor;

(c)   make staff and other facilities available to the Monitor.

(8)   The Secretary of State may appoint more than one person to act jointly as Monitor (in which case they shall divide or share functions in accordance with the terms of their appointment and, subject to that, by agreement between them).

(9)   A person who is employed within a government department may not be appointed as Monitor of Accommodation Centres.

Initial Commencement
To be appointed: see s 162(1).

35   Ancillary provisions

(1)   The following provisions of the Immigration and Asylum Act 1999 (c 33) shall apply for the purposes of this Part as they apply for the purposes of Part VI of that Act (support for asylum-seeker)—

- (a)   section 105 (false representation),
- (b)   section 106 (dishonest representation),
- (c)   section 107 (delay or obstruction),
- (d)   section 108 (failure of sponsor to maintain),
- (e)   section 109 (offence committed by body),
- (f)   section 112 (recovery of expenditure),
- (g)   section 113 (recovery of expenditure from sponsor),
- (h)   section 124 (corporation sole), and
- (i)   section 127 (redirection of post).

(2)   In the application of section 112 a reference to something done under section 95 or 98 of that Act shall be treated as a reference to something done under section 17 or 24 of this Act.

(3)   In the application of section 113 a reference to section 95 of that Act shall be treated as a reference to section 17 of this Act.

Initial Commencement
Sub-s (1)(h): Royal Assent: 7 November 2002: see s 162(2)(g).
Sub-ss (1)(a)–(g), (i), (2), (3): To be appointed: see s 162(1).

36   Education: general

(1)   For the purposes of section 13 of the Education Act 1996 (c 56) (general responsibility of local education authority) a resident of an accommodation centre shall not be treated as part of the population of a local education authority's area.

(2)   A child who is a resident of an accommodation centre may not be admitted to a maintained school or a maintained nursery (subject to section 37).

(3)   But subsection (2) does not prevent a child's admission to a school which is—

- (a)   a community special school or a foundation special school, and
- (b)   named in a statement in respect of the child under section 324 of the Education Act 1996 (c 56) (special educational needs).

(4)   In subsections (2) and (3)—

- (a)   "maintained school" means a maintained school within the meaning of section 20(7) of the School Standards and Framework Act 1998 (c 31) (definition), and
- (b)   "maintained nursery" means a facility for nursery education, within the meaning of section 117 of that Act, provided by a local education authority.

(5) The following shall not apply in relation to a child who is a resident of an accommodation centre (subject to section 37)—

(a) section 86(1) and (2) of the School Standards and Framework Act 1998 (parental preference),
(b) section 94 of that Act (appeal),
(c) section 19 of the Education Act 1996 (education out of school),
(d) section 316(2) and (3) of that Act (child with special educational needs to be educated in mainstream school), and
(e) paragraphs 3 and 8 of Schedule 27 to that Act (special education needs: making of statement: parental preference).

(6) The power of the Special Educational Needs Tribunal under section 326(3) of the Education Act 1996 (appeal against content of statement) is subject to subsection (2) above.

(7) A person exercising a function under this Act or the Education Act 1996 shall (subject to section 37) secure that a child who is a resident of an accommodation centre and who has special educational needs shall be educated by way of facilities provided under section 29(1)(f) of this Act unless that is incompatible with—

(a) his receiving the special educational provision which his learning difficulty calls for,
(b) the provision of efficient education for other children who are residents of the centre, or
(c) the efficient use of resources.

(8) A person may rely on subsection (7)(b) only where there is no action—

(a) which could reasonably be taken by that person or by another person who exercises functions, or could exercise functions, in respect of the accommodation centre concerned, and
(b) as a result of which subsection (7)(b) would not apply.

(9) An accommodation centre is not a school within the meaning of section 4 of the Education Act 1996 (definition); but—

(a) *the School Inspections Act 1996 (c 57)* [Part 1 of the Education Act 2005 (school inspections)] shall apply to educational facilities provided at an accommodation centre as if the centre were a school (for which purpose a reference to the appropriate authority shall be taken as a reference to the person (or persons) responsible for the provision of education at the accommodation centre),
(b) section 329A of the Education Act 1996 (review or assessment of educational needs at request of responsible body) shall have effect as if—
(i) an accommodation centre were a relevant school for the purposes of that section,
(ii) a child for whom education is provided at an accommodation centre under section 29(1)(f) were a registered pupil at the centre, and
(iii) a reference in section 329A to the responsible body in relation to an accommodation centre were a reference to any person providing education at the centre under section 29(1)(f), and
(c) section 140 of the Learning and Skills Act 2000 (c 21) (learning difficulties: assessment of post-16 needs) shall have effect as if an accommodation centre were a school.

(10) Subsections (1), (2) and (5) shall not apply in relation to an accommodation centre if education is not provided for children who are residents of the centre under section 29(1)(f).

(11) An expression used in this section and in the Education Act 1996 (c 56) shall have the same meaning in this section as in that Act.

Initial Commencement
To be appointed: see s 162(1).

Amendment
Sub-s (9): in para (a) words "the School Inspections Act 1996 (c 57)" in italics repealed and subsequent words in square brackets substituted by the Education Act 2005, s 61, Sch 9, para 30. Date in force: to be appointed: see the Education Act 2005, ss 125(4), 126(1), (2)(c).

37   Education: special cases

(1) This section applies to a child if a person who provides education to residents of an accommodation centre recommends in writing to the local education authority for the area in which the centre is that this section should apply to the child on the grounds that his special circumstances call for provision that can only or best be arranged by the authority.

(2) A local education authority may—

    (a) arrange for the provision of education for a child to whom this section applies;

    (b) disapply a provision of section 36 in respect of a child to whom this section applies.

(3) In determining whether to exercise a power under subsection (2) in respect of a child a local education authority shall have regard to any relevant guidance issued by the Secretary of State.

(4) The governing body of a maintained school shall comply with a requirement of the local education authority to admit to the school a child to whom this section applies.

(5) Subsection (4) shall not apply where compliance with a requirement would prejudice measures taken for the purpose of complying with a duty arising under section 1(6) of the School Standards and Framework Act 1998 (c 31) (limit on infant class size).

(6) A local education authority may not impose a requirement under subsection (4) in respect of a school unless the authority has consulted the school in accordance with regulations made by the Secretary of State.

(7) In the case of a maintained school for which the local education authority are the admission authority, the authority may not arrange for the admission of a child to whom this section applies unless the authority has notified the school in accordance with regulations made by the Secretary of State.

(8) In this section—

    (a) "maintained school" means a maintained school within the meaning of section 20(7) of the School Standards and Framework Act 1998 (definition), and

    (b) an expression which is also used in the Education Act 1996 (c 56) shall have the same meaning as it has in that Act.

Initial Commencement
To be appointed: see s 162(1).

38 Local authority

(1) A local authority may in accordance with arrangements made by the Secretary of State—

    (a) assist in arranging for the provision of an accommodation centre;
    (b) make premises available for an accommodation centre;
    (c) provide services in connection with an accommodation centre.

(2) In particular, a local authority may—

    (a) incur reasonable expenditure;
    (b) provide services outside its area;
    (c) provide services jointly with another body;
    (d) form a company;
    (e) tender for or enter into a contract;
    (f) do anything (including anything listed in paragraphs (a) to (e)) for a preparatory purpose.

(3) In this section "local authority" means—

    (a) a local authority within the meaning of section 94 of the Immigration and Asylum Act 1999 (c 33), and
    (b) a Northern Ireland authority within the meaning of section 110 of that Act and an Education and Library Board established under Article 3 of the Education and Libraries (Northern Ireland) Order 1986 (SI 1986/ 594 (NI 3)).

Initial Commencement
Royal Assent: 7 November 2002: see s 162(2)(h).

39 "Prescribed": orders and regulations

(1) In this Part "prescribed" means prescribed by the Secretary of State by order or regulations.

(2) An order or regulations under this Part may—

    (a) make provision which applies generally or only in specified cases or circumstances (which may be determined wholly or partly by reference to location);
    (b) make different provision for different cases or circumstances;
    (c) include consequential, transitional or incidental provision.

(3) An order or regulations under this Part must be made by statutory instrument.

(4) An order or regulations under any of the following provisions of this Part shall be subject to annulment in pursuance of a resolution of either House of Parliament—

    (a) section 17,
    (b) section 19,
    (c) section 20,
    (d) section 21,
    (e) section 26,
    (f) section 29,
    (g) section 31,
    (h) section 32,
    (i) section 33,
    (j) section 37,
    (k) section 40, and
    (l) section 41.

(5) An order under section 25 or regulations under section 30 may not be made unless a draft has been laid before and approved by resolution of each House of Parliament.

Initial Commencement
To be appointed: see s 162(1).

40   Scotland

(1) The Secretary of State may not make arrangements under section 16 for the provision of premises in Scotland unless he has consulted the Scottish Ministers.

(2) The Secretary of State may by order make provision in relation to the education of residents of accommodation centres in Scotland.

(3) An order under subsection (2) may, in particular—

(a) apply, disapply or modify the effect of an enactment (which may include a provision made by or under an Act of the Scottish Parliament);
(b) make provision having an effect similar to the effect of a provision of section 36 or 37.

Initial Commencement
Sub-s (1): Royal Assent: 7 November 2002: see s 162(2)(i).
Sub-ss (2), (3): To be appointed: see s 162(1).

41   Northern Ireland

(1) The Secretary of State may not make arrangements under section 16 for the provision of premises in Northern Ireland unless he has consulted the First Minister and the deputy First Minister.

(2) The Secretary of State may by order make provision in relation to the education of residents of accommodation centres in Northern Ireland.

(3) An order under subsection (2) may, in particular—

(a) apply, disapply or modify the effect of an enactment (which may include a provision made by or under Northern Ireland legislation);
(b) make provision having an effect similar to the effect of a provision of section 36 or 37.

Initial Commencement
Sub-s (1): Royal Assent: 7 November 2002: see s 162(2)(j).
Sub-ss (2), (3): To be appointed: see s 162(1).

42   Wales

The Secretary of State may not make arrangements under section 16 for the provision of premises in Wales unless he has consulted the National Assembly for Wales.

Initial Commencement
Royal Assent: 7 November 2002: see s 162(2)(k).

PART 3
OTHER SUPPORT AND ASSISTANCE

43   Asylum-seeker: form of support

(1) The Secretary of State may make an order restricting the application of section 96(1)(b) of the Immigration and Asylum Act 1999 (c 33) (support for asylum-seeker: essential living needs)—

1630

(a)　in all circumstances, to cases in which support is being provided under section 96(1)(a) (accommodation), or

(b)　in specified circumstances only, to cases in which support is being provided under section 96(1)(a).

(2)　An order under subsection (1)(b) may, in particular, make provision by reference to—

(a)　location;

(b)　the date of an application.

(3)　An order under subsection (1) may include transitional provision.

(4)　An order under subsection (1)—

(a)　must be made by statutory instrument, and

(b)　may not be made unless a draft has been laid before and approved by resolution of each House of Parliament.

Initial Commencement
Royal Assent: 7 November 2002: see s 162(2)(l).

44　Destitute asylum-seeker

(1)　Section 94 of the Immigration and Asylum Act 1999 (c 33) (support for destitute asylum-seeker) shall be amended as follows.

(2)　In subsection (1) for the definition of "asylum-seeker" substitute—

""asylum-seeker" means a person—
(a)　who is at least 18 years old,
(b)　who is in the United Kingdom,
(c)　who has made a claim for asylum at a place designated by the Secretary of State,
(d)　whose claim has been recorded by the Secretary of State, and
(e)　whose claim has not been determined;".

(3)　In subsection (1) for the definition of "dependant" substitute—

""dependant" in relation to an asylum-seeker or a supported person means a person who—
(a)　is in the United Kingdom, and
(b)　is within a prescribed class;".

(4)　For subsection (3) substitute—

"(3)　A claim for asylum shall be treated as determined for the purposes of subsection (1) at the end of such period as may be prescribed beginning with—

(a)　the date on which the Secretary of State notifies the claimant of his decision on the claim, or

(b)　if the claimant appeals against the Secretary of State's decision, the date on which the appeal is disposed of.

(3A)　A person shall continue to be treated as an asylum-seeker despite paragraph (e) of the definition of "asylum-seeker" in subsection (1) while—

(a)　his household includes a dependant child who is under 18, and

(b)　he does not have leave to enter or remain in the United Kingdom."

(5)　Omit subsections (5) and (6).

(6)　The following shall be substituted for section 95(2) to (8) of the Immigration and Asylum Act 1999 (c 33) (support for destitute asylum-seeker: interpretation)—

"(2)   Where a person has dependants, he and his dependants are destitute for the purpose of this section if they do not have and cannot obtain both—

    (a)   adequate accommodation, and
    (b)   food and other essential items.

(3)   Where a person does not have dependants, he is destitute for the purpose of this section if he does not have and cannot obtain both—

    (a)   adequate accommodation, and
    (b)   food and other essential items.

(4)   In determining whether accommodation is adequate for the purposes of subsection (2) or (3) the Secretary of State must have regard to any matter prescribed for the purposes of this subsection.

(5)   In determining whether accommodation is adequate for the purposes of subsection (2) or (3) the Secretary of State may not have regard to—

    (a)   whether a person has an enforceable right to occupy accommodation,
    (b)   whether a person shares all or part of accommodation,
    (c)   whether accommodation is temporary or permanent,
    (d)   the location of accommodation, or
    (e)   any other matter prescribed for the purposes of this subsection.

(6)   The Secretary of State may by regulations specify items which are or are not to be treated as essential items for the purposes of subsections (2) and (3).

(7)   The Secretary of State may by regulations—

    (a)   provide that a person is not to be treated as destitute for the purposes of this Part in specified circumstances;
    (b)   enable or require the Secretary of State in deciding whether a person is destitute to have regard to income which he or a dependant of his might reasonably be expected to have;
    (c)   enable or require the Secretary of State in deciding whether a person is destitute to have regard to support which is or might reasonably be expected to be available to the person or a dependant of his;
    (d)   enable or require the Secretary of State in deciding whether a person is destitute to have regard to assets of a prescribed kind which he or a dependant of his has or might reasonably be expected to have;
    (e)   make provision as to the valuation of assets."

Initial Commencement
To be appointed: see s 162(1).

45   Section 44: supplemental

(1)   The following shall be substituted for section 96(1)(b) of the Immigration and Asylum Act 1999 (ways of providing support)—

    "(b) by providing the supported person and his dependants (if any) with food and other essential items;".

(2)   In section 97 of the Immigration and Asylum Act 1999 (c 33) (support: supplemental)—

    (a)   in subsection (4) for "essential living needs" there shall be substituted "food and other essential items",
    (b)   in subsection (5) for "essential living needs" there shall be substituted "food and other essential items", and
    (c)   in subsection (6) for "living needs" there shall be substituted "items".

(3)   Paragraphs 2 and 6 of Schedule 8 to the Immigration and Asylum Act 1999 (support: regulations) shall cease to have effect.

(4)   In paragraph 3 of Schedule 9 to the Immigration and Asylum Act 1999 (support: interim provision)—

(a)   for "Subsections (3) to (8) of section 95" substitute "Subsections (2) to (6) of section 95", and

(b)   for "subsections (5) and (7)" substitute "subsections (4) and (5)".

(5)   The following shall be substituted for section 21(1B) of the National Assistance Act 1948 (c 29) (duty of local authority to provide accommodation: exclusion of destitute asylum-seeker: interpretation)—

"(1B)   Section 95(2) to (7) of that Act shall apply for the purposes of subsection (1A) above; and for that purpose a reference to the Secretary of State in section 95(4) or (5) shall be treated as a reference to a local authority."

(6)   The following shall be substituted for section 45(4B) of the Health Services and Public Health Act 1968 (c 46) (local authority promotion of welfare of elderly: exclusion of destitute asylum-seeker: interpretation)—

"(4B)   Section 95(2) to (7) of that Act shall apply for the purposes of subsection (4A) above; and for that purpose a reference to the Secretary of State in section 95(4) or (5) shall be treated as a reference to a local authority."

(7)   The following shall be substituted for paragraph 2(2B) of Schedule 8 to the National Health Service Act 1977 (c 49) (local authority arrangements for prevention and care: exclusion of asylum-seeker: interpretation)—

"(2B)   Section 95(2) to (7) of that Act shall apply for the purposes of sub-paragraph (2A) above; and for that purpose a reference to the Secretary of State in section 95(4) or (5) shall be treated as a reference to a local social services authority."

Initial Commencement
To be appointed: see s 162(1).

46   Section 44: supplemental: Scotland and Northern Ireland

(1)   The following shall be substituted for section 12(2B) of the Social Work (Scotland) Act 1968 (c 49)(general social welfare services of local authorities – exclusion of destitute asylum seeker: interpretation)—

"(2B)   Section 95(2) to (7) of that Act shall apply for the purposes of subsection (2A) of this section; and for that purpose a reference to the Secretary of State in section 95(4) or (5) shall be treated as a reference to a local authority."

(2)   The following shall be substituted for section 13A(5) of that Act (provision of residential accommodation with nursing – exclusion of destitute asylum seeker: interpretation)—

"(5)   Section 95(2) to (7) of that Act shall apply for the purposes of subsection (4) of this section; and for that purpose a reference to the Secretary of State in section 95(4) or (5) shall be treated as a reference to a local authority."

(3)   The following shall be substituted for section 13B(4) of that Act (provision of care and after-care – exclusion of destitute asylum seeker: interpretation)—

"(4)   Section 95(2) to (7) of that Act shall apply for the purposes of subsection (3) of this section; and for that purpose a reference to the Secretary of State in section 95(4) or (5) shall be treated as a reference to a local authority."

(4)   The following shall be substituted for section 7(4) of the Mental Health (Scotland) Act 1984 (c 36)(functions of local authorities – exclusion of destitute asylum seeker: interpretation)—

"(4)   Section 95(2) to (7) of that Act shall apply for the purposes of subsection (3) of this section; and for that purpose a reference to the Secretary of State in section 95(4) or (5) shall be treated as a reference to a local authority."

(5)   The following shall be substituted for section 8(5) of that Act (provision of after-care services – exclusion of destitute asylum seeker: interpretation)—

"(5)   Section 95(2) to (7) of that Act shall apply for the purposes of subsection (4) of this section; and for that purpose a reference to the Secretary of State in section 95(4) or (5) shall be treated as a reference to a local authority."

(6)   The following shall be substituted for Article 7(3A) of the Health and Personal Social Services (Northern Ireland) Order 1972 (SI 1972/1265 (NI 14)) (prevention of illness, care and after-care: exclusion of asylum-seeker: interpretation)—

"(3A)   Section 95(2) to (7) of that Act shall apply for the purpose of paragraph (3); and for that purpose a reference to the Secretary of State in section 95(4) or (5) shall be treated as a reference to the Department."

(7)   The following shall be substituted for Article 15(7) of that Order (general social welfare: exclusion of destitute asylum-seeker: interpretation)—

"(7)   Section 95(2) to (7) of that Act shall apply for the purpose of paragraph (6); and for that purpose a reference to the Secretary of State in section 95(4) or (5) shall be treated as a reference to the Department."

Initial Commencement
To be appointed: see s 162(1).

47   Asylum-seeker: family with children

The following shall be substituted for section 122 of the Immigration and Asylum Act 1999 (c 33) (destitute asylum-seeker with child: duty to support)—

"122   Family with children

(1)   This section applies where a person ("the asylum-seeker") applies for support under section 95 of this Act or section 17 of the Nationality, Immigration and Asylum Act 2002 (accommodation centres) if—

  (a)   the Secretary of State thinks that the asylum-seeker is eligible for support under either or both of those sections, and
  (b)   the asylum-seeker's household includes a dependant child who is under 18.

(2)   The Secretary of State must offer the provision of support for the child, as part of the asylum-seeker's household, under one of the sections mentioned in subsection (1).

(3)   A local authority (or, in Northern Ireland, an authority) may not provide assistance for a child if—

  (a)   the Secretary of State is providing support for the child in accordance with an offer under subsection (2),
  (b)   an offer by the Secretary of State under subsection (2) remains open in respect of the child, or
  (c)   the Secretary of State has agreed that he would make an offer in respect of the child under subsection (2) if an application were made as described in subsection (1).

(4)   In subsection (3) "assistance" means assistance under—

(a) section 17 of the Children Act 1989 (c 41) (local authority support),
(b) section 22 of the Children (Scotland) Act 1995 (c 36) (similar provision for Scotland), or
(c) Article 18 of the Children (Northern Ireland) Order 1995 (SI 1995/755 (NI 2)) (similar provision for Northern Ireland).

(5) The Secretary of State may by order disapply subsection (3) in specified circumstances.

(6) Where subsection (3) ceases to apply to a child because the Secretary of State stops providing support, no local authority may provide assistance for the child except the authority for the area within which the support was provided."

Initial Commencement
To be appointed: see s 162(1).

48 Young asylum-seeker

The following provisions of the Immigration and Asylum Act 1999 (c 33) shall have effect as if the definition of asylum-seeker in section 94(1) of that Act did not exclude persons who are under 18—

(a) section 110 (local authority expenditure on asylum-seekers), and
(b) section 111 (grants to voluntary organisations).

Initial Commencement
Royal Assent: 7 November 2002: see s 162(2)(m).

49 Failed asylum-seeker

(1) The following shall be added at the end of section 4 of the Immigration and Asylum Act 1999 (accommodation for person on temporary admission or release)—

"(2) The Secretary of State may provide, or arrange for the provision of, facilities for the accommodation of a person if—

(a) he was (but is no longer) an asylum-seeker, and
(b) his claim for asylum was rejected.

(3) The Secretary of State may provide, or arrange for the provision of, facilities for the accommodation of a dependant of a person for whom facilities may be provided under subsection (2).

(4) The following expressions have the same meaning in this section as in Part VI of this Act (as defined in section 94)—

(a) asylum-seeker,
(b) claim for asylum, and
(c) dependant."

(2) The present section 4 of the Immigration and Asylum Act 1999 (c 33) becomes subsection (1) (and its heading becomes "Accommodation").

Initial Commencement
Royal Assent: 7 November 2002: see s 162(2)(n).

50 Conditions of support

(1) The following shall be inserted after section 95(9) of the Immigration and Asylum Act 1999 (support for asylum-seeker: condition)—

"(9A) A condition imposed under subsection (9) may, in particular, relate to—

(a) any matter relating to the use of the support provided, or

(b) compliance with a restriction imposed under paragraph 21 of Schedule 2 to the 1971 Act (temporary admission or release from detention) or paragraph 2 or 5 of Schedule 3 to that Act (restriction pending deportation)."

(2) The following shall be inserted after paragraph 6 of Schedule 9 to that Act (asylum-seeker: interim support)—

"6A   The regulations may, in particular, require support to be provided subject to a condition of compliance with any restriction imposed under paragraph 21 of Schedule 2 to the 1971 Act (temporary admission or release from detention) or paragraph 2 or 5 of Schedule 3 to that Act (restriction pending deportation)."

Initial Commencement
Royal Assent: 7 November 2002: see s 162(2)(o).

51   Choice of form of support

(1) The Secretary of State may refuse to provide support for a person under a provision specified in subsection (2) on the grounds that an offer has been made to the person of support under another provision specified in that subsection.

(2) The provisions are—

(a) sections 17 and 24 of this Act,

(b) section 4 of the Immigration and Asylum Act 1999 (accommodation for person temporarily admitted or released from detention), and

(c) sections 95 and 98 of that Act (support for destitute asylum-seeker).

(3) In deciding under which of the provisions listed in subsection (2) to offer support to a person the Secretary of State may—

(a) have regard to administrative or other matters which do not concern the person's personal circumstances;

(b) regard one of those matters as conclusive;

(c) apply different criteria to different persons for administrative reasons (which may include the importance of testing the operation of a particular provision).

Initial Commencement
To be appointed: see s 162(1).

52   Back-dating of benefit for refugee

In section 123(7) of the Immigration and Asylum Act 1999 (c 33) (back-dating of benefit for refugee: deduction for support received) after "under this Part" there shall be inserted "or Part 2 of the Nationality, Immigration and Asylum Act 2002 (accommodation centres)".

Initial Commencement
To be appointed: see s 162(1).

Amendment
Repealed by the Asylum and Immigration (Treatment of Claimants, etc) Act 2004, s 47, Sch 4.
Date in force: to be appointed: see the Asylum and Immigration (Treatment of Claimants, etc) Act 2004, s 48(3)–(6).

53   Asylum-seeker: appeal against refusal to support

The following shall be substituted for section 103 of the Immigration and Asylum Act 1999 (asylum support appeal)—

"103   Appeals: general

(1) This section applies where a person has applied for support under—

    (a)   section 95,

    (b)   section 17 of the Nationality, Immigration and Asylum Act 2002, or

    (c)   both.

(2) The person may appeal to an adjudicator against a decision that the person is not qualified to receive the support for which he has applied.

(3) The person may also appeal to an adjudicator against a decision to stop providing support under a provision mentioned in subsection (1).

(4) But subsection (3) does not apply—

    (a)   to a decision to stop providing support under one of the provisions mentioned in subsection (1) if it is to be replaced immediately by support under the other provision, or

    (b)   to a decision taken on the ground that the person is no longer an asylum-seeker or the dependant of an asylum-seeker.

(5) On an appeal under this section an adjudicator may—

    (a)   require the Secretary of State to reconsider a matter;

    (b)   substitute his decision for the decision against which the appeal is brought;

    (c)   dismiss the appeal.

(6) An adjudicator must give his reasons in writing.

(7) If an appeal under this section is dismissed the Secretary of State shall not consider any further application by the appellant for support under a provision mentioned in subsection (1)(a) or (b) unless the Secretary of State thinks there has been a material change in circumstances.

(8) An appeal under this section may not be brought or continued by a person who is outside the United Kingdom.

103A   Appeals: location of support under section 95

(1) The Secretary of State may by regulations provide for a decision as to where support provided under section 95 is to be provided to be appealable to an adjudicator under this Part.

(2) Regulations under this section may provide for a provision of section 103 to have effect in relation to an appeal under the regulations with specified modifications.

103B   Appeals: travelling expenses

The Secretary of State may pay reasonable travelling expenses incurred by an appellant in connection with attendance for the purposes of an appeal under or by virtue of section 103 or 103A."

Initial Commencement
To be appointed: see s 162(1).

54   Withholding and withdrawal of support

Schedule 3 (which makes provision for support to be withheld or withdrawn in certain circumstances) shall have effect.

Appendix 1   Legislation and materials

Appointment
Appointment (for remaining purposes): 8 January 2003: see SI 2002/2811, art 2, Schedule.
Appointment (for certain purposes): 8 December 2002: see SI 2002/2811, art 2, Schedule.

Subordinate Legislation
Withholding and Withdrawal of Support (Travel Assistance and Temporary Accommodation)
Regulations 2002, SI 2002/3078.

55   Late claim for asylum: refusal of support

(1)   The Secretary of State may not provide or arrange for the provision of support to
a person under a provision mentioned in subsection (2) if—

   (a)   the person makes a claim for asylum which is recorded by the Secretary of
State, and
   (b)   the Secretary of State is not satisfied that the claim was made as soon as
reasonably practicable after the person's arrival in the United Kingdom.

(2)   The provisions are—

   (a)   sections 4, 95 and 98 of the Immigration and Asylum Act 1999 (c 33)
(support for asylum-seeker, &c), and
   (b)   sections 17 and 24 of this Act (accommodation centre).

(3)   An authority may not provide or arrange for the provision of support to a person
under a provision mentioned in subsection (4) if—

   (a)   the person has made a claim for asylum, and
   (b)   the Secretary of State is not satisfied that the claim was made as soon as
reasonably practicable after the person's arrival in the United Kingdom.

(4)   The provisions are—

   (a)   section 29(1)(b) of the Housing (Scotland) Act 1987 (c 26) (accommodation
pending review),
   (b)   section 188(3) or 204(4) of the Housing Act 1996 (c 52) (accommodation
pending review or appeal), and
   (c)   section 2 of the Local Government Act 2000 (c 22) (promotion of well-being).

(5)   This section shall not prevent—

   (a)   the exercise of a power by the Secretary of State to the extent necessary for the
purpose of avoiding a breach of a person's Convention rights (within the
meaning of the Human Rights Act 1998 (c 42)),
   (b)   the provision of support under section 95 of the Immigration and Asylum
Act 1999 (c 33) or section 17 of this Act in accordance with section 122 of
that Act (children), or
   (c)   the provision of support under section 98 of the Immigration and Asylum
Act 1999 or section 24 of this Act (provisional support) to a person under the
age of 18 and the household of which he forms part.

(6)   An authority which proposes to provide or arrange for the provision of support to
a person under a provision mentioned in subsection (4)—

   (a)   must inform the Secretary of State if the authority believes that the person has
made a claim for asylum,
   (b)   must act in accordance with any guidance issued by the Secretary of State to
determine whether subsection (3) applies, and
   (c)   shall not be prohibited from providing or arranging for the provision of
support if the authority has complied with paragraph (a) and (b) and
concluded that subsection (3) does not apply.

(7)   The Secretary of State may by order—

1638

    (a)   add, remove or amend an entry in the list in subsection (4);

    (b)   provide for subsection (3) not to have effect in specified cases or circumstances.

(8)   An order under subsection (7)—

    (a)   may include transitional, consequential or incidental provision,

    (b)   must be made by statutory instrument, and

    (c)   may not be made unless a draft has been laid before and approved by resolution of each House of Parliament.

(9)   For the purposes of this section "claim for asylum" has the same meaning as in section 18.

(10)   A decision of the Secretary of State that this section prevents him from providing or arranging for the provision of support to a person is not a decision that the person does not qualify for support for the purpose of section 103 of the Immigration and Asylum Act 1999 (appeals).

(11)   This section does not prevent a person's compliance with a residence restriction imposed in reliance on section 70 (induction).

Appointment
Appointment: 8 January 2003: see SI 2002/2811, art 2, Schedule.

56   Provision of support by local authority

(1)   Section 99 of the Immigration and Asylum Act 1999 (provision of support by local authority) shall be amended as follows.

(2)   In subsection (1)—

    (a)   after "local authority" insert "or Northern Ireland authority", and

    (b)   at the end add "or 98".

(3)   For subsections (2) and (3) substitute—

"(2)   Support may be provided by an authority in accordance with arrangements made with the authority or with another person.

(3)   Support may be provided by an authority in accordance with arrangements made under section 95 only in one or more of the ways mentioned in section 96(1) and (2)."

(4)   In subsection (4)—

    (a)   for "A local authority" substitute "An authority", and

    (b)   at the end add "or 98".

(5)   In subsection (5)—

    (a)   for "a local authority" substitute "an authority", and

    (b)   in paragraph (b) for "bodies who are not local authorities" substitute "other bodies".

Initial Commencement
Royal Assent: 7 November 2002: see s 162(2)(p).

57   Application for support: false or incomplete information

At the end of paragraph 12(c) of Schedule 8 to the Immigration and Asylum Act 1999 (c 33) (asylum-seeker support: procedure: disregarding of application) there shall be inserted "(which may, in particular, provide for an application not to be entertained where the Secretary of State is not satisfied that the information provided is complete or accurate or that the applicant is co-operating with enquiries under paragraph (d))".

Appendix 1   Legislation and materials

Appointment

Appointment: 8 December 2002: see SI 2002/2811, art 2, Schedule.

58   Voluntary departure from United Kingdom

(1)   A person is a "voluntary leaver" for the purposes of this section if—

(a)   he is not a British citizen or an EEA national,

(b)   he leaves the United Kingdom for a place where he hopes to take up permanent residence (his "new place of residence"), and

(c)   the Secretary of State thinks that it is in the person's interest to leave the United Kingdom and that the person wishes to leave.

(2)   The Secretary of State may make arrangements to—

(a)   assist voluntary leavers;

(b)   assist individuals to decide whether to become voluntary leavers.

(3)   The Secretary of State may, in particular, make payments (whether to voluntary leavers or to organisations providing services for them) which relate to—

(a)   travelling and other expenses incurred by or on behalf of a voluntary leaver, or a member of his family or household, in leaving the United Kingdom;

(b)   expenses incurred by or on behalf of a voluntary leaver, or a member of his family or household, on or shortly after arrival in his new place of residence;

(c)   the provision of services designed to assist a voluntary leaver, or a member of his family or household, to settle in his new place of residence;

(d)   expenses in connection with a journey undertaken by a person (with or without his family or household) to prepare for, or to assess the possibility of, his becoming a voluntary leaver.

(4)   In subsection (1)(a) "EEA national" means a national of a State which is a contracting party to the Agreement on the European Economic Area signed at Oporto on 2nd May 1992 (as it has effect from time to time).

(5)   The following provisions of the Immigration Act 1971 (c 77) shall cease to have effect—

(a)   section 29 (contributions to expenses of persons returning abroad), and

(b)   section 31(d) (expenses).

Initial Commencement

Royal Assent: 7 November 2002: see s 162(2)(q).

59   International projects

(1)   The Secretary of State may participate in a project which is designed to—

(a)   reduce migration,

(b)   assist or ensure the return of migrants,

(c)   facilitate co-operation between States in matters relating to migration,

(d)   conduct or consider research about migration, or

(e)   arrange or assist the settlement of migrants (whether in the United Kingdom or elsewhere).

(2)   In particular, the Secretary of State may—

(a)   provide financial support to an international organisation which arranges or participates in a project of a kind described in subsection (1);

(b)   provide financial support to an organisation in the United Kingdom or another country which arranges or participates in a project of that kind;

(c) provide or arrange for the provision of financial or other assistance to a migrant who participates in a project of that kind;
(d) participate in financial or other arrangements which are agreed between Her Majesty's Government and the government of one or more other countries and which are or form part of a project of that kind.

(3) In this section—

(a) "migrant" means a person who leaves the country where he lives hoping to settle in another country (whether or not he is a refugee within the meaning of any international Convention), and
(b) "migration" shall be construed accordingly.

(4) Subsection (1) does not—

(a) confer a power to remove a person from the United Kingdom, or
(b) affect a person's right to enter or remain in the United Kingdom.

Initial Commencement
Royal Assent: 7 November 2002: see s 162(2)(r).

60 Northern Ireland authorities

(1) In section 110(9) of the Immigration and Asylum Act 1999 (c 33) (support: payment to local authority: Northern Ireland authority) after paragraph (b) there shall be added—

"; or
(c) a Health and Social Services trust established under the Health and Personal Social Services (Northern Ireland) Order 1991 (SI 1991/194 (NI 1)."

(2) In section 94(1) of that Act (support: interpretation) after the definition of "local authority" there shall be inserted—

""Northern Ireland authority" has the meaning given by section 110(9)."

Appointment
Appointment: 10 February 2003: see SI 2003/1, art 2, Schedule.

61 Repeal of spent provisions

The following provisions of the Immigration and Asylum Act 1999 shall cease to have effect—

(a) section 96(4) to (6) (which relate to a provision about support for asylum-seekers which has been repealed by order), and
(b) section 166(4)(e) (order under section 96(5): procedure).

Initial Commencement
Royal Assent: 7 November 2002: see s 162(2)(s).

PART 4
DETENTION AND REMOVAL

Detention

62 Detention by Secretary of State

(1) A person may be detained under the authority of the Secretary of State pending—

(a) a decision by the Secretary of State whether to give directions in respect of the person under paragraph 10, 10A or 14 of Schedule 2 to the Immigration Act 1971 (c 77) (control of entry: removal), or

(b) removal of the person from the United Kingdom in pursuance of directions given by the Secretary of State under any of those paragraphs.

(2) Where the Secretary of State is empowered under section 3A of that Act (powers of Secretary of State) to examine a person or to give or refuse a person leave to enter the United Kingdom, the person may be detained under the authority of the Secretary of State pending—

(a) the person's examination by the Secretary of State,

(b) the Secretary of State's decision to give or refuse the person leave to enter,

(c) a decision by the Secretary of State whether to give directions in respect of the person under paragraph 8 or 9 of Schedule 2 to that Act (removal), or

(d) removal of the person in pursuance of directions given by the Secretary of State under either of those paragraphs.

(3) A provision of Schedule 2 to that Act about a person who is detained or liable to detention under that Schedule shall apply to a person who is detained or liable to detention under this section: and for that purpose—

(a) a reference to paragraph 16 of that Schedule shall be taken to include a reference to this section,

(b) a reference in paragraph 21 of that Schedule to an immigration officer shall be taken to include a reference to the Secretary of State, and

(c) a reference to detention under that Schedule or under a provision or Part of that Schedule shall be taken to include a reference to detention under this section.

(4) In the case of a restriction imposed under paragraph 21 of that Schedule by virtue of this section—

(a) a restriction imposed by an immigration officer may be varied by the Secretary of State, and

(b) a restriction imposed by the Secretary of State may be varied by an immigration officer.

(5) In subsection (1) the reference to paragraph 10 of that Schedule includes a reference to that paragraph as applied by virtue of section 10 of the Immigration and Asylum Act 1999 (c 33) (persons unlawfully in United Kingdom: removal).

(6) Subsection (5) is without prejudice to the generality of section 159.

(7) A power under this section which is exercisable pending a decision of a particular kind by the Secretary of State is exercisable where the Secretary of State has reasonable grounds to suspect that he may make a decision of that kind.

(8) At the end of section 11(1) of the Immigration Act 1971 (c 77) (person not deemed to have entered United Kingdom while detained, &c) there shall be inserted "or section 62 of the Nationality, Immigration and Asylum Act 2002".

(9) In section 24(1)(e) of the Immigration Act 1971 (offence: failure to comply with restriction) for "or to an immigration officer" there shall be substituted ", to an immigration officer or to the Secretary of State".

(10) In the Mental Health Act 1983 (c 20)—

(a) at the end of section 48(2)(d) (detained persons susceptible to transfer for mental treatment: immigration) there shall be added "or under section 62 of the Nationality, Immigration and Asylum Act 2002 (detention by Secretary of State)", and

(b) in the heading of section 53 (supplemental provision) the reference to the Immigration Act 1971 becomes a reference to the Immigration Acts.

(11)   In the Mental Health (Scotland) Act 1984 (c 36)—

(a)   at the end of section 71(2)(c) (detained persons who may be transferred to hospital for mental treatment) there shall be added "or under section 62 of the Nationality, Immigration and Asylum Act 2002 (detention by the Secretary of State)", and

(b)   at the end of section 74(1)(b) (further provision about such persons) there shall be added "or under section 62 of the Nationality, Immigration and Asylum Act 2002 (detention by the Secretary of State)".

(12)   In the Mental Health (Northern Ireland) Order 1986 (SI 1986/595 (NI 4))—

(a)   at the end of Article 54(2)(d) (detained persons susceptible to transfer for mental treatment: immigration) there shall be added "or under section 62 of the Nationality, Immigration and Asylum Act 2002 (detention by Secretary of State)", and

(b)   in the heading of Article 59 (supplemental provision) the reference to the Immigration Act 1971 becomes a reference to the Immigration Acts.

(13)   Section 53 of the Immigration and Asylum Act 1999 (c 33) (bail) shall be amended as follows—

(a)   at the end of subsection (1) add "or under section 62 of the Nationality, Immigration and Asylum Act 2002", and

(b)   at the end of subsection (3)(a) add "or under section 62 of the Nationality, Immigration and Asylum Act 2002".

(14)   In section 147 of that Act (detention centres: interpretation) at the end of the definition of "detained persons" there shall be inserted "or under section 62 of the Nationality, Immigration and Asylum Act 2002 (detention by Secretary of State);".

(15)   ...

(16)   ...

Appointment
Appointment: 10 February 2003: see SI 2003/1, art 2, Schedule.

Amendment
Sub-ss (15), (16): repealed by the Prevention of Terrorism Act 2005, s 16(2)(c).
Date in force: 14 March 2005: see the Prevention of Terrorism Act 2005, s 16(3).

63   Control of entry to United Kingdom, &c: use of force

In paragraph 17(2) of Schedule 2 to the Immigration Act 1971 (c 77) (control of entry, &c: person liable to detention: use of force) for "if need be by force" there shall be substituted "if need be by reasonable force".

Appointment
Appointment: 10 February 2003: see SI 2003/1, art 2, Schedule.

64   Escorts

The following shall be added after paragraph 17(2) of Schedule 2 to the Immigration Act 1971 (detention for examination or removal: right to enter premises)—

"(3)   Sub-paragraph (4) applies where an immigration officer or constable—

(a)   enters premises in reliance on a warrant under sub-paragraph (2), and
(b)   detains a person on the premises.

(4)   A detainee custody officer may enter the premises, if need be by reasonable force, for the purpose of carrying out a search.

1643

(5) In sub-paragraph (4)—

"detainee custody officer" means a person in respect of whom a certificate of authorisation is in force under section 154 of the Immigration and Asylum Act 1999 (c 33) (detained persons: escort and custody), and

"search" means a search under paragraph 2(1)(a) of Schedule 13 to that Act (escort arrangements: power to search detained person)."

Appointment
Appointment: 10 February 2003: see SI 2003/1, art 2, Schedule.

65   Detention centres: custodial functions

(1) The following shall be substituted for section 154(5) of the Immigration and Asylum Act 1999 (power to confer functions of detainee custody officers on prison officers and prisoner custody officers)—

"(5) The Secretary of State may confer functions of detainee custody officers on prison officers or prisoner custody officers."

(2) The following shall be added at the end of Schedule 11 to that Act (detainee custody officers)—

"**8   Prison officers and prisoner custody officers**

A reference in this Schedule to a detainee custody officer includes a reference to a prison officer or prisoner custody officer exercising custodial functions."

(3) The following shall be added at the end of Schedule 12 to that Act (discipline at detention centre)—

"**9   Prison officers and prisoner custody officers**

A reference in this Schedule to a detainee custody officer includes a reference to a prison officer or prisoner custody officer exercising custodial functions."

Appointment
Appointment: 10 February 2003: see SI 2003/1, art 2, Schedule.

66   Detention centres: change of name

(1) In section 147 of the Immigration and Asylum Act 1999 (c 33) (Part VIII: interpretation)—

(a) the definition of "detention centre" shall cease to have effect, and

(b) the following shall be inserted after the definition of "prisoner custody officer"—

""removal centre" means a place which is used solely for the detention of detained persons but which is not a short-term holding facility, a prison or part of a prison;".

(2) In the provisions listed in subsection (3) (and any relevant headings)—

(a) for the words "detention centre" there shall be substituted the words "removal centre", and

(b) for the words "detention centres" there shall be substituted the words "removal centres".

(3) The provisions are—

(a) in section 147 of the Immigration and Asylum Act 1999 (Part VIII: interpretation), the definitions of "contracted out detention centre", "contractor", "custodial functions", "detention centre contract", "detention centre rules", and "directly managed detention centre",

(b) section 148 of that Act (management of centre),
(c) sections 149 and 150 of that Act (contracting out),
(d) section 151 of that Act (intervention by Secretary of State),
(e) section 152 of that Act (visiting committee),
(f) section 153 of that Act (rules),
(g) section 155 of that Act (custodial functions),
(h) section 157 of that Act (short-term holding facility),
(i) section 158 of that Act (disclosure of information),
(j) section 159 of that Act (power of constable),
(k) Schedule 11 to that Act (detainee custody officer),
(l) Schedule 12 to that Act (procedure at detention centre),
(m) Schedule 13 to that Act (escort),
(n) section 141(5)(e) and (6) of that Act (fingerprinting),
(o) section 5A(5A) of the Prison Act 1952 (c 52) (Chief Inspector of Prisons), and
(p) paragraph 13 of Schedule 4A to the Water Industry Act 1991 (c 56) (disconnection).

(4) A reference in an enactment or instrument to a detention centre within the meaning of Part VIII of the Immigration and Asylum Act 1999 (c 33) shall be construed as a reference to a removal centre within the meaning of that Part.

Appointment
Appointment: 10 February 2003: see SI 2003/1, art 2, Schedule.

67 Construction of reference to person liable to detention

(1) This section applies to the construction of a provision which—

(a) does not confer power to detain a person, but
(b) refers (in any terms) to a person who is liable to detention under a provision of the Immigration Acts.

(2) The reference shall be taken to include a person if the only reason why he cannot be detained under the provision is that—

(a) he cannot presently be removed from the United Kingdom, because of a legal impediment connected with the United Kingdom's obligations under an international agreement,
(b) practical difficulties are impeding or delaying the making of arrangements for his removal from the United Kingdom, or
(c) practical difficulties, or demands on administrative resources, are impeding or delaying the taking of a decision in respect of him.

(3) This section shall be treated as always having had effect.

Initial Commencement
Royal Assent: 7 November 2002: see s 162(2)(t); for effect see sub-s (3) above.

Temporary release

68 Bail

(1) This section applies in a case where an immigration officer not below the rank of chief immigration officer has sole or shared power to release a person on bail in accordance with—

(a) a provision of Schedule 2 to the Immigration Act 1971 (c 77) (control of entry) (including a provision of that Schedule applied by a provision of that Act or by another enactment), or

(b) section 9A of the Asylum and Immigration Appeals Act 1993 (c 23) (pending appeal from Immigration Appeal Tribunal).

(2) In respect of an application for release on bail which is instituted after the expiry of the period of eight days beginning with the day on which detention commences, the power to release on bail—

(a) shall be exercisable by the Secretary of State (as well as by any person with whom the immigration officer's power is shared under the provision referred to in subsection (1)), and

(b) shall not be exercisable by an immigration officer (except where he acts on behalf of the Secretary of State).

(3) In relation to the exercise by the Secretary of State of a power to release a person on bail by virtue of subsection (2), a reference to an immigration officer shall be construed as a reference to the Secretary of State.

(4) The Secretary of State may by order amend or replace subsection (2) so as to make different provision for the circumstances in which the power to release on bail may be exercised by the Secretary of State and not by an immigration officer.

(5) An order under subsection (4)—

(a) may include consequential or transitional provision,
(b) must be made by statutory instrument, and
(c) may not be made unless a draft has been laid before and approved by resolution of each House of Parliament.

(6) The following provisions of Part III of the Immigration and Asylum Act 1999 (c 33) (Bail) shall cease to have effect—

(a) sections 44 to 52 (routine bail hearings),
(b) section 53(5) (bail under regulations to match bail under Part III), and
(c) section 55 (grants to advisory organisations).

Appointment

Sub-ss (1)–(5): Appointment: 1 April 2003: see SI 2003/754, art 2(1), Sch 1.
Sub-s (6): Appointment: 10 February 2003: see SI 2003/1, art 2, Schedule.

69   Reporting restriction: travel expenses

(1) The Secretary of State may make a payment to a person in respect of travelling expenses which the person has incurred or will incur for the purpose of complying with a reporting restriction.

(2) In subsection (1) "reporting restriction" means a restriction which—

(a) requires a person to report to the police, an immigration officer or the Secretary of State, and
(b) is imposed under a provision listed in subsection (3).

(3) Those provisions are—

(a) paragraph 21 of Schedule 2 to the Immigration Act 1971 (c 77) (temporary admission or release from detention),
(b) paragraph 29 of that Schedule (bail), and
(c) paragraph 2 or 5 of Schedule 3 to that Act (pending deportation).

Initial Commencement
Royal Assent: 7 November 2002: see s 162(2)(u).

70   Induction

(1)   A residence restriction may be imposed on an asylum-seeker or a dependant of an asylum-seeker without regard to his personal circumstances if—

(a)   it requires him to reside at a specified location for a period not exceeding 14 days, and

(b)   the person imposing the residence restriction believes that a programme of induction will be made available to the asylum-seeker at or near the specified location.

(2)   In subsection (1) "residence restriction" means a restriction imposed under—

(a)   paragraph 21 of Schedule 2 to the Immigration Act 1971 (temporary admission or release from detention), or

(b)   paragraph 2(5) of Schedule 3 to that Act (control pending deportation).

(3)   In this section—

"asylum-seeker" has the meaning given by section 18 of this Act but disregarding section 18(1)(a),

"dependant of an asylum-seeker" means a person who appears to the Secretary of State to be making a claim or application in respect of residence in the United Kingdom by virtue of being a dependant of an asylum-seeker, and

"programme of induction" means education about the nature of the asylum process.

(4)   Regulations under subsection (3)—

(a)   may make different provision for different circumstances,
(b)   must be made by statutory instrument, and
(c)   shall be subject to annulment in pursuance of a resolution of either House of Parliament.

(5)   Subsection (6) applies where the Secretary of State arranges for the provision of a programme of induction (whether or not he also provides other facilities to persons attending the programme and whether or not all the persons attending the programme are subject to residence restrictions).

(6)   A local authority may arrange for or participate in the provision of the programme or other facilities.

(7)   In particular, a local authority may—

(a)   incur reasonable expenditure;
(b)   provide services outside its area;
(c)   provide services jointly with another body;
(d)   form a company;
(e)   tender for or enter into a contract;
(f)   do anything (including anything listed in paragraphs (a) to (e)) for a preparatory purpose.

(8)   In this section "local authority" means—

(a)   a local authority within the meaning of section 94 of the Immigration and Asylum Act 1999 (c 33), and

(b)   a Northern Ireland authority within the meaning of section 110 of that Act.

Initial Commencement
Royal Assent: 7 November 2002: see s 162(2)(v).

71   Asylum-seeker: residence, &c restriction

(1) This section applies to—

(a) a person who makes a claim for asylum at a time when he has leave to enter or remain in the United Kingdom, and

(b) a dependant of a person within paragraph (a).

(2) The Secretary of State or an immigration officer may impose on a person to whom this section applies any restriction which may be imposed under paragraph 21 of Schedule 2 to the Immigration Act 1971 (c 77) (control of entry: residence, reporting and occupation restrictions) on a person liable to detention under paragraph 16 of that Schedule.

(3) Where a restriction is imposed on a person under subsection (2)—

(a) the restriction shall be treated for all purposes as a restriction imposed under paragraph 21 of that Schedule, and

(b) if the person fails to comply with the restriction he shall be liable to detention under paragraph 16 of that Schedule.

(4) A restriction imposed on a person under this section shall cease to have effect if he ceases to be an asylum-seeker or the dependant of an asylum-seeker.

(5) In this section—

"asylum-seeker" has the same meaning as in section 70,

"claim for asylum" has the same meaning as in section 18, and

"dependant" means a person who appears to the Secretary of State to be making a claim or application in respect of residence in the United Kingdom by virtue of being a dependant of another person.

(6) Regulations under subsection (5)—

(a) may make different provision for different circumstances,

(b) must be made by statutory instrument, and

(c) shall be subject to annulment in pursuance of a resolution of either House of Parliament.

Appointment
Appointment: 10 February 2003: see SI 2003/1, art 2, Schedule.

Removal

72   Serious criminal

(1) This section applies for the purpose of the construction and application of Article 33(2) of the Refugee Convention (exclusion from protection).

(2) A person shall be presumed to have been convicted by a final judgment of a particularly serious crime and to constitute a danger to the community of the United Kingdom if he is—

(a) convicted in the United Kingdom of an offence, and

(b) sentenced to a period of imprisonment of at least two years.

(3) A person shall be presumed to have been convicted by a final judgment of a particularly serious crime and to constitute a danger to the community of the United Kingdom if—

(a) he is convicted outside the United Kingdom of an offence,

(b) he is sentenced to a period of imprisonment of at least two years, and

   (c) he could have been sentenced to a period of imprisonment of at least two years had his conviction been a conviction in the United Kingdom of a similar offence.

(4) A person shall be presumed to have been convicted by a final judgment of a particularly serious crime and to constitute a danger to the community of the United Kingdom if—

   (a) he is convicted of an offence specified by order of the Secretary of State, or

   (b) he is convicted outside the United Kingdom of an offence and the Secretary of State certifies that in his opinion the offence is similar to an offence specified by order under paragraph (a).

(5) An order under subsection (4)—

   (a) must be made by statutory instrument, and

   (b) shall be subject to annulment in pursuance of a resolution of either House of Parliament.

(6) A presumption under subsection (2), (3) or (4) that a person constitutes a danger to the community is rebuttable by that person.

(7) A presumption under subsection (2), (3) or (4) does not apply while an appeal against conviction or sentence—

   (a) is pending, or

   (b) could be brought (disregarding the possibility of appeal out of time with leave).

(8) Section 34(1) of the Anti-terrorism, Crime and Security Act 2001 (c 24) (no need to consider gravity of fear or threat of persecution) applies for the purpose of considering whether a presumption mentioned in subsection (6) has been rebutted as it applies for the purpose of considering whether Article 33(2) of the Refugee Convention applies.

(9) Subsection (10) applies where—

   (a) a person appeals under section 82, 83 or 101 of this Act or under section 2 of the Special Immigration Appeals Commission Act 1997 (c 68) wholly or partly on the ground that to remove him from or to require him to leave the United Kingdom would breach the United Kingdom's obligations under the Refugee Convention, and

   (b) the Secretary of State issues a certificate that presumptions under subsection (2), (3) or (4) apply to the person (subject to rebuttal).

(10) The ... Tribunal or Commission hearing the appeal—

   (a) must begin substantive deliberation on the appeal by considering the certificate, and

   (b) if in agreement that presumptions under subsection (2), (3) or (4) apply (having given the appellant an opportunity for rebuttal) must dismiss the appeal in so far as it relies on the ground specified in subsection (9)(a).

(11) For the purposes of this section—

   (a) "the Refugee Convention" means the Convention relating to the Status of Refugees done at Geneva on 28th July 1951 and its Protocol, and

   (b) a reference to a person who is sentenced to a period of imprisonment of at least two years—

      (i) does not include a reference to a person who receives a suspended sentence (unless at least two years of the sentence are not suspended),

    (ii) includes a reference to a person who is sentenced to detention, or ordered or directed to be detained, in an institution other than a prison (including, in particular, a hospital or an institution for young offenders), and

    (iii) includes a reference to a person who is sentenced to imprisonment or detention, or ordered or directed to be detained, for an indeterminate period (provided that it may last for two years).

Appointment

Sub-ss (1)–(8), (11): Appointment: 10 February 2003: see SI 2003/1, art 2, Schedule.

Sub-ss (9), (10): Appointment: 1 April 2003: see SI 2003/754, art 2(1), Sch 1; for transitional provisions see art 3(1) thereof.

Amendment

Sub-s (10): word omitted repealed by the Asylum and Immigration (Treatment of Claimants, etc) Act 2004, ss 26(7), 47, Sch 2, Pt 1, paras 16, 17, Sch 4. Date in force: 4 April 2005: see SI 2005/565, art 2(d); for transitional provisions in relation to pending appeals which were made to an adjudicator before 4 April 2005 and in relation to further appeals and applications in such cases see arts 3–9 thereof.

Subordinate Legislation

Nationality, Immigration and Asylum Act 2002 (Specification of Particularly Serious Crimes) Order 2004, SI 2004/1910 (made under sub-s (4)(a)).

73   Family

(1) The following shall be inserted after paragraph 10 of Schedule 2 to the Immigration Act 1971 (c 77) (control of entry: removal)—

"**10A** Where directions are given in respect of a person under any of paragraphs 8 to 10 above, directions to the same effect may be given under that paragraph in respect of a member of the person's family."

(2) Section 10 of the Immigration and Asylum Act 1999 (c 33) (removal of person unlawfully in United Kingdom) shall be amended as follows.

(3) In subsection (1)(c) omit—

    (a) "("the first directions")", and

    (b) "("the other person")".

(4) The following shall be substituted for subsections (3) to (5) (removal of family)—

"(3) Directions for the removal of a person may not be given under subsection (1)(c) unless the Secretary of State has given the person written notice of the intention to remove him.

(4) A notice under subsection (3) may not be given if—

    (a) the person whose removal under subsection (1)(a) or (b) is the cause of the proposed directions under subsection (1)(c) has left the United Kingdom, and

    (b) more than eight weeks have elapsed since that person's departure.

(5) If a notice under subsection (3) is sent by first class post to a person's last known address, that subsection shall be taken to be satisfied at the end of the second day after the day of posting.

(5A) Directions for the removal of a person under subsection (1)(c) cease to have effect if he ceases to belong to the family of the person whose removal under subsection (1)(a) or (b) is the cause of the directions under subsection (1)(c)."

(5) In paragraph 16(2) of Schedule 2 to the Immigration Act 1971 (c 77) (control of entry, &c: detention) for the words "8 to 10" there shall be substituted "8 to 10A".

Appointment
Appointment: 10 February 2003: see SI 2003/1, art 2, Schedule.

74 Deception

In section 10(1) of the Immigration and Asylum Act 1999 (c 33) (removal) the following shall be substituted for paragraph (b)—

"(b) he uses deception in seeking (whether successfully or not) leave to remain;".

Appointment
Appointment: 10 February 2003: see SI 2003/1, art 2, Schedule.

75 Exemption from deportation

(1) Section 7 of the Immigration Act 1971 (existing residents exempt from deportation) shall be amended as follows.

(2) Subsection (1)(a) (which is redundant) shall cease to have effect.

(3) The following shall be substituted for subsection (1)(b)—

"(b) shall not be liable to deportation under section 3(5) if at the time of the Secretary of State's decision he had for the last five years been ordinarily resident in the United Kingdom and Islands;".

(4) The following shall be added at the end of section 10 of the Immigration and Asylum Act 1999 (removal)—

"(10) A person shall not be liable to removal from the United Kingdom under this section at a time when section 7(1)(b) of the Immigration Act 1971 (Commonwealth and Irish citizens ordinarily resident in United Kingdom) would prevent a decision to deport him."

Appointment
Appointment: 10 February 2003: see SI 2003/1, art 2, Schedule.

76 Revocation of leave to enter or remain

(1) The Secretary of State may revoke a person's indefinite leave to enter or remain in the United Kingdom if the person—

(a) is liable to deportation, but
(b) cannot be deported for legal reasons.

(2) The Secretary of State may revoke a person's indefinite leave to enter or remain in the United Kingdom if—

(a) the leave was obtained by deception,
(b) the person would be liable to removal because of the deception, but
(c) the person cannot be removed for legal or practical reasons.

(3) The Secretary of State may revoke a person's indefinite leave to enter or remain in the United Kingdom if the person, or someone of whom he is a dependant, ceases to be a refugee as a result of—

(a) voluntarily availing himself of the protection of his country of nationality,
(b) voluntarily re-acquiring a lost nationality,
(c) acquiring the nationality of a country other than the United Kingdom and availing himself of its protection, or
(d) voluntarily establishing himself in a country in respect of which he was a refugee.

(4) In this section—

"indefinite leave" has the meaning given by section 33(1) of the Immigration Act 1971 (c 77) (interpretation),

"liable to deportation" has the meaning given by section 3(5) and (6) of that Act (deportation),

"refugee" has the meaning given by the Convention relating to the Status of Refugees done at Geneva on 28th July 1951 and its Protocol, and

"removed" means removed from the United Kingdom under—

    (a) paragraph 9 or 10 of Schedule 2 to the Immigration Act 1971 (control of entry: directions for removal), or

    (b) section 10(1)(b) of the Immigration and Asylum Act 1999 (c 33) (removal of persons unlawfully in United Kingdom: deception).

(5) A power under subsection (1) or (2) to revoke leave may be exercised—

    (a) in respect of leave granted before this section comes into force;

    (b) in reliance on anything done before this section comes into force.

(6) A power under subsection (3) to revoke leave may be exercised—

    (a) in respect of leave granted before this section comes into force, but

    (b) only in reliance on action taken after this section comes into force.

(7) In section 10(1) of the Immigration and Asylum Act 1999 (removal of persons unlawfully in United Kingdom) after paragraph (b) (and before the word "or") there shall be inserted—

    "(ba)his indefinite leave to enter or remain has been revoked under section 76(3) of the Nationality, Immigration and Asylum Act 2002 (person ceasing to be refugee);".

Appointment
Appointment: 10 February 2003: see SI 2003/1, art 2, Schedule.

77   No removal while claim for asylum pending

(1) While a person's claim for asylum is pending he may not be—

    (a) removed from the United Kingdom in accordance with a provision of the Immigration Acts, or

    (b) required to leave the United Kingdom in accordance with a provision of the Immigration Acts.

(2) In this section—

    (a) "claim for asylum" means a claim by a person that it would be contrary to the United Kingdom's obligations under the Refugee Convention to remove him from or require him to leave the United Kingdom, and

    (b) a person's claim is pending until he is given notice of the Secretary of State's decision on it.

(3) In subsection (2) "the Refugee Convention" means the Convention relating to the Status of Refugees done at Geneva on 28th July 1951 and its Protocol.

(4) Nothing in this section shall prevent any of the following while a claim for asylum is pending—

    (a) the giving of a direction for the claimant's removal from the United Kingdom,

    (b) the making of a deportation order in respect of the claimant, or

    (c) the taking of any other interim or preparatory action.

(5) Section 15 of the Immigration and Asylum Act 1999 (c 33) (protection from removal or deportation) shall cease to have effect.

Appointment

Appointment: 1 April 2003: see SI 2003/754, art 2(1) Sch 1; for transitional provisons see art 3(2), Sch 2, para 1(2) thereto.

78   No removal while appeal pending

(1)   While a person's appeal under section 82(1) is pending he may not be—

   (a)   removed from the United Kingdom in accordance with a provision of the Immigration Acts, or

   (b)   required to leave the United Kingdom in accordance with a provision of the Immigration Acts.

(2)   In this section "pending" has the meaning given by section 104.

(3)   Nothing in this section shall prevent any of the following while an appeal is pending—

   (a)   the giving of a direction for the appellant's removal from the United Kingdom,

   (b)   the making of a deportation order in respect of the appellant (subject to section 79), or

   (c)   the taking of any other interim or preparatory action.

(4)   This section applies only to an appeal brought while the appellant is in the United Kingdom in accordance with section 92.

Appointment

Appointment: 1 April 2003: see SI 2003/754, art 2(1), Sch 1; for transitional provisions see art 3(2), Sch 2, para 1(3) thereto.

79   Deportation order: appeal

(1)   A deportation order may not be made in respect of a person while an appeal under section 82(1) against the decision to make the order—

   (a)   could be brought (ignoring any possibility of an appeal out of time with permission), or

   (b)   is pending.

(2)   In this section "pending" has the meaning given by section 104.

Appointment

Appointment: 1 April 2003: see SI 2003/754, art 2(1), Sch 1; for transitional provisions see art 3(2), Sch 2, para 1(4) thereto.

80   ...

...

Amendment

Repealed by the Asylum and Immigration (Treatment of Claimants, etc) Act 2004, ss 33(3)(a), 47, Sch 4. Date in force: 1 October 2004 (except in relation to a person subject to a certificate under the Immigration and Asylum Act 1999, ss 11, 12 issued by the Secretary of State before that date): see SI 2004/2523, arts 2, 3, Schedule.

PART 5

IMMIGRATION AND ASYLUM APPEALS

[Appeal to Tribunal]

[81   The Asylum and Immigration Tribunal]

[(1)   There shall be a tribunal to be known as the Asylum and Immigration Tribunal.

(2)   Schedule 4 (which makes provision about the Tribunal) shall have effect.

(3)   A reference in this Part to the Tribunal is a reference to the Asylum and Immigration Tribunal.]

Amendment
Substituted by the Asylum and Immigration (Treatment of Claimants, etc) Act 2004, s 26(1); for transitional provisions see s 26(7), Sch 2, Pt 2, paras 26, 27 and 29 thereto. Date in force: 4 April 2005: see SI 2005/565, art 2(a); for transitional provisions in relation to pending appeals which were made to an adjudicator before 4 April 2005 and in relation to further appeals and applications in such cases see arts 3–9 thereof.

82   Right of appeal: general

(1)   Where an immigration decision is made in respect of a person he may appeal [to the Tribunal].

(2)   In this Part "immigration decision" means—

   (a)   refusal of leave to enter the United Kingdom,
   (b)   refusal of entry clearance,
   (c)   refusal of a certificate of entitlement under section 10 of this Act,
   (d)   refusal to vary a person's leave to enter or remain in the United Kingdom if the result of the refusal is that the person has no leave to enter or remain,
   (e)   variation of a person's leave to enter or remain in the United Kingdom if when the variation takes effect the person has no leave to enter or remain,
   (f)   revocation under section 76 of this Act of indefinite leave to enter or remain in the United Kingdom,
   (g)   a decision that a person is to be removed from the United Kingdom by way of directions under section 10(1)(a), (b) or (c) of the Immigration and Asylum Act 1999 (c 33) (removal of person unlawfully in United Kingdom),
   (h)   a decision that an illegal entrant is to be removed from the United Kingdom by way of directions under paragraphs 8 to 10 of Schedule 2 to the Immigration Act 1971 (c 77) (control of entry: removal),
   (i)   a decision that a person is to be removed from the United Kingdom by way of directions given by virtue of paragraph 10A of that Schedule (family),
   [(ia)   a decision that a person is to be removed from the United Kingdom by way of directions under paragraph 12(2) of Schedule 2 to the Immigration Act 1971 (c 77) (seamen and aircrews),]
   (j)   a decision to make a deportation order under section 5(1) of that Act, and
   (k)   refusal to revoke a deportation order under section 5(2) of that Act.

(3)   A variation or revocation of the kind referred to in subsection (2)(e) or (f) shall not have effect while an appeal under subsection (1) against that variation or revocation—

   (a)   could be brought (ignoring any possibility of an appeal out of time with permission), or
   (b)   is pending.

(4)   The right of appeal under subsection (1) is subject to the exceptions and limitations specified in this Part.

Appointment
Appointment: 1 April 2003: see SI 2003/754, art 2(1), Sch 1; for transitional provisions see art 3(1) thereof.

Amendment
Sub-s (1): words "to the Tribunal" in square brackets substituted by the Asylum and Immigration (Treatment of Claimants, etc) Act 2004, s 26(2). Date in force: 4 April 2005: see SI 2005/565,

art 2(a); for transitional provisions in relation to pending appeals which were made to an adjudicator before 4 April 2005 and in relation to further appeals and applications in such cases see arts 3–9 thereof.

Sub-s (2): para (ia) inserted by the Asylum and Immigration (Treatment of Claimants, etc) Act 2004, s 31. Date in force: 1 October 2004: see SI 2004/2523, art 2, Schedule.

83 Appeal: asylum claim

(1) This section applies where a person has made an asylum claim and—

    (a) his claim has been rejected by the Secretary of State, but

    (b) he has been granted leave to enter or remain in the United Kingdom for a period exceeding one year (or for periods exceeding one year in aggregate).

(2) The person may appeal [to the Tribunal] against the rejection of his asylum claim.

Appointment

Appointment: 1 April 2003: see SI 2003/754, art 2(1), Sch 1; for transitional provisions see art 3(1) thereof.

Amendment

Sub-s (2): words "to the Tribunal" in square brackets substituted by the Asylum and Immigration (Treatment of Claimants, etc) Act 2004, s 26(3). Date in force: 4 April 2005: see SI 2005/565, art 2(a); for transitional provisions in relation to pending appeals which were made to an adjudicator before 4 April 2005 and in relation to further appeals and applications in such cases see arts 3–9 thereof.

84 Grounds of appeal

(1) An appeal under section 82(1) against an immigration decision must be brought on one or more of the following grounds—

    (a) that the decision is not in accordance with immigration rules;

    (b) that the decision is unlawful by virtue of section 19B of the Race Relations Act 1976 (c 74) [or Article 20A of the Race Relations (Northern Ireland) Order 1997] (discrimination by public authorities);

    (c) that the decision is unlawful under section 6 of the Human Rights Act 1998 (c 42) (public authority not to act contrary to Human Rights Convention) as being incompatible with the appellant's Convention rights;

    (d) that the appellant is an EEA national or a member of the family of an EEA national and the decision breaches the appellant's rights under the Community Treaties in respect of entry to or residence in the United Kingdom;

    (e) that the decision is otherwise not in accordance with the law;

    (f) that the person taking the decision should have exercised differently a discretion conferred by immigration rules;

    (g) that removal of the appellant from the United Kingdom in consequence of the immigration decision would breach the United Kingdom's obligations under the Refugee Convention or would be unlawful under section 6 of the Human Rights Act 1998 as being incompatible with the appellant's Convention rights.

(2) In subsection (1)(d) "EEA national" means a national of a State which is a contracting party to the Agreement on the European Economic Area signed at Oporto on 2nd May 1992 (as it has effect from time to time).

(3) An appeal under section 83 must be brought on the grounds that removal of the appellant from the United Kingdom would breach the United Kingdom's obligations under the Refugee Convention.

Appointment

Appointment: 1 April 2003: see SI 2003/754, art 2(1), Sch 1; for transitional provisions see art 3(1) thereof.

Amendment
Sub-s (1): in para (b) words "or Article 20A of the Race Relations (Northern Ireland) Order 1997" in square brackets inserted by the Race Relations Order (Amendment) Regulations (Northern Ireland) 2003, SR 2003/341, art 60. Date in force: 19 July 2003: see the Race Relations Order (Amendment) Regulations (Northern Ireland) 2003, SR 2003/341, art 1(1).

85   Matters to be considered

(1)   An appeal under section 82(1) against a decision shall be treated by [the Tribunal] as including an appeal against any decision in respect of which the appellant has a right of appeal under section 82(1).

(2)   If an appellant under section 82(1) makes a statement under section 120, [the Tribunal] shall consider any matter raised in the statement which constitutes a ground of appeal of a kind listed in section 84(1) against the decision appealed against.

(3)   Subsection (2) applies to a statement made under section 120 whether the statement was made before or after the appeal was commenced.

(4)   On an appeal under section 82(1) or 83(2) against a decision [the Tribunal] may consider evidence about any matter which [it] thinks relevant to the substance of the decision, including evidence which concerns a matter arising after the date of the decision.

(5)   But in relation to an appeal under section 82(1) against refusal of entry clearance or refusal of a certificate of entitlement under section 10—

  (a)   subsection (4) shall not apply, and
  (b)   [the Tribunal] may consider only the circumstances appertaining at the time of the decision to refuse.

Appointment
Appointment: 1 April 2003: see SI 2003/754, art 2(1), Sch 1; for transitional provisions see art 3(1) thereof.

Amendment
Sub-s (1): words "the Tribunal" square brackets substituted by the Asylum and Immigration (Treatment of Claimants, etc) Act 2004, s 26(7), Sch 2, Pt 1, paras 16, 18(1)(b), (2)(a); for transitional provisions see s 26(7), Sch 2, Pt 2 thereto. Date in force: 4 April 2005: see SI 2005/565, art 2(d); for transitional provisions in relation to pending appeals which were made to an adjudicator before 4 April 2005 and in relation to further appeals and applications in such cases see arts 3–9 thereof.
Sub-s (2): words "the Tribunal" in square brackets substituted by the Asylum and Immigration (Treatment of Claimants, etc) Act 2004, s 26(7), Sch 2, Pt 1, paras 16, 18(1)(b), (2)(a); for transitional provisions see s 26(7), Sch 2, Pt 2 thereto. Date in force: 4 April 2005: see SI 2005/565, art 2(d); for transitional provisions in relation to pending appeals which were made to an adjudicator before 4 April 2005 and in relation to further appeals and applications in such cases see arts 3–9 thereof.
Sub-s (4): words "the Tribunal" in square brackets substituted by the Asylum and Immigration (Treatment of Claimants, etc) Act 2004, s 26(7), Sch 2, Pt 1, paras 16, 18(1)(a), (2)(a); for transitional provisions see s 26(7), Sch 2, Pt 2 thereto. Date in force: 4 April 2005: see SI 2005/565, art 2(d); for transitional provisions in relation to pending appeals which were made to an adjudicator before 4 April 2005 and in relation to further appeals and applications in such cases see arts 3–9 thereof.
Sub-s (4): word "it" in square brackets substituted by the Asylum and Immigration (Treatment of Claimants, etc) Act 2004, s 26(7), Sch 2, Pt 1, paras 16, 18(1)(c), (2)(a); for transitional provisions see s 26(7), Sch 2, Pt 2 thereto. Date in force: 4 April 2005: see SI 2005/565, art 2(d); for transitional provisions in relation to pending appeals which were made to an adjudicator before 4 April 2005 and in relation to further appeals and applications in such cases see arts 3–9 thereof.
Sub-s (5): in para (b) words "the Tribunal" in square brackets substituted by the Asylum and Immigration (Treatment of Claimants, etc) Act 2004, s 26(7), Sch 2, Pt 1, paras 16, 18(1)(b),

(2)(a); for transitional provisions see s 26(7), Sch 2, Pt 2 thereto. Date in force: 4 April 2005: see SI 2005/565, art 2(d); for transitional provisions in relation to pending appeals which were made to an adjudicator before 4 April 2005 and in relation to further appeals and applications in such cases see arts 3–9 thereof.

86 Determination of appeal

(1) This section applies on an appeal under section 82(1) or 83.

(2) [The Tribunal] must determine—

(a) any matter raised as a ground of appeal (whether or not by virtue of section 85(1)), and

(b) any matter which section 85 requires [it] to consider.

(3) [The Tribunal] must allow the appeal in so far as [it] thinks that—

(a) a decision against which the appeal is brought or is treated as being brought was not in accordance with the law (including immigration rules), or

(b) a discretion exercised in making a decision against which the appeal is brought or is treated as being brought should have been exercised differently.

(4) For the purposes of subsection (3) a decision that a person should be removed from the United Kingdom under a provision shall not be regarded as unlawful if it could have been lawfully made by reference to removal under another provision.

(5) In so far as subsection (3) does not apply, [the Tribunal] shall dismiss the appeal.

(6) Refusal to depart from or to authorise departure from immigration rules is not the exercise of a discretion for the purposes of subsection (3)(b).

Appointment
Appointment: 1 April 2003: see SI 2003/754, art 2(1), Sch 1; for transitional provisions see art 3(1) thereof.

Amendment
Sub-s (2): words "The Tribunal" in square brackets substituted by the Asylum and Immigration (Treatment of Claimants, etc) Act 2004, s 26(7), Sch 2, Pt 1, paras 16, 18(1)(b), (2)(b); for transitional provisions see s 26(7), Sch 2, Pt 2 thereto. Date in force: 4 April 2005: see SI 2005/565, art 2(d); for transitional provisions in relation to pending appeals which were made to an adjudicator before 4 April 2005 and in relation to further appeals and applications in such cases see arts 3–9 thereof.
Sub-s (2): in para (b) word "it" in square brackets substituted by the Asylum and Immigration (Treatment of Claimants, etc) Act 2004, s 26(7), Sch 2, Pt 1, paras 16, 18(1)(d), (2)(b); for transitional provisions see s 26(7), Sch 2, Pt 2 thereto. Date in force: 4 April 2005: see SI 2005/565, art 2(d); for transitional provisions in relation to pending appeals which were made to an adjudicator before 4 April 2005 and in relation to further appeals and applications in such cases see arts 3–9 thereof.
Sub-s (3): words "The Tribunal" in square brackets substituted by the Asylum and Immigration (Treatment of Claimants, etc) Act 2004, s 26(7), Sch 2, Pt 1, paras 16, 18(1)(b), (2)(b); for transitional provisions see s 26(7), Sch 2, Pt 2 thereto. Date in force: 4 April 2005: see SI 2005/565, art 2(d); for transitional provisions in relation to pending appeals which were made to an adjudicator before 4 April 2005 and in relation to further appeals and applications in such cases see arts 3–9 thereof.
Sub-s (3): word "it" in square brackets substituted by the Asylum and Immigration (Treatment of Claimants, etc) Act 2004, s 26(7), Sch 2, Pt 1, paras 16, 18(1)(c), (2)(b); for transitional provisions see s 26(7), Sch 2, Pt 2 thereto. Date in force: 4 April 2005: see SI 2005/565, art 2(d); for transitional provisions in relation to pending appeals which were made to an adjudicator before 4 April 2005 and in relation to further appeals and applications in such cases see arts 3–9 thereof.
Sub-s (5): words "the Tribunal" in square brackets substituted by the Asylum and Immigration (Treatment of Claimants, etc) Act 2004, s 26(7), Sch 2, Pt 1, paras 16, 18(1)(b), (2)(b); for transitional provisions see s 26(7), Sch 2, Pt 2 thereto. Date in force: 4 April 2005: see

SI 2005/565, art 2(d); for transitional provisions in relation to pending appeals which were made to an adjudicator before 4 April 2005 and in relation to further appeals and applications in such cases see arts 3–9 thereof.

87   Successful appeal: direction

(1)   If [the Tribunal] allows an appeal under section 82 or 83 [it] may give a direction for the purpose of giving effect to [its] decision.

(2)   A person responsible for making an immigration decision shall act in accordance with any relevant direction under subsection (1).

[(3)   But a direction under this section shall not have effect while—

(a)   an application under section 103A(1) (other than an application out of time with permission) could be made or is awaiting determination,

(b)   reconsideration of an appeal has been ordered under section 103A(1) and has not been completed,

(c)   an appeal has been remitted to the Tribunal and is awaiting determination,

(d)   an application under section 103B or 103E for permission to appeal (other than an application out of time with permission) could be made or is awaiting determination,

(e)   an appeal under section 103B or 103E is awaiting determination, or

(f)   a reference under section 103C is awaiting determination.]

(4)   *A direction under subsection (1) shall be treated* [*as part of the Tribunal's decision on the appeal for the purposes of section 103A*].

Appointment
Appointment: 1 April 2003: see SI 2003/754, art 2(1), Sch 1; for transitional provisions see art 3(1) thereof.

Amendment
Sub-s (1): words "the Tribunal" in square brackets substituted by the Asylum and Immigration (Treatment of Claimants, etc) Act 2004, s 26(7), Sch 2, Pt 1, paras 16, 18(1)(a), (2)(c); for transitional provisions see s 26(7), Sch 2, Pt 2 thereto. Date in force: 4 April 2005: see SI 2005/565, art 2(d); for transitional provisions in relation to pending appeals which were made to an adjudicator before 4 April 2005 and in relation to further appeals and applications in such cases see arts 3–9 thereof.
Sub-s (1): word "it" in square brackets substituted by the Asylum and Immigration (Treatment of Claimants, etc) Act 2004, s 26(7), Sch 2, Pt 1, paras 16, 18(1)(c), (2)(c); for transitional provisions see s 26(7), Sch 2, Pt 2 thereto. Date in force: 4 April 2005: see SI 2005/565, art 2(d); for transitional provisions in relation to pending appeals which were made to an adjudicator before 4 April 2005 and in relation to further appeals and applications in such cases see arts 3–9 thereof.
Sub-s (1): word "its" in square brackets substituted by the Asylum and Immigration (Treatment of Claimants, etc) Act 2004, s 26(7), Sch 2, Pt 1, paras 16, 18(1)(e), (2)(c); for transitional provisions see s 26(7), Sch 2, Pt 2 thereto. Date in force: 4 April 2005: see SI 2005/565, art 2(d); for transitional provisions in relation to pending appeals which were made to an adjudicator before 4 April 2005 and in relation to further appeals and applications in such cases see arts 3–9 thereof.
Sub-s (3): substituted by the Asylum and Immigration (Treatment of Claimants, etc) Act 2004, s 26(7), Sch 2, Pt 1, paras 16, 19(a); for transitional provisions see s 26(7), Sch 2, Pt 2 thereto. Date in force: 4 April 2005: see SI 2005/565, art 2(d); for transitional provisions in relation to pending appeals which were made to an adjudicator before 4 April 2005 and in relation to further appeals and applications in such cases see arts 3–9 thereof.
Sub-s (4): repealed by the Asylum and Immigration (Treatment of Claimants, etc) Act 2004, s 47, Sch 4. Date in force: to be appointed: see the Asylum and Immigration (Treatment of Claimants, etc) Act 2004, s 48(3)–(6).
Sub-s (4): words "as part of the Tribunal's decision on the appeal for the purposes of section 103A" in square brackets substituted by the Asylum and Immigration (Treatment of Claimants, etc) Act 2004, s 26(7), Sch 2, Pt 1, paras 16, 19(b); for transitional provisions see s 26(7), Sch 2, Pt 2 thereto. Date in force: 4 April 2005: see SI 2005/565, art 2(d); for transitional

provisions in relation to pending appeals which were made to an adjudicator before 4 April 2005 and in relation to further appeals and applications in such cases see arts 3–9 thereof.

Exceptions and limitations

88   Ineligibility

(1) This section applies to an immigration decision of a kind referred to in section 82(2)(a), (b), (d) or (e).

(2) A person may not appeal under section 82(1) against an immigration decision which is taken on the grounds that he or a person of whom he is a dependant—

(a)   does not satisfy a requirement as to age, nationality or citizenship specified in immigration rules,

(b)   does not have an immigration document of a particular kind (or any immigration document),

(c)   is seeking to be in the United Kingdom for a period greater than that permitted in his case by immigration rules, or

(d)   is seeking to enter or remain in the United Kingdom for a purpose other than one for which entry or remaining is permitted in accordance with immigration rules.

(3) In subsection (2)(b) "immigration document" means—

(a)   entry clearance,

(b)   a passport,

(c)   a work permit or other immigration employment document within the meaning of section 122, and

(d)   a document which relates to a national of a country other than the United Kingdom and which is designed to serve the same purpose as a passport.

(4) Subsection (2) does not prevent the bringing of an appeal on any or all of the grounds referred to in section 84(1)(b), (c) and (g).

Appointment
Appointment: 1 April 2003: see SI 2003/754, art 2(1), Sch 1; for transitional provisions see art 3(1) thereof.

[88A   Ineligibility: entry clearance]

[(1) A person may not appeal under section 82(1) against refusal of entry clearance if the decision to refuse is taken on grounds which—

(a)   relate to a provision of immigration rules, and

(b)   are specified for the purpose of this section by order of the Secretary of State.

(2) Subsection (1)—

(a)   does not prevent the bringing of an appeal on either or both of the grounds referred to in section 84(1)(b) and (c), and

(b)   is without prejudice to the effect of section 88 in relation to an appeal under section 82(1) against refusal of entry clearance.]

Amendment
Inserted by the Asylum and Immigration (Treatment of Claimants, etc) Act 2004, s 29(1). Date in force: 1 October 2004: see SI 2004/2523, art 2, Schedule.

89   Visitor or student without entry clearance

(1) This section applies to a person who applies for leave to enter the United Kingdom—

(a)   as a visitor,
(b)   in order to follow a course of study for which he has been accepted and which will not last more than six months,
(c)   in order to study but without having been accepted for a course, or
(d)   as the dependant of a person who applies for leave to enter as a visitor or for a purpose described in paragraph (b) or (c).

(2)   A person may not appeal under section 82(1) against refusal of leave to enter the United Kingdom if at the time of the refusal he does not have entry clearance.

(3)   Subsection (2) does not prevent the bringing of an appeal on any or all of the grounds referred to in section 84(1)(b), (c) and (g).

Appointment
Appointment: 1 April 2003: see SI 2003/754, art 2(1), Sch 1; for transitional provisions see art 3(1) thereof.

90   Non-family visitor

(1)   A person who applies for entry clearance for the purpose of entering the United Kingdom as a visitor may appeal under section 82(1) against refusal of entry clearance only if the application was made for the purpose of visiting a member of the applicant's family.

(2)   In subsection (1) the reference to a member of the applicant's family shall be construed in accordance with regulations.

(3)   Regulations under subsection (2) may, in particular, make provision wholly or partly by reference to the duration of two individuals' residence together.

(4)   Subsection (1) does not prevent the bringing of an appeal on either or both of the grounds referred to in section 84(1)(b) and (c).

Appointment
Appointment: 1 April 2003: see SI 2003/754, art 2(1), Sch 1; for transitional provisions see art 3(1) thereof.

91   Student

(1)   A person may not appeal under section 82(1) against refusal of entry clearance if he seeks it—

(a)   in order to follow a course of study for which he has been accepted and which will not last more than six months,
(b)   in order to study but without having been accepted for a course, or
(c)   as the dependant of a person seeking entry clearance for a purpose described in paragraph (a) or (b).

(2)   Subsection (1) does not prevent the bringing of an appeal on either or both of the grounds referred to in section 84(1)(b) and (c).

Appointment
Appointment: 1 April 2003: see SI 2003/754, art 2(1), Sch 1; for transitional provisions see art 3(1) thereof.

92   Appeal from within United Kingdom: general

(1)   A person may not appeal under section 82(1) while he is in the United Kingdom unless his appeal is of a kind to which this section applies.

(2)   This section applies to an appeal against an immigration decision of a kind specified in section 82(2)(c), (d), (e), (f) and (j).

[(3) This section also applies to an appeal against refusal of leave to enter the United Kingdom if—

(a) at the time of the refusal the appellant is in the United Kingdom, and
(b) on his arrival in the United Kingdom the appellant had entry clearance.

(3A) But this section does not apply by virtue of subsection (3) if subsection (3B) or (3C) applies to the refusal of leave to enter.

(3B) This subsection applies to a refusal of leave to enter which is a deemed refusal under paragraph 2A(9) of Schedule 2 to the Immigration Act 1971 (c 77) resulting from cancellation of leave to enter by an immigration officer—

(a) under paragraph 2A(8) of that Schedule, and
(b) on the grounds specified in paragraph 2A(2A) of that Schedule.

(3C) This subsection applies to a refusal of leave to enter which specifies that the grounds for refusal are that the leave is sought for a purpose other than that specified in the entry clearance.

(3D) This section also applies to an appeal against refusal of leave to enter the United Kingdom if at the time of the refusal the appellant—

(a) is in the United Kingdom,
(b) has a work permit, and
(c) is any of the following (within the meaning of the British Nationality Act 1981 (c 61))—
    (i) a British overseas territories citizen,
    (ii) a British Overseas citizen,
    (iii) a British National (Overseas),
    (iv) a British protected person, or
    (v) a British subject.]

(4) This section also applies to an appeal against an immigration decision if the appellant—

(a) has made an asylum claim, or a human rights claim, while in the United Kingdom, or
(b) is an EEA national or a member of the family of an EEA national and makes a claim to the Secretary of State that the decision breaches the appellant's rights under the Community Treaties in respect of entry to or residence in the United Kingdom.

Appointment
Appointment: 1 April 2003: see SI 2003/754, art 2(1), Sch 1; for transitional provisions see art 3(1) thereof.

Amendment
Sub-ss (3), (3A)–(3D): substituted, for sub-s (3) as originally enacted, by the Asylum and Immigration (Treatment of Claimants, etc) Act 2004, s 28. Date in force: 1 October 2004: see SI 2004/2523, art 2, Schedule.

93   ...

...

Amendment
Repealed by the Asylum and Immigration (Treatment of Claimants, etc) Act 2004, ss 33(3)(b), 47, Sch 4. Date in force: 1 October 2004 (except in relation to a person subject to a certificate under the Immigration and Asylum Act 1999, ss 11, 12 issued by the Secretary of State before that date): see SI 2004/2523, arts 2, 3, Schedule.

94   Appeal from within United Kingdom: unfounded human rights or asylum claim

(1)   This section applies to an appeal under section 82(1) where the appellant has made an asylum claim or a human rights claim (or both).

[(1A)   A person may not bring an appeal against an immigration decision of a kind specified in section 82(2)(c), (d) or (e) in reliance on section 92(2) if the Secretary of State certifies that the claim or claims mentioned in subsection (1) above is or are clearly unfounded.]

(2)   A person may not bring an appeal to which this section applies [in reliance on section 92(4)(a)] if the Secretary of State certifies that the claim or claims mentioned in subsection (1) is or are clearly unfounded.

(3)   If the Secretary of State is satisfied that an asylum claimant or human rights claimant is entitled to reside in a State listed in subsection (4) he shall certify the claim under subsection (2) unless satisfied that it is not clearly unfounded.

(4)   Those States are—

    (a)   ...
    (b)   ...
    (c)   ...
    (d)   ...
    (e)   ...
    (f)   ...
    (g)   ...
    (h)   ...
    (i)   ...
    (j)   ...
    [(k)   the Republic of Albania,
    (l)   Bulgaria,
    (m)   Serbia and Montenegro,
    (n)   Jamaica,
    (o)   Macedonia,
    (p)   the Republic of Moldova, ...
    (q)   Romania],
    [(r)   ...
    (s)   Bolivia,
    (t)   Brazil,
    (u)   Ecuador,
    (v)   Sri Lanka,
    (w)   South Africa, and
    (x)   Ukraine],
    [(y)   India].

(5)   The Secretary of State may by order add a State, or part of a State, to the list in subsection (4) if satisfied that—

    (a)   there is in general in that State or part no serious risk of persecution of persons entitled to reside in that State or part, and
    (b)   removal to that State or part of persons entitled to reside there will not in general contravene the United Kingdom's obligations under the Human Rights Convention.

[(5A)   If the Secretary of State is satisfied that the statements in subsection (5) (a) and (b) are true of a State or part of a State in relation to a description of person, an order under subsection (5) may add the State or part to the list in subsection (4) in respect of that description of person.

(5B) Where a State or part of a State is added to the list in subsection (4) in respect of a description of person, subsection (3) shall have effect in relation to a claimant only if the Secretary of State is satisfied that he is within that description (as well as being satisfied that he is entitled to reside in the State or part).

(5C) A description for the purposes of subsection (5A) may refer to—

(a) gender,
(b) language,
(c) race,
(d) religion,
(e) nationality,
(f) membership of a social or other group,
(g) political opinion, or
(h) any other attribute or circumstance that the Secretary of State thinks appropriate.]

[(6) The Secretary of State may by order amend the list in subsection (4) so as to omit a State or part added under subsection (5); and the omission may be—

(a) general, or
(b) effected so that the State or part remains listed in respect of a description of person.]

[(6A) Subsection (3) shall not apply in relation to an asylum claimant or human rights claimant who—

(a) is the subject of a certificate under section 2 or 70 of the Extradition Act 2003 (c 41),
(b) is in custody pursuant to arrest under section 5 of that Act,
(c) is the subject of a provisional warrant under section 73 of that Act,
(d) is the subject of an authority to proceed under section 7 of the Extradition Act 1989 (c 33) or an order under paragraph 4(2) of Schedule 1 to that Act, or
(e) is the subject of a provisional warrant under section 8 of that Act or of a warrant under paragraph 5(1)(b) of Schedule 1 to that Act.]

(7) A person may not bring an appeal to which this section applies in reliance on section 92(4) if the Secretary of State certifies that—

(a) it is proposed to remove the person to a country of which he is not a national or citizen, and
(b) there is no reason to believe that the person's rights under the Human Rights Convention will be breached in that country.

(8) In determining whether a person in relation to whom a certificate has been issued under subsection (7) may be removed from the United Kingdom, the country specified in the certificate is to be regarded as—

(a) a place where a person's life and liberty is not threatened by reason of his race, religion, nationality, membership of a particular social group, or political opinion, and
(b) a place from which a person will not be sent to another country otherwise than in accordance with the Refugee Convention.

(9) Where a person in relation to whom a certificate is issued under this section subsequently brings an appeal under section 82(1) while outside the United Kingdom, the appeal shall be considered as if he had not been removed from the United Kingdom.

Appointment
Sub-ss (1)–(4), (6)–(9): Appointment: 1 April 2003: see SI 2003/754, art 2(1), Sch 1; for transitional provisions see art 3(1) thereof.

Sub-s (5): Appointment (for the purpose of enabling the Secretary of State to exercise the power to make subordinate legislation): 10 February 2003: see SI 2003/249, art 2, Schedule.
Sub-s (5): Appointment (for remaining purposes): 1 April 2003: see SI 2003/754, art 2(1), Sch 1; for transitional provisions see art 3(1) thereof.

Amendment
Sub-s (1A): inserted by the Asylum and Immigration (Treatment of Claimants, etc) Act 2004, s 27(1), (2). Date in force: 1 October 2004: see SI 2004/2523, art 2, Schedule.
Sub-s (2): words "in reliance on section 92(4)(a)" in square brackets substituted by the Asylum and Immigration (Treatment of Claimants, etc) Act 2004, s 27(1), (3). Date in force: 1 October 2004: see SI 2004/2523, art 2, Schedule.
Sub-s (4): paras (a)–(j) repealed by the Asylum and Immigration (Treatment of Claimants, etc) Act 2004, ss 27(1), (4), 47, Sch 4. Date in force: 1 October 2004: see SI 2004/2523, art 2, Schedule.
Sub-s (4): paras (k)–(q) inserted by SI 2003/970, art 3. Date in force: 1 April 2003 (being the date on which sub-s (4) above came into force): see SI 2003/754, art 2, Sch 1 and SI 2003/970, art 2.
Sub-s (4): in para (p) word omitted repealed by virtue of SI 2003/1919, art 2. Date in force: 23 July 2003 (except in relation to an asylum claim or human rights claim made before that date): see SI 2003/1919, art 1.
Sub-s (4): paras (r)–(x) inserted by SI 2003/1919, art 2. Date in force: 23 July 2003 (except in relation to an asylum claim or human rights claim made before that date): see SI 2003/1919, art 1.
Sub-s (4): para (r) repealed by SI 2005/1016, art 2. Date in force: 22 April 2005: see SI 2005/1016, art 1.
Sub-s (4): para (y) inserted by SI 2005/330, art 2. Date in force: 15 February 2005 (except in relation to an asylum claim or human rights claim made before that date): see SI 2005/330, art 1.
Sub-ss (5A)–(5C): inserted by the Asylum and Immigration (Treatment of Claimants, etc) Act 2004, s 27(1), (5). Date in force: 1 October 2004: see SI 2004/2523, art 2, Schedule.
Sub-s (6): substituted by the Asylum and Immigration (Treatment of Claimants, etc) Act 2004, s 27(1), (6). Date in force: 1 October 2004: see SI 2004/2523, art 2, Schedule.
Sub-s (6A): inserted by the Asylum and Immigration (Treatment of Claimants, etc) Act 2004, s 27(1), (7). Date in force: 1 October 2004: see SI 2004/2523, art 2, Schedule.

Subordinate Legislation
Asylum (Designated States) Order 2003, SI 2003/970 (made under sub-s (5)).
Asylum (Designated States) (No 2) Order 2003, SI 2003/1919 (made under sub-s (5)).
Asylum (Designated States) Order 2005, SI 2005/330 (made under sub-s (5)).
Asylum (Designated States) (Amendment) Order 2005, SI 2005/1016 (made under sub-s (6)).

95 Appeal from outside United Kingdom: removal

A person who is outside the United Kingdom may not appeal under section 82(1) on the ground specified in section 84(1)(g) (except in a case to which section 94(9) applies).

Appointment
Appointment: 1 April 2003: see SI 2003/754, art 2(1), Sch 1; for transitional provisions see art 3(1) thereof.

96 Earlier right of appeal

[(1) An appeal under section 82(1) against an immigration decision ("the new decision") in respect of a person may not be brought if the Secretary of State or an immigration officer certifies—

    (a) that the person was notified of a right of appeal under that section against another immigration decision ("the old decision") (whether or not an appeal was brought and whether or not any appeal brought has been determined),

    (b) that the claim or application to which the new decision relates relies on a matter that could have been raised in an appeal against the old decision, and

(c) that, in the opinion of the Secretary of State or the immigration officer, there is no satisfactory reason for that matter not having been raised in an appeal against the old decision.

(2) An appeal under section 82(1) against an immigration decision ("the new decision") in respect of a person may not be brought if the Secretary of State or an immigration officer certifies—

(a) that the person received a notice under section 120 by virtue of an application other than that to which the new decision relates or by virtue of a decision other than the new decision,

(b) that the new decision relates to an application or claim which relies on a matter that should have been, but has not been, raised in a statement made in response to that notice, and

(c) that, in the opinion of the Secretary of State or the immigration officer, there is no satisfactory reason for that matter not having been raised in a statement made in response to that notice.]

(4) In subsection (1) "notified" means notified in accordance with regulations under section 105.

(5) [Subsections (1) and (2) apply to prevent] a person's right of appeal whether or not he has been outside the United Kingdom since an earlier right of appeal arose or since a requirement under section 120 was imposed.

(6) In this section a reference to an appeal under section 82(1) includes a reference to an appeal under section 2 of the Special Immigration Appeals Commission Act 1997 (c 68) which is or could be brought by reference to an appeal under section 82(1).

[(7) A certificate under subsection (1) or (2) shall have no effect in relation to an appeal instituted before the certificate is issued.]

Appointment
Appointment: 1 April 2003: see SI 2003/754, art 2(1), Sch 1; for transitional provisions see art 3(1) thereof.

Amendment
Sub-ss (1), (2): substituted, for sub-ss (1)–(3) as originally enacted, by the Asylum and Immigration (Treatment of Claimants, etc) Act 2004, s 30(1), (2). Date in force: 1 October 2004: see SI 2004/2523, art 2, Schedule.
Sub-s (5): words "Subsections (1) and (2) apply to prevent" in square brackets substituted by the Asylum and Immigration (Treatment of Claimants, etc) Act 2004, s 30(1), (3). Date in force: 1 October 2004: see SI 2004/2523, art 2, Schedule.
Sub-s (7): inserted by the Asylum and Immigration (Treatment of Claimants, etc) Act 2004, s 30(1), (4). Date in force: 1 October 2004: see SI 2004/2523, art 2, Schedule.

97 National security, &c

(1) An appeal under section 82(1) or 83(2) against a decision in respect of a person may not be brought or continued if the Secretary of State certifies that the decision is or was taken—

(a) by the Secretary of State wholly or partly on a ground listed in subsection (2), or

(b) in accordance with a direction of the Secretary of State which identifies the person to whom the decision relates and which is given wholly or partly on a ground listed in subsection (2).

(2) The grounds mentioned in subsection (1) are that the person's exclusion or removal from the United Kingdom is—

(a) in the interests of national security, or

(b)   in the interests of the relationship between the United Kingdom and another country.

(3)   An appeal under section 82(1) or 83(2) against a decision may not be brought or continued if the Secretary of State certifies that the decision is or was taken wholly or partly in reliance on information which in his opinion should not be made public—

(a)   in the interests of national security,
(b)   in the interests of the relationship between the United Kingdom and another country, or
(c)   otherwise in the public interest.

(4)   In subsections (1)(a) and (b) and (3) a reference to the Secretary of State is to the Secretary of State acting in person.

Appointment
Appointment: 1 April 2003: see SI 2003/754, art 2(1), Sch 1; for transitional provisions see art 3(1) thereof.

98   Other grounds of public good

(1)   This section applies to an immigration decision of a kind referred to in section 82(2)(a) or (b).

(2)   An appeal under section 82(1) against an immigration decision may not be brought or continued if the Secretary of State certifies that the decision is or was taken—

(a)   by the Secretary of State wholly or partly on the ground that the exclusion or removal from the United Kingdom of the person to whom the decision relates is conducive to the public good, or
(b)   in accordance with a direction of the Secretary of State which identifies the person to whom the decision relates and which is given wholly or partly on that ground.

(3)   In subsection (2)(a) and (b) a reference to the Secretary of State is to the Secretary of State acting in person.

(4)   Subsection (2) does not prevent the bringing of an appeal on either or both of the grounds referred to in section 84(1)(b) and (c).

(5)   Subsection (2) does not prevent the bringing of an appeal against an immigration decision of the kind referred to in section 82(2)(a) on the grounds referred to in section 84(1)(g).

Appointment
Appointment: 1 April 2003: see SI 2003/754, art 2(1), Sch 1; for transitional provisions see art 3(1) thereof.

99   Sections 96 to 98: appeal in progress

(1)   This section applies where a certificate is issued under section 96(1) or (2), 97 or 98 in respect of a pending appeal.

(2)   The appeal shall lapse.

Appointment
Appointment: 1 April 2003: see SI 2003/754, art 2(1), Sch 1; for transitional provisions see art 3(1) thereof.

100 ...

...

Amendment

Repealed by the Asylum and Immigration (Treatment of Claimants, etc) Act 2004, ss 26(5)(a), 47, Sch 4; for transitional provisions see s 26(7), Sch 2, Pt 2 thereto. Date in force: 4 April 2005: see SI 2005/565, art 2(a); for transitional provisions in relation to pending appeals which were made to an adjudicator before 4 April 2005 and in relation to further appeals and applications in such cases see arts 3–9 thereof.

101 ...

...

Amendment

Repealed by the Asylum and Immigration (Treatment of Claimants, etc) Act 2004, ss 26(5)(a), 47, Sch 4; for transitional provisions see s 26(7), Sch 2, Pt 2 thereto. Date in force: 4 April 2005: see SI 2005/565, art 2(a); for transitional provisions in relation to pending appeals which were made to an adjudicator before 4 April 2005 and in relation to further appeals and applications in such cases see arts 3–9 thereof.

102 ...

...

Amendment

Repealed by the Asylum and Immigration (Treatment of Claimants, etc) Act 2004, ss 26(5)(a), 47, Sch 4; for transitional provisions see s 26(7), Sch 2, Pt 2 thereto. Date in force: 4 April 2005: see SI 2005/565, art 2(a); for transitional provisions in relation to pending appeals which were made to an adjudicator before 4 April 2005 and in relation to further appeals and applications in such cases see arts 3–9 thereof.

103 ...

...

Amendment

Repealed by the Asylum and Immigration (Treatment of Claimants, etc) Act 2004, ss 26(5)(a), 47, Sch 4; for transitional provisions see s 26(7), Sch 2, Pt 2 thereto. Date in force: 4 April 2005: see SI 2005/565, art 2(a); for transitional provisions in relation to pending appeals which were made to an adjudicator before 4 April 2005 and in relation to further appeals and applications in such cases see arts 3–9 thereof.

Procedure

[103A   Review of Tribunal's decision]

[(1)   A party to an appeal under section 82 or 83 may apply to the appropriate court, on the grounds that the Tribunal made an error of law, for an order requiring the Tribunal to reconsider its decision on the appeal.

(2)   The appropriate court may make an order under subsection (1)—

(a)   only if it thinks that the Tribunal may have made an error of law, and
(b)   only once in relation to an appeal.

(3)   An application under subsection (1) must be made—

(a)   in the case of an application by the appellant made while he is in the United Kingdom, within the period of 5 days beginning with the date on which he is treated, in accordance with rules under section 106, as receiving notice of the Tribunal's decision,

(b)   in the case of an application by the appellant made while he is outside the United Kingdom, within the period of 28 days beginning with the date on which he is treated, in accordance with rules under section 106, as receiving notice of the Tribunal's decision, and

(c)   in the case of an application brought by a party to the appeal other than the appellant, within the period of 5 days beginning with the date on which he is treated, in accordance with rules under section 106, as receiving notice of the Tribunal's decision.

(4)   But—

(a)   rules of court may specify days to be disregarded in applying subsection (3)(a), (b) or (c), and

(b)   the appropriate court may permit an application under subsection (1) to be made outside the period specified in subsection (3) where it thinks that the application could not reasonably practicably have been made within that period.

(5)   An application under subsection (1) shall be determined by reference only to—

(a)   written submissions of the applicant, and

(b)   where rules of court permit, other written submissions.

(6)   A decision of the appropriate court on an application under subsection (1) shall be final.

(7)   In this section a reference to the Tribunal's decision on an appeal does not include a reference to—

(a)   a procedural, ancillary or preliminary decision, or

(b)   a decision following remittal under section 103B, 103C or 103E.

(8)   This section does not apply to a decision of the Tribunal where its jurisdiction is exercised by three or more legally qualified members.

(9)   In this section "the appropriate court" means—

(a)   in relation to an appeal decided in England or Wales, the High Court,

(b)   in relation to an appeal decided in Scotland, the Court of Session, and

(c)   in relation to an appeal decided in Northern Ireland, the High Court in Northern Ireland.

(10)   An application under subsection (1) to the Court of Session shall be to the Outer House.]

Amendment
Inserted by the Asylum and Immigration (Treatment of Claimants, etc) Act 2004, s 26(6); for transitional provisions see s 26(7), Sch 2, Pt 2 thereto. Date in force: 4 April 2005: see SI 2005/565, art 2(b); for transitional provisions in relation to pending appeals which were made to an adjudicator before 4 April 2005 and in relation to further appeals and applications in such cases see arts 3–9 thereof.

Subordinate Legislation
Civil Procedure (Amendment) Rules 2005, SI 2005/352 (made under sub-s (4)(a)).
Act of Sederunt (Rules of the Court of Session Amendment No 6) (Asylum and Immigration (Treatment of Claimants, etc) Act 2004) 2005, SSI 2005/198 (made under sub-s (4)(a)).

[103B   Appeal from Tribunal following reconsideration]

[(1) Where an appeal to the Tribunal has been reconsidered, a party to the appeal may bring a further appeal on a point of law to the appropriate appellate court.

(2) In subsection (1) the reference to reconsideration is to reconsideration pursuant to—

(a) an order under section 103A(1), or
(b) remittal to the Tribunal under this section or under section 103C or 103E.

(3) An appeal under subsection (1) may be brought only with the permission of—

(a) the Tribunal, or
(b) if the Tribunal refuses permission, the appropriate appellate court.

(4) On an appeal under subsection (1) the appropriate appellate court may—

(a) affirm the Tribunal's decision;
(b) make any decision which the Tribunal could have made;
(c) remit the case to the Tribunal;
(d) affirm a direction under section 87;
(e) vary a direction under section 87;
(f) give a direction which the Tribunal could have given under section 87.

(5) In this section "the appropriate appellate court" means—

(a) in relation to an appeal decided in England or Wales, the Court of Appeal,
(b) in relation to an appeal decided in Scotland, the Court of Session, and
(c) in relation to an appeal decided in Northern Ireland, the Court of Appeal in Northern Ireland.

(6) An appeal under subsection (1) to the Court of Session shall be to the Inner House.]

Amendment

Inserted by the Asylum and Immigration (Treatment of Claimants, etc) Act 2004, s 26(6); for transitional provisions see s 26(7), Sch 2, Pt 2 thereto. Date in force: 4 April 2005: see SI 2005/565, art 2(b); for transitional provisions in relation to pending appeals which were made to an adjudicator before 4 April 2005 and in relation to further appeals and applications in such cases see arts 3–9 thereof.

[103C   Appeal from Tribunal instead of reconsideration]

[(1) On an application under section 103A in respect of an appeal the appropriate court, if it thinks the appeal raises a question of law of such importance that it should be decided by the appropriate appellate court, may refer the appeal to that court.

(2) On a reference under subsection (1) the appropriate appellate court may—

(a) affirm the Tribunal's decision;
(b) make any decision which the Tribunal could have made;
(c) remit the case to the Tribunal;
(d) affirm a direction under section 87;
(e) vary a direction under section 87;
(f) give a direction which the Tribunal could have given under section 87;
(g) restore the application under section 103A to the appropriate court.

(3) In this section—

"the appropriate court" has the same meaning as in section 103A, and
"the appropriate appellate court" has the same meaning as in section 103B.

(4)   A reference under subsection (1) to the Court of Session shall be to the Inner House.]

Amendment
Inserted by the Asylum and Immigration (Treatment of Claimants, etc) Act 2004, s 26(6); for transitional provisions see s 26(7), Sch 2, Pt 2 thereto. Date in force: 4 April 2005: see SI 2005/565, art 2(b); for transitional provisions in relation to pending appeals which were made to an adjudicator before 4 April 2005 and in relation to further appeals and applications in such cases see arts 3–9 thereof.

[103D   Reconsideration: legal aid]

[(1)   On the application of an appellant under section 103A, the appropriate court may order that the appellant's costs in respect of the application under section 103A shall be paid out of the Community Legal Service Fund established under section 5 of the Access to Justice Act 1999 (c 22).

(2)   Subsection (3) applies where the Tribunal has decided an appeal following reconsideration pursuant to an order made—

(a)   under section 103A(1), and
(b)   on the application of the appellant.

(3)   The Tribunal may order that the appellant's costs—

(a)   in respect of the application for reconsideration, and
(b)   in respect of the reconsideration,

shall be paid out of that Fund.

(4)   The Secretary of State may make regulations about the exercise of the powers in subsections (1) and (3).

(5)   Regulations under subsection (4) may, in particular, make provision—

(a)   specifying or providing for the determination of the amount of payments;
(b)   about the persons to whom the payments are to be made;
(c)   restricting the exercise of the power (whether by reference to the prospects of success in respect of the appeal at the time when the application for reconsideration was made, the fact that a reference has been made under section 103C(1), the circumstances of the appellant, the nature of the appellant's legal representatives, or otherwise).

(6)   Regulations under subsection (4) may make provision—

(a)   conferring a function on the Legal Services Commission;
(b)   modifying a duty or power of the Legal Services Commission in respect of compliance with orders under subsection (3);
(c)   applying (with or without modifications), modifying or disapplying a provision of, or of anything done under, an enactment relating to the funding of legal services.

(7)   Before making regulations under subsection (4) the Secretary of State shall consult such persons as he thinks appropriate.

(8)   This section has effect only in relation to an appeal decided in—

(a)   England,
(b)   Wales, or
(c)   Northern Ireland.

(9)   In relation to an appeal decided in Northern Ireland this section shall have effect—

(a)　as if a reference to the Community Legal Service Fund were to the fund established under paragraph 4(2)(a) of Schedule 3 to the Access to Justice (Northern Ireland) Order 2003 (SI 2003/ 435 (NI 10)), and

(b)　with any other necessary modifications.]

Amendment
Inserted by the Asylum and Immigration (Treatment of Claimants, etc) Act 2004, s 26(6); for transitional provisions see s 26(7), Sch 2, Pt 2 thereto. Date in force (in relation to England and Wales): 4 April 2005: see SI 2005/565, art 2(b); for transitional provisions in relation to pending appeals which were made to an adjudicator before 4 April 2005 and in relation to further appeals and applications in such cases see arts 3–9 thereof.. Date in force (in relation to Northern Ireland): to be appointed: see the Asylum and Immigration (Treatment of Claimants, etc) Act 2004, s 48(3)–(6).

Subordinate Legislation
Community Legal Service (Asylum and Immigration Appeals) Regulations 2005, SI 2005/966.

[103E　Appeal from Tribunal sitting as panel]

[(1)　This section applies to a decision of the Tribunal on an appeal under section 82 or 83 where its jurisdiction is exercised by three or more legally qualified members.

(2)　A party to the appeal may bring a further appeal on a point of law to the appropriate appellate court.

(3)　An appeal under subsection (2) may be brought only with the permission of—

(a)　the Tribunal, or
(b)　if the Tribunal refuses permission, the appropriate appellate court.

(4)　On an appeal under subsection (2) the appropriate appellate court may—

(a)　affirm the Tribunal's decision;
(b)　make any decision which the Tribunal could have made;
(c)　remit the case to the Tribunal;
(d)　affirm a direction under section 87;
(e)　vary a direction under section 87;
(f)　give a direction which the Tribunal could have given under section 87.

(5)　In this section "the appropriate appellate court" means—

(a)　in relation to an appeal decided in England or Wales, the Court of Appeal,
(b)　in relation to an appeal decided in Scotland, the Court of Session, and
(c)　in relation to an appeal decided in Northern Ireland, the Court of Appeal in Northern Ireland.

(6)　A further appeal under subsection (2) to the Court of Session shall be to the Inner House.

(7)　In this section a reference to the Tribunal's decision on an appeal does not include a reference to—

(a)　a procedural, ancillary or preliminary decision, or
(b)　a decision following remittal under section 103B or 103C.]

Amendment
Inserted by the Asylum and Immigration (Treatment of Claimants, etc) Act 2004, s 26(6); for transitional provisions see s 26(7), Sch 2, Pt 2 thereto. Date in force: 4 April 2005: see SI 2005/565, art 2(b); for transitional provisions in relation to pending appeals which were made to an adjudicator before 4 April 2005 and in relation to further appeals and applications in such cases see arts 3–9 thereof.

104   Pending appeal

(1)   An appeal under section 82(1) is pending during the period—

   (a)   beginning when it is instituted, and
   (b)   ending when it is finally determined, withdrawn or abandoned (or when it
          lapses under section 99).

[(2)   An appeal under section 82(1) is not finally determined for the purposes of
subsection (1)(b) while—

   (a)   an application under section 103A(1) (other than an application out of time
          with permission) could be made or is awaiting determination,
   (b)   reconsideration of an appeal has been ordered under section 103A(1) and has
          not been completed,
   (c)   an appeal has been remitted to the Tribunal and is awaiting determination,
   (d)   an application under section 103B or 103E for permission to appeal (other
          than an application out of time with permission) could be made or is awaiting
          determination,
   (e)   an appeal under section 103B or 103E is awaiting determination, or
   (f)   a reference under section 103C is awaiting determination.]

(3)   …

(4)   An appeal under section 82(1) shall be treated as abandoned if the appellant—

   (a)   is granted leave to enter or remain in the United Kingdom, or
   (b)   leaves the United Kingdom.

(5)   An appeal under section 82(2)(a), (c), (d), (e) or (f) shall be treated as finally
determined if a deportation order is made against the appellant.

Appointment
Appointment: 1 April 2003: see SI 2003/754, art 2(1), Sch 1; for transitional provisions see
art 3(1) thereof.

Amendment
Sub-s (2): substituted by the Asylum and Immigration (Treatment of Claimants, etc) Act 2004,
s 26(7), Sch 2, Pt 1, paras 16, 20(a); for transitional provisions see s 26(7), Sch 2, Pt 2 thereto.
Date in force: 4 April 2005: see SI 2005/565, art 2(d); for transitional provisions in relation to
pending appeals which were made to an adjudicator before 4 April 2005 and in relation to further
appeals and applications in such cases see arts 3–9 thereof.
Sub-s (3): repealed by the Asylum and Immigration (Treatment of Claimants, etc) Act 2004,
ss 26(7), 47, Sch 2, Pt 1, paras 16, 20(b), Sch 4. Date in force: 4 April 2005: see SI 2005/565,
art 2(d); for transitional provisions in relation to pending appeals which were made to an
adjudicator before 4 April 2005 and in relation to further appeals and applications in such cases
see arts 3–9 thereof.

105   Notice of immigration decision

(1)   The Secretary of State may make regulations requiring a person to be given
written notice where an immigration decision is taken in respect of him.

(2)   The regulations may, in particular, provide that a notice under subsection (1) of a
decision against which the person is entitled to appeal under section 82(1) must state—

   (a)   that there is a right of appeal under that section, and
   (b)   how and when that right may be exercised.

(3)   The regulations may make provision (which may include presumptions) about
service.

Appointment
Appointment: 1 April 2003: see SI 2003/754, art 2(1), Sch 1.

Subordinate Legislation
Immigration (Notices) Regulations 2003, SI 2003/658.

106   Rules

(1)   The Lord Chancellor may make rules—

  (a)   regulating the exercise of the right of appeal under section 82 [or 83 or by virtue of section 109];
  (b)   prescribing procedure to be followed in connection with proceedings under section 82 [or 83 or by virtue of section 109].

[(1A)   In making rules under subsection (1) the Lord Chancellor shall aim to ensure—

  (a)   that the rules are designed to ensure that proceedings before the Tribunal are handled as fairly, quickly and efficiently as possible, and
  (b)   that the rules where appropriate confer on members of the Tribunal responsibility for ensuring that proceedings before the Tribunal are handled as fairly, quickly and efficiently as possible.]

(2)   In particular, rules under subsection (1)—

  (a)   must entitle an appellant to be legally represented at any hearing of his appeal;
  (b)   may enable or require an appeal to be determined without a hearing;
  (c)   may enable or require an appeal to be dismissed without substantive consideration where practice or procedure has not been complied with;
  (d)   may enable or require [the Tribunal] to treat an appeal as abandoned in specified circumstances;
  (e)   may enable or require ... the Tribunal to determine an appeal in the absence of parties in specified circumstances;
  (f)   may enable or require ... the Tribunal to determine an appeal by reference only to written submissions in specified circumstances;
  (g)   may make provision about the adjournment of an appeal by [the Tribunal] (which may include provision prohibiting [the Tribunal] from adjourning except in specified circumstances);
  (h)   may make provision about the treatment of adjourned appeals by [the Tribunal] (which may include provision requiring [the Tribunal] to determine an appeal within a specified period);
  (i)   may make provision about the use of electronic communication in the course of or in connection with a hearing;
  (j)   ...
  (k)   ...
  (l)   may enable the Tribunal to set aside a decision of the Tribunal;
  (m)   must make provision about the consolidation of appeals ...;
  (n)   may make provision (which may include presumptions) about service;
  (o)   may confer ancillary powers on ... the Tribunal;
  (p)   may confer a discretion on ... the Tribunal;
  (q)   may require ... the Tribunal to give notice of a determination to a specified person;
  (r)   may require or enable notice of a determination to be given on behalf of ... the Tribunal;
  (s)   may make provision about the grant of bail by ... the Tribunal (which may, in particular, include provision which applies or is similar to any enactment);
  [(t)   may make provision about the number of members exercising the Tribunal's jurisdiction;

    (u)   may make provision about the allocation of proceedings among members of the Tribunal (which may include provision for transfer);

    (v)   may make provision about reconsideration of a decision pursuant to an order under section 103A(1) (which may, in particular, include provision about the action that may be taken on reconsideration and about the matters and evidence to which the Tribunal may have regard);

    (w)   shall provide that a party to an appeal is to be treated as having received notice of the Tribunal's decision, unless the contrary is shown, at such time as may be specified in, or determined in accordance with, the rules;

    (x)   may make provision about proceedings under paragraph 30 of Schedule 2 to the Asylum and Immigration (Treatment of Claimants, etc) Act 2004 (transitional filter of applications for reconsideration from High Court to Tribunal) (and may, in particular, make provision of a kind that may be made by rules of court under section 103A(5)(b));

    (y)   may make provision about the form and content of decisions of the Tribunal].

(3)   Rules under subsection (1)—

    (a)   may enable ... the Tribunal to make an award of costs or expenses,

    (b)   may make provision (which may include provision conferring discretion on a court) for the taxation or assessment of costs or expenses,

    (c)   may make provision about interest on an award of costs or expenses (which may include provision conferring a discretion or providing for interest to be calculated in accordance with provision made by the rules),

    (d)   may enable ... the Tribunal to disallow all or part of a representative's costs or expenses,

    (e)   may enable ... the Tribunal to require a representative to pay specified costs or expenses, and

    [(f)   may enable the Tribunal to certify that an appeal had no merit (and shall make provision for the consequences of the issue of a certificate)].

(4)   A person commits an offence if without reasonable excuse he fails to comply with a requirement imposed in accordance with rules under subsection (1) to attend before ... the Tribunal—

    (a)   to give evidence, or

    (b)   to produce a document.

(5)   A person who is guilty of an offence under subsection (4) shall be liable on summary conviction to a fine not exceeding level 3 on the standard scale.

Appointment
Appointment: 1 April 2003: see SI 2003/754, art 2(1), Sch 1.

Amendment
Sub-s (1): in para (a) words "or 83 or by virtue of section 109" in square brackets substituted by the Asylum and Immigration (Treatment of Claimants, etc) Act 2004, s 26(7), Sch 2, Pt 1, paras 16, 21(a). Date in force: 4 April 2005: see SI 2005/565, art 2(d); for transitional provisions in relation to pending appeals which were made to an adjudicator before 4 April 2005 and in relation to further appeals and applications in such cases see arts 3–9 thereof.
Sub-s (1): in para (b) words "or 83 or by virtue of section 109" in square brackets substituted by the Asylum and Immigration (Treatment of Claimants, etc) Act 2004, s 26(7), Sch 2, Pt 1, paras 16, 21(b). Date in force: 4 April 2005: see SI 2005/565, art 2(d); for transitional provisions in relation to pending appeals which were made to an adjudicator before 4 April 2005 and in relation to further appeals and applications in such cases see arts 3–9 thereof.
Sub-s (1A): inserted by the Asylum and Immigration (Treatment of Claimants, etc) Act 2004, s 26(7), Sch 2, Pt 1, paras 16, 21(c); for transitional provisions see s 26(7), Sch 2, Pt 2 thereto. Date in force: 4 April 2005: see SI 2005/565, art 2(d); for transitional provisions in relation to pending appeals which were made to an adjudicator before 4 April 2005 and in relation to further appeals and applications in such cases see arts 3–9 thereof.

Sub-s (2): in para (d) words "the Tribunal" in square brackets substituted by the Asylum and Immigration (Treatment of Claimants, etc) Act 2004, s 26(7), Sch 2, Pt 1, paras 16, 21(d); for transitional provisions see s 26(7), Sch 2, Pt 2 thereto. Date in force: 4 April 2005: see SI 2005/565, art 2(d); for transitional provisions in relation to pending appeals which were made to an adjudicator before 4 April 2005 and in relation to further appeals and applications in such cases see arts 3–9 thereof.

Sub-s (2): in paras (e), (f) words omitted repealed by the Asylum and Immigration (Treatment of Claimants, etc) Act 2004, ss 26(7), 47, Sch 2, Pt 1, paras 16, 21(e), Sch 4. Date in force: 4 April 2005: see SI 2005/565, art 2(d); for transitional provisions in relation to pending appeals which were made to an adjudicator before 4 April 2005 and in relation to further appeals and applications in such cases see arts 3–9 thereof.

Sub-s (2): in para (g) words "the Tribunal" in square brackets in both places they occur substituted by the Asylum and Immigration (Treatment of Claimants, etc) Act 2004, s 26(7), Sch 2, Pt 1, paras 16, 21(f); for transitional provisions see s 26(7), Sch 2, Pt 2 thereto. Date in force: 4 April 2005: see SI 2005/565, art 2(d); for transitional provisions in relation to pending appeals which were made to an adjudicator before 4 April 2005 and in relation to further appeals and applications in such cases see arts 3–9 thereof.

Sub-s (2): in para (h) words "the Tribunal" in square brackets in both places they occur substituted by the Asylum and Immigration (Treatment of Claimants, etc) Act 2004, s 26(7), Sch 2, Pt 1, paras 16, 21(g); for transitional provisions see s 26(7), Sch 2, Pt 2 thereto. Date in force: 4 April 2005: see SI 2005/565, art 2(d); for transitional provisions in relation to pending appeals which were made to an adjudicator before 4 April 2005 and in relation to further appeals and applications in such cases see arts 3–9 thereof.

Sub-s (2): paras (j), (k) repealed by the Asylum and Immigration (Treatment of Claimants, etc) Act 2004, ss 26(7), 47, Sch 2, Pt 1, paras 16, 21(h), Sch 4. Date in force: 4 April 2005: see SI 2005/565, art 2(d); for transitional provisions in relation to pending appeals which were made to an adjudicator before 4 April 2005 and in relation to further appeals and applications in such cases see arts 3–9 thereof.

Sub-s (2): in para (m) words omitted repealed by the Asylum and Immigration (Treatment of Claimants, etc) Act 2004, ss 26(7), 47, Sch 2, Pt 1, paras 16, 21(i), Sch 4. Date in force: 4 April 2005: see SI 2005/565, art 2(d); for transitional provisions in relation to pending appeals which were made to an adjudicator before 4 April 2005 and in relation to further appeals and applications in such cases see arts 3–9 thereof.

Sub-s (2): in para (o) words omitted repealed by the Asylum and Immigration (Treatment of Claimants, etc) Act 2004, ss 26(7), 47, Sch 2, Pt 1, paras 16, 21(j), Sch 4. Date in force: 4 April 2005: see SI 2005/565, art 2(d); for transitional provisions in relation to pending appeals which were made to an adjudicator before 4 April 2005 and in relation to further appeals and applications in such cases see arts 3–9 thereof.

Sub-s (2): in para (p) words omitted repealed by the Asylum and Immigration (Treatment of Claimants, etc) Act 2004, ss 26(7), 47, Sch 2, Pt 1, paras 16, 21(k), Sch 4. Date in force: 4 April 2005: see SI 2005/565, art 2(d); for transitional provisions in relation to pending appeals which were made to an adjudicator before 4 April 2005 and in relation to further appeals and applications in such cases see arts 3–9 thereof.

Sub-s (2): in para (q) words omitted repealed by the Asylum and Immigration (Treatment of Claimants, etc) Act 2004, ss 26(7), 47, Sch 2, Pt 1, paras 16, 21(l), Sch 4. Date in force: 4 April 2005: see SI 2005/565, art 2(d); for transitional provisions in relation to pending appeals which were made to an adjudicator before 4 April 2005 and in relation to further appeals and applications in such cases see arts 3–9 thereof.

Sub-s (2): in para (r) words omitted repealed by the Asylum and Immigration (Treatment of Claimants, etc) Act 2004, ss 26(7), 47, Sch 2, Pt 1, paras 16, 21(m), Sch 4. Date in force: 4 April 2005: see SI 2005/565, art 2(d); for transitional provisions in relation to pending appeals which were made to an adjudicator before 4 April 2005 and in relation to further appeals and applications in such cases see arts 3–9 thereof.

Sub-s (2): in para (s) words omitted repealed by the Asylum and Immigration (Treatment of Claimants, etc) Act 2004, ss 26(7), 47, Sch 2, Pt 1, paras 16, 21(n), Sch 4. Date in force: 4 April 2005: see SI 2005/565, art 2(d); for transitional provisions in relation to pending appeals which were made to an adjudicator before 4 April 2005 and in relation to further appeals and applications in such cases see arts 3–9 thereof.

Sub-s (2): paras (t)–(y) inserted by the Asylum and Immigration (Treatment of Claimants, etc) Act 2004, s 26(7), Sch 2, Pt 1, paras 16, 21(o); for transitional provisions see s 26(7), Sch 2, Pt 2 thereto. Date in force: 4 April 2005: see SI 2005/565, art 2(d); for transitional provisions in relation to pending appeals which were made to an adjudicator before 4 April 2005 and in relation to further appeals and applications in such cases see arts 3–9 thereof.

Sub-s (3): in para (a) words omitted repealed by the Asylum and Immigration (Treatment of Claimants, etc) Act 2004, ss 26(7), 47, Sch 2, Pt 1, paras 16, 21(p), Sch 4. Date in force: 4 April 2005: see SI 2005/565, art 2(d); for transitional provisions in relation to pending appeals which were made to an adjudicator before 4 April 2005 and in relation to further appeals and applications in such cases see arts 3–9 thereof.

Sub-s (3): in para (d) words omitted repealed by the Asylum and Immigration (Treatment of Claimants, etc) Act 2004, ss 26(7), 47, Sch 2, Pt 1, paras 16, 21(q), Sch 4. Date in force: 4 April 2005: see SI 2005/565, art 2(d); for transitional provisions in relation to pending appeals which were made to an adjudicator before 4 April 2005 and in relation to further appeals and applications in such cases see arts 3–9 thereof.

Sub-s (3): in para (e) words omitted repealed by the Asylum and Immigration (Treatment of Claimants, etc) Act 2004, ss 26(7), 47, Sch 2, Pt 1, paras 16, 21(r), Sch 4. Date in force: 4 April 2005: see SI 2005/565, art 2(d); for transitional provisions in relation to pending appeals which were made to an adjudicator before 4 April 2005 and in relation to further appeals and applications in such cases see arts 3–9 thereof.

Sub-s (3): para (f) substituted by the Asylum and Immigration (Treatment of Claimants, etc) Act 2004, s 26(7), Sch 2, Pt 1, paras 16, 21(s); for transitional provisions see s 26(7), Sch 2, Pt 2 thereto. Date in force: 4 April 2005: see SI 2005/565, art 2(d); for transitional provisions in relation to pending appeals which were made to an adjudicator before 4 April 2005 and in relation to further appeals and applications in such cases see arts 3–9 thereof.

Sub-s (4): words omitted repealed by the Asylum and Immigration (Treatment of Claimants, etc) Act 2004, ss 26(7), 47, Sch 2, Pt 1, paras 16, 21(t), Sch 4. Date in force: 4 April 2005: see SI 2005/565, art 2(d); for transitional provisions in relation to pending appeals which were made to an adjudicator before 4 April 2005 and in relation to further appeals and applications in such cases see arts 3–9 thereof.

Subordinate Legislation

Immigration and Asylum Appeals (Fast Track Procedure) (Amendment) Rules 2004, SI 2004/1891 (made under sub-ss (1)–(3)).

Asylum and Immigration Tribunal (Procedure) Rules 2005, SI 2005/230 (made under sub-ss (1)–(3)).

Asylum and Immigration Tribunal (Fast Track Procedure) Rules 2005, SI 2005/560 (made under sub-ss (1), (1A), (2), (3)).

Asylum and Immigration Tribunal (Procedure) (Amendment) Rules 2005, SI 2005/569 (made under sub-ss (1)–(3)).

107   Practice directions

(1)   The President of [the Tribunal] may give directions as to the practice to be followed by the Tribunal.

(2)   ...

[(3)   A practice direction may, in particular, require the Tribunal to treat a specified decision of the Tribunal as authoritative in respect of a particular matter.]

Appointment

Appointment: 1 April 2003: see SI 2003/754, art 2(1), Sch 1.

Amendment

Sub-s (1): words "the Tribunal" in square brackets substituted by the Asylum and Immigration (Treatment of Claimants, etc) Act 2004, s 26(7), Sch 2, Pt 1, paras 16, 22(1)(a); for transitional provisions see s 26(7), Sch 2, Pt 2 thereto. Date in force: 4 April 2005: see SI 2005/565, art 2(d); for transitional provisions in relation to pending appeals which were made to an adjudicator before 4 April 2005 and in relation to further appeals and applications in such cases see arts 3–9 thereof.

Sub-s (2): repealed by the Asylum and Immigration (Treatment of Claimants, etc) Act 2004, ss 26(7), 47, Sch 2, Pt 1, paras 16, 22(1)(b), Sch 4. Date in force: 4 April 2005: see SI 2005/565, art 2(d); for transitional provisions in relation to pending appeals which were made to an adjudicator before 4 April 2005 and in relation to further appeals and applications in such cases see arts 3–9 thereof.

Sub-s (3): inserted by the Asylum and Immigration (Treatment of Claimants, etc) Act 2004, s 26(7), Sch 2, Pt 1, paras 16, 21(1)(c), (2); for transitional provisions see s 26(7), Sch 2, Pt 2 thereto. Date in force: 4 April 2005: see SI 2005/565, art 2(d); for transitional provisions in relation to pending appeals which were made to an adjudicator before 4 April 2005 and in relation to further appeals and applications in such cases see arts 3–9 thereof.

108 Forged document: proceedings in private

(1) This section applies where it is alleged—

    (a) that a document relied on by a party to an appeal under section 82 [or 83] is a forgery, and

    (b) that disclosure to that party of a matter relating to the detection of the forgery would be contrary to the public interest.

(2) [The Tribunal]—

    (a) must investigate the allegation in private, and

    (b) may proceed in private so far as necessary to prevent disclosure of the matter referred to in subsection (1)(b).

Appointment
Appointment: 1 April 2003: see SI 2003/754, art 2(1), Sch 1.

Amendment
Sub-s (1): in para (a) words "or 83" in square brackets substituted by the Asylum and Immigration (Treatment of Claimants, etc) Act 2004, s 26(7), Sch 2, Pt 1, paras 16, 23(a). Date in force: 4 April 2005: see SI 2005/565, art 2(d); for transitional provisions in relation to pending appeals which were made to an adjudicator before 4 April 2005 and in relation to further appeals and applications in such cases see arts 3–9 thereof.
Sub-s (2): words "The Tribunal" in square brackets substituted by the Asylum and Immigration (Treatment of Claimants, etc) Act 2004, s 26(7), Sch 2, Pt 1, paras 16, 23(b); for transitional provisions see s 26(7), Sch 2, Pt 2 thereto. Date in force: 4 April 2005: see SI 2005/565, art 2(d); for transitional provisions in relation to pending appeals which were made to an adjudicator before 4 April 2005 and in relation to further appeals and applications in such cases see arts 3–9 thereof.

General

109 European Union and European Economic Area

(1) Regulations may provide for, or make provision about, an appeal against an immigration decision taken in respect of a person who has or claims to have a right under any of the Community Treaties.

(2) The regulations may—

    (a) apply a provision of this Act or the Special Immigration Appeals Commission Act 1997 (c 68) with or without modification;

    (b) make provision similar to a provision made by or under this Act or that Act;

    (c) disapply or modify the effect of a provision of this Act or that Act.

(3) In subsection (1) "immigration decision" means a decision about—

    (a) a person's entitlement to enter or remain in the United Kingdom, or

    (b) removal of a person from the United Kingdom.

Appointment
Appointment: 1 April 2003: see SI 2003/754, art 2(1), Sch 1.

Appendix 1   Legislation and materials

Subordinate Legislation
Immigration (European Economic Area) (Amendment No 2) Regulations 2003, SI 2003/3188.
Immigration (European Economic Area) and Accession (Amendment) Regulations 2004, SI 2004/1236.
Immigration (European Economic Area) (Amendment) Regulations 2005, SI 2005/47.
Immigration (European Economic Area) (Amendment) (No 2) Regulations 2005, SI 2005/671.

110   Grants

(1)   The Secretary of State may make a grant to a voluntary organisation which provides—

(a)   advice or assistance to persons who have a right of appeal under this Part;
(b)   other services for the welfare of those persons.

(2)   A grant under this section may be subject to terms or conditions (which may include conditions as to repayment).

Appointment
Appointment: 1 April 2003: see SI 2003/754, art 2(1), Sch 1.

111   Monitor of certification of claims as unfounded

(1)   The Secretary of State shall appoint a person to monitor the use of the powers under sections 94(2) and 115(1).

(2)   The person appointed under this section shall make a report to the Secretary of State—

(a)   once in each calendar year, and
(b)   on such occasions as the Secretary of State may request.

(3)   Where the Secretary of State receives a report under subsection (2)(a) he shall lay a copy before Parliament as soon as is reasonably practicable.

(4)   The person appointed under this section shall hold and vacate office in accordance with the terms of his appointment (which may include provision about retirement, resignation or dismissal).

(5)   The Secretary of State may—

(a)   pay fees and allowances to the person appointed under this section;
(b)   defray expenses of the person appointed under this section.

(6)   A person who is employed within a government department may not be appointed under this section.

Appointment
Appointment: 1 April 2003: see SI 2003/754, art 2(1), Sch 1.

112   Regulations, &c

(1)   Regulations under this Part shall be made by the Secretary of State.

(2)   Regulations and rules under this Part[, other than regulations under section 103D(4),]—

(a)   must be made by statutory instrument, and
(b)   shall be subject to annulment in pursuance of a resolution of either House of Parliament.

(3)   Regulations and rules under this Part—

    (a)   may make provision which applies generally or only in a specified case or in specified circumstances,

    (b)   may make different provision for different cases or circumstances,

    (c)   may include consequential, transitional or incidental provision, and

    (d)   may include savings.

[(3A)   An order under section 88A—

    (a)   must be made by statutory instrument,

    (b)   may not be made unless a draft has been laid before and approved by resolution of each House of Parliament, and

    (c)   may include transitional provision.]

(4)   An order under section 94(5) or 115(8)—

    (a)   must be made by statutory instrument,

    (b)   may not be made unless a draft has been laid before and approved by resolution of each House of Parliament, and

    (c)   may include transitional provision.

(5)   An order under section 94(6) or 115(9)—

    (a)   must be made by statutory instrument,

    (b)   shall be subject to annulment in pursuance of a resolution of either House of Parliament, and

    (c)   may include transitional provision.

[(5A)   If an instrument makes provision under section 94(5) and 94(6)—

    (a)   subsection (4)(b) above shall apply, and

    (b)   subsection (5)(b) above shall not apply.]

[(6)   Regulations under section 103D(4)—

    (a)   must be made by statutory instrument, and

    (b)   shall not be made unless a draft has been laid before and approved by resolution of each House of Parliament.

(7)   An order under paragraph 4 of Schedule 4—

    (a)   may include consequential or incidental provision (which may include provision amending, or providing for the construction of, a reference in an enactment, instrument or other document to a member of the Asylum and Immigration Tribunal),

    (b)   must be made by statutory instrument, and

    (c)   shall be subject to annulment in pursuance of a resolution of either House of Parliament.]

Appointment
Appointment: 10 February 2003: see SI 2003/249, art 2, Schedule.

Amendment
Sub-s (2): words ", other than regulations under section 103D(4)," in square brackets inserted by the Asylum and Immigration (Treatment of Claimants, etc) Act 2004, s 26(7), Sch 2, Pt 1, paras 16, 24(1), (2). Date in force: 4 April 2005: see SI 2005/565, art 2(d); for transitional provisions in relation to pending appeals which were made to an adjudicator before 4 April 2005 and in relation to further appeals and applications in such cases see arts 3–9 thereof.
Sub-s (3A): inserted by the Asylum and Immigration (Treatment of Claimants, etc) Act 2004, s 29(2). Date in force: 1 October 2004: see SI 2004/2523, art 2, Schedule.
Sub-s (5A): inserted by the Asylum and Immigration (Treatment of Claimants, etc) Act 2004, s 27(8). Date in force: 1 October 2004: see SI 2004/2523, art 2, Schedule.
Sub-ss (6), (7): substituted, for sub-s (6) as originally enacted, by the Asylum and Immigration (Treatment of Claimants, etc) Act 2004, s 26(7), Sch 2, Pt 1, paras 16, 24(1), (3); for transitional

provisions see s 26(7), Sch 2, Pt 2 thereto. Date in force: 4 April 2005: see SI 2005/565, art 2(d); for transitional provisions in relation to pending appeals which were made to an adjudicator before 4 April 2005 and in relation to further appeals and applications in such cases see arts 3–9 thereof.

113   Interpretation

(1)   In this Part, unless a contrary intention appears—

"asylum claim" means a claim made by a person to the Secretary of State at a place designated by the Secretary of State that to remove the person from or require him to leave the United Kingdom would breach the United Kingdom's obligations under the Refugee Convention,

"entry clearance" has the meaning given by section 33(1) of the Immigration Act 1971 (c 77) (interpretation),

"human rights claim" means a claim made by a person to the Secretary of State at a place designated by the Secretary of State that to remove the person from or require him to leave the United Kingdom would be unlawful under section 6 of the Human Rights Act 1998 (c 42) (public authority not to act contrary to Convention) as being incompatible with his Convention rights,

"the Human Rights Convention" has the same meaning as "the Convention" in the Human Rights Act 1998 and "Convention rights" shall be construed in accordance with section 1 of that Act,

"illegal entrant" has the meaning given by section 33(1) of the Immigration Act 1971,

"immigration rules" means rules under section 1(4) of that Act (general immigration rules),

"prescribed" means prescribed by regulations,

"the Refugee Convention" means the Convention relating to the Status of Refugees done at Geneva on 28th July 1951 and its Protocol,

"visitor" means a visitor in accordance with immigration rules, and

"work permit" has the meaning given by section 33(1) of the Immigration Act 1971 (c 77) (interpretation).

(2)   A reference to varying leave to enter or remain in the United Kingdom does not include a reference to adding, varying or revoking a condition of leave.

Appointment
Appointment: 10 February 2003: see SI 2003/249, art 2, Schedule.

114   Repeal

(1)   Part IV of the Immigration and Asylum Act 1999 (c 33) (appeals) shall cease to have effect.

(2)   Schedule 6 (which makes transitional provision in connection with the repeal of Part IV of that Act and its replacement by this Part) shall have effect.

(3)   Schedule 7 (consequential amendments) shall have effect.

Initial Commencement
Sub-s (3): Royal Assent (for certain purposes): 7 November 2002: see s 162(2)(w).
Sub-ss (1), (2): To be appointed: see s 162(1).
Sub-s (3): To be appointed (for remaining purposes): see s 162(1).

Appointment
Sub-ss (1), (2): Appointment: 1 April 2003: see SI 2003/754, art 2(1), Sch 1; for transitional provisions see art 3, Sch 2, para 6(4) thereto.
Sub-s (3): Appointment (for certain purposes): 10 February 2003: see SI 2003/1, art 2, Schedule.

115   Appeal from within United Kingdom: unfounded human rights or asylum claim: transitional provision

(1)   A person may not bring an appeal under section 65 or 69 of the Immigration and Asylum Act 1999 (human rights and asylum) while in the United Kingdom if—

    (a)   the Secretary of State certifies that the appeal relates to a human rights claim or an asylum claim which is clearly unfounded, and

    (b)   the person does not have another right of appeal while in the United Kingdom under Part IV of that Act.

(2)   A person while in the United Kingdom may not bring an appeal under section 69 of that Act, or raise a question which relates to the Human Rights Convention under section 77 of that Act, if the Secretary of State certifies that—

    (a)   it is proposed to remove the person to a country of which he is not a national or citizen, and

    (b)   there is no reason to believe that the person's rights under the Human Rights Convention will be breached in that country.

(3)   A person while in the United Kingdom may not bring an appeal under section 65 of that Act (human rights) if the Secretary of State certifies that—

    (a)   it is proposed to remove the person to a country of which he is not a national or citizen, and

    (b)   there is no reason to believe that the person's rights under the Human Rights Convention will be breached in that country.

(4)   In determining whether a person in relation to whom a certificate has been issued under subsection (2) or (3) may be removed from the United Kingdom, the country specified in the certificate is to be regarded as—

    (a)   a place where a person's life and liberty is not threatened by reason of his race, religion, nationality, membership of a particular social group, or political opinion, and

    (b)   a place from which a person will not be sent to another country otherwise than in accordance with the Refugee Convention.

(5)   Where a person in relation to whom a certificate is issued under this section subsequently brings an appeal or raises a question under section 65, 69 or 77 of that Act while outside the United Kingdom, the appeal or question shall be considered as if he had not been removed from the United Kingdom.

(6)   If the Secretary of State is satisfied that a person who makes a human rights claim or an asylum claim is entitled to reside in a State listed in subsection (7), he shall issue a certificate under subsection (1) unless satisfied that the claim is not clearly unfounded.

(7)   Those States are—

    (a)   the Republic of Cyprus,

    (b)   the Czech Republic,

    (c)   the Republic of Estonia,

    (d)   the Republic of Hungary,

    (e)   the Republic of Latvia,

    (f)   the Republic of Lithuania,

    (g)   the Republic of Malta,

    (h)   the Republic of Poland,

    (i)   the Slovak Republic,

    (j)   the Republic of Slovenia,

    [(k)   the Republic of Albania,

    (l)   Bulgaria,
    (m) Serbia and Montenegro,
    (n)   Jamaica,
    (o)   Macedonia,
    (p)   the Republic of Moldova, and
    (q)   Romania].

(8)   The Secretary of State may by order add a State, or part of a State, to the list in subsection (7) if satisfied that—

    (a)   there is in general in that State or part no serious risk of persecution of persons entitled to reside in that State or part, and
    (b)   removal to that State or part of persons entitled to reside there will not in general contravene the United Kingdom's obligations under the Human Rights Convention.

(9)   The Secretary of State may by order remove from the list in subsection (7) a State or part added under subsection (8).

(10)   In this section "asylum claim" and "human rights claim" have the meanings given by section 113 but—

    (a)   a reference to a claim in that section shall be treated as including a reference to an allegation, and
    (b)   a reference in that section to making a claim at a place designated by the Secretary of State shall be ignored.

Initial Commencement
Royal Assent: 7 November 2002: see s 162(2)(w).

Amendment
Sub-s (7): paras (k)–(q) inserted by SI 2003/970, art 4. Date in force: 1 April 2003: see SI 2003/970, art 2(1).

See Further
See further, in relation to to continued application of this section in respect of any person who made an asylum claim or human rights claim (as defined in sub-s (10) hereof) on or after 1 April 2003: the Nationality, Immigration and Asylum Act 2002 (Commencement No 4) Order 2003, SI 2003/754, art 3(2), Sch 2, para 1(5).

Subordinate Legislation
Asylum (Designated States) Order 2003, SI 2003/970 (made under sub-s (8)).

116   Special Immigration Appeals Commission: Community Legal Service

In paragraph 2(1) of Schedule 2 to the Access to Justice Act 1999 (c 22) (Community Legal Service: courts and tribunals in which advocacy may be funded) the following shall be inserted after paragraph (h) (and before the word "or" which appears immediately after that paragraph)—

"(ha)the Special Immigration Appeals Commission,".

Appointment
Appointment: 1 April 2003: see SI 2003/754, art 2(1), Sch 1.

117   Northern Ireland appeals: legal aid

(1)   In Part 1 of Schedule 1 to the Legal Aid, Advice and Assistance (Northern Ireland) Order 1981 (SI 1981/228 (NI 8)) (proceedings for which legal aid may be given under Part II of that Order) the following shall be inserted after paragraph 6—

"6A   Proceedings before an adjudicator appointed for the purposes of Part 5 of the Nationality, Immigration and Asylum Act 2002, the Immigration Appeal Tribunal or the Special Immigration Appeals Commission."

(2)   The amendment made by subsection (1) is without prejudice to the power to make regulations under Article 10(2) of the Legal Aid, Advice and Assistance (Northern Ireland) Order 1981 amending or revoking the provision inserted by that subsection.

Appointment
Appointment: 1 April 2003: see SI 2003/754, art 2(1), Sch 1; for transitional provisions see art 3(1) thereof.

Amendment
Repealed by SI 2003/435, art 49(2), Sch 5. Date in force: to be appointed: see SI 2003/435, art 1(2).

PART 6
IMMIGRATION PROCEDURE

Applications

118   Leave pending decision on variation application

The following shall be substituted for section 3C of the Immigration Act 1971 (c 77) (continuation of leave to enter or remain pending decision on application for variation)—

"3C   Continuation of leave pending variation decision

(1)   This section applies if—

    (a)   a person who has limited leave to enter or remain in the United Kingdom applies to the Secretary of State for variation of the leave,

    (b)   the application for variation is made before the leave expires, and

    (c)   the leave expires without the application for variation having been decided.

(2)   The leave is extended by virtue of this section during any period when—

    (a)   the application for variation is neither decided nor withdrawn,

    (b)   an appeal under section 82(1) of the Nationality, Asylum and Immigration Act 2002 could be brought against the decision on the application for variation (ignoring any possibility of an appeal out of time with permission), or

    (c)   an appeal under that section against that decision is pending (within the meaning of section 104 of that Act).

(3)   Leave extended by virtue of this section shall lapse if the applicant leaves the United Kingdom.

(4)   A person may not make an application for variation of his leave to enter or remain in the United Kingdom while that leave is extended by virtue of this section.

(5)   But subsection (4) does not prevent the variation of the application mentioned in subsection (1)(a).

(6)   In this section a reference to an application being decided is a reference to notice of the decision being given in accordance with regulations under section 105 of that Act (notice of immigration decision)."

Appointment
Appointment: 1 April 2003: see SI 2003/754, art 2(1), Sch 1; for transitional provisions see art 3(2), Sch 2, para 2(2) thereto (as amended by SI 2003/1040, art 2).

119   Deemed leave on cancellation of notice

In paragraph 6(3) of Schedule 2 to the Immigration Act 1971 (c 77) (deemed leave on cancellation of notice of refusal) after "and the immigration officer does not at the same time give him indefinite or limited leave to enter" there shall be inserted "or require him to submit to further examination".

Appointment
Appointment: 8 January 2003: see SI 2002/2811, art 2, Schedule.

120   Requirement to state additional grounds for application

(1)   This section applies to a person if—

   (a)   he has made an application to enter or remain in the United Kingdom, or
   (b)   an immigration decision within the meaning of section 82 has been taken or may be taken in respect of him.

(2)   The Secretary of State or an immigration officer may by notice in writing require the person to state—

   (a)   his reasons for wishing to enter or remain in the United Kingdom,
   (b)   any grounds on which he should be permitted to enter or remain in the United Kingdom, and
   (c)   any grounds on which he should not be removed from or required to leave the United Kingdom.

(3)   A statement under subsection (2) need not repeat reasons or grounds set out in—

   (a)   the application mentioned in subsection (1)(a), or
   (b)   an application to which the immigration decision mentioned in subsection (1)(b) relates.

Appointment
Appointment: 1 April 2003: see SI 2003/754, art 2(1), Sch 1.

121   Compliance with procedure

The following shall be inserted after section 31A(3) of the Immigration Act 1971 (procedural requirements for application)—

"(3A)   Regulations under this section may provide that a failure to comply with a specified requirement of the regulations—

   (a)   invalidates an application,
   (b)   does not invalidate an application, or
   (c)   invalidates an application in specified circumstances (which may be described wholly or partly by reference to action by the applicant, the Secretary of State, an immigration officer or another person)."

Appointment
Appointment: 10 February 2003: see SI 2003/1, art 2, Schedule.

Work permit

122   Fee for work permit, &c

(1)   The Secretary of State may by regulations require an application for an immigration employment document to be accompanied by a fee prescribed in the regulations.

(2) In subsection (1) "immigration employment document" means—

(a) a work permit, and

(b) any other document which relates to employment and is issued for a purpose of immigration rules or in connection with leave to enter or remain in the United Kingdom.

(3) Regulations under subsection (1)—

(a) may make provision which applies generally or only in specified cases or circumstances (or except in specified cases or circumstances), and

(b) may make different provision for different cases or circumstances.

(4) In particular, regulations by virtue of subsection (3)(a) which create an exception may make provision by reference to an arrangement with the Secretary of State under which a payment is made in respect of—

(a) a specified number or class of applications, or

(b) a specified period of time.

(5) Regulations under subsection (1)—

(a) must be made by statutory instrument, and

(b) shall be subject to annulment in pursuance of a resolution of either House of Parliament.

(6) In this section—

"immigration rules" has the meaning given by section 33(1) of the Immigration Act 1971 (c 77) (interpretation), and

"work permit" has the meaning given by that section.

Appointment
Appointment: 10 February 2003: see SI 2003/1, art 2, Schedule.

Subordinate Legislation
Immigration Employment Document (Fees) Regulations 2003, SI 2003/541.
Immigration Employment Document (Fees) (Amendment) Regulations 2003, SI 2003/1277.
Immigration Employment Document (Fees) (Amendment No 2) Regulations 2003, SI 2003/2447.
Immigration Employment Document (Fees) (Amendment No 3) Regulations 2003, SI 2003/2626.
Immigration Employment Document (Fees) (Amendment) Regulations 2004, SI 2004/1044.
Immigration Employment Document (Fees) (Amendment) (No 2) Regulations 2004, SI 2004/1485.
Immigration Employment Document (Fees) (Amendment) Regulations 2005, SI 2005/627.

123 Advice about work permit, &c

(1) Section 82 of the Immigration and Asylum Act 1999 (c 33) (immigration advice and services: interpretation) shall be amended as follows.

(2) In the definition of "relevant matters" in subsection (1), after paragraph (b) there shall be inserted—

"(ba)an application for an immigration employment document;".

(3) At the end of the section add—

"(3) In the definition of "relevant matters" in subsection (1) "immigration employment document" means—

(a) a work permit (within the meaning of section 33(1) of the Immigration Act 1971 (interpretation)), and

1685

(b)   any other document which relates to employment and is issued for a purpose of immigration rules or in connection with leave to enter or remain in the United Kingdom."

Appointment
Appointment: 1 April 2004: see SI 2003/754, art 2(1), Sch 1 (as amended by SI 2003/1339, art 3 and SI 2003/2993, art 3).

Authority-to-carry scheme

124   Authority to carry

(1)   Regulations made by the Secretary of State may authorise him to require a person (a "carrier") to pay a penalty if the carrier brings a passenger to the United Kingdom and—

(a)   the carrier was required by an authority-to-carry scheme to seek authority under the scheme to carry the passenger, and

(b)   the carrier did not seek authority before the journey to the United Kingdom commenced or was refused authority under the scheme.

(2)   An "authority-to-carry scheme" is a scheme operated by the Secretary of State which requires carriers to seek authority to bring passengers to the United Kingdom.

(3)   An authority-to-carry scheme must specify—

(a)   the class of carrier to which it applies (which may be defined by reference to a method of transport or otherwise), and

(b)   the class of passenger to which it applies (which may be defined by reference to nationality, the possession of specified documents or otherwise).

(4)   The Secretary of State may operate different authority-to-carry schemes for different purposes.

(5)   Where the Secretary of State makes regulations under subsection (1) he must—

(a)   identify in the regulations the authority-to-carry scheme to which they refer, and

(b)   lay the authority-to-carry scheme before Parliament.

(6)   Regulations under subsection (1) may, in particular—

(a)   apply or make provision similar to a provision of sections 40 to 43 of and Schedule 1 to the Immigration and Asylum Act 1999 (c 33) (charge for passenger without document);

(b)   do anything which may be done under a provision of any of those sections;

(c)   amend any of those sections.

(7)   Regulations by virtue of subsection (6)(a) may, in particular—

(a)   apply a provision with modification;

(b)   apply a provision which confers power to make legislation.

(8)   The grant or refusal of authority under an authority-to-carry scheme shall not be taken to determine whether a person is entitled or permitted to enter the United Kingdom.

(9)   Regulations under this section—

(a)   must be made by statutory instrument, and

(b)   may not be made unless a draft has been laid before and approved by resolution of each House of Parliament.

Initial Commencement
To be appointed: see s 162(1).

Evasion of procedure

125   Carriers' liability

Schedule 8 (which amends Part II of the Immigration and Asylum Act 1999 (carriers' liability)) shall have effect.

Appointment
Appointment (for the purpose of enabling the Secretary of State to exercise the power to make subordinate legislation under the Immigration and Asylum Act 1999, ss 32(2A), 35(5), (7), (9), (12), (13), 37(5B), (7) and 40A(4), (6)): 14 November 2002: see SI 2002/2811, art 2, Schedule; for transitional provisions see art 4 thereof.
Appointment (for the purpose of enabling the Secretary of State to exercise the power under the Immigration and Asylum Act 1999, s 32A(1), (3), (4) to lay a draft code of practice before Parliament and bring the code of practice into force): 14 November 2002: see SI 2002/2811, art 2, Schedule; for transitional provisions see art 4 thereof.
Appointment (for the purposes of clandestine entrants (within the meaning of the Immigration and Asylum Act 1999, s 32(1)) who arrive in the United Kingdom concealed in a vehicle or a rail freight wagon): 8 December 2002: see SI 2002/2811, art 2, Schedule; for transitional provisions see art 4 thereof.
Appointment (for certain purposes): 8 December 2002: see SI 2002/2811, art 2, Schedule; for transitional provisions see art 4 thereof.

Provision of information by traveller

126   Physical data: compulsory provision

(1)   The Secretary of State may by regulations—

(a)   require an immigration application to be accompanied by specified information about external physical characteristics of the applicant;
(b)   enable an authorised person to require an individual who makes an immigration application to provide information about his external physical characteristics;
(c)   enable an authorised person to require an entrant to provide information about his external physical characteristics.

(2)   In subsection (1) "immigration application" means an application for—

(a)   entry clearance,
(b)   leave to enter or remain in the United Kingdom, or
(c)   variation of leave to enter or remain in the United Kingdom.

(3)   Regulations under subsection (1) may not—

(a)   impose a requirement in respect of a person to whom section 141 of the Immigration and Asylum Act 1999 (c 33) (fingerprinting) applies, during the relevant period within the meaning of that section, or
(b)   enable a requirement to be imposed in respect of a person to whom that section applies, during the relevant period within the meaning of that section.

(4)   Regulations under subsection (1) may, in particular—

(a)   require, or enable an authorised person to require, the provision of information in a specified form;
(b)   require an individual to submit, or enable an authorised person to require an individual to submit, to a specified process by means of which information is obtained or recorded;

    (c)   make provision about the effect of failure to provide information or to submit to a process (which may, in particular, include provision for an application to be disregarded or dismissed if a requirement is not satisfied);

    (d)   confer a function (which may include the exercise of a discretion) on an authorised person;

    (e)   require an authorised person to have regard to a code (with or without modification);

    (f)   require an authorised person to have regard to such provisions of a code (with or without modification) as may be specified by direction of the Secretary of State;

    (g)   make provision about the use and retention of information provided (which may include provision permitting the use of information for specified purposes which do not relate to immigration);

    (h)   make provision which applies generally or only in specified cases or circumstances;

    (i)   make different provision for different cases or circumstances.

(5)   Regulations under subsection (1) must—

    (a)   include provision about the destruction of information obtained or recorded by virtue of the regulations,

    (b)   require the destruction of information at the end of the period of ten years beginning with the day on which it is obtained or recorded in a case for which destruction at the end of another period is not required by or in accordance with the regulations, and

    (c)   include provision similar to section 143(2) and (10) to (13) of the Immigration and Asylum Act 1999 (c 33) (fingerprints: destruction of copies and electronic data).

(6)   In so far as regulations under subsection (1) require an individual under the age of 16 to submit to a process, the regulations must make provision similar to section 141(3) to (5) and (13) of the Immigration and Asylum Act 1999 (fingerprints: children).

(7)   In so far as regulations under subsection (1) enable an authorised person to require an individual under the age of 16 to submit to a process, the regulations must make provision similar to section 141(3) to (5), (12) and (13) of that Act (fingerprints: children).

(8)   Regulations under subsection (1)—

    (a)   must be made by statutory instrument, and

    (b)   shall not be made unless a draft of the regulations has been laid before and approved by resolution of each House of Parliament.

(9)   In this section—

    "authorised person" has the meaning given by section 141(5) of the Immigration and Asylum Act 1999 (authority to take fingerprints),

    "code" has the meaning given by section 145(6) of that Act (code of practice),

    "entrant" has the meaning given by section 33(1) of the Immigration Act 1971 (c 77) (interpretation),

    "entry clearance" has the meaning given by section 33(1) of that Act, and

    "external physical characteristics" includes, in particular, features of the iris or any other part of the eye.

Appointment

Appointment: 1 April 2003: see SI 2003/754, art 2(1), Sch 1.

Subordinate Legislation
Immigration (Provision of Physical Data) Regulations 2003, SI 2003/1875 (made under sub-s (1)).
Immigration (Provision of Physical Data) (Amendment) Regulations 2004, SI 2004/474 (made under sub-s (1)).
Immigration (Provision of Physical Data) (Amendment) (No 2) Regulations 2004, SI 1998/1834 (made under sub-s (1)).

127 Physical data: voluntary provision

(1) The Secretary of State may operate a scheme under which an individual may supply, or submit to the obtaining or recording of, information about his external physical characteristics to be used (wholly or partly) in connection with entry to the United Kingdom.

(2) In particular, the Secretary of State may—

(a) require an authorised person to use information supplied under a scheme;
(b) make provision about the collection, use and retention of information supplied under a scheme (which may include provision requiring an authorised person to have regard to a code);
(c) charge for participation in a scheme.

(3) In this section the following expressions have the same meaning as in section 126—

(a) "authorised person",
(b) "code", and
(c) "external physical characteristics".

Appointment
Appointment: 10 December 2004: see SI 2004/2998, art 2.

128 Data collection under Immigration and Asylum Act 1999

(1) The following shall be added at the end of section 144 of the Immigration and Asylum Act 1999 (c 33) (collection of data about external physical characteristics) (which becomes subsection (1))—

"(2) In subsection (1) "external physical characteristics" includes, in particular, features of the iris or any other part of the eye."

(2) The following shall be inserted after section 145(2) of that Act (codes of practice)—

"(2A) A person exercising a power under regulations made by virtue of section 144 must have regard to such provisions of a code as may be specified."

Appointment
Appointment: 10 February 2003: see SI 2003/1, art 2, Schedule.

Disclosure of information by public authority

129 Local authority

(1) The Secretary of State may require a local authority to supply information for the purpose of establishing where a person is if the Secretary of State reasonably suspects that—

(a) the person has committed an offence under section 24(1)(a), (b), (c), (e) or (f), 24A(1) or 26(1)(c) or (d) of the Immigration Act 1971 (c 77) (illegal entry, deception, &c), and
(b) the person is or has been resident in the local authority's area.

(2)   A local authority shall comply with a requirement under this section.

(3)   In the application of this section to England and Wales "local authority" means—

   (a)   a county council,
   (b)   a county borough council,
   (c)   a district council,
   (d)   a London borough council,
   (e)   the Common Council of the City of London, and
   (f)   the Council of the Isles of Scilly.

(4)   In the application of this section to Scotland "local authority" means a council constituted under section 2 of the Local Government etc (Scotland) Act 1994 (c 39).

(5)   In the application of this section to Northern Ireland—

   (a)   a reference to a local authority shall be taken as a reference to the Northern Ireland Housing Executive, and
   (b)   the reference to a local authority's area shall be taken as a reference to Northern Ireland.

Appointment
Appointment: 30 July 2003: see SI 2003/1747, art 2(a).

130   Inland Revenue

(1)   The Commissioners of Inland Revenue may supply the Secretary of State with information for the purpose of establishing where a person is if the Secretary of State reasonably suspects—

   (a)   that the person does not have leave to enter or remain in the United Kingdom, and
   (b)   that the person does not have permission to work in accordance with section 1(2) of the Immigration Act 1971 (c 77) (general principles).

(2)   The Commissioners of Inland Revenue may supply the Secretary of State with information for the purpose of establishing where a person is if the Secretary of State reasonably suspects that the person has undertaken employment in the United Kingdom in breach of—

   (a)   a condition attached to leave to enter or remain in the United Kingdom,
   (b)   a restriction imposed under paragraph 21 of Schedule 2 to the Immigration Act 1971 (control of entry), or
   (c)   a restriction imposed under paragraph 2 of Schedule 3 to that Act (deportation).

(3)   The Commissioners of Inland Revenue may supply the Secretary of State with information for the purpose of determining whether an applicant for naturalisation under the British Nationality Act 1981 (c 61) is of good character.

(4)   The Commissioners of Inland Revenue may supply the Secretary of State with information for the purpose of applying, in the case of an applicant for entry clearance within the meaning of section 33 of the Immigration Act 1971, a provision of rules under section 3 of that Act relating to maintenance or accommodation.

(5)   Information supplied to the Secretary of State under any of subsections (1) to (4) may be supplied by him to another person only—

   (a)   for a purpose specified in any of those subsections,
   (b)   for the purpose of legal proceedings, or

(c)   with consent (which may be general or specific) of the Commissioners of Inland Revenue, for a purpose for which the Commissioners could supply the information.

(6)   A power of the Commissioners of Inland Revenue under this section—

(a)   may be exercised on their behalf only by a person authorised (generally or specifically) for the purpose, and

(b)   may be exercised despite any statutory or other requirement of confidentiality.

Appointment
Appointment: 1 April 2003: see SI 2003/754, art 2(1), Sch 1.

131   Police, &c

Information may be supplied under section 20 of the Immigration and Asylum Act 1999 (c 33) (supply of information to Secretary of State) for use for the purpose of determining whether an applicant for naturalisation under the British Nationality Act 1981 is of good character.

Appointment
Appointment: 10 February 2003: see SI 2003/1, art 2, Schedule.

132   Supply of document, &c to Secretary of State

(1)   Section 20 of the Immigration and Asylum Act 1999 (supply of information to Secretary of State) shall be amended as follows.

(2)   After subsection (1) insert—

"(1A)   This section also applies to a document or article which—

(a)   comes into the possession of a person listed in subsection (1) or someone acting on his behalf, or

(b)   is discovered by a person listed in subsection (1) or someone acting on his behalf."

(3)   In subsection (2) after "information" insert ", document or article".

(4)   After subsection (2) insert—

"(2A)   The Secretary of State may—

(a)   retain for immigration purposes a document or article supplied to him under subsection (2), and

(b)   dispose of a document or article supplied to him under subsection (2) in such manner as he thinks appropriate (and the reference to use in subsection (2) includes a reference to disposal)."

(5)   In subsection (6) after "information" insert ", documents or articles".

Appointment
Appointment: 10 February 2003: see SI 2003/1, art 2, Schedule.

133   Medical inspectors

(1)   This section applies to a person if an immigration officer acting under Schedule 2 to the Immigration Act 1971 (c 77) (control on entry, &c) has brought the person to the attention of—

(a)   a medical inspector appointed under paragraph 1(2) of that Schedule, or

(b)   a person working under the direction of a medical inspector appointed under that paragraph.

(2) A medical inspector may disclose to a health service body—

(a) the name of a person to whom this section applies,
(b) his place of residence in the United Kingdom,
(c) his age,
(d) the language which he speaks,
(e) the nature of any disease with which the inspector thinks the person may be infected,
(f) relevant details of the person's medical history,
(g) the grounds for an opinion mentioned in paragraph (e) (including the result of any test or examination which has been carried out), and
(h) the inspector's opinion about action which the health service body should take.

(3) A disclosure may be made under subsection (2) only if the medical inspector thinks it necessary for the purpose of—

(a) preventative medicine,
(b) medical diagnosis,
(c) the provision of care or treatment, or
(d) the management of health care services.

(4) For the purposes of this section "health service body" in relation to a person means a body which carries out functions in an area which includes his place of residence and which is—

(a) in relation to England—
 (i) a Primary Care Trust established under section 16A of the National Health Service Act 1977 (c 49),
 (ii) a National Health Service Trust established under section 5 of the National Health Service and Community Care Act 1990 (c 19),
 [(iia) an NHS foundation trust,]
 (iii) a Strategic Health Authority established under section 8 of the National Health Service Act 1977, [or]
 (iv) a Special Health Authority established under section 11 of that Act, ...
 (v) ..., [or
 (vi) the Health Protection Agency]
(b) in relation to Wales—
 (i) a Health Authority or Local Health Board established under section 8 or 16BA of that Act, [or]
 (ii) a National Health Service Trust established under section 5 of the National Health Service and Community Care Act 1990, ...
 (iii) ...[or]
 [(iv) the Health Protection Agency]
(c) in relation to Scotland—
 (i) a Health Board, Special Health Board or National Health Service Trust established under section 2 or 12A of the National Health Service (Scotland) Act 1978 (c 29), ...
 (ii) the Common Services Agency for the Scottish Health Service established under section 10 of that Act, or
 [(iii) the Health Protection Agency, or]
(d) in relation to Northern Ireland—
 (i) a Health and Social Services Board established under the Health and Personal Social Services (Northern Ireland) Order 1972 (SI 1972/1265 (NI 14)),
 (ii) a Health and Social Services trust established under the Health and Personal Social Services (Northern Ireland) Order 1991 (SI 1991/194 (NI 1)), ...

(iii) the Department of Health, Social Services and Public Safety, [or
(iv) the Health Protection Agency].

Appointment
Appointment: 10 February 2003: see SI 2003/1, art 2, Schedule.

Amendment
Sub-s (4): para (a)(iia) inserted by the Health and Social Care (Community Health and Standards) Act 2003, s 34, Sch 4, paras 127, 128. Date in force: 1 April 2004: see SI 2004/759, art 2.
Sub-s (4): in para (a)(iii) word "or" in square brackets inserted by the Health and Social Care (Community Health and Standards) Act 2003, s 190(2), Sch 13, para 12(a). Date in force: 1 April 2005: see SI 2005/457, art 2(1)(a).
Sub-s (4): para (a)(v) and word omitted immediately preceding it repealed by the Health and Social Care (Community Health and Standards) Act 2003, ss 190(2), 196, Sch 13, para 12(a), Sch 14, Pt 7. Date in force: 1 April 2005: see SI 2005/457, art 2(1)(a), (b).
Sub-s (4): para (a)(vi) and word "or" immediately preceding it inserted by the Health Protection Agency Act 2004, s 11(1), Sch 3, para 17(1), (2). Date in force: 1 April 2005: see SI 2005/121, art 2(2).
Sub-s (4): in para (b)(i) word "or" in square brackets inserted by the Health and Social Care (Community Health and Standards) Act 2003, s 190(2), Sch 13, para 12(b). Date in force: 1 April 2005: see SI 2005/457, art 2(1)(a).
Sub-s (4): para (b)(iii) and word omitted immediately preceding it repealed by the Health and Social Care (Community Health and Standards) Act 2003, ss 190(2), 196, Sch 13, para 12(b), Sch 14, Pt 7. Date in force: 1 April 2005: see SI 2005/457, art 2(1)(a), (b).
Sub-s (4): para (b)(iv) and word "or" immediately preceding it inserted by the Health Protection Agency Act 2004, s 11(1), Sch 3, para 17(1), (3). Date in force: 1 April 2005: see SI 2005/121, art 2(2).
Sub-s (4): in para (c)(i) word omitted repealed by the Health Protection Agency Act 2004, s 11(1), (2), Sch 3, para 17(1), (4)(a), Sch 4. Date in force: 1 April 2005: see SI 2005/121, art 2(2).
Sub-s (4): para (c)(iii) inserted by the Health Protection Agency Act 2004, s 11(1), Sch 3, para 17(1), (4)(b). Date in force: 1 April 2005: see SI 2005/121, art 2(2).
Sub-s (4): in para (d)(ii) word omitted repealed by the Health Protection Agency Act 2004, s 11(1), (2), Sch 3, para 17(1), (5)(a), Sch 4. Date in force: 1 April 2005: see SI 2005/121, art 2(2).
Sub-s (4): para (d)(iv) and word "or" immediately preceding it inserted by the Health Protection Agency Act 2004, s 11(1), Sch 3, para 17(1), (5)(b). Date in force: 1 April 2005: see SI 2005/121, art 2(2).

Disclosure of information by private person

134   Employer

(1)   The Secretary of State may require an employer to supply information about an employee whom the Secretary of State reasonably suspects of having committed an offence under—

(a) section 24(1)(a), (b), (c), (e) or (f), 24A(1) or 26(1)(c) or (d) of the Immigration Act 1971 (c 77) (illegal entry, deception, &c),
(b) section 105(1)(a), (b) or (c) of the Immigration and Asylum Act 1999 (c 33) (support for asylum-seeker: fraud), or
(c) section 106(1)(a), (b) or (c) of that Act (support for asylum-seeker: fraud).

(2)   The power under subsection (1) may be exercised to require information about an employee only if the information—

(a) is required for the purpose of establishing where the employee is, or
(b) relates to the employee's earnings or to the history of his employment.

(3)   In this section a reference to an employer or employee—

(a) includes a reference to a former employer or employee, and
(b) shall be construed in accordance with section 8(8) of the Asylum and Immigration Act 1996 (c 49) (restrictions on employment).

(4) Where—

    (a) a business (the "employment agency") arranges for one person (the "worker") to provide services to another (the "client"), and

    (b) the worker is not employed by the employment agency or the client,

this section shall apply as if the employment agency were the worker's employer while he provides services to the client.

Appointment
Appointment: 30 July 2003: see SI 2003/1747, art 2(b).

135   Financial institution

(1) The Secretary of State may require a financial institution to supply information about a person if the Secretary of State reasonably suspects that—

    (a) the person has committed an offence under section 105(1)(a), (b) or (c) or 106(1)(a), (b) or (c) of the Immigration and Asylum Act 1999 (c 33) (support for asylum-seeker: fraud),

    (b) the information is relevant to the offence, and

    (c) the institution has the information.

(2) In this section "financial institution" means—

    (a) a person who has permission under Part 4 of the Financial Services and Markets Act 2000 (c 8) to accept deposits, and

    (b) a building society (within the meaning given by the Building Societies Act 1986 (c 53)).

Appointment
Appointment: 30 July 2003: see SI 2003/1747, art 2(b).

136   Notice

(1) A requirement to provide information under section 134 or 135 must be imposed by notice in writing specifying—

    (a) the information,

    (b) the manner in which it is to be provided, and

    (c) the period of time within which it is to be provided.

(2) A period of time specified in a notice under subsection (1)(c)—

    (a) must begin with the date of receipt of the notice, and

    (b) must not be less than ten working days.

(3) A person on whom a notice is served under subsection (1) must provide the Secretary of State with the information specified in the notice.

(4) Information provided under subsection (3) must be provided—

    (a) in the manner specified under subsection (1)(b), and

    (b) within the time specified under subsection (1)(c).

(5) In this section "working day" means a day which is not—

    (a) Saturday,

    (b) Sunday,

    (c) Christmas Day,

    (d) Good Friday, or

    (e) a day which is a bank holiday under the Banking and Financial Dealings Act 1971 (c 80) in any part of the United Kingdom.

Appointment
Appointment: 30 July 2003: see SI 2003/1747, art 2(b).

137   Disclosure of information: offences

(1)   A person commits an offence if without reasonable excuse he fails to comply with section 136(3).

(2)   A person who is guilty of an offence under subsection (1) shall be liable on summary conviction to—

    (a)   imprisonment for a term not exceeding *three months* [51 weeks],
    (b)   a fine not exceeding level 5 on the standard scale, or
    (c)   both.

Appointment
Appointment: 30 July 2003: see SI 2003/1747, art 2(b).

Amendment
Sub-s (2): in para (a) words "3 months" in italics repealed and subsequent words in square brackets substituted by the Criminal Justice Act 2003, s 280(2), (3), Sch 26, para 58. Date in force: to be appointed: see the Criminal Justice Act 2003, s 336(3).

138   Offence by body

(1)   Subsection (2) applies where an offence under section 137 is committed by a body corporate and it is proved that the offence—

    (a)   was committed with the consent or connivance of an officer of the body, or
    (b)   was attributable to neglect on the part of an officer of the body.

(2)   The officer, as well as the body, shall be guilty of the offence.

(3)   In this section a reference to an officer of a body corporate includes a reference to—

    (a)   a director, manager or secretary,
    (b)   a person purporting to act as a director, manager or secretary, and
    (c)   if the affairs of the body are managed by its members, a member.

(4)   Where an offence under section 137 is committed by a partnership (other than a limited partnership), each partner shall be guilty of the offence.

(5)   Subsection (1) shall have effect in relation to a limited partnership as if—

    (a)   a reference to a body corporate were a reference to a limited partnership, and
    (b)   a reference to an officer of the body were a reference to a partner.

Appointment
Appointment: 30 July 2003: see SI 2003/1747, art 2(b).

139   Privilege against self-incrimination

(1)   Information provided by a person pursuant to a requirement under section 134 or 135 shall not be admissible in evidence in criminal proceedings against that person.

(2)   This section shall not apply to proceedings for an offence under section 137.

Appointment
Appointment: 30 July 2003: see SI 2003/1747, art 2(b).

Immigration services

140   Immigration Services Commissioner

(1)   The following shall be inserted after paragraph 7(1) of Schedule 5 to the Immigration and Asylum Act 1999 (c 33) (investigation by Commissioner: power of entry)—

"(1A)   This paragraph also applies if the Commissioner is investigating a matter under paragraph 5(5) and—

(a)   the matter is of a kind described in paragraph 5(3)(a), (b) or (d) (for which purpose a reference to an allegation shall be treated as a reference to a suspicion of the Commissioner), and

(b)   there are reasonable grounds for believing that particular premises are being used in connection with the provision of immigration advice or immigration services by a registered person."

(2)   The following shall be inserted after paragraph 3 of Schedule 6 to the Immigration and Asylum Act 1999 (c 33) (registration by Commissioner)—

"**3A   Variation of registration**

The Commissioner may vary a person's registration—

(a)   so as to make it have limited effect in any of the ways mentioned in paragraph 2(2); or

(b)   so as to make it have full effect."

(3)   The following shall be inserted after section 87(3)(e) of the Immigration and Asylum Act 1999 (Immigration Services Tribunal: jurisdiction) (before the word "or")—

"(ea)to vary a registration under paragraph 3A of that Schedule;".

Appointment
Appointment: 8 January 2003: see SI 2002/2811, art 2, Schedule; for transitional provisions in relation to sub-s (1) above, see art 5 thereof.

Immigration control

141   EEA ports: juxtaposed controls

(1)   The Secretary of State may by order make provision for the purpose of giving effect to an international agreement which concerns immigration control at an EEA port (whether or not it also concerns other aspects of frontier control at the port).

(2)   An order under this section may make any provision which appears to the Secretary of State—

(a)   likely to facilitate implementation of the international agreement (including those aspects of the agreement which relate to frontier control other than immigration control), or

(b)   appropriate as a consequence of provision made for the purpose of facilitating implementation of the agreement.

(3)   In particular, an order under this section may—

(a)   provide for a law of England and Wales to have effect, with or without modification, in relation to a person in a specified area or anything done in a specified area;

(b) provide for a law of England and Wales not to have effect in relation to a person in a specified area or anything done in a specified area;

(c) provide for a law of England and Wales to be modified in its effect in relation to a person in a specified area or anything done in a specified area;

(d) disapply or modify an enactment in relation to a person who has undergone a process in a specified area;

(e) disapply or modify an enactment otherwise than under paragraph (b), (c) or (d);

(f) make provision conferring a function (which may include—
  (i) provision conferring a discretionary function;
  (ii) provision conferring a function on a servant or agent of the government of a State other than the United Kingdom);

(g) create or extend the application of an offence;

(h) impose or permit the imposition of a penalty;

(i) require the payment of, or enable a person to require the payment of, a charge or fee;

(j) make provision about enforcement (which may include—
  (i) provision conferring a power of arrest, detention or removal from or to any place;
  (ii) provision for the purpose of enforcing the law of a State other than the United Kingdom);

(k) confer jurisdiction on a court or tribunal;

(l) confer immunity or provide for indemnity;

(m) make provision about compensation;

(n) impose a requirement, or enable a requirement to be imposed, for a person to co-operate with or to provide facilities for the use of another person who is performing a function under the order or under the international agreement (which may include a requirement to provide facilities without charge);

(o) make provision about the disclosure of information.

(4) An order under this section may—

(a) make provision which applies generally or only in specified circumstances;

(b) make different provision for different circumstances;

(c) amend an enactment.

(5) An order under this section—

(a) must be made by statutory instrument,

(b) may not be made unless the Secretary of State has consulted with such persons as appear to him to be appropriate, and

(c) may not be made unless a draft has been laid before and approved by resolution of each House of Parliament.

(6) In this section—

"EEA port" means a port in an EEA State from which passengers are commonly carried by sea to or from the United Kingdom,

"EEA State" means a State which is a contracting party to the Agreement on the European Economic Area signed at Oporto on 2nd May 1992 (as it has effect from time to time),

"frontier control" means the enforcement of law which relates to, or in so far as it relates to, the movement of persons or goods into or out of the United Kingdom or another State,

"immigration control" means arrangements made in connection with the movement of persons into or out of the United Kingdom or another State,

"international agreement" means an agreement made between Her Majesty's Government and the government of another State, and "specified area" means an area (whether of the United Kingdom or of another State) specified in an international agreement.

Appointment
Appointment: 8 January 2003: see SI 2002/2811, art 2, Schedule.

Subordinate Legislation
Nationality, Immigration and Asylum Act 2002 (Juxtaposed Controls) Order 2003, SI 2003/2818.

Country information

142   Advisory Panel on Country Information

(1)   The Secretary of State shall appoint a group of not fewer than ten nor more than 20 individuals (to be known as the Advisory Panel on Country Information).

(2)   The Secretary of State shall appoint one member of the Advisory Panel as its Chairman.

(3)   The function of the Advisory Panel shall be to consider and make recommendations to the Secretary of State about the content of country information.

(4)   In this section "country information" means information about conditions in countries outside the United Kingdom which the Secretary of State compiles and makes available, for purposes connected with immigration, to—

    (a)   immigration officers, and
    (b)   other officers of the Secretary of State.

(5)   The function of the Advisory Panel shall be shared among its members in accordance with arrangements made by the Chairman.

(6)   A member of the Advisory Panel shall hold and vacate office in accordance with the terms of his appointment (which may include provision about retirement, resignation or dismissal).

(7)   The Secretary of State may—

    (a)   pay fees and allowances to members of the Advisory Panel;
    (b)   defray expenses of members of the Advisory Panel;
    (c)   make staff and other facilities available to the Advisory Panel.

Appointment
Appointment: 1 April 2003: see SI 2003/754, art 2(1), Sch 1.

PART 7
OFFENCES

Substance

143   Assisting unlawful immigration, &c

The following shall be substituted for section 25 of the Immigration Act 1971 (c 77) (assisting illegal entry)—

"25   Assisting unlawful immigration to member State

(1)   A person commits an offence if he—

    (a)   does an act which facilitates the commission of a breach of immigration law by an individual who is not a citizen of the European Union,
    (b)   knows or has reasonable cause for believing that the act facilitates the commission of a breach of immigration law by the individual, and

1698

   (c) knows or has reasonable cause for believing that the individual is not a citizen of the European Union.

(2) In subsection (1) "immigration law" means a law which has effect in a member State and which controls, in respect of some or all persons who are not nationals of the State, entitlement to—

   (a) enter the State,
   (b) transit across the State, or
   (c) be in the State.

(3) A document issued by the government of a member State certifying a matter of law in that State—

   (a) shall be admissible in proceedings for an offence under this section, and
   (b) shall be conclusive as to the matter certified.

(4) Subsection (1) applies to anything done—

   (a) in the United Kingdom,
   (b) outside the United Kingdom by an individual to whom subsection (5) applies, or
   (c) outside the United Kingdom by a body incorporated under the law of a part of the United Kingdom.

(5) This subsection applies to—

   (a) a British citizen,
   (b) a British overseas territories citizen,
   (c) a British National (Overseas),
   (d) a British Overseas citizen,
   (e) a person who is a British subject under the British Nationality Act 1981 (c 61), and
   (f) a British protected person within the meaning of that Act.

(6) A person guilty of an offence under this section shall be liable—

   (a) on conviction on indictment, to imprisonment for a term not exceeding 14 years, to a fine or to both, or
   (b) on summary conviction, to imprisonment for a term not exceeding six months, to a fine not exceeding the statutory maximum or to both.

25A   Helping asylum-seeker to enter United Kingdom

(1) A person commits an offence if—

   (a) he knowingly and for gain facilitates the arrival in the United Kingdom of an individual, and
   (b) he knows or has reasonable cause to believe that the individual is an asylum-seeker.

(2) In this section "asylum-seeker" means a person who intends to claim that to remove him from or require him to leave the United Kingdom would be contrary to the United Kingdom's obligations under—

   (a) the Refugee Convention (within the meaning given by section 167(1) of the Immigration and Asylum Act 1999 (c 33) (interpretation)), or
   (b) the Human Rights Convention (within the meaning given by that section).

(3) Subsection (1) does not apply to anything done by a person acting on behalf of an organisation which—

   (a) aims to assist asylum-seekers, and

(b) does not charge for its services.

(4) Subsections (4) to (6) of section 25 apply for the purpose of the offence in subsection (1) of this section as they apply for the purpose of the offence in subsection (1) of that section.

25B   Assisting entry to United Kingdom in breach of deportation or exclusion order

(1) A person commits an offence if he—

(a) does an act which facilitates a breach of a deportation order in force against an individual who is a citizen of the European Union, and

(b) knows or has reasonable cause for believing that the act facilitates a breach of the deportation order.

(2) Subsection (3) applies where the Secretary of State personally directs that the exclusion from the United Kingdom of an individual who is a citizen of the European Union is conducive to the public good.

(3) A person commits an offence if he—

(a) does an act which assists the individual to arrive in, enter or remain in the United Kingdom,

(b) knows or has reasonable cause for believing that the act assists the individual to arrive in, enter or remain in the United Kingdom, and

(c) knows or has reasonable cause for believing that the Secretary of State has personally directed that the individual's exclusion from the United Kingdom is conducive to the public good.

(4) Subsections (4) to (6) of section 25 apply for the purpose of an offence under this section as they apply for the purpose of an offence under that section.

25C   Forfeiture of vehicle, ship or aircraft

(1) This section applies where a person is convicted on indictment of an offence under section 25, 25A or 25B.

(2) The court may order the forfeiture of a vehicle used or intended to be used in connection with the offence if the convicted person—

(a) owned the vehicle at the time the offence was committed,

(b) was at that time a director, secretary or manager of a company which owned the vehicle,

(c) was at that time in possession of the vehicle under a hire-purchase agreement,

(d) was at that time a director, secretary or manager of a company which was in possession of the vehicle under a hire-purchase agreement, or

(e) was driving the vehicle in the course of the commission of the offence.

(3) The court may order the forfeiture of a ship or aircraft used or intended to be used in connection with the offence if the convicted person—

(a) owned the ship or aircraft at the time the offence was committed,

(b) was at that time a director, secretary or manager of a company which owned the ship or aircraft,

(c) was at that time in possession of the ship or aircraft under a hire-purchase agreement,

(d) was at that time a director, secretary or manager of a company which was in possession of the ship or aircraft under a hire-purchase agreement,

(e) was at that time a charterer of the ship or aircraft, or

(f) committed the offence while acting as captain of the ship or aircraft.

(4)   But in a case to which subsection (3)(a) or (b) does not apply, forfeiture may be ordered only—

(a)   in the case of a ship, if subsection (5) or (6) applies;
(b)   in the case of an aircraft, if subsection (5) or (7) applies.

(5)   This subsection applies where—

(a)   in the course of the commission of the offence, the ship or aircraft carried more than 20 illegal entrants, and
(b)   a person who, at the time the offence was committed, owned the ship or aircraft or was a director, secretary or manager of a company which owned it, knew or ought to have known of the intention to use it in the course of the commission of an offence under section 25, 25A or 25B.

(6)   This subsection applies where a ship's gross tonnage is less than 500 tons.

(7)   This subsection applies where the maximum weight at which an aircraft (which is not a hovercraft) may take off in accordance with its certificate of airworthiness is less than 5,700 kilogrammes.

(8)   Where a person who claims to have an interest in a vehicle, ship or aircraft applies to a court to make representations on the question of forfeiture, the court may not make an order under this section in respect of the ship, aircraft or vehicle unless the person has been given an opportunity to make representations.

(9)   In the case of an offence under section 25, the reference in subsection (5)(a) to an illegal entrant shall be taken to include a reference to—

(a)   an individual who seeks to enter a member State in breach of immigration law (within the meaning of section 25), and
(b)   an individual who is a passenger for the purpose of section 145 of the Nationality, Immigration and Asylum Act 2002 (traffic in prostitution).

(10)   In the case of an offence under section 25A, the reference in subsection (5)(a) to an illegal entrant shall be taken to include a reference to—

(a)   an asylum-seeker (within the meaning of that section), and
(b)   an individual who is a passenger for the purpose of section 145(1) of the Nationality, Immigration and Asylum Act 2002.

(11)   In the case of an offence under section 25B, the reference in subsection (5)(a) to an illegal entrant shall be taken to include a reference to an individual who is a passenger for the purpose of section 145(1) of the Nationality, Immigration and Asylum Act 2002."

Appointment
Appointment: 10 February 2003: see SI 2003/1, art 2, Schedule.

144   Section 143: consequential amendments

(1)   The Immigration Act 1971 (c 77) shall be amended as follows.

(2)   Section 25A (detention of ship, aircraft or vehicle) shall be renumbered as section 25D (and its title becomes "Detention of ship, aircraft or vehicle") and—

(a)   in subsection (1) for "section 25(1)(a) or (b)" substitute "section 25, 25A or 25B",
(b)   in subsections (2) and (4) for "section 25(6)" substitute "section 25C",
(c)   for subsection (3) substitute—

"(3)   A person (other than the arrested person) may apply to the court for the release of a ship, aircraft or vehicle on the grounds that—

  (a)   he owns the ship, aircraft or vehicle,
  (b)   he was, immediately before the detention of the ship, aircraft or vehicle, in possession of it under a hire-purchase agreement, or
  (c)   he is a charterer of the ship or aircraft.", and
  (d)   omit subsection (7).

(3)   In section 28A (arrest without warrant)—

  (a)   in subsection (3)(a) for "section 25(1)" substitute "section 25, 25A or 25B",
  (b)   omit subsection (4),
  (c)   in subsection (10) omit ", (4)(b)", and
  (d)   in subsection (11) omit ", (4)".

(4)   In section 28B(5) (search and arrest by warrant) for ", section 24A or section 25(2)" substitute ", 24A".

(5)   In section 28C(1) (search and arrest without warrant) for "section 25(1)" substitute "section 25, 25A or 25B".

(6)   In section 28D(4) (entry and search of premises) for "section 24A or section 25" substitute "24A, 25, 25A, 25B".

(7)   In section 28F (the title to which becomes "Entry and search of premises following arrest under section 25, 25A or 25B") in subsection (1) for "section 25(1)" substitute "section 25, 25A, 25B".

(8)   After section 33(1) (interpretation) insert—

"(1A)   A reference to being an owner of a vehicle, ship or aircraft includes a reference to being any of a number of persons who jointly own it."

Appointment
Appointment: 10 February 2003: see SI 2003/1, art 2, Schedule.

145   ...

...

Amendment
Repealed by the Sexual Offences Act 2003, ss 139, 140, Sch 6, para 48, Sch 7. Date in force: 1 May 2004: see SI 2004/874, art 2.

146   ...

...

Amendment
Repealed by the Sexual Offences Act 2003, ss 139, 140, Sch 6, para 48, Sch 7. Date in force: 1 May 2004: see SI 2004/874, art 2.

147   Employment

(1)   Section 8 of the Asylum and Immigration Act 1996 (c 49) (employment: offence) shall be amended as follows.

(2)   For subsection (2) (defence) substitute—

"(2)   It is a defence for a person charged with an offence under this section to prove that before the employment began any relevant requirement of an order of the Secretary of State under subsection (2A) was complied with.

(2A)   An order under this subsection may—

(a) require the production to an employer of a document of a specified description;

(b) require the production to an employer of one document of each of a number of specified descriptions;

(c) require an employer to take specified steps to retain, copy or record the content of a document produced to him in accordance with the order;

(d) make provision which applies generally or only in specified circumstances;

(e) make different provision for different circumstances."

(3) After subsection (6) insert—

"(6A) Where an offence under this section is committed by a partnership (other than a limited partnership) each partner shall be guilty of the offence and shall be liable to be proceeded against and punished accordingly.

(6B) Subsection (5) shall have effect in relation to a limited partnership as if—

(a) a reference to a body corporate were a reference to a limited partnership, and

(b) a reference to an officer of the body were a reference to a partner."

(4) At the end of the section add—

"(9) Section 28(1) of the Immigration Act 1971 (c 77) (extended time limit for prosecution) shall apply in relation to an offence under this section.

(10) An offence under this section shall be treated as—

(a) a relevant offence for the purpose of sections 28B and 28D of that Act (search, entry and arrest), and

(b) an offence under Part III of that Act (criminal proceedings) for the purposes of sections 28E, 28G and 28H (search after arrest)."

Appointment

Sub-ss (1), (3), (4): Appointment: 1 April 2003: see SI 2003/754, art 2(1), Sch 1.

Sub-s (2): Appointment (for the purpose of enabling subordinate legislation to be made): 1 April 2003: see SI 2003/754, art 2(1), Sch 1.

Sub-s (2): Appointment (for remaining purposes): 1 May 2004: see SI 2004/1201, art 2.

148   Registration card

The following shall be inserted after section 26 of the Immigration Act 1971 (general offences)—

"26A   Registration card

(1) In this section "registration card" means a document which—

(a) carries information about a person (whether or not wholly or partly electronically), and

(b) is issued by the Secretary of State to the person wholly or partly in connection with a claim for asylum (whether or not made by that person).

(2) In subsection (1) "claim for asylum" has the meaning given by section 18 of the Nationality, Immigration and Asylum Act 2002.

(3) A person commits an offence if he—

(a) makes a false registration card,

(b) alters a registration card with intent to deceive or to enable another to deceive,

(c) has a false or altered registration card in his possession without reasonable excuse,

(d) uses or attempts to use a false registration card for a purpose for which a registration card is issued,

   (e)   uses or attempts to use an altered registration card with intent to deceive,

   (f)   makes an article designed to be used in making a false registration card,

   (g)   makes an article designed to be used in altering a registration card with intent to deceive or to enable another to deceive, or

   (h)   has an article within paragraph (f) or (g) in his possession without reasonable excuse.

(4)   In subsection (3) "false registration card" means a document which is designed to appear to be a registration card.

(5)   A person who is guilty of an offence under subsection (3)(a), (b), (d), (e), (f) or (g) shall be liable—

   (a)   on conviction on indictment, to imprisonment for a term not exceeding ten years, to a fine or to both, or

   (b)   on summary conviction, to imprisonment for a term not exceeding six months, to a fine not exceeding the statutory maximum or to both.

(6)   A person who is guilty of an offence under subsection (3)(c) or (h) shall be liable—

   (a)   on conviction on indictment, to imprisonment for a term not exceeding two years, to a fine or to both, or

   (b)   on summary conviction, to imprisonment for a term not exceeding six months, to a fine not exceeding the statutory maximum or to both.

(7)   The Secretary of State may by order—

   (a)   amend the definition of "registration card" in subsection (1);

   (b)   make consequential amendment of this section.

(8)   An order under subsection (7)—

   (a) . must be made by statutory instrument, and

   (b)   may not be made unless a draft has been laid before and approved by resolution of each House of Parliament."

Appointment
Appointment: 10 February 2003: see SI 2003/1, art 2, Schedule.

149   Immigration stamp

The following shall be inserted after section 26A of the Immigration Act 1971 (c 77) (registration card: falsification, &c) (inserted by section 148 above)—

"26B   Possession of immigration stamp

(1)   A person commits an offence if he has an immigration stamp in his possession without reasonable excuse.

(2)   A person commits an offence if he has a replica immigration stamp in his possession without reasonable excuse.

(3)   In this section—

   (a)   "immigration stamp" means a device which is designed for the purpose of stamping documents in the exercise of an immigration function,

   (b)   "replica immigration stamp" means a device which is designed for the purpose of stamping a document so that it appears to have been stamped in the exercise of an immigration function, and

   (c)   "immigration function" means a function of an immigration officer or the Secretary of State under the Immigration Acts.

(4) A person who is guilty of an offence under this section shall be liable—

(a) on conviction on indictment, to imprisonment for a term not exceeding two years, to a fine or to both, or

(b) on summary conviction, to imprisonment for a term not exceeding six months, to a fine not exceeding the statutory maximum or to both."

Appointment
Appointment: 10 February 2003: see SI 2003/1, art 2, Schedule.

150 Sections 148 and 149: consequential amendments

(1) The following shall be inserted after section 28A(9) of the Immigration Act 1971 (arrest without warrant)—

"(9A) A constable or immigration officer may arrest without warrant a person—

(a) who has committed an offence under section 26A or 26B; or

(b) whom he has reasonable grounds for suspecting has committed an offence under section 26A or 26B."

(2) In section 28B(5) of that Act (search and arrest by warrant) after ", 24A" there shall be inserted ", 26A or 26B.".

(3) In section 28D(4) of that Act (search of premises) after ", 25B" there shall be inserted ", 26A or 26B".

Appointment
Appointment: 10 February 2003: see SI 2003/1, art 2, Schedule.

151 False information

In section 26(3) of the Immigration Act 1971 (general offences: "relevant enactment")—

(a) the word "or" after paragraph (c) shall cease to have effect, and

(b) after paragraph (d) there shall be inserted—
"; or

(e) the Nationality, Immigration and Asylum Act 2002 (apart from Part 5)."

Appointment
Appointment: 10 February 2003: see SI 2003/1, art 2, Schedule.

Procedure

152 Arrest by immigration officer

The following shall be inserted after section 28A of the Immigration Act 1971 (c 77) (arrest without warrant)—

"28AA Arrest with warrant

(1) This section applies if on an application by an immigration officer a justice of the peace is satisfied that there are reasonable grounds for suspecting that a person has committed an offence under—

(a) section 24(1)(d), or

(b) section 8 of the Asylum and Immigration Act 1996 (c 49) (employment: offence).

(2) The justice of the peace may grant a warrant authorising any immigration officer to arrest the person.

(3) In the application of this section to Scotland a reference to a justice of the peace shall be treated as a reference to the sheriff or a justice of the peace."

Appointment
Appointment: 8 January 2003: see SI 2002/2811, art 2, Schedule.

153 Power of entry

(1) The following shall be inserted after section 28C of the Immigration Act 1971 (search and arrest without warrant)—

"28CA   Business premises: entry to arrest

(1) A constable or immigration officer may enter and search any business premises for the purpose of arresting a person—

- (a) for an offence under section 24,
- (b) for an offence under section 24A, or
- (c) under paragraph 17 of Schedule 2.

(2) The power under subsection (1) may be exercised only—

- (a) to the extent that it is reasonably required for a purpose specified in subsection (1),
- (b) if the constable or immigration officer has reasonable grounds for believing that the person whom he is seeking is on the premises,
- (c) with the authority of the Secretary of State (in the case of an immigration officer) or a Chief Superintendent (in the case of a constable), and
- (d) if the constable or immigration officer produces identification showing his status.

(3) Authority for the purposes of subsection (2)(c)—

- (a) may be given on behalf of the Secretary of State only by a civil servant of the rank of at least Assistant Director, and
- (b) shall expire at the end of the period of seven days beginning with the day on which it is given.

(4) Subsection (2)(d) applies—

- (a) whether or not a constable or immigration officer is asked to produce identification, but
- (b) only where premises are occupied.

(5) Subsection (6) applies where a constable or immigration officer—

- (a) enters premises in reliance on this section, and
- (b) detains a person on the premises.

(6) A detainee custody officer may enter the premises for the purpose of carrying out a search.

(7) In subsection (6)—

"detainee custody officer" means a person in respect of whom a certificate of authorisation is in force under section 154 of the Immigration and Asylum Act 1999 (c 33) (detained persons: escort and custody), and
"search" means a search under paragraph 2(1)(a) of Schedule 13 to that Act (escort arrangements: power to search detained person)."

(2) The following shall be substituted for section 146(2) of the Immigration and Asylum Act 1999 (use of force)—

"(2)   A person exercising a power under any of the following may if necessary use reasonable force—

 (a)   section 28CA, 28FA or 28FB of the 1971 Act (business premises: entry to arrest or search),
 (b)   section 141 or 142 of this Act, and
 (c)   regulations under section 144 of this Act."

Appointment
Appointment: 8 January 2003: see SI 2002/2811, art 2, Schedule.

154   Power to search for evidence

The following shall be inserted after section 28F of the Immigration Act 1971 (c 77) (entry and search)—

"28FA   Search for personnel records: warrant unnecessary

(1)   This section applies where—

 (a)   a person has been arrested for an offence under section 24(1) or 24A(1),
 (b)   a person has been arrested under paragraph 17 of Schedule 2,
 (c)   a constable or immigration officer reasonably believes that a person is liable to arrest for an offence under section 24(1) or 24A(1), or
 (d)   a constable or immigration officer reasonably believes that a person is liable to arrest under paragraph 17 of Schedule 2.

(2)   A constable or immigration officer may search business premises where the arrest was made or where the person liable to arrest is if the constable or immigration officer reasonably believes—

 (a)   that a person has committed an immigration employment offence in relation to the person arrested or liable to arrest, and
 (b)   that employee records, other than items subject to legal privilege, will be found on the premises and will be of substantial value (whether on their own or together with other material) in the investigation of the immigration employment offence.

(3)   A constable or officer searching premises under subsection (2) may seize and retain employee records, other than items subject to legal privilege, which he reasonably suspects will be of substantial value (whether on their own or together with other material) in the investigation of—

 (a)   an immigration employment offence, or
 (b)   an offence under section 105 or 106 of the Immigration and Asylum Act 1999 (c 33) (support for asylum-seeker: fraud).

(4)   The power under subsection (2) may be exercised only—

 (a)   to the extent that it is reasonably required for the purpose of discovering employee records other than items subject to legal privilege,
 (b)   if the constable or immigration officer produces identification showing his status, and
 (c)   if the constable or immigration officer reasonably believes that at least one of the conditions in subsection (5) applies.

(5)   Those conditions are—

 (a)   that it is not practicable to communicate with a person entitled to grant access to the records,
 (b)   that permission to search has been refused,
 (c)   that permission to search would be refused if requested, and

(d)   that the purpose of a search may be frustrated or seriously prejudiced if it is not carried out in reliance on subsection (2).

(6)   Subsection (4)(b) applies—

(a)   whether or not a constable or immigration officer is asked to produce identification, but
(b)   only where premises are occupied.

(7)   In this section "immigration employment offence" means an offence under section 8 of the Asylum and Immigration Act 1996 (c 49) (employment).

28FB   Search for personnel records: with warrant

(1)   This section applies where on an application made by an immigration officer in respect of business premises a justice of the peace is satisfied that there are reasonable grounds for believing—

(a)   that an employer has provided inaccurate or incomplete information under section 134 of the Nationality, Immigration and Asylum Act 2002 (compulsory disclosure by employer),
(b)   that employee records, other than items subject to legal privilege, will be found on the premises and will enable deduction of some or all of the information which the employer was required to provide, and
(c)   that at least one of the conditions in subsection (2) is satisfied.

(2)   Those conditions are—

(a)   that it is not practicable to communicate with a person entitled to grant access to the premises,
(b)   that it is not practicable to communicate with a person entitled to grant access to the records,
(c)   that entry to the premises or access to the records will not be granted unless a warrant is produced, and
(d)   that the purpose of a search may be frustrated or seriously prejudiced unless an immigration officer arriving at the premises can secure immediate entry.

(3)   The justice of the peace may issue a warrant authorising an immigration officer to enter and search the premises.

(4)   Subsection (7)(a) of section 28D shall have effect for the purposes of this section as it has effect for the purposes of that section.

(5)   An immigration officer searching premises under a warrant issued under this section may seize and retain employee records, other than items subject to legal privilege, which he reasonably suspects will be of substantial value (whether on their own or together with other material) in the investigation of—

(a)   an offence under section 137 of the Nationality, Immigration and Asylum Act 2002 (disclosure of information: offences) in respect of a requirement under section 134 of that Act, or
(b)   an offence under section 105 or 106 of the Immigration and Asylum Act 1999 (c 33) (support for asylum-seeker: fraud)."

Appointment
Appointment: 8 January 2003 (except in relation to the insertion of s 28FB above): see SI 2002/2811, art 2, Schedule; for transitional provisions see art 6 thereof.

155   Sections 153 and 154: supplemental

The following shall be added at the end of section 28L of the Immigration Act 1971 (c 77) (interpretation) (which becomes subsection (1))—

"(2) In this Part "business premises" means premises (or any part of premises) not used as a dwelling.

(3) In this Part "employee records" means records which show an employee's—

    (a) name,
    (b) date of birth,
    (c) address,
    (d) length of service,
    (e) rate of pay, or
    (f) nationality or citizenship.

(4) The Secretary of State may by order amend section 28CA(3)(a) to reflect a change in nomenclature.

(5) An order under subsection (4)—

    (a) must be made by statutory instrument, and
    (b) shall be subject to annulment in pursuance of a resolution of either House of Parliament."

Appointment
Appointment: 8 January 2003: see SI 2002/2811, art 2, Schedule.

156 Time limit on prosecution

(1) In section 28(1) of the Immigration Act 1971 (c 77) (extended time limit for prosecution) the words ", 24A, 25" shall cease to have effect.

(2) Section 24A(4) of that Act (deception: application of extended time limit) shall cease to have effect.

Appointment
Appointment: 10 February 2003: see SI 2003/1, art 2, Schedule.

PART 8
GENERAL

157 Consequential and incidental provision

(1) The Secretary of State may by order make consequential or incidental provision in connection with a provision of this Act.

(2) An order under this section may, in particular—

    (a) amend an enactment;
    (b) modify the effect of an enactment.

(3) An order under this section must be made by statutory instrument.

(4) An order under this section which amends an enactment shall not be made unless a draft has been laid before and approved by resolution of each House of Parliament.

(5) Any other order under this section shall be subject to annulment pursuant to a resolution of either House of Parliament.

Initial Commencement
Royal Assent: 7 November 2002: see s 162(2)(x).

Subordinate Legislation
Nationality, Immigration and Asylum Act 2002 (Consequential and Incidental Provisions) Order 2003, SI 2003/1016 (made under sub-s (1)).

158   Interpretation: "the Immigration Acts"

[(1)   A reference to "the Immigration Acts" shall be construed in accordance with section 44 of the Asylum and Immigration (Treatment of Claimants, etc) Act 2004.]

(3)   The following shall be substituted for section 32(5) of the Immigration Act 1971—

"(5)   In subsection (4) "the Immigration Acts" has the meaning given by section 158 of the Nationality, Immigration and Asylum Act 2002."

(4)   The following shall be substituted for the definition of "the Immigration Acts" in section 167(1) of the Immigration and Asylum Act 1999—

""the Immigration Acts" has the meaning given by section 158 of the Nationality, Immigration and Asylum Act 2002."

Appointment
Appointment: 10 February 2003: see SI 2003/1, art 2, Schedule.

Amendment
Sub-s (1): substituted, for sub-ss (1), (2) as originally enacted, by the Asylum and Immigration (Treatment of Claimants, etc) Act 2004, s 44(3). Date in force: 1 October 2004: see SI 2004/2523, art 2, Schedule.

159   Applied provision

(1)   Subsection (2) applies where this Act amends or refers to a provision which is applied by, under or for purposes of—

(a)   another provision of the Act which contains the provision, or
(b)   another Act.

(2)   The amendment or reference shall have effect in relation to the provision as applied.

(3)   Where this Act applies a provision of another Act, a reference to that provision in any enactment includes a reference to the provision as applied by this Act.

Appointment
Appointment: 10 February 2003: see SI 2003/1, art 2, Schedule.

160   Money

(1)   Expenditure of the Secretary of State or the Lord Chancellor in connection with a provision of this Act shall be paid out of money provided by Parliament.

(2)   An increase attributable to this Act in the amount payable out of money provided by Parliament under another enactment shall be paid out of money provided by Parliament.

(3)   A sum received by the Secretary of State or the Lord Chancellor in connection with a provision of this Act shall be paid into the Consolidated Fund.

Initial Commencement
Royal Assent: 7 November 2002: see s 162(2)(y).

161   Repeals

The provisions listed in Schedule 9 are hereby repealed to the extent specified.

Initial Commencement
Royal Assent (for certain purposes): 7 November 2002: see s 162(2)(w).
To be appointed (for remaining purposes): see s 162(1).

Appointment
Appointment (for certain purposes): 10 February 2003: see SI 2003/1, art 2, Schedule.
Appointment (for certain purposes): 1 April 2003: see SI 2003/754, art 2(1), Sch 1; for transitional provisions see art 3, Sch 2, para 6(4) thereto.
Appointment (for certain purposes): 8 December 2002: see SI 2002/2811, art 2, Schedule.

162   Commencement

(1)   Subject to subsections (2) to (5), the preceding provisions of this Act shall come into force in accordance with provision made by the Secretary of State by order.

(2)   The following provisions shall come into force on the passing of this Act—

    (a)   section 6,
    (b)   section 7,
    (c)   section 10(1) to (4) and (6),
    (d)   section 11,
    (e)   section 15 (and Schedule 2),
    (f)   section 16,
    (g)   section 35(1)(h),
    (h)   section 38,
    (i)   section 40(1),
    (j)   section 41(1),
    (k)   section 42,
    (l)   section 43,
    (m)   section 48,
    (n)   section 49,
    (o)   section 50,
    (p)   section 56,
    (q)   section 58,
    (r)   section 59,
    (s)   section 61,
    (t)   section 67,
    (u)   section 69,
    (v)   section 70,
    (w)   section 115 and paragraph 29 of Schedule 7 (and the relevant entry in Schedule 9),
    (x)   section 157, and
    (y)   section 160.

(3)   Section 5 shall have effect in relation to—

    (a)   an application made after the passing of this Act, and
    (b)   an application made, but not determined, before the passing of this Act.

(4)   Section 8 shall have effect in relation to—

    (a)   an application made on or after a date appointed by the Secretary of State by order, and
    (b)   an application made, but not determined, before that date.

(5)   Section 9 shall have effect in relation to a child born on or after a date appointed by the Secretary of State by order.

(6)   An order under subsection (1) may—

    (a)   make provision generally or for a specified purpose only (which may include the purpose of the application of a provision to or in relation to a particular place or area);

    (b)   make different provision for different purposes;

    (c)   include transitional provision;

    (d)   include savings;

    (e)   include consequential provision;

    (f)   include incidental provision.

(7)   An order under this section must be made by statutory instrument.

Initial Commencement
Royal Assent: 7 November 2002: (no specific commencement provision).

Subordinate Legislation
Nationality, Immigration and Asylum Act 2002 (Commencement No 1) Order 2002, SI 2002/2811 (made under sub-ss (1), (6)).
Nationality, Immigration and Asylum Act 2002 (Commencement No 2) Order 2003, SI 2003/1 (made under sub-ss (1), (6)).
Nationality, Immigration and Asylum Act 2002 (Commencement No 3) Order 2003, SI 2003/249 (made under sub-ss (1), (6)).
Nationality, Immigration and Asylum Act 2002 (Commencement No 4) Order 2003, SI 2003/754 (made under sub-ss (1), (4), (6)).
Nationality, Immigration and Asylum Act 2002 (Commencement No 4) (Amendment of Transitional Provisions) Order 2003, SI 2003/1040 (made under sub-ss (1), (6)).
Nationality, Immigration and Asylum Act 2002 (Commencement No 4) (Amendment) (No 2) Order 2003, SI 2003/1339 (made under sub-ss (1), (6)).
Nationality, Immigration and Asylum Act 2002 (Commencement No 4) (Amendment) (No 2) Order 2003, SI 2003/1339 (made under sub-ss (1), (6)).
Nationality, Immigration and Asylum Act 2002 (Commencement No 5) Order 2003, SI 2003/1747 (made under sub-s (1)).
Nationality, Immigration and Asylum Act 2002 (Commencement No 4) (Amendment) (No 3) Order 2003, SI 2003/2993 (made under sub-ss (1), (6)).
Nationality, Immigration and Asylum Act 2002 (Commencement No 6) Order 2003, SI 2003/3156 (made under sub-ss (1), (6)).
Nationality, Immigration and Asylum Act 2002 (Commencement No 7) Order 2004, SI 2004/1201 (made under sub-ss (1), (6)).
Nationality, Immigration and Asylum Act 2002 (Commencement No 8) Order 2004, SI 2004/1707 (made under sub-ss (1), (6)).
Nationality, Immigration and Asylum Act 2002 (Commencement No 9) Order 2004, SI 2004/2998 (made under sub-ss (1), (6)).

163   Extent

(1)   A provision of this Act which amends or repeals a provision of another Act or inserts a provision into another Act has the same extent as the provision amended or repealed or as the Act into which the insertion is made (ignoring, in any case, extent by virtue of an Order in Council).

(2)   Sections 145 and 146 extend only to—

    (a)   England and Wales, and

    (b)   Northern Ireland.

(3)   A provision of this Act to which neither subsection (1) nor subsection (2) applies extends to—

    (a)   England and Wales,

    (b)   Scotland, and

    (c)   Northern Ireland.

(4) Her Majesty may by Order in Council direct that a provision of this Act is to extend, with or without modification or adaptation, to—

(a) any of the Channel Islands;
(b) the Isle of Man.

(5) Subsection (4) does not apply in relation to the extension to a place of a provision which extends there by virtue of subsection (1).

Initial Commencement
Royal Assent: 7 November 2002: (no specific commencement provision).

164 Short title

This Act may be cited as the Nationality, Immigration and Asylum Act 2002.

Initial Commencement
Royal Assent: 7 November 2002: (no specific commencement provision).

SCHEDULE 1
CITIZENSHIP CEREMONY, OATH AND PLEDGE

Section 3

1 The following shall be substituted for section 42 of the British Nationality Act 1981 (c 61) (registration and naturalisation: fee and oath)—

"42 Registration and naturalisation: citizenship ceremony, oath and pledge

(1) A person of full age shall not be registered under this Act as a British citizen unless he has made the relevant citizenship oath and pledge specified in Schedule 5 at a citizenship ceremony.

(2) A certificate of naturalisation as a British citizen shall not be granted under this Act to a person of full age unless he has made the relevant citizenship oath and pledge specified in Schedule 5 at a citizenship ceremony.

(3) A person of full age shall not be registered under this Act as a British overseas territories citizen unless he has made the relevant citizenship oath and pledge specified in Schedule 5.

(4) A certificate of naturalisation as a British overseas territories citizen shall not be granted under this Act to a person of full age unless he has made the relevant citizenship oath and pledge specified in Schedule 5.

(5) A person of full age shall not be registered under this Act as a British Overseas citizen or a British subject unless he has made the relevant citizenship oath specified in Schedule 5.

(6) Where the Secretary of State thinks it appropriate because of the special circumstances of a case he may—

(a) disapply any of subsections (1) to (5), or
(b) modify the effect of any of those subsections.

(7) Sections 5 and 6 of the Oaths Act 1978 (c 19) (affirmation) apply to a citizenship oath; and a reference in this Act to a citizenship oath includes a reference to a citizenship affirmation.

42A   Registration and naturalisation: fee

(1)   A person shall not be registered under a provision of this Act as a citizen of any description or as a British subject unless any fee payable by virtue of this Act in connection with the registration has been paid.

(2)   A certificate of naturalisation shall not be granted to a person under a provision of this Act unless any fee payable by virtue of this Act in connection with the grant of the certificate has been paid.

42B   Registration and naturalisation: timing

(1)   A person who is registered under this Act as a citizen of any description or as a British subject shall be treated as having become a citizen or subject—

(a)   immediately on making the required citizenship oath and pledge in accordance with section 42, or

(b)   where the requirement for an oath and pledge is disapplied, immediately on registration.

(2)   A person granted a certificate of naturalisation under this Act as a citizen of any description shall be treated as having become a citizen—

(a)   immediately on making the required citizenship oath and pledge in accordance with section 42, or

(b)   where the requirement for an oath and pledge is disapplied, immediately on the grant of the certificate.

(3)   In the application of subsection (1) to registration as a British Overseas citizen or as a British subject the reference to the citizenship oath and pledge shall be taken as a reference to the citizenship oath."

2   The following shall be substituted for Schedule 5 to the British Nationality Act 1981 (c 61)—

"SCHEDULE 5
CITIZENSHIP OATH AND PLEDGE

1   The form of citizenship oath and pledge is as follows for registration of or naturalisation as a British citizen—

Oath

"I, *[name]*, swear by Almighty God that, on becoming a British citizen, I will be faithful and bear true allegiance to Her Majesty Queen Elizabeth the Second, Her Heirs and Successors according to law."

Pledge

"I will give my loyalty to the United Kingdom and respect its rights and freedoms. I will uphold its democratic values. I will observe its laws faithfully and fulfil my duties and obligations as a British citizen."

2   The form of citizenship oath and pledge is as follows for registration of or naturalisation as a British overseas territories citizen—

Oath

"I, *[name]*, swear by Almighty God that, on becoming a British overseas territories citizen, I will be faithful and bear true allegiance to Her Majesty Queen Elizabeth the Second, Her Heirs and Successors according to law."

Pledge

"I will give my loyalty to *[name of territory]* and respect its rights and freedoms. I will uphold its democratic values. I will observe its laws faithfully and fulfil my duties and obligations as a British overseas territories citizen."

3 The form of citizenship oath is as follows for registration of a British Overseas citizen—

I, *[name]*, swear by Almighty God that, on becoming a British Overseas citizen, I will be faithful and bear true allegiance to Her Majesty Queen Elizabeth the Second, Her Heirs and Successors according to law."

4 The form of citizenship oath is as follows for registration of a British subject—

"I, *[name]*, swear by Almighty God that, on becoming a British subject, I will be faithful and bear true allegiance to Her Majesty Queen Elizabeth the Second, Her Heirs and Successors according to law."."

3 Section 41 of the British Nationality Act 1981 (c 61) (regulations) shall be amended as follows.

4 For subsection (1)(d) substitute—

"(d) for the time within which an obligation to make a citizenship oath and pledge at a citizenship ceremony must be satisfied;
(da) for the time within which an obligation to make a citizenship oath or pledge must be satisfied;
(db) for the content and conduct of a citizenship ceremony;
(dc) for the administration and making of a citizenship oath or pledge;
(dd) for the registration and certification of the making of a citizenship oath or pledge;
(de) for the completion and grant of a certificate of registration or naturalisation;".

5 In subsection (2)(c)—

(a) for "the taking there of any oath of allegiance" substitute "the making there of a citizenship oath or pledge", and
(b) for "granted or taken" substitute "or granted".

6 In subsection (3)(a) for "taking of oaths of allegiance" substitute "making of oaths and pledges of citizenship".

7 After subsection (3) insert—

"(3A) Regulations under subsection (1)(d) to (de) may, in particular—

(a) enable the Secretary of State to designate or authorise a person to exercise a function (which may include a discretion) in connection with a citizenship ceremony or a citizenship oath or pledge;
(b) require, or enable the Secretary of State to require, a local authority to provide specified facilities and to make specified arrangements in connection with citizenship ceremonies;
(c) impose, or enable the Secretary of State to impose, a function (which may include a discretion) on a local authority or on a registrar.

(3B) In subsection (3A)—

"local authority" means—
(a) in relation to England and Wales, a county council, a county borough council, a metropolitan district council, a London Borough Council and the Common Council of the City of London, and
(b) in relation to Scotland, a council constituted under section 2 of the Local Government etc (Scotland) Act 1994 (c 39), and
"registrar" means—

(a)   in relation to England and Wales, a superintendent registrar of births, deaths and marriages (or, in accordance with section 8 of the Registration Service Act 1953 (c 37), a deputy superintendent registrar), and

(b)   in relation to Scotland, a district registrar within the meaning of section 7(12) of the Registration of Births, Deaths and Marriages (Scotland) Act 1965 (c 49)."

8   The Secretary of State may make a payment to a local authority in respect of anything done by the authority in accordance with regulations made by virtue of section 41(3A) of the British Nationality Act 1981 (c 61).

9   (1)   A local authority must—

(a)   comply with a requirement imposed on it by regulations made by virtue of that section, and

(b)   carry out a function imposed on it by regulations made by virtue of that section.

(2)   A local authority on which a requirement or function is imposed by regulations made by virtue of that section—

(a)   may provide facilities or make arrangements in addition to those which it is required to provide or make, and

(b)   may make a charge for the provision of facilities or the making of arrangements under paragraph (a) which does not exceed the cost of providing the facilities or making the arrangements.

Appointment
Appointment: 1 January 2004 (except in relation to any application for registration or naturalisation made before that date): see SI 2003/3156, arts 2(a), 3, 4.

SCHEDULE 2
NATIONALITY: REPEAL OF SPENT PROVISIONS

Section 15

1   The following provisions of the British Nationality Act 1981 (c 61) shall cease to have effect—

(a)   section 7 (registration as British citizen by virtue of residence or employment),

(b)   section 8 (registration as British citizen by virtue of marriage),

(c)   section 9 (registration as British citizen by virtue of father's status),

(d)   section 19 (registration as British Dependent Territories citizen by virtue of residence),

(e)   section 20 (registration as British Dependent Territories citizen by virtue of marriage),

(f)   section 21 (registration as British Dependent Territories citizen by virtue of father's status),

(g)   section 27(2) (entitlement of minor to registration as British Overseas citizen),

(h)   section 28 (registration as British Overseas citizen by virtue of marriage), and

(i)   section 33 (registration as British subject of certain women by virtue of earlier entitlement).

2   Nothing in this Schedule has any effect in relation to a registration made under a provision before its repeal.

Initial Commencement
Royal Assent: 7 November 2002: see s 162(2)(e).

SCHEDULE 3
WITHHOLDING AND WITHDRAWAL OF SUPPORT

Section 54

Ineligibility for support

1 (1) A person to whom this paragraph applies shall not be eligible for support or assistance under—

 (a) section 21 or 29 of the National Assistance Act 1948 (c 29) (local authority: accommodation and welfare),

 (b) section 45 of the Health Services and Public Health Act 1968 (c 46) (local authority: welfare of elderly),

 (c) section 12 or 13A of the Social Work (Scotland) Act 1968 (c 49) (social welfare services),

 (d) Article 7 or 15 of the Health and Personal Social Services (Northern Ireland) Order 1972 (SI 1972/1265 (NI 14)) (prevention of illness, social welfare, &c),

 (e) section 21 of and Schedule 8 to the National Health Service Act 1977 (c 49) (social services),

 (f) section 29(1)(b) of the Housing (Scotland) Act 1987 (c 26) (interim duty to accommodate in case of apparent priority need where review of a local authority decision has been requested),

 (g) section 17, 23C, 24A or 24B of the Children Act 1989 (c 41) (welfare and other powers which can be exercised in relation to adults),

 (h) Article 18, 35 or 36 of the Children (Northern Ireland) Order 1995 (SI 1995/755 (NI 2)) (welfare and other powers which can be exercised in relation to adults),

 (i) sections 22, 29 and 30 of the Children (Scotland) Act 1995 (c 36) (provisions analogous to those mentioned in paragraph (g)),

 (j) section 188(3) or 204(4) of the Housing Act 1996 (c 52) (accommodation pending review or appeal),

 (k) section 2 of the Local Government Act 2000 (c 22) (promotion of well-being),

 (l) a provision of the Immigration and Asylum Act 1999 (c 33), or

 (m) a provision of this Act.

(2) A power or duty under a provision referred to in sub-paragraph (1) may not be exercised or performed in respect of a person to whom this paragraph applies (whether or not the person has previously been in receipt of support or assistance under the provision).

(3) An approval or directions given under or in relation to a provision referred to in sub-paragraph (1) shall be taken to be subject to sub-paragraph (2).

Exceptions

2 (1) Paragraph 1 does not prevent the provision of support or assistance—

 (a) to a British citizen, or

 (b) to a child, or

 (c) under or by virtue of regulations made under paragraph 8, 9 or 10 below, or

 (d) in a case in respect of which, and to the extent to which, regulations made by the Secretary of State disapply paragraph 1, or

 (e) in circumstances in respect of which, and to the extent to which, regulations made by the Secretary of State disapply paragraph 1.

(2) Regulations under sub-paragraph (1)(d) may confer a discretion on the Secretary of State.

(3)   Regulations under sub-paragraph (1)(e) may, in particular, disapply paragraph 1 to the provision of support or assistance by a local authority to a person where the authority—

  (a)   has taken steps in accordance with guidance issued by the Secretary of State to determine whether paragraph 1 would (but for the regulations) apply to the person, and
  (b)   has concluded on the basis of those steps that there is no reason to believe that paragraph 1 would apply.

(4)   Regulations under sub-paragraph (1)(d) or (e) may confer a discretion on an authority.

(5)   A local authority which is considering whether to give support or assistance to a person under a provision listed in paragraph 1(1) shall act in accordance with any relevant guidance issued by the Secretary of State under sub-paragraph (3)(a).

(6)   A reference in this Schedule to a person to whom paragraph 1 applies includes a reference to a person in respect of whom that paragraph is disapplied to a limited extent by regulations under sub-paragraph (1)(d) or (e), except in a case for which the regulations provide otherwise.

3   Paragraph 1 does not prevent the exercise of a power or the performance of a duty if, and to the extent that, its exercise or performance is necessary for the purpose of avoiding a breach of—

  (a)   a person's Convention rights, or
  (b)   a person's rights under the Community Treaties.

First class of ineligible person: refugee status abroad

4   (1)   Paragraph 1 applies to a person if he—

  (a)   has refugee status abroad, or
  (b)   is the dependant of a person who is in the United Kingdom and who has refugee status abroad.

(2)   For the purposes of this paragraph a person has refugee status abroad if—

  (a)   he does not have the nationality of an EEA State, and
  (b)   the government of an EEA State other than the United Kingdom has determined that he is entitled to protection as a refugee under the Refugee Convention.

Second class of ineligible person: citizen of other EEA State

5   Paragraph 1 applies to a person if he—

  (a)   has the nationality of an EEA State other than the United Kingdom, or
  (b)   is the dependant of a person who has the nationality of an EEA State other than the United Kingdom.

Third class of ineligible person: failed asylum-seeker

6   (1)   Paragraph 1 applies to a person if—

  (a)   he was (but is no longer) an asylum-seeker, and
  (b)   he fails to cooperate with removal directions issued in respect of him.

(2)   Paragraph 1 also applies to a dependant of a person to whom that paragraph applies by virtue of sub-paragraph (1).

Fourth class of ineligible person: person unlawfully in United Kingdom

7 Paragraph 1 applies to a person if—

(a) he is in the United Kingdom in breach of the immigration laws within the meaning of section 11, and

(b) he is not an asylum-seeker.

[Fifth class of ineligible person: failed asylum-seeker with family

7A (1) Paragraph 1 applies to a person if—

(a) he—
    (i) is treated as an asylum-seeker for the purposes of Part VI of the Immigration and Asylum Act 1999 (c 33) (support) by virtue only of section 94(3A) (failed asylum-seeker with dependent child), or
    (ii) is treated as an asylum-seeker for the purposes of Part 2 of this Act by virtue only of section 18(2),

(b) the Secretary of State has certified that in his opinion the person has failed without reasonable excuse to take reasonable steps—
    (i) to leave the United Kingdom voluntarily, or
    (ii) to place himself in a position in which he is able to leave the United Kingdom voluntarily,

(c) the person has received a copy of the Secretary of State's certificate, and

(d) the period of 14 days, beginning with the date on which the person receives the copy of the certificate, has elapsed.

(2) Paragraph 1 also applies to a dependant of a person to whom that paragraph applies by virtue of sub-paragraph (1).

(3) For the purpose of sub-paragraph (1)(d) if the Secretary of State sends a copy of a certificate by first class post to a person's last known address, the person shall be treated as receiving the copy on the second day after the day on which it was posted.

(4) The Secretary of State may by regulations vary the period specified in sub-paragraph (1)(d).]

Travel assistance

8 The Secretary of State may make regulations providing for arrangements to be made enabling a person to whom paragraph 1 applies by virtue of paragraph 4 or 5 to leave the United Kingdom.

Temporary accommodation

9 (1) The Secretary of State may make regulations providing for arrangements to be made for the accommodation of a person to whom paragraph 1 applies pending the implementation of arrangements made by virtue of paragraph 8.

(2) Arrangements for a person by virtue of this paragraph—

(a) may be made only if the person has with him a dependent child, and

(b) may include arrangements for a dependent child.

10 (1) The Secretary of State may make regulations providing for arrangements to be made for the accommodation of a person if—

(a) paragraph 1 applies to him by virtue of paragraph 7, and

(b) he has not failed to cooperate with removal directions issued in respect of him.

(2) Arrangements for a person by virtue of this paragraph—

(a) may be made only if the person has with him a dependent child, and

(b) may include arrangements for a dependent child.

Assistance and accommodation: general

11 Regulations under paragraph 8, 9 or 10 may—

(a) provide for the making of arrangements under a provision referred to in paragraph 1(1) or otherwise;
(b) confer a function (which may include the exercise of a discretion) on the Secretary of State, a local authority or another person;
(c) provide that arrangements must be made in a specified manner or in accordance with specified principles;
(d) provide that arrangements may not be made in a specified manner;
(e) require a local authority or another person to have regard to guidance issued by the Secretary of State in making arrangements;
(f) require a local authority or another person to comply with a direction of the Secretary of State in making arrangements.

12 (1) Regulations may, in particular, provide that if a person refuses an offer of arrangements under paragraph 8 or fails to implement or cooperate with arrangements made for him under that paragraph—

(a) new arrangements may be made for him under paragraph 8, but
(b) new arrangements may not be made for him under paragraph 9.

(2) Regulations by virtue of this paragraph may include exceptions in the case of a person who—

(a) has a reason of a kind specified in the regulations for failing to implement or cooperate with arrangements made under paragraph 8, and
(b) satisfies any requirements of the regulations for proof of the reason.

Offences

13 (1) A person who leaves the United Kingdom in accordance with arrangements made under paragraph 8 commits an offence if he—

(a) returns to the United Kingdom, and
(b) requests that arrangements be made for him by virtue of paragraph 8, 9 or 10.

(2) A person commits an offence if he—

(a) requests that arrangements be made for him by virtue of paragraph 8, 9 or 10, and
(b) fails to mention a previous request by him for the making of arrangements under any of those paragraphs.

(3) A person who is guilty of an offence under this paragraph shall be liable on summary conviction to imprisonment for a term not exceeding six months.

Information

14 (1) If it appears to a local authority that paragraph 1 applies or may apply to a person in the authority's area by virtue of [paragraph 6, 7 or 7A], the authority must inform the Secretary of State.

(2) A local authority shall act in accordance with any relevant guidance issued by the Secretary of State for the purpose of determining whether paragraph 1 applies or may apply to a person in the authority's area by virtue of [paragraph 6, 7 or 7A].

Power to amend Schedule

15   The Secretary of State may by order amend this Schedule so as—

(a)   to provide for paragraph 1 to apply or not to apply to a class of person;
(b)   to add or remove a provision to or from the list in paragraph 1(1);
(c)   to add, amend or remove a limitation of or exception to paragraph 1.

Orders and regulations

16   (1)   An order or regulations under this Schedule must be made by statutory instrument.

(2)   An order or regulations under this Schedule may—

(a)   make provision which applies generally or only in specified cases or circumstances or only for specified purposes;
(b)   make different provision for different cases, circumstances or purposes;
(c)   make transitional provision;
(d)   make consequential provision (which may include provision amending a provision made by or under this or another Act).

(3)   An order under this Schedule, regulations under paragraph 2(1)(d) or (e) or other regulations which include consequential provision amending an enactment shall not be made unless a draft has been laid before and approved by resolution of each House of Parliament.

(4)   Regulations under this Schedule to which sub-paragraph (3) does not apply shall be subject to annulment in pursuance of a resolution of either House of Parliament.

Interpretation

17   (1)   In this Schedule—

"asylum-seeker" means a person—
(a)   who is at least 18 years old,
(b)   who has made a claim for asylum (within the meaning of section 18(3)), and
(c)   whose claim has been recorded by the Secretary of State but not determined,

"Convention rights" has the same meaning as in the Human Rights Act 1998 (c 42),

"child" means a person under the age of eighteen,

"dependant" and "dependent" shall have such meanings as may be prescribed by regulations made by the Secretary of State,

"EEA State" means a State which is a contracting party to the Agreement on the European Economic Area signed at Oporto on 2nd May 1992 (as it has effect from time to time),

"local authority"—
(a)   in relation to England and Wales, has the same meaning as in section 129(3),
(b)   in relation to Scotland, has the same meaning as in section 129(4), and
(c)   in relation to Northern Ireland, means a health service body within the meaning of section 133(4)(d) and the Northern Ireland Housing Executive (for which purpose a reference to the authority's area shall be taken as a reference to Northern Ireland),

"the Refugee Convention" means the Convention relating to the status of Refugees done at Geneva on 28th July 1951 and its Protocol, and "removal directions" means directions under Schedule 2 to the Immigration Act 1971 (c 77) (control of entry, &c), under Schedule 3 to that Act (deportation) or under section 10 of the Immigration and Asylum Act 1999 (c 33) (removal of person unlawfully in United Kingdom).

(2)   For the purpose of the definition of "asylum-seeker" in sub-paragraph (1) a claim is determined if—

(a)   the Secretary of State has notified the claimant of his decision,
(b)   no appeal against the decision can be brought (disregarding the possibility of an appeal out of time with permission), and
(c)   any appeal which has already been brought has been disposed of.

(3)   For the purpose of sub-paragraph (2)(c) an appeal is disposed of when it is no longer pending for the purpose of—

(a)   Part 5 of this Act, or
(b)   the Special Immigration Appeals Commission Act 1997 (c 68).

(4)   The giving of directions in respect of a person under a provision of the Immigration Acts is not the provision of assistance to him for the purposes of this Schedule.

Appointment
Paras 1, 3–7, 13, 14, 17: Appointment: 8 January 2003: see SI 2002/2811, art 2, Schedule.
Paras 2, 8–12, 15, 16: Appointment (for the purpose of enabling the Secretary of State to exercise the power to make subordinate legislation): 8 December 2002: see SI 2002/2811, art 2, Schedule.
Paras 2, 8–12, 15, 16: Appointment (for remaining purposes): 8 January 2003: see SI 2002/2811, art 2, Schedule.

Amendment
Para 7A: inserted by the Asylum and Immigration (Treatment of Claimants, etc) Act 2004, s 9(1). Date in force: 1 December 2004: see SI 2004/2999, art 2, Schedule; for transitional provision and further effect in relation to appeals under the Immigration and Asylum Act 1999, s 103 see art 4 thereof and the Asylum and Immigration (Treatment of Claimants, etc) Act 2004, s 9(3), (4).
Para 14: words "paragraph 6, 7 or 7A" in square brackets in both places they occur substituted by the Asylum and Immigration (Treatment of Claimants, etc) Act 2004, s 9(2). Date in force: 1 December 2004: see SI 2004/2999, art 2, Schedule; for transitional provision and further effect in relation to appeals under the Immigration and Asylum Act 1999, s 103 see art 4 thereof and the Asylum and Immigration (Treatment of Claimants, etc) Act 2004, s 9(3), (4).

See Further
By virtue of the Asylum and Immigration (Treatment of Claimants, etc) Act 2004 (Commencement No 2) Order 2004, SI 2004/2999, art 3, reference to "section 94(3A)" in para 7A(1)(a)(i) above shall be construed as a reference to "section 94(5)" until s 44 to this Act comes into force.

Subordinate Legislation
Withholding and Withdrawal of Support (Travel Assistance and Temporary Accommodation) Regulations 2002, SI 2002/3078 (made under paras 8–12, 16(2), 17).

[SCHEDULE 4
THE ASYLUM AND IMMIGRATION TRIBUNAL]

[Section 81]

[Membership

1   The Lord Chancellor shall appoint the members of the Asylum and Immigration Tribunal.

2   (1)   A person is eligible for appointment as a member of the Tribunal only if he—

(a) has a seven year general qualification within the meaning of section 71 of the Courts and Legal Services Act 1990 (c 41),

(b) is an advocate or solicitor in Scotland of at least seven years' standing,

(c) is a member of the Bar of Northern Ireland, or a solicitor of the Supreme Court of Northern Ireland, of at least seven years' standing,

(d) in the Lord Chancellor's opinion, has legal experience which makes him as suitable for appointment as if he satisfied paragraph (a), (b) or (c), or

(e) in the Lord Chancellor's opinion, has non-legal experience which makes him suitable for appointment.

(2) A person appointed under sub-paragraph (1)(a) to (d) shall be known as a legally qualified member of the Tribunal.

3 (1) A member—

(a) may resign by notice in writing to the Lord Chancellor,

(b) shall cease to be a member on reaching the age of 70, and

(c) otherwise, shall hold and vacate office in accordance with the terms of his appointment (which may include provision—
　(i) about the training, appraisal and mentoring of members of the Tribunal by other members, and
　(ii) for removal).

(2) Sub-paragraph (1)(b) is subject to section 26(4) to (6) of the Judicial Pensions and Retirement Act 1993 (c 8) (extension to age 75).

4 The Lord Chancellor may by order make provision for the title of members of the Tribunal.

Presidency

5 (1) The Lord Chancellor shall appoint—

(a) a member of the Tribunal, who holds or has held high judicial office within the meaning of the Appellate Jurisdiction Act 1876 (c 59), as President of the Tribunal, and

(b) one or more members of the Tribunal as Deputy President.

(2) A Deputy President—

(a) may act for the President if the President is unable to act or unavailable, and

(b) shall perform such functions as the President may delegate or assign to him.

Proceedings

6 The Tribunal shall sit at times and places determined by the Lord Chancellor.

7 (1) The jurisdiction of the Tribunal shall be exercised by such number of its members as the President, having regard to the complexity and other circumstances of particular cases or classes of case, may direct.

(2) A direction under this paragraph—

(a) may relate to the whole or part of specified proceedings or to the whole or part of proceedings of a specified kind,

(b) may enable jurisdiction to be exercised by a single member,

(c) may require or permit the transfer of the whole or part of proceedings—
　(i) from one member to another,
　(ii) from one group of members to another,
　(iii) from one member to a group of members, or
　(iv) from a group of members to one member,

(d) may be varied or revoked by a further direction, and

(e)   is subject to rules under section 106.

8   (1)   The President may make arrangements for the allocation of proceedings to members of the Tribunal.

(2)   Arrangements under this paragraph—

(a)   may permit allocation by the President or another member of the Tribunal,
(b)   may permit the allocation of a case to a specified member or to a specified class of member,
(c)   may include provision for transfer, and
(d)   are subject to rules under section 106.

Staff

9   The Lord Chancellor may appoint staff for the Tribunal.

Money

10   The Lord Chancellor—

(a)   may pay remuneration and allowances to members of the Tribunal,
(b)   may pay remuneration and allowances to staff of the Tribunal, and
(c)   may defray expenses of the Tribunal.

11   The Lord Chancellor may pay compensation to a person who ceases to be a member of the Tribunal if the Lord Chancellor thinks it appropriate because of special circumstances.]

Amendment
Substituted by the Asylum and Immigration (Treatment of Claimants, etc) Act 2004, s 26(4), Sch 1; for transitional provisions see s 26(7), Sch 2, Pt 2 thereto. Date in force: 4 April 2005: see SI 2005/565, art 2(c); for transitional provisions in relation to pending appeals which were made to an adjudicator before 4 April 2005 and in relation to further appeals and applications in such cases see arts 3–9 thereof.

Subordinate Legislation
Asylum and Immigration Tribunal (Judicial Titles) Order 2005, SI 2005/227 (made under para 4).

SCHEDULE 5
...

...

Amendment
Repealed by the Asylum and Immigration (Treatment of Claimants, etc) Act 2004, ss 26(5)(b), 47, Sch 4; for transitional provisions see s 26(7), Sch 2, Pt 2 thereto. Date in force: 4 April 2005: see SI 2005/565, art 2(a); for transitional provisions in relation to pending appeals which were made to an adjudicator before 4 April 2005 and in relation to further appeals and applications in such cases see arts 3–9 thereof.

SCHEDULE 6
IMMIGRATION AND ASYLUM APPEALS: TRANSITIONAL PROVISION

Section 114

"Commencement"

1   In this Schedule "commencement" means the coming into force of Part 5 of this Act.

Adjudicator

2 Where a person is an adjudicator under section 57 of the Immigration and Asylum Act 1999 (c 33) immediately before commencement his appointment shall have effect after commencement as if made under section 81 of this Act.

Tribunal

3 (1) Where a person is a member of the Immigration Appeal Tribunal immediately before commencement his appointment shall have effect after commencement as if made under Schedule 5.

(2) Where a person is a member of staff of the Immigration Appeal Tribunal immediately before commencement his appointment shall have effect after commencement as if made under Schedule 5.

Earlier appeal

4 In the application of section 96—

    (a) a reference to an appeal or right of appeal under a provision of this Act includes a reference to an appeal or right of appeal under the Immigration and Asylum Act 1999,

    (b) a reference to a requirement imposed under this Act includes a reference to a requirement of a similar nature imposed under that Act,

    (c) a reference to a statement made in pursuance of a requirement imposed under a provision of this Act includes a reference to anything done in compliance with a requirement of a similar nature under that Act, and

    (d) a reference to notification by virtue of this Act includes a reference to notification by virtue of any other enactment.

Saving

5 (1) This Schedule is without prejudice to the power to include transitional provision in an order under section 162.

(2) An order under that section may, in particular, provide for a reference to a provision of Part 5 of this Act to be treated as being or including a reference (with or without modification) to a provision of the Immigration and Asylum Act 1999 (c 33).

Appointment
Appointment: 1 April 2003: see SI 2003/754, art 2(1), Sch 1; for transitional provisions see art 3(1) thereof.

SCHEDULE 7
IMMIGRATION AND ASYLUM APPEALS: CONSEQUENTIAL AMENDMENTS

Section 114

Immigration Act 1971 (c 77)

1 In section 33(4) of the Immigration Act 1971 (c 77) (pending appeal: interpretation) for paragraphs (a) and (b) substitute "in accordance with section 104 of the Nationality, Immigration and Asylum Act 2002 (pending appeals)".

2 In paragraph 2A(9) of Schedule 2 to that Act (control of entry: person with continuing leave) for "Part IV of the Immigration and Asylum Act 1999" substitute "Part 5 of the Nationality, Immigration and Asylum Act 2002 (immigration and asylum appeals)".

3 In paragraph 4(4) of that Schedule (examination and detention of documents) for "an appeal under this Act" substitute "an appeal under the Nationality, Immigration and Asylum Act 2002".

4 In paragraph 8(2) of that Schedule (time within which directions may be given) after "United Kingdom" insert "(ignoring any period during which an appeal by him under the Immigration Acts is pending)".

5 In paragraph 25 of that Schedule (rules) for "section 22 of this Act" substitute "section 106 of the Nationality, Immigration and Asylum Act 2002 (appeals)".

6 In paragraph 29 of that Schedule (bail pending appeal)—

    (a)   in sub-paragraph (1), for the words from "section" to "1999" substitute "Part 5 of the Nationality, Immigration and Asylum Act 2002", and

    (b)   for the words "Appeal Tribunal" substitute, in each place, "Immigration Appeal Tribunal".

7 In paragraph 2(2) of Schedule 3 to that Act (deportation) for "section 18 of this Act" substitute "section 105 of the Nationality, Immigration and Asylum Act 2002 (notice of decision)".

8 For paragraph 3 of that Schedule (deportation: effect of appeal) substitute—

"3 So far as they relate to an appeal under section 82(1) of the Nationality, Immigration and Asylum Act 2002 against a decision of the kind referred to in section 82(2)(j) or (k) of that Act (decision to make deportation order and refusal to revoke deportation order), paragraphs 29 to 33 of Schedule 2 to this Act shall apply for the purposes of this Schedule as if the reference in paragraph 29(1) to Part I of that Schedule were a reference to this Schedule."

House of Commons Disqualification Act 1975 (c 24)

9 In Part III of Schedule 1 to the House of Commons Disqualification Act 1975 (disqualifying offices) for "Adjudicator appointed for the purposes of the Immigration and Asylum Act 1999." substitute "Adjudicator appointed for the purposes of Part 5 of the Nationality, Immigration and Asylum Act 2002.".

Northern Ireland Assembly Disqualification Act 1975 (c 25)

10 In Part III of Schedule 1 to the Northern Ireland Assembly Disqualification Act 1975 (disqualifying offices) for "Adjudicator appointed for the purposes of the Immigration and Asylum Act 1999." substitute "Adjudicator appointed for the purposes of Part 5 of the Nationality, Immigration and Asylum Act 2002.".

Race Relations Act 1976 (c 74)

11 In section 53(1) (restriction of proceedings) for "Part IV of the Immigration and Asylum Act 1999" substitute "Part 5 of the Nationality, Immigration and Asylum Act 2002".

12 Section 57A (immigration cases) shall be amended as follows—

    (a)   in subsection (1)(a) for "Part IV of the 1999 Act" substitute "Part 5 of the 2002 Act",

    (b)   in subsection (5) for the definition of "the Immigration Acts" substitute—
""the Immigration Acts" has the meaning given by section 158 of the 2002 Act;",

    (c)   in that subsection in the definition of "immigration appellate body" for "the 1999 Act" substitute "Part 5 of the 2002 Act",

    (d)   in that subsection for the definition of "immigration authority" substitute—

""immigration authority" means the Secretary of State, an immigration officer or a person responsible for the grant or refusal of entry clearance (within the meaning of section 33(1) of the Immigration Act 1971 (c 77));",

(e) in that subsection in the definition of "pending" for "Part IV of the 1999 Act" substitute "Part 5 of the 2002 Act",

(f) in that subsection in the definition of "relevant decision" for "Part IV of the 1999 Act" substitute "Part 5 of the 2002 Act",

(g) in that subsection in the definition of "relevant immigration proceedings" for "Part IV of the 1999 Act" substitute "Part 5 of the 2002 Act", and

(h) in that subsection for the definition of "the 1999 Act" substitute—

""the 2002 Act" means the Nationality, Immigration and Asylum Act 2002;".

13 In section 62(1)(ba) (persistent discrimination) for "Part IV of the Immigration and Asylum Act 1999" substitute "Part 5 of the Nationality, Immigration and Asylum Act 2002".

14 In section 65(7)(b) (help for aggrieved person) for "Part IV of the Immigration and Asylum Act 1999" substitute "Part 5 of the Nationality, Immigration and Asylum Act 2002".

15 In section 66 (assistance by Commission)—

(a) in subsection (8) for "Part IV of the Immigration and Asylum Act 1999" substitute "Part 5 of the Nationality, Immigration and Asylum Act 2002", and

(b) in subsection (9)—

(i) for "Part IV of the Act of 1999" substitute "Part 5 of the Act of 2002",

(ii) for "rules under section 5 or 8 of that Act;" substitute "rules under that Act;", and

(iii) for "rules under paragraph 3 or 4 of Schedule 4 to that Act." substitute "rules under that Act.".

Courts and Legal Services Act 1990 (c 41)

16 In Schedule 11 to the Courts and Legal Services Act 1990 (judges &c barred from legal practice) for "Adjudicator for the purposes of the Immigration and Asylum Act 1999 (other than Asylum Support Adjudicator)" substitute "Adjudicator appointed for the purposes of Part 5 of the Nationality, Immigration and Asylum Act 2002".

Tribunals and Inquiries Act 1992 (c 53)

17 In paragraph 22 of Schedule 1 to the Tribunals and Inquiries Act 1992 (tribunals under the supervision of the Council on Tribunals)—

(a) in sub-paragraph (a), for "section 57 of the Immigration and Asylum Act 1999" substitute "section 81 of the Nationality, Immigration and Asylum Act 2002", and

(b) in sub-paragraph (b), for "section 56 of that Act" substitute "section 100 of that Act".

Judicial Pensions and Retirement Act 1993 (c 8)

18 In Part II of Schedule 1 to the Judicial Pensions and Retirement Act 1993 (offices which may be qualifying judicial offices) for "Adjudicator for the purposes of the Immigration and Asylum Act 1999 (other than Asylum Support Adjudicator)" substitute "Adjudicator appointed for the purposes of Part 5 of the Nationality, Immigration and Asylum Act 2002".

19 In Schedule 5 to that Act (retirement provisions: the relevant offices) for "Adjudicator for the purposes of the Immigration and Asylum Act 1999 (other than

Asylum Support Adjudicator)" substitute "Adjudicator appointed for the purposes of Part 5 of the Nationality, Immigration and Asylum Act 2002".

Special Immigration Appeals Commission Act 1997 (c 68)

20   The following shall be substituted for section 2 of the Special Immigration Appeals Commission Act 1997 (jurisdiction: appeals)—

"2   Jurisdiction: appeals

(1)   A person may appeal to the Special Immigration Appeals Commission against a decision if—

    (a)   he would be able to appeal against the decision under section 82(1) or 83(2) of the Nationality, Immigration and Asylum Act 2002 but for a certificate of the Secretary of State under section 97 of that Act (national security, &c), or

    (b)   an appeal against the decision under section 82(1) or 83(2) of that Act lapsed under section 99 of that Act by virtue of a certificate of the Secretary of State under section 97 of that Act.

(2)   The following provisions shall apply, with any necessary modifications, in relation to an appeal against an immigration decision under this section as they apply in relation to an appeal under section 82(1) of the Nationality, Immigration and Asylum Act 2002—

    (a)   section 3C of the Immigration Act 1971 (c 77) (continuation of leave pending variation decision),

    (b)   section 78 of the Nationality, Immigration and Asylum Act 2002 (no removal while appeal pending),

    (c)   section 79 of that Act (deportation order: appeal),

    (d)   section 82(3) of that Act (variation or revocation of leave to enter or remain: appeal),

    (e)   section 84 of that Act (grounds of appeal),

    (f)   section 85 of that Act (matters to be considered),

    (g)   section 86 of that Act (determination of appeal),

    (h)   section 87 of that Act (successful appeal: direction),

    (i)   section 96 of that Act (earlier right of appeal),

    (j)   section 104 of that Act (pending appeal),

    (k)   section 105 of that Act (notice of immigration decision), and

    (l)   section 110 of that Act (grants).

(3)   The following provisions shall apply, with any necessary modifications, in relation to an appeal against the rejection of a claim for asylum under this section as they apply in relation to an appeal under section 83(2) of the Nationality, Immigration and Asylum Act 2002—

    (a)   section 85(4) of that Act (matters to be considered),

    (b)   section 86 of that Act (determination of appeal),

    (c)   section 87 of that Act (successful appeal: direction), and

    (d)   section 110 of that Act (grants).

(4)   An appeal against the rejection of a claim for asylum under this section shall be treated as abandoned if the appellant leaves the United Kingdom.

(5)   A person may bring or continue an appeal against an immigration decision under this section while he is in the United Kingdom only if he would be able to bring or continue the appeal while he was in the United Kingdom if it were an appeal under section 82(1) of that Act.

(6) In this section "immigration decision" has the meaning given by section 82(2) of the Nationality, Immigration and Asylum Act 2002."

21 Section 2A of that Act (human rights) shall cease to have effect.

22 Section 4 of that Act (determination of appeals) shall cease to have effect.

23 In section 5 of that Act (procedure)—

(a) in subsections (1)(a) and (b) and (2) omit "or 2A", and
(b) after subsection (2) insert—

"(2A) Rules under this section may, in particular, do anything which may be done by rules under section 106 of the Nationality, Immigration and Asylum Act 2002 (appeals: rules)."

24 Section 7A of that Act (pending appeals) shall cease to have effect.

25 In paragraph 5 of Schedule 1 to that Act—

(a) in sub-paragraph (b)(i), for "section 57(2) of the Immigration and Asylum Act 1999" substitute "section 81(3)(a) of the Nationality, Immigration and Asylum Act 2002", and
(b) in sub-paragraph (b)(ii), for "paragraph 1(3) of Schedule 2" substitute "paragraph 11 of Schedule 5".

26 Schedule 2 to that Act shall cease to have effect.

Immigration and Asylum Act 1999 (c 33)

27 In section 23(1) of the Immigration and Asylum Act 1999 (monitoring refusal of entry clearance) for "section 60(5)" there shall be substituted "section 90 or 91 of the Nationality, Immigration and Asylum Act 2002".

28 In section 53(4) of that Act (bail) for "this Act" there shall be substituted "the Nationality, Immigration and Asylum Act 2002".

29 (1) Paragraph 9 of Schedule 4 to that Act (appeals: procedure: Convention cases) shall be amended as follows—

(a) in sub-paragraph (1)(a), omit "(4), (5)", and
(b) omit sub-paragraphs (4) and (5).

(2) This paragraph is without prejudice to—

(a) the effect after commencement of this paragraph of a certificate issued before commencement, or
(b) the power of the Secretary of State after the commencement of this paragraph to issue a certificate in respect of a claim made before commencement.

...

30 ...

Proceeds of Crime Act 2002 (c 29)

31 The following shall be substituted for paragraph 4 of Schedule 2 to the Proceeds of Crime Act 2002 (lifestyle offences: England and Wales: people trafficking)—

"**4** (1) An offence under section 25, 25A or 25B of the Immigration Act 1971 (c 77) (assisting unlawful immigration etc).

(2) An offence under section 145 of the Nationality, Immigration and Asylum Act 2002 (traffic in prostitution)."

32   In paragraph 4 of Schedule 4 to that Act (lifestyle offences: Scotland: people trafficking) for "section 25(1) of the Immigration Act 1971 (assisting illegal entry etc)" there shall be substituted "section 25, 25A or 25B of the Immigration Act 1971 (assisting unlawful immigration etc)".

33   The following shall be substituted for paragraph 4 of Schedule 5 to that Act (lifestyle offences: Northern Ireland: people trafficking)—

"**4**   (1)   An offence under section 25, 25A or 25B of the Immigration Act 1971 (assisting unlawful immigration etc).

(2)   An offence under section 145 of the Nationality, Immigration and Asylum Act 2002 (traffic in prostitution)."

Initial Commencement
Para 29: Royal Assent: 7 November 2002: see s 162(2)(w).
Paras 1–28, 30–33: To be appointed: see s 162(1).

Appointment
Paras 1–28, 30: Appointment: 1 April 2003: see SI 2003/754, art 2(1), Sch 1; for transitional provisions see art 3, Sch 2, para 5 thereto.
Paras 31–33: Appointment: 10 February 2003: see SI 2003/1, art 2, Schedule.

Amendment
Para 30: repealed by the Prevention of Terrorism Act 2005, s 16(2)(c). Date in force: 14 March 2005: see the Prevention of Terrorism Act 2005, s 16(3).

SCHEDULE 8
CARRIERS' LIABILITY

Section 125

1   The Immigration and Asylum Act 1999 (c 33) shall be amended as follows.

2   (1)   Section 32 (penalty for carrying clandestine entrant) shall be amended as follows.

(2)   After subsection (1)(a) insert—

"(aa)he arrives in the United Kingdom concealed in a rail freight wagon,".

(3)   For subsection (2) substitute—

"(2)   The Secretary of State may require a person who is responsible for a clandestine entrant to pay—

(a)   a penalty in respect of the clandestine entrant;
(b)   a penalty in respect of any person who was concealed with the clandestine entrant in the same transporter.

(2A)   In imposing a penalty under subsection (2) the Secretary of State—

(a)   must specify an amount which does not exceed the maximum prescribed for the purpose of this paragraph,
(b)   may, in respect of a clandestine entrant or a concealed person, impose separate penalties on more than one of the persons responsible for the clandestine entrant, and
(c)   may not impose penalties in respect of a clandestine entrant or a concealed person which amount in aggregate to more than the maximum prescribed for the purpose of this paragraph."

(4)   For subsection (4) substitute—

"(4)   Where a penalty is imposed under subsection (2) on the driver of a vehicle who is an employee of the vehicle's owner or hirer—

    (a)   the employee and the employer shall be jointly and severally liable for the penalty imposed on the driver (irrespective of whether a penalty is also imposed on the employer), and

    (b)   a provision of this Part about notification, objection or appeal shall have effect as if the penalty imposed on the driver were also imposed on the employer (irrespective of whether a penalty is also imposed on the employer in his capacity as the owner or hirer of the vehicle).

(4A)   In the case of a detached trailer, subsection (4) shall have effect as if a reference to the driver were a reference to the operator."

(5)   In subsection (5)—

    (a)   in paragraph (a) for the second "or" substitute "and", and

    (b)   in paragraphs (b) and (c) for "or" substitute "and".

(6)   After subsection (5) insert—

"(5A)   In the case of a clandestine entrant to whom subsection (1)(aa) applies, the responsible person is—

    (a)   where the entrant arrived concealed in a freight train, the train operator who, at the train's last scheduled stop before arrival in the United Kingdom, was responsible for certifying it as fit to travel to the United Kingdom, or

    (b)   where the entrant arrived concealed in a freight shuttle wagon, the operator of the shuttle-train of which the wagon formed part."

(7)   In subsection (6)(a) and (b) for "or" substitute "and".

(8)   After subsection (6) insert—

"(6A)   Where a person falls within the definition of responsible person in more than one capacity, a separate penalty may be imposed on him under subsection (2) in respect of each capacity."

3   After section 32 insert—

"32A   Level of penalty: code of practice

(1)   The Secretary of State shall issue a code of practice specifying matters to be considered in determining the amount of a penalty under section 32.

(2)   The Secretary of State shall have regard to the code (in addition to any other matters he thinks relevant)—

    (a)   when imposing a penalty under section 32, and

    (b)   when considering a notice of objection under section 35(4).

(3)   Before issuing the code the Secretary of State shall lay a draft before Parliament.

(4)   After laying the draft code before Parliament the Secretary of State may bring the code into operation by order.

(5)   The Secretary of State may from time to time revise the whole or any part of the code and issue the code as revised.

(6)   Subsections (3) and (4) also apply to a revision or proposed revision of the code."

4   The heading of section 33 (code of practice) becomes "Prevention of clandestine entrants: code of practice".

5   In section 33(2)(b) omit "both Houses of".

6   (1)   Section 34 (defence) shall be amended as follows.

(2)   For subsection (1) substitute—

"(1)   A person ("the carrier") shall not be liable to the imposition of a penalty under section 32(2) if he has a defence under this section."

(3)   In subsection (3)(c) omit the first "that".

(4)   After subsection (3) insert—

"(3A)   It is also a defence for the carrier to show that—

    (a)   he knew or suspected that a clandestine entrant was or might be concealed in a rail freight wagon, having boarded after the wagon began its journey to the United Kingdom;

    (b)   he could not stop the train or shuttle-train of which the wagon formed part without endangering safety;

    (c)   an effective system for preventing the carriage of clandestine entrants was in operation in relation to the train or shuttle-train; and

    (d)   on the occasion in question the person or persons responsible for operating the system did so properly."

(5)   Omit subsection (5).

(6)   For subsection (6) substitute—

"(6)   Where a person has a defence under subsection (2) in respect of a clandestine entrant, every other responsible person in respect of the clandestine entrant is also entitled to the benefit of the defence."

7   (1)   Section 35 (notification and objection) shall be amended as follows.

(2)   In subsection (2)(d)(i) for "must" substitute "may".

(3)   For subsections (3) to (8) substitute—

"(3)   Subsection (4) applies where a person to whom a penalty notice is issued objects on the ground that—

    (a)   he is not liable to the imposition of a penalty, or

    (b)   the amount of the penalty is too high.

(4)   The person may give a notice of objection to the Secretary of State.

(5)   A notice of objection must—

    (a)   be in writing,

    (b)   give the objector's reasons, and

    (c)   be given before the end of such period as may be prescribed.

(6)   Where the Secretary of State receives a notice of objection to a penalty in accordance with this section he shall consider it and—

    (a)   cancel the penalty,

    (b)   reduce the penalty,

    (c)   increase the penalty, or

    (d)   determine to take no action under paragraphs (a) to (c).

(7)   Where the Secretary of State considers a notice of objection under subsection (6) he shall—

    (a)   inform the objector of his decision before the end of such period as may be prescribed or such longer period as he may agree with the objector,

    (b)   if he increases the penalty, issue a new penalty notice under subsection (1), and

    (c)   if he reduces the penalty, notify the objector of the reduced amount."

(4)   In subsection (9)—

    (a)   for the first "served" substitute "issued", and
    (b)   for "served on" substitute "issued to".

(5)   At the end add—

"(11)   In proceedings for enforcement of a penalty under subsection (10) no question may be raised as to—

    (a)   liability to the imposition of the penalty, or
    (b)   its amount.

(12)   A document which is to be issued to or served on a person outside the United Kingdom for the purpose of subsection (1) or (7) or in the course of proceedings under subsection (10) may be issued or served—

    (a)   in person,
    (b)   by post,
    (c)   by facsimile transmission, or
    (d)   in another prescribed manner.

(13)   The Secretary of State may by regulations provide that a document issued or served in a manner listed in subsection (12) in accordance with the regulations is to be taken to have been received at a time specified by or determined in accordance with the regulations."

8   After section 35 insert—

"35A   Appeal

(1)   A person may appeal to the court against a penalty imposed on him under section 32 on the ground that—

    (a)   he is not liable to the imposition of a penalty, or
    (b)   the amount of the penalty is too high.

(2)   On an appeal under this section the court may—

    (a)   allow the appeal and cancel the penalty,
    (b)   allow the appeal and reduce the penalty, or
    (c)   dismiss the appeal.

(3)   An appeal under this section shall be a re-hearing of the Secretary of State's decision to impose a penalty and shall be determined having regard to—

    (a)   any code of practice under section 32A which has effect at the time of the appeal,
    (b)   the code of practice under section 33 which had effect at the time of the events to which the penalty relates, and
    (c)   any other matters which the court thinks relevant (which may include matters of which the Secretary of State was unaware).

(4)   Subsection (3) has effect despite any provision of Civil Procedure Rules.

(5)   An appeal may be brought by a person under this section against a penalty whether or not—

    (a)   he has given notice of objection under section 35(4);
    (b)   the penalty has been increased or reduced under section 35(6)."

9   (1)   Section 36 (detention of vehicle) shall be amended as follows.

(2)   In subsection (1)—

    (a)   for "given" substitute "issued",
    (b)   after paragraph (b) omit "or", and
    (c)   after paragraph (c) insert
"or
    (d)   rail freight wagon,".

(3)   After subsection (2) insert—

"(2A)   A vehicle may be detained under subsection (1) only if—

    (a)   the driver of the vehicle is an employee of its owner or hirer,
    (b)   the driver of the vehicle is its owner or hirer, or
    (c)   a penalty notice is issued to the owner or hirer of the vehicle.

(2B)   A senior officer may detain a relevant vehicle, small ship, small aircraft or rail freight wagon pending—

    (a)   a decision whether to issue a penalty notice,
    (b)   the issue of a penalty notice, or
    (c)   a decision whether to detain under subsection (1).

(2C)   That power may not be exercised in any case—

    (a)   for longer than is necessary in the circumstances of the case, or
    (b)   after the expiry of the period of 24 hours beginning with the conclusion of the first search of the vehicle, ship, aircraft or wagon by an immigration officer after it arrived in the United Kingdom."

10   After section 36 insert—

"36A   Detention in default of payment

(1)   This section applies where a person to whom a penalty notice has been issued under section 35 fails to pay the penalty before the date specified in accordance with section 35(2)(c).

(2)   The Secretary of State may make arrangements for the detention of any vehicle, small ship, small aircraft or rail freight wagon which the person to whom the penalty notice was issued uses in the course of a business.

(3)   A vehicle, ship, aircraft or wagon may be detained under subsection (2) whether or not the person to whom the penalty notice was issued owns it.

(4)   But a vehicle may be detained under subsection (2) only if the person to whom the penalty notice was issued—

    (a)   is the owner or hirer of the vehicle, or
    (b)   was an employee of the owner or hirer of the vehicle when the penalty notice was issued.

(5)   The power under subsection (2) may not be exercised while an appeal against the penalty under section 35A is pending or could be brought (ignoring the possibility of an appeal out of time with permission).

(6)   The Secretary of State shall arrange for the release of a vehicle, ship, aircraft or wagon detained under this section if the person to whom the penalty notice was issued pays—

    (a)   the penalty, and
    (b)   expenses reasonably incurred in connection with the detention."

11 (1) Section 37 (effect of detention of transporter) shall be amended as follows.

(2) In subsection (1) for "section 36" substitute "section 36(1)".

(3) In subsection (2) for "claiming an interest in the transporter," substitute "whose interests may be affected by detention of the transporter,".

(4) In subsection (3)(c) omit "and the applicant has a compelling need to have the transporter released".

(5) After subsection (3) insert—

"(3A) The court may also release the transporter on the application of the owner of the transporter under subsection (2) if—

    (a) a penalty notice was not issued to the owner or an employee of his, and
    (b) the court considers it right to release the transporter.

(3B) In determining whether to release a transporter under subsection (3A) the court shall consider—

    (a) the extent of any hardship caused by detention,
    (b) the extent (if any) to which the owner is responsible for the matters in respect of which the penalty notice was issued, and
    (c) any other matter which appears to the court to be relevant (whether specific to the circumstances of the case or of a general nature)."

(6) After subsection (5) insert—

"(5A) The power of sale under subsection (4) may be exercised only when no appeal against the imposition of the penalty is pending or can be brought (ignoring the possibility of an appeal out of time with permission).

(5B) The power of sale under subsection (4) shall lapse if not exercised within a prescribed period."

(7) After subsection (6) add—

"(7) This section applies to a transporter detained under section 36A as it applies to a transporter detained under section 36(1); but for that purpose—

    (a) the court may release the transporter only if the court considers that the detention was unlawful or under subsection (3A) (and subsection (3) shall not apply), and
    (b) the reference in subsection (4) to the period of 84 days shall be taken as a reference to a period prescribed for the purpose of this paragraph."

12 Section 39 (rail freight) shall cease to have effect.

13 For section 40 (charge in respect of passenger without proper documents) substitute—

"40 Charge in respect of passenger without proper documents

(1) This section applies if an individual requiring leave to enter the United Kingdom arrives in the United Kingdom by ship or aircraft and, on being required to do so by an immigration officer, fails to produce—

    (a) an immigration document which is in force and which satisfactorily establishes his identity and his nationality or citizenship, and
    (b) if the individual requires a visa, a visa of the required kind.

(2) The Secretary of State may charge the owner of the ship or aircraft, in respect of the individual, the sum of £2,000.

(3) The charge shall be payable to the Secretary of State on demand.

(4) No charge shall be payable in respect of any individual who is shown by the owner to have produced the required document or documents to the owner or his employee or agent when embarking on the ship or aircraft for the voyage or flight to the United Kingdom.

(5) For the purpose of subsection (4) an owner shall be entitled to regard a document as—

    (a) being what it purports to be unless its falsity is reasonably apparent, and

    (b) relating to the individual producing it unless it is reasonably apparent that it does not relate to him.

(6) For the purposes of this section an individual requires a visa if—

    (a) under the immigration rules he requires a visa for entry into the United Kingdom, or

    (b) as a result of section 41 he requires a visa for passing through the United Kingdom.

(7) The Secretary of State may by order amend this section for the purpose of applying it in relation to an individual who—

    (a) requires leave to enter the United Kingdom, and

    (b) arrives in the United Kingdom by train.

(8) An order under subsection (7) may provide for the application of this section—

    (a) except in cases of a specified kind;

    (b) subject to a specified defence.

(9) In this section "immigration document" means—

    (a) a passport, and

    (b) a document which relates to a national of a country other than the United Kingdom and which is designed to serve the same purpose as a passport.

(10) The Secretary of State may by order substitute a sum for the sum in subsection (2).

40A Notification and objection

(1) If the Secretary of State decides to charge a person under section 40, the Secretary of State must notify the person of his decision.

(2) A notice under subsection (1) (a "charge notice") must—

    (a) state the Secretary of State's reasons for deciding to charge the person,

    (b) state the amount of the charge,

    (c) specify the date before which, and the manner in which, the charge must be paid,

    (d) include an explanation of the steps that the person may take if he objects to the charge, and

    (e) include an explanation of the steps that the Secretary of State may take under this Part to recover any unpaid charge.

(3) Where a person on whom a charge notice is served objects to the imposition of the charge on him, he may give a notice of objection to the Secretary of State.

(4) A notice of objection must—

    (a) be in writing,

    (b) give the objector's reasons, and

(c)   be given before the end of such period as may be prescribed.

(5)   Where the Secretary of State receives a notice of objection to a charge in accordance with this section, he shall—

(a)   consider it, and
(b)   determine whether or not to cancel the charge.

(6)   Where the Secretary of State considers a notice of objection, he shall inform the objector of his decision before the end of—

(a)   such period as may be prescribed, or
(b)   such longer period as he may agree with the objector.

(7)   Any sum payable to the Secretary of State as a charge under section 40 may be recovered by the Secretary of State as a debt due to him.

(8)   In proceedings for enforcement of a charge under subsection (7) no question may be raised as to the validity of the charge.

(9)   Subsections (12) and (13) of section 35 shall have effect for the purpose of this section as they have effect for the purpose of section 35(1), (7) and (10).

40B   Appeal

(1)   A person may appeal to the court against a decision to charge him under section 40.

(2)   On an appeal under this section the court may—

(a)   allow the appeal and cancel the charge, or
(b)   dismiss the appeal.

(3)   An appeal under this section—

(a)   shall be a re-hearing of the Secretary of State's decision to impose a charge, and
(b)   may be determined having regard to matters of which the Secretary of State was unaware.

(4)   Subsection (3)(a) has effect despite any provision of Civil Procedure Rules.

(5)   An appeal may be brought by a person under this section against a decision to charge him whether or not he has given notice of objection under section 40A(3)."

14   Section 42 (power to detain vehicle, &c carrying person without proper travel documents) shall cease to have effect.

15   In section 43 (interpretation) (which becomes subsection (1))—

(a)   in the definition of "concealed" for "or aircraft" substitute ", aircraft or rail freight wagon",
(b)   omit the definition of "court",
(c)   after the definition of "equipment" insert—
""freight shuttle wagon" means a wagon which—
    (a)   forms part of a shuttle-train, and
    (b)   is designed to carry commercial goods vehicles;
"freight train" means any train other than—
    (a)   a train engaged on a service for the carriage of passengers, or
    (b)   a shuttle-train;",
(d)   in the definition of "owner" omit paragraph (b) and the word "and" immediately preceding it,
(e)   for the definition of "rail freight wagon" substitute—
""rail freight wagon" means—

(a) any rolling stock, other than a locomotive, which forms part of a freight train, or

(b) a freight shuttle wagon,

and for the purpose of this definition, "rolling stock" and "locomotive" have the meanings given by section 83 of the Railways Act 1993 (c 43);",

(f) after the definition of "ship" insert—

""shuttle-train" has the meaning given by section 1(9) of the Channel Tunnel Act 1987 (c 53);",

(g) in the definition of "transporter" for "or aircraft" substitute ", aircraft or rail freight wagon", and

(h) at the end insert—

"(2) A reference in this Part to "the court" is a reference—

(a) in England and Wales, to a county court,

(b) in Scotland, to the sheriff, and

(c) in Northern Ireland, to a county court.

(3) But—

(a) a county court may transfer proceedings under this Part to the High Court, and

(b) the sheriff may transfer proceedings under this Part to the Court of Session."

16 (1) Schedule 1 (sale of transporter) shall be amended as follows.

(2) In paragraph 1(2)(a) omit "or charge".

(3) After paragraph 2 insert—

"2A Where the owner of a transporter is a party to an application for leave to sell it, in determining whether to give leave the court shall consider—

(a) the extent of any hardship likely to be caused by sale,

(b) the extent (if any) to which the owner is responsible for the matters in respect of which the penalty notice was issued, and

(c) any other matter which appears to the court to be relevant (whether specific to the circumstances of the case or of a general nature)."

(4) In paragraph 5(1) omit "or 42".

(5) In paragraph 5(2)(d) omit "or charge".

17 (1) This paragraph applies to a code of practice which—

(a) has effect, before the coming into force of paragraph 12 of this Schedule, by virtue of sections 33 and 39 of the Immigration and Asylum Act 1999 (c 33) (power to apply provisions about carriers' liability to rail freight), and

(b) could be issued under section 33 of that Act after the coming into force of paragraph 2 of this Schedule.

(2) A code of practice to which this paragraph applies—

(a) shall continue to have effect after the coming into force of paragraph 12 of this Schedule, and

(b) shall be treated after that time as if made and brought into operation under section 33 alone.

Initial Commencement
To be appointed: see s 162(1).

Appointment

Paras 1, 2, 7, 11, 13: Appointment (for the purpose of enabling the Secretary of State to exercise the power to make subordinate legislation under the Immigration and Asylum Act 1999, ss 32(2A), 35(5), (7), (9), (12), (13), 37(5B), (7) and 40A(4), (6)): 14 November 2002: see SI 2002/2811, art 2, Schedule; for transitional provisions in relation to paras 1, 2, 7 and 11 see art 4 thereof.

Para 1: Appointment (for the purposes of para 3 below): 14 November 2002: by virtue of SI 2002/2811, art 2, Schedule; for transitional provisions see art 4 thereof.

Para 1: Appointment (for the purposes of paras 13–15 below): 8 December 2002: by virtue of SI 2002/2811, art 2, Schedule; for transitional provisions in relation to para 15 see art 4 thereof.

Paras 1–12, 16: Appointment (for the purposes of clandestine entrants (within the meaning of the Immigration and Asylum Act 1999, s 32(1)) who arrive in the United Kingdom concealed in a vehicle or a rail freight wagon): 8 December 2002: see SI 2002/2811, art 2, Schedule; for transitional provisions see art 4 thereof.

Para 3: Appointment (for the purpose of enabling the Secretary of State to exercise the power under the Immigration and Asylum Act 1999, s 32A(1), (3), (4) to lay a draft code of practice before Parliament and bring the code of practice into force): 14 November 2002: see SI 2002/2811, art 2, Schedule; for transitional provisions see art 4 thereof.

Para 13: Appointment (for remaining purposes): 8 December 2002: see SI 2002/2811, art 2, Schedule.

Paras 14, 15: Appointment: 8 December 2002: see SI 2002/2811, art 2, Schedule; for transitional provisions in relation to para 15 see art 4 thereof.

Para 17: Appointment: 8 December 2002: see SI 2002/2811, art 2, Schedule; for transitional provisions see art 4 thereof.

SCHEDULE 9
REPEALS

Section 161

Short title and chapter	Extent of repeal
Immigration Act 1971 (c 77)	In section 3(9)(b), the words "issued by or on behalf of the Government of the United Kingdom certifying that he has such a right of abode". Section 7(1)(a). Section 24A(4). Section 25A(7). In section 26(3) the word "or" after paragraph (c). In section 28(1) the words ", 24A, 25". In section 28A— subsection (4), in subsection (10), ", (4)(b)", and in subsection (11), ", (4)". Section 29. Section 31(d).
Race Relations Act 1976 (c 74)	Section 19E(7). In section 71A(1), the words "(within the meaning of section 19D(1))".
British Nationality Act 1981 (c 61)	In section 3(6), paragraph (c) and the word "and" immediately preceding it. Sections 7 to 9. In section 10— in subsection (1), the words ", if a woman,", and in subsection (2), the words "if a woman,".

In section 17(6), paragraph (c) and the word "and" immediately preceding it.

Sections 19 to 21.

In section 22—

in subsection (1), the words ", if a woman,", and

in subsection (2), the words "if a woman,".

Section 27(2).

Section 28.

Section 33.

Section 44(2) and (3).

Section 47.

In Schedule 1—

in paragraph 4(c), the words "and (e)", and

in paragraph 8(c), the words "and (e)".

In Schedule 2—

in paragraphs 1(1)(b) and 2(1)(b), the words "he is born legitimate and", and

in paragraph 3(1)(b), the words "had attained the age of ten but".

In Schedule 4—

in paragraph 2, in the second column of the Table, the entry relating to section 29(1) of the Immigration Act 1971, and paragraph 6.

British Nationality (Falkland Islands) Act 1983 (c 6)	Section 4(3)(b).
British Nationality (Hong Kong) Act 1990 (c 34)	Section 1(5).
Asylum and Immigration Act 1996 (c 49)	Section 5.
Special Immigration Appeals Commission Act 1997 (c 68)	Section 2A. Section 4. In section 5(1)(a) and (b) and (2), the words "or 2A". Section 7A. Schedule 2.
Immigration and Asylum Act 1999 (c 33)	In section 10(1)(c), the words "("the first directions")" and "("the other person")". Section 15. Section 29. In section 33(2)(b), the words "both Houses of". In section 34— in subsection (3)(c), the first "that", and subsection (5). In section 36(1), the word "or" immediately preceding paragraph (c). In section 37(3)(c), the words "and the applicant has a compelling need to have the transporter released". Section 38(1) and (3). Section 39. Section 42.

	In section 43, in the definition of "owner" paragraph (b) and the word "and" immediately preceding it.
	Sections 44 to 52.
	Section 53(5).
	Section 55.
	Sections 56 to 81.
	Section 94(5) and (6).
	Section 96(4) to (6).
	In section 147, the definition of "detention centre".
	Section 166(4)(e).
	In Schedule 1—
	in paragraph 1(2)(a), the words "or charge",
	in paragraph 5(1), the words "or 42", and
	in paragraph 5(2)(d), the words "or charge".
	In paragraph 9 of Schedule 4, the words "(4), (5)" in sub-paragraph (1)(a), and sub-paragraphs (4) and (5).
	Schedules 2 to 4.
	In Schedule 8, paragraphs 2 and 6.
	In Schedule 14, paragraphs 46(a), 51, 53, 66, 96, 98(2) and (3), 120 to 121 and 126 to 129.
Race Relations (Amendment) Act 2000 (c 34)	In Schedule 2, paragraphs 23 to 29 and 32 to 40.

Initial Commencement

Royal Assent (in part): 7 November 2002: see s 162(2).
To be appointed (remainder): see s 162(1).

Appointment

Appointment (in part): 1 April 2003: see SI 2003/754, art 2(1), Sch 1; for transitional provisions see art 3, Sch 2, para 6(4) thereto.
Appointment (in part): 8 December 2002: see SI 2002/2811, art 2, Schedule.
Appointment (in part): 10 February 2003: see SI 2003/1, art 2, Schedule.

ASYLUM AND IMMIGRATION (TREATMENT OF CLAIMANTS, ETC) ACT 2004

2004 CHAPTER 19

An Act to make provision about asylum and immigration.

[22nd July 2004]

Be it enacted by the Queen's most Excellent Majesty, by and with the advice and consent of the Lords Spiritual and Temporal, and Commons, in this present Parliament assembled, and by the authority of the same, as follows:—

Offences

1   Assisting unlawful immigration

(1)   At the end of section 25 of the Immigration Act 1971 (c 77) (offence of assisting unlawful immigration to member State) add—

"(7)   In this section—

(a)   a reference to a member State includes a reference to a State on a list prescribed for the purposes of this section by order of the Secretary of State (to be known as the "Section 25 List of Schengen Acquis States"), and

(b)   a reference to a citizen of the European Union includes a reference to a person who is a national of a State on that list.

(8)   An order under subsection (7)(a)—

(a)   may be made only if the Secretary of State thinks it necessary for the purpose of complying with the United Kingdom's obligations under the Community Treaties,

(b)   may include transitional, consequential or incidental provision,

(c)   shall be made by statutory instrument, and

(d)   shall be subject to annulment in pursuance of a resolution of either House of Parliament."

(2)   In section 25C(9)(a) of that Act (forfeiture of vehicle, ship or aircraft) for "(within the meaning of section 25)" substitute "(for which purpose "member State" and "immigration law" have the meanings given by section 25(2) and (7))".

Appointment
Appointment: 1 October 2004: see SI 2004/2523, art 2, Schedule.

2   Entering United Kingdom without passport, &c

(1)   A person commits an offence if at a leave or asylum interview he does not have with him an immigration document which—

(a)   is in force, and

(b)   satisfactorily establishes his identity and nationality or citizenship.

(2)   A person commits an offence if at a leave or asylum interview he does not have with him, in respect of any dependent child with whom he claims to be travelling or living, an immigration document which—

(a)   is in force, and

(b)   satisfactorily establishes the child's identity and nationality or citizenship.

(3)   But a person does not commit an offence under subsection (1) or (2) if—

(a)   the interview referred to in that subsection takes place after the person has entered the United Kingdom, and

(b)   within the period of three days beginning with the date of the interview the person provides to an immigration officer or to the Secretary of State a document of the kind referred to in that subsection.

(4)   It is a defence for a person charged with an offence under subsection (1)—

(a)   to prove that he is an EEA national,

(b)   to prove that he is a member of the family of an EEA national and that he is exercising a right under the Community Treaties in respect of entry to or residence in the United Kingdom,

(c)   to prove that he has a reasonable excuse for not being in possession of a document of the kind specified in subsection (1),

(d)   to produce a false immigration document and to prove that he used that document as an immigration document for all purposes in connection with his journey to the United Kingdom, or

(e)   to prove that he travelled to the United Kingdom without, at any stage since he set out on the journey, having possession of an immigration document.

(5)   It is a defence for a person charged with an offence under subsection (2) in respect of a child—

(a)   to prove that the child is an EEA national,

(b)   to prove that the child is a member of the family of an EEA national and that the child is exercising a right under the Community Treaties in respect of entry to or residence in the United Kingdom,

(c)   to prove that the person has a reasonable excuse for not being in possession of a document of the kind specified in subsection (2),

(d)   to produce a false immigration document and to prove that it was used as an immigration document for all purposes in connection with the child's journey to the United Kingdom, or

(e)   to prove that he travelled to the United Kingdom with the child without, at any stage since he set out on the journey, having possession of an immigration document in respect of the child.

(6)   Where the charge for an offence under subsection (1) or (2) relates to an interview which takes place after the defendant has entered the United Kingdom—

(a)   subsections (4)(c) and (5)(c) shall not apply, but

(b)   it is a defence for the defendant to prove that he has a reasonable excuse for not providing a document in accordance with subsection (3).

(7)   For the purposes of subsections (4) to (6)—

(a)   the fact that a document was deliberately destroyed or disposed of is not a reasonable excuse for not being in possession of it or for not providing it in accordance with subsection (3), unless it is shown that the destruction or disposal was—

(i)   for a reasonable cause, or

(ii)   beyond the control of the person charged with the offence, and

(b)   in paragraph (a)(i) "reasonable cause" does not include the purpose of—

(i)   delaying the handling or resolution of a claim or application or the taking of a decision,

(ii)   increasing the chances of success of a claim or application, or

(iii)   complying with instructions or advice given by a person who offers advice about, or facilitates, immigration into the United Kingdom, unless in the circumstances of the case it is unreasonable to expect non-compliance with the instructions or advice.

(8)   A person shall be presumed for the purposes of this section not to have a document with him if he fails to produce it to an immigration officer or official of the Secretary of State on request.

(9)   A person guilty of an offence under this section shall be liable—

(a)   on conviction on indictment, to imprisonment for a term not exceeding two years, to a fine or to both, or

(b)   on summary conviction, to imprisonment for a term not exceeding twelve months, to a fine not exceeding the statutory maximum or to both.

(10)   If *a constable or* [an] immigration officer reasonably suspects that a person has committed an offence under this section he may arrest the person without warrant.

(11)   An offence under this section shall be treated as—

(a)   a relevant offence for the purposes of sections 28B and 28D of the Immigration Act 1971 (c 77) (search, entry and arrest), and

(b)   an offence under Part III of that Act (criminal proceedings) for the purposes of sections 28(4), 28E, 28G and 28H (search after arrest, &c) of that Act.

(12)   In this section—

"EEA national" means a national of a State which is a contracting party to the Agreement on the European Economic Area signed at Oporto on 2nd May 1992 (as it has effect from time to time),

"immigration document" means—

(a)   a passport, and

(b)   a document which relates to a national of a State other than the United Kingdom and which is designed to serve the same purpose as a passport, and

"leave or asylum interview" means an interview with an immigration officer or an official of the Secretary of State at which a person—

(a)   seeks leave to enter or remain in the United Kingdom, or

(b)   claims that to remove him from or require him to leave the United Kingdom would breach the United Kingdom's obligations under the Refugee Convention or would be unlawful under section 6 of the Human Rights Act 1998 (c 42) as being incompatible with his Convention rights.

(13)   For the purposes of this section—

(a)   a document which purports to be, or is designed to look like, an immigration document, is a false immigration document, and

(b)   an immigration document is a false immigration document if and in so far as it is used—

(i)   outside the period for which it is expressed to be valid,

(ii)   contrary to provision for its use made by the person issuing it, or

(iii)   by or in respect of a person other than the person to or for whom it was issued.

(14)   Section 11 of the Immigration Act 1971 (c 77) shall have effect for the purpose of the construction of a reference in this section to entering the United Kingdom.

(15)   In so far as this section extends to England and Wales, subsection (9)(b) shall, until the commencement of section 154 of the Criminal Justice Act 2003 (c 44) (increased limit on magistrates' power of imprisonment), have effect as if the reference to twelve months were a reference to six months.

(16)   In so far as this section extends to Scotland, subsection (9)(b) shall have effect as if the reference to twelve months were a reference to six months.

(17)   In so far as this section extends to Northern Ireland, subsection (9)(b) shall have effect as if the reference to twelve months were a reference to six months.

Initial Commencement
Specified date: 22 September 2004: see s 48(1).

Amendment
Sub-s (10): words "a constable or" in italics repealed and subsequent word in square brackets substituted by the Serious Organised Crime and Police Act 2005, s 111, Sch 7, Pt 4, para 63(a). Date in force: to be appointed: see the Serious Organised Crime and Police Act 2005, s 178(8).

3   Immigration documents: forgery

(1)   Section 5 of the Forgery and Counterfeiting Act 1981 (c 45) (offences relating to various documents) shall be amended as follows.

(2)   After subsection (5)(f) (passports) insert—

"(fa) immigration documents;" .

(3)   After subsection (8) add—

"(9)   In subsection (5)(fa) "immigration document" means a card, adhesive label or other instrument which satisfies subsection (10) or (11).

(10)   A card, adhesive label or other instrument satisfies this subsection if it—

(a)   is designed to be given, in the exercise of a function under the Immigration Acts (within the meaning of section 44 of the Asylum and Immigration (Treatment of Claimants, etc) Act 2004), to a person who has been granted leave to enter or remain in the United Kingdom, and

(b)   carries information (whether or not wholly or partly electronically) about the leave granted.

(11)   A card, adhesive label or other instrument satisfies this subsection if it is given to a person to confirm a right of his under the Community Treaties in respect of entry to or residence in the United Kingdom."

Appointment
Appointment: 1 October 2004: see SI 2004/2523, art 2, Schedule.

4   Trafficking people for exploitation

(1)   A person commits an offence if he arranges or facilitates the arrival in the United Kingdom of an individual (the "passenger") and—

(a)   he intends to exploit the passenger in the United Kingdom or elsewhere, or

(b)   he believes that another person is likely to exploit the passenger in the United Kingdom or elsewhere.

(2)   A person commits an offence if he arranges or facilitates travel within the United Kingdom by an individual (the "passenger") in respect of whom he believes that an offence under subsection (1) may have been committed and—

(a)   he intends to exploit the passenger in the United Kingdom or elsewhere, or

(b)   he believes that another person is likely to exploit the passenger in the United Kingdom or elsewhere.

(3)   A person commits an offence if he arranges or facilitates the departure from the United Kingdom of an individual (the "passenger") and—

    (a) he intends to exploit the passenger outside the United Kingdom, or

    (b) he believes that another person is likely to exploit the passenger outside the United Kingdom.

(4) For the purposes of this section a person is exploited if (and only if)—

    (a) he is the victim of behaviour that contravenes Article 4 of the Human Rights Convention (slavery and forced labour),

    (b) he is encouraged, required or expected to do anything as a result of which he or another person would commit an offence under the Human Organ Transplants Act 1989 (c 31) or *the Human Organ Transplants (Northern Ireland) Order 1989 (SI 1989/2408 (NI 21))* [under section 32 or 33 of the Human Tissue Act 2004],

    (c) he is subjected to force, threats or deception designed to induce him—

        (i) to provide services of any kind,

       (ii) to provide another person with benefits of any kind, or

      (iii) to enable another person to acquire benefits of any kind, or

    (d) he is requested or induced to undertake any activity, having been chosen as the subject of the request or inducement on the grounds that—

        (i) he is mentally or physically ill or disabled, he is young or he has a family relationship with a person, and

       (ii) a person without the illness, disability, youth or family relationship would be likely to refuse the request or resist the inducement.

(5) A person guilty of an offence under this section shall be liable—

    (a) on conviction on indictment, to imprisonment for a term not exceeding 14 years, to a fine or to both, or

    (b) on summary conviction, to imprisonment for a term not exceeding twelve months, to a fine not exceeding the statutory maximum or to both.

Appointment

Appointment (in relation to Scotland): 1 December 2004: see SSI 2004/494, art 2.
Appointment (in relation to England, Wales and Northern Ireland): 1 December 2004: see SI 2004/2999, art 2, Schedule.

Amendment

Sub-s (4): in para (b) words "the Human Organ Transplants (Northern Ireland) Order 1989 (SI 1989/2408 (NI 21))" in italics repealed and subsequent words in square brackets substituted by the Human Tissue Act 2004, s 56, Sch 6, para 7. Date in force: to be appointed: see the Human Tissue Act 2004, s 60(2).

See Further

By virtue of s 5(11)–(13) to this Act, reference to "twelve months" in sub-s (5)(b) above shall be construed as a reference to "six months" in relation to England and Wales until the Criminal Justice Act 2003, s 154 comes into force and in relation to Scotland and Northern Ireland.

5   Section 4: supplemental

(1) Subsections (1) to (3) of section 4 apply to anything done—

    (a) in the United Kingdom,

    (b) outside the United Kingdom by an individual to whom subsection (2) below applies, or

    (c) outside the United Kingdom by a body incorporated under the law of a part of the United Kingdom.

(2) This subsection applies to—

    (a) a British citizen,

    (b) a British overseas territories citizen,

  (c)   a British National (Overseas),
  (d)   a British Overseas citizen,
  (e)   a person who is a British subject under the British Nationality Act 1981 (c 61), and
  (f)   a British protected person within the meaning of that Act.

(3) In section 4(4)(a) "the Human Rights Convention" means the Convention for the Protection of Human Rights and Fundamental Freedoms agreed by the Council of Europe at Rome on 4th November 1950.

(4) Sections 25C and 25D of the Immigration Act 1971 (c 77) (forfeiture or detention of vehicle, &c) shall apply in relation to an offence under section 4 of this Act as they apply in relation to an offence under section 25 of that Act.

(5) At the end of section 25C(9)(b), (10)(b) and (11) of that Act add "or section 4 of the Asylum and Immigration (Treatment of Claimants, etc) Act 2004 (trafficking people for exploitation).".

(6) After paragraph 2(n) of Schedule 4 to the Criminal Justice and Court Services Act 2000 (c 43) (offence against child) insert—

    "(o) an offence under section 4 of the Asylum and Immigration (Treatment of Claimants, etc) Act 2004 (trafficking people for exploitation).".

(7) At the end of paragraph 4 of Schedule 2 to the Proceeds of Crime Act 2002 (c 29) (lifestyle offences: England and Wales: people trafficking) add—

    "(3) An offence under section 4 of the Asylum and Immigration (Treatment of Claimants, etc) Act 2004 (exploitation).".

(8) At the end of paragraph 4 of Schedule 4 to the Proceeds of Crime Act 2002 (lifestyle offences: Scotland: people trafficking) add "or under section 4 of the Asylum and Immigration (Treatment of Claimants, etc) Act 2004 (exploitation)".

(9) At the end of paragraph 4 of Schedule 5 to the Proceeds of Crime Act 2002 (lifestyle offences: Northern Ireland: people trafficking) add—

    "(3) An offence under section 4 of the Asylum and Immigration (Treatment of Claimants, etc) Act 2004 (exploitation).".

(10) After paragraph 2(l) of the Schedule to the Protection of Children and Vulnerable Adults (Northern Ireland) Order 2003 (SI 2003/417 (NI 4)) (offence against child) insert—

    "(m) an offence under section 4 of the Asylum and Immigration (Treatment of Claimants, etc) Act 2004 (trafficking people for exploitation).".

(11) In so far as section 4 extends to England and Wales, subsection (5)(b) shall, until the commencement of section 154 of the Criminal Justice Act 2003 (c 44) (increased limit on magistrates' power of imprisonment), have effect as if the reference to twelve months were a reference to six months.

(12) In so far as section 4 extends to Scotland, subsection (5)(b) shall have effect as if the reference to twelve months were a reference to six months.

(13) In so far as section 4 extends to Northern Ireland, subsection (5)(b) shall have effect as if the reference to twelve months were a reference to six months.

Appointment
Appointment (in relation to Scotland): 1 December 2004: see SSI 2004/494, art 2.
Appointment (in relation to England, Wales and Northern Ireland): 1 December 2004: see SI 2004/2999, art 2, Schedule.

Appendix 1   Legislation and materials

6   Employment

(1)   For section 8(4) of the Asylum and Immigration Act 1996 (c 49) (employment: penalty) substitute—

"(4)   A person guilty of an offence under this section shall be liable—

    (a)   on conviction on indictment, to a fine, or

    (b)   on summary conviction, to a fine not exceeding the statutory maximum.".

(2)   Section 8(9) of that Act (extension of time limit for prosecution) shall cease to have effect.

Appointment
Appointment: 1 October 2004: see SI 2004/2523, art 2, Schedule.

7   Advice of Director of Public Prosecutions

In section 3(2) of the Prosecution of Offences Act 1985 (c 23) (functions of Director of Public Prosecutions) after paragraph (eb) insert—

    "(ec) to give, to such extent as he considers appropriate, advice to immigration officers on matters relating to criminal offences;".

Appointment
Appointment: 1 December 2004: see SI 2004/2999, art 2, Schedule.

Treatment of claimants

8   Claimant's credibility

(1)   In determining whether to believe a statement made by or on behalf of a person who makes an asylum claim or a human rights claim, a deciding authority shall take account, as damaging the claimant's credibility, of any behaviour to which this section applies.

(2)   This section applies to any behaviour by the claimant that the deciding authority thinks—

    (a)   is designed or likely to conceal information,

    (b)   is designed or likely to mislead, or

    (c)   is designed or likely to obstruct or delay the handling or resolution of the claim or the taking of a decision in relation to the claimant.

(3)   Without prejudice to the generality of subsection (2) the following kinds of behaviour shall be treated as designed or likely to conceal information or to mislead—

    (a)   failure without reasonable explanation to produce a passport on request to an immigration officer or to the Secretary of State,

    (b)   the production of a document which is not a valid passport as if it were,

    (c)   the destruction, alteration or disposal, in each case without reasonable explanation, of a passport,

    (d)   the destruction, alteration or disposal, in each case without reasonable explanation, of a ticket or other document connected with travel, and

    (e)   failure without reasonable explanation to answer a question asked by a deciding authority.

(4)   This section also applies to failure by the claimant to take advantage of a reasonable opportunity to make an asylum claim or human rights claim while in a safe country.

1748

(5) This section also applies to failure by the claimant to make an asylum claim or human rights claim before being notified of an immigration decision, unless the claim relies wholly on matters arising after the notification.

(6) This section also applies to failure by the claimant to make an asylum claim or human rights claim before being arrested under an immigration provision, unless—

    (a)   he had no reasonable opportunity to make the claim before the arrest, or

    (b)   the claim relies wholly on matters arising after the arrest.

(7) In this section—

"asylum claim" has the meaning given by section 113(1) of the Nationality, Immigration and Asylum Act 2002 (c 41) (subject to subsection (9) below),

"deciding authority" means—

    (a)   an immigration officer,

    (b)   the Secretary of State,

    (c)   the Asylum and Immigration Tribunal, or

    (d)   the Special Immigration Appeals Commission,

"human rights claim" has the meaning given by section 113(1) of the Nationality, Immigration and Asylum Act 2002 (subject to subsection (9) below),

"immigration decision" means—

    (a)   refusal of leave to enter the United Kingdom,

    (b)   refusal to vary a person's leave to enter or remain in the United Kingdom,

    (c)   grant of leave to enter or remain in the United Kingdom,

    (d)   a decision that a person is to be removed from the United Kingdom by way of directions under section 10(1)(a), (b), (ba) or (c) of the Immigration and Asylum Act 1999 (c 33) (removal of persons unlawfully in United Kingdom),

    (e)   a decision that a person is to be removed from the United Kingdom by way of directions under paragraphs 8 to 12 of Schedule 2 to the Immigration Act 1971 (c 77) (control of entry: removal),

    (f)   a decision to make a deportation order under section 5(1) of that Act, and

    (g)   a decision to take action in relation to a person in connection with extradition from the United Kingdom,

"immigration provision" means—

    (a)   sections 28A, 28AA, 28B, 28C and 28CA of the Immigration Act 1971 (immigration offences: enforcement),

    (b)   paragraph 17 of Schedule 2 to that Act (control of entry),

    (c)   section 14 of this Act, and

    (d)   a provision of the Extradition Act 1989 (c 33) or 2003 (c 41),

"notified" means notified in such manner as may be specified by regulations made by the Secretary of State,

"passport" includes a document which relates to a national of a country other than the United Kingdom and which is designed to serve the same purpose as a passport, and

"safe country" means a country to which Part 2 of Schedule 3 applies.

(8) A passport produced by or on behalf of a person is valid for the purposes of subsection (3)(b) if it—

    (a)   relates to the person by whom or on whose behalf it is produced,

    (b)   has not been altered otherwise than by or with the permission of the authority who issued it, and

    (c)   was not obtained by deception.

(9)   In subsection (4) a reference to an asylum claim or human rights claim shall be treated as including a reference to a claim of entitlement to remain in a country other than the United Kingdom made by reference to the rights that a person invokes in making an asylum claim or a human rights claim in the United Kingdom.

(10)   Regulations under subsection (7) specifying a manner of notification may, in particular—

    (a)   apply or refer to regulations under section 105 of the Nationality, Immigration and Asylum Act 2002 (c 41) (notice of immigration decisions);

    (b)   make provision similar to provision that is or could be made by regulations under that section;

    (c)   modify a provision of regulations under that section in its effect for the purpose of regulations under this section;

    (d)   provide for notice to be treated as received at a specified time if sent to a specified class of place in a specified manner.

(11)   Regulations under subsection (7) specifying a manner of notification—

    (a)   may make incidental, consequential or transitional provision,

    (b)   shall be made by statutory instrument, and

    (c)   shall be subject to annulment in pursuance of a resolution of either House of Parliament.

(12)   This section shall not prevent a deciding authority from determining not to believe a statement on the grounds of behaviour to which this section does not apply.

(13)   Before the coming into force of section 26 a reference in this section to the Asylum and Immigration Tribunal shall be treated as a reference to—

    (a)   an adjudicator appointed, or treated as if appointed, under section 81 of the Nationality, Immigration and Asylum Act 2002 (c 41) (appeals), and

    (b)   the Immigration Appeal Tribunal.

Appointment
Sub-ss (1)–(6), (8), (9), (12), (13): Appointment: 1 January 2005: see SI 2004/3398, art 2.
Sub-ss (7), (10), (11): Appointment (for the purposes of making subordinate legislation): 1 October 2004: see SI 2004/2523, art 2, Schedule.
Sub-ss (7), (10), (11): Appointment (for remaining purposes): 1 January 2005: see SI 2004/3398, art 2.

Subordinate Legislation
Immigration (Claimant's Credibility) Regulations 2004, SI 2004/3263 (made under sub-ss (7), (10), (11)).

9   Failed asylum seekers: withdrawal of support

(1)   In Schedule 3 to the Nationality, Immigration and Asylum Act 2002 (withholding and withdrawal of support) after paragraph 7 insert—

"7A   Fifth class of ineligible person: failed asylum-seeker with family

(1)   Paragraph 1 applies to a person if—

    (a)   he—

        (i)   is treated as an asylum-seeker for the purposes of Part VI of the Immigration and Asylum Act 1999 (c 33) (support) by virtue only of section 94(3A) (failed asylum-seeker with dependent child), or

        (ii)   is treated as an asylum-seeker for the purposes of Part 2 of this Act by virtue only of section 18(2),

(b)   the Secretary of State has certified that in his opinion the person has failed without reasonable excuse to take reasonable steps—
    (i) to leave the United Kingdom voluntarily, or
    (ii) to place himself in a position in which he is able to leave the United Kingdom voluntarily,
(c)   the person has received a copy of the Secretary of State's certificate, and
(d)   the period of 14 days, beginning with the date on which the person receives the copy of the certificate, has elapsed.

(2) Paragraph 1 also applies to a dependant of a person to whom that paragraph applies by virtue of sub-paragraph (1).

(3) For the purpose of sub-paragraph (1)(d) if the Secretary of State sends a copy of a certificate by first class post to a person's last known address, the person shall be treated as receiving the copy on the second day after the day on which it was posted.

(4) The Secretary of State may by regulations vary the period specified in sub-paragraph (1)(d).".

(2) In paragraph 14(1) and (2) of Schedule 3 to the Nationality, Immigration and Asylum Act 2002 (local authority to notify Secretary of State) for "paragraph 6 or 7" substitute "paragraph 6, 7 or 7A".

(3) No appeal may be brought under section 103 of the Immigration and Asylum Act 1999 (asylum support appeal) against a decision—

(a)   that by virtue of a provision of Schedule 3 to the Nationality, Immigration and Asylum Act 2002 (c 41) other than paragraph 7A a person is not qualified to receive support, or
(b)   on the grounds of the application of a provision of that Schedule other than paragraph 7A, to stop providing support to a person.

(4) On an appeal under section 103 of the Immigration and Asylum Act 1999 (c 33) against a decision made by virtue of paragraph 7A of Schedule 3 to the Nationality, Immigration and Asylum Act 2002 the adjudicator may, in particular—

(a)   annul a certificate of the Secretary of State issued for the purposes of that paragraph;
(b)   require the Secretary of State to reconsider the matters certified.

(5) An order under section 48 providing for this section to come into force may, in particular, provide for this section to have effect with specified modifications before the coming into force of a provision of the Nationality, Immigration and Asylum Act 2002.

Appointment
Appointment: 1 December 2004: see SI 2004/2999, art 2, Schedule; for transitional provision see art 4 thereof.

See Further
By virtue of the Asylum and Immigration (Treatment of Claimants, etc) Act 2004 (Commencement No 2) Order 2004, SI 2004/2999, art 3, reference to "section 94(3A)" in sub-s (1) above shall be construed as a reference to "section 94(5)" until the Nationality, Immigration and Asylum Act 2002, s 44 comes into force.

Subordinate Legislation
Asylum and Immigration (Treatment of Claimants, etc) Act 2004 (Commencement No 2) Order 2004, SI 2004/2999 (made under sub-s (5)).

10   Failed asylum seekers: accommodation

(1) At the end of section 4 of the Immigration and Asylum Act 1999 (provision of accommodation for failed asylum seekers, &c) add—

"(5) The Secretary of State may make regulations specifying criteria to be used in determining—

- (a) whether or not to provide accommodation, or arrange for the provision of accommodation, for a person under this section;
- (b) whether or not to continue to provide accommodation, or arrange for the provision of accommodation, for a person under this section.

(6) The regulations may, in particular—

- (a) provide for the continuation of the provision of accommodation for a person to be conditional upon his performance of or participation in community activities in accordance with arrangements made by the Secretary of State;
- (b) provide for the continuation of the provision of accommodation to be subject to other conditions;
- (c) provide for the provision of accommodation (or the continuation of the provision of accommodation) to be a matter for the Secretary of State's discretion to a specified extent or in a specified class of case.

(7) For the purposes of subsection (6)(a)—

- (a) "community activities" means activities that appear to the Secretary of State to be beneficial to the public or a section of the public, and
- (b) the Secretary of State may, in particular—
  - (i) appoint one person to supervise or manage the performance of or participation in activities by another person;
  - (ii) enter into a contract (with a local authority or any other person) for the provision of services by way of making arrangements for community activities in accordance with this section;
  - (iii) pay, or arrange for the payment of, allowances to a person performing or participating in community activities in accordance with arrangements under this section.

(8) Regulations by virtue of subsection (6)(a) may, in particular, provide for a condition requiring the performance of or participation in community activities to apply to a person only if the Secretary of State has made arrangements for community activities in an area that includes the place where accommodation is provided for the person.

(9) A local authority or other person may undertake to manage or participate in arrangements for community activities in accordance with this section.".

(2) In section 166(5) of that Act (regulations: affirmative instrument) before paragraph (a) insert—

"(za) section 4(5),".

(3) In section 103 of the Immigration and Asylum Act 1999 (c 33) (support for asylum-seekers: appeal) as it has effect before the commencement of section 53 of the Nationality, Immigration and Asylum Act 2002 (c 41)—

- (a) after subsection (2) insert—

"(2A) If the Secretary of State decides not to provide accommodation for a person under section 4, or not to continue to provide accommodation for a person under section 4, the person may appeal to an adjudicator.", and

- (b) in subsections (6) and (7) for "section 95" substitute "section 4 or 95".

(4) In section 103 of the Immigration and Asylum Act 1999 (support for asylum-seekers: appeal) as it has effect after the commencement of section 53 of the Nationality, Immigration and Asylum Act 2002—

(a)   for subsection (1) substitute—

"(1)   This section applies where a person has applied for support under all or any of the following provisions—

(a)   section 4,
(b)   section 95, and
(c)   section 17 of the Nationality, Immigration and Asylum Act 2002.",

(b)   in subsection (4)(a) for "the other provision" substitute "another of those provisions", and

(c)   in subsection (7) for "subsection (1)(a) or (b)" substitute "subsection (1)".

(5)   In section 103A of the Immigration and Asylum Act 1999 (appeal about location of support) in subsection (1) (and in the heading) for "section 95" substitute "section 4 or 95".

(6)   In an amendment made by this section a reference to providing accommodation includes a reference to arranging for the provision of accommodation.

(7)   Regulations under section 4(5)(b) of the Immigration and Asylum Act 1999 (c 33) (as inserted by subsection (1) above) may apply to persons receiving support under section 4 when the regulations come into force.

Appointment
Sub-ss (1), (2), (6), (7): Appointment: 1 December 2004: see SI 2004/2999, art 2, Schedule.
Sub-ss (3)–(5): Appointment: 31 March 2005: see SI 2005/372, art 2.

11   Accommodation for asylum seekers: local connection

(1)   At the end of section 199 of the Housing Act 1996 (c 52) (local connection) add—

"(6)   A person has a local connection with the district of a local housing authority if he was (at any time) provided with accommodation in that district under section 95 of the Immigration and Asylum Act 1999 (support for asylum seekers).

(7)   But subsection (6) does not apply—

(a)   to the provision of accommodation for a person in a district of a local housing authority if he was subsequently provided with accommodation in the district of another local housing authority under section 95 of that Act, or
(b)   to the provision of accommodation in an accommodation centre by virtue of section 22 of the Nationality, Immigration and Asylum Act 2002 (c 41) (use of accommodation centres for section 95 support).".

(2)   Subsection (3) applies where—

(a)   a local housing authority would (but for subsection (3)) be obliged to secure that accommodation is available for occupation by a person under section 193 of the Housing Act 1996 (homeless persons),
(b)   the person was (at any time) provided with accommodation in a place in Scotland under section 95 of the Immigration and Asylum Act 1999 (support for asylum seekers),
(c)   the accommodation was not provided in an accommodation centre by virtue of section 22 of the Nationality, Immigration and Asylum Act 2002 (use of accommodation centres for section 95 support), and
(d)   the person has neither—
   (i)   a local connection with the district of a local housing authority (in England or Wales) within the meaning of section 199 of the Housing Act 1996 as amended by subsection (1) above, nor
   (ii)   a local connection with a district (in Scotland) within the meaning of section 27 of the Housing (Scotland) Act 1987 (c 26).

(3) Where this subsection applies—

(a) the duty of the local housing authority under section 193 of the Housing Act 1996 in relation to the person shall not apply, but

(b) the local housing authority—

    (i) may secure that accommodation is available for occupation by the person for a period giving him a reasonable opportunity of securing accommodation for his occupation, and

    (ii) may provide the person (or secure that he is provided with) advice and assistance in any attempts he may make to secure that accommodation becomes available for his occupation.

Appointment
Appointment: 4 January 2005: see SI 2004/2999, art 2, Schedule.

12   Refugee: back-dating of benefits

(1) Section 123 of the Immigration and Asylum Act 1999 (c 33) (back-dating of benefits for refugees) shall cease to have effect.

(2) Accordingly (and without prejudice to any other implied repeal, revocation or amendment) the following (each of which concerns the treatment of refugees) lapse—

(a) in the Income Support (General) Regulations 1987 (SI 1987/1967)—

    (i) regulation 21ZB,

    (ii) paragraph 18A of Schedule 1B, and

    (iii) paragraph 57 of Schedule 9,

(b) in the Income Support (General) Regulations (Northern Ireland) 1987 (SR 1987 No 459)—

    (i) regulation 21A,

    (ii) paragraph 18A of Schedule 1B, and

    (iii) paragraph 57 of Schedule 9,

(c) in the Social Security (Claims and Payments) Regulations 1987 (SI 1987/1968)—

    (i) regulation 4(3C),

    (ii) regulation 6(4D), and

    (iii) regulation 19(8),

(d) in the Social Security (Claims and Payments) Regulations (Northern Ireland) 1987 (SR 1987 No 465)—

    (i) regulation 4(3C),

    (ii) regulation 6(4D), and

    (iii) regulation 19(8),

(e) in the Housing Benefit (General) Regulations 1987 (SI 1987/1971)—

    (i) regulation 7B,

    (ii) Schedule A1,

    (iii) paragraphs 61 and 62 of Schedule 4, and

    (iv) paragraphs 50 and 51 of Schedule 5,

(f) in the Housing Benefit (General) Regulations (Northern Ireland) 1987 (SR 1987 No 461)—

    (i) regulation 7B,

    (ii) Schedule A1,

    (iii) paragraphs 62 and 63 of Schedule 4, and

    (iv) paragraphs 48 and 49 of Schedule 5, and

(g) in the Council Tax Benefit (General) Regulations 1992 (SI 1992/1814)—

    (i) regulation 4D,

    (ii) Schedule A1,

    (iii) paragraphs 60 and 61 of Schedule 4, and

    (iv) paragraphs 50 and 51 of Schedule 5.

(3) Regulation 12(1) and (2) of the Social Security (Immigration and Asylum) Consequential Amendments Regulations 2000 (SI 2000/636) (which save for transitional purposes the effect of provision made for back-payment of benefits for refugees under section 11(2) of the Asylum and Immigration Act 1996 (c 49)) shall cease to have effect.

(4) Regulation 11(1) and (2) of the Social Security (Immigration and Asylum) Consequential Amendments Regulations (Northern Ireland) 2000 (SR2000 No 71) (which make similar transitional savings) shall cease to have effect.

(5) An order under section 48 bringing this section into force may, in particular, provide for this section to have effect in relation to persons recorded as refugees after a specified date (irrespective of when the process resulting in the record was begun).

Initial Commencement
To be appointed: see s 48(3)–(6).

13   Integration loan for refugees

(1) The Secretary of State may make regulations enabling him to make loans to refugees.

(2) A person is a refugee for the purpose of subsection (1) if the Secretary of State has—

    (a) recorded him as a refugee within the meaning of the Convention relating to the Status of Refugees done at Geneva on 28 July 1951, and

    (b) granted him indefinite leave to enter or remain in the United Kingdom (within the meaning of section 33(1) of the Immigration Act 1971 (c 77)).

(3) Regulations under subsection (1)—

    (a) shall specify matters which the Secretary of State shall, in addition to other matters appearing to him to be relevant, take into account in determining whether or not to make a loan (and those matters may, in particular, relate to—
        (i) a person's income or assets,
        (ii) a person's likely ability to repay a loan, or
        (iii) the length of time since a person was recorded as a refugee),

    (b) shall enable the Secretary of State to specify (and vary from time to time) a minimum and a maximum amount of a loan,

    (c) shall prevent a person from receiving a loan if—
        (i) he is under the age of 18,
        (ii) he is insolvent, within a meaning given by the regulations, or
        (iii) he has received a loan under the regulations,

    (d) shall make provision about repayment of a loan (and may, in particular, make provision—
        (i) about interest;
        (ii) for repayment by deduction from a social security benefit or similar payment due to the person to whom the loan is made),

    (e) shall enable the Secretary of State to attach conditions to a loan (which may include conditions about the use of the loan),

    (f) shall make provision about—
        (i) the making of an application for a loan, and
        (ii) the information, which may include information about the intended use of a loan, to be provided in or with an application,

    (g) may make provision about steps to be taken by the Secretary of State in establishing an applicant's likely ability to repay a loan,

(h)   may make provision for a loan to be made jointly to more than one refugee, and

(i)   may confer a discretion on the Secretary of State.

(4)   Regulations under this section—

(a)   shall be made by statutory instrument, and

(b)   may not be made unless a draft has been laid before and approved by resolution of each House of Parliament.

Initial Commencement
To be appointed: see s 48(3)–(6).

Enforcement powers

14   Immigration officer: power of arrest

(1)   Where an immigration officer in the course of exercising a function under the Immigration Acts forms a reasonable suspicion that a person has committed or attempted to commit an offence listed in subsection (2), he may arrest the person without warrant.

(2)   Those offences are—

(a)   the offence of conspiracy at common law (in relation to conspiracy to defraud),

(b)   at common law in Scotland, any of the following offences—
  (i)   fraud,
  (ii)   conspiracy to defraud,
  (iii)   uttering and fraud,
  (iv)   bigamy,
  (v)   theft, and
  (vi)   reset,

(c)   an offence under section 57 of the Offences against the Person Act 1861 (c 100) (bigamy),

(d)   an offence under section 3 or 4 of the Perjury Act 1911 (c 6) (false statements),

(e)   an offence under section 7 of that Act (aiding, abetting &c.) if it relates to an offence under section 3 or 4 of that Act,

(f)   an offence under section 53 of the Registration of Births, Deaths and Marriages (Scotland) Act 1965 (c 49) (knowingly giving false information to district registrar, &c),

(g)   an offence under any of the following provisions of the Theft Act 1968 (c 60)—
  (i)   section 1 (theft),
  (ii)   section 15 (obtaining property by deception),
  (iii)   section 16 (obtaining pecuniary advantage by deception),
  (iv)   section 17 (false accounting), and
  (v)   section 22 (handling stolen goods),

(h)   an offence under section 1, 15, 16, 17 or 21 of the Theft Act (Northern Ireland) 1969 (c 16) (NI),

(i)   an offence under section 1 or 2 of the Theft Act 1978 (c 31) (obtaining services, or evading liability, by deception),

(j)   an offence under Article 3 or 4 of the Theft (Northern Ireland) Order 1978 (SI 1978/1407 (NI 23)),

(k)   an offence under Article 8 or 9 of the Perjury (Northern Ireland) Order 1979 (SI 1979/1714 (NI 19)),

(l) an offence under Article 12 of that Order if it relates to an offence under Article 8 or 9 of that Order,

(m) an offence under any of the following provisions of the Forgery and Counterfeiting Act 1981 (c 45)—

   (i) section 1 (forgery),

  (ii) section 2 (copying false instrument),

 (iii) section 3 (using false instrument),

 (iv) section 4 (using copy of false instrument), and

  (v) section 5(1) and (3) (false documents),

(n) an offence under any of sections 57 to 59 of the Sexual Offences Act 2003 (c 42) (trafficking for sexual exploitation),

(o) an offence under section 22 of the Criminal Justice (Scotland) Act 2003 (asp 7) (trafficking in prostitution), and

(p) an offence under section 4 of this Act.

(3) The following provisions of the Immigration Act 1971 (c 77) shall have effect for the purpose of making, or in connection with, an arrest under this section as they have effect for the purpose of making, or in connection with, arrests for offences under that Act—

(a) section 28C (entry and search before arrest),

(b) sections 28E and 28F (entry and search after arrest),

(c) sections 28G and 28H (search of arrested person), and

(d) section 28I (seized material).

(4) In section 19D(5)(a) of the Race Relations Act 1976 (c 74) (permitted discrimination)—

(a) for "(within the meaning of section 158 of the Nationality, Immigration and Asylum Act 2002)" substitute "(within the meaning of section 44 of the Asylum and Immigration (Treatment of Claimants, etc) Act 2004)", and

(b) at the end add "and excluding section 14 of the Asylum and Immigration (Treatment of Claimants, etc) Act 2004".

Appointment
Appointment: 1 December 2004: see SI 2004/2999, art 2, Schedule.

15   Fingerprinting

(1) Section 141 of the Immigration and Asylum Act 1999 (c 33) (fingerprinting) shall be amended as follows.

(2) In subsection (7) for paragraph (c) substitute—

"(c) any person ("C") in respect of whom a relevant immigration decision has been made;".

(3) In subsection (8) for paragraph (c) substitute—

"(c) for C, on the service on him of notice of the relevant immigration decision by virtue of section 105 of the Nationality, Immigration and Asylum Act 2002 (c 41);".

(4) In subsection (9) for paragraph (c) substitute—

"(c) for C—

  (i) the time when the relevant immigration decision ceases to have effect, whether as a result of an appeal or otherwise, or

 (ii) if a deportation order has been made against him, its revocation or its otherwise ceasing to have effect;".

(5) After subsection (15) add—

1757

"(16)   "Relevant immigration decision" means a decision of the kind mentioned in section 82(2)(g), (h), (i), (j) or (k) of the Nationality, Immigration and Asylum Act 2002 (c 41).".

Appointment
Appointment: 1 October 2004: see SI 2004/2523, art 2, Schedule.

16   Information about passengers

In paragraph 27B of Schedule 2 to the Immigration Act 1971 (c 77) (control on entry: provision of information about passengers) after sub-paragraph (4) insert—

"(4A)   The officer may ask the carrier to provide a copy of all or part of a document that relates to a passenger and contains passenger information.".

Initial Commencement
To be appointed: see s 48(3)–(6).

17   Retention of documents

Where a document comes into the possession of the Secretary of State or an immigration officer in the course of the exercise of an immigration function, the Secretary of State or an immigration officer may retain the document while he suspects that—

   (a)   a person to whom the document relates may be liable to removal from the United Kingdom in accordance with a provision of the Immigration Acts, and
   (b)   retention of the document may facilitate the removal.

Appointment
Appointment: 1 December 2004: see SI 2004/2999, art 2, Schedule.

18   Control of entry

After paragraph 2A(2) of Schedule 2 to the Immigration Act 1971 (control of entry: persons arriving with leave to enter) insert—

"(2A)   Where the person's leave to enter derives, by virtue of section 3A(3), from an entry clearance, he may also be examined by an immigration officer for the purpose of establishing whether the leave should be cancelled on the grounds that the person's purpose in arriving in the United Kingdom is different from the purpose specified in the entry clearance.".

Appointment
Appointment: 1 October 2004: see SI 2004/2523, art 2, Schedule.

Procedure for marriage

19   England and Wales

(1)   This section applies to a marriage—

   (a)   which is to be solemnised on the authority of certificates issued by a superintendent registrar under Part III of the Marriage Act 1949 (c 76), and
   (b)   a party to which is subject to immigration control.

(2)   In relation to a marriage to which this section applies, the notices under section 27 of the Marriage Act 1949—

(a) shall be given to the superintendent registrar of a registration district specified for the purpose of this paragraph by regulations made by the Secretary of State,

(b) shall be delivered to the superintendent registrar in person by the two parties to the marriage,

(c) may be given only if each party to the marriage has been resident in a registration district for the period of seven days immediately before the giving of his or her notice (but the district need not be that in which the notice is given and the parties need not have resided in the same district), and

(d) shall state, in relation to each party, the registration district by reference to which paragraph (c) is satisfied.

(3) The superintendent registrar shall not enter in the marriage notice book notice of a marriage to which this section applies unless satisfied, by the provision of specified evidence, that the party subject to immigration control—

(a) has an entry clearance granted expressly for the purpose of enabling him to marry in the United Kingdom,

(b) has the written permission of the Secretary of State to marry in the United Kingdom, or

(c) falls within a class specified for the purpose of this paragraph by regulations made by the Secretary of State.

(4) For the purposes of this section—

(a) a person is subject to immigration control if—
    (i) he is not an EEA national, and
    (ii) under the Immigration Act 1971 (c 77) he requires leave to enter or remain in the United Kingdom (whether or not leave has been given),

(b) "EEA national" means a national of a State which is a contracting party to the Agreement on the European Economic Area signed at Oporto on 2nd May 1992 (as it has effect from time to time),

(c) "entry clearance" has the meaning given by section 33(1) of the Immigration Act 1971, and

(d) "specified evidence" means such evidence as may be specified in guidance issued by the Registrar General.

Appointment
Sub-s (1): Appointment: 1 February 2005: see SI 2004/3398, art 3.
Sub-ss (2)–(4): Appointment (for certain purposes): 1 December 2004: see SI 2004/2999, art 2, Schedule.
Sub-ss (2)–(4): Appointment (for remaining purposes): 1 February 2005: see SI 2004/3398, art 3.

Subordinate Legislation
Immigration (Procedure for Marriage) Regulations 2005, SI 2005/15 (made under sub-ss (2)(a), (3)(c)).

20 England and Wales: supplemental

(1) The Marriage Act 1949 (c 76) shall have effect in relation to a marriage to which section 19 applies—

(a) subject to that section, and

(b) with any necessary consequential modification.

(2) In particular—

(a) section 28(1)(b) of that Act (declaration: residence) shall have effect as if it required a declaration that—

> (i) the notice of marriage is given in compliance with section 19(2) above, and
>
> (ii) the party subject to immigration control satisfies section 19(3)(a), (b) or (c), and

(b) section 48 of that Act (proof of certain matters not essential to validity of marriage) shall have effect as if the list of matters in section 48(1)(a) to (e) included compliance with section 19 above.

(3) Regulations of the Secretary of State under section 19(2)(a) or (3)(c)—

(a) may make transitional provision,

(b) shall be made by statutory instrument, and

(c) shall be subject to annulment in pursuance of a resolution of either House of Parliament.

(4) Before making regulations under section 19(2)(a) the Secretary of State shall consult the Registrar General.

(5) An expression used in section 19 or this section and in Part III of the Marriage Act 1949 (c 76) has the same meaning in section 19 or this section as in that Part.

(6) An order under the Regulatory Reform Act 2001 (c 6) may include provision—

(a) amending section 19, this section or section 25 in consequence of other provision of the order, or

(b) repealing section 19, this section and section 25 and re-enacting them with modifications consequential upon other provision of the order.

Appointment
Sub-ss (1), (2), (5), (6): Appointment: 1 February 2005: see SI 2004/3398, art 3.
Sub-ss (3), (4): Appointment (for certain purposes): 1 December 2004: see SI 2004/2999, art 2, Schedule.
Sub-ss (3), (4): Appointment (for remaining purposes): 1 February 2005: see SI 2004/3398, art 3.

21   Scotland

(1) This section applies to a marriage—

(a) which is intended to be solemnised in Scotland, and

(b) a party to which is subject to immigration control.

(2) In relation to a marriage to which this section applies, notice under section 3 of the Marriage (Scotland) Act 1977 (c 15)—

(a) may be submitted to the district registrar of a registration district prescribed for the purposes of this section, and

(b) may not be submitted to the district registrar of any other registration district.

(3) Where the district registrar to whom notice is submitted by virtue of subsection (2) is the district registrar for the registration district in which the marriage is to be solemnised, he shall not make an entry under section 4, or complete a Marriage Schedule under section 6, of the Marriage (Scotland) Act 1977 in respect of the marriage unless satisfied, by the provision of specified evidence, that the party subject to immigration control—

(a) has an entry clearance granted expressly for the purpose of enabling him to marry in the United Kingdom,

(b) has the written permission of the Secretary of State to marry in the United Kingdom, or

(c) falls within a class specified for the purpose of this paragraph by regulations made by the Secretary of State.

(4)   Where the district registrar to whom notice is submitted by virtue of subsection (2) (here the "notified registrar") is not the district registrar for the registration district in which the marriage is to be solemnised (here the "second registrar")—

(a)   the notified registrar shall, if satisfied as is mentioned in subsection (3), send the notices and any fee, certificate or declaration which accompanied them, to the second registrar, and

(b)   the second registrar shall be treated as having received the notices from the parties to the marriage on the dates on which the notified registrar received them.

(5)   Subsection (4) of section 19 applies for the purposes of this section as it applies for the purposes of that section except that for the purposes of this section the reference in paragraph (d) of that subsection to guidance issued by the Registrar General shall be construed as a reference to guidance issued by the Secretary of State after consultation with the Registrar General for Scotland.

Appointment
Sub-ss (1), (4): Appointment: 1 February 2005: see SI 2004/3398, art 3.
Sub-ss (2), (3), (5): Appointment (for certain purposes): 1 December 2004: see SI 2004/2999, art 2, Schedule.
Sub-ss (2), (3), (5): Appointment (for remaining purposes): 1 February 2005: see SI 2004/3398, art 3.

Subordinate Legislation
Immigration (Procedure for Marriage) Regulations 2005, SI 2005/15 (made under sub-ss (2)(a), (3)(c)).

22   Scotland: supplemental

(1)   The Marriage (Scotland) Act 1977 shall have effect in relation to a marriage to which section 21 applies—

(a)   subject to that section, and
(b)   with any necessary consequential modification.

(2)   In subsection (2)(a) of that section "prescribed" means prescribed by regulations made by the Secretary of State after consultation with the Registrar General for Scotland; and other expressions used in subsections (1) to (4) of that section and in the Marriage (Scotland) Act 1977 have the same meaning in those subsections as in that Act.

(3)   Regulations made by of the Secretary of State under subsection (2)(a) or (3)(c) of that section—

(a)   may make transitional provision,
(b)   shall be made by statutory instrument, and
(c)   shall be subject to annulment in pursuance of a resolution of either House of Parliament.

Appointment
Sub-s (1): Appointment: 1 February 2005: see SI 2004/3398, art 3.
Sub-ss (2), (3): Appointment (for certain purposes): 1 December 2004: see SI 2004/2999, art 2, Schedule.
Sub-ss (2), (3): Appointment (for remaining purposes): 1 February 2005: see SI 2004/3398, art 3.

23   Northern Ireland

(1)   This section applies to a marriage—

(a)   which is intended to be solemnised in Northern Ireland, and

(b)   a party to which is subject to immigration control.

(2)   In relation to a marriage to which this section applies, the marriage notices—

(a)   shall be given only to a prescribed registrar, and
(b)   shall, in prescribed cases, be given by both parties together in person at a prescribed register office.

(3)   The prescribed registrar shall not act under Article 4 or 7 of the Marriage (Northern Ireland) Order 2003 (SI 2003/413 (NI 3)) (marriage notice book, list of intended marriages and marriage schedule) unless he is satisfied, by the provision of specified evidence, that the party subject to immigration control—

(a)   has an entry clearance granted expressly for the purpose of enabling him to marry in the United Kingdom,
(b)   has the written permission of the Secretary of State to marry in the United Kingdom, or
(c)   falls within a class specified for the purpose of this paragraph by regulations made by the Secretary of State.

(4)   Subject to subsection (5), if the prescribed registrar is not the registrar for the purposes of Article 4 of that Order, the prescribed registrar shall send him the marriage notices and he shall be treated as having received them from the parties to the marriage on the dates on which the prescribed registrar received them.

(5)   The prescribed registrar shall not act under subsection (4) unless he is satisfied as mentioned in subsection (3).

(6)   For the purposes of this section—

(a)   a person is subject to immigration control if—
  (i)   he is not an EEA national, and
  (ii)   under the Immigration Act 1971 (c 77) he requires leave to enter or remain in the United Kingdom (whether or not leave has been given),
(b)   "EEA national" means a national of a State which is a contracting party to the Agreement on the European Economic Area signed at Oporto on 2nd May 1992 (as it has effect from time to time),
(c)   "entry clearance" has the meaning given by section 33(1) of the Immigration Act 1971, and
(d)   "specified evidence" means such evidence as may be specified in guidance issued by the Secretary of State after consulting the Registrar General for Northern Ireland.

Appointment
Sub-ss (1), (4), (5): Appointment: 1 February 2005: see SI 2004/3398, art 3.
Sub-ss (2), (3), (6): Appointment (for certain purposes): 1 December 2004: see SI 2004/2999, art 2, Schedule.
Sub-ss (2), (3), (6): Appointment (for remaining purposes): 1 February 2005: see SI 2004/3398, art 3.

Subordinate Legislation
Immigration (Procedure for Marriage) Regulations 2005, SI 2005/15 (made under sub-ss (2)(a), (3)(c)).

24   Northern Ireland: supplemental

(1)   The Marriage (Northern Ireland) Order 2003 (SI 2003/413 (NI 3)) shall have effect in relation to a marriage to which section 23 applies—

(a)   subject to section 23, and
(b)   with any necessary consequential modification.

(2) In section 23 "prescribed" means prescribed for the purposes of that section by regulations made by the Secretary of State after consulting the Registrar General for Northern Ireland and other expressions used in that section or this section and the Marriage (Northern Ireland) Order 2003 have the same meaning in section 23 or this section as in that Order.

(3) Section 18(3) of the Interpretation Act (Northern Ireland) 1954 (c 33 (NI)) (provisions as to holders of offices) shall apply to section 23 as if that section were an enactment within the meaning of that Act.

(4) Regulations of the Secretary of State under section 23—

    (a)   may make transitional provision,

    (b)   shall be made by statutory instrument, and

    (c)   shall be subject to annulment in pursuance of a resolution of either House of Parliament.

Appointment
Sub-ss (1), (3): Appointment: 1 February 2005: see SI 2004/3398, art 3.
Sub-ss (2), (4): Appointment (for certain purposes): 1 December 2004: see SI 2004/2999, art 2, Schedule.
Sub-ss (2), (4): Appointment (for remaining purposes): 1 February 2005: see SI 2004/3398, art 3.

25   Application for permission under section 19(3)(b), 21(3)(b) or 23(3)(b)

(1) The Secretary of State may make regulations requiring a person seeking permission under section 19(3)(b), 21(3)(b) or 23(3)(b)—

    (a)   to make an application in writing, and

    (b)   to pay a fee.

(2) The regulations shall, in particular, specify—

    (a)   the information to be contained in or provided with the application,

    (b)   the amount of the fee, and

    (c)   how and to whom the fee is to be paid.

(3) The regulations may, in particular, make provision—

    (a)   excepting a specified class of persons from the requirement to pay a fee;

    (b)   permitting a specified class of persons to pay a reduced fee;

    (c)   for the refund of all or part of a fee in specified circumstances.

(4) Regulations under this section—

    (a)   shall be made by statutory instrument, and

    (b)   shall be subject to annulment in pursuance of a resolution of either House of Parliament.

Appointment
Appointment: 1 December 2004: see SI 2004/2999, art 2, Schedule.

Subordinate Legislation
Immigration (Procedure for Marriage) Regulations 2005, SI 2005/15.

Appeals

26   Unification of appeal system

(1) For section 81 of the Nationality, Immigration and Asylum Act 2002 (c 41) (appeals: adjudicators) substitute—

81   The Asylum and Immigration Tribunal

(1)   There shall be a tribunal to be known as the Asylum and Immigration Tribunal.

(2)   Schedule 4 (which makes provision about the Tribunal) shall have effect.

(3)   A reference in this Part to the Tribunal is a reference to the Asylum and Immigration Tribunal.".

(2)   In section 82(1) of that Act (right of appeal: general) for "to an adjudicator" substitute "to the Tribunal".

(3)   In section 83(2) of that Act (appeal: asylum claim) for "to an adjudicator" substitute "to the Tribunal".

(4)   For Schedule 4 to that Act (adjudicators) substitute the Schedule set out in Schedule 1 to this Act (Asylum and Immigration Tribunal).

(5)   The following provisions of that Act shall cease to have effect—

   (a)   sections 100 to 103 (Immigration Appeal Tribunal), and
   (b)   Schedule 5 (Immigration Appeal Tribunal).

(6)   Before section 104 of that Act (pending appeal) insert—

"103A   Review of Tribunal's decision

(1)   A party to an appeal under section 82 or 83 may apply to the appropriate court, on the grounds that the Tribunal made an error of law, for an order requiring the Tribunal to reconsider its decision on the appeal.

(2)   The appropriate court may make an order under subsection (1)—

   (a)   only if it thinks that the Tribunal may have made an error of law, and
   (b)   only once in relation to an appeal.

(3)   An application under subsection (1) must be made—

   (a)   in the case of an application by the appellant made while he is in the United Kingdom, within the period of 5 days beginning with the date on which he is treated, in accordance with rules under section 106, as receiving notice of the Tribunal's decision,
   (b)   in the case of an application by the appellant made while he is outside the United Kingdom, within the period of 28 days beginning with the date on which he is treated, in accordance with rules under section 106, as receiving notice of the Tribunal's decision, and
   (c)   in the case of an application brought by a party to the appeal other than the appellant, within the period of 5 days beginning with the date on which he is treated, in accordance with rules under section 106, as receiving notice of the Tribunal's decision.

(4)   But—

   (a)   rules of court may specify days to be disregarded in applying subsection (3)(a), (b) or (c), and
   (b)   the appropriate court may permit an application under subsection (1) to be made outside the period specified in subsection (3) where it thinks that the application could not reasonably practicably have been made within that period.

(5)   An application under subsection (1) shall be determined by reference only to—

(a) written submissions of the applicant, and
(b) where rules of court permit, other written submissions.

(6) A decision of the appropriate court on an application under subsection (1) shall be final.

(7) In this section a reference to the Tribunal's decision on an appeal does not include a reference to—

(a) a procedural, ancillary or preliminary decision, or
(b) a decision following remittal under section 103B, 103C or 103E.

(8) This section does not apply to a decision of the Tribunal where its jurisdiction is exercised by three or more legally qualified members.

(9) In this section "the appropriate court" means—

(a) in relation to an appeal decided in England or Wales, the High Court,
(b) in relation to an appeal decided in Scotland, the Court of Session, and
(c) in relation to an appeal decided in Northern Ireland, the High Court in Northern Ireland.

(10) An application under subsection (1) to the Court of Session shall be to the Outer House.

103B Appeal from Tribunal following reconsideration

(1) Where an appeal to the Tribunal has been reconsidered, a party to the appeal may bring a further appeal on a point of law to the appropriate appellate court.

(2) In subsection (1) the reference to reconsideration is to reconsideration pursuant to—

(a) an order under section 103A(1), or
(b) remittal to the Tribunal under this section or under section 103C or 103E.

(3) An appeal under subsection (1) may be brought only with the permission of—

(a) the Tribunal, or
(b) if the Tribunal refuses permission, the appropriate appellate court.

(4) On an appeal under subsection (1) the appropriate appellate court may—

(a) affirm the Tribunal's decision;
(b) make any decision which the Tribunal could have made;
(c) remit the case to the Tribunal;
(d) affirm a direction under section 87;
(e) vary a direction under section 87;
(f) give a direction which the Tribunal could have given under section 87.

(5) In this section "the appropriate appellate court" means—

(a) in relation to an appeal decided in England or Wales, the Court of Appeal,
(b) in relation to an appeal decided in Scotland, the Court of Session, and
(c) in relation to an appeal decided in Northern Ireland, the Court of Appeal in Northern Ireland.

(6) An appeal under subsection (1) to the Court of Session shall be to the Inner House.

103C Appeal from Tribunal instead of reconsideration

(1) On an application under section 103A in respect of an appeal the appropriate court, if it thinks the appeal raises a question of law of such importance that it should be decided by the appropriate appellate court, may refer the appeal to that court.

(2)   On a reference under subsection (1) the appropriate appellate court may—

(a)   affirm the Tribunal's decision;
(b)   make any decision which the Tribunal could have made;
(c)   remit the case to the Tribunal;
(d)   affirm a direction under section 87;
(e)   vary a direction under section 87;
(f)   give a direction which the Tribunal could have given under section 87;
(g)   restore the application under section 103A to the appropriate court.

(3)   In this section—

"the appropriate court" has the same meaning as in section 103A, and
"the appropriate appellate court" has the same meaning as in section 103B.

(4)   A reference under subsection (1) to the Court of Session shall be to the Inner House.

103D   Reconsideration: legal aid

(1)   On the application of an appellant under section 103A, the appropriate court may order that the appellant's costs in respect of the application under section 103A shall be paid out of the Community Legal Service Fund established under section 5 of the Access to Justice Act 1999 (c 22).

(2)   Subsection (3) applies where the Tribunal has decided an appeal following reconsideration pursuant to an order made—

(a)   under section 103A(1), and
(b)   on the application of the appellant.

(3)   The Tribunal may order that the appellant's costs—

(a)   in respect of the application for reconsideration, and
(b)   in respect of the reconsideration,

shall be paid out of that Fund.

(4)   The Secretary of State may make regulations about the exercise of the powers in subsections (1) and (3).

(5)   Regulations under subsection (4) may, in particular, make provision—

(a)   specifying or providing for the determination of the amount of payments;
(b)   about the persons to whom the payments are to be made;
(c)   restricting the exercise of the power (whether by reference to the prospects of success in respect of the appeal at the time when the application for reconsideration was made, the fact that a reference has been made under section 103C(1), the circumstances of the appellant, the nature of the appellant's legal representatives, or otherwise).

(6)   Regulations under subsection (4) may make provision—

(a)   conferring a function on the Legal Services Commission;
(b)   modifying a duty or power of the Legal Services Commission in respect of compliance with orders under subsection (3);
(c)   applying (with or without modifications), modifying or disapplying a provision of, or of anything done under, an enactment relating to the funding of legal services.

(7)   Before making regulations under subsection (4) the Secretary of State shall consult such persons as he thinks appropriate.

(8)   This section has effect only in relation to an appeal decided in—

  (a) England,
  (b) Wales, or
  (c) Northern Ireland.

(9) In relation to an appeal decided in Northern Ireland this section shall have effect—

  (a) as if a reference to the Community Legal Service Fund were to the fund established under paragraph 4(2)(a) of Schedule 3 to the Access to Justice (Northern Ireland) Order 2003 (SI 2003/ 435 (NI 10)), and
  (b) with any other necessary modifications.

103E Appeal from Tribunal sitting as panel

(1) This section applies to a decision of the Tribunal on an appeal under section 82 or 83 where its jurisdiction is exercised by three or more legally qualified members.

(2) A party to the appeal may bring a further appeal on a point of law to the appropriate appellate court.

(3) An appeal under subsection (2) may be brought only with the permission of—

  (a) the Tribunal, or
  (b) if the Tribunal refuses permission, the appropriate appellate court.

(4) On an appeal under subsection (2) the appropriate appellate court may—

  (a) affirm the Tribunal's decision;
  (b) make any decision which the Tribunal could have made;
  (c) remit the case to the Tribunal;
  (d) affirm a direction under section 87;
  (e) vary a direction under section 87;
  (f) give a direction which the Tribunal could have given under section 87.

(5) In this section "the appropriate appellate court" means—

  (a) in relation to an appeal decided in England or Wales, the Court of Appeal,
  (b) in relation to an appeal decided in Scotland, the Court of Session, and
  (c) in relation to an appeal decided in Northern Ireland, the Court of Appeal in Northern Ireland.

(6) A further appeal under subsection (2) to the Court of Session shall be to the Inner House.

(7) In this section a reference to the Tribunal's decision on an appeal does not include a reference to—

  (a) a procedural, ancillary or preliminary decision, or
  (b) a decision following remittal under section 103B or 103C.".

(7) Schedule 2 (which makes amendments consequential on this section, and transitional provision) shall have effect.

(8) The Lord Chancellor may by order vary a period specified in—

  (a) section 103A(3)(a), (b) or (c) of the Nationality, Immigration and Asylum Act 2002 (c 41) (review of Tribunal's decision) (as inserted by subsection (6) above), or
  (b) paragraph 30(5)(b) of Schedule 2 to this Act.

(9) An order under subsection (8)—

  (a) may make provision generally or only for specified cases or circumstances,
  (b) may make different provision for different cases or circumstances,

(c)   shall be made by statutory instrument, and
(d)   shall be subject to annulment in pursuance of a resolution of either House of Parliament.

(10)   Before making an order under subsection (8) the Lord Chancellor shall consult—

(a)   the Lord Chief Justice, if the order affects proceedings in England and Wales,
(b)   the Lord President of the Court of Session, if the order affects proceedings in Scotland, and
(c)   the Lord Chief Justice of Northern Ireland, if the order affects proceedings in Northern Ireland.

Appointment
Sub-ss (1)–(5), (7)–(10): Appointment: 4 April 2005: see SI 2005/565, art 2(a); for transitional provisions see arts 3–9 thereof.
Sub-s (6): Appointment (except in so far as it inserts 2002 c 41, s 103D in relation to Northern Ireland): 4 April 2005: see SI 2005/565, art 2(b); for transitional provisions see arts 3–9 thereof.

Subordinate Legislation
Asylum and Immigration (Fast Track Time Limits) Order 2005, SI 2005/561 (made under sub-ss (8), (9)).

27   Unfounded human rights or asylum claim

(1)   Section 94 of the Nationality, Immigration and Asylum Act 2002 (c 41) (no appeal from within United Kingdom for unfounded human rights or asylum claim) shall be amended as follows.

(2)   After subsection (1) insert—

"(1A)   A person may not bring an appeal against an immigration decision of a kind specified in section 82(2)(c), (d) or (e) in reliance on section 92(2) if the Secretary of State certifies that the claim or claims mentioned in subsection (1) above is or are clearly unfounded.".

(3)   In subsection (2) for "in reliance on section 92(4)" substitute "in reliance on section 92(4)(a)".

(4)   In subsection (4) omit paragraphs (a) to (j).

(5)   After subsection (5) insert—

"(5A)   If the Secretary of State is satisfied that the statements in subsection (5) (a) and (b) are true of a State or part of a State in relation to a description of person, an order under subsection (5) may add the State or part to the list in subsection (4) in respect of that description of person.

(5B)   Where a State or part of a State is added to the list in subsection (4) in respect of a description of person, subsection (3) shall have effect in relation to a claimant only if the Secretary of State is satisfied that he is within that description (as well as being satisfied that he is entitled to reside in the State or part).

(5C)   A description for the purposes of subsection (5A) may refer to—

(a)   gender,
(b)   language,
(c)   race,
(d)   religion,
(e)   nationality,
(f)   membership of a social or other group,
(g)   political opinion, or

(h) any other attribute or circumstance that the Secretary of State thinks appropriate.".

(6) For subsection (6) substitute—

"(6) The Secretary of State may by order amend the list in subsection (4) so as to omit a State or part added under subsection (5); and the omission may be—

(a) general, or

(b) effected so that the State or part remains listed in respect of a description of person.".

(7) After subsection (6) insert—

"(6A) Subsection (3) shall not apply in relation to an asylum claimant or human rights claimant who—

(a) is the subject of a certificate under section 2 or 70 of the Extradition Act 2003 (c 41),

(b) is in custody pursuant to arrest under section 5 of that Act,

(c) is the subject of a provisional warrant under section 73 of that Act,

(d) is the subject of an authority to proceed under section 7 of the Extradition Act 1989 (c 33) or an order under paragraph 4(2) of Schedule 1 to that Act, or

(e) is the subject of a provisional warrant under section 8 of that Act or of a warrant under paragraph 5(1)(b) of Schedule 1 to that Act.".

(8) After section 112(5) of that Act (orders, &c) insert—

"(5A) If an instrument makes provision under section 94(5) and 94(6)—

(a) subsection (4)(b) above shall apply, and

(b) subsection (5)(b) above shall not apply.".

Appointment
Appointment: 1 October 2004: see SI 2004/2523, art 2, Schedule.

28 Appeal from within United Kingdom

For section 92(3) of the Nationality, Immigration and Asylum Act 2002 (c 41) (appeal from within United Kingdom: person with entry clearance or work permit) substitute—

"(3) This section also applies to an appeal against refusal of leave to enter the United Kingdom if—

(a) at the time of the refusal the appellant is in the United Kingdom, and

(b) on his arrival in the United Kingdom the appellant had entry clearance.

(3A) But this section does not apply by virtue of subsection (3) if subsection (3B) or (3C) applies to the refusal of leave to enter.

(3B) This subsection applies to a refusal of leave to enter which is a deemed refusal under paragraph 2A(9) of Schedule 2 to the Immigration Act 1971 (c 77) resulting from cancellation of leave to enter by an immigration officer—

(a) under paragraph 2A(8) of that Schedule, and

(b) on the grounds specified in paragraph 2A(2A) of that Schedule.

(3C) This subsection applies to a refusal of leave to enter which specifies that the grounds for refusal are that the leave is sought for a purpose other than that specified in the entry clearance.

(3D) This section also applies to an appeal against refusal of leave to enter the United Kingdom if at the time of the refusal the appellant—

(a) is in the United Kingdom,

(b) has a work permit, and
(c) is any of the following (within the meaning of the British Nationality Act 1981 (c 61))—
    (i) a British overseas territories citizen,
    (ii) a British Overseas citizen,
    (iii) a British National (Overseas),
    (iv) a British protected person, or
    (v) a British subject.".

Appointment
Appointment: 1 October 2004: see SI 2004/2523, art 2, Schedule.

29   Entry clearance

(1) After section 88 of the Nationality, Immigration and Asylum Act 2002 (c 41) (appeal: ineligibility) insert—

"88A   Ineligibility: entry clearance

(1) A person may not appeal under section 82(1) against refusal of entry clearance if the decision to refuse is taken on grounds which—

(a) relate to a provision of immigration rules, and
(b) are specified for the purpose of this section by order of the Secretary of State.

(2) Subsection (1)—

(a) does not prevent the bringing of an appeal on either or both of the grounds referred to in section 84(1)(b) and (c), and
(b) is without prejudice to the effect of section 88 in relation to an appeal under section 82(1) against refusal of entry clearance.".

(2) In section 112 of that Act (regulations, &c) after subsection (3) insert—

"(3A) An order under section 88A—

(a) must be made by statutory instrument,
(b) may not be made unless a draft has been laid before and approved by resolution of each House of Parliament, and
(c) may include transitional provision.".

Appointment
Appointment: 1 October 2004: see SI 2004/2523, art 2, Schedule.

30   Earlier right of appeal

(1) Section 96 of the Nationality, Immigration and Asylum Act 2002 (earlier right of appeal) shall be amended as follows.

(2) For subsections (1) to (3) substitute—

"(1) An appeal under section 82(1) against an immigration decision ("the new decision") in respect of a person may not be brought if the Secretary of State or an immigration officer certifies—

(a) that the person was notified of a right of appeal under that section against another immigration decision ("the old decision") (whether or not an appeal was brought and whether or not any appeal brought has been determined),
(b) that the claim or application to which the new decision relates relies on a matter that could have been raised in an appeal against the old decision, and

   (c)   that, in the opinion of the Secretary of State or the immigration officer, there is no satisfactory reason for that matter not having been raised in an appeal against the old decision.

(2) An appeal under section 82(1) against an immigration decision ("the new decision") in respect of a person may not be brought if the Secretary of State or an immigration officer certifies—

   (a)   that the person received a notice under section 120 by virtue of an application other than that to which the new decision relates or by virtue of a decision other than the new decision,

   (b)   that the new decision relates to an application or claim which relies on a matter that should have been, but has not been, raised in a statement made in response to that notice, and

   (c)   that, in the opinion of the Secretary of State or the immigration officer, there is no satisfactory reason for that matter not having been raised in a statement made in response to that notice.".

(3) In subsection (5) for "Subsections (1) to (3) apply to prevent or restrict" substitute "Subsections (1) and (2) apply to prevent".

(4) At the end add—

"(7) A certificate under subsection (1) or (2) shall have no effect in relation to an appeal instituted before the certificate is issued.".

Appointment
Appointment: 1 October 2004: see SI 2004/2523, art 2, Schedule.

31   Seamen and aircrews: right of appeal

In section 82(2) of the Nationality, Immigration and Asylum Act 2002 (c 41) after paragraph (i) insert—
   "(ia) a decision that a person is to be removed from the United Kingdom by way of directions under paragraph 12(2) of Schedule 2 to the Immigration Act 1971 (c 77) (seamen and aircrews),".

Appointment
Appointment: 1 October 2004: see SI 2004/2523, art 2, Schedule.

32   ...

...

Amendment
Repealed by the Prevention of Terrorism Act 2005, s 16(2)(d). Date in force: 14 March 2005: see the Prevention of Terrorism Act 2005, s 16(3).

Removal and detention

33   Removing asylum seeker to safe country

(1) Schedule 3 (which concerns the removal of persons claiming asylum to countries known to protect refugees and to respect human rights) shall have effect.

(2) Sections 11 and 12 of the Immigration and Asylum Act 1999 (c 33) (removal of asylum claimant to country under standing or other arrangements) shall cease to have effect.

(3) The following provisions of the Nationality, Immigration and Asylum Act 2002 (c 41) shall cease to have effect—

   (a)   section 80 (new section 11 of 1999 Act), and
   (b)   section 93 (appeal from within United Kingdom: "third country" removal).

Appointment
Appointment: 1 October 2004: see SI 2004/2523, art 2, Schedule; for transitional provisions see art 3 thereof.

34   Detention pending deportation

(1)   In paragraph 2(1) of Schedule 3 to the Immigration Act 1971 (c 77) (detention pending deportation on recommendation by court) for the words "and that person is neither detained in pursuance of the sentence or order of any court nor for the time being released on bail by any court having power so to release him" substitute "and that person is not detained in pursuance of the sentence or order of any court".

(2)   In paragraph 2(2) of that Schedule (detention following notice of deportation) for the words "and he is neither detained in pursuance of the sentence or order of a court nor for the time being released on bail by a court having power so to release him" substitute "and he is not detained in pursuance of the sentence or order of a court".

Appointment
Appointment: 1 October 2004: see SI 2004/2523, art 2, Schedule.

35   Deportation or removal: cooperation

(1)   The Secretary of State may require a person to take specified action if the Secretary of State thinks that—

   (a)   the action will or may enable a travel document to be obtained by or for the person, and
   (b)   possession of the travel document will facilitate the person's deportation or removal from the United Kingdom.

(2)   In particular, the Secretary of State may require a person to—

   (a)   provide information or documents to the Secretary of State or to any other person;
   (b)   obtain information or documents;
   (c)   provide fingerprints, submit to the taking of a photograph or provide information, or submit to a process for the recording of information, about external physical characteristics (including, in particular, features of the iris or any other part of the eye);
   (d)   make, or consent to or cooperate with the making of, an application to a person acting for the government of a State other than the United Kingdom;
   (e)   cooperate with a process designed to enable determination of an application;
   (f)   complete a form accurately and completely;
   (g)   attend an interview and answer questions accurately and completely;
   (h)   make an appointment.

(3)   A person commits an offence if he fails without reasonable excuse to comply with a requirement of the Secretary of State under subsection (1).

(4)   A person guilty of an offence under subsection (3) shall be liable—

   (a)   on conviction on indictment, to imprisonment for a term not exceeding two years, to a fine or to both, or
   (b)   on summary conviction, to imprisonment for a term not exceeding twelve months, to a fine not exceeding the statutory maximum or to both.

(5)   If *a constable or* [an] immigration officer reasonably suspects that a person has committed an offence under subsection (3) he may arrest the person without warrant.

(6) An offence under subsection (3) shall be treated as—

    (a) a relevant offence for the purposes of sections 28B and 28D of the Immigration Act 1971 (c 77) (search, entry and arrest), and

    (b) an offence under Part III of that Act (criminal proceedings) for the purposes of sections 28(4), 28E, 28G and 28H (search after arrest, &c) of that Act.

(7) In subsection (1)—

    "travel document" means a passport or other document which is issued by or for Her Majesty's Government or the government of another State and which enables or facilitates travel from the United Kingdom to another State, and

    "removal from the United Kingdom" means removal under—

        (a) Schedule 2 to the Immigration Act 1971 (control on entry) (including a provision of that Schedule as applied by another provision of the Immigration Acts),

        (b) section 10 of the Immigration and Asylum Act 1999 (c 33) (removal of person unlawfully in United Kingdom), or

        (c) Schedule 3 to this Act.

(8) While sections 11 and 12 of the Immigration and Asylum Act 1999 continue to have effect, the reference in subsection (7)(c) above to Schedule 3 to this Act shall be treated as including a reference to those sections.

(9) In so far as subsection (3) extends to England and Wales, subsection (4)(b) shall, until the commencement of section 154 of the Criminal Justice Act 2003 (c 44) (increased limit on magistrates' power of imprisonment), have effect as if the reference to twelve months were a reference to six months.

(10) In so far as subsection (3) extends to Scotland, subsection (4)(b) shall have effect as if the reference to twelve months were a reference to six months.

(11) In so far as subsection (3) extends to Northern Ireland, subsection (4)(b) shall have effect as if the reference to twelve months were a reference to six months.

Amendment

Sub-s (5): words "a constable or" in italics repealed and subsequent word in square brackets substituted by the Serious Organised Crime and Police Act 2005, s 111, Sch 7, Pt 4, para 63(b). Date in force: to be appointed: see the Serious Organised Crime and Police Act 2005, s 178(8).

36 Electronic monitoring

(1) In this section—

    (a) "residence restriction" means a restriction as to residence imposed under—

        (i) paragraph 21 of Schedule 2 to the Immigration Act 1971 (c 77) (control on entry) (including that paragraph as applied by another provision of the Immigration Acts), or

        (ii) Schedule 3 to that Act (deportation),

    (b) "reporting restriction" means a requirement to report to a specified person imposed under any of those provisions,

    (c) "employment restriction" means a restriction as to employment or occupation imposed under any of those provisions, and

    (d) "immigration bail" means—

        (i) release under a provision of the Immigration Acts on entry into a recognizance or bail bond,

        (ii) bail granted in accordance with a provision of the Immigration Acts by a court, a justice of the peace, the sheriff, the Asylum and Immigration Tribunal, the Secretary of State or an immigration officer (but not by a police officer), and

(iii) bail granted by the Special Immigration Appeals Commission.

(2) Where a residence restriction is imposed on an adult—

(a) he may be required to cooperate with electronic monitoring, and
(b) failure to comply with a requirement under paragraph (a) shall be treated for all purposes of the Immigration Acts as failure to observe the residence restriction.

(3) Where a reporting restriction could be imposed on an adult—

(a) he may instead be required to cooperate with electronic monitoring, and
(b) the requirement shall be treated for all purposes of the Immigration Acts as a reporting restriction.

(4) Immigration bail may be granted to an adult subject to a requirement that he cooperate with electronic monitoring; and the requirement may (but need not) be imposed as a condition of a recognizance or bail bond.

(5) In this section a reference to requiring an adult to cooperate with electronic monitoring is a reference to requiring him to cooperate with such arrangements as the person imposing the requirement may specify for detecting and recording by electronic means the location of the adult, or his presence in or absence from a location—

(a) at specified times,
(b) during specified periods of time, or
(c) throughout the currency of the arrangements.

(6) In particular, arrangements for the electronic monitoring of an adult—

(a) may require him to wear a device;
(b) may require him to make specified use of a device;
(c) may prohibit him from causing or permitting damage of or interference with a device;
(d) may prohibit him from taking or permitting action that would or might prevent the effective operation of a device;
(e) may require him to communicate in a specified manner and at specified times or during specified periods of time;
(f) may involve the performance of functions by persons other than the person imposing the requirement to cooperate with electronic monitoring (and those functions may relate to any aspect or condition of a residence restriction, of a reporting restriction, of an employment restriction, of a requirement under this section or of immigration bail).

(7) In this section "adult" means an individual who is at least 18 years old.

(8) The Secretary of State—

(a) may make rules about arrangements for electronic monitoring for the purposes of this section, and
(b) when he thinks that satisfactory arrangements for electronic monitoring are available in respect of an area, shall notify persons likely to be in a position to exercise power under this section in respect of the area.

(9) Rules under subsection (8)(a) may, in particular, require that arrangements for electronic monitoring impose on a person of a specified description responsibility for specified aspects of the operation of the arrangements.

(10) A requirement to cooperate with electronic monitoring—

(a) shall comply with rules under subsection (8)(a), and

(b) may not be imposed in respect of an adult who is or is expected to be in an area unless the person imposing the requirement has received a notification from the Secretary of State under subsection (8)(b) in respect of that area.

(11) Rules under subsection (8)(a)—

(a) may include incidental, consequential or transitional provision,

(b) may make provision generally or only in relation to specified cases, circumstances or areas,

(c) shall be made by statutory instrument, and

(d) shall be subject to annulment in pursuance of a resolution of either House of Parliament.

(12) Before the commencement of section 26 a reference in this section to the Asylum and Immigration Tribunal shall be treated as a reference to—

(a) a person appointed, or treated as if appointed, as an adjudicator under section 81 of the Nationality, Immigration and Asylum Act 2002 (c 41) (appeals), and

(b) the Immigration Appeal Tribunal.

Appointment
Appointment: 1 October 2004: see SI 2004/2523, art 2, Schedule.

Immigration services

37 Provision of immigration services

(1) For section 84(2) and (3) of the Immigration and Asylum Act 1999 (c 33) (person qualified to provide immigration services) substitute—

"(2) A person is a qualified person if he is—

(a) a registered person,

(b) authorised by a designated professional body to practise as a member of the profession whose members the body regulates,

(c) the equivalent in an EEA State of—

(i) a registered person, or

(ii) a person within paragraph (b),

(d) a person permitted, by virtue of exemption from a prohibition, to provide in an EEA State advice or services equivalent to immigration advice or services, or

(e) acting on behalf of, and under the supervision of, a person within any of paragraphs (a) to (d) (whether or not under a contract of employment).

(3) Subsection (2)(a) and (e) are subject to any limitation on the effect of a person's registration imposed under paragraph 2(2) of Schedule 6.".

(2) In section 85(1) of that Act (registration by the Commissioner) omit "and (b)".

(3) In section 89 of that Act (disciplinary charge upheld by Immigration Services Tribunal)—

(a) for subsections (2) and (3) substitute—

"(2) If the person charged is a registered person or acts on behalf of a registered person, the Tribunal may—

(a) direct the Commissioner to record the charge and the Tribunal's decision for consideration in connection with the registered person's next application for continued registration;

1775

(b) direct the registered person to apply for continued registration as soon as is reasonably practicable.", and

(b) in subsection (8) for "employed by him or working" substitute "acting on his behalf or".

(4) In section 90(4) of that Act (orders by disciplinary bodies) for "works under the supervision of" substitute "is acting on behalf of".

(5) In Schedule 5 to that Act (Immigration Services Commissioner)—

(a) for paragraph 1(1)(b) substitute—
"(b) those acting on behalf of registered persons,",
(b) for paragraph 1(3)(b) substitute—
"(b) any person acting on behalf of that person.",
(c) for paragraph 3(3)(b) substitute—
"(b) a person who is acting on behalf of a person who is within paragraph (a);",
(d) for paragraph 4(1)(b) substitute—
"(b) persons acting on behalf of persons who are within paragraph (a).",
(e) in paragraph 5(3)(b) for "employed by, or working under the supervision of," substitute "acting on behalf of",
(f) for paragraph 5(3)(e) substitute—
"(e) an alleged breach of a rule of a relevant regulatory body,",
(g) for paragraph 6(3)(c) substitute—
"(c) in any other case, refer the matter to any relevant regulatory body.",
(h) in paragraphs 9(1)(a) and (b) for "or a person employed by, or working under the supervision of," substitute "or is acting on behalf of",
(i) for paragraph 9(1)(c) substitute—
"(c) refer the complaint and his decision on it to a relevant regulatory body;",
(j) for paragraphs 9(3)(a) and (b) substitute—
"(a) imposing restrictions on the provision of immigration advice or immigration services by the relevant person or by a person acting on his behalf or under his supervision;
(b) prohibiting the provision of immigration advice or immigration services by the relevant person or a person acting on his behalf or under his supervision.", and
(k) for paragraphs 9(4)(b) to (d) substitute—
"(b) a person acting on behalf of a registered person;".

(6) In Schedule 6 to that Act (registration)—

(a) in paragraph 1(1) omit "or (b)", and
(b) in paragraph 3(7)(a) for "section 89(3)(b)" substitute "section 89(2)(b)".

Appointment
Appointment: 1 October 2004: see SI 2004/2523, art 2, Schedule.

38   Immigration Services Commissioner: power of entry

(1) After section 92 of the Immigration and Asylum Act 1999 (c 33) (offences: enforcement) insert—

"92A   Investigation of offence: power of entry

(1) On an application made by the Commissioner a justice of the peace may issue a warrant authorising the Commissioner to enter and search premises.

(2) A justice of the peace may issue a warrant in respect of premises only if satisfied that there are reasonable grounds for believing that—

(a) an offence under section 91 has been committed,

(b)   there is material on the premises which is likely to be of substantial value (whether by itself or together with other material) to the investigation of the offence, and

(c)   any of the conditions specified in subsection (3) is satisfied.

(3)   Those conditions are—

(a)   that it is not practicable to communicate with a person entitled to grant entry to the premises,

(b)   that it is not practicable to communicate with a person entitled to grant access to the evidence,

(c)   that entry to the premises will be prevented unless a warrant is produced, and

(d)   that the purpose of a search may be frustrated or seriously prejudiced unless the Commissioner can secure immediate entry on arrival at the premises.

(4)   The Commissioner may seize and retain anything for which a search is authorised under this section.

(5)   A person commits an offence if without reasonable excuse he obstructs the Commissioner in the exercise of a power by virtue of this section.

(6)   A person guilty of an offence under subsection (5) shall be liable on summary conviction to—

(a)   imprisonment for a term not exceeding six months,

(b)   a fine not exceeding level 5 on the standard scale, or

(c)   both.

(7)   In this section—

(a)   a reference to the Commissioner includes a reference to a member of his staff authorised in writing by him,

(b)   a reference to premises includes a reference to premises used wholly or partly as a dwelling, and

(c)   a reference to material—

   (i)   includes material subject to legal privilege within the meaning of the Police and Criminal Evidence Act 1984 (c 60),

   (ii)   does not include excluded material or special procedure material within the meaning of that Act, and

   (iii)   includes material whether or not it would be admissible in evidence at a trial.

(8)   In the application of this section to Scotland—

(a)   a reference to a justice of the peace shall be taken as a reference to the sheriff,

(b)   for sub-paragraph (i) of subsection (7)(c) there is substituted—

"(i)   includes material comprising items subject to legal privilege (as defined by section 412 of the Proceeds of Crime Act 2002 (c 29))," and

(c)   sub-paragraph (ii) of subsection (7)(c) shall be ignored.

(9)   In the application of this section to Northern Ireland the reference to the Police and Criminal Evidence Act 1984 shall be taken as a reference to the Police and Criminal Evidence (Northern Ireland) Order 1989 (SI 1989/1341 (NI 12)).".

(2)   In paragraph 7 of Schedule 5 to the Immigration and Asylum Act 1999 (c 33) (investigation of complaints, &c: power of entry)—

(a)   in sub-paragraph (1)(b) after "(b)" insert ", (c)",

(b)   in sub-paragraph (1)(c) for "registered person." substitute "registered or exempt person.",

(c)   in sub-paragraph (1A)(a) after "(b)" insert ", (c)",

(d) in sub-paragraph (1A)(b) for "registered person." substitute "registered or exempt person.", and
(e) after sub-paragraph (8) insert—

"(9) Sub-paragraphs (7) and (8) shall apply to an exempt person as they apply to a registered person, but with a reference to cancellation of registration being treated as a reference to withdrawal of exemption.

(10) In this paragraph "exempt person" means a person certified by the Commissioner as exempt under section 84(4)(a).".

Appointment
Appointment: 1 October 2004: see SI 2004/2523, art 2, Schedule.

39   Offence of advertising services

After section 92A of the Immigration and Asylum Act 1999 (c 33) (inserted by section 38 above) insert—

"92B   Advertising

(1) A person commits an offence if—

(a) he offers to provide immigration advice or immigration services, and
(b) provision by him of the advice or services would constitute an offence under section 91.

(2) For the purpose of subsection (1) a person offers to provide advice or services if he—

(a) makes an offer to a particular person or class of person,
(b) makes arrangements for an advertisement in which he offers to provide advice or services, or
(c) makes arrangements for an advertisement in which he is described or presented as competent to provide advice or services.

(3) A person guilty of an offence under this section shall be liable on summary conviction to a fine not exceeding level 4 on the standard scale.

(4) Subsections (3) to (7) of section 91 shall have effect for the purposes of this section as they have effect for the purposes of that section.

(5) An information relating to an offence under this section may in England and Wales be tried by a magistrates' court if—

(a) it is laid within the period of six months beginning with the date (or first date) on which the offence is alleged to have been committed, or
(b) it is laid—
(i) within the period of two years beginning with that date, and
(ii) within the period of six months beginning with a date certified by the Immigration Services Commissioner as the date on which the commission of the offence came to his notice.

(6) In Scotland, proceedings for an offence under this section may be commenced—

(a) at any time within the period of six months beginning with the date (or first date) on which the offence is alleged to have been committed, or
(b) at any time within both—
(i) the period of two years beginning with that date, and

(ii) the period of six months beginning with a date specified, in a certificate signed by or on behalf of the procurator fiscal, as the date on which evidence sufficient in his opinion to warrant such proceedings came to his knowledge,

and any such certificate purporting to be so signed shall be deemed so signed unless the contrary is proved and be conclusive as to the facts stated in it.

(7) Subsection (3) of section 136 of the Criminal Procedure (Scotland) Act 1995 (c 46) (date on which proceedings are deemed commenced) has effect to the purposes of subsection (6) as it has effect for the purposes of that section.

(8) A complaint charging the commission of an offence under this section may in Northern Ireland be heard and determined by a magistrates' court if—

(a) it is made within the period of six months beginning with the date (or first date) on which the offence is alleged to have been committed, or
(b) it is made—
    (i) within the period of two years beginning with that date, and
    (ii) within the period of six months beginning with a date certified by the Immigration Services Commissioner as the date on which the commission of the offence came to his notice.".

Appointment
Appointment: 1 October 2004: see SI 2004/2523, art 2, Schedule.

40 Appeal to Immigration Services Tribunal

Section 87(3)(f) of the Immigration and Asylum Act 1999 (c 33) (appeal to Tribunal against deferral of decision) shall cease to have effect.

Appointment
Appointment: 1 October 2004: see SI 2004/2523, art 2, Schedule.

41 Professional bodies

(1) Section 86 of the Immigration and Asylum Act 1999 (designated professional bodies) shall be amended as follows.

(2) For subsection (2) substitute—

"(2) The Secretary of State may by order remove a body from the list in subsection (1) if he considers that the body—

(a) has failed to provide effective regulation of its members in their provision of immigration advice or immigration services, or
(b) has failed to comply with a request of the Commissioner for the provision of information (whether general or in relation to a particular case or matter).".

(3) For subsection (9)(b) substitute—

"(b) report to the Secretary of State if the Commissioner considers that a designated professional body—
    (i) is failing to provide effective regulation of its members in their provision of immigration advice or immigration services, or
    (ii) has failed to comply with a request of the Commissioner for the provision of information (whether general or in relation to a particular case or matter).".

(4) After subsection (9) insert—

"(9A) A designated professional body shall comply with a request of the Commissioner for the provision of information (whether general or in relation to a specified case or matter).".

(5) In section 166(2) of the Immigration and Asylum Act 1999 (c 33) (regulations and orders) after "in relation to" insert "orders made under section 90(1),".

(6) For paragraph 21(2) of Schedule 5 to the Immigration and Asylum Act 1999 (Commissioner: annual report) substitute—

"(2) The report must, in particular, set out the Commissioner's opinion as to the extent to which each designated professional body has—

(a) provided effective regulation of its members in their provision of immigration advice or immigration services, and

(b) complied with requests of the Commissioner for the provision of information.".

Appointment
Appointment: 1 October 2004: see SI 2004/2523, art 2, Schedule.

Fees

42   Amount of fees

(1) In prescribing a fee for an application or process under a provision specified in subsection (2) the Secretary of State may, with the consent of the Treasury, prescribe an amount which is intended to—

(a) exceed the administrative costs of determining the application or undertaking the process, and

(b) reflect benefits that the Secretary of State thinks are likely to accrue to the person who makes the application, to whom the application relates or by or for whom the process is undertaken, if the application is successful or the process is completed.

(2) Those provisions are—

(a) section 41(2) of the British Nationality Act 1981 (c 61) (fees for applications, &c under that Act),

(b) section 5(1)(a) and (b) of the Immigration and Asylum Act 1999 (fees for application for leave to remain, &c), and

(c) sections 10 and 122 of the Nationality, Immigration and Asylum Act 2002 (c 41) (certificate of entitlement to right of abode; and fees for work permit, &c).

(3) An Order in Council under section 1 of the Consular Fees Act 1980 (c 23) (fees) which prescribes a fee in relation to an application for the issue of a certificate under section 10 of the Nationality, Immigration and Asylum Act 2002 (right of abode: certificate of entitlement) may prescribe an amount which is intended to—

(a) exceed the administrative costs of determining the application, and

(b) reflect benefits that in the opinion of Her Majesty in Council are likely to accrue to the applicant if the application is successful.

(4) Where an instrument prescribes a fee in reliance on this section it may include provision for the refund, where an application is unsuccessful or a process is not completed, of that part of the fee which is intended to reflect the matters specified in subsection (1)(b) or (3)(b).

(5) Provision included by virtue of subsection (4)—

    (a) may determine, or provide for the determination of, the amount to be refunded;

    (b) may confer a discretion on the Secretary of State or another person (whether in relation to determining the amount of a refund or in relation to determining whether a refund should be made).

(6) An instrument may not be made in reliance on this section unless the Secretary of State has consulted with such persons as appear to him to be appropriate.

(7) An instrument may not be made in reliance on this section unless a draft has been laid before and approved by resolution of each House of Parliament (and any provision making the instrument subject to annulment in pursuance of a resolution of either House of Parliament shall not apply).

(8) This section is without prejudice to the power to make an order under section 102 of the Finance (No 2) Act 1987 (c 51) (government fees and charges) in relation to a power under a provision specified in this section.

Appointment
Appointment: 1 October 2004: see SI 2004/2523, art 2, Schedule.

43   Transfer of leave stamps

(1) Section 5 of the Immigration and Asylum Act 1999 (c 33) (charges) shall be amended as follows.

(2) For subsection (1)(c) (transfer of indefinite leave stamp to new document) substitute—

    "(c) the fixing of a limited leave stamp or indefinite leave stamp on a passport or other document issued to the applicant where the stamp was previously fixed on another passport or document issued to the applicant.".

(3) For subsection (5) substitute—

"(5) In this section—

    (a) "limited leave stamp" means a stamp, sticker or other attachment which indicates that a person has been granted limited leave to enter or remain in the United Kingdom, and

    (b) "indefinite leave stamp" means a stamp, sticker or other attachment which indicates that a person has been granted indefinite leave to enter or remain in the United Kingdom.".

Appointment
Appointment: 1 October 2004: see SI 2004/2523, art 2, Schedule.

General

44   Interpretation: "the Immigration Acts"

(1) A reference to "the Immigration Acts" is to—

    (a) the Immigration Act 1971 (c 77),
    (b) the Immigration Act 1988 (c 14),
    (c) the Asylum and Immigration Appeals Act 1993 (c 23),
    (d) the Asylum and Immigration Act 1996 (c 49),
    (e) the Immigration and Asylum Act 1999,
    (f) the Nationality, Immigration and Asylum Act 2002 (c 41), and
    (g) this Act.

(2)   This section has effect in relation to a reference in this Act or any other enactment (including an enactment passed or made before this Act).

(3)   For section 158(1) and (2) of the Nationality, Immigration and Asylum Act 2002 (c 41) substitute—

"(1)   A reference to "the Immigration Acts" shall be construed in accordance with section 44 of the Asylum and Immigration (Treatment of Claimants, etc) Act 2004.".

(4)   In the following provisions for "section 158 of the Nationality, Immigration and Asylum Act 2002" substitute "section 44 of the Asylum and Immigration (Treatment of Claimants, etc) Act 2004"—

(a)   section 32(5) of the Immigration Act 1971 (c 77), and
(b)   section 167(1) of the Immigration and Asylum Act 1999 (c 33).

Appointment
Appointment: 1 October 2004: see SI 2004/2523, art 2, Schedule.

45   Interpretation: immigration officer

In this Act "immigration officer" means a person appointed by the Secretary of State as an immigration officer under paragraph 1 of Schedule 2 to the Immigration Act 1971.

Appointment
Appointment: 1 October 2004: see SI 2004/2523, art 2, Schedule.

46   Money

There shall be paid out of money provided by Parliament—

(a)   any expenditure incurred by a Minister of the Crown in connection with this Act, and
(b)   any increase attributable to this Act in the sums payable under any other enactment out of money provided by Parliament.

Appointment
Appointment: 1 October 2004: see SI 2004/2523, art 2, Schedule.

47   Repeals

The enactments listed in Schedule 4 are hereby repealed to the extent specified.

Appointment
Appointment (for certain purposes): 1 October 2004: see SI 2004/2523, art 2, Schedule.

48   Commencement

(1)   Sections 2, 32(2) and 35 shall come into force at the end of the period of two months beginning with the date on which this Act is passed.

(2)   Section 32(1) shall have effect in relation to determinations of the Special Immigration Appeals Commission made after the end of the period of two months beginning with the date on which this Act is passed.

(3)   The other preceding provisions of this Act shall come into force in accordance with provision made—

(a)   in the case of section 26 or Schedule 1 or 2, by order of the Lord Chancellor,
(b)   in the case of sections 4 and 5 in so far as they extend to Scotland, by order of the Scottish Ministers, and
(c)   in any other case, by order of the Secretary of State.

(4) An order under subsection (3)—

(a) may make transitional or incidental provision,
(b) may make different provision for different purposes, and
(c) shall be made by statutory instrument.

(5) Transitional provision under subsection (4)(a) in relation to the commencement of section 26 may, in particular, make provision in relation to proceedings which, immediately before commencement—

(a) are awaiting determination by an adjudicator appointed, or treated as if appointed, under section 81 of the Nationality, Immigration and Asylum Act 2002 (c 41),
(b) are awaiting determination by the Immigration Appeal Tribunal,
(c) having been determined by an adjudicator could be brought before the Immigration Appeal Tribunal,
(d) are awaiting the determination of a further appeal brought in accordance with section 103 of that Act,
(e) having been determined by the Immigration Appeal Tribunal could be brought before another court by way of further appeal under that section,
(f) are or could be made the subject of an application under section 101 of that Act (review of decision on permission to appeal to Tribunal), or
(g) are or could be made the subject of another kind of application to the High Court or the Court of Session.

(6) Provision made under subsection (5) may, in particular—

(a) provide for the institution or continuance of an appeal of a kind not generally available after the commencement of section 26,
(b) provide for the termination of proceedings, or
(c) make any other provision that the Lord Chancellor thinks appropriate.

Initial Commencement
Royal Assent: 22 July 2004: (no specific commencement provision).

Subordinate Legislation
Asylum and Immigration (Treatment of Claimants, etc) Act 2004 (Commencement No 1) Order 2004, SI 2004/2523 (made under sub-ss (3), (4)).
Asylum and Immigration (Treatment of Claimants, etc) Act 2004 (Commencement No 2) Order 2004, SI 2004/2999 (made under sub-ss (3), (4)).
Asylum and Immigration (Treatment of Claimants, etc) Act 2004 (Commencement No 3) Order 2004, SI 2004/3398 (made under sub-ss (3), (4)).
Asylum and Immigration (Treatment of Claimants, etc) Act 2004 (Commencement No 4) Order 2005, SI 2005/372 (made under sub-s (3)).
Asylum and Immigration (Treatment of Claimants, etc) Act 2004 (Commencement No 5 and Transitional Provisions) Order 2005, SI 2005/565 (made under sub-ss (3)(a), (4)–(6)).
Asylum and Immigration (Treatment of Claimants etc) Act 2004 (Commencement) (Scotland) Order 2004, SSI 2004/494 (made under sub-s (3)).

49 Extent

(1) This Act extends (subject to subsection (2)) to—

(a) England and Wales,
(b) Scotland, and
(c) Northern Ireland.

(2) An amendment effected by this Act has the same extent as the enactment, or as the relevant part of the enactment, amended (ignoring extent by virtue of an Order in Council).

(3)   Her Majesty may by Order in Council direct that a provision of this Act is to extend, with or without modification or adaptation, to—

(a)   any of the Channel Islands;
(b)   the Isle of Man.

Initial Commencement
Royal Assent: 22 July 2004: (no specific commencement provision).

50   Short title

This Act may be cited as the Asylum and Immigration (Treatment of Claimants, etc) Act 2004.

Initial Commencement
Royal Assent: 22 July 2004: (no specific commencement provision).

SCHEDULE 1
NEW SCHEDULE 4 TO THE NATIONALITY, IMMIGRATION AND ASYLUM ACT 2002

Section 26

"SCHEDULE 4
THE ASYLUM AND IMMIGRATION TRIBUNAL

Membership

1   The Lord Chancellor shall appoint the members of the Asylum and Immigration Tribunal.

2   (1)   A person is eligible for appointment as a member of the Tribunal only if he—

(a)   has a seven year general qualification within the meaning of section 71 of the Courts and Legal Services Act 1990 (c 41),
(b)   is an advocate or solicitor in Scotland of at least seven years' standing,
(c)   is a member of the Bar of Northern Ireland, or a solicitor of the Supreme Court of Northern Ireland, of at least seven years' standing,
(d)   in the Lord Chancellor's opinion, has legal experience which makes him as suitable for appointment as if he satisfied paragraph (a), (b) or (c), or
(e)   in the Lord Chancellor's opinion, has non-legal experience which makes him suitable for appointment.

(2)   A person appointed under sub-paragraph (1)(a) to (d) shall be known as a legally qualified member of the Tribunal.

3   (1)   A member—

(a)   may resign by notice in writing to the Lord Chancellor,
(b)   shall cease to be a member on reaching the age of 70, and
(c)   otherwise, shall hold and vacate office in accordance with the terms of his appointment (which may include provision—
(i)   about the training, appraisal and mentoring of members of the Tribunal by other members, and
(ii)   for removal).

(2)   Sub-paragraph (1)(b) is subject to section 26(4) to (6) of the Judicial Pensions and Retirement Act 1993 (c 8) (extension to age 75).

4   The Lord Chancellor may by order make provision for the title of members of the Tribunal.

Presidency

5   (1)   The Lord Chancellor shall appoint—

(a)   a member of the Tribunal, who holds or has held high judicial office within the meaning of the Appellate Jurisdiction Act 1876 (c 59), as President of the Tribunal, and

(b)   one or more members of the Tribunal as Deputy President.

(2)   A Deputy President—

(a)   may act for the President if the President is unable to act or unavailable, and

(b)   shall perform such functions as the President may delegate or assign to him.

Proceedings

6   The Tribunal shall sit at times and places determined by the Lord Chancellor.

7   (1)   The jurisdiction of the Tribunal shall be exercised by such number of its members as the President, having regard to the complexity and other circumstances of particular cases or classes of case, may direct.

(2)   A direction under this paragraph—

(a)   may relate to the whole or part of specified proceedings or to the whole or part of proceedings of a specified kind,

(b)   may enable jurisdiction to be exercised by a single member,

(c)   may require or permit the transfer of the whole or part of proceedings—

(i)   from one member to another,

(ii)   from one group of members to another,

(iii)   from one member to a group of members, or

(iv)   from a group of members to one member,

(d)   may be varied or revoked by a further direction, and

(e)   is subject to rules under section 106.

8   (1)   The President may make arrangements for the allocation of proceedings to members of the Tribunal.

(2)   Arrangements under this paragraph—

(a)   may permit allocation by the President or another member of the Tribunal,

(b)   may permit the allocation of a case to a specified member or to a specified class of member,

(c)   may include provision for transfer, and

(d)   are subject to rules under section 106.

Staff

9   The Lord Chancellor may appoint staff for the Tribunal.

Money

10   The Lord Chancellor—

(a)   may pay remuneration and allowances to members of the Tribunal,

(b)   may pay remuneration and allowances to staff of the Tribunal, and

(c)   may defray expenses of the Tribunal.

11   The Lord Chancellor may pay compensation to a person who ceases to be a member of the Tribunal if the Lord Chancellor thinks it appropriate because of special circumstances."

Appendix 1   Legislation and materials

Appointment
Appointment: 4 April 2005: see SI 2005/565, art 2(c); for transitional provisions see arts 3–9 thereof.

SCHEDULE 2
ASYLUM AND IMMIGRATION TRIBUNAL: CONSEQUENTIAL AMENDMENTS AND
TRANSITIONAL PROVISION

Section 26

PART 1
CONSEQUENTIAL AMENDMENTS
Immigration Act 1971 (c 77)

1 (1)   Schedule 2 to the Immigration Act 1971 (control on entry) shall be amended as follows.

(2)   In the following provisions for "adjudicator" (or "an adjudicator" or "the adjudicator") substitute "the Asylum and Immigration Tribunal"—

    (a)   paragraph 22(1A), (2) and (3),
    (b)   paragraph 23(1) and (2),
    (c)   paragraph 24(2), and
    (d)   paragraph 25.

(3)   In paragraph 24(3) for "An adjudicator, justice of the peace or sheriff before whom a person is brought by virtue of sub-paragraph (2)(a) above" substitute "Where a person is brought before the Asylum and Immigration Tribunal, a justice of the peace or the sheriff by virtue of sub-paragraph (2)(a), the Tribunal, justice of the peace or sheriff".

(4)   In paragraph 29—

    (a)   in sub-paragraph (2) for "an adjudicator or the Immigration Appeal Tribunal" substitute "the Asylum and Immigration Tribunal",
    (b)   in sub-paragraph (3)—
        (i)   for "An adjudicator" substitute "The Asylum and Immigration Tribunal",
        (ii)   for "that or any other adjudicator" substitute "the Tribunal",
        (iii)   omit the words from "and where an adjudicator dismisses" to the end,
    (c)   omit sub-paragraph (4), and
    (d)   in sub-paragraph (6)—
        (i)   for "an adjudicator or the Tribunal" substitute "the Asylum and Immigration Tribunal",
        (ii)   for "the adjudicator or Tribunal" substitute "the Tribunal", and
        (iii)   for "the adjudicator or the Tribunal" substitute "the Tribunal".

(5)   In paragraphs 30, 31, 32 and 33—

    (a)   for "an adjudicator and the Tribunal" substitute "the Tribunal",
    (b)   for "an adjudicator or the Tribunal" substitute "the Tribunal",
    (c)   for "the adjudicator or the Tribunal, as the case may be" substitute "the Tribunal",
    (d)   for "the adjudicator or Tribunal" substitute "the Tribunal",
    (e)   for "the adjudicator or the Tribunal" substitute "the Tribunal",
    (f)   for "an adjudicator or Tribunal" substitute "the Tribunal", and
    (g)   for "before an adjudicator or before the Tribunal" substitute "before the Tribunal".

(6)   In paragraph 33—

(a) in sub-paragraph (2)(a) for "before an adjudicator" substitute "before the Tribunal",

(b) in sub-paragraph (2)(b) for "before that adjudicator or before the Tribunal, as the case may be" substitute "before it", and

(c) in sub-paragraph (3) for "An adjudicator, justice of the peace or sheriff before whom a person is brought by virtue of sub-paragraph (2)(a) above" substitute "Where a person is brought before the Asylum and Immigration Tribunal, a justice of the peace or the sheriff by virtue of sub-paragraph (2)(a), the Tribunal, justice of the peace or sheriff".

House of Commons Disqualification Act 1975 (c 24)

2 (1) Schedule 1 to the House of Commons Disqualification Act 1975 (disqualifying offices) shall be amended as follows.

(2) In Part II for the entry relating to the Immigration Appeal Tribunal substitute—

"The Asylum and Immigration Tribunal."

(3) In Part III omit the entry relating to immigration adjudicators.

Northern Ireland Assembly Disqualification Act 1975 (c 25)

3 (1) Schedule 1 to the Northern Ireland Assembly Disqualification Act 1975 (disqualifying offices) shall be amended as follows.

(2) In Part II for the entry relating to the Immigration Appeal Tribunal substitute—

"The Asylum and Immigration Tribunal."

(3) In Part III omit the entry relating to immigration adjudicators.

British Nationality Act 1981 (c 61)

4 In section 40A of the British Nationality Act 1981 (deprivation of citizenship: appeal)—

(a) in subsection (1) for "an adjudicator appointed under section 81 of the Nationality, Immigration and Asylum Act 2002 (immigration appeal)" substitute "the Asylum and Immigration Tribunal",

(b) for subsections (3) to (5) substitute—

"(3) The following provisions of the Nationality, Immigration and Asylum Act 2002 (c 41) shall apply in relation to an appeal under this section as they apply in relation to an appeal under section 82 or 83 of that Act—

(a) section 87 (successful appeal: direction) (for which purpose a direction may, in particular, provide for an order under section 40 above to be treated as having had no effect),

(b) sections 103A to 103E (review and appeal),

(c) section 106 (rules), and

(d) section 107 (practice directions).", and

(c) omit subsections (6) to (8).

Legal Aid, Advice and Assistance (Northern Ireland) Order 1981 (SI 1981/228 (NI 8))

5 (1) For paragraph 6A of Part 1 of Schedule 1 to the Legal Aid, Advice and Assistance (Northern Ireland) Order 1981 (proceedings for which legal aid may be given under Part II of that Order) substitute—

"**6A** Proceedings before the Asylum and Immigration Tribunal or the Special Immigration Appeals Commission.".

(2) The amendment made by sub-paragraph (1) is without prejudice to any power to amend or revoke the provision inserted by that sub-paragraph.

Courts and Legal Services Act 1990 (c 41)

6 In Schedule 11 to the Courts and Legal Services Act 1990 (judges barred from legal practice) for the entries relating to the Immigration Appeal Tribunal and immigration adjudicators substitute—

"President or other member of the Asylum and Immigration Tribunal".

Tribunals and Inquiries Act 1992 (c 53)

7 (1) The Tribunals and Inquiries Act 1992 shall be amended as follows.

(2) In section 7 (dismissal) omit subsection (3).

(3) In Schedule 1 (tribunals under supervision of Council) for the entry for immigration appeals substitute—

| "Immigration and asylum | 22 The Asylum and Immigration Tribunal constituted under section 81 of the Nationality, Immigration and Asylum Act 2002." |

Judicial Pensions and Retirement Act 1993 (c 8)

8 (1) The Judicial Pensions and Retirement Act 1993 shall be amended as follows.

(2) In Schedule 1 (qualifying judicial offices) for the entries relating to the Immigration Appeal Tribunal and immigration adjudicators substitute (in the place occupied by the first of those entries)—

"President or other member of the Asylum and Immigration Tribunal".

(3) In Schedule 5 (retirement: relevant offices) for the entries relating to the Immigration Appeal Tribunal and immigration adjudicators substitute—

"President or other member of the Asylum and Immigration Tribunal".

Asylum and Immigration Appeals Act 1993 (c 23)

9 Section 9A of the Asylum and Immigration Appeals Act 1993 (bail) shall cease to have effect.

Special Immigration Appeals Commission Act 1997 (c 68)

10 The Special Immigration Appeals Commission Act 1997 shall be amended as follows.

11 At the end of section 2B (deprivation of citizenship) insert "(and section 40A(3)(a) shall have effect in relation to appeals under this section).".

12 (1) In Schedule 1 (constitution, &c) for paragraph 5(b) substitute—

"(b) at least one is or has been a legally qualified member of the Asylum and Immigration Tribunal.".

(2) A person is qualified for the purposes of paragraph 5(b) of that Schedule as it has effect after the commencement of sub-paragraph (1) above if he is qualified for the purposes of paragraph 5(b) as it had effect at any time since its commencement.

13   (1)   Schedule 3 (bail) shall be amended as follows.

(2)   In paragraph 1(2) for ""adjudicator"" substitute ""Tribunal"".

(3)   In paragraph 1(3)(a) for "adjudicator"" substitute "the Asylum and Immigration Tribunal"".

(4)   In paragraph 1(3)(b) for "adjudicator"" substitute "the Asylum and Immigration Tribunal"".

(5)   In paragraph 1(4)(a) and (b) for "adjudicator"" substitute "the Asylum and Immigration Tribunal"".

(6)   In paragraph 2(2)(a) for ""an adjudicator"" substitute ""the Asylum and Immigration Tribunal"".

(7)   In paragraph 2(2)(b) for ""the adjudicator"" substitute ""the Asylum and Immigration Tribunal"".

(8)   In paragraph 2(3)(a) for ""an adjudicator"" substitute ""the Asylum and Immigration Tribunal"".

(9)   In paragraph 2(3)(b) for ""the adjudicator"" substitute ""the Asylum and Immigration Tribunal"".

(10)   In paragraph 6(2)(a) for ""an adjudicator or the Tribunal"" substitute ""the Tribunal"".

(11)   In paragraph 6(2)(b) for ""the adjudicator or the Tribunal, as the case may be,"" substitute ""the Tribunal"".

(12)   In paragraph 6(2)(c) for ""the adjudicator or Tribunal"" substitute ""the Tribunal"".

(13)   In paragraph 6(3)(a) for ""an adjudicator or the Tribunal"" substitute ""the Tribunal"".

(14)   In paragraph 6(3)(b) for ""the adjudicator or Tribunal"" substitute ""the Tribunal"".

(15)   In paragraph 7(a) for ""an adjudicator or the Tribunal"" substitute ""the Tribunal"".

(16)   In paragraph 7(b) for ""the adjudicator or Tribunal"" substitute ""the Tribunal"".

(17)   In paragraph 7(c) for ""the adjudicator or the Tribunal"" substitute ""the Tribunal"".

Access to Justice Act 1999 (c 22)

14   For paragraph 2(1)(h) of Schedule 2 to the Access to Justice Act 1999 (Community Legal Service: excluded services) substitute—

"(h) the Asylum and Immigration Tribunal,".

Immigration and Asylum Act 1999 (c 33)

15   In section 156(3) of the Immigration and Asylum Act 1999 (escorts and custody) for paragraphs (a) and (b) substitute—

"(a) the Asylum and Immigration Tribunal;".

Nationality, Immigration and Asylum Act 2002 (c 41)

16   The Nationality, Immigration and Asylum Act 2002 shall be amended as follows.

17   In section 72(10) (serious criminal) omit "adjudicator,".

18   (1)   In the provisions listed in sub-paragraph (2)—

    (a)   for "an adjudicator" substitute "the Tribunal",
    (b)   for "the adjudicator" substitute "the Tribunal",
    (c)   for "he" in relation to an adjudicator substitute "it",
    (d)   for "him" in relation to an adjudicator substitute "it", and
    (e)   for "his" in relation to an adjudicator substitute "its".

(2)   The provisions are—

    (a)   section 85 (matters to be considered),
    (b)   section 86 (determination of appeal), and
    (c)   section 87 (successful appeal: direction).

19   In section 87—

    (a)   for subsection (3) substitute—

"(3)   But a direction under this section shall not have effect while—

    (a)   an application under section 103A(1) (other than an application out of time with permission) could be made or is awaiting determination,
    (b)   reconsideration of an appeal has been ordered under section 103A(1) and has not been completed,
    (c)   an appeal has been remitted to the Tribunal and is awaiting determination,
    (d)   an application under section 103B or 103E for permission to appeal (other than an application out of time with permission) could be made or is awaiting determination,
    (e)   an appeal under section 103B or 103E is awaiting determination, or
    (f)   a reference under section 103C is awaiting determination.", and
    (b)   in subsection (4) for "as part of the determination of the appeal for the purposes of section 101" substitute "as part of the Tribunal's decision on the appeal for the purposes of section 103A".

20   In section 104 (pending appeal)—

    (a)   for subsection (2) substitute—

"(2)   An appeal under section 82(1) is not finally determined for the purposes of subsection (1)(b) while—

    (a)   an application under section 103A(1) (other than an application out of time with permission) could be made or is awaiting determination,
    (b)   reconsideration of an appeal has been ordered under section 103A(1) and has not been completed,
    (c)   an appeal has been remitted to the Tribunal and is awaiting determination,
    (d)   an application under section 103B or 103E for permission to appeal (other than an application out of time with permission) could be made or is awaiting determination,
    (e)   an appeal under section 103B or 103E is awaiting determination, or
    (f)   a reference under section 103C is awaiting determination.", and
    (b)   omit subsection (3) (remittal to adjudicator).

21   In section 106 (rules)—

    (a)   in subsection (1)(a) for ", 83 or 101" substitute "or 83 or by virtue of section 109",
    (b)   in subsection (1)(b) for ", 83, 101(1) or 103" substitute "or 83 or by virtue of section 109",
    (c)   after subsection (1) insert—

"(1A) In making rules under subsection (1) the Lord Chancellor shall aim to ensure—

(a) that the rules are designed to ensure that proceedings before the Tribunal are handled as fairly, quickly and efficiently as possible, and

(b) that the rules where appropriate confer on members of the Tribunal responsibility for ensuring that proceedings before the Tribunal are handled as fairly, quickly and efficiently as possible.",

(d) in subsection (2)(d) for "an adjudicator or the Immigration Appeal Tribunal" substitute "the Tribunal",

(e) in subsection (2)(e) and (f) omit "an adjudicator or",

(f) in subsection (2)(g) for "an adjudicator" substitute, in each place, "the Tribunal",

(g) in subsection (2)(h) for "an adjudicator" substitute, in each place, "the Tribunal",

(h) omit subsection (2)(j) and (k),

(i) in subsection (2)(m) omit the words from "(which may" to the end,

(j) in subsection (2)(o) omit "an adjudicator or",

(k) in subsection (2)(p) omit "an adjudicator or",

(l) in subsection (2)(q) omit "an adjudicator or",

(m) in subsection (2)(r) omit "an adjudicator or",

(n) in subsection (2)(s) omit "an adjudicator or",

(o) after subsection (2)(s) insert—

"(t) may make provision about the number of members exercising the Tribunal's jurisdiction;

(u) may make provision about the allocation of proceedings among members of the Tribunal (which may include provision for transfer);

(v) may make provision about reconsideration of a decision pursuant to an order under section 103A(1) (which may, in particular, include provision about the action that may be taken on reconsideration and about the matters and evidence to which the Tribunal may have regard);

(w) shall provide that a party to an appeal is to be treated as having received notice of the Tribunal's decision, unless the contrary is shown, at such time as may be specified in, or determined in accordance with, the rules;

(x) may make provision about proceedings under paragraph 30 of Schedule 2 to the Asylum and Immigration (Treatment of Claimants, etc) Act 2004 (transitional filter of applications for reconsideration from High Court to Tribunal) (and may, in particular, make provision of a kind that may be made by rules of court under section 103A(5)(b));

(y) may make provision about the form and content of decisions of the Tribunal.",

(p) in subsection (3)(a) omit "an adjudicator or",

(q) in subsection (3)(d) omit "an adjudicator or",

(r) in subsection (3)(e) omit "an adjudicator or",

(s) for subsection (3)(f) substitute—

"(f) may enable the Tribunal to certify that an appeal had no merit (and shall make provision for the consequences of the issue of a certificate).", and

(t) in subsection (4) omit "an adjudicator or".

22 (1) In section 107 (practice directions)—

(a) for "the Immigration Appeal Tribunal" substitute "the Tribunal",

(b) omit subsection (2), and

(c) at the end add—

"(3) A practice direction may, in particular, require the Tribunal to treat a specified decision of the Tribunal as authoritative in respect of a particular matter.".

(2)   The reference to a decision of the Tribunal in section 107(3) (as added by sub-paragraph (1) above) shall be treated as including a reference to a decision of the Immigration Appeal Tribunal.

23   In section 108 (forged document: proceedings in private)—

   (a)   in subsection (1)(a) for ", 83 or 101" substitute "or 83", and
   (b)   in subsection (2) for "The adjudicator or the Immigration Appeal Tribunal" substitute "The Tribunal".

24   (1)   Section 112 (regulations, &c) shall be amended as follows.

(2)   In subsection (2) after "Regulations and rules under this Part" insert ", other than regulations under section 103D(4),".

(3)   For subsection (6) substitute—

"(6)   Regulations under section 103D(4)—

   (a)   must be made by statutory instrument, and
   (b)   shall not be made unless a draft has been laid before and approved by resolution of each House of Parliament.

(7)   An order under paragraph 4 of Schedule 4—

   (a)   may include consequential or incidental provision (which may include provision amending, or providing for the construction of, a reference in an enactment, instrument or other document to a member of the Asylum and Immigration Tribunal),
   (b)   must be made by statutory instrument, and
   (c)   shall be subject to annulment in pursuance of a resolution of either House of Parliament.".

Access to Justice (Northern Ireland) Order 2003 (SI 2003/435 (NI 10))

25   (1)   For paragraph 2(i) of Schedule 2 to the Access to Justice (Northern Ireland) Order 2003 (civil legal services: excluded services) substitute—

"(i)   proceedings before the Asylum and Immigration Tribunal or the Special Immigration Appeals Commission,".

(2)   The amendment made by sub-paragraph (1) is without prejudice to any power to amend or revoke the provision inserted by that sub-paragraph.

Appointment
Appointment: 4 April 2005: see SI 2005/565, art 2(d); for transitional provisions see arts 3–9 thereof.

PART 2
TRANSITIONAL PROVISION

26   In this Part "commencement" means the coming into force of section 26.

27   A person who immediately before commencement is, or is to be treated as, an adjudicator appointed under section 81 of the Nationality, Immigration and Asylum Act 2002 (c 41) (appeals) (as it has effect before commencement) shall be treated as having been appointed as a member of the Asylum and Immigration Tribunal under paragraph 1 of Schedule 4 to that Act (as it has effect after commencement) immediately after commencement.

28   Where immediately before commencement a person is a member of the Immigration Appeal Tribunal—

    (a) he shall be treated as having been appointed as a member of the Asylum and Immigration Tribunal under paragraph 1 of Schedule 4 to that Act immediately after commencement, and

    (b) if he was a legally qualified member of the Immigration Appeal Tribunal (within the meaning of Schedule 5 to that Act) he shall be treated as having been appointed as a legally qualified member of the Asylum and Immigration Tribunal.

29 A person who immediately before commencement is a member of staff of adjudicators appointed or treated as appointed under section 81 of the Nationality, Immigration and Asylum Act 2002 (c 41) or of the Immigration Appeal Tribunal shall be treated as having been appointed as a member of the staff of the Asylum and Immigration Tribunal under paragraph 9 of Schedule 4 to the Nationality, Immigration and Asylum Act 2002 immediately after commencement.

30 (1) This paragraph shall have effect in relation to applications under section 103A(1) or for permission under section 103A(4)(b) made—

    (a) during the period beginning with commencement and ending with such date as may be appointed by order of the Lord Chancellor, and

    (b) during any such later period as may be appointed by order of the Lord Chancellor.

(2) An application in relation to which this paragraph has effect shall be considered by a member of the Asylum and Immigration Tribunal (in accordance with arrangements under paragraph 8(1) of Schedule 4 to the Nationality, Immigration and Asylum Act 2002 (inserted by Schedule 1 above)).

(3) For the purposes of sub-paragraph (2)—

    (a) references in section 103A to the appropriate court shall be taken as references to the member of the Tribunal who is considering the application or who is to consider the application,

    (b) rules of court made for the purpose of section 103A(4)(a) in relation to the court to which an application is made shall have effect in relation to the application despite the fact that it is considered outside the appropriate court, and

    (c) section 103A(6) shall be subject to sub-paragraph (5) below.

(4) Where a member of the Tribunal considers an application under section 103A(1) or 103A(4)(b) by virtue of this paragraph—

    (a) he may make an order under section 103A(1) or grant permission under section 103A(4)(b), and

    (b) if he does not propose to make an order or grant permission, he shall notify the appropriate court and the applicant.

(5) Where notice is given under sub-paragraph (4)(b)—

    (a) the applicant may notify the appropriate court that he wishes the court to consider his application under section 103A(1) or 103A(4)(b),

    (b) the notification must be given within the period of 5 days beginning with the date on which the applicant is treated, in accordance with rules under section 106 of the Nationality, Immigration and Asylum Act 2002, as receiving the notice under sub-paragraph (4)(b) above, and

    (c) the appropriate court shall consider the application under section 103A(1) or 103A(4)(b) if—

        (i) the applicant has given notice in accordance with paragraphs (a) and (b) above, or

      (ii)   the applicant has given notice under paragraph (a) above outside the period specified in paragraph (b) above, but the appropriate court concludes that the application should be considered on the grounds that the notice could not reasonably practicably have been given within that period.

(6)   Rules of court may specify days to be disregarded in applying sub-paragraph (5)(b).

(7)   A member of the Tribunal considering an application under section 103A(1) by virtue of this paragraph may not make a reference under section 103C

(8)   An order under sub-paragraph (1)(a) or (b)—

   (a)   shall be made by statutory instrument,
   (b)   shall not be made unless the Lord Chancellor has consulted such persons as he thinks appropriate, and
   (c)   shall not be made unless a draft has been laid before and approved by resolution of each House of Parliament.

Appointment
Appointment: 4 April 2005: see SI 2005/565, art 2(d); for transitional provisions see arts 3–9 thereof.

Subordinate Legislation
Civil Procedure (Amendment) Rules 2005, SI 2005/352 (made under para 30(6)).

SCHEDULE 3
REMOVAL OF ASYLUM SEEKER TO SAFE COUNTRY

Section 33

PART 1
INTRODUCTORY

1   (1)   In this Schedule—

"asylum claim" means a claim by a person that to remove him from or require him to leave the United Kingdom would breach the United Kingdom's obligations under the Refugee Convention,

"Convention rights" means the rights identified as Convention rights by section 1 of the Human Rights Act 1998 (c 42) (whether or not in relation to a State that is a party to the Convention),

"human rights claim" means a claim by a person that to remove him from or require him to leave the United Kingdom would be unlawful under section 6 of the Human Rights Act 1998 (public authority not to act contrary to Convention) as being incompatible with his Convention rights,

"immigration appeal" means an appeal under section 82(1) of the Nationality, Immigration and Asylum Act 2002 (c 41) (appeal against immigration decision), and

"the Refugee Convention" means the Convention relating to the Status of Refugees done at Geneva on 28th July 1951 and its Protocol.

(2)   In this Schedule a reference to anything being done in accordance with the Refugee Convention is a reference to the thing being done in accordance with the principles of the Convention, whether or not by a signatory to it.

Appointment
Appointment: 1 October 2004: see SI 2004/2523, art 2, Schedule.

PART 2
FIRST LIST OF SAFE COUNTRIES (REFUGEE CONVENTION AND HUMAN RIGHTS (1))

2   This Part applies to—

    (a)   Austria,
    (b)   Belgium,
    (c)   Republic of Cyprus,
    (d)   Czech Republic,
    (e)   Denmark,
    (f)   Estonia,
    (g)   Finland,
    (h)   France,
    (i)   Germany,
    (j)   Greece,
    (k)   Hungary,
    (l)   Iceland,
    (m)   Ireland,
    (n)   Italy,
    (o)   Latvia,
    (p)   Lithuania,
    (q)   Luxembourg,
    (r)   Malta,
    (s)   Netherlands,
    (t)   Norway,
    (u)   Poland,
    (v)   Portugal,
    (w)   Slovak Republic,
    (x)   Slovenia,
    (y)   Spain, and
    (z)   Sweden.

3   (1)   This paragraph applies for the purposes of the determination by any person, tribunal or court whether a person who has made an asylum claim or a human rights claim may be removed—

    (a)   from the United Kingdom, and
    (b)   to a State of which he is not a national or citizen.

(2)   A State to which this Part applies shall be treated, in so far as relevant to the question mentioned in sub-paragraph (1), as a place—

    (a)   where a person's life and liberty are not threatened by reason of his race, religion, nationality, membership of a particular social group or political opinion,
    (b)   from which a person will not be sent to another State in contravention of his Convention rights, and
    (c)   from which a person will not be sent to another State otherwise than in accordance with the Refugee Convention.

4   Section 77 of the Nationality, Immigration and Asylum Act 2002 (c 41) (no removal while claim for asylum pending) shall not prevent a person who has made a claim for asylum from being removed—

    (a)   from the United Kingdom, and
    (b)   to a State to which this Part applies;

provided that the Secretary of State certifies that in his opinion the person is not a national or citizen of the State.

5   (1)   This paragraph applies where the Secretary of State certifies that—

(a)   it is proposed to remove a person to a State to which this Part applies, and

(b)   in the Secretary of State's opinion the person is not a national or citizen of the State.

(2)   The person may not bring an immigration appeal by virtue of section 92(2) or (3) of that Act (appeal from within United Kingdom: general).

(3)   The person may not bring an immigration appeal by virtue of section 92(4)(a) of that Act (appeal from within United Kingdom: asylum or human rights) in reliance on—

(a)   an asylum claim which asserts that to remove the person to a specified State to which this Part applies would breach the United Kingdom's obligations under the Refugee Convention, or

(b)   a human rights claim in so far as it asserts that to remove the person to a specified State to which this Part applies would be unlawful under section 6 of the Human Rights Act 1998 because of the possibility of removal from that State to another State.

(4)   The person may not bring an immigration appeal by virtue of section 92(4)(a) of that Act in reliance on a human rights claim to which this sub-paragraph applies if the Secretary of State certifies that the claim is clearly unfounded; and the Secretary of State shall certify a human rights claim to which this sub-paragraph applies unless satisfied that the claim is not clearly unfounded.

(5)   Sub-paragraph (4) applies to a human rights claim if, or in so far as, it asserts a matter other than that specified in sub-paragraph (3)(b).

6   A person who is outside the United Kingdom may not bring an immigration appeal on any ground that is inconsistent with treating a State to which this Part applies as a place—

(a)   where a person's life and liberty are not threatened by reason of his race, religion, nationality, membership of a particular social group or political opinion,

(b)   from which a person will not be sent to another State in contravention of his Convention rights, and

(c)   from which a person will not be sent to another State otherwise than in accordance with the Refugee Convention.

Appointment
Appointment: 1 October 2004: see SI 2004/2523, art 2, Schedule.

PART 3
SECOND LIST OF SAFE COUNTRIES (REFUGEE CONVENTION AND HUMAN RIGHTS (2))

7   (1)   This Part applies to such States as the Secretary of State may by order specify.

(2)   An order under this paragraph—

(a)   shall be made by statutory instrument, and

(b)   shall not be made unless a draft has been laid before and approved by resolution of each House of Parliament.

8   (1)   This paragraph applies for the purposes of the determination by any person, tribunal or court whether a person who has made an asylum claim may be removed—

(a)   from the United Kingdom, and

(b)   to a State of which he is not a national or citizen.

(2) A State to which this Part applies shall be treated, in so far as relevant to the question mentioned in sub-paragraph (1), as a place—

  (a) where a person's life and liberty are not threatened by reason of his race, religion, nationality, membership of a particular social group or political opinion, and

  (b) from which a person will not be sent to another State otherwise than in accordance with the Refugee Convention.

9 Section 77 of the Nationality, Immigration and Asylum Act 2002 (c 41) (no removal while claim for asylum pending) shall not prevent a person who has made a claim for asylum from being removed—

  (a) from the United Kingdom, and

  (b) to a State to which this Part applies;

provided that the Secretary of State certifies that in his opinion the person is not a national or citizen of the State.

10 (1) This paragraph applies where the Secretary of State certifies that—

  (a) it is proposed to remove a person to a State to which this Part applies, and

  (b) in the Secretary of State's opinion the person is not a national or citizen of the State.

(2) The person may not bring an immigration appeal by virtue of section 92(2) or (3) of that Act (appeal from within United Kingdom: general).

(3) The person may not bring an immigration appeal by virtue of section 92(4)(a) of that Act (appeal from within United Kingdom: asylum or human rights) in reliance on an asylum claim which asserts that to remove the person to a specified State to which this Part applies would breach the United Kingdom's obligations under the Refugee Convention.

(4) The person may not bring an immigration appeal by virtue of section 92(4)(a) of that Act in reliance on a human rights claim if the Secretary of State certifies that the claim is clearly unfounded; and the Secretary of State shall certify a human rights claim where this paragraph applies unless satisfied that the claim is not clearly unfounded.

11 A person who is outside the United Kingdom may not bring an immigration appeal on any ground that is inconsistent with treating a State to which this Part applies as a place—

  (a) where a person's life and liberty are not threatened by reason of his race, religion, nationality, membership of a particular social group or political opinion, and

  (b) from which a person will not be sent to another State otherwise than in accordance with the Refugee Convention.

Appointment
Appointment: 1 October 2004: see SI 2004/2523, art 2, Schedule.

PART 4
THIRD LIST OF SAFE COUNTRIES (REFUGEE CONVENTION ONLY)

12 (1) This Part applies to such States as the Secretary of State may by order specify.

(2) An order under this paragraph—

  (a) shall be made by statutory instrument, and

  (b) shall not be made unless a draft has been laid before and approved by resolution of each House of Parliament.

13 (1) This paragraph applies for the purposes of the determination by any person, tribunal or court whether a person who has made an asylum claim may be removed—

(a) from the United Kingdom, and
(b) to a State of which he is not a national or citizen.

(2) A State to which this Part applies shall be treated, in so far as relevant to the question mentioned in sub-paragraph (1), as a place—

(a) where a person's life and liberty are not threatened by reason of his race, religion, nationality, membership of a particular social group or political opinion, and
(b) from which a person will not be sent to another State otherwise than in accordance with the Refugee Convention.

14 Section 77 of the Nationality, Immigration and Asylum Act 2002 (c 41) (no removal while claim for asylum pending) shall not prevent a person who has made a claim for asylum from being removed—

(a) from the United Kingdom, and
(b) to a State to which this Part applies;

provided that the Secretary of State certifies that in his opinion the person is not a national or citizen of the State.

15 (1) This paragraph applies where the Secretary of State certifies that—

(a) it is proposed to remove a person to a State to which this Part applies, and
(b) in the Secretary of State's opinion the person is not a national or citizen of the State.

(2) The person may not bring an immigration appeal by virtue of section 92(2) or (3) of that Act (appeal from within United Kingdom: general).

(3) The person may not bring an immigration appeal by virtue of section 92(4)(a) of that Act (appeal from within United Kingdom: asylum or human rights) in reliance on an asylum claim which asserts that to remove the person to a specified State to which this Part applies would breach the United Kingdom's obligations under the Refugee Convention.

(4) The person may not bring an immigration appeal by virtue of section 92(4)(a) of that Act in reliance on a human rights claim if the Secretary of State certifies that the claim is clearly unfounded.

16 A person who is outside the United Kingdom may not bring an immigration appeal on any ground that is inconsistent with treating a State to which this Part applies as a place—

(a) where a person's life and liberty are not threatened by reason of his race, religion, nationality, membership of a particular social group or political opinion, and
(b) from which a person will not be sent to another State otherwise than in accordance with the Refugee Convention.

Appointment
Appointment: 1 October 2004: see SI 2004/2523, art 2, Schedule.

PART 5
COUNTRIES CERTIFIED AS SAFE FOR INDIVIDUALS

17 This Part applies to a person who has made an asylum claim if the Secretary of State certifies that—

(a) it is proposed to remove the person to a specified State,
(b) in the Secretary of State's opinion the person is not a national or citizen of the specified State, and
(c) in the Secretary of State's opinion the specified State is a place—
  (i) where the person's life and liberty will not be threatened by reason of his race, religion, nationality, membership of a particular social group or political opinion, and
  (ii) from which the person will not be sent to another State otherwise than in accordance with the Refugee Convention.

18 Where this Part applies to a person section 77 of the Nationality, Immigration and Asylum Act 2002 (c 41) (no removal while claim for asylum pending) shall not prevent his removal to the State specified under paragraph 17.

19 Where this Part applies to a person—

(a) he may not bring an immigration appeal by virtue of section 92(2) or (3) of that Act (appeal from within United Kingdom: general),
(b) he may not bring an immigration appeal by virtue of section 92(4)(a) of that Act (appeal from within United Kingdom: asylum or human rights) in reliance on an asylum claim which asserts that to remove the person to the State specified under paragraph 17 would breach the United Kingdom's obligations under the Refugee Convention,
(c) he may not bring an immigration appeal by virtue of section 92(4)(a) of that Act in reliance on a human rights claim if the Secretary of State certifies that the claim is clearly unfounded, and
(d) he may not while outside the United Kingdom bring an immigration appeal on any ground that is inconsistent with the opinion certified under paragraph 17(c).

Appointment
Appointment: 1 October 2004: see SI 2004/2523, art 2, Schedule.

PART 6
AMENDMENT OF LISTS

20 (1) The Secretary of State may by order add a State to the list specified in paragraph 2.

(2) The Secretary of State may by order—

(a) add a State to a list specified under paragraph 7 or 12, or
(b) remove a State from a list specified under paragraph 7 or 12.

21 (1) An order under paragraph 20(1) or (2)(a)—

(a) shall be made by statutory instrument,
(b) shall not be made unless a draft has been laid before and approved by resolution of each House of Parliament, and
(c) may include transitional provision.

(2) An order under paragraph 20(2)(b)—

(a) shall be made by statutory instrument,
(b) shall be subject to annulment in pursuance of a resolution of either House of Parliament, and
(c) may include transitional provision.

Appointment
Appointment: 1 October 2004: see SI 2004/2523, art 2, Schedule.

SCHEDULE 4
REPEALS

Section 47

Short title and chapter	Extent of repeal
Immigration Act 1971 (c 77)	In Schedule 2— (a) in paragraph 29(3), the words from "and where an adjudicator dismisses" to the end, and (b) paragraph 29(4).
House of Commons Disqualification Act 1975 (c 24)	In Part III of Schedule 1, the entry relating to immigration adjudicators.
Northern Ireland Assembly Disqualification Act 1975 (c 25)	In Part III of Schedule 1, the entry relating to immigration adjudicators.
British Nationality Act 1981 (c 61)	Section 40A(6) to (8).
Tribunals and Inquiries Act 1992 (c 53)	Section 7(3).
Asylum and Immigration Appeals Act 1993 (c 23)	Section 9A.
Asylum and Immigration Act 1996 (c 49)	Section 8(9).
Immigration and Asylum Act 1999 (c 33)	Sections 11 and 12.
	In section 72(10), "adjudicator". In section 85(1), "and (b)". Section 87(3)(f). Section 123. In Schedule 6, in paragraph 1(1), "or (b)".
State Pension Credit Act 2002 (c 16)	In Schedule 2, paragraph 42.
Tax Credits Act 2002 (c 21)	In Schedule 4, paragraph 22.
Nationality, Immigration and Asylum Act 2002 (c 41)	Section 52.
	Section 80. Section 87(4). Section 93. Section 94(4)(a) to (j). Sections 100 to 103. Section 104(3). In section 106— (a) in subsection (2)(e) and (f), "an adjudicator or", (b) subsection (2)(j) and (k), (c) in subsection (2)(m), the words from " (which may" to the end, and (d) in subsections (2)(o), (p), (q), (r) and (s), (3)(a), (d), (e) and (4), "an adjudicator or". Section 107(2). Schedule 5.
State Pension Credit Act (Northern Ireland) 2002 (c 14 (NI))	In Schedule 2, paragraph 31.

Appointment
Appointment (in part): 1 October 2004: see SI 2004/2523, art 2, Schedule.

OTHER RELEVANT LEGISLATION

NATIONAL ASSISTANCE ACT 1948

1948 CHAPTER 29

An Act to terminate the existing poor law and to provide in lieu thereof for the assistance of persons in need by the National Assistance Board and by local authorities; to make further provision for the welfare of disabled, sick, aged and other persons and for regulating homes for disabled and aged persons and charities for disabled persons; to amend the law relating to non-contributory old age pensions; to make provision as to the burial or cremation of deceased persons; and for purposes connected with the matters aforesaid

[13th May 1948]

PART III
LOCAL AUTHORITY SERVICES
Provision of Accommodation

21 Duty of local authorities to provide accommodation

(1) [Subject to and in accordance with the provisions of this Part of this Act, a local authority may with the approval of the Secretary of State, and to such extent as he may direct shall, make arrangements for providing]—

    (a) residential accommodation for persons [aged eighteen or over] who by reason of age, [illness, disability] or any other circumstances are in need of care and attention which is not otherwise available to them; [and

    (aa) residential accommodation for expectant and nursing mothers who are in need of care and attention which is not otherwise available to them.]

    (b) ...

[(1A) A person to whom section 115 of the Immigration and Asylum Act 1999 (exclusion from benefits) applies may not be provided with residential accommodation under subsection (1)(a) if his need for care and attention has arisen solely—

    (a) because he is destitute; or

    (b) because of the physical effects, or anticipated physical effects, of his being destitute.

(1B) Subsections (3) and (5) to (8) of section 95 of the Immigration and Asylum Act 1999, and paragraph 2 of Schedule 8 to that Act, apply for the purposes of subsection (1A) as they apply for the purposes of that section, but for the references in subsections (5) and (7) of that section and in that paragraph to the Secretary of State substitute references to a local authority.

[(1B) Section 95(2) to (7) of that Act shall apply for the purposes of subsection (1A) above; and for that purpose a reference to the Secretary of State in section 95(4) or (5) shall be treated as a reference to a local authority.]]

(2) In [making any such arrangements] a local authority shall have regard to the welfare of all persons for whom accommodation is provided, and in particular to the need for providing accommodation of different descriptions suited to different descriptions of such persons as are mentioned in the last foregoing subsection.

[(2A) In determining for the purposes of paragraph (a) or (aa) of subsection (1) of this section whether care and attention are otherwise available to a person, a local authority shall disregard so much of the person's resources as may be specified in, or determined in accordance with, regulations made by the Secretary of State for the purposes of this subsection.

(2B)   In subsection (2A) of this section the reference to a person's resources is a reference to his resources within the meaning of regulations made for the purposes of that subsection.]

(3)   ...

(4)   [Subject to the provisions of section 26 of this Act] accommodation provided by a local authority in the exercise of their [functions under this section] shall be provided in premises managed by the authority or, to such extent as may be [determined in accordance with the arrangements] under this section, in such premises managed by another local authority as may be agreed between the two authorities and on such terms, including terms as to the reimbursement of expenditure incurred by the said other authority, as may be so agreed.

(5)   References in this Act to accommodation provided under this Part thereof shall be construed as references to accommodation provided in accordance with this and the five next following sections, and as including references to board and other services, amenities and requisites provided in connection with the accommodation except where in the opinion of the authority managing the premises their provision is unnecessary.

(6)   References in this Act to a local authority providing accommodation shall be construed, in any case where a local authority agree with another local authority for the provision of accommodation in premises managed by the said other authority, as references to the first-mentioned local authority.

(7)   Without prejudice to the generality of the foregoing provisions of this section, a local authority may—

(a)   provide, in such cases as they may consider appropriate, for the conveyance of persons to and from premises in which accommodation is provided for them under this Part of the Act;

[(b)   make arrangements for the provision on the premises in which accommodation is being provided of such other services as appear to the authority to be required.]

...

(8)   ... nothing in this section shall authorise or require a local authority to make any provision authorised or required to be made (whether by that or by any other authority) by or under any enactment not contained in this Part of this Act [or authorised or required to be provided under the National Health Service Act 1977].

Appointment
Appointment (in relation to England and Wales): 5 July 1948: see SI 1948/1218, art 2.

Amendment
Repealed in relation to Scotland by the Social Work (Scotland) Act 1968, s 95(2), Sch 9, Pt I.
Sub-s (1): first words in square brackets substituted by the Local Government Act 1972, s 195, Sch 23, para 2; second words in square brackets inserted by the Children Act 1989, s 108(5), Sch 13, para 11(1); third words in square brackets substituted, and final words in square brackets inserted, by the National Health Service and Community Care Act 1990, s 42(1); para (b) repealed by the Housing (Homeless Persons) Act 1977, s 20(4), Schedule.
Sub-ss (1A), (1B): inserted by the Immigration and Asylum Act 1999, s 116; for transitional provisions see Sch 15, para 5 thereto. Date in force: 6 December 1999: see SI 1999/3190, art 2, Schedule.
Sub-s (1B): substituted by the Nationality, Immigration and Asylum Act 2002, s 45(5). Date in force: to be appointed: see the Nationality, Immigration and Asylum Act 2002, s 162(1).

Sub-s (2): words "making any such arrangements" in square brackets substituted by the Local Government Act 1972, s 195, Sch 23, para 2.
Sub-ss (2A), (2B) (as inserted by the Community Care (Residential Accommodation) Act 1998, s 1): substituted by the Health and Social Care Act 2001, s 53. Date in force (in relation to England): 1 October 2001: see SI 2001/3167, art 2, Schedule. Date in force (in relation to Wales): 1 April 2003: see SI 2003/939, art 2, Sch 1.
Sub-s (3): repealed by the Local Government Act 1972, ss 195, 272, Sch 23, para 2, Sch 30.
Sub-s (4): first words in square brackets inserted by the National Health Service and Community Care Act 1990, s 66(1), Sch 9, para 5(1); other words in square brackets substituted by the Local Government Act 1972, s 195, Sch 23, para 2.
Sub-s (7): para (b) substituted, for paras (b), (c) as originally enacted, by the National Health Service and Community Care Act 1990, s 66(1), Sch 9, para 5(2); words omitted repealed by the National Health Service Reorganisation Act 1973, s 58, Sch 5.
Sub-s (8): words omitted repealed, and words in square brackets inserted, by the National Health Service and Community Care Act 1990, s 66(1), (2), Sch 9, para 5(3), Sch 10.

Transfer of Functions
Functions of a Minister of the Crown, so far as exercisable in relation to Wales, transferred to the National Assembly for Wales, by the National Assembly for Wales (Transfer of Functions) Order 1999, SI 1999/672, art 2, Sch 1.

Subordinate Legislation
National Assistance (Residential Accommodation) (Disregarding of Resources) (England) Regulations 2001, SI 2001/3067 (made under sub-s (2A)).
National Assistance (Residential Accommodation) (Disregarding of Resources) (Wales) Regulations 2003, SI 2003/969 (made under sub-s (2A)).

Welfare Services

29 Welfare arrangements for blind, deaf, dumb and crippled persons, etc

(1) A local authority [may, with the approval of the Secretary of State, and to such extent as he may direct in relation to persons ordinarily resident in the area of the local authority shall] make arrangements for promoting the welfare of persons to whom this section applies, that is to say persons [aged eighteen or over] who are blind, deaf or dumb [or who suffer from mental disorder of any description], and other persons [aged eighteen or over] who are substantially and permanently handicapped by illness, injury, or congenital deformity or such other disabilities as may be prescribed by the Minister.

(2), (3) ...

(4) Without prejudice to the generality of the provisions of subsection (1) of this section, arrangements may be made thereunder—

(a) for informing persons to whom arrangements under that subsection relate of the services available for them thereunder;

(b) for giving such persons instruction in their own homes or elsewhere in methods of overcoming the effects of their disabilities;

(c) for providing workshops where such persons may be engaged (whether under a contract of service or otherwise) in suitable work, and hostels where persons engaged in the workshops, and other persons to whom arrangements under subsection (1) of this section relate and for whom work or training is being provided in pursuance of the Disabled Persons (Employment) Act 1944 [or the Employment and Training Act 1973] may live;

(d) for providing persons to whom arrangements under subsection (1) of this section relate with suitable work (whether under a contract of service or otherwise) in their own homes or elsewhere;

(e) for helping such persons in disposing of the produce of their work;

(f) for providing such persons with recreational facilities in their own homes or elsewhere;

(g) for compiling and maintaining classified registers of the persons to whom arrangements under subsection (1) of this section relate.

[(4A) Where accommodation in a hostel is provided under paragraph (c) of subsection (4) of this section—

(a) if the hostel is managed by a local authority, section 22 of this Act shall apply as it applies where accommodation is provided under section 21;

(b) if the accommodation is provided in a hostel managed by a person other than a local authority under arrangements made with that person, subsections (2) to (4A) of section 26 of this Act shall apply as they apply where accommodation is provided under arrangements made by virtue of that section; and

(c) sections 32 and 43 of this Act shall apply as they apply where accommodation is provided under sections 21 to 26;

and in this subsection references to "accommodation" include references to board and other services, amenities and requisites provided in connection with the accommodation, except where in the opinion of the authority managing the premises or, in the case mentioned in paragraph (b) above, the authority making the arrangements their provision is unnecessary.]

(5) ...

(6) Nothing in the foregoing provisions of this section shall authorise or require—

(a) the payment of money to persons to whom this section applies, other than persons for whom work is provided under arrangements made by virtue of paragraph (c) or paragraph (d) of subsection (4) of this section or who are engaged in work which they are enabled to perform in consequence of anything done in pursuance of arrangements made under this section; or

(b) the provision of any accommodation or services required to be provided under the [National Health Service Act 1977] ...

(7) A person engaged in work in a workshop provided under paragraph (c) of subsection (4) of this section, or a person in receipt of a superannuation allowance granted on his retirement from engagement in any such workshop, shall be deemed for the purposes of this Act to continue to be ordinarily resident in the area in which he was ordinarily resident immediately before he [was accepted for work in that workshop; and for the purposes of this subsection a course of training in such a workshop shall be deemed to be work in that workshop].

Appointment
Appointment (in relation to England and Wales): 5 July 1948: see SI 1948/1218, art 2.

Amendment
Repealed in relation to Scotland by the Social Work (Scotland) Act 1968, s 95(2), Sch 9, Part I.
Sub-s (1): first words in square brackets substituted by the Local Government Act 1972, s 195, Sch 23, para 2; second and final words in square brackets inserted by the Children Act 1989, s 108(5), (6), Sch 13, para 11(2), Sch 14, para 1; third words in square brackets substituted by the Mental Health (Scotland) Act 1960, ss 113(1), 114, Sch 4.
Sub-ss (2), (3): repealed by the Local Government Act 1972, ss 195, 272(1), Sch 23, para 2, Sch 30.
Sub-s (4): words in square brackets inserted by the Employment and Training Act 1973, s 14(1), Sch 3, para 3.
Sub-s (4A): inserted by the National Health Service and Community Care Act 1990, s 44(7).
Sub-s (5): repealed by the Health and Social Services and Social Security Adjudications Act 1983, s 30, Sch 10, Part I.
Sub-s (6): words in square brackets substituted by the National Health Service Act 1977, s 129, Sch 15, para 6; words omitted repealed by the Social Work (Scotland) Act 1968, s 95(2), Sch 9, Part I.

Sub-s (7): words in square brackets substituted retrospectively by the National Assistance (Amendment) Act 1959, s 1(2).

Transfer of Functions
Functions of the Minister of Health transferred to the Secretary of State for Health by virtue of the Secretary of State for Social Services Order 1968, SI 1968/1699, and the Transfer of Functions (Health and Social Services) Order 1988, SI 1988/1843.
Functions under this section, so far as exercisable in relation to Wales, transferred to the National Assembly for Wales, by the National Assembly for Wales (Transfer of Functions) Order 1999, SI 1999/672, art 2, Sch 1.

EUROPEAN COMMUNITIES ACT 1972

1972 CHAPTER 68

An Act to make provision in connection with the enlargement of the European Communities to include the United Kingdom, together with (for certain purposes) the Channel Islands, the Isle of Man and Gibraltar

[17th October 1972]

BE IT ENACTED by the Queen's most Excellent Majesty, by and with the advice and consent of the Lords Spiritual and Temporal, and Commons, in this present Parliament assembled, and by the authority of the same, as follows

PART I
GENERAL PROVISIONS

1   Short title and interpretation[1]

(1)   This Act may be cited as the European Communities Act 1972.

(2)   In this Act ... —

"the Communities" means the European Economic Community, the European Coal and Steel Community and the European Atomic Energy Community;
"the Treaties" or "the Community Treaties" means, subject to subsection (3) below, the pre-accession treaties, that is to say, those described in Part I of Schedule 1 to this Act, taken with—
(a)   the treaty relating to the accession of the United Kingdom to the European Economic Community and to the European Atomic Energy Community, signed at Brussels on the 22nd January 1972; and
(b)   the decision, of the same date, of the Council of the European Communities relating to the accession of the United Kingdom to the European Coal and Steel Community; [and
(c)   the treaty relating to the accession of the Hellenic Republic to the European Economic Community and to the European Atomic Energy Community, signed at Athens on 28th May 1979; and
(d)   the decision, of 24th May 1979, of the Council relating to the accession of the Hellenic Republic to the European Coal and Steel Community;] [and

(e) the decisions of the Council of 7th May 1985, 24th June 1988, 31st October 1994 and 29th September 2000, on the Communities' system of own resources; and]

[(g) the treaty relating to the accession of the Kingdom of Spain and the Portuguese Republic to the European Economic Community and to the European Atomic Energy Community, signed at Lisbon and Madrid on 12th June 1985; and

(h) the decision, of 11th June 1985, of the Council relating to the accession of the Kingdom of Spain and the Portuguese Republic to the European Coal and Steel Community;] [and

(j) the following provisions of the Single European Act signed at Luxembourg and The Hague on 17th and 28th February 1986, namely Title II (amendment of the treaties establishing the Communities) and, so far as they relate to any of the Communities or any Community institution, the preamble and Titles I (common provisions) and IV (general and final provisions);] [and

(k) Titles II, III and IV of the Treaty on European Union signed at Maastricht on 7th February 1992, together with the other provisions of the Treaty so far as they relate to those Titles, and the Protocols adopted at Maastricht on that date and annexed to the Treaty establishing the European Community with the exception of the Protocol on Social Policy on page 117 of Cm 1934] [and

(l) the decision, of 1st February 1993, of the Council amending the Act concerning the election of the representatives of the European Parliament by direct universal suffrage annexed to Council Decision 76/787/ECSC, EEC, Euratom of 20th September 1976] [and

(m) the Agreement on the European Economic Area signed at Oporto on 2nd May 1992 together with the Protocol adjusting that Agreement signed at Brussels on 17th March 1993] [and

(n) the treaty concerning the accession of the Kingdom of Norway, the Republic of Austria, the Republic of Finland and the Kingdom of Sweden to the European Union, signed at Corfu on 24th June 1994;] [and

(o) the following provisions of the Treaty signed at Amsterdam on 2nd October 1997 amending the Treaty on European Union, the Treaties establishing the European Communities and certain related Acts—
  (i) Articles 2 to 9,
  (ii) Article 12, and
  (iii) the other provisions of the Treaty so far as they relate to those Articles,
and the Protocols adopted on that occasion other than the Protocol on Article J.7 of the Treaty on European Union] [and

(p) the following provisions of the Treaty signed at Nice on 26th February 2001 amending the Treaty on European Union, the Treaties establishing the European Communities and certain related Acts—
  (i) Articles 2 to 10, and
  (ii) the other provisions of the Treaty so far as they relate to those Articles,
and the Protocols adopted on that occasion;]
and any other treaty entered into by any of the Communities, with or without any of the member States, or entered into, as a treaty ancillary to any of the Treaties, by the United Kingdom; [and

(q) the treaty concerning the accession of the Czech Republic, the Republic of Estonia, the Republic of Cyprus, the Republic of Latvia, the Republic of Lithuania, the Republic of Hungary, the Republic of Malta, the Republic of Poland, the Republic of Slovenia and the Slovak Republic to the European Union, signed at Athens on 16th April 2003;]

and any expression defined in Schedule 1 to this Act has the meaning there given to it.

(3)   If Her Majesty by Order in Council declares that a treaty specified in the Order is to be regarded as one of the Community Treaties as herein defined, the Order shall be conclusive that it is to be so regarded; but a treaty entered into by the United Kingdom after the 22nd January 1972, other than a pre-accession treaty to which the United Kingdom accedes on terms settled on or before that date, shall not be so regarded unless it is so specified, nor be so specified unless a draft of the Order in Council has been approved by resolution of each House of Parliament.

(4)   For purposes of subsections (2) and (3) above, "treaty" includes any international agreement, and any protocol or annex to a treaty or international agreement.

Note
Section 1 has been amended by a number of acts passed to give effect to amendments in the EC Treaty:
  (i)   the European Communities (Spanish and Portuguese Accession) Act 1985 (to include Spain and Portugal in the Member States of the European Economic Community, as it was then known);
  (ii)   the European Communities (Amendment) Act 1986 (to incorporate the provisions of the Single European Act 1986);
  (iii) the European Communities (Amendment) Act 1986 (to include the provisions of the Maastricht Treaty, signed on 7 February 1992);
  (iv)   the European Economic Area Act 1993 (incorporating the provisions of the European Economic Area Agreement signed in Oporto on 2 May 1992, so that the 1972 Act will apply to the EEA where appropriate);
  (v)   the European Union Accessions Act 1994 (to include the Treaty concerning the accession of Norway, Austria, Finland and Sweden to the Economic Union within the definition of 'Treaties' in s 1);
  (vi)   the European Communities (Amendment) Act 1998 (making consequential provisions following amendments made to the EU and EC Treaties by the Amsterdam Treaty signed on 2 October 1997);
  (vii) the European Communities (Amendment) Act 2002 (making consequential amendments following amendments to the EU and EC Treaties by the Treaty of Nice signed on 26 February 2001).
NB – the European Union (Accessions) Act 2003, which also amends the ECA 1972, is printed separately.

Initial Commencement
This Act received Royal Assent on 17 October 1972 but did not have practical effect until 1 January 1973 (the date on which the United Kingdom joined the European Communities).

Amendment
Sub-s (2): words omitted repealed by the Interpretation Act 1978, s 25(1), Sch 3.
Sub-s (2): in definition ""the Treaties" or "the Community Treaties"" paras (c), (d) inserted by the European Communities (Greek Accession) Act 1979, s 1.
Sub-s (2): in definition ""the Treaties" or "the Community Treaties"" para (e) substituted for existing paras (e), (f) (as inserted by the European Communities (Finance) Act 1985, s 1), by the European Communities (Finance) Act 1995, s 1.
Sub-s (2): in definition ""the Treaties" or "the Community Treaties"" para (e) and word "and" immediately preceding it substituted by the European Communities (Finance) Act 2001, s 1. Date in force: this amendment came into force on 4 December 2001 (date of Royal Assent of the European Communities (Finance) Act 2001) in the absence of any specific commencement provision.
Sub-s (2): in definition ""the Treaties" or "the Community Treaties"" paras (g), (h) inserted by the European Communities (Spanish and Portuguese Accession) Act 1985, s 1.
Sub-s (2): in definition ""the Treaties" or "the Community Treaties"" para (j) inserted by the European Communities (Amendment) Act 1986, s 1.
Sub-s (2): in definition ""the Treaties" or "the Community Treaties"" para (k) inserted by the European Communities (Amendment) Act 1993, s 1(1).

Sub-s (2): in definition ""the Treaties" or "the Community Treaties"" para (l) and word "and" immediately preceding it inserted by the European Parliamentary Elections Act 1993, s 3(2): amendment continued by the European Parliamentary Elections Act 2002, s 15, Sch 3, para 1.
Sub-s (2): in definition ""the Treaties" or "the Community Treaties"" para (m) inserted by the European Economic Area Act 1993, s 1.
Sub-s (2): in definition ""the Treaties" or "the Community Treaties"" para (n) inserted by the European Union (Accessions) Act 1994, s 1.
Sub-s (2): in definition ""the Treaties" or "the Community Treaties"" para (o) inserted by the European Communities (Amendment) Act 1998, s 1. Date in force: this amendment came into force on 11 June 1998 (date of Royal Assent of the European Communities (Amendment) Act 1998) in the absence of any specific commencement provision.
Sub-s (2): in definition ""the Treaties" or "the Community Treaties"" para (p) inserted by the European Communities (Amendment) Act 2002, s 1(1). Date in force: this amendment came into force on 26 February 2002 (date of Royal Assent of the European Communities (Amendment) Act 2002) in the absence of any specific commencement provision.
Sub-s (2): in definition ""the Treaties" or "the Community Treaties"" para (q) and word "and" immediately preceding it inserted by the European Union (Accessions) Act 2003, s 1(1). Date in force: this amendment came into force on 13 November 2003 (date of Royal Assent of the European Union (Accessions) Act 2003) in the absence of any specific commencement provision.

Subordinate Legislation
European Communities (Definition of Treaties) Order 1972, SI 1972/1993 (made under sub-s (3)).
European Communities (Definition of Treaties) Order 1973, SI 1973/1314 (made under sub-s (3)).
European Communities (Definition of Treaties) (No 2) Order 1973, SI 1973/2154 (made under sub-s (3)).
European Communities (Definition of Treaties) Order 1974, SI 1974/1263 (made under sub-s (3)).
European Communities (Definition of Treaties) Order 1975, SI 1975/408 (made under sub-s (3)).
European Communities (Definition of Treaties) (No 2) Order 1975, SI 1975/2162 (made under sub-s (3)).
European Communities (Definition of Treaties) Order 1976, SI 1976/217 (made under sub-s (3)).
European Communities (Definition of Treaties) (No 2) Order 1976, SI 1976/218 (made under sub-s (3)).
European Communities (Definition of Treaties) Order 1977, SI 1977/822 (made under sub-s (3)).
European Communities (Definition of Treaties) (No 2) Order 1977, SI 1977/823 (made under sub-s (3)).
European Communities (Definition of Treaties) (No 3) Order 1977, SI 1977/2144 (made under sub-s (3)).
European Communities (Definition of Treaties) (No 4) Order 1977, SI 1977/2145 (made under sub-s (3)).
European Communities (Definition of Treaties) (No 5) Order 1977, SI 1977/2146 (made under sub-s (3)).
European Communities (Definition of Treaties) (No 6) Order 1977, SI 1977/2147 (made under sub-s (3)).
European Communities (Definition of Treaties) Order 1978, SI 1978/617 (made under sub-s (3)).
European Communities (Definition of Treaties) (No 2) Order 1978, SI 1978/618 (made under sub-s (3)).
European Communities (Definition of Treaties) (No 3) Order 1978, SI 1978/619 (made under sub-s (3)).
European Communities (Definition of Treaties) (No 4) Order 1978, SI 1978/781 (made under sub-s (3)).
European Communities (Definition of Treaties) (No 5) (Joint European Torus) Order 1978, SI 1978/1032 (made under sub-s (3)).
European Communities (Definition of Treaties) (No 6) (International Development Association) Order 1978, SI 1978/1103 (made under sub-s (3)).
European Communities (Definition of Treaties) (No 7) (International Wheat Agreement) Order 1978, SI 1978/1104 (made under sub-s (3)).
European Communities (Definition of Treaties) (ECSC Decision on Supplementary Revenues) Order 1979, SI 1979/292 (made under sub-s (3)).

European Communities (Definition of Treaties) (ECSC Decision of 9th April 1979 on Supplementary Revenues) Order 1979, SI 1979/932 (made under sub-s (3)).
European Communities (Definition of Treaties) (International Wheat Agreement) Order 1979, SI 1979/1446 (made under sub-s (3)).
European Communities (Definition of Treaties) (Multilateral Trade Negotiations) Order 1980, SI 1980/191 (made under sub-s (3)).
European Communities (Definition of Treaties) (Second ACP-EEC Convention of Lomé) Order 1980, SI 1980/1077 (made under sub-s (3)).
European Communities (Definition of Treaties) (ECSC Decision of 18th March 1980 on Supplementary Revenue) Order 1980, SI 1980/1090 (made under sub-s (3)).
European Communities (Definition of Treaties) (International Railway Tariffs Agreements) Order 1980, SI 1980/1094 (made under sub-s (3)).
European Communities (Definition of Treaties) (Accession of the Republic of Zimbabwe to the Second ACP-EEC Convention of Lomé) Order 1981, SI 1981/835 (made under sub-s (3)).
European Communities (Definition of Treaties) (Yugoslavia Agreements) Order 1981, SI 1981/1125 (made under sub-s (3)).
European Communities (Definition of Treaties) (ECSC Decision of 7th December 1981 on Supplementary Revenue) Order 1982, SI 1982/341 (made under sub-s (3)).
European Communities (Definition of Treaties) (International Railway Tariffs Agreements) Order 1982, SI 1982/707 (made under sub-s (3)).
European Communities (Definition of Treaties) (International Railway Tariffs Agreements) Order 1982, SI 1982/707 (made under sub-s (3)).
European Communities (Definition of Treaties) (Change in Status of Greenland) Order 1984, SI 1984/1820 (made under sub-s (3)).
European Communities (Definition of Treaties) (Third ACP-EEC Convention of Lomé) Order 1985, SI 1985/1198 (made under sub-s (3)).
European Communities (Definition of Treaties) (International Convention on the Harmonised Commodity Description and Coding System) Order 1987, SI 1987/2040.
European Communities (Definition of Treaties) (European School) Order 1990, SI 1990/236 (made under sub-s (3)).
European Communities (Definition of Treaties) (Fourth ACP-EEC Convention of Lomé) Order 1991, SI 1991/758.
European Communities (Definition of Treaties) (Europe Agreement establishing an Association between the European Communities and their Member States and the Republic of Hungary) Order 1992, SI 1992/2871 (made under sub-s (3)).
European Communities (Definition of Treaties) (Europe Agreement establishing an Association between the European Communities and their Member States and the Republic of Poland) Order 1992, SI 1992/2872 (made under sub-s (3)).
European Communities (Definition of Treaties) (International Railway Tariffs Agreements) Order 1993, SI 1993/944 (made under sub-s (3)).
European Communities (Definition of Treaties) (Agreement on Customs Union and Co-operation between the European Economic Community and the Republic of San Marino) Order 1993, SI 1993/1783 (made under sub-s (3)).
European Communities (Definition of Treaties) (European Investment Fund) Order 1993, SI 1993/3157 (made under sub-s (3)).
European Communities (Definition of Treaties) (Europe Agreement establishing an Association between the European Communities and their Member States and the Republic of Bulgaria) Order 1994, SI 1994/758 (made under sub-s (3)).
European Communities (Definition of Treaties) (Europe Agreement establishing an Association between the European Communities and their Member States and the Czech Republic) Order 1994, SI 1994/759 (made under sub-s (3)).
European Communities (Definition of Treaties) (Europe Agreement establishing an Association between the European Communities and their Member States and Romania) Order 1994, SI 1994/760 (made under sub-s (3)).
European Communities (Definition of Treaties) (Europe Agreement establishing an Association between the European Communities and their Member States and the Slovak Republic) Order 1994, SI 1994/761 (made under sub-s (3)).
European Communities (Definition of Treaties) (The Agreement Establishing the World Trade Organisation) Order 1995, SI 1995/265 (made under sub-s (3)).
European Communities (Definition of Treaties) (Partnership and Co-operation Agreement between the European Communities and their Member States and the Russian Federation) Order 1995, SI 1995/1618 (made under sub-s (3)).

Appendix 1 Legislation and materials

European Communities (Definition of Treaties) (Partnership and Co-operation Agreement between the European Communities and their Member States, and Ukraine) Order 1995, SI 1995/1619 (made under sub-s (3)).

European Communities (Definition of Treaties) (Statute of the European Schools) Order 1996, SI 1996/267 (made under sub-s (3)).

European Communities (Definition of Treaties) (The Energy Charter Treaty) Order 1996, SI 1996/1639 (made under sub-s (3)).

European Communities (Definition of Treaties) (Europe Agreement establishing an Association between the European Communities and their Member States and the Republic of Estonia) Order 1997, SI 1997/269 (made under sub-s (3)).

European Communities (Definition of Treaties) (Europe Agreement establishing an Association between the European Communities and their Member States and the Republic of Latvia) Order 1997, SI 1997/270 (made under sub-s (3)).

European Communities (Definition of Treaties) (Europe Agreement establishing an Association between the European Communities and their Member States and the Republic of Lithuania) Order 1997, SI 1997/271 (made under sub-s (3)).

European Communities (Definition of Treaties) (Euro-Mediterranean Agreement establishing an Association between the European Communities and their Member States and the State of Israel) Order 1997, SI 1997/863 (made under sub-s (3)).

European Communities (Definition of Treaties) (Framework Cooperation Agreement between the European Community and its Member States and the Republic of Chile) Order 1997, SI 1997/2576 (made under sub-s (3)).

European Communities (Definition of Treaties) (Euro-Mediterranean Agreement Establishing an Association between the European Communities and their Member States and the Kingdom of Morocco) Order 1997, SI 1997/2577 (made under sub-s (3)).

European Communities (Definition of Treaties) (Inter-regional Framework Co-operation Agreement between the European Community and its Member States and the Southern Common Market and its Party States) Order 1997, SI 1997/2603 (made under sub-s (3)).

European Communities (Definition of Treaties) (European Police Office) Order 1997, SI 1997/2972 (made under sub-s (3)).

European Communities (Definition of Treaties) (Partnership and Co-operation Agreement between the European Communities and their Member States and Georgia) Order 1998, SI 1998/1059 (made under sub-s (3)).

European Communities (Definition of Treaties) (Partnership and Co-operation Agreement between the European Communities and their Member States and the Republic of Armenia) Order 1998, SI 1998/1060 (made under sub-s (3)).

European Communities (Definition of Treaties) (Partnership and Co-operation Agreement between the European Communities and their Member States and the Republic of Azerbaijan) Order 1998, SI 1998/1061 (made under sub-s (3)).

European Communities (Definition of Treaties) (Europe Agreement establishing an Association between the European Communities and their Member States, and the Republic of Slovenia) Order 1998, SI 1998/1062 (made under sub-s (3)).

European Communities (Definition of Treaties) (Partnership and Co-operation Agreement between the European Communities and their Member States and the Republic of Uzbekistan) Order 1998, SI 1998/1063 (made under sub-s (3)).

European Communities (Definition of Treaties) (North-East Atlantic Fisheries Commission) Order 1999, SI 1999/279 (made under sub-s (3)).

European Communities (Definition of Treaties) (Economic Partnership, Political Coordination and Cooperation Agreement between the European Community and its Member States and the United Mexican States) Order 1999, SI 1999/1738 (made under sub-s (3)).

European Communities (Definition of Treaties) (EuroMediterranean Agreement establishing an Association between the European Communities and their Member States and the Hashemite Kingdom of Jordan) Order 1999, SI 1999/1739 (made under sub-s (3)).

European Communities (Definition of Treaties) (Framework Agreement for Trade and Cooperation between the European Community and its Member States and the Republic of Korea) Order 1999, SI 1999/1740 (made under sub-s (3)).

European Communities (Definition of Treaties) (Agreement between the European Community and its Member States and the Swiss Confederation on the Free Movement of Persons) Order 2000, SI 2000/3269 (made under sub-s (3)).

European Communities (Definition of Treaties) (The Convention on Mutual Assistance and Co-operation between Customs Administrations (Naples II)) Order 2001, SI 2001/413 (made under sub-s (3)).

European Communities (Definition of Treaties) (European School) Order 2001, SI 2001/3671 (made under sub-s (3)).
European Communities (Definition of Treaties) (North Atlantic Salmon Conservation Organization) Order 2001, SI 2001/3672 (made under sub-s (3)).
European Communities (Definition of Treaties) (Partnership Agreement between the Members of the African, Caribbean and Pacific Group of States and the European Community and its Member States (The Cotonou Agreement)) Order 2001, SI 2001/3935 (made under sub-s (3)).
European Communities (Definition of Treaties) (Stabilisation and Association Agreement between the European Communities and their Member States, and the Former Yugoslav Republic of Macedonia) Order 2002, SI 2002/2841 (made under sub-s (3)).
European Communities (Definition of Treaties) (Agreement on Trade, Development and Co-operation between the European Community and its Member States and the Republic of South Africa) Order 2002, SI 2002/3139 (made under sub-s (3)).
European Communities (Definition of Treaties) (Euro-Mediterranean Agreement establishing an Association between the European Communities and their Member States and the Arab Republic of Egypt) Order 2003, SI 2003/1554 (made under sub-s (3)).
European Communities (Definition of Treaties) (Agreement establishing an association between the European Community and its Member States and the Republic of Chile) Order 2003, SI 2003/1556 (made under sub-s (3)).
European Communities (Definition of Treaties) (Database Protection Agreement between the United Kingdom on behalf of the Isle of Man and the European Community) Order 2003, SI 2003/1891 (made under sub-s (3)).
European Communities (Definition of Treaties) (Common Electoral Principles) Order 2004, SI 2004/304 (made under sub-s (3)).
European Communities (Definition of Treaties) (Euro-Mediterranean Agreement establishing an Association between the European Communities and their Member States and the People's Democratic Republic of Algeria) Order 2004, SI 2004/345 (made under sub-s (3)).
European Communities (Definition of Treaties) (Agreement on Enlargement of the European Economic Area) Order 2004, SI 2004/1499 (made under sub-s (3)).
European Communities (Definition of Treaties) (Stabilisation and Association Agreement between the European Communities and their Member States, and the Republic of Croatia) Order 2004, SI 2004/2037 (made under sub-s (3)).
European Communities (Definition of Treaties) (European Police Office) Order 2004, SI 2004/3331 (made under sub-s (3)).

2 General implementation of Treaties

(1) All such rights, powers, liabilities, obligations and restrictions from time to time created or arising by or under the Treaties, and all such remedies and procedures from time to time provided for by or under the Treaties, as in accordance with the Treaties are without further enactment to be given legal effect or used in the United Kingdom shall be recognised and available in law, and be enforced, allowed and followed accordingly; and the expression "enforceable Community right" and similar expressions shall be read as referring to one to which this subsection applies.

(2) Subject to Schedule 2 to this Act, at any time after its passing Her Majesty may by Order in Council, and any designated Minister or department may by regulations, make provision—

    (a) for the purpose of implementing any Community obligation of the United Kingdom, or enabling any such obligation to be implemented, or of enabling any rights enjoyed or to be enjoyed by the United Kingdom under or by virtue of the Treaties to be exercised; or

    (b) for the purpose of dealing with matters arising out of or related to any such obligation or rights or the coming into force, or the operation from time to time, of subsection (1) above;

and in the exercise of any statutory power or duty, including any power to give directions or to legislate by means of orders, rules, regulations or other subordinate instrument, the person entrusted with the power or duty may have regard to the objects of the Communities and to any such obligation or rights as aforesaid.

In this subsection "designated Minister or department" means such Minister of the Crown or government department as may from time to time be designated by Order in Council in relation to any matter or for any purpose, but subject to such restrictions or conditions (if any) as may be specified by the Order in Council.

(3)   There shall be charged on and issued out of the Consolidated Fund or, if so determined by the Treasury, the National Loans Fund the amounts required to meet any Community obligation to make payments to any of the Communities or member States, or any Community obligation in respect of contributions to the capital or reserves of the European Investment Bank or in respect of loans to the Bank, or to redeem any notes or obligations issued or created in respect of any such Community obligation; and, except as otherwise provided by or under any enactment,—

    (a)   any other expenses incurred under or by virtue of the Treaties or this Act by any Minister of the Crown or government department may be paid out of moneys provided by Parliament; and

    (b)   any sums received under or by virtue of the Treaties or this Act by any Minister of the Crown or government department, save for such sums as may be required for disbursements permitted by any other enactment, shall be paid into the Consolidated Fund or, if so determined by the Treasury, the National Loans Fund.

(4)   The provision that may be made under subsection (2) above includes, subject to Schedule 2 to this Act, any such provision (of any such extent) as might be made by Act of Parliament, and any enactment passed or to be passed, other than one contained in this Part of this Act, shall be construed and have effect subject to the foregoing provisions of this section; but, except as may be provided by any Act passed after this Act, Schedule 2 shall have effect in connection with the powers conferred by this and the following sections of this Act to make Orders in Council and regulations.

(5)   ... and the references in that subsection to a Minister of the Crown or government department and to a statutory power or duty shall include a Minister or department of the Government of Northern Ireland and a power or duty arising under or by virtue of an Act of the Parliament of Northern Ireland.

(6)   A law passed by the legislature of any of the Channel Islands or of the Isle of Man, or a colonial law (within the meaning of the Colonial Laws Validity Act 1865) passed or made for Gibraltar, if expressed to be passed or made in the implementation of the Treaties and of the obligations of the United Kingdom thereunder, shall not be void or inoperative by reason of any inconsistency with or repugnancy to an Act of Parliament, passed or to be passed, that extends to the Island or Gibraltar or any provision having the force and effect of an Act there (but not including this section), nor by reason of its having some operation outside the Island or Gibraltar; and any such Act or provision that extends to the Island or Gibraltar shall be construed and have effect subject to the provisions of any such law.

Initial Commencement
This Act received Royal Assent on 17 October 1972 but did not have practical effect until 1 January 1973 (the date on which the United Kingdom joined the European Communities).

Amendment
Sub-s (5): words omitted repealed by the Northern Ireland Constitution Act 1973, s 41(1), Sch 6, Part I.

Modification
Modified by the Scotland Act 1998, s 125, Sch 8, para 15.
The Northern Ireland Act 1998 makes new provision for the government of Northern Ireland for the purpose of implementing the Belfast Agreement (the agreement reached at multi-party talks on Northern Ireland and set out in Command Paper 3883). As a consequence of that Act, any

reference in this section to the Parliament of Northern Ireland or the Assembly established under the Northern Ireland Assembly Act 1973, s 1, certain office-holders and Ministers, and any legislative act and certain financial dealings thereof, shall, for the period specified, be construed in accordance with Sch 12, paras 1–11 to the 1998 Act.

Transfer of Functions
Functions under this section: certain functions under this section are transferred, in so far as they are exercisable in or as regards Scotland, to the Scottish Ministers, by the Scotland Act 1998 (Transfer of Functions to the Scottish Ministers etc) Order 2005, SI 2005/849, arts 2, 6, Schedule. Functions under this section: by the Scotland Act 1998 (Transfer of Functions to the Scottish Ministers etc) Order 1999, SI 1999/1750, art 3, Sch 2, certain functions under sub-s (2) which were exercisable by a Minister of the Crown are, in so far as they are exercisable in or as regards Scotland, exercisable by the Scottish Ministers acting concurrently with the Minister of the Crown concerned. See also art 7(4) of the 1999 Order.

3   Decisions on, and proof of, Treaties and Community instruments, etc

(1)   For the purposes of all legal proceedings any question as to the meaning or effect of any of the Treaties, or as to the validity, meaning or effect of any Community instrument, shall be treated as a question of law (and, if not referred to the European Court, be for determination as such in accordance with the principles laid down by and any relevant [decision of the European Court or any court attached thereto)].

(2)   Judicial notice shall be taken of the Treaties, of the Official Journal of the Communities and of any decision of, or expression of opinion by, the European Court [or any court attached thereto] on any such question as aforesaid; and the Official Journal shall be admissible as evidence of any instrument or other act thereby communicated of any of the Communities or of any Community institution.

(3)   Evidence of any instrument issued by a Community institution, including any judgment or order of the European Court [or any court attached thereto], or of any document in the custody of a Community institution, or any entry in or extract from such a document, may be given in any legal proceedings by production of a copy certified as a true copy by an official of that institution; and any document purporting to be such a copy shall be received in evidence without proof of the official position or handwriting of the person signing the certificate.

(4)   Evidence of any Community instrument may also be given in any legal proceedings—

  (a)   by production of a copy purporting to be printed by the Queen's Printer;
  (b)   where the instrument is in the custody of a government department (including a department of the Government of Northern Ireland), by production of a copy certified on behalf of the department to be a true copy by an officer of the department generally or specially authorised so to do;

and any document purporting to be such a copy as is mentioned in paragraph (b) above of an instrument in the custody of a department shall be received in evidence without proof of the official position or handwriting of the person signing the certificate, or of his authority to do so, or of the document being in the custody of the department.

(5)   ...

Initial Commencement
This Act received Royal Assent on 17 October 1972 but did not have practical effect until 1 January 1973 (the date on which the United Kingdom joined the European Communities).

Amendment
Sub-ss (1)–(3): words in square brackets substituted or inserted by the European Communities (Amendment) Act 1986, s 2.

Sub-s (5): applies to Scotland only.

Modification
Modified, so as to have effect as if references to a government department include any part of the Scottish Administration, by the Scotland Act 1998, s 125, Sch 8, para 15(4).

See Further
See further, in relation to the application of sub-ss (2)–(5) to the EFTA Court and the EFTA Surveillance Authority: the European Economic Area Act 1993, s 4.

PART II
AMENDMENT OF LAW

4   General provision for repeal and amendment

(1)   The enactments mentioned in Schedule 3 to this Act (being enactments that are superseded or to be superseded by reason of Community obligations and of the provision made by this Act in relation thereto or are not compatible with Community obligations) are hereby repealed, to the extent specified in column 3 of the Schedule, with effect from the entry date or other date mentioned in the Schedule; and in the enactments mentioned in Schedule 4 to this Act there shall, subject to any transitional provision there included, be made the amendments provided for by that Schedule.

(2)   Where in any Part of Schedule 3 to this Act it is provided that repeals made by that Part are to take effect from a date appointed by order, the orders shall be made by statutory instrument, and an order may appoint different dates for the repeal of different provisions to take effect, or for the repeal of the same provision to take effect for different purposes; and an order appointing a date for a repeal to take effect may include transitional and other supplementary provisions arising out of that repeal, including provisions adapting the operation of other enactments included for repeal but not yet repealed by that Schedule, and may amend or revoke any such provisions included in a previous order.

(3)   Where any of the following sections of this Act, or any paragraph of Schedule 4 to this Act, affects or is construed as one with an Act or Part of an Act similar in purpose to provisions having effect only in Northern Ireland, then—

    (a)   unless otherwise provided by Act of the Parliament of Northern Ireland, the Governor of Northern Ireland may by Order in Council make provision corresponding to any made by the section or paragraph, and amend or revoke any provision so made; and

    (b)   ...

(4)   Where Schedule 3 or 4 to this Act provides for the repeal or amendment of an enactment that extends or is capable of being extended to any of the Channel Islands or the Isle of Man, the repeal or amendment shall in like manner extend or be capable of being extended thereto.

Initial Commencement
This Act received Royal Assent on 17 October 1972 but did not have practical effect until 1 January 1973 (the date on which the United Kingdom joined the European Communities).

Amendment
Sub-s (3): para (b) repealed by the Northern Ireland Constitution Act 1973, s 41(1), Sch 6, Part I.

Modification
The Northern Ireland Act 1998 makes new provision for the government of Northern Ireland for the purpose of implementing the Belfast Agreement (the agreement reached at multi-party talks on Northern Ireland and set out in Command Paper 3883). As a consequence of that Act, any reference in this section to the Parliament of Northern Ireland or the Assembly established under

the Northern Ireland Assembly Act 1973, s 1, certain office-holders and Ministers, and any legislative act and certain financial dealings thereof, shall, for the period specified, be construed in accordance with Sch 12, paras 1–11 to the 1998 Act.

Appointed Day
Appointed Day, for the purposes of sub-s (2): 16 August 1982 (for certain purposes), see SI 1982/1048; 1 September 1981 (for certain purposes), see SI 1981/1192; 1 September 1978 (for certain purposes), see SI 1978/1003; 1 January 1978 (for certain purposes), see SI 1977/2028; 1 December 1976 (for certain purposes), see SI 1976/2016; 1 September 1976 (for certain purposes), see SI 1976/1304; 5 May 1976 (for certain purposes), see SI 1976/548; 1 August 1975 (for certain purposes), see SI 1975/1164; 1 January 1974 (for certain purposes), see SI 1973/2176; 1 July 1973 (for certain purposes), see SI 1973/1019; 1 February 1973 (for remaining purposes), see SI 1973/135.

RACE RELATIONS ACT 1976

1976 CHAPTER 74

An Act to make fresh provision with respect to discrimination on racial grounds and relations between people of different racial groups; and to make in the Sex Discrimination Act 1975 amendments for bringing provisions in that Act relating to its administration and enforcement into conformity with the corresponding provisions in this Act

[22nd November 1976]

BE IT ENACTED by the Queen's most Excellent Majesty, by and with the advice and consent of the Lords Spiritual and Temporal, and Commons, in this present Parliament assembled, and by the authority of the same, as follows:–

PART I
DISCRIMINATION TO WHICH ACT APPLIES

1   Racial discrimination

(1)   A person discriminates against another in any circumstances relevant for the purposes of any provision of this Act if—

(a)   on racial grounds he treats that other less favourably than he treats or would treat other persons; or

(b)   he applies to that other a requirement or condition which he applies or would apply equally to persons not of the same racial group as that other but—

(i)   which is such that the proportion of persons of the same racial group as that other who can comply with it is considerably smaller than the proportion of persons not of that racial group who can comply with it; and

(ii)   which he cannot show to be justifiable irrespective of the colour, race, nationality or ethnic or national origins of the person to whom it is applied; and

(iii)   which is to the detriment of that other because he cannot comply with it.

[(1A)   A person also discriminates against another if, in any circumstances relevant for the purposes of any provision referred to in subsection (1B), he applies to that other a provision, criterion or practice which he applies or would apply equally to persons not of the same race or ethnic or national origins as that other, but—

    (a)   which puts or would put persons of the same race or ethnic or national origins as that other at a particular disadvantage when compared with other persons,

    (b)   which puts that other at that disadvantage, and

    (c)   which he cannot show to be a proportionate means of achieving a legitimate aim.

(1B)   The provisions mentioned in subsection (1A) are—

    (a)   Part II;

    (b)   sections 17 to 18D;

    (c)   section 19B, so far as relating to -

        (i)   any form of social security;

        (ii) health care;

        (iii) any other form of social protection; and

        (iv) any form of social advantage;

    which does not fall within section 20;

    (d)   sections 20 to 24;

    (e)   sections 26A and 26B;

    (f)   sections 76 and 76ZA; and

    (g)   Part IV, in its application to the provisions referred to in paragraphs (a) to (f).

(1C)   Where, by virtue of subsection (1A), a person discriminates against another, subsection (1)(b) does not apply to him.]

(2)   It is hereby declared that, for the purposes of this Act, segregating a person from other persons on racial grounds is treating him less favourably than they are treated.

Appointment
Sub-ss (1)(a), (2): Appointment: 13 June 1977: see SI 1977/840, art 3.
Sub-s (1)(b): Appointment (except in relation to discrimination in the field of education): 13 June 1977: see SI 1977/840, arts 3, 4.
Sub-s (1)(b): Appointment (in relation to discrimination in the field of education): 1 September 1977: see SI 1977/840, art 4.

Amendment
Sub-ss (1A)–(1C): inserted by SI 2003/1626, reg 3. Date in force: 19 July 2003: see SI 2003/1626, reg 1(1).

3   Meaning of "racial grounds", "racial group" etc

(1)   In this Act, unless the context otherwise requires—

    "racial grounds" means any of the following grounds, namely colour, race, nationality or ethnic or national origins;

    "racial group" means a group of persons defined by reference to colour, race, nationality or ethnic or national origins, and references to a person's racial group refer to any racial group into which he falls.

(2)   The fact that a racial group comprises two or more distinct racial groups does not prevent it from constituting a particular racial group for the purposes of this Act.

(3)   In this Act—

    (a)   references to discrimination refer to any discrimination falling within section 1 or 2; and

    (b)   references to racial discrimination refer to any discrimination falling within section 1,

and related expressions shall be construed accordingly.

(4)   A comparison of the case of a person of a particular racial group with that of a person not of that group under section 1(1) [or (1A)] must be such that the relevant circumstances in the one case are the same, or not materially different, in the other.

Appointment
Appointment: 13 June 1977: see SI 1977/840, art 3.

Amendment
Sub-s (4): words "or (1A)" in square brackets inserted by SI 2003/1626, reg 4. Date in force: 19 July 2003: see SI 2003/1626, reg 1(1).

PART III
DISCRIMINATION IN OTHER FIELDS

[Public authorities]

[19B   Public authorities]

[(1)   It is unlawful for a public authority in carrying out any functions of the authority to do any act which constitutes discrimination.

[(1A)   It is unlawful for a public authority to subject a person to harassment in the course of carrying out any functions of the authority which consist of the provision of—

(a)   any form of social security;
(b)   healthcare;
(c)   any other form of social protection; or
(d)   any form of social advantage,

which does not fall within section 20.]

(2)   In this section "public authority"—

(a)   includes any person certain of whose functions are functions of a public nature; but
(b)   does not include any person mentioned in subsection (3).

(3)   The persons mentioned in this subsection are—

(a)   either House of Parliament;
(b)   a person exercising functions in connection with proceedings in Parliament;
(c)   the Security Service;
(d)   the Secret Intelligence Service;
(e)   the Government Communications Headquarters; and
(f)   any unit or part of a unit of any of the naval, military or air forces of the Crown which is for the time being required by the Secretary of State to assist the Government Communications Headquarters in carrying out its functions.

(4)   In relation to a particular act, a person is not a public authority by virtue only of subsection (2)(a) if the nature of the act is private.

(5)   This section is subject to sections 19C to 19F.

(6)   Nothing in this section makes unlawful any act of discrimination [or harassment] which—

(a)   is made unlawful by virtue of any other provision of this Act; or
(b)   would be so made but for any provision made by or under this Act.]

Amendment
Section heading: words omitted repealed by SI 2003/1626, reg 20(1). Date in force: 19 July 2003: see SI 2003/1626, reg 1(1).

Inserted by the Race Relations (Amendment) Act 2000, s 1. Date in force: 2 April 2001: see SI 2001/566, art 2(1).
Sub-s (1A): inserted by SI 2003/1626, reg 20(2)(a). Date in force: 19 July 2003: see SI 2003/1626, reg 1(1).
Sub-s (6): words "or harassment" in square brackets inserted by SI 2003/1626, reg 20(2)(b). Date in force: 19 July 2003: see SI 2003/1626, reg 1(1).

[19C   Exceptions or further exceptions from section 19B for judicial and legislative acts etc]

[(1)   Section 19B does not apply to—

(a)   any judicial act (whether done by a court, tribunal or other person); or
(b)   any act done on the instructions, or on behalf, of a person acting in a judicial capacity.

(2)   Section 19B does not apply to any act of, or relating to, making, confirming or approving any enactment or Order in Council or any instrument made by a Minister of the Crown under an enactment.

(3)   Section 19B does not apply to any act of, or relating to, making or approving arrangements, or imposing requirements or conditions, of a kind [excepted by] section 41.

(4)   Section 19B does not apply to any act of, or relating to, imposing a requirement, or giving an express authorisation, of a kind mentioned in section 19D(3) in relation to the carrying out of [immigration functions].

(5)   In this section—

"[immigration functions]" has the meaning given in section 19D; and
"Minister of the Crown" includes the National Assembly for Wales and a member of the Scottish Executive.]

Amendment
Inserted by the Race Relations (Amendment) Act 2000, s 1. Date in force: 2 April 2001: see SI 2001/566, art 2(1).
Sub-s (3): words "excepted by" in square brackets substituted by SI 2003/1626, reg 21. Date in force: 19 July 2003: see SI 2003/1626, reg 1(1).
Sub-s (4): words "immigration functions" in square brackets substituted by SI 2003/1016, art 3, Schedule, para 2. Date in force: 4 April 2003: see SI 2003/1016, art 2(2).
Sub-s (5): words "immigration functions" in square brackets substituted by SI 2003/1016, art 3, Schedule, para 2. Date in force: 4 April 2003: see SI 2003/1016, art 2(2).

[19D   Exception from section 19B for certain acts in immigration and nationality cases]

[(1)   Section 19B does not make it unlawful for a relevant person to discriminate against another person on grounds of nationality or ethnic or national origins in carrying out [immigration functions].

(2)   For the purposes of subsection (1), "relevant person" means—

(a)   a Minister of the Crown acting personally; or
(b)   any other person acting in accordance with a relevant authorisation.

(3)   In subsection (2), "relevant authorisation" means a requirement imposed or express authorisation given—

(a)   with respect to a particular case or class of case, by a Minister of the Crown acting personally;
(b)   with respect to a particular class of case—
      (i)   by any of the enactments mentioned in subsection (5); or

(ii) by any instrument made under or by virtue of any of those enactments.

[(4)   In subsection (1) "immigration functions" means functions exercisable by virtue of any of the enactments mentioned in subsection (5).

(5)   Those enactments are—

(a)   the Immigration Acts [(within the meaning of section 44 of the Asylum and Immigration (Treatment of Claimants, etc) Act 2004)] excluding sections 28A to 28K of the Immigration Act 1971 (c 77) so far as they relate to offences under Part III of that Act [and excluding section 14 of the Asylum and Immigration (Treatment of Claimants, etc) Act 2004];

(b)   the Special Immigration Appeals Commission Act 1997 (c 68);

(c)   provision made under section 2(2) of the European Communities Act 1972 (c 68) which relates to immigration or asylum; and

(d)   any provision of Community law which relates to immigration or asylum.]]

Amendment

Inserted by the Race Relations (Amendment) Act 2000, s 1. Date in force (for the purpose of the imposition of requirements or giving of express authorisations by a Minister of the Crown acting personally in accordance with sub-s (3) above): 26 March 2001: see SI 2001/566, art 2(2). Date in force (for remaining purposes): 2 April 2001: see SI 2001/566, art 2(1).

Sub-s (1): words "immigration functions" in square brackets substituted by the Nationality, Immigration and Asylum Act 2002, s 6(1), (2). Date in force: 7 November 2002: see the Nationality, Immigration and Asylum Act 2002, s 162(2)(a).

Sub-ss (4), (5): substituted by the Nationality, Immigration and Asylum Act 2002, s 6(1), (3). Date in force: 7 November 2002: see the Nationality, Immigration and Asylum Act 2002, s 162(2)(a).

Sub-s (5): in para (a) words "(within the meaning of section 44 of the Asylum and Immigration (Treatment of Claimants, etc) Act 2004)" in square brackets substituted by the Asylum and Immigration (Treatment of Claimants, etc) Act 2004, s 14(4)(a). Date in force: 1 December 2004: see SI 2004/2999, art 2, Schedule.

Sub-s (5): in para (a) words "and excluding section 14 of the Asylum and Immigration (Treatment of Claimants, etc) Act 2004" in square brackets inserted by the Asylum and Immigration (Treatment of Claimants, etc) Act 2004, s 14(4)(b). Date in force: 1 December 2004: see SI 2004/2999, art 2, Schedule.

[19E   Monitoring of exception in relation to immigration and nationality cases]

[(1)   The Secretary of State shall appoint a person who is not a member of his staff to act as a monitor.

(2)   Before appointing any such person, the Secretary of State shall consult the Commission.

(3)   The person so appointed shall monitor, in such manner as the Secretary of State may determine—

(a)   the likely effect on the operation of the exception in section 19D of any relevant authorisation relating to the carrying out of [immigration functions] which has been given by a Minister of the Crown acting personally; and

(b)   the operation of that exception in relation to acts which have been done by a person acting in accordance with such an authorisation.

(4)   The monitor shall make an annual report on the discharge of his functions to the Secretary of State.

(5)   The Secretary of State shall lay a copy of any report made to him under subsection (4) before each House of Parliament.

(6)   The Secretary of State shall pay to the monitor such fees and allowances (if any) as he may determine.

(7)   ...]

Amendment
Inserted by the Race Relations (Amendment) Act 2000, s 1. Date in force: 2 April 2001: see SI 2001/566, art 2(1).
Sub-s (3): in para (a) words "immigration functions" in square brackets substituted by the Nationality, Immigration and Asylum Act 2002, s 6(4)(a). Date in force: 7 November 2002: see the Nationality, Immigration and Asylum Act 2002, s 162(2)(a).
Sub-s (7): repealed by the Nationality, Immigration and Asylum Act 2002, ss 6(4)(b), 161, Sch 9. Date in force: 7 November 2002: see the Nationality, Immigration and Asylum Act 2002, s 162(2)(a).

PART X
SUPPLEMENTAL

[71   Specified authorities: general statutory duty]

[(1)   Every body or other person specified in Schedule 1A or of a description falling within that Schedule shall, in carrying out its functions, have due regard to the need—

(a)   to eliminate unlawful racial discrimination; and
(b)   to promote equality of opportunity and good relations between persons of different racial groups.

(2)   The Secretary of State may by order impose, on such persons falling within Schedule 1A as he considers appropriate, such duties as he considers appropriate for the purpose of ensuring the better performance by those persons of their duties under subsection (1).

(3)   An order under subsection (2)—

(a)   may be made in relation to a particular person falling within Schedule 1A, any description of persons falling within that Schedule or every person falling within that Schedule;
(b)   may make different provision for different purposes.

(4)   Before making an order under subsection (2), the Secretary of State shall consult the Commission.

(5)   The Secretary of State may by order amend Schedule 1A; but no such order may extend the application of this section unless the Secretary of State considers that the extension relates to a person who exercises functions of a public nature.

(6)   An order under subsection (2) or (5) may contain such incidental, supplementary or consequential provision as the Secretary of State considers appropriate (including provision amending or repealing provision made by or under this Act or any other enactment).

(7)   This section is subject to section 71A and 71B and is without prejudice to the obligation of any person to comply with any other provision of this Act.]

Amendment
Substituted, together with ss 71A–71E, for this section as originally enacted, by the Race Relations (Amendment) Act 2000, s 2(1). Date in force: 2 April 2001: see SI 2001/566, art 2(1).

CHILDREN ACT 1989

1989 CHAPTER 41

An Act to reform the law relating to children; to provide for local authority services for children in need and others; to amend the law with respect to children's homes, community homes, voluntary homes and voluntary organisations; to make provision with respect to fostering, child minding and day care for young children and adoption; and for connected purposes

[16th November 1989]

BE IT ENACTED by the Queen's most Excellent Majesty, by and with the advice and consent of the Lords Spiritual and Temporal, and Commons, in this present Parliament assembled, and by the authority of the same, as follows:-

PART III

LOCAL AUTHORITY SUPPORT FOR CHILDREN AND FAMILIES

Provision of services for children and their families

17   Provision of services for children in need, their families and others

(1)   It shall be the general duty of every local authority (in addition to the other duties imposed on them by this Part)—

(a)   to safeguard and promote the welfare of children within their area who are in need; and

(b)   so far as is consistent with that duty, to promote the upbringing of such children by their families,

by providing a range and level of services appropriate to those children's needs.

(2)   For the purpose principally of facilitating the discharge of their general duty under this section, every local authority shall have the specific duties and powers set out in Part I of Schedule 2.

(3)   Any service provided by an authority in the exercise of functions conferred on them by this section may be provided for the family of a particular child in need or for any member of his family, if it is provided with a view to safeguarding or promoting the child's welfare.

(4)   The Secretary of State may by order amend any provision of Part I of Schedule 2 or add any further duty or power to those for the time being mentioned there.

[(4A)   Before determining what (if any) services to provide for a particular child in need in the exercise of functions conferred on them by this section, a local authority shall, so far as is reasonably practicable and consistent with the child's welfare—

(a)   ascertain the child's wishes and feelings regarding the provision of those services; and

(b)   give due consideration (having regard to his age and understanding) to such wishes and feelings of the child as they have been able to ascertain.]

(5)   Every local authority—

(a)   shall facilitate the provision by others (including in particular voluntary organisations) of services which the authority have power to provide by virtue of this section, or section 18, 20, [23, 23B to 23D, 24A or 24B]; and

(b)   may make such arrangements as they see fit for any person to act on their behalf in the provision of any such service.

(6)   The services provided by a local authority in the exercise of functions conferred on them by this section may include [providing accommodation and] giving assistance in kind or, in exceptional circumstances, in cash.

(7)   Assistance may be unconditional or subject to conditions as to the repayment of the assistance or of its value (in whole or in part).

(8)   Before giving any assistance or imposing any conditions, a local authority shall have regard to the means of the child concerned and of each of his parents.

(9)   No person shall be liable to make any repayment of assistance or of its value at any time when he is in receipt of income support [under] [Part VII of the Social Security Contributions and Benefits Act 1992][, of any element of child tax credit other than the family element, of working tax credit] [or of an income-based jobseeker's allowance].

(10)   For the purposes of this Part a child shall be taken to be in need if—

(a)   he is unlikely to achieve or maintain, or to have the opportunity of achieving or maintaining, a reasonable standard of health or development without the provision for him of services by a local authority under this Part;
(b)   his health or development is likely to be significantly impaired, or further impaired, without the provision for him of such services; or
(c)   he is disabled,

and "family", in relation to such a child, includes any person who has parental responsibility for the child and any other person with whom he has been living.

(11)   For the purposes of this Part, a child is disabled if he is blind, deaf or dumb or suffers from mental disorder of any kind or is substantially and permanently handicapped by illness, injury or congenital deformity or such other disability as may be prescribed; and in this Part—

"development" means physical, intellectual, emotional, social or behavioural development; and

"health" means physical or mental health.

[(12)   The Treasury may by regulations prescribe circumstances in which a person is to be treated for the purposes of this Part (or for such of those purposes as are prescribed) as in receipt of any element of child tax credit other than the family element or of working tax credit.]

Appointment
Appointment: 14 October 1991: see SI 1991/828, art 3(2).

Amendment
Sub-s (4A): inserted by the Children Act 2004, s 53(1). Date in force (in relation to England): 1 March 2005: see SI 2005/394, art 2(1)(g). Date in force (in relation to Wales): to be appointed: see the Children Act 2004, s 67(7)(e).
Sub-s (5): in para (a) words "23, 23B to 23D, 24A or 24B" in square brackets substituted by the Children (Leaving Care) Act 2000, s 7(1), (2). Date in force (in relation to England): 1 October 2001: see SI 2001/2878, art 2. Date in force (in relation to Wales): 1 October 2001: see SI 2001/2191, art 2.
Sub-s (6): words "providing accommodation and" in square brackets inserted by the Adoption and Children Act 2002, s 116(1). Date in force: this amendment came into force on 7 November 2002 (date of Royal Assent of the Adoption and Children Act 2002) in the absence of any specific commencement provision.

Sub-s (9): word "under" in square brackets substituted by the Tax Credits Act 2002, s 47, Sch 3, paras 15, 16(1), (2)(a). Date in force: 6 April 2003: see SI 2003/962, art 2(1), (3)(b), (d)(iii); for savings and transitional provisions see arts 3–5 thereof.

Sub-s (9): words "Part VII of the Social Security Contributions and Benefits Act 1992" in square brackets substituted by the Social Security (Consequential Provisions) Act 1992, s 4, Sch 2, para 108(a).

Sub-s (9): words from ", of any element" to "working tax credit" in square brackets inserted by the Tax Credits Act 2002, s 47, Sch 3, paras 15, 16(1), (2)(b). Date in force: 6 April 2003: see SI 2003/962, art 2(1), (3)(b), (d)(iii); for savings and transitional provisions see arts 3–5 thereof.

Sub-s (9): words "or of an income-based jobseeker's allowance" in square brackets inserted by the Jobseekers Act 1995, s 41(4), Sch 2, para 19(2).

Sub-s (12): inserted by the Tax Credits Act 2002, s 47, Sch 3, paras 15, 16(1), (3). Date in force: 6 April 2003: see SI 2003/962, art 2(1), (3)(b), (d)(iii); for savings and transitional provisions see arts 3–5 thereof.

Transfer of Functions
Functions of the Secretary of State, so far as exercisable in relation to Wales, transferred to the National Assembly for Wales, by the National Assembly for Wales (Transfer of Functions) Order 1999, SI 1999/672, art 2, Sch 1.

Subordinate Legislation
Children Act 1989 (Amendment) (Children's Services Planning) Order 1996, SI 1996/785 (made under sub-s (4)).
Children Act 1989, Section 17(12) Regulations 2003, SI 2003/2077 (made under sub-s (2)).

Extent
This section does not extend to Scotland: see s 108(11).

Provision of accommodation for children

20   Provision of accommodation for children: general

(1)   Every local authority shall provide accommodation for any child in need within their area who appears to them to require accommodation as a result of—

   (a)   there being no person who has parental responsibility for him;
   (b)   his being lost or having been abandoned; or
   (c)   the person who has been caring for him being prevented (whether or not permanently, and for whatever reason) from providing him with suitable accommodation or care.

(2)   Where a local authority provide accommodation under subsection (1) for a child who is ordinarily resident in the area of another local authority, that other local authority may take over the provision of accommodation for the child within—

   (a)   three months of being notified in writing that the child is being provided with accommodation; or
   (b)   such other longer period as may be prescribed.

(3)   Every local authority shall provide accommodation for any child in need within their area who has reached the age of sixteen and whose welfare the authority consider is likely to be seriously prejudiced if they do not provide him with accommodation.

(4)   A local authority may provide accommodation for any child within their area (even though a person who has parental responsibility for him is able to provide him with accommodation) if they consider that to do so would safeguard or promote the child's welfare.

(5)   A local authority may provide accommodation for any person who has reached the age of sixteen but is under twenty-one in any community home which takes children who have reached the age of sixteen if they consider that to do so would safeguard or promote his welfare.

Appendix 1   Legislation and materials

(6)   Before providing accommodation under this section, a local authority shall, so far as is reasonably practicable and consistent with the child's welfare—

   (a)   ascertain the child's wishes [and feelings] regarding the provision of accommodation; and

   (b)   give due consideration (having regard to his age and understanding) to such wishes [and feelings] of the child as they have been able to ascertain.

(7)   A local authority may not provide accommodation under this section for any child if any person who—

   (a)   has parental responsibility for him; and

   (b)   is willing and able to—

     (i)   provide accommodation for him; or

     (ii)   arrange for accommodation to be provided for him,

objects.

(8)   Any person who has parental responsibility for a child may at any time remove the child from accommodation provided by or on behalf of the local authority under this section.

(9)   Subsections (7) and (8) do not apply while any person—

   (a)   in whose favour a residence order is in force with respect to the child; *or*

   [(aa) who is a special guardian of the child; or]

   (b)   who has care of the child by virtue of an order made in the exercise of the High Court's inherent jurisdiction with respect to children,

agrees to the child being looked after in accommodation provided by or on behalf of the local authority.

(10)   Where there is more than one such person as is mentioned in subsection (9), all of them must agree.

(11)   Subsections (7) and (8) do not apply where a child who has reached the age of sixteen agrees to being provided with accommodation under this section.

Appointment
Appointment: 14 October 1991: see SI 1991/828, art 3(2).

Amendment
Sub-s (6): in paras (a), (b) words "and feelings" in square brackets inserted by the Children Act 2004, s 53(2). Date in force (in relation to England): 1 March 2005: see SI 2005/394, art 2(1)(g). Date in force (in relation to Wales): to be appointed: see the Children Act 2004, s 67(7)(e).
Sub-s (9): in para (a) word "or" in italics repealed by the Adoption and Children Act 2002, s 139(1), (3), Sch 3, paras 54, 59, Sch 5. Date in force: to be appointed: see the Adoption and Children Act 2002, s 148(1), (2).
Sub-s (9): para (aa) inserted by the Adoption and Children Act 2002, s 139(1), Sch 3, paras 54, 59. Date in force: to be appointed: see the Adoption and Children Act 2002, s 148(1), (2).

Extent
This section does not extend to Scotland: see s 108(11).

Duties of local authorities in relation to children looked after by them

22   General duty of local authority in relation to children looked after by them

(1)   In this Act, any reference to a child who is looked after by a local authority is a reference to a child who is—

   (a)   in their care; or

(b) provided with accommodation by the authority in the exercise of any functions (in particular those under this Act) which [are social services functions within the meaning of] the Local Authority Social Services Act 1970[, apart from functions under sections [17], 23B and 24B].

(2) In subsection (1) "accommodation" means accommodation which is provided for a continuous period of more than 24 hours.

(3) It shall be the duty of a local authority looking after any child—

(a) to safeguard and promote his welfare; and
(b) to make such use of services available for children cared for by their own parents as appears to the authority reasonable in his case.

[(3A) The duty of a local authority under subsection (3)(a) to safeguard and promote the welfare of a child looked after by them includes in particular a duty to promote the child's educational achievement.]

(4) Before making any decision with respect to a child whom they are looking after, or proposing to look after, a local authority shall, so far as is reasonably practicable, ascertain the wishes and feelings of—

(a) the child;
(b) his parents;
(c) any person who is not a parent of his but who has parental responsibility for him; and
(d) any other person whose wishes and feelings the authority consider to be relevant,

regarding the matter to be decided.

(5) In making any such decision a local authority shall give due consideration—

(a) having regard to his age and understanding, to such wishes and feelings of the child as they have been able to ascertain;
(b) to such wishes and feelings of any person mentioned in subsection (4)(b) to (d) as they have been able to ascertain; and
(c) to the child's religious persuasion, racial origin and cultural and linguistic background.

(6) If it appears to a local authority that it is necessary, for the purpose of protecting members of the public from serious injury, to exercise their powers with respect to a child whom they are looking after in a manner which may not be consistent with their duties under this section, they may do so.

(7) If the Secretary of State considers it necessary, for the purpose of protecting members of the public from serious injury, to give directions to a local authority with respect to the exercise of their powers with respect to a child whom they are looking after, he may give such directions to the authority.

(8) Where any such directions are given to an authority they shall comply with them even though doing so is inconsistent with their duties under this section.

Appointment
Appointment: 14 October 1991: see SI 1991/828, art 3(2).

Amendment
Sub-s (1): in para (b) words "are social services functions within the meaning of" in square brackets substituted by the Local Government Act 2000, s 107, Sch 5, para 19. Date in force (in relation to England): 26 October 2000: see SI 2000/2849, art 2(f). Date in force (in relation to

Wales): 28 July 2001 (unless the National Assembly for Wales by order provides for this amendment to come into force before that date): see the Local Government Act 2000, s 108(4), (6)(b).

Sub-s (1): in para (b) words ", apart from functions under sections 23B and 24B" in square brackets inserted by the Children (Leaving Care) Act 2000, s 2(1), (2). Date in force (in relation to England): 1 October 2001: see SI 2001/2878, art 2. Date in force (in relation to Wales): 1 October 2001: see SI 2001/2191, art 2.

Sub-s (1): in para (b) reference to "17" in square brackets inserted by the Adoption and Children Act 2002, s 116(2). Date in force: this amendment came into force on 7 November 2002 (date of Royal Assent of the Adoption and Children Act 2002) in the absence of any specific commencement provision.

Sub-s (3A): inserted by the Children Act 2004, s 52. Date in force (in relation to England): 1 July 2005: see SI 2005/394, art 2(3)(b). Date in force (in relation to Wales): to be appointed: see the Children Act 2004, s 67(7)(e).

Modification
Sub-ss (4)(b), (c), (5)(b): modified, in relation to England, in so far as relating to adoption, by the Adoption Agencies Regulations 2005, SI 2005/389, reg 45(1), (2)(a)–(c).
Sub-ss (4)(b), (c), (5)(b): modified, in relation to Wales, in so far as relating to adoption, by the Adoption Agencies (Wales) Regulations 2005, SI 2005/1313, reg 46(1), (2)(a)–(c).

Transfer of Functions
Functions of the Secretary of State, so far as exercisable in relation to Wales, transferred to the National Assembly for Wales, by the National Assembly for Wales (Transfer of Functions) Order 1999, SI 1999/672, art 2, Sch 1.

Extent
This section does not extend to Scotland: see s 108(11).

HUMAN RIGHTS ACT 1998

1998 CHAPTER 42

An Act to give further effect to rights and freedoms guaranteed under the European Convention on Human Rights; to make provision with respect to holders of certain judicial offices who become judges of the European Court of Human Rights; and for connected purposes.

[9th November 1998]

BE IT ENACTED by the Queen's most Excellent Majesty, by and with the advice and consent of the Lords Spiritual and Temporal, and Commons, in this present Parliament assembled, and by the authority of the same, as follows:—

Introduction

1   The Convention Rights

(1)   In this Act "the Convention rights" means the rights and fundamental freedoms set out in—

(a)   Articles 2 to 12 and 14 of the Convention,
(b)   Articles 1 to 3 of the First Protocol, and
(c)   [Article 1 of the Thirteenth Protocol],

as read with Articles 16 to 18 of the Convention.

(2) Those Articles are to have effect for the purposes of this Act subject to any designated derogation or reservation (as to which see sections 14 and 15).

(3) The Articles are set out in Schedule 1.

(4) The [Secretary of State] may by order make such amendments to this Act as he considers appropriate to reflect the effect, in relation to the United Kingdom, of a protocol.

(5) In subsection (4) "protocol" means a protocol to the Convention—

    (a) which the United Kingdom has ratified; or
    (b) which the United Kingdom has signed with a view to ratification.

(6) No amendment may be made by an order under subsection (4) so as to come into force before the protocol concerned is in force in relation to the United Kingdom.

Appointment
Appointment: 2 October 2000: see SI 2000/1851, art 2.

Amendment
Sub-s (1): in para (c) words "Article 1 of the Thirteenth Protocol" in square brackets substituted by SI 2004/1574, art 2(1). Date in force: 22 June 2004: see SI 2004/1574, art 1.
Sub-s (4): words "Secretary of State" in square brackets substituted by SI 2003/1887, art 9, Sch 2, para 10(1). Date in force: 19 August 2003: see SI 2003/1887, art 1(2).

Subordinate Legislation
Human Rights Act 1998 (Amendment) Order 2004, SI 2004/1574 (made under sub-s (4)).

2 Interpretation of Convention rights

(1) A court or tribunal determining a question which has arisen in connection with a Convention right must take into account any—

    (a) judgment, decision, declaration or advisory opinion of the European Court of Human Rights,
    (b) opinion of the Commission given in a report adopted under Article 31 of the Convention,
    (c) decision of the Commission in connection with Article 26 or 27(2) of the Convention, or
    (d) decision of the Committee of Ministers taken under Article 46 of the Convention,

whenever made or given, so far as, in the opinion of the court or tribunal, it is relevant to the proceedings in which that question has arisen.

(2) Evidence of any judgment, decision, declaration or opinion of which account may have to be taken under this section is to be given in proceedings before any court or tribunal in such manner as may be provided by rules.

(3) In this section "rules" means rules of court or, in the case of proceedings before a tribunal, rules made for the purposes of this section—

    (a) by ... the Secretary of State, in relation to any proceedings outside Scotland;
    (b) by the Secretary of State, in relation to proceedings in Scotland; or
    (c) by a Northern Ireland department, in relation to proceedings before a tribunal in Northern Ireland—
        (i) which deals with transferred matters; and
        (ii) for which no rules made under paragraph (a) are in force.

Appointment

Appointment: 2 October 2000: see SI 2000/1851, art 2.

Amendment

Sub-s (3): in para (a) words omitted repealed by SI 2003/1887, art 9, Sch 2, para 10(2). Date in force: 19 August 2003: see SI 2003/1887, art 1(2).

Legislation

3   Interpretation of legislation

(1)   So far as it is possible to do so, primary legislation and subordinate legislation must be read and given effect in a way which is compatible with the Convention rights.

(2)   This section—

- (a)   applies to primary legislation and subordinate legislation whenever enacted;
- (b)   does not affect the validity, continuing operation or enforcement of any incompatible primary legislation; and
- (c)   does not affect the validity, continuing operation or enforcement of any incompatible subordinate legislation if (disregarding any possibility of revocation) primary legislation prevents removal of the incompatibility.

Appointment

Appointment: 2 October 2000: see SI 2000/1851, art 2.

4   Declaration of incompatibility

(1)   Subsection (2) applies in any proceedings in which a court determines whether a provision of primary legislation is compatible with a Convention right.

(2)   If the court is satisfied that the provision is incompatible with a Convention right, it may make a declaration of that incompatibility.

(3)   Subsection (4) applies in any proceedings in which a court determines whether a provision of subordinate legislation, made in the exercise of a power conferred by primary legislation, is compatible with a Convention right.

(4)   If the court is satisfied—

- (a)   that the provision is incompatible with a Convention right, and
- (b)   that (disregarding any possibility of revocation) the primary legislation concerned prevents removal of the incompatibility,

it may make a declaration of that incompatibility.

(5)   In this section "court" means—

- (a)   the House of Lords;
- (b)   the Judicial Committee of the Privy Council;
- (c)   the Courts-Martial Appeal Court;
- (d)   in Scotland, the High Court of Justiciary sitting otherwise than as a trial court or the Court of Session;
- (e)   in England and Wales or Northern Ireland, the High Court or the Court of Appeal;
- [(f)   the Court of Protection, in any matter being dealt with by the President of the Family Division, the Vice-Chancellor or a puisne judge of the High Court].

(6)   A declaration under this section ("a declaration of incompatibility")—

- (a)   does not affect the validity, continuing operation or enforcement of the provision in respect of which it is given; and
- (b)   is not binding on the parties to the proceedings in which it is made.

Appointment
Appointment: 2 October 2000: see SI 2000/1851, art 2.

Amendment
Sub-s (5): para (f) inserted by the Mental Capacity Act 2005, s 67(1), Sch 6, para 43. Date in force: to be appointed: see the Mental Capacity Act 2005, s 68(1).

5 Right of Crown to intervene

(1) Where a court is considering whether to make a declaration of incompatibility, the Crown is entitled to notice in accordance with rules of court.

(2) In any case to which subsection (1) applies—

(a) a Minister of the Crown (or a person nominated by him),
(b) a member of the Scottish Executive,
(c) a Northern Ireland Minister,
(d) a Northern Ireland department,

is entitled, on giving notice in accordance with rules of court, to be joined as a party to the proceedings.

(3) Notice under subsection (2) may be given at any time during the proceedings.

(4) A person who has been made a party to criminal proceedings (other than in Scotland) as the result of a notice under subsection (2) may, with leave, appeal to the House of Lords against any declaration of incompatibility made in the proceedings.

(5) In subsection (4)—

"criminal proceedings" includes all proceedings before the Courts-Martial Appeal Court; and
"leave" means leave granted by the court making the declaration of incompatibility or by the House of Lords.

Appointment
Appointment: 2 October 2000: see SI 2000/1851, art 2.

Transfer of Functions
The function under sub-s (2) shall be exercisable by the National Assembly for Wales concurrently with any Minister of the Crown by whom it is exercisable, in so far as it relates to any proceedings in which a court is considering whether to make a declaration of incompatibility within the meaning of s 4 of this Act, in respect of subordinate legislation made by the National Assembly, and subordinate legislation made, in relation to Wales, by a Minister of the Crown in the exercise of a function which is exercisable by the National Assembly: see the National Assembly for Wales (Transfer of Functions) (No 2) Order 2000, SI 2000/1830, art 2.

Public authorities

6 Acts of public authorities

(1) It is unlawful for a public authority to act in a way which is incompatible with a Convention right.

(2) Subsection (1) does not apply to an act if—

(a) as the result of one or more provisions of primary legislation, the authority could not have acted differently; or
(b) in the case of one or more provisions of, or made under, primary legislation which cannot be read or given effect in a way which is compatible with the Convention rights, the authority was acting so as to give effect to or enforce those provisions.

(3)   In this section "public authority" includes—

(a)   a court or tribunal, and
(b)   any person certain of whose functions are functions of a public nature,

but does not include either House of Parliament or a person exercising functions in connection with proceedings in Parliament.

(4)   In subsection (3) "Parliament" does not include the House of Lords in its judicial capacity.

(5)   In relation to a particular act, a person is not a public authority by virtue only of subsection (3)(b) if the nature of the act is private.

(6)   "An act" includes a failure to act but does not include a failure to—

(a)   introduce in, or lay before, Parliament a proposal for legislation; or
(b)   make any primary legislation or remedial order.

Appointment
Appointment: 2 October 2000: see SI 2000/1851, art 2.

7   Proceedings

(1)   A person who claims that a public authority has acted (or proposes to act) in a way which is made unlawful by section 6(1) may—

(a)   bring proceedings against the authority under this Act in the appropriate court or tribunal, or
(b)   rely on the Convention right or rights concerned in any legal proceedings,

but only if he is (or would be) a victim of the unlawful act.

(2)   In subsection (1)(a) "appropriate court or tribunal" means such court or tribunal as may be determined in accordance with rules; and proceedings against an authority include a counterclaim or similar proceeding.

(3)   If the proceedings are brought on an application for judicial review, the applicant is to be taken to have a sufficient interest in relation to the unlawful act only if he is, or would be, a victim of that act.

(4)   If the proceedings are made by way of a petition for judicial review in Scotland, the applicant shall be taken to have title and interest to sue in relation to the unlawful act only if he is, or would be, a victim of that act.

(5)   Proceedings under subsection (1)(a) must be brought before the end of—

(a)   the period of one year beginning with the date on which the act complained of took place; or
(b)   such longer period as the court or tribunal considers equitable having regard to all the circumstances,

but that is subject to any rule imposing a stricter time limit in relation to the procedure in question.

(6)   In subsection (1)(b) "legal proceedings" includes—

(a)   proceedings brought by or at the instigation of a public authority; and
(b)   an appeal against the decision of a court or tribunal.

(7)   For the purposes of this section, a person is a victim of an unlawful act only if he would be a victim for the purposes of Article 34 of the Convention if proceedings were brought in the European Court of Human Rights in respect of that act.

(8)   Nothing in this Act creates a criminal offence.

(9) In this section "rules" means—

    (a) in relation to proceedings before a court or tribunal outside Scotland, rules made by ... the Secretary of State for the purposes of this section or rules of court,

    (b) in relation to proceedings before a court or tribunal in Scotland, rules made by the Secretary of State for those purposes,

    (c) in relation to proceedings before a tribunal in Northern Ireland—
        (i) which deals with transferred matters; and
        (ii) for which no rules made under paragraph (a) are in force,
    rules made by a Northern Ireland department for those purposes,

and includes provision made by order under section 1 of the Courts and Legal Services Act 1990.

(10) In making rules, regard must be had to section 9.

(11) The Minister who has power to make rules in relation to a particular tribunal may, to the extent he considers it necessary to ensure that the tribunal can provide an appropriate remedy in relation to an act (or proposed act) of a public authority which is (or would be) unlawful as a result of section 6(1), by order add to—

    (a) the relief or remedies which the tribunal may grant; or
    (b) the grounds on which it may grant any of them.

(12) An order made under subsection (11) may contain such incidental, supplemental, consequential or transitional provision as the Minister making it considers appropriate.

(13) "The Minister" includes the Northern Ireland department concerned.

Appointment
Appointment: 2 October 2000: see SI 2000/1851, art 2.

Amendment
Sub-s (9): in para (a) words omitted repealed by SI 2003/1887, art 9, Sch 2, para 10(2). Date in force: 19 August 2003: see SI 2003/1887, art 1(2).

8 Judicial remedies

(1) In relation to any act (or proposed act) of a public authority which the court finds is (or would be) unlawful, it may grant such relief or remedy, or make such order, within its powers as it considers just and appropriate.

(2) But damages may be awarded only by a court which has power to award damages, or to order the payment of compensation, in civil proceedings.

(3) No award of damages is to be made unless, taking account of all the circumstances of the case, including—

    (a) any other relief or remedy granted, or order made, in relation to the act in question (by that or any other court), and
    (b) the consequences of any decision (of that or any other court) in respect of that act,

the court is satisfied that the award is necessary to afford just satisfaction to the person in whose favour it is made.

(4) In determining—

    (a) whether to award damages, or
    (b) the amount of an award,

the court must take into account the principles applied by the European Court of Human Rights in relation to the award of compensation under Article 41 of the Convention.

(5)   A public authority against which damages are awarded is to be treated—

(a)   in Scotland, for the purposes of section 3 of the Law Reform (Miscellaneous Provisions) (Scotland) Act 1940 as if the award were made in an action of damages in which the authority has been found liable in respect of loss or damage to the person to whom the award is made;

(b)   for the purposes of the Civil Liability (Contribution) Act 1978 as liable in respect of damage suffered by the person to whom the award is made.

(6)   In this section—

"court" includes a tribunal;
"damages" means damages for an unlawful act of a public authority; and
"unlawful" means unlawful under section 6(1).

Appointment
Appointment: 2 October 2000: see SI 2000/1851, art 2.

9   Judicial acts

(1)   Proceedings under section 7(1)(a) in respect of a judicial act may be brought only—

(a)   by exercising a right of appeal;
(b)   on an application (in Scotland a petition) for judicial review; or
(c)   in such other forum as may be prescribed by rules.

(2)   That does not affect any rule of law which prevents a court from being the subject of judicial review.

(3)   In proceedings under this Act in respect of a judicial act done in good faith, damages may not be awarded otherwise than to compensate a person to the extent required by Article 5(5) of the Convention.

(4)   An award of damages permitted by subsection (3) is to be made against the Crown; but no award may be made unless the appropriate person, if not a party to the proceedings, is joined.

(5)   In this section—

"appropriate person" means the Minister responsible for the court concerned, or a person or government department nominated by him;
"court" includes a tribunal;
"judge" includes a member of a tribunal, a justice of the peace [(or, in Northern Ireland, a lay magistrate)] and a clerk or other officer entitled to exercise the jurisdiction of a court;
"judicial act" means a judicial act of a court and includes an act done on the instructions, or on behalf, of a judge; and
"rules" has the same meaning as in section 7(9).

Appointment
Appointment: 2 October 2000: see SI 2000/1851, art 2.

Amendment
Sub-s (5): in definition "judge" words "(or, in Northern Ireland, a lay magistrate)" in square brackets inserted by the Justice (Northern Ireland) Act 2002, s 10(6), Sch 4, para 39. Date in force: 1 April 2005: see the Justice (Northern Ireland) Act 2002 (Commencement No 8) Order 2005, SR 2005/109, art 2, Schedule.

Remedial action

10   Power to take remedial action

(1)   This section applies if—

(a)   a provision of legislation has been declared under section 4 to be incompatible with a Convention right and, if an appeal lies—

(i)   all persons who may appeal have stated in writing that they do not intend to do so;

(ii)   the time for bringing an appeal has expired and no appeal has been brought within that time; or

(iii)   an appeal brought within that time has been determined or abandoned; or

(b)   it appears to a Minister of the Crown or Her Majesty in Council that, having regard to a finding of the European Court of Human Rights made after the coming into force of this section in proceedings against the United Kingdom, a provision of legislation is incompatible with an obligation of the United Kingdom arising from the Convention.

(2)   If a Minister of the Crown considers that there are compelling reasons for proceeding under this section, he may by order make such amendments to the legislation as he considers necessary to remove the incompatibility.

(3)   If, in the case of subordinate legislation, a Minister of the Crown considers—

(a)   that it is necessary to amend the primary legislation under which the subordinate legislation in question was made, in order to enable the incompatibility to be removed, and

(b)   that there are compelling reasons for proceeding under this section,

he may by order make such amendments to the primary legislation as he considers necessary.

(4)   This section also applies where the provision in question is in subordinate legislation and has been quashed, or declared invalid, by reason of incompatibility with a Convention right and the Minister proposes to proceed under paragraph 2(b) of Schedule 2.

(5)   If the legislation is an Order in Council, the power conferred by subsection (2) or (3) is exercisable by Her Majesty in Council.

(6)   In this section "legislation" does not include a Measure of the Church Assembly or of the General Synod of the Church of England.

(7)   Schedule 2 makes further provision about remedial orders.

Appointment
Appointment: 2 October 2000: see SI 2000/1851, art 2.

Other rights and proceedings

11   Safeguard for existing human rights

A person's reliance on a Convention right does not restrict—

(a)   any other right or freedom conferred on him by or under any law having effect in any part of the United Kingdom; or

(b)   his right to make any claim or bring any proceedings which he could make or bring apart from sections 7 to 9.

Appendix 1 Legislation and materials

Appointment
Appointment: 2 October 2000: see SI 2000/1851, art 2.

12 Freedom of expression

(1) This section applies if a court is considering whether to grant any relief which, if granted, might affect the exercise of the Convention right to freedom of expression.

(2) If the person against whom the application for relief is made ("the respondent") is neither present nor represented, no such relief is to be granted unless the court is satisfied—

    (a) that the applicant has taken all practicable steps to notify the respondent; or
    (b) that there are compelling reasons why the respondent should not be notified.

(3) No such relief is to be granted so as to restrain publication before trial unless the court is satisfied that the applicant is likely to establish that publication should not be allowed.

(4) The court must have particular regard to the importance of the Convention right to freedom of expression and, where the proceedings relate to material which the respondent claims, or which appears to the court, to be journalistic, literary or artistic material (or to conduct connected with such material), to—

    (a) the extent to which—
        (i) the material has, or is about to, become available to the public; or
        (ii) it is, or would be, in the public interest for the material to be published;
    (b) any relevant privacy code.

(5) In this section—

"court" includes a tribunal; and
"relief" includes any remedy or order (other than in criminal proceedings).

Appointment
Appointment: 2 October 2000: see SI 2000/1851, art 2.

13 Freedom of thought, conscience and religion

(1) If a court's determination of any question arising under this Act might affect the exercise by a religious organisation (itself or its members collectively) of the Convention right to freedom of thought, conscience and religion, it must have particular regard to the importance of that right.

(2) In this section "court" includes a tribunal.

Appointment
Appointment: 2 October 2000: see SI 2000/1851, art 2.

Derogations and reservations

14 Derogations

(1) In this Act "designated derogation" means—

    ...

    any derogation by the United Kingdom from an Article of the Convention, or of any protocol to the Convention, which is designated for the purposes of this Act in an order made by the [Secretary of State].

(2) ...

1836

(3) If a designated derogation is amended or replaced it ceases to be a designated derogation.

(4) But subsection (3) does not prevent the [Secretary of State] from exercising his power under subsection (1)... to make a fresh designation order in respect of the Article concerned.

(5) The [Secretary of State] must by order make such amendments to Schedule 3 as he considers appropriate to reflect—

    (a) any designation order; or
    (b) the effect of subsection (3).

(6) A designation order may be made in anticipation of the making by the United Kingdom of a proposed derogation.

Appointment
Appointment: 2 October 2000: see SI 2000/1851, art 2.

Amendment
Sub-s (1): words omitted repealed by SI 2001/1216, art 2(a). Date in force: 1 April 2001: see SI 2001/1216, art 1.
Sub-s (1): words "Secretary of State" in square brackets substituted by SI 2003/1887, art 9, Sch 2, para 10(1). Date in force: 19 August 2003: see SI 2003/1887, art 1(2).
Sub-s (2): repealed by SI 2001/1216, art 2(b). Date in force: 1 April 2001: see SI 2001/1216, art 1.
Sub-s (4): words "Secretary of State" in square brackets substituted by SI 2003/1887, art 9, Sch 2, para 10(1). Date in force: 19 August 2003: see SI 2003/1887, art 1(2).
Sub-s (4): reference omitted repealed by SI 2001/1216, art 2(c). Date in force: 1 April 2001: see SI 2001/1216, art 1.
Sub-s (5): words "Secretary of State" in square brackets substituted by SI 2003/1887, art 9, Sch 2, para 10(1). Date in force: 19 August 2003: see SI 2003/1887, art 1(2).

15 Reservations

(1) In this Act "designated reservation" means—

    (a) the United Kingdom's reservation to Article 2 of the First Protocol to the Convention; and
    (b) any other reservation by the United Kingdom to an Article of the Convention, or of any protocol to the Convention, which is designated for the purposes of this Act in an order made by the [Secretary of State].

(2) The text of the reservation referred to in subsection (1)(a) is set out in Part II of Schedule 3.

(3) If a designated reservation is withdrawn wholly or in part it ceases to be a designated reservation.

(4) But subsection (3) does not prevent the [Secretary of State] from exercising his power under subsection (1)(b) to make a fresh designation order in respect of the Article concerned.

(5) The [Secretary of State] must by order make such amendments to this Act as he considers appropriate to reflect—

    (a) any designation order; or
    (b) the effect of subsection (3).

Appointment
Appointment: 2 October 2000: see SI 2000/1851, art 2.

Amendment
Sub-s (1): in para (b) words "Secretary of State" in square brackets substituted by SI 2003/1887, art 9, Sch 2, para 10(1). Date in force: 19 August 2003: see SI 2003/1887, art 1(2).
Sub-s (4): words "Secretary of State" in square brackets substituted by SI 2003/1887, art 9, Sch 2, para 10(1). Date in force: 19 August 2003: see SI 2003/1887, art 1(2).
Sub-s (5): words "Secretary of State" in square brackets substituted by SI 2003/1887, art 9, Sch 2, para 10(1). Date in force: 19 August 2003: see SI 2003/1887, art 1(2).

16   Period for which designated derogations have effect

(1)   If it has not already been withdrawn by the United Kingdom, a designated derogation ceases to have effect for the purposes of this Act—

...

at the end of the period of five years beginning with the date on which the order designating it was made.

(2)   At any time before the period—

(a)   fixed by subsection (1)..., or
(b)   extended by an order under this subsection,

comes to an end, the [Secretary of State] may by order extend it by a further period of five years.

(3)   An order under section 14(1)... ceases to have effect at the end of the period for consideration, unless a resolution has been passed by each House approving the order.

(4)   Subsection (3) does not affect—

(a)   anything done in reliance on the order; or
(b)   the power to make a fresh order under section 14(1)...

(5)   In subsection (3) "period for consideration" means the period of forty days beginning with the day on which the order was made.

(6)   In calculating the period for consideration, no account is to be taken of any time during which—

(a)   Parliament is dissolved or prorogued; or
(b)   both Houses are adjourned for more than four days.

(7)   If a designated derogation is withdrawn by the United Kingdom, the [Secretary of State] must by order make such amendments to this Act as he considers are required to reflect that withdrawal.

Appointment
Appointment: 2 October 2000: see SI 2000/1851, art 2.

Amendment
Sub-s (1): words omitted repealed by SI 2001/1216, art 3(a). Date in force: 1 April 2001: see SI 2001/1216, art 1.
Sub-s (2): in para (b) words omitted repealed by SI 2001/1216, art 3(b). Date in force: 1 April 2001: see SI 2001/1216, art 1.
Sub-s (2): words "Secretary of State" in square brackets substituted by SI 2003/1887, art 9, Sch 2, para 10(1). Date in force: 19 August 2003: see SI 2003/1887, art 1(2).
Sub-s (3): reference omitted repealed by SI 2001/1216, art 3(c). Date in force: 1 April 2001: see SI 2001/1216, art 1.
Sub-s (4): in para (b) reference omitted repealed by SI 2001/1216, art 3(d). Date in force: 1 April 2001: see SI 2001/1216, art 1.
Sub-s (7): words "Secretary of State" in square brackets substituted by SI 2003/1887, art 9, Sch 2, para 10(1). Date in force: 19 August 2003: see SI 2003/1887, art 1(2).

17 Periodic review of designated reservations

(1) The appropriate Minister must review the designated reservation referred to in section 15(1)(a)—

(a) before the end of the period of five years beginning with the date on which section 1(2) came into force; and

(b) if that designation is still in force, before the end of the period of five years beginning with the date on which the last report relating to it was laid under subsection (3).

(2) The appropriate Minister must review each of the other designated reservations (if any)—

(a) before the end of the period of five years beginning with the date on which the order designating the reservation first came into force; and

(b) if the designation is still in force, before the end of the period of five years beginning with the date on which the last report relating to it was laid under subsection (3).

(3) The Minister conducting a review under this section must prepare a report on the result of the review and lay a copy of it before each House of Parliament.

Appointment
Appointment: 2 October 2000: see SI 2000/1851, art 2.

Judges of the European Court of Human Rights

18 Appointment to European Court of Human Rights

(1) In this section "judicial office" means the office of—

(a) Lord Justice of Appeal, Justice of the High Court or Circuit judge, in England and Wales;

(b) judge of the Court of Session or sheriff, in Scotland;

(c) Lord Justice of Appeal, judge of the High Court or county court judge, in Northern Ireland.

(2) The holder of a judicial office may become a judge of the European Court of Human Rights ("the Court") without being required to relinquish his office.

(3) But he is not required to perform the duties of his judicial office while he is a judge of the Court.

(4) In respect of any period during which he is a judge of the Court—

(a) a Lord Justice of Appeal or Justice of the High Court is not to count as a judge of the relevant court for the purposes of section 2(1) or 4(1) of the Supreme Court Act 1981 (maximum number of judges) nor as a judge of the Supreme Court for the purposes of section 12(1) to (6) of that Act (salaries etc);

(b) a judge of the Court of Session is not to count as a judge of that court for the purposes of section 1(1) of the Court of Session Act 1988 (maximum number of judges) or of section 9(1)(c) of the Administration of Justice Act 1973 ("the 1973 Act") (salaries etc);

(c) a Lord Justice of Appeal or judge of the High Court in Northern Ireland is not to count as a judge of the relevant court for the purposes of section 2(1) or 3(1) of the Judicature (Northern Ireland) Act 1978 (maximum number of judges) nor as a judge of the Supreme Court of Northern Ireland for the purposes of section 9(1)(d) of the 1973 Act (salaries etc);

(d) a Circuit judge is not to count as such for the purposes of section 18 of the Courts Act 1971 (salaries etc);

(e)   a sheriff is not to count as such for the purposes of section 14 of the Sheriff Courts (Scotland) Act 1907 (salaries etc);

(f)   a county court judge of Northern Ireland is not to count as such for the purposes of section 106 of the County Courts Act (Northern Ireland) 1959 (salaries etc).

(5)   If a sheriff principal is appointed a judge of the Court, section 11(1) of the Sheriff Courts (Scotland) Act 1971 (temporary appointment of sheriff principal) applies, while he holds that appointment, as if his office is vacant.

(6)   Schedule 4 makes provision about judicial pensions in relation to the holder of a judicial office who serves as a judge of the Court.

(7)   The Lord Chancellor or the Secretary of State may by order make such transitional provision (including, in particular, provision for a temporary increase in the maximum number of judges) as he considers appropriate in relation to any holder of a judicial office who has completed his service as a judge of the Court.

Initial Commencement
Royal Assent: 9 November 1998: see s 22(2).

Parliamentary procedure

19   Statements of compatibility

(1)   A Minister of the Crown in charge of a Bill in either House of Parliament must, before Second Reading of the Bill—

(a)   make a statement to the effect that in his view the provisions of the Bill are compatible with the Convention rights ("a statement of compatibility"); or

(b)   make a statement to the effect that although he is unable to make a statement of compatibility the government nevertheless wishes the House to proceed with the Bill.

(2)   The statement must be in writing and be published in such manner as the Minister making it considers appropriate.

Appointment
Appointment: 24 November 1998: see SI 1998/2882, art 2.

Supplemental

20   Orders etc under this Act

(1)   Any power of a Minister of the Crown to make an order under this Act is exercisable by statutory instrument.

(2)   The power of ... the Secretary of State to make rules (other than rules of court) under section 2(3) or 7(9) is exercisable by statutory instrument.

(3)   Any statutory instrument made under section 14, 15 or 16(7) must be laid before Parliament.

(4)   No order may be made by ... the Secretary of State under section 1(4), 7(11) or 16(2) unless a draft of the order has been laid before, and approved by, each House of Parliament.

(5)   Any statutory instrument made under section 18(7) or Schedule 4, or to which subsection (2) applies, shall be subject to annulment in pursuance of a resolution of either House of Parliament.

(6)   The power of a Northern Ireland department to make—

(a) rules under section 2(3)(c) or 7(9)(c), or
(b) an order under section 7(11),

is exercisable by statutory rule for the purposes of the Statutory Rules (Northern Ireland) Order 1979.

(7) Any rules made under section 2(3)(c) or 7(9)(c) shall be subject to negative resolution; and section 41(6) of the Interpretation Act (Northern Ireland) 1954 (meaning of "subject to negative resolution") shall apply as if the power to make the rules were conferred by an Act of the Northern Ireland Assembly.

(8) No order may be made by a Northern Ireland department under section 7(11) unless a draft of the order has been laid before, and approved by, the Northern Ireland Assembly.

Initial Commencement
Royal Assent: 9 November 1998: see s 22(2).

Amendment
Sub-s (2): words omitted repealed by SI 2003/1887, art 9, Sch 2, para 10(2). Date in force: 19 August 2003: see SI 2003/1887, art 1(2).
Sub-s (4): words omitted repealed by SI 2003/1887, art 9, Sch 2, para 10(2). Date in force: 19 August 2003: see SI 2003/1887, art 1(2).

21   Interpretation, etc

(1) In this Act—
"amend" includes repeal and apply (with or without modifications);
"the appropriate Minister" means the Minister of the Crown having charge of the appropriate authorised government department (within the meaning of the Crown Proceedings Act 1947);
"the Commission" means the European Commission of Human Rights;
"the Convention" means the Convention for the Protection of Human Rights and Fundamental Freedoms, agreed by the Council of Europe at Rome on 4th November 1950 as it has effect for the time being in relation to the United Kingdom;
"declaration of incompatibility" means a declaration under section 4;
"Minister of the Crown" has the same meaning as in the Ministers of the Crown Act 1975;
"Northern Ireland Minister" includes the First Minister and the deputy First Minister in Northern Ireland;
"primary legislation" means any—
(a) public general Act;
(b) local and personal Act;
(c) private Act;
(d) Measure of the Church Assembly;
(e) Measure of the General Synod of the Church of England;
(f) Order in Council—
(i) made in exercise of Her Majesty's Royal Prerogative;
(ii) made under section 38(1)(a) of the Northern Ireland Constitution Act 1973 or the corresponding provision of the Northern Ireland Act 1998; or
(iii) amending an Act of a kind mentioned in paragraph (a), (b) or (c);
and includes an order or other instrument made under primary legislation (otherwise than by the National Assembly for Wales, a member of the Scottish Executive, a Northern Ireland Minister or a Northern Ireland department) to the extent to which it operates to bring one or more provisions of that legislation into force or amends any primary legislation;

"the First Protocol" means the protocol to the Convention agreed at Paris on 20th March 1952;

...

"the Eleventh Protocol" means the protocol to the Convention (restructuring the control machinery established by the Convention) agreed at Strasbourg on 11th May 1994;

["the Thirteenth Protocol" means the protocol to the Convention (concerning the abolition of the death penalty in all circumstances) agreed at Vilnius on 3rd May 2002;]

"remedial order" means an order under section 10;

"subordinate legislation" means any—

- (a) Order in Council other than one—
    - (i) made in exercise of Her Majesty's Royal Prerogative;
    - (ii) made under section 38(1)(a) of the Northern Ireland Constitution Act 1973 or the corresponding provision of the Northern Ireland Act 1998; or
    - (iii) amending an Act of a kind mentioned in the definition of primary legislation;
- (b) Act of the Scottish Parliament;
- (c) Act of the Parliament of Northern Ireland;
- (d) Measure of the Assembly established under section 1 of the Northern Ireland Assembly Act 1973;
- (e) Act of the Northern Ireland Assembly;
- (f) order, rules, regulations, scheme, warrant, byelaw or other instrument made under primary legislation (except to the extent to which it operates to bring one or more provisions of that legislation into force or amends any primary legislation);
- (g) order, rules, regulations, scheme, warrant, byelaw or other instrument made under legislation mentioned in paragraph (b), (c), (d) or (e) or made under an Order in Council applying only to Northern Ireland;
- (h) order, rules, regulations, scheme, warrant, byelaw or other instrument made by a member of the Scottish Executive, a Northern Ireland Minister or a Northern Ireland department in exercise of prerogative or other executive functions of Her Majesty which are exercisable by such a person on behalf of Her Majesty;

"transferred matters" has the same meaning as in the Northern Ireland Act 1998; and

"tribunal" means any tribunal in which legal proceedings may be brought.

(2) The references in paragraphs (b) and (c) of section 2(1) to Articles are to Articles of the Convention as they had effect immediately before the coming into force of the Eleventh Protocol.

(3) The reference in paragraph (d) of section 2(1) to Article 46 includes a reference to Articles 32 and 54 of the Convention as they had effect immediately before the coming into force of the Eleventh Protocol.

(4) The references in section 2(1) to a report or decision of the Commission or a decision of the Committee of Ministers include references to a report or decision made as provided by paragraphs 3, 4 and 6 of Article 5 of the Eleventh Protocol (transitional provisions).

(5) Any liability under the Army Act 1955, the Air Force Act 1955 or the Naval Discipline Act 1957 to suffer death for an offence is replaced by a liability to imprisonment for life or any less punishment authorised by those Acts; and those Acts shall accordingly have effect with the necessary modifications.

Initial Commencement
Sub-s (5): Royal Assent: 9 November 1998: see s 22(2).

Appointment
Sub-ss (1)–(4): Appointment: 2 October 2000: see SI 2000/1851, art 2.

Amendment
Sub-s (1): definition "the Sixth Protocol" (omitted) repealed by SI 2004/1574, art 2(2). Date in force: 22 June 2004: see SI 2004/1574, art 1.
Sub-s (1): definition "the Thirteenth Protocol" inserted by SI 2004/1574, art 2(2). Date in force: 22 June 2004: see SI 2004/1574, art 1.

22 Short title, commencement, application and extent

(1) This Act may be cited as the Human Rights Act 1998.

(2) Sections 18, 20 and 21(5) and this section come into force on the passing of this Act.

(3) The other provisions of this Act come into force on such day as the Secretary of State may by order appoint; and different days may be appointed for different purposes.

(4) Paragraph (b) of subsection (1) of section 7 applies to proceedings brought by or at the instigation of a public authority whenever the act in question took place; but otherwise that subsection does not apply to an act taking place before the coming into force of that section.

(5) This Act binds the Crown.

(6) This Act extends to Northern Ireland.

(7) Section 21(5), so far as it relates to any provision contained in the Army Act 1955, the Air Force Act 1955 or the Naval Discipline Act 1957, extends to any place to which that provision extends.

Initial Commencement
Royal Assent: 9 November 1998: see s 22(2).

Subordinate Legislation
Human Rights Act 1998 (Commencement) Order 1998, SI 1998/2882 (made under sub-s (3)).
Human Rights Act 1998 (Commencement No 2) Order 2000, SI 2000/1851 (made under sub-s (3)).

SCHEDULE 1
THE ARTICLES

Section 1(3)

PART I
THE CONVENTION

RIGHTS AND FREEDOMS

Article 2
Right to life

1 Everyone's right to life shall be protected by law. No one shall be deprived of his life intentionally save in the execution of a sentence of a court following his conviction of a crime for which this penalty is provided by law.

2 Deprivation of life shall not be regarded as inflicted in contravention of this Article when it results from the use of force which is no more than absolutely necessary:

(a) in defence of any person from unlawful violence;
(b) in order to effect a lawful arrest or to prevent the escape of a person lawfully detained;
(c) in action lawfully taken for the purpose of quelling a riot or insurrection.

Article 3
Prohibition of torture

No one shall be subjected to torture or to inhuman or degrading treatment or punishment.

Article 4
Prohibition of slavery and forced labour

1 No one shall be held in slavery or servitude.

2 No one shall be required to perform forced or compulsory labour.

3 For the purpose of this Article the term "forced or compulsory labour" shall not include:

(a) any work required to be done in the ordinary course of detention imposed according to the provisions of Article 5 of this Convention or during conditional release from such detention;
(b) any service of a military character or, in case of conscientious objectors in countries where they are recognised, service exacted instead of compulsory military service;
(c) any service exacted in case of an emergency or calamity threatening the life or well-being of the community;
(d) any work or service which forms part of normal civic obligations.

Article 5
Right to liberty and security

1 Everyone has the right to liberty and security of person. No one shall be deprived of his liberty save in the following cases and in accordance with a procedure prescribed by law:

(a) the lawful detention of a person after conviction by a competent court;
(b) the lawful arrest or detention of a person for non-compliance with the lawful order of a court or in order to secure the fulfilment of any obligation prescribed by law;
(c) the lawful arrest or detention of a person effected for the purpose of bringing him before the competent legal authority on reasonable suspicion of having committed an offence or when it is reasonably considered necessary to prevent his committing an offence or fleeing after having done so;
(d) the detention of a minor by lawful order for the purpose of educational supervision or his lawful detention for the purpose of bringing him before the competent legal authority;
(e) the lawful detention of persons for the prevention of the spreading of infectious diseases, of persons of unsound mind, alcoholics or drug addicts or vagrants;
(f) the lawful arrest or detention of a person to prevent his effecting an unauthorised entry into the country or of a person against whom action is being taken with a view to deportation or extradition.

2   Everyone who is arrested shall be informed promptly, in a language which he understands, of the reasons for his arrest and of any charge against him.

3   Everyone arrested or detained in accordance with the provisions of paragraph 1(c) of this Article shall be brought promptly before a judge or other officer authorised by law to exercise judicial power and shall be entitled to trial within a reasonable time or to release pending trial. Release may be conditioned by guarantees to appear for trial.

4   Everyone who is deprived of his liberty by arrest or detention shall be entitled to take proceedings by which the lawfulness of his detention shall be decided speedily by a court and his release ordered if the detention is not lawful.

5   Everyone who has been the victim of arrest or detention in contravention of the provisions of this Article shall have an enforceable right to compensation.

Article 6
Right to a fair trial

1   In the determination of his civil rights and obligations or of any criminal charge against him, everyone is entitled to a fair and public hearing within a reasonable time by an independent and impartial tribunal established by law. Judgment shall be pronounced publicly but the press and public may be excluded from all or part of the trial in the interest of morals, public order or national security in a democratic society, where the interests of juveniles or the protection of the private life of the parties so require, or to the extent strictly necessary in the opinion of the court in special circumstances where publicity would prejudice the interests of justice.

2   Everyone charged with a criminal offence shall be presumed innocent until proved guilty according to law.

3   Everyone charged with a criminal offence has the following minimum rights:

(a)   to be informed promptly, in a language which he understands and in detail, of the nature and cause of the accusation against him;

(b)   to have adequate time and facilities for the preparation of his defence;

(c)   to defend himself in person or through legal assistance of his own choosing or, if he has not sufficient means to pay for legal assistance, to be given it free when the interests of justice so require;

(d)   to examine or have examined witnesses against him and to obtain the attendance and examination of witnesses on his behalf under the same conditions as witnesses against him;

(e)   to have the free assistance of an interpreter if he cannot understand or speak the language used in court.

Article 7
No punishment without law

1   No one shall be held guilty of any criminal offence on account of any act or omission which did not constitute a criminal offence under national or international law at the time when it was committed. Nor shall a heavier penalty be imposed than the one that was applicable at the time the criminal offence was committed.

2   This Article shall not prejudice the trial and punishment of any person for any act or omission which, at the time when it was committed, was criminal according to the general principles of law recognised by civilised nations.

Article 8
Right to respect for private and family life

1   Everyone has the right to respect for his private and family life, his home and his correspondence.

2   There shall be no interference by a public authority with the exercise of this right except such as is in accordance with the law and is necessary in a democratic society in the interests of national security, public safety or the economic well-being of the country, for the prevention of disorder or crime, for the protection of health or morals, or for the protection of the rights and freedoms of others.

Article 9
Freedom of thought, conscience and religion

1   Everyone has the right to freedom of thought, conscience and religion; this right includes freedom to change his religion or belief and freedom, either alone or in community with others and in public or private, to manifest his religion or belief, in worship, teaching, practice and observance.

2   Freedom to manifest one's religion or beliefs shall be subject only to such limitations as are prescribed by law and are necessary in a democratic society in the interests of public safety, for the protection of public order, health or morals, or for the protection of the rights and freedoms of others.

Article 10
Freedom of expression

1   Everyone has the right to freedom of expression. This right shall include freedom to hold opinions and to receive and impart information and ideas without interference by public authority and regardless of frontiers. This Article shall not prevent States from requiring the licensing of broadcasting, television or cinema enterprises.

2   The exercise of these freedoms, since it carries with it duties and responsibilities, may be subject to such formalities, conditions, restrictions or penalties as are prescribed by law and are necessary in a democratic society, in the interests of national security, territorial integrity or public safety, for the prevention of disorder or crime, for the protection of health or morals, for the protection of the reputation or rights of others, for preventing the disclosure of information received in confidence, or for maintaining the authority and impartiality of the judiciary.

Article 11
Freedom of assembly and association

1   Everyone has the right to freedom of peaceful assembly and to freedom of association with others, including the right to form and to join trade unions for the protection of his interests.

2   No restrictions shall be placed on the exercise of these rights other than such as are prescribed by law and are necessary in a democratic society in the interests of national security or public safety, for the prevention of disorder or crime, for the protection of health or morals or for the protection of the rights and freedoms of others. This Article shall not prevent the imposition of lawful restrictions on the exercise of these rights by members of the armed forces, of the police or of the administration of the State.

Article 12
Right to marry
Men and women of marriageable age have the right to marry and to found a family, according to the national laws governing the exercise of this right.

Article 14
Prohibition of discrimination
The enjoyment of the rights and freedoms set forth in this Convention shall be secured without discrimination on any ground such as sex, race, colour, language,

religion, political or other opinion, national or social origin, association with a national minority, property, birth or other status.

Article 16
Restrictions on political activity of aliens
Nothing in Articles 10, 11 and 14 shall be regarded as preventing the High Contracting Parties from imposing restrictions on the political activity of aliens.

Article 17
Prohibition of abuse of rights
Nothing in this Convention may be interpreted as implying for any State, group or person any right to engage in any activity or perform any act aimed at the destruction of any of the rights and freedoms set forth herein or at their limitation to a greater extent than is provided for in the Convention.

Article 18
Limitation on use of restrictions on rights
The restrictions permitted under this Convention to the said rights and freedoms shall not be applied for any purpose other than those for which they have been prescribed.

Appointment
Appointment: 2 October 2000: see SI 2000/1851, art 2.

PART II
THE FIRST PROTOCOL

Article 1
Protection of property
Every natural or legal person is entitled to the peaceful enjoyment of his possessions. No one shall be deprived of his possessions except in the public interest and subject to the conditions provided for by law and by the general principles of international law.

The preceding provisions shall not, however, in any way impair the right of a State to enforce such laws as it deems necessary to control the use of property in accordance with the general interest or to secure the payment of taxes or other contributions or penalties.

Article 2
Right to education
No person shall be denied the right to education. In the exercise of any functions which it assumes in relation to education and to teaching, the State shall respect the right of parents to ensure such education and teaching in conformity with their own religious and philosophical convictions.

Article 3
Right to free elections
The High Contracting Parties undertake to hold free elections at reasonable intervals by secret ballot, under conditions which will ensure the free expression of the opinion of the people in the choice of the legislature.

Appointment
Appointment: 2 October 2000: see SI 2000/1851, art 2.

Appendix 1 Legislation and materials

[PART III
ARTICLE 1 OF THE THIRTEENTH PROTOCOL]

[Abolition of the Death Penalty

The death penalty shall be abolished. No one shall be condemned to such penalty or executed.]

Amendment
Substituted by SI 2004/1574, art 2(3). Date in force: 22 June 2004: see SI 2004/1574, art 1.

SCHEDULE 2
REMEDIAL ORDERS

Section 10

Orders

1   (1)   A remedial order may—

(a)   contain such incidental, supplemental, consequential or transitional provision as the person making it considers appropriate;
(b)   be made so as to have effect from a date earlier than that on which it is made;
(c)   make provision for the delegation of specific functions;
(d)   make different provision for different cases.

(2)   The power conferred by sub-paragraph (1)(a) includes—

(a)   power to amend primary legislation (including primary legislation other than that which contains the incompatible provision); and
(b)   power to amend or revoke subordinate legislation (including subordinate legislation other than that which contains the incompatible provision).

(3)   A remedial order may be made so as to have the same extent as the legislation which it affects.

(4)   No person is to be guilty of an offence solely as a result of the retrospective effect of a remedial order.

Procedure

2   No remedial order may be made unless—

(a)   a draft of the order has been approved by a resolution of each House of Parliament made after the end of the period of 60 days beginning with the day on which the draft was laid; or
(b)   it is declared in the order that it appears to the person making it that, because of the urgency of the matter, it is necessary to make the order without a draft being so approved.

Orders laid in draft

3   (1)   No draft may be laid under paragraph 2(a) unless—

(a)   the person proposing to make the order has laid before Parliament a document which contains a draft of the proposed order and the required information; and
(b)   the period of 60 days, beginning with the day on which the document required by this sub-paragraph was laid, has ended.

(2)   If representations have been made during that period, the draft laid under paragraph 2(a) must be accompanied by a statement containing—

(a)   a summary of the representations; and
(b)   if, as a result of the representations, the proposed order has been changed, details of the changes.

Urgent cases

4   (1)   If a remedial order ("the original order") is made without being approved in draft, the person making it must lay it before Parliament, accompanied by the required information, after it is made.

(2)   If representations have been made during the period of 60 days beginning with the day on which the original order was made, the person making it must (after the end of that period) lay before Parliament a statement containing—

(a)   a summary of the representations; and
(b)   if, as a result of the representations, he considers it appropriate to make changes to the original order, details of the changes.

(3)   If sub-paragraph (2)(b) applies, the person making the statement must—

(a)   make a further remedial order replacing the original order; and
(b)   lay the replacement order before Parliament.

(4)   If, at the end of the period of 120 days beginning with the day on which the original order was made, a resolution has not been passed by each House approving the original or replacement order, the order ceases to have effect (but without that affecting anything previously done under either order or the power to make a fresh remedial order).

Definitions

5   In this Schedule—

"representations" means representations about a remedial order (or proposed remedial order) made to the person making (or proposing to make) it and includes any relevant Parliamentary report or resolution; and
"required information" means—
(a)   an explanation of the incompatibility which the order (or proposed order) seeks to remove, including particulars of the relevant declaration, finding or order; and
(b)   a statement of the reasons for proceeding under section 10 and for making an order in those terms.

Calculating periods

6   In calculating any period for the purposes of this Schedule, no account is to be taken of any time during which—

(a)   Parliament is dissolved or prorogued; or
(b)   both Houses are adjourned for more than four days.

[**7**   (1)   This paragraph applies in relation to—

(a)   any remedial order made, and any draft of such an order proposed to be made,—
    (i)   by the Scottish Ministers; or
    (ii)   within devolved competence (within the meaning of the Scotland Act 1998) by Her Majesty in Council; and
(b)   any document or statement to be laid in connection with such an order (or proposed order).

(2)   This Schedule has effect in relation to any such order (or proposed order), document or statement subject to the following modifications.

(3)   Any reference to Parliament, each House of Parliament or both Houses of Parliament shall be construed as a reference to the Scottish Parliament.

(4)   Paragraph 6 does not apply and instead, in calculating any period for the purposes of this Schedule, no account is to be taken of any time during which the Scottish Parliament is dissolved or is in recess for more than four days.]

Appointment
Appointment: 2 October 2000: see SI 2000/1851, art 2.

Amendment
Para 7: inserted by SI 2000/2040, art 2(1), Schedule, Pt I, para 21. Date in force: 27 July 2000: see SI 2000/2040, art 1(1).

SCHEDULE 3
DEROGATION AND RESERVATION

Sections 14 and 15

PART I
...

Amendment
Repealed by SI 2001/1216, art 4. Date in force: 1 April 2001: see SI 2001/1216, art 1.

[PART I
...]

Amendment
Inserted by SI 2001/4032, art 2, Schedule. Date in force: 20 December 2001: see SI 2001/4032, art 1.
Repealed by SI 2005/1071, art 2. Date in force: 8 April 2005: see SI 2005/1071, art 1.

PART II
RESERVATION

At the time of signing the present (First) Protocol, I declare that, in view of certain provisions of the Education Acts in the United Kingdom, the principle affirmed in the second sentence of Article 2 is accepted by the United Kingdom only so far as it is compatible with the provision of efficient instruction and training, and the avoidance of unreasonable public expenditure.

Dated 20 March 1952. Made by the United Kingdom Permanent Representative to the Council of Europe.

Appointment
Appointment: 2 October 2000: see SI 2000/1851, art 2.

SCHEDULE 4
JUDICIAL PENSIONS

Section 18(6)

Duty to make orders about pensions

1   (1)   The appropriate Minister must by order make provision with respect to pensions payable to or in respect of any holder of a judicial office who serves as an ECHR judge.

(2) A pensions order must include such provision as the Minister making it considers is necessary to secure that—

   (a) an ECHR judge who was, immediately before his appointment as an ECHR judge, a member of a judicial pension scheme is entitled to remain as a member of that scheme;

   (b) the terms on which he remains a member of the scheme are those which would have been applicable had he not been appointed as an ECHR judge; and

   (c) entitlement to benefits payable in accordance with the scheme continues to be determined as if, while serving as an ECHR judge, his salary was that which would (but for section 18(4)) have been payable to him in respect of his continuing service as the holder of his judicial office.

Contributions

2 A pensions order may, in particular, make provision—

   (a) for any contributions which are payable by a person who remains a member of a scheme as a result of the order, and which would otherwise be payable by deduction from his salary, to be made otherwise than by deduction from his salary as an ECHR judge; and

   (b) for such contributions to be collected in such manner as may be determined by the administrators of the scheme.

Amendments of other enactments

3 A pensions order may amend any provision of, or made under, a pensions Act in such manner and to such extent as the Minister making the order considers necessary or expedient to ensure the proper administration of any scheme to which it relates.

Definitions

4 In this Schedule—

"appropriate Minister" means—
      (a) in relation to any judicial office whose jurisdiction is exercisable exclusively in relation to Scotland, the Secretary of State; and
      (b) otherwise, the Lord Chancellor;

"ECHR judge" means the holder of a judicial office who is serving as a judge of the Court;

"judicial pension scheme" means a scheme established by and in accordance with a pensions Act;

"pensions Act" means—
      (a) the County Courts Act (Northern Ireland) 1959;
      (b) the Sheriffs' Pensions (Scotland) Act 1961;
      (c) the Judicial Pensions Act 1981; or
      (d) the Judicial Pensions and Retirement Act 1993; and

"pensions order" means an order made under paragraph 1.

Initial Commencement
Royal Assent: 9 November 1998: see s 22(2).

EUROPEAN UNION (ACCESSIONS) ACT 2003

2003 CHAPTER 35

An Act to make provision consequential on the treaty concerning the accession of the Czech Republic, the Republic of Estonia, the Republic of Cyprus, the Republic of Latvia, the Republic of Lithuania, the Republic of Hungary, the Republic of Malta, the Republic of Poland, the Republic of Slovenia and the Slovak Republic to the European Union, signed at Athens on 16th April 2003; and to make provision in relation to the entitlement of nationals of certain acceding States to enter or reside in the United Kingdom as workers.

[13th November 2003]

Be it enacted by the Queen's most Excellent Majesty, by and with the advice and consent of the Lords Spiritual and Temporal, and Commons, in this present Parliament assembled, and by the authority of the same, as follows:—

1   Accession treaty

(1)   In section 1(2) of the European Communities Act 1972 (c 68), in the definition of "the Treaties" and "the Community Treaties", after paragraph (p), insert

"and
(q)   the treaty concerning the accession of the Czech Republic, the Republic of Estonia, the Republic of Cyprus, the Republic of Latvia, the Republic of Lithuania, the Republic of Hungary, the Republic of Malta, the Republic of Poland, the Republic of Slovenia and the Slovak Republic to the European Union, signed at Athens on 16th April 2003;".

(2)   For the purpose of section 12 of the European Parliamentary Elections Act 2002 (c 24) (ratification of treaties), the treaty concerning the accession of the Czech Republic, the Republic of Estonia, the Republic of Cyprus, the Republic of Latvia, the Republic of Lithuania, the Republic of Hungary, the Republic of Malta, the Republic of Poland, the Republic of Slovenia and the Slovak Republic to the European Union, signed at Athens on 16th April 2003, is approved.

Initial Commencement
Royal Assent: 13 November 2003: (no specific commencement provision).

2   Freedom of movement for workers

(1)   The Secretary of State may by regulations provide that a specified enactment relating to—

(a)   the entitlement of a national of an EEA State to enter or reside in the United Kingdom as a worker, or
(b)   any matter ancillary to that entitlement,

applies in relation to a national of a relevant acceding State as it applies in relation to a national of an EEA State.

(2)   Regulations under this section in respect of a specified enactment may apply that enactment subject to specified exceptions or modifications.

(3)   Regulations under this section—

(a)   may include incidental, supplementary, consequential or transitional provision;

(b) may make different provision for different cases.

(4) Regulations under this section do not have effect so as to apply an enactment in relation to a national of a relevant acceding State which has not ratified the treaty mentioned in section 1(2).

(5) The power to make regulations under this section is exercisable by statutory instrument.

(6) Regulations may not be made under this section unless a draft has been laid before and approved by a resolution of each House of Parliament.

(7) But, in the case of regulations other than the first set of regulations under this section, subsection (6) does not apply if it appears to the Secretary of State that by reason of urgency they should be made without being approved in draft.

(8) Where by virtue of subsection (7) regulations are made without being approved in draft, the regulations—

(a) must be laid before Parliament, and
(b) cease to have effect at the end of the period mentioned in subsection (9) unless they are approved during that period by resolution of each House of Parliament.

(9) The period referred to in subsection (8)(b) is the period of 40 days—

(a) beginning with the day on which the regulations are made, and
(b) ignoring any period during which Parliament is dissolved or prorogued or during which both Houses are adjourned for more than four days.

(10) The fact that regulations cease to have effect by virtue of subsection (8)—

(a) does not affect the lawfulness of anything done before the regulations cease to have effect, and
(b) does not prevent the making of new regulations.

(11) In this section—

"EEA State" means a State (other than the United Kingdom) which is a contracting party to the Agreement on the European Economic Area signed at Oporto on 2nd May 1992, as adjusted by the Protocol signed at Brussels on 17th March 1993;
"enactment" includes an enactment comprised in subordinate legislation (within the meaning of the Interpretation Act 1978 (c 30));
"relevant acceding State" means any of the following—
(a) the Czech Republic,
(b) the Republic of Estonia,
(c) the Republic of Latvia,
(d) the Republic of Lithuania,
(e) the Republic of Hungary,
(f) the Republic of Poland,
(g) the Republic of Slovenia,
(h) the Slovak Republic;
"specified" means specified in regulations under this section; and
"worker" means the same as it does for the purposes of Article 39 of the Treaty establishing the European Community.

Initial Commencement
Royal Assent: 13 November 2003: (no specific commencement provision).

Subordinate Legislation
Accession (Immigration and Worker Registration) Regulations 2004, SI 2004/1219.

Appendix 1   Legislation and materials

3   Short title

This Act may be cited as the European Union (Accessions) Act 2003.

Initial Commencement
Royal Assent: 13 November 2003: (no specific commencement provision).

IMMIGRATION RULES

IMMIGRATION RULES

STATEMENT OF CHANGES IN IMMIGRATION RULES (HC 395)

Date Laid before Parliament 23 May 1994.

Authority Immigration Act 1971, s 3(2).

Note
This incorporates amending Statements laid before, or presented to, Parliament on 20 September 1994 (Cmnd 2663), 26 October 1995 (HC 797), 4 January 1996 (Cmnd 3073), 7 March 1996 (HC 274), 2 April 1996 (HC 329), 30 August 1996 (Cmnd 3365), 31 October 1996 (HC 31), 27 February 1997 (HC 338), 29 May 1997 (Cmnd 3669), 5 June 1997 (HC 26), 30 July 1997 (HC 161), 11 May 1998 (Cmnd 3953), 8 October 1998 (Cmnd 4065), 18 November 1999 (HC 22), 28 July 2000 (HC 704), 20 September 2000 (Cmnd 4851), 27 August 2001 (Cmnd 5253), 16 April 2002 (HC 735), 27 August 2002 (Cmnd 5597), 7 November 2002 (HC 1301), 26 November 2002 (HC 104), 8 January 2003 (HC 180), 10 February 2003 (HC 389), 31 March 2003 (HC 538), 30 May 2003 (Cmnd 5829), 25 August 2003 (Cm 5949), 12 November 2003 (HC 1224), 17 December 2003 (HC 95), 12 January 2004 (HC 176), 26 February 2004 (HC 370), 31 March 2004 (HC 464), 1 May 2004 (HC 523), 3 August 2004 (Cm 6297), 24 September 2004 (Cm 6339), 18 October 2004 (HC 1112), 20 December 2004 (HC 164), 11 January 2005 (HC 194), 7 February 2005 (HC 302), 22 February 2005 (HC 346), 24 March 2005 (HC 486), 15 June 2005 (HC 104) and 12 July 2005 (HC 299).

CONTENTS

1857

Appendix 1   Legislation and materials

Part 2: Persons seeking to enter or remain in the United Kingdom for visits
Visitors (rr 40–46)
Visitors in transit (rr 47–50)
Visitors seeking to enter or remain for private medical treatment (rr 51–56)
Parent of a child at school (rr 56A–56C)
Visitors seeking to enter for the purposes of marriage (rr 56D–56F)
Visitors seeking leave to enter under the Approved Destination Status (ADS) Agreement with China (rr 56G–56J)

Part 3: Persons seeking to enter or remain in the United Kingdom for studies
Students (rr 57–62)
Student nurses (rr 63–69)
Re-sits of examinations (rr 69A–69F)
Writing up a thesis (rr 69G–69L)
Postgraduate doctors and dentists (rr 70–75M)
Spouses of students (rr 76–78)
Children of students (rr 79–81)
Prospective students (rr 82–87)
Student Union sabbatical officers (rr 87A–87F)

Part 4: Persons seeking to enter or remain in the United Kingdom in an 'au pair' placement, as a working holidaymaker or for training or work experience
'Au pair' placements (rr 88–94)
Working holidaymakers (rr 95–100)
Children of working holidaymakers (rr 101–103)
Seasonal workers at agricultural camps (rr 104–109)
Teachers and language assistants coming to the United Kingdom under approved exchange schemes (rr 110–115)
Home Office approved training or work experience (rr 116–121)
Spouses of persons with limited leave to enter or remain under paragraphs 110–121 (rr 122–124)
Children of persons admitted or allowed to remain under paragraphs 110–121 (rr 125–127)

Part 5: Persons seeking to enter or remain in the United Kingdom for employment
Work permit employment (rr 128–135)
Highly skilled migrants (rr 135A–135H)
Sectors-based scheme (rr 135I–135N)
Science and Engineering Graduates Scheme (rr 135O–135T)
Representatives of overseas newspapers, news agencies and broadcasting organisations (rr 136–143F)
Representatives of overseas firms which have no branch, subsidiary or other representative in the United Kingdom (sole representatives) (rr 144–151)
Private servants in diplomatic households (rr 152–159)
Domestic workers in private households (rr 159A–159H)
Overseas government employees (rr 160–168)
Ministers of religion, missionaries and members of religious orders (rr 169–177)
Airport-based operational ground staff of overseas-owned airlines (rr 178–185)
Persons with United Kingdom ancestry (rr 186–193)
Spouses of persons with limited leave to enter or remain under paragraphs 128–193 (but not paragraphs 135I–135K) (rr 194–196)
Children of persons with limited leave to enter or remain in the United Kingdom under paragraphs 128–193 (but not paragraphs 135I–135K) (rr 197–199)
Multiple-entry work permit employment (rr 199A–199C)

Part 6: Persons seeking to enter or remain in the United Kingdom as a businessman, self-employed person, investor, writer, composer or artist
Persons intending to establish themselves in business (rr 200–210)
Innovators (rr 210A–210H)

1858

Children born in the United Kingdom who are not British citizens (rr 304–309)
Adopted children (rr 309A–316F)
Parents, grandparents and other dependent relatives of persons present and settled in the United Kingdom (rr 317–319)
Part 9: General grounds for the refusal of entry clearance, leave to enter or variation of leave to enter or remain in the United Kingdom
Refusal of entry clearance or leave to enter the United Kingdom (rr 320–321A)
Refusal of variation of leave to enter or remain or curtailment of leave (rr 322–324)
Part 10: Registration with the police (rr 324A–326)
Part 11: Asylum (rr 327–352F)
Part 12: Procedure (r 353)
Part 11A: Temporary Protection (rr 354–356B)
Part 11B (rr 357–361)
Part 13: Deportation [and Administrative Removal under Section 10 of the 1999 Act] (rr 362–395F)
Appendix 1: Visa requirements for the United Kingdom
Appendix 2: Countries or territories whose nationals or citizens are relevant foreign nationals for the purposes of Part 10 of these rules (registration with the police)
Appendix 3: Specified Nationals – Entry Clearance requirements for the United Kingdom

Introduction

1 The Home Secretary has made changes in the Rules laid down by him as to the practice to be followed in the administration of the Immigration Acts for regulating entry into and the stay of persons in the United Kingdom and contained in the statement laid before Parliament on 23 March 1990 (HC 251) (as amended). This statement contains the Rules as changed and replaces the provisions of HC 251 (as amended).
2 Immigration Officers, Entry Clearance Officers and all staff of the Home Office Immigration and Nationality [Directorate] will carry out their duties without regard to the race, colour or religion of persons seeking to enter or remain in the United Kingdom [and in compliance with the provisions of the Human Rights Acts 1998].
3 In these Rules words importing the masculine gender include the feminine unless the contrary intention appears.

Note
Words in square brackets inserted by Cm 4851.

Implementation and transitional provisions

4 These Rules come into effect on 1 October 1994 and will apply to all decisions taken on or after that date save that any application made before 1 October 1994 for entry clearance, leave to enter or remain or variation of leave to enter or remain [, other than an application for leave by a person seeking asylum,] shall be decided under the provisions of HC 251, as amended, as if these Rules had not been made.

Application

[5 Save where expressly indicated, these Rules do not apply to those persons who are entitled to enter or remain in the United Kingdom by virtue of the provisions of the Immigration (European Economic Area) Regulations 2000 or Commission Regulation 1251/70. But any person who is not entitled to rely on the provisions of those Regulations is covered by these Rules.]

Note
Substituted by Cm 4851.

Interpretation

6 In these Rules the following interpretations apply:

'the Immigration Acts' mean the Immigration Act 1971 and the Immigration Act 1988.
'the 1993 Act' is the Asylum and Immigration Appeals Act 1993.
['the 1996 Act' is the Asylum and Immigration Act 1996.]
['the 2000 EEA Regulations' are the Immigration (European Area) regulations 2000.]
['Accession State national' means a national of the Czech Republic, the Republic of Cyprus, the Republic of Estonia, the Republic of Latvia, the Republic of Lithuania, the Republic of Hungary, the Republic of Malta, the Republic of Poland, the Republic of Slovenia or the Slovak Republic.]
['EEA National' has the meaning set out in paragraph 257.]
['adoption' unless the contrary intention appears, includes a de facto adoption in accordance with the requirements of paragraph 309A of these Rules, and 'adopted' and 'adoptive parent' should be construed accordingly.]
['Approved Destination Status Agreement with China' means the Memorandum of Understanding on visa and related issues concerning tourist groups from the People's Republic of China to the United Kingdom as a approved destination, signed on 21 January 2005.]
['degree level study' means a course which leads to a recognised United Kingdom degree at bachelor's level or above, or an equivalent qualification at level 6 or above of the revised National Qualifications Framework, or levels 9 or above of the Scottish Credit and Qualifications Framework;]
'United Kingdom passport' bears the meaning it has in the Immigration Act 1971.
'Immigration Officer' includes a Customs Officer acting as an Immigration Officer.
['public funds' means

(a)   housing under Part VI or VII of the Housing Act 1996 and under Part II of the Housing Act 1985, Part I or II of the Housing (Scotland) Act 1987, Part II of the Housing (Northern Ireland) Order 1981 or Part II of the Housing (Northern Ireland) Order 1988;

(b)   attendance allowance, severe disablement allowance, [carer's allowance] and disability living allowance under Part III of the Social Security Contribution and Benefits Act 1992;, income support ... council tax benefit ... and housing benefit under Part VII of that Act; a social fund payment under Part VIII of that Act; child benefit under Part IX of that Act; income based jobseeker's allowance under the Jobseekers Act 1995[; state pension credit under the State Pension Credit Act 2002; or child tax credit and working tax credit under Part 1 of the Tax Credits Act 2002].

(c)   attendance allowance, severe disablement allowance, [carer's allowance] and disability living allowance under Part III of the Social Security Contribution and Benefits (Northern Ireland) Act 1992;, income support ... council tax benefit ... housing benefit under Part VII of that Act; a social fund payment under Part VIII of that Act; child benefit under Part IX of that Act; or income based jobseeker's allowance under the Jobseekers (Northern Ireland) Order 1995.

(d)   ...]

[...]

'settled in the United Kingdom' means that the person concerned:

(a)   is free from any restriction on the period for which he may remain save that a person entitled to an exemption under Section 8 of the Immigration Act 1971 (otherwise than as a member of the home forces) is not to be regarded as settled in the United Kingdom except in so far as Section 8(5A) so provides; and

(b)   is either:

(i)   ordinarily resident in the United Kingdom without having entered or remained in breach of the immigration laws; or

(ii)   despite having entered or remained in breach of the immigration laws, has subsequently entered lawfully or has been granted leave to remain and is ordinarily resident.

'a parent' includes:

(a)   the stepfather of a child whose father is dead;

(b)   the stepmother of a child whose mother is dead;

(c)   the father as well as the mother of an illegitimate child where he is proved to be the father;

[(d)   an adoptive parent, where a child was adopted in accordance with a decision taken by the competent administrative authority or court in a country whose adoption orders are recognised by the United Kingdom or where a child is the subject of a de facto adoption in accordance with the requirements of paragraph 309A of these Rules (except that an adopted child or child who is the subject of a de facto adoption may not make an application for leave to enter or remain in order to accompany, join or remain with an adoptive parent under paragraphs 297–303); and]

(e)   in the case of a child born in the United Kingdom who is not a British citizen, a person to whom there has been a genuine transfer of parental responsibility on the ground of the original parent(s)' inability to care for the child.

['intention to live permanently with the other' means an intention to live together, evidenced by a clear commitment from both parties that they will live together permanently in the United Kingdom immediately following the outcome of the application in question or as soon as circumstances permit thereafter, and 'intends to live permanently with the other' shall be construed accordingly;]

['present and settled' means that the person concerned is settled in the United Kingdom, and, at the time that an application under these Rules is made, is physically present here or is coming here with or to join the applicant and intends to make the United Kingdom their home with the applicant if the application is successful;]

['sponsor' means the person in relation to whom an applicant is seeking leave to enter or remain as their spouse, fiancé, unmarried partner or dependent relative, as the case may be, under paragraphs 277 to 295O or 317 to 319;]

'visa nationals' are the persons specified in the [Appendix 1] to these Rules who need a visa for the United Kingdom.

['specified national' is a person specified in Appendix 3 to these Rules who seeks leave to enter the United Kingdom for a period of more than six months.]

'employment', unless the contrary intention appears, includes paid and unpaid employment, self-employment and engaging in business or any professional activity.

[....]

['the Human Rights Convention' means the Convention for the Protection of Human Rights and Fundamental Freedoms, agreed by the Council of Europe at Rome on 4th November 1950 as it has effect for the time being in relation to the United Kingdom.]

['Immigration employment document' means a work permit or any other document which relates to employment and is issued for the purpose of these Rules or in connection with leave to enter or remain in the United Kingdom.]

Note

Frequent amendments to this paragraph makes it important to note the following. Before 4 April 1996 the definition covered: housing under the Housing Act 1985; income support family credit, council tax benefit and housing benefit. After 3 April 1996, HC 329 added: attendance allowance, severe disablement allowance, invalid care allowance, disability living allowance, disability working allowance. The position (as at March 1997) is that since 30 October 1996 HC 31 has added child benefit. It also replaces income support with income-based jobseeker's allowance

(JSA). This definition does not include contributions-based JSA. The definition of 'visa national' was amended with effect from 11 May 1998 (Cmnd 3953). On each occasion the definitions have included the equivalent provisions under legislation for Scotland and Northern Ireland.
Words in square brackets beginning 'the 2000 EEA Regulations' substituted by Cm 4851.
Definition of 'family member' omitted by Cm 4851.
Words in square brackets beginning 'the Human Rights Convention' inserted by Cm 4851.
Definition of 'Department of Employment' following definition of 'public funds' deleted by Cmnd 5253.
Definitions of 'EEA National', 'Immigration employment document' and 'Public funds' inserted by Cm 5597.
In definition 'Public funds' words in square brackets inserted and words deleted by HC 346.
Definition of 'adoption' inserted and sub-paragraph (*d*) in definition of 'a parent' substituted by HC 538.
Definitions of 'intention to live permanently with the other' and 'present and settled' inserted by HC 538.
Definition of 'specified national' inserted by HC 1224.
Definition of 'Accession State national' inserted by HC 523.
Definition of 'degree level study' inserted and definition of 'sponsor' substituted by Cm 6339.
Definition of 'Approved Destination Status Agreement with China' inserted by HC 486.

[6A For the purpose of these Rules, a person is not to be regarded as having (or potentially having) recourse to public funds merely because he is (or will be) reliant in whole or in part on public funds provided to his sponsor, unless, as a result of his presence in the United Kingdom, the sponsor is (or would be) entitled to increased or additional public funds).]

Note
Inserted by Cm 4851.

[6B A person shall not be regarded as having recourse to public funds if he is a person who is not excluded from specified benefits under section 115 of the Immigration and Asylum Act 1999 by virtue of regulations made under sub-sections (3) and (4) of that section or section 42 of the Tax Credits Act 2002.]

Note
Inserted by HC 346.

PART 1
GENERAL PROVISIONS REGARDING LEAVE TO ENTER OR REMAIN IN THE UNITED KINGDOM

Leave to enter the United Kingdom

[7 A person who is neither a British citizen nor a Commonwealth citizen with the right of abode nor a person who is entitled to enter or remain in the United Kingdom by virtue of the provisions of the Immigration (European Economic Area) Regulations 2000 or Commission Regulation 1251/70 requires leave to enter the United Kingdom.]

Note
Substituted by Cm 4851.

[8 Under Sections 3 and 4 of the Immigration Act 1971 an Immigration Officer when admitting to the United Kingdom a person subject to control under that Act may give leave to enter for a limited period and, if he does, may impose all or any of the following conditions:

(i)   a condition restricting employment or occupation in the United Kingdom;
(ii)   a condition requiring the person to maintain and accommodate himself, and any dependants of his, without recourse to public funds; and
(iii) a condition requiring the person to register with the police.

He may also require him to report to the appropriate Medical Officer of Environmental Health. Under Section 24 of the 1971 Act it is an offence knowingly to remain beyond the time limit or to fail to comply with such a condition or requirement.]

[9 The time limit and any conditions attached will normally be made known to the person concerned:

(i)   by written notice given to him or endorsed by the immigration officer in his passport or travel document; or
(ii)   in any other manner permitted by the Immigration (Leave to Enter and Remain) Order 2000.]

Note
Paragraph 9 substituted by HC 704.

[Exercise of the power to refuse leave to enter the United Kingdom or to cancel leave to enter or remain which is in force]

10 The power to refuse leave to enter the United Kingdom [or to cancel leave to enter or remain which is already in force] is not to be exercised by an Immigration Officer acting on his own. The authority of a Chief Immigration Officer or of an Immigration Inspector must always be obtained.

[Suspension of leave to enter or remain in the United Kingdom

10A Where a person has arrived in the United Kingdom with leave to enter or remain which is in force but which was given to him before his arrival he may be examined by an Immigration Officer under paragraph 2A of Schedule 2 to the Immigration Act 1971. An Immigration Officer examining a person under paragraph 2A may suspend that person's leave to enter or remain in the United Kingdom until the examination is completed.

Cancellation of leave to enter or remain in the United Kingdom

10B Where a person arrived in the United Kingdom with leave to enter or remain in the United Kingdom which is already in force, an Immigration Officer may cancel that leave.]

Note
Sub-heading of paragraph 10 substituted, words in square brackets in paragraph 10 inserted and paragraphs 10A and 10B inserted by HC 704.

Requirement for persons arriving in the United Kingdom or seeking entry through the Channel Tunnel to produce evidence of identity and nationality

11 A person must, on arrival in the United Kingdom or when seeking entry through the Channel Tunnel, produce on request by the Immigration Officer:

(i)   a valid national passport or other document satisfactorily establishing his identity and nationality; and

(ii)   such information as may be required to establish whether he requires leave to enter the United Kingdom and, if so, whether and on what terms leave to enter should be given.

Note

This paragraph reproduces the powers of Immigration Officers contained in the Immigration Act 1971, Sch 2, para 4.

Requirement for a person not requiring leave to enter the United Kingdom to prove that he has the right of abode

12 A person claiming to be a British citizen must prove that he has the right of abode in the United Kingdom by producing either:

(i)   a United Kingdom passport describing him as a British citizen or as a citizen of the United Kingdom and Colonies having the right of abode in the United Kingdom; or

(ii)   a certificate of entitlement duly issued by or on behalf of the Government of the United Kingdom certifying that he has the right of abode.

13 A person claiming to be a Commonwealth citizen with the right of abode in the United Kingdom must prove that he has the right of abode by producing a certificate of entitlement duly issued to him by or on behalf of the Government of the United Kingdom certifying that he has the right of abode.

14 A Commonwealth citizen who has been given limited leave to enter the United Kingdom may later claim to have the right of abode. The time limit on his stay may be removed if he is able to establish a claim to the right of abode, for example by showing that:

(i)   immediately before the commencement of the British Nationality Act 1981 he was a Commonwealth citizen born to or legally adopted by a parent who at the time of his birth had citizenship of the United Kingdom and Colonies by his birth in the United Kingdom or any of the Islands; and

(ii)   he has not ceased to be a Commonwealth citizen in the meanwhile.

Common Travel Area

15 The United Kingdom, the Channel Islands, the Isle of Man and the Republic of Ireland collectively form a common travel area. A person who has been examined for the purpose of immigration control at the point at which he entered the area does not normally require leave to enter any other part of it. However certain persons subject to the Immigration (Control of Entry through the Republic of Ireland)Order 1972 (as amended) who enter the United Kingdom through the Republic of Ireland do require leave to enter. This includes:

(i)   those who merely passed through the Republic of Ireland;

(ii)   persons requiring visas;

(iii)   persons who entered the Republic of Ireland unlawfully;

(iv)   persons who are subject to directions given by the Secretary of State for their exclusion from the United Kingdom on the ground that their exclusion is conducive to the public good;

(v)   persons who entered the Republic from the United Kingdom and Islands after entering there unlawfully or overstaying their leave.

Admission of certain British passport holders

16 A person in any of the following categories may be admitted freely to the United Kingdom on production of a United Kingdom passport issued in the United Kingdom and Islands or the Republic of Ireland prior to 1 January 1973, unless his passport has been endorsed to show that he was subject to immigration control:

(i)   a British Dependent Territories citizen;
(ii)   a British National (Overseas);
(iii)   a British Overseas citizen;
(iv)   a British protected person;
(v)   a British subject by virtue of Section 30(a) of the British Nationality Act 1981, (who, immediately before the commencement of the 1981 Act, would have been a British subject not possessing citizenship of the United Kingdom and Colonies or the citizenship of any other Commonwealth country or territory).

17 British Overseas citizens who hold United Kingdom passports wherever issued and who satisfy the Immigration Officer that they have, since 1 March 1968, been given indefinite leave to enter or remain in the United Kingdom may be given indefinite leave to enter.

[Persons outside the United Kingdom

17A Where a person is outside the United Kingdom but wishes to travel to the United Kingdom an Immigration Officer may give or refuse him leave to enter. An Immigration Officer may exercise these powers whether or not he is, himself, in the United Kingdom. However, an Immigration Officer is not obliged to consider an application for leave to enter from a person outside the United Kingdom.

17B Where a person, having left the common travel area, has leave to enter the United Kingdom which remains in force under article 13 of the Immigration (Leave to Enter and Remain) Order 2000, an Immigration Officer may cancel that leave. An Immigration Officer mat exercise these powers whether or not he is, himself, in the United Kingdom. If a person outside the United Kingdom has leave to remain in the United Kingdom which is in force in this way, the Secretary of State may cancel that leave.]

Note
Paragraphs 17A and B inserted by HC 704.

Returning residents

18 A person seeking leave to enter the United Kingdom as a returning resident may be admitted for settlement provided the Immigration Officer is satisfied that the person concerned:

(i)   had indefinite leave to enter or to remain in the United Kingdom when he last left; and
(ii)   has not been away from the United Kingdom for more than 2 years; and

(iii)   did not receive assistance from public funds towards the cost of leaving the United Kingdom; and

(iv)   now seeks admission for the purpose of settlement.

19 A person who does not benefit from the preceding paragraph by reason only of having been away from the United Kingdom too long may nevertheless be admitted as a returning resident if, for example, he has lived here for most of his life.

[19A Where a person who has indefinite leave to enter or remain in the United Kingdom accompanies, on a tour of duty abroad, a spouse or unmarried partner who is a member of HM Forces serving overseas, or a permanent member of HM Diplomatic Service, or a comparable United Kingdom-based staff member of the British Council, or a staff member of the Department for International Development who is a British Citizen or is settled in the United Kingdom, sub-paragraphs (ii) and (iii) of paragraph 18 shall not apply.]

Note
Substituted by Cm 5597.

20 The leave of a person whose stay in the United Kingdom is subject to a time limit lapses on his going to a country or territory outside the common travel area [if the leave was given for a period of six months or less or conferred by a visit visa. In other cases, leave lapses on the holder remaining outside the United Kingdom for a continuous period of more than two years]. [A person whose leave has lapsed and] who returns after a temporary absence abroad within the period of this earlier leave has no claim to admission as a returning resident. His application to re-enter the United Kingdom should be considered in the light of all the relevant circumstances. The same time limit and any conditions attached will normally be reimposed if he meets the requirements of these Rules, unless he is seeking admission in a different capacity from the one in which he was last given leave to enter or remain.

Note
Words in first set of square brackets in paragraph 20 inserted and those in second set of square brackets substituted by HC 704.

[Non-lapsing leave

20A Leave to enter or remain in the United Kingdom will usually lapse on the holder going to a country or territory outside the common travel area. However, under article 13 of the Immigration (Leave to Enter and Remain) Order 2000 such leave will not lapse where it was given for a period exceeding six months or where it was conferred by means of an entry clearance (other than a visit visa).]

Note
Inserted by HC 704.

Holders of restricted travel documents and passports

21 The leave to enter or remain in the United Kingdom of the holder of a passport or travel document whose permission to enter another country has to be exercised before a given date may be restricted so as to terminate at least 2 months before that date.

22 If his passport or travel document is endorsed with a restriction on the period for which he may remain outside his country of normal residence, his leave to enter or remain in the United Kingdom may be limited so as not to extend beyond the period of authorised absence.

23 The holder of a travel document issued by the Home Office should not be given leave to enter or remain for a period extending beyond the validity of that document. This paragraph and paragraphs 21–22 do not apply to a person who is eligible for admission for settlement or to a spouse who is eligible for admission under paragraph 282 or to a person who qualifies for the removal of the time limit on his stay.

[**23A** A person who is not a visa national, not a specified national or who is seeking entry for a purpose for which prior entry clearance is not required under these Rules may ascertain in advance whether he is eligible for admission to the United Kingdom by applying for an entry clearance in accordance with paragraphs 24–30. A person who seeks leave to enter on arrival in the United Kingdom may be granted such leave, irrespective of the purpose or period of time for which he seeks entry, for a period not exceeding 6 months.]

Note
Paragraph 23A inserted by HC 1224.

Entry clearance

24 A visa national[, a specified national] and any other person who is seeking entry for a purpose for which prior entry clearance is required under these Rules must produce to the Immigration Officer a valid passport or other identity document endorsed with a United Kingdom entry clearance issued to him for the purpose for which he seeks entry. Such a person will be refused leave to enter if he has no such current entry clearance. Any other person who wishes to ascertain in advance whether he is eligible for admission to the United Kingdom may apply for the issue of an entry clearance.

25 Entry clearance takes the form of a visa (for visa nationals) or an entry certificate (for non-visa nationals). These documents are to be taken as evidence of the holder's eligibility for entry into the United Kingdom, and accordingly accepted as 'entry clearances' within the meaning of the Immigration Act 1971.

[**25A** An entry clearance which satisfies the requirements set out in article 3 of the Immigration (Leave to Enter and Remain) Order 2000 will have effect as leave to enter the United Kingdom. The requirements are that the entry clearance must specify the purpose for which the holder wants to enter the United Kingdom and should be endorsed with the conditions to which it is subject or with a statement that it has effect as indefinite leave to enter the United Kingdom. The holder of such an entry clearance will not require leave to enter on arrival in the United Kingdom and, for the purposes of the Rules, will be treated as a person who has arrived in the United Kingdom with leave to enter the United Kingdom which is in force but which was given to him before his arrival.]

Note
Words in square brackets in paragraph 24 inserted by HC 1224. Paragraph 25A inserted by HC 704.

26 An application for entry clearance will be considered in accordance with the provisions in these Rules governing the grant or refusal of leave to enter. Where appropriate, the term 'Entry Clearance Officer' should be substituted for 'Immigration Officer'.

27 An application of entry clearance is to be decided in the light of the circumstances existing at the time of the decision, except that an applicant will not be refused an entry clearance where entry is sought in one of the categories contained in paragraphs 296–316 solely on account of his attaining the age of 18 years between receipt of his application and the date of the decision on it.

28 An applicant for an entry clearance must be outside the United Kingdom and Islands at the time of the application. An applicant for an entry clearance who is seeking entry as a visitor must apply to a post designated by the Secretary of State to accept applications for entry clearance for that purpose and from that category of applicant. Any other application must be made to the post in the country or territory where the applicant is living which has been designated by the Secretary of State to accept applications for entry clearance for that purpose and from that category of applicant. Where there is no such post the applicant must apply to the appropriate designated post outside the country or territory where he is living.

29 For the purposes of paragraph 28 'post' means a British Diplomatic Mission, British Consular post or the office of any person outside the United Kingdom and Islands who has been authorised by the Secretary of State to accept applications for entry clearance. A list of designated posts is published by the Foreign and Commonwealth Office.

30 An application for an entry clearance is not made until any fee required to be paid under the Consular Fees Act 1980 (including any Regulations or Orders made under that Act) has been paid.

[30A An entry clearance may be revoked if the Entry Clearance Officer is satisfied that:

(i) whether or not to the holder's knowledge, false representations were employed or material facts were not disclosed, either in writing or orally, for the purpose of obtaining the entry clearance; or

(ii) a change in circumstances since the entry clearance was issued has removed the basis of the holder's claim to be admitted to the United Kingdom, except where the change of circumstances amounts solely to his exceeding the age for entry in one of the categories contained in paragraphs 296–316 of these Rules since the issue of the entry clearance; or

(iii) the holder's exclusion from the United Kingdom would be conducive to the public good.]

[30B An entry clearance shall cease to have effect where the entry clearance has effect as leave to enter and an Immigration Officer cancels that leave in accordance with paragraph 2A(8) of Schedule 2 to the Immigration Act 1971.

30C An Immigration Officer may cancel an entry clearance which is capable of having effect as leave to enter if the holder arrives in the United Kingdom before the day on which the entry clearance becomes effective of if the holder seeks to enter the United Kingdom for a purpose other than the purpose specified in the entry clearance.]

Note
Paragraph 30A inserted by HC 31. Paragraphs 30B and 30C inserted by HC 704.

Variation of leave to enter or remain in the United Kingdom

31 Under Section 3(3) of the 1971 Act a limited leave to enter or remain in the United Kingdom may be varied by extending or restricting its duration, by adding, varying or revoking conditions or by removing the time limit (whereupon any condition attached to the leave ceases to apply). When leave to enter or remain is varied an entry is to be made in the applicant's passport or travel document (and his registration certificate where appropriate) or the decision may be made known in writing or some other appropriate way.

[**31A** Where a person has arrived in the United Kingdom with leave to enter or remain in the United Kingdom which is in force but was given to him before his arrival, he may apply, on arrival at a port of entry in the United Kingdom, for variation of that leave. An Immigration Officer acting on behalf of the Secretary of State may vary the leave at the port of entry but is not obliged to consider an application for variation made at the port of entry. If an Immigration Officer acting on behalf of the Secretary of State has declined to consider an application for variation of leave at a port of entry but the leave has not been cancelled under paragraph 2A(8) of Schedule 2 to the Immigration Act 1971, the person seeking variation should apply to the Home Office under paragraph 32.]

Note
Paragraph 31A inserted by HC 704.

32 After admission to the United Kingdom any application for an extension of the time limit on or variation of conditions attached to a person's stay in the United Kingdom must be made to the Home Office before the applicant's current leave to enter or remain expires.

[With the exception of applications made under [paragraph 31A (applications at the port of entry),] paragraph 33 (work permits), [33A (applications made outside the United Kingdom),] paragraphs 255 to 257 (EEA nationals) and Part 11 (asylum), all applications for variation of leave to enter or remain must be made using the form prescribed for the purpose by the Secretary of State, which must be completed in the manner required by the form and be accompanied by the documents and photographs specified in the form. An application for such a variation made in any other way is not valid.]

33 Where the application is in respect of employment for which a work permit or a permit for training or work experience is required or is in respect of the spouse or child or a person who is making such an application, the application should be made direct to the [Work permits (UK) at the Home Office].

[**33A** Where a person, having left the common travel area, has leave to enter or remain in the United Kingdom which remains in force under article 13 of the Immigration (Leave to Enter and Remain) Order 2000, his leave may be varied (including any conditions to which it is subject) in such form and manner as permitted for the giving of leave to enter. However, the Secretary of State is not obliged to consider an application for variation of leave to enter or remain from a person outside the United Kingdom.]

Note
Words in first set of square brackets in paragraph 32 added by HC 329, para 2 with effect from 3 June 1996. Words in square brackets within first set in paragraph 32, and the whole of paragraph 33A, inserted by HC 704. Words in square brackets in paragraph 33 substituted by Cmnd 5253.

Withdrawn applications for variation of leave to enter or remain in the United Kingdom

34 Where a person whose application for variation of leave to enter or remain is being considered requests the return of his passport for the purpose of travel outside the common travel area, the application for variation of leave shall, provided it has not already been determined, be treated as withdrawn as soon as the passport is returned in response to that request [...].

Note
Words deleted by Cm 4851.

Undertakings

35 A sponsor of a person seeking leave to enter or variation of leave to enter or remain in the United Kingdom may be asked to give an undertaking in writing to be responsible for that person's maintenance and accommodation for the period of any leave granted, including any further variation. Under the Social Security Administration Act 1992 and the Social Security Administration (Northern Ireland) Act 1992, the Department of Social Security or, as the case may be, the Department of Health and Social Services in Northern Ireland may seek to recover from the person giving such an undertaking any income support paid to meet the needs of the person in respect of whom the undertaking has been given.

[Under the Immigration and Asylum Act 1999 the Home Office may seek to recover from the person giving such an undertaking amounts attributable to any support provided under section 95 of the Immigration and Asylum Act 1999 (support for asylum seekers) to, or in respect of, the person in respect of whom the undertaking has been given. Failure by the sponsor to maintain that person on accordance with the undertaking, may also be an offence under section 105 of the Social Security Administration Act 1992 and/or under section 108 of the Immigration and Asylum Act 1999 if, as a consequence asylum support and/or income support is provided to or in respect of, that person.]

Note
Words in square brackets inserted by Cm 4851.

Medical

36 A person who intends to remain in the United Kingdom for more than 6 months should normally be referred to the Medical Inspector for examination. If he produces a medical certificate he should be advised to hand it to the Medical Inspector. Any person seeking entry who mentions health or medical treatment as a reason for his visit, or who appears not to be in good mental or physical health, should also be referred to the Medical Inspector; and the Immigration Officer has discretion, which should be exercised sparingly, to refer for examination in any other case.

37 Where the Medical Inspector advises that a person seeking entry is suffering from a specified disease or condition which may interfere with his ability to support himself or his dependants, the Immigration Officer should take account of this, in conjunction with other factors, in deciding whether to admit that person. The Immigration Officer should also take account of the Medical Inspector's assessment of the likely course of treatment in deciding whether a person seeking entry for private medical treatment has sufficient means at his disposal.

38 A returning resident should not be refused leave to enter [or have existing leave to enter or remain cancelled] on medical grounds. But where a person would be refused leave to enter [or to cancel existing leave to enter or remain] on medical grounds if he were not a returning resident, or in any case where it is decided on compassionate grounds not to exercise the power to refuse leave to enter, or in any other case where the Medical Inspector so recommends, the Immigration Officer should give the person concerned a notice requiring him to report to the Medical Officer of Environmental Health designated by the Medical Inspector with a view to further examination and any necessary treatment.

39 The Entry Clearance Officer has the same discretion as an Immigration Officer to refer applicants for entry clearance for medical examination and the same principles will apply to the decision whether or not to issue an entry clearance.

Note
Paragraphs 7–39 replace HC 251, paras 6–21 and 58–60. Words in square brackets in paragraph 38 inserted by HC 704.

[Students

39A An application for a variation of leave to enter or remain made by a student who is sponsored by a government or international sponsorship agency may be refused if the sponsor has not given written consent to the proposed variation.]

PART 2
PERSONS SEEKING TO ENTER OR REMAIN IN THE UNITED KINGDOM
FOR VISITS

VISITORS

Requirements for leave to enter as a visitor

40 For the purpose of paragraphs 41–46 a visitor includes a person living and working outside the United Kingdom who comes to the United Kingdom to transact business (such as attending meetings and briefings, fact finding, negotiating or making contracts with United Kingdom businesses to buy or sell goods or services). A visitor seeking leave to enter or remain for private medical treatment must meet the requirements of paragraphs 51 or 54.

[A visitor seeking leave to enter for the purposes of marriage must meet the requirements of paragraph 56D.]

Note
Words in square brackets in paragraph 40 inserted by HC 346.

41 The requirements to be met by a person seeking leave to enter the United Kingdom as a visitor are that he:

  (i)   is genuinely seeking entry as a visitor for a limited period as stated by him, not exceeding 6 months; and
  (ii) intends to leave the United Kingdom at the end of the period of the visit as stated by him; and
  (iii) does not intend to take employment in the United Kingdom; and
  (iv) does not intend to produce goods or provide services within the United Kingdom, including the selling of goods or services direct to members of the public; and
  (v)   does not intend to study at a maintained school; and
  (vi) will maintain and accommodate himself and any dependants adequately out of resources available to him without recourse to public funds or taking employment; or will, with any dependants, be maintained and accommodated adequately by relatives or friends; and
  (vii) can meet the cost of the return or onward journey.

Leave to enter as a visitor

42 A person seeking leave to enter the United Kingdom as a visitor may be admitted for a period not exceeding 6 months, subject to a condition prohibiting employment, provided the Immigration Officer is satisfied that each or the requirements of paragraph 41 is met.

Refusal of leave to enter as a visitor

43 Leave to enter as a visitor is to be refused if the Immigration Officer is not satisfied that each of the requirements of paragraph 41 is met.

Requirements for an extension of stay as a visitor

44 Six months is the maximum permitted leave which may be granted to a visitor. The requirements for an extension of stay as a visitor are that the applicant:

  (i)   meets the requirements of paragraph 41(ii)–(vii); and
  (ii) has not already spent, or would not as a result of an extension of stay spend, more than 6 months in total in the United Kingdom as a visitor.

Any period spent as a seasonal agricultural worker is to be counted as a period spent as a visitor.

[and

  (iii) was not last admitted to the United Kingdom under the Approved Destination Status Agreement with China.]

Note
Words in square brackets inserted by HC 486.

Appendix 1 Legislation and materials

Extension of stay as a visitor

45 An extension of stay as a visitor may be granted, subject to a condition prohibiting employment, provided the Secretary of State is satisfied that each of the requirements of paragraph 44 is met.

Refusal of extension of stay as a visitor

46 An extension of stay as a visitor is to be refused if the Secretary of State is not satisfied that each of the requirements of paragraph 44 is met.

Note
Paragraphs 40–46 replace HC 251, paras 22, 24, 104 and 105.

VISITORS IN TRANSIT

Requirements for admission as a visitor in transit to another country

47 The requirements to be met by a person (not being a member of the crew of a ship, aircraft, hovercraft, hydrofoil or train) seeking leave to enter the United Kingdom as visitor in transit to another country are that he:

(i)   is in transit to a country outside the common travel area; and
(ii)   has both the means and the intention of proceeding at once to another country; and
(iii) is assured of entry there; and
(iv)   intends and is able to leave the United Kingdom within 48 hours.

Leave to enter as a visitor in transit

48 A person seeking leave to enter the United Kingdom as a visitor in transit may be admitted for a period not exceeding 48 hours with a prohibition on employment provided the Immigration Officer is satisfied that each of the requirements of paragraph 47 is met.

Refusal of leave to enter as a visitor in transit

49 Leave to enter as a visitor in transit is to be refused if the Immigration Officer is not satisfied that each of the requirements of paragraph 47 is met.

Extension of stay as a visitor in transit

50 The maximum permitted leave which may be granted to a visitor in transit is 48 hours. An application for an extension of stay beyond 48 hours from a person admitted in this category is to be refused.

VISITORS SEEKING TO ENTER OR REMAIN FOR PRIVATE MEDICAL TREATMENT

Requirements for leave to enter as a visitor for private medical treatment

51 The requirements to be met by a person seeking leave to enter the United Kingdom as a visitor for private medical treatment are that he:

(i)   meets the requirements set out in paragraph 41(iii)–(vii) for entry as a visitor; and

(ii)   in the case of a person suffering from a communicable disease, has satisfied the Medical Inspector that there is no danger to public health; and

(iii)   can show, if required to do so, that any proposed course of treatment is of finite duration; and

(iv)   intends to leave the United Kingdom at the end of his treatment; and

(v)   can produce satisfactory evidence, if required to do so, of:

    (a)   the medical condition requiring consultation or treatment; and

    (b)   satisfactory arrangements for the necessary consultation or treatment at his own expense; and

    (c)   the estimated costs of such consultation or treatment; and

    (d)   the likely duration of his visit; and

    (e)   sufficient funds available to him in the United Kingdom to meet the estimated costs of his undertaking to do so.

Leave to enter as a visitor for private medical treatment

52 A person seeking leave to enter the United Kingdom as a visitor for private medical treatment may be admitted for a period not exceeding 6 months, subject to a condition prohibiting employment, provided the Immigration Officer is satisfied that each of the requirements of paragraph 51 is met.

Refusal of leave to enter as a visitor for private medical treatment

53 Leave to enter as a visitor for private medical treatment is to be refused if the Immigration Officer is not satisfied that each of the requirements of paragraph 51 is met.

Requirements for an extension of stay as a visitor for private medical treatment

54 The requirements for an extension of stay as a visitor to undergo or continue private medical treatment are that the applicant:

(i)   meets the requirements set out in paragraph 41(ii)–(vii) and paragraph 51(ii)–(v); and

[(ii)   has produced evidence from a registered medical practitioner who holds an NHS consultant post or who appears in the Specialist Register of the General Medical Council of satisfactory arrangements for private medical consultation or treatment and its likely duration; and, where treatment has already begun, evidence as to its progress; and]

(iii)   can show that he has met, out of the resources available to him, any costs and expenses incurred in relation to his treatment in the United Kingdom; and

(iv)   has sufficient funds available to him in the United Kingdom to meet the likely costs of his treatment and intends to meet those costs; [and

1875

(v)   was not last admitted to the United Kingdom under the Approved Destination Status Agreement with China.]

Note
Paragraph 54(ii) substituted by Cm 4851. Paragraph 54(v) inserted by HC 486.

Extension of stay as a visitor for private medical treatment

55 An extension of stay to undergo or continue private medical treatment may be granted, with a prohibition on employment, provided the Secretary of State is satisfied that each of the requirements of paragraph 54 is met.

Refusal of extension of stay as a visitor for private medical treatment

56 An extension of stay as a visitor to undergo or continue private medical treatment is to be refused if the Secretary of State is not satisfied that each of the requirements of paragraph 54 is met.

[PARENT OF A CHILD AT SCHOOL

Requirements for leave to enter or remain as the parent of a child at school

56A The requirements to be met by a person seeking leave to enter or remain in the United Kingdom as the parent of a child at school are that:

(i)   the parent meets the requirements set out in paragraph 41 (ii)–(iv); and
(ii)   the child is attending an independent fee paying day school and meets the requirements set out in paragraph 57 (i)–(vi); and
(iii)   the child is under 12 years of age; and
(iv)   the parent can provide satisfactory evidence of adequate and reliable funds for maintaining a second home in the United Kingdom; and
(v)   the parent is not seeking to make the United Kingdom his main home; [and
(vi)   the parent was not last admitted to the United Kingdom under the Approved Destination Status Agreement with China.]

Note
Paragraph 56A(vi) inserted by HC 486.

Leave to enter or remain as the parent of a child at school

56B A person seeking leave to enter or remain in the United Kingdom as the parent of a child at school may be admitted or allowed to remain for a period not exceeding 12 months, subject to a condition prohibiting employment, providing the Immigration Officer or, in the case of an application for limited leave to remain, the Secretary of State is satisfied that each of the requirements of paragraph 56A is met.

Refusal of leave to enter or remain as the parent of a child at school

56C Leave to enter or remain in the United Kingdom as the parent of a child at school is to be refused if the Immigration Office or, in the case of an application for limited leave to remain, the Secretary of State, is not satisfied that each of the requirements of paragraph 56A is met.]

Note
Words in square brackets inserted by Cm 4851.

[VISITORS SEEKING TO ENTER FOR THE PURPOSES OF MARRIAGE]

[Requirements for leave to enter as a visitor for marriage]

[56D The requirements to be met by a person seeking leave to enter the United Kingdom as a visitor for marriage are that he:

  (i)   meets the requirements set out in paragraph 41 for entry as a visitor; and
  (ii)   can show that he intends to give notice of marriage, or marry, in the United Kingdom within the period for which entry is sought; and
  (iii)   can produce satisfactory evidence, if required to do so, of the arrangements for giving notice of marriage, or for his wedding ceremony to take place, in the United Kingdom during the period for which entry is sought; and
  (iv)   holds a valid United Kingdom entry clearance for entry in this capacity.]

Note
Inserted by HC 346.

[Leave to enter as a visitor for marriage]

[56E A person seeking leave to enter the United Kingdom as a visitor for marriage may be admitted for a period not exceeding 6 months, subject to a condition prohibiting employment, provided the Immigration Officer is satisfied that each of the requirements of paragraph 56D is met.]

Note
Inserted by HC 346.

[Refusal of leave to enter as a visitor for marriage]

[56F Leave to enter as a visitor for marriage is to be refused if the Immigration Officer is not satisfied that each of the requirements of paragraph 56D is met.]

Note
Inserted by HC 346.

Appendix 1   Legislation and materials

[Requirements for leave to enter as a visitor under the Approved Destination Status Agreement with China ('ADS Agreement')]

[56G The requirements to be met by a person seeking leave to enter the United Kingdom as a visitor under the ADS agreement with China are that he:

   (i)   meets the requirements set out in paragraph 41 (ii)–(vii) ; and
   (ii)   is a national of the People's Republic of China; and
   (iii) is genuinely seeking entry as a visitor for a limited period as stated by him, not exceeding 30 days; and
   (iv)   intends to enter, leave and travel within the territory of the United Kingdom as a member of a tourist group under the ADS agreement; and
   (v)   holds a valid ADS agreement visit visa.]

Note
Inserted by HC 486.

[Leave to enter as a visitor under the ADS agreement with China]

[56H A person seeking leave to enter the United Kingdom as a visitor under the ADS Agreement may be admitted for a period not exceeding 30 days, subject to a condition prohibiting employment, provided they hold an ADS Agreement visit visa.]

Note
Inserted by HC 486.

[Refusal of leave to enter as a visitor under the ADS agreement with China]

[56I Leave to enter as a visitor under the ADS agreement with China is to be refused if the person does not hold an ADS Agreement visit visa.]

Note
Inserted by HC 486.

[Extension of stay as a visitor under the ADS agreement with China]

[56J Any application for an extension of stay as a visitor under the ADS Agreement with China is to be refused.]

Note
Inserted by HC 486.

PART 3
PERSONS SEEKING TO ENTER OR REMAIN IN THE UNITED KINGDOM
FOR STUDIES

STUDENTS

Requirements for leave to enter as a student

57 The requirements to be met by a person seeking leave to enter the United Kingdom as a student are that he:

[(i)   has been accepted for a course of study which is to be provided by an organisation which is included on the Department for Education and Skill' Register of Education and Training Providers, and is at either:
(a)   a publicly funded institution of further or higher education; or
(b)   a bona fide private education institution which maintains satisfactory records of enrolment and attendance; or
(c)   an independent fee paying school outside the maintained sector; and]
(ii)   is able and intends to follow either:
(a)   a recognised full-time degree course at a publicly funded institution of further or higher education; or
(b)   a weekday full-time course involving attendance at a single institution for a minimum of 15 hours organised daytime study per week of a single subject or directly related subjects; or
(c)   a full-time course of study at an independent fee paying school; and
(iii)   if under the age of 16 years is enrolled at an independent fee paying school on a full-time course of studies which meets the requirements of the Education Act 1944; and
(iv)   intends to leave the United Kingdom at the end of his studies; and
(v)   does not intend to engage in business or to take employment, except part-time or vacation work undertaken with the consent of the Secretary of State for Employment; and
(vi)   is able to meet the costs of his course and accommodation and the maintenance of himself and any dependants without taking employment or engaging in business or having recourse to public funds.

Note
[Paragraphs 57–62 replace HC 251, paras 26, 27 and 108–112.]
Sub-paragraphs (i)(a)–(c) substituted by HC 164, in force 1 January 2005.

Leave to enter as a student

58 A person seeking leave to enter the United Kingdom as a student may be admitted for an appropriate period depending on the length of his course of study and his means, and with a condition restricting his freedom to take employment, provided the Immigration Officer is satisfied that each of the requirements of paragraph 57 is met.

Refusal of leave to enter as a student

59 Leave to enter as a student is to be refused if the Immigration Officer is not satisfied that each of the requirements of paragraph 57 is met.

Appendix 1   Legislation and materials

Requirements for an extension of stay as student

60 The requirements for an extension of stay as a student are that the applicant:

[(i)   either–
- (a)   he is a person specified in Appendix 1 to these Rules and he was last admitted to the United Kingdom in possession of a valid student entry clearance, or valid prospective student entry clearance in accordance with paragraphs 82 to 87 of these Rules; or
- (b)   he is not a person specified in Appendix 1 to these Rules and he has been accepted for a course of study at degree level or above; or
- (c)   he is not a person specified in Appendix 1 to these Rules and he was last admitted to the United Kingdom in possession of a valid student entry clearance, or valid prospective student entry clearance in accordance with paragraphs 82 to 87 of these Rules, if he has been accepted for a course of study below degree level; and]
- (ii)   meets the requirements for admission as a student set out in paragraph 57(i)–(vi); and
- (iii)   has produced evidence of his enrolment on a course which meets the requirements of paragraph 57; and
- (iv)   can produce satisfactory evidence of regular attendance during any course which he has already begun; or any other course for which he has been enrolled in the past; and
- (v)   can show evidence of satisfactory progress in his course of study including the taking and passing of any relevant examinations; and
- (vi)   would not, as a result of an extension of stay, spend more than [2] years on short courses [below degree level] (ie courses of less than [1] years duration, or longer courses broken off before completion); and
- (vii)   has not come to the end of a period of government or international scholarship agency sponsorship, or has the written consent of his [official] sponsor for a further period of study in the United Kingdom and satisfactory evidence that sufficient sponsorship funding is available.

Note
Words in square brackets in paragraph 60(vii) substituted by Cm 4851. Paragraph 60(i) substituted by Cm 6339. Words in square brackets in paragraph 60(vi) substituted by Cm 6339.

Extension of stay as a student

61 An extension of stay as a student may be granted, subject to a restriction on his freedom to take employment, provided the Secretary of State is satisfied that the applicant meets each of the requirements of paragraph 60.

Refusal of extension of stay as a student

62 an extension of stay as a student is to be refused if the Secretary of State is not satisfied that each of the requirements of paragraph 60 is met.

STUDENT NURSES

Definition of student nurse

63 For the purposes of these Rules the term student nurse means a person accepted for training as a student nurse or midwife leading to a registered nursing qualification; or

1880

an overseas nurse or midwife who has been accepted on an adaptation course leading to registration as a nurse with the United Kingdom Central Council for Nursing, Midwifery and Health Visiting.

Requirements for leave to enter as a student nurse

64 The requirements to be met by a person seeking leave to enter the United Kingdom as a student nurse are that the person:

   (i)   comes within the definition set out in paragraph 63 above; and
   (ii) has been accepted for a course of study in a recognised nursing educational establishment offering nursing training which meets the requirements of the United Kingdom Central Council for Nursing, Midwifery and Health Visiting; and
   (iii) did not obtain acceptance by misrepresentation; and
   (iv) is able and intends to follow the course; and
   (v)   does not intend to engage in business or take employment except in connection with the training course; and
   (vi) intends to leave the United Kingdom at the end of the course; and
   (vii) has sufficient funds available for accommodation and maintenance for himself and any dependants without engaging in business or taking employment (except in connection with the training course) or having recourse to public funds. The possession of a Department of Health bursary may be taken into account in assessing whether the student meets the maintenance requirement.

Leave to enter the United Kingdom as a student nurse

65 A person seeking leave to enter the United Kingdom as a student nurse may be admitted for the duration of the training course, with a restriction on his freedom to take employment, provided the Immigration Officer is satisfied that each of the requirements of paragraph 64 is met.

Refusal of leave to enter as a student nurse

66 Leave to enter as a student nurse is to be refused if the Immigration Officer is not satisfied that each of the requirements of paragraph 64 is met.

Requirements for an extension of stay as a student nurse

67 The requirements for an extension of stay as a student nurse are that the applicant:

[(i)   was last admitted to the United Kingdom in possession of a valid student entry clearance, or valid prospective student entry clearance in accordance with paragraphs 82 to 87 of these Rules, if he is a person specified in Appendix 1 to these Rules; and]
   (ii) meets the requirements set out in paragraphs 64(i)–(vii); and
   (iii) has produced evidence of enrolment at a recognised nursing educational establishment; and
   (iv) can provide satisfactory evidence of regular attendance during any course which he has already begun; or any other course for which he has been enrolled in the past; and

1881

(v)   would not, as a result of an extension of stay, spend more than 4 years in obtaining the relevant qualification; and

(vi)   has not come to the end of a period of government or international scholarship agency sponsorship, or has the written consent of his [official] sponsor for a further period of study in the United Kingdom and evidence that sufficient sponsorship funding is available.

Note
Words in square brackets in paragraph 67(vi) substituted by Cm 4851. Paragraph 67(i) substituted by Cm 5597.

Extension of stay as a student nurse

68 An extension of stay as a student nurse may be granted, subject to a restriction on his freedom to take employment, provided the Secretary of State is satisfied that the applicant meets each of the requirements of paragraph 67.

Refusal of extension of stay as student nurse

69 An extension of stay as a student nurse is to be refused if the Secretary of State is not satisfied that each of the requirements of paragraph 67 is met.

[RE-SITS OF EXAMINATIONS

Requirements for leave to enter to re-sit an examination

69A The requirements to be met by a person seeking leave to enter the United Kingdom in order to re-sit an examination are that the applicant:

(i)
    (a)   meets the requirements for admission as a student set out in paragraph 57(i)–(vi); or
    (b)   met the requirements for admission as a student set out in paragraph 57(i)–(iii) in the previous academic year and continues to meet the requirements of paragraph 57(iv)–(vi); and

(ii)   has produced written confirmation from the education institution or independent fee paying school which he attends or attended in the previous academic year that he is required to re-sit an examination; and

(iii) can provide satisfactory evidence of regular attendance during any course which he has already begun; or any other course for which he has been enrolled in the past; and

(iv)   has not come to the end of a period of government or international scholarship agency sponsorship, or has the written consent of his official sponsor for a further period of study in the United Kingdom and satisfactory evidence that sufficient sponsorship funding is available; and

(v)   has not previously been granted leave to re-sit the examination.

Leave to enter to re-sit an examination

69B A person seeking leave to enter the United Kingdom in order to re-sit an examination may be admitted for a period sufficient to enable him to re-sit the examination at the first available opportunity with a condition restricting his freedom to take employment, provided the Immigration Officer is satisfied that each of the requirements of paragraph 69A is met.

Refusal of leave to enter to re-sit an examination

69C Leave to enter to re-sit an examination is to be refused if the Immigration Officer is not satisfied that each of the requirements of paragraph 69A is met.

Requirements for an extension of stay to re-sit an examination

69D The requirements for an extension of stay to re-sit an examination are that the applicant:

(i)   was admitted to the United Kingdom with a valid student entry clearance if he was then a visa national; and
(ii)   meets the requirements set out in paragraph 69A(i)–(v).

Extension of stay to re-sit an examination

69E An extension of stay to re-sit an examination may be granted for a period sufficient to enable the applicant to re-sit the examination at the first available opportunity, subject to a restriction on his freedom to take employment, provided the Secretary of State is satisfied that the applicant meets each of the requirements of paragraph 69D.

Refusal of extension of stay to re-sit an examination

69F An extension of stay to re-sit an examination is to be refused if the Secretary of State is not satisfied that each of the requirements of paragraph 69D is met.

WRITING UP A THESIS

Requirements for leave to enter to write up a thesis

69G The requirements to be met by a person seeking leave to enter the United Kingdom in order to write up a thesis are that the applicant:

(i)
  (a)   meets the requirements for admission as a student set out in paragraph 57(i)–(vi); or
  (b)   met the requirements for admission as a student set out in paragraph 57(i)–(iii) in the previous academic year and continues to meet the requirements of paragraph 57(iv)–(vi); and
(ii)   can provide satisfactory evidence that he is a postgraduate student enrolled at an education institution as either a full time, part time or writing up student; and
(iii) can demonstrate that his application is supported by the education institution; and

(iv)   has not come to the end of a period of government or international scholarship agency sponsorship, or has the written consent of his official sponsor for a further period of study in the United Kingdom and satisfactory evidence that sufficient sponsorship funding is available; and

(v)   has not previously been granted 12 months leave to write up the same thesis.

Leave to enter to write up a thesis

69H A person seeking leave to enter the United Kingdom in order to write up a thesis may be admitted for 12 months with a condition restricting his freedom to take employment, provided the Immigration Officer is satisfied that each of the requirements of paragraph 69G is met.

Refusal of leave to enter to write up a thesis

69I Leave to enter to write up a thesis is to be refused if the Immigration Officer is not satisfied that each of the requirements of paragraph 69G is met.

Requirements for an extension of stay to write up a thesis

69J The requirements for an extension of stay to write up a thesis are that the applicant:

(i)   was admitted to the United Kingdom with a valid student entry clearance if he was then a visa national; and

(ii)   meets the requirements set out in paragraph 69G(i)–(v).

Extension of stay to write up a thesis

69K An extension of stay to write up a thesis may be granted for 12 months subject to a restriction on his freedom to take employment, provided the Secretary of State is satisfied that the applicant meets each of the requirements of paragraph 69J.

Refusal of extension of stay to write up a thesis

69L An extension of stay to write up a thesis is to be refused if the Secretary of State is not satisfied that each of the requirements of paragraph 69J is met.]

Note
[Paragraphs 63–69 replace HC 251, para 29.]
Paragraphs 69A to 69L inserted by Cm 4851.

[POSTGRADUATE DOCTORS AND DENTISTS]

[Requirements for leave to enter the United Kingdom as a postgraduate doctor or dentist

70 The requirements for leave to enter the United Kingdom for the purpose of training as a doctor or dentist are that the applicant:

(i)
  (a)   is a graduate from a medical school or dental school who has a confirmed place on a recognised Foundation Programme to continue their training as a doctor or dentist in the UK; or
  (b)   is a doctor or dentist who has full, limited or temporary registration with the General Medical Council or General Dental Council or who is eligible for the same and who intends to undertake basic or higher specialist training in the United Kingdom in a hospital or the Community Health services or in General Practice, or in a combination of these; and
(ii)   holds a letter from the Postgraduate Dean responsible for their training in the UK approving the applicant's training plan and recommending the duration of leave that should be granted; and
(iii) is able to maintain and accommodate himself and any dependants without recourse to public funds; and
(iv)   intends to leave the United Kingdom if, on expiry of his leave under this paragraph, he has not been granted leave to remain in the United Kingdom as:
  (a)   a doctor or dentist undertaking a period of clinical attachment or a dental observer post in accordance with paragraphs 75G to 75M of these Rules; or
  (b)   a work permit holder in accordance with paragraphs 128 to 135 of these Rules; or
  (c)   a highly skilled migrant in accordance with paragraphs 135A to 135H of these Rules; or
  (d)   a person intending to establish themselves in business in accordance with paragraphs 200 to 210 of these Rules; or
  (e)   an innovator in accordance with paragraphs 210A to 210H of these Rules; and
(v)   if his study at medical school or dental school, or any subsequent studies he has undertaken, were sponsored by a government or international scholarship agency, he has the written consent of his sponsor to enter or remain in the United Kingdom as a postgraduate doctor or dentist; and
(vi)   if he has previously been granted leave as a postgraduate doctor or dentist, is not seeking leave to enter or remain which, when amalgamated with any previous periods of leave in this category, would total more than:
  (a)   26 months to complete a Foundation Programme; or
  (b)   3 years to complete basic specialist training, if the applicant has already completed a Foundation Programme; or
  (c)   4 years to complete basic specialist training, if the applicant has not already completed a Foundation Programme; and
(vii) holds a valid entry clearance for entry in this capacity except where he is a British National (Overseas), a British overseas territories citizen, a British Overseas citizen, a British protected person or a person who under the British Nationality Act 1981 is a British subject.]

Note

Paragraphs 70–75 substituted by HC 104. Further substituted by HC 299.

[Leave to enter as a postgraduate doctor or dentist

71 Leave to enter the United Kingdom as a postgraduate doctor or dentist may be granted:

(i)   to undertake a Foundation Programme, for a period not exceeding 26 months; or

(ii)   to undertake postgraduate training as a doctor or dentist in a hospital or the
Community Health services or in General Practice, or in a combination of
these, for a period not exceeding 3 years at a time;

provided the Immigration Officer is satisfied that each of the requirements of
paragraph 70 is met.]

Note
Paragraphs 70–75 substituted by HC 104. Further substituted by HC 299.

[Refusal of leave to enter as a postgraduate doctor or dentist

72 Leave to enter as a postgraduate doctor or dentist is to be refused if the
Immigration Officer is not satisfied that each of the requirements of paragraph 70 is
met.]

Note
Paragraphs 70–75 substituted by HC 104. Further substituted by HC 299.

[Requirements for extension of stay as a postgraduate doctor or dentist

73 The requirements to be met by a person seeking an extension of stay as a
postgraduate doctor or dentist are that the applicant:

(i)   meets the requirements of paragraph 70(i)–(vi); and
(ii)   has leave to enter or remain in the United Kingdom as either:
  (a)   a student in accordance with paragraphs 57 to 69L of these Rules; or
  (b)   as a postgraduate doctor or dentist in accordance with paragraphs 70 to
          75 of these Rules; or
  (c)   as a doctor taking the PLAB Test in accordance with paragraphs 75A to
          75F of these Rules; or
  (d)   as a doctor or dentist undertaking a period of clinical attachment or a
          dental observer post in accordance with paragraphs 75G to 75M of
          these Rules; or
  (e)   as a work permit holder in accordance with paragraphs 128 to 135 of
          these Rules.]

Note
Paragraphs 70–75 substituted by HC 104. Further substituted by HC 299.

[Extension of stay as a postgraduate doctor or dentist

74 An extension of stay as a postgraduate doctor or dentist may be granted:

(i)   to undertake a Foundation Programme, for a period not exceeding 26 months;
        or
(ii)   to undertake postgraduate training as a doctor or dentist in a hospital or the
        Community Health services or in General Practice, or in a combination of
        these, for a period not exceeding 3 years at a time;

provided the Secretary of State is satisfied that each of the requirements of paragraph 73 is met.]

Note
Paragraphs 70–75 substituted by HC 104. Further substituted by HC 299.

[Refusal of extension of stay as a postgraduate doctor or dentist

75 An extension of stay as a postgraduate doctor or dentist is to be refused if the Secretary of State is not satisfied that each of the requirements of paragraph 73 is met.]

Note
Paragraphs 70–75 substituted by HC 104. Further substituted by HC 299.

[Requirements for leave to enter the United Kingdom to take the PLAB Test]

[**75A** The requirements to be met by a person seeking leave to enter in order to take the PLAB Test are that the applicant:

(i)   is a graduate from a medical school and intends to take the PLAB Test in the United Kingdom; and

(ii)   can provide documentary evidence of a confirmed test date or of his eligibility to take the PLAB Test; and

(iii)   meets the requirements of paragraph 41 (iii)–(vii) for entry as a visitor; and

(iv)   intends to leave the United Kingdom at the end of his leave granted under this paragraph unless he is successful in the PLAB Test and granted leave to remain:

    (a)   as a postgraduate doctor or trainee general practitioner in accordance with paragraphs 70 to 75; or

    (b)   to undertake a clinical attachment in accordance with paragraphs 75G to 75M of these Rules; or

    (c)   as a work permit holder for employment in the United Kingdom as a doctor in accordance with paragraphs 128 to 135; or

    (d)   as a doctor under the highly skilled migrant programme in accordance with paragraphs 135A to 135H.]

Note
Paragraphs 75A–75M inserted by HC 346.

[Leave to enter to take the PLAB Test]

[**75B** A person seeking leave to enter the United Kingdom to take the PLAB Test may be admitted for a period not exceeding 6 months, provided the Immigration Officer is satisfied that each of the requirements of paragraph 75A is met.]

Note
Paragraphs 75A–75M inserted by HC 346.

[Refusal of leave to enter to take the PLAB Test]

[**75C** Leave to enter the United Kingdom to take the PLAB Test is to be refused if the Immigration Officer is not satisfied that each of the requirements of paragraph 75A is met.]

Note
Paragraphs 75A–75M inserted by HC 346.

Appendix 1   Legislation and materials

[Requirements for an extension of stay in order to take the PLAB Test]

[75D The requirements for an extension of stay in the United Kingdom in order to take the PLAB Test are that the applicant:

(i)   was given leave to enter the United Kingdom for the purposes of taking the PLAB Test in accordance with paragraph 75B of these Rules; and

(ii)   intends to take the PLAB Test and can provide documentary evidence of a confirmed test date; and

(iii)   meets the requirements set out in paragraph 41(iii)–(vii); and

(iv)   intends to leave the United Kingdom at the end of his leave granted under this paragraph unless he is successful in the PLAB Test and granted leave to remain:

(a)   as a postgraduate doctor or trainee general practitioner in accordance with paragraphs 70 to 75; or

(b)   to undertake a clinical attachment in accordance with paragraphs 75G to 75M of these Rules; or

(c)   as a work permit holder for employment in the United Kingdom as a doctor in accordance with paragraphs 128 to 135; or

(d)   as a doctor under the highly skilled migrant programme in accordance with paragraphs 135A to 135H; and

(v)   would not as a result of an extension of stay spend more than 18 months in the United Kingdom for the purpose of taking the PLAB Test.]

Note
Paragraphs 75A–75M inserted by HC 346.

[Extension of stay to take the PLAB Test]

[75E A person seeking leave to remain in the United Kingdom to take the PLAB Test may be granted an extension of stay for a period not exceeding 6 months, provided the Secretary of State is satisfied that each of the requirements of paragraph 75D is met.]

Note
Paragraphs 75A–75M inserted by HC 346.

[Refusal of extension of stay to take the PLAB Test]

[75F Leave to remain in the United Kingdom to take the PLAB Test is to be refused if the Secretary of State is not satisfied that each of the requirements of paragraph 75D is met.

Requirements for leave to enter to undertake a clinical attachment or dental observer post 75G. The requirements to be met by a person seeking leave to enter to undertake a clinical attachment or dental observer post are that the applicant:

(i)   is a graduate from a medical or dental school and intends to undertake a clinical attachment or dental observer post in the United Kingdom; and

(ii)   can provide documentary evidence of the clinical attachment or dental observer post which will:
(a)   be unpaid; and
(b)   only involve observation, not treatment, of patients; and

(iii)   meets the requirements of paragraph 41(iii)–(vii) of these Rules; and

(iv)   intends to leave the United Kingdom at the end of his leave granted under this paragraph unless he is granted leave to remain:

(a)   as a postgraduate doctor, dentist or trainee general practitioner in accordance with paragraphs 70 to 75;

(b)   as a work permit holder for employment in the United Kingdom as a doctor or dentist in accordance with paragraphs 128 to 135; or

(c)   as a General Practitioner under the highly skilled migrant programme in accordance with paragraphs 135A to 135H.]

Note
Paragraphs 75A–75M inserted by HC 346.

[Leave to enter to undertake a clinical attachment or dental observer post]

[75H A person seeking leave to enter the United Kingdom to undertake a clinical attachment or dental observer post may be admitted for the period of the clinical attachment or dental observer post, up to a maximum of 12 months, provided the Immigration Officer is satisfied that each of the requirements of paragraph 75G is met.]

Note
Paragraphs 75A–75M inserted by HC 346.

[Refusal of leave to enter to undertake a clinical attachment or dental observer post]

[75J Leave to enter the United Kingdom to undertake a clinical attachment or dental observer post is to be refused if the Immigration Officer is not satisfied that each of the requirements of paragraph 75G is met.]

Note
Paragraphs 75A–75M inserted by HC 346.

[Requirements for an extension of stay in order to undertake a clinical attachment or dental observer post]

[75K The requirements to be met by a person seeking an extension of stay to undertake a clinical attachment or dental observer post are that the applicant:

(i)   was given leave to enter or remain in the United Kingdom to undertake a clinical attachment or dental observer post or:

    (a)   for the purposes of taking the PLAB Test in accordance with paragraphs 75A to 75F and has passed both parts of the PLAB Test;

    (b)   as a postgraduate doctor, dentist or trainee general practitioner in accordance with paragraphs 70 to 75; or

    (c)   as a work permit holder for employment in the UK as a doctor or dentist in accordance with paragraphs 128 to 135; and

(ii)   is a graduate from a medical or dental school and intends to undertake a clinical attachment or dental observer post in the United Kingdom; and

(iii)   can provide documentary evidence of the clinical attachment or dental observer post which will:

    (a)   be unpaid; and

    (b)   only involve observation, not treatment, of patients; and

(iv)   intends to leave the United Kingdom at the end of his period of leave granted under this paragraph unless he is granted leave to remain:

    (a)   as a postgraduate doctor, dentist or trainee general practitioner in accordance with paragraphs 70 to 75; or

Appendix 1   Legislation and materials

    (b)   as a work permit holder for employment in the United Kingdom as a doctor or dentist in accordance with paragraphs 128 to 135; or

    (c)   as a General Practitioner under the highly skilled migrant programme in accordance with paragraphs 135A to 135H.; and

(v)   meets the requirements of paragraph 41(iii)–(vii) of these Rules.]

Note
Paragraphs 75A–75M inserted by HC 346.

[Extension of stay to undertake a clinical attachment or dental observer post]

[75L A person seeking leave to remain in the United Kingdom to undertake a clinical attachment or dental observer post may be granted an extension of stay for the period of their clinical attachment or dental observer post, provided that the Secretary of State is satisfied that each of the requirements of paragraph 75K is met.]

Note
Paragraphs 75A–75M inserted by HC 346.

[Refusal of extension of stay to undertake a clinical attachment or dental observer post]

[75M Leave to remain in the United Kingdom to undertake a clinical attachment or dental observer post is to be refused if the Secretary of State is not satisfied that each of the requirements of paragraph 75K is met.]

Note
Paragraphs 75A–75M inserted by HC 346.

Spouses of students

Requirements for leave to enter or remain as the spouse of a student [or prospective student]

76 The requirements to be met by a person seeking leave to enter or remain in the United Kingdom as the spouse of a student are that:

(i)   the applicant is married to a person admitted to or allowed to remain in the United Kingdom under paragraphs 57–75 [or 82–87]; and

(ii)   each of the parties intends to live with the other as his or her spouse during the applicant's stay and the marriage is subsisting; and

(iii)   there will be adequate accommodation for the parties and any dependants without recourse to public funds; and

(iv)   the parties will be able to maintain themselves and any dependants adequately without recourse to public funds; and

(v)   the applicant does not intend to take employment except as permitted under paragraph 77 below; and

(vi)   the applicant intends to leave the United Kingdom at the end of any period of leave granted to him.

1890

Leave to enter or remain as the spouse of a student [or prospective student]

77 A person seeking leave to enter or remain in the United Kingdom as the spouse of a student may be admitted or allowed to remain for a period not in excess of that granted to the student provided the Immigration Officer or, in the case of an application for limited leave to remain, the Secretary of State, is satisfied that each of the requirements of paragraph 76 is met. [Employment may be permitted] where the period of leave being granted is [, or was,] 12 months or more.

Note
Words in square brackets substituted and inserted by Cm 4851.

Refusal of leave to enter or remain as the spouse of a student [or prospective student]

78 Leave to enter or remain as the spouse of a student is to be refused if the Immigration Officer or, in the case of an application for limited leave to remain, the Secretary of State is not satisfied that each of the requirements of paragraph 76 is met.

CHILDREN OF STUDENTS

Requirements for leave to enter or remain as the child of a student [or prospective student]

79 The requirements to be met by a person seeking leave to enter or remain in the United Kingdom as the child of a student are that he:

(i)   is the child of a parent admitted to or allowed to remain in the United Kingdom as a student under the paragraphs 57–75 [or 82–87]; and

(ii)   is under the age of 18 or has current leave to enter or remain in this capacity; and

(iii)   is unmarried, has not formed an independent family unit and is not leading an independent life; and

(iv)   can, and will, be maintained and accommodated adequately without recourse to public funds; and

(v)   will not stay in the United Kingdom beyond any period of leave granted to his parent.

Leave to enter or remain as the child of a student [or prospective student]

[80 A person seeking leave to enter or remain in the United Kingdom as the child of a student may be admitted or allowed to remain for a period not in excess of that granted to the student provided the Immigration Officer or, in the case of an application for limited leave to remain, the Secretary of State is satisfied that each of the requirements of paragraph 79 is met. Employment may be permitted where the period of leave being granted is, or was, 12 months or more.]

Note
Substituted by Cm 4851.

Refusal of leave to enter or remain as the child of a student [or prospective student]

81 Leave to enter or remain in the United Kingdom as the child of a student is to be refused if the Immigration Officer or, in the case of an application for limited leave to remain, the Secretary of State, is not satisfied that each of the requirements of paragraph 79 is met.

Note
[Paragraphs 76–81 replace HC 251, paras 31 and 116.]

PROSPECTIVE STUDENTS

Requirements for leave to enter as a prospective student

82 The requirements to be met by a person seeking leave to enter the United Kingdom as a prospective student are that he:

   (i)   can demonstrate a genuine and realistic intention of undertaking, within 6 months of his date of entry, a course of study which would meet the requirements for an extension of stay as a student set out in paragraphs 60 or 67; and

   (ii)   intends to leave the United Kingdom on completion of his studies or on the expiry of his leave to enter if he is not able to meet the requirements for an extension of stay as a student set out in paragraphs 60 or 67; and

   (iii) is able without working or recourse to public funds to meet the costs of his intended course and accommodation and the maintenance of himself and any dependants while making arrangements to study and during the course of his studies.

Leave to enter as a prospective student

83 A person seeking leave to enter the United Kingdom as a prospective student may be admitted for a period not exceeding 6 months with a condition prohibiting employment, provided the Immigration Officer is satisfied that each of the requirements of paragraph 82 is met.

Refusal of leave to enter as a prospective student

84 Leave to enter as a prospective student is to be refused if the Immigration Officer is not satisfied that each of the requirements of paragraph 82 is met.

Requirements for extension of stay as a prospective student

85 Six months is the maximum permitted leave which may be granted to a prospective student. The requirements for an extension of stay as a prospective student are that the applicant:

   (i)   was admitted to the United Kingdom with a valid prospective student entry clearance if he is a person specified in [Appendix 1] to these Rules; and

   (ii)   meets the requirements of paragraph 82; and

(iii)   would not, as a result of an extension of stay, spend more than 6 months in the United Kingdom.

Note
Paragraph 85(i) amended with effect from 11 May 1998 (Cmnd 3953).
Paragraph 85(i) of HC 395 of 1994 shall not apply to any application for an extension of stay for the purpose of studying made by a national of the Slovak Republic whose current leave to enter and remain was granted before 8 October 1998 or by a national of the Republic of Croatia whose current leave to enter and remain was granted before 19 November 1999.

Extension of stay as a prospective student

86 An extension of stay as a prospective student may be granted, with a prohibition on employment, provided the Secretary of State is satisfied that each of the requirements of paragraph 85 is met.

Refusal of extension of stay as a prospective student

87 An extension of stay as a prospective student is to be refused if the Secretary of State is not satisfied that each of the requirements of paragraph 85 is met.

[STUDENTS' UNIONS SABBATICAL OFFICERS]

Requirements for leave to enter as a sabbatical officer

87A The requirements to be met by a person seeking leave to enter the United Kingdom as a sabbatical officer are that the person:

(i)   has been elected to a full-time salaried post as a sabbatical officer at an educational establishment at which he is registered as a student;

(ii)   meets the requirements set out in paragraph 57 (i)–(ii) or met the requirements set out in paragraph 57 (i)–(ii) in the academic year prior to the one in which he took up or intends to take up sabbatical office; and

(iii)   does not intend to engage in business or take employment except in connection with his sabbatical post; and

(iv)   is able to maintain and accommodate himself and any dependants adequately without recourse to public funds; and

(v)   at the end of the sabbatical post he intends to:
  (a)   complete a course of study which he has already begun; or
  (b)   take up a further course of study which has been deferred to enable the applicant to take up the sabbatical post; or
  (c)   leave the United Kingdom; and

(vi)   has not come to the end of a period of government or international scholarship agency sponsorship, or has the written consent of his official sponsor to take up a sabbatical post in the United Kingdom; and

(vii)   has not already completed 2 years as a sabbatical officer.

1893

Appendix 1 Legislation and materials

Leave to enter the United Kingdom as a sabbatical officer

87B A person seeking leave to enter the United Kingdom as a sabbatical officer may be admitted for a period not exceeding 12 months on conditions specifying his employment provided the Immigration Officer is satisfied that each of the requirements of paragraph 87A is met.

Refusal of leave to enter the United Kingdom as a sabbatical officer

87C Leave to enter as a sabbatical officer is to be refused if the Immigration Officer is not satisfied that each of the requirements of paragraph 87A is met.

Requirements for an extension of stay as a sabbatical officer

87D The requirements for an extension of stay as a sabbatical officer are that the applicant:

- (i)   was admitted to the United Kingdom with a valid student entry clearance if he was then a visa national; and
- (ii)   meets the requirements set out in paragraph 87A(i)–(vi); and
- (iii) would not, as a result of an extension of stay, remain in the United Kingdom as a sabbatical officer to a date beyond 2 years from the date on which he was first given leave to enter the United Kingdom in this capacity.

Extension of stay as a sabbatical officer

87E An extension of stay as a sabbatical officer may be granted for a period not exceeding 12 months on conditions specifying his employment provided the Secretary of State is satisfied that the applicant meets each of the requirements of paragraph 87D.

Refusal of extension of stay as a sabbatical officer

87F An extension of stay as a sabbatical officer is to be refused if the Secretary of State is not satisfied that each of the requirements of paragraph 87D is met.]

Note
Paragraphs 87A–87F inserted by Cm 4851.

PART 4
PERSONS SEEKING TO ENTER OR REMAIN IN THE UNITED KINGDOM IN AN 'AU PAIR' PLACEMENT, AS A WORKING HOLIDAYMAKER, OR FOR TRAINING OR WORK EXPERIENCE

'AU PAIR' PLACEMENTS

Definition of an 'au pair' placement

88 For the purposes of these Rules an 'au pair' placement is an arrangement whereby a young person:

(a)   comes to the United Kingdom for the purpose of learning the English language; and
(b)   lives for a time as a member of an English speaking family with appropriate opportunities for study; and
(c)   helps in the home for a maximum of 5 hours per day in return for a reasonable allowance and with two free days per week.

Requirements for leave to enter as an 'au pair'

89 The requirements to be met by a person seeking leave to enter the United Kingdom as an 'au pair' are that he:

  (i)   is seeking entry for the purpose of taking up an arranged placement which can be shown to fall within the definition set out in paragraph 88; and
  (ii)   is aged between 17–27 inclusive or was so aged when first given leave to enter in this capacity; and
  (iii) is unmarried; and
  (iv)   is without dependants; and
[(v)   is a national of one of the following countries: Andorra, Bosnia-Herzegovina, Republic of Bulgaria, Croatia, The Faroes, Greenland, Macedonia, Monaco, Romania, San Marino or Turkey; and]
  (vi)   does not intend to stay in the United Kingdom for more than 2 years as an 'au pair'; and
  (vii) intends to leave the United Kingdom on completion of his stay as an 'au pair'; and
  (viii) if he has previously spent time in the United Kingdom as an 'au pair', is not seeking leave to enter to a date beyond 2 years from the date on which he was first given leave to enter the United Kingdom in this capacity; and
  (ix)   is able to maintain and accommodate himself without recourse to public funds.

Note
Sub-paragraph (v) substituted by HC 523.

Leave to enter as an 'au pair'

90 A person seeking leave to enter the United Kingdom as an 'au pair' may be admitted for a period not exceeding 2 years with a prohibition on employment except as an 'au pair', provided the Immigration Officer is satisfied that each of the requirements of paragraph 89 is met. (A non-visa national who wishes to ascertain in advance whether a proposed 'au pair' placement is likely to meet the requirements of paragraph 89 is advised to obtain entry clearance before travelling to the United Kingdom).

Refusal of leave to enter as an 'au pair'

91 An application for leave to enter as an 'au pair' is to be refused if the Immigration Officer is not satisfied that each of the requirements of paragraph 89 is met.

Requirements for an extension of stay as an 'au pair'

92 The requirements for an extension of stay as an 'au pair' are that the applicant:

   (i)   was given leave to enter the United Kingdom as an 'au pair' under paragraph 90; and

  (ii)   is undertaking an arranged 'au pair' placement which can be shown to fall within the definition set out in paragraph 88; and

 (iii)   meets the requirements of paragraph [89(ii)–(ix)]; and

 (iv)   would not, as a result of an extension to stay, remain in the United Kingdom as an 'au pair' to a date beyond 2 years from the date on which he was first given leave to enter the United Kingdom in this capacity.

Extension of stay as an 'au pair'

93 An extension of stay as an 'au pair' may be granted with a prohibition on employment except as an 'au pair', provided the Secretary of State is satisfied that each of the requirements of paragraph 92 is met.

Refusal of extension of stay as an 'au pair'

94 An extension of stay as an 'au pair' is to be refused if the Secretary of State is not satisfied that each of the requirements of paragraph 92 is met.

WORKING HOLIDAYMAKERS

Requirements for leave to enter as a working holidaymaker

[95 The requirements to be met by a person seeking leave to enter the United Kingdom as a working holidaymaker are that he:

   (i)   is a national or citizen of a country listed in Appendix 3 of these Rules, or a British Overseas Citizen; a British Overseas Territories Citizen; or a British National (Overseas); and

  (ii)   is aged between 17 and 30 inclusive or was so aged at the date of his application for leave to enter; and

 (iii)   is unmarried or is married to a person who meets the requirements of this paragraph and the parties to the marriage intend to take a working holiday together; and

 (iv)   has the means to pay for his return or onward journey; and

  (v)   is able and intends to maintain and accommodate himself without recourse to public funds; and

 (vi)   is intending only to take employment incidental to a holiday, and not to engage in business, or to provide services as a professional sportsperson, and in any event not to work for more than 12 months during his stay; and

 (vii)   does not have dependent children any of whom are 5 years of age or over or who will reach 5 years of age before the applicant completes his working holiday; and

(viii)   intends to leave the UK at the end of his working holiday: and

 (ix)   has not spent time in the United Kingdom on a previous working holidaymaker entry clearance; and

[(x)   holds a valid United Kingdom entry clearance, granted for a limited period not exceeding 2 years, for entry in this capacity.]]

Note

Substituted by HC 302. Sub-paragraph (x) substituted by HC 104.

Leave to enter as a working holidaymaker

[96 A person seeking to enter the United Kingdom as a working holidaymaker may be admitted provided he is able to produce on arrival a valid United Kingdom entry clearance granted for a period not exceeding 2 years for entry in this capacity.]

Note
Substituted by HC 302. Further substituted by HC 104.

Refusal of leave to enter as a working holidaymaker

97 Leave to enter as a working holidaymaker is to be refused if a valid United Kingdom entry clearance for entry in this capacity is not produced to the Immigration Officer on arrival.

98–100...

Note
Deleted by HC 302.

CHILDREN OF WORKING HOLIDAYMAKERS

[Requirements for leave to enter or remain as the child of a working holidaymaker

[101 The requirements to be met by a person seeking leave to enter or remain in the United Kingdom as the child of a working holidaymaker are that:
- (i) he is the child of a parent admitted to, and currently present in, the United Kingdom as a working holidaymaker; and
- (ii) he is under the age of 5 and will leave the United Kingdom before reaching that age; and
- (iii) he can and will be maintained and accommodated adequately without recourse to public funds or without his parent(s) engaging in employment except as provided by paragraph 95 above; and
- (iv) both parents are being or have been admitted to the United Kingdom, save where:
  - (a) the parent he is accompanying or joining is his sole surviving parent; or
  - (b) the parent he is accompanying or joining has had sole responsibility for his upbringing; or
  - (c) there are serious and compelling family or other considerations which make exclusion from the United Kingdom undesirable and suitable arrangements have been made for his care; and

(v) he holds a valid United Kingdom entry clearance for entry in this capacity or, if seeking leave to remain, was admitted with a valid United Kingdom entry clearance for entry in this capacity, and is seeking leave to a date not beyond the date to which his parent(s) have leave to enter in the working holidaymaker category.]

Note
Substituted by HC 302.

Leave to enter [or remain] as the child of a working holidaymaker

[102 A person seeking to enter the United Kingdom as the child of working holidaymaker/s must be able to produce on arrival a valid United Kingdom entry clearance for entry in this capacity.]

Note
Substituted by HC 302.

Refusal of leave to enter or remain as the child of a working holidaymaker

103 Leave to enter or remain in the United Kingdom as the child of a working holidaymaker is to be refused if, in relation to an application for leave to enter, a valid United Kingdom entry clearance for entry in this capacity is not produced to the Immigration Officer on arrival or, in the case of an application for leave to remain, the applicant was not admitted with a valid United Kingdom entry clearance for entry in this capacity or is unable to satisfy the Secretary of State that each of the requirements of paragraph 101(i)–(iv) is met.

[SEASONAL WORKERS AT AGRICULTURAL CAMPS]

Requirements for leave to enter as a [seasonal agricultural worker]

104 The requirements to be met by a person seeking leave to enter the United Kingdom as a [seasonal agricultural worker] ... are that he:
- (i)   is a student in full-time education aged [18 or over]; and
- (ii)   holds [an immigration employment document in the form of] a valid Home Office work card issued by the operator of a scheme approved by the Secretary of State; and
- (iii) intends to leave the United Kingdom at the end of his period of leave as a [seasonal agricultural worker]; and
- (iv)   does not intend to take employment except [as permitted by his work card and within the terms of this paragraph].
- [(v) is not seeking leave to enter on a date less than 3 months from the date on which an earlier period of leave to enter or remain granted to him in this capacity expired; and]
- [(vi)] is able to maintain and accommodate himself ... without recourse to public funds.

Note
Words deleted by HC 538. Words 'seasonal agricultural worker' and words in square brackets in sub-paragraphs (i), (ii), (iv), (v) and (vi) substituted HC 1224.

Leave to enter as a [seasonal agricultural worker]

[105 A person seeking leave to enter the United Kingdom as a seasonal agricultural worker may be admitted with a condition restricting his freedom to take employment for a period not exceeding 6 months providing the Immigration Officer is satisfied that each of the requirements of paragraph 104 is met.]

Note
Words 'seasonal agricultural worker' and paragraph 105 substituted by HC 1224.

Refusal of leave to enter as a [seasonal agricultural worker]

106 Leave to enter the United Kingdom as a [seasonal agricultural worker] ... is to be refused if the Immigration Officer is not satisfied that each of the requirements of paragraph 104 is met.

Note
Words deleted by HC 538. Words 'seasonal agricultural worker' substituted by HC 1224.

Requirements for extension of stay as a [seasonal agricultural worker]

[**107** The requirements for an extension of stay as a seasonal agricultural worker are that the applicant:

  (i)   entered the United Kingdom as a seasonal agricultural worker under paragraph 105; and
  (ii)   meets the requirements of paragraph 104(iii)–(vi); and
  (iii) would not, as a result of an extension of stay sought, remain in the United Kingdom as a seasonal agricultural worker beyond 6 months from the date on which he was given leave to enter the United Kingdom on this occasion in this capacity.]

Note
Words 'seasonal agricultural worker' and paragraph 107 substituted by HC 1224.

Extension of stay as a [seasonal agricultural worker]

[**108** An extension of stay as a seasonal agricultural worker may be granted with a condition restricting his freedom to take employment for a period which does not extend beyond 6 months from the date on which he was given leave to enter the United Kingdom on this occasion in this capacity, provided the Secretary of State is satisfied that the applicant meets each of the requirements of paragraph 107.]

Note
Words 'seasonal agricultural worker' and paragraph 108 substituted by HC 1224.

Refusal of extension of stay as a [seasonal agricultural worker]

109 An extension of stay as a [seasonal agricultural worker] ... is to be refused if the Secretary of State is not satisfied that each of the requirements of paragraph 107 is met.

Note
Words deleted by HC 538. Words 'seasonal agricultural worker' substituted by HC 1224.

Appendix 1   Legislation and materials

TEACHERS AND LANGUAGE ASSISTANTS COMING TO THE UNITED KINGDOM UNDER
APPROVED EXCHANGE SCHEMES

**Requirements for leave to enter as a teacher or language assistant under an approved
exchange scheme**

110 The requirements to be met by a person seeking leave to enter the United
Kingdom as a teacher or language assistant on an approved exchange scheme are that
he:

[(i)   is coming to an educational establishment in the United Kingdom under an
           exchange scheme approved by the Department for Education and Skills, the
           Scottish or Welsh Office of Education or the Department of Education,
           Northern Ireland, or administered by the British Council's Education and
           Training Group or the League for the Exchange of Commonwealth Teachers;
           and]
  (ii)   intends to leave the United Kingdom at the end of his exchange period; and
  (iii)   does not intend to take employment except in the terms of this paragraph; and
  (iv)   is able to maintain and accommodate himself and any dependants without
           recourse to public funds; and
  (v)   holds a valid United Kingdom entry clearance for entry in this capacity.

Note
Sub-paragraph (i) substituted by Cm 6339.

Leave to enter as a teacher or language assistant under an exchange scheme

111 A person seeking leave to enter the United Kingdom as a teacher or language
assistant under an approved exchange scheme may be given leave to enter for a period
not exceeding 12 months provided he is able to produce to the Immigration Officer, on
arrival, a valid United Kingdom entry clearance for entry in this capacity.

**Refusal of leave to enter as a teacher or language assistant under an approved
exchange scheme**

112 Leave to enter the United Kingdom as a teacher or language assistant under an
approved exchange scheme is to be refused if a valid United Kingdom entry clearance
for entry in this capacity is not produced to the Immigration Officer on arrival.

**Requirements for extension of stay as a teacher or language assistant under an
approved exchange scheme**

113 The requirements for an extension of stay as a teacher or language assistant under
an approved exchange scheme are that the applicant:

  (i)   entered the United Kingdom with a valid United Kingdom entry clearance as a
           teacher or language assistant; and
  (ii)   is still engaged in the employment for which his entry clearance was granted;
           and
  (iii)   is still required for the employment in question, as certified by the employer;
           and
  (iv)   meets the requirements of paragraph 110(ii)–(iv); and

1900

(v)   would not, as a result of an extension of stay, remain in the United Kingdom as an exchange teacher or language assistant for more than 2 years from the date on which he was first given leave to enter the United Kingdom in this capacity.

Extension of stay as a teacher or language assistant under an approved exchange scheme

114 An extension of stay as a teacher or language assistant under an approved exchange scheme may be granted for a further period not exceeding 12 months provided the Secretary of State is satisfied that each of the requirements of paragraph 113 is met.

Refusal of extension of stay as a teacher or language assistant under an approved exchange scheme

115 An extension of stay as a teacher or language assistant under an approved exchange scheme is to be refused if the Secretary of State is not satisfied that each of the requirements of paragraph 113 is met.

[HOME OFFICE] APPROVED TRAINING OR WORK EXPERIENCE

Requirements for leave to enter for [Home Office] approved training or work experience

116 The requirements to be met by a person seeking leave to enter the United Kingdom for [Home Office] approved training or work experience are that he:

(i)   holds a valid work permit from the [Home Office] issued under the Training and Work Experience Scheme; and

[...]

(iii)   is capable of undertaking the training or work experience as specified in his work permit; and

(iv)   intends to leave the United Kingdom on the completion of his training or work experience; and

(v)   does not intend to take employment except as specified in his work permit; and

(vi)   is able to maintain and accommodate himself and any dependants adequately without recourse to public funds[; and

[(vii)   holds a valid United Kingdom entry clearance for entry in this capacity except where he holds a work permit valid for 6 months or less [...] [or he is a British National (Overseas), a British overseas territories citizen, a British Overseas citizen, a British protected person or a person who under the British Nationality Act 1981 is a British subject].]

Note
Words in square brackets in paragraph 116 and sub-paragraph (i) substituted by Cmnd 5253. Sub-paragraph (ii) deleted by HC 538. Sub-paragraph (vii) inserted by HC 1224. Words in square brackets within sub-paragraph (vii) inserted by HC 176. Words in sub-paragraph (vii) deleted by HC 523.

Appendix 1   Legislation and materials

Leave to enter for [Home Office] approved training or work experience

[**117** A person seeking leave to enter the United Kingdom for the purpose of approved training or approved work experience under the Training or Work Experience Scheme may be admitted to the United Kingdom for a period not exceeding the period of training or work experience approved by the Home Office for this purpose (as specified in his work permit), subject to a condition restricting him to that approved employment, provided he is able to produce to the Immigration Officer, on arrival, a valid United Kingdom entry clearance for entry in this capacity or, where entry clearance is not required, provided the Immigration Officer is satisfied that each of the requirements of paragraph 116(i)–(vi) is met.]

Note
Paragraph 117 substituted by HC 1224.

Refusal of leave to enter for [Home Office] approved training or work experience

[**118** Leave to enter the United Kingdom for Home Office approved training or work experience under the Training and Work Experience scheme is to be refused if a valid United Kingdom entry clearance for entry in this capacity is not produced to the Immigration Officer on arrival or, where entry clearance is not required, if the Immigration Officer is not satisfied that each of the requirements of paragraph 116(i)–(vi) is met.]

Note
Words 'Home Office' in square brackets substituted by Cmnd 5253. Paragraph 118 substituted by HC 1224.

Requirements for extension of stay for [Home Office] approved training or work experience

119 The requirements for an extension of stay for [Home Office] approved training or work experience are that the applicant:

(i)   entered the United Kingdom with a valid work permit under paragraph 117 or was admitted or allowed to remain in the United Kingdom as a student; and

(ii)   has written approval from the [Home Office] for an extension of stay in this category; and

(iii)   meets the requirements of paragraph 116(ii)–(vi); and

(iv)   ...

Note
Words in square brackets substituted by Cmnd 5253. Sub-paragraph (iv) deleted by Cm 5597.

Extension of stay for [Home Office] approved training or work experience

[**120** An extension of stay for approved training or approved work experience under the Training and Work Experience scheme may be granted for a further period not exceeding the extended period of training or work experience approved by the Home Office for this purpose (as specified in his work permit), provided that in each case the Secretary of State is satisfied that the requirements of paragraph 119 are met. An extension of stay is to be subject to a condition permitting the applicant to take or change employment only with the permission of the Home Office.]

1902

Note
Words 'Home Office' in square brackets substituted by Cmnd 5253. Paragraph 120 substituted by HC 1224.

Refusal of extension of stay for [Home Office] approved training or work experience

[121 An extension of stay for approved training or approved work experience under the Training and Work Experience scheme is to be refused if the Secretary of State is not satisfied that each of the requirements of paragraph 119 is met.]

Note
Words 'Home Office' in square brackets substituted by Cmnd 5253. Paragraph 121 substituted by HC 1224.

SPOUSES OF PERSONS WITH LIMITED LEAVE TO ENTER OR REMAIN UNDER
PARAGRAPHS 110–121

Requirements for leave to enter or remain as the spouse of a person with limited leave to enter or remain in the United Kingdom under paragraphs 110–121

122 The requirements to be met by a person seeking leave to enter or remain in the United Kingdom as the spouse of a person with limited leave to enter or remain in the United Kingdom under paragraphs 110–121 are that:

(i)   the applicant is married to a person with limited leave to enter or remain in the United Kingdom under paragraphs 110–121; and

(ii)   each or the parties intends to live with the other as his or her spouse during the applicant's stay and the marriage is subsisting; and

(iii)   there will be adequate accommodation for the parties and any dependants without recourse to public funds in accommodation which they own or occupy exclusively; and

(iv)   the parties will be able to maintain themselves and any dependants adequately without recourse to public funds; and

(v)   the applicant does not intend to stay in the United Kingdom beyond any period of leave granted to his spouse; and

(vi)   if seeking leave to enter, the applicant holds a valid United Kingdom entry clearance for entry in this capacity or, if seeking leave to remain, was admitted with a valid United Kingdom entry clearance for entry in this capacity.

Leave to enter or remain as the spouse of a person with limited leave to enter or remain in the United Kingdom under paragraphs 110–121

123 A person seeking leave to enter or remain in the United Kingdom as the spouse of a person with limited leave to enter or remain in the United Kingdom under paragraphs 110–121 may be given leave to enter or remain in the United Kingdom for a period of leave not in excess of that granted to the person with limited leave to enter or remain under paragraphs 110–121 provided that, in relation to an application for leave to enter, he is able, on arrival, to produce to the Immigration Officer a valid United Kingdom entry clearance for entry in this capacity or, in the case of an application for limited leave to remain, was admitted with a valid United Kingdom entry clearance for entry in this capacity and is able to satisfy the Secretary of State that each of the requirements of paragraph 122(i)–(v) is met.

Refusal of leave to enter or remain as the spouse of a person with limited leave to enter or remain in the United Kingdom under paragraphs 110–121

124 Leave to enter or remain in the United Kingdom as the spouse of a person with limited leave to enter or remain in the United Kingdom under paragraphs 110–121 is to be refused if, in relation to an application for leave to enter, a valid United Kingdom entry clearance for entry in this capacity is not produced the the Immigration Officer on arrival or, in the case of an application for limited leave to remain, if the applicant was not admitted with a valid United Kingdom entry clearance for entry in this capacity or is unable to satisfy the Secretary of State that each of the requirements of paragraph 122(i)–(v) is met.

CHILDREN OF PERSONS ADMITTED OR ALLOWED TO REMAIN UNDER
PARAGRAPHS 110–121

Requirements for leave to enter or remain as the child of a person with limited leave to enter or remain in the United Kingdom under paragraphs 110–121

125 The requirements to be met by a person seeking leave to enter or remain in the United Kingdom as the child of a person with limited leave to enter or remain in the United Kingdom under paragraphs 110–121 are that:

(i)   he is the child of a parent who has limited leave to enter or remain in the United Kingdom under paragraphs 110–121; and

(ii)   he is under the age of 18 or has current leave to enter or remain in this capacity; and

(iii)   he is unmarried, has not formed an independent family unit and is not leading an independent life; and

(iv)   he can, and will, be maintained and accommodated adequately without recourse to public funds in accommodation which his parent(s) own or occupy exclusively; and

(v)   he will not stay in the United Kingdom beyond any period of leave granted to his parent(s); and

(vi)   both parents are being or have been admitted to or allowed to remain in the United Kingdom save where:

(a)   the parent he is accompanying or joining is his sole surviving parent; or

(b)   the parent he is accompanying or joining has had sole responsibility for his upbringing; or

(c)   there are serious and compelling family or other considerations which make exclusion from the United Kingdom undesirable and suitable arrangements have been made for his care; and

(vii)   if seeking leave to enter, he holds a valid United Kingdom entry clearance for entry in this capacity of, if seeking leave to remain, was admitted with a valid United Kingdom entry clearance for entry in this capacity.

Leave to enter or remain as the child of a person with limited leave to enter or remain in the United Kingdom under paragraphs 110–121

126 A person seeking leave to enter or remain in the United Kingdom as the child of a person with limited leave to enter or remain in the United Kingdom under paragraphs 110–121 may be given leave to enter or remain in the United Kingdom for a period of leave not in excess of that granted to the person with limited leave to enter or remain under paragraphs 110–121 provided that, in relation to an application for leave to enter, he is able, on arrival, to produce to the Immigration Officer a valid United Kingdom entry clearance for entry in this capacity or, in the case of an application for limited leave to remain, he was admitted with a valid United Kingdom entry clearance for entry in this capacity and is able to satisfy the Secretary of State that each of the requirements of paragraph 125(i)–(vi) is met.

Refusal of leave to enter or remain as the child of a person with limited leave to enter or remain in the United Kingdom under paragraphs 110–121

127 Leave to enter or remain in the United Kingdom as the child of a person with limited leave to enter or remain in the United Kingdom under paragraphs 110–121 is to be refused if, in relation to an application for leave to enter, a valid United Kingdom entry clearance for entry in this capacity is not produced to the Immigration Officer on arrival or, in the case of an application for limited leave to remain, if the applicant was not admitted with a valid United Kingdom entry clearance for entry in this capacity or is unable to satisfy the Secretary of State that each of the requirements of paragraph 125(i)–(vi) is met.

PART 5
PERSONS SEEKING TO ENTER OR REMAIN IN THE UNITED KINGDOM FOR EMPLOYMENT

WORK PERMIT EMPLOYMENT

Requirements for leave to enter the United Kingdom for work permit employment

128 The requirements to be met by a person coming to the United Kingdom to seek or take employment (unless he is otherwise eligible for admission for employment under these Rules or is eligible for admission as a seaman under contract to join a ship due to leave British waters) are that he:

(i) holds a valid [Home Office] work permit; and
(ii) is not of an age which puts him outside the limits for employment; and
(iii) is capable of undertaking the employment specified in the work permit; and
(iv) does not intend to take employment except as specified in his work permit; and
(v) is able to maintain and accommodate himself and any dependants adequately without recourse to public funds; and
(vi) in the case of a person in possession of a work permit which is valid for a period of 12 months or less, intends to leave the United Kingdom at the end of his approved employment[; and]
[(vii) holds a valid United Kingdom entry clearance for entry in this capacity except where he holds a work permits valid for 6 months' or less […] [or he is a British National (Overseas), a British overseas territories citizen, a British Overseas citizen, a British protected person or a person who under the British Nationality Act 1981 is a British subject].]

Note
Words 'Home Office' in square brackets substituted by Cmnd 5253. Sub-paragraph (vii) inserted by HC 1224. Words in square brackets within sub-paragraph (vii) inserted by HC 176. Words in sub-paragraph (vii) deleted by HC 523.

Appendix 1   Legislation and materials

Leave to enter for work permit employment

[129 A person seeking leave to enter the United Kingdom for the purpose of work permit employment may be admitted for a period not exceeding the period of employment approved by the Home Office (as specified in his work permit), subject to a condition restricting him to that approved employment, provided he is able to produce to the Immigration Officer, on arrival, a valid United Kingdom entry clearance for entry in this capacity or, where entry clearance is not required, provided the Immigration Officer is satisfied that each of the requirements of paragraph 128(i)–(vi) is met.]

Note
Paragraph 129 substituted by HC 1224.

Refusal of leave to enter for employment

[130 Leave to enter for the purpose of work permit employment is to be refused if a valid United Kingdom entry clearance for entry in this capacity is not produced to the Immigration Officer on arrival or, where entry clearance is not required, if the Immigration Officer is not satisfied that each of the requirements of paragraph 128(i)–(vi) is met.]

Note
Paragraph 130 substituted by HC 1224.

Requirements for an extension of stay for work permit employment

131 The requirements for an extension of stay to seek or take employment (unless the applicant is otherwise eligible for an extension of stay for employment under these Rules) are that the applicant:
  (i)   entered the United Kingdom with a valid work permit under paragraph 129 [...]; and
  (ii)   has written approval from the [Home Office] for the continuation of his employment; and
  (iii) meets the requirements of paragraph 128(ii)–(v).

Note
Words in first square brackets deleted by Cmnd 5829. Words in second square brackets substituted by Cmnd 5253.

[131A The requirements for an extension of stay to take employment (unless the applicant is otherwise eligible for an extension of stay for employment under these Rules) for a student are that the applicant:
  (i)   entered the United Kingdom or was given leave to remain as a student in accordance with paragraphs 57 to 62 of these Rules; and
  (ii)   has [obtained a degree qualification on] a recognised degree course at either a United Kingdom publicly funded further or higher education institution or a bona fide [United Kingdom] private education institution which maintains satisfactory records of enrolment and attendance; and
  (iii) holds a valid Home Office immigration employment document for employment; and

1906

(iv)   has the written consent of his official sponsor to such employment if he is a member of a government or international scholarship agency sponsorship and that sponsorship is either ongoing or has recently come to an end at the time of the requested extension; and

(v)   meets each of the requirements of paragraph 128 (ii) to (vi).]

Note
Paragraph 131A inserted by Cmnd 5597. Words in square brackets in sub-paragraph (ii) substituted by HC 104.

[**131B** The requirements for an extension of stay to take employment (unless the applicant is otherwise eligible for an extension of stay for employment under these Rules) for a student nurse, postgraduate doctor or postgraduate dentist are that the applicant:

(i)   entered the United Kingdom or was given leave to remain as a student nurse in accordance with paragraphs 63 to 69 of these Rules; or

(ii)   entered the United Kingdom or was given leave to remain as a postgraduate doctor or a postgraduate dentist in accordance with paragraphs 70 to 75 of these Rules; and

(iii)   holds a valid Home Office immigration employment document for employment as a nurse, doctor or dentist; and

(iv)   has the written consent of his official sponsor to such employment if he is a member of a government or international scholarship agency sponsorship and that sponsorship is either ongoing or has recently come to an end at the time of the requested extension; and

(v)   meets each of the requirements of paragraph 128 (ii) to (vi).]

Note
Inserted by Cmnd 5597.

[**131C** The requirements for an extension of stay to take employment for a Science and Engineering Graduate Scheme participant are that the applicant:

(i)   entered the United Kingdom or was given leave to remain as a Science and Engineering Graduate Scheme participant in accordance with paragraphs 135O to 135T of these Rules; and

(ii)   holds a valid Home Office immigration employment document for employment; and

(iii)   meets each of the requirements of paragraph 128 (ii) to (vi).]

Note
Substituted by Cm 6339.

[**131D** The requirements for an extension of stay to take employment (unless the applicant is otherwise eligible for an extension of stay for employment under these Rules) for a working holidaymaker are that the applicant:

(i)   entered the United Kingdom as a working holidaymaker in accordance with paragraphs 95 to 96 of these Rules; and

(ii)   he has spent more than 12 months in total in the UK in this capacity; and

(iii)   holds a valid Home Office immigration employment document for employment in an occupation listed on the Work Permits (UK) shortage occupations list; and

(iv)   meets each of the requirements of paragraph 128 (ii) to (vi).]

Note
Substituted by HC 302.

1907

Appendix 1   Legislation and materials

[**131E** The requirements for an extension of stay to take employment for a highly skilled migrant are that the applicant:

(i)   entered the United Kingdom or was given leave to remain as a highly skilled migrant in accordance with paragraphs 135A to 135E of these Rules; and

(ii)   holds a valid work permit; and

(iii) meets each of the requirements of paragraph 128(ii) to (vi).]

Note
Inserted by Cm 6339.

[**131F** The requirements for an extension of stay to take employment (unless the applicant is otherwise eligible for an extension of stay for employment under these Rules) for an Innovator are that the applicant:

(i)   entered the United Kingdom or was given leave to remain as an Innovator in accordance with paragraphs 210A to 210E of these Rules; and

(ii)   holds a valid Home Office immigration employment document for employment; and

(iii) meets each of the requirements of paragraph 128(ii) to (vi).]

Note
Inserted by Cm 6339.

[**131G** The requirements for an extension of stay to take employment (unless the applicant is otherwise eligible for an extension of stay for employment under these Rules) for an individual who has leave to enter or leave to remain in the United Kingdom to take the PLAB Test or to undertake a clinical attachment or dental observer post are that the applicant:

(i)   entered the United Kingdom or was given leave to remain for the purposes of taking the PLAB Test in accordance with paragraphs 75A to 75F of these Rules; or

(ii)   entered the United Kingdom or was given leave to remain to undertake a clinical attachment or dental observer post in accordance with paragraphs 75G to 75M of these Rules; and

(iii) holds a valid Home Office immigration employment document for employment as a doctor or dentist; and

(iv) meets each of the requirements of paragraph 128 (ii) to (vi).]

Note
Inserted by HC 346.

[**131H** The requirements for an extension of stay to take employment (unless the applicant is otherwise eligible for an extension of stay for employment under these Rules) in the case of a person who has leave to enter or remain as a Fresh Talent: Working in Scotland scheme participant are that the applicant:

(i)   entered the United Kingdom or was given leave to remain as a Fresh Talent: Working in Scotland scheme participant in accordance with paragraphs 143A to 143F of these Rules; and

(ii)   holds a valid Home Office immigration employment document for employment in Scotland; and

(iii) has the written consent of his official sponsor to such employment if the studies which led to him being granted leave under the Fresh Talent: Working in Scotland scheme in accordance with paragraphs 143A to 143F of these Rules, or any studies he has subsequently undertaken, were sponsored by a government or international scholarship agency; and

(iv)   meets each of the requirements of paragraph 128(ii) to (vi).]

Note
Inserted by HC 346.

Extension of stay for work permit employment

[132 An extension of stay for work permit employment may be granted for a period not exceeding the period of approved employment recommended by the Home Office provided the Secretary of State is satisfied that each of the requirements of paragraphs 131, 131A, 131B, 131C, 131D, 131E, 131F, 131G or 131H is met. An extension of stay is to be subject to a condition restricting the applicant to employment approved by the Home Office.]

Note
Substituted by HC 346. Further substituted by HC 104.

Refusal of extension of stay for employment

[133 An extension of stay for employment is to be refused if the Secretary of State is not satisfied that each of the requirements of paragraphs 131, 131A, 131B, 131C, 131D, 131E, 131F, 131G or 131H is met (unless the applicant is otherwise eligible for an extension of stay for employment under these Rules).]

Note
Substituted by HC 346. Further substituted by HC 104.

Indefinite leave to remain for a work permit holder

134 Indefinite leave to remain may be granted, on application, to a person admitted as a work permit holder provided:

(i)   he has spent a continuous period of 4 years in the United Kingdom in this capacity; and
[(ii)   he has met the requirements of paragraph 131, 131A, 131B, 131C, 131D, 131E or 131F throughout the 4 year period; and]
(iii)   he is still required for the employment in question, as certified by his employer.

Note
Sub-paragraph (ii) substituted by HC 1112.

Refusal of indefinite leave to remain for a work permit holder

135 Indefinite leave to remain in the United Kingdom for a work permit holder is to be refused if the Secretary of State is not satisfied that each of the requirements of paragraph 134 is met.

Appendix 1   Legislation and materials

[HIGHLY SKILLED MIGRANTS]

[Requirements for leave to enter the United Kingdom as a highly skilled migrant

135A The requirements to be met by a person seeking leave to enter as a highly skilled migrant are that the applicant:

   (i)   must produce a valid document issued by the Home Office confirming that he meets, at the time of the issue of that document, the criteria specified by the Secretary of State for entry to the United Kingdom under the Highly Skilled Migrant Programme; and
  (ii)   intends to make the United Kingdom his main home; and
 (iii)   is able to maintain and accommodate himself and any dependants adequately without recourse to public funds; and
  (iv)   holds a valid United Kingdom entry clearance for entry in this capacity.]

Note
Inserted by HC 538.

[Leave to enter as a highly skilled migrant

135B A person seeking leave to enter the United Kingdom as a highly skilled migrant may be admitted for a period not exceeding 12 months, provided the Immigration Officer is satisfied that each of the requirements of paragraph 135A is met.]

Note
Inserted by HC 538.

[Refusal of leave to enter as a highly skilled migrant

135C Leave to enter as a highly skilled migrant is to be refused if the Immigration Officer is not satisfied that each of the requirements of paragraph 135A is met.]

Note
Inserted by HC 538.

[Requirements for an extension of stay as a highly skilled migrant

[135D The requirements for an extension of stay as a highly skilled migrant, in the case of a person who was granted leave to enter under paragraph 135A, are that the applicant:

   (i)   entered the United Kingdom with a valid United Kingdom entry clearance as a highly skilled migrant; and
  (ii)   has already taken during his period of leave all reasonable steps to become lawfully economically active in the United Kingdom in employment, self-employment or a combination of both; and
 (iii)   meets the requirements of paragraph 135A(i)–(iii).]

Note
Substituted by Cm 6339.

[**135DA** The requirements for an extension of stay as a highly skilled migrant in the case of a person who has leave to remain for work permit employment are that the applicant:

(i)   entered the United Kingdom or was given leave to remain as a work permit holder in accordance with paragraphs 128 to 132 of these Rules; and

(ii)   meets the requirements of paragraph 135A (i)–(iii).]

Note
Inserted by Cm 6339.

[**135DB** The requirements for an extension of stay as a highly skilled migrant in the case of a person who has leave to remain as a student are that the applicant:

(i)   entered the United Kingdom or was given leave to remain as a student in accordance with paragraphs 57 to 62 of these Rules; and

(ii)   has obtained a degree qualification on a recognised degree course at either a United Kingdom publicly funded further or higher education institution or a bona fide United Kingdom private education institution which maintains satisfactory records of enrolment and attendance; and

(iii)   has the written consent of his official sponsor to remain as a highly skilled migrant if he is a member of a government or international scholarship agency sponsorship and that sponsorship is either ongoing or has recently come to an end at the time of the requested extension; and

(iv)   meets the requirements of paragraph 135A(i)–(iii).]

Note
Inserted by Cm 6339.

[**135DC** The requirements for an extension of stay as a highly skilled migrant in the case of a person who has leave to remain as a postgraduate doctor or postgraduate dentist [or trainee general practitioner] are that the applicant:

(i)   entered the United Kingdom or was given leave to remain as a postgraduate doctor or a postgraduate dentist [or trainee general practitioner] in accordance with paragraphs 70 to 75 of these Rules; and

(ii)   has the written consent of his official sponsor to such employment if he is a member of a government or international scholarship agency sponsorship and that sponsorship is either ongoing or has recently come to an end at the time of the requested extension; and

(iii)   meets the requirements of paragraph 135A(i)–(iii).]

Note
Paragraph 135DC inserted by Cm 6339. Words in square brackets inserted HC 1112.

[**135DD** The requirements for an extension of stay as a highly skilled migrant for a working holidaymaker are that the applicant:

(i)   entered the United Kingdom as a working holidaymaker in accordance with paragraphs 95 to 96 of these Rules; and

(ii)   meets the requirements of paragraph 135A(i)–(iii).]

Note
Inserted by Cm 6339.

[**135DE** The requirements for an extension of stay as a highly skilled migrant for a participant in the Science and Engineering Graduate Scheme are that the applicant:

(i) entered the United Kingdom or was given leave to remain as a participant in the Science and Engineering Graduate Scheme in accordance with paragraphs 135O to 135T of these Rules; and

(ii) meets the requirements of paragraph 135A(i)–(iii).]

Note
Inserted by HC 1112.

[135DF The requirements for an extension of stay as a highly skilled migrant for an innovator are that the applicant:

(i) entered the United Kingdom or was given leave to remain as an innovator in accordance with paragraphs 210A to 210E of these Rules; and

(ii) meets the requirements of paragraph 135A(i)–(iii).]

Note
Inserted by HC 1112.

[135DG The requirements for an extension of stay as a highly skilled migrant in the case of a person who has leave to enter or leave to remain in the United Kingdom to take the PLAB Test or to undertake a clinical attachment are that the applicant:

(i) entered the United Kingdom or was given leave to remain for the purposes of taking the PLAB Test in accordance with paragraphs 75A to 75F of these Rules; or

(ii) entered the United Kingdom or was given leave to remain to undertake a clinical attachment in accordance with paragraphs 75G to 75M of these Rules; and

(iii) holds a valid document issued by the Home Office confirming that he meets, at the time of the issue of that document, the criteria specified by the Secretary of State for entry to the United Kingdom under the Highly Skilled Migrant Programme under the priority application process for general practitioners; and

(iv) meets the requirements of paragraph 135A(ii)–(iii).]

Note
Inserted by HC 346.

[135DH The requirements for an extension of stay as a highly skilled migrant in the case of a person who has leave to enter or remain as a Fresh Talent: Working in Scotland scheme participant are that the applicant:

(i) entered the United Kingdom or was given leave to remain as a Fresh Talent: Working in Scotland scheme participant in accordance with paragraphs 143A to 143F of these Rules; and

(ii) has the written consent of his official sponsor to such employment if the studies which led to him being granted leave under the Fresh Talent: Working in Scotland scheme in accordance with paragraphs 143A to 143F of these Rules, or any studies he has subsequently undertaken, were sponsored by a government or international scholarship agency; and

(iii) meets the requirements of paragraph 135A(i)–(iii).]

Note
Inserted by HC 104.

[Extension of stay as a highly skilled migrant

[135E An extension of stay as a highly skilled migrant may be granted for a period not exceeding 3 years, provided that the Secretary of State is satisfied that each of the requirements of paragraph 135D, 135DA, 135DB, 135DC, 135DD, 135DE, 135DF, 135DG or 135DH is met.]

Note
Substituted by HC 346. Further substituted by HC 104.

[Refusal of extension of stay as a highly skilled migrant

[135F An extension of stay as a highly skilled migrant is to be refused if the Secretary of State is not satisfied that each of the requirements of paragraph 135D, 135DA, 135DB, 135DC, 135DD, 135DE, 135DF, 135DG or 135DH is met.]

Note
Substituted by HC 346. Further substituted by HC 104.

[Indefinite leave to remain as a highly skilled migrant

135G Indefinite leave to remain may be granted,, on application, to a person currently with leave as a highly skilled migrant, provided that he:

(i)   has had a continuous period of at least 4 years' leave to enter or remain in the United Kingdom in this capacity or has had a continuous period of at least 4 years' leave to enter or remain in the United Kingdom which includes periods of leave to enter or remain granted under paragraphs 128 to 319 of these Rules; and
(ii)   for the period of leave as a highly skilled migrant, has met the requirements of paragraph 135A (i)–(iii); and
(iii)   for any period of leave not in this capacity, has not had recourse to public funds; and
(iv)   is lawfully economically active in the United Kingdom in employment, self-employment or a combination of both.]

Note
Inserted by HC 538.

[Requirements for an extension of stay as a highly skilled migrant

135H Indefinite leave to remain in the United Kingdom to a person currently with leave as a highly skilled migrant is to be refused if the Secretary of State is not satisfied that each of the requirements of paragraph 135G is met.]

Note
Inserted by HC 538.

Appendix 1   Legislation and materials

[Requirements for leave to enter the United Kingdom for the purpose of employment under the Sectors-Based Scheme

135I The requirements to be met by a person seeking leave to enter the United Kingdom for the purpose of employment under the Sectors-Based Scheme are that he:

   (i)   holds a valid Home Office immigration employment document issued under the Sectors-Based Scheme; and

  (ii) is not of an age which puts him outside the limits for employment; and

 (iii) is capable of undertaking the employment specified in the immigration employment document; and

 (iv) does not intend to take employment except as specified in his immigration employment document; and

  (v) is able to maintain and accommodate himself adequately without recourse to public funds; and

 (vi) intends to leave the United Kingdom at the end of his approved employment; and

[(vii) holds a valid United Kingdom entry clearance for entry in this capacity.]

Note
Paragraphs 135I–135K inserted by Cmnd 5829. Sub-paragraph (vii) substituted by HC 523.

[Leave to enter for the purpose of employment under the Sectors-Based Scheme

135J A person seeking leave to enter the United Kingdom for the purpose of employment under the Sectors-Based Scheme may be admitted for a period not exceeding 12 months (normally as specified in his work permit), subject to a condition restricting him to employment approved by the Home Office, provided the Immigration Officer is satisfied that each of the requirements of paragraph 135I is met.]

Note
Paragraphs 135I–135K inserted by Cmnd 5829.

[Refusal of leave to enter for the purpose of employment under the Sectors-Based Scheme

135K Leave to enter the United Kingdom for the purpose of employment under the Sectors-Based Scheme is to be refused if the Immigration Officer is not satisfied that each of the requirements of paragraph 135I is met.]

Note
Paragraphs 135I–135K inserted by Cmnd 5829.

[Requirements for an extension of stay for Sector-Based employment

135L The requirements for an extension of stay for Sector-Based employment are that the applicant:

  (i)   entered the United Kingdom with a valid Home Office immigration employment document issued under the sectors-Based Scheme and;

(ii)   has written approval from the Home Office for the continuation of his employment under the Sectors-Based Scheme; and
(iii) meets the requirements of paragraph 135I (ii) to (vi); and
(iv)   would not, as a result of the extension of stay sought, remain in the United Kingdom for Sector-Based Scheme employment to a date beyond 12 months from the date on which he was given leave to enter the United Kingdom on this occasion in this capacity.]

Note
Paragraphs 135L–135N inserted by HC 464.

[Extension of stay for Sectors-Based Scheme employment

135M An extension of stay for Sectors-Based Scheme employment may be granted for a period not exceeding the period of approved employment recommended by the Home Office provided the Secretary of State is satisfied that each of the requirements of paragraph 135L are met. An extension of stay is to be subject to a condition restricting the applicant to employment approved by the Home Office.]

Note
Paragraphs 135L–135N inserted by HC 464.

[Refusal of extension of stay for Sectors-Based Scheme employment

135N An extension of stay for Sector-Based Scheme employment is to be refused if the Secretary of State is not satisfied that each of the requirements of paragraph 135L is met.]

Note
Paragraphs 135L–135N inserted by HC 464.

[SCIENCE AND ENGINEERING GRADUATES SCHEME]

[Requirements for leave to enter as a participant in the Science and Engineering Graduates Scheme]

[135O The requirements to be met by a person seeking leave to enter as a participant in the Science and Engineering Graduates Scheme are that he:

(i)   has successfully completed and obtained a degree (with second class honours or above), masters degree or PhD in a subject approved by the Department for Education and Skills at either:
   (a)   a publicly funded institution of further or higher education; or
   (b)   a bona fide private education institution which maintains satisfactory records of enrolment and attendance.
(ii) intends to seek and take work during the period for which leave is granted in this capacity;
(iii) can maintain and accommodate himself and any dependants without recourse to public funds;
(iv) completed his degree, masters or PhD in the approved subject in the last 12 months;

(v)   if he has previously spent time in the UK as a participant in the Science and Engineering Graduates Scheme, is not seeking leave to enter to a date beyond 12 months from the date he was first given leave to enter or remain in this capacity;

(vi)   intends to leave the United Kingdom if, on expiry of his leave under this scheme, he has not been granted leave to remain in the United Kingdom in accordance with paragraphs 128–135H or 200–210H of these Rules;

(vii)   has the written consent of his official sponsor to enter or remain in the United Kingdom under the Science and Engineering Graduate Scheme if his approved studies, or any studies he has subsequently undertaken, were sponsored by a government or international scholarship agency; and

(viii)   holds a valid entry clearance for entry in this capacity except where he is a British National (Overseas), a British overseas territories citizen, a British Overseas citizen, a British protected person or a person who under the British Nationality Act 1981 is a British subject.]

Note
Paragraphs 135O–135T inserted by Cm 6339.

[Leave to enter as a participant in the Science and Engineering Graduates Scheme]

[135P A person seeking leave to enter the United Kingdom as a participant in the Science and Engineering Graduates Scheme may be admitted for a period not exceeding 12 months provided he is able to produce to the Immigration Officer, on arrival, a valid United Kingdom entry clearance for entry in this capacity.]

Note
Paragraphs 135O–135T inserted by Cm 6339.

[Refusal of leave to enter as a participant in the Science and Engineering Graduates Scheme]

[135Q Leave to enter as a participant in the Science and Engineering Graduates Scheme is to be refused if the Immigration Officer is not satisfied that each of the requirements of paragraph 135O is met.]

Note
Paragraphs 135O–135T inserted by Cm 6339.

[Requirements for leave to remain as a participant in the Science and Engineering Graduates Scheme]

[135R The requirements to be met by a person seeking leave to remain as a participant in the Science and Engineering Graduates Scheme are that he:

(i)   meets the requirements of paragraph 135O(i) to (vii); and

(ii)   has leave to enter or remain as a student or as a participant in the Science and Engineering Graduates Scheme in accordance with paragraphs 57–69L or 135O–135T of these Rules;

(iii)   would not, as a result of an extension of stay, remain in the United Kingdom as a participant in the Science and Engineering Graduates Scheme to a date beyond 12 months from the date on which he was first given leave to enter or remain in this capacity.]

Note
Paragraphs 135O–135T inserted by Cm 6339.

[Leave to remain as a participant in the Science and Engineering Graduates Scheme]

[135S Leave to remain as a participant in the Science and Engineering Graduates Scheme may be granted if the Secretary of State is satisfied that the applicant meets each of the requirements of paragraph 135R.]

Note
Paragraphs 135O–135T inserted by Cm 6339.

[Refusal of leave to remain as a participant in the Science and Engineering Graduates Scheme]

[135T Leave to remain as a participant in the Science and Engineering Graduates Scheme is to be refused if the Secretary of State is not satisfied that each of the requirements of paragraph 135R is met.]

Note
Paragraphs 135O to 135T inserted by Cm 6339.

REPRESENTATIVES OF OVERSEAS NEWSPAPERS, NEWS AGENCIES AND BROADCASTING ORGANISATIONS

Requirements for leave to enter as a representative of an overseas newspaper, news agency or broadcasting organisation

136 The requirements to be met by a person seeking leave to enter the United Kingdom as a representative of an overseas newspaper, news agency or broadcasting organisation are that he:

(i)   has been engaged by that organisation outside the United Kingdom and is being posted to the United Kingdom on a long-term assignment as a representative; and

(ii)   intends to work full-time as a representative of that overseas newspaper, news agency or broadcasting organisation; and

(iii)   does not intend to take employment except within the terms of this paragraph; and

(iv)   can maintain and accommodate himself and any dependants adequately without recourse to public funds; and

(v)   holds a valid United Kingdom entry clearance for entry in this capacity.

Leave to enter as a representative of an overseas newspaper, news agency or broadcasting organisation

137 A person seeking leave to enter the United Kingdom as a representative of an overseas newspaper, news agency or broadcasting organisation may be admitted for a period not exceeding 12 months provided he is able to produce to the Immigration Officer, on arrival, a valid United Kingdom entry clearance for entry in this capacity.

Appendix 1 Legislation and materials

Refusal of leave to enter as a representative of an overseas newspaper, news agency or broadcasting organisation

138 Leave to enter as a representative of an overseas newspaper, news agency or broadcasting organisation is to be refused if a valid United Kingdom entry clearance for entry in this capacity is not produced to the Immigration Officer on arrival.

Requirements for an extension of stay as a representative of an overseas newspaper, news agency or broadcasting organisation

139 The requirements for an extension of stay as a representative of an overseas newspaper, news agency or broadcasting organisation are that the applicant:

(i)   entered the United Kingdom with a valid United Kingdom entry clearance as a representative of an overseas newspaper, news agency or broadcasting organisation; and

(ii)   is still engaged in the employment for which his entry clearance was granted; and

(iii)   is still required for the employment in question, as certified by his employer; and

(iv)   meets the requirements of paragraph 136(ii)–(iv).

Extension of stay as a representative of an overseas newspaper, newsagency or broadcasting organisation

140 An extension of stay as a representative of an overseas newspaper, news agency or broadcasting organisation may be granted for a period not exceeding 3 years provided the Secretary of State is satisfied that each of the requirements of paragraph 139 is met.

Refusal of extension of stay as a representative of an overseas newspaper, news agency or broadcasting organisation

141 An extension of stay as a representative of an overseas newspaper, news agency or broadcasting organisation is to be refused if the Secretary of State is not satisfied that each of the requirements of paragraph 139 is met.

Indefinite leave to remain for a representative of an overseas newspaper, news agency or broadcasting organisation

142 Indefinite leave to remain may be granted, on application, to a representative of an overseas newspaper, news agency or broadcasting organisation provided:

(i)   he has spent a continuous period of 4 years in the United Kingdom in this capacity; and

(ii)   he has met the requirements of paragraph 139 throughout the 4 year period; and

(iii)   he is still required for the employment in question, as certified by his employer.

1918

Refusal of indefinite leave to remain for a representative of an overseas newspaper, news agency or broadcasting organisation

143 Indefinite leave to remain in the United Kingdom for a representative of an overseas newspaper, news agency or broadcasting organisation is to be refused if the Secretary of State is not satisfied that each of the requirements of paragraph 142 is met.

[**Requirements for leave to enter the United Kingdom as a Fresh Talent: Working in Scotland scheme participant**

143A The requirements to be met by a person seeking leave to enter as a Fresh Talent: Working in Scotland scheme participant are that the applicant:

(i)   has been awarded an HND, or a UK recognised undergraduate degree, Master's degree or PhD by either:
    (a)   a Scottish publicly funded institution of further or higher education; or
    (b)   a Scottish bona fide private education institution which maintains satisfactory records of enrolment and attendance; and

(ii)   has lived in Scotland for an appropriate period of time whilst studying for the HND, undergraduate degree, Master's degree or PhD referred to in (i) above; and

(iii)   intends to seek and take employment in Scotland during the period of leave granted under this paragraph; and

(iv)   is able to maintain and accommodate himself and any dependants adequately without recourse to public funds; and

(v)   has completed the HND, undergraduate degree, Masters' degree or PhD referred to in (i) above in the last 12 months; and

(vi)   intends to leave the United Kingdom if, on expiry of his leave under this paragraph, he has not been granted leave to remain in the United Kingdom as:
    (a)   a work permit holder in accordance with paragraphs 128–135 of these Rules; or
    (b)   under the highly skilled migrant programme in accordance with paragraphs 135A–135H of these Rules; or
    (c)   a person intending to establish themselves in business in accordance with paragraphs 200–210 of these Rules; or
    (d)   an innovator in accordance with paragraphs 210A–210H of these Rules; and

(vii)   has the written consent of his official sponsor to enter or remain in the United Kingdom as a Fresh Talent: Working in Scotland scheme participant, if the studies which led to his qualification under (i) above (or any studies he has subsequently undertaken) were sponsored by a government or international scholarship agency; and

(viii)   if he has previously been granted leave as either:
    (a)   a Fresh Talent: Working in Scotland scheme participant in accordance with this paragraph; and/or
    (b)   a participant in the Science and Engineering Graduates Scheme in accordance with paragraphs 135O–135T of these Rules is not seeking leave to enter under this paragraph which, when amalgamated with any previous periods of leave granted in either of these two categories, would total more than 24 months; and

(ix)   holds a valid entry clearance for entry in this capacity except where he is a British National (Overseas), a British overseas territories citizen, a British Overseas citizen, a British protected person or a person who under the British Nationality Act 1981 is a British subject.]

Appendix 1   Legislation and materials

Note
Inserted by HC 104.

[Leave to enter as a Fresh Talent: Working in Scotland scheme participant

143B A person seeking leave to enter the United Kingdom as a Fresh Talent: Working in Scotland scheme participant may be admitted for a period not exceeding 24 months provided the Immigration Officer is satisfied that each of the requirements of paragraph 143A is met.]

Note
Inserted by HC 104.

[Refusal of leave to enter as a Fresh Talent: Working in Scotland scheme participant

143C Leave to enter as a Fresh Talent: Working in Scotland scheme participant is to be refused if the Immigration Officer is not satisfied that each of the requirements of paragraph 143A is met.]

Note
Inserted by HC 104.

[Requirements for an extension of stay as a Fresh Talent: Working in Scotland scheme participant

143D The requirements to be met by a person seeking an extension of stay as a Fresh Talent: Working in Scotland scheme participant are that the applicant:
  (i)   meets the requirements of paragraph 143A(i) to (vii); and
  (ii)   has leave to enter or remain in the United Kingdom as either:
          (a)   a student in accordance with paragraphs 57–69L of these Rules; or
          (b)   a participant in the Science and Engineering Graduates Scheme in accordance with paragraphs 135O–135T of these Rules; or
          (c)   a Fresh Talent: Working in Scotland scheme participant in accordance with paragraphs 143A–143F of these Rules; and
  (iii)   if he has previously been granted leave as either:
          (a)   a Fresh Talent: Working in Scotland scheme participant in accordance with paragraphs 143A–143F of these Rules; and/or
          (b)   a Science and Engineering Graduates Scheme participant in accordance with paragraphs 135O–135T of these Rules is not seeking leave to remain under this paragraph which, when amalgamated with any previous periods of leave granted in either of these two categories, would total more than 24 months.]

Note
Inserted by HC 104.

[Extension of stay as a Fresh Talent: Working in Scotland scheme participant

143E An extension of stay as a Fresh Talent: Working in Scotland scheme participant may be granted for a period not exceeding 24 months if the Secretary of State is satisfied that each of the requirements of paragraph 143D is met.]

1920

Note
Inserted by HC 104.

[Refusal of an extension of stay as a Fresh Talent: Working in Scotland scheme participant

143F An extension of stay as a Fresh Talent: Working in Scotland scheme participant is to be refused if the Secretary of State is not satisfied that each of the requirements of paragraph 143D is met.]

Note
Inserted by HC 104.

REPRESENTATIVES OF OVERSEAS FIRMS WHICH HAVE NO BRANCH, SUBSIDIARY OR OTHER REPRESENTATIVE IN THE UNITED KINGDOM (SOLE REPRESENTATIVES)

Requirements for leave to enter as a sole representative

144 The requirements to be met by a person seeking leave to enter the United Kingdom as a sole representative are that he:

  (i) has been recruited and taken on as an employee outside the United Kingdom as a representative of a firm which has its headquarters and principal place of business outside the United Kingdom and which has no branch, subsidiary or other representative in the United Kingdom; and

  (ii) seeks entry to the United Kingdom as a senior employee with full authority to take operational decisions on behalf of the overseas firm for the purpose of representing it in the United Kingdom by establishing and operating a registered branch or wholly owned subsidiary of that overseas firm; and

  (iii) intends to be employed full time as a representative of that overseas firm; and

  (iv) is not a majority shareholder in that overseas firm; and

  (v) does not intend to take employment except within the terms of this paragraph; and

  (vi) can maintain and accommodate himself and any dependants adequately without recourse to public funds; and

  (vii) holds a valid United Kingdom entry clearance for entry in this capacity.

Leave to enter as a sole representative

145 A person seeking leave to enter the United Kingdom as a sole representative may be admitted for a period not exceeding 12 months provided he is able to produce to the Immigration Officer, on arrival, a valid United Kingdom entry clearance for entry in this capacity.

Refusal of leave to enter as a sole representative

146 Leave to enter as a sole representative is to be refused if a valid United Kingdom entry clearance for entry in this capacity is not produced to the Immigration Officer on arrival.

Appendix 1   Legislation and materials

Requirements for an extension of stay as a sole representative

147 The requirements for an extension of stay as a sole representative are that the applicant:

(i)   entered the United Kingdom with a valid United Kingdom entry clearance as a sole representative of an overseas firm; and

(ii) can show that the overseas firm still has its headquarters and principal place of business outside the United Kingdom; and

(iii) is employed full-time as a representative of that overseas firm and has established and is in charge of its registered branch or wholly-owned subsidiary; and

(iv) is still required for the employment in question, as certified by his employer; and

(v)   meets the requirements of paragraph 144(iii)–(vi).

Extension of stay as a sole representative

148 An extension of stay not exceeding 3 years as a sole representative may be granted provided the Secretary of State is satisfied that each of the requirements of paragraph 147 is met.

Refusal of extension of stay as a sole representative

149 An extension of stay as a sole representative is to be refused if the Secretary of State is not satisfied that each of the requirements of paragraph 147 is met.

Indefinite leave to remain for a sole representative

150 Indefinite leave to remain may be granted, on application, to a sole representative provided:

(i)   he has spent a continuous period of 4 years in the United Kingdom in this capacity; and

(ii) he has met the requirements of paragraph 147 throughout the 4 year period; and

(iii) he is still required for the employment in question, as certified by his employer.

Refusal of indefinite leave to remain for a sole representative

151 Indefinite leave to remain in the United Kingdom for a sole representative is to be refused if the Secretary of State is not satisfied that each of the requirements of paragraph 150 is met.

PRIVATE SERVANTS IN DIPLOMATIC HOUSEHOLDS

Requirements for leave to enter as a private servant in a diplomatic household

152 The requirements to be met by a person seeking leave to enter the United Kingdom as a private servant in a diplomatic household are that he:

1922

(i)   is aged 18 or over; and

(ii)   is employed as a private servant in the household of a member of staff of a diplomatic or consular mission who enjoys diplomatic privileges and immunity within the meaning of the Vienna Convention on Diplomatic and Consular Relations or a member of the family forming part of the household of such a person; and

(iii)   intends to work full-time as a private servant within the terms of this paragraph; and

(iv)   does not intend to take employment except within the terms of this paragraph; and

(v)   can maintain and accommodate himself and any dependants adequately without recourse to public funds; and

(vi)   holds a valid United Kingdom entry clearance for entry in this capacity.

Leave to enter as a private servant in a diplomatic household

153 A person seeking leave to enter the United Kingdom as a private servant in a diplomatic household may be given leave to enter for a period not exceeding 12 months provided he is able to produce to the Immigration Officer, on arrival, a valid United Kingdom entry clearance for entry in this capacity.

Refusal of leave to enter as a private servant in a diplomatic household

154 Leave to enter as a private servant in a diplomatic household is to be refused if a valid United Kingdom entry clearance for entry in this capacity is not produced to the Immigration Officer on arrival.

Requirements for an extension of stay as a private servant in a diplomatic household

155 The requirements for an extension of stay as a private servant in a diplomatic household are that the applicant:

(i)   entered the United Kingdom with a valid United Kingdom entry clearance as a private servant in a diplomatic household; and

(ii)   is still engaged in the employment for which his entry clearance was granted; and

(iii)   is still required for the employment in question, as certified by the employer; and

(iv)   meets the requirements of paragraph 152(iii)–(v).

Extension of stay as a private servant in a diplomatic household

156 An extension of stay as a private servant in a diplomatic household may be granted for a period not exceeding 12 months provided the Secretary of State is satisfied that each of the requirements of paragraph 155 is met.

Refusal of extension of stay as a private servant in a diplomatic household

157 An extension of stay as a private servant in a diplomatic household is to be refused if the Secretary of State is not satisfied that each of the requirements of paragraph 155 is met.

Appendix 1   Legislation and materials

Indefinite leave to remain for a servant in a diplomatic household

158 Indefinite leave to remain may be granted, on application, to a private servant in a diplomatic household provided:

(i)   he has spent a continuous period of 4 years in the United Kingdom in this capacity; and

(ii)   he has met the requirements of paragraph 155 throughout the 4 year period; and

(iii)   he is still required for the employment in question, as certified by his employer.

Refusal of indefinite leave to remain for a servant in a diplomatic household

159 Indefinite leave to remain in the United Kingdom for a private servant in a diplomatic household is to be refused if the Secretary of State is not satisfied that each of the requirements of paragraph 158 is met.

[DOMESTIC WORKERS IN PRIVATE HOUSEHOLDS]

[Requirements for leave to enter as a domestic worker in a private household

159A The requirements to be met by a person seeking leave to enter the United Kingdom as a domestic worker in a private household are that he:

(i)   is aged 18–65 inclusive;

(ii)   has been employed as a domestic worker for one year or more immediately prior to application for entry clearance under the same roof as his employer or in a household that the employer uses for himself on a regular basis and where there is evidence that there is a connection between employer and employee;

(iii)   that he intends to travel to the United Kingdom in the company of his employer, his employer's spouse or his employer's minor child;

(iv)   intends to work full time as a domestic worker under the same roof as his employer or in a household that the employer uses for himself on a regular basis and where there is evidence that there is a connection between employer and employee;

(v)   does not intend to take employment except within the terms of this paragraph; and

(vi)   can maintain and accommodate himself adequately without recourse to public funds; and

(vii)   holds a valid United Kingdom entry clearance for entry in this capacity.]

Note
Main heading and paragraphs 159A–159H inserted by Cm 5597.

[Leave to enter as a domestic worker in a private household

159B A person seeking leave to enter the United Kingdom as a domestic worker in a private household may be given leave to enter for that purpose for a period not exceeding 12 months provided he is able to produce to the Immigration Officer, on arrival, a valid United Kingdom entry clearance for entry in this capacity.]

Note
Main heading and paragraphs 159A–159H inserted by Cm 5597.

[Refusal of leave to enter as a domestic worker in a private household

159C Leave to enter as a domestic worker in a private household is to be refused if a valid United Kingdom entry clearance for entry in this capacity is not produced to the Immigration Officer on arrival.]

Note
Main heading and paragraphs 159A–159H inserted by Cm 5597.

[Requirements for extension of stay as a domestic worker in a private household

159D The requirements for an extension of stay as a domestic worker in a private household are that the applicant:

(i)   entered the United Kingdom with a valid United Kingdom entry clearance as a domestic worker in a private household; and

(ii) has continued to be employed for the duration of his leave as a domestic worker in a private household; and

(iii) continues to be required for employment for the period of the extension sought as a domestic worker in a private household within the terms of paragraph 159A as certified by his current employer; and

(iv) meets each of the requirements of paragraph 159A(i) to (vi).]

Note
Main heading and paragraphs 159A–159H inserted by Cm 5597.

[Extension of stay as a domestic worker in a private household

159E An extension of stay as a domestic worker in a private household may be granted for a period not exceeding 12 months provided the Secretary of State is satisfied that each of the requirements of paragraph 159D is met.]

Note
Main heading and paragraphs 159A–159H inserted by Cm 5597.

[Refusal of extension of stay as a domestic worker in a private household

159F An extension of stay as a domestic worker may be refused if the Secretary of State is not satisfied that each of the requirements of paragraph 159D is met.]

Note
Main heading and paragraphs 159A–159H inserted by Cm 5597.

[Indefinite leave to remain for a domestic worker in a private household

159G Indefinite leave to remain may be granted, on application, to a domestic worker in a private household provided that:

(i)   he has spent a continuous period of 4 years in the United Kingdom employed in this capacity; and

(ii) he has met the requirements of paragraph 159A throughout the 4 year period; and

(iii)   he is still required for employment as a domestic worker in a private household, as certified by the current employer.]

Note
Main heading and paragraphs 159A–159H inserted by Cm 5597.

[Refusal of indefinite leave to remain for a domestic worker in a private household

159H Indefinite leave to remain in the United Kingdom for a domestic worker in a private household is to be refused if the Secretary of State is not satisfied that each of the requirements of paragraph 159G is met.]

Note
Main heading and paragraphs 159A–159H inserted by Cm 5597.

OVERSEAS GOVERNMENT EMPLOYEES

Requirements for leave to enter as an overseas government employee

160 For the purposes of these Rules an overseas government employee means a person coming for employment by an overseas government or employed by the United Nations Organisation or other international organisation of which the United Kingdom is a member.

161 The requirements to be met by a person seeking leave to enter the United Kingdom as an overseas government employee are that he:

(i)   is able to produce either a valid United Kingdom entry clearance for entry in this capacity or satisfactory documentary evidence of his status as an overseas government employee; and
(ii)   intends to work full time for the government or organisation concerned; and
(iii) does not intend to take employment except within the terms of this paragraph; and
(iv)   can maintain and accommodate himself and any dependants adequately without recourse to public funds.

Leave to enter as an overseas government employee

162 A person seeking leave to enter the United Kingdom as an overseas government employee may be given leave to enter for a period not exceeding 12 months, provided he is able, on arrival, to produce to the Immigration Officer a valid United Kingdom entry clearance for entry in this capacity or satisfy the Immigration Officer that each of the requirements of paragraph 161 is met.

Refusal of leave to enter as an overseas government employee

163 Leave to enter as an overseas government employee is to be refused if a valid United Kingdom entry clearance for entry in this capacity is not produced to the Immigration Officer on arrival or if the Immigration Officer is not satisfied that each of the requirements of paragraph 161 is met.

Requirements for an extension of stay as an overseas government employee

164 The requirements to be met by a person seeking an extension of stay as an overseas government employee are that the applicant:

(i)   was given leave to enter the United Kingdom under paragraph 162 as an overseas government employee; and

(ii)   is still engaged in the employment in question; and

(iii)   is still required for the employment is question, as certified by the employer; and

(iv)   meets the requirements of paragraph 161(ii)–(iv).

Extension of stay as an overseas government employee

165 An extension of stay as an overseas government employee may be granted for a period not exceeding 3 years provided the Secretary of State is satisfied that each of the requirements of paragraph 164 is met.

Refusal of extension of stay as an overseas government employee

166 An extension of stay as an overseas government employee is to be refused if the Secretary of State is not satisfied that each of the requirements of paragraph 164 is met.

Indefinite leave to remain for an overseas government employee

167 Indefinite leave to remain may be granted, on application, to an overseas government employee provided:

(i)   he has spent a continuous period of 4 years in the United Kingdom in this capacity; and

(ii)   he has met the requirements of paragraph 164 throughout the 4 year period; and

(iii)   he is still required for the employment in question, as certified by his employer.

Refusal of indefinite leave to remain for an overseas government employee

168 Indefinite leave to remain in the United Kingdom for an overseas government employee is to be refused if the Secretary of State is not satisfied that each of the requirements of paragraph 167 is met.

MINISTERS OF RELIGION, MISSIONARIES AND MEMBERS OF RELIGIOUS ORDERS

169 For the purposes of these Rules:

(i)   a minister of religion means a religious functionary whose main regular duties comprise the leading of a congregation in performing the rites and rituals of the faith and in preaching the essentials of the creed;

(ii)   a missionary means a person who is directly engaged in spreading a religious doctrine and whose work is not in essence administrative or clerical;

(iii)   a member of a religious order means a person who is coming to live in a community run by that order.

Requirements for leave to enter as a minister or religion, missionary or member of a religious order

170 The requirements to be met by a person seeking leave to enter the United Kingdom as a minister of religion, missionary or member of a religious order are that he:

(i)
    (a)   if seeking leave to enter as a minister of religion has either been working for at least one year as a minister of religion [in any of the 5 years immediately prior to the date on which the application is made] or, where ordination is prescribed by a religious faith as the sole means of entering the ministry, has been ordained as a minister of religion following at least one year's full-time or two years' part-time training for the ministry; or

    (b)   if seeking leave to enter as a missionary has been trained as a missionary or has worked as a missionary and is being sent to the United Kingdom by an overseas organisation; or

    (c)   if seeking leave to enter as a member of a religious order is coming to live in a community maintained by the religious order of which he is a member and, if intending to teach, does not intend to do so save at an establishment maintained by his order; and

(ii)   intends to work full-time as a minister of religion, missionary or for the religious order of which he is a member; and

(iii)   does not intend to take employment except within the terms of this paragraph; and

(iv)   can maintain and accommodate himself and any dependants adequately without recourse to public funds; and

[(iva)   if seeking entry as a minister of religion, can produce an International English Language Testing System certificate issued to him to certify that he has achieved level 4 competence in spoken English and that is dated not more than two years prior to the date on which the application is made;]

(v)   holds a valid United Kingdom entry clearance for entry in this capacity.

Note
Words in square brackets in sub paragraph (i)(a) and (iva) inserted by Cm 6297.

Leave to enter as a minister or religion, missionary or member of a religious order

171 A person seeking leave to enter the United Kingdom as a minister of religion, missionary or member of a religious order may be admitted for a period not exceeding 12 months provided he is able to produce to the Immigration Officer, on arrival, a valid United Kingdom entry clearance for entry in this capacity.

Refusal of leave to enter as a minister of religion, missionary or member of a religious order

172 Leave to enter as a minister of religion, missionary or member of a religious order is to be refused if a valid United Kingdom entry clearance for entry in this capacity is not produced to the Immigration Officer on arrival.

[Requirements for an extension of stay as a minister of religion where entry to the United Kingdom was granted in that capacity]

173 The requirements for an extension of stay as a minister of religion [where entry to the United Kingdom was granted in that capacity], missionary or member of a religious order are that the applicant:

(i) entered the United Kingdom with a valid United Kingdom entry clearance as a minister of religion, missionary or member of a religious order; and

(ii) is still engaged in the employment for which his entry clearance was granted; and

(iii) is still required for the employment in question as certified by the leadership of his congregation, his employer or the head of his religious order; and

[(iv)

    (a) if he entered the United Kingdom as a minister of religion in accordance with sub-paragraph (i) prior to 23rd August 2004 or as a missionary or member of a religious order, meets the requirements of paragraph 170(ii)–(iv);

    (b) if he entered the United Kingdom as a minister of religion in accordance with sub-paragraph (i) after 23rd August 2004, or was granted leave to remain in accordance with paragraph 174B after that date, meets the requirements of paragraph 170(ii)–(iva); or]

Note
Words in square brackets in heading, paragraph 173 and sub-paragraph (iv)(*a*) and (*b*) inserted by Cm 6297.

Extension of stay as a minister of religion, missionary or member of a religious order

174 An extension of stay as a minister of religion, missionary or member of a religious order may be granted for a period not exceeding 3 years provided the Secretary of State is satisfied that each of the requirements of paragraph 173 is met.

[Requirements for an extension of stay as a minister of religion where entry to the United Kingdom was not granted in that capacity]

[174A The requirements for an extension of stay as a minister of religion for an applicant who did not enter the United Kingdom in that capacity are that he:

(i) entered the United Kingdom, or was given an extension of stay, in accordance with these Rules, except as a minister of religion or as a visitor under paragraphs 40–56 of these Rules, and has spent a continuous period of at least 12 months here pursuant to that leave immediately prior to the application being made; and

(ii) has either been working for at least one year as a minister of religion in any of the 5 years immediately prior to the date on which the application is made (provided that, when doing so, he was not in breach of a condition of any subsisting leave to enter or remain) or, where ordination is prescribed by a religious faith as the sole means of entering the ministry, has been ordained as a minister of religion following at least one year's full-time or two years part-time training for the ministry; and

(iii) is imminently to be appointed, or has been appointed, to a position as a minister of religion in the United Kingdom and is suitable for such a position, as certified by the leadership of his prospective congregation; and

(iv)   meets the requirements of paragraph 170(ii)–(iva).]

Note
Heading and paragraph 174A inserted by Cm 6297.

[Extension of stay as a minister of religion where leave to enter was not granted in that capacity]

[174B An extension of stay as a minister of religion may be granted for a period not exceeding 12 months provided the Secretary of State is satisfied that each of the requirements of paragraph 174A is met.]

Note
Heading and paragraph 174B inserted by Cm 6297.

Refusal of extension of stay as a minister of religion, missionary or member of a religious order

175 An extension of stay as a minister of religion, missionary or member of a religious order is to be refused if the Secretary of State is not satisfied that each of the requirements of paragraph 173 [or 174A] is met.

Note
Words in square brackets inserted by Cm 6297.

Indefinite leave to remain for a minister of religion, missionary or member of a religious order

176 Indefinite leave to remain may be granted, on application, to a person admitted as a minister of religion, missionary or member of a religious order provided:

(i)   he has spent a continuous period of 4 years in the United Kingdom in this capacity; and
(ii)   he has met the requirements of paragraph 173 [or 174A] throughout the 4 year period; and
(iii)   he is still required for the employment in question as certified by the leadership of his congregation, his employer or the head of the religious order to which he belongs.

Note
Words in square brackets inserted by Cm 6297.

Refusal of indefinite leave to remain for a minister of religion, missionary or member of a religious order

177 Indefinite leave to remain in the United Kingdom for a minister of religion, missionary or member of a religious order is to be refused if the Secretary of State is not satisfied that each of the requirements of paragraph 176 is met.

Requirements for leave to enter the United Kingdom as a member of the operational ground staff of an overseas-owned airline

178 The requirements to be met by a person seeking leave to enter the United Kingdom as a member of the operational ground staff of an overseas-owned airline are that he:

(i) has been transferred to the United Kingdom by an overseas-owned airline operating services to and from the United Kingdom to take up duty at an international airport as station manager, security manager or technical manager; and

(ii) intends to work full-time for the airline concerned; and

(iii) does not intend to take employment except within the terms of this paragraph; and

(iv) can maintain and accommodate himself and any dependants without recourse to public funds; and

(v) holds a valid United Kingdom entry clearance for entry in this capacity.

Leave to enter as a member of the operational ground staff of an overseas-owned airline

179 A person seeking leave to enter the United Kingdom as a member of the operational staff of an overseas-owned airline may be given leave to enter for a period not exceeding 12 months, provided he is able to produce to the Immigration Officer, on arrival, a valid United Kingdom entry clearance for entry in this capacity.

Refusal of leave to enter as a member of the operational ground staff of an overseas-owned airline

180 Leave to enter as a member of the operational ground staff of an overseas-owned airline is to be refused if a valid United Kingdom entry clearance for entry in this capacity is not produced to the Immigration Officer on arrival.

Requirements for an extension of stay as a member of the operational ground staff of an overseas-owned airline

181 The requirements to be met by a person seeking an extension of stay as a member of the operational ground staff of an overseas-owned airline are that the applicant:

(i) entered the United Kingdom with a valid United Kingdom entry clearance as a member of the operational ground staff of an overseas-owned airline; and

(ii) is still engaged in the employment for which entry was granted; and

(iii) is still required for the employment in question, as certified by the employer; and

(iv) meets the requirements of paragraph 178(ii)–(iv).

1931

Extension of stay as a member of the operational ground staff of an overseas-owned airline

182 An extension of stay as a member of the operational ground staff of an overseas-owned airline may be granted for a period not exceeding 3 years, provided the Secretary of State is satisfied that each of the requirements of paragraph 181 is met.

Refusal of extension of stay as a member of the operational ground staff of an overseas-owned airline

183 An extension of stay as a member of the operational staff of an overseas-owned airline is to be refused if the Secretary of State is not satisfied that each of the requirements of paragraph 181 is met.

Indefinite leave to remain for a member of the operational ground staff of an overseas-owned airline

184 Indefinite leave to remain may be granted, on application, to a member of the operational ground staff of an overseas-owned airline provided:

(i) he has spent a continuous period of 4 years in the United Kingdom in this capacity; and

(ii) he has met the requirements of paragraph 181 throughout the 4 year period; and

(iii) he is still required for the employment in question, as certified by the employer.

Refusal of indefinite leave to remain for a member of the operational ground staff of an overseas-owned airline

185 Indefinite leave to remain in the United Kingdom for a member of the operational ground staff of an overseas-owned airline is to be refused if the Secretary of State is not satisfied that each of the requirements of paragraph 184 is met.

PERSONS WITH UNITED KINGDOM ANCESTRY

Requirements for leave to enter on the grounds of United Kingdom ancestry

186 The requirements to be met by a person seeking leave to enter the United Kingdom on the grounds of his United Kingdom ancestry are that he:

(i) is a Commonwealth citizen; and

(ii) is aged 17 or over; and

(iii) is able to provide proof that one of his grandparents was born in the United Kingdom and Islands [and that any such grandparent is the applicant's blood grandparent or grandparent by reason of an adoption recognised by the laws of the United Kingdom relating to adoption]; and

(iv) is able to work and intends to take or seek employment in the United Kingdom; and

(v) will be able to maintain and accommodate himself and any dependants adequately without recourse to public funds; and

(vi) holds a valid United Kingdom entry clearance for entry in this capacity.

Note
Words in square brackets in sub-paragraph (iii) inserted by Cm 5949.

Leave to enter the United Kingdom on the grounds of United Kingdom ancestry

187 A person seeking leave to enter the United Kingdom on the grounds of his United Kingdom ancestry may be given leave to enter for a period not exceeding 4 years provided he is able to produce to the Immigration Officer, on arrival, a valid United Kingdom entry clearance for entry in this capacity.

Refusal of leave to enter on the grounds of United Kingdom ancestry

188 Leave to enter the United Kingdom on the grounds of United Kingdom ancestry is to be refused if a valid United Kingdom entry clearance for entry in this capacity is not produced to the Immigration Officer on arrival.

Requirements for an extension of stay on the grounds of United Kingdom ancestry

[189 The requirements to be met by a person seeking an extension of stay on the grounds of United Kingdom ancestry are that:

(i)   he is able to meet each of the requirements of paragraph 186(i)–(v); and
(ii) he was admitted to the United Kingdom on the grounds of United Kingdom ancestry in accordance with paragraphs 186 to 188 or has been granted an extension of stay in this capacity.]

Note
Paragraph 189 substituted by HC 1112.

Extension of stay on the grounds of United Kingdom ancestry

190 An extension of stay on the grounds of United Kingdom ancestry may be granted for a period not exceeding 4 years provided the Secretary of State is satisfied that each of the requirements of [paragraph 189] is met.

Note
Words in square brackets substituted by HC 1112.

Refusal of extension of stay on the grounds of United Kingdom ancestry

191 An extension of stay on the grounds of United Kingdom ancestry is to be refused if the Secretary of State is not satisfied that each of the requirements of [paragraph 189] is met.

Note
Words in square brackets substituted by HC 1112.

Appendix 1 Legislation and materials

Indefinite leave to remain on the grounds of United Kingdom ancestry

192 Indefinite leave to remain may be granted, on application, to a Commonwealth citizen with a United Kingdom born grandparent provided:

(i) he meets the requirements of paragraph 186(i)–(v); and
(ii) he has spent a continuous period of 4 years in the United Kingdom in this capacity.

Refusal of indefinite leave to remain on the grounds of United Kingdom ancestry

193 Indefinite leave to remain in the United Kingdom on the grounds of a United Kingdom born grandparent is to be refused if the Secretary of State is not satisfied that each of the requirements of paragraph 192 is met.

SPOUSES OF PERSONS WITH LIMITED LEAVE TO ENTER OR REMAIN UNDER PARAGRAPHS 128–193 [(BUT NOT PARAGRAPHS 135I–135K)]

Requirements for leave to enter or remain as the spouse of a person with limited leave to enter or remain in the United Kingdom under paragraphs 128–193 [(but not paragraphs 135I–135K)]

194 The requirements to be met by a person seeking leave to enter or remain in the United Kingdom as the spouse of a person with limited leave to enter or remain in the United Kingdom under paragraphs 128–193 [(but not paragraphs 135I–135K)] are that:

(i) the applicant is married to a person with limited leave to enter or remain in the United Kingdom under paragraphs 128–193 [(but not paragraphs 135I–135K)]; and
(ii) each of the parties intends to live with the other as his or her spouse during the applicant's stay and the marriage is subsisting; and
(iii) there will be adequate accommodation for the parties and any dependants without recourse to public funds in accommodation which they own or occupy exclusively; and
(iv) the parties will be able to maintain themselves and any dependants adequately without recourse to public funds; and
(v) the applicant does not intend to stay in the United Kingdom beyond any period of leave granted to his spouse; and
(vi) if seeking leave to enter, the applicant holds a valid United Kingdom entry clearance for entry in this capacity or, if seeking leave to remain, was admitted with a valid United Kingdom entry clearance for entry in this capacity.

Note
Words in square brackets inserted by Cmnd 5829.

Leave to enter or remain as the spouse of a person with limited leave to enter or remain in the United Kingdom under paragraphs 128–193 [(but not paragraphs 135I–135K)]

195 A person seeking leave to enter or remain in the United Kingdom as the spouse of a person with limited leave to enter or remain in the United Kingdom under

paragraphs 128–193 [(but not paragraphs 135I–135K)] may be given leave to enter or remain in the United Kingdom for a period of leave not in excess of that granted to the person with limited leave to enter or remain under paragraphs 128–193 [(but not paragraphs 135I–135K)] provided that, in relation to an application for leave to enter, he is able, on arrival, to produce to the Immigration Officer a valid United Kingdom entry clearance for entry in this capacity or, in the case of an application for limited leave to remain, he was admitted with a valid United Kingdom entry clearance for entry in this capacity and is able to satisfy the Secretary of State that each of the requirements of paragraph 194(i)–(v) is met. An application for indefinite leave to remain in this category may be granted provided the applicant was admitted with a valid United Kingdom entry clearance for entry in this capacity and is able to satisfy the Secretary of State that each of the requirements of paragraph 194(i)–(v) is met and provided indefinite leave to remain is, at the same time, being granted to the person with limited leave to enter or remain under paragraphs 128–193 [(but not paragraphs 135I–135K)].

Note
Words in square brackets inserted by Cmnd 5829.

Refusal of leave to enter or remain as the spouse of a person with limited leave to enter or remain in the United Kingdom under paragraphs 128–193 [(but not paragraphs 135I–135K)]

196 Leave to enter or remain in the United Kingdom as the spouse of a person with limited leave to enter or remain in the United Kingdom under paragraphs 128–193 [(but not paragraphs 135I–135K)] is to be refused if, in relation to an application for leave to enter, a valid United Kingdom entry clearance for entry in this capacity is not produced to the Immigration Officer on arrival or, in the case of an application for limited leave to remain, if the applicant was not admitted with a valid United Kingdom entry clearance for entry in this capacity or is unable to satisfy the Secretary of State that each of the requirements of paragraph 194(i)–(v) is met. An application for indefinite leave to remain in this category is to be refused if the applicant was not admitted with a valid United Kingdom entry clearance for entry in this capacity or is unable to satisfy the Secretary of State that each of the requirements of paragraph 194(i)–(v) is met or if indefinite leave to remain is not, at the same time, being granted to the person with limited leave to enter or remain under paragraphs 128–193 [(but not paragraphs 135I–135K)].

Note
Words in square brackets inserted by Cmnd 5829.

CHILDREN OF PERSONS WITH LIMITED LEAVE TO ENTER OR REMAIN IN THE UNITED KINGDOM UNDER PARAGRAPHS 128–193 [(BUT NOT PARAGRAPHS 135I–135K)]

Requirements for leave to enter or remain as the child of a person with limited leave to enter or remain in the United Kingdom under paragraphs 128–193 [(but not paragraphs 135I–135K)]

197 The requirements to be met by a person seeking leave to enter or remain in the United Kingdom as a child of a person with limited leave to enter or remain in the United Kingdom under paragraphs 128–193 [(but not paragraphs 135I–135K)] are that:

Appendix 1   Legislation and materials

(i)   he is the child of a parent with limited leave to enter or remain in the United Kingdom under paragraphs 128–193 [(but not paragraphs 135I–135K)]; and

(ii)   he is under the age of 18 or has current leave to enter or remain in this capacity; and

(iii)   he is unmarried, has not formed an independent family unit and is not leading an independent life; and

(iv)   he can and will be maintained and accommodated adequately without recourse to public funds in accommodation which his parent(s) own or occupy exclusively; and

(v)   he will not stay in the United Kingdom beyond any period of leave granted to his parent(s); and

(vi)   both parents are being or have been admitted to or allowed to remain in the United Kingdom save where:

   (a)   the parent he is accompanying or joining is his sole surviving parent; or

   (b)   the parent he is accompanying or joining has had sole responsibility for his upbringing; or

   (c)   there are serious and compelling family or other considerations which make exclusion from the United Kingdom undesirable and suitable arrangements have been made for his care; and

(vii)   if seeking leave to enter, he holds a valid United Kingdom entry clearance for entry in this capacity or, if seeking leave to remain, was admitted with a valid United Kingdom entry clearance for entry in this capacity.

Note
Words in square brackets inserted by Cmnd 5829.

Leave to enter or remain as the child of a person with limited leave to enter or remain in the United Kingdom under paragraphs 128–193 [(but not paragraphs 135I–135K)]

198   A person seeking leave to enter or remain in the United Kingdom as the child of a person with limited leave to enter or remain in the United Kingdom under paragraphs 128–193 [(but not paragraphs 135I–135K)] may be given leave to enter or remain in the United Kingdom for a period of leave not in excess of that granted to the person with limited leave to enter or remain under paragraphs 128–193 [(but not paragraphs 135I–135K)] provided that, in relation to an application for leave to enter, he is able to produce to the Immigration Officer, on arrival, a valid United Kingdom entry clearance for entry in this capacity or, in the case of an application for limited leave to remain, he was admitted with a valid United Kingdom entry clearance for entry in this capacity and is able to satisfy the Secretary of State that each of the requirements of paragraph 197(i)–(vi) is met. An application for indefinite leave to remain in this category may be granted provided the applicant was admitted with a valid United Kingdom entry clearance for entry in this capacity and is able to satisfy the Secretary of State that each of the requirements of paragraph 197(i)–(vi) is met and provided indefinite leave to remain is, at the same time, being granted to the person with limited leave to enter or remain under paragraphs 128–193 [(but not paragraphs 135I–135K)].

Note
Words in square brackets inserted by Cmnd 5829.

Refusal of leave to enter or remain as the child of a person with limited leave to enter or remain in the United Kingdom under paragraphs 128–193 [(but not paragraphs 135I–135K)]

199   Leave to enter or remain in the United Kingdom as the child of a person with limited leave to enter or remain in the United Kingdom under paragraphs 128–193

[(but not paragraphs 135I–135K)] is to be refused if, in relation to an application for leave to enter, a valid United Kingdom entry clearance for entry in this capacity is not produced to the Immigration Officer on arrival or, in the case of an application for limited leave to remain, if the applicant was not admitted with a valid United Kingdom entry clearance for entry in this capacity or is unable to satisfy the Secretary of State that each of the requirements of paragraph 197(i)–(vi) is met. An application for indefinite leave to remain in this category is to be refused if the applicant was not admitted with a valid United Kingdom entry clearance for entry in this capacity or is unable to satisfy the Secretary of State that each of the requirements of paragraph 197(i)–(vi) is met or if indefinite leave to remain is not, at the same time, being granted to the person with limited leave to enter or remain under paragraphs 128–193 [(but not paragraphs 135I–135K)].

Note
Words in square brackets inserted by Cmnd 5829.

[MULTIPLE ENTRY WORK PERMIT EMPLOYMENT]

[Requirements for leave to enter for Multiple Entry work permit employment

199A The requirements to be met by a person coming to the United Kingdom to seek or take Multiple Entry work permit employment are that he:

  (i)   holds a valid work permit;
  (ii) is not of an age which puts him outside the limits for employment;
  (iii) is capable of undertaking the employment specified in the work permit;
  (iv) does not intend to take employment except as specified in his work permit;
  (v)   is able to maintain and accommodate himself adequately without recourse to public funds; and
  (vi) intends to leave the United Kingdom at the end of the employment covered by the Multiple Entry work permit.]
[(vii) intends to leave the United Kingdom at the end of the employment covered by the Multiple Entry work permit and holds a valid United Kingdom Entry clearance for entry into this capacity except where he holds a work permit valid for 6 months or less [...] or he is a British National (Overseas), a British overseas territories citizen, a British Overseas citizen, a British protected person or a person who under the British Nationality Act 1981 is a British subject.]

Note
Main heading and paragraphs 199A–199C inserted by Cm 5597. Sub-paragraph (vii) inserted by HC 176. Words in sub-paragraph (vii) deleted by HC 523.

[Leave to enter for Multiple Entry work permit employment

199B A person seeking leave to enter the United Kingdom for the purpose of Multiple Entry work permit employment may be admitted for a period not exceeding 2 years provided that the Immigration Officer is satisfied that each of the requirements of paragraph 199A are met.]

Note
Main heading and paragraphs 199A–199C inserted by Cm 5597.

Appendix 1   Legislation and materials

[Refusal of leave to enter for Multiple Entry work permit employment

199C Leave to enter for the purpose of Multiple Entry work permit employment is to be refused if the Immigration Officer is not satisfied that each of the requirements of paragraph 199A is met.]

Note
Main heading and paragraphs 199A–199C inserted by Cm 5597.

PART 6
PERSONS SEEKING TO ENTER OR REMAIN IN THE UNITED KINGDOM AS A BUSINESSMAN, SELF-EMPLOYED PERSON, INVESTOR, WRITER, COMPOSER OR ARTIST

PERSONS INTENDING TO ESTABLISH THEMSELVES IN BUSINESS

Requirements for leave to enter the United Kingdom as a person intending to establish himself in business

200 For the purpose of paragraphs 201–210 a business means an enterprise as:

- a sole trader; or
- a partnership; or
- a company registered in the United Kingdom.

201 The requirements to be met by a person seeking leave to enter the United Kingdom to establish himself in business are:

(i) that he satisfies the requirements of either paragraph 202 or paragraph 203; and

(ii) that he has not less than £200,000 of his own money under his control and disposable in the United Kingdom which is held in his own name and not by a trust or other investment vehicle and which he will be investing in the business in the United Kingdom; and

(iii) that until his business provides him with an income he will have sufficient additional funds to maintain and accommodate himself and any dependants without recourse to employment (other than his work for the business) or to public funds; and

(iv) that he will be actively involved full-time in trading or providing services on his own account or in partnership, or in the promotion and management of the company as a director; and

(v) that his level of financial investment will be proportional to his interest in the business; and

(vi) that he will have either a controlling or equal interest in the business and that any partnership or directorship does not amount to disguised employment; and

(vii) that he will be able to bear his share of liabilities; and

(viii) that there is a genuine need for his investment and services in the United Kingdom; and

(ix) that his share of the profits of the business will be sufficient to maintain and accommodate himself and any dependants without recourse to employment (other than his work for the business) or to public funds; and

(x) that he does not intend to supplement his business activities by taking or seeking employment in the United Kingdom other than his work for the business; and

(xi) that he holds a valid United Kingdom entry clearance for entry in this capacity.

202 Where a person intends to take over or join as a partner or director an existing business in the United Kingdom he will need, in addition to meeting the requirements at paragraph 201, to produce:

  (i)   a written statement of the terms on which he is to take over or join the business; and
  (ii)   audited accounts for the business for previous years; and
  (iii) evidence that his services and investment will result in a net increase in the employment provided by the business to persons settled here to the extent of creating at least 2 new full-time jobs.

203 Where a person intends to establish a new business in the United Kingdom he will need, in addition to meeting the requirements at paragraph 201 above, to produce evidence:

  (i)   that he will be bringing into the country sufficient funds of his own to establish a business; and
  (ii)   that the business will create full-time paid employment for at least 2 persons already settled in the United Kingdom.

Leave to enter the United Kingdom as a person seeking to establish himself in business

204 A person seeking leave to enter the United Kingdom to establish himself in business may be admitted for a period not exceeding 12 months with a condition restricting his freedom to take employment provided he is able to produce to the Immigration Officer, on arrival, a valid United Kingdom entry clearance for entry in this capacity.

Refusal of leave to enter the United Kingdom as a person seeking to establish himself in business

205 Leave to enter the United Kingdom as a person seeking to establish himself in business is to be refused if a valid United Kingdom entry clearance for entry in this capacity is not produced to the Immigration Officer on arrival.

Requirements for an extension of stay in order to remain in business

206 The requirements for an extension to stay in order to remain in business in the United Kingdom are that the applicant can show:

  (i)   that he entered the United Kingdom with a valid United Kingdom entry clearance as a businessman; and
  (ii)   audited accounts which show the precise financial position of the business and which confirm that he has invested not less than £200,000 of his own money directly into the business in the United Kingdom; and
  (iii) that he is actively involved on a full-time basis in trading or providing services on his own account or in partnership or in the promotion and management of the company as a director; and
  (iv)   that his level of financial investment is proportional to his interest in the business; and
  (v)   that he has either a controlling or equal interest in the business and that any partnership or directorship does not amount to disguised employment; and

(vi)   that he is able to bear his share of any liability the business may incur; and

(vii) that there is a genuine need for his investment and services in the United Kingdom; and

(viii)

  (a)   that where he has established a new business, new full-time paid employment has been created in the business for at least 2 persons settled in the United Kingdom; or

  (b)   that where he has taken over or joined an existing business, his services and investment have resulted in a net increase in the employment provided by the business to persons settled here to the extent of creating at least 2 new full-time jobs; and

(ix)   that his share of the profits of the business is sufficient to maintain and accommodate him and any dependants without recourse to employment (other than his work for the business) or to public funds; and

(x)   that he does not and will not have to supplement his business activities by taking or seeking employment in the United Kingdom other than his work for the business.

[206A The requirements for an extension of stay as a person intending to establish himself in business in the United Kingdom for a person who has leave to enter or remain for work permit employment are that the applicant:

(i)   entered the United Kingdom or was given leave to remain as a work permit holder in accordance with paragraphs 128 to 133 of these Rules; and

(ii)   meets each of the requirements of paragraph 201(i)–(x).]

Note
Paragraphs 206A–206F inserted by HC 346.

[206B The requirements for an extension of stay as a person intending to establish himself in business in the United Kingdom for a highly skilled migrant are that the applicant:

(i)   entered the United Kingdom or was given leave to remain as a highly skilled migrant in accordance with paragraphs 135A to 135F of these Rules; and

(ii)   meets each of the requirements of paragraph 201 (i)–(x).]

Note
Paragraphs 206A–206F inserted by HC 346.

[206C The requirements for an extension of stay as a person intending to establish himself in business in the United Kingdom for a participant in the Science and Engineering Graduates Scheme are that the applicant:

(i)   entered the United Kingdom or was given leave to remain as a participant in the Science and Engineering Graduates Scheme in accordance with paragraphs 135O to 135T of these Rules; and

(ii)   meets each of the requirements of paragraph 201(i)–(x).]

Note
Paragraphs 206A–206F inserted by HC 346.

[206D The requirements for an extension of stay as a person intending to establish himself in business in the United Kingdom for an innovator are that the applicant:

(i)   entered the United Kingdom or was given leave to remain as an innovator in accordance with paragraphs 210A to 210F of these Rules; and

(ii)   meets each of the requirements of paragraph 201(i)–(x).]

Note
Paragraphs 206A–206F inserted by HC 346.

[206E The requirements for an extension of stay as a person intending to establish himself in business in the United Kingdom for a student are that the applicant:

(i)   entered the United Kingdom or was given leave to remain as a student in accordance with paragraphs 57 to 62 of these Rules; and

(ii)   has obtained a degree qualification on a recognised degree course at either a United Kingdom publicly funded further or higher education institution or a bona fide United Kingdom private education institution which maintains satisfactory records of enrolment and attendance; and

(iii)   has the written consent of his official sponsor to such self employment if he is a member of a government or international scholarship agency sponsorship and that sponsorship is either ongoing or has recently come to an end at the time of the requested extension; and

(iv)   meets each of the requirements of paragraph 201(i)–(x).]

Note
Paragraphs 206A–206F inserted by HC 346.

[206F The requirements for an extension of stay as a person intending to establish himself in business in the United Kingdom for a working holidaymaker are that the applicant:

(i)   entered the United Kingdom or was given leave to remain as a working holidaymaker in accordance with paragraphs 95 to 100 of these Rules; and

(ii)   has spent more than 12 months in total in the UK in this capacity; and

(iii)   meets each of the requirements of paragraph 201(i)–(x).]

Note
Paragraphs 206A–206F inserted by HC 346.

[206G The requirements for an extension of stay as a person intending to establish himself in business in the United Kingdom in the case of a person who has leave to enter or remain as a Fresh Talent: Working in Scotland scheme participant are that the applicant:

(i)   entered the United Kingdom or was given leave to remain as a Fresh Talent: Working in Scotland scheme participant in accordance with paragraphs 143A to 143F of these Rules; and

(ii)   has the written consent of this official sponsor to such employment if the studies which led to him being granted leave under the Fresh Talent: Working in Scotland scheme in accordance with paragraphs 143A to 143F of these Rules, or any studies he has subsequently undertaken, were sponsored by a government or international scholarship agency; and

(iii)   meets each of the requirements of paragraph 201(i)–(x).]

Note
Inserted by HC 104.

Extension of stay in order to remain in business

[207 An extension of stay in order to remain in business with a condition restricting his freedom to take employment may be granted for a period not exceeding 3 years

1941

provided the Secretary of State is satisfied that each of the requirements of para-graph 206, 206A, 206B, 206C, 206D, 206E, 206F or 206G is met.]

Note
Substituted by HC 346. Further substituted by HC 104.

Refusal of extension of stay in order to remain in business

[208 An extension of stay in order to remain in business is to be refused if the Secretary of State is not satisfied that each of the requirements of paragraph 206, 206A, 206B, 206C, 206D, 206E, 206F or 206G is met.]

Note
Substituted by HC 346. Further substituted by HC 104.

Indefinite leave to remain for a person established in business

209 Indefinite leave to remain may be granted, on application, to a person established in business provided he:

(i)   has spent a continuous period of 4 years in the United Kingdom in this capacity and is still engaged in the business in question; and
(ii)   has met the requirements of paragraph 206 throughout the 4 year period; and
(iii)   submits audited accounts for the first 3 years of trading and management accounts for the 4th year.

Refusal of indefinite leave to remain for a person established in business

210 Indefinite leave to remain in the United Kingdom for a person established in business is to be refused if the Secretary of State is not satisfied that each of the requirements of paragraph 209 is met.

INNOVATORS

[Requirements for leave to enter the United Kingdom as an innovator

210A The requirements to be met by a person seeking leave to enter as an innovator are that the applicant:

(i)   is approved by the Home Office as a person who meets the criteria specified by the Secretary of State for entry under the innovator scheme at the time that approval is sought under that scheme;
(ii)   intends to set up a business that will create full-time paid employment for at least 2 persons already settled in the UK; and
(iii)   intends to maintain a minimum five per cent shareholding of the equity capital in that business, once it has been set up, throughout the period of his stay as an innovator; and
(iv)   will be able to maintain and accommodated himself and any dependants adequately without recourse to public funds or to other employment; and
(v)   holds a valid United Kingdom entry clearance for entry in this capacity.]

Note
Inserted by HC 538.

[**Leave to enter as an innovator**

210B A person seeking leave to enter the United Kingdom as an innovator may be admitted for a period not exceeding 18 months, provided the Immigration Officer is satisfied that each of the requirements of paragraph 210A is met.]

Note
Inserted by HC 538.

[**Refusal of leave to enter as an innovator**

210C Leave to enter as an innovator is to be refused if the Immigration Officer is not satisfied that each of the requirements of paragraph 210A are met.]

Note
Inserted by HC 538.

Requirements for an extension of stay as an innovator

[**210D** The requirements for an extension of stay in the United Kingdom as an innovator, in the case of a person who was granted leave to enter under paragraph 210A, are that the applicant:

(i)   has established a viable trading business, by reference to the audited accounts and trading records of that business; and

(ii)   continues to meet the requirements of paragraph 210A (i) and (iv); and

has set up a business that will create full-time paid employment for at least 2 persons already settled in the UK; and

(iii)   has maintained a minimum five per cent shareholding of the equity capital in that business, once it has been set up, throughout the period of his stay.]

Note
Substituted by Cm 6339.

[**210DA** The requirements for an extension of stay in the United Kingdom as an innovator, in the case of a person who has leave for the purpose of work permit employment are that the applicant:

(i)   entered the United Kingdom or was given leave to remain as a work permit holder in accordance with paragraphs 128 to 132 of these Rules; and

(ii)   meets the requirements of paragraph 210A(i)–(iv).]

Note
Inserted by Cm 6339.

[**210DB** The requirements for an extension of stay in the United Kingdom as an innovator in the case of a person who has leave as a student are that the applicant:

(i)   entered the United Kingdom or was given leave to remain as a student in accordance with paragraphs 57 to 62 of these Rules; and

(ii)   has obtained a degree qualification on a recognised degree course at either a United Kingdom publicly funded further or higher education institution or a bona fide United Kingdom private education institution which maintains satisfactory records of enrolment and attendance; and

(iii)   has the written consent of his official sponsor to remain under the Innovator category if he is a member of a government or international scholarship agency sponsorship and that sponsorship is either ongoing or has recently come to an end at the time of the requested extension; and

(iv)   meets the requirements of paragraph 210(i)–(iv).]

Note
Inserted by Cm 6339.

[**210DC** The requirements to be met for an extension of stay as an innovator, for a person who has leave as a working holidaymaker are that the applicant:

(i)   entered the United Kingdom as a working holidaymaker in accordance with paragraphs 95 to 96 of these Rules; and

(ii)   meets the requirements of paragraph 210A(i)–(iv).]

Note
Inserted by Cm 6339.

[**210DD** The requirements to be met for an extension of stay as an innovator, for a postgraduate doctor, postgraduate dentist or trainee general practitioner are that the applicant:

(i)   entered the United Kingdom or was given leave to remain as a postgraduate doctor, postgraduate dentist or trainee general practitioner in accordance with paragraphs 70 to 75 of these Rules; and

(ii)   has the written consent of his official sponsor to remain under the innovator category if he is a member of a government or international scholarship agency sponsorship and that sponsorship is either ongoing or has recently come to an end at the time of the requested extension; and

(iii)   meets the requirements of paragraph 210(i)–(iv).]

Note
Inserted by HC 1112.

[**210DE** The requirements to be met for an extension of stay as an innovator, for a participant in the Science and Engineering Graduate Scheme are that the applicant:

(i)   entered the United Kingdom or was given leave to remain as a participant in the Science and Engineering Graduate Scheme in accordance with paragraphs 135O to 135T of these Rules; and

(ii)   meets the requirements of paragraph 210A(i)–(iv).]

Note
Inserted by HC 1112.

[**210DF** The requirements to be met for an extension of stay as an innovator, for a highly skilled migrant are that the applicant:

(i)   entered the United Kingdom or was given leave to remain as a highly skilled migrant in accordance with paragraphs 135A to 135E of these Rules; and

(ii)   meets the requirements of paragraph 210A(i)–(iv).]

Note
Inserted by HC 1112

[**210DG** The requirements to be met for an extension of stay as an innovator, for a person in the United Kingdom to establish themselves or remain in business are that the applicant:

(i) entered the United Kingdom or was granted leave to remain as a person intending to establish themselves or remain in business in accordance with paragraphs 201–208 of these Rules; and

(ii) meets the requirements of paragraph 210(i)–(iv).]

Note
Inserted by HC 346.

[**210DH** The requirements to be met for an extension of stay as an innovator, in the case of a person who has leave to enter or remain as a Fresh Talent: Working in Scotland scheme participant are that the applicant:

(i) entered the United Kingdom or was given leave to remain as a Fresh Talent: Working in Scotland scheme participant in accordance with paragraphs 143A to 143F of these Rules; and

(ii) has the written consent of his official sponsor to such employment if the studies which led to him being granted leave under the Fresh Talent: Working in Scotland scheme in accordance with paragraphs 143A to 143F of these Rules, or any studies he has subsequently undertaken, were sponsored by a government or international scholarship agency; and

(iii) meets each of the requirements of paragraph 210(i)–(iv).]

Note
Inserted by HC 104.

[**Extension of stay as an innovator**

210E An extension of stay as an innovator may be granted for a period not exceeding 30 months provided the Secretary of State is satisfied that each of the requirements of paragraph 210D, 210DA, 210DB, 210DC, 210DD, 210DE, 210DF, 210DG or 210DH is met.]

Note
Substituted by HC 346. Further substituted by HC 104.

[**Refusal of extension to stay as an innovator**

210F An extension of stay as an innovator is to be refused if the Secretary of State is not satisfied that each of the requirements of paragraph 210D, 210DA, 210DB, 210DC, 210DD, 210DE, 210DF, 210DG or 210DH is met.]

Note
Substituted by HC 346. Further substituted by HC 104.

Appendix 1   Legislation and materials

[Indefinite leave to remain for an innovator

210G Indefinite leave to remain may be granted, on application, to a person currently with leave as an innovator provided that he:

(i)   has spent a continuous period of at least 4 years leave in the United Kingdom in this capacity; and
(ii) has met the requirements of paragraph 210D throughout the 4 years period.]

Note
Inserted by HC 538.

[Refusal of indefinite leave to remain as an innovator

210H Indefinite leave to remain in the United Kingdom as a person currently with leave as a innovator is to be refused if the Secretary of State is not satisfied that each of the requirements of paragraph 210G is met.]

Note
Inserted by HC 538.

PERSONS INTENDING TO ESTABLISH THEMSELVES IN BUSINESS UNDER PROVISIONS OF EC ASSOCIATION AGREEMENTS

Requirements for leave to enter the United Kingdom as a person intending to establish himself in business under the provisions of an EC Association Agreement

211 For the purpose of paragraphs 212–223 a business means an enterprise as:

–   a sole trader; or
–   a partnership; or
–   a company registered in the United Kingdom.

212 The requirements to be met by a person seeking leave to enter the United Kingdom to establish himself in business are that:

(i)   he satisfies the requirements of either paragraph 213 or paragraph 214; and
(ii)   the money he is putting into the business is under his control and sufficient to establish himself in business in the United Kingdom; and
(iii) until his business provides him with an income he will have sufficient additional funds to maintain and accommodate himself and any dependants without recourse to employment (other than his work for the business) or to public funds; and
(iv)   his share of the profits of the business will be sufficient to maintain and accommodate himself and any dependants without recourse to employment (other than his work for the business) or to public funds; and
(v)   he does not intend to supplement his business activities by taking or seeking employment in the United Kingdom other than his work for the business; and
(vi)   he holds a valid United Kingdom entry clearance for entry in this capacity.

213 Where a person intends to establish himself in a company in the United Kingdom which he effectively controls he will need, in addition to meeting the requirements at paragraph 212, to show:

[(i)   that he is a national of Bulgaria or Romania; and]

1946

(ii)   that he will have a controlling interest in the company; and
(iii)   that he will be actively involved in the promotion and management of the company; and
(iv)   that the company will be registered in the United Kingdom and be trading or providing services in the United Kingdom; and
(v)   that the company will be the owner of the assets of the business; and
(vi)   where he is taking over an existing company, a written statement of the terms on which he is to take over the business and audited accounts for the business for previous years.

Note
Paragraph 213(i) substituted by HC 523.

214 Where a person intends to establish himself in self-employment or in partnership in the United Kingdom he will need, in addition to meeting the requirements at 212 above, to show:

[(i)   that he is a national of Bulgaria or Romania; and]
(ii)   that he will be actively involved in trading or providing services on his own account or in partnership in the United Kingdom; and
(iii)   that he, or he together with his partners, will be the owner of the assets of the business; and
(iv)   in the case of a partnership, that his part in the business will not amount to disguised employment; and
(v)   where he is taking over or joining an existing business a written statement of the terms on which he is to take over or join the business and audited accounts for the business for previous years.

Note
Paragraph 214(i) substituted by HC 523.

Leave to enter the United Kingdom as a person seeking to establish himself in business under the provisions of an EC Association Agreement

215 A person seeking leave to enter the United Kingdom to establish himself in business may be admitted for a period not exceeding 12 months with a condition restricting his freedom to take employment provided he is able to produce to the Immigration Officer, on arrival, a valid United Kingdom entry clearance for entry in this capacity.

Refusal of leave to enter the United Kingdom as a person seeking to establish himself in business under the provisions of an EC Association Agreement

216 Leave to enter the United Kingdom as a person seeking to establish himself in business is to be refused if a valid United Kingdom entry clearance for entry in this capacity is not produced to the Immigration Officer on arrival.

Requirements for an extension of stay in order to remain in business under the provisions of an EC Association Agreement

217 The requirements for an extension of stay in order to remain in business in the United Kingdom are that the applicant can show that:

[(i)   he entered the United Kingdom with a valid United Kingdom entry clearance as a person intending to establish himself in business under the provisions of an EC Association Agreement; and

(ia)   he has established himself in business in the United Kingdom; and]

(ii)   his share of the profits of the business is sufficient to maintain and accommodate himself and any dependants without recourse to employment (other than his work for the business) or to public funds; and

(iii)   he does not and will not supplement his business activities by taking or seeking employment in the United Kingdom other than his work for the business; and

(iv)   in addition he satisfies the requirements of either paragraph 218 or paragraph 219.

Note
Sub-paragraphs (i) and (ia) substituted by Cm 6297.

218 Where a person has established himself in a company in the United Kingdom which he effectively controls he will need, in addition to meeting the requirements at paragraph 217 above, to show:

[(i)   that he is a national of Bulgaria or Romania; and]

(ii)   that he is actively involved in the promotion and management of the company; and

(iii)   that he has a controlling interest in the company; and

(iv)   that the company is registered in the United Kingdom and trading or providing services in the United Kingdom; and

(v)   that the company is the owner of the assets of the business; and

(vi)   the current financial position in the form of audited accounts for the company.

Note
Paragraph 218(i) substituted by HC 523.

219 Where a person has established himself as a sole trader or in partnership in the United Kingdom he will need, in addition to meeting the requirements at 217 above, to show:

[(i)   that he is a national of Bulgaria or Romania; and]

(ii)   that he is actively involved in trading or providing services on his own account or in partnership in the United Kingdom; and

(iii)   that he, or he together with his partners, is the owner of the assets of the business; and

(iv)   in the case of a partnership, that his part in the business does not amount to disguised employment; and

(v)   the current financial position in the form of audited accounts for the business.

Note
Paragraph 219(i) substituted by HC 523.

Extension of stay in order to remain in business under the provisions of an EC Association Agreement

220 An extension of stay in order to remain in business with a condition restricting his freedom to take employment may be granted for a period not exceeding 3 years provided the Secretary of State is satisfied that each of the requirements of paragraphs 217 and 218 or 219 is met.

Refusal of extension of stay in order to remain in business under the provisions of an EC Association Agreement

221 An extension of stay in order to remain in business is to be refused if the Secretary of State is not satisfied that each of the requirements of paragraphs 217 and 218 or 219 is met.

Indefinite leave to remain for a person established in business under the provisions of an EC Association Agreement

222 Indefinite leave to remain may be granted, on application, to a person established in business provided he:

    (i)   has spent a continuous period of 4 years in the United Kingdom in this capacity and is still so engaged; and

    (ii)   has met the requirements of paragraphs 217 and 218 or 219 throughout the 4 years; and

    (iii)   submits audited accounts for the first 3 years of trading and management accounts for the 4th year.

Refusal of indefinite leave to remain for a person established in business under the provisions of an EC Association Agreement

223 Indefinite leave to remain in the United Kingdom for a person established in business is to be refused if the Secretary of State is not satisfied that each of the requirements of paragraph 222 is met.

INVESTORS

Requirements for leave to enter the United Kingdom as an investor

224 The requirements to be met by a person seeking leave to enter the United Kingdom as an investor are that he:

[(i)

    (a)   has money of his own under his control in the United Kingdom amounting to no less than £1 million; or

    (b)

        (i)   owns personal assets which, taking into account any liabilities to which he is subject, have a value exceeding £2 million; and

        (ii)   has money under his control in the United Kingdom amounting to no less than £1 million, which may include money loaned to him provided that it was loaned by a financial institution regulated by the Financial Services Authority; and]

    (ii)   intends to invest not less than £750,000 of his capital in the United Kingdom by way of United Kingdom Government bonds, share capital or loan capital in active and trading United Kingdom registered companies (other than those principally engaged in property investment and excluding investment by the applicant by way of deposits with a bank, building society or other enterprise whose normal course of business includes the acceptance of deposits); and

    (iii)   intends to make the United Kingdom his main home; and

(iv)   is able to maintain and accommodate himself and any dependants without taking employment (other than self-employment or business) or recourse to public funds; and

(v)   holds a valid United Kingdom entry clearance for entry in this capacity.

Note
Sub-paragraph (i) substituted by HC 176.

Leave to enter as an investor

225 A person seeking leave to enter the United Kingdom as an investor may be admitted for a period not exceeding 12 months with a restriction on his right to take employment, provided he is able to produce to the Immigration Officer, on arrival, a valid United Kingdom entry clearance for entry in this capacity.

Refusal of leave to enter as an investor

226 Leave to enter as an investor is to be refused if a valid United Kingdom entry clearance for entry in this capacity is not produced to the Immigration Officer on arrival.

Requirements for an extension of stay as an investor

227 The requirements for an extension of stay as an investor are that the applicant:

(i)   entered the United Kingdom with a valid United Kingdom entry clearance as an investor; and

(ii)   has no less than £1 million of his own money under his control in the United Kingdom; and

(iii)   has invested not less than £750,000 of his capital in the United Kingdom on the terms set out in paragraph 224(ii) above and intends to maintain that investment on the terms set out in paragraph 224(ii); and

(iv)   has made the United Kingdom his main home; and

(v)   is able to maintain and accommodate himself and any dependants without taking employment (other than his self-employment or business) or recourse to public funds.

[227A The requirements to be met for an extension of stay as an investor, for a person who has leave to enter or remain in the United Kingdom as a work permit holder are that the applicant:

(i)   entered the United Kingdom or was granted leave to remain as a work permit holder in accordance with paragraphs 128 to 133 of these Rules; and

(ii)   meets the requirements of paragraph 224(i)–(iv).]

Note
Paragraphs 227A–227D inserted by HC 346.

[227B The requirements to be met for an extension of stay as an investor, for a person in the United Kingdom as a highly skilled migrant are that the applicant:

(i)   entered the United Kingdom or was granted leave to remain as a highly skilled migrant in accordance with paragraphs 135A to 135F of these Rules; and

(ii)   meets the requirements of paragraph 224(i)–(iv).]

Note
Paragraphs 227A–227D inserted by HC 346.

[227C The requirements to be met for an extension of stay as an investor, for a person in the United Kingdom to establish themselves or remain in business are that the applicant:

(i)   entered the United Kingdom or was granted leave to remain as a person intending to establish themselves or remain in business in accordance with paragraphs 201 to 208 of these Rules; and
(ii)   meets the requirements of paragraph 224(i)–(iv).]

Note
Paragraphs 227A–227D inserted by HC 346.

[227D The requirements to be met for an extension of stay as an investor, for a person in the United Kingdom as an innovator are that the applicant:

(i)   entered the United Kingdom or was granted leave to remain as an innovator in accordance with paragraphs 210A to 210F of these Rules; and
(ii)   meets the requirements of paragraph 224(i)–(iv).]

Note
Paragraphs 227A–227D inserted by HC 346.

Extension of stay as an investor

[228 An extension of stay as an investor, with a restriction on the taking of employment, may be granted for a maximum period of 3 years, provided the Secretary of State is satisfied that each of the requirements of paragraph 227, 227A, 227B, 227C or 227D is met.]

Note
Substituted by HC 346.

Refusal of extension of stay as an investor

[229 An extension of stay as an investor is to be refused if the Secretary of State is not satisfied that each of the requirements of paragraph 227, 227A, 227B, 227C or 227D is met.]

Note
Substituted by HC 346.

Indefinite leave to remain for an investor

230 Indefinite leave to remain may be granted, on application, to a person admitted as an investor provided he:

(i)   has spent a continuous period of 4 years in the United Kingdom in this capacity; and

(ii)   has met the requirements of paragraph 227 throughout the 4 year period including the requirement as to the investment of £750,000 and continues to do so.

Refusal of indefinite leave to remain for an investor

231 Indefinite leave to remain in the United Kingdom for an investor is to be refused if the Secretary of State is not satisfied that each of the requirements of paragraph 230 is met.

WRITERS, COMPOSERS AND ARTISTS

Requirements for leave to enter the United Kingdom as a writer, composer or artist

232 The requirements to be met by a person seeking leave to enter the United Kingdom as a writer, composer or artist are that he:

(i)   has established himself outside the United Kingdom as a writer, composer or artist primarily engaged in producing original work which has been published (other than exclusively in newspapers or magazines), performed or exhibited for its literary, musical or artistic merit; and

(ii)   does not intend to work except as related to his self-employment as a writer, composer or artist; and

(iii)   has for the preceding year been able to maintain and accommodate himself and any dependants from his own resources without working except as a writer, composer or artist; and

(iv)   will be able to maintain and accommodate himself and any dependants from his own resources without working except as a writer, composer or artist and without recourse to public funds; and

(v)   holds a valid United Kingdom entry clearance for entry in this capacity.

Leave to enter as a writer, composer or artist

233 A person seeking leave to enter the United Kingdom as a writer, composer or artist may be admitted for a period not exceeding 12 months, subject to a condition restricting his freedom to take employment, provided he is able to produce to the Immigration Officer, on arrival, a valid United Kingdom entry clearance for entry in this capacity.

Refusal of leave to enter as a writer, composer or artist

234 Leave to enter as a writer, composer or artist is to be refused if a valid United Kingdom entry clearance for entry in this capacity is not produced to the Immigration Officer on arrival.

Requirements for an extension of stay as a writer, composer or artist

235 The requirements for an extension of stay as a writer, composer or artist are that the applicant:

(i)   entered the United Kingdom with a valid United Kingdom entry clearance as a writer, composer or artist; and

(ii)   meets the requirements of paragraph 232(ii)–(iv).

Extension of stay as a writer, composer or artist

236 An extension of stay as writer, composer or artist may be granted for a period not exceeding 3 years with a restriction on his freedom to take employment, provided the Secretary of State is satisfied that each of the requirements of paragraph 235 is met.

Refusal of extension of stay as a writer, composer or artist

237 An extension of stay as a writer, composer or artist is to be refused if the Secretary of State is not satisfied that each of the requirements of paragraph 235 is met.

Indefinite leave to remain for a writer, composer or artist

238 Indefinite leave to remain may be granted, on application, to a person admitted as a writer, composer or artist provided he:

(i)   has spent a continuous period of 4 years in the United Kingdom in this capacity; and

(ii)   has met the requirements of paragraph 235 throughout the 4 year period.

Refusal of indefinite leave to remain for a writer, composer or artist

239 Indefinite leave to remain for a writer, composer or artist is to be refused if the Secretary of State is not satisfied that each of the requirements of paragraph 238 is met.

SPOUSES OF PERSONS WITH LIMITED LEAVE TO ENTER OR REMAIN UNDER PARAGRAPHS 200–239

Requirements for leave to enter or remain as the spouse of a person with limited leave to enter or remain under paragraphs 200–239

240 The requirements to be met by a person seeking leave to enter or remain in the United Kingdom as the spouse of a person with limited leave to enter or remain in the United Kingdom under paragraphs 200–239 are that:

(i)   the applicant is married to a person with limited leave to enter or remain in the United Kingdom under paragraphs 200–239; and

(ii)   each of the parties intends to live with the other as his or her spouse during the applicant's stay and the marriage is subsisting; and

(iii) there will be adequate accommodation for the parties and any dependants without recourse to public funds in accommodation which they own or occupy exclusively; and

(iv) the parties will be able to maintain themselves and any dependants adequately without recourse to public funds; and

(v)   the applicant does not intend to stay in the United Kingdom beyond any period of leave granted to his spouse; and

(vi)   if seeking leave to enter, the applicant holds a valid United Kingdom entry clearance for entry in this capacity or, if seeking leave to remain, was admitted with a valid United Kingdom entry clearance for entry in this capacity.

Leave to enter or remain as the spouse of a person with limited leave to enter or remain in the United Kingdom under paragraphs 200–239

241 A person seeking leave to enter or remain in the United Kingdom as the spouse of a person with limited leave to enter or remain in the United Kingdom under paragraphs 200–239 may be given leave to enter or remain in the United Kingdom for a period of leave not in excess of that granted to the person with limited leave to enter or remain under paragraphs 200–239 provided that, in relation to an application for leave to enter, he is able, on arrival, to produce to the Immigration Officer a valid United Kingdom entry clearance for entry in this capacity or, in the case of an application for limited leave to remain, he was admitted with a valid United Kingdom entry clearance for entry in this capacity and is able the satisfy the Secretary of State that each of the requirements of paragraph 240(i)–(v) is met. An application for indefinite leave to remain in this category may be granted provided the applicant was admitted with a valid United Kingdom entry clearance for entry in this capacity and is able to satisfy the Secretary of State that each of the requirements of paragraph 240(i)–(v) is met and provided indefinite leave to remain is, at the same time, being granted to the person with limited leave to remain under paragraphs 200–239.

Refusal of leave to enter or remain as the spouse of a person with limited leave to enter or remain in the United Kingdom under paragraphs 200–239

242 Leave to enter or remain in the United Kingdom as the spouse of a person with limited leave to enter or remain in the United Kingdom under paragraphs 200–239 is to be refused if, in relation to an application for leave to enter, a valid United Kingdom entry clearance for entry in this capacity is not produced to the Immigration Officer on arrival or, in the case of an application for limited leave to remain, if the applicant was not admitted with a valid United Kingdom entry clearance for entry in this capacity or is unable to satisfy the Secretary of State that each of the requirements of paragraph 240(i)–(v) is met. An application for indefinite leave to remain in this category is to be refused if the applicant was not admitted with a valid United Kingdom entry clearance for entry in this capacity or is unable to satisfy the Secretary of State that each of the requirements of paragraph 240(i)–(v) is met or if indefinite leave to remain is not, at the same time, being granted to the person with limited leave to remain under paragraphs 200–239.

CHILDREN OF PERSONS WITH LIMITED LEAVE TO ENTER OR REMAIN UNDER PARAGRAPHS 200–239

Requirements for leave to enter or remain as the child of a person with limited leave to enter or remain in the United Kingdom under paragraphs 200–239

243 The requirements to be met by a person seeking leave to enter or remain in the United Kingdom as a child of a person with limited leave to enter or remain in the United Kingdom under paragraphs 200–239 are that:

(i)   he is the child of a parent who has leave to enter or remain in the United Kingdom under paragraphs 200–239; and

(ii)   he is under the age of 18 or has current leave to enter or remain in this capacity; and
(iii)   he is unmarried, has not formed an independent family unit and is not leading an independent life; and
(iv)   he can and will be maintained and accommodated adequately without recourse to public funds in accommodation which his parent(s) own or occupy exclusively; and
(v)   he will not stay in the United Kingdom beyond any period of leave granted to his parent(s); and
(vi)   both parents are being or have been admitted to or allowed to remain in the United Kingdom save where:
   (a)   the parent he is accompanying or joining is his sole surviving parent; or
   (b)   the parent he is accompanying or joining has had sole responsibility for his upbringing; or
   (c)   there are serious and compelling family or other considerations which make exclusion from the United Kingdom undesirable and suitable arrangements have been made for his care; and
(vii)   if seeking leave to enter, he holds a valid United Kingdom entry clearance for entry in this capacity or, if seeking leave to remain, was admitted with a valid United Kingdom entry clearance for entry in this capacity.

Leave to enter or remain as the child of a person with limited leave to enter or remain in the United Kingdom under paragraphs 200–239

244 A person seeking leave to enter or remain in the United Kingdom as the child of a person with limited leave to enter or remain in the United Kingdom under paragraphs 200–239 may be admitted to or allowed to remain in the United Kingdom for the same period of leave as that granted to the person given limited leave to enter or remain under paragraphs 200–239 provided that, in relation to an application for leave to enter, he is able to produce to the Immigration Officer, on arrival, a valid United Kingdom entry clearance for entry in this capacity or, in the case of an application for limited leave to remain, he was admitted with a valid United Kingdom entry clearance for entry in this capacity and is able the satisfy the Secretary of State that each of the requirements of paragraph 243(i)–(vi) is met. An application for indefinite leave to remain in this category may be granted provided the applicant was admitted with a valid United Kingdom entry clearance for entry in this capacity and is able to satisfy the Secretary of State that each of the requirements of paragraph 243(i)–(vi) is met and provided indefinite leave to remain is, at the same time, being granted to the person with limited leave to remain under paragraphs 200–239.

Refusal of leave to enter or remain as the child of a person with limited leave to enter or remain in the United Kingdom under paragraphs 200–239

245 Leave to enter or remain in the United Kingdom as the child of a person with limited leave to enter or remain in the United Kingdom under paragraphs 200–239 is to be refused if, in relation to an application for leave to enter, a valid United Kingdom entry clearance for entry in this capacity is not produced to the Immigration Officer on arrival or, in the case of an application for limited leave to remain, if the applicant was not admitted with a valid United Kingdom entry clearance for entry in this capacity or is unable to satisfy the Secretary of State that each of the requirements of paragraph 243(i)–(vi) is met. An application for indefinite leave to remain in this capacity is to be refused if the applicant was not admitted with a valid United Kingdom entry clearance for entry in this capacity or is unable to satisfy the Secretary of State that each of the requirements of paragraph 243(i)–(vi) is met or if indefinite leave to remain is not, at the same time, being granted to the person with limited leave to remain under paragraphs 200–239.

PART 7
OTHER CATEGORIES

PERSONS EXERCISING RIGHTS OF ACCESS TO A CHILD RESIDENT IN THE
UNITED KINGDOM

[Requirements for leave to enter the United Kingdom as a person exercising rights of access to a child resident in the United Kingdom

246 The requirements to be met by a person seeking leave to enter the United Kingdom to exercise access rights to a child resident in the United Kingdom are that:

  (i)   the applicant is the parent of a child who is resident in the United Kingdom; and
  (ii)   the parent or carer with whom the child permanently resides is resident in the United Kingdom; and
  (iii) the applicant produces evidence that he has access rights to the child in the form of:
         (a)   a Residence Order or a Contact Order granted by a Court in the United Kingdom; or
         (b)   a certificate issued by a district judge confirming the applicant's intention to maintain contact with the child; and
  (iv)   the applicant intends to continue to take an active role in the child's upbringing; and
  (v)   the child is under the age of 18; and
  (vi)   there will be adequate accommodation for the applicant and any dependants without recourse to public funds in accommodation which the applicant owns or occupies exclusively; and
  (vii) the applicant will be able to maintain himself and any dependants adequately without recourse to public funds; and
  (viii) the applicant holds a valid United Kingdom entry clearance for entry in this capacity.

Leave to enter the United Kingdom as a person exercising rights of access to a child resident in the United Kingdom

247 Leave to enter as a person exercising access rights to a child resident in the United Kingdom may be granted for 12 months in the first instance, provided that a valid United Kingdom entry clearance for entry in this capacity is produced to the Immigration Officer on arrival.

Refusal of leave to enter the United Kingdom as a person exercising rights of access to a child resident in the United Kingdom

248 Leave to enter as a person exercising rights of access to a child resident in the United Kingdom is to be refused if a valid United Kingdom entry clearance for entry in this capacity is not produced to the Immigration Officer on arrival.]

[Requirements for leave to remain in the United Kingdom as a person exercising rights of access to a child resident in the United Kingdom

248A The requirements to be met by a person seeking leave to remain in the United Kingdom to exercise access rights to a child resident in the United Kingdom are that:

(i) the applicant is the parent of a child who is resident in the United Kingdom; and

(ii) the parent or carer with whom the child permanently resides is resident in the United Kingdom; and

(iii) the applicant produces evidence that he has access rights to the child in the form of:
    (a) a Residence Order or a Contact Order granted by a Court in the United Kingdom; or
    (b) a certificate issued by a district judge confirming the applicant's intention to maintain contact with the child; or
    (c) a statement from the child's other parent (or, if contact is supervised, from the supervisor) that the applicant is maintaining contact with the child; and

(iv) the applicant takes and intends to continue to take an active role in the child's upbringing; and

(v) the child visits or stays with the applicant on a frequent and regular basis and the applicant intends this to continue; and

(vi) the child is under the age of 18; and

(vii) the applicant has limited leave to remain in the United Kingdom as the spouse or unmarried partner of a person present and settled in the United Kingdom who is the other parent of the child; and

(viii) the applicant has not remained in breach of the immigration laws; and

(ix) there will be adequate accommodation for the applicant and any dependants without recourse to public funds in accommodation which the applicant owns or occupies exclusively; and

(x) the applicant will be able to maintain himself and any dependants adequately without recourse to public funds.

Leave to remain in the United Kingdom as a person exercising rights of access to a child resident in the United Kingdom

248B Leave to remain as a person exercising access rights to a child resident in the United Kingdom may be granted for 12 months in the first instance, provided the Secretary of State is satisfied that each of the requirements of paragraph 248A is met.

Refusal of leave to remain in the United Kingdom as a person exercising rights of access to a child resident in the United Kingdom

248C Leave to remain as a person exercising rights of access to a child resident in the United Kingdom is to be refused if the Secretary of State is not satisfied that each of the requirements of paragraph 248A is met.

Indefinite leave to remain in the United Kingdom as a person exercising rights of access to a child resident in the United Kingdom

248D The requirements for indefinite leave to remain in the United Kingdom as a person exercising rights of access to a child resident in the United Kingdom are that:

Appendix 1   Legislation and materials

(i) the applicant was admitted to the United Kingdom or granted leave to remain in the United Kingdom for a period of 12 months as a person exercising rights of access to a child and has completed a period of 12 months as a person exercising rights of access to a child; and

(ii) the applicant takes and intends to continue to take an active role in the child's upbringing; and

(iii) the child visits or stays with the applicant on a frequent and regular basis and the applicant intends this to continue; and

(iv) there will be adequate accommodation for the applicant and any dependants without recourse to public funds in accommodation which the applicant owns or occupies exclusively; and

(v) the applicant will be able to maintain himself and any dependants adequately without recourse to public funds; and

(vi) the child is under 18 years of age.

Indefinite leave to remain as a person exercising rights of access to a child resident in the United Kingdom

248E Indefinite leave to remain as a person exercising rights of access to a child may be granted provided the Secretary of State is satisfied that each of the requirements of paragraph 248D is met.

Refusal of indefinite leave to remain in the United Kingdom as a person exercising rights of access to a child resident in the United Kingdom

248F Indefinite leave to remain as a person exercising rights of access to a child is to be refused if the Secretary of State is not satisfied that each of the requirements of paragraph 248D is met.]

Note
Paragraphs 246–248 substituted by Cm 4851. Paragraphs 248A–248F inserted by Cm 4851.

HOLDERS OF SPECIAL VOUCHERS

249–254 [...]

Note
Paragraphs 249–254 deleted by Cm 5597.

EEA NATIONALS AND THEIR FAMILIES

Settlement

[255 Any person (other than a student) who under, either the Immigration (European Economic Area) Order 1994, or the 2000 EEA Regulations has been issued with a residence permit or residence document valid for 5 years, and who has remained in the United Kingdom in accordance with the provisions of that Order or those Regulations (as the case may be) for 4 years and continues to do so may, on application, have his residence permit or residence document (as the case may be) endorsed to show permission to remain in the United Kingdom indefinitely.]

Note
Substituted by Cm 4851.

[255A This paragraph applies where a Swiss national has been issued with a residence permit under the 2000 EEA Regulations and, prior to 1st June 2002, remained in the United Kingdom in accordance with the provisions of these Rules and in a capacity which would have entitled that Swiss national to apply for indefinite leave to remain after a continuous period of 4 years in that capacity in the United Kingdom. Where this paragraph applies, the period during which the Swiss national remained in the United Kingdom prior to 1st June 2002 shall be treated as a period during which he remained in the United Kingdom in accordance with the 2000 EEA Regulations for the purpose of calculating the 4 year period referred to in paragraph 255.]

Note
Paragraph 255A inserted by Cm 5597.

[255B This paragraph applies where an Accession State national has been issued with a residence permit under the 2000 EEA Regulations and, prior to 1st May 2004, remained in the United Kingdom in accordance with the provisions of these Rules and in a capacity which would have entitled that Accession State national to apply for indefinite leave to remain after a continuous period of 4 years in that capacity in the United Kingdom.

Where this paragraph applies, the period during which the Accession State national remained in the United Kingdom prior to 1st May 2004 shall be treated as a period during which he remained in the United Kingdom in accordance with the 2000 EEA Regulations for the purpose of calculating the 4 year period referred to in paragraph 255.]

Note
Paragraph 255B inserted by HC 523.

256 [...]

Note
Paragraph 256 deleted by Cm 4851.

257 In addition, the following persons will be permitted to remain in the United Kingdom indefinitely [in accordance with Commission Regulation 1251/70]:

(i)   an EEA national who has been continuously resident in the United Kingdom for at least 3 years, has been in employment in the United Kingdom or any other Member State of the EEA for the preceding 12 months, and has reached the age of entitlement to a state retirement pension;

(ii)   an EEA national who has ceased to be employed owing to a permanent incapacity for work arising out of an accident at work or an occupational disease entitling him to a state disability pension;

(iii) an EEA national who has been continuously resident in the United Kingdom for at least 2 years, and who has ceased to be employed owing to a permanent incapacity for work;

(iv)   a member of the family of an EEA national [...] to whom (i), (ii) or (iii) above applies;

(v)   a member of the family of an EEA national [...] who dies during his working life after having resided continuously in the United Kingdom for at least 2 years, or whose death results from an accident at work or an occupational disease.

Appendix 1   Legislation and materials

[For the purposes of this paragraph:

[(a) EEA national means a national of a Member State, other than the United Kingdom, or Norway, Iceland or Liechtenstein, but for the purposes of (iv) and (v) includes a national of the United Kingdom where the conditions set out in regulation 11 of the 2000 EEA Regulations are satisfied. A Swiss national shall also be treated as an EEA national for the purposes of these Rules; and]

A 'member of the family' is a family member as defined in regulation 6 of the 2000 EEA Regulations, or a person whom it has been decided to treat as a family member in accordance with the principles set out in regulation 10 of those Regulations. [So far as this paragraph relates to a Swiss national no account will be taken of any period of residence before 1st June 2002, a cessation of employment before that date, or a death before that date.]]

[(b) So far as this paragraph relates to an Accession State national no account will be taken of any period of residence before 1st May 2004, a cessation of employment before that date, or a death before that date.]

Note
Words deleted and words in square brackets inserted by Cm 4851. Words in square brackets in definition of 'member of the family' inserted by Cm 5597. Definition of 'EEA national' substituted and sub-paragraph (b) inserted by HC 523.

[257A This paragraph applies where a Swiss national was admitted to the United Kingdom before 1st June 2002 for an initial period not exceeding 12 months pursuant to paragraph 282 and on or after that date became a qualified person or the family member of a qualified person under the 2000 EEA Regulations. Where this paragraph applies the Swiss national may, on application, have his residence permit endorsed to show permission to remain in the United Kingdom indefinitely if he meets the requirements set out in paragraph 287.]

Note
Paragraph 257A inserted by Cm 5597.

[257B This paragraph applies where an Accession State national was admitted to the United Kingdom before 1st May 2004 for an initial period not exceeding 12 months pursuant to paragraph 282 and on or after that date became a qualified person or the family member of a qualified person under the 2000 EEA Regulations. Where this paragraph applies the Accession State national may, on application, have his residence permit endorsed to show permission to remain in the United Kingdom indefinitely if he meets the requirements set out in paragraph 287.]

Note
Paragraph 257B inserted by HC 523.

[Requirements for leave to enter or remain as the primary carer or relative of an EEA national self-sufficient child]

[257C The requirements to be met by a person seeking leave to enter or remain as the primary carer or relative of an EEA national self-sufficient child are that the applicant:

   (i)   is:
       (a)   the primary carer; or
       (b)   the parent; or

(c)   the sibling,

of an EEA national under the age of 18 who has a right of residence in the United Kingdom under the 2000 EEA Regulations as a self-sufficient person; and

(ii)   is living with the EEA national or is seeking entry to the United Kingdom in order to live with the EEA national; and

(iii)   in the case of a sibling of the EEA national:
         (a)   is under the age of 18 or has current leave to enter or remain in this capacity; and
         (b)   is unmarried, has not formed an independent family unit and is not leading an independent life; and

(iv)   can, and will, be maintained and accommodated without taking employment or having recourse to public funds; and

(v)   if seeking leave to enter, holds a valid United Kingdom entry clearance for entry in this capacity.

In this paragraph, 'sibling', includes a half-brother or half-sister and a stepbrother or stepsister.]

Note
Paragraphs 257C–257E inserted by HC 164, in force 1 January 2005.

[Leave to enter or remain as the primary carer or relative of an EEA national self-sufficient child]

[257D Leave to enter or remain in the United Kingdom as the primary carer or relative of an EEA national self-sufficient child may be granted for a period not exceeding five years or the remaining period of validity of any residence permit held by the EEA national under the 2000 EEA Regulations, whichever is the shorter, provided that, in the case of an application for leave to enter, the applicant is able to produce to the Immigration Officer, on arrival a valid entry clearance for entry in this capacity or, in the case of an application for leave to remain, the applicant is able to satisfy the Secretary of State that each of the requirements of paragraph 257C(i) to (iv) is met. Leave to enter or remain is to be subject to a condition prohibiting employment and recourse to public funds.]

Note
Paragraphs 257C–257E inserted by HC 164, in force 1 January 2005.

[Refusal of leave to enter or remain as the primary carer or relative of an EEA national self-sufficient child]

[257E Leave to enter or remain in the United Kingdom as the primary carer or relative of an EEA national self-sufficient child is to be refused if, in the case of an application for leave to enter, the applicant is unable to produce to the Immigration Officer on arrival a valid United Kingdom entry clearance for entry in this capacity or, in the case of an application for leave to remain, if the applicant is unable to satisfy the Secretary of State that each of the requirements of paragraph 257C(i) to (iv) is met.]

Note
Paragraphs 257C–257E inserted by HC 164, in force 1 January 2005.

258–261 [...]

Appendix 1   Legislation and materials

Note
Paragraph 258–281deleted by Cm 4851.

Registration with the police for family members of EEA nationals

262 [*Deleted with effect from 11 May 1998 by Cmnd 3953.*]

RETIRED PERSONS OF INDEPENDENT MEANS

Requirements for leave to enter the United Kingdom as a retired person of independent means

263 The requirements to be met by a person seeking leave to enter the United Kingdom as a retired person of independent means are that he:

(i)   is at least 60 years old; and
(ii)   has under his control and disposable in the United Kingdom an income of his own of not less than £25,000 per annum; and
(iii) is able and willing to maintain and accommodate himself and any dependants indefinitely in the United Kingdom from his own resources with no assistance from any other person and without taking employment or having recourse to public funds; and
(iv)   can demonstrate a close connection with the United Kingdom; and
(v)   intends to make the United Kingdom his main home; and
(vi)   holds a valid United Kingdom entry clearance for entry in this capacity.

Leave to enter as a retired person of independent means

264 A person seeking leave to enter the United Kingdom as a retired person of independent means may be admitted subject to a condition prohibiting employment for a period not exceeding 4 years, provided he is able to produce to the Immigration Officer, on arrival, a valid United Kingdom entry clearance for entry in this capacity.

Refusal of leave to enter as a retired person of independent means

265 Leave to enter as a retired person of independent means is to be refused if a valid United Kingdom entry clearance for entry in this capacity is not produced to the Immigration Officer on arrival.

Requirements for an extension of stay as a retired person of independent means

266 The requirements for an extension of stay as a retired person of independent means are that the applicant:

(i)   entered the United Kingdom with a valid United Kingdom entry clearance as a retired person of independent means; and
(ii)   meets the requirements of paragraph 263(ii)–(iv); and
(iii) has made the United Kingdom his main home.

[Extension of stay as a retired person of independent means]

[266A The requirements for an extension of stay as a retired person of independent means for a person in the United Kingdom as a work permit holder are that the applicant:

(i) entered the United Kingdom or was granted leave to remain as a work permit holder in accordance with paragraphs 128 to 133 of these Rules; and

(ii) meets the requirements of paragraph 263 (i)–(v).]

Note
Paragraphs 266A–266D inserted by HC 346.

[266B The requirements for an extension of stay as a retired person of independent means for a person in the United Kingdom as a highly skilled migrant are that the applicant:

(i) entered the United Kingdom or was granted leave to remain as a highly skilled migrant in accordance with paragraphs 135A to 135F of these Rules; and

(ii) meets the requirements of paragraph 263(i)–(v).]

Note
Paragraphs 266A–266D inserted by HC 346.

[266C The requirements for an extension of stay as a retired person of independent means for a person in the United Kingdom to establish themselves or remain in business are that the applicant:

(i) entered the United Kingdom or was granted leave to remain as a person intending to establish themselves or remain in business in accordance with paragraphs 201 to 208 of these Rules; and

(ii) meets the requirements of paragraph 263(i)–(v).]

Note
Paragraphs 266A–266D inserted by HC 346.

[266D The requirements for an extension of stay as a retired person of independent means for a person in the United Kingdom as an innovator are that the applicant:

(i) entered the United Kingdom or was granted leave to remain as an innovator in accordance with paragraphs 210A to 210F of these Rules; and

(ii) meets the requirements of paragraph 263(i)–(v).]

Note
Paragraphs 266A–266D inserted by HC 346.

[267 An extension of stay as a retired person of independent means, with a prohibition on the taking of employment, may be granted so as to bring the person's stay in this category up to a maximum of 4 years in aggregate, provided the Secretary of State is satisfied that each of the requirements of paragraph 266 is met. An extension of stay as a retired person of independent means, with a prohibition on the taking of employment, may be granted for a maximum period of 4 years, provided the Secretary of State is satisfied that each of the requirements of paragraph 266A, 266B, 266C or 266D is met.]

Note
Substituted by HC 346.

Appendix 1 Legislation and materials

Refusal of extension of stay as a retired person of independent means

[268 An extension of stay as a retired person of independent means is to be refused if the Secretary of State is not satisfied that each of the requirements of paragraph 266, 266A, 266B, 266C or 266D is met.]

Note
Substituted by HC 346.

Indefinite leave to remain for a retired person of independent means

269 Indefinite leave to remain may be granted, on application, to a person admitted as a retired person of independent means provided he:

(i) has spent a continuous period of 4 years in the United Kingdom in this capacity; and

(ii) has met the requirements of paragraph 266 throughout the 4 year period and continues to do so.

Refusal of indefinite leave to remain for a retired person of independent means

270 Indefinite leave to remain in the United Kingdom for a retired person of independent means is to be refused if the Secretary of State is not satisfied that each of the requirements of paragraph 26[9] is met.

SPOUSES OF PERSONS WITH LIMITED LEAVE TO ENTER OR REMAIN IN THE UNITED KINGDOM AS RETIRED PERSONS OF INDEPENDENT MEANS

Requirements for leave to enter or remain as the spouse of a person with limited leave to enter or remain in the United Kingdom as a retired person of independent means

271 The requirements to be met by a person seeking leave to enter or remain in the United Kingdom as the spouse of a person with limited leave to enter or remain in the United Kingdom as a retired person of independent means are that:

(i) the applicant is married to a person with limited leave to enter or remain in the United Kingdom as a retired person of independent means; and

(ii) each of the parties intends to live with the other as his or her spouse during the applicant's stay and the marriage is subsisting; and

(iii) there will be adequate accommodation for the parties and any dependants without recourse to public funds in accommodation which they own or occupy exclusively; and

(iv) the parties will be able to maintain themselves and any dependants adequately without recourse to public funds; and

(v) the applicant does not intend to stay in the United Kingdom beyond any period of leave granted to his spouse; and

(vi) if seeking leave to enter, the applicant holds a valid United Kingdom entry clearance for entry in this capacity or, if seeking leave to remain, was admitted with a valid United Kingdom entry clearance for entry in this capacity.

Leave to enter or remain as the spouse of a person with limited leave to enter or remain in the United Kingdom as a retired person of independent means

272 A person seeking leave to enter or remain in the United Kingdom as the spouse of a person with limited leave to enter or remain in the United Kingdom as a retired person of independent means may be given leave to enter or remain in the United Kingdom for a period not in excess of that granted to the person given limited leave to enter or remain as a retired person of independent means provided that, in relation to an application for leave to enter, he is able to produce to the Immigration Officer, on arrival, a valid United Kingdom entry clearance for entry in this capacity, or, in the case of an application for limited leave to remain, he was admitted with a valid United Kingdom entry clearance for entry in this capacity and is able to satisfy the Secretary of State that each of the requirements of paragraph 271(i)–(v) is met. An application for indefinite leave to remain in this category may be granted provided the applicant was admitted with a valid United Kingdom entry clearance for entry in this capacity and is able to satisfy the Secretary of State that each of the requirements of paragraph 271(i)–(v) is met and provided indefinite leave to remain is, at the same time, being granted to the person with limited leave to enter or remain as a retired person of independent means. Leave to enter or remain is to be subject to a condition prohibiting employment except in relation to the grant of indefinite leave to remain.

Refusal of leave to enter or remain as the spouse of a person with limited leave to enter or remain in the United Kingdom as a retired person of independent means

273 Leave to enter or remain in the United Kingdom as the spouse of a person with limited leave to enter or remain in the United Kingdom as a retired person of independent means is to be refused if, in relation to an application for leave to enter, a valid United Kingdom entry clearance for entry in this capacity is not produced to the Immigration Officer on arrival or, in the case of an application for limited leave to remain, if the applicant was not admitted with a valid United Kingdom entry clearance for entry in this capacity or is unable to satisfy the Secretary of State that each of the requirements of paragraph 271(i)–(v) is met. An application for indefinite leave to remain in this category is to be refused if the applicant was not admitted with a valid United Kingdom entry clearance for entry in this capacity or is unable to satisfy the Secretary of State that each of the requirements of paragraph 271(i)–(v) is met or if indefinite leave to remain is not, at the same time, being granted to the person with limited leave to enter or remain as a retired person of independent means.

CHILDREN OF PERSONS WITH LIMITED LEAVE TO ENTER OR REMAIN IN THE UNITED KINGDOM AS RETIRED PERSONS OF INDEPENDENT MEANS

Requirements for leave to enter or remain as the child of a person with limited leave to enter or remain in the United Kingdom as a retired person of independent means

274 The requirements to be met by a person seeking leave to enter or remain in the United Kingdom as the child of a person with limited leave to enter or remain in the United Kingdom as a retired person of independent means are that:

(i)   he is the child of a parent who has been admitted to or allowed to remain in the United Kingdom as a retired person of independent means; and

(ii)   he is under the age of 18 or has current leave to enter or remain in this capacity; and

(iii)   he is unmarried, has not formed an independent family unit and is not leading an independent life; and

(iv)   he can, and will, be maintained and accommodated adequately without recourse to public funds in accommodation which his parent(s) own or occupy exclusively; and

(v)   he will not stay in the United Kingdom beyond any period of leave granted to his parent(s); and

(vi)   both parents are being or have been admitted to or allowed to remain in the United Kingdom save where:

(a)   the parent he is accompanying or joining is his sole surviving parent; or

(b)   the parent he is accompanying or joining has had sole responsibility for his upbringing; or

(c)   there are serious and compelling family or other considerations which make exclusion from the United Kingdom undesirable and suitable arrangements have been made for his care; and

(vii)   if seeking leave to enter, he holds a valid United Kingdom entry clearance for entry in this capacity or, if seeking leave to remain, was admitted with a valid United Kingdom entry clearance for entry in this capacity.

Leave to enter or remain as the child of a person with limited leave to enter or remain in the United Kingdom as a retired person of independent means

275 A person seeking leave to enter or remain in the United Kingdom as the child of a person with limited leave to enter or remain in the United Kingdom as a retired person of independent means may be given leave to enter or remain in the United Kingdom for a period of leave not in excess of that granted to the person with limited leave to enter or remain as a retired person of independent means provided that, in relation to an application for leave to enter, he is able to produce to the Immigration Officer, on arrival, a valid United Kingdom entry clearance for entry in this capacity or, in the case of an application for limited leave to remain, he was admitted with a valid United Kingdom entry clearance for entry in this capacity and is able to satisfy the Secretary of State that each of the requirements of paragraph 274(i)–(vi) is met. An application for indefinite leave to remain in this category may be granted provided the applicant was admitted to the United Kingdom with a valid United Kingdom entry clearance for entry in this capacity and is able to satisfy the Secretary of State that each of the requirements of paragraph 274(i)–(vi) is met and provided indefinite leave to remain is, at the same time, being granted to the person with limited leave to enter or remain as a retired person of independent means. Leave to enter or remain is to be subject to a condition prohibiting employment except in relation to the grant of indefinite leave to remain.

Refusal of leave to enter or remain as the child of a person with limited leave to enter or remain in the United Kingdom as a retired person of independent means

276 Leave to enter or remain in the United Kingdom as the child of a person with limited leave to enter or remain in the United Kingdom as a retired person of independent means is to be refused if, in relation to an application for leave to enter, a valid United Kingdom entry clearance for entry in this capacity is not produced to the Immigration Officer on arrival, or in the case of an application for limited leave to remain, if the applicant was not admitted with a valid United Kingdom entry clearance for entry in this capacity or is unable to satisfy the Secretary of State that each of the requirements of paragraph 274(i)–(vi) is met. An application for indefinite leave to remain in this category is to be refused if the applicant was not admitted with a valid

United Kingdom entry clearance for entry in this capacity or is unable to satisfy the Secretary of State that each of the requirements of paragraph 274(i)–(vi) is met or if indefinite leave to remain is not, at the same time, being granted to the person with limited leave to enter or remain as a retired person of independent means.

LONG RESIDENCE

[**Long residence in the United Kingdom**

276A For the purposes of paragraphs 276B to 276D:

(a)   continuous residence' means residence in the United Kingdom for an unbroken period, and for these purposes a period shall not be considered to have been broken where an applicant is absent from the United Kingdom for a period of 6 months or less at any one time, provided that the applicant in question has existing limited leave to enter or remain upon their departure and return, but shall be considered to have been broken if the applicant:

    (i)   has been removed under Schedule 2 of the 1971 Act, section 10 of the 1999 Act, has been deported or has left the United Kingdom having been refused leave to enter or remain here; or

    (ii)   has left the United Kingdom and, on doing so, evidenced a clear intention not to return; or

    (iii)   left the United Kingdom in circumstances in which he could have had no reasonable expectation at the time of leaving that he would lawfully be able to return; or

    (iv)   has been convicted of an offence and was sentenced to a period of imprisonment or was directed to be detained in an institution other than a prison (including, in particular, a hospital or an institution for young offenders), provided that the sentence in question was not a suspended sentence; or

    (v)   has spent a total of more than 18 months absent from the United Kingdom during the period in question.

(b)   'lawful residence' means residence which is continuous residence pursuant to:

    (i)   existing leave to enter or remain; or

    (ii)   temporary admission within section 11 of the 1971 Act where leave to enter or remain is subsequently granted; or

    (iii)   an exemption from immigration control, including where an exemption ceases to apply if it is immediately followed by a grant of leave to enter or remain.]

Note
Inserted by HC 538.

Requirements for indefinite leave to remain on the ground of long residence in the United Kingdom

276B The requirements to be met by an applicant for indefinite leave to remain on the ground of long residence in the United Kingdom are that:

(i)

    (a)   he has had at least 10 years continuous lawful residence in the United Kingdom; or

    [(b)   he has had at least 14 years continuous residence in the United Kingdom, excluding any period spent in the United Kingdom following service of notice of liability to removal or notice of a decision to remove by way of directions under paragraphs 8 to 10A, or 12 to 14, of Schedule 2 to the Immigration Act 1971 or section 10 of the Immigration and Asylum Act 1999 Act, or of a notice of intention to deport him from the United Kingdom; and]

(ii)   having regard to the public interest there are no reasons why it would be undesirable for him to be given indefinite leave to remain on the ground of long residence, taking into account his:

(a)   age; and

(b)   strength of connections in the United Kingdom; and

(c)   personal history, including character, conduct, associations and employment record; and

(d)   domestic circumstances; and

(e)   previous criminal record and the nature of any offence of which the person has been convicted; and

(f)   compassionate circumstances; and

(g)   any representations received on the person's behalf.]

Note
Inserted by HC 538. Sub-paragraph (i)(*b*) substituted by Cm 6339.

[Indefinite leave to remain on the ground of long residence in the United Kingdom

276C Indefinite leave to remain on the ground of long residence in the United Kingdom may be granted provided that the Secretary of State is satisfied that each of the requirements of paragraph 276B is met.]

Note
Inserted by HC 538.

[Refusal of indefinite leave to remain on the ground of long residence in the United Kingdom

276D Indefinite leave to remain on the ground of long residence in the United Kingdom is to be refused if the Secretary of State is not satisfied that each of the requirements of paragraph 276B is met.]

Note
Inserted by HC 538.

[HM FORCES]

[Definition of Gurkha]

[276E For the purposes of these Rules the term 'Gurkha' means a citizen or national of Nepal who has served in the Brigade of Gurkhas of the British Army under the Brigade of Gurkhas? terms and conditions of service.]

Note
Inserted by HC 1112.

1968

[LEAVE TO ENTER OR REMAIN IN THE UNITED KINGDOM AS A GURKHA DISCHARGED FROM THE BRITISH ARMY]

[Requirements for indefinite leave to enter the United Kingdom as a Gurkha discharged from the British Army]

[276F The requirements for indefinite leave to enter the United Kingdom as a Gurkha discharged from the British Army are that:

(i)   the applicant has completed at least four years? service as a Gurkha with the British Army; and
(ii)   was discharged from the British Army in Nepal on completion of engagement on or after 1 July 1997; and
(iii)   was not discharged from the British Army more than 2 years prior to the date on which the application is made; and
(iv)   holds a valid United Kingdom entry clearance for entry in this capacity.]

Note
Inserted by HC 1112.

[Indefinite leave to enter the United Kingdom as a Gurkha discharged from the British Army]

[276G A person seeking indefinite leave to enter the United Kingdom as a Gurkha discharged from the British Army may be granted indefinite leave to enter provided a valid United Kingdom entry clearance for entry in this capacity is produced to the Immigration Officer on arrival.]

Note
Inserted by HC 1112.

[Refusal of indefinite leave to enter the United Kingdom as a Gurkha discharged from the British Army]

[276H Indefinite leave to enter the United Kingdom as a Gurkha discharged from the British Army is to be refused if a valid United Kingdom entry clearance for entry in this capacity is not produced to the Immigration Officer on arrival.]

Note
Inserted by HC 1112.

[Requirements for indefinite leave to remain in the United Kingdom as a Gurkha discharged from the British Army]

[276I The requirements for indefinite leave to remain in the United Kingdom as a Gurkha discharged from the British Army are that:

(i)   the applicant has completed at least four years' service as a Gurkha with the British Army; and
(ii)   was discharged from the British Army in Nepal on completion of engagement on or after 1 July 1997; and
(iii)   was not discharged from the British Army more than 2 years prior to the date on which the application is made; and

(iv)   on the date of application has leave to enter or remain in the United Kingdom.]

Note
Inserted by HC 1112.

[Indefinite leave to remain in the United Kingdom as a Gurkha discharged from the British Army]

[276J A person seeking indefinite leave to remain in the United Kingdom as a Gurkha discharged from the British Army may be granted indefinite leave to remain provided the Secretary of State is satisfied that each of the requirements of paragraph 276I is met.]

Note
Inserted by HC 1112.

[Refusal of indefinite leave to remain in the United Kingdom as a Gurkha discharged from the British Army]

[276K Indefinite leave to remain in the United Kingdom as a Gurkha discharged from the British Army is to be refused if the Secretary of State is not satisfied that each of the requirements of paragraph 276I is met.]

Note
Inserted by HC 1112.

[LEAVE TO ENTER OR REMAIN IN THE UNITED KINDGOM AS A FOREIGN OR COMMONWEALTH CITIZEN DISCHARGED FROM HM FORCES]

[Requirements for indefinite leave to enter the United Kingdom as a foreign or Commonwealth citizen discharged from HM Forces]

[276L The requirements for indefinite leave to enter the United Kingdom as a foreign or Commonwealth citizen discharged from HM Forces are that:

(i)   the applicant has completed at least four years' service with HM Forces; and
(ii)   was discharged from HM Forces on completion of engagement; and
(iii)   was not discharged from HM Forces more than 2 years prior to the date on which the application is made; and
(iv)   holds a valid United Kingdom entry clearance for entry in this capacity.]

Note
Inserted by HC 1112.

[Indefinite leave to enter the United Kingdom as a foreign or Commonwealth citizen discharged from HM Forces]

[276M A person seeking indefinite leave to enter the United Kingdom as a foreign or Commonwealth citizen discharged from HM Forces may be granted indefinite leave to enter provided a valid United Kingdom entry clearance for entry in this capacity is produced to the Immigration Officer on arrival.]

Note
Inserted by HC 1112.

[Refusal of indefinite leave to enter the United Kingdom as a foreign or Commonwealth citizen discharged from HM Forces]

[276N Indefinite leave to enter the United Kingdom as a foreign or Commonwealth citizen discharged from HM Forces is to be refused if a valid United Kingdom entry clearance for entry in this capacity is not produced to the Immigration Officer on arrival.]

Note
Inserted by HC 1112.

[Requirements for indefinite leave to remain in the United Kingdom as a foreign or Commonwealth citizen discharged from HM Forces]

[276O The requirements for indefinite leave to remain in the United Kingdom as a foreign or Commonwealth citizen discharged from HM Forces are that:

(i)   the applicant has completed at least four years' service with HM Forces; and
(ii)   was discharged from HM Forces on completion of engagement; and
(iii)   was not discharged from HM Forces more than 2 years prior to the date on which the application is made; and
(iv)   on the date of application has leave to enter or remain in the United Kingdom.]

Note
Inserted by HC 1112.

[Indefinite leave to remain in the United Kingdom as a foreign or Commonwealth citizen discharged from HM Forces]

[276P A person seeking indefinite leave to remain in the United Kingdom as a foreign or Commonwealth citizen discharged from HM Forces may be granted indefinite leave to remain provided the Secretary of State is satisfied that each of the requirements of paragraph 276O is met.]

Note
Inserted by HC 1112.

[Refusal of indefinite leave to remain in the United Kingdom as a foreign or Commonwealth citizen discharged from HM Forces]

[276Q Indefinite leave to remain in the United Kingdom as a foreign or Commonwealth citizen discharged from HM Forces is to be refused if the Secretary of State is not satisfied that each of the requirements of paragraph 276O is met.]

Note
Inserted by HC 1112.

Appendix 1   Legislation and materials

[SPOUSES OF PERSONS SETTLED OR SEEKING SETTLEMENT IN THE UNITED KINGDOM IN ACCORDANCE WITH PARAGRAPHS 276E TO 276Q (HM FORCES RULES)]

[Leave to enter or remain in the UK as the spouse of a person present and settled in the United Kingdom or being granted settlement on the same occasion in accordance with paragraphs 276E to 276Q]

[Requirements for indefinite leave to enter the United Kingdom as the spouse of a person present and settled in the United Kingdom or being admitted on the same occasion for settlement under paragraphs 276E to 276Q]

[276R The requirements to be met by a person seeking indefinite leave to enter the United Kingdom as the spouse of a person present and settled in the United Kingdom or being admitted on the same occasion for settlement in accordance with paragraphs 276E to 276Q are that:

(i)   the applicant is married to a person present and settled in the United Kingdom or who is being admitted on the same occasion for settlement in accordance with paragraphs 276E to 276Q; and

(ii)   the parties to the marriage have met; and

(iii) the parties were married at least 2 years ago; and

(iv)   each of the parties intends to live permanently with the other as his or her spouse and

(v)   the marriage is subsisting; and

(vi)   the applicant holds a valid United Kingdom entry clearance for entry in this capacity.]

Note
Paragraphs 276R–276Z and 276AA–276AC inserted by HC 164, in force 1 January 2005.

[Indefinite leave to enter the United Kingdom as the spouse of a person present and settled in the United Kingdom or being admitted on the same occasion for settlement in accordance with paragraphs 276E to 276Q]

[276S A person seeking leave to enter the United Kingdom as the spouse of a person present and settled in the United Kingdom or being admitted on the same occasion for settlement in accordance with paragraphs 276E to 276Q may be granted indefinite leave to enter provided a valid United Kingdom entry clearance for entry in this capacity is produced to the Immigration Officer on arrival.]

Note
Paragraphs 276R–276Z and 276AA–276AC inserted by HC 164, in force 1 January 2005.

[Refusal of indefinite leave to enter the United Kingdom as the spouse of a person present and settled in the UK or being admitted on the same occasion for settlement in accordance with paragraphs 276E to 276Q]

[276T Leave to enter the United Kingdom as the spouse of a person present and settled in the United Kingdom or being admitted on the same occasion for settlement in accordance with paragraphs 276E to 276Q is to be refused if a valid United Kingdom entry clearance for entry in this capacity is not produced to the Immigration Officer on arrival.]

Note
Paragraphs 276R–276Z and 276AA–276AC inserted by HC 164, in force 1 January 2005.

[Requirements for indefinite leave to remain in the United Kingdom as the spouse of a person present and settled in the United Kingdom or being granted settlement on the same occasion in accordance with paragraphs 276E to 276Q]

[276U The requirements to be met by a person seeking indefinite leave to remain in the United Kingdom as the spouse of a person present and settled in the United Kingdom or being granted settlement on the same occasion in accordance with paragraphs 276E to 276Q are that:

(i)   the applicant is married to a person present and settled in the United Kingdom or being granted settlement on the same occasion in accordance with paragraphs 276E to 276Q; and
(ii)   the parties to the marriage have met; and
(iii) the parties were married at least 2 years ago; and
(iv)   each of the parties intends to live permanently with the other as his or her spouse; and
(v)   the marriage is subsisting; and
(vi)   has leave to enter or remain in the United Kingdom.]

Note
Paragraphs 276R–276Z and 276AA–276AC inserted by HC 164, in force 1 January 2005.

[Indefinite leave to remain in the United Kingdom as the spouse of a person present and settled in the United Kingdom or being granted settlement on the same occasion in accordance with paragraphs 276E to 276Q]

[276V Indefinite leave to remain in the United Kingdom as the spouse of a person present and settled in the United Kingdom or being granted settlement on the same occasion in accordance with paragraphs 276E to 276Q may be granted provided the Secretary of State is satisfied that each of the requirements of paragraph 276U is met.]

Note
Paragraphs 276R–276Z and 276AA–276AC inserted by HC 164, in force 1 January 2005.

[Refusal of indefinite leave to remain in the United Kingdom as the spouse of a person present and settled in the United Kingdom or being granted settlement on the same occasion in accordance with paragraphs 276E to 276Q]

[276W Indefinite leave to remain in the United Kingdom as the spouse of a person present and settled in the United Kingdom or being granted settlement on the same occasion in accordance with paragraphs 276E to 276Q is to be refused if the Secretary of State is not satisfied that each of the requirements of paragraph 276U is met.]

Note
Paragraphs 276R–276Z and 276AA–276AC inserted by HC 164, in force 1 January 2005.

Appendix 1   Legislation and materials

[CHILDREN OF A PARENT, PARENTS OR A RELATIVE SETTLED OR SEEKING SETTLEMENT IN THE UNITED KINGDOM UNDER PARAGRAPHS 276E TO 276Q (HM FORCES RULES)]

[Leave to enter or remain in the United Kingdom as the child of a parent, parents or a relative present and settled in the United Kingdom or being granted settlement on the same occasion in accordance with paragraphs 276E to 276Q]

[Requirements for indefinite leave to enter the United Kingdom as the child of a parent, parents or a relative present and settled in the United Kingdom or being admitted for settlement on the same occasion in accordance with paragraphs 276E to 276Q]

[276X The requirements to be met by a person seeking indefinite leave to enter the United Kingdom as the child of a parent, parents or a relative present and settled in the United Kingdom or being admitted for settlement on the same occasion in accordance with paragraphs 276E to 276Q are that:

(i) the applicant is seeking indefinite leave to enter to accompany or join a parent, parents or a relative in one of the following circumstances:
  (a) both parents are present and settled in the United Kingdom; or
  (b) both parents are being admitted on the same occasion for settlement; or
  (c) one parent is present and settled in the United Kingdom and the other is being admitted on the same occasion for settlement; or
  (d) one parent is present and settled in the United Kingdom or being admitted on the same occasion for settlement and the other parent is dead; or
  (e) one parent is present and settled in the United Kingdom or being admitted on the same occasion for settlement and has had sole responsibility for the child's upbringing; or
  (f) one parent or a relative is present and settled in the United Kingdom or being admitted on the same occasion for settlement and there are serious and compelling family or other considerations which make exclusion of the child undesirable and suitable arrangements have been made for the child's care; and
(ii) is under the age of 18; and
(iii) is not leading an independent life, is unmarried, and has not formed an independent family unit; and
(iv) holds a valid United Kingdom entry clearance for entry in this capacity.]

Note
Paragraphs 276R–276Z and 276AA–276AC inserted by HC 164, in force 1 January 2005.

[Indefinite leave to enter the United Kingdom as the child of a parent, parents or a relative present and settled in the United Kingdom or being admitted for settlement on the same occasion in accordance with paragraphs 276E to 276Q]

[276Y Indefinite leave to enter the United Kingdom as the child of a parent, parents or a relative present and settled in the United Kingdom or being admitted for settlement on the same occasion in accordance with paragraphs 276E to 276Q may be granted provided a valid United Kingdom entry clearance for entry in this capacity is produced to the Immigration Officer on arrival.]

Note
Paragraphs 276R–276Z and 276AA–276AC inserted by HC 164, in force 1 January 2005.

1974

[Refusal of indefinite leave to enter the United Kingdom as the child of a parent, parents or a relative present and settled in the United Kingdom or being admitted for settlement on the same occasion in accordance with paragraphs 276E to 276Q]

[276Z Indefinite leave to enter the United Kingdom as the child of a parent, parents, or a relative present and settled in the United Kingdom or being admitted for settlement on the same occasion in accordance with paragraphs 276E to 276Q is to be refused if a valid United Kingdom entry clearance for entry in this capacity is not produced to the Immigration Officer on arrival.]

Note
Paragraphs 276R–276Z and 276AA–276AC inserted by HC 164, in force 1 January 2005.

[Requirements for indefinite leave to remain in the United Kingdom as the child of a parent, parents or a relative present and settled in the United Kingdom or being granted settlement on the same occasion in accordance with paragraphs 276E to 276Q]

[276AA The requirements to be met by a person seeking indefinite leave to remain in the United Kingdom as the child of a parent, parents or a relative present and settled in the United Kingdom or being granted settlement on the same occasion in accordance with paragraphs 276E to 276Q are that:

(i)   the applicant is seeking indefinite leave to remain with a parent, parents or a relative in one of the following circumstances:
   (a)   both parents are present and settled in the United Kingdom or being granted settlement on the same occasion; or
   (b)   one parent is present and settled in the United Kingdom or being granted settlement on the same occasion and the other parent is dead; or
   (c)   one parent is present and settled in the United Kingdom or being granted settlement on the same occasion and has had sole responsibility for the child's upbringing; or
   (d)   one parent or a relative is present and settled in the United Kingdom or being granted settlement on the same occasion and there are serious and compelling family or other considerations which make exclusion of the child undesirable and suitable arrangements have been made for the child's care; and
(ii)   is under the age of 18; and
(iii)   is not leading an independent life, is unmarried, and has not formed an independent family unit; and
(iv)   has leave to enter or remain in the United Kingdom.]

Note
Paragraphs 276R–276Z and 276AA–276AC inserted by HC 164, in force 1 January 2005.

[Indefinite leave to remain in the United Kingdom as the child of a parent, parents or a relative present and settled in the United Kingdom or being granted settlement on the same occasion in accordance with paragraphs 276E to 276Q]

[276AB Indefinite leave to remain in the United Kingdom as the child of a parent, parents or a relative present and settled in the United Kingdom or being granted settlement on the same occasion in accordance with paragraphs 276E to 276Q may be granted if the Secretary of State is satisfied that each of the requirements of paragraph 276AA is met.]

Appendix 1   Legislation and materials

Note
Paragraphs 276R–276Z and 276AA–276AC inserted by HC 164, in force 1 January 2005.

[Refusal of indefinite leave to remain in the United Kingdom as the child of a parent, parents or a relative present and settled in the United Kingdom or being granted settlement on the same occasion in accordance with paragraphs 276E to 276Q]

[276AC Indefinite leave to remain in the United Kingdom as the child of a parent, parents or a relative present and settled in the United Kingdom or being granted settlement on the same occasion in accordance with paragraphs 276E to 276Q is to be refused if the Secretary of State is not satisfied that each of the requirements of paragraph 276AA is met.]

Note
Paragraphs 276R–276Z and 276AA–276AC inserted by HC 164, in force 1 January 2005.

SPOUSES OF ARMED FORCES MEMBERS WHO ARE EXEMPT FROM IMMIGRATION CONTROL UNDER SECTION 8(4) OF THE IMMIGRATION ACT 1971]

[Requirements for leave to enter or remain as the spouse of an armed forces member who is exempt from immigration control under section 8(4) of the Immigration Act 1971]

[276AD The requirements to be met by a person seeking leave to enter or remain in the United Kingdom as the spouse of an armed forces member who is exempt from immigration control under section 8(4) of the Immigration Act 1971 are that:

  (i)   the applicant is married to an armed forces member who is exempt from immigration control under section 8(4) of the Immigration Act 1971; and
  (ii) each of the parties intends to live with the other as his or her spouse during the applicant's stay and the marriage is subsisting; and
  (iii) there will be adequate accommodation for the parties and any dependants without recourse to public funds in accommodation which they own or occupy exclusively; and
  (iv) the parties will be able to maintain themselves and any dependants adequately without recourse to public funds; and
  (v)   the applicant does not intend to stay in the United Kingdom beyond his or her spouse's enlistment in the home forces, or period of posting or training in the United Kingdom.]

Note
Paragraphs 276AD–276AI inserted by HC 346.

[Leave to enter or remain as the spouse of an armed forces member who is exempt from immigration control under section 8(4) of the Immigration Act 1971]

[276AE A person seeking leave to enter or remain in the United Kingdom as the spouse of an armed forces member who is exempt from immigration control under section 8(4) of the Immigration Act 1971 may be given leave to enter or remain in the United Kingdom for a period not exceeding 4 years or the duration of the enlistment, posting or training of his or her spouse, whichever is shorter, provided that the Immigration Officer, or in the case of an application for leave to remain, the Secretary of State, is satisfied that each of the requirements of paragraph 276AD(i)–(v) is met.]

Note
Paragraphs 276AD–276AI inserted by HC 346.

[Refusal of leave to enter or remain as the spouse of an armed forces member who is exempt from immigration control under section 8(4) of the Immigration Act 1971]

[**276AF** Leave to enter or remain in the United Kingdom as the spouse an armed forces member who is exempt from immigration control under section 8(4) of the Immigration Act 1971 is to be refused if the Immigration Officer, or in the case of an application for leave to remain, the Secretary of State, is not satisfied that each of the requirements of paragraph 276AD (i)–(v) is met.]

Note
Paragraphs 276AD–276AI inserted by HC 346.

[CHILDREN OF ARMED FORCES MEMBERS WHO ARE EXEMPT FROM IMMIGRATION CONTROL UNDER SECTION 8(4) OF THE IMMIGRATION ACT 1971]

[Requirements for leave to enter or remain as the child of an armed forces member exempt from immigration control under section 8(4) of the Immigration Act 1971]

[**276AG** The requirements to be met by a person seeking leave to enter or remain in the United Kingdom as the child of an armed forces member exempt from immigration control under section 8(4) of the Immigration Act 1971 are that:

(i)   he is the child of a parent who is an armed forces member exempt from immigration control under section 8(4) of the Immigration Act 1971; and

(ii)   he is under the age of 18 or has current leave to enter or remain in this capacity; and

(iii)   he is unmarried, has not formed an independent family unit and is not leading an independent life; and (iv) he can and will be maintained and accommodated adequately without recourse to public funds in accommodation which his parent(s) own or occupy exclusively; and

(v)   he will not stay in the United Kingdom beyond the period of his parent's enlistment in the home forces, or posting or training in the United Kingdom; and

(vi)   his other parent is being or has been admitted to or allowed to remain in the United Kingdom save where:

    (a)   the parent he is accompanying or joining is his sole surviving parent; or

    (b)   the parent he is accompanying or joining has had sole responsibility for his upbringing; or

    (c)   there are serious and compelling family or other considerations which make exclusion from the United Kingdom undesirable and suitable arrangements have been made for his care.]

Note
Paragraphs 276AD–276AI inserted by HC 346.

[Leave to enter or remain as the child of an armed forces member exempt from immigration control under section 8(4) of the Immigration Act 1971]

[**276AH** A person seeking leave to enter or remain in the United Kingdom as the child of an armed forces member exempt from immigration control under section 8(4) of the

Appendix 1   Legislation and materials

Immigration Act 1971 may be given leave to enter or remain in the United Kingdom for a period not exceeding 4 years or the duration of the enlistment, posting or training of his parent, whichever is the shorter, provided that the Immigration Officer, or in the case of an application for leave to remain, the Secretary of State, is satisfied that each of the requirements of 276AG(i)–(vi) is met.]

Note
Paragraphs 276AD–276AI inserted by HC 346.

[**Refusal of leave to enter or remain as the child of an armed forces member exempt from immigration control under section 8(4) of the Immigration Act 1971**]

[**276AI** Leave to enter or remain in the United Kingdom as the child of an armed forces member exempt from immigration control under section 8(4) of the Immigration Act 1971 is to be refused if the Immigration Officer, or in the case of an application for leave to remain, the Secretary of State, is not satisfied that each of the requirements of paragraph 276AG(i)–(vi) is met.]

Note
Paragraphs 276AD–276AI inserted by HC 346.

PART 8
FAMILY MEMBERS

SPOUSES

277 Nothing in these Rules shall be construed as permitting a person to be granted entry clearance, leave to enter, leave to remain or variation of leave as a spouse of another if [either the applicant] [or the sponsor will be aged under 18] on the date of arrival in the United Kingdom or (as the case may be) on the date on which the leave to remain or variation of leave would be granted.

[278 Nothing in these Rules shall be construed as allowing a person to be granted entry clearance, leave to enter, leave to remain or variation of leave as the spouse of a man or woman (the sponsor) if:

(i)   his or her marriage to the sponsor is polygamous; and
(ii)   there is another person living who is the husband or wife of the sponsor and who:
       (a)   is, or at any time since his or her marriage to the sponsor has been, in the United Kingdom; or
       (b)   has been granted a certificate of entitlement in respect of the right of abode mentioned in Section 2(1)(a) of the Immigration Act 1988 or an entry clearance to enter the United Kingdom as the husband or wife of the sponsor.

For the purpose of this paragraph a marriage may be polygamous although at its inception neither party had any other spouse.]

Note
In paragraph 277 words in first square brackets substituted by HC 164; words in second square brackets substituted and inserted by HC 538. Paragraph 278 substituted by Cm 4851.

[279 Paragraph 278 does not apply to any person who seeks entry clearance, leave to enter, leave to remain or variation of leave where:

(i)   he or she has been in the United Kingdom before 1 August 1988 having been admitted for the purpose of settlement as the husband or wife of the sponsor; or

(ii)   he or she has, since their marriage to the sponsor, been in the United Kingdom at any time when there was no such other spouse living as is mentioned in paragraph 278 (ii).

But where a person claims that paragraph 278 does not apply to them because they have been in the United Kingdom in circumstances which cause them to fall within sub-paragraphs (i) or (ii) of that paragraph, it shall be for them to prove that fact.]

Note
Paragraph 279 substituted by Cm 4851.

[280 For the purposes of paragraphs 278 and 279 the presence of any wife or husband in the United Kingdom in any of the following circumstances shall be disregarded:

(i)   as a visitor; or
(ii)   an illegal entrant; or
(iii)   in circumstances whereby a person is deemed by Section 11(1) of the Immigration Act 1971 not to have entered the United Kingdom.]

Note
Paragraph 280 substituted by Cm 4851.

SPOUSES OF PERSONS PRESENT AND SETTLED IN THE UNITED KINGDOM OR BEING ADMITTED ON THE SAME OCCASION FOR SETTLEMENT

Requirements for leave to enter the United Kingdom with a view to settlement as the spouse of a person present and settled in the United Kingdom or being admitted on the same occasion for settlement

[281 The requirements to be met by a person seeking leave to enter the United Kingdom with a view to settlement as the spouse of a person present and settled in the United Kingdom or who is on the same occasion being admitted for settlement are that:

[(i)

    (a)   the applicant is married to a person present and settled in the United Kingdom or who is on the same occasion being admitted for settlement; or

    (b)   the applicant is married to a person who has a right of abode in the United Kingdom or indefinite leave to enter or remain in the United Kingdom and is on the same occasion seeking admission to the United Kingdom for the purposes of settlement and the parties were married at least 4 years ago, since which time they have been living together outside the United Kingdom; and]

(ii)   the parties to the marriage have met; and
(iii)   each of the parties intends to live permanently with the other as his or her spouse and the marriage is subsisting; and
(iv)   there will be adequate accommodation for the parties and any dependants without recourse to public funds in accommodation which they own or occupy exclusively; and

(v)   the parties will be able to maintain themselves and any dependants adequately without recourse to public funds; and

(vi) the applicant holds a valid United Kingdom entry clearance for entry in this capacity.

[For the purposes of this paragraph and paragraphs 282–289 a member of HM Forces serving overseas, or a permanent member of HM Diplomatic Service or a comparable UK-based staff member of the British Council on a tour of duty abroad, or a staff member of the Department for International Development who is a British Citizen or is settled in the United Kingdom, is to be regarded as present and settled in the United Kingdom.]

Note
Substituted by HC 26, para 1 with effect from 5 June 1997. Words in first set of square brackets substituted by HC 538. Words in second set of square brackets substituted by Cm 5597.

Leave to enter as the spouse of a person present and settled in the United Kingdom or being admitted for settlement on the same occasion

282 A person seeking leave to enter the United Kingdom as the spouse of a person present and settled in the United Kingdom or who is on the same occasion being admitted for settlement may[, in the case of a person within paragraph 281(i)(a),] be admitted for an initial period not exceeding [2 years or, in the case of a person within paragraph 281(i)(b), indefinte leave to enter may be granted] provided a valid United Kingdom entry clearance for entry [[in] the appropriate] capacity is produced to the Immigration Officer on arrival.

Note
Words in square brackets inserted by HC 538. Word 'in' in final square brackets substituted by Cm 5949.

Refusal of leave to enter as the spouse of a person present and settled in the United Kingdom or being admitted on the same occasion for settlement

283 Leave to enter the United Kingdom as the spouse of a person present and settled in the United Kingdom or who is on the same occasion being admitted for settlement is to be refused if a valid United Kingdom entry clearance for entry in this capacity is not produced to the Immigration Officer on arrival.

Requirements for an extension of stay as the spouse of a person present and settled in the United Kingdom

[**284** The requirements for an extension of stay as the spouse of a person present and settled in the United Kingdom are that:

[(i)   the applicant has limited leave to enter or remain in the United Kingdom [which was given in accordance with any of the provisions of these Rules], other than where as a result of that leave he would not have been in the United Kingdom beyond 6 months from the date on which he was admitted to the United Kingdom on this occasion in accordance with these Rules, unless the leave in question is limited leave to enter as a fiance; and]

   (ii) is married to a person present and settled in the United Kingdom; and

   (iii) the parties to the marriage have met; and

(iv)   the applicant has not remained in breach of the immigration laws; and
(v)   the marriage has not taken place after a decision has been made to deport the applicant or he has been recommended for deportation or been given notice under Section 6(2) of the Immigration Act 1971; and
(vi)   each of the parties intends to live permanently with the other as his or her spouse and the marriage is subsisting; and
(vii)   there will be adequate accommodation for the parties and any dependants without recourse to public funds in accommodation which they own or occupy exclusively; and
(viii)   the parties will be able to maintain themselves and any dependants adequately without recourse to public funds.]

Note
Substituted by HC 26, para 2 with effect from 5 June 1997. Sub-paragraph (i) substituted by Cm 5949. Words in square brackets within sub-paragraph (i) inserted by Cm 6339.

Extension of stay as the spouse of a person present and settled in the United Kingdom

285 An extension of stay as the spouse of a person present and settled in the United Kingdom may be granted for a period of [2 years] in the first instance, provided the Secretary of State is satisfied that each of the requirements of paragraph 284 is met.

Note
Words in square brackets inserted by HC 538.

Refusal of extension of stay as the spouse of a person present and settled in the United Kingdom

286 An extension of stay as the spouse of a person present and settled in the United Kingdom is to be refused if the Secretary of State is not satisfied that each of the requirements of paragraph 284 is met.

Requirements for indefinite leave to remain for the spouse of a person present and settled in the United Kingdom

[287

(a)   The requirements for indefinite leave to remain for the spouse of a person present and settled in the United Kingdom are that:
  [(i)
      (a)   the applicant was admitted to the United Kingdom or given an extension of stay for a period of 2 years in accordance with paragraphs 281 to 286 of these Rules and has completed a period of 2 years as the spouse of a person present and settled in the United Kingdom; or
      (b)   the applicant was admitted to the United Kingdom or given an extension of stay for a period of 2 years in accordance with paragraphs 295AA to 295F of these Rules and during that 2 year period married the person whom he or she was admitted or granted an extension of stay to join and has completed a period of 2 years as the unmarried partner and then the spouse of a person present and settled in the United Kingdom; and]

(ii)   the applicant is still the spouse of the person he or she was admitted or granted an extension of stay to join and the marriage is subsisting; and

(iii)   each of the parties intends to live permanently with the other as his or her spouse; and

(iv)   there will be adequate accommodation for the parties and any dependants without recourse to public funds in accommodation which they own or occupy exclusively; and

(v)   the parties will be able to maintain themselves and any dependants adequately without recourse to public funds.

(b)   The requirements for indefinite leave to remain for the bereaved spouse of a person who was present and settled in the United Kingdom are that:

[(i)

(a)   the applicant was admitted to the United Kingdom or given an extension of stay for a period of 2 years as the spouse of a person present and settled in the United Kingdom in accordance with paragraphs 281 to 286 of these Rules; or

(b)   the applicant was admitted to the United Kingdom or given an extension of stay for a period of 2 years as the unmarried partner of a person present and settled in the United Kingdom in accordance with paragraphs 295AA to 295F of these Rules and during that 2 year period married the person whom he or she was admitted or granted an extension of stay to join; and]

(ii)   the person whom the applicant was admitted or granted an extension of stay to join died during that [2 years] period; and

(iii)   the applicant was still the spouse of the person he or she was admitted or granted an extension of stay to join at the time of the death; and

(iv)   each of the parties intended to live permanently with the other as his or her spouse and the marriage was subsisting at the time of the death.]

Note

Paragraph 287 substituted by Cm 4851. Words in square brackets substituted by HC 538. Sub-paragraph (a)(i)(a), (b) substituted by Cm 6339. Sub-paragraph (b)(i)(a), (b) substituted by Cm 6339.

Indefinite leave to remain for the spouse of a person present and settled in the United Kingdom

288 Indefinite leave to remain for the spouse of a person present and settled in the United Kingdom may be granted provided the Secretary of State is satisfied that each of the requirements of paragraph 287 is met.

Refusal of indefinite leave to remain for the spouse of a person present and settled in the United Kingdom

289 Indefinite leave to remain for the spouse of a person present and settled in the United Kingdom is to be refused if the Secretary of State is not satisfied that each of the requirements of paragraph 287 is met.

[Refusal of indefinite leave to remain in the United Kingdom as the victim of domestic violence

289A The requirements to be met by a person who is the victim of domestic violence and who is seeking indefinite leave to remain in the United Kingdom are that the applicant:

(i)   was admitted to the United Kingdom or given an extension of stay for a period of [2 years] as the spouse of a person present and settled here; or

(ii)   was admitted to the United Kingdom or given an extension of stay for a period of 2 years as the unmarried partner of a person present and settled here; and

(iii) the relationship with their spouse or unmarried partner, as appropriate, was subsisting at the beginning of the relevant period of leave or extension of stay referred to in (i) or (ii) above; and

(iv)   is able to produce such evidence as may be required by the Secretary of State to establish that the relationship was caused to permanently break down before the end of that period as a result of domestic violence.]

Note
Inserted by HC 104. Words in brackets substituted by HC 538.

[Indefinite leave to remain as the victim of domestic violence

289B Indefinite leave to remain as the victim of domestic violence may be granted provided the Secretary of State is satisfied that each of the requirements of paragraph 289A is met.]

Note
Inserted by HC 538.

[Refusal of indefinite leave to remain as the victim of domestic violence

289C Indefinite leave to remain as the victim of domestic violence is to be refused if the Secretary of State is not satisfied that each of the requirements of paragraph 287A is met.]

Note
Inserted by HC 538.

FIANCÉ(E)S

[**289AA** Nothing in these Rules shall be construed as permitting a person to be granted entry clearance, leave to enter or variation of leave as a fiancé(e) if [either the applicant] or the sponsor will aged under 18 on the date of arrival of the applicant in the United Kingdom or (as the case may be) on the date on which the leave to enter or variation of leave would be granted.]

Note
Paragraph 289AA inserted by HC 538. Words in square brackets substituted by HC 164.

Requirements for leave to enter the United Kingdom as a fiancé(e) (ie with a view to marriage and permanent settlement in the United Kingdom)

[**290** The requirements to be met by a person seeking leave to enter the United Kingdom as a fiancé(e) are that:

(i)   the applicant is seeking leave to enter the United Kingdom for marriage to a person present and settled in the United Kingdom or who is on the same occasion being admitted for settlement; and

  (ii)   the parties to the proposed marriage have met; and

 (iii)   each of the parties intends to live permanently with the other as his or her spouse after the marriage; and

 (iv)   adequate maintenance and accommodation without recourse to public funds will be available for the applicant until the date of the marriage; and

  (v)   there will, after the marriage, be adequate accommodation for the parties and any dependants without recourse to public funds in accommodation which they own or occupy exclusively; and

 (vi)   the parties will be able after the marriage to maintain themselves and any dependants adequately without recourse to public funds; and

 (vii)   the applicant holds a valid United Kingdom entry clearance for entry in this capacity.]

Note
Substituted by HC 26, para 3 with effect from 5 June 1997.

[**290A** For the purposes of paragraph 290 and paragraphs 291–295, an EEA national who, under either the Immigration (European Economic Area) Order 1994 or the 2000 EEA Regulations, has been issued with a residence permit valid for 5 years is to be regarded as present and settled in the United Kingdom even if that EEA national has not been granted permission to remain in the United Kingdom indefinitely.]

Note
Paragraph 290A inserted by Cm 5597.

Leave to enter as a fiancé(e)

291 A person seeking leave to enter the United Kingdom as a fiancé(e) may be admitted, with a prohibition on employment, for a period not exceeding 6 months to enable the marriage to take place provided a valid United Kingdom entry clearance for entry in this capacity is produced to the Immigration Officer on arrival.

Refusal of leave to enter as a fiancé(e)

292 Leave to enter the United Kingdom as a fiancé(e) is to be refused if a valid United Kingdom entry clearance for entry in this capacity is not produced to the Immigration Officer on arrival.

Requirements for an extension of stay as a fiancé(e)

293 The requirements for an extension of stay as a fiancé(e) are that:

  (i)   the applicant was admitted to the United Kingdom with a valid United Kingdom entry clearance as a fiancé(e); and

 (ii)   good cause is shown why the marriage did not take place within the initial period of leave granted under paragraph 291; and

 (iii)   there is satisfactory evidence that the marriage will take place at an early date; and

 (iv)   the requirements of paragraph 290(ii)–(vi) are met.]

Note
Sub-paragraph (iv) substituted by HC 26, para 4 with effect from 5 June 1997.

Extension of stay as a fiancé(e)

294 An extension of stay as a fiancé(e) may be granted for an appropriate period with a prohibition on employment to enable the marriage to take place provided the Secretary of State is satisfied that each of the requirements of paragraph 293 is met.

Refusal of extension of stay as a fiancé(e)

295 An extension of stay is to be refused if the Secretary of State is not satisfied that each of the requirements of paragraph 293 is met.

[LEAVE TO ENTER AS THE UNMARRIED PARTNER OF A PERSON PRESENT AND SETTLED IN THE UNITED KINGDOM OR BEING ADMITTED ON THE SAME OCCASION FOR SETTLEMENT

[**295AA** Nothing in these Rules shall be construed as permitting a person to be granted entry clearance, leave to enter or variation of leave as an unmarried partner if [either the applicant] or the sponsor will aged under 18 on the date of arrival of the applicant in the United Kingdom or (as the case may be) on the date on which the leave to enter or variation of leave would be granted.]

Note
Paragraph 295AA inserted by HC 538. Words in square brackets substituted by HC 164.

Requirements for leave to enter the United Kingdom with a view to settlement as the unmarried partner of a person present and settled in the United Kingdom or being admitted on the same occasion for settlement

295A The requirements to be met by a person seeking leave to enter the United Kingdom with a view to settlement as the unmarried partner of a person present and settled in the United Kingdom or being admitted on the same occasion for settlement, are that:

[(i)
    (a)   the applicant is the unmarried partner of a person present and settled in the United Kingdom or who is on the same occasion being admitted for settlement and the parties have been living together in a relationship akin to marriage which has subsisted for two years or more; or
    (b)   the applicant is the unmarried partner of a person who has a right of abode in the United Kingdom or indefinite leave to enter or remain in the United Kingdom and is on the same occasion seeking admission to the United Kingdom for the purposes of settlement and the parties have been living together outside the United Kingdom in a relationship akin to marriage which has subsisted for 4 years or more; and]
  (ii) any previous marriage (or similar relationship) by either partner has permanently broken down; and
[(iii) the parties are not involved in a consanguineous relationship with one another; and]
[...]
  (v) there will be adequate accommodation for the parties and any dependants without recourse to public funds in accommodation which they own or occupy exclusively; and

(vi)   the parties will be able to maintain themselves and any dependants adequately without recourse to public funds; and

(vii) the parties intend to live together permanently; and

(viii) the applicant holds a valid United Kingdom entry clearance for entry in this capacity.

[For the purposes of this paragraph and paragraphs 295B–295I, a member of HM Forces serving overseas, or a permanent member of HM Diplomatic Service or a comparable UK-based staff member of the British Council on a tour of duty abroad, or a staff member of the Department for International Development who is a British Citizen or is settled in the United Kingdom, is to be regarded as present and settled in the United Kingdom.]

Note
Sub-paragraph (i)(a) and (b) substituted and sub-paragraph (iv) deleted by HC 538. Sub-paragraph (iii) inserted by Cm 5949. Final paragraph inserted by Cm 5597.

Leave to enter the United Kingdom with a view to settlement as the unmarried partner of a person present and settled in the United Kingdom or being admitted on the same occasion for settlement

295B Leave to enter the United Kingdom with a view to settlement as the unmarried partner of a person present and settled in the United Kingdom or being admitted on the same occasion for settlement may [, or in the case of a person within paragraph 295A(i)(a),] be granted for an initial period not exceeding 2 years [or, in the case of a person within paragraph 295A(i)(b), indefinite leave to enter may be granted] provided that a valid United Kingdom entry clearance for entry [[in] the appropriate] capacity is produced to the Immigration Officer on arrival.

Note
Words in square brackets inserted and substituted by HC 538. Word 'in' in last square brackets substituted by Cm 5949.

Refusal of leave to enter the United Kingdom with a view to settlement as the unmarried partner of a person present and settled in the United Kingdom or being admitted on the same occasion for settlement

295C Leave to enter the United Kingdom with a view to settlement as the unmarried partner of a person present and settled in the United Kingdom or being admitted on the same occasion for settlement, is to be refused if a valid United Kingdom entry clearance for entry in this capacity is not produced to the Immigration Officer on arrival.

LEAVE TO REMAIN AS THE UNMARRIED PARTNER OF A PERSON PRESENT AND SETTLED IN THE UNITED KINGDOM

Requirements for leave to remain as the unmarried partner of a person present and settled in the United Kingdom

295D The requirements to be met by a person seeking leave to remain as the unmarried partner of a person present and settled in the United Kingdom are that:

  (i)   the applicant has limited leave to remain in the United Kingdom [which was given in accordance with any of the provisions of these Rules]; and

  (ii) any previous marriage (or similar relationship) by either partner has permanently broken down; and

 (iii) the applicant is the unmarried partner of a person who is present and settled in the United Kingdom; and

 (iv) the applicant has not remained in breach of the immigration laws; and

[(v) the parties are not involved in a consanguineous relationship with one another; and]

 (vi) the parties have been living together in a relationship akin to marriage which has subsisted for two years or more; and

 (vii) the parties' relationship pre-dates any decision to deport the applicant, recommend him for deportation, give him notice under Section 6(2) of the Immigration Act 1971, or give directions for his removal under section 10 of the Immigration and Asylum Act 1999; and

(viii) there will be adequate accommodation for the parties and any dependants without recourse to public funds in accommodation which they own or occupy exclusively; and -

 (ix) the parties will be able to maintain themselves and any dependants adequately without recourse to public funds; and

  (x) the parties intend to live together permanently.

Note
Sub-paragraph (v) inserted by Cm 5949. Words in square brackets in sub-paragraph (i) inserted by Cm 6339.

Leave to remain as the unmarried partner of a person present and settled in the United Kingdom

295E Leave to remain as the unmarried partner of a person present and settled in the United Kingdom may be granted for a period of 2 years in the first instance provided that the Secretary of State is satisfied that each of the requirements of paragraph 295D are met.

Refusal of leave to remain as the unmarried partner of a person present and settled in the United Kingdom

295F Leave to remain as the unmarried partner of a person present and settled in the United Kingdom is to be refused if the Secretary of State is not satisfied that each of the requirements of paragraph 295D is met.

INDEFINITE LEAVE TO REMAIN AS THE UNMARRIED PARTNER OF A PERSON PRESENT AND SETTLED IN THE UNITED KINGDOM

Requirements for indefinite leave to remain as the unmarried partner of a person present and settled in the United Kingdom

295G The requirements to be met by a person seeking indefinite leave to remain as the unmarried partner of a person present and settled in the United Kingdom are that:

   (i)   the applicant was admitted to the United Kingdom or given an extension of stay for a period of 2 years [in accordance with paragraphs 295AA to 295F of these Rules] and has completed a period of 2 years as the unmarried partner of a person present and settled here; and

  (ii)   the applicant is still the unmarried partner of the person he was admitted or granted an extension of stay to join and the relationship is still subsisting; and

 (iii)   each of the parties intends to live permanently with the other as his partner; and

 (iv)   there will be adequate accommodation for the parties and any dependants without recourse to public funds in accommodation which they own or occupy exclusively; and

  (v)   the parties will be able to maintain themselves and any dependants adequately without recourse to public funds.

Note
Words in square brackets in sub paragraph (i) inserted by Cm 6339.

Indefinite leave to remain as the unmarried partner of a person present and settled in the United Kingdom

295H Indefinite leave to remain as the unmarried partner of a person present and settled in the United Kingdom may be granted provided that the Secretary of State is satisfied that each of the requirements of paragraph 295G is met.

Refusal of indefinite leave to remain as the unmarried partner of a person present and settled in the United Kingdom

295I Indefinite leave to remain as the unmarried partner of a person present and settled in the United Kingdom is to be refused if the Secretary of State is not satisfied that each of the requirements of paragraph 295G is met.

LEAVE TO ENTER OR REMAIN AS THE UNMARRIED PARTNER OF A PERSON WITH LIMITED LEAVE TO ENTER OR REMAIN IN THE UNITED KINGDOM UNDER PARAGRAPHS 128–193; 200–239; OR 263–270

Requirements for leave to enter or remain as the unmarried partner of a person with limited leave to enter or remain in the United Kingdom under paragraphs 128–193; 200–239; or 263–270

295J The requirements to be met by a person seeking leave to enter or remain as the unmarried partner of a person with limited leave to enter or remain in the United Kingdom under paragraphs 128–193; 200–239; or 263–270; are that:

   (i)   the applicant is the unmarried partner of a person who has limited leave to enter or remain in the United Kingdom under paragraphs 128–193; 200–239; or 263–270; and

  (ii)   any previous marriage (or similar relationship) by either partner has permanently broken down; and

[(iii)   the parties are not involved in a consanguineous relationship with one another; and]

 (iv)   the parties have been living together in a relationship akin to marriage which has subsisted for 2 years or more; and

(v)   each of the parties intends to live with the other as his partner during the applicant's stay; and

(vi)   there will be adequate accommodation for the parties and any dependants without recourse to public funds in accommodation which they own or occupy exclusively; and

(vii)   the parties will be able to maintain themselves and any dependants adequately without recourse to public funds; and

(viii)   the applicant does not intend to stay in the United Kingdom beyond any period of leave granted to his partner; and

(ix)   if seeking leave to enter, the applicant holds a valid United Kingdom entry clearance for entry in this capacity or, if seeking leave to remain, was admitted with a valid United Kingdom entry clearance for entry in this capacity.

Note
Sub-paragraph (iii) inserted by Cm 5949.

Leave to enter or remain as the unmarried partner of a person with limited leave to enter or remain in the United Kingdom under paragraphs 128–193; 200–239; or 263–270

295K Leave to enter as the unmarried partner of a person with limited leave to enter or remain in the United Kingdom under paragraphs 128–193; 200–239; or 263–270; may be granted provided that a valid United Kingdom entry clearance for entry in this capacity is produced to the Immigration Officer on arrival. Leave to remain as the unmarried partner of a person with limited leave to enter or remain in the United Kingdom under paragraphs 128–193; 200–239; or 263–270; may be granted provided that the Secretary of State is satisfied that each of the requirements of paragraph 295J is met.

Refusal of leave to enter or remain as the unmarried partner of a person with limited leave to enter or remain in the United Kingdom under paragraphs 128–193; 200–239; or 263–270

295L Leave to enter as the unmarried partner of a person with limited leave to enter or remain in the United Kingdom under paragraphs 128–193; 200–239; or 263–270; is to be refused if a valid United Kingdom entry clearance for entry in this capacity is not produced to the Immigration Officer on arrival. Leave to remain as the unmarried partner of a person with limited leave to enter or remain in the United Kingdom under paragraphs 128–193; 200–239; or 263–270; is to be refused if the Secretary of State is not satisfied that each of the requirements of paragraph 295J is met.

INDEFINITE LEAVE TO REMAIN FOR THE BEREAVED UNMARRIED PARTNER OF A PERSON PRESENT AND SETTLED IN THE UNITED KINGDOM

Requirements for indefinite leave to remain for the bereaved unmarried partner of a person present and settled in the United Kingdom

295M The requirements to be met by a person seeking indefinite leave to remain as the bereaved unmarried partner of a person present and settled in the United Kingdom, are that:

(i)   the applicant was admitted to the United Kingdom or given an extension of stay for a period of 2 years [in accordance with paragraphs 295AA to 295F of these Rules] as the unmarried partner of a person present and settled in the United Kingdom; and

(ii)   the person whom the applicant was admitted or granted an extension of stay to join died during that 2 year period; and

(iii)   the applicant was still the unmarried partner of the person he was admitted or granted extension of stay to join at the time of the death; and

(iv)   each of the parties intended to live permanently with the other as his partner and the relationship was subsisting at the time of the death.

Note
Words in square brackets in sub-paragraph (i) inserted by Cm 6339.

Indefinite leave to remain for the bereaved unmarried partner of a person present and settled in the United Kingdom

295N Indefinite leave to remain for the bereaved unmarried partner of a person present and settled in the United Kingdom, may be granted provided that the Secretary of State is satisfied that each of the requirements of paragraph 295M is met.

Refusal of indefinite leave to remain for the bereaved unmarried partner of a person present and settled in the United Kingdom

295O Indefinite leave to remain for the bereaved unmarried partner of a person present and settled in the United Kingdom, is to be refused if the Secretary of State is not satisfied that each of the requirements of paragraph 295M is met.]

Note
Paragraphs 295A–295O inserted by Cm 4851.

CHILDREN

[296 Nothing in these Rules shall be construed as permitting a child to be granted entry clearance, leave to enter or remain, or variation of leave where his mother is party to a polygamous marriage and any application by that parent for admission or leave to remain for settlement or with a view to settlement would be refused pursuant to paragraphs 278 or 278A].

Note
Paragraphs 296 substituted by Cm 4851.

LEAVE TO ENTER OR REMAIN IN THE UNITED KINGDOM AS THE CHILD OF A PARENT, PARENTS OR A RELATIVE PRESENT AND SETTLED OR BEING ADMITTED FOR SETTLEMENT IN THE UNITED KINGDOM

Requirements for indefinite leave to enter the United Kingdom as the child of a parent, parents or a relative present and settled or being admitted for settlement in the United Kingdom

297 The requirements to be met by a person seeking indefinite leave to enter the United Kingdom as the child of a parent, parents or a relative present and settled or being admitted for settlement in the United Kingdom are that he:

(i)   is seeking leave to enter to accompany or join a parent, parents or a relative in one of the following circumstances:

    (a)   both parents are present and settled in the United Kingdom; or

    (b)   both parents are being admitted on the same occasion for settlement; or

    (c)   one parent is present and settled in the United Kingdom and the other is being admitted on the same occasion for settlement; or

    (d)   one parent is present and settled in the United Kingdom or being admitted on the same occasion for settlement and the other parent is dead; or

    (e)   one parent is present and settled in the United Kingdom or being admitted on the same occasion for settlement and has had sole responsibility for the child's upbringing; or

    (f)   one parent or a relative is present and settled in the United Kingdom or being admitted on the same occasion for settlement and there are serious and compelling family or other considerations which make exclusion of the child undesirable and suitable arrangements have been made for the child's care; and

(ii)   is under the age of 18; and

(iii)   is not leading an independent life, is unmarried, and has not formed an independent family unit; and

[(iv)   can, and will, be accommodated adequately by the parent, parents or relative the child is seeking to join without recourse to public funds in accommodation which the parent, parents or relative the child is seeking to join, own or occupy exclusively; and

(v)   can, and will, be maintained adequately by the parent, parents or relative the child is seeking to join, without recourse to public funds; and

(vi)   holds a valid United Kingdom entry clearance for entry in this capacity.]

Note
Paragraph 297 (iv)–(v) substituted and paragraph 297 (vi) inserted by Cm 485

Requirements for indefinite leave to remain in the United Kingdom as the child of a parent, parents or a relative present and settled or being admitted for settlement in the United Kingdom

298 The requirements to be met by a person seeking indefinite leave to remain in the United Kingdom as the child of a parent, parents or a relative present and settled in the United Kingdom are that he:

(i)   is seeking to remain with a parent, parents or a relative in one of the following circumstances:

    (a)   both parents are present and settled in the United Kingdom; or

    (b)   one parent is present and settled in the United Kingdom and the other parent is dead; or

    (c)   one parent is present and settled in the United Kingdom and has had sole responsibility for the child's upbringing; or

    (d)   one parent or a relative is present and settled in the United Kingdom and there are serious and compelling family or other considerations which make exclusion of the child undesirable and suitable arrangements have been made for the child's care; and

(ii)   has limited leave to enter or remain in the United Kingdom, and

    (a)   is under the age of 18; or

    (b)   was given leave to enter or remain with a view to settlement under paragraph 302; and

(iii)   is not leading an independent life, is unmarried, and has not formed an independent family unit; and

[(iv)   can, and will, be accommodated adequately by the parent, parents or relative the child was admitted to join, without recourse to public funds in accommodation which the parent, parents or relative the child was admitted to join, own or occupy exclusively; and

(v)   can, and will, be maintained adequately by the parent, parents or relative the child was admitted to join, without recourse to public funds.]

Note
Paragraph 298 (iv) substituted and paragraph 298 (v) inserted by Cm 4851.

Indefinite leave to enter or remain in the United Kingdom as the child of a parent, parents or a relative present and settled or being admitted for settlement in the United Kingdom

299   Indefinite leave to enter the United Kingdom as the child of a parent, parents or a relative present and settled or being admitted for settlement in the United Kingdom may be granted provided a valid United Kingdom entry clearance for entry in this capacity is produced to the Immigration Officer on arrival. Indefinite leave to remain in the United Kingdom as the child of a parent, parents or a relative present and settled in the United Kingdom may be granted provided the Secretary of State is satisfied that each of the requirements of paragraph 298 is met.

Refusal of indefinite leave to enter or remain in the United Kingdom as the child of a parent, parents or a relative present and settled or being admitted for settlement in the United Kingdom

300   Indefinite leave to enter the United Kingdom as the child of a parent, parents or a relative present and settled or being admitted for settlement in the United Kingdom is to be refused if a valid United Kingdom entry clearance for entry in this capacity is not produced to the Immigration Officer on arrival. Indefinite leave to remain in the United Kingdom as the child of a parent, parents or a relative present and settled in the United Kingdom is to be refused if the Secretary of State is not satisfied that each of the requirements of paragraph 298 is met.

Requirements for limited leave to enter or remain in the United Kingdom with a view to settlement as the child of a parent or parents given limited leave to enter or remain in the United Kingdom with a view to settlement

301   The requirements to be met by a person seeking limited leave to enter or remain in the United Kingdom with a view to settlement as the child of a parent or parents given limited leave to enter or remain in the United Kingdom with a view to settlement are that he:

(i)   is seeking leave to enter to accompany or join or remain with a parent or parents in one of the following circumstances:

   (a)   one parent is present and settled in the United Kingdom or being admitted on the same occasion for settlement and the other parent is being or has been given limited leave to enter or remain in the United Kingdom with a view to settlement; or

    (b)   one parent is being or has been given limited leave to enter or remain in the United Kingdom with a view to settlement and has had sole responsibility for the child's upbringing; or

    (c)   one parent is being or has been given limited leave to enter or remain in the United Kingdom with a view to settlement and there are serious and compelling family or other considerations which make exclusion of the child undesirable and suitable arrangements have been made for the child's care; and

(ii)   is under the age of 18; and

(iii)   is not leading an independent life, is unmarried, and has not formed an independent family unit; and

[(iv)   can, and will, be accommodated adequately without recourse to public funds, in accommodation which the parent or parents own or occupy exclusively; and

(iva)   can, and will, be maintained adequately by the parent or parents without recourse to public funds; and]

(v)   (where an application is made for limited leave to remain with a view to settlement) has limited leave to enter or remain in the United Kingdom; and

(vi)   if seeking leave to enter, holds a valid United Kingdom entry clearance for entry in this capacity or, if seeking leave to remain, was admitted with a valid United Kingdom entry clearance for entry in this capacity.

Note
Paragraph 301(iv) substituted and paragraph 301(iva) inserted by Cm 4851.

Limited leave to enter or remain in the United Kingdom with a view to settlement as the child of a parent or parents given limited leave to enter or remain in the United Kingdom with a view to settlement

302 A person seeking limited leave to enter the United Kingdom with a view to settlement as the child of a parent or parents given limited leave to enter or remain in the United Kingdom with a view to settlement may be admitted for a period not exceeding [24 months] provided he is able, on arrival, to produce to the Immigration Officer a valid United Kingdom entry clearance for entry in this capacity. A person seeking limited leave to remain in the United Kingdom with a view to settlement as the child of a parent or parents given limited leave to enter or remain in the United Kingdom with a view to settlement may be given limited leave to remain for a period not exceeding 12 months provided the Secretary of State is satisfied that each of the requirements of paragraph 301(i)–(v) is met.

Note
Words in square brackets substituted by HC 1224.

Refusal of limited leave to enter or remain in the United Kingdom with a view to settlement as the child of a parent or parents given limited leave to enter or remain in the United Kingdom with a view to settlement

303 Limited leave to enter the United Kingdom with a view to settlement as the child of a parent or parents given limited leave to enter or remain in the United Kingdom with a view to settlement is to be refused if a valid United Kingdom entry clearance for entry in this capacity is not produced to the Immigration Officer on arrival. Limited leave to remain in the United Kingdom with a view to settlement as the child of a parent or parents given limited leave to enter or remain in the United Kingdom with a

view to settlement is to be refused if the Secretary of State is not satisfied that each of the requirements of paragraph 301(i)–(v) is met.

[LEAVE TO ENTER AND EXTENSION OF STAY IN THE UNITED KINGDOM AS THE CHILD OF A PARENT WHO IS BEING, OR HAS BEEN ADMITTED TO THE UNITED KINGDOM AS A FIANCÉ(E)

Requirements for limited leave to enter the United Kingdom as the child of a fiancé(e)

303A The requirements to be met by a person seeking limited leave to enter the United Kingdom as the child of a fiancé(e), are that:

(i)   he is seeking to accompany or join a parent who is, on the same occasion that the child seeks admission, being admitted as a fiancé(e), or who has been admitted as a fiancé(e); and

(ii)   he is under the age of 18; and

(iii)   he is not leading an independent life, is unmarried, and has not formed an independent family unit; and

(iv)   he can, and will, be maintained and accommodated adequately without recourse to public funds with the parent admitted or being admitted as a fiancé(e); and

(v)   there are serious and compelling family or other considerations which make the child's exclusion undesirable, that suitable arrangements have been made for his care in the United Kingdom, and there is no other person outside the United Kingdom who could reasonably be expected to care for him; and

(vi)   he holds a valid United Kingdom entry clearance for entry in this capacity.

Limited leave to enter the United Kingdom as the child of a parent who is being, or has been admitted to the United Kingdom as a fiancé(e)

303B A person seeking limited leave to enter the United Kingdom as the child of a fiancé(e), may be granted limited leave to enter the United Kingdom for a period not in excess of that granted to the fiancé(e), provided that a valid United Kingdom entry clearance for entry in this capacity is produced to the Immigration Officer on arrival. Where the period of limited leave granted to a fiancé(e) will expire in more than 6 months, a person seeking limited leave to enter as the child of the fiancé(e) should be granted leave for a period not exceeding six months.

Refusal of limited leave to enter the United Kingdom as the child of a parent who is being, or has been admitted to the United Kingdom as a fiancé(e)

303C Limited leave to enter the United Kingdom as the child of a fiancé(e), is to be refused if a valid United Kingdom entry clearance for entry in this capacity is not produced to the Immigration Officer on arrival.

Requirements for an extension of stay in the United Kingdom as the child of a fiancé(e)

303D The requirements to be met by a person seeking an extension of stay in the United Kingdom as the child of a fiancé(e) are that:

(i)   the applicant was admitted with a valid United Kingdom entry clearance as the child of a fiancé(e); and

(ii)   the applicant is the child of a parent who has been granted limited leave to enter, or an extension of stay, as a fiancé(e); and

(iii)   the requirements of paragraph 303A(ii)–(v) are met.

Extension of stay in the United Kingdom as the child of a fiancé(e)

303E An extension of stay as the child of a fiancé(e) may be granted provided that the Secretary of State is satisfied that each of the requirements of paragraph 303D is met.

Refusal of an extension of stay in the United Kingdom as the child of a fiancé(e)

303F An extension of stay as the child of a fiancé(e) is to be refused if the Secretary of State is not satisfied that each of the requirements of paragraph 303D is met.]

Note
Paragraphs 303A-303F inserted by Cm 4851.

CHILDREN BORN IN THE UNITED KINGDOM WHO ARE NOT BRITISH CITIZENS

304 This paragraph and paragraphs 305–309 apply only to unmarried dependent children under 18 years of age who were born in the United Kingdom on or after 1 January 1983 (when the British Nationality Act 1981 came into force) but who, because neither of their parents was a British citizen or settled in the United Kingdom at the time of their birth, are not British citizens and are therefore subject to immigration control. Such a child requires leave to enter where admission to the United Kingdom is sought, and leave to remain where permission is sought for the child to be allowed to stay in the United Kingdom. If he qualifies for entry clearance, leave to enter or leave to remain under any other part of these Rules, a child who was born in the United Kingdom but is not a British citizen may be granted entry clearance, leave to enter or leave to remain in accordance with the provisions of that other part.

Requirements for leave to enter or remain in the United Kingdom as the child of a parent or parents given leave to enter or remain in the United Kingdom

305 The requirements to be met by a child born in the United Kingdom who is not a British citizen who seeks leave to enter or remain in the United Kingdom as the child of a parent or parents given leave to enter or remain in the United Kingdom are that he:

(i)
  (a)   is accompanying or seeking to join or remain with a parent or parents who have, or are given, leave to enter or remain in the United Kingdom; or

  (b)   is accompanying or seeking to join or remain with a parent or parents one of whom is a British citizen or has the right of abode in the United Kingdom; or

  (c)   is a child in respect of whom the parental rights and duties are vested solely in a local authority; and

(ii)   is under the age of 18; and

(iii)   was born in the United Kingdom; and

(iv)   is not leading an independent life, is unmarried, and has not formed an independent family unit; and

(v)   (where an application is made for leave to enter) has not been away from the United Kingdom for more than 2 years.

Leave to enter or remain in the United Kingdom

306 A child born in the United Kingdom who is not a British citizen and who requires leave to enter or remain in the circumstances set out in paragraph 304 may be given leave to enter for the same period as his parent or parents where paragraph 305(i)(a) applies, provided the Immigration Officer is satisfied that each of the requirements of paragraph 305(ii)–(v) is met. Where leave to remain in sought, the child may be granted leave to remain for the same period as his parent or parents where paragraph 305(i)(a) applies, provided the Secretary of State is satisfied that each of the requirements of paragraph 305(ii)–(iv) is met. Where the parent or parents have or are given periods of leave of different duration, the child may be given leave to whichever period is longer except that if the parents are living apart the child should be given leave for the same period as the parent who has day to day responsibility for him.

307 If a child does not qualify for leave to enter or remain because neither of his parents has a current leave (and neither of them is a British citizen or has the right of abode), he will normally be refused leave to enter or remain, even if each of the requirements of paragraph 305(ii)–(v) has been satisfied. However, he may be granted leave to enter or remain for a period not exceeding 3 months if both of his parents are in the United Kingdom and it appears unlikely that they will be removed in the immediate future, and there is no other person outside the United Kingdom who could reasonably be expected to care for him.

308 A child born in the United Kingdom who is not a British citizen and who requires leave to enter or remain in the United Kingdom in the circumstances set out in paragraph 304 may be given indefinite leave to enter where paragraph 305(i)(b) or (i)(c) applies provided the Immigration Officer is satisfied that each of the requirements of paragraph 305(ii)–(v) is met. Where an application is for leave to remain, such a child may be granted indefinite leave to remain where paragraph 305(i)(b) or (i)(c) applies, provided the Secretary of State is satisfied that each of the requirements of paragraph 305(ii)–(iv) is met.

Refusal of leave to enter or remain in the United Kingdom

309 Leave to enter the United Kingdom where the circumstances set out in paragraph 304 apply is to be refused if the Immigration Officer is not satisfied that each of the requirements of paragraph 305 is met. Leave to remain for such a child is to be refused if the Secretary of State is not satisfied that each of the requirements of paragraph 305(i)–(iv) is met.

ADOPTED CHILDREN

[309A For the purposes of adoption under paragraphs 310–316C a de facto adoption shall be regarded as having taken place if:

(a)   at the time immediately preceding the making of the application for entry clearance under these Rules the adoptive parent or parents have been living abroad (in applications involving two parents both must have lived abroad together) for at least a period of time equal to the first period mentioned in sub-paragraph (b)(i) and must have cared for the child for at least a period of time equal to the second period material in that sub-paragraph; and

(b)   during their time abroad, the adoptive parent or parents have:

    (i)   lived together for a minimum period of 18 months, of which the 12 months immediately preceding the application for entry clearance must have been spent living together with the child; and

    (ii)   have assumed the role of the child's parents, since the beginning of the 18 month period, so that there has been a genuine transfer of parental responsibility.]

Note
Inserted by HC 538.

Requirements for indefinite leave to enter the United Kingdom as the adopted child of a parent or parents present and settled or being admitted for settlement in the United Kingdom

310 The requirements to be met in the case of a child seeking indefinite leave to enter the United Kingdom as the adopted child of a parent or parents present and settled or being admitted for settlement in the United Kingdom are that he:

(i)   is seeking leave to enter to accompany or join an adoptive parent or parents in one of the following circumstances:

    (a)   both parents are present and settled in the United Kingdom; or

    (b)   both parents are being admitted on the same occasion for settlement; or

    (c)   one parent is present and settled in the United Kingdom and the other is being admitted on the same occasion for settlement; or

    (d)   one parent is present and settled in the United Kingdom or being admitted on the same occasion for settlement and the other parent is dead; or

    (e)   one parent is present and settled in the United Kingdom or being admitted on the same occasion for settlement and has had sole responsibility for the child's upbringing; or

    (f)   one parent is present and settled in the United Kingdom or being admitted on the same occasion for settlement and there are serious and compelling family or other considerations which make exclusion of the child undesirable and suitable arrangements have been made for the child's care; [or]

    [(g)   in the case of a de facto adoption one parent has a right of abode in the United Kingdom or indefinite leave to enter or remain in the United Kingdom and is seeking admission to the United Kingdom on the same occasion for the purposes of settlement; and]

(ii)   is under the age of 18; and

(iii)   is not leading an independent life, is unmarried, and has not formed an independent family unit; and

[(iv)   can, and will, be accommodated [and maintained] adequately without recourse to public funds in accommodation which the adoptive parent or parents own or occupy exclusively; and]

...

[(vi)

    (a)   was adopted in accordance with a decision taken by the competent administrative authority or court in his country of origin or the country

in which he is resident[, being a country whose adoption orders are recognised by the United Kingdom]; or
    (b)   is the subject of a de facto adoption; and]
(vii)   was adopted at a time when:
        (a)   both adoptive parents were resident together abroad; or
        (b)   either or both adoptive parents were settled in the United Kingdom; and
(viii)   has the same rights and obligations as any other child of the [adoptive parent's or parents' family]; and
(ix)   was adopted due to the inability of the original parent(s) or current carer(s) to care for him and there has been a genuine transfer of parental responsibility to the adoptive parents; and
(x)   has lost or broken his ties with his family of origin; and
(xi)   was adopted, but the adoption is not one of convenience arranged to facilitate his admission to or remaining in the United Kingdom; and
(xii)   holds a valid United Kingdom entry clearance for entry in this capacity.

Note
Paragraph 310(iv) substituted, paragraph 310(v) inserted and subsequent paragraphs renumbered by Cm 4851. Words in square brackets in sub-paragraph (i)(*f*), (i)(*g*), (iv), (vi) and (viii) substituted and sub-paragraph (v) deleted by HC 538. Words in square brackets in (vi)(*a*) inserted by Cm 5253.

Requirements for indefinite leave to remain in the United Kingdom as the adopted child of a parent or parents present and settled in the United Kingdom

311 The requirements to be met in the case of a child seeking indefinite leave to remain in the United Kingdom as the adopted child of a parent or parents present and settled in the United Kingdom are that he:

(i)   is seeking to remain with an adoptive parent or parents in one of the following circumstances:
    (a)   both parents are present and settled in the United Kingdom; or
    (b)   one parent is present and settled in the United Kingdom and the other parent is dead; or
    (c)   one parent is present and settled in the United Kingdom and has had sole responsibility for the child's upbringing; or
    (d)   one parent is present and settled in the United Kingdom and there are serious and compelling family or other considerations which make exclusion of the child undesirable and suitable arrangements have been made for the child's care; [or]
    [(e)   in the case of a de facto adoption one parent has a right of abode in the United Kingdom or indefinite leave to enter or remain in the United Kingdom and is seeking admission to the United Kingdom on the same occasion for the purpose of settlement; and]
(ii)   has limited leave to enter or remain in the United Kingdom, and
    (a)   is under the age of 18; or
    (b)   was given leave to enter or remain with a view to settlement under paragraph 315 [or paragraph 316B]; and
(iii)   is not leading an independent life, is unmarried, and has not formed an independent family unit; and
[(iv)   can, and will, be accommodated [and maintained] adequately without recourse to public funds in accommodation which the adoptive parent or parents own or occupy exclusively; and]
[(vi)

(a)   was adopted in accordance with a decision taken by the competent administrative authority or court in his country of origin or the country in which he is resident[, being a country whose adoption orders are recognised by the United Kingdom]; or

(b)   is the subject of a de facto adoption; and]

(vii)   was adopted at a time when:

(a)   both adoptive parents were resident together abroad; or

(b)   either or both adoptive parents were settled in the United Kingdom; and

(viii)   has the same rights and obligations as any other child of the [adoptive parent's or parents' family]; and

(ix)   was adopted due to the inability of the original parent(s) or current carer(s) to care for him and there has been a genuine transfer of parental responsibility to the adoptive parents; and

(x)   has lost or broken his ties with his family of origin; and

(ix)   was adopted, but the adoption is not one of convenience arranged to facilitate his admission to or remaining in the United Kingdom.

Note
Words in square brackets in paragraph 311(ii)(b) inserted, paragraph 311(iv) substituted and subsequent paragraphs renumbered by Cm 4851. Words in square brackets in sub-paragraph (i)(d), (i)(e), (iv), (vi) and (viii) substituted and (v) deleted by HC 538. Words in square brackets in (vi)(a) inserted by Cm 5253.

Indefinite leave to enter or remain in the United Kingdom as the adopted child of a parent or parents present and settled or being admitted for settlement in the United Kingdom

312 Indefinite leave to enter the United Kingdom as the adopted child of a parent or parents present and settled or being admitted for settlement in the United Kingdom may be granted provided a valid United Kingdom entry clearance for entry in this capacity is produced to the Immigration Officer on arrival. Indefinite leave to remain in the United Kingdom as the adopted child of a parent or parents present and settled in the United Kingdom may be granted provided the Secretary of State is satisfied that each of the requirements of paragraph 311 is met.

Refusal of indefinite leave to enter or remain in the United Kingdom as the adopted child of a parent or parents present and settled or being admitted for settlement in the United Kingdom

313 Indefinite leave to enter the United Kingdom as the adopted child of a parent or parents present and settled or being admitted for settlement in the United Kingdom is to be refused if a valid United Kingdom entry clearance for entry in this capacity is not produced to the Immigration Officer on arrival. Indefinite leave to remain in the United Kingdom as the adopted child of a parent or parents present and settled in the United Kingdom is to be refused if the Secretary of State is not satisfied that each of the requirements of paragraph 311 is met.

Requirements for limited leave to enter or remain in the United Kingdom with a view to settlement as the adopted child of a parent or parents given limited leave to enter or remain in the United Kingdom with a view to settlement

314 The requirements to be met in the case of a child seeking limited leave to enter or remain in the United Kingdom with a view to settlement as the adopted child of a parent or parents given limited leave to enter or remain in the United Kingdom with a view to settlement are that he:

(i)   is seeking leave to enter to accompany or join or remain with a parent or parents in one of the following circumstances:

    (a)   one parent is present and settled in the United Kingdom or being admitted on the same occasion for settlement and the other parent is being or has been given limited leave to enter or remain in the United Kingdom with a view to settlement; or

    (b)   one parent is being or has been given limited leave to enter or remain in the United Kingdom with a view to settlement and has had sole responsibility for the child's upbringing; or

    (c)   one parent is being or has been given limited leave to enter or remain in the United Kingdom with a view to settlement and there are serious and compelling family or other considerations which make exclusion of the child undesirable and suitable arrangements have been made for the child's care; or

    [(d)   in the case of a de facto adoption one parent has a right of abode in the United Kingdom or indefinite leave to enter or remain in the United Kingdom and is seeking admission to the United Kingdom on the same occasion for the purpose of settlement; and]

(ii)   is under the age of 18; and

(iii)   is not leading an independent life, is unmarried, and has not formed an independent family unit; and

[(iv)   can, and will, be accommodated [and maintained] adequately without recourse to public funds in accommodation which the adoptive parent or parents own or occupy exclusively; and]

[(v)

    (a)   was adopted in accordance with a decision taken by the competent administrative authority or court in his country of origin or the country in which he is resident[, being a country whose adoption orders are recognised by the United Kingdom]; or

    (b)   is the subject of a de facto adoption; and]

(vi)   was adopted at a time when:

    (a)   both adoptive parents were resident together abroad; or

    (b)   either or both adoptive parents were settled in the United Kingdom; and

(vii)   has the same rights and obligations as any other child of the [adoptive parent's or parents' family]; and

(viii) was adopted due to the inability of the original parent(s) or current carer(s) to care for him and there has been a genuine transfer of parental responsibility to the adoptive parents; and

(ix)   has lost or broken his ties with his family of origin; and

(x)   was adopted, but the adoption is not one of convenience arranged to facilitate his admission to the United Kingdom; and

(xi)   (where an application is made for limited leave to remain with a view to settlement) has limited leave to enter or remain in the United Kingdom; and

(xii)   if seeking leave to enter, holds a valid United Kingdom entry clearance for entry in this capacity.

Note

Paragraph 314(iv) substituted by Cm 4851. Words in square brackets in sub-paragraph (i)(c), (i)(d), (iv), (v) and (vii) substituted and (iva) deleted by HC 538. Words in square brackets in (v)(a) inserted by Cm 5253.

Limited leave to enter or remain in the United Kingdom with a view to settlement as the adopted child of a parent or parents given limited leave to enter or remain in the United Kingdom with a view to settlement

315 A person seeking limited leave to enter the United Kingdom with a view to settlement as the adopted child of a parent or parents given limited leave to enter or remain in the United Kingdom with a view to settlement may be admitted for a period not exceeding 12 months provided he is able, on arrival, to produce to the Immigration Officer a valid United Kingdom entry clearance for entry in this capacity. A person seeking limited leave to remain in the United Kingdom with a view to settlement as the adopted child of a parent or parents given limited leave to enter or remain in the United Kingdom with a view to settlement may be granted limited leave for a period not exceeding 12 months provided the Secretary of State is satisfied that each of the requirements of paragraph 314(i)–(xi) is met.

Refusal of limited leave to enter or remain in the United Kingdom with a view to settlement as the adopted child of a parent or parents given limited leave to enter or remain in the United Kingdom with a view to settlement

316 Limited leave to enter the United Kingdom with a view to settlement as the adopted child of a parent or parents given limited leave to enter or remain in the United Kingdom with a view to settlement is to be refused if a valid United Kingdom entry clearance for entry in this capacity is not produced to the Immigration Officer on arrival. Limited leave to remain in the United Kingdom with a view to settlement as the adopted child of a parent or parents given limited leave to enter or remain in the United Kingdom with a view to settlement is to be refused if the Secretary of State is not satisfied that each of the requirements of paragraph 314(i)–(xi) is met.

[Requirements for limited leave to enter the United Kingdom with a view to settlement as a child for adoption

316A The requirements to be satisfied in the case of a child seeking limited leave to enter the United Kingdom for the purpose of being adopted [(which, for the avoidance of doubt, does not include a de facto adoption)] in the United Kingdom are that he:

(i)   is seeking limited leave to enter to accompany or join a person or persons who wish to adopt him in the United Kingdom (the 'prospective parent(s)'), in one of the following circumstances:

    (a)   both prospective parents are present and settled in the United Kingdom; or

    (b)   both prospective parents are being admitted for settlement on the same occasion that the child is seeking admission; or

    (c)   one prospective parent is present and settled in the United Kingdom and the other is being admitted for settlement on the same occasion that the child is seeking admission; or

    (d)   one prospective parent is present and settled in the United Kingdom and the other is being given limited leave to enter or remain in the United Kingdom with a view to settlement on the same occasion that the child is seeking admission, or has previously been given such leave; or

    (e)   one prospective parent is being admitted for settlement on the same occasion that the other is being granted limited leave to enter with a view to settlement, which is also on the same occasion that the child is seeking admission; or

(f)   one prospective parent is present and settled in the United Kingdom or is being admitted for settlement on the same occasion that the child is seeking admission, and has had sole responsibility for the child's upbringing; or

(g)   one prospective parent is present and settled in the United Kingdom or is being admitted for settlement on the same occasion that the child is seeking admission, and there are serious and compelling family or other considerations which would make the child's exclusion undesirable, and suitable arrangements have been made for the child's care; and

(ii)   is under the age of 18; and

(iii)   is not leading an independent life, is unmarried, and has not formed an independent family unit; and

(iv)   can, and will, be maintained and accommodated adequately without recourse to public funds in accommodation which the prospective parent or parents own or occupy exclusively; and

(v)   will have the same rights and obligations as any other child of the marriage; and

(vi)   is being adopted due to the inability of the original parent(s) or current carer(s) (or those looking after him immediately prior to him being physically transferred to his prospective parent or parents) to care for him, and there has been a genuine transfer of parental responsibility to the prospective parent or parents; and

(vii) has lost or broken or intends to lose or break his ties with his family of origin; and

(viii) will be adopted in the United Kingdom by his prospective parent or parents [in accordance with the law relating to adoption in the United Kingdom], but the proposed adoption is not one of convenience arranged to facilitate his admission to the United Kingdom.

Note
Words in square brackets inserted by HC 538.

Limited leave to enter the United Kingdom with a view to settlement as a child for adoption

316B A person seeking limited leave to enter the United Kingdom with a view to settlement as a child for adoption may be admitted for a period not exceeding [24 months] provided he is able, on arrival, to produce to the Immigration Officer a valid United Kingdom entry clearance for entry in this capacity.

Note
Words in square brackets inserted by Cmnd 5829.

Refusal of limited leave to enter the United Kingdom with a view to settlement as a child for adoption

316C Limited leave to enter the United Kingdom with a view to settlement as a child for adoption is to be refused if a valid United Kingdom entry clearance for entry in this capacity is not produced to the Immigration Officer on arrival.]

Note
Paragraphs 316A–316C inserted by Cm 4851.

[Requirements for limited leave to enter the United Kingdom with a view to settlement as a child for adoption under the Hague Convention

316D The requirements to be satisfied in the case of a child seeking limited leave to enter the United Kingdom for the purpose of being adopted in the United Kingdom under the Hague Convention are that he:

(i)   is seeking limited leave to enter to accompany one or two people each of whom are habitually resident in the United Kingdom and who wish to adopt him under the Hague Convention ("the prospective parents");

(ii)   s the subject of an agreement made under Article 17(c) of the Hague Convention; and

(iii)   has been entrusted to the prospective parents by the competent administrative authority of the country from which he is coming to the United Kingdom for adoption under the Hague Convention; and

(iv)   is under the age of 18; and

(v)*   can, and will, be maintained and accommodated adequately without recourse to public funds in accommodation which the prospective parent or parents own or occupy exclusively; and

(vi)*   holds a valid United Kingdom entry clearance for entry in this capacity.]

Note
Paragraphs 316D–316F inserted by Cmnd 5829.
* Please note that in the printed version of Cmnd 5829 these points appear in error numbered as an alternative version of 316D (iii) and (iv).

[Limited leave to enter the United Kingdom with a view to settlement as a child for adoption under the Hague Convention

316E A person seeking limited leave to enter the United Kingdom with a view to settlement as a child for adoption under the Hague Convention may be admitted for a period not exceeding 24 months provided he is able, on arrival, to produce to the Immigration Officer a valid United Kingdom entry clearance for entry in this capacity.]

Note
Paragraphs 316D–316F inserted by Cmnd 5829.

[Refusal of limited leave to enter the United Kingdom with a view to settlement as a child for adoption under the Hague Convention

316F Limited leave to enter the United Kingdom with a view to settlement as a child for adoption under the Hague Convention is to be refused if a valid United Kingdom entry clearance for entry in this capacity is not produced to the Immigration Officer on arrival.]

Note
Paragraphs 316D–316F inserted by Cmnd 5829.

PARENTS, GRANDPARENTS AND OTHER DEPENDENT RELATIVES OF PERSONS PRESENT
AND SETTLED IN THE UNITED KINGDOM

**Requirements for indefinite leave to enter or remain in the United Kingdom as the
parent, grandparent or other dependent relative of a person present and settled in the
United Kingdom**

317 The requirements to be met by a person seeking indefinite leave to enter or remain
in the United Kingdom as the parent, grandparent or other dependent relative of a
person present and settled in the United Kingdom are that the person:

(i)   is related to a person present and settled in the United Kingdom in one of the
        following ways:
        (a)   mother or grandmother who is a widow aged 65 years or over; or
        (b)   father or grandfather who is a widower aged 65 years or over; or
        (c)   parent or grandparents travelling together of whom at least one is aged
               65 or over; or
        (d)   a parent or grandparent aged 65 or over who has remarried but cannot
               look to the spouse or children of the second marriage for financial
               support; and where the person settled in the United Kingdom is able and
               willing to maintain the parent or grandparent and any spouse or child of
               the second marriage who would be admissible as a dependent; or
        (e)   a parent or grandparent under the age of 65 if living alone outside the
               United Kingdom in the most exceptional compassionate circumstances
               and mainly dependent financially on relatives settled in the United
               Kingdom; or
        (f)   the son, daughter, sister, brother, uncle or aunt over the age of 18 if
               living alone outside the United Kingdom in the most exceptional
               compassionate circumstances and mainly dependent financially on rela-
               tives settled in the United Kingdom; and
(ii)   is joining or accompanying a person who is present and settled in the United
        Kingdom or who is on the same occasion being admitted for settlement; and
(iii)   is financially wholly or mainly dependent on the relative present and settled in
        the United Kingdom; and
[(iv)   can, and will, be accommodated adequately, together with any dependants,
        without recourse to public funds, in accommodation which the sponsor owns
        or occupies exclusively; and
(iva)   can, and will, be maintained adequately, together with any dependants, without
        recourse to public funds; and]
(v)   has no other close relatives in his own country to whom he could turn for
        financial support; and
(vi)   if seeking leave to enter, holds a valid United Kingdom entry clearance for entry
        in this capacity.

Note
Paragraph 317(iv) substituted and paragraph 317(iva) inserted by Cm 4851.

**Indefinite leave to enter or remain as the parent, grandparent or other dependent
relative of a person present and settled in the United Kingdom**

318 Indefinite leave to enter the United Kingdom as the parent, grandparent or other
dependent relative of a person present and settled in the United Kingdom may be
granted provided a valid United Kingdom entry clearance for entry in this capacity is
produced to the Immigration Officer on arrival. Indefinite leave to remain in the
United Kingdom as the parent, grandparent or other dependent relative of a person

present and settled in the United Kingdom may be granted provided the Secretary of State is satisfied that each of the requirements of paragraph 317(i)–(v) is met.

Refusal of indefinite leave to enter or remain in the United Kingdom as the parent, grandparent or other dependent relative of a person present and settled in the United Kingdom

319 Indefinite leave to enter the United Kingdom as the parent, grandparent or other dependent relative of a person settled in the United Kingdom is to be refused if a valid United Kingdom entry clearance for entry in this capacity is not produced to the Immigration Officer on arrival. Indefinite leave to remain in the United Kingdom as the parent, grandparent or other dependent relative of a person present and settled in the United Kingdom is to be refused if the Secretary of State is not satisfied that each of the requirements of paragraph 317(i)–(v) is met.

PART 9
GENERAL GROUNDS FOR THE REFUSAL OF ENTRY CLEARANCE, LEAVE TO ENTER OR VARIATION OF LEAVE TO ENTER OR REMAIN IN THE UNITED KINGDOM

REFUSAL OF ENTRY CLEARANCE OR LEAVE TO ENTER THE UNITED KINGDOM

320 In addition to the grounds for refusal of entry clearance or leave to enter set out in Parts 2–8 of these Rules, and subject to paragraph 321 below, the following grounds for the refusal of entry clearance or leave to enter apply:

Grounds on which entry clearance or leave to enter the United Kingdom is to be refused

(1) the fact that entry is being sought for a purpose not covered by these Rules;
(2) the fact that the person seeking entry to the United Kingdom is currently the subject of a deportation order;
(3) failure by the person seeking entry to the United Kingdom to produce to the Immigration Officer a valid national passport or other document satisfactorily establishing his identity and nationality;
(4) failure to satisfy the Immigration Officer, in the case of a person arriving in the United Kingdom or seeking entry through the Channel Tunnel with the intention of entering any other part of the common travel area, that he is acceptable to the immigration authorities there;
(5) failure, in the case of a visa national, to produce to the Immigration Officer a passport or other identity document endorsed with a valid and current United Kingdom entry clearance issued for the purpose for which entry is sought;
(6) where the Secretary of State has personally directed that the exclusion of a person from the United Kingdom is conducive to the public good;
(7) save in relation to a person settled in the United Kingdom or where the Immigration Officer is satisfied that there are strong compassionate reasons justifying admission, confirmation from the Medical Inspector that, for medical reasons, it is undesirable to admit a person seeking leave to enter the United Kingdom.

Appendix 1   Legislation and materials

Grounds on which entry clearance or leave to enter the United Kingdom should normally be refused

(8)   failure by a person arriving in the United Kingdom to furnish the Immigration Officer with such information as may be required for the purpose of deciding whether he requires leave to enter and, if so, whether and on what terms leave should be given;

[(8A)   where the person seeking leave is outside the United Kingdom, failure by him to supply any information, documents, copy documents or medical report requested by an Immigration Officer;]

(9)   failure by a person seeking leave to enter as a returning resident to satisfy the Immigration Officer that he meets the requirements of paragraph 18 of these Rules [or that he seeks leave to enter for the same purpose as that for which his earlier leave was granted];

(10)   production by the person seeking leave to enter the United Kingdom of a national passport or travel document issued by a territorial entity or authority which is not recognised by Her Majesty's Government as a state or is not dealt with as a government by them, or which does not accept valid United Kingdom passports for the purpose of its own immigration control; or a passport or travel document which does not comply with international passport practice;

(11)   failure to observe the time limit or conditions attached to any grant of leave to enter or remain in the United Kingdom;

(12)   the obtaining of a previous leave to enter or remain by deception;

(13)   failure, except by a person eligible for admission to the United Kingdom for settlement or a spouse eligible for admission under paragraph 282, to satisfy the Immigration Officer that he will be admitted to another country after a stay in the United Kingdom;

(14)   refusal by a sponsor of a person seeking leave to enter the United Kingdom to give, if requested to do so, an undertaking in writing to be responsible for that person's maintenance and accommodation for the period of any leave granted;

(15)   whether or not to the holder's knowledge, the making of false representations or the failure to disclose any material fact for the purpose of obtaining [an immigration employment document];

(16)   failure, in the case of a child under the age of 18 years seeking leave to enter the United Kingdom otherwise than in conjunction with an application made by his parent(s) or legal guardian, to provide the Immigration Officer, if required to do so, with written consent to the application from his parent(s) or legal guardian; save that the requirement as to written consent does not apply in the case of a child seeking admission to the United Kingdom as an asylum seeker;

(17)   save in relation to a person settled in the United Kingdom, refusal to undergo a medical examination when required to do so by the Immigration Officer;

(18)   save where the Immigration Officer is satisfied that admission would be justified for strong compassionate reasons, conviction in any country including the United Kingdom of an offence which, if committed in the United Kingdom, is punishable with imprisonment for a term of 12 months or any greater punishment or, if committed outside the United Kingdom, would be so punishable if the conduct constituting the offence had occurred in the United Kingdom;

(19)   where from information available to the Immigration Officer, it seems right to refuse leave to enter on the ground that exclusion from the United Kingdom is conducive to the public good; if, for example, in the light of the character, conduct or associations of the person seeking leave to enter it is undesirable to give him leave to enter.

[(20) failure by a person seeking entry into the United Kingdom to comply with a requirement relating to the provision of physical data to which he is subject by regulations made under section 126 of the Nationality, Immigration and Asylum Act 2002.]

[(21) Whether or not to the applicant's knowledge, the submission of a false document in support of an application.]

Note

Sub-paragraph (8A) inserted by HC 704. Sub-paragraph (20) inserted by HC 370. Words in square brackets in sub-paragraph (15) substituted by Cm 6339. Sub-paragraph (21) inserted by HC 1112.

Refusal of leave to enter in relation to a person in possession of an entry clearance

321 A person seeking leave to enter the United Kingdom who holds an entry clearance which was duly issued to him and is still current may be refused leave to enter only where the Immigration Officer is satisfied that:

(i) whether or not to the holder's knowledge, false representations were employed or material facts were not disclosed, either in writing or orally, for the purpose of obtaining the entry clearance; or

(ii) a change of circumstances since it was issued has removed the basis of the holder's claim to admission, except where the change of circumstances amounts solely to the person becoming over age for entry in one of the categories contained in paragraphs 296–316 of these Rules since the issue of the entry clearance; or

(iii) refusal is justified on grounds of restricted returnability; on medical grounds; on grounds of criminal record; because the person seeking leave to enter is the subject of a deportation order or because exclusion would be conducive to the public good.

[Grounds on which leave to enter or remain which is in force is to be cancelled at port or while the holder is outside the United Kingdom

321A The following grounds for the cancellation of a person's leave to enter or remain which is in force on his arrival in, or whilst he is outside, the United Kingdom apply:

(1) there has been such a change in the circumstances of that person's case, since the leave was given, that it should be cancelled; or

(2) the leave was obtained as a result of false information given by that person or by that person's failure to disclose material facts; or

(3) save in relation to a person settled in the United Kingdom or where the Immigration Officer or the Secretary of State is satisfied that there are strong compassionate reasons justifying admission, where it is apparent that, for medical reasons, it is undesirable to admit that person to the United Kingdom; or

(4) where the Secretary of State has personally directed that the exclusion of that person from the United Kingdom is conducive to the public good; or

(5) where from information available to the Immigration officer or the Secretary of State, it seems right to cancel leave on the ground that exclusion from the United Kingdom is conducive to public good; if, for example, in the light of the character, conduct or associations of that person it is undesirable for him to have leave to enter the United Kingdom; or

(6)   where that person is outside the United Kingdom, failure by that person to supply any information, documents, copy documents or medical report requested by an Immigration Officer or the Secretary of State.]

Note
Paragraph 321 replaces HC 251, para 17, which did not come under the sub-heading General in Pt IX of HC 251. Paragraph 321A inserted by HC 704.

REFUSAL OF VARIATION OF LEAVE TO ENTER OR REMAIN OR CURTAILMENT OF LEAVE

322 In addition to the grounds for refusal of extension of stay set out in Parts 2–8 of these Rules, the following provisions apply in relation to the refusal of an application for variation of leave to enter or remain or, where appropriate, the curtailment of leave:

Grounds on which an application to vary leave to enter or remain in the United Kingdom is to be refused

(1)   the fact that variation of leave to enter or remain is being sought for a purpose not covered by these Rules.

Grounds on which an application to vary leave to enter or remain in the United Kingdom should normally be refused

(2)   the making of false representations or the failure to disclose any material fact for the purpose of obtaining leave to enter or a previous variation of leave;

(3)   failure to comply with any conditions attached to the grant of leave to enter or remain;

(4)   failure by the person concerned to maintain or accommodate himself and any dependants without recourse to public funds;

(5)   the undesirability of permitting the person concerned to remain in the United Kingdom in the light of his character, conduct or associations or the fact that he represents a threat to national security;

(6)   refusal by a sponsor of the person concerned to give, if requested to do so, an undertaking in writing to be responsible for his maintenance and accommodation in the United Kingdom or failure to honour such an undertaking once given;

(7)   failure by the person concerned to honour any declaration or undertaking given orally or in writing as to the intended duration and/or purpose of his stay;

(8)   failure, except by a person who qualifies for settlement in the United Kingdom or by the spouse of a person settled in the United Kingdom, to satisfy the Secretary of State that he will be returnable to another country if allowed to remain in the United Kingdom for a further period;

[(9)   failure by an applicant to produce within a reasonable time information, documents or other evidence required by the Secretary of State to establish his claim to remain under these Rules;]

(10)   failure, without providing a reasonable explanation, to comply with a request made on behalf of the Secretary of State to attend for interview;

(11)   failure, in the case of a child under the age of 18 years seeking a variation of his leave to enter or remain in the United Kingdom otherwise than in conjunction with an application by his parent(s) or legal guardian, to provide the Secretary of State, if required to do so, with written consent to the application from his

parent(s) or legal guardian; save that the requirement as to written consent does not apply in the case of a child who has been admitted to the United Kingdom as an asylum seeker.

Note
Sub-paragraph (9) substituted by HC 104. Sub-paragraphs (10) and (11) are also new.

Grounds on which leave to enter or remain may be curtailed

[323 A person's leave to enter or remain may be curtailed:

(i)   on any of the grounds set out in paragraph 322(2)–(5) above; or
(ii)   if he ceases to meet the requirements of the Rules under which his leave to enter or remain was granted; or
(iii) if he is the dependant, or is seeking leave to remain as the dependant, of an asylum applicant whose claim has been refused and whose leave has been curtailed under section 7 of the 1993 Act, and he does not qualify for leave to remain in his own right.]

Crew members

324 A person who has been given leave to enter to join a ship, aircraft, hovercraft, hydrofoil or international train service as a member of its crew, or a crew member who has been given leave to enter for hospital treatment, repatriation or transfer to another ship, aircraft, hovercraft, hydrofoil or international train service in the United Kingdom, is to be refused leave to remain unless an extension of stay is necessary to fulfil the purpose for which he was given leave to enter or unless he meets the requirements for an extension of stay as a spouse in paragraph 284.

Note
Paragraphs 320–324 replace HC 251, paras 78–86, 99–102.

PART 10
REGISTRATION WITH THE POLICE

[324A ...

325 For the purposes of paragraph 326, a 'relevant foreign national' is a person aged 16 or over who is:

(i)   a national or citizen of a country or territory listed in Appendix 2 to these Rules;
(ii)   a stateless person; or
(iii) a person holding a non-national travel document.

326 (1) Subject to sub-paragraph (2) below, a condition requiring registration with the police should normally
be imposed on any relevant foreign national who is:

(i)   given limited leave to enter the United Kingdom for longer than six months; or
(ii)   given limited leave to remain which has the effect of allowing him to remain in the United Kingdom for longer than six months, reckoned from the date of his arrival (whether or not such a condition was imposed when he arrived).

(2) Such a condition should not normally be imposed where the leave is given:

   (i)   as a seasonal agricultural worker;
   (ii)   as a private servant in a diplomatic household;
   (iii) as a minister of religion, missionary or member of a religious order;
   (iv)   on the basis of marriage to a person settled in the United Kingdom or as the unmarried partner of a person settled in the United Kingdom;
   (v)   as a person exercising access rights to a child resident in the United Kingdom;
   (vi)   as the parent of a child at school; or
   (vii) following the grant of asylum.

(3) Such a condition should also be imposed on any foreign national given limited leave to enter the United Kingdom where, exceptionally, the Immigration Officer considers it necessary to ensure that he complies with the terms of the leave.]

Note
Paragraph 324A deleted and paragraphs 325 and 326 substituted by HC 194, in force 4 February 2005.

PART 11
ASYLUM

Definition of asylum applicant

327 Under these Rules an asylum applicant is a person who claims that it would be contrary to the United Kingdom's obligations under the United Nations Convention and Protocol relating to the Status of Refugees for him to be removed from or required to leave the United Kingdom. All such cases are referred to in these Rules as asylum applications.

Applications for asylum

328 All asylum applications will be determined by the Secretary of State in accordance with the United Kingdom's obligations under the United Nations Convention and Protocol relating to the Status of Refugees. Every asylum application made by a person at a port or airport in the United Kingdom will be referred by the Immigration Officer for determination by the Secretary of State in accordance with these Rules.

[329 Until an asylum application has been determined by the Secretary of State or the Secretary of State has issued a certificate under Part 2, 3, 4 or 5 of Schedule 3 to the Asylum and Immigration (Treatment of Claimants, etc) Act 2004 no action will be taken to require the departure of the asylum applicant or his dependants from the United Kingdom.]

Note
Paragraph 329 substituted by HC 1112.

330 If the Secretary of State decides to grant asylum and the person has not yet been given leave to enter, the Immigration Officer will grant limited leave to enter.

[331 [If a person seeking leave to enter is refused asylum, the Immigration Officer will consider whether or not he is in a position to decide to give or refuse leave to enter without interviewing the person further. If the Immigration Officer decides that a further interview is not required he may serve the notice giving or refusing leave to enter by post. If the Immigration Officer decides that a further interview is required, he will then resume his examination to determine whether or not to grant the person] leave to enter under any other provision of these Rules. If the person fails at any time to comply with a requirement to report to an Immigration Officer for examination, the Immigration Officer may direct that the person's examination shall be treated as concluded at that time. The Immigration Officer will then consider any outstanding applications for entry on the basis of any evidence before him.]

Note
Paragraph 331 substituted by Cm 3365. Words in further square brackets inserted by HC 704.

332 If a person who has been refused leave to enter applies for asylum and that application is refused, leave to enter will again be refused unless the applicant qualifies for admission under any other provision of these Rules.

333 ...

Note
Paragraph 333 deleted by Cm 4851.

Grant of asylum

334 An asylum applicant will be granted asylum in the United Kingdom if the Secretary of State is satisfied that:

(i)   he is in the United Kingdom or has arrived at a port of entry in the United Kingdom; and
(ii) he is a refugee, as defined by the Convention and Protocol; and
(iii) refusing his application would result in his being required to go (whether immediately or after the time limited by an existing leave to enter or remain) in breach of the Convention and Protocol, to a country in which his life or freedom would be threatened on account of his race, religion, nationality, political opinion or membership of a particular social group.

335 If the Secretary of State decides to grant asylum to a person who has been given leave to enter (whether or not the leave has expired) or to a person who has entered without leave, the Secretary of State will vary the existing leave or grant limited leave to remain.

Refusal of asylum

336 An application which does not meet the criteria set out in paragraph 334 will be refused.

337 ...

338 When a person in the United Kingdom is notified that asylum has been refused he may, if he is liable to removal as an illegal entrant [, removal under section 10 of the Immigration and Asylum Act 1999] or to deportation, at the same time be notified of removal directions, served with a notice of intention to make a deportation order, or served with a deportation order, as appropriate.

Appendix 1 Legislation and materials

339 ...

[Consideration of asylum applications and human rights claims]

340 A failure, without reasonable explanation, to make a prompt and full disclosure of material facts, either orally or in writing, or otherwise to assist the Secretary of State in establishing the facts of the case may lead to refusal of an asylum application [or a human rights claim]. This includes failure to comply with a notice issued by the Secretary of State or an Immigration Officer requiring the applicant [or claimant] to report to a designated place to be fingerprinted, or failure to complete an asylum questionnaire, or failure to comply with a request to attend an interview concerning the application [or claim], or failure to comply with a requirement to report to an Immigration Officer for examination.

[341 In determining an asylum or human rights claim, the Secretary of State will have regard to matters which may damage a claimant's credibility. Among such matters are:

(i)   that the claimant has adduced manifestly false evidence in support of his claim, or has otherwise made false representations, either orally or in writing;
(ii) that the applicant has lodged concurrent claims for asylum in the United Kingdom or in another country.

If the Secretary of State concludes for these or any other reasons that a claimant's account is not credible, the claim will be refused.]

342 The actions of anyone acting as an agent of the asylum applicant [or human rights claimant] may also be taken into account in regard to the matters set out in paragraphs 340 and 341.

343 If there is a part of the country from which the applicant claims to be a refugee in which he would not have a well-founded fear of persecution, and to which it would be reasonable to expect him to go, the application may be refused.

344 Cases will normally be considered on an individual basis but if an applicant is part of a group whose claims are clearly not related to the criteria for refugee status in the Convention and Protocol he may be refused without examination of his individual claim. However, the Secretary of State will have regard to any evidence produced by an individual to show that his claim should be distinguished from those of the rest of the group.

Third country cases

[345

(1)   In a case where the Secretary of State is satisfied that the conditions set out in paragraphs 4 and 5(1), 9 and 10(1), 14 and 15(1) or 17 of Schedule 3 to the Asylum and Immigration (Treatment of Claimants, etc) Act 2004 are fulfilled, he will normally decline to examine the asylum application substantively and issue a certificate under Part 2, 3, 4 or 5 of Schedule 3 to the Asylum and Immigration (Treatment of Claimants, etc) Act 2004 as appropriate.

(2)   The Secretary of State shall not issue a certificate under Part 2, 3, 4 or 5 of Schedule 3 to the Asylum and Immigration (Treatment of Claimants, etc) Act 2004 unless:

   (i)   the asylum applicant has not arrived in the United Kingdom directly from the country in which he claims to fear persecution and has had an opportunity at the border or within the third country or territory to make contact with the authorities of that third country or territory in order to seek their protection; or

   (ii)   there is other clear evidence of his admissibility to a third country or territory.

Provided that he is satisfied that a case meets these criteria, the Secretary of State is under no obligation to consult the authorities of the third country or territory before the removal of an asylum applicant to that country or territory.

(3)   Where a certificate is issued under Part 2, 3, 4 or 5 of Schedule 3 to the Asylum and Immigration (Treatment of Claimants, etc) Act 2004 in relation to the asylum claim and the person is seeking leave to enter the Immigration Officer will consider whether or not he is in a position to decide to give or refuse leave to enter without interviewing the person further. If the Immigration Officer decides that a further interview is not required he may serve the notice giving or refusing leave to enter by post. If the Immigration Officer decides that a further interview is required, he will then resume his examination to determine whether or not to grant the person leave to enter under any other provision of these Rules. If the person fails at any time to comply with a requirement to report to an Immigration Officer for examination, the Immigration Officer may direct that the person's examination shall be treated as concluded at that time. The Immigration Officer will then consider any outstanding applications for entry on the basis of any evidence before him.

(4)   Where a certificate is issued under Part 2, 3, 4 or 5 of Schedule 3 to the Asylum and Immigration (Treatment of Claimants, etc) Act 2004 the person may, if liable to removal as an illegal entrant, or removal under section 10 of the Immigration and Asylum Act 1999 or to deportation, at the same time be notified of removal directions, served with a notice of intention to make a deportation order, or served with a deportation order, as appropriate.]

Note
Paragraph 345 substituted by HC 1112.

Previously rejected applications

346 ...

347 ...

Appendix 1   Legislation and materials

Note
Paragraph 346 deleted by HC 1112.

Rights of appeal

348 ...

Note
Paragraph 348 deleted by Cm 4851.

Dependants

[349 A spouse or minor child accompanying a principal applicant may be included in his application for asylum as his dependant. A spouse or minor child may also claim asylum in his own right. If the principal applicant is granted asylum and leave to enter or remain any spouse or minor child will be granted leave to enter or remain for the same duration. The case of any dependant who claims asylum in his own right will be considered individually in accordance with paragraph 334 above. An applicant under this paragraph, including an accompanied child, may be interviewed where he makes a claim as a dependant or in his own right. If the spouse or minor child in question has a claim in his own right, that claim should be made at the earliest opportunity. Any failure to do so will be taken into account and may damage credibility if no reasonable explanation for it is given. Where an asylum application is unsuccessful, at the same time that asylum is refused the applicant may be notified of removal directions or served with a notice of the Secretary of State's intention to deport him, as appropriate. In this paragraph and paragraphs 350–352 a child means a person who is under 18 years of age or who, in the absence of documentary evidence establishing age, appears to be under that age.]

Note
Paragraph 324 substituted by Cm 5597.

Unaccompanied children

350 Unaccompanied children may also apply for asylum and, in view of their potential vulnerability, particular priority and care is to be given to the handling of their cases.

351 A person of any age may qualify for refugee status under the Convention and the criteria in paragraph 334 apply to all cases. However, account should be taken of the applicant's maturity and in assessing the claim of a child more weight should be given to objective indications of risk than to the child's state of mind and understanding of his situation. An asylum application made on behalf of a child should not be refused solely because the child is too young to understand his situation or to have formed a well founded fear of persecution. Close attention should be given to the welfare of the child at all times.

352 [An accompanied or unaccompanied child who has claimed asylum in his own right may be interviewed about the substance of his claim or to determine his age and identity.] When an interview is necessary it should be conducted in the presence of a parent, guardian, representative or another adult who for the time being takes responsibility for the child and is not an Immigration Officer, an officer of the Secretary of State or a police officer. The interviewer should have particular regard to

the possibility that a child will feel inhibited or alarmed. The child should be allowed to express himself in his own way and at his own speed. If he appears tired or distressed, the interview should be stopped.

Note
Words in square brackets substituted by Cm 5597.

[352A The requirements to be met by a person seeking leave to enter or remain in the United Kingdom as the spouse of a refugee are that:

   (i)   the applicant is married to a person granted asylum in the United Kingdom; and

   (ii)   the marriage did not take place after the person granted asylum left the country of his former habitual residence in order to seek asylum; and

   (iii) the applicant would not be excluded from protection by virtue of article 1F of the United Nations Convention and Protocol relating to the Status of Refugees if he were to seek asylum in his own right; and

[(iv)   each of the parties intends to live permanently with the other as his or her spouse and the marriage is subsisting; and]

[(v)]   if seeking leave to enter, the applicant holds a valid United Kingdom entry clearance for entry in this capacity.

352B Limited leave to enter the United Kingdom as the spouse of a refugee may be granted provided a valid United Kingdom entry clearance for entry in this capacity is produced to the Immigration Officer on arrival. Limited leave to remain in the United Kingdom as the spouse of a refugee may be granted provided the Secretary of State is satisfied that each of the requirements of paragraph 352A(i)–(iii) are met.

352C Limited leave to enter the United Kingdom as the spouse of a refugee is to be refused if a valid United Kingdom entry clearance for entry in this capacity is not produced to the Immigration Officer on arrival. Limited leave to remain as the spouse of a refugee is to be refused if the Secretary of State is not satisfied that each of the requirements of paragraph 352A(i)–(iii) are met.

352D The requirements to be met by a person seeking leave to enter or remain in the United Kingdom [in order to join or remain with the parent who has been granted asylum in the United Kingdom] are that the applicant:

   (i)   is the child of a parent who has been granted asylum in the United Kingdom; and

   (ii)   is under the age of 18, and

   (iii) is not leading an independent life, is unmarried, and has not formed an independent family unit; and

   (iv) was part of the family unit of the person granted asylum at the time that the person granted asylum left the country of his habitual residence in order to seek asylum; and

   (v)   would not be excluded from protection by virtue of article 1F of the United Nations Convention and Protocol relating to the Status of Refugees if he were to seek asylum in his own right; and

   (vi) if seeking leave to enter, holds a valid United Kingdom entry clearance for entry in this capacity.

352E Limited leave to enter the United Kingdom as the child of a refugee may be granted provided a valid United Kingdom entry clearance for entry in this capacity is produced to the Immigration Officer on arrival. Limited leave to remain in the United Kingdom as the child of a refugee may be granted provided the Secretary of State is satisfied that each of the requirements of paragraph 352D(i)–(v) are met.

352F Limited leave to enter the United Kingdom as the child of a refugee is to be refused if a valid United Kingdom entry clearance for entry in this capacity is not produced to the Immigration Officer on arrival. Limited leave to remain as the child of a refugee is to be refused if the Secretary of State is not satisfied that each of the requirements of paragraph 352D (i)–(v) are met.]

Note
Paragraphs 352A–352F inserted by Cm 4851. In paragraph 352A, sub-paragraph (iv) inserted and (v) renumbered by Cm 5597. Words in square brackets in 352D substituted by Cm 5597.

[PART 12
PROCEDURE]

[Fresh Claims]

[353 When a human rights or asylum claim has been refused and any appeal relating to that claim is no longer pending, the decision maker will consider any further submissions and, if rejected, will then determine whether they amount to a fresh claim. The submissions will amount to a fresh claim if they are significantly different from the material that has previously been considered. The submissions will only be significantly different if the content:

(i)   had not already been considered; and
(ii)   taken together with the previously considered material, created a realistic prospect of success, notwithstanding its rejection.

This paragraph does not apply to claims made overseas.]

354–361 [...]

Note
Paragraphs 354–361 deleted by Cm 4851. Paragraph 353 inserted by HC 1112.

[PART 11A
TEMPORARY PROTECTION]

[Definition of Temporary Protection Directive]

[354 For the purposes of paragraphs 355 to 356B, 'Temporary Protection Directive' means Council Directive 2001/55/EC of 20 July 2001 regarding the giving of temporary protection by Member States in the event of a mass influx of displaced persons.]

Note
Paragraphs 354–356B inserted by HC 164.

[Grant of temporary protection]

[355 An applicant for temporary protection will be granted temporary protection if the Secretary of State is satisfied that:

(i)   the applicant is in the United Kingdom or has arrived at a port of entry in the United Kingdom; and

(ii)   the applicant is a person entitled to temporary protection as defined by, and in accordance with, the Temporary Protection Directive; and

(iii)   the applicant does not hold an extant grant of temporary protection entitling him to reside in another Member State of the European Union. This requirement is subject to the provisions relating to dependants set out in paragraphs 356 to 356B and to any agreement to the contrary with the Member State in question; and

(iv)   the applicant is not excluded from temporary protection under the provisions in paragraph 355A.

355A An applicant or a dependant may be excluded from temporary protection if:

(i)   there are serious reasons for considering that:

    (a)   he has committed a crime against peace, a war crime, or a crime against humanity, as defined in the international instruments drawn up to make provision in respect of such crimes; or

    (b)   he has committed a serious non-political crime outside the United Kingdom prior to his application for temporary protection; or

    (c)   he has committed acts contrary to the purposes and principles of the United Nations, or

(ii)   there are reasonable grounds for regarding the applicant as a danger to the security of the United Kingdom or, having been convicted by a final judgment of a particularly serious crime, to be a danger to the community of the United Kingdom.

Consideration under this paragraph shall be based solely on the personal conduct of the applicant concerned. Exclusion decisions or measures shall be based on the principle of proportionality.

355B If temporary protection is granted to a person who has been given leave to enter or remain (whether or not the leave has expired) or to a person who has entered without leave, the Secretary of State will vary the existing leave or grant limited leave to remain.

355C A person to whom temporary protection is granted will be granted limited leave to enter or remain, which is not to be subject to a condition prohibiting employment, for a period not exceeding 12 months. On the expiry of this period, he will be entitled to apply for an extension of this limited leave for successive periods of 6 months thereafter.

355D A person to whom temporary protection is granted will be permitted to return to the United Kingdom from another Member State of the European Union during the period of a mass influx of displaced persons as established by the Council of the European Union pursuant to Article 5 of the Temporary Protection Directive.

355E A person to whom temporary protection is granted will be provided with a document in a language likely to be understood by him in which the provisions relating to temporary protection and which are relevant to him are set out. A person with temporary protection will also be provided with a document setting out his temporary protection status.

355F The Secretary of State will establish and maintain a register of those granted temporary protection. The register will record the name, nationality, date and place of birth and marital status of those granted temporary protection and their family relationship to any other person who has been granted temporary protection.

355G If a person who makes an asylum application is also eligible for temporary protection, the Secretary of State may decide not to consider the asylum application until the applicant ceases to be entitled to temporary protection.]

Note
Paragraphs 354–356B inserted by HC 164.

[Dependants]

[356 In this part:

'dependant' means a family member or a close relative.
'family member' means:
- (i) the spouse of an applicant for, or a person who has been granted, temporary protection; or
- (ii) the unmarried partner of an applicant for, or a person who has been granted, temporary protection where the parties have been living together in a relationship akin to marriage which has subsisted for 2 years or more; or
- (iii) the unmarried minor child of an applicant for, or a person who has been granted, temporary protection or his spouse,

who lived with the principal applicant as part of the family unit in the country of origin immediately prior to the mass influx.
'close relative' means:
- (i) the parent, grandparent or unmarried adult child of an applicant for, or person who has been granted, temporary protection; or
- (ii) the unmarried sibling or the uncle or aunt of an applicant for, or person who has been granted, temporary protection, who lived with the principal applicant as part of the family unit in the country of origin immediately prior to the mass influx and was wholly or mainly dependent upon the principal applicant at that time, and would face extreme hardship if reunification with the principal applicant did not take place.

356A A dependant may apply for temporary protection. Where the dependant falls within paragraph 356 and does not fall to be excluded under paragraph 355A, he will be granted temporary protection for the same duration and under the same conditions as the principal applicant.

356B When considering any application by a dependant child, the Secretary of State shall take into consideration the best interests of that child.]

Note
Paragraphs 354–356B inserted by HC 164.

[PART 11B]

[Reception Conditions for non-EU asylum applicants]

[357 Part 11B only applies to asylum applicants (within the meaning of these Rules) who are not nationals of a member State.]

Note
Paragraphs 357–361 inserted by HC 194.

[Information to be provided to asylum applicants]

[358 The Secretary of State shall inform asylum applicants within a reasonable time not exceeding fifteen days after their claim for asylum has been recorded of the benefits and services that they may be eligible to receive and of the rules and procedures with which they must comply relating to them. The Secretary of State shall also provide information on non-governmental organisations and persons that provide legal assistance to asylum applicants and which may be able to help asylum applicants or provide information on available benefits and services.

358A The Secretary of State shall ensure that the information referred to in paragraph 358 is available in writing and, to the extent possible, will provide the information in a language that asylum applicants may reasonably be supposed to understand. Where appropriate, the Secretary of State may also arrange for this information to be supplied orally.]

Note
Paragraphs 357–361 inserted by HC 194.

[Information to be provided by asylum applicants]

[358B An asylum applicant must notify the Secretary of State of his current address and of any change to his address or residential status. If not notified beforehand, any change must be notified to the Secretary of State without delay after it occurs.]

Note
Paragraphs 357–361 inserted by HC 194.

[Documentation]

[359 The Secretary of State shall ensure that, within three working days of recording an asylum application, a document is made available to that asylum applicant, issued in his own name, certifying his status as an asylum
applicant or testifying that he is allowed to remain in the United Kingdom while his asylum application is pending. For the avoidance of doubt, in cases where the Secretary of State declines to examine an application it will no longer be pending for the purposes of this rule.

359A The obligation in paragraph 359 above shall not apply where the asylum applicant is detained under the Immigration Acts, the Immigration and Asylum Act 1999 or the Nationality, Immigration and Asylum Act 2002.

359B A document issued to an asylum applicant under paragraph 359 does not constitute evidence of the asylum applicant's identity.

359C In specific cases the Secretary of State or an Immigration Officer may provide an asylum applicant with evidence equivalent to that provided under rule 359. This might be, for example, in circumstances in which it is only possible or desirable to issue a time-limited document.]

Appendix 1   Legislation and materials

Note
Paragraphs 357–361 inserted by HC 194.

[Right to request permission to take up employment]

[360 An asylum applicant may apply to the Secretary of State for permission to take up employment which shall not include permission to become self employed or to engage in a business or professional activity if a decision at first instance has not been taken on the applicant's asylum application within one year of the date on which it was recorded. The Secretary of State shall only consider such an application if, in his opinion, any delay in reaching a decision at first instance cannot be attributed to the applicant.

360A If an asylum applicant is granted permission to take up employment under rule 360 this shall only be until such time as his asylum application has been finally determined.]

Note
Paragraphs 357–361 inserted by HC 194.

[Interpretation]

[361 For the purposes of this Part:
(a)   'working day' means any day other than a Saturday or Sunday, a bank holiday, Christmas day or Good Friday;
(b)   'member State' has the same meaning as in Schedule 1 to the European Communities Act 1972.]

Note
Paragraphs 357–361 inserted by HC 194.

PART 13
DEPORTATION [AND ADMINISTRATIVE REMOVAL UNDER SECTION 10 OF THE 1999 ACT]

A deportation order

362 A deportation order requires the subject to leave the United Kingdom and authorises his detention until he is removed. It also prohibits him from re-entering the country for as long as it is in force and invalidates any leave to enter or remain in the United Kingdom given him before the order was made or while it is in force.

[363 The circumstances in which a person is liable to deportation include:
(i)   where the Secretary of State deems the person's deportation to be conducive the public good;
(ii)   where the person is the spouse or child under 18 of a person ordered to be deported; and
(iii)   where a court recommends deportation in the case of a person over the age of 17 who has been convicted of an offence punishable with imprisonment.]

[363A Prior to 2 October 2000, a person would have been liable to deportation in certain circumstances in which he is now liable to administrative removal. These circumstances are listed in paragraph 394B below. However, such a person remains liable to deportation, rather than administrative removal where:

(i)   a decision to make a deportation order against him was taken before 2 October 2000; or

(ii) the person has made a valid application under the Immigration (Regularisation Period for Overstayers) Regulations 2000.]

364 [Subject to paragraph 380] in considering whether deportation is the right course on the merits, the public interest will be balanced against any compassionate circumstances of the case. While each case will be considered in the light of the particular circumstances, the aim is an exercise of the power of deportation which is consistent and fair as between one person and another, although one case will rarely be identical with another in all material respects.

[In the cases detailed in paragraph 363A,] deportation will normally be the proper course where a person has failed to comply with or has contravened a condition or has remained without authority. Before a decision to deport is reached the Secretary of State will take into account all relevant factors known to him including:

(i)   age;
(ii)   length of residence in the United Kingdom;
(iii) strength of connections with the United Kingdom;
(iv)   personal history, including character, conduct and employment record;
(v)   domestic circumstances;
(vi)   previous criminal record and the nature of any offence of which the person has been convicted;
(vii) compassionate circumstances;
(viii) any representations received on the person's behalf.

Note
Words in square brackets in the title to Part 13 inserted by Cm 4851. Paragraph 363 substituted and paragraph 363A and words in square brackets in paragraph 364 inserted by Cm 4851.

Deportation of family members

[365 Section 5 of the Immigration Act 1971 gives the Secretary of State power in certain circumstances to make a deportation order against the spouse or child of a person against whom a deportation order has been made. The Secretary of State will not normally decide to deport the spouse of a deportee where:

(i)   he has qualified for settlement in his own right; or
(ii) he has been living apart from the deportee.]

[366 The Secretary of State will not normally decide to deport the child of a deportee where:

(i)   he and his mother or father are living apart from the deportee; or
(ii)   he has left home and established himself on an independent basis; or
(iii) he married before deportation came into prospect.]

[367 In considering whether to require a spouse or child to leave with the deportee, the Secretary of State will take account of the factors listed in paragraph 364 as well as the following:

(i)   the ability of the spouse to maintain herself and any children in the United Kingdom, or to be maintained by relatives or friends without charge to public funds, not merely for a short period but for the foreseeable future; and
(ii)   in the case of a child of school age, the effect of removal on his education; and
(iii)   the practicability of any plans for a child's care and maintenance in this country if one or both of his parents were deported; and
(iv)   any representations made by or on behalf of the spouse or child.]

368 Where the Secretary of State decides that it would be appropriate to deport a member of a family as such, the decision, and the right of appeal, will be notified and it will at the same time be explained that it is open to the member of the family to leave the country voluntarily if he does not wish to appeal or if he appeals and his appeal is dismissed.

369–374 [...].

Note
Paragraphs 369–374 deleted by Cm 4851.

Hearing of appeals

376 [...]

377 [...]

[378 A deportation order may not be made while it is still open to the person to appeal against the Secretary of State's decision, or while an appeal is pending. There is no appeal within the immigration appeal system against the making of a deportation order on the recommendation of a court; but there is a right of appeal to a higher court against the recommendation itself. A deportation order may not be made while it is still open to the person to appeal against the relevant conviction, sentence or recommendation, or while such an appeal is pending.]

Note
Paragraph 377 deleted and paragraph 378 substituted by Cm 4851.

Persons who have claimed asylum

379–379A [...]

Note
Paragraphs 379 and 379A deleted by Cm 4851.

380 A deportation order will not be made against any person if his removal in pursuance of the order would be contrary to the United Kingdom's obligations under the Convention and Protocol relating to the Status of Refugees [or the Human Rights Convention].

Note
Words in square brackets inserted by Cm 4851.

Procedure

381 When a decision to make a deportation order has been taken (otherwise than on the recommendation of a court) a notice will be given to the person concerned informing him of the decision and of his right of appeal [...].

382 [Following the issue of such a notice the Secretary of State may authorise detention or make an order restricting a person as to residence, employment or occupation and requiring him to report to the police, pending the making of a deportation order.]

383 [...].

384 If a notice of appeal is given within the period allowed, a summary of the facts of the case on the basis of which the decision was taken will be sent to the [appropriate] appellate authorities, who will notify the appellant of the arrangements for the appeal to be heard.

Note
Words in paragraph 381 deleted, paragraph 382 substituted, paragraph 383 deleted and words in square brackets in paragraph 384 inserted by Cm 4851.

Arrangements for removal

385 A person against whom a deportation order has been made will normally be removed from the United Kingdom. The power is to be exercised so as to secure the person's return to the country of which he is a national, or which has most recently provided him with a travel document, unless he can show that another country will receive him. In considering any departure from the normal arrangements, regard will be had to the public interest generally, and to any additional expense that may fall on public funds.

386 The person will not be removed as the subject of a deportation order while an appeal may be brought against the removal directions or such an appeal is pending.

Supervised departure

387 [...]

Note
Paragraph 387 deleted by Cm 4851.

Returned deportees

388 Where a person returns to this country when a deportation order is in force against him, he may be deported under the original order. The Secretary of State will consider every such case in the light of all the relevant circumstances before deciding whether to enforce the order.

Appendix 1 Legislation and materials

Returned family members

389 Persons deported in the circumstances set out in paragraph 365–368 above (deportation of family members) may be able to seek re-admission to the United Kingdom under the Immigration Rules where:

(i)   a child reaches 18 (when he ceases to be subject to the deportation order); or
(ii)   in the case of a wife, the marriage comes to an end.

Revocation of deportation order

390 An application for revocation of a deportation order will be considered in the light of all the circumstances including the following:

(i)   the grounds on which the order was made;
(ii)   any representations made in support of revocation;
(iii)   the interests of the community, including the maintenance of an effective immigration control;
(iv)   the interests of the applicant, including any compassionate circumstances.

391 In the case of an applicant with a serious criminal record continued exclusion for a long term of years will normally be the proper course. In other cases revocation of the order will not normally be authorised unless the situation has been materially altered, either by a change of circumstances since the order was made, or by fresh information coming to light which was not before the court which made the recommendation or the appellate authorities or the Secretary of State. The passage of time since the person was deported may also in itself amount to such a change of circumstances as to warrant revocation of the order. However, save in the most exceptional circumstances, the Secretary of State will not revoke the order unless the person has been absent from the United Kingdom for a period of at least 3 years since it was made.

392 Revocation of a deportation order does not entitle the person concerned to re-enter the United Kingdom; it renders him eligible to apply for admission under the Immigration Rules. Application for revocation of the order may be made to the Entry Clearance Officer or direct to the Home Office.

Rights of appeal in relation to a decision not to revoke a deportation order

393–394 [...]

395 [There may be a right of appeal against refusal to revoke a deportation order.] Where an appeal does lie the right of appeal will be notified at the same time as the decision to refuse to revoke the order.

[Administrative Removal

395A A person is now liable to administrative removal in certain circumstances in which he would, prior to 2 October 2000, have been liable to deportation.

395B These circumstances are set out in section 10 of the 1999 Act. They are:

(i) failure to comply with a condition attached to his leave to enter or remain, or remaining beyond the time limited by the leave;
(ii) where the person has obtained leave to remain by deception; and
(iii) where the person is the spouse or child under 18 of someone in respect of whom directions for removal have been given under section 10.

[395C Before a decision to remove under section 10 is given, regard will be had to all the relevant factors known to the Secretary of State, as listed in paragraph 364. In the case of family members, the factors listed in paragraphs 365–368 must also be taken into account.]

Note
Substituted by Cm 6339.

395D No one shall be removed under section 10 if his removal' would be contrary to the United Kingdom's obligations under the Convention and Protocol relating to the Status of Refugees or under the Human Rights Convention.

Procedure

[395E When a decision that a person is to be removed under section 10 has been given, a notice will be given to the person concerned informing him of the decision and of any right of appeal.]

Note
Substituted by Cm 6339.

395F Following the issue of such a notice an Immigration Officer may authorise detention or make an order restricting a person as to residence, employment or occupation and requiring him to report to the police, pending the removal.]

Note
[Paragraphs 362–395 replace HC 251, paras 155–180.] Paragraphs 393 and 394 deleted, words in square brackets in paragraph 395 inserted and paragraphs 395A to 395F inserted by Cm 4851.

[APPENDIX 1]

[VISA REQUIREMENTS FOR THE UNITED KINGDOM

1 Subject to paragraph 2 below the following persons need a visa for the United Kingdom:

(a) Nationals or citizens of the following countries or territorial entities:

Afghanistan	Georgia	Philippines
Albania	Ghana	Qatar
Algeria	Guinea	Romania
Angola	Guinea-Bissau	Russia
Armenia	Guyana	Rwanda
Azerbaijan	Haiti	Sao Tome e Principe
Bahrain	India	Saudi Arabia
Bangladesh	Indonesia	Senegal
Belarus	Iran	Sierra Leone

Appendix 1   Legislation and materials

Benin	Iraq	[...]
Bhutan	Ivory Coast	Somalia
Bosnia-Herzegovina	Jamaica	Sri Lanka
Bulgaria	Jordan	Sudan
Burkina Faso	Kazakhstan	Surinam
Burma	Kenya	Syria
Burundi	Kirgizstan	Taiwan
Cambodia	Korea (North)	Tajikistan
Cameroon	Laos	Tanzania
Cape Verde	Lebanon	Thailand
Central African Republic	Liberia	Togo
Chad	Libya	Tunisia
[People's Republic of	Macedonia	Turkey
China (except those		
referred to in		
sub-paragraph 2(d) and		
(e) of this Appendix]		
[Colombia]	Madagascar	Turkmenistan
Comoros	...	Uganda
Congo	Mali	Ukraine
[Republic of Croatia]	Mauritania	United Arab Emirates
Cuba	Moldova	Uzbekistan
[Democratic Republic of	Mongolia	Vietnam
the Congo (Zaire)]		
Djibouti	Morocco	Yemen
Dominican Republic	Mozambique	The territories formerly
		comprising the Socialist
		Federal Republic of
		Yugoslavia excluding
		Croatia and Slovenia.
Ecuador	Nepal	Zambia
Egypt	Niger	Zimbabwe
Equatorial Guinea	Nigeria	
Eritrea	Oman	
Ethiopia	Pakistan	
Fiji	...	
Gabon	Peru	

(b)   Persons who hold passports or travel documents issued by the former Soviet Union or by the former Socialist Federal Republic of Yugoslavia.

(c)   Stateless persons.

(d)   Persons who hold non-national documents.

2 The following persons do not need a visa for the United Kingdom:

(a)   those who qualify for admission to the United Kingdom as returning residents in accordance with paragraph 18;

[(b)   those who seek leave to enter the United Kingdom within the period of their earlier leave and for the same purpose as that for which leave was granted, unless it:

    (i)   was for a period of six months or less; or

    (ii)   was extended by statutory instrument [or by section 3C of the Immigration Act 1971 (inserted by section 3 of the Immigration and Asylum Act 1999];]

...

[(d) those nationals or citizens of the People's Republic of China holding passports issued by Hong Kong Special Administrative Region; or

(e) those nationals or citizens of the People's Republic of China holding passports issued by Macao Special Administrative Region.]

[(f) those who arrive in the United Kingdom with leave to enter which is in force but which was given before arrival so long as those in question arrive within the period of their earlier leave and for the same purpose as that for which leave was granted, unless that leave—

    (i) was for a period of six months or less, or

    (ii) was extended by statutory instrument or by section 3C of the Immigration Act 1971 (inserted by section 3 of the Immigration and Asylum Act 1999).]

Note

Appendix amended by Statement of Changes in Immigration Rules with effect from 4 April 1996. Renamed Appendix 1 with effect from 11 May 1998 (Cmnd 3953). Republic of Croatia added by HC 22. People's Republic of China amended by HC 735. Maldives, Mauritius and Papua New Guinea deleted by HC 104. Jamaica inserted by HC 180. Zimbabwe inserted by HC 1301. Slovak Republic deleted by HC 95. Sub-paragraphs 2(d) and (e) inserted by HC 735. Sub-paragraph 2(c) deleted by HC 389. Words in square brackets in 2(b)(ii) and sub-paragraph (f)(i) and (ii) inserted by HC 104.

Readers are warned that in relation to this Appendix in particular amendments are made periodically and often without prior warning.

[APPENDIX 2

COUNTRIES OR TERRITORIES WHOSE NATIONALS OR CITIZENS ARE RELEVANT FOREIGN NATIONALS FOR THE PURPOSES OF PART 10 OF THESE RULES (REGISTRATION WITH THE POLICE)

(Paragraph 324A)

Afghanistan	Iran	Qatar
Algeria	Iraq	Russia
Argentina	Israel	Saudi Arabia
Armenia	Jordan	Sudan
Azerbaijan	Kazakhstan	Syria
Bahrain	Kirgizstan	Tajikistan
Belarus	Kuwait	Tunisia
Bolivia	Lebanon	Turkey
Bhutan	Libya	Turkmenistan
Brazil	Moldova	United Arab Emirates
China	Morocco	Ukraine
Colombia	North Korea	Uzbekistan
Cuba	Oman	Yemen]
Egypt	Palestine	
Georgia	Peru	

Note

Appendix 2 added with effect from 11 May 1998 by Cmnd 3953.

Appendix 1 Legislation and materials

[APPENDIX 3]

[SPECIFIED NATIONALS: ENTRY CLEARANCE REQUIREMENTS FOR THE
UNITED KINGDOM

Nationals or citizens of the following countries who seek leave to enter the United
Kingdom for a period of more than 6 months need an entry clearance for the United
Kingdom issued for the purpose for which entry is sought:

Australia,
Canada,
Hong Kong (other than British Nationals (Overseas) under section 2(1) of the Hong
Kong Act 1985),
Japan,
Malaysia,
New Zealand,
Singapore,
South Africa,
South Korea,
United States of America.]

[List of countries participating in the Working Holidaymaker scheme

Antigua and Barbuda,
Australia,
The Bahamas,
Bangladesh,
Barbados,
Belize,
Botswana,
Brunei Darussalam,
Canada,
Cameroon,
Dominica,
Fiji Islands,
The Gambia,
Ghana,
Grenada,
Guyana,
India,
Jamaica,
Kenya,
Kiribati,
Malawi,
Malaysia,
Maldives,
Mauritius,
Mozambique,
Namibia,
Nauru,
New Zealand,
Nigeria,
Pakistan,

2028

Papua New Guinea,
Saint Christopher and Nevis,
Saint Lucia,
Saint Vincent and the Grenadines,
Seychelles,
Sierra Leone,
Singapore,
Solomon Islands,
South Africa,
Sri Lanka,
Swaziland,
Tanzania, United Republic of,
Tonga,
Trinidad and Tobago,
Tuvalu,
Uganda,
Vanuatu,
Western Samoa,
Zambia,
Zimbabwe.]

Note
Appendix 3 inserted by HC 1224. List of countries participating in the Working Holidaymaker scheme inserted by HC 302.

PROCEDURE RULES, PRACTICE DIRECTIONS ETC

CIVIL PROCEDURE RULES 1998

1998 No 3132

Made . . . .*10th December 1998*

Laid before Parliament . . . .*17th December 1998*

Coming into force . . . .*26th April 1999*

The Civil Procedure Rule Committee, having power under section 2 of the Civil Procedure Act 1997 to make rules of court under section 1 of that Act, make the following rules which may be cited as the Civil Procedure Rules 1998:

PART 54
JUDICIAL REVIEW AND STATUTORY REVIEW

[SECTION II—STATUTORY REVIEW UNDER THE NATIONALITY, IMMIGRATION AND ASYLUM ACT 2002]

[Rule   54.21   Scope and interpretation]

[(1)   This Section of this Part contains rules about applications to the High Court under section 101(2) of the Nationality, Immigration and Asylum Act 2002 for a review of a decision of the Immigration Appeal Tribunal on an application for permission to appeal from an adjudicator.

(2)   In this Section—

   (a)   "the Act" means the Nationality, Immigration and Asylum Act 2002;

   (b)   "adjudicator" means an adjudicator appointed for the purposes of Part 5 of the Act;

   (c)   "applicant" means a person applying to the High Court under section 101(2) of the Act;

   (d)   "other party" means the other party to the proceedings before the Tribunal; and

   (e)   "Tribunal" means the Immigration Appeal Tribunal.]

Amendment
Inserted by SI 2003/364, r 5(f), Schedule, Pt 2. Date in force: 1 April 2003 (being the date on which the Nationality, Immigration and Asylum Act 2002, ss 81–117 came into force): see SI 2003/364, r 1 and SI 2003/754, art 2(1), Sch 1; for transitional provisions see SI 2003/754, art 3, and Sch 2, para 1(4A), (4B) (as amended by SI 2003/1339, art 4) and (5).

[Rule   54.22   Application for review]

[(1)   An application under section 101(2) of the Act must be made to the Administrative Court.

(2)   The application must be made by filing an application notice.

(3)   The applicant must file with the application notice—

   [(a)   the immigration or asylum decision to which the proceedings relate, and any document giving reasons for that decision;]

   (b)   the grounds of appeal to the adjudicator;

   (c)   the adjudicator's determination;

   (d)   the grounds of appeal to the Tribunal together with any documents sent with them;

   (e)   the Tribunal's determination on the application for permission to appeal; and

(f)   any other documents material to the application which were before the adjudicator.

(4)   The applicant must also file with the application notice written submissions setting out—

(a)   the grounds upon which it is contended that the Tribunal made an error of law; and
(b)   reasons in support of those grounds.

(5)   ...]

Amendment
Inserted by SI 2003/364, r 5(f), Schedule, Pt 2. Date in force: 1 April 2003 (being the date on which the Nationality, Immigration and Asylum Act 2002, ss 81–117 came into force): see SI 2003/364, r 1 and SI 2003/754, art 2(1), Sch 1; for transitional provisions see SI 2003/754, art 3, and Sch 2, para 1(4A), (4B) (as amended by SI 2003/1339, art 4) and (5).
Para (3): sub-para (a) substituted by SI 2003/1329, r 4(a). Date in force: 9 June 2003: see SI 2003/1329, r 1.
Para (5): revoked by SI 2003/1329, r 4(b). Date in force: 9 June 2003: see SI 2003/1329, r 1.

[Rule   54.23   Time limit for application]

[(1)   The application notice must be filed not later than 14 days after the applicant is deemed to have received notice of the Tribunal's decision in accordance with rules made under section 106 of the Act.

(2)   The court may extend the time limit in paragraph (1) in exceptional circumstances.

(3)   An application to extend the time limit must be made in the application notice and supported by written evidence verified by a statement of truth.]

Amendment
Inserted by SI 2003/364, r 5(f), Schedule, Pt 2. Date in force: 1 April 2003 (being the date on which the Nationality, Immigration and Asylum Act 2002, ss 81–117 came into force): see SI 2003/364, r 1 and SI 2003/754, art 2(1), Sch 1; for transitional provisions see SI 2003/754, art 3, and Sch 2, para 1(4A), (4B) (as amended by SI 2003/1339, art 4) and (5).

[Rule   54.24   Service of application]

[(1)   The applicant must serve on the [Asylum and Immigration Tribunal] copies of the application notice and written submissions.

(2)   Where an application is for review of a decision by the Tribunal to grant permission to appeal, the applicant must serve on the other party copies of—

(a)   the application notice;
(b)   the written submissions; and
(c)   all the documents filed in support of the application, except for documents which come from or have already been served on that party.

(3)   Where documents are required to be served under paragraphs (1) and (2), they must be served as soon as practicable after they are filed.]

Amendment
Inserted by SI 2003/364, r 5(f), Schedule, Pt 2. Date in force: 1 April 2003 (being the date on which the Nationality, Immigration and Asylum Act 2002, ss 81–117 came into force): see SI 2003/364, r 1 and SI 2003/754, art 2(1), Sch 1; for transitional provisions see SI 2003/754, art 3, and Sch 2, para 1(4A), (4B) (as amended by SI 2003/1339, art 4) and (5).
Para (1): words "Asylum and Immigration Tribunal" in square brackets substituted by SI 2005/352, r 4. Date in force: 4 April 2005: see SI 2005/352, r 1; for transitional provisions see r 9 thereof.

[Rule   54.25   Determining the application]

[(1)   The application will be determined by a single judge without a hearing, and by reference only to the written submissions and the documents filed with them.

(2)   If the applicant relies on evidence which was not submitted to the adjudicator or the Tribunal, the court will not consider that evidence unless it is satisfied that there were good reasons why it was not submitted to the adjudicator or the Tribunal.]

[(3)   The court may—

    (a)   affirm the Tribunal's decision to refuse permission to appeal;
    (b)   reverse the Tribunal's decision to grant permission to appeal; or
    (c)   order the Asylum and Immigration Tribunal to reconsider the adjudicator's decision on the appeal.

(4)   Where the Tribunal refused permission to appeal, the court will order the Asylum and Immigration Tribunal to reconsider the adjudicator's decision on the appeal only if it is satisfied that—

    (a)   the Tribunal may have made an error of law; and
    (b)   there is a real possibility that the Asylum and Immigration Tribunal would make a different decision from the adjudicator on reconsidering the appeal (which may include making a different direction under section 87 of the 2002 Act).

(5)   Where the Tribunal granted permission to appeal, the court will reverse the Tribunal's decision only if it is satisfied that there is no real possibility that the Asylum and Immigration Tribunal, on reconsidering the adjudicator's decision on the appeal, would make a different decision from the adjudicator.

(6)   The court's decision shall be final and there shall be no appeal from that decision or renewal of the application.]

Amendment
Inserted by SI 2003/364, r 5(f), Schedule, Pt 2. Date in force: 1 April 2003 (being the date on which the Nationality, Immigration and Asylum Act 2002, ss 81–117 came into force): see SI 2003/364, r 1 and SI 2003/754, art 2(1), Sch 1; for transitional provisions see SI 2003/754, art 3, and Sch 2, para 1(4A), (4B) (as amended by SI 2003/1339, art 4) and (5).
Paras (3)–(6): substituted, for paras (3)–(7) as originally enacted, by SI 2005/352, r 5. Date in force: 4 April 2005: see SI 2005/352, r 1; for transitional provisions see r 9 thereof.

[Rule   54.26   Service of order]

[(1)   The court will send copies of its order to—

    (a)   the applicant, except where paragraph (2) applies;
    (b)   the other party; and
    (c)   the [Asylum and Immigration Tribunal].

(2)   Where—

    (a)   the application relates, in whole or in part, to a claim for asylum;
    (b)   the Tribunal refused permission to appeal; and
    (c)   the court affirms the Tribunal's decision,

the court will send a copy of its order to the Secretary of State, who must serve the order on the applicant.

(3)   Where the Secretary of State has served an order in accordance with paragraph (2), he must notify the court on what date and by what method the order was served.

(4)   If the court issues a certificate under section 101(3)(d) of the Act, it will send a copy of the certificate together with the order to—

    (a)   the persons to whom it sends the order under paragraphs (1) and (2); and

    (b)   if the applicant is in receipt of public funding, the Legal Services Commission.]

Amendment
Inserted by SI 2003/364, r 5(f), Schedule, Pt 2. Date in force: 1 April 2003 (being the date on which the Nationality, Immigration and Asylum Act 2002, ss 81–117 came into force): see SI 2003/364, r 1 and SI 2003/754, art 2(1), Sch 1; for transitional provisions see SI 2003/754, art 3, and Sch 2, para 1(4A), (4B) (as amended by SI 2003/1339, art 4) and (5).
Para (1): in sub-para (c) words "Asylum and Immigration Tribunal" in square brackets substituted by SI 2005/352, r 6. Date in force: 4 April 2005: see SI 2005/352, r 1; for transitional provisions see r 9 thereof.

[Rule   54.27   Costs]

[The court may reserve the costs of the application to be determined by the [A]sylum and Immigration Tribunal].

Amendment
Inserted by SI 2003/364, r 5(f), Schedule, Pt 2. Date in force: 1 April 2003 (being the date on which the Nationality, Immigration and Asylum Act 2002, ss 81–117 came into force): see SI 2003/364, r 1 and SI 2003/754, art 2(1), Sch 1; for transitional provisions see SI 2003/754, art 3, and Sch 2, para 1(4A), (4B) (as amended by SI 2003/1339, art 4) and (5).
Words "Asylum and Immigration Tribunal" in square brackets substituted by SI 2005/352, r 6. Date in force: 4 April 2005: see SI 2005/352, r 1; for transitional provisions see r 9 thereof.

[SECTION III—APPLICATIONS FOR STATUTORY REVIEW UNDER SECTION 103A OF THE NATIONALITY, IMMIGRATION AND ASYLUM ACT 2002]

[54.28   Scope and interpretation]

[(1)   This Section of this Part contains rules about applications to the High Court under section 103A of the Nationality, Immigration and Asylum Act 2002 for an order requiring the Asylum and Immigration Tribunal to reconsider its decision on an appeal.

(2)   In this Section—

    (a)   "the 2002 Act" means the Nationality, Immigration and Asylum Act 2002;

    (b)   "the 2004 Act" means the Asylum and Immigration (Treatment of Claimants, etc) Act 2004;

    (c)   "appellant" means the appellant in the proceedings before the Tribunal;

    (d)   "applicant" means a person applying to the High Court under section 103A;

    (e)   "asylum claim" has the meaning given in section 113(1) of the 2002 Act;

    (f)   "filter provision" means paragraph 30 of Schedule 2 to the 2004 Act;

    (g)   "order for reconsideration" means an order under section 103A(1) requiring the Tribunal to reconsider its decision on an appeal;

    (h)   "section 103A" means section 103A of the 2002 Act;

    (i)   "Tribunal" means the Asylum and Immigration Tribunal.

(3)   Any reference in this Section to a period of time specified in—

    (a)   section 103A(3) for making an application for an order under section 103A(1); or

    (b)   paragraph 30(5)(b) of Schedule 2 to the 2004 Act for giving notice under that paragraph,

includes a reference to that period as varied by any order under section 26(8) of the 2004 Act.

(4)   Rule 2.8 applies to the calculation of the periods of time specified in—

(a)   section 103A(3); and
(b)   paragraph 30(5)(b) of Schedule 2 to the 2004 Act.

(5)   Save as provided otherwise, the provisions of this Section apply to an application under section 103A regardless of whether the filter provision has effect in relation to that application.]

Amendment
Inserted by SI 2005/352, r 7, Schedule, Pt II. Date in force: 4 April 2005: see SI 2005/352, r 1; for transitional provisions see r 9 thereof.

[54.29   Application for review]

[(1)   Subject to paragraph (4), an application for an order for reconsideration must be made by filing an application notice—

(a)   during a period in which the filter provision has effect, with the Tribunal at the address specified in the relevant practice direction; and
(b)   at any other time, at the Administrative Court Office.

(2)   The applicant must file with the application notice—

(a)   the notice of the immigration, asylum or nationality decision to which the appeal related;
(b)   any other document which was served on the appellant giving reasons for that decision;
(c)   the grounds of appeal to the Tribunal;
(d)   the Tribunal's determination on the appeal; and
(e)   any other documents material to the application which were before the Tribunal.

(3)   The applicant must also file with the application notice written submissions setting out—

(a)   the grounds upon which it is contended that the Tribunal made an error of law which may have affected its decision; and
(b)   reasons in support of those grounds.

(4)   Where the applicant—

(a)   was the respondent to the appeal; and
(b)   was required to serve the Tribunal's determination on the appellant,

the application notice must contain a statement of the date on which, and the means by which, the determination was served.

(5)   Where the applicant is in detention under the Immigration Acts, the application may be made either—

(a)   in accordance with paragraphs (1) to (3); or
(b)   by serving the documents specified in paragraphs (1) to (3) on the person having custody of him.

(6)   Where an application is made in accordance with paragraph (5)(b), the person on whom the application notice is served must—

(a)   endorse on the notice the date that it is served on him;
(b)   give the applicant an acknowledgment in writing of receipt of the notice; and
(c)   forward the notice and documents within 2 days—
      (i)   during a period in which the filter provision has effect, to the Tribunal; and

2037

(ii) at any other time, to the Administrative Court Office.]

Amendment
Inserted by SI 2005/352, r 7, Schedule, Pt II. Date in force: 4 April 2005: see SI 2005/352, r 1; for transitional provisions see r 9 thereof.

[54.30 Application to extend time limit]

[An application to extend the time limit for making an application under section 103A(1) must—

(a) be made in the application notice;
(b) set out the grounds on which it is contended that the application notice could not reasonably practicably have been filed within the time limit; and
(c) be supported by written evidence verified by a statement of truth.]

Amendment
Inserted by SI 2005/352, r 7, Schedule, Pt II. Date in force: 4 April 2005: see SI 2005/352, r 1; for transitional provisions see r 9 thereof.

[54.31 Procedure while filter provision has effect]

[(1) This rule applies during any period in which the filter provision has effect.

(2) Where the applicant receives notice from the Tribunal that it—

(a) does not propose to make an order for reconsideration; or
(b) does not propose to grant permission for the application to be made outside the relevant time limit,

and the applicant wishes the court to consider the application, the applicant must file a notice in writing at the Administrative Court Office in accordance with paragraph 30(5)(b) of Schedule 2 to the 2004 Act.

(3) Where the applicant—

(a) was the respondent to the appeal; and
(b) was required to serve the notice from the Tribunal mentioned in paragraph (2) on the appellant,

the notice filed in accordance with paragraph 30(5)(b) of Schedule 2 to the 2004 Act must contain a statement of the date on which, and the means by which, the notice from the Tribunal was served.

(4) A notice which is filed outside the period specified in paragraph 30(5)(b) must—

(a) set out the grounds on which it is contended that the notice could not reasonably practicably have been filed within that period; and
(b) be supported by written evidence verified by a statement of truth.

(5) If the applicant wishes to respond to the reasons given by the Tribunal for its decision that it—

(a) does not propose to make an order for reconsideration; or
(b) does not propose to grant permission for the application to be made outside the relevant time limit,

the notice filed in accordance with paragraph 30(5)(b) of Schedule 2 to the 2004 Act must be accompanied by written submissions setting out the grounds upon which the applicant disputes any of the reasons given by the Tribunal and giving reasons in support of those grounds.]

Amendment
Inserted by SI 2005/352, r 7, Schedule, Pt II. Date in force: 4 April 2005: see SI 2005/352, r 1; for transitional provisions see r 9 thereof.

[54.32   Procedure in fast track cases while filter provision does not have effect]

[(1)   This rule applies only during a period in which the filter provision does not have effect.

(2)   Where a fast track order applies to an application under section 103A—

  (a)   the court will serve copies of the application notice and written submissions on the other party to the appeal; and
  (b)   the other party to the appeal may file submissions in response to the application not later than 2 days after being served with the application.

(3)   In this Rule, a "fast track order" means an order made under section 26(8) of the 2004 Act which replaces a period of time specified in section 103A(3) of the 2002 Act with a period shorter than 5 days.]

Amendment
Inserted by SI 2005/352, r 7, Schedule, Pt II. Date in force: 4 April 2005: see SI 2005/352, r 1; for transitional provisions see r 9 thereof.

[54.33   Determination of the application by the Administrative Court]

[(1)   This rule, and rules 54.34 and 54.35, apply to applications under section 103A which are determined by the Administrative Court.

(2)   The application will be considered by a single judge without a hearing.

(3)   Unless it orders otherwise, the court will not receive evidence which was not submitted to the Tribunal.

(4)   Subject to paragraph (5), where the court determines an application for an order for reconsideration, it may—

  (a)   dismiss the application;
  (b)   make an order requiring the Tribunal to reconsider its decision on the appeal under section 103A(1) of the 2002 Act; or
  (c)   refer the appeal to the Court of Appeal under section 103C of the 2002 Act.

(5)   The court will only make an order requiring the Tribunal to reconsider its decision on an appeal if it thinks that—

  (a)   the Tribunal may have made an error of law; and
  (b)   there is a real possibility that the Tribunal would make a different decision on reconsidering the appeal (which may include making a different direction under section 87 of the 2002 Act).

(6)   Where the Court of Appeal has restored the application to the court under section 103C(2)(g) of the 2002 Act, the court may not refer the appeal to the Court of Appeal.

(7)   The court's decision shall be final and there shall be no appeal from that decision or renewal of the application.]

Amendment
Inserted by SI 2005/352, r 7, Schedule, Pt II. Date in force: 4 April 2005: see SI 2005/352, r 1; for transitional provisions see r 9 thereof.

Appendix 1   Legislation and materials

[54.34   Service of order]

[(1)   The court will send copies of its order to—

    (a)   the applicant and the other party to the appeal, except where paragraph (2) applies; and

    (b)   the Tribunal.

(2)   Where the application relates, in whole or in part, to an asylum claim, the court will send a copy of its order to the Secretary of State.

(3)   Where the court sends an order to the Secretary of State under paragraph (2), the Secretary of State must—

    (a)   serve the order on the appellant; and

    (b)   immediately after serving the order, notify the court on what date and by what method the order was served.

(4)   The Secretary of State must provide the notification required by paragraph (3)(b) no later than 28 days after the date on which the court sends him a copy of its order.

(5)   If, 28 days after the date on which the court sends a copy of its order to the Secretary of State in accordance with paragraph (2), the Secretary of State has not provided the notification required by paragraph (3)(b), the court may serve the order on the appellant.

(6)   If the court makes an order under section 103D(1) of the 2002 Act, it will send copies of that order to—

    (a)   the appellant's legal representative; and

    (b)   the Legal Services Commission.

(7)   Where paragraph (2) applies, the court will not serve copies of an order under section 103D(1) of the 2002 Act until either—

    (a)   the Secretary of State has provided the notification required by paragraph (3)(b); or

    (b)   28 days after the date on which the court sent a copy of its order to the Secretary of State,

whichever is the earlier.]

Amendment
Inserted by SI 2005/352, r 7, Schedule, Pt II. Date in force: 4 April 2005: see SI 2005/352, r 1; for transitional provisions see r 9 thereof.

[54.35   Costs]

[The court shall make no order as to the costs of an application under this Section except, where appropriate, an order under section 103D(1) of the 2002 Act.]

Amendment
Inserted by SI 2005/352, r 7, Schedule, Pt II. Date in force: 4 April 2005: see SI 2005/352, r 1; for transitional provisions see r 9 thereof.

PRACTICE DIRECTION 54B

APPLICATIONS FOR STATUTORY REVIEW UNDER SECTION 103A OF THE NATIONALITY, IMMIGRATION AND ASYLUM ACT 2002

(THIS PRACTICE DIRECTION SUPPLEMENTS SECTION III OF CPR PART 54)

REFERRAL   TO COURT OF APPEAL

1   Attention is drawn to:

- Sections 103A, 103C and 103D of the Nationality, Immigration and Asylum Act 2002 (inserted by section 26(6) of the Asylum and Immigration (Treatment of Claimants, etc) Act 2004); and
- Paragraph 30 of Schedule 2 to the 2004 Act.

THE COURT

2.1   Applications for review under section 103A(1) of the 2002 Act are dealt with in the Administrative Court, subject to the transitional filter provision in paragraph 30 of Schedule 2 of the 2004 Act which provides that they shall initially be considered by a member of the Tribunal.

2.2   During any period in which the filter provision has effect, the address for filing section 103A applications shall be the Asylum and Immigration Tribunal, P.O. Box 6987, Leicester LE1 6ZX.

2.3   Where a fast track order within the meaning of Rule 54.32(3) applies to a section 103A application, paragraph 2.2 shall not apply and the address for filing the application shall be the address specified in the Tribunal's determination of the appeal.

ACCESS   TO COURT ORDERS SERVED ON THE APPELLANT BY THE SECRETARY OF STATE

3.1   Where the court sends a copy of its order on a section 103A application to the Secretary of State but not the appellant in accordance with Rule 54.34(2), then Rules 5.4(3)(b) and 5.4(5)(a)(ii) are modified as follows.

3.2   Neither the appellant nor any other person may obtain from the records of the court a copy of the court's order on the section 103A application, or of any order made under section 103D(1) of the 2002 Act in relation to that application, until either the Secretary of State has given the court the notification required by Rule 54.34(3)(b) or 28 days after the date on which the court sent a copy of the order to the Secretary of State, whichever is the earlier.

REFERRAL   TO COURT OF APPEAL

4.1   Where the court refers an appeal to the Court of Appeal, its order will set out the question of law raised by the appeal which is of such importance that it should be decided by the Court of Appeal.

4.2   Paragraph 21.7A of the practice direction supplementing Part 52 makes provision about appeals which are referred to the Court of Appeal.

ASYLUM SUPPORT APPEALS (PROCEDURE) RULES 2000

2000 No 541

Made . . . . *2nd March 2000*

Laid before Parliament . . . . *10th March 2000*

Coming into force . . . . *3rd April 2000*

The Secretary of State, in exercise of the powers conferred on him by sections 104 and 166(3) of the Immigration and Asylum Act 1999, after consultation with the Council on Tribunals in accordance with section 8 of the Tribunals and Inquiries Act 1992, and having regard to the desirability of securing, so far as is reasonably practicable, that appeals are brought and disposed of with the minimum of delay, hereby makes the following Rules:

General

1   Title and commencement

These Rules may be cited as the Asylum Support Appeals (Procedure) Rules 2000 and shall come into force on 3rd April 2000.

Initial Commencement
Specified date: 3 April 2000: see above.

2   Interpretation

(1)   In these Rules—

"the Act" means the Immigration and Asylum Act 1999;

"adjudication" means a decision of an adjudicator made in accordance with section 103(3) of the Act;

"appeal bundle" means a bundle prepared by the Secretary of State containing copies of the following documents:

(a)   the form on which the appellant made a claim for support under section 95 of the Act, if the appeal is made under section 103(1) of the Act;

(b)   any supporting documentation attached to that form;

(c)   the decision letter; and

(d)   other material relied on by the Secretary of State in reaching his decision;

"appellant" means a person who appeals under section 103 of the Act against a decision of the Secretary of State;

"bank holiday" means a day that is specified in, or appointed under, the Banking and Financial Dealings Act 1971;

"consideration day" has the meaning given to it by rule 4(4);

"decision letter" means a letter from the Secretary of State giving notice of a decision that gives rise to a right to appeal under section 103;

"excluded day" means a Saturday, a Sunday, a bank holiday, Christmas Day or Good Friday;

"member of the adjudicators' staff" means a person appointed by the Secretary of State under paragraph 5(1) of Schedule 10 to the Act;

"notice of appeal" has the meaning given to it by rule 3(1); and

"party" includes the appellant and the Secretary of State.

(2)   Any reference in these Rules:

(a) to an adjudicator, in relation to the sending, giving or receiving of notices or other documents, whether by an adjudicator or a party to the appeal, includes a reference to a member of the adjudicators' staff;

(b) to an adjudicator, in relation to the receiving of a notice of appeal by him, includes a reference to the offices occupied by the adjudicators;

(c) to the appellant, in relation to the sending or giving of notices or other documents by the adjudicator or the Secretary of State, is also a reference to his representative, if he has one; and

(d) to a representative is to be construed in accordance with rule 15.

(3) For the purposes of these Rules, an appeal is determined when an adjudicator gives his adjudication.

Initial Commencement
Specified date: 3 April 2000: see r 1.

Procedure before determination of appeal

3 Notice of appeal

(1) A person who wishes to appeal under section 103 of the Act must give notice to an adjudicator by completing in full, and in English, the form for the time being issued by the Secretary of State for the purpose ("notice of appeal"); and any form so issued is to be in the form shown in the Schedule to these Rules or a form to like effect.

(2) The notice of appeal must be signed by the appellant or his representative.

(3) Subject to paragraph (4), the notice of appeal must be received by the adjudicator not later than [3 days] after the day on which the appellant received the decision letter.

(4) The adjudicator may extend the time limit for receiving the notice of appeal (either before or after its expiry) if:

(a) he considers that it is in the interests of justice to do so; and

(b) he is satisfied that:
  (i) the appellant; or
  (ii) his representative (if he has one);
was prevented from complying with the time limit by circumstances beyond his control.

Initial Commencement
Specified date: 3 April 2000: see r 1.

Amendment
Para (3): words "3 days" in square brackets substituted by SI 2003/1735, rr 2, 3. Date in force: 11 August 2003 (except in relation to decision letters received by appellants before that date): see SI 2003/1735, r 1.

Amendment

4 Procedure after receiving notice of appeal

(1) On the day that the adjudicator receives notice of appeal or, if not reasonably practicable, as soon as possible on the following day, he must send a copy of the notice of appeal, and any supporting documents, to the Secretary of State by fax.

(2) [2 days after the day] on which the adjudicator receives notice of appeal, the Secretary of State must send the appeal bundle to the adjudicator by fax or by hand and to the appellant by first class post or by fax.

(3) On consideration day, the adjudicator must:

    (a)   decide in accordance with rule 5 whether there should be an oral hearing;
    (b)   set the date for determining the appeal in accordance with rule 6;
    (c)   if there is to be an oral hearing, give notice to the Secretary of State and the appellant, in accordance with rule 7, of the date on which it is to be held.

(4)   "Consideration day" means the day after the day on which the Secretary of State sends the appeal bundle to the adjudicator in accordance with paragraph (2).

Initial Commencement
Specified date: 3 April 2000: see r 1.

Amendment
Para (2): words "2 days after the day" in square brackets substituted by SI 2003/1735, rr 2, 4. Date in force: 11 August 2003 (except in relation to decision letters received by appellants before that date): see SI 2003/1735, r 1.

5   Whether there should be an oral hearing

(1)   The adjudicator must decide to hold an oral hearing:

    (a)   where the appellant has requested an oral hearing in his notice of appeal; or
    (b)   if the adjudicator considers that it is necessary for the appeal to be disposed of justly.

(2)   In all other cases, the appeal may be determined without an oral hearing.

Initial Commencement
Specified date: 3 April 2000: see r 1.

6   Date for determination of appeal

(1)   If there is to be an oral hearing, the hearing must be held and the appeal determined [not later than 5 days] after consideration day.

(2)   In all other cases, the appeal must be determined on consideration day, or as soon as possible thereafter, but in any event not later than [5 days] after consideration day.

Initial Commencement
Specified date: 3 April 2000: see r 1.

Amendment
Para (1): words "not later than 5 days" in square brackets substituted by SI 2003/1735, rr 2, 5. Date in force: 11 August 2003 (except in relation to decision letters received by appellants before that date): see SI 2003/1735, r 1.
Para (2): words "5 days" in square brackets substituted by SI 2003/1735, rr 2, 6. Date in force: 11 August 2003 (except in relation to decision letters received by appellants before that date): see SI 2003/1735, r 1.

7   Notification of date of oral hearing

If there is to be an oral hearing, the adjudicator must send a notice to the appellant and to the Secretary of State informing them of the date, time and place of the hearing.

Initial Commencement
Specified date: 3 April 2000: see r 1.

8   Further evidence provided before the determination of the appeal

(1)   Where the appellant sends to the adjudicator evidence to which this paragraph applies, the appellant must at the same time send a copy of such evidence to the Secretary of State.

(2) Paragraph (1) applies to evidence which is sent after the appellant has sent notice of appeal to the adjudicator but before the appeal has been determined.

(3) Where the Secretary of State sends to the adjudicator evidence to which this paragraph applies, the Secretary of State must at the same time send a copy of such evidence to the appellant.

(4) Paragraph (3) applies to evidence which is sent after the Secretary of State has sent the appeal bundle to the adjudicator but before the appeal has been determined.

Initial Commencement
Specified date: 3 April 2000: see r 1.

Determination of appeal

9 Hearing of appeal in absence of either party

(1) If an appellant has indicated in his notice of appeal that he does not want to attend, or be represented at, an oral hearing, the hearing may proceed in his absence.

(2) Where:

    (a) an appellant has indicated in his notice of appeal that he wants to attend, or be represented at, an oral hearing;
    (b) he has been notified of the date, time and place of the hearing in accordance with rule 7; and
    (c) neither he nor his representative (if he has one) attends the hearing;

the hearing may proceed in his absence.

(3) Where neither the Secretary of State nor his representative (if he has one) attends the hearing, it may proceed in his absence.

Initial Commencement
Specified date: 3 April 2000: see r 1.

10 Evidence

(1) Paragraph (2) applies to all appeals.

(2) The adjudicator may take into account any matters which he considers to be relevant to the appeal (including matters arising after the date on which the decision appealed against was taken).

(3) Paragraphs (4) to (6) apply to oral hearings only.

(4) No person may be compelled to give any evidence or produce any document which he could not be compelled to give or produce on the trial of an action.

(5) The adjudicator may require any witness to give evidence on oath or affirmation, and for that purpose an oath or affirmation in due form may be administered.

(6) When the adjudicator takes into consideration documentary evidence at an oral hearing, a party present at the hearing is to be given an opportunity of inspecting and considering that evidence and taking copies if copies have not been provided previously to that party in accordance with these Rules.

Initial Commencement
Specified date: 3 April 2000: see r 1.

11 Record of proceedings

A record of the proceedings at an oral hearing before the adjudicator is to be made.

Initial Commencement
Specified date: 3 April 2000: see r 1.

12   Exclusion of public

(1)   Subject to the provisions of this rule, oral hearings are to take place in public.

(2)   Subject to the provisions of paragraph (3), the adjudicator may exclude a member of the public or members of the public generally from a hearing or from part of a hearing if, and to the extent that, he considers it necessary to do so in the public interest.

(3)   But nothing in this rule is to prevent a member of the Council on Tribunals, a member of the Scottish Committee of that Council, the Chief Asylum Support Adjudicator or the Deputy Chief Asylum Support Adjudicator, in their capacity as such, from attending an oral hearing.

Initial Commencement
Specified date: 3 April 2000: see r 1.

13   Adjudication

(1)   Where an oral hearing is held:

   (a)   the adjudicator must inform all persons present of his adjudication at the conclusion of the hearing;

   (b)   if neither the appellant nor his representative (if he has one) is present at the conclusion of the hearing, the adjudicator must send notice of his adjudication on the same day to the appellant;

   (c)   if the Secretary of State is not present at the conclusion of the hearing, the adjudicator must send notice of his adjudication on the same day to the Secretary of State; and

   (d)   not later than [3 days] after the day on which the appeal is determined, the adjudicator must send a reasons statement to the appellant and the Secretary of State.

(2)   Where there is no oral hearing, the adjudicator must on the day that the appeal is determined:

   (a)   send notice of his adjudication to the appellant and the Secretary of State; and

   (b)   send a reasons statement to them.

(3)   An adjudication takes effect from the day on which it is made.

(4)   A "reasons statement" is a written statement giving reasons for the adjudication.

Initial Commencement
Specified date: 3 April 2000: see r 1.

Amendment
Para (1): in sub-para (d) words "3 days" in square brackets substituted by SI 2003/1735, rr 2, 7.
Date in force: 11 August 2003 (except in relation to decision letters received by appellants before that date): see SI 2003/1735, r 1.

Miscellaneous

14   Directions

The adjudicator may give directions on any matter arising in connection with an appeal if he considers it necessary or desirable to do so in the interests of justice.

Initial Commencement
Specified date: 3 April 2000: see r 1.

15 Representation

A party to the appeal may be represented by any other person.

Initial Commencement
Specified date: 3 April 2000: see r 1.

16 Withdrawal of decision

(1) Where the Secretary of State withdraws the decision which is appealed against, he must give notice to the adjudicator and the appellant forthwith.

(2) Where the appellant withdraws his appeal, he must give notice to the adjudicator and the Secretary of State forthwith.

(3) Where paragraph (1) or (2) applies, the appeal is to be treated for all purposes as at an end.

Initial Commencement
Specified date: 3 April 2000: see r 1.

17 Notices

In the absence of express provision, any notice or other document required or authorised by these Rules to be sent or given by any party may be sent by first class post, by fax or by hand.

Initial Commencement
Specified date: 3 April 2000: see r 1.

18 Time

(1) Subject to paragraph (2), for the purposes of these Rules, a notice or other document is to be taken to have been received on the day on which it was in fact received.

(2) Where a notice or other document is sent by first class post by the Secretary of State or by the adjudicator, it is to be taken to have been received 2 days after the day on which it was sent, unless the contrary is proven.

(3) Where reference is made in these Rules to a specified number of days after an event, the number of days is to be calculated from the expiry of the day on which the event occurred.

(4) Where these Rules provide that an act is to be done or to be taken to have been done:

    (a) not later than a specified number of days after an event; or
    (b) a specified number of days after an event;

and that number of days:

    (c) expires on an excluded day, the act is to be taken to have been done as required if done on the next working day;
    (d) includes an excluded day, that day is to be discounted.

(5) Where these Rules provide that an act is to be done or to be taken to have been done on a certain day and that day is an excluded day, the act is to be taken to have been done as required if done on the next working day.

Initial Commencement
Specified date: 3 April 2000: see r 1.

19 Irregularities

(1) Any irregularity resulting from failure to comply with these Rules before the adjudicator has determined the appeal is not by itself to render the proceedings void.

(2) But the adjudicator must, if he considers that either party may have been prejudiced, take such steps as he thinks fit to remove or reduce the prejudice.

Initial Commencement
Specified date: 3 April 2000: see r 1.

[SCHEDULE
NOTICE OF APPEAL]

[Rule 3(1)]

[Please see the Guidance Note at the end of this document for further information on completing this form.

Section one
Give your personal details
Full Name:
Date of Birth: Nationality:
Your NASS reference number:

Section two
Give an address in the United Kingdom where the Asylum Support Adjudicators can write you:

Give a daytime fax or telephone number in the United Kingdom (if you have one) where the Asylum Support Adjudicators can contact you:

Section three
Give the date of the decision letter against which you are appealing:
Please attach a copy of that decision letter to this form.

Section four

	Tick appropriate box	
I want my appeal determined on the papers.	Yes	No
I want an oral hearing of my appeal.	Yes	No
I want to attend the oral hearing of my appeal.	Yes	No
If you want to attend the hearing, will you need an interpreter?	Yes	No
If so, in what language?		
Are you to be represented in this appeal?	Yes	No

If so you must give full details of your representative: name and address, and telephone and fax numbers if available, together with any reference number the representative has given your case.

Will your representative attend any oral hearing of your appeal?	Yes		No

Section five
You must complete this section. Failure to do so may result in your appeal being treated as invalid.
What are the grounds of your appeal?
What matters in the decision letter do you disagree with? (*Please use a separate sheet if required.*)

Signed: Date:
[Appellant/Representative]

Guidance Note

If you have further information which you would like the Adjudicators to take into account when makin a decision about your appeal, you should send this together with copies of any documents with this form.

Please ensure that you complete all sections as fully as possible.

If you have requested an oral hearing, it is in your interests to atend.

You must include your grounds of appeal at section five or your appeal may be treated as invalid.

The Migrant Helpline may be able to help you in completing this form. You can contact them at:

Migrant Helpline
45 Friends Road
Croydon
Surrey CR0 1ED
Telephone number: (020) 8774 0002.

There may be a local office near you.

Return this form to:

Asylum Support Adjudicators

Christopher Wren House

113 High Street

Croydon CR0 1QG.

You may also return this form by fax. The ASA's fax number is (020) 8688 6075.

The ASA freephone number for appellants who wish to discuss any aspect of the appeal process is (0800) 389 7913.

Further information about the ASA is available on www.asylum-support-adjudicators.org.uk.]

Amendment
Substituted by SI 2003/1735, rr 2, 8, Schedule. Date in force: 11 August 2003 (except in relation to decision letters received by appellants before that date): see SI 2003/1735, r 1.

SPECIAL IMMIGRATION APPEALS COMMISSION (PROCEDURE) RULES 2003

2003 No 1034

Made . . . . *1st April 2003*
Coming into force in accordance with rule 1

The Lord Chancellor, in exercise of the powers conferred by sections 5 and 8 of the Special Immigration Appeals Commission Act 1997 and sections 24(3) and 27(5) of the Anti-terrorism, Crime and Security Act 2001, makes the following Rules a draft of which has, in accordance with sections 5(9) and 8(4) of the Special Immigration Appeals Commission Act 1997, been laid before and approved by resolution of each House of Parliament:

PART 1
INTRODUCTION

1   Citation and commencement

These Rules may be cited as the Special Immigration Appeals Commission (Procedure) Rules 2003 and shall come into force forthwith.

Initial Commencement
Specified date: 1 April 2003: see above.

2   Interpretation

(1)   In these Rules—

"the 1997 Act" means the Special Immigration Appeals Commission Act 1997;
"the 2001 Act" means the Anti-terrorism, Crime and Security Act 2001;
"the 2002 Act" means the Nationality, Immigration and Asylum Act 2002;
"appellant" means a person appealing to the Commission, and in Part 7 is to be interpreted as additionally including—
    (i)   in relation to applications for permission to appeal or applications for bail, the applicant; and
    (ii)   in relation to reviews, the person certified;
"certification" means certification of a person by the Secretary of State under section 21(1) of the 2001 Act and, unless the context requires otherwise, "certified" and "certificate" are to be interpreted accordingly;
"chairman" means the chairman of the Commission;
"Commission" means the Special Immigration Appeals Commission;

"Immigration Acts" means the Acts referred to in section 158(1) of the 2002 Act;
"proceedings" means any appeal or application to, or review held by, the
Commission;
"relevant law officer" has the meaning given by section 6(2) of the 1997 Act;
"review" means a review of certification by the Commission under section 26 of
the 2001 Act;
"special advocate" means a person appointed under section 6(1) of the 1997 Act to
represent the interests of a party to proceedings;
"United Kingdom Representative" means the United Kingdom Representative of
the United Nations High Commissioner for Refugees.

(2) In relation to an appeal to the Commission under section 2B of the 1997 Act
against a decision which was made by a person exercising the functions of the
Secretary of State pursuant to section 43 of the British Nationality Act 1981, references
in these Rules to the Secretary of State are to be read as if they referred to the person
who made the decision.

Initial Commencement
Specified date: 1 April 2003: see r 1.

3   Scope of these Rules

These Rules apply to the following proceedings—

- (a) appeals to the Commission;
- (b) reviews;
- (c) applications to the Commission for leave to appeal to the Court of Appeal, the
  Court of Session or the Court of Appeal in Northern Ireland; and
- (d) applications to the Commission for bail.

Initial Commencement
Specified date: 1 April 2003: see r 1.

4   General duty of Commission

(1) When exercising its functions, the Commission shall secure that information is
not disclosed contrary to the interests of national security, the international relations of
the United Kingdom, the detection and prevention of crime, or in any other circumstances where disclosure is likely to harm the public interest.

(2) Where these Rules require information not to be disclosed contrary to the public
interest, that requirement is to be interpreted in accordance with paragraph (1).

(3) Subject to paragraphs (1) and (2), the Commission must satisfy itself that the
material available to it enables it properly to determine proceedings.

Initial Commencement
Specified date: 1 April 2003: see r 1.

5   Delegated powers

(1) The powers of the Commission under the following provisions of these Rules may
be exercised by the chairman or by any other member of the Commission who falls
within paragraph 5(a) or (b) of Schedule 1 to the 1997 Act—

- (a) rule 8(5) (extensions of time for appealing);
- (b) rules 11(1) and 17(1) (applications for leave to vary grounds of appeal);
- (c) rule 15(2) (applications for leave to appeal against certification);
- (d) Part 5 (applications for leave to appeal to Court of Appeal, Court of Session
  or Court of Appeal in Northern Ireland);

- (e)   Part 6 (bail);
- (f)   rule 37(5) (applications for leave to amend or supplement material filed by Secretary of State);
- (g)   rule 39 (directions);
- (h)   rule 40(1) (orders upon failure to comply with directions);
- (i)   rule 45 (issue of witness summons); and
- (j)   rule 46 (orders that two or more proceedings be heard together).

(2)   Anything of an administrative nature which is required or permitted to be done by the Commission under these Rules may be done by a member of the Commission's staff.

Initial Commencement
Specified date: 1 April 2003: see r 1.

PART 2
APPEALS TO THE COMMISSION UNDER THE 1997 ACT

6   Scope of this Part

This Part applies to appeals to the Commission under section 2 or 2B of the 1997 Act.

Initial Commencement
Specified date: 1 April 2003: see r 1.

7   Starting an appeal

(1)   An appeal to the Commission under the 1997 Act must be made by giving notice of appeal in accordance with these Rules.

(2)   Subject to paragraph (3), notice of appeal must be given by filing it with the Commission.

(3)   A person who is in detention under the Immigration Acts or the 2001 Act may give notice of appeal either—

- (a)   in accordance with paragraph (2); or
- (b)   by serving it on the person having custody of him.

(4)   When a person files a notice of appeal in accordance with paragraph (2), he must at the same time serve a copy of the notice and any accompanying documents on the Secretary of State.

(5)   Where notice of appeal is given in accordance with paragraph (3)(b)—

- (a)   the person having custody of the appellant must endorse on the notice the date that it is served on him and forward it to the Commission; and
- (b)   the Commission must serve a copy of the notice and any accompanying documents on the Secretary of State.

Initial Commencement
Specified date: 1 April 2003: see r 1.

8   Time limit for appealing

(1)   Subject to the following paragraphs of this rule, a notice of appeal to the Commission under the 1997 Act must be given—

- (a)   if the appellant is in detention under the Immigration Acts or the 2001 Act when he is served with notice of the decision against which he wishes to appeal, not later than 5 days after he is served with that notice;
- (b)   otherwise—

    (i) if the appellant is in the United Kingdom, not later than 10 days; or

    (ii) if the appellant is outside the United Kingdom, not later than 28 days,

after the appellant is served with notice of the decision against which he wishes to appeal.

(2) Where the appellant—

(a) is in the United Kingdom when he is served with notice of the decision against which he wishes to appeal; and

(b) may not appeal against the decision while in the United Kingdom by reason of section 2(5) of the 1997 Act,

a notice of appeal against the decision must be given not later than 28 days after his departure from the United Kingdom.

(3) Paragraph (4) applies where—

(a) the appellant has given notice of appeal under Part 5 of the 2002 Act against a decision ("the previous appeal"); and

(b) the previous appeal has lapsed due to a certificate being issued under section 97 of the 2002 Act while the appeal was pending.

(4) Where this paragraph applies, a notice of appeal to the Commission against the decision which was the subject of the previous appeal must be given—

(a) if the appellant is in detention under the Immigration Acts or the 2001 Act when he is served with notice that the previous appeal has lapsed, not later than 5 days after he is served with that notice;

(b) otherwise—

    (i) if the appellant is in the United Kingdom, not later than 10 days; or

    (ii) if the appellant is outside the United Kingdom, not later than 28 days,

after the appellant is served with notice that the previous appeal has lapsed.

(5) The Commission may extend the time limits in this rule if satisfied that by reason of special circumstances it would be unjust not to do so.

Initial Commencement
Specified date: 1 April 2003: see r 1.

9   Contents of notice of appeal

(1) The notice of appeal must set out the grounds for the appeal and give reasons in support of those grounds.

(2) The notice of appeal must state the name and address of—

(a) the appellant; and

(b) any representative of the appellant.

(3) The notice of appeal must be signed by the appellant or his representative, and dated.

(4) If the notice of appeal is signed by the appellant's representative, the representative must certify in the notice of appeal that he has completed the notice of appeal in accordance with the appellant's instructions.

(5) The appellant must attach to the notice of appeal a copy of the notice of decision against which he is appealing and any other document which was served on him containing reasons for that decision.

Initial Commencement
Specified date: 1 April 2003: see r 1.

10   Secretary of State's reply

(1)   If the Secretary of State intends to oppose an appeal, he must as soon as reasonably practicable file with the Commission a statement of the evidence upon which he relies in opposition to the appeal.

(2)   Unless the Secretary of State objects to the statement being disclosed to the appellant or his representative, he must serve a copy of the statement of evidence on the appellant at the same time as filing it.

(3)   Where the Secretary of State objects to a statement filed under paragraph (1) being disclosed to the appellant or his representative, rules 37 and 38 shall apply.

Initial Commencement
Specified date: 1 April 2003: see r 1.

11   Variation of grounds of appeal

(1)   Subject to section 85(2) of the 2002 Act, the appellant may vary the grounds of appeal only with the leave of the Commission.

(2)   The appellant must file any proposed variation of the grounds of appeal with the Commission and serve a copy on the Secretary of State.

Initial Commencement
Specified date: 1 April 2003: see r 1.

12   Hearing of appeal

Every appeal must be determined at a hearing before the Commission, except where—

   (a)   the appeal—
      (i)   is treated as abandoned pursuant to section 2(4) of the 1997 Act or section 104(4) of the 2002 Act;
      (ii)   is treated as finally determined pursuant to section 104(5) of the 2002 Act; or
      (iii)   is withdrawn by the appellant;
   (b)   the Secretary of State consents to the appeal being allowed; or
   (c)   the appellant is outside the United Kingdom or it is impracticable to give him notice of a hearing and, in either case, he is unrepresented.

Initial Commencement
Specified date: 1 April 2003: see r 1.

PART 3
CERTIFICATION: APPEALS

13   Scope of this Part

This Part contains rules about appeals under section 25 of the 2001 Act against certification.

Initial Commencement
Specified date: 1 April 2003: see r 1.

14   Notice of appeal

(1)   An appeal against certification must be made by giving notice of appeal in accordance with these Rules.

(2)   Subject to paragraph (3), notice of appeal must be given by filing it with the Commission.

(3)   A person who is in detention under the Immigration Acts or the 2001 Act may give notice of appeal either—

(a)   in accordance with paragraph (2); or
(b)   by serving it on the person having custody of him.

(4)   When a person files a notice of appeal in accordance with paragraph (2), he must at the same time serve a copy of the notice and any accompanying documents on the Secretary of State.

(5)   Where notice of appeal is given in accordance with paragraph (3)(b)—

(a)   the person having custody of the appellant must endorse on the notice the date that it is served on him and forward it to the Commission; and
(b)   the Commission must serve a copy of the notice and any accompanying documents on the Secretary of State.

(6)   The notice of appeal must—

(a)   set out the grounds for the appeal; and
(b)   state the name and address of—
    (i)   the appellant; and
    (ii)   any representative of the appellant.

(7)   The notice of appeal must be signed by the appellant or his representative, and dated.

Initial Commencement
Specified date: 1 April 2003: see r 1.

15   Time limit for appealing

(1)   A notice of appeal to the Commission against certification must be given—

(a)   within the period of three months beginning with the date on which the certificate is issued; or
(b)   subject to paragraph (2), after the end of that period but before the commencement of the first review of the certification.

(2)   Where a notice of appeal is given during the period specified in paragraph (1)(b)—

(a)   the appeal may proceed only with the leave of the Commission; and
(b)   the notice of appeal shall be treated as including an application for leave to appeal, and must state the grounds on which the appellant applies for such leave.

Initial Commencement
Specified date: 1 April 2003: see r 1.

16   Secretary of State's reply

(1)   If the Secretary of State intends to oppose an appeal, he must as soon as practicable file with the Commission a statement of the evidence upon which he relies in opposition to the appeal.

(2)   Unless the Secretary of State objects to the statement being disclosed to the appellant or his representative, he must serve a copy of the statement on the appellant at the same time as filing it.

(3)   Where the Secretary of State objects to a statement filed under paragraph (1) being disclosed to the appellant or his representative, rules 37 and 38 shall apply.

Initial Commencement
Specified date: 1 April 2003: see r 1.

17   Variation of grounds of appeal

(1)   The appellant may vary the grounds of appeal only with the leave of the Commission.

(2)   The appellant must file any proposed variation of the grounds of appeal with the Commission and serve a copy on the Secretary of State.

Initial Commencement
Specified date: 1 April 2003: see r 1.

18   Hearing of appeal

Every appeal must be determined at a hearing before the Commission, except where—

- (a)   the appeal is withdrawn by the appellant;
- (b)   the Secretary of State consents to the appeal being allowed; or
- (c)   the appellant is outside the United Kingdom or it is impracticable to give him notice of a hearing and, in either case, he is unrepresented.

Initial Commencement
Specified date: 1 April 2003: see r 1.

19   Determination of appeal

Where the Commission dismisses an appeal against certification—

- (a)   it must serve on the parties, together with its determination, notice of when it is going to commence the first review of the certificate; and
- (b)   it may serve on the parties directions relating to that review.

Initial Commencement
Specified date: 1 April 2003: see r 1.

PART 4
CERTIFICATION: REVIEWS

20   Scope of this Part

This Part contains rules about reviews of certification.

Initial Commencement
Specified date: 1 April 2003: see r 1.

21   Commencement of first review

(1)   Before the Commission holds the first review of a certificate under section 26 of the 2001 Act—

- (a)   it must serve on the person certified, the Secretary of State and the relevant law officer notice of when it is going to commence the review, unless it has already served on them a notice under rule 19; and
- (b)   it may give directions in relation to the review.

(2) A notice under paragraph (1)(a) must be served not later than 42 days before the commencement of the review, unless the Commission orders otherwise.

Initial Commencement
Specified date: 1 April 2003: see r 1.

22 Application for review

(1) An application for a review under section 26(4) of the 2001 Act—

(a) must be made in writing; and

(b) must state the grounds of the application, including details of the matters relied upon as constituting a change of circumstances for the purpose of section 26(4)(b).

(2) An application under paragraph (1) must be filed with the Commission, and a copy of the application must at the same time be served on the Secretary of State.

(3) If the Secretary of State objects to a review being held, he must file any written representations with the Commission within 5 days of being served with the application.

(4) If the Commission decides to hold a review—

(a) it must send notice of when it is going to commence a review to the person certified, the Secretary of State and the relevant law officer; and

(b) it may give directions in relation to the review.

Initial Commencement
Specified date: 1 April 2003: see r 1.

23 Method of conducting review

(1) The Commission shall conduct a review as soon as reasonably practicable after the date notified to the parties as the date of commencement of the review.

(2) Subject to paragraph (3), a review shall be conducted without an oral hearing unless the Commission orders otherwise.

(3) The first review of a certificate shall, unless the Commission orders otherwise, be conducted at an oral hearing if there has not previously been an oral hearing of an appeal against the certificate.

(4) Where paragraph (3) does not apply, a party or the special advocate may apply to the Commission for a review to be conducted at an oral hearing.

(5) An application under paragraph (4)—

(a) must be made in writing; and

(b) must state the applicant's reasons for requesting an oral hearing.

Initial Commencement
Specified date: 1 April 2003: see r 1.

24 Evidence and written submissions

(1) Subject to any directions given by the Commission, the parties must file and serve any evidence and written submissions for a review, and the special advocate must file and serve any written submissions, in accordance with this rule.

(2) The person certified must, not later than 28 days before the review is to commence, file with the Commission and serve on the Secretary of State—

(a) any written evidence which he wishes the Commission to take into account upon the review; and
(b) any written submissions.

(3) The Secretary of State must, not later than 14 days before the review is to commence, file with the Commission—

(a) a statement of the reasons for the continuation of the certificate;
(b) any written evidence upon which the Secretary of State relies to support the continuation of the certificate, other than evidence already filed upon a previous appeal against or review of the certificate;
(c) if he relies upon evidence already filed, a statement identifying that evidence and confirming that it remains true; and
(d) any written submissions.

(4) Unless the Secretary of State objects to the material filed under paragraph (3) being disclosed to the person certified or his representative, he must serve a copy of the material on the person certified at the same time as filing it.

(5) Where the Secretary of State objects to material filed under paragraph (3) being disclosed to the person certified or his representative, rules 37 and 38 shall apply.

(6) The person certified may, not later than the date on which the review is to commence, file with the Commission and serve on the Secretary of State any evidence or written submissions in reply to the material served by the Secretary of State.

(7) Where a special advocate is appointed for the purposes of a review he may, not later than the date on which the review is to commence, file with the Commission and serve on the Secretary of State any written submissions.

Initial Commencement
Specified date: 1 April 2003: see r 1.

25   Determination of review

Where, upon holding a review, the Commission upholds a certificate—

(a) it shall send to the parties, together with its determination, notice of when it is going to commence the next review of the certificate; and
(b) it may send to the parties directions in relation to that review.

Initial Commencement
Specified date: 1 April 2003: see r 1.

PART 5
APPLICATIONS FOR LEAVE TO APPEAL FROM COMMISSION

26   Scope of this Part

This Part applies to applications to the Commission for leave to appeal on a question of law to the Court of Appeal, the Court of Session or the Court of Appeal in Northern Ireland, from a final determination by the Commission of an appeal or review.

Initial Commencement
Specified date: 1 April 2003: see r 1.

27   Application for leave to appeal

(1) An application for leave to appeal must be made by filing with the Commission an application in writing.

(2) The application must be filed—

Special Immigration Appeals Commission (Procedure) Rules 2003

(a) If the applicant is in detention under the Immigration Acts or the 2001 Act when he is served with written notice of the Commission's determination, not later than 5 days after he is served with that determination.

(b) otherwise, not later than 10 days after he is served with written notice of the Commission's determination.

(3) The application must—

(a) state the grounds of appeal; and
(b) be signed by the applicant or his representative, and dated.

(4) The applicant must serve a copy of the application notice on every other party.

(5) The Commission may decide an application for leave without a hearing unless it considers that there are special circumstances which make a hearing necessary or desirable.

Initial Commencement
Specified date: 1 April 2003: see r 1.

PART 6
BAIL

28   Scope of this Part and interpretation

This Part applies to applications to the Commission under—

(a) the Immigration Acts; or
(b) section 24 of the 2001 Act,

by persons detained under those Acts, to be released on bail.

Initial Commencement
Specified date: 1 April 2003: see r 1.

29   Application for bail

(1) An application to be released on bail must be made by filing with the Commission an application in writing.

(2) The application must contain the following details—

(a) the applicant's—
   (i) full name;
   (ii) date of birth; and
   (iii) date of arrival in the United Kingdom;
(b) the address of the place where the applicant is detained;
(c) whether there are pending before the Commission any proceedings to which the applicant is a party;
(d) the address where the applicant will reside if his application for bail is granted or, if he is unable to give such an address, the reason why an address is not given;
(e) the amount of the recognizance in which he will agree to be bound;
(f) the full names, addresses, occupations and dates of birth of any persons who have agreed to act as sureties for the applicant if bail is granted, and the amounts of the recognizances in which they will agree to be bound;
(g) the grounds on which the application is made and, where a previous application has been refused, full details of any change in circumstances which has occurred since the refusal; and
(h) whether the applicant requires an interpreter at the hearing and, if so, for what language and dialect.

(3)   The application must be signed by the applicant or his representative or, in the case of an applicant who is a child or is for any other reason incapable of acting, by a person acting on his behalf.

Initial Commencement
Specified date: 1 April 2003: see r 1.

30   Bail hearing and decision

(1)   Where an application for bail is filed, the Commission must—

  (a)   as soon as reasonably practicable, serve a copy of the application on the Secretary of State; and
  (b)   fix a hearing.

(2)   If the Secretary of State wishes to contest the application, he must file with the Commission a written statement of his reasons for doing so—

  (a)   not later than 2.00 pm the day before the hearing; or
  (b)   where he received notice of the hearing less than 24 hours before that time, as soon as reasonably practicable.

(3)   If the Secretary of State objects to a statement filed under paragraph (2) being disclosed to the applicant or his representative, rules 37 and 38 shall apply.

(4)   The Commission must serve written notice of—

  (a)   its decision upon an application for bail; and
  (b)   if and to the extent that it is possible to do so without disclosing information contrary to the public interest, the reasons for its decision,

on the applicant, the Secretary of State, and the person having custody of the applicant.

(5)   Where bail is granted, the notice must include—

  (a)   the conditions of bail; and
  (b)   the amounts in which the applicant and any sureties are to be bound.

(6)   The recognizance of the applicant or of a surety must be in writing and must state—

  (a)   the amount in which he agrees to be bound; and
  (b)   that he has read and understood the bail decision and that he agrees to pay that amount of money if the applicant fails to comply with the conditions set out in the bail decision.

(7)   The recognizance must be—

  (a)   signed by the applicant or surety; and
  (b)   filed with the Commission.

(8)   The person having custody of an applicant must release him upon—

  (a)   being served with a copy of the decision to grant bail; and
  (b)   being satisfied that any recognizances required as a condition of that decision have been entered into.

Initial Commencement
Specified date: 1 April 2003: see r 1.

31   Application of this Part to Scotland

(1)   Rules 29 and 30 shall apply to Scotland with the following modifications—

  (a)   in rule 29, in paragraph (2), for sub-paragraphs (e) and (f) substitute—

"(e) the amount, if any, to be deposited if bail is granted;
(f) the full names, addresses, occupations and dates of birth of any persons offering to act as cautioners if the application for bail is granted;";
(b) in rule 30—
(i) in paragraph (5), for sub-paragraph (b) substitute—
"(b) the amount (if any) to be deposited by the applicant and any cautioners.";
(ii) paragraphs (6) and (7) do not apply; and
(iii) in paragraph (8), for sub-paragraph (b) substitute—
"(b) being satisfied that the amount to be deposited, if any, has been deposited.".

Initial Commencement
Specified date: 1 April 2003: see r 1.

PART 7
GENERAL PROVISIONS

32 Parties

(1) Subject to rule 2(2) and to paragraph (2) of this rule, the parties to proceedings shall be the appellant and the Secretary of State.

(2) The United Kingdom Representative may give written notice to the Commission that he wishes to be treated as a party to proceedings, and where he gives such notice he shall be treated as a party from the date of the notice.

(3) Any restriction imposed by or under these Rules in relation to the appellant as to—

(a) the disclosure of material;
(b) attendance at hearings;
(c) notification of orders, directions or determinations; and
(d) communication from the special advocate,

shall also apply to the United Kingdom Representative where he is a party.

Initial Commencement
Specified date: 1 April 2003: see r 1.

33 Representation of parties

(1) The appellant may act in person or be represented by—

(a) a person having a qualification referred to in section 6(3) of the 1997 Act;
(b) a person appointed by any voluntary organisation for the time being in receipt of a grant under section 110 of the 2002 Act; or
(c) with the leave of the Commission, any other person,

provided that the person referred to in sub-paragraphs (a) to (c) is not prohibited from providing immigration services by section 84 of the Immigration and Asylum Act 1999.

(2) The Secretary of State and the United Kingdom Representative may be represented by any person authorised by them to act on their behalf.

Initial Commencement
Specified date: 1 April 2003: see r 1.

34 Appointment of special advocate

(1) Subject to paragraph (2), the Secretary of State must, upon being served with a copy of a notice of appeal or application under these Rules, give notice of the proceedings to the relevant law officer.

(2) Paragraph (1) applies unless—

    (a) the Secretary of State does not intend to—
        (i) oppose the appeal or application; or
        (ii) object to the disclosure of any material to the appellant; or
    (b) a special advocate has already been appointed to represent the interests of the appellant in the proceedings.

(3) Where notice is given to the relevant law officer under paragraph (1), the relevant law officer may appoint a special advocate to represent the interests of the appellant in proceedings before the Commission.

(4) Where any proceedings before the Commission are pending but no special advocate has been appointed, the appellant or the Secretary of State may at any time request the relevant law officer to appoint a special advocate.

Initial Commencement
Specified date: 1 April 2003: see r 1.

35 Functions of special advocate

The functions of a special advocate are to represent the interests of the appellant by—

    (a) making submissions to the Commission at any hearings from which the appellant and his representatives are excluded;
    (b) cross-examining witnesses at any such hearings; and
    (c) making written submissions to the Commission.

Initial Commencement
Specified date: 1 April 2003: see r 1.

36 Special advocate: communicating about proceedings

(1) The special advocate may communicate with the appellant or his representative at any time before the Secretary of State serves material on him which he objects to being disclosed to the appellant.

(2) After the Secretary of State serves material on the special advocate as mentioned in paragraph (1), the special advocate must not communicate with any person about any matter connected with the proceedings, except in accordance with paragraph (3) or a direction of the Commission pursuant to a request under paragraph (4).

(3) The special advocate may, without directions from the Commission, communicate about the proceedings with—

    (a) the Commission;
    (b) the Secretary of State, or any person acting for him;
    (c) the relevant law officer, or any person acting for him;
    (d) any other person, except for the appellant or his representative, with whom it is necessary for administrative purposes for him to communicate about matters not connected with the substance of the proceedings.

(4) The special advocate may request directions from the Commission authorising him to communicate with the appellant or his representative or with any other person.

(5) Where the special advocate makes a request for directions under paragraph (4)—

    (a) the Commission must notify the Secretary of State of the request; and
    (b) the Secretary of State must, within a period specified by the Commission, file with the Commission and serve on the special advocate notice of any objection which he has to the proposed communication, or to the form in which it is proposed to be made.

(6) Paragraph (2) does not prohibit the appellant from communicating with the special advocate after the Secretary of State has served material on him as mentioned in paragraph (1), but—

(a) the appellant may only communicate with the special advocate through a legal representative in writing; and

(b) the special advocate must not reply to the communication other than in accordance with directions of the Commission, except that he may without such directions send a written acknowledgment of receipt to the appellant's legal representative.

Initial Commencement
Specified date: 1 April 2003: see r 1.

37 Closed material

(1) In this rule, "closed material" means material upon which the Secretary of State wishes to rely in any proceedings before the Commission, but which the Secretary of State objects to disclosing to the appellant or his representative.

(2) The Secretary of State may not rely upon closed material unless a special advocate has been appointed to represent the interests of the appellant.

(3) Where the Secretary of State wishes to rely upon closed material and a special advocate has been appointed, the Secretary of State must file with the Commission and serve on the special advocate—

(a) a copy of the closed material;

(b) a statement of his reasons for objecting to its disclosure; and

(c) if and to the extent that it is possible to do so without disclosing information contrary to the public interest, a statement of the material in a form which can be served on the appellant.

(4) The Secretary of State must, at the same time as filing it, serve on the appellant any statement filed under paragraph (3)(c).

(5) The Secretary of State may, with the leave of the Commission, at any time amend or supplement material filed under this rule.

Initial Commencement
Specified date: 1 April 2003: see r 1.

38 Consideration of Secretary of State's objection

(1) Where the Secretary of State makes an objection under rule 36(5)(b) or rule 37, the Commission must decide in accordance with this rule whether to uphold the objection.

(2) The Commission must fix a hearing for the Secretary of State and the special advocate to make oral representations, unless—

(a) the special advocate gives notice to the Commission that he does not challenge the objection;

(b) the Commission has previously considered an objection by the Secretary of State to the disclosure of the same or substantially the same material, and is satisfied that it would be just to uphold the objection without a hearing; or

(c) the Secretary of State and the special advocate consent to the Commission deciding the issue without an oral hearing.

(3) If the special advocate does not challenge the objection, he must give notice of that fact to the Commission and the Secretary of State within 14 days after the Secretary of State serves on him a notice under rule 36(5)(b) or material under rule 37(3).

(4) Where the Commission fixes a hearing under this rule, the Secretary of State and the special advocate must before the hearing file with the Commission a schedule identifying the issues which cannot be agreed between them, which must—

    (a) list the items or issues in dispute;
    (b) give brief reasons for their contentions on each; and
    (c) set out any proposals for the Commission to resolve the issues in contention.

(5) A hearing under this rule shall take place in the absence of the appellant and his representative.

(6) The Commission may—

    (a) uphold or overrule the Secretary of State's objection; and
    (b) where the Secretary of State has made an objection under rule 37(3), direct him to serve on the appellant all or part of the material which he has filed with the Commission but not served on the appellant, either in the form in which it was filed or in a different form.

(7) Where the Commission overrules the Secretary of State's objection or directs him to serve any material on the appellant, the Secretary of State shall not be required to serve the material if he chooses not to rely upon it in the proceedings.

Initial Commencement
Specified date: 1 April 2003: see r 1.

39　Directions

(1) The Commission may give directions relating to the conduct of any proceedings.

(2) The power to give directions is to be exercised subject to—

    (a) these Rules, including in particular the obligation in rule 4(1) to ensure that information is not disclosed contrary to the public interest; and
    (b) any decision which the Commission makes under rule 38(6).

(3) Directions under this rule may be given orally or in writing.

(4) Subject to rule 48, the Commission must serve notice of any written directions on every party.

(5) Directions given under this rule may in particular—

    (a) specify the length of time allowed for anything to be done;
    (b) vary any time limit;
    (c) require any party to file and serve—
        (i) further details of his case, or any other information which appears to be necessary for the determination of the appeal or application;
        (ii) witness statements;
        (iii) written submissions;
        (iv) a statement of any interpretation requirements; or
        (v) any other document;
    (d) provide for—
        (i) a particular matter to be dealt with as a preliminary issue; or
        (ii) a pre-hearing review to be held;
    (e) relate to any matter concerning the preparation for a hearing;
    (f) specify—

      (i) the manner in which any evidence is to be given; and

      (ii) the witnesses, if any, to be heard;

  (g) provide for a hearing to be conducted or evidence given or representations made by video link or by other electronic means; and

  (h) make provision to secure the anonymity of the appellant or a witness.

(6) The power to give directions may be exercised in the absence of the parties.

Initial Commencement
Specified date: 1 April 2003: see r 1.

40   Failure to comply with directions

(1) Where a party or the special advocate fails to comply with a direction, the Commission may serve on him a notice which states—

  (a) the respect in which he has failed to comply with the direction;

  (b) a time limit for complying with the direction; and

  (c) that the Commission may proceed to determine the appeal on the material available to it if the party or the special advocate fails to comply with the relevant direction within the time specified.

(2) Where a party or special advocate fails to comply with such a notice, the Commission may proceed in accordance with paragraph (1)(c).

Initial Commencement
Specified date: 1 April 2003: see r 1.

41   Notification of hearing

Unless the Commission orders otherwise, it must serve notice of the date, time and place fixed for any hearing on—

  (a) every party, whether or not entitled to attend that hearing; and

  (b) the special advocate, if one has been appointed.

Initial Commencement
Specified date: 1 April 2003: see r 1.

42   Adjournment of hearing

The Commission may adjourn the hearing of any proceedings.

Initial Commencement
Specified date: 1 April 2003: see r 1.

43   Hearings in private

(1) If the Commission considers it necessary for the appellant and his representative to be excluded from a hearing or part of a hearing in order to secure that information is not disclosed contrary to the public interest, it must—

  (a) direct accordingly; and

  (b) conduct the hearing, or that part of it from which the appellant and his representative are excluded, in private.

(2) The Commission may conduct a hearing or part of a hearing in private for any other good reason.

Initial Commencement
Specified date: 1 April 2003: see r 1.

44   Evidence

(1)   Subject to these Rules, the evidence of witnesses may be given either—

    (a)   orally, before the Commission;

    (b)   in writing, in which case it shall be given in such a manner and at such time as the Commission directs.

(2)   The Commission may also receive evidence in documentary or any other form.

(3)   The Commission may receive evidence that would not be admissible in a court of law.

(4)   No person shall be compelled to give evidence or produce a document which he could not be compelled to give or produce on the trial of a civil claim in the part of the United Kingdom in which the proceedings before the Commission are taking place.

(5)   Every party shall be entitled to adduce evidence and to cross-examine witnesses during any part of a hearing from which he and his representative are not excluded.

(6)   The Commission may require a witness to give evidence on oath.

Initial Commencement
Specified date: 1 April 2003: see r 1.

45   Summoning of witnesses

(1)   Subject to these Rules, the Commission may, by issuing a summons, require any person in the United Kingdom—

    (a)   to attend as a witness at the hearing of any proceedings before the Commission; and

    (b)   at the hearing, to answer any questions or produce any documents in his custody or under his control which relate to any matter in issue in the proceedings.

(2)   No person shall be required to attend a hearing in compliance with a summons issued under paragraph (1) unless—

    (a)   the summons is served on him; and

    (b)   the necessary expenses of his attendance are paid or tendered to him.

(3)   Where a summons is issued at the request of a party, that party must pay or tender the expenses of the witness.

Initial Commencement
Specified date: 1 April 2003: see r 1.

46   Hearing two or more proceedings together

(1)   Where two or more appeals, applications or reviews are pending at the same time, the Commission may direct them to be heard together if—

    (a)   some common question of law or fact arises in each of them;

    (b)   they relate to decisions or action taken in respect of persons who are members of the same family; or

    (c)   for some other reason it is desirable for the proceedings to be heard together.

(2)   Except where section 27(7) and (8) of the 2001 Act applies, the Commission must give all the parties who would be entitled to attend the hearing of the proceedings an opportunity to make representations before hearing proceedings together under this rule.

Initial Commencement
Specified date: 1 April 2003: see r 1.

47 Giving of determination

(1) This rule applies when the Commission determines any proceedings.

(2) The Commission must record its decision and the reasons for it.

(3) The Commission must serve on the parties a written determination containing its decision and, if and to the extent that it is possible to do so without disclosing information contrary to the public interest, the reasons for it.

(4) Where the determination under paragraph (3) does not include the full reasons for its decision, the Commission must serve on the Secretary of State and the special advocate a separate determination including those reasons.

Initial Commencement
Specified date: 1 April 2003: see r 1.

48 Application by Secretary of State for reconsideration of decision

(1) This rule applies where the Commission proposes to serve notice on the appellant of—

(a) any order or direction made or given in the absence of the Secretary of State; or

(b) its determination of the proceedings.

(2) Before the Commission serves any such notice on the appellant, it must first serve notice on the Secretary of State of its intention to do so.

(3) The Secretary of State may, within 5 days of being served with notice under paragraph (2), apply to the Commission to reconsider the order or direction or to review the proposed determination if he considers that—

(a) his compliance with the order or direction; or

(b) the notification to the appellant of any matter contained in the order, direction or determination,

would cause information to be disclosed contrary to the public interest.

(4) Where the Secretary of State makes an application under paragraph (3), he must at the same time serve a copy of it on the special advocate, if one has been appointed.

(5) Rule 38, except for paragraphs (6)(b) and (7) of that rule, shall, if a special advocate has been appointed, apply with any necessary modifications to the consideration of an application under paragraph (3) of this rule.

(6) The Commission must not serve notice on the appellant as mentioned in paragraph (1) before the time for the Secretary of State to make an application under paragraph (3) has expired.

Initial Commencement
Specified date: 1 April 2003: see r 1.

49 Filing and service of documents

(1) Any document which is required or permitted by these Rules or by an order of the Commission to be filed with the Commission or served on any person may be—

(a) delivered or sent by post to an address;

(b) sent by fax to a fax number; or

(c) sent by e-mail to an e-mail address,

specified for that purpose by the Commission or the person to which the document is directed.

(2)   A document to be served on an individual may be served personally by leaving it with that individual.

(3)   Subject to paragraph (4), if any document is served on a person who has notified the Commission that he is acting as the representative of a party, it shall be deemed to have been served on that party.

(4)   Paragraph (3) does not apply if the Commission directs that a document is to be served on both a party and his representative.

(5)   Any document that is served on a person in accordance with this rule shall, unless the contrary is proved, be deemed to be served—

(a)   where the document is sent by post from and to a place within the United Kingdom, on the second day after it was sent;

(b)   where the document is sent by post from or to a place outside the United Kingdom, on the twenty-eighth day after it was sent; and

(c)   in any other case, on the day on which the document was sent or delivered to, or left with, that person.

(6)   Any document which is filed with the Commission shall be treated as being filed on the day on which it is received by the Commission.

Initial Commencement
Specified date: 1 April 2003: see r 1.

50   Address for service

(1)   Every party, and any person representing a party or acting as special advocate, must notify the Commission of a postal address at which documents may be served on him and of any changes to that address.

(2)   Until a party, representative or special advocate notifies the Commission of a change of address, any document served on him at the most recent address he has given to the Commission shall be deemed to have been properly served on him.

Initial Commencement
Specified date: 1 April 2003: see r 1.

51   Calculation of time

(1)   Where a period of time for doing any act is specified by these Rules or by a direction of the Commission, that period is to be calculated—

(a)   excluding the day on which the period begins; and

(b)   where the period is 10 days or less, excluding any day which is not a business day.

(2)   Where the time specified by these Rules or by a direction of the Commission for doing any act ends on a day which is not a business day, that act is done in time if it is done on the next business day.

(3)   In this rule, "business day" means any day other than a Saturday or Sunday, a bank holiday, Christmas Day, 27th to 31st December or Good Friday.

Initial Commencement
Specified date: 1 April 2003: see r 1.

52   Signature of documents

Any requirement in these Rules for a document to be signed shall be satisfied, in the case of a document which is filed or served by e-mail in accordance with these Rules, by the person who is required to sign the document typing his name in it.

Initial Commencement
Specified date: 1 April 2003: see r 1.

53   Errors of procedure

Where in any proceedings, before they have been determined by the Commission, there has been an error of procedure such as a failure to comply with a rule—

(a)   subject to these Rules, the error does not invalidate any step taken in the proceedings unless the Commission so orders; and
(b)   the Commission may make an order or take any other step that it considers appropriate to remedy the error.

Initial Commencement
Specified date: 1 April 2003: see r 1.

54   Correction of orders and determinations

(1)   The Commission may at any time amend an order or determination to correct a clerical error or other accidental slip or omission.

(2)   Where an order or determination is amended under this rule—

(a)   the Commission must serve the amended order or determination on every person on whom the original order or determination was served; and
(b)   the time within which a party may apply for permission to appeal against an amended determination runs from the date on which the party is served with the amended determination.

Initial Commencement
Specified date: 1 April 2003: see r 1.

PART 8
REVOCATIONS AND TRANSITIONAL PROVISIONS

55   Revocations

The following Rules are revoked—

(a)   the Special Immigration Appeals Commission (Procedure) Rules 1998 ("the 1998 Rules"); and
(b)   the Special Immigration Appeals Commission (Procedure) (Amendment) Rules 2000.

Initial Commencement
Specified date: 1 April 2003: see r 1.

56   Transitional provisions

(1)   These Rules shall apply—

(a)   with appropriate modifications, to any proceedings pending on the date on which they come into force, to which immediately before that date the 1998 Rules applied; and

(b)   to any appeal under section 2B of the 1997 Act pending on the date on which these Rules come into force.

(2)   In relation to any proceedings pending on the date on which these Rules come into force, anything done or any direction given before that date under the 1998 Rules or under any other powers of the Commission shall be treated as if done or given under these Rules.

(3)   If—

(a)   a notice of appeal is given or an application is made to the Commission within 5 days of the date on which these Rules come into force; and

(b)   the notice of appeal or application would have been given or made in time if these Rules had not come into force,

the notice of appeal or application shall be treated as being given or made in time, notwithstanding any time limit in these Rules.

Initial Commencement
Specified date: 1 April 2003: see r 1.

ASYLUM AND IMMIGRATION TRIBUNAL (PROCEDURE) RULES 2005

2005 No 230

Made . . . . *6th February 2005*

Laid before Parliament . . . . *8th February 2005*

Coming into force . . . . *4th April 2005*

The Lord Chancellor, in exercise of the powers conferred by sections 106(1)–(3) and 112(3) of the Nationality, Immigration and Asylum Act 2002 and section 40A(3) of the British Nationality Act 1981, after consulting with the Council on Tribunals in accordance with section 8 of the Tribunals and Inquiries Act 1992, makes the following Rules:

PART 1
INTRODUCTION

1   Citation and commencement

These Rules may be cited as the Asylum and Immigration Tribunal (Procedure) Rules 2005 and shall come into force on 4th April 2005.

Initial Commencement
Specified date: 4 April 2005: see above.

2   Interpretation

In these Rules—

"the 2002 Act" means the Nationality, Immigration and Asylum Act 2002;
"the 2004 Act" means the Asylum and Immigration (Treatment of Claimants, etc) Act 2004;

"appellant" means a person who has given a notice of appeal to the Tribunal against a relevant decision in accordance with these Rules;

"appropriate appellate court" has the meaning given in sections 103B(5) and 103E(5) of the 2002 Act;

"apropriate court" has the meaning given in section 103A(9) of the 2002 Act;

"appropriate prescribed form" means the appropriate form in the Schedule to these Rules, or that form with any variations that the circumstances may require;

"asylum claim" has the meaning given in section 113(1) of the 2002 Act;

"business day" means any day other than a Saturday or Sunday, a bank holiday, 25th to 31st December or Good Friday;

"determination", in relation to an appeal, means a decision by the Tribunal in writing to allow or dismiss the appeal, and does not include a procedural, ancillary or preliminary decision;

"the Immigration Acts" means the Acts referred to in section 44(1) of the 2004 Act;

"immigration decision" means a decision of a kind listed in section 82(2) of the 2002 Act;

"immigration rules" means the rules referred to in section 1(4) of the Immigration Act 1971;

"order for reconsideration" means an order under section 103A(1) or any other statutory provision requiring the Tribunal to reconsider its decision on an appeal;

"President" means the President of the Tribunal;

"relevant decision" means a decision against which there is an exercisable right of appeal to the Tribunal;

"respondent" means the decision maker specified in the notice of decision against which a notice of appeal has been given;

"section 103A" means section 103A of the 2002 Act (Review of Tribunal's decision) and "section 103A application" means an application under section 103A;

"Tribunal" means the Asylum and Immigration Tribunal;

"United Kingdom Representative" means the United Kingdom Representative of the United Nations High Commissioner for Refugees.

Initial Commencement
Specified date: 4 April 2005: see r 1.

3   Scope of these Rules

(1)   These Rules apply to the following proceedings—

(a)   appeals to the Tribunal;

(b)   section 103A applications which are considered by a member of the Tribunal in accordance with paragraph 30 of Schedule 2 to the 2004 Act;

(c)   reconsideration of appeals by the Tribunal;

(d)   applications to the Tribunal for permission to appeal to the Court of Appeal, the Court of Session, or the Court of Appeal in Northern Ireland; ...

(e)   applications to the Tribunal for bail[; and

(f)   proceedings incidental to any of the above proceedings, including in particular applications relating to the Tribunal's exercise of its powers under section 103D of the 2002 Act (Reconsideration: legal aid)].

(2)   These Rules apply subject to any other Rules made under section 106 of the 2002 Act which apply to specific classes of proceedings.

Initial Commencement
Specified date: 4 April 2005: see r 1.

Appendix 1   Legislation and materials

Amendment
Para (1): in sub-para (d) word omitted revoked by SI 2005/569, r 2(a). Date in force: 4 April 2005: see SI 2005/569, r 1(1).
Para (1): sub-para (f) and word "; and" immediately preceding it inserted by SI 2005/569, r 2(b). Date in force: 4 April 2005: see SI 2005/569, r 1(1).

4   Overriding objective

The overriding objective of these Rules is to secure that proceedings before the Tribunal are handled as fairly, quickly and efficiently as possible; and, where appropriate, that members of the Tribunal have responsibility for ensuring this, in the interests of the parties to the proceedings and in the wider public interest.

Initial Commencement
Specified date: 4 April 2005: see r 1.

PART 2

APPEALS TO THE TRIBUNAL

5   Scope of this Part

This Part applies to appeals to the Tribunal.

Initial Commencement
Specified date: 4 April 2005: see r 1.

6   Giving notice of appeal

(1)   An appeal to the Tribunal may only be instituted by giving notice of appeal against a relevant decision in accordance with these Rules.

(2)   Subject to paragraphs (3) and (4), notice of appeal must be given by filing it with the Tribunal in accordance with rule 55(1).

(3)   A person who is in detention under the Immigration Acts may give notice of appeal either—

   (a)   in accordance with paragraph (2); or
   (b)   by serving it on the person having custody of him.

(4)   A person who is outside the United Kingdom and wishes to appeal against a decision of an entry clearance officer may give notice of appeal either—

   (a)   in accordance with paragraph (2); or
   (b)   by serving it on the entry clearance officer.

(5)   Where a notice of appeal is served on a custodian under paragraph (3)(b), that person must—

   (a)   endorse on the notice the date that it is served on him; and
   (b)   forward it to the Tribunal within 2 days.

(6)   Where a notice of appeal is served on an entry clearance officer under paragraph (4)(b), the officer must—

   (a)   endorse on the notice the date that it is served on him;
   (b)   forward it to the Tribunal as soon as reasonably practicable, and in any event within 10 days; and
   (c)   if it is practicable to do so within the time limit in sub-paragraph (b), send to the Tribunal with the notice of appeal a copy of the documents listed in rule 13(1).

Initial Commencement
Specified date: 4 April 2005: see r 1.

7 Time limit for appeal

(1) A notice of appeal by a person who is in the United Kingdom must be given—

    (a) if the person is in detention under the Immigration Acts when he is served with notice of the decision against which he is appealing, not later than 5 days after he is served with that notice; and

    (b) in any other case, not later than 10 days after he is served with notice of the decision.

(2) A notice of appeal by a person who is outside the United Kingdom must be given—

    (a) if the person—

        (i) was in the United Kingdom when the decision against which he is appealing was made; and

        (ii) may not appeal while he is the United Kingdom by reason of a provision of the 2002 Act,

    not later than 28 days after his departure from the United Kingdom; or

    (b) in any other case, not later than 28 days after he is served with notice of the decision.

(3) Where a person—

    (a) is served with notice of a decision to reject an asylum claim; and

    (b) on the date of being served with that notice does not satisfy the condition in section 83(1)(b) of the 2002 Act, but later satisfies that condition,

paragraphs (1) and (2)(b) apply with the modification that the time for giving notice of appeal under section 83(2) runs from the date on which the person is served with notice of the decision to grant him leave to enter or remain in the United Kingdom by which he satisfies the condition in section 83(1)(b).

Initial Commencement
Specified date: 4 April 2005: see r 1.

8 Form and contents of notice of appeal

(1) The notice of appeal must be in the appropriate prescribed form and must—

    (a) state the name and address of the appellant; and

    (b) state whether the appellant has authorised a representative to act for him in the appeal and, if so, give the representative's name and address;

    (c) set out the grounds for the appeal;

    (d) give reasons in support of those grounds; and

    (e) so far as reasonably practicable, list any documents which the appellant intends to rely upon as evidence in support of the appeal.

(2) The notice of appeal must if reasonably practicable be accompanied by the notice of decision against which the appellant is appealing, or a copy of it.

(3) The notice of appeal must be signed by the appellant or his representative, and dated.

(4) If a notice of appeal is signed by the appellant's representative, the representative must certify in the notice of appeal that he has completed it in accordance with the appellant's instructions.

Initial Commencement
Specified date: 4 April 2005: see r 1.

9   Rejection of invalid notice of appeal

(1)   Where—

(a)   a person has given a notice of appeal to the Tribunal; and
(b)   there is no relevant decision,

the Tribunal shall not accept the notice of appeal.

(2)   Where the Tribunal does not accept a notice of appeal, it must—

(a)   notify the person giving the notice of appeal and the respondent; and
(b)   take no further action.

Initial Commencement
Specified date: 4 April 2005: see r 1.

10   Late notice of appeal

(1)   If a notice of appeal is given outside the applicable time limit, it must include an application for an extension of time for appealing, which must—

(a)   include a statement of the reasons for failing to give the notice within that period; and
(b)   be accompanied by any written evidence relied upon in support of those reasons.

(2)   If a notice of appeal appears to the Tribunal to have been given outside the applicable time limit but does not include an application for an extension of time, unless the Tribunal extends the time for appealing of its own initiative, it must notify the person giving notice of appeal in writing that it proposes to treat the notice of appeal as being out of time.

(3)   Where the Tribunal gives notification under paragraph (2), if the person giving notice of appeal contends that—

(a)   the notice of appeal was given in time, or
(b)   there were special circumstances for failing to give the notice of appeal in time which could not reasonably have been stated in the notice of appeal,

he may file with the Tribunal written evidence in support of that contention.

(4)   Written evidence under paragraph (3) must be filed—

(a)   if the person giving notice of appeal is in the United Kingdom, not later than 3 days; or
(b)   if the person giving notice of appeal is outside the United Kingdom, not later than 10 days,

after notification is given under paragraph (2).

(5)   Where the notice of appeal was given out of time, the Tribunal may extend the time for appealing if satisfied that by reason of special circumstances it would be unjust not to do so.

(6)   The Tribunal must decide any issue as to whether a notice of appeal was given in time, or whether to extend the time for appealing, as a preliminary decision without a hearing, and in doing so may only take account of—

(a)   the matters stated in the notice of appeal;

(b) any evidence filed by the person giving notice of appeal in accordance with paragraph (1) or (3); and

(c) any other relevant matters of fact within the knowledge of the Tribunal.

(7) Subject to paragraphs (8) and (9), the Tribunal must serve written notice of any decision under this rule on the parties.

(8) Where—

(a) a notice of appeal under section 82 of the 2002 Act which relates in whole or in part to an asylum claim was given out of time;

(b) the person giving notice of appeal is in the United Kingdom; and

(c) the Tribunal refuses to extend the time for appealing,

the Tribunal must serve written notice of its decision on the respondent, which must—

(i) serve the notice of decision on the person giving notice of appeal not later than 28 days after receiving it from the Tribunal; and

(ii) as soon as practicable after serving the notice of decision, notify the Tribunal on what date and by what means it was served.

(9) Where paragraph (8) applies, if the respondent does not give the Tribunal notification under sub-paragraph (ii) within 29 days after the Tribunal serves the notice of decision on it, the Tribunal must serve the notice of decision on the person giving notice of appeal as soon as reasonably practicable thereafter.

Initial Commencement
Specified date: 4 April 2005: see r 1.

11 Special provisions for imminent removal cases

(1) This rule applies in any case in which the respondent notifies the Tribunal that removal directions have been issued against a person who has given notice of appeal, pursuant to which it is proposed to remove him from the United Kingdom within 5 calendar days of the date on which the notice of appeal was given.

(2) The Tribunal must, if reasonably practicable, make any preliminary decision under rule 10 before the date and time proposed for his removal.

(3) Rule 10 shall apply subject to the modifications that the Tribunal may—

(a) give notification under rule 10(2) orally, which may include giving it by telephone;

(b) shorten the time for giving evidence under rule 10(3); and

(c) direct that any evidence under rule 10(3) is to be given orally, which may include requiring the evidence to be given by telephone, and hold a hearing or telephone hearing for the purpose of receiving such evidence.

Initial Commencement
Specified date: 4 April 2005: see r 1.

12 Service of notice of appeal on respondent

(1) Subject to paragraph (2), when the Tribunal receives a notice of appeal it shall serve a copy upon the respondent as soon as reasonably practicable.

(2) Paragraph (1) does not apply where the notice of appeal was served on an entry clearance officer under rule 6(4)(b).

Initial Commencement
Specified date: 4 April 2005: see r 1.

13   Filing of documents by respondent

(1)   When the respondent is served with a copy of a notice of appeal, it must (unless it has already done so) file with the Tribunal a copy of—

    (a)   the notice of the decision to which the notice of appeal relates, and any other document served on the appellant giving reasons for that decision;

    (b)   any—

        (i)   statement of evidence form completed by the appellant; and

        (ii)   record of an interview with the appellant,

in relation to the decision being appealed;

    (c)   any other unpublished document which is referred to in a document mentioned in sub-paragraph (a) or relied upon by the respondent; and

    (d)   the notice of any other immigration decision made in relation to the appellant in respect of which he has a right of appeal under section 82 of the 2002 Act.

(2)   Subject to paragraph (3), the respondent must file the documents listed in paragraph (1)—

    (a)   in accordance with any directions given by the Tribunal; and

    (b)   if no such directions are given, as soon as reasonably practicable and in any event not later than 2.00 pm on the business day before the earliest date appointed for any hearing of or in relation to the appeal.

(3)   If the Tribunal considers the timeliness of a notice of appeal as a preliminary issue under rule 10, the respondent must file the documents listed in paragraph (1) as soon as reasonably practicable after being served with a decision of the Tribunal allowing the appeal to proceed, and in any event not later than 2.00 pm on the business day before the earliest date appointed for any hearing of or in relation to the appeal following that decision.

(4)   The respondent must, at the same time as filing them, serve on the appellant a copy of all the documents listed in paragraph (1), except for documents which the respondent has already sent to the appellant.

Initial Commencement
Specified date: 4 April 2005: see r 1.

14   Variation of grounds of appeal

Subject to section 85(2) of the 2002 Act, the appellant may vary his grounds of appeal only with the permission of the Tribunal.

Initial Commencement
Specified date: 4 April 2005: see r 1.

15   Method of determining appeal

(1)   Every appeal must be considered by the Tribunal at a hearing, except where—

    (a)   the appeal—

        (i)   lapses pursuant to section 99 of the 2002 Act;

        (ii)   is treated as abandoned pursuant to section 104(4) of the 2002 Act;

        (iii)   is treated as finally determined pursuant to section 104(5) of the 2002 Act; or

        (iv)   is withdrawn by the appellant or treated as withdrawn in accordance with rule 17;

    (b)   paragraph (2) of this rule applies; or

(c) any other provision of these Rules or of any other enactment permits or requires the Tribunal to dispose of an appeal without a hearing.

(2) The Tribunal may determine an appeal without a hearing if—

(a) all the parties to the appeal consent;

(b) the appellant is outside the United Kingdom or it is impracticable to give him notice of a hearing and, in either case, he is unrepresented;

(c) a party has failed to comply with a provision of these Rules or a direction of the Tribunal, and the Tribunal is satisfied that in all the circumstances, including the extent of the failure and any reasons for it, it is appropriate to determine the appeal without a hearing; or

(d) subject to paragraph (3), the Tribunal is satisfied, having regard to the material before it and the nature of the issues raised, that the appeal can be justly determined without a hearing.

(3) Where paragraph (2)(d) applies, the Tribunal must not determine the appeal without a hearing without first giving the parties notice of its intention to do so, and an opportunity to make written representations as to whether there should be a hearing.

Initial Commencement
Specified date: 4 April 2005: see r 1.

16 Certification of pending appeal

(1) If the Secretary of State or an immigration officer issues a certificate under section 97 or 98 of the 2002 Act which relates to a pending appeal, he must file notice of the certification with the Tribunal.

(2) Where a notice of certification is filed under paragraph (1), the Tribunal must—

(a) notify the parties; and

(b) take no further action in relation to the appeal.

Initial Commencement
Specified date: 4 April 2005: see r 1.

17 Withdrawal of appeal

(1) An appellant may withdraw an appeal—

(a) orally, at a hearing; or

(b) at any time, by filing written notice with the Tribunal.

(2) An appeal shall be treated as withdrawn if the respondent notifies the Tribunal that the decision (or, where the appeal relates to more than one decision, all of the decisions) to which the appeal relates has been withdrawn.

(3) If an appeal is withdrawn or treated as withdrawn, the Tribunal must serve on the parties a notice that the appeal has been recorded as having been withdrawn.

Initial Commencement
Specified date: 4 April 2005: see r 1.

18 Abandonment of appeal

(1) Any party to a pending appeal must notify the Tribunal if they are aware that an event specified in—

(a) section 104(4) or (5) of the 2002 Act; or

(b) regulation 33(1A) of the Immigration (European Economic Area) Regulations 2000 ("the 2000 Regulations"), has taken place.

(2)   Where an appeal is treated as abandoned pursuant to section 104(4) of the 2002 Act or regulation 33(1A) of the 2000 Regulations, or finally determined pursuant to section 104(5) of the 2002 Act, the Tribunal must—

   (a)   serve on the parties a notice informing them that the appeal is being treated as abandoned or finally determined; and

   (b)   take no further action in relation to the appeal.

Initial Commencement
Specified date: 4 April 2005: see r 1.

19   Hearing appeal in absence of a party

(1)   The Tribunal must hear an appeal in the absence of a party or his representative, if satisfied that the party or his representative—

   (a)   has been given notice of the date, time and place of the hearing, and

   (b)   has given no satisfactory explanation for his absence.

(2)   Where paragraph (1) does not apply, the Tribunal may hear an appeal in the absence of a party if satisfied that—

   (a)   a representative of the party is present at the hearing;

   (b)   the party is outside the United Kingdom;

   (c)   the party is suffering from a communicable disease or there is a risk of him behaving in a violent or disorderly manner;

   (d)   the party is unable to attend the hearing because of illness, accident or some other good reason;

   (e)   the party is unrepresented and it is impracticable to give him notice of the hearing; or

   (f)   the party has notified the Tribunal that he does not wish to attend the hearing.

Initial Commencement
Specified date: 4 April 2005: see r 1.

20   Hearing two or more appeals together

Where two or more appeals are pending at the same time, the Tribunal may direct them to be heard together if it appears that—

   (a)   some common question of law or fact arises in each of them;

   (b)   they relate to decisions or action taken in respect of persons who are members of the same family; or

   (c)   for some other reason it is desirable for the appeals to be heard together.

Initial Commencement
Specified date: 4 April 2005: see r 1.

21   Adjournment of appeals

(1)   Where a party applies for an adjournment of a hearing of an appeal, he must—

   (a)   if practicable, notify all other parties of the application;

   (b)   show good reason why an adjournment is necessary; and

   (c)   produce evidence of any fact or matter relied upon in support of the application.

(2)   The Tribunal must not adjourn a hearing of an appeal on the application of a party, unless satisfied that the appeal cannot otherwise be justly determined.

(3)   The Tribunal must not, in particular, adjourn a hearing on the application of a party in order to allow the party more time to produce evidence, unless satisfied that—

(a)   the evidence relates to a matter in dispute in the appeal;
(b)   it would be unjust to determine the appeal without permitting the party a further opportunity to produce the evidence; and
(c)   where the party has failed to comply with directions for the production of the evidence, he has provided a satisfactory explanation for that failure.

(4)   Where the hearing of an appeal is adjourned, the Tribunal will fix a new hearing date which—

(a)   shall be not more than 28 days after the original hearing date, unless the Tribunal is satisfied that because of exceptional circumstances the appeal cannot justly be heard within that time; and
(b)   shall in any event be not later than is strictly required by the circumstances necessitating the adjournment.

Initial Commencement
Specified date: 4 April 2005: see r 1.

22   Giving of determination

(1)   Except in cases to which rule 23 applies, where the Tribunal determines an appeal it must serve on every party a written determination containing its decision and the reasons for it.

(2)   The Tribunal must send its determination—

(a)   if the appeal is considered at a hearing, not later than 10 days after the hearing finishes; or
(b)   if the appeal is determined without a hearing, not later than 10 days after it is determined.

Initial Commencement
Specified date: 4 April 2005: see r 1.

23   Special procedures and time limits in asylum appeals

(1)   This rule applies to appeals under section 82 of the 2002 Act where—

(a)   the appellant is in the United Kingdom; and
(b)   the appeal relates, in whole or in part, to an asylum claim.

(2)   Subject to paragraph (3)—

(a)   where an appeal is to be considered by the Tribunal at a hearing, the hearing must be fixed for a date not more than 28 days after the later of—
    (i)   the date on which the Tribunal receives the notice of appeal; or
    (ii) if the Tribunal makes a preliminary decision under rule 10 (late notice of appeal), the date on which notice of that decision is served on the appellant; and
(b)   where an appeal is to be determined without a hearing, the Tribunal must determine it not more than 28 days after the later of those dates.

(3)   If the respondent does not file the documents specified in rule 13(1) within the time specified in rule 13 or directions given under that rule—

(a)   paragraph (2) does not apply; and
(b)   the Tribunal may vary any hearing date that it has already fixed in accordance with paragraph (2)(a), if it is satisfied that it would be unfair to the appellant to proceed with the hearing on the date fixed.

(4)   The Tribunal must serve its determination on the respondent—

    (a)   if the appeal is considered at a hearing, by sending it not later than 10 days after the hearing finishes; or

    (b)   if the appeal is determined without a hearing, by sending it not later than 10 days after it is determined.

(5)   The respondent must—

    (a)   serve the determination on the appellant—

        (i)   if the respondent makes a section 103A application or applies for permission to appeal under section 103B or 103E of the 2002 Act, by sending, delivering or personally serving the determination not later than the date on which it makes that application; and

        (ii)   otherwise, not later than 28 days after receiving the determination from the Tribunal; and

    (b)   as soon as practicable after serving the determination, notify the Tribunal on what date and by what means it was served.

(6)   If the respondent does not give the Tribunal notification under paragraph (5)(b) within 29 days after the Tribunal serves the determination on it, the Tribunal must serve the determination on the appellant as soon as reasonably practicable thereafter.

(7)   In paragraph (2) of this rule, references to a hearing do not include a case management review hearing or other preliminary hearing.

Initial Commencement
Specified date: 4 April 2005: see r 1.

PART 3
RECONSIDERATION OF APPEALS ETC

24   Scope of this Part

(1)   Section 1 of this Part applies to section 103A applications made during any period in which paragraph 30 of Schedule 2 to the 2004 Act has effect, which are considered by an immigration judge in accordance with that paragraph.

(2)   Section 2 of this Part applies to reconsideration of appeals by the Tribunal pursuant to—

    (a)   an order under section 103A(1) made by—
        (i)   the appropriate court; or
        (ii)   an immigration judge in accordance with paragraph 30 of Schedule 2 to the 2004 Act; and

    (b)   remittal by the appropriate appellate court under section 103B(4)(c), 103C(2)(c) or 103E(4)(c) of the 2002 Act.

(3)   Section 3 of this Part applies to applications for permission to appeal to the appropriate appellate court.

Initial Commencement
Specified date: 4 April 2005: see r 1.

SECTION 1
SECTION 103A APPLICATIONS CONSIDERED BY MEMBERS OF THE TRIBUNAL

25   Procedure for applying for review

Where paragraph 30 of Schedule 2 to the 2004 Act has effect in relation to a section 103A application, the application must be made in accordance with relevant rules of court (including any practice directions supplementing those rules).

Initial Commencement
Specified date: 4 April 2005: see r 1.

26 Deciding applications for review

(1)   A section 103A application shall be decided by an immigration judge authorised by the President to deal with such applications.

(2)   The immigration judge shall decide the application without a hearing, and by reference only to the applicant's written submissions and the documents filed with the application notice.

(3)   The immigration judge is not required to consider any grounds for ordering the Tribunal to reconsider its decision other than those set out in the application notice.

(4)   The application must be decided not later than 10 days after the Tribunal receives the application notice.

(5)   In deciding a section 103A application, the immigration judge may—

   (a)   in relation to an application for permission under section 103A(4)(b), either—
      (i)   permit the application to be made outside the period specified in section 103A(3); or
      (ii)   record that he does not propose to grant permission; and
   (b)   in relation to an application for an order under section 103A(1), either—
      (i)   make an order for reconsideration; or
      (ii)   record that he does not propose to make such an order.

(6)   The immigration judge may make an order for reconsideration only if he thinks that—

   (a)   the Tribunal may have made an error of law; and
   (b)   there is a real possibility that the Tribunal would decide the appeal differently on reconsideration.

Initial Commencement
Specified date: 4 April 2005: see r 1.

27 Form and service of decision

(1)   Where an immigration judge decides a section 103A application, he must give written notice of his decision, including his reasons which may be in summary form.

(2)   Where an immigration judge makes an order for reconsideration—

   (a)   his notice of decision must state the grounds on which the Tribunal is ordered to reconsider its decision on the appeal; and
   (b)   he may give directions for the reconsideration of the decision on the appeal which may—
      (i)   provide for any of the matters set out in rule 45(4) which he considers appropriate to such reconsideration; and
      (ii)   specify the number or class of members of the Tribunal to whom the reconsideration shall be allocated.

(3)   The Tribunal must, except in cases to which paragraph (5) applies—

   (a)   serve a copy of the notice of decision and any directions on every party to the appeal to the Tribunal; and
   (b)   where the immigration judge makes an order for reconsideration, serve on the party to the appeal other than the party who made the section 103A application a copy of the application notice and any documents which were attached to it.

(4) Paragraph (5) applies to reviews of appeals under section 82 of the 2002 Act where—

    (a)   the appellant is in the United Kingdom; and
    (b)   the appeal relates, in whole or in part, to an asylum claim.

(5) In cases to which this paragraph applies—

    (a)   the Tribunal must send to the respondent to the appeal—
        (i)   the notice of decision,
        (ii)   any directions, and
        (iii)   the application notice and any documents which were attached to it (unless the respondent to the appeal made the application for reconsideration);
    (b)   the respondent must serve on the appellant—
        (i)   the notice of decision and any directions; and
        (ii)   the application notice and any documents which were attached to it (unless the appellant made the application for reconsideration),
not later than 28 days after receiving them from the Tribunal;
    (c)   the respondent must, as soon as practicable after serving the documents mentioned in sub-paragraph (b), notify the Tribunal on what date and by what means they were served; and
    (d)   if the respondent does not give the Tribunal notification under sub-paragraph (c) within 29 days after the Tribunal serves the notice of decision on it, the Tribunal must serve the documents mentioned in sub-paragraph (b) on the appellant as soon as reasonably practicable thereafter.

Initial Commencement
Specified date: 4 April 2005: see r 1.

28   Sending notice of decision to the appropriate court

The Tribunal must send to the appropriate court copies of—

    (a)   the notice of decision; and
    (b)   the application notice and any documents which were attached to it,

upon being requested to do so by the appropriate court.

Initial Commencement
Specified date: 4 April 2005: see r 1.

[28A   Orders for funding on section 103A applications]

[(1) This rule applies where a section 103A application has been made by an appellant in relation to an appeal decided in England, Wales or Northern Ireland.

(2) If an immigration judge, when he considers a section 103A application, makes an order under section 103D(1) of the 2002 Act, the Tribunal must send a copy of that order to—

    (a)   the appellant's representative; and
    (b)   the relevant funding body.

(3) If, pursuant to regulations under section 103D of the 2002 Act, the appellant's representative applies for an order under section 103D(1) of the 2002 Act where an immigration judge has made an order for reconsideration of an appeal but the reconsideration does not proceed—

    (a)   the immigration judge may decide that application without a hearing; and
    (b)   the Tribunal must send notice of his decision to—

    (i) the appellant's representative; and

    (ii) if he makes an order under section 103D(1), the relevant funding body.

(4) In a case to which rule 27(5) applies, the Tribunal must not send an order or decision under this rule to the appellant's representative until either—

    (a) the respondent has notified the Tribunal under rule 27(5)(c) that it has served the documents mentioned in rule 27(5)(b) on the appellant; or

    (b) the Tribunal has served those documents on the appellant under rule 27(5)(d).

(5) In this rule, "relevant funding body" has the same meaning as in rule 33.]

Amendment

Inserted by SI 2005/569, r 3. Date in force: 4 April 2005: see SI 2005/569, r 1(1).

SECTION 2
RECONSIDERATION OF APPEALS

29   Rules applicable on reconsideration of appeal

Rules 15 to 23, except for rule 23(2) and (3), and Part 5 of these Rules apply to the reconsideration of an appeal as they do to the initial determination of an appeal, and references in those rules to an appeal shall be interpreted as including proceedings for the reconsideration of an appeal.

Initial Commencement

Specified date: 4 April 2005: see r 1.

30   Reply

(1) When the other party to the appeal is served with an order for reconsideration, he must, if he contends that the Tribunal should uphold the initial determination for reasons different from or additional to those given in the determination, file with the Tribunal and serve on the applicant a reply setting out his case.

(2) The other party to the appeal must file and serve any reply not later than 5 days before the earliest date appointed for any hearing of or in relation to the reconsideration of the appeal.

(3) In this rule, "other party to the appeal" means the party other than the party on whose application the order for reconsideration was made.

Initial Commencement

Specified date: 4 April 2005: see r 1.

31   Procedure for reconsideration of appeal

(1) Where an order for reconsideration has been made, the Tribunal must reconsider an appeal as soon as reasonably practicable after that order has been served on both parties to the appeal.

(2) Where the reconsideration is pursuant to an order under section 103A—

    (a) the Tribunal carrying out the reconsideration must first decide whether the original Tribunal made a material error of law; and

    (b) if it decides that the original Tribunal did not make a material error of law, the Tribunal must order that the original determination of the appeal shall stand.

(3) Subject to paragraph (2), the Tribunal must substitute a fresh decision to allow or dismiss the appeal.

(4) In carrying out the reconsideration, the Tribunal—

(a) may limit submissions or evidence to one or more specified issues; and

(b) must have regard to any directions given by the immigration judge or court which ordered the reconsideration.

(5)   In this rule, a "material error of law" means an error of law which affected the Tribunal's decision upon the appeal.

Initial Commencement
Specified date: 4 April 2005: see r 1.

32   Evidence on reconsideration of appeal

(1)   The Tribunal may consider as evidence any note or record made by the Tribunal of any previous hearing at which the appeal was considered.

(2)   If a party wishes to ask the Tribunal to consider evidence which was not submitted on any previous occasion when the appeal was considered, he must file with the Tribunal and serve on the other party written notice to that effect, which must—

(a) indicate the nature of the evidence; and

(b) explain why it was not submitted on any previous occasion.

(3)   A notice under paragraph (2) must be filed and served as soon as practicable after the parties have been served with the order for reconsideration.

(4)   If the Tribunal decides to admit additional evidence, it may give directions as to—

(a) the manner in which; and

(b) the time by which,

the evidence is to be given or filed.

Initial Commencement
Specified date: 4 April 2005: see r 1.

33   Orders for funding on reconsideration

(1)   This rule applies where—

(a) the Tribunal has reconsidered an appeal following a section 103A application made by the appellant in relation to an appeal decided in England, Wales or Northern Ireland; and

(b) the appellant's representative has specified that he seeks an order under section 103D of the 2002 Act for his costs to be paid out of the relevant fund.

(2)   The Tribunal must make a separate determination ("the funding determination") stating whether it orders that the appellant's costs—

(a) in respect of the application for reconsideration; and

(b) in respect of the reconsideration,

are to be paid out of the relevant fund.

(3)   The Tribunal must send the funding determination to—

(a) the appellant's representative; and

(b) if the Tribunal has made an order under section 103D, the relevant funding body.

(4)   Where the determination of the reconsidered appeal ("the principal determination") is served in accordance with rule 23, the Tribunal must not send the funding determination to the appellant's representative until—

(a)   the respondent has notified the Tribunal under rule 23(5)(b) that it has served the principal determination on the appellant; or

(b)   the Tribunal has served the principal determination on the appellant under rule 23(6).

[(4A)   Where, in accordance with regulations under section 103D of the 2002 Act, a senior immigration judge reviews a decision by the Tribunal not to make an order under section 103D(3), the Tribunal must send notice of the decision upon that review to—

(a)   the appellant's representative; and

(b)   if the senior immigration judge makes an order under section 103D(3), the relevant funding body.]

(5)   In this Rule—

(a)   "relevant fund" means—
   (i)   in relation to an appeal decided in England or Wales, the Community Legal Service Fund established under section 5 of the Access to Justice Act 1999;
   (ii)   in relation to an appeal decided in Northern Ireland, the fund established under paragraph 4(2)(a) of Schedule 3 to the Access to Justice (Northern Ireland) Order 2003; and

(b)   "relevant funding body" means—
   (i)   in relation to an appeal decided in England or Wales, the Legal Services Commission;
   (ii)   in relation to an appeal decided in Northern Ireland, the Northern Ireland Legal Services Commission.

Initial Commencement
Specified date: 4 April 2005: see r 1.

Amendment
Para (4A): inserted by SI 2005/569, r 4. Date in force: 4 April 2005: see SI 2005/569, r 1(1).

SECTION 3
APPLICATIONS FOR PERMISSION TO APPEAL TO THE APPROPRIATE APPELLATE COURT

34   Applying for permission to appeal

(1)   An application to the Tribunal under this Section must be made by filing with the Tribunal an application notice for permission to appeal.

(2)   The application notice for permission to appeal must—

(a)   be in the appropriate prescribed form;

(b)   state the grounds of appeal; and

(c)   be signed by the applicant or his representative, and dated.

(3)   If the application notice is signed by the applicant's representative, the representative must certify in the application notice that he has completed the application notice in accordance with the applicant's instructions.

(4)   As soon as practicable after an application notice for permission to appeal is filed, the Tribunal must notify the other party to the appeal to the Tribunal that it has been filed.

Initial Commencement
Specified date: 4 April 2005: see r 1.

35   Time limit for application

(1)   In application notice for permission to appeal must be filed in accordance with rule 34—

(a)   if the applicant is in detention under the Immigration Acts when he is served with the Tribunal's determination, not later than 5 days after he is served with that determination;

(b)   in any other case, not later than 10 days after he is served with the Tribunal's determination.

(2)   The Tribunal may not extend the time limits in paragraph (1).

Initial Commencement
Specified date: 4 April 2005: see r 1.

36   Determining the application

(1)   An application for permission to appeal must be determined by a senior immigration judge without a hearing.

(2)   The Tribunal may either grant or refuse permission to appeal.

(3)   Where the Tribunal intends to grant permission to appeal it may, if it thinks that the Tribunal has made an administrative error in relation to the proceedings, instead set aside the Tribunal's determination and direct that the proceedings be reheard by the Tribunal.

(4)   The Tribunal must serve on every party written notice of its decision, including its reasons, which may be in summary form.

Initial Commencement
Specified date: 4 April 2005: see r 1.

PART 4
BAIL

37   Scope of this Part and interpretation

(1)   This Part applies to applications under the Immigration Acts to the Tribunal, by persons detained under those Acts, to be released on bail.

(2)   In this Part, "applicant" means a person applying to the Tribunal to be released on bail.

(3)   The parties to a bail application are the applicant and the Secretary of State.

Initial Commencement
Specified date: 4 April 2005: see r 1.

38   Applications for bail

(1)   An application to be released on bail must be made by filing with the Tribunal an application notice in the appropriate prescribed form.

(2)   The application notice must contain the following details—

(a)   the applicant's—
  (i)   full name;
  (ii)   date of birth; and
  (iii)   date of arrival in the United Kingdom;
(b)   the address of the place where the applicant is detained;
(c)   whether an appeal by the applicant to the Tribunal is pending;

(d)   the address where the applicant will reside if his application for bail is granted, or, if he is unable to give such an address, the reason why an address is not given;

(e)   where the applicant is aged 18 or over, whether he will, if required, agree as a condition of bail to co-operate with electronic monitoring under section 36 of the 2004 Act;

(f)   the amount of the recognizance in which he will agree to be bound;

(g)   the full names, addresses, occupations and dates of birth of any persons who have agreed to act as sureties for the applicant if bail is granted, and the amounts of the recognizances in which they will agree to be bound;

(h)   the grounds on which the application is made and, where a previous application has been refused, full details of any change in circumstances which has occurred since the refusal; and

(i)   whether an interpreter will be required at the hearing, and in respect of what language or dialect.

(3)   The application must be signed by the applicant or his representative or, in the case of an applicant who is a child or is for any other reason incapable of acting, by a person acting on his behalf.

Initial Commencement
Specified date: 4 April 2005: see r 1.

39   Bail hearing

(1)   Where an application for bail is filed, the Tribunal must—

(a)   as soon as reasonably practicable, serve a copy of the application on the Secretary of State; and

(b)   fix a hearing.

(2)   If the Secretary of State wishes to contest the application, he must file with the Tribunal and serve on the applicant a written statement of his reasons for doing so—

(a)   not later than 2.00 pm on the business day before the hearing; or

(b)   if he was served with notice of the hearing less than 24 hours before that time, as soon as reasonably practicable.

(3)   The Tribunal must serve written notice of its decision on—

(a)   the parties; and

(b)   the person having custody of the applicant.

(4)   Where bail is granted, the notice must include—

(a)   the conditions of bail; and

(b)   the amount in which the applicant and any sureties are to be bound.

(5)   Where bail is refused, the notice must include reasons for the refusal.

Initial Commencement
Specified date: 4 April 2005: see r 1.

40   Recognizances

(1)   The recognizance of an applicant or a surety must be in writing and must state—

(a)   the amount in which he agrees to be bound; and

(b)   that he has read and understood the bail decision and that he agrees to pay that amount of money if the applicant fails to comply with the conditions set out in the bail decision.

(2) The recognizance must be—

(a) signed by the applicant or surety; and
(b) filed with the Tribunal.

Initial Commencement
Specified date: 4 April 2005: see r 1.

41 Release of applicant

The person having custody of the applicant must release him upon—

(a) being served with a copy of the decision to grant bail; and
(b) being satisfied that any recognizances required as a condition of that decision have been entered into.

Initial Commencement
Specified date: 4 April 2005: see r 1.

42 Application of this Part to Scotland

This Part applies to Scotland with the following modifications—

(a) in rule 38, for paragraph (2)(f) and (g) substitute—
"(f) the amount, if any, to be deposited if bail is granted;
(g) the full names, addresses and occupations of any persons offering to act as cautioners if the application for bail is granted;";
(b) in rule 39, for paragraph (4)(b) substitute—
"(b) the amount (if any) to be deposited by the applicant and any cautioners.";
(c) rule 40 does not apply; and
(d) in rule 41, for sub-paragraph (b) substitute—
"(b) being satisfied that the amount to be deposited, if any, has been deposited.".

Initial Commencement
Specified date: 4 April 2005: see r 1.

PART 5
GENERAL PROVISIONS

43 Conduct of appeals and applications

(1) The Tribunal may, subject to these Rules, decide the procedure to be followed in relation to any appeal or application.

(2) Anything of a formal or administrative nature which is required or permitted to be done by the Tribunal under these Rules may be done by a member of the Tribunal's staff.

Initial Commencement
Specified date: 4 April 2005: see r 1.

44 Constitution of the Tribunal

(1) The Tribunal shall be under no duty to consider any representations by a party about the number or class of members of the Tribunal which should exercise the jurisdiction of the Tribunal.

(2) Where the President directs that the Tribunal's jurisdiction shall be exercised by more than one member, unless the President's direction specifies otherwise a single immigration judge may—

(a) conduct a case management review hearing;
(b) give directions to the parties; and
(c) deal with any other matter preliminary or incidental to the hearing of an appeal or application.

Initial Commencement
Specified date: 4 April 2005: see r 1.

45 Directions

(1) The Tribunal may give directions to the parties relating to the conduct of any appeal or application.

(2) The power to give directions is to be exercised subject to any specific provision of these Rules.

(3) Directions must be given orally or in writing to every party.

(4) Directions of the Tribunal may, in particular—

(a) relate to any matter concerning the preparation for a hearing;
(b) specify the length of time allowed for anything to be done;
(c) vary any time limit in these Rules or in directions previously given by the Tribunal for anything to be done by a party;
(d) provide for—
  (i) a particular matter to be dealt with as a preliminary issue;
  (ii) a case management review hearing to be held;
  (iii) a party to provide further details of his case, or any other information which appears to be necessary for the determination of the appeal;
  (iv) the witnesses, if any, to be heard;
  (v) the manner in which any evidence is to be given (for example, by directing that witness statements are to stand as evidence in chief);
(e) require any party to file and serve—
  (i) statements of the evidence which will be called at the hearing;
  (ii) a paginated and indexed bundle of all the documents which will be relied on at the hearing;
  (iii) a skeleton argument which summarises succinctly the submissions which will be made at the hearing and cites all the authorities which will be relied on, identifying any particular passages to be relied on;
  (iv) a time estimate for the hearing;
  (v) a list of witnesses whom any party wishes to call to give evidence;
  (vi) a chronology of events; and
  (vii) details of whether an interpreter will be required at the hearing, and in respect of what language and dialect;
(f) limit—
  (i) the number or length of documents upon which a party may rely at a hearing;
  (ii) the length of oral submissions;
  (iii) the time allowed for the examination and cross-examination of witnesses; and
  (iv) the issues which are to be addressed at a hearing; and
(g) require the parties to take any steps to enable two or more appeals to be heard together under rule 20.
(h) provide for a hearing to be conducted or evidence given or representations made by video link or by other electronic means; and
(i) make provision to secure the anonymity of a party or a witness.

(5) The Tribunal must not direct an unrepresented party to do something unless it is satisfied that he is able to comply with the direction.

(6)   The President may direct that, in individual cases or in such classes of case as he shall specify, any time period in these Rules for the Tribunal to do anything shall be extended by such period as he shall specify.

Initial Commencement
Specified date: 4 April 2005: see r 1.

46   Notification of hearings

(1)   When the Tribunal fixes a hearing it must serve notice of the date, time and place of the hearing on every party.

(2)   The Tribunal may vary the date of a hearing, but must serve notice of the new date, time and place of the hearing on every party.

Initial Commencement
Specified date: 4 April 2005: see r 1.

47   Adjournment

Subject to any provision of these Rules, the Tribunal may adjourn any hearing.

Initial Commencement
Specified date: 4 April 2005: see r 1.

48   Representation

(1)   An appellant or applicant for bail may act in person or be represented by any person not prohibited from representing him by section 84 of the Immigration and Asylum Act 1999.

(2)   A respondent to an appeal, the Secretary of State or the United Kingdom Representative may be represented by any person authorised to act on his behalf.

(3)   If a party to whom paragraph (1) applies is represented by a person not permitted by that paragraph to represent him, any determination given or other step taken by the Tribunal in the proceedings shall nevertheless be valid.

(4)   Where a representative begins to act for a party, he must immediately notify the Tribunal and the other party of that fact.

(5)   Where a representative is acting for a party, he may on behalf of that party do anything that these Rules require or permit that party to do.

(6)   Where a representative is acting for an appellant, the appellant is under a duty—

  (a)   to maintain contact with his representative until the appeal is finally determined; and
  (b)   to notify the representative of any change of address.

(7)   Where a representative ceases to act for a party, the representative and the party must immediately notify the Tribunal and the other party of that fact, and of the name and address of any new representative (if known).

(8)   Notification under paragraph (4) or (7)—

  (a)   may be given orally at a hearing to the Tribunal and to any other party present at that hearing; but
  (b)   must otherwise be given in writing.

(9)   Until the Tribunal is notified that a representative has ceased to act for a party, any document served on that representative shall be deemed to be properly served on the party he was representing.

Initial Commencement
Specified date: 4 April 2005: see r 1.

49 United Kingdom Representative

(1) The United Kingdom Representative may give notice to the Tribunal that he wishes to participate in any proceedings where the appellant has made an asylum claim.

(2) Where the United Kingdom Representative has given notice under paragraph (1)—

  (a) rules 54(6) and 55(7) shall apply; and
  (b) the Tribunal must permit him to make representations in the proceedings if he wishes to do so, and may give directions for that purpose.

Initial Commencement
Specified date: 4 April 2005: see r 1.

50 Summoning of witnesses

(1) The Tribunal may, by issuing a summons ("a witness summons"), require any person in the United Kingdom—

  (a) to attend as a witness at the hearing of an appeal; and
  (b) subject to rule 51(2), at the hearing to answer any questions or produce any documents in his custody or under his control which relate to any matter in issue in the appeal.

(2) A person is not required to attend a hearing in obedience to a witness summons unless—

  (a) the summons is served on him; and
  (b) the necessary expenses of his attendance are paid or tendered to him.

(3) If a witness summons is issued at the request of a party, that party must pay or tender the expenses referred to in paragraph (2)(b).

Initial Commencement
Specified date: 4 April 2005: see r 1.

51 Evidence

(1) The Tribunal may allow oral, documentary or other evidence to be given of any fact which appears to be relevant to an appeal or an application for bail, even if that evidence would be inadmissible in a court of law.

(2) The Tribunal may not compel a party or witness to give any evidence or produce any document which he could not be compelled to give or produce at the trial of a civil claim in the part of the United Kingdom in which the hearing is taking place.

(3) The Tribunal may require the oral evidence of a witness to be given on oath or affirmation.

(4) Where the Tribunal has given directions setting time limits for the filing and serving of written evidence, it must not consider any written evidence which is not filed or served in accordance with those directions unless satisfied that there are good reasons to do so.

(5) Where a party seeks to rely upon a copy of a document as evidence, the Tribunal may require the original document to be produced.

(6) In an appeal to which section 85(5) of the 2002 Act applies, the Tribunal must only consider evidence relating to matters which it is not prevented by that section from considering.

(7) Subject to section 108 of the 2002 Act, the Tribunal must not take account of any evidence that has not been made available to all the parties.

Initial Commencement
Specified date: 4 April 2005: see r 1.

52   Language of documents

(1) Subject to paragraph (2)—

  (a) any notice of appeal or application notice filed with the Tribunal must be completed in English; and
  (b) any other document filed with the Tribunal must be in English, or accompanied by a translation into English signed by the translator to certify that the translation is accurate.

(2) In proceedings in or having a connection with Wales, a document may be filed with the Tribunal in Welsh.

(3) The Tribunal shall be under no duty to consider a document which is not in English (or, where paragraph (2) applies, in Welsh), or accompanied by a certified translation.

Initial Commencement
Specified date: 4 April 2005: see r 1.

53   Burden of proof

(1) If an appellant asserts that a relevant decision ought not to have been taken against him on the ground that the statutory provision under which that decision was taken does not apply to him, it is for that party to prove that the provision does not apply to him.

(2) If—

  (a) an appellant asserts any fact; and
  (b) by virtue of an Act, statutory instrument or immigration rules, if he had made such an assertion to the Secretary of State, an immigration officer or an entry clearance officer, it would have been for him to satisfy the Secretary of State or officer that the assertion was true,

it is for the appellant to prove that the fact asserted is true.

Initial Commencement
Specified date: 4 April 2005: see r 1.

54   Admission of public to hearings

(1) Subject to the following provisions of this rule, every hearing before the Tribunal must be held in public.

(2) Where the Tribunal is considering an allegation referred to in section 108 of the 2002 Act—

  (a) all members of the public must be excluded from the hearing, and
  (b) any party or representative of a party may be excluded from the hearing.

(3) The Tribunal may exclude any or all members of the public from any hearing or part of a hearing if it is necessary—

(a) in the interests of public order or national security; or

(b) to protect the private life of a party or the interests of a minor.

(4) The Tribunal may also, in exceptional circumstances, exclude any or all members of the public from any hearing or part of a hearing to ensure that publicity does not prejudice the interests of justice, but only if and to the extent that it is strictly necessary to do so.

(5) A member of the Council on Tribunals or of its Scottish Committee acting in that capacity is entitled to attend any hearing and may not be excluded pursuant to paragraph (2), (3) or (4) of this rule.

(6) The United Kingdom Representative, where he has given notice to the Tribunal under rule 49, is entitled to attend any hearing except where paragraph (2) applies, and may not be excluded pursuant to paragraph (3) or (4) of this rule.

Initial Commencement
Specified date: 4 April 2005: see r 1.

55   Filing and service of documents

(1) Any document which is required or permitted by these Rules or by a direction of the Tribunal to be filed with the Tribunal, or served on any person may be—

(a) delivered, or sent by post, to an address;

(b) sent via a document exchange to a document exchange number or address;

(c) sent by fax to a fax number; or

(d) sent by e-mail to an e-mail address,

specified for that purpose by the Tribunal or person to whom the document is directed.

(2) A document to be served on an individual may be served personally by leaving it with that individual.

(3) Where a person has notified the Tribunal that he is acting as the representative of an appellant and has given an address for service, if a document is served on the appellant, a copy must also at the same time be sent to the appellant's representative.

(4) If any document is served on a person who has notified the Tribunal that he is acting as the representative of a party, it shall be deemed to have been served on that party.

(5) Subject to paragraph (6), any document that is served on a person in accordance with this rule shall, unless the contrary is proved, be deemed to be served—

(a) where the document is sent by post or document exchange from and to a place within the United Kingdom, on the second day after it was sent;

(b) where the document is sent by post or document exchange from or to a place outside the United Kingdom, on the twenty-eighth day after it was sent; and

(c) in any other case, on the day on which the document was sent or delivered to, or left with, that person.

(6) Any notice of appeal which is served on a person under rule 6(3)(b) or 6(4)(b) shall be treated as being served on the day on which it is received by that person.

(7) Where the United Kingdom Representative has given notice to the Tribunal under rule 49 in relation to any proceedings, any document which is required by these Rules or by a direction of the Tribunal to be served on a party in those proceedings must also be served on the United Kingdom Representative.

Initial Commencement
Specified date: 4 April 2005: see r 1.

56   Address for service

(1)   Every party, and any person representing a party, must notify the Tribunal in writing of a postal address at which documents may be served on him and of any changes to that address.

(2)   Until a party or representative notifies the Tribunal of a change of address, any document served on him at the most recent address which he has notified to the Tribunal shall be deemed to have been properly served on him.

Initial Commencement
Specified date: 4 April 2005: see r 1.

57   Calculation of time

(1)   Where a period of time for doing any act is specified by these Rules or by a direction of the Tribunal, that period is to be calculated—

   (a)   excluding the day on which the period begins; and
   (b)   where the period is 10 days or less, excluding any day which is not a business day (unless the period is expressed as a period of calendar days).

(2)   Where the time specified by these Rules or by a direction of the Tribunal for doing any act ends on a day which is not a business day, that act is done in time if it is done on the next business day.

Initial Commencement
Specified date: 4 April 2005: see r 1.

58   Signature of documents

Any requirement in these Rules for a document to be signed by a party or his representative shall be satisfied, in the case of a document which is filed or served electronically in accordance with these rules, by the person who is required to sign the document typing his name or producing it by computer or other mechanical means.

Initial Commencement
Specified date: 4 April 2005: see r 1.

59   Errors of procedure

(1)   Where, before the Tribunal has determined an appeal or application, there has been an error of procedure such as a failure to comply with a rule—

   (a)   subject to these Rules, the error does not invalidate any step taken in the proceedings, unless the Tribunal so orders; and
   (b)   the Tribunal may make any order, or take any other step, that it considers appropriate to remedy the error.

(2)   In particular, any determination made in an appeal or application under these Rules shall be valid notwithstanding that—

   (a)   a hearing did not take place; or
   (b)   the determination was not made or served,

within a time period specified in these Rules.

Initial Commencement
Specified date: 4 April 2005: see r 1.

60   Correction of orders and determinations

(1)   The Tribunal may at any time amend an order, notice of decision or determination to correct a clerical error or other accidental slip or omission.

(2)   Where an order, notice of decision or determination is amended under this rule—

  (a)   the Tribunal must serve an amended version on the party or parties on whom it served the original; and
  (b)   if rule 10(8) and (9), rule 23(5) and (6) or rule 27(5)(b)–(d) applied in relation to the service of the original, it shall also apply in relation to the service of the amended version.

(3)   The time within which a party may apply for permission to appeal against, or for a review of, an amended determination runs from the date on which the party is served with the amended determination.

Initial Commencement
Specified date: 4 April 2005: see r 1.

PART 6
REVOCATION AND TRANSITIONAL PROVISIONS

61   Revocation

The Immigration and Asylum Appeals (Procedure) Rules 2003 are revoked.

Initial Commencement
Specified date: 4 April 2005: see r 1.

62   Transitional provisions

(1)   Subject to the following paragraphs of this rule, these Rules apply to any appeal or application to an adjudicator or the Immigration Appeal Tribunal which was pending immediately before 4th April 2005, and which continues on or after that date as if it had been made to the Tribunal by virtue of a transitional provisions order.

(2)   Where a notice of a relevant decision has been served before 4th April 2005 and the recipient gives notice of appeal against the decision on or after 4th April 2005—

  (a)   rules 6–8, 12 and 13 of these Rules shall not apply; and
  (b)   rules 6–9 of the 2003 Rules shall continue to apply as if those Rules had not been revoked, but subject to the modifications in paragraph (4).

(3)   Where a notice of appeal to an adjudicator has been given before 4th April 2005, but the respondent has not filed the notice of appeal with the appellate authority in accordance with rule 9 of the 2003 Rules—

  (a)   rules 12 and 13 of these Rules shall not apply; and
  (b)   rule 9 of the 2003 Rules shall continue to apply as if it had not been revoked, but subject to the modifications in paragraph (4).

(4)   The modifications referred to in paragraphs (2)(b) and (3)(b) are that—

  (a)   references to an adjudicator or the appellate authority shall be treated as referring to the Tribunal;
  (b)   in rule 9(1) of the 2003 Rules—
      (i)   the words "Subject to rule 10" shall be omitted; and
      (ii)   for "together with" there shall be substituted "and must also when directed by the Asylum and Immigration Tribunal file"; and
  (c)   for rule 9(2) of the 2003 Rules there shall be substituted—

"(2)   The respondent must, as soon as practicable after filing the notice of appeal, serve on the appellant—

    (a)   a copy of all the documents listed in paragraph (1), except for documents which the respondent has already sent to the appellant; and

    (b)   notice of the date on which the notice of appeal was filed.".

(5)   Where, pursuant to a transitional provisions order, the Tribunal considers a section 103A application for a review of an adjudicator's determination of an appeal, Section 1 of Part 3 of these Rules shall apply subject to the modifications that—

    (a)   in rules 26(3) and 27(2), the references to "its decision" shall be interpreted as referring to the adjudicator's decision; and

    (b)   in rules 26(6)(a) and 27(3)(a), the references to "the Tribunal" shall be interpreted as referring to the adjudicator.

(6)   Where, pursuant to a transitional provisions order, the Tribunal reconsiders an appeal which was originally determined by an adjudicator, Section 2 of Part 3 shall apply to the reconsideration, subject to paragraph (7).

(7)   Where—

    (a)   a party has been granted permission to appeal to the Immigration Appeal Tribunal against an adjudicator's determination before 4th April 2005, but the appeal has not been determined by that date; and

    (b)   by virtue of a transitional provisions order the grant of permission to appeal is treated as an order for the Tribunal to reconsider the adjudicator's determination,

the reconsideration shall be limited to the grounds upon which the Immigration Appeal Tribunal granted permission to appeal.

(8)   Any time limit in these Rules for the Tribunal to do anything shall not apply in relation to proceedings to which these Rules apply by virtue of paragraph (1) of this rule.

(9)   In relation to proceedings which were pending immediately before 4th April 2005—

    (a)   unless the Tribunal directs otherwise—

        (i)   anything done or any directions given before 4th April 2005 under the 2003 Rules (including anything which, pursuant to rule 61(3) of those Rules, was treated as if done or given under those Rules) shall continue to have effect on and after that date;

        (ii)   anything done or any directions given by the appellate authority shall be treated as if done or given by the Tribunal; and

        (iii)   any document served on the appellate authority shall be treated as if served on the Tribunal;

    (b)   unless the context requires otherwise, any reference in a document to an adjudicator, the Immigration Appeal Tribunal or the appellate authority shall, insofar as it relates to an event on or after 4th April 2005, be treated as a reference to the Tribunal.

(10)   In this rule—

    (a)   "the 2003 Rules" means the Immigration and Asylum Appeals (Procedure) Rules 2003;

    (b)   "adjudicator" and "appellate authority" have the same meaning as in the 2003 Rules; and

    (c)   "a transitional provisions order" means an order under section 48(3)(a) of the 2004 Act containing transitional provisions.

Initial Commencement
Specified date: 4 April 2005: see r 1.

SCHEDULE
FORMS

Rule 2

[The text of these forms is currently unavailable. Please see the originals]

Initial Commencement
Specified date: 4 April 2005: see r 1.

ASYLUM AND IMMIGRATION TRIBUNAL (FAST TRACK PROCEDURE) RULES 2005

2005 No 560

Made	*7th March 2005*
Laid before Parliament	*10th March 2005*
Coming into force	*4th April 2005*

The Lord Chancellor, in exercise of the powers conferred by sections 106(1)–(3) and 112(3) of the Nationality, Immigration and Asylum Act 2002 and section 40A(3) of the British Nationality Act 1981, after consulting with the Council on Tribunals in accordance with section 8 of the Tribunals and Inquiries Act 1992, hereby makes the following Rules:

PART 1
INTRODUCTION

1   Citation and commencement

These Rules may be cited as the Asylum and Immigration Tribunal (Fast Track Procedure) Rules 2005 and shall come into force on 4th April 2005.

Initial Commencement
Specified date: 4 April 2005: see above.

2   Interpretation

(1)   In these Rules, "the Principal Rules" means the Asylum and Immigration Tribunal (Procedure) Rules 2005.

(2)   Subject to paragraph (3), words and expressions used in these Rules which are defined in rule 2 of the Principal Rules have the same meaning in these Rules as in the Principal Rules.

(3)   In these Rules, and in any provision of the Principal Rules which applies by virtue of these Rules, "business day" means any day other than a Saturday or Sunday, a bank holiday, 24th to 31st December, Maundy Thursday, Good Friday or the Tuesday after the last Monday in May.

(4)   In a provision of the Principal Rules which applies by virtue of these Rules, a reference to an "appropriate prescribed form" means, in relation to a notice of appeal or an application notice for permission to appeal to the appropriate appellate court, the appropriate form in Schedule 1 to these Rules, or that form with any variations that the circumstances may require.

(5)   Where a provision of the Principal Rules applies by virtue of these Rules—

(a)   any reference in that provision to the Principal Rules is to be interpreted as including a reference to these Rules; and

(b)   any reference in that provision to a specific Part or rule in the Principal Rules is to be interpreted as including a reference to any equivalent Part or rule in these Rules.

Initial Commencement
Specified date: 4 April 2005: see r 1.

3   Scope of these Rules

(1)   Part 2 of these Rules applies to appeals to the Tribunal in the circumstances specified in rule 5.

(2)   Part 3 applies to proceedings before the Tribunal of the types described in rule 24 of the Principal Rules in the circumstances specified in rule 15.

(3)   Part 4 applies to proceedings before the Tribunal to which Part 2 or 3 applies.

(4)   Part 5 applies to proceedings before the Tribunal to which Part 2 or 3 applies or has applied.

(5)   For the purpose of rules 5 and 15, a party does not cease to satisfy a condition that he must have been continuously in detention under the Immigration Acts at a place or places specified in Schedule 2 to these Rules by reason only of—

(a)   being transported from one place of detention specified in that Schedule to another place which is so specified; or

(b)   leaving and returning to such a place of detention for any purpose between the hours of 6am and 10pm.

Initial Commencement
Specified date: 4 April 2005: see r 1.

4   Application of the Principal Rules

(1)   Rule 4 of the Principal Rules (Overriding objective) applies to these Rules.

(2)   Where Part 2 or 3 of these Rules applies to proceedings before the Tribunal, the Principal Rules also apply to the extent specified in rules 6, 16, 20, 24 and 27 of these Rules.

Initial Commencement
Specified date: 4 April 2005: see r 1.

PART 2
APPEALS TO THE TRIBUNAL

5   Scope of this Part

(1)   This Part applies to an appeal to the Tribunal where the person giving notice of appeal—

    (a)   was in detention under the Immigration Acts at a place specified in Schedule 2 when he was served with notice of the immigration decision against which he is appealing; and

    (b)   has been continuously in detention under the Immigration Acts at a place or places specified in Schedule 2 since that notice was served on him.

(2)   This Part shall cease to apply if the Tribunal makes an order under rule 30(1).

Initial Commencement
Specified date: 4 April 2005: see r 1.

6   Application of Part 2 of the Principal Rules

Where this Part applies to an appeal, the following provisions of Part 2 of the Principal Rules apply—

    (a)   rule 6(1) to (3), omitting the reference to rule 6(4) in rule 6(2);
    (b)   rule 8;
    (c)   rule 10(1);
    (d)   rule 13(1) and (4);
    (e)   rule 14; and
    (f)   rules 17 to 19.

Initial Commencement
Specified date: 4 April 2005: see r 1.

7   Giving notice of appeal

Where a notice of appeal is served on a custodian under rule 6(3)(b) of the Principal Rules, the custodian must—

    (a)   endorse on the notice the date that it is served on him; and
    (b)   forward it to the Tribunal immediately.

Initial Commencement
Specified date: 4 April 2005: see r 1.

8   Time limit

(1)   A person who wishes to appeal must give a notice of appeal not later than 2 days after the day on which he is served with notice of the immigration decision against which he is appealing.

(2)   Where a notice of appeal is given outside the time limit in paragraph (1), the Tribunal must not extend the time for appealing unless it is satisfied that, because of circumstances outside the control of the person giving notice of appeal or his representative, it was not practicable for the notice of appeal to be given within that time limit.

Initial Commencement
Specified date: 4 April 2005: see r 1.

9   Service of notice of appeal on respondent

When the Tribunal receives a notice of appeal it shall immediately serve a copy upon the respondent.

Initial Commencement
Specified date: 4 April 2005: see r 1.

10   Filing of documents by respondent

The respondent must file the documents listed in rule 13(1) of the Principal Rules not later than 2 days after the day on which the Tribunal serves the respondent with the notice of appeal.

Initial Commencement
Specified date: 4 April 2005: see r 1.

11   Listing

(1)   The Tribunal shall fix a hearing date which is—

    (a)   not later than 2 days after the day on which the respondent files the documents under rule 10; or

    (b)   if the Tribunal is unable to arrange a hearing within that time, as soon as practicable thereafter.

(2)   The Tribunal must serve notice of the date, time and place of the hearing on every party as soon as practicable, and in any event not later than noon on the business day before the hearing.

Initial Commencement
Specified date: 4 April 2005: see r 1.

12   Deciding timeliness issues

(1)   The Tribunal shall consider any issue as to—

    (a)   whether a notice of appeal was given outside the applicable time limit; and

    (b)   whether to extend the time for appealing where the notice of appeal was given outside that time limit,

as a preliminary issue at the hearing fixed under rule 11, subject to paragraph (2) of this rule.

(2)   Rule 13 applies to the consideration and decision of such an issue as it applies to the consideration and determination of an appeal.

(3)   Where the notice of appeal was given outside the applicable time limit and the Tribunal does not grant an extension of time, the Tribunal must take no further action in relation to the notice of appeal, except that it must serve written notice of its decision under this rule on the parties not later than 1 day after the day on which that decision is made.

Initial Commencement
Specified date: 4 April 2005: see r 1.

13   Method of determining appeal

The Tribunal must consider the appeal at the hearing fixed under rule 11 except where—

    (a)   the appeal—
        (i)   lapses pursuant to section 99 of the 2002 Act;
        (ii)   is treated as abandoned pursuant to section 104(4) of the 2002 Act;
        (iii)   is treated as finally determined pursuant to section 104(5) of the 2002 Act; or
        (iv)   is withdrawn by the appellant or treated as withdrawn in accordance with rule 17 of the Principal Rules;
    (b)   the Tribunal adjourns the hearing under rule 28 or 30(2)(a) of these Rules; or

(c)   all of the parties to the appeal consent to the Tribunal determining the appeal without a hearing.

Initial Commencement
Specified date: 4 April 2005: see r 1.

14   Giving of determination

(1)   Where the Tribunal determines an appeal, it must give a written determination containing its decision and the reasons for it.

(2)   The Tribunal must serve its determination on every party to the appeal—

(a)   if the appeal is considered at a hearing, not later than 2 days after the day on which the hearing of the appeal finishes; or

(b)   if the appeal is determined without a hearing, not later than 2 days after the day on which it is determined.

Initial Commencement
Specified date: 4 April 2005: see r 1.

PART 3
RECONSIDERATION OF APPEALS, ETC

15   Scope of this Part

(1)   This Part applies to proceedings before the Tribunal of a type specified in rule 24 of the Principal Rules, where—

(a)   Part 2 of these Rules applied at all times to the appeal to the Tribunal;

(b)   Part 3 of these Rules applied at all times to any other proceedings before the Tribunal of a type specified in rule 24 of the Principal Rules which related to that appeal; and

(c)   the appellant has been continuously in detention under the Immigration Acts at a place or places specified in Schedule 2 to these Rules since being served with notice of the immigration decision against which he is appealing.

(2)   This Part shall cease to apply if the Tribunal makes an order under rule 30(1).

Initial Commencement
Specified date: 4 April 2005: see r 1.

SECTION 1
SECTION 103A APPLICATIONS CONSIDERED BY MEMBERS OF THE TRIBUNAL

16   Application of Section 1 of Part 3 of the Principal Rules

Where this Part applies to a section 103A application, the following provisions of Section 1 of Part 3 of the Principal Rules apply—

(a)   rule 25;

(b)   rule 26, omitting paragraphs (2) and (4) of that rule;

(c)   rule 27(1) and (2); and

(d)   rule 28.

Initial Commencement
Specified date: 4 April 2005: see r 1.

17   Service of application and response

Where a section 103A application to which this Part applies is filed with the Tribunal—

(a)   the Tribunal must serve copies of the application notice and any documents which were attached to it on the party to the appeal other than the party who made the section 103A application as soon as practicable; and

(b)   the party to the appeal other than the party who made the section 103A application may file submissions in response to the application not later than 1 day after the day on which it is served with the application.

Initial Commencement
Specified date: 4 April 2005: see r 1.

18   Method of deciding applications for review

The immigration judge shall decide the application without a hearing, and by reference only to—

(a)   the applicant's written submissions and the documents filed with the application notice; and

(b)   any submissions filed in response to the application under rule 17(b).

Initial Commencement
Specified date: 4 April 2005: see r 1.

19   Service of decision

The Tribunal must serve a copy of the notice of decision and any directions given under rule 27(2)(b) of the Principal Rules on every party to the appeal—

(a)   if submissions were filed in response to the application under rule 17(b), not later than 1 day after they were filed; or

(b)   if no submissions were filed within the period specified in rule 17(b), not later than 1 day after the end of that period.

Initial Commencement
Specified date: 4 April 2005: see r 1.

SECTION 2
RECONSIDERATION OF APPEALS

20   Application of the Principal Rules

(1)   Where this Part applies to the reconsideration of an appeal, the following provisions of Section 2 of Part 3 of the Principal Rules apply—

(a)   rule 31(2) to (5); and

(b)   rule 32(1).

(2)   Rules 17 to 19 and Part 5 of the Principal Rules apply, with any necessary modifications, to the reconsideration of an appeal under this Part to the extent that they would apply to the initial determination of an appeal under Part 2 of these Rules.

Initial Commencement
Specified date: 4 April 2005: see r 1.

21   Procedure for reconsideration of appeal

(1)   Where an order for reconsideration has been made, the Tribunal must fix a hearing date for the reconsideration of its decision on the appeal which is—

(a)   not later than 2 days after the day on which that order has been served on both parties to the appeal; or

(b)   if the Tribunal is unable to arrange a hearing within that time, as soon as practicable thereafter.

(2)   The Tribunal must serve notice of the date, time and place of the reconsideration hearing on every party not later than noon on the business day before the hearing.

Initial Commencement
Specified date: 4 April 2005: see r 1.

22   Fresh evidence on reconsideration of appeal

(1)   If a party wishes to ask the Tribunal to consider evidence which was not submitted on any previous occasion when it considered the appeal, he must notify the Tribunal and the other party of—

(a)   the nature of the evidence; and

(b)   the reasons why it was not submitted on any previous occasion.

(2)   Wherever practicable, notification under paragraph (1) must be given before the date fixed for the reconsideration hearing under rule 21.

Initial Commencement
Specified date: 4 April 2005: see r 1.

23   Determination on reconsideration

(1)   The Tribunal must reconsider its decision on the appeal at the hearing fixed under rule 21 except where—

(a)   any of the circumstances set out in rule 13 applies;

(b)   a party has failed to comply with a provision of these Rules or a direction of the Tribunal, and the Tribunal is satisfied that in all the circumstances, including the extent of the failure and any reasons for it, it is appropriate to reconsider its decision on the appeal without a hearing; or

(c)   the Tribunal is satisfied, having regard to the material before it and the nature of the issues raised, that its decision on the appeal can be justly reconsidered without a hearing.

(2)   Rule 14 applies to the reconsideration of an appeal as it applies to the initial determination of an appeal.

Initial Commencement
Specified date: 4 April 2005: see r 1.

SECTION 3
APPLICATIONS FOR PERMISSION TO APPEAL TO THE APPROPRIATE APPELLATE COURT

24   Application of Section 3 of Part 3 of the Principal Rules

Where this Part applies to an application for permission to appeal to the appropriate appellate court, the following provisions of Section 3 of Part 3 of the Principal Rules apply—

(a)   rule 34(1) to (3); and

(b)   rule 36.

Initial Commencement
Specified date: 4 April 2005: see r 1.

25   Time limits for filing and serving application

(1)   An application notice for permission to appeal must be filed not later than 2 days after the day on which the appellant is served with the Tribunal's determination.

(2)   The Tribunal may not extend the time limit in paragraph (1).

(3)   Immediately upon an application notice for permission to appeal being filed, the Tribunal must notify the other party to the appeal to the Tribunal that it has been filed.

Initial Commencement
Specified date: 4 April 2005: see r 1.

26   Time limit for determining the application

The Tribunal must determine the application for permission to appeal, and serve its determination on every party, not later than 1 day after the day on which the Tribunal receives the application notice.

Initial Commencement
Specified date: 4 April 2005: see r 1.

PART 4

GENERAL PROVISIONS

27   Application of Part 5 of the Principal Rules

Where this Part applies, Part 5 of the Principal Rules applies, except that—

    (a)   rule 47 applies subject to rule 28 of these Rules; and
    (b)   rule 60(2) does not apply.

Initial Commencement
Specified date: 4 April 2005: see r 1.

28   Adjournment

The Tribunal may only adjourn a hearing where—

    (a)   it is necessary to do so because there is insufficient time to hear the appeal or application which is before the Tribunal;
    (b)   a party has not been served with notice of the hearing in accordance with these Rules;
    (c)   the Tribunal is satisfied by evidence filed or given by or on behalf of a party that—
        (i)   the appeal or application cannot be justly determined on the date on which it is listed for hearing; and
        (ii)   there is an identifiable future date, not more than 10 days after the date on which the appeal or application is listed for hearing, by which it can be justly determined; or
    (d)   the Tribunal makes an order under rule 30.

Initial Commencement
Specified date: 4 April 2005: see r 1.

29   Correction of orders and determinations

Where an order, notice of decision or determination is amended under rule 60(1) of the Principal Rules, the Tribunal must, not later than 1 day after making the amendment, serve an amended version on every party on whom it served the original.

Initial Commencement
Specified date: 4 April 2005: see r 1.

PART 5
REMOVAL OF PENDING PROCEEDINGS FROM FAST TRACK

30   Transfer out of fast track procedure

(1)   Where Part 2 or 3 of these Rules applies to an appeal or application, the Tribunal must order that that Part shall cease to apply—

- (a)   if all the parties consent;
- (b)   if it is satisfied by evidence filed or given by or on behalf of a party that there are exceptional circumstances which mean that the appeal or application cannot otherwise be justly determined; or
- (c)   if—
    - (i)   the respondent to the appeal has failed to comply with a provision of these Rules, or the Principal Rules as applied by these Rules, or a direction of the Tribunal; and
    - (ii)   the Tribunal is satisfied that the appellant would be prejudiced by that failure if the appeal or application were determined in accordance with these Rules.

(2)   When making an order under paragraph (1), the Tribunal may—

- (a)   adjourn any hearing of the appeal or application; and
- (b)   give directions relating to the further conduct of the appeal or application.

(3)   Where the Tribunal adjourns a hearing under paragraph (2)(a)—

- (a)   it must fix a new date, time and place for the hearing; and
- (b)   in the case of an adjournment of an appeal, rule 21(4) of the Principal Rules shall apply.

Initial Commencement
Specified date: 4 April 2005: see r 1.

31   Application of the Principal Rules on transfer out of fast track

(1)   This rule applies where Part 2 or 3 of these Rules ceases to apply to an appeal or application because—

- (a)   the conditions in rule 5 or 15 cease to apply; or
- (b)   the Tribunal makes an order under rule 30(1).

(2)   Subject to paragraph (3), the Principal Rules shall apply to the appeal or application from the date on which these Rules cease to apply.

(3)   Where—

- (a)   a period of time for doing something has started to run under a provision of these Rules; and
- (b)   that provision ceases to apply,

if the Principal Rules contain a time limit for doing the same thing, the time limit in the Principal Rules shall apply, and the relevant period of time shall be treated as running from the date on which the period of time under these Rules started to run.

Initial Commencement
Specified date: 4 April 2005: see r 1.

PART 6
REVOCATION AND TRANSITIONAL PROVISIONS

32   Revocation

The Immigration and Asylum Appeals (Fast Track Procedure) Rules 2003 are revoked.

Initial Commencement
Specified date: 4 April 2005: see r 1.

33   Transitional provisions

(1)   Subject to the following paragraphs of this rule, these Rules apply to any pending appeal or application to an adjudicator or the Immigration Appeal Tribunal which was subject to the 2003 Fast Track Rules immediately before 4th April 2005, and which continues on or after that date as if it had been made to the Tribunal by virtue of a transitional provisions order.

(2)   Where a notice of a relevant decision has been served before 4th April 2005 and the recipient gives notice of appeal against the decision on or after 4th April 2005—

    (a)   rules 7 to 10 of these Rules, and rules 6(1) to (3), 8 and 13(1) and (4) of the Principal Rules, shall not apply; and

    (b)   rule 6 of the 2003 Fast Track Rules and rules 6 and 8 of the 2003 Principal Rules shall continue to apply as if those rules had not been revoked, with the modification that references to an adjudicator or the appellate authority shall be treated as referring to the Tribunal.

(3)   Where a notice of appeal to an adjudicator has been given before 4th April 2005, but the respondent has not filed the notice of appeal with the appellate authority in accordance with rule 6(3)(a) of the 2003 Fast Track Rules—

    (a)   rules 9 and 10 of these Rules, and rule 13(1) and (4) of the Principal Rules, shall not apply; and

    (b)   rule 6(3) of the 2003 Fast Track Rules shall continue to apply as if it had not been revoked, with the modification that the reference to the appellate authority shall be treated as referring to the Tribunal.

(4)   Where, pursuant to a transitional provisions order, the Tribunal reconsiders an appeal which was originally determined by an adjudicator, Section 2 of Part 3 shall apply to the reconsideration, subject to paragraph (5).

(5)   Where—

    (a)   a party has been granted permission to appeal to the Immigration Appeal Tribunal against an adjudicator's determination before 4th April 2005, but the appeal has not been determined by that date; and

    (b)   by virtue of a transitional provisions order the grant of permission to appeal is treated as an order for the Tribunal to reconsider the adjudicator's determination,

the reconsideration shall be limited to the grounds upon which the Immigration Appeal Tribunal granted permission to appeal.

(6) In relation to proceedings which were pending immediately before 4th April 2005—

  (a) unless the Tribunal directs otherwise—
      (i) anything done or any directions given before 4th April 2005 under the 2003 Fast Track Rules shall continue to have effect on and after that date;
      (ii) anything done or any directions given by the appellate authority shall be treated as if done or given by the Tribunal; and
      (iii) any document served on the appellate authority shall be treated as if served on the Tribunal;
  (b) unless the context requires otherwise, any reference in a document to an adjudicator, the Immigration Appeal Tribunal or the appellate authority shall, insofar as it relates to an event on or after 4th April 2005, be treated as a reference to the Tribunal.

(7) In this rule—

  (a) "the 2003 Fast Track Rules" means the Immigration and Asylum Appeals (Fast Track Procedure) Rules 2003;
  (b) "the 2003 Principal Rules" means the Immigration and Asylum Appeals (Procedure) Rules 2003;
  (c) "adjudicator" and "appellate authority" have the same meaning as in the 2003 Fast Track Rules and 2003 Principal Rules; and
  (d) "a transitional provisions order" means an order under section 48(3)(a) of the 2004 Act containing transitional provisions.

Initial Commencement
Specified date: 4 April 2005: see r 1.

SCHEDULE 1
FORMS

Rule 2(4)

[The text of these forms is currently unavailable. Please see the originals]

Initial Commencement
Specified date: 4 April 2005: see r 1.

SCHEDULE 2
SPECIFIED PLACES OF DETENTION

Rules 5 and 15

Campsfield House Immigration Removal Centre, Kidlington, Oxfordshire

Colnbrook House Immigration Removal Centre, Harmondsworth, Middlesex

Harmondsworth Immigration Removal Centre, Harmondsworth, Middlesex

Yarls Wood Immigration Removal Centre, Clapham, Bedfordshire

Initial Commencement
Specified date: 4 April 2005: see r 1.

ASYLUM AND IMMIGRATION (FAST TRACK TIME LIMITS) ORDER 2005

2005 No 561

Made . . . . *7th March 2005*

Laid before Parliament . . . . *10th March 2005*

Coming into force . . . . *4th April 2005*

The Lord Chancellor, in exercise of the powers conferred upon him by sections 26(8) and (9) of the Asylum and Immigration (Treatment of Claimants, etc) Act 2004, after consulting in accordance with section 26(10) of that Act, hereby makes the following Order:

1   Citation and commencement

This Order may be cited as the Asylum and Immigration (Fast Track Time Limits) Order 2005 and shall come into force on 4th April 2005.

Initial Commencement
Specified date: 4 April 2005: see above.

2   Interpretation

(1)   In this Order—

    (a)   "the 2002 Act" means the Nationality, Immigration and Asylum Act 2002;

    (b)   "the 2004 Act" means the Asylum and Immigration (Treatment of Claimants, etc) Act 2004;

    (c)   "the Fast Track Procedure Rules" means the Asylum and Immigration Tribunal (Fast Track Procedure) Rules 2005;

    (d)   "the Tribunal" means the Asylum and Immigration Tribunal.

(2)   Rule 3(5) of the Fast Track Procedure Rules applies for the purpose of articles 3 and 4 of this Order as it applies for the purpose of rules 5 and 15 of those Rules.

Initial Commencement
Specified date: 4 April 2005: see art 1.

3   Time limit for making review application

(1)   This article applies in relation to an application under section 103A(1) of the 2002 Act for a review of the Tribunal's decision on an appeal where—

    (a)   Part 2 of the Fast Track Procedure Rules applied at all times to the appeal to the Tribunal; and

    (b)   the appellant has been continuously in detention under the Immigration Acts at a place or places specified in Schedule 2 to the Fast Track Procedure Rules since being served with notice of the immigration decision against which he is appealing.

(2)   The period of time within which the application must be made in the cases specified in section 103A(3)(a) and (c) of the 2002 Act shall be 2 days beginning with the date on which the applicant is treated in accordance with rules under section 106 of the 2002 Act as receiving notice of the Tribunal's decision.

Initial Commencement
Specified date: 4 April 2005: see art 1.

4   Time limit for notifying appropriate court following review by Tribunal member

(1)   This article applies in relation to an application under section 103A of the 2002 Act for a review of the Tribunal's decision on an appeal where—

(a)   Section 1 of Part 3 of the Fast Track Procedure Rules applied at all times to the consideration of the application by a member of the Tribunal under paragraph 30(2) of Schedule 2 to the 2004 Act; and

(b)   the appellant has been continuously in detention under the Immigration Acts at a place or places specified in Schedule 2 to the Fast Track Procedure Rules since being served with notice of the immigration decision against which he is appealing.

(2)   The period of time within which the applicant must give notification to the appropriate court under paragraph 30(5)(b) of Schedule 2 to the 2004 Act shall be 2 days beginning with the date on which the applicant is treated in accordance with rules under section 106 of the 2002 Act as receiving notice under paragraph 30(4)(b) of that Schedule.

Initial Commencement
Specified date: 4 April 2005: see art 1.

ASYLUM AND IMMIGRATION TRIBUNAL

Practice Direction 1/2005 (April)

The Asylum and Immigration Tribunal ('the Tribunal') is created by the Asylum and Immigration (Treatment of Claimants, etc) Act 2004 ('the 2004 Act'). It replaces the Immigration Appellate Authority ('the IAA'), which consisted of two tiers: adjudicators and the Immigration Appeal Tribunal ('the IAT').

As a result of the replacement of the IAA by the Tribunal, all practice directions made by the Chief Adjudicator and by the President of the IAT cease to have effect as at 4 April 2005, when the Tribunal is established, except to such extent as may be necessary for the purpose of giving effect to any transitional provisions under the 2004 Act.

The directions which follow are intended to regulate the proceedings, practice and procedure of the Tribunal from its inception on 4 April 2005. The directions must be read in conjunction with the Nationality, Immigration and Asylum Act 2002 (as amended by the 2004 Act) and the subordinate legislation made thereunder, in particular the Asylum and Immigration Tribunal (Procedure) Rules 2005 ('the Rules').

Certain of the directions operate not only in relation to notices of appeal given on or after 4 April 2005 but also in relation to notices given before that date, including cases where, for example, an appeal to an adjudicator or to the IAT was pending immediately before that date. Reference should be made to the transitional provisions contained in the primary and secondary legislation.

A number of Guidance Notes were issued by the Chief Adjudicator (and Deputy Chief Adjudicator) between 2001 and 2004, covering issues such as sitting by part-time adjudicators, unrepresented appellants and bail proceedings.

Appendix 1 Legislation and materials

Unless and until the Tribunal issues its own guidance, members of the Tribunal will have regard to these Guidance Notes, subject to any qualifications or modifications necessary as a result of the creation of the Tribunal and of any changes in the relevant legislation.

A list of the Guidance Notes is contained in Annex C.

Notes: The directions which follow are made under section 107 of the 2002 Act and paragraph 7 of Schedule 4 to that Act.

Any failure to comply with these directions does not of itself invalidate any decision made by the Tribunal.

1 Interpretation

1.1 In these directions:

'the 2002 Act' means the Nationality, Immigration and Asylum Act 2002 (as amended); and any reference in these directions to a numbered section or Schedule, without more, is a reference to the relevant section or Schedule in the 2002 Act;

'the 2004 Act' means the Asylum and Immigration (Treatment of Claimants, etc.) Act 2004;

'adjudicator' means an adjudicator appointed, or treated as appointed, under section 81;

'the Commencement Order' means the Asylum and Immigration (Treatment of Claimants, etc.) Act 2004 (Commencement No. 5 and Transitional Provisions) Order 2005;

'CMR hearing' means a case management review hearing;

'fast track appeal' means an appeal to which Part 2 of the Fast Track Rules applies;

'the Fast Track Rules' means the Asylum and Immigration Tribunal (Fast Track Procedure) Rules 2005;

'the Fast Track Time Limits Order' means the Asylum and Immigration (Fast Track Time Limits) Order 2005;

'the IAT' means the Immigration Appeal Tribunal;

'legally qualified member of the Tribunal' has the meaning given by paragraph 2 of Schedule 4;

'the President' means the President of the Tribunal;

'the Rules' means the Asylum and Immigration Tribunal (Procedure) Rules 2005 (as amended); and any reference in these directions to a numbered rule, without more, is a reference to the relevant provision of the Rules;

'the Tribunal' means the Asylum and Immigration Tribunal.

1.2 Other expressions used in these directions have the same meaning as in the Rules or the 2002 Act.

2 Proceedings of Tribunal

2.1 The President has under paragraph 7 of Schedule 4 made directions relating to the proceedings of the Tribunal to the following effect.

2.2 Subject to paragraph 2.3, the jurisdiction of the Tribunal in dealing with the matters specified in the first column below shall be exercised by the number and type of members specified in the second column.

(1) Decisions as to whether notice of appeal given in time/whether to extend time for appealing (including imminent removal)/rejection of invalid notice of appeal	A legally qualified member

(2)	All appeals in which no specific direction is given or which are not specified below	A legally qualified member or two or more members, at least one of whom is legally qualified
(3)	Reconsiderations of appeals where no specific direction is given (including decisions on orders for funding)	A legally qualified member or two or more members, at least one of whom is legally qualified
(4)	Appeals which have to be reheard if two members disagree	Three or more members (but so that there is an odd number of members sitting) at least one of whom is legally qualified
(5)	Case management review hearings and other interlocutory hearings, the giving of any directions concerning appeals or applications (whether or not at such hearings) and adjournments (except where a specific direction for the appeal to be heard by a group of members provides otherwise)	A legally qualified member
(6)	Appeals which are to be determined without a hearing	A legally qualified member
(7)	Applications for bail	A legally qualified member
(8)	The issue of a witness summons	A legally qualified member
(9)	Applications for review	An immigration judge authorised by the President to deal with such applications
(10)	Any determination that an appeal be dismissed as abandoned or finally determined	A legally qualified member
(11)	Reviews of decisions not to make funding order	A senior immigration judge who was not involved in the decision being reviewed

2.3 Any of the matters specified in paragraph 2.2(5), (6), (7), (8) or (10) above may be dealt with by a Tribunal hearing an appeal as specified in paragraph 2.2(2) to (4) above.

3 Rejection of invalid notice of appeal

3.1 Rule 9 (rejection of invalid notice of appeal) imposes a duty on the Tribunal not to accept an invalid notice of appeal and to serve notice to this effect on both the person who gave the notice of appeal and the respondent.

3.2 The Tribunal will scrutinise a notice of appeal as soon as practicable after it has been given. Rule 9 makes no provision for the issue of validity to be determined by means of a hearing or by reference to any representations of the parties.

3.3 Once the Tribunal has served the notice described in paragraph 3.1, rule 9 provides that the Tribunal shall take no further action in relation to the notice of appeal.

3.4 The fact that a hearing date may have been given to the parties does not mean that the appeal must be treated as valid. The Tribunal will therefore act accordingly if at a hearing (including a CMR hearing) it transpires that the notice of appeal does not relate to a decision against which there is an exercisable right of appeal.

3.5 Rule 9 does not apply in the case of a fast track appeal and any issue as to the validity of any such appeal will be dealt with at the hearing.

2111

Appendix 1 Legislation and materials

4 Late notice of appeal

4.1 An important consequence of appeals being made directly to the Tribunal, rather than being given to the Home Office or Entry Clearance Officer (as was the position with the former Immigration Appellate Authority), is that the Tribunal will have to consider in every case whether a notice of appeal was given in time.

4.2 Attention is drawn to rule 10 (late notice of appeal), which requires a notice of appeal given outside the applicable time limit to include an application for an extension of time for appealing. That application must give reasons for lateness and be accompanied by any written evidence relied upon in support of those reasons.

4.3 Where no such application is made but it appears to the Tribunal, upon receipt of the notice of appeal, that that notice is out of time, the Tribunal must notify the person giving the notice that it is proposed to treat the notice as out of time. That person then has three days (or ten days if outside the United Kingdom) in which to file evidence to show the notice was given in time or that there are special circumstances for failing to do so, which could not reasonably have been stated in the notice of appeal.

4.4 The obligation on the Tribunal to give such notification does not arise if the Tribunal extends time for appealing of its own initiative (rule 10(2)). Parties must **not** assume that the existence of this power means that the limits specified in rule 7 (time limit for appeal) can in practice be ignored. The power is intended to be used where, for instance, a disruption of the postal service delays notices that would otherwise have been received in time.

4.5 Except as described in paragraph 4.4, the Tribunal may extend time for appealing if satisfied that by reason of special circumstances it would be unjust not to do so (rule 10(5)). That issue must be decided without a hearing. The Tribunal's decision cannot be the subject of an application for reconsideration under section 103A; nor can it be appealed.

4.6 The preceding provisions of this paragraph do not apply in the case of a fast track appeal. Instead, any issue of timeliness will be decided as a preliminary issue at the hearing (rule 12 of the Fast Track Rules).

5 Imminent removal

5.1 Rule 11 (special provisions for imminent removal cases) requires the Tribunal, if reasonably practicable and except in the case of a fast track appeal, to make a preliminary decision under rule 10 (late notice of appeal) before the date and time of a person's proposed removal from the United Kingdom where:

  (a) that person has given notice of appeal; and
  (b) removal directions have been issued to take effect within five calendar days of the date on which such notice of appeal was given.

5.2 In such a case, the Tribunal may decide that notification under rule 10(2) may be given orally (including by telephone), that the three day period for giving evidence under rule 10(4) should be shortened and that any such evidence should be given orally, including by telephone. The Tribunal's decision under rule 10 must still, however, be served in writing.

5.3 Imminent removal cases under rule 11 will normally be dealt with by senior immigration judges on a 'rota' basis. It will be for the senior immigration judge concerned to decide whether to exercise all or any of the powers conferred by rule 11(3), having regard to the circumstances of the particular case. These may include whether the person concerned is able to give evidence by telephone, in particular where that person's language is not English, and, where that person is represented, the practicability of receiving submissions from the representative. The judge may decide to hold a hearing or a telephone hearing for the purpose of receiving evidence.

6 Case management review hearings and directions

6.1 Except where the Tribunal directs otherwise, a CMR hearing shall be held in respect of every asylum appeal (other than a fast track appeal and an appeal in respect of which the determination of the Tribunal is ordered to be reconsidered), where the appellant:

    (a) is present in the United Kingdom; and
    (b) has a right of appeal whilst in the United Kingdom.

6.2 It is important that the parties and their representatives understand that a CMR hearing or similar first hearing is a hearing in the appeal and that the appeal may be determined by the Tribunal under rule 15(2) (determination of an appeal without a hearing) or rule 19 (hearing of appeal in the absence of a party) if a party does not appear and is not represented at that hearing.

6.3 In addition to any information required by rule 8 (form and contents of notice of appeal), the appellant must provide the Tribunal and the respondent at the CMR hearing with:

    (a) particulars of any application for permission to vary the grounds of appeal (see rule 14 (variation of grounds of appeal));
    (b) particulars of any amendments to the reasons in support of the grounds of appeal;
    (c) particulars of any witnesses to be called or whose written statement or report is proposed to be relied upon at the full hearing; and
    (d) a draft of any directions that the appellant is requesting the Tribunal to make at the CMR hearing.

6.4 In addition to any documents required by rule 13 (filing of documents by the respondent), the respondent must provide the Tribunal and the appellant at the CMR hearing with:

    (a) any amendment that has been made or that is proposed to be made to the notice of decision to which the appeal relates or to any other document served on the appellant giving reasons for that decision; and
    (b) a draft of any directions that the respondent is requesting the Tribunal to make at the CMR hearing.

6.5 In most cases, including those appeals where a CMR hearing is to be held, the Tribunal will normally have given to the parties the following directions with the notice of hearing:

    (a) not later than 5 working days before the full hearing the appellant shall serve on the Tribunal and the respondent:
    (i)witness statements of the evidence to be called at the hearing, such statements to stand as evidence in chief at the hearing;
    (ii)a paginated and indexed bundle of all the documents to be relied upon at the hearing with a schedule identifying the essential passages;
    (iii)a skeleton argument, identifying all relevant issues including human rights claims and citing all the authorities relied upon; and
    (iv)a chronology of events;
    (b) not later than 5 working days before the full hearing the respondent shall serve on the Tribunal and the appellant a paginated and indexed bundle of all the documents to be relied on at the hearing, with a schedule identifying the relevant passages, and a list of any authorities relied upon.

6.6 At the end of the CMR hearing, the Tribunal will give to the parties any further written directions relating to the conduct of the appeal.

6.7 Although in normal circumstances a witness statement should stand as evidence in chief, there may be cases where it will be appropriate for appellants or witnesses to have the opportunity of adding to or supplementing their witness statements. Parties are referred to the judgment of the Court of Appeal in *R v Secretary of State for the Home Department ex parte Singh* [1998] INLR 608.

6.8 If at the CMR hearing the Tribunal considers that the circumstances are such that the jurisdiction of the Tribunal at the full hearing should be exercised by a group of members the Tribunal may give a direction to that effect at the CMR hearing.

6.9 In addition to the directions referred to above, at the end of the CMR hearing the Tribunal shall also give to the parties written confirmation of:

(a)   any issues that have been agreed at the CMR hearing as being relevant to the determination of the appeal; and

(b)   any concessions made at the CMR hearing by a party.

6.10 In paragraph 6.1, 'asylum appeal' means an appeal that relates, in whole or part, to an asylum claim.

7 Standard directions in fast track appeals

7.1 In the case of a fast track appeal, the appellant and the respondent shall respectively serve the materials specified in direction 6.5(a) and (b) either at the hearing or, if practicable, on the business day immediately preceding the date of the hearing.

7.2 Subject to the point made in paragraph 6.7, witness statements served in pursuance of paragraph 7.1 shall stand as evidence in chief at the hearing.

8 Trial bundles

8.1 The parties shall have regard to paragraph 8.2 to 8.6 in the preparation of trial bundles for hearings before the Tribunal.

8.2 The best practice for the preparation of bundles is as follows:

(a)   all documents must be relevant, be presented in logical order and be legible;

(b)   where the document is not in the English language, a typed translation of the document signed by the translator in accordance with rule 52 (language of documents) to certify that the translation is accurate, must be inserted in the bundle next to the copy of the original document, together with details of the identity and qualifications of the translator;

(c)   if it is necessary to include a lengthy document, that part of the document on which reliance is placed should, unless the passages are outlined in any skeleton argument, be highlighted or clearly identified by reference to page and/or paragraph number;

(d)   bundles submitted must have an index showing the page numbers of each document in the bundle;

(e)   the skeleton argument or written submission should define and confine the areas at issue in a numbered list of brief points and each point should refer to any documentation in the bundle on which the appellant proposes to rely (together with its page number);

(f)   where reliance is placed on a particular case or text, photocopies of the case or text must be provided in full for the Tribunal and the other party; and

(g)   large bundles should be contained in a ring binder or lever arch file, capable of lying flat when opened.

8.3 The Tribunal recognises the constraints on those representing the parties in appeals in relation to the preparation of trial bundles and this direction does not therefore make it mandatory in every case that bundles in exactly the form prescribed must be prepared. Where the issues are particularly complex it is of the highest importance that comprehensive bundles are prepared. If parties to appeals fail in individual cases to present documentation in a way which complies with the direction, it will be for the Tribunal to deal with any such issue.

8.4 Much evidence in asylum and immigration appeals is in documentary form. Representatives preparing bundles need to be aware of the position of the Tribunal, which may be coming to the case for the first time. The better a bundle has been prepared, the greater it will assist the Tribunal. Bundles should contain all the documents that the Tribunal will require to enable it to reach a decision without the need to refer to any other file or document. The Tribunal will not be assisted by repetitious, outdated or irrelevant material.

8.5 It may not be practical in many appeals to require there to be an agreed trial bundle but it nevertheless remains vital that the parties inform each other at an early stage of all and any documentation upon which they intend to rely.

8.6 The parties cannot rely on the Tribunal having judicial notice of any country information or background reports in relation to the case in question. If either party wishes to rely on such country or background information, copies of the relevant documentation must be produced.

9 Adjournments

9.1 Applications for the adjournment of appeals (other than fast track appeals) listed for hearing before the Tribunal must be made not later than 4.00 pm one clear working day before the date of the hearing.

9.2 For the avoidance of doubt, where a case is listed for hearing on, for example, a Friday, the application must be received by 4.00 pm on the Wednesday.

9.3 The application for an adjournment must be supported by full reasons and must be made in accordance with rule 21 (adjournment of appeals).

9.4 Any application made later than the end of the period mentioned in paragraph 9.1 must be made to the Tribunal at the hearing and will require the attendance of the party or the representative of the party seeking the adjournment.

9.5 It will be only in the most exceptional circumstances that late applications for adjournments will be considered without the attendance of a party or representative.

9.6 Parties must not assume that an application, even if made in accordance with paragraph 9.1, will be successful and they must always check with the Tribunal as to the outcome of the application. This is particularly important, given the restrictions imposed by rule 21 on the Tribunal's power to adjourn appeal hearings.

9.7 Any application for the adjournment of a fast track appeal must be made to the Tribunal at the hearing and will be considered by the Tribunal under rule 28 (adjournment) of the Fast Track Rules (see also rule 30(2)(a) of those Rules).

9.8 If an adjournment is not granted and a party fails to attend the hearing, the Tribunal is required by rule 19 (hearing appeal in absence of a party) to proceed with the hearing, if satisfied that valid notice of the hearing has been given and that there has been no satisfactory explanation for absence.

10 Determinations where jurisdiction of Tribunal exercised by more than one member

10.1 Where, in respect of any appeal, the jurisdiction of the Tribunal is exercised by more than one member, the determination is that reached by the majority of those members.

10.2 It is accordingly inappropriate that a dissenting view should be expressed or that the determination should indicate that it is that of a majority.

10.3 Such a determination will therefore not disclose whether it is unanimous or by a majority nor will any minority or dissenting views be included in it or otherwise communicated.

11 Record of Proceedings

11.1 The Tribunal shall keep a proper record of proceedings of any hearing.

11.2 That record should be signed and dated by the member of the Tribunal responsible for taking the record and be attached to the Tribunal's case file.

12 Transfer of proceedings

12.1 Where:

    (a)   the Tribunal ('the original Tribunal') has started to hear an appeal but has not completed the hearing or given its determination; and

    (b)   a senior immigration judge or designated immigration judge decides that it is not practicable for the original Tribunal to complete the hearing or to give its determination justly or without undue delay,

the senior immigration judge or designated immigration judge may direct the appeal to be heard by a differently constituted Tribunal ('the new Tribunal').

12.2 Where an appeal is transferred under paragraph 12.1:

    (a)   any documents sent to or given by the original Tribunal shall be deemed to have been sent to or given by the new Tribunal; and

    (b)   the new Tribunal shall have power to deal with the appeal as if it had been commenced before it.

12.3 The Tribunal may transfer proceedings regarding the reconsideration of an appeal in the circumstances described in paragraph 14.2 and 14.9.

12.4 Where proceedings are transferred under paragraph 12.3, any documents sent to or given by the Tribunal which transferred the proceedings shall be deemed to have been sent to or given by the Tribunal to which those proceedings are transferred.

13 Review

13.1 It is an important feature of the single-tier Tribunal that a party dissatisfied by a determination may, in certain circumstances, apply for that determination to be reconsidered by the Tribunal.

13.2 The relevant statutory provisions concerning reconsideration of appeals are to be found in:

    (a)   section 103A (as inserted by section 26(6) of the 2004 Act);

    (b)   paragraph 30 of Schedule 2 to the 2004 Act ('the filter provision');

    (c)   rules 24 to 33;

    (d)   rules 16 to 23 of the Fast Track Rules (in the case of fast track appeals); and

    (e)   rules 54.28 to 54.35 of the Civil Procedure Rules 1998 ('CPR') (as inserted by rule 7 of the Civil Procedure (Amendment) Rules 2005).

13.3 For an unspecified period beginning with 4 April 2005, an application for an order requiring the Tribunal to review its decision on an appeal will be considered initially by the Tribunal itself under the filter provision, with a right to apply to the High Court where the immigration judge decides not to order reconsideration.

13.4 A reconsideration order may not be made in respect of a determination of the Tribunal:

(a) where such an order has previously been made in relation to the appeal (section 103A(2)(b)); or

(b) where the jurisdiction of the Tribunal was exercised by three or more legally qualified members (section 103A(8)).

13.5 In those cases, sections 103B and 103E provide for an appeal to the Court of Appeal/Court of Session/ Court of Appeal in Northern Ireland.

13.6 The time limits for applying for an order for reconsideration are contained in section 103A(3) or, in the case of fast track appeals, in rule 3 of the Fast Track Time Limits Order. The requirements for filing the application are contained in CPR 54.29. An application outside the relevant time limit may be entertained if the immigration judge thinks that the application could not reasonably practicably have been made within that period (section 103A(4)(b)).

13.7 The immigration judge may make an order for reconsideration only if that judge thinks that the original Tribunal may have made an error of law **and** that there is a real possibility that the Tribunal would decide the appeal differently on reconsideration (rule 26(6)).

13.8 The effect of rule 26(6) is that, as with applications for permission to appeal to the IAT under section 101 (now repealed), a party seeking to adduce evidence that was not before the original Tribunal must explain in the application the significance of that evidence with regard to **both** of the requirements specified in paragraph 13.7 (see *E&R* [2004] EWCA Civ 49; CA [2004] EWCA Civ 1165).

13.9 The immigration judge who has decided to make an order for reconsideration:

(a) must state the grounds on which the Tribunal is ordered to reconsider its decision (rule 27(2)(a)); and

(b) will (amongst other things) decide under rule 27(2)(b) whether to direct that a CMR hearing be held before the reconsideration hearing takes place and whether to make a direction as to the evidence to be adduced at the hearing initially fixed for the reconsideration (as to which, see paragraph 14).

13.10 The references in paragraph 13.7 and 13.8 to the original Tribunal include references to an adjudicator in any case where, by virtue of article 6 of the Commencement Order, the order under section 103A is made in respect of the decision of an adjudicator.

14 Procedure on reconsideration

14.1 Subject to paragraph 14.12, where an appeal has been ordered under section 103A to be reconsidered, then, unless and to the extent that they are directed otherwise, the parties to the appeal should assume that the issues to be considered at the hearing fixed for the reconsideration will be whether the original Tribunal made a material error of law (see rule 31(2)) and, if so, whether, on the basis of the original Tribunal's findings of fact, the appeal should be allowed or dismissed.

14.2 Where the Tribunal decides that the original Tribunal made a material error of law but that the Tribunal cannot proceed under rule 31(3) to substitute a fresh decision to allow or dismiss the appeal because findings of fact are needed which the Tribunal is not in a position to make, the Tribunal will make arrangements for the adjournment of the hearing or for the transfer of the proceedings under paragraph 12.3 so as to enable evidence to be adduced for that purpose.

14.3 Where the Tribunal acting under paragraph 14.2 adjourns the hearing, its determination, produced after the adjourned hearing has taken place, will contain the Tribunal's reasons for finding that the original Tribunal made a material error of law.

14.4 Where the Tribunal acting under paragraph 14.2 transfers the proceedings, it shall prepare written reasons for its finding that the original Tribunal made a material error of law and those written reasons shall be attached to, and form part of, the determination of the Tribunal which substitutes a fresh decision to allow or dismiss the appeal.

14.5 The references in paragraph 14.1 to 14.4 to the original Tribunal include references to an adjudicator in any case where, by virtue of article 6 of the Commencement Order, the order under section 103A is made in respect of the decision of an adjudicator.

14.6 Under article 5 of the Commencement Order, any appeal that was pending before the IAT immediately before 4 April 2005 shall on and after that date be dealt with in the same manner as if the Tribunal had originally decided the appeal and was reconsidering its decision.

14.7 Rule 62(7) provides that, in the case of an appeal described in paragraph 14.6, the reconsideration shall be limited to the grounds upon which the IAT granted permission to appeal. In most cases, those grounds will require the Tribunal to decide whether the adjudicator made a material error of law.

14.8 Subject to paragraph 14.12, on and after 4 April 2005, and in the absence of any direction to the contrary, the parties to any appeal that falls to be dealt with as described in paragraph 14.6 should assume that the issues to be considered at the hearing will be whether the adjudicator made a material error of law and, if so, whether, on the basis of that adjudicator's findings of fact, the appeal should be allowed or dismissed.

14.9 Where the Tribunal decides that the adjudicator made a material error of law but that the Tribunal cannot proceed under rule 31(3) to substitute a fresh decision to allow or dismiss the appeal because findings of fact are needed which the Tribunal is not in a position to make, the Tribunal will make arrangements for the adjournment of the hearing or for the transfer of the proceedings under paragraph 12.3 so as to enable evidence to be adduced for that purpose.

14.10 The provisions of paragraph 14.3 and 14.4 shall apply in relation to paragraph 14.9 as they apply in relation to paragraph 14.2 but with the modification that the references to the original Tribunal shall be interpreted as referring to the adjudicator.

14.11 Where, immediately before 4 April 2005, an appeal was pending before an adjudicator, having been remitted to an adjudicator by a court or the IAT, it will already have been decided that the original adjudicator's determination cannot stand. The Tribunal will accordingly proceed to re-hear the appeal.

14.12 In the case of a reconsideration of a fast track appeal, the Tribunal reconsidering the appeal is required by rule 23 of the Fast Track Rules to reconsider its decision on the appeal at the reconsideration hearing, subject to the qualifications described in rule 23(1) of those Rules. The Tribunal's power to adjourn a fast track appeal that remains as such is governed by rule 28 of those Rules.

14.13 The parties to any fast track appeal which is being reconsidered by the Tribunal on or after 4 April 2005 will be expected to attend with all necessary witnesses and evidence that may be required if the Tribunal should decide that it is necessary to re-hear the appeal. It will be unusual for the Tribunal to adjourn the reconsideration hearing but, if it does so, paragraph 14.4 will, so far as appropriate, apply.

14.14 The preceding provisions of this paragraph and paragraph 13 are subject to article 9 of the Commencement Order in the case of certain 'old' appeals, where the issue is not restricted to whether the adjudicator made an error of law.

15 Legal aid on reconsideration

15.1 The relevant statutory provisions concerning the provision of legal aid in respect of the reconsideration of appeals (other than fast track appeals) decided in England and Wales are to be found in:

(a) section 103D (as inserted by section 26(6) of the 2004 Act);
(b) rule 28A (orders for funding of section 103A applications) (as inserted by the Asylum and Immigration Tribunal (Procedure) (Amendment) Rules 2005) and rule 33 (orders for funding on reconsideration);
(c) the Community Legal Service (Asylum and Immigration Appeals) Regulations 2005 ('the CLS Regulations').

15.2 On an application under section 103A which is dealt with by an immigration judge under the filter provision referred to in paragraph 13.3, the immigration judge has power to make an order under section 103D for the appellant's costs to be paid out of the CLS fund ('a funding order'). That power is, however, exercisable only in the following circumstances:

(a) where the immigration judge dismisses or makes no order on the section 103A application, that judge may make a funding order only where there has been a change in relevant circumstances or a change in the law since the application was made **and** at the time the application was made, there was a significant prospect that the appeal would be allowed upon reconsideration (regulation 5(4));
(b) where the immigration judge makes an order for reconsideration but, in the event, no reconsideration takes place (eg because the immigration decision appealed against is withdrawn) (regulation 5(5)).

15.3 A funding order of the kind described in paragraph 15.2(b) can be made only on application by a supplier (as defined in the CLS Regulations) or counsel instructed by the supplier (regulation 5(5)).

15.4 Rule 33 (orders for funding on reconsideration) requires the Tribunal that has reconsidered an appeal to make a funding determination, where the appellant's representative has specified in the application for reconsideration that he is seeking a funding order. The funding determination is separate from the determination of the appeal itself.

15.5 Unless it directs otherwise, the Tribunal shall hear any submissions as to such an order at the conclusion of the proceedings on the reconsideration.

15.6 If the Tribunal allows the appeal on reconsideration, it is required by regulation 6(2) to make a funding order. If it does not allow the appeal, the Tribunal must not make a funding order unless it is satisfied that, **at the time when the appellant made the section 103A application**, there was a **significant prospect** that the appeal would be allowed upon reconsideration (regulation 6(3)).

15.7 The Tribunal must give reasons where it decides not to make a funding order, following a reconsideration of an appeal (regulation 6(4)). A supplier, or counsel instructed by a supplier, may apply under regulation 7 for a review of such a decision. The review will be carried out by a senior immigration judge, who will decide whether to hold a hearing, if one is requested.

15.8 It should be noted that the power to make a funding order in the circumstances described in paragraph 15.2(b) covers only the costs in respect of the review application; not any costs incurred in connection with preparing for a reconsideration that does not, in the event, take place. In certain circumstances, it may be inappropriate for a supplier or counsel to be denied a funding order which would cover the costs of preparing for the reconsideration. In an appropriate case, therefore, the Tribunal will consider representations as to whether it should make a decision by consent on the appeal following reconsideration (whether or not involving a hearing), so as to enable the Tribunal to make a funding order under section 103D(3) in respect of the review application and the reconsideration, notwithstanding that it may not otherwise have been necessary to undertake the reconsideration.

15.9 A funding order can only be made where there has been an application for an order under section 103A(1) (see section 103D(2)(b)). Accordingly, a funding order may not be made in a case described in paragraph 14.6 or paragraph 14.11. Nor can such an order be made in a case described in paragraph 14.1 where a pending application to the IAT is treated as an application under section 103A(1) (see paragraph 14.5 and article 6(5) of the Commencement Order).

16 Format of determinations

16.1 In order to ensure consistency in the formatting of determinations, the member of the Tribunal who is preparing the determination shall:

  (a)   use the front sheet format set out in Annex A as appropriate for the case;
  (b)   number sequentially each paragraph of the determination;
  (c)   conclude each determination under a heading 'Decision' in the manner set out in Annex B, adapting the wording as necessary; and
  (d)   sign and date the determination at the end of the document or employ such electronic methods as the President may approve for signifying that the determination is finalised.

17 Citation of determinations

17.1 A determination of the Tribunal to which this sub-paragraph applies will be either 'reported' or 'unreported'. The decision whether to report a case is that of the Tribunal and is not perceived to be an issue in which the parties to the appeal have an interest.

17.2 Paragraph 17.1 applies to any determination that is promulgated following a hearing at which the jurisdiction of the Tribunal was exercised by a senior immigration judge (whether sitting alone or with another member or members).

17.3 No determination will be reportable which follows a hearing before a single member of the Tribunal other than the President or a Deputy President of the Tribunal.

17.4 Reported determinations will receive a neutral citation number of the form [2005] UKAIT 0000 and will be widely available (including being available on the Tribunal's website). They will be anonymised and will be cited by the neutral citation number. Determinations without such a number are unreported. Anonymised versions of unreported determinations will be deposited in the Supreme Court Library and treated as unreported determinations for the purposes of the Tribunal's website.

17.5 Other determinations will receive no neutral citation number. They will be sent to the parties (in accordance with the Rules) but will not be published.

17.6 A determination of the Tribunal which has not been reported may not be cited in proceedings before the Tribunal unless either:

(a) the appellant in the present proceedings, or a member of his family, was a party to the proceedings in which the previous determination was issued; or

(b) the Tribunal gives permission.

17.7 Permission under paragraph 17.6 will be given only in exceptional cases, and even more rarely in the case of determinations promulgated following a hearing before a single member of the Tribunal.

17.8 An application for permission to cite a determination which has not been reported must:

(a) include a **full** transcript of the determination;

(b) identify the proposition for which the determination is to be cited;

(c) certify that the proposition is not found in any reported determination of the Tribunal or of the IAT and has not been superseded by a decision of a higher authority; and

(d) be accompanied by a summary analysis of all other decisions of the Tribunal and all available decisions of higher authority, relating to the same issue, promulgated in the period beginning six months before the date of the decision proposed to be cited and ending two weeks before the date of the hearing. (This analysis is intended to show the trend of Tribunal decisions on the issue.)

17.9 The provisions of paragraph 17.6 to 17.8 apply to unreported determinations of the IAT and to determinations of Adjudicators as those provisions apply to unreported determinations of the Tribunal and to determinations promulgated following a hearing by a single member of the Tribunal.

17.10 Until 4 October 2005, the references in paragraph 17.8(d) to decisions of the Tribunal shall be construed as including references to decisions of the IAT.

17.11 A party citing a determination of the IAT bearing a neutral citation number prior to [2003] (including all series of 'bracket numbers') must be in a position to certify that the matter or proposition for which the determination is cited has not been the subject of more recent, reported, determinations of the IAT or of the Tribunal.

18 Starred and Country Guidance determinations

18.1 Reported determinations of the Tribunal and of the IAT which are 'starred' shall be treated by the Tribunal as authoritative in respect of the matter to which the 'starring' relates, unless inconsistent with other authority that is binding on the Tribunal.

18.2 A reported determination of the Tribunal or of the IAT bearing the letters 'CG' shall be treated as an authoritative finding on the country guidance issue identified in the determination, based upon the evidence before the members of the Tribunal or the IAT that determined the appeal. As a result, unless it has been expressly superseded or replaced by any later 'CG' determination, or is inconsistent with other authority that is binding on the Tribunal, such a country guidance case is authoritative in any subsequent appeal, so far as that appeal:

(a) relates to the country guidance issue in question; and

(b) depends upon the same or similar evidence.

18.3 A list of current CG cases will be maintained on the Tribunal website. Both the respondent and any representative of the appellant in an appeal concerning a particular country will be expected to be conversant with the current 'CG' determinations relating to that country.

18.4 Because of the principle that like cases should be treated in like manner, any failure to follow a clear, apparently applicable country guidance case or to show why it does not apply to the case in question is likely to be regarded as grounds for review or appeal on a point of law.

19 Bail applications

19.1 An application for bail shall if practicable be listed for hearing within three working days of receipt by the Tribunal of the notice of application.

19.2 Any such notice which is received by the Tribunal after 3.30pm on a particular day shall be treated for the purposes of this paragraph as if it were received on the next business day.

20 Discrimination

20.1 Section 84(1)(b) makes it a ground of appeal against an immigration decision that that decision is unlawful by virtue of section 19B of the Race Relations Act 1976 (discrimination by public authorities).

20.2 In cases where there is a finding of discrimination, the person affected can bring a claim in the County Court. On that claim, both the claimant and the court are bound by the decision in the immigration appeal (section 57A of the Race Relations Act 1976).

20.3 Accordingly, in a case where discrimination is raised as a ground of appeal, it is particularly important that the Tribunal is aware of its duty under section 86(2)(a) to determine any matter raised as a ground of appeal and that it makes a finding on that ground, even if the alleged discrimination is not relevant to the ultimate outcome of the appeal (see *Bibi* [2005] EWHC 386 (Admin)).

21 Council on Tribunals

21.1 Under rule 54(5), members of the Council on Tribunals (and its Scottish equivalent) are entitled to attend hearings of cases before the Tribunal.

21.2 Although that rule does not specifically envisage that such a member should have access to discussions between members of the Tribunal before and after the hearing (where the jurisdiction of the Tribunal is being exercised by more than one of its members), a member of the Council visiting in an official capacity should be invited to observe the whole of the Tribunal's work if that member wishes to do so.

21.3 In order to avoid any misunderstanding, the parties (including their representatives) present at a hearing should be informed that the member of the Council will retire with the Tribunal and will observe (but not take part in or communicate) the Tribunal's deliberations.

MR JUSTICE HODGE
PRESIDENT
4 April 2005

ANNEX A
Front sheet of determination

Asylum and Immigration Tribunal   Appeal number:

THE IMMIGRATION ACTS

Heard at   Determination Promulgated
On

Before

[XXXX NAME[S] XXXX]
[TITLE[S]]

Between

[Appellant's names – as in AIT file]
Appellant
and
[THE SECRETARY OF STATE FOR THE HOME DEPARTMENT]
[or]
[ENTRY CLEARANCE OFFICER, (City)]
[or]
[IMMIGRATION OFFICER]
Respondent

Representation:
For the Appellant:
For the Respondent:

DETERMINATION AND REASONS

ANNEX B
Concluding words of determination

1 In asylum/human rights appeals
DECISION
The appeal is allowed/dismissed on asylum grounds
The appeal is allowed/dismissed on human rights grounds
Signed/ Official crest
Dated
Immigration Judge/Designated Immigration Judge/Senior Immigration Judge

2 In immigration/human rights appeals
DECISION
The appeal in respect of the Immigration Rules is allowed/dismissed
The appeal is allowed/dismissed on human rights grounds
Signed/Official Crest
Dated
Immigration Judge/Designated Immigration Judge/Senior Immigration Judge

3 On reconsideration of an appeal
DECISION
The original Tribunal did not make a material error of law and the original
determination of the appeal shall stand

Appendix 1   Legislation and materials

The original Tribunal made a material error of law.

The following decision is accordingly substituted:

[see 1 and 2 above]

Signed/Official Crest

Dated

Immigration Judge/Designated Immigration Judge/Senior Immigration Judge

[insert wording from section 1, 2 or 3 above as appropriate and subject to any necessary amendment]

ANNEX C
Guidance Notes

- Guidance Note No 1 (November 2001) – Guidance on sitting for part-time adjudicators
- Guidance Note No 2 (May 2002) – Guidance on transfer of proceedings
- Guidance Note No 3 (May 2002) – Pre-hearing introduction
- Guidance Note No 4 (February 2003) – Delayed promulgations
- Guidance Note No 5 (April 2003) – Unrepresented appellants
- Bail guidance notes for Adjudicators (May 2003) (Third edition)
- Guidance Note No 6 (June 2003) – Guidance for adjudicators on deposit of recognizances
- Guidance Note No 7 (July 2003) – Guidance for adjudicators on withdrawals
- Guidance Note No 8 (April 2004) – Unaccompanied children
- Guidance note (August 2004) – Unrepresented appellants who do not understand English

STATUTORY INSTRUMENTS

IMMIGRATION (CONTROL OF ENTRY THROUGH REPUBLIC OF IRELAND) ORDER 1972

1972 No 1610

Made . . . . *23rd October 1972*

Authority: Immigration Act 1971, s 9(2), (6)

1

This Order may be cited as the Immigration (Control of Entry through Republic of Ireland) Order 1972 and shall come into operation on 1st January 1973.

2

(1) In this Order—

"the Act" means the Immigration Act 1971; and

"visa national" means a person who, in accordance with the immigration rules, is required on entry into the United Kingdom to produce a passport or other document of identity endorsed with a United Kingdom visa and includes a stateless person.

(2) In this Order any reference to an Article shall be construed as a reference to an Article of this Order and any reference in an Article to a paragraph as a reference to a paragraph of that Article.

(3) The Interpretation Act 1889 shall apply to the interpretation of this Order as it applies to the interpretation of an Act of Parliament.

3

(1) This Article applies to—

(a) any person (other than a citizen of the Republic of Ireland) who arrives in the United Kingdom on an aircraft which began its flight in that Republic if he entered that Republic in the course of a journey to the United Kingdom which began outside the common travel area and was not given leave to land in that Republic in accordance with the law in force there;

(b) any person (other than a person to whom sub-paragraph (a) of this paragraph applies) who arrives in the United Kingdom on a local journey from the Republic of Ireland if he satisfies any of the following conditions, that is to say:—

(i) he is a visa national who has no valid visa for his entry into the United Kingdom;

(ii) he entered that Republic unlawfully from a place outside the common travel area;

(iii) he entered that Republic from a place in the United Kingdom and Islands after entering there unlawfully, [or, if he had a limited leave to enter or remain there, after the expiry of the leave, provided that in either case] he has not subsequently been given leave to enter or remain in the United Kingdom or any of the Islands; or

(iv) he is a person in respect of whom directions have been given by the Secretary of State for him not to be given entry to the United Kingdom on the ground that his exclusion is conducive to the public good.

2127

(2)   In relation only to persons to whom this Article applies, the Republic of Ireland shall be excluded from section 1(3) of the Act (provisions relating to persons travelling on local journeys in the common travel area).

Amendment
Para (1): words in square brackets substituted by SI 1979/730, art 2.

4

(1)   Subject to paragraph (2), this Article applies to [any person who does not have the right of abode in the United Kingdom under section 2 of the Act] and is not a citizen of the Republic of Ireland who enters the United Kingdom on a local journey from the Republic of Ireland after having entered that Republic—

    (a)   on coming from a place outside the common travel area; or
    (b)   after leaving the United Kingdom whilst having a limited leave to enter or remain there which has since expired.

(2)   This Article shall not apply to any person [who arrives in the United Kingdom with leave to enter or remain in the United Kingdom which is in force but which was given to him before his arrival or] who requires leave to enter the United Kingdom by virtue of Article 3 or section 9(4) of the Act.

(3)   A person to whom this Article applies by virtue only of paragraph (1)(a) shall, unless he is a visa national who has a visa containing the words "short visit", be subject to the restriction and to the condition set out in paragraph (4).

(4)   The restriction and the condition referred to in paragraph (3) are—

    (a)   the period for which he may remain in the United Kingdom shall not be more than three months from the date on which he entered the United Kingdom; and
    [(b)   unless he is a national of a state which is a member of the European Economic Community he shall not engage in any occupation for reward; and
    (c)   unless he is a national of a state which is a member of the European Economic Community other than ... [, Portugal or Spain] he shall not engage in any employment.]

(5)   In relation to a person who is a visa national and has a visa containing the words "short visit" the restriction and the conditions set out in paragraph (6) shall have effect instead of the provisions contained in paragraph (4).

(6)   The restriction and the conditions referred to in paragraph (5) are—

    (a)   the period for which he may remain in the United Kingdom shall not be more than one month from the date on which he entered the United Kingdom;
    (b)   he shall not engage in any occupation for reward or any employment; and
    (c)   he shall, unless he is under the age of 16 years, be required to register with the police.

(7)   The preceding provisions of this Article shall have effect in relation to a person to whom this Article applies by virtue of sub-paragraph (b) of paragraph (1) (whether or not he is also a person to whom this Article applies by virtue of sub-paragraph (a) thereof) as they have effect in relation to a person to whom this Article applies by virtue only of the said sub-paragraph (a), but as if for the references in paragraphs (4) and (6) to three months and one month respectively there were substituted a reference to seven days.

Amendment
Para (1): words in square brackets substituted by SI 1982/1028, art 2.

Para (2): words from "who arrives in" to "his arrival or" in square brackets inserted by SI 2000/1776, art 2. Date in force: 30 July 2000: see SI 2000/1776, art 1.
Para (4): sub-paras (b), (c) substituted by SI 1980/1859, art 2; in para (c), word omitted revoked by SI 1987/2092, art 2, words in square brackets inserted by SI 1985/1854, art 2.

IMMIGRATION (EXEMPTION FROM CONTROL) ORDER 1972

1972 No 1613

Made – – – 24th October 1972

Authority: Immigration Act 1971, s 8(2)

1

This Order may be cited as the Immigration (Exemption from Control) Order 1972 and shall come into operation on 1st January 1973.

2

(1) In this Order—

"the Act" means the Immigration Act 1971; and
"consular employee" and "consular officer" have the meanings respectively assigned to them by Article 1 of the Vienna Convention on Consular Relations as set out in Schedule 1 to the Consular Relations Act 1968.

(2) In this Order any reference to an Article or to the Schedule shall be construed as a reference to an Article of this Order or, as the case may be, to the Schedule thereto and any reference in an Article to a paragraph as a reference to a paragraph of that Article.

(3) In this Order any reference to an enactment is a reference to it as amended, and includes a reference to it as applied, by or under any other enactment and any reference to an instrument made under or by virtue of any enactment is a reference to any such instrument for the time being in force.

(4) The Interpretation Act 1889 shall apply to the interpretation of this Order as it applies to the interpretation of an Act of Parliament.

3

(1) The following persons shall be exempt from any provision of the Act relating to those who are not [British citizens], that is to say:—

    (a) any consular officer in the service of any of the states specified in the Schedule (being states with which consular conventions have been concluded by Her Majesty);

    (b) any consular employee in such service as is mentioned in sub-paragraph (a) of this paragraph; and

    (c) any member of the family of a person exempted under sub-paragraph (a) or (b) of this paragraph forming part of his household.

2129

(2) In paragraph (1) and in Article 4 any reference to a consular employee shall be construed as a reference to such an employee who is in the full-time service of the state concerned and is not engaged in the United Kingdom in any private occupation for gain.

Amendment
Para (1): words in square brackets substituted by SI 1982/1649, art 2.

4

The following persons shall be exempt from any provision of the Act relating to those who are not [British citizens] except any provision relating to deportation, that is to say:—

(a) unless the Secretary of State otherwise directs, any member of the government of a country or territory outside the United Kingdom and Islands who is visiting the United Kingdom on the business of that government;

(b) any person entitled to immunity from legal process with respect to acts performed by him in his official capacity under any Order in Council made under section 3(1) of the Bretton Woods Agreements Act 1945 (which empowers Her Majesty by Order in Council to make provision relating to the immunities and privileges of the governors, executive directors, alternates, officers and employees of the International Monetary Fund and the International Bank for Reconstruction and Development);

(c) any person entitled to immunity from legal process with respect to acts performed by him in his official capacity under any Order in Council made under section 3(1) of the International Finance Corporation Act 1955 (which empowers Her Majesty by Order in Council to make provision relating to the immunities and privileges of the governors, directors, alternates, officers and employees of the International Finance Corporation);

(d) any person entitled to immunity from legal process with respect to acts performed by him in his official capacity under any Order in Council made under section 3(1) of the International Development Association Act 1960 (which empowers Her Majesty by Order in Council to make provision relating to the immunities and privileges of the governors, directors, alternates, officers and employees of the International Development Association);

(e) any person (not being a person to whom section 8(3) of the Act applies) who is the representative or a member of the official staff of the representative of the government of a country to which section 1 of the Diplomatic Immunities (Conferences with Commonwealth Countries and Republic of Ireland) Act 1961 applies (which provides for representatives of certain Commonwealth countries and their staff attending conferences in the United Kingdom to be entitled to diplomatic immunity) so long as he is included in a list compiled and published in accordance with that section;

(f) any person on whom any immunity from jurisdiction is conferred by any Order in Council made under section 12(1) of the Consular Relations Act 1968 (which empowers Her Majesty by Order in Council to confer on certain persons connected with the service of the government of Commonwealth countries or the Republic of Ireland all or any of the immunities and privileges which are conferred by or may be conferred under that Act on persons connected with consular posts);

(g) any person (not being a person to whom section 8(3) of the Act applies) on whom any immunity from suit and legal process is conferred by any Order in Council made under section 1(2), 5(1) or 6(2) of the International Organisations Act 1968 (which empower Her Majesty by Order in Council to confer certain immunities and privileges on persons connected with certain international organisations and international tribunals and on representatives of foreign countries and their staffs attending certain conferences in the United Kingdom) except any such person as is mentioned in section 5(2)(c) to (e) of the said Act of 1968 [or by any Order in Council continuing to have effect by virtue of section 12(5) of the said Act of 1968];

(h) any consular officer (not being an honorary consular officer) in the service of a state other than such a state as is mentioned in the Schedule;

(i) any consular employee in such service as is mentioned in paragraph (h);

[(j) any officer or servant of the Commonwealth Secretariat falling within paragraph 6 of the Schedule to the Commonwealth Secretariat Act 1966 (which confers certain immunities on those members of the staff of the Secretariat who are not entitled to full diplomatic immunity);

[(k) any person to whom any immunity from suit and legal process is conferred by the European Communities (Immunities and Privileges of the North Atlantic Salmon Conservation Organisation) Order 1985 (which confers certain immunities and privileges on the representatives and officers of the North Atlantic Salmon Conservation Organisation);

[(l) any member of the Hong Kong Economic and Trade Office as defined by paragraph 8 of the Schedule to the Hong Kong Economic and Trade Office Act 1996,

[(m)
    (i) Any member or servant of the Independent International Commission on Decommissioning ("the Commission") established under an Agreement between the Government of the United Kingdom of Great Britain and Northern Ireland and the Government of the Republic of Ireland concluded on 26th August 1997,

    (ii) in sub-paragraph (i) above, "servant" includes any agent of or person carrying out work for or giving advice to the Commission,

(n) any member of the family of a person exempted under any of the preceding paragraphs forming part of his household;]]]]

[(o) any person falling within article 4A below].

Amendment
Words "British citizens" in square brackets substituted by SI 1982/1649, art 2.
In para (g) words "or by any Order in Council continuing to have effect by virtue of section 12(5) of the said Act of 1968" in square brackets inserted by SI 1977/693, art 3(a).
Paras (j), (k) substituted for para (j) as originally enacted, by SI 1977/693, art 3(b).
Paras (k), (l) substituted for existing para (k), by SI 1985/1809, art 4.
Paras (l), (m) substituted for existing para (l), by SI 1997/1402, art 3.
Paras (m), (n) prospectively substituted for existing para (m), by SI 1997/2207, art 3, as from 1 September 1997.
Para (o) inserted by SI 2004/3171, art 2(1), (2). Date in force: this amendment shall come into force on the date on which the Agreement on the Privileges and Immunities of the International Criminal Court done at New York on 9 September 2002 enters into force in respect of the United Kingdom: see SI 2004/3171, art 1.

[4A

[(1) In relation to the court ("the ICC") established by the Rome Statute of the International Criminal Court done at Rome on 17th July 1998 ("the Rome Statute");

(a) except in so far as in any particular case the exemption given by this article is waived by the State or intergovernmental organisation they represent,
    (i) any representative of a State party to the Rome Statute attending meetings of the Assembly or one of its subsidiary organs,
    (ii) any representative of another State attending meetings of the Assembly or one of its subsidiary organs as an observer, and
    (iii) any representative of a State or of an intergovernmental organisation invited to a meeting of the Assembly or one of its subsidiary organs,

while exercising their official functions and during their journey to and from the place of the meeting;

(b) except in so far as in any particular case the exemption given by this article is waived by the State they represent, any representative of a State participating in the proceedings of the ICC while exercising their official functions and during their journeys to and from the place of the proceedings of the ICC;

(c) except in so far as in any particular case the exemption given by this article is waived by an absolute majority of the judges, any judge and the Prosecutor, when engaged on or with respect to the business of the ICC;

(d) except in so far as in any particular case the exemption given by this article is waived by the Prosecutor, any Deputy Prosecutor, when engaged on or with respect to the business of the ICC;

(e) except in so far as in any particular case the exemption given by this article is waived by the Presidency, the Registrar, when engaged on or with respect to the business of the ICC;

(f) except in so far as in any particular case the exemption given by this article is waived by the Registrar, the Deputy Registrar, so far as necessary for the performance of his functions;

(g) except in so far as in any particular case the exemption given by this article is waived by the Prosecutor, any member of the staff of the office of the Prosecutor, so far as necessary for the performance of their functions;

(h) except in so far as in any particular case the exemption given by this article is waived by the Registrar, any member of the staff of the Registry, so far as necessary for the performance of their functions;

(i) except in so far as in any particular case the exemption given by this article is waived by the Presidency and subject to the production of the certificate under seal of the Registrar provided to counsel and persons assisting defence counsel upon appointment, counsel and any person assisting defence counsel, so far as necessary for the performance of their functions;

(j) except in so far as in any particular case the exemption given by this article is waived by the Presidency and subject to the production of a document provided by the ICC certifying that the person's appearance before the ICC is required by the ICC and specifying a time period during which such appearance is necessary, any witness, to the extent necessary for their appearance before the ICC for the purposes of giving evidence;

(k) except in so far as in any particular case the exemption given by this article is waived by the Presidency and subject to the production of a document provided by the ICC certifying the participation of the person in the proceedings of the ICC and specifying a time period for that participation, any victim, to the extent necessary for their appearance before the ICC;

(l) except in so far as in any particular case the exemption given by this article is waived by the head of the organ of the ICC appointing the person and subject to the production of a document provided by the ICC certifying that the person is performing functions for the ICC and specifying a time period during which those functions will last, any expert performing functions for the ICC, to the extent necessary for the exercise of those functions;

(m) any member of the family of a person exempted under any of paragraphs (c) to (h) above forming part of their household.

(2) In paragraph (1) above:

"the Assembly" means the assembly of State parties to the Rome Statute;
"the Presidency" means the organ of the ICC composed of the president and the first and second vice-presidents of the ICC elected in accordance with article 38, paragraph 1, of the Rome Statute;

"the Prosecutor" and "Deputy Prosecutors" mean the prosecutor and deputy prosecutors respectively elected by the assembly of State parties to the Rome Statute in accordance with article 42, paragraph 4, of the Rome Statute;
"the Registrar" and "the Deputy Registrar" mean the registrar and deputy registrar respectively elected by the ICC in accordance with article 43, paragraph 4, of the Rome Statute.]

Amendment
Inserted by SI 2004/3171, art 2(1), (3). Date in force: this amendment shall come into force on the date on which the Agreement on the Privileges and Immunities of the International Criminal Court done at New York on 9 September 2002 enters into force in respect of the United Kingdom: see SI 2004/3171, art 1.

5

(1) Subject to the provisions of this Article the following persons who are not [British citizens] shall, on arrival in the United Kingdom, be exempt from the provisions of section 3(1)(a) of the Act (which requires persons who are not [British citizens] to obtain leave to enter the United Kingdom), that is to say—

    (a) any citizen of the United Kingdom and Colonies who holds a passport issued to him in the United Kingdom and Islands and expressed to be a British Visitor's Passport;

    (b) any Commonwealth citizen who is included in a passport issued in the United Kingdom by the Government of the United Kingdom or in one of the Islands by the Lieutenant-Governor thereof which is expressed to be a Collective Passport;

    (c) any Commonwealth citizen or citizen of the Republic of Ireland returning to the United Kingdom from an excursion to France or Belgium [or the Netherlands] who holds a valid document of identity issued in accordance with arrangements approved by the United Kingdom Government and in a form authorised by the Secretary of State and enabling him to travel on such an excursion without a passport;

    (d) any Commonwealth citizen who holds a British seaman's card or any citizen of the Republic of Ireland if (in either case) he was engaged as a member of the crew of a ship in a place within the common travel area and, on arrival in the United Kingdom, is, or is to be, discharged from his engagement;

    (e) any person who, having left the United Kingdom after having been given a limited leave to enter, returns to the United Kingdom within the period for which he had leave as a member of the crew of an aircraft under an engagement requiring him to leave on that or another aircraft as a member of its crew within a period exceeding seven days.

(2) Paragraph (1) shall not apply so as to confer any exemption on any person against whom there is a deportation order in force or who has previously entered the United Kingdom unlawfully and has not subsequently been given leave to enter or remain in the United Kingdom and sub-paragraphs (d) and (e) of that paragraph shall not apply to a person who is required by an immigration officer to submit to examination in accordance with Schedule 2 to the Act.

(3) In this Article any reference to a Commonwealth citizen shall be construed as including a reference to a British protected person and in paragraph (1)(d) "British seaman's card" means a valid card issued under any regulations in force under section 70 of the Merchant Shipping Act 1970 or any card having effect by virtue of the said regulations as a card so issued and "holder of a British seaman's card" has the same meaning as in the said regulations.

Appendix 1 Legislation and materials

Amendment
Para (1): first and second words in square brackets substituted by SI 1982/1649, art 2; final words in square brackets inserted by SI 1975/617, art 2.

[6

[(1) For the purposes of section 1(1) of the British Nationality Act 1981 (which relates to acquisition of British citizenship by birth in the United Kingdom), a person to whom a child is born in the United Kingdom on or after 1st January 1983 is to be regarded (notwithstanding the preceding provisions of this Order) as settled in the United Kingdom at the time of the birth if—

(a) he would fall to be so regarded but for his being at that time entitled to an exemption by virtue of this Order; and

(b) immediately before he became entitled to that exemption he was settled in the United Kingdom; and

(c) he was ordinarily resident in the United Kingdom from the time when he became entitled to that exemption to the time of the birth;

but this Article shall not apply if at the time of the birth the child's father or mother is a person on whom any immunity from jurisdiction is conferred by or under the Diplomatic Privileges Act 1964.

(2) Expressions used in this Article shall be construed in accordance with section 50 of the British Nationality Act 1981.]

Amendment
Inserted by SI 1982/1649, art 3.

SCHEDULE
STATES WITH WHICH CONSULAR CONVENTIONS HAVE BEEN CONCLUDED BY
HER MAJESTY

Articles 3, 4

Austria

Belgium

Bulgaria

[Czechoslovakia]

Denmark

France

[German Democratic Republic]

Greece

Federal Republic of Germany

Hungary

Italy

Japan

Mexico

[Mongolia]

Norway

Poland

Roumania

Sweden

Spain

Union of Soviet Socialist Republics

United States of America

Yugoslavia

Amendment
Words in square brackets inserted by SI 1977/693, art 4.

IMMIGRATION (PARTICULARS OF PASSENGERS AND CREW) ORDER 1972

1972 No 1667

Made . . . . *1st November 1972*

Authority: Immigration Act 1971, Sch 2, para 27(2)

1

This Order may be cited as the Immigration (Particulars of Passengers and Crew) Order 1972 and shall come into operation on 1st January 1973.

2

The Interpretation Act 1889 shall apply to the interpretation of this Order as it applies to the interpretation of an Act of Parliament[; and in this Order the expressions "shuttle train", "through train" and "train manager" have the same meanings as in the Channel Tunnel (International Arrangements) Order 1993].

Amendment
Words in square brackets inserted by SI 1993/1813, art 8, Sch 5, Part II, para 1(a).

3

(1) This Article applies to a ship which arrives in the United Kingdom from or after calling at a place outside the common travel area or an aircraft which arrives there from or after calling at a place outside the United Kingdom and Islands.

[(1A) This article also applies to through trains and shuttle trains arriving in the United Kingdom.]

(2) Subject to the following provisions of this Article, the captain of a ship or aircraft to which this Article applies shall—

    (a) if so required by an immigration officer, furnish to that officer a list of the names and nationalities of all passengers arriving on the ship or aircraft, as the case may be; and

    (b)

    (i) in the case of a ship, furnish to an immigration officer within 12 hours of the arrival of the ship, a return in the form set out in the Schedule to this Order containing particulars of all members of the crew arriving on the ship;

    (ii) in the case of an aircraft, if so required by an immigration officer, furnish to that officer a list of the names, dates of birth and nationalities of all members of the crew arriving on the aircraft as soon as practicable after the arrival of the aircraft.

(3)   In relation to an aircraft which started its flight in the Republic of Ireland, paragraph (2) of this Article shall have effect as if—

(a)   for the reference in sub-paragraph (a) to all passengers arriving on the aircraft there were substituted a reference to any passengers so arriving (not being citizens of that Republic) who entered that Republic in the course of a journey to the United Kingdom which began outside the common travel area and were not given leave to land in that Republic in accordance with the law in force there; and

(b)   sub-paragraph (b)(ii) were omitted.

[(3A)   In relation to a train to which this article applies, paragraph [(2) of this article shall have effect as if the reference to the captain of a ship or aircraft were a reference to the train manager, and—

(a)   in the case of a shuttle train, as if sub-paragraph (a) were omitted;

(b)   in the case of a through train, as if the reference in sub-paragraph (a) to the ship or aircraft were a reference to the train; and

(c)   in each case, as if the reference in sub-paragraph (b)(ii) to an aircraft were a reference to a through train or as the case may be a shuttle train and references to the aircraft were references to the train.]

(4)   An immigration officer may by notice given to the captain of a ship or aircraft [or the train manager of a train] dispense with the requirements of paragraph (2)(b) of this Article either in respect of all members of the crew or in respect of such classes of persons as he may specify.

(5)   Any passenger on a ship or aircraft [or through train] shall furnish to the captain of the ship or aircraft [or the train manager of a train], as the case may be, any information required by him for the purpose of complying with the provisions of this Article.

Amendment
Paras (1A), (3A): inserted by SI 1993/1813, art 8, Sch 5, Part II, para 1(b), (c).
Paras (4), (5): words in square brackets inserted by SI 1993/1813, art 8, Sch 5, Part II, para 1(d), (e).

[SCHEDULE
PARTICULARS OF MEMBERS OF THE CREW OF A SHIP ARRIVING IN THE UNITED KINGDOM]

Article 3

[(This Form deals with the return required by an immigration officer. Due to its complexity, it has proved impossible to obtain a satisfactory reproduction on the database. It has therefore been omitted. Please see the original.)]

Amendment
Substituted by SI 1975/980, art 2, Schedule.

IMMIGRATION (HOTEL RECORDS) ORDER 1972

1972 No 1689

Made . . . .*7th November 1972*

Authority: Immigration Act 1971, s 4(4)

1   Citation and commencement

This Order may be cited as the Immigration (Hotel Records) Order 1972 and shall come into operation on 1st January 1973.

2   Interpretation and transitional provisions

(1)   In this Order the following expressions have the meanings hereby respectively assigned to them, that is to say:—

"alien" has the same meaning as in the [British Nationality Act 1981];

"certificate of registration" means a certificate issued, or treated as issued, in pursuance of regulations from time to time in force under section 4(3) of the Immigration Act 1971;

"keeper", in relation to any premises, includes any person who for reward receives any other person to stay in the premises, whether on his own behalf or as manager or otherwise on behalf of any other person;

"nationality" includes the status of a stateless alien;

"stay" means lodge or sleep, for one night or more, in accommodation provided for reward.

(2)   The Interpretation Act 1889 shall apply to the interpretation of this Order as it applies to the interpretation of an Act of Parliament.

(3)   Any information required by this Order to be given by or to any person may be given by or to any other person acting on his behalf.

(4)   Anything done under, or for the purposes of, Article 19 of the Aliens Order 1953, as amended, shall have effect as if done under, or for the purposes of, this Order and, in particular, any information given or record maintained under or for the purposes of the said Article 19 shall be treated as if it had been given or maintained under, or for the purposes of, this Order.

Amendment
Para (1): in definition "alien" words in square brackets substituted by SI 1982/1025, art 2.

3   Application of Order

This Order shall apply in the case of any hotel or other premises, whether furnished or unfurnished, where lodging or sleeping accommodation is provided for reward, not being premises certified by the chief officer of police of the area in which they are situate to be occupied for the purposes of a school, hospital, club or other institution or association.

4   Provision of information by visitors

(1)   Every person of or over the age of 16 years who stays at any premises to which this Order applies shall, on arriving at the premises, inform the keeper of the premises of his full name and nationality.

(2)   Every such person who is an alien shall also—

(a) on arriving at the premises, inform the keeper of the premises of the number and place of issue of his passport, certificate of registration or other document establishing his identity and nationality; and

(b) on or before his departure from the premises, inform the keeper of the premises of his next destination and, if it is known to him, his full address there.

5   Records to be maintained by keeper of premises

The keeper of any premises to which this Order applies shall—

(a) require all persons of or over the age of 16 years who stay at the premises to comply with their obligations under the foregoing Article; and

(b) keep for a period of at least 12 months a record in writing of the date of arrival of every such person and of all information given to him by any such person in pursuance of the foregoing Article;

and every record shall at all times be open to inspection by any constable or by any person authorised by the Secretary of State.

IMMIGRATION (REGISTRATION WITH POLICE) REGULATIONS 1972

1972 No 1758

Made . . . . *14th November 1972*

Authority: Immigration Act 1971, s 4(3)

1   Citation and commencement

These Regulations may be cited as the Immigration (Registration with Police) Regulations 1972 and shall come into operation on 1st January 1973.

2   Interpretation and transitional provisions

(1) In these Regulations, except where the context otherwise requires, the following expressions have the meanings hereby respectively assigned to them, that is to say:—

"the Act" means the Immigration Act 1971;

"alien" has the same meaning as in the [British Nationality Act 1981];

"certificate of registration" means a certificate issued in pursuance of Regulation 10(1) to the alien concerned;

"local register" means a register kept in pursuance of Regulation 4;

"nationality" includes the status of a stateless alien;

"registration officer" and "appropriate registration officer" have the meanings assigned thereto by Regulation 4;

"a residence" means a person's private dwelling-house or other premises in which he is ordinarily resident but does not include any premises in which he is not ordinarily resident.

(2) In these Regulations any reference to a Regulation is a reference to a Regulation contained therein and any reference in a Regulation to a paragraph is a reference to a paragraph of that Regulation.

(3)   Where an alien has failed to comply with any requirement made by a provision of these Regulations within a period specified in that provision he shall, without prejudice to any liability in respect of that failure under section 26(1)(f) of the Act, continue to be subject to that requirement notwithstanding the expiry of that period.

(4)   The Interpretation Act 1889 shall apply to the interpretation of these Regulations as it applies to the interpretation of an Act of Parliament.

(5)   Anything done, or having effect as if done, under or for the purposes of, any provision of the Aliens Order 1953, as amended, corresponding to a provision of these Regulations shall have effect as if done under, or for the purposes of, that corresponding provision and, in particular—

    (a)   any register kept under Article 13 of the said Order shall be treated as part of the local register kept under Regulation 4(2);

    (b)   particulars furnished under Article 14(2) of the said Order shall be treated as furnished under Regulation 5, and

    (c)   a certificate of registration supplied in pursuance of Article 13(3)(b) of the said Order shall be treated as a certificate of registration issued in pursuance of Regulation 10(1).

Amendment
Para (1): in definition "alien" words in square brackets substituted by SI 1982/1024, reg 2.

3   Application of Regulations

These Regulations shall apply in the case of an alien who has a limited leave to enter or remain in the United Kingdom which is for the time being subject to a condition requiring him to register with the police and in the case of an alien who, by virtue of section 34 of the Act or paragraph 1 of Schedule 4 thereto, is treated as having such a limited leave.

4   Registration officers etc

(1)   For the purposes of these Regulations the chief officer of police for each police area shall be the registration officer for that area, and the police area shall be the registration area; and any reference to the appropriate registration officer is a reference—

    (a)   in the case of an alien who has a residence in the United Kingdom, to the registration officer for the area in which that residence is situated;

    (b)   in any other case, to the registration officer for the area in which, for the time being, he happens to be.

(2)   Every registration officer shall keep for his registration district a local register of aliens containing the particulars specified in the Schedule hereto:
Provided that if a registration officer is not satisfied as to the nationality of an alien he may describe that alien in the local register as being of uncertain nationality or may describe him as having such nationality as appears to that officer to be the probable nationality of the alien.

(3)   Anything required or authorised by these Regulations to be done by or to a registration officer may be done by or to any constable or other person who is authorised by that officer to act for the purposes of these Regulations.

5   Duty to register etc

(1)   Within 7 days of these Regulations becoming applicable to him, an alien shall, subject to Regulation 6, attend at the office of the appropriate registration officer and furnish to that officer such information, documents and other particulars (including a

recent photograph) relating to him as are required by that officer for the purposes of the local register kept by him or the issue of a certificate of registration to the alien.

(2)   Without prejudice to the generality of paragraph (1) an alien attending as aforesaid shall either—

(a)   produce to the appropriate registration officer a passport furnished with a photograph of himself or some other document satisfactorily establishing his identity and nationality; or

(b)   give to that officer a satisfactory explanation of the circumstances which prevent him from producing such a passport or document.

6   Exemption from registration in certain cases

(1)   An alien shall not be required to attend and furnish particulars under Regulation 5 if—

(a)   immediately before these Regulations becoming applicable to him, he was ordinarily resident in the United Kingdom, and

(b)   he had previously, during that period of ordinary residence, attended and furnished particulars under Regulation 5.

(2)   Without prejudice to paragraph (1) or the provisions of Regulation 2(5), an alien shall not be required to attend and furnish particulars under Regulation 5 if—

(a)   on the coming into operation of these Regulations they become applicable to him,

(b)   immediately before their coming into operation he was resident in the United Kingdom, and

(c)   he had previously, during that period of residence, attended and furnished particulars under Article 14(2) of the Aliens Order 1953, as amended.

7   Duty to notify changes of residence or address etc

(1)   Every alien to whom these Regulations apply who has furnished particulars under Regulation 5 shall be under a duty to notify any changes therein in accordance with this Regulation.

(2)   Such an alien who for the time being has a residence in the United Kingdom shall, if he adopts a new residence within the United Kingdom, report his arrival at his new residence to the appropriate registration officer before the expiration of the period of 7 days beginning with the day of his arrival.

(3)   Such an alien who for the time being has a residence in the United Kingdom, if he is absent from his residence for a continuous period exceeding 2 months (without adopting a new residence)—

(a)   shall forthwith notify the appropriate registration officer of his address for the time being (whether within or outside the United Kingdom);

(b)   subject to paragraph (5), shall notify the appropriate registration officer of any subsequent change of address within the United Kingdom before the expiration of 8 days beginning with the day of his arrival at the new address; and

(c)   shall, on returning to his residence, notify the appropriate registration officer of his return (whether or not he has throughout the period of absence remained in the United Kingdom).

(4)   Subject to paragraphs (5) and (6), such an alien who for the time being has not a residence in the United Kingdom shall, if he moves from one address to another (in the same or a different registration district), notify the appropriate registration officer of his arrival thereat before the expiration of 8 days beginning with the day of his arrival.

(5) Such an alien need not, under paragraph (3)(b) or (4), notify the appropriate registration officer of his address unless he remains or intends to remain at that address for a longer period than 7 days beginning with the day of his arrival thereat.

(6) If such an alien who for the time being has not a residence in the United Kingdom supplies to a registration officer the name and address of a referee, being a person resident within the United Kingdom who is willing to act, and in the opinion of that officer is a suitable person to act, as a referee under this paragraph, the officer shall include the referee's name and address among the entries relating to the alien in the local register kept by him; and in such case, the following provisions shall apply in substitution for those of paragraph (4), that is to say:—

(a) the alien shall keep the referee informed as to his address from time to time and shall notify the registration officer of any change in the referee's address; and

(b) the referee shall, if so required by the registration officer, furnish to that officer any information in his possession as to the alien which is required by that officer for the purposes of his duties under these Regulations.

8   Duty to notify other changes in particulars etc

Every alien to whom these Regulations apply who has furnished particulars under Regulation 5—

(a) shall notify the appropriate registration officer of any change in his case in the particulars specified as items 1, 3, 5, 6, 7 and 14 in the Schedule hereto, before the expiration of 8 days beginning with that on which the change, or the event occasioning the change, occurs; and

(b) if so required by the appropriate registration officer, shall furnish to that officer by such date as he may specify such information, documents and other particulars (including, where so required, a recent photograph) relating to him which are required by that officer for the purposes of his duties under these Regulations.

9   Provisions supplemental to Regulations 5, 7 and 8

(1) An alien required under Regulation 5(1) or 8(b) to furnish a photograph of himself shall furnish 2 copies of the same photograph; and, if he fails to furnish such copies, the registration officer may cause him to be photographed.

(2) An alien required under Regulation 7 or 8(a) to notify the appropriate registration officer of any change in his residence or address or of any change in his case in the particulars mentioned in Rule 8(a) shall either attend for the purpose at the office of the registration officer or send written notice of the change to that officer by post so, however, that where written notice is given the alien shall also send to the registration officer his certificate of registration.

(3) An alien required under Regulation 8(b) to furnish information, documents or other particulars to the appropriate registration officer (whether or not in connection with a change of which written notice has been given in pursuance of paragraph (2)) shall attend for the purpose at the office of the registration officer if that officer so requires.

[10   Issue of registration certificates]

[(1) Every registration officer shall issue certificates of registration to aliens of whom particulars are entered in the local register kept by him.

(2) A certificate of registration shall be independent of, and shall not be included in, any other document.

2141

(3)   An alien to whom a certificate of registration is issued shall pay to the registration officer concerned a fee of [£34] except where the requirement to register is a condition of leave granted to an alien after an absence from the United Kingdom of a period of less than one year immediately following an earlier period of leave which was subject to the same condition.]

Amendment
Substituted by SI 1990/400, reg 2.
Para (3): sum in square brackets substituted by SI 1995/2928, reg 2.

11   Production of registration certificates

(1)   On the making of any alteration or addition to the local register, the registration officer may require the alien concerned to produce his certificate of registration in order that any necessary amendment may be made thereto.

(2)   Any immigration officer or constable may—

   (a)   require an alien to whom these Regulations apply, forthwith, to either produce a certificate of registration or give to the officer or constable a satisfactory reason for his failure to produce it;

   (b)   where the alien fails to produce a certificate of registration in pursuance of such a requirement (whether or not he gives a satisfactory reason for his failure), require him, within the following 48 hours, to produce a certificate of registration at a police station specified by the officer or constable,

so, however, that a requirement under sub-paragraph (b) to produce a certificate of registration at a police station shall have effect in substitution for the requirement under sub-paragraph (a) so as to cause that previous requirement to cease to have effect.

SCHEDULE
PARTICULARS TO BE ENTERED IN LOCAL REGISTER

1   Name in full.

2   Sex.

3   Matrimonial status (married or single).

4
   (a)   Date of birth.
   (b)   Country of birth.

5
   (a)   Present nationality.
   (b)   How and when acquired.
   (c)   Previous nationality (if any).

6   Particulars of passport or other document establishing nationality.

7   Business, profession or occupation.

8   Residence in the United Kingdom (or address if no residence).

9   Name and address of referee (if any) supplied under Regulation 7(b).

10   Last residence outside the United Kingdom.

11
   (a)   Date of arrival in the United Kingdom.
   (b)   Place of arrival in the United Kingdom.
   (c)   Mode of arrival in the United Kingdom.

12   Duration of limited leave and conditions attached thereto.

13   Restrictions or conditions, if any, applicable by virtue of section 9(2) of the Act.

14
   (a)   If employed in the United Kingdom—
      (i)   name and address of employer;
      (ii)   address at which employed, if different.
   (b)   If engaged in business or profession in the United Kingdom—
      (i)   name under which business or profession is carried on;
      (ii)   address at which business or profession is carried on.

15   Signature (or fingerprints if unable to write in the characters of the English language).

16   Photograph.

IMMIGRATION (PORTS OF ENTRY) ORDER 1987

1987 No 177

Made . . . . *10th February 1987*
Authority: Immigration Act 1971, s 33(3)

1

(1)   This Order may be cited as the Immigration (Ports of Entry) Order 1987 and shall come into force on 1st March 1987.

(2)   ...

Amendment
Para (2): revokes SI 1972/1668, SI 1975/2221 and SI 1979/1635.

2

The ports specified in the Schedule to this Order shall be ports of entry for the purposes of the Immigration Act 1971.

SCHEDULE
PORTS OF ENTRY

Article 2

Seaports and Hoverports

Dover	Plymouth
Felixstowe	Portsmouth
Folkestone	Ramsgate
Harwich	Sheerness
Hull	Southampton
London	Tyne
Newhaven	

Airports

Aberdeen	Leeds/Bradford
Belfast	Liverpool
Birmingham	Luton
Bournemouth (Hurn)	Manchester
Bristol	Newcastle
Cardiff (Wales)	Norwich
East Midlands	Prestwick
Edinburgh	Southampton
Gatwick–London	Southend
Glasgow	Stansted–London
Heathrow–London	Tees-side

CHANNEL TUNNEL (INTERNATIONAL ARRANGEMENTS) ORDER 1993

1993 No 1813

Made . . . . *16th July 1993*

Whereas a draft of this Order has been approved by resolution of each House of Parliament;

Now, therefore, in exercise of the powers conferred on the appropriate Minister by section 11 of the Channel Tunnel Act 1987, the Lord Chancellor, the Secretary of State for the Home Department, the Secretary of State for Health, the Minister of Agriculture, Fisheries and Food and the Commissioners of Customs and Excise hereby make the following Order:

1   Citation and commencement

This Order may be cited as the Channel Tunnel (International Arrangements) Order 1993 and shall come into force on the date on which the Protocol between the Government of the United Kingdom of Great Britain and Northern Ireland and the Government of the French Republic Concerning Frontier Controls and Policing, Co-operation in Criminal Justice, Public Safety and Mutual Assistance Relating to the Channel Fixed Link enters into force. That date will be notified in the London, Edinburgh and Belfast Gazettes.

2   Interpretation

(1)   In this Order, except for the purpose of construing the international articles [or the supplementary articles], and in any enactment as applied by it with modifications, any expression for which there is an entry in the first column of Schedule 1 has the meaning given against it in the second column.

(2)   In this Order "the authorised purposes" means—

(a)   purposes for which provision is authorised by any of paragraphs (a), (d) and (g), and

(b)   purposes connected with any matter in relation to or with respect to or for regulating which provision is authorised by any of paragraphs (c), (e), (f) and (h), of section 11(1) of the Channel Tunnel Act 1987.

(3)   In this Order "the international articles" means the provisions set out in Schedule 2 (being Articles or parts of Articles of the Protocol mentioned in article 1 above); and in the international articles the expression "the Fixed Link" shall for the purposes of this Order be taken to have the same meaning as is given to "the tunnel system" by section 1(7) of the Channel Tunnel Act 1987.

[(4)   In this Order "the supplementary articles" means the provisions set out in Schedule 2A (being Articles of the Additional Protocol between the Government of the United Kingdom of Great Britain and Northern Ireland and the Government of the French Republic), and in the supplementary articles "the Protocol signed at Sangatte" and "the Sangatte Protocol" mean the Protocol mentioned in article 1 above.

(5)   In paragraph (4) and in the supplementary articles, "Additional Protocol" means the Additional Protocol to the Sangatte Protocol on the Establishment of Bureaux Responsible for Controls on Persons Travelling by Train between France and the United Kingdom, signed at Brussels on 29th May 2000.]

Amendment
Para (1): words "or the supplementary articles" in square brackets inserted by SI 2001/1544, arts 2, 3(1). Date in force: 25 May 2001: see SI 2001/1544, art 1(2), and the London Gazette, 20 July 2001.
Paras (4), (5): inserted by SI 2001/1544, arts 2, 3(2). Date in force: 25 May 2001: see SI 2001/1544, art 1(2), and the London Gazette, 20 July 2001.

3   Application of international articles

(1)   The international articles shall have the force of law in the United Kingdom—

  (a)   within the tunnel system,
  (b)   within a control zone, and
  (c)   elsewhere for the authorised purposes only.

(2)   Without prejudice to paragraph (1) officers belonging to the French Republic shall to the extent specified in the international articles have rights and obligations and powers to carry out functions in the United Kingdom.

(3)   For the purpose of giving full effect to Article 34 of the international articles (accommodation, ETC, for authorities of adjoining State) the appropriate Minister may by written notice require any occupier or person concerned with the management of a terminal control point to provide [free of charge] such accommodation, installations and equipment as may be necessary to satisfy requirements determined under Article 33 of the Protocol mentioned in article 1 above (which requires the competent authorities of the two States to determine their respective requirements in consultation with one another).

Amendment
Para (3): words "free of charge" in square brackets inserted by SI 2001/3707, arts 2, 3(1). Date in force: 10 December 2001: see SI 2001/3707, art 1(1).

[3A   Application of supplementary articles]

[(1)   The supplementary articles shall have the force of law in the United Kingdom within a supplementary control zone.

(2)   Without prejudice to paragraph (1), officers belonging to the French Republic who are responsible for immigration controls shall to the extent specified in the supplementary articles have rights and obligations and powers to carry out functions in the United Kingdom.

[(3)   For the purpose of enabling the authorities of the French Republic to make use in the United Kingdom of the accommodation, installations and equipment necessary for the performance of their functions under the supplementary articles, the Secretary of State for the Home Department may by written notice require any occupier or person concerned with the management of a terminal control point to provide free of charge such accommodation, installations and equipment as may be necessary to satisfy requirements determined by the authorities of the French Republic in consultation with the authorities of the United Kingdom.]]

Amendment
Inserted by SI 2001/1544, arts 2, 3(3). Date in force: 25 May 2001: see SI 2001/1544, art 1(2), and the London Gazette, 20 July 2001.
Para (3): substituted by SI 2001/3707, arts 2, 3(2). Date in force: 10 December 2001: see SI 2001/3707, art 1(1).

4   Application of enactments

(1)   All frontier control enactments [except those relating to transport and road traffic controls] shall for the purpose of enabling officers belonging to the United Kingdom to carry out frontier controls extend to France within a control zone.

[(1A)   All frontier control enactments relating to transport and road traffic controls shall for the purpose of enabling officers belonging to the United Kingdom to carry out such controls extend to France within the control zone in France within the tunnel system.]

[(1B)   All immigration control enactments shall, for the purpose of enabling immigration officers to carry out immigration controls, extend to France within a supplementary control zone.]

[(1C)   The Race Relations Act 1976 shall apply to the carrying out by immigration officers of their functions in a control zone or a supplementary control zone outside the United Kingdom as it applies to the carrying out of their functions within the United Kingdom.]

[(2)   For the purposes of section 5 of the Data Protection Act 1998 ("the 1998 Act"), data which are—

    (a)   processed within a control zone in France in connection with the carrying out of frontier controls by an officer belonging to the United Kingdom, or
    (b)   processed within a supplementary control zone in France in connection with the carrying out of immigration controls by an immigration officer,

shall be treated as processed by a data controller established in the United Kingdom in the context of that establishment (and the 1998 Act shall accordingly apply in respect of such data).]

[(3)   For the purposes of section 5 of the 1998 Act, data which are—

    (a)   processed within a control zone in the United Kingdom in connection with the carrying out of frontier controls by an officer belonging to the French Republic, or
    (b)   processed within a supplementary control zone in the United Kingdom in connection with the carrying out of immigration controls by such an officer,

shall be treated as processed by a data controller established in France in the context of that establishment (and the 1998 Act shall accordingly not apply in respect of such data).]

Amendment
Para (1): words in square brackets inserted by SI 1996/2283, art 2(b).
Para (1A): inserted by SI 1996/2283, art 2(b).

Para (1B): inserted by SI 2001/1544, arts 2, 3(4). Date in force: 25 May 2001: see SI 2001/1544, art 1(2), and the London Gazette, 20 July 2001.
Para (1C): inserted by SI 2001/3707, arts 2, 4. Date in force: 10 December 2001: see SI 2001/3707, art 1(1).
Para (2): substituted by SI 2001/1544, arts 2, 3(5). Date in force: 25 May 2001: see SI 2001/1544, art 1(2), and the London Gazette, 20 July 2001.
Para (3): substituted by SI 2001/1544, arts 2, 3(6). Date in force: 25 May 2001: see SI 2001/1544, art 1(2), and the London Gazette, 20 July 2001.

5 Application of criminal law

(1) Any act or omission which—

(a) takes place outside the United Kingdom in a control zone, and
(b) would, if taking place in England, constitute an offence under a frontier control enactment,

[or any act or omission which—

(c) takes place outside the United Kingdom in a supplementary control zone, and
(d) would, if taking place in England, constitute an offence under an immigration control enactment,]

shall be treated for the purposes of that enactment as taking place in England.

[(1A) Summary proceedings for anything that is by virtue of paragraph (1) an offence triable summarily or triable either way may be taken, and the offence may for all incidental purposes be treated as having been committed, in the county of Kent or in the inner London area as defined in section 2(1)(a) of the Justices of the Peace Act 1979.]

(2) Any jurisdiction conferred by virtue of [paragraphs (1) and (1A)] on any court is without prejudice to any jurisdiction exercisable apart from this article by that or any other court.

(3) Where it is proposed to institute proceedings in respect of an alleged offence in any court and a question as to the court's jurisdiction arises under Article 38(2)(a) of the international articles, it shall be presumed, unless the contrary is proved, that the court has jurisdiction by virtue of that Article.

Amendment
Para (1): sub-paras (c), (d) and words "or any act or omission which—" immediately preceding them inserted by SI 2001/1544, arts 2, 3(7). Date in force: 25 May 2001: see SI 2001/1544, art 1(2), and the London Gazette, 20 July 2001.
Para (1A): inserted by SI 1994/1405, art 8, Sch 4, para 9(a).
Para (2): words "paragraphs (1) and (1A)" in square brackets substituted by SI 1994/1405, art 8, Sch 4, para 9(b).

[5A Persons boarding a through train]

[For the purposes of the exercise of any power of an immigration officer in a supplementary control zone in France, any person who seeks to board a through train shall be deemed to be seeking to arrive in the United Kingdom through the tunnel system.]

Amendment
Inserted by SI 2001/1544, arts 2, 3(8). Date in force: 25 May 2001: see SI 2001/1544, art 1(2), and the London Gazette, 20 July 2001.

6 Powers of officers and supplementary controls

Schedule 3 (which contains in Part I provision as to powers exercisable by constables and other officers and in Part II provision for meeting obligations under Article 25 of the Protocol mentioned in article 1 above concerning the prevention of animals from straying into the Fixed Link) shall have effect.

7   Enactments modified

(1)   Without prejudice to the generality of [articles 4(1), 4(1B) and 5(1)], the frontier control enactments mentioned in Schedule 4 shall—

- (a)   in their application to France by virtue of article 4(1) [or article 4(1B)], and
- (b)   in their application to the United Kingdom—
  - (i)   within the tunnel system, and
  - (ii)   elsewhere for the authorised purposes,

have effect with the modifications set out in Schedule 4.

(2)   Subject to paragraph (3), within a control zone [or a supplementary control zone] and on trains within the tunnel system section 54(3) of the Firearms Act 1968 (application to Crown servants) shall have effect as if the reference to a member of a police force included a reference to an officer belonging to the French Republic exercising functions as mentioned in Article 28(2) of the international articles [or functions under Article 3 of the supplementary articles].

(3)   As respects officers exercising their functions in a control zone paragraph (2) applies only to the agreed number of specified officers mentioned in Article 28(2)(b) of the international articles.

[(3A)   As respects officers exercising their functions in a supplementary control zone paragraph (2) applies only to the number of specified officers agreed in pursuance of the supplementary articles.]

[(4)   The frontier control enactments relating to transport and road traffic controls in their application to France within the control zone in France within the tunnel system by virtue of article 4(1A) shall have effect as if any reference therein to a "public road" or "road" were a reference to any part of that control zone.]

Amendment
Para (1): words "articles 4(1), 4(1B) and 5(1)" in square brackets substituted by SI 2001/1544, arts 2, 3(9)(a). Date in force: 25 May 2001: see SI 2001/1544, art 1(2), and the London Gazette, 20 July 2001.
Para (1): in sub-para (a) words "or article 4(1B)" in square brackets inserted by SI 2001/1544, arts 2, 3(9)(b). Date in force: 25 May 2001: see SI 2001/1544, art 1(2), and the London Gazette, 20 July 2001.
Para (2): words "or a supplementary control zone" and "or functions under Article 3 of the supplementary articles" in square brackets inserted by SI 2001/1544, arts 2, 3(10). Date in force: 25 May 2001: see SI 2001/1544, art 1(2), and the London Gazette, 20 July 2001.
Para (3A): inserted by SI 2001/1544, arts 2, 3(11). Date in force: 25 May 2001: see SI 2001/1544, art 1(2), and the London Gazette, 20 July 2001.
Para (4): inserted by SI 1996/2283, art 2(c).

8   Amendments of enactments and instruments

(1)   The enactments mentioned in Part I of Schedule 5 shall have effect subject to the amendments there specified.

(2)   The instruments mentioned in Part II of Schedule 5 shall have effect subject to the amendments there specified.

9   Repeals and revocations

(1)   The enactments mentioned in Part I of Schedule 6 are repealed to the extent there specified.

(2)   The Orders mentioned in Part II of Schedule 6 are revoked to the extent there specified.

SCHEDULE 1
EXPRESSIONS DEFINED

Article 2(1)

Expression	*Meaning*
"The Concessionaires"	The meaning given by section 1(8) (read with section 3(3)) of the Channel Tunnel Act 1987.
"Control zone"	A control zone within the meaning of the international articles.
"Frontier controls"	So far as they constitute frontier controls within the meaning of the international articles and are controls in relation to persons or goods, police, immigration, customs, health, veterinary and phytosanitary[, and transport and road traffic] controls.
"Frontier control enactment"	An Act, or an instrument made under an Act, for the time being in force, which contains provision relating to frontier controls.
["Immigration control enactment"	An Act, or an instrument made under an Act, for the time being in force, which contains provision relating to immigration controls.]
["Immigration officer"	The same meaning as in the Immigration Act 1971.]
"The international articles"	The meaning given by article 2(3) above.
"International service"	The meaning given in section 13(6) of the Channel Tunnel Act 1987.
"Shuttle train"	The meaning given in section 1(9) of the Channel Tunnel Act 1987.
["State of arrival"	The meaning given by the supplementary articles.]
["State of departure"	The meaning given by the supplementary articles.]
["The supplementary articles"	The meaning given by article 2(4) above.]
["Supplementary control zone"	[The part of the territory of the State of departure, determined by mutual agreement between the Governments of the State of departure and the State of arrival, within which the officers of the State of arrival are empowered to effect controls under the supplementary articles.]]
"Terminal control point"	A place which is an authorised terminal control point for international services for the purposes of sections 11 and 12 of the Channel Tunnel Act 1987.

2149

"Through train"	A train, other than a shuttle train, which for the purposes of sections 11 and 12 of the Channel Tunnel Act 1987 is engaged on an international service.
"Train manager"	In relation to a through train or shuttle train, the person designated as train manager by the person operating the international service on which the train is engaged.
"The tunnel system"	The meaning given by section 1(7) of the Channel Tunnel Act 1987.

Amendment
In definition "Frontier controls" words in square brackets inserted by SI 1996/2283, art 2(a).
Definition "Immigration control enactment" inserted by SI 2001/1544, arts 2, 4(1). Date in force: 25 May 2001: see SI 2001/1544, art 1(2), and the London Gazette, 20 July 2001.
Definition "Immigration officer" inserted by SI 2001/1544, arts 2, 4(1). Date in force: 25 May 2001: see SI 2001/1544, art 1(2), and the London Gazette, 20 July 2001.
Definition "State of arrival" inserted by SI 2001/3707, arts 2, 5(2). Date in force: 10 December 2001: see SI 2001/3707, art 1(1).
Definition "State of departure" inserted by SI 2001/3707, arts 2, 5(2). Date in force: 10 December 2001: see SI 2001/3707, art 1(1).
Definition "The supplementary articles" inserted by SI 2001/1544, arts 2, 4(1). Date in force: 25 May 2001: see SI 2001/1544, art 1(2), and the London Gazette, 20 July 2001.
Definition "Supplementary control zone" inserted by SI 2001/1544, arts 2, 4(1). Date in force: 25 May 2001: see SI 2001/1544, art 1(2), and the London Gazette, 20 July 2001.
In definition "Supplementary control zone" words from "The part of the" to "under the supplementary articles." in square brackets substituted by SI 2001/3707, arts 2, 5(1). Date in force: 10 December 2001: see SI 2001/3707, art 1(1).

SCHEDULE 2
INTERNATIONAL ARTICLES

Article 2(3)

ARTICLE 1
Definitions

(1) Any term defined in the Treaty shall have the same meaning in this Protocol.

(2) Otherwise for the purposes of this Protocol the expression:

(a) "frontier controls" means police, immigration, customs, health, veterinary and phytosanitary, consumer protection, and transport and road traffic controls, as well as any other controls provided for in national or European Community laws and regulations;

(b) "host State" means the State in whose territory the controls of the other State are effected;

(c) "adjoining State" means the other State;

(d) "officers" means persons responsible for policing and frontier controls who are under the command of the persons or authorities designated in accordance with Article 2(1);

(e) "rescue services" means the authorities and organisations whose functions are provided for in the emergency arrangements referred to in Part VII of this Protocol who are under the command of the persons or authorities designated in accordance with Article 2(1);

(g) "control zone" means the part of the territory of the host State determined by mutual agreement between the two Governments within which the officers of the adjoining State are empowered to effect controls;

(h) "restricted zone" means the part of the Fixed Link situated in each State subject to special protective security measures;

(i) "through trains" means trains travelling the Fixed Link but originating and terminating outside it, as opposed to "shuttle trains" which are trains travelling solely within the Fixed Link.

PART I
AUTHORITIES AND GENERAL PRINCIPLES OF CO-OPERATION

ARTICLE 2

(1) Each of the Governments shall designate the authorities or the persons having charge of the services which in its territory have responsibility for the exercise of frontier controls, the maintenance of law and order and fire fighting and rescue within the Fixed Link.

PART II
FRONTIER CONTROLS AND POLICE: GENERAL

ARTICLE 5

(1) In order to simplify and speed up the formalities relating to entry into the State of arrival and exit from the State of departure, the two Governments agree to establish juxtaposed national control bureaux in the terminal installations situated at Frethun in French territory and at Folkestone in British territory. These bureaux shall be so arranged that, for each direction of travel, the frontier controls shall be carried out in the terminal in the State of departure.

(2) Supplementary frontier controls may exceptionally be carried out in the Fixed Link by officers of the State of arrival on its own territory.

ARTICLE 6

The competence of those juxtaposed national control bureaux shall extend to all cross-frontier movements with the exception of customs clearance of commercial traffic.

ARTICLE 7

(1) For through trains, each state may carry out its frontier controls during the journey and may authorise the officers of the other State to carry out their frontier controls in its territory.

(2) The two States may agree to an extension of the control zones for through trains, as far as London and Paris, respectively.

ARTICLE 8

Within the Fixed Link, each Government shall permit officers of the other State to carry out their functions in its own territory in application of their powers relating to frontier controls.

ARTICLE 9

The laws and regulations relating to frontier controls of the adjoining State shall be applicable in the control zone situated in the host State and shall be put into effect by the officers of the adjoining State in the same way as in their own territory.

ARTICLE 10

(1) The officers of the adjoining State shall, in exercise of their national powers, be permitted in the control zone situated in the host State to detain or arrest persons in

accordance with the laws and regulations relating to frontier controls of the adjoining State or persons sought by the authorities of the adjoining State. These officers shall also be permitted to conduct such persons to the territory of the adjoining State.

(2)   However, except in exceptional circumstances, no person may be held more than 24 hours in the areas reserved, in the host State, for the frontier controls of the adjoining State. Any such detention shall be subject to the requirements and procedures laid down by the legislation of the adjoining State.

(3)   In exceptional circumstances the 24 hour period of detention may be extended for a further period of 24 hours in accordance with the legislation of the adjoining State. The extension of the period of detention shall be notified to the authorities of the host State.

ARTICLE 11
Breaches of the laws and regulations relating to frontier controls of the adjoining State which are detected in the control zone situated in the host State shall be subject to the laws and regulations of the adjoining State, as if the breaches had occurred in the latter's own territory.

ARTICLE 12
(1)   The frontier controls of the State of departure shall normally be effected before those of the State of arrival.

(2)   The officers of the State of arrival are not authorised to begin to carry out such controls before the end of controls of the State of departure. Any form of relinquishment of such controls shall be considered as a control.

(3)   The officers of the State of departure may no longer carry out their controls when the officers of the State of arrival have begun their own operations except with the consent of the competent officers of the State of arrival.

(4)   If exceptionally, in the course of the frontier controls, the sequence of operations provided for in paragraph (1) of this Article is modified, the officers of the State of arrival may not proceed to detentions, arrests or seizures until the frontier controls of the State of departure are completed. In such a case, these officers shall escort the persons, vehicles, merchandise, animals or other goods, for which the frontier controls of the State of departure are not yet completed, to the officers of that State. If these latter then wish to proceed to detentions, arrests or seizures, they shall have priority.

ARTICLE 14
The detailed plans for the Fixed Link and its means of access, shall, in accordance with the relevant provisions of the Concession, delimit among other things:

  (a)   the control zones;
  (b)   the restricted zones and their sub-divisions;
  (c)   railway lines and their means of access included in the control zones;
  (d)   the area of the frontier control installations and their means of access.

ARTICLE 16
Where investigations and proceedings concern offences committed in the Fixed Link or having a connection with the Fixed Link, the authorities of the host State shall, at the request of the authorities of the adjoining State, undertake official enquiries, the examination of witnesses and experts and the notification to accused persons of summonses and administrative decisions.

ARTICLE 17

The assistance provided for in Article 16 shall be furnished in accordance with the laws, regulations and procedures in force in the State providing the assistance, and with international agreements to which that State is a party.

ARTICLE 18

If the State of arrival refuses admission to persons, vehicles, animals or goods, or if persons decide not to pass through the frontier controls of the State of arrival, or send or take back any vehicles, animals or goods which are accompanying them, the authorities of the State of departure may not refuse to accept back such persons, vehicles, animals or goods. However, the authorities of the State of departure may take any measures to deal with them in accordance with national law and in a way which does not impose obligations on the other State.

ARTICLE 19

(2) In an emergency, the local representatives of the authorities concerned may by mutual agreement, provisionally bring into effect alterations to the delimitation of the control zones which may prove necessary. Any arrangement so reached shall come into effect immediately.

PART III

HEALTH, VETERINARY AND PHYTOSANITARY CONTROLS

ARTICLE 20

Controls on persons for the purpose of safeguarding public health shall be carried out in the control zone situated in the host State by the competent authorities of the adjoining State in conformity with the regulations applicable in that State.

ARTICLE 21

The bringing into each of the two States of living animals, animal products, plants, plant products and foodstuffs for human or animal consumption shall be subject to controls by the competent authorities of the importing State in conformity with the regulations applicable in that State.

ARTICLE 22

The frontier controls referred to in Article 21 shall be carried out by the competent authorities of the two States either before or during Customs clearance.

ARTICLE 23

(1) The frontier controls referred to in Article 21 shall include:

(a) inspection of certificates or accompanying documents, termed documentary inspection;
(b) physical examination, including where necessary the taking of samples;
(c) inspection of means of transport.

(2) Such controls may be limited to documentary inspection, while physical examination may be undertaken as considered necessary.

ARTICLE 24

Veterinary inspection of living animals shall be without prejudice to any subsequent quarantine measures which may be imposed by the importing State.

PART IV

OFFICERS

ARTICLE 26

Officers of both States shall be permitted to circulate freely in the whole of the Fixed Link for official purposes. In carrying out their functions they shall be authorised to pass through the frontier controls simply by producing appropriate evidence of their identity and status.

ARTICLE 28

(1) Officers of the adjoining State may wear their national uniform or visible distinctive insignia in the host State.

(2) In accordance with the laws, regulations and procedures governing the carriage and use of firearms in the host State, the competent authorities of that State will issue permanent licences to carry arms:

(a) to officers of the adjoining State exercising their official functions on board trains within the Fixed Link; and
(b) to an agreed number of specified officers of the adjoining State exercising their functions within the control zone of the host State.

ARTICLE 29

(1) The authorities of the host State shall grant the same protection and assistance to officers of the adjoining State, in the exercise of their functions, as they grant to their own officers.

(2) The provisions of the criminal law in force in the host State for the protection of officers in the exercise of their functions shall be equally applicable to the punishment of offences committed against officers of the adjoining State in the exercise of their functions.

ARTICLE 30

(1) Without prejudice to the application of the provisions of Article 46, claims for compensation for loss, injury or damage caused by or to officers of the adjoining State in the exercise of their functions in the host State shall be subject to the law and jurisdiction of the adjoining State as if the circumstance giving rise to the claim had occurred in that State.

(2) Officers of the adjoining State may not be prosecuted by authorities of the host State for any acts performed in the control zone or within the Fixed Link whilst in the exercise of their functions. In such a case, they shall come under the jurisdiction of the adjoining State, as if the act had been committed in that State.

(3) The judicial authorities or the police of the host State, having taken steps to record the complaint and to assemble the facts relating thereto, shall communicate all the particulars and evidence thereof to the competent authorities of the other State for the purposes of a possible prosecution according to the laws in force in the latter.

ARTICLE 31

(1) Officers of the adjoining State shall be permitted freely to transfer to that State sums of money levied on behalf of their Government in the control zone situated in the host State, as well as merchandise and other goods seized there.

(2) They may equally sell such merchandise and other goods in the host State in conformity with the provisions in force in the host State, and transfer the proceeds to the adjoining State.

PART V
FACILITIES

ARTICLE 34

The authorities of the adjoining State shall be able to make use in the host State of the accommodation, installations and equipment necessary for the performance of their functions.

ARTICLE 35

(1) The officers of the adjoining State are empowered to keep order within the accommodation appointed for their exclusive use in the host State.

(2) The officers of the host State shall not have access to such accommodation, except at the request of the officers of the adjoining State or in accordance with the laws of the host State applicable to entry into and searches of private premises.

ARTICLE 36

All goods which are necessary to enable the officers of the adjoining State to carry out their functions in the host State shall be exempt from all taxes and dues on entry and exit.

ARTICLE 37

(1) The officers of the adjoining State whilst exercising their functions in the host State shall be authorised to communicate with their national authorities.

PART VI
CO-OPERATION IN CRIMINAL JUSTICE

ARTICLE 38

(1) Without prejudice to the provisions of Articles 11 and 30(2), when an offence is committed in the territory of one of the two States, including that lying within the Fixed Link up to its frontier, that State shall have jurisdiction.

(2)
- (a) Within the Fixed Link, each State shall have jurisdiction and shall apply its own law:
  - (i) when it cannot be ascertained with certainty where an offence has been committed; or
  - (ii) when an offence committed in the territory of one State is related to an offence committed on the territory of the other State; or
  - (iii) when an offence has begun in or has been continued into its own territory;
- (b) however, the State which first receives the person suspected of having committed such an offence (in this Article referred to as "the receiving State") shall have priority in exercising jurisdiction.

(3) When the receiving State decides not to exercise its priority jurisdiction under paragraph (2) of this Article it shall inform the other State without delay. If the latter decides not to exercise its jurisdiction, the receiving State shall be obliged to exercise its jurisdiction in accordance with its own national law.

ARTICLE 39

Where an arrest has been made for an offence in respect of which a State has jurisdiction under Article 38, that arrest shall not be affected by the fact that it continues in the territory of the other State.

ARTICLE 40

Without prejudice to the application of Article 3 of the Treaty and of Part II of this Protocol, the police and customs officers of one State may in accordance with their own national laws make arrests on the territory of the other State in cases where a person is found committing, attempting to commit, or just having committed an offence:

(a)   on board any train which has commenced its journey from one State to the other and is within the Fixed Link; or

(b)   within any tunnel described in Article 1(2) of the Treaty.

ARTICLE 41

In the case of arrests covered by Articles 39 and 40:

(a)   the person arrested shall be presented without delay to the competent authorities of the State of arrival for that State to be responsible for determining the exercise of jurisdiction as required by Article 38; and

(b)   where jurisdiction shall be exercised by the other State in accordance with Article 38, the person arrested may be transferred to the territory of that State. However, any such transfer shall take place within 48 hours of the presentation under paragraph (a) of this Article. Moreover, each State reserves the right not to transfer its nationals.

PART VII
PUBLIC SAFETY AND RESCUE

ARTICLE 42

(1)   In case of need the rescue services of the two countries may be committed to joint interventions within the Fixed Link; the rescue services of the adjoining State shall in that case be placed at the disposal of the competent authorities of the host State.

(2)   The rescue services so committed shall however remain under their own internal command.

ARTICLE 43

(1)   In the case of a joint intervention, the competent authorities of each State shall be responsible for the costs incurred by their own rescue services. Any costs which may be recovered from any person or organisation shall be shared in proportion to their actual costs incurred by the rescue services of the two countries.

(2)   The conditions under which the rescue services of the two countries may intervene shall be determined by the emergency arrangements established jointly by the competent authorities of the two States.

ARTICLE 44

(1)   Without prejudice to the application of the provisions of Article 46, if, during a rescue operation in the territory of the host State, damage is caused to a third party by a member of the rescue services of the adjoining State, the competent authorities of the

host State shall make reparations in respect of the damage according to the arrangements which would have applied had the damage been caused by its own rescue services.

(2)   In the case of the death of, or personal injury to, the personnel of the rescue services of the adjoining State, that State shall waive any claim against the host State.

(3)   Whilst in the exercise of their official functions, members of the rescue services shall:

> (a)   benefit in the same way as officers from the provisions of Articles 28(1), 29 and 30(2);
>
> (b)   in the case of a joint intervention, be permitted to circulate freely in the whole of the Fixed Link;
>
> (c)   except in circumstances provided for in sub-paragraph (b) and after agreement by the competent authorities of the two States, be granted access where necessary to that part of the Fixed Link lying within the territory of the adjoining State.

PART VIII
FINAL CLAUSES

ARTICLE 46

(1)   Without prejudice to the application of Articles 15 and 16 of the Treaty in any case covered by those two Articles, in the case of claims for compensation resulting from the application of this Protocol the following provisions shall apply:

> (a)   each State shall waive any claim which it may have against the other State for compensation in respect of damage caused to its officers or its property;
>
> (b)   claims by the Concessionaires shall be dealt with in accordance with the provisions of the Concession.

(2)   The provisions of this Article do not affect in any way the rights of third parties under the laws of each State.

ARTICLE 47

The procedures for the implementation of this Protocol may, as far as necessary, be the subject of technical or administrative arrangements between the competent authorities of the two States.

[SCHEDULE 2A
SUPPLEMENTARY ARTICLES]

[Article 2(4)]

[ARTICLE 1

Any terms defined in Article 1 of the Protocol signed at Sangatte have the same meaning in this Additional Protocol. For the purposes of this Additional Protocol, the following definitions shall be added:

"State of departure" means the State in which the persons board the train;
"State of arrival" means the State in which the persons alight from the train.

ARTICLE 2

The authorities of the two States shall jointly put in place control bureaux, for persons using through trains and wishing to travel to the State of arrival, in the stations of London–Waterloo, London–St Pancras and Ashford on British territory, and the stations of Paris–Gare du Nord, Calais, and Lille–Europe on French territory.

The provisions of the Protocol signed at Sangatte concerning the officers of the adjoining State shall be applicable, under the same conditions, to the officers of the State of arrival who are on duty in the stations mentioned in the preceding paragraph.

ARTICLE 3

The purpose of the controls carried out by the authorities of the State of departure shall be to check whether the person can leave its territory.

The purpose of the controls carried out by the authorities of the State of arrival shall be to check whether the person is in possession of the necessary travel documents and fulfils the other conditions for entry to its territory. If this is not the case, the person shall be immediately handed over to the authorities of the State of departure who shall apply their domestic law procedures.

The authorities of the State of departure and of the State of arrival shall carry out their controls in accordance with this Additional Protocol, with their laws and regulations and with their international obligations.

The controls mentioned in the preceding paragraphs are without prejudice to customs and security controls.

ARTICLE 4

Notwithstanding the third paragraph of Article 3 of this Additional Protocol, when a person submits a request for refugee status or any other kind of protection provided for in international law or in the domestic law of the State of departure during a control carried out at the station of the State of departure by the officers of the State of arrival, this request shall be examined by the authorities of the State of departure in accordance with the rules and procedures of its domestic law.

The same provisions shall be applicable when the request is submitted after the person has passed through this control and before the train doors close at the last scheduled stop at a station located in the territory of the State of departure. If such a request is made after the train doors have closed, it shall be processed by the State of arrival in accordance with the rules and procedures of its domestic law.

ARTICLE 5

The controls referred to in Article 3 of this Additional Protocol shall be carried out in accordance with Article 12 of the Sangatte Protocol.

ARTICLE 6

The procedures for the implementation of this Additional Protocol may, as far as necessary, be the subject of technical or administrative arrangements between the competent authorities of the two States.]

Amendment
Inserted by SI 2001/1544, arts 2, 4(2). Date in force: 25 May 2001: see SI 2001/1544, art 1(2), and the London Gazette, 20 July 2001.

SCHEDULE 3

Article 6

PART I
POWERS OF OFFICERS

1   Power to assist French authorities

(1) Where—

   (a)   an officer belonging to the French Republic has in a control zone in the United Kingdom [or in a supplementary control zone in the United Kingdom] arrested or detained a person as permitted by Article 10(1) of the international articles [and Article 2 of the supplementary articles], and

(b) such an officer so requests,

a constable or an officer commissioned by the Commissioners of Customs and Excise under section 6(3) of the Customs and Excise Management Act 1979(a) (in this Schedule referred to as a "customs officer") may make arrangements for the person to be taken into temporary custody.

(2) A person taken into temporary custody under sub-paragraph (1)—

(a) shall be treated for all purposes as being in lawful custody, and

(b) may be taken to a police station or such other place as may be appropriate in the circumstances, and shall in that case be treated as being a person in whose case sections 36(7) and (8), 54 to 56 and 58 of the Police and Criminal Evidence Act 1984 (in this Schedule referred to as "the 1984 Act"), and in the case of a child or young person section 34(2) to (7), (8) and (9) of the Children and Young Persons Act 1933, apply, and

(c) must be returned, before the end of the period for which he could in the circumstances be detained in the United Kingdom under Article 10 of the international articles [or Article 2 of the supplementary articles], to a place where detention under that Article could be resumed.

[(3) Where a person falls to be treated as mentioned in sub-paragraph (2)(b) section 56 of the 1984 Act shall be taken to apply as if he were detained for a serious arrestable offence.]

2 Powers of arrest outside United Kingdom

(1) A constable may in a control zone in France—

(a) exercise any power of arrest conferred by a frontier control enactment or conferred by the 1984 Act in respect of an offence under such an enactment,

(b) make any arrest authorised by a warrant issued by a court in the United Kingdom, and

(c) arrest any person whose name or description or both, together with particulars of an arrestable offence (within the meaning of section 24 of the 1984 Act) of which there are reasonable grounds for suspecting him to be guilty, have been made available by a chief officer of police to other such officers.

(2) For the purposes of sub-paragraph (1)(a) the reference in sub-paragraph (1) to a constable shall be construed—

(a) in relation to the powers of arrest conferred by [section 28A(1) and (3)] of and paragraph 17(1) of Schedule 2 to the Immigration Act 1971, as including a reference both—
   (i) to an immigration officer appointed for the purposes of that Act under paragraph 1 of that Schedule, and
   (ii) to an officer of customs and excise who is the subject of arrangements for the employment of such officers as immigration officers made under that paragraph by the Secretary of State,
[and where this sub-paragraph applies, the reference in sub-paragraph (1) to a control zone in France shall be construed as including a reference to a supplementary control zone in France,] and

(b) ...

(c) in relation to any arrest that may be made by a customs officer by virtue of section 138 of the Customs and Excise Management Act 1979 and an arrest for a drug trafficking offence as defined in section 38(1) of the Drug Trafficking Offences Act 1986, as including a reference to a customs officer.

Appendix 1   Legislation and materials

(3) A customs officer may in a control zone in France arrest any person whose name or description or both, together with particulars of an arrestable offence (within the meaning of section 24 of the 1984 Act) which is an offence in relation to an assigned matter as defined in section 1(1) of the Customs and Excise Management Act 1979 and of which there are reasonable grounds for suspecting him to be guilty, have been made available to customs officers generally under the authority of the Commissioners of Customs and Excise.

(4) For the purpose of enabling constables to make arrests in France in the cases described in Article 40 of the international articles sections 24 and 25 of the 1984 Act shall extend to France.

(5) Where—

(a) an arrest has been made for an offence of the kind mentioned in Article 39 of the international articles, and
(b) it falls to the competent authorities in France to determine the exercise of jurisdiction in accordance with Article 38,

the person arrested shall be treated as continuing to be under arrest while in France until he is presented to those authorities as required by Article 41(a).

(6) Where—

(a) an arrest falling within sub-paragraph (4) or (5) above has been made, and
(b) the competent authorities in France determine under Article 4I of the international articles that jurisdiction is to be exercised by the United Kingdom,

the person arrested shall be treated as having continued to be under arrest throughout, even if he was for some period in the custody of those authorities, and sections 30 and 41 of the 1984 Act shall apply accordingly.

(7) Any power conferred by an enactment to search an arrested person may be exercised following an arrest authorised by this paragraph as if the person had been arrested in the United Kingdom.

3   Arrested persons held in France

(1) Where—

(a) an arrest of any kind authorised by paragraph 2 above has been made in a control zone in France [or in a supplementary control zone in France], or
(b) an arrest of any such kind has been made in the United Kingdom and the person arrested enters such a control zone while under arrest,

the person arrested may be held in France for a period of not more than 24 hours and, if there are exceptional circumstances and an officer belonging to the French Republic is notified of the extension, for a further such period.

(2) Subject to sub-paragraphs (3) and (4), the person arrested shall be treated as if the place where he is held were for the purposes of the provisions mentioned in paragraph 1(2)(b) above and those of sections 61 to 63 of the 1984 Act a police station, or where the arrest was made by a customs officer, a customs office, in England, not being a police station or customs office designated under section 35 of the 1984 Act.

(3) Where—

(a) an arrest falling within paragraph 2(1)(a) or (3) above has been made by a customs officer, and

(b) the person arrested is held in France in a place within the tunnel system which would if it were in England be a customs office within the meaning of the 1984 Act,

sections 34(1) to (5), 36, 37, 39 to 42, 50, 54, 55, 56(1) to (9), 58 (1) to (11), 62, 63 and 64(1) to (6) of the 1984 Act and in the case of a child or young person section 34(2) to (7), (8) and (9) of the Children and Young Persons Act 1933, shall apply as if the place where he is held were a customs office in England designated under section 35 of the 1984 Act.

(4) ...

4 [Arrested persons arriving in the United Kingdom]

[(1) Where—

(a) an arrest falling within Article 39 or 40 of the international articles has been made, and

(b) the person arrested enters the United Kingdom while under arrest,

the person arrested shall be taken to a police station.]

(2) The custody officer at the police station to which the person is taken shall determine—

(a) whether the offence is one over which the United Kingdom has jurisdiction by virtue of Article 38(1), and

(b) if he determines that it is not, whether it is one over which the United Kingdom may exercise jurisdiction by virtue of Article 38(2) and if so whether jurisdiction is to be exercised,

and may for the purpose of determining those questions detain the person at the police station for not longer than the permitted period.

(3) The permitted period is the period of 48 hours beginning at the time at which the person arrives at the police station.

(4) Subject to sub-paragraph (6), the person shall be treated—

(a) as not being detained at the police station for the purposes of section 37 of the 1984 Act, and

(b) as not being in police detention for the purposes of sections 40 to 43 of the 1984 Act.

(5) Where the custody officer determines that the United Kingdom does not have jurisdiction by virtue of Article 38(1) and—

(a) that jurisdiction is not exercisable by virtue of Article 38(2), or

(b) that jurisdiction is exercisable by virtue of Article 38(2) but is not to be exercised,

he shall immediately inform the competent French authorities of his determination and shall arrange for the person to be transferred to France within the permitted period.

(6) Where the custody officer determines that the United Kingdom has jurisdiction by virtue of Article 38(1) or that jurisdiction is exercisable by virtue of Article 38(2) and is to be exercised—

(a) he shall immediately inform the person of his determination,

(b) the person shall be treated as being in police detention for all purposes of Part IV of the 1984 Act, and

(c) that Part shall have effect in relation to him as if the relevant time mentioned in section 41(1) were the time at which he is informed of the determination.

(7)   Where the police station to which the person is taken is not a police station designated under section 35 of the 1984 Act, references in this paragraph to the custody officer are to be construed as references to an officer not below the rank of sergeant.

5   Arrests of French officers

(1)   This paragraph applies where an officer belonging to the French Republic ("the officer") is arrested for an act performed in the United Kingdom in the tunnel system or a control zone [or supplementary control zone].

(2)   If the officer enters France while under arrest—

(a)   he shall without delay be handed over for custody to the competent French authorities and shall be treated as continuing to be under arrest until he has been handed over, and

(b)   if after consultation with those authorities it is then determined that the act was not performed by the officer whilst in the exercise of his functions and he accordingly does not by virtue of Article 30(2) of the international articles come under French jurisdiction, he shall be treated as having continued to be under arrest until sub-paragraph (3) has been complied with.

(3)   Where—

(a)   sub-paragraph (2)(b) applies, or
(b)   the officer does not enter France while under arrest,

he shall be taken to a police station designated under section 35 of the 1984 Act.

(4)   Sub-paragraphs (5) to (9) apply in a case falling within sub-paragraph (3)(b).

(5)   The custody officer at the police station to which the officer is taken shall after consultation with the competent French authorities determine whether the act was performed by the officer whilst in the exercise of his functions, and may for the purpose of determining that question detain the officer at the police station for not longer than the permitted period.

(6)   The permitted period is the period of 48 hours beginning at the time at which the officer arrives at the police station.

(7)   Subject to sub-paragraph (9), the officer shall be treated—

(a)   as not being detained at the police station for the purposes of section 37 of the 1984 Act, and
(b)   as not being in police detention for the purposes of sections 40 to 43 of the 1984 Act.

(8)   Where the custody officer determines that the act was performed by the officer whilst in the exercise of his functions and the officer accordingly comes under French jurisdiction by virtue of Article 30(2), he shall immediately inform the competent French authorities and shall arrange for the officer to be transferred to France within the permitted period.

(9)   In any other case—

(a)   the custody officer shall immediately inform the officer of his determination,
(b)   the officer shall be treated as being in police detention for all purposes of Part IV of the 1984 Act, and
(c)   that Part shall have effect in relation to him as if the relevant time mentioned in section 41(1) were the time at which he is informed of the determination.

6   Arrests of United Kingdom officers

(1)   This paragraph applies where an officer belonging to the United Kingdom ("the officer") is arrested for an act performed in France in the tunnel system or a control zone [or supplementary control zone].

(2)   If—

(a)   the officer does not enter the United Kingdom while under arrest, and

(b)   the competent French authorities determine that the act was performed by the officer whilst in the exercise of his functions and he accordingly comes under United Kingdom jurisdiction by virtue of Article 30(2) of the international articles,

he shall on being handed over by those authorities to a constable be treated as having been arrested by the constable.

(3)   Where—

(a)   sub-paragraph (2)(b) applies, or

(b)   the officer enters the United Kingdom while under the original arrest,

he shall be taken to a police station designated under section 35 of the 1984 Act.

(4)   Sub-paragraphs (5) to (9) apply in a case falling within sub-paragraph (3)(b).

(5)   The custody officer at the police station to which the officer is taken shall—

(a)   immediately invite the competent French authorities to determine whether the act was performed by the officer whilst in the exercise of his functions, and

(b)   afford those authorities any assistance they may require in determining that question, and may for the purpose of enabling that question to be determined detain the officer at the police station for not longer than the permitted period.

(6)   The permitted period is the period of 48 hours beginning at the time at which the officer arrives at the police station.

(7)   Subject to sub-paragraph (9), the officer shall be treated—

(a)   as not being detained at the police station for the purposes of section 37 of the 1984 Act, and

(b)   as not being in police detention for the purposes of sections 40 to 43 of the 1984 Act.

(8)   Where the competent French authorities determine that the act was not performed by the officer whilst in the exercise of his functions and the officer accordingly does not by virtue of Article 30(2) come under United Kingdom jurisdiction, the custody officer shall arrange for the officer to be transferred to France within the permitted period.

(9)   In any other case—

(a)   the custody officer shall immediately inform the officer of the determination,

(b)   the officer shall be treated as being in police detention for all purposes of Part IV of the 1984 Act, and

(c)   that Part shall have effect in relation to him as if the relevant time mentioned in section 41(1) were the time at which he is informed of the determination.

Amendment
Para 1: in sub-para (1)(a) words "or in a supplementary control zone in the United Kingdom" and "and Article 2 of the supplementary articles" in square brackets inserted by SI 2001/1544, arts 2, 5(1), (2). Date in force: 25 May 2001: see SI 2001/1544, art 1(2), and the London Gazette, 20 July 2001.

Appendix 1   Legislation and materials

Para 1: in sub-para (2)(c) words "or Article 2 of the supplementary articles" in square brackets inserted by SI 2001/1544, arts 2, 5(1), (3). Date in force: 25 May 2001: see SI 2001/1544, art 1(2), and the London Gazette, 20 July 2001.

Para 1: sub-para (3) inserted by SI 1994/1405, art 8, Sch 4, para 10(a).

Para 2: in sub-para (2)(a) words "section 28A(1) and (3)" in square brackets substituted by SI 2001/1544, arts 2, 5(1), (4). Date in force: 25 May 2001: see SI 2001/1544, art 1(2), and the London Gazette, 20 July 2001.

Para 2: in sub-para (2)(a) words from "and where this sub-paragraph" to "control zone in France," in square brackets inserted by SI 2001/1544, arts 2, 5(1), (4). Date in force: 25 May 2001: see SI 2001/1544, art 1(2), and the London Gazette, 20 July 2001.

Para 2: sub-para (2)(b) revoked by SI 2001/178, art 3(a). Date in force: 19 February 2001: see SI 2001/178, art 1.

Para 3: in sub-para (1)(a) words "or in a supplementary control zone in France" in square brackets inserted by SI 2001/1544, arts 2, 5(1), (5). Date in force: 25 May 2001: see SI 2001/1544, art 1(2), and the London Gazette, 20 July 2001.

Para 3: sub-para (4) revoked by SI 2001/178, art 3(b). Date in force: 19 February 2001: see SI 2001/178, art 1.

Para 4: para-heading and sub-para (1) substituted by SI 1994/1405, art 8, Sch 4, para 10(b), (c).

Para 5: in sub-para (1) words "or supplementary control zone" in square brackets inserted by SI 2001/1544, arts 2, 5(1), (6). Date in force: 25 May 2001: see SI 2001/1544, art 1(2), and the London Gazette, 20 July 2001.

Para 6: in sub-para (1) words "or supplementary control zone" in square brackets inserted by SI 2001/1544, arts 2, 5(1), (6). Date in force: 25 May 2001: see SI 2001/1544, art 1(2), and the London Gazette, 20 July 2001.

PART II
SUPPLEMENTARY CONTROLS OVER ANIMALS

1   Extent

This Part does not extend to France.

2   Interpretation

In this Part "animal" means a four-footed mammal capable of carrying the rabies virus, except one which—

(a) is lawfully being transported through the tunnel system, or

(b) enters the tunnel system for purposes connected with law enforcement or security and is under the control of a person approved in writing by the appropriate Minister,

and "tunnel", except in the expression "tunnel system", means a tunnel mentioned in section 1(7)(a) of the Channel Tunnel Act 1987.

3   Duties of Concessionaires

The Concessionaires shall—

[(a) construct and maintain fencing around the entrance to each tunnel, except at places where gaps are necessary to allow the passage of vehicles through the tunnel, of such material and of such a height above and depth below the surface of the ground as to ensure, so far as is practicable, that an animal cannot cross it, and]

(b) comply with the requirements imposed by paragraph 5.

4   ...

5   Requirements

The requirements mentioned in paragraph 3(b) are—

(a) to ensure, so far as is practicable, that any animal which has entered a tunnel is removed from the tunnel system,

(b) to operate a system of surveillance that will ensure, so far as is practicable, that the passage of any animal through a tunnel is detected,

(c) to take effective measures for the control of rodents, including monitoring each tunnel for the presence of rodents and laying poisoned bait for them,

(d) so far as is practicable, to keep each tunnel free of waste food, urine, faeces and every other substance likely to attract animals,

(e) to ensure that all points of access to a tunnel, other than the entrance to the tunnel and any ventilation shafts, are sealed when not in use,

(f) to ensure that all tunnel ventilation shafts are so constructed as effectively to deter animals from passing through them, and

(g) to keep records of the taking of any bait laid as mentioned in sub-paragraph (c) and of the detection of the presence of any animal in a tunnel or within the fencing [described in paragraph 3(a)].

6 Unauthorised interference

Unless authorised in writing by the Concessionaires, no person shall intentionally—

(a) remove or in any way impair the effectiveness of [the fencing described in paragraph 3(a)], or

(b) do anything which might in any way impair the effectiveness of any measures taken to comply with the requirements described in paragraph 5.

7 Enforcement

A person authorised by the appropriate Minister may, on producing, if required to do so, some duly authenticated document showing his authority—

(a) enter any part of the tunnel system for the purpose of ascertaining whether there is or has been any breach of a requirement or prohibition imposed by this Part, and

(b) for that purpose inspect any relevant document or computer record.

8 Offences

A person who contravenes any of paragraphs 3 to 6 or obstructs the exercise of powers by an authorised person under paragraph 7 shall be guilty of an offence and shall be liable—

(a) on conviction on indictment to a fine, and

(b) on summary conviction to a fine not exceeding the statutory maximum.

Amendment
Para 3: sub-para (a) substituted by SI 2003/2799, art 2(1), (2). Date in force: 30 November 2003: see SI 2003/2799, art 1.
Para 4: revoked by SI 2003/2799, art 2(1), (3). Date in force: 30 November 2003: see SI 2003/2799, art 1.
Para 5: in sub-para (g) words "described in paragraph 3(a)" in square brackets substituted by SI 2003/2799, art 2(1), (4). Date in force: 30 November 2003: see SI 2003/2799, art 1.
Para 6: in sub-para (a) words "the fencing described in paragraph 3(a)" in square brackets substituted by SI 2003/2799, art 2(1), (5). Date in force: 30 November 2003: see SI 2003/2799, art 1.

SCHEDULE 4
ENACTMENTS MODIFIED

Article 7(1)

Immigration Act 1971

1   (1)   In this paragraph "the 1971 Act" means the Immigration Act 1971.

(2)   In section 3 of the 1971 Act (general provision for regulation and control)—

(a)   after subsection (4) insert—

"(4A)   For the purposes of subsection (4) above a person seeking to leave the United Kingdom through the tunnel system who is refused admission to France shall be treated as having gone to a country outside the common travel area.";
and
(b)   after subsection (7) insert—

"(7A)   Any reference in an Order in Council under subsection (7) above to embarking or being about to embark shall be construed as including a reference to leaving or seeking to leave the United Kingdom through the tunnel system.".

(3)   In section 4 of the 1971 Act (administration of control) in subsection (2)—

(a)   for the words "the United Kingdom by ship or aircraft" substitute ", or seeking to arrive in or leave, the United Kingdom through the tunnel system"; and
(b)   for the words after "arrive as" substitute "members of the crews of through trains or shuttle trains".

(4)   In section 8 of the 1971 Act (exceptions for seamen etc) in subsection (1)—

(a)   for the words from "of a ship" to "its crew" substitute "of a through train or shuttle train under an engagement requiring him to leave within seven days as a member of the crew of that or another such train"; and
(b)   for the words "departure of the ship or aircraft" substitute "departure of the through train or shuttle train".

(5)   In section 11 of the 1971 Act (construction of references to entry etc)—

(a)   in subsection (1)—
(i)   for the words "by ship or aircraft" substitute "through the tunnel system", and
(ii)   for the words from "he disembarks" to "immigration officer" substitute—
"(a)   he leaves any control area designated under paragraph 26 of Schedule 2 to this Act, or
(b)   he remains on a through train after it has ceased to be such a control area";
(b)   omit subsections (2) and (3); and
(c)   in subsection (4) omit the words after "section 1(3)".

(6)   In section 13 of the 1971 Act (appeals against exclusion from United Kingdom) in subsection (3) omit the words "at a port of entry and".

(7)   In section 24 of the 1971 Act (illegal entry and similar offences)—

(a)   in subsection (1)(f) for the words from "disembarks" to "aircraft" substitute "leaves a train in the United Kingdom"; and
(b)   in subsection (1)(g) for the word "embarks" substitute "leaves or seeks to leave the United Kingdom through the tunnel system".

(8)   In section 25 of the 1971 Act (assisting illegal entry and harbouring)—

(a) ...

(b) for subsection (6) substitute—

"(6) Where a person convicted on indictment of an offence under subsection (1) above is at the time of the offence—

(a) the owner or one of the owners of a through train, shuttle train or vehicle used or intended to be used in carrying out the arrangements in respect of which the offence is committed; or

(b) a director or manager of a company which is the owner or one of the owners of any such train or vehicle; or

(c) the train manager of any such train;

then subject to subsections (7) and (8) below the court before which he is convicted may order the forfeiture of the train or vehicle.

In this subsection (but not in subsection (7) below)—

"owner" in relation to a train or vehicle which is the subject of a hire-purchase agreement includes the person in possession of it under that agreement, and in relation to a train, includes a charterer; and "vehicle" includes a railway vehicle capable of being uncoupled from a train and a road vehicle carried on a train.";

(c) in subsection (7)—

    (i) for the words "ship or aircraft", wherever occurring, substitute "train",

    (ii) omit paragraph (a), and

    (iii) omit the words from "In this subsection" to "in respect of the aircraft"; and

(d) in subsection (8) for the words "ship, aircraft", wherever occurring, substitute "train".

(9) In section 27 of the 1971 Act (offences by persons connected with ships etc)—

(a) in paragraph (a)—

    (i) for the words "captain of a ship or aircraft" substitute "train manager of a through train or shuttle train", and

    (ii) in sub-paragraph (i) for the word "disembark" substitute "leave the train";

(b) in paragraph (b)—

    (i) for the words "as owner or agent of a ship or aircraft" substitute "as, or as agent of, a person operating an international service",

    (ii) in sub-paragraph (i) for the words from "the ship" to "port of entry" substitute "a through train to stop at a place other than a terminal control point [or an international station]"; and

(c) in paragraph (c)—

    (i) for the words from "as owner" to "port" substitute "as, or as agent of, a person operating an international service, or as an occupier or person concerned with the management of a terminal control point [or an international station]", and

    (ii) for the words "the embarkation or disembarkation of passengers" substitute "persons arriving or seeking to arrive in, or leaving or seeking to leave, the United Kingdom through the tunnel system".

[(9A) In section 28A of the 1971 Act (arrest without warrant), in subsection (3) after the words "immigration officer" insert "or a constable".]

(10) In section 33 of the 1971 Act (interpretation)—

(a) in subsection (1)—

    (i) omit the definitions of "airport" and "port",

(ii) in the definition of "crew" after the word "captain," insert "and in relation to a through train or a shuttle train, means all persons on the train who are actually employed in its service or working, including the train manager," and

(iii) in the definition of "illegal entrant" after the words "unlawfully entering or seeking" insert "(whether or not he has arrived in the United Kingdom)"; and

[(b) in subsection (3) for the words "ports of entry for purposes of this Act" substitute "international stations for purposes of this Act shall be such railway stations as may from time to time be designated by order of the Secretary of State].

(11) In Schedule 2 to the 1971 Act (administrative provisions as to control on entry etc)—

(a) in paragraph 1(4) and where first occurring in paragraph 1(5) for the words "ship or aircraft" substitute "through train or shuttle train";

(b) in paragraph 1(5) for the words after "vehicle" substitute

"which—

(a) is in a control zone in France within the tunnel system, or

(b) has arrived in, or is seeking to leave, the United Kingdom through the tunnel system.";

(c) in paragraph 2(1) for the words from "in the United Kingdom" to "seeking to enter the United Kingdom)" substitute ", or who are seeking to arrive, in the United Kingdom through the tunnel system";

[(d) after paragraph 2(1) insert—

"(1A) The power conferred by sub-paragraph (1) is exercisable—

(a) as respects persons who have arrived in the United Kingdom, in a control area, and

(b) as respects persons seeking to arrive in the United Kingdom (who may first be questioned to ascertain whether they are seeking to do so), in a control zone in France or Belgium, or in a supplementary control zone in France.";]

(e) in paragraph 2(3) [after the words "further examination" insert "(or, if examined by an immigration officer in a supplementary control zone, may be required to submit to a [further examination before or after arrival] in the United Kingdom)" and]—

(i) for the words "crew of a ship or aircraft" substitute "crew of a through train or shuttle train",

(ii) after the words "joining a ship or aircraft" insert "or a shuttle train or through train", and

(iii) after the words "intended ship or aircraft" insert "or train";

[[(ea)after paragraph 2A(1) insert—

"(1A) This paragraph also applies to a person who seeks to arrive in the United Kingdom and who is in a control zone in France or Belgium, or in a supplementary control zone in France]

(eb) in paragraph 2A(6)—

(i) [after the words "sub-paragraph (5)" insert "or sub-paragraph (5A)", and] for the words "crew of a ship or aircraft" substitute "crew of a through train or shuttle train";

(ii) after the words "joining a ship or aircraft" insert "or a shuttle train or through train"; and

(iii) after the words "intended ship or aircraft", insert "or train";]

(f) in paragraph 3(1) and (2) for the words "embarking or seeking to embark in the United Kingdom" substitute "leaving or seeking to leave the United Kingdom through the tunnel system";

(g) in paragraph 5—

    (i) for the words from "requiring passengers" to "such passengers" substitute "requiring persons, or any class of persons, arriving in or leaving, or seeking to arrive in or leave, the United Kingdom through the tunnel system", and

    (ii) for the words after "and for requiring" substitute "persons operating international services to supply such cards to those persons.";

(h) in paragraph 8(1)—

    (i) after the words "in the United Kingdom" insert "through the tunnel system", and

    (ii) for the words after "sub-paragraph (2) below" substitute

"give the person operating the international service by which he arrived ("the carrier") directions requiring the carrier—

(a) to remove him from the United Kingdom through the tunnel system; or

(b) to make arrangements for his removal from the United Kingdom in any ship or aircraft specified or indicated in the directions to a country or territory so specified, being either—

    (i) a country of which he is a national or citizen; or

    (ii) a country or territory in which he has obtained a passport or other document of identity; or

    (iii) the country from which he departed for the United Kingdom; or

    (iv) a country or territory to which there is reason to believe he will be admitted.";

(i) after paragraph 8(1) insert—

"(1A) Where a person seeking to arrive in the United Kingdom through the tunnel system is refused leave to enter and is then in a control zone in France within the tunnel system, an immigration officer may give the Concessionaires directions requiring them to secure that the person is taken out of the control zone to a place where he may be accepted back by the competent French authorities as provided in Article 18 of the international articles.";

(j) in paragraph 8(2)—

    (i) for the words "sub-paragraph (1)(b) or (c)" substitute "sub-paragraph (1)", and

    (ii) for the words "the owners or agents in question" substitute "the carrier";

(k) in paragraph 9 for the words after "an immigration officer" substitute

"may—

(a) if the illegal entrant has arrived in the United Kingdom, give such directions in respect of him as in a case within sub-paragraph (1) of paragraph 8 above are authorised by that sub-paragraph, or

(b) if the illegal entrant is in a control zone in France within the tunnel system, give such directions in respect of him as in a case within sub-paragraph (1A) of paragraph 8 above are authorised by that sub-paragraph.";

(l) in paragraph 10(1)—

    (i) omit the words from "either" to "or (b)",

    (ii) for the words "owners or agents of any ship or aircraft" substitute "person operating the international service by which he arrived", and

    (iii) for the words "paragraph 8(1)(c)" substitute "paragraph 8(1)";

(m) in paragraph 11 after the words "ship or aircraft" insert "or through train or shuttle train";

    (n) in paragraph 13 omit sub-paragraph (1) and in sub-paragraph (2)—
        (i) for the words "crew of a ship or aircraft, and either" substitute "crew of a through train or shuttle train, and",
       (ii) omit the words from "or (B)" to "do so", and
      (iii) for the words after "an immigration officer may" substitute—
"(a) give the train manager of the train in which that person ("the crew member") arrived directions requiring the train manager to remove him from the United Kingdom in that train; or
  (b) give the person operating the international service on which that train is engaged directions requiring that person to remove the crew member from the United Kingdom in any train specified or indicated in the directions, being a train engaged on that international service; or
  (c) give that person directions requiring him to make arrangements for the removal of the crew member from the United Kingdom in any ship or aircraft or through train or shuttle train specified in the directions to a country or territory so specified, being either—
        (i) a country of which he is a national or citizen; or
       (ii) a country or territory in which he has obtained a passport or other document of identity; or
      (iii) the country from which he departed for the United Kingdom; or
      (iv) a country or territory in which he was engaged as a member of the crew of the through train or shuttle train in which he arrived in the United Kingdom; or
       (v) a country or territory to which there is reason to believe he will be admitted.";
    (o) in paragraph 15 after the words "ship or aircraft" insert "or through train or shuttle train";
    (p) in paragraph 16—
        (i) in sub-paragraph (2) for the words "his removal in pursuance of" substitute "the taking of any action in respect of him required by",
       (ii) for sub-paragraph (3) substitute—

"(3) A person may under the authority of an immigration officer be removed for detention under this paragraph—

    (a) from a vehicle in a control zone in the tunnel system in France; or
    (b) from a train or vehicle in which he arrives in the United Kingdom through the tunnel system.",
         and
      (iii) after sub-paragraph (4) insert—

"(5) Where a person has under paragraph 11 or 15 above been placed on a through train or shuttle train sub-paragraph (4) of this paragraph has effect with the substitution—

    (a) for the word "captain", wherever occurring, of the words "train manager"; and
    (b) for the words "ship or aircraft", wherever occurring, of the word "train"; and
    (c) for the word "disembarking", of the words "leaving the train".".
    (q) in paragraphs 19(1) and 20(1) for the words "owners or agents of the ship or aircraft in" substitute "person operating the international service by"; ...
    (r) for paragraphs 26 and 27 substitute—

"26 (1) Persons operating international services shall not, without the approval of the Secretary of State, arrange for any through train to stop for the purpose of enabling passengers to leave it except at a terminal control point [or an international station].

(2) The Secretary of State may from time to time give written notice to persons operating international services designating all or any through trains as control areas while they are within any area in the United Kingdom specified in the notice or while they constitute a control zone.

(3) The Secretary of State may from time to time give written notice designating a control area—

(a) to the Concessionaires as respects any part of the tunnel system in the United Kingdom or of a control zone within the tunnel system in France, or

(b) to any occupier or person concerned with the management of a terminal control point in the United Kingdom [or of an international station].

(4) A notice under sub-paragraph (2) or (3) above may specify conditions and restrictions to be observed in a control area, and any person to whom such a notice is given shall take all reasonable steps to secure that any such conditions or restrictions are observed.

27 (1) The train manager of a through train or shuttle train arriving in the United Kingdom—

(a) shall take such steps as may be necessary to secure that persons, other than members of the crew who may lawfully enter the United Kingdom by virtue of section 8(1) of this Act, do not leave the train except in accordance with any arrangements approved by an immigration officer; and

(b) where persons are to be examined by an immigration officer on the train, shall take such steps as may be necessary to secure that they are ready for examination.

(2) The Secretary of State may by order made by statutory instrument make provision for train managers of through trains or shuttle trains arriving in the United Kingdom to furnish to immigration officers—

(a) in the case of a through train, a passenger list showing the names and nationality or citizenship of passengers arriving in the train;

(b) in any case, particulars of members of the crew of the train;

and for enabling an immigration officer to dispense with the furnishing of any such list or particulars.".

[(s) In paragraph 27B (passenger information)—
  (i) in sub-paragraph (1) for the words "ships or aircraft" substitute "through trains or shuttle trains";
  (ii) in sub-paragraph (2) for the words "owner or agent ("the carrier") of a ship or aircraft" substitute "person operating an international service or his agent ("the carrier")";
  (iii) in sub-paragraph (3)(a) for the words "ship or particular aircraft" substitute "train";
  (iv) in sub-paragraph (3)(b) and (c) for the words "ships or aircraft" substitute "trains"; and
  (v) in sub-paragraphs (4) and (9) for the words "ship or aircraft", wherever occurring, substitute "train"; and
(t) In paragraph 27C (notification of non-EEA arrivals)—
  (i) in sub-paragraph (1)—
    (a) for the words "owner or agent ("the carrier") of a ship or aircraft" substitute "person operating an international service other than a shuttle service or his agent ("the carrier")", and
    (b) for the second occurrence of the words "ship or aircraft" substitute "through train";

> (ii) in sub-paragraph (2)(a) for the words "ship or particular aircraft" substitute "through train";
> (iii) in sub-paragraph (2)(b) and (c) for the words "ships or aircraft" substitute "through trains"; and
> (d) in sub-paragraphs (6), (7) and (9) for the words "ship or aircraft" substitute "through train".]

(12)   In Schedule 3 to the 1971 Act (supplementary provisions as to deportation)—

(a) in paragraph 1(1) after the words "any person" insert "who arrived in the United Kingdom through the tunnel system";
(b) in paragraph 1(2) after sub-paragraph (b) insert—

"(bb)directions to the person operating the international service by which the person in question arrived ("the carrier") requiring the carrier to make arrangements for the removal of the person in question through the tunnel system; or";

and

(c) in paragraph 1(4) after the word "voyage" insert "or journey".

Public Health (Control of Disease) Act 1984

2   In the Public Health (Control of Disease) Act 1984, in section 13 (regulations for control of certain diseases)—

(a) in subsection (1)—
   (i) omit the words from ", as respects" to "coastal waters,",
   (ii) in paragraph (b) for the words after "public health" substitute "from through trains or shuttle trains whose journey terminates in the United Kingdom", and
   (iii) in paragraph (c) for the words "vessel or aircraft leaving any place" substitute "through train or shuttle train whose journey begins in the United Kingdom";
(b) after subsection (2) insert—

"(2A)   Regulations made under this section may provide for the Secretary of State from time to time—

(a) to give written notice to persons operating international services designating all or any through trains as control areas while they are within any area in the United Kingdom specified in the notice or while they constitute a control zone; and
(b) to give written notice designating a control area—
   (i) to the Concessionaires as respects any part of the tunnel system in the United Kingdom or of a control zone within the tunnel system in France, or
   (ii) to any occupier or person concerned with the management of a terminal control point in the United Kingdom or of a place in the United Kingdom which is a customs approved area within the meaning of the Channel Tunnel (Customs and Excise) Order 1990 [or of a railway station which is an international station for the purposes of the Immigration Act 1971];

and references in subsections (2B), (3) and (5) below to a control area are to a control area so designated.

(2B)   Regulations made under this section may—

(a) provide that a notice given as mentioned in subsection (2A) above may specify conditions and restrictions to be observed in a control area; and
(b) require any person to whom such a notice is given to take all reasonable steps to secure that any such conditions or restrictions are observed.";

(c)　in subsection (3)—
　　(i)　omit paragraph (a),
　　(ii)　for paragraph (b) substitute—
"(b)　the questions to be answered in a control area by train managers of through trains and shuttle trains and other persons on such trains, as to cases of epidemic, endemic or infectious disease in the train,",
　　(iii)　in paragraph (c) for the words "alighting from aircraft to answer substitute "on or alighting from such trains to answer in a control area",
　　(iv)　for paragraph (d) substitute—
"(d)　the detention of such trains and of persons on them,",
　　　and
　　(v)　in paragraph (e) for the words after "diseases" substitute "by train managers of and other persons on such trains,";
(d)　in subsection (4) after paragraph (a) insert—
"(aa)may, notwithstanding paragraph (a) above, specify the Secretary of State as an authority, or as the sole authority, by whom they are to be enforced and executed, and";
　and
(e)　in subsection (5)—
　　(i)　in paragraph (a) after the words "subsection (4)(a)" insert "or (aa)", and
　　(ii)　for the words ",vessel or aircraft" substitute "and any through train or shuttle train while it is in or constitutes a control area,".

[Terrorism Act 2000]

3　In the Terrorism Act 2000—

(a)　in Schedule 7 (Port and Border Controls)—
　　(i)　in paragraph 1(2) omit the references to "the border area", "captain", "ship" and "vehicle" and for the words "an airport or hoverport" substitute the words
"a railway station or other place where

(a)　persons embark or disembark or
(b)　goods are loaded or unloaded,

on or from a through train or shuttle train, as the case may be";
　　(ii)　in paragraph 1(3) for the words "ship or aircraft" wherever occurring, substitute "through train or shuttle train";
　　(iii)　in paragraph 2(2), omit the words "or in the border area", "or in the area" and "or Northern Ireland";
　　(iv)　in paragraph 2(3) for the words "ship or aircraft" substitute "through train or shuttle train" and omit the words "or Northern Ireland";
　　(v)　after paragraph 2(3) insert—
"3A　An examination under sub-paragraph (1) may be commenced in a train during the period when it is a control area.";
　　(vi)　omit paragraphs 3 and 4;
　　(vii)　in paragraph 5 omit the words "or 3";
　　(viii)in paragraph 6, in sub-paragraph (1), for the word "vehicle" substitute "through train or shuttle train" and, in sub-paragraph (2), for the words "ship, aircraft or vehicle" substitute "through train or shuttle train";
　　(ix)　in paragraph 7 for the words "ship or aircraft", wherever occurring, substitute "through train or shuttle train";
　　(x)　in paragraph 8 for the words "ship or aircraft", wherever occurring, substitute the words "through train or shuttle train", and omit sub-paragraph (2);

(xi) in paragraph 9, in sub-paragraph (2), omit the words "or in Northern Ireland" and for the words "ship, aircraft or vehicle" substitute "through train or shuttle train" and, in sub-paragraph (4), for the words "ship or aircraft or enter a vehicle" substitute the words "through train or shuttle train";

(xii) omit paragraph 12;

(xiii) in paragraph 13 for the words "ships or aircraft" and the words "ship or aircraft", wherever occurring, substitute "a through train or shuttle train" and for the words "United Kingdom" substitute the words "Tunnel System";

(xiv) for paragraph 14 substitute—

"14   (1)   The Secretary of State may from time to time give written notice to persons operating international services designating all or any through trains as control areas while they are within any area in the UK specified in the notice or while they constitute a control zone.

(2)   The Secretary of State may from time to time give written notice designating a control area—

(i) to the Concessionaires as respects any part of the tunnel system in the UK or of a control zone within the tunnel system in France or Belgium, or

(ii) to any occupier or person concerned with the management of a terminal control point in the UK.

(3)   A notice under sub-paragraph (1) or (2) above may specify facilities to be provided and conditions and restrictions to be observed in a control area, and any persons to whom such a notice is given shall take all reasonable steps to secure that any such facilities, conditions or restrictions are provided or observed.";

(xv) omit paragraphs 15, 16 and 17, and

(xvi) omit the Table of Designated Ports, and

(b)   in Schedule 14 (Exercise of Officers' Powers) in paragraphs 5 and 6 after the words "this Act", in each place where they occur, insert "or the Channel Tunnel (International Arrangements) Order 1993".]

[The Immigration (Leave to Enter and Remain) Order 2000]

[4   In the Immigration (Leave to Enter and Remain) Order 2000—

(a)   in article 4(2)—

(i) after the words "arrives in the United Kingdom", insert "or enters a control zone in France or Belgium, or a supplementary control zone in France, seeking to arrive in the United Kingdom through the tunnel system";

(ii) after the words "before arrival", insert "or entry into the control zone or supplementary control zone"; and

(iii) after the words "date of arrival", insert "or entry into the control zone or supplementary control zone";

(b)   in article 4(3)—

(i) after the words "on arrival in the United Kingdom", insert "or entry into a control zone in France or Belgium, or a supplementary control zone in France, seeking to arrive in the United Kingdom through the tunnel system"; and

(ii) after the words "before arrival", insert "or entry into the control zone or supplementary control zone"; and

(c)   in article 6(2)(a) after the words "arrives in the United Kingdom", insert "or enters a control zone in France or Belgium, or a supplementary control zone in France, seeking to arrive in the United Kingdom through the tunnel system".]

[The Immigration (European Economic Area) Regulations 2000

5   In the Immigration (European Economic Area) Regulations 2000—

(a)   after regulation 12(2) insert—

"(3)   Any passport, identity card, family permit, residence document or document proving family membership which is required to be produced under this regulation as a condition for admission to the United Kingdom ("the required documents") may, for the same purpose, be required to be produced in a control zone or a supplementary control zone.";

(b)   in regulations 21(2) after the word "arrival", in regulation 22(3) after the words "EEA national", and in regulation 22(4) after the words "United Kingdom", insert "or the time of his production of the required documents in a control zone or a supplementary control zone".]

Amendment
Para 1: sub-para (8)(a) revoked by SI 2001/1544, arts 2, 6(1), (2). Date in force: 25 May 2001: see SI 2001/1544, art 1(2), and the London Gazette, 20 July 2001.
Para 1: in sub-para (9)(b)(ii), (c)(i) words "or an international station" in square brackets inserted by SI 1994/1405, art 8, Sch 4, para 11.
Para 1: sub-para (9A) inserted by SI 2001/1544, arts 2, 6(1), (2). Date in force: 25 May 2001: see SI 2001/1544, art 1(2), and the London Gazette, 20 July 2001.
Para 1: sub-para (10)(b) substituted by SI 1994/1405, art 8, Sch 4, para 11.
Para 1: sub-para (11)(d) substituted by SI 2001/1544, arts 2, 6(1), (3). Date in force: 25 May 2001: see SI 2001/1544, art 1(2), and the London Gazette, 20 July 2001.
Para 1: in sub-para (11)(e) words from "after the words" to "United Kingdom)" and" in square brackets inserted by SI 2001/1544, arts 2, 6(1), (4). Date in force: 25 May 2001: see SI 2001/1544, art 1(2), and the London Gazette, 20 July 2001.
Para 1: in sub-para (11)(e) words "further examination before or after arrival" in square brackets substituted by SI 2001/3707, arts 2, 6(1). Date in force: 10 December 2001: see SI 2001/3707, art 1(1).
Para 1: sub-para (11)(ea) substituted by SI 2001/1544, arts 2, 6(1), (5). Date in force: 25 May 2001: see SI 2001/1544, art 1(2), and the London Gazette, 20 July 2001.
Para 1: sub-para (11)(ea), (eb) inserted by SI 2000/1775, art 2(1), (2). Date in force: 30 July 2000: see SI 2000/1775, art 1.
Para 1: in sub-para (11)(eb)(i) words "after the words "sub-paragraph (5)" insert "or sub-paragraph (5A)", and" in square brackets inserted by SI 2001/1544, arts 2, 6(1), (6). Date in force: 25 May 2001: see SI 2001/1544, art 1(2), and the London Gazette, 20 July 2001.
Para 1: in sub-para (11)(q) word omitted revoked by SI 2000/913, art 2(1), (2). Date in force: 28 April 2000: see SI 2000/913, art 1.
Para 1: in sub-para (11)(r) words "or an international station" in square brackets inserted by SI 1994/1405, art 8, Sch 4, para 11.
Para 1: in sub-para (11)(r) words "or of an international station" in square brackets inserted by SI 1994/1405, art 8, Sch 4, para 11.
Para 1: sub-para (11)(s), (t) inserted by SI 2000/913, art 2(1), (3). Date in force: 28 April 2000: see SI 2000/913, art 1.
Para 2: words in square brackets in sub-para (b) inserted by SI 1994/1405, art 8, Sch 4, para 11.
Para 3: substituted by SI 2001/178, art 4. Date in force: 19 February 2001: see SI 2001/178, art 1.
Para 4: inserted by SI 2000/1775, art 2(1), (3). Date in force: 30 July 2000: see SI 2000/1775, art 1.
Para 4: substituted by SI 2001/1544, arts 2, 7. Date in force: 25 May 2001: see SI 2001/1544, art 1(2), and the London Gazette, 20 July 2001.
Para 5: inserted by SI 2001/3707, arts 2, 7. Date in force: 10 December 2001: see SI 2001/3707, art 1(1).

SCHEDULE 5
AMENDMENTS OF ENACTMENTS AND INSTRUMENTS

Article 8

PART I
ENACTMENTS

1 ...

2 ...

3 ...

Amendment
Para 1: amends the Immigration Act 1971, Sch 2, paras 1, 2
Para 2: amends the Animal Health Act 1981, s 10(7).
Para 3: revoked by SI 2001/178, art 5. Date in force: 19 February 2001: see SI 2001/178, art 1.

PART II
INSTRUMENTS

1–4 ...

[5 The Immigration (Places of Detention) (No 2) Direction 2000 is amended—
   (a) in article 2, by inserting after the words "control zone" the words ", supplementary control zone"; and
   (b) in article 3(2)(a)(i) by inserting after the words "control zone" the words "or supplementary control zone".]

[Code of practice for examining officers under the Terrorism Act 2000

6 The code of practice for examining officers under the Terrorism Act 2000 is amended—
   (a) in paragraph 4 by inserting after the words—
""port" and "border area" have the same meaning as in the Schedule"
the words—
"but, by virtue of the Channel Tunnel (International Arrangements) (Amendment No 2) Order 2001, "port" also includes a railway station or other place where—
      (a) persons embark or disembark; or
      (b) goods are loaded or unloaded,
on or, as the case may be, from a through train or shuttle train within the meaning of article 2(1) of the Channel Tunnel (International Arrangements) Order 1993", and
   (b) in paragraph 7 by inserting after the words "(see paragraph 2(3) of the Schedule)" the words "or on a through train or shuttle train which has arrived in Great Britain through the Channel Tunnel system.".

Code of practice for authorised officers under the Terrorism Act 2000

6A The code of practice for authorised officers under the Terrorism Act 2000 is amended—
   (a) in paragraph 3, by inserting after the words—
""Port" has the same meaning as in Schedule 7 of the Act"
the words—
"but, by virtue of the Channel Tunnel (International Arrangements) (Amendment No 2) Order 2001, also includes a railway station or other place where—

    (a)   persons embark or disembark; or

    (b)   goods are loaded or unloaded,

on or, as the case may be, from a through train or shuttle train within the meaning of article 2(1) of the Channel Tunnel (International Arrangements) Order 1993", and

(b)   in paragraph 10, by inserting after the words "includes an airport and a hoverport" the words—

"and, by virtue of the Channel Tunnel (International Arrangements) (Amendment No 2) Order 2001, includes a railway station or other place where—

    (a)   persons embark or disembark; or

    (b)   goods are loaded or unloaded,

on or, as the case may be, from a through train or shuttle train within the meaning of article 2(1) of the Channel Tunnel (International Arrangements) Order 1993.]

7–33 ...

Amendment

Paras 1–4, 7–33: amend SI 1972/1667, arts 2, 3, SI 1974/2211, art 2, SI 1975/65, art 4, SI 1984/2041, rr 2, 4, 6 and SI 1990/2167, arts 2, 3, 5, Schedule.

Para 5: substituted by SI 2001/1544, arts 2, 8. Date in force: 25 May 2001: see SI 2001/1544, art 1(2), and the London Gazette, 20 July 2001.

Paras 6, 6A: substituted, for para 6 as originally enacted, by SI 2001/418, art 3. Date in force: 19 February 2001: see SI 2001/418, art 1.

SCHEDULE 6
REPEALS AND REVOCATIONS

Article 9

PART I
REPEALS

Chapter	*Short title*	*Extent of repeal*
1971 c 77.	The Immigration Act 1971.	In section 4(2)(b) and wherever occurring in section 10(1), the words "or through the tunnel system"; section 11(1A); section 27(d); in section 33(1), the definitions of "Concessionaires" and "tunnel system"; in Schedule 2, in paragraph 3(1) and (2) the words from "or leaving" to "tunnel system", in paragraph 8(1)(c) the words from "or where" to "Concessionaires", paragraph 16(4A), in paragraphs 19(1) and 20(1) the words from "or, where" to "Concessionaires", and paragraph 27A.
1988 c 14.	The Immigration Act 1988.	Section 8(8).
...	...	...

Amendment
Entry relating to "The Prevention of Terrorism (Temporary Provisions) Act 1989" (omitted) revoked by SI 2001/178, art 6. Date in force: 19 February 2001: see SI 2001/178, art 1.

PART II
REVOCATIONS

Orders revoked	*References*	*Extent of revocation*
The Channel Tunnel (Customs and Excise) Order.	SI 1990/2167.	Article 5(2) to (4) and (7); in the Schedule, paragraphs 7 and 25.
The Channel Tunnel (Fire Services, Immigration and Prevention of Terrorism) Order 1990.	SI 1990/2227.	Articles 3 and 4 and Schedules 1 and 2.

ASYLUM SUPPORT (INTERIM PROVISIONS) REGULATIONS 1999

1999 No 3056

Made . . . . *13th November 1999*

Laid before Parliament . . . . *15th November 1999*

Coming into force . . . . *6th December 1999*

The Secretary of State, in exercise of the powers conferred on him by sections 94 and 166 of, and paragraphs 1, 2, 4 to 7, 9, 11 and 13 to 15 of Schedule 9 to, the Immigration and Asylum Act 1999, hereby makes the following Regulations:

1 Citation, commencement and extent

(1) These Regulations may be cited as the Asylum Support (Interim Provisions) Regulations 1999 and shall come into force on 6th December 1999.

(2) These Regulations do not extend to Scotland or Northern Ireland.

Initial Commencement
Specified date: 6 December 1999: see para (1) above.

2 Interpretation

(1) In these Regulations—

"assisted person" means an asylum-seeker, or a dependant of an asylum-seeker, who has applied for support and for whom support is provided;

"dependant", in relation to an asylum-seeker, an assisted person or a person claiming support, means a person in the United Kingdom who:

(a) is his spouse;

(b) is a child of his, or of his spouse, who is under 18 and dependent on him;

(c) is under 18 and is a member of his, or his spouse's, close family;

(d) is under 18 and had been living as part of his household:

(i) for at least six of the 12 months before the day on which his claim for support was made; or

(ii) since birth;

(e) is in need of care and attention from him or a member of his household by reason of a disability and would fall within sub-paragraph (c) or (d) but for the fact that he is not under 18;

(f) had been living with him as a member of an unmarried couple for at least two of the three years before the day on which his claim for support was made;

(g) is a person living as part of his household who was receiving assistance from a local authority under section 17 of the Children Act 1989 immediately before the beginning of the interim period;

(h) has made a claim for leave to enter or remain in the United Kingdom, or for variation of any such leave, which is being considered on the basis that he is dependent on the asylum-seeker; or

(i) in relation to an assisted person or a person claiming support who is himself a dependant of an asylum-seeker, is the asylum-seeker;

"eligible persons" means asylum-seekers or their dependants who appear to be destitute or to be likely to become destitute within 14 days;

"local authority" means:

2179

    (a) in England, a county council, a metropolitan district council, a district council with the functions of a county council, a London borough council, the Common Council of the City of London or the Council of the Isles of Scilly;

    (b) in Wales, a county council or a county borough council.

(2) Any reference in these Regulations to support is to support under these Regulations.

(3) Any reference in these Regulations to assistance under section 21 of the National Assistance Act 1948 is to assistance, the need for which has arisen solely:

    (a) because of destitution; or

    (b) because of the physical effects, or anticipated physical effects, of destitution.

(4) Any reference in these Regulations to assistance under section 17 of the Children Act 1989 is to the provision of accommodation or of any essential living needs.

(5) The interim period begins on the day on which these Regulations come into force and ends on [3rd April 2006].

[(6) The period prescribed under section 94(3) of the Immigration and Asylum Act 1999 (day on which a claim for asylum is determined) for the purposes of Part VI of that Act is 28 days where paragraph (7) below applies, and 21 days in any other case.

(7) This paragraph applies where:

    (a) the Secretary of State notifies the claimant that his decision is to accept the asylum claim;

    (b) the Secretary of State notifies the claimant that his decision is to reject the asylum claim but at the same time notifies him that he is giving him limited leave to enter or remain in the United Kingdom; or

    (c) an appeal by the claimant against the Secretary of State's decision has been disposed of by being allowed.]

Initial Commencement
Specified date: 6 December 1999: see reg 1(1).

Amendment
Para (5): words "3rd April 2006" in square brackets substituted by SI 2005/595, reg 2. Date in force: 3 April 2005: see SI 2005/595, reg 1.
Paras (6), (7): substituted, for para (6) as originally enacted, by SI 2002/471, reg 4. Date in force: 8 April 2002: see SI 2002/471, reg 1(2).

Extent
These Regulations do not extend to Scotland; see reg 1(2).

3   Requirement to provide support

(1) Subject to regulations 7 and 8:

    (a) the local authority concerned, or

    (b) the local authority to whom responsibility for providing support is transferred under regulation 9,

must provide support during the interim period to eligible persons.

(2) The question whether a person is an eligible person is to be determined by the local authority concerned.

(3) For the purposes of these Regulations, the local authority concerned are the local authority to whom a claim for support is made, except where a claim for support is

transferred by a local authority in accordance with regulation 9, in which case the local authority concerned are the local authority to whom the claim is transferred.

Initial Commencement
Specified date: 6 December 1999: see reg 1(1).

Extent
These Regulations do not extend to Scotland; see reg 1(2).

4 Temporary support

(1) This regulation applies to support to be provided before it has been determined whether a person is an eligible person ("temporary support").

(2) Temporary support is to be provided to a person claiming support:

(a) by the local authority to whom the claim is made until such time (if any) as the claim is transferred under regulation 9;
(b) where the claim is so transferred, by the local authority to whom the claim is transferred.

(3) Temporary support must appear to the local authority by whom it is provided to be adequate for the needs of the person claiming support and his dependants (if any).

Initial Commencement
Specified date: 6 December 1999: see reg 1(1).

Extent
These Regulations do not extend to Scotland; see reg 1(2).

5 Provision of support

(1) Subject to paragraph (2), support is to be provided by providing:

(a) accommodation appearing to the local authority by whom it is provided to be adequate for the needs of the assisted person and his dependants (if any) ("accommodation"); and
(b) what appear to the local authority by whom it is provided to be essential living needs of the assisted person and his dependants (if any) ("essential living needs").

(2) Where an assisted person's household includes a child who is under 18 and a dependant of his, support is to be provided:

(a) in accordance with paragraph (1);
(b) by providing accommodation; or
(c) by providing essential living needs.

(3) Support is to be provided to enable the assisted person (if he is the asylum-seeker) to meet reasonable travel expenses incurred in attending:

(a) a hearing of an appeal on his claim for asylum; or
(b) an interview in connection with his claim for asylum which has been requested by the Secretary of State.

(4) Where the circumstances of a particular case are exceptional, support is to be provided in such other ways as are necessary to enable the assisted person and his dependants (if any) to be supported.

(5) ...

(6) A local authority may provide support subject to conditions.

(7) Such conditions are to be set out in writing.

(8) A copy of the conditions is to be given to the assisted person.

Initial Commencement
Specified date: 6 December 1999: see reg 1(1).

Amendment
Para (5): revoked by SI 2002/471, reg 5. Date in force: 8 April 2002: see SI 2002/471, reg 1(2).

Extent
These Regulations do not extend to Scotland; see reg 1(2).

6   Matters to which the local authority are to have regard

(1) In providing support, the local authority are to have regard to:

(a) income which the assisted person has, or his dependants (if any) have, or might reasonably be expected to have;

(b) support which is, or assets which are, or might reasonably be expected to be, available to the assisted person, or to his dependants (if any);

(c) the welfare of the assisted person and his dependants (if any); and

(d) the cost of providing support.

(2) In providing accommodation under these Regulations, the local authority are not to have regard to any preference that the assisted person or his dependants (if any) may have as to:

(a) the locality in which the accommodation is to be provided;

(b) the nature of the accommodation to be provided; or

(c) the nature and standard of fixtures and fittings in that accommodation.

Initial Commencement
Specified date: 6 December 1999: see reg 1(1).

Extent
These Regulations do not extend to Scotland; see reg 1(2).

7   Refusal of support

(1) Unless this paragraph does not apply, support must be refused in the following circumstances:

(a) where the person claiming support has intentionally made himself and his dependants (if any) destitute;

(b) where the person claiming support has made a claim for support to another local authority, except where the claim is one to which regulation 9 applies;

(c) where the claim for support is made by a person to a local authority other than one to whom, in the previous 12 months, he has made a claim for assistance under section 21 of the National Assistance Act 1948 or under section 17 of the Children Act 1989;

(d) where the person claiming support—

(i) is an asylum-seeker within the meaning of paragraph (3A)(a) or (aa) of regulation 70 of the Income Support (General) Regulations 1987 who has not ceased to be an asylum-seeker by virtue of sub-paragraph (b) of that paragraph;

(ii) is a person who became an asylum-seeker under paragraph (3A)(a) of regulation 70 of the Income Support (General) Regulations 1987 and who has not ceased to be an asylum-seeker by virtue of sub-para-graph (b) of that paragraph, as saved by regulation 12(1) of the Social Security (Persons from Abroad) Miscellaneous Amendments Regula-tions 1996;

(iii) is not a person from abroad within the meaning of sub-paragraph (a) of regulation 21(3) of the Income Support (General) Regulations 1987 by virtue of the exclusions specified in that sub-paragraph;

(e) where neither the person claiming support nor any of his dependants is an asylum-seeker or has made a claim for leave to enter or remain in the United Kingdom, or for variation of any such leave, which is being considered on the basis that he is dependent on an asylum-seeker.

(2) For the purposes of paragraph (1)(a), a person has intentionally made himself destitute if he appears to be, or likely within 14 days to become, destitute as a result of an act or omission deliberately done or made by him or any dependant of his without reasonable excuse while in the United Kingdom.

(3) Paragraph (1) does not apply where the local authority concerned did not know, or could not with reasonable diligence have known, of any circumstance set out in that paragraph.

Initial Commencement
Specified date: 6 December 1999: see reg 1(1).

Extent
These Regulations do not extend to Scotland; see reg 1(2).

8 Suspension and discontinuation of support

(1) Support for the assisted person and his dependants (if any) must be discontinued as soon as the local authority by whom it is provided become aware of any circumstance which, if they had known of it when the claim was made, would have led to the claim being refused in accordance with regulation 7(1).

(2) Support may be suspended or discontinued:

(a) where the assisted person, or any dependant of his, fails without reasonable excuse to comply with any condition subject to which the support is provided;

(b) where the assisted person, or any dependant of his, leaves accommodation provided as part of such support for more than seven consecutive days without reasonable excuse.

Initial Commencement
Specified date: 6 December 1999: see reg 1(1).

Extent
These Regulations do not extend to Scotland; see reg 1(2).

9 Transfer of a claim for support or responsibility for providing support by a local authority

A local authority may transfer a claim for support made to them, or responsibility for providing support, to another local authority on such terms as may be agreed between the two authorities.

Initial Commencement
Specified date: 6 December 1999: see reg 1(1).

Extent
These Regulations do not extend to Scotland; see reg 1(2).

Appendix 1   Legislation and materials

10   Assistance to those providing support

Reasonable assistance to a local authority providing support is to be given by:

    (a)   any district council for an area any part of which lies within the area of the local authority providing support, and

    (b)   any registered social landlord, within the meaning of Part I of the Housing Act 1996, which manages any house or other property which is in the area of the local authority providing support,

who is requested to provide such assistance by the local authority providing support.

Initial Commencement
Specified date: 6 December 1999: see reg 1(1).

Extent
These Regulations do not extend to Scotland; see reg 1(2).

11   Transitional provision

Where an asylum-seeker or a dependant of an asylum-seeker is receiving assistance from a local authority under section 21 of the National Assistance Act 1948 or under section 17 of the Children Act 1989 immediately before the beginning of the interim period, he is to be taken to have been accepted for support by the local authority providing such assistance.

Initial Commencement
Specified date: 6 December 1999: see reg 1(1).

Extent
These Regulations do not extend to Scotland; see reg 1(2).

12   Entitlement to claim support

A person entitled to support under these Regulations is not entitled to assistance under section 17 of the Children Act 1989.

Initial Commencement
Specified date: 6 December 1999: see reg 1(1).

Extent
These Regulations do not extend to Scotland; see reg 1(2).

TRAVEL DOCUMENTS (FEES) REGULATIONS 1999

1999 No 3339

Made . . . . *13th December 1999*

Laid before Parliament . . . . *14th December 1999*

Coming into force . . . . *16th December 1999*

The Secretary of State, in exercise of the powers conferred on him by sections 27 and 166 of the Immigration and Asylum Act 1999 and section 56(1) of the Finance Act 1973, and with the approval of the Treasury, hereby makes the following Regulations:

1 Title and commencement

These Regulations may be cited as the Travel Documents (Fees) Regulations 1999 and shall come into force on 16th December 1999.

Initial Commencement
Specified date: 16 December 1999: see above.

2 Interpretation

In these Regulations—

"Convention travel document" means a travel document issued in accordance with Article 28 of the Refugee Convention (travel documents) or Article 28 of the Stateless Persons Convention (travel documents);
"document of identity" means a travel document issued in the United Kingdom to a person who is not a British citizen which enables the holder to make one journey out of the United Kingdom;
"the Refugee Convention" means the Convention relating to the Status of Refugees done at Geneva on 28th July 1951 and the Protocol to the Convention; and
"the Stateless Persons Convention" means the Convention relating to the Status of Stateless Persons done at New York on 28th September 1954.

Initial Commencement
Specified date: 16 December 1999: see reg 1.

3 Prescription of fees

[(1) In connection with an application to the Secretary of State for a Convention travel document or a document of identity, the fee which is to be paid is:

(a) in a case where the person in respect of whom the application is made has not, at the date of the application, attained the age of sixteen years, £25;
(b) in any other case, £42.

(2) In connection with an application to the Secretary of State for any other Home Office travel document, other than an application falling with paragraph (3), the fee which is to be paid is:

(a) in a case where the person in respect of whom the application is made has not, at the date of the application, attained the age of sixteen years, £115;
(b) in any other case, £195.]

[(3)   An application falls within this paragraph where the application is stated as being made in order to enable the applicant to participate in a project operated or approved by the Secretary of State for the purpose of enabling a person in the United Kingdom to make a single trip to a country outside the United Kingdom in order to assist the reconstruction of that country or to decide whether to resettle there.]

Amendment
Paras (1), (2): substituted by SI 2005/653, reg 2. Date in force: 1 April 2005: see SI 2005/653, reg 1.
Para (3): inserted by SI 2002/2155, regs 2, 4. Date in force: 10 September 2002: see SI 2002/2155, reg 1.

4   Payment into the Consolidated Fund

A fee received by the Secretary of State under these Regulations is to be paid into the Consolidated Fund.

Initial Commencement
Specified date: 16 December 1999: see reg 1.

5   Revocation

The Travel Documents (Refugees and Stateless Persons) (Fees) Regulations 1999 are hereby revoked.

Initial Commencement
Specified date: 16 December 1999: see reg 1.

IMMIGRATION (REGULARISATION PERIOD FOR OVERSTAYERS) REGULATIONS 2000

2000 No 265

Made . . . . *7th February 2000*

Coming into force . . . . *8th February 2000*

Whereas a draft of these Regulations has been laid before Parliament and approved by a resolution of each House in accordance with section 166(5) of the Immigration and Asylum Act 1999;

Now, therefore, the Secretary of State, in exercise of the powers conferred upon him by sections 9(1), (2) and (3), 166(3) and 167 of that Act, hereby makes the following Regulations:

1   Citation, commencement and interpretation

(1)   These Regulations may be cited as the Immigration (Regularisation Period for Overstayers) Regulations 2000 and shall come into force on the day after the day on which they are made.

(2)   In these Regulations "the Act" means the Immigration and Asylum Act 1999.

Initial Commencement
Specified date: 8 February 2000: see para (1) above.

2   Manner of application

(1)   An application under section 9(1) of the Act shall be made in the following manner.

(2)   The application shall be made in writing, setting out the information required by paragraph (4), and attaching the material required by paragraph (5).

(3)   The application shall either:

    (a)   be sent by post to the following address:
        Regularisation Scheme for Overstayers
        Initial Consideration Unit
        Immigration and Nationality Directorate
        Block C
        Whitgift Centre
        Croydon
        CR9 1AT; or
    (b)   be delivered by hand to the Home Office at:
        The Public Caller Unit
        Immigration and Nationality Directorate
        Block C
        Whitgift Centre
        Wellesley Road
        Croydon.

(4)   The information referred to in paragraph (2) is:

    (a)   the applicant's full name, date of birth and nationality;
    (b)   the applicant's home address or, if none, an address where he may be contacted;
    (c)   the name and address of any representative who is acting on behalf of the applicant;
    (d)   the date of each occasion on which leave to enter or remain has been granted to the applicant since his first arrival in the United Kingdom, if known;
    (e)   in relation to each date specified in accordance with sub-paragraph (d), the period for which leave was granted, if known;
    (f)   the applicant's Home Office reference, if known;
    (g)   the fact that the application is made under section 9 of the Act; and
    (h)   all the circumstances which the applicant wishes the Secretary of State to take into account when considering his application, including:
        (i)   his length of residence in the United Kingdom;
        (ii)   the strength of his connections with the United Kingdom;
        (iii)   his personal history, including character, conduct and employment record;
        (iv)   his domestic circumstances; and
        (v)   any compassionate circumstances.

(5)   The material referred to in paragraph (2) is:

    (a)   the applicant's current passport, if he has one and it is available to him;
    (b)   any other passports (whether expired or not) which have been used by the applicant and which are available to him; and
    (c)   any document or copy document which the applicant considers is evidence supporting his application.

Initial Commencement
Specified date: 8 February 2000: see reg 1(1).

3   Prescribed days

(1)   The day prescribed for the purposes of section 9(2) of the Act (the start of the regularisation period) is the day on which these Regulations come into force or, if later, 1st February 2000.

(2)   The day prescribed for the purposes of section 9(3) of the Act (the end of the regularisation period in certain circumstances) is 1st October 2000.

Initial Commencement
Specified date: 8 February 2000: see reg 1(1).

4   Delivery of applications

(1)   Paragraph (2) applies to an application sent by recorded delivery, addressed to the address set out in regulation 2(3)(a).

(2)   Such an application shall be taken to have been delivered for the purposes of these Regulations and section 9 of the Act on the second day after the day on which it was posted, if not received earlier.

Initial Commencement
Specified date: 8 February 2000: see reg 1(1).

SOCIAL SECURITY (IMMIGRATION AND ASYLUM) CONSEQUENTIAL AMENDMENTS REGULATIONS 2000

2000 No 636

Made . . . . *7th March 2000*

Laid before Parliament . . . . *13th March 2000*

Coining into force . . . . *3rd April 2000*

The Secretary of State for Social Security, in exercise of the powers conferred upon him by sections 115(3), (4) and (7), 123(5) and (6), 166(3) and 167 of the Immigration and Asylum Act 1999, sections 64(1), 68(4), 70(4), 71(6), 123(1)(a), (d) and (e), 135(1), 136(3) and (4), 137(1) and (2)(i), and 175(1), (3) and (4) of the Social Security Contributions and Benefits Act 1992, section 5(1)(a) and (b), 189(1) and (4) and 191 of the Social Security Administration Act 1992, sections 12(1) and (2), 35(1) and 36(2) and (4) of the Jobseekers Act 1995 and of all other powers enabling him in that behalf, by this Instrument, which contains only regulations made by virtue of, or consequential upon, the Immigration and Asylum Act 1999 and which is made before the end of the period of six months beginning with the coming into force of that Act and, in so far as they relate to housing benefit and council tax benefit, with the agreement of such organisations appearing to him to be representative of the authorities concerned that consultation should not be undertaken hereby make the following Regulations:

1   Citation, commencement and interpretation

(1)   These Regulations may be cited as the Social Security (Immigration and Asylum) Consequential Amendments Regulations 2000.

2188

(2)   These Regulations shall come into force on 3rd April 2000.

(3)   In these Regulations—

"the Act" means the Immigration and Asylum Act 1999;

"the Attendance Allowance Regulations" means the Social Security (Attendance Allowance) Regulations 1991;

"the Claims and Payments Regulations" means the Social Security (Claims and Payments) Regulations 1987;

"the Contributions and Benefits Act" means the Social Security Contributions and Benefits Act 1992;

"the Council Tax Benefit Regulations" means the Council Tax Benefit (General) Regulations 1992;

"the Disability Living Allowance Regulations" means the Social Security (Disability Living Allowance) Regulations 1991;

"the Housing Benefit Regulations" means the Housing Benefit (General) Regulations 1987;

"the Income Support Regulations" means the Income Support (General) Regulations 1987;

"the Invalid Care Allowance Regulations" means the Social Security (Invalid Care Allowance) Regulations 1976;

"the Jobseeker's Allowance Regulations" means the Jobseeker's Allowance Regulations 1996;

"the Persons from Abroad Regulations" means the Social Security (Persons from Abroad) Miscellaneous Amendments Regulations 1996;

"the Severe Disablement Allowance Regulations" means the Social Security (Severe Disablement Allowance) Regulations 1984.

(4)   In these Regulations, unless the context otherwise requires, a reference—

(a)   to a numbered regulation or Schedule is to the regulation in, or the Schedule to, these Regulations bearing that number;

(b)   in a regulation or Schedule to a numbered paragraph is to the paragraph in that regulation or Schedule bearing that number.

Initial Commencement
Specified date: 3 April 2000: see para (2) above.

Amendment
Para (3): definition "the Claims and Payments Regulations" revoked, in so far as it relates to child benefit or guardian's allowance, by SI 2003/492, reg 43, Sch 3, Pt 1; for transitional provisions see reg 44 thereof. Date in force: 7 April 2003: see SI 2003/492, reg 1(1).

2   Persons not excluded from specified benefits under section 115 of the Immigration and Asylum Act 1999

(1)   For the purposes of entitlement to income-based jobseeker's allowance, income support, a social fund payment, housing benefit or council tax benefit under the Contributions and Benefits Act, [or state pension credit under the State Pension Credit Act 2002,] as the case may be, a person falling within a category or description of persons specified in Part I of the Schedule is a person to whom section 115 of the Act does not apply.

(2)   For the purposes of entitlement to attendance allowance, severe disablement allowance, [carer's allowance], disability living allowance, a social fund payment or child benefit under the Contributions and Benefits Act, as the case may be, a person falling within a category or description of persons specified in Part II of the Schedule is a person to whom section 115 of the Act does not apply.

(3) For the purposes of entitlement to child benefit, attendance allowance or disability living allowance under the Contributions and Benefits Act, as the case may be, a person in respect of whom there is an Order in Council made under section 179 of the Social Security Administration Act 1992 giving effect to a reciprocal agreement in respect of one of those benefits, as the case may be, is a person to whom section 115 of the Act does not apply.

(4) For the purposes of entitlement to—

(a) income support, a social fund payment, housing benefit or council tax benefit under the Contributions and Benefits Act, as the case may be, a person who is entitled to or is receiving benefit by virtue of paragraph (1) or (2) of regulation 12 of the Persons from Abroad Regulations is a person to whom section 115 of the Act does not apply;

(b) attendance allowance, disability living allowance, [carer's allowance], severe disablement allowance, a social fund payment or child benefit under the Contributions and Benefits Act, as the case may be, a person who is entitled to or is receiving benefit by virtue of paragraph (10) of regulation 12 is a person to whom section 115 of the Act does not apply;

[(c) state pension credit under the State Pension Credit Act 2002, a person to whom sub-paragraph (a) would have applied but for the fact that they have attained the qualifying age for the purposes of state pension credit, is a person to whom section 115 of the Act does not apply].

(5) For the purposes of entitlement to income support by virtue of regulation 70 of the Income Support Regulations (urgent cases), to jobseeker's allowance by virtue of regulation 147 of the Jobseeker's Allowance Regulations (urgent cases) or to a social fund payment under the Contributions and Benefits Act, as the case may be, a person to whom regulation 12(3) applies is a person to whom section 115 of the Act does not apply.

(6) For the purposes of entitlement to housing benefit, council tax benefit or a social fund payment under the Contributions and Benefits Act, as the case may be, a person to whom regulation 12(6) applies is a person to whom section 115 of the Act does not apply.

[(7) For the purposes of entitlement to state pension credit under the State Pension Credit Act 2002, a person to whom paragraph (5) would have applied but for the fact that they have attained the qualifying age for the purposes of state pension credit, is a person to whom section 115 of the Act does not apply.

(8) Where paragraph 1 of Part I of the Schedule to these Regulations applies in respect of entitlement to state pension credit, the period for which a claimant's state pension credit is to be calculated shall be any period, or the aggregate of any periods, not exceeding 42 days during any one period of leave to which paragraph 1 of Part I of the Schedule to these Regulations applies.]

Initial Commencement
Specified date: 3 April 2000: see reg 1(2).

Amendment
Para (1): words "or state pension credit under the State Pension Credit Act 2002," in square brackets inserted by SI 2003/2274, reg 6(1), (2). Date in force: 6 October 2003: see SI 2003/2274, reg 1.
Para (2): words "carer's allowance" in square brackets substituted by SI 2002/2497, reg 3, Sch 2, paras 1, 2. Date in force: 1 April 2003: see SI 2002/2497, reg 1(b).
Para (4): in sub-para (b) words "carer's allowance" in square brackets substituted by SI 2002/2497, reg 3, Sch 2, paras 1, 2. Date in force: 1 April 2003: see SI 2002/2497, reg 1(b).
Para (4): sub-para (c) inserted by SI 2003/2274, reg 6(1), (3). Date in force: 6 October 2003: see SI 2003/2274, reg 1.

Paras (7), (8): inserted by SI 2003/2274, reg 6(1), (4). Date in force: 6 October 2003: see SI 2003/2274, reg 1.

3 Amendment of the Income Support Regulations

(1) The Income Support Regulations shall be amended in accordance with the following provisions of this regulation.

(2) In regulation 2(1) (interpretation)—

(a) after the definition of "housing benefit expenditure" there shall be inserted the following definition—
""Immigration and Asylum Act" means the Immigration and Asylum Act 1999;" and

(b) the definition of "immigration authorities" shall be omitted.

(3) In paragraph (3)(a) of regulation 4ZA, for the words "regulation 70(3)(a)" there shall be substituted the words "paragraph 1 of Part I of the Schedule to the Social Security (Immigration and Asylum) Consequential Amendments Regulations 2000".

(4) In regulation 21 (special cases)—

(a) in paragraph (1) for the words "regulation 21ZA" there shall be substituted the words "regulation 21ZB";
(b) in paragraph (3) the first definition of "person from abroad" shall be omitted;
(c) in paragraph (3), after the opening words, there shall be inserted the following definition—
""partner of a person subject to immigration control" means a person—
  (i) who is not subject to immigration control within the meaning of section 115(9) of the Immigration and Asylum Act; or
  (ii) to whom section 115 of that Act does not apply by virtue of regulation 2 of the Social Security (Immigration and Asylum) Consequential Amendments Regulations 2000; and
  (iii) who is a member of a couple and his partner is subject to immigration control within the meaning of section 115(9) of that Act and section 115 of that Act applies to her for the purposes of exclusion from entitlement to income support;"; and
(d) in paragraph (3) in the second definition of "person from abroad" the word "also" shall be omitted.

(5) For regulation 21ZA (treatment of refugees) after the heading there shall be substituted the following regulation—

"21ZB (1) This paragraph applies to a person who has submitted a claim for asylum on or after 3rd April 2000 and who is notified that he has been recorded by the Secretary of State as a refugee within the definition in Article 1 of the Convention relating to the Status of Refugees done at Geneva on 28th July 1951 as extended by Article 1(2) of the Protocol relating to the Status of Refugees done at New York on 31st January 1967.

(2) Subject to paragraph (3), a person to whom paragraph (1) applies, who claims income support within 28 days of receiving the notification referred to in paragraph (1), shall have his claim for income support determined as if he had been recorded as a refugee on the date when he submitted his claim for asylum.

(3) The amount of support provided under section 95 or 98 of the Immigration and Asylum Act, including support provided by virtue of regulations made under Schedule 9 to that Act, by the Secretary of State in respect of essential living needs of the claimant and his dependants (if any) as specified in regulations made under paragraph 3 of Schedule 8 to the Immigration and Asylum Act shall be deducted from any award of income support due to the claimant by virtue of paragraph (2).".

(6)   In regulation 40 (calculation of income other than earnings)—

    (a)   at the beginning of paragraph (4) there shall be inserted the words "Subject to paragraph (5)";

    (b)   in paragraph (4) for the words following "paragraph (1)" there shall be substituted the following sub-paragraphs—

"(a)   any payment to which regulation 35(2)(a) or 37(2) (payments not earnings) applies; or

    (b)   in the case of a claimant who is receiving support provided under section 95 or 98 of the Immigration and Asylum Act including support provided by virtue of regulations made under Schedule 9 to that Act, the amount of such support provided in respect of essential living needs of the claimant and his dependants (if any) as is specified in regulations made under paragraph 3 of Schedule 8 to the Immigration and Asylum Act;";

    (c)   after paragraph (4) there shall be added the following paragraph—

"(5)   In the case of a claimant who is the partner of a person subject to immigration control and whose partner is receiving support provided under section 95 or 98 of the Immigration and Asylum Act including support provided by virtue of regulations made under Schedule 9 to that Act, there shall not be included as income to be taken into account under paragraph (1) the amount of support provided in respect of essential living needs of the partner of the claimant and his dependants (if any) as is specified in regulations made under paragraph 3 of Schedule 8 to the Immigration and Asylum Act.".

(7)   In regulation 70 (urgent cases)—

    (a)   in paragraph (2) for sub-paragraph (a) there shall be substituted the following sub-paragraph—

"(a)   a claimant to whom paragraph (2A) applies (persons not excluded from income support under section 115 of the Immigration and Asylum Act);";

    (b)   after paragraph (2) there shall be inserted the following paragraph—

"(2A)   This paragraph applies to a person not excluded from entitlement to income support under section 115 of the Immigration and Asylum Act by virtue of regulation 2 of the Social Security (Immigration and Asylum) Consequential Amendments Regulations 2000 except for a person to whom paragraphs 3 and 4 of Part I of the Schedule to those Regulations applies."; and

    (c)   paragraphs (3), (3A) and (3B) shall be omitted.

(8)   In regulation 71 (applicable amounts in urgent cases)—

    (a)   in paragraph (1)(d), for the words "paragraph 17" there shall be substituted the words "paragraph 16A"; and

    (b)   in paragraph (2), for the words "paragraph (3)" in each place where they occur, there shall be substituted the words "paragraph 2A".

(9)   In Schedule 1B (prescribed categories of person)—

    (a)   after paragraph 18, there shall be inserted the following paragraph—

"18A   A person to whom regulation 21ZB (treatment of refugees) applies by virtue of regulation 21ZB(2) from the date his claim for asylum is made until the date the Secretary of State makes a decision on that claim.";

    (b)   in paragraph 21, for the words "regulation 70(3)" there shall be substituted the words "regulation 70(2A)".

(10)   After paragraph 16 of Schedule 7 (applicable amounts in special cases)—

    (a)   in column (1) there shall be inserted the following paragraph—

"Partner of a person subject to immigration control

16A

   (a)   A claimant who is the partner of a person subject to immigration control.

   (b)   Where regulation 18 (polygamous marriages) applies and the claimant is a person—

       (i)   who is not subject to immigration control within the meaning of section 115(9) of the Immigration and Asylum Act; or

     (ii)   to whom section 115 of that Act does not apply by virtue of regulation 2 of the Social Security (Immigration and Asylum) Consequential Amendments Regulations 2000; and

    (iii)   who is a member of a couple and one or more of his partners is subject to immigration control within the meaning of section 115(9) of that Act and section 115 of that Act applies to her for the purposes of exclusion from entitlement to income support.";

   (b)   in column (2) there shall be inserted the following paragraph—

"16A

   (a)   The amount applicable in respect of the claimant only under regulation 17(1)(a) plus that in respect of any child or young person who is a member of his family and who is not a person subject to immigration control within the meaning of section 115(9) of the Immigration and Asylum Act, and to whom section 115 of that Act does not apply for the purposes of exclusion from entitlement to income support, any amounts which may be applicable to him under regulation 17(1)(b), (c) or (d) plus the amount applicable to him under regulation 17(1)(e), (f) and (g) or, as the case may be, regulation 19 or 21.

   (b)   The amount determined in accordance with that regulation or regulation 19 or 21 in respect of the claimant and any partners of his and any child or young person for whom he or his partner is treated as responsible, who are not subject to immigration control within the meaning of section 115(9) of the Immigration and Asylum Act and to whom section 115 of that Act does not apply for the purposes of exclusion from entitlement to income support.".

(11)   In paragraph 17 of Schedule 7 (applicable amounts in special cases) for the words in column (1) there shall be substituted the words "person from abroad" and for the words in column (2) there shall be substituted the word "nil".

(12)   In paragraph 21 of Schedule 9 (treatment of income in kind)—

   (a)   in sub-paragraph (1) for the words "Subject to sub-paragraph (2)" there shall be substituted the words "Subject to sub-paragraphs (2) and (3)";

   (b)   in sub-paragraph (1) after the words "except where" there shall be added the following words—

"regulation 40(4)(b) (provision of support under section 95 or 98 of the Immigration and Asylum Act including support provided by virtue of regulations made under Schedule 9 to that Act in the calculation of income other than earnings) or";

   (c)   after sub-paragraph (2) there shall be added the following sub-paragraph—

"(3)   The first exception under sub-paragraph (1) shall not apply where the claimant is the partner of a person subject to immigration control and whose partner is receiving support provided under section 95 or 98 of the Immigration and Asylum Act including support provided by virtue of regulations made under Schedule 9 to that Act and the income in kind is support provided in respect of essential living needs of the partner of the claimant and his dependants (if any) as is specified in regulations made under paragraph 3 of Schedule 8 to the Immigration and Asylum Act.".

(13)   In paragraph 57 of Schedule 9 (disregards in the calculation of income other than earnings) and paragraph 49 of Schedule 10 (capital to be disregarded) for the words "regulation 21ZA" there shall be substituted the words "regulation 21ZB".

Initial Commencement
Specified date: 3 April 2000: see reg 1(2).

4   Amendment of the Jobseeker's Allowance Regulations

(1)   The Jobseeker's Allowance Regulations shall be amended in accordance with the following provisions of this regulation.

(2)   In regulation 1(3) (interpretation) after the definition of "housing benefit expenditure" there shall be inserted the following definition—

    ""Immigration and Asylum Act" means the Immigration and Asylum Act 1999;".

(3)   In regulation 85(4) (special cases)—

    (a)   the first definition of "person from abroad" shall be omitted;
    (b)   in the second definition of "person from abroad" the word "also" shall be omitted; and
    (c)   at the beginning of paragraph (4), after the opening words, there shall be inserted the following definition—
    ""partner of a person subject to immigration control" means a person—
        (i)   who is not subject to immigration control within the meaning of section 115(9) of the Immigration and Asylum Act; or
        (ii)   to whom section 115 of that Act does not apply by virtue of regulation 2 of the Social Security (Immigration and Asylum) Consequential Amendments Regulations 2000; and
        (iii)   who is a member of a couple and his partner is subject to immigration control within the meaning of section 115(9) of that Act and section 115 of that Act applies to her for the purposes of exclusion from entitlement to jobseeker's allowance;".

(4)   In regulation 103(6) (calculation of income other than earnings) for the words following "paragraph (1)" there shall be substituted the following sub-paragraphs—

    "(a)   any payment to which regulation 98(2)(a) to (e) or 100(2) (payments not earnings) applies; or
    (b)   in the case of a claimant who is receiving support under section 95 or 98 of the Immigration and Asylum Act including support provided by virtue of regulations made under Schedule 9 to that Act, the amount of such support provided in respect of essential living needs of the claimant and his dependants (if any) as is specified in regulations made under paragraph 3 of Schedule 8 to the Immigration and Asylum Act.".

(5)   In regulation 147 (urgent cases)—

    (a)   in paragraph (2) for sub-paragraph (a) there shall be substituted the following sub-paragraph—
    "(a)   a claimant to whom paragraph (2A) applies (persons not excluded from income-based jobseeker's allowance under section 115 of the Immigration and Asylum Act);";
    (b)   after paragraph (2) there shall be inserted the following paragraph—

"(2A)   This paragraph applies to a person not excluded from entitlement to income-based jobseeker's allowance under section 115 of the Immigration and Asylum Act by virtue of regulation 2 of the Social Security (Immigration and Asylum) Consequential Amendments Regulations 2000 except for a person to whom paragraphs 3 and 4 of Part I to the Schedule to those Regulations applies."; and

(b) in the case of a claimant who is receiving support under section 95 or 98 of the Immigration and Asylum Act including support provided by virtue of regulations made under Schedule 9 to that Act, the amount of such support provided in respect of essential living needs of the claimant and his dependants (if any) as is specified in regulations made under paragraph 3 of Schedule 8 to the Immigration and Asylum Act.".

(5) In Schedule A1 (treatment of claims for housing benefit by refugees)—

(a) in paragraph 1(1)(b) for the words following paragraph (ii) there shall be substituted the following words "his claim for housing benefit shall be treated as having been made on the date specified in sub-paragraph (2)";

(b) in paragraph 1(2) for heads (a) and (b), there shall be substituted the following words—
"on the date on which his claim for asylum was recorded by the Secretary of State as having been made.";

(c) after paragraph 1 there shall be inserted the following paragraph—

2A

"Appropriate authority to whom a claim for housing benefit by a refugee shall be made and time for making a claim

(1) A claim for housing benefit made by a refugee on or after 3rd April 2000 for the relevant period may be made to the appropriate authority for the area in which the dwelling which the claimant occupied as his home was situate and in respect of which he was liable to make payments.

(2) Where the claimant has occupied more than one dwelling as his home in the relevant period, only one claim for housing benefit shall be made in respect of that period and such a claim shall be made to the authority for the area in which the dwelling occupied by the refugee is situate and in respect of which he was liable to make payments when, after he is notified that he has been recorded by the Secretary of State as a refugee, he makes a claim for housing benefit.

(3) The appropriate authority to which a claim for housing benefit is made in accordance with this paragraph, shall determine the claimant's entitlement to that benefit for the whole of the relevant period.

(4) A claim for housing benefit to which this paragraph refers, shall be made within 28 days of a claimant receiving notification from the Secretary of State that he has been recorded as a refugee.

(5) Regulation 72(15) of these Regulations (backdating of claims) shall not have effect with respect to claims to which this Schedule applies."; and

(d) paragraph 2 shall be omitted.

(6) In paragraph 21 of Schedule 4 (treatment of income in kind) after the words "income in kind" there shall be added the following words—

"except where regulation 33(4)(b) (provision of support under section 95 or 98 of the Immigration and Asylum Act in the calculation of income other than earnings) applies".

(7) In paragraph 62 of Schedule 4 and paragraph 51 of Schedule 5 for the words "regulation 21ZA" there shall be substituted the words "regulation 21ZB".

Initial Commencement
Specified date: 3 April 2000: see reg 1(2).

Appendix 1   Legislation and materials

7   Amendment of the Council Tax Benefit Regulations

(1)   The Council Tax Benefit Regulations shall be amended in accordance with the following provisions of this regulation.

(2)   In regulation 2(1) (interpretation) after the definition of "housing benefit" there shall be inserted the following definition—

""Immigration and Asylum Act" means the Immigration and Asylum Act 1999;".

(3)   In regulation 4A—

(a)   paragraphs (2), (3), (4)(a), (b), (c), (d), (e)(iv), (v) and (vi), (f) and (g), (4A), (5)(a), (b) and (c) and (5A) shall be omitted;

(b)   in paragraph (6) the words "paragraphs (3)(b) and (4A)" shall be substituted by the words "Paragraph 1 of Part I of the Schedule to, and regulation 2 as it applies to that paragraph of, the Social Security (Immigration and Asylum) Consequential Amendments Regulations 2000."; and

(c)   in paragraph (7) the definitions of the "Common Travel Area" and the "Convention relating to the Status of Refugees" shall be omitted.

(4)   In paragraph (5) of regulation 24 (calculation of income other than earnings) for the words following "paragraph (1)" there shall be substituted the following sub-paragraphs—

"(a)   any payment to which regulation 19(2) (payments not earnings) applies; or

(b)   in the case of a claimant who is receiving support under section 95 or 98 of the Immigration and Asylum Act including support provided by virtue of regulations made under Schedule 9 to that Act, the amount of such support provided in respect of essential living needs of the claimant and his dependants (if any) as is specified in regulations made under paragraph 3 of Schedule 8 to the Immigration and Asylum Act.".

(5)   In Schedule A1 (treatment of claims for council tax benefit by refugees)—

(a)   in paragraph 1(1)(b) for the words following head (ii) there shall be substituted the following words "his claim for council tax benefit shall be treated as having been made on the date specified in sub-paragraph (2)";

(b)   in paragraph 1(2) for sub-paragraphs (a) and (b), there shall be substituted the following words—
"on the date on which his claim for asylum was recorded by the Secretary of State as having been made.";

(c)   after paragraph 1 there shall be inserted the following paragraph—

2A

"Appropriate authority to whom a claim for council tax benefit by a refugee shall be made and time for making a claim

(1)   A claim for council tax benefit made by a refugee on or after 3rd April 2000 for the relevant period may be made to the appropriate authority for the area in which the dwelling which the claimant occupied as his home was situate and in respect of which he was liable for council tax.

(2)   Where the claimant has occupied more than one dwelling as his home in the relevant period, only one claim for council tax benefit shall be made in respect of that period and such a claim shall be made to the authority for the area in which the dwelling occupied by the refugee is situate and in respect of which he was liable to make payments when, after he is notified that he has been recorded by the Secretary of State as a refugee, he makes a claim for council tax benefit.

(3) The appropriate authority to which a claim for council tax benefit is made in accordance with this paragraph, shall determine the claimant's entitlement to that benefit for the whole of the relevant period.

(4) A claim for council tax benefit to which this paragraph refers, shall be made within 28 days of a claimant receiving notification from the Secretary of State that he has been recorded as a refugee.

(5) Regulation 72(15) of these Regulations (backdating of claims) shall not have effect with respect to claims to which this Schedule applies."; and

    (d) paragraph 2 shall be omitted.

(6) In paragraph 22 of Schedule 4 (treatment of income in kind) after the words "income in kind" there shall be added the following words—

"except where regulation 24(5) (provision of support under section 95 or 98 of the Immigration and Asylum Act in the calculation of income other than earnings) applies".

(7) In paragraph 62 of Schedule 4 and paragraph 51 of Schedule 5 for the words "regulation 21ZA" there shall be substituted the words "regulation 21ZB".

Initial Commencement
Specified date: 3 April 2000: see reg 1(2).

8   Amendment of the Invalid Care Allowance Regulations

(1) The Invalid Care Allowance Regulations shall be amended in accordance with the following provisions of this regulation.

(2) In regulation 9(1) for sub-paragraph (aa) there shall be substituted the following sub-paragraph—

    "(ia) he is not a person subject to immigration control within the meaning of section 115(9) of the Immigration and Asylum Act 1999 or section 115 of that Act does not apply to him for the purposes of entitlement to invalid care allowance by virtue of regulation 2 of the Social Security (Immigration and Asylum) Consequential Amendments Regulations 2000, and".

(3) Paragraph (1A) of regulation 9 shall be omitted.

Initial Commencement
Specified date: 3 April 2000: see reg 1(2).

9   Amendment of the Severe Disablement Allowance Regulations

(1) The Severe Disablement Allowance Regulations shall be amended in accordance with the following provisions of this regulation.

(2) In regulation 3(1) for head (ia) of sub-paragraph (a) there shall be substituted the following head—

    "(ib) he is not a person subject to immigration control within the meaning of section 115(9) of the Immigration and Asylum Act 1999 or section 115 of that Act does not apply to him for the purposes of entitlement to severe disablement allowance by virtue of regulation 2 of the Social Security (Immigration and Asylum) Consequential Amendments Regulations 2000, and".

(3) Paragraph (1B) of regulation 3 shall be omitted.

Initial Commencement
Specified date: 3 April 2000: see reg 1(2).

10 Amendment of the Attendance Allowance Regulations

(1) The Attendance Allowance Regulations shall be amended in accordance with the following provisions of this regulation.

(2) In regulation 2(1) for head (ia) of sub-paragraph (a) there shall be substituted the following head—

"(ib) he is not a person subject to immigration control within the meaning of section 115(9) of the Immigration and Asylum Act 1999 or section 115 of that Act does not apply to him for the purposes of entitlement to attendance allowance by virtue of regulation 2 of the Social Security (Immigration and Asylum) Consequential Amendments Regulations 2000, and".

(3) Paragraph (1A) of regulation 2 shall be omitted.

Initial Commencement
Specified date: 3 April 2000: see reg 1(2).

11 Amendment of the Disability Living Allowance Regulations

(1) The Disability Living Allowance Regulations shall be amended in accordance with the following provisions of this regulation.

(2) In regulation 2(1) for head (ia) of sub-paragraph (a) there shall be substituted the following head—

"(ib) he is not a person subject to immigration control within the meaning of section 115(9) of the Immigration and Asylum Act 1999 or section 115 of that Act does not apply to him for the purposes of entitlement to disability living allowance by virtue of regulation 2 of the Social Security (Immigration and Asylum) Consequential Amendments Regulations 2000, and".

(3) Paragraph (1A) of regulation 2 shall be omitted.

Initial Commencement
Specified date: 3 April 2000: see reg 1(2).

12 Transitional arrangements and savings

(1) *Paragraph (2) shall apply where, in relation to a claim for income support, a social fund payment, housing benefit or council tax benefit, as the case may be, a person has submitted a claim for asylum on or before 2nd April 2000 and is notified that he has been recorded by the Secretary of State as a refugee within the definition in Article 1 of the Convention relating to the Status of Refugees done at Geneva on 28th July 1951 as extended by Article 1(2) of the Protocol relating to the Status of Refugees done at New York on 31st January 1967.*

(2) *Where this paragraph applies—*

  (a) *regulation 21ZA of the Income Support Regulations (treatment of refugees) shall continue to have effect as if regulation 3(4)(a), (5) and (9) had not been made;*

  (b) *regulations 4(3C), 6(4D) and 19(8) of the Claims and Payments Regulations shall continue to have effect as if regulation 5 had not been made;*

  (c) *paragraphs 1 and 2 of Schedule A1, paragraph 62 of Schedule 4 and paragraph 51 of Schedule 5 to the Housing Benefit Regulations (treatment of claims for housing benefit by refugees) shall continue to have effect as if regulation 6(5) and (7) had not been made; and*

(d) *paragraphs 1 and 2 of Schedule A1, paragraph 62 of Schedule 4 and paragraph 51 of Schedule 5 to the Council Tax Benefit Regulations (treatment of claims for council tax benefit by refugees) shall continue to have effect as if regulation 7(5) and (7) had not been made.*

(3) Regulation 70 of the Income Support Regulations and regulation 147 of the Jobseeker's Allowance Regulations, as the case may be, shall apply to a person who is an asylum seeker within the meaning of paragraph (4) who has not ceased to be an asylum seeker by virtue of paragraph (5).

(4) An asylum seeker within the meaning of this paragraph is a person who—

(a) submits on his arrival (other than on his re-entry) in the United Kingdom from a country outside the Common Travel Area a claim for asylum on or before 2nd April 2000 to the Secretary of State that it would be contrary to the United Kingdom's obligations under the Convention for him to be removed or required to leave, the United Kingdom and that claim is recorded by the Secretary of State as having been made before that date; or

(b) on or before 2nd April 2000 becomes, while present in Great Britain, an asylum seeker when—
  (i) the Secretary of State makes a declaration to the effect that the country of which he is a national is subject to such a fundamental change of circumstances that he would not normally order the return of a person to that country; and
  (ii) he submits, within a period of three months from the date that declaration was made, a claim for asylum to the Secretary of State under the Convention relating to the Status of Refugees, and
  (iii) his claim for asylum under that Convention is recorded by the Secretary of State as having been made; and

(c) in the case of a claim for jobseeker's allowance, holds a work permit or has written authorisation from the Secretary of State permitting him to work in the United Kingdom.

(5) A person ceases to be an asylum seeker for the purposes of this paragraph when his claim for asylum is recorded by the Secretary of State as having been decided (other than on appeal) or abandoned.

(6) For the purposes of regulation 7A of the Housing Benefit Regulations and regulation 4A of the Council Tax Benefit Regulations, a person who is an asylum seeker within the meaning of paragraph (7) who has not ceased to be an asylum seeker by virtue of paragraph (8), is not a person from abroad within the meaning of paragraph (1) of those regulations.

(7) An asylum seeker within the meaning of this paragraph is a person who—

(a) submits on his arrival (other than on his re-entry) in the United Kingdom from a country outside the Common Travel Area a claim for asylum on or before 2nd April 2000 to the Secretary of State that it would be contrary to the United Kingdom's obligations under the Convention for him to be removed or required to leave, the United Kingdom and that claim is recorded by the Secretary of State as having been made before that date, or

(b) on or before 2nd April 2000 becomes, while present in Great Britain, an asylum seeker when—
  (i) the Secretary of State makes a declaration to the effect that the country of which he is a national is subject to such a fundamental change of circumstances that he would not normally order the return of a person to that country; and

   (ii) he submits, within a period of three months from the date that declaration was made, a claim for asylum to the Secretary of State under the Convention relating to the Status of Refugees; and

   (iii) his claim for asylum under that Convention is recorded by the Secretary of State as having been made.

(8)   A person ceases to be an asylum seeker for the purposes of this paragraph when his claim for asylum is recorded by the Secretary of State as having been decided (other than on appeal) or abandoned.

(9)   In paragraphs (4) and (7) "the Common Travel Area" means the United Kingdom, the Channel Islands, the Isle of Man and the Republic of Ireland collectively and "the Convention" means the Convention relating to the Status of Refugees done at Geneva on 28th July 1951 as extended by Article 2(1) of the Protocol relating to the Status of Refugees done at New York on 31st January 1967.

(10)   Where, before the coming into force of these Regulations, a person has claimed benefit to which he is entitled or is receiving benefit by virtue of regulation 12(3) of the Persons from Abroad Regulations or regulation 14B(g) of the Child Benefit (General) Regulations 1976, as the case may be, those provisions shall continue to have effect, for the purposes of entitlement to attendance allowance, disability living allowance, [carer's allowance], severe disablement allowance or child benefit, as the case may be, until such time as—

   (a)   his claim for asylum (if any) is recorded by the Secretary of State as having been decided or abandoned; or

   (b)   his entitlement to that benefit is revised or superseded under section 9 or 10 of the Social Security Act 1998, if earlier,

as if regulations 8, 9, 10 and 11 and paragraph (2) or paragraph (3), as the case may be, of regulation 13, had not been made.

(11)   In the Persons from Abroad Regulations—

   (a)   in paragraph (1) of regulation 12, after the words "shall continue to have effect" there shall be inserted the words "(both as regards him and as regards persons who are members of his family at the coming into force of these Regulations)"; and

   (b)   notwithstanding the amendments and revocations in regulations 3, 6 and 7, regulations 12(1) and (2) of the Persons from Abroad Regulations shall continue to have effect as they had effect before those amendments and revocations came into force.

Initial Commencement
Specified date: 3 April 2000: see reg 1(2).

Amendment
Paras (1), (2): revoked by the Asylum and Immigration (Treatment of Claimants, etc) Act 2004, s 12(3). Date in force: to be appointed: see the Asylum and Immigration (Treatment of Claimants, etc) Act 2004, s 48(3)–(6).
Para (10): words "carer's allowance" in square brackets substituted by SI 2002/2497, reg 3, Sch 2, paras 1, 2. Date in force: 1 April 2003: see SI 2002/2497, reg 1(b).

13   Revocations

(1)   The provisions specified in the following paragraphs of this regulation are revoked.

(2)   Regulation 12(3) of the Persons from Abroad Regulations.

(3)   Regulation 14B of the Child Benefit (General) Regulations 1976.

Initial Commencement
Specified date: 3 April 2000: see reg 1(2).

SCHEDULE
PERSONS NOT EXCLUDED FROM CERTAIN BENEFITS UNDER SECTION 115 OF THE
IMMIGRATION AND ASYLUM ACT 1999

Regulation 2

PART I
PERSONS NOT EXCLUDED UNDER SECTION 115 OF THE IMMIGRATION AND ASYLUM
ACT FROM ENTITLEMENT TO INCOME-BASED JOBSEEKER'S ALLOWANCE, INCOME
SUPPORT, A SOCIAL FUND PAYMENT, HOUSING BENEFIT OR COUNCIL TAX BENEFIT

1   A person who—

(a)   has limited leave (as defined in section 33(1) of the Immigration Act 1971) to
       enter or remain in the United Kingdom which was given in accordance with
       the immigration rules (as defined in that section) relating to—
       (i)   there being or there needing to be, no recourse to public funds, or
       (ii) there being no charge on public funds,
       during that period of limited leave; and
(b)   having, during any one period of limited leave (including any such period as
       extended), supported himself without recourse to public funds, other than any
       such recourse by reason of the previous application of this sub-paragraph, is
       temporarily without funds during that period of leave because remittances to
       him from abroad have been disrupted, provided there is a reasonable
       expectation that his supply of funds will be resumed.

2   A person who has been given leave to enter or remain in, the United Kingdom by
the Secretary of State upon an undertaking by another person or persons pursuant to
the immigration rules within the meaning of the Immigration Act 1971, to be
responsible for his maintenance and accommodation and who has not been resident in
the United Kingdom for a period of at least five years beginning on the date of entry or
the date on which the undertaking was given in respect of him, whichever date is the
later and the person or persons who gave the undertaking to provide for his
maintenance and accommodation has, or as the case may be, have died.

3   A person who—

(a)   has been given leave to enter or remain in, the United Kingdom by the
       Secretary of State upon an undertaking by another person or persons pursuant
       to the immigration rules within the meaning of the Immigration Act 1971, to
       be responsible for his maintenance and accommodation; and
(b)   has been resident in the United Kingdom for a period of at least five years
       beginning on the date of entry or the date on which the undertaking was given
       in respect of him, whichever date is the later.

4   A person who is a national of a state which has ratified the European Convention
on Social and Medical Assistance (done in Paris on 11th December 1953) or a state
which has ratified the Council of Europe Social Charter (signed in Turin on 18th
October 1961) and who is lawfully present in the United Kingdom.

Initial Commencement
Specified date: 3 April 2000: see reg 1(2).

PART II
PERSONS NOT EXCLUDED UNDER SECTION 115 OF THE IMMIGRATION AND ASYLUM ACT FROM ENTITLEMENT TO ATTENDANCE ALLOWANCE, SEVERE DISABLEMENT ALLOWANCE, [CARER'S ALLOWANCE], DISABILITY LIVING ALLOWANCE, A SOCIAL FUND PAYMENT OR CHILD BENEFIT

1   A member of a family of a national of a State contracting party to the Agreement on the European Economic Area signed at Oporto on 2nd May 1992 as adjusted by the Protocol signed at Brussels on 17th March 1993.

2   A person who is lawfully working in Great Britain and is a national of a State with which the Community has concluded an agreement under Article 310 of the Treaty of Amsterdam amending the Treaty on European Union, the Treaties establishing the European Communities and certain related Acts providing, in the field of social security, for the equal treatment of workers who are nationals of the signatory State and their families.

3   A person who is a member of a family of, and living with, a person specified in paragraph 2.

4   A person who has been given leave to enter, or remain in, the United Kingdom by the Secretary of State upon an undertaking by another person or persons pursuant to the immigration rules within the meaning of the Immigration Act 1971, to be responsible for his maintenance and accommodation.

Initial Commencement
Specified date: 3 April 2000: see reg 1(2).

Amendment
Part heading: words "Carer's Allowance" in square brackets substituted by SI 2002/2497, reg 3, Sch 2, paras 1, 2. Date in force: 1 April 2003: see SI 2002/2497, reg 1(b).

ASYLUM SUPPORT REGULATIONS 2000

2000 No 704

Made . . . . *6th March 2000*

Laid before Parliament . . . . *13th March 2000*

Coming into force . . . . *3rd April 2000*

The Secretary of State, in exercise of the powers conferred on him by sections 94, 95, 97, 114, 166 and 167 of and Schedule 8 to the Immigration and Asylum Act 1999, hereby makes the following Regulations:

General

1   Citation and commencement
These Regulations may be cited as the Asylum Support Regulations 2000 and shall come into force on 3rd April 2000.

Initial Commencement
Specified date: 3 April 2000: see above.

2   Interpretation

(1)   In these Regulations—

"the Act" means the Immigration and Asylum Act 1999;

"asylum support" means support provided under section 95 of the Act;

"dependant" has the meaning given by paragraphs (4) and (5);

"the interim Regulations" means the Asylum Support (Interim Provisions) Regulations 1999;

"married couple" means a man and woman who are married to each other and are members of the same household; and

"unmarried couple" means a man and woman who, though not married to each other, are living together as if married.

[(2)   The period prescribed under section 94(3) of the Act (day on which a claim for asylum is determined) for the purposes of Part VI of the Act is 28 days where paragraph (2A) applies, and 21 days in any other case.

(2A)   This paragraph applies where:

(a)   the Secretary of State notifies the claimant that his decision is to accept the asylum claim;

(b)   the Secretary of State notifies the claimant that his decision is to reject the asylum claim but at the same time notifies him that he is giving him limited leave to enter or remain in the United Kingdom; or

(c)   an appeal by the claimant against the Secretary of State's decision has been disposed of by being allowed.]

(3)   Paragraph (2) does not apply in relation to a case to which the interim Regulations apply (for which case, provision corresponding to paragraph (2) is made by regulation 2(6) of those Regulations).

(4)   In these Regulations "dependant", in relation to an asylum-seeker, a supported person or an applicant for asylum support, means, subject to paragraph (5), a person in the United Kingdom ("the relevant person") who—

(a)   is his spouse;

(b)   is a child of his or of his spouse, is dependant on him and is, or was at the relevant time, under 18;

(c)   is a member of his or his spouse's close family and is, or was at the relevant time, under 18;

(d)   had been living as part of his household—

(i)   for at least six of the twelve months before the relevant time, or

(ii)   since birth,

and is, or was at the relevant time, under 18;

(e)   is in need of care and attention from him or a member of his household by reason of a disability and would fall within sub-paragraph (c) or (d) but for the fact that he is not, and was not at the relevant time, under 18;

(f)   had been living with him as a member of an unmarried couple for at least two of the three years before the relevant time;

(g)   is living as part of his household and was, immediately before 6th December 1999 (the date when the interim Regulations came into force), receiving assistance from a local authority under section 17 of the Children Act 1989;

(h)   is living as part of his household and was, immediately before the coming into force of these Regulations, receiving assistance from a local authority under—

(i)   section 22 of the Children (Scotland) Act 1995; or

(ii)   Article 18 of the Children (Northern Ireland) Order 1995; or

(i)   has made a claim for leave to enter or remain in the United Kingdom, or for variation of any such leave, which is being considered on the basis that he is dependant on the asylum-seeker;

and in relation to a supported person, or an applicant for asylum support, who is himself a dependant of an asylum-seeker, also includes the asylum-seeker if in the United Kingdom.

(5) Where a supported person or applicant for asylum support is himself a dependant of an asylum-seeker, a person who would otherwise be a dependant of the supported person, or of the applicant, for the purposes of these Regulations is not such a dependant unless he is also a dependant of the asylum-seeker or is the asylum-seeker.

(6) In paragraph (4), "the relevant time", in relation to the relevant person, means—

(a) the time when an application for asylum support for him was made in accordance with regulation 3(3); or

(b) if he has joined a person who is already a supported person in the United Kingdom and sub-paragraph (a) does not apply, the time when he joined that person in the United Kingdom.

(7) Where a person, by falling within a particular category in relation to an asylum-seeker or supported person, is by virtue of this regulation a dependant of the asylum-seeker or supported person for the purposes of these Regulations, that category is also a prescribed category for the purposes of paragraph (c) of the definition of "dependant" in section 94(1) of the Act and, accordingly, the person is a dependant of the asylum-seeker or supported person for the purposes of Part VI of the Act.

(8) Paragraph (7) does not apply to a person who is already a dependant of the asylum-seeker or supported person for the purposes of Part VI of the Act because he falls within either of the categories mentioned in paragraphs (a) and (b) of the definition of "dependant" in section 94(1) of the Act.

(9) Paragraph (7) does not apply for the purposes of any reference to a "dependant" in Schedule 9 to the Act.

Initial Commencement
Specified date: 3 April 2000: see reg 1.

Amendment
Paras (2), (2A): substituted, for para (2) as originally enacted, by SI 2002/472, reg 3. Date in force: 8 April 2002: see SI 2002/472, reg 1.

Initial application for support

3   Initial application for support: individual and group applications

(1) Either of the following—

(a) an asylum-seeker, or

(b) a dependant of an asylum-seeker,

may apply to the Secretary of State for asylum support.

(2) An application under this regulation may be—

(a) for asylum support for the applicant alone; or

(b) for asylum support for the applicant and one or more dependants of his.

(3) The application must be made by completing in full and in English the form for the time being issued by the Secretary of State for the purpose; and any form so issued shall be the form shown in the Schedule to these Regulations or a form to the like effect.

[(4) The application may not be entertained by the Secretary of State—

(a) where it is made otherwise than in accordance with paragraph (3); or

(b) where the Secretary of State is not satisfied that the information provided is complete or accurate or that the applicant is co-operating with enquiries made under paragraph (5).]

(5) The Secretary of State may make further enquiries of the applicant about any matter connected with the application.

[(5A) Where the Secretary of State makes further enquiries under paragraph (5) the applicant shall reply to those enquiries within five working days of his receipt of them.

(5B) The Secretary of State shall be entitled to conclude that the applicant is not co-operating with his enquiries under paragraph (5) if he fails, without reasonable excuse, to reply within the period prescribed by paragraph (5A).

(5C) In cases where the Secretary of State may not entertain an application for asylum support he shall also discontinue providing support under section 98 of the Act.]

(6) Paragraphs (3) and (4) do not apply where a person is already a supported person and asylum support is sought for a dependant of his for whom such support is not already provided (for which case, provision is made by regulation 15).

[(7) For the purposes of this regulation, working day means any day other than a Saturday, a Sunday, Christmas Day, Good Friday or a day which is a bank holiday under section 1 of the Banking and Financial Dealings Act 1971 in the locality in which the applicant is living.]

Initial Commencement
Specified date: 3 April 2000: see reg 1.

Amendment
Para (4): substituted by SI 2002/3110, reg 2. Date in force: 8 January 2003: see SI 2002/3110, reg 1.
Paras (5A)–(5C): inserted by SI 2005/11, regs 2, 3(a). Date in force: 5 February 2005: see SI 2005/11, reg 1.
Para (7): inserted by SI 2005/11, regs 2, 3(b). Date in force: 5 February 2005: see SI 2005/11, reg 1.

4 Persons excluded from support

(1) The following circumstances are prescribed for the purposes of subsection (2) of section 95 of the Act as circumstances where a person who would otherwise fall within subsection (1) of that section is excluded from that subsection (and, accordingly, may not be provided with asylum support).

(2) A person is so excluded if he is applying for asylum support for himself alone and he falls within paragraph (4) by virtue of any sub-paragraph of that paragraph.

(3) A person is so excluded if—

(a) he is applying for asylum support for himself and other persons, or he is included in an application for asylum support made by a person other than himself;

(b) he falls within paragraph (4) (by virtue of any sub-paragraph of that paragraph); and

(c) each of the other persons to whom the application relates also falls within paragraph (4) (by virtue of any sub-paragraph of that paragraph).

(4) A person falls within this paragraph if at the time when the application is determined—

(a) he is a person to whom interim support applies; or

   (b) he is a person to whom social security benefits apply; or

   (c) he has not made a claim for leave to enter or remain in the United Kingdom, or for variation of any such leave, which is being considered on the basis that he is an asylum-seeker or dependent on an asylum-seeker.

(5) For the purposes of paragraph (4), interim support applies to a person if—

   (a) at the time when the application is determined, he is a person to whom, under the interim Regulations, support under regulation 3 of those Regulations must be provided by a local authority;

   (b) sub-paragraph (a) does not apply, but would do so if the person had been determined by the local authority concerned to be an eligible person; or

   (c) sub-paragraph (a) does not apply, but would do so but for the fact that the person's support under those Regulations was (otherwise than by virtue of regulation 7(1)(d) of those Regulations) refused under regulation 7, or suspended or discontinued under regulation 8, of those Regulations;

and in this paragraph "local authority", "local authority concerned" and "eligible person" have the same meanings as in the interim Regulations.

(6) For the purposes of paragraph (4), a person is a person to whom social security benefits apply if he is—

   (a) a person who by virtue of regulation 2 of the Social Security (Immigration and Asylum) Consequential Amendments Regulations 2000 is not excluded by section 115(1) of the Act from entitlement to—
      (i) income-based jobseeker's allowance under the Jobseekers Act 1995; or
     (ii) income support, housing benefit or council tax benefit under the Social Security Contributions and Benefits Act 1992;

   (b) a person who, by virtue of regulation 2 of the Social Security (Immigration and Asylum) Consequential Amendments Regulations (Northern Ireland) 2000 is not excluded by section 115(2) of the Act from entitlement to—
      (i) income-based jobseeker's allowance under the Jobseekers (Northern Ireland) Order 1995; or
     (ii) income support or housing benefit under the Social Security Contributions and Benefits (Northern Ireland) Act 1992;

(7) A person is not to be regarded as falling within paragraph (2) or (3) if, when asylum support is sought for him, he is a dependant of a person who is already a supported person.

(8) The circumstances prescribed by paragraphs (2) and (3) are also prescribed for the purposes of section 95(2), as applied by section 98(3), of the Act as circumstances where a person who would otherwise fall within subsection (1) of section 98 is excluded from that subsection (and, accordingly, may not be provided with temporary support under section 98).

(9) For the purposes of paragraph (8), paragraphs (2) and (3) shall apply as if any reference to an application for asylum support were a reference to an application for support under section 98 of the Act.

Initial Commencement
Specified date: 3 April 2000: see reg 1.

Determining whether persons are destitute

5   Determination where application relates to more than one person, etc

(1) Subject to paragraph (2), where an application in accordance with regulation 3(3) is for asylum support for the applicant and one or more dependants of his, in applying

section 95(1) of the Act the Secretary of State must decide whether the applicant and all those dependants, taken together, are destitute or likely to become destitute within the period prescribed by regulation 7.

(2) Where a person is a supported person, and the question falls to be determined whether asylum support should in future be provided for him and one or more other persons who are his dependants and are—

(a) persons for whom asylum support is also being provided when that question falls to be determined; or

(b) persons for whom the Secretary of State is then considering whether asylum support should be provided,

in applying section 95(1) of the Act the Secretary of State must decide whether the supported person and all those dependants, taken together, are destitute or likely to become destitute within the period prescribed by regulation 7.

Initial Commencement
Specified date: 3 April 2000: see reg 1.

6 Income and assets to be taken into account

(1) This regulation applies where it falls to the Secretary of State to determine for the purposes of section 95(1) of the Act whether—

(a) a person applying for asylum support, or such an applicant and any dependants of his, or

(b) a supported person, or such a person and any dependants of his,

is or are destitute or likely to become so within the period prescribed by regulation 7.

(2) In this regulation "the principal" means the applicant for asylum support (where paragraph (1)(a) applies) or the supported person (where paragraph (1)(b) applies).

(3) The Secretary of State must ignore—

(a) any asylum support, and

(b) any support under section 98 of the Act,

which the principal or any dependant of his is provided with or, where the question is whether destitution is likely within a particular period, might be provided with in that period.

(4) But he must take into account—

(a) any other income which the principal, or any dependant of his, has or might reasonably be expected to have in that period;

(b) any other support which is available to the principal or any dependant of his, or might reasonably be expected to be so available in that period; and

(c) any assets mentioned in paragraph (5) (whether held in the United Kingdom or elsewhere) which are available to the principal or any dependant of his otherwise than by way of asylum support or support under section 98, or might reasonably be expected to be so available in that period.

(5) Those assets are—

(a) cash;

(b) savings;

(c) investments;

(d) land;

(e) cars or other vehicles; and

(f) goods held for the purpose of a trade or other business.

(6)   The Secretary of State must ignore any assets not mentioned in paragraph (5).

Initial Commencement
Specified date: 3 April 2000: see reg 1.

7   Period within which applicant must be likely to become destitute

The period prescribed for the purposes of section 95(1) of the Act is—

    (a) where the question whether a person or persons is or are destitute or likely to become so falls to be determined in relation to an application for asylum support and sub-paragraph (b) does not apply, 14 days beginning with the day on which that question falls to be determined;

    (b) where that question falls to be determined in relation to a supported person, or in relation to persons including a supported person, 56 days beginning with the day on which that question falls to be determined.

Initial Commencement
Specified date: 3 April 2000: see reg 1.

8   Adequacy of existing accommodation

(1)   Subject to paragraph (2), the matters mentioned in paragraph (3) are prescribed for the purposes of subsection (5)(a) of section 95 of the Act as matters to which the Secretary of State must have regard in determining for the purposes of that section whether the accommodation of—

    (a) a person applying for asylum support, or

    (b) a supported person for whom accommodation is not for the time being provided by way of asylum support,

is adequate.

(2)   The matters mentioned in paragraph (3)(a) and (d) to (g) are not so prescribed for the purposes of a case where the person indicates to the Secretary of State that he wishes to remain in the accommodation.

(3)   The matters referred to in paragraph (1) are—

    (a) whether it would be reasonable for the person to continue to occupy the accommodation;

    (b) whether the accommodation is affordable for him;

    (c) whether the accommodation is provided under section 98 of the Act, or otherwise on an emergency basis, only while the claim for asylum support is being determined;

    (d) whether the person can secure entry to the accommodation;

    (e) where the accommodation consists of a moveable structure, vehicle or vessel designed or adapted for human habitation, whether there is a place where the person is entitled or permitted both to place it and reside in it;

    (f) whether the accommodation is available for occupation by the person's dependants together with him;

    (g) whether it is probable that the person's continued occupation of the accommodation will lead to domestic violence against him or any of his dependants.

(4)   In determining whether it would be reasonable for a person to continue to occupy accommodation, regard may be had to the general circumstances prevailing in relation to housing in the district of the local housing authority where the accommodation is.

(5)   In determining whether a person's accommodation is affordable for him, the Secretary of State must have regard to—

   (a)   any income, or any assets mentioned in regulation 6(5) (whether held in the United Kingdom or elsewhere), which is or are available to him or any dependant of his otherwise than by way of asylum support or support under section 98 of the Act, or might reasonably be expected to be so available;

   (b)   the costs in respect of the accommodation; and

   (c)   the person's other reasonable living expenses.

(6) In this regulation—

   (a)   "domestic violence" means violence from a person who is or has been a close family member, or threats of violence from such a person which are likely to be carried out; and

   (b)   "district of the local housing authority" has the meaning given by section 217(3) of the Housing Act 1996.

(7) The reference in paragraph (1) to subsection (5)(a) of section 95 of the Act does not include a reference to that provision as applied by section 98(3) of the Act.

Initial Commencement
Specified date: 3 April 2000: see reg 1.

9   Essential living needs

(1) The matter mentioned in paragraph (2) is prescribed for the purposes of subsection (7)(b) of section 95 of the Act as a matter to which the Secretary of State may not have regard in determining for the purposes of that section whether a person's essential living needs (other than accommodation) are met.

(2) That matter is his personal preference as to clothing (but this shall not be taken to prevent the Secretary of State from taking into account his individual circumstances as regards clothing).

(3) None of the items and expenses mentioned in paragraph (4) is to be treated as being an essential living need of a person for the purposes of Part VI of the Act.

(4) Those items and expenses are—

   (a)   the cost of faxes;

   (b)   computers and the cost of computer facilities;

   (c)   the cost of photocopying;

   (d)   travel expenses, except the expense mentioned in paragraph (5);

   (e)   toys and other recreational items;

   (f)   entertainment expenses.

(5) The expense excepted from paragraph (4)(d) is the expense of an initial journey from a place in the United Kingdom to accommodation provided by way of asylum support or (where accommodation is not so provided) to an address in the United Kingdom which has been notified to the Secretary of State as the address where the person intends to live.

(6) Paragraph (3) shall not be taken to affect the question whether any item or expense not mentioned in paragraph (4) or (5) is, or is not, an essential living need.

(7) The reference in paragraph (1) to subsection (7)(b) of section 95 of the Act includes a reference to that provision as applied by section 98(3) of the Act and, accordingly, the reference in paragraph (1) to "that section" includes a reference to section 98.

Initial Commencement
Specified date: 3 April 2000: see reg 1.

Appendix 1   Legislation and materials

Provision of support

10   Kind and levels of support for essential living needs

(1)   This regulation applies where the Secretary of State has decided that asylum support should be provided in respect of the essential living needs of a person.

[(2)   As a general rule, asylum support in respect of the essential living needs of that person may be expected to be provided weekly in the form of [cash, equal to] the amount shown in the second column of the following Table opposite the entry in the first column which for the time being describes that person ...]

[TABLE

Qualifying couple	£61.71
Lone parent aged 18 or over	£39.34
Single person aged 25 or over	£39.34
Single person aged at least 18 but under 25	£31.15
Person aged at least 16 but under 18 (except a member of a qualifying couple)	£33.85
Person aged under 16	£43.88]

(3)   In paragraph (1) and the provisions of paragraph (2) preceding the Table, "person" includes "couple".

(4)   In this regulation—

    (a)   "qualifying couple" means a married or unmarried couple at least one of whom is aged 18 or over and neither of whom is aged under 16;

    (b)   "lone parent" means a parent who is not a member of a married or unmarried couple;

    (c)   "single person" means a person who is not a parent or a member of a qualifying couple; and

    (d)   "parent" means a parent of a relevant child, that is to say a child who is aged under 18 and for whom asylum support is provided.

(5)   Where the Secretary of State has decided that accommodation should be provided for a person (or couple) by way of asylum support, and the accommodation is provided in a form which also meets other essential living needs (such as bed and breakfast, or half or full board), the amounts shown in the Table in paragraph (2) shall be treated as reduced accordingly.

(6)   ...

Initial Commencement
Specified date: 3 April 2000: see reg 1.

Amendment
Para (2): substituted by SI 2002/472, reg 4(1). Date in force: 8 April 2002: see SI 2002/472, reg 1.
Para (2): words "cash, equal to" in square brackets substituted by SI 2004/1313, reg 2(a). Date in force: 4 June 2004: see SI 2004/1313, reg 1.
Para (2): words omitted revoked by SI 2004/1313, reg 2(b). Date in force: 4 June 2004: see SI 2004/1313, reg 1.
Para (2): table substituted by SI 2005/738, reg 2. Date in force: 11 April 2005: see SI 2005/738, reg 1.
Para (6): revoked by SI 2002/472, reg 4(2). Date in force: 8 April 2002: see SI 2002/472, reg 1.

[10A   Additional support for pregnant women and children under 3]

[(1)   In addition to the [cash support which the Secretary of State may be expected to provide weekly as] described in regulation 10(2), in the case of any pregnant woman or child aged under 3 for whom the Secretary of State has decided asylum support should be provided, there shall, as a general rule, be added to the [cash support] for any week the amount shown in the second column of the following table opposite the entry in the first column which for the time being describes that person.

TABLE

Pregnant woman	£3.00
Child aged under 1	£5.00
Child aged at least 1 and under 3	£3.00

(2)   In this regulation, "pregnant woman" means a woman who has provided evidence to satisfy the Secretary of State that she is pregnant.]

Amendment
Inserted by SI 2003/241, reg 2. Date in force: 3 March 2003: see SI 2003/241, reg 1.
Para (1): words "cash support which the Secretary of State may be expected to provide weekly as" in square brackets substituted by SI 2004/1313, reg 3(a). Date in force: 4 June 2004: see SI 2004/1313, reg 1.
Para (1): words "cash support" in square brackets substituted by SI 2004/1313, reg 3(b). Date in force: 4 June 2004: see SI 2004/1313, reg 1.

11   ...

Amendment
Revoked by SI 2004/1313, reg 4. Date in force: 4 June 2004 (except in relation to payments to a person whose qualifying period ends on or before that date): see SI 2004/1313, regs 1, 4(2).

12   Income and assets to be taken into account in providing support

(1)   This regulation applies where it falls to the Secretary of State to decide the level or kind of asylum support to be provided for—

(a)   a person applying for asylum support, or such an applicant and any dependants of his; or
(b)   a supported person, or such a person and any dependants of his.

(2)   In this regulation "the principal" means the applicant for asylum support (where paragraph (1)(a) applies) or the supported person (where paragraph (1)(b) applies).

(3)   The Secretary of State must take into account—

(a)   any income which the principal or any dependant of his has or might reasonably be expected to have,
(b)   support which is or might reasonably be expected to be available to the principal or any dependant of his, and
(c)   any assets mentioned in regulation 6(5) (whether held in the United Kingdom or elsewhere) which are or might reasonably be expected to be available to the principal or any dependant of his,

otherwise than by way of asylum support.

Initial Commencement
Specified date: 3 April 2000: see reg 1.

13   Accommodation

(1) The matters mentioned in paragraph (2) are prescribed for the purposes of subsection (2)(b) of section 97 of the Act as matters to which regard may not be had when exercising the power under section 95 of the Act to provide accommodation for a person.

(2) Those matters are—

   (a) his personal preference as to the nature of the accommodation to be provided; and
   (b) his personal preference as to the nature and standard of fixtures and fittings;

but this shall not be taken to prevent the person's individual circumstances, as they relate to his accommodation needs, being taken into account.

Initial Commencement
Specified date: 3 April 2000: see reg 1.

14   Services

(1) The services mentioned in paragraph (2) may be provided or made available by way of asylum support to persons who are otherwise receiving such support, but may be so provided only for the purpose of maintaining good order among such persons.

(2) Those services are—

   (a) education, including English language lessons,
   (b) sporting or other developmental activities.

Initial Commencement
Specified date: 3 April 2000: see reg 1.

Change of circumstances

15   Change of circumstances

(1) If a relevant change of circumstances occurs, the supported person concerned or a dependant of his must, without delay, notify the Secretary of State of that change of circumstances.

(2) A relevant change of circumstances occurs where a supported person or a dependant of his—

   (a) is joined in the United Kingdom by a dependant or, as the case may be, another dependant, of the supported person;
   (b) receives or gains access to any money, or other asset mentioned in regulation 6(5), that has not previously been declared to the Secretary of State;
   (c) becomes employed;
   (d) becomes unemployed;
   (e) changes his name;
   (f) gets married;
   (g) starts living with a person as if married to that person;
   (h) gets divorced;
   (i) separates from a spouse, or from a person with whom he has been living as if married to that person;
   (j) becomes pregnant;
   (k) has a child;
   (l) leaves school;
   (m) starts to share his accommodation with another person;
   (n) moves to a different address, or otherwise leaves his accommodation;

   (o)   goes into hospital;
   (p)   goes to prison or is otherwise held in custody;
   (q)   leaves the United Kingdom; or
   (r)   dies.

(3)   If, on being notified of a change of circumstances, the Secretary of State considers that the change may be one—

   (a)   as a result of which asylum support should be provided for a person for whom it was not provided before, or
   (b)   as a result of which asylum support should no longer be provided for a person, or
   (c)   which may otherwise affect the asylum support which should be provided for a person,

he may make further enquiries of the supported person or dependant who gave the notification.

(4)   The Secretary of State may, in particular, require that person to provide him with such information as he considers necessary to determine whether, and if so, what, asylum support should be provided for any person.

Initial Commencement
Specified date: 3 April 2000: see reg 1.

Contributions

16   Contributions

(1)   This regulation applies where, in deciding the level of asylum support to be provided for a person who is or will be a supported person, the Secretary of State is required to take into account income, support or assets as mentioned in regulation 12(3).

(2)   The Secretary of State may—

   (a)   set the asylum support for that person at a level which does not reflect the income, support or assets; and
   (b)   require from that person payments by way of contributions towards the cost of the provision for him of asylum support.

(3)   A supported person must make to the Secretary of State such payments by way of contributions as the Secretary of State may require under paragraph (2).

(4)   Prompt payment of such contributions may be made a condition (under section 95(9) of the Act) subject to which asylum support for that person is provided.

Initial Commencement
Specified date: 3 April 2000: see reg 1.

Recovery of sums by Secretary of State

17   Recovery where assets become realisable

(1)   This regulation applies where it appears to the Secretary of State at any time (the relevant time)—

   (a)   that a supported person had, at the time when he applied for asylum support, assets of any kind in the United Kingdom or elsewhere which were not capable of being realised; but

(b)   that those assets have subsequently become, and remain, capable of being realised.

(2)   The Secretary of State may recover from that person a sum not exceeding the recoverable sum.

(3)   Subject to paragraph (5), the recoverable sum is a sum equal to whichever is the less of—

(a)   the monetary value of all the asylum support provided to the person up to the relevant time; and

(b)   the monetary value of the assets concerned.

(4)   As well as being recoverable as mentioned in paragraph 11(2)(a) of Schedule 8 to the Act, an amount recoverable under this regulation may be recovered by deduction from asylum support.

(5)   The recoverable sum shall be treated as reduced by any amount which the Secretary of State has by virtue of this regulation already recovered from the person concerned (whether by deduction or otherwise) with regard to the assets concerned.

Initial Commencement
Specified date: 3 April 2000: see reg 1.

[17A   Recovery of asylum support]

[(1)   The Secretary of State may require a supported person to refund asylum support if it transpires that at any time during which asylum support was being provided for him he was not destitute.

(2)   If a supported person has dependants, the Secretary of State may require him to refund asylum support if it transpires that at any time during which asylum support was being provided for the supported person and his dependants they were not destitute.

(3)   The refund required shall not exceed the monetary value of all the asylum support provided to the supported person or to the supported person and his dependants for the relevant period.

(4)   In this regulation the relevant period is the time during which asylum support was provided for the supported person or the supported person and his dependants and during which he or they were not destitute.

(5)   If not paid within a reasonable period, the refund required may be recovered from the supported person as if it were a debt due to the Secretary of State.]

Amendment
Inserted by SI 2005/11, regs 2, 4. Date in force: 5 February 2005: see SI 2005/11, reg 1.

18   Overpayments: method of recovery

As well as being recoverable as mentioned in subsection (3) of section 114 of the Act, an amount recoverable under subsection (2) of that section may be recovered by deduction from asylum support.

Initial Commencement
Specified date: 3 April 2000: see reg 1.

Breach of conditions and suspension and discontinuation of support

19   Breach of conditions: decision whether to provide support

(1)   When deciding—

(a) whether to provide, or to continue to provide, asylum support for any person or persons, or

(b) the level or kind of support to be provided for any person or persons,

the Secretary of State may take into account [the extent to which a] relevant condition has been complied with.

[(2) A relevant condition is one which makes the provision of asylum support subject to actual residence by the supported person or a dependant of his for whom support is being provided in a specific place or location.]

Initial Commencement
Specified date: 3 April 2000: see reg 1.

Amendment
Para (1): words "the extent to which a" in square brackets substituted by SI 2005/11, regs 2, 5(a). Date in force: 5 February 2005: see SI 2005/11, reg 1.
Para (2): substituted by SI 2005/11, regs 2, 5(b). Date in force: 5 February 2005: see SI 2005/11, reg 1.

[20   Suspension or discontinuation of support]

[(1) Asylum support for a supported person and any dependant of his or for one or more dependants of a supported person may be suspended or discontinued if—

(a) support is being provided for the supported person or a dependant of his in collective accommodation and the Secretary of State has reasonable grounds to believe that the supported person or his dependant has committed a serious breach of the rules of that accommodation;

(b) the Secretary of State has reasonable grounds to believe that the supported person or a dependant of his for whom support is being provided has committed an act of seriously violent behaviour whether or not that act occurs in accommodation provided by way of asylum support or at the authorised address or elsewhere;

(c) the supported person or a dependant of his has committed an offence under Part VI of the Act;

(d) the Secretary of State has reasonable grounds to believe that the supported person or any dependant of his for whom support is being provided has abandoned the authorised address without first informing the Secretary of State or, if requested, without permission;

(e) the supported person has not complied within a reasonable period, which shall be no less than five working days beginning with the day on which the request was received by him, with requests for information made by the Secretary of State and which relate to the supported person's or his dependant's eligibility for or receipt of asylum support including requests made under regulation 15;

(f) the supported person fails, without reasonable excuse, to attend an interview requested by the Secretary of State relating to the supported person's or his dependant's eligibility for or receipt of asylum support;

(g) the supported person or, if he is an asylum seeker, his dependant, has not complied within a reasonable period, which shall be no less than ten working days beginning with the day on which the request was received by him, with a request for information made by the Secretary of State relating to his claim for asylum;

(h) the Secretary of State has reasonable grounds to believe that the supported person or a dependant of his for whom support is being provided has concealed financial resources and that the supported person or a dependant of his or both have therefore unduly benefited from the receipt of asylum support;

2217

   (i)   the supported person or a dependant of his for whom support is being provided has not complied with a reporting requirement;

   (j)   the Secretary of State has reasonable grounds to believe that the supported person or a dependant of his for whom support is being provided has made a claim for asylum ("the first claim") and before the first claim has been determined makes or seeks to make a further claim for asylum not being part of the first claim in the same or a different name; or

   (k)   the supported person or a dependant of his for whom support is being provided has failed without reasonable excuse to comply with a relevant condition.

(2)   If a supported person is asked to attend an interview of the type referred to in paragraph (1)(f) he shall be given no less than five working days notice of it.

(3)   Any decision to discontinue support in the circumstances referred to in paragraph (1) above shall be taken individually, objectively and impartially and reasons shall be given. Decisions will be based on the particular situation of the person concerned and particular regard shall be had to whether he is a vulnerable person as described by Article 17 of Council Directive 2003/9/EC of 27th January 2003 laying down minimum standards for the reception of asylum seekers.

(4)   No person's asylum support shall be discontinued before a decision is made under paragraph (1).

(5)   Where asylum support for a supported person or his dependant is suspended or discontinued under paragraph (1)(d) or (i) and the supported person or his dependant are traced or voluntarily report to the police, the Secretary of State or an immigration officer, a duly motivated decision based on the reasons for the disappearance shall be taken as to the reinstatement of some or all of the supported person's or his dependant's or both of their asylum support.

(6)   For the purposes of this regulation—

   (a)   the authorised address is—
      (i)   the accommodation provided for the supported person and his dependants (if any) by way of asylum support; or
     (ii)   if no accommodation is so provided, the address notified by the supported person to the Secretary of State in his application for asylum support or, where a change of address has been notified to the Secretary of State under regulation 15 or under the Immigration Rules or both, the address for the time being so notified;

   (b)   "collective accommodation" means accommodation which a supported person or any dependant of his for whom support is being provided shares with any other supported person and includes accommodation in which only facilities are shared;

   (c)   "relevant condition" has the same meaning as in regulation 19(2);

   (d)   "reporting requirement" is a condition or restriction which requires a person to report to the police, an immigration officer or the Secretary of State and is imposed under—
      (i)   paragraph 21 of Schedule 2 to the Immigration Act 1971 (temporary admission or release from detention);
     (ii)   paragraph 22 of that Schedule; or
    (iii)   paragraph 2 or 5 of Schedule 3 to that Act (pending deportation).

   (e)   "working day" has the same meaning as in regulation 3(7) save that the reference to the applicant shall be a reference to the supported person or his dependant.]

Amendment
Substituted by SI 2005/11, regs 2, 6. Date in force: 5 February 2005: see SI 2005/11, reg 1.

[20A   Temporary Support]

[Regulations 19 and 20 shall apply to a person or his dependant who is provided with temporary support under section 98 of the Act in the same way as they apply to a person and his dependant who is in receipt of asylum support and any reference to asylum support in regulations 19 and 20 shall include a reference to temporary support under section 98.]

Amendment
Inserted by SI 2005/11, regs 2, 7. Date in force: 5 February 2005: see SI 2005/11, reg 1.

21   Effect of previous suspension or discontinuation

(1)   [Subject to regulation 20(5) where—]

(a)   an application for asylum support is made,

(b)   the applicant or any other person to whom the application relates has previously had his asylum support suspended or discontinued under regulation 20, and

(c)   there has been no material change of circumstances since the suspension or discontinuation,

the application need not be entertained unless the Secretary of State considers that there are exceptional circumstances which justify its being entertained.

(2)   A material change of circumstances is one which, if the applicant were a supported person, would have to be notified to the Secretary of State under regulation 15.

(3)   This regulation is without prejudice to the power of the Secretary of State to refuse the application even if he has entertained it.

Initial Commencement
Specified date: 3 April 2000: see reg 1.

Amendment
Para (1): words "Subject to regulation 20(5) where—" in square brackets substituted by SI 2005/11, regs 2, 8. Date in force: 5 February 2005: see SI 2005/11, reg 1.

Notice to quit

22   Notice to quit

(1)   If—

(a)   as a result of asylum support, a person has a tenancy or licence to occupy accommodation,

(b)   one or more of the conditions mentioned in paragraph (2) is satisfied, and

(c)   he is given notice to quit in accordance with paragraph (3) or (4),

his tenancy or licence is to be treated as ending with the period specified in that notice, regardless of when it could otherwise be brought to an end.

(2)   The conditions are that—

(a)   the asylum support is suspended or discontinued as a result of any provision of regulation 20;

(b)   the relevant claim for asylum has been determined;

(c)   the supported person has ceased to be destitute; or

(d)   he is to be moved to other accommodation.

(3)   A notice to quit is in accordance with this paragraph if it is in writing and—

(a) in a case where sub-paragraph (a), (c) or (d) of paragraph (2) applies, specifies as the notice period a period of not less than seven days; or

(b) in a case where the Secretary of State has notified his decision on the relevant claim for asylum to the claimant, specifies as the notice period a period at least as long as whichever is the greater of—

(i) seven days; or

(ii) the period beginning with the date of service of the notice to quit and ending with the date of determination of the relevant claim for asylum (found in accordance with section 94(3) of the Act).

(4) A notice to quit is in accordance with this paragraph if—

(a) it is in writing;

(b) it specifies as the notice period a period of less than seven days; and

(c) the circumstances of the case are such that that notice period is justified.

Initial Commencement
Specified date: 3 April 2000: see reg 1.

Meaning of "destitute" for certain other purposes

23   Meaning of "destitute" for certain other purposes

(1) In this regulation "the relevant enactments" means—

(a) section 21(1A) of the National Assistance Act 1948;

(b) section 45(4A) of the Health Services and Public Health Act 1968;

(c) paragraph 2(2A) of Schedule 8 to the National Health Service Act 1977;

(d) sections 12(2A), 13A(4) and 13B(3) of the Social Work (Scotland) Act 1968;

(e) sections 7(3) and 8(4) of the Mental Health (Scotland) Act 1984; and

(f) Articles 7(3) and 15(6) of the Health and Personal Social Services (Northern Ireland) Order 1972.

(2) The following provisions of this regulation apply where it falls to an authority, or the Department, to determine for the purposes of any of the relevant enactments whether a person is destitute.

(3) Paragraphs (3) to (6) of regulation 6 apply as they apply in the case mentioned in paragraph (1) of that regulation, but as if references to the principal were references to the person whose destitution or otherwise is being determined and references to the Secretary of State were references to the authority or (as the case may be) Department.

(4) The matters mentioned in paragraph (3) of regulation 8 (read with paragraphs (4) to (6) of that regulation) are prescribed for the purposes of subsection (5)(a) of section 95 of the Act, as applied for the purposes of any of the relevant enactments, as matters to which regard must be had in determining for the purposes of any of the relevant enactments whether a person's accommodation is adequate.

(5) The matter mentioned in paragraph (2) of regulation 9 is prescribed for the purposes of subsection (7)(b) of section 95 of the Act, as applied for the purposes of any of the relevant enactments, as a matter to which regard may not be had in determining for the purposes of any of the relevant enactments whether a person's essential living needs (other than accommodation) are met.

(6) Paragraphs (3) to (6) of regulation 9 shall apply as if the reference in paragraph (3) to Part VI of the Act included a reference to the relevant enactments.

(7) The references in regulations 8(5) and 9(2) to the Secretary of State shall be construed, for the purposes of this regulation, as references to the authority or (as the case may be) Department.

Initial Commencement
Specified date: 3 April 2000: see reg 1.

SCHEDULE
APPLICATION FORM AND NOTES

Regulation 3(3)

(The full text of this form is currently unavailable. Please see the original which can be viewed at http://www.opsi.gov.uk/si/si2000/SI000704.pdf)

IMMIGRATION (ELIGIBILITY FOR ASSISTANCE) (SCOTLAND AND NORTHERN IRELAND) REGULATIONS 2000

2000 No 705

Made	*6th March 2000*
Laid before Parliament	*13th March 2000*
Coming into force	*3rd April 2000*

In exercise of the powers conferred on him by sections 115(3) and (4), 122(11), 166 and 167 of the Immigration and Asylum Act 1999, the Secretary of State hereby makes the following Regulations:

1 Citation, commencement, interpretation and extent

(1) These Regulations may be cited as the Immigration (Eligibility for Assistance) (Scotland and Northern Ireland) Regulations 2000 and shall come into force on 3rd April 2000.

(2) In these Regulations, "the 1999 Act" means the Immigration and Asylum Act 1999.

(3) Regulation 3 does not extend to Northern Ireland.

(4) Regulation 4 does not extend to Scotland.

Initial Commencement
Specified date: 3 April 2000: see para (1) above.

2 Eligibility for social assistance—Scotland and Northern Ireland

(1) Subject to paragraphs (2) and (3), any asylum-seeker who made a claim for asylum before 3rd April 2000 and any dependant of such an asylum-seeker shall be treated—

(a) in Scotland, for the purposes prescribed by regulation 3 only;
(b) in Northern Ireland, for the purposes prescribed by regulation 4 only;

as not being a person to whom section 115 of the 1999 Act (exclusion from benefits of persons subject to immigration control) applies.

(2) Paragraph (1)(a) does not apply where the person who made the claim for asylum is a person who, by virtue of regulation 2 of the Social Security (Immigration and

2221

Asylum) Consequential Amendments Regulations 2000 is not excluded by section 115(1) of the 1999 Act from entitlement to—

    (a)   income-based jobseeker's allowance under the Jobseekers Act 1995; or

    (b)   income support, housing benefit or council tax benefit under the Social Security Contributions and Benefits Act 1992.

(3)   Paragraph (1)(b) does not apply where the person who made the claim for asylum is a person, who by virtue of regulation 2 of the Social Security (Immigration and Asylum) Consequential Amendments Regulations (Northern Ireland) 2000 is not excluded by section 115(2) of the 1999 Act from entitlement to—

    (a)   income-based jobseeker's allowance under the Jobseekers (Northern Ireland) Order 1995; or

    (b)   income support or housing benefit under the Social Security Contributions and Benefits (Northern Ireland) Act 1992.

Initial Commencement
Specified date: 3 April 2000: see reg 1(1).

3   Eligibility for social assistance—Scottish provisions

Regulation 2(1)(a) applies only for the purposes of the following provisions—

    (a)   sections 12, 13A and 13B of the Social Work (Scotland) Act 1968;

    (b)   sections 7 and 8 of the Mental Health (Scotland) Act 1984.

Initial Commencement
Specified date: 3 April 2000: see reg 1(1).

Extent
This provision does not extend to Northern Ireland: see reg 1(3).

4   Eligibility for social assistance—Northern Ireland provisions

Regulation 2(1)(b) applies only for the purposes of Articles 7 and 15 of the Health and Personal Social Services (Northern Ireland) Order 1972.

Initial Commencement
Specified date: 3 April 2000: see reg 1(1).

Extent
This provision does not extend to Northern Ireland: see reg 1(3).

5   Eligibility for support for children—Scotland and Northern Ireland

Subsection (5) of section 122 of the 1999 Act (support for children) does not apply in relation to any person or family in respect of whom or which a relevant authority was, immediately before 3rd April 2000, providing assistance under—

    (a)   section 22 of the Children (Scotland) Act 1995 (local authority support in Scotland for children and their families); or

    (b)   Article 18 of the Children (Northern Ireland) Order 1995 (equivalent provision for Northern Ireland).

Initial Commencement
Specified date: 3 April 2000: see reg 1(1).

PERSONS SUBJECT TO IMMIGRATION CONTROL (HOUSING AUTHORITY ACCOMMODATION AND HOMELESSNESS) ORDER 2000

2000 No 706

Made . . . . *7th March 2000*

Laid before Parliament . . . . *13th March 2000*

Coming into force . . . . *3rd April 2000*

In exercise of the powers conferred on him by sections 118, 119 and 166(3) of the Immigration and Asylum Act 1999, the Secretary of State hereby makes the following Order:

1 Citation, commencement and extent

(1) This Order may be cited as the Persons subject to Immigration Control (Housing Authority Accommodation and Homelessness) Order 2000 and shall come into force on 3rd April 2000.

(2) This Order does not extend to Wales.

(3) Article 4 extends to England only.

(4) Articles 5 and 8 extend to Northern Ireland only.

(5) Articles 6 and 9 extend to Scotland only.

(6) Article 7 extends to Scotland and Northern Ireland only.

Initial Commencement
Specified date: 3 April 2000: see para (1) above.

Extent
This Order does not extend to Wales: see para (2) above.

2 Interpretation

In this Order—

"the 1971 Act" means the Immigration Act 1971;
"the 1985 Act" means the Housing Act 1985;
"the 1995 Act" means the Jobseekers Act 1995;
"the 1999 Act" means the Immigration and Asylum Act 1999;
"asylum-seeker" means a person who is not under 18 and who made a claim for asylum which is recorded by the Secretary of State as having been made on or before 2nd April 2000 but which has not been determined;
"child in need" means a child—
    (a) who is unlikely to achieve or maintain, or to have the opportunity of achieving or maintaining, a reasonable standard of health or development without the provision for him of services by a local authority under Part III of the Children Act 1989 (local authority support for children and families);
    (b) whose health or development is likely to be significantly impaired, or further impaired, without the provision for him of such services; or

2223

    (c)   who is blind, deaf or dumb or suffers from mental disorder of any kind or is substantially and permanently handicapped by illness, injury or congenital deformity or such other disability as may be prescribed by regulations made under section 17 of the Children Act 1989 (provision of services for children in need, their families and others);

"claim for asylum" means a claim that it would be contrary to the United Kingdom's obligations under the Refugee Convention for the claimant to be removed from, or required to leave, the United Kingdom;

"Common Travel Area" means the United Kingdom, the Channel Islands, the Isle of Man and the Republic of Ireland collectively;

"designated course" means a course of any kind designated by regulations made by the Secretary of State for the purposes of paragraph 10 of Schedule 1 to the 1985 Act (student lettings which are not secure tenancies);

"development" means physical, intellectual, emotional, social or behavioural development;

"educational establishment" means a university or institution which provides further education or higher education (or both); and for the purposes of this definition "further education" has the same meaning as in section 2 of the Education Act 1996 (definition of further education) and "higher education" means education provided by means of a course of any description mentioned in Schedule 6 to the Education Reform Act 1988 (courses of higher education);

"family", in relation to a child in need, includes any person who has parental responsibility for the child and any other person with whom he has been living;

"full-time course" means a course normally involving not less than 15 hours attendance a week in term time for the organised day-time study of a single subject or related subjects;

"health" means physical or mental health;

"the immigration rules" means the rules laid down as mentioned in section 3(2) of the 1971 Act (general provisions for regulation and control);

"limited leave" means leave under the 1971 Act to enter or remain in the United Kingdom which is limited as to duration;

"the Refugee Convention" means the Convention relating to the Status of Refugees done at Geneva on 28th July 1951 as extended by Article 1(2) of the Protocol relating to the Status of Refugees done at New York on 31st January 1967;

"specified education institution" means—

    (a)   a university or other institution within the higher education sector within the meaning of section 91(5) of the Further and Higher Education Act 1992 (interpretation of Education Acts), in respect of a university or other institution in England, or section 56(2) of the Further and Higher Education (Scotland) Act 1992 (interpretation of Part II), in respect of a university or other institution in Scotland;

    (b)   an institution in England within the further education sector within the meaning of section 91(3) of the Further and Higher Education Act 1992;

    (c)   a college of further education in Scotland which is under the management of an education authority or which is managed by a board of management in terms of Part I of the Further and Higher Education (Scotland) Act 1992 (further education in Scotland);

    (d)   a central institution in Scotland within the meaning of section 135(1) of the Education (Scotland) Act 1980 (interpretation);

    (e)   an institution in England which provides a course qualifying for funding under Part I of the Education Act 1994 (teaching training);

    (f)   a higher education institution in Northern Ireland within the meaning of Article 30(3) of the Education and Libraries (Northern Ireland) Order 1993 (funding by Department of higher education); or

(g) an institution of further education in Northern Ireland within the meaning of Article 3 of the Further Education (Northern Ireland) Order 1997 (definition of "further education").

Initial Commencement
Specified date: 3 April 2000: see art 1(1).

Extent
This Order does not extend to Wales: see para (2) above.

3   Housing authority accommodation—England, Scotland and Northern Ireland

The following are classes of persons specified for the purposes of section 118(1) of the 1999 Act (housing authority accommodation) in respect of England, Scotland and Northern Ireland—

(a) Class A—a person recorded by the Secretary of State as a refugee within the definition in Article 1 of the Refugee Convention;

(b) Class B—a person—
  (i) who has been granted by the Secretary of State exceptional leave to enter or remain in the United Kingdom outside the provisions of the immigration rules; and
  (ii) whose leave is not subject to a condition requiring him to maintain and accommodate himself, and any person who is dependent on him, without recourse to public funds;

(c) Class C—a person who has current leave to enter or remain in the United Kingdom which is not subject to any limitation or condition and who is habitually resident in the Common Travel Area other than a person—
  (i) who has been given leave to enter or remain in the United Kingdom upon an undertaking given by another person (his "sponsor") in writing in pursuance of the immigration rules to be responsible for his maintenance and accommodation;
  (ii) who has been resident in the United Kingdom for less than five years beginning on the date of entry or the date on which the undertaking was given in respect of him, whichever date is the later; and
  (iii) whose sponsor or, where there is more than one sponsor, at least one of whose sponsors, is still alive;

(d) Class D—a person who left the territory of Montserrat after 1st November 1995 because of the effect on that territory of a volcanic eruption;

(e) Class E—a person who is—
  (i) a national of a state which has ratified the European Convention on Social and Medical Assistance done at Paris on 11th December 1953 or a state which has ratified the European Social Charter done at Turin on 18th October 1961;
  (ii) lawfully present in the United Kingdom; and
  (iii) habitually resident in the Common Travel Area;

(f) Class F—a person who is attending a full-time course at a specified education institution in a case where the housing accommodation which is or may be provided to him—
  (i) is let by a housing authority to that specified education institution for the purposes of enabling that institution to provide accommodation for students attending a full-time course at that institution; and
  (ii) would otherwise be difficult for that housing authority to let on terms which, in the opinion of the housing authority, are satisfactory.

Initial Commencement
Specified date: 3 April 2000: see art 1(1).

4   Housing authority accommodation—England

(1)   The following are classes of persons specified for the purposes of section 118(1) of the 1999 Act in respect of England—

(a)   Class G—a person who is owed a duty under section 21 of the National Assistance Act 1948 (duty of local authorities to provide accommodation);

(b)   Class H—a person who is either a child in need or a member of the family of a child in need;

(c)   Class I—a person—

(i)   who is owed a duty under section 63(1) (interim duty to accommodate in case of apparent priority need), 65(2) or (3) (duties to persons found to be homeless) or 68(1) or (2) (duties to persons whose applications are referred) of the 1985 Act;

(ii)   who is owed a duty under section 188(1) (interim duty to accommodate in case of apparent priority need), 190(2) (duties to persons becoming homeless intentionally), 193(2) (duty to persons with priority need who are not homeless intentionally), 195(2) (duties in case of threatened homelessness) or 200(1), (3) or (4) (duties to applicant whose case is considered for referral or referred) of the Housing Act 1996; or

(iii)   in respect of whom a local housing authority are exercising their power under section 194(1) (power exercisable after minimum period of duty under section 193) of the Housing Act 1996;

(d)   Class J—an asylum-seeker to whom, or a dependant of an asylum-seeker to whom, a local authority is required to provide support in accordance with regulations made under Schedule 9 to the 1999 Act (asylum support: interim provisions);

(e)   Class K—a person who is attending a designated course, which is a full-time course, at an educational establishment in a case where the housing accommodation which is or may be provided to him by a local housing authority—

(i)   is not and will not be let to him as a secure tenancy by virtue of paragraph 10 of Schedule 1 to the 1985 Act (student lettings which are not secure tenancies); and

(ii)   would otherwise be difficult for that local housing authority to let on terms which, in the opinion of the local housing authority, are satisfactory;

(f)   Class L—a person who has a secure tenancy within the meaning of section 79 of the 1985 Act (secure tenancies).

(2)   "Dependant", in relation to an asylum-seeker within paragraph (1)(d) (Class J), means a person in the United Kingdom who—

(a)   is his spouse;

(b)   is a child of his, or of his spouse, who is under 18 and dependent on him; or

(c)   falls within such additional category as may be prescribed under section 94(1) of the 1999 Act (interpretation of Part VI—support for asylum-seekers), for the purposes of regulations made under Schedule 9 to the 1999 Act (asylum support: interim provisions), in relation to an asylum-seeker.

Initial Commencement
Specified date: 3 April 2000: see art 1(1).

5   Housing authority accommodation—Northern Ireland

The following are classes of persons specified for the purposes of section 118(1) of the 1999 Act in respect of Northern Ireland—

   (a)   Class M—a person who is a secure tenant of the Northern Ireland Housing Executive or a registered housing association within the meaning of Article 25 of the Housing (Northern Ireland) Order 1983 (secure tenancies);

   (b)   Class N—a person who is owed a duty under Article 8 (interim duty to accommodate in case of apparent priority need), 10(2) or (3) (duties to persons found to be homeless) or 11(2) (duties to persons found to be threatened with homelessness) of the Housing (Northern Ireland) Order 1988.

Initial Commencement
Specified date: 3 April 2000: see art 1(1).

6   Housing authority accommodation—Scotland

The following are classes of persons specified for the purposes of section 118(1) of the 1999 Act in respect of Scotland—

   (a)   Class O—a person who is a secure tenant within the meaning of Part III of the Housing (Scotland) Act 1987 (rights of public sector tenants);

   (b)   Class P—a person who is owed a duty under section 29 (interim duty to accommodate in case of apparent priority need), 31 (duties to persons found to be homeless), 32 (duties to persons found to be threatened with homelessness) or 34 (duties to persons whose applications are referred to another local authority) of the Housing (Scotland) Act 1987.

Initial Commencement
Specified date: 3 April 2000: see art 1(1).

7   Homelessness—Scotland and Northern Ireland

(1)   The following are classes of persons specified for the purposes of section 119(1) of the 1999 Act (homelessness: Scotland and Northern Ireland) in respect of Scotland and Northern Ireland—

   (a)   the classes specified in article 3(a) to (e) (Class A, Class B, Class C, Class D and Class E);

   (b)   Class Q—a person who is an asylum-seeker and who made a claim for asylum—

      (i)   which is recorded by the Secretary of State as having been made on his arrival (other than on re-entry) in the United Kingdom from a country outside the Common Travel Area; and

      (ii) which has not been recorded by the Secretary of State as having been either decided (other than on appeal) or abandoned;

   (c)   Class R—a person who is an asylum-seeker and—

      (i)   who made a relevant claim for asylum on or before 4th February 1996; and

      (ii) who was, on 4th February 1996, entitled to benefit under regulation 7A of the Housing Benefit (General) Regulations 1987 (persons from abroad) or regulation 7A of the Housing Benefit (General) Regulations (Northern Ireland) 1987 (persons from abroad).

(2)   In paragraph (1)(c)(i), a relevant claim for asylum is a claim for asylum which—

   (a)   has not been recorded by the Secretary of State as having been either decided (other than on appeal) or abandoned; or

   (b)   has been recorded as having been decided (other than on appeal) on or before 4th February 1996 and in respect of which an appeal is pending which—

      (i)   was pending on 5th February 1996; or

      (ii) was made within the time limits specified in the rules of procedure made under section 22 of the 1971 Act (procedure).

Appendix 1   Legislation and materials

Initial Commencement
Specified date: 3 April 2000: see art 1(1).

8   Homelessness—Northern Ireland

(1)   The following are classes of persons specified for the purposes of section 119(1) of the 1999 Act in respect of Northern Ireland—

   [(a)   Class S—a person who is on an income-based jobseeker's allowance or in receipt of income support and is eligible for that benefit other than because—

      (i)   he has limited leave to enter or remain in the United Kingdom which was given in accordance with the relevant immigration rules and he is temporarily without funds because remittances to him from abroad have been disrupted; or

      (ii)   he has been deemed by regulation 3 of the Displaced Persons (Temporary Protection) Regulations 2005 to have been granted leave to enter or remain in the United Kingdom exceptionally for the purposes of the provision of means of subsistence;]

   (b)   Class T—a person who is an asylum-seeker and—

      (i)   who was in Northern Ireland when the Secretary of State made a declaration to the effect that the country of which that person is a national is subject to such a fundamental change in circumstances that he would not normally order the return of a person to that country;

      (ii)   who made a claim for asylum which is recorded by the Secretary of State as having been made within a period of three months from the day on which that declaration was made; and

      (iii)   whose claim for asylum has not been recorded by the Secretary of State as having been either decided (other than on appeal) or abandoned.

(2)   For the purposes of paragraph (1)(a) (Class S)—

   (a)   "an income-based jobseeker's allowance" means a jobseeker's allowance which is payable under the Jobseekers (Northern Ireland) Order 1995 and entitlement to which is based on the claimant satisfying conditions which include those set out in Article 5 of that Order (the income-based conditions);

   (b)   "income support" has the same meaning as in section 123 of the Social Security Contributions and Benefits (Northern Ireland) Act 1992 (income support);

   (c)   "relevant immigration rules" means the immigration rules relating to—

      (i)   there being or there needing to be no recourse to public funds; or

      (ii)   there being no charge on public funds; and

   (d)   a person is on an income-based jobseeker's allowance on any day in respect of which an income-based jobseeker's allowance is payable to him and on any day—

      (i)   in respect of which he satisfies the conditions for entitlement to an income-based jobseeker's allowance but where the allowance is not paid in accordance with Article 21 of the Jobseekers (Northern Ireland) Order 1995 (circumstances in which a jobseeker's allowance is not payable); or

      (ii)   which is a waiting day for the purposes of paragraph 4 of Schedule 1 to that Order (waiting days) and which falls immediately before a day in respect of which an income-based jobseeker's allowance is payable to him or would be payable to him but for Article 21 of that Order.

[(3)   In paragraph (1)(a) (Class S), "means of subsistence" has the same meaning as in regulation 4 of the Displaced Persons (Temporary Protection) Regulations 2005.]

Initial Commencement
Specified date: 3 April 2000: see art 1(1).

Amendment
Para (1): sub-para (a) substituted by SI 2005/1379, Schedule, paras 10, 11. Date in force: 15 June 2005: see SI 2005/1379, reg 1.
Para (3): inserted by SI 2005/1379, Schedule, paras 10, 12. Date in force: 15 June 2005: see SI 2005/1379, reg 1.

9 Homelessness—Scotland

(1) The following are classes of persons specified for the purposes of section 119(1) of the 1999 Act in respect of Scotland—

[(a) Class U—a person who is on an income-based jobseeker's allowance or in receipt of income support and is eligible for that benefit other than because—
  (i) he has limited leave to enter or remain in the United Kingdom which was given in accordance with the relevant immigration rules and he is temporarily without funds because remittances to him from abroad have been disrupted; or
  (ii) he has been deemed by regulation 3 of the Displaced Persons (Temporary Protection) Regulations 2005 to have been granted leave to enter or remain in the United Kingdom exceptionally for the purposes of the provision of means of subsistence;]
(b) Class V—a person who is an asylum-seeker and—
  (i) who was in Great Britain when the Secretary of State made a declaration to the effect that the country of which that person is a national is subject to such a fundamental change in circumstances that he would not normally order the return of a person to that country;
  (ii) who made a claim for asylum which is recorded by the Secretary of State as having been made within a period of three months from the day on which that declaration was made; and
  (iii) whose claim for asylum has not been recorded by the Secretary of State as having been either decided (other than on appeal) or abandoned.

(2) For the purposes of paragraph (1)(a) (Class U)—

(a) "an income-based jobseeker's allowance" means a jobseeker's allowance which is payable under the 1995 Act and entitlement to which is based on the claimant satisfying conditions which include those set out in section 3 of the 1995 Act (the income-based conditions);
(b) "income support" has the same meaning as in section 124 of the Social Security Contributions and Benefits Act 1992 (income support);
(c) "relevant immigration rules" means the immigration rules relating to—
  (i) there being or there needing to be no recourse to public funds; or
  (ii) there being no charge on public funds; and
(d) a person is on an income-based jobseeker's allowance on any day in respect of which an income-based jobseeker's allowance is payable to him and on any day—
  (i) in respect of which he satisfies the conditions for entitlement to an income-based jobseeker's allowance but where the allowance is not paid in accordance with section 19 of the 1995 Act (circumstances in which jobseeker's allowance is not payable); or
  (ii) which is a waiting day for the purposes of paragraph 4 of Schedule 1 to the 1995 Act (waiting days) and which falls immediately before a day in respect of which an income-based jobseeker's allowance is payable to him or would be payable to him but for section 19 of the 1995 Act;
[(e) in paragraph (1)(a) (Class U), "means of subsistence" has the same meaning as in regulation 4 of the Displaced Persons (Temporary Protection) Regulations 2005].

Initial Commencement
Specified date: 3 April 2000: see art 1(1).

Amendment
Para (1): sub-para (a) substituted by SI 2005/1379, Schedule, paras 10, 13. Date in force: 15 June 2005: see SI 2005/1379, reg 1.
Para (2): sub-para (e) inserted by SI 2005/1379, Schedule, paras 10, 14. Date in force: 15 June 2005: see SI 2005/1379, reg 1.

10   Revocation

The following Orders are revoked—

 (a) the Housing Accommodation and Homelessness (Persons subject to Immigration Control) Order 1996, in so far as it extends to England and Scotland;
 (b) the Homelessness (Persons subject to Immigration Control) (Amendment) Order 1997, in so far as it extends to England and Scotland;
 (c) the Housing Accommodation and Homelessness (Persons subject to Immigration Control) (Amendment) Order 1998, in so far as it extends to England;
 (d) the Housing Accommodation and Homelessness (Persons subject to Immigration Control) (Northern Ireland) Order 1998;
 (e) the Housing Accommodation and Homelessness (Persons subject to Immigration Control) (Amendment) (Scotland) Order 1999; and
 (f) the Housing Accommodation (Persons subject to Immigration Control) (Amendment) (England) Order 1999.

Initial Commencement
Specified date: 3 April 2000: see art 1(1).

Extent
This Order does not extend to Wales: see art 1(2).

IMMIGRATION (PASSENGER INFORMATION) ORDER 2000

2000 No 912

Made . . . . *29th March 2000*

Laid before Parliament . . . . *6th April 2000*

Coming into force . . . . *28th April 2000*

The Secretary of State, in exercise of the powers conferred upon him by paragraph 27B(9) and (10) of Schedule 2 to the Immigration Act 1971, hereby makes the following Order:

1

This Order may be cited as the Immigration (Passenger Information) Order 2000 and shall come into force on 28th April 2000.

Initial Commencement
Specified date: 28 April 2000: see above.

2

(1)   Subject to paragraph (2), the information listed in the Schedule to this Order is specified for the purposes of paragraph 27B(9) of Schedule 2 to the Immigration Act 1971 (definition of "passenger information").

(2)   The information listed in Part II of the Schedule to this Order is so specified only to the extent that it is known to the carrier.

Initial Commencement
Specified date: 28 April 2000: see art 1.

SCHEDULE
PASSENGER INFORMATION

Article 2

PART I
INFORMATION RELATING TO A PASSENGER AS GIVEN ON OR SHOWN BY THE PASSENGER'S PASSPORT OR OTHER TRAVEL DOCUMENT

Full name.
Gender.
Date of birth.
Nationality.
The type of travel document held by the passenger and its number.
If the passenger has a United Kingdom visa or other form of United Kingdom entry clearance, its expiry date.

Initial Commencement
Specified date: 28 April 2000: see art 1.

PART II
OTHER INFORMATION RELATING TO A PASSENGER

Name as it appears on the passenger's reservation.
Ticket number.
Date and place of issue of the ticket.
If not the carrier, the identity of the person who made the passenger's reservation on behalf of the carrier.
Method of payment for the ticket.
Travel itinerary.
Names of all other passengers appearing on the passenger's reservation.
If the passenger is travelling with a car or other vehicle, the vehicle registration number and, if the vehicle has a trailer, the trailer registration number (if different to the vehicle registration number).

Initial Commencement
Specified date: 28 April 2000: see art 1.

PERSONS SUBJECT TO IMMIGRATION CONTROL (HOUSING AUTHORITY ACCOMMODATION) (WALES) ORDER 2000

2000 No 1036

Made . . . . *30th March 2000*

Coming into force . . . . *1st April 2000*

The National Assembly for Wales makes the following Order in exercise of the powers conferred on the Secretary of State by sections 118 and 166(3) of the Immigration and Asylum Act 1999 which are vested in the National Assembly for Wales so far as exercisable in Wales.

1 Citation, commencement and application

(1) This Order may be cited as the Persons Subject to Immigration Control (Housing Authority Accommodation) (Wales) Order 2000 and shall come into force on 1st April 2000.

(2) This Order applies to Wales only.

Initial Commencement
Specified date: 1 April 2000: see para (1) above.

2 Housing authority accommodation

The classes of persons specified in Articles 3 and 4 of the Persons subject to Immigration Control (Housing Authority Accommodation and Homelessness) Order 2000 are specified for the purposes of Section 118(1) of the Immigration and Asylum Act 1999 in relation to Wales and expressions used in those Articles have the meaning given to them by Article 2 of that Order.

Initial Commencement
Specified date: 1 April 2000: see art 1(1).

3 Revocation

The Housing Accommodation (Persons Subject to Immigration Control) (Amendment) (Wales) Order 1999 is revoked and the orders specified in paragraphs (a), (b) and (c) of Article 10 of the Persons Subject to Immigration Control (Housing Authority Accommodation and Homelessness) Order 2000 are revoked in relation to Wales.

Initial Commencement
Specified date: 1 April 2000: see art 1(1).

IMMIGRATION (LEAVE TO ENTER AND REMAIN) ORDER 2000

2000 No 1161

Made . . . . *19th April 2000*

Coming into force
Articles 1 to 12, 14 and 15(1) in accordance with article 1(2)
Articles 13 and 15(2) . . . . *30th July 2000*

Whereas a draft of this Order has been laid before Parliament and approved by a resolution of each House in accordance with sections 3A(13) and 3B(6) of the Immigration Act 1971;

Now, therefore, the Secretary of State, in exercise of the powers conferred upon him by sections 3A(1), (2), (3), (4), (6) and (10) and 3B(2)(a) and (c) and (3)(a) of the Immigration Act 1971, hereby makes the following Order:

PART I
GENERAL

1   Citation, commencement and interpretation

(1)   This Order may be cited as the Immigration (Leave to Enter and Remain) Order 2000.

(2)   Articles 1 to 12, 14 and 15(1) of this Order shall come into force on 28th April 2000 or, if later, on the day after the day on which it is made and articles 13 and 15(2) shall come into force on 30th July 2000.

(3)   In this Order—

"the Act" means the Immigration Act 1971;
"control port" means a port in which a control area is designated under paragraph 26(3) of Schedule 2 to the Act;
["convention travel document" means a travel document issued pursuant to Article 28 of the Refugee Convention, except where that travel document was issued by the United Kingdom Government;]
"the Immigration Acts" means:
    (a)   the Act;
    (b)   the Immigration Act 1988;
    (c)   the Asylum and Immigration Appeals Act 1993;
    (d)   the Asylum and Immigration Act 1996; and
    (e)   the Immigration and Asylum Act 1999;
["Refugee Convention" means the Convention relating to the Status of Refugees done at Geneva on 28th July 1951 and its Protocol;]
"responsible third party" means a person appearing to an immigration officer to be:
    (a)   in charge of a group of people arriving in the United Kingdom together or intending to arrive in the United Kingdom together;
    (b)   a tour operator;
    (c)   the owner or agent of a ship, aircraft, train, hydrofoil or hovercraft;
    (d)   the person responsible for the management of a control port or his agent; or
    (e)   an official at a British Diplomatic Mission or at a British Consular Post or at the office of any person outside the United Kingdom and Islands who has been authorised by the Secretary of State to accept applications for entry clearance;

"tour operator" means a person who, otherwise than occasionally, organises and provides holidays to the public or a section of it; and

"visit visa" means an entry clearance granted for the purpose of entry to the United Kingdom as a visitor under the immigration rules.

Initial Commencement
Specified date: 28 April 2000: see para (2) above.

Amendment
Para (3): definition "convention travel document" inserted by SI 2004/475, arts 2, 3(a). Date in force: 27 February 2004: see SI 2004/475, art 1.
Para (3): definition "Refugee Convention" inserted by SI 2004/475, arts 2, 3(b). Date in force: 27 February 2004: see SI 2004/475, art 1.

PART II
ENTRY CLEARANCE AS LEAVE TO ENTER

2   Entry clearance as Leave to Enter

Subject to article 6(3), an entry clearance which complies with the requirements of article 3 shall have effect as leave to enter the United Kingdom to the extent specified in article 4, but subject to the conditions referred to in article 5.

Initial Commencement
Specified date: 28 April 2000: see art 1(2).

3   Requirements

[(1)   Subject to paragraph (4), an entry clearance shall only have effect as leave to enter if it complies with the requirements of this article.]

(2)   The entry clearance must specify the purpose for which the holder wishes to enter the United Kingdom.

(3)   The entry clearance must be endorsed with:

(a)   the conditions to which it is subject; or
(b)   a statement that it is to have effect as indefinite leave to enter the United Kingdom.

[(4)   Subject to paragraph (5), an entry clearance shall not have effect as leave to enter if it is endorsed on a convention travel document.

(5)   An entry clearance endorsed on a convention travel document before 27th February 2004 shall have effect as leave to enter.]

Initial Commencement
Specified date: 28 April 2000: see art 1(2).

Amendment
Para (1): substituted by SI 2004/475, arts 2, 4(a). Date in force: 27 February 2004: see SI 2004/475, art 1.
Paras (4), (5): inserted by SI 2004/475, arts 2, 4(b). Date in force: 27 February 2004: see SI 2004/475, art 1.

4   Extent to which Entry Clearance is to be Leave to Enter

(1)   A visit visa, during its period of validity, shall have effect as leave to enter the United Kingdom on an unlimited number of occasions, in accordance with paragraph (2).

(2) On each occasion the holder arrives in the United Kingdom, he shall be treated for the purposes of the Immigration Acts as having been granted, before arrival, leave to enter the United Kingdom for a limited period beginning on the date of arrival, being:

    (a) six months if six months or more remain of the visa's period of validity; or

    (b) the visa's remaining period of validity, if less than six months.

(3) In the case of any other form of entry clearance, it shall have effect as leave to enter the United Kingdom on one occasion during its period of validity; and, on arrival in the United Kingdom, the holder shall be treated for the purposes of the Immigration Acts as having been granted, before arrival, leave to enter the United Kingdom:

    (a) in the case of an entry clearance which is endorsed with a statement that it is to have effect as indefinite leave to enter the United Kingdom, for an indefinite period; or

    (b) in the case of an entry clearance which is endorsed with conditions, for a limited period, being the period beginning on the date on which the holder arrives in the United Kingdom and ending on the date of expiry of the entry clearance.

(4) In this article "period of validity" means the period beginning on the day on which the entry clearance becomes effective and ending on the day on which it expires.

Initial Commencement
Specified date: 28 April 2000: see art 1(2).

Modification
Modified, in its application to the Channel Tunnel, by the Channel Tunnel (International Arrangements) Order 1993, SI 1993/1813, art 7(1), Sch 4, para 4.

5 Conditions

An entry clearance shall have effect as leave to enter subject to any conditions, being conditions of a kind that may be imposed on leave to enter given under section 3 of the Act, to which the entry clearance is subject and which are endorsed on it.

Initial Commencement
Specified date: 28 April 2000: see art 1(2).

6 Incidental, supplementary and consequential provisions

(1) Where an immigration officer exercises his power to cancel leave to enter under paragraph 2A(8) of Schedule 2 to the Act or article 13(7) below in respect of an entry clearance which has effect as leave to enter, the entry clearance shall cease to have effect.

(2) If the holder of an entry clearance—

    (a) arrives in the United Kingdom before the day on which it becomes effective; or

    (b) seeks to enter the United Kingdom for a purpose other than the purpose specified in the entry clearance,

an immigration officer may cancel the entry clearance.

(3) If the holder of an entry clearance which does not, at the time, have effect as leave to enter the United Kingdom seeks leave to enter the United Kingdom at any time before his departure for, or in the course of his journey to, the United Kingdom and is refused leave to enter under article 7, the entry clearance shall not have effect as leave to enter.

Appendix 1   Legislation and materials

Initial Commencement
Specified date: 28 April 2000: see art 1(2).

Modification
Modified, in its application to the Channel Tunnel, by the Channel Tunnel (International Arrangements) Order 1993, SI 1993/1813, art 7(1), Sch 4, para 4.

PART III

FORM AND MANNER OF GIVING AND REFUSING LEAVE TO ENTER

7   Grant and refusal of leave to enter before arrival in the United Kingdom

(1)   An immigration officer, whether or not in the United Kingdom, may give or refuse a person leave to enter the United Kingdom at any time before his departure for, or in the course of his journey to, the United Kingdom.

(2)   In order to determine whether or not to give leave to enter under this article (and, if so, for what period and subject to what conditions), an immigration officer may seek such information, and the production of such documents or copy documents, as an immigration officer would be entitled to obtain in an examination under paragraph 2 or 2A of Schedule 2 to the Act.

(3)   An immigration officer may also require the person seeking leave to supply an up to date medical report.

(4)   Failure by a person seeking leave to supply any information, documents, copy documents or medical report requested by an immigration officer under this article shall be a ground, in itself, for refusal of leave.

Initial Commencement
Specified date: 28 April 2000: see art 1(2).

8   Grant or refusal of leave otherwise than by notice in writing

(1)   A notice giving or refusing leave to enter may, instead of being given in writing as required by section 4(1) of the Act, be given as follows.

(2)   The notice may be given by facsimile or electronic mail.

(3)   In the case of a notice giving or refusing leave to enter the United Kingdom as a visitor, it may be given orally, including by means of a telecommunications system.

(4)   In paragraph (3), "leave to enter the United Kingdom as a visitor" means leave to enter as a visitor under the immigration rules for a period not exceeding six months, subject to conditions prohibiting employment and recourse to public funds (within the meaning of the immigration rules).

Initial Commencement
Specified date: 28 April 2000: see art 1(2).

9   Grant or refusal of leave by notice to a responsible third party

(1)   Leave to enter may be given or refused to a person by means of a notice given (in such form and manner as permitted by the Act or this Order for a notice giving or refusing leave to enter) to a responsible third party acting on his behalf.

(2)   A notice under paragraph (1) may refer to a person to whom leave is being granted or refused either by name or by reference to a description or category of persons which includes him.

Initial Commencement
Specified date: 28 April 2000: see art 1(2).

10   Notice of refusal of leave

(1)   Where a notice refusing leave to enter to a person is given under article 8(3) or 9, an immigration officer shall as soon as practicable give to him a notice in writing stating that he has been refused leave to enter the United Kingdom and stating the reasons for the refusal.

(2)   Where an immigration officer serves a notice under the Immigration (Appeals) Notices Regulations 1984 or under regulations made under paragraph 1 of Schedule 4 to the Immigration and Asylum Act 1999 in respect of the refusal, he shall not be required to serve a notice under paragraph (1).

(3)   Any notice required by paragraph (1) to be given to any person may be delivered, or sent by post to—

    (a)   that person's last known or usual place of abode; or
    (b)   any address provided by him for receipt of the notice.

Initial Commencement
Specified date: 28 April 2000: see art 1(2).

11   Burden of proof

Where any question arises under the Immigration Acts as to whether a person has leave to enter the United Kingdom and he alleges that he has such leave by virtue of a notice given under article 8(3) or 9, the onus shall lie upon him to show the manner and date of his entry into the United Kingdom.

Initial Commencement
Specified date: 28 April 2000: see art 1(2).

12

(1)   This article applies where—

    (a)   an immigration officer has commenced examination of a person ("the applicant") under paragraph 2(1)(c) of Schedule 2 to the Act (examination to determine whether or not leave to enter should be given);
    (b)   that examination has been adjourned, or the applicant has been required (under paragraph 2(3) of Schedule 2 to the Act) to submit to a further examination, whilst further inquiries are made (including, where the applicant has made an asylum claim, as to the Secretary of State's decision on that claim); and
    (c)   upon the completion of those inquiries, an immigration officer considers he is in a position to decide whether or not to give or refuse leave to enter without interviewing the applicant further.

(2)   Where this article applies, any notice giving or refusing leave to enter which is on any date thereafter sent by post to the applicant (or is communicated to him in such form or manner as is permitted by this Order) shall be regarded, for the purposes of the Act, as having been given within the period of 24 hours specified in paragraph 6(1) of Schedule 2 to the Act (period within which notice giving or refusing leave to enter must be given after completion of examination).

Initial Commencement
Specified date: 28 April 2000: see art 1(2).

PART IV
LEAVE WHICH DOES NOT LAPSE ON TRAVEL OUTSIDE COMMON TRAVEL AREA

13

(1)   In this article "leave" means—

(a)   leave to enter the United Kingdom (including leave to enter conferred by means of an entry clearance under article 2); and
(b)   leave to remain in the United Kingdom.

(2)   Subject to paragraph (3), where a person has leave which is in force and which was:

(a)   conferred by means of an entry clearance (other than a visit visa) under article 2; or
(b)   given by an immigration officer or the Secretary of State for a period exceeding six months,

such leave shall not lapse on his going to a country or territory outside the common travel area.

(3)   Paragraph (2) shall not apply:

(a)   where a limited leave has been varied by the Secretary of State; and
(b)   following the variation the period of leave remaining is six months or less.

(4)   Leave which does not lapse under paragraph (2) shall remain in force either indefinitely (if it is unlimited) or until the date on which it would otherwise have expired (if limited), but—

(a)   where the holder has stayed outside the United Kingdom for a continuous period of more than two years, the leave (where the leave is unlimited) or any leave then remaining (where the leave is limited) shall thereupon lapse; and
(b)   any conditions to which the leave is subject shall be suspended for such time as the holder is outside the United Kingdom.

(5)   For the purposes of paragraphs 2 and 2A of Schedule 2 to the Act (examination by immigration officers, and medical examination), leave to remain which remains in force under this article shall be treated, upon the holder's arrival in the United Kingdom, as leave to enter which has been granted to the holder before his arrival.

(6)   Without prejudice to the provisions of section 4(1) of the Act, where the holder of leave which remains in force under this article is outside the United Kingdom, the Secretary of State may vary that leave (including any conditions to which it is subject) in such form and manner as permitted by the Act or this Order for the giving of leave to enter.

(7)   Where a person is outside the United Kingdom and has leave which is in force by virtue of this article, that leave may be cancelled:

(a)   in the case of leave to enter, by an immigration officer; or
(b)   in the case of leave to remain, by the Secretary of State.

(8)   In order to determine whether or not to vary (and, if so, in what manner) or cancel leave which remains in force under this article and which is held by a person who is outside the United Kingdom, an immigration officer or, as the case may be, the Secretary of State may seek such information, and the production of such documents or copy documents, as an immigration officer would be entitled to obtain in an examination under paragraph 2 or 2A of Schedule 2 to the Act and may also require the holder of the leave to supply an up to date medical report.

(9)   Failure to supply any information, documents, copy documents or medical report requested by an immigration officer or, as the case may be, the Secretary of State under this article shall be a ground, in itself, for cancellation of leave.

(10)   Section 3(4) of the Act (lapsing of leave upon travelling outside the common travel area) shall have effect subject to this article.

Initial Commencement
Specified date: 28 April 2000: see art 1(2).

PART V
CONSEQUENTIAL AND TRANSITIONAL PROVISIONS

14

Section 9(2) of the Act (further provisions as to common travel area: conditions applicable to certain arrivals on a local journey) shall have effect as if, after the words "British Citizens", there were inserted "and do not hold leave to enter or remain granted to them before their arrival".

Initial Commencement
Specified date: 28 April 2000: see art 1(2).

15

(1)   Article 12 shall apply where an applicant's examination has begun before the date that article comes into force, as well as where it begins on or after that date.

(2)   Article 13 shall apply with respect to leave to enter or remain in the United Kingdom which is in force on the date that article comes into force, as well as to such leave given after that date.

Initial Commencement
Para (1): Specified date: 28 April 2000: see art 1(2).
Para (2): Specified date: 30 July 2000: see art 1(2).

IMMIGRATION (REMOVAL DIRECTIONS) REGULATIONS 2000

2000 No 2243

Made . . . . *16th August 2000*

Laid before Parliament . . . . *24th August 2000*

Coming into force . . . . *2nd October 2000*

The Secretary of State, in exercise of the powers conferred upon him by sections 10, 166(3) and 167 of the Immigration and Asylum Act 1999, hereby makes the following Regulations:

1   Citation and commencement

These Regulations may be cited as the Immigration (Removal Directions) Regulations 2000 and shall come into force on 2nd October 2000.

2239

Appendix 1   Legislation and materials

Initial Commencement
Specified date: 2 October 2000: see above.

2   Interpretation

(1)   In these Regulations—

> "the Act" means the Immigration and Asylum Act 1999;
> "aircraft" includes hovercraft;
> "captain" means master (of a ship) or commander (of an aircraft);
> "international service" has the meaning given by section 13(6) of the Channel
> Tunnel Act 1987;
> "ship" includes every description of vessel used in navigation; and
> "the tunnel system" has the meaning given by section 1(7) of the Channel Tunnel
> Act 1987.

(2)   In these Regulations, a reference to a section number is a reference to a section of the Act.

Initial Commencement
Specified date: 2 October 2000: see reg 1.

3   Persons to whom directions may be given

For the purposes of section 10(6)(a) (classes of person to whom directions may be given), the following classes of person are prescribed—

    (a)   owners of ships;
    (b)   owners of aircraft;
    (c)   agents of ships;
    (d)   agents of aircraft;
    (e)   captains of ships about to leave the United Kingdom;
    (f)   captains of aircraft about to leave the United Kingdom; and
    (g)   persons operating an international service.

Initial Commencement
Specified date: 2 October 2000: see reg 1.

4   Requirements that may be imposed by directions

(1)   For the purposes of section 10(6)(b) (requirements that may be imposed by directions), the following kinds of requirements are prescribed—

    (a)   in the case where directions are given to a captain of a ship or aircraft about to leave the United Kingdom, a requirement to remove the relevant person from the United Kingdom in that ship or aircraft;
    (b)   in the case where directions are given to a person operating an international service, a requirement to make arrangements for the removal of the relevant person through the tunnel system;
    (c)   in the case where directions are given to any other person who falls within a class prescribed in regulation 3, a requirement to make arrangements for the removal of the relevant person in a ship or aircraft specified or indicated in the directions; and
    (d)   in all cases, a requirement to remove the relevant person in accordance with arrangements to be made by an immigration officer.

(2)   Paragraph (1) only applies if the directions specify that the relevant person is to be removed to a country or territory being—
        (i)   a country of which he is a national or citizen; or

(ii) a country or territory to which there is reason to believe that he will be admitted.

(3) Paragraph (1)(b) only applies if the relevant person arrived in the United Kingdom through the tunnel system.

(4) "Relevant person" means a person who may be removed from the United Kingdom in accordance with section 10(1).

Initial Commencement
Specified date: 2 October 2000: see reg 1.

ASYLUM (DESIGNATED SAFE THIRD COUNTRIES) ORDER 2000

2000 No 2245

Made . . . . *16th August 2000*

Laid before Parliament . . . . *24th August 2000*

Coming into force . . . . *2nd October 2000*

The Secretary of State, in exercise of the powers conferred upon him by section 12(1)(b) of the Immigration and Asylum Act 1999, hereby makes the following Order:

1

This Order may be cited as the Asylum (Designated Safe Third Countries) Order 2000 and shall come into force on 2nd October 2000.

Initial Commencement
Specified date: 2 October 2000: see above.

2

The Asylum (Designated Countries of Destination and Designated Safe Third Countries) Order 1996 is hereby revoked.

Initial Commencement
Specified date: 2 October 2000: see art 1.

3

The following countries are designated for the purposes of section 12(1)(b) of the Immigration and Asylum Act 1999 (designation of countries other than EU Member States for the purposes of appeal rights):

Canada
Norway
Switzerland
United States of America.

Initial Commencement
Specified date: 2 October 2000: see art 1.

IMMIGRATION (EUROPEAN ECONOMIC AREA) REGULATIONS 2000

2000 No 2326

Made	*30th August 2000*
Laid before Parliament	*1st September 2000*
Coming into force	*2nd October 2000*

The Secretary of State, being a Minister designated for the purposes of section 2(2) of the European Communities Act 1972 in relation to measures relating to rights of entry into, and residence in, the United Kingdom, in exercise of the powers conferred on him by the said section 2(2), and of the powers conferred on him by section 80 of the Immigration and Asylum Act 1999, hereby makes the following Regulations:

PART I
INTERPRETATION ETC

1   Citation, commencement and revocation

(1)   These Regulations may be cited as the Immigration (European Economic Area) Regulations 2000 and shall come into force on 2nd October 2000.

(2)   Subject to paragraph (3), the Immigration (European Economic Area) Order 1994 is hereby revoked.

(3)   Article 19 of the Order continues to have effect until the commencement of the repeal by the 1999 Act of the Immigration (Carriers' Liability) Act 1987.

Initial Commencement
Specified date: 2 October 2000: see para (1) above.

Interpretation of Regulations

2   General

(1)   In these Regulations—

"the 1971 Act" means the Immigration Act 1971;
"the 1999 Act" means the Immigration and Asylum Act 1999;
["the Accession Regulations 2004" means the Accession (Immigration and Worker Registration) Regulations 2004;]
["the 2002 Act" means the Nationality, Immigration and Asylum Act 2002;]
"decision-maker" means the Secretary of State, an immigration officer or an entry clearance officer (as the case may be);
["EEA decision" means a decision under these Regulations, or under Regulation 1251/70, which concerns a person's—
   (a)   removal from the United Kingdom;
   (b)   entitlement to be admitted to the United Kingdom; or
   (c)   entitlement to be issued with or to have renewed, or not to have revoked, a residence permit or residence document;]
"EEA family permit" means a document issued to a person, in accordance with regulation 10 or 13, in connection with his admission to the United Kingdom;
"EEA national" means a national of an EEA State;
["EEA State" means a Member State, other than the United Kingdom, or Norway, Iceland or Liechtenstein;]

"economic activity" means activity as a worker or self-employed person, or as a provider or recipient of services;

"entry clearance officer" means a person responsible for the grant or refusal of entry clearances;

"military service" means service in the armed forces of an EEA State;

"Regulation 1251/70" means Commission Regulation (EEC) No 1251/70 on the right of workers to remain in the territory of a Member State after having been employed in that State;

"residence document" means a document issued to a person who is not an EEA national, in accordance with regulation 10 or 15, as proof of the holder's right of residence in the United Kingdom;

"residence permit" means a permit issued to an EEA national, in accordance with regulation 10 or 15, as proof of the holder's right of residence in the United Kingdom;

"spouse" does not include a party to a marriage of convenience;

"United Kingdom national" means a person who falls to be treated as a national of the United Kingdom for the purposes of the Community Treaties;

"visa national" means a person who requires a visa for the United Kingdom because he is a national or citizen of one of the countries or territorial entities for the time being specified in the immigration rules.

(2)   In these Regulations unless the context otherwise requires a reference to a regulation is a reference to a regulation of these Regulations; and within a regulation a reference to a paragraph is to a paragraph of that regulation.

Initial Commencement
Specified date: 2 October 2000: see reg 1(1).

Amendment
Para (1): definition "the Accession Regulations 2004" inserted by SI 2004/1236, reg 2(1), (2). Date in force: 1 May 2004: see SI 2004/1236, reg 1.
Para (1): definition "the 2002 Act" inserted by SI 2003/549, reg 2(1), (2)(a). Date in force: 1 April 2003: see SI 2003/549, reg 1.
Para (1): definition "EEA decision" inserted by SI 2003/549, reg 2(1), (2)(b). Date in force: 1 April 2003: see SI 2003/549, reg 1.
Para (1): definition "EEA State" substituted by SI 2004/1219, reg 3. Date in force: 1 May 2004: see SI 2004/1219, reg 1(1).

See Further
See further, in relation to the application of this regulation, with modifications, in relation to Swiss nationals, their family members and posted workers: the Immigration (Swiss Free Movement of Persons) (No 3) Regulations 2002, SI 2002/1241, reg 2, Schedule, para 1.

3   "Worker", "self-employed person", "provider" and "recipient" of services, "self-sufficient person", "retired person" and "student"

(1)   In these Regulations—

   (a)   "worker" means a worker within the meaning of Article 39 of the EC Treaty;
   (b)   "self-employed person" means a person who establishes himself in order to pursue activity as a self-employed person in accordance with Article 43 of the EC Treaty, or who seeks to do so;
   (c)   "provider of services" means a person who provides, or seeks to provide, services within the meaning of Article 50 of the EC Treaty;
   (d)   "recipient of services" means a person who receives, or seeks to receive, services within the meaning of Article 50 of the EC Treaty;
   (e)   "self-sufficient person" means a person who—

        (i) has sufficient resources to avoid his becoming a burden on the social assistance system of the United Kingdom; and
      (ii) is covered by sickness insurance in respect of all risks in the United Kingdom;

  (f) "retired person" means a person who—
       (i) has pursued an activity as an employed or self-employed person;
      (ii) is in receipt of—
          (aa) an invalidity or early retirement pension;
          (bb) old age benefits;
          (cc) survivor's benefits; or
          (dd) a pension in respect of an industrial accident or disease;
          sufficient to avoid his becoming a burden on the social security system of the United Kingdom; and
     (iii) is covered by sickness insurance in respect of all risks in the United Kingdom;

  (g) "student" means a person who—
       (i) is enrolled at a recognised educational establishment in the United Kingdom for the principal purpose of following a vocational training course;
      (ii) assures the Secretary of State by means of a declaration, or by such alternative means as he may choose that are at least equivalent, that he has sufficient resources to avoid him becoming a burden on the social assistance system of the United Kingdom; and
     (iii) is covered by sickness insurance in respect of all risks in the United Kingdom.

[(2) For the purposes of paragraph (1)(e), where family members of the person concerned reside in the United Kingdom and their right to so reside is dependent upon their being family members of that person—

  (a) the requirement for that person to have sufficient resources to avoid becoming a burden on the social assistance system of the United Kingdom shall only be satisfied if his resources and those of the family members are sufficient to avoid him and the family members becoming such a burden;
  (b) the requirement for that person to be covered by sickness insurance in respect of all risks in the United Kingdom shall only be satisfied if he and the family members are so covered.

(3) For the purposes of paragraph (1)(f) where family members of the person concerned reside in the United Kingdom and their right to so reside is dependent upon their being family members of that person—

  (a) the requirement for that person to be in receipt of a pension or benefits sufficient to avoid his becoming a burden on the social security system of the United Kingdom shall only be satisfied if that pension or those benefits are sufficient to avoid him and the family members becoming such a burden;
  (b) the requirement for that person to be covered by sickness insurance in respect of all risks in the United Kingdom shall only be satisfied if he and the family members are so covered.

(4) For the purposes of paragraph (1)(g), where family members of the person concerned reside in the United Kingdom and their right to so reside is dependent upon their being family members of that person, the requirement for that person to assure the Secretary of State that he has sufficient resources to avoid him becoming a burden on the social assistance system of the United Kingdom shall only be satisfied if he assures the Secretary of State that his resources and those of the family members are sufficient to avoid him and the family members becoming such a burden.

(5) For the purposes of paragraph (1)(e) and (f) and paragraphs (2) and (3) the resources of the person concerned and, where applicable, any family members are to be regarded as sufficient if they exceed the level below which social assistance might be granted under the United Kingdom benefit system to a United Kingdom national in the same circumstances.]

Initial Commencement
Specified date: 2 October 2000: see reg 1(1).

Amendment
Paras (2)–(5): substituted, for para (2) as originally enacted, by SI 2004/1236, reg 2(1), (3). Date in force: 1 May 2004: see SI 2004/1236, reg 1.

See Further
See further, in relation to the application of this regulation, with modifications, in relation to Swiss nationals, their family members and posted workers: the Immigration (Swiss Free Movement of Persons) (No 3) Regulations 2002, SI 2002/1241, reg 2, Schedule, para 2.

4 "Self-employed person who has ceased activity"

(1) In these Regulations, "self-employed person who has ceased activity" means—

(a) a person who—
  (i) on the day on which he terminates his activity as a self-employed person has reached the age at which he is entitled to a state pension;
  (ii) has pursued such activity in the United Kingdom for at least the twelve months prior to its termination; and
  (iii) has resided continuously in the United Kingdom for more than three years;
(b) a person who—
  (i) has resided continuously in the United Kingdom for more than two years; and
  (ii) has terminated his activity [there] as a self-employed person as a result of a permanent incapacity to work;
(c) a person who—
  (i) has resided and pursued activity as a self-employed person in the United Kingdom;
  (ii) has terminated that activity as a result of a permanent incapacity to work; and
  (iii) such incapacity is the result of an accident at work or an occupational illness which entitles him to a pension payable in whole or in part by the state;
(d) a person who—
  (i) has been continuously resident and continuously active as a self-employed person in the United Kingdom for three years; and
  (ii) is active as a self-employed person in the territory of an EEA State but resides in the United Kingdom and returns to his residence at least once a week.

(2) But, if the person is the spouse of a United Kingdom national—

(a) the conditions as to length of residence and activity in paragraph (1)(a) do not apply; and
(b) the condition as to length of residence in paragraph (1)(b) does not apply.

(3) For the purposes of [paragraph (1)(a), (b) and (c)] periods of activity completed in an EEA State by a person to whom paragraph (1)(d)(ii) applies are to be considered as having been completed in the United Kingdom.

(4)   For the purposes of paragraph (1)—

    (a)   periods of absence from the United Kingdom which do not exceed three months in any year or periods of absence from the United Kingdom on military service are not to be taken into account; and

    (b)   periods of inactivity caused by circumstances outside the control of the self-employed person and periods of inactivity caused by illness or accident are to be treated as periods of activity as a self-employed person.

Initial Commencement
Specified date: 2 October 2000: see reg 1(1).

Amendment
Para (1): in sub-para (b)(ii) word "there" in square brackets inserted by SI 2001/865, regs 2, 3(1). Date in force: 2 April 2001: see SI 2001/865, reg 1.
Para (3): words "paragraph (1)(a), (b) and (c)" in square brackets substituted by SI 2001/865, regs 2, 3(2). Date in force: 2 April 2001: see SI 2001/865, reg 1.

5   "Qualified person"

(1)   In these Regulations, "qualified person" means a person who is an EEA national and in the United Kingdom as—

    (a)   a worker;
    (b)   a self-employed person;
    (c)   a provider of services;
    (d)   a recipient of services;
    (e)   a self-sufficient person;
    (f)   a retired person;
    (g)   a student; or
    (h)   a self-employed person who has ceased activity;

or who is a person to whom paragraph (4) applies.

(2)   A worker does not cease to be a qualified person solely because—

    (a)   he is temporarily incapable of work as a result of illness or accident; or

    (b)   he is involuntarily unemployed, if that fact is duly recorded by the relevant employment office.

(3)   A self-employed person does not cease to be a qualified person solely because he is temporarily incapable of work as a result of illness or accident.

(4)   This paragraph applies to—

    (a)   the family member of a qualified person referred to in paragraph (1)(h), if—
        (i)   the qualified person has died; and
        (ii)   the family member was residing with him in the United Kingdom immediately before his death;

    (b)   the family member of a qualified person referred to in paragraph 1(b) where—
        (i)   the qualified person has died;
        (ii)   the family member resided with him immediately before his death; and
        (iii)   either—
            (aa)   the qualified person had resided continuously in the United Kingdom for at least the two years immediately before his death; or
            (bb)   the death was the result of an accident at work or an occupational disease; or
            (cc)   his surviving spouse is a United Kingdom national.

    (5)   For the purposes of paragraph (4)(b), periods of absence from the United Kingdom which do not exceed three months in any year or periods of absence from the United Kingdom on military service are not to be taken into account.

Initial Commencement
Specified date: 2 October 2000: see reg 1(1).

Amendment
Paras (2)–(5): substituted, for para (2) as originally enacted, by SI 2004/1236, reg 2(1), (3). Date in force: 1 May 2004: see SI 2004/1236, reg 1.

See Further
See further, in relation to the application of this regulation, with modifications, in relation to an accession State worker requiring registration: the Accession (Immigration and Worker Registration) Regulations 2004, SI 2004/1219, reg 5.

6 "Family member"

(1) In these Regulations, paragraphs (2) to (4) apply in order to determine the persons who are family members of another person.

(2) If the other person is a student, the persons are—

    (a)   his spouse; and
    (b)   his dependent children.

[(2A) If the other person has divorced his spouse, the person is his divorced spouse provided she is the primary carer of their dependent child who is under 19 and attending an educational course in the United Kingdom.

(2B) If the other person has ceased to be a qualified person on ceasing to reside in the United Kingdom, the persons are—

    (a)   his spouse or his divorced spouse, provided she is the primary carer of their dependent child who is under 19 and attending an educational course in the United Kingdom; and
    [(b)   descendants of his or of his spouse who are under 21 or are their dependants, provided that they were attending an educational course in the United Kingdom when the qualified person was residing in the United Kingdom and are continuing to attend such a course].

(2C) For the purposes of paragraphs (2A) and (2B), "educational course" means a course within the scope of Article 12 of Regulation (EEC) No 1612/68 of the Council of the European Communities on freedom of movement for workers within the Community.

(2D) For the purposes of these Regulations, a person to whom paragraph (2B) applies shall be treated as the family member of a qualified person, notwithstanding that the other person has ceased to be a qualified person.]

(3) ...

(4) In any other case, the persons are—

    (a)   his spouse;
    (b)   descendants of his or of his spouse who are under 21 or are their dependants;
    (c)   dependent relatives in his ascending line or that of his spouse.

Initial Commencement
Specified date: 2 October 2000: see reg 1(1).

Amendment
Paras (2A)–(2D): inserted by SI 2003/549, reg 2(1), (3). Date in force: 1 April 2003: see SI 2003/549, reg 1.
Para (2B): sub-para (b) substituted by SI 2003/3188, reg 2(1), (2). Date in force: 1 January 2004: see SI 2003/3188, reg 1(1).
Para (3): revoked by SI 2001/865, regs 2, 4. Date in force: 2 April 2001: see SI 2001/865, reg 1.

Appendix 1 Legislation and materials

Interpretation of other legislation

7   Carriers' liability

For the purposes of satisfying a requirement to produce a visa under section 40(1)(b) of the 1999 Act (charges to carriers in respect of passengers without proper documents), a "valid visa of the required kind" includes a family permit or residence document required for admission as a visa national under regulation 12.

Initial Commencement
Specified date: 2 October 2000: see reg 1(1).

See Further
See further, in relation to the application of this regulation, with modifications, in relation to Swiss nationals, their family members and posted workers: the Immigration (Swiss Free Movement of Persons) (No 3) Regulations 2002, SI 2002/1241, reg 2, Schedule, para 3.

8   Persons not subject to restriction on the period for which they may remain

(1)   For the purposes of the 1971 Act and the British Nationality Act 1981, the following are to be regarded as persons who are in the United Kingdom without being subject under the immigration laws to any restriction on the period for which they may remain—

   (a)   a self-employed person who has ceased activity;
   (b)   the family member of such a person who was residing with that person in the United Kingdom immediately before that person ceased his activity in the United Kingdom;
   (c)   a family member to whom regulation 5(4) applies;
   (d)   a person who has rights under Regulation 1251/70;
   (e)   a person who has been granted permission to remain in the United Kingdom indefinitely.

(2)   However, a qualified person or family member who is not mentioned in paragraph (1) is not, by virtue of his status as a qualified person or the family member of a qualified person, to be so regarded for those purposes.

Initial Commencement
Specified date: 2 October 2000: see reg 1(1).

PART II
SCOPE OF REGULATIONS

9   General

Subject to regulations 10 and 11 (and to regulations 24(1), 25(1), 26(1)[, 28 and 33]) these Regulations apply solely to EEA nationals and their family members.

Initial Commencement
Specified date: 2 October 2000: see reg 1(1).

Amendment
Words ", 28 and 33" in square brackets substituted by SI 2003/549, reg 2(1). (4). Date in force: 1 April 2003: see SI 2003/549, reg 1.

See Further
See further, in relation to the application of this regulation, with modifications, in relation to Swiss nationals, their family members and posted workers: the Immigration (Swiss Free Movement of Persons) (No 3) Regulations 2002, SI 2002/1241, reg 2, Schedule, para 4.

10   Dependants and members of the household of EEA nationals

(1) If a person satisfies any of the conditions in paragraph (4), and if in all the circumstances it appears to the decision-maker appropriate to do so, the decision-maker may issue to that person an EEA family permit, a residence permit or a residence document (as the case may be).

(2) Where a permit or document has been issued under paragraph (1), these Regulations apply to the holder of the permit or document as if he were the family member of an EEA national and the permit or document had been issued to him under regulation 13 or 15.

(3) Without prejudice to regulation 22, a decision-maker may revoke (or refuse to renew) a permit or document issued under paragraph (1) if he decides that the holder no longer satisfies any of the conditions in paragraph (4).

(4) The conditions are that the person [is a relative of an EEA national or his spouse and]—

  (a) is dependent on the EEA national or his spouse;
  (b) is living as part of the EEA national's household outside the United Kingdom; or
  (c) was living as part of the EEA national's household before the EEA national came to the United Kingdom.

(5) However, for those purposes "EEA national" does not include—

  (a) an EEA national who is in the United Kingdom as a self-sufficient person, a retired person or a student;
  (b) an EEA national who, when he is in the United Kingdom, will be a person referred to in sub-paragraph (a).

Initial Commencement
Specified date: 2 October 2000: see reg 1(1).

Amendment
Para (4): words "is a relative of an EEA national or his spouse and" in square brackets inserted by SI 2001/865, regs 2, 5. Date in force: 2 April 2001: see SI 2001/865, reg 1.

See Further
See further, in relation to the application of this regulation, with modifications, in relation to Swiss nationals, their family members and posted workers: the Immigration (Swiss Free Movement of Persons) (No 3) Regulations 2002, SI 2002/1241, reg 2, Schedule, para 5.

11   Family members of United Kingdom nationals

(1) If the conditions in paragraph (2) are satisfied, these Regulations apply to a person who is the family member of a United Kingdom national returning to the United Kingdom as if that person were the family member of an EEA national.

(2) The conditions are that—

  (a) after leaving the United Kingdom, the United Kingdom national resided in an EEA State and—
    (i) was employed there (other than on a transient or casual basis); or
    (ii) established himself there as a self-employed person;
  [(b) the family member of the United Kingdom national is lawfully resident in an EEA State;]
  (c) on his return to the United Kingdom, the United Kingdom national would, if he were an EEA national, be a qualified person; and

(d) if the family member of the United Kingdom national is his spouse, the marriage took place, and the parties lived together in an EEA State, before the United Kingdom national returned to the United Kingdom.

Initial Commencement
Specified date: 2 October 2000: see reg 1(1).

Amendment
Para (2): sub-para (b) substituted by SI 2005/47, reg 2(1), (2). Date in force: 7 February 2005: see SI 2005/47, reg 1; for transitional provisions see reg 3(1) thereof.

PART III

EEA RIGHTS

12   Right of admission to the United Kingdom

(1) Subject to regulation 21(1), an EEA national must be admitted to the United Kingdom if he produces, on arrival, a valid national identity card or passport issued by an EEA State.

(2) Subject to regulation 21(1) and (2), a family member of an EEA national who is not himself an EEA national must be admitted to the United Kingdom if he produces, on arrival—

(a) a valid national identity card issued by an EEA State, or a valid passport; and
(b) either—
   (i) where the family member is a visa national or a person who seeks to be admitted to instal himself with a qualified person, a valid EEA family permit or residence document; or
   (ii) in all other cases (but only where required by an immigration officer) a document proving that he is a family member of a qualified person.

Initial Commencement
Specified date: 2 October 2000: see reg 1(1).

Modification
Modified, in its application to the Channel Tunnel, by the Channel Tunnel (International Arrangements) Order 1993, SI 1993 1813, Sch 4 (as amended by SI 2001/3707, arts 2, 7).

See Further
See further, in relation to the application of this regulation, with modifications, in relation to Swiss nationals, their family members and posted workers: the Immigration (Swiss Free Movement of Persons) (No 3) Regulations 2002, SI 2002/1241, reg 2, Schedule, paras 6, 22.

13   Issue of EEA family permit

(1) An entry clearance officer must issue an EEA family permit, free of charge, to a person who applies for one if he is a family member of—

(a) a qualified person; or
(b) a person who is not a qualified person, where that person—
   (i) will be travelling to the United Kingdom with the person who has made the application within [six months] of the date of the application; and
   (ii) will be a qualified person on arrival in the United Kingdom.

(2) But paragraph (1) does not apply if—

(a) the applicant; or
(b) the person whose family member he is

falls to be excluded from the United Kingdom on grounds of public policy, public security or public health.

[(3)Paragraph (1) also does not apply if the applicant applies for a family permit in an EEA State and is not lawfully resident in any EEA State.]

Initial Commencement
Specified date: 2 October 2000: see reg 1(1).

Amendment
Para (1): in sub-para (b)(i) words "six months" in square brackets substituted by SI 2005/47, reg 2(1), (3). Date in force: 7 February 2005: see SI 2005/47, reg 1; for transitional provisions see reg 3(2) thereof.
Para (3): inserted by SI 2005/47, reg 2(1), (4). Date in force: 7 February 2005: see SI 2005/47, reg 1; for transitional provisions see reg 3(2) thereof.

14 Right of residence

(1) A qualified person is entitled to reside in the United Kingdom, without the requirement for leave to remain under the 1971 Act, for as long as he remains a qualified person.

(2) A family member of a qualified person is entitled to reside in the United Kingdom, without the requirement for such leave, for as long as he remains the family member of a qualified person.

(3) A qualified person and the family member of such a person may reside and pursue economic activity in the United Kingdom notwithstanding that his application for a residence permit or residence document (as the case may be) has not been determined by the Secretary of State.

(4) However, this regulation is subject to regulation 21(3)(b).

Initial Commencement
Specified date: 2 October 2000: see reg 1(1).

See Further
See further, in relation to the application of this regulation, with modifications, in relation to Swiss nationals, their family members and posted workers: the Immigration (Swiss Free Movement of Persons) (No 3) Regulations 2002, SI 2002/1241, reg 2, Schedule, para 8.

PART IV
RESIDENCE PERMITS AND DOCUMENTS

15 Issue of residence permits and residence documents

(1) Subject to regulations 16 and 22(1), the Secretary of State must issue a residence permit to a qualified person on application and production of—

    (a)   a valid identity card or passport issued by an EEA State; and
    (b)   the proof that he is a qualified person.

(2) Subject to regulation 22(1), the Secretary of State must issue a residence permit to a family member of a qualified person (or, where the family member is not an EEA national, a residence document) on application and production of—

    (a)   a valid identity card issued by an EEA State or a valid passport;
    (b)   in the case of a family member who required an EEA family permit for admission to the United Kingdom, such a permit; and
    (c)   in the case of a person not falling within sub-paragraph (b), proof that he is a family member of a qualified person.

(3) In the case of a worker, confirmation of the worker's engagement from his employer or a certificate of employment is sufficient proof for the purposes of paragraph (1)(b).

Initial Commencement
Specified date: 2 October 2000: see reg 1(1).

See Further
See further, in relation to the application of this regulation, with modifications, in relation to Swiss nationals, their family members and posted workers: the Immigration (Swiss Free Movement of Persons) (No 3) Regulations 2002, SI 2002/1241, reg 2, Schedule, para 9.

16   Where no requirement to issue residence permit

(1) The Secretary of State is not required to grant a residence permit to—

  (a) a worker whose employment in the United Kingdom is limited to three months and who holds a document from his employer certifying that his employment is so limited;

  (b) a worker who is employed in the United Kingdom but who resides in the territory of an EEA State and who returns to his residence at least once a week;

  (c) a seasonal worker whose contract of employment has been approved by the Department for Education and Employment; or

  (d) a provider or recipient of services if the services are to be provided for no more than three months.

(2) The requirement in paragraph (1)(a) to hold a document does not apply to workers coming within the provisions of Council Directive 64/224/EEC of 25 February 1964 concerning the attainment of freedom of establishment and freedom to provide services in respect of activities of intermediaries in commerce, industry and small craft industries.

Initial Commencement
Specified date: 2 October 2000: see reg 1(1).

See Further
See further, in relation to the application of this regulation, with modifications, in relation to Swiss nationals, their family members and posted workers: the Immigration (Swiss Free Movement of Persons) (No 3) Regulations 2002, SI 2002/1241, reg 2, Schedule, para 10.

17   Form of residence permit and residence document

(1) The residence permit issued to a worker or a worker's family member who is an EEA national must be in the following form:

  "Residence Permit for a National of an EEA State
    This permit is issued pursuant to Regulation (EEC) No 1612/68 of the Council of the European Communities of 15 October 1968 and to the measures taken in implementation of the Council Directive of 15 October 1968.
    In accordance with the provisions of the above-mentioned Regulation, the holder of this permit has the right to take up and pursue an activity as an employed person in the territory of the United Kingdom under the same conditions as United Kingdom national workers.".

(2) A residence document issued to a family member who is not an EEA national may take the form of a stamp in that person's passport.

Initial Commencement
Specified date: 2 October 2000: see reg 1(1).

Immigration (European Economic Area) Regulations 2000

See Further
See further, in relation to the application of this regulation, with modifications, in relation to Swiss nationals, their family members and posted workers: the Immigration (Swiss Free Movement of Persons) (No 3) Regulations 2002, SI 2002/1241, reg 2, Schedule, para 12.

18 Duration of residence permit

(1) Subject to the following paragraphs and to regulations 20 and 22(2), a residence permit must be valid for at least five years from the date of issue.

(2) In the case of a worker who is to be employed in the United Kingdom for less than twelve but more than three months, the validity of the residence permit may be limited to the duration of the employment.

(3) In the case of a seasonal worker who is to be employed for more than three months, the validity of the residence permit may be limited to the duration of the employment if the duration is indicated in the document confirming the worker's engagement or in a certificate of employment.

(4) In the case of a provider or recipient of services, the validity of the residence permit may be limited to the period during which the services are to be provided.

(5) In the case of a student, the residence permit is to be valid for a period which does not exceed the duration of the course of study; but where the course lasts for more than one year the validity of the residence permit may be limited to one year.

(6) In the case of a retired person or a self-sufficient person, the Secretary of State may, if he deems it necessary, require the revalidation of the residence permit at the end of the first two years of residence.

(7) The validity of a residence permit is not to be affected by absence from the United Kingdom for periods of no more than six consecutive months or absence from the United Kingdom on military service.

Initial Commencement
Specified date: 2 October 2000: see reg 1(1).

See Further
See further, in relation to the application of this regulation, with modifications, in relation to Swiss nationals, their family members and posted workers: the Immigration (Swiss Free Movement of Persons) (No 3) Regulations 2002, SI 2002/1241, reg 2, Schedule, para 13.

19 Renewal of residence permit

(1) Subject to paragraphs (2) and (3) and to regulations 20 and 22(2), a residence permit must be renewed on application.

(2) On the occasion of the first renewal of a worker's residence permit the validity may be limited to one year if the worker has been involuntarily unemployed in the United Kingdom for more than one year.

(3) In the case of a student whose first residence permit is limited to one year by virtue of regulation 18(5), renewal may be for periods limited to one year.

Initial Commencement
Specified date: 2 October 2000: see reg 1(1).

20 Duration and renewal of residence permit or residence document granted to a family member

[(1) Subject to paragraph (2),] the family member of an EEA national is entitled to a residence permit or residence document of the same duration as the residence permit granted to the qualified person of whose family he is a member; and the family member's residence permit or residence document is subject to the same terms as to renewal.

[(2)   In the case of a family member of an EEA national to whom regulation 6(2A) or 6(2B)(a) applies, the validity of the residence permit or residence document may be limited to the period during which the family member is the primary carer of the dependent child who is under 19 and attending an educational course in the United Kingdom.]

Initial Commencement
Specified date: 2 October 2000: see reg 1(1).

Amendment
Para (1): numbered as such and words "Subject to paragraph (2)," in square brackets inserted by SI 2003/549, reg 2(1), (5)(a). Date in force: 1 April 2003: see SI 2003/549, reg 1.
Para (2): inserted by SI 2003/549, reg 2(1), (5)(b). Date in force: 1 April 2003: see SI 2003/549, reg 1.

PART V
WITHDRAWAL OF EEA RIGHTS

21   Exclusion and removal from the United Kingdom

(1)   A person is not entitled to be admitted to the United Kingdom by virtue of regulation 12 if his exclusion is justified on grounds of public policy, public security or public health.

(2)   A person is not entitled to be admitted to the United Kingdom by virtue of regulation 12(2) if, at the time of his arrival, he is not the family member of a qualified person.

(3)   A person may be removed from the United Kingdom—

    (a)   if he is not, or has ceased to be—
        (i) a qualified person; or
        (ii) the family member of a qualified person;
    (b)   if he is a qualified person or the family member of such a person, but the Secretary of State has decided that his removal is justified on the grounds of public policy, public security or public health.

Initial Commencement
Specified date: 2 October 2000: see reg 1(1).

Modification
Modified, in its application to the Channel Tunnel, by the Channel Tunnel (International Arrangements) Order 1993, SI 1993 1813, Sch 4 (as amended by SI 2001/3707, arts 2, 7).

See Further
See further, in relation to the application of this regulation, with modifications, in relation to Swiss nationals, their family members and posted workers: the Immigration (Swiss Free Movement of Persons) (No 3) Regulations 2002, SI 2002/1241, reg 2, Schedule, paras 15, 22.

22   Refusal to issue or renew residence permit or residence document, and revocation of residence permit, residence document or EEA family permit

(1)   The Secretary of State may refuse to issue a residence permit or residence document (as the case may be) if the refusal is justified on grounds of public policy, public security or public health.

(2)   The Secretary of State may revoke, or refuse to renew, a residence permit or residence document if—

(a)   the revocation or refusal is justified on grounds of public policy, public security or public health; or

(b)   the person to whom the residence permit or residence document was issued—
   (i)   is not, or has ceased to be, a qualified person;
   (ii)   is not, or has ceased to be, the family member of a qualified person.

(3)   An immigration officer may, at the time of the arrival in the United Kingdom of a person who is not an EEA national, revoke that person's residence document if he is not at that time the family member of a qualified person.

(4)   An immigration officer may, at the time of a person's arrival in the United Kingdom, revoke that person's EEA family permit if—

(a)   the revocation is justified on grounds of public policy, public security or public health; or

(b)   the person is not at that time the family member of a qualified person.

Initial Commencement
Specified date: 2 October 2000: see reg 1(1).

Modification
Modified, in its application to the Channel Tunnel, by the Channel Tunnel (International Arrangements) Order 1993, SI 1993 1813, Sch 4 (as amended by SI 2001/3707, arts 2, 7).

See Further
See further, in relation to the application of this regulation, with modifications, in relation to Swiss nationals, their family members and posted workers: the Immigration (Swiss Free Movement of Persons) (No 3) Regulations 2002, SI 2002/1241, reg 2, Schedule, paras 16, 22.

23   Public policy, public security and public health

Decisions taken on grounds of public policy, public security or public health ("the relevant grounds") must be taken in accordance with the following principles—

(a)   the relevant grounds must not be invoked to secure economic ends;

(b)   a decision taken on one or more of the relevant grounds must be based exclusively on the personal conduct of the individual in respect of whom the decision is taken;

(c)   a person's previous criminal convictions do not, in themselves, justify a decision on grounds of public policy or public security;

(d)   a decision to refuse admission to the United Kingdom, or to refuse to grant the first residence permit or residence document, to a person on the grounds that he has a disease or disability may be justified only if the disease or disability is of a type specified in Schedule 1 to these Regulations;

(e)   a disease or disability contracted after a person has been granted a first residence permit or first residence document does not justify a decision to refuse to renew the permit or document or a decision to remove him;

(f)   a person is to be informed of the grounds of public policy, public security or public health upon which the decision taken in his case is based unless it would be contrary to the interests of national security to do so.

Initial Commencement
Specified date: 2 October 2000: see reg 1(1).

PART VI
APPLICATION OF THE 1971 ACT AND THE 1999 ACT

24   Persons claiming right of admission

(1)   This regulation applies to a person who claims a right of admission to the United Kingdom under regulation 12 as—

(a)   the family member of an EEA national, where he is not himself an EEA national; or

(b)   an EEA national, where there is reason to believe that he may fall to be excluded from the United Kingdom on grounds of public policy, public security or public health.

(2)   A person to whom this regulation applies is to be treated as if he were a person seeking leave to enter the United Kingdom under the 1971 Act and paragraphs 2 to 4, 7, 16 to 18 and 21 to 24 of Schedule 2 to the 1971 Act (administrative provisions as to control on entry etc) apply accordingly, except that—

(a)   the reference in paragraph 2(1) to the purpose for which the immigration officer may examine any persons who have arrived in the United Kingdom is to be read as a reference to the purpose of determining whether he is a person who is to be granted admission under these Regulations; and

(b)   the references in paragraph 4(2A) and in paragraph 7 to a person who is, or may be, given leave to enter are to be read as references to a person who is, or may be, granted admission under these Regulations.

(3)   For so long as a person to whom this regulation applies is detained, or temporarily admitted or released while liable to detention, under the powers conferred by Schedule 2 to the 1971 Act, he is deemed not to have been admitted to the United Kingdom.

Initial Commencement
Specified date: 2 October 2000: see reg 1(1).

See Further
See further, in relation to the application of this regulation, with modifications, in relation to Swiss nationals, their family members and posted workers: the Immigration (Swiss Free Movement of Persons) (No 3) Regulations 2002, SI 2002/1241, reg 2, Schedule, para 17.

25   Persons refused admission

(1)   This regulation applies to a person who is in the United Kingdom and has been refused admission to the United Kingdom—

(a)   because he does not meet the requirements of regulation 12 (including where he does not meet those requirements because his residence document or EEA family permit has been revoked by an immigration officer in accordance with regulation 22); or

(b)   in accordance with regulation 21(1) or (2).

(2)   A person to whom this regulation applies is to be treated as if he were a person refused leave to enter under the 1971 Act, and the provisions set out in paragraph (3) apply accordingly.

(3)   Those provisions are—

(a)   paragraphs 8, 10, 11, 16 to 18 and 21 to 24 of Schedule 2 to the 1971 Act;

(b)   paragraph 19 of Schedule 2 to the 1971 Act, except that the reference in that paragraph to a certificate of entitlement, entry clearance or work permit is to be read as a reference to an EEA family permit or residence document; and

(c) ...

Initial Commencement
Specified date: 2 October 2000: see reg 1(1).

Amendment
Para (3): sub-para (c) revoked by SI 2003/549, reg 2(1), (6). Date in force: 1 April 2003: see
SI 2003/549, reg 1.

See Further
See further, in relation to the application of this regulation, with modifications, in relation to
Swiss nationals, their family members and posted workers: the Immigration (Swiss Free Move-
ment of Persons) (No 3) Regulations 2002, SI 2002/1241, reg 2, Schedule, para 18.

26 Persons subject to removal

(1) This regulation applies to a person whom it has been decided to remove from the
United Kingdom in accordance with regulation 21(3).

(2) Where the decision is under sub-paragraph (a) of regulation 21(3), the person is
to be treated as if he were a person to whom section 10(1)(a) of the 1999 Act applied,
and section 10 of that Act (removal of certain persons unlawfully in the United
Kingdom) is to apply accordingly.

(3) Where the decision is under sub-paragraph (b) of regulation 21(3), the person is
to be treated as if he were a person to whom section 3(5)(a) of the 1971 Act (liability
to deportation) applied, and section 5 of that Act (procedure for deportation) and
Schedule 3 to that Act (supplementary provisions as to deportation) are to apply
accordingly.

Initial Commencement
Specified date: 2 October 2000: see reg 1(1).

See Further
See further, in relation to the application of this regulation, with modifications, in relation to
Swiss nationals, their family members and posted workers: the Immigration (Swiss Free Move-
ment of Persons) (No 3) Regulations 2002, SI 2002/1241, reg 2, Schedule, para 19.

[26A Requirement to state grounds under section 120 of the 2002 Act]

[Section 120 of the 2002 Act shall apply to a person if an EEA decision has been taken
or may be taken in respect of him and, accordingly, the Secretary of State or an
immigration officer may require a statement from that person under subsection (2) of
that section.]

Amendment
Inserted by SI 2003/549, reg 2(1), (7). Date in force: 1 April 2003: see SI 2003/549, reg 1.

[PART VII
APPEALS UNDER THESE REGULATIONS]

[27 Interpretation of Part VII]

[(1) In this Part—

"[Asylum and Immigration Tribunal]" has the same meaning as in the 2002 Act;
"Commission" has the same meaning as in the Special Immigration Appeals
Commission Act 1997;
"the Human Rights Convention" has the same meaning as "the Convention" in the
Human Rights Act 1998; and

"the Refugee Convention" means the Convention relating to the Status of Refugees done at Geneva on 28th July 1951 and its Protocol.

(2)   For the purposes of this Part, and subject to paragraphs (3) and (4), an appeal is to be treated as pending during the period beginning when notice of appeal is given and ending when the appeal is finally determined, withdrawn or abandoned.

(3)   An appeal is not to be treated as finally determined while a further appeal may be brought; and, if such a further appeal is brought, the original appeal is not to be treated as finally determined until the further appeal is determined, withdrawn or abandoned.

(4)   A pending appeal is not to be treated as abandoned solely because the appellant leaves the United Kingdom.]

Amendment

Substituted, together with regs 28–32, for regs 27–36 as originally enacted, by SI 2003/549, regs 2(1), (8). Date in force: 1 April 2003 (except in relation to appeals against decisions made before that date): see SI 2003/549, regs 1, 3.
Para (1): in definition "Asylum and Immigration Tribunal" (definition "adjudicator" as originally enacted) words "Asylum and Immigration Tribunal" in square brackets substituted by SI 2005/671, reg 2(1), (2). Date in force: 4 April 2005: see SI 2005/671, reg 1.

[28   Scope of Part VII]

[This Part applies to persons who have, or who claim to have, rights under these Regulations or under Regulation 1251/70.]

Amendment

Substituted, together with regs 27, 29–32, for regs 27–36 as originally enacted, by SI 2003/549, regs 2(1), (8). Date in force: 1 April 2003 (except in relation to appeals against decisions made before that date): see SI 2003/549, regs 1, 3.

[29   Appeal rights]

[(1)   Subject to paragraphs (2) to (4), a person may appeal under these Regulations against an EEA decision.

(2)   If a person claims to be an EEA national, he may not appeal under these Regulations unless he produces—

(a)   a valid national identity card; or
(b)   a valid passport, issued by an EEA State.

(3)   If a person claims to be the family member of another person, he may not appeal under these Regulations unless he produces—

(a)   an EEA family permit; or
(b)   other proof that he is related as claimed to that other person.

(4)   For the purposes of paragraphs (2) and (3), a document—

(a)   is to be regarded as being what it purports to be provided that this is reasonably apparent; and
(b)   is to be regarded as relating to the person producing it unless it is reasonably apparent that it relates to another person.

(5)   A person may not rely on a ground in an appeal under these Regulations if the Secretary of State or an immigration officer certifies that the ground was considered in a previous appeal brought by that person under these Regulations or under section 82(1) of the 2002 Act.

(6) Except where an appeal lies to the Commission, an appeal under these Regulations lies to [the Asylum and Immigration Tribunal].

(7) The sections of the 2002 Act set out in Schedule 2 shall have effect for the purposes of appeals under these Regulations to [the Asylum and Immigration Tribunal] in accordance with that Schedule.]

Amendment
Substituted, together with regs 27, 28, 30–32, for regs 27–36 as originally enacted, by SI 2003/549, regs 2(1), (8). Date in force: 1 April 2003 (except in relation to appeals against decisions made before that date): see SI 2003/549, regs 1, 3.
Para (6): words "the Asylum and Immigration Tribunal" in square brackets substituted by SI 2005/671, reg 2(1), (3). Date in force: 4 April 2005: see SI 2005/671, reg 1.
Para (7): words "the Asylum and Immigration Tribunal" in square brackets substituted by SI 2005/671, reg 2(1), (3). Date in force: 4 April 2005: see SI 2005/671, reg 1.

[30   Out-of-country appeals]

[(1) Regulation 29 does not entitle a person to appeal while he is in the United Kingdom against an EEA decision—

    (a)   to refuse to admit him to the United Kingdom;
    (b)   to refuse to revoke a deportation order made against him;
    (c)   to refuse to issue him with an EEA family permit.

(2) Paragraph (1) also applies to a decision to remove someone from the United Kingdom which is consequent upon a refusal to admit him.

(3) But paragraphs (1)(a) and (2) do not apply—

    (a)   ...
    (b)   where a ground of the appeal is that, in taking the decision, the decision-maker acted in breach of the appellant's rights under the Human Rights Convention or the Refugee Convention; or
    (c)   where the person held an EEA family permit, or a residence permit or residence document, on his arrival in the United Kingdom.]

Amendment
Substituted, together with regs 27–29, 31, 32, for regs 27–36 as originally enacted, by SI 2003/549, regs 2(1), (8). Date in force: 1 April 2003 (except in relation to appeals against decisions made before that date): see SI 2003/549, regs 1, 3.
Para (3): sub-para (a) revoked by SI 2005/47, reg 2(1), (5). Date in force: 7 February 2005: see SI 2005/47, reg 1; for transitional provisions see reg 3(3) thereof.

[31   Appeals to the Commission]

[(1) An appeal against an EEA decision lies to the Commission where paragraphs (2) and (4) applies.

(2) This paragraph applies if the Secretary of State certifies that the EEA decision was taken—

    (a)   by the Secretary of State wholly or partly on a ground listed in paragraph (3), or
    (b)   in accordance with a direction of the Secretary of State which identifies the person to whom the decision relates and which is given wholly or partly on a ground listed in paragraph (3).

(3) The grounds mentioned in paragraph (2) are that the person's exclusion or removal from the United Kingdom is—

    (a)   in the interests of national security, or

(b) in the interests of the relationship between the United Kingdom and another country.

(4) This paragraph applies if the Secretary of State certifies that the EEA decision was taken wholly or partly in reliance on information which in his opinion should not be made public—

(a) in the interests of national security,
(b) in the interests of the relationship between the United Kingdom and another country, or
(c) otherwise in the public interest.

(5) In paragraphs (2) and (4) a reference to the Secretary of State is to the Secretary of State acting in person.

(6) Where a certificate is issued under paragraph (2) or (3) in respect of a pending appeal to [the Asylum and Immigration Tribunal] the appeal shall lapse.

(7) An appeal against an EEA decision lies to the Commission where an appeal lapses by virtue of paragraph (6).

(8) The Special Immigration Appeals Commission Act 1997 shall apply to an appeal to the Commission under these Regulations as it applies to an appeal under section 2 of that Act to which subsection (2) of that section applies (appeals against an immigration decision) but paragraph (i) of that subsection shall not apply in relation to such an appeal.]

Amendment
Substituted, together with regs 27–30, 32, for regs 27–36 as originally enacted, by SI 2003/549, regs 2(1), (8). Date in force: 1 April 2003 (except in relation to appeals against decisions made before that date): see SI 2003/549, regs 1, 3.
Para (6): words "the Asylum and Immigration Tribunal" in square brackets substituted by SI 2005/671, reg 2(1), (3). Date in force: 4 April 2005: see SI 2005/671, reg 1.

[32   Effect of appeals to] [the Asylum and Immigration Tribunal]

[(1) If a person in the United Kingdom appeals under these Regulations against an EEA decision to refuse to admit him to the United Kingdom, any directions previously given by virtue of the refusal for his removal from the United Kingdom cease to have effect, except in so far as they have already been carried out, and no directions may be so given while the appeal is pending.

(2) If a person appeals under these Regulations against an EEA decision to remove him from the United Kingdom, any directions given under section 10 of the 1999 Act or Schedule 3 to the 1971 Act for his removal from the United Kingdom are to have no effect, except in so far as they have already been carried out, while the appeal is pending.

(3) But the provisions of Part I of Schedule 2, or as the case may be, Schedule 3 to the 1971 Act with respect to detention and persons liable to detention apply to a person appealing under these Regulations against a refusal to admit him or a decision to remove him as if there were in force directions for his removal from the United Kingdom, except that he may not be detained on board a ship or aircraft so as to compel him to leave the United Kingdom while the appeal is pending.

(4) In calculating the period of two months limited by paragraph 8(2) of Schedule 2 to the 1971 Act for—

(a) the giving of directions under that paragraph for the removal of a person from the United Kingdom, and
(b) the giving of a notice of intention to give such directions,

any period during which there is pending an appeal by him under these Regulations is to be disregarded.

(5) If a person appeals under these Regulations against an EEA decision to remove him from the United Kingdom, a deportation order is not to be made against him under section 5 of the 1971 Act while the appeal is pending.

(6) Paragraph 29 of Schedule 2 to the 1971 Act (grant of bail pending appeal) applies to a person who has an appeal pending under these Regulations as it applies to a person who has an appeal pending under section 82(1) of the 2002 Act.

(7) This regulation does not apply to an appeal which lies to the Commission.]

Amendment
Provision heading: words "the Asylum and Immigration Tribunal" in square brackets substituted by SI 2005/671, reg 2(1), (3). Date in force: 4 April 2005: see SI 2005/671, reg 1.
Substituted, together with regs 27–31, for regs 27–36 as originally enacted, by SI 2003/549, regs 2(1), (8). Date in force: 1 April 2003 (except in relation to appeals against decisions made before that date): see SI 2003/549, regs 1, 3.

33 ...

Amendment
Substituted, together with regs 27–32, 34–36, by new regs 27–32, by SI 2003/549, reg 2(1), (8). Date in force: 1 April 2003 (except in relation to appeals against decisions made before that date): see SI 2003/549, regs 1, 3.

34 ...

Amendment
Substituted, together with regs 27–33, 35, 36, by new regs 27–32, by SI 2003/549, reg 2(1), (8). Date in force: 1 April 2003 (except in relation to appeals against decisions made before that date): see SI 2003/549, regs 1, 3.

35 ...

Amendment
Substituted, together with regs 27–34, 36, by new regs 27–32, by SI 2003/549, reg 2(1), (8). Date in force: 1 April 2003 (except in relation to appeals against decisions made before that date): see SI 2003/549, regs 1, 3.

36 ...

Amendment
Substituted, together with regs 27–35, by new regs 27–32, by SI 2003/549, reg 2(1), (8). Date in force: 1 April 2003 (except in relation to appeals against decisions made before that date): see SI 2003/549, regs 1, 3.

[PART VIII
APPEALS UNDER THE 2002 ACT]

[33   Appeals under the 2002 Act]

[(1A)   A person who has been issued with a residence permit, a residence document or a registration certificate or whose passport has been stamped with a family member residence stamp shall have no right of appeal under section 82(1) of the 2002 Act. Any existing appeal shall be treated as abandoned.]

[[(1B)   Subject to paragraph (1C), a person may appeal to [the Asylum and Immigration Tribunal] under section 83(2) of the 2002 Act against the rejection of his asylum claim where—

(a)   that claim has been rejected, but
(b)   he has a right to reside in the United Kingdom under these Regulations.

(1C)   Paragraph (1B) shall not apply if the person is an EEA national and the Secretary of State certifies that the asylum claim is clearly unfounded.

(1D)   The Secretary of State shall certify the claim under paragraph (1C) unless satisfied that it is not clearly unfounded.]

(2)   In addition to the national of a State which is a contracting party to the Agreement referred to in section 84(2) of the 2002 Act, the national of a State which is a contracting party to any other agreement forming part of the Community Treaties which confers rights of entry to or residence in the United Kingdom shall also be treated as an EEA national for the purposes of section 84(1)(d) of that Act.

(3)   An appeal under these Regulations against an EEA decision made on or after 1st April 2003 shall be treated as an appeal under section 82(1) of the 2002 Act against an immigration decision for the purposes of sections 96(1)(a), (2)(a) and (2)(c) of the 2002 Act and such an EEA decision shall be treated as an immigration decision for the purposes of section 96(2)(b) of that Act.

(4)   A ground considered in an appeal under these Regulations against an EEA decision made on or after 1st April 2003 shall be treated as a ground considered in an appeal under section 82(1) of the 2002 Act for the purposes of section 96(3) of that Act.]

[(5)   In paragraph (1A),

(a)   "registration certificate" has the same meaning as in regulation 1(2)(h) of the Accession Regulations 2004;
(b)   "family member residence stamp" means a stamp in the passport of a family member who is not an EEA national confirming that the family member of an accession state worker requiring registration has a right of residence under these Regulations as the family member of that worker; and in this paragraph reference to family member is to a family member who is not an EEA national and "accession state worker requiring registration" has the same meaning as in regulation 2 of the Accession Regulations 2004.]

Amendment
Para (1A) (as inserted by SI 2003/3188, reg 2(1), (3)(a)): substituted by SI 2004/1236, reg 2(1), (4)(a). Date in force: 1 May 2004: see SI 2004/1236, reg 1.
Paras (1B)–(1D): substituted, for para (1) as originally enacted, by SI 2003/3188, reg 2(1), (3)(b). Date in force: 1 January 2004 (except in relation to the rejection of an asylum claim before that date): see SI 2003/3188, reg 1.
Para (1B): words "the Asylum and Immigration Tribunal" in square brackets substituted by SI 2005/671, reg 2(1), (3). Date in force: 4 April 2005: see SI 2005/671, reg 1.
Inserted by SI 2003/549, reg 2(1), (9). Date in force: 1 April 2003: see SI 2003/549, reg 1.
Para (5): inserted by SI 2004/1236, reg 2(1), (4)(b). Date in force: 1 May 2004: see SI 2004/1236, reg 1.

SCHEDULE 1
SPECIFIED DISEASES AND DISABILITIES

Regulation 23(d)

1   The following diseases may justify a decision taken on grounds of public health—

   (a) diseases subject to quarantine listed in International Health Regulation No 2 of the World Health Organisation of 25th May 1951;

   (b) tuberculosis of the respiratory system in an active state or showing a tendency to develop;

   (c) syphilis;

   (d) other infectious diseases or contagious parasitic diseases, if they are the subject of provisions for the protection of public health in the United Kingdom.

2   The following diseases or disabilities may justify a decision taken on grounds of public policy or public security—

   (a) drug addiction;

   (b) profound mental disturbance; manifest conditions of psychotic disturbance with agitation, delirium, hallucinations or confusion.

Initial Commencement
Specified date: 2 October 2000: see reg 1(1).

[SCHEDULE 2
APPEALS TO] [THE ASYLUM AND IMMIGRATION TRIBUNAL]

[Regulation 29(4)]

[The following provisions of, or made under, the 2002 Act have effect in relation to an appeal under these Regulations to [the Asylum and Immigration Tribunal] as if it were an appeal against an immigration decision under section 82(1) of that Act:

section 84(1) (except paragraphs (a) and (f)) and (2);
sections 85 to 87;
[sections 103A to 103E];
section 105 and any regulations made under that section; and
section 106 and any rules made under that section.]

Amendment
Substituted by SI 2003/3188, reg 2(1), (4). Date in force: 1 January 2004: see SI 2003/3188, reg 1(1).
Words "the Asylum and Immigration Tribunal" in square brackets substituted by SI 2005/671, reg 2(1), (3). Date in force: 4 April 2005: see SI 2005/671, reg 1.
Words "sections 103A to 103E" in square brackets substituted by SI 2005/671, reg 2(1), (4). Date in force: 4 April 2005: see SI 2005/671, reg 1.

IMMIGRATION (DESIGNATION OF TRAVEL BANS) ORDER 2000

2000 No 2724

Made . . . .*3rd October 2000*

Laid before Parliament . . . .*9th October 2000*

Coming into force . . . .*10th October 2000*

The Secretary of State, in exercise of the powers conferred upon him by section 8B(5) and (6) of the Immigration Act 1971, hereby makes the following Order:

1

This Order may be cited as the Immigration (Designation of Travel Bans) Order 2000 and shall come into force on 10th October 2000.

Initial Commencement
Specified date: 10 October 2000: see above.

2

The instruments listed in the Schedule to this Order are designated for the purposes of section 8B(4) and (5) of the Immigration Act 1971.

Initial Commencement
Specified date: 10 October 2000: see art 1.

3

Section 8B(1), (2) and (3) of the Immigration Act 1971 shall not apply in any case where:

(a) failure to apply these provisions would not be contrary to the United Kingdom's obligations under any of the instruments designated by article 2 of this Order,

(b) to apply these provisions would be contrary to the United Kingdom's obligations under the Convention for the Protection of Human Rights and Fundamental Freedoms, agreed by the Council of Europe at Rome on 4th November 1950, or

(c) to apply these provisions would be contrary to the United Kingdom's obligations under the Convention relating to the Status of Refugees done at Geneva on 28th July 1951 and the Protocol to that Convention.

Initial Commencement
Specified date: 10 October 2000: see art 1.

[SCHEDULE
DESIGNATED INSTRUMENTS]

[Article 2]

[PART 1
RESOLUTIONS OF THE SECURITY COUNCIL OF THE UNITED NATIONS]

[Resolution 1390 (2002) of 16th January 2002 (Al Qa'ida and the Taliban).

Resolution 1455 (2003) of 17th January 2003 (Al Qa'ida and the Taliban).

[Resolution 1521 (2003) of 22nd December 2003 (Liberia).]

Resolution 1171 (1998) of 5th June 1998 (Sierra Leone).]

Amendment
Substituted by SI 2003/3285, art 2, Sch 1. Date in force: 19 December 2003: see SI 2003/3285, art 1.
Entry in relation to "Resolution 1521 (2003)" substituted, for entries in relation to "Resolution 1343 (2001)" and "Resolution 1478 (2003)" as originally enacted, by SI 2004/3316, art 2(1), (2). Date in force: 16 December 2004: see SI 2004/3316, art 1.

[PART 2
INSTRUMENTS MADE BY THE COUNCIL OF THE EUROPEAN UNION]

[[Common Position 2002/402/CFSP of 27th May 2002 (Al Qa'ida and the Taliban).

Common Position 2004/661/CFSP of 24th September 2004 (Belarus).]

Common Position 97/193/CFSP (Bosnia-Herzegovina).

[Common Position 2004/423/CFSP of 26th April 2004 (Burma) as amended by Common Position 2004/730/CFSP of 25th October 2004 (Burma).]

Common Position 98/240/CFSP of 19th March 1998 (Federal Republic of Yugoslavia).

Common Position 99/318/CFSP of 10th May 1999 (Federal Republic of Yugoslavia).

Common Position 2000/56/CFSP of 24th January 2000 (Federal Republic of Yugoslavia).

Common Position 2000/696/CFSP of 10th November 2000 (Federal Republic of Yugoslavia).

Common Position 2001/155/CFSP of 26th February 2001 (Federal Republic of Yugoslavia).

[Common Position 2004/133/CFSP of 10th February 2004 (Former Yugoslav Republic of Macedonia).]

[Common Position 2004/293/CFSP of 30th March 2004 (International Criminal Tribunal of the former Yugoslavia).

Common Position 2004/528/CFSP of 28th June 2004 (International Criminal Tribunal of the former Yugoslavia).]

[Common Position 2004/137/CFSP of 10th February 2004 (Liberia).]

[Common Position 2004/179/CFSP of 23rd February 2004 (Moldovan Republic) as amended by Common Position 2004/622/CFSP of 26th August 2004 (Modovan Republic).]

Common Position 98/409/CFSP of 29th June 1998 (Sierra Leone).

[Common Position 2004/161/CFSP of 19th February 2004 (Zimbabwe).]]

Amendment
Entries in relation to "Common Position 2002/402/CFSP" and "Common Position 2004/661/CFSP" inserted by SI 2004/3316, art 2(1), (3)(a). Date in force: 16 December 2004: see SI 2004/3316, art 1.
Substituted by SI 2003/3285, art 2, Sch 1. Date in force: 19 December 2003: see SI 2003/3285, art 1.
Entry in relation to "Common Position 2004/423/CFSP" substituted, for entry in relation to "Common Position 2003/297/CFSP" as originally enacted, by SI 2004/3316, art 2(1), (3)(b). Date in force: 16 December 2004: see SI 2004/3316, art 1.
Entry in relation to "Common Position 2004/133/CFSP" inserted by SI 2004/3316, art 2(1), (3)(c). Date in force: 16 December 2004: see SI 2004/3316, art 1.

Entries relating to "Common Position 2004/293/CFSP" and "Common Position 2004/528/CFSP" substituted, for entries relating to "Common Position 2003/280/CFSP" and "Common Position 2003/484/CFSP" as originally enacted, by SI 2004/3316, art 2(1), (3)(d). Date in force: 16 December 2004: see SI 2004/3316, art 1.

Entry in relation to "Common Position 2004/137/CFSP" substituted, for entries in relation to "Common Position 2001/357/CFSP", "Common Position 2002/457CFSP" and "Common Position 2003/365/CFSP" as originally enacted, by SI 2004/3316, art 2(1), (3)(e). Date in force: 16 December 2004: see SI 2004/3316, art 1.

Entry in relation to "Common Position 2004/622/CFSP" substituted, for entry in relation to "Common Position 2003/139/CFSP" as originally enacted, by SI 2004/3316, art 2(1), (3)(f). Date in force: 16 December 2004: see SI 2004/3316, art 1.

Entry in relation to "Common Position 2004/161/CFSP" substituted, for entries in relation to "Common Position 2002/145/CFSP", "Common Position 2002/754/CFSP" and "Common Position 2003/115/CFSP" as originally enacted, by SI 2004/3316, art 2(1), (3)(g). Date in force: 16 December 2004: see SI 2004/3316, art 1.

IMMIGRATION (LEAVE TO ENTER) ORDER 2001

2001 No 2590

Made . . . . *17th July 2001*

Coming into force . . . . *18th July 2001*

Whereas a draft of this Order has been laid before Parliament and approved by a resolution of each House in accordance with section 3A(13) of the Immigration Act 1971;

Now, therefore, the Secretary of State, in exercise of the powers conferred upon him by section 3A(1), (7), (8) and (10) of the Immigration Act 1971, hereby makes the following Order:

1

(1) This Order may be cited as the Immigration (Leave to Enter) Order 2001 and shall come into force on the day after the day on which it is made.

(2) In this Order—

    (a) "the 1971 Act" means the Immigration Act 1971; and

    (b) "claim for asylum" and "the Human Rights Convention" have the meanings assigned by section 167 of the Immigration and Asylum Act 1999.

Initial Commencement
Specified date: 18 July 2001: see para (1) above.

2

(1) Where this article applies to a person, the Secretary of State may give or refuse him leave to enter the United Kingdom.

(2) This article applies to a person who seeks leave to enter the United Kingdom and who—

    (a) has made a claim for asylum; or

(b) has made a claim that it would be contrary to the United Kingdom's obligations under the Human Rights Convention for him to be removed from, or required to leave, the United Kingdom.

(3) This article also applies to a person who seeks leave to enter the United Kingdom for a purpose not covered by the immigration rules or otherwise on the grounds that those rules should be departed from in his case.

(4) In deciding whether to give or refuse leave under this article the Secretary of State may take into account any additional grounds which a person has for seeking leave to enter the United Kingdom.

(5) The power to give or refuse leave to enter the United Kingdom under this article shall be exercised by notice in writing to the person affected or in such manner as is permitted by the Immigration (Leave to Enter and Remain) Order 2000.

Initial Commencement
Specified date: 18 July 2001: see art 1(1).

3

In relation to the giving or refusing of leave to enter by the Secretary of State under article 2, paragraphs 2 (examination by immigration officers, and medical examination), 4 (information and documents), 7(1), (3) and (4) (power to require medical examination after entry), 8 (removal of persons refused leave to enter), 9 (removal of illegal entrants) and 21 (temporary admission of persons liable to detention) of Schedule 2 to the 1971 Act shall be read as if references to an immigration officer included references to the Secretary of State.

Initial Commencement
Specified date: 18 July 2001: see art 1(1).

4

(1) This article applies where—

(a) an immigration officer has commenced examination of a person ("the applicant") under paragraph 2(1)(c) of Schedule 2 to the 1971 Act (examination to determine whether or not leave to enter should be given);
(b) that examination has been adjourned, or the applicant has been required (under paragraph 2(3) of Schedule 2 to the Immigration Act 1971) to submit to a further examination;
(c) the Secretary of State subsequently examines the applicant or conducts a further examination in relation to him; and
(d) the Secretary of State thereafter gives or refuses the applicant leave to enter.

(2) Where this article applies, the notice giving or refusing leave to enter shall be regarded for the purposes of the 1971 Act as having been given within the period of 24 hours specified in paragraph 6(1) of Schedule 2 to that Act (period within which notice giving or refusing leave to enter must be given after completion of examination by an immigration officer).

Initial Commencement
Specified date: 18 July 2001: see art 1(1).

IMMIGRATION (SWISS FREE MOVEMENT OF PERSONS) (NO 3) REGULATIONS 2002

2002 No 1241

Made . . . . *1st May 2002*

Laid . . . . *9th May 2002*

Coming into force . . . . *1st June 2002*

The Secretary of State, being a Minister designated for the purposes of section 2(2) of the European Communities Act 1972 in relation to measures relating to rights of entry into, and residence in, the United Kingdom, in exercise of the powers conferred on him by that section, hereby makes the following Regulations:

1 Citation, commencement and interpretation

(1) These Regulations may be cited as the Immigration (Swiss Free Movement of Persons) (No 3) Regulations 2002 and shall come into force on 1st June 2002.

(2) The "2000 Regulations" means the Immigration (European Economic Area) Regulations 2000.

Initial Commencement
Specified date: 1 June 2002: see para (1) above.

2 Application of 2000 Regulations to Swiss nationals, their family members and posted workers

(1) The 2000 Regulations shall apply in relation to a Swiss national, and to any person related to that national, as if the Swiss national were an EEA national and Switzerland an EEA state.

(2) The 2000 Regulations shall also apply to a posted worker.

(3) In the application of the 2000 Regulations to a Swiss national or to any person related to a Swiss national or to a posted worker those Regulations shall have effect subject to the modifications set out in the Schedule to these Regulations.

(4) In this regulation—

    (a) "EEA national" and "EEA state" have the same meaning as in regulation 2(1) of the 2000 Regulations;

    (b) "posted worker" has the same meaning as in regulation 3(1) of the 2000 Regulations, as modified by the Schedule to these Regulations;

    (c) a person is related to a Swiss national if that person—

        (i) is a family member of that Swiss national (as determined in accordance with regulation 6 of the 2000 Regulations); or

        (ii) would satisfy any of the conditions in regulation 10(4) of the 2000 Regulations in relation to the Swiss national if the Swiss national were an EEA national.

Initial Commencement
Specified date: 1 June 2002: see reg 1(1).

SCHEDULE

MODIFICATION OF 2000 REGULATIONS IN THEIR APPLICATION TO SWISS NATIONALS

Regulation 2(3)

1 In regulation 2(1),

(a)   after the definition of "the 1999 Act" insert—

" "control zone" and "supplementary control zone" have the same meaning as in the Channel Tunnel (International Arrangements) Order 1993";

(b)   after the definition of "military service" insert—

" "posted worker authorisation" means a document issued to a person, in accordance with regulation 13A, in connection with his admission to the United Kingdom;";

(c)   after the definition of "Regulation 1251/70" insert—

" "required documents" means the documents referred to in regulation 12(3);".

2   In regulation 3 of the 2000 Regulations—

(a)   after paragraph (1)(b) insert—

"(ba)"posted worker" means a person who is not an EEA national and—

(i)   is the employee of a Swiss national or Swiss company that provides or seeks to provide services in the United Kingdom;

(ii)   is posted to the United Kingdom for the purpose of providing those services on behalf of his employer; and

(iii)   prior to the posting, is integrated into the regular labour market of an EEA State,

and, for the purpose of this definition, "services" has the same meaning as in Article 50 of the EC Treaty, and "Swiss company" means a company that is formed in accordance with the law of Switzerland and has its registered office, central administration or principal place of business in Switzerland;";

(b)   delete paragraph (1)(f);

(c)   for paragraph (2) substitute—

"(2)   For the purposes of paragraph (1)(e)—

(a)   resources are to be regarded as sufficient if they exceed the level in respect of which the recipient would qualify for social assistance;

(b)   where the person concerned has been employed in the United Kingdom for less than one year, any unemployment benefit to which he is entitled by virtue of having paid national insurance contributions shall be treated as the resources of that person.".

3   At the end of regulation 7 insert "and, in the case of a posted worker, a valid posted worker authorisation".

4   At the end of regulation 9 insert "and posted workers".

5   In regulation 10, delete paragraph (5).

6   In regulation 12, after paragraph (2) insert—

"(3)   Subject to regulation 21(1) and (2A), a posted worker must be admitted to the United Kingdom if he produces, on arrival—

(a)   a valid passport; and

(b)   a valid posted worker authorisation.

(4)   Any passport, identity card, family permit, residence document, posted worker authorisation or document proving family membership which is required to be produced under this regulation as a condition for admission to the United Kingdom may, for the same purpose, be required to be produced in a control zone or a supplementary control zone.".

7   After regulation 13 insert—

"13A   Issue of posted worker authorisation

(1)   A person may apply to an entry clearance officer for a posted worker authorisation authorising him to enter and reside in the United Kingdom in a calendar year if—

2269

(a) he is to be posted to the United Kingdom by his employer during that calendar year;

(b) he will be a posted worker on arrival in the United Kingdom; and

(c) he has not already been authorised to enter and reside in the United Kingdom under this regulation for 90 days or more in that calendar year.

(2) A posted worker authorisation issued under paragraph (1) shall specify the period during which the posted worker is authorised to enter and reside in the United Kingdom.

(3) A person who applies under paragraph (1) shall be entitled to be issued in relation to any calendar year with a single posted worker authorisation which individually, or with a number of authorisations which collectively, authorise him to enter and reside in the United Kingdom for at least 90 days in that calendar year.

(4) Paragraph (3) shall not apply if the applicant falls to be excluded from the United Kingdom on grounds of public policy, public security or public health.".

8 In regulation 14, after paragraph (3) insert—

"(4) A posted worker is entitled to reside in the United Kingdom without the requirement for leave to remain under the 1971 Act for as long as he has a valid posted worker authorisation and the period of authorised entry and residence specified in that authorisation has not expired.".

9 In regulation 15, after paragraph (2) insert—

"(2A) Subject to regulation 16A and 22 (1), the Secretary of State must issue a residence document to a posted worker on application and production of—

(a) a valid passport; and

(b) a valid posted worker authorisation".

10 In regulation 16—

(a) in paragraph (1)—
  (i) in sub-paragraph (b), after "worker who is employed" insert ", or self-employed person who is established,";
  (ii) delete sub-paragraph (c);
(b) delete paragraph (2).

11 After regulation 16 insert—

"16A   Where no requirement to issue residence document

The Secretary of State is not required to issue a residence document to a posted worker if the period of authorised entry and residence specified in his posted worker authorisation is 90 days or less.".

12 Delete regulation 17.

13 In regulation 18—

(a) delete paragraph (3);
(b) in paragraph (6) delete "a retired person or".

14 After regulation 20 insert—

"20A   Duration of residence document granted to a posted worker

In the case of a posted worker the validity of the resident document may be limited to the period of authorised entry and residence specified in his posted worker authorisation.".

15   In regulation 21—

(a)   in paragraph (2), after "arrival" insert "or the time of his production of the required documents in a control zone or supplementary control zone";

(b)   after paragraph (2) insert—

"(2A)   A person is not entitled to be admitted to the United Kingdom by virtue of regulation 12(3) if, at the time of his arrival, he is not a posted worker.";

(c)   in paragraph (3)(b), after "such a person" insert "or a posted worker";

(d)   after paragraph (3) insert—

"(4)   A person who was admitted to the United Kingdom as a posted worker may be removed from the United Kingdom if—

(a)   he ceases to be a posted worker or the period of authorised entry and residence specified in his posted worker authorisation has expired; and

(b)   he is not a qualified person or the family member of a qualified person.".

16   In regulation 22—

(a)   in paragraph (2), after paragraph (b) insert—

"or

(c)   the person to whom the residence document was issued was admitted to the United Kingdom as a posted worker and—

(i)   he has ceased to be a posted worker; and

(ii)   he is not a qualified person or the family member of a qualified person.";

(b)   in paragraph (3), after "EEA national" insert ", or the time of his production of the required documents in a control zone or supplementary control zone," and at the end of that paragraph insert "or a posted worker";

(c)   in paragraph (4), after "United Kingdom" insert ", or the time of his production of the required documents in a control zone or supplementary control zone,";

(d)   after paragraph (4) insert—

"(5)   An immigration officer may, at the time of a person's arrival in the United Kingdom, or the time of his production of the required documents in a control zone or supplementary control zone, revoke that person's posted worker authorisation if—

(a)   the revocation is justified on the grounds of public policy, public security or public health; or

(b)   the person is not at that time a posted worker.".

17   In regulation 24(1), after paragraph (a) insert—

"(aa)a posted worker; or".

18   In regulation 25—

(a)   in paragraph (1)—
(i)   in sub-paragraph (a), after "EEA family permit" insert "or posted worker authorisation";
(ii)   in sub-paragraph (b), for "or (2)" insert ", (2) or (2A)";

(b)   in paragraph (3)—
(i)   in sub-paragraph (b), after "EEA family permit" insert ", posted worker authorisation";
(ii)   in sub-paragraph (c), after "EEA family permit" insert ", posted worker authorisation".

19   In regulation 26—

(a)   in paragraph (1), at the end insert "or (4)";
(b)   in paragraph (2), after "regulation 21(3)" insert "or regulation 21(4)".

20 In regulation 30(3)(c), after "EEA family permit" insert "or posted worker authorisation".

21 For regulation 35 and 36 substitute—

"35 Transitional provisions

(1) Where before 1st June 2002 a qualified person or the family member of a qualified person has been given limited leave to enter or remain in the United Kingdom under section 3 of the 1971 Act subject to conditions, those conditions shall cease to have effect on and after that date.

(2) Where before 1st June 2002 directions have been given for the removal of a qualified person or the family member of a qualified person under paragraphs 8 to 10 of Schedule 2 to the 1971 Act or section 10 of the 1999 Act, those directions shall cease to have effect on and after that date.

(3) Where before 1st June 2002 the Secretary of State has made a decision to make a deportation order against a qualified person or the family member of a qualified person under section 5(1) of the 1971 Act—

    (a) that decision shall, on and after 1st June 2002, be treated as if it were a decision under regulation 21(3)(b); and

    (b) any appeal against that decision, or against the refusal by the Secretary of State to revoke the deportation order, made under section 63 of the 1999 Act before 1st June 2002 shall, on and after that date, be treated as if it had been made under regulation 29.

(4) Any reference in this regulation to a qualified person or to the family member of a qualified person is a reference to a person who becomes a qualified person or the family member of a qualified person, as the case may be, on or after 1st June 2002 by virtue of these Regulations.".

22 The modifications of the 2000 Regulations set out in paragraph 5 of Schedule 4 to the Channel Tunnel (International Arrangements) Order 1993 shall not apply.

Initial Commencement
Specified date: 1 June 2002: see reg 1(1).

WITHHOLDING AND WITHDRAWAL OF SUPPORT (TRAVEL ASSISTANCE AND TEMPORARY ACCOMMODATION) REGULATIONS 2002

2002 No 3078

Made . . . . *13th December 2002*

Laid before Parliament . . . . *17th December 2002*

Coming into force . . . . *8th January 2003*

The Secretary of State, in exercise of the powers conferred on him by section 54 of and paragraphs 8, 9, 10, 11, 12, 16(2) and 17 of Schedule 3 to the Nationality, Immigration and Asylum Act 2002, hereby makes the following Regulations:

1 Citation and commencement

These Regulations may be cited as the Withholding and Withdrawal of Support (Travel Assistance and Temporary Accommodation) Regulations 2002 and shall come into force on 8th January 2003.

Initial Commencement
Specified date: 8 January 2003: see above.

2 Interpretation

(1) In these Regulations—

"the Act" means the Nationality, Immigration and Asylum Act 2002,
"person with refugee status abroad" means a person to whom paragraph 1 of Schedule 3 to the Act applies by virtue of paragraph 4 of that Schedule,
"EEA national" means a person to whom paragraph 1 of Schedule 3 to the Act applies by virtue of paragraph 5 of that Schedule,
"person unlawfully in the United Kingdom" means a person to whom paragraph 1 of Schedule 3 to the Act applies by virtue of paragraph 7 of that Schedule,
"relevant EEA State" means—
    (a)   in relation to a person with refugee status abroad, the EEA State the government of which has determined that he, or a person on whom he is dependent, is entitled to protection as a refugee under the Refugee Convention;
    (b)   in relation to an EEA national, the EEA State of which he, or a person on whom he is dependent, is a national;
"travel arrangements" means arrangements made under regulation 3(1).

(2) In these Regulations and for the purposes of Schedule 3 to the Act, a "dependant" of a person means a person who at the relevant time—

    (a)   is his spouse;
    (b)   is a child of his or of his spouse;
    (c)   is a member of his or his spouse's close family and is under 18;
    (d)   has been living as part of his household—
        (i)   for at least six of the twelve months before the relevant time, or
        (ii) since birth,
and is under 18;

    (e)   is in need of care and attention from him or a member of his household by reason of a disability and would fall under (c) or (d) but for the fact that he is not under 18;

    (f)   has been living with him as an unmarried couple for at least two of the three years before the relevant time,

and "dependent" has the corresponding meaning.

(3)   In paragraph (2)—

"relevant time" means, in relation to any arrangements made by a local authority in respect of a person, the time when the local authority begins to make those arrangements;

"unmarried couple" means a man and woman who, though not married to each other, are living together as if married.

Initial Commencement
Specified date: 8 January 2003: see reg 1.

3   Power for local authorities to arrange travel and provide accommodation

(1)   A local authority may make arrangements ("travel arrangements") enabling a person with refugee status abroad or who is an EEA national to leave the United Kingdom to travel to the relevant EEA State.

(2)   A local authority may make arrangements for the accommodation of a person in respect of whom travel arrangements have been or are to be made pending the implementation of those arrangements.

(3)   A local authority may make arrangements for the accommodation of a person unlawfully in the United Kingdom who has not failed to co-operate with removal directions issued in respect of him.

(4)   Arrangements for a person by virtue of paragraph (2) or (3)—

    (a)   may be made only if the person has with him a dependent child, and

    (b)   may include arrangements for that child.

Initial Commencement
Specified date: 8 January 2003: see reg 1.

4   Requirements relating to travel and accommodation arrangements

(1)   Travel arrangements and arrangements for accommodation must be made so as to secure implementation of those arrangements at the lowest practicable cost to the local authority.

(2)   Subject to the requirements in paragraph (1), travel arrangements made in respect of a person must be made so that the person leaves the United Kingdom as soon as practicable.

(3)   Travel arrangements and arrangements for accommodation may not include cash payments to a person in respect of whom the arrangements are made and must be made in such a way as to prevent the obtaining of services or benefits other than those specified in the arrangements.

(4)   A local authority must have regard to guidance issued by the Secretary of State in making travel arrangements and arrangements for accommodation.

Initial Commencement
Specified date: 8 January 2003: see reg 1.

5   Failure to implement travel arrangements

Where a person with refugee status abroad or an EEA national refuses an offer of travel arrangements or fails to implement or co-operate with travel arrangements, a local authority may make new travel arrangements for him to travel to the relevant EEA State.

Initial Commencement
Specified date: 8 January 2003: see reg 1.

6

(1)   Where a person with refugee status abroad or an EEA national in respect of whom travel arrangements have been made by a local authority fails to implement or co-operate with those travel arrangements, neither that local authority nor any other local authority may make arrangements for the accommodation of that person except in accordance with the following provisions of this regulation.

(2)   Where paragraph (1) applies to a person because of his failure to travel as arranged, the relevant local authority or another local authority may make further arrangements for the accommodation of that person pending the implementation of revised travel arrangements if, but only if, the local authority considers that—

(a)   the failure was for one or both of the reasons set out in paragraph (3) and for no other reason, and

(b)   the person took all reasonable steps to travel as arranged,

and the person has provided or taken all reasonable steps to provide the explanations and evidence requested by the local authority as regards the matters referred to in sub-paragraphs (a) and (b).

(3)   The reasons referred to in paragraph (2) are—

(a)   that the applicant or a person within his family group was medically unfit to travel as arranged;

(b)   that despite his having taken all reasonable steps to ensure that he travelled as arranged, he was prevented from doing so by failure of a transport service.

(4)   Arrangements for accommodation pursuant to this regulation may only be made in accordance with the provisions of these Regulations, including this regulation.

(5)   In this regulation—

(a)   "family group" in relation to a person means that person and those of his dependants who are to travel with him under arrangements made under these Regulations;

(b)   "transport service" means a public transport service or any transport provided or arranged by the local authority.

Initial Commencement
Specified date: 8 January 2003: see reg 1.

IMMIGRATION APPEALS (FAMILY VISITOR) REGULATIONS 2003

2003 No 518

Made . . . . *5th March 2003*

Laid before Parliament . . . . *10th March 2003*

Coming into force . . . . *1st April 2003*

The Secretary of State, in exercise of the powers conferred on him by sections 90(2) and (3) and 112(1), (2) and (3) of the Nationality, Immigration and Asylum Act 2002, hereby makes the following Regulations:

1

These Regulations may be cited as the Immigration Appeals (Family Visitor) Regulations 2003 and shall come into force on 1st April 2003.

Initial Commencement
Specified date: 1 April 2003: see above.

2

(1)   For the purposes of section 90(1) of the Nationality, Immigration and Asylum Act 2002, a "member of the applicant's family" is any of the following persons—

    (a)   the applicant's spouse, father, mother, son, daughter, grandfather, grandmother, grandson, granddaughter, brother, sister, uncle, aunt, nephew, niece or first cousin;

    (b)   the father, mother, brother or sister of the applicant's spouse;

    (c)   the spouse of the applicant's son or daughter;

    (d)   the applicant's stepfather, stepmother, stepson, stepdaughter, stepbrother or stepsister; or

    (e)   a person with whom the applicant has lived as a member of an unmarried couple for at least two of the three years before the day on which his application for entry clearance was made.

(2)   In these Regulations, "first cousin" means, in relation to a person, the son or daughter of his uncle or aunt.

Initial Commencement
Specified date: 1 April 2003: see above.

IMMIGRATION EMPLOYMENT DOCUMENT (FEES) REGULATIONS 2003

2003 No 541

Made . . . . *6th March 2003*

Laid before Parliament . . . . *11th March 2003*

Coming into force . . . . *1st April 2003*

In exercise of the powers conferred upon him by section 122 of the Nationality, Immigration and Asylum Act 2002, the Secretary of State hereby makes the following Regulations:

1   Citation, commencement and interpretation

These Regulations may be cited as the Immigration Employment Document (Fees) Regulations 2003.

Initial Commencement
Specified date: 1 April 2003: see reg 2.

2

These Regulations shall come into force on 1st April 2003.

Initial Commencement
Specified date: 1 April 2003: see above.

3

In these Regulations:

"application" means an application for an immigration employment document;

...

"Highly Skilled Migrant Programme" means a programme operated by the Secretary of State for highly skilled migrants under the immigration rules; and

"school teacher" has the meaning given by section 5 of the School Teachers' Pay and Conditions Act 1991;

...

Initial Commencement
Specified date: 1 April 2003: see reg 2.

Amendment
Definition "excepted country" (omitted) revoked by SI 2004/1044, reg 2(1), (2). Date in force: 1 May 2004: see SI 2004/1044, reg 1.
Definition "the Sectors-Based Scheme" (omitted) inserted by SI 2003/1277, reg 2(1), (2). Date in force: 30 May 2003: see SI 2003/1277, reg 1.
Definition "the Sectors-Based Scheme" (omitted) revoked by SI 2004/1485, reg 2(1), (2). Date in force: 2 July 2004: see SI 2004/1485, reg 1.

4   Payment of a fee

An application shall, subject to regulations [4A, ...] [4C,] [4D,] 5 and 6, be accompanied by a fee of [£153].

Initial Commencement
Specified date: 1 April 2003: see reg 2.

Appendix 1   Legislation and materials

Amendment
Reference in square brackets beginning "4A," inserted by SI 2003/1277, reg 2(1), (3). Date in force: 30 May 2003: see SI 2003/1277, reg 1.
Reference omitted revoked by SI 2004/1485, reg 2(1), (3)(a). Date in force: 2 July 2004: see SI 2004/1485, reg 1.
Reference to "4C," in square brackets inserted by SI 2003/2447, reg 2(1), (2). Date in force: 20 October 2003: see SI 2003/2447, reg 1.
Reference to "4D," in square brackets inserted by SI 2003/2626, reg 2(1), (2). Date in force: 31 October 2003: see SI 2003/2626, reg 1.
Sum "£153" in square brackets substituted by SI 2004/1485, reg 2(1), (3)(b). Date in force: 2 July 2004: see SI 2004/1485, reg 1.

[4A   Fee in relation to a group application]

[(1)   Subject to paragraph (3), where an application is made by a single employer in respect of a number of persons who form a group, each of whom is seeking to enter, or remain, in the United Kingdom as a person to whom paragraph (2) applies, a single fee of £95 is payable in relation to that application.

(2)   This paragraph applies to a person who is seeking to enter, or remain, in the United Kingdom—

(a)   as a person employed by a ballet or other dance group, theatre group, circus troupe, or orchestra or other group of musicians; and
(b)   for the purpose of fulfilling a contractual obligation to perform in that capacity in the United Kingdom.

(3)   Regulation 5 will only except an application referred to in paragraph (1) from the requirement that it be accompanied by a fee if every person in respect of whom the application is made is a person to whom regulation 5(a) applies.]

Amendment
Inserted by SI 2003/1277, reg 2(1), (4). Date in force: 30 May 2003: see SI 2003/1277, reg 1.

[4B
[...]

Amendment
Inserted by SI 2003/1277, reg 2(1), (4). Date in force: 30 May 2003: see SI 2003/1277, reg 1.
Revoked by SI 2004/1485, reg 2(1), (4). Date in force: 2 July 2004: see SI 2004/1485, reg 1.

[4C   Fee in relation to an application made in respect of a seasonal agricultural worker

[Subject to regulation 5(a), an application made in respect of a person seeking to enter, or remain, in the United Kingdom as a seasonal agricultural worker under the immigration rules shall be accompanied by a fee of £12.]

Amendment
Inserted by SI 2003/2447, reg 2(1), (3). Date in force: 20 October 2003: see SI 2003/2447, reg 1.

[4D   Fee in relation to an application made in respect of a highly skilled migrant]

[Subject to regulation 5(a), an application made in respect of a person seeking to enter, or remain, in the United Kingdom under the Highly Skilled Migrant Programme shall be accompanied by a fee of [£315]].

Amendment
Inserted by SI 2003/2626, reg 2(1), (3). Date in force: 31 October 2003: see SI 2003/2626, reg 1.

Sum "£315" in square brackets substituted by SI 2005/627, reg 2. Date in force: 1 April 2005: see SI 2005/627, reg 1.

[5 Exception]

[An application need not be accompanied by a fee if it is made in respect of a person who is a national of a state which has ratified the Council Of Europe Social Charter (signed in Turin on 18th October 1961) or the Council of Europe Revised Social Charter (signed in Strasbourg on 3rd May 1996).]

Amendment
Substituted by SI 2004/1044, reg 2(1), (3). Date in force: 1 May 2004: see SI 2004/1044, reg 1.

6 Provision in respect of school teachers in England

An application that is not excepted by regulation [5] and which is made in respect of a person seeking to enter, or remain, in the United Kingdom as a school teacher employed in England need not be accompanied by a fee but shall be subject to the special payment arrangement referred to in regulation 7.

Initial Commencement
Specified date: 1 April 2003: see reg 2.

Amendment
Reference to "5" in square brackets substituted by SI 2004/1044, reg 2(1), (4). Date in force: 1 May 2004: see SI 2004/1044, reg 1.

7 Special payment arrangement

Payment of a fee in respect of an application referred to in regulation 6 shall be made in accordance with an arrangement entered into for this purpose between the Secretary of State for the Home Department and the Secretary of State for the Department for Education and Skills.

Initial Commencement
Specified date: 1 April 2003: see reg 2.

SCHEDULE
...

Amendment
Revoked by SI 2004/1044, reg 2(1), (5). Date in force: 1 May 2004: see SI 2004/1044, reg 1.

NATIONALITY, IMMIGRATION AND ASYLUM ACT 2002 (COMMENCEMENT NO 4) ORDER 2003

2003 No 754

Made . . . . *14th March 2003*

In exercise of the powers conferred upon him by section 162(1), (4) and (6) of the Nationality, Immigration and Asylum Act 2002, the Secretary of State hereby makes the following Order:

1 Citation and interpretation

(1) This Order may be cited as the Nationality, Immigration and Asylum Act 2002 (Commencement No 4) Order 2003.

(2) In this Order—

"the 1971 Act" means the Immigration Act 1971;
"the 1988 Act" means the Immigration Act 1988;
"the 1993 Act" means the Asylum and Immigration Appeals Act 1993;
"the 1997 Act" means the Special Immigration Appeals Commission Act 1997;
"the 1999 Act" means the Immigration and Asylum Act 1999; and
"the 2002 Act" means the Nationality, Immigration and Asylum Act 2002.

Initial Commencement
Date made: 14 March 2003: (no specific commencement provision).

2 Commencement and appointed date provisions

(1) The provisions of the 2002 Act specified in column 1 of Schedule 1 to this Order shall come into force on the date specified in column 2 of that Schedule, but where a particular purpose is specified in relation to any such provision in column 3 of that Schedule, the provision concerned shall come into force on that date only for that purpose.

(2) The date appointed under section 162(4) of the 2002 Act for the purposes of section 8 of that Act is 1st April 2003.

Initial Commencement
Date made: 14 March 2003: (no specific commencement provision).

3 Transitional provisions

(1) Subject to Schedule 2, the new appeals provisions are not to have effect in relation to events which took place before 1st April 2003 and, notwithstanding their repeal by the provisions of the 2002 Act commenced by this Order, the old appeals provisions are to continue to have effect in relation to such events.

(2) Schedule 2, which makes further transitional provisions, has effect.

Initial Commencement
Date made: 14 March 2003: (no specific commencement provision).

4 Definitions for transitional provisions

(1) In this Order—

2280

(a) "the new appeals provisions" means sections 82 to 99 and sections 101 to 103 of the 2002 Act; together with any provision (including subordinate legislation) of—
  (i) the 2002 Act;
  (ii) the 1971 Act, the 1997 Act and the 1999 Act (all as amended by the 2002 Act);
which refer to those provisions;

(b) "the old appeals provisions" means—
  (i) sections 13 to 17 of the 1971 Act;
  (ii) subsections (1) to (4) of section 8 of the 1993 Act;
  (iii) the 1997 Act (without the amendments made by the 2002 Act);
  (iv) Part IV of, and Schedule 4 (except paragraphs 10 to 20 and 23) to, the 1999 Act;
  (v) section 115 of the 2002 Act;
together with—
  (vi) any subordinate legislation which applies to those provisions (unless specific provision is made to the contrary); and
  (vii) any provision of the old Immigration Acts which refers to those provisions;

(c) "the old Immigration Acts" means the 1971 Act, the 1988 Act, the 1993 Act, the 1996 Act, the 1997 Act and the 1999 Act, all without the amendments made by the 2002 Act.

(3) For the purposes of article 3 and Schedule 2, an event has taken place under the old Immigration Acts where—

(a) a notice was served;
(b) a decision was made or taken;
(c) directions were given; and
(d) a certificate was issued.

(4) For the purposes of this Order—

(a) a notice was served;
(b) a decision was made or taken;
(c) directions were given; and
(d) a certificate was issued;

on the day on which it was or they were sent to the person concerned, if sent by post or by fax, or delivered to that person, if delivered by hand.

(5) In this article—

(a) "the person concerned" means the person who is the subject of the notice, decision, directions or certificate or the person who appears to be his representative; and
(b) a reference to the issue of a certificate is a reference to the issue of a certificate under section 11, 12 or 72(2) of the 1999 Act or section 115 of the 2002 Act.

Initial Commencement
Date made: 14 March 2003: (no specific commencement provision).

SCHEDULE 1

Article 2

Column 1	Column 2	Column 3
Section 4 (deprivation of citizenship).	1st April 2003	

Section 12 (British citizenship: registration of certain persons without other citizenship).	30th April 2003	
Section 13 (British citizenship: registration of certain persons born between 1961 and 1983).	30th April 2003	
Section 68 (1) to (5) (bail).	1st April 2003	
Section 72 (9) and (10) (serious criminal).	1st April 2003	
Section 77 (no removal while claim for asylum pending).	1st April 2003	
Section 78 (no removal while appeal pending).	1st April 2003	
Section 79 (deportation order: appeal).	1st April 2003	
Section 80 (removal of asylum-seeker to third country).	1st April 2003	So far as not already in force.
Section 81 (adjudicators).	1st April 2003	
Section 82 (right of appeal: general).	1st April 2003	
Section 83 (appeal: asylum claim).	1st April 2003	
Section 84 (grounds of appeal).	1st April 2003	
Section 85 (matters to be considered).	1st April 2003	
Section 86 (determination of appeal).	1st April 2003	
Section 87 (successful appeal: direction).	1st April 2003	
Section 88 (ineligibility).	1st April 2003	
Section 89 (visitor or student without entry clearance).	1st April 2003	
Section 90 (non-family visitor).	1st April 2003	
Section 91 (student).	1st April 2003	
Section 92 (appeal from within United Kingdom: general).	1st April 2003	
Section 93 (appeal from within United Kingdom: "third country" removal).	1st April 2003	
Section 94 (appeal from within United Kingdom: unfounded human rights or asylum claim).	1st April 2003	
Section 95 (appeal from outside United Kingdom: removal).	1st April 2003	
Section 96 (earlier right of appeal).	1st April 2003	
Section 97 (national security, &c.)	1st April 2003	
Section 98 (other grounds of public good).	1st April 2003	
Section 99 (sections 96 to 98: appeal in progress).	1st April 2003	
Section 100 (Immigration Appeal Tribunal).	1st April 2003	
Section 101 (appeal to Tribunal).	1st April 2003	
Section 102 (decision).	1st April 2003	
Section 103 (appeal from Tribunal).	1st April 2003	
Section 104 (pending appeal).	1st April 2003	
Section 105 (notice of immigration decision).	1st April 2003	
Section 106 (rules).	1st April 2003	
Section 107 (practice directions).	1st April 2003	
Section 108 (forged document: proceedings in private).	1st April 2003	
Section 109 (European Union and European Economic Area).	1st April 2003	
Section 110 (grants).	1st April 2003	
Section 111 (monitor of certification of claims as unfounded).	1st April 2003	

Section 114 (1) and (2) (repeal).	1st April 2003	
Section 116 (Special Immigration Appeals Commission: Community Legal Service).	1st April 2003	
Section 117 (Northern Ireland appeals: legal aid).	1st April 2003	
Section 118 (leave pending decision on variation application).	1st April 2003	
Section 120 (requirement to state additional grounds for application).	1st April 2003	
Section 123 (advice about work permit, &c.).	[1st April 2004]	
Section 126 (physical data: compulsory provision).	1st April 2003	
Section 130 (Inland Revenue).	1st April 2003	
Section 142 (Advisory Panel on Country Information).	1st April 2003	
Section 147(1), (3) and (4) (employment).	1st April 2003	
Section 147(2) (employment).	1st April 2003	For the purpose of enabling subordinate legislation to be made under it.
Schedule 4 (Immigration and Asylum Appeals: Adjudicators).	1st April 2003	
Schedule 5 (The Immigration Appeal Tribunal).	1st April 2003	
Schedule 6 (Immigration and Asylum Appeals: Transitional Provision).	1st April 2003	
Schedule 7 (Immigration and Asylum Appeals: Consequential Amendments).	1st April 2003	So far as not already in force.
Section 161 and Schedule 9 (repeals) (the entries relating to sections 3(9)(b), 29 and 31(d) of the Immigration Act 1971; to sections 19E(7) and 71A(1) of the Race Relations Act 1976; to sections 7 to 9, 10, 19 to 21, 22, 27(2), 28, 33, 44(2) and (3) of and Schedule 2 paragraph 3(1)(b) and Schedule 4 to the British Nationality Act 1981; to section 4(3)(b) of the British Nationality (Falkland Islands) Act 1983; to section 1(5) of the British Nationality (Hong Kong) Act 1990; to sections 2A, 4, 5(1)(a) and (b) and (2) and 7A of, and Schedule 2 to, the Special Immigration Appeals Commission Act 1997; to sections 15, and 56 to 81, of, and Schedules 2 to 4, and 14, to, the 1999 Act; and to Schedule 2 to the Race Relations Amendment Act 2000.	1st April 2003	

Initial Commencement
Date made: 14 March 2003: (no specific commencement provision).

Amendment
In entry relating to the Nationality, Immigration and Asylum Act 2002, s 123, in column 2 words "1st April 2004" in square brackets substituted by SI 2003/2993, art 3. Date in force: 19 November 2003: see SI 2003/2993, art 2.

SCHEDULE 2

Article 3

1   Transitional provisions relating to the 2002 Act

(1) In this paragraph, a reference to a section or to a Schedule is to be read as a reference to a section of, or to a Schedule to, the 2002 Act, unless otherwise specified.

(2) Section 77 (no removal while claim for asylum pending) shall have effect in relation to a claim for asylum pending on 31st March 2003 as it has effect in relation to a claim for asylum pending under the 2002 Act.

(3) Section 78 (no removal while appeal pending) shall have effect in relation to an appeal pending under the old appeals provisions as it has effect in relation to an appeal pending under section 82(1) of the 2002 Act.

(4) Section 79 (deportation order: appeal) shall have effect in relation to an appeal pending under the old appeals provisions as it has effect in relation to an appeal pending under section 82(1) of the 2002 Act.

[(4A) Section 101(1) shall apply to a party to an appeal to an adjudicator under Part 4 of the 1999 Act which is determined on or after 9th June 2003, as it applies to a party to an appeal to an adjudicator under section 82 or 83.

(4B) Where section 101(1) applies by virtue of sub-paragraph (4A) above—

(a) sections 101(2) and (3), 102 and 103 shall apply in relation to any appeal or application for permission to appeal under section 101(1) subject to the modifications that—
   (i) in section 102(1)(d), the reference to section 87 shall be treated as being a reference to paragraph 21 of Schedule 4 to the 1999 Act; and
   (ii) in section 102(3), the reference to section 82 shall be treated as being a reference to Part 4 of the 1999 Act; and
(b) paragraphs 7, 22 and 23 of Schedule 4 to the 1999 Act shall not apply.]

(5) Section 115 (appeal from within the United Kingdom: unfounded human rights claim or asylum claim: transitional provision) shall continue to have effect in relation to any person who made an asylum claim or human rights claim (as defined in subsection (10)) on or after 1st April 2003.

2   Transitional provisions relating to the appeals provisions of the 1971 Act

(1) In this paragraph, a reference to a section or to a Schedule is to be read as a reference to a section of, or to a Schedule to, the 1971 Act, unless otherwise specified.

[(2) Section 3C of the 1971 Act (continuation of leave pending variation decision), as substituted by section 118 of the 2002 Act, shall apply in relation to an application made before 1st April 2003, in respect of which no decision has been made on or before 1st April 2003, as it applies to such an application made after 1st April 2003.]

(3) Section 5 (procedure for, and further provisions as to, deportation) is to continue to have effect in relation to—

(a) any person on whom the Secretary of State has, before 2nd October 2000, served a notice of his decision to make a deportation order; and
(b) any person—
   (i) who applied during the regularisation period fixed by section 9 of the 1999 Act, in accordance with the Immigration (Regularisation Period for Overstayers) Regulations 2000, for leave to remain in the United Kingdom; and

(ii) on whom the Secretary of State has since served a notice of his decision to make a deportation order;

and, for the purposes of section 5, such a person is to be taken to be a person who is liable to deportation under section 3(5).

(4) Section 13 (appeals against exclusions from the United Kingdom) is to continue to have effect where the decision to refuse leave to enter the United Kingdom, or to refuse a certificate of entitlement or an entry clearance, was made before 2nd October 2000.

(5) Section 14 (appeals against conditions) is to continue to have effect where the decision to vary, or to refuse to vary, the limited leave to enter or remain was made before 2nd October 2000.

(6) Section 15 (appeals in respect of deportation orders) is to continue to have effect in relation to—

(a) any person on whom the Secretary of State has, before 2nd October 2000, served a notice of his decision to make a deportation order; and

(b) any person—
   (i) who applied during the regularisation period fixed by section 9 of the 1999 Act, in accordance with the Immigration (Regularisation Period for Overstayers) Regulations 2000, for leave to remain in the United Kingdom; and
   (ii) on whom the Secretary of State has since served a notice of his decision to make a deportation order.

(7) Section 16 (appeals against validity of directions for removal) is to continue to have effect where the directions for a person's removal from the United Kingdom were given before 2nd October 2000.

(8) Section 17 (appeals against removal on objection to destination) is to continue to have effect—

(a) where the directions for a person's removal from the United Kingdom were given, or the notice specifying the destination of his removal was served, before 2nd October 2000; and

(b) in relation to any person—
   (i) who applied during the regularisation period fixed by section 9 of the 1999 Act, in accordance with the Immigration (Regularisation Period for Overstayers) Regulations 2000, for leave to remain in the United Kingdom; and
   (ii) on whom the Secretary of State has since served a notice of his decision to make a deportation order.

(9) Section 21 (references of cases by Secretary of State for further consideration) (including that section as applied by paragraph 4 of Schedule 2 to the 1993 Act) is to continue to have effect where the Secretary of State has referred a matter for consideration under that section before 2nd October 2000.

(10) Where an appeal is made under Part II (including that Part as it applies by virtue of Schedule 2 to the 1993 Act)—

(a) paragraph 28 of Schedule 2 (stay on directions for removal) (including that paragraph as applied by paragraph 9 of Schedule 2 to the 1993 Act) is to continue to have effect;

(b) the following provisions are not to have effect—
   (i) paragraph 29(1) of Schedule 2 (grant of bail pending appeal) (including that paragraph as applied by paragraph 9 of Schedule 2 to the 1993 Act and by section 3(6) of the 1996 Act), as amended by paragraph 66 of Schedule 14 to the 1999 Act;

2285

(ii) paragraph 3 of Schedule 3 (effect of appeals) including that paragraph as applied by paragraph 9 of Schedule 2 to the 1993 Act), as amended by paragraph 69 of Schedule 14 to the 1999 Act.

3   Transitional provision relating to the appeals provisions of the 1988 Act

Section 5 (restricted right of appeal against deportation in cases of breach of limited leave) is to continue to have effect—

(a) where the directions for a person's removal from the United Kingdom were given, or the notice specifying the destination of his removal was served, before 2nd October 2000,

(b) in relation to any person—

(i) who applied during the regularisation period fixed by section 9 of the 1999 Act, in accordance with the Immigration (Regularisation Period for Overstayers) Regulations 2000, for leave to remain in the United Kingdom; and

(ii) on whom the Secretary of State has since served a notice of his decision to make a deportation order.

4   Transitional provisions relating to the appeals provisions of the 1993 Act

(1) In this paragraph, a reference to a section or to a Schedule is to be read as a reference to a section of, or to a Schedule to, the 1993 Act, unless otherwise specified.

(2) In section 8 (asylum appeals)—

(a) subsection (1) is to continue to have effect where the decision to refuse leave to enter was made before 2nd October 2000;

(b) subsection (2) is to continue to have effect where the decision to vary, or to refuse to vary, the limited leave to enter or remain was made before 2nd October 2000;

(c) subsection (3) is to continue to have effect where the decision to make a deportation order, or the decision to refuse to revoke a deportation order, was made before 2nd October 2000;

(d) subsection (4) is to continue to have effect where the directions for a person's removal from the United Kingdom were given before 2nd October 2000.

(3) Where an appeal is made under Part II of the 1971 Act (including that Part as it applies by virtue of Schedule 2)—

(a) section 9A (bail pending appeal from Immigration Appeal Tribunal), as amended by paragraphs 105 and 106 of Schedule 14 to the 1999 Act, is not to have effect;

(b) the reference in section 9A (without the amendments made by the 1999 Act) to section 9 (appeals from Immigration Appeal Tribunal) is to include a reference to paragraph 23 of Schedule 4 to the 1999 Act (appeals from Immigration Appeal Tribunal).

(4) Where an appeal is made under section 8, the section 8 appeals provisions are to continue to have effect.

(5) In this paragraph "the section 8 appeals provisions" means—

(a) paragraph 1 of Schedule 2 (asylum appeal rights to replace rights under the 1971 Act);

(b) paragraph 2 of Schedule 2 (scope of asylum rights of appeal);

(c) paragraph 3 of Schedule 2 (other grounds for appeal);

(d) paragraph 5 of Schedule 2 (special appeals procedures for claims without foundation);

(e) paragraph 6 of Schedule 2 (exception for national security);

(f) paragraph 7 of Schedule 2 (suspension of variation of limited leave pending appeal);

(g) paragraph 8 of Schedule 2 (deportation order not to be made while appeal pending);

(h) paragraph 9 of Schedule 2 (stay of removal directions pending appeal and bail).

(6) Where an appeal is made under section 8, the reference in paragraph 5 of Schedule 2 to section 20(1) of the 1971 Act (appeals to the Immigration Appeal Tribunal) is to include a reference to paragraph 22(1) of Schedule 4 to the 1999 Act (appeals to the Immigration Appeal Tribunal).

5   Transitional provision relating to the 1997 Act

(1) The amendments to the 1997 Act made by the provisions of the 2002 Act commenced by this Order are not to have effect in relation to an appeal which is pending, by virtue of section 7A of the 1997 Act, on 1st April 2003 and, notwithstanding their amendment by the provisions commenced by this Order, the old appeal provisions are to continue to have effect in relation to such an appeal.

6   Transitional provisions relating to the 1999 Act

(1) In this paragraph, a reference to a section or to a Schedule is to be read as a reference to a section of, or to a Schedule to, the 1999 Act, unless otherwise specified.

(2) Section 10 (removal of certain persons unlawfully in the United Kingdom) is not to have effect in relation to—

(a) any person on whom the Secretary of State has, before 2nd October 2000, served a notice of his intention to make a deportation order; and

(b) any person—

(i) who applied during the regularisation period fixed by section 9 of the 1999 Act, in accordance with the Immigration (Regularisation Period for Overstayers) Regulations 2000 for leave to remain in the United Kingdom; and

(ii) on whom the Secretary of State has since served a notice of his decision to make a deportation order;

and, for the purposes of section 5, such a person is to be taken to be a person who is liable to deportation under section 3(5).

(3) Where a certificate is issued under section 11 (removal of asylum-seeker to third country), as substituted by section 80 of the 2002 Act, before 1st April 2003 and an allegation is made after 1st April the allegation may be certified under section 72(2) of the 1999 Act, notwithstanding its repeal by the provisions of the 2002 Act commenced by this Order, and that certification shall have effect for the purposes of an appeal under the old appeal provisions.

(4) Subject to the provisions of the Order and any other enactment sections 59 to 78 and Schedules 2 to 4 shall continue to have effect in relation to events which took place before 1st April 2003.

(5) Where a decision has been taken under the Immigration Acts relating to a person's entitlement to enter or remain in the United Kingdom before 1st April 2003 there shall only be a right of appeal under section 65(1) where an allegation is made before 1st July 2003.

Initial Commencement
Date made: 14 March 2003: (no specific commencement provision).

Amendment
Para 1: sub-paras (4A), (4B) inserted by SI 2003/1339, art 4. Date in force: 9 June 2003: see SI 2003/1339, art 2(2).
Para 2: sub-para (2) substituted by SI 2003/1040, art 2. Date in force: 8 April 2003: see SI 2003/1040, art 1.

ASYLUM (DESIGNATED STATES) ORDER 2003

2003 No 970

Made . . . . *31st March 2003*

Coming into force in accordance with article 2

Whereas a draft of this Order has been laid before and approved by resolution of each House of Parliament;

And whereas the Secretary of State is satisfied that there is in general in the States listed in articles 3 and 4 no serious risk of persecution of persons entitled to reside in those States and that removal to those States of persons entitled to reside there will not in general contravene the United Kingdom's obligations under the Human Rights Convention;

Now, therefore, in exercise of the powers conferred on him by sections 94(5) and 115(8) of the Nationality, Immigration and Asylum Act 2002, the Secretary of State hereby makes the following Order:

1   Citation and interpretation

(1)   This Order may be cited as the Asylum (Designated States) Order 2003.

(2)   In this Order, "the 2002 Act" means the Nationality, Immigration and Asylum Act 2002.

Initial Commencement
Specified date: 1 April 2003: see art 2(1).

2   Commencement

(1)   This Order, except article 3, shall come into force on the day after the day on which this Order is made.

(2)   Article 3 shall come into force on the day on which section 94(4) of the 2002 Act comes into force.

Initial Commencement
Specified date: 1 April 2003: see para (1) above.

3   Designated States

The States listed below shall be added to the list of States in section 94(4) of the 2002 Act:

"(k) the Republic of Albania,
(l)   Bulgaria,
(m) Serbia and Montenegro,
(n)   Jamaica,
(o)   Macedonia,

(p) the Republic of Moldova, and
(q) Romania.".

Appointment
Appointment: 1 April 2003: see SI 2003/754, art 2, Sch 1.

4

The States listed below shall be added to the list of States in section 115(7) of the 2002 Act:

"(k) the Republic of Albania,
(l) Bulgaria,
(m) Serbia and Montenegro,
(n) Jamaica,
(o) Macedonia,
(p) the Republic of Moldova, and
(q) Romania.".

Initial Commencement
Specified date: 1 April 2003: see para (1) above.

IMMIGRATION (PASSENGER TRANSIT VISA) ORDER 2003

2003 No 1185

Made . . . . *30th April 2003*

Laid before Parliament . . . . *1st May 2003*

Coming into force . . . . *2nd May 2003*

In exercise of the powers conferred upon him by section 41 of the Immigration and Asylum Act 1999 the Secretary of State hereby makes the following Order:

1 Citation, commencement and interpretation
This order may be cited as the Immigration (Passenger Transit Visa) Order 2003 and shall come into force on 2nd May 2003.

Initial Commencement
Specified date: 2 May 2003: see above.

2

(1) Subject to paragraph (4), in this Order a "transit passenger" means a person to whom paragraph (2) or (3) applies and who on arrival in the United Kingdom passes through to another country or territory without entering the United Kingdom.

(2) This paragraph applies to a person who is a citizen or national of a country or territory listed in Schedule 1 to this Order.

(3) This paragraph applies to a person holding a travel document issued by:

(a) the purported "Turkish Republic of Northern Cyprus";

(b)   the former Socialist Republic of Yugoslavia;
(c)   the former Federal Republic of Yugoslavia; or
(d)   the former Zaire.

(4)   A person to whom paragraph (2) or (3) applies will not be a transit passenger if he:

(a)   has the right of abode in the United Kingdom under the Immigration Act 1971;
(b)   is a national of an EEA State; or
(c)   in the case of a national or citizen of the People's Republic of China, holds a passport issued by either the Hong Kong Special Administrative Region or the Macao Special Administrative Region.

(5)   In [this Order] "EEA State" means a country which is a contracting party to the Agreement on the European Economic Area signed at Oporto on 2nd May 1992 as adjusted by the Protocol signed at Brussels on 17th March 1993.

Initial Commencement
Specified date: 2 May 2003: see art 1.

Amendment
Para (5): words "this Order" in square brackets substituted by SI 2003/2628, art 2(1), (2). Date in force: 16 October 2003: see SI 2003/2628, art 1.

3   Requirement for a transit passenger to hold a transit visa

[Subject to article 3A, a] transit passenger is required to hold a transit visa.

Initial Commencement
Specified date: 2 May 2003: see art 1.

Amendment
Words "Subject to article 3A, a" in square brackets substituted by SI 2003/2628, art 2(1), (3). Date in force: 16 October 2003: see SI 2003/2628, art 1.

[3A   Exemption from the requirement for a transit passenger to hold a transit visa]

[(1)   A transit passenger is not required to hold a transit visa if he holds or a person with whom he arrives in the United Kingdom holds on his behalf:

(a)   a valid visa for entry to [Australia, Canada, New Zealand or the United States of America] and a valid airline ticket for travel via the United Kingdom [as part of a journey] from another country or territory to the country in respect of which the visa is held;
[(ab) a valid visa for entry to Australia, Canada, New Zealand or the United States of America and a valid airline ticket for travel via the United Kingdom as part of a journey from the country in respect of which the visa is held to another country or territory;]
[(b)   a valid airline ticket for travel via the United Kingdom as part of a journey from Australia, Canada, New Zealand or the United States of America to another country or territory, provided that the transit passenger does not seek to travel via the United Kingdom on a date more than six months from the date on which he last entered Australia, Canada, New Zealand or the United States of America with a valid visa for entry to that country;]
(c)   a valid USA I-551 Permanent Resident Card issued on or after 21st April 1998;
(d)   a valid Canadian Permanent Resident Card issued on or after 28th June 2002;

(e)   a valid common format Category D visa for entry to an EEA State;

(f)   a valid common format residence permit issued by an EEA State pursuant to Council Regulation (EC) No 1030/2002;

(g)   a diplomatic or service passport issued by the People's Republic of China; ...

(h)   a diplomatic or official passport issued by India[; or

(i)   a diplomatic or official passport issued by Vietnam].

(2)   ...]

Amendment
Inserted by SI 2003/2628, art 2(1), (4). Date in force: 16 October 2003: see SI 2003/2628, art 1.
Para (1): in sub-para (a) words "Australia, Canada, New Zealand or the United States of America" in square brackets substituted by SI 2005/492, art 2(1), (2)(a). Date in force: 9 March 2005: see SI 2005/492, art 1.
Para (1): in sub-para (a) words "as part of a journey" in square brackets inserted by SI 2004/1304, art 2(1), (2)(a). Date in force: 13 May 2004: see SI 2004/1304, art 1.
Para (1): sub-para (ab) inserted by SI 2005/492, art 2(1), (2)(b). Date in force: 9 March 2005: see SI 2005/492, art 1.
Para (1): sub-para (b) substituted by SI 2005/492, art 2(1), (2)(c). Date in force: 9 March 2005: see SI 2005/492, art 1.
Para (1): in sub-para (g) word omitted revoked by virtue of SI 2004/1304, art 2(1), (2)(c). Date in force: 13 May 2004: see SI 2004/1304, art 1.
Para (1): sub-para (i) and word "; or" immediately preceding it inserted by virtue of SI 2004/1304, art 2(1), (2)(c). Date in force: 13 May 2004: see SI 2004/1304, art 1.
Para (2): revoked by SI 2004/1304, art 2(1), (2)(d). Date in force: 13 May 2004: see SI 2004/1304, art 1.

4   Method of application for a transit visa

An application for a transit visa may be made to any British High Commission, Embassy or Consulate which accepts such applications.

Initial Commencement
Specified date: 2 May 2003: see art 1.

5 Revocations

The Orders specified in Schedule 2 to this Order are hereby revoked.

Initial Commencement
Specified date: 2 May 2003: see art 1.

[SCHEDULE 1
COUNTRIES OR TERRITORIES WHOSE NATIONALS OR CITIZENS NEED TRANSIT VISAS]

[Article 2]

[Afghanistan

Albania

Algeria

Angola

Bangladesh

Belarus

Burma

Burundi

Cameroon

Appendix 1   Legislation and materials

Colombia

[Congo]

Democratic Republic of the Congo

Ecuador

Eritrea

Ethiopia

Former Yugoslav Republic of Macedonia

Gambia

Ghana

[Guinea

Guinea-Bissau]

India

Iran

Iraq

Ivory Coast

[Kenya]

Lebanon

Liberia

Moldova

[Mongolia]

Nepal

Nigeria

Pakistan

Palestinian Territories

People's Republic of China

Rwanda

Senegal

Serbia and Montenegro

Sierra Leone

Somalia

Sri Lanka

Sudan

[Tanzania]

Turkey

Uganda

Vietnam

Zimbabwe]

2292

Amendment
Substituted by SI 2003/2628, art 2(1), (5), Schedule. Date in force: 16 October 2003: see SI 2003/2628, art 1.
Entry "Congo" inserted by SI 2005/492, art 2(1), (3)(a). Date in force: 9 March 2005: see SI 2005/492, art 1.
Entries "Guinea" and "Guinea-Bissau" inserted by SI 2005/492, art 2(1), (3)(b). Date in force: 9 March 2005: see SI 2005/492, art 1.
Entry "Kenya" inserted by SI 2004/1304, art 2(1), (3)(a). Date in force: 13 May 2004: see SI 2004/1304, art 1.
Entry "Mongolia" inserted by SI 2005/492, art 2(1), (3)(c). Date in force: 9 March 2005: see SI 2005/492, art 1.
Entry "Tanzania" inserted by SI 2004/1304, art 2(1), (3)(b). Date in force: 13 May 2004: see SI 2004/1304, art 1.

SCHEDULE 2
REVOCATIONS

Article 5

(1) Orders revoked	(2) References
The Immigration (Transit Visa) Order 1993	SI 1993/1678
The Immigration (Transit Visa) (Amendment) Order 1998	SI 1998/55
The Immigration (Transit Visa) (Amendment No 2) Order 1998	SI 1998/1014
The Immigration (Transit Visa) (Amendment) Order 2000	SI 2000/1381
The Immigration (Transit Visa) (Amendment) Order 2002	SI 2002/825
The Immigration (Transit Visa) (Amendment No 2) Order 2002	SI 2002/2758

Initial Commencement
Specified date: 2 May 2003: see art 1.

IMMIGRATION (LEAVE TO REMAIN) (FEES) REGULATIONS 2003

2003 No 1711

Made . . . . *9th July 2003*

Laid before Parliament . . . . *10th July 2003*

Coming into force . . . . *1st August 2003*

The Secretary of State, in exercise of the powers conferred on him by sections 5(1), (3)(b) and (7) and 166(3) of the Immigration and Asylum Act 1999, having regard to the meaning of "prescribed" in section 167(1), with the approval of the Treasury, hereby makes the following Regulations:

1

These Regulations may be cited as the Immigration (Leave to Remain) (Fees) Regulations 2003 and shall come into force on 1st August 2003.

Appendix 1   Legislation and materials

Initial Commencement
Specified date: 1 August 2003: see above.

2

In these Regulations:

"application" means an application for—
  (a) leave to remain in the United Kingdom,
  (b) the variation of leave to enter, or remain in, the United Kingdom, or
  [(c) the fixing of a limited leave stamp or indefinite leave stamp on a passport or other document issued to the applicant where the stamp was previously fixed on another passport or document issued to the applicant];
["assistance" means assistance, accommodation or maintenance provided under—
  (a) section 17, 20 or 23 of the Children Act 1989,
  (b) section 22, 25 or 26 of the Children (Scotland) Act 1995, or
  (c) Article 18, 21 or 27 of the Children (Northern Ireland) Order 1995;]
"dependant", of a person, means—
  (a) the spouse or unmarried partner, or
  (b) a child under the age of eighteen,
of that person;
  ...
"immigration rules" has the same meaning as in section 33(1) of the Immigration Act 1971; and
"the 1999 Act" means the Immigration and Asylum Act 1999.

Initial Commencement
Specified date: 1 August 2003: see above.

Amendment
In definition "application" para (c) substituted by SI 2005/654, regs 2, 3. Date in force: 1 April 2005: see SI 2005/654, reg 1.
Definition "assistance" inserted by SI 2004/3105, regs 2, 3(a). Date in force: 17 December 2004: see SI 2004/3105, reg 1.
Definition "immigration employment document" (omitted) revoked by SI 2004/3105, regs 2, 3(b). Date in force: 17 December 2004: see SI 2004/3105, reg 1.

[3

[(1) Subject to section 5(3)(a) of the 1999 Act and regulations 3A, 4 and 5 below, the fee to be paid in connection with an application falling within paragraphs (a) or (b) of the definition of "application" in regulation 2 shall be—

  (a) £500 for an application made in person at a Public Enquiry Office of the Immigration and Nationality Directorate of the Home Office; or
  (b) £335 for an application made by post or courier.

(2) Subject to section 5(3)(a) of the 1999 Act, the fee to be paid in connection with an application falling within paragraph (c) of the definition of "application" in regulation 2 shall be—

  (a) £500 for an application made in person at a Public Enquiry Office of the Immigration and Nationality Directorate of the Home Office; or
  (b) £160 for an application made by post.]

Amendment
Substituted by SI 2005/654, regs 2, 4. Date in force: 1 April 2005: see SI 2005/654, reg 1.

[3A

[(1)   Regulation 3(1) does not apply to an application falling within paragraph (a) or (b) of the definition of "application" in regulation 2 above where the application is for leave to remain in the United Kingdom:

  (a)   as a student,
  (b)   as a student nurse,
  (c)   to re-sit an examination,
  (d)   to write up a thesis,
  (e)   as a student union sabbatical officer, or
  (f)   as a prospective student, under the immigration rules.

(2)   The fee to be paid in connection with an application referred to in paragraph (1) shall be—

  (a)   £500 for an application made in person at a Public Enquiry Office of the Immigration and Nationality Directorate of the Home Office; or
  (b)   £250 for an application made by post.]

Amendment
Substituted (for this regulation as inserted by SI 2004/580, regs 2, 4) by SI 2005/654, regs 2, 5. Date in force: 1 April 2005: see SI 2005/654, reg 1.

4

Where an application is made by an applicant in respect of himself and one or more of his dependants, a single fee is payable in connection with that application.

Initial Commencement
Specified date: 1 August 2003: see reg 1.

5

No fee shall be payable in connection with an application falling within paragraph (a) or (b) of the definition of "application" in regulation 2 above in any of the following circumstances—

  (a)   the application is made under the terms of a European Community Association Agreement;
  [(b)   the application is made in respect of a person seeking a variation of leave to enter or remain in the United Kingdom for a period of up to 6 months where the application is made to an immigration officer on arrival at a port of entry in the United Kingdom;
  (c)   the application is an application [for leave to remain in the United Kingdom:
    (i)   for work permit employment,
    (ii)   as a highly skilled migrant,
    (iii)   as a seasonal agricultural worker,
    (iv)   for the purposes of employment under the Sectors-Based scheme, or
    (v)   for Home Office approved training or work experience,
under the immigration rules] and is made in respect of a person who is a national of a state which has ratified the Council of Europe Social Charter (signed in Turin on 18th October 1961) or the Council of Europe Revised Social Charter (signed in Strasbourg on 3rd May 1996);]
  [(d)   the application is made in respect of a person who, at the time of making the application—
    (i)   is a child under the age of eighteen and is being provided with assistance by a local authority (or, in Northern Ireland, an authority); or

     (ii) has limited leave to enter or remain in the United Kingdom which was granted outside the provisions of the immigration rules when he was under the age of eighteen on the rejection of his claim for asylum, and is seeking further leave to remain in the United Kingdom outside the provisions of the immigration rules; ...]

  (e) the application is made in respect of a person seeking indefinite leave to remain in the United Kingdom on grounds of domestic violence under the immigration rules where, at the time of making the application, the applicant appears to the Secretary of State to be destitute[; or

  (f) the application is made in respect of a person who, at the time of making the application, has limited leave to enter or remain in the United Kingdom which was granted outside the provisions of the immigration rules on the rejection of his asylum claim and is seeking further leave to remain in the United Kingdom outside the provisions of the immigration rules].

Initial Commencement
Specified date: 1 August 2003: see reg 1.

Amendment
Paras (b), (c) substituted, for paras (b)–(d) as originally enacted, by SI 2004/580, regs 2, 5. Date in force: 1 April 2004: see SI 2004/580, reg 1.
In para (c) words from "for leave to" to "the immigration rules" in square brackets substituted by SI 2005/654, regs 2, 6. Date in force: 1 April 2005: see SI 2005/654, reg 1.
Para (d) inserted by SI 2004/3105, regs 2, 4. Date in force: 17 December 2004: see SI 2004/3105, reg 1.
In para (d) word omitted revoked by SI 2005/654, regs 2, 7(a). Date in force: 1 April 2005: see SI 2005/654, reg 1.
Para (f) and word "; or" immediately preceding it inserted by SI 2005/654, regs 2, 7(b). Date in force: 1 April 2005: see SI 2005/654, reg 1.

6

For the purposes of section 5(3)(a)(ii) of the 1999 Act, a "dependant" of a person making a claim for asylum means—

  (a) the spouse or unmarried partner, or
  (b) a child under the age of eighteen,

of such a person.

Initial Commencement
Specified date: 1 August 2003: see reg 1.

IMMIGRATION (PROVISION OF PHYSICAL DATA) REGULATIONS 2003

2003 No 1875

Made . . . . *17th July 2003*

Coming into force . . . . *18th July 2003*

Whereas a draft of these Regulations has been laid before and approved by resolution of each House of Parliament;

Now, therefore, in exercise of the powers conferred upon him by section 126(1) of the Nationality, Immigration and Asylum Act 2002, the Secretary of State hereby makes the following Regulations:

1 Citation, commencement and interpretation

These Regulations may be cited as the Immigration (Provision of Physical Data) Regulations 2003 and shall come into force on the day after they are made.

Initial Commencement
Specified date: 18 July 2003: see above.

2

In these Regulations:

["application" means:

(a) an application for entry clearance made at a British Diplomatic mission or a British Consular post listed in the Schedule to these Regulations; or

(b) an application for leave to enter the United Kingdom where the person seeking leave to enter presents a convention travel document endorsed with an entry clearance;]

"applicant" means a person who makes an application and is aged five or over at the date of making that application;

["convention travel document" means a travel document issued pursuant to Article 28 of the Refugee Convention, except where that travel document was issued by the United Kingdom Government; and

"Refugee Convention" means the Convention relating to the Status of Refugees done at Geneva on 28th July 1951 and its Protocol].

Initial Commencement
Specified date: 18 July 2003: see reg 1.

Amendment
Definition "application" substituted by SI 2004/474, regs 2, 3(a). Date in force: 27 February 2004: see SI 2004/474, reg 1.
Definitions "convention travel document" and "Refugee Convention" inserted by SI 2004/474, regs 2, 3(b). Date in force: 27 February 2004: see SI 2004/474, reg 1.

3 Requirement for an application to be accompanied by a record of fingerprints

An application shall, subject to regulation 4, be accompanied by a record of the fingerprints of the applicant.

Initial Commencement
Specified date: 18 July 2003: see reg 1.

4   Provision in relation to applicants under the age of sixteen

(1)   An applicant under the age of sixteen shall not be required to provide a record of their fingerprints except in the presence of a person aged 18 or over who is—

(a)   the child's parent or guardian; or
(b)   a person who for the time being takes responsibility for the child.

(2)   The person mentioned in sub-paragraph (1)(b) may not be—

(a)   an officer of the Secretary of State who is not an authorised person; or
(b)   an authorised person.

(3)   An applicant under the age of sixteen shall not be required to provide a record of their fingerprints unless it has been confirmed by an authorised person that the applicant's decision to provide it will comply with regulations 4(1) and (2) and that confirmation has been ratified by a person designated for the purpose by the Secretary of State.

(4)   This regulation shall not apply if the authorised person reasonably believes that the applicant is aged sixteen or over.

Initial Commencement
Specified date: 18 July 2003: see reg 1.

[5   Consequences of failure to comply with these Regulations

(1)   Subject to paragraphs (2) and (3), where an application is not accompanied by a record of the applicant's fingerprints it may be treated as invalid.

(2)   An application shall not be treated as invalid under paragraph (1) if it is for leave to enter the United Kingdom where the person seeking leave to enter presents a convention travel document endorsed with an entry clearance.

(3)   Where an application is of a type described in paragraph (2) and is not accompanied by a record of the applicant's fingerprints it may be refused.]

Amendment
Substituted by SI 2004/474, regs 2, 4. Date in force: 27 February 2004: see SI 2004/474, reg 1.

6   Use of fingerprints

The Secretary of State may, in particular, supply information, including copies of fingerprints provided pursuant to these Regulations to any of the persons to whom, and for any of the purposes for which, he may supply information under section 21 of the Immigration and Asylum Act 1999.

Initial Commencement
Specified date: 18 July 2003: see reg 1.

7   Destruction of information

Subject to regulation 8, any record of fingerprints and copies of fingerprints provided by an applicant pursuant to these Regulations must be destroyed by the Secretary of State at the end of ten years from the date on which they were provided.

Initial Commencement
Specified date: 18 July 2003: see reg 1.

8

If an applicant proves that he is—

(a) a British citizen; or
(b) a Commonwealth citizen who has right of abode in the United Kingdom as a result of section 2(1)(b) of the Immigration Act 1971,

any record of fingerprints provided pursuant to these Regulations and any copies of fingerprints must be destroyed as soon as reasonably practicable.

Initial Commencement
Specified date: 18 July 2003: see reg 1.

9

The Secretary of State must take all reasonably practicable steps to secure:

(a) that data held in electronic form which relate to any record of fingerprints which are to be destroyed in accordance with regulation 7 are destroyed or erased; or
(b) that access to such data is blocked.

Initial Commencement
Specified date: 18 July 2003: see reg 1.

10

The applicant to whom the data relates is entitled, on written request, to a certificate issued by the Secretary of State to the effect that he has taken the steps required by regulation 9.

Initial Commencement
Specified date: 18 July 2003: see reg 1.

11

A certificate issued under regulation 10 must be issued within three months of the date on which the request was received by the Secretary of State.

Initial Commencement
Specified date: 18 July 2003: see reg 1.

SCHEDULE
COUNTRIES IN WHICH AN APPLICATION FOR ENTRY CLEARANCE IS AN
"APPLICATION" UNDER THESE REGULATIONS

Regulation 2

[Djibouti

Eritrea

Ethiopia]

[Kenya]

[Rwanda]

Sri Lanka

[Tanzania

Uganda]

Initial Commencement
Specified date: 18 July 2003: see reg 1.

Amendment
Entries "Djibouti", "Eritrea" and "Ethiopia" inserted by SI 2004/474, regs 2, 5(a). Date in force: 27 February 2004: see SI 2004/474, reg 1.
Entry "Kenya" inserted by SI 2004/1834, reg 2(b). Date in force: 1 September 2004: see SI 2004/1834, reg 1(2).
Entry "Rwanda" inserted by SI 2004/1834, reg 2(a). Date in force: 1 August 2004: see SI 2004/1834, reg 1(2).
Entries "Tanzania" and "Uganda" inserted by SI 2004/474, regs 2, 5(b). Date in force: 27 February 2004: see SI 2004/474, reg 1.

NATIONALITY, IMMIGRATION AND ASYLUM ACT 2002 (JUXTAPOSED CONTROLS) ORDER 2003

2003 No 2818

Made . . . . *4th November 2003*

Coming into force in accordance with article 1(2)

Whereas the Secretary of State has consulted with such persons as appear to him to be appropriate;

And whereas a draft of this Order has been approved by a resolution of each House of Parliament;

Now, therefore, in exercise of the powers conferred on him by section 141 of the Nationality, Immigration and Asylum Act 2002, the Secretary of State hereby makes the following Order:

PART 1
INTRODUCTION

1 Citation and commencement

(1) This Order may be cited as the Nationality, Immigration and Asylum Act 2002 (Juxtaposed Controls) Order 2003.

(2) Save for article 10 of this Order which shall come into force on the day after the day on which the Order is made, this Order shall come into force on the date on which the Treaty between the Government of the United Kingdom of Great Britain and Northern Ireland and the Government of the French Republic concerning the Implementation of Frontier Controls at the Sea Ports of Both Countries on the Channel and North Sea enters into force.

Initial Commencement
Specified date (for certain purposes): 5 November 2003: see para (2) above.

Appointment
Appointment (for remaining purposes): 1 February 2004: see the London Gazette, 30 January 2004.

2 Interpretation

In this Order, and in any enactment applied with modifications by Schedule 2 to this Order—

2300

"Control Zone" means the part of the territory of the State of Departure within a port designated in Schedule 1 to this Order within which the officers of the State of Arrival are authorised to carry out immigration control under the Treaty;

"immigration control" means arrangements made in connection with the movement of persons into or out of the United Kingdom or another State and includes the investigation of offences relating to immigration;

"immigration officer" means an officer appointed by the Secretary of State under paragraph 1 of Schedule 2 to the 1971 Act;

"officer belonging to the French Republic" means an officer given responsibility by the Government of the French Republic for the exercise of immigration control in accordance with the Treaty;

"State of Departure" means the State upon whose territory the immigration control of the other State is carried out, and "State of Arrival" means the other State;

"the 1971 Act" means the Immigration Act 1971;

"the 1984 Act" means the Police and Criminal Evidence Act 1984; and

"Treaty" means the Treaty mentioned in article 1 (2).

Initial Commencement
Specified date (for certain purposes): 5 November 2003: see art 1(2).

Appointment
Appointment (for remaining purposes): 1 February 2004: see the London Gazette, 30 January 2004.

PART 2

PROVISIONS RELATING TO THE EXERCISE OF POWERS BY FRENCH OFFICERS IN A CONTROL ZONE IN THE UNITED KINGDOM

3   Exercise of functions by French officers

(1)   An officer belonging to the French Republic shall be permitted to carry out his functions in a Control Zone in the United Kingdom in application of his powers relating to immigration control.

(2)   The offence in section 26 (1)(g) of the 1971 Act of obstructing, without reasonable excuse, an immigration officer or other person lawfully acting in the execution of the 1971 Act shall apply to an officer belonging to the French Republic carrying out his functions in accordance with paragraph (1) as it applies to such an immigration officer or other person.

Appointment
Appointment: 1 February 2004: see the London Gazette, 30 January 2004.

4   Powers of arrest and detention by French officers

(1)   An officer belonging to the French Republic may arrest and hold for questioning in a Control Zone in the United Kingdom a person who is being examined for the purposes of immigration control.

(2)   The arrested person may be detained for a period of not more than 24 hours and, if there are exceptional circumstances and an immigration officer or a constable is notified of the extension, for a further such period.

Appointment
Appointment: 1 February 2004: see the London Gazette, 30 January 2004.

5   Detention of arrested persons by a constable

(1)   Where—

(a) an officer belonging to the French Republic has in a Control Zone in the United Kingdom arrested or detained a person in accordance with article 4 (1), and

(b) such an officer so requests,

a constable may make arrangements for the person to be taken into temporary custody.

(2) A person taken into temporary custody under paragraph (1)—

(a) shall be treated for all purposes as being in lawful custody, and

(b) may be taken to a police station or such other place as may be appropriate in the circumstances, and shall in that case be treated as being a person in whose case sections 36(7) and (8), 54, 55, 56 and 58 of the 1984 Act and, in the case of a child or young person, section 34(2) to (7), (8) and (9) of the Children and Young Persons Act 1933 apply, and

(c) must be returned to an officer belonging to the French Republic before the end of the period referred to in article 4(2), to a place where detention can be resumed under that article.

(3) Where a person falls to be treated as mentioned in paragraph (2)(b), section 56 of the 1984 Act shall be taken to apply as if he were detained for a serious arrestable offence.

Appointment
Appointment: 1 February 2004: see the London Gazette, 30 January 2004.

6   Immunity from prosecution

An officer belonging to the French Republic shall not be prosecuted for any offence committed in the exercise of his functions in a Control Zone in the United Kingdom.

Appointment
Appointment: 1 February 2004: see the London Gazette, 30 January 2004.

7   Arrest of French officer

(1) Where an officer belonging to the French Republic is arrested for an act performed in a Control Zone in the United Kingdom, the officer shall be taken to a police station designated under section 35 of the 1984 Act.

(2) The custody officer at the police station to which the officer is taken shall, after consultation with the competent French authorities, determine whether the act was performed by the officer whilst in the exercise of his functions, and may for the purpose of determining that question detain the officer at the police station for not longer than the permitted period.

(3) The permitted period is the period of 48 hours beginning at the time at which the officer arrives at the police station.

(4) Subject to paragraph (6), the officer shall be treated—

(a) as not being detained at the police station for the purposes of section 37 of the 1984 Act, and

(b) as not being in police detention for the purposes of sections 40 to 43 of the 1984 Act.

(5) Where the custody officer determines that the act was performed by the officer whilst in the exercise of his functions, he shall immediately inform the competent French authorities and shall make arrangements within the permitted period for the transfer of the officer to France.

(6) In any other case—

(a) the custody officer shall immediately inform the officer of his determination,
(b) the officer shall be treated as being in police detention for all purposes of Part IV of the 1984 Act, and
(c) that Part shall have effect in relation to him as if the relevant time mentioned in section 41(2) were the time at which he is informed of the determination.

Appointment
Appointment: 1 February 2004: see the London Gazette, 30 January 2004.

8 Disapplication of law of England and Wales

(1) The law of England and Wales shall not have effect in relation to any claim for compensation which may be alleged against, or by, an officer belonging to the French Republic for loss or injury in the exercise of his functions in a Control Zone in the United Kingdom and any such claim shall be subject to the law of the French Republic as if the circumstances giving rise to the claim had occurred in France.

(2) The Data Protection Act 1998 shall not have effect in relation to data which are processed within a Control Zone in the United Kingdom in connection with the carrying out of immigration control by an officer belonging to the French Republic.

(3) No charge shall be payable under section 40(2) of the Immigration and Asylum Act 1999 (charge in respect of passenger without proper documents) by the owner of a ship in respect of any individual who is shown by the owner to have embarked on the ship for the voyage to the United Kingdom after having passed through a Control Zone in France.

Appointment
Appointment: 1 February 2004: see the London Gazette, 30 January 2004.

9 Carrying of firearms by French officers

Section 54(3) of the Firearms Act 1968 (application to Crown servants) shall have effect in relation to an officer belonging to the French Republic exercising his functions within a Control Zone in the United Kingdom as if the reference to a member of a police force included a reference to such an officer.

Appointment
Appointment: 1 February 2004: see the London Gazette, 30 January 2004.

10 Provision of facilities for French officers

The Secretary of State may by written notice require any person concerned with the management of a port in the United Kingdom which is designated in Schedule 1 to this Order to provide free of charge such accommodation, installations and equipment as may be necessary to enable officers belonging to the French Republic to perform their functions in a Control Zone in the United Kingdom.

Initial Commencement
Specified date: 5 November 2003: see art 1(2).

PART 3

PROVISIONS RELATING TO THE EXERCISE OF POWERS BY UNITED KINGDOM
IMMIGRATION OFFICERS AND CONSTABLES IN A CONTROL ZONE IN FRANCE

11 Enactments having effect in a Control Zone in France

(1) For the purpose of enabling immigration officers to exercise immigration control in a Control Zone in France, the following shall have effect in relation to a person in a Control Zone in France, or anything done in that Zone, with the modifications set out in Schedule 2 to this Order—

Appendix 1   Legislation and materials

    (a)   the 1971 Act;
    (b)   Schedules 7, 8 and 14 to the Terrorism Act 2000;
    (c)   the Code of Practice for examining officers under The Terrorism Act 2000;
    (d)   the Immigration (Leave to Enter and Remain) Order 2000; and
    (e)   the Immigration (European Economic Area) Regulations 2000.

(2)   Paragraphs 2 (powers and duties of detainee custody officers) and 3 (short-term holding facilities) of Schedule 11, and paragraph 2 of Schedule 13 (powers and duties of detainee custody officers), to the Immigration and Asylum Act 1999 shall have effect in relation to a detainee custody officer in a Control Zone in France as they have effect in relation to such an officer in the United Kingdom and, in the definition of "short-term holding facility" in section 147 of that Act, the reference to "a place" includes a place in a Control Zone in France.

(3)   Sections 19B (discrimination by public authorities) and 19D (exception from section 19B for certain acts in immigration and nationality cases) of the Race Relations Act 1976 shall have effect in relation to immigration officers carrying out their functions in a Control Zone in France as they have effect in relation to such officers carrying out their functions in England and Wales and Scotland.

(4)   The Data Protection Act 1998 shall have effect in relation to data which are processed in a Control Zone in France in connection with the carrying out of immigration control by an immigration officer or a constable, or the exercise of a power of arrest by a constable under article 13 (3) of this Order, as if, for the purposes of section 5 of that Act, the data were processed by a data controller established in the United Kingdom in the context of that establishment.

(5)   The law of England and Wales shall have effect in relation to any claim for compensation which may be alleged against, or by, a constable or an immigration officer for loss or injury in the exercise of his functions in a Control Zone in France as if the circumstances giving rise to the claim had occurred in England.

Appointment
Appointment: 1 February 2004: see the London Gazette, 30 January 2004.

12   Application of criminal law to a Control Zone in France

(1)   An act or omission which constitutes an offence under one of the following provisions of the 1971 Act shall also be an offence if it takes place in a Control Zone in France—

    (a)   section 24A (1)(a) and (3) (deception);
    (b)   section 25 (assisting unlawful immigration to member state), but as if subsections (4) and (5) were omitted;
    (d)   section 25A (helping asylum seeker to enter United Kingdom);
    (e)   section 25B (assisting entry to United Kingdom in breach of deportation or exclusion order);
    (f)   section 26 (general offences in connection with administration of Act); and
    (g)   section 27(c) (offences by persons connected with ships or aircraft or with ports) but as if the words "or aircraft" and "or disembarkation" were omitted.

(2)   An act or omission which constitutes an offence under the law of England and Wales if committed by a constable or an immigration officer in the exercise of his functions shall also be an offence if it takes place in a Control Zone in France by such an officer in the exercise of his functions.

(3) An act or omission which constitutes an offence under paragraph 4 (assaulting a detainee custody officer) or paragraph 5 (obstructing detainee custody officers) of Schedule 11 to the Immigration and Asylum Act 1999 shall also be an offence if it takes place in a Control Zone in France.

(4) An act or omission which constitutes an offence under paragraph 18 of Schedule 7 to the Terrorism Act 2000 shall also be an offence if it takes place in a Control Zone in France.

(5) A provision of the criminal law in force in England and Wales for the protection of constables or immigration officers, or their property (including property in their possession or control), shall apply also in a Control Zone in France.

(6) Summary proceedings for an offence committed in a Control Zone in France by virtue of this article and which is an offence triable summarily or triable either way may be taken, and the offence may for all incidental purposes be treated as having been committed, in the county of Kent or in the inner London area as defined in article 2(3) of the Justices of the Peace (Commission Areas) Order 1999.

Appointment
Appointment: 1 February 2004: see the London Gazette, 30 January 2004.

13 Powers of arrest and search outside United Kingdom

(1) An immigration officer may in a Control Zone in France exercise the powers of arrest conferred by—

(a) section 28A (1), (3) and (5) of the 1971 Act; and
(b) paragraph 17(1) of Schedule 2 to the 1971 Act,

in respect of an offence under that Act or in respect of an offence under that Act as applied by this Order.

(2) Where an immigration officer makes a request to a police officer of the rank of sergeant or above for assistance in arresting a person in a Control Zone in France in respect of an offence under the 1971 Act or in respect of an offence under that Act as applied by article 12(1) of this Order, a constable of the police force of which that officer is a member may in such a Control Zone exercise any power of arrest conferred by the 1971 Act or by the 1984 Act, and any such request shall be recorded in writing at the time it is made or as soon as practicable afterwards.

(3) A constable may in a Control Zone in France exercise any power of arrest conferred by the 1984 Act in respect of an offence as applied by article 12(2) to (5) of this Order which is committed in a Control Zone in France.

(4) Any power conferred by the 1971 Act or the 1984 Act to search an arrested person or a vehicle or to seize anything following an arrest authorised by this article may be exercised as if the person had been arrested in England.

Appointment
Appointment: 1 February 2004: see the London Gazette, 30 January 2004.

14 Arrested persons held in France

(1) Where an arrest of any kind provided for by article 13 has been made in a Control Zone in France, the person arrested may be detained in France for a period of not more than 24 hours and, if there are exceptional circumstances and an officer belonging to the French Republic is notified of the extension, for a further such period.

(2) Where a constable exercises a power of arrest pursuant to article 13(2) or (3), the person arrested shall be treated as if the place where he is held were, for the purposes

of sections 36(7) and (8), 54, 55, 56, 58 and 61 to 63 of the 1984 Act and, in the case of a child or young person, section 34(2) to (7), (8) and (9) of the Children and Young Persons Act 1933, a police station in England, not being a police station designated under section 35 of the 1984 Act.

Appointment
Appointment: 1 February 2004: see the London Gazette, 30 January 2004.

15   Arrested persons arriving in the United Kingdom

(1)   Where—

(a)   an arrest has been made by a constable or an immigration officer in a Control Zone in France, and

(b)   the person arrested enters the United Kingdom while under arrest,

the person arrested shall be taken to a police station.

(2)   The person arrested shall be treated as being in police detention for all purposes of Part IV of the 1984 Act, and that Part shall have effect in relation to him as if the relevant time mentioned in section 41(2) were the time at which he arrives in the United Kingdom.

Appointment
Appointment: 1 February 2004: see the London Gazette, 30 January 2004.

16   Arrests of constables and immigration officers

(1)   This article applies where a constable or an immigration officer is arrested in respect of an act performed in a Control Zone in France.

(2)   If the competent French authorities determine that the act was performed by the officer whilst in the exercise of his functions he shall, on being handed over by those authorities to a constable, be treated as having been arrested by the constable.

(3)   The officer shall be taken to a police station designated under section 35 of the 1984 Act.

(4)   The officer shall be treated as being in police detention for all purposes of Part IV of the 1984 Act, and that Part shall have effect in relation to him as if the relevant time mentioned in section 41(2) were the time at which he arrives in the United Kingdom.

Appointment
Appointment: 1 February 2004: see the London Gazette, 30 January 2004.

SCHEDULE 1
DESIGNATION OF PORTS

Articles 2 and 10

United Kingdom	France
Dover	Calais
	Boulogne
	Dunkirk

Initial Commencement
Specified date: 5 November 2003: see art 1(2).

SCHEDULE 2
MODIFICATION OF APPLIED ENACTMENTS

Article 11(1)

1   Immigration Act 1971

(1)   In section 4 of the 1971 Act (administration of control) in subsection (2)—for the words "the United Kingdom by ship or aircraft" substitute ", or seeking to arrive in, the United Kingdom by entering a Control Zone".

(2)   In section 33 of the 1971 Act (interpretation) in subsection (1)—

(i)   after the definition of "certificate of entitlement" insert—

""Control Zone" means a Control Zone in France in which immigration officers exercise immigration control pursuant to the Treaty between the Government of the United Kingdom of Great Britain and Northern Ireland and the Government of the French Republic concerning the Implementation of Frontier Controls at the Sea Ports of Both Countries on the Channel and North Sea;"; and

(ii)   in the definition of "illegal entrant" after the words "unlawfully entering or seeking" insert " (whether or not he has arrived in the United Kingdom)".

(3)   In Schedule 2 to the 1971 Act (administrative provisions as to control on entry etc)—

(a)   in paragraph 1(5) for the words after "vehicle" substitute "which is in a Control Zone.";

(b)   in paragraph 2(1) for the words from "in the United Kingdom" to "seeking to enter the United Kingdom)" substitute ", or who are seeking to arrive, in the United Kingdom by entering a Control Zone";

(c)   after paragraph 2(1) insert—

"(1A)   The power conferred by sub-paragraph (1) is exercisable as respects persons seeking to arrive in the United Kingdom (who may first be questioned to ascertain whether they are seeking to do so), in a Control Zone, but where it has not been possible to examine such persons in a Control Zone then the power conferred by sub-paragraph (1) shall apply.";

(d)   after paragraph 8(1) insert—

"(1A)   Where a person seeking to arrive in the United Kingdom is refused leave to enter and is then in a Control Zone, an immigration officer may request the competent French authorities to secure that the person is taken out of the Control Zone.";

(e)   in paragraph 9(1) for the words after "an immigration officer" substitute

"may—

(a)   if the illegal entrant has arrived in the United Kingdom, give such directions in respect of him as in a case within sub-paragraph (1) of paragraph 8 above are authorised by that sub-paragraph, or

(b)   if the illegal entrant is in a Control Zone, make such requests in respect of him as in a case within sub-paragraph (1A) of paragraph 8 above are authorised by that sub-paragraph.";

(f)   in paragraph 16—
(a)   in sub-paragraph (2) for the words "his removal in pursuance of" substitute "the taking of any action in respect of him pursuant to any request made to the competent French authorities authorised under paragraph 8(1A)",
(b)   after sub-paragraph (3) insert—

"(3A)   A person may under the authority of an immigration officer be removed for detention under this paragraph from a vehicle in a Control Zone."; and

(g)   for paragraph 26(2) and (3) there is substituted—

"(2)   The Secretary of State may from time to time give written notice to the owners or agents of ships designating control areas for the embarkation of passengers in a Control Zone and specifying the conditions and restrictions (if any) to be observed in any control area; and where by notice given to any owners or agents a control area is for the time being designated for the embarkation of passengers in a Control Zone, the owners or agents shall take all reasonable steps to secure that, in the case of their ships, passengers do not embark in the Control Zone outside the control area and that any conditions or restrictions notified to them are observed.

(3)   The Secretary of State may also from time to time give to any persons concerned with the management of a port in a Control Zone written notice designating control areas in the Control Zone and specifying conditions or restrictions to be observed in any control area; and any such person shall take all reasonable steps to secure that any conditions or restrictions as notified to him are observed.".

2   The Terrorism Act 2000

(1)   In Schedule 7 to the Terrorism Act 2000—

    (a)   in paragraph 1—
        (i)   in sub-paragraph (1)(a), insert at the beginning "subject to sub-paragraph (1A),",
        (ii)   omit sub-paragraph (1)(c),
        (iii)   after sub-paragraph (1) insert—

"(1A)   A constable shall only exercise the powers in this Schedule in a Control Zone where an immigration officer has made a request to a police officer of the rank of sergeant or above in the same police force of which the constable is a member, for assistance in exercising the powers in question in a particular case, and any such request shall be recorded in writing at the time it is made or as soon as practicable afterwards.",
        (iv)   for sub-paragraph (2) substitute—
"In this Schedule "Control Zone" means a Control Zone in France in which immigration officers exercise immigration control pursuant to the Treaty between the Government of the United Kingdom of Great Britain and Northern Ireland and the Government of the French Republic concerning the Implementation of Frontier Controls at the Sea Ports of Both Countries on the Channel and North Sea.", and
        (v)   omit sub-paragraph (3);
    (b)   in paragraph 2—
        (i)   for sub-paragraph (2) substitute "This paragraph applies to a person if he is in a Control Zone.", and
        (ii)   omit sub-paragraph (3);
    (c)   omit paragraphs 3 and 4;
    (d)   in paragraph 5 omit the words "or 3";
    (e)   in paragraph 6, omit the words "or 3" and in sub-paragraph (2) the word "aircraft";
    (f)   in paragraph 7, omit the words "or aircraft" in each place where they occur;
    (g)   in paragraph 8, in sub-paragraph (1) omit the words "or aircraft" in each place where they occur and omit sub-paragraph (2);
    (h)   in paragraph 9—
        (i)   for sub-paragraph (2) substitute "This paragraph applies to goods which have arrived in or are about to leave a Control Zone on a ship or in a vehicle.", and

      (ii) in sub-paragraph (4) omit the words "or aircraft"; and
  (i) omit paragraphs 12 to 17 and the Table of Designated Ports at the end of the Schedule".

(2) In Schedule 8 to the Terrorism Act 2000—

  (a) in paragraph 1—
    (i) in sub-paragraph (1), omit the words "or section 41", and
    (ii) omit sub-paragraphs (2), (4) and (6);
  (b) in paragraph 2, omit sub-paragraph (2)(b) and (c); and
  (c) omit paragraphs 3, 4 and 6 to 37.

(3) In Schedule 14 to the Terrorism Act 2000—

  (a) in paragraph 1, omit sub-paragraph (a);
  (b) in paragraph 2, after the word "may" insert "in a Control Zone (as defined in Schedule 7)" and omit " (within the meaning of section 121)"; and
  (c) in paragraph 3, omit the words "and 3".

3   The Code of Practice for examining officers under the Terrorism Act 2000

In the Code of Practice for examining officers under the Terrorism Act 2000

  (a) in paragraph 3—
    (i) omit the words "or customs officer designated for the purpose of the Schedule by the Secretary of State and the Commissioners of Customs and Excise",
    (ii) omit the words "or designated customs officers" and
    (iii) omit the words from "or the Customs and Excise Management Act 1979" to the end of that paragraph;
  (b) for paragraph 4 substitute—
"— 'Control Zone' means a Control Zone in France in which immigration officers exercise immigration control in pursuance of the Treaty between the Government of the United Kingdom of Great Britain and Northern Ireland and the Government of the French Republic concerning the Implementation of Frontier Controls at the Sea Ports of Both Countries on the Channel and North Sea
  — A "juvenile" means anyone who appears to be under the age of 17 in the absence of clear evidence that he/she is older.";
  (c) in paragraph 5, for the words "at ports or in the border area" substitute "in the Control Zone" and omit "and customs officers";
  (d) for paragraph 6 substitute—

"The functions under the Schedule and under Schedules 8 and 14 of the Act should only be carried out by a constable in a Control Zone where an immigration officer makes a request to a police officer of the rank of sergeant or above in the police force of which the constable is a member, for assistance in exercising the powers in question in a particular case, and any such request shall be recorded in writing at the time it is made or as soon as practicable afterwards.";

  (e) for paragraph 7 substitute "The power to examine someone under the Schedule applies to a person who is in a Control Zone.";
  (f) omit paragraph 8 and the Note for guidance on paragraph 8;
  (g) in the Note for guidance on paragraph 10—
    (i) for the words "under the port and border area powers" and "at the port or the area" substitute in each case "in the Control Zone", and
    (ii) for the words "at individual ports or parts of the border area" substitute "within the Control Zone";
  (h) in paragraph 12, omit the words "at the port, or in the border area, a police station";

(i) in paragraph 13, for the words "at the port or at a specified police station" and "at the port or, in the border area, at a police station" substitute "in the Control Zone";

(j) in the Note for guidance on paragraph 13, for the words "at a port or at a police station in the border area" substitute "in the Control Zone";

(k) in paragraph 14, omit the words " (or in Scotland, a child)" and "/child";

(l) in paragraph 19, for the words "at the port or, in the case of the border area, that location" substitute "in the Control Zone";

(m) in paragraph 21, omit the words from "; and should bear in mind that people travelling to and from Northern Ireland" to the end of that paragraph;

(n) omit the Note for guidance on paragraph 23;

(o) in paragraph 29, for the words "at the port" substitute "in the Control Zone";

(p) paragraphs 33 and 34 shall be omitted; and

(q) in the Annex—

    (i) for the words in the first set of square brackets substitute "in the Control Zone" and omit the words in the second set of square brackets, and

    (ii) omit the paragraph beginning "You may also be asked, or have been asked".

4   The Immigration (Leave to Enter and Remain) Order 2000

In the Immigration (Leave to Enter and Remain) Order 2000—

(a) in article 1(3), after the definition of "control port" insert—

""Control Zone" means a Control Zone in France in which immigration officers exercise immigration control in pursuance of the Treaty between the United Kingdom of Great Britain and Northern Ireland and the Government of the French Republic concerning the Implementation of Frontier Controls at the Sea Ports of Both Countries on the Channel and North Sea;";

(b) in article 4(2)—

    (i) after the words "arrives in the United Kingdom", insert "or enters a Control Zone",

    (ii) after the words "before arrival", insert "or entry into the Control Zone", and

    (iii) after the words "date of arrival", insert "or entry into the Control Zone";

(c) in article 4(3)—

    (i) after the words "on arrival in the United Kingdom", insert "or entry into a Control Zone", and

    (ii) after the words "before arrival", insert "or entry into the Control Zone"; and

(d) in article 6(2)(a) after the words "arrives in the United Kingdom", insert "or enters a Control Zone".

5   The Immigration (European Economic Area) Regulations 2000

In the Immigration (European Economic Area) Regulations 2000—

(a) in regulation 2, at the beginning insert—

""Control Zone" means a Control Zone in France in which immigration officers exercise immigration control in pursuance of the Treaty between the Government of the United Kingdom of Great Britain and Northern Ireland and the Government of the French Republic concerning the Implementation of Frontier Controls at the Sea Ports of Both Countries on the Channel and North Sea;";

(b) after regulation 12(2) insert—

"(3) Any passport, identity card, family permit, residence document or document proving family membership which is required to be produced under this regulation as a condition for admission to the United Kingdom ("the required documents") may, for the same purpose, be required to be produced in a Control Zone."; and

(c) in regulation 21(2) after the word "arrival", in regulation 22(3) after the words "EEA national", and in regulation 22(4) after the words "United Kingdom", insert "or the time of his production of the required documents in a Control Zone".

Appointment

Appointment: 1 February 2004: see the London Gazette, 30 January 2004.

ACCESSION (IMMIGRATION AND WORKER REGISTRATION) REGULATIONS 2004

2004 No 1219

Made . . . . *28th April 2004*

Coming into force . . . . *1st May 2004*

The Secretary of State, being a Minister designated for the purposes of section 2(2) of the European Communities Act 1972 in relation to measures relating to the right of entry into, and residence in, the United Kingdom and access to the labour market of the United Kingdom, in exercise of the powers conferred on him by section 2(2), and in exercise of the powers conferred upon him by section 2 of the European Union (Accessions) Act 2003, hereby makes the following Regulations, a draft of which has been approved by resolution of each House of Parliament:

PART 1
GENERAL

1   Citation, commencement and interpretation

(1) These Regulations may be cited as the Accession (Immigration and Worker Registration) Regulations 2004 and shall come into force on 1st May 2004.

(2) In these Regulations—

(a) "the 1971 Act" means the Immigration Act 1971;

(b) "the 2000 Regulations" means the Immigration (European Economic Area) Regulations 2000;

(c) "accession period" means the period beginning on 1st May 2004 and ending on 30th April 2009;

(d) "accession State worker requiring registration" shall be interpreted in accordance with regulation 2;

(e) "authorised employer" shall be interpreted in accordance with regulation 7;

(f) "EEA State" means a Member State, other than the United Kingdom, or Norway, Iceland or Liechtenstein, and "EEA national" means a national of an EEA State;

(g) "employer" means, in relation to a worker, the person who directly pays the wage or salary of that worker;

(h)   "registration certificate" means a certificate issued under regulation 8 authorising an accession State worker requiring registration to work for an employer;

(i)   "relevant accession State" means the Czech Republic, the Republic of Estonia, the Republic of Latvia, the Republic of Lithuania, the Republic of Hungary, the Republic of Poland, the Republic of Slovenia and the Slovak Republic;

(j)   "self-sufficient person" has the same meaning as in regulation 3 of the 2000 Regulations;

(k)   "worker" means a worker within the meaning of Article 39 of the Treaty establishing the European Community, and "work" and "working" shall be construed accordingly.

Initial Commencement
Specified date: 1 May 2004: see para (1) above.

2   "Accession State worker requiring registration"

(1)   Subject to the following paragraphs of this regulation, "accession State worker requiring registration" means a national of a relevant accession State working in the United Kingdom during the accession period.

(2)   A national of a relevant accession State is not an accession State worker requiring registration if on 30th April 2004 he had leave to enter or remain in the United Kingdom under the 1971 Act and that leave was not subject to any condition restricting his employment.

(3)   A national of a relevant accession State is not an accession State worker requiring registration if he was legally working in the United Kingdom on 30th April 2004 and had been legally working in the United Kingdom without interruption throughout the period of 12 months ending on that date.

(4)   A national of a relevant accession State who legally works in the United Kingdom without interruption for a period of 12 months falling partly or wholly after 30th April 2004 shall cease to be an accession State worker requiring registration at the end of that period of 12 months.

(5)   A national of a relevant accession State is not an accession State worker requiring registration during any period in which he is also a national of—

(a)   the United Kingdom;
(b)   another EEA State, other than a relevant accession State; or
(c)   Switzerland.

(6)   A national of a relevant accession State is not an accession State worker requiring registration during any period in which he is—

(a)   a posted worker; or
[(b)   a family member of a Swiss or EEA national who is in the United Kingdom as—
  (i)   a worker, other than as an accession State worker requiring registration;
  (ii)   a self-sufficient person;
  (iii)   a retired person;
  (iv)   a self-employed person; or
  (v)   a student].

(7)   For the purpose of this regulation—

(a)   a person working in the United Kingdom during a period falling before 1st May 2004 was legally working in the United Kingdom during that period if—

      (i) he had leave to enter or remain in the United Kingdom under the 1971 Act for that period, that leave allowed him to work in the United Kingdom, and he was working in accordance with any condition on that leave restricting his employment; or

     (ii) he was entitled to reside in the United Kingdom for that period under the 2000 Regulations without the requirement for such leave;

  (b) a person working in the United Kingdom on or after 1st May 2004 is legally working during any period in which he is working in the United Kingdom for an authorised employer;

  (c) a person shall also be treated as legally working in the United Kingdom on or after 1st May 2004 during any period in which he falls within paragraph (5) or (6).

(8) For the purpose of paragraphs (3) and (4), a person shall be treated as having worked in the United Kingdom without interruption for a period of 12 months if he was legally working in the United Kingdom at the beginning and end of that period and any intervening periods in which he was not legally working in the United Kingdom do not, in total, exceed 30 days.

(9) In this regulation—

  (a) "retired person" and "student" have the same meaning as in regulation 3 of the 2000 Regulations;

  (b) "posted worker" means a person whose employer is not established in the United Kingdom and who works for that employer in the United Kingdom for the purpose of providing services on his employer's behalf;

  (c) "family member" means—

    [(i) in relation to a worker or a self-employed person, his spouse and his children who are under 21 or dependent on him;]

    (ii) in relation to any other person, his spouse and his children who are dependent on him.

Initial Commencement
Specified date: 1 May 2004: see reg 1(1).

Amendment
Para (6): sub-para (b) substituted by SI 2004/1236, reg 3(1), (2)(a). Date in force: 1 May 2004: see SI 2004/1236, reg 1.
Para (9): sub-para (c)(i) substituted by SI 2004/1236, reg 3(1), (2)(b). Date in force: 1 May 2004: see SI 2004/1236, reg 1.

PART 2

IMMIGRATION

3   Amendment of the 2000 Regulations

In regulation 2(1) of the 2000 Regulations, for the definition of "EEA State" substitute—

    ""EEA State" means a Member State, other than the United Kingdom, or Norway, Iceland or Liechtenstein.".

Initial Commencement
Specified date: 1 May 2004: see reg 1(1).

4   Right of residence of work seekers and workers from relevant acceding States during the accession period

(1) This regulation derogates during the accession period from Article 39 of the Treaty establishing the European Community, Articles 1 to 6 of Regulation (EEC)

Appendix 1 Legislation and materials

No 1612/68 on freedom of movement for workers within the Community and Council Directive (EEC) No 68/360 on the abolition of restrictions on movement and residence within the Community for workers of Member States and their families.

(2) A national of a relevant accession State shall not be entitled to reside in the United Kingdom for the purpose of seeking work by virtue of his status as a work seeker if he would be an accession State worker requiring registration if he began working in the United Kingdom.

(3) Paragraph (2) is without prejudice to the right of a national of a relevant accession State to reside in the United Kingdom under the 2000 Regulations as a self-sufficient person whilst seeking work in the United Kingdom.

(4) An accession State worker requiring registration shall only be entitled to reside in the United Kingdom in accordance with the 2000 Regulations as modified by regulation 5.

Initial Commencement
Specified date: 1 May 2004: see reg 1(1).

5 Application of 2000 Regulations in relation to an accession State worker requiring registration

(1) The 2000 Regulations shall apply in relation to an accession State worker requiring registration subject to the modifications set out in this regulation.

(2) An accession State worker requiring registration shall be treated as a worker for the purpose of the definition of "qualified person" in regulation 5(1) of the 2000 Regulations only during a period in which he is working in the United Kingdom for an authorised employer.

(3) Subject to paragraph (4), regulation 5(2) of the 2000 Regulations shall not apply to an accession State worker requiring registration who ceases to work.

(4) Where an accession State worker requiring registration—

    (a) begins working for an authorised employer on or after 1st May 2004; and
    (b) ceases working for that employer in the circumstances mentioned in regulation 5(2) of the 2000 Regulations during the one month period beginning on the date on which the work begins,

that regulation shall apply to that worker during the remainder of that one month period.

(5) An accession State worker requiring registration shall not be treated as an EEA national for the purpose of the power in regulation 10 of the 2000 Regulations (dependants and members of the household of EEA nationals) to issue a residence permit or a residence document to a relative of an EEA national or his spouse.

(6) An accession State worker requiring registration shall not be treated as a qualified person for the purpose of regulation 15 of the 2000 Regulations (issue of residence permits and residence documents).

Initial Commencement
Specified date: 1 May 2004: see reg 1(1).

6 Transitional provisions applying to the application of the 2000 Regulations to nationals of the accession States and their family members

(1) Where before 1st May 2004 a qualified person or the family member of a qualified person has been given leave to enter or remain in the United Kingdom under the 1971 Act subject to conditions, those conditions shall cease to have effect on and after that date.

2314

(2) Where before 1st May 2004 directions have been given for the removal of a qualified person or the family member of a qualified person under paragraphs 8 to 10A of Schedule 2 to the 1971 Act or section 10 of the 1999 Act, those directions shall cease to have effect on and after that date.

(3) Where before 1st May 2004 the Secretary of State has made a decision to make a deportation order against a qualified person or the family member of a qualified person under section 5(1) of the 1971 Act—

(a) that decision shall, on and after 1st May 2004, be treated as if it were a decision under regulation 21(3)(b) of the 2000 Regulations; and

(b) any appeal against that decision, or against the refusal by the Secretary of State to revoke the deportation order, made under section 63 of the 1999 Act or section 82(2)(j) or (k) of the 2002 Act before 1st May 2004 shall, on and after that date, be treated as if it had been made under regulation 29 of the 2000 Regulations.

(4) In this regulation—

(a) "the 1999 Act" means the Immigration and Asylum Act 1999

(b) "the 2002 Act" means the Nationality, Immigration and Asylum Act 2002;

(c) regulation 6 of the 2000 Regulations shall apply for the purpose of determining whether a person is the family member of another person;

(d) any reference to a qualified person or to the family member of a qualified person is a reference to a person who becomes for the purpose of the 2000 Regulations a qualified person or the family member of a qualified person, as the case may be, on 1st May 2004 by virtue of regulation 3.

Initial Commencement
Specified date: 1 May 2004: see reg 1(1).

PART 3
ACCESSION STATE WORKER REGISTRATION

7   Requirement for an accession State worker requiring registration to be authorised to work

(1) By way of derogation from Article 39 of the Treaty establishing the European Community and Articles 1 to 6 of Regulation (EEC) No 1612/68 on freedom of movement for workers within the Community, an accession State worker requiring registration shall only be authorised to work in the United Kingdom for an authorised employer.

(2) An employer is an authorised employer in relation to a worker if—

(a) the worker was legally working for that employer on 30th April 2004 and has not ceased working for that employer after that date;

(b) the worker—

(i) during the one month period beginning on the date on which he begins working for the employer, applies for a registration certificate authorising him to work for that employer in accordance with regulation 8; and

(ii) has not received a valid registration certificate or notice of refusal under regulation 8 in relation to that application or ceased working for that employer since the application was made;

(c) the worker has received a valid registration certificate authorising him to work for that employer and that certificate has not expired under paragraph (5); or

(d) the employer is an authorised employer in relation to that worker under paragraph (3) or (4).

(3)   Where a worker begins working for an employer on or after 1st May 2004 that employer is an authorised employer in relation to that worker during the one month period beginning on the date on which the work begins.

(4)   Where a worker was, before 1st May 2004, issued with leave to enter the United Kingdom under the 1971 Act as a seasonal worker at an agricultural camp and the worker begins working for an employer on or after 1st May 2004 as a seasonal worker at such a camp, that employer is an authorised employer in relation to that worker during the period beginning on the date on which the work begins and ending on the date on which the worker ceases working for that employer, or on 31st December 2004, which ever is the earlier.

(5)   A registration certificate—

    (a)   is invalid if the worker is no longer working for the employer specified in the certificate on the date on which it is issued;

    (b)   expires on the date on which the worker ceases working for that employer.

(6)   Regulation 2(7)(a) shall apply for the purpose of determining whether a person is legally working on 30th April 2004 for the purpose of this regulation.

Initial Commencement
Specified date: 1 May 2004: see reg 1(1).

8   Registration card and registration certificate

(1)   An application for a registration certificate authorising an accession State worker requiring registration to work for an employer may only be made by an applicant who is working for that employer at the date of the application.

(2)   The application shall be in writing and shall be made to the Secretary of State.

(3)   The application shall state—

    (a)   the name, address, and date of birth of the applicant;

    (b)   the name and address of the head or main office of the employer;

    (c)   the date on which the applicant began working for that employer;

    (d)   where the applicant has been issued with a registration card, the reference number of that card.

(4)   Unless the applicant has been issued with a registration card under paragraph (5), the application shall be accompanied by—

    (a)   a registration fee of £50;

    (b)   two passport size photographs of the applicant;

    (c)   the applicant's national identity card or passport issued by the applicant's State;

    (d)   a letter from the employer concerned confirming that the applicant began working for the employer on the date specified in the application.

(5)   In the case of an application by an applicant who has not been issued with a registration card under this paragraph, the Secretary of State shall, where he is satisfied that the application is made in accordance with this regulation and that the applicant—

    (a)   is an accession State worker requiring registration; and

    (b)   began working for the employer on the date specified in the application,

send the applicant a registration card and a registration certificate authorising the worker to work for the employer specified in the application, and shall return the applicant's national identity card or passport.

(6)   In the case of any other application, the Secretary of State shall, if he is satisfied as mentioned in paragraph (5), send the applicant a registration certificate authorising the worker to work for the employer specified in the application.

(7)   A registration card issued under paragraph (5) shall contain—

(a)   the name, nationality and date of birth of the applicant;
(b)   a photograph of the applicant;
(c)   a reference number.

(8)   A registration certificate issued under paragraph (5) or (6) shall contain—

(a)   the name of the applicant;
(b)   the reference number of the applicant's registration card;
(c)   the name and address of the head or main office of the employer, as specified in the application;
(d)   the date on which the applicant began working for the employer, as specified in the application; and
(e)   the date on which the certificate is issued.

(9)   Where the Secretary of State receives an application made in accordance with this regulation and he is not satisfied as mentioned in paragraph (5), he shall—

(a)   send the applicant a notice of refusal; and
(b)   return any documents and fee that accompanied the application to the applicant.

(10)   Where the Secretary of State sends a registration certificate or notice of refusal to an applicant under this regulation he shall, at the same time, send a copy of the certificate or notice to the employer concerned at the address specified in the application for that employer.

(11)   Certificates and notices, and copies of these documents, sent under this regulation shall be sent by post.

Initial Commencement
Specified date: 1 May 2004: see reg 1(1).

9   Restriction on employers of relevant accession State workers requiring registration

(1)   Subject to paragraph (2), if an employer employs an accession State worker requiring registration during a period in which the employer is not an authorised employer in relation to that worker, the employer shall be guilty of an offence.

(2)   Subject to paragraph (4), in proceedings under this regulation it shall be a defence to prove that—

(a)   there was produced to the employer during the one month period beginning on the date on which the worker began working for the employer a document that appeared to him to establish that the worker was not an accession State worker requiring registration; and
(b)   the employer took and retained a copy of that document.

(3)   Subject to paragraph (4), in proceedings under this regulation it shall be a defence to prove that—

(a)   there was produced to the employer during the one month period beginning on the date on which the worker began working for the employer a document that appeared to him to establish that the worker had applied for a registration certificate in accordance with regulation 8 authorising the worker to work for that employer;

(b)   the employer took and retained a copy of that document; and

(c)   the employer has not received a copy of a registration certificate or notice of refusal in relation to that application.

(4)   The defence afforded by paragraph (2) or (3) shall not be available in any case where the employer knew that his employment of the worker would constitute an offence under this regulation.

(5)   A person guilty of an offence under this regulation shall be liable on summary conviction to a fine not exceeding level 5 on the standard scale.

(6)   Where an offence under this regulation committed by a body corporate is proved to have been committed with the consent or connivance of, or to be attributable to any neglect on the part of—

(a)   any director, manager, secretary or other similar officer of the body corporate; or

(b)   any person purporting to act in such a capacity,

he as well as the body corporate shall be guilty of the offence and shall be liable to be proceeded against and punished accordingly.

(7)   Where the affairs of a body corporate are managed by its members, paragraph (6) shall apply in relation to the acts and defaults of a member in connection with his functions of management as if he were a director of the body corporate.

(8)   Where an offence under this regulation is committed by a partnership (other than a limited partnership) each partner shall be guilty of the offence and shall be liable to be proceeded against and punished accordingly.

(9)   Paragraph (6) shall have effect in relation to a limited partnership as if—

(a)   a reference to a body corporate were a reference to a limited partnership; and

(b)   a reference to an officer of the body corporate were a reference to a partner.

(10)   Section 28(1) of the 1971 Act (extended time limit for prosecution) shall apply in relation to an offence under this regulation.

(11)   An offence under this regulation shall be treated as—

(a)   a relevant offence for the purpose of sections 28B and 28D of that Act (search, entry and arrest); and

(b)   an offence under Part III of that Act (criminal proceedings) for the purposes of sections 28E, 28G and 28H(search after arrest).

Initial Commencement
Specified date: 1 May 2004: see reg 1(1).

SOCIAL SECURITY (HABITUAL RESIDENCE) AMENDMENT REGULATIONS 2004

2004 No 1232

Made . . . . *28th April 2004*

Laid before Parliament . . . . *30th April 2004*

Coming into force . . . . *1st May 2004*

The Secretary of State for Work and Pensions, in exercise of the powers conferred upon him by sections 123(1)(a), (d) and (e), 131(3)(b), 135(1) and (2), 137(1) and (2)(i) and 175(1), (3) and (4) of the Social Security Contributions and Benefits Act 1992, sections 4(5), 35(1) and 36(2) and (4) of the Jobseekers Act 1995 and section 1(5)(a) and 17(1) of the State Pension Credit Act 2002 and of all other powers enabling him in that behalf, after consultation with such organisations appearing to him to be representative of the authorities concerned in so far as they relate to housing benefit and council tax benefit and after reference to the Social Security Advisory Committee, hereby makes the following Regulations:

1 Citation, commencement and interpretation

(1) These Regulations shall be cited as the Social Security (Habitual Residence) Amendment Regulations 2004 and shall come into force on 1st May 2004.

(2) In these Regulations—

"the Council Tax Benefit Regulations" means the Council Tax Benefit (General) Regulations 1992;
"the Housing Benefit Regulations" means the Housing Benefit (General) Regulations 1987;
"the Income Support Regulations" means the Income Support (General) Regulations 1987;
"the Jobseeker's Allowance Regulations" means the Jobseeker's Allowance Regulations 1996;
"the State Pension Credit Regulations" means the State Pension Credit Regulations 2002.

Initial Commencement
Specified date: 1 May 2004: see para (1) above.

2 Amendment of the Council Tax Benefit Regulations and of the Housing Benefit Regulations

In both regulation 4A of the Council Tax Benefit Regulations and regulation 7A of the Housing Benefit Regulations (persons from abroad)—

(a) in paragraph (4)(e)(i) after "No 73/148/EEC" add "or a person who is an accession State worker requiring registration who is treated as a worker for the purpose of the definition of "qualified person" in regulation 5(1) of the Immigration (European Economic Area) Regulations 2000 pursuant to regulation 5 of the Accession (Immigration and Worker Registration) Regulations 2004.";

(b) after paragraph (4) insert the following paragraph—

"(4B) In this regulation, for the purposes of the definition of a person from abroad no person shall be treated as habitually resident in the United Kingdom, the Channel

Islands, the Isle of Man or the Republic of Ireland if he does not have a right to reside in the United Kingdom, the Channel Islands, the Isle of Man or the Republic of Ireland.".

Initial Commencement
Specified date: 1 May 2004: see reg 1(1).

3   Amendment of the Income Support Regulations

In regulation 21 of the Income Support Regulations (special cases)—

   (a)   in paragraph (3), for "Subject to paragraph (3F)" substitute "Subject to paragraphs (3F) and (3G)";
   (b)   in the definition of "person from abroad" in paragraph (3) in sub-paragraph (a) after "No 73/148/EEC" add "or a person who is an accession State worker requiring registration who is treated as a worker for the purpose of the definition of "qualified person" in regulation 5(1) of the Immigration (European Economic Area) Regulations 2000 pursuant to regulation 5 of the Accession (Immigration and Worker Registration) Regulations 2004.";
   (c)   after paragraph (3F) insert the following paragraph—

"(3G)   In paragraph (3), for the purposes of the definition of a person from abroad no person shall be treated as habitually resident in the United Kingdom, the Channel Islands, the Isle of Man or the Republic of Ireland if he does not have a right to reside in the United Kingdom, the Channel Islands, the Isle of Man or the Republic of Ireland.".

Initial Commencement
Specified date: 1 May 2004: see reg 1(1).

4   Amendment of the Jobseeker's Allowance Regulations

In regulation 85 of the Jobseeker's Allowance Regulations (special cases)—

   (a)   in paragraph (4), for "Subject to paragraph (4A)" substitute "Subject to paragraphs (4A) and (4B)";
   (b)   in the definition of "person from abroad" in paragraph (4) in sub-paragraph (a) after "No 73/148/EEC" add "or a person who is an accession State worker requiring registration who is treated as a worker for the purpose of the definition of "qualified person" in regulation 5(1) of the Immigration (European Economic Area) Regulations 2000 pursuant to regulation 5 of the Accession (Immigration and Worker Registration) Regulations 2004.";
   (c)   after paragraph (4A) insert the following paragraph—

"(4B)   In paragraph (4), for the purposes of the definition of a person from abroad no person shall be treated as habitually resident in the United Kingdom, the Channel Islands, the Isle of Man or the Republic of Ireland if he does not have a right to reside in the United Kingdom, the Channel Islands, the Isle of Man or the Republic of Ireland.".

Initial Commencement
Specified date: 1 May 2004: see reg 1(1).

5   Amendment of the State Pension Credit Regulations

In regulation 2 of the State Pension Credit Regulations (persons not in Great Britain)—

   (a)   at the beginning insert "(1) Subject to paragraph (2),";
   (b)   in sub-paragraph (a) after "No 73/148/EEC" add "or a person who is an accession State worker requiring registration who is treated as a worker for

the purpose of the definition of "qualified person" in regulation 5(1) of the Immigration (European Economic Area) Regulations 2000 pursuant to regulation 5 of the Accession (Immigration and Worker Registration) Regulations 2004."

(c) after sub-paragraph (e) insert the following paragraph—

"(2) For the purposes of treating a person as not in Great Britain in paragraph (1), no person shall be treated as habitually resident in the United Kingdom, the Channel Islands, the Isle of Man or the Republic of Ireland if he does not have a right to reside in the United Kingdom, the Channel Islands, the Isle of Man or the Republic of Ireland.".

Initial Commencement
Specified date: 1 May 2004: see reg 1(1).

6 Transitional arrangements and savings

(1) Paragraph (2) shall apply where a person—

(a) is entitled to a specified benefit in respect of a period which includes 30th April 2004;

(b) claims a specified benefit on or after 1st May 2004 and it is subsequently determined that he is entitled to that benefit in respect of a period which includes 30th April 2004;

(c) claims a specified benefit on or after 1st May 2004 and it is subsequently determined that he is entitled to such a benefit in respect of a period which is continuous with a period of entitlement to the same or another specified benefit which includes 30th April 2004;

(d) claims jobseeker's allowance on or after 1st May 2004 and it is subsequently determined that he is entitled to jobseeker's allowance in respect of a period of entitlement to that benefit which is linked to a previous period of entitlement which includes 30th April 2004 by virtue of regulations made under paragraph 3 of Schedule 1 to the Jobseekers Act 1995.

(2) Where this paragraph applies—

(a) regulation 4A of the Council Tax Benefit Regulations and regulation 7A of the Housing Benefit Regulations shall continue to have effect as if regulation 2 had not been made;

(b) regulation 21 of the Income Support Regulations shall continue to have effect as if regulation 3 had not been made;

(c) regulation 85 of the Jobseeker's Allowance Regulations shall continue to have effect as if regulation 4 had not been made; and

(d) regulation 2 of the State Pension Credit Regulations shall continue to have effect as if regulation 5 had not been made.

(3) The provisions saved by paragraph (2) shall continue to have effect until the date on which entitlement to a specified benefit for the purposes of paragraph (1) ceases, and if there is more than one such specified benefit, until the last date on which such entitlement ceases.

(4) In this regulation "specified benefit" means income support, housing benefit, council tax benefit, jobseeker's allowance and state pension credit.

Initial Commencement
Specified date: 1 May 2004: see reg 1(1).

NATIONALITY, IMMIGRATION AND ASYLUM ACT 2002 (SPECIFICATION OF PARTICULARLY SERIOUS CRIMES) ORDER 2004

2004 No 1910

Made . . . . *20th July 2004*

Laid before Parliament . . . . *22nd July 2004*

Coming into force . . . . *12th August 2004*

In exercise of the powers conferred upon him by section 72(4)(a) of the Nationality, Immigration and Asylum Act 2002, the Secretary of State hereby makes the following Order:

1

This Order may be cited as the Nationality, Immigration and Asylum Act 2002 (Specification of Particularly Serious Crimes) Order 2004 and shall come into force on 12th August 2004.

Initial Commencement
Specified date: 12 August 2004: see above.

2

An offence of a description set out in any of Schedules 1 to 6 to this Order is hereby specified for the purposes of section 72(4)(a) of the Nationality, Immigration and Asylum Act 2002.

Initial Commencement
Specified date: 12 August 2004: see art 1.

SCHEDULE 1
STATUTORY OFFENCES THAT APPLY THROUGHOUT THE UNITED KINGDOM

Offences under the Explosive Substances Act 1883

Section 2 (unlawfully and maliciously causing an explosion likely to endanger life or cause serious injury to property).

Section 3(1)(a) (unlawfully and maliciously doing an act, intending or conspiring to cause an explosion likely to endanger life or cause serious injury to property).

Section 3(1)(b) (unlawfully and maliciously making, possessing, or having under control, an explosive substance intending to endanger life or cause serious injury to property).

Section 4 (making, or knowingly possessing, an explosive substance in circumstances that lead to reasonable suspicion that such making or possession is for an unlawful object).

Offences under the Misuse of Drugs Act 1971

Section 4(3)(a) (supplying or offering to supply a controlled drug, where the offence in question is in respect of a Class A drug or Class B drug controlled by the Misuse of Drugs Act 1971).

Section 4(3)(b) (being concerned in the supply of a controlled drug, where the offence in question is in respect of a Class A drug or Class B drug controlled by the Misuse of Drugs Act 1971).

Section 4(3)(c) (being concerned in the making of an offer to supply a controlled drug, where the offence in question is in respect of a Class A drug or Class B drug controlled by the Misuse of Drugs Act 1971).

Section 5(3) (possessing a controlled drug intending to supply it to another, where the offence in question is in respect of a Class A drug or Class B drug controlled by the Misuse of Drugs Act 1971).

Section 8(a) (occupying or managing premises where the production or attempted production of a controlled drug is knowingly permitted on those premises).

Section 8(b) (occupying or managing premises where the supply, or attempted supply, of or the offer to supply a controlled drug is knowingly permitted on those premises).

Section 9(a) (smoking or otherwise using opium).

Section 9(b) (frequenting a place used for opium smoking).

Section 9(c)(i) (possessing pipes or utensils for use in connection with opium smoking which have been used, permitted or intended for use, for that purpose).

Section 9(c)(ii) (possessing utensils for use in connection with preparing opium for smoking which have been used, permitted or intended for use for that purpose).

Section 20 (assisting or inducing, while in the United Kingdom, the commission of an offence under a corresponding law outside the United Kingdom).

Offences under the Immigration Act 1971

Section 25(1)(a) (facilitating the breach of immigration law by a person who is not a citizen of the European Union).

Section 25A (facilitating, for gain, the arrival in the United Kingdom of an asylum seeker).

Section 25B (facilitating a breach of a deportation or exclusion order in force against a citizen of the European Union).

Offences under the Biological Weapons Act 1974

Section 1(1)(a) (developing, producing, stockpiling, acquiring or retaining a biological agent or toxin in a quantity that has no justification for peaceful purposes).

Section 1(1)(b) (developing, producing, stockpiling, acquiring or retaining a weapon, equipment or means of delivery designed to use a biological agent or toxin for hostile purposes or in an armed conflict).

Section 1(1A)(a) (transferring a biological agent or toxin for non-peaceful purposes or entering into an agreement to do so).

Section 1(1A)(b) (making arrangements for the transfer of a biological agent or toxin for non-peaceful purposes or entering into an agreement to do so).

Offences under the Customs and Excise Act 1979

Section 50(3) (importing or being concerned in importing goods contrary to any prohibition or restriction, intending to evade that prohibition or restriction, where the offence in question is in respect of a Class A drug or Class B drug controlled by the Misuse of Drugs Act 1971).

Appendix 1   Legislation and materials

Section 68(1) (exporting or shipping as stores, or bringing to the United Kingdom for the purpose of exporting or shipping as stores, goods contrary to any prohibition or restriction, where the offence in question is in respect of a Class A drug or Class B drug controlled by the Misuse of Drugs Act 1971).

Section 68(2) (knowingly being concerned in exporting, or shipping as stores, any goods, intending to evade a prohibition or restriction, where the offence in question is in respect of a Class A or Class B drug controlled by the Misuse of Drugs Act 1971).

Section 170(2)(b) (knowingly being concerned in the fraudulent evasion of any prohibition or restriction in relation to goods, where the offence in question is in respect of a Class A or Class B drug controlled by the Misuse of Drugs Act 1971).

Offences under the Taking of Hostages Act 1982

Section 1(1) (detaining a person and threatening to kill, injure or continue to detain that person in order to compel a State, international governmental organisation or person to do, or abstain from doing, any act).

Offences under the Aviation Security Act 1982

Section 1(1) (unlawfully seizing, or exercising control of, an aircraft by using force or threats).

Section 2(1)(a) (unlawfully and intentionally destroying an aircraft in service or damaging such an aircraft so as to render it incapable of flight or endanger its safety in flight).

Section 2(1)(b) (unlawfully and intentionally committing an act of violence on board an aircraft in flight likely to endanger its safety).

Section 3(1) (unlawfully and intentionally destroying, damaging or interfering with any property used for the provision of air navigation facilities where such destruction, damage or interference is likely to endanger the safety of aircraft in flight).

Section 3(3) (intentionally communicating materially false, misleading or deceptive information which endangers, or is likely to endanger, the safety of an aircraft in flight).

Section 4(1)(a) (possessing, without lawful authority or reasonable excuse, a firearm or explosive, or article having the appearance of either, or any article made or adapted for injuring a person or destroying or damaging property, in any aircraft registered in the United Kingdom).

Section 4(1)(b) (possessing, without lawful authority or reasonable excuse, a firearm, explosive or article having the appearance of either or any article made or adapted for injuring a person or destroying or damaging property in any aircraft not registered in the United Kingdom when it is in, or flying over, the United Kingdom).

Section 4(1)(c) (possessing, without lawful authority or reasonable excuse, a firearm, explosive or article having the appearance of either or any article made or adapted for injuring a person or destroying or damaging property in an aerodrome in the United Kingdom).

Section 4(1)(d) (possessing, without lawful authority or reasonable excuse, a firearm, explosive or article having the appearance of either or any article made or adapted for injuring a person or destroying or damaging property in any air navigation installation in the United Kingdom).

Offences under the Nuclear Materials (Offences) Act 1983

Section 2(2)(a) (receiving, holding or dealing with nuclear material intending to do an act which is an offence referred to in section 1(1)(a) or (b) of the Nuclear Materials (Offences) Act 1983).

Section 2(2)(b) (receiving, holding or dealing with nuclear material being reckless as to whether another would do an act which is an offence referred to in section 1(1)(a) or (b) of the Nuclear Materials (Offences) Act 1983).

Section 2(3) (making a threat to do an act by means of nuclear material which is an offence referred to in section 1(1)(a) or (b) of the Nuclear Materials (Offences) Act 1983, intending that the person to whom the threat is made shall fear that it will be carried out).

Section 2(4) (threatening to obtain nuclear material by an act which is an offence referred to in section 1(1)(c) of the Nuclear Materials (Offences) Act 1983 in order to compel a state, international governmental organisation or person to do, or abstain from doing, an act).

Offences under the Criminal Justice Act 1988

Section 134(1) (intentionally inflicting severe pain or suffering on another, where the offender is a public official or person acting in an official capacity who does such acts in performance, or purported performance, of his official duties).

Section 134(2) (intentionally inflicting severe pain or suffering on another at the instigation, consent or acquiescence of a public official or person acting in an official capacity who at the time of such instigation, consent or acquiescence is acting in performance, or purported performance, of his official duties).

Offences under the Criminal Justice (International Co-operation) Act 1990

Section 12(1) (manufacturing or supplying a scheduled substance, knowing or suspecting that the substance is to be used for the unlawful production of a controlled drug).

Offences under the Aviation and Maritime Security Act 1990

Section 1(1) (intentionally committing an act of violence at an aerodrome serving international civil aviation with any device, substance or weapon which causes, or is likely to cause, serious personal injury or death and endangers the safe operation of that aerodrome or the safety of persons there).

Section 1(2)(a)(i) (unlawfully and intentionally destroying or seriously damaging property used for the provision of any facilities at an aerodrome serving international civil aviation with any device, substance or weapon in a way that endangers, or is likely to endanger, the safe operation of that aerodrome or the safety of persons there).

Section 1(2)(a)(ii) (unlawfully and intentionally destroying or seriously damaging an out of service aircraft at an aerodrome serving international civil aviation with any device, substance or weapon in a way that endangers, or is likely to endanger, the safe operation of that aerodrome or the safety of persons there).

Section 1(2)(b) (unlawfully and intentionally disrupting the services of an aerodrome serving international civil aviation with any device, substance or weapon in a way that endangers, or is likely to endanger, the safe operation of that aerodrome or the safety of persons there).

Section 9 (unlawfully seizing, or exercising of control, of a ship by force or with threats).

Section 13(1) (threatening to do an act to a ship or fixed platform which is an offence under section 11(1) of the Aviation and Maritime Security Act 1990).

Section 13(2) (threatening to do an act which is an offence under section 12(1) of the Aviation and Maritime Security Act 1990).

Offences under the Channel Tunnel (Security) Order 1994

Article 4(1) (unlawfully seizing, or exercising control, of a Channel Tunnel train by using force or threats).

Article 5(1) (unlawfully seizing, or exercising control, of the tunnel system by using force or threats).

Article 6(1)(a) (unlawfully and intentionally destroying a Channel Tunnel train or the tunnel system or any goods on a train or within the tunnel system so as to endanger, or to be likely to endanger, the safe operation of the train or the safety of the tunnel system).

Article 6(1)(b) (unlawfully and intentionally damaging a Channel Tunnel train or the tunnel system or any goods on a train or within the tunnel system so as to endanger, or to be likely to endanger, the safe operation of the train or the safety of the tunnel system).

Article 6(1)(c) (committing an act of violence on board a Channel Tunnel train or within the tunnel system likely to endanger the safe operation of the train or the safety of the tunnel system).

Article 6(2)(a) (unlawfully and intentionally placing a device or substance on a Channel Tunnel train likely to destroy or damage it, or goods on it, so as to endanger its safe operation).

Article 6(2)(b) (unlawfully and intentionally placing a device or substance in the tunnel system likely to destroy or damage it so as to endanger its safety).

Article 7(1) (unlawfully and intentionally destroying, damaging, or interfering with, the operation of property referred to in article 7(2) of the Channel Tunnel (Security) Order 1994 likely to endanger the safe operation of any Channel Tunnel train or the safety of the tunnel system).

Article 7(3) (intentionally communicating information, knowing it to be false in a material particular, which endangers the safe operation of any Channel Tunnel train or the safety of the tunnel system).

Article 8(1) (threatening to commit an offence under article 6(1) of the Channel Tunnel (Security) Order 1994 in order to compel a person to do, or abstain from doing, any act, where the making of such a threat is likely to endanger the safe operation of a train or the safety of the tunnel system).

Article 8(2) (threatening to commit an offence under article 7(1) of the Channel Tunnel (Security) Order 1994 in order to compel a person to do, or abstain from doing, any act, where the making of such a threat is likely to endanger the safe operation of a train or the safety of the tunnel system).

Offences under the Chemical Weapons Act 1996

Section 2(1)(a) (using a chemical weapon).

Section 2(1)(b) (developing or producing a chemical weapon).

Section 2(1)(c) (possessing a chemical weapon).

Section 2(1)(d) (participating in the transfer of a chemical weapon).

Section 2(1)(e) (engaging in military preparations, intending to use a chemical weapon).

Section 11(1)(a) (constructing premises, intending them to be used for producing a chemical weapon).

Section 11(1)(b) (altering premises, intending them to be used for producing a chemical weapon).

Section 11(1)(c) (installing or constructing equipment, intending it to be used for producing a chemical weapon).

Section 11(1)(d) (altering equipment, intending it to be used for producing a chemical weapon).

Section 11(1)(e) (occupying land and permitting construction of premises on it, intending those premises to be used for producing a chemical weapon).

Section 11(1)(f) (occupying land and permitting premises to be altered on it, intending those premises to be used for producing a chemical weapon).

Section 11(1)(g) (occupying land and permitting installation or construction on it of equipment, intending that equipment to be used for producing a chemical weapon).

Section 11(1)(h) (occupying land and permitting equipment to be altered on it, intending that equipment to be used for producing a chemical weapon).

Offences under the Terrorism Act 2000

Section 11(1) (belonging, or professing to belong, to a proscribed organisation).

Section 12(1) (inviting support for a proscribed organisation that is not restricted to the provision of money or property).

Section 12(2)(a) (arranging, managing or assisting in the arrangement or management of a meeting, knowing that it supports a proscribed organisation).

Section 12(2)(b) (arranging, managing or assisting in the arrangement or management of a meeting, knowing that it furthers the activities of a proscribed organisation).

Section 12(2)(c) (arranging, managing or assisting in the arrangement or management of a meeting, knowing that it is to be addressed by a member or professed member of a proscribed organisation).

Section 12(3) (addressing a meeting for the purpose of encouraging support or furthering the activities of a proscribed organisation).

Section 15(1) (inviting another to provide money or property, intending, or having reasonable cause to suspect, that it may be used for terrorist purposes).

Section 15(2) (receiving money or property, intending, or having reasonable cause to suspect, that it may be used for terrorist purposes).

Section 15(3) (providing money or property, intending, or having reasonable cause to suspect, that it may be used for terrorist purposes).

Section 16(1) (using money or property for terrorist purposes).

Section 16(2) (possessing money or property, intending, or having reasonable cause to suspect, that it may be used for terrorist purposes).

Section 17(1) (entering into, or becoming concerned in, an arrangement where money or other property is made available knowing, or having reasonable cause to suspect, that it may be used for terrorist purposes).

Appendix 1 Legislation and materials

Section 18(1)(a) (entering into, or becoming concerned in, an arrangement facilitating the retention or control of terrorist property by concealment).

Section 18(1)(b) (entering into, or becoming concerned in, an arrangement facilitating the retention or control of terrorist property by removal from the jurisdiction).

Section 18(1)(c) (entering into, or becoming concerned in, an arrangement facilitating the retention or control of terrorist property by transfer to nominees).

Section 18(1)(d) (entering into, or becoming concerned in, an arrangement facilitating the retention or control of terrorist property in any other way).

Section 19(2) (not disclosing as soon as reasonably practicable a belief or suspicion, and the information on which the belief or suspicion is based, that an offence has been committed under sections 15 to 18 of the Terrorism Act 2000).

Section 38B(1)(a) (not disclosing information, knowing or believing it to be of material assistance in preventing an act of terrorism).

Section 38B(1)(b) (not disclosing information, knowing or believing it to be of material assistance in securing the apprehension, prosecution or conviction of a person for a terrorist offence).

Section 54(1)(a) (providing instruction or training in the making or use of a firearm).

Section 54(1)(aa) (providing instruction or training in the making or use of a radioactive material or weapon designed or adapted to discharge it).

Section 54(1)(b) (providing instruction or training in the making or use of an explosive).

Section 54(1)(c) (providing instruction or training in the making or use of a chemical, biological or nuclear weapon).

Section 54(2)(a) (receiving instruction or training in the making or use of a radioactive material or weapon designed or adapted to discharge it).

Section 54(2)(aa) (receiving instruction or training in the making or use of a radioactive material or weapon designed or adapted to discharge it).

Section 54(2)(b) (receiving instruction or training in the making or use of an explosive).

Section 54(2)(c) (receiving instruction or training in the making or use of a chemical, biological or nuclear weapon).

Section 54(3)(a) (inviting another to receive instruction or training where receipt would constitute an offence under section 54(2) of the Terrorism Act 2000).

Section 54(3)(b) (inviting another to receive instruction or training where receipt would constitute an offence under section 54(2) of the Terrorism Act 2000 but for the fact that it would take place outside the United Kingdom).

Section 56(1) (directing the activities of an organisation at any level which is concerned in the commission of a terrorist act).

Section 57(1) (possessing an article giving rise to a reasonable suspicion that possessing it is connected with the commission, preparation or instigation of a terrorist act).

Section 58(1)(a) (collecting or making a record of information of a kind likely to be useful to a person committing or preparing a terrorist act).

Section 58(1)(b) (possessing a record of information of a kind likely to be useful to a person committing or preparing a terrorist act).

Offences under the Anti-terrorism, Crime and Security Act 2001

Section 47(1)(a) (knowingly causing a nuclear weapon explosion).

Section 47(1)(b) (developing or producing a nuclear weapon, or participating in either activity).

Section 47(1)(c) (possessing a nuclear weapon).

Section 47(1)(d) (participating in the transfer of a nuclear weapon).

Section 47(1)(e) (engaging in military preparations intending, or threatening, to use a nuclear weapon).

Section 113(1) (using a noxious substance or thing in a way which causes serious violence or serious damage to property, endangers human life, creates a serious risk to health or safety or induces in the public a fear that such an act will endanger their lives or health or safety, and which is designed to influence the government or intimidate the public).

Section 114(1) (placing or sending a substance or thing, intending to induce a belief that it is a noxious substance or thing likely to endanger human life or create a serious risk to human health).

Section 114(2) (communicating information knowing or believing it to be false, intending to induce a belief that a noxious substance or thing is present in any place, thereby to endanger human life or create a serious risk to human health).

Offences under the Proceeds of Crime Act 2002

Section 327(1)(a) (concealing criminal property).

Section 327(1)(b) (disguising criminal property).

Section 327(1)(c) (converting criminal property).

Section 327(1)(d) (transferring criminal property).

Section 327(1)(e) (removing criminal property from England and Wales, Scotland or Northern Ireland).

Section 328(1) (entering into, or becoming concerned in, an arrangement, knowing or suspecting that it will facilitate the acquisition, retention, use, or control of criminal property).

Section 329(1)(a) (acquiring criminal property).

Section 329(1)(b) (using criminal property).

Section 329(1)(c) (possessing criminal property).

Section 332(1) (failing, as a nominated person, to disclose known or suspected money laundering as soon as reasonably practicable after the information on which that knowledge or suspicion is based is obtained in consequence of a disclosure under section 337 or 338 of the Proceeds of Crime Act 2002).

Section 333 (disclosing information likely to prejudice any investigation that might be conducted following the disclosure of information by a nominated person under section 337 or 338 of the Proceeds of Crime Act 2002).

Initial Commencement
Specified date: 12 August 2004: see art 1.

Appendix 1   Legislation and materials

SCHEDULE 2
OFFENCES UNDER THE COMMON LAW OF ENGLAND AND WALES AND STATUTORY
OFFENCES THAT APPLY ONLY IN ENGLAND AND WALES

1

Offences under the Common Law of England and Wales.

Manslaughter.

2

Statutory offences that apply only in England and Wales.

Offences under the Infant Life (Preservation) Act 1929)

Section 1 (doing a wilful act, intending to destroy the life of a child capable of being born alive that causes a child to die before it is born).

Offences under the Infanticide Act 1938

Section 1 (doing a wilful act causing the death of a child before it is over 12 months old, where that act is done by the mother of the child and her balance of mind is disturbed for reasons relating to lactation or the birth of the child).

Offences under the Theft Act 1968

Section 1(1) (dishonestly appropriating another's property, intending to permanently deprive him of it).

Section 8(1) (stealing, and before or at the time of doing so, using force or putting another in fear of being there and then subjected to force).

Section 9(1)(a) (entering a building as a trespasser, intending to steal, inflict or attempt to inflict grievous bodily harm or rape).

Section 9(1)(b) (having entered a building as a trespasser, stealing or attempting to steal or inflicting or attempting to inflict grievous bodily harm).

Section 10(1) (committing burglary with a firearm, imitation firearm, weapon of offence or explosive).

Section 12A (aggravated taking of a vehicle).

Offences under the Criminal Damage Act 1971

Section 1(1) (destroying or damaging, without lawful excuse, another's property intending to destroy or damage it or being reckless as to that).

Section 1(2) (destroying or damaging, without lawful excuse, property, intending, or being reckless as to whether, that destruction or damage would result and intending that damage or destruction to endanger the life of another or being reckless as to that).

Section 2 (threatening, without lawful excuse, to destroy or damage property, knowing that such a threat is likely to endanger another's life).

Section 3(a) (having in custody or under control anything intending, without lawful excuse, to use, or permit use of, it to destroy or damage another's property).

Section 3(b) (having in custody or under control anything, intending, without lawful excuse, to use, or permit use of, it to destroy or damage property knowing that such an act is likely to endanger another's life).

Offences under the Criminal Law Act 1977

Section 1 (agreeing to pursue a course of conduct which, if carried out as intended, necessarily amounts to the commission of an offence or would do so but for the fact that such commission is impossible, provided that the offence in question is an offence described either in Schedule 1 to this Order or this Schedule).

Section 51(1) (placing or dispatching an article, intending to induce a belief that it will explode or ignite and cause personal injury or property damage).

Section 51(2) (communicating information, knowing or believing it to be false intending to induce a belief that a bomb or other thing is liable to explode in a place) .

Offences under the Magistrates Courts Act 1980

Section 44 (aiding, abetting, counselling or procuring the commission of a summary offence, provided that the offence in question is described in Schedule 1 to this Order or this Schedule).

Offences under the Criminal Attempts Act 1981

Section 1(1) (intending to commit an offence and doing an act that is more than merely preparatory to the commission of that offence, provided that the offence in question is described in Schedule 1 to this Order or this Schedule) .

Offences under the Public Order Act 1986

Section 1(1) (being in a group of 12 or more people who use, or threaten, unlawful violence for a common purpose so as to cause a person of reasonable firmness present at the scene to fear for his safety).

Section 2(1) (being in a group of 3 or more people who use, or threaten, unlawful violence for a common purpose so as to cause a person of reasonable firmness present at the scene to fear for his safety).

Section 3(1) (using, or threatening, unlawful violence so as to cause a person of reasonable firmness present at the scene to fear for his safety).

Offences under the Protection from Harassment Act 1997

Section 4(1) (causing fear in another on at least two occasions that violence will be used against him, where the offender knows, or ought to know, that his course of conduct will cause such fear on each occasion).

Offences under the Crime and Disorder Act 1998

Section 29(1)(a) (maliciously wounding or causing grievous bodily harm so as to constitute an offence under section 20 of the Offences Against the Person Act 1861 that is racially or religiously aggravated).

Section 29(1)(b) (causing actual bodily harm so as to constitute an offence under section 47 of the Offences Against the Person Act 1861 that is racially or religiously aggravated).

Section 29(1)(c) (committing a common assault that is racially or religiously aggravated).

Section 31(1)(a) (committing an offence under section 4(1) of the Public Order Act 1986 that is racially or religiously aggravated).

Section 31(1)(b) (committing an offence under section 4A(1) of the Public Order Act 1986 that is racially or religiously aggravated).

Offences under the Sexual Offences Act 2003

Section 1(1) (intentionally penetrating the vagina, anus or mouth of another with a penis, where the victim does not consent and the offender does not reasonably believe that there is consent).

Section 2(1) (intentionally sexually penetrating the vagina or anus of another with a part of the body or anything else, where the victim does not consent and the offender does not reasonably believe that there is consent).

Section 3(1) (intentionally sexually touching another, where the victim does not consent and the offender does not reasonably believe that there is consent).

Section 4(1) (intentionally causing another to engage in sexual activity, where the victim does not consent and the offender does not reasonably believe that there is consent).

Section 5(1) (intentionally sexually penetrating the vagina, anus or mouth of another with a penis, where the victim is under 13).

Section 6(1) (intentionally sexually penetrating the vagina or anus of another who is under 13 with a part of the body or anything else).

Section 7(1) (intentionally sexually touching a person who is under 13) .

Section 8(1) (intentionally causing or inciting another who is under 13 to engage in sexual activity).

Section 9(1) (intentionally sexually touching another who is 13 or under, or is 16 or under and the offender, who is 18 or over, does not believe that the victim is 16 or over) .

Section 10(1) (intentionally causing or inciting another to engage in sexual activity, where the victim is 13 or under, or is 16 or under and the offender, who is 18 or over, does not believe that the victim is 16 or over).

Section 11(1) (intentionally engaging, for the purpose of sexual gratification, in sexual activity in a place where another is present or can observe and the offender, who is 18 or over, knows, believes or intends the victim to be there and the victim is 13 or under, or is under 16 and the offender does not reasonably believe that the victim is 16 or over).

Section 12(1) (intentionally causing, for the purpose of sexual gratification, another to watch or look at an image of a third person engaging in sexual activity, where the victim is 13 or under, or is under 16 and the offender does not reasonably believe that the victim is 16 or over).

Section 13(1) (committing an offence under section 9 to 12 of the Sexual Offences Act 2003 which would be an offence if the offender was 18).

Section 14(1) (intentionally arranging or facilitating something in any part of the world that, if done, would involve the commission of any offence under sections 9 to 13 of the Sexual Offences Act 2003).

Section 25 (intentionally sexually touching a family member, where the offender could reasonably be expected to know that the victim is a family member, and the victim is 13, or is under 18 and the offender does not reasonably believe that the victim is 18 or over).

Section 26 (intentionally inciting a family member to touch or allow himself to be touched sexually where the offender could reasonably be expected to know that the victim is a family member, and the victim is 13 or under, or is under 18 and the offender does not reasonably believe that the victim is 18 or over).

Section 30(1) (intentionally sexually touching another where the victim is unable to refuse by reason of a mental disorder and the offender could reasonably be expected to know that the victim has a mental disorder that is likely to render him unable to refuse).

Section 31(1) (intentionally inciting another to engage in sexual activity where the victim is unable to refuse by reason of a mental disorder and the offender could reasonably be expected to know that the victim has a mental disorder that is likely to render him unable to refuse).

Section 32(1) (intentionally engaging in sexual activity for sexual gratification in a place where a person who is unable to refuse by reason of a mental disorder observes it or the offender knows, believes or intends the victim to observe it and the offender knows or could reasonably be expected to know that the victim has a mental disorder that is likely to render him unable to refuse).

Section 33(1) (intentionally causing, for sexual gratification, another to watch, or look at an image of, a third person engaging in sexual activity, where the victim is unable to refuse by reason of mental disorder and the offender knows or could reasonably be expected to know that the victim has a mental disorder that is likely to render him unable to refuse).

Section 34(1) (intentionally sexually touching another with a mental disorder, where the victim agrees and such agreement is obtained by inducement, threat, or deception and the offender knows, or could reasonably be expected to know, about that mental disorder).

Section 35(1) (intentionally causing another with a mental disorder, by inducement, threat, or deception, to engage in sexual activity and the victim has a mental disorder which the offender knows, or could reasonably be expected to know, about).

Section 36(1) (intentionally engaging in sexual activity, for the purpose of sexual gratification, in a place where another with a mental disorder is present or observes it, or the offender knows, believes or intends the victim to observe it, because of inducement, threat or deception and the offender knows, or could reasonably be expected to know, that the victim has a mental disorder).

Section 37(1) (intentionally causing another with a mental disorder, by inducement, threat or deception, to watch or look, for the purposes of sexual gratification, at an image of a third person engaging in sexual activity, and the offender knows, or could reasonably be expected to know, that the victim has a mental disorder).

Section 38(1) (intentionally sexually touching another with a mental disorder which the offender knows, or could reasonably be expected to know, about, where the offender is involved in the victim's care).

Section 39(1) (intentionally causing or inciting another with a mental disorder to engage in sexual activity, where the offender knows or could reasonably be expected to know that the victim has a mental disorder and the offender is involved in the victim's care).

Section 61(1) (intentionally administering a substance to another knowing that the victim does not consent, with the intention of stupefying or overpowering the victim so that sexual activity can be engaged in with the victim).

Section 62(1) (committing an offence intending to commit a sexual offence under Part I of the Sexual Offences Act 2003).

Section 63(1) (trespassing on premises, knowing that, or being reckless as to whether, trespass is taking place and intending to commit a sexual offence under Part I of the Sexual Offences Act 2003).

Initial Commencement
Specified date: 12 August 2004: see art 1.

SCHEDULE 3
OFFENCES UNDER THE COMMON LAW OF SCOTLAND AND STATUTORY OFFENCES
THAT APPLY ONLY IN SCOTLAND

1

Offences under the Common Law of Scotland.

Abduction.
Abduction of women or girls with intent to rape.
Aiding and abetting an offence under the Common Law of Scotland (provided that the offence in question is described in this paragraph of this Schedule).
Assault with intent to rape or ravish.
Assault and robbery.
Attempted murder.
Breach of the peace inferring personal violence.
Clandestine injury to women.
Conspiracy (in respect of an offence described in Schedule 1 to this Order or this Schedule).
Culpable homicide.
Culpable and reckless fire-raising.
Indecent assault.
Malicious mischief.
Mobbing and rioting.
Rape.
Robbery.
Theft by housebreaking.
Threatening personal violence.
Wilful fire-raising.
Wrongful imprisonment.

2

Statutory offences that apply only in Scotland.

Offences under the Children and Young Persons (Scotland) Act 1937

Section 12 (ill-treating, neglecting, abandoning or exposing a child under 16, or causing such, where the offender is 16 and has parental responsibility for the victim or has charge or care of him).

Offences under the Civic Government (Scotland) Act 1982

Section 52 (taking and distributing indecent images of children).

Section 52A (possessing indecent images of children).

Offences under the Prohibition of Female Circumcision Act 1985

Section 1(1)(a) (excising, infibulating or otherwise mutilating the labia or clitoris of another).

Offences under the Criminal Law (Consolidation) (Scotland) Act 1995

Section 3(1) (having sexual intercourse with a member of the same household who is 16 or under where the offender is in a position of trust).

Section 5(1) (having sexual intercourse with a girl under 13).

Section 6 (engaging in lewd, indecent or libidinous behaviour towards a girl between 12 and 16, where that behaviour would have constituted a common law offence had that girl been under 12).

Section 50A(1)(a) (pursuing a racially aggravated course of conduct amounting to harassment that is intended to harass or which occurs in circumstances where it would appear to a reasonable person to constitute harassment).

Section 50A(1)(b) (acting in a racially aggravated manner which causes, or is intended to cause, alarm or distress).

Section 52(1) (wilfully or recklessly destroying or damaging property).

Offences under the Criminal Procedure (Scotland) Act 1995

Section 293(2) (aiding, abetting, counselling, procuring or inciting the commission of an offence against the provisions of any enactment, provided that the offence in question is described in Schedule 1 to this Order or in this paragraph of this Schedule).

Section 294 (attempting to commit an indictable offence, provided that the offence in question is described in Schedule 1 to this Order or this Schedule).

Offences under the Sexual Offences (Amendment) Act 2000

Section 3 (having sexual intercourse, or engaging in other sexual activity with, a person under 18, where the offender is 18 or over and is in a position of trust).

Offences under the International Criminal Court (Scotland) Act 2001

Section 1 (committing genocide, a crime against humanity or a war crime).

Offences under the Criminal Justice (Scotland) Act 2003

Section 22(1)(a)(i) (arranging or facilitating the arrival or travel in the United Kingdom of a person and intending to exercise control over prostitution of the victim or involving the victim in the production of obscene or indecent material).

Section 22(1)(a)(ii) (arranging or facilitating the arrival or travel in the United Kingdom of a person and believing that another will exercise control over prostitution of the victim or involving the victim in the production of obscene or indecent material).

Section 22(1)(b)(i) (arranging or facilitating the departure from the United Kingdom of a person and intending to exercise control over prostitution of the victim or involving the victim in the production of obscene or indecent material).

Section 22(1)(b)(ii) (arranging or facilitating the departure from the United Kingdom of a person and believing that another will exercise control over prostitution of the victim or involving the victim in the production of obscene or indecent material).

Initial Commencement
Specified date: 12 August 2004: see art 1.

SCHEDULE 4
OFFENCES UNDER THE COMMON LAW OF NORTHERN IRELAND AND STATUTORY
OFFENCES THAT APPLY ONLY IN NORTHERN IRELAND

1

Offences under the Common Law of Northern Ireland.

Affray.
Rape.
Rioting.

2

Statutory offences that apply only in Northern Ireland.

Offences under the Offences Against the Person Act 1861

Section 52 (indecently assaulting a woman or a girl under 16).

Section 53 (abducting a woman by force, intending to have sexual intercourse with her).

Offences under the Criminal Law (Amendment) Act 1885

Section 4 (having unlawful sexual intercourse with a girl under 13).

Section 5 (having unlawful sexual intercourse with a girl under 16).

Offences under the Infanticide Act (Northern Ireland) 1939

Section 1(1) (doing a wilful act causing the death of a child before it is over 12 months old, where that act is done by the mother of the child and her balance of mind is disturbed for reasons relating to lactation or the birth of the child).

Offences under the Criminal Justice Act (Northern Ireland) 1945

Section 25(1) (doing a wilful act, intending to destroy the life of a child capable of being born alive that causes the child to die before it is born).

Offences under the Attempted Rape Act (Northern Ireland) 1960

Section 2 (committing assault intending to commit rape).

Offences under the Children and Young Persons Act (Northern Ireland) 1968

Section 20(1) (wilfully assaulting, ill-treating, neglecting, abandoning or exposing, or causing such, of a child of 16 where the offender has responsibility for the victim, in a manner likely to cause the victim unnecessary suffering or injury to health).

Section 22 (committing an act of gross indecency with or towards a child or inciting a child to perform such an act).

Offences under the Theft Act (Northern Ireland) 1969

Section 1(1) (dishonestly appropriating another's property, intending to permanently deprive him of it).

Section 8(1) (stealing, and before or at the time of doing so, using force or putting another in fear of being there and then subjected to force).

Section 9(1)(a) (entering a building as a trespasser, intending to steal, inflict or attempt to inflict grievous bodily harm or rape).

Section 9(1)(b) (having entered a building as a trespasser, stealing or attempting to steal or inflicting or attempting to inflict grievous bodily harm).

Section 10(1) (committing burglary with a firearm or imitation firearm, a weapon of offence or an explosive).

Offences under the Protection of the Person and Property Act (Northern Ireland) 1969

Section 3 (throwing, placing, attaching or using a petrol bomb, intending to destroy, or damage, the property of another, or to cause personal injury to another, or to give another reasonable cause to fear any destruction of property or personal injury or being reckless in regard to causing any such destruction, damage, injury or fear).

Offences under the Criminal Damage (Northern Ireland) Order 1977

Article 3(1) (destroying or damaging, without lawful excuse, another's property, intending to destroy or damage it or being reckless as to that).

Article 3(2) (destroying or damaging, without lawful excuse, property, intending, or being reckless as to whether, that destruction or damage would result and intending that damage or destruction to endanger the life of another or being reckless as to that).

Article 4 (threatening, without lawful excuse, to destroy or damage property, knowing that such a threat is likely to endanger another's life).

Section 5(a) (having in custody or under control anything, intending, without lawful excuse, to use, or permit use of, it to destroy or damage another's property).

Section 5(b) (having in custody or under control anything, intending, without lawful excuse, to use, or permit use of, it to destroy or damage property knowing that such an act is likely to endanger another's life).

Offences under the Criminal Law (Amendment) (Northern Ireland) Order 1977

Article 3(1) (placing or sending an article, intending to induce a belief that it is likely to explode or ignite and cause personal injury or damage to property).

Article 3(2) (communicating information, knowing or believing it to be false and intending to induce a false belief that a bomb or other explosive device is present).

Offences under the Firearms (Northern Ireland) Order 1981

Article 6(1) (possessing, purchasing, acquiring, manufacturing, selling or transferring any of the items referred to in Article 6(1) of the Firearms (Northern Ireland) Order 1981).

Article 6(1A) (possessing, purchasing, acquiring, manufacturing, selling or transferring any of the items referred to in article 6(1A) of the Firearms (Northern Ireland) Order 1981).

Article 17 (possessing a firearm or ammunition, intending to endanger life or cause serious injury to property or to enable another to do so).

Article 17A (possessing a firearm or imitation firearm, intending to cause, or enable another to cause, a person to believe that he will be the victim of unlawful violence).

Article 18(1) (making or attempting to make use of a firearm or imitation firearm, intending to resist or prevent the lawful arrest or detention of himself or any other person).

Appendix 1 Legislation and materials

Article 18(2) (committing, or being arrested for, an offence specified in Schedule 1 of the Firearms (Northern Ireland) Order 1981 and possessing a firearm or imitation firearm without lawful object).

Article 19(1) (having a firearm or imitation firearm, intending to commit an indictable offence, or to resist arrest or to prevent the arrest of another).

Article 20(1) (having, without lawful authority or reasonable excuse, in public a loaded shot gun, loaded air weapon or any other firearm together with ammunition suitable for use in that firearm).

Article 21(1) (having a firearm, or imitation firearm when trespassing in a building without reasonable excuse).

Article 21(2) (having a firearm, or imitation firearm when trespassing on land without reasonable excuse).

Article 23 (possessing a firearm or ammunition giving rise to a reasonable suspicion that such possession is not for a lawful object).

Offences under the Magistrates Courts (Northern Ireland) Order 1981

Article 59 (aiding, abetting, counselling or procuring the commission of a summary offence, provided that the offence in question is described in Schedule 1 to this Order or this Schedule).

Offences under the Criminal Attempts and Conspiracy (Northern Ireland) Order 1983

Article 3 (intending to commit an offence and doing an act that is more than merely preparatory to the commission of that offence, provided that the offence in question is described in Schedule 1 to this Order or this Schedule).

Article 9 (agreeing to pursue a course of conduct which, if carried out as intended, necessarily amounts to the commission of an offence to, or would do so but for the fact that such commission is impossible, provided that the offence in question is described in Schedule 1 to this Order or this Schedule).

Offences under the Public Order (Northern Ireland) Order 1987

Article 18 (using threatening, abusive, or insulting words or behaviour, displaying anything, doing any act or, being the owner or occupier of any land or premises, causing or permitting anything to be displayed or any act to be done, intending to provoke a breach of the peace or by which a breach of the peace or public disorder is likely to be occasioned).

Offences under the Road Traffic (Northern Ireland) Order 1995

Article 9 (causing the death of, or grievous bodily injury to, another by driving a mechanically propelled vehicle dangerously on a road or other public place) .

Article 14(1)(a) (causing the death of, or grievous bodily injury to, another by driving without due care and attention, or without reasonable consideration, and being unfit to drive through drink or drugs).

Article 14(1)(b) (causing the death of, or grievous bodily injury to, another by driving without due care and attention, or without reasonable consideration, having consumed so much alcohol that the proportion of it in his breath, blood or urine exceeds the prescribed limit).

Article 14(1)(c) (causing the death of, or grievous bodily injury to, another by driving without due care and attention or without reasonable consideration and failing, without reasonable excuse, to provide a specimen in pursuance of Article 18 of the Road Traffic (Northern Ireland) Order 1995 within 18 hours of that incident).

Offences under the Protection from Harassment (Northern Ireland) Order 1997

Article 6 (causing fear in another on at least two occasions that violence will be used against him, where the offender knows or ought to know that his course of conduct will cause such fear on each of those occasions).

Offences under the Criminal Justice (Northern Ireland) Order 2003

Article 20 (committing assault, intending to commit buggery).

Article 21(1) (indecently assaulting a man).

Initial Commencement
Specified date: 12 August 2004: see art 1.

SCHEDULE 5
STATUTORY OFFENCES THAT APPLY ONLY IN ENGLAND AND WALES AND SCOTLAND

Offences under the Firearms Act 1968

Section 5(1) (possessing, purchasing, acquiring, manufacturing, selling or transferring, without authorisation, any item listed in section 5(1) of the Firearms Act 1968).

Section 16 (possessing a firearm or ammunition, intending to endanger, or enable another to endanger, life).

Section 16A (possessing a firearm or imitation firearm, intending to cause, or to enable another to cause, a belief that unlawful violence will be used).

Section 17(1) (using, or attempting to use, a firearm, intending to prevent or resist lawful arrest or detention).

Section 17(2) (unlawfully possessing a firearm or imitation firearm while committing an offence listed in Schedule 1 to the Firearms Act 1968).

Section 18(1) (having a firearm or imitation forearm, intending to commit an indictable offence or to resist or prevent arrest).

Section 19 (unlawfully or unreasonably possessing, without lawful authority or reasonable excuse, a loaded shot gun or air weapon or any other firearm, whether loaded or not, together with ammunition suitable for use in that firearm).

Offences under the Road Traffic Act 1988

Section 1 (causing the death of another by driving a mechanically propelled vehicle dangerously on a road or other public place).

Section 3A(1)(a) (causing the death of another by driving without due care and attention, or without reasonable consideration, and being unfit to drive through drink or drugs).

Article 3A(1)(b) (causing the death of another by driving without due care and attention, or without reasonable consideration, having consumed so much alcohol that the proportion of it in his breath, blood or urine exceeds the prescribed limit).

Article 3A(1)(c) (causing the death of another by driving without due care and attention or without reasonable consideration and failing, without reasonable excuse, to provide a specimen in pursuance of section 7 of the Road Traffic Act 1988 within 18 hours of that incident).

Appendix 1 Legislation and materials

Initial Commencement
Specified date: 12 August 2004: see art 1.

SCHEDULE 6

OFFENCES UNDER THE COMMON LAW OF ENGLAND AND WALES AND NORTHERN
IRELAND AND STATUTORY OFFENCES THAT APPLY ONLY IN ENGLAND AND WALES
AND NORTHERN IRELAND

1

Offences under Common Law of England and Wales and Northern Ireland.

> False Imprisonment.
> Kidnapping.

2

Statutory offences that apply only in England and Wales and Northern Ireland.

Offences under the Accessories and Abettors Act 1861

Section 8 (aiding, abetting, counselling or procuring the commission of an indictable offence, provided that the offence in question is described in Schedule 1, Schedule 2 or Schedule 4 to this Order or this Schedule).

Offences under the Offences Against the Person Act 1861

Section 4 (soliciting, encouraging, persuading, endeavouring to persuade or proposing murder).

Section 16 (unlawfully threatening to kill, intending that the subject of the threat would fear that it would be carried out).

Section 18 (unlawfully and maliciously wounding or causing grievous bodily harm, intending to cause grievous bodily harm or to resist or prevent lawful apprehension or detention).

Section 20 (unlawfully and maliciously wounding or inflicting grievous bodily harm).

Section 21 (attempting to choke, suffocate or strangle another or attempting, by means calculated to choke, suffocate or strangle, to render that person insensible, unconscious or incapable of resistance and intending to commit an indictable offence).

Section 22 (applying or administering a stupefying or overpowering drug, matter or thing intending to commit an indictable offence).

Section 23 (unlawfully and maliciously administering a poison or destructive or noxious thing so as to endanger life or inflict grievous bodily harm).

Section 27 (unlawfully abandoning or exposing a child under 2 so as to endanger life or cause permanent injury).

Section 28 (unlawfully and maliciously exploding a substance causing burning, maiming, disfigurement, disablement or grievous bodily harm).

Section 29 (unlawfully and maliciously causing an explosion or sending or delivering an explosive substance, or placing or throwing a corrosive, destructive or explosive substance, intending to burn, maim, disfigure, disable or do grievous bodily harm).

Section 30 (unlawfully and maliciously placing or throwing an explosive substance on or near a building, ship or vessel intending to do bodily injury).

Section 32 (unlawfully and maliciously placing an obstruction on a railway or interfering with railway equipment intending to endanger safety).

Section 33 (unlawfully and maliciously throwing any object at a railway vehicle intending to injure or endanger the safety of any person in that vehicle).

Section 47 (committing assault occasioning actual bodily harm).

Offences under the International Criminal Court Act 2001

Section 51 (committing genocide, a crime against humanity or a war crime against the laws of England and Wales).

Section 58 (committing genocide, a crime against humanity or a war crime against the laws of Northern Ireland).

Offences under the Nationality, Immigration and Asylum Act 2002

Section 145(1) (arranging or facilitating the arrival or travel in the United Kingdom of a person, intending to exercise control over prostitution of the victim or involving the victim in the production of obscene or indecent material).

Section 145(2) (arranging or facilitating the travel within the United Kingdom by a passenger, believing an offence to have been committed under section 145(1) of the Nationality, Immigration and Asylum Act 2002 and intending to exercise control over prostitution of him or believing that another person will exercise such control).

Section 145(3) (arranging or facilitating the departure from the United Kingdom of a passenger, intending to exercise control over prostitution of him outside the United Kingdom or believing that another person will exercise such control outside the United Kingdom).

Offences under the Female Genital Mutilation Act 2003

Section 1(1) (excising, infibulating or otherwise mutilating the whole or part of a girl's labia majora, labia minora or clitoris).

Offences under the Sexual Offences Act 2003

Section 15(1) (meeting, or travelling, intending to meet a person under 16 who has been met or communicated with on two previous occasions, where the offender intends to do something that would constitute a relevant offence (as defined in section 15(2)(b) of the Sexual Offences Act 2003) and does not believe the victim to be over 16).

Section 16(1) (intentionally sexually touching a person under 13, or under 18, where the offender is in a position of trust in relation to the victim and does not reasonably believe that the victim is over 18).

Section 17(1) (intentionally causing or inciting another to engage in sexual activity, where the offender is a person who is 18 or over and is in a position of trust in relation to the victim, and the victim is under 13, or is under 18 and the offender does not reasonably believe that the victim is 18 or over).

Section 47(1) (intentionally obtaining the sexual services of a person under 13, or under 18 and the offender does not reasonably believe that the victim is 18 or over, where the offender has made or promised payment for those services or knows that another has made or promised payment).

Section 48(1) (intentionally causing or inciting another to become a prostitute or be involved in pornography, where the victim is under 13, or is under 18 and the offender does not reasonably believe that the victim is 18 or over).

Section 49(1) (intentionally controlling any activities of another relating to the latter's prostitution or involvement in pornography, where the victim is under 13, or is under 18 and the offender does not reasonably believe that the victim is 18 or over).

Section 50(1) (intentionally arranging or facilitating the prostitution or involvement in pornography of another, where the victim is under 13, or is under 18 and the offender does not reasonably believe that the victim is 18 or over).

Section 57(1)(a) (intentionally arranging or facilitating the arrival in the United Kingdom of another and intending to do something in respect of that person after arrival that would constitute an offence specified under section 60 of the Sexual Offences Act 2003).

Section 57(1)(b) (intentionally arranging or facilitating the arrival in the United Kingdom of another and believing that a third party is likely to do something in respect of that person after arrival that would constitute an offence specified under section 60 of the Sexual Offences Act 2003).

Section 58(1)(a) (intentionally arranging or facilitating travel within the United Kingdom by another and intending to do something in respect of that person during or after the journey that would constitute an offence specified under section 60 of the Sexual Offences Act 2003).

Section 58(1)(b) (intentionally arranging or facilitating travel within the United Kingdom by another and believing that a third party is likely to do something during or after the journey in respect of that person that would constitute an offence specified under section 60 of the Sexual Offences Act 2003).

Initial Commencement
Specified date: 12 August 2004: see art 1.

ASYLUM AND IMMIGRATION (TREATMENT OF CLAIMANTS, ETC) ACT 2004 (COMMENCEMENT NO 1) ORDER 2004

2004 No 2523

Made . . . . *22nd September 2004*

The Secretary of State, in exercise of the powers conferred upon him by section 48(3) and (4) of the Asylum and Immigration (Treatment of Claimants, etc) Act 2004, hereby makes the following Order:

1   Citation and interpretation

(1)   This Order may be cited as the Asylum and Immigration (Treatment of Claimants, etc) Act 2004 (Commencement No 1) Order 2004.

(2)   In this Order, "the 1999 Act" means the Immigration and Asylum Act 1999 and "the 2004 Act" means the Asylum and Immigration (Treatment of Claimants, etc) Act 2004.

Initial Commencement
Date made: 22 September 2004: (no specific commencement provision).

2   Commencement

The provisions of the 2004 Act specified in column 1 of the Schedule to this Order shall come into force on 1st October 2004, but where a particular purpose is specified

2342

in relation to any such provision in column 2 of that Schedule, the provision concerned shall come into force on that date only for that purpose.

Initial Commencement
Date made: 22 September 2004: (no specific commencement provision).

3   Transitional provision

Notwithstanding their repeal by section 33 of the 2004 Act (removing asylum-seeker to safe country), sections 11 (removal of asylum claimant under standing arrangement with member States) and 12 (removal of asylum claimants in other circumstances) of the 1999 Act and sections 80 (removal of asylum-seeker to third country) and 93 (appeal from within the United Kingdom: "third country" removal) of the Nationality, Immigration and Asylum Act 2002 shall continue to have effect in relation to a person who is subject to a certificate under section 11(2) or section 12(2) or (5) of the 1999 Act which was issued by the Secretary of State before 1st October 2004.

Initial Commencement
Date made: 22 September 2004: (no specific commencement provision).

SCHEDULE

Article 2

Column 1	Column 2
Section 1 (assisting unlawful immigration)	
Section 3 (immigration documents: forgery)	
Section 6 (employment)	
Section 8(7), (10) and (11) (claimant's credibility)	For the purpose of enabling the Secretary of State to exercise the power to make subordinate legislation under section 8(7)
Section 15 (fingerprinting)	
Section 18 (control of entry)	
Section 27 (unfounded human rights or asylum claim)	
Section 28 (appeal from within the United Kingdom)	
Section 29 (entry clearance)	
Section 30 (earlier right of appeal)	
Section 31 (seamen and aircrews: right of appeal)	
Section 33 (removing asylum-seeker to safe country) and Schedule 3 (removal of asylum-seeker to safe country)	
Section 34 (detention pending deportation)	
Section 36 (electronic monitoring)	
Section 37 (provision of immigration services)	
Section 38 (Immigration Services Commissioner: power of entry)	
Section 39 (offence of advertising services)	

Section 40 (appeal to Immigration
Services Tribunal)
Section 41 (professional bodies)
Section 42 (amount of fees)
Section 43 (transfer of leave stamps)
Section 44 (interpretation: "the
Immigration Acts")
Section 45 (interpretation: immigration
officer)
Section 46 (money)
Section 47 and Schedule 4 (repeals), the
entries relating to section 8(9) of the
Asylum and Immigration Act 1996,
sections 11, 12, 85(1) and 87(3)(f) of
the Immigration and Asylum Act 1999
and paragraph 1(1) of Schedule 6 to
that Act and sections 80, 93 and
94(4)(a) to (j) of the Nationality,
Immigration and Asylum Act 2002

Initial Commencement
Date made: 22 September 2004: (no specific commencement provision).

IMMIGRATION (CLAIMANT'S CREDIBILITY) REGULATIONS 2004

2004 No 3263

Made . . . . *8th December 2004*

Laid before Parliament . . . . *10th December 2004*

Coming into force . . . . *1st January 2005*

The Secretary of State, in exercise of the powers conferred on him by section 8(7), (10) and (11) of the Asylum and Immigration (Treatment of Claimants, etc) Act 2004, hereby makes the following Regulations:

1   Citation and commencement

These Regulations may be cited as the Immigration (Claimant's Credibility) Regulations 2004 and shall come into force on the 1st January 2005.

Initial Commencement
Specified date: 1 January 2005: see above.

2   Interpretation

In these Regulations —

"the 2004 Act" means the Asylum and Immigration (Treatment of Claimants, etc) Act 2004;
"representative" means a person who appears to the decision maker —

(a) to be the representative of a person; and
(b) not to be prohibited from acting as a representative by section 84 of the Immigration and Asylum 1999 Act .

Initial Commencement
Specified date: 1 January 2005: see reg 1.

3 Manner of notifying immigration decision

(1) For the purpose of section 8(5) of the 2004 Act a person may be notified of an immigration decision in any of the following ways —

(a) orally, including by means of a telecommunications system;
(b) in writing given by hand; or
(c) in writing
  (i) sent by fax to a fax number;
  (ii) sent by electronic mail to an electronic mail address; or
  (iii) delivered or sent by postal service to an address,
provided for correspondence by the person or his representative.

(2) Where no fax number, electronic mail or postal address for correspondence has been provided by the person, notice of an immigration decision under paragraph (1)(c) may be delivered or sent by postal service to the last known or usual place of abode or place of business of the person or his representative.

(3) Notice given in accordance with paragraph (1) or (2) to the representative of the person, is to be taken to have been given to the person.

(4) In the case of a minor who does not have a representative, notice given in accordance with paragraph (1) or (2) to the parent, guardian or another adult who for the time being takes responsibility for the minor is taken to have been given to the minor.

Initial Commencement
Specified date: 1 January 2005: see reg 1.

4 Presumptions about receipt of notice

(1) For the purpose of section 8(5) of the 2004 Act notice of an immigration decision shall, unless the contrary is proved, be treated as received;

(a) where the notice is sent by postal service in which delivery or receipt is recorded to an address, on the recorded date of delivery or receipt, or on the second day after the day it was posted, whichever is the earlier;
(b) in any other case in which the notice is sent by postal service on the second day after the day it was posted; or
(c) in any other case, on the day and time that it was communicated orally, given by hand or sent by electronic mail or fax.

(2) For the purposes of determining the second day after a notice is posted under paragraph (1) (a) and (b) any day which is not a business day shall be excluded.

(3) In this regulation "business day" means any day other than Saturday or Sunday, a day which is a bank holiday under the Banking and Financial Dealings Act 1971 in the part of the United Kingdom from or to which the notice is sent, Christmas Day or Good Friday.

Initial Commencement
Specified date: 1 January 2005: see reg 1.

ASYLUM SEEKERS (RECEPTION CONDITIONS) REGULATIONS 2005

2005 No 7

Made . . . . *10th January 2005*

Laid before Parliament . . . . *14th January 2005*

Coming into force . . . . *5th February 2005*

The Secretary of State, being a Minister designated for the purposes of section 2(2) of the European Communities Act 1972 in relation to measures relating to immigration, asylum, refugees and displaced persons, in exercise of the powers conferred upon him by that section, hereby makes the following Regulations:

1   Citation and commencement

(1)   These Regulations may be cited as the Asylum Seekers (Reception Conditions) Regulations 2005 and shall come into force on 5th February 2005.

(2)   These Regulations shall only apply to a person whose claim for asylum is recorded on or after 5th February 2005.

Initial Commencement
Specified date: 5 February 2005 (in relation to a person whose claim for asylum is recorded on or after that date): see above.

2   Interpretation

(1)   In these Regulations—

   (a)   "the 1999 Act" means the Immigration and Asylum Act 1999;
   (b)   "asylum seeker" means a person who is at least 18 years old who has made a claim for asylum which has been recorded by the Secretary of State but not yet determined;
   (c)   "claim for asylum" means a claim made by a third country national or a stateless person that to remove him or require him to leave the United Kingdom would be contrary to the United Kingdom's obligations under the Convention relating to the Status of Refugees done at Geneva on 28th July 1951 and its Protocol;
   (d)   "family members" means, in so far as the family already existed in the country of origin, the following members of the asylum seeker's family who are present in the United Kingdom and who are asylum seekers or dependants on the asylum seeker's claim for asylum:
      (i)   the spouse of the asylum seeker or his unmarried partner in a stable relationship;
      (ii)   the minor child of the couple referred to in paragraph (2)(d)(i) or of the asylum seeker as long as the child is unmarried and dependent on the asylum seeker;
   (e)   "Immigration Acts" has the same meaning as in section 44 of the Asylum and Immigration (Treatment of Claimants, etc) Act 2004; and
   (f)   "third country national" means a person who is not a national of a member State.

(2)   For the purposes of these Regulations—

2346

(a) a claim is determined on the date on which the Secretary of State notifies the asylum seeker of his decision on his claim or, if the asylum seeker appeals against the Secretary of State's decision, the date on which that appeal is disposed of; and

(b) an appeal is disposed of when it is no longer pending for the purposes of the Immigration Acts.

Initial Commencement
Specified date: 5 February 2005 (in relation to a person whose claim for asylum is recorded on or after that date): see reg 1.

3 Families

(1) When the Secretary of State is providing or arranging for the provision of accommodation for an asylum seeker and his family members under section 95 or 98 of the 1999 Act, he shall have regard to family unity and ensure, in so far as it is reasonably practicable to do so, that family members are accommodated together.

(2) Paragraph (1) shall only apply to those family members who confirm to the Secretary of State that they agree to being accommodated together.

(3) This regulation shall not apply in respect of a child when the Secretary of State is providing or arranging for the provision of accommodation for that child under section 122 of the 1999 Act.

Initial Commencement
Specified date: 5 February 2005 (in relation to a person whose claim for asylum is recorded on or after that date): see reg 1.

4 Provisions for persons with special needs

(1) This regulation applies to an asylum seeker or the family member of an asylum seeker who is a vulnerable person.

(2) When the Secretary of State is providing support or considering whether to provide support under section 95 or 98 of the 1999 Act to an asylum seeker or his family member who is a vulnerable person, he shall take into account the special needs of that asylum seeker or his family member.

(3) A vulnerable person is—

(a) a minor;
(b) a disabled person;
(c) an elderly person;
(d) a pregnant woman;
(e) a lone parent with a minor child; or
(f) a person who has been subjected to torture, rape or other serious forms of psychological, physical or sexual violence;

who has had an individual evaluation of his situation that confirms he has special needs.

(4) Nothing in this regulation obliges the Secretary of State to carry out or arrange for the carrying out of an individual evaluation of a vulnerable person's situation to determine whether he has special needs.

Initial Commencement
Specified date: 5 February 2005 (in relation to a person whose claim for asylum is recorded on or after that date): see reg 1.

5 Asylum support under section 95 or 98 of the 1999 Act

(1) If an asylum seeker or his family member applies for support under section 95 of the 1999 Act and the Secretary of State thinks that the asylum seeker or his family member is eligible for support under that section he must offer the provision of support to the asylum seeker or his family member.

(2) If the Secretary of State thinks that the asylum seeker or his family member is eligible for support under section 98 of the 1999 Act he must offer the provision of support to the asylum seeker or his family member.

Initial Commencement
Specified date: 5 February 2005 (in relation to a person whose claim for asylum is recorded on or after that date): see reg 1.

6 Tracing family members of unaccompanied minors

(1) So as to protect an unaccompanied minor's best interests, the Secretary of State shall endeavour to trace the members of the minor's family as soon as possible after the minor makes his claim for asylum.

(2) In cases where there may be a threat to the life or integrity of the minor or the minor's close family, the Secretary of State shall take care to ensure that the collection, processing and circulation of information concerning the minor or his close family is undertaken on a confidential basis so as not to jeopardise his or their safety.

(3) For the purposes of this regulation—

    (a) an unaccompanied minor means a person below the age of eighteen who arrives in the United Kingdom unaccompanied by an adult responsible for him whether by law or custom and makes a claim for asylum;

    (b) a person shall be an unaccompanied minor until he is taken into the care of such an adult or until he reaches the age of 18 whichever is the earlier;

    (c) an unaccompanied minor also includes a minor who is left unaccompanied after he arrives in or enters the United Kingdom but before he makes his claim for asylum.

Initial Commencement
Specified date: 5 February 2005 (in relation to a person whose claim for asylum is recorded on or after that date): see reg 1.

IMMIGRATION (PROCEDURE FOR MARRIAGE) REGULATIONS 2005

2005 No 15

Made . . . . *10th January 2005*

Laid before Parliament . . . . *11th January 2005*

Coming into force . . . . *1st February 2005*

Whereas the Secretary of State has consulted with the Registrar General, the Registrar General for Scotland and the Registrar General for Northern Ireland in accordance with sections 20(4), 22(2) and 24(2) of the Asylum and Immigration (Treatment of Claimants, etc) Act 2004:

Now, therefore, the Secretary of State, in exercise of the powers conferred upon him by sections 19(2)(a) and (3)(c), 21(2)(a) and (3)(c), 23(2)(a) and (3)(c) and 25 of that Act, having regard to the meanings of "prescribed" in sections 22(2) and 24(2), hereby makes the following Regulations:

1 Citation, commencement and interpretation

These Regulations may be cited as the Immigration (Procedure for Marriage) Regulations 2005 and shall come into force on 1st February 2005.

Initial Commencement
Specified date: 1 February 2005: see above.

2

In these Regulations, "the 2004 Act" means the Asylum and Immigration (Treatment of Claimants, etc) Act 2004.

Initial Commencement
Specified date: 1 February 2005: see reg 1.

3 Specified registration districts in England and Wales

The registration districts in England and Wales listed in Schedule 1 are specified for the purposes of section 19(2)(a) of the 2004 Act.

Initial Commencement
Specified date: 1 February 2005: see reg 1.

4 Prescribed registration districts in Scotland

Every registration district in Scotland is prescribed for the purposes of section 21(2)(a) of the 2004 Act.

Initial Commencement
Specified date: 1 February 2005: see reg 1.

5 Prescribed registrars in Northern Ireland

The registrar of every register office in Northern Ireland is prescribed for the purposes of section 23(2)(a) of the 2004 Act.

Initial Commencement
Specified date: 1 February 2005: see reg 1.

Appendix 1   Legislation and materials

6   Specified classes of person

(1)   A person who is settled in the United Kingdom is hereby specified for the purpose of sections 19(3)(c), 21(3)(c) and 23(3)(c) of the 2004 Act.

(2)   In this regulation, "settled in the United Kingdom" has the meaning given in paragraph 6 of the immigration rules (which are the rules laid before Parliament under section 3(2) of the Immigration Act 1971).

Initial Commencement
Specified date: 1 February 2005: see reg 1.

7   Application for permission

(1)   A person seeking the permission of the Secretary of State to marry in the United Kingdom under section 19(3)(b), 21(3)(b) or 23(3)(b) of the 2004 Act shall—

(a)   make an application in writing; and
(b)   pay a fee on the submission of the application in accordance with regulation 8.

(2)   The information set out in Schedule 2 is to be contained in or provided with the application.

Initial Commencement
Specified date: 1 February 2005: see reg 1.

8

(1)   The fee to be paid in connection with the application is £135.

(2)   The fee is to be paid to the Immigration and Nationality Directorate of the Home Office—

(a)   by a cheque or postal order crossed and made payable to "Home Office Certificate of Approval"; or
(b)   by means of any debit card or credit card which that Directorate accepts.

Initial Commencement
Specified date: 1 February 2005: see reg 1.

SCHEDULE 1
SPECIFIED REGISTRATION DISTRICTS IN ENGLAND AND WALES

Regulation 3

Aberconwy	Lambeth
Barking and Dagenham	Leeds
Barnet	Leicester
Birmingham	Lewisham
Blackburn with Darwen	Lincolnshire
Brent	Liverpool
Brighton and Hove	Luton
Bristol	Manchester
Bury St Edmunds	Merton
Cambridge	Middlesbrough
Camden	Mid Powys
Cardiff	Milton Keynes
Cardiganshire North	Newcastle upon Tyne
Carlisle	Newham

<table>
<tr><td>Colchester</td><td>Northampton</td></tr>
<tr><td>Coventry</td><td>North Surrey</td></tr>
<tr><td>Crawley</td><td>Norwich</td></tr>
<tr><td>Croydon</td><td>Nottingham</td></tr>
<tr><td>Dacorum</td><td>Oxfordshire</td></tr>
<tr><td>Ealing</td><td>Pembrokeshire</td></tr>
<tr><td>Enfield</td><td>Peterborough</td></tr>
<tr><td>Exeter</td><td>Plymouth</td></tr>
<tr><td>Gloucester</td><td>Reading</td></tr>
<tr><td>Greenwich</td><td>Redbridge</td></tr>
<tr><td>Hackney</td><td>Sheffield</td></tr>
<tr><td>Hammersmith and Fulham</td><td>Shrewsbury</td></tr>
<tr><td>Hampshire North</td><td>Slough</td></tr>
<tr><td>Haringey</td><td>Southampton</td></tr>
<tr><td>Harrow</td><td>Southwark</td></tr>
<tr><td>Havering</td><td>Stoke on Trent</td></tr>
<tr><td>Hillingdon</td><td>Swansea</td></tr>
<tr><td>Hounslow</td><td>Swindon</td></tr>
<tr><td>Hull</td><td>Tower Hamlets</td></tr>
<tr><td>Islington</td><td>Truro</td></tr>
<tr><td>Kendal</td><td>Waltham Forest</td></tr>
<tr><td>Kensington and Chelsea</td><td>Wandsworth</td></tr>
<tr><td>Kent</td><td>Westminster</td></tr>
<tr><td>Kingston upon Thames</td><td>Wrexham</td></tr>
</table>

Initial Commencement
Specified date: 1 February 2005: see reg 1.

SCHEDULE 2
INFORMATION TO BE CONTAINED IN OR PROVIDED WITH AN APPLICATION FOR PERMISSION TO MARRY IN THE UNITED KINGDOM

Regulation 7

(a) Information to be provided in respect of the applicant

Name

Date of birth

Name at birth (if different)

Nationality

Full postal address

Daytime telephone number

Passport or travel document number

Home Office reference number

Current immigration status

Date on which current leave to enter or remain in the United Kingdom was granted

Date on which that leave expires

Whether he has previously been married, and if so, information showing that he is now free to marry

Two passport-sized photographs

Passport or travel document

(b) *Information to be provided in respect of the other party to the intended marriage*

Name

Date of birth

Name at birth (if different)

Nationality

Full postal address

Daytime telephone number

Passport or travel document number

Whether he is subject to immigration control, and if so:

   Home Office reference number
   Current immigration status
   Date on which current leave to enter or remain in the United Kingdom was granted
   Date on which that leave expires

Whether he has previously been married, and if so, information showing that he is now free to marry

Two passport-sized photographs

Passport or travel document

Initial Commencement
Specified date: 1 February 2005: see reg 1.

ASYLUM AND IMMIGRATION (TREATMENT OF CLAIMANTS, ETC) ACT 2004 (COMMENCEMENT NO 5 AND TRANSITIONAL PROVISIONS) ORDER 2005

2005 No 565

Made . . . . *7th March 2005*

The Lord Chancellor, in exercise of the powers conferred upon him by section 48(3)(a), (4), (5) and (6) of the Asylum and Immigration (Treatment of Claimants, etc) Act 2004, makes the following Order:

1   Citation and interpretation

(1)   This Order may be cited as the Asylum and Immigration (Treatment of Claimants, etc) Act 2004 (Commencement No 5 and Transitional Provisions) Order 2005.

(2)   In this Order—

   "the 2002 Act" means the Nationality, Immigration and Asylum Act 2002;
   "the 2004 Act" means the Asylum and Immigration (Treatment of Claimants, etc) Act 2004;

"adjudicator" means an adjudicator appointed, or treated as if appointed, under section 81 of the 2002 Act;

"appropriate appellate court" has the meaning given in section 103B(5) of the 2002 Act;

"appropriate court" has the meaning given in section 103A(9) of the 2002 Act;

"commencement" means the commencement date in article 2 of this Order;

"the old appeals provisions" means the following provisions, insofar as they continued to have effect immediately before commencement in relation to a pending appeal—

    (i) Part IV of, and Schedule 4 to, the Immigration and Asylum Act 1999;

    (ii) section 8(1) to (4) of the Asylum and Immigration Act 1993;

    (iii) sections 13 to 17 of the Immigration Act 1971.

(3) In this Order, references to a section by number alone are to the section so numbered in the 2002 Act.

Initial Commencement
Date made: 7 March 2005: (no specific commencement provision).

2 Commencement provisions

The following provisions of the 2004 Act shall come into force on 4th April 2005—

    (a) section 26(1) to (5) and (7) to (10),

    (b) section 26(6), except that the insertion of section 103D into the 2002 Act shall not come into force in Northern Ireland;

    (c) Schedule 1; and

    (d) Schedule 2.

Initial Commencement
Date made: 7 March 2005: (no specific commencement provision).

3 Transitional provisions: general

(1) Where, immediately before commencement, an adjudicator or the Immigration Appeal Tribunal—

    (a) has completed the hearing of an appeal, but has not produced his or its written determination; or

    (b) has produced a written determination of an appeal but that determination has not been served on all the parties,

the appeal shall continue after commencement as an appeal to an adjudicator or the Immigration Appeal Tribunal, as the case may be, until the determination has been served on all the parties.

(2) A member of the Asylum and Immigration Tribunal who, immediately before commencement was—

    (a) an adjudicator; or

    (b) a member of the Immigration Appeal Tribunal,

shall, notwithstanding section 26(1), (4) and (5) of the 2004 Act, be deemed to remain an adjudicator or member of the Immigration Appeal Tribunal after commencement, to the extent necessary for the purpose of completing the determination of an appeal in the circumstances specified in paragraph (1) of this article.

Initial Commencement
Date made: 7 March 2005: (no specific commencement provision).

4

Subject to article 3—

(a) any appeal or application to an adjudicator which is pending immediately before commencement shall continue after commencement as an appeal or application to the Asylum and Immigration Tribunal; and

(b) any appeal to the Immigration Appeal Tribunal which is pending immediately before commencement shall continue after commencement as an appeal to the Asylum and Immigration Tribunal.

Initial Commencement
Date made: 7 March 2005: (no specific commencement provision).

5

(1) This article applies, subject to article 3, in relation to any appeal which immediately before commencement is—

(a) pending before an adjudicator, having been remitted to an adjudicator by a court or the Immigration Appeal Tribunal; or

(b) pending before the Immigration Appeal Tribunal.

(2) The Asylum and Immigration Tribunal shall, after commencement, subject to rules under section 106 of the 2002 Act deal with the appeal in the same manner as if it had originally decided the appeal and it was reconsidering its decision .

(3) Following the determination of the appeal by the Asylum and Immigration Tribunal, a party—

(a) may not apply to the appropriate court under section 103A(1); but

(b) may, subject to section 103B(3), bring a further appeal on a point of law to the appropriate appellate court under section 103B(1).

Initial Commencement
Date made: 7 March 2005: (no specific commencement provision).

6

(1) Where an application for permission to appeal to the Immigration Appeal Tribunal against an adjudicator's decision is pending immediately before commencement, it shall be treated after commencement as an application under section 103A(1) (subject to paragraph (4) and to article 9(4) below) for an order requiring the Asylum and Immigration Tribunal to reconsider the adjudicator's decision on the appeal.

(2) Where—

(a) an adjudicator has determined an appeal; and

(b) no application for permission to appeal to the Immigration Appeal Tribunal is pending immediately before commencement,

a party to the appeal may after commencement apply under section 103A(1) (as modified by paragraph (4) below) for an order requiring the Asylum and Immigration Tribunal to reconsider the adjudicator's decision on the appeal.

(3) Where, in a case to which paragraph (2) applies, a time period specified in rules under section 106 for applying for permission to appeal to the Immigration Appeal Tribunal has started to run before 4th April 2005, an application under section 103A(1) may, notwithstanding section 103A(3), be made at any time before the expiry of that time period.

(4)   In relation to an application which, by virtue of this article, is made or treated as made under section 103A, that section shall apply with the modifications that—

- (a)   references to the Tribunal, except for the second such reference in section 103A(1), shall be interpreted as referring to the adjudicator who determined the appeal;
- (b)   references to the Tribunal's decision shall be interpreted as referring to the adjudicator's decision.

(5)   Section 103D shall not apply in relation to a pending application which is treated as an application under section 103A by virtue of paragraph (1) of this article.

Initial Commencement
Date made: 7 March 2005: (no specific commencement provision).

7

(1)   An application to a court under section 101(2) (review of Immigration Appeal Tribunal's decision upon application for permission to appeal) which is pending immediately before commencement shall continue after commencement as if that section had not been repealed.

(2)   A party who, immediately before commencement, was entitled to make an application to a court under section 101(2), may make such an application after commencement as if that section had not been repealed.

(3)   Where, by virtue of this article, an application under section 101(2) is made or continues after commencement—

- (a)   paragraphs (a) and (c) of section 101(3) shall apply in relation to the application, as if they had not been repealed; and
- (b)   the judge determining the application may—
  - (i)   affirm the Immigration Appeal Tribunal's decision to refuse permission to appeal;
  - (ii)   reverse the Immigration Appeal Tribunal's decision to grant permission to appeal; or
  - (iii)   order the Asylum and Immigration Tribunal to reconsider the adjudicator's decision on the appeal.

Initial Commencement
Date made: 7 March 2005: (no specific commencement provision).

8

(1)   An appeal to the Court of Appeal or Court of Session under section 103 (appeal from Immigration Appeal Tribunal), or an application to the Court of Appeal or Court of Session for permission to appeal under section 103, which is pending immediately before commencement shall continue after commencement as if that section had not been repealed.

(2)   Where, immediately before commencement, an application to the Immigration Appeal Tribunal for permission to appeal under section 103 is pending—

- (a)   the application shall, following commencement, be determined by the Asylum and Immigration Tribunal; and
- (b)   section 103 shall continue to apply in relation to the application as if it had not been repealed, but with the modification in paragraph (5) below.

(3)   A party who—

- (a)   is granted permission to appeal under section 103; or

(b)   immediately before commencement, was entitled to apply to the Court of Appeal or Court of Session for permission to appeal under section 103,

may, after commencement, appeal or apply for permission to appeal under section 103 (as the case may be) as if that section had not been repealed.

(4)   A party who, immediately before commencement, was entitled to apply to the Immigration Appeal Tribunal for permission to appeal under section 103, may apply to the Asylum and Immigration Tribunal for permission to appeal under that section; and section 103 shall continue to apply in relation to the application as if it had not been repealed, but with the modification in paragraph (5) below.

(5)   In relation to an application for permission to appeal under section 103 which is made to or determined by the Asylum and Immigration Tribunal pursuant to paragraph (2) or (4), section 103 shall apply with the modification that the references to the Tribunal in section 103(2) shall be interpreted as referring to the Asylum and Immigration Tribunal.

(6)   Where, after commencement, the Court of Appeal or Court of Session determines an appeal under section 103, section 103B(4) shall apply in relation to the appeal as it would in relation to an appeal under section 103B(1), but with the modification that the references to the Tribunal in paragraphs (a), (b) and (f) shall be interpreted as references to the Immigration Appeal Tribunal.

Initial Commencement
Date made: 7 March 2005: (no specific commencement provision).

9   Further transitional provisions: appeals under the old appeals provisions

(1)   Where, immediately before commencement, an appeal to an adjudicator is pending to which any of the old appeals provisions apply, those provisions shall continue to apply to the appeal after commencement, subject (except where article 3 applies) to the modification that any reference in those provisions to an adjudicator shall be treated as a reference to the Asylum and Immigration Tribunal.

(2)   Subject to paragraphs (3) to (5), any provision in the old appeals provisions about appeals or applications to the Immigration Appeal Tribunal or to a court shall not have effect after commencement, and instead sections 103A to 103E shall have effect in relation to appeals decided under the old appeals provisions.

(3)   Where sections 103A to 103E have effect by virtue of paragraph (2), they shall do so with the modification that references to section 82 or 83 shall be treated as including a reference to the old appeals provisions.

(4)   Where an appeal or application for permission to appeal to the Immigration Appeal Tribunal under the old appeals provisions is pending immediately before commencement—

(a)   articles 4(b) and 5, or article 6(1), of this Order (as appropriate) shall apply; but

(b)   if, under the old appeals provisions, the appeal or application was not restricted to the ground that the adjudicator made an error of law, then it shall not be so restricted following commencement.

(5)   In relation to an appeal which has been determined by the Immigration Appeal Tribunal under the old appeals provisions before commencement, article 8 of this Order shall apply with the references to section 103 being treated as including references to corresponding provisions in the old appeals provisions.

Initial Commencement
Date made: 7 March 2005: (no specific commencement provision).

IMMIGRATION (APPLICATION FEES) ORDER 2005

2005 No 582

Made . . . . *9th March 2005*

Coming into force . . . . *10th March 2005*

Whereas a draft of this Order has been approved by resolution of the House of Commons in pursuance of section 102(5) of the Finance (No 2) Act 1987;

Now, therefore, in exercise of the powers conferred on him by sections 102(3) and (4) of that Act, the Secretary of State hereby makes the following Order:

1 Citation, commencement and interpretation

(1) This Order may be cited as the Immigration (Application Fees) Order 2005 and shall come into force on the day after it is made.

(2) In this Order—

"the 1987 Act" means the Finance (No 2) Act 1987;
"the 1999 Act" means the Immigration and Asylum Act 1999;
"the 2002 Act" means the Nationality, Immigration and Asylum Act 2002.

Initial Commencement
Specified date: 10 March 2005: see para (1) above.

2 Functions to be taken into account in fixing fees for leave to remain applications and variation of leave to enter or remain applications

(1) In relation to each of the powers to fix fees specified in paragraph (2), the functions listed in paragraph (3) are hereby specified for the purposes of section 102(3) of the 1987 Act as functions, the costs of which are to be taken into account in determining the amount of those fees.

(2) The powers to fix fees are those in—

(a) section 5(1)(a) of the 1999 Act to prescribe fees for leave to remain applications; and

(b) section 5(1)(b) of the 1999 Act to prescribe fees for applications for the variation of leave to enter or remain.

(3) The functions are the functions of operating an appeals system in respect of decisions for which application fees are prescribed under the powers in paragraph (2) including, without prejudice to the generality of the foregoing—

(a) handling and processing appeals, including preparation for and presentation of cases; and

(b) providing and running the appeals system.

Initial Commencement
Specified date: 10 March 2005: see art 1(1).

3 Matters to be taken into account in fixing fees for all relevant applications

(1) In relation to any functions, the costs of which fall to be taken into account in the exercise of each of the powers to fix fees listed in paragraph (2), the recovery of any deficits incurred before as well as after the date when this Order was made, is hereby

specified for the purposes of section 102(4) of the 1987 Act as a matter to be taken into account in determining the amount of those fees.

(2)   The powers to fix fees are those in—

   (a)   section 5(1)(a) of the 1999 Act to prescribe fees for leave to remain applications;

   (b)   section 5(1)(b) of the 1999 Act to prescribe fees for applications for the variation of leave to enter or remain;

   (c)   section 5(1)(c) of the 1999 Act to prescribe fees for the transfer of limited or indefinite leave stamps to a new document;

   (d)   section 122(1) of the 2002 Act to prescribe fees for applications for immigration employment documents;

   (e)   section 41(2) of the British Nationality Act 1981 to make provision for fees in connection with any applications made under that Act; and

   (f)   section 1 of the Consular Fees Act 1980 and section 10 of the 2002 Act to prescribe fees for a certificate showing that the applicant has a right of abode in the United Kingdom.

Initial Commencement
Specified date: 10 March 2005: see art 1(1).

IMMIGRATION (LEAVE TO REMAIN) (PRESCRIBED FORMS AND PROCEDURES) REGULATIONS 2005

2005 No 771

Made . . . . *16th March 2005*

Laid before Parliament . . . . *17th March 2005*

Coming into force . . . . *1st April 2005*

The Secretary of State, in exercise of the powers conferred upon him by section 31A of the Immigration Act 1971, hereby makes the following Regulations:

1   Citation, commencement and interpretation

These Regulations may be cited as the Immigration (Leave to Remain) (Prescribed Forms and Procedures) Regulations 2005 and shall come into force on 1st April 2005.

Initial Commencement
Specified date: 1 April 2005: see above.

2

In these Regulations:

   "asylum claimant" means a person making a claim for asylum (within the meaning given in section 94(1) of the Immigration and Asylum Act 1999) which claim either has not been determined or has been granted; and

   "dependant", of a person, means—

      (a)   the spouse or unmarried partner, or

(b)   a child under the age of eighteen,
of that person.

Initial Commencement
Specified date: 1 April 2005: see reg 1.

3   Prescribed forms

(1)   Subject to paragraph (2) below, the form set out in Schedule 1 is hereby prescribed for an application for limited or indefinite leave to remain in the United Kingdom:

(a)   as a business person,
(b)   as a sole representative,
(c)   as a retired person of independent means,
(d)   as an investor, or
(e)   as an innovator,

for the purposes of the immigration rules.

(2)   Paragraph (1) does not apply to an application for limited or indefinite leave to remain in the United Kingdom as a business person where the application is made under the terms of a European Community Association Agreement.

Initial Commencement
Specified date: 1 April 2005: see reg 1.

4

The form set out in Schedule 2 is hereby prescribed for an application for limited leave to remain in the United Kingdom:

(a)   for work permit employment,
(b)   as a highly skilled migrant,
(c)   as a seasonal agricultural worker,
(d)   for the purpose of employment under the Sectors-Based Scheme, or
(e)   for Home Office approved training or work experience,

for the purposes of the immigration rules.

Initial Commencement
Specified date: 1 April 2005: see reg 1.

5

The form set out in Schedule 3 is hereby prescribed for an application for limited leave to remain in the United Kingdom:

(a)   as the spouse of a person present and settled in the United Kingdom, or
(b)   as the unmarried partner of a person present and settled in the United Kingdom,

for the purposes of the immigration rules.

Initial Commencement
Specified date: 1 April 2005: see reg 1.

6

The form set out in Schedule 4 is hereby prescribed for an application for limited leave to remain in the United Kingdom:

- (a) as a student,
- (b) as a student nurse,
- (c) to re-sit an examination, or
- (d) to write up a thesis,

for the purposes of the immigration rules.

Initial Commencement
Specified date: 1 April 2005: see reg 1.

7

The form set out in Schedule 5 is hereby prescribed for an application for limited leave to remain in the United Kingdom as a participant in the Science and Engineering Graduates Scheme for the purposes of the immigration rules.

Initial Commencement
Specified date: 1 April 2005: see reg 1.

8

(1)   The form set out in Schedule 6 is hereby prescribed for an application for limited leave to remain in the United Kingdom:

- (a) as a visitor,
- (b) as a visitor seeking to undergo or continue private medical treatment,
- (c) as a postgraduate doctor or dentist or a trainee general practitioner,
- (d) as an au pair,
- (e) as a teacher or language assistant under an approved exchange scheme,
- (f) as a representative of an overseas newspaper, news agency or broadcasting organisation,
- (g) as a private servant in a diplomatic household,
- (h) as a domestic worker in a private household,
- (i) as an overseas government employee,
- (j) as a minister of religion, missionary or member of a religious order,
- (k) as a member of the operational ground staff of an overseas-owned airline,
- (l) as a person with United Kingdom ancestry,
- (m) as a writer, composer or artist,
- (n) as a member of the crew of a ship, aircraft, hovercraft, hydrofoil or international train service, or
- (o) as the spouse or child of an armed forces member who is exempt from immigration control under section 8(4) of the Immigration Act 1971,

for the purposes of the immigration rules.

(2)   Further to paragraph (1) and subject to paragraph (3) below, the form set out in Schedule 6 is hereby prescribed for an application for limited leave to remain in the United Kingdom for any other reason or purpose for which provision is made in the immigration rules but which is not covered by the forms prescribed in regulations 3 to 7 above.

(3)   Paragraph (2) does not apply to an application for limited leave to remain in the United Kingdom where:

- (a) the application is made under the terms of a European Community Association Agreement, or
- (b) the basis on which the application is made is that the applicant is an asylum claimant or a dependant of an asylum claimant.

Initial Commencement
Specified date: 1 April 2005: see reg 1.

9

The form set out in Schedule 7 is hereby prescribed for an application for indefinite leave to remain in the United Kingdom:

(a) as the spouse of a person present and settled in the United Kingdom, or

(b) as the unmarried partner of a person present and settled in the United Kingdom,

for the purposes of the immigration rules.

Initial Commencement
Specified date: 1 April 2005: see reg 1.

10

The form set out in Schedule 8 is hereby prescribed for an application for indefinite leave to remain in the United Kingdom:

(a) as the child under the age of eighteen of a parent, parents or relative present and settled in the United Kingdom,

(b) as the adopted child under the age of eighteen of a parent or parents present and settled in the United Kingdom, or

(c) as the parent, grandparent or other dependent relative of a person present and settled in the United Kingdom,

for the purposes of the immigration rules.

Initial Commencement
Specified date: 1 April 2005: see reg 1.

11

(1) The form set out in Schedule 9 is hereby prescribed for an application for indefinite leave to remain in the United Kingdom:

(a) as a work permit holder,

(b) as a highly skilled migrant,

(c) 204 as a representative of an overseas newspaper, news agency or broadcasting organisation,

(d) as a private servant in a diplomatic household,

(e) as a domestic worker in a private household,

(f) as an overseas government employee,

(g) as a minister of religion, missionary or member of a religious order,

(h) as a member of the operational ground staff of an overseas-owned airline,

(i) as a person with United Kingdom ancestry,

(j) as a writer, composer or artist,

(k) on the basis of long residence in the United Kingdom,

(l) as a victim of domestic violence, or

(m) as a foreign or Commonwealth citizen discharged from HM Forces,

for the purposes of the immigration rules.

(2) Further to paragraph (1) and subject to paragraph (3) below, the form set out in Schedule 9 is hereby prescribed for an application for indefinite leave to remain in the United Kingdom for any other reason or purpose for which provision is made in the immigration rules but which is not covered by the forms prescribed in regulations 9 or 10 above.

(3)   Paragraph (2) does not apply to an application for indefinite leave to remain in the United Kingdom where:

(a)   the application is made under the terms of a European Community Association Agreement, or

(b)   the basis on which the application is made is that the applicant is an asylum claimant or a dependant of an asylum claimant.

Initial Commencement
Specified date: 1 April 2005: see reg 1.

12

An application for leave to remain in the United Kingdom which is made by a person ("the main applicant") on a form prescribed in any of the regulations 3 to 11 above may include an application in respect of any person applying for leave to remain in the United Kingdom as a dependent of the main applicant, insofar as this is permitted by the immigration rules.

Initial Commencement
Specified date: 1 April 2005: see reg 1.

13   Prescribed procedures

(1)   The following procedures are hereby prescribed in relation to an application for which a form is prescribed in regulation 3 above:

(a)   the form shall be signed and dated by the applicant, save that where the applicant is under the age of eighteen, the form may be signed and dated by the parent or legal guardian of the applicant on behalf of the applicant;

(b)   the application shall be accompanied by such documents and photographs as specified in the form; and

(c)   the application shall be sent by prepaid post or by courier to the Immigration and Nationality Directorate of the Home Office. It may not be submitted in person at a Public Enquiry Office of the Immigration and Nationality Directorate of the Home Office.

(2)   The following procedures are hereby prescribed in relation to an application for which a form is prescribed in regulation 4 above:

(a)   the form shall be signed and dated by the applicant, save that where the applicant is under the age of eighteen, the form may be signed and dated by the parent or legal guardian of the applicant on behalf of the applicant;

(b)   the application shall be accompanied by such documents and photographs as specified in the form; and

(c)   the application shall be:

(i)   sent by prepaid post or by courier to Work Permits (UK) at the Immigration and Nationality Directorate of the Home Office, or

(ii)   submitted in person at the Croydon Public Enquiry Office (but no other public enquiry office) of the Immigration and Nationality Directorate of the Home Office;

save that an application for which a form is prescribed in regulation 4(b) above (application for limited leave to remain in the United Kingdom as a highly skilled migrant) shall be sent by prepaid post or by courier to Work Permits (UK) at the Immigration and Nationality Directorate of the Home Office and may not be submitted in person at a Public Enquiry Office.

(3)   The following procedures are hereby prescribed in relation to an application for which a form is prescribed in regulations 5 to 11 above:

(a) the form shall be signed and dated by the applicant, save that where the applicant is under the age of eighteen, the form may be signed and dated by the parent or legal guardian of the applicant on behalf of the applicant;

(b) the application shall be accompanied by such documents and photographs as specified in the form; and

(c) the application shall be:
  (i) sent by prepaid post to the Immigration and Nationality Directorate of the Home Office, or
  (ii) submitted in person at a Public Enquiry Office of the Immigration and Nationality Directorate of the Home Office.

Initial Commencement
Specified date: 1 April 2005: see reg 1.

14

(1) A failure to comply with any of the requirements of regulation 13(1)(a) or (b), 13(2)(a) or (b), or 13(3)(a) or (b) above to any extent will only invalidate an application if:

(a) the applicant does not provide, when making the application, an explanation for the failure which the Secretary of State considers to be satisfactory,

(b) the Secretary of State notifies the applicant, or the person who appears to the Secretary of State to represent the applicant, of the failure within 21 days of the date on which the application is made, and

(c) the applicant does not comply with the requirements within a reasonable time, and in any event within 28 days, of being notified by the Secretary of State of the failure.

(2) For the purposes of this regulation, the date on which the application is made is:

(a) in the case of an application sent by post, the date of posting,

(b) in the case of an application submitted in person, the date on which the application is delivered to, and accepted by, a Public Enquiry Office of the Immigration and Nationality Directorate of the Home Office, and

(c) in the case of an application sent by courier, the date on which the application is delivered to Work Permits (UK) at the Immigration and Nationality Directorate of the Home Office.

Initial Commencement
Specified date: 1 April 2005: see reg 1.

15   Revocation

(1) The Regulations referred to in paragraph (2) are hereby revoked.

(2) Those Regulations are:

(a) the Immigration (Leave to Remain) (Prescribed Forms and Procedures) Regulations 2003;

(b) the Immigration (Leave to Remain) (Prescribed Forms and Procedures) (Amendment) Regulations 2004; and

(c) the Immigration (Leave to Remain) (Prescribed Forms and Procedures) (Amendment No 2) Regulations 2004.

Initial Commencement
Specified date: 1 April 2005: see reg 1.

Appendix 1   Legislation and materials

SCHEDULE 1

Regulation 3

[The text of this form is currently unavailable. Please see the original]

Initial Commencement
Specified date: 1 April 2005: see reg 1.

SCHEDULE 2

Regulation 4

[The text of this form is currently unavailable. Please see the original]

Initial Commencement
Specified date: 1 April 2005: see reg 1.

SCHEDULE 3

Regulation 5

[The text of this form is currently unavailable. Please see the original]

Initial Commencement
Specified date: 1 April 2005: see reg 1.

SCHEDULE 4

Regulation 6

[The text of this form is currently unavailable. Please see the original]

Initial Commencement
Specified date: 1 April 2005: see reg 1.

SCHEDULE 5

Regulation 7

[The text of this form is currently unavailable. Please see the original]

Initial Commencement
Specified date: 1 April 2005: see reg 1.

SCHEDULE 6

Regulation 8

[The text of this form is currently unavailable. Please see the original]

Initial Commencement
Specified date: 1 April 2005: see reg 1.

SCHEDULE 7

Regulation 9

[The text of this form is currently unavailable. Please see the original]

Initial Commencement
Specified date: 1 April 2005: see reg 1.

SCHEDULE 8

Regulation 10

[The text of this form is currently unavailable. Please see the original]

Initial Commencement
Specified date: 1 April 2005: see reg 1.

SCHEDULE 9

Regulation 11

[The text of this form is currently unavailable. Please see the original]

Initial Commencement
Specified date: 1 April 2005: see reg 1.

IMMIGRATION AND ASYLUM (PROVISION OF ACCOMMODATION TO FAILED ASYLUM-SEEKERS) REGULATIONS 2005

2005 No 930

Made . . . .*24th March 2005*
Coming into force . . . .*31st March 2005*

Whereas a draft of these Regulations has been laid before Parliament in accordance with section 166(5) of the Immigration and Asylum Act 1999 and approved by a resolution of each House of Parliament:

Now, the Secretary of State, in exercise of the powers conferred upon him by sections 4(5) and 166(3) of the Immigration and Asylum Act 1999 hereby makes the following Regulations:

1   Citation and commencement

(1)   These Regulations may be cited as the Immigration and Asylum (Provision of Accommodation to Failed Asylum-Seekers) Regulations 2005 and shall come into force on 31st March 2005.

(2)   These Regulations apply to a person who is receiving accommodation when these Regulations come into force to the same extent as they apply to a person provided with accommodation after these Regulations come into force.

Initial Commencement
Specified date: 31 March 2005: see para (1) above.

2   Interpretation

In these Regulations—

   "the 1999 Act" means the Immigration and Asylum Act 1999;
   "destitute" is to be construed in accordance with section 95(3) of the 1999 Act; and

"reporting requirement" means a condition or restriction which requires a person to report to the police, an immigration officer or the Secretary of State, and is imposed under—

(a) paragraph 21 of Schedule 2 to the Immigration Act 1971 (temporary admission or release from detention),

(b) paragraph 22 of that Schedule, or

(c) paragraph 2 or 5 of Schedule 3 to that Act (pending deportation).

Initial Commencement
Specified date: 31 March 2005: see reg 1(1).

3   Eligibility for and provision of accommodation to a failed asylum-seeker

(1) Subject to regulations 4 and 6, the criteria to be used in determining the matters referred to in paragraphs (a) and (b) of section 4(5) of the 1999 Act in respect of a person falling within section 4(2) or (3) of that Act are—

(a) that he appears to the Secretary of State to be destitute, and

(b) that one or more of the conditions set out in paragraph (2) are satisfied in relation to him.

(2) Those conditions are that—

(a) he is taking all reasonable steps to leave the United Kingdom or place himself in a position in which he is able to leave the United Kingdom, which may include complying with attempts to obtain a travel document to facilitate his departure;

(b) he is unable to leave the United Kingdom by reason of a physical impediment to travel or for some other medical reason;

(c) he is unable to leave the United Kingdom because in the opinion of the Secretary of State there is currently no viable route of return available;

(d) he has made an application for judicial review of a decision in relation to his asylum claim—

    (i) in England and Wales, and has been granted permission to proceed pursuant to Part 54 of the Civil Procedure Rules 1998,

    (ii) in Scotland, pursuant to Chapter 58 of the Rules of the Court of Session 1994 or

    (iii) in Northern Ireland, and has been granted leave pursuant to Order 53 of the Rules of Supreme Court (Northern Ireland) 1980; or

(e) the provision of accommodation is necessary for the purpose of avoiding a breach of a person's Convention rights, within the meaning of the Human Rights Act 1998.

Initial Commencement
Specified date: 31 March 2005: see reg 1(1).

4   Community activities: general

(1) Where the Secretary of State so determines, the continued provision of accommodation to a person falling within section 4(2) or (3) of the 1999 Act is to be conditional upon that person's performance of or participation in such community activity as is described in this regulation and is from time to time notified to the person in accordance with regulation 5.

(2) In making the determination referred to in paragraph (1), regard will be had to the following matters—

(a) the length of time that he believes the person will continue to be eligible for accommodation,

(b)   the arrangements that have been made for the performance of or participation in community activities in the area in which the person is being provided with accommodation,

(c)   any relevant health and safety standards which are agreed between the Secretary of State and a person with whom he has made arrangements for the provision of community activities in the person's area,

(d)   whether the person is in the Secretary of State's belief unable to perform or participate in community activities because of a physical or mental impairment or for some other medical reason,

(e)   whether the person is in the Secretary of State's belief unable to perform or participate in community activities because of a responsibility for the care of a dependant child or of a dependant who because of a physical or mental impairment is unable to look after himself, and

(f)   any relevant information provided to the Secretary of State, regarding the person's suitability to perform or participate in particular tasks, activities or a range of tasks or activities.

(3)   Paragraph (1) does not apply in relation to a person who is under the age of 18.

(4)   No condition on the continued provision of accommodation will require a person to perform or participate in community activities for more than 35 hours in any week, including the weekend.

Initial Commencement
Specified date: 31 March 2005: see reg 1(1).

5   Community activities: Relevant information

A notice under regulation 4(1) falls within this regulation if it contains the following information—

(a)   the task, activity or range of tasks or activities in the area in which the person lives which are to be performed or participated in as community activities,

(b)   the geographical location at which the community activities will be performed or participated in,

(c)   the maximum number of hours per week that the person will be expected to perform or participate in community activities, where it is possible for the Secretary of State to so specify, and

(d)   the date upon which the task, activity or range of tasks or activities to be performed or participated in as community activities will commence and, where it is possible for the Secretary of State to so specify, the length of time such community activities will last.

Initial Commencement
Specified date: 31 March 2005: see reg 1(1).

6   Other conditions on continued provision of accommodation

(1)   The continued provision of accommodation to a person falling within section 4(2) or (3) of the 1999 Act is to be subject to such other conditions falling within paragraph (2) as—

(a)   the Secretary of State may from time to time determine, and

(b)   are set out in a notice to that person in writing.

(2)   A condition falls within this paragraph to the extent that it relates to—

(a)   complying with specified standards of behaviour,

(b)   complying with a reporting requirement,

(c)   complying with a requirement—

      (i) to reside at an authorised address, or

     (ii) if he is absent from an authorised address without the permission of the Secretary of State, to ensure that that absence is for no more than seven consecutive days and nights or for no more than a total of fourteen days and nights in any six month period, or

  (d) complying with specified steps to facilitate his departure from the United Kingdom.

Initial Commencement
Specified date: 31 March 2005: see reg 1(1).

EUROPEAN LEGISLATION

CONSOLIDATED VERSION OF THE TREATY ON EUROPEAN UNION

OJ C325/5, 24 December 2002

His Majesty the King of the Belgians, Her Majesty the Queen of Denmark, the President of the Federal Republic of Germany, the President of the Hellenic Republic, His Majesty the King of Spain, the President of the French Republic, the President of Ireland, the President of the Italian Republic, His Royal Highness the Grand Duke of Luxembourg, Her Majesty the Queen of the Netherlands, the President of the Portuguese Republic, Her Majesty the Queen of the United Kingdom of Great Britain and Northern Ireland,

Resolved to mark a new stage in the process of European integration undertaken with the establishment of the European Communities,

Recalling the historic importance of the ending of the division of the European continent and the need to create firm bases for the construction of the future Europe,

Confirming their attachment to the principles of liberty, democracy and respect for human rights and fundamental freedoms and of the rule of law,

Confirming their attachment to fundamental social rights as defined in the European Social Charter signed at Turin on 18 October 1961 and in the 1989 Community Charter of the Fundamental Social Rights of Workers,

Desiring to deepen the solidarity between their peoples while respecting their history, their culture and their traditions,

Desiring to enhance further the democratic and efficient functioning of the institutions so as to enable them better to carry out, within a single institutional framework, the tasks entrusted to them,

Resolved to achieve the strengthening and the convergence of their economies and to establish an economic and monetary union including, in accordance with the provisions of this Treaty, a single and stable currency,

Determined to promote economic and social progress for their peoples, taking into account the principle of sustainable development and within the context of the accomplishment of the internal market and of reinforced cohesion and environmental protection, and to implement policies ensuring that advances in economic integration are accompanied by parallel progress in other fields,

Resolved to establish a citizenship common to nationals of their countries,

Resolved to implement a common foreign and security policy including the progressive framing of a common defence policy, which might lead to a common defence in accordance with the provisions of Article 17, thereby reinforcing the European identity and its independence in order to promote peace, security and progress in Europe and in the world,

Resolved to facilitate the free movement of persons, while ensuring the safety and security of their peoples, by establishing an area of freedom, security and justice, in accordance with the provisions of this Treaty,

Resolved to continue the process of creating an ever closer union among the peoples of Europe, in which decisions are taken as closely as possible to the citizen in accordance with the principle of subsidiarity,

In view of further steps to be taken in order to advance European integration,

Have decided to establish a European Union and to this end have designated as their Plenipotentiaries:

(*List of plenipotentiaries not reproduced*)

Who, having exchanged their full powers, found in good and due form, have agreed as follows.

TITLE I
COMMON PROVISIONS

Article 1

By this Treaty, the HIGH CONTRACTING PARTIES establish among themselves a EUROPEAN UNION, hereinafter called 'the Union'.

This Treaty marks a new stage in the process of creating an ever closer union among the peoples of Europe, in which decisions are taken as openly as possible and as closely as possible to the citizen.

The Union shall be founded on the European Communities, supplemented by the policies and forms of cooperation established by this Treaty. Its task shall be to organise, in a manner demonstrating consistency and solidarity, relations between the Member States and between their peoples.

Article 2

The Union shall set itself the following objectives:

— to promote economic and social progress and a high level of employment and to achieve balanced and sustainable development, in particular through the creation of an area without internal frontiers, through the strengthening of economic and social cohesion and through the establishment of economic and monetary union, ultimately including a single currency in accordance with the provisions of this Treaty,

— to assert its identity on the international scene, in particular through the implementation of a common foreign and security policy including the progressive framing of a common defence policy, which might lead to a common defence, in accordance with the provisions of Article 17,

— to strengthen the protection of the rights and interests of the nationals of its Member States through the introduction of a citizenship of the Union,

— to maintain and develop the Union as an area of freedom, security and justice, in which the free movement of persons is assured in conjunction with appropriate measures with respect to external border controls, asylum, immigration and the prevention and combating of crime,

— to maintain in full the acquis communautaire and build on it with a view to considering to what extent the policies and forms of cooperation introduced by this Treaty may need to be revised with the aim of ensuring the effectiveness of the mechanisms and the institutions of the Community.

The objectives of the Union shall be achieved as provided in this Treaty and in accordance with the conditions and the timetable set out therein while respecting the principle of subsidiarity as defined in Article 5 of the Treaty establishing the European Community.

Article 3

The Union shall be served by a single institutional framework which shall ensure the consistency and the continuity of the activities carried out in order to attain its objectives while respecting and building upon the acquis communautaire.

The Union shall in particular ensure the consistency of its external activities as a whole in the context of its external relations, security, economic and development policies. The Council and the Commission shall be responsible for ensuring such consistency and shall cooperate to this end. They shall ensure the implementation of these policies, each in accordance with its respective powers.

Article 4

The European Council shall provide the Union with the necessary impetus for its development and shall define the general political guidelines thereof.

The European Council shall bring together the Heads of State or Government of the Member States and the President of the Commission. They shall be assisted by the Ministers for Foreign Affairs of the Member States and by a Member of the Commission. The European Council shall meet at least twice a year, under the chairmanship of the Head of State or Government of the Member State which holds the Presidency of the Council.

The European Council shall submit to the European Parliament a report after each of its meetings and a yearly written report on the progress achieved by the Union.

Article 5

The European Parliament, the Council, the Commission, the Court of Justice and the Court of Auditors shall exercise their powers under the conditions and for the purposes provided for, on the one hand, by the provisions of the Treaties establishing the European Communities and of the subsequent Treaties and Acts modifying and supplementing them and, on the other hand, by the other provisions of this Treaty.

Article 6

1. The Union is founded on the principles of liberty, democracy, respect for human rights and fundamental freedoms, and the rule of law, principles which are common to the Member States.

2. The Union shall respect fundamental rights, as guaranteed by the European Convention for the Protection of Human Rights and Fundamental Freedoms signed in Rome on 4 November 1950 and as they result from the constitutional traditions common to the Member States, as general principles of Community law.

3. The Union shall respect the national identities of its Member States.

4. The Union shall provide itself with the means necessary to attain its objectives and carry through its policies.

Article 7

1. On a reasoned proposal by one third of the Member States, by the European Parliament or by the Commission, the Council, acting by a majority of four fifths of its members after obtaining the assent of the European Parliament, may determine that there is a clear risk of a serious breach by a Member State of principles mentioned in Article 6(1), and address appropriate recommendations to that State. Before making such a determination, the Council shall hear the Member State in question and, acting in accordance with the same procedure, may call on independent persons to submit within a reasonable time limit a report on the situation in the Member State in question.

The Council shall regularly verify that the grounds on which such a determination was made continue to apply.

2.   The Council, meeting in the composition of the Heads of State or Government and acting by unanimity on a proposal by one third of the Member States or by the Commission and after obtaining the assent of the European Parliament, may determine the existence of a serious and persistent breach by a Member State of principles mentioned in Article 6(1), after inviting the government of the Member State in question to submit its observations.

3.   Where a determination under paragraph 2 has been made, the Council, acting by a qualified majority, may decide to suspend certain of the rights deriving from the application of this Treaty to the Member State in question, including the voting rights of the representative of the government of that Member State in the Council. In doing so, the Council shall take into account the possible consequences of such a suspension on the rights and obligations of natural and legal persons.

The obligations of the Member State in question under this Treaty shall in any case continue to be binding on that State.

4.   The Council, acting by a qualified majority, may decide subsequently to vary or revoke measures taken under paragraph 3 in response to changes in the situation which led to their being imposed.

5.   For the purposes of this Article, the Council shall act without taking into account the vote of the representative of the government of the Member State in question. Abstentions by members present in person or represented shall not prevent the adoption of decisions referred to in paragraph 2. A qualified majority shall be defined as the same proportion of the weighted votes of the members of the Council concerned as laid down in Article 205(2) of the Treaty establishing the European Community.

This paragraph shall also apply in the event of voting rights being suspended pursuant to paragraph 3.

6.   For the purposes of paragraphs 1 and 2, the European Parliament shall act by a two-thirds majority of the votes cast, representing a majority of its Members.

CONSOLIDATED VERSION OF THE TREATY ESTABLISHING THE EUROPEAN COMMUNITY

OJ C325/33, 24 December 2002

Note
Only provisions relevant to this work are printed below.

His Majesty the King of the Belgians, the President of the Federal Republic of Germany, the President of the French Republic, the President of the Italian Republic, His Royal Highness The Grand Duke of Luxembourg, Her Majesty the Queen of the Netherlands[1],

Determined to lay the foundations of an ever closer union among the peoples of Europe,

Resolved to ensure the economic and social progress of their countries by common action to eliminate the barriers which divide Europe,

Affirming as the essential objective of their efforts the constant improvements of the living and working conditions of their peoples,

Recognising that the removal of existing obstacles calls for concerted action in order to guarantee steady expansion, balanced trade and fair competition,

Anxious to strengthen the unity of their economies and to ensure their harmonious development by reducing the differences existing between the various regions and the backwardness of the less favoured regions,

Desiring to contribute, by means of a common commercial policy, to the progressive abolition of restrictions on international trade,

Intending to confirm the solidarity which binds Europe and the overseas countries and desiring to ensure the development of their prosperity, in accordance with the principles of the Charter of the United Nations,

Resolved by thus pooling their resources to preserve and strengthen peace and liberty, and calling upon the other peoples of Europe who share their ideal to join in their efforts,

Determined to promote the development of the highest possible level of knowledge for their peoples through a wide access to education and through its continuous updating,

Have decided to create a *European Community* and to this end have designated as their Plenipotentiaries:

(*List of plenipotentiaries not reproduced*)

Who, having exchanged their full powers, found in good and due form, have agreed as follows.

¹ The Kingdom of Denmark, the Hellenic Republic, the Kingdom of Spain, Ireland, the Republic of Austria, the Portuguese Republic, the Republic of Finland, the Kingdom of Sweden and the United Kingdom of Great Britain and Northern Ireland have since become members of the European Community.

PART ONE
PRINCIPLES

Article 3

1. For the purposes set out in Article 2, the activities of the Community shall include, as provided in this Treaty and in accordance with the timetable set out therein:

(a) the prohibition, as between Member States, of customs duties and quantitative restrictions on the import and export of goods, and of all other measures having equivalent effect;

(b) a common commercial policy;

(c) an internal market characterised by the abolition, as between Member States, of obstacles to the free movement of goods, persons, services and capital;

(d) measures concerning the entry and movement of persons as provided for in Title IV;

(e) a common policy in the sphere of agriculture and fisheries;

(f) a common policy in the sphere of transport;

(g) a system ensuring that competition in the internal market is not distorted;

(h) the approximation of the laws of Member States to the extent required for the functioning of the common market;

(i) the promotion of coordination between employment policies of the Member States with a view to enhancing their effectiveness by developing a coordinated strategy for employment;

(j) a policy in the social sphere comprising a European Social Fund;

(k) the strengthening of economic and social cohesion;

(l) a policy in the sphere of the environment;

(m) the strengthening of the competitiveness of Community industry;
(n) the promotion of research and technological development;
(o) encouragement for the establishment and development of trans-European networks;
(p) a contribution to the attainment of a high level of health protection;
(q) a contribution to education and training of quality and to the flowering of the cultures of the Member States;
(r) a policy in the sphere of development cooperation;
(s) the association of the overseas countries and territories in order to increase trade and promote jointly economic and social development;
(t) a contribution to the strengthening of consumer protection;
(u) measures in the spheres of energy, civil protection and tourism.

2.   In all the activities referred to in this Article, the Community shall aim to eliminate inequalities, and to promote equality, between men and women.

Article   5

The Community shall act within the limits of the powers conferred upon it by this Treaty and of the objectives assigned to it therein.

In areas which do not fall within its exclusive competence, the Community shall take action, in accordance with the principle of subsidiarity, only if and in so far as the objectives of the proposed action cannot be sufficiently achieved by the Member States and can therefore, by reason of the scale or effects of the proposed action, be better achieved by the Community.

Any action by the Community shall not go beyond what is necessary to achieve the objectives of this Treaty.

Article   12

Within the scope of application of this Treaty, and without prejudice to any special provisions contained therein, any discrimination on grounds of nationality shall be prohibited.

The Council, acting in accordance with the procedure referred to in Article 251, may adopt rules designed to prohibit such discrimination.

Article   13

1.   Without prejudice to the other provisions of this Treaty and within the limits of the powers conferred by it upon the Community, the Council, acting unanimously on a proposal from the Commission and after consulting the European Parliament, may take appropriate action to combat discrimination based on sex, racial or ethnic origin, religion or belief, disability, age or sexual orientation.

2.   By way of derogation from paragraph 1, when the Council adopts Community incentive measures, excluding any harmonisation of the laws and regulations of the Member States, to support action taken by the Member States in order to contribute to the achievement of the objectives referred to in paragraph 1, it shall act in accordance with the procedure referred to in Article 251.

Article   14

1.   The Community shall adopt measures with the aim of progressively establishing the internal market over a period expiring on 31 December 1992, in accordance with the provisions of this Article and of Articles 15, 26, 47(2), 49, 80, 93 and 95 and without prejudice to the other provisions of this Treaty.

2.   The internal market shall comprise an area without internal frontiers in which the free movement of goods, persons, services and capital is ensured in accordance with the provisions of this Treaty.

3.   The Council, acting by a qualified majority on a proposal from the Commission, shall determine the guidelines and conditions necessary to ensure balanced progress in all the sectors concerned.

PART TWO
CITIZENSHIP OF THE UNION

Article   17

1.   Citizenship of the Union is hereby established. Every person holding the nationality of a Member State shall be a citizen of the Union. Citizenship of the Union shall complement and not replace national citizenship.

2.   Citizens of the Union shall enjoy the rights conferred by this Treaty and shall be subject to the duties imposed thereby.

Article   18

1.   Every citizen of the Union shall have the right to move and reside freely within the territory of the Member States, subject to the limitations and conditions laid down in this Treaty and by the measures adopted to give it effect.

2.   If action by the Community should prove necessary to attain this objective and this Treaty has not provided the necessary powers, the Council may adopt provisions with a view to facilitating the exercise of the rights referred to in paragraph 1. The Council shall act in accordance with the procedure referred to in Article 251.

3.   Paragraph 2 shall not apply to provisions on passports, identity cards, residence permits or any other such document or to provisions on social security or social protection.

TITLE III
FREE MOVEMENT OF PERSONS, SERVICES AND CAPITAL

Chapter 1 – Workers

Article   39

1.   Freedom of movement for workers shall be secured within the Community.

2.   Such freedom of movement shall entail the abolition of any discrimination based on nationality between workers of the Member States as regards employment, remuneration and other conditions of work and employment.

3.   It shall entail the right, subject to limitations justified on grounds of public policy, public security or public health:

(a)   to accept offers of employment actually made;
(b)   to move freely within the territory of Member States for this purpose;
(c)   to stay in a Member State for the purpose of employment in accordance with the provisions governing the employment of nationals of that State laid down by law, regulation or administrative action;
(d)   to remain in the territory of a Member State after having been employed in that State, subject to conditions which shall be embodied in implementing regulations to be drawn up by the Commission.

4.   The provisions of this article shall not apply to employment in the public service.

Article   40

The Council shall, acting in accordance with the procedure referred to in Article 251 and after consulting the Economic and Social Committee, issue directives or make regulations setting out the measures required to bring about freedom of movement for workers, as defined in Article 39, in particular:

(a) by ensuring close cooperation between national employment services;

(b) by abolishing those administrative procedures and practices and those quali-fying periods in respect of eligibility for available employment, whether resulting from national legislation or from agreements previously concluded between Member States, the maintenance of which would form an obstacle to liberalisation of the movement of workers;

(c) by abolishing all such qualifying periods and other restrictions provided for either under national legislation or under agreements previously concluded between Member States as imposed on workers of other Member States conditions regarding the free choice of employment other than those imposed on workers of the State concerned;

(d) by setting up appropriate machinery to bring offers of employment into touch with applications for employment and to facilitate the achievement of a balance between supply and demand in the employment market in such a way as to avoid serious threats to the standard of living and level of employment in the various regions and industries.

Article   41

Member States shall, within the framework of a joint programme, encourage the exchange of young workers.

Article   42

The Council shall, acting in accordance with the procedure referred to in Article 251, adopt such measures in the field of social security as are necessary to provide freedom of movement for workers; to this end, it shall make arrangements to secure for migrant workers and their dependants:

(a) aggregation, for the purpose of acquiring and retaining the right to benefit and of calculating the amount of benefit, of all periods taken into account under the laws of the several countries;

(b) payment of benefits to persons resident in the territories of Member States.

Chapter 2 – Right of establishment

Article   43

Within the framework of the provisions set out below, restrictions on the freedom of establishment of nationals of a Member State in the territory of another Member State shall be prohibited. Such prohibition shall also apply to restrictions on the setting-up of agencies, branches or subsidiaries by nationals of any Member State established in the territory of any Member State.

Freedom of establishment shall include the right to take up and pursue activities as self-employed persons and to set up and manage undertakings, in particular companies or firms within the meaning of the second paragraph of Article 48, under the conditions laid down for its own nationals by the law of the country where such establishment is effected, subject to the provisions of the chapter relating to capital.

Article   44

1. In order to attain freedom of establishment as regards a particular activity, the Council, acting in accordance with the procedure referred to in Article 251 and after consulting the Economic and Social Committee, shall act by means of directives.

2. The Council and the Commission shall carry out the duties devolving upon them under the preceding provisions, in particular:

(a)   by according, as a general rule, priority treatment to activities where freedom of establishment makes a particularly valuable contribution to the development of production and trade;

(b)   by ensuring close cooperation between the competent authorities in the Member States in order to ascertain the particular situation within the Community of the various activities concerned;

(c)   by abolishing those administrative procedures and practices, whether resulting from national legislation or from agreements previously concluded between Member States, the maintenance of which would form an obstacle to freedom of establishment;

(d)   by ensuring that workers of one Member State employed in the territory of another Member State may remain in that territory for the purpose of taking up activities therein as self-employed persons, where they satisfy the conditions which they would be required to satisfy if they were entering that State at the time when they intended to take up such activities;

(e)   by enabling a national of one Member State to acquire and use land and buildings situated in the territory of another Member State, in so far as this does not conflict with the principles laid down in Article 33(2);

(f)   by effecting the progressive abolition of restrictions on freedom of establishment in every branch of activity under consideration, both as regards the conditions for setting up agencies, branches or subsidiaries in the territory of a Member State and as regards the subsidiaries in the territory of a Member State and as regards the conditions governing the entry of personnel belonging to the main establishment into managerial or supervisory posts in such agencies, branches or subsidiaries;

(g)   by coordinating to the necessary extent the safeguards which, for the protection of the interests of members and other, are required by Member States of companies or firms within the meaning of the second paragraph of Article 48 with a view to making such safeguards equivalent throughout the Community;

(h)   by satisfying themselves that the conditions of establishment are not distorted by aids granted by Member States.

Article   45

The provisions of this chapter shall not apply, so far as any given Member State is concerned, to activities which in that State are connected, even occasionally, with the exercise of official authority.

The Council may, acting by a qualified majority on a proposal from the Commission, rule that the provisions of this chapter shall not apply to certain activities.

Article   46

1. The provisions of this chapter and measures taken in pursuance thereof shall not prejudice the applicability of provisions laid down by law, regulation or administrative action providing for special treatment for foreign nationals on grounds of public policy, public security or public health.

2. The Council shall, acting in accordance with the procedure referred to in Article 251, issue directives for the coordination of the abovementioned provisions.

Article   47

1. In order to make it easier for persons to take up and pursue activities as self-employed persons, the Council shall, acting in accordance with the procedure referred to in Article 251, issue directives for the mutual recognition of diplomas, certificates and other evidence of formal qualifications.

2. For the same purpose, the Council shall, acting in accordance with the procedure referred to in Article 251, issue directives for the coordination of the provisions laid down by law, regulation or administrative action in Member States concerning the taking-up and pursuit of activities as self-employed persons. The Council, acting unanimously throughout the procedure referred to in Article 251, shall decide on directives the implementation of which involves in at least one Member State amendment of the existing principles laid down by law governing the professions with respect to training and conditions of access for natural persons. In other cases the Council shall act by qualified majority.

3. In the case of the medical and allied and pharmaceutical professions, the progressive abolition of restrictions shall be dependent upon coordination of the conditions for their exercise in the various Member States.

Article   48

Companies or firms formed in accordance with the law of a Member State and having their registered office, central administration or principal place of business within the Community shall, for the purposes of this Chapter, be treated in the same way as natural persons who are nationals of Member States.

'Companies or firms' means companies or firms constituted under civil or commercial law, including cooperative societies, and other legal persons governed by public or private law, save for those which are non-profit-making.

Chapter 3 – Services

Article   49

Within the framework of the provisions set out below, restrictions on freedom to provide services within the Community shall be prohibited in respect of nationals of Member States who are established in a State of the Community other than that of the person for whom the services are intended.

The Council may, acting by a qualified majority on a proposal from the Commission, extend the provisions of the Chapter to nationals of a third country who provide services and who are established within the Community.

Article   50

Services shall be considered to be 'services' within the meaning of this Treaty where they are normally provided for remuneration, in so far as they are not governed by the provisions relating to freedom of movement for goods, capital and persons.

'Services' shall in particular include:

(a) activities of an industrial character;
(b) activities of a commercial character;
(c) activities of craftsmen;
(d) activities of the professions.

Without prejudice to the provisions of the chapter relating to the right of establishment, the person providing a service may, in order to do so, temporarily pursue his activity in the State where the service is provided, under the same conditions as are imposed by that State on its own nationals.

Article 51

1. Freedom to provide services in the field of transport shall be governed by the provisions of the title relating to transport.

2. The liberalisation of banking and insurance services connected with movements of capital shall be effected in step with the liberalisation of movement of capital.

Article 52

1. In order to achieve the liberalisation of a specific service, the Council shall, on a proposal from the Commission and after consulting the Economic and Social Committee and the European Parliament, issue directives acting by a qualified majority.

2. As regards the directives referred to in paragraph 1, priority shall as a general rule be given to those services which directly affect production costs or the liberalisation of which helps to promote trade in goods.

Article 53

The Member States declare their readiness to undertake the liberalisation of services beyond the extent required by the directives issued pursuant to Article 52(1), if their general economic situation and the situation of the economic sector concerned so permit.

To this end, the Commission shall make recommendations to the Member States concerned.

Article 54

As long as restrictions on freedom to provide services have not been abolished, each Member State shall apply such restrictions without distinction on grounds of nationality or residence to all persons providing services within the meaning of the first paragraph of Article 49.

Article 55

The provisions of Articles 45 to 48 shall apply to the matters covered by this chapter.

TITLE IV
VISAS, ASYLUM, IMMIGRATION AND OTHER POLICIES RELATED TO FREE MOVEMENT OF PERSONS

Article 61

In order to establish progressively an area of freedom, security and justice, the Council shall adopt:

    (a) within a period of five years after the entry into force of the Treaty of Amsterdam, measures aimed at ensuring the free movement of persons in accordance with Article 14, in conjunction with directly related flanking measures with respect to external border controls, asylum and immigration, in accordance with the provisions of Article 62(2) and (3) and Article 63(1)(a) and (2)(a), and measures to prevent and combat crime in accordance with the provisions of Article 31(e) of the Treaty on European Union;

(b)   other measures in the fields of asylum, immigration and safeguarding the rights of nationals of third countries, in accordance with the provisions of Article 63;

(c)   measures in the field of judicial cooperation in civil matters as provided for in Article 65;

(d)   appropriate measures to encourage and strengthen administrative cooperation, as provided for in Article 66;

(e)   measures in the field of police and judicial cooperation in criminal matters aimed at a high level of security by preventing and combating crime within the Union in accordance with the provisions of the Treaty on European Union.

Article   62

The Council, acting in accordance with the procedure referred to in Article 67, shall, within a period of five years after the entry into force of the Treaty of Amsterdam, adopt:

(1)   measures with a view to ensuring, in compliance with Article 14, the absence of any controls on persons, be they citizens of the Union or nationals of third countries, when crossing internal borders;

(2)   measures on the crossing of the external borders of the Member States which shall establish:

   (a)   standards and procedures to be followed by Member States in carrying out checks on persons at such borders;

   (b)   rules on visas for intended stays of no more than three months, including:

      (i)   the list of third countries whose nationals must be in possession of visas when crossing the external borders and those whose nationals are exempt from that requirement;

      (ii)   the procedures and conditions for issuing visas by Member States;

      (iii)   a uniform format for visas;

      (iv)   rules on a uniform visa;

(3)   measures setting out the conditions under which nationals of third countries shall have the freedom to travel within the territory of the Member States during a period of no more than three months.

Article   63

The Council, acting in accordance with the procedure referred to in Article 67, shall, within a period of five years after the entry into force of the Treaty of Amsterdam, adopt:

(1)   measures on asylum, in accordance with the Geneva Convention of 28 July 1951 and the Protocol of 31 January 1967 relating to the status of refugees and other relevant treaties, within the following areas:

   (a)   criteria and mechanisms for determining which Member State is responsible for considering an application for asylum submitted by a national of a third country in one of the Member States,

   (b)   minimum standards on the reception of asylum seekers in Member States,

   (c)   minimum standards with respect to the qualification of nationals of third countries as refugees,

   (d)   minimum standards on procedures in Member States for granting or withdrawing refugee status;

(2)   measures on refugees and displaced persons within the following areas:

   (a)   minimum standards for giving temporary protection to displaced persons from third countries who cannot return to their country of origin and for persons who otherwise need international protection,

(b) promoting a balance of effort between Member States in receiving and bearing the consequences of receiving refugees and displaced persons;

(3) measures on immigration policy within the following areas:

(a) conditions of entry and residence, and standards on procedures for the issue by Member States of long-term visas and residence permits, including those for the purpose of family reunion,

(b) illegal immigration and illegal residence, including repatriation of illegal residents;

(4) measures defining the rights and conditions under which nationals of third countries who are legally resident in a Member State may reside in other Member States.

Measures adopted by the Council pursuant to points 3 and 4 shall not prevent any Member State from maintaining or introducing in the areas concerned national provisions which are compatible with this Treaty and with international agreements.

Measures to be adopted pursuant to points 2(b), 3(a) and 4 shall not be subject to the five-year period referred to above.

Article 64

1. This title shall not affect the exercise of the responsibilities incumbent upon Member States with regard to the maintenance of law and order and the safeguarding of internal security.

2. In the event of one or more Member States being confronted with an emergency situation characterised by a sudden inflow of nationals of third countries and without prejudice to paragraph 1, the Council may, acting by qualified majority on a proposal from the Commission, adopt provisional measures of a duration not exceeding six months for the benefit of the Member States concerned.

Article 65

Measures in the field of judicial cooperation in civil matters having cross-border implications, to be taken in accordance with Article 67 and in so far as necessary for the proper functioning of the internal market, shall include:

(a) improving and simplifying:
  – the system for cross-border service of judicial and extrajudicial documents,
  – cooperation in the taking of evidence,
  – the recognition and enforcement of decisions in civil and commercial cases, including decisions in extrajudicial cases;

(b) promoting the compatibility of the rules applicable in the Member States concerning the conflict of laws and of jurisdiction;

(c) eliminating obstacles to the good functioning of civil proceedings, if necessary by promoting the compatibility of the rules on civil procedure applicable in the Member States.

Article 66

The Council, acting in accordance with the procedure referred to in Article 67, shall take measures to ensure cooperation between the relevant departments of the administrations of the Member States in the areas covered by this title, as well as between those departments and the Commission.

Article   67

1. During a transitional period of five years following the entry into force of the Treaty of Amsterdam, the Council shall act unanimously on a proposal from the Commission or on the initiative of a Member State and after consulting the European Parliament.

2. After this period of five years:

—   the Council shall act on proposals from the Commission; the Commission shall examine any request made by a Member State that it submit a proposal to the Council,

—   the Council, acting unanimously after consulting the European Parliament, shall take a decision with a view to providing for all or parts of the areas covered by this title to be governed by the procedure referred to in Article 251 and adapting the provisions relating to the powers of the Court of Justice.

3. By derogation from paragraphs 1 and 2, measures referred to in Article 62(2)(b) (i) and (iii) shall, from the entry into force of the Treaty of Amsterdam, be adopted by the Council acting by a qualified majority on a proposal from the Commission and after consulting the European Parliament.

4. By derogation from paragraph 2, measures referred to in Article 62(2)(b) (ii) and (iv) shall, after a period of five years following the entry into force of the Treaty of Amsterdam, be adopted by the Council acting in accordance with the procedure referred to in Article 251.

5. By derogation from paragraph 1, the Council shall adopt, in accordance with the procedure referred to in Article 251:

—   the measures provided for in Article 63(1) and (2)(a) provided that the Council has previously adopted, in accordance with paragraph 1 of this article, Community legislation defining the common rules and basic principles governing these issues,

—   the measures provided for in Article 65 with the exception of aspects relating to family law.

Article   68

1. Article 234 shall apply to this title under the following circumstances and conditions: where a question on the interpretation of this title or on the validity or interpretation of acts of the institutions of the Community based on this title is raised in a case pending before a court or a tribunal of a Member State against whose decisions there is no judicial remedy under national law, that court or tribunal shall, if it considers that a decision on the question is necessary to enable it to give judgment, request the Court of Justice to give a ruling thereon.

2. In any event, the Court of Justice shall not have jurisdiction to rule on any measure or decision taken pursuant to Article 62(1) relating to the maintenance of law and order and the safeguarding of internal security.

3. The Council, the Commission or a Member State may request the Court of Justice to give a ruling on a question of interpretation of this title or of acts of the institutions of the Community based on this title. The ruling given by the Court of Justice in response to such a request shall not apply to judgments of courts or tribunals of the Member States which have become res judicata.

Article   69

The application of this title shall be subject to the provisions of the Protocol on the position of the United Kingdom and Ireland and to the Protocol on the position of

2384

Denmark and without prejudice to the Protocol on the application of certain aspects of Article 14 of the Treaty establishing the European Community to the United Kingdom and to Ireland.

COUNCIL DIRECTIVE (64/221/EEC) of 25 February 1964
on the co-ordination of special measures concerning the movement and residence of foreign nationals which are justified on grounds of public policy, public security or public health

OJ P 56, 4 April 1964, p.850

THE COUNCIL OF THE EUROPEAN ECONOMIC COMMUNITY,

Having regard to the Treaty establishing the European Economic Community, and in particular Article 56(2) thereof;

Having regard to Council Regulation of 16 August 1961[1] on initial measures to bring about free movement of workers within the Community, and in particular Article 47 thereof;

Having regard to Council Directive of 16 August 1961[2] on administrative procedures and practices governing the entry into and employment and residence in a member state of workers and their families from other member states of the Community;

Having regard to the General Programme[3] for the abolition of restrictions on freedom of establishment and on freedom to provide services, and in particular Title II of each such programme;

Having regard to the Council Directive of 25 February 1964[4] on the abolition of restrictions on movement and residence within the Community for nationals of member states with regard to establishment and the provision of services;

Having regard to the proposal from the Commission;

Having regard to the Opinion of the European Parliament[5];

Having regard to the Opinion of the Economic and Social Committee[6];

Whereas co-ordination of provisions laid down by law, regulation or administrative action which provide for special treatment for foreign nationals on grounds of public policy, public security or public health should in the first place deal with the conditions for entry and residence of nationals of member states moving within the Community either in order to pursue activities as employed or self-employed persons, or as recipients of services;

Whereas such co-ordination presupposes in particular an approximation of the procedures followed in each member state when invoking grounds of public policy, public security or public health in matters connected with the movement or residence of foreign nationals;

Whereas in each member state, nationals of other member states should have adequate legal remedies available to them in respect of the decisions of the administration in such matters;

Whereas it would be of little practical use to compile a list of diseases and disabilities which might endanger public health, public policy or public security and it would be difficult to make such a list exhaustive; whereas it is sufficient to classify such diseases and disabilities in groups;

[1]   OJ No 57, 26.8.1961, p 1073/61.
[2]   OJ No 80, 13.12.1961, p 1513/61.

³   OJ No 2, 15.1.1962, pp 32/62 and 36/62.
⁴   OJ No 56, 4.4.1964, p 845/64.
⁵   OJ No 134,14.12.1967, p2861/62.
⁶   OJ No 56, 4.4.1964, p 856/64.

Has adopted this Directive:

Article   1

1   The provisions of this Directive shall apply to any national of a member state who resides in or travels to another member state of the Community, either in order to pursue an activity as an employed or self-employed person, or as a recipient of services.

2   These provisions shall apply also to the spouse and to members of the family who come within the provisions of the regulations and directives adopted in this field in pursuance of the Treaty.

Article   2

1   This Directive relates to all measures concerning entry into their territory, issue or renewal of residence permits, or expulsion from their territory, taken by member states on grounds of public policy, public security or public health.

2   Such grounds shall not be invoked to service economic ends.

Article   3

1   Measures taken on grounds of public policy or of public security shall be based exclusively on the personal conduct of the individual concerned.

2   Previous criminal convictions shall not in themselves constitute grounds for the taking of such measures.

3   Expiry of the identity card or passport used by the person concerned to enter the host country and to obtain a residence permit shall not justify expulsion from the territory.

4   The state which issued the identity card or passport shall allow the holder of such document to re-enter its territory without any formality even if the document is no longer valid or the nationality of the holder is in dispute.

Article   4

1   The only diseases or disabilities justifying refusal of entry into a territory or refusal to issue a first residence permit shall be those listed in the Annex to this Directive.

2   Diseases or disabilities occurring after a first residence permit has been issued shall not justify refusal to renew the residence permit or expulsion from the territory.

3   Member states shall not introduce new provisions or practices which are more restrictive than those in force at the date of notification of this Directive.

Article   5

1   A decision to grant or to refuse a first residence permit shall be taken as soon as possible and in any event not later than six months from the date of application for the permit.

The person concerned shall be allowed to remain temporarily in the territory pending a decision either to grant or to refuse a residence permit.

2   The host country may, in cases where this is considered essential, request the member state of origin of the applicant, and if need be other member states, to provide

information concerning any previous police record. Such enquiries shall not be made as a matter of routine. The member state consulted shall give its reply within two months.

Article 6

The person concerned shall be informed of the grounds of public policy, public security, or public health upon which the decision taken in his case is based, unless this is contrary to the interests of the security of the state involved.

Article 7

The person concerned shall be officially notified of any decision to refuse the issue or renewal of a residence permit or to expel him from the territory. The period allowed for leaving the territory shall be stated in this notification. Save in cases of urgency, this period shall be not less than fifteen days if the person concerned has not yet been granted a residence permit and not less than one month in all other cases.

Article 8

The person concerned shall have the same legal remedies in respect of any decision concerning entry, or refusing the issue or renewal of a residence permit, or ordering expulsion from the territory, as are available to nationals of the state concerned in respect of acts of the administration.

Article 9

1 Where there is no right of appeal to a court of law, or where such appeal may be only in respect of the legal validity of the decision, or where the appeal cannot have suspensory effect, a decision refusing renewal of a residence permit or ordering the expulsion of the holder of a residence permit from the territory shall not be taken by the administrative authority, save in cases of urgency, until an opinion has been obtained from a competent authority of the host country before which the person concerned enjoys such rights of defence and of assistance or representation as the domestic law of that country provides for.

This authority shall not be the same as that empowered to take the decision refusing renewal of the residence permit or ordering expulsion.

2 Any decision refusing the issue of a first residence permit or ordering expulsion of the person concerned before the issue of the permit shall, where that person so requests, be referred for consideration to the authority whose prior opinion is required under paragraph 1. The person concerned shall then be entitled to submit his defence in person, except where this would be contrary to the interests of national security.

Article 10

1 Member states shall within six months of notification of this Directive put into force the measures necessary to comply with its provisions and shall forthwith inform the Commission thereof.

2 Member states shall ensure that the texts of the main provisions of national law which they adopt in the field governed by this Directive are communicated to the Commission.

Article 11

This Directive is addressed to the member states.

Done at Brussels, 25 February 1964.

ANNEX

A   **Diseases which might endanger public health:**

1   Diseases subject to quarantine listed in International Health Regulation No 2 of the World Health Organisation of 25 May 1951;

2   Tuberculosis of the respiratory system in an active state or showing a tendency to develop;
3   Syphilis;
4   Other infectious diseases or contagious parasitic diseases if they are the subject of provisions for the protection of nationals of the host country.

B   **Diseases and disabilities which might threaten public policy or public security:**

1   Drug addiction;
2   Profound mental disturbance; manifest conditions of psychotic disturbance with agitation, delirium, hallucinations or confusion.

REGULATION (EEC) 1612/68 OF THE COUNCIL of
15 October 1968 on freedom of movement for workers within the Community

OJ L 257, 19 October 1968, p.2

THE COUNCIL OF THE EUROPEAN COMMUNITIES,

Having regard to the Treaty establishing the European Economic Community, and in particular Article 49 thereof;

Having regard to the proposal from the Commission;

Having regard to the Opinion of the European Parliament[1];

Having regard to the Opinion of the Economic and Social Committee[2];

Whereas freedom of movement for workers should be secured within the Community by the end of the transitional period at the latest; whereas the attainment of this objective entails the abolition of any discrimination based on nationality between workers of the member states as regards employment, remuneration and other conditions of work and employment, as well as the right of such workers to move freely within the Community in order to pursue activities as employed persons subject to any limitations justified on grounds of public policy, public security or public health;

Whereas by reason in particular of the early establishment of the customs union and in order to ensure the simultaneous completion of the principal foundations of the Community, provisions should be adopted to enable the objectives laid down in Articles 48 and 49 of the Treaty in the field of freedom of movement to be achieved and to perfect measures adopted successively under Regulation No 15[3] on the first steps for attainment of freedom of movement and under Council Regulation No 38/EEC[4] of 25 March 1964 on freedom of movement for workers within the Community;

Whereas freedom of movement constitutes a fundamental right of workers and their families; whereas mobility of labour within the Community must be one of the means by which the worker is guaranteed the possibility of improving his living and working conditions and promoting his social advancement, while helping to satisfy the requirements of the economies of the member states; whereas the right of all workers in the member states to pursue the activity of their choice within the Community should be affirmed;

Whereas such right must be enjoyed without discrimination by permanent, seasonal and frontier workers and by those who pursue their activities for the purpose of providing services;

Whereas the right of freedom of movement, in order that it may be exercised, by objective standards, in freedom and dignity, requires that equality of treatment shall be ensured in fact and in law in respect of all matters relating to the actual pursuit of activities as employed persons and to eligibility for housing, and also that obstacles to the mobility of workers shall be eliminated, in particular as regards the worker's right to be joined by his family and the conditions for the integration of that family into the host country;

Whereas the principle of non-discrimination between Community workers entails that all nationals of member states have the same priority as regards employment as is enjoyed by national workers;

Whereas it is necessary to strengthen the machinery for vacancy clearance, in particular by developing direct co-operation between the central employment services and also between the regional services, as well as by increasing and co-ordinating the exchange of information in order to ensure in a general way a clearer picture of the labour market; whereas workers wishing to move should also be regularly informed of living and working conditions; whereas, furthermore, measures should be provided for the case where a member state undergoes or foresees disturbances on its labour market which may seriously threaten the standard of living and level of employment in a region or an industry; whereas for this purpose the exchange of information, aimed at discouraging workers from moving to such a region or industry, constitutes the method to be applied in the first place but, where necessary, it should be possible to strengthen the results of such exchange of information by temporarily suspending the above-mentioned machinery, any such decision to be taken at Community level;

Whereas close links exist between freedom of movement for workers, employment and vocational training, particularly where the latter aims at putting workers in a position to take up offers of employment from other regions of the Community; whereas such links make it necessary that the problems arising in this connection should no longer be studied in isolation but viewed as inter-dependent, account also being taken of the problems of employment at the regional level; and whereas it is therefore necessary to direct the efforts of member states toward coordinating their employment policies at Community level;

Whereas the Council, by its Decision of 15 October 1968[5] made Article 48 and 49 of the Treaty and also the measures taken in implementation thereof applicable to the French overseas departments;

1   OJ No 268, 6.11.1967, p 9.
2   ON No 298, 7.12.1967, p 10.
3   OJ No 57, 26.8.1961, p 1073/61.
4   OJ No 62, 17.4.1964, p 965/64.
5   OJ No 257, 19.10.1968, p 1.

Has adopted this Regulation:

PART I
EMPLOYMENT AND WORKERS' FAMILIES

TITLE I
ELIGIBILITY FOR EMPLOYMENT

Article   1

1   Any national of a member state, shall, irrespective of his place of residence, have the right to take up an activity as an employed person, and to pursue such activity, within the territory of another member state in accordance with the provisions laid down by law, regulation or administrative action governing the employment of nationals of that state.

2   He shall, in particular, have the right to take up available employment in the territory of another member state with the same priority as nationals of that state.

Appendix 1 Legislation and materials

Article 2

Any national of a member state and any employer pursuing an activity in the territory of a member state may exchange their applications for and offers of employment, and may conclude and perform contracts of employment in accordance with the provisions in force laid down by law, regulation or administrative action, without any discrimination resulting therefrom.

Article 3

1 Under this Regulation, provisions laid down by law, regulation or administrative action or administrative practices of a member state shall not apply:

— where they limit application for and offers of employment, or the right of foreign nationals to take up and pursue employment or subject these to conditions not applicable in respect of their own nationals; or
— where, though applicable irrespective of nationality, their exclusive or principal aim or effect is to keep nationals of other member states away from the employment offered.

This provision shall not apply to conditions relating to linguistic knowledge required by reason of the nature of the post to be filled.

2 There shall be included in particular among the provisions or practices of a member state referred to in the first subparagraph of paragraph 1 those which:

(a) prescribe a special recruitment procedure for foreign nationals;
(b) limit or restrict the advertising of vacancies in the press or through any other medium or subject it to conditions other than those applicable in respect of employers pursuing their activities in the territory of that member state;
(c) subject eligibility for employment to conditions of registration with employment offices or impede recruitment of individual workers, where persons who do not reside in the territory of that state are concerned.

Article 4

1 Provisions laid down by law, regulation or administrative action of the member states which restrict by number or percentage the employment of foreign nationals in any undertaking, branch of activity or region, or at a national level, shall not apply to nationals of the other member states.

2 When in a member state the granting of any benefit to undertakings is subject to a minimum percentage of national workers being employed, nationals of the other member states shall be counted as national workers, subject to the provisions of the Council Directive of 15 October 1963[1].

[1] OJ No 159, 2.11.63, p 2661/63.

Article 5

A national of a member state who seeks employment in the territory of another member state shall receive the same assistance there as that afforded by the employment offices in that state to their own nationals seeking employment.

Article 6

1 The engagement and recruitment of a national of one member state for a post in another member state shall not depend on medical, vocational or other criteria which are discriminatory on grounds of nationality by comparison with those applied to nationals of the other member state who wish to pursue the same activity.

2 Nevertheless, a national who holds an offer in his name from an employer in a member state other than that of which he is a national may have to undergo a vocational test, if the employer expressly requests this when making his offer of employment.

TITLE II

EMPLOYMENT AND EQUALITY OF TREATMENT

Article   7

1 A worker who is a national of a member state may not, in the territory of another member state, be treated differently from national workers by reason of his nationality in respect of any conditions of employment and work, in particular as regards remuneration, dismissal, and should he become unemployed, reinstatement or re-employment;

2 He shall enjoy the same social and tax advantages as national workers.

3 He shall also, by virtue of the same right and under the same conditions as national workers, have access to training in vocational schools and retraining centres.

4 Any clause of a collective or individual agreement or of any other collective regulation concerning eligibility for employment, employment remuneration and other conditions of work or dismissal shall be null and void in so far as it lays down or authorises discriminatory conditions in respect of workers who are nationals of the other member states.

Article   8

1 A worker who is a national of a member state and who is employed in the territory of another member state shall enjoy equality of treatment as regards membership of trade unions and the exercise of rights attaching thereto, including the right to vote [and to be eligible for the administration or management posts of a trade union][1]; he may be excluded from taking part in the management of bodies governed by public law and from holding an office governed by public law. Furthermore, he shall have the right of eligibility for workers' representative bodies in the undertaking. The provisions of this Article shall not affect law or regulations in certain member states which grant more extensive rights to workers coming from the other member states.

[Paragraph deleted by Council Regulation (EEC) 312/76 OJL39 14.2.76, p 2.]

[1]   Amended by Council Regulation (EEC) 312/76 OJL39 14.2.76, p 2.

Article   9

1 A worker who is a national of a member state and who is employed in the territory of another member state shall enjoy all the rights and benefits accorded to national workers in matters of housing, including ownership of the housing he needs.

2 Such a worker may, with the same right as nationals, put his name down on the housing lists in the region in which he is employed, where such lists exist; he shall enjoy the resultant benefits and priorities.

If his family has remained in the country whence he came, they shall be considered for this purpose as residing in the said region, where national workers benefit from a similar presumption.

TITLE III

WORKERS' FAMILIES

Article   10

1   The following shall, irrespective of their nationality, have the right to install themselves with a worker who is a national of one member state and who is employed in the territory of another member state.

   (a)   his spouse and their descendants who are under the age of 21 years or are dependants;

   (b)   dependent relatives in the ascending line of the worker and his spouse.

2   Member states shall facilitate the admission of any member of the family not coming within the provisions of paragraph 1 if dependent on the worker referred to above or living under his roof in the country whence he comes.

3   For the purposes of paragraphs 1 and 2, the worker must have available for his family housing considered as normal for national workers in the region where he is employed; this provision, however must not give rise to discrimination between national workers and workers from the other member states.

Article   11

Where a national of a member state is pursuing an activity as an employed or self-employed person in the territory of another member state, his spouse and those of the children who are under the age of 21 years or dependent on him shall have the right to take up any activity as an employed person throughout the territory of that same state, even if they are not nationals of any member state.

Article   12

The children of a national of a member state who is or has been employed in the territory of another member state shall be admitted to that state's general educational, apprenticeship and vocational training courses under the same conditions as the nationals of that state, if such children are residing in its territory.

Member states shall encourage all efforts to enable such children to attend these courses under the best possible conditions.

PART II

CLEARANCE OF VACANCIES AND APPLICATIONS FOR EMPLOYMENT

TITLE I

CO-OPERATION BETWEEN THE MEMBER STATES AND WITH THE COMMISSION

Article   13

1   The member states or the Commission shall instigate or together undertake any study of employment or unemployment which they consider necessary for securing freedom of movement for workers within the Community.

The central employment services of the member states shall co-operate closely with each other and with the Commission with a view to acting jointly as regards the clearing of vacancies and applications for employment within the Community and the resultant placing of workers in employment.

2   To this end the member states shall designate specialist services which shall be entrusted with organising work in the fields referred to above and co-operating with each other and with the departments of the Commission.

The member states shall notify the Commission of any change in the designation of such services; the Commission shall publish details thereof for information in the *Official Journal of the European Communities*.

Article 14

1 The member states shall send to the Commission information on problems arising in connection with the freedom of movement and employment of workers and particulars of the state and development of employment ... [1].

2 [The Commission, taking the utmost account of the opinion of the Technical Committee, shall determine the manner in which the information referred to in paragraph 1 is to be drawn up][2].

3 In accordance with the procedure laid down by the Commission [taking the utmost account of the opinion of the Technical Committee][3], the specialist service of each member state shall send to the specialist services of the other member states and to the European Co-ordination Office such information concerning living and working conditions and the state of the labour market as is likely to be of guidance to workers from the other member states. Such information shall be brought up to date regularly.

The specialist services of the other member states shall ensure that wide publicity is given to such information, in particular by circulating it among the appropriate employment services and by all suitable means of communication for informing the workers concerned.

[1] Some words deleted in para 1 by Council Regulation (EEC) 2434 OJL245 26.8.92 p 1.
[2] Amended by Council Regulation (EEC) 2434 OJL245 26.8.92 p 1.
[3] Amended by Council Regulation (EEC) 2434 OJL245 26.8.92 p 1.

TITLE II
MACHINERY FOR VACANCY CLEARANCE

Article 15

1 [The specialist service of each member state shall regularly send to the specialist services of the other member states and to the European Co-ordination Office:

(a) details of vacancies which could be filled by nationals of other member states;
(b) details of vacancies addressed to non-member states;
(c) details of applications for employment by those who have formally expressed a wish to work in another member state;
(d) information, by region and by branch of activity, on applicants who have declared themselves actually willing to accept employment in another country.

The specialist service of each member state shall forward this information to the appropriate employment services and agencies as soon as possible.

2 The details of vacancies and applications referred to in paragraph 1 shall be circulated according to a uniform system to be established by the European Coordination Office in collaboration with the Technical Committee.

If necessary, the European Co-ordination Office may adapt this system in collaboration with the Technical Committee][1].

[1] Amended by Council Regulation (EEC) 2434 OJL245 26.8.92 p 1 and p 2.

Article 16

1 [Any vacancy within the meaning of Article 15 communicated to the employment services of a member state shall be notified to and processed by the competent employment services of the other member states concerned.

Such services shall forward to the services of the first member state the details of suitable applications.

2   The applications for employment referred to in Article 15(1)(c) shall be responded to by the relevant services of the member states within a reasonable period, not exceeding one month.

3   The employment services shall grant workers who are nationals of the member states the same priority as the relevant measures grant to nationals *vis-à-vis* workers from non-member states.][1]

[1]   Amended by Council Regulation (EEC) 2434 OJL245 26.8.92 p 2.

Article   17

1   The provisions of Article 16 shall be implemented by the specialist services. However, in so far as they have been authorised by the central services and in so far as the organisation of the employment services of a member state and the placing techniques employed make it possible:

   (a)   the regional employment services of the member states shall:
      (i)   on the basis of the [details][1] referred to in Article 15, on which appropriate action will be taken, directly bring together and clear vacancies and applications for employment;
      (ii)   establish direct relations for clearance:
         —   of vacancies offered to a named worker;
         —   of individual applications for employment sent either to a specific employment service or to an employer pursuing his activity within the area covered by such a service;
         —   where the clearing operations concern seasonal workers who must be recruited as quickly as possible;
   (b)   [the services territorially responsible for the border regions of two or more member states shall regularly exchange data relating to vacancies and applications for employment in their area and, acting in accordance with their arrangements with the other employment services of their countries, shall directly bring together and clear vacancies and applications for employment.
   If necessary, the services territorially responsible for border regions shall also set up co-operation and service structures to provide:
         —   users with as much practical information as possible on the various aspects of mobility; and
         —   management and labour, social services (in particular public, private or those of public interest) and all institutions concerned, with a framework of coordinated measures relating to mobility];[2]
   (c)   official employment services which specialise in certain occupations or specific categories of persons shall co-operate directly with each other.

2   The member states concerned shall forward to the Commission the list, drawn up by common accord, of services referred to in paragraph 1; the Commission shall publish such list, and any amendment thereto, in the *Official Journal of the European Communities*.

[1]   Amended by Council Regulation (EEC) 2434 OJL245 26.8.92 p 2.
[2]   Para 1(b) as amended by Council Regulations (EEC) 2434 OJL245 26.8.92 p 2.

Article   18

Adoption of recruiting procedures as applied by the implementing bodies provided for under agreements concluded between two or more member states shall not be obligatory.

TITLE III
MEASURES FOR CONTROLLING THE BALANCE OF THE LABOUR MARKET

Article 19

[1 On the basis of a report from the Commission drawn up from information supplied by the member states, the latter and the Commission shall at least once a year analyse jointly the results of Community arrangements regarding vacancies and applications.]¹

2 The member states shall examine with the Commission all the possibilities of giving priority to nationals of member states when filing employment vacancies in order to achieve a balance between vacancies and applications for employment within the Community. They shall adopt all measures necessary for this purpose.

[3 Every two years the Commission shall submit a report to the European Parliament, the Council and the Economic and Social Committee on the implementation of Part II of this Regulation, summarising the information required and the data obtained from the studies and research carried out and highlighting any useful points with regard to developments on the Community's labour market.]²

¹ Amended by Council Regulation (EEC) 2434 OJL245 26.8.92 p 2.
² Added by Council Regulation (EEC) 2434 OJL245 26.8.92 p 2.

Article 20

[Article 20 deleted by Council Regulation (EEC) 2434 OJ245 26.8.92 p 2.]

TITLE IV
EUROPEAN CO-ORDINATION OFFICE

Article 21

The European Office for Co-ordinating the Clearance of Vacancies and Applications for Employment, established within the Commission (called in this Regulation the 'European Co-ordination Office', shall have the general task of promoting vacancy clearance at Community level. It shall be responsible in particular for all the technical duties in this field which, under the provisions of this Regulation, are assigned to the Commission, and especially for assisting the national employment services.

It shall summarise the information referred to in Articles 14 and 15 and the data arising out of the studies and research carried out pursuant to Article 13, so as to bring to light any useful facts about foreseeable developments on the Community labour market; such facts shall be communicated to the specialist services of the member states and to the Advisory and Technical Committees.

Article 22

1 The European Co-ordination Office shall be responsible, in particular, for:

(a) co-ordinating the practical measures necessary for vacancy clearance at Community level and for analysing the resulting movements of workers;

(b) contributing to such objectives by implementing, in co-operation with the Technical Committee, joint methods of action at administrative and technical levels;

(c) carrying out, where a special need arises, and in agreement with the specialist services, the bringing together of vacancies and applications for employment for clearance by these specialist services.

2 It shall communicate to the specialist services vacancies and applications for employment sent directly to the Commission, and shall be informed of the action taken thereon.

Article 23

The Commission may, in agreement with the competent authority of each member state, and in accordance with the conditions and procedures which it shall determine on the basis of the Opinion of the Technical Committee, organise visits and assignments for officials of other member states, and also advanced programmes for specialist personnel.

PART III

COMMITTEES FOR ENSURING CLOSE CO-OPERATION BETWEEN THE MEMBER STATES IN MATTERS CONCERNING THE FREEDOM OF MOVEMENT OF WORKERS AND THEIR EMPLOYMENT

TITLE I
THE ADVISORY COMMITTEE

Article 24

The Advisory Committee shall be responsible for assisting the Commission in the examination of any questions arising from the application of the Treaty and measures taken in pursuance thereof, in matters concerning the freedom of movement of workers and their employment.

Article 25

The Advisory Committee shall be responsible in particular for:

(a) examining problems concerning freedom of movement and employment within the framework of national manpower policies, with a view to co-ordinating the employment policies of the member states at Community level, thus contributing to the development of the economies and to an improved balance of the labour market;

(b) making a general study of the effects of implementing this Regulation and any supplementary measures;

(c) submitting to the Commission any reasoned proposals for revising this Regulation;

(d) delivering, either at the request of the Commission or on its own initiative, reasoned opinions on general questions or on questions of principle, in particular on exchange of information concerning developments in the labour market, on the movement of workers between member states, on programmes or measures to develop vocational guidance and vocational training which are likely to increase the possibilities of freedom of movement and employment, and on all forms of assistance to workers and their families, including social assistance and the housing of workers.

Article 26

1 The Advisory Committee shall be composed of six members for each member state, two of whom shall represent the government, two the trade unions and two the employers' associations.

2 For each of the categories referred to in paragraph 1, one alternate member shall be appointed by each member state.

2396

3 The term of office of the members and their alternates shall be two years. Their appointments shall be renewable.

On expiry of their term of office, the members and their alternates shall remain in office until replaced or until their appointments are renewed.

Article 27

The members of the Advisory Committee and their alternates shall be appointed by the Council which shall endeavour, when selecting representatives of trade unions and employers' associations, to achieve adequate representation on the Committee of the various economic sectors concerned.

The list of members and their alternates shall be published by the Council for information in the *Official Journal of the European Communities*.

Article 28

The Advisory Committee shall be chaired by a member of the Commission or his alternate. The Chairman shall not vote. The Committee shall meet at least twice a year. It shall be convened by its Chairman, either on his own initiative, or at the request of at least one third of the members. Secretarial services shall be provided for the Committee by the Commission.

Article 29

The chairman may invite individuals or representatives of bodies with wide experience in the field of employment or movement of workers to take part in meetings as observers or as experts. The Chairman may be assisted by expert advisers.

Article 30

1 An opinion delivered by the Committee shall not be valid unless two-thirds of the members are present.

2 Opinions shall state the reasons on which they are based; they shall be delivered by an absolute majority of the votes validly cast; they shall be accompanied by a written statement of the views expressed by the minority, when the latter so requests.

Article 31

The Advisory Committee shall establish its working methods by rules of procedure which shall enter into force after the Council, having received an opinion from the Commission, has given its approval. The entry into force of any amendment that the Committee decides to make thereto shall be subject to the same procedure.

TITLE II
THE TECHNICAL COMMITTEE

Article 32

The Technical Committee shall be responsible for assisting the Commission to prepare, promote and follow up all technical work and measures for giving effect to this Regulation and any supplementary measures.

Article 33

The Technical Committee shall be responsible in particular for:

(a) promoting and advancing co-operation between the public authorities concerned in the member states on all technical questions relating to freedom of movement of workers and their employment;

(b) formulating procedures for the organisation of the joint activities of the public authorities concerned;

(c) facilitating the gathering of information likely to be of use to the Commission and for the studies and research provided for in this Regulation, and encouraging exchange of information and experience between the administrative bodies concerned;

(d) investigating at a technical level the harmonisation of the criteria by which member states assess the state of their labour markets.

Article   34

1   The Technical Committee shall be composed of representatives of the Governments of the member states. Each Government shall appoint as member of the Technical Committee one of the members who represent it on the Advisory Committee.

2   Each government shall appoint an alternate from among its other representatives—members or alternates—on the Advisory Committee.

Article   35

The Technical Committee shall be chaired by a member of the Commission or his representative. The Chairman shall not vote. The Chairman and the members of the Committee may be assisted by expert advisers.

Secretarial services shall be provided for the Committee by the Commission.

Article   36

The proposals and opinions formulated by the Technical Committee shall be submitted to the Commission, and the Advisory Committee shall be informed thereof. Any such proposals and opinions shall be accompanied by a written statement of the views expressed by the various members of the Technical Committee, when the latter so request.

Article   37

The Technical Committee shall establish its working methods by rules of procedure which shall enter into force after the Council, having received an opinion from the Commission, has given its approval. The entry into force of any amendment which the Committee decides to make thereto shall be subject to the same procedure.

PART IV
TRANSITIONAL AND FINAL PROVISIONS

TITLE I
TRANSITIONAL PROVISIONS

Article   38

Until the adoption by the Commission of the uniform system referred to in Article 15(2), the European Co-ordination Office shall propose any measures likely to be of use in drawing up and circulating the returns referred to in Article 15(1).

Article   39

The rules of procedure of the Advisory Committee and the Technical Committee in force at the time of entry into force of this Regulation shall continue to apply.

Article   40

Until the entry into force of the measures to be taken by member states in pursuance of the Council Directive of 15 October 1968[1] and where, under the measures taken by the member states in pursuance of the Council Directive of 25 March 1964[2] the work permit provided for in Article 22 of Regulation No 38/64/EEC is necessary to determine the period of validity and extension of the residence permit, written confirmation of engagement from the employer or a certificate of employment stating the period of employment may be substituted for such work permit. Any written confirmation by the employer or certificate of employment showing that the worker has been engaged for an indefinite period shall have the same effect as that of a permanent work permit.

[1]   OJ No 257 19.10.1968, p 13.
[2]   OJ No 62, 17.4.1964, p 981/64.

Article   41

If, by reason of the abolition of the work permit, a member state can no longer compile certain statistics on the employment of foreign nationals such member state may, for statistical purposes, retain the work permit in respect of nationals of the other member states until new statistical methods are introduced, but no later than 31 December 1969. The work permit must be issued automatically and must be valid until the actual abolition of work permit in such member state.

TITLE II
FINAL PROVISIONS

Article   42

1   This Regulation shall not affect the provisions of the Treaty establishing the European Coal and Steel Community which relate to workers with recognised qualifications in coalmining or steelmaking, nor those of the Treaty establishing the European Atomic Energy Community which deal with eligibility for skilled employment in the field of nuclear energy, nor any measures taken in pursuance of those Treaties.

Nevertheless, this Regulation shall apply to categories of workers referred to in the first subparagraph and to members of their families in so far as their legal position is not governed by the above-mentioned Treaties or measures.

2   This Regulation shall not affect measures taken in accordance with Article 51 of the Treaty.

3   This Regulation shall not affect the obligations of member states arising out of:

— special relations or future agreements with certain non-European countries or territories, based on institutional ties existing at the time of the entry into force of this Regulation; or

— agreements in existence at the time of the entry into force of this Regulation with certain non-European countries or territories, based on institutional ties between them.

Workers from such countries or territories who, in accordance with this provision, are pursuing activities as employed persons in the territory of one of those member states may not invoke the benefit of the provisions of this Regulation in the territory of the other member states.

Article   43

Member states shall, for information purposes, communicate to the Commission the texts of agreements, conventions or arrangements concluded between them in the manpower field between the date of their being signed and that of their entry into force.

Article   44

The Commission shall adopt measures pursuant to this Regulation for its implementation. To this end it shall act in close co-operation with the central public authorities of the member states.

Article   45

The Commission shall submit to the Council proposals aimed at abolishing, in accordance with the conditions of the Treaty, restrictions on eligibility for employment of workers who are nationals of member states, where the absence of mutual recognition of diplomas, certificates or other evidence of formal qualifications may prevent freedom of movement for workers.

Article   46

The administrative expenditure of the Committees referred to in Part III shall be included in the budget of the European Communities in the section relating to the Commission.

Article   47

This Regulation shall apply to the territories of the member states and to their nationals, without prejudice to Articles 2, 3, 10 and 11.

Article   48

Regulation No 38/64/EEC shall cease to have effect when this Regulation enters into force.

This Regulation shall be binding in its entirety and directly applicable in all member states.

Done at Luxembourg, 15 October 1968.

ANNEX

[Annex deleted by Council Regulation (EEC) 2434 OJ L245 36.8.92 p 2.]

COUNCIL DIRECTIVE (68/360/EEC) on the abolition of restrictions on movement and residence within the Community for workers of member states and their families

OJ L 257, 19 October 1968, p.13

THE COUNCIL OF THE EUROPEAN COMMUNITIES,

Having regard to the Treaty establishing the European Economic Community, and in particular Article 49 thereof;

Having regard to the proposal from the Commission;

Having regard to the Opinion of the European Parliament;

Having regard to the Opinion of the Economic and Social Committee;

Whereas Council Regulation (EEC) No 1612/68 fixed the provisions governing freedom of movement for workers within the Community; whereas, consequently, measures should be adopted for the abolition of restrictions which still exist concerning movement and residence within the Community, which conform to the rights and privileges accorded by the said Regulation to nationals of any member state who move in order to pursue activities as employed persons and to members of their families;

Whereas the rules applicable to residence should, as far as possible, bring the position of workers from other member states and members of their families into line with that of nationals;

Whereas the co-ordination of special measures relating to the movement and residence of foreign nationals, justified on grounds of public policy, public security or public health, is the subject of the Council Directive of 25 February 1964 adopted in application of Article 56(2) of the Treaty;

Has adopted this Directive:

Article 1

Member states shall, acting as provided in this Directive, abolish restrictions on the movement and residence of nationals of the said states and of members of their families to whom Regulation (EEC) No 1612/68 applies.

Article 2

1 Member states shall grant the nationals referred to in Article 1 the right to leave their territory in order to take up activities as employed persons and to pursue such activities in the territory of another member state. Such right shall be exercised simply on production of a valid identity card or passport. Members of the family shall enjoy the same right as the national on whom they are dependent.

2 Member states shall, acting in accordance with their laws, issue to such nationals, or renew, an identity card or passport, which shall state in particular the holder's nationality.

3 The passport must be valid at least for all member states and for countries through which the holder must pass when travelling between member states. Where a passport is the only document on which the holder may lawfully leave the country, its period of validity shall be not less than five years.

4 Member states may not demand from the nationals referred to in Article 1 any exit visa or any equivalent document.

Article   3

1   Member states shall allow the persons referred to in Article 1 to enter their territory simply on production of a valid identity card or passport.

2   No entry visa or equivalent document may be demanded save from members of the family who are not nationals of a member state. Member states shall accord to such persons every facility for obtaining any necessary visas.

Article   4

1   Member states shall grant the right of residence in their territory to the persons referred to in Article 1 who are able to produce the documents listed in paragraph 3.

2   As proof of the right of residence, a document entitled 'Residence permit for a national of a member state of the EEC' shall be issued. This document must include a statement that it has been issued pursuant to Regulation (EEC) No 1612/68 and to the measures taken by the member states for the implementation of the present Directive. The text of such statement is given in the Annex to this Directive.

3   For the issue of a residence permit for a national of a member state of the EEC, member states may require only the production of the following documents;

   — by the worker:
     (a)   the document with which he entered their territory;
     (b)   a confirmation of engagement from the employer or a certificate of employment;
   — by the members of the worker's family:
     (c)   the document with which they entered the territory;
     (d)   a document issued by the competent authority of the state of origin or the state whence they came, proving their relationship;
     (e)   in the cases referred to in Article 10(1) and (2) of Regulation (EEC) No 1612/68, a document issued by the competent authority of the state of origin or the state whence they came, testifying that they are dependent on the worker or that they live under his roof in such country.

4   A member of the family who is not a national of a member state shall be issued with a residence document which shall have the same validity as that issued to the worker on whom he is dependent.

Article   5

Completion of the formalities for obtaining a residence permit shall not hinder the immediate beginning of employment under a contract concluded by the applicants.

Article   6

1   The residence permit:

     (a)   must be valid throughout the territory of the member state which issued it;
     (b)   must be valid for at least five years from the date of issue and be automatically renewable.

2   Breaks in residence not exceeding six consecutive months and absence on military service shall not affect the validity of a residence permit.

3   Where a worker is employed for a period exceeding three months but not exceeding a year in the service of an employer in the host state or in the employ of a person providing services, the host member state shall issue him a temporary residence permit, the validity of which may be limited to the expected period of the employment.

Subject to the provisions of Article 8(1)(*c*), a temporary residence permit shall be issued also to a seasonal worker employed for a period of more than three months. The period of employment must be shown in the documents referred to in paragraph 4(3)(*b*).

Article 7

1   A valid residence permit may not be withdrawn from a worker solely on the grounds that he is no longer in employment, either because he is temporarily incapable of work as a result of illness or accident, or because he is involuntarily unemployed, this being duly confirmed by the competent employment office.

2   When the residence permit is renewed for the first time, the period of residence may be restricted, but not to less than twelve months, where the worker has been involuntarily unemployed in the member state for more than twelve consecutive months.

Article 8

1   Member states shall, without issuing a residence permit, recognise the right of residence in their territory of:

(a)   a worker pursuing an activity as an employed person, where the activity is not expected to last for more than three months. The document with which the person concerned entered the territory and a statement by the employer on the expected duration of the employment shall be sufficient to cover his stay; a statement by the employer shall not, however, be required in the case of workers coming within the provisions of the Council Directive of 25 February 1964 on the attainment of freedom of establishment and freedom to provide services in respect of the activities of intermediaries in commerce, industry and small craft industries.

(b)   a worker who, while having his residence in the territory of a member state to which he returns as a rule, each day or at least once a week, is employed in the territory of another member state. The competent authority of the state where he is employed may issue such worker with a special permit valid for five years and automatically renewable;

(c)   a seasonal worker who holds a contract of employment stamped by the competent authority of the member state on whose territory he has come to pursue his activity.

2   In all cases referred to in paragraph 1, the competent authorities of the host member state may require the worker to report his presence in the territory.

Article 9

1   The residence documents granted to nationals of a member state of the EEC referred to in this Directive shall be issued and renewed free of charge or on payment of an amount not exceeding the dues and taxes charged for the issue of identity cards to nationals.

2   The visa referred to in Article 3(2) and the stamp referred to in Article 8(1)(*c*) shall be free of charge.

3   Member states shall take the necessary steps to simplify as much as possible the formalities and procedure for obtaining the documents mentioned in paragraph 1.

Article 10

Member states shall not derogate from the provisions of this Directive save on grounds of public policy, public security or public health.

2403

Appendix 1   Legislation and materials

Article   11

1   This Directive shall not affect the provisions of the Treaty establishing the European Coal and Steel Community which relate to workers with recognised skills in coal mining and steel making, or the provisions of the Treaty establishing the European Atomic Energy Community which deal with the right to take up skilled employment in the field of nuclear energy, or any measures taken in implementation of those Treaties.

2   Nevertheless, this Directive shall apply to the categories of workers referred to in paragraph 1, and to members of their families, in so far as their legal position is not governed by the abovementioned Treaties or measures.

Article   12

1   Member states shall, within nine months of notification of this Directive, bring into force the measures necessary to comply with its provisions and shall forthwith inform the Commission thereof.

2   They shall notify the Commission of amendments made to provisions imposed by law, regulation or administrative action for the simplification of the formalities and procedure for issuing such documents as are still necessary for the entry, exit and residence of workers and members of their families.

Article   13

1   The Council Directive of 25 March 1964 on the abolition of restrictions on movement and on residence within the Community of workers and their families shall continue to have effect until this Directive is implemented by the member states.

2   Residence permits issued pursuant to the Directive referred to in paragraph 1 shall remain valid until the date on which they next expire.

Article   14

This Directive is addressed to the member states

Done at Luxembourg, 15 October 1968.

ANNEX

Text of the statement referred to in Article 4(2):

'This permit is issued pursuant to Regulation (EEC) No 1612/68 of the Council of the European Communities of 15 October 1968 and to the measures taken in implementation of the Council Directive of 15 October 1968.

In accordance with the provisions of the above-mentioned Regulation, the holder of this permit has the right to take up and pursue an activity as an employed person in ... . territory under the same conditions as ... .* workers.'

*   Belgian, Danish, German, Greek, Spanish, French, Irish, Italian, Luxembourg, Dutch, Portuguese, United Kingdom, depending on which country issues the card.

REGULATION (EEC) 1251/70 OF
THE COMMISSION of 29 June 1970 on the right of workers to remain in the territory of a member state after having been employed in that state

OJ L 142, 30 June 1970, p.24

THE COMMISSION OF THE EUROPEAN COMMUNITIES,

Having regard to the Treaty establishing the European Economic Community, and in particular Article 48(3)(*d*) thereof, and Article 2 of the Protocol on the Grand Duchy of Luxembourg;

Having regard to the Opinion of the European Parliament[1];

Whereas Council Regulation (EEC) No 1612/68[2] of 15 October 1968 and Council Directive No 68/360/EEC of 15 October 1968[3] enabled freedom of movement for workers to be secured at the end of a series of measures to be achieved progressively; whereas the right of residence acquired by workers in active employment has as a corollary the right, granted by the Treaty to such workers, to remain in the territory of a member state after having been employed in that state; whereas it is important to lay down the conditions for the exercise of such right;

Whereas the said Council Regulation and Council Directive contain the appropriate provisions concerning the right of workers to reside in the territory of a member state for the purposes of employment; whereas the right to remain, referred to in Article 48(3)(*d*) of the Treaty is interpreted therefore as the right of the worker to maintain his residence in the territory of a member state when he ceases to be employed there;

Whereas the mobility of labour in the Community requires that workers may be employed successively in several member states without thereby being placed at a disadvantage;

Whereas it is important, in the first place, to guarantee to the worker residing in the territory of a member state the right to remain in that territory when he ceases to be employed in that state because he has reached retirement age or by reason of permanent incapacity to work; whereas, however, it is equally important to ensure that right for the worker who, after a period of employment and residence in the territory of a member state, works as an employed person in the territory of another member state, while still retaining his residence in the territory of the first state;

Whereas, to determine the conditions under which the right to remain arises, account should be taken of the reasons which have led to the termination of employment in the territory of the member state concerned and, in particular, of the difference between retirement, the normal and foreseeable end of working life, and incapacity to work which leads to a premature and unforeseeable termination of activity; whereas special conditions must be laid down where termination of activity is the result of an accident at work or occupational disease, or where the worker's spouse is or was a national of the member state concerned;

Whereas the worker who has reached the end of his working life should have sufficient time in which to decide where he wishes to establish his final residence;

Whereas the exercise by the worker of the right to remain entails that such right shall be extended to members of his family; whereas in the case of the death of the worker during his working life, maintenance of the right of residence of the members of his family must also be recognised and be the subject of special conditions;

2405

Appendix 1   Legislation and materials

Whereas persons to whom the right to remain applies must enjoy equality of treatment with national workers who have ceased their working lives;

¹   OJ No C65, 5.6.1970, p 16.
²   OJ No L 257, 19.10.1968, p 2.
³   OJ No L 257, 19.10.1968, p 13.

Has adopted this Regulation:

Article   1

The provisions of this Regulation shall apply to nationals of a member state who have worked as employed persons in the territory of another member state and to members of their families, as defined in Article 10 of Council Regulation (EEC) No 1612/68 on freedom of movement for workers within the Community.

Article   2

1   The following shall have the right to remain permanently in the territory of a member state:

(a)   a worker who, at the time of termination of his activity, has reached the age laid down by the law of that member state for entitlement to an old-age pension and who has been employed in that state for at least the last twelve months and has resided there continuously for more than three years;

(b)   a worker who, having resided continuously in the territory of that state for more than two years, ceases to work there as an employed person as a result of permanent incapacity to work. If such incapacity is the result of an accident at work or an occupational disease entitling him to a pension for which an institution of that state is entirely or partially responsible, no condition shall be imposed as to length of residence;

(c)   a worker who, after three years' continuous employment and residence in the territory of that state, works as an employed person in the territory of another member state, while retaining his residence in the territory of the first state, to which he returns, as a rule, each day or at least once a week.

Periods of employment completed in this way in the territory of the other member state shall, for the purposes of entitlement to the rights referred to in subparagraphs (a) and (b), be considered as having been completed in the territory of the state of residence.

2   The conditions as to length of residence and employment laid down in paragraph 1(a) and the conditions as to length of residence laid down in paragraph 1(b) shall not apply if the worker's spouse is a national of the member state concerned or has lost the nationality of that state by marriage to that worker.

Article   3

1   The members of a worker's family referred to in Article 1 of this Regulation who are residing with him in the territory of a member state shall be entitled to remain there permanently if the worker has acquired the right to remain in the territory of that state in accordance with Article 2, and to do so even after his death.

2   If, however, the worker dies during his working life and before having acquired the right to remain in the territory of the state concerned, members of his family shall be entitled to remain there permanently on condition that:

—   the worker, on the date of his decease, had resided continuously in the territory of that member state for at least 2 years; or

—   his death resulted from an accident at work or an occupational disease; or

—   the surviving spouse is a national of the state of residence or lost the nationality of that state by marriage to that worker.

Article 4

1 Continuity of residence as provided for in Articles 2(1)and 3(2) may be attested by any means of proof in use in the country of residence. It shall not be affected by temporary absences not exceeding a total of three months per year, nor by longer absences due to compliance with the obligations of military service.

2 Periods of involuntary unemployment, duly recorded by the competent employment office, and absences due to illness or accident shall be considered as periods of employment within the meaning of Article 2(1).

Article 5

1 The person entitled to the right to remain shall be allowed to exercise it within two years from the time of becoming entitled to such right pursuant to Article 2(1)(*a*) and (*b*) and Article 3. During such period he may leave the territory of the member state without adversely affecting such right.

2 No formality shall be required on the part of the person concerned in respect of the exercise of the right to remain.

Article 6

1 Persons coming under the provisions of this Regulation shall be entitled to a residence permit which:

   (a) shall be issued and renewed free of charge or on payment of a sum not exceeding the dues and taxes payable by nationals for the issue or renewal identity documents;
   (b) must be valid throughout the territory of the Member State issuing it;
   (c) must be valid for at least five years and must be renewable automatically.

2 Periods of non-residence not exceeding six consecutive months shall not affect the validity of the residence permit.

Article 7

The right to equality of treatment, established by Council Regulation (EEC) No 1612/68, shall apply to persons coming under the provisions of this Regulation.

Article 8

1 This Regulation shall not affect any provisions laid down by law, regulation or administrative action of one Member State which would be more favourable to nationals of other Member States.

2 Member States shall facilitate re-admission to their territories of workers who have left those territories after having resided there permanently for a long period and having been employed there and who wish to return there when they have reached retirement age or are permanently incapacitated for work.

Article 9

1 The Commission may, taking account of developments in the demographic situation of the Grand Duchy of Luxembourg, lay down, at the request of that State, different conditions from those provided for in this Regulation, in respect of the exercise of the right to remain in Luxembourg territory.

2 Within two months after the request supplying all appropriate details has been put before it, the Commission shall take a decision, stating the reasons on which it is based.

It shall notify the Grand Duchy of Luxembourg of such decision and inform the other Member States thereof;

This Regulation shall be binding in its entirety and directly applicable in all Member States.

Done at Brussels, 29 June 1970.

COUNCIL DIRECTIVE (73/148/EEC) of 21 May 1973 on the abolition of restrictions on movements and residence within the Community for nationals of member states with regard to establishment and the provision of services

OJ L 172, 28 June 1973, p.14

THE COUNCIL OF THE EUROPEAN ECONOMIC COMMUNITY,

Having regard to the Treaty establishing the European Economic Community, and in particular Articles 54(2) and 63(2) thereof;

Having regard to the General Programmes for the abolition of restrictions on freedom of establishment and freedom to provide services[1], and in particular Title II thereof;

Having regard to the proposal from the commission;

Having regard to the Opinion of the European Parliament[2];

Having regard to the Opinion of the Economic and Social Committee[3];

Whereas freedom of movement of persons as provided for in the Treaty and the General Programmes for the abolition of restrictions on freedom of establishment and on freedom to provide services entails the abolition of restrictions on movement and residence within the Community for nationals of member states wishing to establish themselves or to provide services within the territory of another member state;

Whereas freedom of establishment can be fully attained only if a right of permanent residence is granted to the persons who are to enjoy freedom of establishment; whereas freedom to provide services entails that persons providing and receiving services should have the right of residence for the time during which the services are being provided;

Whereas this Directive does not affect measures justified on grounds of public policy, public security or public health; whereas, in pursuance of Article 56(2) of the Treaty, co-ordination of such measures is to be dealt with in a separate Directive;

Whereas Council Directive of 25 February 1964[4] on the abolition of restrictions on movement and residence within the Community for nationals of member states with regard to establishment and the provision of services laid down the rules applicable in this area to activities as self-employed persons;

Whereas Council Directive of 15October 1968[5] on the abolition of restrictions on movement and residence within the Community for workers of member states and their families, which replaced the Directive of 25 March 1964[6] bearing the same title, has in the meantime amended the rules applicable to employed persons;

Whereas the provisions concerning movement and residence within the Community of self-employed persons and their families should likewise be improved;

Whereas the co-ordination of special measures concerning the movement and residence of foreign nationals, justified on grounds of public policy, public security or public health, is already the subject of the Council Directive of 25 February 1964[7];

[1]   OJ No 2, 15.1.1962, pp 32/62 and 36/62.
[2]   OJ No 19, 28.2.1972, p 5.

3   OJ No C 67, 24.6.1972, p 7.
4   OJ No 56, 4.4.1964, p 845/64.
5   OJ No L 257, 19.10.1968, p 13.
6   OJ No 62, 17.4.1964, p 981/64.
7   OJ No 56, 4.4.1964, p 850/64.

Has adopted this directive:

Article 1

1   Member states shall, acting as provided in this Directive, abolish restrictions on the movement and residence of:

(a)   nationals of a member state who are established or who wish to establish themselves in another member state in order to pursue activities as self-employed persons, or who wish to provide services in that state;

(b)   nationals of member states wishing to go to another member state as recipients of services;

(c)   the spouse and the children under twenty-one years of age of such nationals, irrespective of their nationality;

(d)   the relatives in the ascending and descending lines of such nationals and of the spouse of such nationals, whose relatives are dependent on them, irrespective of their nationality.

2   Member states shall favour the admission of any other member of the family of a national referred to in paragraph 1(*a*) or (*b*) or of the spouse of that national, which member is dependent on that national or who in the country of origin was living under the same roof.

Article 2

1   Member states shall grant the persons referred to in Article 1 the right to leave their territory. Such right shall be exercised simply on production of a valid identity card or passport. Members of the family shall enjoy the same right as the national on whom they are dependent.

2   Member states shall, acting in accordance with their laws, issue to their nationals, or renew, an identity card or passport, which shall state in particular the holder's nationality.

3   The passport must be valid at least for all member states and for countries through which the holder must pass when travelling between member states. Where a passport is the only document on which the holder may lawfully leave the country, its period of validity shall not be less than five years.

4   Member states may not demand from the persons referred to in Article 1 any exit visa or any equivalent requirement.

Article 3

1   Member states shall grant to the persons referred to in Article 1 right to enter their territory merely on production of a valid identity card or passport.

2   No entry visa or equivalent requirement may be demanded save in respect of members of the family who do have the nationality of a member state. Member states shall afford to such persons every facility for obtaining any necessary visas.

2409

Appendix 1   Legislation and materials

Article   4

1   Each member state shall grant the right of permanent residence to nationals of other member states who establish themselves within its territory in order to pursue activities as self-employed persons, when the restrictions on these activities have been abolished pursuant to the Treaty.

As proof of the right of residence, a document entitled 'Residence Permit for a national of a member state of the European Communities' shall be issued. This document shall be valid for not less than five years from the date of issue and shall be automatically renewable.

Breaks in residence not exceeding six consecutive months and absence on military service shall not affect the validity of a residence permit.

A valid residence permit may not be withdrawn from a national referred to in Article 1(1)(a) solely on the grounds that he is no longer in employment because he is temporarily incapable of work as a result of illness or accident.

Any national of a member state who is not specified in the first subparagraph but who is authorised under the laws of another member state to pursue an activity within its territory shall be granted a right of abode for a period not less than that of the authorisation granted for the pursuit of the activity in question.

However, any national referred to in subparagraph 1 and to whom the provisions of the preceding subparagraph apply as a result of a change of employment shall retain his residence permit until the date on which it expires.

2   The right of residence for persons providing and receiving services shall be of equal duration with the period during which the services are provided.

Where such period exceeds three months, the member state in the territory of which the services are performed shall issue a right of abode as proof of the right of residence.

Where the period does not exceed three months, the identity card or passport with which the person concerned entered the territory shall be sufficient to cover his stay. The member state may, however, require the person concerned to report his presence in the territory.

3   A member of the family who is not a national of a member state shall be issued with a residence document which shall have the same validity as that issued to the national on whom he is dependent.

Article   5

The right of residence shall be effective throughout the territory of the member state concerned.

Article   6

An applicant for a residence permit or right of abode shall not be required by a member state to produce anything other than the following, namely:

(a)   the identity card or passport with which he or she entered its territory;
(b)   proof that he or she comes within one of the classes of person referred to in Articles 1 and 4.

Article   7

1   The residence documents granted to nationals of a member state shall be issued and renewed free of charge or on payment of an amount not exceeding the dues and taxes

2410

charged for the issue of identity cards to nationals. These provisions shall also apply to documents and certificates required for the issue and renewal of such residence documents.

2 The visas referred to in Article 3(2) shall be free of charge.

3 Member states shall take the necessary steps to simplify as much as possible the formalities and the procedure for obtaining the documents mentioned in paragraph 1.

Article 8

Member states shall not derogate from the provisions of this Directive save on grounds of public security or public health.

Article 9

1 Member states shall within six months of notification of this Directive bring into force the measures necessary to comply with its provisions and shall forthwith inform the Commission thereof.

2 They shall notify the Commission of amendments made to provisions imposed by law, regulation or administrative action for the simplification with regard to establishment and the provision of services of the formalities and procedure for issuing such documents as are still necessary for the movement and residence of persons referred to in Article 1.

Article 10

1 The Council Directive of 25 February 1964 on the abolition of restrictions on movement and residence within the Community for nationals of member states with regard to establishment and the provision of services shall remain applicable until this Directive is implemented by the member states.

2 Residence documents issued pursuant to the Directive referred to in paragraph 1 shall remain valid until the date on which they next expire.

Article 11

This Directive is addressed to the member states.

Done at Brussels, 21 May 1973.

COUNCIL DIRECTIVE (75/34/EEC) of 17 December 1974

concerning the right of nationals of a member state to remain in the territory of another member state after having pursued therein an activity in a self-employed capacity

OJ L 014, 20 January 1975, p.10

THE COUNCIL OF THE EUROPEAN COMMUNITIES,

Having regard to the Treaty establishing the European Economic Community, and in particular Article 235 thereof;

Having regard to the General Programme for the abolition of restrictions on freedom of establishment[1], and in particular Title II thereof;

Having regard to the proposal from the Commission;

Having regard to the Opinion of the European Parliament[2];

Having regard to the Opinion of the Economic and Social Committee[3];

Whereas pursuant to Council Directive No 73/148/EEC[4] of 21 May 1973 on the abolition of restrictions on movement and residence within the Community for nationals of member states with regard to establishment and the provision of services, each member state grants the right of permanent residence to nationals of other member states who establish themselves within its territory in order to pursue activities as self-employed persons, when the restrictions on these activities have been abolished pursuant to the Treaty;

Whereas it is normal for a person to prolong a period of permanent residence in the territory of a member state by remaining there after having pursued an activity there; whereas the absence of a right so to remain in such circumstances is an obstacle to the attainment of freedom of establishment; whereas, as regards employed persons, the conditions under which such a right may be exercised have already been laid down by Regulation (EEC) No 1251/70[5];

Whereas Article 48(3)(*d*) of the Treaty recognises the right of workers to remain in the territory of a member state after having been employed in that state; whereas Article 54(2) does not expressly provide a similar right for self-employed persons; whereas, nevertheless, the nature of establishment, together with attachments formed to the countries in which they have pursued their activities, means that such persons have a definite interest in enjoying the same right to remain as that granted to workers; whereas in justification of this measure reference should be made to the Treaty provision enabling it to be taken;

Whereas freedom of establishment within the Community requires that nationals of member states may pursue self-employed activities in several member states in succession without thereby being placed at a disadvantage;

Whereas a national of a member state residing in the territory of another member state should be guaranteed the right to remain in that territory when he ceases to pursue an activity as a self-employed person in that state because he has reached retirement age or by reason of permanent incapacity to work; whereas such a right should also be guaranteed to the national of a member state who, after a period of activity in a self-employed capacity and residence in the territory of a second member state, while still retaining his residence in the territory of the second state;

Whereas, to determine the conditions under which the right to remain arises, account should be taken of the reasons which have led to the termination of activity in the territory of the member state concerned and, in particular, of the difference between retirement, the normal and foreseeable end of working life, and permanent incapacity to work which leads to a premature and unforeseeable termination of activity; whereas special conditions must be laid down where the spouse is or was a national of the member state concerned, or where termination of activity is the result of an accident at work or occupational illness;

Whereas a national of a member state who has reached the end of his working life, after working in self-employed capacity in the territory of another member state, should have sufficient time in which to decide where he wishes to establish his final residence;

Whereas the exercise of the right to remain by a national of a member state working in a self-employed capacity entails extension of such right to the members of his family; whereas in the case of the death of a national of a member state working in a self-employed capacity during his working life the right of residence of the members of his family must also be recognised and be the subject of special conditions;

Whereas persons to whom the right to remain applies must enjoy equality of treatment with nationals of the state concerned who have reached the end of their working lives;

¹   OJ No 2, 15.1.1962, p 36/62.
²   OJ No C 14, 27.3.1973, p 20.
³   OJ No C 142, 31.12.1972, p 12.
⁴   OJ No L 172, 28.6.1973, p 14.
⁵   OJ No L 142, 30.6.1970, p 24.

Has adopted this Directive:

Article   1

Member states shall, under the conditions laid down in this Directive, abolish restrictions on the right to remain in their territory in favour of nationals of another member state who have pursued activities as self-employed persons in their territory, and members of their families, as defined in Article 1 of Directive No 73/148/EEC.

Article   2

1   Each member state shall recognise the right to remain permanently in its territory of:

(a)   any person who, at the time of termination of his activity, has reached the age laid down by the law of that state for entitlement to an old-age pension and who has pursued his activity in that state for at least the previous twelve months and has resided there continuously for more than three years.
Where the law of that member state does not grant the right to an old-age pension to certain categories of self-employed workers, the age requirement shall be considered as satisfied when the beneficiary reaches 65 years of age;

(b)   any person who, having resided continuously in the territory of that state for more than two years, ceases to pursue his activity there as a result of permanent incapacity to work.
If such incapacity is the result of an accident at work or an occupational illness entitling him to a pension which is payable in whole or in part by an institution of that state no condition shall be imposed as to length of residence;

(c)   any person who, after three years' continuous activity and residence in the territory of that state, pursues his activity in the territory of another member state, while retaining his residence in the territory of the first state, to which he returns, as a rule, each day or at least once a week.
Periods of activity so completed in the territory of the other member state shall, for the purposes of entitlement to the rights referred to in (*a*) and (*b*), be considered as having been completed in the territory of the state of residence.

2413

2   The conditions as to length of residence and activity laid down in paragraph 1(*a*) and the condition as to length of residence laid down in paragraph 1(*b*) shall not apply if the spouse of the self-employed person is a national of the member state concerned or has lost the nationality of that state by marriage to that person.

Article   3

1   Each member state shall recognise the right of the members of the self-employed person's family referred to in Article 1 who are residing with him in the territory of that state to remain there permanently, if the person concerned has acquired the right to remain in the territory of that state in accordance with Article 2. This provision shall continue to apply even after the death of the person concerned.

2   If, however, the self-employed person dies during his working life and before having acquired the right to remain in the territory of the state concerned, that state shall recognise the right of the members of his family to remain there permanently on condition that:

— the person concerned, on the date of his decease, had resided continuously in its territory for at least two years; or
— his death resulted from an accident at work or an occupational illness; or
— the surviving spouse is a national of that state or lost such nationality by marriage to the person concerned.

Article   4

1   Continuity of residence as provided for in Articles 2(1) and 3(2) may be attested by any means of proof in use in the country of residence. It may not be affected by temporary absences not exceeding a total of three months per year, nor by longer absences due to compliance with the obligations of military service.

2   Periods of inactivity due to circumstances outside the control of the person concerned or of inactivity owing to illness or accident must be considered as periods of activity within the meaning of Article 2(1).

Article   5

1   Member states shall allow the person entitled to the right to remain to exercise such right within two years from the time of becoming entitled thereto pursuant to Article 2(1)(*a*) and (*b*) and Article 3. During this period the beneficiary must be able to leave the territory of the member state without adversely affecting such right.

2   Member states shall not require the person concerned to comply with any particular formality in order to exercise the right to remain.

Article   6

1   Member states shall recognise the right of persons having the right to remain in their territory to a residence permit, which must:

(a)   be issued and renewed free of charge or on payment of a sum not exceeding the dues and taxes payable by nationals for the issue or renewal of identity cards;
(b)   be valid throughout the territory of the member state issuing it;
(c)   be valid for five years and renewable automatically.

2   Periods of non-residence not exceeding six consecutive months and longer absences due to compliance with the obligations of military service may not affect the validity of a residence permit.

Article 7

Member states shall apply to persons having the right to remain in their territory the right of equality of treatment recognised by the Council Directives on the abolition of restrictions on freedom of establishment pursuant to Title III of the General Programme which provides for such abolition.

Article 8

1 This Directive shall not affect any provisions laid down by law, regulation or administrative action of any member state which would be more favourable to nationals of other member states.

2 Member states shall facilitate re-admission to their territories of self-employed persons who left those territories after having resided there permanently for a long period while pursuing an activity there and who wish to return when they have reached retirement age as defined in Article 2(1)(*a*) or are permanently incapacitated for work.

Article 9

Member states may not derogate from the provisions of this Directive save on grounds of public policy, public security or public health.

Article 10

1 Member states shall, within twelve months of notification of this Directive, bring into force the measures necessary to comply with its provisions and shall forthwith inform the Commission thereof.

2 Following notification of this Directive, member states shall further ensure that the Commission is informed, in sufficient time for it to submit its comments, of all proposed laws, regulations or administrative provisions which they intend to adopt in the field covered by this Directive.

Article 11

This Directive is addressed to the member states.

Done at Brussels, 17 December 1974.

COUNCIL DIRECTIVE (75/35/EEC) of 17 December 1974

extending the scope of Directive No 64/221/EEC on the co-ordination of special measures concerning the movement and residence of foreign nationals which are justified on grounds of public policy, public security or public health to include nationals of a member state who exercise the right to remain in the territory of another member state after having pursued therein an activity in a self-employed capacity

OJ L 014, 20 January 1975, p.14

THE COUNCIL OF THE EUROPEAN COMMUNITIES,

Having regard to the Treaty establishing the European Economic Community, and in particular Article 56(2) and Article 235 thereof;

Having regard to the proposal from the Commission;

Having regard to the Opinion of the European Parliament[1];

Having regard to the Opinion of the Economic and Social Committee[2];

Whereas Directive No 64/221/EEC[3] co-ordinated special measures concerning the movement and residence of foreign nationals which are justified on grounds of public policy, public security or public health and whereas Directive No 75/34/EEC[4] laid down conditions for the exercise of the right of nationals of a member state to remain in the territory of another member state after having pursued therein an activity in a self-employed capacity;

Whereas Directive No 64/221/EEC should therefore apply to persons to whom Directive No 75/34/EEC applies;

[1]   OJ No C 14, 27.3.1973, p 21.
[2]   OJ No C 142, 31.12.1972, p 10.
[3]   OJ No 56, 4.4.1964, p 850/64.
[4]   See p 10 of this Official Journal.

Has adopted this Directive:

Article   1

Directive No 64/221/EEC shall apply to nationals of member states and members of their families who have the right to remain in the territory of a member state pursuant to Directive No 75/34/EEC.

Article   2

Member states shall, within twelve months of notification of this Directive, bring into force the measures necessary to comply with its provisions and shall forthwith inform the Commission thereof.

Article   3

This Directive is addressed to the member states.

Done at Brussels, 17 December 1974.

COUNCIL DIRECTIVE (90/364/EEC) of 28 June 1990 on the right of residence

OJ L 180, 13 July 1990, p.26

THE COUNCIL OF THE EUROPEAN COMMUNITIES,

Having regard to the Treaty establishing the European Economic Community, and in particular Article 235 thereof;

Having regard to the proposal from the Commission[1];

Having regard to the Opinion of the European Parliament[2];

Having regard to the Opinion of the Economic and Social Committee[3];

Whereas Article 3(c) of the Treaty provides that the activities of the Community shall include, as provided in the Treaty, the abolition, as between member states, of obstacles to freedom of movement for persons;

Whereas Article 8(a) of the Treaty provides that the internal market must be established by 31 December 1992; whereas the internal market comprises an area without internal frontiers in which the free movement of goods, persons, services and capital is ensured in accordance with the provisions of the Treaty;

Whereas national provisions on the right of nationals of the member states to reside in a member state other than their own must be harmonised to ensure such freedom of movement;

Whereas beneficiaries of the right of residence must not become an unreasonable burden on the public finances of the host member state;

Whereas this right can only be genuinely exercised if it is also granted to members of the family;

Whereas the beneficiaries of this Directive should be covered by administrative arrangements similar to those laid down in particular in Directive 68/360/EEC[4] and Directive 64/221/EEC[5];

Whereas the Treaty does not provide, for the action concerned, powers other than those of Article 235;

[1] OJ No C 191, 28.7.1989, p 5; and OJ No C 26, 3.2.1990, p 22.
[2] Opinion delivered on 13 June 1990 (not yet published in official Journal).
[3] OJ No C 329, 30.12.1989, p 25.
[4] OJ No L257, 19.10.1968, p 13.
[5] OJ No 56, 4.4.1964, p 850/40.

Has adopted this Directive:

Article   1

1   Member states shall grant the right of residence to nationals of member states who do not enjoy this right under other provisions of Community law and to members of their families as defined in paragraph 2, provided that they themselves and the members of their families are covered by sickness insurance in respect of all risks in the host member state and have sufficient resources to avoid becoming a burden on the social assistance system of the host member state during their period of residence.

The resources referred to in the first subparagraph shall be deemed sufficient where they are higher than the level of resources below which the host member state may grant social assistance to its nationals, taking into account the personal circumstances of the applicant and, where appropriate, the personal circumstances of persons admitted pursuant to paragraph 2.

Where the second subparagraph cannot be applied in a member state, the resources of the applicant shall be deemed sufficient if they are higher than the level of the minimum social security pension paid by the host member state.

2   The following shall, irrespective of their nationality, have the right to install themselves in another member state with the holder of the right of residence:

(a)   his or her spouse and their descendants who are dependents;
(b)   dependent relatives in the ascending line of the holder of the right of residence and his or her spouse.

Article   2

1   Exercise of the right of residence shall be evidenced by means of the issue of a document known as a 'Residence permit for a national of a member state of the EEC', the validity of which may be limited to five years on a renewable basis. However, the member states may, when they deem it to be necessary, require revalidation of the permit at the end of the first two years of residence. Where a member of the family does not hold the nationality of a member state, he or she shall be issued with a residence document of the same validity as that issued to the national on whom he or she depends.

For the purpose of issuing the residence permit or document, the member state may require only that the applicant present a valid identity card or passport and provide proof that he or she meets the conditions laid down in Article 1.

2   Articles 2, 3, 6(1)(*a*) and (2) and Article 9 of Directive 68/360/EEC shall apply *mutatis mutandis* to the beneficiaries of this Directive.

The spouse and the dependent children of a national of a member state entitled to the right of residence within the territory of a member state shall be entitled to take up any employed or self-employed activity anywhere within the territory of that member state, even if they are not nationals of a member state.

Member states shall not derogate from the provisions of this Directive save on grounds of public policy, public security or public health. In that event, Directive 64/221/EEC shall apply.

3   This Directive shall not affect existing law on the acquisition of second homes.

Article   3

The right of residence shall remain for as long as beneficiaries of that right fulfil the conditions laid down in Article 1.

Article   4

The Commission shall, not more than three years after the date of implementation of this Directive, and at three-yearly intervals thereafter, draw up a report on the application of this Directive and submit it to the European Parliament and the Council.

Article   5

Member states shall bring into force the laws, regulations and administrative provisions necessary to comply with this Directive not later than 30 June 1992. They shall forthwith inform the Commission thereof.

Article 6

This Directive is addressed to the member states.

Done at Luxembourg, 28 June 1990.

COUNCIL DIRECTIVE (90/365/EEC) of 28 June 1990 on the right of residence for employees and self-employed persons who have ceased their occupational activity

OJ L 180, 13 July 1990, p.28

THE COUNCIL OF THE EUROPEAN COMMUNITIES,

Having regard to the Treaty establishing the European Economic Community, and in particular Article 235 thereof;

Having regard to the proposal from the Commission[1];

Having regard to the opinion of the European Parliament[2];

Having regard to the opinion of the Economic and Social Committee[3];

Whereas Article 3(c) of the Treaty provides that the activities of the Community shall include, as provided in the Treaty, the abolition, as between member states, of obstacles to freedom of movement for persons;

Whereas Article 8(a) of the Treaty provides that the internal market must be established by 31 December 1992; whereas the internal market comprises an area without internal frontiers in which the free movement of goods, persons, services and capital is ensured, in accordance with the provisions of the Treaty;

Whereas Articles 48 and 52 of the Treaty provide for freedom of movement for workers and self-employed persons, which entails the right of residence in the member states in which they pursue their occupational activity; whereas it is desirable that this right of residence also be granted to persons who have ceased their occupational activity even if they have not exercised their right to freedom of movement during their working life;

Whereas beneficiaries of the right of residence must not become an unreasonable burden on the public finances of the host member state;

Whereas under Article 10 of Regulation (EEC) No 1408/71[4], as amended by Regulation (EEC)No 1390/81[5], recipients of invalidity or old age cash benefits or pensions for accidents at work or occupational diseases are entitled to continue to receive these benefits and pensions even if they reside in the territory of a member state other than that in which the institution responsible for payment is situated;

Whereas this right can only be genuinely exercised if it is also granted to members of the family;

Whereas the beneficiaries of this Directive should be covered by administrative arrangements similar to those laid down in particular in Directive 68/630/EEC[6] and Directive 64/221/EEC[7];

Whereas the Treaty does not provide, for the action concerned, powers other than those of Article 235;

[1]   OJ No C 191, 28.7.1989, p 3; and OJ No C 26, 3.2.1990, p 19.
[2]   Opinion delivered on 13 June 1990 (not yet published in Official Journal).
[3]   OJ No C 329, 30.12.1989, p 25.
[4]   OJ No L 149, 5.7.1971, p 2.

5   OJ No L 143, 29.5.1981, p 1.
6   OJ No L257, 19.10.1968, p 13.
7   OJ No 56, 4.4.1964, p 850/64.

Has adopted this Directive:

Article   1

1   Member states shall grant the right of residence to nationals of member states who have pursued an activity as an employee or self-employed person and to members of their families as defined in paragraph 2, provided that they are recipients of an invalidity or early retirement pension, or old age benefits, or of a pension in respect of an industrial accident or disease of an amount sufficient to avoid becoming a burden on the social security system of the host member state during their period of residence and provided they are covered by sickness insurance in respect of all risks in the host member state.

The resources of the applicant shall be deemed sufficient where they are higher than the level of resources below which the host member state may grant social assistance to its nationals, taking into account the personal circumstances of persons admitted pursuant to paragraph 2.

Where the second subparagraph cannot be applied in a member state, the resources of the applicant shall be deemed sufficient if they are higher than the level of the minimum social security pension paid by the host member state.

2   The following shall, irrespective of their nationality, have the right to install themselves in another member state with the holder of the right of residence:

    (a)   his or her spouse and their descendants who are dependents;
    (b)   dependent relatives in the ascending line of the holder of the right of residence and his or her spouse.

Article   2

1   Exercise of the right of residence shall be evidenced by means of the issue of a document known as a 'Residence permit for a national of a member state of the EEC', whose validity may be limited to five years on a renewable basis. However, the member states may, when they deem it to be necessary, require revalidation of the permit at the end of the first two years of residence. Where a member of the family does not hold the nationality of a member state, he or she shall be issued with a residence document of the same validity as that issued to the national on whom he or she depends.

For the purposes of issuing the residence permit or document, the member state may require only that the applicant present a valid identity card or passport and provide proof that he or she meets the conditions laid down in Article 1.

2   Articles 2, 3, 6(1)(a) and (2) and Article 9 of Directive 68/360/EEC shall apply *mutatis mutandis* to the beneficiaries of this Directive.

The spouse and the dependent children of a national of a member state entitled to the right of residence within the territory of a member state shall be entitled to take up any employed or self-employed activity anywhere within the territory of that member state, even if they are not nationals of a member state.

Member states shall not derogate from the provisions of this Directive save on grounds of public policy, public security or public health. In that event, Directive 64/221/EEC shall apply.

3   This Directive shall not affect existing law on the acquisition of second homes.

Article   3

The right of residence shall remain for as long as beneficiaries of that right fulfil the conditions laid down in Article 1.

Article   4

The Commission shall, not more than three years after the date of implementation of this Directive, and at three-yearly intervals thereafter, draw up a report on the application of this Directive and submit it to the European Parliament and the Council.

Article   5

Member states shall bring into force the laws, regulations and administrative provisions necessary to comply with this Directive not later than 30 June 1992. They shall forthwith inform the Commission thereof.

Article   6

This Directive is addressed to the member states.

Done at Luxembourg, 28 June 1990.

COUNCIL DIRECTIVE (93/96/EEC) of 29 October 1993 on
the right of residence for students

OJ L 317, 18 December 1993, p.59

THE COUNCIL OF THE EUROPEAN COMMUNITIES,

Having regard to the Treaty establishing the European Economic Community, and in particular the second paragraph of Article 7 thereof;

Having regard to the proposal from the Commission[1];

In cooperation with the European Parliament[2];

Having regard to the opinion of the Economic and Social Committee[3];

Whereas Article 3(c) of the Treaty provides that the activities of the Community shall include, as provided in the Treaty, the abolition, as between member states, of obstacles to freedom of movement for persons;

Whereas Article 8(a) of the Treaty provides that the internal market must be established by 31 December 1992; whereas the internal market comprises an area without internal frontiers in which the free movement of goods, persons, services and capital is ensured in accordance with the provisions of the Treaty;

Whereas, as the Court of Justice has held, Articles 128 and 7 of the Treaty prohibit any discrimination between nationals of the member states as regards access to vocational training in the Community; whereas access by a national of one member state to vocational training in another member state implies, for that national, a right of residence in that other member state;

Whereas, accordingly, in order to guarantee access to vocational training, the conditions likely to facilitate the effective exercise of that right of residence should be laid down;

Whereas the right of residence for students forms part of a set of related measures designed to promote vocational training;

2421

Whereas beneficiaries of the right of residence must not become an unreasonable burden on the public finances of the host member state;

Whereas, in the present state of Community law, as established by the case law of the Court of Justice, assistance granted to students, does not fall within the scope of the Treaty within the meaning of Article 7 thereof;

Whereas the right of residence can only be genuinely exercised if it is also granted to the spouse and their dependent children;

Whereas the beneficiaries of this Directive should be covered by administrative arrangements similar to those laid down in particular in Council Directive 68/360/EEC of 15 October 1968 on the abolition of restrictions on movement and residence within the Community for workers of member states and their families[4] and Council Directive 64/221/EEC of 25 February 1964 on the co-ordination of special measures concerning the movement and residence of foreign nationals which are justified on grounds of public policy, public security or public health[5];

Whereas this Directive does not apply to students who enjoy the right of residence by virtue of the fact that they are or have been effectively engaged in economic activities or are members of the family of a migrant worker;

Whereas, by its judgment of 7 July 1992 in Case C–295/90, the Court of Justice annulled Council Directive 90/366/EEC of 28 June 1990 on the right of residence for students 'while maintaining the effects of the annulled Directive until the entry into force of a Directive adopted on the appropriate legal basis';

Whereas the effects of Directive 90/366/EEC should be maintained during the period up to 31 December 1993, the date by which member states are to have adopted the laws, regulations and administrative provisions necessary to comply with this Directive;

[1]   OJ No C166, 17.6.1993, p 16.
[2]   OJ No C255, 20.9.1993, p 70 and OJ No C315, 22.1.1993.
[3]   OJ No C304, 10.11.1993, p 1.
[4]   OJ No L257, 19.10.1968, p 13. Directive as last amended by the Act of Accession of 1985.
[5]   OJ No 56, 4.4.1964, p 850/64.
[6]   OJ No L180, 13.7.1990, p 30.

Has adopted this directive:

Article   1

In order to lay down conditions to facilitate the exercise of the right of residence and with a view to guaranteeing access to vocational training in a non-discriminatory manner for a national of a member state who has been accepted to attend a vocational training course in another member state, the member states shall recognise the right of residence for any student who is a national of a member state and who does not enjoy that right under other provisions of Community law, and for the student's spouse and their dependent children, where the student assures the relevant national authority, by means of a declaration or by such alternative means as the student may choose that are at least equivalent, that he has sufficient resources to avoid becoming a burden on the social assistance system of the host member state during their period of residence, provided that the student is enrolled in a recognised educational establishment for the principal purpose of following a vocational training course there and that he is covered by sickness insurance in respect of all risks in the host member state.

1   The right of residence shall be restricted to the duration of the course of studies in question.

The right of residence shall be evidenced by means of the issue of a document known as a 'residence permit for a national of a member state of the Community', the validity of which may be limited to the duration of the course of studies or to one year where the course lasts longer; in the latter event it shall be renewable annually. Where a member of the family does not hold the nationality of a member state, he or she shall be issued with a residence document of the same validity as that issued to the national on whom he or she depends.

For the purpose of issuing the residence permit or document, the member state may require only that the applicant present a valid identity card or passport and provide proof that he or she meets the conditions laid down in Article 1.

2 Articles 2, 3 and 9 of Directive 68/360/EEC shall apply *mutatis mutandis* to the beneficiaries of this Directive.

The spouse and dependent children of a national of a member state entitled to the right of residence within the territory of a member state shall be entitled to take up any employed or self-employed activity anywhere within the territory of that member state, even if they are not nationals of a member state.

Member states shall not derogate from the provisions of this Directive save on grounds of public policy, public security or public health; in that event, Articles 2 to 9 of Directive 64/221/EEC shall apply.

Article 3

This Directive shall not establish any entitlement to the payment of maintenance grants by the host member state on the part of students benefiting from the right of residence.

Article 4

The right of residence shall remain for as long as beneficiaries of that right fulfil the conditions laid down in Article 1.

Article 5

The Commission shall, not more than three years after the date of implementation of this Directive, and at three-yearly intervals thereafter, draw up a report on the application of this Directive and submit it to the European Parliament and the Council.

The Commission shall pay particular attention to any difficulties which the implementation of Article 1 might give rise in the member states; it shall, if appropriate, submit proposals to the Council with the aim of remedying such difficulties.

Article 6

Member states shall bring into force the laws, regulations and administrative provisions necessary to comply with this Directive not later than 31 December 1993. They shall forthwith inform the Commission thereof.

For the period preceding that date, the effects of Directive 90/366/EEC shall be maintained.

When member states adopt those measures, they shall contain a reference to this Directive or shall be accompanied by such a reference on the occasion of their official publication. The methods of making such references shall be laid down by the member states.

Article 7

This Directive is addressed to the member states.

Done at Brussels, 29 October 1993.

COUNCIL DIRECTIVE (2001/55/EC) of 20 July 2001 on minimum standards for giving temporary protection in the event of a mass influx of displaced persons and on measures promoting a balance of efforts between Member States in receiving such persons and bearing the consequences thereof

OJ L 212, 7 August 2001, p.12

THE COUNCIL OF THE EUROPEAN UNION,

Having regard to the Treaty establishing the European Community, and in particular point 2(a) and (b) of Article 63 thereof,

Having regard to the proposal from the Commission[1],

Having regard to the opinion of the European Parliament[2],

Having regard to the opinion of the Economic and Social Committee[3],

Having regard to the opinion of the Committee of the Regions[4],

Whereas:

(1) The preparation of a common policy on asylum, including common European arrangements for asylum, is a constituent part of the European Union's objective of establishing progressively an area of freedom, security and justice open to those who, forced by circumstances, legitimately seek protection in the European Union.

(2) Cases of mass influx of displaced persons who cannot return to their country of origin have become more substantial in Europe in recent years. In these cases it may be necessary to set up exceptional schemes to offer them immediate temporary protection.

(3) In the conclusions relating to persons displaced by the conflict in the former Yugoslavia adopted by the Ministers responsible for immigration at their meetings in London on 30 November and 1 December 1992 and Copenhagen on 1 and 2 June 1993, the Member States and the Community institutions expressed their concern at the situation of displaced persons.

(4) On 25 September 1995 the Council adopted a Resolution on burden-sharing with regard to the admission and residence of displaced persons on a temporary basis[5], and, on 4 March 1996, adopted Decision 96/198/JHA on an alert and emergency procedure for burden-sharing with regard to the admission and residence of displaced persons on a temporary basis[6].

(5) The Action Plan of the Council and the Commission of 3 December 1998[7] provides for the rapid adoption, in accordance with the Treaty of Amsterdam, of minimum standards for giving temporary protection to displaced persons from third countries who cannot return to their country of origin and of measures promoting a balance of effort between Member States in receiving and bearing the consequences of receiving displaced persons.

(6) On 27 May 1999 the Council adopted conclusions on displaced persons from Kosovo. These conclusions call on the Commission and the Member States to learn the lessons of their response to the Kosovo crisis in order to establish the measures in accordance with the Treaty.

(7) The European Council, at its special meeting in Tampere on 15 and 16 October 1999, acknowledged the need to reach agreement on the issue of temporary protection for displaced persons on the basis of solidarity between Member States.

(8) It is therefore necessary to establish minimum standards for giving temporary protection in the event of a mass influx of displaced persons and to take measures to promote a balance of efforts between the Member States in receiving and bearing the consequences of receiving such persons.

(9) Those standards and measures are linked and interdependent for reasons of effectiveness, coherence and solidarity and in order, in particular, to avert the risk of secondary movements. They should therefore be enacted in a single legal instrument.

(10) This temporary protection should be compatible with the Member States' international obligations as regards refugees. In particular, it must not prejudice the recognition of refugee status pursuant to the Geneva Convention of 28 July 1951 on the status of refugees, as amended by the New York Protocol of 31 January 1967, ratified by all the Member States.

(11) The mandate of the United Nations High Commissioner for Refugees regarding refugees and other persons in need of international protection should be respected, and effect should be given to Declaration No 17, annexed to the Final Act to the Treaty of Amsterdam, on Article 63 of the Treaty establishing the European Community which provides that consultations are to be established with the United Nations High Commissioner for Refugees and other relevant international organisations on matters relating to asylum policy.

(12) It is in the very nature of minimum standards that Member States have the power to introduce or maintain more favourable provisions for persons enjoying temporary protection in the event of a mass influx of displaced persons.

(13) Given the exceptional character of the provisions established by this Directive in order to deal with a mass influx or imminent mass influx of displaced persons from third countries who are unable to return to their country of origin, the protection offered should be of limited duration.

(14) The existence of a mass influx of displaced persons should be established by a Council Decision, which should be binding in all Member States in relation to the displaced persons to whom the Decision applies. The conditions for the expiry of the Decision should also be established.

(15) The Member States' obligations as to the conditions of reception and residence of persons enjoying temporary protection in the event of a mass influx of displaced persons should be determined. These obligations should be fair and offer an adequate level of protection to those concerned.

(16) With respect to the treatment of persons enjoying temporary protection under this Directive, the Member States are bound by obligations under instruments of international law to which they are party and which prohibit discrimination.

(17) Member States should, in concert with the Commission, enforce adequate measures so that the processing of personal data respects the standard of protection of Directive 95/46/EC of the European Parliament and the Council of 24 October 1995 on the protection of individuals with regard to the processing of personal data and on the free movement of such data[8].

(18) Rules should be laid down to govern access to the asylum procedure in the context of temporary protection in the event of a mass influx of displaced persons, in conformity with the Member States' international obligations and with the Treaty.

(19) Provision should be made for principles and measures governing the return to the country of origin and the measures to be taken by Member States in respect of persons whose temporary protection has ended.

(20) Provision should be made for a solidarity mechanism intended to contribute to the attainment of a balance of effort between Member States in receiving and bearing the consequences of receiving displaced persons in the event of a mass influx. The mechanism should consist of two components. The first is financial and the second concerns the actual reception of persons in the Member States.

(21) The implementation of temporary protection should be accompanied by administrative cooperation between the Member States in liaison with the Commission.

(22) It is necessary to determine criteria for the exclusion of certain persons from temporary protection in the event of a mass influx of displaced persons.

(23) Since the objectives of the proposed action, namely to establish minimum standards for giving temporary protection in the event of a mass influx of displaced persons and measures promoting a balance of efforts between the Member States in receiving and bearing the consequences of receiving such persons, cannot be sufficiently attained by the Member States and can therefore, by reason of the scale or effects of the proposed action, be better achieved at Community level, the Community may adopt measures in accordance with the principle of subsidiarity as set out in Article 5 of the Treaty. In accordance with the principle of proportionality as set out in that Article, this Directive does not go beyond what is necessary in order to achieve those objectives.

(24) In accordance with Article 3 of the Protocol on the position of the United Kingdom and Ireland, annexed to the Treaty on European Union and to the Treaty establishing the European Community, the United Kingdom gave notice, by letter of 27 September 2000, of its wish to take part in the adoption and application of this Directive.

(25) Pursuant to Article 1 of the said Protocol, Ireland is not participating in the adoption of this Directive. Consequently and without prejudice to Article 4 of the aforementioned Protocol, the provisions of this Directive do not apply to Ireland.

(26) In accordance with Articles 1 and 2 of the Protocol on the position of Denmark, annexed to the Treaty on European Union and to the Treaty establishing the European Community, Denmark is not participating in the adoption of this Directive, and is therefore not bound by it nor subject to its application,

1   OJ C 311 E, 31.10.2000, p. 251.
2   Opinion delivered on 13 March 2001 (not yet published in the Official Journal).
3   OJ C 155, 29.5.2001, p. 21.
4   Opinion delivered on 13 June 2001 (not yet published in the Official Journal).
5   OJ C 262, 7.10.1995, p. 1.
6   OJ L 63, 13.3.1996, p. 10.
7   OJ C 19, 20.1.1999, p. 1.
8   OJ L 281, 23.11.1995, p. 31.

Has adopted this Directive:

CHAPTER I
GENERAL PROVISIONS

Article   1

The purpose of this Directive is to establish minimum standards for giving temporary protection in the event of a mass influx of displaced persons from third countries who are unable to return to their country of origin and to promote a balance of effort between Member States in receiving and bearing the consequences of receiving such persons.

Article 2

For the purposes of this Directive:

(a) 'temporary protection' means a procedure of exceptional character to provide, in the event of a mass influx or imminent mass influx of displaced persons from third countries who are unable to return to their country of origin, immediate and temporary protection to such persons, in particular if there is also a risk that the asylum system will be unable to process this influx without adverse effects for its efficient operation, in the interests of the persons concerned and other persons requesting protection;

(b) 'Geneva Convention' means the Convention of 28 July 1951 relating to the status of refugees, as amended by the New York Protocol of 31 January 1967;

(c) 'displaced persons' means third-country nationals or stateless persons who have had to leave their country or region of origin, or have been evacuated, in particular in response to an appeal by international organisations, and are unable to return in safe and durable conditions because of the situation prevailing in that country, who may fall within the scope of Article 1A of the Geneva Convention or other international or national instruments giving international protection, in particular:

   (i) persons who have fled areas of armed conflict or endemic violence;
   (ii) persons at serious risk of, or who have been the victims of, systematic or generalised violations of their human rights;

(d) 'mass influx' means arrival in the Community of a large number of displaced persons, who come from a specific country or geographical area, whether their arrival in the Community was spontaneous or aided, for example through an evacuation programme;

(e) 'refugees' means third-country nationals or stateless persons within the meaning of Article 1A of the Geneva Convention;

(f) 'unaccompanied minors' means third-country nationals or stateless persons below the age of eighteen, who arrive on the territory of the Member States unaccompanied by an adult responsible for them whether by law or custom, and for as long as they are not effectively taken into the care of such a person, or minors who are left unaccompanied after they have entered the territory of the Member States;

(g) 'residence permit' means any permit or authorisation issued by the authorities of a Member State and taking the form provided for in that State's legislation, allowing a third country national or a stateless person to reside on its territory;

(h) 'sponsor' means a third-country national enjoying temporary protection in a Member State in accordance with a decision taken under Article 5 and who wants to be joined by members of his or her family.

Article 3

1. Temporary protection shall not prejudge recognition of refugee status under the Geneva Convention.

2. Member States shall apply temporary protection with due respect for human rights and fundamental freedoms and their obligations regarding non-refoulement.

3. The establishment, implementation and termination of temporary protection shall be the subject of regular consultations with the Office of the United Nations High Commissioner for Refugees (UNHCR) and other relevant international organisations.

4. This Directive shall not apply to persons who have been accepted under temporary protection schemes prior to its entry into force.

5. This Directive shall not affect the prerogative of the Member States to adopt or retain more favourable conditions for persons covered by temporary protection.

CHAPTER II
DURATION AND IMPLEMENTATION OF TEMPORARY PROTECTION

Article   4

1. Without prejudice to Article 6, the duration of temporary protection shall be one year. Unless terminated under the terms of Article 6(1)(b), it may be extended automatically by six monthly periods for a maximum of one year.

2. Where reasons for temporary protection persist, the Council may decide by qualified majority, on a proposal from the Commission, which shall also examine any request by a Member State that it submit a proposal to the Council, to extend that temporary protection by up to one year.

Article   5

1. The existence of a mass influx of displaced persons shall be established by a Council Decision adopted by a qualified majority on a proposal from the Commission, which shall also examine any request by a Member State that it submit a proposal to the Council.

2. The Commission proposal shall include at least:

  (a) a description of the specific groups of persons to whom the temporary protection will apply;
  (b) the date on which the temporary protection will take effect;
  (c) an estimation of the scale of the movements of displaced persons.

3. The Council Decision shall have the effect of introducing temporary protection for the displaced persons to which it refers, in all the Member States, in accordance with the provisions of this Directive. The Decision shall include at least:

  (a) a description of the specific groups of persons to whom the temporary protection applies;
  (b) the date on which the temporary protection will take effect;
  (c) information received from Member States on their reception capacity;
  (d) information from the Commission, UNHCR and other relevant international organisations.

4. The Council Decision shall be based on:

  (a) an examination of the situation and the scale of the movements of displaced persons;
  (b) an assessment of the advisability of establishing temporary protection, taking into account the potential for emergency aid and action on the ground or the inadequacy of such measures;
  (c) information received from the Member States, the Commission, UNHCR and other relevant international organisations.

5. The European Parliament shall be informed of the Council Decision.

Article   6

1. Temporary protection shall come to an end:

  (a) when the maximum duration has been reached; or

(b) at any time, by Council Decision adopted by a qualified majority on a proposal from the Commission, which shall also examine any request by a Member State that it submit a proposal to the Council.

2. The Council Decision shall be based on the establishment of the fact that the situation in the country of origin is such as to permit the safe and durable return of those granted temporary protection with due respect for human rights and fundamental freedoms and Member States' obligations regarding non-refoulement. The European Parliament shall be informed of the Council Decision.

Article 7

1. Member States may extend temporary protection as provided for in this Directive to additional categories of displaced persons over and above those to whom the Council Decision provided for in Article 5 applies, where they are displaced for the same reasons and from the same country or region of origin. They shall notify the Council and the Commission immediately.

2. The provisions of Articles 24, 25 and 26 shall not apply to the use of the possibility referred to in paragraph 1, with the exception of the structural support included in the European Refugee Fund set up by Decision 2000/596/EC[9], under the conditions laid down in that Decision.

[9] OJ L 252, 6.10.2000, p. 12.

CHAPTER III
OBLIGATIONS OF THE MEMBER STATES TOWARDS PERSONS ENJOYING
TEMPORARY PROTECTION

Article 8

1. The Member States shall adopt the necessary measures to provide persons enjoying temporary protection with residence permits for the entire duration of the protection. Documents or other equivalent evidence shall be issued for that purpose.

2. Whatever the period of validity of the residence permits referred to in paragraph 1, the treatment granted by the Member States to persons enjoying temporary protection may not be less favourable than that set out in Articles 9 to 16.

3. The Member States shall, if necessary, provide persons to be admitted to their territory for the purposes of temporary protection with every facility for obtaining the necessary visas, including transit visas. Formalities must be reduced to a minimum because of the urgency of the situation. Visas should be free of charge or their cost reduced to a minimum.

Article 9

The Member States shall provide persons enjoying temporary protection with a document, in a language likely to be understood by them, in which the provisions relating to temporary protection and which are relevant to them are clearly set out.

Article 10

To enable the effective application of the Council Decision referred to in Article 5, Member States shall register the personal data referred to in Annex II, point (a), with respect to the persons enjoying temporary protection on their territory.

Article 11

A Member State shall take back a person enjoying temporary protection on its territory, if the said person remains on, or, seeks to enter without authorisation onto, the territory of another Member State during the period covered by the Council Decision referred to in Article 5. Member States may, on the basis of a bilateral agreement, decide that this Article should not apply.

Article   12

The Member States shall authorise, for a period not exceeding that of temporary protection, persons enjoying temporary protection to engage in employed or self-employed activities, subject to rules applicable to the profession, as well as in activities such as educational opportunities for adults, vocational training and practical work-place experience. For reasons of labour market policies, Member States may give priority to EU citizens and citizens of States bound by the Agreement on the European Economic Area and also to legally resident third-country nationals who receive unemployment benefit. The general law in force in the Member States applicable to remuneration, access to social security systems relating to employed or self-employed activities and other conditions of employment shall apply.

Article   13

1. The Member States shall ensure that persons enjoying temporary protection have access to suitable accommodation or, if necessary, receive the means to obtain housing.

2. The Member States shall make provision for persons enjoying temporary protection to receive necessary assistance in terms of social welfare and means of subsistence, if they do not have sufficient resources, as well as for medical care. Without prejudice to paragraph 4, the assistance necessary for medical care shall include at least emergency care and essential treatment of illness.

3. Where persons enjoying temporary protection are engaged in employed or self-employed activities, account shall be taken, when fixing the proposed level of aid, of their ability to meet their own needs.

4. The Member States shall provide necessary medical or other assistance to persons enjoying temporary protection who have special needs, such as unaccompanied minors or persons who have undergone torture, rape or other serious forms of psychological, physical or sexual violence.

Article   14

1. The Member States shall grant to persons under 18 years of age enjoying temporary protection access to the education system under the same conditions as nationals of the host Member State The Member States may stipulate that such access must be confined to the state education system.

2. The Member States may allow adults enjoying temporary protection access to the general education system.

Article   15

1. For the purpose of this Article, in cases where families already existed in the country of origin and were separated due to circumstances surrounding the mass influx, the following persons shall be considered to be part of a family:

(a)   the spouse of the sponsor or his/her unmarried partner in a stable relationship, where the legislation or practice of the Member State concerned treats unmarried couples in a way comparable to married couples under its law relating to aliens; the minor unmarried children of the sponsor or of his/her spouse, without distinction as to whether they were born in or out of wedlock or adopted;

(b) other close relatives who lived together as part of the family unit at the time of the events leading to the mass influx, and who were wholly or mainly dependent on the sponsor at the time.

2. In cases where the separate family members enjoy temporary protection in different Member States, Member States shall reunite family members where they are satisfied that the family members fall under the description of paragraph 1(a), taking into account the wish of the said family members. Member States may reunite family members where they are satisfied that the family members fall under the description of paragraph 1(b), taking into account on a case by case basis the extreme hardship they would face if the reunification did not take place.

3. Where the sponsor enjoys temporary protection in one Member State and one or some family members are not yet in a Member State, the Member State where the sponsor enjoys temporary protection shall reunite family members, who are in need of protection, with the sponsor in the case of family members where it is satisfied that they fall under the description of paragraph 1(a). The Member State may reunite family members, who are in need of protection, with the sponsor in the case of family members where it is satisfied that they fall under the description of paragraph 1(b), taking into account on a case by case basis the extreme hardship which they would face if the reunification did not take place.

4. When applying this Article, the Member States shall taken into consideration the best interests of the child.

5. The Member States concerned shall decide, taking account of Articles 25 and 26, in which Member State the reunification shall take place.

6. Reunited family members shall be granted residence permits under temporary protection. Documents or other equivalent evidence shall be issued for that purpose. Transfers of family members onto the territory of another Member State for the purposes of reunification under paragraph 2, shall result in the withdrawal of the residence permits issued, and the termination of the obligations towards the persons concerned relating to temporary protection, in the Member State of departure.

7. The practical implementation of this Article may involve cooperation with the international organisations concerned.

8. A Member State shall, at the request of another Member State, provide information, as set out in Annex II, on a person receiving temporary protection which is needed to process a matter under this Article.

Article   16

1. The Member States shall as soon as possible take measures to ensure the necessary representation of unaccompanied minors enjoying temporary protection by legal guardianship, or, where necessary, representation by an organisation which is responsible for the care and well-being of minors, or by any other appropriate representation.

2. During the period of temporary protection Member States shall provide for unaccompanied minors to be placed:

(a) with adult relatives;
(b) with a foster-family;
(c) in reception centres with special provisions for minors, or in other accommodation suitable for minors;
(d) with the person who looked after the child when fleeing.

The Member States shall take the necessary steps to enable the placement. Agreement by the adult person or persons concerned shall be established by the Member States. The views of the child shall be taken into account in accordance with the age and maturity of the child.

2431

CHAPTER IV
ACCESS TO THE ASYLUM PROCEDURE IN THE CONTEXT OF TEMPORARY PROTECTION

Article   17

1. Persons enjoying temporary protection must be able to lodge an application for asylum at any time.

2. The examination of any asylum application not processed before the end of the period of temporary protection shall be completed after the end of that period.

Article   18

The criteria and mechanisms for deciding which Member State is responsible for considering an asylum application shall apply. In particular, the Member State responsible for examining an asylum application submitted by a person enjoying temporary protection pursuant to this Directive, shall be the Member State which has accepted his transfer onto its territory.

Article   19

1. The Member States may provide that temporary protection may not be enjoyed concurrently with the status of asylum seeker while applications are under consideration.

2. Where, after an asylum application has been examined, refugee status or, where applicable, other kind of protection is not granted to a person eligible for or enjoying temporary protection, the Member States shall, without prejudice to Article 28, provide for that person to enjoy or to continue to enjoy temporary protection for the remainder of the period of protection.

CHAPTER V
RETURN AND MEASURES AFTER TEMPORARY PROTECTION HAS ENDED

Article   20

When the temporary protection ends, the general laws on protection and on aliens in the Member States shall apply, without prejudice to Articles 21, 22 and 23.

Article   21

1. The Member States shall take the measures necessary to make possible the voluntary return of persons enjoying temporary protection or whose temporary protection has ended. The Member States shall ensure that the provisions governing voluntary return of persons enjoying temporary protection facilitate their return with respect for human dignity.

The Member State shall ensure that the decision of those persons to return is taken in full knowledge of the facts. The Member States may provide for exploratory visits.

2. For such time as the temporary protection has not ended, the Member States shall, on the basis of the circumstances prevailing in the country of origin, give favourable consideration to requests for return to the host Member State from persons who have enjoyed temporary protection and exercised their right to a voluntary return.

3. At the end of the temporary protection, the Member States may provide for the obligations laid down in CHAPTER III to be extended individually to persons who have been covered by temporary protection and are benefiting from a voluntary return programme. The extension shall have effect until the date of return.

Article 22

1. The Member States shall take the measures necessary to ensure that the enforced return of persons whose temporary protection has ended and who are not eligible for admission is conducted with due respect for human dignity.

2. In cases of enforced return, Member States shall consider any compelling humanitarian reasons which may make return impossible or unreasonable in specific cases.

Article 23

1. The Member States shall take the necessary measures concerning the conditions of residence of persons who have enjoyed temporary protection and who cannot, in view of their state of health, reasonably be expected to travel; where for example they would suffer serious negative effects if their treatment was interrupted. They shall not be expelled so long as that situation continues.

2. The Member States may allow families whose children are minors and attend school in a Member State to benefit from residence conditions allowing the children concerned to complete the current school period.

CHAPTER VI
SOLIDARITY

Article 24

The measures provided for in this Directive shall benefit from the European Refugee Fund set up by Decision 2000/596/EC, under the terms laid down in that Decision.

Article 25

1. The Member States shall receive persons who are eligible for temporary protection in a spirit of Community solidarity. They shall indicate – in figures or in general terms – their capacity to receive such persons. This information shall be set out in the Council Decision referred to in Article 5. After that Decision has been adopted, the Member States may indicate additional reception capacity by notifying the Council and the Commission. This information shall be passed on swiftly to UNHCR.

2. The Member States concerned, acting in cooperation with the competent international organisations, shall ensure that the eligible persons defined in the Council Decision referred to in Article 5, who have not yet arrived in the Community have expressed their will to be received onto their territory.

3. When the number of those who are eligible for temporary protection following a sudden and massive influx exceeds the reception capacity referred to in paragraph 1, the Council shall, as a matter of urgency, examine the situation and take appropriate action, including recommending additional support for Member States affected.

Article 26

1. For the duration of the temporary protection, the Member States shall cooperate with each other with regard to transferral of the residence of persons enjoying temporary protection from one Member State to another, subject to the consent of the persons concerned to such transferral.

2. A Member State shall communicate requests for transfers to the other Member States and notify the Commission and UNHCR. The Member States shall inform the requesting Member State of their capacity for receiving transferees.

3.   A Member State shall, at the request of another Member State, provide information, as set out in Annex II, on a person enjoying temporary protection which is needed to process a matter under this Article.

4.   Where a transfer is made from one Member State to another, the residence permit in the Member State of departure shall expire and the obligations towards the persons concerned relating to temporary protection in the Member State of departure shall come to an end. The new host Member State shall grant temporary protection to the persons concerned.

5.   The Member States shall use the model pass set out in Annex I for transfers between Member States of persons enjoying temporary protection.

CHAPTER VII
ADMINISTRATIVE COOPERATION

Article   27

1.   For the purposes of the administrative cooperation required to implement temporary protection, the Member States shall each appoint a national contact point, whose address they shall communicate to each other and to the Commission. The Member States shall, in liaison with the Commission, take all the appropriate measures to establish direct cooperation and an exchange of information between the competent authorities.

2.   The Member States shall, regularly and as quickly as possible, communicate data concerning the number of persons enjoying temporary protection and full information on the national laws, regulations and administrative provisions relating to the implementation of temporary protection.

CHAPTER VIII
SPECIAL PROVISIONS

Article   28

1.   The Member States may exclude a person from temporary protection if:

  (a)   there are serious reasons for considering that:
    (i)   he or she has committed a crime against peace, a war crime, or a crime against humanity, as defined in the international instruments drawn up to make provision in respect of such crimes;
    (ii)   he or she has committed a serious non-political crime outside the Member State of reception prior to his or her admission to that Member State as a person enjoying temporary protection. The severity of the expected persecution is to be weighed against the nature of the criminal offence of which the person concerned is suspected. Particularly cruel actions, even if committed with an allegedly political objective, may be classified as serious non-political crimes. This applies both to the participants in the crime and to its instigators;
    (iii)   he or she has been guilty of acts contrary to the purposes and principles of the United Nations;
  (b)   there are reasonable grounds for regarding him or her as a danger to the security of the host Member State or, having been convicted by a final judgment of a particularly serious crime, he or she is a danger to the community of the host Member State.

2.   The grounds for exclusion referred to in paragraph 1 shall be based solely on the personal conduct of the person concerned. Exclusion decisions or measures shall be based on the principle of proportionality.

CHAPTER IX
FINAL PROVISIONS

Article 29

Persons who have been excluded from the benefit of temporary protection or family reunification by a Member State shall be entitled to mount a legal challenge in the Member State concerned.

Article 30

The Member States shall lay down the rules on penalties applicable to infringements of the national provisions adopted pursuant to this Directive and shall take all measures necessary to ensure that they are implemented. The penalties provided for must be effective, proportionate and dissuasive.

Article 31

1. Not later than two years after the date specified in Article 32, the Commission shall report to the European Parliament and the Council on the application of this Directive in the Member States and shall propose any amendments that are necessary. The Member States shall send the Commission all the information that is appropriate for drawing up this report.

2. After presenting the report referred to at paragraph 1, the Commission shall report to the European Parliament and the Council on the application of this Directive in the Member States at least every five years.

Article 32

1. The Member States shall bring into force the laws, regulations and administrative provisions necessary to comply with this Directive by 31 December 2002 at the latest. They shall forthwith inform the Commission thereof.

2. When the Member States adopt these measures, they shall contain a reference to this Directive or shall be accompanied by such reference on the occasion of their official publication. The methods of making such a reference shall be laid down by the Member States.

Article 33

This Directive shall enter into force on the day of its publication in the Official Journal of the European Communities.

Article 34

This Directive is addressed to the Member States in accordance with the Treaty establishing the European Community.

Done at Brussels, 20 July 2001.

ANNEX I

MODEL PASS FOR THE TRANSFER OF PERSONS ENJOYING TEMPORARY PROTECTION

[The full text of this form is currently unavailable – please refer to the original document]

ANNEX II

The information referred to in Articles 10, 15 and 26 of the Directive includes to the extent necessary one or more of the following documents or data:

(a) personal data on the person concerned (name, nationality, date and place of birth, marital status, family relationship);

(b) identity documents and travel documents of the person concerned;

(c) documents concerning evidence of family ties (marriage certificate, birth certificate, certificate of adoption);

(d) other information essential to establish the person's identity or family relationship;

(e) residence permits, visas or residence permit refusal decisions issued to the person concerned by the Member State, and documents forming the basis of decisions;

(f) residence permit and visa applications lodged by the person concerned and pending in the Member State, and the stage reached in the processing of these.

The providing Member State shall notify any corrected information to the requesting Member State.

COUNCIL DIRECTIVE (2003/9/EC) of 27 January 2003
laying down minimum standards for the reception of asylum seekers

OJ L 31, 6 February 2003, p.18

THE COUNCIL OF THE EUROPEAN UNION,

Having regard to the Treaty establishing the European Community, and in particular point (1)(b) of the first subparagraph of Article 63 thereof,

Having regard to the proposal from the Commission[1],

Having regard to the opinion of the European Parliament[2],

Having regard to the opinion of the Economic and Social Committee[3],

Having regard to the opinion of the Committee of the Regions[4]),

Whereas:

(1) A common policy on asylum, including a Common European Asylum System, is a constituent part of the European Union's objective of progressively establishing an area of freedom, security and justice open to those who, forced by circumstances, legitimately seek protection in the Community.

(2) At its special meeting in Tampere on 15 and 16 October 1999, the European Council agreed to work towards establishing a Common European Asylum System, based on the full and inclusive application of the Geneva Convention relating to the Status of Refugees of 28 July 1951, as supplemented by the New York Protocol of 31 January 1967, thus maintaining the principle of non-refoulement.

(3) The Tampere Conclusions provide that a Common European Asylum System should include, in the short term, common minimum conditions of reception of asylum seekers.

(4) The establishment of minimum standards for the reception of asylum seekers is a further step towards a European asylum policy.

(5) This Directive respects the fundamental rights and observes the principles recognised in particular by the Charter of Fundamental Rights of the

European Union. In particular, this Directive seeks to ensure full respect for human dignity and to promote the application of Articles 1 and 18 of the said Charter.

(6) With respect to the treatment of persons falling within the scope of this Directive, Member States are bound by obligations under instruments of international law to which they are party and which prohibit discrimination.

(7) Minimum standards for the reception of asylum seekers that will normally suffice to ensure them a dignified standard of living and comparable living conditions in all Member States should be laid down.

(8) The harmonisation of conditions for the reception of asylum seekers should help to limit the secondary movements of asylum seekers influenced by the variety of conditions for their reception.

(9) Reception of groups with special needs should be specifically designed to meet those needs.

(10) Reception of applicants who are in detention should be specifically designed to meet their needs in that situation.

(11) In order to ensure compliance with the minimum procedural guarantees consisting in the opportunity to contact organisations or groups of persons that provide legal assistance, information should be provided on such organisations and groups of persons.

(12) The possibility of abuse of the reception system should be restricted by laying down cases for the reduction or withdrawal of reception conditions for asylum seekers.

(13) The efficiency of national reception systems and cooperation among Member States in the field of reception of asylum seekers should be secured.

(14) Appropriate coordination should be encouraged between the competent authorities as regards the reception of asylum seekers, and harmonious relationships between local communities and accommodation centres should therefore be promoted.

(15) It is in the very nature of minimum standards that Member States have the power to introduce or maintain more favourable provisions for third-country nationals and stateless persons who ask for international protection from a Member State.

(16) In this spirit, Member States are also invited to apply the provisions of this Directive in connection with procedures for deciding on applications for forms of protection other than that emanating from the Geneva Convention for third country nationals and stateless persons.

(17) The implementation of this Directive should be evaluated at regular intervals.

(18) Since the objectives of the proposed action, namely to establish minimum standards on the reception of asylum seekers in Member States, cannot be sufficiently achieved by the Member States and can therefore, by reason of the scale and effects of the proposed action, be better achieved by the Community, the Community may adopt measures in accordance with the principles of subsidiarity as set out in Article 5 of the Treaty. In accordance with the principle of proportionality, as set out in that Article, this Directive does not go beyond what is necessary in order to achieve those objectives.

(19) In accordance with Article 3 of the Protocol on the position of the United Kingdom and Ireland, annexed to the Treaty on European Union and to the Treaty establishing the European Community, the United Kingdom gave notice, by letter of 18 August 2001, of its wish to take part in the adoption and application of this Directive.

(20) In accordance with Article 1 of the said Protocol, Ireland is not participating in the adoption of this Directive. Consequently, and without prejudice to Article 4 of the aforementioned Protocol, the provisions of this Directive do not apply to Ireland.

(21) In accordance with Articles 1 and 2 of the Protocol on the position of Denmark, annexed to the Treaty on European Union and to the Treaty establishing the European Community, Denmark is not participating in the adoption of this Directive and is therefore neither bound by it nor subject to its application,

¹ OJ C 213 E, 31.7.2001, p. 286.
² Opinion delivered on 25 April 2002 (not yet published in the Official Journal).
³ OJ C 48, 21.2.2002, p. 63.
⁴ OJ C 107, 3.5.2002, p. 85.

Has adopted this Directive:

CHAPTER I
PURPOSE, DEFINITIONS AND SCOPE

Article   1   Purpose

The purpose of this Directive is to lay down minimum standards for the reception of asylum seekers in Member States.

Article   2   Definitions

For the purposes of this Directive:

(a) 'Geneva Convention' shall mean the Convention of 28 July 1951 relating to the status of refugees, as amended by the New York Protocol of 31 January 1967;

(b) 'application for asylum' shall mean the application made by a third-country national or a stateless person which can be understood as a request for international protection from a Member State, under the Geneva Convention. Any application for international protection is presumed to be an application for asylum unless a third-country national or a stateless person explicitly requests another kind of protection that can be applied for separately;

(c) 'applicant' or 'asylum seeker' shall mean a third country national or a stateless person who has made an application for asylum in respect of which a final decision has not yet been taken;

(d) 'family members' shall mean, in so far as the family already existed in the country of origin, the following members of the applicant's family who are present in the same Member State in relation to the application for asylum:

   (i) the spouse of the asylum seeker or his or her unmarried partner in a stable relationship, where the legislation or practice of the Member State concerned treats unmarried couples in a way comparable to married couples under its law relating to aliens;

   (ii) the minor children of the couple referred to in point (i) or of the applicant, on condition that they are unmarried and dependent and regardless of whether they were born in or out of wedlock or adopted as defined under the national law;

(e) 'refugee' shall mean a person who fulfils the requirements of Article 1(A) of the Geneva Convention;

(f) 'refugee status' shall mean the status granted by a Member State to a person who is a refugee and is admitted as such to the territory of that Member State;

(g) 'procedures' and 'appeals', shall mean the procedures and appeals established by Member States in their national law;

(h) 'unaccompanied minors' shall mean persons below the age of eighteen who arrive in the territory of the Member States unaccompanied by an adult responsible for them whether by law or by custom, and for as long as they are not effectively taken into the care of such a person; it shall include minors who are left unaccompanied after they have entered the territory of Member States;

(i) 'reception conditions' shall mean the full set of measures that Member States grant to asylum seekers in accordance with this Directive;

(j) 'material reception conditions' shall mean the reception conditions that include housing, food and clothing, provided in kind, or as financial allowances or in vouchers, and a daily expenses allowance;

(k) 'detention' shall mean confinement of an asylum seeker by a Member State within a particular place, where the applicant is deprived of his or her freedom of movement;

(l) 'accommodation centre' shall mean any place used for collective housing of asylum seekers.

Article 3 Scope

1. This Directive shall apply to all third country nationals and stateless persons who make an application for asylum at the border or in the territory of a Member State as long as they are allowed to remain on the territory as asylum seekers, as well as to family members, if they are covered by such application for asylum according to the national law.

2. This Directive shall not apply in cases of requests for diplomatic or territorial asylum submitted to representations of Member States.

3. This Directive shall not apply when the provisions of Council Directive 2001/55/EC of 20 July 2001 on minimum standards for giving temporary protection in the event of a mass influx of displaced persons and on measures promoting a balance of efforts between Member States in receiving such persons and bearing the consequences thereof[5] are applied.

4. Member States may decide to apply this Directive in connection with procedures for deciding on applications for kinds of protection other than that emanating from the Geneva Convention for third-country nationals or stateless persons who are found not to be refugees.

[5] OJ L 212, 7.8.2001, p. 12.

Article 4 More favourable provisions

Member States may introduce or retain more favourable provisions in the field of reception conditions for asylum seekers and other close relatives of the applicant who are present in the same Member State when they are dependent on him or for humanitarian reasons insofar as these provisions are compatible with this Directive.

CHAPTER II
GENERAL PROVISIONS ON RECEPTION CONDITIONS

Article 5 Information

1. Member States shall inform asylum seekers, within a reasonable time not exceeding fifteen days after they have lodged their application for asylum with the competent authority, of at least any established benefits and of the obligations with which they must comply relating to reception conditions.

Member States shall ensure that applicants are provided with information on organisations or groups of persons that provide specific legal assistance and organisations that might be able to help or inform them concerning the available reception conditions, including health care.

2. Member States shall ensure that the information referred to in paragraph 1 is in writing and, as far as possible, in a language that the applicants may reasonably be supposed to understand. Where appropriate, this information may also be supplied orally.

Article   6   Documentation

1. Member States shall ensure that, within three days after an application is lodged with the competent authority, the applicant is provided with a document issued in his or her own name certifying his or her status as an asylum seeker or testifying that he or she is allowed to stay in the territory of the Member State while his or her application is pending or being examined.

If the holder is not free to move within all or a part of the territory of the Member State, the document shall also certify this fact.

2. Member States may exclude application of this Article when the asylum seeker is in detention and during the examination of an application for asylum made at the border or within the context of a procedure to decide on the right of the applicant legally to enter the territory of a Member State. In specific cases, during the examination of an application for asylum, Member States may provide applicants with other evidence equivalent to the document referred to in paragraph 1.

3. The document referred to in paragraph 1 need not certify the identity of the asylum seeker.

4. Member States shall adopt the necessary measures to provide asylum seekers with the document referred to in paragraph 1, which must be valid for as long as they are authorised to remain in the territory of the Member State concerned or at the border thereof.

5. Member States may provide asylum seekers with a travel document when serious humanitarian reasons arise that require their presence in another State.

Article   7   Residence and freedom of movement

1. Asylum seekers may move freely within the territory of the host Member State or within an area assigned to them by that Member State. The assigned area shall not affect the unalienable sphere of private life and shall allow sufficient scope for guaranteeing access to all benefits under this Directive.

2. Member States may decide on the residence of the asylum seeker for reasons of public interest, public order or, when necessary, for the swift processing and effective monitoring of his or her application.

3. When it proves necessary, for example for legal reasons or reasons of public order, Member States may confine an applicant to a particular place in accordance with their national law.

4. Member States may make provision of the material reception conditions subject to actual residence by the applicants in a specific place, to be determined by the Member States. Such a decision, which may be of a general nature, shall be taken individually and established by national legislation.

5. Member States shall provide for the possibility of granting applicants temporary permission to leave the place of residence mentioned in paragraphs 2 and 4 and/or the assigned area mentioned in paragraph 1. Decisions shall be taken individually, objectively and impartially and reasons shall be given if they are negative.

The applicant shall not require permission to keep appointments with authorities and courts if his or her appearance is necessary.

6.   Member States shall require applicants to inform the competent authorities of their current address and notify any change of address to such authorities as soon as possible.

Article   8   Families

Member States shall take appropriate measures to maintain as far as possible family unity as present within their territory, if applicants are provided with housing by the Member State concerned. Such measures shall be implemented with the asylum seeker's agreement.

Article   9   Medical screening

Member States may require medical screening for applicants on public health grounds.

Article   10   Schooling and education of minors

1.   Member States shall grant to minor children of asylum seekers and to asylum seekers who are minors access to the education system under similar conditions as nationals of the host Member State for so long as an expulsion measure against them or their parents is not actually enforced. Such education may be provided in accommodation centres.

The Member State concerned may stipulate that such access must be confined to the State education system.

Minors shall be younger than the age of legal majority in the Member State in which the application for asylum was lodged or is being examined. Member States shall not withdraw secondary education for the sole reason that the minor has reached the age of majority.

2.   Access to the education system shall not be postponed for more than three months from the date the application for asylum was lodged by the minor or the minor's parents. This period may be extended to one year where specific education is provided in order to facilitate access to the education system.

3.   Where access to the education system as set out in paragraph 1 is not possible due to the specific situation of the minor, the Member State may offer other education arrangements.

Article   11   Employment

1.   Member States shall determine a period of time, starting from the date on which an application for asylum was lodged, during which an applicant shall not have access to the labour market.

2.   If a decision at first instance has not been taken within one year of the presentation of an application for asylum and this delay cannot be attributed to the applicant, Member States shall decide the conditions for granting access to the labour market for the applicant.

3.   Access to the labour market shall not be withdrawn during appeals procedures, where an appeal against a negative decision in a regular procedure has suspensive effect, until such time as a negative decision on the appeal is notified.

4.   For reasons of labour market policies, Member States may give priority to EU citizens and nationals of States parties to the Agreement on the European Economic Area and also to legally resident third-country nationals.

Article 12 Vocational training

Member States may allow asylum seekers access to vocational training irrespective of whether they have access to the labour market.

Access to vocational training relating to an employment contract shall depend on the extent to which the applicant has access to the labour market in accordance with Article 11.

Article 13 General rules on material reception conditions and health care

1. Member States shall ensure that material reception conditions are available to applicants when they make their application for asylum.

2. Member States shall make provisions on material reception conditions to ensure a standard of living adequate for the health of applicants and capable of ensuring their subsistence.

Member States shall ensure that that standard of living is met in the specific situation of persons who have special needs, in accordance with Article 17, as well as in relation to the situation of persons who are in detention.

3. Member States may make the provision of all or some of the material reception conditions and health care subject to the condition that applicants do not have sufficient means to have a standard of living adequate for their health and to enable their subsistence.

4. Member States may require applicants to cover or contribute to the cost of the material reception conditions and of the health care provided for in this Directive, pursuant to the provision of paragraph 3, if the applicants have sufficient resources, for example if they have been working for a reasonable period of time.

If it transpires that an applicant had sufficient means to cover material reception conditions and health care at the time when these basic needs were being covered, Member States may ask the asylum seeker for a refund.

5. Material reception conditions may be provided in kind, or in the form of financial allowances or vouchers or in a combination of these provisions.

Where Member States provide material reception conditions in the form of financial allowances or vouchers, the amount thereof shall be determined in accordance with the principles set out in this Article.

Article 14 Modalities for material reception conditions

1. Where housing is provided in kind, it should take one or a combination of the following forms:

   (a) premises used for the purpose of housing applicants during the examination of an application for asylum lodged at the border;
   (b) accommodation centres which guarantee an adequate standard of living;
   (c) private houses, flats, hotels or other premises adapted for housing applicants.

2. Member States shall ensure that applicants provided with the housing referred to in paragraph 1(a), (b) and (c) are assured:

   (a) protection of their family life;
   (b) the possibility of communicating with relatives, legal advisers and representatives of the United Nations High Commissioner for Refugees (UNHCR) and non-governmental organisations (NGOs) recognised by Member States.

Member States shall pay particular attention to the prevention of assault within the premises and accommodation centres referred to in paragraph 1(a) and (b).

3.   Member States shall ensure, if appropriate, that minor children of applicants or applicants who are minors are lodged with their parents or with the adult family member responsible for them whether by law or by custom.

4.   Member States shall ensure that transfers of applicants from one housing facility to another take place only when necessary. Member States shall provide for the possibility for applicants to inform their legal advisers of the transfer and of their new address.

5.   Persons working in accommodation centres shall be adequately trained and shall be bound by the confidentiality principle as defined in the national law in relation to any information they obtain in the course of their work.

6.   Member States may involve applicants in managing the material resources and non-material aspects of life in the centre through an advisory board or council representing residents.

7.   Legal advisors or counsellors of asylum seekers and representatives of the United Nations High Commissioner for Refugees or non-governmental organisations designated by the latter and recognised by the Member State concerned shall be granted access to accommodation centres and other housing facilities in order to assist the said asylum seekers. Limits on such access may be imposed only on grounds relating to the security of the centres and facilities and of the asylum seekers.

8.   Member States may exceptionally set modalities for material reception conditions different from those provided for in this Article, for a reasonable period which shall be as short as possible, when:

   –   an initial assessment of the specific needs of the applicant is required,
   –   material reception conditions, as provided for in this Article, are not available in a certain geographical area,
   –   housing capacities normally available are temporarily exhausted,
   –   the asylum seeker is in detention or confined to border posts.

These different conditions shall cover in any case basic needs.

Article   15   Health care

1.   Member States shall ensure that applicants receive the necessary health care which shall include, at least, emergency care and essential treatment of illness.

2.   Member States shall provide necessary medical or other assistance to applicants who have special needs.

CHAPTER III
REDUCTION OR WITHDRAWAL OF RECEPTION CONDITIONS

Article   16   Reduction or withdrawal of reception conditions

1.   Member States may reduce or withdraw reception conditions in the following cases:

   (a)   where an asylum seeker:
       –   abandons the place of residence determined by the competent authority without informing it or, if requested, without permission, or
       –   does not comply with reporting duties or with requests to provide information or to appear for personal interviews concerning the asylum procedure during a reasonable period laid down in national law, or
       –   has already lodged an application in the same Member State.
       When the applicant is traced or voluntarily reports to the competent authority, a duly motivated decision, based on the reasons for the disappearance, shall be taken on the reinstallation of the grant of some or all of the reception conditions;

(b)   where an applicant has concealed financial resources and has therefore unduly benefited from material reception conditions.

If it transpires that an applicant had sufficient means to cover material reception conditions and health care at the time when these basic needs were being covered, Member States may ask the asylum seeker for a refund.

2.   Member States may refuse conditions in cases where an asylum seeker has failed to demonstrate that the asylum claim was made as soon as reasonably practicable after arrival in that Member State.

3.   Member States may determine sanctions applicable to serious breaching of the rules of the accommodation centres as well as to seriously violent behaviour.

4.   Decisions for reduction, withdrawal or refusal of reception conditions or sanctions referred to in paragraphs 1, 2 and 3 shall be taken individually, objectively and impartially and reasons shall be given. Decisions shall be based on the particular situation of the person concerned, especially with regard to persons covered by Article 17, taking into account the principle of proportionality. Member States shall under all circumstances ensure access to emergency health care.

5.   Member States shall ensure that material reception conditions are not withdrawn or reduced before a negative decision is taken.

CHAPTER IV
PROVISIONS FOR PERSONS WITH SPECIAL NEEDS

Article   17   General principle

1.   Member States shall take into account the specific situation of vulnerable persons such as minors, unaccompanied minors, disabled people, elderly people, pregnant women, single parents with minor children and persons who have been subjected to torture, rape or other serious forms of psychological, physical or sexual violence, in the national legislation implementing the provisions of Chapter II relating to material reception conditions and health care.

2.   Paragraph 1 shall apply only to persons found to have special needs after an individual evaluation of their situation.

Article   18   Minors

1.   The best interests of the child shall be a primary consideration for Member States when implementing the provisions of this Directive that involve minors.

2.   Member States shall ensure access to rehabilitation services for minors who have been victims of any form of abuse, neglect, exploitation, torture or cruel, inhuman and degrading treatment, or who have suffered from armed conflicts, and ensure that appropriate mental health care is developed and qualified counselling is provided when needed.

Article   19   Unaccompanied minors

1.   Member States shall as soon as possible take measures to ensure the necessary representation of unaccompanied minors by legal guardianship or, where necessary, representation by an organisation which is responsible for the care and well-being of minors, or by any other appropriate representation. Regular assessments shall be made by the appropriate authorities.

2.   Unaccompanied minors who make an application for asylum shall, from the moment they are admitted to the territory to the moment they are obliged to leave the host Member State in which the application for asylum was made or is being examined, be placed:

(a) with adult relatives;
(b) with a foster-family;
(c) in accommodation centres with special provisions for minors;
(d) in other accommodation suitable for minors.

Member States may place unaccompanied minors aged 16 or over in accommodation centres for adult asylum seekers.

As far as possible, siblings shall be kept together, taking into account the best interests of the minor concerned and, in particular, his or her age and degree of maturity. Changes of residence of unaccompanied minors shall be limited to a minimum.

3. Member States, protecting the unaccompanied minor's best interests, shall endeavour to trace the members of his or her family as soon as possible. In cases where there may be a threat to the life or integrity of the minor or his or her close relatives, particularly if they have remained in the country of origin, care must be taken to ensure that the collection, processing and circulation of information concerning those persons is undertaken on a confidential basis, so as to avoid jeopardising their safety.

4. Those working with unaccompanied minors shall have had or receive appropriate training concerning their needs, and shall be bound by the confidentiality principle as defined in the national law, in relation to any information they obtain in the course of their work.

Article   20   Victims of torture and violence

Member States shall ensure that, if necessary, persons who have been subjected to torture, rape or other serious acts of violence receive the necessary treatment of damages caused by the aforementioned acts.

CHAPTER V
APPEALS

Article   21   Appeals

1. Member States shall ensure that negative decisions relating to the granting of benefits under this Directive or decisions taken under Article 7 which individually affect asylum seekers may be the subject of an appeal within the procedures laid down in the national law. At least in the last instance the possibility of an appeal or a review before a judicial body shall be granted.

2. Procedures for access to legal assistance in such cases shall be laid down in national law.

CHAPTER VI
ACTIONS TO IMPROVE THE EFFICIENCY OF THE RECEPTION SYSTEM

Article   22   Cooperation

Member States shall regularly inform the Commission on the data concerning the number of persons, broken down by sex and age, covered by reception conditions and provide full information on the type, name and format of the documents provided for by Article 6.

Article   23   Guidance, monitoring and control system

Member States shall, with due respect to their constitutional structure, ensure that appropriate guidance, monitoring and control of the level of reception conditions are established.

Article   24   Staff and resources

1. Member States shall take appropriate measures to ensure that authorities and other organisations implementing this Directive have received the necessary basic training with respect to the needs of both male and female applicants.

2. Member States shall allocate the necessary resources in connection with the national provisions enacted to implement this Directive.

CHAPTER VII
FINAL PROVISIONS

Article   25   Reports

By 6 August 2006, the Commission shall report to the European Parliament and the Council on the application of this Directive and shall propose any amendments that are necessary.

Member States shall send the Commission all the information that is appropriate for drawing up the report, including the statistical data provided for by Article 22 by 6 February 2006.

After presenting the report, the Commission shall report to the European Parliament and the Council on the application of this Directive at least every five years.

Article   26   Transposition

1. Member States shall bring into force the laws, regulations and administrative provisions necessary to comply with this Directive by 6 February 2005. They shall forthwith inform the Commission thereof.

When the Member States adopt these measures, they shall contain a reference to this Directive or shall be accompanied by such a reference on the occasion of their official publication. Member States shall determine how such a reference is to be made.

2. Member States shall communicate to the Commission the text of the provisions of national law which they adopt in the field relating to the enforcement of this Directive.

Article   27   Entry into force

This Directive shall enter into force on the day of its publication in the Official Journal of the European Union.

Article   28   Addressees

This Directive is addressed to the Member States in accordance with the Treaty establishing the European Union.

Done at Brussels, 27 January 2003.

COUNCIL REGULATION (EC) NO 343/2003 of

18 February 2003 establishing the criteria and mechanisms for determining the Member State responsible for examining an asylum application lodged in one of the Member States by a third-country national

OJ L 50, 25 February 2003, p.1

THE COUNCIL OF THE EUROPEAN UNION,

Having regard to the Treaty establishing the European Community, and in particular Article 63, first paragraph, point (1)(a),

Having regard to the proposal from the Commission[1],

Having regard to the opinion of the European Parliament[2],

Having regard to the opinion of the European Economic and Social Committee[3],

Whereas:

(1) A common policy on asylum, including a Common European Asylum System, is a constituent part of the European Union's objective of progressively establishing an area of freedom, security and justice open to those who, forced by circumstances, legitimately seek protection in the Community.

(2) The European Council, at its special meeting in Tampere on 15 and 16 October 1999, agreed to work towards establishing a Common European Asylum System, based on the full and inclusive application of the Geneva Convention relating to the Status of Refugees of 28 July 1951, as supplemented by the New York Protocol of 31 January 1967, thus ensuring that nobody is sent back to persecution, i.e. maintaining the principle of non-refoulement. In this respect, and without affecting the responsibility criteria laid down in this Regulation, Member States, all respecting the principle of non-refoulement, are considered as safe countries for third-country nationals.

(3) The Tampere conclusions also stated that this system should include, in the short term, a clear and workable method for determining the Member State responsible for the examination of an asylum application.

(4) Such a method should be based on objective, fair criteria both for the Member States and for the persons concerned. It should, in particular, make it possible to determine rapidly the Member State responsible, so as to guarantee effective access to the procedures for determining refugee status and not to compromise the objective of the rapid processing of asylum applications.

(5) As regards the introduction in successive phases of a common European asylum system that should lead, in the longer term, to a common procedure and a uniform status, valid throughout the Union, for those granted asylum, it is appropriate at this stage, while making the necessary improvements in the light of experience, to confirm the principles underlying the Convention determining the State responsible for examining applications for asylum lodged in one of the Member States of the European Communities[4], signed in Dublin on 15 June 1990 (hereinafter referred to as the Dublin Convention), whose implementation has stimulated the process of harmonising asylum policies.

(6) Family unity should be preserved in so far as this is compatible with the other objectives pursued by establishing criteria and mechanisms for determining the Member State responsible for examining an asylum application.

(7) The processing together of the asylum applications of the members of one family by a single Member State makes it possible to ensure that the applications are examined thoroughly and the decisions taken in respect of them are consistent. Member States should be able to derogate from the

2447

      responsibility criteria, so as to make it possible to bring family members together where this is necessary on humanitarian grounds.

(8) The progressive creation of an area without internal frontiers in which free movement of persons is guaranteed in accordance with the Treaty establishing the European Community and the establishment of Community policies regarding the conditions of entry and stay of third country nationals, including common efforts towards the management of external borders, makes it necessary to strike a balance between responsibility criteria in a spirit of solidarity.

(9) The application of this Regulation can be facilitated, and its effectiveness increased, by bilateral arrangements between Member States for improving communications between competent departments, reducing time limits for procedures or simplifying the processing of requests to take charge or take back, or establishing procedures for the performance of transfers.

(10) Continuity between the system for determining the Member State responsible established by the Dublin Convention and the system established by this Regulation should be ensured. Similarly, consistency should be ensured between this Regulation and Council Regulation (EC) No 2725/2000 of 11 December 2000 concerning the establishment of 'Eurodac' for the comparison of fingerprints for the effective application of the Dublin Convention[5].

(11) The operation of the Eurodac system, as established by Regulation (EC) No 2725/2000 and in particular the implementation of Articles 4 and 8 contained therein should facilitate the implementation of this Regulation.

(12) With respect to the treatment of persons falling within the scope of this Regulation, Member States are bound by obligations under instruments of international law to which they are party.

(13) The measures necessary for the implementation of this Regulation should be adopted in accordance with Council Decision 1999/468/EC of 28 June 1999 laying down the procedures for the exercise of implementing powers conferred on the Commission[6].

(14) The application of the Regulation should be evaluated at regular intervals.

(15) The Regulation observes the fundamental rights and principles which are acknowledged in particular in the Charter of Fundamental Rights of the European Union[7]. In particular, it seeks to ensure full observance of the right to asylum guaranteed by Article 18.

(16) Since the objective of the proposed measure, namely the establishment of criteria and mechanisms for determining the Member State responsible for examining an asylum application lodged in one of the Member States by a third-country national, cannot be sufficiently achieved by the Member States and, given the scale and effects, can therefore be better achieved at Community level, the Community may adopt measures in accordance with the principle of subsidiarity as set out in Article 5 of the Treaty. In accordance with the principle of proportionality, as set out in that Article, this Regulation does not go beyond what is necessary in order to achieve that objective.

(17) In accordance with Article 3 of the Protocol on the position of the United Kingdom and Ireland, annexed to the Treaty on European Union and to the Treaty establishing the European Community, the United Kingdom and Ireland gave notice, by letters of 30 October 2001, of their wish to take part in the adoption and application of this Regulation.

(18) In accordance with Articles 1 and 2 of the Protocol on the position of Denmark, annexed to the Treaty on European Union and to the Treaty establishing the European Community, Denmark does not take part in the adoption of this Regulation and is not bound by it nor subject to its application.

(19) The Dublin Convention remains in force and continues to apply between Denmark and the Member States that are bound by this Regulation until such time an agreement allowing Denmark's participation in the Regulation has been concluded,

1   OJ C 304 E, 30.10.2001, p. 192.
2   Opinion of 9 April 2002.
3   OJ C 125, 27.5.2002, p. 28.
4   OJ C 254, 19.8.1997, p. 1.
5   OJ L 316, 15.12.2000, p. 1.
6   OJ L 184, 17.7.1999, p. 23.
7   OJ C 364, 18.12.2000, p. 1.
8   OJ L 281, 23.11.1995, p. 31.

Has adopted this Regulation:

CHAPTER I
SUBJECT-MATTER AND DEFINITIONS

Article   1

This Regulation lays down the criteria and mechanisms for determining the Member State responsible for examining an application for asylum lodged in one of the Member States by a third-country national.

Article   2

For the purposes of this Regulation:

(a) 'third-country national' means anyone who is not a citizen of the Union within the meaning of Article 17(1) of the Treaty establishing the European Community;

(b) 'Geneva Convention' means the Convention of 28 July 1951 relating to the status of refugees, as amended by the New York Protocol of 31 January 1967;

(c) 'application for asylum' means the application made by a third-country national which can be understood as a request for international protection from a Member State, under the Geneva Convention. Any application for international protection is presumed to be an application for asylum, unless a third-country national explicitly requests another kind of protection that can be applied for separately;

(d) 'applicant' or 'asylum seeker' means a third country national who has made an application for asylum in respect of which a final decision has not yet been taken;

(e) 'examination of an asylum application' means any examination of, or decision or ruling concerning, an application for asylum by the competent authorities in accordance with national law except for procedures for determining the Member State responsible in accordance with this Regulation;

(f) 'withdrawal of the asylum application' means the actions by which the applicant for asylum terminates the procedures initiated by the submission of his application for asylum, in accordance with national law, either explicitly or tacitly;

(g) 'refugee' means any third-country national qualifying for the status defined by the Geneva Convention and authorised to reside as such on the territory of a Member State;

(h) 'unaccompanied minor' means unmarried persons below the age of eighteen who arrive in the territory of the Member States unaccompanied by an adult responsible for them whether by law or by custom, and for as long as they are not effectively taken into the care of such a person; it includes minors who are left unaccompanied after they have entered the territory of the Member States;

(i) 'family members' means insofar as the family already existed in the country of origin, the following members of the applicant's family who are present in the territory of the Member States:

   (i) the spouse of the asylum seeker or his or her unmarried partner in a stable relationship, where the legislation or practice of the Member State concerned treats unmarried couples in a way comparable to married couples under its law relating to aliens;

   (ii) the minor children of couples referred to in point (i) or of the applicant, on condition that they are unmarried and dependent and regardless of whether they were born in or out of wedlock or adopted as defined under the national law;

   (iii) the father, mother or guardian when the applicant or refugee is a minor and unmarried;

(j) 'residence document' means any authorisation issued by the authorities of a Member State authorising a third-country national to stay in its territory, including the documents substantiating the authorisation to remain in the territory under temporary protection arrangements or until the circumstances preventing a removal order from being carried out no longer apply, with the exception of visas and residence authorisations issued during the period required to determine the responsible Member State as established in this Regulation or during examination of an application for asylum or an application for a residence permit;

(k) 'visa' means the authorisation or decision of a Member State required for transit or entry for an intended stay in that Member State or in several Member States. The nature of the visa shall be determined in accordance with the following definitions:

   (i) 'long-stay visa' means the authorisation or decision of a Member State required for entry for an intended stay in that Member State of more than three months;

   (ii) 'short-stay visa' means the authorisation or decision of a Member State required for entry for an intended stay in that State or in several Member States for a period whose total duration does not exceed three months;

   (iii) 'transit visa' means the authorisation or decision of a Member State for entry for transit through the territory of that Member State or several Member States, except for transit at an airport;

   (iv) 'airport transit visa' means the authorisation or decision allowing a third-country national specifically subject to this requirement to pass through the transit zone of an airport, without gaining access to the national territory of the Member State concerned, during a stopover or a transfer between two sections of an international flight.

CHAPTER II
GENERAL PRINCIPLES

Article 3

1. Member States shall examine the application of any third-country national who applies at the border or in their territory to any one of them for asylum. The application shall be examined by a single Member State, which shall be the one which the criteria set out in Chapter III indicate is responsible.

2. By way of derogation from paragraph 1, each Member State may examine an application for asylum lodged with it by a third-country national, even if such examination is not its responsibility under the criteria laid down in this Regulation. In such an event, that Member State shall become the Member State responsible within the meaning of this Regulation and shall assume the obligations associated with that

responsibility. Where appropriate, it shall inform the Member State previously responsible, the Member State conducting a procedure for determining the Member State responsible or the Member State which has been requested to take charge of or take back the applicant.

3. Any Member State shall retain the right, pursuant to its national laws, to send an asylum seeker to a third country, in compliance with the provisions of the Geneva Convention.

4. The asylum seeker shall be informed in writing in a language that he or she may reasonably be expected to understand regarding the application of this Regulation, its time limits and its effects.

Article 4

1. The process of determining the Member State responsible under this Regulation shall start as soon as an application for asylum is first lodged with a Member State.

2. An application for asylum shall be deemed to have been lodged once a form submitted by the applicant for asylum or a report prepared by the authorities has reached the competent authorities of the Member State concerned. Where an application is not made in writing, the time elapsing between the statement of intention and the preparation of a report should be as short as possible.

3. For the purposes of this Regulation, the situation of a minor who is accompanying the asylum seeker and meets the definition of a family member set out in Article 2, point (i), shall be indissociable from that of his parent or guardian and shall be a matter for the Member State responsible for examining the application for asylum of that parent or guardian, even if the minor is not individually an asylum seeker. The same treatment shall be applied to children born after the asylum seeker arrives in the territory of the Member States, without the need to initiate a new procedure for taking charge of them.

4. Where an application for asylum is lodged with the competent authorities of a Member State by an applicant who is in the territory of another Member State, the determination of the Member State responsible shall be made by the Member State in whose territory the applicant is present. The latter Member State shall be informed without delay by the Member State which received the application and shall then, for the purposes of this Regulation, be regarded as the Member State with which the application for asylum was lodged.

The applicant shall be informed in writing of this transfer and of the date on which it took place.

5. An asylum seeker who is present in another Member State and there lodges an application for asylum after withdrawing his application during the process of determining the Member State responsible shall be taken back, under the conditions laid down in Article 20, by the Member State with which that application for asylum was lodged, with a view to completing the process of determining the Member State responsible for examining the application for asylum.

This obligation shall cease, if the asylum seeker has in the meantime left the territories of the Member States for a period of at least three months or has obtained a residence document from a Member State.

CHAPTER III
HIERARCHY OF CRITERIA

Article 5

1. The criteria for determining the Member State responsible shall be applied in the order in which they are set out in this Chapter.

2.   The Member State responsible in accordance with the criteria shall be determined on the basis of the situation obtaining when the asylum seeker first lodged his application with a Member State.

Article   6

Where the applicant for asylum is an unaccompanied minor, the Member State responsible for examining the application shall be that where a member of his or her family is legally present, provided that this is in the best interest of the minor.

In the absence of a family member, the Member State responsible for examining the application shall be that where the minor has lodged his or her application for asylum.

Article   7

Where the asylum seeker has a family member, regardless of whether the family was previously formed in the country of origin, who has been allowed to reside as a refugee in a Member State, that Member State shall be responsible for examining the application for asylum, provided that the persons concerned so desire.

Article   8

If the asylum seeker has a family member in a Member State whose application has not yet been the subject of a first decision regarding the substance, that Member State shall be responsible for examining the application for asylum, provided that the persons concerned so desire.

Article   9

1.   Where the asylum seeker is in possession of a valid residence document, the Member State which issued the document shall be responsible for examining the application for asylum.

2.   Where the asylum seeker is in possession of a valid visa, the Member State which issued the visa shall be responsible for examining the application for asylum, unless the visa was issued when acting for or on the written authorisation of another Member State. In such a case, the latter Member State shall be responsible for examining the application for asylum. Where a Member State first consults the central authority of another Member State, in particular for security reasons, the latter's reply to the consultation shall not constitute written authorisation within the meaning of this provision.

3.   Where the asylum seeker is in possession of more than one valid residence document or visa issued by different Member States, the responsibility for examining the application for asylum shall be assumed by the Member States in the following order:

(a)   the Member State which issued the residence document conferring the right to the longest period of residency or, where the periods of validity are identical, the Member State which issued the residence document having the latest expiry date;
(b)   the Member State which issued the visa having the latest expiry date where the various visas are of the same type;
(c)   where visas are of different kinds, the Member State which issued the visa having the longest period of validity, or, where the periods of validity are identical, the Member State which issued the visa having the latest expiry date.

4.   Where the asylum seeker is in possession only of one or more residence documents which have expired less than two years previously or one or more visas which have expired less than six months previously and which enabled him actually to enter the

territory of a Member State, paragraphs 1, 2 and 3 shall apply for such time as the applicant has not left the territories of the Member States.

Where the asylum seeker is in possession of one or more residence documents which have expired more than two years previously or one or more visas which have expired more than six months previously and enabled him actually to enter the territory of a Member State and where he has not left the territories of the Member States, the Member State in which the application is lodged shall be responsible.

5. The fact that the residence document or visa was issued on the basis of a false or assumed identity or on submission of forged, counterfeit or invalid documents shall not prevent responsibility being allocated to the Member State which issued it. However, the Member State issuing the residence document or visa shall not be responsible if it can establish that a fraud was committed after the document or visa had been issued.

Article 10

1. Where it is established, on the basis of proof or circumstantial evidence as described in the two lists mentioned in Article 18(3), including the data referred to in Chapter III of Regulation (EC) No 2725/2000, that an asylum seeker has irregularly crossed the border into a Member State by land, sea or air having come from a third country, the Member State thus entered shall be responsible for examining the application for asylum. This responsibility shall cease 12 months after the date on which the irregular border crossing took place.

2. When a Member State cannot or can no longer be held responsible in accordance with paragraph 1, and where it is established, on the basis of proof or circumstantial evidence as described in the two lists mentioned in Article 18(3), that the asylum seeker – who has entered the territories of the Member States irregularly or whose circumstances of entry cannot be established – at the time of lodging the application has been previously living for a continuous period of at least five months in a Member State, that Member State shall be responsible for examining the application for asylum.

If the applicant has been living for periods of time of at least five months in several Member States, the Member State where this has been most recently the case shall be responsible for examining the application.

Article 11

1. If a third-country national enters into the territory of a Member State in which the need for him or her to have a visa is waived, that Member State shall be responsible for examining his or her application for asylum.

2. The principle set out in paragraph 1 does not apply, if the third-country national lodges his or her application for asylum in another Member State, in which the need for him or her to have a visa for entry into the territory is also waived. In this case, the latter Member State shall be responsible for examining the application for asylum.

Article 12

Where the application for asylum is made in an international transit area of an airport of a Member State by a third-country national, that Member State shall be responsible for examining the application.

Article 13

Where no Member State responsible for examining the application for asylum can be designated on the basis of the criteria listed in this Regulation, the first Member State with which the application for asylum was lodged shall be responsible for examining it.

Article   14

Where several members of a family submit applications for asylum in the same Member State simultaneously, or on dates close enough for the procedures for determining the Member State responsible to be conducted together, and where the application of the criteria set out in this Regulation would lead to them being separated, the Member State responsible shall be determined on the basis of the following provisions:

(a)   responsibility for examining the applications for asylum of all the members of the family shall lie with the Member State which the criteria indicate is responsible for taking charge of the largest number of family members;

(b)   failing this, responsibility shall lie with the Member State which the criteria indicate is responsible for examining the application of the oldest of them.

CHAPTER IV
HUMANITARIAN CLAUSE

Article   15

1.   Any Member State, even where it is not responsible under the criteria set out in this Regulation, may bring together family members, as well as other dependent relatives, on humanitarian grounds based in particular on family or cultural considerations. In this case that Member State shall, at the request of another Member State, examine the application for asylum of the person concerned. The persons concerned must consent.

2.   In cases in which the person concerned is dependent on the assistance of the other on account of pregnancy or a new-born child, serious illness, severe handicap or old age, Member States shall normally keep or bring together the asylum seeker with another relative present in the territory of one of the Member States, provided that family ties existed in the country of origin.

3.   If the asylum seeker is an unaccompanied minor who has a relative or relatives in another Member State who can take care of him or her, Member States shall if possible unite the minor with his or her relative or relatives, unless this is not in the best interests of the minor.

4.   Where the Member State thus approached accedes to the request, responsibility for examining the application shall be transferred to it.

5.   The conditions and procedures for implementing this Article including, where appropriate, conciliation mechanisms for settling differences between Member States concerning the need to unite the persons in question, or the place where this should be done, shall be adopted in accordance with the procedure referred to in Article 27(2).

CHAPTER V
TAKING CHARGE AND TAKING BACK

Article   16

1.   The Member State responsible for examining an application for asylum under this Regulation shall be obliged to:

(a)   take charge, under the conditions laid down in Articles 17 to 19, of an asylum seeker who has lodged an application in a different Member State;

(b)   complete the examination of the application for asylum;

(c)   take back, under the conditions laid down in Article 20, an applicant whose application is under examination and who is in the territory of another Member State without permission;

(d) take back, under the conditions laid down in Article 20, an applicant who has withdrawn the application under examination and made an application in another Member State;

(e) take back, under the conditions laid down in Article 20, a third-country national whose application it has rejected and who is in the territory of another Member State without permission.

2. Where a Member State issues a residence document to the applicant, the obligations specified in paragraph 1 shall be transferred to that Member State.

3. The obligations specified in paragraph 1 shall cease where the third-country national has left the territory of the Member States for at least three months, unless the third-country national is in possession of a valid residence document issued by the Member State responsible.

4. The obligations specified in paragraph 1(d) and (e) shall likewise cease once the Member State responsible for examining the application has adopted and actually implemented, following the withdrawal or rejection of the application, the provisions that are necessary before the third-country national can go to his country of origin or to another country to which he may lawfully travel.

Article 17

1. Where a Member State with which an application for asylum has been lodged considers that another Member State is responsible for examining the application, it may, as quickly as possible and in any case within three months of the date on which the application was lodged within the meaning of Article 4(2), call upon the other Member State to take charge of the applicant.

Where the request to take charge of an applicant is not made within the period of three months, responsibility for examining the application for asylum shall lie with the Member State in which the application was lodged.

2. The requesting Member State may ask for an urgent reply in cases where the application for asylum was lodged after leave to enter or remain was refused, after an arrest for an unlawful stay or after the service or execution of a removal order and/or where the asylum seeker is held in detention.

The request shall state the reasons warranting an urgent reply and the period within which a reply is expected. This period shall be at least one week.

3. In both cases, the request that charge be taken by another Member State shall be made using a standard form and including proof or circumstantial evidence as described in the two lists mentioned in Article 18(3) and/or relevant elements from the asylum seeker's statement, enabling the authorities of the requested Member State to check whether it is responsible on the basis of the criteria laid down in this Regulation.

The rules on the preparation of and the procedures for transmitting requests shall be adopted in accordance with the procedure referred to in Article 27(2).

Article 18

1. The requested Member State shall make the necessary checks, and shall give a decision on the request to take charge of an applicant within two months of the date on which the request was received.

2. In the procedure for determining the Member State responsible for examining the application for asylum established in this Regulation, elements of proof and circumstantial evidence shall be used.

3. In accordance with the procedure referred to in Article 27(2) two lists shall be established and periodically reviewed, indicating the elements of proof and circumstantial evidence in accordance with the following criteria:

   (a) Proof:
       (i) This refers to formal proof which determines responsibility pursuant to this Regulation, as long as it is not refuted by proof to the contrary.
       (ii) The Member States shall provide the Committee provided for in Article 27 with models of the different types of administrative documents, in accordance with the typology established in the list of formal proofs.
   (b) Circumstantial evidence:
       (i) This refers to indicative elements which while being refutable may be sufficient, in certain cases, according to the evidentiary value attributed to them.
       (ii) Their evidentiary value, in relation to the responsibility for examining the application for asylum shall be assessed on a case-by-case basis.

4. The requirement of proof should not exceed what is necessary for the proper application of this Regulation.

5. If there is no formal proof, the requested Member State shall acknowledge its responsibility if the circumstantial evidence is coherent, verifiable and sufficiently detailed to establish responsibility.

6. Where the requesting Member State has pleaded urgency, in accordance with the provisions of Article 17(2), the requested Member State shall make every effort to conform to the time limit requested. In exceptional cases, where it can be demonstrated that the examination of a request for taking charge of an applicant is particularly complex, the requested Member State may give the reply after the time limit requested, but in any case within one month. In such situations the requested Member State must communicate its decision to postpone a reply to the requesting Member State within the time limit originally requested.

7. Failure to act within the two-month period mentioned in paragraph 1 and the one-month period mentioned in paragraph 6 shall be tantamount to accepting the request, and entail the obligation to take charge of the person, including the provisions for proper arrangements for arrival.

Article 19

1. Where the requested Member State accepts that it should take charge of an applicant, the Member State in which the application for asylum was lodged shall notify the applicant of the decision not to examine the application, and of the obligation to transfer the applicant to the responsible Member State.

2. The decision referred to in paragraph 1 shall set out the grounds on which it is based. It shall contain details of the time limit for carrying out the transfer and shall, if necessary, contain information on the place and date at which the applicant should appear, if he is travelling to the Member State responsible by his own means. This decision may be subject to an appeal or a review. Appeal or review concerning this decision shall not suspend the implementation of the transfer unless the courts or competent bodies so decide on a case by case basis if national legislation allows for this.

3. The transfer of the applicant from the Member State in which the application for asylum was lodged to the Member State responsible shall be carried out in accordance with the national law of the first Member State, after consultation between the Member States concerned, as soon as practically possible, and at the latest within six

months of acceptance of the request that charge be taken or of the decision on an appeal or review where there is a suspensive effect.

If necessary, the asylum seeker shall be supplied by the requesting Member State with a laissez passer of the design adopted in accordance with the procedure referred to in Article 27(2).

The Member State responsible shall inform the requesting Member State, as appropriate, of the safe arrival of the asylum seeker or of the fact that he did not appear within the set time limit.

4. Where the transfer does not take place within the six months' time limit, responsibility shall lie with the Member State in which the application for asylum was lodged. This time limit may be extended up to a maximum of one year if the transfer could not be carried out due to imprisonment of the asylum seeker or up to a maximum of eighteen months if the asylum seeker absconds.

5. Supplementary rules on carrying out transfers may be adopted in accordance with the procedure referred to in Article 27(2).

Article 20

1. An asylum seeker shall be taken back in accordance with Article 4(5) and Article 16(1)(c), (d) and (e) as follows:

(a) the request for the applicant to be taken back must contain information enabling the requested Member State to check that it is responsible;

(b) the Member State called upon to take back the applicant shall be obliged to make the necessary checks and reply to the request addressed to it as quickly as possible and under no circumstances exceeding a period of one month from the referral. When the request is based on data obtained from the Eurodac system, this time limit is reduced to two weeks;

(c) where the requested Member State does not communicate its decision within the one month period or the two weeks period mentioned in subparagraph (b), it shall be considered to have agreed to take back the asylum seeker;

(d) a Member State which agrees to take back an asylum seeker shall be obliged to readmit that person to its territory. The transfer shall be carried out in accordance with the national law of the requesting Member State, after consultation between the Member States concerned, as soon as practically possible, and at the latest within six months of acceptance of the request that charge be taken by another Member State or of the decision on an appeal or review where there is a suspensive effect;

(e) the requesting Member State shall notify the asylum seeker of the decision concerning his being taken back by the Member State responsible. The decision shall set out the grounds on which it is based. It shall contain details of the time limit on carrying out the transfer and shall, if necessary, contain information on the place and date at which the applicant should appear, if he is travelling to the Member State responsible by his own means. This decision may be subject to an appeal or a review. Appeal or review concerning this decision shall not suspend the implementation of the transfer except when the courts or competent bodies so decide in a case-by-case basis if the national legislation allows for this.

If necessary, the asylum seeker shall be supplied by the requesting Member State with a laissez passer of the design adopted in accordance with the procedure referred to in Article 27(2).

The Member State responsible shall inform the requesting Member State, as appropriate, of the safe arrival of the asylum seeker or of the fact that he did not appear within the set time limit.

2.   Where the transfer does not take place within the six months' time limit, responsibility shall lie with the Member State in which the application for asylum was lodged. This time limit may be extended up to a maximum of one year if the transfer or the examination of the application could not be carried out due to imprisonment of the asylum seeker or up to a maximum of eighteen months if the asylum seeker absconds.

3.   The rules of proof and evidence and their interpretation, and on the preparation of and the procedures for transmitting requests, shall be adopted in accordance with the procedure referred to in Article 27(2).

4.   Supplementary rules on carrying out transfers may be adopted in accordance with the procedure referred to in Article 27(2).

CHAPTER VI
ADMINISTRATIVE COOPERATION

Article   21

1.   Each Member State shall communicate to any Member State that so requests such personal data concerning the asylum seeker as is appropriate, relevant and non-excessive for:

(a)   the determination of the Member State responsible for examining the application for asylum;
(b)   examining the application for asylum;
(c)   implementing any obligation arising under this Regulation.

2.   The information referred to in paragraph 1 may only cover:

(a)   personal details of the applicant, and, where appropriate, the members of his family (full name and where appropriate, former name; nicknames or pseudonyms; nationality, present and former; date and place of birth);
(b)   identity and travel papers (references, validity, date of issue, issuing authority, place of issue, etc.);
(c)   other information necessary for establishing the identity of the applicant, including fingerprints processed in accordance with Regulation (EC) No 2725/2000;
(d)   places of residence and routes travelled;
(e)   residence documents or visas issued by a Member State;
(f)   the place where the application was lodged;
(g)   the date any previous application for asylum was lodged, the date the present application was lodged, the stage reached in the proceedings and the decision taken, if any.

3.   Furthermore, provided it is necessary for the examination of the application for asylum, the Member State responsible may request another Member State to let it know on what grounds the asylum seeker bases his application and, where applicable, the grounds for any decisions taken concerning the applicant. The Member State may refuse to respond to the request submitted to it, if the communication of such information is likely to harm the essential interests of the Member State or the protection of the liberties and fundamental rights of the person concerned or of others. In any event, communication of the information requested shall be subject to the written approval of the applicant for asylum.

4.   Any request for information shall set out the grounds on which it is based and, where its purpose is to check whether there is a criterion that is likely to entail the responsibility of the requested Member State, shall state on what evidence, including relevant information from reliable sources on the ways and means asylum seekers enter the territories of the Member States, or on what specific and verifiable part of the

applicant's statements it is based. It is understood that such relevant information from reliable sources is not in itself sufficient to determine the responsibility and the competence of a Member State under this Regulation, but it may contribute to the evaluation of other indications relating to the individual asylum seeker.

5. The requested Member State shall be obliged to reply within six weeks.

6. The exchange of information shall be effected at the request of a Member State and may only take place between authorities whose designation by each Member State has been communicated to the Commission, which shall inform the other Member States thereof.

7. The information exchanged may only be used for the purposes set out in paragraph 1. In each Member State such information may, depending on its type and the powers of the recipient authority, only be communicated to the authorities and courts and tribunals entrusted with:

(a) the determination of the Member State responsible for examining the application for asylum;

(b) examining the application for asylum;

(c) implementing any obligation arising under this Regulation.

8. The Member State which forwards the information shall ensure that it is accurate and up-to-date. If it transpires that that Member State has forwarded information which is inaccurate or which should not have been forwarded, the recipient Member States shall be informed thereof immediately. They shall be obliged to correct such information or to have it erased.

9. The asylum seeker shall have the right to be informed, on request, of any data that is processed concerning him.

If he finds that this information has been processed in breach of this Regulation or of Directive 95/46/EC of the European Parliament and the Council of 24 October 1995 on the protection of individuals with regard to the processing of personal data and on the free movement of such data(8), in particular because it is incomplete or inaccurate, he is entitled to have it corrected, erased or blocked.

The authority correcting, erasing or blocking the data shall inform, as appropriate, the Member State transmitting or receiving the information.

10. In each Member State concerned, a record shall be kept, in the individual file for the person concerned and/or in a register, of the transmission and receipt of information exchanged.

11. The data exchanged shall be kept for a period not exceeding that which is necessary for the purposes for which it is exchanged.

12. Where the data is not processed automatically or is not contained, or intended to be entered, in a file, each Member State should take appropriate measures to ensure compliance with this Article through effective checks.

Article 22

1. Member States shall notify the Commission of the authorities responsible for fulfilling the obligations arising under this Regulation and shall ensure that those authorities have the necessary resources for carrying out their tasks and in particular for replying within the prescribed time limits to requests for information, requests to take charge of and requests to take back asylum seekers.

2. Rules relating to the establishment of secure electronic transmission channels between the authorities mentioned in paragraph 1 for transmitting requests and

ensuring that senders automatically receive an electronic proof of delivery shall be established in accordance with the procedure referred to in Article 27(2).

Article 23

1. Member States may, on a bilateral basis, establish administrative arrangements between themselves concerning the practical details of the implementation of this Regulation, in order to facilitate its application and increase its effectiveness. Such arrangements may relate to:

(a) exchanges of liaison officers;
(b) simplification of the procedures and shortening of the time limits relating to transmission and the examination of requests to take charge of or take back asylum seekers;

2. The arrangements referred to in paragraph 1 shall be communicated to the Commission. The Commission shall verify that the arrangements referred to in paragraph 1(b) do not infringe this Regulation.

CHAPTER VII
TRANSITIONAL PROVISIONS AND FINAL PROVISIONS

Article 24

1. This Regulation shall replace the Convention determining the State responsible for examining applications for asylum lodged in one of the Member States of the European Communities, signed in Dublin on 15 June 1990 (Dublin Convention).

2. However, to ensure continuity of the arrangements for determining the Member State responsible for an application for asylum, where an application has been lodged after the date mentioned in the second paragraph of Article 29, the events that are likely to entail the responsibility of a Member State under this Regulation shall be taken into consideration, even if they precede that date, with the exception of the events mentioned in Article 10(2).

3. Where, in Regulation (EC) No 2725/2000 reference is made to the Dublin Convention, such reference shall be taken to be a reference made to this Regulation.

Article 25

1. Any period of time prescribed in this Regulation shall be calculated as follows:

(a) where a period expressed in days, weeks or months is to be calculated from the moment at which an event occurs or an action takes place, the day during which that event occurs or that action takes place shall not be counted as falling within the period in question;
(b) a period expressed in weeks or months shall end with the expiry of whichever day in the last week or month is the same day of the week or falls on the same date as the day during which the event or action from which the period is to be calculated occurred or took place. If, in a period expressed in months, the day on which it should expire does not occur in the last month, the period shall end with the expiry of the last day of that month;
(c) time limits shall include Saturdays, Sundays and official holidays in any of the Member States concerned.

2. Requests and replies shall be sent using any method that provides proof of receipt.

Article 26

As far as the French Republic is concerned, this Regulation shall apply only to its European territory.

Article 27

1. The Commission shall be assisted by a committee.

2. Where reference is made to this paragraph, Articles 5 and 7 of Decision 1999/468/EC shall apply.

The period laid down in Article 5(6) of Decision 1999/468/EC shall be set at three months.

3. The Committee shall draw up its rules of procedure.

Article 28

At the latest three years after the date mentioned in the first paragraph of Article 29, the Commission shall report to the European Parliament and the Council on the application of this Regulation and, where appropriate, shall propose the necessary amendments. Member States shall forward to the Commission all information appropriate for the preparation of that report, at the latest six months before that time limit expires.

Having submitted that report, the Commission shall report to the European Parliament and the Council on the application of this Regulation at the same time as it submits reports on the implementation of the Eurodac system provided for by Article 24(5) of Regulation (EC) No 2725/2000.

Article 29

This Regulation shall enter into force on the 20th day following that of its publication in the Official Journal of the European Union.

It shall apply to asylum applications lodged as from the first day of the sixth month following its entry into force and, from that date, it will apply to any request to take charge of or take back asylum seekers, irrespective of the date on which the application was made. The Member State responsible for the examination of an asylum application submitted before that date shall be determined in accordance with the criteria set out in the Dublin Convention.

This Regulation shall be binding in its entirety and directly applicable in the Member States in conformity with the Treaty establishing the European Community.

Done at Brussels, 18 February 2003.

DIRECTIVE 2004/38/EC OF THE EUROPEAN PARLIAMENT AND OF THE COUNCIL of 29 April 2004

on the right of citizens of the Union and their family members to move and reside freely within the territory of the Member States amending Regulation (EEC) No 1612/68 and repealing Directives 64/221/EEC, 68/360/EEC, 72/194/EEC, 73/148/EEC, 75/34/EEC, 75/35/EEC, 90/364/EEC, 90/365/EEC and 93/96/EEC

OJ L 158, 30 April 2004, p.77

THE EUROPEAN PARLIAMENT AND THE COUNCIL OF THE EUROPEAN UNION,

Having regard to the Treaty establishing the European Community, and in particular Articles 12, 18, 40, 44 and 52 thereof,

Having regard to the proposal from the Commission[1],

Having regard to the Opinion of the European Economic and Social Committee[2],

Having regard to the Opinion of the Committee of the Regions[3],

Acting in accordance with the procedure laid down in Article 251 of the Treaty[4],

Whereas:

(1) Citizenship of the Union confers on every citizen of the Union a primary and individual right to move and reside freely within the territory of the Member States, subject to the limitations and conditions laid down in the Treaty and to the measures adopted to give it effect.

(2) The free movement of persons constitutes one of the fundamental freedoms of the internal market, which comprises an area without internal frontiers, in which freedom is ensured in accordance with the provisions of the Treaty.

(3) Union citizenship should be the fundamental status of nationals of the Member States when they exercise their right of free movement and residence. It is therefore necessary to codify and review the existing Community instruments dealing separately with workers, self-employed persons, as well as students and other inactive persons in order to simplify and strengthen the right of free movement and residence of all Union citizens.

(4) With a view to remedying this sector-by-sector, piecemeal approach to the right of free movement and residence and facilitating the exercise of this right, there needs to be a single legislative act to amend Council Regulation (EEC) No 1612/68 of 15 October 1968 on freedom of movement for workers within the Community[5], and to repeal the following acts: Council Directive 68/360/EEC of 15 October 1968 on the abolition of restrictions on movement and residence within the Community for workers of Member States and their families[6], Council Directive 73/148/EEC of 21 May 1973 on the abolition of restrictions on movement and residence within the Community for nationals of Member States with regard to establishment and the provision of services[7], Council Directive 90/364/EEC of 28 June 1990 on the right of residence[8], Council Directive 90/365/EEC of 28 June 1990 on the right of residence for employees and self-employed persons who have ceased their occupational activity[9] and Council Directive 93/96/EEC of 29 October 1993 on the right of residence for students[10].

(5) The right of all Union citizens to move and reside freely within the territory of the Member States should, if it is to be exercised under objective conditions of freedom and dignity, be also granted to their family members, irrespective of

nationality. For the purposes of this Directive, the definition of 'family member' should also include the registered partner if the legislation of the host Member State treats registered partnership as equivalent to marriage.

(6) In order to maintain the unity of the family in a broader sense and without prejudice to the prohibition of discrimination on grounds of nationality, the situation of those persons who are not included in the definition of family members under this Directive, and who therefore do not enjoy an automatic right of entry and residence in the host Member State, should be examined by the host Member State on the basis of its own national legislation, in order to decide whether entry and residence could be granted to such persons, taking into consideration their relationship with the Union citizen or any other circumstances, such as their financial or physical dependence on the Union citizen.

(7) The formalities connected with the free movement of Union citizens within the territory of Member States should be clearly defined, without prejudice to the provisions applicable to national border controls.

(8) With a view to facilitating the free movement of family members who are not nationals of a Member State, those who have already obtained a residence card should be exempted from the requirement to obtain an entry visa within the meaning of Council Regulation (EC) No 539/2001 of 15 March 2001 listing the third countries whose nationals must be in possession of visas when crossing the external borders and those whose nationals are exempt from that requirement[11] or, where appropriate, of the applicable national legislation.

(9) Union citizens should have the right of residence in the host Member State for a period not exceeding three months without being subject to any conditions or any formalities other than the requirement to hold a valid identity card or passport, without prejudice to a more favourable treatment applicable to job-seekers as recognised by the case-law of the Court of Justice.

(10) Persons exercising their right of residence should not, however, become an unreasonable burden on the social assistance system of the host Member State during an initial period of residence. Therefore, the right of residence for Union citizens and their family members for periods in excess of three months should be subject to conditions.

(11) The fundamental and personal right of residence in another Member State is conferred directly on Union citizens by the Treaty and is not dependent upon their having fulfilled administrative procedures.

(12) For periods of residence of longer than three months, Member States should have the possibility to require Union citizens to register with the competent authorities in the place of residence, attested by a registration certificate issued to that effect.

(13) The residence card requirement should be restricted to family members of Union citizens who are not nationals of a Member State for periods of residence of longer than three months.

(14) The supporting documents required by the competent authorities for the issuing of a registration certificate or of a residence card should be comprehensively specified in order to avoid divergent administrative practices or interpretations constituting an undue obstacle to the exercise of the right of residence by Union citizens and their family members.

(15) Family members should be legally safeguarded in the event of the death of the Union citizen, divorce, annulment of marriage or termination of a registered partnership. With due regard for family life and human dignity, and in certain conditions to guard against abuse, measures should therefore be taken to ensure that in such circumstances family members already residing within the territory of the host Member State retain their right of residence exclusively on a personal basis.

(16) As long as the beneficiaries of the right of residence do not become an unreasonable burden on the social assistance system of the host Member State they should not be expelled. Therefore, an expulsion measure should not be the automatic consequence of recourse to the social assistance system. The host Member State should examine whether it is a case of temporary difficulties and take into account the duration of residence, the personal circumstances and the amount of aid granted in order to consider whether the beneficiary has become an unreasonable burden on its social assistance system and to proceed to his expulsion. In no case should an expulsion measure be adopted against workers, self-employed persons or job-seekers as defined by the Court of Justice save on grounds of public policy or public security.

(17) Enjoyment of permanent residence by Union citizens who have chosen to settle long term in the host Member State would strengthen the feeling of Union citizenship and is a key element in promoting social cohesion, which is one of the fundamental objectives of the Union. A right of permanent residence should therefore be laid down for all Union citizens and their family members who have resided in the host Member State in compliance with the conditions laid down in this Directive during a continuous period of five years without becoming subject to an expulsion measure.

(18) In order to be a genuine vehicle for integration into the society of the host Member State in which the Union citizen resides, the right of permanent residence, once obtained, should not be subject to any conditions.

(19) Certain advantages specific to Union citizens who are workers or self-employed persons and to their family members, which may allow these persons to acquire a right of permanent residence before they have resided five years in the host Member State, should be maintained, as these constitute acquired rights, conferred by Commission Regulation (EEC) No 1251/70 of 29 June 1970 on the right of workers to remain in the territory of a Member State after having been employed in that State[12] and Council Directive 75/34/EEC of 17 December 1974 concerning the right of nationals of a Member State to remain in the territory of another Member State after having pursued therein an activity in a self-employed capacity[13].

(20) In accordance with the prohibition of discrimination on grounds of nationality, all Union citizens and their family members residing in a Member State on the basis of this Directive should enjoy, in that Member State, equal treatment with nationals in areas covered by the Treaty, subject to such specific provisions as are expressly provided for in the Treaty and secondary law.

(21) However, it should be left to the host Member State to decide whether it will grant social assistance during the first three months of residence, or for a longer period in the case of job-seekers, to Union citizens other than those who are workers or self-employed persons or who retain that status or their family members, or maintenance assistance for studies, including vocational training, prior to acquisition of the right of permanent residence, to these same persons.

(22) The Treaty allows restrictions to be placed on the right of free movement and residence on grounds of public policy, public security or public health. In order to ensure a tighter definition of the circumstances and procedural safeguards subject to which Union citizens and their family members may be denied leave to enter or may be expelled, this Directive should replace Council Directive 64/221/EEC of 25 February 1964 on the coordination of special measures concerning the movement and residence of foreign nationals, which are justified on grounds of public policy, public security or public health[14].

(23) Expulsion of Union citizens and their family members on grounds of public policy or public security is a measure that can seriously harm persons who, having availed themselves of the rights and freedoms conferred on them by the Treaty, have become genuinely integrated into the host Member State. The

scope for such measures should therefore be limited in accordance with the principle of proportionality to take account of the degree of integration of the persons concerned, the length of their residence in the host Member State, their age, state of health, family and economic situation and the links with their country of origin.

(24) Accordingly, the greater the degree of integration of Union citizens and their family members in the host Member State, the greater the degree of protection against expulsion should be. Only in exceptional circumstances, where there are imperative grounds of public security, should an expulsion measure be taken against Union citizens who have resided for many years in the territory of the host Member State, in particular when they were born and have resided there throughout their life. In addition, such exceptional circumstances should also apply to an expulsion measure taken against minors, in order to protect their links with their family, in accordance with the United Nations Convention on the Rights of the Child, of 20 November 1989.

(25) Procedural safeguards should also be specified in detail in order to ensure a high level of protection of the rights of Union citizens and their family members in the event of their being denied leave to enter or reside in another Member State, as well as to uphold the principle that any action taken by the authorities must be properly justified.

(26) In all events, judicial redress procedures should be available to Union citizens and their family members who have been refused leave to enter or reside in another Member State.

(27) In line with the case-law of the Court of Justice prohibiting Member States from issuing orders excluding for life persons covered by this Directive from their territory, the right of Union citizens and their family members who have been excluded from the territory of a Member State to submit a fresh application after a reasonable period, and in any event after a three year period from enforcement of the final exclusion order, should be confirmed.

(28) To guard against abuse of rights or fraud, notably marriages of convenience or any other form of relationships contracted for the sole purpose of enjoying the right of free movement and residence, Member States should have the possibility to adopt the necessary measures.

(29) This Directive should not affect more favourable national provisions.

(30) With a view to examining how further to facilitate the exercise of the right of free movement and residence, a report should be prepared by the Commission in order to evaluate the opportunity to present any necessary proposals to this effect, notably on the extension of the period of residence with no conditions.

(31) This Directive respects the fundamental rights and freedoms and observes the principles recognised in particular by the Charter of Fundamental Rights of the European Union. In accordance with the prohibition of discrimination contained in the Charter, Member States should implement this Directive without discrimination between the beneficiaries of this Directive on grounds such as sex, race, colour, ethnic or social origin, genetic characteristics, language, religion or beliefs, political or other opinion, membership of an ethnic minority, property, birth, disability, age or sexual orientation,

1 OJ C 270 E, 25.9.2001, p. 150.
2 OJ C 149, 21.6.2002, p. 46.
3 OJ C 192, 12.8.2002, p. 17.
4 Opinion of the European Parliament of 11 February 2003 (OJ C 43 E, 19.2.2004, p.42), Council Common Position of 5 December 2003 (OJ C 54 E, 2.3.2004, p.12) and Position of the European Parliament of 10 March 2004 (not yet published in the Official Journal).
5 OJ L 257, 19.10.1968, p. 2. Regulation as last amended by Regulation (EEC) No 2434/92 (OJ L 245, 26.8.1992, p. 1).
6 OJ L 257, 19.10.1968, p. 13. Directive as last amended by the 2003 Act of Accession.
7 OJ L 172, 28.6.1973, p. 14.

[8]   OJ L 180, 13.7.1990, p. 26.
[9]   OJ L 180, 13.7.1990, p. 28.
[10] OJ L 317, 18.12.1993, p. 59.
[11] OJ L 81, 21.3.2001, p. 1. Regulation as last amended by Regulation (EC) No 453/2003 (OJ L 69, 13.3.2003, p. 10).
[12] OJ L 142, 30.6.1970, p. 24.
[13] OJ L 14, 20.1.1975, p. 10.
[14] OJ 56, 4.4.1964, p. 850. Directive as last amended by Directive 75/35/EEC (OJ 14, 20.1.1975, p. 14).

Have adopted this Directive:

CHAPTER I
GENERAL PROVISIONS

Article   1   Subject

This Directive lays down:

(a)   the conditions governing the exercise of the right of free movement and residence within the territory of the Member States by Union citizens and their family members;

(b)   the right of permanent residence in the territory of the Member States for Union citizens and their family members;

(c)   the limits placed on the rights set out in (a) and (b) on grounds of public policy, public security or public health.

Article   2   Definitions

For the purposes of this Directive:

(1)   'Union citizen' means any person having the nationality of a Member State;

(2)   'Family member' means:

(a)   the spouse;

(b)   the partner with whom the Union citizen has contracted a registered partnership, on the basis of the legislation of a Member State, if the legislation of the host Member State treats registered partnerships as equivalent to marriage and in accordance with the conditions laid down in the relevant legislation of the host Member State;

(c)   the direct descendants who are under the age of 21 or are dependants and those of the spouse or partner as defined in point (b);

(d)   the dependent direct relatives in the ascending line and those of the spouse or partner as defined in point (b);

(3)   'Host Member State' means the Member State to which a Union citizen moves in order to exercise his/her right of free movement and residence.

Article   3   Beneficiaries

1.   This Directive shall apply to all Union citizens who move to or reside in a Member State other than that of which they are a national, and to their family members as defined in point 2 of Article 2 who accompany or join them.

2.   Without prejudice to any right to free movement and residence the persons concerned may have in their own right, the host Member State shall, in accordance with its national legislation, facilitate entry and residence for the following persons:

(a)   any other family members, irrespective of their nationality, not falling under the definition in point 2 of Article 2 who, in the country from which they have come, are dependants or members of the household of the Union citizen

having the primary right of residence, or where serious health grounds strictly require the personal care of the family member by the Union citizen;
(b) the partner with whom the Union citizen has a durable relationship, duly attested.

The host Member State shall undertake an extensive examination of the personal circumstances and shall justify any denial of entry or residence to these people.

CHAPTER II
RIGHT OF EXIT AND ENTRY

Article   4   Right of exit

1. Without prejudice to the provisions on travel documents applicable to national border controls, all Union citizens with a valid identity card or passport and their family members who are not nationals of a Member State and who hold a valid passport shall have the right to leave the territory of a Member State to travel to another Member State.

2. No exit visa or equivalent formality may be imposed on the persons to whom paragraph 1 applies.

3. Member States shall, acting in accordance with their laws, issue to their own nationals, and renew, an identity card or passport stating their nationality.

4. The passport shall be valid at least for all Member States and for countries through which the holder must pass when travelling between Member States. Where the law of a Member State does not provide for identity cards to be issued, the period of validity of any passport on being issued or renewed shall be not less than five years.

Article   5   Right of entry

1. Without prejudice to the provisions on travel documents applicable to national border controls, Member States shall grant Union citizens leave to enter their territory with a valid identity card or passport and shall grant family members who are not nationals of a Member State leave to enter their territory with a valid passport.

No entry visa or equivalent formality may be imposed on Union citizens.

2. Family members who are not nationals of a Member State shall only be required to have an entry visa in accordance with Regulation (EC) No 539/2001 or, where appropriate, with national law. For the purposes of this Directive, possession of the valid residence card referred to in Article 10 shall exempt such family members from the visa requirement.

Member States shall grant such persons every facility to obtain the necessary visas. Such visas shall be issued free of charge as soon as possible and on the basis of an accelerated procedure.

3. The host Member State shall not place an entry or exit stamp in the passport of family members who are not nationals of a Member State provided that they present the residence card provided for in Article 10.

4. Where a Union citizen, or a family member who is not a national of a Member State, does not have the necessary travel documents or, if required, the necessary visas, the Member State concerned shall, before turning them back, give such persons every reasonable opportunity to obtain the necessary documents or have them brought to them within a reasonable period of time or to corroborate or prove by other means that they are covered by the right of free movement and residence.

5.   The Member State may require the person concerned to report his/her presence within its territory within a reasonable and non-discriminatory period of time. Failure to comply with this requirement may make the person concerned liable to proportionate and non-discriminatory sanctions.

CHAPTER III
RIGHT OF RESIDENCE

Article   6   Right of residence for up to three months

1.   Union citizens shall have the right of residence on the territory of another Member State for a period of up to three months without any conditions or any formalities other than the requirement to hold a valid identity card or passport.

2.   The provisions of paragraph 1 shall also apply to family members in possession of a valid passport who are not nationals of a Member State, accompanying or joining the Union citizen.

Article   7   Right of residence for more than three months

1.   All Union citizens shall have the right of residence on the territory of another Member State for a period of longer than three months if they:

(a)   are workers or self-employed persons in the host Member State; or

(b)   have sufficient resources for themselves and their family members not to become a burden on the social assistance system of the host Member State during their period of residence and have comprehensive sickness insurance cover in the host Member State; or

(c)

– are enrolled at a private or public establishment, accredited or financed by the host Member State on the basis of its legislation or administrative practice, for the principal purpose of following a course of study, including vocational training; and

– have comprehensive sickness insurance cover in the host Member State and assure the relevant national authority, by means of a declaration or by such equivalent means as they may choose, that they have sufficient resources for themselves and their family members not to become a burden on the social assistance system of the host Member State during their period of residence; or

(d)   are family members accompanying or joining a Union citizen who satisfies the conditions referred to in points (a), (b) or (c).

2.   The right of residence provided for in paragraph 1 shall extend to family members who are not nationals of a Member State, accompanying or joining the Union citizen in the host Member State, provided that such Union citizen satisfies the conditions referred to in paragraph 1(a), (b) or (c).

3.   For the purposes of paragraph 1(a), a Union citizen who is no longer a worker or self-employed person shall retain the status of worker or self-employed person in the following circumstances:

(a)   he/she is temporarily unable to work as the result of an illness or accident;

(b)   he/she is in duly recorded involuntary unemployment after having been employed for more than one year and has registered as a job-seeker with the relevant employment office;

(c)   he/she is in duly recorded involuntary unemployment after completing a fixed-term employment contract of less than a year or after having become involuntarily unemployed during the first twelve months and has registered as a job-seeker with the relevant employment office. In this case, the status of worker shall be retained for no less than six months;

(d) he/she embarks on vocational training. Unless he/she is involuntarily unemployed, the retention of the status of worker shall require the training to be related to the previous employment.

4. By way of derogation from paragraphs 1(d) and 2 above, only the spouse, the registered partner provided for in Article 2(2)(b) and dependent children shall have the right of residence as family members of a Union citizen meeting the conditions under 1(c) above. Article 3(2) shall apply to his/her dependent direct relatives in the ascending lines and those of his/her spouse or registered partner.

Article 8 Administrative formalities for Union citizens

1. Without prejudice to Article 5(5), for periods of residence longer than three months, the host Member State may require Union citizens to register with the relevant authorities.

2. The deadline for registration may not be less than three months from the date of arrival. A registration certificate shall be issued immediately, stating the name and address of the person registering and the date of the registration. Failure to comply with the registration requirement may render the person concerned liable to proportionate and non-discriminatory sanctions.

3. For the registration certificate to be issued, Member States may only require that:

- Union citizens to whom point (a) of Article 7(1) applies present a valid identity card or passport, a confirmation of engagement from the employer or a certificate of employment, or proof that they are self-employed persons;
- Union citizens to whom point (b) of Article 7(1) applies present a valid identity card or passport and provide proof that they satisfy the conditions laid down therein;
- Union citizens to whom point (c) of Article 7(1) applies present a valid identity card or passport, provide proof of enrolment at an accredited establishment and of comprehensive sickness insurance cover and the declaration or equivalent means referred to in point (c) of Article 7(1). Member States may not require this declaration to refer to any specific amount of resources.

4. Member States may not lay down a fixed amount which they regard as 'sufficient resources' but they must take into account the personal situation of the person concerned. In all cases this amount shall not be higher than the threshold below which nationals of the host Member State become eligible for social assistance, or, where this criterion is not applicable, higher than the minimum social security pension paid by the host Member State.

5. For the registration certificate to be issued to family members of Union citizens, who are themselves Union citizens, Member States may require the following documents to be presented:

(a) a valid identity card or passport;
(b) a document attesting to the existence of a family relationship or of a registered partnership;
(c) where appropriate, the registration certificate of the Union citizen whom they are accompanying or joining;
(d) in cases falling under points (c) and (d) of Article 2(2), documentary evidence that the conditions laid down therein are met;
(e) in cases falling under Article 3(2)(a), a document issued by the relevant authority in the country of origin or country from which they are arriving certifying that they are dependants or members of the household of the Union

citizen, or proof of the existence of serious health grounds which strictly require the personal care of the family member by the Union citizen;

(f) in cases falling under Article 3(2)(b), proof of the existence of a durable relationship with the Union citizen.

Article 9   Administrative formalities for family members who are not nationals of a Member State

1. Member States shall issue a residence card to family members of a Union citizen who are not nationals of a Member State, where the planned period of residence is for more than three months.

2. The deadline for submitting the residence card application may not be less than three months from the date of arrival.

3. Failure to comply with the requirement to apply for a residence card may make the person concerned liable to proportionate and non-discriminatory sanctions.

Article 10   Issue of residence cards

1. The right of residence of family members of a Union citizen who are not nationals of a Member State shall be evidenced by the issuing of a document called 'Residence card of a family member of a Union citizen' no later than six months from the date on which they submit the application. A certificate of application for the residence card shall be issued immediately.

2. For the residence card to be issued, Member States shall require presentation of the following documents:

(a) a valid passport;

(b) a document attesting to the existence of a family relationship or of a registered partnership;

(c) the registration certificate or, in the absence of a registration system, any other proof of residence in the host Member State of the Union citizen whom they are accompanying or joining;

(d) in cases falling under points (c) and (d) of Article 2(2), documentary evidence that the conditions laid down therein are met;

(e) in cases falling under Article 3(2)(a), a document issued by the relevant authority in the country of origin or country from which they are arriving certifying that they are dependants or members of the household of the Union citizen, or proof of the existence of serious health grounds which strictly require the personal care of the family member by the Union citizen;

(f) in cases falling under Article 3(2)(b), proof of the existence of a durable relationship with the Union citizen.

Article 11   Validity of the residence card

1. The residence card provided for by Article 10(1) shall be valid for five years from the date of issue or for the envisaged period of residence of the Union citizen, if this period is less than five years.

2. The validity of the residence card shall not be affected by temporary absences not exceeding six months a year, or by absences of a longer duration for compulsory military service or by one absence of a maximum of twelve consecutive months for important reasons such as pregnancy and childbirth, serious illness, study or vocational training, or a posting in another Member State or a third country.

Article   12   Retention of the right of residence by family members in the event of death or departure of the Union citizen

1.   Without prejudice to the second subparagraph, the Union citizen's death or departure from the host Member State shall not affect the right of residence of his/her family members who are nationals of a Member State.

Before acquiring the right of permanent residence, the persons concerned must meet the conditions laid down in points (a), (b), (c) or (d) of Article 7(1).

2.   Without prejudice to the second subparagraph, the Union citizen's death shall not entail loss of the right of residence of his/her family members who are not nationals of a Member State and who have been residing in the host Member State as family members for at least one year before the Union citizen's death.

Before acquiring the right of permanent residence, the right of residence of the persons concerned shall remain subject to the requirement that they are able to show that they are workers or self-employed persons or that they have sufficient resources for themselves and their family members not to become a burden on the social assistance system of the host Member State during their period of residence and have comprehensive sickness insurance cover in the host Member State, or that they are members of the family, already constituted in the host Member State, of a person satisfying these requirements. 'Sufficient resources' shall be as defined in Article 8(4).

Such family members shall retain their right of residence exclusively on a personal basis.

3.   The Union citizen's departure from the host Member State or his/her death shall not entail loss of the right of residence of his/her children or of the parent who has actual custody of the children, irrespective of nationality, if the children reside in the host Member State and are enrolled at an educational establishment, for the purpose of studying there, until the completion of their studies.

Article   13   Retention of the right of residence by family members in the event of divorce, annulment of marriage or termination of registered partnership

1.   Without prejudice to the second subparagraph, divorce, annulment of the Union citizen's marriage or termination of his/her registered partnership, as referred to in point 2(b) of Article 2 shall not affect the right of residence of his/her family members who are nationals of a Member State.

Before acquiring the right of permanent residence, the persons concerned must meet the conditions laid down in points (a), (b), (c) or (d) of Article 7(1).

2.   Without prejudice to the second subparagraph, divorce, annulment of marriage or termination of the registered partnership referred to in point 2(b) of Article 2 shall not entail loss of the right of residence of a Union citizen's family members who are not nationals of a Member State where:

(a)   prior to initiation of the divorce or annulment proceedings or termination of the registered partnership referred to in point 2(b) of Article 2, the marriage or registered partnership has lasted at least three years, including one year in the host Member State; or

(b)   by agreement between the spouses or the partners referred to in point 2(b) of Article 2 or by court order, the spouse or partner who is not a national of a Member State has custody of the Union citizen's children; or

(c)   this is warranted by particularly difficult circumstances, such as having been a victim of domestic violence while the marriage or registered partnership was subsisting; or

(d) by agreement between the spouses or partners referred to in point 2(b) of Article 2 or by court order, the spouse or partner who is not a national of a Member State has the right of access to a minor child, provided that the court has ruled that such access must be in the host Member State, and for as long as is required.

Before acquiring the right of permanent residence, the right of residence of the persons concerned shall remain subject to the requirement that they are able to show that they are workers or self-employed persons or that they have sufficient resources for themselves and their family members not to become a burden on the social assistance system of the host Member State during their period of residence and have comprehensive sickness insurance cover in the host Member State, or that they are members of the family, already constituted in the host Member State, of a person satisfying these requirements. 'Sufficient resources' shall be as defined in Article 8(4).

Such family members shall retain their right of residence exclusively on personal basis.

Article   14   Retention of the right of residence

1. Union citizens and their family members shall have the right of residence provided for in Article 6, as long as they do not become an unreasonable burden on the social assistance system of the host Member State.

2. Union citizens and their family members shall have the right of residence provided for in Articles 7, 12 and 13 as long as they meet the conditions set out therein.

In specific cases where there is a reasonable doubt as to whether a Union citizen or his/her family members satisfies the conditions set out in Articles 7, 12 and 13, Member States may verify if these conditions are fulfilled. This verification shall not be carried out systematically.

3. An expulsion measure shall not be the automatic consequence of a Union citizen's or his or her family member's recourse to the social assistance system of the host Member State.

4. By way of derogation from paragraphs 1 and 2 and without prejudice to the provisions of Chapter VI, an expulsion measure may in no case be adopted against Union citizens or their family members if:

(a) the Union citizens are workers or self-employed persons, or
(b) the Union citizens entered the territory of the host Member State in order to seek employment. In this case, the Union citizens and their family members may not be expelled for as long as the Union citizens can provide evidence that they are continuing to seek employment and that they have a genuine chance of being engaged.

Article   15   Procedural safeguards

1. The procedures provided for by Articles 30 and 31 shall apply by analogy to all decisions restricting free movement of Union citizens and their family members on grounds other than public policy, public security or public health.

2. Expiry of the identity card or passport on the basis of which the person concerned entered the host Member State and was issued with a registration certificate or residence card shall not constitute a ground for expulsion from the host Member State.

3. The host Member State may not impose a ban on entry in the context of an expulsion decision to which paragraph 1 applies.

CHAPTER IV
RIGHT OF PERMANENT RESIDENCE

SECTION I
ELIGIBILITY

Article 16 General rule for Union citizens and their family members

1. Union citizens who have resided legally for a continuous period of five years in the host Member State shall have the right of permanent residence there. This right shall not be subject to the conditions provided for in Chapter III.

2. Paragraph 1 shall apply also to family members who are not nationals of a Member State and have legally resided with the Union citizen in the host Member State for a continuous period of five years.

3. Continuity of residence shall not be affected by temporary absences not exceeding a total of six months a year, or by absences of a longer duration for compulsory military service, or by one absence of a maximum of twelve consecutive months for important reasons such as pregnancy and childbirth, serious illness, study or vocational training, or a posting in another Member State or a third country.

4. Once acquired, the right of permanent residence shall be lost only through absence from the host Member State for a period exceeding two consecutive years.

Article 17 Exemptions for persons no longer working in the host Member State and their family members

1. By way of derogation from Article 16, the right of permanent residence in the host Member State shall be enjoyed before completion of a continuous period of five years of residence by:

(a) workers or self-employed persons who, at the time they stop working, have reached the age laid down by the law of that Member State for entitlement to an old age pension or workers who cease paid employment to take early retirement, provided that they have been working in that Member State for at least the preceding twelve months and have resided there continuously for more than three years.

If the law of the host Member State does not grant the right to an old age pension to certain categories of self-employed persons, the age condition shall be deemed to have been met once the person concerned has reached the age of 60;

(b) workers or self-employed persons who have resided continuously in the host Member State for more than two years and stop working there as a result of permanent incapacity to work.

If such incapacity is the result of an accident at work or an occupational disease entitling the person concerned to a benefit payable in full or in part by an institution in the host Member State, no condition shall be imposed as to length of residence;

(c) workers or self-employed persons who, after three years of continuous employment and residence in the host Member State, work in an employed or self-employed capacity in another Member State, while retaining their place of residence in the host Member State, to which they return, as a rule, each day or at least once a week.

For the purposes of entitlement to the rights referred to in points (a) and (b), periods of employment spent in the Member State in which the person concerned is working shall be regarded as having been spent in the host Member State.

Periods of involuntary unemployment duly recorded by the relevant employment office, periods not worked for reasons not of the person's own making and absences from work or cessation of work due to illness or accident shall be regarded as periods of employment.

2. The conditions as to length of residence and employment laid down in point (a) of paragraph 1 and the condition as to length of residence laid down in point (b) of paragraph 1 shall not apply if the worker's or the self-employed person's spouse or partner as referred to in point 2(b) of Article 2 is a national of the host Member State or has lost the nationality of that Member State by marriage to that worker or self-employed person.

3. Irrespective of nationality, the family members of a worker or a self-employed person who are residing with him in the territory of the host Member State shall have the right of permanent residence in that Member State, if the worker or self-employed person has acquired himself the right of permanent residence in that Member State on the basis of paragraph 1.

4. If, however, the worker or self-employed person dies while still working but before acquiring permanent residence status in the host Member State on the basis of paragraph 1, his family members who are residing with him in the host Member State shall acquire the right of permanent residence there, on condition that:

   (a) the worker or self-employed person had, at the time of death, resided continuously on the territory of that Member State for two years; or

   (b) the death resulted from an accident at work or an occupational disease; or

   (c) the surviving spouse lost the nationality of that Member State following marriage to the worker or self-employed person.

Article 18 Acquisition of the right of permanent residence by certain family members who are not nationals of a Member State

Without prejudice to Article 17, the family members of a Union citizen to whom Articles 12(2) and 13(2) apply, who satisfy the conditions laid down therein, shall acquire the right of permanent residence after residing legally for a period of five consecutive years in the host Member State.

SECTION II
ADMINISTRATIVE FORMALITIES

Article 19 Document certifying permanent residence for Union citizens

1. Upon application Member States shall issue Union citizens entitled to permanent residence, after having verified duration of residence, with a document certifying permanent residence.

2. The document certifying permanent residence shall be issued as soon as possible.

Article 20 Permanent residence card for family members who are not nationals of a Member State

1. Member States shall issue family members who are not nationals of a Member State entitled to permanent residence with a permanent residence card within six months of the submission of the application. The permanent residence card shall be renewable automatically every ten years.

2. The application for a permanent residence card shall be submitted before the residence card expires. Failure to comply with the requirement to apply for a permanent residence card may render the person concerned liable to proportionate and non-discriminatory sanctions.

2474

3. Interruption in residence not exceeding two consecutive years shall not affect the validity of the permanent residence card.

Article 21 Continuity of residence

For the purposes of this Directive, continuity of residence may be attested by any means of proof in use in the host Member State. Continuity of residence is broken by any expulsion decision duly enforced against the person concerned.

CHAPTER V
PROVISIONS COMMON TO THE RIGHT OF RESIDENCE AND THE RIGHT OF
PERMANENT RESIDENCE

Article 22 Territorial scope

The right of residence and the right of permanent residence shall cover the whole territory of the host Member State. Member States may impose territorial restrictions on the right of residence and the right of permanent residence only where the same restrictions apply to their own nationals.

Article 23 Related rights

Irrespective of nationality, the family members of a Union citizen who have the right of residence or the right of permanent residence in a Member State shall be entitled to take up employment or self-employment there.

Article 24 Equal treatment

1. Subject to such specific provisions as are expressly provided for in the Treaty and secondary law, all Union citizens residing on the basis of this Directive in the territory of the host Member State shall enjoy equal treatment with the nationals of that Member State within the scope of the Treaty. The benefit of this right shall be extended to family members who are not nationals of a Member State and who have the right of residence or permanent residence.

2. By way of derogation from paragraph 1, the host Member State shall not be obliged to confer entitlement to social assistance during the first three months of residence or, where appropriate, the longer period provided for in Article 14(4)(b), nor shall it be obliged, prior to acquisition of the right of permanent residence, to grant maintenance aid for studies, including vocational training, consisting in student grants or student loans to persons other than workers, self-employed persons, persons who retain such status and members of their families.

Article 25 General provisions concerning residence documents

1. Possession of a registration certificate as referred to in Article 8, of a document certifying permanent residence, of a certificate attesting submission of an application for a family member residence card, of a residence card or of a permanent residence card, may under no circumstances be made a precondition for the exercise of a right or the completion of an administrative formality, as entitlement to rights may be attested by any other means of proof.

2. All documents mentioned in paragraph 1 shall be issued free of charge or for a charge not exceeding that imposed on nationals for the issuing of similar documents.

Article 26 Checks

Member States may carry out checks on compliance with any requirement deriving from their national legislation for non-nationals always to carry their registration certificate or residence card, provided that the same requirement applies to their own nationals as regards their identity card. In the event of failure to comply with this requirement, Member States may impose the same sanctions as those imposed on their own nationals for failure to carry their identity card.

CHAPTER VI

RESTRICTIONS ON THE RIGHT OF ENTRY AND THE RIGHT OF RESIDENCE ON GROUNDS OF PUBLIC POLICY, PUBLIC SECURITY OR PUBLIC HEALTH

Article   27   General principles

1.   Subject to the provisions of this Chapter, Member States may restrict the freedom of movement and residence of Union citizens and their family members, irrespective of nationality, on grounds of public policy, public security or public health. These grounds shall not be invoked to serve economic ends.

2.   Measures taken on grounds of public policy or public security shall comply with the principle of proportionality and shall be based exclusively on the personal conduct of the individual concerned. Previous criminal convictions shall not in themselves constitute grounds for taking such measures.

The personal conduct of the individual concerned must represent a genuine, present and sufficiently serious threat affecting one of the fundamental interests of society. Justifications that are isolated from the particulars of the case or that rely on considerations of general prevention shall not be accepted.

3.   In order to ascertain whether the person concerned represents a danger for public policy or public security, when issuing the registration certificate or, in the absence of a registration system, not later than three months from the date of arrival of the person concerned on its territory or from the date of reporting his/her presence within the territory, as provided for in Article 5(5), or when issuing the residence card, the host Member State may, should it consider this essential, request the Member State of origin and, if need be, other Member States to provide information concerning any previous police record the person concerned may have. Such enquiries shall not be made as a matter of routine. The Member State consulted shall give its reply within two months.

4.   The Member State which issued the passport or identity card shall allow the holder of the document who has been expelled on grounds of public policy, public security, or public health from another Member State to re-enter its territory without any formality even if the document is no longer valid or the nationality of the holder is in dispute.

Article   28   Protection against expulsion

1.   Before taking an expulsion decision on grounds of public policy or public security, the host Member State shall take account of considerations such as how long the individual concerned has resided on its territory, his/her age, state of health, family and economic situation, social and cultural integration into the host Member State and the extent of his/her links with the country of origin.

2.   The host Member State may not take an expulsion decision against Union citizens or their family members, irrespective of nationality, who have the right of permanent residence on its territory, except on serious grounds of public policy or public security.

3.   An expulsion decision may not be taken against Union citizens, except if the decision is based on imperative grounds of public security, as defined by Member States, if they:

   (a)   have resided in the host Member State for the previous ten years; or

(b) are a minor, except if the expulsion is necessary for the best interests of the child, as provided for in the United Nations Convention on the Rights of the Child of 20 November 1989.

Article 29 Public health

1. The only diseases justifying measures restricting freedom of movement shall be the diseases with epidemic potential as defined by the relevant instruments of the World Health Organisation and other infectious diseases or contagious parasitic diseases if they are the subject of protection provisions applying to nationals of the host Member State.

2. Diseases occurring after a three-month period from the date of arrival shall not constitute grounds for expulsion from the territory.

3. Where there are serious indications that it is necessary, Member States may, within three months of the date of arrival, require persons entitled to the right of residence to undergo, free of charge, a medical examination to certify that they are not suffering from any of the conditions referred to in paragraph 1. Such medical examinations may not be required as a matter of routine.

Article 30 Notification of decisions

1. The persons concerned shall be notified in writing of any decision taken under Article 27(1), in such a way that they are able to comprehend its content and the implications for them.

2. The persons concerned shall be informed, precisely and in full, of the public policy, public security or public health grounds on which the decision taken in their case is based, unless this is contrary to the interests of State security.

3. The notification shall specify the court or administrative authority with which the person concerned may lodge an appeal, the time limit for the appeal and, where applicable, the time allowed for the person to leave the territory of the Member State. Save in duly substantiated cases of urgency, the time allowed to leave the territory shall be not less than one month from the date of notification.

Article 31 Procedural safeguards

1. The persons concerned shall have access to judicial and, where appropriate, administrative redress procedures in the host Member State to appeal against or seek review of any decision taken against them on the grounds of public policy, public security or public health.

2. Where the application for appeal against or judicial review of the expulsion decision is accompanied by an application for an interim order to suspend enforcement of that decision, actual removal from the territory may not take place until such time as the decision on the interim order has been taken, except:
- where the expulsion decision is based on a previous judicial decision; or
- where the persons concerned have had previous access to judicial review; or
- where the expulsion decision is based on imperative grounds of public security under Article 28(3).

3. The redress procedures shall allow for an examination of the legality of the decision, as well as of the facts and circumstances on which the proposed measure is based. They shall ensure that the decision is not disproportionate, particularly in view of the requirements laid down in Article 28.

4. Member States may exclude the individual concerned from their territory pending the redress procedure, but they may not prevent the individual from submitting his/her

defence in person, except when his/her appearance may cause serious troubles to public policy or public security or when the appeal or judicial review concerns a denial of entry to the territory.

Article 32 Duration of exclusion orders

1. Persons excluded on grounds of public policy or public security may submit an application for lifting of the exclusion order after a reasonable period, depending on the circumstances, and in any event after three years from enforcement of the final exclusion order which has been validly adopted in accordance with Community law, by putting forward arguments to establish that there has been a material change in the circumstances which justified the decision ordering their exclusion.

The Member State concerned shall reach a decision on this application within six months of its submission.

2. The persons referred to in paragraph 1 shall have no right of entry to the territory of the Member State concerned while their application is being considered.

Article 33 Expulsion as a penalty or legal consequence

1. Expulsion orders may not be issued by the host Member State as a penalty or legal consequence of a custodial penalty, unless they conform to the requirements of Articles 27, 28 and 29.

2. If an expulsion order, as provided for in paragraph 1, is enforced more than two years after it was issued, the Member State shall check that the individual concerned is currently and genuinely a threat to public policy or public security and shall assess whether there has been any material change in the circumstances since the expulsion order was issued.

CHAPTER VII
FINAL PROVISIONS

Article 34 Publicity

Member States shall disseminate information concerning the rights and obligations of Union citizens and their family members on the subjects covered by this Directive, particularly by means of awareness-raising campaigns conducted through national and local media and other means of communication.

Article 35 Abuse of rights

Member States may adopt the necessary measures to refuse, terminate or withdraw any right conferred by this Directive in the case of abuse of rights or fraud, such as marriages of convenience. Any such measure shall be proportionate and subject to the procedural safeguards provided for in Articles 30 and 31.

Article 36 Sanctions

Member States shall lay down provisions on the sanctions applicable to breaches of national rules adopted for the implementation of this Directive and shall take the measures required for their application. The sanctions laid down shall be effective and proportionate. Member States shall notify the Commission of these provisions not later than ... * and as promptly as possible in the case of any subsequent changes.

* Two years from the date of entry into force of this Directive.

Article 37 More favourable national provisions

The provisions of this Directive shall not affect any laws, regulations or administrative provisions laid down by a Member State which would be more favourable to the persons covered by this Directive.

Article 38 Repeals

1. Articles 10 and 11 of Regulation (EEC) No 1612/68 shall be repealed with effect from ... *

2. Directives 64/221/EEC, 68/360/EEC, 72/194/EEC, 73/148/EEC, 75/34/EEC, 75/35/EEC, 90/364/EEC, 90/365/EEC and 93/96/EEC shall be repealed with effect from ... *

3. References made to the repealed provisions and Directives shall be construed as being made to this Directive.

* Two years from the date of entry into force of this Directive.

Article 39 Report

No later than ... * the Commission shall submit a report on the application of this Directive to the European Parliament and the Council, together with any necessary proposals, notably on the opportunity to extend the period of time during which Union citizens and their family members may reside in the territory of the host Member State without any conditions. The Member States shall provide the Commission with the information needed to produce the report.

* Four years from the date of entry into force of this Directive.

Article 40 Transposition

1. Member States shall bring into force the laws, regulations and administrative provisions necessary to comply with this Directive by ... *.

When Member States adopt those measures, they shall contain a reference to this Directive or shall be accompanied by such a reference on the occasion of their official publication. The methods of making such reference shall be laid down by the Member States.

* Two years from the date of entry into force of this Directive.

2. Member States shall communicate to the Commission the text of the provisions of national law which they adopt in the field covered by this Directive together with a table showing how the provisions of this Directive correspond to the national provisions adopted.

Article 41 Entry into force

This Directive shall enter into force on the day of its publication in the Official Journal of the European Union.

2479

Article 42 Addressees

This Directive is addressed to the Member States.

Done at Strasbourg, 29 April 2004.

COUNCIL DIRECTIVE (2004/83/EC) of 29 April 2004 on

minimum standards for the qualification and status of third country nationals or stateless persons as refugees or as persons who otherwise need international protection and the content of the protection granted

OJ L 304, 30 September 2004, p.12

THE COUNCIL OF THE EUROPEAN UNION,

Having regard to the Treaty establishing the European Community, and in particular points 1(*c*), 2(*a*) and 3(*a*) of Article 63 thereof,

Having regard to the proposal from the Commission[1],

Having regard to the opinion of the European Parliament[2],

Having regard to the opinion of the European Economic and Social Committee[3],

Having regard to the opinion of the Committee of the Regions[4],

Whereas:

(1) A common policy on asylum, including a Common European Asylum System, is a constituent part of the European Union's objective of progressively establishing an area of freedom, security and justice open to those who, forced by circumstances, legitimately seek protection in the Community.

(2) The European Council at its special meeting in Tampere on 15 and 16 October 1999 agreed to work towards establishing a Common European Asylum System, based on the full and inclusive application of the Geneva Convention relating to the Status of Refugees of 28 July 1951 (Geneva Convention), as supplemented by the New York Protocol of 31 January 1967 (Protocol), thus affirming the principle of non-refoulement and ensuring that nobody is sent back to persecution.

(3) The Geneva Convention and Protocol provide the cornerstone of the international legal regime for the protection of refugees.

(4) The Tampere conclusions provide that a Common European Asylum System should include, in the short term, the approximation of rules on the recognition of refugees and the content of refugee status.

(5) The Tampere conclusions also provide that rules regarding refugee status should be complemented by measures on subsidiary forms of protection, offering an appropriate status to any person in need of such protection.

(6) The main objective of this Directive is, on the one hand, to ensure that Member States apply common criteria for the identification of persons genuinely in need of international protection, and, on the other hand, to ensure that a minimum level of benefits is available for these persons in all Member States.

(7) The approximation of rules on the recognition and content of refugee and subsidiary protection status should help to limit the secondary movements of applicants for asylum between Member States, where such movement is purely caused by differences in legal frameworks.

(8) It is in the very nature of minimum standards that Member States should have the power to introduce or maintain more favourable provisions for third

country nationals or stateless persons who request international protection from a Member State, where such a request is understood to be on the grounds that the person concerned is either a refugee within the meaning of Article 1(A) of the Geneva Convention, or a person who otherwise needs international protection.

(9) Those third country nationals or stateless persons, who are allowed to remain in the territories of the Member States for reasons not due to a need for international protection but on a discretionary basis on compassionate or humanitarian grounds, fall outside the scope of this Directive.

(10) This Directive respects the fundamental rights and observes the principles recognised in particular by the Charter of Fundamental Rights of the European Union. In particular this Directive seeks to ensure full respect for human dignity and the right to asylum of applicants for asylum and their accompanying family members.

(11) With respect to the treatment of persons falling within the scope of this Directive, Member States are bound by obligations under instruments of international law to which they are party and which prohibit discrimination.

(12) The 'best interests of the child' should be a primary consideration of Member States when implementing this Directive.

(13) This Directive is without prejudice to the Protocol on asylum for nationals of Member States of the European Union as annexed to the Treaty Establishing the European Community.

(14) The recognition of refugee status is a declaratory act.

(15) Consultations with the United Nations High Commissioner for Refugees may provide valuable guidance for Member States when determining refugee status according to Article 1 of the Geneva Convention.

(16) Minimum standards for the definition and content of refugee status should be laid down to guide the competent national bodies of Member States in the application of the Geneva Convention.

(17) It is necessary to introduce common criteria for recognising applicants for asylum as refugees within the meaning of Article 1 of the Geneva Convention.

(18) In particular, it is necessary to introduce common concepts of protection needs arising sur place; sources of harm and protection; internal protection; and persecution, including the reasons for persecution.

(19) Protection can be provided not only by the State but also by parties or organisations, including international organisations, meeting the conditions of this Directive, which control a region or a larger area within the territory of the State.

(20) It is necessary, when assessing applications from minors for international protection, that Member States should have regard to child-specific forms of persecution.

(21) It is equally necessary to introduce a common concept of the persecution ground 'membership of a particular social group'.

(22) Acts contrary to the purposes and principles of the United Nations are set out in the Preamble and Articles 1 and 2 of the Charter of the United Nations and are, amongst others, embodied in the United Nations Resolutions relating to measures combating terrorism, which declare that 'acts, methods and practices of terrorism are contrary to the purposes and principles of the United Nations' and that 'knowingly financing, planning and inciting terrorist acts are also contrary to the purposes and principles of the United Nations'.

(23) As referred to in Article 14, 'status' can also include refugee status.

(24) Minimum standards for the definition and content of subsidiary protection status should also be laid down. Subsidiary protection should be complementary and additional to the refugee protection enshrined in the Geneva Convention.

(25) It is necessary to introduce criteria on the basis of which applicants for international protection are to be recognised as eligible for subsidiary protection. Those criteria should be drawn from international obligations under human rights instruments and practices existing in Member States.

(26) Risks to which a population of a country or a section of the population is generally exposed do normally not create in themselves an individual threat which would qualify as serious harm.

(27) Family members, merely due to their relation to the refugee, will normally be vulnerable to acts of persecution in such a manner that could be the basis for refugee status.

(28) The notion of national security and public order also covers cases in which a third country national belongs to an association which supports international terrorism or supports such an association.

(29) While the benefits provided to family members of beneficiaries of subsidiary protection status do not necessarily have to be the same as those provided to the qualifying beneficiary, they need to be fair in comparison to those enjoyed by beneficiaries of subsidiary protection status.

(30) Within the limits set out by international obligations, Member States may lay down that the granting of benefits with regard to access to employment, social welfare, health care and access to integration facilities requires the prior issue of a residence permit.

(31) This Directive does not apply to financial benefits from the Member States which are granted to promote education and training.

(32) The practical difficulties encountered by beneficiaries of refugee or subsidiary protection status concerning the authentication of their foreign diplomas, certificates or other evidence of formal qualification should be taken into account.

(33) Especially to avoid social hardship, it is appropriate, for beneficiaries of refugee or subsidiary protection status, to provide without discrimination in the context of social assistance the adequate social welfare and means of subsistence.

(34) With regard to social assistance and health care, the modalities and detail of the provision of core benefits to beneficiaries of subsidiary protection status should be determined by national law. The possibility of limiting the benefits for beneficiaries of subsidiary protection status to core benefits is to be understood in the sense that this notion covers at least minimum income support, assistance in case of illness, pregnancy and parental assistance, in so far as they are granted to nationals according to the legislation of the Member State concerned.

(35) Access to health care, including both physical and mental health care, should be ensured to beneficiaries of refugee or subsidiary protection status.

(36) The implementation of this Directive should be evaluated at regular intervals, taking into consideration in particular the evolution of the international obligations of Member States regarding non-refoulement, the evolution of the labour markets in the Member States as well as the development of common basic principles for integration.

(37) Since the objectives of the proposed Directive, namely to establish minimum standards for the granting of international protection to third country nationals and stateless persons by Member States and the content of the protection granted, cannot be sufficiently achieved by the Member States and can therefore, by reason of the scale and effects of the Directive, be better achieved at Community level, the Community may adopt measures, in accordance with the principle of subsidiarity as set out in Article 5 of the Treaty. In accordance with the principle of proportionality, as set out in that Article, this Directive does not go beyond what is necessary in order to achieve those objectives.

(38) In accordance with Article 3 of the Protocol on the position of the United Kingdom and Ireland, annexed to the Treaty on European Union and to the Treaty establishing the European Community, the United Kingdom has notified, by letter of 28 January 2002 , its wish to take part in the adoption and application of this Directive.

(39) In accordance with Article 3 of the Protocol on the position of the United Kingdom and Ireland, annexed to the Treaty on European Union and to the Treaty establishing the European Community, Ireland has notified, by letter of 13 February 2002 , its wish to take part in the adoption and application of this Directive.

(40) In accordance with Articles 1 and 2 of the Protocol on the position of Denmark, annexed to the Treaty on European Union and to the Treaty establishing the European Community, Denmark is not taking part in the adoption of this Directive and is not bound by it or subject to its application,

1 OJ C 51 E, 26.2.2002, p 325.
2 OJ C 300 E, 11.12.2003, p 25.
3 OJ C 221, 17.9.2002, p 43.
4 OJ C 278, 14.11.2002, p 44.

Has adopted this Directive,

CHAPTER I
GENERAL PROVISIONS

Article   1   Subject matter and scope

The purpose of this Directive is to lay down minimum standards for the qualification of third country nationals or stateless persons as refugees or as persons who otherwise need international protection and the content of the protection granted.

Article   2   Definitions

For the purposes of this Directive:

(a) 'international protection' means the refugee and subsidiary protection status as defined in (d) and (f);

(b) Geneva Convention' means the Convention relating to the status of refugees done at Geneva on 28 July 1951, as amended by the New York Protocol of 31 January 1967;

(c) 'refugee' means a third country national who, owing to a well-founded fear of being persecuted for reasons of race, religion, nationality, political opinion or membership of a particular social group, is outside the country of nationality and is unable or, owing to such fear, is unwilling to avail himself or herself of the protection of that country, or a stateless person, who, being outside of the country of former habitual residence for the same reasons as mentioned above, is unable or, owing to such fear, unwilling to return to it, and to whom Article 12 does not apply;

(d) 'refugee status' means the recognition by a Member State of a third country national or a stateless person as a refugee;

(e) 'person eligible for subsidiary protection' means a third country national or a stateless person who does not qualify as a refugee but in respect of whom substantial grounds have been shown for believing that the person concerned, if returned to his or her country of origin, or in the case of a stateless person, to his or her country of former habitual residence, would face a real risk of suffering serious harm as defined in Article 15, and to whom Article 17(1) and (2) do not apply, and is unable, or, owing to such risk, unwilling to avail himself or herself of the protection of that country;

(f) 'subsidiary protection status' means the recognition by a Member State of a third country national or a stateless person as a person eligible for subsidiary protection;

(g) 'application for international protection' means a request made by a third country national or a stateless person for protection from a Member State, who can be understood to seek refugee status or subsidiary protection status, and who does not explicitly request another kind of protection, outside the scope of this Directive, that can be applied for separately;

(h) 'family members' means, insofar as the family already existed in the country of origin, the following members of the family of the beneficiary of refugee or subsidiary protection status who are present in the same Member State in relation to the application for international protection:

— the spouse of the beneficiary of refugee or subsidiary protection status or his or her unmarried partner in a stable relationship, where the legislation or practice of the Member State concerned treats unmarried couples in a way comparable to married couples under its law relating to aliens,

— the minor children of the couple referred to in the first indent or of the beneficiary of refugee or subsidiary protection status, on condition that they are unmarried and dependent and regardless of whether they were born in or out of wedlock or adopted as defined under the national law;

(i) 'unaccompanied minors' means third-country nationals or stateless persons below the age of 18, who arrive on the territory of the Member States unaccompanied by an adult responsible for them whether by law or custom, and for as long as they are not effectively taken into the care of such a person; it includes minors who are left unaccompanied after they have entered the territory of the Member States;

(j) 'residence permit' means any permit or authorisation issued by the authorities of a Member State, in the form provided for under that State's legislation, allowing a third country national or stateless person to reside on its territory;

(k) 'country of origin' means the country or countries of nationality or, for stateless persons, of former habitual residence.

Article   3   More favourable standards

Member States may introduce or retain more favourable standards for determining who qualifies as a refugee or as a person eligible for subsidiary protection, and for determining the content of international protection, in so far as those standards are compatible with this Directive.

CHAPTER II
ASSESSMENT OF APPLICATIONS FOR INTERNATIONAL PROTECTION

Article   4   Assessment of facts and circumstances

1. Member States may consider it the duty of the applicant to submit as soon as possible all elements needed to substantiate the application for international protection. In cooperation with the applicant it is the duty of the Member State to assess the relevant elements of the application.

2. The elements referred to in of paragraph 1 consist of the applicant's statements and all documentation at the applicants disposal regarding the applicant's age, background, including that of relevant relatives, identity, nationality(ies), country(ies) and place(s) of previous residence, previous asylum applications, travel routes, identity and travel documents and the reasons for applying for international protection.

3. The assessment of an application for international protection is to be carried out on an individual basis and includes taking into account:

(a) all relevant facts as they relate to the country of origin at the time of taking a decision on the application; including laws and regulations of the country of origin and the manner in which they are applied;

(b) the relevant statements and documentation presented by the applicant including information on whether the applicant has been or may be subject to persecution or serious harm;

(c) the individual position and personal circumstances of the applicant, including factors such as background, gender and age, so as to assess whether, on the basis of the applicant's personal circumstances, the acts to which the applicant has been or could be exposed would amount to persecution or serious harm;

(d) whether the applicant's activities since leaving the country of origin were engaged in for the sole or main purpose of creating the necessary conditions for applying for international protection, so as to assess whether these activities will expose the applicant to persecution or serious harm if returned to that country;

(e) whether the applicant could reasonably be expected to avail himself of the protection of another country where he could assert citizenship.

4. The fact that an applicant has already been subject to persecution or serious harm or to direct threats of such persecution or such harm, is a serious indication of the applicant's well-founded fear of persecution or real risk of suffering serious harm, unless there are good reasons to consider that such persecution or serious harm will not be repeated.

5. Where Member States apply the principle according to which it is the duty of the applicant to substantiate the application for international protection and where aspects of the applicant's statements are not supported by documentary or other evidence, those aspects shall not need confirmation, when the following conditions are met:

(a) the applicant has made a genuine effort to substantiate his application;

(b) all relevant elements, at the applicant's disposal, have been submitted, and a satisfactory explanation regarding any lack of other relevant elements has been given;

(c) the applicant's statements are found to be coherent and plausible and do not run counter to available specific and general information relevant to the applicant's case;

(d) the applicant has applied for international protection at the earliest possible time, unless the applicant can demonstrate good reason for not having done so; and

(e) the general credibility of the applicant has been established.

Article 5 International protection needs arising sur place

1. A well-founded fear of being persecuted or a real risk of suffering serious harm may be based on events which have taken place since the applicant left the country of origin.

2. A well-founded fear of being persecuted or a real risk of suffering serious harm may be based on activities which have been engaged in by the applicant since he left the country of origin, in particular where it is established that the activities relied upon constitute the expression and continuation of convictions or orientations held in the country of origin.

3. Without prejudice to the Geneva Convention, Member States may determine that an applicant who files a subsequent application shall normally not be granted refugee status, if the risk of persecution is based on circumstances which the applicant has created by his own decision since leaving the country of origin.

Article 6   Actors of persecution or serious harm

Actors of persecution or serious harm include:

(*a*) the State;

(*b*) parties or organisations controlling the State or a substantial part of the territory of the State;

(*c*) non-State actors, if it can be demonstrated that the actors mentioned in (a) and (b), including international organisations, are unable or unwilling to provide protection against persecution or serious harm as defined in Article 7.

Article   7   Actors of protection

1.   Protection can be provided by:

(a) the State; or

(b) parties or organisations, including international organisations, controlling the State or a substantial part of the territory of the State.

2.   Protection is generally provided when the actors mentioned in paragraph 1 take reasonable steps to prevent the persecution or suffering of serious harm, inter alia, by operating an effective legal system for the detection, prosecution and punishment of acts constituting persecution or serious harm, and the applicant has access to such protection.

3.   When assessing whether an international organisation controls a State or a substantial part of its territory and provides protection as described in paragraph 2, Member States shall take into account any guidance which may be provided in relevant Council acts.

Article   8   Internal protection

1.   As part of the assessment of the application for international protection, Member States may determine that an applicant is not in need of international protection if in a part of the country of origin there is no well-founded fear of being persecuted or no real risk of suffering serious harm and the applicant can reasonably be expected to stay in that part of the country.

2.   In examining whether a part of the country of origin is in accordance with paragraph 1, Member States shall at the time of taking the decision on the application have regard to the general circumstances prevailing in that part of the country and to the personal circumstances of the applicant.

3.   Paragraph 1 may apply notwithstanding technical obstacles to return to the country of origin.

CHAPTER III
QUALIFICATION FOR BEING A REFUGEE

Article   9   Acts of persecution

1.   Acts of persecution within the meaning of article 1 A of the Geneva Convention must:

(a) be sufficiently serious by their nature or repetition as to constitute a severe violation of basic human rights, in particular the rights from which derogation cannot be made under Article 15(2) of the European Convention for the Protection of Human Rights and Fundamental Freedoms; or

(b) be an accumulation of various measures, including violations of human rights which is sufficiently severe as to affect an individual in a similar manner as mentioned in (a).

CHAPTER IV
REFUGEE STATUS

Article 13 Granting of refugee status

Member States shall grant refugee status to a third country national or a stateless person, who qualifies as a refugee in accordance with Chapters II and III.

Article 14 Revocation of, ending of or refusal to renew refugee status

1. Concerning applications for international protection filed after the entry into force of this Directive, Member States shall revoke, end or refuse to renew the refugee status of a third country national or a stateless person granted by a governmental, administrative, judicial or quasi-judicial body, if he or she has ceased to be a refugee in accordance with Article 11.

2. Without prejudice to the duty of the refugee in accordance with Article 4(1) to disclose all relevant facts and provide all relevant documentation at his/her disposal, the Member State, which has granted refugee status, shall on an individual basis demonstrate that the person concerned has ceased to be or has never been a refugee in accordance with paragraph 1 of this Article.

3. Member States shall revoke, end or refuse to renew the refugee status of a third country national or a stateless person, if, after he or she has been granted refugee status, it is established by the Member State concerned that:

   (a) he or she should have been or is excluded from being a refugee in accordance with Article 12;
   (b) his or her misrepresentation or omission of facts, including the use of false documents, were decisive for the granting of refugee status.

4. Member States may revoke, end or refuse to renew the status granted to a refugee by a governmental, administrative, judicial or quasi-judicial body, when:

   (a) there are reasonable grounds for regarding him or her as a danger to the security of the Member State in which he or she is present;
   (b) he or she, having been convicted by a final judgement of a particularly serious crime, constitutes a danger to the community of that Member State.

5. In situations described in paragraph 4, Member States may decide not to grant status to a refugee, where such a decision has not yet been taken.

6. Persons to whom paragraphs 4 or 5 apply are entitled to rights set out in or similar to those set out in Articles 3, 4, 16, 22, 31 and 32 and 33 of the Geneva Convention in so far as they are present in the Member State.

CHAPTER V
QUALIFICATION FOR SUBSIDIARY PROTECTION

Article 15 Serious harm

Serious harm consists of:

   (a) death penalty or execution; or
   (b) torture or inhuman or degrading treatment or punishment of an applicant in the country of origin; or
   (c) serious and individual threat to a civilian's life or person by reason of indiscriminate violence in situations of international or internal armed conflict.

Article 16 Cessation

1. A third country national or a stateless person shall cease to be eligible for subsidiary protection when the circumstances which led to the granting of subsidiary protection status have ceased to exist or have changed to such a degree that protection is no longer required.

2. In applying paragraph 1, Member States shall have regard to whether the change of circumstances is of such a significant and non-temporary nature that the person eligible for subsidiary protection no longer faces a real risk of serious harm.

Article 17 Exclusion

1. A third country national or a stateless person is excluded from being eligible for subsidiary protection where there are serious reasons for considering that:

(a) he or she has committed a crime against peace, a war crime, or a crime against humanity, as defined in the international instruments drawn up to make provision in respect of such crimes;

(b) he or she has committed a serious crime;

(c) he or she has been guilty of acts contrary to the purposes and principles of the United Nations set out in the Preamble and Articles 1 and 2 of the Charter of the United Nations;

(d) he or she constitutes a danger to the community or to the security of the Member State in which he or she is present.

2. Paragraph 1 applies to persons who instigate or otherwise participate in the commission of the crimes or acts mentioned therein.

3. Member States may exclude a third country national or a stateless person from being eligible for subsidiary protection, if he or she prior to his or her admission to the Member State has committed one or more crimes, outside the scope of paragraph 1, which would be punishable by imprisonment, had they been committed in the Member State concerned, and if he or she left his or her country of origin solely in order to avoid sanctions resulting from these crimes.

CHAPTER VI
SUBSIDIARY PROTECTION STATUS

Article 18 Granting of subsidiary protection status

Member States shall grant subsidiary protection status to a third country national or a stateless person eligible for subsidiary protection in accordance with Chapters II and V.

Article 19 Revocation of, ending of or refusal to renew subsidiary protection status

1. Concerning applications for international protection filed after the entry into force of this Directive, Member States shall revoke, end or refuse to renew the subsidiary protection status of a third country national or a stateless person granted by a governmental, administrative, judicial or quasi-judicial body, if he or she has ceased to be eligible for subsidiary protection in accordance with Article 16.

2. Member States may revoke, end or refuse to renew the subsidiary protection status of a third country national or a stateless person granted by a governmental, administrative, judicial or quasi-judicial body, if after having been granted subsidiary protection status, he or she should have been excluded from being eligible for subsidiary protection in accordance with Article 17(3).

3. Member States shall revoke, end or refuse to renew the subsidiary protection status of a third country national or a stateless person, if:

(a) he or she, after having been granted subsidiary protection status, should have been or is excluded from being eligible for subsidiary protection in accordance with Article 17(1) and (2);

(b) his or her misrepresentation or omission of facts, including the use of false documents, were decisive for the granting of subsidiary protection status.

4. Without prejudice to the duty of the third country national or stateless person in accordance with Article 4(1) to disclose all relevant facts and provide all relevant documentation at his/her disposal, the Member State, which has granted the subsidiary protection status, shall on an individual basis demonstrate that the person concerned has ceased to be or is not eligible for subsidiary protection in accordance with paragraphs 1, 2 and 3 of this Article.

CHAPTER VII
CONTENT OF INTERNATIONAL PROTECTION

Article   20   General rules

1. This Chapter shall be without prejudice to the rights laid down in the Geneva Convention.

2. This Chapter shall apply both to refugees and persons eligible for subsidiary protection unless otherwise indicated.

3. When implementing this Chapter, Member States shall take into account the specific situation of vulnerable persons such as minors, unaccompanied minors, disabled people, elderly people, pregnant women, single parents with minor children and persons who have been subjected to torture, rape or other serious forms of psychological, physical or sexual violence.

4. Paragraph 3 shall apply only to persons found to have special needs after an individual evaluation of their situation.

5. The best interest of the child shall be a primary consideration for Member States when implementing the provisions of this Chapter that involve minors.

6. Within the limits set out by the Geneva Convention, Member States may reduce the benefits of this Chapter, granted to a refugee whose refugee status has been obtained on the basis of activities engaged in for the sole or main purpose of creating the necessary conditions for being recognised as a refugee.

7. Within the limits set out by international obligations of Member States, Member States may reduce the benefits of this Chapter, granted to a person eligible for subsidiary protection, whose subsidiary protection status has been obtained on the basis of activities engaged in for the sole or main purpose of creating the necessary conditions for being recognised as a person eligible for subsidiary protection.

Article   21   Protection from refoulement

1. Member States shall respect the principle of non-refoulement in accordance with their international obligations.

2. Where not prohibited by the international obligations mentioned in paragraph 1, Member States may refoule a refugee, whether formally recognised or not, when:

(a) there are reasonable grounds for considering him or her as a danger to the security of the Member State in which he or she is present; or

(b)   he or she, having been convicted by a final judgement of a particularly serious crime, constitutes a danger to the community of that Member State.

3.   Member States may revoke, end or refuse to renew or to grant the residence permit of (or to) a refugee to whom paragraph 2 applies.

Article   22   Information

Member States shall provide persons recognised as being in need of international protection, as soon as possible after the respective protection status has been granted, with access to information, in a language likely to be understood by them, on the rights and obligations relating to that status.

Article   23   Maintaining family unity

1.   Member States shall ensure that family unity can be maintained.

2.   Member States shall ensure that family members of the beneficiary of refugee or subsidiary protection status, who do not individually qualify for such status, are entitled to claim the benefits referred to in Articles 24 to 34, in accordance with national procedures and as far as it is compatible with the personal legal status of the family member.

In so far as the family members of beneficiaries of subsidiary protection status are concerned, Member States may define the conditions applicable to such benefits.

In these cases, Member States shall ensure that any benefits provided guarantee an adequate standard of living.

3.   Paragraphs 1 and 2 are not applicable where the family member is or would be excluded from refugee or subsidiary protection status pursuant to Chapters III and V.

4.   Notwithstanding paragraphs 1 and 2, Member States may refuse, reduce or withdraw the benefits referred therein for reasons of national security or public order.

5.   Member States may decide that this Article also applies to other close relatives who lived together as part of the family at the time of leaving the country of origin, and who were wholly or mainly dependent on the beneficiary of refugee or subsidiary protection status at that time.

Article   24   Residence permits

1.   As soon as possible after their status has been granted, Member States shall issue to beneficiaries of refugee status a residence permit which must be valid for at least three years and renewable unless compelling reasons of national security or public order otherwise require, and without prejudice to Article 21(3).

Without prejudice to Article 23(1), the residence permit to be issued to the family members of the beneficiaries of refugee status may be valid for less than three years and renewable.

2.   As soon as possible after the status has been granted, Member States shall issue to beneficiaries of subsidiary protection status a residence permit which must be valid for at least one year and renewable, unless compelling reasons of national security or public order otherwise require.

Article   25   Travel document

1.   Member States shall issue to beneficiaries of refugee status travel documents in the form set out in the Schedule to the Geneva Convention, for the purpose of travel outside their territory unless compelling reasons of national security or public order otherwise require.

2. Member States shall issue to beneficiaries of subsidiary protection status who are unable to obtain a national passport, documents which enable them to travel, at least when serious humanitarian reasons arise that require their presence in another State, unless compelling reasons of national security or public order otherwise require.

Article 26 Access to employment

1. Member States shall authorise beneficiaries of refugee status to engage in employed or self-employed activities subject to rules generally applicable to the profession and to the public service, immediately after the refugee status has been granted.

2. Member States shall ensure that activities such as employment-related education opportunities for adults, vocational training and practical workplace experience are offered to beneficiaries of refugee status, under equivalent conditions as nationals.

3. Member States shall authorise beneficiaries of subsidiary protection status to engage in employed or self-employed activities subject to rules generally applicable to the profession and to the public service immediately after the subsidiary protection status has been granted. The situation of the labour market in the Member States may be taken into account, including for possible prioritisation of access to employment for a limited period of time to be determined in accordance with national law. Member States shall ensure that the beneficiary of subsidiary protection status has access to a post for which the beneficiary has received an offer in accordance with national rules on prioritisation in the labour market.

4. Member States shall ensure that beneficiaries of subsidiary protection status have access to activities such as employment-related education opportunities for adults, vocational training and practical workplace experience, under conditions to be decided by the Member States.

5. The law in force in the Member States applicable to remuneration, access to social security systems relating to employed or self-employed activities and other conditions of employment shall apply.

Article 27 Access to education

1. Member States shall grant full access to the education system to all minors granted refugee or subsidiary protection status, under the same conditions as nationals.

2. Member States shall allow adults granted refugee or subsidiary protection status access to the general education system, further training or retraining, under the same conditions as third country nationals legally resident.

3. Member States shall ensure equal treatment between beneficiaries of refugee or subsidiary protection status and nationals in the context of the existing recognition procedures for foreign diplomas, certificates and other evidence of formal qualifications.

Article 28 Social welfare

1. Member States shall ensure that beneficiaries of refugee or subsidiary protection status receive, in the Member State that has granted such statuses, the necessary social assistance, as provided to nationals of that Member State.

2. By exception to the general rule laid down in paragraph 1, Member States may limit social assistance granted to beneficiaries of subsidiary protection status to core benefits which will then be provided at the same levels and under the same eligibility conditions as nationals.

Article   29   Health care

1.   Member States shall ensure that beneficiaries of refugee or subsidiary protection status have access to health care under the same eligibility conditions as nationals of the Member State that has granted such statuses.

2.   By exception to the general rule laid down in paragraph 1, Member States may limit health care granted to beneficiaries of subsidiary protection to core benefits which will then be provided at the same levels and under the same eligibility conditions as nationals.

3.   Member States shall provide, under the same eligibility conditions as nationals of the Member State that has granted the status, adequate health care to beneficiaries of refugee or subsidiary protection status who have special needs, such as pregnant women, disabled people, persons who have undergone torture, rape or other serious forms of psychological, physical or sexual violence or minors who have been victims of any form of abuse, neglect, exploitation, torture, cruel, inhuman and degrading treatment or who have suffered from armed conflict.

Article   30   Unaccompanied minors

1.   As soon as possible after the granting of refugee or subsidiary protection status Member States shall take the necessary measures, to ensure the representation of unaccompanied minors by legal guardianship or, where necessary, by an organisation responsible for the care and well-being of minors, or by any other appropriate representation including that based on legislation or Court order.

2.   Member States shall ensure that the minor's needs are duly met in the implementation of this Directive by the appointed guardian or representative. The appropriate authorities shall make regular assessments.

3.   Member States shall ensure that unaccompanied minors are placed either:

   (a)   with adult relatives; or
   (b)   with a foster family; or
   (c)   in centres specialised in accommodation for minors; or
   (d)   in other accommodation suitable for minors.

In this context, the views of the child shall be taken into account in accordance with his or her age and degree of maturity.

4.   As far as possible, siblings shall be kept together, taking into account the best interests of the minor concerned and, in particular, his or her age and degree of maturity. Changes of residence of unaccompanied minors shall be limited to a minimum.

5.   Member States, protecting the unaccompanied minor's best interests, shall endeavour to trace the members of the minor's family as soon as possible. In cases where there may be a threat to the life or integrity of the minor or his or her close relatives, particularly if they have remained in the country of origin, care must be taken to ensure that the collection, processing and circulation of information concerning those persons is undertaken on a confidential basis.

6.   Those working with unaccompanied minors shall have had or receive appropriate training concerning their needs.

Article   31   Access to accommodation

The Member States shall ensure that beneficiaries of refugee or subsidiary protection status have access to accommodation under equivalent conditions as other third country nationals legally resident in their territories.

Article   32   **Freedom of movement within the Member State**

Member States shall allow freedom of movement within their territory to beneficiaries of refugee or subsidiary protection status, under the same conditions and restrictions as those provided for other third country nationals legally resident in their territories.

Article   33   **Access to integration facilities**

1.   In order to facilitate the integration of refugees into society, Member States shall make provision for integration programmes which they consider to be appropriate or create pre-conditions which guarantee access to such programmes.

2.   Where it is considered appropriate by Member States, beneficiaries of subsidiary protection status shall be granted access to integration programmes.

Article   34   **Repatriation**

Member States may provide assistance to beneficiaries of refugee or subsidiary protection status who wish to repatriate.

CHAPTER VIII
ADMINISTRATIVE COOPERATION

Article   35   **Cooperation**

Member States shall each appoint a national contact point, whose address they shall communicate to the Commission, which shall communicate it to the other Member States.

Member States shall, in liaison with the Commission, take all appropriate measures to establish direct cooperation and an exchange of information between the competent authorities.

Article   36   **Staff**

Member States shall ensure that authorities and other organisations implementing this Directive have received the necessary training and shall be bound by the confidentiality principle, as defined in the national law, in relation to any information they obtain in the course of their work.

CHAPTER IX
FINAL PROVISIONS

Article   37   **Reports**

1.   By 10 April 2008, the Commission shall report to the European Parliament and the Council on the application of this Directive and shall propose any amendments that are necessary. These proposals for amendments shall be made by way of priority in relation to Articles 15, 26 and 33. Member States shall send the Commission all the information that is appropriate for drawing up that report by 10 October 2007 .

2.   After presenting the report, the Commission shall report to the European Parliament and the Council on the application of this Directive at least every five years.

Article   38   **Transposition**

1.   The Member States shall bring into force the laws, regulations and administrative provisions necessary to comply with this Directive before 10 October 2006. They shall forthwith inform the Commission thereof.

Appendix 1   Legislation and materials

When the Member States adopt those measures, they shall contain a reference to this Directive or shall be accompanied by such a reference on the occasion of their official publication. The methods of making such reference shall be laid down by Member States.

2.   Member States shall communicate to the Commission the text of the provisions of national law which they adopt in the field covered by this Directive.

Article   39   Entry into force

This Directive shall enter into force on the twentieth day following that of its publication in the Official Journal of the European Union.

Article   40   Addressees

This Directive is addressed to the Member States in accordance with the Treaty establishing the European Community.

Done at Luxembourg, 29 April 2004.

INTERNATIONAL MATERIALS

CONVENTION RELATING TO THE STATUS OF REFUGEES

Done at Geneva on 28 July 1951

Entry into force . . . . *22 April 1954, in accordance with Article 43*

Text . . . . *United Nations Treaty Series No 2545, Vol 189, p 137*

PREAMBLE

The High Contracting Parties

Considering that the Charter of the United Nations and the Universal Declaration of Human Rights approved on 10 December 1948 by the General Assembly have affirmed the principle that human beings shall enjoy fundamental rights and freedoms without discrimination,

Considering that the United Nations has, on various occasions, manifested its profound concern for refugees and endeavoured to assure refugees the widest possible exercise of these fundamental rights and freedoms,

Considering that it is desirable to revise and consolidate previous international agreements relating to the status of refugees and to extend the scope of and the protection accorded by such instruments by means of a new agreement.

Considering that the grant of asylum may place unduly heavy burdens on certain countries, and that a satisfactory solution of a problem of which the United Nations has recognised the international scope and nature cannot therefore be achieved without international co-operation,

Expressing the wish that all states, recognizing the social and humanitarian nature of the problem of refugees, will do everything within their power to prevent this problem from becoming a cause of tension between states,

Noting that the United Nations High Commissioner for Refugees is charged with the task of supervising international conventions providing for the protection of refugees, and recognising that the effective co-ordination of measures taken to deal with this problem will depend upon the co-operation of states with the High Commissioner,

Have agreed as follows:

Note

The Convention was adopted by the United Nations Conference of Plenipotentiaries on the Status of Refugees and Stateless Persons, held at Geneva from 2 to 25 July 1951. The Conference was convened pursuant to resolution 429(V), adopted by the General Assembly of the United Nations on 14 December 1950. For the text of this resolution, see Official Records of the General Assembly, Fifth Session, Supplement No 20(A/1775), p 48, The Text of the Final Act of the Conference is reproduced in the Appendix.

CHAPTER 1
GENERAL PROVISIONS

Article 1 Definition of the term 'Refugee'

A For the purposes of the present Convention, the term 'refugee' shall apply to any person who:

(1)   Has been considered a refugee under the Arrangements of 12 May 1926 and 30 June 1928 or under the Conventions of 28 October 1933 and 10 February 1938, the Protocol of 14 September 1939 or the Constitution of the International Refugee Organization;

Decisions of non-eligibility taken by the International Refugee Organization during the period of its activities shall not prevent the status of refugee being accorded to persons who fulfil the conditions of paragraph 2 of this section;

(2)   As a result of events occurring before 1 January 1951 and owing to well-founded fear of being persecuted for reasons of race, religion, nationality, membership of a particular social group or political opinion, is outside the country of his nationality and is unable or, owing to such fear, is unwilling to avail himself of the protection of that country; or who, not having a nationality and being outside the country of his former habitual residence as a result of such events, is unable or, owing to such fear, is unwilling to return to it.

In the case of a person who has more than one nationality, the term 'the country of his nationality' shall mean each of the countries of which he is a national, and a person shall not be deemed to be lacking the protection of the country of his nationality if, without any valid reason based on well-founded fear, he has not availed himself of the protection of one of the countries of which he is a national.

B

(1)   For the purposes of this Convention, the words 'events occurring before 1 January 1951' in Article 1, Section A, shall be understood to mean either

(a)   'events occurring in Europe before 1 January 1951'; or

(b)   'events occurring in Europe or elsewhere before 1 January 1951', and each contracting state shall make a declaration at the time of signature, ratification or accession, specifying which of these meanings it applies for the purpose of its obligations under this Convention.

(2)   Any contracting state which has adopted alternative (a) may at any time extend its obligations by adopting alternative (b) by means of a notification addressed to the Secretary-General of the United Nations.

C   This Convention shall cease to apply to any person falling under the terms of section A if:

(1)   He has voluntarily re-availed himself of the protection of the country of his nationality; or

(2)   Having lost his nationality, he has voluntarily re-acquired it, or

(3)   He has acquired a new nationality, and enjoys the protection of the country of his new nationality; or

(4)   He has voluntarily re-established himself in the country which he left or outside which he remained owing to fear of persecution; or

(5)   He can no longer, because the circumstances in connection with which he has been recognized as a refugee have ceased to exist, continue to refuse to avail himself of the protection of the country of his nationality;

Provided that this paragraph shall not apply to a refugee falling under section A(1) of this Article who is able to invoke compelling reasons arising out of previous persecution for refusing to avail himself of the protection of the country of nationality;

(6)   Being a person who has no nationality he is, because the circumstances in connection with which he has been recognized as a refugee have ceased to exist, able to return to the country of his former habitual residence;

Provided that this paragraph shall not apply to a refugee falling under section A(1) of this Article who is able to invoke compelling reasons arising out of previous persecution for refusing to return to the country of his former habitual residence.

D This Convention shall not apply to persons who are at present receiving from organs or agencies of the United Nations other than the United Nations High Commissioner for Refugees protection or assistance.

When such protection or assistance has ceased for any reason, without the position of such persons being definitely settled in accordance with the relevant resolutions adopted by the General Assembly of the United Nations, these persons shall *ipso facto* be entitled to the benefits of this Convention.

E This Convention shall not apply to a person who is recognized by the competent authorities of the country in which he has taken residence as having the rights and obligations which are attached to the possession of the nationality of that country.

F The provisions of this Convention shall not apply to any person with respect to whom there are serious reasons for considering that:

   (a) he has committed a crime against peace, a war crime, or a crime against humanity, as defined in the international instruments drawn up to make provision in respect of such crimes;

   (b) he has committed a serious non-political crime outside the country of refuge prior to his admission to that country as a refugee;

   (c) he has been guilty of acts contrary to the purposes and principles of the United Nations.

Article 2 General obligations

Every refugee has duties to the country in which he finds himself, which require in particular that he conform to its laws and regulations as well as to measures taken for the maintenance of public order.

Article 3 Non-discrimination

The contracting states shall apply the provisions of this Convention to refugees without discrimination as to race, religion or country of origin.

Article 4 Religion

The contracting states shall accord to refugees within their territories treatment at least as favourable as that accorded to their nationals with respect to freedom to practise their religion and freedom as regards the religious education of their children.

Article 5 Rights granted apart from this Convention

Nothing in this Convention shall be deemed to impair any rights and benefits granted by a contracting state to refugees apart from this Convention.

Article 6 The term 'in the same circumstances'

For the purpose of this Convention, the term 'in the same circumstances' implies that any requirements (including requirements as to length and conditions of sojourn or residence) which the particular individual would have to fulfil for the enjoyment of the right in question, if he were not a refugee, must be fulfilled by him, with the exception of requirements which by their nature a refugee is incapable of fulfilling.

Article 7 Exemption from reciprocity

1 Except where this Convention contains more favourable provisions, a contracting state shall accord to refugees the same treatment as is accorded to aliens generally.

2 After a period of three years' residence, all refugees shall enjoy exemption from legislative reciprocity in the territory of the contracting states.

3 Each contracting state shall continue to accord to refugees the rights and benefits to which they were already entitled, in the absence of reciprocity, at the date of entry into force of this Convention for that state.

4 The contracting states shall consider favourably the possibility of according to refugees, in the absence of reciprocity, rights and benefits beyond those to which they are entitled according to paragraphs 2 and 3, and to extending exemption from reciprocity to refugees who do not fulfil the conditions provided for in paragraphs 2 and 3.

5 The provisions of paragraphs 2 and 3 apply both to the rights and benefits referred to in Articles 13, 18, 19, 21 and 22 of this Convention and to rights and benefits for which this Convention does not provide.

Article 8 Exemption from exceptional measures

With regard to exceptional measures which may be taken against the person, property or interests of nationals of a foreign state, the contracting states shall not apply such measures to a refugee who is formally a national of the said state solely on account of such nationality. Contracting states which, under their legislation, are prevented from applying the general principle expressed in this Article, shall, in appropriate cases, grant exemptions in favour of such refugees.

Article 9 Provisional measures

Nothing in this Convention shall prevent a contracting state, in time of war or other grave and exceptional circumstances, from taking provisionally measures which it considers to be essential to the national security in the case of a particular person, pending a determination by the contracting state that that person is in fact a refugee and that the continuance of such measures is necessary in his case in the interests of national security.

Article 10 Continuity of residence

1 Where a refugee has been forcibly displaced during the Second World War and removed to the territory of a contracting state, and is resident there, the period of such enforced sojourn shall be considered to have been lawful residence within that territory.

2 Where a refugee has been forcibly displaced during the Second World War from the territory of a contracting state and has, prior to the date of entry into force of this Convention, returned there for the purpose of taking up residence, the period of residence before and after such enforced displacement shall be regarded as one uninterrupted period for any purposes for which uninterrupted residence is required.

Article 11 Refugee seamen

In the case of refugees regularly serving as crew members on board a ship flying the flag of a contracting state, that state shall give sympathetic consideration to their establishment on its territory and the issue of travel documents to them or their temporary admission to its territory particularly with a view to facilitating their establishment in another country.

CHAPTER II
JURIDICAL STATUS

Article   12   Personal status

1   The personal status of a refugee shall be governed by the law of the country of his domicile or, if he has no domicile, by the law of the country of his residence.

2   Rights previously acquired by a refugee and dependent on personal status, more particularly rights attaching to marriage, shall be respected by a contracting state, subject to compliance, if this be necessary, with the formalities required by the law of that state, provided that the right in question is one which would have been recognized by the law of that state had he not become a refugee.

Article   13   Movable and immovable property

The contracting states shall accord to a refugee treatment as favourable as possible and, in any event, not less favourable than that accorded to aliens generally in the same circumstances, as regards the acquisition of movable and immovable property and other rights pertaining thereto, and to leases and other contracts relating to movable and immovable property.

Article   14   Artistic rights and industrial property

In respect of the protection of industrial property, such as inventions, designs or models, trade marks, trade names, and of rights in literary, artistic and scientific works, a refugee shall be accorded in the country in which he has his habitual residence the same protection as is accorded to nationals of that country. In the territory of any other contracting state, he shall be accorded the same protection as is accorded in that territory to nationals of the country in which he has his habitual residence.

Article   15   Right of association

As regards non-political and non-profit-making associations and trade unions the contracting states shall accord to refugees lawfully staying in their territory the most favourable treatment accorded to nationals of a foreign country, in the same circumstances.

Article   16   Access to courts

1   A refugee shall have free access to the courts of law on the territory of all contracting states.

2   A refugee shall enjoy in the contracting state in which he has his habitual residence the same treatment as a national in matters pertaining to access to the Courts, including legal assistance and exemption from *cautio judicatum solvi*.

3   A refugee shall be accorded in the matters referred to in paragraph 2 in countries other than that in which he has his habitual residence the treatment granted to a national of the country of his habitual residence.

CHAPTER III
GAINFUL EMPLOYMENT

Article   17   Wage-earning employment

1   The contracting state shall accord to refugees lawfully staying in their territory the most favourable treatment accorded to nationals of a foreign country in the same circumstances, as regards the right to engage in wage-earning employment.

2   In any case, restrictive measures imposed on aliens or the employment of aliens for the protection of the national labour market shall not be applied to a refugee who was already exempt from them at the date of entry into force of this Convention for the contracting state concerned, or who fulfils one of the following conditions:

(a) He has completed three years' residence in the country,
(b) He has a spouse possessing the nationality of the country of residence. A refugee may not invoke the benefits of this provision if he has abandoned his spouse,
(c) He has one or more children possessing the nationality of the country of residence.

3   The contracting states shall give sympathetic consideration to assimilating the rights of all refugees with regard to wage-earning employment to those of nationals, and in particular of those refugees who have entered their territory pursuant to programmes of labour recruitment or under immigration schemes.

Article   18   Self-employment

The contracting states shall accord to a refugee lawfully in their territory treatment as favourable as possible and, in any event, not less favourable than that accorded to aliens generally in the same circumstances, as regards the right to engage on his own account in agriculture, industry, handicrafts and commerce and to establish commercial and industrial companies.

Article   19   Liberal professions

1   Each contracting state shall accord to refugees lawfully staying in their territory who hold diplomas recognized by the competent authorities of that state, and who are desirous of practising a liberal profession, treatment as favourable as possible and, in any event, not less favourable than that accorded to aliens generally in the same circumstances.

2   The contracting states shall use their best endeavours consistently with their laws and constitutions to secure the settlement of such refugees in the territories, other than the metropolitan territory, for whose international relations they are responsible.

CHAPTER IV
WELFARE

Article   20   Rationing

Where a rationing system exists, which applies to the population at large and regulates the general distribution of products in short supply, refugees shall be accorded the same treatment as nationals.

Article   21   Housing

As regards housing, the contracting states, in so far as the matter is regulated by laws or regulations or is subject to the control of public authorities, shall accord to refugees lawfully staying in their territory treatment as favourable as possible and, in any event, not less favourable than that accorded to aliens generally in the same circumstances.

Article   22   Public education

1   The contracting states shall accord to refugees the same treatment as is accorded to nationals with respect to elementary education.

2   The contracting states shall accord to refugees treatment as favourable as possible, and, in any event, not less favourable than that accorded to aliens generally in the same

2504

circumstances, with respect to education other than elementary education and, in particular, as regards access to studies, the recognition of foreign school certificates, diplomas and degrees, the remission of fees and charges and the award of scholarships.

Article 23 Public relief

The contracting states shall accord to refugees lawfully staying in their territory the same treatment with respect to public relief and assistance as is accorded to their nationals.

Article 24 Labour legislation and social security

1 The contracting states shall accord to refugees lawfully staying in their territory the same treatment as is accorded to nationals in respect of the following matters:

(a) In so far as such matters are governed by laws or regulations or are subject to the control of administrative authorities: remuneration, including family allowances where these form part of remuneration, hours of work, overtime arrangements, holidays with pay, restrictions on home work, minimum age of employment, apprenticeship and training, women's work and the work of young persons, and the enjoyment of the benefits of collective bargaining;

(b) Social security (legal provisions in respect of employment injury, occupational diseases, maternity, sickness, disability, old age, death, unemployment, family responsibilities and any other contingency which, according to national laws or regulations, is covered by a social security scheme), subject to the following limitations:

(i) There may be appropriate arrangements for the maintenance of acquired rights and rights in course of acquisition;

(ii) National laws or regulations of the country of residence may prescribe special arrangements concerning benefits or portions of benefits which are payable wholly out of public funds, and concerning allowances paid to persons who do not fulfil the contribution conditions prescribed for the award of a normal pension.

2 The right to compensation for the death of a refugee resulting from employment injury or from occupational disease shall not be affected by the fact that the residence of the beneficiary is outside the territory of the contracting state.

3 The contracting states shall extend to refugees the benefits of agreements concluded between them, or which may be concluded between them in the future, concerning the maintenance of acquired rights and rights in the process of acquisition in regard to social security, subject only to the conditions which apply to nationals of the states signatory to the agreements in question.

4 The contracting states will give sympathetic consideration to extending to refugees so far as possible the benefits of similar agreements which may at any time be in force between such contracting states and non-contracting states.

CHAPTER V
ADMINISTRATIVE MEASURES

Article 25 Administrative assistance

1 When the exercise of a right by a refugee would normally require the assistance of authorities of a foreign country to whom he cannot have recourse, the contracting states in whose territory he is residing shall arrange that such assistance be afforded to him by their own authorities or by an international authority.

2   The authority or authorities mentioned in paragraph 1 shall deliver or cause to be delivered under their supervision to refugees such documents or certifications as would normally be delivered to aliens by or through their national authorities.

3   Documents or certifications so delivered shall stand in the stead or the official instruments delivered to aliens by or through their national authorities, and shall be given credence in the absence of proof to the contrary.

4   Subject to such exceptional treatment as may be granted to indigent persons, fees may be charged for the services mentioned herein, but such fees shall be moderate and commensurate with those charged to nationals for similar services.

5   The provisions of this Article shall be without prejudice to Articles 27 and 28.

Article   26   Freedom of movement

Each contracting state shall accord to refugees lawfully in its territory the right to choose their place of residence and to move freely within its territory, subject to any regulations applicable to aliens generally in the same circumstances.

Article   27   Identity papers

The contracting states shall issue identity papers to any refugee in their territory who does not possess a valid travel document.

Article   28   Travel documents

1   The contracting states shall issue to refugees lawfully staying in their territory travel documents for the purpose of travel outside their territory unless compelling reasons of national security or public order otherwise require, and the provisions of the Schedule to this Convention shall apply with respect to such documents. The contracting states may issue such a travel document to any other refugee in their territory, they shall in particular give sympathetic consideration to the issue of such a travel document to refugees in their territory who are unable to obtain a travel document from the country of their lawful residence.

2   Travel documents issued to refugees under previous international agreements by parties thereto shall be recognized and treated by the contracting states in the same way as if they had been issued pursuant to this article.

Article   29   Fiscal charges

1   The contracting states shall not impose upon refugees duties, charges or taxes, of any description whatsoever, other or higher than those which are or may be levied on their nationals in similar situations.

2   Nothing in the above paragraph shall prevent the application to refugees of the laws and regulations concerning charges in respect of the issue to aliens of administrative documents including identity papers.

Article   30   Transfer of assets

1   A contracting state shall, in conformity with its laws and regulations, permit refugees to transfer assets which they have brought into its territory, to another country where they have been admitted for the purposes of resettlement.

2   A contracting state shall give sympathetic consideration to the application of refugees for permission to transfer assets wherever they may be and which are necessary for their resettlement in another country to which they have been admitted.

Article   31   Refugees unlawfully in the country of refuge

1   The contracting states shall not impose penalties, on account of their illegal entry or presence, on refugees who, coming directly from a territory where their life or freedom was threatened in the sense of Article 1, enter or are present in their territory without authorisation, provided they present themselves without delay to the authorities and show good cause for their illegal entry or presence.

2   The contracting states shall not apply to the movements of such refugees restrictions other than those which are necessary and such restrictions shall only be applied until their status in the country is regularised or they obtain admission into another country. The contracting states shall allow such refugees a reasonable period and all the necessary facilities to obtain admission into another country.

Article   32   Expulsion

1   The contracting states shall not expel a refugee lawfully in their territory save on grounds of national security or public order.

2   The expulsion of such a refugee shall be only in pursuance of a decision reached in accordance with due process of law. Except where compelling reasons of national security otherwise require, the refugee shall be allowed to submit evidence to clear himself, and to appeal to and be represented for the purpose before competent authority or a person or persons specially designated by the competent authority.

3   The contracting states shall allow such a refugee a reasonable period within which to seek legal admission into another country. The contracting states reserve the right to apply during that period such internal measures as they may deem necessary.

Article   33   Prohibition of expulsion or return ('refoulement')

1   No contracting state shall expel or return ('refouler') a refugee in any manner whatsoever to the frontiers of territories where his life or freedom would be threatened on account of his race, religion, nationality, membership of a particular social group or political opinion.

2   The benefit of the present provision may not, however, be claimed by a refugee whom there are reasonable grounds for regarding as a danger to the security of the country in which he is, or who, having been convicted by a final judgment of a particularly serious crime, constitutes a danger to the community of that country.

Article   34   Naturalisation

The contracting states shall as far as possible facilitate the assimilation and naturalisation of refugees. They shall in particular make every effort to expedite naturalisation proceedings and to reduce as far as possible the charges and costs of such proceedings.

CHAPTER VI
EXECUTORY AND TRANSITORY PROVISIONS

Article   35   Co-operation of the national authorities with the United Nations

1   The contracting states undertake to co-operate with the Office of the United Nations High Commissioner for Refugees, or any other agency of the United Nations which may succeed it, in the exercise of its functions, and shall in particular facilitate its duty of supervising the application of the provisions of this Convention.

2   In order to enable the Office of the High Commissioner or any other agency of the United Nations which may succeed it, to make reports to the competent organs of the

United Nations, the contracting states undertake to provide them in the appropriate form with information and statistical data requested concerning:

(a) the condition of refugees,
(b) the implementation of this Convention, and
(c) laws, regulations and decrees which are, or may hereafter be, in force relating to refugees.

Article   36   Information on national legislation

The contracting states shall communicate to the Secretary-General of the United Nations the laws and regulations which they may adopt to ensure the application of this Convention.

Article   37   Relation to previous Conventions

Without prejudice to Article 28, paragraph 2, of this Convention, this Convention replaces, as between parties to it, the Arrangements of 5 July 1922, 31 May 1924, 12 May 1926, 30 June 1928 and 30 July 1935, the Conventions of 28 October 1933 and 10 February 1938, the Protocol of 14 September 1939 and the Agreement of 15 October 1946.

CHAPTER VII
FINAL CLAUSES

Article   38   Settlement of disputes

Any dispute between parties to this Convention relating to its interpretation or application, which cannot be settled by other means, shall be referred to the International Court of Justice at the request of any one of the parties to the dispute.

Article   39   Signature, ratification and accession

1 This Convention shall be opened for signature at Geneva on 28 July 1951 and shall thereafter be deposited with the Secretary-General of the United Nations. It shall be open for signature at the European Office of the United Nations from 28 July to 31 August 1951 and shall be re-opened for signature at the Headquarters of the United Nations from 17 September 1951 to 31 December 1952.

2 This Convention shall be open for signature on behalf of all states members of the United Nations, and also on behalf of any other state invited to attend the Conference of Plenipotentiaries on the Status of Refugees and Stateless Persons or to which an invitation to sign will have been addressed by the General Assembly. It shall be ratified and the instruments of ratification shall be deposited with the Secretary-General of the United Nations.

3 This Convention shall be open from 28 July 1951 for accession by the states referred to in paragraph 2 of this Article. Accession shall be effected by the deposit of an instrument of accession with the Secretary-General of the United Nations.

Article   40   Territorial application clause

1 Any state may, at the time of signature, ratification or accession, declare that this Convention shall extend to all or any of the territories for the international relations of which it is responsible. Such a declaration shall take effect when the Convention enters into force for the state concerned.

2 At any time thereafter any such extension shall be made by notification addressed to the Secretary-General of the United Nations and shall take effect as from the

ninetieth day after the day of receipt by the Secretary-General of the United Nations of this notification, or as from the date of entry into force of the Convention for the state concerned, whichever is later.

3   With respect to those territories to which this Convention is not extended at the time of signature, ratification or accession, each state concerned shall consider the possibility of taking the necessary steps in order to extend the application of this Convention to such territories, subject, where necessary for constitutional reasons, to the consent of the governments of such territories.

Article   41   Federal clause

In the case of a federal or non-unitary state, the following provisions shall apply:

(a)   With respect to those Articles of this Convention that come within the legislative jurisdiction of the federal legislative authority, the obligations of the Federal Government shall to this extent be the same as those of Parties which are not federal states,

(b)   With respect to those Articles of this Convention that come within the legislative jurisdiction of constituent states, provinces or cantons which are not, under the constitutional system of the federation, bound to take legislative action, the Federal Government shall bring such Articles with a favourable recommendation to the notice of the appropriate authorities of states, provinces or cantons at the earliest possible moment.

(c)   A federal state party to this Convention shall, at the request of any other contracting state transmitted through the Secretary-General of the United Nations, supply a statement of the law and practice of the Federation and its constituent units in regard to any particular provision of the Convention showing the extent to which effect has been given to that provision by legislative or other action.

Article   42   Reservations

1   At the time of signature, ratification or accession, any state may make reservations to articles of the Convention other than to Articles 1, 3, 4, 16(1), 33, 36–46 inclusive.

2   Any state making a reservation in accordance with paragraph 1 of this article may at any time withdraw the reservation by a communication to that effect addressed to the Secretary-General of the United Nations.

Article   43   Entry into force

1   This Convention shall come into force on the ninetieth day following the day of deposit of the sixth instrument of ratification or accession.

2   For each state ratifying or acceding to the Convention after the deposit of the sixth instrument of ratification or accession, the Convention shall enter into force on the ninetieth day following the date of deposit by such state of its instrument of ratification or accession.

Article   44   Denunciation

1   Any contracting state may denounce this Convention at any time by a notification addressed to the Secretary-General of the United Nations.

2   Such denunciation shall take effect for the contracting state concerned one year from the date upon which it is received by the Secretary-General of the United Nations.

3   Any state which has made a declaration or notification under Article 40 may, at any time thereafter, by a notification to the Secretary-General of the United Nations,

declare that the Convention shall cease to extend to such territory one year after the date of receipt of the notification by the Secretary-General.

Article   45   Revision

1   Any contracting state may request revision of this Convention at any time by a notification addressed to the Secretary-General of the United Nations.

2   The General Assembly of the United Nations shall recommend the steps, if any, to be taken in respect of such request.

Article   46   Notifications by the Secretary-General of the United Nations

The Secretary-General of the United Nations shall inform all Members of the United Nations and non-member states referred to in Article 39:

(a)   of declarations and notifications in accordance with Section B of Article 1;
(b)   of signatures, ratifications and accessions in accordance with Article 39;
(c)   of declarations and notifications in accordance with Article 40;
(d)   of reservations and withdrawals in accordance with Article 42;
(e)   of the date on which this Convention will come into force in accordance with Article 43;
(f)   of denunciations and notifications in accordance with Article 44;
(g)   of requests for revision in accordance with Article 45.

In Faith Whereof the undersigned, duly authorized, have signed this Convention on behalf of their respective Governments,

DONE at Geneva, this twenty-eighth day of July, one thousand nine hundred and fifty-one, in a single copy, of which the English and French texts are equally authentic and which shall remain deposited in the archives of the United Nations, and certified true copies of which shall be delivered to all Members of the United Nations and to the non-member states referred to in Article 39.

SCHEDULE

Paragraph   1

1   The travel document referred to in Article 28 of this Convention shall be similar to the specimen annexed hereto.

2   The document shall be made out in at least two languages, one of which shall be English or French.

Paragraph   2

Subject to the regulations obtaining in the country of issue, children may be included in the travel document of a parent or, in exceptional circumstances, of another adult refugee.

Paragraph   3

The fees charged for issue of the document shall not exceed the lowest scale of charges for national passports.

Paragraph   4

Save in special or exceptional cases, the document shall be made valid for the largest possible number of countries.

Paragraph 5

The document shall have a validity of either one or two years, at the discretion of the issuing authority.

Paragraph 6

1 The renewal or extension of the validity of the document is a matter for the authority which issued it, so long as the holder has not established lawful residence in another territory and resides lawfully in the territory of the said authority. The issue of a new document is, under the same conditions, a matter for the authority which issued the former document.

2 Diplomatic or consular authorities, specially authorised for the purpose, shall be empowered to extend, for a period not exceeding six months, the validity of travel documents issued by their Governments.

3 The contracting states shall give sympathetic consideration to renewing or extending the validity of travel documents or issuing new documents to refugees no longer lawfully resident in their territory who are unable to obtain a travel document from the country of their lawful residence.

Paragraph 7

The contracting states shall recognise the validity of the documents issued in accordance with the provisions of Article 28 of this Convention.

Paragraph 8

The competent authorities of the country to which the refugee desires to proceed shall, if they are prepared to admit him and if a visa is required, affix a visa on the document of which he is the holder.

Paragraph 9

1 The contracting states undertake to issue transit visas to refugees who have obtained visas for a territory of final destination.

2 The issue of such visas may be refused on grounds which would justify refusal of a visa to any alien.

Paragraph 10

The fees for the issue of exit, entry or transit visas shall not exceed the lowest scale of charges for visas on foreign passports.

Paragraph 11

When a refugee has lawfully taken up residence in the territory of another contracting state, the responsibility for the issue of a new document, under the terms and conditions of Article 28, shall be that of the competent authority of that territory, to which the refugee shall be entitled to apply.

Paragraph 12

The authority issuing a new document shall withdraw the old document and shall return it to the country of issue, if it is stated in the document that it should be so returned; otherwise it shall withdraw and cancel the document.

Paragraph 13

1 Each contracting state undertakes that the holder of a travel document issued by it in accordance with Article 28 of this Convention shall be re-admitted to its territory at any time during the period of its validity.

2 Subject to the provisions of the preceding sub-paragraph, a contracting state may require the holder of the document to comply with such formalities as may be prescribed in regard to exit from or return to its territory.

3 The contracting states reserve the right, in exceptional cases, or in cases where the refugee's stay is authorised for a specific period, when issuing the document, to limit the period during which the refugee may return to a period of not less than three months.

Paragraph 14

Subject only to the terms of paragraph 13, the provisions of this Schedule in no way affect the laws and regulations governing the conditions of admission to, transit through, residence and establishment in, and departure from, the territories of the contracting states.

Paragraph 15

Neither the issue of the document nor the entries made thereon determine or affect the status of the holder, particularly as regards nationality.

Paragraph 16

The issue of the document does not in any way entitle the holder to the protection of the diplomatic or consular authorities of the country of issue, and does not confer on these authorities a right of protection.

ANNEX

Specimen Travel Document

The document will be in booklet form (approximately 15 x 10 centimetres).

It is recommended that it be so printed that any erasure or alteration by chemical or other means can be readily detected, and that the words 'Convention of 28 July 1951' be printed in continuous repetition on each page, in the language of the issuing country.

(Cover of booklet)
TRAVEL DOCUMENT
(Convention of 28 July 1951)
No. ...

(1)
TRAVEL DOCUMENT
(Convention of 28 July 1951)

This document expires on ... unless its validity is extended or renewed.
Name ...
Forename(s) ...
Accompanied by ... child (children)

2512

Convention Relating to the Status of Refugees (28/7/1951)

1. This document is issued solely with a view to providing the holder with a travel document which can serve in lieu of a national passport. It is without prejudice to and in no way affects the holder's nationality.

2. The holder is authorized to return to ... [state here the country whose authorities are issuing the document] on or before ... unless some later date is hereafter specified.

[The period during which the holder is allowed to return must not be less than three months]

3. Should the holder take up residence in a country other than that which issued the present document, he must, if he wishes to travel again, apply to the competent authorities of his country of residence for a new document. [The old travel document shall be withdrawn by the authority issuing the new document and returned to the authority which issued it.]¹

(This document contains ... pages, exclusive of cover.)

¹ The sentence in brackets to be inserted by Governments which so desire.

(2)

Place and date of birth ...
Occupation ...
Present residence ...
* Maiden name and forename(s) of wife ...
* Name of forename(s) of husband ...

Description
Height ...
Hair ...
Colour of eyes ...
Nose ...
Shape of face ...
Complexion ...
Special peculiarities ...

Children accompanying holder

Name	Forename(s)	Place and date of birth	Sex
...	...	...	...
...	...	...	...
...	...	...	...
...	...	...	...

* Strike out whichever does not apply.
(This document contains ... pages, exclusive of cover.)

(3)

Photograph of holder and stamp of issuing authority
Finger-prints of holder (if required)
Signature of holder ...
(This document contains ... pages, exclusive of cover.)

(4)

1. This document is valid for the following countries:
   ...
   ...
   ...

...

2. Document or documents on the basis of which the present document is issues:

...

...

...

...

Issued at ...

Date ...

Signature and stamp of authority issuing the document

Fee paid:

(This document contains ... pages, exclusive of cover.)

(5)

Extension or renewal of validity

Fee paid:	From ...
	To ...
Done at:	Date ...

Signature and stamp of authority extending or renewing the validity of the document:

Extension or renewal of validity

Fee paid:	From ...
	To ...
Done at:	Date ...

Signature and stamp of authority extending or renewing the validity of the document:

(This document contains ... pages, exclusive of cover.)

(6)

Extension or renewal of validity

Fee paid:	From ...
	To ...
Done at:	Date ...

Signature and stamp of authority extending or renewing the validity of the document:

Extension or renewal of validity

Fee paid:	From ...
	To ...
Done at:	Date ...

Signature and stamp of authority extending or renewing the validity of the document:

(This document contains ... pages, exclusive of cover.)

(7–32)

Visas

The name of the holder of the document must be repeated in each visa.

(This document contains ... pages, exclusive of cover.)

2514

APPENDIX

FINAL ACT OF THE 1951 UNITED NATIONS CONFERENCE OF PLENIPOTENTIARIES ON THE STATUS OF REFUGEES AND STATELESS PERSONS

I   The General Assembly of the United Nations, by Resolution 429(V) of 14 December 1950, decided to convene in Geneva a Conference of Plenipotentiaries to complete the drafting of, and to sign, a Convention relating to the Status of Refugees and a Protocol relating to the Status of Stateless Persons.

The Conference met at the European Office of the United Nations in Geneva from 2 to 25 July 1951.

The Governments of the following twenty-six states were represented by delegates who all submitted satisfactory credentials or other communications of appointment authorizing them to participate in the Conference:

Australia	Israel
Austria	Italy
Belgium	Luxembourg
Brazil	Monaco
Canada	Netherlands
Colombia	Norway
Denmark	Sweden
Egypt	Switzerland (the Swiss delegation also represented Liechtenstein)
France	Turkey
Germany, Federal Republic of	United Kingdom of Great Britain and Northern Ireland
Greece	United States of America
Holy See	Venezuela
Iraq	Yugoslavia

The Governments of the following two states were represented by observers:

Cuba	Iran

Pursuant to the request of the General Assembly, the United Nations High Commissioner for Refugees participated, without the right to vote, in the deliberations of the Conference.

The International Labour Organisation and the International Refugee Organization were represented at the Conference without the right to vote.

The Conference invited a representative of the Council of Europe to be represented at the Conference without the right to vote.

Representatives of the following Non-Governmental Organizations in consultative relationship with the Economic and Social Council were also present as observers:

Category   A

International Confederation of Free Trade Unions

International Federation of Christian Trade Unions

Inter-Parliamentary Union

Category   B

Agudas Israel World Organization

Caritas Internationalis

2515

Appendix 1   Legislation and materials

Catholic International Union for Social Service

Commission of the Churches on International Affairs

Consultative Council of Jewish Organizations

Co-ordinating Board of Jewish Organizations

Friends' World Committee for Consultation

International Association of Penal Law

International Bureau for the Unification of Penal Law

International Committee of the Red Cross

International Council of Women

International Federation of Friends of Young Women

International League for the Rights of Man

International Social Service

International Union for Child Welfare

International Union of Catholic Women's Leagues

Pax Romana

Women's International League for Peace and Freedom

World Jewish Congress

World Union for Progressive Judaism

World Young Women's Christian Association

Register

International Relief Committee for Intellectual Workers

League of Red Cross Societies

Standing Conference of Voluntary Agencies

World Association of Girl Guides and Girl Scouts

World University Service

Representatives of Non-Governmental Organizations which have been granted consultative status by the Economic and Social Council as well as those entered by the Secretary-General on the Register referred to in Resolution 288 B(X) of the Economic and Social Council, paragraph 17, had under the rules of procedure adopted by the Conference the right to submit written or oral statements to the Conference.

The Conference elected Mr. Knud Larsen, of Denmark, as President, and Mr A Herment, of Belgium, and Mr Talat Miras, of Turkey, as Vice-Presidents.

At its second meeting, the Conference, acting on a proposal of the representative of Egypt, unanimously decided to address an invitation to the Holy See to designate a plenipotentiary representative to participate in its work. A representative of the Holy See took his place at the Conference on 10 July 1951.

The Conference adopted as its agenda the Provisional Agenda drawn up by the Secretary-General (A/CONF 2/2/Rev 1). It also adopted the Provisional Rules of Procedure drawn up by the Secretary-General, with the addition of a provision which authorized a representative of the Council of Europe to be present at the Conference without the right to vote and to submit proposals (A/CONF 2/3/Rev 1).

2516

Convention Relating to the Status of Refugees (28/7/1951)

In accordance with the Rules of Procedure of the Conference, the President and Vice-Presidents examined the credentials of representatives and on 17 July 1951 reported to the Conference the results of such examination, the Conference adopting the report.

The Conference used as the basis of its discussions the draft Convention relating to the Status of Refugees and the draft Protocol relating to the Status of Stateless Persons prepared by the *ad hoc* Committee on Refugees and Stateless Persons at its second session held in Geneva from 14 to 25 August 1950, with the exception of the preamble and Article 1 (Definition of the term 'refugee') of the draft Convention. The text of the preamble before the Conference was that which was adopted by the Economic and Social Council on 11 August 1950 in Resolution 319 B II(XI). The text of Article 1 before the Conference was that recommended by the General Assembly on 14 December 1950 and contained in the Annex to Resolution 429(V). The latter was a modification of the text as it had been adopted by the Economic and Social Council in Resolution 319 B II(XI)[1].

The Conference adopted the Convention relating to the Status of Refugees in two readings. Prior to its second reading it established a Style Committee composed of the President and the representatives of Belgium, France, Israel, Italy, the United Kingdom of Great Britain and Northern Ireland and the United States of America, together with the High Commissioner for Refugees, which elected as its Chairman Mr. G. Warren, of the United States of America. The Style Committee re-drafted the text which had been adopted by the Conference on first reading, particularly from the point of view of language and of concordance between the English and French texts.

The Convention was adopted on 25 July by 24 votes to none with no abstentions and opened for signature at the European Office of the United Nations from 28 July to 31 August 1951. It will be re-opened for signature at the permanent headquarters of the United Nations in New York from 17 September 1951 to 31 December 1952.

The English and French texts of the Convention, which are equally authentic, are appended to this Final Act.

[1] The texts referred to in the paragraph above are contained in document A/CONF 2/1.

II The Conference decided, by 17 votes to 3 with 3 abstentions, that the titles of the chapters and of the articles of the Convention are included for practical purposes and do not constitute an element of interpretation.

III With respect to the draft Protocol relating to the Status of Stateless Persons, the Conference adopted the following resolution:

The Conference,
 Having considered the draft Protocol relating to the Status of Stateless Persons,
 Considering that the subject still requires more detailed study,
 Decides not to take a decision on the subject at the present Conference and refers the draft Protocol back to the appropriate organs of the United Nations for further study.

IV The Conference adopted unanimously the following recommendations:

A
(Facilitation of refugee travels)[1]

The Conference,
Considering that the issue and recognition of travel documents is necessary to facilitate the movement of refugees, and in particular their resettlement,

Urges Governments which are parties to the Inter-Governmental Agreement on Refugee Travel Documents signed in London on 15 October 1946, or which recognize travel documents issued in accordance with the Agreement, to continue to issue or to recognize such travel documents, and to extend the issue of such documents to refugees as defined in Article 1 of the Convention relating to the Status of Refugees or to recognize the travel documents so issued to such persons, until they shall have undertaken obligations under Article 28 of the said Convention.

¹   Headline added.

B

(Principle of unity of the family)¹

The Conference,

Considering that the unity of the family, the natural and fundamental group unit of society, is an essential right of the refugee, and that such unity is constantly threatened, and

Noting with satisfaction that, according to the official commentary of the *ad hoc* Committee on Statelessness and Related Problems (E/1618, p. 40) the rights granted to a refugee are extended to members of his family,

Recommends Governments to take the necessary measures for the protection of the refugee's family, especially with a view to:

(1)   Ensuring that the unity of the refugee's family is maintained particularly in cases where the head of the family has fulfilled the necessary conditions for admission to a particular country,

(2)   The protection of refugees who are minors, in particular unaccompanied children and girls, with special reference to guardianship and adoption.

¹   Headline added.

C

(Welfare services)¹

The Conference,

Considering that, in the moral, legal and material spheres, refugees need the help of suitable welfare services, especially that of appropriate non-governmental organizations,

Recommends Governments and inter-governmental bodies to facilitate, encourage and sustain the efforts of properly qualified organizations.

¹   Headline added.

D

(International co-operation in the field of asylum and resettlement)

The Conference,

Considering that many persons still leave their country of origin for reasons of persecution and are entitled to special protection on account of their position,

Recommends that Governments continue to receive refugees in their territories and that they act in concert in a true spirit of international co-operation in order that these refugees may find asylum and the possibility of resettlement.

E

(Extension of treatment provided by the Convention)

The Conference,

Expresses the hope that the Convention relating to the Status of Refugees will have value as an example exceeding its contractual scope and that all nations will be guided by it in granting so far as possible to persons in their territory as refugees and who would not be covered by the terms of the Convention, the treatment for which it provides.

In Witness Whereof the President, Vice-Presidents and the Executive Secretary of the Conference have signed this Final Act.

Done at Geneva this twenty-eighth day of July one thousand nine hundred and fifty-one in a single copy in the English and French languages, each text being equally authentic. Translations of this Final Act into Chinese, Russian and Spanish will be prepared by the Secretary-General of the United Nations, who will, on request, send copies thereof to each of the Governments invited to attend the Conference.

The President of the Conference:	Knud Larsen
The Vice-Presidents of the Conference:	A Herment
	Talat Miras
The Executive Secretary of the Conference:	John P Humphrey

PROTOCOL RELATING TO THE STATUS OF REFUGEES OF 31 JANUARY 1967

Entry into force . . . . *4 October 1967, in accordance with Article VIII*

Text . . . . *United Nations Treaty Series No 8791, Vol 606, p 267*

The States Parties to the present Protocol,

Considering that the Convention relating to the Status of Refugees done at Geneva on 28 July 1951 (hereinafter referred to as the Convention) covers only those persons who have become refugees as a result of events occurring before 1 January, 1951,

Considering that new refugee situations have arisen since the Convention was adopted and that the refugees concerned may therefore not fall within the scope of the Convention,

Considering that it is desirable that equal status should be enjoyed by all refugees covered by the definition in the Convention irrespective of the dateline 1 January 1951,

Have agreed as follows:

Article   I   General provision

1   The states parties to the present Protocol undertake to apply Articles 2 to 34 inclusive of the Convention to refugees as hereinafter defined.

2   For the purpose of the present Protocol, the term 'refugee' shall, except as regards the application of paragraph 3 of this Article, mean any person within the definition of Article 1 of the Convention as if the words 'As a result of events occurring before 1 January 1951 and ...' and the words '... as a result of such events', in Article 1 A (2) were omitted.

3   The present Protocol shall be applied by the states parties hereto without any geographic limitation, save that existing declarations made by states already Parties to

the Convention in accordance with Article 1 B (1)(a) of the Convention, shall, unless extended under Article 1 B (2) thereof, apply also under the present Protocol.

Notes
The Protocol was signed by the President of the General Assembly and by the Secretary-General on 31 January 1967. The text of the General Assembly Resolution 2198 (XXI) of 16 December 1966 concerning the accession to the 1967 Protocol relating to the Status of Refugees is reproduced in Appendix.

Article   II   Co-operation of the national authorities with the United Nations

1   The states parties to the present Protocol undertake to co-operate with the Office of the United Nations High Commissioner for Refugees, or any other agency of the United Nations which may succeed it, in the exercise of its functions, and shall in particular facilitate its duty of supervising the application of the provisions of the present Protocol.

2   In order to enable the Office of the High Commissioner, or any other agency of the United Nations which may succeed it, to make reports to the competent organs of the United Nations, the states parties to the present Protocol undertake to provide them with the information and statistical data requested, in the appropriate form, concerning:

(a)   The condition of refugees;
(b)   The implementation of the present Protocol;
(c)   Laws, regulations and decrees which are, or may hereafter be, in force relating to refugees.

Article   III   Information on national legislation

The states parties to the present Protocol shall communicate to the Secretary-General of the United Nations the laws and regulations which they may adopt to ensure the application of the present Protocol.

Article   IV   Settlement of disputes

Any dispute between states parties to the present Protocol which relates to its interpretation or application and which cannot be settled by other means shall be referred to the International Court of Justice at the request of any one of the parties to the dispute.

Article   V   Accession

The present Protocol shall be open for accession on behalf of all states parties to the Convention and of any other State Member of the United Nations or member of any of the specialized agencies or to which an invitation to accede may have been addressed by the General Assembly of the United Nations. Accession shall be effected by the deposit of an instrument of accession with the Secretary-General of the United Nations.

Article   VI   Federal clause

In the case of a federal or non-unitary state, the following provisions shall apply:

(a)   With respect to those articles of the Convention to be applied in accordance with Article 1, paragraph 1, of the present Protocol that come within the legislative jurisdiction of the federal legislative authority, the obligations of the Federal Government shall to this extent be the same as those of states parties which are not federal states;
(b)   With respect to those articles of the Convention to be applied in accordance with Article I, paragraph 1, of the present Protocol that come within the

legislative jurisdiction of constituent states, provinces or cantons which are not, under the constitutional system of the federation, bound to take legislative action, the Federal Government shall bring such articles with a favourable recommendation to the notice of the appropriate authorities of states, provinces or cantons at the earliest possible moment;

(c) A Federal State Party to the present Protocol shall, at the request of any other state party hereto transmitted through the Secretary-General of the United Nations, supply a statement of the law and practice of the Federation and its constituent units in regard to any particular provision of the Convention to be applied in accordance with Article I, paragraph 1, of the present Protocol, showing the extent to which effect has been given to that provision by legislative or other action.

Article VII Reservations and declarations

1 At the time of accession, any state may make reservations in respect of Article IV of the present Protocol and in respect of the application in accordance with Article I of the present Protocol of any provisions of the Convention other than those contained in Articles 1, 3, 4, 16(1) and 33 thereof, provided that in the case of a state party to the Convention reservations made under this Article shall not extend to refugees in respect of whom the Convention applies.

2 Reservations made by states parties to the Convention in accordance with Article 42 thereof shall, unless withdrawn, be applicable in relation to their obligations under the present Protocol.

3 Any state making a reservation in accordance with paragraph 1 of this Article may at any time withdraw such reservation by a communication to that effect addressed to the Secretary-General of the United Nations.

4 Declarations made under Article 40, paragraphs 1 and 2, of the Convention by a state party thereto which accedes to the present Protocol shall be deemed to apply in respect of the present Protocol, unless upon accession a notification to the contrary is addressed by the state party concerned to the Secretary-General of the United Nations. The provisions of Article 40, paragraphs 2 and 3, and of Article 44, paragraph 3, of the Convention shall be deemed to apply *mutatis mutandis* to the present Protocol.

Article VIII Entry into force

1 The present Protocol shall come into force on the day of deposit of the sixth instrument of accession.

2 For each state acceding to the Protocol after the deposit of the sixth instrument of accession, the Protocol shall come into force on the date of deposit by such state of its instrument of accession.

Article IX Denunciation

1 Any state party hereto may denounce this Protocol at any time by a notification addressed to the Secretary-General of the United Nations.

2 Such denunciation shall take effect for the state party concerned one year from the date on which it is received by the Secretary-General of the United Nations.

Article X Notifications by the Secretary-General of the United Nations

The Secretary-General of the United Nations shall inform the states referred to in Article V above of the date of entry into force, accessions, reservations and withdrawals of reservations to and denunciations of the present Protocol, and of declarations and notifications relating hereto.

Article   XI   Deposit in the archives of the Secretariat of the United Nations

A copy of the present Protocol, of which the Chinese, English, French, Russian and Spanish texts are equally authentic, signed by the President of the General Assembly and by the Secretary-General of the United Nations, shall be deposited in the archives of the Secretariat of the United Nations. The Secretary-General will transmit certified copies thereof to all states members of the United Nations and to the other states referred to in Article V above.

APPENDIX

GENERAL ASSEMBLY RESOLUTION 2198 (XXI)

Protocol   relating to the Status of Refugees

The General Assembly,
    Considering that the Convention relating to the Status of Refugees, signed at Geneva on 28 July 1951[1], covers only those persons who have become refugees as a result of events occurring before 1 January 1951,
    Considering that new refugee situations have arisen since the Convention was adopted and that the refugees concerned may therefore not fall within the scope of the Convention,
    Considering that it is desirable that equal status should be enjoyed by all refugees covered by the definition in the Convention, irrespective of the date-line of 1 January 1951,
    Taking note of the recommendation of the Executive Committee of the Programme of the United Nations High Commissioner for Refugees[2] that the draft Protocol relating to the Status of Refugees should be submitted to the General Assembly after consideration by the Economic and Social Council, in order that the Secretary-General might be authorised to open the Protocol for accession by Governments within the shortest possible time,
    Considering that the Economic and Social Council, in its resolution 1186 (XLI) of 18 November 1966, took note with approval of the draft Protocol contained in the addendum to the report of the United Nations High Commissioner for Refugees and concerning measures to extend the personal scope of the Convention[3] and transmitted the addendum to the General Assembly,
    1*Takes note* of the Protocol relating to the Status of Refugees, the text of which is contained in the addendum to the report of the United Nations High Commissioner for Refugees;
    2*Requests* the Secretary-General to transmit the text of the Protocol to the States mentioned in article V thereof, with a view to enabling them to accede to the Protocol[4].

1495th plenary meeting,

16 December 1966.

Notes

[1]   United Nations, *Treaty Series*, vol 189 (1954), No 2545.
[2]   See A/6311/Rev 1/Add 1, part two, para 38.
[3]   *Ibid*, part one, para 2.
[4]   The Protocol was signed by the President of the General Assembly and by the Secretary-General on 31 January 1967.

Convention relating to the status of refugees, 28 July 1951 (UNTS, vol 189, p 137); entry into force: 22 April 1954.

UK GOVERNMENT RESERVATION TO THE 1951 CONVENTION RELATING TO THE STATUS OF REFUGEES

(i)   The Government of the United Kingdom of Great Britain and Northern Ireland understand articles 8 and 9 as not preventing them from taking in time of war or other grave and exceptional circumstances measures in the interests of national security in the case of a refugee on the ground of his nationality. The provision of article 8 shall not prevent the Government of the United Kingdom of Great Britain and Northern Ireland from exercising any rights over property or interests which they may acquire or have acquired as an Allied or Associated Power under a Treaty of Peace or other agreement or arrangement for the restoration of peace which has been or may be completed as a result of the Second World War. Furthermore, the provision of article 8 shall not affect the treatment to be accorded to any property or interests which, at the date of entry into force of this Convention for the United Kingdom of Great Britain and Northern Ireland, are under the control of the Government of the United Kingdom of Great Britain and Northern Ireland by reason of a state of war which exists or existed between them and any other state.

(ii) The Government of the United Kingdom of Great Britain and Northern Ireland accept article 17, paragraph 2, with the substitution of 'four years' for 'three years' in subparagraph (a) and with the omission of subparagraph (c).

(iii) The Government of the United Kingdom of Great Britain and Northern Ireland cannot undertake to give effect to the obligations contained in article 25, paragraphs 1 and 2, and can only undertake to apply the provision of paragraph 3 so far as the law allows.

UK GOVERNMENT COMMENTARY:

In connection with article 24, paragraph 1, subparagraph (b) relating to certain matters within the scope of the National Health Service, the National Health Service (Amendment) Act, 1949, contains powers for charges to be made to persons not ordinarily resident in Great Britain (which category would include refugees) who receive treatment under the Service. While these powers have not yet been exercised it is possible that this might have to be done at some future date. In Northern Ireland the Health Services are restricted to persons ordinarily resident in the country except where regulations are made to extend the Service to others. It is for these reasons that the Government of the United Kingdom while they are prepared in the future, as in the past, to give the most sympathetic consideration to the situation of refugees, find it necessary to make a reservation to article 24, paragraph 1, subparagraph (b), of the Convention.

The scheme of Industrial Injuries Insurance in Great Britain does not meet the requirements of article 24, paragraph 2, of the Convention. Where an insured person has died as the result of an industrial accident or a disease due to the nature of his employment, benefit cannot generally be paid to his dependants who are abroad unless they are in any part of the British Commonwealth, in the Irish Republic or in a country with which the United Kingdom has made a reciprocal agreement concerning the payment of industrial injury benefits. There is an exception to this rule in favour of the dependants of certain seamen who die as a result of industrial accidents happening to them while they are in the service of British ships. In this matter refugees are treated in the same way as citizens of the United Kingdom and Colonies and by reason of article 24, paragraphs 3 and 4, of the Convention, the dependants of refugees will be able to take advantage of reciprocal agreements which provide for the payment of United Kingdom industrial injury benefits in other countries. By reason of article 24, paragraphs 3 and 4, refugees will enjoy under the scheme of National Insurance and Industrial Injuries Insurance certain rights which are withheld from British subjects who are not citizens of the United Kingdom and Colonies.

No arrangements exist in the United Kingdom for the administrative assistance for which provision is made in article 25 nor have any such arrangements been found necessary in the case of refugees. Any need for the documents or certifications mentioned in paragraph 2 of that article would be met by affidavits.

CONVENTION RELATING TO THE STATUS OF STATELESS PERSONS

Adopted on . . . . *28 September 1954*

Entry into force . . . . *6 June 1960, in accordance with article 39*

PREAMBLE

The High Contracting Parties,

Considering that the Charter of the United Nations and the Universal Declaration of Human Rights approved on 10 December 1948 by the General Assembly of the United Nations have affirmed the principle that human beings shall enjoy fundamental rights and freedoms without discrimination,

Considering that the United Nations has, on various occasions, manifested its profound concern for stateless persons and endeavoured to assure stateless persons the widest possible exercise of these fundamental rights and freedoms,

Considering that only those stateless persons who are also refugees are covered by the Convention relating to the Status of Refugees of 28 July 1951, and that there are many stateless persons who are not covered by that Convention,

Considering that it is desirable to regulate and improve the status of stateless persons by an international agreement,

Have agreed as follows:

CHAPTER I
GENERAL PROVISIONS

Article 1 Definition of the term 'Stateless Person'

1 For the purpose of this Convention, the term 'stateless person' means a person who is not considered as a national by any State under the operation of its law.

2 This Convention shall not apply:

(i) To persons who are at present receiving from organs or agencies of the United Nations other than the United Nations High Commissioner for Refugees protection or assistance so long as they are receiving such protection or assistance;

(ii) To persons who are recognized by the competent authorities of the country in which they have taken residence as having the rights and obligations which are attached to the possession of the nationality of that country;

(iii) To persons with respect to whom there are serious reasons for considering that:

(a) They have committed a crime against peace, a war crime, or a crime against humanity, as defined in the international instruments drawn up to make provisions in respect of such crimes;

(b) They have committed a serious non-political crime outside the country of their residence prior to their admission to that country;

(c) They have been guilty of acts contrary to the purposes and principles of the United Nations.

Article 2 General obligations

Every stateless person has duties to the country in which he finds himself, which require in particular that he conform to its laws and regulations as well as to measures taken for the maintenance of public order.

Article 3 Non-discrimination

The Contracting States shall apply the provisions of this Convention to stateless persons without discrimination as to race, religion or country of origin.

Article 4 Religion

The Contracting States shall accord to stateless persons within their territories treatment at least as favourable as that accorded to their nationals with respect to freedom to practise their religion and freedom as regards the religious education of their children.

Article 5 Rights granted apart from this Convention

Nothing in this Convention shall be deemed to impair any rights and benefits granted by a Contracting State to stateless persons apart from this Convention.

Article 6 The term 'in the same circumstances'

For the purpose of this Convention, the term 'in the same circumstances' implies that any requirements (including requirements as to length and conditions of sojourn or residence) which the particular individual would have to fulfil for the enjoyment of the right in question, if he were not a stateless person, must be fulfilled by him, with the exception of requirements which by their nature a stateless person is incapable of fulfilling.

Article 7 Exemption from reciprocity

1 Except where this Convention contains more favourable provisions, a Contracting State shall accord to stateless persons the same treatment as is accorded to aliens generally.

2 After a period of three years' residence, all stateless persons shall enjoy exemption from legislative reciprocity in the territory of the Contracting States.

3 Each Contracting State shall continue to accord to stateless persons the rights and benefits to which they were already entitled, in the absence of reciprocity, at the date of entry into force of this Convention for that State.

4 The Contracting States shall consider favourably the possibility of according to stateless persons, in the absence of reciprocity, rights and benefits beyond those to which they are entitled according to paragraphs 2 and 3, and to extending exemption from reciprocity to stateless persons who do not fulfil the conditions provided for in paragraphs 2 and 3.

5 The provisions of paragraphs 2 and 3 apply both to the rights and benefits referred to in articles 13, 18, 19, 21 and 22 of this Convention and to rights and benefits for which this Convention does not provide.

Article   8   Exemption from exceptional measures

With regard to exceptional measures which may be taken against the person, property or interests of nationals or former nationals of a foreign State, the Contracting States shall not apply such measures to a stateless person solely on account of his having previously possessed the nationality of the foreign State in question. Contracting States which, under their legislation, are prevented from applying the general principle expressed in this article shall, in appropriate cases, grant exemptions in favour of such stateless persons.

Article   9   Provisional measures

Nothing in this Convention shall prevent a Contracting State, in time of war or other grave and exceptional circumstances, from taking provisionally measures which it considers to be essential to the national security in the case of a particular person, pending a determination by the Contracting State that that person is in fact a stateless person and that the continuance of such measures is necessary in his case in the interests of national security.

Article   10   Continuity of residence

1   Where a stateless person has been forcibly displaced during the Second World War and removed to the territory of a Contracting State, and is resident there, the period of such enforced sojourn shall be considered to have been lawful residence within that territory.

2   Where a stateless person has been forcibly displaced during the Second World War from the territory of a Contracting State and has, prior to the date of entry into force of this Convention, returned there for the purpose of taking up residence, the period of residence before and after such enforced displacement shall be regarded as one uninterrupted period for any purposes for which uninterrupted residence is required.

Article   11   Stateless seamen

In the case of stateless persons regularly serving as crew members on board a ship flying the flag of a Contracting State, that State shall give sympathetic consideration to their establishment on its territory and the issue of travel documents to them or their temporary admission to its territory particularly with a view to facilitating their establishment in another country.

CHAPTER II
JURIDICAL STATUS

Article   12   Personal status

1   The personal status of a stateless person shall be governed by the law of the country of his domicile or, if he has no domicile, by the law of the country of his residence.

2   Rights previously acquired by a stateless person and dependent on personal status, more particularly rights attaching to marriage, shall be respected by a Contracting State, subject to compliance, if this be necessary, with the formalities required by the law of that State, provided that the right in question is one which would have been recognized by the law of that State had he not become stateless.

Article   13   Movable and immovable property

The Contracting States shall accord to a stateless person treatment as favourable as possible and, in any event, not less favourable than that accorded to aliens generally in the same circumstances, as regards the acquisition of movable and immovable property and other rights pertaining thereto, and to leases and other contracts relating to movable and immovable property.

Article   14   Artistic rights and industrial property

In respect of the protection of industrial property, such as inventions, designs or models, trade marks, trade names, and of rights in literary, artistic and scientific works, a stateless person shall be accorded in the country in which he has his habitual residence the same protection as is accorded to nationals of that country. In the territory of any other Contracting State, he shall be accorded the same protection as is accorded in that territory to nationals of the country in which he has his habitual residence.

Article   15   Right of association

As regards non-political and non-profit-making associations and trade unions the Contracting States shall accord to stateless persons lawfully staying in their territory treatment as favourable as possible, and in any event, not less favourable than that accorded to aliens generally in the same circumstances.

Article   16   Access to courts

1   A stateless person shall have free access to the courts of law on the territory of all Contracting States.

2   A stateless person shall enjoy in the Contracting State in which he has his habitual residence the same treatment as a national in matters pertaining to access to the courts, including legal assistance and exemption from cautio judicatum solvi.

3   A stateless person shall be accorded in the matters referred to in paragraph 2 in countries other than that in which he has his habitual residence the treatment granted to a national of the country of his habitual residence.

CHAPTER III
GAINFUL EMPLOYMENT

Article   17   Wage-earning employment

1   The Contracting States shall accord to stateless persons lawfully staying in their territory treatment as favourable as possible and, in any event, not less favourable that that accorded to aliens generally in the same circumstances, as regards the right to engage in wage-earning employment.

2   The Contracting States shall give sympathetic consideration to assimilating the rights of all stateless persons with regard to wage-earning employment to those of nationals, and in particular of those stateless persons who have entered their territory pursuant to programmes of labour recruitment or under immigration schemes.

Article   18   Self-employment

The Contracting States shall accord to a stateless person lawfully in their territory treatment as favourable as possible and, in any event, not less favourable than that accorded to aliens generally in the same circumstances, as regards the right to engage on his own account in agriculture, industry, handicrafts and commerce and to establish commercial and industrial companies.

Article   19   Liberal professions

Each Contracting State shall accord to stateless persons lawfully staying in their territory who hold diplomas recognized by the competent authorities of that State, and who are desirous of practising a liberal profession, treatment as favourable as possible and, in any event, not less favourable than that accorded to aliens generally in the same circumstances.

CHAPTER IV
WELFARE

Article   20   Rationing

Where a rationing system exists, which applies to the population at large and regulates the general distribution of products in short supply, stateless persons shall be accorded the same treatment as nationals.

Article   21   Housing

As regards housing, the Contracting States, in so far as the matter is regulated by laws or regulations or is subject to the control of public authorities, shall accord to stateless persons lawfully staying in their territory treatment as favourable as possible and, in any event, not less favourable than that accorded to aliens generally in the same circumstances.

Article   22   Public education

1   The Contracting States shall accord to stateless persons the same treatment as is accorded to nationals with respect to elementary education.

2   The Contracting States shall accord to stateless persons treatment as favourable as possible and, in any event, not less favourable than that accorded to aliens generally in the same circumstances, with respect to education other than elementary education and, in particular, as regards access to studies, the recognition of foreign school certificates, diplomas and degrees, the remission of fees and charges and the award of scholarships.

Article   23   Public relief

The Contracting States shall accord to stateless persons lawfully staying in their territory the same treatment with respect to public relief and assistance as is accorded to their nationals.

Article   24   Labour legislation and social security

1   The Contracting States shall accord to stateless persons lawfully staying in their territory the same treatment as is accorded to nationals in respect of the following matters:

(a)   In so far as such matters are governed by laws or regulations or are subject to the control of administrative authorities; remuneration, including family allowances where these form part of remuneration, hours of work, overtime arrangements, holidays with pay, restrictions on home work, minimum age of employment, apprenticeship and training, women's work and the work of young persons, and the enjoyment of the benefits of collective bargaining;

(b)   Social security (legal provisions in respect of employment injury, occupational diseases, maternity, sickness, disability, old age, death, unemployment, family responsibilities and any other contingency which, according to national laws or regulations, is covered by a social security scheme), subject to the following limitations:

(i)   There may be appropriate arrangements for the maintenance of acquired rights and rights in course of acquisition;

(ii) National laws or regulations of the country of residence may prescribe special arrangements concerning benefits or portions of benefits which are payable wholly out of public funds, and concerning allowances paid to persons who do not fulfil the contribution conditions prescribed for the award of a normal pension.

2 The right to compensation for the death of a stateless person resulting from employment injury or from occupational disease shall not be affected by the fact that the residence of the beneficiary is outside the territory of the Contracting State.

3 The Contracting States shall extend to stateless persons the benefits of agreements concluded between them, or which may be concluded between them in the future, concerning the maintenance of acquired rights and rights in the process of acquisition in regard to social security, subject only to the conditions which apply to nationals of the States signatory to the agreements in question.

4 The Contracting States will give sympathetic consideration to extending to stateless persons so far as possible the benefits of similar agreements which may at any time be in force between such Contracting States and non-contracting States.

CHAPTER V
ADMINISTRATIVE MEASURES

Article 25 Administrative assistance

1 When the exercise of a right by a stateless person would normally require the assistance of authorities of a foreign country to whom he cannot have recourse, the Contracting State in whose territory he is residing shall arrange that such assistance be afforded to him by their own authorities.

2 The authority or authorities mentioned in paragraph I shall deliver or cause to be delivered under their supervision to stateless persons such documents or certifications as would normally be delivered to aliens by or through their national authorities.

3 Documents or certifications so delivered shall stand in the stead of the official instruments delivered to aliens by or through their national authorities and shall be given credence in the absence of proof to the contrary.

4 Subject to such exceptional treatment as may be granted to indigent persons, fees may be charged for the services mentioned herein, but such fees shall be moderate and commensurate with those charged to nationals for similar services.

5 The provisions of this article shall be without prejudice to articles 27 and 28.

Article 26 Freedom of movement

Each Contracting State shall accord to stateless persons lawfully in its territory the right to choose their place of residence and to move freely within its territory, subject to any regulations applicable to aliens generally in the same circumstances.

Article 27 Identity papers

The Contracting States shall issue identity papers to any stateless person in their territory who does not possess a valid travel document.

Article 28 Travel documents

The Contracting States shall issue to stateless persons lawfully staying in their territory travel documents for the purpose of travel outside their territory, unless compelling reasons of national security or public order otherwise require, and the provisions of the schedule to this Convention shall apply with respect to such documents. The

Contracting States may issue such a travel document to any other stateless person in their territory; they shall in particular give sympathetic consideration to the issue of such a travel document to stateless persons in their territory who are unable to obtain a travel document from the country of their lawful residence.

Article 29 Fiscal charges

1 The Contracting States shall not impose upon stateless persons duties, charges or taxes, of any description whatsoever, other or higher than those which are or may be levied on their nationals in similar situations.

2 Nothing in the above paragraph shall prevent the application to stateless persons of the laws and regulations concerning charges in respect of the issue to aliens of administrative documents including identity papers.

Article 30 Transfer of assets

1 A Contracting State shall, in conformity with its laws and regulations, permit stateless persons to transfer assets which they have brought into its territory, to another country where they have been admitted for the purposes of resettlement.

2 A Contracting State shall give sympathetic consideration to the application of stateless persons for permission to transfer assets wherever they may be and which are necessary for their resettlement in another country to which they have been admitted.

Article 31 Expulsion

1 The Contracting States shall not expel a stateless person lawfully in their territory save on grounds of national security or public order.

2 The expulsion of such a stateless person shall be only in pursuance of a decision reached in accordance with due process of law. Except where compelling reasons of national security otherwise require, the stateless person shall be allowed to submit evidence to clear himself, and to appeal to and be represented for the purpose before competent authority or a person or persons specially designated by the competent authority.

3 The Contracting States shall allow such a stateless person a reasonable period within which to seek legal admission into another country. The Contracting States reserve the right to apply during that period such internal measures as they may deem necessary.

Article 32 Naturalization

The Contracting States shall as far as possible facilitate the assimilation and naturalization of stateless persons. They shall in particular make every effort to expedite naturalization proceedings and to reduce as far as possible the charges and costs of such proceedings.

CHAPTER VI
FINAL CLAUSES

Article 33 Information on national legislation

The Contracting States shall communicate to the Secretary-General of the United Nations the laws and regulations which they may adopt to ensure the application of this Convention.

2530

Article   34   Settlement of disputes

Any dispute between Parties to this Convention relating to its interpretation or application, which cannot be settled by other means, shall be referred to the International Court of Justice at the request of any one of the parties to the dispute.

Article   35   Signature, ratification and accession

1   This Convention shall be open for signature at the Headquarters of the United Nations until 31 December 1955.

2   It shall be open for signature on behalf of:

   (a)   Any State Member of the United Nations;

   (b)   Any other State invited to attend the United Nations Conference on the Status of Stateless Persons; and

   (c)   Any State to which an invitation to sign or to accede may be addressed by the General Assembly of the United Nations.

3   It shall be ratified and the instruments of ratification shall be deposited with the Secretary-General of the United Nations.

4   It shall be open for accession by the States referred to in paragraph 2 of this article. Accession shall be effected by the deposit of an instrument of accession with the Secretary-General of the United Nations.

Article   36   Territorial application clause

1   Any State may, at the time of signature, ratification or accession, declare that this Convention shall extend to all or any of the territories for the international relations of which it is responsible. Such a declaration shall take effect when the Convention enters into force for the State concerned.

2   At any time thereafter any such extension shall be made by notification addressed to the Secretary-General of the United Nations and shall take effect as from the ninetieth day after the day of receipt by the Secretary-General of the United Nations of this notification, or as from the date of entry into force of the Convention for the State concerned, whichever is the later.

3   With respect to those territories to which this Convention is not extended at the time of signature, ratification or accession, each State concerned shall consider the possibility of taking the necessary steps in order to extend the application of this Convention to such territories, subject, where necessary for constitutional reasons, to the consent of the Governments of such territories.

Article   37   Federal clause

In the case of a Federal or non-unitary State, the following provisions shall apply

   (a)   With respect to those articles of this Convention that come within the legislative jurisdiction of the federal legislative authority, the obligations of the Federal Government shall to this extent be the same as those of Parties which are not Federal States;

   (b)   With respect to those articles of this Convention that come within the legislative jurisdiction of constituent States, provinces or cantons which are not, under the constitutional system of the Federation, bound to take legislative action, the Federal Government shall bring such articles with a favourable recommendation to the notice of the appropriate authorities of States, provinces or cantons at the earliest possible moment;

   (c)   A Federal State Party to this Convention shall, at the request of any other Contracting State transmitted through the Secretary-General of the United

Nations, supply a statement of the law and practice of the Federation and its constituent units in regard to any particular provision of the Convention showing the extent to which effect has been given to that provision by legislative or other action.

Article   38   Reservations

1   At the time of signature, ratification or accession, any State may make reservations to articles of the Convention other than to articles 1, 3, 4, 16 (1) and 33 to 42 inclusive.

2   Any State making a reservation in accordance with paragraph I of this article may at any time withdraw the reservation by a communication to that effect addressed to the Secretary-General of the United Nations.

Article   39   Entry into force

1   This Convention shall come into force on the ninetieth day following the day of deposit of the sixth instrument of ratification or accession.

2   For each State ratifying or acceding to the Convention after the deposit of the sixth instrument of ratification or accession, the Convention shall enter into force on the ninetieth day following the date of deposit by such State of its instrument of ratification or accession.

Article   40   Denunciation

1   Any Contracting State may denounce this Convention at any time by a notification addressed to the Secretary-General of the United Nations.

2   Such denunciation shall take effect for the Contracting State concerned one year from the date upon which it is received by the Secretary-General of the United Nations.

3   Any State which has made a declaration or notification under article 36 may, at any time thereafter, by a notification to the Secretary- General of the United Nations, declare that the Convention shall cease to extend to such territory one year after the date of receipt of the notification by the Secretary-General.

Article   41   Revision

1   Any Contracting State may request revision of this Convention at any time by a notification addressed to the Secretary-General of the United Nations.

2   The General Assembly of the United Nations shall recommend the steps, if any, to be taken in respect of such request.

Article   42   Notifications by the Secretary-General of the United Nations

The Secretary-General of the United Nations shall inform all Members of the United Nations and non-member States referred to in article 35:

   (a)   Of signatures, ratifications and accessions in accordance with article 35;
   (b)   Of declarations and notifications in accordance with article 36;
   (c)   Of reservations and withdrawals in accordance with article 38;
   (d)   Of the date on which this Convention will come into force in accordance with article 39;
   (e)   Of denunciations and notifications in accordance with article 40;
   (f)   Of request for revision in accordance with article 41.

Appendix 2

OFFICIAL ADDRESSES

(NB – telephone contact details within the Home Office and Immigration Service are subject to frequent change)

Immigration & Nationality Directorate
Lunar House
40 Wellesley Road
Croydon
CR9 2BY

tel (Immigration and Nationality Enquiry Bureau (INEB)): 0870 606 7766
tel (asylum enquries): 0151 237 8016
tel (NASS): 020 8633 0154
tel (Nationality Directorate): 0151 237 5444
tel (Nationality enquiries): 0845 010 5200
tel (Work Permits UK): 0114 259 4074
tel (Ports, Enforcement, Removal Centres): 020 8760 2127
tel (complaints about UKIS): 020 8745 2350
tel (complaints about IND): 020 8760 8190
email (IND Public Enquiries): indpublicenquiries@ind.homeoffice.gsi.gov.uk
email (nationality enquiries): nationalityenquiries@ind.homeoffice.gsi.gov.uk
email (Worker Registration Scheme): wrs@ind.homeoffice.gsi.gov.uk
website: www.ind.homeoffice.gov.uk

PEO Reps Same-Day Service
First Floor, Lunar House
40 Wellesley Road
Croydon
CR9 2BY

tel (Birmingham): 0121 704 5450
tel (Glasgow): 0141 555 1258
tel (Liverpool): 0151 237 0473

Initial Consideration Unit (Immigration and Nationality Directorate)
PO Box 3615
Walsall Road
Cannock
WS11 0WS

Nationality Policy and Special Cases Unit
India Buildings
Water Street
Liverpool
L2 0QN

tel: 0151 237 5200
fax: 0151 237 5386

(for applications) Managed Migration Directorate (Nationality Group)
Casework Support Unit
PO Box 12
Liverpool
L69 2UX

NASS
Voyager House
30 Wellesley Road
Croydon
CR0 2AD

tel (support enquiries): 0845 6000 914
tel (telephone enquiry bureau): 0845 602 1739
tel (Sodexho Helpline): 01252 369 799
fax: 020 8633 0129

2533

Appendix 2   Official addresses

Work Permits (UK)
PO Box 3468
Sheffield

tel: 0114 259 4074
fax: 0114 259 3776
email:
    customrel.workpermits@wpuk.gov.uk
website: www.workingintheuk.gov.uk

IMMIGRATION SERVICE ENFORCEMENT UNITS: CONTACT NUMBERS

Apex House

tel: 01474 352 308
fax: 01474 534 731

Becket House

tel: 020 7238 1300
tel (casework): 020 7238 1486/3950
fax: 020 7378 9110/1426

Bristol (Portishead)

tel: 01275 815 020
fax: 01275 818 680

Croydon

tel: 020 8760 3838/3821
fax: 020 8760 3082

Dover

tel: 01304 200 400/401
fax: 01304 216 303

East Midlands Airport

tel: 01332 812 000
fax: 01332 811 569

Glasgow

tel: 0141 847 5300
fax: 0141 889 0062

Leeds/Bradford

tel: 0113 391 3000
fax: 0113 391 3007

Midlands Enforcement Unit

tel: 0121 606 7300
fax: 0121 704 5056

North West Enforcement Unit

tel: 0161 489 2367
fax: 0161 489 2370

Stansted Enforcement Unit

tel: 01279 680 691
fax: 01279 680 041

Status Park Enforcement Unit

tel: 020 8745 2400
fax: 020 8745 2407

AIRPORTS AND PORTS

UK Immigration Service

Aberdeen Airport
Dyce
Aberdeen
AB21 7DU

tel: 01124 722 890

Belfast International Airport
Belfast
BT29 4AB

tel (public): 028 9448 4323
tel (terminal office): 028 9442 2500
fax: 028 9445 9211

2534

Biggin Hill
Kent
TN16 5BN

tel:/fax: 01959 572 225

Birmingham International Airport
Birmingham
B26 3QZ

tel: 0121 606 7350/7359/7361
fax: 0121 782 0006

Blackpool Airport Ltd
Blackpool
Lancs
FY4 2QY

tel: 01253 348 035 (covered by UKIS
Liverpool enforcement)

Bournemouth International Airport
(post to Poole office)

tel: 01202 572 515

Bristol Airport
(post to Portishead office)

tel:/fax: 01275 472 843

Terminal Building – RAF Brize Norton
Oxon
OX18 3LX

tel:/fax: 01993 845 992

Cambridge Airport
Newmarket Road
Cambridge
CB5 8RX

tel: 01223 294 213

Cardiff International Airport
Rhoose
Barry
Vale of Glamorgan
CF6 4NW

tel (general): 01446 710 485
tel (casework): 029 20710 485
fax: 029 20710 606

**Carlisle Airport (covered by Manchester
TN 1)**
Crosby on Eden
Carlisle
Cumbria
CA6 4NW

tel: 01228 573 641

**Coventry Airport (covered by
Birmingham)**
Baginton
Coventry
CV 3AZ

tel: 02476 301 717

East Midlands Airport
Ground Floor
Pembroke House
Pegasus Business Park
Castle Donington
Derby
DE74 2SA

tel (general): 01332 817 100
tel (casework): 013332 812 000

Edinburgh Airport
Edinburgh
EH12 9DN

tel: 01313 484 026

Exeter Airport
(post to Plymouth)

tel:/fax: 01392 366 492

Gatwick Airport (North Terminal)
West Sussex
RH6 0PJ

tel: 01293 507 075
fax: 01293 507 097

Gatwick Airport (South Terminal)
West Sussex
RH6 0NP

tel: 01293 502 019
fax: 01293 553 643

Glasgow Airport
Paisley
Renfrewshire
PA3 2TD

tel: 0141 847 5300
fax: 0141 887 1566

2535

Appendix 2   Official addresses

Heathrow Airport (Terminal 1)
Hounslow
Middlesex
TW6 1BN

tel: 020 8745 6800
tel (casework): 020 8745 6809
fax (asylum/non-asylum cases/temporary
    admission/bail cases): 020 8745 6814
fax (detained cases/new arrivals): 020
    8745 2514
fax (general): 020 8745 6828

Heathrow Airport (Terminal 2)
Hounslow
Middlesex
TW6 1EN

tel (general): 020 8745 6850
tel (casework): 020 8745 6860
tel (asylum desk): 020 8745 6870/73
fax: 020 8745 6867/77

Heathrow Airport (Terminal 3)
Hounslow
Middlesex
TW6 1ND

tel (general): 020 8745 6900
tel (casework): 020 8745 6932
fax: 020 8745 6943

Heathrow Airport (Terminal 4)
Hounslow
Middlesex
TW6 3XB

tel (switchboard): 020 8745 4700/1
tel (casework): 020 8745 4724
tel (asylum): 020 8745 4722
fax: 020 8745 4705

Humberside International Airport
Kirmington
Ulceby
North Lincolnshire
DN39 6YH

Inverness Airport
Inverness
IV1 2JB

tel: 01667 462 470

Kent International Airport Ltd
PO Box 500
Manston
Kent
CT12 5BP

tel (switchboard): 01843 823 333

Leeds/Bradford International Airport
Whitehouse Lane
Yeadon
West Yorkshire
LS19 7TZ

tel: 0113 202 9380
fax: 0113 202 9381

Liverpool Airport
Terminal Building
Liverpool

tel: 0151 448 1448

London City Airport
Royal Docks
Silvertown
London
E16 2PX

tel: 020 7474 1390
tel (casework): 020 7474 1395
fax: 020 7511 2363

Luton Airport
Luton
Bedfordshire
LU2 9LU

tel: 01582 439 030
tel (casework): 01582 421 891
fax: 01582 405 215

Manchester Airport (Terminal 1)
6th Floor
Tower Block
Manchester
M90 2AA

tel: 0161 489 3000
tel (casework): 0161 489 2652
fax: 0161 499 2346

Manchester Airport (Terminal 2)
Wythenshawe
Manchester
M90 4HH

tel: 0161 489 6230
fax: 0161 489 6231

Manchester Airport (Terminal 3)

tel: 0161 489 6045

Newcastle International Airport
Woolsington
Newcastle upon Tyne
NE13 8BZ

tel: 0191 214 2700/2701

Norwich Airport
Amsterdam Way
Norwich
NR6 6EP

tel: 01603 268 960

Prestwick Airport
Ayrshire
KA9 2PQ

tel:/fax: 01292 478 675

Sheffield City Airport
Europa Link
Sheffield
South Yorkshire
S9 1XZ

tel: 0114 201 5316

Shetland Islands

tel: (mobile) 07721 466 190
tel: via Aberdeen 01224 722 890

Shoreham Airport
(covered by Gatwick South)
Shoreham-by-Sea
West Sussex
BN43 5FF

tel: 01273 592 664

IMMIGRATION REMOVAL CENTRES

Campsfield House IRC
(Global Solutions Limited)
Langford Lane
Kidlington
Oxfordshire
OX5 1RE

tel: 01865 377712
fax: 01865 377723

Southampton International Airport
Wide Lane
Eastleigh
Southampton
SO18 2NL

tel: 02380 627 107

Stansted Passenger Terminal
Bassingbourn Road
Stansted
Essex
CM24 1RW

tel: 01279 680 118
fax: 01279 680 145

Teesside International Airport
Middleton St George
Darlington
Co Durham
DL2 1LU

tel: 01325 331 400

Dover East
tel: 01304 244 900
fax: 01304 213 594

Harwich
tel: 01255 504 371
fax: 01255 240 233

Waterloo International Terminal
tel: 020 7919 5910
fax: 020 7919 5918

Colnbrook IRC
(Premier Custodial Group)
Colnbrook Bypass
Harmondsworth
West Drayton
Middlesex
UB7 0FX

tel: 020 8607 5200
fax: 020 8607 5388

Dover IRC
(HM Prison Service)
The Citadel
Western Heights
Dover
CT17 9DR

tel: 01304 246400
fax: 01304 246407

Dungavel IRC
(Premier Detention Services)
Dungavel
Strathaven
South Lanarkshire
ML10 6RF

tel: 01698 395000
fax: 01698 395076

Gatwick Airport (Holding Centre)
2 Holding Rooms

tel (North Terminal): 01293 507803
tel (South Terminal): 01293 502640

Harmondsworth IRC
(United Kingdom Detention Services)
Colnbrook Bypass
Longford
West Drayton
Middlesex
UB7 0HB

tel: 020 8283 3850
fax: 020 8283 3851

Haslar IRC
(HM Prison Service)
Dolphin Way
Gosport
PO12 2AW

tel: 023 9258 0381
fax: 023 9251 0266

Lindholme IRC
(HM Prison Service)
Bawtry Road
Hattield
Woodhouse
Doncaster
DN7 6EE

tel: 01302 848666
fax: 01302 848620

Manchester Airport IRC
(Global Solutions Limited)
Terminal 2
Manchester Airport
M90 4HH

tel: 0161 489 5701
fax: 0161 489 5701

Queens buildings (Holding centre)
(Premier Custodial Group)
Heathrow Airport

tel: 020 8564 9726 or 020 8564 9727

Oakington Reception Centre
(Global Solutions Limited)
Longstanton
Cambridgeshire
CB4 4EJ

tel: 01954 783000 or 01954 783091

Rochester Detention Centre
HMP Rochester
1 Fort Road
Rochester
Kent
ME1 3SQ

tel (switchboard): 01634 838100
fax: 01634 838101

Tinsley House Detention Centre
Perimeter Road South
Gatwick Airport
West Sussex
RH6 OPQ

tel (switchboard): 01293 434800
fax (for legal visits): 01293 423221
fax (for detainees): 01293 434825

Yarl's Wood IRC
(Global Solutions Limited)
Twinwood Road
Clapham
Bedfordshire
MK41 6HL

tel: 01234 821800
tel (for detainees): 01234 821000
fax: 01234 821 026

RECEPTION CENTRES

Oakington Reception Centre
Rampton Road
Longstanton
Cambridge
CB4 4EJ

tel: 01954 783 300
fax: 01954 789 505

HOME OFFICE PRESENTING OFFICERS' UNITS

Central London
2nd floor
Building 1
Angel Square
1 Torrens Street
London
EC1V 1NY

tel: 020 7239 1701
fax: 020 7239 1702/1616

Glasgow
10th Floor
Eagle Building
215 Bothwell Street
Glasgow
G2 7ED

tel: 0141 221 4218
fax: 0141 204 5987

Feltham
Hanover House
Plane Tree Crescent
Feltham
Middlesex
TW13 7JJ

tel: 020 8917 2039
fax: 020 8890 6489

Leeds
2nd Floor Springfield House
76 Wellington Street
Leeds
LS1 2AY

tel: 0113 244 4205
fax: 0113 245 3472

Manchester
15th Floor West Point
501 Chester Road
Old Trafford
Manchester
M15 9HU

tel: 0161 261 0937
fax: 0161 261 0992

Birmingham
1st Floor
2308 Coventry Road
Sheldon
Birmingham
B26 3JS

tel: 0121 700 1616
fax: 0121 700 1696

Newcastle
2nd Floor
Link House
Melbourne Street
Newcastle
NE1 2JQ

tel: 0191 376 2900
fax: 0191 376 2894

Stoke on Trent
2nd Floor
Bennett House
Town Road
Hanley
Stoke on Trent
ST1 2QB

tel: 0178 246 3571
fax: 0178 246 3560

ASYLUM AND IMMIGRATION TRIBUNAL

tel: 0845 6000 877

Appendix 2 Official addresses

Postal addresses:
PO Box 6987
Leicester
LE1 6ZX
fax: 0116 249 4130 / 4131 (general
    correspondence)
website: www.ait.gov.uk
PO Box 7866
Loughborough
LE11 2XZ
fax: 01509 221699 (appeal forms)

Hearing Centres:

tel for all centres (customer service):
    0845 600 0877

London
Taylor House
88 Rosebery Avenue
London
EC1R 4QU

London
Field House
15 Breams Buildings
London
EC4A 1DZ

London
York House
2–3 Dukes Green Avenue
Feltham
Middlesex
TW14 0LS

London
Gloucester House
4 Dukes Green Avenue
Feltham
Middlesex
TW14 0LR

Belfast
The Old Town Hall Building
80 Victoria Street
Belfast
BT1 3FA

Birmingham
Sheldon Court
1 Wagon Lane
Birmingham
West Midlands
B26 3DU

Bradford
Phoenix House
Rushton Avenue
Thornbury
Bradford
BD3 7BH

Bromley
Bromley Magistrates Court
1st Floor, 1 London Road
Bromley
Kent
BR1 1RA

Croydon
Croydon Magistrates Court
Barclay Road
Croydon
Surrey
CR9 3NG

Glasgow
4th Floor, Eagle Building
215 Bothwell Street
Glasgow
G2 7EZ

Manchester
1st Floor, Piccadilly Exchange
Piccadilly Plaza
Manchester
M1 4AH

Newport
Columbus House
Langstone Business Park
Chepstowe Road
Newport
NP18 2LX

North Shields
Kings Court
Royal Quays
Earl Grey Way
North Shields
NE29 6AR

Nottingham
Nottingham Magistrates Court
Carrington Street
Nottingham
NG2 1EE

Stoke on Trent
Bennett House
Town Road
Hanley
Stoke-on-Trent
ST1 2QB

Surbiton
Sessions House
17 Ewell Road
Surbiton
Surrey
KT6 6AQ

Walsall
2nd floor, Bridge House
47 Bridge Street
Walsall
WS1 1HZ

OTHER OFFICIAL ADDRESSES

Commission for Racial Equality
St Dunstan's House
201–211 Borough High Street
London
SE1 1GZ

tel: 020 7939 0000
website: www.cre.gov.uk

European Commission (England)
8 Storey's Gate
London
SW1P 3AT

tel: 020 7973 1992

European Commission (N. Ireland)
9–15 Bedford Street
Belfast
BT2 7EG

tel: 028 9024 0708

European Commission (Scotland)
9 Alva Street
Edinburgh
EH2 4PH

tel: 0131 225 2058

European Commission (Wales)
2 Caspian Point/2 Pentir Caspian
Caspian Way/Ffordd Caspian
Cardiff/Caerdydd
CF10 4QQ

tel: 029 20895020
website: www.cec.eu.int

European Court of Human Rights
Council of Europe
F – 67075
Strasbourg-Cedex

tel: (+0033) (0)3 88 41 20 18
website: www.echr.coe.int

Foreign and Commonwealth Office
King Charles Street
London
SW1A 2AH

tel: (visa enquiries) 020 7008 8438
website: www.fco.gov.uk or
     www.ukvisas.gov.uk

Legal Services Commission
85 Gray's Inn Road
London
WC1X 8TX

tel: 020 7759 0000
fax: 020 7759 0534

Legal Services Commission (Immigration Services Team)
4th Floor, 12 Roger Street
London
WC1N 2JL

tel: 020 7759 1471
fax: 020 7759 1469

Office of the Immigration Service Commissioner
Fleetbank House
2–6 Salisbury Square
London
EC4Y 8JX

tel: 020 7211 1500
fax: 020 7211 1553
website: www.oisc.gov.uk

Appendix 2 Official addresses

Overseas Visitors Records Office
(registration with police)

Brandon House
180 Borough High Street
London
SE1 1LH

tel: 020 7230 1208

Royal Courts of Justice
Strand
London
WC2A 2LL

tel: 020 7947 6000
tel (Admin Court): 020 7947 6359
tel (Civil Appeals): 020 7947 7882
website: www.hmcourts-service.gov.uk

USEFUL CONTACTS

Advice Services Alliance
12th Floor, New London Bridge House
25 London Bridge Street
London
SE1 9ST

tel: 020 7378 6428
website: www.asauk.org.uk

AIRE Centre (Advice on Individual
Rights in Europe)
3rd Floor, 17 Red Lion Square
London
WC1R 4QH

tel (Administration): 020 7831 4276
tel (advice line): 020 7831 3850
website: www.airecentre.org

Amnesty International UK
The Human Rights Action Centre
17–25 New Inn Yard
London
EC2A 3EA

tel: 020 7033 1500
website: www.amnesty.org.uk

United Nations High Commissioner for
Refugees (UNHCR)
Case Postale 2500
CH-1211 Genève 2 Dépôt
Switzerland

tel: 00 41 22 739 8111
website: www.unhcr.ch

United Nations High Commissioner for
Refugees (UNHCR) (UK)
The Office of the Representative for the
United Kingdom
21st Floor, Millbank Tower
Millbank
London
SW1P 4QP

tel: 020 7828 9191
fax: 020 7630 5349
email: gbrloea@unhcr.ch
website: www.unhcr.org.uk

Asylum Aid
28 Commercial Street
London
E1 6LS

tel: 020 7377 5123
tel (advice line): 020 7247 8741
website: www.asylumaid.org.uk

Bail for Immigration Detainees (BID)
28 Commercial Street
London
E1 6LS

tel: 020 7247 3590
website: www.biduk.org

Campaign Against Criminalising
Communities (CAMPACC)
website: www.cacc.org.uk

Cellmark Diagnostics
PO Box 265
Abingdon
Oxfordshire
OX14 1YX

tel: 0123 552 8000
website: www.cellmark.co.uk

Children's Legal Centre
Wivenhoe Park
University of Essex
Colchester
Essex
CO4 3SQ

tel (admin): 01206 872466
tel (advice): 01206 873873
website: www.childrenslegalcentre.com

Citizen's Advice
Myddelton House,
115–123 Pentonville Road
London
N1 9LZ

tel: 020 7833 2181
website: www.citizensadvice.org.uk

Citizen's Advice
The Corner House
Station Road
Sturminster Newton
Dorset
DT10 1YJ

tel: 0845 330 7928 / 01258 473795
website: www.thecornerhouse.org.uk

Detention Advice Service

308 Seven Sisters Road
London
N4 2AG

tel: 020 8802 3422
email: das@das.ndirect.co.uk

Educational Grants Advisory Service
501–505 Kingsland Road
London
E8 4AU

tel (advice): 020 7254 6251

website: www.egas-online.org

Electronic Immigration Network
The Progress Centre
Charlton Place
Manchester
M12 6HS

tel: 0845 458 4151 (0161 2737515)
website: www.ein.org.uk

European Council on Refugees and Exiles (ECRE)
103 Worship Street
London
EC2A 4DF

tel: 020 7377 7556
fax: 020 7377 7586

Foundation for Public Service Interpreting
1 St Clements Court
London
EC4N 7HB

tel: 020 7626 0220
email: mkiddle@aol.com

Free Representation Unit
6th Floor, 289–293 High Holborn
London
WC1V 7HZ

tel: 0207 611 9555
website: www.fru.org.uk

Greater Manchester Immigration Aid Unit
1 Delaunays Road
Crumpsall Green
Manchester
M8 4QS

tel: 0161 740 7722
email: gmiau@ein.org.uk

Human Rights Watch (UK office)
2nd Floor, 2–12 Pentonville Road
London

N1 9HF

tel: 020 7713 1995
website: www.hrw.org

Immigration Advisory Service
County House Great Dover Street
London
SE1 4YB

tel: 020 7967 1200
website: www.iasuk.org

Appendix 2   Official addresses

Immigration Law Practitioners Association
Lindsey House
40–42 Charterhouse Street
London
EC1M 6JN

tel: 020 7251 8383
website: www.ilpa.org.uk

Institute of Race Relations
2–6 Leeke Street
London
WC1X 9HS

tel: 020 7837 0041
website: www.irr.org.uk

Interights
Lancaster House
33 Islington High Street
London
N1 9LH

tel: 020 7278 3230
website: www.interights.org

International Social Service (UK)
3rd Floor, Cranmer House
39 Brixton Road
London
SW9 6DD
email: help@issuk.org.uk

Joint Council for the Welfare of Immigrants
115 Old Street
London
EC1V 9RT

tel: 020 7251 8708
tel (advice line): 020 7251 8706
fax: 020 7251 8707
website: www.jcwi.org.uk

Justice
59 Carter Lane
London
EC4V 5AQ

tel: 020 7329 5100
website: www.justice.org.uk

Kalayaan (Justice for Domestic Workers)
St Francis Centre
13 Hippodrome Place
London
W11 4SF

tel: 020 7243 2942
email: kalayaanuk@aol.com

Language Line
Swallow House
11–21 Northdown Street
London
N1 9BN

tel: 0800 169 2879 / 020 7520 1430
website: www.languageline.co.uk

Law Centres Federation
Duchess House
18–19 Warren Street
London
W1T 5LR

tel: 020 7387 8570
website: www.lawcentres.org.uk

Legal Action Group
242 Pentonville Road
London
N1 9UN

tel: 020 7833 7434/7429
website: www.lag.org.uk

Liberty
21 Tabard Street
London
SE1 4LA

tel: 020 7403 3888
website:
    www.liberty-human-rights.org.uk

Medical Foundation for the Care of Victims of Torture (London)
111 Isledon Road
London
N7 7JW

tel: 020 7697 7777

2544

Medical Foundation for the Care of Victims of Torture (Northwest Office)
1st Floor North Square
11–13 Spear Street
Manchester
M1 1JU

tel: 0161 839 8090

Medical Foundation for the Care of Victims of Torture (Scotland)
2nd Floor
73 Robertson Street
Glasgow
G2 8QD

tel: 0141 847 0012
website: www.torturecare.org.uk

Minority Rights Group International
54 Commercial Street
London
E1 6LT

tel: 020 7422 4200
website: www.minorityrights.org

National Coalition of Anti-Deportation Campaigns (NCADC)
1 Delaunays Road
Crumpsall
Manchester
M8 4QS

tel: 0121 554 6947
website: www.ncadc.org.uk

National Union of Students
Nelson Mandela House
461 Holloway Road
London
N7 6LJ
website: www.nusonline.co.uk

North of England Refugee Service
2 Jesmond Road West
Newcastle Upon Tyne
NE2 4PQ

tel: 0191 245 7311
website: www.refugee.org.uk

Panel of Advisers for Unaccompanied Refugee Children
240–250 Ferndale Road
London
SW9 8BB

tel: 020 7346 1134
website: www.refugeecouncil.org.uk

Praxis
Pott Street
London
E2 0EF

tel: 020 7729 7985
website: www.praxis.org.uk

Refugee Action
The Old Fire Station
150 Waterloo Road
London
SE1 8SB

tel: 020 7654 7700
website: www.refugee-action.org.uk

Refugee Arrivals Project
41b Cross Lances Road
Hounslow
Middlesex
TW3 2AD

tel: 020 8607 6888
Refugee Arrivals Project (Reception)
Room 1116, 1st Floor
Queen's Building
Heathrow Airport
Hounslow
Middlesex
TW6 1DN

tel: 020 8759 5740
website: www.refugee-arrivals.org.uk

Refugee Council (Head Office)
240–250 Ferndale Road
London
SW9 8BB

tel: 020 7346 6700
tel (advice): 020 7346 6777

Refugee Council (Training & Employment Section)
3–9 Bondway
London
SW8 1SJ

tel: 020 7840 4488

Appendix 2 Official addresses

Refugee Council (Oakington Detention Centre)
Building 25 Reception
Oakington Barracks
Longstanton
Cambridge
CB4 4EJ

tel: 01954 789444
website: www.refugeecouncil.org.uk

Refugee Education Training Advisory Service (RETAS)
Education Action International
14 Dufferin Street
London
EC1Y 8PD

tel: 020 7426 5800
website: www.education-action.org

Refugee Legal Centre
153–157 Commercial Road
London
E1 2DA

tel: 020 7780 3200
website: www.refugee-legal-centre.org.uk

Refugee Studies Centre
Queen Elizabeth House
Oxford University
21 St Giles
Oxford
OX1 3LA

tel: 01865 270 722
website: www.rsc.ox.ac.uk

Refugee Women's Legal Group
c/o ILPA
Lindsey House
40–42 Charterhouse Street
London
EC1M 6JN
website: www.rwlg.org.uk

Refugee Women's Legal Project
website: www.asylumaid.org.uk

Save the Children (UK)
17 Grove Lane
London
SE5 8RD

tel: 020 7703 5400
website: www.savethechildren.org.uk

Scottish Refugee Council
5 Cadogan Square
(170 Blythswood Court)
Glasgow
G2 7PH

tel: 0141 248 9799
website:
    www.scottishrefugeecouncil.org.uk

Statewatch
PO Box 1516
London
N16 0EW

tel: 020 8802 1882
website: www.statewatch.org

Women's Resource Centre
76 Wentworth Street
London
E1 7SA

tel: 020 7377 0088
website: www.wrc.org.uk

Appendix 3

LEGAL AND COUNTRY INFORMATION WEBSITES

- Amnesty International – www.amnesty.org
- Asylumlaw.org – http://asylumlaw.org/
- Australian Legal Information Institute – www.austlii.org
- Australian Refugee Review Tribunal – www.rrt.gov.au
- British and Irish Legal Information Institute – www.bailii.org
- Canada Immigration and Refugee Board – www.irb-cisr.gc.ca
- Civil Procedure Rules – www.dca.gov.uk/civil/procrules_fin/menus/rules.htm
- Commonwealth courts – www.legalresearch.org
- Electronic Immigration Network – www.ein.org.uk
- Euro Legal Services – www.eurolegal.org
- European Court of Human Rights – www.echr.coe.int
- European Court of Justice – www.curia.eu.int
- European Union – www.europa.eu.int
- Federal Court of Canada – www.fja.gc.ca/en
- Hansard – www.parliament.uk/hansard
- HMSO – www.hmso.gov.uk
- Home Office Country Information – www.ind.homeoffice.gov.uk/ind/en/home/laws___policy/country_information.html
- House of Lords Judgments – www.parliament.uk/judicial_work
- Human Rights Watch – www.hrw.org
- Immigration and Nationality Directorate (Immigration Rules) – www.ind.homeoffice.gov.uk/ind/en/home/laws___policy/immigration_rules.html
- Inter-American Commission on Human Rights – www.iachr.org
- International Committee of the Red Cross (international humanitarian law) – www.icrc.org
- International Court of Justice – www.icj-cij.org
- Joint Committee on Human Rights (parliament) – www.publications.parliament.uk/pa/jt/jtrights.htm
- New Zealand Refugee Law – www.refugee.org.nz
- Organisation for Security and Co-operation in Europe – www.osce.org
- Rightsnet (welfare benefits, NASS etc) – www.rightsnet.org.uk
- UK Acts – www.opsi.gov.uk/acts.htm
- UK Statutory Instruments – www.opsi.gov.uk/stat.htm
- UN General Assembly resolutions – www.un.org/Depts/dhl/resguide/resins.htm
- UN Office of the High Commissioner for Human Rights – www.ohchr.org/english
- UNHCR – www.unhcr.ch/
- UNHCR UK – www.unhcr.org.uk
- University of Michigan Refugee Case Law Site – www.refugeecaselaw.org
- US Committee for Refugees and Immigrants (USRI) – www.refugees.org
- US Department of State – www.state.gov
- War Resisters International – www.wri-irg.org

Appendix 4
GLOSSARY

AAPD	Asylum and Appeals Procedures Unit
AC	Administrative Court
AC	Appeal Cases (Law Reports)
ACD	Asylum Casework Directorate
ACU	Asylum Coordination Unit
ACPI	Advisory Panel on Country Information
ADSU	Asylum Decision Service Unit
AFIS	Automated Fingerprint Identification System
AI	Amnesty International
AIT	Asylum and Immigration Tribunal
AJRU	Appeal and Judicial Review Unit
All ER	All England Law Reports
AN	Application form for naturalisation as a British citizen
AO	Adjudication Officer
APC	Appeals Processing Centre
API	Asylum Policy Instructions
APIS	Advance Passenger Information System
APU	Asylum Policy Unit
APPU	Asylum Processes and Procedures Unit
ARC	Asylum/Application Registration Card
ASA	Asylum Support Adjudicator
ASU	Asylum Screening Unit
BC	British citizen
BCU	Business Cases Unit
BDTC	British Dependent Territories citizen (now BOTC)
BID	Bail for Immigration Detainees
BOC	British Overseas citizen
BOTC	British Overseas Territories citizen
BPP	British Protected Person
BS	British subject
BUS	Application form for leave to remain as business person, sole representative, retired person of independent means, investor or innovator
CA	Court of Appeal
CAC	Complaints Audit Committee (Home Office)
CAC	House of Commons Constitutional Affairs Committee
CAST	Complete Action Service Team (Home Office)
CD	Communications Directorate (Home Office)
CE/CoE	Council of Europe
CEDAW	UN Convention for the Elimination of Discrimination against Women
CEHR	Commission for Equality and Human Rights
CERA	Certificate of Entitlement to the Right of Abode
CERD	UN Convention for the Elimination of All Forms of Racial Discrimination
CFAPT	Children and Fairness Asylum Policy Team (Home Office)
CIO	Chief Immigration Officer

CIPU	Country Information and Policy Unit (Home Office)
CIREA	Centre for Information, Discussion and Exchange on Asylum
CLR	Controlled Legal Representation
CLS	Community Legal Service
CLT	Central Law Training
Cm	House of Commons Command Paper
Cmnd	House of Commons Command Paper
CMOPU	Contact Management Operational Policy Unit (Home Office)
CMT	Case Management Team (Home Office)
CMT+	Case Management Team Plus (Home Office)
COA (Marriage)	Certificate of Authorisation for Marriage, and application form for obtaining it
COROC/CRC	UN Convention on the Rights of the Child
CTA	Common Travel Area
CW4BO	Close Working for Better Outcomes (Home Office)
DCA	Department for Constitutional Affairs
DEPMU	Detention Escorting and Population Management Unit (Home Office)
DIJ	Designated Immigration Judge
DL	Discretionary leave
DO	Deportation Order
DSP	Diplomatic Service Procedures
DSPU	Detention Services Policy Unit (Home Office)
E&E	Evidence and Enquiry
EC	European Community
EC	Entry clearance
ECAA	EC Association Agreement
ECCA Main	Application form for FLR/ILR as a self-employed person under the EC Association Agreement with Bulgaria or Romania
ECHR	European Convention on Human Rights
ECSMA	European Convention on Social and Medical Assistance
ECtHR	European Court of Human Rights
ECIP	Entry clearance Issuing Post
ECO	Entry clearance officer
ECJ	European Court of Justice
EDI	European Directorate Instructions
EEA	European Economic Area
EEC	European Economic Community
EEC1	Application form for residence permit for EEA national
EEC2	Application form for indefinite leave to remain for EEA national or family member
EEC3	Application form for residence stamp for non-EEA family member of accession worker
EFTA	European Free Trade Area
ELR	Exceptional leave to remain; application form for ILR for person granted ELR
EO	Enforcement Officer
EPU	Enforcement Policy Unit (Home Office)
ERCU	Enforcement and Removals Coordination Unit (Home Office)
ERD	Enforcement and Removals Directorate (Home Office)
EU	European Union
Eurodac	European Central Database System for Fingerprinting Asylum seekers and other aliens
EWCA Civ	England and Wales Court of Appeal Civil Division (case citation)

EWHC (Admin)	England and Wales High Court (Administrative Court) (case citation)
EWS	Early Warning system (EC)
FLR	Further leave to remain
FLR(M)	Application form for further leave to remain based on marriage
FLR(O)	Application form for further leave to remain for other purposes
FLR(S)	Application form for further leave to remain as a student
FLR(SEGS)	Application form for further leave to remain under the Science and Engineering Graduate Scheme
FCO	Foreign and Commonwealth Office
FOI	Freedom of Information
FSJ	Freedom, Security and Justice
HC	House of Commons Paper
HOPO	Home Office Presenting Officer
HP	Humanitarian protection
HRW	Human Rights Watch
HSMP	Highly Skilled Migrant Programme, and application form to remain in programme
ICCPR	International Covenant on Civil and Political Rights
ICESCR	International Covenant on Economic, Social and Cultural Rights
IDI	Immigration Directorates' Instructions
IED	Immigration employment document
IFB	Immigration Fingerprint Bureau (Home Office)
IJ	Immigration Judge
ILR	Indefinite leave to remain
IM2	Application form for entry clearance
Imm AR	Immigration Appeal Reports
IND	Immigration and Nationality Department (Home Office)
INDIS	IND Intelligence Section (Home Office)
INLR	Immigration and Nationality Law Reports
INDP	IND Policy Unit (Home Office)
INEB	Immigration and Nationality Enquiry Bureau
IO	Immigration Officer
IOM	International Organisation for Migration
IRIS	Iris Recognition Information System
IS	Immigration Service (Home Office)
IS96	Immigration Service Form 96 (temporary admission)
IS151	Immigration Service Form 151 (continued detention)
ISTDU	Immigration Service Training and Development Unit
JCHR	Parliamentary Joint Committee on Human Rights
JECU	Joint Entry Clearance Unit (Home and Foreign Office)
JHA	Justice and Home Affairs (European Council)
JIC	Joint Intelligence Cell
LAB	Legal Advisers' Branch (Home Office)
LEO	Local Enforcement Office (Home Office)
LSC	Legal Services Commission
LTE	Leave to enter
LTR	Leave to remain
MAU	Multiple Applications Unit (Home Office)
MCU	Ministerial Correspondence Unit (Home Office)
MMD	Managed Migration Directorate
MMSR	Managed Migration Strategy and Review (Home Office)
MODCU	Management of Detained Cases Unit (Home Office)
NASS	National Asylum Support Service (Home Office)

NEAT	NASS Eligibility and Assessment Team (Home Office)
NI	Nationality Instructions
NIU	National Intelligence Unit
NSA	Non-suspensive appeal
NTL	Endorsement of 'no time limit' in passport; application form for transfer of stamp to new passport
NWCIS	North West Consortia Induction Service (Home Office)
NWP	North West Project (asylum process) (Home Office)
OASIS	Operational Advisory Service for Immigration Service
OEM	Operational Enforcement Manual
OISC	Office of the Immigration Service Commissioner
PEO	Public Enquiry Office (Home Office)
PNC	Police National Computer
PNR	Passenger Name Record
POU	Presenting Officers' Unit (Home Office)
QBD	Queens Bench Division (Divisional Court)
RANS	Restricted Access to NASS Support (Home Office)
RCU	Residual Casework Unit (Home Office)
RESCU	Removals Strategy/Resettlement and Coordination Unit (Home Office)
RFRL	Reasons for refusal letter
RLE	Refusal of leave to enter
ROA	Right of abode
RRU	Residual Registry Unit (Home Office)
SAB	Subject Access Bureau
SEF	Statement of Evidence Form
SEGS	Science and Engineering Graduates Scheme
SET(M)	Application form for settlement on the basis of marriage
SET(O)	Application form for settlement in all other cases
SI	Statutory Instrument
SIJ	Senior Immigration Judge
SSHD	Secretary of State for the Home Department
STANA	Superfast Track and Non-suspensive Appeal (Home Office)
TOC	Transfer of conditions of leave into new passport; application form for transfer
TP	Temporary Protection
UASC	Unaccompanied asylum seeking child
UDHR	Universal Declaration of Human Rights
UFV	Uniform Format Visa (EC)
UKHL	United Kingdom House of Lords (case citation)
UKRP	United Kingdom Residence Permit
UNCAT	United Nations Convention Against Torture
UNCHR	United Nations Commission for Human Rights
UNHCR	United Nations High Commission(er) for Refugees
VARP	Voluntary Assisted Returns Programme
VWL	Visa Warnings List
WICU	Warnings Index Computerised Unit (reports on overstayers etc) (Home Office)
WLR	Weekly Law Reports
WP	Work permit
WSU	Workflow Support Unit (Home Office)

Index

Index

Index

Index